Bloomsbury
Crossword
Key

Bloomsbury
Crossword
Key

Second Edition

BLOOMSBURY

A BLOOMSBURY REFERENCE BOOK
www.bloomsbury.com/reference

Editors
S.M.H. Collin
P.H. Collin

First edition published 2000, 2001 by
Peter Collin Publishing Ltd

Second edition published 2004 by
Bloomsbury Publishing Plc
38 Soho Square
London W1D 3HB

British Library Cataloguing-in-Publication Data
A catalogue record for this book is available from the British Library

ISBN 0 7475 7224 0

All papers used by Bloomsbury Publishing are natural, recyclable
products made from wood grown in well-managed forests. The
manufacturing processes conform to the environmental regulations of
the country of origin.

Computer processing and typesetting by Bloomsbury
Printed in Italy by Legoprint

Preface

This dictionary lists over 390,000 words of four to fifteen letters, each organised into chapters according to the length of the word, then sorted according to each letter's position within the word.

The words within this dictionary have been selected from the wide range of dictionaries that Bloomsbury publishes, to ensure that the terms cover all aspects of English that might be used by the person setting the puzzle.

We created this dictionary as a companion volume to the *Bloomsbury Crossword Solver's Dictionary* (ISBN 0-7475-6642-9). While the *Crossword Solver's Dictionary* provides possible answers to cryptic crossword clues, this *Crossword Key* can be used to help solve cryptic crosswords, but is also very useful for any type of crossword, word puzzle or game.

How to use the Crossword Key

This book lists words in two ways. Firstly, the words are organised into chapters by length (the number of letters that they contain). Within each of these chapters, the words are then sorted alphabetically by each letter in each position.

For example, all the four-letter words are listed four times: alphabetically by the first letter in each word, then by the second letter, then the third, then the fourth.

This repeated listing makes it very easy to find the group of words that fits the space in your crossword puzzle or word game.

As an example, here is the way to find an eight-letter word, with 'b' as the third letter and 'n' as the last letter:

Word required: ☐☐ **B** ☐☐☐☐ **N**

1. Turn to the chapter for eight-letter words (p.245)

2. Turn to the section listing eight-letter words organised by third letter (p.274)

3. Look down the list until you find words with 'B' (column 4 of p.275)

4. Within this group, look for the words that have the letter 'N' as the last letter.

You have now found the following words as possible solutions:

ALBANIAN	EMBOLDEN	ROBINSON	UNBEATEN
AMBITION	LIBATION	SIBERIAN	UNBIDDEN
ANBUSSON	LIBERIAN	SUBHUMAN	UNBROKEN
BOBBYPIN	NOBLEMAN	SUBURBAN	UNBURDEN
CABOCHON	PUBLICAN	TOBOGGAN	UNBUTTON
EMBLAZON			

4:1									
AGUE	ANAL	ASTI	BALI	BENE	BLUB	BRAY	CADE	CHAN	
AALU	AHAB	ANAN	ASUR	BALK	BENJ	BLUE	BRED	CADI	CHAP
AARU	AHEM	ANAS	ATAP	BALL	BENN	BLUR	BREE	CAEN	CHAR
ABAC	AHOY	ANCE	ATAR	BALM	BENT	BLUT	BREN	CAFÉ	CHAT
ABAS	AIDA	ANDA	ATEN	BALT	BENZ	BOAK	BRER	CAGE	CHAW
ABBA	AIDE	ANEW	ATLI	BALU	BERE	BOAR	BREW	CAIN	CHAY
ABBE	AIDS	ANFO	ATOC	BANC	BERG	BOAT	BRIE	CAKE	CHEF
ABED	AÎNÉ	ANIL	ATOK	BAND	BERK	BOAZ	BRIG	CALC	CHER
ABEL	AINT	ANKH	ATOM	BANE	BERM	BOBA	BRIM	CALF	CHEW
ABER	AINU	ANNA	ATOP	BANG	BERN	BOCK	BRIO	CALK	CHIC
ABET	AIRE	ANNE	ATTO	BANI	BESS	BODE	BRIS	CALL	CHIK
ABIB	AIRN	ANNO	ATTU	BANK	BEST	BODY	BRIT	CALM	CHIL
ABLE	AIRS	ANOA	ATUA	BANT	BETA	BOER	BRIX	CALP	CHIN
ABLY	AIRT	ANON	ATUM	BAPU	BETE	BOFF	BRNO	CALX	CHIP
ABRI	AIRY	ANTA	AUDE	BARB	BÊTE	BOGY	BROD	CAMA	CHIT
ABSE	AITU	ANTE	AUDI	BARD	BETH	BOIL	BROG	CAME	CHOC
ABUS	AJAR	ANTI	AULA	BARE	BEVY	BOKE	BRON	CAMP	CHON
ABUT	AJAX	ANTS	AULD	BARF	BHEL	BOKO	BROO	CANA	CHOP
ABYE	AJEE	ANUS	AUNE	BARI	BIAS	BOLD	BROS	CANE	CHOU
ABZU	AKEE	APAY	AUNT	BARK	BIBB	BOLE	BROW	CANN	CHOW
ACAS	AKIN	APEX	AURA	BARM	BICE	BOLL	BRUM	CANS	CHOY
ACCT	ALAI	APIA	AUTO	BARN	BIDE	BOLO	BRUT	CANT	CHUB
AC/DC	ALAN	APIS	AVAL	BARP	BIEN	BOLT	BUAT	CAPA	CHUG
ACER	ALAR	APSE	AVER	BARS	BIER	BOMA	BUBA	CAPE	CHUM
ACES	ALAS	APUS	AVES	BART	BIFF	BOMB	BUBO	CAPH	CHUT
ACHE	ALAY	AQUA	AVID	BASE	BIGA	BONA	BUCK	CAPO	CIAO
ACHT	ALBE	ARAB	AVON	BASH	BIGG	BOND	BUDD	CAPT	CIEL
ACID	ALBI	ARAK	AVOW	BASK	BIKE	BONE	BUDE	CARD	CIGS
ACIS	ALEC	ARAL	AWAY	BASS	BILE	BONG	BUDO	CARE	CILL
ACME	ALEW	ARAM	AWDL	BAST	BILK	BONK	BUFF	CARK	CINE
ACNE	ALEX	ARAN	AWED	BATE	BILL	BONN	BUFO	CARL	CION
ACOL	ALFA	ARAR	AWOL	BATH	BIMM	BONY	BUGS	CARP	CIRÉ
ACRE	ALGA	ARCH	AWRY	BATS	BIND	BOOB	BUHL	CARR	CIRL
ACRI	ALIA	ARCO	AXIL	BATT	BINE	BOOK	BUIK	CART	CIST
ACRO	ALIF	AREA	AXIS	BAUD	BING	BOOL	BUKE	CARY	CITE
ACTA	ALKY	AREG	AXLE	BAUK	BINK	BOOM	BULB	CASA	CITO
ACTS	ALLO	ARES	AXON	BAUR	BINT	BOON	BULK	CASE	CITS
ADAD	ALLY	ARET	AYAH	BAWD	BIRD	BOOR	BULL	CASH	CITY
ADAM	ALMA	AREW	AYER	BAWL	BIRK	BOOT	BUMF	CASK	CIVE
ADAR	ALMS	ARGO	AYES	BAWN	BIRL	BORA	BUMP	CAST	CLAD
ADAW	ALOD	ARIA	AYIN	BAWR	BIRO	BORD	BUNA	CATE	CLAG
ADEN	ALOE	ARID	AYMÉ	BAYE	BIRR	BORE	BUND	CATO	CLAM
ADES	ALOW	ARIL	AYRE	BAYS	BISE	BORN	BUNG	CATS	CLAN
ADIT	ALPH	ARIS	AZAN	BAYT	BISH	BORO	BUNK	CAUK	CLAP
ADUR	ALPS	ARLY	AZOV	BCOM	BISK	BORS	BUNT	CAUL	CLAT
ADZE	ALSO	ARMS	BAAL	BEAD	BISP	BOSH	BUOY	CAUM	CLAW
AEON	ALTA	ARMY	BAAS	BEAK	BITE	BOSS	BURD	CAUP	CLAY
AERO	ALTE	ARNA	BABA	BEAM	BITO	BOTE	BURG	CAVE	CLEF
AESC	ALTO	ARNE	BABE	BEAN	BITS	BOTH	BURK	CAVY	CLEG
AFAR	ALUM	ARNO	BABI	BEAR	BITT	BOTS	BURL	CAWK	CLEM
AFFY	ALVA	ARRU	BABU	BEAT	BLAB	BOTT	BURN	CCTV	CLEW
AFRO	AMAH	ARRY	BABY	BEAU	BLAD	BOUK	BURP	CEDE	CLIO
AGAG	AMBO	ARSE	BACA	BECK	BLAE	BOUN	BURR	CEDI	CLIP
AGAR	AMEN	ARTA	BACH	BEDE	BLAG	BOUT	BURT	CEIL	CLOD
AGED	AMES	ARTS	BACK	BEDS	BLAH	BOWL	BURY	CELL	CLOG
AGEE	AMID	ARTY	BADE	BEDU	BLAT	BOWR	BUSH	CELT	CLOP
AGEN	AMIE	ARUM	BAEL	BEEB	BLAY	BOYG	BUSK	CENS	CLOS
AGES	AMIN	ARUN	BAFF	BEEF	BLEB	BOYO	BUSS	CENT	CLOT
AGHA	AMIR	ARVO	BAFT	BEEN	BLED	BOYS	BUST	CERE	CLOU
AGIN	AMIS	ARYL	BAGS	BEEP	BLEE	BOZO	BUSY	CERO	CLOW
AGIO	AMLA	ASAP	BAHT	BEER	BLET	BRAD	BUTE	CERT	CLOY
AGIS	AMMO	ASAR	BAIL	BEES	BLEW	BRAE	BUTT	CESS	CLUB
AGLU	AMOK	ASAS	BAIT	BEET	BLEY	BRAG	BUZZ	CETE	CLUE
AGMA	AMOS	ASCH	BAJU	BEGO	BLIN	BRAK	BYKE	CEYX	COAL
AGNI	AMOY	ASHE	BAKE	BEIN	BLIP	BRAM	BYNG	CFAF	COAT
AGOG	AMUN	ASHY	BAKU	BELL	BLOB	BRAN	BYRD	CHAD	COAX
AGON	AMUR	ASIA	BALA	BELT	BLOC	BRAS	BYRE	CHAI	COBB
AGRA	AMYL	ASKE	BALD	BEMA	BLOT	BRAT	BYTE	CHAL	COBH
	ANAK	ASKR	BALE	BEND	BLOW	BRAW	CABA	CHAM	COCA

COCH	CRAG	DANK	DIAL	DOPA	DUNS	ELIA	EVAN	FELT	FLOE
COCK	CRAM	DARD	DIAS	DOPE	DUNT	ELIS	EVEN	FEME	FLOG
COCO	CRAN	DARE	DIAZ	DORA	DUPE	ELKS	EVER	FEND	FLOP
CODA	CRAP	DARG	DIBS	DORÉ	DURA	ELLA	EVET	FENI	FLOR
CODE	CRAW	DARI	DICE	DORM	DURE	ELLE	EVIL	FENT	FLOW
CODY	CRAX	DARK	DICH	DORP	DURN	ELMO	EVOE	FEOD	FLOX
COED	CRAY	DARN	DICK	DORR	DURO	ELOI	EWER	FERE	FLUB
COFF	CRED	DART	DICY	DORT	DUSE	ELSA	EWES	FERM	FLUE
COIF	CREE	DASH	DIDO	DORY	DUSH	ELSE	EXAM	FERN	FLUX
COIL	CREW	DATA	DIEB	DOSE	DUSK	ELUL	EXES	FEST	FOAL
COIN	CRIB	DATE	DIED	DOSH	DUST	EMEU	EXIT	FETA	FOAM
COIR	CRIT	DATO	DIES	DOSS	DUTY	EMIC	EXON	FETE	FOCH
COIT	CROP	DAUB	DIET	DOTE	DYAD	EMIR	EXOR	FETT	FOEN
COKE	CROW	DAUD	DIEU	DOTH	DYAK	EMIT	EXPO	FEUD	FOGG
COLA	CRUD	DAUR	DIGS	DOTS	DYER	EMMA	EXUL	FEZE	FOGY
COLD	CRUE	DAUT	DIKA	DOUC	DYKE	EMMY	EYAS	FIAT	FOIL
COLE	CRUX	DAWD	DIKE	DOUM	DYNE	EMYS	EYER	FICO	FOIN
COLL	CRYO	DAWK	DILL	DOUP	EACH	ENDS	EYES	FIDE	FOLD
COLT	CUBA	DAWN	DIMA	DOUR	EALE	ENEW	EYNE	FIDO	FOLK
COLY	CUBE	DAWT	DIME	DOUT	EARD	ENID	EYOT	FIEF	FOND
COMA	CUBS	DAYS	DINE	DOVE	EARL	ENNA	EYRA	FIFA	FONE
COMB	CUFF	DAZE	DING	DOWF	EARN	ENOL	EYRE	FIFE	FONS
COME	CUIF	DBLE	DINK	DOWN	EARP	ENOS	EYRY	FIGO	FONT
COMM	CUIT	DEAD	DINT	DOWT	EARS	ENOW	EZRA	FIJI	FOOD
COMO	CULL	DEAF	DIOL	DOXY	EASE	ENSI	FACE	FIKE	FOOL
COMP	CULM	DEAL	DIOR	DOZE	EAST	ENVY	FACT	FIKY	FOON
CONE	CULT	DEAN	DIRE	DOZY	EASY	EOAN	FADE	FILE	FOOT
CONK	CUMA	DEAR	DIRK	DRAB	EATS	EOKA	FADO	FILL	FORB
CONN	CUNT	DEAW	DIRL	DRAD	EBBW	EORL	FAFF	FILM	FORD
CONS	CUPS	DEBT	DIRT	DRAG	EBOR	EPEE	FAHD	FILO	FORE
CONT	CURB	DECA	DISA	DRAM	EBRO	EPHA	FAIL	FILS	FORK
CONY	CURD	DECK	DISC	DRAT	ECAD	EPIC	FAIN	FIND	FORM
COOF	CURE	DECO	DISH	DRAW	ECCE	EPOS	FAIR	FINE	FORT
COOK	CURK	DEED	DISK	DRAY	ECCO	ERAT	FAIX	FINK	FOSS
COOL	CURL	DEEK	DISS	DREE	ECHE	ERGO	FAKE	FINN	FOUD
COOM	CURN	DEEM	DITA	DREG	ECHO	ERIA	FALA	FINO	FOUG
COON	CURR	DEEN	DITE	DREW	ECHT	ERIC	FALL	FIRE	FOUL
COOP	CURT	DEEP	DITT	DREY	ECRU	ERIE	FALX	FIRK	FOUR
COOT	CUSH	DEER	DIVA	DRIB	EDAL	ERIK	FAME	FIRM	FOWL
COPE	CUSK	DEEV	DIVE	DRIP	EDAM	ERIN	FAND	FIRN	FOXY
COPS	CUSP	DEFT	DIXY	DROP	EDDA	ERIS	FANE	FISC	FOZY
COPY	CUSS	DEIL	DOAB	DROW	EDDO	ERNE	FANG	FISH	FRAB
CORD	CUTE	DEKE	DOAT	DRUB	EDDY	EROS	FANK	FISK	FRAE
CORE	CUYP	DELE	DOCK	DRUG	EDEN	ERSE	FANS	FIST	FRAG
CORF	CYAN	DELF	DODO	DRUM	EDER	ERTÉ	FARD	FITT	FRAP
CORK	CYMA	DELI	DOEK	DUAD	EDGE	ERYX	FARE	FITZ	FRAU
CORM	CYME	DELL	DOER	DUAL	EDGY	ESAU	FARM	FIVE	FRAY
CORN	CYST	DEME	DOES	DUAN	EDIT	ESKY	FARO	FIZZ	FREE
CORY	CYTE	DEMI	DOFF	DUAR	EDOM	ESLA	FARR	FLAB	FRET
COSE	CZAR	DEMO	DOGE	DUBS	EECH	ESME	FART	FLAG	FRIG
COSH	DABS	DEMY	DOGS	DUCE	EELS	ESNE	FASH	FLAK	FRIT
COSS	DACE	DENE	DOGY	DUCK	EFIK	ESPY	FASO	FLAM	FROE
COST	DADA	DENT	DOHA	DUCT	EGAD	ESSE	FAST	FLAN	FROG
COSY	DADD	DENY	DOIT	DUDE	EGAL	ESTE	FATE	FLAP	FROM
COTE	DADO	DEPT	DOJO	DUDS	EGER	ESTH	FATS	FLAT	FROW
COTH	DAFF	DERE	DOLE	DUEL	EGGS	ETCH	FAUN	FLAW	FUEL
COTT	DAFT	DERM	DOLL	DUES	EGIS	ETEN	FAWN	FLAX	FUFF
COTY	DAGO	DERN	DOLT	DUET	EGMA	ETHE	FAZE	FLAY	FUJI
COUE	DAHL	DERO	DOME	DUFF	EHEU	ETIC	FEAL	FLEA	FULA
COUP	DAIL	DERV	DONA	DUKE	EIGG	ETNA	FEAR	FLED	FULL
COUR	DAIS	DESK	DONE	DULE	EILD	ETON	FEAT	FLEE	FUME
COVE	DAKS	DEVA	DONG	DULL	EINE	ETTA	FECK	FLEG	FUND
COWL	DALE	DEVI	DONT	DULY	EIRE	ETTY	FEED	FLEW	FUNG
COWP	DALI	DEWY	DOOB	DUMA	EKKA	ETUI	FEEL	FLEX	FUNK
COWS	DAME	DHAK	DOOK	DUMB	ELAM	EUGE	FEER	FLEY	FUNS
COZE	DAMN	DHAL	DOOL	DUMP	ELAN	EUGH	FEET	FLIC	FURL
COZY	DAMP	DHOW	DOOM	DUNE	ELAT	EUOI	FEGS	FLIP	FURR
CPRS	DANE		DOON	DUNG	ELBA	EURE	FEIS	FLIT	FURY
CRAB	DANG		DOOR	DUNK	ELBE	EURO	FELL	FLIX	FUSE

FUSS	GENS	GOEY	GULL	HARZ	HING	HUME	IOTA	JINX	KANT
FUST	GENT	GOFF	GULP	HASE	HINT	HUMF	IOWA	JIRD	KAON
FUZE	GENU	GOGO	GUMP	HASH	HIPT	HUMP	IPOH	JISM	KAPH
FUZZ	GERE	GOLD	GUNK	HASK	HIRE	HUNG	IPSE	JIZZ	KARA
FYKE	GERM	GOLE	GUNN	HASP	HISH	HUNK	IRAN	JOAN	KARD
FYRD	GEST	GOLF	GUNS	HATE	HISS	HUNT	IRAQ	JOBE	KARL
GABY	GETA	GONE	GUNZ	HATH	HIST	HUON	IRAS	JOCK	KART
GADE	GETT	GONG	GURL	HAUD	HIVE	HURL	IRID	JOCO	KATA
GADI	GEUM	GONK	GURN	HAUL	HMSO	HURT	IRIS	JODO	KATE
GAEA	GHAN	GOOD	GURU	HAUT	HOAR	HUSH	IRON	JOEL	KATI
GAEL	GHAT	GOOF	GUSH	HAVE	HOAX	HUSK	IRUS	JOEY	KAVA
GAFF	GHEE	GOOG	GUST	HAWK	HOBO	HUSO	ISAR	JOHN	KAYO
GAGA	GIBE	GOOK	GUTS	HAWM	HOCK	HUSS	ISER	JOIN	KEAN
GAGE	GIDE	GOOL	GUYS	HAZE	HOGG	HUTU	ISIS	JOKE	KECK
GAIA	GIER	GOON	GWYN	HAZY	HOGH	HWYL	ISLE	JOLE	KEEK
GAID	GIFT	GOOP	GYAL	HEAD	HOKE	HYDE	ISMY	JOLL	KEEL
GAIN	GIGA	GOOR	GYBE	HEAL	HOKI	HYKE	ISNT	JOLO	KEEN
GAIR	GIGI	GORE	GYMP	HEAP	HOLD	HYLA	ITCH	JOLT	KEEP
GAIT	GILA	GORM	GYNT	HEAR	HOLE	HYLE	ITEM	JOMO	KEIR
GAJO	GILD	GORP	GYRE	HEAT	HOLI	HYMN	ITYS	JOOK	KELL
GALA	GILL	GORY	GYRO	HEBE	HOLM	HYPE	IVAN	JOSE	KELP
GALE	GILT	GOSH	GYTE	HECH	HOLT	HYPO	IVES	JOSH	KELT
GALL	GIMP	GOSS	GYVE	HECK	HOLY	IAGO	IVOR	JOSS	KEMB
GAMB	GING	GOTA	HAAF	HECT	HOMA	IAMB	IVRY	JOTA	KEMP
GAME	GINK	GOTH	HAAL	HEED	HOME	IBEX	IWIS	JOUK	KENO
GAMP	GIRD	GOUK	HAAR	HEEL	HOMO	IBID	IYAR	JOVE	KENT
GAMY	GIRL	GOUT	HABU	HEEP	HOND	IBIS	IYNX	JOWL	KEPI
GANG	GIRN	GOWF	HACK	HEFT	HONE	ICED	IZAR	JUAN	KEPT
GANT	GIRO	GOWK	HADE	HEIL	HONG	ICEL	JAAP	JUBA	KERB
GAOL	GIRR	GOWL	HADJ	HEIR	HONI	ICKY	JACK	JUBE	KERF
GAPE	GIRT	GOWN	HAEM	HELA	HONK	ICON	JADE	JUDE	KERN
GAPO	GISM	GOYA	HAET	HELD	HOOD	IDEA	JAGG	JUDO	KESH
GARB	GIST	GRAB	HAFF	HELE	HOOF	IDÉE	JAGS	JUDY	KEST
GARE	GITE	GRAD	HAFT	HELL	HOOK	IDEM	JAIL	JUJU	KETA
GART	GIVE	GRAF	HAGG	HELM	HOON	IDES	JAIN	JUKE	KEYS
GARY	GIZZ	GRAM	HAGH	HELO	HOOP	IDLE	JAKE	JULY	KHAN
GASH	GLAD	GRAN	HAHA	HELP	HOOT	IDLY	JAMB	JUMA	KHAT
GASP	GLAM	GRAS	HAIG	HEME	HOPE	IDOL	JANE	JUMP	KHOR
GAST	GLEE	GRAT	HAIK	HEMI	HOPI	IFFY	JANN	JUNE	KHUD
GATE	GLEG	GRAV	HAIL	HEMP	HOPS	IFOR	JAPE	JUNG	KIBE
GATH	GLEI	GRAY	HAIN	HEND	HORE	IGAD	JARK	JUNK	KICK
GATT	GLEN	GREE	HAIR	HENT	HORN	IGBO	JARL	JUNO	KIDD
GAUD	GLEY	GREW	HAIT	HEPT	HORS	IGOR	JARP	JURA	KIEL
GAUL	GLIA	GREY	HAKA	HERA	HOSE	IKAT	JASS	JURE	KIER
GAUM	GLIB	GRID	HAKE	HERB	HOSS	IKON	JATO	JURY	KIEV
GAUP	GLID	GRIG	HALE	HERD	HOST	ILEX	JAUP	JUST	KIKE
GAUR	GLIM	GRIM	HALF	HERE	HOTE	ILIA	JAVA	JUTE	KILL
GAVE	GLIT	GRIN	HALL	HERL	HOUR	ILKA	JAWI	JYNX	KILN
GAWD	GLOB	GRIP	HALM	HERM	HOUT	ILLE	JAWS	KADE	KILO
GAWK	GLOM	GRIS	HALO	HERN	HOVA	ILLY	JAZZ	KADI	KILP
GAWP	GLOP	GRIT	HALS	HERO	HOVE	IMAM	JEAT	KAGO	KILT
GAZA	GLOW	GROG	HALT	HERR	HOWE	IMPI	JEEL	KAID	KINA
GAZE	GLUE	GROT	HAME	HERS	HOWK	INBY	JEEP	KAIE	KIND
GCSE	GLUM	GROW	HAMS	HERY	HOWL	INCA	JEER	KAIF	KINE
GDAY	GLUT	GRUB	HAND	HERZ	HOYA	INCH	JEFF	KAIL	KING
GEAL	GNAR	GRUE	HANG	HESP	HUCK	INDY	JEHU	KAIM	KINK
GEAN	GNAT	GRUG	HANK	HESS	HUER	INES	JELL	KAIN	KINO
GEAR	GNAW	GRUM	HANS	HEST	HUEY	INFO	JENA	KAKI	KIPE
GEAT	GOAD	GRUS	HANT	HETE	HUFF	INGE	JERK	KALE	KIPP
GECK	GOAF	GSOH	HAPI	HETH	HUGE	INGO	JESS	KALI	KIRI
GEED	GOAL	GUAM	HARD	HICK	HUGH	INKY	JEST	KAMA	KIRK
GEEK	GOAT	GUAN	HARE	HIDE	HUGO	INLY	JETÉ	KAME	KIRN
GEEP	GOBI	GUAR	HARK	HIGH	HUHU	INNS	JEWS	KAMI	KISH
GEEZ	GOBO	GUFF	HARL	HIKE	HUIA	INRI	JIAO	KANA	KISS
GEIT	GOBY	GUGA	HARM	HILL	HULA	INRO	JIBE	KANE	KIST
GELD	GODS	GUID	HARN	HILO	HULE	INST	JILL	KANG	KITE
GELT	GOEL	GULA	HARO	HILT	HULK	INTI	JILT	KANO	KITH
GEMS	GOER	GULE	HARP	HINC	HULL	INTO	JIMP	KANS	KIVA
GENE	GOES	GULF	HART	HIND	HUMA	IONA	JINK		KIWI

KLAN	LAMP	LIAS	LOLA	LYLE	MATT	MING	MOUE	NAZI	NOPE
KLEE	LANA	LIBS	LOLL	LYLY	MATY	MINI	MOUL	NEAL	NORE
KNAG	LAND	LICE	LOMA	LYME	MAUD	MINK	MOUP	NEAP	NORI
KNAP	LANE	LICH	LOME	LYNX	MAUL	MINO	MOVE	NEAR	NORK
KNAR	LANG	LICK	LONE	LYON	MAUT	MINT	MOVY	NEAT	NORM
KNEE	LANK	LIDE	LONG	LYRA	MAWK	MINX	MOWA	NEBO	NORN
KNEW	LANT	LIDO	LOOF	LYRE	MAWR	MIRA	MOXA	NECK	NOSE
KNIT	LANX	LIED	LOOK	LYSE	MAXI	MIRE	MOYA	NEED	NOSH
KNOB	LAON	LIEF	LOOM	LYTE	MAYA	MIRK	MOYL	NEEM	NOSY
KNOP	LAOS	LIEN	LOON	MAAM	MAYO	MIRO	MOZE	NEEP	NOTE
KNOT	LAPP	LIES	LOOP	MAAR	MAZE	MIRV	MOZZ	NEIF	NOTT
KNOW	LARD	LIEU	LOOR	MAAS	MEAD	MISC	MUCH	NEIL	NOUN
KNOX	LARE	LIFE	LOOS	MAAT	MEAL	MISE	MUCK	NELL	NOUP
KNUB	LARK	LIFT	LOOT	MACE	MEAN	MISO	MUFF	NEMO	NOUS
KNUR	LARN	LIKE	LOPE	MACH	MEAT	MISS	MUID	NENE	NOUT
KNUT	LASH	LILL	LORD	MACK	MEDE	MIST	MUIL	NEON	NOVA
KOAN	LASS	LILO	LORE	MADE	MEED	MITE	MUIR	NERD	NOVO
KOBE	LAST	LILT	LORI	MAGE	MEEK	MITT	MULE	NERK	NOWL
KOBO	LATE	LILY	LORN	MAGG	MEER	MOAN	MULL	NERO	NOWT
KOEL	LATH	LIMA	LORY	MAGI	MEET	MOAT	MUMP	NESH	NOWY
KOFF	LATS	LIMB	LOSE	MAHU	MEGA	MOBY	MUNG	NESS	NUDD
KOHL	LAUD	LIME	LOSH	MAIA	MEIN	MOCH	MUON	NEST	NUDE
KOKO	LAUF	LIMN	LOSS	MAID	MEIR	MOCK	MURE	NETE	NUER
KOLA	LAVA	LIMO	LOST	MAIK	MELA	MODE	MURK	NETS	NUKE
KOLO	LAVE	LIMP	LOTE	MAIL	MELD	MODO	MURL	NETT	NULL
KOND	LAWN	LIMY	LOTH	MAIM	MELL	MODS	MUSA	NEUK	NUMA
KONG	LAZE	LIND	LOTI	MAIN	MELT	MOHR	MUSE	NEVA	NUMB
KONK	LAZY	LINE	LOTO	MAKE	MEMO	MOHS	MUSH	NEVE	NUNC
KOOK	LEAD	LING	LOTS	MAKO	MEND	MOIL	MUSK	NEWS	NURD
KORA	LEAF	LINK	LOUD	MALE	MENE	MOIT	MUSO	NEWT	NURL
KORE	LEAK	LINN	LOUP	MALI	MENG	MOJO	MUSS	NEXT	NURR
KOSS	LEAL	LINO	LOUR	MALL	MENT	MOKE	MUST	NIBS	NUTS
KOTO	LEAM	LINT	LOUT	MALM	MENU	MOKI	MUTE	NICE	NUUK
KRAB	LEAN	LION	LOVE	MALO	MEOW	MOKO	MUTI	NICK	NYAS
KRIS	LEAP	LIPS	LOWE	MALT	MERE	MOLA	MUTT	NIDE	NYET
KROO	LEAR	LIRA	LOZI	MAMA	MERI	MOLD	MYAL	NIEF	NYOS
KSAR	LEAT	LIRK	LUAU	MAME	MERK	MOLE	MYTH	NIFE	OAHU
KUDU	LECH	LISA	LUBA	MANA	MERL	MOLL	MZEE	NIFF	OAKS
KUKU	LEDA	LISK	LUCE	MANE	MERU	MOLT	NAAM	NIGH	OAKY
KUNA	LEEK	LISP	LUCK	MANG	MESA	MOLY	NAAN	NIKE	OARS
KURD	LEEP	LIST	LUCY	MANI	MESE	MOME	NABK	NILE	OAST
KURI	LEER	LITE	LUDD	MANN	MESH	MONA	NADA	NILL	OATH
KURU	LEES	LITH	LUDO	MANO	MESO	MONG	NAFF	NINA	OATS
KWAI	LEET	LIVE	LUES	MANS	MESS	MONK	NAGA	NINE	OBAN
KWIC	LEFT	LIVY	LUEZ	MANU	META	MONO	NAIA	NINO	OBEY
KYAT	LEGO	LIZA	LUFF	MANX	METE	MONS	NAIK	NIPA	OBIA
KYLE	LEGS	LLYR	LUGE	MANY	MEVE	MONY	NAIL	NIRL	OBIT
KYPE	LEHR	LNER	LUGH	MAPS	MEWL	MOOD	NAIN	NISI	OBOE
KYTE	LEIR	LOAD	LUGS	MARA	MEWS	MOOG	NAIR	NITH	OBOL
LACE	LELY	LOAF	LUIT	MARC	MEZE	MOOI	NAJA	NIXY	OCHE
LACK	LEME	LOAM	LUKE	MARE	MICA	MOOL	NALA	NKVD	OCTA
LACY	LEND	LOAN	LULL	MARG	MICE	MOON	NAME	NOAH	ODAL
LADA	LENG	LOBE	LULU	MARI	MICK	MOOP	NANA	NOCK	ODDS
LADE	LENO	LOBO	LUMP	MARK	MICO	MOOR	NAND	NODE	ODER
LADY	LENS	LOCH	LUNA	MARL	MIDI	MOOT	NANO	NOEL	ODIN
LAER	LENT	LOCK	LUNE	MARM	MIEN	MOPE	NAOS	NOES	ODOR
LAHN	LERP	LOCO	LUNG	MARO	MIFF	MOPP	NAPE	NOGO	ODSO
LAIC	LESS	LODE	LUNT	MARS	MIKE	MORE	NARC	NOIL	ODYL
LAID	LEST	LOFT	LURE	MART	MILD	MORI	NARD	NOLE	OETA
LAIK	LETO	LOGE	LURK	MARY	MILE	MORN	NARE	NOLL	OFAY
LAIN	LETS	LOGO	LUSH	MASA	MILK	MORO	NARK	NOLO	OFFA
LAIR	LETT	LOGS	LUSK	MASE	MILL	MORS	NARY	NOMA	OGAM
LAIS	LEVA	LOGY	LUST	MASH	MILO	MORT	NASA	NOME	OGEE
LAKE	LEVE	LOID	LUTE	MASK	MILT	MOSS	NASH	NONE	OGEN
LAKH	LEVI	LOIN	LUTZ	MASS	MIME	MOST	NASO	NONG	OGLE
LALO	LEVY	LOIR	LUXE	MAST	MIMI	MOTE	NATO	NONO	OGPU
LAMA	LEWD	LOIS	LWEI	MASU	MINA	MOTH	NAVE	NOOK	OGRE
LAMB	LIAM	LOKE	LYAM	MATE	MIND	MOTT	NAVY	NOON	OHIO
LAME	LIAR	LOKI	LYCH	MATH	MINE	MOTU	NAZE	NOOP	OILS

OILY	OUCH	PAVO	PIMP	POOD	PUNA	RAPE	RIEL	ROSS	SALK
OINK	OUDS	PAWA	PINA	POOF	PUNG	RAPT	RIEM	ROSY	SALP
OINT	OULK	PAWK	PINE	POOH	PUNK	RARE	RIFE	ROTA	SALT
OISE	OUMA	PAWL	PING	POOK	PUNT	RASC	RIFF	ROTE	SAMA
OKAY	OUPA	PAWN	PINK	POOL	PUNY	RASE	RIFT	ROTI	SAME
OKRA	OUPH	PAYE	PINS	POON	PUPA	RASH	RIGA	ROTL	SAMI
OKRO	OURS	PEAG	PINT	POOP	PURE	RASP	RIGG	ROUD	SAMP
OKTA	OUST	PEAK	PION	POOR	PURI	RAST	RIGI	ROUÉ	SAND
OLAF	OUZO	PEAL	PIPA	POOT	PURL	RATA	RILE	ROUL	SANE
OLDS	OVAL	PEAN	PIPE	POPE	PURR	RATE	RILL	ROUM	SANG
OLEA	OVEL	PEAR	PIPI	PORE	PUSH	RATH	RIMA	ROUP	SANK
OLEO	OVEN	PEAS	PIRL	PORK	PUSS	RATS	RIME	ROUT	SANS
OLID	OVER	PEAT	PIRN	PORN	PUTT	RATU	RIMU	ROUX	SANT
OLIM	OVID	PEBA	PIRO	PORT	PUTZ	RAUN	RIND	ROVE	SARD
OLIO	OVRA	PECH	PISE	POSE	PYAT	RAVE	RINE	ROWE	SARI
OLLA	OVUM	PECK	PISH	POSH	PYET	RAWN	RING	ROWT	SARK
OLPE	OWED	PEDI	PISO	POSS	PYOT	RAYS	RINK	RSVP	SASA
OMAN	OWEN	PEEK	PISS	POST	PYRE	RAZE	RINT	RUBE	SASH
OMAR	OWLS	PEEL	PITA	POSY	PYRO	RAZZ	RIOT	RUBY	SASS
OMBU	OWLY	PEEN	PITH	POTE	QADI	READ	RIPE	RUCK	SATE
OMEN	OWNS	PEEP	PITT	POTS	QING	REAK	RIPP	RUDD	SATI
OMER	OWRE	PEER	PITY	POTT	QOPH	REAL	RIPS	RUDE	SATS
OMIT	OXEN	PEGH	PIUM	POUF	QUAD	REAM	RISE	RUFF	SAUK
OMNI	OXER	PEIN	PIUS	POUK	QUAG	REAN	RISK	RUGA	SAUL
ONCE	OXON	PEKE	PIXY	POUR	QUAT	REAP	RISP	RUHR	SAUT
ONER	OXUS	PELA	PIZE	POUT	QUAY	REAR	RISS	RUIN	SAVE
ONE'S	OYER	PELE	PLAN	POWN	QUEP	RECD	RITA	RUKH	SAWN
ONGO	OYEZ	PELF	PLAP	POXY	QUEY	RECK	RITE	RULE	SAXE
ONLY	PAAL	PELL	PLAT	PRAD	QUID	REDD	RITT	RULY	SAYE
ONST	PACA	PELT	PLAY	PRAM	QUIM	REDE	RITZ	RUME	SCAB
ONTO	PACE	PEND	PLEA	PRAT	QUIN	REDO	RIVA	RUMI	SCAD
ONUS	PACK	PENE	PLEB	PRAU	QUIP	REED	RIVE	RUMP	SCAG
ONYX	PACO	PENH	PLED	PRAY	QUIT	REEF	RIVO	RUND	SCAM
OONS	PACT	PENI	PLEW	PREE	QUIZ	REEK	RIZA	RUNE	SCAN
OONT	PAGE	PENK	PLIÉ	PREP	QUOD	REEL	ROAD	RUNG	SCAR
OOPS	PAID	PENN	PLIM	PREY	QUOP	REEN	ROAM	RUNS	SCAT
OORT	PAIK	PENT	PLOD	PRIG	RABI	REFT	ROAN	RUNT	SCAW
OOSE	PAIL	PEON	PLOP	PRIM	RACA	REIF	ROAR	RURP	SCOG
OOZE	PAIN	PEPO	PLOT	PRIX	RACE	REIK	ROBE	RURU	SCOP
OOZY	PAIR	PÈRE	PLOW	PROA	RACK	REIN	ROCA	RUSA	SCOT
OPAH	PAIS	PERI	PLOY	PROD	RACY	REIS	ROCH	RUSE	SCOW
OPAL	PALE	PERK	PLUE	PROF	RADA	REJA	ROCK	RUSH	SCRY
OPEC	PALI	PERM	PLUG	PROG	RAFF	REKE	RODE	RUSK	SCUD
OPEL	PALK	PERN	PLUM	PROM	RAFT	RELY	ROIL	RUST	SCUG
OPEN	PALL	PERT	PLUS	PROO	RAGA	REME	ROIN	RUTA	SCUL
OPIE	PALM	PERU	PNYX	PROP	RAGE	REMS	ROJI	RUTE	SCUM
OPPO	PALP	PESO	POCK	PROW	RAGG	REND	ROKE	RUTH	SCUR
OPUS	PAND	PEST	PODS	PRUH	RAGI	RENE	ROLE	RYAL	SCUT
ORAL	PANE	PHEW	POEM	PSBR	RAGS	RENO	ROLF	RYAN	SCYE
ORAN	PANG	PHIL	POET	PTAH	RAHU	RENT	ROLL	RYFE	SEAL
ORBY	PANT	PHIZ	POGO	PUCA	RAID	RENY	ROME	RYND	SEAM
ORCA	PAPA	PHOH	POKE	PUCE	RAIK	REPP	ROMP	RYOT	SEAN
ORFE	PARA	PHOT	POKY	PUCK	RAIL	REPS	RONE	RYVE	SEAR
ORFF	PARD	PHUT	POLE	PUDU	RAIN	RESH	RONG	SABA	SEAS
ORGE	PARE	PIAF	POLK	PUER	RAIT	REST	RONT	SACK	SEAT
ORGY	PARK	PICA	POLL	PUFF	RAKE	RETE	ROOD	SADE	SECH
ORLE	PARP	PICE	POLO	PUGH	RAKI	RETT	ROOF	SAFE	SECT
ORLY	PARR	PICK	POLT	PUJA	RAKU	REVD	ROOK	SAGA	SEED
ORNE	PART	PICT	POLY	PULA	RAKY	RHEA	ROOM	SAGE	SEEK
ORRA	PASE	PIED	POME	PULE	RALE	RHUS	ROON	SAGO	SEEL
ORTS	PASH	PIER	POMO	PULI	RAMA	RHYS	ROOP	SAIC	SEEM
ORYX	PASS	PIES	POMP	PULK	RAMI	RIAL	ROOT	SAID	SEEN
OSLO	PAST	PIET	POND	PULL	RAMP	RIBS	ROPE	SAIL	SEEP
OSSA	PATE	PIGS	PONE	PULP	RANA	RICA	ROPY	SAIM	SEER
OTHO	PATH	PIKA	PONG	PULU	RAND	RICE	RORE	SAIN	SEGO
OTIC	PATU	PIKE	PONK	PULY	RANG	RICH	RORO	SAIR	SEIF
OTIS	PAUA	PILE	PONS	PUMA	RANI	RICK	RORT	SAKE	SEIL
OTTO	PAUL	PILI	PONT	PUMP	RANK	RICO	RORY	SAKI	SEIR
OTUS	PAVE	PILL	PONY	PUMY	RANT	RIDE	ROSE	SALE	SEJM

SEKT	SIGN	SLIM	SORD	STYX	TAKE	TETE	TOFT	TRIP	ULNA
SELE	SIJO	SLIP	SORE	SUCH	TALA	TETH	TOFU	TROD	UMBO
SELF	SIKA	SLIT	SORN	SUCK	TALC	TEXT	TOGA	TROG	UMPH
SELL	SIKE	SLOB	SORT	SUDD	TALE	THAE	TOGE	TRON	UNAU
SEMI	SIKH	SLOE	SOSS	SUDS	TALK	THAI	TOGO	TROP	UNBE
SENA	SILA	SLOG	SOUK	SUER	TALL	THAN	TOGS	TROT	UNCE
SEND	SILD	SLOP	SOUL	SUET	TAME	THAR	TOHO	TROU	UNCO
SENS	SILE	SLOT	SOUM	SUEY	TAMP	THAT	TOIL	TROW	UNDE
SENT	SILK	SLOW	SOUP	SUEZ	TANA	THAW	TOJO	TROY	UNDO
SEPS	SILL	SLUB	SOUR	SUFI	TANE	THEA	TOKE	TRUE	UNIO
SEPT	SILO	SLUE	SOWM	SUIT	TANG	THEE	TOKO	TRUG	UNIT
SERA	SILT	SLUG	SOWP	SULK	TANH	THEM	TOLA	TRYE	UNTO
SERB	SIMA	SLUM	SOYA	SULU	TANK	THEN	TOLD	TSAR	UPAS
SERE	SIMI	SLUR	SPAE	SUMO	TAPA	THEW	TOLE	TSHI	UPGO
SERF	SIMP	SLUT	SPAG	SUMP	TAPE	THEY	TOLL	TUAN	UPON
SERK	SIND	SMEE	SPAM	SUMS	TAPS	THIN	TOLT	TUBA	UPSY
SESE	SINE	SMEW	SPAN	SUNG	TAPU	THIR	TOLU	TUBE	URAL
SESS	SING	SMIT	SPAR	SUNK	TARA	THIS	TOMB	TUCK	URAO
SETA	SINK	SMOG	SPAT	SUNN	TARE	THON	TOME	TUES	URDÉ
SETT	SINO	SMUG	SPAW	SURA	TARN	THOR	TONE	TUFA	URDU
SEUL	SION	SMUR	SPAY	SURD	TARO	THOS	TONG	TUFF	URDY
SEVE	SIPE	SMUT	SPEC	SURE	TART	THOU	TONK	TUFT	UREA
SEWN	SIRE	SNAG	SPED	SURF	TASH	THRU	TONS	TULE	URGE
SEXT	SIRI	SNAP	SPEE	SUSA	TASK	THUD	TONY	TULI	URIC
SEXY	SISS	SNEB	SPET	SUSS	TASS	THUG	TOOK	TULL	URIM
SHAD	SIST	SNED	SPEW	SUSU	TATA	THUN	TOOL	TUMP	URSA
SHAG	SITE	SNEE	SPEY	SUVA	TATE	THUS	TOOM	TUMS	URUS
SHAH	SITU	SNIB	SPIC	SWAB	TATH	TICE	TOON	TUNA	URVA
SHAM	SIUM	SNIG	SPIF	SWAD	TATI	TICH	TOOT	TUND	USAK
SHAN	SIVA	SNIP	SPIK	SWAG	TATT	TICK	TOPE	TUNE	USED
SHAP	SIZE	SNIT	SPIN	SWAM	TATU	TIDE	TOPI	TUNG	USER
SHAW	SKAG	SNOB	SPIT	SWAN	TAUT	TIDY	TOPS	TUPI	USES
SHAY	SKAT	SNOD	SPIV	SWAP	TAWA	TIED	TORC	TURD	USSR
SHEA	SKAW	SNOG	SPOT	SWAT	TAWS	TIER	TORE	TURF	UTAH
SHED	SKED	SNOT	SPRY	SWAY	TAWT	TIFF	TORN	TURK	UTAS
SHEM	SKEG	SNOW	SPUD	SWEE	TAXA	TIFT	TORR	TURM	UTIS
SHET	SKEN	SNUB	SPUE	SWEY	TAXI	TIGE	TORT	TURN	UVEA
SHIA	SKEO	SNUG	SPUN	SWIG	TEAK	TIKA	TORY	TUSH	VAAL
SHIE	SKEP	SNYE	SPUR	SWIM	TEAL	TIKE	TOSA	TUSK	VACH
SHIM	SKER	SOAK	STAB	SWIZ	TEAM	TIKI	TOSE	TUTU	VADE
SHIN	SKET	SOAP	STAG	SWOB	TEAN	TILE	TOSH	TUZZ	VAIL
SHIP	SKEW	SOAR	STAN	SWOP	TEAR	TILL	TOSS	TWAE	VAIN
SHIT	SKIA	SOAY	STAP	SWOT	TEAT	TILT	TOST	TWAL	VAIR
SHIV	SKID	SOCA	STAR	SWUM	TECH	TIME	TOTE	TWAT	VALE
SHOA	SKIM	SOCK	STAT	SYCE	TEDY	TINA	TOTO	TWAY	VALI
SHOD	SKIN	SODA	STAW	SYEN	TEEM	TIND	TOUK	TWEE	VAMP
SHOE	SKIO	SOFA	STAY	SYKE	TEEN	TINE	TOUN	TWIG	VANE
SHOG	SKIP	SOFI	STED	SYNC	TEER	TING	TOUR	TWIN	VANG
SHOO	SKIT	SOFT	STEM	SYND	TEES	TINK	TOUT	TWIT	VARA
SHOP	SKOL	SOHO	STEN	SYNE	TEFF	TINT	TOVE	TYKE	VARE
SHOT	SKRY	SOIL	STEP	SYPE	TEGG	TINY	TOWN	TYMP	VARY
SHOW	SKUA	SOJA	STET	TAAL	TEHR	TIPI	TOWT	TYNE	VASE
SHRI	SKUG	SOLA	STEW	TABI	TEIL	TIPU	TOYS	TYPE	VAST
SHUL	SKYE	SOLD	STEY	TABU	TELA	TIRE	TOZE	TYPO	VATU
SHUN	SKYR	SOLE	STIE	TACE	TELE	TIRL	TRAD	TYRE	VAUD
SHUT	SLAB	SOLO	STIM	TACH	TELL	TIRO	TRAM	TYRO	VAUT
SHWA	SLAE	SOMA	STIR	TACK	TEME	TIRR	TRAP	TYTE	VAYU
SIAL	SLAG	SOME	STOA	TACO	TEMP	TITE	TRAY	TZAR	VEAL
SIAM	SLAM	SONE	STOB	TACT	TEND	TITI	TREE	UBER	VEDA
SIAN	SLAP	SONG	STOL	TAEL	TENE	TITO	TREK	UCCA	VEEP
SIBB	SLAT	SOOK	STOP	TAFF	TENG	TOAD	TRET	UDAD	VEER
SICE	SLAV	SOOL	STOT	TAFT	TENT	TOBY	TREW	UDAL	VEGA
SICH	SLAW	SOOM	STOW	TAHA	TERA	TOCO	TREY	UFFA	VEHM
SICK	SLAY	SOON	STUB	TAHR	TERF	TODD	TREZ	UGLI	VEIL
SIDA	SLED	SOOP	STUD	TAIG	TERM	TODO	TRIE	UGLY	VEIN
SIDE	SLEE	SOOT	STUM	TAIL	TERN	TODY	TRIG	UIST	VELA
SIEN	SLEW	SOPH	STUN	TAIN	TERR	TOEA	TRIM	ULAD	VELE
SIFT	SLEY	SORA	STUR	TAIT	TESS	TOEY	TRIN	ULAN	VELL
SIGH	SLID	SORB	STYE	TAKA	TEST	TOFF	TRIO	ULEX	VENA

VEND	WAND	WHIN	XEMA	YORE	BABI	CAGE	DARI	GAFF	HALS
VENN	WANE	WHIP	XERO	YORK	BABU	CAIN	DARK	GAGA	HALT
VENT	WANG	WHIR	XIAN	YOUD	BABY	CAKE	DARN	GAGE	HAME
VERA	WANK	WHIT	XMAS	YOUK	BACA	CALC	DART	GAIA	HAMS
VERB	WANT	WHIZ	XOSA	YOUR	BACH	CALF	DASH	GAID	HAND
VERS	WARB	WHOA	XYST	YOWE	BACK	CALK	DATA	GAIN	HANG
VERT	WARD	WHOM	YACK	YOWL	BADE	CALL	DATE	GAIR	HANK
VERY	WARE	WHOP	YAFF	YOYO	BAEL	CALM	DATO	GAIT	HANS
VEST	WARK	WHOT	YAGI	YUAN	BAFF	CALP	DAUB	GAJO	HANT
VETO	WARM	WICE	YALE	YUCA	BAFT	CALX	DAUD	GALA	HAPI
VETS	WARN	WICK	YALU	YUCK	BAGS	CAMA	DAUR	GALE	HARD
VIAL	WARP	WIDE	YAMA	YUEN	BAHT	CAME	DAUT	GALL	HARE
VIBS	WART	WIEL	YANG	YUFT	BAIL	CAMP	DAVY	GAMB	HARK
VICE	WARY	WIEN	YANK	YUGA	BAIT	CANA	DAWD	GAME	HARL
VIDE	WASE	WIFE	YAPP	YUKE	BAJU	CANE	DAWK	GAMP	HARM
VIED	WASH	WILD	YARD	YUKO	BAKE	CANN	DAWN	GAMY	HARN
VIES	WASP	WILE	YARE	YULE	BAKU	CANS	DAWT	GANG	HARO
VIEW	WAST	WILI	YARN	YUMP	BALA	CANT	DAYS	GANT	HARP
VIGO	WATE	WILL	YARR	YUNX	BALD	CAPA	DAZE	GAOL	HART
VILE	WATT	WILT	YATE	YWIS	BALE	CAPE	EACH	GAPE	HARZ
VILL	WAUL	WILY	YAUD	ZACK	BALI	CAPH	EALE	GAPO	HASE
VIMY	WAUR	WIMP	YAUP	ZAMA	BALK	CAPO	EARD	GARB	HASH
VINA	WAVE	WIND	YAWL	ZANY	BALL	CAPT	EARL	GARE	HASK
VINE	WAVY	WINE	YAWN	ZARF	BALM	CARD	EARN	GART	HASP
VINO	WAWA	WING	YAWP	ZATI	BALT	CARE	EARP	GARY	HATE
VINT	WAWL	WINK	YAWS	ZBUD	BALU	CARK	EARS	GASH	HATH
VIOL	WAXY	WINN	YAWY	ZEAL	BANC	CARL	EASE	GASP	HAUD
VIRL	WAYS	WINO	YBET	ZEBU	BAND	CARP	EAST	GAST	HAUL
VISA	WEAK	WIPE	YEAD	ZEIN	BANE	CARR	EASY	GATE	HAUT
VISE	WEAL	WIRE	YEAH	ZENO	BANG	CART	EATS	GATH	HAVE
VITA	WEAN	WIRY	YEAR	ZERO	BANI	CARY	FACE	GATT	HAWK
VITE	WEAR	WISE	YEDE	ZEST	BANK	CASA	FACT	GAUD	HAWM
VIVA	WEBB	WISH	YEED	ZETA	BANT	CASE	FADE	GAUL	HAZE
VIVE	WEED	WISP	YEGG	ZEUS	BAPU	CASH	FADO	GAUM	HAZY
VIVO	WEEK	WIST	YELD	ZEZE	BARB	CASK	FAFF	GAUP	IAGO
VLEI	WEEL	WITE	YELL	ZIFF	BARD	CAST	FAHD	GAUR	IAMB
VOAR	WEEM	WITH	YELP	ZILA	BARE	CATE	FAIL	GAVE	JAAP
VOCE	WEEN	WITS	YELT	ZIMB	BARF	CATO	FAIN	GAWD	JACK
VOID	WEEP	WIVE	YERK	ZINC	BARI	CATS	FAIR	GAWK	JADE
VOLA	WEET	WOAD	YESK	ZING	BARK	CAUK	FAIX	GAWP	JAGG
VOLE	WEFT	WOCK	YEST	ZION	BARM	CAUL	FAKE	GAZA	JAGS
VOLT	WEGG	WOKE	YETI	ZITI	BARN	CAUM	FALA	GAZE	JAIL
VOTE	WEID	WOLD	YETT	ZIZZ	BARP	CAUP	FALL	HAAF	JAIN
VRIL	WEIR	WOLF	YEUK	ZOBO	BARS	CAVE	FALX	HAAL	JAKE
VTOL	WEKA	WOMB	YEVE	ZOBU	BART	CAVY	FAME	HAAR	JAMB
VULN	WELD	WONG	YGOE	ZOEA	BASE	CAWK	FAND	HABU	JANE
WACK	WELK	WONT	YIKE	ZOIC	BASH	DABS	FANE	HACK	JANN
WADD	WELL	WOOD	YILL	ZOID	BASK	DACE	FANG	HADE	JAPE
WADE	WELT	WOOF	YIPS	ZOLA	BASS	DADA	FANK	HADJ	JARK
WADI	WEMB	WOOL	YIRD	ZOMO	BAST	DADD	FANS	HAEM	JARL
WADY	WEND	WOON	YIRK	ZONA	BATE	DADO	FARD	HAET	JARP
WAFD	WENT	WOOT	YIRR	ZONE	BATH	DAFF	FARE	HAFF	JASS
WAFF	WEPT	WORD	YITE	ZOOM	BATS	DAFT	FARM	HAFT	JATO
WAFT	WERE	WORE	YLEM	ZOOT	BATT	DAGO	FARO	HAGG	JAUP
WAGE	WERT	WORK	YLKE	ZORI	BAUD	DAHL	FARR	HAGH	JAVA
WAIF	WEST	WORM	YMIR	ZOUK	BAUK	DAIL	FART	HAHA	JAWI
WAIL	WEVE	WORN	YMPE	ZULU	BAUR	DAIS	FASH	HAIG	JAWS
WAIN	WHAM	WORT	YOCK	ZUNI	BAWD	DAKS	FASO	HAIK	JAZZ
WAIT	WHAP	WOVE	YODH	ZUPA	BAWL	DALE	FAST	HAIL	KADE
WAKA	WHAT	WOWF	YOGA	ZURF	BAWN	DALI	FATE	HAIN	KADI
WAKE	WHAU	WRAP	YOGH	ZYME	BAWR	DAME	FATS	HAIR	KAGO
WAKF	WHEE	WREN	YOGI	4:2	BAYE	DAMN	FAUN	HAIT	KAID
WALD	WHEN	WRIT	YOKE	AALU	BAYS	DAMP	FAWN	HAKA	KAIE
WALE	WHET	WULL	YOLK	AARU	BAYT	DANE	FAZE	HAKE	KAIF
WALI	WHEW	WURM	YOMP	BAAL	CABA	DANG	GABY	HALE	KAIL
WALK	WHEY	WUSS	YOND	BAAS	CADE	DANK	GADE	HALF	KAIM
WALL	WHID	WYND	YONI	BABA	CADI	DARD	GADI	HALL	KAIN
WALY	WHIG	WYNN	YOOF	BABE	CAEN	DARE	GAEA	HALM	KAKI
WAME	WHIM	WYTE	YOOP		CAFÉ	DARG	GAEL	HALO	KALE

KALI	MAAM	MAYO	PARP	RAYS	TALE	WAKF	ABET	SCOT	BEGO
KAMA	MAAR	MAZE	PARR	RAZE	TALK	WALD	ABIB	SCOW	BEIN
KAME	MAAS	NAAM	PART	RAZZ	TALL	WALE	ABLE	SCRY	BELL
KAMI	MAAT	NAAN	PASE	SABA	TAME	WALI	ABLY	SCUD	BELT
KANA	MACE	NABK	PASH	SACK	TAMP	WALK	ABRI	SCUG	BEMA
KANE	MACH	NADA	PASS	SADE	TANA	WALL	ABSE	SCUL	BEND
KANG	MACK	NAFF	PAST	SAFE	TANE	WALY	ABUS	SCUM	BENE
KANO	MADE	NAGA	PATE	SAGA	TANG	WAME	ABUT	SCUR	BENJ
KANS	MAGE	NAIA	PATH	SAGE	TANH	WAND	ABYE	SCUT	BENN
KANT	MAGG	NAIK	PATU	SAGO	TANK	WANE	ABZU	SCYE	BENT
KAON	MAGI	NAIL	PAUA	SAIC	TAPA	WANG	DBLE	UCCA	BENZ
KAPH	MAHU	NAIN	PAUL	SAID	TAPE	WANK	EBBW	ADAD	BERE
KARA	MAIA	NAIR	PAVE	SAIL	TAPS	WANT	EBOR	ADAM	BERG
KARD	MAID	NAJA	PAVO	SAIM	TAPU	WARB	EBRO	ADAR	BERK
KARL	MAIK	NALA	PAWA	SAIN	TARA	WARD	IBEX	ADAW	BERM
KART	MAIL	NAME	PAWK	SAIR	TARE	WARE	IBID	ADES	BERN
KATA	MAIM	NANA	PAWL	SAKE	TARN	WARK	IBIS	ADIT	BESS
KATE	MAIN	NAND	PAWN	SAKI	TARO	WARM	OBAN	ADUR	BEST
KATI	MAKE	NANO	PAYE	SALE	TART	WARN	OBEY	ADZE	BETA
KAVA	MAKO	NAOS	QADI	SALK	TASH	WARP	OBIA	EDAL	BETE
KAYO	MALE	NAPE	RABI	SALP	TASK	WART	OBIT	EDAM	BÊTE
LACE	MALI	NARC	RACA	SALT	TASS	WARY	OBOE	EDDA	BETH
LACK	MALL	NARD	RACE	SAMA	TATA	WASE	OBOL	EDDO	BEVY
LACY	MALM	NARE	RACK	SAME	TATE	WASH	UBER	EDDY	CEDE
LADA	MALO	NARK	RACY	SAMI	TATH	WASP	YBET	EDEN	CEDI
LADE	MALT	NARY	RADA	SAMP	TATI	WAST	ZBUD	EDER	CEIL
LADY	MAMA	NASA	RAFF	SAND	TATT	WATE	ACAS	EDGE	CELL
LAER	MAME	NASH	RAFT	SANE	TATU	WATT	ACCT	EDGY	CELT
LAHN	MANA	NASO	RAGA	SANG	TAUT	WAUL	AC/DC	EDIT	CENS
LAIC	MANE	NATO	RAGE	SANK	TAWA	WAUR	ACER	EDOM	CENT
LAID	MANG	NAVE	RAGG	SANS	TAWS	WAVE	ACES	GDAY	CERE
LAIK	MANI	NAVY	RAGI	SANT	TAWT	WAVY	ACHE	IDEA	CERO
LAIN	MANN	NAZE	RAGS	SARD	TAXA	WAWA	ACHT	IDÉE	CERT
LAIR	MANO	NAZI	RAHU	SARI	TAXI	WAWL	ACID	IDEM	CESS
LAIS	MANS	OAHU	RAID	SARK	VAAL	WAXY	ACIS	IDES	CETE
LAKE	MANU	OAKS	RAIK	SASA	VACH	WAYS	ACME	IDLE	CEYX
LAKH	MANX	OAKY	RAIL	SASH	VADE	YACK	ACNE	IDLY	DEAD
LALO	MANY	OARS	RAIN	SASS	VAIL	YAFF	ACOL	IDOL	DEAF
LAMA	MAPS	OAST	RAIT	SATE	VAIN	YAGI	ACRE	ODAL	DEAL
LAMB	MARA	OATH	RAKE	SATI	VAIR	YALE	ACRI	ODDS	DEAN
LAME	MARC	OATS	RAKI	SATS	VALE	YALU	ACRO	ODER	DEAR
LAMP	MARE	PAAL	RAKU	SAUK	VALI	YAMA	ACTA	ODIN	DEAW
LANA	MARG	PACA	RAKY	SAUL	VAMP	YANG	ACTS	ODOR	DEBT
LAND	MARI	PACE	RALE	SAUT	VANE	YANK	BCOM	ODSO	DECA
LANE	MARK	PACK	RAMA	SAVE	VANG	YAPP	CCTV	ODYL	DECK
LANG	MARL	PACO	RAMI	SAWN	VARA	YARD	ECAD	UDAD	DECO
LANK	MARM	PACT	RAMP	SAXE	VARE	YARE	ECCE	UDAL	DEED
LANT	MARO	PAGE	RANA	SAYE	VARY	YARN	ECCO	AEON	DEEK
LANX	MARS	PAID	RAND	TAAL	VASE	YARR	ECHE	AERO	DEEM
LAON	MART	PAIK	RANG	TABI	VAST	YATE	ECHO	AESC	DEEN
LAOS	MARY	PAIL	RANI	TABU	VATU	YAUD	ECHT	BEAD	DEEP
LAPP	MASA	PAIN	RANK	TACE	VAUD	YAUP	ECRU	BEAK	DEER
LARD	MASE	PAIR	RANT	TACH	VAUT	YAWL	GCSE	BEAM	DEEV
LARE	MASH	PAIS	RAPE	TACK	VAYU	YAWN	ICED	BEAN	DEFT
LARK	MASK	PALE	RAPT	TACO	WACK	YAWP	ICEL	BEAR	DEFY
LARN	MASS	PALI	RARE	TACT	WADD	YAWS	ICKY	BEAT	DEIL
LASH	MAST	PALK	RASC	TAEL	WADE	YAWY	ICON	BEAU	DEKE
LASS	MASU	PALL	RASE	TAFF	WADI	ZACK	OCHE	BECK	DELE
LAST	MATE	PALM	RASH	TAFT	WADY	ZAMA	OCTA	BEDE	DELF
LATE	MATH	PALP	RASP	TAHA	WAFD	ZANY	SCAB	BEDS	DELI
LATH	MATT	PAND	RAST	TAHR	WAFF	ZARF	SCAD	BEDU	DELL
LATS	MATY	PANE	RATA	TAIG	WAFT	ZATI	SCAG	BEEB	DEME
LAUD	MAUD	PANG	RATE	TAIL	WAGE	ABAC	SCAM	BEEF	DEMI
LAUF	MAUL	PANT	RATH	TAIN	WAIF	ABAS	SCAN	BEEN	DEMO
LAVA	MAUT	PAPA	RATS	TAIT	WAIL	ABBA	SCAR	BEEP	DEMY
LAVE	MAWK	PARA	RATU	TAKA	WAIN	ABBE	SCAT	BEER	DENE
LAWN	MAWR	PARD	RAUN	TAKE	WAIT	ABED	SCAW	BEES	DENT
LAZE	MAXI	PARE	RAVE	TALA	WAKA	ABEL	SCOG	BEET	DENY
LAZY	MAYA	PARK	RAWN	TALC	WAKE	ABER	SCOP		DEPT

DERE	HEED	KEST	MERU	PENH	SEER	VEER	ZEBU	CHEW	SHWA
DERM	HEEL	KETA	MESA	PENI	SEGO	VEGA	ZEIN	CHIC	THAE
DERN	HEEP	KEYS	MESE	PENK	SEIF	VEHM	ZENO	CHIK	THAI
DERO	HEFT	LEAD	MESH	PENN	SEIL	VEIL	ZERO	CHIL	THAN
DERV	HEIL	LEAF	MESO	PENT	SEIR	VEIN	ZEST	CHIN	THAR
DESK	HEIR	LEAK	MESS	PEON	SEJM	VELA	ZETA	CHIP	THAT
DEVA	HELA	LEAL	META	PEPO	SEKT	VELE	ZEUS	CHIT	THAW
DEVI	HELD	LEAM	METE	PÈRE	SELE	VELL	ZEZE	CHOC	THEA
DEWY	HELE	LEAN	MEVE	PERI	SELF	VENA	AFAR	CHON	THEE
EECH	HELL	LEAP	MEWL	PERK	SELL	VEND	AFFY	CHOP	THEM
EELS	HELM	LEAR	MEWS	PERM	SEMI	VENN	AFRO	CHOU	THEN
FEAL	HELO	LEAT	MEZE	PERN	SENA	VENT	CFAF	CHOW	THEW
FEAR	HELP	LECH	NEAL	PERT	SEND	VERA	EFIK	CHOY	THEY
FEAT	HEME	LEDA	NEAP	PERU	SENS	VERB	IFFY	CHUB	THIN
FECK	HEMI	LEEK	NEAR	PESO	SENT	VERS	IFOR	CHUG	THIR
FEED	HEMP	LEEP	NEAT	PEST	SEPS	VERT	OFAY	CHUM	THIS
FEEL	HEND	LEER	NEBO	READ	SEPT	VERY	OFFA	CHUT	THON
FEER	HENT	LEES	NECK	REAK	SERA	VEST	UFFA	DHAK	THOR
FEET	HEPT	LEET	NEED	REAL	SERB	VETO	AGAG	DHAL	THOS
FEGS	HERA	LEFT	NEEM	REAM	SERE	VETS	AGAR	DHOW	THOU
FEIS	HERB	LEGO	NEEP	REAN	SERF	WEAK	AGED	EHEU	THRU
FELL	HERD	LEGS	NEIF	REAP	SERK	WEAL	AGEE	GHAN	THUD
FELT	HERE	LEHR	NEIL	REAR	SESE	WEAN	AGEN	GHAT	THUG
FEME	HERL	LEIR	NELL	RECD	SESS	WEAR	AGES	GHEE	THUN
FEND	HERM	LELY	NEMO	RECK	SETA	WEBB	AGHA	KHAN	THUS
FENI	HERN	LEME	NENE	REDD	SETT	WEED	AGIN	KHAT	WHAM
FENT	HERO	LEND	NEON	REDE	SEUL	WEEK	AGIO	KHOR	WHAP
FEOD	HERR	LENG	NERD	REDO	SEVE	WEEL	AGIS	KHUD	WHAT
FERE	HERS	LENO	NERK	REED	SEWN	WEEM	AGLU	OHIO	WHAU
FERM	HERY	LENS	NERO	REEF	SEXT	WEEN	AGMA	PHEW	WHEE
FERN	HERZ	LENT	NESH	REEK	SEXY	WEEP	AGNI	PHIL	WHEN
FEST	HESP	LERP	NESS	REEL	TEAK	WEET	AGOG	PHIZ	WHET
FETA	HESS	LESS	NEST	REEN	TEAL	WEFT	AGON	PHOH	WHEW
FETE	HEST	LEST	NETE	REFT	TEAM	WEGG	AGRA	PHOT	WHEY
FETT	HETE	LETO	NETS	REIF	TEAN	WEID	AGUE	PHUT	WHID
FEUD	HETH	LETS	NETT	REIK	TEAR	WEIR	EGAD	RHEA	WHIG
FEZE	JEAT	LETT	NEUK	REIN	TEAT	WEKA	EGAL	RHUS	WHIM
GEAL	JEEL	LEVA	NEVA	REIS	TECH	WELD	EGER	RHYS	WHIN
GEAN	JEEP	LEVE	NEVE	REJA	TEDY	WELK	EGIS	SHAD	WHIP
GEAR	JEER	LEVI	NEWS	REKE	TEEM	WELL	EGMA	SHAG	WHIR
GEAT	JEFF	LEVY	NEWT	RELY	TEEN	WELT	IGAD	SHAH	WHIT
GECK	JEHU	LEWD	NEXT	REME	TEER	WEMB	IGBO	SHAM	WHIZ
GEED	JELL	MEAD	OETA	REMS	TEES	WEND	IGOR	SHAN	WHOA
GEEK	JENA	MEAL	PEAG	REND	TEFF	WENT	OGAM	SHAP	WHOM
GEEP	JERK	MEAN	PEAK	RENE	TEGG	WEPT	OGEE	SHAW	WHOP
GEEZ	JESS	MEAT	PEAL	RENO	TEHR	WERE	OGEN	SHAY	WHOT
GEIT	JEST	MEDE	PEAN	RENT	TEIL	WERT	OGLE	SHEA	AIDA
GELD	JETÉ	MEED	PEAR	RENY	TELA	WEST	OGPU	SHED	AIDE
GELT	JEWS	MEEK	PEAS	REPP	TELE	WEVE	OGRE	SHEM	AIDS
GEMS	KEAN	MEER	PEAT	REPS	TELL	XEMA	UGLI	SHET	AÎNÉ
GENE	KECK	MEET	PEBA	RESH	TEME	XERO	UGLY	SHIA	AINT
GENS	KEEK	MEGA	PECH	REST	TEMP	YEAD	YGOE	SHIE	AINU
GENT	KEEL	MEIN	PECK	RETE	TEND	YEAH	AHAB	SHIM	AIRE
GENU	KEEN	MEIR	PEDI	RETT	TENE	YEAR	AHEM	SHIN	AIRN
GERE	KEEP	MELA	PEEK	REVD	TENG	YEDE	AHOY	SHIP	AIRS
GERM	KEIR	MELD	PEEL	SEAL	TENT	YEED	BHEL	SHIT	AIRT
GEST	KELL	MELL	PEEN	SEAM	TERA	YEGG	CHAD	SHIV	AIRY
GETA	KELP	MELT	PEEP	SEAN	TERF	YELD	CHAI	SHOA	AITU
GETT	KELT	MEMO	PEER	SEAR	TERM	YELL	CHAL	SHOD	BIAS
GEUM	KEMB	MEND	PEGH	SEAS	TERN	YELP	CHAM	SHOE	BIBB
HEAD	KEMP	MENE	PEIN	SEAT	TERR	YELT	CHAN	SHOG	BICE
HEAL	KENO	MENG	PEKE	SECH	TESS	YERK	CHAP	SHOO	BIDE
HEAP	KENT	MENT	PELA	SECT	TEST	YESK	CHAR	SHOP	BIEN
HEAR	KEPI	MENU	PELE	SEED	TETE	YEST	CHAT	SHOT	BIER
HEAT	KEPT	MEOW	PELF	SEEK	TETH	YETI	CHAW	SHOW	BIFF
HEBE	KERB	MERE	PELL	SEEL	TEXT	YETT	CHAY	SHRI	BIGA
HECH	KERF	MERI	PELT	SEEM	VEAL	YEUK	CHEF	SHUL	BIGG
HECK	KERN	MERK	PEND	SEEN	VEDA	YEVE	CHER	SHUN	BIKE
HECT	KESH	MERL	PENE	SEEP	VEEP	ZEAL		SHUT	BILE

BILK	DISS	HIDE	LIES	MISS	QING	SIMP	VISE	SKEG	BLUB
BILL	DITA	HIGH	LIEU	MIST	RIAL	SIND	VITA	SKEN	BLUE
BIMM	DITE	HIKE	LIFE	MITE	RIBS	SINE	VITE	SKEO	BLUR
BIND	DITT	HILL	LIFT	MITT	RICA	SING	VIVA	SKEP	BLUT
BINE	DIVA	HILO	LIKE	NIBS	RICE	SINK	VIVO	SKER	CLAD
BING	DIVE	HILT	LILL	NICE	RICH	SINO	VIVE	SKET	CLAG
BINK	DIXY	HINC	LILO	NICK	RICK	SION	WICE	SKEW	CLAM
BINT	EIGG	HIND	LILT	NIDE	RICO	SIPE	WICK	SKIA	CLAN
BIRD	EILD	HING	LILY	NIEF	RIDE	SIRE	WIDE	SKID	CLAP
BIRK	EINE	HINT	LIMA	NIFE	RIEL	SIRI	WIEL	SKIM	CLAT
BIRL	EIRE	HIPT	LIMB	NIFF	RIEM	SISS	WIEN	SKIN	CLAW
BIRO	FIAT	HIRE	LIME	NIGH	RIFE	SIST	WIFE	SKIO	CLAY
BIRR	FICO	HISH	LIMN	NIKE	RIFF	SITE	WILD	SKIP	CLEF
BISE	FIDE	HISS	LIMO	NILE	RIFT	SITU	WILE	SKIT	CLEG
BISH	FIDO	HIST	LIMP	NILL	RIGA	SIUM	WILI	SKOL	CLEM
BISK	FIEF	HIVE	LIMY	NINA	RIGG	SIVA	WILL	SKRY	CLEW
BISP	FIFA	JIAO	LIND	NINE	RIGI	SIZE	WILT	SKUA	CLIO
BITE	FIFE	JIBE	LINE	NINO	RILE	TICE	WILY	SKUG	CLIP
BITO	FIGO	JILL	LING	NIPA	RILL	TICH	WIMP	SKYE	CLOD
BITS	FIJI	JILT	LINK	NIRL	RIMA	TICK	WIND	SKYR	CLOG
BITT	FIKE	JIMP	LINN	NISI	RIME	TIDE	WINE	ALAI	CLOP
CIAO	FIKY	JINK	LINO	NITH	RIMU	TIDY	WING	ALAN	CLOS
CIEL	FILE	JINX	LINT	NIXY	RIND	TIED	WINK	ALAR	CLOT
CIGS	FILL	JIRD	LION	OILS	RINE	TIER	WINN	ALAS	CLOU
CILL	FILM	JISM	LIPS	OILY	RING	TIFF	WINO	ALAY	CLOW
CINE	FILO	JIVE	LIRA	OINK	RINK	TIFT	WIPE	ALBE	CLOY
CION	FILS	JIZZ	LIRK	OINT	RINT	TIGE	WIRE	ALBI	CLUB
CIRÉ	FIND	KIBE	LISA	OISE	RIOT	TIKA	WIRY	ALEC	CLUE
CIRL	FINE	KICK	LISK	PIAF	RIPE	TIKE	WISE	ALEW	ELAM
CIST	FINK	KIDD	LISP	PICA	RIPP	TIKI	WISH	ALEX	ELAN
CITE	FINN	KIEL	LIST	PICE	RIPS	TILE	WISP	ALFA	ELAT
CITO	FINO	KIER	LITE	PICK	RISE	TILL	WIST	ALGA	ELBA
CITS	FIRE	KIEV	LITH	PICT	RISK	TILT	WITE	ALIA	ELBE
CITY	FIRK	KIKE	LIVE	PIED	RISP	TIME	WITH	ALIF	ELIA
CIVE	FIRM	KILL	LIVY	PIER	RISS	TINA	WITS	ALKY	ELIS
DIAL	FIRN	KILN	LIZA	PIES	RITA	TIND	WIVE	ALLO	ELKS
DIAS	FISC	KILO	MICA	PIET	RITE	TINE	XIAN	ALLY	ELLA
DIAZ	FISH	KILP	MICE	PIGS	RITT	TING	YIKE	ALMA	ELLE
DIBS	FISK	KILT	MICK	PIKA	RITZ	TINK	YILL	ALMS	ELMO
DICE	FIST	KINA	MICO	PIKE	RIVA	TINT	YIPS	ALOD	ELOI
DICH	FITT	KIND	MIDI	PILE	RIVE	TINY	YIRD	ALOE	ELSA
DICK	FITZ	KINE	MIEN	PILI	RIVO	TIPI	YIRK	ALOW	ELSE
DICY	FIVE	KING	MIFF	PILL	RIZA	TIPU	YIRR	ALPH	ELUL
DIDO	FIZZ	KINK	MIKE	PIMP	SIAL	TIRE	YITE	ALPS	FLAB
DIEB	GIBE	KINO	MILD	PINA	SIAM	TIRL	ZIFF	ALSO	FLAG
DIED	GIDE	KIPE	MILE	PINE	SIAN	TIRO	ZILA	ALTA	FLAK
DIES	GIER	KIPP	MILK	PING	SIBB	TIRR	ZIMB	ALTE	FLAM
DIET	GIFT	KIRI	MILL	PINK	SICE	TITE	ZINC	ALTO	FLAN
DIEU	GIGA	KIRK	MILO	PINS	SICH	TITI	ZING	ALUM	FLAP
DIGS	GIGI	KIRN	MILT	PINT	SICK	TITO	ZION	ALVA	FLAT
DIKA	GILA	KISH	MIME	PION	SIDA	UIST	ZITI	BLAB	FLAW
DIKE	GILD	KISS	MIMI	PIPA	SIDE	VIAL	ZIZZ	BLAD	FLAX
DILL	GILL	KIST	MINA	PIPE	SIEN	VIBS	AJAR	BLAE	FLAY
DIMA	GILT	KITE	MIND	PIPI	SIFT	VICE	AJAX	BLAG	FLEA
DIME	GIMP	KITH	MINE	PIRL	SIGH	VIDE	AJEE	BLAH	FLED
DINE	GING	KIVA	MING	PIRN	SIGN	VIED	AKEE	BLAT	FLEE
DING	GINK	KIWI	MINI	PIRO	SIJO	VIES	AKIN	BLAY	FLEG
DINK	GIRD	LIAM	MINK	PISE	SIKA	VIEW	EKKA	BLEB	FLEW
DINT	GIRL	LIAR	MINO	PISH	SIKE	VIGO	IKAT	BLED	FLEX
DIOL	GIRN	LIAS	MINT	PISO	SIKH	VILE	IKON	BLEE	FLEY
DIOR	GIRO	LIBS	MINX	PISS	SILA	VILL	NKVD	BLET	FLIC
DIRE	GIRR	LICE	MIRA	PITA	SILD	VIMY	OKAY	BLEW	FLIP
DIRK	GIRT	LICH	MIRE	PITH	SILE	VINA	OKRA	BLEY	FLIT
DIRL	GISM	LICK	MIRK	PITT	SILK	VINE	OKRO	BLIN	FLIX
DIRT	GIST	LIDE	MIRO	PITY	SILL	VINO	OKTA	BLIP	FLOE
DISA	GITE	LIDO	MIRV	PIUM	SILO	VINT	SKAG	BLOB	FLOG
DISC	GIVE	LIED	MISC	PIUS	SILT	VIOL	SKAT	BLOC	FLOP
DISH	GIZZ	LIEF	MISE	PIXY	SIMA	VIRL	SKAW	BLOT	FLOR
DISK	HICK	LIEN	MISO	PIZE	SIMI	VISA	SKED	BLOW	FLOW

FLOX	SLEE	XMAS	ONGO	BORD	CORE	DOUP	GOOL	JOBE	LOON
FLUB	SLEW	YMIR	ONLY	BORE	CORF	DOUR	GOON	JOCK	LOOP
FLUE	SLEY	YMPE	ONST	BORN	CORK	DOUT	GOOP	JOCO	LOOR
FLUX	SLID	ANAK	ONTO	BORO	CORM	DOVE	GOOR	JODO	LOOS
GLAD	SLIM	ANAL	ONUS	BORS	CORN	DOWF	GORE	JOEL	LOOT
GLAM	SLIP	ANAN	ONYX	BOSH	CORY	DOWN	GORM	JOEY	LOPE
GLEE	SLIT	ANAS	PNYX	BOSS	COSE	DOWT	GORP	JOHN	LORD
GLEG	SLOB	ANCE	SNAG	BOTE	COSH	DOXY	GORY	JOIN	LORE
GLEI	SLOE	ANDA	SNAP	BOTH	COSS	DOZE	GOSH	JOKE	LORI
GLEN	SLOG	ANEW	SNEB	BOTS	COST	DOZY	GOSS	JOLE	LORN
GLEY	SLOP	ANFO	SNED	BOTT	COSY	EOAN	GOTA	JOLL	LORY
GLIA	SLOT	ANIL	SNEE	BOUK	COTE	EOKA	GOTH	JOLO	LOSE
GLIB	SLOW	ANKH	SNIB	BOUN	COTH	EORL	GOUK	JOLT	LOSH
GLID	SLUB	ANNA	SNIG	BOUT	COTT	FOAL	GOUT	JOMO	LOSS
GLIM	SLUE	ANNE	SNIP	BOWL	COTY	FOAM	GOWF	JOOK	LOST
GLIT	SLUG	ANNO	SNIT	BOWR	COUE	FOCH	GOWK	JOSE	LOTE
GLOB	SLUM	ANOA	SNOB	BOYG	COUP	FOEN	GOWL	JOSH	LOTH
GLOM	SLUR	ANON	SNOD	BOYO	COUR	FOGG	GOWN	JOSS	LOTI
GLOP	SLUT	ANTA	SNOG	BOYS	COVE	FOGY	GOYA	JOTA	LOTO
GLOW	ULAD	ANTE	SNOT	BOZO	COWL	FOIL	HOAR	JOUK	LOTS
GLUE	ULAN	ANTI	SNOW	COAL	COWP	FOIN	HOAX	JOVE	LOUD
GLUM	ULEX	ANTS	SNUB	COAT	COWS	FOLD	HOBO	JOWL	LOUP
GLUT	ULNA	ANUS	SNUG	COAX	COZE	FOLK	HOCK	KOAN	LOUR
ILEX	VLEI	ENDS	SNYE	COBB	COZY	FOND	HOGG	KOBE	LOUT
ILIA	YLEM	ENEW	UNAU	COBH	DOAB	FONE	HOGH	KOBO	LOVE
ILKA	YLKE	ENID	UNBE	COCA	DOAT	FONS	HOKE	KOEL	LOWE
ILLE	AMAH	ENNA	UNCE	COCH	DOCK	FONT	HOKI	KOFF	LOZI
ILLY	AMBO	ENOL	UNCO	COCK	DODO	FOOD	HOLD	KOHL	MOAN
KLAN	AMEN	ENOS	UNDE	COCO	DOEK	FOOL	HOLE	KOKO	MOAT
KLEE	AMES	ENOW	UNDO	CODA	DOER	FOON	HOLI	KOLA	MOBY
LLYR	AMID	ENSI	UNIO	CODE	DOES	FOOT	HOLM	KOLO	MOCH
OLAF	AMIE	ENVY	UNIT	CODY	DOFF	FORB	HOLT	KOND	MOCK
OLDS	AMIN	GNAR	UNTO	COED	DOGE	FORD	HOLY	KONG	MODE
OLEA	AMIR	GNAT	BOAK	COFF	DOGS	FORE	HOMA	KONK	MODO
OLEO	AMIS	GNAW	BOAR	COIF	DOGY	FORK	HOME	KOOK	MODS
OLID	AMLA	INBY	BOAT	COIL	DOHA	FORM	HOMO	KORA	MOHR
OLIM	AMMO	INCA	BOAZ	COIN	DOIT	FORT	HOND	KORE	MOHS
OLIO	AMOK	INCH	BOBA	COIR	DOJO	FOSS	HONE	KOSS	MOIL
OLLA	AMOS	INDY	BOCK	COIT	DOLE	FOUD	HONG	KOTO	MOIT
OLPE	AMOY	INES	BODE	COKE	DOLL	FOUG	HONI	LOAD	MOJO
PLAN	AMUN	INFO	BODY	COLA	DOLT	FOUL	HONK	LOAF	MOKE
PLAP	AMUR	INGE	BOER	COLD	DOME	FOUR	HOOD	LOAM	MOKI
PLAT	AMYL	INGO	BOFF	COLE	DONA	FOWL	HOOF	LOAN	MOKO
PLAY	EMEU	INKY	BOGY	COLL	DONE	FOXY	HOOK	LOBE	MOLA
PLEA	EMIC	INLY	BOIL	COLT	DONG	FOZY	HOON	LOBO	MOLD
PLEB	EMIR	INNS	BOKE	COLY	DONT	GOAD	HOOP	LOCH	MOLE
PLED	EMIT	INRI	BOKO	COMA	DOOB	GOAF	HOOT	LOCK	MOLL
PLEW	EMMA	INRO	BOLD	COMB	DOOK	GOAL	HOPE	LOCO	MOLT
PLIÉ	EMMY	INST	BOLE	COME	DOOL	GOAT	HOPI	LODE	MOLY
PLIM	EMYS	INTI	BOLL	COMM	DOOM	GOBI	HOPS	LOFT	MOME
PLOD	HMSO	INTO	BOLO	COMO	DOON	GOBO	HORE	LOGE	MONA
PLOP	IMAM	KNAG	BOLT	COMP	DOOR	GOBY	HORN	LOGO	MONG
PLOT	IMPI	KNAP	BOMA	CONE	DOPA	GODS	HORS	LOGS	MONK
PLOW	OMAN	KNAR	BOMB	CONK	DOPE	GOEL	HOSE	LOGY	MONO
PLOY	OMAR	KNEE	BONA	CONN	DORA	GOER	HOSS	LOID	MONS
PLUE	OMBU	KNEW	BOND	CONS	DORÉ	GOES	HOST	LOIN	MONY
PLUG	OMEN	KNIT	BONE	CONT	DORM	GOEY	HOTE	LOIR	MOOD
PLUM	OMER	KNOB	BONG	CONY	DORP	GOFF	HOUR	LOIS	MOOG
PLUS	OMIT	KNOP	BONK	COOF	DORR	GOGO	HOUT	LOKE	MOOI
SLAB	OMNI	KNOT	BONN	COOK	DORT	GOLD	HOVA	LOKI	MOOL
SLAE	SMEE	KNOW	BONY	COOL	DORY	GOLE	HOVE	LOLA	MOON
SLAG	SMEW	KNOX	BOOB	COOM	DOSE	GOLF	HOWE	LOLL	MOOP
SLAM	SMIT	KNUB	BOOK	COON	DOSH	GONE	HOWK	LOMA	MOOR
SLAP	SMOG	KNUR	BOOL	COOP	DOSS	GONG	HOWL	LOME	MOOT
SLAT	SMUG	KNUT	BOOM	COOT	DOTE	GONK	HOYA	LONE	MOPE
SLAV	SMUR	LNER	BOON	COPE	DOTH	GOOD	IONA	LONG	MOPP
SLAW	SMUT	ONCE	BOOR	COPS	DOTS	GOOF	IOTA	LOOF	MORE
SLAY	UMBO	ONER	BOOT	COPY	DOUC	GOOG	IOWA	LOOK	MORI
SLED	UMPH	ONE'S	BORA	CORD	DOUM	GOOK	JOAN	LOOM	MORN

11

MORO	POGO	ROOD	SOUR	VOID	EPIC	ARSE	DRIB	KRIS	URGE
MORS	POKE	ROOF	SOWM	VOLA	EPOS	ARTA	DRIP	KROO	URIC
MORT	POKY	ROOK	SOWP	VOLE	IPOH	ARTS	DROP	ORAL	URIM
MOSS	POLE	ROOM	SOYA	VOLT	IPSE	ARTY	DROW	ORAN	URSA
MOST	POLK	ROON	TOAD	VOTE	OPAH	ARUM	DRUB	ORBY	URUS
MOTE	POLL	ROOP	TOBY	WOAD	OPAL	ARUN	DRUG	ORCA	URVA
MOTH	POLO	ROOT	TOCO	WOCK	OPEC	ARVO	DRUM	ORFE	VRIL
MOTT	POLT	ROPE	TODD	WOKE	OPEL	ARYL	ERAT	ORFF	WRAP
MOTU	POLY	ROPY	TODO	WOLD	OPEN	BRAD	ERGO	ORGE	WREN
MOUE	POME	RORE	TODY	WOLF	OPIE	BRAE	ERIA	ORGY	WRIT
MOUL	POMO	RORO	TOEA	WOMB	OPPO	BRAG	ERIC	ORLE	ASAP
MOUP	POMP	RORT	TOEY	WONG	OPUS	BRAK	ERIE	ORLY	ASAR
MOVE	POND	RORY	TOFF	WONT	SPAE	BRAM	ERIK	ORNE	ASAS
MOVY	PONE	ROSE	TOFT	WOOD	SPAG	BRAN	ERIN	ORRA	ASCH
MOWA	PONG	ROSS	TOFU	WOOF	SPAM	BRAS	ERIS	ORTS	ASHE
MOXA	PONK	ROSY	TOGA	WOOL	SPAN	BRAT	ERNE	ORYX	ASHY
MOYA	PONS	ROTA	TOGE	WOON	SPAR	BRAW	EROS	PRAD	ASIA
MOYL	PONT	ROTE	TOGO	WOOT	SPAT	BRAY	ERSE	PRAM	ASKE
MOZE	PONY	ROTI	TOGS	WORD	SPAW	BRED	ERTÉ	PRAT	ASKR
MOZZ	POOD	ROTL	TOHO	WORE	SPAY	BREE	ERYX	PRAU	ASTI
NOAH	POOF	ROUD	TOIL	WORK	SPEC	BREN	FRAB	PRAY	ASUR
NOCK	POOH	ROUÉ	TOJO	WORM	SPED	BRER	FRAE	PREE	ESAU
NODE	POOK	ROUL	TOKE	WORN	SPEE	BREW	FRAG	PREP	ESKY
NOEL	POOL	ROUM	TOKO	WORT	SPET	BRIE	FRAP	PREY	ESLA
NOES	POON	ROUP	TOLA	WOVE	SPEW	BRIG	FRAU	PRIG	ESME
NOGO	POOP	ROUT	TOLD	WOWF	SPEY	BRIM	FRAY	PRIM	ESNE
NOIL	POOR	ROUX	TOLE	XOSA	SPIC	BRIO	FREE	PRIX	ESPY
NOLE	POOT	ROVE	TOLL	YOCK	SPIF	BRIS	FRET	PROA	ESSE
NOLL	POPE	ROWE	TOLT	YODH	SPIK	BRIT	FRIG	PROD	ESTE
NOLO	PORE	ROWT	TOLU	YOGA	SPIN	BRIX	FRIT	PROF	ESTH
NOMA	PORK	SOAK	TOMB	YOGH	SPIT	BRNO	FROE	PROG	GSOH
NOME	PORN	SOAP	TOME	YOGI	SPIV	BROD	FROG	PROM	ISAR
NONE	PORT	SOAR	TONE	YOKE	SPOT	BROG	FROM	PROO	ISER
NONG	POSE	SOAY	TONG	YOLK	SPRY	BRON	FROW	PROP	ISIS
NONO	POSH	SOCA	TONK	YOMP	SPUD	BROO	GRAB	PROW	ISLE
NOOK	POSS	SOCK	TONS	YOND	SPUE	BROS	GRAD	PRUH	ISMY
NOON	POST	SODA	TONY	YONI	SPUN	BROW	GRAF	TRAD	ISNT
NOOP	POSY	SOFA	TOOK	YOOF	SPUR	BRUM	GRAM	TRAM	KSAR
NOPE	POTE	SOFI	TOOL	YOOP	UPAS	BRUT	GRAN	TRAP	OSLO
NORE	POTS	SOFT	TOOM	YORE	UPGO	CRAB	GRAS	TRAY	OSSA
NORI	POTT	SOHO	TOON	YORK	UPON	CRAG	GRAT	TREE	PSBR
NORK	POUF	SOIL	TOOT	YOUD	UPSY	CRAM	GRAV	TREK	RSVP
NORM	POUK	SOJA	TOPE	YOUK	AQUA	CRAN	GRAY	TRET	TSAR
NORN	POUR	SOLA	TOPI	YOUR	ARAB	CRAP	GREE	TREW	TSHI
NOSE	POUT	SOLD	TOPS	YOWE	ARAK	CRAW	GREW	TREY	USAK
NOSH	POWN	SOLE	TORC	YOWL	ARAL	CRAX	GREY	TREZ	USED
NOSY	POXY	SOLO	TORE	YOYO	ARAM	CRAY	GRID	TRIE	USER
NOTE	QOPH	SOMA	TORN	ZOBO	ARAN	CRED	GRIG	TRIG	USES
NOTT	ROAD	SOME	TORR	ZOBU	ARAR	CREE	GRIM	TRIM	USSR
NOUN	ROAM	SONE	TORT	ZOEA	ARCH	CREW	GRIN	TRIN	ATAP
NOUP	ROAN	SONG	TORY	ZOIC	ARCO	CRIB	GRIP	TRIO	ATAR
NOUS	ROAR	SOOK	TOSA	ZOID	AREA	CRIT	GRIS	TRIP	ATEN
NOUT	ROBE	SOOL	TOSE	ZOLA	AREG	CROP	GRIT	TROD	ATLI
NOVA	ROCA	SOOM	TOSH	ZOMO	ARES	CROW	GROG	TROG	ATOC
NOVO	ROCH	SOON	TOSS	ZONA	ARET	CRUD	GROT	TRON	ATOK
NOWL	ROCK	SOOP	TOST	ZONE	AREW	CRUE	GROW	TROP	ATOM
NOWT	RODE	SOOT	TOTE	ZOOM	ARGO	CRUX	GRUB	TROT	ATOP
NOWY	ROIL	SOPH	TOTO	ZOOT	ARIA	CRYO	GRUE	TROU	ATTO
OONS	ROIN	SORA	TOUK	ZORI	ARID	DRAB	GRUG	TROW	ATTU
OONT	ROJI	SORB	TOUN	ZOUK	ARIL	DRAD	GRUM	TROY	ATUA
OOPS	ROKE	SORD	TOUR	APAY	ARIS	DRAG	GRUS	TRUE	ATUM
OORT	ROLE	SORE	TOUT	APEX	ARLY	DRAM	IRAN	TRUG	ETCH
OOSE	ROLF	SORN	TOVE	APIA	ARMS	DRAT	IRAQ	TRYE	ETEN
OOZE	ROLL	SORT	TOWN	APIS	ARMY	DRAW	IRAS	URAL	ETHE
OOZY	ROME	SOSS	TOWT	APSE	ARNA	DRAY	IRID	URAO	ETIC
POCK	ROMP	SOUK	TOYS	APUS	ARNE	DREE	IRIS	URDÉ	ETNA
PODS	RONE	SOUL	TOZE	CPRS	ARNO	DREG	IRON	URDU	ETON
POEM	RONG	SOUM	VOAR	EPEE	ARRU	DREW	IRUS	URDY	ETTA
POET	RONT	SOUP	VOCE	EPHA	ARRY	DREY	KRAB	UREA	ETTY

ETUI
ITCH
ITEM
ITYS
OTHO
OTIC
OTIS
OTTO
OTUS
PTAH
STAB
STAG
STAN
STAP
STAR
STAT
STAW
STAY
STED
STEM
STEN
STEP
STET
STEW
STEY
STIE
STIM
STIR
STOA
STOB
STOL
STOP
STOT
STOW
STUB
STUD
STUM
STUN
STUR
STYE
STYX
UTAH
UTAS
UTIS
VTOL
AUDE
AUDI
AULA
AULD
AUNE
AUNT
AURA
AUTO
BUAT
BUBA
BUBO
BUCK
BUDD
BUDE
BUDO
BUFF
BUFO
BUGS
BUHL
BUIK
BUKE
BULB
BULK
BULL

BUMF
BUMP
BUNA
BUND
BUNG
BUNK
BUNT
BUOY
BURD
BURG
BURK
BURL
BURN
BURP
BURR
BURT
BURY
BUSH
BUSK
BUSS
BUST
BUSY
BUTE
BUTT
BUZZ
CUBA
CUBE
CUBS
CUFF
CUIF
CUIT
CULL
CULM
CULT
CUMA
CUNT
CUPS
CURB
CURD
CURE
CURK
CURL
CURN
CURR
CURT
CUSH
CUSK
CUSP
CUSS
CUTE
CUYP
DUAD
DUAL
DUAN
DUAR
DUBS
DUCE
DUCK
DUCT
DUDE
DUDS
DUEL
DUES
DUET
DUFF
DUKE
DULE
DULL
DULY

DUMA
DUMB
DUMP
DUNE
DUNG
DUNK
DUNS
DUNT
DUPE
DURA
DURE
DURN
DURO
DUSE
DUSH
DUSK
DUST
DUTY
EUGE
EUGH
EUOI
EURE
EURO
FUEL
FUFF
FUJI
FULA
FULL
FUME
FUND
FUNG
FUNK
FUNS
FURL
FURR
FURY
FUSE
FUSS
FUST
FUZE
FUZZ
GUAM
GUAN
GUAR
GUFF
GUGA
GUID
GULA
GULE
GULF
GULL
GULP
GUMP
GUNK
GUNN
GUNS
GUNZ
GURL
GURN
GURU
GUSH
GUST
GUTS
GUYS
HUCK
HUER
HUEY
HUFF
HUGE

HUGH
HUGO
HUHU
HUIA
HULA
HULE
HULK
HULL
HUMA
HUME
HUMF
HUMP
HUNG
HUNK
HUNT
HUON
HURL
HURT
HUSH
HUSK
HUSO
HUSS
HUTU
JUAN
JUBA
JUBE
JUDE
JUDO
JUDY
JUJU
JUKE
JULY
JUMA
JUMP
JUNE
JUNG
JUNK
JUNO
JURA
JURE
JURY
JUST
JUTE
KUDU
KUKU
KUNA
KURD
KURI
KURU
LUAU
LUBA
LUCE
LUCK
LUCY
LUDD
LUDO
LUES
LUEZ
LUFF
LUGE
LUGH
LUGS
LUIT
LUKE
LULL
LULU
LUMP
LUNA
LUNE

LUNG
LUNT
LURE
LURK
LUSH
LUSK
LUST
LUTE
LUTZ
LUXE
MUCH
MUCK
MUFF
MUID
MUIL
MUIR
MULE
MULL
MUMP
MUNG
MUON
MURE
MURK
MURL
MUSA
MUSE
MUSH
MUSK
MUSO
MUSS
MUST
MUTE
MUTI
MUTT
NUDD
NUDE
NUER
NUKE
NULL
NUMA
NUMB
NUNC
NURD
NURL
NURR
NUTS
NUUK
OUCH
OUDS
OULK
OUMA
OUPA
OUPH
OURS
OUST
OUZO
PUCA
PUCE
PUCK
PUDU
PUER
PUFF
PUGH
PUJA
PUKE
PULA
PULE
PULI
PULL

PULP
PULU
PULY
PUMA
PUMP
PUMY
PUNA
PUNG
PUNK
PUNT
PUNY
PUPA
PURE
PURI
PURL
PURR
PUSH
PUSS
PUTT
PUTZ
QUAD
QUAG
QUAT
QUAY
QUEP
QUEY
QUID
QUIM
QUIN
QUIP
QUIT
QUIZ
QUOD
QUOP
RUBE
RUBY
RUCK
RUDD
RUDE
RUFF
RUGA
RUHR
RUIN
RUKH
RULE
RULY
RUME
RUMI
RUMP
RUND
RUNE
RUNG
RUNS
RUNT
RURP
RURU
RUSA
RUSE
RUSH
RUSK
RUST
RUTA
RUTE
RUTH
SUCH
SUCK
SUDD
SUDS
SUER

SUET
SUEY
SUEZ
SUFI
SUIT
SULK
SULU
SUMO
SUMP
SUMS
SUNG
SUNK
SUNN
SURA
SURD
SURE
SURF
SUSA
SUSS
SUSU
SUVA
TUAN
TUBA
TUBE
TUCK
TUES
TUFA
TUFF
TUFT
TULE
TULI
TULL
TUMP
TUMS
TUNA
TUND
TUNE
TUNG
TUPI
TURD
TURF
TURK
TURM
TURN
TUSH
TUSK
TUTU
TUZZ
VULN
WULL
WURM
WUSS
YUAN
YUCA
YUCK
YUEN
YUFT
YUGA
YUKE
YUKO
YULE
YUMP
YUNX
ZULU
ZUNI
ZUPA
ZURF
AVAL
AVER

AVES
AVID
AVON
AVOW
EVAN
EVEN
EVER
EVET
EVIL
EVOE
IVAN
IVES
IVOR
IVRY
OVAL
OVEL
OVEN
OVER
OVID
OVRA
OVUM
UVEA
AWAY
AWDL
AWED
AWOL
AWRY
EWER
EWES
GWYN
HWYL
IWIS
KWAI
KWIC
LWEI
OWED
OWEN
OWLS
OWLY
OWNS
OWRE
SWAB
SWAD
SWAG
SWAM
SWAN
SWAP
SWAT
SWAY
SWEE
SWEY
SWIG
SWIM
SWIZ
SWOB
SWOP
SWOT
SWUM
TWAE
TWAL
TWAT
TWAY
TWEE
TWIG
TWIN
TWIT
YWIS
AXIL
AXIS

AXLE
AXON
EXAM
EXES
EXIT
EXON
EXOR
EXPO
EXUL
OXEN
OXER
OXON
OXUS
AYAH
AYER
AYES
AYIN
AYMÉ
AYRE
BYKE
BYNG
BYRD
BYRE
BYTE
CYAN
CYMA
CYME
CYST
CYTE
DYAD
DYAK
DYER
DYKE
DYNE
EYAS
EYER
EYES
EYNE
EYOT
EYRA
EYRE
EYRY
FYKE
FYRD
GYAL
GYBE
GYMP
GYNT
GYRE
GYRO
GYTE
GYVE
HYDE
HYKE
HYLA
HYLE
HYMN
HYPE
HYPO
IYAR
IYNX
JYNX
KYAT
KYLE
KYPE
KYTE
LYAM
LYCH
LYLE

LYLY
LYME
LYNX
LYON
LYRA
LYRE
LYSE
LYTE
MYAL
MYTH
NYAS
NYET
NYOS
OYER
OYEZ
PYAT
PYET
PYOT
PYRE
PYRO
RYAL
RYAN
RYFE
RYND
RYOT
RYVE
SYCE
SYEN
SYKE
SYNC
SYND
SYNE
SYPE
TYKE
TYMP
TYNE
TYPE
TYPO
TYRE
TYRO
TYTE
WYND
WYNN
WYTE
XYST
ZYME
AZAN
AZOV
CZAR
EZRA
IZAR
MZEE
TZAR

4:3

ABAC
ABAS
ACAS
ADAD
ADAM
ADAR
ADAW
AFAR
AGAG
AGAR
AHAB
AJAR
AJAX
ALAI

ALAN	CLAD	FLAN	KHAN	PIAF	SOAK	WEAL	OMBU	INCA	RUCK
ALAR	CLAG	FLAP	KHAT	PLAN	SOAP	WEAN	ORBY	INCH	SACK
ALAS	CLAM	FLAT	KLAN	PLAP	SOAR	WEAR	PEBA	ITCH	SECH
ALAY	CLAN	FLAW	KNAG	PLAT	SOAY	WHAM	PSBR	JACK	SECT
AMAH	CLAP	FLAX	KNAP	PLAY	SPAE	WHAP	RABI	JOCK	SICE
ANAK	CLAT	FLAY	KNAR	PRAD	SPAG	WHAT	RIBS	JOCO	SICH
ANAL	CLAW	FOAL	KOAN	PRAM	SPAM	WHAU	ROBE	KECK	SICK
ANAN	CLAY	FOAM	KRAB	PRAT	SPAN	WOAD	RUBE	KICK	SOCA
ANAS	COAL	FRAB	KSAR	PRAU	SPAR	WRAP	RUBY	LACE	SOCK
APAY	COAT	FRAE	KWAI	PRAY	SPAT	XIAN	SABA	LACK	SUCH
ARAB	COAX	FRAG	KYAT	PTAH	SPAW	XMAS	SIBB	LACY	SUCK
ARAK	CRAB	FRAP	LEAD	PYAT	STAB	YEAD	TABI	LECH	SYCE
ARAL	CRAG	FRAU	LEAF	QUAD	STAG	YEAH	TABU	LICE	TACE
ARAM	CRAM	FRAY	LEAK	QUAG	STAN	YEAR	TOBY	LICH	TACH
ARAN	CRAN	GDAY	LEAL	QUAT	STAP	YUAN	TUBA	LICK	TACK
ARAR	CRAP	GEAL	LEAM	QUAY	STAR	ZEAL	TUBE	LOCH	TACO
ASAP	CRAW	GEAN	LEAN	READ	STAT	ABBA	UMBO	LOCK	TACT
ASAR	CRAX	GEAR	LEAP	REAK	STAW	ABBE	UNBE	LOCO	TECH
ASAS	CRAY	GEAT	LEAR	REAL	STAY	ALBE	VIBS	LUCE	TICE
ATAP	CYAN	GHAN	LEAT	REAM	SWAB	ALBI	WEBB	LUCK	TICH
ATAR	CZAR	GHAT	LIAM	REAN	SWAD	AMBO	ZEBU	LUCY	TICK
AVAL	DEAD	GLAD	LIAR	REAP	SWAG	BABA	ZOBO	LYCH	TOCO
AWAY	DEAF	GLAM	LIAS	REAR	SWAM	BABE	ZOBU	MACE	TUCK
AYAH	DEAL	GNAR	LOAD	RIAL	SWAN	BABI	ACCT	MACH	UCCA
AZAN	DEAN	GNAT	LOAF	ROAD	SWAP	BABU	ANCE	MACK	UNCE
BAAL	DEAR	GNAW	LOAM	ROAM	SWAT	BABY	ARCH	MICA	UNCO
BAAS	DEAW	GOAD	LOAN	ROAN	SWAY	BIBB	ARCO	MICE	VACH
BEAD	DHAK	GOAF	LUAU	ROAR	TAAL	BOBA	ASCH	MICK	VICE
BEAK	DHAL	GOAL	LYAM	RYAL	TEAK	BUBA	BACA	MICO	VOCE
BEAM	DIAL	GOAT	MAAM	RYAN	TEAL	BUBO	BACH	MOCH	WACK
BEAN	DIAS	GRAB	MAAR	SCAB	TEAM	CABA	BACK	MOCK	WICE
BEAR	DIAZ	GRAD	MAAS	SCAD	TEAN	COBB	BECK	MUCH	WICK
BEAT	DOAB	GRAF	MAAT	SCAG	TEAR	COBH	BICE	MUCK	WOCK
BEAU	DOAT	GRAM	MEAD	SCAM	TEAT	CUBA	BOCK	NECK	YACK
BIAS	DRAB	GRAN	MEAL	SCAN	THAE	CUBE	BUCK	NICE	YOCK
BLAB	DRAD	GRAS	MEAN	SCAR	THAI	CUBS	COCA	NICK	YUCA
BLAD	DRAG	GRAT	MEAT	SCAT	THAN	DABS	COCH	NOCK	YUCK
BLAE	DRAM	GRAV	MOAN	SCAW	THAR	DEBT	COCO	ONCE	ZACK
BLAG	DRAT	GRAY	MOAT	SEAL	THAT	DIBS	DACE	ORCA	AC/DC
BLAH	DRAW	GUAM	MYAL	SEAM	THAW	DUBS	DECA	OUCH	AIDA
BLAT	DRAY	GUAN	NAAM	SEAN	TOAD	EBBW	DECK	PACA	AIDE
BLAY	DUAD	GUAR	NAAN	SEAR	TRAD	ELBA	DECO	PACE	AIDS
BOAK	DUAL	GYAL	NEAL	SEAS	TRAM	ELBE	DICE	PACK	ANDA
BOAR	DUAN	HAAF	NEAP	SEAT	TRAP	GABY	DICH	PACO	AUDE
BOAT	DUAR	HAAL	NEAR	SHAD	TRAY	GIBE	DICK	PACT	AUDI
BOAZ	DYAD	HAAR	NEAT	SHAG	TSAR	GOBI	DICY	PECH	AWDL
BRAD	DYAK	HEAD	NOAH	SHAH	TUAN	GOBO	DOCK	PECK	BADE
BRAE	ECAD	HEAL	NYAS	SHAM	TWAE	GOBY	DUCE	PICA	BEDE
BRAG	EDAL	HEAP	OBAN	SHAN	TWAL	GYBE	DUCK	PICE	BEDS
BRAK	EDAM	HEAR	ODAL	SHAP	TWAT	HABU	DUCT	PICK	BEDU
BRAM	EGAD	HEAT	OFAY	SHAW	TWAY	HEBE	EACH	PICT	BIDE
BRAN	EGAL	HOAR	OGAM	SHAY	TZAR	HOBO	ECCE	POCK	BODE
BRAS	ELAM	HOAX	OKAY	SIAL	UDAD	IGBO	ECCO	PUCA	BODY
BRAT	ELAN	IGAD	OLAF	SIAM	UDAL	INBY	EECH	PUCE	BUDD
BRAW	ELAT	IKAT	OMAN	SIAN	ULAD	JIBE	ETCH	PUCK	BUDE
BRAY	EOAN	IMAM	OMAR	SKAG	ULAN	JOBE	FACE	RACA	BUDO
BUAT	ERAT	IRAN	OPAH	SKAT	UNAU	JUBA	FACT	RACE	CADE
CFAF	ESAU	IRAQ	OPAL	SKAW	UPAS	JUBE	FECK	RACK	CADI
CHAD	EVAN	IRAS	ORAL	SLAB	URAL	KIBE	FICO	RACY	CEDE
CHAI	EXAM	ISAR	ORAN	SLAE	URAO	KOBE	FOCH	RECD	CEDI
CHAL	EYAS	IYAR	OVAL	SLAG	USAK	KOBO	GECK	RECK	CODA
CHAM	FEAL	IZAR	PAAL	SLAM	UTAH	LIBS	HACK	RICA	CODE
CHAN	FEAR	JAAP	PEAG	SLAP	UTAS	LOBE	HECH	RICE	CODY
CHAP	FEAT	JEAT	PEAK	SLAT	VAAL	LOBO	HECK	RICH	DADA
CHAR	FIAT	JIAO	PEAL	SLAV	VEAL	LUBA	HECT	RICK	DADD
CHAT	FLAB	JOAN	PEAN	SLAW	VIAL	MOBY	HICK	RICO	DADO
CHAW	FLAG	JUAN	PEAR	SLAY	VOAR	NABK	HOCK	ROCA	DIDO
CHAY	FLAK	KEAN	PEAS	SNAG	WEAK	NEBO	HOCK	ROCH	DODO
CIAO	FLAM		PEAT	SNAP		NIBS	HUCK	ROCK	DUDE

DUDS	TIDE	BLEY	FLEX	LIEN	REEL	TREE	HEFT	EDGE	SIGN
EDDA	TIDY	BOER	FLEY	LIES	REEN	TREK	HUFF	EDGY	TEGG
EDDO	TODD	BRED	FOEN	LIEU	RHEA	TRET	IFFY	EGGS	TIGE
EDDY	TODO	BREE	FREE	LNER	RIEL	TREW	INFO	EIGG	TOGA
ENDS	TODY	BREN	FRET	LUES	RIEM	TREY	JEFF	ERGO	TOGE
FADE	UNDE	BRER	FUEL	LUEZ	SEED	TREZ	KOFF	EUGE	TOGO
FADO	UNDO	BREW	GAEA	LWEI	SEEK	TUES	LEFT	EUGH	TOGS
FIDE	URDÉ	CAEN	GAEL	MEED	SEEL	TWEE	LIFE	FEGS	UPGO
FIDO	URDU	CHEF	GEED	MEEK	SEEM	UBER	LIFT	FIGO	URGE
GADE	URDY	CHER	GEEK	MEER	SEEN	ULEX	LOFT	FOGG	VEGA
GADI	VADE	CHEW	GEEP	MEET	SEEP	UREA	LUFF	FOGY	VIGO
GIDE	VEDA	CIEL	GEEZ	MIEN	SEER	USED	MIFF	GAGA	WAGE
GODS	VIDE	CLEF	GHEE	MZEE	SHEA	USER	MUFF	GAGE	WEGG
HADE	WADD	CLEG	GIER	NEED	SHED	USES	NAFF	GIGA	YAGI
HADJ	WADE	CLEM	GLEE	NEEM	SHEM	UVEA	NIFE	GIGI	YEGG
HIDE	WADI	CLEW	GLEG	NEEP	SHET	VEEP	NIFF	GOGO	YOGA
HYDE	WADY	COED	GLEI	NIEF	SIEN	VEER	OFFA	GUGA	YOGH
INDY	WIDE	CRED	GLEN	NOEL	SKED	VIED	ORFE	HAGG	YOGI
JADE	YEDE	CREE	GLEY	NOES	SKEG	VIES	ORFF	HAGH	YUGA
JODO	YODH	CREW	GOEL	NUER	SKEN	VIEW	PUFF	HIGH	ACHE
JUDE	ABED	DEED	GOER	NYET	SKEO	WEED	RAFF	HOGG	ACHT
JUDO	ABEL	DEEK	GOES	OBEY	SKEP	WEEK	RAFT	HOGH	AGHA
JUDY	ABER	DEEM	GOEY	ODER	SKER	WEEL	REFT	HUGE	ASHE
KADE	ABET	DEEN	GREE	OGEE	SKET	WEEM	RIFE	HUGH	ASHY
KADI	ACER	DEEP	GREW	OGEN	SKEW	WEEN	RIFF	HUGO	BAHT
KIDD	ACES	DEER	GREY	OLEA	SLED	WEEP	RIFT	IAGO	BUHL
KUDU	ADEN	DEEV	HAEM	OLEO	SLEE	WEET	RUFF	INGE	DAHL
LADA	ADES	DIEB	HAET	OMEN	SLEW	WHEE	RYFE	INGO	DOHA
LADE	AGED	DIED	HEED	OMER	SLEY	WHEN	SAFE	JAGG	ECHE
LADY	AGEE	DIES	HEEL	ONER	SMEE	WHET	SOFA	JAGS	ECHO
LEDA	AGEN	DIET	HEEP	ONE'S	SMEW	WHEW	SOFI	KAGO	ECHT
LIDE	AGES	DIEU	HUER	OPEC	SNEB	WHEY	SOFT	LEGO	EPHA
LIDO	AHEM	DOEK	HUEY	OPEL	SNED	WIEL	SUFI	LEGS	ETHE
LODE	AJEE	DOER	IBEX	OPEN	SNEE	WIEN	TAFF	LOGE	FAHD
LUDD	AKEE	DOES	ICED	OVEL	SPEC	WREN	TAFT	LOGO	HAHA
LUDO	ALEC	DREE	ICEL	OVEN	SPED	YBET	TEFF	LOGS	HUHU
MADE	ALEW	DREG	IDEA	OVER	SPEE	YEED	TIFF	LOGY	JEHU
MEDE	ALEX	DREW	IDÉE	OWED	SPET	YLEM	TIFT	LUGE	JOHN
MIDI	AMEN	DREY	IDEM	OWEN	SPEW	YUEN	TOFF	LUGH	KOHL
MODE	AMES	DUEL	IDES	OXEN	SPEY	ZOEA	TOFT	LUGS	LAHN
MODO	ANEW	DUES	ILEX	OXER	STED	AFFY	TOFU	MAGE	LEHR
MODS	APEX	DUET	INES	OYER	STEM	ALFA	TUFF	MAGG	MAHU
NADA	AREA	DYER	ISER	OYEZ	STEN	ANFO	TUFT	MAGI	MOHR
NIDE	AREG	EDEN	ITEM	PEEK	STEP	BAFF	UFFA	MEGA	MOHS
NODE	ARES	EDER	IVES	PEEL	STET	BAFT	WAFF	NAGA	OAHU
NUDD	ARET	EGER	JEEL	PEEN	STEW	BIFF	WAFT	NIGH	OCHE
NUDE	AREW	EHEU	JEEP	PEEP	STEY	BOFF	WEFT	NOGO	OTHO
ODDS	ATEN	EMEU	JEER	PEER	SUER	BUFF	WIFE	ONGO	RAHU
OLDS	AVER	ENEW	JOEL	PHEW	SUET	BUFO	YAFF	ORGE	RUHR
OUDS	AVES	EPEE	JOEY	PIED	SUEY	CAFÉ	YUFT	ORGY	SOHO
PEDI	AWED	ETEN	KEEK	PIER	SUEZ	COFF	ZIFF	PAGE	TAHA
PODS	AYER	EVEN	KEEL	PIES	SWEE	CUFF	ALGA	PEGH	TAHR
PUDU	AYES	EVER	KEEN	PIET	SWEY	DAFF	ARGO	PIGS	TEHR
QADI	BAEL	EVET	KEEP	PLEA	SYEN	DAFT	BAGS	POGO	TOHO
RADA	BEEB	EWER	KIEL	PLEB	TAEL	DEFT	BEGO	PUGH	TSHI
REDD	BEEF	EWES	KIER	PLED	TEEM	DEFY	BEGS	RAGA	VEHM
REDE	BEEN	EXES	KIEV	PLEW	TEEN	DOFF	BIGA	RAGE	ABIB
REDO	BEEP	EYER	KLEE	POEM	TEER	DUFF	BIGG	RAGG	ACID
RIDE	BEER	EYES	KNEE	POET	TEES	EFFS	BOGS	RAGI	ACIS
RODE	BEES	FEED	KNEW	PREE	THEA	FAFF	BOGY	RAGS	ADIT
RUDD	BEET	FEEL	KOEL	PREP	THEE	FIFA	BUGS	RIGA	AGIN
RUDE	BHEL	FEER	LAER	PREY	THEM	FIFE	CAGE	RIGG	AGIO
SADE	BIEN	FEET	LEEK	PUER	THEN	FUFF	CIGS	RIGI	AGIS
SIDA	BIER	FIEF	LEEP	PYET	THEW	GAFF	DAGO	RUGA	AKIN
SIDE	BLEB	FLEA	LEER	QUEP	THEY	GIFT	DIGS	SAGA	ALIA
SODA	BLED	FLED	LEES	QUEY	TIED	GOFF	DOGE	SAGE	ALIF
SUDD	BLEE	FLEE	LEET	REED	TIER	GUFF	DOGS	SAGO	AMID
SUDS	BLET	FLEG	LIED	REEF	TOEA	HAFF	DOGY	SEGO	AMIE
TEDY	BLEW	FLEW	LIEF	REEK	TOEY	HAFT	DUGS	SIGH	AMIN

AMIR	ETIC	LAIS	ROIL	URIC	FIKE	YLKE	DULL	IDLY	NULL
AMIS	EVIL	LEIR	ROIN	URIM	FIKY	YOKE	DULY	ILLE	OGLE
ANIL	EXIT	LOID	RUIN	UTIS	FYKE	YUKE	EALE	ILLY	OILS
APIA	FAIL	LOIN	SAIC	VAIL	HAKA	YUKO	EELS	INLY	OILY
APIS	FAIN	LOIR	SAID	VAIN	HAKE	AALU	EILD	ISLE	OLLA
ARIA	FAIR	LOIS	SAIL	VAIR	HIKE	ABLE	ELLA	JELL	ONLY
ARID	FAIX	LUIT	SAIM	VEIL	HOKE	ABLY	ELLE	JILL	ORLE
ARIL	FEIS	MAIA	SAIN	VEIN	HOKI	AGLU	ESLA	JILT	ORLY
ARIS	FLIC	MAID	SAIR	VOID	HYKE	ALLO	FALA	JOLE	OSLO
ASIA	FLIP	MAIK	SEIF	VRIL	ICKY	ALLY	FALL	JOLL	OULK
AVID	FLIT	MAIL	SEIL	WAIF	ILKA	AMLA	FALX	JOLO	OWLS
AXIL	FLIX	MAIM	SEIR	WAIL	INKY	ARLY	FELL	JOLT	OWLY
AXIS	FOIL	MAIN	SHIA	WAIN	JAKE	ATLI	FELT	JULY	PALE
AYIN	FOIN	MEIN	SHIE	WAIT	JOKE	AULA	FILE	KALE	PALI
BAIL	FRIG	MEIR	SHIM	WEID	JUKE	AULD	FILL	KALI	PALK
BAIT	FRIT	MOIL	SHIN	WEIR	KAKI	AXLE	FILM	KELL	PALL
BEIN	GAIA	MOIT	SHIP	WHID	KIKE	BALA	FILO	KELP	PALM
BLIN	GAID	MUID	SHIT	WHIG	KOKO	BALD	FILS	KELT	PALP
BLIP	GAIN	MUIL	SHIV	WHIM	KUKU	BALE	FOLD	KILL	PELA
BOIL	GAIR	MUIR	SKIA	WHIN	LAKE	BALI	FOLK	KILN	PELE
BRIE	GAIT	NAIA	SKID	WHIP	LAKH	BALK	FULA	KILO	PELF
BRIG	GEIT	NAIK	SKIM	WHIR	LIKE	BALL	FULL	KILP	PELL
BRIM	GLIA	NAIL	SKIN	WHIT	LOKE	BALM	GALA	KILT	PELT
BRIO	GLIB	NAIN	SKIO	WHIZ	LOKI	BALT	GALE	KOLA	PILE
BRIS	GLID	NAIR	SKIP	WRIT	LUKE	BALU	GELD	KOLO	PILI
BRIT	GLIM	NEIF	SKIT	YMIR	MAKE	BELL	GELT	KYLE	PILL
BRIX	GLIT	NEIL	SLID	YWIS	MAKO	BELT	GILA	LALO	POLE
BUIK	GRID	NOIL	SLIM	ZEIN	MIKE	BILE	GILD	LELY	POLK
CAIN	GRIG	OBIA	SLIP	ZOIC	MOKE	BILK	GILL	LILL	POLL
CEIL	GRIM	OBIT	SLIT	ZOID	MOKI	BILL	GILT	LILO	POLO
CHIC	GRIN	ODIN	SMIT	BAJU	MOKO	BOLD	GOLD	LILT	POLT
CHIK	GRIP	OHIO	SNIB	DOJO	NIKE	BOLE	GOLE	LILY	POLY
CHIL	GRIS	OLID	SNIG	FIJI	NUKE	BOLL	GOLF	LOLA	PULA
CHIN	GRIT	OLIM	SNIP	FUJI	OAKS	BOLO	GULA	LOLL	PULE
CHIP	GUID	OLIO	SNIT	GAJO	OAKY	BOLT	GULE	LULU	PULI
CHIT	HAIG	OMIT	SOIL	JUJU	PEKE	BULB	GULF	LYLE	PULL
CLIO	HAIK	OPIE	SPIC	MOJO	PIKA	BULK	GULP	LYLY	PULP
CLIP	HAIL	OTIC	SPIF	NAJA	PIKE	BULL	HALE	MALE	PULU
COIF	HAIN	OTIS	SPIK	PUJA	POKE	CALC	HALF	MALI	PULY
COIL	HAIR	OVID	SPIN	REJA	POKY	CALF	HALL	MALL	RALE
COIN	HAIT	PAID	SPIT	ROJI	PUKE	CALK	HALM	MALM	RELY
COIR	HEIL	PAIK	SPIV	SEJM	RAKE	CALL	HALO	MALO	RILE
COIT	HEIR	PAIL	STIE	SIJO	RAKI	CALM	HALS	MALT	RILL
CRIB	HUIA	PAIN	STIM	SOJA	RAKU	CALP	HALT	MELA	ROLE
CRIT	IBID	PAIR	STIR	TOJO	RAKY	CALX	HELA	MELD	ROLF
CUIF	IBIS	PAIS	SUIT	ALKY	REKE	CELL	HELD	MELL	ROLL
CUIT	ILIA	PEIN	SWIG	ANKH	ROKE	CELT	HELE	MELT	RULE
DAIL	IRID	PHIL	SWIM	ASKE	RUKH	CILL	HELL	MILD	RULY
DAIS	IRIS	PHIZ	SWIZ	ASKR	SAKE	COLA	HELM	MILE	SALE
DEIL	ISIS	PLIÉ	TAIG	BAKE	SAKI	COLD	HELO	MILK	SALK
DOIT	IWIS	PLIM	TAIL	BAKU	SEKT	COLE	HELP	MILL	SALP
DRIB	JAIL	PRIG	TAIN	BIKE	SIKA	COLL	HILL	MILO	SALT
DRIP	JAIN	PRIM	TAIT	BOKE	SIKE	COLT	HILO	MILT	SELE
EDIT	JOIN	PRIX	TEIL	BOKO	SIKH	COLY	HILT	MOLA	SELF
EFIK	KAID	QUID	THIN	BUKE	SYKE	CULL	HOLD	MOLE	SELL
EGIS	KAIE	QUIM	THIR	BYKE	TAKA	CULM	HOLE	MOLL	SILA
ELIA	KAIF	QUIN	THIS	CAKE	TAKE	CULT	HOLI	MOLT	SILD
ELIS	KAIL	QUIP	TOIL	COKE	TIKA	DALE	HOLM	MOLY	SILE
EMIC	KAIM	QUIT	TRIE	DAKS	TIKE	DALI	HOLT	MULE	SILK
EMIR	KAIN	QUIZ	TRIG	DEKE	TIKI	DBLE	HOLY	MULL	SILL
EMIT	KEIR	RAID	TRIM	DIKA	TOKE	DELE	HULA	NALA	SILO
ENID	KNIT	RAIK	TRIN	DIKE	TOKO	DELF	HULE	NELL	SILT
EPIC	KRIS	RAIT	TRIO	DUKE	TYKE	DELI	HULK	NILE	SOLA
ERIA	KWIC	RAIL	TRIP	DYKE	WAKA	DELL	HULL	NILL	SOLD
ERIC	LAIC	REIF	TWIG	EKKA	WAKE	DILL	HYLA	NOLE	SOLE
ERIE	LAID	REIK	TWIN	ELKS	WAKF	DOLE	HYLE	NOLL	SOLO
ERIK	LAIK	REIN	TWIT	EOKA	WEKA	DOLL	IDLE	NOLE	SULK
ERIN	LAIN	REIS	UNIO	ESKY	WOKE	DOLT	IDLE	NOLL	SULU
ERIS	LAIR	REIS	UNIT	FAKE	YIKE	DULE	IDLE	NOLO	TALA

16

TALC	ARMY	KAMA	TAMP	CANE	GONE	LENS	PEND	SUNK	ZONE
TALE	AYMÉ	KAME	TEME	CANN	GONG	LENT	PENE	SUNN	ZUNI
TALK	BEMA	KAMI	TEMP	CANS	GONK	LINE	PENH	SYNC	ACOL
TALL	BIMM	KEMB	TIME	CANT	GUNK	LING	PENI	SYND	AEON
TELA	BOMA	KEMP	TOMB	CENS	GUNN	LINK	PENK	SYNE	AGOG
TELE	BOMB	LAMA	TOME	CENT	GUNS	LINN	PENN	TANA	AGON
TELL	BUMF	LAMB	TUMP	CINE	GUNZ	LINO	PENT	TANE	AHOY
TILE	BUMP	LAME	TUMS	CONE	GYNT	LINT	PINA	TANG	ALOD
TILL	CAMA	LAMP	TYMP	CONK	HAND	LONE	PINE	TANH	ALOE
TILT	CAME	LEME	VAMP	CONN	HANG	LONG	PING	TANK	ALOW
TOLA	CAMP	LIMA	VIMY	CONS	HANK	LUNA	PINK	TEND	AMOK
TOLD	COMA	LIMB	WAME	CONT	HANS	LUNE	PINS	TENE	AMOS
TOLE	COMB	LIME	WEMB	CONY	HANT	LUNG	PINT	TENG	AMOY
TOLL	COME	LIMN	WIMP	CUNT	HEND	LUNT	POND	TENT	ANOA
TOLT	COMM	LIMO	WOMB	DANE	HENT	LYNX	PONE	TINA	ANON
TOLU	COMO	LIMP	XEMA	DANG	HINC	MANA	PONG	TIND	ATOC
TULE	COMP	LIMY	YAMA	DANK	HIND	MANE	PONK	TINE	ATOK
TULI	CUMA	LOMA	YOMP	DENE	HING	MANG	PONS	TING	ATOM
TULL	CYMA	LOME	YUMP	DENT	HINT	MANI	PONT	TINK	ATOP
UGLI	CYME	LUMP	ZAMA	DENY	HOND	MANN	PONY	TINT	AVON
UGLY	DAME	LYME	ZIMB	DINE	HONE	MANO	PUNA	TINY	AVOW
VALE	DAMN	MAMA	ZOMO	DING	HONG	MANS	PUNG	TONE	AWOL
VALI	DAMP	MAME	ZYME	DINK	HONI	MANU	PUNK	TONG	AXON
VELA	DEME	MEMO	ACNE	DINT	HONK	MANX	PUNT	TONK	AZOV
VELE	DEMI	MIME	AGNI	DONA	HUNG	MANY	PUNY	TONS	BCOM
VELL	DEMO	MIMI	AÎNÉ	DONE	HUNK	MEND	QING	TONY	BLOB
VILE	DEMY	MOME	AINT	DONG	HUNT	MENE	RANA	TUNA	BLOC
VILL	DIMA	MUMP	AINU	DONT	INNS	MENG	RAND	TUND	BLOT
VOLA	DIME	NAME	ANNA	DUNE	IONA	MENT	RANG	TUNE	BLOW
VOLE	DOME	NEMO	ANNE	DUNG	ISNT	MENU	RANI	TUNG	BOOB
VOLT	DUMA	NOMA	ANNO	DUNK	IYNX	MINA	RANK	TYNE	BOOK
VULN	DUMB	NOME	ARNA	DUNS	JANE	MIND	RANT	ULNA	BOOL
WALD	DUMP	NUMA	ARNE	DUNT	JANN	MINE	REND	VANE	BOOM
WALE	EGMA	NUMB	ARNO	DYNE	JENA	MING	RENE	VANG	BOON
WALI	ELMO	OUMA	AUNE	EINE	JINK	MINI	RENO	VENA	BOOR
WALK	EMMA	PIMP	AUNT	ENNA	JINX	MINK	RENT	VEND	BOOT
WALL	EMMY	POME	BANC	ERNE	JUNE	MINO	RENY	VENN	BROD
WALY	ESME	POMO	BAND	ESNE	JUNG	MINT	RIND	VENT	BROG
WELD	FAME	POMP	BANE	ETNA	JUNK	MINX	RINE	VINA	BRON
WELK	FEME	PUMA	BANG	EYNE	JUNO	MONA	RING	VINE	BROO
WELL	FUME	PUMP	BANI	FAND	JYNX	MONG	RINK	VINO	BROS
WELT	GAMB	PUMY	BANK	FANE	KANA	MONK	RINT	VINT	BROW
WILD	GAME	RAMA	BANT	FANG	KANE	MONO	RONE	WAND	BUOY
WILE	GAMP	RAMI	BEND	FANK	KANG	MONS	RONG	WANE	CHOC
WILI	GAMY	RAMP	BENE	FANS	KANO	MONY	RONT	WANG	CHON
WILL	GEMS	REME	BENJ	FEND	KANS	MUNG	RUND	WANK	CHOP
WILT	GIMP	REMS	BENN	FENI	KANT	MYNA	RUNE	WANT	CHOU
WILY	GUMP	RIMA	BENT	FENT	KENO	NANA	RUNG	WEND	CHOW
WOLD	GYMP	RIME	BENZ	FIND	KENT	NAND	RUNS	WENT	CHOY
WOLF	HAME	RIMU	BIND	FINE	KINA	NANO	RUNT	WIND	CION
WULL	HAMS	ROME	BINE	FINK	KIND	NENE	RYND	WINE	CLOD
YALE	HEME	ROMP	BING	FINN	KINE	NINA	SAND	WING	CLOG
YALU	HEMI	RUME	BINK	FINO	KING	NINE	SANE	WINK	CLOP
YELD	HEMP	RUMI	BINT	FOND	KINK	NINO	SANG	WINN	CLOS
YELL	HOMA	RUMP	BONA	FONE	KINO	NONA	SANK	WINO	CLOT
YELP	HOME	SAMA	BOND	FONS	KOND	NONE	SANS	WONG	CLOU
YELT	HOMO	SAME	BONE	FONT	KONG	NONG	SANT	WONT	CLOW
YILL	HUMA	SAMI	BONG	FUND	KONK	NONO	SENA	WYND	CLOY
YOLK	HUME	SAMP	BONK	FUNG	KUNA	NUNC	SEND	WYNN	COOF
YULE	HUMF	SEMI	BONN	FUNK	LANA	OINK	SENS	YANG	COOK
ZILA	HUMP	SIMA	BONY	FUNS	LAND	OINT	SENT	YANK	COOL
ZOLA	HYMN	SIMI	BRNO	GANG	LANE	OONS	SIND	YOND	COOM
ZULU	IAMB	SIMP	BUNA	GANT	LANG	OONT	SINE	YONI	COON
ACME	ISMY	SOMA	BUND	GENE	LANK	ORNE	SING	YUNX	COOP
AGMA	JAMB	SOME	BUNG	GENS	LANT	OWNS	SINK	ZANY	COOT
ALMA	JIMP	SUMO	BUNK	GENT	LANX	PAND	SINO	ZENO	CROP
ALMS	JOMO	SUMP	BUNT	GENU	LEND	PANE	SONE	ZINC	CROW
AMMO	JUMA	SUMS	BYNG	GING	LENG	PANG	SONG	ZING	DHOW
ARMS	JUMP	TAME	CANA	GINK	LENO	PANT	SUNG	ZONA	DIOL

DIOR	IVOR	PYOT	TROW	OUPA	BARP	DERO	GORP	LORE	PARP
DOOB	JOOK	QUOD	TROY	OUPH	BARS	DERV	GORY	LORI	PARR
DOOK	KAON	QUOP	UPON	PAPA	BART	DIRE	GURL	LORN	PART
DOOL	KHOR	RIOT	VIOL	PEPO	BERE	DIRK	GURN	LORY	PÈRE
DOOM	KNOB	ROOD	VTOL	PIPA	BERG	DIRL	GURU	LURE	PERI
DOON	KNOP	ROOF	WHOA	PIPE	BERK	DIRT	GYRE	LURK	PERK
DOOR	KNOT	ROOK	WHOM	PIPI	BERM	DORA	GYRO	LYRA	PERM
DROP	KNOW	ROOM	WHOP	POPE	BERN	DORÉ	HARD	LYRE	PERN
DROW	KNOX	ROON	WHOT	PUPA	BIRD	DORM	HARE	MARA	PERT
EBOR	KOOK	ROOP	WOOD	QOPH	BIRK	DORP	HARK	MARC	PERU
EDOM	KROO	ROOT	WOOF	RAPE	BIRL	DORR	HARL	MARG	PIRL
ELOI	LAON	RYOT	WOOL	RAPT	BIRO	DORT	HARM	MARI	PIRN
ENOL	LAOS	SCOG	WOON	REPP	BIRR	DORY	HARN	MARK	PIRO
ENOS	LION	SCOP	WOOT	REPS	BORA	DURA	HARO	MARL	PORE
ENOW	LOOF	SCOW	YGOE	RIPE	BORD	DURE	HARP	MARM	PORK
EPOS	LOOK	SHOA	YOOF	RIPP	BORE	DURN	HART	MARO	PORN
EROS	LOOM	SHOD	YOOP	RIPS	BORN	DURO	HARZ	MARS	PORT
ETON	LOON	SHOE	ZION	ROPE	BORO	EARD	HERA	MART	PURE
EUOI	LOOP	SHOG	ZOOM	ROPY	BORS	EARL	HERB	MARY	PURI
EVOE	LOOR	SHOO	ZOOT	SEPS	BURD	EARN	HERD	MERE	PURL
EXON	LOOS	SHOP	ALPH	SEPT	BURG	EARP	HERE	MERI	PURR
EXOR	LOOT	SHOT	ALPS	SIPE	BURK	EARS	HERL	MERK	PYRE
EYOT	LYON	SHOW	BAPU	SOPH	BURL	EBRO	HERM	MERL	PYRO
FEOD	MEOW	SION	CAPA	SYPE	BURN	ECRU	HERN	MERU	RARE
FLOE	MOOD	SKOL	CAPE	TAPA	BURP	EIRE	HERO	MIRA	RORE
FLOG	MOOG	SLOB	CAPH	TAPE	BURR	EORL	HERR	MIRE	RORO
FLOP	MOOI	SLOE	CAPO	TAPS	BURT	EURE	HERS	MIRK	RORT
FLOR	MOOL	SLOG	CAPT	TAPU	BURY	EURO	HERY	MIRO	RORY
FLOW	MOON	SLOP	COPE	TIPI	BYRD	EYRA	HERZ	MIRV	RURP
FLOX	MOOP	SLOT	COPS	TIPU	BYRE	EYRE	HIRE	MORE	RURU
FOOD	MOOR	SLOW	COPY	TOPE	CARD	EYRY	HORE	MORI	SARD
FOOL	MOOT	SMOG	CUPS	TOPI	CARE	EZRA	HORN	MORN	SARI
FOON	MUON	SNOB	DEPT	TOPS	CARK	FARD	HORS	MORO	SARK
FOOT	NAOS	SNOD	DOPA	TUPI	CARL	FARE	HURL	MORS	SCRY
FROE	NEON	SNOG	DOPE	TYPE	CARP	FARM	HURT	MORT	SERA
FROG	NOOK	SNOT	DUPE	TYPO	CARR	FARO	INRI	MURE	SERB
FROM	NOON	SNOW	ESPY	UMPH	CART	FARR	INRO	MURK	SERE
FROW	NOOP	SOOK	EXPO	WEPT	CARY	FART	IVRY	MURL	SERF
GAOL	NYOS	SOOL	GAPE	WIPE	CERE	FERE	JARK	NARC	SERK
GLOB	OBOE	SOOM	GAPO	YAPP	CERO	FERM	JARL	NARD	SHRI
GLOM	OBOL	SOON	HAPI	YIPS	CERT	FERN	JARP	NARE	SIRE
GLOP	ODOR	SOOP	HEPT	YMPE	CIRÉ	FIRE	JERK	NARK	SIRI
GLOW	OXON	SOOT	HIPT	ZUPA	CIRL	FIRK	JIRD	NARY	SKRY
GOOD	PEON	SPOT	HOPE	AARU	CORD	FIRM	JURA	NERD	SORA
GOOF	PHOH	STOA	HOPI	ABRI	CORE	FIRN	JURE	NERK	SORB
GOOG	PHOT	STOB	HOPS	ACRE	CORF	FORB	JURY	NERO	SORD
GOOK	PION	STOL	HYPE	ACRI	CORK	FORD	KARA	NIRL	SORE
GOOL	PLOD	STOP	HYPO	ACRO	CORM	FORE	KARD	NORE	SORN
GOON	PLOP	STOT	IMPI	AERO	CORN	FORK	KARL	NORI	SORT
GOOP	PLOT	STOW	JAPE	AFRO	CORY	FORM	KART	NORK	SPRY
GOOR	PLOW	SWOB	KAPH	AGRA	CPRS	FORT	KERB	NORM	SURA
GROG	PLOY	SWOP	KEPI	AIRE	CURB	FURL	KERF	NORN	SURD
GROT	POOD	SWOT	KEPT	AIRN	CURD	FURR	KERN	NURD	SURE
GROW	POOF	THON	KIPE	AIRS	CURE	FURY	KIRI	NURL	SURF
GSOH	POOH	THOR	KIPP	AIRT	CURK	FYRD	KIRK	NURR	TARA
HOOD	POOK	THOS	KYPE	AIRY	CURL	GARB	KIRN	OARS	TARE
HOOF	POOL	THOU	LAPP	ARRU	CURN	GARE	KORA	OGRE	TARN
HOOK	POON	TOOK	LIPS	ARRY	CURR	GART	KORE	OKRA	TARO
HOON	POOP	TOOL	LOPE	AURA	CURT	GARY	KURD	OKRO	TART
HOOP	POOR	TOOM	MAPS	AWRY	DARD	GERE	KURI	OORT	TERA
HOOT	POOT	TOON	MOPE	AYRE	DARE	GERM	KURU	ORRA	TERF
HUON	PROA	TOOT	MOPP	BARB	DARG	GIRD	LARD	OURS	TERM
ICON	PROD	TROD	NAPE	BARD	DARI	GIRL	LARE	OVRA	TERN
IDOL	PROF	TROG	NIPA	BARE	DARK	GIRN	LARK	OWRE	TERR
IFOR	PROG	TRON	NOPE	BARF	DARN	GIRO	LARN	PARA	THRU
IGOR	PROM	TROP	OGPU	BARI	DART	GIRR	LERP	PARD	TIRE
IKON	PROO	TROT	OLPE	BARK	DERE	GIRT	LIRA	PARE	TIRL
IPOH	PROP	TROU	OOPS	BARM	DERM	GORE	LIRK	PARK	TIRO
IRON	PROW	TROW	OPPO	BARN	DERN	GORM	LORD	PARK	TIRR

TORC	BISE	GOSH	MISO	SESS	BITO	JOTA	PUTZ	APUS	GOUT
TORE	BISH	GOSS	MISS	SISS	BITS	JUTE	RATA	AQUA	GRUB
TORN	BISK	GUSH	MIST	SIST	BITT	KATA	RATE	ARUM	GRUE
TORR	BISP	GUST	MOSS	SOSS	BOTE	KATE	RATH	ARUN	GRUG
TORT	BOSH	HASE	MOST	SUSA	BOTH	KATI	RATS	ASUR	GRUM
TORY	BOSS	HASH	MUSA	SUSS	BOTS	KETA	RATU	ATUA	GRUS
TURD	BUSH	HASK	MUSE	SUSU	BOTT	KITE	RETE	ATUM	HAUD
TURF	BUSK	HASP	MUSH	TASH	BUTE	KITH	RETT	BAUD	HAUL
TURK	BUSS	HESP	MUSK	TASK	BUTT	KOTO	RITA	BAUK	HAUT
TURM	BUST	HESS	MUSO	TASS	BYTE	KYTE	RITE	BAUR	HOUR
TURN	BUSY	HEST	MUSS	TESS	CATE	LATE	RITT	BLUB	HOUT
TYRE	CASA	HISH	MUST	TEST	CATO	LATH	RITZ	BLUE	IRUS
TYRO	CASE	HISS	NASA	TOSA	CATS	LATS	ROTA	BLUR	JAUP
VARA	CASH	HIST	NASH	TOSE	CCTV	LETO	ROTE	BLUT	JOUK
VARE	CASK	HMSO	NASO	TOSH	CETE	LETS	ROTI	BOUK	KHUD
VARY	CAST	HOSE	NESH	TOSS	CITE	LETT	ROTL	BOUN	KNUB
VERA	CESS	HOSS	NESS	TOST	CITO	LITE	RUTA	BOUT	KNUR
VERB	CIST	HOST	NEST	TUSH	CITS	LITH	RUTE	BRUM	KNUT
VERS	COSE	HUSH	NISI	TUSK	CITY	LOTE	RUTH	BRUT	LAUD
VERT	COSH	HUSK	NOSE	UIST	COTE	LOTH	SATE	CAUK	LAUF
VERY	COSS	HUSO	NOSH	UPSY	COTH	LOTI	SATI	CAUL	LOUD
VIRL	COST	HUSS	NOSY	URSA	COTT	LOTO	SATS	CAUM	LOUP
WARB	COSY	INST	OAST	USSR	COTY	LOTS	SETA	CAUP	LOUR
WARD	CUSH	IPSE	ODSO	VASE	CUTE	LUTE	SETT	CHUB	LOUT
WARE	CUSK	JASS	OISE	VAST	CYTE	LUTZ	SITE	CHUG	MAUD
WARK	CUSP	JESS	ONST	VEST	DATA	LYTE	SITU	CHUM	MAUL
WARM	CUSS	JEST	OOSE	VISA	DATE	MATE	TATA	CHUT	MAUT
WARN	CYST	JISM	OSSA	VISE	DATO	MATH	TATE	CLUB	MOUE
WARP	DASH	JOSE	OUST	WASE	DITA	MATT	TATH	CLUE	MOUL
WART	DESK	JOSH	PASE	WASH	DITE	MATY	TATI	COUE	MOUP
WARY	DISA	JOSS	PASH	WASP	DITT	META	TATT	COUP	NEUK
WERE	DISC	JUST	PASS	WAST	DOTE	METE	TATU	COUR	NOUN
WERT	DISH	KESH	PAST	WEST	DOTH	MITE	TETE	CRUD	NOUP
WIRE	DISK	KEST	PESO	WISE	DOTS	MITT	TETH	CRUE	NOUS
WIRY	DISS	KISH	PEST	WISH	DUTY	MOTE	TITE	CRUX	NOUT
WORD	DOSE	KISS	PISE	WISP	EATS	MOTH	TITI	DAUB	NUUK
WORE	DOSH	KIST	PISH	WIST	ERTÉ	MOTT	TITO	DAUD	ONUS
WORK	DOSS	KOSS	PISO	WUSS	ESTE	MOTU	TOTE	DAUR	OPUS
WORM	DUSE	LASH	PISS	XOSA	ESTH	MUTE	TOTO	DAUT	OTUS
WORN	DUSH	LASS	POSE	XYST	ETTA	MUTI	TUTU	DOUC	OVUM
WORT	DUSK	LAST	POSH	YESK	ETTY	MUTT	TYTE	DOUM	OXUS
WURM	DUST	LESS	POSS	YEST	FATE	MYTH	UNTO	DOUP	PAUA
XERO	EASE	LEST	POST	ZEST	FATS	NATO	VATU	DOUR	PAUL
YARD	EAST	LISA	POSY	ACTA	FETA	NETE	VETO	DOUT	PHUT
YARE	EASY	LISK	PUSH	ACTS	FETE	NETS	VETS	DRUB	PIUM
YARN	ELSA	LISP	PUSS	AITU	FETT	NETT	VITA	DRUG	PIUS
YARR	ELSE	LIST	RASC	ALTA	FITT	NITH	VITE	DRUM	PLUE
YERK	ENSI	LOSE	RASE	ALTE	FITZ	NOTE	VOTE	ELUL	PLUG
YIRD	ERSE	LOSH	RASH	ALTO	GATE	NOTT	WATE	ETUI	PLUM
YIRK	ESSE	LOSS	RASP	ANTA	GATH	NUTS	WATT	EXUL	PLUS
YIRR	FASH	LOST	RAST	ANTE	GATT	OATH	WITE	FAUN	POUF
YORE	FASO	LUSH	RESH	ANTI	GETA	OATS	WITH	FEUD	POUK
YORK	FAST	LUSK	REST	ANTS	GETT	OCTA	WITS	FLUB	POUR
ZARF	FEST	LUST	RISE	ARTA	GITE	OETA	WYTE	FLUE	POUT
ZERO	FISC	LYSE	RISK	ARTS	GOTA	OKTA	YATE	FLUX	PRUH
ZORI	FISH	MASA	RISP	ARTY	GOTH	ONTO	YETI	FOUD	RAUN
ZURF	FISK	MASE	RISS	ASTI	GUTS	ORTS	YETT	FOUG	RHUS
ABSE	FIST	MASH	ROSE	ATTO	GYTE	OTTO	YITE	FOUL	ROUD
AESC	FOSS	MASK	ROSS	ATTU	HATE	PATE	ZATI	FOUR	ROUÉ
ALSO	FUSE	MASS	ROSY	AUTO	HATH	PATH	ZETA	GAUD	ROUL
APSE	FUSS	MASU	RUSA	BATE	HETE	PATU	ZITI	GAUL	ROUM
ARSE	FUST	MESA	RUSE	BATH	HETH	PITA	ABUS	GAUM	ROUP
BASE	GASH	MESE	RUSH	BATS	HOTE	PITH	ABUT	GAUP	ROUT
BASH	GASP	MESH	RUSK	BATT	HUTU	PITT	ADUR	GAUR	ROUX
BASK	GAST	MESO	RUST	BETA	INTI	PITY	AGUE	GEUM	SAUK
BASS	GCSE	MESS	SASA	BETE	INTO	POTE	ALUM	GLUE	SAUL
BAST	GEST	MESS	SASH	BÊTE	IOTA	POTS	AMUN	GLUM	SAUT
BESS	GISM	MISC	SASS	BETH	JATO	POTT	AMUR	GLUT	SCUD
BEST	GIST	MISE	SESE	BITE	JETÉ	PUTT	ANUS	GOUK	SCUG

SCUL	DAVY	BOWR	YAWP	YOYO	ARTA	GALA	META	RIVA	VENA
SCUM	DEVA	CAWK	YAWS	ABZU	ASIA	GAZA	MICA	RIZA	VERA
SCUR	DEVI	COWL	YAWY	ADZE	ATUA	GETA	MINA	ROCA	VINA
SCUT	DIVA	COWP	YOWE	BOZO	AULA	GIGA	MIRA	ROTA	VISA
SEUL	DIVE	COWS	YOWL	BUZZ	AURA	GILA	MOLA	RUGA	VITA
SHUL	DOVE	DAWD	DIXY	COZE	BABA	GLIA	MONA	RUSA	VIVA
SHUN	ENVY	DAWK	DOXY	COZY	BACA	GOTA	MOWA	RUTA	VOLA
SHUT	FIVE	DAWN	FOXY	DAZE	BALA	GOYA	MOXA	SABA	WAKA
SIUM	GAVE	DAWT	LUXE	DOZE	BEMA	GUGA	MOYA	SAGA	WAWA
SKUA	GIVE	DEWY	MAXI	DOZY	BETA	GULA	MUSA	SAMA	WEKA
SKUG	GYVE	DOWF	MOXA	FAZE	BIGA	HAHA	NADA	SASA	WHOA
SLUB	HAVE	DOWN	NEXT	FEZE	BOBA	HAKA	NAGA	SENA	XEMA
SLUE	HIVE	DOWT	NIXY	FIZZ	BOMA	HELA	NAIA	SERA	XOSA
SLUG	HOVA	FAWN	PIXY	FOZY	BONA	HERA	NAJA	SETA	YAMA
SLUM	HOVE	FOWL	POXY	FUZE	BORA	HOMA	NALA	SHEA	YOGA
SLUR	JAVA	GAWD	SAXE	FUZZ	BUBA	HOVA	NANA	SHIA	YUCA
SLUT	JIVE	GAWK	SEXT	GAZA	BUNA	HOYA	NASA	SHOA	YUGA
SMUG	JOVE	GAWP	SEXY	GAZE	CABA	HUIA	NEVA	SHWA	ZAMA
SMUR	KAVA	GOWF	TAXA	GIZZ	CAMA	HULA	NINA	SIDA	ZETA
SMUT	KIVA	GOWK	TAXI	HAZE	CANA	HUMA	NIPA	SIKA	ZILA
SNUB	LAVA	GOWL	TEXT	HAZY	CAPA	HYLA	NOMA	SILA	ZOEA
SNUG	LAVE	GOWN	WAXY	JAZZ	CASA	IDEA	NOVA	SIMA	ZOLA
SOUK	LEVA	HAWK	ABYE	JIZZ	COCA	ILIA	NUMA	SIVA	ZONA
SOUL	LEVE	HAWM	AMYL	LAZE	CODA	ILKA	OBIA	SKIA	ZUPA
SOUM	LEVI	HOWE	ARYL	LAZY	COLA	INCA	OCTA	SKUA	ABIB
SOUP	LEVY	HOWK	BAYE	LIZA	COMA	IONA	OETA	SOCA	AHAB
SOUR	LIVE	HOWL	BAYS	LOZI	CUBA	IOTA	OFFA	SODA	ARAB
SPUD	LIVY	IOWA	BAYT	MAZE	CUMA	IOWA	OKRA	SOFA	BARB
SPUE	LOVE	JAWI	BOYG	MEZE	CYMA	JAVA	OKTA	SOJA	BEEB
SPUN	MEVE	JAWS	BOYO	MOZE	DADA	JENA	OLEA	SOLA	BIBB
SPUR	MOVE	JEWS	BOYS	MOZZ	DATA	JOTA	OLLA	SOMA	BLAB
STUB	MOVY	JOWL	CEYX	NAZE	DECA	JUBA	ORCA	SORA	BLEB
STUD	NAVE	KIWI	CRYO	NAZI	DEVA	JUMA	ORRA	SOYA	BLOB
STUM	NAVY	LAWN	CUYP	OOZE	DIKA	JURA	OSSA	STOA	BLUB
STUN	NEVA	LEWD	DAYS	OOZY	DIMA	KAMA	OUMA	SURA	BOMB
STUR	NEVE	LOWE	EMYS	OUZO	DISA	KANA	OUPA	SUSA	BOOB
SWUM	NKVD	MAWK	ERYX	PIZE	DITA	KARA	OVRA	SUVA	BULB
TAUT	NOVA	MAWR	GOYA	RAZE	DIVA	KATA	PACA	TAHA	CHUB
THUD	NOVO	MEWL	GUYS	RAZZ	DOHA	KAVA	PAPA	TAKA	CLUB
THUG	PAVE	MEWS	GWYN	RIZA	DONA	KETA	PARA	TALA	COBB
THUN	PAVO	MOWA	HOYA	SIZE	DOPA	KINA	PAUA	TANA	COMB
THUS	RAVE	NEWS	HWYL	TOZE	DORA	KIVA	PAWA	TAPA	CRAB
TOUK	REVD	NEWT	ITYS	TUZZ	DUMA	KOLA	PEBA	TARA	CRIB
TOUN	RIVA	NOWL	KAYO	ZEZE	DURA	KORA	PELA	TATA	CURB
TOUR	RIVE	NOWT	KEYS	ZIZZ	EDDA	KUNA	PICA	TAWA	DAUB
TOUT	RIVO	NOWY	LLYR		EGMA	LADA	PIKA	TAXA	DIEB
TRUE	ROVE	PAWA	MAYA	4:4	EKKA	LAMA	PINA	TELA	DOAB
TRUG	RSVP	PAWK	MAYO	ABBA	ELBA	LANA	PIPA	TERA	DOOB
URUS	RYVE	PAWL	MOYA	ACTA	ELIA	LAVA	PITA	THEA	DRAB
VAUD	SAVE	PAWN	MOYL	AGHA	ELLA	LEDA	PLEA	TIKA	DRIB
VAUT	SEVE	POWN	ODYL	AGMA	ELSA	LEVA	PROA	TINA	DRUB
WAUL	SIVA	RAWN	ONYX	AGRA	EMMA	LIMA	PUCA	TOEA	DUMB
WAUR	SUVA	ROWE	ORYX	AIDA	ENNA	LIRA	PUJA	TOGA	FLAB
YAUD	TOVE	ROWT	PAYE	ALFA	EOKA	LISA	PULA	TOLA	FLUB
YAUP	URVA	SAWN	PNYX	ALGA	EPHA	LIZA	PUMA	TOSA	FORB
YEUK	VIVA	SEWN	RAYS	ALIA	ERIA	LOLA	PUNA	TUBA	FRAB
YOUD	VIVE	SHWA	RHYS	ALMA	ESLA	LOMA	PUPA	TUFA	GAMB
YOUK	VIVO	SOWM	SAYE	ALTA	ETNA	LUBA	RACA	TUNA	GARB
YOUR	WAVE	SOWP	SCYE	ALVA	ETTA	LUNA	RADA	UCCA	GLIB
ZBUD	WAVY	TAWA	SKYE	AMLA	EYRA	LYRA	RAGA	UFFA	GLOB
ZEUS	WEVE	TAWS	SKYR	ANDA	EZRA	MAIA	RAMA	ULNA	GRAB
ZOUK	WIVE	TAWT	SNYE	ANOA	FALA	MAMA	RANA	UREA	GRUB
ALVA	WOVE	TOWN	SOYA	ANTA	FETA	MANA	RATA	URSA	HERB
ARVO	YEVE	TOWT	STYE	APIA	FIFA	MARA	REJA	URVA	IAMB
BEVY	BAWD	WAWA	STYX	AQUA	FLEA	MASA	RHEA	UVEA	JAMB
CAVE	BAWL	WAWL	TOYS	AREA	FULA	MAYA	RICA	VARA	KEMB
CAVY	BAWN	WOWF	TRYE	ARIA	GAEA	MEGA	RIGA	VEDA	KERB
CIVE	BAWR	YAWL	VAYU	ARNA	GAGA	MELA	RIMA	VEGA	KNOB
COVE	BOWL	YAWN	WAYS		GAIA	MESA	RITA	VELA	KNUB

KRAB	ALOD	GAUD	NURD	TROD	AYRE	COVE	ETHE	HAME	KOBE
LAMB	AMID	GAWD	OLID	TUND	BABE	COZE	EUGE	HARE	KORE
LIMB	ARID	GEED	OVID	TURD	BADE	CREE	EURE	HASE	KYLE
NUMB	AULD	GELD	OWED	UDAD	BAKE	CRUE	EVOE	HATE	KYPE
PLEB	AVID	GILD	PAID	ULAD	BALE	CUBE	EYNE	HAVE	KYTE
SCAB	AWED	GIRD	PAND	USED	BANE	CURE	EYRE	HAZE	LACE
SERB	BALD	GLAD	PARD	VAUD	BARE	CUTE	FACE	HEBE	LADE
SIBB	BAND	GLID	PEND	VEND	BASE	CYME	FADE	HELE	LAKE
SLAB	BARD	GOAD	PIED	VIED	BATE	CYTE	FAKE	HEME	LAME
SLOB	BAUD	GOLD	PLED	VOID	BAYE	DACE	FAME	HERE	LANE
SLUB	BAWD	GOOD	PLOD	WADD	BEDE	DALE	FANE	HETE	LARE
SNEB	BEAD	GRAD	POND	WAFD	BENE	DAME	FARE	HIDE	LATE
SNIB	BEND	GRID	POOD	WALD	BERE	DANE	FATE	HIKE	LAVE
SNOB	BIND	GUID	PRAD	WAND	BETE	DARE	FAZE	HIRE	LAZE
SNUB	BIRD	HAND	PROD	WARD	BÊTE	DATE	FEME	HIVE	LEME
SORB	BLAD	HARD	QUAD	WEED	BICE	DAZE	FERE	HOKE	LEVE
STAB	BLED	HAUD	QUID	WEID	BIDE	DBLE	FETE	HOLE	LICE
STOB	BOLD	HEAD	QUOD	WELD	BIKE	DEKE	FEZE	HOME	LIDE
STUB	BOND	HEED	RAID	WEND	BILE	DELE	FIDE	HONE	LIFE
SWAB	BORD	HELD	RAND	WHID	BINE	DEME	FIFE	HOPE	LIKE
SWOB	BRAD	HEND	READ	WILD	BISE	DENE	FIKE	HORE	LIME
TOMB	BRED	HERD	RECD	WIND	BITE	DERE	FILE	HOSE	LINE
VERB	BROD	HIND	REDD	WOAD	BLAE	DICE	FINE	HOTE	LITE
WARB	BUDD	HOLD	REED	WOLD	BLEE	DIKE	FIRE	HOVE	LIVE
WEBB	BUND	HOND	REND	WOOD	BLUE	DIME	FIVE	HOWE	LOBE
WEMB	BURD	HOOD	REVD	WORD	BODE	DINE	FLEE	HUGE	LODE
WOMB	BYRD	IBID	RIND	WYND	BOKE	DIRE	FLOE	HULE	LOGE
ZIMB	CARD	ICED	ROAD	YARD	BOLE	DITE	FLUE	HUME	LOKE
ABAC	CHAD	IGAD	ROOD	YAUD	BONE	DIVE	FONE	HYDE	LOME
AC/DC	CLAD	IRID	ROUD	YEAD	BORE	DOGE	FORE	HYKE	LONE
AESC	CLOD	JIRD	RUDD	YEED	BOTE	DOLE	FRAE	HYLE	LOPE
ALEC	COED	KAID	RUND	YELD	BRAE	DOME	FREE	HYPE	LORE
ATOC	COLD	KARD	RYND	YIRD	BREE	DONE	FROE	IDÉE	LOSE
BANC	CORD	KHUD	SAID	YOND	BRIE	DOPE	FUME	IDLE	LOTE
BLOC	CRED	KIDD	SAND	YOUD	BUDE	DORÉ	FUSE	ILLE	LOVE
CALC	CRUD	KIND	SARD	ZBUD	BUKE	DOSE	FUZE	INGE	LOWE
CHIC	CURD	KOND	SCAD	ZOID	BUTE	DOTE	FYKE	IPSE	LUCE
CHOC	DADD	KURD	SCUD	ABBE	BYKE	DOVE	GADE	ISLE	LUGE
DISC	DARD	LAID	SEED	ABLE	BYRE	DOZE	GAGE	JADE	LUKE
DOUC	DAUD	LAND	SEND	ABSE	BYTE	DREE	GALE	JAKE	LUNE
EMIC	DAWD	LARD	SHAD	ABYE	CADE	DUCE	GAME	JANE	LURE
EPIC	DEAD	LAUD	SHED	ACHE	CAFÉ	DUDE	GAPE	JAPE	LUTE
ERIC	DEED	LEAD	SHOD	ACME	CAGE	DUKE	GARE	JETÉ	LUXE
ETIC	DIED	LEND	SILD	ACNE	CAKE	DULE	GATE	JIBE	LYLE
FISC	DRAD	LEWD	SIND	ACRE	CAME	DUNE	GAVE	JIVE	LYME
FLIC	DUAD	LIED	SKED	ADZE	CANE	DUPE	GAZE	JOBE	LYRE
HINC	DYAD	LIND	SKID	AGEE	CAPE	DURE	GCSE	JOKE	LYSE
KWIC	EARD	LOAD	SLED	AGUE	CARE	DUSE	GENE	JOLE	LYTE
LAIC	ECAD	LOID	SLID	AIDE	CASE	DYKE	GERE	JOSE	MACE
MARC	EGAD	LORD	SNED	AÎNÉ	CATE	DYNE	GHEE	JOVE	MADE
MISC	EILD	LOUD	SNOD	AIRE	CAVE	EALE	GIBE	JUBE	MAGE
NARC	ENID	LUDD	SOLD	AJEE	CEDE	EASE	GIDE	JUDE	MAKE
NUNC	FAHD	MAID	SORD	AKEE	CERE	ECCE	GITE	JUKE	MALE
OPEC	FAND	MAUD	SPED	ALBE	CETE	ECHE	GIVE	JUNE	MAME
OTIC	FARD	MEAD	SPUD	ALOE	CINE	EDGE	GLEE	JURE	MANE
RASC	FEED	MEED	STED	ALTE	CIRÉ	EINE	GLUE	JUTE	MARE
SAIC	FEND	MELD	STUD	AMIE	CITE	EIRE	GOLE	KADE	MASE
SPEC	FEOD	MEND	SUDD	ANCE	CIVE	ELBE	GONE	KAIE	MATE
SPIC	FEUD	MILD	SURD	ANNE	CLUE	ELLE	GORE	KALE	MAZE
SYNC	FIND	MIND	SWAD	ANTE	CODE	ELSE	GREE	KAME	MEDE
TALC	FLED	MOLD	SYND	APSE	COKE	EPEE	GRUE	KANE	MENE
TORC	FOLD	MOOD	TEND	ARNE	COLE	ERIE	GULE	KATE	MERE
URIC	FOND	MUID	THUD	ARSE	COME	ERNE	GYBE	KIBE	MESE
ZINC	FOOD	NAND	TIED	ASHE	CONE	ERSE	GYRE	KIKE	METE
ZOIC	FORD	NARD	TIND	ASKE	COPE	ERTÉ	GYTE	KINE	MEVE
ABED	FOUD	NEED	TOAD	AUDE	CORE	ESME	GYVE	KIPE	MEZE
ACID	FUND	NERD	TODD	AUNE	COSE	ESNE	HADE	KITE	MICE
ADAD	FYRD	NKVD	TOLD	AXLE	COTE	ESSE	HAKE	KLEE	MIKE
AGED	GAID	NUDD	TRAD	AYMÉ	COUE	ESTE	HALE	KNEE	MILE

21

MIME	PEKE	RUNE	TICE	WIDE	HALF	BRIG	PRIG	BOSH	NASH
MINE	PELE	RUSE	TIDE	WIFE	HOOF	BROG	PROG	BOTH	NESH
MIRE	PENE	RUTE	TIGE	WILE	HUFF	BUNG	PUNG	BUSH	NIGH
MISE	PÈRE	RYFE	TIKE	WINE	HUMF	BURG	QING	CAPH	NITH
MITE	PICE	RYVE	TILE	WIPE	JEFF	BYNG	QUAG	CASH	NOAH
MODE	PIKE	SADE	TIME	WIRE	KAIF	CHUG	RAGG	COBH	NOSH
MOKE	PILE	SAFE	TINE	WISE	KERF	CLAG	RANG	COCH	OATH
MOLE	PINE	SAGE	TIRE	WITE	KOFF	CLEG	RIGG	COSH	OPAH
MOME	PIPE	SAKE	TITE	WIVE	LAUF	CLOG	RING	COTH	OUCH
MOPE	PISE	SALE	TOGE	WOKE	LEAF	CRAG	RONG	CUSH	OUPH
MORE	PIZE	SAME	TOKE	WORE	LIEF	DANG	RUNG	DASH	PASH
MOTE	PLIÉ	SANE	TOLE	WOVE	LOAF	DARG	SANG	DICH	PATH
MOUE	PLUE	SATE	TOME	WYTE	LOOF	DING	SCAG	DISH	PECH
MOVE	POKE	SAVE	TONE	YALE	LUFF	DONG	SCOG	DOSH	PEGH
MOZE	POLE	SAXE	TOPE	YARE	MIFF	DRAG	SCUG	DOTH	PENH
MULE	POME	SAYE	TORE	YATE	MUFF	DREG	SHAG	DUSH	PHOH
MURE	PONE	SCYE	TOSE	YEDE	NAFF	DRUG	SHOG	EACH	PISH
MUSE	POPE	SELE	TOTE	YEVE	NEIF	DUNG	SING	EECH	PITH
MUTE	PORE	SERE	TOVE	YGOE	NIEF	EIGG	SKAG	ETCH	POOH
MZEE	POSE	SESE	TOZE	YIKE	NIFF	FANG	SKEG	EUGH	POSH
NAME	POTE	SEVE	TREE	YITE	OLAF	FLAG	SKUG	FASH	PRUH
NAPE	PREE	SHIE	TRIE	YLKE	ORFF	FLEG	SLAG	FISH	PTAH
NARE	PUCE	SHOE	TRUE	YMPE	PELF	FLOG	SLOG	FOCH	PUGH
NAVE	PUKE	SICE	TRYE	YOKE	PIAF	FOGG	SLUG	GASH	PUSH
NAZE	PULE	SIDE	TUBE	YORE	POOF	FOUG	SMOG	GATH	QOPH
NENE	PURE	SIKE	TULE	YOWE	POUF	FRAG	SMUG	GOSH	RASH
NETE	PYRE	SILE	TUNE	YUKE	PROF	FRIG	SNAG	GOTH	RATH
NEVE	RACE	SINE	TYPE	YULE	PUFF	FROG	SNIG	GSOH	RESH
NICE	RAGE	SIPE	TYRE	ZEZE	RAFF	FUNG	SNOG	GUSH	RICH
NIDE	RAKE	SIRE	TYTE	ZONE	REEF	GANG	SNUG	HAGH	ROCH
NIFE	RALE	SITE	TYNE	ZYME	REIF	GING	SONG	HASH	RUKH
NIKE	RAPE	SIZE	TYPE	ALIF	RIFF	GLEG	SPAG	HATH	RUSH
NILE	RARE	SKYE	TYRE	BAFF	ROLF	GONG	STAG	HECH	RUTH
NINE	RASE	SLAE	TYTE	BARF	ROOF	GOOG	SUNG	HETH	SASH
NODE	RATE	SLEE	UNBE	BEEF	RUFF	GRIG	SWAG	HIGH	SECH
NOLE	RAVE	SLOE	UNCE	BIFF	SEIF	GROG	SWIG	HISH	SICH
NOME	RAZE	SLUE	UNDE	BOFF	SELF	GRUG	TAIG	HOGH	SIGH
NONE	REDE	SMEE	URDÉ	BUFF	SERF	HAGG	TANG	HUGH	SIKH
NOPE	REKE	SNEE	URGE	BUMF	SPIF	HAIG	TEGG	HUSH	SOPH
NORE	REME	SNYE	VADE	CALF	SURF	HANG	TENG	INCH	SUCH
NOSE	RENE	SOLE	VALE	CFAF	TAFF	HING	THUG	IPOH	TACH
NOTE	RETE	SOME	VANE	CHEF	TEFF	HOGG	TING	ITCH	TANH
NUDE	RICE	SONE	VARE	CLEF	TERF	HONG	TONG	JOSH	TASH
NUKE	RIDE	SORE	VASE	COFF	TIFF	HUNG	TRIG	KAPH	TATH
OBOE	RIFE	SPAE	VELE	COIF	TOFF	JAGG	TROG	KESH	TECH
OCHE	RILE	SPEE	VICE	COOF	TUFF	JUNG	TRUG	KISH	TETH
OGEE	RIME	SPUE	VIDE	CORF	TURF	KANG	TUNG	KITH	TICH
OGLE	RINE	STIE	VILE	CUFF	WAFF	KING	TWIG	LAKH	TOSH
OGRE	RIPE	STYE	VINE	CUIF	WAIF	KNAG	VANG	LASH	TUSH
OISE	RISE	SURE	VISE	DAFF	WAKF	KONG	WANG	LATH	UMPH
OLPE	RITE	SWEE	VITE	DEAF	WOLF	LANG	WEGG	LECH	UTAH
ONCE	RIVE	SYCE	VIVE	DELF	WOOF	LENG	WHIG	LICH	VACH
OOSE	ROBE	SYKE	VOCE	DOFF	WOWF	LING	WING	LITH	WASH
OOZE	RODE	SYNE	VOLE	DOWF	YAFF	LONG	WONG	LOCH	WISH
OPIE	ROKE	SYPE	VOTE	DUFF	YOOF	LUNG	YANG	LOSH	WITH
ORFE	ROLE	TACE	WADE	FAFF	ZARF	MAGG	YEGG	LOTH	YEAH
ORGE	ROME	TAKE	WAGE	FIEF	ZIFF	MANG	ZING	LUGH	YODH
ORLE	RONE	TALE	WAKE	FUFF	ZURF	MARG	ALPH	LUSH	YOGH
ORNE	ROPE	TAME	WALE	GAFF	AGAG	MENG	AMAH	LYCH	ABRI
OWRE	RORE	TANE	WAME	GOAF	AGOG	MING	ANKH	MACH	ACRI
PACE	ROSE	TAPE	WANE	GOFF	AREG	MONG	ARCH	MASH	AGNI
PAGE	ROTE	TARE	WARE	GOLF	BANG	MOOG	ASCH	MATH	ALAI
PALE	ROUÉ	TATE	WASE	GOOF	BERG	MUNG	AYAH	MESH	ALBI
PANE	ROVE	TELE	WATE	GOWF	BIGG	NONG	BACH	MOCH	ANTI
PARE	ROWE	TEME	WAVE	GRAF	BING	PANG	BASH	MOTH	ASTI
PASE	RUBE	TENE	WERE	GUFF	BLAG	PEAG	BATH	MUCH	ATLI
PATE	RUDE	TETE	WEVE	GULF	BONG	PING	BETH	MUSH	AUDI
PAVE	RULE	THAE	WHEE	HAAF	BOYG	PLUG	BISH	MYTH	BABI
PAYE	RUME	THEE	WICE	HAFF	BRAG	PONG	BLAH		

BALI	PILI	BOCK	HOCK	PALK	WEAK	DELL	JOEL	REAL	ADAM
BANI	PIPI	BONK	HONK	PARK	WEEK	DHAL	JOLL	REEL	AHEM
BARI	PULI	BOOK	HOOK	PAWK	WELK	DIAL	JOWL	RIAL	ALUM
CADI	PURI	BOUK	HOWK	PEAK	WICK	DILL	KAIL	RIEL	ARAM
CEDI	QADI	BRAK	HUCK	PECK	WINK	DIOL	KARL	RILL	ARUM
CHAI	RABI	BUCK	HULK	PEEK	WOCK	DIRL	KEEL	ROIL	ATOM
DALI	RAGI	BUIK	HUNK	PENK	WORK	DOLL	KELL	ROLL	ATUM
DARI	RAKI	BULK	HUSK	PERK	YACK	DOOL	KIEL	ROTL	BALM
DELI	RAMI	BUNK	JACK	PICK	YANK	DUAL	KILL	ROUL	BARM
DEMI	RANI	BURK	JARK	PINK	YERK	DUEL	KOEL	RYAL	BCOM
DEVI	RIGI	BUSK	JERK	POCK	YESK	DULL	KOHL	SAIL	BEAM
ELOI	ROJI	CALK	JINK	POLK	YEUK	EARL	LEAL	SAUL	BERM
ENSI	ROTI	CARK	JOCK	PONK	YIRK	EDAL	LILL	SCUL	BIMM
ETUI	RUMI	CASK	JOOK	POOK	YOCK	EGAL	LOLL	SEAL	BOOM
EUOI	SAKI	CAUK	JOUK	PORK	YOLK	ELUL	LULL	SEEL	BRAM
FENI	SAMI	CAWK	JUNK	POUK	YOUK	ENOL	MAIL	SEIL	BRIM
FIJI	SARI	CHIK	KECK	PUCK	YORK	EORL	MALL	SELL	BRUM
FUJI	SATI	COCK	KEEK	PUNK	YUCK	EVIL	MARL	SEUL	CALM
GADI	SEMI	CONK	KICK	RACK	ZACK	EXUL	MAUL	SHUL	CAUM
GIGI	SHRI	COOK	KINK	RAIK	ZOUK	FAIL	MEAL	SIAL	CHAM
GLEI	SIMI	CORK	KIRK	RANK	ABEL	FALL	MELL	SILL	CHUM
GOBI	SIRI	CURK	KONK	REAK	ACOL	FEAL	MERL	SKOL	CLAM
HAPI	SOFI	CUSK	KOOK	RECK	AMYL	FEEL	MEWL	SOIL	CLEM
HEMI	SUFI	DANK	LACK	REEK	ANAL	FELL	MILL	SOOL	COMM
HOKI	TABI	DARK	LAIK	REIK	ANIL	FILL	MOIL	SOUL	COOM
HOLI	TATI	DAWK	LANK	RICK	ARAL	FOAL	MOLL	STOL	CORM
HONI	TAXI	DECK	LARK	RINK	ARIL	FOIL	MOOL	TAAL	CRAM
HOPI	THAI	DEEK	LEAK	RISK	ARYL	FOOL	MOUL	TAEL	CULM
IMPI	TIKI	DESK	LEEK	ROCK	AVAL	FOUL	MOYL	TAIL	DEEM
INRI	TIPI	DHAK	LICK	ROOK	AWDL	FOWL	MUIL	TALL	DERM
INTI	TITI	DICK	LINK	RUCK	AWOL	FUEL	MULL	TEAL	DOOM
JAWI	TOPI	DINK	LIRK	RUSK	AXIL	FULL	MURL	TEIL	DORM
KADI	TSHI	DIRK	LISK	SACK	BAAL	FURL	MYAL	TELL	DOUM
KAKI	TULI	DISK	LOCK	SALK	BAEL	GAEL	NAIL	TILL	DRAM
KALI	TUPI	DOCK	LOOK	SANK	BAIL	GALL	NEAL	TIRL	DRUM
KAMI	UGLI	DOEK	LUCK	SARK	BALL	GAOL	NEIL	TOIL	EDAM
KATI	VALI	DOOK	LURK	SAUK	BAWL	GAUL	NELL	TOLL	EDOM
KEPI	VLEI	DUCK	LUSK	SEEK	BELL	GEAL	NILL	TOOL	ELAM
KIRI	WADI	DUNK	MACK	SERK	BHEL	GILL	NIRL	TULL	EXAM
KIWI	WALI	DUSK	MAIK	SICK	BILL	GIRL	NOEL	TWAL	FARM
KURI	WILI	DYAK	MARK	SILK	BIRL	GOAL	NOIL	UDAL	FERM
KWAI	YAGI	EFIK	MASK	SINK	BOIL	GOEL	NOLL	URAL	FILM
LEVI	YETI	ERIK	MAWK	SOAK	BOLL	GOOL	NOWL	VAAL	FIRM
LOKI	YOGI	FANK	MEEK	SOCK	BOOL	GOWL	NULL	VAIL	FLAM
LORI	YONI	FECK	MERK	SOOK	BOWL	GULL	NURL	VEAL	FOAM
LOTI	ZATI	FINK	MICK	SOUK	BUHL	GURL	OBOL	VEIL	FORM
LOZI	ZITI	FIRK	MILK	SPIK	BULL	GYAL	ODAL	VELL	FROM
LWEI	ZORI	FISK	MINK	SUCK	BURL	HAAL	ODYL	VIAL	GAUM
MAGI	ZUNI	FLAK	MIRK	SULK	CALL	HAIL	OPAL	VILL	GERM
MALI	BENJ	FOLK	MOCK	SUNK	CARL	HALL	OPEL	VIOL	GEUM
MANI	HADJ	FORK	MONK	TACK	CAUL	HARL	ORAL	VIRL	GISM
MARI	AMOK	FUNK	MUCK	TALK	CEIL	HAUL	OVAL	VRIL	GLAM
MAXI	ANAK	GAWK	MURK	TANK	CELL	HEAL	OVEL	VTOL	GLIM
MERI	ARAK	GECK	MUSK	TASK	CHAL	HEEL	PAAL	WAIL	GLOM
MIDI	ATOK	GEEK	NABK	TEAK	CHIL	HEIL	PAIL	WALL	GLUM
MIMI	BACK	GINK	NAIK	TICK	CIEL	HELL	PALL	WAUL	GORM
MINI	BALK	GONK	NARK	TINK	CILL	HERL	PAUL	WAWL	GRAM
MOKI	BANK	GOOK	NECK	TONK	CIRL	HILL	PAWL	WEAL	GRIM
MOOI	BARK	GOUK	NERK	TOOK	COAL	HOWL	PEAL	WEEL	GRUM
MORI	BASK	GOWK	NEUK	TOUK	COIL	HULL	PEEL	WELL	GUAM
MUTI	BAUK	GUNK	NICK	TREK	COLL	HURL	PELL	WIEL	HAEM
NAZI	BEAK	HACK	NOCK	TUCK	COOL	HWYL	PHIL	WILL	HALM
NISI	BECK	HAIK	NOOK	TURK	COWL	ICEL	PILL	WOOL	HARM
NORI	BERK	HANK	NORK	TUSK	CULL	IDOL	PIRL	WULL	HAWM
OMNI	BILK	HARK	NUUK	USAK	CURL	JAIL	POLL	YAWL	HELM
PALI	BINK	HASK	OINK	WACK	DAHL	JARL	POOL	YELL	HERM
PEDI	BIRK	HAWK	OULK	WALK	DAIL	JEEL	PULL	YILL	HOLM
PENI	BISK	HECK	PACK	WANK	DEAL	JELL	PURL	YOWL	IDEM
PERI	BOAK	HICK	PAIK	WARK	DEIL	JILL	RAIL	ZEAL	IMAM

ITEM	WEEM	DURN	LIMN	SIAN	AMMO	HMSO	NOGO	XERO	JARP
JISM	WHAM	EARN	LINN	SIEN	ANFO	HOBO	NOLO	YOYO	JAUP
KAIM	WHIM	EDEN	LION	SIGN	ANNO	HOMO	NONO	YUKO	JEEP
LEAM	WHOM	ELAN	LOAN	SION	ARCO	HUGO	NOVO	ZENO	JIMP
LIAM	WORM	EOAN	LOIN	SKEN	ARGO	HUSO	ODSO	ZERO	JUMP
LOAM	WURM	ERIN	LOON	SKIN	ARNO	HYPO	OHIO	ZOBO	KEEP
LOOM	YLEM	ETEN	LORN	SOON	ARVO	IAGO	OKRO	ZOMO	KELP
LYAM	ZOOM	ETON	LYON	SORN	ATTO	IGBO	OLEO	ASAP	KEMP
MAAM	ADEN	EVAN	MAIN	SPAN	AUTO	INFO	OLIO	ATAP	KILP
MAIM	AEON	EVEN	MANN	SPIN	BEGO	INGO	ONGO	ATOP	KIPP
MALM	AGEN	EXON	MEAN	SPUN	BIRO	INRO	ONTO	BARP	KNAP
MARM	AGIN	FAIN	MEIN	STAN	BITO	INTO	OPPO	BEEP	KNOP
NAAM	AGON	FAUN	MIEN	STEN	BOKO	JATO	OSLO	BISP	LAMP
NEEM	AIRN	FAWN	MOAN	STUN	BOLO	JIAO	OTHO	BLIP	LAPP
NORM	AKIN	FERN	MOON	SUNN	BORO	JOCO	OTTO	BUMP	LEAP
OGAM	ALAN	FINN	MORN	SWAN	BOYO	JODO	OUZO	BURP	LEEP
OLIM	AMEN	FIRN	MUON	SYEN	BOZO	JOLO	PACO	CALP	LERP
OVUM	AMIN	FLAN	NAAN	TAIN	BRIO	JOMO	PAVO	CAMP	LIMP
PALM	AMUN	FOEN	NAIN	TARN	BRNO	JUDO	PEPO	CARP	LISP
PERM	ANAN	FOIN	NEON	TEAN	BROO	JUNO	PESO	CAUP	LOOP
PIUM	ANON	FOON	NOON	TEEN	BUBO	KAGO	PIRO	CHAP	LOUP
PLIM	ARAN	GAIN	NORN	TERN	BUDO	KANO	PISO	CHIP	LUMP
PLUM	ARUN	GEAN	NOUN	THAN	BUFO	KAYO	POGO	CHOP	MOOP
POEM	ATEN	GHAN	OBAN	THEN	CAPO	KENO	POLO	CLAP	MOPP
PRAM	AVON	GIRN	ODIN	THIN	CATO	KILO	POMO	CLIP	MOUP
PRIM	AXON	GLEN	OGEN	THON	CERO	KINO	PROO	CLOP	MUMP
PROM	AYIN	GOON	OMAN	THUN	CIAO	KOBO	PYRO	COMP	NEAP
QUIM	AZAN	GOWN	OMEN	TOON	CITO	KOKO	REDO	COOP	NEEP
REAM	BARN	GRAN	OPEN	TORN	CLIO	KOLO	RENO	COUP	NOOP
RIEM	BAWN	GRIN	ORAN	TOUN	COCO	KOTO	RICO	COWP	NOUP
ROAM	BEAN	GUAN	OVEN	TOWN	COMO	KROO	RIVO	CRAP	PALP
ROOM	BEEN	GUNN	OWEN	TRIN	CRYO	LALO	RORO	CROP	PARP
ROUM	BEIN	GURN	OXEN	TRON	DADO	LEGO	SAGO	CUSP	PEEP
SAIM	BENN	GWYN	OXON	TUAN	DAGO	LENO	SEGO	CUYP	PIMP
SCAM	BERN	HAIN	PAIN	TURN	DATO	LETO	SHOO	DAMP	PLAP
SCUM	BIEN	HARN	PAWN	TWIN	DECO	LIDO	SIJO	DEEP	PLOP
SEAM	BLIN	HERN	PEAN	ULAN	DEMO	LILO	SILO	DORP	POMP
SEEM	BONN	HOON	PEEN	UPON	DERO	LIMO	SINO	DOUP	POOP
SEJM	BOON	HORN	PEIN	VAIN	DIDO	LINO	SKEO	DRIP	PREP
SHAM	BORN	HUON	PENN	VEIN	DODO	LOBO	SKIO	DROP	PROP
SHEM	BOUN	HYMN	PEON	VENN	DOJO	LOCO	SOHO	DUMP	PULP
SHIM	BRAN	ICON	PERN	VULN	DURO	LOGO	SOLO	EARP	PUMP
SIAM	BREN	IKON	PION	WAIN	EBRO	LOTO	SUMO	FLAP	QUEP
SIUM	BRON	IRAN	PIRN	WARN	ECCO	LUDO	TACO	FLIP	QUIP
SKIM	BURN	IRON	PLAN	WEAN	ECHO	MAKO	TARO	FLOP	QUOP
SLAM	CAEN	IVAN	POON	WEEN	EDDO	MALO	TIRO	FRAP	RAMP
SLIM	CAIN	JAIN	PORN	WHEN	ELMO	MANO	TITO	GAMP	RASP
SLUM	CANN	JANN	POWN	WHIN	ERGO	MARO	TOCO	GASP	REAP
SOOM	CHAN	JOAN	QUIN	WIEN	EURO	MAYO	TODO	GAUP	REPP
SOUM	CHIN	JOHN	RAIN	WINN	EXPO	MEMO	TOGO	GAWP	RIPP
SOWM	CHON	JOIN	RAUN	WOON	FADO	MESO	TOHO	GEEP	RISP
SPAM	CION	JUAN	RAWN	WORN	FARO	MICO	TOJO	GIMP	ROMP
STEM	CLAN	KAIN	REAN	WREN	FASO	MILO	TOKO	GLOP	ROOP
STIM	COIN	KAON	REEN	WYNN	FICO	MINO	TOTO	GOOP	ROUP
STUM	CONN	KEAN	REIN	XIAN	FIDO	MIRO	TRIO	GORP	RSVP
SWAM	COON	KEEN	ROAN	YARN	FIGO	MISO	TYPO	GRIP	RUMP
SWIM	CORN	KERN	ROIN	YAWN	FILO	MODO	TYRO	GULP	RURP
SWUM	CRAN	KHAN	ROON	YUAN	FINO	MOJO	UMBO	GUMP	SALP
TEAM	CURN	KILN	RUIN	YUEN	GAJO	MOKO	UNCO	GYMP	SAMP
TEEM	CYAN	KIRN	RYAN	ZEIN	GAPO	MONO	UNDO	HARP	SCOP
TERM	DAMN	KLAN	SAIN	ZION	GIRO	MORO	UNIO	HASP	SEEP
THEM	DARN	KOAN	SAWN	ACRO	GOBO	MUSO	UNTO	HEAP	SHAP
TOOM	DAWN	LAHN	SCAN	AERO	GOGO	NANO	UPGO	HEEP	SHIP
TRAM	DEAN	LAIN	SEAN	AFRO	GYRO	NASO	URAO	HELP	SHOP
TRIM	DEEN	LAON	SEEN	AGIO	HALO	NATO	VETO	HEMP	SIMP
TURM	DERN	LARN	SEWN	ALLO	HARO	NEBO	VIGO	HESP	SKEP
URIM	DOON	LAWN	SHAN	ALSO	HELO	NEMO	VINO	HOOP	SKIP
VEHM	DOWN	LEAN	SHIN	ALTO	HERO	NERO	VIVO	HUMP	SLAP
WARM	DUAN	LIEN	SHUN	AMBO	HILO	NINO	WINO	JAAP	SLIP

SLOP	CARR	LIAR	TZAR	CESS	HERS	NOUS	THUS	CART	FLAT
SNAP	CHAR	LLYR	UBER	CIGS	HESS	NUTS	TOGS	CAST	FLIT
SNIP	CHER	LNER	USER	CITS	HISS	NYAS	TONS	CELT	FONT
SOAP	COIR	LOIR	USSR	CLOS	HOPS	NYOS	TOPS	CENT	FOOT
SOOP	COUR	LOOR	VAIR	CONS	HORS	OAKS	TOSS	CERT	FORT
SOUP	CURR	LOUR	VEER	COPS	HOSS	OARS	TOYS	CHAT	FRET
SOWP	CZAR	MAAR	VOAR	COSS	HUSS	OATS	TUES	CHIT	FRIT
STAP	DAUR	MAWR	WAUR	COWS	IBIS	ODDS	TUMS	CHUT	FUST
STEP	DEAR	MEER	WEAR	CPRS	IDES	OILS	UPAS	CIST	GAIT
STOP	DEER	MEIR	WEIR	CUBS	INES	OLDS	URUS	CLAT	GANT
SUMP	DIOR	MOHR	WHIR	CUPS	INNS	ONE'S	USES	CLOT	GART
SWAP	DOER	MOOR	YARR	CUSS	IRAS	ONUS	UTAS	COAT	GAST
SWOP	DOOR	MUIR	YEAR	DABS	IRIS	OONS	UTIS	COIT	GATT
TAMP	DORR	NAIR	YIRR	DAIS	IRUS	OOPS	VERS	COLT	GEAT
TEMP	DOUR	NEAR	YMIR	DAKS	ISIS	OPUS	VETS	CONT	GEIT
TRAP	DUAR	NUER	YOUR	DAYS	ITYS	ORTS	VIBS	COOT	GELT
TRIP	DYER	NURR	ABAS	DIAS	IVES	OTIS	VIES	COST	GENT
TROP	EBOR	ODER	ABUS	DIBS	IWIS	OTUS	WAYS	COTT	GEST
TUMP	EDER	ODOR	ACAS	DIES	JAGS	OUDS	WITS	CRIT	GETT
TYMP	EGER	OMAR	ACES	DIGS	JASS	OURS	WUSS	CUIT	GHAT
VAMP	EMIR	OMER	ACIS	DISS	JAWS	OWLS	XMAS	CULT	GIFT
VEEP	EVER	ONER	ACTS	DOES	JESS	OWNS	YAWS	CUNT	GILT
WARP	EWER	OVER	ADES	DOGS	JEWS	OXUS	YIPS	CURT	GIRT
WASP	EXOR	OXER	AGES	DOSS	JOSS	PAIS	YWIS	CYST	GIST
WEEP	EYER	OYER	AGIS	DOTS	KANS	PASS	ZEUS	DAFT	GLIT
WHAP	FAIR	PAIR	AIDS	DUBS	KEYS	PEAS	ABET	DART	GLUT
WHIP	FARR	PARR	AIRS	DUDS	KISS	PIES	ABUT	DAUT	GNAT
WHOP	FEAR	PEAR	ALAS	DUES	KOSS	PIGS	ACCT	DAWT	GOAT
WIMP	FEER	PEER	ALMS	DUNS	KRIS	PINS	ACHT	DEBT	GOUT
WISP	FLOR	PIER	ALPS	EARS	LAIS	PISS	ADIT	DEFT	GRAT
WRAP	FOUR	POOR	AMES	EATS	LAOS	PIUS	AINT	DENT	GRIT
YAPP	FURR	POUR	AMIS	EELS	LASS	PLUS	AIRT	DEPT	GROT
YAUP	GAIR	PSBR	AMOS	EGGS	LATS	PODS	ARET	DIET	GUST
YAWP	GAUR	PUER	ANAS	EGIS	LEES	PONS	AUNT	DINT	GYNT
YELP	GEAR	PURR	ANTS	ELIS	LEGS	POSS	BAFT	DIRT	HAET
YOMP	GIER	REAR	ANUS	ELKS	LENS	POTS	BAHT	DITT	HAFT
YOOP	GIRR	ROAR	APIS	EMYS	LESS	PUSS	BAIT	DOAT	HAIT
YUMP	GNAR	RUHR	APUS	ENDS	LETS	RAGS	BALT	DOIT	HALT
IRAQ	GOER	SAIR	ARES	ENOS	LIAS	RATS	BANT	DOLT	HANT
ABER	GOOR	SCAR	ARIS	EPOS	LIBS	RAYS	BART	DONT	HART
ACER	GUAR	SCUR	ARMS	ERIS	LIES	REIS	BAST	DORT	HAUT
ADAR	HAAR	SEAR	ARTS	EROS	LIPS	REMS	BATT	DOUT	HEAT
ADUR	HAIR	SEER	ASAS	EWES	LOGS	REPS	BAYT	DOWT	HECT
AFAR	HEAR	SEIR	AVES	EXES	LOIS	RHUS	BEAT	DRAT	HEFT
AGAR	HEIR	SKER	AXIS	EYAS	LOOS	RHYS	BEET	DUCT	HENT
AJAR	HERR	SKYR	AYES	EYES	LOSS	RIBS	BELT	DUET	HEPT
ALAR	HOAR	SLUR	BAAS	FANS	LOTS	RIPS	BENT	DUNT	HEST
AMIR	HOUR	SMUR	BAGS	FATS	LUES	RISS	BEST	DUST	HILT
AMUR	HUER	SOAR	BARS	FEGS	LUGS	ROSS	BINT	EAST	HINT
ARAR	IFOR	SOUR	BASS	FEIS	MAAS	RUNS	BITT	ECHT	HIPT
ASAR	IGOR	SPAR	BATS	FILS	MANS	SANS	BLAT	EDIT	HIST
ASKR	ISAR	SPUR	BAYS	FONS	MAPS	SASS	BLET	ELAT	HOLT
ASUR	ISER	STAR	BEDS	FOSS	MARS	SATS	BLOT	EMIT	HOOT
ATAR	IVOR	STIR	BEES	FUNS	MASS	SEAS	BLUT	ERAT	HOST
AVER	IYAR	STUR	BESS	FUSS	MESS	SENS	BOAT	EVET	HOUT
AYER	IZAR	SUER	BIAS	GEMS	MEWS	SEPS	BOLT	EXIT	HUNT
BAUR	JEER	TAHR	BITS	GENS	MISS	SESS	BOOT	EYOT	HURT
BAWR	KEIR	TEAR	BORS	GODS	MODS	SISS	BOTT	FACT	IKAT
BEAR	KHOR	TEER	BOSS	GOES	MOHS	SOSS	BOUT	FART	INST
BEER	KIER	TEHR	BOTS	GOSS	MONS	SUDS	BRAT	FAST	ISNT
BIER	KNAR	TERR	BOYS	GRAS	MORS	SUMS	BRIT	FEAT	JEAT
BIRR	KNUR	THAR	BRAS	GRIS	MOSS	SUSS	BRUT	FEET	JEST
BLUR	KSAR	THIR	BRIS	GRUS	MUSS	TAPS	BUAT	FELT	JILT
BOAR	LAER	THOR	BROS	GUNS	NAOS	TASS	BUNT	FENT	JOLT
BOER	LAIR	TIER	BUGS	GUTS	NESS	TAWS	BURT	FEST	JUST
BOOR	LEAR	TIRR	BUSS	GUYS	NETS	TEES	BUST	FETT	KANT
BOWR	LEER	TORR	CANS	HALS	NEWS	TESS	BUTT	FIAT	KART
BRER	LEHR	TOUR	CATS	HAMS	NIBS	THIS	CANT	FIST	KELT
BURR	LEIR	TSAR	CENS	HANS	NOES	THOS	CAPT	FITT	KENT

25

KEPT	OORT	SEPT	VENT	KUDU	BREW	FAIX	COTY	LELY	SPRY
KEST	OUST	SETT	VERT	KUKU	BROW	FALX	COZY	LEVY	STAY
KHAT	PACT	SEXT	VEST	KURU	CHAW	FLAX	CRAY	LILY	STEY
KILT	PANT	SHET	VINT	LIEU	CHEW	FLEX	DAVY	LIMY	SUEY
KIST	PART	SHIT	VOLT	LUAU	CHOW	FLIX	DEFY	LIVY	SWAY
KNIT	PAST	SHOT	WAFT	LULU	CLAW	FLOX	DEMY	LOGY	SWEY
KNOT	PEAT	SHUT	WAIT	MAHU	CLEW	FLUX	DENY	LORY	TEDY
KNUT	PELT	SIFT	WANT	MANU	CLOW	HOAX	DEWY	LUCY	THEY
KYAT	PENT	SILT	WART	MASU	CRAW	IBEX	DICY	LYLY	TIDY
LANT	PERT	SIST	WAST	MENU	CREW	ILEX	DIXY	MANY	TINY
LAST	PEST	SKAT	WATT	MERU	CROW	IYNX	DOGY	MARY	TOBY
LEAT	PHOT	SKET	WEET	MOTU	DEAW	JINX	DORY	MATY	TODY
LEET	PHUT	SKIT	WEFT	OAHU	DHOW	JYNX	DOXY	MOBY	TOEY
LEFT	PICT	SLAT	WELT	OGPU	DRAW	KNOX	DOZY	MOLY	TONY
LENT	PIET	SLIT	WENT	OMBU	DREW	LANX	DRAY	MONY	TORY
LEST	PINT	SLOT	WEPT	PATU	DROW	LYNX	DREY	MOVY	TRAY
LETT	PITT	SLUT	WERT	PERU	EBBW	MANX	DULY	NARY	TREY
LIFT	PLAT	SMIT	WEST	PRAU	ENEW	MINX	DUTY	NAVY	TROY
LILT	PLOT	SMUT	WHAT	PUDU	ENOW	ONYX	EASY	NIXY	TWAY
LINT	POET	SNIT	WHET	PULU	FLAW	ORYX	EDDY	NOSY	UGLY
LIST	POLT	SNOT	WHIT	RAHU	FLEW	PNYX	EDGY	NOWY	UPSY
LOFT	PONT	SOFT	WHOT	RAKU	FLOW	PRIX	EMMY	OAKY	URDY
LOOT	POOT	SOOT	WILT	RATU	FROW	ROUX	ENVY	OBEY	VARY
LOST	PORT	SORT	WIST	RIMU	GLOW	STYX	ESKY	OFAY	VERY
LOUT	POST	SPAT	WONT	RURU	GNAW	ULEX	ESPY	OILY	VIMY
LUIT	POTT	SPET	WOOT	SITU	GREW	YUNX	ETTY	OKAY	WADY
LUNT	POUT	SPIT	WORT	SULU	GROW	ABLY	EYRY	ONLY	WALY
LUST	PRAT	SPOT	WRIT	SUSU	KNEW	AFFY	FIKY	OOZY	WARY
MAAT	PUNT	STAT	XYST	TABU	KNOW	AHOY	FLAY	ORBY	WAVY
MALT	PUTT	STET	YBET	TAPU	MEOW	AIRY	FLEY	ORGY	WAXY
MART	PYAT	STOT	YELT	TATU	PHEW	ALAY	FOGY	ORLY	WHEY
MAST	PYET	SUET	YEST	THOU	PLEW	ALKY	FOXY	OWLY	WILY
MATT	PYOT	SUIT	YETT	THRU	PLOW	ALLY	FOZY	PITY	WIRY
MAUT	QUAT	SWAT	YUFT	TIPU	PROW	AMOY	FRAY	PIXY	YAWY
MEAT	QUIT	SWOT	ZEST	TOFU	SCAW	APAY	FURY	PLAY	ZANY
MEET	RAFT	TACT	ZOOT	TOLU	SCOW	ARLY	GABY	PLOY	BENZ
MELT	RAIT	TAFT	AALU	TROU	SHAW	ARMY	GAMY	POKY	BOAZ
MENT	RANT	TAIT	AARU	TUTU	SHOW	ARRY	GARY	POLY	BUZZ
MILT	RAPT	TART	ABZU	UNAU	SKAW	ARTY	GDAY	PONY	DIAZ
MINT	RAST	TATT	AGLU	URDU	SKEW	ASHY	GLEY	POSY	FITZ
MIST	REFT	TAUT	AINU	VATU	SLAW	AWAY	GOBY	POXY	FIZZ
MITT	RENT	TAWT	AITU	VAYU	SLEW	AWRY	GOEY	PRAY	FUZZ
MOAT	REST	TEAT	ARRU	WHAU	SLOW	BABY	GORY	PREY	GEEZ
MOIT	RETT	TENT	ATTU	YALU	SMEW	BEVY	GRAY	PULY	GIZZ
MOLT	RIFT	TEST	BABU	ZEBU	SNOW	BLAY	GREY	PUMY	GUNZ
MOOT	RINT	TEXT	BAJU	ZOBU	SPAW	BLEY	HAZY	PUNY	HARZ
MORT	RIOT	THAT	BAKU	ZULU	SPEW	BODY	HERY	QUAY	HERZ
MOST	RITT	TIFT	BALU	AZOV	STAW	BOGY	HOLY	QUEY	JAZZ
MOTT	RONT	TILT	BAPU	CCTV	STEW	BONY	HUEY	RACY	JIZZ
MUST	ROOT	TINT	BEAU	DEEV	STOW	BRAY	ICKY	RAKY	LUEZ
MUTT	RORT	TOFT	BEDU	DERV	THAW	BUOY	IDLY	RELY	LUTZ
NEAT	ROUT	TOLT	CHOU	GRAV	THEW	BURY	IFFY	RENY	MOZZ
NEST	ROWT	TOOT	CLOU	KIEV	TREW	BUSY	ILLY	ROPY	OYEZ
NETT	RUNT	TORT	DIEU	MIRV	TROW	CARY	INBY	RORY	PHIZ
NEWT	RUST	TOST	ECRU	SHIV	VIEW	CAVY	INDY	ROSY	PUTZ
NEXT	RYOT	TOUT	EHEU	SLAV	WHEW	CHAY	INKY	RUBY	QUIZ
NOTT	SALT	TOWT	EMEU	SPIV	AJAX	CHOY	INLY	RULY	RAZZ
NOUT	SANT	TRET	ESAU	ADAW	ALEX	CITY	ISMY	SCRY	RITZ
NOWT	SAUT	TROT	FRAU	ALEW	APEX	CLAY	IVRY	SEXY	SUEZ
NYET	SCAT	TWAT	GENU	ALOW	BRIX	CLOY	JOEY	SHAY	SWIZ
OAST	SCOT	TWIT	GURU	ANEW	CALX	CODY	JUDY	SKRY	TREZ
OBIT	SCUT	UIST	HABU	AREW	CEYX	COLY	JULY	SLAY	TUZZ
OINT	SEAT	UNIT	HUHU	AVOW	COAX	CONY	JURY	SLEY	WHIZ
OMIT	SECT	VAST	HUTU	BLEW	CRAX	COPY	LACY	SOAY	ZIZZ
ONST	SEKT	VAUT	JEHU	BLOW	CRUX	CORY	LADY	SPAY	
OONT	SENT		JUJU	BRAW	ERYX	COSY	LAZY	SPEY	

5:1									
	ADULT	ALIEN	ANGUS	ARHAT	AUDEN	BALMY	BEGAN	BLACK	BONUS
AARON	AEDES	ALIGN	ANIGH	ARIAN	AUDIO	BALOO	BEGET	BLADE	BONZE
ABABA	AEGIS	ALIKE	ANIMA	ARICA	AUDIT	BALOR	BEGIN	BLAIR	BOOBY
ABACK	AESOP	ALIVE	ANION	ARIEL	AUGER	BALSA	BEGUM	BLAKE	BOONE
ABACO	AFEAR	ALLAH	ANISE	ARIES	AUGHT	BAMBI	BEGUN	BLAME	BOONG
ABAFT	AFFIX	ALLAN	ANITA	ARISE	AUGUR	BANAL	BEHAN	BLANC	BOOST
ABASE	AFIRE	ALLAY	ANJOU	ARISH	AULIC	BANCO	BEIGE	BLAND	BOOTH
ABASH	AFOOT	ALLEN	ANKER	ARIST	AULIS	BANDA	BEING	BLANK	BOOTS
ABATE	AFORE	ALLEY	ANKLE	ARITA	AUNTY	BANDS	BEKAA	BLARE	BOOTY
ABBAS	AFOUL	ALLOT	ANKUS	ARKLE	AURAL	BANDY	BELAY	BLASÉ	BOOZE
ABBEY	AFRIT	ALLOW	ANNAL	ARLES	AURIC	BANJO	BELCH	BLAST	BOOZY
ABBOT	AFTER	ALLOY	ANNAM	ARMED	AUXIN	BANKS	BELGA	BLAZE	BORAX
ABDAR	AGAIN	ALLYL	ANNEX	ARMET	AVAIL	BANNS	BELIE	BLEAK	BORED
ABDUL	AGAMI	ALNUS	ANNIE	ARMOR	AVANT	BANTU	BELLE	BLEAR	BOREE
ABEAM	AGAPE	ALOES	ANNOY	AROID	AVAST	BARGE	BELLS	BLEAT	BORER
ABEAR	AGATE	ALOFT	ANNUL	AROMA	AVENA	BARMY	BELLY	BLEED	BORIC
ABELE	AGAVE	ALOHA	ANODE	AROSE	AVENS	BARON	BELOW	BLEEP	BORIS
ABHOR	AGENT	ALONE	ANOLE	ARRAN	AVERT	BARRA	BEMBA	BLEND	BORNE
ABIDE	AGGER	ALONG	ANOMY	ARRAS	AVIAN	BARRE	BENCH	BLESS	BORON
ABIES	AGGRO	ALOOF	ANSON	ARRAY	AVION	BARRY	BENDS	BLEST	BOSCH
ABLER	AGILE	ALOUD	ANTAR	ARRÊT	AVISO	BARTS	BENDY	BLIGH	BOSEY
ABLOW	AGING	ALPHA	ANTIC	ARRIS	AVOID	BASAL	BENET	BLIMP	BOSKY
ABODE	AGIST	ALTAI	ANTON	ARROW	AVOUÉ	BASAN	BENIN	BLIND	BOSOM
ABORT	AGLEE	ALTAR	ANVIL	ARSIS	AWAIT	BASES	BENNE	BLINI	BOSSY
ABOUT	AGLET	ALTER	ANZAC	ARSON	AWAKE	BASHO	BEROB	BLINK	BOSUN
ABOVE	AGLEY	ALULA	AORTA	ARTIE	AWARD	BASIC	BERRY	BLISS	BOTCH
ABRAM	AGLOW	ALURE	APACE	ARUBA	AWARE	BASIL	BERTH	BLITZ	BOTHA
ABRAY	AGNES	ALVIS	APAGE	ARVAL	AWARN	BASIN	BERYL	BLOAT	BOTHY
ABRIM	AGONE	AMAIN	APAID	ARYAN	AWASH	BASIS	BESET	BLOCK	BOTTE
ABSIT	AGONY	AMANT	APART	ASAPH	AWEEL	BASLE	BESOM	BLOKE	BOUGH
ABUJA	AGORA	AMASS	APEAK	ASCII	AWFUL	BASRA	BESOT	BLOND	BOULE
ABUNA	AGREE	AMAZE	APERT	ASCOT	AWOKE	BASSO	BETEL	BLOOD	BOUND
ABUSE	AHEAD	AMBER	APHID	ASCUS	AXIAL	BASTA	BETON	BLOOM	BOURG
ABYSM	AHMED	AMBIT	APHIS	ASDIC	AXIOM	BASTE	BETTE	BLOOP	BOWED
ABYSS	AIDAN	AMBLE	APODE	ASHEN	AXOID	BASTO	BETTY	BLOWN	BOWEL
ACCRA	AIDOS	AMEBA	APOOP	ASHER	AYRIE	BATCH	BEVEL	BLOWY	BOWER
ACERB	AIKEN	AMEND	APPAL	ASHES	AZOIC	BATED	BEVIS	BLUES	BOWIE
ACINI	AINEE	AMENE	APPAY	ASHET	AZOTE	BATES	BÉVUE	BLUEY	BOWLS
ACOCK	AIOLI	AMENT	APPEL	ASIAN	AZTEC	BATHE	BEVVY	BLUFF	BOXED
ACORN	AIRER	AMICE	APPLE	ASIDE	AZURE	BATHS	BEZEL	BLUNT	BOXER
ACRES	AIRES	AMIEL	APPLY	ASKER	AZYME	BATIK	BHANG	BLURB	BOYAR
ACRID	AISLE	AMIGO	APPRO	ASKEW	BABAR	BATON	BIBBY	BLURT	BOYAU
ACTIN	AITCH	AMINE	APPUI	ASOKA	BABEL	BATTY	BIBLE	BLUSH	BOYCE
ACTON	AKARA	AMINO	APRIL	ASPEN	BABOO	BAULK	BIDDY	BOARD	BOYLE
ACTOR	AKBAR	AMISH	APRON	ASPER	BABUL	BAWDY	BIDET	BOAST	BOYNE
ACUTE	AKELA	AMISS	APSIS	ASPIC	BACCY	BAYER	BIFID	BOCHE	BRACE
ADAGE	AKENE	AMITY	APTLY	ASSAI	BACKS	BAYLE	BIGHT	BODES	BRACK
ADAMS	ALACK	AMMAN	AQABA	ASSAM	BACON	BAYOU	BIGOT	BODGE	BRACT
ADAPT	ALAMO	AMNIO	ARABA	ASSAY	BADDY	BAZOO	BIJOU	BOGEY	BRADY
ADDED	ALANS	AMONG	ARBOR	ASSET	BADEN	BEACH	BIKER	BOGGY	BRAID
ADDER	ALAPA	AMORT	ARCOT	ASTER	BADGE	BEADS	BILGE	BOGIE	BRAIN
ADDIO	ALARM	AMOUR	ARCUS	ASTIR	BADLY	BEADY	BILLY	BOGLE	BRAKE
ADDIS	ALATE	AMPLE	ARDEA	ASTON	BAFFY	BEALE	BIMBO	BOGUS	BRAND
ADDLE	ALBAN	AMPLY	ARDEB	ASTRA	BAGEL	BEAMY	BINGE	BOHEA	BRANK
ADEEM	ALBEE	AMUCK	ARDEN	ASWAN	BAGGY	BEANO	BINGO	BOING	BRASH
ADEPT	ALBUM	AMUSE	ARDIL	ATHOS	BAHAI	BEANS	BIONT	BOLAS	BRASS
ADIEU	ALDAN	ANANA	ARDOR	ATILT	BAHUT	BEARD	BIPED	BOLUS	BRAVA
ADIGE	ALDER	ANDES	ARECA	ATLAS	BAIRD	BEAST	BIPOD	BOMBE	BRAVE
ADIOS	ALDIS	ANEAR	AREDE	ATLIN	BAIRN	BEAUT	BIRCH	BOMBO	BRAVO
ADLIB	ALEPH	ANELE	ARENA	ATMAN	BAIZE	BEBOP	BIRDS	BONAR	BRAWL
ADMIN	ALERT	ANEND	ARENE	ATOLL	BAJRI	BECKY	BIRTH	BONCE	BRAWN
ADMIT	ALEUT	ANENT	ARENT	ATOMY	BAKED	BEDAD	BISON	BONDI	BREAD
ADMIX	ALFIE	ANGEL	ARETE	ATONE	BAKER	BEDEW	BITCH	BONDS	BREAK
ADOBE	ALGAE	ANGER	ARGIL	ATONY	BAKHA	BEECH	BITER	BONER	BREAM
ADOPT	ALGID	ANGLE	ARGON	ATOPY	BALAN	BEEFY	BITTE	BONES	BREDA
ADORE	ALGOL	ANGLO	ARGOT	ATRIP	BALER	BEERY	BITTY	BONEY	BREDE
ADORN	ALIAS	ANGRY	ARGUE	ATTAR	BALFE	BEFIT		BONGO	BREED
ADSUM	ALIBI	ANGST	ARGUS	ATTIC	BALLS	BEFOG		BONNY	BREEM
	ALICE			ATTLE	BALLY	BEGAD			BREME

BRENT	BURMA	CARAT	CHEER	CIRCA	CODED	COURB	CRORE	DAKAR	DEPTH
BREST	BURNS	CARDS	CHEKA	CIRCE	CODEX	COURT	CROSS	DALEK	DERAY
BREVE	BURNT	CARER	CHERE	CISCO	CODON	COUTH	CROUP	DALIT	DERBY
BRIAN	BUROO	CARET	CHERT	CISSY	COHOE	COVEN	CROWD	DALLE	DERMA
BRIAR	BURRO	CAREW	CHESS	CIVET	COIGN	COVER	CROWN	DALLY	DERRY
BRIBE	BURSA	CAREY	CHEST	CIVIC	COKES	COVET	CROZE	DAMAN	DESEX
BRICK	BURST	CARIB	CHEVY	CIVIL	COLET	COVEY	CRUCK	DAMME	DESSE
BRIDE	BUSBY	CARLE	CHEWA	CIVVY	COLEY	COWAN	CRUDE	DAMON	DETER
BRIEF	BUSHY	CAROB	CHEWY	CLACK	COLIC	COWER	CRUEL	DANAE	DETOX
BRIER	BUSTY	CAROL	CHIAO	CLAIM	COLIN	COWRY	CRUET	DANCE	DEUCE
BRILL	BUTCH	CARRY	CHICA	CLAMP	COLLY	COXAL	CRUMB	DANDO	DEVIL
BRINE	BUTTE	CARTA	CHICK	CLANG	COLON	COXED	CRUMP	DANDY	DEWAN
BRING	BUTTY	CARTE	CHICO	CLANK	COLOR	COYLY	CRUOR	DANES	DEWAR
BRINK	BUXOM	CARVE	CHIDE	CLARA	COLTS	COYNE	CRUSE	DANTE	DEWEY
BRINY	BUYER	CARVY	CHIEF	CLARE	COLZA	COYPU	CRUSH	DARBY	DHABI
BRISK	BWANA	CASCA	CHILD	CLARK	COMBE	COZEN	CRUST	DARCY	DHOBI
BRIZE	BWAZI	CASCO	CHILE	CLARY	COMBO	CRABS	CRWTH	DARTS	DHOTI
BROAD	BYLAW	CASES	CHILI	CLASH	COMBS	CRACK	CRYPT	DATED	DIALS
BROCK	BYRON	CASTE	CHILL	CLASP	COMET	CRAFT	CUBAN	DATER	DIANA
BROIL	BYWAY	CATCH	CHIME	CLASS	COMFY	CRAIG	CUBBY	DATES	DIARY
BROKE	CABAL	CATER	CHIMP	CLAUS	COMIC	CRAKE	CUBEB	DATUK	DIAZO
BRONX	CABAS	CATES	CHINA	CLAVE	COMMA	CRAMP	CUBED	DATUM	DICEY
BROOD	CABBY	CATTY	CHINE	CLEAN	COMPO	CRANE	CUBIC	DAUBE	DICKY
BROOK	CABER	CAULD	CHING	CLEAR	COMTE	CRANK	CUBIT	DAUNT	DIDNT
BROOL	CABIN	CAULK	CHINK	CLEAT	COMUS	CRAPE	CUDDY	DAVID	DIEGO
BROOM	CABLE	CAUSE	CHINO	CLECK	CONAN	CRAPS	CUFFS	DAVIS	DIGHT
BROSE	CABOB	CAVAN	CHIPS	CLEEK	CONCH	CRARE	CUFFY	DAVIT	DIGIT
BROTH	CABOT	CAVIL	CHIRK	CLEEP	CONDE	CRASH	CUFIC	DAYAK	DIKER
BROWN	CACAO	CDROM	CHIRL	CLEFT	CONDO	CRASS	CULET	DAZED	DILDO
BRUCE	CACHE	CEASE	CHIRP	CLEPE	CONEY	CRATE	CULEX	DEATH	DIMLY
BRUIN	CADDY	CECIL	CHIRR	CLERK	CONGÉ	CRAVE	CULLY	DEBAG	DINAR
BRUIT	CADET	CECUM	CHIRT	CLICK	CONGO	CRAWL	CUMIN	DEBAR	DINER
BRULE	CADGE	CEDAR	CHIVE	CLIFF	CONIC	CRAZE	CUPAR	DEBEL	DINGE
BRUME	CADGY	CELEB	CHIVY	CLIFT	CONTE	CRAZY	CUPEL	DEBIT	DINGO
BRUNO	CADRE	CELLA	CHLOE	CLIMB	COOEE	CREAK	CUPID	DEBUG	DINGY
BRUNT	CAGEY	CELLO	CHOCK	CLIME	COOKS	CREAM	CUPPA	DEBUT	DINKA
BRUSH	CAGOT	CELLS	CHOCO	CLING	COOMB	CRECY	CURDS	DECAL	DINKY
BRUTE	CAINE	CENCI	CHOIR	CLINK	COOPT	CREDO	CURED	DECAY	DIODE
BUBBY	CAIRN	CENSE	CHOKE	CLINT	COPER	CREED	CURER	DECCA	DIOTA
BUCCA	CAIRO	CENTO	CHOKO	CLIVE	COPPY	CREEK	CURIA	DECKO	DIPPY
BUCKO	CAIUS	CEORL	CHOKY	CLOAK	COPRA	CREEL	CURIE	DECON	DIRGE
BUCKS	CAJUN	CERES	CHOMP	CLOCK	COPSE	CREEP	CURIO	DECOR	DIRTY
BUDDY	CALEB	CERNE	CHOOK	CLOMP	CORAL	CREME	CURLY	DECOY	DISCO
BUDGE	CALIX	CESAR	CHOPS	CLONE	CORAM	CREON	CURRY	DECRY	DISHY
BUFFO	CALOR	CETUS	CHORD	CLOOT	CORDS	CREPE	CURSE	DEEDS	DITAL
BUFFS	CALPE	CHACO	CHORE	CLOSE	CORED	CREPT	CURST	DEFER	DITCH
BUGGY	CALVE	CHAFE	CHOSE	CLOTH	CORER	CRESS	CURVE	DEFOE	DITTO
BUGLE	CALYX	CHAFF	CHOTA	CLOUD	CORFE	CREST	CURVY	DEGAS	DITTY
BUICK	CAMAS	CHAIN	CHOTT	CLOUT	CORFU	CRETE	CUSHY	DEIGN	DIVAN
BUILD	CAMEL	CHAIR	CHUBB	CLOVE	CORGI	CREWE	CUTCH	DEIST	DIVER
BUILT	CAMEO	CHALK	CHUCK	CLOWN	CORIN	CRICK	CUTEY	DEITY	DIVES
BULGE	CAMIS	CHAMP	CHUFF	CLOZE	CORKY	CRIED	CUTIE	DEKKO	DIVOT
BULKY	CAMPO	CHANT	CHUMP	CLUBS	CORNY	CRIER	CUTIS	DELAY	DIVVY
BULLA	CAMUS	CHAOS	CHUNK	CLUCK	COROT	CRIES	CUTTY	DELFT	DIWAN
BULLS	CANAL	CHAPE	CHURL	CLUMP	CORPS	CRIME	CYCAD	DELHI	DIXIE
BULLY	CANDY	CHAPS	CHURN	CLUNG	CORSE	CRIMP	CYCLE	DELOS	DIZZY
BULOW	CANES	CHARD	CHURR	CLUNK	CORSO	CRISE	CYMRU	DELPH	DOBBY
BUMPH	CANNA	CHARK	CHUTE	CLYDE	CORVO	CRISP	CYMRY	DELTA	DOBRO
BUMPY	CANNY	CHARM	CHYLE	COACH	COSEC	CROAK	CYNIC	DELVE	DOCKS
BUNCE	CANOE	CHART	CHYME	COADE	COSMO	CROAT	CYRUS	DEMOB	DODDY
BUNCH	CANON	CHARY	CHYND	COAST	COSTA	CROCE	CZECH	DEMON	DODGE
BUNCO	CANTO	CIBOL	CIDER	COATI	COSTS	CROCK	DACCA	DEMOS	DODGO
BUNDY	CAPER	CHASE	CIGAR	COBIA	COTTA	CROFT	DACHA	DEMUR	DODGY
BUNGY	CAPET	CHASM	CIGGY	COBOL	COUCH	CROME	DADDY	DENIM	DOGGO
BUNNY	CAPIZ	CHEAP	CILIA	COBRA	COUDÉ	CRONE	DAFFY	DENIS	DOGGY
BURGH	CAPON	CHEAT	CILLA	COCCI	COUGH	CRONK	DAGON	DENSE	DOGMA
BURIN	CAPOT	CHECK	CINCH	COCKY	COULD	CRONY	DAILY	DENYS	DOILY
BURKE	CAPRI	CHEEK	CINNA	COCOA	COUNT	CROOK	DAIRY	DEPOT	DOING
BURLY	CAPUT	CHEEP		COCOS	COUPE	CROPS	DAISY		DOLCE
									DOLIN

DOLLY	DROOP	EERIE	ENJOY	EXACT	FECAL	FLAKY	FORTH	FUSTY	GEODE
DOMED	DROPS	EGDON	ENMEW	EXALT	FECES	FLAME	FORTY	FUTON	GERBE
DONAR	DROSS	EGEST	ENNUI	EXCEL	FECIT	FLANK	FORUM	FUZEE	GESSE
DONAT	DROVE	EGGAR	ENOCH	EXEAT	FEIGN	FLARE	FOSSA	FUZZY	GESSO
DONEE	DROWN	EGRET	ENORM	EXERT	FEINT	FLASH	FOSSE	FYLDE	GESTE
DONNA	DRUGS	EGYPT	ENROL	EXILE	FELIS	FLASK	FOUET	GABBY	GETUP
DONNE	DRUID	EIDER	ENSEW	EXINE	FELIX	FLATS	FOULÉ	GABLE	GHANA
DONOR	DRUNK	EIGER	ENSOR	EXIST	FELLA	FLECK	FOUND	GABON	GHATS
DOONE	DRUPE	EIGHT	ENSUE	EXODE	FELON	FLEET	FOUNT	GADGE	GHAZI
DOORN	DRURY	EIKON	ENTER	EXPEL	FEMTO	FLESH	FOURS	GADUS	GHOST
DOORS	DRUZE	EILAT	ENTRY	EXTOL	FEMUR	FLEUR	FOVEA	GAFFE	GHOUL
DOPEY	DRYAD	EJECT	ENUGU	EXTRA	FENCE	FLEWS	FOXED	GAILY	GHYLL
DORAS	DRYER	ELAND	ENURE	EXUDE	FENNY	FLICK	FOYER	GAINS	GIANT
DOREE	DRYLY	ELATE	ENVOI	EXULT	FEOFF	FLIER	FOYLE	GAIUS	GIBBY
DORIC	DUALA	ELBOW	ENVOY	EXURB	FERAL	FLIES	FRACK	GALAM	GIBUS
DORIS	DUBAI	ELDER	EOLIC	EYRIE	FERIA	FLING	FRACT	GALBA	GIDDY
DORMY	DUCAT	ELECT	EOSIN	EYTIE	FERMI	FLINT	FRAIL	GALEA	GIFTS
DORTS	DUCHY	ELEGY	EPHOD	FABER	FERRY	FLIRT	FRAME	GALEN	GIGLI
DOTTY	DUCKS	ELENE	EPHOR	FABLE	FESSE	FLOAT	FRANC	GALOP	GIGOT
DOUAI	DUCKY	ELFIN	EPOCH	FABRÉ	FESTA	FLOCK	FRANK	GAMAY	GIGUE
DOUAR	DUDDY	ELGAR	EPODE	FACER	FESTE	FLONG	FRANS	GAMBA	GILES
DOUAY	DUKAS	ELGIN	EPOXY	FACET	FETAL	FLOOD	FRANZ	GAMBO	GILET
DOUBT	DUKES	ELIAD	EPSOM	FACIA	FETCH	FLOOR	FRAUD	GAMES	GILLS
DOUCE	DULAC	ELIAS	EQUAL	FACTO	FETID	FLOPS	FREAK	GAMIC	GILTS
DOUGH	DUMAS	ELIDE	EQUIP	FACTS	FETOR	FLORA	FREED	GAMMA	GIMEL
DOUMA	DUMMY	ELIHU	ERARD	FADDY	FETUS	FLOSS	FREON	GAMMY	GIMPY
DOURA	DUMPS	ELIOT	ERASE	FADED	FEVER	FLOTA	FRESH	GAMUT	GIPPO
DOURO	DUMPY	ELITE	ERATO	FADGE	FEWER	FLOUR	FREUD	GANDA	GIPSY
DOUSE	DUNCE	ELLEN	ERECT	FAERY	FIBER	FLOUT	FRIAR	GANJA	GIRLS
DOVER	DUNNO	ELLIS	ERGOT	FAGOT	FIBRE	FLOWN	FRIED	GANNY	GIRLY
DOWDY	DUOMO	ELMER	ERICA	FAGUS	FIBRO	FLUFF	FRIES	GAPER	GIRTH
DOWEL	DUPIN	ELOGE	ERICK	FAINS	FICHE	FLUID	FRILL	GARBO	GISMO
DOWER	DUPLE	ELOGY	ERNIE	FAINT	FICHU	FLUKE	FRISK	GARDA	GIVEN
DOWNS	DURER	ELOPE	ERNST	FAIRY	FIDEL	FLUME	FRIST	GARNI	GIVER
DOWNY	DUROY	ELSAN	ERODE	FAITH	FIDES	FLUMP	FRITH	GARTH	GIZMO
DOWRY	DURRY	ELTON	ERROR	FAKER	FIELD	FLUNG	FRITZ	GARUM	GLACE
DOWSE	DURST	ELUDE	ERUCA	FAKIR	FIEND	FLUNK	FROCK	GASES	GLADE
DOYEN	DURUM	ELVAN	ERUCT	FALDO	FIERE	FLUON	FROND	GASPÉ	GLAIR
DOYLE	DUSKY	ELVER	ERUPT	FALLA	FIERY	FLUSH	FRONT	GASSY	GLAND
DOYLY	DUSTY	ELVES	ESCOT	FALLS	FIFTH	FLUTE	FROST	GATED	GLANS
DOZEN	DUTCH	ELVIS	ESKER	FALSE	FIFTY	FLYER	FROTH	GAUDE	GLASS
DRACO	DUVAL	EMAIL	ESROM	FAMED	FIGHT	FLYTE	FROWN	GAUDY	GLAZE
DRAFT	DUVET	EMBED	ESSAY	FANAL	FILCH	FOAMY	FROWY	GAUGE	GLEAM
DRAIN	DWARF	EMBER	ESTER	FANCY	FILET	FOCAL	FROZE	GAULT	GLEAN
DRAKE	DWELL	EMBOW	ESTOC	FANNY	FILLY	FOCUS	FRUIT	GAUNT	GLEBE
DRAMA	DYFED	EMBOX	ESTOP	FANON	FILMS	FOEHN	FRUMP	GAUSS	GLEEK
DRANK	DYING	EMBUS	ETAGE	FARAD	FILMY	FOGEY	FUBSY	GAUZE	GLEET
DRAPE	DYKER	EMCEE	ETAIN	FARCE	FILTH	FOGGY	FUCHS	GAUZY	GLIDE
DRAWL	DYLAN	EMDEN	ETAPE	FARCI	FINAL	FOIST	FUDGE	GAVEL	GLIFF
DRAWN	DYULA	EMEND	ETATS	FARCY	FINCH	FOLIC	FUERO	GAWKY	GLINT
DREAD	EAGER	EMERY	ETHAL	FARGO	FINER	FOLIE	FUGAL	GAYAL	GLISK
DREAM	EAGLE	EMILE	ETHER	FARNE	FINIS	FOLIO	FUGGY	GAZON	GLITZ
DREAR	EARLY	EMILY	ETHIC	FAROE	FINKS	FOLKS	FUGUE	GÉANT	GLOAT
DREGS	EARTH	EMLYN	ETHOS	FARSE	FIORD	FOLLY	FULLY	GEARE	GLOBE
DRERE	EASEL	EMMER	ETHYL	FARSI	FIRMA	FONDA	FUMED	GEBER	GLOGG
DRESS	EATER	EMMET	ETUDE	FATAL	FIRST	FONDS	FUMES	GECKO	GLOOM
DRIED	EAVES	EMOTE	ETWEE	FATED	FIRTH	FOODS	FUMET	GEESE	GLORY
DRIER	EBOLA	EMOVE	EULER	FATES	FISHY	FOOLS	FUNDI	GEIST	GLOSS
DRIES	EBONY	EMPTY	EVADE	FATTY	FITCH	FOOTS	FUNDS	GELID	GLOVE
DRIFT	ECLAT	EMRYS	EVANS	FATWA	FIVER	FOOTY	FUNDY	GEMMA	GLUCK
DRILL	EDEMA	EMURE	EVENS	FAULT	FIVES	FORAY	FUNKY	GEMMY	GLUED
DRILY	EDGAR	ENACT	EVENT	FAUNA	FIXED	FORCE	FUNNY	GENET	GLUEY
DRINK	EDGED	ENARM	EVERT	FAURE	FIXER	FOREL	FURAN	GENIC	GLUME
DRIVE	EDGER	ENATE	EVERY	FAUST	FIZZY	FORGE	FUROR	GENIE	GLUON
DROIT	EDICT	ENDED	EVIAN	FAUVE	FJORD	FORGO	FURRY	GENOA	GLYPH
DROLL	EDIFY	ENDOW	EVICT	FAVOR	FLACK	FORKS	FURZE	GENRE	GNARL
DROME	EDILE	ENDUE	EVITA	FAVUS	FLAIL	FORME	FUSED	GENTS	GNASH
DRONE	EDUCE	ENEMA	EVITE	FEARE	FLAIR	FORMS	FUSEE	GENTY	GNOME
DROOL	EDWIN	ENEMY	EVOKE	FEAST	FLAKE	FORTE	FUSSY	GENUS	GOATY

GOBBO	GRIME	HABIT	HEART	HODGE	HUTCH	INGLE	JAVEL	KANAK	KNIFE
GODET	GRIMM	HÁ{\C}	HEATH	HOGAN	HUZZA	INGOT	JAZZY	KANDY	KNOCK
GODLY	GRIMY	EK	HEAVE	HOICK	HYDRA	INIGO	JEANS	KANGA	KNOLL
GOFER	GRIND	HACEK	HEAVY	HOIST	HYDRO	INION	JEBEL	KANJI	KNOUT
GOGOL	GRIOT	HADES	HECHT	HOKEY	HYENA	INIUM	JEHAD	KAPOK	KNOWN
GOING	GRIPE	HADJI	HECTO	HOKUM	HYLUM	INJUN	JELAB	KAPPA	KNURL
GOLAN	GRIST	HADNT	HEDDA	HOLED	HYMEN	INLAW	JELLO	KAPUT	KNURR
GOLEM	GRITS	HAFIZ	HEDGE	HOLEY	HYOID	INLAY	JELLY	KARAT	KOALA
GOLGI	GROAN	HAGUE	HEELS	HOLLA	HYPER	INLET	JEMMY	KARMA	KODAK
GOLLY	GROAT	HAIDA	HEFTY	HOLLY	HYPHA	INNER	JENNY	KARNO	KOFTA
GOMBO	GROIN	HAIFA	HEGEL	HOLST	HYRAX	INNES	JEREZ	KARRI	KOINE
GONAD	GROOM	HAIKU	HEIGH	HOMER	HYTHE	INPUT	JERKS	KARST	KOKUM
GONER	GROPE	HAIRS	HEINE	HOMME	IBERT	INSET	JERKY	KARSY	KONGO
GONNA	GROSS	HAIRY	HEIST	HONAN	IBIZA	INTER	JERRY	KASHA	KOOKY
GONZO	GROSZ	HAITI	HELEN	HONDO	IBSEN	INTRA	JESSE	KAURI	KOORI
GOODS	GROUP	HAKKA	HELGA	HONEY	ICENI	INTRO	JESUS	KAYAK	KOPJE
GOODY	GROUT	HALER	HELIO	HONKY	ICHOR	INUIT	JETTY	KEBAB	KOPPA
GOOEY	GROVE	HALFA	HELIX	HONOR	ICILY	INURE	JEWEL	KEBEL	KORAN
GOOFY	GROWL	HALLÉ	HELLO	HOOCH	ICING	INWIT	JEWRY	KEBLE	KOREA
GOOLY	GROWN	HALLO	HELOT	HOOEY	ICKER	IONIC	JIFFY	KEBOB	KORMA
GOOSE	GRUEL	HALMA	HELVE	HOOKY	ICTUS	IQBAL	JIHAD	KEDAR	KOTOW
GOPAK	GRUFE	HALON	HENCE	HOOSH	IDAHO	IRAQI	JIMMU	KEDGE	KRAAL
GORED	GRUFF	HALSE	HENGE	HOOVE	IDEAL	IRATE	JIMMY	KEDGY	KRAFT
GORGE	GRUME	HALVE	HENNA	HORAH	IDEAS	IRENA	JIMPY	KEECH	KRANG
GORKY	GRUMP	HAMMY	HENRY	HORDE	IDIOM	IRENE	JINGO	KEELS	KRANS
GORSE	GRUNT	HANAP	HERBS	HOREB	IDIOT	IRGUN	JINKS	KEEPS	KRANZ
GOSHT	GUACO	HANCE	HERMA	HORNE	IDLER	IRISH	JINNI	KEFIR	KRAUT
GOSSE	GUANA	HANCH	HERNE	HORNY	IDRIS	IROKO	JIRGA	KELIM	KRIEG
GOTCH	GUANO	HANDS	HEROD	HORSA	IDYLL	IRONS	JOCKO	KELLS	KRILL
GOTHA	GUARD	HANDY	HERON	HORSE	IGAPO	IRONY	JOINT	KELLY	KRONA
GOTTA	GUAVA	HANKY	HERSE	HORSY	IGLOO	ISAAC	JOIST	KEMPE	KRONE
GOUDA	GUELF	HANOI	HERTS	HORUS	ILEAC	ISERE	JOKER	KENDO	KUALA
GOUGE	GUESS	HANSE	HERTZ	HOSEA	ILEUM	ISLAM	JOLLY	KENGA	KUDOS
GOURD	GUEST	HAPPY	HESSE	HOSEN	ILEUS	ISLAY	JONAH	KENYA	KUDZU
GOUTY	GUEUX	HARDY	HETTY	HOSTA	ILIAC	ISLES	JONES	KERAL	KUFIC
GOWAN	GUIDE	HAREM	HEUGH	HOTCH	ILIAD	ISLET	JONTY	KERMA	KUKRI
GOWER	GUILD	HARPO	HEVEA	HOTEL	ILIUM	ISMET	JORIS	KERNE	KULAK
GRAAL	GUILE	HARPY	HEWER	HOTLY	IMAGE	ISOLA	JORUM	KETCH	KURMA
GRACE	GUILT	HARRY	HEXAD	HOTTY	IMAGO	ISSUE	JOUAL	KEVIN	KUTCH
GRADE	GUIMP	HARSH	HEXAM	HOUGH	IMARI	ITALA	JOULE	KEYED	KVASS
GRAFF	GUISE	HARTY	HEXYL	HOUND	IMAUM	ITALY	JOUNT	KEYES	KYANG
GRAFT	GULAG	HASNT	HEYER	HOURI	IMBED	ITCHY	JOUST	KHAKI	KYLIE
GRAIL	GULCH	HASTA	HIKER	HOURS	IMBUE	IVIED	JOYCE	KHAYA	KYLIN
GRAIN	GULES	HASTE	HILAR	HOUSE	IMMER	IVORY	JUDAS	KHAZI	KYLIX
GRAND	GULLS	HASTY	HILDA	HOVEL	IMMEW	IXION	JUDGE	KIANG	KYLOE
GRANT	GULLY	HATCH	HILLS	HOVER	IMPEL	IZARD	JUGAL	KIDDY	KYRIE
GRAPE	GULPH	HATHI	HILLY	HOWBE	IMPLY	IZMIR	JUICE	KIDGE	LABDA
GRAPH	GUMBO	HATTY	HILUM	HOWDY	IMPOT	IZZAT	JUICY	KILDA	LABEL
GRASP	GUMMA	HAUGH	HINDI	HOYLE	IMSHI	JABOT	JULEP	KILIM	LABIS
GRASS	GUMMY	HAULM	HINDU	HUBBY	INANE	JACKS	JUMAR	KIMBO	LABOR
GRATE	GUNGE	HAULT	HINGE	HUFFY	INAPT	JACOB	JUMBO	KINGS	LACET
GRAVE	GUNNY	HAUNT	HINNY	HULKS	INARI	JADED	JUMBY	KINKY	LACKS
GRAVY	GUPPY	HAUSA	HIPPO	HULLO	INARM	JADIS	JUMNA	KIOSK	LADEN
GRAYS	GUSHY	HAUSE	HIPPY	HULME	INCLE	JAFFA	JUMPS	KIPPS	LADLE
GRAZE	GUSTO	HAUTE	HIRAM	HUMAN	INCUR	JAGGY	JUMPY	KIRBY	LAGAN
GREAT	GUSTY	HAVEL	HIRED	HUMID	INCUS	JAKES	JUNCO	KIROV	LAGER
GREBE	GUTSY	HAVEN	HIRER	HUMOR	INDEW	JALAP	JUNTA	KITTY	LAGOS
GREED	GUTTA	HAVER	HITCH	HUMPH	INDEX	JAMBE	JUNTO	KIWIS	LAIRD
GREEK	GUYED	HAVOC	HITHE	HUMUS	INDIA	JAMBO	JUPON	KLANG	LAIRY
GREEN	GUYON	HAWSE	HIVER	HUNCH	INDIC	JAMES	JURAT	KLEIN	LAITH
GREER	GUYOT	HAYDN	HIVES	HUNKS	INDRA	JAMMY	JUROR	KLIEG	LAITY
GREET	GYGES	HAYLE	HMONG	HUNKY	INDRE	JANTY	KAABA	KLOOF	LAMED
GREGG	GYMNO	HAZAN	HOARD	HUNTS	INDRI	JANUS	KABOB	KNACK	LAMIA
GRETA	GYNAE	HAZEL	HOARE	HURON	INDUE	JAPAN	KABUL	KNARL	LAMMY
GREYS	GYPPO	HEADS	HOARY	HURRY	INDUS	JASEY	KAFIR	KNAVE	LAMPS
GRIEF	GYPSY	HEADY	HOAST	HURST	INEPT	JASON	KAFKA	KNEAD	LANCE
GRIEG	GYRUS	HEALD	HOBBS	HUSKS	INERT	JASPÉ	KALIF	KNEEL	LANDE
GRIFF	HABET	HEAPS	HOBBY	HUSKY	INFER	JAUNT	KAMME	KNELL	LANKA
GRILL		HEARD	HOCUS	HUSSY	INFRA	JAVAN	KAMPF	KNELT	LANKY

LAPEL	LERNA	LOAMY	LUNAR	MAMMY	MEDIC	MINOR	MOTEL	NACHO	NEVIS
LAPIS	LERNE	LOATH	LUNCH	MANCH	MEDOC	MINOS	MOTET	NACHT	NEWEL
LAPSE	LESHY	LOBAR	LUNDY	MANED	MEETS	MINOT	MOTHS	NACRE	NEWLY
LARCH	LETHE	LOBBY	LUNED	MANES	MEITH	MINSK	MOTIF	NADER	NEWSY
LARGE	LEVEE	LOBED	LUNGE	MANET	MELBA	MINUS	MOTOR	NADIR	NEWTS
LARGO	LEVEL	LOCAL	LUNGI	MANGE	MELEE	MIRTH	MOTTE	NADPH	NEXUS
LARKS	LEVEN	LOCKE	LUNGS	MANGO	MELIA	MIRZA	MOTTO	NAGAS	NGAIO
LARNE	LEVER	LOCKS	LUPIN	MANGY	MELIC	MISER	MOUCH	NAGOR	NICAD
LARRY	LEVIN	LOCUM	LUPUS	MANIA	MELON	MISSA	MOULD	NAHUM	NICHE
LARVA	LEVIS	LOCUS	LURCH	MANIC	MELOS	MISSY	MOULS	NAIAD	NICOL
LASER	LEWES	LODEN	LURGY	MANLY	MENAI	MISTY	MOULT	NAILS	NIDOR
LASKI	LEWIS	LODGE	LURID	MANNA	MENGE	MITES	MOUND	NAIRA	NIDUS
LASSA	LEXIS	LOESS	LUSHY	MANOR	MENSA	MITRE	MOUNT	NAIVE	NIECE
LASSO	LHASA	LOFTY	LUSTY	MANSE	MERAK	MIXED	MOURN	NAKED	NIEVE
LATCH	LIANA	LOGAN	LUTIN	MANTA	MERCY	MIXER	MOUSE	NAMED	NIFTY
LATEN	LIANE	LOGIC	LUTON	MANUL	MERGE	MIXTE	MOUSY	NAMES	NIGEL
LATER	LIANG	LOGOS	LUZON	MANUS	MERIL	MIXUP	MOUTH	NAMIB	NIGER
LATEX	LIARD	LOINS	LYCÉE	MAORI	MERIT	MOCHA	MOVED	NANCE	NIGHT
LATHE	LIBEL	LOIRE	LYCRA	MAPLE	MERLE	MODAL	MOVER	NANCY	NIHIL
LATHI	LIBER	LOLLY	LYDIA	MARAT	MERRY	MODEL	MOVIE	NANDI	NINJA
LATIN	LIBRA	LOMAN	LYING	MARCH	MESIC	MODEM	MOWER	NANDU	NINNY
LATTE	LIBYA	LONER	LYMPH	MARCO	MESNE	MODER	MOYLE	NANNA	NINON
LAUDS	LICHT	LONGS	LYNCH	MARDI	MESON	MODUS	MUCID	NANNY	NINTH
LAUGH	LICIT	LOOBY	LYRIC	MARGE	MESSY	MOGGY	MUCIN	NANTZ	NIOBE
LAURA	LIEGE	LOOFA	LYSIN	MARIA	MESTO	MOGUL	MUCKY	NAPPA	NIPPY
LAVER	LIFER	LOONS	LYSIS	MARIE	METAL	MOIRA	MUCRO	NAPPE	NISAN
LAVRA	LIGER	LOONY	LYSOL	MARLE	METER	MOIRE	MUCUS	NAPPY	NISUS
LAWKS	LIGGE	LOOPY	LYTHE	MARLY	METHS	MOIST	MUDDY	NARES	NITID
LAYBY	LIGHT	LOOSE	MACAW	MARNE	METIC	MOLAR	MUDGE	NARKS	NITON
LAYER	LIKED	LORCA	MACER	MAROT	METIF	MOLLY	MUFTI	NARKY	NITRE
LAZAR	LIKEN	LORDS	MACHO	MARRY	METIS	MOLTO	MUGGY	NASAL	NITRO
LAZZO	LIKES	LORIS	MACLE	MARSH	METOL	MOMMA	MULCH	NASHE	NIVAL
LEACH	LILAC	LORNA	MACON	MASAI	METRE	MOMMY	MULCT	NASTY	NIXON
LEADS	LILLY	LORNE	MACRO	MASER	METRO	MONAD	MULLA	NATAL	NIZAM
LEAFY	LIMAX	LORRY	MADAM	MASHY	MEUSE	MONAL	MULSE	NATES	NOBBY
LEAKY	LIMBO	LOSER	MADGE	MASON	MEYER	MONDO	MULTI	NATTY	NOBEL
LEANT	LIMER	LOTOS	MADLY	MASSA	MEZZE	MONET	MUMMY	NATUS	NOBLE
LEAPT	LIMES	LOTTO	MAEVE	MASSE	MEZZO	MONEY	MUMPS	NAURU	NOBLY
LEARN	LIMEY	LOTUS	MAFIA	MASUS	MIAMI	MONKS	MUNCH	NAVAL	NODAL
LEASE	LIMIT	LOUGH	MAGHA	MATAI	MIAOU	MONTE	MUNDA	NAVEL	NODDY
LEASH	LINCH	LOUIE	MAGIC	MATCH	MIAOW	MONTH	MUNGO	NAVEW	NODES
LEAST	LINED	LOUIS	MAGMA	MATER	MIAUL	MONZA	MUNRO	NAVVY	NODUS
LEAVE	LINEN	LOUPE	MAGNA	MATES	MICAH	MOOCH	MURAL	NAWAB	NOISE
LECOQ	LINER	LOUSE	MAGOG	MATEY	MICHE	MOODY	MUREX	NAXOS	NOISY
LEDGE	LINES	LOUSY	MAGOT	MATHS	MICRO	MOOLI	MURKY	NAZIR	NOMAD
LEECH	LINGO	LOUTH	MAGUS	MATIN	MIDAS	MOONY	MURRE	NEAGH	NOMEN
LEEDS	LININ	LOVAT	MAHDI	MATLO	MIDDY	MOORE	MURRY	NEALE	NOMIC
LEERY	LINKS	LOVER	MAHOE	MATTE	MIDGE	MOOSE	MUSCA	NEBEL	NONCE
LEESE	LINUS	LOWAN	MAHUA	MAUND	MIDST	MOPED	MUSCI	NEDDY	NONES
LEFTY	LIONS	LOWER	MAHWA	MAUVE	MIFFY	MOPER	MUSES	NEEDS	NONET
LEGAL	LIPID	LOWLY	MAIKO	MAVIN	MIGHT	MOPSY	MUSHA	NEEDY	NONNY
LEGER	LIPPI	LOWRY	MAILE	MAVIS	MILAN	MORAL	MUSHY	NEGEV	NOOKY
LEGGE	LISLE	LOYAL	MAINE	MAXIM	MILCH	MORAN	MUSIC	NEGRO	NOOSE
LEGGY	LISTS	LOZEN	MAINS	MAYBE	MILER	MORAT	MUSIT	NEGUS	NORAH
LEGIT	LISZT	LUBRA	MAIRE	MAYOR	MILES	MORAY	MUSKY	NEHRU	NORIA
LEHAR	LITAS	LUCAN	MAIZE	MAZER	MILKY	MOREL	MUSSE	NEIGH	NORMA
LEIGH	LITER	LUCIA	MAJOR	MCCOY	MILLI	MORES	MUSSY	NELLY	NORSE
LEISH	LITHE	LUCID	MAKAR	MEALS	MILLS	MORIA	MUSTY	NEPAL	NORTH
LEITH	LITRE	LUCIO	MAKER	MEALY	MILNE	MORIN	MUTED	NEPER	NOSER
LEMAN	LIVED	LUCKY	MALAR	MEANS	MIMER	MORNE	MUZAK	NERVA	NOSEY
LEMMA	LIVEN	LUCRE	MALAY	MEANT	MIMIC	MORON	MUZZY	NERVE	NOTAL
LEMON	LIVER	LUDIC	MALFI	MEATH	MIMUS	MORPH	MVULE	NERVI	NOTCH
LEMUR	LIVES	LUFFA	MALIK	MEATS	MINCE	MORSE	MYNAH	NERVO	NOTED
LENIN	LIVID	LUGER	MALMO	MEATY	MINCH	MORUS	MYOMA	NERVY	NOTES
LENTO	LIVRE	LULLY	MALTA	MEBBE	MINER	MOSEY	MYRON	NESSA	NOTTS
LEONE	LLAMA	LUMEN	MAMBA	MECCA	MINGY	MOSES	MYRRH	NESTA	NOTUM
LEPER	LLANO	LUMME	MAMBO	MEDAL	MINHO	MOSSI	NAAFI	NEVEL	NOVEL
LEPID	LLANO	LUMMY	MAMEY	MEDEA	MINIM	MOSSO	NABOB	NEVER	NOVUM
LEPUS	LLOYD	LUMPY	MAMMA	MEDIA	MINKE	MOSSY	NACHE		NOWAY

NOXAL	OMEGA	OXBOW	PATCH	PHLOX	PLATH	POTOO	PUGIN	QUOTH	REDON
NOYAU	ONCER	OXEYE	PATER	PHNOM	PLATO	POTTO	PUKKA	QURAN	REDOX
NOYES	ONCUS	OXIDE	PATIO	PHOBE	PLATY	POTTY	PULEX	RABAT	REECH
NSPCC	ONION	OXIME	PATNA	PHONE	PLATZ	POUCH	PULPY	RABBI	REEDE
NUBIA	ONKUS	OXLIP	PATSY	PHONY	PLAYA	POULE	PULSE	RABID	REEDS
NUCHA	ONSET	OXTER	PATTI	PHOTO	PLAZA	POULT	PUNCH	RACER	REEDY
NUDGE	OOMPH	OZARK	PATTY	PHYLE	PLEAD	POUND	PUNIC	RACES	REEVE
NULLA	OPERA	OZONE	PAUSA	PIANO	PLEAT	POUPE	PUNTO	RADAR	REFER
NUMEN	OPHIR	PABLO	PAUSE	PIAVE	PLEBS	POWAN	PUNTY	RADHA	REFIT
NUNKY	OPINE	PACER	PAVID	PICEA	PLEIN	POWER	PUPAL	RADIO	REGAL
NURSE	OPIUM	PACEY	PAWKY	PICOT	PLICA	POWYS	PUPIL	RADIX	REGAN
NUTTY	OPTIC	PACHA	PAYEE	PICUS	PLIER	PRADO	PUPPY	RADON	REGIA
NYALA	ORANG	PADDY	PAYER	PIECE	PLINY	PRAHU	PUREE	RAGED	RÉGIE
NYASA	ORATE	PADMA	PEACE	PIERS	PLONK	PRANA	PURGE	RAGGA	REGIS
NYLON	ORBIT	PADRE	PEACH	PIERT	PLOTS	PRANG	PURIM	RAGGY	RÈGLE
NYMPH	ORCUS	PAEAN	PEAKY	PIETA	PLUCK	PRANK	PURSE	RAHAB	REICH
NYSSA	ORDER	PAGAN	PEARL	PIETY	PLUMB	PRATE	PURSY	RAINE	REIGN
OAKEN	ORFEO	PAGER	PEASE	PIEZO	PLUME	PRAWL	PUSHY	RAINY	REINS
OAKER	ORGAN	PAGES	PEATY	PIGGY	PLUMP	PRAWN	PUSLE	RAISE	REIST
OAKUM	ORGUE	PAINE	PECAN	PIGMY	PLUNK	PREEN	PUSSY	RAJAB	REITH
OASIS	ORIEL	PAINS	PEDAL	PILAF	PLUSH	PRESA	PUTID	RAJAH	REJIG
OATEN	ORION	PAINT	PEDRO	PILAU	PLUTO	PRESS	PUTTO	RAKED	RELAX
OATES	ORLON	PAIRE	PEERS	PILCH	POACH	PREST	PUTTY	RAKEE	RELAY
OBEAH	ORLOP	PAIRS	PEEVE	PILED	PODEX	PRIAL	PYGMY	RAKER	RELIC
OBESE	ORMER	PAISA	PEGGY	PILES	PODGE	PRIAM	PYLON	RAKES	REMIT
OBIAH	ORMUZ	PALEA	PEKAN	PILLS	PODGY	PRICE	PYREX	RALLY	REMUE
OBIIT	ORNIS	PALES	PEKIN	PILOT	POEMS	PRICK	PYRUS	RALPH	REMUS
OBOTE	OROMO	PALET	PEKOE	PILUM	POESY	PRIDE	PYXIS	RAMAN	RENAL
OCCAM	ORPEN	PALIO	PELEE	PILUS	POETS	PRILL	PZAZZ	RAMBO	RENAN
OCCUR	ORRIS	PALLY	PELLA	PINCH	POILU	PRIMA	QAJAR	RAMUS	RENEW
OCEAN	ORTHO	PALMY	PELMA	PINES	POINT	PRIME	QATAR	RANCE	RENTE
OCHER	ORTON	PALSY	PENAL	PINGO	POISE	PRIMO	QUACK	RANCH	REPAY
OCHRE	ORTUS	PAMIR	PENCE	PINKO	POKER	PRIMP	QUADS	RANDY	REPEL
OCKER	ORVAL	PANDA	PENIS	PINKY	POKEY	PRINT	QUAFF	RANEE	REPLY
OCNUS	OSAGE	PANDY	PENNA	PINNA	POLAR	PRION	QUAIL	RANGE	REPOT
OCREA	OSAKA	PANEL	PENNE	PINNY	POLIO	PRIOR	QUAKE	RANGY	REPRO
OCTAD	OSCAR	PANGA	PENNY	PINON	POLKA	PRISE	QUALM	RANKE	RERUN
OCTAL	OSIER	PANIC	PEONY	PIÑON	POLLY	PRISM	QUANT	RANKS	RESET
OCTET	OSMAN	PANNE	PEPPY	PINOT	POLYP	PRIVY	QUARK	RAPID	RESIN
ODDER	OSSIA	PANSY	PEPSI	PINTA	POMMY	PRIZE	QUART	RAREE	RESIT
ODDLY	OSTIA	PANTO	PEPYS	PINTO	PONCE	PROBE	QUASH	RASTA	RESTS
ODEON	OTARY	PANTS	PERAI	PIOUS	PONDS	PROKE	QUASI	RATCH	RETCH
ODETS	OTHER	PANTY	PERCE	PIPAL	PONEY	PROLE	QUEEN	RATEL	RETRO
ODIUM	OTIUM	PAOLO	PERCH	PIPER	PONGA	PROMO	QUEER	RATES	REVEL
ODOUR	OTTAR	PAPAL	PERCY	PIPIT	PONGO	PRONE	QUELL	RATIO	REVET
OFFAL	OTTER	PAPAW	PERDU	PIPPA	PONTY	PRONG	QUERN	RATTY	REVIE
OFFAS	OTWAY	PAPER	PERIL	PIPUL	POOCH	PROOF	QUERY	RAVEL	REVUE
OFFER	OUGHT	PARCH	PERKS	PIQUE	POOLS	PROSE	QUEST	RAVEN	REYES
OFLAG	OUIDA	PARDY	PERKY	PIROG	POORI	PROSY	QUEUE	RAVER	RHEIN
OFTEN	OUIJA	PAREO	PERON	PISKY	POPES	PROUD	QUICK	RAYED	RHETT
OGGIN	OUNCE	PAREU	PERRY	PISTE	POPOV	PROUT	QUIDS	RAYLE	RHEUM
OGHAM	OUSEL	PARIS	PERSE	PITCH	POPPA	PROVE	QUIET	RAYON	RHINE
OGIER	OUTBY	PARKA	PESKY	PITHY	POPPY	PROVO	QUIFF	RAZOR	RHINO
OGIVE	OUTDO	PARKY	PESTO	PITON	POPSY	PROWL	QUILL	REACH	RHODO
OILED	OUTER	PARMA	PETAL	PITOT	POPUP	PROXY	QUILP	REACT	RHOMB
OILER	OUTGO	PARRY	PETER	PITTA	PORCH	PRUDE	QUILT	READE	RHONE
OKAPI	OUTRE	PARSE	PETIT	PIVOT	PORGY	PRUNE	QUINS	READY	RHUMB
OLDEN	OUZEL	PARSI	PETRA	PIXEL	PORNO	PSALM	QUINT	REALM	RHYME
OLDER	OVARY	PARTI	PETRE	PIXIE	PORTA	PSEUD	QUIRE	REAMS	RIANT
OLDIE	OVATE	PARTS	PETRI	PIZZA	PORTE	PSHAW	QUIRK	REARM	RICAN
OLEIC	OVERT	PARTY	PETTO	PLACE	PORTO	PSOAS	QUITE	REBBE	RICIN
OLEIN	OVINE	PARVO	PETTY	PLACK	PORTS	PSORA	QUITO	REBEL	RIDER
OLEUM	OVOID	PASCH	PHARE	PLAID	POSED	PSYCH	QUITS	REBUS	RIDGE
OLIVE	OVOLO	PASEO	PHASE	PLAIN	POSER	PUBIC	QUOIF	REBUT	RIFLE
OLLIE	OVULE	PASHA	PHEBE	PLAIT	POSIT	PUBIS	QUOIN	RECAP	RIGHT
OMAGH	OWING	PASSE	PHENO	PLANE	POSSE	PUDGE	QUOIT	RECCE	RIGID
OMANI	OWLER	PASTA	PHEON	PLANK	POSTE	PUDGY	QUORN	RECTO	RIGOR
OMBER	OWLET	PASTE	PHIAL	PLANT	POTIN	PUDOR	QUOTA	RECUR	RILEY
OMBRE	OWNER	PASTY	PHILE	PLATE	POTIN	PUFFY	QUOTE	REDAN	RILKE

RILLE	ROUGH	SALAD	SCALP	SELIM	SHIRK	SIXER	SMARM	SOLUS	SPIKE
RINSE	ROULE	SALEM	SCALY	SELLE	SHIRR	SIXTH	SMART	SOLVE	SPIKY
RIOJA	ROUND	SALEP	SCAMP	SELVA	SHIRT	SIXTY	SMASH	SOMME	SPILE
RIOTS	ROUSE	SALES	SCANT	SEMEN	SHITE	SIZAR	SMEAR	SONAR	SPILL
RIPEN	ROUST	SALIC	SCAPA	SEMIS	SHIVA	SKATE	SMEEK	SONDE	SPILT
RIPER	ROUTE	SALIX	SCAPE	SENNA	SHIVE	SKEAN	SMELL	SONIC	SPINA
RIPON	ROVER	SALLE	SCARE	SENOR	SHLEP	SKEER	SMELT	SONNY	SPINE
RISEN	ROWAN	SALLY	SCARF	SENSE	SHOAH	SKEET	SMILE	SOOTH	SPINY
RISER	ROWDY	SALMI	SCARP	SENZA	SHOAL	SKEIN	SMIRK	SOOTY	SPIRE
RISKY	ROWEL	SALON	SCARY	SEOUL	SHOCK	SKELM	SMITE	SOPHY	SPITE
RISUS	ROWER	SALSA	SCATH	SEPAL	SHOJI	SKELP	SMITH	SOPPY	SPITZ
RITES	ROYAL	SALSE	SCAUP	SEPIA	SHOLA	SKIER	SMOCK	SOPRA	SPLAT
RITZY	ROZET	SALTS	SCAUR	SEPOY	SHONA	SKIFF	SMOKE	SORBO	SPLAY
RIVAL	RSPCA	SALTY	SCENE	SERAI	SHONE	SKILL	SMOKY	SORDO	SPLIT
RIVEN	RUBIN	SALVE	SCENT	SERGE	SHOOK	SKIMP	SMOLT	SOREX	SPODE
RIVER	RUBLE	SALVO	SCHWA	SERIF	SHOOT	SKINK	SMOTE	SORGO	SPOHR
RIVET	RUCHE	SAMBA	SCIFI	SERIN	SHOPS	SKINS	SMUTS	SORRY	SPOIL
RIYAL	RUDDY	SAMBO	SCION	SERRA	SHORE	SKINT	SNACK	SORTS	SPOKE
ROACH	RUDGE	SAMFU	SCLIM	SERRE	SHORN	SKIRL	SNAFU	SOTTO	SPOOF
ROAST	RUFFE	SAMMY	SCOFF	SERUM	SHORT	SKIRR	SNAGS	SOUGH	SPOOK
ROBES	RUFUS	SAMOA	SCOLD	SERVE	SHOTS	SKIRT	SNAIL	SOULS	SPOOL
ROBEY	RUGBY	SAMOS	SCONE	SERVO	SHOUT	SKIVE	SNAKE	SOUND	SPOON
ROBIN	RUING	SAMSO	SCOOP	SETUP	SHOVE	SKOAL	SNAKY	SOUSA	SPOOR
ROBOT	RUINS	SANDS	SCOOT	SEVEN	SHOWN	SKRIM	SNAPS	SOUSE	SPORE
ROCKS	RULER	SANDY	SCOPE	SEVER	SHOWY	SKULK	SNARE	SOUTH	SPORT
ROCKY	RULES	SANTA	SCOPS	SEWER	SHRED	SKULL	SNARK	SOWER	SPOTS
RODEO	RUMBA	SANTO	SCORE	SHACK	SHREW	SKUNK	SNARL	SOWLE	SPOUT
RODIN	RUMEN	SAPID	SCORN	SHADE	SHROW	SLACK	SNASH	SOWND	SPRAG
ROGER	RUMEX	SAPOR	SCOTS	SHADY	SHRUB	SLADE	SNEAD	SOWTH	SPRAT
ROGET	RUMMY	SAPPY	SCOTT	SHAFT	SHRUG	SLAIN	SNEAK	SOYUZ	SPRAY
ROGUE	RUMOR	SARAH	SCOUP	SHAKE	SHUCK	SLAKE	SNECK	SPACE	SPREE
ROHAN	RUMPY	SARAN	SCOUR	SHAKO	SHUNT	SLANG	SNEER	SPADE	SPRIG
ROIST	RUNCH	SARGE	SCOUT	SHAKY	SHUSH	SLANT	SNICK	SPADO	SPRIT
ROKER	RUNES	SARIN	SCOWL	SHALE	SHUTE	SLASH	SNIDE	SPAHI	SPROD
ROLFE	RUNIC	SAROS	SCOWP	SHALL	SHUTS	SLATE	SNIFF	SPAIN	SPROG
ROLLO	RUNNY	SARUS	SCRAB	SHALT	SHYLY	SLATS	SNIFT	SPALD	SPRUE
ROLLS	RUNUP	SASHA	SCRAG	SHAME	SIBYL	SLATY	SNIPE	SPALL	SPUME
ROMAN	RUPEE	SASSE	SCRAM	SHANG	SIDHA	SLAVE	SNOBS	SPALT	SPUNK
ROMEO	RUPIA	SASSY	SCRAP	SHANK	SIDLE	SLEEK	SNOEK	SPANK	SPURN
ROMER	RURAL	SCRAT	SCRAT	SHANT	SIDON	SLEEP	SNOOD	SPARE	SPURS
RONDE	RUSHY	SATAN	SCRAW	SHAPE	SIEGE	SLEET	SNOOK	SPARK	SPURT
RONDO	RUSSE	SATAY	SCRAY	SHARD	SIEVE	SLEPT	SNOOP	SPART	SQUAB
RONEO	RUSSO	SATED	SCREE	SHARE	SIGHS	SLICE	SNOOT	SPASM	SQUAD
RONNE	RUSTY	SATEM	SCREW	SHARK	SIGHT	SLICK	SNORE	SPATE	SQUAT
ROOKY	RYDAL	SATIE	SCRIM	SHARP	SIGIL	SLIDE	SNORT	SPATS	SQUAW
ROOMS	SABAL	SATIN	SCRIP	SHAUN	SIGLA	SLIGO	SNOUT	SPAWN	SQUIB
ROOMY	SABER	SATIS	SCROD	SHAVE	SIGMA	SLIME	SNOWY	SPEAK	SQUID
ROOPY	SABIN	SATYR	SCROG	SHAWL	SIGNS	SLIMY	SNUFF	SPEAR	SQUIT
ROOST	SABLE	SAUCE	SCROW	SHAWM	SILAS	SLING	SOANE	SPECK	STACK
ROOTS	SABOT	SAUCH	SCRUB	SHCHI	SILEX	SLINK	SOAPY	SPECS	STADE
ROOTY	SABRA	SAUCY	SCRUM	SHEAF	SILKY	SLIPE	SOARE	SPEED	STAFF
ROPED	SABRE	SAUDI	SCUBA	SHEAR	SILLY	SLIPS	SOBER	SPEER	STAGE
ROPER	SACHA	SAUGH	SCUFF	SHEBA	SILVA	SLOAN	SOCKS	SPEKE	STAGY
ROPES	SACHS	SAULT	SCULL	SHEEL	SIMBA	SLOOP	SOCLE	SPELL	STAID
ROPEY	SACKS	SAUNA	SCULP	SHEEN	SIMON	SLOPE	SODOM	SPELT	STAIN
ROQUE	SADHE	SAURY	SCURF	SHEEP	SINAI	SLOPS	SODOR	SPEND	STAIR
RORIC	SADHU	SAUTE	SCUTE	SHEER	SINCE	SLOSH	SOFIA	SPENS	STAKE
RORKE	SADIE	SAVER	SEALS	SHEET	SINEW	SLOTH	SOFTY	SPENT	STALE
RORTY	SADLY	SAVOR	SEAMY	SHEIK	SINGE	SLUGS	SOGGY	SPERM	STALK
ROSCO	SAFAR	SAVOY	SEARE	SHELF	SINUS	SLUMP	SOKEN	SPICA	STALL
ROSES	SAGES	SAVVY	SECCO	SHELL	SIREN	SLUNG	SOKOL	SPICE	STAMP
ROSET	SAGGY	SAXON	SEDAN	SHERD	SISAL	SLUNK	SOLAN	SPICK	STAND
ROSIN	SAHEL	SAYER	SEDGE	SHERE	SISSY	SLURB	SOLAR	SPICY	STANK
ROSIT	SAHIB	SAYSO	SEDUM	SHIEL	SITAR	SLURP	SOLDE	SPIED	STAPH
ROSSE	SAICE	SCADS	SEEDY	SHIFT	SITIN	SLUSH	SOLFA	SPIEL	STARE
ROSSI	SAILS	SCAFF	SEGUE	SHILL	SITKA	SLYLY	SOLID	SPIES	STARK
ROTOR	SAINE	SCALA	SEINE	SHINE	SITTA	SLYPE	SOLON	SPIEL	STARR
ROUEN	SAINT	SCALD	SEISM	SHINY	SITUP	SMACK	SOLTI	SPIFF	STARS
ROUGE	SAKER	SCALE	SEIZE	SHIRE	SIVAN	SMALL	SOLUM	SPIFF	START

33

STASH	STREP	SWEAT	TANKA	TERSE	TIGHT	TOTTY	TSUGA	UNBED	VANCE
STASI	STREW	SWEDE	TANSY	TESLA	TIGON	TOUCH	TUBBY	UNCAP	VANDA
STATE	STRIA	SWEEP	TAPAS	TESSA	TIKKA	TOUGH	TUBER	UNCLE	VANYA
STAVE	STRIP	SWEET	TAPER	TESTA	TILDE	TOWEL	TUDOR	UNCUS	VAPID
STAYS	STROP	SWELL	TAPET	TESTS	TILED	TOWER	TUFFE	UNCUT	VAPOR
STEAD	STRUM	SWELT	TAPIR	TESTY	TILER	TOWNS	TULIP	UNDAM	VAREC
STEAK	STRUT	SWEPT	TAPIS	TETON	TILES	TOWSE	TULLE	UNDER	VARIX
STEAL	STUCK	SWIFT	TARDY	TETRA	TILIA	TOWZE	TULLY	UNDID	VARUS
STEAM	STUDY	SWILL	TARGE	TEVET	TILTH	TOXIC	TUMID	UNDUE	VAULT
STEED	STUFF	SWINE	TAROT	TEXAN	TIMER	TOXIN	TUMMY	UNFED	VAUNT
STEEK	STUKA	SWING	TARRY	TEXAS	TIMES	TRACE	TUMOR	UNFIT	VEDDA
STEEL	STUMP	SWIPE	TARTY	TEXEL	TIMID	TRACK	TUNER	UNGET	VEDIC
STEEN	STUNG	SWIRE	TASSE	TEXTS	TIMON	TRACT	TUNIC	UNIAT	VEERY
STEEP	STUNK	SWIRL	TASSO	THAIS	TIMOR	TRADE	TUNIS	UNIFY	VEGAN
STEER	STUNT	SWISH	TASTE	THANE	TINEA	TRAIL	TUNKU	UNION	VELAR
STEIN	STUPA	SWISS	TASTY	THANK	TINGE	TRAIN	TUNNY	UNITA	VELDT
STELA	STUPE	SWIZZ	TATAR	THECA	TINNY	TRAIT	TUQUE	UNITE	VELUM
STELE	STURT	SWOON	TATER	THEFT	TIPPY	TRAMP	TURBO	UNITS	VENAL
STENT	STYLE	SWOOP	TATIN	THEGN	TIPSY	TRANS	TURCO	UNITY	VENDA
STEPS	STYLO	SWORD	TATRA	THEIR	TIRED	TRANT	TURIN	UNLAW	VENIN
STERN	STYME	SWORE	TATTY	THEMA	TIREE	TRAPS	TURKI	UNLAY	VENOM
STEVE	SUAVE	SWORN	TAUBE	THEME	TIROS	TRASH	TURKU	UNLIT	VENUE
STEWS	SUCKS	SWUNG	TAUNT	THERE	TITAN	TRAWL	TURPS	UNMAN	VENUS
STEWY	SUCRE	SYBIL	TAUON	THERM	TITCH	TREAD	TUTOR	UNMIX	VERDI
STICK	SUDAN	SYCEE	TAUPE	THESE	TITHE	TREAT	TUTSI	UNPEN	VEREY
STIFF	SUDOR	SYLPH	TAVAH	THETA	TITLE	TRECK	TUTTI	UNPIN	VERGE
STILE	SUEDE	SYNGE	TAWNY	THETE	TITRE	TREEN	TWAIN	UNRIG	VERNE
STILL	SUETY	SYNOD	TAWSE	THEWS	TITTY	TREES	TWANG	UNRIP	VERSA
STILT	SUGAN	SYNTH	TAXED	THICK	TITUS	TREMA	TWANK	UNSAY	VERSE
STIME	SUGAR	SYRAH	TAXIN	THIEF	TIZZY	TREND	TWEAK	UNTIE	VERSO
STIMY	SUITE	SYRIA	TAXIS	THIGH	TOADY	TRENT	TWEED	UNTIL	VERST
STING	SUITS	SYRUP	TAXOL	THILL	TOAST	TRESS	TWEET	UNWED	VERTU
STINK	SULFA	TABBY	TAXON	THINE	TOBIT	TREVI	TWERP	UNZIP	VERVE
STINT	SULKS	TABER	TAXUS	THING	TODAY	TREWS	TWICE	UPEND	VESPA
STIPE	SULKY	TABES	TAZZA	THINK	TODDY	TRIAD	TWIGS	UPPER	VESTA
STIRP	SULLA	TABLA	TEACH	THIOL	TOILE	TRIAL	TWILL	UPSET	VETCH
STOAT	SULLY	TABLE	TEARS	THIRD	TOILS	TRIBE	TWILT	UPSEY	VEXED
STOCK	SUMMA	TABOO	TEASE	THIRL	TOISE	TRICE	TWINE	UPTON	VIAND
STOEP	SUNDA	TABOR	TEAZE	THOFT	TOKAY	TRICK	TWINS	URALS	VIBES
STOGA	SUNNI	TACHE	TEDDY	THOLE	TOKEN	TRIED	TWIRL	URATE	VICAR
STOGY	SUNNY	TACIT	TEENS	THONG	TOKYO	TRIER	TWIRP	URBAN	VICHY
STOIC	SUOMI	TACKY	TEENY	THORN	TOLAR	TRIES	TWIST	UREDO	VIDEO
STOKE	SUPER	TAFFY	TEETH	THOSE	TOMAN	TRIKE	TWIXT	URIAH	VIGIL
STOLA	SUPPE	TAGUS	TEHEE	THOTH	TOMMY	TRILL	TWOER	URINE	VIGOR
STOLE	SUPRA	TAIGA	TEIGN	THREE	TONAL	TRINE	TYING	URITE	VILLA
STOLL	SURGE	TAILS	TELEX	THREW	TONDO	TRIPE	TYLER	URSON	VILLI
STOMA	SURLY	TAINE	TELIC	THRID	TONER	TRITE	TYNED	USAGE	VINYL
STOMP	SURYA	TAINO	TELLY	THRIP	TONGA	TROIC	TYPED	USHER	VIOLA
STONE	SUSAN	TAINT	TELOS	THROB	TONGS	TROLL	TYPES	USING	VIPER
STONY	SUSHI	TAKEN	TEMPE	THROE	TONIC	TROMP	TYPHA	USTED	VIRAL
STOOD	SUTCH	TAKER	TEMPO	THROW	TONNE	TROON	TYROL	USUAL	VIREO
STOOK	SUTOR	TALAQ	TEMPT	THRUM	TONUS	TROOP	UDALL	USURE	VIRGA
STOOL	SUTRA	TALAR	TENCH	THUGS	TOOLS	TROPE	UDDER	USURP	VIRGO
STOOP	SUVLA	TALEA	TENDS	THUJA	TOOTH	TROTH	UGRIC	USURY	VIRID
STOOR	SUZIE	TALES	TENET	THULE	TOPAZ	TROTS	UHLAN	UTHER	VIRTU
STOPE	SWAIN	TALKS	TENON	THUMB	TOPEE	TROUT	UHURU	UTTER	VIRUS
STORE	SWALE	TALLY	TENOR	THUMP	TOPER	TROVE	UKASE	UTURN	VISBY
STORK	SWAMI	TALMA	TENSE	THUNK	TOPIC	TRUCE	ULCER	UVULA	VISIT
STORM	SWAMP	TALON	TENTH	THUYA	TOPSY	TRUCK	ULEMA	UZBEK	VISNA
STORY	SWANK	TALUS	TENUE	THYME	TOQUE	TRULL	ULNAR	VADUZ	VISON
STOUP	SWANS	TAMAR	TEPEE	TIARA	TORAH	TRULY	ULTRA	VAGUE	VISOR
STOUR	SWARD	TAMER	TEPID	TIBBS	TORCH	TRUMP	UMBEL	VAGUS	VISTA
STOUT	SWARF	TAMIL	TERCE	TIBBY	TORII	TRUNK	UMBER	VAILS	VITAE
STOVE	SWARM	TAMIS	TEREK	TIBER	TORSO	TRURO	UMBLE	VALET	VITAL
STOWE	SWASH	TAMMY	TERES	TIBET	TORTE	TRUSS	UMBRA	VALID	VITIS
STRAD	SWATH	TAMPA	TERMS	TIBIA	TORUS	TRUST	UMPTY	VALOR	VITUS
STRAP	SWATS	TANGA	TERNE	TIDAL	TOSCA	TRUTH	UNAPT	VALSE	VIVAT
STRAW	SWAZI	TANGO	TERRA	TIDDY	TOTAL	TRYST	UNARM	VALUE	VIVID
STRAY	SWEAR	TANGY	TERRY	TIGER	TOTEM	TSUBA	UNBAR	VALVE	VIVID

VIXEN	WEIGH	WITTY	YEAST	BAHUT	CABOT	CAVAN	FALSE	GAUZY	HAZEL
VIZOR	WEILL	WIVES	YEATS	BAIRD	CACAO	CAVIL	FAMED	GAVEL	JABOT
VLACH	WEIRD	WODEN	YEMEN	BAIRN	CACHE	DACCA	FANAL	GAWKY	JACKS
VNECK	WELCH	WODGE	YERBA	BAIZE	CADDY	DACHA	FANCY	GAYAL	JACOB
VOCAB	WELLS	WOKEN	YEZDI	BAJRI	CADET	DADDY	FANNY	GAZON	JADED
VOCAL	WELLY	WOMAN	YIELD	BAKED	CADGE	DAFFY	FANON	HABET	JADIS
VODKA	WELSH	WOMEN	YIKES	BAKER	CADGY	DAGON	FARAD	HABIT	JAFFA
VOGUE	WENCH	WONGA	YIPPY	BAKHA	CADRE	DAILY	FARCE	HÁ{\C}	JAGGY
VOICE	WENDY	WONKY	YOBBO	BALAN	CAGEY	DAIRY	FARCI	EK	JAKES
VOILA	WESER	WOODS	YODEL	BALER	CAGOT	DAISY	FARCY	HACEK	JALAP
VOILE	WHACK	WOODY	YOICK	BALFE	CAINE	DAKAR	FARGO	HADES	JAMBE
VOLET	WHALE	WOOER	YOKEL	BALLS	CAIRN	DALEK	FARNE	HADJI	JAMBO
VOLGA	WHANG	WOOFY	YONKS	BALLY	CAIRO	DALIT	FAROE	HADNT	JAMES
VOLTA	WHARF	WOOLF	YONNE	BALMY	CAIUS	DALLE	FARSE	HAFIZ	JAMMY
VOLTE	WHAUP	WOOLY	YOULL	BALOO	CAJUN	DALLY	FARSI	HAGUE	JANTY
VOLVA	WHAUR	WOOZY	YOUNG	BALOR	CALEB	DAMAN	FATAL	HAIDA	JANUS
VOLVO	WHEAL	WORCS	YOURS	BALSA	CALIX	DAMME	FATED	HAIFA	JAPAN
VOMER	WHEAT	WORDS	YOURT	BAMBI	CALOR	DAMON	FATES	HAIKU	JASEY
VOMIT	WHEEL	WORDY	YOUTH	BANAL	CALPE	DANAE	FATTY	HAIRS	JASON
VOTER	WHEEN	WORKS	YOUVE	BANCO	CALVE	DANCE	FATWA	HAIRY	JASPÉ
VOTES	WHELK	WORLD	YPRES	BANDA	CALYX	DANDO	FAULT	HAITI	JAUNT
VOUCH	WHELP	WORMS	YUCCA	BANDS	CAMAS	DANDY	FAUNA	HAKKA	JAVAN
VOWEL	WHERE	WORMY	YUCKY	BANDY	CAMEL	DANES	FAURE	HALER	JAVEL
VOZHD	WHICH	WORRY	YUKKY	BANJO	CAMEO	DANTE	FAUST	HALFA	JAZZY
VROOM	WHIFF	WORSE	YUKON	BANKS	CAMIS	DARBY	FAUVE	HALLÉ	KAABA
VULGO	WHIFT	WORST	YULAN	BANNS	CAMPO	DARCY	FAVOR	HALLO	KABOB
VULVA	WHILE	WORTH	YUMMY	BANTU	CAMUS	DARTS	FAVUS	HALMA	KABUL
WACKY	WHIMS	WOULD	YUPIK	BARGE	CANAL	DATED	GABBY	HALON	KAFIR
WADER	WHINE	WOUND	YUPPY	BARMY	CANDY	DATER	GABLE	HALSE	KAFKA
WAFER	WHIPS	WOVEN	ZABRA	BARON	CANES	DATES	GABON	HALVE	KALIF
WAGER	WHIRL	WRACK	ZADOK	BARRA	CANNA	DATUK	GADGE	HAMMY	KAMME
WAGES	WHIRR	WRATH	ZAIRE	BARRE	CANNY	DATUM	GADUS	HANAP	KAMPF
WAGGA	WHISH	WREAK	ZAKAT	BARRY	CANOE	DAUBE	GAFFE	HANCE	KANAK
WAGON	WHISK	WRECK	ZAMBO	BARTS	CANON	DAUNT	GAILY	HANCH	KANDY
WAIST	WHIST	WREST	ZANTE	BASAL	CANTO	DAVID	GAINS	HANDS	KANGA
WAITS	WHITE	WRING	ZAYIN	BASAN	CAPER	DAVIS	GAIUS	HANDY	KANJI
WAIVE	WHIZZ	WRIST	ZEBRA	BASES	CAPET	DAVIT	GALAM	HANKY	KAPOK
WAKEN	WHOLE	WRITE	ZENOS	BASHO	CAPIZ	DAYAK	GALBA	HANOI	KAPPA
WAKES	WHOOP	WRITS	ZEPPO	BASIC	CAPON	DAZED	GALEA	HANSE	KAPUT
WALDO	WHOOT	WRONG	ZERDA	BASIL	CAPOT	EAGER	GALEN	HAPPY	KARAT
WALER	WHORE	WROTE	ZIGAN	BASIN	CAPRI	EAGLE	GALOP	HARDY	KARMA
WALES	WHORL	WROTH	ZILCH	BASIS	CAPUT	EARLY	GAMAY	HAREM	KARNO
WALLY	WHOSE	WRUNG	ZINCO	BASLE	CARAT	EARTH	GAMBA	HARPO	KARRI
WALTZ	WIDEN	WRYLY	ZINEB	BASRA	CARDS	EASEL	GAMBO	HARPY	KARST
WANED	WIDOW	WURST	ZIPPY	BASSO	CARER	EATER	GAMES	HARRY	KARSY
WANLY	WIDTH	WYMAN	ZLOTY	BASTA	CARET	EAVES	GAMIC	HARSH	KASHA
WARES	WIELD	XEBEC	ZOHAR	BASTE	CAREW	FABER	GAMMA	HARTY	KAURI
WARTY	WIGAN	XENIA	ZOMBI	BASTO	CAREY	FABLE	GAMMY	HASNT	KAYAK
WASHY	WIGHT	XENON	ZONAL	BATCH	CARGO	FABRÉ	GAMUT	HASTA	LABDA
WASNT	WILDE	XERES	ZORBA	BATED	CARIB	FACER	GANDA	HASTE	LABEL
WASTE	WILDS	XEROX	ZORRO	BATES	CARLE	FACET	GANJA	HASTY	LABIS
WATCH	WILES	XHOSA	**5:2**	BATHE	CAROB	FACIA	GANNY	HATCH	LABOR
WATER	WILGA	XYLEM	AARON	BATHS	CAROL	FACTO	GAPER	HATHI	LACET
WATTS	WILLY	XYRIS	BABAR	BATIK	CARRY	FACTS	GARBO	HATTY	LACKS
WAUGH	WILTS	YACHT	BABEL	BATON	CARTA	FADDY	GARDA	HAUGH	LADEN
WAVED	WIMPY	YAHOO	BABOO	BATTY	CARTE	FADED	GARNI	HAULM	LADLE
WAVER	WINCE	YAHVE	BABUL	BAULK	CARVE	FADGE	GARTH	HAULT	LAGAN
WAVES	WINCH	YAKKA	BACCY	BAWDY	CARVY	FAERY	GARUM	HAUNT	LAGER
WAXEN	WINDY	YAKUT	BACKS	BAYER	CASCA	FAGOT	GASES	HAUSA	LAGOS
WEALD	WINEY	YALTA	BACON	BAYLE	CASCO	FAGUS	GASPÉ	HAUSE	LAIRD
WEARY	WINGS	YAMEN	BADDY	BAYOU	CASES	FAINS	GASSY	HAUTE	LAIRY
WEAVE	WIPER	YAPOK	BADEN	BAZOO	CASTE	FAINT	GATED	HAVEL	LAITH
WEBER	WIRED	YARFA	BADGE	CABAL	CATCH	FAIRY	GAUDE	HAVEN	LAITY
WEDGE	WIRES	YARNS	BADLY	CABAS	CATER	FAITH	GAUDY	HAVER	LAMED
WEEDS	WISPY	YARRA	BAFFY	CABBY	CATES	FAKER	GAUGE	HAVOC	LAMIA
WEEDY	WITAN	YARTA	BAGEL	CABER	CATTY	FAKIR	GAULT	HAWSE	LAMMY
WEEKS	WITCH	YATES	BAGGY	CABIN	CAULD	FALDO	GAUNT	HAYDN	LAMPS
WEENY	WITHE	YCLAD	BAHAI	CABLE	CAULK	FALLA	GAUSS	HAYLE	LANCE
WEEPY	WITHY	YEARN		CABOB	CAUSE	FALLS	GAUZE	HAZAN	LANDE
		YEARS							

LANKA	MALMO	NADIR	PALLY	RAINE	SALMI	TAILS	VANCE	ABBAS	SCALD
LANKY	MALTA	NADPH	PALMY	RAINY	SALON	TAINE	VANDA	ABBEY	SCALE
LAPEL	MAMBA	NAGAS	PALSY	RAISE	SALSA	TAINO	VANYA	ABBOT	SCALP
LAPIS	MAMBO	NAGOR	PAMIR	RAJAB	SALSE	TAINT	VAPID	ABDAR	SCALY
LAPSE	MAMEY	NAHUM	PANDA	RAJAH	SALTS	TAKEN	VAPOR	ABDUL	SCAMP
LARCH	MAMMA	NAIAD	PANDY	RAKED	SALTY	TAKER	VAREC	ABEAM	SCANT
LARGE	MAMMY	NAILS	PANEL	RAKEE	SALVE	TALAQ	VARIX	ABEAR	SCAPA
LARGO	MANCH	NAIRA	PANGA	RAKER	SALVO	TALAR	VARUS	ABELE	SCAPE
LARKS	MANED	NAIVE	PANIC	RAKES	SAMBA	TALEA	VAULT	ABHOR	SCARE
LARNE	MANES	NAKED	PANNE	RALLY	SAMBO	TALES	VAUNT	ABIDE	SCARF
LARRY	MANET	NAMED	PANSY	RALPH	SAMFU	TALKS	WACKY	ABIES	SCARP
LARVA	MANGE	NAMES	PANTO	RAMAN	SAMOA	TALLY	WADER	ABLER	SCARY
LASER	MANGO	NAMIB	PANTS	RAMBO	SAMOS	TALMA	WAFER	ABLOW	SCATH
LASKI	MANGY	NANCE	PANTY	RAMUS	SAMSO	TALON	WAGER	ABODE	SCAUP
LASSA	MANIA	NANCY	PAOLO	RANCE	SANDS	TALUS	WAGES	ABORT	SCAUR
LASSO	MANIC	NANDI	PAPAL	RANCH	SANDY	TAMAR	WAGGA	ABOUT	SCENE
LATCH	MANLY	NANDU	PAPAW	RANDY	SANTA	TAMER	WAGON	ABOVE	SCENT
LATEN	MANNA	NANNA	PAPER	RANEE	SANTO	TAMIL	WAIST	ABRAM	SCHWA
LATER	MANOR	NANNY	PARCH	RANGE	SAPID	TAMIS	WAITS	ABRAY	SCIFI
LATEX	MANSE	NANTZ	PARDY	RANGY	SAPOR	TAMMY	WAIVE	ABRIM	SCION
LATHE	MANTA	NAPPA	PAREO	RANKE	SAPPY	TAMPA	WAKEN	ABSIT	SCLIM
LATHI	MANUL	NAPPE	PAREU	RANKS	SARAH	TANGA	WAKES	ABUJA	SCOFF
LATIN	MANUS	NAPPY	PARIS	RAPID	SARAN	TANGO	WALDO	ABUNA	SCOLD
LATTE	MAORI	NARES	PARKA	RAREE	SARGE	TANGY	WALER	ABUSE	SCONE
LAUDS	MAPLE	NARKS	PARKY	RASTA	SARIN	TANKA	WALES	ABYSM	SCOOP
LAUGH	MARAT	NARKY	PARMA	RATCH	SARKY	TANSY	WALLY	ABYSS	SCOOT
LAURA	MARCH	NASAL	PARRY	RATEL	SAROS	TAPAS	WALTZ	EBOLA	SCOPE
LAVER	MARCO	NASHE	PARSE	RATES	SARUS	TAPER	WANED	EBONY	SCOPS
LAVRA	MARDI	NASTY	PARSI	RATIO	SASHA	TAPET	WANLY	IBERT	SCORE
LAWKS	MARGE	NATAL	PARTI	RATTY	SASSE	TAPIR	WARES	IBIZA	SCORN
LAYBY	MARIA	NATCH	PARTS	RAVEL	SASSO	TAPIS	WARTY	IBSEN	SCOTS
LAYER	MARIE	NATES	PARTY	RAVEN	SASSY	TARDY	WASHY	OBEAH	SCOTT
LAZAR	MARLE	NATTY	PARVO	RAVER	SATAN	TARGE	WASNT	OBESE	SCOUP
LAZZO	MARLY	NATUS	PASCH	RAYED	SATAY	TAROT	WATCH	OBIAH	SCOUR
MACAW	MARNE	NAURU	PASEO	RAYLE	SATED	TARRY	WATER	OBIIT	SCOUT
MACER	MAROT	NAVAL	PASHA	RAYON	SATEM	TARTY	WATTS	OBOTE	SCOWL
MACHO	MARRY	NAVEL	PASSE	RAZOR	SATIE	TASSE	WAUGH	ACCRA	SCOWP
MACLE	MARSH	NAVEW	PASTA	SABAL	SATIN	TASSO	WAVED	ACERB	SCRAB
MACON	MASAI	NAVVY	PASTE	SABER	SATIS	TASTE	WAVER	ACINI	SCRAG
MACRO	MASER	NAXOS	PASTY	SABIN	SATYR	TATAR	WAVES	ACOCK	SCRAM
MADAM	MASHY	NAZIR	PATCH	SABLE	SAUCE	TATER	WAXEN	ACORN	SCRAP
MADGE	MASON	OAKEN	PATER	SABOT	SAUCH	TATIN	YACHT	ACRES	SCRAT
MADLY	MASSA	OAKER	PATIO	SABRA	SAUCY	TATRA	YAHOO	ACRID	SCRAW
MAEVE	MASSE	OAKUM	PATNA	SABRE	SAUDI	TATTY	YAHVE	ACTIN	SCRAY
MAFIA	MASUS	OASIS	PATSY	SACHA	SAUGH	TAUBE	YAKKA	ACTON	SCREE
MAGHA	MATAI	OATEN	PATTI	SACHS	SAULT	TAUNT	YAKUT	ACTOR	SCREW
MAGIC	MATCH	OATES	PATTY	SACKS	SAURY	TAUON	YALTA	ACUTE	SCRIM
MAGMA	MATER	PABLO	PAUSA	SADHE	SAUTE	TAUPE	YAMEN	ECLAT	SCRIP
MAGNA	MATES	PACER	PAUSE	SADHU	SAVER	TAVAH	YAPOK	ICENI	SCROD
MAGOG	MATEY	PACEY	PAVID	SADIE	SAVOR	TAWNY	YARFA	ICHOR	SCROG
MAGOT	MATHS	PACHA	PAWKY	SADLY	SAVOY	TAWSE	YARNS	ICILY	SCROW
MAGUS	MATIN	PADDY	PAYEE	SAFAR	SAVVY	TAXED	YARRA	ICING	SCRUB
MAHDI	MATLO	PADMA	PAYER	SAGES	SAXON	TAXIN	YARTA	ICKER	SCRUM
MAHOE	MATTE	PADRE	QAJAR	SAGGY	SAYER	TAXIS	YATES	ICTUS	SCUBA
MAHUA	MAUND	PAEAN	QATAR	SAHEL	SAYSO	TAXOL	ZABRA	MCCOY	SCUFF
MAHWA	MAUVE	PAGAN	RABAT	SAHIB	TABBY	TAXON	ZADOK	OCCAM	SCULL
MAIKO	MAVIN	PAGER	RABBI	SAICE	TABER	TAXUS	ZAIRE	OCCUR	SCULP
MAILE	MAVIS	PAGES	RABID	SAILS	TABES	TAZZA	ZAKAT	OCEAN	SCURF
MAINE	MAXIM	PAINE	RACER	SAINE	TABLA	VADUZ	ZAMBO	OCHER	SCUTE
MAINS	MAYBE	PAINS	RACES	SAINT	TABLE	VAGUE	ZANTE	OCHRE	YCLAD
MAIRE	MAYOR	PAINT	RADAR	SAKER	TABOO	VAGUS	ZAYIN	OCKER	ADAGE
MAIZE	MAZER	PAIRE	RADHA	SALAD	TABOR	VAILS	ABABA	OCNUS	ADAMS
MAJOR	NAAFI	PAIRS	RADIO	SALEM	TACHE	VALET	ABACO	OCREA	ADAPT
MAKAR	NABOB	PAISA	RADIX	SALEP	TACIT	VALID	ABACK	OCTAD	ADDED
MAKER	NACHE	PALEA	RADON	SALES	TACKY	VALOR	ABAFT	OCTAL	ADDER
MALAR	NACHO	PALES	RAGED	SALIC	TAFFY	VALSE	ABASE	OCTET	ADDIO
MALAY	NACHT	PALET	RAGGA	SALIX	TAGUS	VALUE	ABASH	SCADS	ADDIS
MALFI	NACRE	PALIO	RAGGY	SALLE	TAIGA	VALVE	ABATE	SCAFF	ADDLE
MALIK	NADER		RAHAB	SALLY				SCALA	ADEEM

ADEPT	BEIGE	DEFER	GÉANT	HEYER	LEITH	METRO	PERKY	RESIT	TENSE
ADIEU	BEING	DEFOE	GEARE	JEANS	LEMAN	MEUSE	PERON	RESTS	TENTH
ADIGE	BEKAA	DEGAS	GEBER	JEBEL	LEMMA	MEYER	PERRY	RETCH	TENUE
ADIOS	BELAY	DEIFY	GECKO	JEHAD	LEMON	MEZZE	PERSE	RETRO	TEPEE
ADLIB	BELCH	DEIGN	GEESE	JELAB	LEMUR	MEZZO	PESKY	REVEL	TEPID
ADMIN	BELGA	DEIST	GEIST	JELLO	LENIN	NEAGH	PESTO	REVET	TERCE
ADMIT	BELIE	DEITY	GELID	JELLY	LENTO	NEALE	PETAL	REVIE	TEREK
ADMIX	BELLE	DEKKO	GEMMA	JEMMY	LEONE	NEBEL	PETER	REVUE	TERES
ADOBE	BELLS	DELAY	GEMMY	JENNY	LEPER	NEDDY	PETIT	REYES	TERMS
ADOPT	BELLY	DELFT	GENET	JEREZ	LEPID	NEEDS	PETRA	SEALS	TERNE
ADORE	BELOW	DELHI	GENIC	JERKS	LEPUS	NEEDY	PETRE	SEAMY	TERRA
ADORN	BEMBA	DELOS	GENIE	JERKY	LERNA	NEGEV	PETRI	SEARE	TERRY
ADSUM	BENCH	DELPH	GENOA	JERRY	LERNE	NEGRO	PETTO	SECCO	TERSE
ADULT	BENDS	DELTA	GENRE	JESSE	LESHY	NEGUS	PETTY	SEDAN	TESLA
CDROM	BENDY	DELVE	GENTS	JESUS	LETHE	NEHRU	REACH	SEDGE	TESSA
EDEMA	BENET	DEMOB	GENTY	JETTY	LEVEE	NEIGH	REACT	SEDUM	TESTA
EDGAR	BENIN	DEMON	GENUS	JEWEL	LEVEL	NELLY	READE	SEEDY	TESTS
EDGED	BENNE	DEMOS	GEODE	JEWRY	LEVEN	NEPAL	READY	SEGUE	TESTY
EDGER	BEPAT	DEMUR	GERBE	KEBAB	LEVER	NEPER	REALM	SEINE	TETON
EDICT	BERET	DENIM	GESSE	KEBEL	LEVIN	NERVA	REAMS	SEISM	TETRA
EDIFY	BERIA	DENIS	GESSO	KEBLE	LEVIS	NERVE	REARM	SEIZE	TEVET
EDILE	BEROB	DENSE	GESTE	KEBOB	LEWES	NERVI	REBBE	SELIM	TEXAN
EDUCE	BERRY	DENYS	GETUP	KEDAR	LEWIS	NERVO	REBEL	SELLE	TEXAS
EDWIN	BERTH	DEPOT	HEADS	KEDGE	LEXIS	NERVY	REBUS	SELVA	TEXEL
IDAHO	BERYL	DEPTH	HEADY	KEDGY	MEALS	NESSA	REBUT	SEMEN	TEXTS
IDEAL	BESET	DERAY	HEALD	KEECH	MEALY	NESTA	RECAP	SEMIS	VEDDA
IDEAS	BESOM	DERBY	HEAPS	KEELS	MEANS	NEVEL	RECCE	SENNA	VEDIC
IDIOM	BESOT	DERMA	HEARD	KEEPS	MEANT	NEVER	RECTO	SENOR	VEERY
IDIOT	BETEL	DERRY	HEART	KEFIR	MEATH	NEVIS	RECUR	SENSE	VEGAN
IDLER	BETON	DESEX	HEATH	KELIM	MEATS	NEWEL	REDAN	SENZA	VEINS
IDRIS	BETTE	DESSE	HEAVE	KELLS	MEATY	NEWLY	REDON	SEOUL	VELAR
IDYLL	BETTY	DETER	HEAVY	KELLY	MEBBE	NEWSY	REDOX	SEPAL	VELDT
ODDER	BEVEL	DETOX	HECHT	KEMPE	MECCA	NEWTS	REECH	SEPIA	VELUM
ODDLY	BEVIS	DEUCE	HECTO	KENDO	MEDAL	NEXUS	REEDE	SEPOY	VENAL
ODEON	BÉVUE	DEVIL	HEDDA	KENGA	MEDEA	PEACE	REEDS	SERAI	VENDA
ODETS	BÉVVY	DEWAN	HEDGE	KENYA	MEDIA	PEACH	REEDY	SERGE	VENIN
ODIUM	BEZEL	DEWAR	HEELS	KERAL	MEDIC	PEAKY	REFER	SERIF	VENOM
ODOUR	CEASE	DEWEY	HEFTY	KERMA	MEDOC	PEARL	REFIT	SERIN	VENUE
UDALL	CECIL	EERIE	HEGEL	KERNE	MEETS	PEASE	REGAL	SERRA	VENUS
UDDER	CECUM	FEARE	HEIGH	KETCH	MEITH	PEATY	REGAN	SERRE	VERDI
AEDES	CEDAR	FEAST	HEINE	KEVIN	MELBA	PECAN	REGIA	SERUM	VEREY
AEGIS	CELEB	FECAL	HEIST	KEYED	MELEE	PEDAL	RÉGIE	SERVE	VERGE
AESOP	CELLA	FECES	HELEN	KEYES	MELIA	PEDRO	REGIS	SERVO	VERNE
BEACH	CELLO	FECIT	HELGA	LEACH	MELIC	PEERS	RÈGLE	SETUP	VERSA
BEADS	CELLS	FEIGN	HELIO	LEADS	MELON	PEEVE	REICH	SEVEN	VERSE
BEADY	CENCI	FEINT	HELIX	LEAFY	MELOS	PEGGY	REIGN	SEVER	VERSO
BEALE	CENSE	FELIS	HELLO	LEAKY	MENAI	PEKAN	REINS	SEWER	VERST
BEAMY	CENTO	FELIX	HELOT	LEANT	MENGE	PEKIN	REIST	TEACH	VERTU
BEANO	CEORL	FELLA	HELVE	LEAPT	MENSA	PEKOE	REITH	TEARS	VERVE
BEANS	CERES	FELON	HENCE	LEARN	MERAK	PELEE	REJIG	TEASE	VESPA
BEARD	CERNE	FEMTO	HENGE	LEASE	MERCY	PELLA	RELAX	TEAZE	VESTA
BEAST	CESAR	FEMUR	HENNA	LEASH	MERGE	PELMA	RELAY	TEDDY	VETCH
BEAUT	CETUS	FENCE	HENRY	LEAST	MERIL	PENAL	RELIC	TEENS	VEXED
BEBOP	DEATH	FENNY	HERBS	LEAVE	MERIT	PENCE	REMIT	TEENY	WEALD
BECKY	DEBAG	FEOFF	HERMA	LECOQ	MERLE	PENIS	REMUE	TEETH	WEARY
BEDAD	DEBAR	FERAL	HERNE	LEDGE	MERRY	PENNA	REMUS	TEHEE	WEAVE
BEDEW	DEBEL	FERIA	HEROD	LEECH	MESIC	PENNE	RENAL	TEIGN	WEBER
BEECH	DEBIT	FERMI	HERON	LEEDS	MESNE	PENNY	RENAN	TELEX	WEDGE
BEEFY	DEBUG	FERRY	HERSE	LEERY	MESON	PEONY	RENEW	TELIC	WEEDS
BEERY	DEBUT	FESSE	HERTS	LEESE	MESSY	PEPPY	RENTE	TELLY	WEEDY
BEFIT	DECAL	FESTA	HERTZ	LEFTY	MESTO	PEPSI	REPAY	TELOS	WEEKS
BEFOG	DECAY	FESTE	HESSE	LEGAL	METAL	PEPYS	REPEL	TEMPE	WEENY
BEGAD	DECCA	FETAL	HETTY	LEGER	METER	PERAI	REPLY	TEMPO	WEEPY
BEGAN	DECKO	FETCH	HEUGH	LEGGE	METHS	PERCE	REPOT	TEMPT	WEIGH
BEGET	DECON	FETID	HEVEA	LEGGY	METIC	PERCH	REPRO	TENCH	WEILL
BEGIN	DECOR	FETOR	HEWER	LEGIT	METIF	PERCY	RERUN	TENDS	WEIRD
BEGUM	DECOY	FETUS	HEXAD	LEHAR	METIS	PERDU	RESET	TENET	WELCH
BEGUN	DECRY	FEVER	HEXAM	LEIGH	METOL	PERIL	RESIN	TENON	WELLS
BEHAN	DEEDS	FEWER	HEXYL	LEISH	METRE	PERKS	RESIT	TENOR	WELLY

WELSH	CHACO	CHOSE	SHARK	THEMA	WHOLE	DIMLY	GIBBY	LIBER	MIMIC
WENCH	CHAFE	CHOTA	SHARP	THEME	WHOOP	DINAR	GIBUS	LIBRA	MIMUS
WENDY	CHAFF	CHOTT	SHAUN	THERE	WHOOT	DINER	GIDDY	LIBYA	MINCE
WESER	CHAIN	CHUBB	SHAVE	THERM	WHORE	DINGE	GIFTS	LICHT	MINCH
XEBEC	CHAIR	CHUCK	SHAWL	THESE	WHORL	DINGO	GIGLI	LICIT	MINER
XENIA	CHALK	CHUFF	SHAWM	THETA	WHOSE	DINGY	GIGOT	LIEGE	MINGY
XENON	CHAMP	CHUMP	SHCHI	THETE	XHOSA	DINKA	GIGUE	LIFER	MINHO
XERES	CHANT	CHUNK	SHEAF	THEWS	AIDAN	DINKY	GILES	LIGER	MINIM
XEROX	CHAOS	CHURL	SHEAR	THICK	AIDOS	DIODE	GILET	LIGGE	MINKE
YEARN	CHAPE	CHURN	SHEBA	THIEF	AIKEN	DIOTA	GILLS	LIGHT	MINOR
YEARS	CHAPS	CHURR	SHEEL	THIGH	AINEE	DIPPY	GILTS	LIKED	MINOS
YEAST	CHARD	CHUTE	SHEEN	THILL	AIOLI	DIRGE	GIMEL	LIKEN	MINOT
YEATS	CHARK	CHYLE	SHEEP	THINE	AIRER	DIRTY	GIMPY	LIKES	MINSK
YEMEN	CHARM	CHYME	SHEER	THING	AIRES	DISCO	GIPPO	LILAC	MINUS
YERBA	CHART	CHYND	SHEET	THINK	AISLE	DISHY	GIPSY	LILLE	MIRTH
YEZDI	CHARY	DHABI	SHEIK	THIOL	AITCH	DITAL	GISMO	LILLY	MIRZA
ZEBRA	CHASE	DHOBI	SHELF	THIRD	BIBBY	DITCH	GIRLS	LIMAX	MISER
ZENOS	CHASM	DHOTI	SHELL	THIRL	BIBLE	DITTO	GIRLY	LIMBO	MISSA
ZEPPO	CHEAP	GHANA	SHERD	THOFT	BIDDY	DITTY	GIRTH	LIMER	MISSY
ZERDA	CHEAT	GHATS	SHERE	THOLE	BIDET	DIVAN	GISMO	LIMES	MISTY
AFEAR	CHECK	GHAZI	SHIEL	THONG	BIFID	DIVER	GIVEN	LIMEY	MITES
AFFIX	CHEEK	GHOST	SHIFT	THORN	BIGHT	DIVES	GIVER	LIMIT	MITRE
AFIRE	CHEEP	GHOUL	SHILL	THOSE	BIGOT	DIVOT	GIZMO	LINCH	MIXED
AFOOT	CHEER	GHYLL	SHINE	THOTH	BIJOU	DIVVY	HIKER	LINED	MIXER
AFORE	CHEKA	KHAKI	SHINY	THREE	BIKER	DIWAN	HILAR	LINEN	MIXTE
AFOUL	CHERE	KHAYA	SHIRE	THREW	BILGE	DIXIE	HILDA	LINER	MIXUP
AFRIT	CHERT	KHAZI	SHIRK	THRID	BILLY	DIZZY	HILLS	LINES	NICAD
AFTER	CHESS	LHASA	SHIRR	THRIP	BIMBO	EIDER	HILLY	LINGO	NICHE
OFFAL	CHEST	PHARE	SHIRT	THROB	BINGE	EIGER	HILUM	LININ	NICOL
OFFAS	CHEVY	PHASE	SHITE	THROE	BINGO	EIGHT	HINDI	LINKS	NIDOR
OFFER	CHEWA	PHEBE	SHIVA	THROW	BIONT	EIKON	HINDU	LINUS	NIDUS
OFLAG	CHEWY	PHENO	SHIVE	THRUM	BIPED	EILAT	HINGE	LIONS	NIECE
OFTEN	CHIAO	PHEON	SHLEP	THUGS	BIPOD	FIBER	HINNY	LIPID	NIEVE
AGAIN	CHICA	PHIAL	SHOAH	THUJA	BIRCH	FIBRE	HIPPO	LIPPI	NIFTY
AGAMI	CHICK	PHILE	SHOAL	THULE	BIRDS	FIBRO	HIPPY	LISLE	NIGEL
AGAPE	CHICO	PHLOX	SHOCK	THUMB	BIRTH	FICHE	HIRAM	LISTS	NIGER
AGATE	CHIDE	PHNOM	SHOJI	THUMP	BISON	FICHU	HIRED	LISZT	NIGHT
AGAVE	CHIEF	PHOBE	SHOLA	THUNK	BITCH	FIDEL	HIRER	LITAS	NIHIL
AGENT	CHILD	PHONE	SHONA	THUYA	BITER	FIDES	HITCH	LITER	NINJA
AGGER	CHILE	PHONY	SHONE	THYME	BITTE	FIELD	HITHE	LITHE	NINNY
AGGRO	CHILI	PHOTO	SHOOK	UHLAN	BITTY	FIEND	HIVER	LITRE	NINON
AGILE	CHILL	PHYLE	SHOOT	UHURU	CIBOL	FIERE	HIVES	LIVED	NINTH
AGING	CHIME	RHEIN	SHOPS	WHACK	CIDER	FIERY	JIFFY	LIVEN	NIOBE
AGIST	CHIMP	RHETT	SHORE	WHALE	CIGAR	FIFTH	JIHAD	LIVER	NIPPY
AGLEE	CHINA	RHEUM	SHORN	WHANG	CIGGY	FIFTY	JIMMU	LIVES	NISAN
AGLET	CHINE	RHINE	SHORT	WHARF	CILIA	FIGHT	JIMMY	LIVID	NISUS
AGLEY	CHING	RHINO	SHOTS	WHAUP	CILLA	FILCH	JIMPY	LIVRE	NITID
AGLOW	CHINK	RHODO	SHOUT	WHAUR	CINCH	FILET	JINGO	MIAMI	NITON
AGNES	CHINO	RHOMB	SHOVE	WHEAL	CINNA	FILLY	JINKS	MIAOU	NITRE
AGONE	CHIPS	RHONE	SHOWN	WHEAT	CIRCA	FILMS	JINNI	MIAOW	NITRO
AGONY	CHIRK	RHUMB	SHOWY	WHEEL	CIRCE	FILMY	JIRGA	MIAUL	NIVAL
AGORA	CHIRL	RHYME	SHRED	WHEEN	CISCO	FILTH	KIANG	MICAH	NIXON
AGREE	CHIRP	SHACK	SHREW	WHELK	CISSY	FINAL	KIDDY	MICHE	NIZAM
EGDON	CHIRR	SHADE	SHROW	WHELP	CIVET	FINCH	KIDGE	MICRO	OILED
EGEST	CHIRT	SHADY	SHRUB	WHERE	CIVIC	FINER	KILDA	MIDAS	OILER
EGGAR	CHIVE	SHAFT	SHRUG	WHICH	CIVIL	FINIS	KILIM	MIDDY	PIANO
EGRET	CHIVY	SHAKE	SHUCK	WHIFF	CIVVY	FINKS	KIMBO	MIDGE	PIAVE
EGYPT	CHLOE	SHAKO	SHUNT	WHIFT	DIALS	FIORD	KINGS	MIDST	PICEA
IGAPO	CHOCK	SHAKY	SHUSH	WHILE	DIANA	FIRMA	KINKY	MIFFY	PICOT
IGLOO	CHOCO	SHALE	SHUTE	WHIMS	DIARY	FIRST	KIOSK	MIGHT	PICUS
NGAIO	CHOIR	SHALL	SHUTS	WHINE	DIAZO	FIRTH	KIPPS	MILAN	PIECE
OGGIN	CHOKE	SHALT	SHYLY	WHIPS	DICEY	FISHY	KIRBY	MILCH	PIERS
OGHAM	CHOKO	SHAME	THAIS	WHIRL	DICKY	FITCH	KIROV	MILER	PIERT
OGIER	CHOKY	SHANG	THANE	WHIRR	DIDNT	FIVER	KITTY	MILES	PIETA
OGIVE	CHOMP	SHANK	THANK	WHISH	DIEGO	FIVES	KIWIS	MILKY	PIETY
UGRIC	CHOOK	SHANT	THECA	WHISK	DIGHT	FIXED	LIANA	MILLI	PIEZO
AHEAD	CHOPS	SHAPE	THEFT	WHIST	DIGIT	FIXER	LIANE	MILLS	PIGGY
AHMED	CHORD	SHARD	THEGN	WHITE	DIKER	FIZZY	LIANG	MILNE	PIGMY
BHANG	CHORE	SHARE	THEIR	WHIZZ	DILDO	GIANT	LIBEL	MIMER	PILAF

PILAU	SIDHA	TITHE	YIPPY	ALLOT	CLARK	ELVER	GLOOM	SLATE	EMBER
PILCH	SIDLE	TITLE	ZIGAN	ALLOW	CLARY	ELVES	GLORY	SLATS	EMBOW
PILED	SIDON	TITRE	ZILCH	ALLOY	CLASH	ELVIS	GLOSS	SLATY	EMBOX
PILES	SIEGE	TITTY	ZINCO	ALLYL	CLASP	FLACK	GLOVE	SLAVE	EMBUS
PILLS	SIEVE	TITUS	ZINEB	ALNUS	CLASS	FLAIL	GLUCK	SLEEK	EMCEE
PILOT	SIGHS	TIZZY	ZIPPY	ALOES	CLAUS	FLAIR	GLUED	SLEEP	EMDEN
PILUM	SIGHT	VIAND	EJECT	ALOFT	CLAVE	FLAKE	GLUEY	SLEET	EMEND
PILUS	SIGIL	VIBES	FJORD	ALOHA	CLEAN	FLAKY	GLUME	SLEPT	EMERY
PINCH	SIGLA	VICAR	AKARA	ALONE	CLEAR	FLAME	GLUON	SLICE	EMILE
PINES	SIGMA	VICHY	AKBAR	ALONG	CLEAT	FLANK	GLYPH	SLICK	EMILY
PINGO	SIGNS	VIDEO	AKELA	ALOOF	CLECK	FLARE	ILEAC	SLIDE	EMLYN
PINKO	SILAS	VIGIL	AKENE	ALOUD	CLEEK	FLASH	ILEUM	SLIGO	EMMER
PINKY	SILEX	VIGOR	OKAPI	ALPHA	CLEEP	FLASK	ILEUS	SLIME	EMMET
PINNA	SILKY	VILLA	SKATE	ALTAI	CLEFT	FLATS	ILIAC	SLIMY	EMOTE
PINNY	SILLY	VILLI	SKEAN	ALTAR	CLEPE	FLECK	ILIAD	SLING	EMOVE
PINON	SILVA	VINYL	SKEER	ALTER	CLERK	FLEET	ILIUM	SLINK	EMPTY
PIÑON	SIMBA	VIOLA	SKEET	ALULA	CLICK	FLESH	KLANG	SLIPE	EMRYS
PINOT	SIMON	VIPER	SKEIN	ALURE	CLIFF	FLEUR	KLEIN	SLIPS	EMURE
PINTA	SINAI	VIRAL	SKELM	ALVIS	CLIFT	FLEWS	KLIEG	SLOAN	HMONG
PINTO	SINCE	VIREO	SKELP	BLACK	CLIMB	FLICK	KLOOF	SLOOP	IMAGE
PIOUS	SINEW	VIRGA	SKIER	BLADE	CLIME	FLIER	LLAMA	SLOPE	IMAGO
PIPAL	SINGE	VIRGO	SKIFF	BLAIR	CLING	FLIES	LLANO	SLOPS	IMARI
PIPER	SINUS	VIRID	SKILL	BLAKE	CLINK	FLING	LLOYD	SLOSH	IMAUM
PIPIT	SIREN	VIRTU	SKIMP	BLAME	CLINT	FLINT	OLDEN	SLOTH	IMBED
PIPPA	SISAL	VIRUS	SKINK	BLANC	CLIVE	FLIRT	OLDER	SLUGS	IMBUE
PIPUL	SISSY	VISBY	SKINS	BLAND	CLOAK	FLOAT	OLDIE	SLUMP	IMMER
PIQUE	SITAR	VISIT	SKINT	BLANK	CLOCK	FLOCK	OLEIC	SLUNG	IMMEW
PIROG	SITIN	VISNA	SKIRL	BLARE	CLOMP	FLONG	OLEIN	SLUNK	IMPEL
PISKY	SITKA	VISON	SKIRR	BLASÉ	CLONE	FLOOD	OLEUM	SLURB	IMPLY
PISTE	SITTA	VISOR	SKIRT	BLAST	CLOOT	FLOOR	OLIVE	SLURP	IMPOT
PITCH	SITUP	VISTA	SKIVE	BLAZE	CLOSE	FLOPS	OLLIE	SLUSH	IMSHI
PITHY	SIVAN	VITAE	SKOAL	BLEAK	CLOTH	FLORA	PLACE	SLYLY	OMAGH
PITON	SIXER	VITAL	SKRIM	BLEAR	CLOUD	FLOSS	PLACK	SLYPE	OMANI
PITOT	SIXTH	VITIS	SKULK	BLEAT	CLOUT	FLOTA	PLAID	ULCER	OMBER
PITTA	SIXTY	VITUS	SKULL	BLEED	CLOVE	FLOUR	PLAIN	ULEMA	OMBRE
PIVOT	SIZAR	VIVAT	SKUNK	BLEEP	CLOWN	FLOUT	PLAIT	ULMAR	OMEGA
PIXEL	TIARA	VIVID	UKASE	BLEND	CLOZE	FLOWN	PLANE	ULTRA	SMACK
PIXIE	TIBBS	VIXEN	ALACK	BLESS	CLUBS	FLUFF	PLANK	VLACH	SMALL
PIZZA	TIBBY	VIZOR	ALAMO	BLEST	CLUCK	FLUID	PLANT	ZLOTY	SMARM
RIANT	TIBER	WIDEN	ALANS	BLIGH	CLUMP	FLUKE	PLATE	AMAIN	SMART
RICAN	TIBET	WIDOW	ALAPA	BLIMP	CLUNG	FLUME	PLATH	AMANT	SMASH
RICIN	TIBIA	WIDTH	ALARM	BLIND	CLUNK	FLUMP	PLATO	AMASS	SMEAR
RIDER	TIDAL	WIELD	ALATE	BLINI	CLYDE	FLUNG	PLATY	AMAZE	SMEEK
RIDGE	TIDDY	WIGAN	ALBAN	BLINK	ELAND	FLUNK	PLATZ	AMBER	SMELL
RIFLE	TIGER	WIGHT	ALBEE	BLISS	ELATE	FLYER	PLAYA	AMBIT	SMELT
RIGHT	TIGHT	WILDE	ALBUM	BLITZ	ELBOW	FLYTE	PLAZA	AMBLE	SMILE
RIGID	TIGON	WILDS	ALDAN	BLOAT	ELDER	GLACE	PLEAD	AMEBA	SMIRK
RIGOR	TIKKA	WILES	ALDER	BLOCK	ELECT	GLADE	PLEAT	AMEND	SMITE
RILEY	TILDE	WILGA	ALDIS	BLOKE	ELEGY	GLAIR	PLEBS	AMENE	SMITH
RILKE	TILED	WILLY	ALEPH	BLOND	ELENE	GLANCE	PLEIN	AMENT	SMOCK
RILLE	TILER	WILTS	ALERT	BLOOD	ELFIN	GLAND	PLICA	AMICE	SMOKE
RINSE	TILES	WIMPY	ALEUT	BLOOM	ELGAR	GLANS	PLIER	AMIEL	SMOKY
RIOJA	TILIA	WINCE	ALFIE	BLOOP	ELGIN	GLARE	PLINY	AMIGO	SMOLT
RIOTS	TILTH	WINCH	ALGAE	BLOWN	ELIAD	GLASS	PLONK	AMINE	SMOTE
RIPEN	TIMER	WINDY	ALGID	BLOWY	ELIAS	GLAZE	PLOTS	AMINO	SMUTS
RIPER	TIMES	WINEY	ALGOL	BLUES	ELIDE	GLEAM	PLUCK	AMISH	UMBEL
RIPON	TIMID	WINGS	ALIAS	BLUEY	ELIHU	GLEAN	PLUMB	AMISS	UMBER
RISEN	TIMON	WIPER	ALIBI	BLUFF	ELIOT	GLEBE	PLUME	AMITY	UMBLE
RISER	TIMOR	WIRED	ALICE	BLUNT	ELITE	GLEEK	PLUMP	AMMAN	UMBRA
RISKY	TINEA	WIRES	ALIEN	BLURB	ELLEN	GLEET	PLUNK	AMNIO	UMPTY
RISUS	TINGE	WISPY	ALIGN	BLURT	ELLIS	GLIDE	PLUSH	AMONG	ANANA
RITES	TINNY	WITAN	ALIKE	BLUSH	ELMER	GLIFF	PLUTO	AMORT	ANDES
RITZY	TIPPY	WITCH	ALIVE	CLACK	ELOGE	GLINT	SLACK	AMOUR	ANEAR
RIVAL	TIPSY	WITHE	ALLAH	CLAIM	ELOGY	GLISK	SLADE	AMPLE	ANELE
RIVEN	TIRED	WITHY	ALLAN	CLAMP	ELOPE	GLITZ	SLAIN	AMPLY	ANEND
RIVER	TIREE	WITTY	ALLAY	CLANG	ELSAN	GLOAT	SLAKE	AMUCK	ANENT
RIVET	TIROS	WIVES	ALLÉE	CLANK	ELTON	GLOBE	SLANG	AMUSE	ANGEL
RIYAL	TITAN	YIELD	ALLEN	CLARA	ELUDE	GLOGG	SLANT	EMAIL	ANGER
SIBYL	TITCH	YIKES	ALLEY	CLARE	ELVAN	GLOGG	SLASH	EMBED	ANGLE

39

ANGLO	INDUS	SNORE	BONNY	COLOR	COYLY	FOLIO	GOWER	JOULE	LOWRY
ANGRY	INEPT	SNORT	BONUS	COLTS	COYNE	FOLKS	HOARD	JOUNT	LOYAL
ANGST	INERT	SNOUT	BONZE	COLZA	COYPU	FOLLY	HOARE	JOUST	LOZEN
ANGUS	INFER	SNOWY	BOOBY	COMBE	COZEN	FONDA	HOARY	JOYCE	MOCHA
ANIGH	INFRA	SNUFF	BOONE	COMBO	DOBBY	FONDS	HOAST	KOALA	MODAL
ANIMA	INGLE	UNAPT	BOONG	COMBS	DOBRO	FOODS	HOBBS	KODAK	MODEL
ANION	INGOT	UNARM	BOOST	COMET	DOCKS	FOOLS	HOBBY	KOFTA	MODEM
ANISE	INIGO	UNBAR	BOOTH	COMFY	DODDY	FOOTS	HOCUS	KOINE	MODER
ANITA	INION	UNBED	BOOTS	COMIC	DODGE	FOOTY	HODGE	KOKUM	MODUS
ANJOU	INIUM	UNCAP	BOOTY	COMMA	DODGY	FORAY	HOGAN	KONGO	MOGGY
ANKER	INJUN	UNCLE	BOOZE	COMPO	DOGGO	FORCE	HOICK	KOOKY	MOGUL
ANKLE	INLAW	UNCUS	BOOZY	COMTE	DOGGY	FOREL	HOIST	KOORI	MOIRA
ANKUS	INLAY	UNCUT	BORAX	COMUS	DOGMA	FORGE	HOKEY	KOPJE	MOIRE
ANNAL	INLET	UNDAM	BORED	CONAN	DOILY	FORGO	HOKUM	KOPPA	MOIST
ANNAM	INNER	UNDER	BOREE	CONCH	DOING	FORKS	HOLED	KORAN	MOLAR
ANNEX	INNES	UNDID	BORER	CONDE	DOLCE	FORME	HOLEY	KOREA	MOLLY
ANNIE	INPUT	UNDUE	BORIC	CONDO	DOLIN	FORMS	HOLLA	KORMA	MOLTO
ANNOY	INSET	UNFED	BORIS	CONEY	DOLLY	FORTE	HOLLY	KOTOW	MOMMA
ANNUL	INTER	UNFIT	BORNE	CONGÉ	DOMED	FORTH	HOLST	LOAMY	MOMMY
ANODE	INTRA	UNGET	BORON	CONGO	DONAR	FORTY	HOMER	LOATH	MONAD
ANOLE	INTRO	UNIAT	BOSCH	CONIC	DONAT	FORUM	HOMME	LOBAR	MONAL
ANOMY	INUIT	UNIFY	BOSEY	CONTE	DONEE	FOSSA	HONAN	LOBBY	MONDO
ANSON	INURE	UNION	BOSKY	COOEE	DONNA	FOSSE	HONDO	LOBED	MONET
ANTAR	INWIT	UNITA	BOSOM	COOKS	DONNE	FOUET	HONEY	LOCAL	MONEY
ANTIC	KNACK	UNITE	BOSSY	COOMB	DONOR	FOULÉ	HONKY	LOCKE	MONKS
ANTON	KNARL	UNITS	BOSUN	COOPT	DOONE	FOUND	HONOR	LOCKS	MONTE
ANVIL	KNAVE	UNITY	BOTCH	COPER	DOORN	FOUNT	HOOCH	LOCUM	MONTH
ANZAC	KNEAD	UNLAW	BOTHA	COPPY	DOORS	FOURS	HOOEY	LOCUS	MONZA
ENACT	KNEEL	UNLAY	BOTHY	COPRA	DOPEY	FOVEA	HOOKY	LODEN	MOOCH
ENARM	KNELL	UNLIT	BOTTE	COPSE	DORAS	FOXED	HOOSH	LODGE	MOODY
ENATE	KNELT	UNMAN	BOUGH	CORAL	DOREE	FOYER	HOOVE	LOESS	MOOLI
ENDED	KNIFE	UNMIX	BOULE	CORAM	DORIC	FOYLE	HORAH	LOFTY	MOONY
ENDOW	KNOCK	UNPEN	BOUND	CORDS	DORIS	GOATY	HORDE	LOGAN	MOORE
ENDUE	KNOLL	UNPIN	BOURG	CORED	DORMY	GOBBO	HOREB	LOGIC	MOOSE
ENEMA	KNOUT	UNRIG	BOWED	CORER	DORTS	GODET	HORNE	LOGOS	MOPED
ENEMY	KNOWN	UNRIP	BOWEL	CORFE	DOTTY	GODLY	HORNY	LOINS	MOPER
ENJOY	KNURL	UNSAY	BOWER	CORFU	DOUAI	GOFER	HORSA	LOIRE	MOPSY
ENMEW	KNURR	UNTIE	BOWIE	CORGI	DOUAR	GOGOL	HORSE	LOLLY	MORAL
ENNUI	ONCER	UNTIL	BOWLS	CORIN	DOUAY	GOING	HORSY	LOMAN	MORAN
ENOCH	ONCUS	UNWED	BOXED	CORKY	DOUBT	GOLAN	HORUS	LONER	MORAT
ENORM	ONION	UNZIP	BOXER	CORNY	DOUCE	GOLEM	HOSEA	LONGS	MORAY
ENROL	ONKUS	VNECK	BOYAR	COROT	DOUGH	GOLGI	HOSEN	LOOBY	MOREL
ENSEW	ONSET	AORTA	BOYAU	CORPS	DOUMA	GOLLY	HOSTA	LOOFA	MORES
ENSOR	AOSTA	AOSTA	BOYCE	CORSE	DOURA	GOMBO	HOTCH	LOONS	MORIA
ENSUE	SNACK	BOARD	BOYLE	CORSO	DOURO	GONAD	HOTEL	LOONY	MORIN
ENTER	SNAFU	BOAST	BOYNE	CORVO	DOUSE	GONER	HOTLY	LOOPY	MORNE
ENTRY	SNAGS	BOBBY	COACH	COSEC	DOVER	GONNA	HOTTY	LOOSE	MORON
ENUGU	SNAIL	BOCHE	COADE	COSMO	DOWDY	GONZO	HOUGH	LORCA	MORPH
ENURE	SNAKE	BODES	COAST	COSTA	DOWEL	GOODS	HOUND	LORDS	MORSE
ENVOI	SNAKY	BODGE	COATI	COSTS	DOWER	GOODY	HOURI	LORIS	MORUS
ENVOY	SNAPS	BOGEY	COBIA	COTTA	DOWNS	GOOEY	HOURS	LORNA	MOSES
GNARL	SNARE	BOGGY	COBOL	COUCH	DOWNY	GOOFY	HOUSE	LORNE	MOSEY
GNASH	SNARK	BOGIE	COBRA	COUDÉ	DOWRY	GOOLY	HOVEL	LORRY	MOSSI
GNOME	SNARL	BOGLE	COCCI	COUGH	DOWSE	GOOSE	HOVER	LOSER	MOSSO
INANE	SNASH	BOGUS	COCKY	COULD	DOYEN	GOPAK	HOWBE	LOTOS	MOSSY
INAPT	SNEAD	BOHEA	COCOA	COUNT	DOYLE	GORED	HOWDY	LOTTO	MOTEL
INARI	SNEAK	BOING	COCOS	COUPE	DOYLY	GORGE	HOYLE	LOTUS	MOTET
INARM	SNECK	BOLAS	CODED	COURB	DOZEN	GORKY	IONIC	LOUGH	MOTHS
INCLE	SNEER	BOLUS	CODEX	COURT	EOLIC	GORSE	JOCKO	LOUIE	MOTIF
INCUR	SNICK	BOMBE	CODON	COUTH	EOSIN	GOSHT	JOINT	LOUIS	MOTOR
INCUS	SNIDE	BOMBO	COHOE	COVEN	FOAMY	GOSSE	JOIST	LOUPE	MOTTE
INDEW	SNIFF	BONAR	COIGN	COVER	FOCAL	GOTCH	JOKER	LOUSE	MOTTO
INDEX	SNIFT	BONCE	COKES	COVET	FOCUS	GOTHA	JOLLY	LOUSY	MOUCH
INDIA	SNIPE	BONDI	COLET	COVEY	FOEHN	GOTTA	JONAH	LOUTH	MOULD
INDIC	SNOBS	BONDS	COLEY	COWAN	FOGEY	GOUDA	JONES	LOVAT	MOULS
INDRA	SNOEK	BONER	COLIC	COWER	FOGGY	GOUGE	JONTY	LOVER	MOULT
INDRE	SNOOD	BONES	COLIN	COWRY	FOIST	GOURD	JORIS	LOWAN	MOUND
INDRI	SNOOK	BONEY	COLLY	COXAL	FOLIC	GOUTY	JORUM	LOWER	MOUNT
INDUE	SNOOT	BONGO	COLON	COXED	FOLIE	GOWAN	JOUAL	LOWLY	MOURN

MOUSE	PONGO	ROPED	SORRY	VOILE	APPAY	SPITZ	ARIAN	BROAD	CRONE
MOUSY	PONTY	ROPER	SORTS	VOLET	APPEL	SPLAT	ARICA	BROCK	CRONK
MOUTH	POOCH	ROPES	SOTTO	VOLGA	APPLE	SPLAY	ARIEL	BROIL	CRONY
MOVED	POOLS	ROPEY	SOUGH	VOLTA	APPLY	SPLIT	ARIES	BROKE	CROOK
MOVER	POORI	ROQUE	SOULS	VOLTE	APPRO	SPODE	ARISE	BRONX	CROPS
MOVIE	POPES	RORIC	SOUND	VOLVA	APPUI	SPOHR	ARISH	BROOD	CRORE
MOWER	POPOV	RORKE	SOUSA	VOLVO	APRIL	SPOIL	ARIST	BROOK	CROSS
MOYLE	POPPA	RORTY	SOUSE	VOMER	APRON	SPOKE	ARITA	BROOL	CROUP
NOBBY	POPPY	ROSCO	SOUTH	VOMIT	APSIS	SPOOF	ARKLE	BROOM	CROWD
NOBEL	POPSY	ROSES	SOWER	VOTER	APTLY	SPOOK	ARLES	BROSE	CROWN
NOBLE	POPUP	ROSET	SOWLE	VOTES	EPHOD	SPOOL	ARMED	BROTH	CROZE
NOBLY	PORCH	ROSIN	SOWND	VOUCH	EPHOR	SPOON	ARMET	BROWN	CRUCK
NODAL	PORGY	ROSIT	SOWTH	VOWEL	EPOCH	SPOOR	ARMOR	BRUCE	CRUDE
NODDY	PORKY	ROSSE	SOYUZ	VOZHD	EPODE	SPORE	AROID	BRUIN	CRUEL
NODES	PORNO	ROSSI	TOADY	WODEN	EPOXY	SPORT	AROMA	BRUIT	CRUET
NODUS	PORTA	ROTOR	TOAST	WODGE	EPSOM	SPOTS	AROSE	BRULE	CRUMB
NOISE	PORTE	ROUEN	TOBIT	WOKEN	OPERA	SPOUT	ARRAN	BRUME	CRUMP
NOISY	PORTO	ROUGE	TODAY	WOMAN	OPHIR	SPRAG	ARRAS	BRUNO	CRUOR
NOMAD	PORTS	ROUGH	TODDY	WOMEN	OPINE	SPRAT	ARRAY	BRUNT	CRUSE
NOMEN	POSED	ROULE	TOILE	WONGA	OPIUM	SPRAY	ARRÊT	BRUSH	CRUSH
NOMIC	POSER	ROUND	TOILS	WONKY	OPTIC	SPREE	ARRIS	BRUTE	CRUST
NONCE	POSIT	ROUSE	TOISE	WOODS	SPACE	SPRIG	ARROW	CRABS	CRWTH
NONES	POSSE	ROUST	TOKAY	WOODY	SPADE	SPRIT	ARSIS	CRACK	CRYPT
NONET	POSTE	ROUTE	TOKEN	WOOER	SPADO	SPROD	ARSON	CRAFT	DRACO
NONNY	POTIN	ROVER	TOKYO	WOOFY	SPAHI	SPROG	ARTIE	CRAIG	DRAFT
NOOKY	POTOO	ROWAN	TOLAR	WOOLF	SPAIN	SPRUE	ARUBA	CRAKE	DRAIN
NOOSE	POTTO	ROWDY	TOMAN	WOOZY	SPALD	SPUME	ARVAL	CRAMP	DRAKE
NORAH	POTTY	ROWEL	TOMMY	WORCS	SPALL	SPUNK	ARYAN	CRANE	DRAMA
NORIA	POUCH	ROWER	TONAL	WORDS	SPALT	SPURN	BRACE	CRANK	DRANK
NORMA	POULE	ROYAL	TONDO	WORDY	SPANK	SPURS	BRACK	CRAPE	DRAPE
NORSE	POULT	ROZET	TONER	WORKS	SPARE	SPURT	BRACT	CRAPS	DRAWL
NORTH	POUND	SOANE	TONGA	WORLD	SPARK	UPEND	BRADY	CRARE	DRAWN
NOSER	POUPE	SOAPY	TONGS	WORMS	SPART	UPPER	BRAID	CRASH	DREAD
NOSEY	POWAN	SOARE	TONIC	WORMY	SPASM	UPSET	BRAIN	CRASS	DREAM
NOTAL	POWER	SOBER	TONNE	WORRY	SPATE	UPSEY	BRAKE	CRATE	DREAR
NOTCH	POWYS	SOCKS	TONUS	WORSE	SPATS	UPTON	BRAND	CRAVE	DREGS
NOTED	ROACH	SOCLE	TOOLS	WORST	SPAWN	YPRES	BRANK	CRAWL	DRERE
NOTES	ROAST	SODOM	TOOTH	WORTH	SPEAK	AQABA	BRASH	CRAZE	DRESS
NOTTS	ROBES	SODOR	TOPAZ	WOULD	SPEAN	EQUAL	BRASS	CRAZY	DRIED
NOTUM	ROBEY	SOFIA	TOPEE	WOUND	SPEAR	EQUIP	BRAVA	CREAK	DRIER
NOVEL	ROBIN	SOFTY	TOPER	WOVEN	SPECK	IQBAL	BRAVE	CREAM	DRIES
NOVUM	ROBOT	SOGGY	TOPIC	YOBBO	SPECS	SQUAB	BRAVO	CRECY	DRIFT
NOWAY	ROCKS	SOKEN	TOPSY	YODEL	SPEED	SQUAD	BRAWL	CREDO	DRILL
NOXAL	ROCKY	SOKOL	TOQUE	YOICK	SPEER	SQUAT	BRAWN	CREED	DRILY
NOYAU	RODEO	SOLAN	TORAH	YOKEL	SPEKE	SQUAW	BREAD	CREEK	DRINK
NOYES	RODIN	SOLAR	TORCH	YONKS	SPELL	SQUIB	BREAK	CREEL	DRIVE
OOMPH	ROGER	SOLDE	TORII	YONNE	SPELT	SQUID	BREAM	CREEP	DROIT
POACH	ROGET	SOLFA	TORSO	YOULL	SPEND	SQUIT	BREDA	CREME	DROLL
PODEX	ROGUE	SOLID	TORTE	YOUNG	SPENS	ARABA	BREDE	CREON	DROME
PODGE	ROHAN	SOLON	TORUS	YOURS	SPENT	ARBOR	BREED	CREPE	DRONE
PODGY	ROIST	SOLTI	TOSCA	YOURT	SPERM	ARCOT	BREEM	CREPT	DROOL
POEMS	ROKER	SOLUM	TOTAL	YOUTH	SPICA	ARCUS	BREME	CRESS	DROOP
POESY	ROLFE	SOLUS	TOTEM	YOUVE	SPICE	ARDEA	BRENT	CREST	DROPS
POETS	ROLLO	SOLVE	TOTTY	ZOHAR	SPICK	ARDEB	BREST	CRETE	DROSS
POILU	ROLLS	SOMME	TOUCH	ZOMBI	SPICY	ARDEN	BREVE	CREWE	DROVE
POINT	ROMAN	SONAR	TOUGH	ZONAL	SPIED	ARDIL	BRIAN	CRICK	DROWN
POISE	ROMEO	SONDE	TOWEL	ZORBA	SPIEL	ARDOR	BRIAR	CRIED	DRUGS
POKER	ROMER	SONIC	TOWER	ZORRO	SPIES	ARECA	BRIBE	CRIER	DRUID
POKEY	RONDE	SONNY	TOWNS	APACE	SPIFF	AREDE	BRICK	CRIES	DRUNK
POLAR	RONDO	SOOTH	TOWSE	APAGE	SPIKE	ARENA	BRIDE	CRIME	DRUPE
POLIO	RONEO	SOOTY	TOWZE	APAID	SPIKY	ARENE	BRIEF	CRIMP	DRURY
POLKA	RONNE	SOPHY	TOXIC	APART	SPILE	ARENT	BRIER	CRISE	DRUZE
POLLY	ROOKY	SOPPY	TOXIN	APEAK	SPILL	ARETE	BRILL	CRISP	DRYAD
POLYP	ROOMS	SOPRA	VOCAB	APERT	SPILT	ARGIL	BRINE	CROAK	DRYER
POMMY	ROOMY	SORBO	VOCAL	APHID	SPINA	ARGON	BRING	CROAT	DRYLY
PONCE	ROOPY	SORDO	VODKA	APHIS	SPINE	ARGOT	BRINK	CROCE	ERARD
PONDS	ROOST	SORES	VOGUE	APODE	SPINY	ARGUE	BRINY	CROCK	ERASE
PONEY	ROOTS	SOREX	VOICE	APOOP	SPIRE	ARGUS	BRISK	CROFT	ERATO
PONGA	ROOTY	SORGO	VOILA	APPAL	SPITE	ARHAT	BRIZE	CROME	ERECT

ERGOT	GREYS	ORTON	TRENT	ASHET	ATRIP	STICK	AUDEN	CULEX	FUNKY
ERICA	GRIEF	ORTUS	TRESS	ASIAN	ATTAR	STIFF	AUDIO	CULLY	FUNNY
ERICK	GRIEG	ORVAL	TREVI	ASIDE	ATTIC	STILE	AUDIT	CUMIN	FURAN
ERNIE	GRIFF	PRADO	TREWS	ASKER	ATTLE	STILL	AUGER	CUPAR	FUROR
ERNST	GRILL	PRAHU	TRIAD	ASKEW	ETAGE	STILT	AUGHT	CUPEL	FURRY
ERODE	GRIME	PRANA	TRIAL	ASOKA	ETAIN	STIME	AUGUR	CUPID	FURZE
ERROR	GRIMM	PRANG	TRIBE	ASPEN	ETAPE	STIMY	AULIC	CUPPA	FUSED
ERUCA	GRIMY	PRANK	TRICE	ASPER	ETATS	STING	AULIS	CURDS	FUSEE
ERUCT	GRIND	PRATE	TRICK	ASPIC	ETHAL	STINK	AUNTY	CURED	FUSSY
ERUPT	GRIOT	PRAWL	TRIED	ASSAI	ETHER	STINT	AURAL	CURER	FUSTY
FRACK	GRIPE	PRAWN	TRIER	ASSAM	ETHIC	STIPE	AURIC	CURIA	FUTON
FRACT	GRIST	PREEN	TRIES	ASSAY	ETHOS	STIRP	AUXIN	CURIE	FUZEE
FRAIL	GRITS	PRESA	TRIKE	ASSET	ETHYL	STOAT	BUBBY	CURIO	FUZZY
FRAME	GROAN	PRESS	TRILL	ASTER	ETUDE	STOCK	BUCCA	CURLY	GUACO
FRANC	GROAT	PREST	TRINE	ASTIR	ETWEE	STOEP	BUCKO	CURRY	GUANA
FRANK	GROIN	PRIAL	TRIPE	ASTON	ITALA	STOGA	BUCKS	CURSE	GUANO
FRANS	GROOM	PRIAM	TRITE	ASTRA	ITALY	STOGY	BUDDY	CURST	GUARD
FRANZ	GROPE	PRICE	TROIC	ASWAN	ITCHY	STOIC	BUDGE	CURVE	GUAVA
FRAUD	GROSS	PRICK	TROLL	ESCOT	OTARY	STOKE	BUFFO	CURVY	GUELF
FREAK	GROSZ	PRIDE	TROMP	ESKER	OTHER	STOLA	BUFFS	CUSHY	GUESS
FREED	GROUP	PRILL	TROON	ESROM	OTIUM	STOLE	BUGGY	CUTCH	GUEST
FREON	GROUT	PRIMA	TROOP	ESSAY	OTTAR	STOLL	BUGLE	CUTEY	GUEUX
FRESH	GROVE	PRIME	TROPE	ESTER	OTTER	STOMA	BUICK	CUTIE	GUIDE
FREUD	GROWL	PRIMO	TROTH	ESTOC	OTWAY	STOMP	BUILD	CUTIS	GUILD
FRIAR	GROWN	PRIMP	TROTS	ESTOP	STACK	STONE	BUILT	CUTTY	GUILE
FRIED	GRUEL	PRINT	TROUT	ISAAC	STADE	STONY	BULGE	DUALA	GUILT
FRIES	GRUFE	PRION	TROVE	ISERE	STAFF	STOOD	BULKY	DUBAI	GUIMP
FRILL	GRUFF	PRIOR	TRUCE	ISLAM	STAGE	STOOK	BULLA	DUCAT	GUISE
FRISK	GRUME	PRISE	TRUCK	ISLAY	STAGY	STOOL	BULLS	DUCHY	GULAG
FRIST	GRUMP	PRISM	TRULL	ISLES	STAID	STOOP	BULLY	DUCKS	GULCH
FRITH	GRUNT	PRIVY	TRULY	ISLET	STAIN	STOOR	BULOW	DUCKY	GULES
FRITZ	IRAQI	PRIZE	TRUMP	ISMET	STAIR	STOPE	BUMPH	DUDDY	GULLS
FROCK	IRATE	PROBE	TRUNK	ISOLA	STAKE	STORE	BUMPY	DUKAS	GULLY
FROND	IRENA	PROKE	TRURO	ISSUE	STALE	STORK	BUNCE	DUKES	GULPH
FRONT	IRENE	PROLE	TRUSS	NSPCC	STALK	STORM	BUNCH	DULAC	GUMBO
FROST	IRGUN	PROMO	TRUST	OSAGE	STALL	STORY	BUNCO	DUMAS	GUMMA
FROTH	IRISH	PRONE	TRUTH	OSAKA	STAMP	STOUP	BUNDY	DUMMY	GUMMY
FROWN	IROKO	PRONG	TRYST	OSCAR	STAND	STOUR	BUNGY	DUMPS	GUNGE
FROWY	IRONS	PROOF	URALS	OSIER	STANK	STOUT	BUNNY	DUMPY	GUNNY
FROZE	IRONY	PROSE	URATE	OSMAN	STAPH	STOVE	BURGH	DUNCE	GUPPY
FRUIT	KRAAL	PROSY	URBAN	OSSIA	STARE	STOWE	BURIN	DUNNO	GUSHY
FRUMP	KRAFT	PROUD	UREDO	OSTIA	STARK	STRAD	BURKE	DUOMO	GUSTO
GRAAL	KRANG	PROUT	URIAH	PSALM	STARR	STRAP	BURLY	DUPIN	GUSTY
GRACE	KRANS	PROVE	URINE	PSEUD	STARS	STRAW	BURMA	DUPLE	GUTSY
GRADE	KRANZ	PROVO	URITE	PSHAW	START	STRAY	BURNS	DURER	GUTTA
GRAFF	KRAUT	PROWL	URSON	PSOAS	STASH	STREP	BURNT	DUROY	GUYED
GRAFT	KRIEG	PROXY	VROOM	PSORA	STASI	STREW	BUROO	DURRY	GUYON
GRAIL	KRILL	PRUDE	WRACK	PSYCH	STATE	STRIA	BURRO	DURST	GUYOT
GRAIN	KRONA	PRUNE	WRATH	RSPCA	STAVE	STRIP	BURSA	DURUM	HUBBY
GRAND	KRONE	TRACE	WREAK	TSUBA	STAYS	STROP	BURST	DUSKY	HUFFY
GRANT	ORANG	TRACK	WRECK	TSUGA	STEAD	STRUM	BURSB...	DUSTY	HULKS
GRAPE	ORATE	TRACT	WREST	USAGE	STEAK	STRUT	BUSBY	DUTCH	HULLO
GRAPH	ORBIT	TRADE	WRING	USHER	STEAL	STUCK	BUSHY	DUVAL	HULME
GRASP	ORCUS	TRAIL	WRIST	USING	STEAM	STUDY	BUSTY	DUVET	HUMAN
GRASS	ORDER	TRAIN	WRITE	USTED	STEED	STUFF	BUTCH	EULER	HUMID
GRATE	ORFEO	TRAIT	WRITS	USUAL	STEEK	STUKA	BUTTE	FUBSY	HUMOR
GRAVE	ORGAN	TRAMP	WRONG	USURE	STEEL	STUMP	BUTTY	FUCHS	HUMPH
GRAVY	ORGUE	TRANS	WROTE	USURP	STEEN	STUNG	BUXOM	FUDGE	HUMUS
GRAYS	ORIEL	TRANT	WROTH	USURY	STEEP	STUNK	BUYER	FUERO	HUNCH
GRAZE	ORION	TRAPS	WRUNG	ATHOS	STEER	STUNT	CUBAN	FUGAL	HUNKS
GREAT	ORLON	TRASH	WRYLY	ATILT	STEIN	STUPA	CUBBY	FUGGY	HUNKY
GREBE	ORLOP	TRAWL	ASAPH	ATLAS	STELA	STUPE	CUBEB	FUGUE	HUNTS
GREED	ORMER	TREAD	ASCII	ATLIN	STELE	STURT	CUBED	FULLY	HURON
GREEK	ORMUZ	TREAT	ASCOT	ATMAN	STENT	STYLE	CUBIC	FUMED	HURRY
GREEN	ORNIS	TRECK	ASCUS	ATOLL	STEPS	STYLO	CUBIT	FUMES	HURST
GREER	OROMO	TREEN	ASDIC	ATOMY	STERN	STYME	CUDDY	FUMET	HUSKS
GREET	ORPEN	TREES	ASHEN	ATONE	STEVE	UTHER	CUFFS	FUNDI	HUSKY
GREGG	ORRIS	TREMA	ASHER	ATONY	STEWS	UTTER	CUFFY	FUNDS	HUSSY
GRETA	ORTHO	TREND	ASHES	ATOPY	STEWY	UTURN	CUFIC	FUNDY	HUTCH

HUZZA	MULCT	PURSE	RUNNY	VULVA	SWARF	OXIDE	RYDAL	AVAIL	CHASE
JUDAS	MULLA	PURSY	RUNUP	WURST	SWARM	OXIME	SYBIL	AVANT	CHASM
JUDGE	MULSE	PUSHY	RUPEE	YUCCA	SWASH	OXLIP	SYCEE	AVAST	CLACK
JUGAL	MULTI	PUSLE	RUPIA	YUCKY	SWATH	OXTER	SYLPH	AWAIT	CLAIM
JUICE	MUMMY	PUSSY	RURAL	YUKKY	SWATS	AYRIE	SYNGE	AWAKE	CLAMP
JUICY	MUMPS	PUTID	RUSHY	YUKON	SWAZI	BYLAW	SYNOD	AWARD	CLANG
JULEP	MUNCH	PUTTO	RUSSE	YULAN	SWEAR	BYRON	SYNTH	AWARE	CLANK
JUMAR	MUNDA	PUTTY	RUSSO	YUMMY	SWEAT	BYWAY	SYRAH	AWARN	CLARA
JUMBO	MUNGO	QUACK	RUSTY	YUPIK	SWEDE	CYCAD	SYRIA	AWASH	CLARE
JUMBY	MUNRO	QUADS	SUAVE	YUPPY	SWEEP	CYCLE	SYRUP	BEACH	CLARK
JUMNA	MURAL	QUAFF	SUCKS	AVAIL	SWEET	CYMRU	TYING	BEADS	CLARY
JUMPS	MUREX	QUAIL	SUCRE	AVANT	SWELL	CYMRY	TYLER	BEADY	CLASH
JUMPY	MURKY	QUAKE	SUDAN	AVAST	SWELT	CYNIC	TYNED	BEALE	CLASP
JUNCO	MURRE	QUALM	SUDOR	AVENA	SWEPT	CYRUS	TYPED	BEAMY	CLASS
JUNTA	MURRY	QUANT	SUEDE	AVENS	SWIFT	DYFED	TYPES	BEANO	CLAUS
JUNTO	MUSCA	QUARK	SUETY	AVERT	SWILL	DYING	TYPHA	BEANS	CLAVE
JUPON	MUSCI	QUART	SUGAN	AVIAN	SWINE	DYKER	TYROL	BEARD	COACH
JURAT	MUSES	QUASH	SUGAR	AVION	SWING	DYLAN	WYMAN	BEAST	COADE
JUROR	MUSHA	QUASI	SUITE	AVISO	SWIPE	DYULA	XYLEM	BEAUT	COAST
KUALA	MUSHY	QUEEN	SUITS	AVOID	SWIRE	EYRIE	XYRIS	BHANG	COATI
KUDOS	MUSIC	QUEER	SULFA	AVOUÉ	SWIRL	EYTIE	AZOIC	BLACK	CRABS
KUDZU	MUSIT	QUELL	SULKS	EVADE	SWISH	FYLDE	AZOTE	BLADE	CRACK
KUFIC	MUSKY	QUERN	SULKY	EVANS	SWISS	GYGES	AZTEC	BLAIR	CRAFT
KUKRI	MUSSE	QUERY	SULLA	EVENS	SWIZZ	GYMNO	AZURE	BLAKE	CRAIG
KULAK	MUSSY	QUEST	SULLY	EVENT	SWOON	GYNAE	AZYME	BLAME	CRAKE
KURMA	MUSTY	QUEUE	SUMMA	EVERT	SWOOP	GYPPO	CZECH	BLANC	CRAMP
KUTCH	MUTED	QUICK	SUNDA	EVERY	SWORD	GYPSY	IZARD	BLAND	CRANE
LUBRA	MUZAK	QUIDS	SUNNI	EVIAN	SWORE	GYRUS	IZMIR	BLANK	CRANK
LUCAN	MUZZY	QUIET	SUNNY	EVICT	SWORN	HYDRA	IZZAT	BLARE	CRAPE
LUCIA	NUBIA	QUIFF	SUOMI	EVITA	SWUNG	HYDRO	OZARK	BLASÉ	CRAPS
LUCID	NUCHA	QUILL	SUPER	EVITE	TWAIN	HYENA	OZONE	BLAST	CRARE
LUCIO	NUDGE	QUILP	SUPPE	EVOKE	TWANG	HYLUM	PZAZZ	BLAZE	CRASH
LUCKY	NULLA	QUILT	SUPRA	IVIED	TWANK	HYMEN	UZBEK	BOARD	CRASS
LUCRE	NUMEN	QUINS	SURGE	IVORY	TWEAK	HYOID		BOAST	CRATE
LUDIC	NUNKY	QUINT	SURLY	KVASS	TWEED	HYPER	**5:3**	BRACE	CRAVE
LUFFA	NURSE	QUIRE	SURYA	MVULE	TWEET	HYPHA	ABABA	BRACK	CRAWL
LUGER	NUTTY	QUIRK	SUSAN	OVARY	TWERP	HYRAX	ABACK	BRACT	CRAZE
LULLY	OUGHT	QUITE	SUSHI	OVATE	TWICE	HYTHE	ABACO	BRADY	CRAZY
LUMEN	OUIDA	QUITO	SUTCH	OVERT	TWIGS	KYANG	ABAFT	BRAID	DEATH
LUMME	OUIJA	QUITS	SUTOR	OVINE	TWILL	KYLIE	ABASE	BRAIN	DHABI
LUMMY	OUNCE	QUOIF	SUTRA	OVOID	TWILT	KYLIN	ABASH	BRAKE	DIALS
LUMPY	OUSEL	QUOIN	SUVLA	OVOLO	TWINE	KYLIX	ABATE	BRAND	DIANA
LUNAR	OUTBY	QUOIT	SUZIE	OVULE	TWINS	KYLOE	ADAGE	BRANK	DIARY
LUNCH	OUTDO	QUORN	TUBBY	UVULA	TWIRL	KYRIE	ADAMS	BRASH	DIAZO
LUNDY	OUTER	QUOTA	TUBER	AWAIT	TWIRP	LYCÉE	ADAPT	BRASS	DRACO
LUNED	OUTGO	QUOTE	TUDOR	AWAKE	TWIST	LYCRA	AGAIN	BRAVA	DRAFT
LUNGE	OUTRE	QUOTH	TUFFE	AWARD	TWIXT	LYDIA	AGAMI	BRAVE	DRAIN
LUNGI	OUZEL	QURAN	TULIP	AWARE	TWOER	LYING	AGAPE	BRAVO	DRAKE
LUNGS	PUBIC	RUBIN	TULLE	AWARN	AXIAL	LYMPH	AGATE	BRAWL	DRAMA
LUPIN	PUBIS	RUBLE	TULLY	AWASH	AXIOM	LYNCH	AGAVE	BRAWN	DRANK
LUPUS	PUDGE	RUCHE	TUMID	AWEEL	AXOID	LYRIC	AKARA	BWANA	DRAPE
LURCH	PUDGY	RUDDY	TUMMY	AWFUL	EXACT	LYSIN	ALACK	BWAZI	DRAWL
LURGY	PUDOR	RUDGE	TUMOR	AWOKE	EXALT	LYSIS	ALAMO	CEASE	DRAWN
LURID	PUFFY	RUFFE	TUNER	BWANA	EXCEL	LYSOL	ALANS	CHACO	DUALA
LUSHY	PUGIN	RUFUS	TUNIC	BWAZI	EXEAT	LYTHE	ALAPA	CHAFE	DWARF
LUSTY	PUKKA	RUGBY	TUNIS	DWARF	EXERT	MYNAH	ALARM	CHAFF	ELAND
LUTIN	PULEX	RUING	TUNKU	DWELL	EXILE	MYOMA	ALATE	CHAIN	ELATE
LUTON	PULPY	RUINS	TUNNY	GWENT	EXINE	MYRON	AMAIN	CHAIR	EMAIL
LUZON	PULSE	RULER	TUQUE	OWING	EXIST	MYRRH	AMANT	CHALK	ENACT
MUCID	PUNCH	RULES	TURBO	OWLER	EXODE	NYALA	AMASS	CHAMP	ENARM
MUCIN	PUNIC	RUMBA	TURCO	OWLET	EXPEL	NYASA	AMAZE	CHANT	ENATE
MUCKY	PUNTO	RUMEN	TURIN	OWNER	EXTOL	NYLON	ANANA	CHAOS	ERARD
MUCRO	PUNTY	RUMEX	TURKI	SWAIN	EXTRA	NYMPH	APACE	CHAPE	ERASE
MUCUS	PUPAL	RUMMY	TURKU	SWALE	EXUDE	NYSSA	APAGE	CHAPS	ERATO
MUDDY	PUPIL	RUMOR	TURPS	SWAMI	EXULT	PYGMY	APAID	CHARD	ETAGE
MUDGE	PUPPY	RUMPY	TUTOR	SWAMP	EXURB	PYLON	APART	CHARK	ETAIN
MUFTI	PUREE	RUNCH	TUTSI	SWANK	IXION	PYREX	AQABA	CHARM	ETAPE
MUGGY	PURGE	RUNES	TUTTI	SWANS	OXBOW	PYRUS	ARABA	CHART	ETATS
MULCH	PURIM	RUNIC	VULGO	SWARD	OXEYE	PYXIS	ASAPH	CHARY	EVADE

EVANS	HEARD	MEATH	QUASH	SMALL	SWARM	BABUL	LABDA	UNBAR	EK
EXACT	HEART	MEATS	QUASI	SMARM	SWASH	BEBOP	LABEL	UNBED	HACEK
EXALT	HEATH	MEATY	REACH	SMART	SWATH	BIBBY	LABIS	URBAN	HECHT
FEARE	HEAVE	MIAMI	REACT	SMASH	SWATS	BIBLE	LABOR	UZBEK	HECTO
FEAST	HEAVY	MIAOU	READE	SNACK	SWAZI	BOBBY	LIBEL	VIBES	HOCUS
FLACK	HOARD	MIAOW	READY	SNAFU	TEACH	BUBBY	LIBER	WEBER	INCLE
FLAIL	HOARE	MIAUL	REALM	SNAGS	TEARS	CABAL	LIBRA	XEBEC	INCUR
FLAIR	HOARY	NAAFI	REAMS	SNAIL	TEASE	CABAS	LIBYA	YOBBO	INCUS
FLAKE	HOAST	NEAGH	REARM	SNAKE	TEAZE	CABBY	LOBAR	ZABRA	ITCHY
FLAKY	IDAHO	NEALE	RIANT	SNAKY	THAIS	CABER	LOBBY	ZEBRA	JACKS
FLAME	IGAPO	NGAIO	ROACH	SNAPS	THANE	CABIN	LOBED	ACCRA	JACOB
FLANK	IMAGE	NYALA	ROAST	SNARE	THANK	CABLE	LUBRA	ARCOT	JOCKO
FLARE	IMAGO	NYASA	SCADS	SNARK	TIARA	CABOB	MEBBE	ARCUS	LACET
FLASH	IMARI	OKAPI	SCAFF	SNARL	TOADY	CABOT	NABOB	ASCII	LACKS
FLASK	IMAUM	OMAGH	SCALA	SNASH	TOAST	CIBOL	NEBEL	ASCOT	LECOQ
FLATS	INANE	OMANI	SCALD	SOANE	TRACE	COBIA	NOBBY	ASCUS	LICHT
FOAMY	INAPT	ORANG	SCALE	SOAPY	TRACK	COBOL	NOBEL	BACCY	LICIT
FRACK	INARI	ORATE	SCALP	SOARE	TRACT	COBRA	NOBLE	BACKS	LOCAL
FRACT	INARM	OSAGE	SCALY	SPACE	TRADE	CUBAN	NOBLY	BACON	LOCKE
FRAIL	IRAQI	OSAKA	SCAMP	SPADE	TRAIL	CUBBY	NUBIA	BECKY	LOCKS
FRAME	IRATE	OTARY	SCANT	SPADO	TRAIN	CUBEB	OMBER	BOCHE	LOCUM
FRANC	ISAAC	OVARY	SCAPA	SPAHI	TRAIT	CUBED	OMBRE	BUCCA	LOCUS
FRANK	ITALA	OVATE	SCAPE	SPAIN	TRAMP	CUBIC	ORBIT	BUCKO	LUCAN
FRANS	ITALY	OZARK	SCARE	SPALD	TRANS	CUBIT	OXBOW	BUCKS	LUCIA
FRANZ	IZARD	PEACE	SCARF	SPALL	TRANT	DEBAG	PABLO	CACAO	LUCID
FRAUD	JEANS	PEACH	SCARP	SPALT	TRAPS	DEBAR	PUBIC	CACHE	LUCIO
GÉANT	KAABA	PEAKY	SCARY	SPANK	TRASH	DEBEL	PUBIS	CECIL	LUCKY
GEARE	KHAKI	PEARL	SCATH	SPARE	TRAWL	DEBIT	RABAT	CECUM	LUCRE
GHANA	KHAYA	PEASE	SCAUP	SPARK	TWAIN	DEBUG	RABBI	COCCI	LYCÉE
GHATS	KHAZI	PEATY	SCAUR	SPART	TWANG	DEBUT	RABID	COCKY	LYCRA
GHAZI	KIANG	PHARE	SEALS	SPASM	TWANK	DOBBY	REBBE	COCOA	MACAW
GIANT	KLANG	PHASE	SEAMY	SPATE	UDALL	DOBRO	REBEL	COCOS	MACER
GLACE	KNACK	PIANO	SEARE	SPATS	UKASE	DUBAI	REBUS	CYCAD	MACHO
GLADE	KNARL	PIAVE	SHACK	SPAWN	UNAPT	ELBOW	REBUT	CYCLE	MACLE
GLAIR	KNAVE	PLACE	SHADE	STACK	UNARM	EMBED	ROBES	DACCA	MACON
GLAND	KOALA	PLACK	SHADY	STADE	URALS	EMBER	ROBEY	DACHA	MACRO
GLANS	KRAAL	PLAID	SHAFT	STAFF	URATE	EMBOW	ROBIN	DECAL	MCCOY
GLASS	KRAFT	PLAIN	SHAKE	STAGE	USAGE	EMBOX	ROBOT	DECAY	MECCA
GLAZE	KRANG	PLAIT	SHAKO	STAGY	VIAND	EMBUS	RUBIN	DECCA	MICAH
GNARL	KRANS	PLANE	SHAKY	STAID	VLACH	FABER	RUBLE	DECKO	MICHE
GNASH	KRANZ	PLANK	SHALE	STAIN	WEALD	FABLE	SABAL	DECON	MICRO
GOATY	KRAUT	PLANT	SHALL	STAIR	WEARY	FABRÉ	SABER	DECOR	MOCHA
GRAAL	KUALA	PLATE	SHALT	STAKE	WEAVE	FIBER	SABIN	DECOY	MUCID
GRACE	KVASS	PLATH	SHAME	STALE	WHACK	FIBRE	SABLE	DECRY	MUCIN
GRADE	KYANG	PLATO	SHANG	STALK	WHALE	FIBRO	SABOT	DICEY	MUCKY
GRAFF	LEACH	PLATY	SHANK	STALL	WHANG	FUBSY	SABRA	DICKY	MUCRO
GRAFT	LEADS	PLATZ	SHANT	STAMP	WHARF	GABBY	SABRE	DOCKS	MUCUS
GRAIL	LEAFY	PLAYA	SHAPE	STAND	WHAUP	GABLE	SIBYL	DUCAT	NACHE
GRAIN	LEAKY	PLAZA	SHARD	STANK	WHAUR	GABON	SOBER	DUCHY	NACHO
GRAND	LEANT	POACH	SHARE	STAPH	WRACK	GEBER	SYBIL	DUCKS	NACHT
GRANT	LEAPT	PRADO	SHARK	STARE	WRATH	GIBBY	TABBY	DUCKY	NACRE
GRAPE	LEARN	PRAHU	SHARP	STARK	YEARN	GIBUS	TABER	EMCEE	NICAD
GRAPH	LEASE	PRANA	SHAUN	STARR	YEARS	GOBBO	TABES	ESCOT	NICHE
GRASP	LEASH	PRANG	SHAVE	STARS	YEAST	HABET	TABLA	EXCEL	NICOL
GRASS	LEAST	PRANK	SHAWL	START	YEATS	HABIT	TABLE	FACER	NUCHA
GRATE	LEAVE	PRATE	SHAWM	STASH	ABBAS	HOBBS	TABOO	FACET	OCCAM
GRAVE	LHASA	PRAWL	SKATE	STASI	ABBEY	HOBBY	TABOR	FACIA	OCCUR
GRAVY	LIANA	PRAWN	SLACK	STATE	ABBOT	HUBBY	TIBBS	FACTO	ONCER
GRAYS	LIANE	PSALM	SLADE	STAVE	AKBAR	IMBED	TIBBY	FACTS	ONCUS
GRAZE	LIANG	PZAZZ	SLAIN	STAYS	ALBAN	IMBUE	TIBER	FECAL	ORCUS
GUACO	LIARD	QUACK	SLAKE	SUAVE	ALBEE	IQBAL	TIBET	FECES	OSCAR
GUANA	LLAMA	QUADS	SLANG	SWAIN	ALBUM	JABOT	TIBIA	FECIT	PACER
GUANO	LLANO	QUAFF	SLANT	SWALE	AMBER	JEBEL	TOBIT	FICHE	PACEY
GUARD	LOAMY	QUAIL	SLASH	SWAMI	AMBIT	KABOB	TUBBY	FICHU	PACHA
GUAVA	LOATH	QUAKE	SLATE	SWAMP	AMBLE	KABUL	TUBER	FOCAL	PECAN
HEADS	MEALS	QUALM	SLATS	SWANK	ARBOR	KEBAB	UMBEL	FOCUS	PICEA
HEADY	MEALY	QUANT	SLATY	SWANS	BABAR	KEBEL	UMBER	GECKO	PICOT
HEALD	MEANS	QUARK	SLAVE	SWARD	BABEL	KEBLE	UMBLE	GECKO	PICUS
HEAPS	MEANT	QUART	SMACK	SWARF	BABOO	KEBOB	UMBRA	HÁ{\C}	RACER

RACES	BUDDY	LODEN	SADLY	AWEEL	DRERE	IRENA	REEDY	STEPS	AWFUL	
RECAP	BUDGE	LODGE	SEDAN	BEECH	DRESS	IRENE	REEVE	STERN	BAFFY	
RECCE	CADDY	LUDIC	SEDGE	BEEFY	DWELL	ISERE	RHEIN	STEVE	BEFIT	
RECTO	CADET	LYDIA	SEDUM	BEERY	EDEMA	KEECH	RHETT	STEWS	BEFOG	
RECUR	CADGE	MADAM	SIDHA	BLEAK	EGEST	KEELS	RHEUM	STEWY	BIFID	
RICAN	CADGY	MADGE	SIDLE	BLEAR	EJECT	KEEPS	SCENE	SUEDE	BUFFO	
RICIN	CADRE	MADLY	SIDON	BLEAT	ELECT	KLEIN	SCENT	SUETY	BUFFS	
ROCKS	CEDAR	MEDAL	SODOM	BLEED	ELEGY	KNEAD	SEEDY	SWEAR	CUFFS	
ROCKY	CIDER	MEDEA	SODOR	BLEEP	ELENE	KNEEL	SHEAF	SWEAT	CUFFY	
RUCHE	CODED	MEDIA	SUDAN	BLEND	EMEND	KNELL	SHEAR	SWEDE	CUFIC	
SACHA	CODEX	MEDIC	SUDOR	BLESS	EMERY	KNELT	SHEBA	SWEEP	DAFFY	
SACHS	CODON	MEDOC	TEDDY	BLEST	ENEMA	LEECH	SHEEL	SWELL	DEFER	
SACKS	CUDDY	MIDAS	TIDAL	BREAD	ENEMY	LEEDS	SHEEN	SWELT	DEFOE	
SECCO	DADDY	MIDDY	TIDDY	BREAK	ERECT	LEERY	SHEEP	SWEPT	DYFED	
SHCHI	DIDNT	MIDGE	TODAY	BREAM	EVENS	LEESE	SHEER	TEENS	ELFIN	
SOCKS	DODDY	MIDST	TODDY	BREDA	EVENT	LIEGE	SHEET	TEENY	FIFTH	
SOCLE	DODGE	MODAL	TUDOR	BREDE	EVERT	LOESS	SHEIK	TEETH	FIFTY	
SUCKS	DODGY	MODEL	UDDER	BREED	EVERY	MAEVE	SHELF	THECA	GAFFE	
SUCRE	DUDDY	MODEM	UNDAM	BREEM	EXEAT	MEETS	SHELL	THEFT	GIFTS	
SYCEE	EGDON	MODER	UNDER	BREME	EXERT	NEEDS	SHERD	THEGN	GOFER	
TACHE	EIDER	MODUS	UNDID	BRENT	FAERY	NEEDY	SHERE	THEIR	HAFIZ	
TACIT	ELDER	MUDDY	UNDUE	BREST	FIELD	NIECE	SIEGE	THEMA	HEFTY	
TACKY	EMDEN	MUDGE	VADUZ	BREVE	FIEND	NIEVE	SIEVE	THEME	HUFFY	
ULCER	ENDED	NADER	VEDDA	CHEAP	FIERE	OBEAH	SKEAN	THERE	INFER	
UNCAP	ENDOW	NADIR	VEDIC	CHEAT	FIERY	OBESE	SKEER	THERM	INFRA	
UNCLE	ENDUE	NADPH	VIDEO	CHECK	FLECK	OCEAN	SKEET	THESE	JAFFA	
UNCUS	FADDY	NEDDY	VODKA	CHEEK	FLEET	ODEON	SKEIN	THETA	JIFFY	
UNCUT	FADED	NIDOR	WADER	CHEEP	FLESH	ODETS	SKELM	THETE	KAFIR	
VICAR	FADGE	NIDUS	WEDGE	CHEER	FLEUR	OLEIC	SKELP	THEWS	KAFKA	
VICHY	FIDEL	NODAL	WIDEN	CHEKA	FLEWS	OLEIN	SLEEK	TREAD	KEFIR	
VOCAB	FIDES	NODDY	WIDOW	CHERE	FOEHN	OLEUM	SLEEP	TREAT	KOFTA	
VOCAL	FUDGE	NODES	WIDTH	CHERT	FREAK	OMEGA	SLEET	TRECK	KUFIC	
WACKY	GADGE	NODUS	WODEN	CHESS	FREED	OPERA	SLEPT	TREEN	LEFTY	
YACHT	GADUS	NUDGE	WODGE	CHEST	FREON	OVERT	SMEAR	TREES	LIFER	
YUCCA	GIDDY	ODDER	YODEL	CHEVY	FRESH	OXEYE	SMEEK	TREMA	LOFTY	
YUCKY	GODET	ODDLY	ZADOK	CHEWA	FREUD	PAEAN	SMELL	TREND	LUFFA	
ABDAR	GODLY	OLDEN	ABEAM	CHEWY	FUERO	PEERS	SMELT	TRENT	MAFIA	
ABDUL	HADES	OLDER	ABEAR	CLEAN	GEESE	PEEVE	SNEAD	TRESS	MIFFY	
ADDED	HADJI	OLDIE	ABELE	CLEAR	GLEAM	PHEBE	SNEAK	TREVI	MUFTI	
ADDER	HADNT	ORDER	ACERB	CLEAT	GLEAN	PHENO	SNECK	TREWS	NIFTY	
ADDIO	HEDDA	PADDY	ADEEM	CLECK	GLEBE	PHEON	SNEER	TWEAK	OFFAL	
ADDIS	HEDGE	PADMA	ADEPT	CLEEK	GLEEK	PIECE	SPEAK	TWEED	OFFAS	
ADDLE	HODGE	PADRE	AFEAR	CLEEP	GLEET	PIERS	SPEAN	TWEET	OFFER	
AEDES	HYDRA	PEDAL	AGENT	CLEFT	GREAT	PIERT	SPEAR	TWERP	ORFEO	
AIDAN	HYDRO	PEDRO	AHEAD	CLEPE	GREBE	PIETA	SPECK	ULEMA	PUFFY	
AIDOS	INDEW	PODEX	AKELA	CLERK	GREED	PIETY	SPECS	UPEND	REFER	
ALDAN	INDEX	PODGE	AKENE	CREAK	GREEK	PIEZO	SPEED	UREDO	REFIT	
ALDER	INDIA	PODGY	ALEPH	CREAM	GREEN	PLEAD	SPEER	VEERY	RIFLE	
ALDIS	INDIC	PUDGE	ALERT	CRECY	GREER	PLEAT	SPEKE	VNECK	RUFFE	
ANDES	INDRA	PUDGY	ALEUT	CREDO	GREET	PLEBS	SPELL	WEEDS	RUFUS	
ARDEA	INDRE	PUDOR	AMEBA	CREED	GREGG	PLEIN	SPELT	WEEDY	SAFAR	
ARDEB	INDRI	RADAR	AMEND	CREEK	GRETA	POEMS	SPEND	WEEKS	SOFIA	
ARDEN	INDUE	RADHA	AMENE	CREEL	GREYS	POESY	SPENS	WEENY	SOFTY	
ARDIL	INDUS	RADIO	AMENT	CREEP	GUELF	POETS	SPENT	WEEPY	TAFFY	
ARDOR	JADED	RADIX	ANEAR	CREME	GUESS	PREEN	SPERM	WHEAL	TUFFE	
ASDIC	JADIS	RADON	ANELE	CREON	GUEST	PRESA	STEAD	WHEAT	UNFED	
AUDEN	JUDAS	REDAN	ANEND	CREPE	GUEUX	PRESS	STEAK	WHEEL	UNFIT	
AUDIO	JUDGE	REDON	ANENT	CREPT	GWENT	PREST	STEAL	WHEEN	WAFER	
AUDIT	KEDAR	REDOX	APEAK	CRESS	HEELS	PSEUD	STEAM	WHELK	AEGIS	
BADDY	KEDGE	RIDER	APERT	CREST	HYENA	QUEEN	STEED	WHELP	AGGER	
BADEN	KEDGY	RIDGE	ARECA	CRETE	IBERT	QUEER	STEEK	WHERE	AGGRO	
BADGE	KIDDY	RODEO	AREDE	CREWE	ICENI	QUELL	STEEL	WIELD	ALGAE	
BADLY	KIDGE	RODIN	ARENA	CZECH	IDEAL	QUERN	STEEN	WREAK	ALGID	
BEDAD	KODAK	RUDDY	ARENE	DEEDS	IDEAS	QUERY	STEEP	WRECK	ALGOL	
BEDEW	KUDOS	RUDGE	ARENT	DIEGO	ILEAC	QUEST	STEER	WREST	ANGEL	
BIDDY	KUDZU	RYDAL	ARETE	DREAD	ILEUM	QUEUE	STEIN	YIELD	ANGER	
BIDET	LADEN	SADHE	AVENA	DREAM	ILEUS	REECH	STELA	AFFIX	ANGLE	
BODES	LADLE	SADHU	AVENS	DREAR	INEPT	REEDE	STELE	ALFIE	ANGLO	
BODGE	LEDGE	SADIE	AVERT	DREGS	INERT	REEDS	STENT		ANGRY	

ANGST	JUGAL	SIGLA	UTHER	BRIER	DRIES	GRITS	OBIIT	SPILL
ANGUS	LAGAN	SIGMA	YAHOO	BRILL	DRIFT	GUIDE	ODIUM	SPILT
ARGIL	LAGER	SIGNS	YAHVE	BRINE	DRILL	GUILD	OGIER	SPINA
ARGON	LAGOS	SOGGY	ZOHAR	BRING	DRILY	GUILE	OGIVE	SPINE
ARGOT	LEGAL	SUGAN	ABIDE	BRINK	DRINK	GUILT	OLIVE	SPINY
ARGUE	LEGER	SUGAR	ABIES	BRINY	DRIVE	GUIMP	ONION	SPIRE
ARGUS	LEGGE	TAGUS	ACINI	BRISK	DYING	GUISE	OPINE	SPITE
AUGER	LEGGY	TIGER	ADIEU	BRIZE	EDICT	HAIDA	OPIUM	SPITZ
AUGHT	LEGIT	TIGHT	ADIGE	BUICK	EDIFY	HAIFA	ORIEL	STICK
AUGUR	LIGER	TIGON	ADIOS	BUILD	EDILE	HAIKU	ORION	STIFF
BAGEL	LIGGE	UNGET	AFIRE	BUILT	ELIAD	HAIRS	OSIER	STILE
BAGGY	LIGHT	VAGUE	AGILE	CAINE	ELIAS	HAIRY	OTIUM	STILL
BEGAD	LOGAN	VAGUS	AGING	CAIRN	ELIDE	HAITI	OUIDA	STILT
BEGAN	LOGIC	VEGAN	AGIST	CAIRO	ELIHU	HEIGH	OUIJA	STIME
BEGET	LOGOS	VIGIL	ALIAS	CAIUS	ELIOT	HEINE	OVINE	STIMY
BEGIN	LUGER	VIGOR	ALIBI	CHIAO	ELITE	HEIST	OWING	STING
BEGUM	MAGHA	VOGUE	ALICE	CHICA	EMILE	HOICK	OXIDE	STINK
BEGUN	MAGIC	WAGER	ALIEN	CHICK	EMILY	HOIST	OXIME	STINT
BIGHT	MAGMA	WAGES	ALIGN	CHICO	ERICA	IBIZA	PAINE	STIPE
BIGOT	MAGNA	WAGGA	ALIKE	CHIDE	ERICK	ICILY	PAINS	STIRP
BOGEY	MAGOG	WAGON	ALIVE	CHIEF	EVIAN	ICING	PAINT	SUITE
BOGGY	MAGOT	WIGAN	AMICE	CHILD	EVICT	IDIOM	PAIRE	SUITS
BOGIE	MAGUS	WIGHT	AMIEL	CHILE	EVITA	IDIOT	PAIRS	SWIFT
BOGLE	MIGHT	ZIGAN	AMIGO	CHILI	EVITE	ILIAC	PAISA	SWILL
BOGUS	MOGGY	ABHOR	AMINE	CHILL	EXILE	ILIAD	PHIAL	SWINE
BUGGY	MOGUL	APHID	AMINO	CHIME	EXINE	ILIUM	PHILE	SWING
BUGLE	MUGGY	APHIS	AMISH	CHIMP	EXIST	INIGO	PLICA	SWIPE
CAGEY	NAGAS	ARHAT	AMISS	CHINA	FAINS	INION	PLIER	SWIRE
CAGOT	NAGOR	ASHEN	AMITY	CHINE	FAINT	INIUM	PLINY	SWIRL
CIGAR	NEGEV	ASHER	ANIGH	CHING	FAIRY	IRISH	POILU	SWISH
CIGGY	NEGRO	ASHES	ANIMA	CHINK	FAITH	IVIED	POINT	SWISS
DAGON	NEGUS	ASHET	ANION	CHINO	FEIGN	IXION	POISE	SWIZZ
DEGAS	NIGEL	ATHOS	ANISE	CHIPS	FEINT	JOINT	PRIAL	TAIGA
DIGHT	NIGER	BAHAI	ANITA	CHIRK	FLICK	JOIST	PRIAM	TAILS
DIGIT	NIGHT	BAHUT	ARIAN	CHIRL	FLIER	JUICE	PRICE	TAINE
DOGGO	OGGIN	BEHAN	ARICA	CHIRP	FLIES	JUICY	PRICK	TAINO
DOGGY	ORGAN	BOHEA	ARIEL	CHIRR	FLING	KLIEG	PRIDE	TAINT
DOGMA	ORGUE	COHOE	ARIES	CHIRT	FLINT	KNIFE	PRILL	TEIGN
EAGER	OUGHT	EPHOD	ARISE	CHIVE	FLIRT	KOINE	PRIMA	THICK
EAGLE	PAGAN	EPHOR	ARISH	CHIVY	FOIST	KRIEG	PRIME	THIEF
EDGAR	PAGER	ETHAL	ARIST	CLICK	FRIAR	KRILL	PRIMO	THIGH
EDGED	PAGES	ETHER	ARITA	CLIFF	FRIED	LAIRD	PRIMP	THILL
EDGER	PEGGY	ETHIC	ASIAN	CLIFT	FRIES	LAIRY	PRINT	THINE
EGGAR	PIGGY	ETHOS	ASIDE	CLIMB	FRILL	LAITH	PRION	THING
EIGER	PIGMY	ETHYL	ATILT	CLIME	FRISK	LAITY	PRIOR	THINK
EIGHT	PUGIN	ICHOR	AVIAN	CLING	FRIST	LEIGH	PRISE	THIOL
ELGAR	PYGMY	JEHAD	AVION	CLINK	FRITH	LEISH	PRISM	THIRD
ELGIN	RAGED	JIHAD	AVISO	CLINT	FRITZ	LEITH	PRIVY	THIRL
ERGOT	RAGGA	LEHAR	AXIAL	CLIVE	GAILY	LOINS	PRIZE	TOILE
FAGOT	RAGGY	MAHDI	AXIOM	COIGN	GAINS	LOIRE	QUICK	TOILS
FAGUS	REGAL	MAHOE	BAIRD	CRICK	GAIUS	LYING	QUIDS	TOISE
FIGHT	REGAN	MAHUA	BAIRN	CRIED	GEIST	MAIKO	QUIET	TRIAD
FOGEY	REGIA	MAHWA	BAIZE	CRIER	GLIDE	MAILE	QUIFF	TRIAL
FOGGY	RÉGIE	NAHUM	BEIGE	CRIES	GLIFF	MAINE	QUILL	TRIBE
FUGAL	REGIS	NEHRU	BEING	CRIME	GLINT	MAINS	QUILP	TRICE
FUGGY	RÈGLE	NIHIL	BLIGH	CRIMP	GLISK	MAIRE	QUILT	TRICK
FUGUE	RIGHT	OCHER	BLIMP	CRISE	GLITZ	MAIZE	QUINS	TRIED
GIGLI	RIGID	OCHRE	BLIND	CRISP	GOING	MEITH	QUINT	TRIER
GIGOT	RIGOR	OGHAM	BLINI	DAILY	GRIEF	MOIRA	QUIRE	TRIES
GIGUE	ROGER	OPHIR	BLINK	DAIRY	GRIEG	MOIRE	QUIRK	TRIKE
GOGOL	ROGET	OTHER	BLISS	DAISY	GRIFF	MOIST	QUITE	TRILL
GYGES	ROGUE	PSHAW	BLITZ	DEIFY	GRILL	NAIAD	QUITO	TRINE
HAGUE	RUGBY	RAHAB	BOING	DEIGN	GRIME	NAILS	QUITS	TRIPE
HEGEL	SAGES	ROHAN	BRIAN	DEIST	GRIMM	NAIRA	RAINE	TRITE
HOGAN	SAGGY	SAHEL	BRIAR	DEITY	GRIMY	NAIVE	RAINY	TWICE
INGLE	SEGUE	SAHIB	BRIBE	DOILY	GRIND	NEIGH	RAISE	TWIGS
INGOT	SIGHS	SCHWA	BRICK	DOING	GRIOT	NOISE	REICH	TWILL
IRGUN	SIGHT	TEHEE	BRIDE	DRIED	GRIPE	NOISY	REIGN	TWILT
JAGGY	SIGIL	USHER	BRIEF	DRIER	GRIST	OBIAH	REINS	TWINE

TWINS	BEKAA	AGLOW	DALEK	HALMA	MILCH	SALAD	UHLAN	COMFY	JIMPY
TWIRL	BIKER	ALLAH	DALIT	HALON	MILER	SALEM	UNLAW	COMIC	JUMAR
TWIRP	COKES	ALLAN	DALLE	HALSE	MILES	SALEP	UNLAY	COMMA	JUMBO
TWIST	DAKAR	ALLAY	DALLY	HALVE	MILKY	SALES	UNLIT	COMPO	JUMBY
TWIXT	DEKKO	ALLÉE	DELAY	HELEN	MILLI	SALIC	VALET	COMTE	JUMNA
TYING	DIKER	ALLEN	DELFT	HELGA	MILLS	SALIX	VALID	COMUS	JUMPS
UNIAT	DUKAS	ALLEY	DELHI	HELIO	MILNE	SALLE	VALOR	CUMIN	JUMPY
UNIFY	DUKES	ALLOT	DELOS	HELIX	MOLAR	SALLY	VALSE	CYMRU	KAMME
UNION	DYKER	ALLOW	DELPH	HELLO	MOLLY	SALMI	VALUE	CYMRY	KAMPF
UNITA	EIKON	ALLOY	DELTA	HELOT	MOLTO	SALON	VALVE	DAMAN	KEMPE
UNITE	ESKER	ALLYL	DELVE	HELVE	MULCH	SALSA	VELAR	DAMME	KIMBO
UNITS	FAKER	ARLES	DILDO	HILAR	MULCT	SALSE	VELDT	DAMON	LAMED
UNITY	FAKIR	ATLAS	DOLCE	HILDA	MULLA	SALTS	VELUM	DAMME	LAMIA
URIAH	HAKKA	ATLIN	DOLIN	HILLS	MULSE	SALTY	VILLA	DEMOB	LAMMY
URINE	HIKER	AULIC	DOLLY	HILLY	MULTI	SALVE	VILLI	DEMON	LAMPS
URITE	HOKEY	AULIS	DULAC	HILUM	NELLY	SALVO	VOLET	DEMOS	LEMAN
USING	HOKUM	BALAN	DYLAN	HOLED	NULLA	SCLIM	VOLGA	DEMUR	LEMMA
VAILS	ICKER	BALER	ECLAT	HOLEY	NYLON	SELIM	VOLTA	DIMLY	LEMON
VEINS	JAKES	BALFE	EILAT	HOLLA	OFLAG	SELLE	VOLTE	DOMED	LEMUR
VOICE	JOKER	BALLS	ELLEN	HOLLY	OILED	SELVA	VOLVA	DUMAS	LIMAX
VOILA	KOKUM	BALLY	ELLIS	HOLST	OILER	SHLEP	VOLVO	DUMMY	LIMBO
VOILE	KUKRI	BALMY	EMLYN	HULKS	OLLIE	SILAS	VULGO	DUMPS	LIMER
WAIST	LIKED	BALOO	EOLIC	HULLO	ORLON	SILEX	VULVA	DUMPY	LIMES
WAITS	LIKEN	BALOR	EULER	HULME	ORLOP	SILKY	WALDO	ELMER	LIMEY
WAIVE	LIKES	BALSA	FALDO	HYLUM	OWLER	SILLY	WALER	EMMER	LIMIT
WEIGH	MAKAR	BELAY	FALLA	IDLER	OWLET	SILVA	WALES	EMMET	LOMAN
WEILL	MAKER	BELCH	FALLS	IGLOO	OXLIP	SOLAN	WALLY	ENMEW	LUMEN
WEIRD	NAKED	BELGA	FALSE	INLAW	PALEA	SOLAR	WALTZ	FAMED	LUMME
WHICH	OAKEN	BELIE	FELIS	INLAY	PALES	SOLDE	WELCH	FEMTO	LUMMY
WHIFF	OAKER	BELLE	FELIX	INLET	PALET	SOLFA	WELLS	FEMUR	LUMPY
WHIFT	OAKUM	BELLS	FELLA	ISLAM	PALIO	SOLID	WELLY	FUMED	LYMPH
WHILE	OCKER	BELLY	FELON	ISLAY	PALLY	SOLON	WELSH	FUMES	MAMBA
WHIMS	ONKUS	BELOW	FILCH	ISLES	PALMY	SOLTI	WILDE	FUMET	MAMBO
WHINE	PEKAN	BILGE	FILET	ISLET	PALSY	SOLUM	WILDS	GAMAY	MAMEY
WHIPS	PEKIN	BILLY	FILLY	JALAP	PELEE	SOLUS	WILES	GAMBA	MAMMA
WHIRL	PEKOE	BOLAS	FILMS	JELAB	PELLA	SOLVE	WILGA	GAMBO	MAMMY
WHIRR	POKER	BOLUS	FILMY	JELLO	PELMA	SPLAT	WILLY	GAMES	MIMER
WHISH	POKEY	BULGE	FILTH	JELLY	PHLOX	SPLAY	WILTS	GAMIC	MIMIC
WHISK	PUKKA	BULKY	FOLIC	JOLLY	PILAF	SPLIT	XYLEM	GAMMA	MIMUS
WHIST	RAKED	BULLA	FOLIE	JULEP	PILAU	SULFA	YALTA	GAMMY	MOMMA
WHITE	RAKEE	BULLS	FOLIO	KALIF	PILCH	SULKS	YCLAD	GEMMA	MOMMY
WHIZZ	RAKER	BULLY	FOLKS	KELIM	PILED	SULKY	YULAN	GEMMY	MUMMY
WRING	RAKES	BULOW	FOLLY	KELLS	PILES	SULLA	ZILCH	GIMEL	MUMPS
WRIST	ROKER	BYLAW	FULLY	KELLY	PILLS	SULLY	ADMIN	GIMPY	NAMED
WRITE	SAKER	CALEB	FYLDE	KILDA	PILOT	SYLPH	ADMIT	GOMBO	NAMES
WRITS	SOKEN	CALIX	GALAM	KILIM	PILUM	TALAQ	ADMIX	GUMBO	NAMIB
YOICK	SOKOL	CALOR	GALBA	KULAK	PILUS	TALAR	AHMED	GUMMA	NOMAD
ZAIRE	TAKER	CALPE	GALEA	KYLIE	POLAR	TALEA	AMMAN	GUMMY	NOMEN
ANJOU	TAKES	CALVE	GALEN	KYLIN	POLIO	TALES	ARMED	GYMNO	NOMIC
BAJRI	TIKKA	CALYX	GALOP	KYLIX	POLKA	TALKS	ARMET	HAMMY	NUMEN
BIJOU	TOKAY	CELEB	GELID	KYLOE	POLLY	TALLY	ARMOR	HOMER	NYMPH
CAJUN	TOKEN	CELLA	GILES	LILAC	POLYP	TALMA	ATMAN	HOMME	OOMPH
ENJOY	TOKYO	CELLO	GILET	LILLE	PULEX	TALON	BAMBI	HUMAN	ORMER
INJUN	WAKEN	CELLS	GILLS	LILLY	PULPY	TALUS	BEMBA	HUMID	ORMUZ
MAJOR	WAKES	CHLOE	GILTS	LOLLY	PULSE	TELEX	BIMBO	HUMOR	OSMAN
QAJAR	WOKEN	CILIA	GOLAN	LULLY	PYLON	TELIC	BOMBE	HUMPH	PAMIR
RAJAB	YAKKA	CILLA	GOLEM	MALAR	RALLY	TELLY	BOMBO	HUMUS	POMMY
RAJAH	YAKUT	COLET	GOLGI	MALAY	RALPH	TELOS	BUMPH	HYMEN	RAMAN
REJIG	YIKES	COLEY	GOLLY	MALFI	RELAX	TILDE	BUMPY	IMMER	RAMBO
AIKEN	YOKEL	COLIC	GULAG	MALIK	RELAY	TILED	CAMAS	IMMEW	RAMUS
ANKER	YUKKY	COLIN	GULCH	MALMO	RELIC	TILER	CAMEL	ISMET	REMIT
ANKLE	YUKON	COLLY	GULES	MALTA	RILEY	TILES	CAMEO	IZMIR	REMUE
ANKUS	ZAKAT	COLON	GULLS	MELBA	RILKE	TILIA	CAMIS	JAMBE	REMUS
ARKLE	ABLER	COLOR	GULLY	MELEE	RILLE	TILTH	CAMPO	JAMBO	ROMAN
ASKER	ABLOW	COLTS	GULPH	MELIA	ROLFE	TOLAR	CAMUS	JAMES	ROMEO
ASKEW	ADLIB	COLZA	HALER	MELIC	ROLLO	TULIP	COMBE	JAMMY	ROMER
BAKED	AGLEE	CULET	HALFA	MELON	ROLLS	TULLE	COMBO	JEMMY	RUMBA
BAKER	AGLET	CULEX	HALLÉ	MELOS	RULER	TULLY	COMBS	JIMMU	RUMEN
BAKHA	AGLEY	CULLY	HALLO	MILAN	RULES	TYLER	COMET	JIMMY	RUMEX

RUMMY	BENDS	DONOR	IONIC	MINER	PIÑON	TENSE	ALOFT	CHOPS	ERODE
RUMOR	BENDY	DUNCE	JANTY	MINGY	PINOT	TENTH	ALOHA	CHORD	EVOKE
RUMPY	BENET	DUNNO	JANUS	MINHO	PINTA	TENUE	ALONE	CHORE	EXODE
SAMBA	BENIN	ENNUI	JENNY	MINIM	PINTO	TINEA	ALONG	CHOSE	FEOFF
SAMBO	BENNE	ERNIE	JINGO	MINKE	PONCE	TINGE	ALOOF	CHOTA	FIORD
SAMFU	BINGE	ERNST	JINKS	MINOR	PONDS	TINNY	ALOUD	CHOTT	FJORD
SAMMY	BINGO	FANAL	JINNI	MINOS	PONEY	TONAL	AMONG	CLOAK	FLOAT
SAMOA	BONAR	FANCY	JONAH	MINOT	PONGA	TONDO	AMORT	CLOCK	FLOCK
SAMOS	BONCE	FANNY	JONES	MINSK	PONGO	TONER	AMOUR	CLOMP	FLONG
SAMSO	BONDI	FANON	JONTY	MINUS	PONTY	TONGA	ANODE	CLONE	FLOOD
SEMEN	BONDS	FENCE	JUNCO	MONAD	PUNCH	TONGS	ANOLE	CLOOT	FLOOR
SEMIS	BONER	FENNY	JUNTA	MONAL	PUNIC	TONIC	ANOMY	CLOSE	FLOPS
SIMBA	BONES	FINAL	JUNTO	MONDO	PUNTO	TONNE	APODE	CLOTH	FLORA
SIMON	BONEY	FINCH	KANAK	MONET	PUNTY	TONUS	APOOP	CLOUD	FLOSS
SOMME	BONGO	FINER	KANDY	MONEY	RANCE	TUNER	AROID	CLOUT	FLOTA
SUMMA	BONNY	FINIS	KANGA	MONKS	RANCH	TUNIC	AROMA	CLOVE	FLOUR
TAMAR	BONUS	FINKS	KANJI	MONTE	RANDY	TUNIS	AROSE	CLOWN	FLOUT
TAMER	BONZE	FONDA	KENDO	MONTH	RANEE	TUNKU	ASOKA	CLOZE	FLOWN
TAMIL	BUNCE	FONDS	KENGA	MONZA	RANGE	TUNNY	ATOLL	COOEE	FOODS
TAMIS	BUNCH	FUNDI	KENYA	MUNCH	RANGY	TYNED	ATOMY	COOKS	FOOLS
TAMMY	BUNCO	FUNDS	KINGS	MUNDA	RANKE	ULNAR	ATONE	COOMB	FOOTS
TAMPA	BUNDY	FUNDY	KINKY	MUNGO	RANKS	VANCE	ATONY	COOPT	FOOTY
TEMPE	BUNGY	FUNKY	KONGO	MUNRO	RENAL	VANDA	ATOPY	CROAK	FROCK
TEMPO	BUNNY	FUNNY	LANCE	MYNAH	RENAN	VANYA	AVOID	CROAT	FROND
TEMPT	CANAL	GANDA	LANDE	NANCE	RENEW	VENAL	AVOUÉ	CROCE	FRONT
TIMER	CANDY	GANJA	LANKA	NANCY	RENTE	VENDA	AWOKE	CROCK	FROST
TIMES	CANES	GANNY	LANKY	NANDI	RINSE	VENIN	AXOID	CROFT	FROTH
TIMID	CANNA	GENET	LENIN	NANDU	RONDE	VENOM	AZOIC	CROME	FROWN
TIMON	CANNY	GENIC	LENTO	NANNA	RONDO	VENUE	AZOTE	CRONE	FROWY
TIMOR	CANOE	GENIE	LINCH	NANNY	RONEO	VENUS	BIONT	CRONK	FROZE
TOMAN	CANON	GENOA	LINED	NANTZ	RONNE	VINYL	BLOAT	CRONY	GEODE
TOMMY	CANTO	GENRE	LINEN	NINJA	RUNCH	WANED	BLOCK	CROOK	GHOST
TUMID	CENCI	GENTS	LINER	NINNY	RUNES	WANLY	BLOKE	CROPS	GHOUL
TUMMY	CENSE	GENTY	LINES	NINON	RUNIC	WENCH	BLOND	CRORE	GLOAT
TUMOR	CENTO	GENUS	LINGO	NINTH	RUNNY	WENDY	BLOOD	CROSS	GLOBE
UNMAN	CINCH	GONAD	LININ	NONCE	RUNUP	WINCE	BLOOM	CROUP	GLOGG
UNMIX	CINNA	GONER	LINKS	NONES	SANDS	WINCH	BLOOP	CROWD	GLOOM
VOMER	CONAN	GONNA	LINUS	NONET	SANDY	WINDY	BLOWN	CROWN	GLORY
VOMIT	CONCH	GONZO	LONER	NONNY	SANTA	WINEY	BLOWY	CROZE	GLOSS
WIMPY	CONDE	GUNGE	LONGS	NUNKY	SANTO	WINGS	BOOBY	DHOBI	GLOVE
WOMAN	CONDO	GUNNY	LUNAR	OCNUS	SENNA	WONGA	BOONE	DHOTI	GNOME
WOMEN	CONEY	GYNAE	LUNCH	ORNIS	SENOR	WONKY	BOONG	DIODE	GOODS
WYMAN	CONGÉ	HANAP	LUNDY	OUNCE	SENSE	XENIA	BOOST	DIOTA	GOODY
YAMEN	CONGO	HANCE	LUNED	OWNER	SENZA	XENON	BOOTH	DOONE	GOOEY
YEMEN	CONIC	HANCH	LUNGE	PANDA	SINAI	YONKS	BOOTS	DOORN	GOOFY
YUMMY	CONTE	HANDS	LUNGI	PANDY	SINCE	YONNE	BOOTY	DOORS	GOOLY
ZAMBO	CYNIC	HANDY	LUNGS	PANEL	SINEW	ZANTE	BOOZE	DROIT	GOOSE
ZOMBI	DANAE	HANKY	LYNCH	PANGA	SINGE	ZENOS	BOOZY	DROLL	GROAN
AGNES	DANCE	HANOI	MANCH	PANIC	SINUS	ZINCO	BROAD	DROME	GROAT
AINEE	DANDO	HANSE	MANED	PANNE	SONAR	ZINEB	BROCK	DRONE	GROIN
ALNUS	DANDY	HENCE	MANES	PANSY	SONDE	ZONAL	BROIL	DROOL	GROOM
AMNIO	DANES	HENGE	MANET	PANTO	SONIC	ABODE	BRONX	DROOP	GROPE
ANNAL	DANTE	HENNA	MANGE	PANTS	SONNY	ABORT	BROOD	DROPS	GROSS
ANNAM	DENIM	HENRY	MANGO	PANTY	SUNDA	ABOUT	BROOK	DROSS	GROSZ
ANNEX	DENIS	HINDI	MANGY	PENAL	SUNNI	ABOVE	BROOL	DROVE	GROUP
ANNIE	DENSE	HINDU	MANIA	PENCE	SUNNY	ACOCK	BROOM	DROWN	GROUT
ANNOY	DENYS	HINGE	MANIC	PENIS	SYNGE	ACORN	BROSE	DUOMO	GROVE
ANNUL	DINAR	HINNY	MANLY	PENNA	SYNOD	ADOBE	BROTH	EBOLA	GROWL
AUNTY	DINER	HONAN	MANNA	PENNE	SYNTH	ADOPT	BROWN	EBONY	GROWN
BANAL	DINGE	HONDO	MANOR	PENNY	TANGA	ADORE	CEORL	ELOGE	HMONG
BANCO	DINGO	HONEY	MANSE	PHNOM	TANGO	ADORN	CHOCK	ELOGY	HOOCH
BANDA	DINGY	HONKY	MANTA	PINCH	TANGY	AFOOT	CHOCO	ELOPE	HOOEY
BANDS	DINKA	HONOR	MANUL	PINES	TANKA	AFORE	CHOIR	EMOTE	HOOKY
BANDY	DINKY	HUNCH	MANUS	PINGO	TANSY	AFOUL	CHOKE	EMOVE	HOOSH
BANJO	DONAR	HUNKS	MENAI	PINKO	TENCH	AGONE	CHOKO	ENOCH	HOOVE
BANKS	DONAT	HUNKY	MENGE	PINKY	TENDS	AGONY	CHOKY	ENORM	HYOID
BANNS	DONEE	HUNTS	MENSA	PINNA	TENET	AGORA	CHOMP	EPOCH	IROKO
BANTU	DONNA	INNER	MINCE	PINNY	TENON	AIOLI	CHOOK	EPODE	IRONS
BENCH	DONNE	INNES	MINCH	PINON	TENOR	ALOES	CHOOK	EPOXY	IRONY

ISOLA	QUOIT	SNOOT	TROTH	GYPSY	ROPED	ARRAY	CORER	FIRTH	JORUM
IVORY	QUORN	SNORE	TROTS	HAPPY	ROPER	ARRÊT	CORFE	FORAY	JURAT
KIOSK	QUOTA	SNORT	TROUT	HIPPO	ROPES	ARRIS	CORFU	FORCE	JUROR
KLOOF	QUOTE	SNOUT	TROVE	HIPPY	ROPEY	ARROW	CORGI	FOREL	KARAT
KNOCK	QUOTH	SNOWY	TWOER	HYPER	RSPCA	ATRIP	CORIN	FORGE	KARMA
KNOLL	RHODO	SOOTH	VIOLA	HYPHA	RUPEE	AURAL	CORKY	FORGO	KARNO
KNOUT	RHOMB	SOOTY	VROOM	IMPEL	RUPIA	AURIC	CORNY	FORKS	KARRI
KNOWN	RHONE	SPODE	WHOLE	IMPLY	SAPID	AYRIE	COROT	FORME	KARST
KOOKY	RIOJA	SPOHR	WHOOP	IMPOT	SAPOR	BARGE	CORPS	FORMS	KARSY
KOORI	RIOTS	SPOIL	WHOOT	INPUT	SAPPY	BARMY	CORSE	FORTE	KERAL
KRONA	ROOKY	SPOKE	WHORE	JAPAN	SEPAL	BARON	CORSO	FORTH	KERMA
KRONE	ROOMS	SPOOF	WHORL	JUPON	SEPIA	BARRA	CORVO	FORTY	KERNE
LEONE	ROOMY	SPOOK	WHOSE	KAPOK	SEPOY	BARRE	CURDS	FORUM	KIRBY
LIONS	ROOPY	SPOOL	WOODS	KAPPA	SOPHY	BARRY	CURED	FURAN	KIROV
LLOYD	ROOST	SPOON	WOODY	KAPUT	SOPPY	BARTS	CURER	FUROR	KORAN
LOOBY	ROOTS	SPOOR	WOOER	KIPPS	SOPRA	BERET	CURIA	FURRY	KOREA
LOOFA	ROOTY	SPORE	WOOFY	KOPJE	SUPER	BERIA	CURIE	FURZE	KORMA
LOONS	SCOFF	SPORT	WOOLF	KOPPA	SUPPE	BEROB	CURIO	GARBO	KURMA
LOONY	SCOLD	SPOTS	WOOZY	LAPEL	SUPRA	BERRY	CURLY	GARDA	KYRIE
LOOPY	SCONE	SPOUT	WRONG	LAPIS	TAPAS	BERTH	CURRY	GARNI	LARCH
LOOSE	SCOOP	STOAT	WROTE	LAPSE	TAPER	BERYL	CURSE	GARTH	LARGE
MAORI	SCOOT	STOCK	WROTH	LEPER	TAPET	BIRCH	CURST	GARUM	LARGO
MOOCH	SCOPE	STOEP	XHOSA	LEPID	TAPIR	BIRDS	CURVE	GERBE	LARKS
MOODY	SCOPS	STOGA	ZLOTY	LEPUS	TAPIS	BIRTH	CURVY	GIRLS	LARNE
MOOLI	SCORE	STOGY	ALPHA	LIPID	TEPEE	BORAX	CYRUS	GIRLY	LARRY
MOONY	SCORN	STOIC	AMPLE	LIPPI	TEPID	BORED	DARBY	GIRTH	LARVA
MOORE	SCOTS	STOKE	AMPLY	LUPIN	TIPPY	BOREE	DARCY	GORED	LERNA
MOOSE	SCOTT	STOLA	APPAL	LUPUS	TIPSY	BORER	DARTS	GORGE	LERNE
MYOMA	SCOUP	STOLE	APPAY	MAPLE	TOPAZ	BORIC	DERAY	GORKY	LORCA
NIOBE	SCOUR	STOLL	APPEL	MOPED	TOPEE	BORIS	DERBY	GORSE	LORDS
NOOKY	SCOUT	STOMA	APPLE	MOPER	TOPER	BORNE	DERMA	GYRUS	LORIS
NOOSE	SCOWL	STOMP	APPLY	MOPSY	TOPIC	BORON	DERRY	HARDY	LORNA
OBOTE	SCOWP	STONE	APPRO	NAPPA	TOPSY	BURGH	DIRGE	HAREM	LORNE
ODOUR	SEOUL	STONY	APPUI	NAPPE	TYPED	BURIN	DIRTY	HARPO	LORRY
OROMO	SHOAH	STOOD	ASPEN	NAPPY	TYPES	BURKE	DORAS	HARPY	LURCH
OVOID	SHOAL	STOOK	ASPER	NEPAL	TYPHA	BURLY	DOREE	HARRY	LURGY
OVOLO	SHOCK	STOOL	ASPIC	NEPER	UMPTY	BURMA	DORIC	HARSH	LURID
OZONE	SHOJI	STOOP	BEPAT	NIPPY	UNPEN	BURNS	DORIS	HARTY	LYRIC
PAOLO	SHOLA	STOOR	BIPED	NSPCC	UNPIN	BURNT	DORMY	HERBS	MARAT
PEONY	SHONA	STOPE	BIPOD	ORPEN	UPPER	BUROO	DORTS	HERMA	MARCH
PHOBE	SHONE	STORE	CAPER	PAPAL	VAPID	BURRO	DURER	HERNE	MARCO
PHONE	SHOOK	STORK	CAPET	PAPAW	VAPOR	BURSA	DUROY	HEROD	MARDI
PHONY	SHOOT	STORM	CAPIZ	PAPER	VIPER	BURST	DURRY	HERON	MARGE
PHOTO	SHOPS	STORY	CAPON	PEPPY	WIPER	BYRON	DURST	HERSE	MARIA
PIOUS	SHORE	STOUP	CAPOT	PEPSI	YAPOK	CARAT	DURUM	HERTS	MARIE
PLONK	SHORN	STOUR	CAPRI	PEPYS	YIPPY	CARDS	EARLY	HERTZ	MARLE
PLOTS	SHORT	STOUT	CAPUT	PIPAL	YUPIK	CARER	EARTH	HIRAM	MARLY
POOCH	SHOTS	STOVE	COPER	PIPER	ZEPPO	CARET	EERIE	HIRED	MARNE
POOLS	SHOUT	STOWE	COPPY	PIPIT	ZIPPY	CAREW	EGRET	HIRER	MAROT
POORI	SHOVE	SUOMI	COPRA	PIPPA	PIQUE	CAREY	EMRYS	HORAH	MARRY
PROBE	SHOWN	SWOON	COPSE	PIPUL	ROQUE	CARGO	ENROL	HORDE	MARSH
PROKE	SHOWY	SWOOP	CUPAR	POPES	TOQUE	CARIB	ERROR	HOREB	MERAK
PROLE	SKOAL	SWORD	CUPEL	POPOV	TUQUE	CARLE	ESROM	HORNE	MERCY
PROMO	SLOAN	SWORE	CUPID	POPPA	AARON	CAROB	EYRIE	HORNY	MERGE
PRONE	SLOOP	SWORN	CUPPA	POPPY	ABRAM	CAROL	FARAD	HORSA	MERIL
PRONG	SLOPE	THOFT	DEPOT	POPSY	ABRAY	CARRY	FARCE	HORSE	MERIT
PROOF	SLOPS	THOLE	DEPTH	POPUP	ABRIM	CARTA	FARCI	HORSY	MERLE
PROSE	SLOSH	THONG	DIPPY	PUPAL	ACRES	CARTE	FARCY	HORUS	MERRY
PROSY	SLOTH	THORN	DOPEY	PUPIL	ACRID	CARVE	FARGO	HURON	MIRTH
PROUD	SMOCK	THOTH	DUPIN	PUPPY	CDROM	CARVY	FARNE	HURRY	MIRZA
PROUT	SMOKE	TOOLS	DUPLE	RAPID	AFRIT	CERES	FAROE	HURST	MORAL
PROVE	SMOKY	TOOTH	EMPTY	REPAY	AGREE	CERNE	FARSE	HYRAX	MORAN
PROVO	SMOLT	TROIC	EXPEL	REPEL	AIRER	CIRCA	FARSI	IDRIS	MORAT
PROWL	SMOTE	TROLL	GAPER	REPLY	AIRES	CIRCE	FERAL	JEREZ	MORAY
PROXY	SNOBS	TROMP	GIPPO	REPOT	AORTA	CORAL	FERIA	JERKS	MOREL
PSOAS	SNOEK	TROON	GIPSY	REPRO	APRIL	CORAM	FERMI	JERKY	MORES
PSORA	SNOOD	TROOP	GOPAK	RIPEN	APRON	CORDS	FERRY	JERRY	MORIA
QUOIF	SNOOK	TROPE	GUPPY	RIPER	ARRAN	CORED	FIRMA	JIRGA	MORIN
QUOIN	SNOOP		GYPPO	RIPON	ARRAS		FIRST	JORIS	MORNE

MORON	QURAN	STRIP	VIRUS	CASCA	LASER	PISKY	ALTAI	ESTOP	MATIN
MORPH	RAREE	STROP	WARES	CASCO	LASKI	PISTE	ALTAR	EXTOL	MATLO
MORSE	RERUN	STRUM	WARTY	CASES	LASSA	POSED	ALTER	EXTRA	MATTE
MORUS	RORIC	STRUT	WIRED	CASTE	LASSO	POSER	ANTAR	EYTIE	METAL
MURAL	RORKE	SURGE	WIRES	CESAR	LESHY	POSIT	ANTIC	FATAL	METER
MUREX	RORTY	SURLY	WORCS	CISCO	LISLE	POSSE	ANTON	FATED	METHS
MURKY	RURAL	SURYA	WORDS	CISSY	LISTS	POSTE	APTLY	FATES	METIC
MURRE	SARAH	SYRAH	WORDY	COSEC	LISZT	PUSHY	ARTIE	FATTY	METIF
MURRY	SARAN	SYRIA	WORKS	COSMO	LOSER	PUSLE	ASTER	FATWA	METIS
MYRON	SARGE	SYRUP	WORLD	COSTA	LUSHY	PUSSY	ASTIR	FETAL	METOL
MYRRH	SARIN	TARDY	WORMS	COSTS	LUSTY	RASTA	ASTON	FETCH	METRE
NARES	SARKY	TARGE	WORMY	CUSHY	LYSIN	RESET	ASTRA	FETID	METRO
NARKS	SAROS	TAROT	WORRY	DESEX	LYSIS	RESIN	ATTAR	FETOR	MITES
NARKY	SARUS	TARRY	WORSE	DESSE	LYSOL	RESIT	ATTIC	FETUS	MITRE
NERVA	SCRAB	TARTY	WORST	DISCO	MASAI	RESTS	ATTLE	FITCH	MOTEL
NERVE	SCRAG	TERCE	WORTH	DISHY	MASER	RISEN	AZTEC	FUTON	MOTET
NERVI	SCRAM	TEREK	WURST	DUSKY	MASHY	RISER	BATCH	GATED	MOTHS
NERVO	SCRAP	TERES	XERES	DUSTY	MASON	RISKY	BATED	GETUP	MOTIF
NERVY	SCRAT	TERMS	XEROX	EASEL	MASSA	RISUS	BATES	GOTCH	MOTOR
NORAH	SCRAW	TERNE	XYRIS	ELSAN	MASSE	ROSCO	BATHE	GOTHA	MOTTE
NORIA	SCRAY	TERRA	YARFA	ENSEW	MASUS	ROSES	BATHS	GOTTA	MOTTO
NORMA	SCREE	TERRY	YARNS	ENSOR	MESIC	ROSET	BATIK	GUTSY	MUTED
NORSE	SCREW	TERSE	YARRA	ENSUE	MESNE	ROSIN	BATON	GUTTA	NATAL
NORTH	SCRIM	THREE	YARTA	EOSIN	MESON	ROSIT	BATTY	HATCH	NATCH
NURSE	SCRIP	THREW	YERBA	EPSOM	MESSY	ROSSE	BETEL	HATHI	NATES
OCREA	SCROD	THRID	YPRES	ESSAY	MESTO	ROSSI	BETON	HATTY	NATTY
ORRIS	SCROG	THRIP	ZERDA	FESSE	MISER	RUSHY	BETTE	HETTY	NATUS
PARCH	SCROW	THROB	ZORBA	FESTA	MISSA	RUSSE	BETTY	HITCH	NITID
PARDY	SCRUB	THROE	ZORRO	FESTE	MISSY	RUSSO	BITCH	HITHE	NITON
PAREO	SCRUM	THROW	ABSIT	FISHY	MISTY	RUSTY	BITER	HOTCH	NITRE
PAREU	SERAI	THRUM	ADSUM	FOSSA	MOSES	SASHA	BITTE	HOTEL	NITRO
PARIS	SERGE	TIRED	AESOP	FOSSE	MOSEY	SASSE	BITTY	HOTLY	NOTAL
PARKA	SERIF	TIREE	AISLE	FUSED	MOSSI	SASSY	BOTCH	HOTTY	NOTCH
PARKY	SERIN	TIROS	ANSON	FUSEE	MOSSO	SISAL	BOTHA	HUTCH	NOTED
PARMA	SERRA	TORAH	AOSTA	FUSSY	MUSCA	SISSY	BOTHY	HYTHE	NOTES
PARRY	SERRE	TORCH	APSIS	FUSTY	MUSCI	SUSAN	BOTTE	ICTUS	NOTTS
PARSE	SERUM	TORII	ARSIS	GASES	MUSES	SUSHI	BUTCH	INTER	NOTUM
PARSI	SERVE	TORSO	ARSON	GASPÉ	MUSHA	TASSE	BUTTE	INTRA	NUTTY
PARTI	SERVO	TORTE	ASSAI	GASSY	MUSHY	TASSO	BUTTY	INTRO	OATEN
PARTS	SHRED	TORUS	ASSAM	GESSE	MUSIC	TASTE	CATCH	JETTY	OATES
PARTY	SHREW	TURBO	ASSAY	GESSO	MUSIT	TASTY	CATER	KETCH	OCTAD
PARVO	SHROW	TURCO	ASSET	GESTE	MUSKY	TESLA	CATES	KITTY	OCTAL
PERAI	SHRUB	TURIN	BASAL	GISMO	MUSSE	TESSA	CATTY	KOTOW	OCTET
PERCE	SHRUG	TURKI	BASAN	GOSHT	MUSSY	TESTA	CETUS	KUTCH	OFTEN
PERCH	SIREN	TURKU	BASES	GOSSE	MUSTY	TESTS	COTTA	LATCH	OPTIC
PERCY	SKRIM	TURPS	BASHO	GUSHY	NASAL	TESTY	CUTCH	LATEN	ORTHO
PERDU	SORBO	TYROL	BASIC	GUSTO	NASHE	TOSCA	CUTEY	LATER	ORTON
PERIL	SORDO	UGRIC	BASIL	GUSTY	NASTY	UNSAY	CUTIE	LATEX	ORTUS
PERKS	SOREX	UNRIG	BASIN	HASNT	NESSA	UPSET	CUTIS	LATHE	OSTIA
PERKY	SORES	UNRIP	BASIS	HASTA	NESTA	UPSEY	CUTTY	LATHI	OTTAR
PERON	SORGO	VAREC	BASLE	HASTE	NISAN	URSON	DATED	LATIN	OTTER
PERRY	SORRY	VARIX	BASRA	HASTY	NISEI	VESPA	DATER	LATTE	OUTBY
PERSE	SORTS	VARUS	BASSO	HESSE	NISUS	VESTA	DATES	LETHE	OUTDO
PIROG	SPRAG	VERDI	BASTA	HOSEA	NOSER	VISBY	DATUK	LITAS	OUTER
PORCH	SPRAT	VEREY	BASTE	HOSEN	NOSEY	VISIT	DATUM	LITER	OUTGO
PORGY	SPRAY	VERGE	BASTO	HOSTA	NYSSA	VISNA	DETER	LITHE	OUTRE
PORKY	SPREE	VERNE	BESET	HUSKS	OASIS	VISON	DETOX	LITRE	OXTER
PORNO	SPRIG	VERSA	BESOM	HUSKY	ONSET	VISOR	DITAL	LOTOS	PATCH
PORTA	SPRIT	VERSE	BESOT	HUSSY	OSSIA	VISTA	DITCH	LOTTO	PATER
PORTE	SPROD	VERSO	BISON	IBSEN	OUSEL	WASHY	DITTO	LOTUS	PATIO
PORTO	SPROG	VERST	BOSCH	IMSHI	PASCH	WASNT	DITTY	LUTIN	PATNA
PORTS	SPRUE	VERTU	BOSEY	INSET	PASEO	WASTE	DOTTY	LUTON	PATSY
PUREE	STRAD	VERVE	BOSKY	ISSUE	PASHA	WESER	DUTCH	LYTHE	PATTI
PURGE	STRAP	VIRAL	BOSOM	JASEY	PASSE	WISPY	EATER	MATAI	PATTY
PURIM	STRAW	VIREO	BOSSY	JASON	PASTA	ACTIN	ELTON	MATCH	PETAL
PURSE	STRAY	VIRGA	BOSUN	JASPÉ	PASTE	ACTON	ENTER	MATER	PETER
PURSY	STREP	VIRGO	BUSBY	JESSE	PASTY	ACTOR	ENTRY	MATES	PETIT
PYREX	STREW	VIRID	BUSHY	JESUS	PESKY	AFTER	ESTER	MATEY	PETRA
PYRUS	STRIA	VIRTU	BUSTY	KASHA	PESTO	AITCH	ESTOC	MATHS	PETRE

PETRI	UTTER	COULD	FOURS	MOUSE	SPUME	ALVIS	LIVID	DOWER	LEXIS
PETTO	VETCH	COUNT	FRUIT	MOUSY	SPUMY	ANVIL	LIVRE	DOWNS	MAXIM
PETTY	VITAE	COUPE	FRUMP	MOUTH	SPUNK	ARVAL	LOVAT	DOWNY	MIXED
PITCH	VITAL	COURB	GAUDE	MVULE	SPURN	BEVEL	LOVER	DOWRY	MIXER
PITHY	VITIS	COURT	GAUDY	NAURU	SPURS	BEVIS	MAVIN	DOWSE	MIXTE
PITON	VITUS	COUTH	GAUGE	OVULE	SPURT	BÉVUE	MAVIS	EDWIN	MIXUP
PITOT	VOTER	CRUCK	GAULT	PAUSA	SQUAB	BEVVY	MOVED	ETWEE	NAXOS
PITTA	VOTES	CRUDE	GAUNT	PAUSE	SQUAD	CAVAN	MOVER	FEWER	NEXUS
POTIN	WATCH	CRUEL	GAUSS	PLUCK	SQUAT	CAVIL	MOVIE	GAWKY	NIXON
POTOO	WATER	CRUET	GAUZE	PLUMB	SQUAW	CIVET	NAVAL	GOWAN	NOXAL
POTTO	WATTS	CRUMB	GAUZY	PLUME	SQUIB	CIVIC	NAVEL	GOWER	PIXEL
POTTY	WITAN	CRUMP	GLUCK	PLUMP	SQUID	CIVIL	NAVEW	HAWSE	PIXIE
PUTID	WITCH	CRUOR	GLUED	PLUNK	SQUIT	CIVVY	NAVVY	HEWER	PYXIS
PUTTO	WITHE	CRUSE	GLUEY	PLUSH	STUCK	COVEN	NEVEL	HOWBE	SAXON
PUTTY	WITHY	CRUSH	GLUME	PLUTO	STUDY	COVER	NEVER	HOWDY	SIXER
QATAR	WITTY	CRUST	GLUON	POUCH	STUFF	COVET	NEVIS	INWIT	SIXTH
RATCH	YATES	DAUBE	GOUDA	POULE	STUMP	COVEY	NIVAL	JEWEL	SIXTY
RATEL	ABUJA	DAUNT	GOUGE	POULT	STUNG	DAVID	NOVEL	JEWRY	TAXED
RATES	ABUNA	DEUCE	GOURD	POUND	STUNK	DAVIS	NOVUM	KIWIS	TAXIN
RATIO	ABUSE	DOUAI	GOUTY	POUPE	STUNT	DAVIT	ORVAL	LAWKS	TAXIS
RATTY	ACUTE	DOUAR	GRUEL	PRUDE	STUPA	DEVIL	PAVID	LEWES	TAXOL
RETCH	ADULT	DOUAY	GRUFE	PRUNE	STUPE	DIVAN	PIVOT	LEWIS	TAXON
RETRO	ALULA	DOUBT	GRUFF	RHUMB	STURT	DIVER	RAVEL	LOWAN	TAXUS
RITES	ALURE	DOUCE	GRUME	ROUEN	SWUNG	DIVES	RAVEN	LOWER	TEXAN
RITZY	AMUCK	DOUGH	GRUMP	ROUGE	TAUBE	DIVOT	RAVER	LOWLY	TEXAS
ROTOR	AMUSE	DOUMA	GRUNT	ROUGH	TAUNT	DIVVY	REVEL	LOWRY	TEXEL
SATAN	ARUBA	DOURA	HAUGH	ROULE	TAUON	DOVER	REVET	MOWER	TEXTS
SATAY	AZURE	DOURO	HAULM	ROUND	TAUPE	DUVAL	REVIE	NAWAB	TOXIC
SATED	BAULK	DRUGS	HAULT	ROUSE	THUGS	DUVET	REVUE	NEWEL	TOXIN
SATEM	BLUES	DRUID	HAUNT	ROUST	THUJA	EAVES	RIVAL	NEWLY	VEXED
SATIE	BLUEY	DRUNK	HAUSA	ROUTE	THULE	ELVAN	RIVEN	NEWSY	VIXEN
SATIN	BLUFF	DRUPE	HAUSE	SAUCE	THUMB	ELVER	RIVER	NEWTS	WAXEN
SATIS	BLUNT	DRURY	HAUTE	SAUCH	THUMP	ELVES	RIVET	NOWAY	ABYSM
SATYR	BLURB	DRUSE	HEUGH	SAUCY	THUNK	ELVIS	ROVER	OTWAY	ABYSS
SETUP	BLURT	DRUZE	HOUGH	SAUDI	THUYA	ENVOI	SAVER	PAWKY	ARYAN
SITAR	BLUSH	DYULA	HOURI	SAUGH	TOUCH	ENVOY	SAVOR	POWAN	AZYME
SITIN	BOUGH	EDUCE	HOURS	SAULT	TOUGH	FAVOR	SAVOY	POWER	BAYER
SITKA	BOUND	ELUDE	HOUSE	SAUNA	TRUCE	FAVUS	SAVVY	POWYS	BAYLE
SITTA	BOURG	EMURE	INUIT	SAURY	TRUCK	FEVER	SEVEN	ROWAN	BAYOU
SITUP	BRUCE	ENUGU	INURE	SAUTE	TRULL	FIVER	SEVER	ROWDY	BOYAR
SOTTO	BRUIN	ENURE	JAUNT	SCUBA	TRULY	FIVES	SIVAN	ROWEL	BOYAU
SUTCH	BRUIT	EQUAL	JOUAL	SCUFF	TRUMP	FOVEA	SUVLA	ROWER	BOYCE
SUTOR	BRULE	EQUIP	JOULE	SCULL	TRUNK	GAVEL	TAVAH	SEWER	BOYLE
SUTRA	BRUME	ERUCA	JOUNT	SCULP	TRURO	GIVEN	TEVET	SOWER	BOYNE
TATAR	BRUNO	ERUCT	JOUST	SCURF	TRUSS	GIVER	VIVAT	SOWLE	BUYER
TATER	BRUNT	ERUPT	KAURI	SCUTE	TRUST	HAVEL	VIVID	SOWND	CHYLE
TATIN	BRUSH	ETUDE	KNURL	SHUCK	TRUTH	HAVEN	WAVED	SOWTH	CHYME
TATRA	BRUTE	EXUDE	KNURR	SHUNT	TSUBA	HAVER	WAVER	TAWNY	CHYND
TATTY	CAULD	EXULT	LAUDS	SHUSH	TSUGA	HAVOC	WAVES	TAWSE	CLYDE
TETON	CAULK	EXURB	LAUGH	SHUTE	UHURU	HEVEA	WIVES	TOWEL	COYLY
TETRA	CAUSE	FAULT	LAURA	SHUTS	USUAL	HIVER	WOVEN	TOWER	COYNE
TITAN	CHUBB	FAUNA	LOUGH	SKULK	USURE	HIVES	ASWAN	TOWNS	COYPU
TITCH	CHUCK	FAURE	LOUIE	SKULL	USURP	HOVEL	BAWDY	TOWSE	CRYPT
TITHE	CHUFF	FAUST	LOUIS	SKUNK	USURY	HOVER	BOWED	TOWZE	DAYAK
TITLE	CHUMP	FAUVE	LOUPE	SLUGS	UTURN	JAVAN	BOWEL	UNWED	DOYEN
TITRE	CHUMS	FLUFF	LOURE	SLUMP	UVULA	JAVEL	BOWER	VOWEL	DOYLE
TITTY	CHUNK	FLUID	LOUSE	SLUNG	VAULT	KEVIN	BOWIE	AUXIN	DOYLY
TITUS	CHURL	FLUKE	LOUSY	SLUNK	VAUNT	LAVER	BOWLS	BOXED	DRYAD
TOTAL	CHURN	FLUKY	LOUTH	SLURB	VOUCH	LAVRA	BYWAY	BOXER	DRYER
TOTEM	CHURR	FLUME	MAUND	SLURP	WAUGH	LEVEE	COWAN	BUXOM	DRYLY
TOTTY	CHUTE	FLUMP	MAUVE	SLUSH	WOULD	LEVEL	COWER	COXAL	EGYPT
TUTOR	CLUBS	FLUNG	MEUSE	SMUTS	WOUND	LEVEN	COWRY	COXED	FLYER
TUTSI	CLUCK	FLUNK	MOUCH	SNUFF	WRUNG	LEVER	CRWTH	DIXIE	FLYTE
TUTTI	CLUMP	FLUSH	MOULD	SOUGH	YOULL	LEVIN	DEWAN	FIXED	FOYER
ULTRA	CLUNG	FLUTE	MOULS	SOULS	YOUNG	LEVIS	DEWAR	FIXER	FOYLE
UNTIE	CLUNK	FOUET	MOULT	SOUND	YOURS	LIVED	DEWEY	FOXED	GAYAL
UNTIL	COUCH	FOULÉ	MOUND	SOUSA	YOURT	LIVEN	DIWAN	HEXAD	GHYLL
UPTON	COUDÉ	FOUND	MOUNT	SOUSE	YOUTH	LIVER	DOWDY	HEXAM	GLYPH
USTED	COUGH	FOUNT	MOURN	SOUTH	YOUVE	LIVES	DOWEL	HEXYL	GUYED

GUYON	MUZZY	BEDAD	DIWAN	HONAN	MIDAS	PUPAL	SPRAG	WHEAL	KIMBO
GUYOT	NAZIR	BEGAD	DONAR	HORAH	MILAN	QAJAR	SPRAT	WHEAT	KIRBY
HAYDN	NIZAM	BEGAN	DONAT	HUMAN	MODAL	QATAR	SPRAY	WIGAN	LAYBY
HAYLE	OUZEL	BEHAN	DORAS	HYRAX	MOLAR	QURAN	SQUAB	WITAN	LIMBO
HEYER	PIZZA	BEKAA	DOUAI	IDEAL	MONAD	RABAT	SQUAD	WOMAN	LOBBY
HOYLE	RAZOR	BELAY	DOUAR	IDEAS	MONAL	RADAR	SQUAT	WREAK	LOOBY
IDYLL	ROZET	BEPAT	DOUAY	ILEAC	MORAL	RAHAB	SQUAW	WYMAN	MAMBA
JOYCE	SIZAR	BLEAK	DREAD	ILIAC	MORAN	RAJAB	STEAD	YCLAD	MAMBO
KAYAK	SUZIE	BLEAR	DREAM	ILIAD	MORAT	RAJAH	STEAK	YULAN	MAYBE
KEYED	TAZZA	BLEAT	DREAR	INLAW	MORAY	RAMAN	STEAL	ZAKAT	MEBBE
KEYES	TIZZY	BLOAT	DRYAD	INLAY	MURAL	RECAP	STEAM	ZIGAN	MELBA
LAYBY	UNZIP	BOLAS	DUBAI	IQBAL	MUZAK	REDAN	STOAT	ZOHAR	NIOBE
LAYER	VIZOR	BONAR	DUCAT	ISAAC	MYNAH	REGAL	STRAD	ZONAL	NOBBY
LOYAL	VOZHD	BORAX	DUKAS	ISLAM	NAGAS	REGAN	STRAP	ABABA	OUTBY
MAYBE	YEZDI	BOYAR	DULAC	ISLAY	NAIAD	RELAX	STRAW	ADOBE	PHEBE
MAYOR	5:4	BOYAU	DUMAS	IZZAT	NASAL	RELAY	STRAY	ALIBI	PHOBE
MEYER	ABBAS	BREAD	DUVAL	JALAP	NATAL	RENAL	SUDAN	AMEBA	PLEBS
MOYLE	ABDAR	BREAK	DYLAN	JAPAN	NAVAL	RENAN	SUGAN	AQABA	PROBE
NOYAU	ABEAM	BREAM	ECLAT	JAVAN	NAWAB	REPAY	SUGAR	ARABA	RABBI
NOYES	ABEAR	BRIAN	EDGAR	JEHAD	NEPAL	RICAN	SUSAN	ARUBA	RAMBO
PAYEE	ABRAM	BRIAR	EGGAR	JELAB	NICAD	RIVAL	SWEAR	BAMBI	REBBE
PAYER	ABRAY	BROAD	EILAT	JIHAD	NISAN	RIYAL	SWEAT	BEMBA	RUGBY
PHYLE	AFEAR	BYLAW	ELGAR	JONAH	NIVAL	ROHAN	SYRAH	BIBBY	RUMBA
PSYCH	AHEAD	BYWAY	ELIAD	JOUAL	NIZAM	ROMAN	TALAQ	BIMBO	SAMBA
RAYED	AIDAN	CABAL	ELIAS	JUDAS	NODAL	ROWAN	TALAR	BOBBY	SAMBO
RAYLE	AKBAR	CABAS	ELSAN	JUGAL	NOMAD	ROYAL	TAMAR	BOMBE	SCUBA
RAYON	ALBAN	CACAO	ELVAN	JUMAR	NORAH	RURAL	TAPAS	BOMBO	SHEBA
REYES	ALDAN	CAMAS	EQUAL	JURAT	NOTAL	RYDAL	TATAR	BOOBY	SIMBA
RHYME	ALGAE	CANAL	ESSAY	KANAK	NOWAY	SABAL	TAVAH	BRIBE	SNOBS
RIYAL	ALIAS	CARAT	ETHAL	KARAT	NOXAL	SAFAR	TEXAN	BUBBY	SORBO
ROYAL	ALLAH	CAVAN	EVIAN	KAYAK	NOYAU	SALAD	TEXAS	BUSBY	TABBY
SAYER	ALLAN	CEDAR	EXEAT	KEBAB	OBEAH	SARAH	TIDAL	CABBY	TAUBE
SAYSO	ALLAY	CESAR	FANAL	KEDAR	OBIAH	SARAN	TITAN	CHUBB	TIBBS
SHYLY	ALTAI	CHEAP	FARAD	KERAL	OCCAM	SATAN	TODAY	CLUBS	TIBBY
SLYLY	ALTAR	CHEAT	FATAL	KNEAD	OCEAN	SATAY	TOKAY	COMBE	TRIBE
SLYPE	AMMAN	CHIAO	FECAL	KODAK	OCTAD	SCRAB	TOLAR	COMBO	TSUBA
SOYUZ	ANEAR	CIGAR	FERAL	KORAN	OCTAL	SCRAG	TOMAN	COMBS	TUBBY
STYLE	ANNAL	CLEAN	FETAL	KRAAL	OFFAL	SCRAM	TONAL	CRABS	TURBO
STYLO	ANNAM	CLEAR	FINAL	KULAK	OFFAS	SCRAP	TOPAZ	CUBBY	VISBY
STYME	ANTAR	CLEAT	FLOAT	LAGAN	OFLAG	SCRAT	TORAH	DARBY	YERBA
THYME	ANZAC	CLOAK	FOCAL	LAZAR	OGHAM	SCRAW	TOTAL	DAUBE	YOBBO
TRYST	APEAK	CONAN	FORAY	LEGAL	ORGAN	SCRAY	TREAD	DERBY	ZAMBO
WRYLY	APPAL	CORAL	FREAK	LEHAR	ORVAL	SEDAN	TREAT	DHABI	ZOMBI
ZAYIN	APPAY	CORAM	FRIAR	LEMAN	OSCAR	SEPAL	TRIAD	DHOBI	ZORBA
ANZAC	ARHAT	COWAN	FUGAL	LILAC	OSMAN	SERAI	TRIAL	DOBBY	ABACK
BAZOO	ARIAN	COXAL	FURAN	LIMAX	OTTAR	SHEAF	TWEAK	DOUBT	ABACO
BEZEL	ARRAN	CREAK	GALAM	LITAS	OTWAY	SHEAR	UHLAN	GABBY	ACOCK
COZEN	ARRAS	CREAM	GAMAY	LOBAR	PAEAN	SHOAH	ULNAR	GALBA	AITCH
DAZED	ARRAY	CROAK	GAYAL	LOCAL	PAGAN	SHOAL	UNBAR	GAMBA	ALACK
DIZZY	ARVAL	CROAT	GLEAM	LOGAN	PAPAL	SILAS	UNCAP	GAMBO	ALICE
DOZEN	ARYAN	CUBAN	GLEAN	LOMAN	PAPAW	SINAI	UNDAM	GARBO	AMICE
FIZZY	ASIAN	CUPAR	GLOAT	LOVAT	PECAN	SISAL	UNIAT	GERBE	AMUCK
FUZEE	ASSAI	CYCAD	GOLAN	LOWAN	PEDAL	SITAR	UNLAW	GIBBY	APACE
FUZZY	ASSAM	DAKAR	GONAD	LOYAL	PEKAN	SIVAN	UNLAY	GLEBE	ARECA
GAZON	ASSAY	DAMAN	GOPAK	LUCAN	PENAL	SIZAR	UNMAN	GLOBE	ARICA
GIZMO	ASWAN	DANAE	GOWAN	LUNAR	PERAI	SKEAN	UNSAY	GOBBO	BACCY
HAZAN	ATLAS	DAYAK	GRAAL	MACAW	PETAL	SKOAL	URBAN	GOMBO	BANCO
HAZEL	ATMAN	DEBAG	GREAT	MADAM	PHIAL	SLOAN	URIAH	GREBE	BATCH
HUZZA	ATTAR	DEBAR	GROAN	MAKAR	PILAF	SMEAR	USUAL	GUMBO	BEACH
IZZAT	AURAL	DECAL	GROAT	MALAR	PILAU	SNEAD	VEGAN	HERBS	BEECH
JAZZY	AVIAN	DECAY	GULAG	MALAY	PIPAL	SNEAK	VELAR	HOBBS	BELCH
LAZAR	AXIAL	DEGAS	GYNAE	MARAT	PLEAD	SOLAN	VENAL	HOBBY	BENCH
LAZZO	BABAR	DELAY	HANAP	MASAI	PLEAT	SOLAR	VICAR	HOWBE	BIRCH
LOZEN	BAHAI	DERAY	HAZAN	MATAI	POLAR	SONAR	VIRAL	HUBBY	BITCH
LUZON	BALAN	DEWAN	HEXAD	MEDAL	POWAN	SPEAK	VITAE	JAMBE	BLACK
MAZER	BANAL	DEWAR	HEXAM	MENAI	PRIAL	SPEAN	VITAL	JAMBO	BLOCK
MEZZE	BASAL	DINAR	HILAR	MERAK	PRIAM	SPEAR	VIVAT	JUMBO	BONCE
MEZZO	BASAN	DITAL	HIRAM	METAL	PSHAW	SPLAT	VOCAB	JUMBY	BOSCH
MUZAK		DIVAN	HOGAN	MICAH	PSOAS	SPLAY	VOCAL	KAABA	BOTCH

```
BOYCE  ERUCT  MUSCA  SPECK  BONDI  HILDA  SPADO  ANKER  BRIEF  DATES
BRACE  EVICT  MUSCI  SPECS  BONDS  HINDI  SPODE  ANNEX  BRIER  DAZED
BRACK  EXACT  NANCE  SPICA  BRADY  HINDU  STADE  APPEL  BUYER  DEBEL
BRACT  FANCY  NANCY  SPICE  BREDA  HONDO  STUDY  ARDEA  CABER  DEFER
BRICK  FARCE  NATCH  SPICK  BREDE  HORDE  SUEDE  ARDEB  CADET  DESEX
BROCK  FARCI  NIECE  SPICY  BRIDE  HOWDY  SUNDA  ARDEN  CAGEY  DETER
BRUCE  FARCY  NONCE  STACK  BUDDY  KANDY  SWEDE  ARIEL  CALEB  DEWEY
BUCCA  FENCE  NOTCH  STICK  BUNDY  KENDO  TARDY  ARIES  CAMEL  DICEY
BUICK  FETCH  NSPCC  STOCK  CADDY  KIDDY  TEDDY  ARLES  CAMEO  DIKER
BUNCE  FILCH  OUNCE  STUCK  CANDY  KILDA  TENDS  ARMED  CANES  DINER
BUNCH  FINCH  PARCH  SUTCH  CARDS  LABDA  TIDDY  ARMET  CAPER  DIVER
BUNCO  FITCH  PASCH  TEACH  CHIDE  LANDE  TILDE  ARRÊT  CAPET  DIVES
BUTCH  FLACK  PATCH  TENCH  CLYDE  LAUDS  TOADY  ASHEN  CARER  DOMED
CASCA  FLECK  PEACE  TERCE  COADE  LEADS  TODDY  ASHER  CARET  DONEE
CASCO  FLICK  PEACH  THECA  CONDE  LEEDS  TONDO  ASHES  CAREW  DOPEY
CATCH  FLOCK  PENCE  THICK  CONDO  LORDS  TRADE  ASHET  CAREY  DOREE
CENCI  FORCE  PERCE  TITCH  CORDS  LUNDY  UREDO  ASKER  CASES  DOVER
CHACO  FRACK  PERCH  TORCH  COUDÉ  MAHDI  VANDA  ASKEW  CATER  DOWEL
CHECK  FRACT  PERCY  TOSCA  CREDO  MARDI  VEDDA  ASPEN  CATES  DOWER
CHICA  FROCK  PIECE  TOUCH  CRUDE  MIDDY  VELDT  ASPER  CELEB  DOWER
CHICK  GLACE  PILCH  TRACE  CUDDY  MONDO  VENDA  ASSET  CERES  DOYEN
CHICO  GLUCK  PINCH  TRACK  CURDS  MOODY  VERDI  ASTER  CHEEK  DOZEN
CHOCK  GOTCH  PITCH  TRACT  DADDY  MUDDY  WALDO  AUDEN  CHEEP  DRIED
CHOCO  GRACE  PLACE  TRECK  DANDO  MUNDA  WEEDS  AUGER  CHEER  DRIER
CHUCK  GUACO  PLACK  TRICE  DANDY  NANDI  WEEDY  AWEEL  CHIEF  DRIES
CINCH  GULCH  PLICA  TRICK  DEEDS  NANDU  WENDY  AZTEC  CIDER  DRYER
CIRCA  HANCE  PLUCK  TRUCE  DILDO  NEDDY  WILDE  BABEL  CIVET  DUKES
CIRCE  HANCH  POACH  TRUCK  DIODE  NEEDS  WILDS  BADEN  CLEEK  DURER
CISCO  HATCH  PONCE  TURCO  DODDY  NEEDY  WINDY  BAGEL  CLEEP  DUVET
CLACK  HENCE  POOCH  TWICE  DOWDY  NODDY  WOODS  BAKED  CODED  DYFED
CLECK  HITCH  PORCH  VANCE  DUDDY  OUIDA  WOODY  BAKER  CODEX  DYKER
CLICK  HOICK  POUCH  VETCH  ELIDE  OUTDO  WORDS  BALER  COKES  EAGER
CLOCK  HOOCH  PRICE  VLACH  ELUDE  OXIDE  WORDY  BASES  COLET  EASEL
CLUCK  HOTCH  PRICK  VNECK  EPODE  PADDY  YEZDI  BATED  COLEY  EATER
COACH  HUNCH  PSYCH  VOICE  ERODE  PANDA  ZERDA  BATES  COMET  EAVES
COCCI  HUTCH  PUNCH  VOUCH  ETUDE  PANDY  ABBEY  BAYER  CONEY  EDGED
CONCH  JOYCE  QUACK  WATCH  EVADE  PARDY  ABIES  BEDEW  COOEE  EDGER
COUCH  JUICE  QUICK  WENCH  EXODE  PERDU  ABLER  BEGET  COPER  EGRET
CRACK  JUICY  RANCE  WHACK  EXUDE  PONDS  ACRES  BENET  CORED  EIDER
CRECY  JUNCO  RANCH  WHICH  FADDY  PRADO  ADDED  BERET  CORER  EIGER
CRICK  KEECH  RATCH  WINCE  FALDO  PRIDE  ADDER  BESET  COSEC  ELDER
CROCE  KETCH  REACH  WINCH  FONDA  PRUDE  ADEEM  BETEL  COVEN  ELLEN
CROCK  KNACK  REACT  WITCH  FONDS  QUADS  ADIEU  BEVEL  COVER  ELMER
CRUCK  KNOCK  RECCE  WORCS  FOODS  QUIDS  AEDES  BEZEL  COVET  ELVER
CUTCH  KUTCH  REECH  YOICK  FUNDI  RANDY  AFTER  BIDET  COVEY  ELVES
CZECH  LANCE  REICH  YUCCA  FUNDS  READE  AGGER  BIKER  COWER  EMBED
DACCA  LARCH  RETCH  ZILCH  FUNDY  READY  AGLEE  BIPED  COXED  EMBER
DANCE  LATCH  ROACH  ZINCO  FYLDE  REEDE  AGLET  BITER  COZEN  EMCEE
DARCY  LEACH  ROSCO  ABIDE  GANDA  REEDS  AGLEY  BLEED  CREED  EMDEN
DECCA  LEECH  RSPCA  ABODE  GARDA  REEDY  AGNES  BLEEP  CREEK  EMMER
DEUCE  LINCH  RUNCH  ANODE  GAUDE  RHODO  AGREE  BLUES  CREEL  EMMET
DISCO  LORCA  SAICE  APODE  GAUDY  RONDE  AHMED  BLUEY  CREEP  ENDED
DITCH  LUNCH  SAUCE  AREDE  GEODE  RONDO  AIKEN  BODES  CRIED  ENSEW
DOLCE  LURCH  SAUCH  ASIDE  GIDDY  ROWDY  AINEE  BOGEY  CRIER  ENTER
DOUCE  LYNCH  SAUCY  BADDY  GLADE  RUDDY  AIRER  BOHEA  CRIES  ESKER
DRACO  MANCH  SECCO  BANDA  GLIDE  SANDS  AIRES  BONER  CRUEL  ESTER
DUNCE  MARCH  SHACK  BANDS  GOODS  SANDY  ALBEE  BONES  CRUET  ETHER
DUTCH  MARCO  SHOCK  BANDY  GOODY  SAUDI  ALDER  BONEY  CUBEB  ETWEE
EDICT  MATCH  SHUCK  BAWDY  GOUDA  SCADS  ALIEN  BORED  CUBED  EULER
EDUCE  MECCA  SINCE  BEADS  GRADE  SEEDY  ALLÉE  BOREE  CULET  EXCEL
EJECT  MERCY  SLACK  BEADY  GUIDE  SHADE  ALLEN  BORER  CULEX  EXPEL
ELECT  MILCH  SLICE  BENDS  HAIDA  SHADY  ALLEY  BOSEY  CUPEL  FABER
ENACT  MINCE  SLICK  BENDY  HANDS  SLADE  ALOES  BOWED  CURED  FACER
ENOCH  MINCH  SMACK  BIDDY  HANDY  SLIDE  ALTER  BOWEL  CURER  FACET
EPOCH  MOOCH  SMOCK  BIRDS  HARDY  SNIDE  AMBER  BOWER  CUTEY  FADED
ERECT  MOUCH  SNACK  BLADE  HAYDN  SOLDE  AMIEL  BOXED  DALEK  FAKER
ERICA  MULCH  SNECK         HEADS  SONDE  ANDES  BOXER  DANES  FAMED
ERICK  MULCT  SNICK         HEADY  SORDO  ANGEL  BREED  DATED  FATED
ERUCA  MUNCH  SPACE         HEDDA  SPADE  ANGER  BREEM  DATER  FATES
```

FECES	EK	KRIEG	MISER	ONSET	RAYED	SHRED	TINEA	WAVES	JAFFA
FEVER	HACEK	LABEL	MITES	ORDER	REBEL	SHREW	TIRED	WAXEN	JIFFY
FEWER	HADES	LACET	MIXED	ORFEO	REFER	SILEX	TIREE	WEBER	KNIFE
FIBER	HALER	LADEN	MIXER	ORIEL	RENEW	SINEW	TIREE	WESER	KRAFT
FIDEL	HAREM	LAGER	MODEL	ORMER	REPEL	SIREN	TOKEN	WHEEL	LEAFY
FIDES	HAVEL	LAMED	MODEM	ORPEN	RESET	SIXER	TONER	WHEEN	LOOFA
FILET	HAVEN	LAPEL	MODER	OSIER	REVEL	SKEER	TOPEE	WIDEN	LUFFA
FINER	HAVER	LASER	MONET	OTHER	REVET	SKEET	TOPER	WILES	MALFI
FIVER	HAZEL	LATEN	MONEY	OTTER	REYES	SKIER	TOTEM	WINEY	MIFFY
FIVES	HEGEL	LATER	MOPED	OUSEL	RIDER	SLEEK	TOWEL	WIPER	NAAFI
FIXED	HELEN	LATEX	MOPER	OUTER	RILEY	SLEEP	TOWER	WIRED	PUFFY
FIXER	HEVEA	LAVER	MOREL	OUZEL	RIPEN	SLEET	TREEN	WIRES	QUAFF
FLEET	HEWER	LAYER	MORES	OWLER	RIPER	SMEEK	TREES	WIVES	QUIFF
FLIER	HEYER	LEGER	MOSES	OWLET	RISEN	SNEER	TRIED	WODEN	ROLFE
FLIES	HIKER	LEPER	MOSEY	OWNER	RISER	SNOEK	TRIER	WOKEN	RUFFE
FLYER	HIRED	LEVEE	MOTEL	OXTER	RITES	SOBER	TRIES	WOMEN	SAMFU
FOGEY	HIRER	LEVEL	MOTET	PACER	RIVEN	SOKEN	TUBER	WOOER	SCAFF
FOREL	HIVER	LEVEN	MOVED	PACEY	RIVER	SORES	TUNER	WOVEN	SCIFI
FOUET	HIVES	LEVER	MOVER	PAGER	RIVET	SOREX	TWEED	XEBEC	SCOFF
FOVEA	HOKEY	LEWES	MOWER	PAGES	ROBES	SOWER	TWEET	XERES	SCUFF
FOXED	HOLED	LIBEL	MUREX	PALEA	ROBEY	SPEED	TWOER	XYLEM	SHAFT
FOYER	HOLEY	LIBER	MUSES	PALES	RODEO	SPEER	TYLER	YAMEN	SHIFT
FREED	HOMER	LIFER	MUTED	PALET	ROGER	SPIED	TYNED	YATES	SKIFF
FRIED	HONEY	LIGER	NADER	PANEL	ROGET	SPIEL	TYPED	YEMEN	SNAFU
FRIES	HOOEY	LIKED	NAKED	PAPER	ROKER	SPIES	TYPES	YIKES	SNIFF
FUMED	HOREB	LIKEN	NAMED	PAREO	ROMEO	SPREE	UDDER	YODEL	SNIFT
FUMES	HOSEA	LIKES	NAMES	PAREU	ROMER	STEED	ULCER	YOKEL	SNUFF
FUMET	HOSEN	LIMER	NARES	PASEO	RONEO	STEEK	UMBEL	YPRES	SOLFA
FUSED	HOTEL	LIMES	NATES	PATER	ROPED	STEEL	UMBER	ZINEB	SPIFF
FUSEE	HOVEL	LIMEY	NAVEL	PAYEE	ROPER	STEEN	UNBED	ABAFT	STAFF
FUZEE	HOVER	LINED	NAVEW	PAYER	ROPES	STEEP	UNDER	ALOFT	STIFF
GALEA	HYMEN	LINEN	NEBEL	PELEE	ROPEY	STEER	UNFED	BAFFY	STUFF
GALEN	HYPER	LINER	NEGEV	PETER	ROSES	STOEP	UNGET	BALFE	SULFA
GAMES	IBSEN	LINES	NEPER	PICEA	ROSET	STREP	UNPEN	BEEFY	SWIFT
GAPER	ICKER	LITER	NEVEL	PILED	ROUEN	STREW	UNWED	BLUFF	TAFFY
GASES	IDLER	LIVED	NEVER	PILES	ROVER	SUPER	UPPER	BUFFO	THEFT
GATED	IMBED	LIVEN	NEWEL	PINES	ROWEL	SWEEP	UPSET	BUFFS	THOFT
GAVEL	IMMER	LIVER	NIGEL	PIPER	ROWER	SWEET	UPSEY	CHAFE	TUFFE
GEBER	IMMEW	LIVES	NIGER	PIXEL	ROZET	SYCEE	USHER	CHAFF	UNIFY
GENET	IMPEL	LOBED	NOBEL	PLIER	RULER	TABER	USTED	CHUFF	WHIFF
GILES	INDEW	LODEN	NODES	PODEX	RULES	TABES	UTHER	CLEFT	WHIFT
GILET	INDEX	LONER	NOMEN	POKER	RUMEN	TAKEN	UTTER	CLIFF	WOOFY
GIMEL	INFER	LOSER	NONES	POKEY	RUMEX	TAKER	UZBEK	CLIFT	YARFA
GIVEN	INLET	LOVER	NONET	PONEY	RUNES	TALEA	VALET	COMFY	ADAGE
GIVER	INNER	LOWER	NOSER	POPES	RUPEE	TALES	VAREC	CORFE	ADIGE
GLEEK	INNES	LOZEN	NOSEY	POSED	SABER	TAMER	VEREY	CORFU	ALIGN
GLEET	INSET	LUGER	NOTED	POSER	SAGES	TAPER	VEXED	CRAFT	AMIGO
GLUED	INTER	LUMEN	NOTES	POWER	SAHEL	TAPET	VIBES	CROFT	ANIGH
GLUEY	ISLES	LUNED	NOVEL	PREEN	SAKER	TATER	VIDEO	CUFFS	APAGE
GODET	ISLET	LYCÉE	NOYES	PULEX	SALEM	TAXED	VIPER	CUFFY	BADGE
GOFER	ISMET	MACER	NUMEN	PUREE	SALEP	TEHEE	VIREO	DAFFY	BAGGY
GOLEM	IVIED	MAKER	OAKEN	PYREX	SALES	TELEX	VIXEN	DEIFY	BARGE
GONER	JADED	MAMEY	OAKER	QUEEN	SATED	TENET	VOLET	DELFT	BEIGE
GOOEY	JAKES	MANED	OATEN	QUEER	SATEM	TEPEE	VOMER	DRAFT	BELGA
GORED	JAMES	MANES	OATES	QUIET	SAVER	TEREK	VOTER	DRIFT	BILGE
GOWER	JASEY	MANET	OCHER	RACER	SAYER	TERES	VOTES	EDIFY	BINGE
GREED	JAVEL	MASER	OCKER	RACES	SCREE	TEVET	VOWEL	FEOFF	BINGO
GREEK	JEBEL	MATER	OCREA	RAGED	SCREW	TEXEL	WADER	FLUFF	BLIGH
GREEN	JEREZ	MATES	OCTET	RAKED	SEMEN	THIEF	WAFER	GAFFE	BODGE
GREER	JEWEL	MATEY	ODDER	RAKEE	SEVEN	THREE	WAGER	GLIFF	BOGGY
GREET	JOKER	MAZER	OFFER	RAKER	SEVER	THREW	WAGES	GOOFY	BONGO
GRIEF	JONES	MEDEA	OFTEN	RAKES	SEWER	TIBER	WAKEN	GRAFF	BOUGH
GRIEG	JULEP	MELEE	OGIER	RANEE	SHEEL	TIBET	WAKES	GRAFT	BUDGE
GRUEL	KEBEL	METER	OILED	RAREE	SHEEN	TIGER	WALER	GRIFF	BUGGY
GULES	KEYED	MEYER	OILER	RATEL	SHEEP	TILED	WALES	GRUFE	BULGE
GUYED	KEYES	MILER	OLDEN	RATES	SHEER	TILER	WANED	GRUFF	BUNGY
GYGES	KLIEG	MILES	OLDER	RAVEL	SHEET	TILES	WARES	HAIFA	BURGH
HABET	KNEEL	MIMER	OMBER	RAVEN	SHIEL	TIMER	WATER	HALFA	CADGE
HÁ{\C}	KOREA	MINER	ONCER	RAVER	SHLEP	TIMES	WAVER	HUFFY	CADGY

CARGO	LEGGY	STOGY	ITCHY	ADDIO	BROIL	FAKIR	LOUIE	OXLIP	SCRIM
CIGGY	LEIGH	SURGE	KASHA	ADDIS	BRUIN	FECIT	LOUIS	PALIO	SCRIP
COIGN	LIEGE	SYNGE	LATHE	ADLIB	BRUIT	FELIS	LUCIA	PAMIR	SELIM
CONGÉ	LIGGE	TAIGA	LATHI	ADMIN	BURIN	FELIX	LUCID	PANIC	SEMIS
CONGO	LINGO	TANGA	LESHY	ADMIT	CABIN	FERIA	LUCIO	PARIS	SEPIA
CORGI	LODGE	TANGO	LETHE	ADMIX	CALIX	FETID	LUDIC	PATIO	SERIF
COUGH	LONGS	TANGY	LICHT	AEGIS	CAMIS	FINIS	LUPIN	PAVID	SERIN
DEIGN	LOUGH	TARGE	LIGHT	AFFIX	CAPIZ	FLAIL	LURID	PEKIN	SHEIK
DIEGO	LUNGE	TEIGN	LITHE	AFRIT	CARIB	FLAIR	LUTIN	PENIS	SIGIL
DINGE	LUNGI	THEGN	LUSHY	AGAIN	CAVIL	FLUID	LYDIA	PERIL	SITIN
DINGO	LUNGS	THIGH	LYTHE	ALDIS	CECIL	FOLIC	LYRIC	PETIT	SKEIN
DINGY	LURGY	TINGE	MACHO	ALFIE	CHAIN	FOLIE	LYSIN	PIPIT	SKRIM
DIRGE	MADGE	TONGA	MAGHA	ALGID	CHAIR	FOLIO	LYSIS	PIXIE	SLAIN
DODGE	MANGE	TONGS	MASHY	ALVIS	CHOIR	FRAIL	MAFIA	PLAID	SNAIL
DODGY	MANGO	TOUGH	MATHS	AMAIN	CILIA	FRUIT	MAGIC	PLAIN	SOFIA
DOGGO	MANGY	TSUGA	METHS	AMBIT	CIVIC	GAMIC	MALIK	PLAIT	SOLID
DOGGY	MARGE	TWIGS	MICHE	AMNIO	CIVIL	GELID	MANIA	PLEIN	SONIC
DOUGH	MENGE	USAGE	MIGHT	ANNIE	CLAIM	GENIC	MANIC	POLIO	SPAIN
DREGS	MERGE	VERGE	MINHO	ANTIC	COBIA	GENIE	MARIA	POSIT	SPLIT
DRUGS	MIDGE	VIRGA	MOCHA	ANVIL	COLIC	GLAIR	MARIE	POTIN	SPOIL
ELEGY	MINGY	VIRGO	MOTHS	APAID	COLIN	GRAIL	MATIN	PUBIC	SPRIG
ELOGE	MOGGY	VOLGA	MUSHA	APHID	COMIC	GRAIN	MAVIN	PUBIS	SPRIT
ELOGY	MUDGE	VULGO	MUSHY	APHIS	CONIC	GROIN	MAVIS	PUGIN	SQUIB
ENUGU	MUGGY	WAGGA	NACHE	APRIL	CORIN	HABIT	MAXIM	PUNIC	SQUID
ETAGE	MUNGO	WAUGH	NACHO	APSIS	CRAIG	HAFIZ	MEDIA	PUPIL	SQUIT
FADGE	NEAGH	WEDGE	NACHT	ARDIL	CUBIC	HELIO	MEDIC	PURIM	STAID
FARGO	NEIGH	WEIGH	NASHE	ARGIL	CUBIT	HELIX	MELIA	PUTID	STAIN
FEIGN	NUDGE	WILGA	NICHE	AROID	CUFIC	HUMID	MELIC	PYXIS	STAIR
FOGGY	OMAGH	WINGS	NIGHT	ARRIS	CUMIN	HYOID	MERIL	QUAIL	STEIN
FORGE	OMEGA	WODGE	NUCHA	ARSIS	CUPID	IDRIS	MERIT	QUOIF	STOIC
FORGO	OSAGE	WONGA	ORTHO	ARTIE	CURIA	INDIA	MESIC	QUOIN	STRIA
FUDGE	OUTGO	ALOHA	OUGHT	ASCII	CURIE	INDIC	METIC	QUOIT	STRIP
FUGGY	PANGA	ALPHA	PACHA	ASDIC	CURIO	INUIT	METIF	RABID	SUZIE
GADGE	PEGGY	AUGHT	PASHA	ASPIC	CUTIE	INWIT	METIS	RADIO	SWAIN
GAUGE	PIGGY	BAKHA	PITHY	ASTIR	CUTIS	IONIC	MIMIC	RADIX	SYBIL
GLOGG	PINGO	BASHO	PRAHU	ATLIN	CYNIC	IZMIR	MINIM	RAPID	SYRIA
GOLGI	PODGE	BATHE	PUSHY	ATRIP	DALIT	JADIS	MORIA	RATIO	TACIT
GORGE	PODGY	BATHS	RADHA	ATTIC	DAVID	JORIS	MORIN	REFIT	TAMIL
GOUGE	PONGA	BIGHT	RIGHT	AUDIO	DAVIS	KAFIR	MOTIF	REGIA	TAMIS
GREGG	PONGO	BOCHE	RUCHE	AUDIT	DAVIT	KALIF	MOVIE	RÉGIE	TAPIR
GUNGE	PORGY	BOTHA	RUSHY	AULIC	DEBIT	KEFIR	MUCID	REGIS	TAPIS
HAUGH	PUDGE	BOTHY	SACHA	AULIS	DENIM	KELIM	MUCIN	REJIG	TATIN
HEDGE	PUDGY	BUSHY	SACHS	AURIC	DENIS	KEVIN	MUSIC	RELIC	TAXIN
HEIGH	PURGE	CACHE	SADHE	AUXIN	DEVIL	KILIM	MUSIT	REMIT	TAXIS
HELGA	RAGGA	CUSHY	SADHU	AVAIL	DIGIT	KIWIS	NADIR	RESIN	TELIC
HENGE	RAGGY	DACHA	SASHA	AVOID	DIXIE	KLEIN	NAMIB	RESIT	TEPID
HEUGH	RANGE	DELHI	SHCHI	AWAIT	DOLIN	KUFIC	NAZIR	REVIE	THAIS
HINGE	RANGY	DIGHT	SIDHA	AXOID	DORIC	KYLIE	NEVIS	RHEIN	THEIR
HODGE	REIGN	DISHY	SIGHS	AYRIE	DORIS	KYLIN	NGAIO	RICIN	THRID
HOUGH	RIDGE	DUCHY	SIGHT	AZOIC	DRAIN	KYLIX	NIHIL	RIGID	THRIP
IMAGE	ROUGE	EIGHT	SOPHY	BASIC	DROIT	KYRIE	NITID	ROBIN	TIBIA
IMAGO	ROUGH	ELIHU	SPAHI	BASIL	DRUID	LABIS	NOMIC	RODIN	TILIA
INIGO	RUDGE	FICHE	SPOHR	BASIN	DUPIN	LAMIA	NORIA	RORIC	TIMID
JAGGY	SAGGY	FICHU	SUSHI	BASIS	EDWIN	LAPIS	NUBIA	ROSIN	TOBIT
JINGO	SARGE	FIGHT	TACHE	BATIK	EERIE	LATIN	OASIS	ROSIT	TONIC
JIRGA	SAUGH	FISHY	TIGHT	BEFIT	ELFIN	LEGIT	OBIIT	RUBIN	TOPIC
JUDGE	SEDGE	FOEHN	TITHE	BEGIN	ELGIN	LENIN	OGGIN	RUNIC	TORII
KANGA	SERGE	FUCHS	TYPHA	BELIE	ELLIS	LEPID	OLDIE	RUPIA	TOXIC
KEDGE	SIEGE	GOSHT	VICHY	BENIN	ELVIS	LEVIN	OLEIC	SABIN	TOXIN
KEDGY	SINGE	GOTHA	VOZHD	BERIA	EMAIL	LEVIS	OLEIN	SADIE	TRAIL
KENGA	SLIGO	HATHI	WASHY	BEVIS	EOLIC	LEWIS	OLLIE	SAHIB	TRAIN
KIDGE	SLUGS	HECHT	WIGHT	BIFID	EOSIN	LEXIS	OPHIR	SALIC	TRAIT
KINGS	SNAGS	HITHE	WITHE	BLAIR	EQUIP	LICIT	OPTIC	SALIX	TROIC
KONGO	SOGGY	HYPHA	WITHY	BOGIE	ERNIE	LIMIT	ORBIT	SAPID	TULIP
LARGE	SORGO	HYTHE	YACHT	BORIC	ETAIN	LININ	ORNIS	SARIN	TUMID
LARGO	SOUGH	IDAHO	ABRIM	BORIS	ETHIC	LIPID	ORRIS	SATIE	TUNIC
LAUGH	STAGE	IMSHI	ABSIT	BOWIE	EYRIE	LIVID	OSSIA	SATIN	TUNIS
LEDGE	STAGY		ACRID	BRAID	EYTIE	LOGIC	OSTIA	SATIS	TURIN
LEGGE	STOGA		ACTIN	BRAIN	FACIA	LORIS	OVOID	SCLIM	TWAIN

UGRIC	DUCKY	PUKKA	ARKLE	EDILE	KNELT	REPLY	SULLA	BARMY	HAMMY
UNDID	DUSKY	QUAKE	ATILT	EMILE	KNOLL	RIFLE	SULLY	BEAMY	HERMA
UNFIT	EVOKE	RANKE	ATOLL	EMILY	KOALA	RILLE	SURLY	BLAME	HOMME
UNLIT	FINKS	RANKS	ATTLE	EXALT	KRILL	RILLO	SUVLA	BLIMP	HULME
UNMIX	FLAKE	RILKE	BADLY	EXILE	KUALA	ROLLO	SWALE	BREME	JAMMY
UNPIN	FLAKY	RISKY	BALLS	EXULT	LADLE	ROLLS	SWELL	BRUME	JEMMY
UNRIG	FLUKE	ROCKS	BALLY	FABLE	LILLE	ROULE	SWELT	BURMA	JIMMU
UNRIP	FOLKS	ROCKY	BASLE	FALLA	LILLY	RUBLE	SWILL	CHAMP	JIMMY
UNTIE	FORKS	ROOKY	BAULK	FALLS	LISLE	SABLE	TABLA	CHIME	KAMME
UNTIL	FUNKY	RORKE	BAYLE	FAULT	LOLLY	SADLY	TABLE	CHIMP	KARMA
UNZIP	GAWKY	SACKS	BEALE	FELLA	LOWLY	SAILS	TAILS	CHOMP	KERMA
VALID	GECKO	SARKY	BELLE	FIELD	LULLY	SALLE	TALLY	CHUMP	KORMA
VAPID	GORKY	SHAKE	BELLS	FILLY	MACLE	SALLY	TELLY	CHYME	KURMA
VARIX	HAIKU	SHAKO	BELLY	FOLLY	MADLY	SAULT	TESLA	CLAMP	LAMMY
VEDIC	HAKKA	SHAKY	BIBLE	FOOLS	MAILE	SCALA	THILL	CLIMB	LEMMA
VENIN	HANKY	SILKY	BILLY	FOULÉ	MANLY	SCALD	THOLE	CLIME	LLAMA
VIGIL	HONKY	SITKA	BOGLE	FOYLE	MAPLE	SCALE	THULE	CLOMP	LOAMY
VIRID	HOOKY	SLAKE	BOULE	FRILL	MARLE	SCALP	TITLE	CLUMP	LUMME
VISIT	HULKS	SMOKE	BOWLS	FULLY	MARLY	SCALY	TOILE	COMMA	LUMMY
VITIS	HUNKS	SMOKY	BOYLE	GABLE	MATLO	SCOLD	TOILS	COOMB	MAGMA
VIVID	HUNKY	SNAKE	BRILL	GAILY	MEALS	SCULL	TOOLS	COSMO	MALMO
VOMIT	HUSKS	SNAKY	BRULE	GAULT	MEALY	SCULP	TRILL	CRAMP	MAMMA
XENIA	HUSKY	SOCKS	BUGLE	GHYLL	MERLE	SEALS	TROLL	CREME	MAMMY
XYRIS	IROKO	SPEKE	BUILD	GIGLI	MILLI	SELLE	TRULL	CRIME	MIAMI
YUPIK	JACKS	SPIKE	BUILT	GILLS	MILLS	SHALE	TWILL	CRIMP	MOMMA
ZAYIN	JERKS	SPIKY	BULLA	GIRLS	MOLLY	SHALL	TWILT	CROME	MOMMY
ABUJA	JERKY	SPOKE	BULLS	GIRLY	MOOLI	SHALT	UDALL	CRUMB	MUMMY
BANJO	JINKS	STAKE	BULLY	GODLY	MOULD	SHELF	UMBLE	CRUMP	MYOMA
GANJA	JOCKO	STOKE	BURLY	GOLLY	MOULS	SHELL	UNCLE	DAMME	NORMA
HADJI	KAFKA	STUKA	CABLE	GOOLY	MOULT	SHILL	URALS	DERMA	OROMO
KANJI	KHAKI	SUCKS	CARLE	GRILL	MOYLE	SHOLA	UVULA	DOGMA	OXIME
KOPJE	KINKY	SULKS	CAULD	GUELF	MULLA	SHYLY	VAILS	DORMY	PADMA
NINJA	KOOKY	SULKY	CAULK	GUILD	MVULE	SIDLE	VAULT	DOUMA	PALMY
OUIJA	LACKS	TACKY	CELLA	GUILE	NAILS	SIGLA	VILLA	DRAMA	PARMA
RIOJA	LANKA	TALKS	CELLO	GUILT	NEALE	SILLY	VILLI	DROME	PELMA
SHOJI	LANKY	TANKA	CELLS	GULLS	NELLY	SKELM	VIOLA	DUMMY	PIGMY
THUJA	LARKS	TIKKA	CHALK	GULLY	NEWLY	SKELP	VOILA	DUOMO	PLUMB
ALIKE	LASKI	TRIKE	CHILD	HALLÉ	NOBLE	SKILL	VOILE	EDEMA	PLUME
ASOKA	LAWKS	TUNKU	CHILE	HALLO	NOBLY	SKULK	WALLY	ENEMA	PLUMP
AWAKE	LEAKY	TURKI	CHILI	HAULM	NULLA	SKULL	WANLY	ENEMY	POEMS
AWOKE	LINKS	TURKU	CHILL	HAULT	NYALA	SLYLY	WEALD	FERMI	POMMY
BACKS	LOCKE	VODKA	CHYLE	HAYLE	ODDLY	SMALL	WEILL	FILMS	PRIMA
BANKS	LOCKS	WACKY	CILLA	HEALD	OVOLO	SMELL	WELLS	FILMY	PRIME
BECKY	LUCKY	WEEKS	COLLY	HEELS	OVULE	SMELT	WELLY	FIRMA	PRIMO
BLAKE	MAIKO	WONKY	COULD	HELLO	PABLO	SMILE	WHALE	FLAME	PRIMP
BLOKE	MILKY	WORKS	COYLY	HILLS	PALLY	SMOLT	WHELK	FLUME	PROMO
BOSKY	MINKE	YAKKA	CULLY	HILLY	PAOLO	SOCLE	WHELP	FLUMP	PYGMY
BRAKE	MONKS	YONKS	CURLY	HOLLA	PELLA	SOULS	WHILE	FOAMY	REAMS
BROKE	MUCKY	YUCKY	CYCLE	HOLLY	PHILE	SOWLE	WHOLE	FORME	RHOMB
BUCKO	MURKY	YUKKY	DAILY	HOTLY	PHYLE	SPALD	WIELD	FORMS	RHUMB
BUCKS	MUSKY	ABELE	DALLE	HOYLE	PILLS	SPALL	WILLY	FRAME	RHYME
BULKY	NARKS	ADDLE	DALLY	HULLO	POILU	SPALT	WOOLF	GAMMA	ROOMS
BURKE	NARKY	ADULT	DIALS	ICILY	POLLY	SPELL	WORLD	GAMMY	ROOMY
CHEKA	NOOKY	AGILE	DIMLY	IDYLL	POOLS	SPELT	WOULD	GEMMA	RUMMY
CHOKE	NUNKY	AIOLI	DOILY	IMPLY	POULE	SPILE	WRYLY	GEMMY	SALMI
CHOKO	OSAKA	AISLE	DOLLY	INCLE	POULT	SPILL	YIELD	GISMO	SAMMY
CHOKY	PARKA	AKELA	DOYLE	INGLE	PRILL	SPILT	YOULL	GIZMO	SCAMP
COCKY	PARKY	ALULA	DOYLY	ISOLA	PROLE	STALE	ADAMS	GLUME	SEAMY
COOKS	PAWKY	AMBLE	DRILL	ITALA	PSALM	STALK	AGAMI	GNOME	SHAME
CORKY	PEAKY	AMPLE	DRILY	ITALY	PUSLE	STALL	ALAMO	GRIME	SIGMA
CRAKE	PERKS	AMPLY	DROLL	JELLO	QUALM	STELA	ANIMA	GRIMM	SKIMP
DECKO	PERKY	ANELE	DRYLY	JELLY	QUELL	STELE	ANOMY	GRIMY	SLIME
DEKKO	PESKY	ANGLE	DUALA	JOLLY	QUILL	STILE	AROMA	GRUME	SLIMY
DICKY	PINKO	ANGLO	DUPLE	JOULE	QUILP	STILL	ATOMY	GRUMP	SLUMP
DINKA	PINKY	ANKLE	DWELL	KEBLE	QUILT	STILT	AZYME	GUIMP	SOMME
DINKY	PISKY	ANOLE	DYULA	KEELS	RALLY	STOLA	BALMY	GUMMA	SPUME
DOCKS	POLKA	APPLE	EAGLE	KELLS	RAYLE	STOLE		GUMMY	STAMP
DRAKE	PORKY	APPLY	EARLY	KELLY	REALM	STOLL		HALMA	STIME
DUCKS	PROKE	APTLY	EBOLA	KNELL	RÈGLE	STYLE			STIMY

STOMA	BLOND	ELENE	JAUNT	PHONY	SPENS	WRUNG	BUROO	ETHOS	MAJOR
STOMP	BLUNT	EMEND	JEANS	PIANO	SPENT	YARNS	BUXOM	EXTOL	MANOR
STUMP	BOING	EVANS	JENNY	PINNA	SPINA	YONNE	BYRON	FAGOT	MAROT
STYME	BONNY	EVENS	JINNI	PINNY	SPINE	YOUNG	CABOB	FANON	MASON
SUMMA	BOONE	EVENT	JOINT	PLANE	SPINY	AARON	CABOT	FAROE	MAYOR
SUOMI	BOONG	EXINE	JOUNT	PLANK	SPUNK	ABBOT	CAGOT	FAVOR	MCCOY
SWAMI	BORNE	FAINS	JUMNA	PLANT	STAND	ABHOR	CALOR	FELON	MEDOC
SWAMP	BOUND	FAINT	KARNO	PLINY	STANK	ABLOW	CANOE	FETOR	MELON
TALMA	BOYNE	FANNY	KERNE	PLONK	STENT	ACTON	CANON	FLOOD	MELOS
TAMMY	BRAND	FARNE	KIANG	PLUNK	STING	ACTOR	CAPON	FLOOR	MESON
TERMS	BRANK	FAUNA	KLANG	POINT	STINK	ADIOS	CAPOT	FLUON	METOL
THEMA	BRENT	FEINT	KOINE	PORNO	STINT	AESOP	CAROB	FREON	MIAOU
THEME	BRINE	FENNY	KRANG	POUND	STONE	AFOOT	CAROL	FUROR	MIAOW
THUMB	BRING	FIEND	KRANS	PRANA	STONY	AGLOW	CDROM	FUTON	MINOR
THUMP	BRINK	FLANK	KRANZ	PRANG	STUNG	AIDOS	CHAOS	GABON	MINOS
THYME	BRINY	FLING	KRONA	PRANK	STUNK	ALGOL	CHLOE	GALOP	MINOT
TOMMY	BRONX	FLINT	KRONE	PRINT	STUNT	ALLOT	CHOOK	GAZON	MORON
TRAMP	BRUNO	FLONG	KYANG	PRONE	SUNNI	ALLOW	CIBOL	GENOA	MOTOR
TREMA	BRUNT	FLUNG	LARNE	PRONG	SUNNY	ALLOY	CLOOT	GIGOT	MYRON
TROMP	BUNNY	FLUNK	LEANT	PRUNE	SWANK	ALOOF	COBOL	GLOOM	NABOB
TRUMP	BURNS	FOUND	LEONE	QUANT	SWANS	ANION	COCOA	GLUON	NAGOR
TUMMY	BURNT	FOUNT	LERNA	QUINS	SWINE	ANJOU	COCOS	GOGOL	NAXOS
ULEMA	BWANA	FRANC	LERNE	QUINT	SWING	ANNOY	CODON	GRIOT	NICOL
WHIMS	CAINE	FRANK	LIANA	RAINE	SWUNG	ANSON	COHOE	GROOM	NIDOR
WORMS	CANNA	FRANS	LIANE	RAINY	TAINE	ANTON	COLON	GUYON	NINON
WORMY	CANNY	FRANZ	LIANG	REINS	TAINO	APOOP	COLOR	GUYOT	NITON
YUMMY	CERNE	FROND	LIONS	RHINE	TAINT	APRON	COROT	HALON	NIXON
ABUNA	CHANT	FRONT	LLANO	RHINO	TAUNT	ARBOR	CREON	HANOI	NYLON
ACINI	CHINA	FUNNY	LOINS	RHONE	TAWNY	ARCOT	CROOK	HAVOC	ODEON
AGENT	CHINE	GAINS	LOONS	RIANT	TEENS	ARDOR	CRUOR	HELOT	ONION
AGING	CHING	GANNY	LOONY	RONNE	TEENY	ARGON	DAGON	HEROD	ORION
AGONE	CHINK	GARNI	LORNA	ROUND	TERNE	ARGOT	DAMON	HERON	ORLON
AGONY	CHINO	GAUNT	LORNE	RUING	THANE	ARMOR	DECON	HONOR	ORLOP
AKENE	CHUNK	GÉANT	LYING	RUINS	THANK	ARROW	DECOR	HUMOR	ORTON
ALANS	CHYND	GHANA	MAGNA	RUNNY	THINE	ARSON	DECOY	HURON	OXBOW
ALONE	CINNA	GIANT	MAINE	SAINE	THING	ASCOT	DEFOE	ICHOR	PEKOE
ALONG	CLANG	GLAND	MAINS	SAINT	THINK	ASTON	DELOS	IDIOM	PERON
AMANT	CLANK	GLANS	MANNA	SAUNA	THONG	ATHOS	DEMOB	IDIOT	PHEON
AMEND	CLING	GLINT	MARNE	SCANT	THUNK	AVION	DEMON	IGLOO	PHLOX
AMENE	CLINK	GOING	MAUND	SCENE	TINNY	AXIOM	DEMOS	IMPOT	PHNOM
AMENT	CLINT	GONNA	MEANS	SCENT	TONNE	BABOO	DEPOT	INGOT	PICOT
AMINE	CLONE	GRAND	MEANT	SCONE	TOWNS	BACON	DETOX	INION	PILOT
AMINO	CLUNG	GRANT	MESNE	SEINE	TRANS	BALOO	DIVOT	IXION	PINON
AMONG	CLUNK	GRIND	MILNE	SENNA	TRANT	BALOR	DONOR	JABOT	PIÑON
ANANA	CORNY	GRUNT	MOONY	SHANG	TREND	BARON	DROOL	JACOB	PINOT
ANEND	COUNT	GUANA	MORNE	SHANK	TRENT	BATON	DROOP	JASON	PIROG
ANENT	COYNE	GUANO	MOUND	SHANT	TRINE	BAYOU	DUROY	JUPON	PITON
ARENA	CRANE	GUNNY	MOUNT	SHINE	TRUNK	BAZOO	EGDON	JUROR	PITOT
ARENE	CRANK	GWENT	NANNA	SHINY	TUNNY	BEBOP	EIKON	KABOB	PIVOT
ARENT	CRONE	GYMNO	NANNY	SHONA	TWANG	BEFOG	ELBOW	KAPOK	POPOV
ATONE	CRONK	HADNT	NINNY	SHONE	TWANK	BELOW	ELIOT	KEBOB	POTOO
ATONY	CRONY	HASNT	NONNY	SHUNT	TWINE	BEROB	ELTON	KIROV	PRION
AVANT	DAUNT	HAUNT	OMANI	SIGNS	TWINS	BESOM	EMBOW	KLOOF	PRIOR
AVENA	DIANA	HEINE	OPINE	SKINK	TYING	BESOT	EMBOX	KOTOW	PROOF
AVENS	DIDNT	HENNA	ORANG	SKINS	UPEND	BETON	ENDOW	KUDOS	PUDOR
BANNS	DOING	HERNE	OVINE	SKINT	URINE	BIGOT	ENJOY	KYLOE	PYLON
BEANO	DONNA	HINNY	OWING	SKUNK	USING	BIJOU	ENROL	LABOR	RADON
BEANS	DONNE	HMONG	OZONE	SLANG	VAUNT	BIPOD	ENSOR	LAGOS	RAYON
BEING	DOONE	HORNE	PAINE	SLANT	VEINS	BISON	ENVOI	LECOQ	RAZOR
BENNE	DOWNS	HORNY	PAINS	SLING	VERNE	BLOOD	ENVOY	LEMON	REDON
BHANG	DOWNY	HOUND	PAINT	SLINK	VIAND	BLOOM	EPHOD	LOGOS	REDOX
BIONT	DRANK	HYENA	PANNE	SLUNG	VISNA	BLOOP	EPHOR	LOTOS	REPOT
BLANC	DRINK	ICENI	PATNA	SLUNK	WASNT	BORON	EPSOM	LUTON	RIGOR
BLAND	DRONE	ICING	PENNA	SOANE	WEENY	BOSOM	ERGOT	LUZON	RIPON
BLANK	DRUNK	INANE	PENNE	SONNY	WHANG	BROOD	ERROR	LYSOL	ROBOT
BLEND	DUNNO	IRENA	PENNY	SOUND	WHINE	BROOK	ESCOT	MACON	ROTOR
BLIND	DYING	IRENE	PEONY	SOWND	WOUND	BROOL	ESROM	MAGOG	RUMOR
BLINI	EBONY	IRONS	PHENO	SPANK	WRING	BROOM	ESTOC	MAGOT	SABOT
BLINK	ELAND	IRONY	PHONE	SPEND	WRONG	BULOW	ESTOP	MAHOE	SALON

SAMOA	TUMOR	GIPPO	SNAPS	BERRY	EXTRA	LEARN	REPRO	SWARD	AVISO
SAMOS	TUTOR	GLYPH	SNIPE	BLARE	EXURB	LEERY	RETRO	SWARF	AWASH
SAPOR	TYROL	GRAPE	SOAPY	BLURB	FABRÉ	LIARD	SABRA	SWARM	BALSA
SAROS	UNION	GRAPH	SOPPY	BLURT	FAERY	LIBRA	SABRE	SWIRE	BASSO
SAVOR	UPTON	GRIPE	STAPH	BOARD	FAIRY	LITRE	SAURY	SWIRL	BEAST
SAVOY	URSON	GROPE	STEPS	BOURG	FAURE	LIVRE	SCARE	SWORD	BLASÉ
SAXON	VALOR	GULPH	STIPE	BURRO	FEARE	LOIRE	SCARF	SWORE	BLAST
SCION	VAPOR	GUPPY	STOPE	CADRE	FERRY	LORRY	SCARP	SWORN	BLESS
SCOOP	VENOM	GYPPO	STUPA	CAIRN	FIBRE	LOWRY	SCARY	TARRY	BLEST
SCOOT	VIGOR	HAPPY	STUPE	CAIRO	FIBRO	LUBRA	SCORE	TATRA	BLISS
SCROD	VISON	HARPO	SUPPE	CAPRI	FIERE	LUCRE	SCORN	TEARS	BLUSH
SCROG	VISOR	HARPY	SWEPT	CARRY	FIERY	LYCRA	SCURF	TERRA	BOAST
SCROW	VIZOR	HEAPS	SWIPE	CEORL	FIORD	MACRO	SEARE	TERRY	BOOST
SENOR	VROOM	HIPPO	SYLPH	CHARD	FJORD	MAIRE	SERRA	TETRA	BOSSY
SEPOY	WAGON	HIPPY	TAMPA	CHARK	FLARE	MAORI	SERRE	THERE	BRASH
SHOOK	WHOOP	HUMPH	TAUPE	CHARM	FLIRT	MARRY	SHARD	THERM	BRASS
SHOOT	WHOOT	IGAPO	TEMPE	CHART	FLORA	MERRY	SHARE	THIRD	BREST
SHROW	WIDOW	INAPT	TEMPO	CHARY	FOURS	METRE	SHARK	THIRL	BRISK
SIDON	XENON	INEPT	TEMPT	CHERE	FUERO	METRO	SHARP	THORN	BROSE
SIMON	XEROX	JASPÉ	TIPPY	CHERT	FURRY	MICRO	SHERD	TIARA	BRUSH
SLOOP	YAHOO	JIMPY	TRAPS	CHIRK	GEARE	MITRE	SHERE	TITRE	BURSA
SNOOD	YAPOK	JUMPS	TRIPE	CHIRL	GENRE	MOIRA	SHIRE	TRURO	BURST
SNOOK	YUKON	JUMPY	TROPE	CHIRP	GLORY	MOIRE	SHIRK	TWERP	CAUSE
SNOOP	ZADOK	KAMPF	TURPS	CHIRR	GNARL	MOORE	SHIRR	TWIRL	CEASE
SNOOT	ZENOS	KAPPA	UNAPT	CHIRT	GOURD	MOURN	SHIRT	TWIRP	CENSE
SODOM	ADAPT	KEEPS	VESPA	CHORD	GUARD	MUCRO	SHORE	UHURU	CHASE
SODOR	ADEPT	KEMPE	WEEPY	CHORE	HAIRS	MUNRO	SHORN	ULTRA	CHASM
SOKOL	ADOPT	KIPPS	WHIPS	CHURL	HAIRY	MURRE	SHORT	UMBRA	CHESS
SOLON	AGAPE	KOPPA	WIMPY	CHURN	HARRY	MURRY	SKIRL	UNARM	CHEST
SPOOF	ALAPA	LAMPS	WISPY	CHURR	HEARD	MYRRH	SKIRR	USURE	CHOSE
SPOOK	ALEPH	LEAPT	YIPPY	CLARA	HEART	NACRE	SKIRT	USURP	CISSY
SPOOL	ASAPH	LIPPI	YUPPY	CLARE	HENRY	NAIRA	SLURB	USURY	CLASH
SPOON	ATOPY	LOOPY	ZEPPO	CLARK	HOARD	NAURU	SLURP	UTURN	CLASP
SPOOR	BUMPH	LOUPE	ZIPPY	CLARY	HOARE	NEGRO	SMARM	VEERY	CLASS
SPROD	BUMPY	LUMPY	IRAQI	CLERK	HOARY	NEHRU	SMART	WEARY	CLOSE
SPROG	CALPA	LYMPH	ABORT	COBRA	HOURI	NITRE	SMIRK	WEIRD	COAST
STOOD	CAMPO	MORPH	ACCRA	COPRA	HOURS	NITRO	SNARE	WHARF	COPSE
STOOK	CHAPE	MUMPS	ACERB	COURB	HURRY	OCHRE	SNARK	WHERE	CORSE
STOOL	CHAPS	NADPH	ACORN	COURT	HYDRA	OMBRE	SNARL	WHIRL	CORSO
STOOP	CHIPS	NAPPA	ADORE	COWRY	HYDRO	OPERA	SNORE	WHIRR	CRASH
STOOR	CHOPS	NAPPE	ADORN	CRARE	IBERT	OTARY	SNORT	WHORE	CRASS
STROP	CLEPE	NAPPY	AFIRE	CRORE	IMARI	OUTRE	SOARE	WHORL	CRESS
SUDOR	COMPO	NIPPY	AFORE	CURRY	INARI	OVARY	SOPRA	WORRY	CREST
SUTOR	COOPT	NYMPH	AGGRO	CYMRU	INARM	OVERT	SORRY	YARRA	CRISE
SWOON	COPPY	OKAPI	AGORA	CYMRY	INDRA	OZARK	SPARE	YEARN	CRISP
SWOOP	CORPS	OOMPH	AKARA	DAIRY	INDRE	PADRE	SPARK	YEARS	CROSS
SYNOD	COUPE	PEPPY	ALARM	DECRY	INDRI	PAIRE	SPART	YOURS	CRUSE
TABOO	COYPU	PIPPA	ALERT	DERRY	INERT	PAIRS	SPERM	YOURT	CRUSH
TABOR	CRAPE	POPPA	ALURE	DIARY	INFRA	PARRY	SPIRE	ZABRA	CRUST
TALON	CRAPS	POPPY	AMORT	DOBRO	INTRA	PEARL	SPORE	ZAIRE	CURSE
TAROT	CREPE	POUPE	ANGRY	DOORN	INTRO	PEDRO	SPORT	ZEBRA	CURST
TAUON	CREPT	PULPY	APART	DOORS	INURE	PEERS	SPURN	ZORRO	DAISY
TAXOL	CROPS	PUPPY	APERT	DOURA	ISERE	PERRY	SPURS	ABASE	DEIST
TAXON	CRYPT	RALPH	APPRO	DOURO	IVORY	PETRA	SPURT	ABASH	DENSE
TELOS	CUPPA	ROOPY	ASTRA	DOWRY	IZARD	PETRE	STARE	ABYSM	DESSE
TENON	DELPH	RUMPY	AVERT	DRERE	JERRY	PETRI	STARK	ABYSS	DOUSE
TENOR	DIPPY	SAPPY	AWARD	DRURY	JEWRY	PHARE	STARR	AGIST	DOWSE
TETON	DRAPE	SCAPA	AWARE	DURRY	KARRI	PIERS	STARS	AMASS	DRESS
THIOL	DROPS	SCAPE	AWARN	DWARF	KAURI	PIERT	START	AMISH	DROSS
THROB	DRUPE	SCOPE	AZURE	EMERY	KNARL	POORI	STERN	AMISS	DURST
THROE	DUMPS	SCOPS	BAIRD	EMURE	KNURL	PSORA	STIRP	AMUSE	EGEST
THROW	DUMPY	SHAPE	BAIRN	ENARM	KNURR	QUARK	STORE	ANGST	ERASE
TIGON	EGYPT	SHOPS	BAJRI	ENORM	KOORI	QUART	STORK	ANISE	ERNST
TIMON	ELOPE	SLEPT	BARRA	ENTRY	KUKRI	QUERN	STORM	ARISE	EXIST
TIMOR	ERUPT	SLIPE	BARRE	ENURE	LAIRD	QUERY	STORY	ARISH	FALSE
TIROS	ETAPE	SLIPS	BARRY	ERARD	LAIRY	QUIRE	STURT	ARIST	FARSE
TROON	FLOPS	SLOPE	BASRA	EVERT	LARRY	QUIRK	SUCRE	AROSE	FARSI
TROOP	GASPÉ	SLOPS	BEARD	EVERY	LAURA	QUORN	SUPRA	AVAST	FAUST
TUDOR	GIMPY	SLYPE	BEERY	EXERT	LAVRA	REARM	SUTRA	AVISO	FEAST

FESSE	LASSA	PROSY	VERSE	CRETE	HAITI	ORATE	SCATH	URITE	CYRUS
FIRST	LASSO	PULSE	VERSO	CRWTH	HARTY	OVATE	SCOTS	VERTU	DATUK
FLASH	LEASE	PURSE	VERST	CUTTY	HASTA	PANTO	SCOTT	VESTA	DATUM
FLASK	LEASH	PURSY	WAIST	DANTE	HASTE	PANTS	SCUTE	VIRTU	DEBUG
FLESH	LEAST	PUSSY	WELSH	DARTS	HASTY	PANTY	SHITE	VISTA	DEBUT
FLOSS	LEESE	QUASH	WHISH	DEATH	HATTY	PARTI	SHOTS	VOLTA	DEMUR
FLUSH	LEISH	QUASI	WHISK	DEITY	HAUTE	PARTS	SHUTE	VOLTE	DURUM
FOIST	LHASA	QUEST	WHIST	DELTA	HEATH	PARTY	SHUTS	WAITS	EMBUS
FOSSA	LOESS	RAISE	WHOSE	DEPTH	HECTO	PASTA	SITTA	WALTZ	ENDUE
FOSSE	LOOSE	REIST	WORSE	DHOTI	HEFTY	PASTE	SIXTH	WARTY	ENNUI
FRESH	LOUSE	RINSE	WORST	DIOTA	HERTS	PASTY	SIXTY	WASTE	ENSUE
FRISK	LOUSY	ROAST	WREST	DIRTY	HERTZ	PATTI	SKATE	WATTS	FAGUS
FRIST	MANSE	ROIST	WRIST	DITTO	HETTY	PATTY	SLATE	WHITE	FAVUS
FROST	MARSH	ROOST	WURST	DITTY	HOSTA	PEATY	SLATS	WIDTH	FEMUR
FUBSY	MASSA	ROSSE	XHOSA	DORTS	HOTTY	PESTO	SLATY	WILTS	FETUS
FUSSY	MASSE	ROSSI	YEAST	DOTTY	HUNTS	PETTO	SLOTH	WITTY	FLEUR
GASSY	MENSA	ROUSE	ABATE	DUSTY	IRATE	PETTY	SMITE	WORTH	FLOUR
GAUSS	MESSY	RUSSE	AGATE	EARTH	JANTY	PHOTO	SMITH	WRATH	FLOUT
GEESE	MEUSE	RUSSO	ALATE	ELATE	JETTY	PIETA	SMOTE	WRITE	FOCUS
GEIST	MIDST	SALSA	AMITY	ELITE	JONTY	PIETY	SMUTS	WRITS	FORUM
GESSE	MINSK	SALSE	ANITA	EMOTE	JUNTA	PINTA	SOFTY	WROTE	FRAUD
GESSO	MISSA	SAMSO	AORTA	EMPTY	JUNTO	PINTO	SOLTI	WROTH	FREUD
GHOST	MISSY	SASSE	AOSTA	ENATE	KITTY	PISTE	SOOTH	YALTA	FUGUE
GIPSY	MOIST	SASSO	ARETE	ERATO	KOFTA	PITTA	SOOTY	YARTA	GADUS
GLASS	MOOSE	SASSY	ARITA	ETATS	LAITH	PLATE	SORTS	YEATS	GAIUS
GLISK	MOPSY	SAYSO	AUNTY	EVITA	LAITY	PLATH	SOTTO	YOUTH	GAMUT
GLOSS	MORSE	SEISM	AZOTE	EVITE	LATTE	PLATO	SOUTH	ZANTE	GARUM
GNASH	MOSSI	SENSE	BANTU	FACTO	LEFTY	PLATY	SOWTH	ZLOTY	GENUS
GOOSE	MOSSO	SHUSH	BARTS	FACTS	LEITH	PLATZ	SPATE	ABDUL	GETUP
GORSE	MOSSY	SISSY	BASTA	FAITH	LENTO	PLOTS	SPATS	ABOUT	GHOUL
GOSSE	MOUSE	SLASH	BASTE	FATTY	LISTS	PLUTO	SPITE	ADSUM	GIBUS
GRASP	MOUSY	SLOSH	BASTO	FEMTO	LOATH	PONTY	SPITZ	AFOUL	GIGUE
GRASS	MULSE	SLUSH	BATTY	FESTA	LOFTY	PORTA	SPOTS	ALBUM	GROUP
GRIST	MUSSE	SMASH	BERTH	FESTE	LOTTO	PORTE	STATE	ALEUT	GROUT
GROSS	MUSSY	SNASH	BETTE	FIFTH	LOUTH	PORTO	SUETY	ALNUS	GUEUX
GROSZ	NESSA	SOUSA	BETTY	FIFTY	LUSTY	PORTS	SUITE	ALOUD	GYRUS
GUESS	NEWSY	SOUSE	BIRTH	FILTH	MALTA	POSTE	SUITS	AMOUR	HAGUE
GUEST	NOISE	SPASM	BITTE	FIRTH	MANTA	POSTO	SWATH	ANGUS	HILUM
GUISE	NOISY	STASH	BITTY	FLATS	MATTE	POTTO	SWATS	ANKUS	HOCUS
GUTSY	NOOSE	STASI	BLITZ	FLOTA	MEATH	POTTY	SYNTH	ANNUL	HOKUM
GYPSY	NORSE	SWASH	BOOTH	FLUTE	MEATS	PRATE	TARTY	APPUI	HORUS
HALSE	NURSE	SWISH	BOOTS	FLYTE	MEATY	PUNTO	TASTE	ARCUS	HUMUS
HANSE	NYASA	SWISS	BOOTY	FOOTS	MEETS	PUNTY	TASTY	ARGUE	HYLUM
HARSH	NYSSA	TANSY	BOTTE	FOOTY	MEITH	PUTTO	TATTY	ARGUS	ICTUS
HAUSA	OBESE	TASSE	BOTTO	FORTE	MESTO	PUTTY	TEETH	ASCUS	ILEUM
HAUSE	PAISA	TASSO	BROTH	FORTH	MIRTH	QUITE	TENTH	AUGUR	ILEUS
HAWSE	PALSY	TAWSE	BRUTE	FORTY	MISTY	QUITO	TESTA	AVOUÉ	ILIUM
HEIST	PANSY	TEASE	BUSTY	FRITH	MIXTE	QUITS	TESTS	AWFUL	IMAMU
HERSE	PARSE	TENSE	BUTTE	FRITZ	MOLTO	QUOTA	TESTY	BABUL	IMBUE
HESSE	PARSI	TERSE	BUTTY	FROTH	MONTE	QUOTE	TEXTS	BAHUT	INCUR
HOAST	PASSE	TESSA	CANTO	FUSTY	MONTH	QUOTH	THETA	BEAUT	INCUS
HOIST	PATSY	THESE	CARTA	GARTH	MOTTE	RASTA	THETE	BEGUM	INDUE
HOLST	PAUSA	THOSE	CARTE	GENTS	MOTTO	RATTY	THOTH	BEGUN	INDUS
HOOSH	PAUSE	TIPSY	CASTE	GENTY	MOUTH	RECTO	TILTH	BÉVUE	INIUM
HORSA	PEASE	TOAST	CATTY	GESTE	MUFTI	REITH	TITTY	BOGUS	INJUN
HORSE	PEPSI	TOISE	CENTO	GHATS	MULTI	RENTE	TOOTH	BOLUS	INPUT
HORSY	PERSE	TOPSY	CHOTA	GIFTS	MUSTY	RESTS	TORTE	BONUS	IRGUN
HOUSE	PHASE	TORSO	CHOTT	GILTS	NANTZ	RHETT	TOTTY	BOSUN	ISSUE
HURST	PLUSH	TOWSE	CHUTE	GIRTH	NASTY	RIOTS	TRITE	CAIUS	JANUS
HUSSY	POESY	TRASH	CLOTH	GLITZ	NATTY	ROOTS	TROTH	CAJUN	JESUS
IRISH	POISE	TRESS	COATI	GOATY	NESTA	ROOTY	TROTS	CAMUS	JORUM
JESSE	POPSY	TRUSS	COLTS	GOTTA	NEWTS	RORTY	TRUTH	CAPUT	KABUL
JOIST	POSSE	TRUST	COMTE	GOUTY	NIFTY	ROUTE	TUTTI	CECUM	KAPUT
JOUST	PRESA	TRYST	CONTE	GRATE	NINTH	RUSTY	UMPTY	CETUS	KNOUT
KARST	PRESS	TUTSI	COSTA	GRETA	NORTH	SALTS	UNITA	CLAUS	KOKUM
KARSY	PREST	TWIST	COSTS	GRITS	NOTTS	SALTY	UNITE	CLOUD	KRAUT
KIOSK	PRISE	UKASE	COTTA	GUSTO	NUTTY	SANTA	UNITS	CLOUT	LEMUR
KVASS	PRISM	VALSE	COUTH	GUSTY	OBOTE	SANTO	UNITY	COMUS	LEPUS
LAPSE	PROSE	VERSA	CRATE	GUTTA	ODETS	SAUTE	URATE	CROUP	LINUS

LOCUM	SCOUP	CHIVY	VERVE	PLAYA	ABUJA	CUPPA	HOLLA	MAMMA	PIZZA
LOCUS	SCOUR	CIVVY	VOLVA	POLYP	ABUNA	CURIA	HORSA	MANIA	PLAYA
LOTUS	SCOUT	CLAVE	VOLVO	POWYS	ACCRA	DACCA	HOSEA	MANNA	PLAZA
LUPUS	SCRUB	CLIVE	VULVA	SATYR	AGORA	DACHA	HOSTA	MANTA	PLICA
MAGUS	SCRUM	CLOVE	WAIVE	SIBYL	AKARA	DECCA	HUZZA	MARIA	POLKA
MAHUA	SEDUM	CORVO	WEAVE	STAYS	AKELA	DELTA	HYDRA	MASSA	PONGA
MANUL	SEGUE	CRAVE	YAHVE	SURYA	ALAPA	DERMA	HYENA	MECCA	POPPA
MANUS	SEOUL	CURVE	YOUVE	THUYA	ALOHA	DIANA	HYPHA	MEDEA	PORTA
MASUS	SERUM	CURVY	BLOWN	TOKYO	ALPHA	DINKA	IBIZA	MEDIA	PRANA
MIAUL	SETUP	DELVE	BLOWY	VANYA	ALULA	DIOTA	INDIA	MELBA	PRESA
MIMUS	SHAUN	DIVVY	BRAWL	VINYL	AMEBA	DOGMA	INDRA	MELIA	PRIMA
MINUS	SHOUT	DRIVE	BRAWN	AMAZE	ANANA	DONNA	INFRA	MENSA	PSORA
MIXUP	SHRUB	DROVE	BROWN	BAIZE	ANIMA	DOUMA	INTRA	MIRZA	PUKKA
MODUS	SHRUG	EMOVE	CHEWA	BLAZE	ANITA	DOURA	IRENA	MISSA	QUOTA
MOGUL	SINUS	FAUVE	CHEWY	BONZE	AORTA	DRAMA	ISOLA	MOCHA	RADHA
MORUS	SITUP	GLOVE	CLOWN	BOOZE	AOSTA	DUALA	ITALA	MOIRA	RAGGA
MUCUS	SNOUT	GRAVE	CRAWL	BOOZY	AQABA	DYULA	JAFFA	MOMMA	RASTA
NAHUM	SOLUM	GRAVY	CREWE	BRIZE	ARABA	EBOLA	JIRGA	MONZA	REGIA
NATUS	SOLUS	GROVE	CROWD	BWAZI	ARDEA	EDEMA	JUMNA	MORIA	RIOJA
NEGUS	SOYUZ	GUAVA	CROWN	CLOZE	ARECA	ENEMA	JUNTA	MULLA	RSPCA
NEXUS	SPOUT	HALVE	DRAWL	COLZA	ARENA	ERICA	KAABA	MUNDA	RUMBA
NIDUS	SPRUE	HEAVE	DRAWN	CRAZE	ARICA	ERUCA	KAFKA	MUSCA	RUPIA
NISUS	STOUP	HEAVY	DROWN	CRAZY	ARITA	EVITA	KANGA	MUSHA	SABRA
NODUS	STOUR	HELVE	FATWA	CROZE	AROMA	EXTRA	KAPPA	MYOMA	SACHA
NOTUM	STOUT	HOOVE	FLEWS	DIAZO	ARUBA	FACIA	KARMA	NAIRA	SALSA
NOVUM	STRUM	KNAVE	FLOWN	DIZZY	ASOKA	FALLA	KASHA	NANNA	SAMBA
OAKUM	STRUT	LARVA	FROWN	DRUZE	ASTRA	FATWA	KENGA	NAPPA	SAMOA
OCCUR	SYRUP	LEAVE	FROWY	FIZZY	AVENA	FAUNA	KERMA	NERVA	SANTA
OCNUS	TAGUS	MAEVE	GROWL	FROZE	BAKHA	FELLA	KHAYA	NESSA	SASHA
ODIUM	TALUS	MAUVE	GROWN	FURZE	BALSA	FERIA	KILDA	NESTA	SAUNA
ODOUR	TAXUS	NAIVE	KNOWN	FUZZY	BANDA	FESTA	KOALA	NINJA	SCALA
OLEUM	TENUE	NAVVY	MAHWA	GAUZE	BARRA	FIRMA	KOFTA	NORIA	SCAPA
ONCUS	THRUM	NERVA	PRAWL	GAUZY	BASRA	FLORA	KOPPA	NORMA	SCHWA
ONKUS	TITUS	NERVE	PRAWN	GHAZI	BASTA	FLOTA	KOREA	NUBIA	SCUBA
OPIUM	TONUS	NERVI	PROWL	GLAZE	BEKAA	FONDA	KORMA	NUCHA	SELVA
ORCUS	TOQUE	NERVO	SCHWA	GONZO	BELGA	FOSSA	KRONA	NULLA	SENNA
ORGUE	TORUS	NERVY	SCOWL	GRAZE	BEMBA	FOVEA	KUALA	NYALA	SENZA
ORMUZ	TROUT	NIEVE	SCOWP	HUZZA	BERIA	GALBA	KURMA	NYASA	SEPIA
ORTUS	TUQUE	OGIVE	SHAWL	IBIZA	BOHEA	GALEA	LABDA	NYSSA	SERRA
OTIUM	UNCUS	OLIVE	SHAWM	JAZZY	BOTHA	GAMBA	LAMIA	OCREA	SHEBA
PICUS	UNCUT	PARVO	SHOWN	KHAZI	BRAVA	GAMMA	LANKA	OMEGA	SHIVA
PILUM	UNDUE	PEEVE	SHOWY	KUDZU	BREDA	GANDA	LARVA	OPERA	SHOLA
PILUS	VADUZ	PIAVE	SNOWY	LAZZO	BUCCA	GANJA	LASSA	OSAKA	SHONA
PIOUS	VAGUE	PRIVY	SPAWN	LISZT	BULLA	GARDA	LAURA	OSSIA	SIDHA
PIPUL	VAGUS	PROVE	STEWS	MAIZE	BURMA	GEMMA	LAVRA	OSTIA	SIGLA
PIQUE	VALUE	PROVO	STEWY	MEZZE	BURSA	GENOA	LEMMA	OUIDA	SIGMA
POPUP	VARUS	REEVE	STOWE	MEZZO	BWANA	GHANA	LERNA	OUIJA	SILVA
PROUD	VELUM	SALVE	THEWS	MIRZA	CANNA	GONNA	LHASA	PACHA	SIMBA
PROUT	VENUE	SALVO	TRAWL	MONZA	CARTA	GOTHA	LIANA	PADMA	SITKA
PSEUD	VENUS	SAVVY	TREWS	MUZZY	CASCA	GOTTA	LIBRA	PAISA	SITTA
PYRUS	VIRUS	SELVA	EPOXY	PIEZO	CELLA	GOUDA	LIBYA	PALEA	SOFIA
QUEUE	VITUS	SERVE	PROXY	PIZZA	CHEKA	GRETA	LLAMA	PANDA	SOLFA
RAMUS	VOGUE	SERVO	TWIXT	PLAZA	CHEWA	GUANA	LOOFA	PANGA	SOPRA
REBUS	WHAUP	SHAVE	ALLYL	PRIZE	CHICA	GUAVA	LORCA	PARKA	SOUSA
REBUT	WHAUR	SHIVA	BERYL	PZAZZ	CHINA	GUMMA	LORNA	PARMA	SPICA
RECUR	YAKUT	SHIVE	CALYX	RITZY	CHOTA	GUTTA	LUBRA	PASHA	SPINA
REMUE	ABOVE	SHOVE	DENYS	SEIZE	CILIA	HAIDA	LUCIA	PASTA	STELA
REMUS	AGAVE	SIEVE	EMLYN	SENZA	CILLA	HAIFA	LUFFA	PATNA	STOGA
RERUN	ALIVE	SILVA	EMRYS	SWAZI	CINNA	HAKKA	LYCRA	PAUSA	STOLA
REVUE	BEVVY	SKIVE	ETHYL	SWIZZ	CIRCA	HALFA	LYDIA	PELLA	STOMA
RHEUM	BRAVA	SLAVE	GRAYS	TAZZA	CLARA	HALMA	MAFIA	PELMA	STRIA
RISUS	BRAVE	SOLVE	GREYS	TEAZE	COBIA	HASTA	MAGHA	PENNA	STUKA
ROGUE	BRAVO	STAVE	HEXYL	TIZZY	COBRA	HAUSA	MAGMA	PETRA	STUPA
ROQUE	BREVE	STEVE	KENYA	TOWZE	COCOA	HEDDA	MAGNA	PICEA	SULFA
RUFUS	CALVE	STOVE	KHAYA	WHIZZ	COLZA	HELGA	MAHUA	PIETA	SULLA
RUNUP	CARVE	SUAVE	LIBYA	WOOZY	COMMA	HENNA	MAHWA	PINNA	SUMMA
SARUS	CARVY	TREVI	LLOYD	**5:5**	COPRA	HERMA	MALTA	PINTA	SUNDA
SCAUP	CHEVY	TROVE	OXEYE		COSTA	HEVEA	MALTA	PIPPA	SUPRA
SCAUR	CHIVE	VALVE	PEPYS	ABABA	COTTA	HILDA	MAMBA	PITTA	SURYA

SUTRA	ZEBRA	ESTOC	BEGAD	FOXED	NOMAD	UNFED	ANODE	BRACE	CONDE
SUVLA	ZERDA	ETHIC	BIFID	FRAUD	NOTED	UNWED	ANOLE	BRAKE	CONGÉ
SYRIA	ZORBA	FOLIC	BIPED	FREED	OCTAD	UPEND	APACE	BRAVE	CONTE
TABLA	ACERB	FRANC	BIPOD	FREUD	OILED	USTED	APAGE	BREDE	COOEE
TAIGA	ADLIB	GAMIC	BLAND	FRIED	OVOID	VALID	APODE	BREME	COPSE
TALEA	ARDEB	GENIC	BLEED	FROND	PAVID	VAPID	APPLE	BREVE	CORFE
TALMA	BEROB	HAVOC	BLEND	FUMED	PILED	VEXED	AREDE	BRIBE	CORSE
TAMPA	BLURB	ILEAC	BLIND	FUSED	PLAID	VIAND	ARENE	BRIDE	COUDÉ
TANGA	CABOB	ILIAC	BLOND	GATED	PLEAD	VIRID	ARETE	BRINE	COUPE
TANKA	CALEB	INDIC	BLOOD	GELID	POSED	VIVID	ARGUE	BRIZE	COYNE
TATRA	CARIB	IONIC	BOARD	GLAND	POUND	VOZHD	ARISE	BROKE	CRAKE
TAZZA	CAROB	ISAAC	BORED	GLUED	PROUD	WANED	ARKLE	BROSE	CRANE
TERRA	CELEB	KUFIC	BOUND	GONAD	PSEUD	WAVED	AROSE	BRUCE	CRAPE
TESLA	CHUBB	LILAC	BOWED	GORED	PUTID	WEALD	ARTIE	BRULE	CRARE
TESSA	CLIMB	LOGIC	BOXED	GOURD	RABID	WEIRD	ASIDE	BRUME	CRATE
TESTA	COOMB	LUDIC	BRAID	GRAND	RAGED	WIELD	ATONE	BRUTE	CRAVE
TETRA	COURB	LYRIC	BRAND	GREED	RAKED	WIRED	ATTLE	BUDGE	CRAZE
THECA	CRUMB	MAGIC	BREAD	GRIND	RAPID	WORLD	AVOUÉ	BUGLE	CREME
THEMA	CUBEB	MANIC	BREED	GUARD	RAYED	WOULD	AWAKE	BULGE	CREPE
THETA	DEMOB	MEDIC	BROAD	GUILD	RIGID	WOUND	AWARE	BUNCE	CRETE
THUJA	EXURB	MEDOC	BROOD	GUYED	ROPED	YCLAD	AWOKE	BURKE	CREWE
THUYA	HOREB	MELIC	BUILD	HEALD	ROUND	YIELD	AYRIE	BUTTE	CRIME
TIARA	JACOB	MESIC	CAULD	HEARD	SALAD	ABASE	AZOTE	CABLE	CRISE
TIBIA	JELAB	METIC	CHARD	HEROD	SAPID	ABATE	AZURE	CACHE	CROCE
TIKKA	KABOB	MIMIC	CHILD	HEXAD	SATED	ABELE	AZYME	CADGE	CROME
TILIA	KEBAB	MUSIC	CHORD	HIRED	SCALD	ABIDE	BADGE	CADRE	CRONE
TINEA	KEBOB	NOMIC	CHYND	HOARD	SCOLD	ABODE	BAIZE	CAINE	CRORE
TONGA	NABOB	NSPCC	CLOUD	HOLED	SCROD	ABOVE	BALFE	CALPE	CROZE
TOSCA	NAMIB	OLEIC	CODED	HOUND	SHARD	ABUSE	BARGE	CALVE	CRUDE
TREMA	NAWAB	OPTIC	CORED	HUMID	SHERD	ACUTE	BARRE	CARLE	CRUSE
TSUBA	PLUMB	PANIC	COULD	HYOID	SHRED	ADAGE	BASLE	CARTE	CURIE
TSUGA	RAHAB	PUBIC	COXED	ILIAD	SNEAD	ADDLE	BASTE	CARVE	CURSE
TYPHA	RAJAB	PUNIC	CREED	IMBED	SNOOD	ADIGE	BATHE	CASTE	CURVE
ULEMA	RHOMB	RELIC	CRIED	IVIED	SOLID	ADOBE	BAYLE	CAUSE	CUTIE
ULTRA	RHUMB	RORIC	CROWD	IZARD	SOUND	ADORE	BEALE	CEASE	CYCLE
UMBRA	SAHIB	RUNIC	CUBED	JADED	SOWND	AFIRE	BEIGE	CENSE	DALLE
UNITA	SCRAB	SALIC	CUPID	JEHAD	SPALD	AFORE	BELIE	CERNE	DAMME
UVULA	SCRUB	SONIC	CURED	JIHAD	SPEED	AGAPE	BELLE	CHAFE	DANAE
VANDA	SHRUB	STOIC	CYCAD	KEYED	SPEND	AGATE	BENNE	CHAPE	DANCE
VANYA	SLURB	TELIC	DATED	KNEAD	SPIED	AGAVE	BETTE	CHASE	DANTE
VEDDA	SQUAB	TONIC	DAVID	LAIRD	SPROD	AGILE	BÉVUE	CHERE	DAUBE
VENDA	SQUIB	TOPIC	DAZED	LAMED	SQUAD	AGLEE	BIBLE	CHIDE	DEFOE
VERSA	THROB	TOXIC	DOMED	LEPID	SQUID	AGONE	BILGE	CHILE	DELVE
VESPA	THUMB	TROIC	DREAD	LIARD	STAID	AGREE	BINGE	CHIME	DENSE
VESTA	VOCAB	TUNIC	DRIED	LIKED	STAND	AINEE	BITTE	CHINE	DESSE
VILLA	ZINEB	UGRIC	DRUID	LINED	STEAD	AISLE	BLADE	CHIVE	DEUCE
VIOLA	ANTIC	VAREC	DRYAD	LIPID	STEED	AKENE	BLAKE	CHLOE	DINGE
VIRGA	ANZAC	VEDIC	DYFED	LIVED	STOOD	ALATE	BLAME	CHOKE	DIODE
VISNA	ASDIC	XEBEC	EDGED	LIVID	STRAD	ALBEE	BLARE	CHORE	DIRGE
VISTA	ASPIC	ACRID	ELAND	LLOYD	SWARD	ALFIE	BLASÉ	CHOSE	DIXIE
VODKA	ATTIC	ADDED	ELIAD	LOBED	SWORD	ALGAE	BLAZE	CHUTE	DODGE
VOILA	AULIC	AHEAD	EMBED	LUCID	SYNOD	ALICE	BLOKE	CHYLE	DONEE
VOLGA	AURIC	AHMED	EMEND	LUNED	TAXED	ALIKE	BOCHE	CHYME	DONNE
VOLTA	AZOIC	ALGID	ENDED	LURID	TEPID	ALIVE	BODGE	CIRCE	DOONE
VOLVA	AZTEC	ALOUD	EPHOD	MANED	THIRD	ALLÉE	BOGIE	CLARE	DOREE
VULVA	BASIC	AMEND	ERARD	MAUND	THRID	ALONE	BOGLE	CLAVE	DOUCE
WAGGA	BLANC	ANEND	FADED	MIXED	TILED	ALURE	BOMBE	CLEPE	DOUSE
WILGA	BORIC	APAID	FAMED	MONAD	TIMID	AMAZE	BONCE	CLIME	DOWSE
WONGA	CIVIC	APHID	FARAD	MOPED	TIRED	AMBLE	BONZE	CLIVE	DOYLE
XENIA	COLIC	ARMED	FATED	MOULD	TREAD	AMENE	BOONE	CLONE	DRAKE
XHOSA	COMIC	AROID	FETID	MOUND	TREND	AMICE	BOOZE	CLOSE	DRAPE
YAKKA	CONIC	AVOID	FIELD	MOVED	TRIAD	AMINE	BOREE	CLOVE	DRERE
YALTA	COSEC	AWARD	FIEND	MUCID	TRIED	AMPLE	BORNE	CLOZE	DRIVE
YARFA	CUBIC	AXOID	FIORD	MUTED	TUMID	AMUSE	BOTTE	CLYDE	DROME
YARRA	CUFIC	BAIRD	FIXED	NAIAD	TWEED	ANELE	BOULE	COADE	DRONE
YARTA	CYNIC	BAKED	FJORD	NAKED	TYNED	ANGLE	BOWIE	COHOE	DROVE
YERBA	DORIC	BATED	FLOOD	NAMED	TYPED	ANISE	BOYCE	COMBE	DRUPE
YUCCA	DULAC	BEARD	FLUID	NICAD	UNBED	ANKLE	BOYLE	COMTE	DRUZE
ZABRA	EOLIC	BEDAD	FOUND	NITID	UNDID	ANNIE	BOYNE		

DUNCE	FOULÉ	HEAVE	LEONE	MOYLE	PHILE	RIDGE	SHOVE	STOPE	TRIBE
DUPLE	FOYLE	HEDGE	LERNE	MUDGE	PHOBE	RIFLE	SHUTE	STORE	TRICE
EAGLE	FRAME	HEINE	LETHE	MULSE	PHONE	RILKE	SIDLE	STOVE	TRIKE
EDILE	FROZE	HELVE	LEVEE	MURRE	PHYLE	RILLE	SIEGE	STOWE	TRINE
EDUCE	FUDGE	HENCE	LIANE	MUSSE	PIAVE	RINSE	SIEVE	STUPE	TRIPE
EERIE	FUGUE	HENGE	LIEGE	MVULE	PIECE	ROGUE	SINCE	STYLE	TRITE
ELATE	FURZE	HERNE	LIGGE	NACHE	PIQUE	ROLFE	SINGE	STYME	TROPE
ELENE	FUSEE	HERSE	LILLE	NACRE	PISTE	RONDE	SKATE	SUAVE	TROVE
ELIDE	FUZEE	HESSE	LISLE	NAIVE	PIXIE	RONNE	SKIVE	SUCRE	TRUCE
ELITE	FYLDE	HINGE	LITHE	NANCE	PLACE	ROQUE	SLADE	SUEDE	TUFFE
ELOGE	GABLE	HITHE	LITRE	NAPPE	PLANE	RORKE	SLAKE	SUITE	TULLE
ELOPE	GADGE	HODGE	LIVRE	NASHE	PLATE	ROSSE	SLATE	SUPPE	TUQUE
ELUDE	GAFFE	HOARE	LOCKE	NEALE	PLUME	ROUGE	SLAVE	SURGE	TWICE
EMCEE	GASPÉ	HOMME	LODGE	NERVE	PODGE	ROULE	SLICE	SUZIE	TWINE
EMILE	GAUDE	HOOVE	LOIRE	NICHE	POISE	ROUSE	SLIDE	SWALE	UKASE
EMOTE	GAUGE	HORDE	LOOSE	NIECE	PONCE	ROUTE	SLIME	SWEDE	UMBLE
EMOVE	GAUZE	HORNE	LORNE	NIEVE	PORTE	RUBLE	SLIPE	SWINE	UNCLE
EMURE	GEARE	HORSE	LOUIE	NIOBE	POSSE	RUCHE	SLOPE	SWIPE	UNDUE
ENATE	GEESE	HOUSE	LOUPE	NITRE	POSTE	RUDGE	SLYPE	SWIRE	UNITE
ENDUE	GENIE	HOWBE	LOUSE	NOBLE	POULE	RUFFE	SMILE	SWORE	UNTIE
ENSUE	GENRE	HOYLE	LUCRE	NOISE	POUPE	RUPEE	SMITE	SYCEE	URATE
ENURE	GEODE	HULME	LUMME	NONCE	PRATE	RUSSE	SMOKE	SYNGE	URINE
EPODE	GERBE	HYTHE	LUNGE	NOOSE	PRICE	SABLE	SMOTE	TABLE	URITE
ERASE	GESSE	IMAGE	LYCÉE	NORSE	PRIDE	SABRE	SNAKE	TACHE	USAGE
ERNIE	GESTE	IMBUE	LYTHE	NUDGE	PRIME	SADHE	SNARE	TAINE	USURE
ERODE	GIGUE	INANE	MACLE	NURSE	PRISE	SADIE	SNIDE	TARGE	VAGUE
ETAGE	GLACE	INCLE	MADGE	OBESE	PRIZE	SAICE	SNIPE	TASSE	VALSE
ETAPE	GLADE	INDRE	MAEVE	OBOTE	PROBE	SAINE	SNORE	TASTE	VALUE
ETUDE	GLAZE	INDUE	MAHOE	OCHRE	PROKE	SALLE	SOANE	TAUBE	VALVE
ETWEE	GLEBE	INGLE	MAILE	OGIVE	PROLE	SALSE	SOARE	TAUPE	VANCE
EVADE	GLIDE	INURE	MAINE	OLDIE	PRONE	SALVE	SOCLE	TAWSE	VENUE
EVITE	GLOBE	IRATE	MAIRE	OLIVE	PROSE	SARGE	SOLDE	TEASE	VERGE
EVOKE	GLOVE	IRENE	MAIZE	OLLIE	PROVE	SASSE	SOLVE	TEAZE	VERNE
EXILE	GLUME	ISERE	MANGE	OMBRE	PRUDE	SATIE	SOMME	TEHEE	VERSE
EXINE	GNOME	ISSUE	MANSE	OPINE	PRUNE	SAUCE	SONDE	TEMPE	VERVE
EXODE	GOOSE	JAMBE	MAPLE	ORATE	PUDGE	SAUTE	SOUSE	TENSE	VITAE
EXUDE	GORGE	JASPÉ	MARGE	ORGUE	PULSE	SCALE	SOWLE	TENUE	VOGUE
EYRIE	GORSE	JESSE	MARIE	OSAGE	PUREE	SCAPE	SPACE	TEPEE	VOICE
EYTIE	GOSSE	JOULE	MARLE	OUNCE	PURGE	SCARE	SPADE	TERCE	VOILE
FABLE	GOUGE	JOYCE	MARNE	OUTRE	PURSE	SCENE	SPARE	TERNE	VOLTE
FABRÉ	GRACE	JUDGE	MASSE	OVATE	PUSLE	SCONE	SPATE	TERSE	WAIVE
FADGE	GRADE	JUICE	MATTE	OVINE	QUAKE	SCOPE	SPEKE	THANE	WASTE
FALSE	GRAPE	KAMME	MAUVE	OVULE	QUEUE	SCORE	SPICE	THEME	WEAVE
FARCE	GRATE	KEBLE	MAYBE	OXEYE	QUIRE	SCREE	SPIKE	THERE	WEDGE
FARNE	GRAVE	KEDGE	MEBBE	OXIDE	QUITE	SCUTE	SPILE	THESE	WHALE
FAROE	GRAZE	KEMPE	MELEE	OXIME	QUOTE	SEARE	SPINE	THETE	WHERE
FARSE	GREBE	KERNE	MENGE	OZONE	RAINE	SEDGE	SPIRE	THINE	WHILE
FAURE	GRIME	KIDGE	MERGE	PADRE	RAISE	SEGUE	SPITE	THOLE	WHINE
FAUVE	GRIPE	KNAVE	MERLE	PAINE	RAKEE	SEINE	SPODE	THOSE	WHITE
FEARE	GROPE	KNIFE	MESNE	PAIRE	RANCE	SEIZE	SPOKE	THREE	WHOLE
FENCE	GROVE	KOINE	METRE	PANNE	RANEE	SELLE	SPORE	THROE	WHORE
FESSE	GRUFE	KOPJE	MEUSE	PARSE	RANGE	SENSE	SPREE	THULE	WHOSE
FESTE	GRUME	KRONE	MEZZE	PASSE	RANKE	SERGE	SPRUE	THYME	WILDE
FIBRE	GUIDE	KYLIE	MICHE	PASTE	RAREE	SERRE	SPUME	TILDE	WINCE
FICHE	GUILE	KYLOE	MIDGE	PAUSE	RAYLE	SERVE	STADE	TINGE	WITHE
FIERE	GUISE	KYRIE	MILNE	PAYEE	READE	SHADE	STAGE	TIREE	WODGE
FLAKE	GUNGE	LADLE	MINCE	PEACE	REBBE	SHAKE	STAKE	TITHE	WORSE
FLAME	GYNAE	LANCE	MINKE	PEASE	RECCE	SHALE	STALE	TITLE	WRITE
FLARE	HAGUE	LANDE	MITRE	PEEVE	REEDE	SHAME	STARE	TITRE	WROTE
FLUKE	HALLÉ	LAPSE	MIXTE	PEKOE	REEVE	SHAPE	STATE	TOILE	YAHVE
FLUME	HALSE	LARGE	MOIRE	PELEE	RÉGIE	SHARE	STAVE	TOISE	YONNE
FLUTE	HALVE	LARNE	MONTE	PENCE	RÈGLE	SHAVE	STELE	TONNE	YOUVE
FLYTE	HANCE	LATHE	MOORE	PENNE	REMUE	SHERE	STEVE	TOPEE	ZAIRE
FOLIE	HANSE	LATTE	MOOSE	PERCE	RENTE	SHINE	STILE	TOQUE	ZANTE
FORCE	HASTE	LEASE	MORNE	PERSE	REVIE	SHIRE	STIME	TORTE	ALOOF
FORGE	HAUSE	LEAVE	MORSE	PETRE	REVUE	SHITE	STIPE	TOWSE	BLUFF
FORME	HAUTE	LEDGE	MOTTE	PHARE	RHINE	SHIVE	STOKE	TOWZE	BRIEF
FORTE	HAWSE	LEESE	MOUSE	PHASE	RHONE	SHONE	STOLE	TRACE	CHAFF
FOSSE	HAYLE	LEGGE	MOVIE	PHEBE	RHYME	SHORE	STONE	TRADE	CHIEF

CHUFF	HMONG	BROTH	JONAH	PUNCH	WHICH	LUNGI	BRICK	KAPOK	STUNK
CLIFF	ICING	BRUSH	KEECH	QUASH	WHISH	MAHDI	BRINK	KAYAK	SWANK
DWARF	KIANG	BUMPH	KETCH	QUOTH	WIDTH	MALFI	BRISK	KIOSK	TEREK
FEOFF	KLANG	BUNCH	KUTCH	RAJAH	WINCH	MAORI	BROCK	KNACK	THANK
FLUFF	KLIEG	BURGH	LAITH	RALPH	WITCH	MARDI	BROOK	KNOCK	THICK
GLIFF	KRANG	BUTCH	LARCH	RANCH	WORTH	MASAI	BUICK	KODAK	THINK
GRAFF	KRIEG	CATCH	LATCH	RATCH	WRATH	MATAI	CAULK	KULAK	THUNK
GRIEF	KYANG	CINCH	LAUGH	REACH	WROTH	MENAI	CHALK	MALIK	TRACK
GRIFF	LIANG	CLASH	LEACH	REECH	YOUTH	MIAMI	CHARK	MERAK	TRECK
GRUFF	LYING	CLOTH	LEASH	REICH	ZILCH	MILLI	CHECK	MINSK	TRICK
GUELF	MAGOG	COACH	LEECH	REITH	ACINI	MOOLI	CHEEK	MUZAK	TRUCK
KALIF	OFLAG	CONCH	LEIGH	RETCH	AGAMI	MOSSI	CHICK	OZARK	TRUNK
KAMPF	ORANG	COUCH	LEISH	ROACH	AIOLI	MUFTI	CHINK	PLACK	TWANK
KLOOF	OWING	COUGH	LEITH	ROUGH	ALIBI	MULTI	CHIRK	PLANK	TWEAK
METIF	PIROG	COUTH	LINCH	RUNCH	ALTAI	MUSCI	CHOCK	PLONK	UZBEK
MOTIF	PRANG	CRASH	LOATH	SARAH	APPUI	NAAFI	CHOOK	PLUCK	VNECK
PILAF	PRONG	CRUSH	LOUGH	SAUCH	ASCII	NANDI	CHUCK	PLUNK	WHACK
PROOF	REJIG	CRWTH	LOUTH	SAUGH	ASSAI	NERVI	CHUNK	PRANK	WHELK
QUAFF	RUING	CUTCH	LUNCH	SCATH	BAHAI	OKAPI	CLACK	PRICK	WHISK
QUIFF	SCRAG	CZECH	LURCH	SHOAH	BAJRI	OMANI	CLANK	QUACK	WRACK
QUOIF	SCROG	DEATH	LYMPH	SHUSH	BAMBI	PARSI	CLARK	QUARK	WREAK
SCAFF	SHANG	DELPH	LYNCH	SIXTH	BLINI	PARTI	CLECK	QUICK	WRECK
SCARF	SHRUG	DEPTH	MANCH	SLASH	BONDI	PATTI	CLEEK	QUIRK	YAPOK
SCOFF	SLANG	DITCH	MARCH	SLOSH	BWAZI	PEPSI	CLERK	SHACK	YOICK
SCUFF	SLING	DOUGH	MARSH	SLOTH	CAPRI	PERAI	CLICK	SHANK	YUPIK
SCURF	SLUNG	DUTCH	MATCH	SLUSH	CENCI	PETRI	CLINK	SHARK	ZADOK
SERIF	SPRAG	EARTH	MEATH	SMASH	CHILI	POORI	CLOAK	SHEIK	ABDUL
SHEAF	SPRIG	ENOCH	MEITH	SMITH	COATI	QUASI	CLOCK	SHIRK	AFOUL
SHELF	SPROG	EPOCH	MICAH	SNASH	COCCI	RABBI	CLUCK	SHOCK	ALGOL
SKIFF	STING	FAITH	MILCH	SOOTH	CORGI	ROSSI	CLUNK	SHOOK	ALLYL
SNIFF	STUNG	FETCH	MINCH	SOUGH	DELHI	SALMI	CRACK	SHUCK	AMIEL
SNUFF	SWING	FIFTH	MIRTH	SOUTH	DHABI	SAUDI	CRANK	SKINK	ANGEL
SPIFF	SWUNG	FILCH	MONTH	SOWTH	DHOBI	SCIFI	CREAK	SKULK	ANNAL
SPOOF	THING	FILTH	MOOCH	STAPH	DHOTI	SERAI	CREEK	SKUNK	ANNUL
STAFF	THONG	FINCH	MORPH	STASH	DOUAI	SHCHI	CRICK	SLACK	ANVIL
STIFF	TWANG	FIRTH	MOUCH	SUTCH	DUBAI	SHOJI	CROAK	SLEEK	APPAL
STUFF	TYING	FITCH	MOUTH	SWASH	ENNUI	SINAI	CROCK	SLICK	APPEL
SWARF	UNRIG	FLASH	MULCH	SWATH	ENVOI	SOLTI	CRONK	SLINK	APRIL
THIEF	USING	FLESH	MUNCH	SWISH	FARCI	SPAHI	CROOK	SLUNK	ARDIL
WHARF	WHANG	FLUSH	MYNAH	SYLPH	FARSI	STASI	CRUCK	SMACK	ARGIL
WHIFF	WRING	FORTH	MYRRH	SYNTH	FERMI	SUNNI	DALEK	SMEEK	ARIEL
WOOLF	WRONG	FRESH	NADPH	SYRAH	FUNDI	SUOMI	DATUK	SMIRK	ARVAL
AGING	WRUNG	FRITH	NATCH	TAVAH	GARNI	SUSHI	DAYAK	SMOCK	ATOLL
ALONG	YOUNG	FROTH	NEAGH	TEACH	GHAZI	SWAMI	DRANK	SNACK	AURAL
AMONG	ABASH	GARTH	NEIGH	TEETH	GIGLI	SWAZI	DRINK	SNARK	AVAIL
BEFOG	AITCH	GIRTH	NINTH	TENCH	GOLGI	TORII	DRUNK	SNEAK	AWEEL
BEING	ALEPH	GLYPH	NORAH	TENTH	HADJI	TREVI	ERICK	SNECK	AWFUL
BHANG	ALLAH	GNASH	NORTH	THIGH	HAITI	TURKI	FLACK	SNICK	AXIAL
BOING	AMISH	GOTCH	NOTCH	THOTH	HANOI	TUTSI	FLANK	SNOEK	BABEL
BOONG	ANIGH	GRAPH	NYMPH	TILTH	HATHI	TUTTI	FLASK	SNOOK	BABUL
BOURG	ARISH	GULCH	OBEAH	TITCH	HINDI	VERDI	FLECK	SPANK	BAGEL
BRING	ASAPH	GULPH	OBIAH	TOOTH	HOURI	VILLI	FLICK	SPARK	BANAL
CHING	AWASH	HANCH	OMAGH	TORAH	ICENI	YEZDI	FLOCK	SPEAK	BASAL
CLANG	BATCH	HARSH	OOMPH	TORCH	IMARI	ZOMBI	FLUNK	SPECK	BASIL
CLING	BEACH	HATCH	PARCH	TOUCH	IMSHI	ABACK	FRACK	SPICK	BERYL
CLUNG	BEECH	HAUGH	PASCH	TOUGH	INARI	ACOCK	FRANK	SPOOK	BETEL
CRAIG	BELCH	HEATH	PATCH	TRASH	INDRI	ALACK	FROCK	SPUNK	BEVEL
DEBAG	BENCH	HEIGH	PEACH	TROTH	IRAQI	AMUCK	FREAK	STACK	BEZEL
DEBUG	BERTH	HEUGH	PERCH	TRUTH	JINNI	APEAK	FRISK	STALK	BOWEL
DOING	BIRCH	HITCH	PILCH	URIAH	KANJI	BATIK	GLEEK	STANK	BRAWL
DYING	BIRTH	HOOCH	PINCH	VETCH	KARRI	BAULK	GLISK	STARK	BRILL
FLING	BITCH	HOOSH	PITCH	VLACH	KAURI	BLACK	GOPAK	STEAK	BROIL
FLONG	BLIGH	HORAH	PLATH	VOUCH	KHAKI	BLANK	GREEK	STEEK	BROOL
FLUNG	BLUSH	HOTCH	PLUSH	WATCH	KHAZI	BLEAK	HÁ{\C}	STICK	CABAL
GLOGG	BOOTH	HOUGH	POACH	WAUGH	KOORI	BLINK	EK	STINK	CAMEL
GOING	BOSCH	HUMPH	POOCH	WEIGH	KUKRI	BLOCK	HACEK	STOCK	CANAL
GREGG	BOTCH	HUNCH	PORCH	WELCH	LASKI	BRACK	HOICK	STOOK	CAROL
GRIEG	BOUGH	HUTCH	POUCH	WELSH	LATHI	BRANK	KANAK	STORK	CAVIL
GULAG	BRASH	IRISH	PSYCH	WENCH	LIPPI	BREAK		STUCK	CECIL

CEORL	JEBEL	PIXEL	THIRL	GALAM	STEAM	BOSUN	FREON	LYSIN	RERUN
CHILL	JEWEL	PRAWL	TIDAL	GARUM	STORM	BRAIN	FROWN	MACON	RESIN
CHIRL	JOUAL	PRIAL	TONAL	GLEAM	STRUM	BRAWN	FURAN	MASON	RHEIN
CHURL	JUGAL	PRILL	TOTAL	GLOOM	SWARM	BRIAN	FUTON	MATIN	RICAN
CIBOL	KABUL	PROWL	TOWEL	GOLEM	THERM	BROWN	GABON	MAVIN	RICIN
CIVIL	KEBEL	PUPAL	TRAIL	GRIMM	THRUM	BRUIN	GALEN	MELON	RIPEN
COBOL	KERAL	PUPIL	TRAWL	GROOM	TOTEM	BURIN	GAZON	MESON	RIPON
CORAL	KNARL	QUAIL	TRIAL	HAREM	UNARM	BYRON	GIVEN	MILAN	RISEN
COXAL	KNEEL	QUELL	TRILL	HAULM	UNDAM	CABIN	GLEAN	MORAN	RIVEN
CRAWL	KNELL	QUILL	TROLL	HEXAM	VELUM	CAIRN	GLUON	MORIN	ROBIN
CREEL	KNOLL	RATEL	TRULL	HILUM	VENOM	CAJUN	GOLAN	MORON	RODIN
CRUEL	KNURL	RAVEL	TWILL	HIRAM	VROOM	CANON	GOWAN	MOURN	ROHAN
CUPEL	KRAAL	REBEL	TWIRL	HOKUM	XYLEM	CAPON	GRAIN	MUCIN	ROMAN
DEBEL	KRILL	REGAL	TYROL	HYLUM	AARON	CAVAN	GREEN	MYRON	ROSIN
DECAL	LABEL	RENAL	UDALL	IDIOM	ACORN	CHAIN	GROAN	NINON	ROUEN
DEVIL	LAPEL	REPEL	UMBEL	ILEUM	ACTIN	CHURN	GROIN	NISAN	ROWAN
DITAL	LEGAL	REVEL	UNTIL	ILIUM	ACTON	CLEAN	GROWN	NITON	RUBIN
DOWEL	LEVEL	RIVAL	USUAL	IMAUM	ADMIN	CLOWN	GUYON	NIXON	RUMEN
DRAWL	LIBEL	RIYAL	VENAL	INARM	ADORN	CODON	HALON	NOMEN	SABIN
DRILL	LOCAL	ROWEL	VIGIL	INIUM	AGAIN	COIGN	HAVEN	NUMEN	SALON
DROLL	LOYAL	ROYAL	VINYL	ISLAM	AIDAN	COLIN	HAYDN	NYLON	SARAN
DROOL	LYSOL	RURAL	VIRAL	JORUM	AIKEN	COLON	HAZAN	OAKEN	SARIN
DUVAL	MANUL	RYDAL	VITAL	KELIM	ALBAN	CONAN	HELEN	OATEN	SATAN
DWELL	MEDAL	SABAL	VOCAL	KILIM	ALDAN	CORIN	HERON	OCEAN	SATIN
EASEL	MERIL	SAHEL	VOWEL	KOKUM	ALIEN	COVEN	HOGAN	ODEON	SAXON
EMAIL	METAL	SCOWL	WEILL	LOCUM	ALIGN	COWAN	HONAN	OFTEN	SCION
ENROL	METOL	SCULL	WHEAL	MADAM	ALLAN	COZEN	HOSEN	OGGIN	SCORN
EQUAL	MIAUL	SEOUL	WHEEL	MAXIM	ALLEN	CREON	HUMAN	OLDEN	SEDAN
ETHAL	MODAL	SEPAL	WHIRL	MINIM	AMAIN	CROWN	HURON	OLEIN	SEMEN
ETHYL	MODEL	SHALL	WHORL	MODEM	AMMAN	CUBAN	HYMEN	ONION	SERIN
EXCEL	MOGUL	SHAWL	YODEL	NAHUM	ANION	CUMIN	IBSEN	ORGAN	SEVEN
EXPEL	MONAL	SHEEL	YOKEL	NIZAM	ANSON	DAGON	INION	ORION	SHAUN
EXTOL	MORAL	SHELL	YOULL	NOTUM	ANTON	DAMAN	INJUN	ORLON	SHEEN
FANAL	MOREL	SHIEL	ZONAL	NOVUM	APRON	DAMON	IRGUN	ORPEN	SHORN
FATAL	MOTEL	SHILL	ABEAM	OAKUM	ARDEN	DECON	IXION	ORTON	SHOWN
FECAL	MURAL	SHOAL	ABRAM	OCCAM	ARGON	DEIGN	JAPAN	OSMAN	SIDON
FERAL	NASAL	SIBYL	ABRIM	ODIUM	ARIAN	DEMON	JASON	PAEAN	SIMON
FETAL	NATAL	SIGIL	ABYSM	OGHAM	ARRAN	DEWAN	JAVAN	PAGAN	SIREN
FIDEL	NAVAL	SISAL	ADEEM	OLEUM	ARSON	DIVAN	JUPON	PECAN	SITIN
FINAL	NAVEL	SKILL	ADSUM	OPIUM	ARYAN	DIWAN	KEVIN	PEKAN	SIVAN
FLAIL	NEBEL	SKIRL	ALARM	OTIUM	ASHEN	DOLIN	KLEIN	PEKIN	SKEAN
FOCAL	NEPAL	SKOAL	ALBUM	PHNOM	ASIAN	DOORN	KNOWN	PERON	SKEIN
FOREL	NEVEL	SKULL	ANNAM	PILUM	ASPEN	DOYEN	KORAN	PHEON	SLAIN
FRAIL	NEWEL	SMALL	AXIOM	PRIAM	ASTON	DOZEN	KYLIN	PINON	SLOAN
FRILL	NICOL	SMELL	ASSAM	PRISM	ASWAN	DRAIN	LADEN	PIÑON	SOKEN
FUGAL	NIGEL	SNAIL	BEGUM	PSALM	ATLIN	DRAWN	LAGAN	PITON	SOLAN
GAVEL	NIHIL	SNARL	BESOM	PURIM	ATMAN	DROWN	LATEN	PLAIN	SOLON
GAYAL	NIVAL	SOKOL	BLOOM	QUALM	AUDEN	DUPIN	LATIN	PLEIN	SPAIN
GHOUL	NOBEL	SPALL	BOSOM	REALM	AUXIN	DYLAN	LEARN	POTIN	SPAWN
GHYLL	NODAL	SPELL	BREAM	REARM	AVIAN	EDWIN	LEMAN	POWAN	SPEAN
GIMEL	NOTAL	SPIEL	BREEM	RHEUM	AVION	EGDON	LEMON	PRAWN	SPOON
GNARL	NOVEL	SPILL	BROOM	SALEM	AWARN	EIKON	LENIN	PREEN	SPURN
GOGOL	NOXAL	SPOIL	BUXOM	SATEM	BACON	ELFIN	LEVEN	PRION	STAIN
GRAAL	OCTAL	SPOOL	CDROM	SCLIM	BADEN	ELGIN	LEVIN	PUGIN	STEEN
GRAIL	OFFAL	STALL	CECUM	SCRAM	BAIRN	ELLEN	LIKEN	PYLON	STEIN
GRILL	ORIEL	STEAL	CHARM	SCRIM	BALAN	ELSAN	LINEN	QUEEN	STERN
GROWL	ORVAL	STEEL	CHASM	SCRUM	BARON	ELTON	LININ	QUERN	SUDAN
GRUEL	OUSEL	STILL	CLAIM	SEDUM	BASAN	ELVAN	LIVEN	QUOIN	SUGAN
HAVEL	OUZEL	STOLL	CORAM	SEISM	BASIN	EMDEN	LODEN	QURAN	SUSAN
HAZEL	PANEL	STOOL	CREAM	SELIM	BATON	EMLYN	LOGAN	RADON	SWAIN
HEGEL	PAPAL	SWELL	DATUM	SERUM	BEGAN	EOSIN	LOMAN	RAMAN	SWOON
HEXYL	PEARL	SWILL	DENIM	SHAWM	BEGIN	ETAIN	LOWAN	RAVEN	SWORN
HOTEL	PEDAL	SWIRL	DREAM	SKELM	BEGUN	EVIAN	LOZEN	RAYON	TAKEN
HOVEL	PENAL	SYBIL	DURUM	SKRIM	BEHAN	FANON	LUCAN	REDAN	TALON
IDEAL	PERIL	TAMIL	ENARM	SMARM	BENIN	FEIGN	LUMEN	REDON	TATIN
IDYLL	PETAL	TAXOL	ENORM	SODOM	BETON	FELON	LUPIN	REGAN	TAUON
IMPEL	PHIAL	TEXEL	EPSOM	SOLUM	BISON	FLOWN	LUTIN	REIGN	TAXIN
IQBAL	PIPAL	THILL	ESROM	SPASM	BLOWN	FLUON	LUTON	RENAN	TAXON
JAVEL	PIPUL	THIOL	FORUM	SPERM	BORON	FOEHN	LUZON		TEIGN

TENON	BEANO	GOMBO	ORFEO	TABOO	POPUP	AFTER	DECOR	GREER	MIMER
TETON	BIMBO	GONZO	OROMO	TAINO	PRIMP	AGGER	DEFER	HALER	MINER
TEXAN	BINGO	GUACO	ORTHO	TANGO	QUILP	AIRER	DEMUR	HAVER	MINOR
THEGN	BOMBO	GUANO	OUTDO	TASSO	RECAP	AKBAR	DETER	HEWER	MISER
THORN	BONGO	GUMBO	OUTGO	TEMPO	RUNUP	ALDER	DEWAR	HEYER	MIXER
TIGON	BRAVO	GUSTO	OVOLO	TOKYO	SALEP	ALTAR	DIKER	HIKER	MODER
TIMON	BRUNO	GYMNO	PABLO	TONDO	SCALP	ALTER	DINAR	HILAR	MOLAR
TITAN	BUCKO	GYPPO	PALIO	TORSO	SCAMP	AMBER	DINER	HIRER	MOPER
TOKEN	BUFFO	HALLO	PANTO	TRURO	SCARP	AMOUR	DIVER	HIVER	MOTOR
TOMAN	BUNCO	HARPO	PAOLO	TURBO	SCAUP	ANEAR	DONAR	HOMER	MOVER
TOXIN	BUROO	HECTO	PAREO	TURCO	SCOOP	ANGER	DONOR	HONOR	MOWER
TRAIN	BURRO	HELIO	PARVO	UREDO	SCOUP	ANKER	DOUAR	HOVER	NADER
TREEN	CACAO	HELLO	PASEO	VERSO	SCOWP	ANTAR	DOVER	HUMOR	NADIR
TROON	CAIRO	HIPPO	PATIO	VIDEO	SCRAP	ARBOR	DOWER	HYPER	NAGOR
TURIN	CAMEO	HONDO	PEDRO	VIREO	SCRIP	ARDOR	DREAR	ICHOR	NAZIR
TWAIN	CAMPO	HULLO	PESTO	VIRGO	SCULP	ARMOR	DRIER	ICKER	NEPER
UHLAN	CANTO	HYDRO	PETTO	VOLVO	SETUP	ASHER	DRYER	IDLER	NEVER
UNION	CARGO	IDAHO	PHENO	VULGO	SHARP	ASKER	DURER	IMMER	NIDOR
UNMAN	CASCO	IGAPO	PHOTO	WALDO	SHEEP	ASPER	DYKER	INCUR	NIGER
UNPEN	CELLO	IGLOO	PIANO	YAHOO	SHLEP	ASTER	EAGER	INFER	NOSER
UNPIN	CENTO	IMAGO	PIEZO	YOBBO	SITUP	ASTIR	EATER	INNER	OAKER
UPTON	CHACO	INIGO	PINGO	ZAMBO	SKELP	ATTAR	EDGAR	INTER	OCCUR
URBAN	CHIAO	INTRO	PINKO	ZEPPO	SKIMP	AUGER	EDGER	IZMIR	OCHER
URSON	CHICO	IROKO	PINTO	ZINCO	SLEEP	AUGUR	EGGAR	JOKER	OCKER
UTURN	CHINO	JAMBO	PLATO	ZORRO	SLOOP	BABAR	EIDER	JUMAR	ODDER
VEGAN	CHOCO	JELLO	PLUTO	AESOP	SLUMP	BAKER	EIGER	JUROR	ODOUR
VENIN	CHOKO	JINGO	POLIO	APOOP	SLURP	BALER	ELDER	KAFIR	OFFER
VISON	CHOKO	JOCKO	PONGO	ATRIP	SNOOP	BALOR	ELGAR	KEDAR	OGIER
VIXEN	CISCO	JUMBO	PORNO	BEBOP	STAMP	BAYER	ELMER	KEFIR	OILER
WAGON	COMBO	JUNCO	PORTO	BLEEP	STEEP	BIKER	ELVER	KNURR	OLDER
WAKEN	COMPO	JUNTO	POTOO	BLIMP	STIRP	BITER	EMBER	LABOR	OMBER
WAXEN	CONDO	KARNO	POTTO	BLOOP	STOEP	BLAIR	EMMER	LAGER	ONCER
WHEEN	CONGO	KENDO	PRADO	CHAMP	STOMP	BLEAR	ENSOR	LASER	OPHIR
WIDEN	CORSO	KIMBO	PRIMO	CHEAP	STOOP	BONAR	ENTER	LATER	ORDER
WIGAN	CORVO	KONGO	PROMO	CHEEP	STOUP	BONER	EPHOR	LAVER	ORMER
WITAN	COSMO	LARGO	PROVO	CHIMP	STRAP	BORER	ERROR	LAYER	OSCAR
WODEN	CREDO	LASSO	PUNTO	CHIRP	STREP	BOWER	ESKER	LAZAR	OSIER
WOKEN	CURIO	LAZZO	PUTTO	CHOMP	STRIP	BOXER	ESTER	LEGER	OTHER
WOMAN	DANDO	LENTO	QUITO	CHUMP	STROP	BOYAR	ETHER	LEHAR	OTTAR
WOMEN	DECKO	LIMBO	RADIO	CLAMP	STUMP	BRIAR	EULER	LEMUR	OTTER
WOVEN	DEKKO	LINGO	RAMBO	CLASP	SWAMP	BRIER	FABER	LEPER	OUTER
WYMAN	DIAZO	LLANO	RATIO	CLEEP	SWEEP	BUYER	FACER	LEVER	OWLER
XENON	DIEGO	LOTTO	RECTO	CLOMP	SWOOP	CABER	FAKER	LIBER	OWNER
YAMEN	DILDO	LUCIO	REPRO	CLUMP	SYRUP	CALOR	FAKIR	LIFER	OXTER
YEARN	DINGO	MACHO	RETRO	CRAMP	THRIP	CAPER	FAVOR	LIGER	PACER
YEMEN	DISCO	MACRO	RHINO	CREEP	THUMP	CARER	FEMUR	LIMER	PAGER
YUKON	DITTO	MAIKO	RHODO	CRIMP	TRAMP	CATER	FETOR	LINER	PAMIR
YULAN	DOBRO	MALMO	RODEO	CRISP	TROMP	CEDAR	FEVER	LITER	PAPER
ZAYIN	DOGGO	MAMBO	ROLLO	CROUP	TROOP	CESAR	FEWER	LIVER	PATER
ZIGAN	DOURO	MANGO	ROMEO	CRUMP	TRUMP	CHAIR	FIBER	LOBAR	PAYER
ABACO	DRACO	MARCO	RONDO	DROOP	TULIP	CHEER	FINER	LONER	PETER
ADDIO	DUNNO	MATLO	RONEO	EQUIP	TWERP	CHIRR	FIVER	LOSER	PIPER
AGGRO	DUOMO	MESTO	ROSCO	ESTOP	TWIRP	CHOIR	FIXER	LOVER	PLIER
ALAMO	ERATO	METRO	RUSSO	FLUMP	UNCAP	CHURR	FLAIR	LOWER	POKER
AMIGO	FACTO	MEZZO	SALVO	FRUMP	UNRIP	CIDER	FLEUR	LUGER	POLAR
AMINO	FALDO	MICRO	SAMBO	GALOP	UNZIP	CIGAR	FLIER	LUNAR	POSER
AMNIO	FARGO	MINHO	SAMSO	GETUP	USURP	CLEAR	FLOOR	MACER	POWER
ANGLO	FEMTO	MOLTO	SANTO	GRASP	WHAUP	COLOR	FLOUR	MAJOR	PRIOR
APPRO	FIBRO	MONDO	SAYSO	GROUP	WHELP	COPER	FLYER	MAKAR	PUDOR
AUDIO	FOLIO	MOSSO	SECCO	GRUMP	WHOOP	CORER	FOYER	MAKER	QAJAR
AVISO	FORGO	MOTTO	SERVO	GUIMP	LECOQ	COVER	FRIAR	MALAR	QATAR
BABOO	FUERO	MUCRO	SHAKO	HANAP	TALAQ	COWER	FUROR	MANOR	QUEER
BALOO	GAMBO	MUNGO	SLIGO	JALAP	ABDAR	CRIER	GAPER	MASER	RACER
BANCO	GARBO	MUNRO	SORBO	JULEP	ABEAR	CRUOR	GEBER	MATER	RADAR
BANJO	GECKO	NACHO	SORDO	MIXUP	ABHOR	CUPAR	GIVER	MAYOR	RAKER
BASHO	GESSO	NEGRO	SORGO	ORLOP	ABLER	CURER	GLAIR	MAZER	RAVER
BASSO	GIPPO	NERVO	SOTTO	OXLIP	ACTOR	DAKAR	GOFER	METER	RAZOR
BASTO	GISMO	NGAIO	SPADO	PLUMP	ADDER	DATER	GONER	MEYER	RECUR
BAZOO	GOBBO	NITRO	STYLO	POLYP	AFEAR	DEBAR	GOWER	MILER	REFER

RIDER	TIBER	AMISS	CHOPS	FAVUS	HORUS	LOONS	ORCUS	SAGES	TEXAS
RIGOR	TIGER	ANDES	CLASS	FECES	HOURS	LORDS	ORNIS	SAILS	TEXTS
RIPER	TILER	ANGUS	CLAUS	FELIS	HULKS	LORIS	ORRIS	SALES	THAIS
RISER	TIMER	ANKUS	CLUBS	FETUS	HUMUS	LOTOS	ORTUS	SALTS	THEWS
RIVER	TIMOR	APHIS	COCOS	FIDES	HUNKS	LOTUS	PAGES	SAMOS	THUGS
ROGER	TOLAR	APSIS	COKES	FILMS	HUNTS	LOUIS	PAINS	SANDS	TIBBS
ROKER	TONER	ARCUS	COLTS	FINIS	HUSKS	LUNGS	PAIRS	SAROS	TILES
ROMER	TOPER	ARGUS	COMBS	FINKS	ICTUS	LUPUS	PALES	SARUS	TIMES
ROPER	TOWER	ARIES	COMUS	FIVES	IDEAS	LYSIS	PANTS	SATIS	TIROS
ROTOR	TRIER	ARLES	COOKS	FLATS	IDRIS	MAGUS	PARIS	SCADS	TITUS
ROVER	TUBER	ARRAS	CORDS	FLEWS	ILEUS	MAINS	PARTS	SCOPS	TOILS
ROWER	TUDOR	ARRIS	CORPS	FLIES	INCUS	MANES	PEERS	SCOTS	TONGS
RULER	TUMOR	ARSIS	COSTS	FLOPS	INDUS	MANUS	PENIS	SEALS	TONUS
RUMOR	TUNER	ASCUS	CRABS	FLOSS	INNES	MASUS	PEPYS	SEMIS	TOOLS
SABER	TUTOR	ASHES	CRAPS	FOCUS	IRONS	MATES	PERKS	SHOPS	TORUS
SAFAR	TWOER	ATHOS	CRASS	FOLKS	ISLES	MATHS	PICUS	SHOTS	TOWNS
SAKER	TYLER	ATLAS	CRESS	FONDS	JACKS	MAVIS	PIERS	SHUTS	TRANS
SAPOR	UDDER	AULIS	CRIES	FOODS	JADIS	MEALS	PILES	SIGHS	TRAPS
SATYR	ULCER	AVENS	CROPS	FOOLS	JAKES	MEANS	PILLS	SIGNS	TREES
SAVER	ULNAR	BACKS	CROSS	FOOTS	JAMES	MEATS	PILUS	SILAS	TRESS
SAVOR	UMBER	BALLS	CUFFS	FORKS	JANUS	MEETS	PINES	SINUS	TREWS
SAYER	UNBAR	BANDS	CURDS	FORMS	JEANS	MELOS	PIOUS	SKINS	TRIES
SCAUR	UNDER	BANKS	CUTIS	FOURS	JERKS	METHS	PLEBS	SLATS	TROTS
SCOUR	UPPER	BANNS	CYRUS	FRANS	JESUS	METIS	PLOTS	SLIPS	TRUSS
SENOR	USHER	BARTS	DANES	FRIES	JINKS	MIDAS	POEMS	SLOPS	TUNIS
SEVER	UTHER	BASES	DARTS	FUCHS	JONES	MILES	POETS	SLUGS	TURPS
SEWER	UTTER	BASIS	DATES	FUMES	JORIS	MILLS	PONDS	SMUTS	TWIGS
SHEAR	VALOR	BATES	DAVIS	FUNDS	JUDAS	MIMUS	POOLS	SNAGS	TWINS
SHEER	VAPOR	BATHS	DEEDS	GADUS	JUMPS	MINOS	POPES	SNAPS	TYPES
SHIRR	VELAR	BEADS	DEGAS	GAINS	KEELS	MINUS	PORTS	SNOBS	UNCUS
SITAR	VICAR	BEANS	DELOS	GAIUS	KEEPS	MITES	POWYS	SOCKS	UNITS
SIXER	VIGOR	BELLS	DEMOS	GAMES	KELLS	MODUS	PRESS	SOLUS	URALS
SIZAR	VIPER	BENDS	DENIS	GASES	KEYES	MONKS	PSOAS	SORES	VAGUS
SKEER	VISOR	BEVIS	DENYS	GAUSS	KINGS	MORES	PUBIS	SORTS	VAILS
SKIER	VIZOR	BIRDS	DIALS	GENTS	KIPPS	MORUS	PYRUS	SOULS	VARUS
SKIRR	VOMER	BLESS	DIVES	GENUS	KIWIS	MOSES	PYXIS	SPATS	VEINS
SMEAR	VOTER	BLISS	DOCKS	GHATS	KRANS	MOTHS	QUADS	SPECS	VENUS
SNEER	WADER	BLUES	DOORS	GIBUS	KUDOS	MOULS	QUIDS	SPENS	VIBES
SOBER	WAFER	BODES	DORAS	GIFTS	KVASS	MUCUS	QUINS	SPIES	VIRUS
SODOR	WAGER	BOGUS	DORIS	GILES	LABIS	MUMPS	QUITS	SPOTS	VITIS
SOLAR	WALER	BOLAS	DORTS	GILLS	LACKS	MUSES	RACES	SPURS	VITUS
SONAR	WATER	BOLUS	DOWNS	GILTS	LAGOS	NAGAS	RAKES	STARS	VOTES
SOWER	WAVER	BONDS	DREGS	GIRLS	LAMPS	NAILS	RAMUS	STAYS	WAGES
SPEAR	WEBER	BONES	DRESS	GLANS	LAPIS	NAMES	RANKS	STEPS	WAITS
SPEER	WESER	BONUS	DRIES	GLASS	LARKS	NARES	RATES	STEWS	WAKES
SPOHR	WHAUR	BOOTS	DROPS	GLOSS	LAUDS	NARKS	REAMS	SUCKS	WALES
SPOOR	WHIRR	BORIS	DROSS	GOODS	LAWKS	NATES	REBUS	SUITS	WARES
STAIR	WIPER	BOWLS	DRUGS	GRASS	LEADS	NATUS	REEDS	SULKS	WATTS
STARR	WOOER	BRASS	DUCKS	GRAYS	LEEDS	NAXOS	REGIS	SWANS	WAVES
STEER	ZOHAR	BUCKS	DUKAS	GREYS	LEPUS	NEEDS	REINS	SWATS	WEEDS
STOOR	ABBAS	BUFFS	DUKES	GRITS	LEVIS	NEGUS	REMUS	SWISS	WEEKS
STOUR	ABIES	BULLS	DUMAS	GROSS	LEWES	NEVIS	RESTS	TABES	WELLS
SUDOR	ABYSS	BURNS	DUMPS	GUESS	LEWIS	NEWTS	REYES	TAGUS	WHIMS
SUGAR	ACRES	CABAS	EAVES	GULES	LEXIS	NEXUS	RIOTS	TAILS	WHIPS
SUPER	ADAMS	CAIUS	ELIAS	GULLS	LIKES	NIDUS	RISUS	TALES	WILDS
SUTOR	ADDIS	CAMAS	ELLIS	GYGES	LIMES	NISUS	RITES	TALKS	WILES
SWEAR	ADIOS	CAMIS	ELVES	GYRUS	LINES	NODES	ROBES	TALUS	WILTS
TABER	AEDES	CAMUS	ELVIS	HADES	LINKS	NODUS	ROCKS	TAMIS	WINGS
TABOR	AEGIS	CANES	EMBUS	HAIRS	LINUS	NONES	ROLLS	TAPAS	WIRES
TAKER	AGNES	CARDS	EMRYS	HANDS	LIONS	NOTES	ROOMS	TAPIS	WIVES
TALAR	AIDOS	CASES	ETATS	HEADS	LISTS	NOTTS	ROOTS	TAXIS	WOODS
TAMAR	AIRES	CATES	ETHOS	HEAPS	LITAS	NOYES	ROPES	TAXUS	WORCS
TAMER	ALANS	CELLS	EVANS	HEELS	LIVES	OASIS	ROSES	TEARS	WORDS
TAPER	ALDIS	CERES	EVENS	HERBS	LOCKS	OATES	RUFUS	TEENS	WORKS
TAPIR	ALIAS	CETUS	FACTS	HERTS	LOCUS	OCNUS	RUINS	TELOS	WORMS
TATAR	ALNUS	CHAOS	FAGUS	HILLS	LOESS	ODETS	RULES	TENDS	WRITS
TATER	ALOES	CHAPS	FAINS	HIVES	LOGOS	OFFAS	RUNES	TERES	XERES
TENOR	ALVIS	CHESS	FALLS	HOBBS	LOINS	ONCUS	SACHS	TERMS	XYRIS
THEIR	AMASS	CHIPS	FATES	HOCUS	LONGS	ONKUS	SACKS	TESTS	YARNS

YATES	BLOAT	DRIFT	GLOAT	LOVAT	ROBOT	TACIT	FICHU	BRONX	BEERY
YEARS	BLUNT	DROIT	GODET	MAGOT	ROGET	TAINT	HAIKU	CALIX	BELAY
YEATS	BLURT	DUCAT	GOSHT	MANET	ROIST	TAPET	HINDU	CALYX	BELLY
YIKES	BOAST	DURST	GRAFT	MARAT	ROOST	TAROT	JIMMU	CODEX	BENDY
YONKS	BOOST	DUVET	GRANT	MAROT	ROSET	TAUNT	KUDZU	CULEX	BERRY
YOURS	BRACT	ECLAT	GREAT	MEANT	ROSIT	TEMPT	MIAOU	DESEX	BETTY
YPRES	BRENT	EDICT	GREET	MERIT	ROUST	TENET	NANDU	DETOX	BEVVY
ZENOS	BREST	EGEST	GRIOT	MIDST	ROZET	TEVET	NAURU	EMBOX	BIBBY
ABAFT	BRUIT	EGRET	GRIST	MIGHT	SABOT	THEFT	NEHRU	FELIX	BIDDY
ABBOT	BRUNT	EGYPT	GROAT	MINOT	SAINT	THOFT	NOYAU	GUEUX	BILLY
ABORT	BUILT	EIGHT	GROUT	MOIST	SAULT	TIBET	PAREU	HELIX	BITTY
ABOUT	BURNT	EILAT	GRUNT	MONET	SCANT	TIGHT	PERDU	HYRAX	BLOWY
ABSIT	BURST	EJECT	GUEST	MORAT	SCENT	TOAST	PILAU	INDEX	BLUEY
ADAPT	CABOT	ELECT	GUILT	MOTET	SCOOT	TOBIT	POILU	KYLIX	BOBBY
ADEPT	CADET	ELIOT	GUYOT	MOULT	SCOTT	TRACT	PRAHU	LATEX	BOGEY
ADMIT	CAGOT	EMMET	HABET	MOUNT	SCOUT	TRAIT	SADHU	LIMAX	BOGGY
ADOPT	CAPET	ENACT	HABIT	MULCT	SCRAT	TRANT	SAMFU	MUREX	BONEY
ADULT	CAPOT	ERECT	HADNT	MUSIT	SHAFT	TREAT	SNAFU	PHLOX	BONNY
AFOOT	CAPUT	ERGOT	HASNT	NACHT	SHALT	TRENT	TUNKU	PODEX	BOOBY
AFRIT	CARAT	ERNST	HAULT	NIGHT	SHANT	TROUT	TURKU	PULEX	BOOTY
AGENT	CARET	ERUCT	HAUNT	NONET	SHEET	TRUST	UHURU	PYREX	BOOZY
AGIST	CHANT	ERUPT	HEART	OBIIT	SHIFT	TRYST	VERTU	RADIX	BOSEY
AGLET	CHART	ESCOT	HECHT	OCTET	SHIRT	TWEET	VIRTU	REDOX	BOSKY
ALERT	CHEAT	EVENT	HEIST	ONSET	SHOOT	TWILT	KIROV	RELAX	BOSSY
ALEUT	CHERT	EVERT	HELOT	ORBIT	SHORT	TWIST	NEGEV	RUMEX	BOTHY
ALLOT	CHEST	EVICT	HOAST	OUGHT	SHOUT	TWIXT	POPOV	SALIX	BRADY
ALOFT	CHIRT	EXACT	HOIST	OVERT	SHUNT	UNAPT	ABLOW	SILEX	BRINY
AMANT	CHOTT	EXALT	HOLST	OWLET	SIGHT	UNCUT	AGLOW	SOREX	BUBBY
AMBIT	CIVET	EXEAT	HURST	PAINT	SKEET	UNFIT	ALLOW	TELEX	BUDDY
AMENT	CLEAT	EXERT	IBERT	PALET	SKINT	UNGET	ARROW	UNMIX	BUGGY
AMORT	CLEFT	EXIST	IDIOT	PETIT	SKIRT	UNIAT	ASKEW	VARIX	BULKY
ANENT	CLIFT	EXULT	IMPOT	PICOT	SLANT	UNLIT	BEDEW	XEROX	BULLY
ANGST	CLINT	FACET	INAPT	PIERT	SLEET	UPSET	BELOW	ABBEY	BUMPY
APART	CLOOT	FAGOT	INEPT	PILOT	SLEPT	VALET	BULOW	ABRAY	BUNDY
APERT	CLOUT	FAINT	INERT	PINOT	SMART	VAULT	BYLAW	AGLEY	BUNGY
ARCOT	COAST	FAULT	INGOT	PIPIT	SMELT	VAUNT	CAREW	AGONY	BUNNY
ARENT	COLET	FAUST	INLET	PITOT	SMOLT	VELDT	ELBOW	ALLAY	BURLY
ARGOT	COMET	FEAST	INPUT	PIVOT	SNIFT	VERST	EMBOW	ALLEY	BUSBY
ARHAT	COOPT	FECIT	INSET	PLAIT	SNOOT	VISIT	ENDOW	ALLOY	BUSHY
ARIST	COROT	FEINT	INUIT	PLANT	SNORT	VIVAT	ENMEW	AMITY	BUSTY
ARMET	COUNT	FIGHT	INWIT	PLEAT	SNOUT	VOLET	ENSEW	AMPLY	BUTTY
ARRÊT	COURT	FILET	ISLET	POINT	SPALT	VOMIT	IMMEW	ANGRY	BYWAY
ASCOT	COVET	FIRST	ISMET	POSIT	SPART	WAIST	INDEW	ANNOY	CABBY
ASHET	CRAFT	FLEET	IZZAT	POULT	SPELT	WASNT	INLAW	ANOMY	CADDY
ASSET	CREPT	FLINT	JABOT	PREST	SPENT	WHEAT	KOTOW	APPAY	CADGY
ATILT	CREST	FLIRT	JAUNT	PRINT	SPILT	WHIFT	MACAW	APPLY	CAGEY
AUDIT	CROAT	FLOAT	JOINT	PROUT	SPLAT	WHIST	MIAOW	APTLY	CANDY
AUGHT	CROFT	FLOUT	JOIST	QUANT	SPLIT	WHOOT	NAVEW	ARRAY	CANNY
AVANT	CRUET	FOIST	JOUNT	QUART	SPORT	WIGHT	OXBOW	ASSAY	CAREY
AVAST	CRUST	FOUET	JOUST	QUEST	SPOUT	WORST	PAPAW	ATOMY	CARRY
AVERT	CRYPT	FOUNT	JURAT	QUIET	SPRAT	WREST	PSHAW	ATONY	CARVY
AWAIT	CUBIT	FRACT	KAPUT	QUILT	SPRIT	WRIST	RENEW	ATOPY	CATTY
BAHUT	CULET	FRIST	KARAT	QUINT	SPURT	WURST	SCRAW	AUNTY	CHARY
BEAST	CURST	FRONT	KARST	QUOIT	SQUAT	YACHT	SCREW	BACCY	CHEVY
BEAUT	DALIT	FROST	KNELT	RABAT	SQUIT	YAKUT	SCROW	BADDY	CHEWY
BEFIT	DAUNT	FRUIT	KNOUT	REACT	START	YEAST	SHREW	BADLY	CHIVY
BEGET	DAVIT	FUMET	KRAFT	REBUT	STENT	YOURT	SHROW	BAFFY	CHOKY
BENET	DEBIT	GAMUT	KRAUT	REFIT	STILT	ZAKAT	SINEW	BAGGY	CIGGY
BEPAT	DEBUT	GAULT	LACET	REIST	STINT	ADIEU	SQUAW	BALLY	CISSY
BERET	DEIST	GAUNT	LEANT	REMIT	STOAT	ANJOU	STRAW	BALMY	CIVVY
BESET	DELFT	GÉANT	LEAPT	REPOT	STOUT	BANTU	STREW	BANDY	CLARY
BESOT	DEPOT	GEIST	LEAST	RESET	STRUT	BAYOU	THREW	BARMY	COCKY
BIDET	DIDNT	GENET	LEGIT	RESIT	STUNT	BIJOU	THROW	BARRY	COLEY
BIGHT	DIGHT	GHOST	LICHT	REVET	STURT	BOYAU	UNLAW	BATTY	COLLY
BIGOT	DIGIT	GIANT	LICIT	RHETT	SWEAT	CORFU	WIDOW	BAWDY	COMFY
BIONT	DIVOT	GIGOT	LIGHT	RIANT	SWEET	COYPU	ADMIX	BEADY	CONEY
BLAST	DONAT	GILET	LIMIT	RIGHT	SWELT	CYMRU	AFFIX	BEAMY	COPPY
BLEAT	DOUBT	GLEET	LISZT	RIVET	SWEPT	ELIHU	ANNEX	BECKY	CORKY
BLEST	DRAFT	GLINT		ROAST	SWIFT	ENUGU	BORAX	BEEFY	CORNY

COVEY	DOYLY	FUZZY	HOLLY	LEERY	MUMMY	PERCY	ROPEY	STOGY	WARTY
COWRY	DRILY	GABBY	HONEY	LEFTY	MURKY	PERKY	RORTY	STONY	WASHY
COYLY	DRURY	GAILY	HONKY	LEGGY	MURRY	PERRY	ROWDY	STORY	WEARY
CRAZY	DRYLY	GAMAY	HOOEY	LESHY	MUSHY	PESKY	RUDDY	STRAY	WEEDY
CRECY	DUCHY	GAMMY	HOOKY	LILLY	MUSKY	PETTY	RUGBY	STUDY	WEENY
CRONY	DUCKY	GANNY	HORNY	LIMEY	MUSSY	PHONY	RUMMY	SUETY	WEEPY
CUBBY	DUDDY	GASSY	HORSY	LOAMY	MUSTY	PIETY	RUMPY	SULKY	WELLY
CUDDY	DUMMY	GAUDY	HOTLY	LOBBY	MUZZY	PIGGY	RUNNY	SULLY	WENDY
CUFFY	DUMPY	GAUZY	HOTTY	LOFTY	NANCY	PIGMY	RUSHY	SUNNY	WILLY
CULLY	DUROY	GAWKY	HOWDY	LOLLY	NANNY	PINKY	RUSTY	SURLY	WIMPY
CURLY	DURRY	GEMMY	HUBBY	LOOBY	NAPPY	PINNY	SADLY	TABBY	WINDY
CURRY	DUSKY	GENTY	HUFFY	LOONY	NARKY	PISKY	SAGGY	TACKY	WINEY
CURVY	DUSTY	GIBBY	HUNKY	LOOPY	NASTY	PITHY	SALLY	TAFFY	WISPY
CUSHY	EARLY	GIDDY	HURRY	LORRY	NATTY	PLATY	SALTY	TALLY	WITHY
CUTEY	EBONY	GIMPY	HUSKY	LOUSY	NAVVY	PLINY	SAMMY	TAMMY	WITTY
CUTTY	EDIFY	GIPSY	HUSSY	LOWLY	NEDDY	PODGY	SANDY	TANGY	WONKY
CYMRY	ELEGY	GIRLY	ICILY	LOWRY	NEEDY	POESY	SAPPY	TANSY	WOODY
DADDY	ELOGY	GLORY	IMPLY	LUCKY	NELLY	POKEY	SARKY	TARDY	WOOFY
DAFFY	EMERY	GLUEY	INLAY	LULLY	NERVY	POLLY	SASSY	TARRY	WOOZY
DAILY	EMILY	GOATY	IRONY	LUMMY	NEWLY	POMMY	SATAY	TARTY	WORDY
DAIRY	EMPTY	GODLY	ISLAY	LUMPY	NEWSY	PONEY	SAUCY	TASTY	WORMY
DAISY	ENEMY	GOLLY	ITALY	LUNDY	NIFTY	PONTY	SAURY	TATTY	WORRY
DALLY	ENJOY	GOODY	ITCHY	LURGY	NINNY	POPPY	SAVOY	TAWNY	WRYLY
DANDY	ENTRY	GOOEY	IVORY	LUSHY	NIPPY	POPSY	SAVVY	TEDDY	YIPPY
DARBY	ENVOY	GOOFY	JAGGY	LUSTY	NOBBY	PORGY	SCALY	TEENY	YUCKY
DARCY	EPOXY	GOOLY	JAMMY	MADLY	NOBLY	PORKY	SCARY	TELLY	YUKKY
DECAY	ESSAY	GORKY	JANTY	MALAY	NODDY	POTTY	SCRAY	TERRY	YUMMY
DECOY	EVERY	GOUTY	JASEY	MAMEY	NOISY	PRIVY	SEAMY	TESTY	YUPPY
DECRY	FADDY	GRAVY	JAZZY	MAMMY	NONNY	PROSY	SEEDY	TIBBY	ZIPPY
DEIFY	FAERY	GRIMY	JELLY		NOOKY	PROXY	SEPOY	TIDDY	ZLOTY
DEITY	FAIRY	GULLY	JEMMY	MANGY	NOSEY	PUDGY	SHADY	TINNY	BLITZ
DELAY	FANCY	GUMMY	JENNY	MANLY	NOWAY	PUFFY	SHAKY	TIPPY	CAPIZ
DERAY	FANNY	GUNNY	JERKY	MARLY	NUNKY	PULPY	SHINY	TIPSY	FRANZ
DERBY	FARCY	GUPPY	JERRY	MARRY	NUTTY	PUNTY	SHOWY	TITTY	FRITZ
DERRY	FATTY	GUSHY	JETTY	MASHY	ODDLY	PUPPY	SHYLY	TIZZY	GLITZ
DEWEY	FENNY	GUSTY	JEWRY	MATEY	OTARY	PURSY	SILKY	TOADY	GROSZ
DIARY	FERRY	GUTSY	JIFFY	MEALY	OTWAY	PUSHY	SILLY	TODAY	HAFIZ
DICEY	FIERY	GYPSY	JIMMY	MEATY	OUTBY	PUSSY	SISSY	TODDY	HERTZ
DICKY	FIFTY	HAIRY	JIMPY	MERCY	OVARY	PUTTY	SIXTY	TOKAY	JEREZ
DIMLY	FILLY	HAMMY	JOLLY	MERRY	PACEY	PYGMY	SLATY	TOMMY	KRANZ
DINGY	FILMY	HANDY	JONTY	MESSY	PADDY	QUERY	SLIMY	TOPSY	NANTZ
DINKY	FISHY	HANKY	JUICY	MIDDY	PALLY	RAGGY	SLYLY	TOTTY	ORMUZ
DIPPY	FIZZY	HAPPY	JUMBY	MIFFY	PALMY	RAINY	SMOKY	TRULY	PLATZ
DIRTY	FLAKY	HARDY	JUMPY	MILKY	PALSY	RALLY	SNAKY	TUBBY	PZAZZ
DISHY	FOAMY	HARPY	KANDY	MINGY	PANDY	RANDY	SNOWY	TULLY	SOYUZ
DITTY	FOGEY	HARRY	KARSY	MISSY	PANSY	RANGY	SOAPY	TUMMY	SPITZ
DIVVY	FOGGY	HARTY	KEDGY	MISTY	PANTY	RATTY	SOFTY	TUNNY	SWIZZ
DIZZY	FOLLY	HASTY	KELLY	MOGGY	PARDY	READY	SOGGY	UMPTY	TOPAZ
DOBBY	FOOTY	HATTY	KIDDY	MOLLY	PARKY	REEDY	SONNY	UNIFY	VADUZ
DODDY	FORAY	HEADY	KINKY	MOMMY	PARRY	RELAY	SOOTY	UNITY	WALTZ
DODGY	FORTY	HEAVY	KIRBY	MONEY	PARTY	REPAY	SOPHY	UNLAY	WHIZZ
DOGGY	FROWY	HEFTY	KITTY	MOODY	PASTY	REPLY	SOPPY	UNSAY	
DOILY	FUBSY	HENRY	KOOKY	MOONY	PATSY	RILEY	SORRY	UPSEY	
DOLLY	FUGGY	HETTY	LAIRY	MOPSY	PATTY	RISKY	SPICY	USURY	
DOPEY	FULLY	HILLY	LAITY	MORAY	PAWKY	RITZY	SPIKY	VEERY	
DORMY	FUNDY	HINNY	LAMMY	MOSEY	PEAKY	ROBEY	SPINY	VEREY	
DOTTY	FUNKY	HIPPY	LANKY	MOSSY	PEATY	ROCKY	SPLAY	VICHY	
DOUAY	FUNNY	HOARY	LARRY	MOUSY	PEGGY	ROOKY	SPRAY	VISBY	
DOWDY	FURRY	HOBBY	LAYBY	MUCKY	PENNY	ROOMY	STAGY	WACKY	
DOWNY	FUSSY	HOKEY	LEAFY	MUDDY	PEONY	ROOPY	STEWY	WALLY	
DOWRY	FUSTY	HOLEY	LEAKY	MUGGY	PEPPY	ROOTY	STIMY	WANLY	

6:1

6:1								
AARONS	ADDEEM	AGUISH	ALWAYS	ANTHER	ARGUED	ASSAIL	AUSSIE	BALKAN
ABACUS	ADDEND	AGUIZE	AMADOU	ANTICS	ARGUTE	ASSART	AUSTEN	BALKIS
ABADAN	ADDICT	AHIMSA	AMAZED	ANTLER	ARGYLE	ASSENT	AUSTER	BALLAD
ABATOR	ADDLED	AIDANT	AMAZON	ANTLIA	ARGYLL	ASSERT	AUSTIN	BALLET
ABATTU	ADDUCE	AIGLET	AMBAGE	ANTONY	ARIOCH	ASSESS	AUTHOR	BALLOT
ABBACY	ADDUCT	AIKIDO	AMBLER	ANTRIM	ARIOSO	ASSETS	AUTISM	BALSAM
ABBESS	ADHERE	AILING	AMBUSH	ANTRUM	ARISTA	ASSIGN	AUTUMN	BALTIC
ABDABS	ADJOIN	AIRBED	AMELIA	ANUBIS	ARISTO	ASSIST	AVALON	BALZAC
ABDIEL	ADJURE	AIRBUS	AMENDE	ANURAN	ARKOSE	ASSIZE	AVATAR	BAMAKO
ABDUCT	ADJUST	AIRGUN	AMENDS	ANYHOW	ARMADA	ASSOIL	AVAUNT	BAMBOO
ABELIA	ADMIRE	AIRILY	AMERCE	ANYONE	ARMAGH	ASSORT	AVENGE	BANANA
ABJECT	ADNATE	AIRING	AMHARA	ANYWAY	ARMFUL	ASSUME	AVENUE	BANDAR
ABJURE	ADONAI	AIRMAN	AMIDOL	AORIST	ARMLET	ASSURE	AVERNO	BANDIT
ABLATE	ADONIS	AIRWAY	AMIDST	AORTAL	ARMORY	ASTART	AVERSE	BANDOG
ABLAUT	ADORER	AKIMBO	AMMINE	AOUDAD	ARMOUR	ASTERN	AVIARY	BANGER
ABLAZE	ADRIAN	ALACUS	AMNION	APACHE	ARMPIT	ASTHMA	AVIATE	BANGLE
ABLOOM	ADRIFT	ALALIA	AMOEBA	APATHY	ARMURE	ASTONE	AVIDLY	BANGUI
ABLUSH	ADROIT	ALARIC	AMORAL	APEPSY	ARNAUT	ASTRAL	AVOCET	BANIAN
ABOARD	ADSORB	ALARUM	AMORCE	APERÇU	ARNHEM	ASTRAY	AVOUCH	BANISH
ABONDE	ADSUKI	ALASKA	AMORET	APHONY	ARNICA	ASTUTE	AVOWAL	BANJAX
ABOUND	ADVENE	ALBANY	AMOUNT	APHTHA	ARNOLD	ASVINA	AVOWED	BANJUL
ABRADE	ADVENT	ALBEDO	AMPERE	APIARY	AROINT	ASWARM	AVULSE	BANKER
ABREGE	ADVERB	ALBEIT	AMTRAK	APICAL	AROLLA	ASYLUM	AWAKEN	BANNED
ABROAD	ADVERT	ALBERT	AMULET	APIECE	AROUET	ATABAL	AWHILE	BANNER
ABROMA	ADVICE	ALBINO	AMUSED	APLITE	AROUND	ATABEG	AWNING	BANNET
ABRUPT	ADVISE	ALBION	AMYCUS	APLOMB	AROUSE	ATAMAN	AWOKEN	BANTAM
ABSEIL	AEDILE	ALBITE	AMYTAL	APNOEA	ARPENT	ATAXIA	AXEMAN	BANTER
ABSENT	AEGEAN	ALBUGO	ANABAS	APOGEE	ARRACK	ATAXIC	AXILLA	BANTRY
ABSORB	AEGEUS	ALCINA	ANADEM	APOLLO	ARRANT	ATHENA	AYESHA	BANYAN
ABSURD	AEGINA	ALCOCK	ANADYR	APORIA	ARREAR	ATHENE	AYMARA	BANZAI
ABULIA	AENEID	ALCOVE	ANALOG	APPALL	ARREST	ATHENS	AZALEA	BAOBAB
ABYDOS	AEOLIC	ALDINE	ANANAS	APPEAL	ARRIAN	ATHROB	AZERTY	BARBED
ACACIA	AEOLIS	ALDOSE	ANCILE	APPEAR	ARRIVE	ATKINS	AZOLLA	BARBEL
ACADIA	AEOLUS	ALDRIN	ANCOME	APPEND	ARROBA	ATOCIA	AZONAL	BARBER
ACAJOU	AERATE	ALECTO	ANCONA	APPIAN	ARROYO	ATOMIC	AZORES	BARBET
ACARID	AEROBE	ALEGAR	ANCORA	APPLES	ARSÈNE	ATONAL	AZOTIC	BARÈGE
ACARUS	AERIAL	ALERCE	ANDEAN	APPORT	ARSINE	ATONIC	AZRAEL	BARELY
ACATES	AFEARS	ALEVIN	ANDREW	APPOSE	ARTAUD	ATRIAL	BABBIT	BARGEE
ACCEDE	AFFAIR	ALEXIA	ANEMIA	AQUILA	ARTERY	ATRIDE	BABBLE	BARHAM
ACCEND	AFFECT	ALEXIN	ANEMIC	ARABIA	ARTFUL	ATRIUM	BABOON	BARING
ACCENT	AFFIRM	ALEXIS	ANGARY	ARABIC	ARTHUR	ATTACH	BACCHI	BARIUM
ACCEPT	AFFORD	ALFRED	ANGELA	ARABIS	ARTIST	ATTACK	BACKER	BARKER
ACCESS	AFFRAY	ALIGHT	ANGELS	ARABLE	ARTURO	ATTAIN	BACKET	BARKIS
ACCORD	AFFRET	ALIPED	ANGERS	ARAFAT	ASADHA	ATTEND	BACKRA	BARLEY
ACCOST	AFGHAN	ALIYAH	ANGICO	ARAGON	ASARUM	ATTEST	BACKUP	BARMAN
ACCRUE	AFIELD	ALKALI	ANGINA	ARALIA	ASCEND	ATTILA	BADGER	BARNES
ACCUSE	AFLAME	ALKANE	ANGLED	ARAMIS	ASCENT	ATTIRE	BADMAN	BARNET
ACEDIA	AFLOAT	ALKENE	ANGLER	ARANDA	ASCHAM	ATTLEE	BAFFIN	BARNEY
ACETIC	AFRAID	ALLEGE	ANGLIA	ARARAT	ASCIAN	ATTONE	BAFFLE	BARNUM
ACHENE	AFREET	ALLELE	ANGOLA	ARBOUR	ASCIUS	ATTORN	BAGFUL	BARODA
ACHING	AFRESH	ALLEYN	ANGORA	ARCADE	ASGARD	ATTRAP	BAGMAN	BARQUE
ACIDIC	AFRICA	ALLIED	ANIMAL	ARCADY	ASHCAN	AUBADE	BAGNIO	BARRED
ACINUS	AFTERS	ALLIER	ANIMUS	ARCANA	ASHDOD	AUBREY	BAGUIO	BARREL
ACKERS	AGADIR	ALLIUM	ANKARA	ARCANE	ASHINE	AUBURN	BAHADA	BARREN
ACORNS	AGAMID	ALLUDE	ANKLET	ARCHED	ASHLAR	AUCUBA	BAHRAM	BARRIE
ACQUIT	AGARIC	ALLURE	ANKOLE	ARCHER	ASHLEY	AUDILE	BAIKAL	BARRIO
ACRAWL	AGATHA	ALMAIN	ANNALS	ARCHES	ASHORE	AUDLEY	BAILEE	BARROW
ACROSS	AGEING	ALMERY	ANNEAL	ARCHIE	ASHPAN	AUDREY	BAILER	BARSAC
ACTING	AGENCY	ALMOND	ANNEXE	ARCHIL	ASHTAR	AUGEAN	BAILEY	BARTER
ACTION	AGENDA	ALMOST	ANNUAL	ARCHON	ASHTON	AUGITE	BAILIE	BARTOK
ACTIUM	AGHAST	ALOGIA	ANOINT	ARCTIC	ASIMOV	AUGURY	BAILLY	BARTON
ACTIVE	AGLAIA	ALONSO	ANONYM	ARDENT	ASKARI	AUGUST	BAKERS	BARUCH
ACTORS	AGNAIL	ALPACA	ANORAK	ARDOUR	ASKING	AUMBRY	BAKERY	BARYTA
ACTUAL	AGNATE	ALPINE	ANOXIA	AREOLA	ASLANT	AUNTIE	BAKING	BASALT
ACUITY	AGONIC	ALPINO	ANOXIC	AREOLE	ASLEEP	AUREUS	BALAAM	BASHER
ACUMEN	AGOUTI	ALTAIR	ANSELM	ARGENT	ASLOPE	AURIGA	BALBOA	BASICS
ADAGIO	AGREED	ALTHEA	ANSWER	ARGHAN	ASMARA	AURORA	BALDER	BASKET
	AGRÉGÉ	ALUDEL	ANTHEM	ARGIVE	ASPECT	AUSPEX	BALDLY	BASQUE
	AGUISE	ALUMNI		ARGOSY	ASPIRE		BALEEN	BASSET

BASUTO	BELIZE	BIGAMY	BODGER	BOTTLE	BROACH	BUREAU	CALAIS	CAPTAN
BATEAU	BELLOC	BIGGER	BODGIE	BOTTOM	BROADS	BURGEE	CALCED	CAPTOR
BATHER	BELLOW	BIGGIN	BODICE	BOUCHE	BROGAN	BURGER	CALICO	CARAFE
BATHOS	BELONG	BIGWIG	BODIES	BOUCLÉ	BROGUE	BURGLE	CALIMA	CARBON
BATMAN	BELSEN	BIKINI	BODILY	BOUFFE	BROKEN	BURIAL	CALIPH	CARBOY
BATTEN	BELTED	BILLET	BODKIN	BOUGHT	BROKER	BURIED	CALKER	CARDAN
BATTER	BELUGA	BILLIE	BODONI	BOULLE	BROLLY	BURKHA	CALKIN	CAREEN
BATTLE	BEMEAN	BILLOW	BOEING	BOUNCE	BRONCO	BURLAP	CALLAS	CAREER
BATTUE	BEMOAN	BILLYO	BOFFIN	BOUNCY	BRONTE	BURLEY	CALLED	CAREME
BAUBLE	BEMOIL	BINARY	BOFORS	BOUNDS	BRONZE	BURNER	CALLER	CARESS
BAUCIS	BEMUSE	BINATE	BOGART	BOUNTY	BROOCH	BURNET	CALLET	CARFAX
BAWBEE	BENAME	BINDER	BOGGLE	BOURÉE	BROODY	BURROW	CALLID	CARIES
BAXTER	BENBOW	BIOGEN	BOGOTA	BOURNE	BROOKE	BURSAR	CALLOP	CARINA
BAYARD	BENDED	BIONIC	BOHUNK	BOURSE	BROOKS	BURTON	CALLOW	CARING
BAYEUX	BENDER	BIOPIC	BOILED	BOUSER	BROWNE	BUSBOY	CALLUP	CARLIN
BAZAAR	BENGAL	BIOPSY	BOILER	BOUTON	BROWSE	BUSHED	CALLUS	CARMEL
BEACHY	BENIGN	BIOTIC	BOLDLY	BOVATE	BRUISE	BUSHEL	CALMLY	CARMEN
BEACON	BENITO	BIOTIN	BOLERO	BOVINE	BRUMAL	BUSILY	CALQUE	CARNAL
BEADED	BENNET	BIRDIE	BOLEYN	BOVRIL	BRUMBY	BUSKER	CALVER	CARNET
BEADLE	BENSON	BIREME	BOLIDE	BOWELS	BRUNCH	BUSKET	CALVIN	CARNOT
BEAGLE	BENUMB	BIRNAM	BOLLEN	BOWERY	BRUNEI	BUSKIN	CAMAIL	CARPAL
BEAKER	BERATE	BISCAY	BOLSHY	BOWFIN	BRUNEL	BUSMAN	CAMBER	CARPEL
BEANIE	BERBER	BISECT	BOLTER	BOWLED	BRUTAL	BUSONI	CAMDEN	CARPER
BEARER	BEREFT	BISHOP	BOMBAY	BOWLER	BRUTUS	BUSTED	CAMERA	CARPET
BEATEN	BERGEN	BISQUE	BOMBER	BOWMAN	BRYANT	BUSTER	CAMION	CARPUS
BEATER	BERING	BISTER	BOMBYX	BOWSER	BRYONY	BUSTLE	CAMISE	CARREL
BEATTY	BERLIN	BISTRE	BONBON	BOWWOW	BUBBLE	BUTANE	CAMOTE	CARROT
BEAUNE	BERTHA	BISTRO	BONDED	BOXCAR	BUBBLY	BUTENE	CAMPED	CARSON
BEAUTY	BERTHE	BITCHY	BONDER	BOXING	BUCCAL	BUTLER	CAMPER	CARTEL
BEAVER	BERTIE	BITING	BONITO	BOYISH	BUCHAN	BUTTER	CAMPUS	CARTER
BECALM	BESANT	BITTEN	BONNET	BRACER	BUCKED	BUTTON	CANAAN	CARTON
BECAME	BESEEM	BITTER	BONNIE	BRACES	BUCKER	BUYERS	CANADA	CARUSO
BECKET	BESIDE	BLACKS	BONSAI	BRAHMA	BUCKET	BUYING	CANAPÉ	CARVED
BECKON	BESORT	BLAISE	BONXIE	BRAHMS	BUCKLE	BUYOUT	CANARD	CARVEL
BECOME	BESSEL	BLAMED	BONZER	BRAINS	BUDDHA	BUZFUZ	CANARY	CARVER
BEDASH	BESSIE	BLANCH	BOOBOO	BRAINY	BUDGET	BUZZER	CANCEL	CASBAH
BEDAUB	BESSUS	BLANCO	BOODLE	BRAISE	BUDGIE	BYEBYE	CANCER	CASEIN
BEDDER	BESTED	BLAZER	BOOGIE	BRAMAH	BUENOS	BYELAW	CANDID	CASHEW
BEDECK	BESTIR	BLAZON	BOOHOO	BRANCH	BUFFER	BYGONE	CANDLE	CASING
BEDLAM	BESTOW	BLEACH	BOOJUM	BRANDY	BUFFET	BYLINE	CANDOR	CASINO
BEDPAN	BETAKE	BLEARY	BOOKED	BRAQUE	BUFFON	BYNAME	CANGUE	CASKET
BEDSIT	BETHEL	BLENCH	BOOKER	BRASSY	BUGGER	BYPASS	CANINE	CASLON
BEEGHA	BETIDE	BLENDE	BOOKIE	BRAWNY	BUGLER	BYRNIE	CANING	CASPAR
BEENAH	BETIME	BLENNY	BOOMER	BRAZEN	BUKSHI	BYSSUS	CANKER	CASQUE
BEEPER	BETISE	BLIGHT	BOOTEE	BRAZIL	BULBIL	BYWORD	CANNAE	CASSIA
BEETLE	BETONY	BLIMEY	BOÖTES	BREACH	BULBUL	CABALE	CANNED	CASSIO
BEETON	BETRAY	BLINKS	BOOTLE	BREAST	BULGAR	CABBIE	CANNEL	CASSIS
BEFALL	BETTER	BLITHE	BOOZER	BREATH	BULGER	CACCIA	CANNON	CASTER
BEFOOL	BETTOR	BLOCKS	BORAGE	BRECHT	BULIMY	CACHET	CANNOT	CASTLE
BEFORE	BEULAH	BLONDE	BORANE	BREECH	BULLER	CACHOU	CANOPY	CASTOR
BEGGAR	BEURRÉ	BLOODY	BORATE	BREEZE	BULLET	CACKLE	CANTAB	CASTRO
BEGONE	BEWAIL	BLOTCH	BORDAR	BREEZY	BUMALO	CACOON	CANTAL	CASUAL
BEHALF	BEWARE	BLOTTO	BORDER	BREGMA	BUMBLE	CACTUS	CANTAR	CATCHY
BEHAVE	BEYOND	BLOUSE	BOREAS	BREMEN	BUMPER	CADDIE	CANTER	CATGUT
BEHEAD	BEZANT	BLOWER	BORGIA	BRETON	BUNCHY	CADDIS	CANTLE	CATHAR
BEHELD	BEZOAR	BLOWUP	BORING	BREVET	BUNDLE	CADETS	CANTON	CATHAY
BEHEST	BEZZLE	BLOWZY	BORNEO	BREWER	BUNGAY	CADGER	CANTOR	CATKIN
BEHIND	BHAJAN	BLUDGE	BORROW	BREWIS	BUNGEE	CADMUS	CANTUS	CATNAP
BEHOLD	BHAJEE	BLUISH	BORSCH	BRIAND	BUNGLE	CAECUM	CANUCK	CATNIP
BEHOOF	BHARAL	BOARDS	BORZOI	BRIARD	BUNION	CAESAR	CANUTE	CATSUP
BEHOVE	BHARAT	BOATER	BOSKET	BRICKS	BUNJEE	CAFARD	CANVAS	CATTLE
BEHRAM	BIASED	BOBBER	BOSSED	BRIDAL	BUNKER	CAFTAN	CANVEY	CAUCUS
BEIRUT	BICARB	BOBBIN	BOSTON	BRIDGE	BUNKUM	CAGILY	CANYON	CAUDEX
BEJADE	BICEPS	BOBBLE	BOSUNS	BRIDIE	BUNSEN	CAHIER	CAPIAS	CAUDLE
BELAMY	BICKER	BOBCAT	BOTANY	BRIDLE	BUNTER	CAHOOT	CAPLET	CAUGHT
BELFRY	BIDDER	BOBWIG	BOTHAM	BRIEFS	BUNYAN	CAIMAN	CAPONE	CAUSAL
BELIAL	BIDENT	BOCAGE	BOTHER	BRIGHT	BURBLE	CAIQUE	CAPOTE	CAUSED
BELIEF	BIFFIN	BODACH	BOTHIE	BRIONY	BURBOT	CAITRA	CAPPED	CAUSEY
BELIKE	BIFOLD	BODEGA	BOTLEY	BRITON	BURDEN	CAJOLE	CAPSID	CAVEAT

CAVEIN	CHEERY	CICADA	COARSE	CONDOR	COSTAR	CRETIN	CULTCH	CYPRUS
CAVELL	CHEESE	CICALA	COATED	CONFAB	COSTER	CREWEL	CULTER	CYRANO
CAVERN	CHEESY	CICELY	COATES	CONFER	COSTLY	CRIANT	CULTUS	CYRENE
CAVITY	CHEMIC	CICERO	COBALT	CONGEE	COTTAR	CRIBLE	CULVER	CYSTIC
CAVORT	CHEMMY	CIERGE	COBBER	CONGER	COTTON	CRIKEY	CUMBER	CYTASE
CAVOUR	CHENET	CILICE	COBBLE	CONICS	COTYLE	CRIMEA	CUMMER	CYTODE
CAYMAN	CHEOPS	CILIUM	COBDEN	CONKER	COUGAR	CRINAL	CUMMIN	CYTOID
CECILS	CHEQUE	CINDER	COBURG	CONMAN	COULEE	CRINGE	CUNEAL	CZAPKA
CECITY	CHERIE	CINEMA	COBWEB	CONNER	COULIS	CRINUM	CUNNER	DABBLE
CEDRIC	CHERRY	CINQUE	COCCID	CONRAD	COUNTY	CRIPES	CUPFUL	DACOIT
CEDULA	CHERUB	CIPHER	COCCUS	CONSUL	COUPLE	CRISIS	CUPMAN	DACTYL
CEEFAX	CHERUP	CIRCLE	COCCYX	CONTRA	COUPON	CRISPY	CUPOLA	DADDLE
CELERY	CHESIL	CIRCUS	COCHIN	CONVEX	COURSE	CRISTA	CUPPED	DAEDAL
CELIAC	CHESTY	CIRQUE	COCKER	CONVEY	COUSIN	CRITIC	CUPPER	DAEMON
CELLAR	CHEVAL	CIRRUS	COCKLE	CONVOY	COVENT	CROAKY	CUPRIC	DAFTIE
CELTIC	CHEVET	CITRIC	COCOON	COOING	COVERT	CROCHE	CUPULE	DAGGER
CEMENT	CHIBOL	CITRIN	CODDLE	COOKED	COVING	CROCKS	CURACY	DAGGLE
CENSER	CHICHI	CITRON	CODGER	COOKER	COWAGE	CROCUS	CURARE	DAHLIA
CENSOR	CHICLE	CITRUS	CODIFY	COOKIE	COWARD	CRONET	CURARI	DAIMIO
CENSUS	CHICON	CIVICS	CODING	COOLER	COWBOY	CRONOS	CURATE	DAINTY
CENTER	CHIGOE	CIVISM	COELOM	COOLIE	COWMAN	CRONUS	CURDLE	DAISHO
CENTRE	CHILDE	CLAGGY	COERCE	COOLLY	COWPAT	CROPPY	CURFEW	DAKOTA
CENTUM	CHILLI	CLAIMS	COEVAL	COOLTH	COWPER	CROSBY	CURIET	DALASI
CERATE	CHILLY	CLAMMY	COFFEE	COOPER	COWPOX	CROSSE	CURIUM	DALETH
CERCAL	CHIMER	CLAMOR	COFFER	COOTIE	COWRIE	CROTAL	CURLER	DALTON
CERCUS	CHIMES	CLAQUE	COFFIN	COPECK	COYOTE	CROTCH	CURLEW	DAMAGE
CEREAL	CHINAR	CLARET	COGENT	COPIED	COZIER	CROTON	CURPEL	DAMASK
CEREUS	CHINCH	CLARTY	COGGER	COPIER	CRABBE	CROUCH	CURRIE	DAMMAR
CERISE	CHINTZ	CLASSY	COGNAC	COPING	CRABBY	CROUPE	CURSAL	DAMMIT
CERIUM	CHIPPY	CLAUDE	COHERE	COPPER	CRADLE	CROUPY	CURSED	DAMNED
CERMET	CHIRON	CLAUSE	COHORT	COPPIN	CRAFTY	CROUSE	CURSOR	DAMPEN
CEROON	CHIRPY	CLAVIS	COHOSH	COPTIC	CRAGGY	CROUTE	CURSUS	DAMPER
CERTES	CHISEL	CLAYEY	COILED	COQUET	CRAMBO	CROUTH	CURTAL	DAMSEL
CERUSE	CHITAL	CLEAVE	COINER	CORALS	CRANCH	CRUELS	CURTAX	DAMSON
CERVIX	CHITIN	CLENCH	COITUS	CORBEL	CRANKY	CRUFTS	CURTLY	DANCER
CESARE	CHITON	CLEOME	COLDLY	CORBIE	CRANNY	CRUISE	CURTSY	DANDER
CESIUM	CHITTY	CLERGY	COLEUS	CORDON	CRANTS	CRUIVE	CURULE	DANDLE
CESTUI	CHIVES	CLERIC	COLLAR	CORIUM	CRAPLE	CRUMBS	CUSCUS	DANGER
CESTUS	CHIVVY	CLERKS	COLLET	CORKED	CRASIS	CRUMEN	CUSHAT	DANGLE
CESURA	CHOANA	CLEVER	COLLIE	CORKER	CRATCH	CRUMMY	CUSSED	DANIEL
CETERA	CHOICE	CLICHÉ	COLLOP	CORMUS	CRATER	CRUNCH	CUSSER	DANISH
CEYLON	CHOKED	CLIENT	COLMAR	CORNEA	CRATON	CRURAL	CUSTER	DANTON
CHADOR	CHOKER	CLIFFS	COLONY	CORNED	CRATUR	CRUSET	CUSTOM	DANUBE
CHAFER	CHOKEY	CLIMAX	COLOUR	CORNEL	CRAVAT	CRUSOE	CUSTOS	DANZIG
CHAINS	CHOLER	CLIMES	COLTER	CORNER	CRAVEN	CRUSTA	CUTCHA	DAPHNE
CHAIRS	CHOOSE	CLINCH	COLUMN	CORNET	CRAYER	CRUSTY	CUTLER	DAPPER
CHAISE	CHOOSY	CLINIC	COMART	CORNUA	CRAYON	CRUTCH	CUTLET	DAPPLE
CHAKRA	CHOPIN	CLIPPY	COMATE	CORNUS	CRAZED	CRYING	CUTOFF	DARGLE
CHALET	CHOPPY	CLIQUE	COMBAT	CORONA	CREACH	CRYPTO	CUTTER	DARIEN
CHALKY	CHORAL	CLOACA	COMBED	CORPSE	CREAGH	CUBAGE	CUTTLE	DARING
CHAMPS	CHOREA	CLOAKS	COMBER	CORPUS	CREAKY	CUBICA	CUTTOE	DARIUS
CHANCE	CHOREE	CLOCHE	COMBLE	CORRAL	CREAMY	CUBISM	CYANIN	DARKEN
CHANCY	CHORUS	CLONIC	COMEDO	CORRIE	CREANT	CUBIST	CYBELE	DARKEY
CHANEY	CHOSEN	CLONUS	COMEDY	CORSET	CREASE	CUBOID	CYBORG	DARKIE
CHANGE	CHOUAN	CLOSED	COMELY	CORTES	CREATE	CUCKOO	CYBRID	DARKLY
CHAPEL	CHOUGH	CLOSER	COMFIT	CORTEX	CRÈCHE	CUDDLE	CYCLIC	DARTER
CHAPKA	CHOWRY	CLOSET	COMICE	CORTEZ	CREDIT	CUDDLY	CYCLUS	DARTLE
CHARGE	CHRISM	CLOTHE	COMING	CORVÉE	CREEPS	CUDGEL	CYDNUS	DARWIN
CHARON	CHRIST	CLOTHO	COMITY	CORVUS	CREEPY	CUEIST	CYESIS	DASHED
CHARTA	CHROMA	CLOUDY	COMMIS	CORYZA	CREESE	CUERPO	CYGNET	DATING
CHASER	CHROME	CLOUGH	COMMIT	COSHER	CREESH	CUESTA	CYGNUS	DATIVE
CHASSE	CHROMO	CLOVEN	COMMON	COSIER	CREMOR	CUFFEE	CYMBAL	DATURA
CHASTE	CHUBBY	CLOVER	COMPEL	COSILY	CRENAL	CUFFIN	CYMRIC	DAUDET
CHATON	CHUFFY	CLOVIS	COMPLY	COSINE	CRENEL	CUISSE	CYNIPS	DAWDLE
CHATTY	CHUKKA	CLUMPS	COMSAT	COSMEA	CREOLE	CUITER	CYPHER	DAWNEY
CHAZAN	CHUMMY	CLUMSY	CONCHA	COSMIC	CRESOL	CULDEE	CYPRID	DAWSON
CHEDER	CHUNKY	CLUNCH	CONCHY	COSMOS	CRESTA	CULLET	CYPRIS	DAYBED
CHEEKY	CHURCH	CLUTCH	CONCUR	COSSET	CRETAN	CULLIS		DAZZLE
CHEERS	CHYPRE	COALER	CONDOM	COSSIE	CRETIC	CULMEN		DEACON

DEADEN	DELVED	DIADEM	DIVIDE	DOUCHE	DUNKER	EGESTA	ENDURE	ERINYS
DEADLY	DEMAIN	DIALOG	DIVINE	DOUGHY	DUNLIN	EGGCUP	ENERGY	ERMINE
DEAFEN	DEMAND	DIANAS	DIVING	DOURLY	DUNLOP	EGMONT	ENFIRE	ERMITE
DEALER	DEMEAN	DIAPER	DIWALI	DOWNAY	DUPLEX	EGOISM	ENFOLD	ERNANI
DEARER	DEMENT	DIATOM	DIYARI	DOWNER	DURANT	EGOIST	ENFREE	ERODED
DEARIE	DEMISE	DIAXON	DIZAIN	DOWSER	DURBAR	EGRESS	ENGAGE	EROICA
DEARLY	DEMIST	DIBBER	DJEBEL	DOWSET	DURESS	EIFFEL	ENGELS	EROTIC
DEARTH	DEMOTE	DIBBLE	DJERBA	DOWSON	DURHAM	EIGHTH	ENGINE	ERRAND
DEBASE	DEMURE	DICAST	DJINNI	DOYLEY	DURIAN	EIGHTY	ENGLUT	ERRANT
DEBATE	DENGUE	DICKER	DOBBIN	DOZENS	DURING	EIRANN	ENGRAM	ERSATZ
DEBILE	DENIAL	DICKEY	DOBSON	DOZING	DURION	EITHER	ENGULF	ESCAPE
DEBRIS	DENIED	DICTUM	DOCENT	DRACHM	DUSTED	ELAINE	ENIGMA	ESCARP
DEBTOR	DENIER	DIDDLE	DOCILE	DRAFTY	DUSTER	ELANCE	ENJOIN	ESCHAR
DEBUNK	DENIMS	DIEPPE	DOCKED	DRAGEE	DVORAK	ELANET	ENLACE	ESCHEW
DECADE	DENNIS	DIESEL	DOCKER	DRAGON	DYADIC	ELAPSE	ENLIST	ESCORT
DECAFF	DENOTE	DIESIS	DOCKET	DRALON	DYBBUK	ELATED	ENMESH	ESCROC
DECAMP	DENTAL	DIETER	DOCTOR	DRAPER	DYEING	ELBRUS	ENMITY	ESCROW
DECANE	DENUDE	DIFFER	DODDER	DRAWER	DYNAMO	ELDERS	ENNIUS	ESCUDO
DECANI	DENVER	DIGEST	DODDLE	DREAMY	DYNAST	ELDEST	ENODAL	ESKIMO
DECANT	DEODAR	DIGGER	DODGEM	DREARY	DZEREN	ELEVEN	ENOSIS	ESPADA
DECCAN	DEPART	DIGLOT	DODGER	DREDGE	EALING	ELFISH	ENOUGH	ESPRIT
DECEIT	DEPEND	DIKDIK	DODOMA	DREGGY	EAMONN	ELICIT	ENRAGE	ESSENE
DECENT	DEPICT	DIKKOP	DOESNT	DRENCH	EARFUL	ELIJAH	ENRAPT	ESTATE
DECIDE	DEPLOY	DIKTAT	DOGGED	DRESSY	EARING	ELISHA	ENRICH	ESTEEM
DÉCIME	DEPONE	DILATE	DOGGER	DRIEST	EARNED	ELIXIR	ENROBE	ESTHER
DECKED	DEPORT	DILUTE	DOINGS	DRIPPY	EARNER	ELLERY	ENROLL	ESTRAY
DECKER	DEPOSE	DIMITY	DOLEUR	DRIVEL	EARTHY	ELLICE	ENSATE	ETALON
DECKLE	DEPTHS	DIMMER	DOLINA	DRIVEN	EARWAX	ELODEA	ENSEAL	ETCHER
DECODE	DEPUTE	DIMPLE	DOLINE	DRIVER	EARWIG	ELOHIM	ENSIGN	ETHANE
DECOKE	DEPUTY	DIMWIT	DOLIUM	DROGUE	EASIER	ELOIGN	ENSILE	ETHENE
DECREE	DERAIL	DINERO	DOLLAR	DROMIO	EASILY	ELOISE	ENSURE	ETHICS
DECREW	DERAIN	DINGHY	DOLLOP	DROMOS	EASING	ELOPER	ENTAIL	ETHIOP
DEDANS	DERGUE	DINGLE	DOLMAN	DRONES	EASTER	ELTCHI	ENTICE	ETHNIC
DEDUCE	DERHAM	DINGLY	DOLMEN	DRONGO	EATAGE	ELUANT	ENTIRE	ETRIER
DEDUCT	DERIDE	DINING	DOLOUR	DROOPY	EATERY	ELUATE	ENTITY	ETYMON
DEEJAY	DERIVE	DINKUM	DOMAIN	DROPSY	EATING	ELUTOR	ENTOMB	EUBOEA
DEEPEN	DERMAL	DINNER	DOMINO	DROSKY	ECARTÉ	ELYSEE	ENTRAP	EUCHRE
DEEPER	DERMIS	DIODON	DONATE	DROVER	ECBOLE	EMBAIL	ENTREE	EUCLID
DEEPLY	DERRIS	DIOXIN	DONGLE	DROVES	ECCLES	EMBALE	ENWRAP	EUGENE
DEFACE	DESCRY	DIPLOE	DONJON	DROWSE	ECHARD	EMBALM	ENZIAN	EULOGY
DEFAME	DESERT	DIPNOI	DONKEY	DROWSY	ECHINO	EMBANK	ENZYME	EUNUCH
DEFEAT	DESIGN	DIPOLE	DONNÉE	DRUDGE	ECLAIR	EMBERS	EOCENE	EUREKA
DEFECT	DESIRE	DIPPER	DONZEL	DRYDEN	ECLOSE	EMBLEM	EOLITH	EUROPA
DEFEND	DESIST	DIQUAT	DOODAD	DRYING	ECONUT	EMBODY	EOTHEN	EUROPE
DEFILE	DESORB	DIRECT	DOODAH	DUBBIN	ECTOPY	EMBOSS	EOZOON	EUSTON
DEFINE	DESPOT	DIRHAM	DOODLE	DUBLIN	ECURIE	EMBRUE	EPARCH	EUTAXY
DEFORM	DETACH	DIRNDL	DOOFER	DUCKED	ECZEMA	EMBRYO	EPAULE	EUXINE
DEFRAG	DETAIL	DISARM	DOOMED	DUCKIE	EDDISH	EMBUSY	EPERDU	EVELYN
DEFRAY	DETAIN	DISBAR	DOPANT	DUDDER	EDGING	EMERGE	EPHEBE	EVENKI
DEFTLY	DETECT	DISBUD	DORADO	DUDEEN	EDIBLE	EMETIC	EPICAL	EVENLY
DEFUSE	DETENT	DISCUS	DORCAS	DUENNA	EDISON	EMEUTE	EPIGON	EVINCE
DÉGAGÉ	DETENU	DISEUR	DORIAN	DUFFEL	EDITED	EMIGRÉ	EPILOG	EVOLUÉ
DEGREE	DETEST	DISHED	DORMER	DUFFER	EDITOR	EMPIRE	EPIRUS	EVOLVE
DEHORN	DETOUR	DISHES	DORRIT	DUFFLE	EDMOND	EMPLOY	EPONYM	EVULSE
DEIDRE	DEVEST	DISMAL	DORSAL	DUGONG	EDMUND	EMULGE	EPOPEE	EVZONE
DEIMOS	DEVICE	DISMAY	DORSET	DUGOUT	EDWARD	EMUNGE	EPPING	EXARCH
DEJECT	DEVILS	DISNEY	DORTER	DULCET	EERILY	ENABLE	EPRISE	EXCEED
DEKKER	DEVISE	DISOWN	DOSAGE	DUMBLY	EEYORE	ENAMEL	EPULIS	EXCEPT
DELATE	DEVOID	DISPEL	DOSSAL	DUMDUM	EFFACE	ENAMOR	EQUALS	EXCESS
DELETE	DEVOTE	DISTAL	DOSSER	DUMONT	EFFECT	ENARCH	EQUANT	EXCISE
DELIAN	DEVOUR	DISTIL	DOTAGE	DUMOSE	EFFETE	ENCALM	EQUATE	EXCITE
DELICE	DEVOUT	DISUSE	DOTARD	DUMPER	EFFIGY	ENCAMP	EQUINE	EXCUSE
DELICT	DEWALI	DITHER	DOTING	DUMPLE	EFFLUX	ENCASE	EQUIPE	EXEDRA
DELISH	DEWITT	DITTOS	DOTTED	DUNBAR	EFFORT	ENCASH	EQUITY	EXEMPT
DELIUS	DEWLAP	DIVALI	DOTTLE	DUNCAN	EFFUSE	ENCODE	ERASED	EXETER
DELPHI	DEXTER	DIVEHI	DOUANE	DUNCES	EFTEST	ENCORE	ERASER	EXEUNT
DELUDE	DHARMA	DIVERS	DOUBLE	DUNDEE	EGBERT	ENDEAR	ERBIUM	EXHALE
DELUGE	DHOOTI	DIVERT	DOUBLY	DUNDER	EGENCY	ENDING	EREBUS	EXHORT
DELUXE	DIACID	DIVEST	DOUCET	DUNELM	EGERIA	ENDIVE	EREMIC	EXHUME

EXISTS	FASCIA	FILIAL	FLIMSY	FORRAD	FUMBLE	GANGER	GERMAN	GLOSSA
EXMOOR	FASTEN	FILING	FLINCH	FORRAY	FUNDED	GANGES	GERUND	GLOSSY
EXOCET	FATHER	FILLED	FLINTY	FORSAY	FUNDUS	GANGLY	GETTER	GLOVED
EXODUS	FATHOM	FILLER	FLITCH	FORTHY	FUNGAL	GANGUE	GEWGAW	GLOWER
EXOGEN	FATIMA	FILLET	FLOOZY	FOSSIL	FUNGUS	GANION	GEYSER	GLUMPS
EXOTIC	FATTEN	FILLIP	FLOPPY	FOSTER	FUNNEL	GANNET	GHARRY	GLUTEN
EXPAND	FAUCES	FILOSE	FLORAL	FOUGHT	FUREUR	GANTRY	GHAZAL	GLYCOL
EXPECT	FAUCET	FILTER	FLORET	FOULLY	FURFUR	GAOLER	GHEBER	GNAWER
EXPEDE	FAULTY	FILTHY	FLORID	FOURTH	FURIES	GAPING	GHERAO	GNEISS
EXPEND	FAUNUS	FILTRÉ	FLORIN	FOUTRE	FURORE	GARAGE	GHETTO	GNOMIC
EXPERT	FAVELA	FIMBRA	FLOSSY	FOWLER	FURPHY	GARBED	GHOSTS	GNOMON
EXPIRE	FAVISM	FINALE	FLOURY	FRACAS	FURROW	GARBLE	GIAOUR	GOALIE
EXPIRY	FAVOSE	FINDER	FLOUSH	FRAGOR	FUSAIN	GARÇON	GIBBER	GOANNA
EXPORT	FAVOUR	FINELY	FLOWER	FRAISE	FUSELI	GARDEN	GIBBET	GOATEE
EXPOSE	FAWKES	FINERY	FLUENT	FRAMED	FUSION	GARETH	GIBBON	GOBBET
EXPUGN	FEALTY	FINEST	FLUFFY	FRANCE	FUSTIC	GARGET	GIBSON	GOBBLE
EXSERT	FECULA	FINGAL	FLUNKY	FRANCK	FUSTOC	GARGLE	GIDDUP	GOBLET
EXTANT	FECUND	FINGER	FLURRY	FRANCO	FUTILE	GARISH	GIDEON	GOBLIN
EXTEND	FEDORA	FINIAL	FLUSHY	FRANZY	FUTURE	GARLIC	GIFTED	GOCART
EXTENT	FEEBLE	FINISH	FLUTED	FRAPPÉ	FUZZLE	GARNER	GIGGLE	GODIVA
EXTERN	FEEBLY	FINITE	FLUTER	FRATER	FYLFOT	GARNET	GIGLET	GODOWN
EXTIRP	FEEDER	FINLAY	FLUTES	FRAYED	GABBLE	GARRET	GIGLOT	GODSON
EXTOLL	FEELER	FINNAN	FLYING	FREELY	GABBRO	GARROT	GIGOLO	GODWIN
EXTORT	FEERIE	FIPPLE	FOCSLE	FREEZE	GABION	GARRYA	GILDAS	GODWIT
EYEFUL	FEINTS	FIRING	FODDER	FRENCH	GABLED	GARTER	GILDED	GOETHE
EYELET	FEISTY	FIRKIN	FOETAL	FRENUM	GADFLY	GARUDA	GILDER	GOFFER
EYELID	FELINE	FIRLOT	FOETID	FRENZY	GADGET	GASBAG	GILEAD	GOGGLE
FABIAN	FELLER	FIRMAN	FOETUS	FRESCO	GADOID	GASCON	GILGAI	GOITER
FABIUS	FELLOE	FIRMER	FOGBOW	FRIAND	GAELIC	GASKET	GILLET	GOITRE
FABLED	FELLOW	FIRMLY	FOIBLE	FRIARY	GAFFER	GASMAN	GILLIE	GOKART
FABLES	FELONY	FISCAL	FOILED	FRIDAY	GAGGLE	GASPAR	GILPIN	GOLDEN
FABRIC	FEMALE	FISHER	FOKINE	FRIDGE	GAGMAN	GASPER	GIMBAL	GOLFER
FACADE	FENCER	FITFUL	FOKKER	FRIEND	GAIETY	GASSER	GIMLET	GOLLOP
FACIAL	FENDER	FITOUT	FOLDED	FRIEZE	GAIJIN	GASTER	GIMMER	GOLOSH
FACIES	FENIAN	FITTED	FOLDER	FRIGGA	GAINER	GASTON	GINGER	GONION
FACILE	FENNEL	FITTER	FOLIAR	FRIGHT	GAINLY	GATEAU	GINGKO	GONIUM
FACING	FERIAL	FIXITY	FOLIOS	FRIGID	GAITER	GATHER	GINKGO	GOOBER
FACTOR	FERMAT	FIZGIG	FOLIOT	FRILLS	GALANT	GAUCHE	GIORGI	GOODLY
FACTUM	FERRET	FIZZED	FOLIUM	FRILLY	GALAXY	GAUCHO	GIOTTO	GOOGIE
FADING	FERRIS	FIZZER	FOLKSY	FRINGE	GALENA	GAUFRE	GIRDER	GOOGLE
FAECAL	FERULA	FIZZLE	FOLLOW	FRIPON	GALERE	GAUGER	GIRDLE	GOOGLY
FAECES	FERULE	FLABBY	FOMENT	FRISKY	GALIOT	GAVAGE	GIRKIN	GOOGOL
FAGGED	FERVID	FLACON	FONDLE	FRIVOL	GALLEN	GAVIAL	GIRLIE	GOOLEY
FAGGOT	FERVOR	FLAGGY	FONDLY	FRIZZY	GALLET	GAWAIN	GIRTON	GOOLIE
FAIBLE	FESCUE	FLAGON	FONDUE	FROLIC	GALLEY	GAZEBO	GITANO	GOPHER
FAINTS	FESTAL	FLAMBÉ	FOOTER	FRONDE	GALLIC	GAZUMP	GIUSTO	GORDON
FAIRLY	FESTER	FLAMEN	FOOTLE	FROSTY	GALLIO	GEASON	GIVING	GORGED
FAKING	FETISH	FLANCH	FOOZLE	FROTHY	GALLON	GEEZER	GIZZEN	GORGES
FALCON	FETTER	FLANGE	FORAGE	FROUDE	GALLOP	GEIGER	GLACIS	GORGET
FALLEN	FETTES	FLANKS	FORBID	FROWST	GALLOW	GEISHA	GLADLY	GORGIA
FALLOW	FETTLE	FLARES	FORÇAT	FROWZY	GALLUP	GELADA	GLAGOL	GORGIO
FALTER	FEUDAL	FLASHY	FORCED	FROZEN	GALLUS	GELATE	GLAIRE	GORGON
FAMILY	FEWEST	FLATLY	FORCES	FRUGAL	GALOOT	GELATO	GLAIVE	GORING
FAMINE	FIACRE	FLATUS	FOREDO	FRUICT	GALORE	GELLER	GLAMIS	GOSPEL
FAMISH	FIANCÉ	FLAUNT	FOREGO	FRUITS	GALOSH	GEMINI	GLAMOR	GOSSIP
FAMOUS	FIASCO	FLAVIN	FOREST	FRUITY	GAMBET	GEMMAN	GLANCE	GOTHAM
FANGLE	FIBBED	FLAVOR	FORGED	FRUMPY	GAMBIA	GENDER	GLASSY	GOTHIC
FANION	FIBBER	FLAWED	FORGER	FRUTEX	GAMBIT	GENERA	GLAZED	GOTTEN
FANTAN	FIBULA	FLAXEN	FORGET	FRYING	GAMBLE	GENEVA	GLIBLY	GOUNOD
FARAND	FICKLE	FLECHE	FORGOT	FUDDLE	GAMBOL	GENIAL	GLIDER	GOURDE
FARCIN	FIDDLE	FLEDGE	FORINT	FUGATO	GAMELY	GENIUS	GLIÈRE	GOURDS
FARDEL	FIDDLY	FLEECE	FORKED	FUHRER	GAMINE	GENOME	GLINKA	GOUTTE
FARDLE	FIDGET	FLEECY	FORMAL	FULANI	GAMING	GENTES	GLIOMA	GOVERN
FARINA	FIELDS	FLENSE	FORMAT	FULFIL	GAMMER	GENTLE	GLITCH	GRABEN
FARMER	FIERCE	FLESHY	FORMER	FULGID	GAMMON	GENTLY	GLITZY	GRACES
FAROFF	FIESTA	FLETCH	FORMIC	FULHAM	GANDER	GEORGE	GLOBAL	GRADED
FAROUK	FIGARO	FLEURY	FORNAX	FULLER	GANDHI	GERBIL	GLOIRE	GRADES
FARROW	FIGURE	FLICKS	FORNIX	FULMAR	GANESH	GERENT	GLOOMY	GRADUS
FASCES	FILFOT	FLIGHT	FORPIT	FUMADO				GRAFIN

GRAHAM	GRUMPH	HALVED	HEATER	HILARY	HORNET	HYPNOS	INDUCT	INWARD
GRAINS	GRUMPS	HALVES	HEAUME	HILTON	HORRID	HYPNUM	INFAME	IODINE
GRAINY	GRUMPY	HAMATE	HEAVED	HIMMEL	HORROR	HYSSOP	INFAMY	IODIZE
GRAMME	GRUNDY	HAMBLE	HEAVEN	HINDER	HORSED	IAMBIC	INFANT	IOLITE
GRAMMY	GRUNGE	HAMITE	HEAVES	HINGED	HOSIER	IAMBUS	INFARE	IONIAN
GRAMPA	GRUTCH	HAMLET	HEBREW	HINGES	HOSING	IBADAN	INFECT	IONIZE
GRAMPS	GRYFON	HAMMAM	HECATE	HIPPED	HOSTEL	IBERIA	INFEST	IPECAC
GRANBY	GUARDI	HAMMER	HECKLE	HIPPUS	HOTAIR	IBIBIO	INFIRM	IRAQIS
GRANGE	GUARDS	HAMOSE	HECTIC	HIRING	HOTBED	IBIDEM	INFLOW	IREFUL
GRANNY	GUBBAH	HAMPER	HECTOR	HIRSEL	HOTPOT	ICARUS	INFLUX	IRETON
GRANTA	GUELPH	HANDEL	HECUBA	HISPID	HOTTER	ICEBOX	INFOLD	IRONED
GRANTH	GUENON	HANDLE	HEDERA	HITECH	HOUDAH	ICECAP	INFORM	IRONIC
GRAPES	GUESTS	HANGAR	HEEDED	HITHER	HOUNDS	ICEMAN	INFUSE	IRRUPT
GRAPPA	GUFFAW	HANGER	HEEHAW	HITLER	HOURLY	ICICLE	INGATE	IRVING
GRASSY	GUGGLE	HANGUP	HEELED	HITMAN	HOUSES	ICONIC	INGEST	IRWELL
GRATED	GUIANA	HANKER	HEGIRA	HITTER	HOWARD	IDIOCY	INGOTS	ISABEL
GRATER	GUIDES	HANKIE	HEIFER	HOARSE	HOWDAH	IFFISH	INGRAM	ISAIAH
GRATIN	GUIDON	HANNAH	HEIGHT	HOAXER	HOWDIE	IGNITE	INGRES	ISCHIA
GRATIS	GUILDS	HANSOM	HEJIRA	HOBART	HOWLER	IGNORE	INGROW	ISEULT
GRAVEL	GUILTY	HAPPEN	HELENA	HOBBES	HOYDEN	IGUANA	INGULF	ISHTAR
GRAVEN	GUINEA	HAPTEN	HELIOS	HOBBLE	HUBBLE	ILKLEY	INHALE	ISLAND
GRAVER	GUITAR	HAPTIC	HELIUM	HOBDAY	HUBBUB	ILLITE	INHERE	ISLETS
GRAVES	GULLAH	HARARE	HELLAS	HOBNOB	HUBRIS	ILLUDE	INHUME	ISOBAR
GRAVID	GULLET	HARASS	HELLER	HOCKEY	HUCKLE	IMBARN	INJECT	ISOLDE
GREASE	GULLEY	HARBOR	HELMET	HODDER	HUDDLE	IMBASE	INJURE	ISOMER
GREASY	GULPER	HARDEN	HELPER	HOGGAR	HUDSON	IMBIBE	INJURY	ISOPOD
GREATS	GUMMED	HARDLY	HEMPEN	HOGGET	HUGELY	IMBOSS	INKJET	ISRAEL
GREAVE	GUNDOG	HARKEN	HENBIT	HOGTIE	HUGHES	IMBRUE	INKPOT	ISSUES
GREECE	GUNGHO	HARLOT	HENLEY	HOIDEN	HUGHIE	IMMUNE	INLAID	ISTRIA
GREEDY	GUNMAN	HARMED	HENNIN	HOLDER	HULLED	IMMURE	INLAND	ITALIC
GREEKS	GUNNEL	HAROLD	HENSON	HOLDUP	HUMANE	IMOGEN	INLAWS	ITCHEN
GREENE	GUNNER	HARPIC	HEPTAD	HOLISM	HUMBER	IMPACT	INLIER	ITERUM
GREENS	GUNTER	HARRIS	HERALD	HOLIST	HUMBLE	IMPAIR	INLINE	ITHACA
GRETNA	GURGLE	HARROW	HERBAL	HOLLER	HUMBUG	IMPALA	INMATE	ITSELF
GREUZE	GURKHA	HARVEY	HERDEN	HOLLOW	HUMECT	IMPALE	INMESH	IZZARD
GRIEVE	GURLET	HASHED	HERDER	HOLMES	HUMITE	IMPART	INMOST	JABBER
GRIGRI	GURNET	HASLET	HEREBY	HOMAGE	HUMMEL	IMPAWN	INNATE	JABBLE
GRILLE	GURNEY	HASSAR	HEREIN	HOMBRE	HUMMER	IMPEDE	INNING	JABIRU
GRILSE	GUSHER	HASSLE	HERERO	HOMELY	HUMMUS	IMPEND	INROAD	JACANA
GRIMES	GUSLAR	HASTEN	HERESY	HOMILY	HUMOUR	IMPISH	INRUSH	JACENT
GRIMLY	GUSSET	HATING	HERETO	HOMING	HUMPED	IMPORT	INSANE	JACKAL
GRIMMS	GUTTER	HATRED	HERIOT	HOMINY	HUMPTY	IMPOSE	INSECT	JACKET
GRINGO	GUTTLE	HATTER	HERMES	HONCHO	HUNGER	IMPOST	INSERT	JACOBS
GRIPES	GUYANA	HAUNCH	HERMIT	HONEST	HUNGRY	IMPUGN	INSIDE	JAEGER
GRIPPE	GUZZLE	HAVANA	HERMON	HONIED	HUNKER	IMPURE	INSIST	JAGGED
GRISLY	GYPSUM	HAVENT	HERNIA	HONOUR	HUNTER	IMPUTE	INSOLE	JAGGER
GRISON	GYRATE	HAVERS	HEROIC	HONSHU	HURDLE	INBORN	INSTAL	JAGUAR
GRITTY	HABILE	HAVING	HEROIN	HOODED	HURLEY	INBRED	INSTAR	JAILER
GROATS	HACHIS	HAWAII	HERONS	HOOFED	HURRAH	INCASE	INSTEP	JAILOR
GROCER	HACKEE	HAWKED	HERPES	HOOFER	HURRAY	INCEDE	INSTIL	JALOPY
GROGGY	HACKER	HAWKER	HERREN	HOOHAH	HURTLE	INCEPT	INSULA	JAMBOK
GROOVE	HACKLE	HAWSER	HESIOD	HOOKAH	HUSHED	INCEST	INSULT	JAMBON
GROOVY	HAEMAL	HAYBOX	HESTIA	HOOKED	HUSSAR	INCHES	INSURE	JAMMED
GROPER	HAEMON	HAYDON	HETERO	HOOKER	HUSSIF	INCHON	INTACT	JAMPOT
GROSSO	HAGDEN	HAYLEY	HETMAN	HOOKEY	HUSTLE	INCISE	INTAKE	JANGLE
GROTTO	HAGGAI	HAYMOW	HEXANE	HOOKUP	HUXLEY	INCITE	INTEND	JANSKY
GROTTY	HAGGIS	HAZARD	HEXOSE	HOOPER	HUZZAH	INCOME	INTENT	JARGON
GROUCH	HAGGLE	HAZILY	HEYDAY	HOOPLA	HYADES	INDABA	INTERN	JARVEY
GROUND	HAILER	HEADED	HIATUS	HOOPOE	HYAENA	INDEED	INTIME	JASPER
GROUPS	HAIRDO	HEADER	HICCUP	HOORAH	HYBRID	INDENT	INTONE	JAUNTY
GROUSE	HALIDE	HEALER	HICKEY	HOORAY	HYBRIS	INDIAN	INTOWN	JAWBOX
GROUTS	HALITE	HEALTH	HIDAGE	HOOTCH	HYDRAX	INDICT	INTRAY	JAZZER
GROUTY	HALLAL	HEAPED	HIDDEN	HOOTER	HYDRIA	INDIES	INTRON	JEEVES
GROVEL	HALLEY	HEARER	HIDING	HOOVER	HYDRUS	INDIGN	INVADE	JEJUNE
GROWER	HALLOO	HEARSE	HIGHER	HOPPER	HYMNAL	INDIGO	INVENT	JEKYLL
GROWTH	HALLOW	HEARTH	HIGHLY	HORACE	HYPATE	INDITE	INVERT	JEMIMA
GROYNE	HALLUX	HEARTS	HIGHUP	HORMUZ	HYPHAL	INDIUM	INVEST	JENNER
GRUBBY	HALOID	HEARTY	HIJACK	HORNED	HYPHEN	INDOOR	INVITE	JENNET
GRUDGE	HALTER	HEATED	HIKING	HORNER	HYPNIC	INDUCE	INVOKE	JERBOA

JEREMY	JUNKER	KEYWAY	KRONER	LARKIN	LENDER	LINKER	LOSING	MADURA
JERKER	JUNKET	KHALAT	KRONOS	LARRUP	LENGTH	LINKUP	LOTION	MADURO
JERKIN	JUNKIE	KHALIF	KRUGER	LARVAE	LENTEL	LINNET	LOUCHE	MAENAD
JEROME	JURANT	KHALSA	KRUMAN	LARVAL	LENTEN	LINTEL	LOUDEN	MAFFIA
JERSEY	JURIST	KHARIF	KUCCHA	LARYNX	LENTIC	LIONEL	LOUDLY	MAGGIE
JESTER	JUSTIN	KHILAT	KUFIAH	LASCAR	LENTIL	LIPARI	LOUNGE	MAGGOT
JESUIT	JUSTLY	KHILIM	KUMARA	LASHED	LENTOR	LIPASE	LOURIE	MAGLEV
JETHRO	KABAKA	KHYBER	KUMERA	LASHER	LEONID	LIPIDE	LOUVER	MAGNES
JETLAG	KABELE	KIAORA	KUMISS	LASKET	LEPTON	LIPOMA	LOUVRE	MAGNET
JETSAM	KABUKI	KIBBLE	KUMMEL	LASSIE	LESBOS	LIPPED	LOVAGE	MAGNON
JETTON	KABYLE	KIBOSH	KVETCH	LASSUS	LESION	LIQUID	LOVELL	MAGNUM
JEWELS	KACCHA	KICKER	KWACHA	LASTLY	LESLIE	LIQUOR	LOVELY	MAGNUS
JEWESS	KAFFER	KIDDIE	KWANZA	LATEEN	LESSEE	LISBON	LOVING	MAGPIE
JEWISH	KAFFIR	KIDDLE	KYBOSH	LATELY	LESSEN	LISPER	LOWBOY	MAGYAR
JIBBAH	KAFTAN	KIDNAP	KYUSHU	LATENT	LESSER	LISSOM	LOWELL	MAHLER
JIGGER	KAISER	KIDNEY	LAAGER	LATEST	LESSON	LISTEL	LOWEST	MAHOUT
JIGGLE	KAKAPO	KIGALI	LABIAL	LATHER	LESSOR	LISTEN	LOWKEY	MAIDAN
JIGSAW	KALMIA	KIKUYU	LABILE	LATONA	LESTER	LISTER	LOYOLA	MAIDEN
JILLET	KALPAK	KILLER	LABIUM	LATRON	LETHAL	LITANY	LUANDA	MAILER
JIMJAM	KANAKA	KILNER	LABLAB	LATTEN	LETOUT	LITCHI	LUBBER	MAINLY
JINGAL	KANGHA	KILTED	LABOUR	LATTER	LETTER	LITHIA	LUBRIC	MAINOR
JINGLE	KANOON	KILTER	LABRUM	LATVIA	LEVANT	LITMUS	LUCENT	MAÎTRE
JINXED	KANSAS	KILTIE	LABRYS	LAUDER	LEVITE	LITTER	LUCIAN	MAJLIS
JISSOM	KANTEN	KIMMER	LACHES	LAUNCE	LEVITY	LITTLE	LUCINA	MAKEUP
JITNEY	KANTHA	KIMONO	LACING	LAUNCH	LEWDLY	LIVELY	LUDWIG	MAKING
JITTER	KANUCK	KINASE	LACKEY	LAUREL	LEXEME	LIVERY	LUGANO	MALAGA
JOANNA	KAOLIN	KINDER	LACTIC	LAURIC	LEYDEN	LIVING	LUGGER	MALATE
JOBBER	KAPUTT	KINDLE	LACUNA	LAURIE	LHOTSE	LIZARD	LUMBAR	MALAWI
JOCKEY	KARATE	KINDLY	LADAKH	LAVABO	LIABLE	LIZZIE	LUMBER	MALDON
JOCOSE	KARIBA	KINGLY	LADDER	LAVAGE	LIAISE	LLOYDS	LUMINA	MALGRE
JOCUND	KARITE	KIPPER	LADDIE	LAVISH	LIBBER	LOADED	LUMMOX	MALIAN
JOGGER	KASBAH	KIRBEH	LADIES	LAWFUL	LIBERO	LOADER	LUMPUR	MALIBU
JOGGLE	KATANA	KIRMAN	LADING	LAWMAN	LIBIDO	LOAFER	LUNACY	MALICE
JOHNNY	KAZAKH	KIRPAN	LADOGA	LAWYER	LIBYAN	LOATHE	LUNARY	MALIGN
JOINER	KEATON	KIRSCH	LAFFER	LAXIST	LICHEN	LOAVES	LUNATE	MALLAM
JOJOBA	KEBELE	KIRTLE	LAGOON	LAXITY	LICTOR	LOCALE	LUNULE	MALLEE
JONSON	KECKSY	KISHKE	LAGUNA	LAYARD	LIEBIG	LOCATE	LUPINE	MALLET
JOPLIN	KEDDAH	KISLEV	LAGUNE	LAYERS	LIEDER	LOCHIA	LURING	MALLOW
JORDAN	KEELER	KISMET	LAICAL	LAYING	LIERNE	LOCKED	LURIST	MALONE
JOSEPH	KEENER	KISSEL	LAISSE	LAYMAN	LIFTED	LOCKER	LUSAKA	MALONY
JOSHUA	KEENLY	KISSER	LALLAN	LAYOFF	LIFTER	LOCKET	LUSTER	MALORY
JOSIAH	KEEPER	KITBAG	LAMBDA	LAYOUT	LIGASE	LOCKUP	LUSTRE	MALTED
JOSKIN	KELLYS	KITCAT	LAMEDH	LAZILY	LIGATE	LOCULE	LUTEAL	MALTHA
JOSSER	KELOID	KITSCH	LAMELY	LEADEN	LIGETI	LOCUST	LUTEIN	MAMMAL
JOSTLE	KELPER	KITTEN	LAMENT	LEADER	LIGGER	LODGED	LUTHER	MAMMON
JOTTER	KELPIE	KITTLE	LAMINA	LEAGUE	LIGHTS	LODGER	LUTINE	MAMZER
JOVIAL	KELTER	KLAXON	LAMMAS	LEALTY	LIGNUM	LOGGER	LUTIST	MANAGE
JOYFUL	KELTIC	KLUDGE	LAMMER	LEANTO	LIGULA	LOGGIA	LUXATE	MANANA
JOYOUS	KELTIE	KNAGGY	LANATE	LEAVEN	LIGULE	LOGJAM	LUXURY	MANATI
JUBATE	KELVIN	KNIGHT	LANCER	LEAVER	LIGURE	LOITER	LUZERN	MANCHE
JUBBAH	KENDAL	KNIVES	LANCET	LEAVES	LIKELY	LOLITA	LYCEUM	MANCHU
JUDDER	KENNEL	KNOBBY	LANCIA	LECHER	LIKING	LOLIUM	LYCHEE	MANEGE
JUDGES	KENNET	KNOTTY	LANDAU	LECTOR	LILIAN	LOLLOP	LYCOSA	MANFUL
JUDICA	KENSAL	KODIAK	LANDED	LEDGER	LILITH	LOMOND	LYDIAN	MANGER
JUDITH	KENYAN	KOMODO	LANDER	LEEWAY	LIMBED	LONDON	LYMPNE	MANGLE
JUGGER	KEPHIR	KOODOO	LANDOR	LEGACY	LIMBER	LONELY	LYRICS	MANIAC
JUGGLE	KEPLER	KOOKIE	LANGUR	LEGATE	LIMBIC	LONGER	LYRIST	MANILA
JUICER	KERALA	KOOLAH	LANUGO	LEGATO	LIMITS	LOOFAH	LYTTON	MANIOC
JUJUBE	KERMES	KOREAN	LAPDOG	LEGEND	LIMNER	LOONIE	MACRON	MANITO
JULIAN	KERMIS	KORUNA	LAPITH	LEGGED	LIMPET	LOOPED	MACULA	MANNER
JULIET	KERNEL	KOSHER	LAPPER	LEGION	LIMPID	LOOPER	MACULE	MANNIN
JULIUS	KETMIR	KOSMOS	LAPPET	LEGIST	LIMPLY	LOOSEN	MADAME	MANQUÉ
JUMADA	KETONE	KOTWAL	LAPSED	LEGLET	LINDEN	LOOTER	MADCAP	MANTIS
JUMBAL	KETOSE	KOUROS	LAPSUS	LEGMAN	LINEAL	LOQUAT	MADDEN	MANTLE
JUMBLE	KETTLE	KOWTOW	LAPTOP	LEGUME	LINEAR	LORCHA	MADDER	MANTRA
JUMPER	KEVLAR	KRAKEN	LAPUTA	LEMNOS	LINEUP	LORDLY	MADEUP	MANTUA
JUNCUS	KEWPIE	KRANTZ	LARDER	LEMONY	LINGER	LORETO	MADMAN	MANUAL
JUNGLE	KEYNES	KRATER	LARDON	LEMUEL	LINGOT	LORICA	MADRAS	MANUKA
JUNIOR	KEYPAD	KRATON	LARIAT	LEMURE	LINING	LORIOT	MADRID	MANURE

MAOIST	MAZUMA	METAGE	MOBILE	MOSAIC	MUSIVE	NEARLY	NINETY	NUTMEG
MAOTAI	MEADOW	METATE	MOBIUS	MOSCOW	MUSKEG	NEATEN	NINIAN	NUTTER
MAPUTO	MEAGER	METEOR	MOCKER	MOSLEM	MUSKET	NEATLY	NIPPER	NUZZER
MAQUIS	MEAGRE	METHOD	MOCKUP	MOSQUE	MUSLIM	NEBBUK	NIPPLE	NUZZLE
MARACA	MEALIE	METHYL	MODELS	MOSSAD	MUSLIN	NEBECK	NIPPON	NYANZA
MARAUD	MEANIE	METIER	MODENA	MOSTLY	MUSSEL	NEBISH	NISSEN	NYLONS
MARBLE	MEANLY	METOPE	MODERN	MOTHER	MUSTER	NEBULA	NITERY	OAFISH
MARCEL	MEASLY	METRIC	MODEST	MOTILE	MUTANT	NEBULE	NITRIC	OAKLEY
MARGIN	MEATUS	METTLE	MODIFY	MOTION	MUTATE	NECKAR	NITRYL	OAKNUT
MARIAN	MEDDLE	MEXICO	MODISH	MOTIVE	MUTELY	NECKED	NITWIT	OARLAP
MARINA	MEDIAL	MIASMA	MODIST	MOTLEY	MUTINY	NECTAR	NIVOSE	OBECHE
MARINE	MEDIAN	MICKEY	MODIUS	MOTOWN	MUTISM	NEEDED	NOBBLE	OBELUS
MARISH	MEDICI	MICKLE	MODULE	MOTTLE	MUTTER	NEEDLE	NOBBUT	OBERON
MARIST	MEDICO	MICMAC	MOGGIE	MOUJIK	MUTTON	NEEDNT	NOBODY	OBIISM
MARKED	MEDINA	MICRON	MOHAIR	MOULDY	MUTUAL	NEFAST	NOCENT	OBITAL
MARKER	MEDISM	MIDDAY	MOHAWK	MOULIN	MUZHIK	NEGATE	NOCTUA	OBITER
MARKET	MEDIUM	MIDDEN	MOHOCK	MOUSER	MUZZLE	NELLIE	NODDED	OBJECT
MARKKA	MEDIUS	MIDDLE	MOIDER	MOUSEY	MYELIN	NELSON	NODDLE	OBLAST
MARKUP	MEDLAR	MIDGET	MOIETY	MOUSSE	MYELON	NEPALI	NODOSE	OBLATE
MARLIN	MEDLEY	MIDWAY	MOIRAI	MOUTAN	MYGALE	NEPETA	NODULE	OBLIGE
MARMOT	MEDUSA	MIGHTY	MOJAVE	MOUTER	MYOGEN	NEPHEW	NOGGIN	OBLONG
MARNER	MEDWAY	MIGNON	MOLECH	MOUTON	MYOPIA	NEREID	NOMADE	OBOIST
MAROON	MEEKLY	MIKADO	MOLEST	MOVIES	MYOPIC	NEREUS	NOMISM	OBOLUS
MARQUE	MEGRIM	MILADY	MOLINE	MOVING	MYOSIN	NERINE	NONAGE	OBSESS
MARRAM	MEJLIS	MILDEW	MOLLAH	MOWING	MYOSIS	NERIUM	NONARY	OBTAIN
MARRON	MEKONG	MILDLY	MOLLIE	MOZART	MYRIAD	NEROLI	NONCOM	OBTECT
MARROW	MELIUS	MILIEU	MOLOCH	MOZZLE	MYRTLE	NERVAL	NOODLE	OBTEND
MARSHY	MELLOW	MILLER	MOLTEN	MUCATE	MYSELF	NERVES	NOOKIE	OBTUND
MARTEL	MELODY	MILLET	MOMENT	MUCKER	MYSORE	NERVII	NORDIC	OBTUSE
MARTEN	MELTED	MILORD	MONACO	MUCKLE	MYSTIC	NESSIE	NORMAL	OBVERT
MARTHA	MELTON	MILTON	MONDAY	MUCOID	MYTHOS	NESSUS	NORMAN	OCCULT
MARTIN	MEMBER	MIMOSA	MONGER	MUCOUS	NAEVUS	NESTLE	NORROY	OCCUPY
MARTYR	MEMNON	MINCER	MONGOL	MUDDER	NAGANA	NESTOR	NORVIC	OCEANS
MARVEL	MEMOIR	MINDED	MUDDLE	MUDDLE	NAGARI	NETHER	NORWAY	OCELOT
MASADA	MEMORY	MINDEL	MONICA	MUESLI	NAILED	NETTLE	NOSILY	OCHONE
MASCOT	MENACE	MINDER	MONISM	MUFFET	NAILER	NEURAL	NOTARY	OCHREA
MASHAM	MENAGE	MINGLE	MONIST	MUFFIN	NALLAH	NEURON	NOTATE	OCKERS
MASHED	MENCAP	MINING	MONKEY	MUFFLE	NAMELY	NEUTER	NOTICE	OCTANE
MASHER	MENDEL	MINION	MONODY	MUFLON	NANDOO	NEVADA	NOTIFY	OCTANS
MASHIE	MENDER	MINNIE	MONROE	MUGGER	NANISM	NEWELL	NOTION	OCTANT
MASKED	MENDES	MINNOW	MONTEM	MULISH	NANKIN	NEWEST	NOUGAT	OCTAVE
MASKER	MENDIP	MINOAN	MONTHS	MULLAH	NANSEN	NEWMAN	NOUGHT	OCTAVO
MASLIN	MENHIR	MINTON	MOOCOW	MULLER	NANTES	NEWTON	NOUNCE	OCTROI
MASQUE	MENIAL	MINUET	MOOLAH	MULLET	NAPALM	NIACIN	NOVENA	OCULAR
MASSED	MENINX	MINUTE	MOOMBA	MULTUM	NAPERY	NIAMEY	NOVIAL	ODDITY
MASSES	MENSAL	MIRAGE	MOPING	MUMBLE	NAPIER	NIBBLE	NOVICE	ODDSON
MASSIF	MENTAL	MIRROR	MOPISH	MUMMER	NAPKIN	NICELY	NOWISE	ODENSE
MASTER	MENTOR	MISÈRE	MOPPET	MUNICH	NAPLES	NICENE	NOYADE	ODESSA
MASTIC	MENTUM	MISERY	MOPSUS	MUNIFY	NAPPER	NICETY	NOYOUS	ODIOUS
MATHIS	MERCAT	MISFIT	MORALE	MUNITE	NARROW	NICKED	NOZZLE	OEDEMA
MATING	MERCER	MISHAP	MORALS	MUNSHI	NASEBY	NICKEL	NUANCE	OENONE
MATINS	MERCIA	MISHIT	MORASS	MUPPET	NASION	NICKER	NUBBIN	OERLAY
MATLOW	MERELY	MISLAY	MORBID	MURAGE	NASSAU	NIDGET	NUBBLE	OEUVRE
MATRIC	MERGER	MISLED	MORBUS	MURALS	NASSER	NIDIFY	NUBILE	OFFCUT
MATRIX	MERINO	MISSAL	MOREEN	MURDER	NASTIC	NIELLO	NUCULE	OFFEND
MATRON	MERKIN	MISSED	MORGAN	MURIEL	NATANT	NIGGER	NUDISM	OFFICE
MATTED	MERLIN	MISSEL	MORGEN	MURINE	NATION	NIGGLE	NUDIST	OFFING
MATTER	MERLOT	MISSIS	MORGUE	MURLIN	NATIVE	NIGGLY	NUDITY	OFFISH
MATURE	MERMAN	MISSUS	MORION	MURMUR	NATRON	NIGHTS	NUDNIK	OFFSET
MAUGRE	MEROPE	MISTER	MORMON	MURPHY	NATTER	NIGHTY	NUGGAR	OGADEN
MAUNDY	MERRIE	MISUSE	MORNAY	MURRAM	NATURE	NIGNOG	NUGGET	OGAMIC
MAUSER	MERROW	MITRAL	MORNED	MURRAY	NAUGHT	NIKKEI	NULLAH	OGRESS
MAWKIN	MERSEY	MITRED	MOROSE	MURRHA	NAUSEA	NILGAI	NUMBER	OILCAN
MAXIMS	MERTON	MITTEN	MORRIS	MURRIN	NAUTCH	NILGAU	NUMBLY	OILERS
MAYBUG	MESAIL	MIZZEN	MORROW	MUSANG	NAVAHO	NILOTE	NUMDAH	OILMAN
MAYDAY	MESCAL	MIZZLE	MORSEL	MUSCAT	NAVAJO	NIMBLE	NUMPTY	OILRIG
MAYFLY	MESIAL	MOANER	MORTAL	MUSCLE	NEAPED	NIMBLY	NUNCIO	OJIBWA
MAYHEM	MESMER	MOATED	MORTAR	MUSEUM	NEARBY	NIMBUS	NUTANT	OLDISH
MAZOUT	MESSRS	MOBCAP	MORTEM	MUSING	NEARER	NIMROD	NUTATE	OLEATE

OLEFIN	ORKNEY	PACIFY	PARKED	PEDDLE	PHENYL	PINXIT	POINTE	POTTLE
OLENUS	ORMOLU	PACKED	PARKER	PEDLAR	PHILIP	PINYIN	POINTS	POUDRE
OLIVER	ORNATE	PACKER	PARKIN	PEELED	PHIZOG	PIPING	POIROT	POUFFE
OLIVET	ORNERY	PACKET	PARLEY	PEELER	PHLEGM	PIPKIN	POISED	POUNCE
OLIVIA	OROIDE	PADANG	PARLOR	PEEPER	PHLEUM	PIPPIN	POISON	POUNDS
OMASUM	ORPHAN	PADDED	PARODY	PEEVED	PHLOEM	PIQUET	POLACK	POURER
OMELET	ORPHIC	PADDLE	PAROLE	PEEWEE	PHOBIA	PIRACY	POLAND	POUTER
OMENTA	ORPINE	PADUAN	PARPEN	PEEWIT	PHOBIC	PIRATE	POLDER	POWDER
OMERTA	ORRERY	PAELLA	PARROT	PEGLEG	PHOBOS	PIRENE	POLICE	POWERS
OMNIUM	ORSINO	PAEONY	PARSEC	PEKING	PHOEBE	PISANO	POLICY	POWNIE
ONAGER	ORTEGA	PAGODA	PARSEE	PELHAM	PHONAL	PISCES	POLISH	POWTER
ONAGRA	ORWELL	PAHARI	PARSON	PELION	PHONEY	PISGAH	POLITE	POWWOW
ONCOME	OSBERT	PAIDUP	PARTLY	PELLET	PHONIC	PISSED	POLITY	PRAGUE
ONCOST	OSCINE	PAINED	PARTON	PELMET	PHOOEY	PISTIL	POLLAN	PRAISE
ONDINE	OSIERY	PAINTS	PARURE	PELOID	PHOTON	PISTOL	POLLED	PRANCE
ONEDIN	OSIRIS	PAINTY	PARVIS	PELOTA	PHRASE	PISTON	POLLEN	PRANKS
ONEGIN	OSMIUM	PAIRER	PASCAL	PELVIC	PHYLLO	PITMAN	POLLEX	PRATER
ONEIDA	OSMOSE	PAKHTI	PASHTO	PELVIS	PHYLUM	PITTED	POLLUX	PRAVDA
ONEMAN	OSPREY	PAKHTO	PASHTU	PENANG	PHYSIC	PITTER	POLONY	PRAXIS
ONEWAY	OSSIAN	PAKHTU	PASQUE	PENCEL	PHYSIO	PLACED	POLYOL	PRAYER
ONIONS	OSSIFY	PALACE	PASSED	PENCIL	PIAFFE	PLACER	POLYPS	PREACE
ONLINE	OSTEND	PALAIS	PASSES	PENMAN	PIAZZA	PLACID	POMACE	PREACH
ONRUSH	OSTIUM	PALATE	PASSIM	PENNAE	PICARD	PLAGAL	POMADE	PRECIS
ONSIDE	OSTLER	PALING	PASTEL	PENNAL	PICKAX	PLAGUE	POMELO	PREFAB
ONWARD	OSTREA	PALLAH	PASTIL	PENNON	PICKED	PLAICE	POMMEL	PREFER
OOCYTE	OSWALD	PALLAS	PASTIS	PENSÉE	PICKER	PLAINS	POMMIE	PREFIX
OODLES	OTALGY	PALLET	PASTON	PENSUM	PICKET	PLAINT	POMONA	PRELIM
OOKPIK	OTELLO	PALLID	PASTOR	PENTAD	PICKLE	PLANCH	POMPEY	PREMED
OOLITE	OTHERS	PALLOR	PASTRY	PENTEL	PICKUP	PLANET	POMPOM	PREPAY
OOLONG	OTIOSE	PALMER	PATACA	PENTUP	PICNIC	PLANKS	POMPON	PREPPY
OOMPAH	OTITIS	PALTRY	PATCHY	PENTYL	PICTOR	PLANKS	PONCHO	PRESTO
OPAQUE	OTTAVA	PAMELA	PATENT	PENURY	PIDDLE	PLAQUE	PONDER	PRETAX
OPENER	OTTAWA	PAMIRS	PATHAN	PEOPLE	PIDGIN	PLASMA	PONENT	PRETTY
OPENLY	OULONG	PAMPAS	PATHIC	PEPLOS	PIECES	PLATED	PONGEE	PREVIN
OPHISM	OUNCES	PAMPER	PATHOS	PEPLUM	PIEDOG	PLATEN	PONGID	PREWAR
OPHITE	OUNDLE	PAMYAT	PATINA	PEPPER	PIEMAN	PLATER	PONTIC	PRICED
OPIATE	OURALI	PANADA	PATMOS	PEPTIC	PIERCE	PLATES	POODLE	PRICEY
OPPOSE	OUTAGE	PANAMA	PATOIS	PEQUOD	PIERIS	PLAYER	POORLY	PRIEST
OPPUGN	OUTBAR	PANDER	PATROL	PERDUE	PIFFLE	PLEACH	POOTER	PRIMAL
OPTICS	OUTBID	PANDIT	PATRON	PERHAP	PIGEON	PLEASE	POPEYE	PRIMED
OPTIMA	OUTCRY	PANFRY	PATTEN	PERILS	PIGLET	PLEDGE	POPLAR	PRIMER
OPTIME	OUTFIT	PANOPE	PATTER	PERIOD	PIGOTT	PLENTY	POPLIN	PRIMLY
OPTION	OUTGAS	PANTER	PATTON	PERISH	PIGPEN	PLENUM	POPPER	PRIMUS
OPTOUT	OUTING	PANTON	PAUNCE	PERKIN	PIGSTY	PLEURA	POPPET	PRINCE
ORACHE	OUTLAW	PANTRY	PAUNCH	PERMIT	PILAFF	PLEXOR	POPPIT	PRIORY
ORACLE	OUTLAY	PANZER	PAUPER	PERNOD	PILAGE	PLEXUS	POPPLE	PRISMS
ORALLY	OUTLET	PAPACY	PAVANE	PERRON	PILATE	PLIANT	PORGIE	PRISON
ORANGE	OUTLIE	PAPAGO	PAVING	PERSON	PILEUM	PLIERS	PORKER	PRISSY
ORATOR	OUTPUT	PAPAYA	PAVLOV	PERUKE	PILEUP	PLIGHT	POROUS	PRIVET
ORBITA	OUTRUN	PAPERS	PAWNEE	PERUSE	PILEUS	PLINTH	PORTAL	PRIZES
ORCHID	OUTSET	PAPERY	PAWPAW	PESADE	PILFER	PLISSÉ	PORTER	PROBIT
ORCHIS	OUTTOP	PAPHOS	PAYDAY	PESETA	PILING	PLONGE	PORTIA	PROFIT
ORCINE	OUTVIE	PAPIST	PAYING	PESHWA	PILLAR	PLOUGH	PORTLY	PROLEG
ORDAIN	OUTWIT	PAPULE	PAYNIM	PESTER	PILLOW	PLOVER	POSADA	PROLIX
ORDEAL	OVERDO	PARADE	PAYOFF	PESTLE	PILOSE	PLUCKY	POSEUR	PROLOG
ORDERS	OVERLY	PARAMO	PAYOLA	PÉTAIN	PIMENT	PLUMED	POSSER	PROMPT
ORDURE	OVIBOS	PARANA	PEAHEN	PETARD	PIMPLE	PLUMMY	POSSET	PRONTO
OREGON	OVISAC	PARAPH	PEAKED	PETARY	PIMPLY	PLUNGE	POSSUM	PROPEL
OREXIS	OWLCAR	PARCAE	PEANUT	PETERS	PINCER	PLURAL	POSTAL	PROPER
ORGANS	OWLISH	PARCEL	PEARLS	PETIPA	PINDAR	PLUTUS	POSTER	PROPYL
ORGASM	OXALIC	PARDIE	PEARLY	PETITE	PINEAL	PLYING	POSTIL	PROSIT
ORGEAT	OXALIS	PARDON	PEBBLE	PETREL	PINERO	PNEUMA	POTASH	PROTEA
ORGONE	OXFORD	PARENT	PEBBLY	PETROL	PINGER	POBBLE	POTATO	PROTON
ORIANO	OXGATE	PARETO	PECKER	PEWTER	PINING	POCKET	POTEEN	PROUST
ORIENT	OXHEAD	PAREVE	PECTEN	PEYOTE	PINION	PODIUM	POTENT	PRUNER
ORIGEN	OXHIDE	PARGET	PECTIN	PHAROS	PINITE	PODSOL	POTHER	PRUSIK
ORIGIN	OXTAIL	PARIAH	PEDALO	PHASIS	PINKIE	PODZOL	POTION	PRYING
ORIOLE	OXYGEN	PARISH	PEDANT	PHASMA	PINTER	POETIC	POTTED	PSALMS
ORISON	OYSTER	PARITY	PEDDER	PHENOL	PINTLE	POETRY	POTTER	PSALMS

PSEUDO	QUAICH	RAMBLE	REBUFF	RELISH	REVIEW	ROBSON	RUCKUS	SALINE
PSYCHE	QUAIGH	RAMEAU	REBUKE	RELIVE	REVILE	ROBUST	RUDDER	SALISH
PSYCHO	QUAINT	RAMIFY	RECALL	REMAIN	REVISE	ROCKER	RUDDLE	SALIVA
PTERIN	QUAKER	RAMJET	RECANT	REMAKE	REVIVE	ROCKET	RUDELY	SALLEE
PTERIS	QUALMS	RAMOSE	RECAST	REMAND	REVOKE	ROCOCO	RUEFUL	SALLET
PTOSIS	QUANGO	RAMOUS	RECEDE	REMARK	REVOLT	RODENT	RUELLE	SALLOW
PUBLIC	QUARRY	RAMROD	RECENT	REMEDY	REWARD	RODHAM	RUFFLE	SALMIS
PUCKER	QUARTO	RANCEL	RECESS	REMIND	REWIND	RODNEY	RUGGED	SALMON
PUDDLE	QUARTZ	RANCHO	RECIFE	REMISS	REWIRE	ROEMER	RUGGER	SALOME
PUDSEY	QUASAR	RANCID	RECIPE	REMORA	REWORD	ROGNON	RUGOSE	SALOON
PUEBLO	QUAVER	RANCOR	RECITE	REMOTE	REWORK	ROGUES	RUGOUS	SALOOP
PUERTO	QUEASY	RANDOM	RECKON	REMOVE	RHAPHE	ROKEBY	RUINED	SALUKI
PUFFED	QUEBEC	RANGER	RECOIL	RENAME	RHEIMS	ROLAND	RULING	SALUTE
PUFFER	QUEENS	RANKED	RECORD	RENDER	RHESUS	ROLLER	RUMBLE	SALVER
PUFFIN	QUELCH	RANKER	RECOUP	RENEGE	RHETOR	ROMANO	RUMKIN	SALVIA
PUISNE	QUENCH	RANKLE	RECTAL	RENNET	RHEUMY	ROMANS	RUMMER	SAMARA
PULLET	QUETCH	RANSOM	RECTOR	RENNIN	RHEXIS	ROMANY	RUMORS	SAMBAL
PULLEY	QUICHE	RANTER	RECTUM	RENOIR	RHODES	ROMISH	RUMOUR	SAMBAR
PULPIT	QUIDAM	RANULA	RECTUS	RENOWN	RHYMER	ROMMEL	RUMPLE	SAMBUR
PULSAR	QUINCE	RAPHIA	REDACT	RENTAL	RHYTHM	ROMNEY	RUMPUS	SAMEKH
PULVER	QUINSY	RAPIDS	REDCAP	RENTER	RIALTO	RONDEL	RUNDLE	SAMFOO
PUMICE	QUINTA	RAPIER	REDCAR	RENVOI	RIBALD	ROOFER	RUNNEL	SAMIAN
PUMMEL	QUIRKY	RAPINE	REDDEN	RENVOY	RIBAND	ROOKIE	RUNNER	SAMIEL
PUNCHY	QUITCH	RAPIST	REDEEM	REOPEN	RIBBED	ROOMER	RUNOFF	SAMIOT
PUNCTO	QUIVER	RAPPED	REDEYE	REPAID	RIBBLE	ROOTED	RUNWAY	SAMITE
PUNDIT	QUOITS	RAPPEL	REDLEG	REPAIR	RIBBON	ROOTER	RUNYON	SAMLET
PUNISH	QUORUM	RAPPER	REDRAW	REPAST	RIBOSE	ROOTLE	RUPEES	SAMOSA
PUNJAB	QUOTED	RAPTLY	REDTOP	REPEAL	RICHES	ROPERY	RUPERT	SAMPAN
PUNKAH	QWERTY	RAPTOR	REDUCE	REPEAT	RICHLY	ROQUET	RUPIAH	SAMPLE
PUNNET	RABATO	RAREFY	REEBOK	REPENT	RICKER	ROSACE	RUPIAS	SAMSON
PUNTER	RABBET	RARELY	REEFER	REPINE	RICKEY	ROSARY	RUSHED	SAMUEL
PUPATE	RABBIT	RARING	REEKIE	REPLAY	RICRAC	ROSCID	RUSKIN	SANCHO
PUPPET	RABBLE	RARITY	REELER	REPORT	RICTAL	ROSCOE	RUSSET	SANDAL
PUPPIS	RABIES	RASCAL	REFACE	REPOSE	RICTUS	ROSERY	RUSSIA	SANDER
PURDAH	RACEME	RASHER	REFECT	REPTON	RIDDLE	ROSINA	RUSTAM	SANELY
PURELY	RACHEL	RASHLY	REFILL	REPUGN	RIDENT	ROSSER	RUSTEM	SANITY
PURIFY	RACHIS	RASPER	REFINE	REPUTE	RIDGED	ROSTER	RUSTIC	SANSEI
PURINE	RACIAL	RASTER	REFLET	REREAD	RIDING	ROSTOV	RUSTLE	SANTAL
PURIST	RACINE	RATBAG	REFLEX	RESALE	RIENZI	ROSYTH	RUSTUM	SANTON
PURITY	RACING	RATHER	REFLUX	RESEAU	RIFFLE	ROTARY	RUTTED	SAPELE
PURLER	RACISM	RATIFY	REFORM	RESECT	RIGGED	ROTATE	RUTTER	SAPHAR
PURLIN	RACIST	RATINE	REFUEL	RESEDA	RIGGER	ROTGUT	RWANDA	SAPIUM
PURPLE	RACKET	RATING	REFUGE	RESENT	RIGHTO	ROTHER	RYOKAN	SAPOTA
PURSED	RADDLE	RATION	REFUND	RESIDE	RIGHTS	ROTHKO	SAANEN	SAPOTE
PURSER	RADIAL	RATOON	REFUSE	RESIGN	RIGOUR	ROTTEN	SABELE	SAPPER
PURSUE	RADIAN	RATTAN	REFUTE	RESIST	RIMINI	ROTTER	SABINE	SAPPHO
PURVEY	RADISH	RATTER	REGAIN	RESORT	RIMMED	ROTULA	SABRES	SARGUS
PUSHER	RADIUM	RATTLE	REGALE	RESULT	RINGED	ROTUND	SACHET	SARNIE
PUSHTU	RADIUS	RATTON	REGARD	RESUME	RINGER	ROUBLE	SACRED	SARONG
PUSHUP	RADULA	RAUNCH	REGENT	RETAIL	RIOTER	ROUGED	SACRUM	SARSEN
PUSSER	RAFALE	RAVAGE	REGEST	RETAIN	RIPOFF	ROUGHY	SADDEN	SARTOR
PUTEAL	RAFFIA	RAVINE	REGGAE	RETAKE	RIPPER	ROUNCE	SADDHU	SARTRE
PUTOIS	RAFFLE	RAVING	REGIME	RETARD	RIPPLE	ROUNDS	SADDLE	SASHAY
PUTOUT	RAFTER	RAVISH	REGINA	RETINA	RIPPON	ROUTER	SADISM	SATEEN
PUTRID	RAGBAG	RAZURE	REGION	RETIRE	RIPSAW	ROVING	SADIST	SATINY
PUTSCH	RAGGED	RAZZIA	REGIUS	RETOOL	RISING	ROWING	SAFARI	SATIRE
PUTTEE	RAGGLE	RAZZLE	REGLET	RETORT	RISQUÉ	ROXANE	SAFELY	SATIVE
PUTTER	RAGING	READER	REGULO	RETOUR	RITUAL	ROYALS	SAFETY	SATORI
PUZZLE	RAGLAN	REALIA	REGRET	RETURN	RIVAGE	ROZZER	SAGELY	SATRAP
PYEDOG	RAGMAN	REALLY	REHASH	REUBEN	RIVERA	RUBBED	SAGGAR	SATURN
PYRENE	RAGOUT	REALTY	REHEAT	REUTER	RIVLIN	RUBBER	SAHARA	SATYRA
PYRITE	RAGTOP	REAMER	REHEEL	REVAMP	RIYADH	RUBBLE	SAILOR	SAUCER
PYRONE	RAGUSA	REAPER	REJECT	REVEAL	ROADIE	RUBBRA	SAINTS	SAUGER
PYROPE	RAIDER	REASON	REJOIN	REVERE	ROAMER	RUBENS	SAITHE	SAURIA
PYRRHO	RAISED	REBATE	RELATE	REVERS	ROARER	RUBIES	SALAAM	SAVAGE
PYTHIA	RAISER	REBECK	RELENT	REVERT	ROBBED	RUBIKS	SALADE	SAVANT
PYTHON	RAISIN	REBITE	RELICS	REVERY	ROBBER	RUBRIC	SALAMI	SAVATE
QUAGGA	RAKING	REBORE	RELICT	RÊVEUR	ROBERT	RUCHED	SALARY	SAVING
QUAHOG	RAKISH	REBORN	RELIEF		ROBING	RUCKLE	SALINA	SAVIOR

SAVOIE	SCRIMP	SENSED	SHARON	SIERRA	SLANGY	SNAZZY	SORROW	SPOTTY
SAVORY	SCRIPT	SENSES	SHARPS	SIESTA	SLATCH	SNEAKY	SORTER	SPOUSE
SAVOUR	SCROLL	SENSOR	SHASTA	SIFFLE	SLATER	SNEATH	SORTES	SPRAIN
SAVVEY	SCROOP	SENTRY	SHAVEN	SIFTER	SLAVER	SNEEZE	SORTIE	SPRANG
SAWDER	SCRUBS	SEPIUM	SHAVER	SIGHTS	SLAVES	SNEEZY	SOUGHT	SPRAWL
SAWNEY	SCRUFF	SEPSIS	SHEARS	SIGNAL	SLAYER	SNIFFY	SOUPER	SPREAD
SAWYER	SCRUNT	SEPTAL	SHEATH	SIGNET	SLEAVE	SNIFTY	SOUPLE	SPRING
SAXONY	SCULPT	SEPTET	SHEAVE	SIGNOR	SLEAZE	SNIPER	SOURCE	SPRINT
SAYERS	SCUMMY	SEPTIC	SHEENY	SIKKIM	SLEAZY	SNIPPY	SOURLY	SPRITE
SAYING	SCUNGE	SEQUEL	SHEERS	SILAGE	SLEDGE	SNITCH	SOUSED	SPRITZ
SBIRRO	SCURRY	SEQUIN	SHEETS	SILENE	SLEEKY	SNIVEL	SOUTER	SPROUT
SCABBY	SCURVY	SERAIL	SHEIKH	SILENT	SLEEPY	SNOOTY	SOVIET	SPRUCE
SCAITH	SCUTCH	SERANG	SHEILA	SILICA	SLEEVE	SNOOZE	SOWBUG	SPRUNG
SCALAR	SCUTUM	SERAPE	SHEKEL	SILKEN	SLEEZY	SNORER	SOWING	SPRYLY
SCALER	SCUZZY	SERAPH	SHELVE	SILVAN	SLEIGH	SNOTTY	SOWSED	SPUNGE
SCALES	SCYLLA	SERBIA	SHERIF	SILVER	SLEUTH	SNOUTY	SOWTER	SPURGE
SCAMPI	SCYTHE	SERDAB	SHERPA	SIMEON	SLEWED	SNOWED	SOZZLE	SPUTUM
SCAMPO	SDEATH	SERENE	SHERRY	SIMIAN	SLICER	SNUDGE	SPACED	SPYING
SCANTY	SEABEE	SERIAL	SHEVAT	SIMILE	SLIDER	SNUGLY	SPACER	SQUAIL
SCAPUS	SEALED	SERIES	SHIELD	SIMKIN	SLIGHT	SOAKED	SPADES	SQUALL
SCARAB	SEAMAN	SERINE	SHIFTY	SIMMER	SLINKY	SOBEIT	SPADIX	SQUAMA
SCARCE	SEAMEN	SERMON	SHIITE	SIMNEL	SLIPPY	SOCAGE	SPARKS	SQUARE
SCARED	SEAMER	SEROSA	SHILOH	SIMONY	SLIPUP	SOCCER	SPARKY	SQUASH
SCARER	SEAMUS	SERVAL	SHIMMY	SIMOOM	SLITHY	SOCIAL	SPARSE	SQUAWK
SCATCH	SEANCE	SERVER	SHINDY	SIMOON	SLIVER	SOCKET	SPARTA	SQUEAK
SCATHE	SEARCH	SESAME	SHINER	SIMPER	SLOANE	SODDEN	SPARTH	SQUEAL
SCATTY	SEASON	SETOSE	SHINNY	SIMPLE	SLOGAN	SODIUM	SPATHE	SQUILL
SCENIC	SEATED	SETTEE	SHINTO	SIMPLY	SLOPES	SODOMY	SPAULD	SQUINT
SCHEMA	SEAWAY	SETTER	SHINTY	SINBAD	SLOPPY	SOFFIT	SPAVIN	SQUIRE
SCHEME	SEBATE	SETTLE	SHIPKA	SINDER	SLOSHY	SOFTEN	SPECIE	SQUIRM
SCHISM	SECANT	SEUMAS	SHIRAZ	SINEWY	SLOUCH	SOFTIE	SPEECH	SQUIRT
SCHIST	SECEDE	SEURAT	SHIRRA	SINFUL	SLOUGH	SOFTLY	SPEEDO	SQUISH
SCHIZO	SECOND	SEVENS	SHIRTY	SINGER	SLOVAK	SOHRAB	SPEEDY	STABLE
SCHLEP	SECRET	SEVERE	SHIVER	SINGLE	SLOVEN	SOIGNÉ	SPEISS	STABLY
SCHMOE	SECTOR	SEVERN	SHODDY	SINGLY	SLOWLY	SOILED	SPENCE	STACKS
SCHOOL	SECURE	·SEVERY	SHOFAR	SINKER	SLUDGE	SOIREE	SPHENE	STAFFA
SCHUSS	SEDATE	SÈVRES	SHOGUN	SINNER	SLUICE	SOLACE	SPHERE	STAGER
SCHUYT	SEDUCE	SEWAGE	SHORTS	SIPHON	SLUMMY	SOLANO	SPHINX	STAGEY
SCILLA	SEEDED	SEWELL	SHOULD	SIPPET	SLURRY	SOLDER	SPICED	STAIRS
SCILLY	SEEDER	SEWING	SHOVEL	SIPPLE	SLUSHY	SOLEIL	SPICER	STAKES
SCIPIO	SEEING	SEXISM	SHOWER	SIRDAR	SMACKS	SOLELY	SPIDER	STALAG
SCIROC	SEEKER	SEXIST	SHRANK	SIRIUS	SMALLS	SOLEMN	SPIGOT	STALIN
SCIRON	SEEMLY	SEXTAN	SHREWD	SIRKAR	SMARMY	SOLENT	SPIKED	STALKS
SCLAFF	SEESAW	SEXTET	SHRIEK	SIRRAH	SMARTY	SOLERA	SPILTH	STALKY
SCLERA	SEETHE	SEXTON	SHRIFT	SIRREE	SMEARY	SOLEUS	SPINAL	STALLS
SCLERE	SEICHE	SEXUAL	SHRIKE	SISKIN	SMEATH	SOLIVE	SPINAR	STAMEN
SCOLEX	SEISIN	SHABBY	SHRILL	SISTER	SMEGMA	SOLUTE	SPINET	STAMPS
SCONCE	SELDOM	SHADED	SHRIMP	SITCOM	SMELLY	SOLVAY	SPIRAL	STANCE
SCOOBS	SELECT	SHADES	SHRINE	SITREP	SMIGHT	SOLVED	SPIRIT	STANCH
SCOOSH	SELENE	SHADOW	SHRINK	SITTER	SMILER	SOLVER	SPITAL	STANZA
SCOPUS	SELFED	SHADUF	SHRIVE	SIZZLE	SMILES	SOMALI	SPLAKE	STAPES
SCORCH	SELJUK	SHAGGY	SHROFF	SKATER	SMILEY	SOMBER	SPLASH	STAPLE
SCORER	SELLBY	SHAKEN	SHROUD	SKATES	SMIRCH	SOMBRE	SPLEEN	STARCH
SCORIA	SELLER	SHAKER	SHROVE	SKELLY	SMITHS	SONANT	SPLENT	STARES
SCORSE	SELSYN	SHAKES	SHRUNK	SKERRY	SMITHY	SONATA	SPLICE	STARRY
SCOTCH	SELWYN	SHALOM	SHTCHI	SKETCH	SMOKER	SONICS	SPLIFF	STARVE
SCOTER	SEMELE	SHAMAN	SHTETL	SKEWED	SMOKEY	SONNET	SPLINT	STASIS
SCOTIA	SEMITE	SHAMBA	SHUDRA	SKEWER	SMOOCH	SONTAG	SPLITS	STATAL
SCOUSE	SEMPRE	SHAMMY	SHUFTI	SKIDOO	SMOOTH	SOONER	SPLOSH	STATED
SCRAMB	SEMTEX	SHAMUS	SHUFTY	SKIING	SMUDGE	SOOTHE	SPOILS	STATEN
SCRAPE	SENATE	SHANDY	SICILY	SKIMPY	SMUDGY	SOPHIA	SPOILT	STATER
SCRAPS	SENDAL	SHANKS	SICKEN	SKINNY	SMUGLY	SORAGE	SPOKEN	STATES
SCRAWL	SENDER	SHANTY	SICKER	SKIVER	SMUTTY	SORBET	SPOKES	STATIC
SCRAWM	SENECA	SHAPED	SICKLE	SKIVVY	SMYRNA	SORDES	SPONGE	STATOR
SCREAM	SENILE	SHARED	SICKLY	SKURRY	SNAGGY	SORDID	SPONGY	STATUE
SCREED	SENIOR	SHARER	SIDDHA	SKYLAB	SNAILY	SORELL	SPOOKY	STATUS
SCREEN	SENLAC	SHARES	SIDING	SKYMAN	SNAKED	SORELY	SPOONY	STAYER
SCREWY	SENNET	SHARIA	SIDNEY	SLACKS	SNAPPY	SORGHO	SPORTS	STEADY
SCRIBE	SENORA	SHARIF	SIENNA	SLALOM	SNATCH	SORREL	SPORTY	STEAMY

STEELE	STRIPE	SUNDRY	TAHITI	TATTOO	TETANY	THROVE	TIVOLI	TRADER
STEELY	STRIPY	SUNHAT	TAIGLE	TAUGHT	TETCHY	THROWN	TIZWAZ	TRADES
STEERS	STRIVE	SUNKEN	TAILLE	TAURUS	TETHER	THRUSH	TMESIS	TRAGIC
STEMMA	STROBE	SUNLIT	TAILOR	TAUTEN	TETHYS	THRUST	TOBAGO	TRAGUS
STENCH	STRODE	SUNRAY	TAIPAN	TAUTLY	TETRAD	THWACK	TOBIAS	TRAJAN
STEPPE	STROKE	SUNSET	TAIPEI	TAUTOG	TETRYL	THWART	TOCSIN	TRALEE
STEREO	STROLL	SUNTAN	TAIWAN	TAVERN	TETTIX	THYMOL	TODDLE	TRANCE
STERIC	STRONG	SUPERB	TAKING	TAWDRY	TEUTON	THYMUS	TOECAP	TRANNY
STERNE	STROUD	SUPINE	TALBOT	TAWPIE	TEVIOT	THYRSE	TOERAG	TRAPES
STEROL	STROUP	SUPLEX	TALCUM	TAXEME	THALER	TICINO	TOETOE	TRASHY
STEVEN	STROVE	SUPPER	TALENT	TAXING	THALES	TICKER	TOFFEE	TRAUMA
STEWED	STRUCK	SUPPLE	TALION	TAXMAN	THALIA	TICKET	TOGGED	TRAVEL
STICKS	STRUNG	SUPPLY	TALKER	TEABAG	THAMES	TICKEY	TOGGLE	TRAVIS
STICKY	STRUNT	SURELY	TALKIE	TEACUP	THANAH	TICKLE	TOILET	TREATY
STIFLE	STUART	SURETÉ	TALLIS	TEAGUE	THANET	TICKLY	TOLEDO	TREBLE
STIGMA	STUBBS	SURETY	TALLOT	TEAPOT	THANKS	TIDBIT	TOLLED	TREBLY
STILTS	STUBBY	SURFER	TALLOW	TEAPOY	THATCH	TIDDLE	TOLLER	TREMOR
STILTY	STUCCO	SURREY	TALMUD	TEASEL	THEAVE	TIDDLY	TOLOSA	TRENCH
STINGO	STUDIO	SURTAX	TAMALE	TEASER	THEBAN	TIDILY	TOLTEC	TRENDY
STINGY	STUMER	SURVEY	TAMANU	TECHNO	THEBES	TIEPIN	TOLUIC	TREPAN
STINKO	STUMPS	SUSSEX	TAMARA	TECKEL	THECAL	TIERCE	TOLUOL	TRESCO
STINKS	STUMPY	SUTLER	TAMARI	TECTUM	THEIRS	TIERED	TOLZEY	TRIAGE
STIPES	STUPID	SUTTEE	TAMELY	TEDIUM	THEISM	TIFFIN	TOMATO	TRIBAL
STITCH	STUPOR	SUTURE	TAMINE	TEENSY	THEIST	TIGHTS	TOMBOY	TRIBES
STOCKS	STURDY	SVELTE	TAMISE	TEEPEE	THEMIS	TIGRIS	TOMCAT	TRICAR
STOCKY	STYLET	SWABIA	TAMMAR	TEETER	THENAR	TILLER	TOMIAL	TRICKS
STODGE	STYLUS	SWAMPY	TAMMUZ	TEETHE	THENCE	TILSIT	TOMIUM	TRICKY
STODGY	STYMIE	SWANEE	TAMPER	TEFLON	THEORY	TIMBER	TOMTOM	TRICOT
STOGIE	STYRAX	SWANKY	TAMPON	TEGMEN	THERMO	TIMBRE	TONANT	TRIFLE
STOKER	SUBDUE	SWARTY	TANDEM	TEGULA	THESIS	TIMELY	TONGAN	TRIGON
STOKES	SUBLET	SWATCH	TANGLE	TEHRAN	THETIC	TIMING	TONGUE	TRILBY
STOLEN	SUBMIT	SWATHE	TANKER	TELEDU	THETIS	TINDER	TONITE	TRIMLY
STOLID	SUBORN	SWEATY	TANKIA	TELEGA	THEYRE	TINGED	TONSIL	TRIODE
STOLON	SUBSET	SWEDEN	TANNAH	TELEGU	THICKY	TINGLE	TONSOR	TRIPLE
STONED	SUBTLE	SWEENY	TANNED	TELLAR	THIERS	TINKER	TOOTER	TRIPOD
STONER	SUBTLY	SWEETS	TANNER	TELLER	THIEVE	TINKLE	TOOTHY	TRIPOS
STONES	SUBURB	SWERVE	TANNIC	TELLUS	THINGS	TINNED	TOOTLE	TRISTE
STOOGE	SUBWAY	SWINGE	TANNIN	TELUGU	THINGY	TINNIE	TOOTSY	TRITON
STOOKS	SUCCOR	SWIPES	TANNOY	TEMPER	THINLY	TINPAN	TOPHUS	TRIVET
STOOLS	SUCCUS	SWITCH	TANTRA	TEMPLE	THIRST	TINPOT	TOPPER	TRIVIA
STORAX	SUCKEN	SWIVEL	TAOISM	TENACE	THIRTY	TINSEL	TOPPLE	TROCAR
STORER	SUCKER	SWIVET	TAOIST	TENANT	THISBE	TINTED	TORERO	TROCHE
STOREY	SUCKET	SWOOSH	TAPPER	TENDER	THOLOS	TINTIN	TORPID	TROIKA
STORMY	SUCKLE	SYDNEY	TAPPET	TENDON	THOLUS	TIPCAT	TORPOR	TROJAN
STOVER	SUDARY	SYLVAN	TAPPIT	TENDRE	THOMAS	TIPOFF	TORQUE	TROMPE
STOWER	SUDATE	SYLVIA	TARCEL	TENGKU	THORAH	TIPPED	TORRES	TROOPS
STRABO	SUDDEN	SYMBOL	TARDIS	TENNER	THORAX	TIPPER	TORRID	TROPHE
STRAFE	SUFFER	SYNCOM	TARGET	TENNIS	THORNE	TIPPET	TORULA	TROPHY
STRAIN	SUFFIX	SYNDIC	TARGUM	TENPIN	THORNY	TIPPLE	TOSHER	TROPIC
STRAIT	SUGARY	SYNTAX	TARIFF	TENSON	THORPE	TIPPOO	TOSSUP	TROPPO
STRAKE	SUITED	SYPHER	TARMAC	TENSOR	THOUGH	TIPTOE	TOTTER	TROUGH
STRAND	SUITOR	SYPHON	TARROW	TENURE	THRALL	TIPTOP	TOTTIE	TROUPE
STRASS	SUIVEZ	SYRIAN	TARSAL	TEOPAN	THRASH	TIPULA	TOUCAN	TROUVÉ
STRATA	SUKKAH	SYRINX	TARSEL	TEPHRA	THRAWN	TIRADE	TOUCHE	TROVER
STRAWS	SULCUS	SYRISM	TARSIA	TERCET	THREAD	TIRANA	TOUCHY	TROWEL
STRAWY	SULFUR	SYRUPY	TARSUS	TERCIO	THREAP	TIRING	TOUPEE	TROYES
STREAK	SULLEN	SYSTEM	TARTAN	TEREDO	THREAT	TISANE	TOUPET	TRUANT
STREAM	SULPHA	SYZYGY	TARTAR	TERESA	THRENE	TISHRI	TOURER	TRUDGE
STREET	SULTAN	TABARD	TARTLY	TERETE	THRESH	TISSOT	TOUSER	TRUISM
STREGA	SULTRY	TABLET	TASMAN	TERGUM	THRICE	TISSUE	TOUSLE	TRUMAN
STRENE	SUMACH	TABULA	TASSEL	TERMES	THRIFT	TITBIT	TOWAGE	TRUMPS
STRESS	SUMMER	TACKET	TASSET	TERMLY	THRILL	TITCHY	TOWARD	TRUNKS
STRICK	SUMMIT	TACKLE	TASSIE	TERNAL	THRIPS	TITFER	TOWBAR	TRUSTY
STRICT	SUMMON	TACOMA	TASTER	TERRAE	THRIST	TITIAN	TOWHEE	TRUTHS
STRIDE	SUNDAE	TACTIC	TATAMI	TERROR	THRIVE	TITLED	TOWNEE	TRYING
STRIFE	SUNDAY	TAENIA	TATERS	TERTIA	THROAT	TITTER	TOWNLY	TSETSE
STRIKE	SUNDER	TAGORE	TATLER	TESTER	THROES	TITTLE	TOWSER	TSHIRT
STRINE	SUNDEW	TAHINA	TATTER	TESTES	THRONE	TITTUP	TOYISH	TSONGA
STRING		TAHINI	TATTLE	TESTIS	THRONG	TITULE	TRACER	TSWANA

TUAREG	UBIETY	UNPAID	USHANT	VERGES	VOMICA	WATERY	WICKED	WORSEN
TUBERS	UCKERS	UNPICK	USURER	VERIFY	VOODOO	WATSON	WICKER	WORTHY
TUBING	UDMURT	UNPLUG	UTERUS	VERILY	VORTEX	WATTLE	WICKET	WORTLE
TUBULE	UFFIZI	UNREAD	UTMOST	VERISM	VOSGES	WAVELL	WIDELY	WOWSER
TUCANA	UGANDA	UNREAL	UTOPIA	VERITY	VOTARY	WAVING	WIDGET	WRAITH
TUCKER	UGARIT	UNREEL	VACANT	VERMIN	VOTING	WAXING	WIDOWS	WRASSE
TUCKET	UGRIAN	UNREST	VACATE	VERMIS	VOTIVE	WAYLAY	WIENER	WREATH
TUFFET	ULCERS	UNRIPE	VACUUM	VERNAL	VOTYAK	WAYOUT	WIFELY	WREKIN
TUFTED	ULITIS	UNROLL	VADOSE	VERNON	VOWELS	WEAKEN	WIGEON	WRENCH
TUGRIK	ULLAGE	UNRULY	VAGARY	VERSAL	VOYAGE	WEAKER	WIGGLE	WRETCH
TUILLE	ULLING	UNSAFE	VAGINA	VERSED	VOYEUR	WEAKLY	WIGGLY	WRIGHT
TULBAN	ULSTER	UNSAID	VAHINE	VERSES	VULCAN	WEALTH	WIGWAM	WRITER
TULIPA	ULTIMA	UNSEAM	VAINLY	VERSET	VULGAR	WEAPON	WILDER	WRITHE
TUMBLE	ULTIMO	UNSEAT	VALENS	VERSUS	VULGUS	WEARER	WILDLY	WYVERN
TUMEFY	UMBLES	UNSEEN	VALETA	VERVET	WABASH	WEASEL	WILFUL	XANADU
TUMOUR	UMBREL	UNSENT	VALGUS	VESICA	WACKER	WEAVER	WILLED	XAVIER
TUMULT	UMBRIA	UNSEXY	VALINE	VESPER	WADDLE	WEBBED	WILLET	XENIAL
TUNDRA	UMBRIL	UNSHOD	VALISE	VESSEL	WADERS	WEDDED	WILLIE	XENIUM
TUNING	UMLAUT	UNSOLD	VALIUM	VESTAL	WADHAM	WEDGED	WILLOW	XEROMA
TUNNEL	UMPIRE	UNSUNG	VALLEY	VESTED	WAFFLE	WEDGIE	WILSON	XERXES
TUPELO	UNABLE	UNSURE	VALLUM	VESTRY	WAFTED	WEEKLY	WIMBLE	XYLENE
TURBAN	UNBEND	UNTIDY	VALOUR	VIABLE	WAGGLE	WEEPER	WIMPLE	XYLOID
TURBID	UNBENT	UNTOLD	VALUER	VIANDS	WAGGON	WEEPIE	WIMSEY	XYLOSE
TURBOT	UNBIND	UNTRUE	VALUTA	VIATOR	WAGNER	WEEVIL	WINDER	YABBER
TUREEN	UNBOLT	UNUSED	VANDAL	VIBRIO	WAGRAM	WEEWEE	WINDOW	YAFFLE
TURGID	UNBORN	UNVEIL	VANISH	VICTIM	WAILER	WEIGHT	WINDUP	YAHWEH
TURKEY	UNBRED	UNWARY	VANITY	VICTOR	WAITER	WEIMAR	WINGED	YAKKER
TURNED	UNBUSY	UNWELL	VAPOUR	VICUNA	WAIVER	WEIRDO	WINGER	YAKUZA
TURNER	UNCAGE	UNWIND	VARECH	VIENNA	WAKING	WELDER	WINKER	YAMMER
TURNIP	UNCIAL	UNWISE	VARESE	VIENNE	WALKER	WELKIN	WINKLE	YANKEE
TURNUP	UNCLAD	UNWRAP	VARIED	VIEWER	WALLAH	WELLER	WINNER	YANKER
TURPIN	UNCOIL	UNYOKE	VARLET	VIGOUR	WALLED	WELLES	WINNIE	YAOURT
TURRET	UNCOOL	UPBEAT	VASSAL	VIKING	WALLER	WELLIE	WINNOW	YARDIE
TURTLE	UNCORK	UPCAST	VASTLY	VILELY	WALLET	WELTER	WINTER	YARROW
TURVES	UNDATE	UPDATE	VATHEK	VILIFY	WALLOP	WELWYN	WINTRY	YATTER
TUSCAN	UNDECK	UPFLOW	VATMAN	VILLUS	WALLOW	WENSUM	WIPERS	YEARLY
TUSKER	UNDIES	UPHELD	VAUNCE	VINERY	WALNUT	WERENT	WIPING	YEASTY
TUSSAH	UNDINE	UPHILL	VECTIS	VINOUS	WALRUS	WESKER	WIRING	YELLOW
TUSSIS	UNDONE	UPHOLD	VECTOR	VIOLET	WALTER	WESLEY	WIRRAL	YEMENI
TUSSLE	UNDULY	UPKEEP	VEDDAH	VIOLIN	WALTON	WESSEX	WISDEN	YEOMAN
TUVALU	UNDYED	UPLAND	VEDISM	VIRAGO	WAMBLE	WETBOB	WISDOM	YEOMEN
TUXEDO	UNEASE	UPLIFT	VEDUTA	VIRGIL	WAMPUM	WETHER	WISELY	YESMAN
TWAITE	UNEASY	UPLINK	VEILED	VIRGIN	WAMPUS	WHACKO	WISHES	YESTER
TWEEDS	UNEVEN	UPPISH	VEINED	VIRILE	WANDER	WHACKY	WITHAL	YEZIDI
TWEEDY	UNFAIR	UPPITY	VELCRO	VIROUS	WANDLE	WHALER	WITHER	YIPPEE
TWEENY	UNFOLD	UPRATE	VELETA	VIRTUE	WANGLE	WHALES	WITHIN	YOGURT
TWEEZE	UNFURL	UPROAR	VELLUM	VISAGE	WANKEL	WHAMMY	WITTED	YOICKS
TWELVE	UNGAIN	UPROOT	VELOCE	VISCID	WANTED	WHARFE	WIVERN	YOKING
TWENTY	UNGULA	UPSHOT	VELOUR	VISHNU	WANTON	WHEELS	WIZARD	YONDER
TWICER	UNHAND	UPSIDE	VELURE	VISIER	WAPITI	WHEELY	WIZIER	YORICK
TWIGGY	UNHOLY	UPTAKE	VELVET	VISION	WARBLE	WHEEZE	WOBBLE	YORKER
TWIGHT	UNHOOK	UPTOWN	VENDEE	VISUAL	WARCRY	WHEEZY	WOBBLY	YORUBA
TWINED	UNHURT	UPTURN	VENDER	VITALS	WARDEN	WHENCE	WOBURN	YUCKER
TWINGE	UNIATE	UPWARD	VENDOR	VIVACE	WARDER	WHERRY	WOEFUL	YUKATA
TWIRLY	UNIQUE	URACIL	VENDUE	VIVIAN	WARHOL	WHILOM	WOLVER	YUMYUM
TWISTY	UNISEX	URANIA	VENEER	VIVIEN	WARILY	WHILST	WOMBAT	YUPPIE
TWITCH	UNISON	URANIC	VENERY	VIZARD	WARMER	WHIMSY	WOMENS	ZAFTIG
TWOBIT	UNITED	URANUS	VENIAL	VIZIER	WARMLY	WHINGE	WONDER	ZAGREB
TYBALT	UNJUST	URBANE	VENICE	VOICED	WARMTH	WHINNY	WONTED	ZAMBIA
TYBURN	UNKIND	URCHIN	VENITE	VOIDED	WARNER	WHISHT	WONTON	ZANDER
TYCOON	UNLACE	URETER	VENOSE	VOIDEE	WARPED	WHISKY	WOODED	ZAPATA
TYMBAL	UNLESS	URGENT	VENOUS	VOIDER	WARREN	WHITBY	WOODEN	ZEALOT
TYMPAN	UNLIKE	URINAL	VENTIL	VOLAGE	WARSAW	WHITED	WOODIE	ZEBECK
TYPHUS	UNLOAD	URSINE	VENTRE	VOLANS	WASHED	WHITEN	WOOFER	ZENANA
TYPIFY	UNLOCK	URSULA	VERBAL	VOLANT	WASHER	WHITES	WOOKEY	ZENDIK
TYPING	UNMADE	URTICA	VERDIN	VOLENS	WASTED	WHOLLY	WOOLEN	ZENITH
TYPIST	UNMASK	USABLE	VERDUN	VOLLEY	WASTEL	WHOOPS	WOOLLY	ZEPHYR
TYRANT	UNMEET	USANCE	VEREIN	VOLUME	WASTER	WHOOSH	WORKED	ZEUGMA
TYRONE	UNPACK	USEFUL	VERGER	VOLUTE	WATERS	WHYDAH	WORKER	ZIGZAG

ZIMMER	BANGUI	CABALE	CANNED	CASSIO	DAPPLE	FANTAN	GAMMER	HALLOW
ZINGER	BANIAN	CABBIE	CANNEL	CASSIS	DARGLE	FARAND	GAMMON	HALLUX
ZINNIA	BANISH	CACCIA	CANNON	CASTER	DARIEN	FARCIN	GANDER	HALOID
ZIPPER	BANJAX	CACHET	CANNOT	CASTLE	DARING	FARDEL	GANDHI	HALTER
ZIRCON	BANJUL	CACHOU	CANOPY	CASTOR	DARIUS	FARDLE	GANESH	HALVED
ZITHER	BANKER	CACKLE	CANTAB	CASTRO	DARKEN	FARINA	GANGER	HALVES
ZODIAC	BANNED	CACOON	CANTAL	CASUAL	DARKEY	FARMER	GANGES	HAMATE
ZOMBIE	BANNER	CACTUS	CANTAR	CATCHY	DARKIE	FAROFF	GANGLY	HAMBLE
ZONING	BANNET	CADDIE	CANTER	CATGUT	DARKLY	FAROUK	GANGUE	HAMITE
ZONKED	BANTAM	CADDIS	CANTLE	CATHAR	DARTER	FARROW	GANION	HAMLET
ZOPHAR	BANTER	CADETS	CANTON	CATHAY	DARTLE	FASCES	GANNET	HAMMAM
ZOSTER	BANTRY	CADGER	CANTOR	CATKIN	DARWIN	FASCIA	GANTRY	HAMMER
ZOUAVE	BANYAN	CADMUS	CANTUS	CATNAP	DASHED	FASTEN	GAOLER	HAMOSE
ZOUNDS	BANZAI	CAECUM	CANUCK	CATNIP	DATING	FATHER	GAPING	HAMPER
ZURICH	BAOBAB	CAESAR	CANUTE	CATSUP	DATIVE	FATHOM	GARAGE	HANDEL
ZYGOMA	BARBED	CAFARD	CANVAS	CATTLE	DATURA	FATIMA	GARBED	HANDLE
ZYGOTE	BARBEL	CAFTAN	CANVEY	CAUCUS	DAUDET	FATTEN	GARBLE	HANGAR
ZYRIAN	BARBER	CAGILY	CANYON	CAUDEX	DAWDLE	FAUCES	GARÇON	HANGER
6:2	BARBET	CAHIER	CAPIAS	CAUDLE	DAWNEY	FAUCET	GARDEN	HANGUP
	BARÈGE	CAHOOT	CAPLET	CAUGHT	DAWSON	FAULTY	GARETH	HANKER
AARONS	BARELY	CAIMAN	CAPONE	CAUSAL	DAYBED	FAUNUS	GARGET	HANKIE
BABBIT	BARGEE	CAIQUE	CAPOTE	CAUSED	DAZZLE	FAVELA	GARGLE	HANNAH
BABBLE	BARHAM	CAITRA	CAPPED	CAUSEY	EALING	FAVISM	GARISH	HANSOM
BABOON	BARING	CAJOLE	CAPSID	CAVEAT	EAMONN	FAVOSE	GARLIC	HAPPEN
BACCHI	BARIUM	CALAIS	CAPTAN	CAVEIN	EARFUL	FAVOUR	GARNER	HAPTEN
BACKER	BARKER	CALCED	CAPTOR	CAVELL	EARING	FAWKES	GARNET	HAPTIC
BACKET	BARKIS	CALICO	CARAFE	CAVERN	EARNED	GABBLE	GARRET	HARARE
BACKRA	BARLEY	CALIMA	CARBON	CAVITY	EARNER	GABBRO	GARROT	HARASS
BACKUP	BARMAN	CALIPH	CARBOY	CAVORT	EARTHY	GABION	GARRYA	HARBOR
BADGER	BARNES	CALKER	CARDAN	CAVOUR	EARWAX	GABLED	GARTER	HARDEN
BADMAN	BARNET	CALKIN	CAREEN	CAYMAN	EARWIG	GADFLY	GARUDA	HARDLY
BAFFIN	BARNEY	CALLAS	CAREER	DABBLE	EASIER	GADGET	GASBAG	HARKEN
BAFFLE	BARNUM	CALLED	CAREME	DACOIT	EASILY	GADOID	GASCON	HARLOT
BAGFUL	BARODA	CALLER	CARESS	DACTYL	EASING	GAELIC	GASKET	HARMED
BAGMAN	BARQUE	CALLET	CARFAX	DADDLE	EASTER	GAFFER	GASMAN	HAROLD
BAGNIO	BARRED	CALLID	CARIES	DAEDAL	EATAGE	GAGGLE	GASPAR	HARPIC
BAGUIO	BARREL	CALLOP	CARINA	DAEMON	EATERY	GAGMAN	GASPER	HARRIS
BAHADA	BARREN	CALLOW	CARING	DAFTIE	EATING	GAIETY	GASSER	HARROW
BAHRAM	BARRIE	CALLUP	CARLIN	DAGGER	FABIAN	GAIJIN	GASTER	HARVEY
BAIKAL	BARRIO	CALLUS	CARMEL	DAGGLE	FABIUS	GAINER	GASTON	HASHED
BAILEE	BARROW	CALMLY	CARMEN	DAHLIA	FABLED	GAINLY	GATEAU	HASLET
BAILER	BARSAC	CALQUE	CARNAL	DAIMIO	FABLES	GAITER	GATHER	HASSAR
BAILEY	BARTER	CALVER	CARNET	DAINTY	FABRIC	GALANT	GAUCHE	HASSLE
BAILIE	BARTOK	CALVIN	CARNOT	DAISHO	FACADE	GALAXY	GAUCHO	HASTEN
BAILLY	BARTON	CAMAIL	CARPAL	DAKOTA	FACIAL	GALENA	GAUFRE	HATING
BAKERS	BARUCH	CAMBER	CARPEL	DALASI	FACIES	GALERE	GAUGER	HATRED
BAKERY	BARYTA	CAMDEN	CARPER	DALETH	FACILE	GALIOT	GAVAGE	HATTER
BAKING	BASALT	CAMERA	CARPET	DALTON	FACING	GALLEN	GAVIAL	HAUNCH
BALAAM	BASHER	CAMION	CARPUS	DAMAGE	FACTOR	GALLET	GAWAIN	HAVANA
BALBOA	BASICS	CAMISE	CARREL	DAMASK	FACTUM	GALLEY	GAZEBO	HAVENT
BALDER	BASKET	CAMOTE	CARROT	DAMMAR	FADING	GALLIC	GAZUMP	HAVERS
BALDLY	BASQUE	CAMPED	CARSON	DAMMIT	FAECAL	GALLIO	HABILE	HAVING
BALEEN	BASSET	CAMPER	CARTEL	DAMNED	FAECES	GALLON	HACHIS	HAWAII
BALKAN	BASUTO	CAMPUS	CARTER	DAMPEN	FAGGED	GALLOP	HACKEE	HAWKED
BALKIS	BATEAU	CANAAN	CARTON	DAMPER	FAGGOT	GALLOW	HACKER	HAWKER
BALLAD	BATHER	CANADA	CARUSO	DAMSEL	FAIBLE	GALLUP	HACKLE	HAWSER
BALLET	BATHOS	CANAPÉ	CARVED	DAMSON	FAINTS	GALLUS	HAEMAL	HAYBOX
BALLOT	BATMAN	CANARD	CARVEL	DANCER	FAIRLY	GALOOT	HAEMON	HAYDON
BALSAM	BATTEN	CANARY	CARVER	DANDER	FAKING	GALORE	HAGDEN	HAYLEY
BALTIC	BATTER	CANCEL	CASBAH	DANDLE	FALCON	GALOSH	HAGGAI	HAYMOW
BALZAC	BATTLE	CANCER	CASEIN	DANGER	FALLEN	GAMBET	HAGGIS	HAZARD
BAMAKO	BATTUE	CANDID	CASHEW	DANGLE	FALLOW	GAMBIA	HAGGLE	HAZILY
BAMBOO	BAUBLE	CANDLE	CASING	DANIEL	FALTER	GAMBIT	HAILER	IAMBIC
BANANA	BAUCIS	CANDOR	CASINO	DANISH	FAMILY	GAMBLE	HAIRDO	IAMBUS
BANDAR	BAWBEE	CANGUE	CASKET	DANTON	FAMINE	GAMBOL	HALIDE	JABBER
BANDIT	BAXTER	CANINE	CASLON	DANUBE	FAMISH	GAMELY	HALITE	JABBLE
BANDOG	BAYARD	CANING	CASPAR	DANZIG	FAMOUS	GAMETE	HALLAL	JABIRU
BANGER	BAYEUX	CANKER	CASQUE	DAPHNE	FANGLE	GAMINE	HALLEY	JACANA
BANGLE	BAZAAR	CANNAE	CASSIA	DAPPER	FANION	GAMING	HALLOO	JACENT

JACKAL	LAGOON	LAXITY	MANCHU	MATING	PAGODA	PARSEE	RAFFLE	RAVING
JACKET	LAGUNA	LAYARD	MANEGE	MATINS	PAHARI	PARSON	RAFTER	RAVISH
JACOBS	LAGUNE	LAYERS	MANFUL	MATLOW	PAIDUP	PARTLY	RAGBAG	RAZURE
JAEGER	LAICAL	LAYING	MANGER	MATRIC	PAINED	PARTON	RAGGED	RAZZIA
JAGGED	LAISSE	LAYMAN	MANGLE	MATRIX	PAINTS	PARURE	RAGGLE	RAZZLE
JAGGER	LALLAN	LAYOFF	MANIAC	MATRON	PAINTY	PARVIS	RAGING	SAANEN
JAGUAR	LAMBDA	LAYOUT	MANILA	MATTED	PAIRER	PASCAL	RAGLAN	SABELE
JAILER	LAMEDH	LAZILY	MANIOC	MATTER	PAKHTI	PASHTO	RAGMAN	SABINE
JAILOR	LAMELY	MACRON	MANITO	MATURE	PAKHTO	PASHTU	RAGOUT	SABRES
JALOPY	LAMENT	MACULA	MANNER	MAUGRE	PAKHTU	PASQUE	RAGTOP	SACHET
JAMBOK	LAMINA	MACULE	MANNIN	MAUNDY	PALACE	PASSED	RAGUSA	SACRED
JAMBON	LAMMAS	MADAME	MANQUÉ	MAUSER	PALAIS	PASSES	RAIDER	SACRUM
JAMMED	LAMMER	MADCAP	MANTIS	MAWKIN	PALATE	PASSIM	RAISED	SADDEN
JAMPOT	LANATE	MADDEN	MANTLE	MAXIMS	PALING	PASTEL	RAISER	SADDHU
JANGLE	LANCER	MADDER	MANTRA	MAYBUG	PALLAH	PASTIL	RAISIN	SADDLE
JANSKY	LANCET	MADEUP	MANTUA	MAYDAY	PALLAS	PASTIS	RAKING	SADISM
JARGON	LANCIA	MADMAN	MANUAL	MAYFLY	PALLET	PASTON	RAKISH	SADIST
JARVEY	LANDAU	MADRAS	MANUKA	MAYHEM	PALLID	PASTOR	RAMBLE	SAFARI
JASPER	LANDED	MADRID	MANURE	MAZOUT	PALLOR	PASTRY	RAMEAU	SAFELY
JAUNTY	LANDER	MADURA	MAOIST	MAZUMA	PALMER	PATACA	RAMIFY	SAFETY
JAWBOX	LANDOR	MADURO	MAOTAI	NAEVUS	PALTRY	PATCHY	RAMJET	SAGELY
JAZZER	LANGUR	MAENAD	MAPUTO	NAGANA	PAMELA	PATENT	RAMOSE	SAGGAR
KABAKA	LANUGO	MAFFIA	MAQUIS	NAGARI	PAMIRS	PATHAN	RAMOUS	SAHARA
KABELE	LAPDOG	MAGGIE	MARACA	NAILED	PAMPAS	PATHIC	RAMROD	SAILOR
KABUKI	LAPITH	MAGGOT	MARAUD	NAILER	PAMPER	PATHOS	RANCEL	SAINTS
KABYLE	LAPPER	MAGLEV	MARBLE	NALLAH	PAMYAT	PATINA	RANCHO	SAITHE
KACCHA	LAPPET	MAGNES	MARCEL	NAMELY	PANADA	PATMOS	RANCID	SALAAM
KAFFER	LAPSED	MAGNET	MARGIN	NANDOO	PANAMA	PATOIS	RANCOR	SALADE
KAFFIR	LAPSUS	MAGNON	MARIAN	NANISM	PANDER	PATROL	RANDOM	SALAMI
KAFTAN	LAPTOP	MAGNUM	MARINA	NANKIN	PANDIT	PATRON	RANGER	SALARY
KAISER	LAPUTA	MAGNUS	MARINE	NANSEN	PANFRY	PATTEN	RANKED	SALINA
KAKAPO	LARDER	MAGPIE	MARISH	NANTES	PANOPE	PATTER	RANKER	SALINE
KALMIA	LARDON	MAGYAR	MARIST	NAPALM	PANTER	PATTON	RANKLE	SALISH
KALPAK	LARIAT	MAHLER	MARKED	NAPERY	PANTON	PAUNCE	RANSOM	SALIVA
KANAKA	LARKIN	MAHOUT	MARKER	NAPIER	PANTRY	PAUNCH	RANTER	SALLEE
KANGHA	LARRUP	MAIDAN	MARKET	NAPKIN	PANZER	PAUPER	RANULA	SALLET
KANOON	LARVAE	MAIDEN	MARKKA	NAPLES	PAPACY	PAVANE	RAPHIA	SALLOW
KANSAS	LARVAL	MAILER	MARKUP	NAPPER	PAPAGO	PAVING	RAPIDS	SALMIS
KANTEN	LARYNX	MAINLY	MARLIN	NARROW	PAPAYA	PAVLOV	RAPIER	SALMON
KANTHA	LASCAR	MAINOR	MARMOT	NASEBY	PAPERS	PAWNEE	RAPINE	SALOME
KANUCK	LASHED	MAÎTRE	MARNER	NASION	PAPERY	PAWPAW	RAPIST	SALOON
KAOLIN	LASHER	MAJLIS	MAROON	NASSAU	PAPHOS	PAYDAY	RAPPED	SALOOP
KAPUTT	LASKET	MAKEUP	MARQUE	NASSER	PAPIST	PAYING	RAPPEL	SALUKI
KARATE	LASSIE	MAKING	MARRAM	NASTIC	PAPULE	PAYNIM	RAPPER	SALUTE
KARIBA	LASSUS	MALAGA	MARRON	NATANT	PARADE	PAYOFF	RAPTLY	SALVER
KARITE	LASTLY	MALATE	MARROW	NATION	PARAMO	PAYOLA	RAPTOR	SALVIA
KASBAH	LATEEN	MALAWI	MARSHY	NATIVE	PARANA	RABATO	RAREFY	SAMARA
KATANA	LATELY	MALDON	MARTEL	NATRON	PARAPH	RABBET	RARELY	SAMBAL
KAZAKH	LATENT	MALGRE	MARTEN	NATTER	PARCAE	RABBIT	RARING	SAMBAR
LAAGER	LATEST	MALIAN	MARTHA	NATURE	PARCEL	RABBLE	RARITY	SAMBUR
LABIAL	LATHER	MALIBU	MARTIN	NAUGHT	PARDIE	RABIES	RASCAL	SAMEKH
LABILE	LATONA	MALICE	MARTYR	NAUSEA	PARDON	RACEME	RASHER	SAMFOO
LABIUM	LATRON	MALIGN	MARVEL	NAUTCH	PARENT	RACHEL	RASHLY	SAMIAN
LABLAB	LATTEN	MALLAM	MASADA	NAVAHO	PARETO	RACHIS	RASPER	SAMIEL
LABOUR	LATTER	MALLEE	MASCOT	NAVAJO	PAREVE	RACIAL	RASTER	SAMIOT
LABRUM	LATVIA	MALLET	MASHAM	OAFISH	PARGET	RACINE	RATBAG	SAMITE
LABRYS	LAUDER	MALLOW	MASHED	OAKLEY	PARIAH	RACING	RATHER	SAMLET
LACHES	LAUNCE	MALONE	MASHER	OAKNUT	PARISH	RACISM	RATIFY	SAMOSA
LACING	LAUNCH	MALONY	MASHIE	OARLAP	PARITY	RACIST	RATINE	SAMPAN
LACKEY	LAUREL	MALORY	MASKED	PACIFY	PARKED	RACKET	RATING	SAMSON
LACTIC	LAURIC	MALTED	MASKER	PACKED	PARKER	RADDLE	RATION	SAMUEL
LACUNA	LAURIE	MALTHA	MASLIN	PACKER	PARKIN	RADIAL	RATOON	SANCHO
LADAKH	LAVABO	MAMMAL	MASQUE	PACKET	PARLEY	RADIAN	RATTAN	SANDAL
LADDER	LAVAGE	MAMMON	MASSED	PADANG	PARLOR	RADISH	RATTER	SANDER
LADDIE	LAVISH	MAMZER	MASSES	PADDED	PARODY	RADIUM	RATTLE	SANDER
LADIES	LAWFUL	MANAGE	MASSIF	PADDLE	PAROLE	RADIUS	RATTON	SANELY
LADING	LAWMAN	MANANA	MASTER	PADUAN	PARPEN	RADULA	RAUNCH	SANITY
LADOGA	LAWYER	MANATI	MASTIC	PAELLA	PARROT	RAFALE	RAVAGE	SANSEI
LAFFER	LAXIST	MANCHE	MATHIS	PAEONY	PARSEC	RAFFIA	RAVINE	SANTAL

83

SANTON	TALMUD	VAGINA	WARMER	ABULIA	ECONUT	SCOTER	ODDSON	BELIKE
SAPELE	TAMALE	VAHINE	WARMLY	ABYDOS	ECTOPY	SCOTIA	ODENSE	BELIZE
SAPHAR	TAMANU	VAINLY	WARMTH	IBADAN	ECURIE	SCOUSE	ODESSA	BELLOC
SAPIUM	TAMARA	VALENS	WARNER	IBERIA	ECZEMA	SCRAMB	ODIOUS	BELLOW
SAPOTA	TAMARI	VALETA	WARPED	IBIBIO	ICARUS	SCRAPE	SDEATH	BELONG
SAPOTE	TAMELY	VALINE	WARREN	IBIDEM	ICEBOX	SCRAPS	UDMURT	BELSEN
SAPPER	TAMINE	VALISE	WARSAW	OBECHE	ICECAP	SCRAWL	AEDILE	BELTED
SAPPHO	TAMISE	VALIUM	WASHED	OBELUS	ICEMAN	SCRAWM	AEGEAN	BELUGA
SARGUS	TAMMAR	VALLEY	WASHER	OBERON	ICICLE	SCREAM	AEGEUS	BEMEAN
SARNIE	TAMMUZ	VALLUM	WASTED	OBIISM	ICONIC	SCREED	AEGINA	BEMOAN
SARONG	TAMPER	VALOUR	WASTEL	OBITAL	OCCULT	SCREEN	AENEID	BEMOIL
SARSEN	TAMPON	VALUER	WASTER	OBITER	OCCUPY	SCREWY	AEOLIC	BEMUSE
SARTOR	TANDEM	VALUTA	WATERS	OBJECT	OCEANS	SCRIBE	AEOLIS	BENAME
SARTRE	TANGLE	VANDAL	WATERY	OBLAST	OCELOT	SCRIMP	AEOLUS	BENBOW
SASHAY	TANKER	VANISH	WATSON	OBLATE	OCHONE	SCRIPT	AERATE	BENDED
SATEEN	TANKIA	VANITY	WATTLE	OBLIGE	OCHREA	SCROLL	AERIAL	BENDER
SATINY	TANNAH	VAPOUR	WAVELL	OBLONG	OCKERS	SCROOP	AEROBE	BENGAL
SATIRE	TANNED	VARECH	WAVING	OBOIST	OCTANE	SCRUBS	BEACHY	BENIGN
SATIVE	TANNER	VARESE	WAXING	OBOLUS	OCTANS	SCRUFF	BEACON	BENITO
SATORI	TANNIC	VARIED	WAYLAY	OBSESS	OCTANT	SCRUNT	BEADED	BENNET
SATRAP	TANNIN	VARLET	WAYOUT	OBTAIN	OCTAVE	SCULPT	BEADLE	BENSON
SATURN	TANNOY	VASSAL	XANADU	OBTECT	OCTAVO	SCUMMY	BEAGLE	BENUMB
SATYRA	TANTRA	VASTLY	XAVIER	OBTEND	OCTROI	SCUNGE	BEAKER	BERATE
SAUCER	TAOISM	VATHEK	YABBER	OBTUND	OCULAR	SCURRY	BEANIE	BERBER
SAUGER	TAOIST	VATMAN	YAFFLE	OBTUSE	SCABBY	SCURVY	BEARER	BEREFT
SAURIA	TAPPER	VAUNCE	YAHWEH	OBVERT	SCAITH	SCUTCH	BEATEN	BERGEN
SAVAGE	TAPPET	WABASH	YAKKER	SBIRRO	SCALAR	SCUTUM	BEATER	BERING
SAVANT	TAPPIT	WACKER	YAKUZA	UBIETY	SCALER	SCUZZY	BEATTY	BERLIN
SAVATE	TARCEL	WADDLE	YAMMER	ACACIA	SCALES	SCYLLA	BEAUNE	BERTHA
SAVING	TARDIS	WADERS	YANKEE	ACADIA	SCAMPI	SCYTHE	BEAUTY	BERTHE
SAVIOR	TARGET	WADHAM	YANKER	ACAJOU	SCAMPO	UCKERS	BEAVER	BERTIE
SAVOIE	TARGUM	WAFFLE	YAOURT	ACARID	SCANTY	ADAGIO	BECALM	BESANT
SAVORY	TARIFF	WAFTED	YARDIE	ACARUS	SCAPUS	ADDEEM	BECAME	BESEEM
SAVOUR	TARMAC	WAGGLE	YARROW	ACATES	SCARAB	ADDEND	BECKET	BESIDE
SAVVEY	TARROW	WAGGON	YATTER	ACCEDE	SCARCE	ADDICT	BECKON	BESORT
SAWDER	TARSAL	WAGNER	ZAFTIG	ACCEND	SCARED	ADDLED	BECOME	BESSEL
SAWNEY	TARSEL	WAGRAM	ZAGREB	ACCENT	SCARER	ADDUCE	BEDASH	BESSIE
SAWYER	TARSIA	WAILER	ZAMBIA	ACCEPT	SCATCH	ADDUCT	BEDAUB	BESSUS
SAXONY	TARSUS	WAITER	ZANDER	ACCESS	SCATHE	ADHERE	BEDDER	BESTED
SAYERS	TARTAN	WAIVER	ZAPATA	ACCORD	SCATTY	ADJOIN	BEDECK	BESTIR
SAYING	TARTAR	WAKING	ABACUS	ACCOST	SCENIC	ADJURE	BEDLAM	BESTOW
TABARD	TARTLY	WALKER	ABADAN	ACCRUE	SCHEMA	ADJUST	BEDPAN	BETAKE
TABLET	TASMAN	WALLAH	ABATOR	ACCUSE	SCHEME	ADMIRE	BEDSIT	BETHEL
TABULA	TASSEL	WALLED	ABATTU	ACEDIA	SCHISM	ADNATE	BEEGHA	BETIDE
TACKET	TASSET	WALLER	ABBACY	ACETIC	SCHIST	ADONAI	BEENAH	BETIME
TACKLE	TASSIE	WALLET	ABBESS	ACHENE	SCHIZO	ADONIS	BEEPER	BETISE
TACOMA	TASTER	WALLOP	ABDABS	ACHING	SCHLEP	ADORER	BEETLE	BETONY
TACTIC	TATAMI	WALLOW	ABDIEL	ACIDIC	SCHMOE	ADRIAN	BEETON	BETRAY
TAENIA	TATERS	WALNUT	ABDUCT	ACINUS	SCHOOL	ADRIFT	BEFALL	BETTER
TAGORE	TATLER	WALRUS	ABELIA	ACKERS	SCHUSS	ADROIT	BEFOOL	BETTOR
TAHINA	TATTER	WALTER	ABJECT	ACORNS	SCHUYT	ADSORB	BEFORE	BEULAH
TAHINI	TATTLE	WALTON	ABJURE	ACQUIT	SCILLA	ADSUKI	BEGGAR	BEURRÉ
TAHITI	TATTOO	WAMBLE	ABLATE	ACRAWL	SCILLY	ADVENE	BEGONE	BEWAIL
TAIGLE	TAUGHT	WAMPUM	ABLAUT	ACROSS	SCIPIO	ADVENT	BEHALF	BEWARE
TAILLE	TAURUS	WAMPUS	ABLAZE	ACTING	SCIROC	ADVERB	BEHAVE	BEYOND
TAILOR	TAUTEN	WANDER	ABLOOM	ACTION	SCIRON	ADVERT	BEHEAD	BEZANT
TAIPAN	TAUTLY	WANDLE	ABLUSH	ACTIUM	SCLAFF	ADVICE	BEHELD	BEZOAR
TAIPEI	TAUTOG	WANGLE	ABOARD	ACTIVE	SCLERA	ADVISE	BEHEST	BEZZLE
TAIWAN	TAVERN	WANKEL	ABONDE	ACTORS	SCLERE	EDDISH	BEHIND	CECILS
TAKING	TAWDRY	WANTED	ABOUND	ACTUAL	SCOLEX	EDGING	BEHOLD	CECITY
TALBOT	TAWPIE	WANTON	ABRADE	ACUITY	SCONCE	EDIBLE	BEHOOF	CEDRIC
TALCUM	TAXEME	WAPITI	ABREGE	ACUMEN	SCOOBS	EDISON	BEHOVE	CEDULA
TALENT	TAXING	WARBLE	ABROAD	ECARTÉ	SCOOSH	EDITED	BEHRAM	CEEFAX
TALION	TAXMAN	WARCRY	ABROMA	ECBOLE	SCOPUS	EDITOR	BEIRUT	CELERY
TALKER	VACANT	WARDEN	ABRUPT	ECCLES	SCORCH	EDMOND	BEJADE	CELIAC
TALKIE	VACATE	WARDER	ABSEIL	ECHARD	SCORER	EDMUND	BELAMY	CELLAR
TALLIS	VACUUM	WARHOL	ABSENT	ECHINO	SCORIA	EDWARD	BELFRY	CELTIC
TALLOT	VADOSE	WARILY	ABSORB	ECLAIR	SCORSE	IDIOCY	BELIAL	CEMENT
TALLOW	VAGARY		ABSURD	ECLOSE	SCOTCH	ODDITY	BELIEF	CENSER

CENSOR	DEFILE	DESORB	GELLER	HEREIN	KETMIR	MEATUS	METTLE	PEEPER
CENSUS	DEFINE	DESPOT	GEMINI	HERERO	KETONE	MEDDLE	MEXICO	PEEVED
CENTER	DEFORM	DETACH	GEMMAN	HERESY	KETOSE	MEDIAL	NEAPED	PEEWEE
CENTRE	DEFRAG	DETAIL	GENDER	HERETO	KETTLE	MEDIAN	NEARBY	PEEWIT
CENTUM	DEFRAY	DETAIN	GENERA	HERIOT	KEVLAR	MEDICI	NEARER	PEGLEG
CERATE	DEFTLY	DETECT	GENEVA	HERMES	KEWPIE	MEDICO	NEARLY	PEKING
CERCAL	DEFUSE	DETENT	GENIAL	HERMIT	KEYNES	MEDINA	NEATEN	PELHAM
CERCUS	DÉGAGÉ	DETENU	GENIUS	HERMON	KEYPAD	MEDISM	NEATLY	PELION
CEREAL	DEGREE	DETEST	GENOME	HERNIA	KEYWAY	MEDIUM	NEBBUK	PELLET
CEREUS	DEHORN	DETOUR	GENTES	HEROIC	LEADEN	MEDIUS	NEBECK	PELMET
CERISE	DEIDRE	DEVEST	GENTLE	HEROIN	LEADER	MEDLAR	NEBISH	PELOID
CERIUM	DEIMOS	DEVICE	GENTLY	HERONS	LEAGUE	MEDLEY	NEBULA	PELOTA
CERMET	DEJECT	DEVILS	GENTRY	HERPES	LEALTY	MEDUSA	NEBULE	PELVIC
CEROON	DELATE	DEVISE	GEORGE	HERREN	LEANTO	MEDWAY	NECKAR	PELVIS
CERTES	DELETE	DEVOID	GERBIL	HESIOD	LEAVEN	MEEKLY	NECKED	PENANG
CERUSE	DELIAN	DEVOTE	GERENT	HESTIA	LEAVER	MEGRIM	NECTAR	PENCEL
CERVIX	DELICE	DEVOUR	GERMAN	HETERO	LEAVES	MEJLIS	NEEDED	PENCIL
CESARE	DELICT	DEVOUT	GERUND	HETMAN	LECHER	MEKONG	NEEDLE	PENMAN
CESIUM	DELISH	DEWALI	GETTER	HEXANE	LECTOR	MELIUS	NEEDNT	PENNAE
CESTUI	DELIUS	DEWITT	GEWGAW	HEXOSE	LEDGER	MELLOW	NEFAST	PENNAL
CESTUS	DELPHI	DEWLAP	GEYSER	HEYDAY	LEEWAY	MELODY	NEGATE	PENNON
CESURA	DELUDE	DEXTER	HEADED	JEEVES	LEGACY	MELTED	NELLIE	PENSÉE
CETERA	DELUGE	EERILY	HEADER	JEJUNE	LEGATE	MELTON	NELSON	PENSUM
CEYLON	DELUXE	EEYORE	HEALER	JEKYLL	LEGATO	MEMBER	NEPALI	PENTAD
DEACON	DELVED	FEALTY	HEALTH	JEMIMA	LEGEND	MEMNON	NEPETA	PENTEL
DEADEN	DEMAIN	FECULA	HEAPED	JENNER	LEGGED	MEMOIR	NEPHEW	PENTUP
DEADLY	DEMAND	FECUND	HEARER	JENNET	LEGION	MEMORY	NEREID	PENTYL
DEAFEN	DEMEAN	FEDORA	HEARSE	JERBOA	LEGIST	MENACE	NEREUS	PENURY
DEALER	DEMENT	FEEBLE	HEARTH	JEREMY	LEGLET	MENAGE	NERINE	PEOPLE
DEARER	DEMISE	FEEBLY	HEARTS	JERKER	LEGMAN	MENCAP	NERIUM	PEPLOS
DEARIE	DEMIST	FEEDER	HEARTY	JERKIN	LEGUME	MENDEL	NEROLI	PEPLUM
DEARLY	DEMOTE	FEELER	HEATED	JEROME	LEMNOS	MENDER	NERVAL	PEPPER
DEARTH	DEMURE	FEERIE	HEATER	JERSEY	LEMONY	MENDES	NERVES	PEPTIC
DEBASE	DENGUE	FEINTS	HEAUME	JESTER	LEMUEL	MENDIP	NERVII	PEQUOD
DEBATE	DENIAL	FEISTY	HEAVED	JESUIT	LEMURE	MENHIR	NESSIE	PERDUE
DEBILE	DENIED	FELINE	HEAVEN	JETHRO	LENDER	MENIAL	NESSUS	PERHAP
DEBRIS	DENIER	FELLER	HEAVES	JETLAG	LENGTH	MENINX	NESTLE	PERILS
DEBTOR	DENIMS	FELLOE	HEBREW	JETSAM	LENTEL	MENSAL	NESTOR	PERIOD
DEBUNK	DENNIS	FELLOW	HECATE	JETTON	LENTEN	MENTAL	NETHER	PERISH
DECADE	DENOTE	FELONY	HECKLE	JEWELS	LENTIC	MENTOR	NETTLE	PERKIN
DECAFF	DENTAL	FEMALE	HECTIC	JEWESS	LENTIL	MENTUM	NEURAL	PERMIT
DECAMP	DENUDE	FENCER	HECTOR	JEWISH	LENTOR	MERCAT	NEURON	PERNOD
DECANE	DENVER	FENDER	HECUBA	KEATON	LEONID	MERCER	NEUTER	PERRON
DECANI	DEODAR	FENIAN	HEDERA	KEBELE	LEPTON	MERCIA	NEVADA	PERSON
DECANT	DEPART	FERIAL	HEEDED	KECKSY	LESBOS	MERELY	NEWELL	PERUKE
DECCAN	DEPEND	FERMAT	HEEHAW	KEDDAH	LESION	MERGER	NEWEST	PERUSE
DECEIT	DEPICT	FERRET	HEELED	KEELER	LESLIE	MERINO	NEWMAN	PESADE
DECENT	DEPLOY	FERRIS	HEGIRA	KEENER	LESSEE	MERKIN	NEWTON	PESETA
DECIDE	DEPONE	FERULA	HEIFER	KEENLY	LESSEN	MERLIN	OEDEMA	PESHWA
DÉCIME	DEPORT	FERULE	HEIGHT	KEEPER	LESSER	MERLOT	OENONE	PESTER
DECKED	DEPOSE	FERVID	HEJIRA	KELLYS	LESSON	MERMAN	OERLAY	PESTLE
DECKER	DEPTHS	FERVOR	HELENA	KELOID	LESSOR	MEROPE	OEUVRE	PÉTAIN
DECKLE	DEPUTE	FESCUE	HELIOS	KELPER	LESTER	MERRIE	PEAHEN	PETARD
DECODE	DEPUTY	FESTAL	HELIUM	KELPIE	LETHAL	MERROW	PEAKED	PETARY
DECOKE	DERAIL	FESTER	HELLAS	KELTER	LETOUT	MERSEY	PEANUT	PETERS
DECREE	DERAIN	FETISH	HELLER	KELTIC	LETTER	MERTON	PEARLS	PETIPA
DECREW	DERGUE	FETTER	HELMET	KELTIE	LEVANT	MESAIL	PEARLY	PETITE
DEDANS	DERHAM	FETTES	HELPER	KELVIN	LEVITE	MESCAL	PEBBLE	PETREL
DEDUCE	DERIDE	FETTLE	HEMPEN	KENDAL	LEVITY	MESIAL	PEBBLY	PETROL
DEDUCT	DERIVE	FEUDAL	HENBIT	KENNEL	LEWDLY	MESMER	PECKER	PEWTER
DEEJAY	DERMAL	FEWEST	HENLEY	KENNET	LEXEME	MESSRS	PECTEN	PEYOTE
DEEPEN	DERMIS	GEASON	HENNIN	KENSAL	LEYDEN	METAGE	PECTIN	READER
DEEPER	DERRIS	GEEZER	HENSON	KENYAN	MEADOW	METATE	PEDALO	REALIA
DEEPLY	DESCRY	GEIGER	HEPTAD	KEPHIR	MEAGER	METEOR	PEDANT	REALLY
DEFACE	DESERT	GEISHA	HERALD	KEPLER	MEAGRE	METHOD	PEDDER	REALTY
DEFAME	DESIGN	GELADA	HERBAL	KERALA	MEALIE	METHYL	PEDDLE	REAMER
DEFEAT	DESIRE	GELATE	HERDEN	KERMES	MEANIE	METIER	PEDLAR	REAPER
DEFECT	DESIST	GELATO	HERDER	KERMIS	MEANLY	METOPE	PEELED	REASON
DEFEND			HEREBY	KERNEL	MEASLY	METRIC	PEELER	REBATE

REBECK	RELENT	REVERS	SENTRY	TEMPER	VERDUN	YESTER	IGNORE	CHIPPY
REBITE	RELICS	REVERT	SEPIUM	TEMPLE	VEREIN	YEZIDI	IGUANA	CHIRON
REBORE	RELICT	REVERY	SEPSIS	TENACE	VERGER	ZEALOT	OGADEN	CHIRPY
REBORN	RELIEF	RÊVEUR	SEPTAL	TENANT	VERGES	ZEBECK	OGAMIC	CHISEL
REBUFF	RELISH	REVIEW	SEPTET	TENDER	VERIFY	ZENANA	OGRESS	CHITAL
REBUKE	RELIVE	REVILE	SEPTIC	TENDON	VERILY	ZENDIK	UGANDA	CHITIN
RECALL	REMAIN	REVISE	SEQUEL	TENDRE	VERISM	ZENITH	UGARIT	CHITON
RECANT	REMAKE	REVIVE	SEQUIN	TENGKU	VERITY	ZEPHYR	UGRIAN	CHITTY
RECAST	REMAND	REVOKE	SERAIL	TENNER	VERMIN	ZEUGMA	AHIMSA	CHIVES
RECEDE	REMARK	REVOLT	SERANG	TENNIS	VERMIS	AFEARS	BHAJAN	CHIVVY
RECENT	REMEDY	REWARD	SERAPE	TENPIN	VERNAL	AFFAIR	BHAJEE	CHOANA
RECESS	REMIND	REWIND	SERAPH	TENSON	VERNON	AFFECT	BHARAL	CHOICE
RECIFE	REMISS	REWIRE	SERBIA	TENSOR	VERSAL	AFFIRM	BHARAT	CHOKED
RECIPE	REMORA	REWORD	SERDAB	TENURE	VERSED	AFFORD	CHADOR	CHOKER
RECITE	REMOTE	REWORK	SERENE	TEOPAN	VERSES	AFFRAY	CHAFER	CHOKEY
RECKON	REMOVE	SEABEE	SERIAL	TEPHRA	VERSET	AFFRET	CHAINS	CHOLER
RECOIL	RENAME	SEALED	SERIES	TERCET	VERSUS	AFGHAN	CHAIRS	CHOOSE
RECORD	RENDER	SEAMAN	SERINE	TERCIO	VERVET	AFIELD	CHAISE	CHOOSY
RECOUP	RENEGE	SEAMEN	SERMON	TEREDO	VESICA	AFLAME	CHAKRA	CHOPIN
RECTAL	RENNET	SEAMER	SEROSA	TERESA	VESPER	AFLOAT	CHALET	CHOPPY
RECTOR	RENNIN	SEAMUS	SERVAL	TERETE	VESSEL	AFRAID	CHALKY	CHORAL
RECTUM	RENOIR	SEANCE	SERVER	TERGUM	VESTAL	AFREET	CHAMPS	CHOREA
RECTUS	RENOWN	SEARCH	SESAME	TERMES	VESTED	AFRESH	CHANCE	CHOREE
REDACT	RENTAL	SEASON	SETOSE	TERMLY	VESTRY	AFRICA	CHANCY	CHORUS
REDCAP	RENTER	SEATED	SETTEE	TERNAL	WEAKEN	AFTERS	CHANEY	CHOSEN
REDCAR	RENVOI	SEAWAY	SETTER	TERRAE	WEAKER	EFFACE	CHANGE	CHOUAN
REDDEN	RENVOY	SEBATE	SETTLE	TERROR	WEAKLY	EFFECT	CHAPEL	CHOUGH
REDEEM	REOPEN	SECANT	SEUMAS	TERTIA	WEALTH	EFFETE	CHAPKA	CHOWRY
REDEYE	REPAID	SECEDE	SEURAT	TESTER	WEAPON	EFFIGY	CHARGE	CHRISM
REDLEG	REPAIR	SECOND	SEVENS	TESTES	WEARER	EFFLUX	CHARON	CHRIST
REDRAW	REPAST	SECRET	SEVERE	TESTIS	WEASEL	EFFORT	CHARTA	CHROMA
REDTOP	REPEAL	SECTOR	SEVERN	TETANY	WEAVER	EFFUSE	CHASER	CHROME
REDUCE	REPEAT	SECURE	SEVERY	TETCHY	WEBBED	EFTEST	CHASSE	CHROMO
REEBOK	REPENT	SEDATE	SÈVRES	TETHER	WEDDED	IFFISH	CHASTE	CHUBBY
REEFER	REPINE	SEDUCE	SEWAGE	TETHYS	WEDGED	OFFCUT	CHATON	CHUFFY
REEKIE	REPLAY	SEEDED	SEWELL	TETRAD	WEDGIE	OFFEND	CHATTY	CHUKKA
REELER	REPORT	SEEDER	SEWING	TETRYL	WEEKLY	OFFICE	CHAZAN	CHUMMY
REFACE	REPOSE	SEEING	SEXISM	TETTIX	WEEPER	OFFING	CHEDER	CHUNKY
REFECT	REPTON	SEEKER	SEXTAN	TEUTON	WEEPIE	OFFISH	CHEEKY	CHURCH
REFILL	REPUGN	SEEMLY	SEXTET	TEVIOT	WEEVIL	OFFSET	CHEERS	CHYPRE
REFINE	REPUTE	SEESAW	SEXTON	VECTIS	WEEWEE	UFFIZI	CHEERY	DHARMA
REFLET	REREAD	SEETHE	SEXUAL	VECTOR	WEIGHT	AGADIR	CHEESE	DHOOTI
REFLEX	RESALE	SEICHE	TEABAG	VEDDAH	WEIMAR	AGAMID	CHEESY	GHARRY
REFLUX	RESCUE	SEISIN	TEACUP	VEDISM	WEIRDO	AGARIC	CHEMIC	GHAZAL
REFORM	RESEAU	SELDOM	TEAGUE	VEDUTA	WELDER	AGATHA	CHEMMY	GHEBER
REFUEL	RESECT	SELECT	TEAPOT	VEILED	WELKIN	AGEING	CHENET	GHERAO
REFUGE	RESEDA	SELENE	TEAPOY	VEINED	WELLER	AGENCY	CHEOPS	GHETTO
REFUND	RESENT	SELFED	TEASEL	VELCRO	WELLES	AGENDA	CHEQUE	GHOSTS
REFUSE	RESIDE	SELJUK	TEASER	VELETA	WELLIE	AGHAST	CHERIE	KHALAT
REFUTE	RESIGN	SELLBY	TECHNO	VELLUM	WELTER	AGLAIA	CHERRY	KHALIF
REGAIN	RESIST	SELLER	TECKEL	VELOCE	WELWYN	AGNAIL	CHERUB	KHALSA
REGALE	RESORT	SELSYN	TECTUM	VELOUR	WENSUM	AGNATE	CHERUP	KHARIF
REGARD	RESULT	SELWYN	TEDIUM	VELURE	WERENT	AGONIC	CHESIL	KHILAT
REGENT	RESUME	SEMELE	TEENSY	VELVET	WESKER	AGOUTI	CHESTY	KHILIM
REGEST	RETAIL	SEMITE	TEEPEE	VENDEE	WESLEY	AGREED	CHEVAL	KHYBER
REGGAE	RETAIN	SEMPRE	TEETER	VENDER	WESSEX	AGRÉGÉ	CHEVET	LHOTSE
REGIME	RETAKE	SEMTEX	TEETHE	VENDOR	WETBOB	AGUISE	CHIBOL	PHAROS
REGINA	RETARD	SENATE	TEFLON	VENDUE	WETHER	AGUISH	CHICHI	PHASIS
REGION	RETINA	SENDAL	TEGMEN	VENEER	XENIAL	AGUIZE	CHICLE	PHASMA
REGIUS	RETIRE	SENDER	TEGULA	VENERY	XENIUM	EGBERT	CHICON	PHENOL
REGLET	RETOOL	SENECA	TEHRAN	VENIAL	XEROMA	EGENCY	CHIGOE	PHENYL
REGRET	RETORT	SENILE	TELEDU	VENICE	XERXES	EGERIA	CHILDE	PHILIP
REGULO	RETOUR	SENIOR	TELEGA	VENITE	YEARLY	EGESTA	CHILLI	PHIZOG
REHASH	RETURN	SENLAC	TELEGU	VENOSE	YEASTY	EGGCUP	CHILLY	PHLEGM
REHEAT	REUBEN	SENNET	TELLAR	VENOUS	YELLOW	EGMONT	CHIMER	PHLEUM
REHEEL	REUTER	SENORA	TELLER	VENTIL	YEMENI	EGOISM	CHIMES	PHLOEM
REJECT	REVAMP	SENSED	TELLUS	VENTRE	YEOMAN	EGOIST	CHINAR	PHOBIA
REJOIN	REVEAL	SENSES	TELSON	VERBAL	YEOMEN	EGRESS	CHINCH	PHOBIC
RELATE	REVERE	SENSOR	TELUGU	VERDIN	YESMAN	IGNITE	CHINTZ	PHOBOS

PHOEBE	SHINNY	THOMAS	AIRING	DIATOM	DIYARI	GIDDUP	JITNEY	LIMITS
PHONAL	SHINTO	THORAH	AIRMAN	DIAXON	DIZAIN	GIDEON	JITTER	LIMNER
PHONEY	SHINTY	THORAX	AIRWAY	DIBBER	EIFFEL	GIFTED	KIAORA	LIMPET
PHONIC	SHIPKA	THORNE	BIASED	DIBBLE	EIGHTH	GIGGLE	KIBBLE	LIMPID
PHOOEY	SHIRAZ	THORNY	BICARB	DICAST	EIGHTY	GIGLET	KIBOSH	LIMPLY
PHOTON	SHIRRA	THORPE	BICEPS	DICKER	EIRANN	GIGLOT	KICKER	LINDEN
PHRASE	SHIRTY	THOUGH	BICKER	DICKEY	EITHER	GIGOLO	KIDDIE	LINEAL
PHYLLO	SHIVER	THRALL	BIDDER	DICTUM	FIACRE	GILDAS	KIDDLE	LINEAR
PHYLUM	SHODDY	THRASH	BIDENT	DIDDLE	FIANCÉ	GILDED	KIDNAP	LINEUP
PHYSIC	SHOFAR	THRAWN	BIFFIN	DIEPPE	FIASCO	GILDER	KIDNEY	LINGER
PHYSIO	SHOGUN	THREAD	BIFOLD	DIESEL	FIBBED	GILEAD	KIGALI	LINGOT
RHAPHE	SHORTS	THREAP	BIGAMY	DIESIS	FIBBER	GILGAI	KIKUYU	LINING
RHEIMS	SHOULD	THREAT	BIGGER	DIETER	FIBULA	GILLET	KILLER	LINKER
RHESUS	SHOVEL	THRENE	BIGGIN	DIFFER	FICKLE	GILLIE	KILNER	LINKUP
RHETOR	SHOWER	THRESH	BIGWIG	DIGEST	FIDDLE	GILPIN	KILTED	LINNET
RHEUMY	SHRANK	THRICE	BIKINI	DIGGER	FIDDLY	GIMBAL	KILTER	LINTEL
RHEXIS	SHREWD	THRIFT	BILLET	DIGLOT	FIDGET	GIMLET	KILTIE	LIONEL
RHODES	SHRIEK	THRILL	BILLIE	DIKDIK	FIELDS	GIMMER	KIMMER	LIPARI
RHYMER	SHRIFT	THRIPS	BILLOW	DIKKOP	FIERCE	GINGER	KIMONO	LIPASE
RHYTHM	SHRIKE	THRIST	BILLYO	DIKTAT	FIESTA	GINGKO	KINASE	LIPIDE
SHABBY	SHRILL	THRIVE	BINARY	DILATE	FIGARO	GINKGO	KINDER	LIPOMA
SHADED	SHRIMP	THROAT	BINATE	DILUTE	FIGURE	GIORGI	KINDLE	LIPPED
SHADES	SHRINE	THROES	BINDER	DIMITY	FILFOT	GIOTTO	KINDLY	LIQUID
SHADOW	SHRINK	THRONE	BIOGEN	DIMMER	FILIAL	GIRDER	KINGLY	LIQUOR
SHADUF	SHRIVE	THRONG	BIONIC	DIMPLE	FILING	GIRDLE	KIPPER	LISBON
SHAGGY	SHROFF	THROVE	BIOPIC	DIMWIT	FILLED	GIRKIN	KIRBEH	LISPER
SHAKEN	SHROUD	THROWN	BIOPSY	DINERO	FILLER	GIRLIE	KIRMAN	LISSOM
SHAKER	SHROVE	THRUSH	BIOTIC	DINGHY	FILLET	GIRTON	KIRPAN	LISTEL
SHAKES	SHRUNK	THRUST	BIOTIN	DINGLE	FILLIP	GITANO	KIRSCH	LISTEN
SHALOM	SHTCHI	THWACK	BIRDIE	DINGLY	FILOSE	GIUSTO	KIRTLE	LISTER
SHAMAN	SHTETL	THWART	BIREME	DINING	FILTER	GIVING	KISHKE	LITANY
SHAMBA	SHUDRA	THYMOL	BIRNAM	DINKUM	FILTHY	GIZZEN	KISLEV	LITCHI
SHAMMY	SHUFTI	THYMUS	BISCAY	DINNER	FILTRÉ	HIATUS	KISMET	LITHIA
SHAMUS	SHUFTY	THYRSE	BISECT	DIODON	FIMBRA	HICCUP	KISSEL	LITMUS
SHANDY	THALER	WHACKO	BISHOP	DIOXIN	FINALE	HICKEY	KISSER	LITTER
SHANKS	THALES	WHACKY	BISQUE	DIPLOE	FINDER	HIDAGE	KITBAG	LITTLE
SHANTY	THALIA	WHALER	BISTER	DIPNOI	FINELY	HIDDEN	KITCAT	LIVELY
SHAPED	THAMES	WHALES	BISTRE	DIPOLE	FINERY	HIDING	KITSCH	LIVERY
SHARED	THANAH	WHAMMY	BISTRO	DIPPER	FINEST	HIGHER	KITTEN	LIVING
SHARER	THANET	WHARFE	BITCHY	DIQUAT	FINGAL	HIGHLY	KITTLE	LIZARD
SHARES	THANKS	WHEELS	BITING	DIRECT	FINGER	HIGHUP	LIABLE	LIZZIE
SHARIA	THEAVE	WHEELY	BITTEN	DIRHAM	FINIAL	HIJACK	LIAISE	MIASMA
SHARIF	THEBAN	WHEEZE	BITTER	DIRNDL	FINISH	HIKING	LIBBER	MICKEY
SHARON	THEBES	WHEEZY	CICADA	DISARM	FINITE	HILARY	LIBERO	MICKLE
SHARPS	THECAL	WHENCE	CICALA	DISBAR	FINLAY	HILTON	LIBIDO	MICMAC
SHASTA	THEIRS	WHERRY	CICELY	DISBUD	FINNAN	HIMMEL	LIBYAN	MICRON
SHAVEN	THEISM	WHILOM	CICERO	DISCUS	FIPPLE	HINDER	LICHEN	MIDDAY
SHAVER	THEIST	WHILST	CIERGE	DISEUR	FIRING	HINGED	LICTOR	MIDDEN
SHEARS	THEMIS	WHIMSY	CILICE	DISHED	FIRKIN	HINGES	LIEBIG	MIDDLE
SHEATH	THENAR	WHINGE	CILIUM	DISHES	FIRLOT	HIPPED	LIEDER	MIDGET
SHEAVE	THENCE	WHINNY	CINDER	DISMAL	FIRMAN	HIPPUS	LIERNE	MIDWAY
SHEENY	THEORY	WHISHT	CINEMA	DISMAY	FIRMER	HIRING	LIFTED	MIGHTY
SHEERS	THERMO	WHISKY	CINQUE	DISNEY	FIRMLY	HIRSEL	LIFTER	MIGNON
SHEETS	THESIS	WHITBY	CIPHER	DISOWN	FISCAL	HISPID	LIGASE	MIKADO
SHEIKH	THETIC	WHITED	CIRCLE	DISPEL	FISHER	HITECH	LIGATE	MILADY
SHEILA	THETIS	WHITEN	CIRCUS	DISTAL	FITFUL	HITHER	LIGETI	MILDEW
SHEKEL	THEYRE	WHITES	CIRQUE	DISTIL	FITOUT	HITLER	LIGGER	MILDLY
SHELVE	THICKY	WHOLLY	CIRRUS	DISUSE	FITTED	HITMAN	LIGHTS	MILIEU
SHERIF	THIERS	WHOOPS	CITRIC	DITHER	FITTER	HITTER	LIGNUM	MILLER
SHERPA	THIEVE	WHOOSH	CITRIN	DITTOS	FIXITY	JIBBAH	LIGULA	MILLET
SHERRY	THINGS	WHYDAH	CITRON	DIVALI	FIZGIG	JIGGER	LIGULE	MILORD
SHEVAT	THINGY	AIDANT	CITRUS	DIVEHI	FIZZED	JIGGLE	LIGURE	MILTON
SHIELD	THINLY	AIGLET	CIVICS	DIVERS	FIZZER	JIGSAW	LIKELY	MIMOSA
SHIFTY	THIRST	AIKIDO	CIVISM	DIVERT	FIZZLE	JILLET	LIKING	MINCER
SHIITE	THIRTY	AILING	DIACID	DIVEST	GIAOUR	JIMJAM	LILIAN	MINDED
SHILOH	THISBE	AIRBED	DIADEM	DIVIDE	GIBBER	JINGAL	LILITH	MINDEL
SHIMMY	THOLOS	AIRBUS	DIALOG	DIVINE	GIBBET	JINGLE	LIMBED	MINDER
SHINDY	THOLUS	AIRGUN	DIANAS	DIVING	GIBBON	JINXED	LIMBER	MINGLE
SHINER		AIRILY	DIAPER	DIWALI	GIBSON	JISSOM	LIMBIC	MINING

MINION	PIAFFE	RIBALD	SIMKIN	TIPPER	WIFELY	SKURRY	BLENNY	ELDERS
MINNIE	PIAZZA	RIBAND	SIMMER	TIPPET	WIGEON	SKYLAB	BLIGHT	ELDEST
MINNOW	PICARD	RIBBED	SIMNEL	TIPPLE	WIGGLE	SKYMAN	BLIMEY	ELEVEN
MINOAN	PICKAX	RIBBLE	SIMONY	TIPPOO	WIGGLY	ALACUS	BLINKS	ELFISH
MINTON	PICKED	RIBBON	SIMOOM	TIPTOE	WIGWAM	ALALIA	BLITHE	ELICIT
MINUET	PICKER	RIBOSE	SIMOON	TIPTOP	WILDER	ALARIC	BLOCKS	ELIJAH
MINUTE	PICKET	RICHES	SIMPER	TIPULA	WILDLY	ALARUM	BLONDE	ELISHA
MIRAGE	PICKLE	RICHLY	SIMPLE	TIRADE	WILFUL	ALASKA	BLOODY	ELIXIR
MIRROR	PICKUP	RICKER	SIMPLY	TIRANA	WILLED	ALBANY	BLOTCH	ELLERY
MISÈRE	PICNIC	RICKEY	SINBAD	TIRING	WILLET	ALBEDO	BLOTTO	ELLICE
MISERY	PICTOR	RICRAC	SINDER	TISANE	WILLIE	ALBEIT	BLOUSE	ELODEA
MISFIT	PIDDLE	RICTAL	SINEWY	TISHRI	WILLOW	ALBERT	BLOWER	ELOHIM
MISHAP	PIDGIN	RICTUS	SINFUL	TISSOT	WILSON	ALBINO	BLOWUP	ELOIGN
MISHIT	PIECES	RIDDLE	SINGER	TISSUE	WIMBLE	ALBION	BLOWZY	ELOISE
MISLAY	PIEDOG	RIDENT	SINGLE	TITBIT	WIMPLE	ALBITE	BLUDGE	ELOPER
MISLED	PIEMAN	RIDGED	SINGLY	TITCHY	WIMSEY	ALBUGO	BLUISH	ELTCHI
MISSAL	PIERCE	RIDING	SINKER	TITFER	WINDER	ALCINA	CLAGGY	ELUANT
MISSED	PIERIS	RIENZI	SINNER	TITIAN	WINDOW	ALCOCK	CLAIMS	ELUATE
MISSEL	PIFFLE	RIFFLE	SIPHON	TITLED	WINDUP	ALCOVE	CLAMMY	ELUTOR
MISSIS	PIGEON	RIGGED	SIPPET	TITTER	WINGED	ALDINE	CLAMOR	ELYSEE
MISSUS	PIGLET	RIGGER	SIPPLE	TITTLE	WINGER	ALDOSE	CLAQUE	FLABBY
MISTER	PIGOTT	RIGHTO	SIRDAR	TITTUP	WINKER	ALDRIN	CLARET	FLACON
MISUSE	PIGPEN	RIGHTS	SIRIUS	TITULE	WINKLE	ALECTO	CLARTY	FLAGGY
MITRAL	PIGSTY	RIGOUR	SIRKAR	TIVOLI	WINNER	ALEGAR	CLASSY	FLAGON
MITRED	PILAFF	RIMINI	SIRRAH	TIZWAZ	WINNIE	ALERCE	CLAUDE	FLAMBÉ
MITTEN	PILAGE	RIMMED	SIRREE	VIABLE	WINNOW	ALEVIN	CLAUSE	FLAMEN
MIZZEN	PILATE	RINGED	SISKIN	VIANDS	WINTER	ALEXIA	CLAVIS	FLANCH
MIZZLE	PILEUM	RINGER	SISTER	VIATOR	WINTRY	ALEXIN	CLAYEY	FLANGE
NIACIN	PILEUP	RIOTER	SITCOM	VIBRIO	WIPERS	ALEXIS	CLEAVE	FLANKS
NIAMEY	PILEUS	RIPOFF	SITREP	VICTIM	WIPING	ALFRED	CLENCH	FLARES
NIBBLE	PILFER	RIPPER	SITTER	VICTOR	WIRING	ALIGHT	CLEOME	FLASHY
NICELY	PILING	RIPPLE	SIZZLE	VICUNA	WIRRAL	ALIPED	CLERGY	FLATLY
NICENE	PILLAR	RIPPON	TICINO	VIENNA	WISDEN	ALIYAH	CLERIC	FLATUS
NICETY	PILLOW	RIPSAW	TICKER	VIENNE	WISDOM	ALKALI	CLERKS	FLAUNT
NICKED	PILOSE	RISING	TICKET	VIEWER	WISELY	ALKANE	CLEVER	FLAVIN
NICKEL	PIMENT	RISQUÉ	TICKEY	VIGOUR	WISHES	ALKENE	CLICHÉ	FLAVOR
NICKER	PIMPLE	RITUAL	TICKLE	VIKING	WITHAL	ALLEGE	CLIENT	FLAWED
NIDGET	PIMPLY	RIVAGE	TICKLY	VILELY	WITHER	ALLELE	CLIFFS	FLAXEN
NIDIFY	PINCER	RIVERA	TIDBIT	VILIFY	WITHIN	ALLEYN	CLIMAX	FLECHE
NIELLO	PINDAR	RIVLIN	TIDDLE	VILLUS	WITTED	ALLIED	CLIMES	FLEDGE
NIGGER	PINEAL	RIYADH	TIDDLY	VINERY	WIVERN	ALLIER	CLINCH	FLEECE
NIGGLE	PINERO	SICILY	TIDILY	VINOUS	WIZARD	ALLIUM	CLINIC	FLEECY
NIGGLY	PINGER	SICKEN	TIEPIN	VIOLET	WIZIER	ALLUDE	CLIPPY	FLENSE
NIGHTS	PINING	SICKER	TIERCE	VIOLIN	YIPPEE	ALLURE	CLIQUE	FLESHY
NIGHTY	PINION	SICKLE	TIERED	VIRAGO	ZIGZAG	ALMAIN	CLOACA	FLETCH
NIGNOG	PINITE	SICKLY	TIFFIN	VIRGIL	ZIMMER	ALMERY	CLOAKS	FLEURY
NIKKEI	PINKIE	SIDDHA	TIGHTS	VIRGIN	ZINGER	ALMOND	CLOCHE	FLICKS
NILGAI	PINTER	SIDING	TIGRIS	VIRILE	ZINNIA	ALMOST	CLONIC	FLIGHT
NILGAU	PINTLE	SIDNEY	TILLER	VIROUS	ZIPPER	ALOGIA	CLONUS	FLIMSY
NILOTE	PINXIT	SIENNA	TILSIT	VIRTUE	ZIRCON	ALONSO	CLOSED	FLINCH
NIMBLE	PINYIN	SIERRA	TIMBER	VISAGE	ZITHER	ALPACA	CLOSER	FLINTY
NIMBLY	PIPING	SIESTA	TIMBRE	VISCID	DJEBEL	ALPINE	CLOSET	FLITCH
NIMBUS	PIPKIN	SIFFLE	TIMELY	VISHNU	DJERBA	ALPINO	CLOTHE	FLOOZY
NIMROD	PIPPIN	SIFTER	TIMING	VISIER	DJINNI	ALTAIR	CLOTHO	FLOPPY
NINETY	PIQUET	SIGHTS	TINDER	VISION	OJIBWA	ALTHEA	CLOUDY	FLORAL
NINIAN	PIRACY	SIGNAL	TINGED	VISUAL	AKIMBO	ALUDEL	CLOUGH	FLORET
NIPPER	PIRATE	SIGNET	TINGLE	VITALS	SKATER	ALUMNI	CLOVEN	FLORID
NIPPLE	PIRENE	SIGNOR	TINKER	VIVACE	SKATES	ALWAYS	CLOVER	FLORIN
NIPPON	PISANO	SIKKIM	TINKLE	VIVIAN	SKELLY	BLACKS	CLOVIS	FLOSSY
NISSEN	PISCES	SILAGE	TINNED	VIVIEN	SKERRY	BLAISE	CLUMPS	FLOURY
NITERY	PISGAH	SILENE	TINNIE	VIZARD	SKETCH	BLAMED	CLUMSY	FLOUSH
NITRIC	PISSED	SILENT	TINPAN	VIZIER	SKEWED	BLANCH	CLUNCH	FLOWER
NITRYL	PISTIL	SILICA	TINPOT	WICKED	SKEWER	BLANCO	CLUTCH	FLUENT
NITWIT	PISTOL	SILKEN	TINSEL	WICKER	SKIDOO	BLAZER	ELAINE	FLUFFY
NIVOSE	PISTON	SILVAN	TINTED	WICKET	SKIING	BLAZON	ELANCE	FLUNKY
OILCAN	PITMAN	SILVER	TINTIN	WIDELY	SKIMPY	BLEACH	ELANET	FLURRY
OILERS	PITTED	SIMEON	TIPCAT	WIDGET	SKINNY	BLEARY	ELAPSE	FLUSHY
OILMAN	PITTER	SIMIAN	TIPOFF	WIDOWS	SKIVER	BLENCH	ELATED	FLUTED
OILRIG	RIALTO	SIMILE	TIPPED	WIENER	SKIVVY	BLENDE	ELBRUS	FLUTER

FLUTES	PLIANT	AMBUSH	SMALLS	ANSELM	GNAWER	INSERT	SNOUTY	UNSEXY
FLYING	PLIERS	AMELIA	SMARMY	ANSWER	GNEISS	INSIDE	SNOWED	UNSHOD
GLACIS	PLIGHT	AMENDE	SMARTY	ANTHEM	GNOMIC	INSIST	SNUDGE	UNSOLD
GLADLY	PLINTH	AMENDS	SMEARY	ANTHER	GNOMON	INSOLE	SNUGLY	UNSUNG
GLAGOL	PLISSÉ	AMERCE	SMEATH	ANTICS	INBORN	INSTAL	UNABLE	UNSURE
GLAIRE	PLONGE	AMHARA	SMEGMA	ANTLER	INBRED	INSTAR	UNBEND	UNTIDY
GLAIVE	PLOUGH	AMIDOL	SMELLY	ANTLIA	INCASE	INSTEP	UNBENT	UNTOLD
GLAMIS	PLOVER	AMIDST	SMIGHT	ANTONY	INCEDE	INSTIL	UNBIND	UNTRUE
GLAMOR	PLUMED	AMMINE	SMILER	ANTRIM	INCEPT	INSULA	UNBOLT	UNUSED
GLANCE	PLUMMY	AMNION	SMILES	ANTRUM	INCEST	INSULT	UNBORN	UNVEIL
GLASSY	PLUNGE	AMOEBA	SMILEY	ANUBIS	INCHES	INSURE	UNBRED	UNWARY
GLAZED	PLURAL	AMORAL	SMIRCH	ANURAN	INCHON	INTACT	UNBUSY	UNWELL
GLIBLY	PLUTUS	AMORCE	SMITHS	ANYHOW	INCISE	INTAKE	UNCAGE	UNWIND
GLIDER	PLYING	AMORET	SMITHY	ANYONE	INCITE	INTEND	UNCIAL	UNWISE
GLIÈRE	SLACKS	AMOUNT	SMOKER	ANYWAY	INCOME	INTENT	UNCLAD	UNWRAP
GLINKA	SLALOM	AMPERE	SMOKEY	ENABLE	INDABA	INTERN	UNCOIL	UNYOKE
GLIOMA	SLANGY	AMTRAK	SMOOCH	ENAMEL	INDEED	INTIME	UNCOOL	AORIST
GLITCH	SLATCH	AMULET	SMOOTH	ENAMOR	INDENT	INTONE	UNCORK	AORTAL
GLITZY	SLATER	AMUSED	SMUDGE	ENARCH	INDIAN	INTOWN	UNDATE	AOUDAD
GLOBAL	SLAVER	AMYCUS	SMUDGY	ENCALM	INDICT	INTRAY	UNDECK	BOARDS
GLOIRE	SLAVES	AMYTAL	SMUGLY	ENCAMP	INDIES	INTRON	UNDINE	BOATER
GLOOMY	SLAYER	EMBAIL	SMUTTY	ENCASE	INDIGN	INVADE	UNDONE	BOBBER
GLORIA	SLEAVE	EMBALE	SMYRNA	ENCASH	INDIGO	INVENT	UNDULY	BOBBIN
GLOSSA	SLEAZE	EMBALM	TMESIS	ENCODE	INDITE	INVERT	UNDYED	BOBBLE
GLOSSY	SLEAZY	EMBARK	UMBELS	ENCORE	INDIUM	INVEST	UNEASE	BOBCAT
GLOVED	SLEDGE	EMBERS	UMBREL	ENDEAR	INDOOR	INVITE	UNEASY	BOBWIG
GLOWER	SLEEKY	EMBLEM	UMBRIA	ENDIVE	INDUCE	INVOKE	UNEVEN	BOCAGE
GLUMPS	SLEEPY	EMBODY	UMBRIL	ENDURE	INDUCT	INWARD	UNFAIR	BODACH
GLUTEN	SLEEVE	EMBOSS	UMLAUT	ENERGY	INFAME	KNAGGY	UNFOLD	BODEGA
GLYCOL	SLEEZY	EMBRUE	UMPIRE	ENFIRE	INFAMY	KNIGHT	UNFURL	BODGER
ILKLEY	SLEIGH	EMBRYO	ANABAS	ENFOLD	INFANT	KNIVES	UNGAIN	BODGIE
ILLITE	SLEUTH	EMBUSY	ANADEM	ENFREE	INFARE	KNOBBY	UNGULA	BODICE
ILLUDE	SLEWED	EMERGE	ANADYR	ENGAGE	INFECT	KNOTTY	UNHAND	BODIES
KLAXON	SLICER	EMETIC	ANALOG	ENGELS	INFEST	ONAGER	UNHOLY	BODILY
KLUDGE	SLIDER	EMEUTE	ANANAS	ENGINE	INFIRM	ONAGRA	UNHOOK	BODKIN
LLOYDS	SLIGHT	EMIGRÉ	ANCHOR	ENGLUT	INFLOW	ONCOME	UNHURT	BODONI
OLDISH	SLINKY	EMPIRE	ANCILE	ENGRAM	INFLUX	ONCOST	UNIATE	BOEING
OLEATE	SLIPPY	EMPLOY	ANCOME	ENGULF	INFOLD	ONDINE	UNIQUE	BOFFIN
OLEFIN	SLIPUP	EMULGE	ANCONA	ENIGMA	INFORM	ONEDIN	UNISEX	BOFORS
OLENUS	SLITHY	EMUNGE	ANCORA	ENJOIN	INFUSE	ONEGIN	UNISON	BOGART
OLIVER	SLIVER	IMBARN	ANDEAN	ENLACE	INGATE	ONEIDA	UNITED	BOGGLE
OLIVET	SLOANE	IMBASE	ANDREW	ENGEST	INGEST	ONEMAN	UNJUST	BOGOTA
OLIVIA	SLOGAN	IMBIBE	ANEMIA	ENLIST	INGOTS	ONEWAY	UNKIND	BOHUNK
PLACED	SLOPES	IMBOSS	ANEMIC	ENMESH	INGRAM	ONIONS	UNLACE	BOILED
PLACER	SLOPPY	IMBRUE	ANGARY	ENMITY	INGRES	ONLINE	UNLESS	BOILER
PLACID	SLOSHY	IMMUNE	ANGELA	ENNIUS	INGROW	ONRUSH	UNLIKE	BOLDLY
PLAGAL	SLOUCH	IMMURE	ANGELS	ENODAL	INGULF	ONSIDE	UNLOAD	BOLERO
PLAGUE	SLOVAK	IMOGEN	ANGERS	ENOSIS	INHALE	ONWARD	UNLOCK	BOLEYN
PLAICE	SLOVEN	IMPACT	ANGICO	ENOUGH	INHERE	PNEUMA	UNMADE	BOLIDE
PLAINS	SLOWLY	IMPAIR	ANGINA	ENRAGE	INHUME	SNAGGY	UNMASK	BOLLEN
PLAINT	SLUDGE	IMPALA	ANGLED	ENRAPT	INJECT	SNAILY	UNMEET	BOLSHY
PLANCH	SLUICE	IMPALE	ANGLER	ENRICH	INJURE	SNAKED	UNPACK	BOLTER
PLANET	SLUMMY	IMPART	ANGLIA	ENROBE	INJURY	SNAPPY	UNPAID	BOMBAY
PLANKS	SLURRY	IMPAWN	ANGOLA	ENROLL	INKJET	SNATCH	UNPICK	BOMBER
PLAQUE	SLUSHY	IMPEDE	ANGORA	ENSATE	INKPOT	SNAZZY	UNPLUG	BOMBYX
PLASMA	ULCERS	IMPEND	ANIMAL	ENSEAL	INLAID	SNEAKY	UNREAD	BONBON
PLATED	ULITIS	IMPISH	ANIMUS	ENSIGN	INLAND	SNEATH	UNREAL	BONDED
PLATEN	ULLAGE	IMPORT	ANKARA	ENSILE	INLAWS	SNEEZE	UNREEL	BONDER
PLATER	ULLING	IMPOSE	ANKLET	ENSURE	INLIER	SNEEZY	UNREST	BONITO
PLATES	ULSTER	IMPOST	ANKOLE	ENTAIL	INLINE	SNIFFY	UNRIPE	BONNET
PLAYER	ULTIMA	IMPUGN	ANNALS	ENTICE	INMATE	SNIFTY	UNROLL	BONNIE
PLEACH	ULTIMO	IMPURE	ANNEAL	ENTIRE	INMESH	SNIPER	UNRULY	BONSAI
PLEASE	OMASUM	IMPUTE	ANNEXE	ENTITY	INMOST	SNIPPY	UNSAFE	BONXIE
PLEDGE	AMADOU	OMELET	ANNUAL	ENTOMB	INNATE	SNITCH	UNSAID	BONZER
PLENTY	AMAZED	OMENTA	ANOINT	ENTRAP	INNING	SNIVEL	UNSEAM	BOOBOO
PLENUM	AMAZON	OMERTA	ANONYM	ENTREE	INROAD	SNOOTY	UNSEAT	BOODLE
PLEURA	AMBAGE	OMNIUM	ANORAK	ENWRAP	INRUSH	SNOOZE	UNSEEN	BOOGIE
PLEXOR	AMBLER	SMACKS	ANOXIA	ENZIAN	INSANE	SNORER	UNSEAT	BOOHOO
PLEXUS			ANOXIC	ENZYME	INSECT	SNOTTY	UNSENT	BOOJUM

BOOKED	COCCID	CONRAD	COUNTY	DOTAGE	FORPIT	HOBDAY	IODIZE	LOOPER
BOOKER	COCCUS	CONSUL	COUPLE	DOTARD	FORRAD	HOBNOB	IOLITE	LOOSEN
BOOKIE	COCCYX	CONTRA	COUPON	DOTING	FORRAY	HOCKEY	IONIAN	LOOTER
BOOMER	COCHIN	CONVEX	COURSE	DOTTED	FORSAY	HODDER	IONIZE	LOQUAT
BOOTEE	COCKER	CONVEY	COUSIN	DOTTLE	FORTHY	HOGGAR	JOANNA	LORCHA
BOÖTES	COCKLE	CONVOY	COVENT	DOUANE	FOSSIL	HOGGET	JOBBER	LORDLY
BOOTLE	COCOON	COOING	COVERT	DOUBLE	FOSTER	HOGTIE	JOCKEY	LORETO
BOOZER	CODDLE	COOKED	COVING	DOUBLY	FOUGHT	HOIDEN	JOCOSE	LORICA
BORAGE	CODGER	COOKER	COWAGE	DOUCET	FOULLY	HOLDER	JOCUND	LORIOT
BORANE	CODIFY	COOKIE	COWARD	DOUCHE	FOURTH	HOLDUP	JOGGER	LOSING
BORATE	CODING	COOLER	COWBOY	DOUGHY	FOUTRE	HOLISM	JOGGLE	LOTION
BORDAR	COELOM	COOLIE	COWMAN	DOURLY	FOWLER	HOLIST	JOHNNY	LOUCHE
BORDER	COERCE	COOLLY	COWPAT	DOWNAY	GOALIE	HOLLER	JOINER	LOUDEN
BOREAS	COEVAL	COOLTH	COWPER	DOWNER	GOANNA	HOLLOW	JOJOBA	LOUDLY
BORGIA	COFFEE	COOPER	COWPOX	DOWSER	GOATEE	HOLMES	JONSON	LOUNGE
BORING	COFFER	COOTIE	COWRIE	DOWSET	GOBBET	HOMAGE	JOPLIN	LOURIE
BORNEO	COFFIN	COPECK	COYOTE	DOWSON	GOBBLE	HOMBRE	JORDAN	LOUVER
BORROW	COGENT	COPIED	COZIER	DOYLEY	GOBLET	HOMELY	JOSEPH	LOUVRE
BORSCH	COGGER	COPIER	DOBBIN	DOZENS	GOBLIN	HOMILY	JOSHUA	LOVAGE
BORZOI	COGNAC	COPING	DOBSON	DOZING	GOCART	HOMING	JOSIAH	LOVELL
BOSKET	COHERE	COPPER	DOCENT	EOCENE	GODIVA	HOMINY	JOSKIN	LOVELY
BOSSED	COHORT	COPPIN	DOCILE	EOLITH	GODOWN	HONCHO	JOSSER	LOVING
BOSTON	COHOSH	COPTIC	DOCKED	EOTHEN	GODSON	HONEST	JOSTLE	LOWBOY
BOSUNS	COILED	COQUET	DOCKER	EOZOON	GODWIN	HONIED	JOTTER	LOWELL
BOTANY	COINER	CORALS	DOCKET	FOCSLE	GODWIT	HONOUR	JOVIAL	LOWEST
BOTHAM	COITUS	CORBEL	DOCTOR	FODDER	GOETHE	HONSHU	JOYFUL	LOWKEY
BOTHER	COLDLY	CORBIE	DODDER	FOETAL	GOFFER	HOODED	JOYOUS	LOYOLA
BOTHIE	COLEUS	CORDON	DODDLE	FOETID	GOGGLE	HOOFED	KODIAK	MOANER
BOTLEY	COLLAR	CORIUM	DODGEM	FOETUS	GOITER	HOOFER	KOMODO	MOATED
BOTTLE	COLLET	CORKED	DODGER	FOGBOW	GOITRE	HOOHAH	KOODOO	MOBCAP
BOTTOM	COLLIE	CORKER	DODOMA	FOIBLE	GOKART	HOOKAH	KOOKIE	MOBILE
BOUCHE	COLLOP	CORMUS	DOESNT	FOILED	GOLDEN	HOOKED	KOOLAH	MOBIUS
BOUCLÉ	COLMAR	CORNEA	DOGGED	FOKINE	GOLFER	HOOKER	KOREAN	MOCKER
BOUFFE	COLONY	CORNED	DOGGER	FOKKER	GOLLOP	HOOKEY	KORUNA	MOCKUP
BOUGHT	COLOUR	CORNEL	DOINGS	FOLDED	GOLOSH	HOOKUP	KOSHER	MODELS
BOULLE	COLTER	CORNER	DOLEUR	FOLDER	GONION	HOOPER	KOSMOS	MODENA
BOUNCE	COLUMN	CORNET	DOLINA	FOLIAR	GONIUM	HOOPLA	KOTWAL	MODERN
BOUNCY	COMART	CORNUA	DOLINE	FOLIOS	GOOBER	HOOPOE	KOUROS	MODEST
BOUNDS	COMATE	CORNUS	DOLIUM	FOLIOT	GOODLY	HOORAH	KOWTOW	MODIFY
BOUNTY	COMBAT	CORONA	DOLLAR	FOLIUM	GOOGIE	HOORAY	LOADED	MODISH
BOURÉE	COMBED	CORPSE	DOLLOP	FOLKSY	GOOGLE	HOOTCH	LOADER	MODIST
BOURNE	COMBER	CORPUS	DOLMAN	FOLLOW	GOOGLY	HOOTER	LOAFER	MODIUS
BOURSE	COMBLE	CORRAL	DOLMEN	FOMENT	GOOGOL	HOOVER	LOATHE	MODULE
BOUSER	COMEDO	CORRIE	DOLOUR	FONDLE	GOOLEY	HOPPER	LOAVES	MOGGIE
BOUTON	COMEDY	CORSET	DOMAIN	FONDLY	GOOLIE	HORACE	LOCALE	MOHAIR
BOVATE	COMELY	CORTES	DOMINO	FONDUE	GOPHER	HORMUZ	LOCATE	MOHAWK
BOVINE	COMFIT	CORTEX	DONATE	FOOTER	GORDON	HORNED	LOCHIA	MOHOCK
BOVRIL	COMICE	CORTEZ	DONGLE	FOOTLE	GORGED	HORNER	LOCKED	MOIDER
BOWELS	COMING	CORVÉE	DONJON	FOOZLE	GORGES	HORNET	LOCKER	MOIETY
BOWERY	COMITY	CORVUS	DONKEY	FORAGE	GORGET	HORRID	LOCKET	MOIRAI
BOWFIN	COMMIS	CORYZA	DONNÉE	FORBID	GORGIA	HORROR	LOCKUP	MOJAVE
BOWLED	COMMIT	COSHER	DONZEL	FORÇAT	GORGIO	HORSED	LOCULE	MOLECH
BOWLER	COMMON	COSIER	DOODAD	FORCED	GORGON	HOSIER	LOCUST	MOLEST
BOWMAN	COMPEL	COSILY	DOODAH	FORCES	GORING	HOSING	LODGED	MOLINE
BOWSER	COMPLY	COSINE	DOODLE	FOREDO	GOSPEL	HOSTEL	LODGER	MOLLAH
BOWWOW	COMSAT	COSMEA	DOOFER	FOREGO	GOSSIP	HOTAIR	LOGGER	MOLLIE
BOXCAR	CONCHA	COSMIC	DOOMED	FOREST	GOTHAM	HOTBED	LOGGIA	MOLOCH
BOXING	CONCHY	COSMOS	DOPANT	FORGED	GOTHIC	HOTPOT	LOGJAM	MOLTEN
BOYISH	CONCUR	COSSET	DORADO	FORGER	GOTTEN	HOTTER	LOITER	MOMENT
COALER	CONDOM	COSSIE	DORCAS	FORGET	GOUNOD	HOUDAH	LOLITA	MONACO
COARSE	CONDOR	COSTAR	DORIAN	FORGOT	GOURDE	HOUNDS	LOLIUM	MONDAY
COATED	CONFAB	COSTER	DORMER	FORINT	GOURDS	HOURLY	LOLLOP	MONGER
COATES	CONFER	COSTLY	DORRIT	FORKED	GOUTTE	HOUSES	LOMOND	MONGOL
COBALT	CONGEE	COTTAR	DORSAL	FORMAL	GOVERN	HOWARD	LONDON	MONIAL
COBBER	CONGER	COTTON	DORSET	FORMAT	HOARSE	HOWDAH	LONELY	MONICA
COBBLE	CONICS	COTYLE	DORTER	FORMER	HOAXER	HOWDIE	LONGER	MONISM
COBDEN	CONKER	COUGAR	DOSAGE	FORMIC	HOBART	HOWLER	LOOFAH	MONIST
COBURG	CONMAN	COULEE	DOSSAL	FORNAX	HOBBES	HOYDEN	LOONIE	MONKEY
COBWEB	CONNER	COULIS	DOSSER	FORNIX	HOBBLE	IODINE	LOOPED	MONODY

MONROE	NONAGE	POMPOM	ROGNON	SOLDER	TOMCAT	WOEFUL	EPRISE	SPOUSE
MONTEM	NONARY	POMPON	ROGUES	SOLEIL	TOMIAL	WOLVER	EPULIS	SPRAIN
MONTHS	NONCOM	PONCHO	ROKEBY	SOLELY	TOMIUM	WOMBAT	IPECAC	SPRANG
MOOCOW	NOODLE	PONDER	ROLAND	SOLEMN	TOMTOM	WOMENS	OPAQUE	SPRAWL
MOOLAH	NOOKIE	PONENT	ROLLER	SOLENT	TONANT	WONDER	OPENER	SPREAD
MOOMBA	NORDIC	PONGEE	ROMANO	SOLERA	TONGAN	WONTED	OPENLY	SPRING
MOPING	NORMAL	PONGID	ROMANS	SOLEUS	TONGUE	WONTON	OPHISM	SPRINT
MOPISH	NORMAN	PONTIC	ROMANY	SOLIVE	TONITE	WOODED	OPHITE	SPRITE
MOPPET	NORROY	POODLE	ROMISH	SOLUTE	TONSIL	WOODEN	OPIATE	SPRITZ
MOPSUS	NORVIC	POORLY	ROMMEL	SOLVAY	TONSOR	WOODIE	OPPOSE	SPROUT
MORALE	NORWAY	POOTER	ROMNEY	SOLVED	TOOTER	WOOFER	OPPUGN	SPRUCE
MORALS	NOSILY	POPEYE	RONDEL	SOLVER	TOOTHY	WOOKEY	OPTICS	SPRUNG
MORASS	NOTARY	POPLAR	ROOFER	SOMALI	TOOTLE	WOOLEN	OPTIMA	SPRYLY
MORBID	NOTATE	POPLIN	ROOKIE	SOMBER	TOOTSY	WOOLLY	OPTIME	SPUNGE
MORBUS	NOTICE	POPPER	ROOMER	SOMBRE	TOPHUS	WORKED	OPTION	SPURGE
MOREEN	NOTIFY	POPPET	ROOTED	SONANT	TOPPER	WORKER	OPTOUT	SPUTUM
MORGAN	NOTION	POPPIT	ROOTER	SONATA	TOPPLE	WORSEN	SPACED	SPYING
MORGEN	NOUGAT	POPPLE	ROOTLE	SONICS	TORERO	WORTHY	SPACER	UPBEAT
MORGUE	NOUGHT	PORGIE	ROPERY	SONNET	TORPID	WORTLE	SPADES	UPCAST
MORION	NOUNCE	PORKER	ROQUET	SONTAG	TORPOR	WOWSER	SPADIX	UPDATE
MORMON	NOVENA	POROUS	ROSACE	SOONER	TORQUE	YOGURT	SPARKS	UPFLOW
MORNAY	NOVIAL	PORTAL	ROSARY	SOOTHE	TORRES	YOICKS	SPARKY	UPHELD
MORNED	NOVICE	PORTER	ROSCID	SOPHIA	TORRID	YOKING	SPARSE	UPHILL
MOROSE	NOWISE	PORTIA	ROSCOE	SORAGE	TORULA	YONDER	SPARTA	UPHOLD
MORRIS	NOYADE	PORTLY	ROSERY	SORBET	TOSHER	YORICK	SPARTH	UPKEEP
MORROW	NOYOUS	POSADA	ROSINA	SORDES	TOSSUP	YORKER	SPATHE	UPLAND
MORSEL	NOZZLE	POSEUR	ROSSER	SORDID	TOTTER	YORUBA	SPAULD	UPLIFT
MORTAL	OOCYTE	POSSER	ROSTER	SORELL	TOTTIE	ZODIAC	SPAVIN	UPLINK
MORTAR	OODLES	POSSET	ROSTOV	SORELY	TOUCAN	ZOMBIE	SPECIE	UPPISH
MORTEM	OOKPIK	POSSUM	ROSYTH	SORGHO	TOUCHE	ZONING	SPEECH	UPPITY
MOSAIC	OOLITE	POSTAL	ROTARY	SORREL	TOUCHY	ZONKED	SPEEDO	UPRATE
MOSCOW	OOLONG	POSTER	ROTATE	SORROW	TOUPEE	ZOPHAR	SPEEDY	UPROAR
MOSLEM	OOMPAH	POSTIL	ROTGUT	SORTER	TOUPET	ZOSTER	SPEISS	UPROOT
MOSQUE	POBBLE	POTASH	ROTHER	SORTES	TOURER	ZOUAVE	SPENCE	UPSHOT
MOSSAD	POCKET	POTATO	ROTHKO	SORTIE	TOUSER	ZOUNDS	SPHENE	UPSIDE
MOSTLY	PODIUM	POTEEN	ROTTEN	SOUGHT	TOUSLE	APACHE	SPHERE	UPTAKE
MOTHER	PODSOL	POTENT	ROTTER	SOUPER	TOWAGE	APATHY	SPHINX	UPTOWN
MOTILE	PODZOL	POTHER	ROTULA	SOUPLE	TOWARD	APEPSY	SPICED	UPTURN
MOTION	POETIC	POTION	ROTUND	SOURCE	TOWBAR	APERÇU	SPICER	UPWARD
MOTIVE	POETRY	POTTED	ROUBLE	SOURLY	TOWHEE	APHONY	SPIDER	AQUILA
MOTLEY	POGROM	POTTER	ROUGED	SOUSED	TOWNEE	APHTHA	SPIGOT	EQUALS
MOTOWN	POINTE	POTTLE	ROUGHY	SOUTER	TOWNLY	APIARY	SPIKED	EQUANT
MOTTLE	POINTS	POUDRE	ROUNCE	SOVIET	TOWSER	APICAL	SPILTH	EQUATE
MOUJIK	POIROT	POUFFE	ROUNDS	SOWBUG	TOYISH	APIECE	SPINAL	EQUINE
MOULDY	POISED	POUNCE	ROUTER	SOWING	VOICED	APLITE	SPINAR	EQUIPE
MOULIN	POISON	POUNDS	ROVING	SOWSED	VOIDED	APLOMB	SPINET	EQUITY
MOUSER	POLACK	POURER	ROWING	SOWTER	VOIDEE	APNOEA	SPIRAL	SQUAIL
MOUSEY	POLAND	POUTER	ROXANE	SOZZLE	VOIDER	APOGEE	SPIRIT	SQUALL
MOUSSE	POLDER	POWDER	ROYALS	TOBAGO	VOLAGE	APOLLO	SPITAL	SQUAMA
MOUTAN	POLICE	POWERS	ROZZER	TOBIAS	VOLANS	APORIA	SPLAKE	SQUARE
MOUTER	POLICY	POWNIE	SOAKED	TOCSIN	VOLANT	APPALL	SPLASH	SQUASH
MOUTON	POLISH	POWTER	SOBEIT	TODDLE	VOLENS	APPEAL	SPLEEN	SQUAWK
MOVIES	POLITE	POWWOW	SOCAGE	TOECAP	VOLLEY	APPEAR	SPLENT	SQUEAK
MOVING	POLITY	ROADIE	SOCCER	TOERAG	VOLUME	APPEND	SPLICE	SQUEAL
MOWING	POLLAN	ROAMER	SOCIAL	TOETOE	VOLUTE	APPIAN	SPLIFF	SQUILL
MOZART	POLLED	ROARER	SOCKET	TOFFEE	VOMICA	APPLES	SPLINT	SQUINT
MOZZLE	POLLEN	ROBBED	SODDEN	TOGGED	VOODOO	APPORT	SPLITS	SQUIRE
NOBBLE	POLLEX	ROBBER	SODIUM	TOGGLE	VORTEX	APPOSE	SPLOSH	SQUIRM
NOBBUT	POLLUX	ROBERT	SODOMY	TOILET	VOSGES	EPARCH	SPOILS	SQUIRT
NOBODY	POLONY	ROBING	SOFFIT	TOLEDO	VOTARY	EPAULE	SPOILT	SQUISH
NOCENT	POLYOL	ROBSON	SOFTEN	TOLLED	VOTING	EPERDU	SPOKEN	ARABIA
NOCTUA	POLYPS	ROBUST	SOFTIE	TOLLER	VOTIVE	EPHEBE	SPOKES	ARABIC
NODDED	POMACE	ROCKER	SOFTLY	TOLOSA	VOTYAK	EPICAL	SPONGE	ARABIS
NODDLE	POMADE	ROCKET	SOHRAB	TOLTEC	VOWELS	EPIGON	SPONGY	ARABLE
NODOSE	POMELO	ROCOCO	SOIGNÉ	TOLUIC	VOYAGE	EPILOG	SPOOKY	ARAFAT
NODULE	POMMEL	RODENT	SOILED	TOLUOL	VOYEUR	EPIRUS	SPOONY	ARAGON
NOGGIN	POMMIE	RODHAM	SOIREE	TOLZEY	WOBBLE	EPONYM	SPORTS	ARALIA
NOMADE	POMONA	RODNEY	SOLACE	TOMATO	WOBBLY	EPOPEE	SPORTY	ARAMIS
NOMISM	POMPEY	ROEMER	SOLANO	TOMBOY	WOBURN	EPPING	SPOTTY	ARANDA

ARARAT	BRAINY	CRANTS	CRUIVE	FRAPPÉ	GRAVID	ORACHE	PRIORY	TROMPE
ARBOUR	BRAISE	CRAPLE	CRUMBS	FRATER	GREASE	ORACLE	PRISMS	TROOPS
ARCADE	BRAMAH	CRASIS	CRUMEN	FRAYED	GREASY	ORALLY	PRISON	TROPHE
ARCADY	BRANCH	CRATCH	CRUMMY	FREELY	GREATS	ORANGE	PRISSY	TROPHY
ARCANA	BRANDY	CRATER	CRUNCH	FREEZE	GREAVE	ORATOR	PRIVET	TROPIC
ARCANE	BRAQUE	CRATON	CRURAL	FRENCH	GREECE	ORBITA	PRIZES	TROPPO
ARCHED	BRASSY	CRATUR	CRUSET	FRENUM	GREEDY	ORCHID	PROBIT	TROUGH
ARCHER	BRAWNY	CRAVAT	CRUSOE	FRENZY	GREEKS	ORCHIS	PROFIT	TROUPE
ARCHES	BRAZEN	CRAVEN	CRUSTA	FRESCO	GREENE	ORCINE	PROLEG	TROUVÉ
ARCHIE	BRAZIL	CRAYER	CRUSTY	FRIAND	GREENS	ORDAIN	PROLIX	TROVER
ARCHIL	BREACH	CRAYON	CRUTCH	FRIARY	GRETNA	ORDEAL	PROLOG	TROWEL
ARCHON	BREAST	CRAZED	CRYING	FRIDAY	GREUZE	ORDERS	PROMPT	TROYES
ARCTIC	BREATH	CREACH	CRYPTO	FRIDGE	GRIEVE	ORDURE	PRONTO	TRUANT
ARDENT	BRECHT	CREAGH	DRACHM	FRIEND	GRIGRI	OREGON	PROPEL	TRUDGE
ARDOUR	BREECH	CREAKY	DRAFTY	FRIEZE	GRILLE	OREXIS	PROPER	TRUISM
AREOLA	BREEZE	CREAMY	DRAGEE	FRIGGA	GRILSE	ORGANS	PROPYL	TRUMAN
AREOLE	BREEZY	CREANT	DRAGON	FRIGHT	GRIMES	ORGASM	PROSIT	TRUMPS
ARGENT	BREGMA	CREASE	DRALON	FRIGID	GRIMLY	ORGEAT	PROTEA	TRUNKS
ARGHAN	BREMEN	CREATE	DRAPER	FRILLS	GRIMMS	ORGONE	PROTON	TRUSTY
ARGIVE	BRETON	CRÈCHE	DRAWER	FRILLY	GRINGO	ORIANO	PROUST	TRUTHS
ARGOSY	BREVET	CREDIT	DREAMY	FRINGE	GRIPES	ORIENT	PROVEN	TRYING
ARGUED	BREWER	CREEPS	DREARY	FRIPON	GRIPPE	ORIGEN	PRUNER	URACIL
ARGUTE	BREWIS	CREEPY	DREDGE	FRISKY	GRISLY	ORIGIN	PRUSIK	URANIA
ARGYLE	BRIAND	CREESE	DREGGY	FRIVOL	GRISON	ORIOLE	PRYING	URANIC
ARGYLL	BRIARD	CREESH	DRENCH	FRIZZY	GRITTY	ORISON	TRACER	URANUS
ARIOCH	BRICKS	CREMOR	DRESSY	FROLIC	GROATS	ORKNEY	TRADER	URBANE
ARIOSO	BRIDAL	CRENAL	DRIEST	FRONDE	GROCER	ORMOLU	TRADES	URCHIN
ARISTA	BRIDGE	CRENEL	DRIPPY	FROSTY	GROGGY	ORNATE	TRAGIC	URETER
ARISTO	BRIDIE	CREOLE	DRIVEL	FROTHY	GROOVE	ORNERY	TRAGUS	URGENT
ARKOSE	BRIDLE	CRESOL	DRIVEN	FROUDE	GROOVY	OROIDE	TRAJAN	URINAL
ARMADA	BRIEFS	CRESTA	DRIVER	FROWST	GROPER	ORPHAN	TRALEE	URSINE
ARMAGH	BRIGHT	CRETAN	DROGUE	FROWZY	GROSSO	ORPHIC	TRANCE	URSULA
ARMFUL	BRIONY	CRETIC	DROMIO	FROZEN	GROTTO	ORPINE	TRANNY	URTICA
ARMLET	BRITON	CRETIN	DROMOS	FRUGAL	GROTTY	ORRERY	TRAPES	WRAITH
ARMORY	BROACH	CREWEL	DRONES	FRUICT	GROUCH	ORSINO	TRASHY	WRASSE
ARMOUR	BROADS	CRIANT	DRONGO	FRUITS	GROUND	ORTEGA	TRAUMA	WREATH
ARMPIT	BROGAN	CRIBLE	DROOPY	FRUITY	GROUPS	ORWELL	TRAVEL	WREKIN
ARMURE	BROGUE	CRIKEY	DROPSY	FRUMPY	GROUSE	PRAGUE	TRAVIS	WRENCH
ARNAUT	BROKEN	CRIMEA	DROSKY	FRUTEX	GROUTS	PRAISE	TREATY	WRETCH
ARNHEM	BROKER	CRINAL	DROVER	FRYING	GROUTY	PRANCE	TREBLE	WRIGHT
ARNICA	BROLLY	CRINGE	DROVES	GRABEN	GROVEL	PRANKS	TREBLY	WRITER
ARNOLD	BRONCO	CRINUM	DROWSE	GRACES	GROWER	PRATER	TREMOR	WRITHE
AROINT	BRONTE	CRIPES	DROWSY	GRADED	GROWTH	PRAVDA	TRENCH	ASADHA
AROLLA	BRONZE	CRISIS	DRUDGE	GRADES	GROYNE	PRAXIS	TRENDY	ASARUM
AROUET	BROOCH	CRISPY	DRYDEN	GRADUS	GRUBBY	PRAYER	TREPAN	ASCEND
AROUND	BROODY	CRISTA	DRYING	GRAFIN	GRUDGE	PREACE	TRESCO	ASCENT
AROUSE	BROOKE	CRITIC	ERASED	GRAHAM	GRUMPH	PREACH	TRIAGE	ASCHAM
ARPENT	BROOKS	CROAKY	ERASER	GRAINS	GRUMPS	PRECIS	TRIBAL	ASCIAN
ARRACK	BROWNE	CROCHE	ERBIUM	GRAINY	GRUMPY	PREFAB	TRIBES	ASCIUS
ARRANT	BROWSE	CROCKS	EREBUS	GRAMME	GRUNDY	PREFER	TRICAR	ASGARD
ARREAR	BRUISE	CROCUS	EREMIC	GRAMMY	GRUNGE	PREFIX	TRICKS	ASHCAN
ARREST	BRUMAL	CRONET	ERINYS	GRAMPA	GRUTCH	PRELIM	TRICKY	ASHDOD
ARRIAN	BRUMBY	CRONOS	ERMINE	GRAMPS	GRYFON	PREMED	TRICOT	ASHINE
ARRIVE	BRUNCH	CRONUS	ERMITE	GRANBY	IRAQIS	PREPAY	TRIFLE	ASHLAR
ARROBA	BRUNEI	CROPPY	ERNANI	GRANGE	IREFUL	PREPPY	TRIGON	ASHLEY
ARROYO	BRUNEL	CROSBY	ERODED	GRANNY	IRETON	PRESTO	TRILBY	ASHORE
ARSÈNE	BRUTAL	CROSSE	EROICA	GRANTA	IRONED	PRETAX	TRIMLY	ASHPAN
ARSINE	BRUTUS	CROTAL	EROTIC	GRANTH	IRONIC	PRETTY	TRIODE	ASHTAR
ARTAUD	BRYANT	CROTCH	ERRAND	GRAPES	IRRUPT	PREVIN	TRIPLE	ASHTON
ARTERY	BRYONY	CROTON	ERRANT	GRAPPA	IRVING	PREWAR	TRIPOD	ASIMOV
ARTFUL	CRABBE	CROUCH	ERSATZ	GRASSY	IRWELL	PRICED	TRIPOS	ASKARI
ARTHUR	CRABBY	CROUPE	FRACAS	GRATED	KRAKEN	PRICEY	TRISTE	ASKING
ARTIST	CRADLE	CROUPY	FRAGOR	GRATER	KRANTZ	PRIEST	TRITON	ASLANT
ARTURO	CRAFTY	CROUSE	FRAISE	GRATIN	KRATER	PRIMAL	TRIVET	ASLEEP
BRACER	CRAGGY	CROUTE	FRAMED	GRATIS	KRATON	PRIMED	TRIVIA	ASLOPE
BRACES	CRAMBO	CROUTH	FRANCE	GRAVEL	KRONER	PRIMER	TROCAR	ASMARA
BRAHMA	CRANCH	CRUELS	FRANCK	GRAVEN	KRONOS	PRIMLY	TROCHE	ASPECT
BRAHMS	CRANKY	CRUFTS	FRANCO	GRAVER	KRUGER	PRIMUS	TROIKA	ASPIRE
BRAINS	CRANNY	CRUISE	FRANZY	GRAVES	KRUMAN	PRINCE	TROJAN	ASSAIL

ASSART	PSYCHO	STAIRS	STOOKS	AUDLEY	BURLAP	CURDLE	DUSTED	GUNTER
ASSENT	TSETSE	STAKES	STOOLS	AUDREY	BURLEY	CURFEW	DUSTER	GURGLE
ASSERT	TSHIRT	STALAG	STORAX	AUGEAN	BURNER	CURIET	EUBOEA	GURKHA
ASSESS	TSONGA	STALIN	STORER	AUGITE	BURNET	CURIUM	EUCHRE	GURLET
ASSETS	TSWANA	STALKS	STOREY	AUGURY	BURROW	CURLER	EUCLID	GURNET
ASSIGN	USABLE	STALKY	STORMY	AUGUST	BURSAR	CURLEW	EUGENE	GURNEY
ASSIST	USANCE	STALLS	STOVER	AUMBRY	BURTON	CURPEL	EULOGY	GUSHER
ASSIZE	USEFUL	STAMEN	STOWER	AUNTIE	BUSBOY	CURRIE	EUNUCH	GUSLAR
ASSOIL	USURER	STAMPS	STRABO	AUREUS	BUSHED	CURSAL	EUREKA	GUSSET
ASSORT	ATABAL	STANCE	STRAFE	AURIGA	BUSHEL	CURSED	EUROPA	GUTTER
ASSUME	ATABEG	STANCH	STRAIN	AURORA	BUSILY	CURSOR	EUROPE	GUTTLE
ASSURE	ATAMAN	STANZA	STRAIT	AUSPEX	BUSKER	CURSUS	EUSTON	GUYANA
ASTART	ATAXIA	STAPES	STRAKE	AUSSIE	BUSKET	CURTAL	EUTAXY	GUZZLE
ASTERN	ATAXIC	STAPLE	STRAND	AUSTEN	BUSKIN	CURTAX	EUXINE	HUBBLE
ASTHMA	ATHENA	STARCH	STRASS	AUSTER	BUSMAN	CURTLY	FUDDLE	HUBBUB
ASTONE	ATHENE	STARES	STRATA	AUSTIN	BUSONI	CURTSY	FUGATO	HUBRIS
ASTRAL	ATHENS	STARRY	STRAWS	AUTHOR	BUSTED	CURULE	FUHRER	HUCKLE
ASTRAY	ATHROB	STARVE	STRAWY	AUTISM	BUSTER	CURVED	FULANI	HUDDLE
ASTUTE	ATKINS	STASIS	STREAK	AUTUMN	BUSTLE	CURVET	FULFIL	HUDSON
ASVINA	ATOCIA	STATAL	STREAM	BUBBLE	BUTANE	CUSCUS	FULGID	HUGELY
ASWARM	ATOMIC	STATED	STREET	BUBBLY	BUTENE	CUSHAT	FULHAM	HUGHES
ASYLUM	ATONAL	STATEN	STREGA	BUCCAL	BUTLER	CUSSED	FULLER	HUGHIE
ESCAPE	ATONIC	STATER	STRENE	BUCHAN	BUTTER	CUSSER	FULMAR	HULLED
ESCARP	ATRIAL	STATES	STRESS	BUCKED	BUTTON	CUSTER	FUMADO	HUMANE
ESCHAR	ATRIDE	STATIC	STRICK	BUCKER	BUYERS	CUSTOM	FUMBLE	HUMBER
ESCHEW	ATRIUM	STATOR	STRICT	BUCKET	BUYING	CUSTOS	FUNDED	HUMBLE
ESCORT	ATTACH	STATUE	STRIDE	BUCKLE	BUYOUT	CUTCHA	FUNDUS	HUMBUG
ESCROC	ATTACK	STATUS	STRIFE	BUDDHA	BUZFUZ	CUTLER	FUNGAL	HUMECT
ESCROW	ATTAIN	STAYER	STRIKE	BUDGET	BUZZER	CUTLET	FUNGUS	HUMITE
ESCUDO	ATTEND	STEADY	STRINE	BUDGIE	CUBAGE	CUTOFF	FUNNEL	HUMMEL
ESKIMO	ATTEST	STEAMY	STRING	BUENOS	CUBICA	CUTTER	FUREUR	HUMMER
ESPADA	ATTILA	STEELE	STRIPE	BUFFER	CUBISM	CUTTLE	FURFUR	HUMMUS
ESPRIT	ATTLEE	STEELY	STRIPY	BUFFET	CUBIST	CUTTOE	FURIES	HUMOUR
ESSENE	ATTIRE	STEERS	STRIVE	BUFFON	CUBOID	DUBBIN	FURORE	HUMPED
ESTATE	ATTONE	STEMMA	STROBE	BUGGER	CUCKOO	DUBLIN	FURPHY	HUMPTY
ESTEEM	ATTORN	STENCH	STRODE	BUGLER	CUDDLE	DUCKED	FURROW	HUNGER
ESTHER	ATTRAP	STEPPE	STROKE	BUKSHI	CUDDLY	DUCKIE	FUSAIN	HUNGRY
ESTRAY	ATTUNE	STEREO	STROLL	BULBIL	CUDGEL	DUDDER	FUSELI	HUNKER
ISABEL	ETALON	STERIC	STRONG	BULBUL	CUEIST	DUDEEN	FUSION	HUNTER
ISAIAH	ETCHER	STERNE	STROUD	BULGAR	CUERPO	DUENNA	FUSTIC	HURDLE
ISCHIA	ETHANE	STEROL	STROUP	BULGER	CUESTA	DUFFEL	FUSTOC	HURLEY
ISEULT	ETHENE	STEVEN	STROVE	BULIMY	CUFFEE	DUFFER	FUTILE	HURRAH
ISHTAR	ETHICS	STEWED	STRUCK	BULLER	CUFFIN	DUFFLE	FUTURE	HURRAY
ISLAND	ETHIOP	STICKS	STRUNG	BULLET	CUISSE	DUGONG	FUZZLE	HURTLE
ISLETS	ETHNIC	STICKY	STRUNT	BUMALO	CUITER	DUGOUT	GUARDI	HUSHED
ISOBAR	ETRIER	STIFLE	STUART	BUMBLE	CULDEE	DULCET	GUARDS	HUSSAR
ISOLDE	ETYMON	STIGMA	STUBBS	BUMPER	CULLET	DUMBLY	GUBBAH	HUSSIF
ISOMER	ITALIC	STILTS	STUBBY	BUNCHY	CULLIS	DUMDUM	GUELPH	HUSTLE
ISOPOD	ITCHEN	STILTY	STUCCO	BUNDLE	CULMEN	DUMONT	GUENON	HUXLEY
ISRAEL	ITERUM	STINGO	STUDIO	BUNGAY	CULTCH	DUMOSE	GUESTS	HUZZAH
ISSUES	ITHACA	STINGY	STUFFY	BUNGEE	CULTER	DUMPER	GUFFAW	JUBATE
ISTRIA	ITSELF	STINKO	STUMER	BUNGLE	CULTUS	DUMPLE	GUGGLE	JUBBAH
OSBERT	OTALGY	STINKS	STUMPS	BUNION	CULVER	DUNBAR	GUIANA	JUDDER
OSCINE	OTELLO	STIPES	STUMPY	BUNJEE	CUMBER	DUNCAN	GUIDES	JUDGES
OSIERY	OTHERS	STITCH	STUPID	BUNKER	CUMMER	DUNCES	GUIDON	JUDICA
OSIRIS	OTIOSE	STOCKS	STUPOR	BUNKUM	CUMMIN	DUNDEE	GUILDS	JUDITH
OSMIUM	OTITIS	STOCKY	STURDY	BUNSEN	CUNEAL	DUNDER	GUILTY	JUGGER
OSMOSE	OTTAVA	STODGE	STYLET	BUNTER	CUNNER	DUNELM	GUINEA	JUGGLE
OSPREY	OTTAWA	STODGY	STYLUS	BUNYAN	CUPFUL	DUNKER	GUITAR	JUICER
OSSIAN	PTERIN	STOGIE	STYMIE	BURBLE	CUPMAN	DUNLIN	GULLAH	JUJUBE
OSSIFY	PTERIS	STOKER	STYRAX	BURBOT	CUPOLA	DUNLOP	GULLET	JULIAN
OSTEND	PTOSIS	STOKES	UTERUS	BURDEN	CUPPED	DUPLEX	GULLEY	JULIET
OSTIUM	STABLE	STOLEN	UTMOST	BUREAU	CUPPER	DURANT	GULPER	JULIUS
OSTLER	STABLY	STOLID	UTOPIA	BURGEE	CUPRIC	DURBAR	GUMMED	JUMADA
OSTREA	STACKS	STOLON	AUBADE	BURGER	CUPULE	DURESS	GUNDOG	JUMBAL
OSWALD	STAFFA	STONED	AUBREY	BURGLE	CURACY	DURHAM	GUNGHO	JUMBLE
PSALMS	STAGER	STONER	AUBURN	BURIAL	CURARE	DURIAN	GUNMAN	JUMPER
PSEUDO	STAGEY	STONES	AUCUBA	BURIED	CURARI	DURING	GUNNEL	JUNCUS
PSYCHE	STAGGY	STOOGE	AUDILE	BURKHA	CURATE	DURION	GUNNER	JUNGLE

JUNIOR	MUNSHI	OUTING	QUAKER	RUSTAM	SUTURE	EVENLY	EXHALE	DYADIC
JUNKER	MUPPET	OUTLAW	QUALMS	RUSTEM	TUAREG	EVINCE	EXHORT	DYBBUK
JUNKET	MURAGE	OUTLAY	QUANGO	RUSTIC	TUBERS	EVOLUÉ	EXHUME	DYEING
JUNKIE	MURALS	OUTLET	QUARRY	RUSTLE	TUBING	EVOLVE	EXISTS	DYNAMO
JURANT	MURDER	OUTLIE	QUARTO	RUSTUM	TUBULE	EVULSE	EXMOOR	DYNAST
JURIST	MURIEL	OUTPUT	QUARTZ	RUTTED	TUCANA	EVZONE	EXOCET	EYEFUL
JUSTIN	MURINE	OUTRUN	QUASAR	RUTTER	TUCKER	KVETCH	EXODUS	EYELET
JUSTLY	MURLIN	OUTSET	QUAVER	SUBDUE	TUCKET	OVERDO	EXOGEN	EYELID
KUCCHA	MURMUR	OUTTOP	QUEASY	SUBLET	TUFFET	OVERLY	EXOTIC	FYLFOT
KUFIAH	MURPHY	OUTVIE	QUEBEC	SUBMIT	TUFTED	OVIBOS	EXPAND	GYPSUM
KUMARA	MURRAM	OUTWIT	QUEENS	SUBORN	TUGRIK	OVISAC	EXPECT	GYRATE
KUMERA	MURRAY	PUBLIC	QUELCH	SUBSET	TUILLE	SVELTE	EXPEDE	HYADES
KUMISS	MURRHA	PUCKER	QUENCH	SUBTLE	TULBAN	AWAKEN	EXPEND	HYAENA
KUMMEL	MURRIN	PUDDLE	QUETCH	SUBTLY	TULIPA	AWHILE	EXPERT	HYBRID
LUANDA	MUSANG	PUDSEY	QUICHE	SUBURB	TUMBLE	AWNING	EXPIRE	HYBRIS
LUBBER	MUSCAT	PUEBLO	QUIDAM	SUBWAY	TUMEFY	AWOKEN	EXPIRY	HYDRAX
LUBRIC	MUSCLE	PUERTO	QUINCE	SUCCOR	TUMOUR	KWACHA	EXPORT	HYDRIA
LUCENT	MUSEUM	PUFFED	QUINSY	SUCCUS	TUMULT	KWANZA	EXPOSE	HYDRUS
LUCIAN	MUSING	PUFFER	QUINTA	SUCKEN	TUNDRA	OWLCAR	EXPUGN	HYMNAL
LUCINA	MUSIVE	PUFFIN	QUIRKY	SUCKER	TUNING	OWLISH	EXSERT	HYPATE
LUDWIG	MUSKEG	PUISNE	QUITCH	SUCKET	TUNNEL	QWERTY	EXTANT	HYPHAL
LUGANO	MUSKET	PULLET	QUIVER	SUCKLE	TUPELO	RWANDA	EXTEND	HYPHEN
LUGGER	MUSLIM	PULLEY	QUOITS	SUDARY	TURBAN	SWABIA	EXTENT	HYPNIC
LUMBAR	MUSLIN	PULPIT	QUORUM	SUDATE	TURBID	SWAMPY	EXTERN	HYPNOS
LUMBER	MUSSEL	PULSAR	QUOTED	SUDDEN	TURBOT	SWANEE	EXTIRP	HYPNUM
LUMINA	MUSTER	PULVER	RUBBED	SUFFER	TUREEN	SWANKY	EXTOLL	HYSSOP
LUMMOX	MUTANT	PUMICE	RUBBER	SUFFIX	TURGID	SWARTY	EXTORT	KYBOSH
LUMPUR	MUTATE	PUMMEL	RUBBLE	SUGARY	TURKEY	SWATCH	OXALIC	KYUSHU
LUNACY	MUTELY	PUNCHY	RUBBRA	SUITED	TURNED	SWATHE	OXALIS	LYCEUM
LUNARY	MUTINY	PUNCTO	RUBENS	SUITOR	TURNER	SWEATY	OXFORD	LYCHEE
LUNATE	MUTISM	PUNDIT	RUBIES	SUIVEZ	TURNIP	SWEDEN	OXGATE	LYCOSA
LUNULE	MUTTER	PUNISH	RUBIKS	SUKKAH	TURNUP	SWEENY	OXHEAD	LYDIAN
LUPINE	MUTTON	PUNJAB	RUBRIC	SULCUS	TURPIN	SWEETS	OXHIDE	LYMPNE
LURING	MUTUAL	PUNKAH	RUCHED	SULFUR	TURRET	SWERVE	OXTAIL	LYRICS
LURIST	MUZHIK	PUNNET	RUCKLE	SULLEN	TURTLE	SWINGE	OXYGEN	LYRIST
LUSAKA	MUZZLE	PUNTER	RUCKUS	SULPHA	TURVES	SWIPES	AYESHA	LYTTON
LUSTER	NUANCE	PUPATE	RUDDER	SULTAN	TUSCAN	SWITCH	AYMARA	MYELIN
LUSTRE	NUBBIN	PUPPET	RUDDLE	SULTRY	TUSKER	SWIVEL	BYEBYE	MYELON
LUTEAL	NUBBLE	PUPPIS	RUDELY	SUMACH	TUSSAH	SWIVET	BYELAW	MYGALE
LUTEIN	NUBILE	PURDAH	RUEFUL	SUMMER	TUSSIS	SWOOSH	BYGONE	MYOGEN
LUTHER	NUCULE	PURELY	RUELLE	SUMMIT	TUSSLE	TWAITE	BYLINE	MYOPIA
LUTINE	NUDISM	PURIFY	RUFFLE	SUMMON	TUVALU	TWEEDS	BYNAME	MYOPIC
LUTIST	NUDIST	PURINE	RUGGED	SUNDAE	TUXEDO	TWEEDY	BYPASS	MYOSIN
LUXATE	NUDITY	PURIST	RUGGER	SUNDAY	VULCAN	TWEENY	BYRNIE	MYOSIS
LUXURY	NUDNIK	PURITY	RUGOSE	SUNDER	VULGAR	TWEEZE	BYSSUS	MYRIAD
LUZERN	NUGGAR	PURLER	RUGOUS	SUNDEW	VULGUS	TWELVE	BYWORD	MYRTLE
MUCATE	NUGGET	PURLIN	RUINED	SUNDRY	YUCKER	TWENTY	CYANIN	MYSELF
MUCKER	NULLAH	PURPLE	RULING	SUNHAT	YUKATA	TWICER	CYBELE	MYSORE
MUCKLE	NUMBER	PURSED	RUMBLE	SUNKEN	YUMYUM	TWIGGY	CYBORG	MYSTIC
MUCOID	NUMBLY	PURSER	RUMKIN	SUNLIT	YUPPIE	TWIGHT	CYBRID	MYTHOS
MUCOUS	NUMDAH	PURSUE	RUMMER	SUNRAY	ZURICH	TWINED	CYCLIC	NYANZA
MUDDER	NUMPTY	PURVEY	RUMORS	SUNSET	AVALON	TWINGE	CYCLUS	NYLONS
MUDDLE	NUNCIO	PUSHER	RUMOUR	SUNTAN	AVATAR	TWIRLY	CYDNUS	OYSTER
MUESLI	NUTANT	PUSHTU	RUMPLE	SUPERB	AVAUNT	TWISTY	CYESIS	PYEDOG
MUFFET	NUTATE	PUSHUP	RUMPUS	SUPINE	AVENGE	TWITCH	CYGNET	PYRENE
MUFFIN	NUTMEG	PUSSER	RUNDLE	SUPLEX	AVENUE	TWOBIT	CYGNUS	PYRITE
MUFFLE	NUTTER	PUTEAL	RUNNEL	SUPPER	AVERNO	AXEMAN	CYMBAL	PYRONE
MUFLON	NUZZER	PUTOIS	RUNNER	SUPPLE	AVERSE	AXILLA	CYMRIC	PYROPE
MUGGER	NUZZLE	PUTOUT	RUNOFF	SUPPLY	AVIARY	EXARCH	CYNIPS	PYRRHO
MULISH	OULONG	PUTRID	RUNWAY	SURELY	AVIATE	EXCEED	CYPHER	PYTHIA
MULLAH	OUNCES	PUTSCH	RUNYON	SURETÉ	AVIDLY	EXCEPT	CYPRID	PYTHON
MULLER	OUNDLE	PUTTEE	RUPEES	SURETY	AVOCET	EXCESS	CYPRIS	RYOKAN
MULLET	OURALI	PUTTER	RUPERT	SURFER	AVOUCH	EXCISE	CYPRUS	SYDNEY
MULTUM	OUTAGE	PUZZLE	RUPIAH	SURREY	AVOWAL	EXCITE	CYRANO	SYLVAN
MUMBLE	OUTBAR	QUAGGA	RUPIAS	SURTAX	AVOWED	EXCUSE	CYRENE	SYLVIA
MUMMER	OUTBID	QUAHOG	RUSHED	SURVEY	AVULSE	EXEDRA	CYSTIC	SYMBOL
MUNICH	OUTCRY	QUAICH	RUSKIN	SUSSEX	DVORAK	EXEMPT	CYTASE	SYNCOM
MUNIFY	OUTFIT	QUAIGH	RUSSET	SUTLER	EVELYN	EXETER	CYTODE	SYNDIC
MUNITE	OUTGAS	QUAINT	RUSSIA	SUTTEE	EVENKI	EXEUNT	CYTOID	SYNTAX

SYPHER	ARABIC	CHAKRA	DIADEM	GLAGOL	ISAIAH	PEAHEN	SCAMPI	SNAZZY	
SYPHON	ARABIS	CHALET	DIALOG	GLAIRE	ITALIC	PEAKED	SCAMPO	SOAKED	
SYRIAN	ARABLE	CHALKY	DIANAS	GLAIVE	JOANNA	PEANUT	SCANTY	SPACED	
SYRINX	ARAFAT	CHAMPS	DIAPER	GLAMIS	KEATON	PEARLS	SCAPUS	SPACER	
SYRISM	ARAGON	CHANCE	DIATOM	GLAMOR	KHALAT	PEARLY	SCARAB	SPADES	
SYRUPY	ARALIA	CHANCY	DIAXON	GLANCE	KHALIF	PHAROS	SCARCE	SPADIX	
SYSTEM	ARAMIS	CHANEY	DRACHM	GLASSY	KHALSA	PHASIS	SCARED	SPARKS	
SYZYGY	ARANDA	CHANGE	DRAFTY	GLAZED	KHARIF	PHASMA	SCARER	SPARKY	
TYBALT	ARARAT	CHAPEL	DRAGEE	GNAWER	KIAORA	PIAFFE	SCATCH	SPARSE	
TYBURN	ASADHA	CHAPKA	DRAGON	GOALIE	KLAXON	PIAZZA	SCATHE	SPARTA	
TYCOON	ASARUM	CHARGE	DRALON	GOANNA	KNAGGY	PLACED	SCATTY	SPARTH	
TYMBAL	ATABAL	CHARON	DRAPER	GOATEE	KRAKEN	PLACER	SEABEE	SPATHE	
TYMPAN	ATABEG	CHARTA	DRAWER	GRABEN	KRANTZ	PLACID	SEALED	SPAULD	
TYPHUS	ATAMAN	CHASER	DYADIC	GRACES	KRATER	PLAGAL	SEAMAN	SPAVIN	
TYPIFY	ATAXIA	CHASSE	ECARTÉ	GRADED	KRATON	PLAGUE	SEAMEN	STABLE	
TYPING	ATAXIC	CHASTE	ELAINE	GRADES	KWACHA	PLAICE	SEAMER	STABLY	
TYPIST	AVALON	CHATON	ELANCE	GRADUS	KWANZA	PLAINS	SEAMUS	STACKS	
TYRANT	AVATAR	CHATTY	ELANET	GRAFIN	LAAGER	PLAINT	SEANCE	STAFFA	
TYRONE	AVAUNT	CHAZAN	ELAPSE	GRAHAM	LEADEN	PLANCH	SEARCH	STAGER	
WYVERN	AWAKEN	CLAGGY	ELATED	GRAINS	LEADER	PLANET	SEASON	STAGEY	
XYLENE	AZALEA	CLAIMS	ENABLE	GRAINY	LEAGUE	PLANKS	SEATED	STAIRS	
XYLOID	BEACHY	CLAMMY	ENAMEL	GRAMME	LEALTY	PLANKS	SEAWAY	STAKES	
XYLOSE	BEACON	CLAMOR	ENAMOR	GRAMMY	LEANTO	PLAQUE	SHABBY	STALAG	
ZYGOMA	BEADED	CLAQUE	ENARCH	GRAMPA	LEAVEN	PLASMA	SHADED	STALIN	
ZYGOTE	BEADLE	CLARET	EPARCH	GRAMPS	LEAVER	PLATED	SHADES	STALKS	
ZYRIAN	BEAGLE	CLARTY	EPAULE	GRANBY	LEAVES	PLATEN	SHADOW	STALKY	
AZALEA	BEAKER	CLASSY	ERASED	GRANGE	LIABLE	PLATER	SHADUF	STALLS	
AZERTY	BEANIE	CLAUDE	ERASER	GRANNY	LIAISE	PLATES	SHAGGY	STAMEN	
AZOLLA	BEARER	CLAUSE	ETALON	GRANTA	LOADED	PLAYER	SHAKEN	STAMPS	
AZONAL	BEATEN	CLAVIS	EXARCH	GRANTH	LOADER	PRAGUE	SHAKER	STANCE	
AZORES	BEATER	CLAYEY	FEALTY	GRAPES	LOAFER	PRAISE	SHAKES	STANCH	
AZOTIC	BEATTY	COALER	FIACRE	GRAPPA	LOATHE	PRANCE	SHALOM	STANZA	
AZRAEL	BEAUNE	COARSE	FIANCÉ	GRASSY	LOAVES	PRANKS	SHAMAN	STAPES	
CZAPKA	BEAUTY	COATED	FIASCO	GRATED	LUANDA	PRATER	SHAMBA	STAPLE	
DZEREN	BEAVER	COATES	FLABBY	GRATER	MEADOW	PRAVDA	SHAMMY	STARCH	
IZZARD	BHAJAN	CRABBE	FLACON	GRATIN	MEAGER	PRAXIS	SHAMUS	STARES	
6:3	BHAJEE	CRABBY	FLAGGY	GRATIS	MEAGRE	PRAYER	SHANDY	STARRY	
	BHARAL	CRADLE	FLAGON	GRAVEL	MEALIE	PSALMS	SHANKS	STARVE	
ABACUS	BHARAT	CRAFTY	FLAMBÉ	GRAVEN	MEANIE	QUAGGA	SHANTY	STASIS	
ABADAN	BIASED	CRAGGY	FLAMEN	GRAVER	MEANLY	QUAHOG	SHAPED	STATAL	
ABATOR	BLACKS	CRAMBO	FLANCH	GRAVES	MEASLY	QUAICH	SHARED	STATED	
ABATTU	BLAISE	CRANCH	FLANGE	GRAVID	MEATUS	QUAIGH	SHARER	STATEN	
ACACIA	BLAMED	CRANKY	FLANKS	GUARDI	MIASMA	QUAINT	SHARES	STATER	
ACADIA	BLANCH	CRANNY	FLARES	GUARDS	MOANER	QUAKER	SHARIA	STATES	
ACAJOU	BLANCO	CRANTS	FLASHY	HEADED	MOATED	QUALMS	SHARIF	STATIC	
ACARID	BLAZER	CRAPLE	FLATLY	HEADER	NEAPED	QUANGO	SHARON	STATOR	
ACARUS	BLAZON	CRASIS	FLATUS	HEALER	NEARBY	QUARRY	SHARPS	STATUE	
ACATES	BOARDS	CRATCH	FLAUNT	HEALTH	NEARER	QUARTO	SHASTA	STATUS	
ADAGIO	BOATER	CRATER	FLAVIN	HEAPED	NEARLY	QUARTZ	SHAVEN	STAYER	
AGADIR	BRACER	CRATON	FLAVOR	HEARER	NEATEN	QUASAR	SHAVER	SWABIA	
AGAMID	BRACES	CRATUR	FLAWED	HEARSE	NEATLY	QUAVER	SKATER	SWAMPY	
AGARIC	BRAHMA	CRAVAT	FLAXEN	HEARTH	NIACIN	READER	SKATES	SWANEE	
AGATHA	BRAHMS	CRAVEN	FRACAS	HEARTS	NIAMEY	REALIA	SLACKS	SWANKY	
ALACUS	BRAINS	CRAYER	FRAGOR	HEARTY	NUANCE	REALLY	SLALOM	SWARTY	
ALALIA	BRAINY	CRAYON	FRAISE	HEATED	NYANZA	REALTY	SLANGY	SWATCH	
ALARIC	BRAISE	CRAZED	FRAMED	HEATER	OGADEN	REAMER	SLATCH	SWATHE	
ALARUM	BRAMAH	CYANIN	FRANCE	HEAUME	OGAMIC	REAPER	SLATER	TEABAG	
ALASKA	BRANCH	CZAPKA	FRANCK	HEAVED	OMASUM	REASON	SLAVER	TEACUP	
AMADOU	BRANDY	DEACON	FRANCO	HEAVEN	ONAGER	RHAPHE	SLAVES	TEAGUE	
AMAZED	BRAQUE	DEADEN	FRANZY	HEAVES	ONAGRA	RIALTO	SLAYER	TEAPOT	
AMAZON	BRASSY	DEADLY	FRAPPÉ	HIATUS	OPAQUE	ROADIE	SMACKS	TEAPOY	
ANABAS	BRAWNY	DEAFEN	FRATER	HOARSE	ORACHE	ROAMER	SMALLS	TEASEL	
ANADEM	BRAZEN	DEALER	FRAYED	HOAXER	ORACLE	ROARER	SMARMY	TEASER	
ANADYR	BRAZIL	DEARER	GEASON	HYADES	ORALLY	RWANDA	SMARTY	THALER	
ANALOG	CHADOR	DEARIE	GHARRY	HYAENA	ORANGE	SAANEN	SNAGGY	THALES	
ANANAS	CHAFER	DEARLY	GHAZAL	IBADAN	ORATOR	SCABBY	SNAILY	THALIA	
APACHE	CHAINS	DEARTH	GIAOUR	ICARUS	OTALGY	SCAITH	SNAKED	THAMES	
APATHY	CHAIRS	DHARMA	GLACIS	IRAQIS	OXALIC	SCALAR	SNAPPY	THANAH	
ARABIA	CHAISE	DIACID	GLADLY	ISABEL	OXALIS	SCALES	SNATCH	THANET	

THANKS	BOBBER	GOBBET	PEBBLE	UNBRED	CACKLE	EUCLID	LOCKET	RACISM
THATCH	BOBBIN	GOBBLE	PEBBLY	UNBUSY	CACOON	EXCEED	LOCKUP	RACIST
TRACER	BOBBLE	GOBLET	POBBLE	UPBEAT	CACTUS	EXCEPT	LOCULE	RACKET
TRADER	BOBCAT	GOBLIN	PUBLIC	URBANE	CECILS	EXCESS	LOCUST	RECALL
TRADES	BOBWIG	GUBBAH	RABATO	VIBRIO	CECITY	EXCISE	LUCENT	RECANT
TRAGIC	BUBBLE	HABILE	RABBET	WABASH	CICADA	EXCITE	LUCIAN	RECAST
TRAGUS	BUBBLY	HEBREW	RABBIT	WEBBED	CICALA	EXCUSE	LUCINA	RECEDE
TRAJAN	CABALE	HOBART	RABBLE	WOBBLE	CICELY	FACADE	LYCEUM	RECENT
TRALEE	CABBIE	HOBBES	RABIES	WOBBLY	CICERO	FACIAL	LYCHEE	RECESS
TRANCE	COBALT	HOBBLE	REBATE	WOBURN	COCCID	FACIES	LYCOSA	RECIFE
TRANNY	COBBER	HOBDAY	REBECK	YABBER	COCCUS	FACILE	MACRON	RECIPE
TRAPES	COBBLE	HOBNOB	REBITE	ZEBECK	COCCYX	FACING	MACULA	RECITE
TRASHY	COBDEN	HUBBLE	REBORE	ACCEDE	COCHIN	FACTOR	MACULE	RECKON
TRAUMA	COBURG	HUBBUB	REBORN	ACCEND	COCKER	FACTUM	MICKEY	RECOIL
TRAVEL	COBWEB	HUBRIS	REBUFF	ACCENT	COCKLE	FECULA	MICKLE	RECORD
TRAVIS	CUBAGE	HYBRID	REBUKE	ACCEPT	COCOON	FECUND	MICMAC	RECOUP
TUAREG	CUBICA	HYBRIS	RIBALD	ACCESS	CUCKOO	FICKLE	MICRON	RECTAL
TWAITE	CUBISM	IMBARN	RIBAND	ACCORD	CYCLIC	FOCSLE	MOCKER	RECTOR
UGANDA	CUBIST	IMBASE	RIBBED	ACCOST	CYCLUS	GOCART	MOCKUP	RECTUM
UGARIT	CUBOID	IMBIBE	RIBBLE	ACCRUE	DACOIT	HACHIS	MUCATE	RECTUS
UNABLE	CYBELE	IMBOSS	RIBBON	ACCUSE	DACTYL	HACKEE	MUCKER	RICHES
URACIL	CYBORG	IMBRUE	RIBOSE	ALCINA	DECADE	HACKER	MUCKLE	RICHLY
URANIA	CYBRID	INBORN	ROBBED	ALCOCK	DECAFF	HACKLE	MUCOID	RICKER
URANIC	DABBLE	INBRED	ROBBER	ALCOVE	DECAMP	HECATE	MUCOUS	RICKEY
URANUS	DEBASE	JABBER	ROBERT	ANCHOR	DECANE	HECKLE	NECKAR	RICRAC
USABLE	DEBATE	JABBLE	ROBING	ANCILE	DECANI	HECTIC	NECKED	RICTAL
USANCE	DEBILE	JABIRU	ROBSON	ANCOME	DECANT	HECTOR	NECTAR	RICTUS
VIABLE	DEBRIS	JIBBAH	ROBUST	ANCONA	DECCAN	HECUBA	NICELY	ROCKER
VIANDS	DEBTOR	JOBBER	RUBBED	ANCORA	DECEIT	HICCUP	NICENE	ROCKET
VIATOR	DEBUNK	JUBATE	RUBBER	ARCADE	DECENT	HICKEY	NICETY	ROCOCO
WEAKEN	DIBBER	JUBBAH	RUBBLE	ARCADY	DECIDE	HOCKEY	NICKED	RUCHED
WEAKER	DIBBLE	KABAKA	RUBBRA	ARCANA	DÉCIME	HUCKLE	NICKEL	RUCKLE
WEAKLY	DOBBIN	KABELE	RUBENS	ARCANE	DECKED	INCASE	NICKER	RUCKUS
WEALTH	DOBSON	KABUKI	RUBIES	ARCHED	DECKER	INCEDE	NOCENT	SACHET
WEAPON	DUBBIN	KABYLE	RUBIKS	ARCHER	DECKLE	INCEPT	NOCTUA	SACRED
WEARER	DUBLIN	KEBELE	RUBRIC	ARCHES	DECODE	INCEST	NUCULE	SACRUM
WEASEL	DYBBUK	KIBBLE	SABELE	ARCHIE	DECOKE	INCHES	OCCULT	SECANT
WEAVER	ECBOLE	KIBOSH	SABINE	ARCHIL	DECREE	INCHON	OCCUPY	SECEDE
WHACKO	EGBERT	KYBOSH	SABRES	ARCHON	DECREW	INCISE	ONCOME	SECOND
WHACKY	ELBRUS	LABIAL	SEBATE	ARCTIC	DICAST	INCITE	ONCOST	SECRET
WHALER	EMBAIL	LABILE	SOBEIT	ASCEND	DICKER	INCOME	OOCYTE	SECTOR
WHALES	EMBALE	LABIUM	SUBDUE	ASCENT	DICKEY	ISCHIA	ORCHID	SECURE
WHAMMY	EMBALM	LABLAB	SUBLET	ASCHAM	DICTUM	ITCHEN	ORCHIS	SICILY
WHARFE	EMBARK	LABOUR	SUBMIT	ASCIAN	DOCENT	JACANA	ORCINE	SICKEN
WRAITH	EMBERS	LABRUM	SUBORN	ASCIUS	DOCILE	JACENT	OSCINE	SICKER
WRASSE	EMBLEM	LABRYS	SUBSET	AUCUBA	DOCKED	JACKAL	PACIFY	SICKLE
YEARLY	EMBODY	LIBBER	SUBTLE	BACCHI	DOCKER	JACKET	PACKED	SICKLY
YEASTY	EMBOSS	LIBERO	SUBTLY	BACKER	DOCKET	JACOBS	PACKER	SOCAGE
ZEALOT	EMBRUE	LIBIDO	SUBURB	BACKET	DOCTOR	JOCKEY	PACKET	SOCCER
ABBACY	EMBRYO	LIBYAN	SUBWAY	BACKRA	DUCKED	JOCOSE	PECKER	SOCIAL
ABBESS	EMBUSY	LUBBER	TABARD	BACKUP	DUCKIE	JOCUND	PECTEN	SOCKET
ALBANY	ERBIUM	LUBRIC	TABLET	BECALM	ECCLES	KACCHA	PECTIN	SUCCOR
ALBEDO	EUBOEA	MOBCAP	TABULA	BECAME	ENCALM	KECKSY	PICARD	SUCCUS
ALBEIT	FABIAN	MOBILE	TOBAGO	BECKET	ENCAMP	KICKER	PICKAX	SUCKEN
ALBERT	FABIUS	MOBIUS	TOBIAS	BECKON	ENCASE	KUCCHA	PICKED	SUCKER
ALBINO	FABLED	NEBBUK	TUBERS	BECOME	ENCASH	LACHES	PICKER	SUCKET
ALBION	FABLES	NEBECK	TUBING	BICARB	ENCODE	LACING	PICKET	SUCKLE
ALBITE	FABRIC	NEBISH	TUBULE	BICEPS	ENCORE	LACKEY	PICKLE	TACKET
ALBUGO	FIBBED	NEBULA	TYBALT	BICKER	EOCENE	LACTIC	PICKUP	TACKLE
AMBAGE	FIBBER	NEBULE	TYBURN	BOCAGE	ESCAPE	LACUNA	PICNIC	TACOMA
AMBLER	FIBULA	NIBBLE	UMBLES	BUCCAL	ESCARP	LECHER	PICTOR	TACTIC
AMBUSH	GABBLE	NOBBLE	UMBREL	BUCHAN	ESCHAR	LECTOR	POCKET	TECHNO
ARBOUR	GABBRO	NOBBUT	UMBRIA	BUCKED	ESCHEW	LICHEN	PUCKER	TECKEL
AUBADE	GABION	NOBODY	UMBRIL	BUCKER	ESCORT	LICTOR	RACEME	TECTUM
AUBREY	GABLED	NUBBIN	UNBEND	BUCKET	ESCROC	LOCALE	RACHEL	TICINO
AUBURN	GIBBER	NUBBLE	UNBENT	BUCKLE	ESCROW	LOCATE	RACHIS	TICKER
BABBIT	GIBBET	NUBILE	UNBIND	CACCIA	ESCUDO	LOCHIA	RACIAL	TICKET
BABBLE	GIBBON	ORBITA	UNBOLT	CACHET	ETCHER	LOCKED	RACINE	TICKEY
BABOON	GIBSON	OSBERT	UNBORN	CACHOU	EUCHRE	LOCKER	RACING	TICKLE

TICKLY	BUDDHA	INDIES	MUDDLE	SEDATE	AYESHA	CRÈCHE	FEERIE	MUESLI
TOCSIN	BUDGET	INDIGN	NIDGET	SEDUCE	AZERTY	CREDIT	FIELDS	MYELIN
TUCANA	BUDGIE	INDIGO	NIDIFY	SIDDHA	BEEGHA	CREEPS	FIERCE	MYELON
TUCKER	CADDIE	INDITE	NODDED	SIDING	BEENAH	CREEPY	FIESTA	NAEVUS
TUCKET	CADDIS	INDIUM	NODDLE	SIDNEY	BEEPER	CREESE	FLECHE	NEEDED
TYCOON	CADETS	INDOOR	NODOSE	SODDEN	BEETLE	CREESH	FLEDGE	NEEDLE
ULCERS	CADGER	INDUCE	NODULE	SODIUM	BEETON	CREMOR	FLEECE	NEEDNT
UNCAGE	CADMUS	INDUCT	NUDISM	SODOMY	BLEACH	CRENAL	FLEECY	NIELLO
UNCIAL	CEDRIC	IODINE	NUDIST	SUDARY	BLEARY	CRENEL	FLENSE	OBECHE
UNCLAD	CEDULA	IODIZE	NUDITY	SUDATE	BLENCH	CREOLE	FLESHY	OBELUS
UNCOIL	CODDLE	JUDDER	NUDNIK	SUDDEN	BLENDE	CRESOL	FLETCH	OBERON
UNCOOL	CODGER	JUDGES	ODDITY	SYDNEY	BLENNY	CRESTA	FLEURY	OCEANS
UNCORK	CODIFY	JUDICA	ODDSON	TEDIUM	BOEING	CRETAN	FOETAL	OCELOT
UPCAST	CODING	JUDITH	OEDEMA	TIDBIT	BREACH	CRETIC	FOETID	ODENSE
URCHIN	CUDDLE	KEDDAH	OLDISH	TIDDLE	BREAST	CRETIN	FOETUS	ODESSA
VACANT	CUDDLY	KIDDIE	ONDINE	TIDDLY	BREATH	CREWEL	FREELY	OLEATE
VACATE	CUDGEL	KIDDLE	OODLES	TIDILY	BRECHT	CUEIST	FREEZE	OLEFIN
VACUUM	CYDNUS	KIDNAP	ORDAIN	TODDLE	BREECH	CUERPO	FRENCH	OLENUS
VECTIS	DADDLE	KIDNEY	ORDEAL	UNDATE	BREEZE	CUESTA	FRENUM	OMELET
VECTOR	DEDANS	KODIAK	ORDERS	UNDECK	BREEZY	CYESIS	FRENZY	OMENTA
VICTIM	DEDUCE	LADAKH	ORDURE	UNDIES	BREGMA	DAEDAL	FRESCO	OMERTA
VICTOR	DEDUCT	LADDER	PADANG	UNDINE	BREMEN	DAEMON	GEEZER	ONEDIN
VICUNA	DIDDLE	LADDIE	PADDED	UNDONE	BRETON	DEEJAY	GHEBER	ONEGIN
WACKER	DODDER	LADIES	PADDLE	UNDULY	BREVET	DEEPEN	GHERAO	ONEIDA
WICKED	DODDLE	LADING	PADUAN	UNDYED	BREWER	DEEPER	GHETTO	ONEMAN
WICKER	DODGEM	LADOGA	PEDALO	UPDATE	BREWIS	DEEPLY	GNEISS	ONEWAY
WICKET	DODGER	LEDGER	PEDANT	VADOSE	BUENOS	DIEPPE	GOETHE	OPENER
YUCKER	DODOMA	LODGED	PEDDER	VEDDAH	BYEBYE	DIESEL	GREASE	OPENLY
ABDABS	DUDDER	LODGER	PEDDLE	VEDISM	BYELAW	DIESIS	GREASY	OREGON
ABDIEL	DUDEEN	LUDWIG	PEDLAR	VEDUTA	CAECUM	DIETER	GREATS	OREXIS
ABDUCT	EDDISH	LYDIAN	PIDDLE	WADDLE	CAESAR	DJEBEL	GREAVE	OTELLO
ADDEEM	ELDERS	MADAME	PIDGIN	WADERS	CEEFAX	DJERBA	GREECE	OVERDO
ADDEND	ELDEST	MADCAP	PODIUM	WADHAM	CHEDER	DOESNT	GREEDY	OVERLY
ADDICT	ENDEAR	MADDEN	PODSOL	WEDDED	CHEEKY	DREAMY	GREEKS	PAELLA
ADDLED	ENDING	MADDER	PODZOL	WEDGED	CHEERS	DREARY	GREENE	PAEONY
ADDUCE	ENDIVE	MADEUP	PUDDLE	WEDGIE	CHEERY	DREDGE	GREENS	PEELED
ADDUCT	ENDURE	MADMAN	PUDSEY	WIDELY	CHEESE	DREGGY	GRETNA	PEELER
AEDILE	FADING	MADRAS	RADDLE	WIDGET	CHEESY	DRENCH	GREUZE	PEEPER
AIDANT	FEDORA	MADRID	RADIAL	WIDOWS	CHEMIC	DRESSY	GUELPH	PEEVED
ALDINE	FIDDLE	MADURA	RADIAN	ZODIAC	CHEMMY	DUENNA	GUENON	PEEWEE
ALDOSE	FIDDLY	MADURO	RADISH	ABELIA	CHENET	DYEING	GUESTS	PEEWIT
ALDRIN	FIDGET	MEDDLE	RADIUM	ACEDIA	CHEOPS	DZEREN	HAEMAL	PHENOL
ANDEAN	FODDER	MEDIAL	RADIUS	ACETIC	CHEQUE	EGENCY	HAEMON	PHENYL
ANDREW	FUDDLE	MEDIAN	RADULA	AFEARS	CHERIE	EGERIA	HEEDED	PIECES
ARDENT	GADFLY	MEDICI	REDACT	AGEING	CHERRY	EGESTA	HEEHAW	PIEDOG
ARDOUR	GADGET	MEDICO	REDCAP	AGENCY	CHERUB	ELEVEN	HEELED	PIEMAN
AUDILE	GADOID	MEDINA	REDCAR	AGENDA	CHERUP	EMERGE	IBERIA	PIERCE
AUDLEY	GIDDUP	MEDISM	REDDEN	ALECTO	CHESIL	EMETIC	ICEBOX	PIERIS
AUDREY	GIDEON	MEDIUM	REDEEM	ALEGAR	CHESTY	EMEUTE	ICECAP	PLEACH
BADGER	GODIVA	MEDIUS	REDEYE	ALERCE	CHEVAL	ENERGY	ICEMAN	PLEASE
BADMAN	GODOWN	MEDLAR	REDLEG	ALEVIN	CHEVET	EPERDU	IPECAC	PLEDGE
BEDASH	GODSON	MEDLEY	REDRAW	ALEXIA	CIERGE	EREBUS	IREFUL	PLENTY
BEDAUB	GODWIN	MEDUSA	REDTOP	ALEXIN	CLEAVE	EREMIC	IRETON	PLENUM
BEDDER	GODWIT	MEDWAY	REDUCE	ALEXIS	CLEOME	EVELYN	ISEULT	PLEURA
BEDECK	HEDERA	MIDDAY	RIDDLE	AMELIA	CLERGY	EVENKI	ITERUM	PLEXOR
BEDLAM	HIDAGE	MIDDEN	RIDENT	AMENDE	CLERIC	EVENLY	JAEGER	PLEXUS
BEDPAN	HIDDEN	MIDDLE	RIDGED	AMENDS	CLERKS	EXEDRA	JEEVES	PNEUMA
BEDSIT	HIDING	MIDGET	RIDING	AMERCE	CLEVER	EXEMPT	KEELER	POETIC
BIDDER	HODDER	MIDWAY	RODENT	ANEMIA	COELOM	EXETER	KEENER	POETRY
BIDENT	HUDDLE	MODELS	RODHAM	ANEMIC	COERCE	EXEUNT	KEENLY	PREACE
BODACH	HUDSON	MODENA	RODNEY	APEPSY	COEVAL	EYEFUL	KEEPER	PREACH
BODEGA	HYDRAX	MODERN	RUDDER	APERÇU	CREACH	EYELET	KVETCH	PRECIS
BODGER	HYDRIA	MODEST	RUDDLE	AREOLA	CREAGH	EYELID	LEEWAY	PREFAB
BODGIE	HYDRUS	MODIFY	RUDELY	AREOLE	CREAKY	FAECAL	LIEBIG	PREFER
BODICE	INDABA	MODISH	SADDEN	AVENGE	CREAMY	FAECES	LIEDER	PREFIX
BODIES	INDEED	MODIST	SADDHU	AVENUE	CREANT	FEEBLE	LIERNE	PRELIM
BODILY	INDENT	MODIUS	SADDLE	AVERNO	CREASE	FEEBLY	MAENAD	PREMED
BODKIN	INDIAN	MODULE	SADISM	AVERSE	CREATE	FEEDER	MEEKLY	PREPAY
BODONI	INDICT	MUDDER	SADIST	AXEMAN	CREATE	FEELER		PREPPY

PRESTO	SLEEZY	TREMOR	DEFEND	RAFTER	AUGURY	HOGGET	NIGGER	TUGRIK
PRETAX	SLEIGH	TRENCH	DEFILE	REFACE	AUGUST	HOGTIE	NIGGLE	UNGAIN
PRETTY	SLEUTH	TRENDY	DEFINE	REFECT	BAGFUL	HUGELY	NIGGLY	UNGULA
PREVIN	SLEWED	TREPAN	DEFORM	REFILL	BAGMAN	HUGHES	NIGHTS	URGENT
PREWAR	SMEARY	TRESCO	DEFRAG	REFINE	BAGNIO	HUGHIE	NIGHTY	VAGARY
PSEUDO	SMEATH	TSETSE	DEFRAY	REFLET	BAGUIO	INGATE	NIGNOG	VAGINA
PTERIN	SMEGMA	TWEEDS	DEFTLY	REFLEX	BEGGAR	INGEST	NOGGIN	VIGOUR
PTERIS	SMELLY	TWEEDY	DEFUSE	REFLUX	BEGONE	INGOTS	NUGGAR	WAGGLE
PUEBLO	SNEAKY	TWEENY	DIFFER	REFORM	BIGAMY	INGRAM	NUGGET	WAGGON
PUERTO	SNEATH	TWEEZE	DUFFEL	REFUEL	BIGGER	INGRES	ORGANS	WAGNER
PYEDOG	SNEEZE	TWELVE	DUFFER	REFUGE	BIGGIN	INGROW	ORGASM	WAGRAM
QUEASY	SNEEZY	TWENTY	DUFFLE	REFUND	BIGWIG	INGULF	ORGEAT	WIGEON
QUEBEC	SPECIE	UNEASE	EFFACE	REFUSE	BOGART	JAGGED	ORGONE	WIGGLE
QUEENS	SPEECH	UNEASY	EFFECT	REFUTE	BOGGLE	JAGGER	OXGATE	WIGGLY
QUELCH	SPEEDO	UNEVEN	EFFETE	RIFFLE	BOGOTA	JAGUAR	PAGODA	WIGWAM
QUENCH	SPEEDY	URETER	EFFIGY	RUFFLE	BUGGER	JIGGER	PEGLEG	YOGURT
QUETCH	SPEISS	USEFUL	EFFLUX	SAFARI	BUGLER	JIGGLE	PIGEON	ZAGREB
QWERTY	SPENCE	UTERUS	EFFORT	SAFELY	BYGONE	JIGSAW	PIGLET	ZIGZAG
REEBOK	STEADY	VIENNA	EFFUSE	SAFETY	CAGILY	JOGGER	PIGOTT	ZYGOMA
REEFER	STEAMY	VIENNE	EIFFEL	SIFFLE	COGENT	JOGGLE	PIGPEN	ZYGOTE
REEKIE	STEELE	VIEWER	ELFISH	SIFTER	COGGER	JUGGER	PIGSTY	ACHENE
REELER	STEELY	WEEKLY	ENFIRE	SOFFIT	COGNAC	JUGGLE	POGROM	ACHING
RHEIMS	STEERS	WEEPER	ENFOLD	SOFTEN	CYGNET	KIGALI	RAGBAG	ADHERE
RHESUS	STEMMA	WEEPIE	ENFREE	SOFTIE	CYGNUS	LAGOON	RAGGED	AGHAST
RHETOR	STENCH	WEEVIL	GAFFER	SOFTLY	DAGGER	LAGUNA	RAGGLE	AMHARA
RHEUMY	STEPPE	WEEWEE	GIFTED	SUFFER	DAGGLE	LAGUNE	RAGING	APHONY
RHEXIS	STEREO	WHEELS	GOFFER	SUFFIX	DÉGAGÉ	LEGACY	RAGLAN	APHTHA
RIENZI	STERIC	WHEELY	GUFFAW	TEFLON	DEGREE	LEGATE	RAGMAN	ASHCAN
ROEMER	STERNE	WHEEZE	IFFISH	TIFFIN	DIGEST	LEGATO	RAGOUT	ASHDOD
RUEFUL	STEROL	WHEEZY	INFAME	TOFFEE	DIGGER	LEGEND	RAGTOP	ASHINE
RUELLE	STEVEN	WHENCE	INFAMY	TUFFET	DIGLOT	LEGGED	RAGUSA	ASHLAR
SCENIC	STEWED	WHERRY	INFANT	TUFTED	DOGGED	LEGION	REGAIN	ASHLEY
SDEATH	SVELTE	WIENER	INFARE	UFFIZI	DOGGER	LEGIST	REGALE	ASHORE
SEEDED	SWEATY	WOEFUL	INFECT	UNFAIR	DUGONG	LEGLET	REGARD	ASHPAN
SEEDER	SWEDEN	WREATH	INFEST	UNFOLD	DUGOUT	LEGMAN	REGENT	ASHTAR
SEEING	SWEENY	WREKIN	INFIRM	UNFURL	EDGING	LEGUME	REGEST	ASHTON
SEEKER	SWEETS	WRENCH	INFLOW	UPFLOW	EGGCUP	LIGASE	REGGAE	ATHENA
SEEMLY	SWERVE	WRETCH	INFLUX	WAFFLE	EIGHTH	LIGATE	REGIME	ATHENE
SEESAW	TAENIA	AFFAIR	INFOLD	WAFTED	EIGHTY	LIGETI	REGINA	ATHENS
SEETHE	TEENSY	AFFECT	INFORM	WIFELY	ENGAGE	LIGGER	REGION	ATHROB
SHEARS	TEEPEE	AFFIRM	INFUSE	YAFFLE	ENGELS	LIGHTS	REGIUS	AWHILE
SHEATH	TEETER	AFFORD	KAFFER	ZAFTIG	ENGINE	LIGNUM	REGLET	BAHADA
SHEAVE	TEETHE	AFFRAY	KAFFIR	AEGEAN	ENGLUT	LIGULA	REGRET	BAHRAM
SHEENY	THEAVE	AFFRET	KAFTAN	AEGEUS	ENGRAM	LIGULE	REGULO	BEHALF
SHEERS	THEBAN	ALFRED	KUFIAH	AEGINA	ENGULF	LIGURE	RIGGED	BEHAVE
SHEETS	THEBES	BAFFIN	LAFFER	AFGHAN	EUGENE	LOGGER	RIGGER	BEHEAD
SHEIKH	THECAL	BAFFLE	LIFTED	AIGLET	FAGGED	LOGGIA	RIGHTO	BEHELD
SHEILA	THEIRS	BEFALL	LIFTER	ANGARY	FAGGOT	LOGJAM	RIGHTS	BEHEST
SHEKEL	THEISM	BEFOOL	MAFFIA	ANGELA	FIGARO	LUGANO	RIGOUR	BEHIND
SHELVE	THEIST	BEFORE	MUFFET	ANGELS	FIGURE	LUGGER	ROGNON	BEHOLD
SHERIF	THEMIS	BIFFIN	MUFFIN	ANGERS	FOGBOW	MAGGIE	ROGUES	BEHOOF
SHERPA	THENAR	BIFOLD	MUFFLE	ANGICO	FUGATO	MAGGOT	RUGGED	BEHOVE
SHERRY	THENCE	BOFFIN	MUFLON	ANGINA	GAGGLE	MAGLEV	RUGGER	BEHRAM
SHEVAT	THEORY	BOFORS	NEFAST	ANGLED	GAGMAN	MAGNES	RUGOSE	BOHUNK
SIENNA	THERMO	BUFFER	OAFISH	ANGLER	GIGGLE	MAGNET	RUGOUS	CAHIER
SIERRA	THESIS	BUFFET	OFFCUT	ANGLIA	GIGLET	MAGNON	SAGELY	CAHOOT
SIESTA	THETIC	BUFFON	OFFEND	ANGOLA	GIGLOT	MAGNUM	SAGGAR	COHERE
SKELLY	THETIS	CAFARD	OFFICE	ANGORA	GIGOLO	MAGNUS	SIGHTS	COHORT
SKERRY	THEYRE	CAFTAN	OFFING	ARGENT	GOGGLE	MAGPIE	SIGNAL	COHOSH
SKETCH	TIEPIN	COFFEE	OFFISH	ARGHAN	GUGGLE	MAGYAR	SIGNET	DAHLIA
SKEWED	TIERCE	COFFER	OFFSET	ARGIVE	HAGDEN	MEGRIM	SIGNOR	DEHORN
SKEWER	TIERED	COFFIN	OXFORD	ARGOSY	HAGGAI	MIGHTY	SUGARY	ECHARD
SLEAVE	TMESIS	CUFFEE	PIFFLE	ARGUED	HAGGIS	MIGNON	TAGORE	ECHINO
SLEAZE	TOECAP	CUFFIN	PUFFED	ARGUTE	HAGGLE	MOGGIE	TEGMEN	EPHEBE
SLEAZY	TOERAG	DAFTIE	PUFFER	ARGYLE	HEGIRA	MUGGER	TEGULA	ETHANE
SLEDGE	TOETOE	DEFACE	PUFFIN	ARGYLL	HIGHER	MYGALE	TIGHTS	ETHENE
SLEEKY	TREATY	DEFAME	RAFALE	ASGARD	HIGHLY	NAGANA	TIGRIS	ETHICS
SLEEPY	TREBLE	DEFEAT	RAFFIA	AUGEAN	HIGHUP	NAGARI	TOGGED	ETHIOP
SLEEVE	TREBLY	DEFECT	RAFFLE	AUGITE	HOGGAR	NEGATE	TOGGLE	ETHNIC

EXHALE	APICAL	CLIQUE	FRILLS	MAÎTRE	RAIDER	SPINET	ULITIS	ASKING
EXHORT	APIECE	COILED	FRILLY	MOIDER	RAISED	SPIRAL	UNIATE	ATKINS
EXHUME	ARIOCH	COINER	FRINGE	MOIETY	RAISER	SPIRIT	UNIQUE	BAKERS
FUHRER	ARIOSO	COITUS	FRIPON	MOIRAI	RAISIN	SPITAL	UNISEX	BAKERY
INHALE	ARISTA	CRIANT	FRISKY	NAILED	RUINED	STICKS	UNISON	BAKING
INHERE	ARISTO	CRIBLE	FRIVOL	NAILER	SAILOR	STICKY	UNITED	BIKINI
INHUME	ASIMOV	CRIKEY	FRIZZY	OBIISM	SAINTS	STIFLE	URINAL	BUKSHI
ISHTAR	AVIARY	CRIMEA	GAIETY	OBITAL	SAITHE	STIGMA	VAINLY	DAKOTA
ITHACA	AVIATE	CRINAL	GAIJIN	OBITER	SBIRRO	STILTS	VEILED	DEKKER
JOHNNY	AVIDLY	CRINGE	GAINER	ODIOUS	SCILLA	STILTY	VEINED	DIKDIK
MAHLER	AXILLA	CRINUM	GAINLY	OJIBWA	SCILLY	STINGO	VOICED	DIKKOP
MAHOUT	BAIKAL	CRIPES	GAITER	OLIVER	SCIPIO	STINGY	VOIDED	DIKTAT
MOHAIR	BAILEE	CRISIS	GEIGER	OLIVET	SCIROC	STINKO	VOIDEE	ESKIMO
MOHAWK	BAILER	CRISPY	GEISHA	OLIVIA	SCIRON	STINKS	VOIDER	FAKING
MOHOCK	BAILEY	CRISTA	GLIBLY	ONIONS	SEICHE	STIPES	WAILER	FOKINE
OCHONE	BAILIE	CRITIC	GLIDER	OPIATE	SEISIN	STITCH	WAITER	FOKKER
OCHREA	BAILLY	CUISSE	GLIÈRE	ORIANO	SHIELD	SUITED	WAIVER	GOKART
OPHISM	BEIRUT	CUITER	GLINKA	ORIENT	SHIFTY	SUITOR	WEIGHT	HIKING
OPHITE	BLIGHT	DAIMIO	GLIOMA	ORIGEN	SHIITE	SUIVEZ	WEIMAR	ILKLEY
OTHERS	BLIMEY	DAISHO	GLITCH	ORIGIN	SHILOH	SWINGE	WEIRDO	INKJET
OXHEAD	BLINKS	DEIDRE	GLITZY	ORIOLE	SHIMMY	SWIPES	WHILOM	INKPOT
OXHIDE	BLITHE	DEIMOS	GOITER	ORISON	SHINDY	SWITCH	WHILST	JEKYLL
PAHARI	BOILED	DJINNI	GOITRE	OSIERY	SHINER	SWIVEL	WHIMSY	KAKAPO
REHASH	BOILER	DOINGS	GRIEVE	OSIRIS	SHINNY	SWIVET	WHINGE	KIKUYU
REHEAT	BRIAND	DRIEST	GRIGRI	OTIOSE	SHINTO	TAIGLE	WHINNY	LIKELY
REHEEL	BRIARD	DRIPPY	GRILLE	OTITIS	SHINTY	TAILLE	WHISHT	LIKING
SAHARA	BRICKS	DRIVEL	GRILSE	OVIBOS	SHIPKA	TAILOR	WHISKY	MAKEUP
SCHEMA	BRIDAL	DRIVEN	GRIMES	OVISAC	SHIRAZ	TAIPAN	WHITBY	MAKING
SCHEME	BRIDGE	DRIVER	GRIMLY	PAIDUP	SHIRRA	TAIPEI	WHITED	MEKONG
SCHISM	BRIDIE	EDIBLE	GRIMMS	PAINED	SHIRTY	TAIWAN	WHITEN	MIKADO
SCHIST	BRIDLE	EDISON	GRINGO	PAINTS	SHIVER	THICKY	WHITES	NIKKEI
SCHIZO	BRIEFS	EDITED	GRIPES	PAINTY	SKIDOO	THIERS	WRIGHT	OAKLEY
SCHLEP	BRIGHT	EDITOR	GRIPPE	PAIRER	SKIING	THIEVE	WRITER	OAKNUT
SCHMOE	BRIONY	ELICIT	GRISLY	PHILIP	SKIVER	THINGS	WRITHE	OCKERS
SCHOOL	BRITON	ELIJAH	GRISON	PHIZOG	SKINNY	THINGY	YOICKS	OOKPIK
SCHUSS	CAIMAN	ELISHA	GRITTY	PLIANT	SKIVER	THINLY	ABJECT	ORKNEY
SCHUYT	CAIQUE	ELIXIR	GUIANA	PLIERS	SKIVVY	THIRST	ABJURE	PAKHTI
SOHRAB	CAITRA	EMIGRÉ	GUIDES	PLIGHT	SLICER	THIRTY	ADJOIN	PAKHTO
SPHENE	CHIBOL	ENIGMA	GUIDON	PLINTH	SLIDER	THISBE	ADJURE	PAKHTU
SPHERE	CHICHI	EPICAL	GUILDS	PLISSÉ	SLIGHT	TOILET	ADJUST	PEKING
SPHINX	CHICLE	EPIGON	GUILTY	POINTE	SLINKY	TRIAGE	BEJADE	RAKING
TAHINA	CHICON	EPILOG	GUINEA	POINTS	SLIPPY	TRIBAL	CAJOLE	RAKISH
TAHINI	CHIGOE	EPIRUS	GUITAR	POIROT	SLIPUP	TRIBES	DEJECT	ROKEBY
TAHITI	CHILDE	ERINYS	HAILER	POISED	SLITHY	TRICAR	ENJOIN	SIKKIM
TEHRAN	CHILLI	EVINCE	HAIRDO	POISON	SLIVER	TRICKS	HEJIRA	SUKKAH
TSHIRT	CHILLY	EXISTS	HEIFER	PRICED	SMIGHT	TRICKY	HIJACK	TAKING
UNHAND	CHIMER	FAIBLE	HEIGHT	PRICEY	SMILER	TRICOT	INJECT	UCKERS
UNHOLY	CHIMES	FAINTS	HOIDEN	PRIEST	SMILES	TRIFLE	INJURE	UNKIND
UNHOOK	CHINAR	FAIRLY	IBIBIO	PRIMAL	SMILEY	TRIGON	INJURY	UPKEEP
UNHURT	CHINCH	FEINTS	IBIDEM	PRIMED	SMIRCH	TRILBY	JEJUNE	VIKING
UPHELD	CHINTZ	FEISTY	ICICLE	PRIMER	SMITHS	TRIMLY	JOJOBA	WAKING
UPHILL	CHIPPY	FLICKS	IDIOCY	PRIMLY	SMITHY	TRIODE	JUJUBE	YAKKER
UPHOLD	CHIRON	FLIGHT	JAILER	PRIMUS	SNIFFY	TRIPLE	MAJLIS	YAKUZA
USHANT	CHIRPY	FLIMSY	JAILOR	PRINCE	SNIFTY	TRIPOD	MEJLIS	YOKING
VAHINE	CHISEL	FLINCH	JOINER	PRIORY	SNIPER	TRIPOS	MOJAVE	YUKATA
YAHWEH	CHITAL	FLINTY	JUICER	PRISMS	SNIPPY	TRISTE	OBJECT	ABLATE
ACIDIC	CHITIN	FLITCH	KAISER	PRISON	SNITCH	TRITON	REJECT	ABLAUT
ACINUS	CHITON	FOIBLE	KHILAT	PRISSY	SNIVEL	TRIVET	REJOIN	ABLAZE
AFIELD	CHITTY	FOILED	KHILIM	PRIVET	SOIGNÉ	TRIVIA	UNJUST	ABLOOM
AHIMSA	CHIVES	FRIAND	KNIGHT	PRIZES	SOILED	TUILLE	ACKERS	ABLUSH
AKIMBO	CHIVVY	FRIARY	KNIVES	PUISNE	SOIREE	TWICER	AIKIDO	AFLAME
ALIGHT	CLICHÉ	FRIDAY	LAICAL	QUICHE	SPICED	TWIGGY	ALKALI	AFLOAT
ALIPED	CLIENT	FRIDGE	LAISSE	QUIDAM	SPICER	TWIGHT	ALKANE	AGLAIA
ALIYAH	CLIFFS	FRIEND	LOITER	QUINCE	SPIDER	TWINED	ALKENE	AILING
AMIDOL	CLIMAX	FRIEZE	MAIDAN	QUINSY	SPIGOT	TWINGE	ANKARA	ALLEGE
AMIDST	CLIMES	FRIGGA	MAIDEN	QUINTA	SPIKED	TWIRLY	ANKLET	ALLELE
ANIMAL	CLINCH	FRIGHT	MAILER	QUIRKY	SPILTH	TWISTY	ANKOLE	ALLEYN
ANIMUS	CLINIC	FRIGID	MAINLY	QUITCH	SPINAL	TWITCH	ARKOSE	ALLIED
APIARY	CLIPPY		MAINOR	QUIVER	SPINAR	UBIETY	ASKARI	ALLIER

ALLIUM	CALQUE	FELLER	HALITE	MALIBU	PALTRY	SALOOP	TELLER	WELKIN
ALLUDE	CALVER	FELLOE	HALLAL	MALICE	PELHAM	SALUKI	TELLUS	WELLER
ALLURE	CALVIN	FELLOW	HALLEY	MALIGN	PELION	SALUTE	TELUGU	WELLES
APLITE	CELERY	FELONY	HALLOO	MALLAM	PELLET	SALVER	TILLER	WELLIE
APLOMB	CELIAC	FILFOT	HALLOW	MALLEE	PELMET	SALVIA	TILSIT	WELTER
ASLANT	CELLAR	FILIAL	HALLUX	MALLET	PELOID	SCLAFF	TOLEDO	WELWYN
ASLEEP	CELTIC	FILING	HALOID	MALLOW	PELOTA	SCLERA	TOLLED	WILDER
ASLOPE	CILICE	FILLED	HALTER	MALONE	PELVIC	SCLERE	TOLLER	WILDLY
BALAAM	CILIUM	FILLER	HALVED	MALONY	PELVIS	SELDOM	TOLOSA	WILFUL
BALBOA	COLDLY	FILLET	HALVES	MALORY	PHLEGM	SELECT	TOLTEC	WILLED
BALDER	COLEUS	FILLIP	HELENA	MALTED	PHLEUM	SELENE	TOLUIC	WILLET
BALDLY	COLLAR	FILOSE	HELIOS	MALTHA	PHLOEM	SELFED	TOLUOL	WILLIE
BALEEN	COLLET	FILTER	HELIUM	MELIUS	PILAFF	SELJUK	TOLZEY	WILLOW
BALKAN	COLLIE	FILTHY	HELLAS	MELLOW	PILAGE	SELLBY	TULBAN	WILSON
BALKIS	COLLOP	FILTRÉ	HELLER	MELODY	PILATE	SELLER	TULIPA	WOLVER
BALLAD	COLMAR	FOLDED	HELMET	MELTED	PILEUM	SELSYN	ULLAGE	XYLENE
BALLET	COLONY	FOLDER	HELPER	MELTON	PILEUP	SELWYN	ULLING	XYLOID
BALLOT	COLOUR	FOLIAR	HILARY	MILADY	PILEUS	SILAGE	UMLAUT	XYLOSE
BALSAM	COLTER	FOLIOS	HILTON	MILDEW	PILFER	SILENE	UNLACE	YELLOW
BALTIC	COLUMN	FOLIOT	HOLDER	MILDLY	PILING	SILENT	UNLESS	ADMIRE
BALZAC	CULDEE	FOLIUM	HOLDUP	MILIEU	PILLAR	SILICA	UNLIKE	ALMAIN
BELAMY	CULLET	FOLKSY	HOLISM	MILLER	PILLOW	SILKEN	UNLOAD	ALMERY
BELFRY	CULLIS	FOLLOW	HOLIST	MILLET	PILOSE	SILVAN	UNLOCK	ALMOND
BELIAL	CULMEN	FULANI	HOLLER	MILORD	POLACK	SILVER	UPLAND	ALMOST
BELIEF	CULTCH	FULFIL	HOLLOW	MILTON	POLAND	SOLACE	UPLIFT	AMMINE
BELIKE	CULTER	FULGID	HOLMES	MOLECH	POLDER	SOLANO	UPLINK	ARMADA
BELIZE	CULTUS	FULHAM	HULLED	MOLEST	POLICE	SOLDER	VALENS	ARMAGH
BELLOC	CULVER	FULLER	ILLITE	MOLINE	POLICY	SOLEIL	VALETA	ARMFUL
BELLOW	DALASI	FULMAR	ILLUDE	MOLLAH	POLISH	SOLELY	VALGUS	ARMLET
BELONG	DALETH	FYLFOT	INLAID	MOLLIE	POLITE	SOLEMN	VALINE	ARMORY
BELSEN	DALTON	GALANT	INLAND	MOLOCH	POLITY	SOLENT	VALISE	ARMOUR
BELTED	DELATE	GALAXY	INLAWS	MOLTEN	POLLAN	SOLERA	VALIUM	ARMPIT
BELUGA	DELETE	GALENA	INLIER	MULISH	POLLED	SOLEUS	VALLEY	ARMURE
BILLET	DELIAN	GALERE	INLINE	MULLAH	POLLEN	SOLIVE	VALLUM	ASMARA
BILLIE	DELICE	GALIOT	IOLITE	MULLER	POLLEX	SOLUTE	VALOUR	AUMBRY
BILLOW	DELICT	GALLEN	ISLAND	MULLET	POLLUX	SOLVAY	VALUER	AYMARA
BILLYO	DELISH	GALLET	ISLETS	MULTUM	POLONY	SOLVED	VALUTA	BAMAKO
BOLDLY	DELIUS	GALLEY	JALOPY	NALLAH	POLYOL	SOLVER	VELCRO	BAMBOO
BOLERO	DELPHI	GALLIC	JILLET	NELLIE	POLYPS	SPLAKE	VELETA	BEMEAN
BOLEYN	DELUDE	GALLIO	JULIAN	NELSON	PULLET	SPLASH	VELLUM	BEMOAN
BOLIDE	DELUGE	GALLON	JULIET	NILGAI	PULLEY	SPLEEN	VELOCE	BEMOIL
BOLLEN	DELUXE	GALLOP	JULIUS	NILGAU	PULPIT	SPLENT	VELOUR	BEMUSE
BOLSHY	DELVED	GALLOW	KALMIA	NILOTE	PULSAR	SPLICE	VELURE	BOMBAY
BOLTER	DILATE	GALLUP	KALPAK	NULLAH	PULVER	SPLIFF	VELVET	BOMBER
BULBIL	DILUTE	GALLUS	KELLYS	NYLONS	RELATE	SPLINT	VILELY	BOMBYX
BULBUL	DOLEUR	GALOOT	KELOID	OBLAST	RELENT	SPLITS	VILIFY	BUMALO
BULGAR	DOLINA	GALORE	KELPER	OBLATE	RELICS	SPLOSH	VILLUS	BUMBLE
BULGER	DOLINE	GALOSH	KELPIE	OBLIGE	RELICT	SULCUS	VOLAGE	BUMPER
BULIMY	DOLIUM	GELADA	KELTER	OBLONG	RELIEF	SULFUR	VOLANS	CAMAIL
BULLER	DOLLAR	GELATE	KELTIC	OILCAN	RELISH	SULLEN	VOLANT	CAMBER
BULLET	DOLLOP	GELATO	KELTIE	OILERS	RELIVE	SULPHA	VOLENS	CAMDEN
BYLINE	DOLMAN	GELLER	KELVIN	OILMAN	ROLAND	SULTAN	VOLLEY	CAMERA
CALAIS	DOLMEN	GILDAS	KILLER	OILRIG	ROLLER	SYLVAN	VOLUME	CAMION
CALCED	DOLOUR	GILDED	KILNER	ONLINE	RULING	SYLVIA	VOLUTE	CAMISE
CALICO	DULCET	GILDER	KILTED	OOLITE	SALAAM	TALBOT	VULCAN	CAMOTE
CALIMA	EALING	GILEAD	KILTER	OOLONG	SALADE	TALCUM	VULGAR	CAMPED
CALIPH	ECLAIR	GILGAI	KILTIE	OULONG	SALAMI	TALENT	VULGUS	CAMPER
CALKER	ECLOSE	GILLET	LALLAN	OWLCAR	SALARY	TALION	WALKER	CAMPUS
CALKIN	ELLERY	GILLIE	LILIAN	OWLISH	SALINA	TALKER	WALLAH	CEMENT
CALLAS	ELLICE	GILPIN	LILITH	PALACE	SALINE	TALKIE	WALLED	COMART
CALLED	ENLACE	GOLDEN	LOLITA	PALAIS	SALISH	TALLIS	WALLER	COMATE
CALLER	ENLIST	GOLFER	LOLIUM	PALATE	SALIVA	TALLOT	WALLET	COMBAT
CALLET	EOLITH	GOLLOP	LOLLOP	PALING	SALLEE	TALLOW	WALLOP	COMBED
CALLID	EULOGY	GOLOSH	MALAGA	PALLAH	SALLET	TALMUD	WALLOW	COMBER
CALLOP	FALCON	GULLAH	MALATE	PALLAS	SALLOW	TELEDU	WALNUT	COMBLE
CALLOW	FALLEN	GULLET	MALAWI	PALLET	SALMIS	TELEGA	WALRUS	COMEDO
CALLUP	FALLOW	GULLEY	MALDON	PALLID	SALMON	TELEGU	WALTER	COMEDY
CALLUS	FALTER	GULPER	MALGRE	PALLOR	SALOME	TELEGU	WALTON	COMELY
CALMLY	FELINE	HALIDE	MALIAN	PALMER	SALOON	TELLAR	WELDER	COMFIT

COMICE	GAMING	LEMNOS	RAMOUS	TAMARA	BANGUI	CANTAB	DINKUM	GINGER
COMING	GAMMER	LEMONY	RAMROD	TAMARI	BANIAN	CANTAL	DINNER	GINGKO
COMITY	GAMMON	LEMUEL	REMAIN	TAMELY	BANISH	CANTAR	DONATE	GINKGO
COMMIS	GEMINI	LEMURE	REMAKE	TAMINE	BANJAX	CANTER	DONGLE	GONION
COMMIT	GEMMAN	LIMBED	REMAND	TAMISE	BANJUL	CANTLE	DONJON	GONIUM
COMMON	GIMBAL	LIMBER	REMARK	TAMMAR	BANKER	CANTON	DONKEY	GUNDOG
COMPEL	GIMLET	LIMBIC	REMEDY	TAMMUZ	BANNED	CANTOR	DONNÉE	GUNGHO
COMPLY	GIMMER	LIMITS	REMIND	TAMPER	BANNER	CANTUS	DONZEL	GUNMAN
COMSAT	GUMMED	LIMNER	REMISS	TAMPON	BANNET	CANUCK	DUNBAR	GUNNEL
CUMBER	HAMATE	LIMPET	REMORA	TEMPER	BANTAM	CANUTE	DUNCAN	GUNNER
CUMMER	HAMBLE	LIMPID	REMOTE	TEMPLE	BANTER	CANVAS	DUNCES	GUNTER
CUMMIN	HAMITE	LIMPLY	REMOVE	TIMBER	BANTRY	CANVEY	DUNDEE	HANDEL
CYMBAL	HAMLET	LOMOND	RIMINI	TIMBRE	BANYAN	CANYON	DUNDER	HANDLE
CYMRIC	HAMMAM	LUMBAR	RIMMED	TIMELY	BANZAI	CENSER	DUNELM	HANGAR
DAMAGE	HAMMER	LUMBER	ROMANO	TIMING	BENAME	CENSOR	DUNKER	HANGER
DAMASK	HAMOSE	LUMINA	ROMANS	TOMATO	BENBOW	CENSUS	DUNLIN	HANGUP
DAMMAR	HAMPER	LUMMOX	ROMANY	TOMBOY	BENDED	CENTER	DUNLOP	HANKER
DAMMIT	HEMPEN	LUMPUR	ROMISH	TOMCAT	BENDER	CENTRE	DYNAMO	HANKIE
DAMNED	HIMMEL	LYMPNE	ROMMEL	TOMIAL	BENGAL	CENTUM	DYNAST	HANNAH
DAMPEN	HOMAGE	MAMMAL	ROMNEY	TOMIUM	BENIGN	CINDER	ENNIUS	HANSOM
DAMPER	HOMBRE	MAMMON	RUMBLE	TOMTOM	BENITO	CINEMA	ERNANI	HENBIT
DAMSEL	HOMELY	MAMZER	RUMKIN	TUMBLE	BENNET	CINQUE	EUNUCH	HENLEY
DAMSON	HOMILY	MEMBER	RUMMER	TUMEFY	BENSON	CONCHA	FANGLE	HENNIN
DEMAIN	HOMING	MEMNON	RUMORS	TUMOUR	BENUMB	CONCHY	FANION	HENSON
DEMAND	HOMINY	MEMOIR	RUMOUR	TUMULT	BINARY	CONCUR	FANTAN	HINDER
DEMEAN	HUMANE	MEMORY	RUMPLE	TYMBAL	BINATE	CONDOM	FENCER	HINGED
DEMENT	HUMBER	MIMOSA	RUMPUS	TYMPAN	BINDER	CONDOR	FENDER	HINGES
DEMISE	HUMBLE	MOMENT	SAMARA	UDMURT	BONBON	CONFAB	FENIAN	HONCHO
DEMIST	HUMBUG	MUMBLE	SAMBAL	UNMADE	BONDED	CONFER	FENNEL	HONEST
DEMOTE	HUMECT	MUMMER	SAMBAR	UNMASK	BONDER	CONGEE	FINALE	HONIED
DEMURE	HUMITE	NAMELY	SAMBUR	UNMEET	BONITO	CONGER	FINDER	HONOUR
DIMITY	HUMMEL	NIMBLE	SAMEKH	UTMOST	BONNET	CONICS	FINELY	HONSHU
DIMMER	HUMMER	NIMBLY	SAMFOO	VOMICA	BONNIE	CONKER	FINERY	HUNGER
DIMPLE	HUMOUR	NIMBUS	SAMIAN	WAMBLE	BONSAI	CONMAN	FINEST	HUNGRY
DIMWIT	HUMPED	NIMROD	SAMIEL	WAMPUM	BONXIE	CONNER	FINGAL	HUNKER
DOMAIN	HUMPTY	NOMADE	SAMIOT	WAMPUS	BONZER	CONRAD	FINGER	HUNTER
DOMINO	HYMNAL	NOMISM	SAMITE	WIMBLE	BUNCHY	CONSUL	FINIAL	IGNITE
DUMBLY	IAMBIC	NUMBER	SAMLET	WIMPLE	BUNDLE	CONTRA	FINISH	IGNORE
DUMDUM	IAMBUS	NUMBLY	SAMOSA	WIMSEY	BUNGAY	CONVEX	FINITE	INNATE
DUMONT	IMMUNE	NUMDAH	SAMPAN	WOMBAT	BUNGEE	CONVEY	FINLAY	INNING
DUMOSE	IMMURE	NUMPTY	SAMPLE	WOMENS	BUNGLE	CONVOY	FINNAN	IONIAN
DUMPER	INMATE	OOMPAH	SAMSON	YAMMER	BUNION	CUNEAL	FONDLE	IONIZE
DUMPLE	INMESH	ORMOLU	SAMUEL	YEMENI	BUNJEE	CYNIPS	FONDLY	JANGLE
EAMONN	INMOST	OSMIUM	SEMELE	YUMYUM	BUNKER	DANCER	FONDUE	JANSKY
EDMOND	JAMBOK	OSMOSE	SEMITE	ZAMBIA	BUNKUM	DANDER	FUNDED	JENNER
EDMUND	JAMBON	PAMELA	SEMPRE	ZIMMER	BUNSEN	DANDLE	FUNDUS	JENNET
EGMONT	JAMMED	PAMIRS	SEMTEX	ZOMBIE	BUNTER	DANGER	FUNGAL	JINGAL
ENMESH	JAMPOT	PAMPAS	SIMEON	ADNATE	BUNYAN	DANGLE	FUNGUS	JINGLE
ENMITY	JEMIMA	PAMPER	SIMIAN	AENEID	BYNAME	DANIEL	FUNNEL	JINXED
ERMINE	JIMJAM	PAMYAT	SIMILE	AGNAIL	CANAAN	DANISH	GANDER	JONSON
ERMITE	JUMADA	PIMENT	SIMKIN	AGNATE	CANADA	DANTON	GANDHI	JUNCUS
EXMOOR	JUMBAL	PIMPLE	SIMMER	AMNION	CANAPÉ	DANUBE	GANESH	JUNGLE
FAMILY	JUMBLE	PIMPLY	SIMNEL	ANNALS	CANARD	DANZIG	GANGER	JUNIOR
FAMINE	JUMPER	POMACE	SIMONY	ANNEAL	CANARY	DENGUE	GANGES	JUNKER
FAMISH	KIMMER	POMADE	SIMOOM	ANNEXE	CANCEL	DENIAL	GANGLY	JUNKET
FAMOUS	KIMONO	POMELO	SIMOON	ANNUAL	CANCER	DENIED	GANGUE	JUNKIE
FEMALE	KOMODO	POMMEL	SIMPER	APNOEA	CANDID	DENIER	GANION	KANAKA
FIMBRA	KUMARA	POMMIE	SIMPLE	ARNAUT	CANDLE	DENIMS	GANNET	KANGHA
FOMENT	KUMERA	POMONA	SIMPLY	ARNHEM	CANDOR	DENNIS	GANTRY	KANOON
FUMADO	KUMISS	POMPEY	SOMALI	ARNICA	CANGUE	DENOTE	GENDER	KANSAS
FUMBLE	KUMMEL	POMPOM	SOMBER	ARNOLD	CANINE	DENTAL	GENERA	KANTEN
GAMBET	LAMBDA	POMPON	SOMBRE	AUNTIE	CANING	DENUDE	GENEVA	KANTHA
GAMBIA	LAMEDH	PUMICE	SUMACH	AWNING	CANKER	DENVER	GENIAL	KANUCK
GAMBIT	LAMELY	PUMMEL	SUMMER	BANANA	CANNAE	DINERO	GENIUS	KENDAL
GAMBLE	LAMENT	RAMBLE	SUMMIT	BANDAR	CANNED	DINGHY	GENOME	KENNEL
GAMBOL	LAMINA	RAMEAU	SUMMON	BANDIT	CANNEL	DINGLE	GENTES	KENNET
GAMELY	LAMMAS	RAMIFY	SYMBOL	BANDOG	CANNON	DINGLY	GENTLE	KENSAL
GAMETE	LAMMER	RAMJET	TAMALE	BANGER	CANNOT	DINING	GENTLY	KENYAN
GAMINE		RAMOSE	TAMANU	BANGLE	CANOPY		GENTRY	KINASE

KINDER	MENHIR	PENNAL	SANDAL	TENSOR	ZANDER	BOOBOO	COOLTH	FLORET
KINDLE	MENIAL	PENNON	SANDER	TENURE	ZENANA	BOODLE	COOPER	FLORID
KINDLY	MENINX	PENSÉE	SANELY	TINDER	ZENDIK	BOOGIE	COOTIE	FLORIN
KINGLY	MENSAL	PENSUM	SANITY	TINGED	ZENITH	BOOHOO	CROAKY	FLOSSY
LANATE	MENTAL	PENTAD	SANSEI	TINGLE	ZINGER	BOOJUM	CROCHE	FLOURY
LANCER	MENTOR	PENTEL	SANTAL	TINKER	ZINNIA	BOOKED	CROCKS	FLOUSH
LANCET	MENTUM	PENTUP	SANTON	TINKLE	ZONING	BOOKER	CROCUS	FLOWER
LANCIA	MINCER	PENTYL	SENATE	TINNED	ZONKED	BOOKIE	CRONET	FOOTER
LANDAU	MINDED	PENURY	SENDAL	TINNIE	ABOARD	BOOMER	CRONOS	FOOTLE
LANDED	MINDEL	PINCER	SENDER	TINPAN	ABONDE	BOOTEE	CRONUS	FOOZLE
LANDER	MINDER	PINDAR	SENECA	TINPOT	ABOUND	BOÖTES	CROPPY	FROLIC
LANDOR	MINGLE	PINEAL	SENILE	TINSEL	ADONAI	BOOTLE	CROSBY	FRONDE
LANGUR	MINING	PINERO	SENIOR	TINTED	ADONIS	BOOZER	CROSSE	FROSTY
LANUGO	MINION	PINGER	SENLAC	TINTIN	ADORER	BROACH	CROTAL	FROTHY
LENDER	MINNIE	PINING	SENNET	TONANT	AEOLIC	BROADS	CROTCH	FROUDE
LENGTH	MINNOW	PINION	SENORA	TONGAN	AEOLIS	BROGAN	CROTON	FROWST
LENTEL	MINOAN	PINITE	SENSED	TONGUE	AEOLUS	BROGUE	CROUCH	FROWZY
LENTEN	MINTON	PINKIE	SENSES	TONITE	AGONIC	BROKEN	CROUPE	FROZEN
LENTIC	MINUET	PINTER	SENSOR	TONSIL	AGOUTI	BROKER	CROUPY	GAOLER
LENTIL	MINUTE	PINTLE	SENTRY	TONSOR	ALOGIA	BROLLY	CROUSE	GEORGE
LENTOR	MONACO	PINXIT	SINBAD	TUNDRA	ALONSO	BRONCO	CROUTE	GHOSTS
LINDEN	MONDAY	PINYIN	SINDER	TUNING	AMOEBA	BRONTE	CROUTH	GIORGI
LINEAL	MONGER	PONCHO	SINEWY	TUNNEL	AMORAL	BRONZE	DEODAR	GIOTTO
LINEAR	MONGOL	PONDER	SINFUL	VANDAL	AMORCE	BROOCH	DHOOTI	GLOBAL
LINEUP	MONIAL	PONENT	SINGER	VANISH	AMORET	BROODY	DIODON	GLOIRE
LINGER	MONICA	PONGEE	SINGLE	VANITY	AMOUNT	BROOKE	DIOXIN	GLOOMY
LINGOT	MONISM	PONGID	SINGLY	VENDEE	ANOINT	BROOKS	DOODAD	GLORIA
LINING	MONIST	PONTIC	SINKER	VENDER	ANONYM	BROWNE	DOODAH	GLOSSA
LINKER	MONKEY	PUNCHY	SINNER	VENDOR	ANORAK	BROWSE	DOODLE	GLOSSY
LINKUP	MONODY	PUNCTO	SONANT	VENDUE	ANOXIA	CHOANA	DOOFER	GLOVED
LINNET	MONROE	PUNDIT	SONATA	VENEER	ANOXIC	CHOICE	DOOMED	GLOWER
LINTEL	MONTEM	PUNISH	SONICS	VENERY	APOGEE	CHOKED	DROGUE	GNOMIC
LONDON	MONTHS	PUNJAB	SONNET	VENIAL	APOLLO	CHOKER	DROMIO	GNOMON
LONELY	MUNICH	PUNKAH	SONTAG	VENICE	APORIA	CHOKEY	DROMOS	GOOBER
LONGER	MUNIFY	PUNNET	SUNDAE	VENITE	AROINT	CHOLER	DRONES	GOODLY
LUNACY	MUNITE	PUNTER	SUNDAY	VENOSE	AROLLA	CHOOSE	DRONGO	GOOGIE
LUNARY	MUNSHI	RANCEL	SUNDER	VENOUS	AROUET	CHOOSY	DROOPY	GOOGLE
LUNATE	NANDOO	RANCHO	SUNDEW	VENTIL	AROUND	CHOPIN	DROSKY	GOOGLY
LUNULE	NANISM	RANCID	SUNDRY	VENTRE	AROUSE	CHOPPY	DROVER	GOOGOL
MANAGE	NANKIN	RANCOR	SUNHAT	VINERY	ATOCIA	CHORAL	DROVES	GOOLEY
MANANA	NANSEN	RANDOM	SUNKEN	VINOUS	ATOMIC	CHOREA	DROWSE	GOOLIE
MANATI	NANTES	RANGER	SUNLIT	WANDER	ATONAL	CHOREE	DROWSY	GROATS
MANCHE	NINETY	RANKED	SUNRAY	WANDLE	ATONIC	CHORUS	DVORAK	GROCER
MANCHU	NINIAN	RANKER	SUNSET	WANGLE	AVOCET	CHOSEN	ECONUT	GROGGY
MANEGE	NONAGE	RANKLE	SUNTAN	WANKEL	AVOUCH	CHOUAN	EGOISM	GROOVE
MANFUL	NONARY	RANSOM	SYNCOM	WANTED	AVOWAL	CHOUGH	EGOIST	GROOVY
MANGER	NONCOM	RANTER	SYNDIC	WANTON	AVOWED	CHOWRY	ELODEA	GROPER
MANGLE	NUNCIO	RANULA	SYNTAX	WENSUM	AWOKEN	CLOACA	ELOHIM	GROSSO
MANIAC	OENONE	RENAME	TANDEM	WINDER	AZOLLA	CLOAKS	ELOIGN	GROTTO
MANILA	OMNIUM	RENDER	TANGLE	WINDOW	AZONAL	CLOCHE	ELOISE	GROTTY
MANIOC	ORNATE	RENEGE	TANKER	WINDUP	AZORES	CLONIC	ELOPER	GROUCH
MANITO	ORNERY	RENNET	TANKIA	WINGED	AZOTIC	CLONUS	ENODAL	GROUND
MANNER	OUNCES	RENNIN	TANNAH	WINGER	BAOBAB	CLOSED	ENOSIS	GROUPS
MANNIN	OUNDLE	RENOIR	TANNED	WINKER	BIOGEN	CLOSER	ENOUGH	GROUSE
MANQUÉ	PANADA	RENOWN	TANNER	WINKLE	BIONIC	CLOSET	EPONYM	GROUTS
MANTIS	PANAMA	RENTAL	TANNIC	WINNER	BIOPIC	CLOTHE	EPOPEE	GROUTY
MANTLE	PANDER	RENTER	TANNIN	WINNIE	BIOPSY	CLOTHO	ERODED	GROVEL
MANTRA	PANDIT	RENVOI	TANNOY	WINNOW	BIOTIC	CLOUDY	EROICA	GROWER
MANTUA	PANFRY	RENVOY	TANTRA	WINTER	BIOTIN	CLOUGH	EROTIC	GROWTH
MANUAL	PANOPE	RINGED	TENACE	WINTRY	BLOCKS	CLOVEN	EVOLUÉ	GROYNE
MANUKA	PANTER	RINGER	TENANT	WONDER	BLONDE	CLOVER	EVOLVE	HOODED
MANURE	PANTON	RONDEL	TENDER	WONTED	BLOODY	CLOVIS	EXOCET	HOOFED
MENACE	PANTRY	RUNDLE	TENDON	WONTON	BLOTCH	COOING	EXODUS	HOOFER
MENAGE	PANZER	RUNNEL	TENDRE	XANADU	BLOTTO	COOKED	EXOGEN	HOOHAH
MENCAP	PENANG	RUNNER	TENGKU	XENIAL	BLOUSE	COOKER	EXOTIC	HOOKAH
MENDEL	PENCEL	RUNOFF	TENNER	XENIUM	BLOWER	COOKIE	FLOOZY	HOOKED
MENDER	PENCIL	RUNWAY	TENNIS	YANKEE	BLOWUP	COOLER	FLOPPY	HOOKER
MENDES	PENMAN	RUNYON	TENPIN	YANKER	BLOWZY	COOLIE	FLORAL	HOOKEY
MENDIP	PENNAE	SANCHO	TENSON	YONDER		COOLLY		HOOKUP

HOOPER	PROLOG	SPOKEN	VIOLIN	DEPUTE	LIPARI	REPEAT	UNPLUG	BARBED
HOOPLA	PROMPT	SPOKES	VOODOO	DEPUTY	LIPASE	REPENT	UPPISH	BARBEL
HOOPOE	PRONTO	SPONGE	WHOLLY	DIPLOE	LIPIDE	REPINE	UPPITY	BARBER
HOORAH	PROPEL	SPONGY	WHOOPS	DIPNOI	LIPOMA	REPLAY	VAPOUR	BARBET
HOORAY	PROPER	SPOOKY	WHOOSH	DIPOLE	LIPPED	REPORT	WAPITI	BARÈGE
HOOTCH	PROPYL	SPOONY	WOODED	DIPPER	LUPINE	REPOSE	WIPERS	BARELY
HOOTER	PROSIT	SPORTS	WOODEN	DOPANT	MAPUTO	REPTON	WIPING	BARGEE
HOOVER	PROTEA	SPORTY	WOODIE	DUPLEX	MOPING	REPUGN	YIPPEE	BARHAM
ICONIC	PROTON	SPOTTY	WOOFER	EMPIRE	MOPISH	REPUTE	YUPPIE	BARING
IMOGEN	PROUST	SPOUSE	WOOKEY	EMPLOY	MOPPET	RIPOFF	ZAPATA	BARIUM
IRONED	PROVEN	STOCKS	WOOLEN	EPPING	MOPSUS	RIPPER	ZEPHYR	BARKER
IRONIC	PTOSIS	STOCKY	WOOLLY	ESPADA	MUPPET	RIPPLE	ZIPPER	BARKIS
ISOBAR	QUOITS	STODGE	YAOURT	ESPRIT	NAPALM	RIPPON	ZOPHAR	BARLEY
ISOLDE	QUORUM	STODGY	YEOMAN	EXPAND	NAPERY	RIPSAW	ACQUIT	BARMAN
ISOMER	QUOTED	STOGIE	YEOMEN	EXPECT	NAPIER	ROPERY	COQUET	BARNES
ISOPOD	REOPEN	STOKER	ALPACA	EXPEDE	NAPKIN	RUPEES	DIQUAT	BARNET
KAOLIN	RHODES	STOKES	ALPINE	EXPEND	NAPLES	RUPERT	LIQUID	BARNEY
KNOBBY	RIOTER	STOLEN	ALPINO	EXPERT	NAPPER	RUPIAH	LIQUOR	BARNUM
KNOTTY	ROOFER	STOLID	AMPERE	EXPIRE	NEPALI	RUPIAS	LOQUAT	BARODA
KOODOO	ROOKIE	STOLON	APPALL	EXPIRY	NEPETA	SAPELE	MAQUIS	BARQUE
KOOKIE	ROOMER	STONED	APPEAL	EXPORT	NEPHEW	SAPHAR	PEQUOD	BARRED
KOOLAH	ROOTED	STONER	APPEAR	EXPOSE	NIPPER	SAPIUM	PIQUET	BARREL
KRONER	ROOTER	STONES	APPEND	EXPUGN	NIPPLE	SAPOTA	ROQUET	BARREN
KRONOS	ROOTLE	STOOGE	APPIAN	FIPPLE	NIPPON	SAPOTE	SEQUEL	BARRIE
LEONID	RYOKAN	STOOKS	APPLES	GAPING	OPPOSE	SAPPER	SEQUIN	BARRIO
LHOTSE	SCOLEX	STOOLS	APPORT	GOPHER	OPPUGN	SAPPHO	AARONS	BARROW
LIONEL	SCONCE	STORAX	APPOSE	GYPSUM	ORPHAN	SEPIUM	ABRADE	BARSAC
LLOYDS	SCOOBS	STORER	ARPENT	HAPPEN	ORPHIC	SEPSIS	ABREGE	BARTER
LOOFAH	SCOOSH	STOREY	ASPECT	HAPTEN	ORPINE	SEPTAL	ABROAD	BARTOK
LOONIE	SCOPUS	STORMY	ASPIRE	HAPTIC	OSPREY	SEPTET	ABROMA	BARTON
LOOPED	SCORCH	STOVER	BYPASS	HEPTAD	PAPACY	SEPTIC	ABRUPT	BARUCH
LOOPER	SCORER	STOWER	CAPIAS	HIPPED	PAPAGO	SIPHON	ACRAWL	BARYTA
LOOSEN	SCORIA	SWOOSH	CAPLET	HIPPUS	PAPAYA	SIPPET	ACROSS	BERATE
LOOTER	SCORSE	TAOISM	CAPONE	HOPPER	PAPERS	SIPPLE	ADRIAN	BERBER
MAOIST	SCOTCH	TAOIST	CAPOTE	HYPATE	PAPERY	SOPHIA	ADRIFT	BEREFT
MAOTAI	SCOTER	TEOPAN	CAPPED	HYPHAL	PAPHOS	SUPERB	ADROIT	BERGEN
MOOCOW	SCOTIA	THOLOS	CAPSID	HYPHEN	PAPIST	SUPINE	AERATE	BERING
MOOLAH	SCOUSE	THOLUS	CAPTAN	HYPNIC	PAPULE	SUPLEX	AERIAL	BERLIN
MOOMBA	SHODDY	THOMAS	CAPTOR	HYPNOS	PEPLOS	SUPPER	AEROBE	BERTHA
MYOGEN	SHOFAR	THORAH	CIPHER	HYPNUM	PEPLUM	SUPPLE	AFRAID	BERTHE
MYOPIA	SHOGUN	THORAX	COPECK	IMPACT	PEPPER	SUPPLY	AFREET	BERTIE
MYOPIC	SHORTS	THORNE	COPIED	IMPAIR	PEPTIC	SYPHER	AFRESH	BIRDIE
MYOSIN	SHOULD	THORNY	COPIER	IMPALA	PIPING	SYPHON	AFRICA	BIREME
MYOSIS	SHOVEL	THORPE	COPING	IMPALE	PIPKIN	TAPPER	AGREED	BIRNAM
NOODLE	SHOWER	THOUGH	COPPER	IMPART	PIPPIN	TAPPET	AGRÉGÉ	BORAGE
NOOKIE	SLOANE	TOOTER	COPPIN	IMPAWN	POPEYE	TAPPIT	AIRBED	BORANE
OBOIST	SLOGAN	TOOTHY	COPTIC	IMPEDE	POPLAR	TEPHRA	AIRBUS	BORATE
OBOLUS	SLOPES	TOOTLE	CUPFUL	IMPEND	POPLIN	TIPCAT	AIRGUN	BORDAR
OROIDE	SLOPPY	TOOTSY	CUPMAN	IMPISH	POPPER	TIPOFF	AIRILY	BORDER
PEOPLE	SLOSHY	TROCAR	CUPOLA	IMPORT	POPPET	TIPPED	AIRING	BOREAS
PHOBIA	SLOUCH	TROCHE	CUPPED	IMPOSE	POPPIT	TIPPER	AIRMAN	BORGIA
PHOBIC	SLOUGH	TROIKA	CUPPER	IMPOST	POPPLE	TIPPET	AIRWAY	BORING
PHOBOS	SLOVAK	TROJAN	CUPRIC	IMPUGN	PUPATE	TIPPLE	AORIST	BORNEO
PHOEBE	SLOVEN	TROMPE	CUPULE	IMPURE	PUPPET	TIPPOO	AORTAL	BORROW
PHONAL	SLOWLY	TROOPS	CYPHER	IMPUTE	PUPPIS	TIPTOE	ARRACK	BORSCH
PHONEY	SMOKER	TROPHE	CYPRID	JOPLIN	RAPHIA	TIPTOP	ARRANT	BORZOI
PHONIC	SMOKEY	TROPHY	CYPRIS	KAPUTT	RAPIDS	TIPULA	ARREAR	BURBLE
PHOOEY	SMOOCH	TROPIC	CYPRUS	KEPHIR	RAPIER	TOPHUS	ARREST	BURBOT
PHOTON	SMOOTH	TROPPO	DAPHNE	KEPLER	RAPINE	TOPPER	ARRIAN	BURDEN
PLONGE	SNOOTY	TROUGH	DAPPER	KIPPER	RAPIST	TOPPLE	ARRIVE	BUREAU
PLOUGH	SNOOZE	TROUPE	DAPPLE	LAPDOG	RAPPED	TUPELO	ARROBA	BURGEE
PLOVER	SNORER	TROUVÉ	DEPART	LAPITH	RAPPEL	TYPHUS	ARROYO	BURGER
POODLE	SNOTTY	TROVER	DEPEND	LAPPER	RAPTOR	TYPIFY	ATRIAL	BURGLE
POORLY	SNOUTY	TROWEL	DEPICT	LAPPET	RAPTLY	TYPING	ATRIDE	BURIAL
POOTER	SNOWED	TROYES	DEPONE	LAPSED	RAPPER	TYPIST	ATRIUM	BURIED
PROBIT	SOONER	TSONGA	DEPORT	LAPSUS	REPAID	UMPIRE	AUREUS	BURKHA
PROFIT	SOOTHE	TWOBIT	DEPOSE	LAPTOP	REPAIR	UNPACK	AURIGA	BURLAP
PROLEG	SPOILS	UTOPIA	DEPTHS	LAPUTA	REPAST	UNPAID	AURORA	BURLEY
PROLIX	SPOILT	VIOLET		LEPTON	REPEAL	UNPICK	AZRAEL	BURNER

BURNET	CORNEL	DORRIT	FORKED	HARROW	LARRUP	MORION	PARROT	SCRIBE
BURROW	CORNER	DORSAL	FORMAL	HARVEY	LARVAE	MORMON	PARSEC	SCRIMP
BURSAR	CORNET	DORSET	FORMAT	HERALD	LARVAL	MORNAY	PARSEE	SCRIPT
BURTON	CORNUA	DORTER	FORMER	HERBAL	LARYNX	MORNED	PARSON	SCROLL
BYRNIE	CORNUS	DURANT	FORMIC	HERDEN	LORCHA	MOROSE	PARTLY	SCROOP
CARAFE	CORONA	DURBAR	FORNAX	HERDER	LORDLY	MORRIS	PARTON	SCRUBS
CARBON	CORPSE	DURESS	FORNIX	HEREBY	LORETO	MORROW	PARURE	SCRUFF
CARBOY	CORPUS	DURHAM	FORPIT	HEREIN	LORICA	MORSEL	PARVIS	SCRUNT
CARDAN	CORRAL	DURIAN	FORRAD	HERERO	LORIOT	MORTAL	PERDUE	SERAIL
CAREEN	CORRIE	DURING	FORRAY	HERESY	LURING	MORTAR	PERHAP	SERANG
CAREER	CORSET	DURION	FORSAY	HERETO	LURIST	MORTEM	PERILS	SERAPE
CAREME	CORTES	EARFUL	FORTHY	HERIOT	LYRICS	MURAGE	PERIOD	SERAPH
CARESS	CORTEX	EARING	FUREUR	HERMES	LYRIST	MURALS	PERISH	SERBIA
CARFAX	CORTEZ	EARNED	FURFUR	HERMIT	MARACA	MURDER	PERKIN	SERDAB
CARIES	CORVÉE	EARNER	FURIES	HERMON	MARAUD	MURIEL	PERMIT	SERENE
CARINA	CORVUS	EARTHY	FURORE	HERNIA	MARBLE	MURINE	PERNOD	SERIAL
CARING	CORYZA	EARWAX	FURPHY	HEROIC	MARCEL	MURLIN	PERRON	SERIES
CARLIN	CURACY	EARWIG	FURROW	HEROIN	MARGIN	MURMUR	PERSON	SERINE
CARMEL	CURARE	EERILY	GARAGE	HERONS	MARIAN	MURPHY	PERUKE	SERMON
CARMEN	CURARI	EGRESS	GARBED	HERPES	MARINA	MURRAM	PERUSE	SEROSA
CARNAL	CURATE	EIRANN	GARBLE	HERREN	MARINE	MURRAY	PHRASE	SERVAL
CARNET	CURDLE	ENRAGE	GARÇON	HIRING	MARISH	MURRHA	PIRACY	SERVER
CARNOT	CURFEW	ENRAPT	GARDEN	HIRSEL	MARIST	MURRIN	PIRATE	SHRANK
CARPAL	CURIET	ENRICH	GARETH	HORACE	MARKED	MYRIAD	PIRENE	SHREWD
CARPEL	CURIUM	ENROBE	GARGET	HORMUZ	MARKER	MYRTLE	PORGIE	SHRIEK
CARPER	CURLER	ENROLL	GARGLE	HORNED	MARKET	NARROW	PORKER	SHRIFT
CARPET	CURLEW	EPRISE	GARISH	HORNER	MARKKA	NEREID	POROUS	SHRIKE
CARPUS	CURPEL	ERRAND	GARLIC	HORNET	MARKUP	NEREUS	PORTAL	SHRILL
CARREL	CURRIE	ERRANT	GARNER	HORRID	MARLIN	NERINE	PORTER	SHRIMP
CARROT	CURSAL	ETRIER	GARNET	HORROR	MARMOT	NERIUM	PORTIA	SHRINE
CARSON	CURSED	EUREKA	GARRET	HORSED	MARNER	NEROLI	PORTLY	SHRINK
CARTEL	CURSOR	EUROPA	GARROT	HURDLE	MAROON	NERVAL	PURDAH	SHRIVE
CARTER	CURSUS	EUROPE	GARRYA	HURLEY	MARQUE	NERVES	PURELY	SHROFF
CARTON	CURTAL	FARAND	GARTER	HURRAH	MARRAM	NERVII	PURIFY	SHROUD
CARUSO	CURTAX	FARCIN	GARUDA	HURRAY	MARRON	NORDIC	PURINE	SHROVE
CARVED	CURTLY	FARDEL	GERBIL	HURTLE	MARROW	NORMAL	PURIST	SHRUNK
CARVEL	CURTSY	FARDLE	GERENT	INROAD	MARSHY	NORMAN	PURITY	SIRDAR
CARVER	CURULE	FARINA	GERMAN	INRUSH	MARTEL	NORROY	PURLER	SIRIUS
CERATE	CURVED	FARMER	GERUND	IRRUPT	MARTEN	NORVIC	PURLIN	SIRKAR
CERCAL	CURVET	FAROFF	GIRDER	ISRAEL	MARTHA	NORWAY	PURPLE	SIRRAH
CERCUS	CYRANO	FAROUK	GIRDLE	JARGON	MARTIN	OARLAP	PURSED	SIRREE
CEREAL	CYRENE	FARROW	GIRKIN	JARVEY	MARTYR	OERLAY	PURSER	SORAGE
CEREUS	DARGLE	FERIAL	GIRLIE	JERBOA	MARVEL	OGRESS	PURSUE	SORBET
CERISE	DARIEN	FERMAT	GIRTON	JEREMY	MERCAT	ONRUSH	PURVEY	SORDES
CERIUM	DARING	FERRET	GORDON	JERKER	MERCER	OURALI	PYRENE	SORDID
CERMET	DARIUS	FERRIS	GORGED	JERKIN	MERCIA	ORRERY	PYRITE	SORELL
CEROON	DARKEN	FERULA	GORGES	JEROME	MERELY	PARADE	PYRONE	SORELY
CERTES	DARKEY	FERULE	GORGET	JERSEY	MERGER	PARAMO	PYROPE	SORGHO
CERUSE	DARKIE	FERVID	GORGIA	JORDAN	MERINO	PARANA	PYRRHO	SORREL
CERVIX	DARKLY	FERVOR	GORGIO	JURANT	MERKIN	PARAPH	RAREFY	SORROW
CHRISM	DARTER	FIRING	GORGON	JURIST	MERLIN	PARCAE	RARELY	SORTER
CHRIST	DARTLE	FIRKIN	GORING	KARATE	MERLOT	PARCEL	RARING	SORTES
CHROMA	DARWIN	FIRLOT	GURGLE	KARIBA	MERMAN	PARDIE	RARITY	SORTIE
CHROME	DERAIL	FIRMAN	GURKHA	KARITE	MEROPE	PARDON	REREAD	SPRAIN
CHROMO	DERAIN	FIRMER	GURLET	KERALA	MERRIE	PARENT	SARGUS	SPRANG
CIRCLE	DERGUE	FIRMLY	GURNET	KERMES	MERROW	PARETO	SARNIE	SPRAWL
CIRCUS	DERHAM	FORAGE	GURNEY	KERMIS	MERSEY	PAREVE	SARONG	SPREAD
CIRQUE	DERIDE	FORBID	GYRATE	KERNEL	MERTON	PARGET	SARSEN	SPRING
CIRRUS	DERIVE	FORÇAT	HARARE	KIRBEH	MIRAGE	PARIAH	SARTOR	SPRINT
CORALS	DERMAL	FORCED	HARASS	KIRMAN	MIRROR	PARISH	SARTRE	SPRITE
CORBEL	DERMIS	FORCES	HARBOR	KIRPAN	MORALE	PARITY	SCRAMB	SPRITZ
CORBIE	DERRIS	FOREDO	HARDEN	KIRSCH	MORALS	PARKED	SCRAPE	SPROUT
CORDON	DIRECT	FOREGO	HARDLY	KIRTLE	MORASS	PARKER	SCRAPS	SPRUCE
CORIUM	DIRHAM	FOREST	HARKEN	KOREAN	MORBID	PARKIN	SCRAWL	SPRUNG
CORKED	DIRNDL	FORGED	HARLOT	KORUNA	MORBUS	PARLEY	SCRAWM	SPRYLY
CORKER	DORADO	FORGER	HARMED	LARDER	MOREEN	PARLOR	SCREAM	STRABO
CORMUS	DORCAS	FORGET	HAROLD	LARDON	MORGAN	PARODY	SCREED	STRAFE
CORNEA	DORIAN	FORGOT	HARPIC	LARIAT	MORGEN	PAROLE	SCREEN	STRAIN
CORNED	DORMER	FORINT	HARRIS	LARKIN	MORGUE	PARPEN	SCREWY	STRAIT

STRAKE	TERTIA	VERGES	ASSIGN	CASUAL	FASTEN	JUSTLY	MOSAIC	POSTER
STRAND	THRALL	VERIFY	ASSIST	CESARE	FESCUE	KASBAH	MOSCOW	POSTIL
STRASS	THRASH	VERILY	ASSIZE	CESIUM	FESTAL	KISHKE	MOSLEM	PUSHER
STRATA	THRAWN	VERISM	ASSOIL	CESTUI	FESTER	KISLEV	MOSQUE	PUSHTU
STRAWS	THREAD	VERITY	ASSORT	CESTUS	FISCAL	KISMET	MOSSAD	PUSHUP
STRAWY	THREAP	VERMIN	ASSUME	CESURA	FISHER	KISSEL	MOSTLY	PUSSER
STREAK	THREAT	VERMIS	ASSURE	COSHER	FOSSIL	KISSER	MUSANG	RASCAL
STREAM	THRENE	VERNAL	AUSPEX	COSIER	FOSTER	KOSHER	MUSCAT	RASHER
STREET	THRESH	VERNON	AUSSIE	COSILY	FUSAIN	KOSMOS	MUSCLE	RASHLY
STREGA	THRICE	VERSAL	AUSTEN	COSINE	FUSELI	LASCAR	MUSEUM	RASPER
STRENE	THRIFT	VERSED	AUSTER	COSMEA	FUSION	LASHED	MUSING	RASTER
STRESS	THRILL	VERSES	AUSTIN	COSMIC	FUSTIC	LASHER	MUSIVE	RESALE
STRICK	THRIPS	VERSET	BASALT	COSMOS	FUSTOC	LASKET	MUSKEG	RESCUE
STRICT	THRIST	VERSUS	BASHER	COSSET	GASBAG	LASSIE	MUSKET	RESEAU
STRIDE	THRIVE	VERVET	BASICS	COSSIE	GASCON	LASSUS	MUSLIM	RESECT
STRIFE	THROAT	VIRAGO	BASKET	COSTAR	GASKET	LASTLY	MUSLIN	RESEDA
STRIKE	THROES	VIRGIL	BASQUE	COSTER	GASMAN	LESBOS	MUSSEL	RESENT
STRINE	THRONE	VIRGIN	BASSET	COSTLY	GASPAR	LESION	MUSTER	RESIDE
STRING	THRONG	VIRILE	BASUTO	CUSCUS	GASPER	LESLIE	MYSELF	RESIGN
STRIPE	THROVE	VIROUS	BESANT	CUSHAT	GASSER	LESSEE	MYSORE	RESIST
STRIPY	THROWN	VIRTUE	BESEEM	CUSSED	GASTER	LESSEN	MYSTIC	RESORT
STRIVE	THRUSH	VORTEX	BESIDE	CUSSER	GASTON	LESSER	NASEBY	RESULT
STROBE	THRUST	WARBLE	BESORT	CUSTER	GOSPEL	LESSON	NASION	RESUME
STRODE	TIRADE	WARCRY	BESSEL	CUSTOM	GOSSIP	LESSOR	NASSAU	RISING
STROKE	TIRANA	WARDEN	BESSIE	CUSTOS	GUSHER	LESTER	NASSER	RISQUÉ
STROLL	TIRING	WARDER	BESSUS	CYSTIC	GUSLAR	LISBON	NASTIC	ROSACE
STRONG	TORERO	WARHOL	BESTED	DASHED	GUSSET	LISPER	NESSIE	ROSARY
STROUD	TORPID	WARILY	BESTIR	DESCRY	HASHED	LISSOM	NESSUS	ROSCID
STROUP	TORPOR	WARMER	BESTOW	DESERT	HASLET	LISTEL	NESTLE	ROSCOE
STROVE	TORQUE	WARMLY	BISCAY	DESIGN	HASSAR	LISTEN	NESTOR	ROSERY
STRUCK	TORRES	WARMTH	BISECT	DESIRE	HASSLE	LISTER	NISSEN	ROSINA
STRUNG	TORRID	WARNER	BISHOP	DESIST	HASTEN	LOSING	NOSILY	ROSSER
STRUNT	TORULA	WARPED	BISQUE	DESORB	HESIOD	LUSAKA	OBSESS	ROSTER
SURELY	TURBAN	WARREN	BISTER	DESPOT	HESTIA	LUSTER	ONSIDE	ROSTOV
SURETÉ	TURBID	WARSAW	BISTRE	DISARM	HISPID	LUSTRE	ORSINO	ROSYTH
SURETY	TURBOT	WERENT	BISTRO	DISBAR	HOSIER	MASADA	OSSIAN	RUSHED
SURFER	TUREEN	WIRING	BOSKET	DISBUD	HOSING	MASCOT	OSSIFY	RUSKIN
SURREY	TURGID	WIRRAL	BOSSED	DISCUS	HOSTEL	MASHAM	OYSTER	RUSSET
SURTAX	TURKEY	WORKED	BOSTON	DISEUR	HUSHED	MASHED	PASCAL	RUSSIA
SURVEY	TURNED	WORKER	BOSUNS	DISHED	HUSSAR	MASHER	PASHTO	RUSTAM
SYRIAN	TURNER	WORSEN	BUSBOY	DISHES	HUSSIF	MASHIE	PASHTU	RUSTEM
SYRINX	TURNIP	WORTHY	BUSHED	DISMAL	HUSTLE	MASKED	PASQUE	RUSTIC
SYRISM	TURNUP	WORTLE	BUSHEL	DISMAY	HYSSOP	MASKER	PASSED	RUSTLE
SYRUPY	TURPIN	XEROMA	BUSILY	DISNEY	INSANE	MASLIN	PASSES	RUSTUM
TARCEL	TURRET	XERXES	BUSKER	DISOWN	INSECT	MASQUE	PASSIM	SASHAY
TARDIS	TURTLE	YARDIE	BUSKET	DISPEL	INSERT	MASSED	PASTEL	SESAME
TARGET	TURVES	YARROW	BUSKIN	DISTAL	INSIDE	MASSES	PASTIL	SISKIN
TARGUM	TYRANT	YORICK	BUSMAN	DISTIL	INSIST	MASSIF	PASTIS	SISTER
TARIFF	TYRONE	YORKER	BUSONI	DISUSE	INSOLE	MASTER	PASTON	SUSSEX
TARMAC	UGRIAN	YORUBA	BUSTED	DOSAGE	INSTAL	MASTIC	PASTOR	SYSTEM
TARROW	UNREAD	ZIRCON	BUSTER	DOSSAL	INSTAR	MESAIL	PASTRY	TASMAN
TARSAL	UNREAL	ZURICH	BUSTLE	DOSSER	INSTEP	MESCAL	PESADE	TASSEL
TARSEL	UNREEL	ZYRIAN	BYSSUS	DUSTED	INSTIL	MESIAL	PESETA	TASSET
TARSIA	UNREST	ABSEIL	CASBAH	DUSTER	INSULA	MESMER	PESHWA	TASSIE
TARSUS	UNRIPE	ABSENT	CASEIN	EASIER	INSULT	MESSRS	PESTER	TASTER
TARTAN	UNROLL	ABSORB	CASHEW	EASILY	INSURE	MISÈRE	PESTLE	TESTER
TARTAR	UNRULY	ABSURD	CASING	EASING	ISSUES	MISERY	PISANO	TESTES
TARTLY	UPRATE	ADSORB	CASINO	EASTER	ITSELF	MISFIT	PISCES	TESTIS
TERCEL	UPROAR	ADSUKI	CASKET	ENSATE	JASPER	MISHAP	PISGAH	TISANE
TERCIO	UPROOT	ANSELM	CASLON	ENSEAL	JESUIT	MISHIT	PISSED	TISHRI
TEREDO	VARECH	ANSWER	CASPAR	ENSIGN	JESTER	MISLAY	PISTIL	TISSOT
TERESA	VARESE	ARSÈNE	CASQUE	ENSILE	JISSOM	MISLED	PISTOL	TISSUE
TERETE	VARIED	ARSINE	CASSIA	ENSURE	JOSEPH	MISSAL	PISTON	TOSHER
TERGUM	VARLET	ASSAIL	CASSIO	ERSATZ	JOSHUA	MISSEL	POSADA	TOSSUP
TERMES	VERBAL	ASSART	CASSIS	ESSENE	JOSIAH	MISSIS	POSEUR	TUSCAN
TERMLY	VERDIN	ASSENT	CASTER	EUSTON	JOSKIN	MISSUS	POSSER	TUSKER
TERNAL	VERDUN	ASSERT	CASTLE	EXSERT	JOSSER	MISTER	POSSET	TUSSAH
TERRAE	VEREIN	ASSESS	CASTOR	FASCES	JOSTLE	MISUSE	POSSUM	TUSSIS
TERROR	VERGER	ASSETS	CASTRO	FASCIA	JUSTIN		POSTAL	TUSSLE

ULSTER	ARTURO	CITRUS	FITTED	LITANY	NUTATE	POTASH	SUTTEE	BAUBLE
UNSAFE	ASTART	COTTAR	FITTER	LITCHI	NUTMEG	POTATO	SUTURE	BAUCIS
UNSAID	ASTERN	COTTON	FUTILE	LITHIA	NUTTER	POTEEN	TATAMI	BEULAH
UNSEAM	ASTHMA	COTYLE	FUTURE	LITMUS	OBTAIN	POTENT	TATERS	BEURRÉ
UNSEAT	ASTONE	CUTCHA	GATEAU	LITTER	OBTECT	POTHER	TATLER	BLUDGE
UNSEEN	ASTRAL	CUTLER	GATHER	LOTION	OBTEND	POTION	TATTER	BLUISH
UNSENT	ASTRAY	CUTLET	GETTER	LUTEAL	OBTUND	POTTED	TATTLE	BOUCHE
UNSEXY	ASTUTE	CUTOFF	GITANO	LUTEIN	OBTUSE	POTTER	TATTOO	BOUCLÉ
UNSHOD	ATTACH	CUTTER	GOTHAM	LUTHER	OCTANE	POTTLE	TETANY	BOUFFE
UNSOLD	ATTACK	CUTTLE	GOTHIC	LUTINE	OCTANS	PUTEAL	TETCHY	BOUGHT
UNSUNG	ATTAIN	CUTTOE	GOTTEN	LUTIST	OCTANT	PUTOIS	TETHER	BOULLE
UNSURE	ATTEND	CYTASE	GUTTER	LYTTON	OCTAVE	PUTOUT	TETHYS	BOUNCE
UPSHOT	ATTEST	CYTODE	GUTTLE	HATING	OCTAVO	PUTRID	TETRAD	BOUNCY
UPSIDE	ATTILA	CYTOID	HATING	MATHIS	OCTROI	PUTSCH	TETRYL	BOUNDS
URSINE	ATTIRE	DATING	HATRED	MATING	OPTICS	PUTTEE	TETTIX	BOUNTY
URSULA	ATTLEE	DATIVE	HATTER	MATINS	OPTIMA	PUTTER	TITBIT	BOURÉE
VASSAL	ATTONE	DATURA	HETERO	MATLOW	OPTIME	PYTHIA	TITCHY	BOURNE
VASTLY	ATTORN	DETACH	HETMAN	MATRIC	OPTION	PYTHON	TITFER	BOURSE
VESICA	ATTRAP	DETAIL	HITECH	MATRIX	OPTOUT	RATBAG	TITIAN	BOUSER
VESPER	ATTUNE	DETAIN	HITHER	MATRON	ORTEGA	RATHER	TITLED	BOUTON
VESSEL	AUTHOR	DETECT	HITLER	MATTED	OSTEND	RATIFY	TITTER	BRUISE
VESTAL	AUTISM	DETENT	HITMAN	MATTER	OSTIUM	RATINE	TITTLE	BRUMAL
VESTED	AUTUMN	DETENU	HITTER	MATURE	OSTLER	RATING	TITTUP	BRUMBY
VESTRY	BATEAU	DETEST	HOTAIR	METAGE	OSTREA	RATION	TITULE	BRUNCH
VISAGE	BATHER	DETOUR	HOTBED	METATE	OTTAVA	RATOON	TOTTER	BRUNEI
VISCID	BATHOS	DITHER	HOTPOT	METEOR	OTTAWA	RATTAN	TOTTIE	BRUNEL
VISHNU	BATMAN	DITTOS	HOTTER	METHOD	OUTAGE	RATTER	ULTIMA	BRUTAL
VISIER	BATTEN	DOTAGE	INTACT	METHYL	OUTBAR	RATTLE	ULTIMO	BRUTUS
VISION	BATTER	DOTARD	INTAKE	METIER	OUTBID	RATTON	UNTIDY	CAUCUS
VISUAL	BATTLE	DOTING	INTEND	METOPE	OUTCRY	RETAIL	UNTOLD	CAUDEX
VOSGES	BATTUE	DOTTED	INTENT	METRIC	OUTFIT	RETAIN	UNTRUE	CAUDLE
WASHED	BETAKE	DOTTLE	INTERN	METTLE	OUTGAS	RETAKE	UPTAKE	CAUGHT
WASHER	BETHEL	EATAGE	INTIME	MITRAL	OUTING	RETARD	UPTOWN	CAUSAL
WASTED	BETIDE	EATERY	INTONE	MITRED	OUTLAW	RETINA	UPTURN	CAUSED
WASTEL	BETIME	EATING	INTOWN	MITTEN	OUTLAY	RETIRE	URTICA	CAUSEY
WASTER	BETISE	ECTOPY	INTRAY	MOTHER	OUTLET	RETOOL	VATHEK	CHUBBY
WESKER	BETONY	EFTEST	INTRON	MOTILE	OUTLIE	RETORT	VATMAN	CHUFFY
WESLEY	BETRAY	EITHER	ISTRIA	MOTION	OUTPUT	RETOUR	VITALS	CHUKKA
WESSEX	BETTER	ELTCHI	JETHRO	MOTIVE	OUTRUN	RETURN	VOTARY	CHUMMY
WISDEN	BETTOR	ENTAIL	JETLAG	MOTLEY	OUTSET	RITUAL	VOTING	CHUNKY
WISDOM	BITCHY	ENTICE	JETSAM	MOTOWN	OUTTOP	ROTARY	VOTIVE	CHURCH
WISELY	BITING	ENTIRE	JETTON	MOTTLE	OUTVIE	ROTATE	VOTYAK	CLUMPS
WISHES	BITTEN	ENTITY	JITNEY	MUTANT	OUTWIT	ROTGUT	WATERS	CLUMSY
YESMAN	BITTER	ENTOMB	JITTER	MUTATE	OXTAIL	ROTHER	WATERY	CLUNCH
YESTER	BOTANY	ENTRAP	JOTTER	MUTELY	PATACA	ROTHKO	WATSON	CLUTCH
ZOSTER	BOTHAM	ENTREE	KATANA	MUTINY	PATCHY	ROTTEN	WATTLE	COUGAR
ACTING	BOTHER	EOTHEN	KETMIR	MUTISM	PATENT	ROTTER	WETBOB	COULEE
ACTION	BOTHIE	ESTATE	KETONE	MUTTER	PATHAN	ROTULA	WETHER	COULIS
ACTIUM	BOTLEY	ESTEEM	KETOSE	MUTTON	PATHIC	ROTUND	WITHAL	COUNTY
ACTIVE	BOTTLE	ESTHER	KETTLE	MUTUAL	PATHOS	RUTTED	WITHER	COUPLE
ACTORS	BOTTOM	ESTRAY	KITBAG	MYTHOS	PATINA	RUTTER	WITHIN	COUPON
ACTUAL	BUTANE	EUTAXY	KITCAT	NATANT	PATOIS	SATEEN	WITTED	COURSE
AFTERS	BUTENE	EXTANT	KITSCH	NATION	PATROL	SATINY	YATTER	COUSIN
ALTAIR	BUTLER	EXTEND	KITTEN	NATIVE	PATRON	SATIRE	ZITHER	CRUELS
ALTHEA	BUTTER	EXTENT	KITTLE	NATRON	PATTEN	SATIVE	ABULIA	CRUFTS
AMTRAK	BUTTON	EXTERN	KOTWAL	NATTER	PATTER	SATORI	ACUITY	CRUISE
ANTHEM	CATCHY	EXTIRP	LATEEN	NATURE	PATTON	SATRAP	ACUMEN	CRUIVE
ANTHER	CATGUT	EXTOLL	LATELY	NETHER	PÉTAIN	SATURN	AGUISE	CRUMBS
ANTICS	CATHAR	EXTORT	LATENT	NETTLE	PETARD	SATYRA	AGUISH	CRUMEN
ANTLER	CATHAY	FATHER	LATEST	NITERY	PETARY	SETOSE	AGUIZE	CRUMMY
ANTLIA	CATKIN	FATHOM	LATHER	NITRIC	PETERS	SETTEE	ALUDEL	CRUNCH
ANTONY	CATNAP	FATIMA	LATONA	NITRYL	PETIPA	SETTER	ALUMNI	CRURAL
ANTRIM	CATNIP	FATTEN	LATRON	NITWIT	PETITE	SETTLE	AMULET	CRUSET
ANTRUM	CATSUP	FETISH	LATTEN	NOTARY	PETREL	SHTCHI	AMUSED	CRUSOE
ARTAUD	CATTLE	FETTER	LATTER	NOTATE	PETROL	SHTETL	ANUBIS	CRUSTA
ARTERY	CETERA	FETTES	LATVIA	NOTICE	PITMAN	SITCOM	ANURAN	CRUSTY
ARTFUL	CITRIC	FETTLE	LETHAL	NOTIFY	PITTED	SITREP	AOUDAD	CRUTCH
ARTHUR	CITRIN	FITFUL	LETOUT	NOTION	PITTER	SITTER	AQUILA	DAUDET
ARTIST	CITRON	FITOUT	LETTER	NUTANT		SUTLER	AVULSE	DOUANE

DOUBLE	JAUNTY	SAUGER	TOUCAN	HAVENT	SEVERE	JAWBOX	BOXCAR	HOYDEN
DOUBLY	KLUDGE	SAURIA	TOUCHE	HAVERS	SEVERN	JEWELS	BOXING	JOYFUL
DOUCET	KOUROS	SCULPT	TOUCHY	HAVING	SEVERY	JEWESS	DEXTER	JOYOUS
DOUCHE	KRUGER	SCUMMY	TOUPEE	INVADE	SÈVRES	JEWISH	EUXINE	KEYNES
DOUGHY	KRUMAN	SCUNGE	TOUPET	INVENT	SOVIET	KEWPIE	FIXITY	KEYPAD
DOURLY	KYUSHU	SCURRY	TOURER	INVERT	TAVERN	KOWTOW	HEXANE	KEYWAY
DRUDGE	LAUDER	SCURVY	TOUSER	INVEST	TEVIOT	LAWFUL	HEXOSE	KHYBER
ECURIE	LAUNCE	SCUTCH	TOUSLE	INVITE	TIVOLI	LAWMAN	HUXLEY	LAYARD
ELUANT	LAUNCH	SCUTUM	TRUANT	INVOKE	TUVALU	LAWYER	LAXIST	LAYERS
ELUATE	LAUREL	SCUZZY	TRUDGE	IRVING	UNVEIL	LEWDLY	LAXITY	LAYING
ELUTOR	LAURIC	SEUMAS	TRUISM	JOVIAL	VIVACE	LOWBOY	LEXEME	LAYMAN
EMULGE	LAURIE	SEURAT	TRUMAN	KEVLAR	VIVIAN	LOWELL	LUXATE	LAYOFF
EMUNGE	LOUCHE	SHUDRA	TRUMPS	LAVABO	VIVIEN	LOWEST	LUXURY	LAYOUT
EPULIS	LOUDEN	SHUFTI	TRUNKS	LAVAGE	WAVELL	LOWKEY	MAXIMS	LEYDEN
EQUALS	LOUDLY	SHUFTY	TRUSTY	LAVISH	WAVING	MAWKIN	MEXICO	LOYOLA
EQUANT	LOUNGE	SKURRY	TRUTHS	LEVANT	WIVERN	MOWING	ROXANE	MAYBUG
EQUATE	LOURIE	SLUDGE	UNUSED	LEVITE	WYVERN	NEWELL	SAXONY	MAYDAY
EQUINE	LOUVER	SLUICE	USURER	LEVITY	XAVIER	NEWEST	SEXISM	MAYFLY
EQUIPE	LOUVRE	SLUMMY	VAUNCE	LIVELY	ALWAYS	NEWMAN	SEXIST	MAYHEM
EQUITY	MAUGRE	SLURRY	ZEUGMA	LIVERY	ASWARM	NEWTON	SEXTAN	NOYADE
EVULSE	MAUNDY	SLUSHY	ZOUAVE	LIVING	BAWBEE	NOWISE	SEXTET	NOYOUS
FAUCES	MAUSER	SMUDGE	ZOUNDS	LOVAGE	BEWAIL	ONWARD	SEXTON	OXYGEN
FAUCET	MOUJIK	SMUDGY	ADVENE	LOVELL	BEWARE	ORWELL	SEXUAL	PAYDAY
FAULTY	MOULDY	SMUGLY	ADVENT	LOVELY	BOWELS	OSWALD	TAXEME	PAYING
FAUNUS	MOULIN	SMUTTY	ADVERB	LOVING	BOWERY	PAWNEE	TAXING	PAYNIM
FEUDAL	MOUSER	SNUDGE	ADVERT	MOVIES	BOWFIN	PAWPAW	TAXMAN	PAYOFF
FLUENT	MOUSEY	SNUGLY	ADVICE	MOVING	BOWLED	PEWTER	TUXEDO	PAYOLA
FLUFFY	MOUSSE	SOUGHT	ADVISE	NAVAHO	BOWLER	POWDER	WAXING	PEYOTE
FLUNKY	MOUTAN	SOUPER	ASVINA	NAVAJO	BOWMAN	POWERS	ABYDOS	PHYLLO
FLURRY	MOUTER	SOUPLE	BOVATE	NEVADA	BOWSER	POWNIE	AMYCUS	PHYLUM
FLUSHY	MOUTON	SOURCE	BOVINE	NIVOSE	BOWWOW	POWTER	AMYTAL	PHYSIC
FLUTED	NAUGHT	SOURLY	BOVRIL	NOVENA	BYWORD	POWWOW	ANYHOW	PHYSIO
FLUTER	NAUSEA	SOUSED	CAVEAT	NOVIAL	COWAGE	REWARD	ANYONE	PLYING
FLUTES	NAUTCH	SOUTER	CAVEIN	NOVICE	COWARD	REWIND	ANYWAY	PRYING
FOUGHT	NEURAL	SPUNGE	CAVELL	OBVERT	COWBOY	REWIRE	ASYLUM	PSYCHE
FOULLY	NEURON	SPURGE	CAVERN	PAVANE	COWMAN	REWORD	BAYARD	PSYCHO
FOURTH	NEUTER	SPUTUM	CAVITY	PAVING	COWPAT	REWORK	BAYEUX	RHYMER
FOUTRE	NOUGAT	SQUAIL	CAVORT	PAVLOV	COWPER	ROWING	BEYOND	RHYTHM
FRUGAL	NOUGHT	SQUALL	CAVOUR	RAVAGE	COWPOX	SAWDER	BOYISH	RIYADH
FRUICT	NOUNCE	SQUAMA	CIVICS	RAVINE	COWRIE	SAWNEY	BRYANT	ROYALS
FRUITS	OCULAR	SQUARE	CIVISM	RAVING	DAWDLE	SAWYER	BRYONY	SAYERS
FRUITY	OEUVRE	SQUASH	COVENT	RAVISH	DAWNEY	SEWAGE	BUYERS	SAYING
FRUMPY	PAUNCE	SQUAWK	COVERT	REVAMP	DAWSON	SEWELL	BUYING	SCYLLA
FRUTEX	PAUNCH	SQUEAK	COVING	REVEAL	DEWALI	SEWING	BUYOUT	SCYTHE
GAUCHE	PAUPER	SQUEAL	DEVEST	REVERE	DEWITT	SOWBUG	CAYMAN	SKYLAB
GAUCHO	PLUCKY	SQUILL	DEVICE	REVERS	DEWLAP	SOWING	CEYLON	SKYMAN
GAUFRE	PLUMED	SQUINT	DEVILS	REVERT	DIWALI	SOWSED	CHYPRE	SMYRNA
GAUGER	PLUMMY	SQUIRE	DEVISE	REVERY	DOWNAY	SOWTER	COYOTE	SPYING
GIUSTO	PLUNGE	SQUIRM	DEVOID	RÊVEUR	DOWNER	TAWDRY	CRYING	STYLET
GLUMPS	PLURAL	SQUIRT	DEVOTE	REVIEW	DOWSER	TAWPIE	CRYPTO	STYLUS
GLUTEN	PLUTUS	SQUISH	DEVOUR	REVILE	DOWSET	THWACK	DAYBED	STYMIE
GOUNOD	POUDRE	STUART	DEVOUT	REVISE	DOWSON	THWART	DIYARI	STYRAX
GOURDE	POUFFE	STUBBS	DIVALI	REVIVE	EDWARD	TOWAGE	DOYLEY	THYMOL
GOURDS	POUNCE	STUBBY	DIVEHI	REVOKE	ENWRAP	TOWARD	DRYDEN	THYMUS
GOUTTE	POUNDS	STUCCO	DIVERS	REVOLT	FAWKES	TOWBAR	DRYING	THYRSE
GRUBBY	POURER	STUDIO	DIVERT	RIVAGE	FEWEST	TOWHEE	EEYORE	TOYISH
GRUDGE	POUTER	STUFFY	DIVEST	RIVERA	FOWLER	TOWNEE	ELYSEE	TRYING
GRUMPH	PRUNER	STUMER	DIVIDE	RIVLIN	GAWAIN	TOWNLY	ETYMON	UNYOKE
GRUMPS	PRUSIK	STUMPS	DIVINE	ROVING	GEWGAW	TOWSER	FLYING	VOYAGE
GRUMPY	RAUNCH	STUMPY	DIVING	SAVAGE	HAWAII	TSWANA	FRYING	VOYEUR
GRUNDY	REUBEN	STUPID	FAVELA	SAVANT	HAWKED	UNWARY	GEYSER	WAYLAY
GRUNGE	REUTER	STUPOR	FAVISM	SAVATE	HAWKER	UNWELL	GLYCOL	WAYOUT
GRUTCH	ROUBLE	STURDY	FAVOSE	SAVING	HAWSER	UNWIND	GRYFON	WHYDAH
HAUNCH	ROUGED	TAUGHT	FAVOUR	SAVIOR	HOWARD	UNWISE	GUYANA	BAZAAR
HOUDAH	ROUGHY	TAURUS	GAVAGE	SAVOIE	HOWDAH	UNWRAP	HAYBOX	BEZANT
HOUNDS	ROUNCE	TAUTEN	GAVIAL	SAVORY	HOWDIE	UPWARD	HAYDON	BEZOAR
HOURLY	ROUNDS	TAUTLY	GIVING	SAVOUR	HOWLER	VOWELS	HAYLEY	BEZZLE
HOUSES	ROUTER	TAUTOG	GOVERN	SAVVEY	INWARD	WOWSER	HAYMOW	BUZFUZ
IGUANA	SAUCER	TEUTON	HAVANA	SEVENS	IRWELL	BAXTER	HEYDAY	BUZZER

COZIER	AFRAID	BICARB	DEBASE	ERRANT	IMPAWN	MARAUD	PAHARI	RETAKE
DAZZLE	AGHAST	BIGAMY	DEBATE	ERSATZ	INCASE	MASADA	PALACE	RETARD
DIZAIN	AGLAIA	BINARY	DECADE	ESCAPE	INDABA	MENACE	PALAIS	REVAMP
DOZENS	AGNAIL	BINATE	DECAFF	ESCARP	INFAME	MENAGE	PALATE	REWARD
DOZING	AGNATE	BLEACH	DECAMP	ESPADA	INFAMY	MESAIL	PANADA	RIBALD
ECZEMA	AIDANT	BLEARY	DECANE	ESTATE	INFANT	METAGE	PANAMA	RIBAND
ENZIAN	ALBANY	BOCAGE	DECANI	ETHANE	INFARE	METATE	PAPACY	RIVAGE
ENZYME	ALKALI	BODACH	DECANT	EUTAXY	INGATE	MIKADO	PAPAGO	RIYADH
EOZOON	ALKANE	BOGART	DEDANS	EXHALE	INHALE	MILADY	PAPAYA	ROLAND
EVZONE	ALMAIN	BORAGE	DEFACE	EXPAND	INLAID	MIRAGE	PARADE	ROMANO
FIZGIG	ALPACA	BORANE	DEFAME	EXTANT	INLAND	MOHAIR	PARAMO	ROMANS
FIZZED	ALTAIR	BORATE	DELATE	FACADE	INLAWS	MOHAWK	PARANA	ROMANY
FIZZER	ALWAYS	BOTANY	DEMAIN	FARAND	INMATE	MOJAVE	PARAPH	ROSACE
FIZZLE	AMBAGE	BOVATE	DEMAND	FEMALE	INNATE	MONACO	PATACA	ROSARY
FUZZLE	AMHARA	BREACH	DEPART	FIGARO	INSANE	MORALE	PAVANE	ROTARY
GAZEBO	ANGARY	BREAST	DERAIL	FINALE	INTACT	MORALS	PEDALO	ROTATE
GAZUMP	ANKARA	BREATH	DERAIN	FORAGE	INTAKE	MORASS	PEDANT	ROXANE
GIZZEN	ANNALS	BRIAND	DETACH	FRIAND	INVADE	MOSAIC	PENANG	ROYALS
GUZZLE	APIARY	BRIARD	DETAIL	FRIARY	INWARD	MOZART	PESADE	SAFARI
HAZARD	APPALL	BROACH	DETAIN	FUGATO	ISLAND	MUCATE	PÉTAIN	SAHARA
HAZILY	ARCADE	BROADS	DEWALI	FULANI	ISRAEL	MURAGE	PETARD	SALAAM
HUZZAH	ARCADY	BRYANT	DICAST	FUMADO	ITHACA	MURALS	PETARY	SALADE
IZZARD	ARCANA	BUMALO	DILATE	FUSAIN	IZZARD	MUSANG	PHRASE	SALAMI
JAZZER	ARCANE	BUTANE	DISARM	GALANT	JACANA	MUTANT	PICARD	SALARY
KAZAKH	ARMADA	BYNAME	DIVALI	GALAXY	JUBATE	MUTATE	PILAFF	SAMARA
LAZILY	ARMAGH	BYPASS	DIWALI	GARAGE	JUMADA	MYGALE	PILAGE	SAVAGE
LIZARD	ARNAUT	CABALE	DIYARI	GAVAGE	JURANT	NAGANA	PILATE	SAVANT
LIZZIE	ARRACK	CAFARD	DIZAIN	GAWAIN	KABAKA	NAGARI	PIRACY	SAVATE
LUZERN	ARRANT	CALAIS	DOMAIN	GELADA	KAKAPO	NAPALM	PIRATE	SCLAFF
MAZOUT	ARTAUD	CAMAIL	DONATE	GELATE	KANAKA	NATANT	PISANO	SCRAMB
MAZUMA	ASGARD	CANAAN	DOPANT	GELATO	KARATE	NAVAHO	PLEACH	SCRAPE
MIZZEN	ASKARI	CANADA	DORADO	GITANO	KATANA	NAVAJO	PLEASE	SCRAPS
MIZZLE	ASLANT	CANAPÉ	DOSAGE	GOCART	KAZAKH	NEFAST	PLIANT	SCRAWL
MOZART	ASMARA	CANARD	DOTAGE	GOKART	KERALA	NEGATE	POLACK	SCRAWM
MOZZLE	ASSAIL	CANARY	DOTARD	GREASE	KIGALI	NEPALI	POLAND	SDEATH
MUZHIK	ASSART	CARAFE	DOUANE	GREASY	KINASE	NEVADA	POMACE	SEBATE
MUZZLE	ASTART	CERATE	DREAMY	GREATS	KUMARA	NOMADE	POMADE	SECANT
NOZZLE	ASWARM	CESARE	DREARY	GREAVE	LADAKH	NONAGE	POSADA	SEDATE
NUZZER	ATTACH	CHOANA	DURANT	GROATS	LANATE	NONARY	POTASH	SENATE
NUZZLE	ATTACK	CICADA	DYNAMO	GUIANA	LAVABO	NOTARY	POTATO	SERAIL
PUZZLE	ATTAIN	CICALA	DYNAST	GUYANA	LAVAGE	NOTATE	PREACE	SERANG
RAZURE	AUBADE	CLEAVE	EATAGE	GYRATE	LAYARD	NOYADE	PREACH	SERAPE
RAZZIA	AVIARY	CLOACA	ECHARD	HAMATE	LEGACY	NUTANT	PUPATE	SERAPH
RAZZLE	AVIATE	CLOAKS	ECLAIR	HARARE	LEGATE	NUTATE	QUEASY	SESAME
ROZZER	AYMARA	COBALT	EDWARD	HARASS	LEGATO	OBLAST	RABATO	SEWAGE
SIZZLE	AZRAEL	COMART	EFFACE	HAVANA	LEVANT	OBLATE	RAFALE	SHEARS
SOZZLE	BAHADA	COMATE	EIRANN	HAWAII	LIGASE	OBTAIN	RAVAGE	SHEATH
SYZYGY	BALAAM	CORALS	ELUANT	HAZARD	LIGATE	OCEANS	REBATE	SHEAVE
TIZWAZ	BAMAKO	COWAGE	ELUATE	HECATE	LIPARI	OCTANE	RECALL	SHRANK
VIZARD	BANANA	COWARD	EMBAIL	HERALD	LIPASE	OCTANS	RECANT	SILAGE
VIZIER	BASALT	CREACH	EMBALE	HEXANE	LITANY	OCTANT	RECAST	SLEAVE
WIZARD	BAYARD	CREAGH	EMBALM	HIDAGE	LIZARD	OCTAVE	REDACT	SLEAZE
WIZIER	BAZAAR	CREAKY	EMBARK	HIJACK	LOCALE	OCTAVO	REFACE	SLEAZY
YEZIDI	BECALM	CREAMY	ENCALM	HILARY	LOCATE	OLEATE	REGAIN	SLOANE
	BECAME	CREANT	ENCAMP	HOBART	LOVAGE	ONWARD	REGALE	SMEARY
6:4	BEDASH	CREASE	ENCASE	HOMAGE	LUGANO	OPIATE	REGARD	SMEATH
ABBACY	BEDAUB	CREATE	ENCASH	HORACE	LUNACY	ORDAIN	REHASH	SNEAKY
ABDABS	BEFALL	CRIANT	ENGAGE	HOTAIR	LUNARY	ORGANS	RELATE	SNEATH
ABLATE	BEHALF	CROAKY	ENLACE	HOWARD	LUNATE	ORGASM	REMAIN	SOCAGE
ABLAUT	BEHAVE	CUBAGE	ENRAGE	HUMANE	LUSAKA	ORIANO	REMAKE	SOLACE
ABLAZE	BEJADE	CURACY	ENRAPT	HYPATE	LUXATE	ORNATE	REMAND	SOLANO
ABOARD	BELAMY	CURARE	ENSATE	IGUANA	MADAME	OSWALD	REMARK	SOMALI
ABRADE	BENAME	CURARI	ENTAIL	IMBARN	MALAGA	OTTAVA	RENAME	SONANT
ACRAWL	BERATE	CURATE	EQUALS	IMBASE	MALATE	OTTAWA	REPAID	SONATA
ADNATE	BESANT	CYRANO	EQUANT	IMPACT	MALAWI	OURALI	REPAIR	SORAGE
AERATE	BETAKE	CYTASE	EQUATE	IMPAIR	MANAGE	OUTAGE	REPAST	SPLAKE
AFEARS	BEWAIL	DALASI	ERNANI	IMPALA	MANANA	OXGATE	RESALE	SPLASH
AFFAIR	BEWARE	DAMAGE	ERRAND	IMPALE	MANATI	OXTAIL	RETAIL	SPRAIN
AFLAME	BEZANT	DAMASK	ERRANT	IMPART	MARACA	PADANG	RETAIN	SPRANG

SPRAWL	UNPACK	BULBUL	GIBBET	NIMBLE	TREBLE	CLOCHE	LAICAL	SEICHE
SQUAIL	UNPAID	BUMBLE	GIBBON	NIMBLY	TREBLY	COCCID	LANCER	SHTCHI
SQUALL	UNSAFE	BURBLE	GIMBAL	NIMBUS	TRIBAL	COCCUS	LANCET	SITCOM
SQUAMA	UNSAID	BURBOT	GLIBLY	NOBBLE	TRIBES	COCCYX	LANCIA	SLACKS
SQUARE	UNWARY	BUSBOY	GLOBAL	NOBBUT	TULBAN	CONCHA	LASCAR	SLICER
SQUASH	UPCAST	BYEBYE	GOBBET	NUBBIN	TUMBLE	CONCHY	LITCHI	SMACKS
SQUAWK	UPDATE	CABBIE	GOBBLE	NUBBLE	TURBAN	CONCUR	LORCHA	SOCCER
STEADY	UPLAND	CAMBER	GOOBER	NUMBER	TURBID	CRÈCHE	LOUCHE	SPACED
STEAMY	UPRATE	CARBON	GRABEN	NUMBLY	TURBOT	CROCHE	MADCAP	SPACER
STRABO	UPTAKE	CARBOY	GRUBBY	OJIBWA	TWOBIT	CROCKS	MANCHE	SPECIE
STRAFE	UPWARD	CASBAH	GUBBAH	OUTBAR	TYMBAL	CROCUS	MANCHU	SPICED
STRAIN	URBANE	CHIBOL	HAMBLE	OUTBID	UNABLE	CUSCUS	MARCEL	SPICER
STRAIT	USHANT	CHUBBY	HARBOR	OVIBOS	USABLE	CUTCHA	MASCOT	STACKS
STRAKE	VACANT	COBBER	HAYBOX	PEBBLE	VERBAL	DANCER	MENCAP	STICKS
STRAND	VACATE	COBBLE	HENBIT	PEBBLY	VIABLE	DEACON	MERCAT	STICKY
STRASS	VAGARY	COMBAT	HERBAL	PHOBIA	WAMBLE	DECCAN	MERCER	STOCKS
STRATA	VIRAGO	COMBED	HOBBES	PHOBIC	WARBLE	DESCRY	MERCIA	STOCKY
STRAWS	VISAGE	COMBER	HOBBLE	PHOBOS	WEBBED	DIACID	MESCAL	STUCCO
STRAWY	VITALS	COMBLE	HOMBRE	POBBLE	WETBOB	DISCUS	MINCER	SUCCOR
STUART	VIVACE	CORBEL	HOTBED	PROBIT	WIMBLE	DORCAS	MOBCAP	SUCCUS
SUDARY	VIZARD	CORBIE	HUBBLE	PUEBLO	WOBBLE	DOUCET	MOOCOW	SULCUS
SUDATE	VOLAGE	COWBOY	HUBBUB	QUEBEC	WOBBLY	DOUCHE	MOSCOW	SYNCOM
SUGARY	VOLANS	CRABBE	HUMBER	RABBET	WOMBAT	DRACHM	MUSCAT	TALCUM
SUMACH	VOLANT	CRABBY	HUMBLE	RABBIT	YABBER	DULCET	MUSCLE	TARCEL
SWEATY	VOTARY	CRIBLE	HUMBUG	RABBLE	ZAMBIA	DUNCAN	NIACIN	TEACUP
TABARD	VOYAGE	CUMBER	IAMBIC	RAGBAG	ZOMBIE	DUNCES	NONCOM	TERCET
TAMALE	WABASH	CYMBAL	IAMBUS	RAMBLE	ABACUS	EGGCUP	NUNCIO	TERCIO
TAMANU	WIZARD	DABBLE	IBIBIO	RATBAG	ACACIA	ELICIT	OBECHE	TETCHY
TAMARA	WREATH	DAYBED	ICEBOX	REEBOK	ALACUS	ELTCHI	OFFCUT	THECAL
TAMARI	XANADU	DIBBER	ISABEL	REUBEN	ALECTO	EPICAL	OILCAN	THICKY
TATAMI	YUKATA	DIBBLE	ISOBAR	RIBBED	AMYCUS	EXOCET	ORACHE	TIPCAT
TENACE	ZAPATA	DISBAR	JABBER	RIBBLE	APACHE	FAECAL	ORACLE	TITCHY
TENANT	ZENANA	DISBUD	JABBLE	RIBBON	APICAL	FAECES	OUNCES	TOECAP
TETANY	ZOUAVE	DJEBEL	JAMBOK	ROBBED	ASHCAN	FALCON	OUTCRY	TOMCAT
THEAVE	AIRBED	DOBBIN	JAMBON	ROBBER	ATOCIA	FARCIN	OWLCAR	TOUCAN
THRALL	AIRBUS	DOUBLE	JAWBOX	ROUBLE	AVOCET	FASCES	PARCAE	TOUCHE
THRASH	ANABAS	DOUBLY	JERBOA	RUBBED	BACCHI	FASCIA	PARCEL	TOUCHY
THRAWN	ANUBIS	DUBBIN	JIBBAH	RUBBER	BAUCIS	FAUCES	PASCAL	TRACER
THWACK	ARABIA	DUMBLY	JOBBER	RUBBLE	BEACHY	FAUCET	PATCHY	TRICAR
THWART	ARABIC	DUNBAR	JUBBAH	RUBBRA	BEACON	FENCER	PENCEL	TRICKS
TIRADE	ARABIS	DURBAR	JUMBAL	RUMBLE	BISCAY	FESCUE	PENCIL	TRICKY
TIRANA	ARABLE	DYBBUK	JUMBLE	SAMBAL	BITCHY	FIACRE	PIECES	TRICOT
TISANE	ATABAL	EDIBLE	KASBAH	SAMBAR	BLACKS	FISCAL	PINCER	TROCAR
TOBAGO	ATABEG	ENABLE	KHYBER	SAMBUR	BLOCKS	FLACON	PISCES	TROCHE
TOMATO	AUMBRY	EREBUS	KIBBLE	SCABBY	BOBCAT	FLECHE	PLACED	TUSCAN
TONANT	BABBIT	FAIBLE	KIRBEH	SEABEE	BOUCHE	FLICKS	PLACER	TWICER
TOWAGE	BABBLE	FEEBLE	KITBAG	SERBIA	BOUCLÉ	FORÇAT	PLACID	URACIL
TOWARD	BALBOA	FEEBLY	KNOBBY	SHABBY	BOXCAR	FORCED	PLUCKY	VELCRO
TREATY	BAMBOO	FIBBED	LAMBDA	SINBAD	BRACER	FORCES	PONCHO	VISCID
TRIAGE	BAOBAB	FIBBER	LESBOS	SOMBER	BRACES	FRACAS	PRECIS	VOICED
TRUANT	BARBED	FIMBRA	LIABLE	SOMBRE	BRECHT	GARÇON	PRICED	VULCAN
TSWANA	BARBEL	FLABBY	LIBBER	SORBET	BRICKS	GASCON	PRICEY	WARCRY
TUCANA	BARBER	FOGBOW	LIEBIG	SOWBUG	BUCCAL	GAUCHE	PSYCHE	WHACKO
TUVALU	BARBET	FOIBLE	LIMBED	STABLE	BUNCHY	GAUCHO	PSYCHO	WHACKY
TYBALT	BAUBLE	FORBID	LIMBER	STABLY	CACCIA	GLACIS	PUNCHY	YOICKS
TYRANT	BAWBEE	FUMBLE	LIMBIC	STUBBS	CAECUM	GLYCOL	PUNCTO	ZIRCON
ULLAGE	BENBOW	GABBLE	LISBON	STUBBY	CALCED	GRACES	QUICHE	ABADAN
UMLAUT	BERBER	GABBRO	LOWBOY	SWABIA	CANCEL	GROCER	RANCEL	ABYDOS
UNCAGE	BOBBER	GAMBET	LUBBER	SYMBOL	CANCER	HICCUP	RANCHO	ACADIA
UNDATE	BOBBIN	GAMBIA	LUMBAR	TALBOT	CATCHY	HONCHO	RANCID	ACEDIA
UNEASE	BOBBLE	GAMBIT	LUMBER	TEABAG	CAUCUS	ICECAP	RANCOR	ACIDIC
UNEASY	BOMBAY	GAMBLE	MARBLE	THEBAN	CERCAL	ICICLE	RASCAL	AGADIR
UNFAIR	BOMBER	GAMBOL	MAYBUG	THEBES	CERCUS	IPECAC	REDCAP	ALUDEL
UNGAIN	BOMBYX	GARBED	MEMBER	TIDBIT	CHICHI	JUICER	REDCAR	AMADOU
UNHAND	BONBON	GARBLE	MORBID	TIMBER	CHICLE	JUNCUS	RESCUE	AMIDOL
UNIATE	BOOBOO	GASBAG	MORBUS	TIMBRE	CHICON	KACCHA	ROSCID	AMIDST
UNLACE	BUBBLE	GERBIL	MUMBLE	TITBIT	CIRCLE	KITCAT	ROSCOE	ANADEM
UNMADE	BUBBLY	GHEBER	NEBBUK	TOMBOY	CIRCUS	KUCCHA	SANCHO	ANADYR
UNMASK	BULBIL	GIBBER	NIBBLE	TOWBAR	CLICHÉ	KWACHA	SAUCER	AOUDAD

ASADHA	DODDLE	HERDER	MILDLY	SENDER	WELDER	ARPENT	CHEERS	ENGELS
ASHDOD	DOODAD	HEYDAY	MINDED	SERDAB	WHYDAH	ARREAR	CHEERY	ENMESH
AVIDLY	DOODAH	HIDDEN	MINDEL	SHADED	WILDER	ARREST	CHEESE	ENSEAL
BALDER	DOODLE	HINDER	MINDER	SHADES	WILDLY	ARSÈNE	CHEESY	EOCENE
BALDLY	DREDGE	HOBDAY	MOIDER	SHADOW	WINDER	ARTERY	CICELY	EPHEBE
BANDAR	DRUDGE	HODDER	MONDAY	SHADUF	WINDOW	ASCEND	CICERO	ESSENE
BANDIT	DRYDEN	HOIDEN	MUDDER	SHODDY	WINDUP	ASCENT	CINEMA	ESTEEM
BANDOG	DUDDER	HOLDER	MUDDLE	SHUDRA	WISDEN	ASLEEP	CLIENT	ETHENE
BEADED	DUMDUM	HOLDUP	MURDER	SIDDHA	WISDOM	ASPECT	COGENT	EUGENE
BEADLE	DUNDEE	HOODED	NANDOO	SINDER	WONDER	ASSENT	COHERE	EUREKA
BEDDER	DUNDER	HOUDAH	NEEDED	SIRDAR	WOODED	ASSERT	COLEUS	EXCEED
BENDED	DYADIC	HOWDAH	NEEDLE	SKIDOO	WOODEN	ASSESS	COMEDO	EXCEPT
BENDER	ELODEA	HOWDIE	NEEDNT	SLEDGE	WOODIE	ASSETS	COMEDY	EXCESS
BIDDER	ENODAL	HUDDLE	NODDED	SLIDER	YARDIE	ASTERN	COMELY	EXPECT
BINDER	ERODED	HURDLE	NODDLE	SLUDGE	YONDER	ATHENA	COPECK	EXPEDE
BIRDIE	EXEDRA	HYADES	NOODLE	SMUDGE	ZANDER	ATHENE	COVENT	EXPEND
BLUDGE	EXODUS	IBADAN	NORDIC	SMUDGY	ZENDIK	ATHENS	COVERT	EXPERT
BOLDLY	FARDEL	IBIDEM	NUMDAH	SNUDGE	ABBESS	ATTEND	CREEPS	EXSERT
BONDED	FARDLE	JORDAN	OGADEN	SODDEN	ABJECT	ATTEST	CREEPY	EXTEND
BONDER	FEEDER	JUDDER	ONEDIN	SOLDER	ABREGE	AUGEAN	CREESE	EXTENT
BOODLE	FENDER	KEDDAH	OUNDLE	SORDES	ABSEIL	AUREUS	CREESH	EXTERN
BORDAR	FEUDAL	KENDAL	PADDED	SORDID	ABSENT	BAKERS	CRUELS	FAVELA
BORDER	FIDDLE	KIDDIE	PADDLE	SPADES	ACCEDE	BAKERY	CUNEAL	FEWEST
BRIDAL	FIDDLY	KIDDLE	PAIDUP	SPADIX	ACCEND	BALEEN	CYBELE	FINELY
BRIDGE	FINDER	KINDER	PANDER	SPIDER	ACCENT	BARÈGE	CYRENE	FINERY
BRIDIE	FLEDGE	KINDLE	PANDIT	STODGE	ACCEPT	BARELY	DALETH	FINEST
BRIDLE	FODDER	KINDLY	PARDIE	STODGY	ACCESS	BATEAU	DECEIT	FLEECE
BUDDHA	FOLDED	KLUDGE	PARDON	STUDIO	ACHENE	BAYEUX	DECENT	FLEECY
BUNDLE	FOLDER	KOODOO	PAYDAY	SUBDUE	ACKERS	BEDECK	DEFEAT	FLUENT
BURDEN	FONDLE	LADDER	PEDDER	SUDDEN	ADDEEM	BEHEAD	DEFECT	FOMENT
CADDIE	FONDLY	LADDIE	PEDDLE	SUNDAE	ADDEND	BEHELD	DEFEND	FOREDO
CADDIS	FONDUE	LANDAU	PERDUE	SUNDAY	ADHERE	BEHEST	DEJECT	FOREGO
CAMDEN	FRIDAY	LANDED	PIDDLE	SUNDER	ADVENE	BEMEAN	DELETE	FOREST
CANDID	FRIDGE	LANDER	PIEDOG	SUNDEW	ADVENT	BEREFT	DEMEAN	FREELY
CANDLE	FUDDLE	LANDOR	PINDAR	SUNDRY	ADVERB	BESEEM	DEMENT	FREEZE
CANDOR	FUNDED	LAPDOG	PLEDGE	SWEDEN	ADVERT	BICEPS	DEPEND	FRIEND
CARDAN	FUNDUS	LARDER	POLDER	SYNDIC	AEGEAN	BIDENT	DESERT	FRIEZE
CAUDEX	GANDER	LARDON	PONDER	TANDEM	AEGEUS	BIREME	DETECT	FUREUR
CAUDLE	GANDHI	LAUDER	POODLE	TARDIS	AENEID	BISECT	DETENT	FUSELI
CHADOR	GARDEN	LEADEN	POUDRE	TAWDRY	AFFECT	BODEGA	DETENU	GAIETY
CHEDER	GENDER	LEADER	POWDER	TENDER	AFIELD	BOLERO	DETEST	GALENA
CINDER	GIDDUP	LENDER	PUDDLE	TENDON	AFREET	BOLEYN	DEVEST	GALERE
COBDEN	GILDAS	LEWDLY	PUNDIT	TENDRE	AFRESH	BOREAS	DIGEST	GAMELY
CODDLE	GILDED	LEYDEN	PURDAH	TIDDLE	AFTERS	BOWELS	DINERO	GAMETE
COLDLY	GILDER	LIEDER	PYEDOG	TIDDLY	AGREED	BOWERY	DIRECT	GANESH
CONDOM	GIRDER	LINDEN	QUIDAM	TINDER	AGRÉGÉ	BREECH	DISEUR	GARETH
CONDOR	GIRDLE	LOADED	RADDLE	TODDLE	ALBEDO	BREEZE	DIVEHI	GATEAU
CORDON	GLADLY	LOADER	RAIDER	TRADER	ALBEIT	BREEZY	DIVERS	GAZEBO
CRADLE	GLIDER	LONDON	RANDOM	TRADES	ALBERT	BRIEFS	DIVERT	GENERA
CREDIT	GOLDEN	LORDLY	READER	TRUDGE	ALKENE	BUREAU	DIVEST	GENEVA
CUDDLE	GOODLY	LOUDEN	REDDEN	TUNDRA	ALLEGE	BUTENE	DOCENT	GERENT
CUDDLY	GORDON	LOUDLY	RENDER	VANDAL	ALLELE	BUYERS	DOLEUR	GIDEON
CULDEE	GRADED	MADDEN	RHODES	VEDDAH	ALLEYN	CADETS	DOZENS	GILEAD
CURDLE	GRADES	MADDER	RIDDLE	VENDEE	ALMERY	CAMERA	DRIEST	GLIÈRE
DADDLE	GRADUS	MAIDAN	ROADIE	VENDER	AMOEBA	CAREEN	DUDEEN	GOVERN
DAEDAL	GRUDGE	MAIDEN	RONDEL	VENDOR	AMPERE	CAREER	DUNELM	GREECE
DANDER	GUIDES	MALDON	RUDDER	VENDUE	ANDEAN	CAREME	DURESS	GREEDY
DANDLE	GUIDON	MAYDAY	RUDDLE	VERDIN	ANGELA	CARESS	EATERY	GREEKS
DAUDET	GUNDOG	MEADOW	RUNDLE	VERDUN	ANGELS	CASEIN	ECZEMA	GREENE
DAWDLE	HAGDEN	MEDDLE	SADDEN	VOIDED	ANGERS	CAVEAT	EFFECT	GREENS
DEADEN	HANDEL	MENDEL	SADDHU	VOIDEE	ANNEAL	CAVEIN	EFFETE	GRIEVE
DEADLY	HANDLE	MENDER	SADDLE	VOIDER	ANNEXE	CAVELL	EFTEST	HAVENT
DEIDRE	HARDEN	MENDES	SANDAL	VOODOO	ANSELM	CAVERN	EGBERT	HAVERS
DEODAR	HARDLY	MENDIP	SANDER	WADDLE	APIECE	CELERY	EGRESS	HEDERA
DIADEM	HAYDON	MIDDAY	SAWDER	WANDER	APPEAL	CEMENT	ELDERS	HELENA
DIDDLE	HEADED	MIDDEN	SEEDED	WANDLE	APPEAR	CEREAL	ELDEST	HEREBY
DIKDIK	HEADER	MIDDLE	SEEDER	WARDEN	APPEND	CEREUS	ELLERY	HEREIN
DIODON	HEEDED	MILDEW	SELDOM	WARDER	ARDENT	CETERA	EMBERS	HERERO
DODDER	HERDEN		SENDAL	WEDDED	ARGENT	CHEEKY	ENDEAR	HERESY

HERETO	LYCEUM	PHLEUM	SAFETY	STRESS	VINERY	FULFIL	TITFER	DARGLE
HETERO	MADEUP	PHOEBE	SAGELY	SUPERB	VOLENS	FURFUR	TOFFEE	DENGUE
HITECH	MAKEUP	PIGEON	SAMEKH	SURELY	VOWELS	FYLFOT	TRIFLE	DERGUE
HOMELY	MANEGE	PILEUM	SANELY	SURETÉ	VOYEUR	GADFLY	TUFFET	DIGGER
HONEST	MERELY	PILEUP	SAPELE	SURETY	WADERS	GAFFER	USEFUL	DINGHY
HUGELY	METEOR	PILEUS	SATEEN	SWEENY	WATERS	GAUFRE	WAFFLE	DINGLE
HUMECT	MISÈRE	PIMENT	SAYERS	SWEETS	WATERY	GOFFER	WILFUL	DINGLY
HYAENA	MISERY	PINEAL	SCHEMA	TALENT	WAVELL	GOLFER	WOEFUL	DODGEM
IMPEDE	MODELS	PINERO	SCHEME	TAMELY	WERENT	GRAFIN	YAFFLE	DODGER
IMPEND	MODENA	PIRENE	SCLERA	TATERS	WHEELS	GRYFON	ADAGIO	DOGGED
INCEDE	MODERN	PLIERS	SCLERE	TAVERN	WHEELY	GUFFAW	AIRGUN	DOGGER
INCEPT	MODEST	POMELO	SCREAM	TAXEME	WHEEZE	HEIFER	ALEGAR	DONGLE
INCEST	MOIETY	PONENT	SCREED	TELEDU	WHEEZY	HOOFED	ALIGHT	DOUGHY
INDEED	MOLECH	POPEYE	SCREEN	TELEGA	WIDELY	HOOFER	ALOGIA	DRAGEE
INDENT	MOLEST	POSEUR	SCREWY	TELEGU	WIFELY	IREFUL	APOGEE	DRAGON
INFECT	MOMENT	POTEEN	SECEDE	TEREDO	WIGEON	JOYFUL	ARAGON	DREGGY
INFEST	MOREEN	POTENT	SELECT	TERESA	WIPERS	KAFFER	BADGER	DROGUE
INGEST	MUSEUM	POWERS	SELENE	TERETE	WISELY	KAFFIR	BANGER	EMIGRÉ
INHERE	MUTELY	PRIEST	SEMELE	THIERS	WIVERN	LAFFER	BANGLE	ENIGMA
INJECT	MYSELF	PURELY	SENECA	THIEVE	WOMENS	LAWFUL	BANGUI	EPIGON
INMESH	NAMELY	PUTEAL	SERENE	THREAD	WYVERN	LOAFER	BARGEE	EXOGEN
INSECT	NAPERY	PYRENE	SEVENS	THREAP	XYLENE	LOOFAH	BEAGLE	FAGGED
INSERT	NASEBY	QUEENS	SEVERE	THREAT	YEMENI	MAFFIA	BEEGHA	FAGGOT
INTEND	NEBECK	RACEME	SEVERN	THRENE	ZEBECK	MANFUL	BEGGAR	FANGLE
INTENT	NEPETA	RAMEAU	SEVERY	THRESH	ARAFAT	MAYFLY	BENGAL	FIDGET
INTERN	NEREID	RAREFY	SEWELL	TIMELY	ARMFUL	MISFIT	BERGEN	FINGAL
INVENT	NEREUS	RARELY	SHEENY	TOLEDO	ARTFUL	MUFFET	BIGGER	FINGER
INVERT	NEWELL	REBECK	SHEERS	TORERO	BAFFIN	MUFFIN	BIGGIN	FIZGIG
INVEST	NEWEST	RECEDE	SHEETS	TUBERS	BAFFLE	MUFFLE	BLIGHT	FLAGGY
IRWELL	NICELY	RECENT	SHIELD	TUMEFY	BAGFUL	OLEFIN	BODGER	FLAGON
ISLETS	NICENE	RECESS	SHREWD	TUPELO	BELFRY	OUTFIT	BODGIE	FLIGHT
ITSELF	NICETY	REDEEM	SHTETL	TUREEN	BIFFIN	PANFRY	BOGGLE	FORGED
JACENT	NINETY	REDEYE	SILENE	TUXEDO	BOFFIN	PIAFFE	BOOGIE	FORGER
JEREMY	NITERY	REFECT	SILENT	TWEEDS	BOUFFE	PIFFLE	BORGIA	FORGET
JEWELS	NOCENT	REGENT	SIMEON	TWEEDY	BOWFIN	PILFER	BOUGHT	FORGOT
JEWESS	NOVENA	REGEST	SINEWY	TWEENY	BUFFER	POUFFE	BREGMA	FOUGHT
JOSEPH	OBJECT	REHEAT	SLEEKY	TWEEZE	BUFFET	PREFAB	BRIGHT	FRAGOR
KABELE	OBSESS	REHEEL	SLEEPY	UBIETY	BUFFON	PREFER	BROGAN	FRIGGA
KEBELE	OBTECT	REJECT	SLEEVE	UCKERS	BUZFUZ	PREFIX	BROGUE	FRIGHT
KOREAN	OBTEND	RELENT	SLEEZY	ULCERS	CARFAX	PROFIT	BUDGET	FRIGID
KUMERA	OBVERT	REMEDY	SNEEZE	UNBEND	CEEFAX	PUFFED	BUGGER	FRUGAL
LAMEDH	OCKERS	RENEGE	SNEEZY	UNBENT	CHAFER	PUFFER	BULGAR	FULGID
LAMELY	OEDEMA	REPEAL	SOBEIT	UNDECK	CHUFFY	PUFFIN	BULGER	FUNGAL
LAMENT	OFFEND	REPEAT	SOLEIL	UNLESS	CLIFFS	RAFFIA	BUNGAY	FUNGUS
LATEEN	OGRESS	REPENT	SOLELY	UNMEET	COFFEE	RAFFLE	BUNGEE	GADGET
LATELY	OILERS	REREAD	SOLEMN	UNREAD	COFFER	REEFER	BUNGLE	GAGGLE
LATENT	ORDEAL	RESEAU	SOLENT	UNREAL	COFFIN	RIFFLE	BURGEE	GANGER
LATEST	ORDERS	RESECT	SOLERA	UNREEL	COMFIT	ROOFER	BURGER	GANGES
LAYERS	ORGEAT	RESEDA	SOLEUS	UNREST	CONFAB	RUEFUL	BURGLE	GANGLY
LEGEND	ORIENT	RESENT	SORELL	UNSEAM	CONFER	RUFFLE	CADGER	GANGUE
LEXEME	ORNERY	REVEAL	SORELY	UNSEAT	CRAFTY	SAMFOO	CANGUE	GARGET
LIBERO	ORRERY	REVERE	SPEECH	UNSEEN	CRUFTS	SELFED	CATGUT	GARGLE
LIGETI	ORTEGA	REVERS	SPEEDO	UNSENT	CUFFEE	SHIFTY	CAUGHT	GAUGER
LIKELY	ORWELL	REVERT	SPEEDY	UNSEXY	CUFFIN	SHOFAR	CHIGOE	GEIGER
LINEAL	OSBERT	REVERY	SPHENE	UNVEIL	CUPFUL	SHUFTI	CLAGGY	GEWGAW
LINEAR	OSIERY	RÊVEUR	SPHERE	UNWELL	CURFEW	SIFFLE	CODGER	GIGGLE
LINEUP	OSTEND	RIDENT	SPLEEN	UPBEAT	DEAFEN	SINFUL	COGGER	GILGAI
LIVELY	OTHERS	RIVERA	SPLENT	UPHELD	DIFFER	SNIFFY	CONGEE	GINGER
LIVERY	OXHEAD	ROBERT	SPREAD	UPKEEP	DOOFER	SNIFTY	CONGER	GINGKO
LONELY	PAMELA	RODENT	SQUEAK	URGENT	DRAFTY	SOFFIT	COUGAR	GLAGOL
LORETO	PAPERS	ROKEBY	SQUEAL	VALENS	DUFFEL	STAFFA	CRAGGY	GOGGLE
LOVELL	PAPERY	ROPERY	STEELE	VALETA	DUFFER	STIFLE	CUDGEL	GOOGIE
LOVELY	PARENT	ROSERY	STEELY	VARECH	DUFFLE	STUFFY	DAGGER	GOOGLE
LOWELL	PARETO	RUBENS	STEERS	VARESE	EARFUL	SUFFER	DAGGLE	GOOGOL
LOWEST	PAREVE	RUDELY	STREAK	VELETA	EIFFEL	SUFFIX	DANGER	GORGED
LUCENT	PATENT	RUPEES	STREAM	VENEER	EYEFUL	SULFUR	DANGLE	GORGES
LUTEAL	PESETA	RUPERT	STREET	VENERY	FILFOT	SURFER		GORGET
LUTEIN	PETERS	SABELE	STREGA	VEREIN	FITFUL	TIFFIN		GORGIA
LUZERN	PHLEGM	SAFELY	STRENE	VILELY	FLUFFY			

GORGIO	MONGER	SORGHO	BATHER	JOSHUA	RODHAM	ALBITE	BODICE	COZIER
GORGON	MONGOL	SOUGHT	BATHOS	KEPHIR	ROTHER	ALCINA	BODIES	CRUISE
GRIGRI	MORGAN	SPIGOT	BETHEL	KISHKE	ROTHKO	ALDINE	BODILY	CRUIVE
GROGGY	MORGEN	STAGER	BISHOP	KOSHER	RUCHED	ALLIED	BOEING	CRYING
GUGGLE	MORGUE	STAGEY	BOOHOO	LACHES	RUSHED	ALLIER	BOLIDE	CUBICA
GUNGHO	MUGGER	STIGMA	BOTHAM	LASHED	SACHET	ALLIUM	BONITO	CUBISM
GURGLE	MYOGEN	STOGIE	BOTHER	LASHER	SAPHAR	ALPINE	BORING	CUBIST
HAGGAI	NAUGHT	TAIGLE	BOTHIE	LATHER	SASHAY	ALPINO	BOVINE	CUEIST
HAGGIS	NIDGET	TANGLE	BRAHMA	LECHER	SIGHTS	AMMINE	BOXING	CURIET
HAGGLE	NIGGER	TARGET	BRAHMS	LETHAL	SIPHON	AMNION	BOYISH	CURIUM
HANGAR	NIGGLE	TARGUM	BUCHAN	LICHEN	SOPHIA	ANCILE	BRAINS	CYNIPS
HANGER	NIGGLY	TAUGHT	BUSHED	LIGHTS	SUNHAT	ANGICO	BRAINY	DANIEL
HANGUP	NILGAI	TEAGUE	BUSHEL	LITHIA	SYPHER	ANGINA	BRAISE	DANISH
HEIGHT	NILGAU	TENGKU	CACHET	LOCHIA	SYPHON	ANOINT	BRUISE	DARIEN
HINGED	NOGGIN	TERGUM	CACHOU	LUTHER	TECHNO	ANTICS	BULIMY	DARING
HINGES	NOUGAT	TINGED	CASHEW	LYCHEE	TEPHRA	AORIST	BUNION	DARIUS
HOGGAR	NOUGHT	TINGLE	CATHAR	MASHAM	TETHER	APLITE	BURIAL	DATING
HOGGET	NUGGAR	TOGGED	CATHAY	MASHED	TETHYS	APPIAN	BURIED	DATIVE
HUNGER	NUGGET	TOGGLE	CIPHER	MASHER	TIGHTS	AQUILA	BUSILY	DEBILE
HUNGRY	ONAGER	TONGAN	COCHIN	MASHIE	TISHRI	ARGIVE	BUYING	DECIDE
IMOGEN	ONAGRA	TONGUE	COSHER	MATHIS	TOPHUS	ARNICA	BYLINE	DÉCIME
JAEGER	ONEGIN	TRAGIC	CUSHAT	MAYHEM	TOSHER	AROINT	CAGILY	DEFILE
JAGGED	OREGON	TRAGUS	CYPHER	MENHIR	TOWHEE	ARRIAN	CAHIER	DEFINE
JAGGER	ORIGEN	TRIGON	DAPHNE	METHOD	TYPHUS	ARRIVE	CALICO	DELIAN
JANGLE	ORIGIN	TURGID	DASHED	METHYL	UNSHOD	ARSINE	CALIMA	DELICE
JARGON	OUTGAS	TWIGGY	DERHAM	MIGHTY	UPSHOT	ARTIST	CALIPH	DELICT
JIGGER	OXYGEN	TWIGHT	DIRHAM	MISHAP	URCHIN	ASCIAN	CAMION	DELISH
JIGGLE	PARGET	VALGUS	DISHED	MISHIT	VATHEK	ASCIUS	CAMISE	DELIUS
JINGAL	PIDGIN	VERGER	DISHES	MOTHER	VISHNU	ASHINE	CANINE	DEMISE
JINGLE	PINGER	VERGES	DITHER	MUZHIK	WADHAM	ASKING	CANING	DEMIST
JOGGER	PISGAH	VIRGIL	DURHAM	MYTHOS	WARHOL	ASPIRE	CAPIAS	DENIAL
JOGGLE	PLAGAL	VIRGIN	EIGHTH	NEPHEW	WASHED	ASSIGN	CARIES	DENIED
JUDGES	PLAGUE	VOSGES	EIGHTY	NETHER	WASHER	ASSIST	CARINA	DENIER
JUGGER	PLIGHT	VULGAR	EITHER	NIGHTS	WETHER	ASSIZE	CARING	DENIMS
JUGGLE	PONGEE	VULGUS	ELOHIM	NIGHTY	WISHES	ASVINA	CASING	DEPICT
JUNGLE	PONGID	WAGGLE	EOTHEN	ORCHID	WITHAL	ATKINS	CASINO	DERIDE
KANGHA	PORGIE	WAGGON	ESCHAR	ORCHIS	WITHER	ATRIAL	CAVITY	DERIVE
KINGLY	PRAGUE	WANGLE	ESCHEW	ORPHAN	WITHIN	ATRIDE	CECILS	DESIGN
KNAGGY	QUAGGA	WEDGED	ESTHER	ORPHIC	ZEPHYR	ATRIUM	CECITY	DESIRE
KNIGHT	RAGGED	WEDGIE	ETCHER	PAKHTI	ZITHER	ATTILA	CELIAC	DESIST
KRUGER	RAGGLE	WEIGHT	EUCHRE	PAKHTO	ZOPHAR	ATTIRE	CERISE	DEVICE
LAAGER	RANGER	WIDGET	FATHER	PAKHTU	ABDIEL	AUDILE	CERIUM	DEVILS
LANGUR	REGGAE	WIGGLE	FATHOM	PAPHOS	ACHING	AUGITE	CESIUM	DEVISE
LEAGUE	RIDGED	WIGGLY	FISHER	PASHTO	ACTING	AURIGA	CHAINS	DEWITT
LEDGER	RIGGED	WINGED	FULHAM	PASHTU	ACTION	AUTISM	CHAIRS	DIMITY
LEGGED	RIGGER	WINGER	GATHER	PATHAN	ACTIUM	AWHILE	CHAISE	DINING
LENGTH	RINGED	WRIGHT	GOPHER	PATHIC	ACTIVE	AWNING	CHOICE	DIVIDE
LIGGER	RINGER	ZEUGMA	GOTHAM	PATHOS	ACUITY	BAKING	CHRISM	DIVINE
LINGER	ROTGUT	ZINGER	GOTHIC	PEAHEN	ADDICT	BANIAN	CHRIST	DIVING
LINGOT	ROUGED	AFGHAN	GRAHAM	PELHAM	ADMIRE	BANISH	CILICE	DOCILE
LODGED	ROUGHY	ALTHEA	GUSHER	PERHAP	ADRIAN	BARING	CILIUM	DOLINA
LODGER	RUGGED	ANCHOR	HACHIS	PESHWA	ADRIFT	BARIUM	CIVICS	DOLINE
LOGGER	RUGGER	ANTHEM	HASHED	POTHER	ADVICE	BASICS	CIVISM	DOLIUM
LOGGIA	SAGGAR	ANTHER	HEEHAW	PUSHER	ADVISE	BEHIND	CLAIMS	DOMINO
LONGER	SARGUS	ANYHOW	HIGHER	PUSHTU	AEDILE	BELIAL	CODIFY	DORIAN
LUGGER	SAUGER	ARCHED	HIGHUP	PUSHUP	AEGINA	BELIEF	CODING	DOTING
MAGGIE	SHAGGY	ARCHER	HITHER	PYTHIA	AERIAL	BELIKE	COMICE	DOZING
MAGGOT	SHOGUN	ARCHES	HOOHAH	PYTHON	AFFIRM	BELIZE	COMING	DRYING
MALGRE	SINGER	ARCHIE	HUGHES	RACHEL	AFRICA	BENIGN	COMITY	DURIAN
MANGER	SINGLE	ARCHIL	HUGHIE	RACHIS	AGEING	BENITO	CONICS	DURING
MANGLE	SINGLY	ARCHON	HUSHED	RAPHIA	AGUISE	BERING	COOING	DURION
MARGIN	SLIGHT	ARGHAN	HYPHAL	RASHER	AGUISH	BESIDE	COPIED	DYEING
MAUGRE	SLOGAN	ARNHEM	HYPHEN	RASHLY	AGUIZE	BETIDE	COPIER	EALING
MEAGER	SMEGMA	ARTHUR	INCHES	RATHER	AIKIDO	BETIME	COPING	EARING
MEAGRE	SMIGHT	ASCHAM	INCHON	RICHES	AILING	BETISE	CORIUM	EASIER
MERGER	SMUGLY	ASTHMA	ISCHIA	RICHLY	AIRILY	BIKINI	COSIER	EASILY
MIDGET	SNAGGY	AUTHOR	ITCHEN	RIGHTO	AIRING	BITING	COSILY	EASING
MINGLE	SNUGLY	BARHAM	JETHRO	RIGHTS	ALBINO	BLAISE	COSINE	EATING
MOGGIE	SOIGNÉ	BASHER	JETHRO	RIGHTS	ALBION	BLUISH	COVING	ECHINO

EDDISH	FINITE	IMPISH	LIVING	MOTILE	OSTIUM	RARING	SAVIOR	STRIDE
EDGING	FIRING	INCISE	LOLITA	MOTION	OUTING	RARITY	SAYING	STRIFE
EERILY	FIXITY	INCITE	LOLIUM	MOTIVE	OWLISH	RATIFY	SCAITH	STRIKE
EFFIGY	FLYING	INDIAN	LORICA	MOVIES	OXHIDE	RATINE	SCHISM	STRINE
EGOISM	FOKINE	INDICT	LORIOT	MOVING	PACIFY	RATING	SCHIST	STRING
EGOIST	FOLIAR	INDIES	LOSING	MOWING	PALING	RATION	SCHIZO	STRIPE
ELAINE	FOLIOS	INDIGN	LOTION	MULISH	PAMIRS	RAVINE	SCRIBE	STRIPY
ELFISH	FOLIOT	INDIGO	LOVING	MUNICH	PAPIST	RAVING	SCRIMP	STRIVE
ELLICE	FOLIUM	INDITE	LUCIAN	MUNIFY	PARIAH	RAVISH	SCRIPT	SUPINE
ELOIGN	FORINT	INDIUM	LUCINA	MUNITE	PARISH	REBITE	SEEING	SYRIAN
ELOISE	FRAISE	INFIRM	LUMINA	MURIEL	PARITY	RECIFE	SEMITE	SYRINX
EMPIRE	FRUICT	INLIER	LUPINE	MURINE	PATINA	RECIPE	SENILE	SYRISM
ENDING	FRUITS	INLINE	LURING	MUSING	PAVING	RECITE	SENIOR	TAHINA
ENDIVE	FRUITY	INNING	LURIST	MUSIVE	PAYING	REFILL	SEPIUM	TAHINI
ENFIRE	FRYING	INSIDE	LUTINE	MUTINY	PEKING	REFINE	SERIAL	TAHITI
ENGINE	FURIES	INSIST	LUTIST	MUTISM	PELION	REGIME	SERIES	TAKING
ENLIST	FUSION	INTIME	LYDIAN	MYRIAD	PERILS	REGINA	SERINE	TALION
ENMITY	FUTILE	INVITE	LYRICS	NANISM	PERIOD	REGION	SEWING	TAMINE
ENNIUS	GABION	IODINE	LYRIST	NAPIER	PERISH	REGIUS	SEXISM	TAMISE
ENRICH	GALIOT	IODIZE	MAKING	NASION	PETIPA	RELICS	SEXIST	TAOISM
ENSIGN	GAMINE	IOLITE	MALIAN	NATION	PETITE	RELICT	SHEIKH	TAOIST
ENSILE	GAMING	IONIAN	MALIBU	NATIVE	PILING	RELIEF	SHEILA	TARIFF
ENTICE	GANION	IONIZE	MALICE	NEBISH	PINING	RELISH	SHIITE	TAXING
ENTIRE	GAPING	IRVING	MALIGN	NERINE	PINION	RELIVE	SHRIEK	TEDIUM
ENTITY	GARISH	ISAIAH	MANIAC	NERIUM	PINITE	REMIND	SHRIFT	TEVIOT
ENZIAN	GAVIAL	JABIRU	MANILA	NIDIFY	PIPING	REMISS	SHRIKE	THEIRS
EOLITH	GEMINI	JEMIMA	MANIOC	NINIAN	PLAICE	REPINE	SHRILL	THEISM
EPPING	GENIAL	JEWISH	MANITO	NOMISM	PLAINS	RESIDE	SHRIMP	THEIST
EPRISE	GENIUS	JOSIAH	MAOIST	NOSILY	PLAINT	RESIGN	SHRINE	THRICE
EQUINE	GIVING	JOVIAL	MARIAN	NOTICE	PLYING	RESIST	SHRINK	THRIFT
EQUIPE	GLAIRE	JUDICA	MARINA	NOTIFY	PODIUM	RETINA	SHRIVE	THRILL
EQUITY	GLAIVE	JUDITH	MARINE	NOTION	POLICE	RETIRE	SICILY	THRIPS
ERBIUM	GLOIRE	JULIAN	MARISH	NOVIAL	POLICY	REVIEW	SIDING	THRIST
ERMINE	GNEISS	JULIET	MARIST	NOVICE	POLISH	REVILE	SILICA	THRIVE
ERMITE	GODIVA	JULIUS	MATING	NOWISE	POLITE	REVISE	SIMIAN	TICINO
EROICA	GONION	JUNIOR	MATINS	NUBILE	POLITY	REVIVE	SIMILE	TIDILY
ESKIMO	GONIUM	JURIST	MAXIMS	NUDISM	POTION	REWIND	SIRIUS	TIMING
ETHICS	GORING	KARIBA	MEDIAL	NUDIST	PRAISE	REWIRE	SKIING	TIRING
ETHIOP	GRAINS	KARITE	MEDIAN	NUDITY	PUMICE	RHEIMS	SLEIGH	TITIAN
ETRIER	GRAINY	KODIAK	MEDICI	OAFISH	PUNISH	RIDING	SLUICE	TOBIAS
EUXINE	HABILE	KUFIAH	MEDICO	OBIISM	PURIFY	RIMINI	SNAILY	TOMIAL
EXCISE	HALIDE	KUMISS	MEDINA	OBLIGE	PURINE	RISING	SOCIAL	TOMIUM
EXCITE	HALITE	LABIAL	MEDISM	OBOIST	PURIST	ROBING	SODIUM	TONITE
EXPIRE	HAMITE	LABILE	MEDIUM	ODDITY	PURITY	ROMISH	SOLIVE	TOYISH
EXPIRY	HATING	LABIUM	MEDIUS	OFFICE	PYRITE	ROSINA	SONICS	TROIKA
EXTIRP	HAVING	LACING	MELIUS	OFFING	QUAICH	ROVING	SOVIET	TRUISM
FABIAN	HAZILY	LADIES	MENIAL	OFFISH	QUAIGH	ROWING	SOWING	TRYING
FABIUS	HEGIRA	LADING	MENINX	OLDISH	RABIES	RUBIES	SPEISS	TSHIRT
FACIAL	HEJIRA	LAMINA	MERINO	OMNIUM	RACIAL	RUBIKS	SPHINX	TUBING
FACIES	HELIOS	LAPITH	MESIAL	ONDINE	RACINE	RULING	SPLICE	TULIPA
FACILE	HELIUM	LARIAT	METIER	ONEIDA	RACING	RUPIAH	SPLIFF	TUNING
FACING	HERIOT	LAVISH	MEXICO	ONLINE	RACISM	RUPIAS	SPLINT	TWAITE
FADING	HESIOD	LAXIST	MILIEU	ONSIDE	RACIST	SABINE	SPLITS	TYPIFY
FAKING	HIDING	LAXITY	MINING	OOLITE	RADIAL	SADISM	SPOILS	TYPING
FAMILY	HIKING	LAYING	MINION	OPHISM	RADIAN	SADIST	SPOILT	TYPIST
FAMINE	HIRING	LAZILY	MOBILE	OPHITE	RADISH	SALINA	SPRING	UFFIZI
FAMISH	HOLISM	LEGION	MOBIUS	OPTICS	RADIUM	SALINE	SPRINT	UGRIAN
FANION	HOLIST	LEGIST	MODIFY	OPTIMA	RADIUS	SALISH	SPRITE	ULLING
FARINA	HOMILY	LESION	MODISH	OPTIME	RAGING	SALIVA	SPRITZ	ULTIMA
FATIMA	HOMING	LEVITE	MODIST	OPTION	RAKING	SAMIAN	SPYING	ULTIMO
FAVISM	HOMINY	LEVITY	MODIUS	ORBITA	RAKISH	SAMIEL	SQUILL	UMPIRE
FELINE	HONIED	LIAISE	MOLINE	ORCINE	RAMIFY	SAMIOT	SQUINT	UNBIND
FENIAN	HOSIER	LIBIDO	MONIAL	OROIDE	RAPIDS	SAMITE	SQUIRE	UNCIAL
FERIAL	HOSING	LIKING	MONICA	ORPINE	RAPIER	SANITY	SQUIRM	UNDIES
FETISH	HUMITE	LILIAN	MONISM	ORSINO	RAPINE	SAPIUM	SQUIRT	UNDINE
FILIAL	IFFISH	LILITH	MONIST	OSCINE	RAPIST	SATINY	SQUISH	UNKIND
FILING	IGNITE	LIMITS	MOPING	OSMIUM	RAPIDS	SATIRE	STAIRS	UNLIKE
FINIAL	ILLITE	LINING	MOPISH	OSSIAN	RAPINE	SATIVE	STRICK	UNPICK
FINISH	IMBIBE	LIPIDE	MORION	OSSIFY	RAPIST	SAVING	STRICT	UNRIPE

UNTIDY	GAIJIN	DECKED	MARKKA	SICKER	ABULIA	CALLID	FABLES	HASLET
UNWIND	INKJET	DECKER	MARKUP	SICKLE	ADDLED	CALLOP	FALLEN	HAYLEY
UNWISE	JIMJAM	DECKLE	MASKED	SICKLY	AEOLIC	CALLOW	FALLOW	HEALER
UPHILL	LOGJAM	DEKKER	MASKER	SIKKIM	AEOLIS	CALLUP	FAULTY	HEALTH
UPLIFT	MOUJIK	DICKER	MAWKIN	SILKEN	AEOLUS	CALLUS	FEALTY	HEELED
UPLINK	PUNJAB	DICKEY	MEEKLY	SIMKIN	AIGLET	CAPLET	FEELER	HELLAS
UPPISH	RAMJET	DIKKOP	MERKIN	SINKER	ALALIA	CARLIN	FELLER	HELLER
UPPITY	SELJUK	DINKUM	MICKEY	SIRKAR	AMBLER	CASLON	FELLOE	HENLEY
UPSIDE	TRAJAN	DOCKED	MICKLE	SISKIN	AMELIA	CELLAR	FELLOW	HITLER
URSINE	TROJAN	DOCKER	MOCKER	SMOKER	AMULET	CEYLON	FIELDS	HOLLER
URTICA	AWAKEN	DOCKET	MOCKUP	SMOKEY	ANALOG	CHALET	FILLED	HOLLOW
VAGINA	AWOKEN	DONKEY	MONKEY	SNAKED	ANGLED	CHALKY	FILLER	HOWLER
VAHINE	BACKER	DUCKED	MUCKER	SOAKED	ANGLER	CHILDE	FILLET	HULLED
VALINE	BACKET	DUCKIE	MUCKLE	SOCKET	ANGLIA	CHILLI	FILLIP	HURLEY
VALISE	BACKRA	DUNKER	MUSKEG	SPIKED	ANKLET	CHILLY	FINLAY	HUXLEY
VALIUM	BACKUP	FAWKES	MUSKET	SPOKEN	ANTLER	CHOLER	FIRLOT	ILKLEY
VANISH	BAIKAL	FICKLE	NANKIN	SPOKES	ANTLIA	COALER	FOILED	INFLOW
VANITY	BALKAN	FIRKIN	NAPKIN	STAKES	APOLLO	COELOM	FOLLOW	INFLUX
VARIED	BALKIS	FOKKER	NECKAR	STOKER	APPLES	COILED	FOULLY	ISOLDE
VEDISM	BANKER	FOLKSY	NECKED	STOKES	ARALIA	COLLAR	FOWLER	ITALIC
VENIAL	BARKER	FORKED	NICKED	SUCKEN	ARMLET	COLLET	FRILLS	JAILER
VENICE	BARKIS	GASKET	NICKEL	SUCKER	AROLLA	COLLIE	FRILLY	JAILOR
VENITE	BASKET	GINKGO	NICKER	SUCKET	ASHLAR	COLLOP	FROLIC	JETLAG
VERIFY	BEAKER	GIRKIN	NIKKEI	SUCKLE	ASHLEY	COOLER	FULLER	JILLET
VERILY	BECKET	GURKHA	NOOKIE	SUKKAH	ASYLUM	COOLIE	GABLED	JOPLIN
VERISM	BECKON	HACKEE	PACKED	SUNKEN	ATTLEE	COOLLY	GAELIC	KAOLIN
VERITY	BICKER	HACKER	PACKER	TACKET	AUDLEY	COOLTH	GALLEN	KEELER
VESICA	BODKIN	HACKLE	PACKET	TACKLE	AVALON	COULEE	GALLET	KELLYS
VIKING	BOOKED	HANKER	PARKED	TALKER	AVULSE	COULIS	GALLEY	KEPLER
VILIFY	BOOKER	HANKIE	PARKER	TALKIE	AXILLA	CULLET	GALLIC	KEVLAR
VIRILE	BOOKIE	HARKEN	PARKIN	TANKER	AZALEA	CULLIS	GALLIO	KHALAT
VISIER	BOSKET	HAWKED	PEAKED	TANKIA	AZOLLA	CURLER	GALLON	KHALIF
VISION	BROKEN	HAWKER	PECKER	TECKEL	BAILEE	CURLEW	GALLOP	KHALSA
VIVIAN	BROKER	HECKLE	PERKIN	TICKER	BAILER	CUTLER	GALLOW	KHILAT
VIVIEN	BUCKED	HICKEY	PICKAX	TICKET	BAILEY	CUTLET	GALLUP	KHILIM
VIZIER	BUCKER	HOCKEY	PICKED	TICKEY	BAILIE	CYCLIC	GALLUS	KILLER
VOMICA	BUCKET	HOOKAH	PICKER	TICKLE	BAILLY	CYCLUS	GAOLER	KISLEV
VOTING	BUCKLE	HOOKED	PICKET	TICKLY	BALLAD	DAHLIA	GARLIC	KOOLAH
VOTIVE	BUNKER	HOOKER	PICKLE	TINKER	BALLET	DEALER	GELLER	LABLAB
WAKING	BUNKUM	HOOKEY	PICKUP	TINKLE	BALLOT	DEPLOY	GIGLET	LALLAN
WAPITI	BURKHA	HUCKLE	PINKIE	TUCKER	BARLEY	DEWLAP	GIGLOT	LEALTY
WARILY	BUSKER	HUNKER	PIPKIN	TUCKET	BEDLAM	DIALOG	GILLET	LEGLET
WAVING	BUSKET	JACKAL	POCKET	TURKEY	BELLOC	DIGLOT	GILLIE	LESLIE
WAXING	BUSKIN	JACKET	PORKER	TUSKER	BELLOW	DIPLOE	GIMLET	LOLLOP
WIPING	CACKLE	JERKER	PUCKER	WACKER	BERLIN	DOLLAR	GIRLIE	MAGLEV
WIRING	CALKER	JERKIN	PUNKAH	WALKER	BEULAH	DOLLOP	GOALIE	MAHLER
WIZIER	CALKIN	JOCKEY	QUAKER	WANKEL	BILLET	DOYLEY	GOBLET	MAILER
WRAITH	CANKER	JOSKIN	RACKET	WEAKEN	BILLIE	DRALON	GOBLIN	MAJLIS
XAVIER	CASKET	JUNKER	RANKED	WEAKER	BILLOW	DUBLIN	GOLLOP	MALLAM
XENIAL	CATKIN	JUNKET	RANKER	WEAKLY	BILLYO	DUNLIN	GOOLEY	MALLEE
XENIUM	CHAKRA	JUNKIE	RANKLE	WEEKLY	BOILED	DUNLOP	GOOLIE	MALLET
YEZIDI	CHOKED	KECKSY	RECKON	WELKIN	BOILER	DUPLEX	GRILLE	MALLOW
YOKING	CHOKER	KICKER	REEKIE	WESKER	BOLLEN	ECCLES	GRILSE	MARLIN
YORICK	CHOKEY	KOOKIE	RICKER	WICKED	BOTLEY	EFFLUX	GUELPH	MASLIN
ZENITH	CHUKKA	KRAKEN	RICKEY	WICKER	BOULLE	EMBLEM	GUILDS	MATLOW
ZODIAC	COCKER	LACKEY	ROCKER	WICKET	BOWLED	EMPLOY	GUILTY	MEALIE
ZONING	COCKLE	LARKIN	ROCKET	WINKER	BOWLER	EMULGE	GULLAH	MEDLAR
ZURICH	CONKER	LASKET	ROOKIE	WINKLE	BROLLY	ENGLUT	GULLET	MEDLEY
ZYRIAN	COOKED	LINKER	RUCKLE	WOOKEY	BUGLER	EPILOG	GULLEY	MEJLIS
ACAJOU	COOKER	LINKUP	RUCKUS	WORKED	BULLER	EPULIS	GURLET	MELLOW
BANJAX	COOKIE	LOCKED	RUMKIN	WORKER	BULLET	ETALON	GUSLAR	MERLIN
BANJUL	CORKED	LOCKER	RUSKIN	WREKIN	BURLAP	EUCLID	HAILER	MERLOT
BHAJAN	CORKER	LOCKET	RYOKAN	YAKKER	BURLEY	EVELYN	HALLAL	MILLER
BHAJEE	CRIKEY	LOCKUP	SEEKER	YANKEE	BUTLER	EVOLUÉ	HALLEY	MILLET
BOOJUM	CUCKOO	LOWKEY	SHAKEN	YANKER	BYELAW	EVOLVE	HALLOO	MISLAY
BUNJEE	DARKEN	MARKED	SHAKER	YORKER	CALLAS	EVULSE	HALLOW	MISLED
DEEJAY	DARKEY	MARKER	SHAKES	YUCKER	CALLED	EYELET	HALLUX	MOLLAH
DONJON	DARKIE	MARKET	SHEKEL	ZONKED	CALLER	EYELID	HAMLET	MOLLIE
ELIJAH	DARKLY	MARKET	SICKEN	ABELIA	CALLET	FABLED	HARLOT	MOOLAH

MOSLEM	PROLEG	SUBLET	ZEALOT	DAIMIO	HETMAN	RIMMED	YEOMAN	CATNAP
MOTLEY	PROLIX	SULLEN	ACUMEN	DAMMAR	HIMMEL	ROAMER	YEOMEN	CATNIP
MOULDY	PROLOG	SUNLIT	AGAMID	DAMMIT	HITMAN	ROEMER	YESMAN	CHANCE
MOULIN	PSALMS	SUPLEX	AHIMSA	DEIMOS	HOLMES	ROMMEL	ABONDE	CHANCY
MUFLON	PUBLIC	SUTLER	AIRMAN	DERMAL	HORMUZ	ROOMER	ACINUS	CHANEY
MULLAH	PULLET	SVELTE	AKIMBO	DERMIS	HUMMEL	RUMMER	ADONAI	CHANGE
MULLER	PULLEY	TABLET	ALUMNI	DIMMER	HUMMER	SALMIS	ADONIS	CHENET
MULLET	PURLER	TAILLE	ANEMIA	DISMAL	ISOMER	SALMON	AGENCY	CHINAR
MURLIN	PURLIN	TAILOR	ANEMIC	DISMAY	JAMMED	SCAMPI	AGENDA	CHINCH
MUSLIM	QUALMS	TALLIS	ANIMAL	DOLMAN	KALMIA	SCAMPO	AGONIC	CHINTZ
MUSLIN	QUELCH	TALLOT	ANIMUS	DOLMEN	KERMES	SCHMOE	ALONSO	CHUNKY
MYELIN	RAGLAN	TALLOW	ARAMIS	DOOMED	KERMIS	SCUMMY	AMENDE	CLENCH
MYELON	REALIA	TATLER	ASIMOV	DORMER	KETMIR	SEAMAN	AMENDS	CLINCH
NAILED	REALLY	TEFLON	ATAMAN	DROMIO	KIMMER	SEAMEN	ANANAS	CLINIC
NAILER	REALTY	TELLAR	ATOMIC	DROMOS	KIRMAN	SEAMER	ANONYM	CLONIC
NALLAH	REDLEG	TELLER	AXEMAN	ENAMEL	KISMET	SEAMUS	ARANDA	CLONUS
NAPLES	REELER	TELLUS	BADMAN	ENAMOR	KOSMOS	SEEMLY	ATONAL	CLUNCH
NELLIE	REFLET	THALER	BAGMAN	EREMIC	KRUMAN	SERMON	ATONIC	COGNAC
NIELLO	REFLEX	THALES	BARMAN	ETYMON	KUMMEL	SEUMAS	AVENGE	COINER
NULLAH	REFLUX	THALIA	BATMAN	EXEMPT	LAMMAS	SHAMAN	AVENUE	CONNER
OAKLEY	REGLET	THOLOS	BLAMED	FARMER	LAMMER	SHAMBA	AZONAL	CORNEA
OARLAP	REPLAY	THOLUS	BLIMEY	FERMAT	LAWMAN	SHAMMY	BAGNIO	CORNED
OBELUS	RIALTO	TILLER	BOOMER	FIRMAN	LAYMAN	SHAMUS	BANNED	CORNEL
OBOLUS	RIVLIN	TITLED	BOWMAN	FIRMER	LEGMAN	SHIMMY	BANNER	CORNER
OCELOT	ROLLER	TOILET	BRAMAH	FIRMLY	LITMUS	SIMMER	BANNET	CORNET
OCULAR	RUELLE	TOLLED	BREMEN	FLAMBÉ	LUMMOX	SKIMPY	BARNES	CORNUA
OERLAY	SAILOR	TOLLER	BRUMAL	FLAMEN	MADMAN	SKYMAN	BARNET	CORNUS
OMELET	SALLEE	TRALEE	BRUMBY	FLIMSY	MAMMAL	SLUMMY	BARNEY	COUNTY
OODLES	SALLET	TRILBY	BUSMAN	FORMAL	MAMMON	STAMEN	BARNUM	CRANCH
ORALLY	SALLOW	TUILLE	CADMUS	FORMAT	MARMOT	STAMPS	BEANIE	CRANKY
OSTLER	SAMLET	TWELVE	CAIMAN	FORMER	MERMAN	STEMMA	BEENAH	CRANNY
OTALGY	SCALAR	UMBLES	CALMLY	FORMIC	MESMER	STUMER	BENNET	CRANTS
OTELLO	SCALER	UNCLAD	CARMEL	FRAMED	MICMAC	STUMPS	BIONIC	CRENAL
OUTLAW	SCALES	UNPLUG	CARMEN	FRUMPY	MOOMBA	STUMPY	BIRNAM	CRENEL
OUTLAY	SCHLEP	UPFLOW	CAYMAN	FULMAR	MORMON	STYMIE	BLANCH	CRINAL
OUTLET	SCILLA	VALLEY	CERMET	GAGMAN	MUMMER	SUBMIT	BLANCO	CRINGE
OUTLIE	SCILLY	VALLUM	CHAMPS	GAMMER	MURMUR	SUMMER	BLENCH	CRINUM
OXALIC	SCOLEX	VARLET	CHEMIC	GAMMON	NEWMAN	SUMMIT	BLENDE	CRONET
OXALIS	SCULPT	VEILED	CHEMMY	GASMAN	NIAMEY	SUMMON	BLENNY	CRONOS
PAELLA	SCYLLA	VELLUM	CHIMER	GEMMAN	NORMAL	SWAMPY	BLINKS	CRONUS
PALLAH	SEALED	VILLUS	CHIMES	GERMAN	NORMAN	TALMUD	BLONDE	CRUNCH
PALLAS	SELLBY	VIOLET	CHUMMY	GIMMER	NUTMEG	TAMMAR	BONNET	CUNNER
PALLET	SELLER	VIOLIN	CLAMMY	GLAMIS	OGAMIC	TAMMUZ	BONNIE	CYANIN
PALLID	SENLAC	VOLLEY	CLAMOR	GLAMOR	OILMAN	TARMAC	BORNEO	CYDNUS
PALLOR	SHALOM	WAILER	CLIMAX	GLUMPS	ONEMAN	TASMAN	BOUNCE	CYGNET
PARLEY	SHELVE	WALLAH	CLIMES	GNOMIC	PALMER	TAXMAN	BOUNDS	CYGNUS
PARLOR	SHILOH	WALLED	CLUMPS	GNOMON	PATMOS	TEGMEN	BOUNTY	DAINTY
PAVLOV	SKELLY	WALLER	CLUMSY	GRAMME	PELMET	TERMES	BRANCH	DAMNED
PEDLAR	SKYLAB	WALLOP	COLMAR	GRAMMY	PENMAN	TERMLY	BRANDY	DAWNEY
PEELED	SLALOM	WALLOW	COMMIS	GRAMPA	PERMIT	THAMES	BRONCO	DENNIS
PEELER	SMALLS	WALLET	COMMIT	GRAMPS	PIEMAN	THEMIS	BRONTE	DIANAS
PEGLEG	SMELLY	WEALTH	COMMON	GRIMES	PITMAN	THOMAS	BRONZE	DINNER
PELLET	SMILER	WELLER	CONMAN	GRIMLY	PLUMED	THYMOL	BRUNCH	DIPNOI
PEPLOS	SMILES	WELLES	CORMUS	GRIMMS	PLUMMY	THYMUS	BRUNEI	DIRNDL
PEPLUM	SMILEY	WELLIE	COSMEA	GRUMPH	POMMEL	TREMOR	BRUNEL	DISNEY
PHILIP	SOILED	WESLEY	COSMIC	GRUMPS	POMMIE	TROMPE	BUENOS	DJINNI
PHYLLO	SPILTH	WHALER	COSMOS	GRUMPY	PREMED	TRUMAN	BURNER	DOINGS
PHYLUM	STALAG	WHALES	COWMAN	GUMMED	PRIMAL	TRUMPS	BURNET	DONNÉE
PIGLET	STALIN	WHILOM	CRAMBO	GUNMAN	PRIMED	VATMAN	BYRNIE	DOWNAY
PILLAR	STALKS	WHILST	CREMOR	HAEMAL	PRIMER	VERMIN	CANNAE	DOWNER
PILLOW	STALKY	WHOLLY	CRIMEA	HAEMON	PRIMLY	VERMIS	CANNED	DRENCH
POLLAN	STALLS	WILLED	CRUMBS	HAMMAM	PRIMUS	WARMER	CANNEL	DRONES
POLLED	STILTS	WILLET	CRUMEN	HAMMER	PROMPT	WARMLY	CANNON	DRONGO
POLLEN	STILTY	WILLIE	CRUMMY	HARMED	PUMMEL	WARMTH	CANNOT	DUENNA
POLLEX	STOLEN	WILLOW	CULMEN	HAYMOW	RAGMAN	WEIMAR	CARNAL	EARNED
POLLUX	STOLID	WOOLEN	CUMMER	HELMET	REAMER	WHAMMY	CARNET	EARNER
POPLAR	STOLON	WOOLLY	CUMMIN	HERMES	RHYMER	WHIMSY	CARNOT	ECONUT
POPLIN	STYLET	YELLOW	CUPMAN	HERMIT		YAMMER		EGENCY
PRELIM	STYLUS		DAEMON	HERMON				ELANCE

ELANET	ICONIC	PAINED	SHINER	TURNER	AREOLE	COLONY	FAROFF	LAYOFF
EMUNGE	IRONED	PAINTS	SHINNY	TURNIP	ARGOSY	COLOUR	FAROUK	LAYOUT
EPONYM	IRONIC	PAINTY	SHINTO	TURNUP	ARIOCH	CORONA	FAVOSE	LEMONY
ERINYS	JAUNTY	PAUNCE	SHINTY	TWENTY	ARIOSO	COYOTE	FAVOUR	LETOUT
ETHNIC	JENNER	PAUNCH	SIDNEY	TWINED	ARKOSE	CREOLE	FEDORA	LIPOMA
EVENKI	JENNET	PAWNEE	SIENNA	TWINGE	ARMORY	CUBOID	FELONY	LOMOND
EVENLY	JITNEY	PAYNIM	SIGNAL	UGANDA	ARMOUR	CUPOLA	FILOSE	LOYOLA
EVINCE	JOANNA	PEANUT	SIGNET	URANIA	ARNOLD	CUTOFF	FITOUT	LYCOSA
FAINTS	JOHNNY	PENNAE	SIGNOR	URANIC	ARROBA	CYBORG	FLOOZY	MAHOUT
FAUNUS	JOINER	PENNAL	SIMNEL	URANUS	ARROYO	CYTODE	FURORE	MALONE
FEINTS	KEENER	PENNON	SINNER	URINAL	ASHORE	CYTOID	GADOID	MALONY
FENNEL	KEENLY	PERNOD	SKINNY	USANCE	ASLOPE	DACOIT	GALOOT	MALORY
FIANCÉ	KENNEL	PHENOL	SLANGY	VAINLY	ASSOIL	DAKOTA	GALORE	MAROON
FINNAN	KENNET	PHENYL	SLINKY	VAUNCE	ASSORT	DECODE	GALOSH	MAZOUT
FLANCH	KERNEL	PHONAL	SONNET	VEINED	ASTONE	DECOKE	GENOME	MEKONG
FLANGE	KEYNES	PHONEY	SOONER	VERNAL	ATTONE	DEFORM	GIAOUR	MELODY
FLANKS	KIDNAP	PHONIC	SPENCE	VERNON	ATTORN	DEHORN	GIGOLO	MEMOIR
FLENSE	KIDNEY	PICNIC	SPINAL	VIANDS	AURORA	DEMOTE	GLIOMA	MEMORY
FLINCH	KILNER	PLANCH	SPINAR	VIENNA	BABOON	DENOTE	GLOOMY	MEROPE
FLINTY	KRANTZ	PLANET	SPINET	VIENNE	BARODA	DEPONE	GODOWN	METOPE
FLUNKY	KRONER	PLANKS	SPONGE	WAGNER	BECOME	DEPORT	GOLOSH	MILORD
FORNAX	KRONOS	PLENTY	SPONGY	WALNUT	BEFOOL	DEPOSE	GROOVE	MIMOSA
FORNIX	KWANZA	PLENUM	SPUNGE	WARNER	BEFORE	DESORB	GROOVY	MINOAN
FRANCE	LAUNCE	PLINTH	STANCE	WHENCE	BEGONE	DETOUR	HALOID	MOHOCK
FRANCK	LAUNCH	PLONGE	STANCH	WHINGE	BEHOLD	DEVOID	HAMOSE	MOLOCH
FRANCO	LEANTO	PLUNGE	STANZA	WHINNY	BEHOOF	DEVOTE	HAROLD	MONODY
FRANZY	LEMNOS	POINTE	STENCH	WIENER	BEHOVE	DEVOUR	HEROIC	MOROSE
FRENCH	LEONID	POINTS	STINGO	WINNER	BELONG	DEVOUT	HEROIN	MOTOWN
FRENUM	LIGNUM	POUNCE	STINGY	WINNIE	BEMOAN	DHOOTI	HERONS	MUCOID
FRENZY	LIMNER	POUNDS	STINKO	WINNOW	BEMOIL	DIPOLE	HEXOSE	MUCOUS
FRINGE	LINNET	POWNIE	STINKS	WRENCH	BESORT	DISOWN	HONOUR	MYSORE
FRONDE	LIONEL	PRANCE	STONED	ZINNIA	BETONY	DODOMA	HUMOUR	NEROLI
FUNNEL	LOONIE	PRANKS	STONER	ZOUNDS	BEYOND	DOLOUR	IDIOCY	NILOTE
GAINER	LOUNGE	PRINCE	STONES	AARONS	BEZOAR	DROOPY	IGNORE	NIVOSE
GAINLY	LUANDA	PRONTO	SWANEE	ABLOOM	BIFOLD	DUGONG	IMBOSS	NOBODY
GANNET	MAENAD	PRUNER	SWANKY	ABROAD	BLOODY	DUGOUT	IMPORT	NODOSE
GARNER	MAGNES	PUNNET	SWINGE	ABROMA	BODONI	DUMONT	IMPOSE	NOYOUS
GARNET	MAGNET	QUANGO	SYDNEY	ABSORB	BOFORS	DUMOSE	IMPOST	NYLONS
GLANCE	MAGNON	QUENCH	TAENIA	ACCORD	BOGOTA	EAMONN	INBORN	OBLONG
GLINKA	MAGNUM	QUINCE	TANNAH	ACCOST	BRIONY	ECBOLE	INCOME	OCHONE
GOANNA	MAGNUS	QUINSY	TANNED	ACROSS	BROOCH	ECLOSE	INDOOR	ODIOUS
GOUNOD	MAINLY	QUINTA	TANNER	ACTORS	BROODY	ECTOPY	INFOLD	OENONE
GRANBY	MAINOR	RAUNCH	TANNIC	ADJOIN	BROOKE	EDMOND	INFORM	ONCOME
GRANGE	MANNER	RENNET	TANNIN	ADROIT	BROOKS	EEYORE	INGOTS	ONCOST
GRANNY	MANNIN	RENNIN	TANNOY	ADSORB	BRYONY	EFFORT	INMOST	ONIONS
GRANTA	MARNER	RIENZI	TEENSY	AEROBE	BUSONI	EGMONT	INROAD	OOLONG
GRANTH	MAUNDY	RODNEY	TENNER	AFFORD	BUYOUT	EMBODY	INSOLE	OPPOSE
GRINGO	MEANIE	ROGNON	TENNIS	AFLOAT	BYGONE	EMBOSS	INTONE	OPTOUT
GRUNDY	MEANLY	ROMNEY	TERNAL	ALCOCK	BYWORD	ENCODE	INTOWN	ORGONE
GRUNGE	MEMNON	ROUNCE	THANAH	ALCOVE	CACOON	ENCORE	INVOKE	ORIOLE
GUENON	MIGNON	ROUNDS	THANET	ALDOSE	CAHOOT	ENFOLD	JACOBS	ORMOLU
GUINEA	MINNIE	RUINED	THANKS	ALMOND	CAJOLE	ENJOIN	JALOPY	OSMOSE
GUNNEL	MINNOW	RUNNEL	THENAR	ALMOST	CAMOTE	ENROBE	JEROME	OTIOSE
GUNNER	MOANER	RUNNER	THENCE	ANCOME	CANOPY	ENROLL	JOCOSE	OULONG
GURNET	MORNAY	RWANDA	THINGS	ANCONA	CAPONE	ENTOMB	JOJOBA	OXFORD
GURNEY	MORNED	SAANEN	THINGY	ANCORA	CAPOTE	EOZOON	JOYOUS	PAEONY
HANNAH	NIGNOG	SAINTS	TINNED	ANGOLA	CAVORT	ESCORT	KANOON	PAGODA
HAUNCH	NOUNCE	SARNIE	TINNIE	ANGORA	CAVOUR	EUBOEA	KELOID	PANOPE
HENNIN	NUANCE	SAWNEY	TOWNEE	ANKOLE	CEROON	EULOGY	KETONE	PARODY
HERNIA	NUDNIK	SCANTY	TOWNLY	ANTONY	CHEOPS	EUROPA	KETOSE	PAROLE
HOBNOB	NYANZA	SCENIC	TRANCE	ANYONE	CHOOSE	EUROPE	KIAORA	PATOIS
HORNED	OAKNUT	SCONCE	TRANNY	APHONY	CHOOSY	EVZONE	KIBOSH	PAYOFF
HORNER	ODENSE	SCUNGE	TRENCH	APLOMB	CHROMA	EXHORT	KIMONO	PAYOLA
HORNET	OLENUS	SEANCE	TRENDY	APNOEA	CHROME	EXMOOR	KOMODO	PELOID
HOUNDS	OMENTA	SENNET	TRUNKS	APPORT	CHROMO	EXPORT	KYBOSH	PELOTA
HYMNAL	OPENER	SHANDY	TSONGA	APPOSE	CLEOME	EXPOSE	LABOUR	PEYOTE
HYPNIC	OPENLY	SHANKS	TUNNEL	ARBOUR	COCOON	EXTOLL	LADOGA	PHLOEM
HYPNOS	ORANGE	SHANTY	TURNED	ARDOUR	COHORT	EXTORT	LAGOON	PHOOEY
HYPNUM	ORKNEY	SHINDY	TURNED	AREOLA	COHOSH	FAMOUS	LATONA	PIGOTT

PILOSE	SIMOOM	VINOUS	DIMPLE	MOPPET	SLIPPY	YIPPEE	BARROW	DERRIS
POLONY	SIMOON	VIROUS	DIPPER	MUPPET	SLIPUP	YUPPIE	BEARER	DHARMA
POMONA	SMOOCH	WAYOUT	DISPEL	MURPHY	SLOPES	ZIPPER	BEHRAM	DJERBA
POROUS	SMOOTH	WHOOPS	DRAPER	MYOPIA	SLOPPY	BARQUE	BETRAY	DORRIT
PRIORY	SNOOTY	WHOOSH	DRIPPY	MYOPIC	SNAPPY	BASQUE	BEURRÉ	DOURLY
PUTOIS	SNOOZE	WIDOWS	DROPSY	NAPPER	SNIPER	BISQUE	BHARAL	DVORAK
PUTOUT	SODOMY	XEROMA	DUMPER	NEAPED	SNIPPY	BRAQUE	BHARAT	DZEREN
PYRONE	SPLOSH	XYLOID	DUMPLE	NIPPER	SOUPER	CAIQUE	BOARDS	ECARTÉ
PYROPE	SPOOKY	XYLOSE	ELAPSE	NIPPLE	SOUPLE	CALQUE	BORROW	ECURIE
RAGOUT	SPOONY	ZYGOMA	ELOPER	NIPPON	STAPES	CASQUE	BOURÉE	EGERIA
RAMOSE	SPROUT	ZYGOTE	EPOPEE	NUMPTY	STAPLE	CHEQUE	BOURNE	ELBRUS
RAMOUS	STOOGE	ALIPED	FIPPLE	OOKPIK	STEPPE	CINQUE	BOURSE	EMBRUE
RATOON	STOOKS	APEPSY	FLOPPY	OOMPAH	STIPES	CIRQUE	BOVRIL	EMBRYO
REBORE	STOOLS	ARMPIT	FORPIT	OUTPUT	STUPID	CLAQUE	BURROW	EMERGE
REBORN	STROBE	ASHPAN	FRAPPÉ	PAMPAS	STUPOR	CLIQUE	CARREL	ENARCH
RECOIL	STRODE	AUSPEX	FRIPON	PAMPER	SULPHA	IRAQIS	CARROT	ENERGY
RECORD	STROKE	BEDPAN	FURPHY	PARPEN	SUPPER	MANQUÉ	CEDRIC	ENFREE
RECOUP	STROLL	BEEPER	GASPAR	PAUPER	SUPPLE	MARQUE	CHARGE	ENGRAM
REFORM	STRONG	BIOPIC	GASPER	PAWPAW	SUPPLY	MASQUE	CHARON	ENTRAP
REJOIN	STROUD	BIOPSY	GILPIN	PEEPER	SWIPES	MOSQUE	CHARTA	ENTREE
REMORA	STROUP	BUMPER	GOSPEL	PEOPLE	TAIPAN	OPAQUE	CHERIE	ENWRAP
REMOTE	STROVE	CAMPED	GRAPES	PEPPER	TAIPEI	PASQUE	CHERRY	EPARCH
REMOVE	SUBORN	CAMPER	GRAPPA	PIGPEN	TAMPER	PLAQUE	CHERUB	EPERDU
RENOIR	SWOOSH	CAMPUS	GRIPES	PIMPLE	TAMPON	RISQUÉ	CHERUP	EPIRUS
RENOWN	TACOMA	CAPPED	GRIPPE	PIMPLY	TAPPER	TORQUE	CHIRON	ESCROC
REPORT	TAGORE	CARPAL	GROPER	PIPPIN	TAPPET	UNIQUE	CHIRPY	ESCROW
REPOSE	THEORY	CARPEL	GULPER	POMPEY	TAPPIT	ACARID	CHORAL	ESPRIT
RESORT	THROAT	CARPER	HAMPER	POMPOM	TAWPIE	ACARUS	CHOREA	ESTRAY
RETOOL	THROES	CARPET	HAPPEN	POMPON	TEAPOT	ACCRUE	CHOREE	EXARCH
RETORT	THRONE	CARPUS	HARPIC	POPPER	TEAPOY	ADORER	CHORUS	FABRIC
RETOUR	THRONG	CASPAR	HEAPED	POPPET	TEEPEE	AFFRAY	CHURCH	FAIRLY
REVOKE	THROVE	CHAPEL	HELPER	POPPIT	TEMPER	AFFRET	CIERGE	FARROW
REVOLT	THROWN	CHAPKA	HEMPEN	POPPLE	TEMPLE	AGARIC	CIRRUS	FEERIE
REWORD	TIPOFF	CHIPPY	HERPES	PREPAY	TENPIN	ALARIC	CITRIN	FERRET
REWORK	TIVOLI	CHOPIN	HIPPED	PREPPY	TEOPAN	ALARUM	CITRON	FERRIS
RIBOSE	TOLOSA	CHOPPY	HIPPUS	PROPEL	TIEPIN	ALDRIN	CITRUS	FIERCE
RIGOUR	TRIODE	CHYPRE	HISPID	PROPER	TINPAN	ALERCE	CLARET	FLARES
RIPOFF	TROOPS	CLIPPY	HOOPER	PROPYL	TINPOT	ALFRED	CLARTY	FLORAL
ROCOCO	TUMOUR	COMPEL	HOOPLA	PULPIT	TIPPED	AMERCE	CLERGY	FLORET
RUGOSE	TYCOON	COMPLY	HOOPOE	PUPPET	TIPPER	AMORAL	CLERIC	FLORID
RUGOUS	TYRONE	COOPER	HOPPER	PUPPIS	TIPPET	AMORCE	CLERKS	FLORIN
RUMORS	UNBOLT	COPPER	HOTPOT	PURPLE	TIPPLE	AMORET	COARSE	FLURRY
RUMOUR	UNBORN	COPPIN	HUMPED	RAPPED	TIPPOO	AMTRAK	COERCE	FORRAD
RUNOFF	UNCOIL	CORPSE	HUMPTY	RAPPER	TOPPER	ANDREW	CONRAD	FORRAY
SALOME	UNCOOL	CORPUS	INKPOT	RASPER	TOPPLE	ANORAK	CORRAL	FOURTH
SALOON	UNCORK	COUPLE	ISOPOD	REAPER	TORPID	ANTRIM	CORRIE	FUHRER
SALOOP	UNDONE	COUPON	JAMPOT	REOPEN	TORPOR	ANTRUM	COURSE	FURROW
SAMOSA	UNFOLD	COWPAT	JASPER	RHAPHE	TOUPEE	ANURAN	COWRIE	GARRET
SAPOTA	UNHOLY	COWPER	JUMPER	RIPPER	TOUPET	APERÇU	CRURAL	GARROT
SAPOTE	UNHOOK	COWPOX	KALPAK	RIPPLE	TRAPES	APORIA	CUERPO	GARRYA
SARONG	UNLOAD	CRAPLE	KEEPER	RIPPON	TREPAN	ARARAT	CUPRIC	GEORGE
SATORI	UNLOCK	CRIPES	KELPER	RUMPLE	TRIPLE	ASARUM	CURRIE	GHARRY
SAVOIE	UNROLL	CROPPY	KELPIE	RUMPUS	TRIPOD	ASTRAL	CYBRID	GHERAO
SAVORY	UNSOLD	CRYPTO	KEWPIE	SAMPAN	TRIPOS	ASTRAY	CYMRIC	GIORGI
SAVOUR	UNTOLD	CUPPED	KEYPAD	SAMPLE	TROPHE	ATHROB	CYPRID	GLORIA
SAXONY	UNYOKE	CUPPER	KIPPER	SAPPER	TROPHY	ATTRAP	CYPRIS	GOURDE
SCHOOL	UPHOLD	CURPEL	KIRPAN	SAPPHO	TROPIC	AUBREY	CYPRUS	GOURDS
SCOOBS	UPROAR	CZAPKA	LAPPER	SCAPUS	TROPPO	AUDREY	DEARER	GUARDI
SCOOSH	UPROOT	DAMPEN	LAPPET	SCIPIO	TURPIN	AVERNO	DEARIE	GUARDS
SCROLL	UPTOWN	DAMPER	LIMPET	SCOPUS	TYMPAN	AVERSE	DEARLY	HAIRDO
SCROOP	UTMOST	DAPPER	LIMPID	SEMPRE	UTOPIA	AZERTY	DEARTH	HARRIS
SECOND	VADOSE	DAPPLE	LIMPLY	SHAPED	VESPER	AZORES	DEBRIS	HARROW
SENORA	VALOUR	DEEPEN	LIPPED	SHIPKA	WAMPUM	BAHRAM	DECREE	HATRED
SEROSA	VAPOUR	DEEPER	LISPER	SIMPER	WAMPUS	BARRED	DECREW	HEARER
SETOSE	VELOCE	DEEPLY	LOOPED	SIMPLE	WARPED	BARREL	DEFRAG	HEARSE
SHROFF	VELOUR	DELPHI	LOOPER	SIMPLY	WEAPON	BARREN	DEFRAY	HEARTH
SHROUD	VENOSE	DESPOT	LUMPUR	SIPPET	WEEPER	BARRIE	DEGREE	HEARTS
SHROVE	VENOUS	DIAPER	LYMPNE	SIPPET	WEEPIE	BARRIO		HEARTY
SIMONY	VIGOUR	DIEPPE	MAGPIE	SIPPLE	WIMPLE			HEBREW

HERREN	NEURON	SECRET	TETRYL	CAESAR	EGESTA	LAPSUS	POISED	TISSUE
HOARSE	NIMROD	SEURAT	THERMO	CAPSID	ELISHA	LASSIE	POISON	TMESIS
HOORAH	NITRIC	SÈVRES	THIRST	CARSON	ELYSEE	LASSUS	POSSER	TOCSIN
HOORAY	NITRYL	SHARED	THIRTY	CASSIA	ENOSIS	LESSEE	POSSET	TONSIL
HORRID	NORROY	SHARER	THORAH	CASSIO	ERASED	LESSEN	POSSUM	TONSOR
HORROR	OBERON	SHARES	THORAX	CASSIS	ERASER	LESSER	PRESTO	TOSSUP
HOURLY	OCHREA	SHARIA	THORNE	CATSUP	EXISTS	LESSON	PRISMS	TOUSER
HUBRIS	OCTROI	SHARIF	THORNY	CAUSAL	FEISTY	LESSOR	PRISON	TOUSLE
HURRAH	OILRIG	SHARON	THORPE	CAUSED	FIASCO	LISSOM	PRISSY	TOWSER
HURRAY	OMERTA	SHARPS	THYRSE	CAUSEY	FIESTA	LOOSEN	PROSIT	TRASHY
HYBRID	OSIRIS	SHERIF	TIERCE	CENSER	FLASHY	MARSHY	PRUSIK	TRESCO
HYBRIS	OSPREY	SHERPA	TIERED	CENSOR	FLESHY	MASSED	PTOSIS	TRISTE
HYDRAX	OSTREA	SHERRY	TIGRIS	CENSUS	FLOSSY	MASSES	PUDSEY	TRUSTY
HYDRIA	OUTRUN	SHIRAZ	TOERAG	CHASER	FLUSHY	MASSIF	PUISNE	TUSSAH
HYDRUS	OVERDO	SHIRRA	TORRES	CHASSE	FOCSLE	MAUSER	PULSAR	TUSSIS
IBERIA	OVERLY	SHIRTY	TORRID	CHASTE	FORSAY	MEASLY	PURSED	TUSSLE
ICARUS	PAIRER	SHORTS	TOURER	CHESIL	FOSSIL	MENSAL	PURSER	TWISTY
IMBRUE	PARROT	SIERRA	TUAREG	CHESTY	FRESCO	MERSEY	PURSUE	UNISEX
INBRED	PATROL	SIRRAH	TUGRIK	CHISEL	GEASON	MESSRS	PUSSER	UNISON
INGRAM	PATRON	SIRREE	TURRET	CHOSEN	GEISHA	MIASMA	QUASAR	UNUSED
INGRES	PEARLS	SITREP	TWIRLY	CLASSY	GEYSER	MISSAL	RAISED	VASSAL
INGROW	PEARLY	SKERRY	UGARIT	CLOSED	GHOSTS	MISSED	RAISER	VERSAL
INTRAY	PERRON	SKURRY	UMBREL	CLOSER	GIBSON	MISSEL	RAISIN	VERSED
INTRON	PETREL	SLURRY	UMBRIA	CLOSET	GIUSTO	MISSIS	RANSOM	VERSES
ISTRIA	PETROL	SMARMY	UMBRIL	COMSAT	GLASSY	MISSUS	REASON	VERSET
ITERUM	PHAROS	SMARTY	UNBRED	CONSUL	GLOSSA	MOPSUS	RHESUS	VERSUS
KHARIF	PIERCE	SMIRCH	UNTRUE	CORSET	GLOSSY	MORSEL	RIPSAW	VESSEL
KOUROS	PIERIS	SMYRNA	UNWRAP	COSSET	GODSON	MOSSAD	ROBSON	WARSAW
LABRUM	PLURAL	SNORER	USURER	COSSIE	GOSSIP	MOUSER	ROSSER	WATSON
LABRYS	POGROM	SOHRAB	UTERUS	COUSIN	GRASSY	MOUSEY	RUSSET	WEASEL
LARRUP	POIROT	SOIREE	VIBRIO	CRASIS	GRISLY	MOUSSE	RUSSIA	WENSUM
LATRON	POORLY	SORREL	WAGRAM	CRESOL	GRISON	MUESLI	SAMSON	WESSEX
LAUREL	POURER	SORROW	WALRUS	CRESTA	GROSSO	MUNSHI	SANSEI	WHISHT
LAURIC	PTERIN	SOURCE	WARREN	CRISIS	GUESTS	MUSSEL	SARSEN	WHISKY
LAURIE	PTERIS	SOURLY	WEARER	CRISPY	GUSSET	MYOSIN	SEASON	WILSON
LIERNE	PUERTO	SPARKS	WEIRDO	CRISTA	GYPSUM	MYOSIS	SEESAW	WIMSEY
LOURIE	PUTRID	SPARKY	WHARFE	CROSBY	HANSOM	NANSEN	SEISIN	WORSEN
LUBRIC	PYRRHO	SPARSE	WHERRY	CROSSE	HASSAR	NASSAU	SELSYN	WOWSER
MACRON	QUARRY	SPARTA	WIRRAL	CRUSET	HASSLE	NASSER	SENSED	WRASSE
MADRAS	QUARTO	SPARTH	YARROW	CRUSOE	HAWSER	NAUSEA	SENSES	YEASTY
MADRID	QUARTZ	SPIRAL	YEARLY	CRUSTA	HENSON	NELSON	SENSOR	ABATOR
MARRAM	QUIRKY	SPIRIT	ZAGREB	CRUSTY	HIRSEL	NESSIE	SEPSIS	ABATTU
MARRON	QUORUM	SPORTS	ALASKA	CUESTA	HONSHU	NESSUS	SHASTA	ACATES
MARROW	QWERTY	SPORTY	AMUSED	CUISSE	HORSED	NISSEN	SIESTA	ACETIC
MATRIC	RAMROD	SPURGE	ARISTA	CURSAL	HOUSES	ODDSON	SLOSHY	AGATHA
MATRIX	REDRAW	STARCH	ARISTO	CURSED	HUDSON	ODESSA	SLUSHY	AMYTAL
MATRON	REGRET	STARES	AUSSIE	CURSOR	HUSSAR	OFFSET	SOUSED	AORTAL
MEGRIM	RICRAC	STARRY	AYESHA	CURSUS	HUSSIF	OMASUM	SOWSED	APATHY
MERRIE	ROARER	STARVE	BALSAM	CUSSED	HYSSOP	ORISON	STASIS	APHTHA
MERROW	RUBRIC	STEREO	BARSAC	CUSSER	JANSKY	OUTSET	SUBSET	ARCTIC
METRIC	SABRES	STERIC	BASSET	CYESIS	JERSEY	OVISAC	SUNSET	ASHTAR
MICRON	SACRED	STERNE	BEDSIT	DAISHO	JETSAM	PARSEC	SUSSEX	ASHTON
MIRROR	SACRUM	STEROL	BELSEN	DAMSEL	JIGSAW	PARSEE	TARSAL	AUNTIE
MITRAL	SATRAP	STORAX	BENSON	DAMSON	JISSOM	PARSON	TARSEL	AUSTEN
MITRED	SAURIA	STORER	BESSEL	DAWSON	JONSON	PASSED	TARSIA	AUSTER
MOIRAI	SBIRRO	STOREY	BESSIE	DIESEL	JOSSER	PASSES	TARSUS	AUSTIN
MONROE	SCARAB	STORMY	BESSUS	DIESIS	KAISER	PASSIM	TASSEL	AVATAR
MORRIS	SCARCE	STURDY	BIASED	DOBSON	KANSAS	PENSÉE	TASSET	AZOTIC
MORROW	SCARED	STYRAX	BOLSHY	DOESNT	KENSAL	PENSUM	TASSIE	BALTIC
MURRAM	SCARER	SUNRAY	BONSAI	DORSAL	KIRSCH	PERSON	TEASEL	BANTAM
MURRAY	SCIROC	SURREY	BORSCH	DORSET	KISSEL	PHASIS	TEASER	BANTER
MURRHA	SCIRON	SWARTY	BOSSED	DOSSAL	KISSER	PHASMA	TENSON	BANTRY
MURRIN	SCORCH	SWERVE	BOUSER	DOSSER	KITSCH	PHYSIC	TENSOR	BARTER
NARROW	SCORER	TARROW	BOWSER	DOWSER	KYUSHU	PHYSIO	THESIS	BARTOK
NATRON	SCORIA	TAURUS	BRASSY	DOWSET	LAISSE	PIGSTY	THISBE	BARTON
NEARBY	SCORSE	TEHRAN	BUKSHI	DOWSON	LAPSED	PISSED	TILSIT	BATTEN
NEARER	SCURRY	TERRAE	BUNSEN	DRESSY		PLASMA	TINSEL	BATTER
NEARLY	SCURVY	TERROR	BURSAR	DROSKY		PLISSÉ	TISSOT	BATTLE
NEURAL	SEARCH	TETRAD	BYSSUS	EDISON		PODSOL		BATTUE

BAXTER	CENTUM	DIKTAT	GIOTTO	KILTIE	MOLTEN	PITTED	RUSTLE	STATUS
BEATEN	CERTES	DISTAL	GIRTON	KIRTLE	MONTEM	PITTER	RUSTUM	STITCH
BEATER	CESTUI	DISTIL	GLITCH	KITTEN	MONTHS	PLATED	RUTTED	SUBTLE
BEATTY	CESTUS	DITTOS	GLITZY	KITTLE	MORTAL	PLATEN	RUTTER	SUBTLY
BEETLE	CHATON	DOCTOR	GLUTEN	KNOTTY	MORTAR	PLATER	SAITHE	SUITED
BEETON	CHATTY	DORTER	GOATEE	KOWTOW	MORTEM	PLATES	SANTAL	SUITOR
BELTED	CHITAL	DOTTED	GOETHE	KRATER	MOSTLY	PLUTUS	SANTON	SULTAN
BERTHA	CHITIN	DOTTLE	GOITER	KRATON	MOTTLE	POETIC	SARTOR	SULTRY
BERTHE	CHITON	DUSTED	GOITRE	KVETCH	MOUTAN	POETRY	SARTRE	SUNTAN
BERTIE	CHITTY	DUSTER	GOTTEN	LACTIC	MOUTER	PONTIC	SCATCH	SURTAX
BESTED	CLOTHE	EARTHY	GOUTTE	LAPTOP	MOUTON	POOTER	SCATHE	SUTTEE
BESTIR	CLOTHO	EASTER	GRATED	LASTLY	MULTUM	PORTAL	SCATTY	SWATCH
BESTOW	CLUTCH	EDITED	GRATER	LATTEN	MUSTER	PORTER	SCOTCH	SWATHE
BETTER	COATED	EDITOR	GRATIN	LATTER	MUTTER	PORTIA	SCOTER	SWITCH
BETTOR	COATES	ELATED	GRATIS	LECTOR	MUTTON	PORTLY	SCOTIA	SYNTAX
BIOTIC	COITUS	ELUTOR	GRETNA	LENTEL	MYRTLE	POSTAL	SCUTCH	SYSTEM
BIOTIN	COLTER	EMETIC	GRITTY	LENTEN	MYSTIC	POSTER	SCUTUM	TACTIC
BISTER	CONTRA	EROTIC	GROTTO	LENTIC	NANTES	POSTIL	SCYTHE	TANTRA
BISTRE	COOTIE	EUSTON	GROTTY	LENTIL	NASTIC	POTTED	SEATED	TARTAN
BISTRO	COPTIC	EXETER	GRUTCH	LENTOR	NATTER	POTTER	SECTOR	TARTAR
BITTEN	CORTES	EXOTIC	GUITAR	LEPTON	NAUTCH	POTTLE	SEETHE	TARTLY
BITTER	CORTEX	FACTOR	GUNTER	LESTER	NEATEN	POUTER	SEMTEX	TASTER
BLITHE	CORTEZ	FACTUM	GUTTER	LETTER	NEATLY	POWTER	SENTRY	TATTER
BLOTCH	COSTAR	FALTER	GUTTLE	LHOTSE	NECTAR	PRATER	SEPTAL	TATTLE
BLOTTO	COSTER	FANTAN	HALTER	LICTOR	NESTLE	PRETAX	SEPTET	TATTOO
BOATER	COSTLY	FASTEN	HAPTEN	LIFTED	NESTOR	PRETTY	SEPTIC	TAUTEN
BOLTER	COTTAR	FATTEN	HAPTIC	LIFTER	NETTLE	PROTEA	SETTEE	TAUTLY
BOOTEE	COTTON	FESTAL	HASTEN	LINTEL	NEUTER	PROTON	SETTER	TAUTOG
BOÖTES	CRATCH	FESTER	HATTER	LISTEL	NEWTON	PUNTER	SETTLE	TECTUM
BOOTLE	CRATER	FETTER	HEATED	LISTEN	NOCTUA	PUTTEE	SEXTAN	TEETER
BOSTON	CRATON	FETTES	HEATER	LISTER	NUTTER	PUTTER	SEXTET	TEETHE
BOTTLE	CRATUR	FETTLE	HECTIC	LITTER	OBITAL	QUETCH	SEXTON	TERTIA
BOTTOM	CRETAN	FILTER	HECTOR	LITTLE	OBITER	QUITCH	SIFTER	TERTIA
BOUTON	CRETIC	FILTHY	HEPTAD	LOATHE	ORATOR	QUOTED	SISTER	TESTER
BRETON	CRETIN	FILTRÉ	HESTIA	LOITER	OTITIS	RAFTER	SITTER	TESTES
BRITON	CRITIC	FITTED	HIATUS	LOOTER	OUTTOP	RAGTOP	SKATER	TESTIS
BRUTAL	CROTAL	FITTER	HILTON	LUSTER	OYSTER	RANTER	SKATES	TETTIX
BRUTUS	CROTCH	FLATLY	HITTER	LUSTRE	PALTRY	RAPTLY	SKETCH	TEUTON
BUNTER	CROTON	FLATUS	HOGTIE	LYTTON	PANTER	RAPTOR	SLATCH	THATCH
BURTON	CRUTCH	FLETCH	HOOTCH	MAÎTRE	PANTON	RASTER	SLATER	THETIC
BUSTED	CUITER	FLITCH	HOOTER	MALTED	PANTRY	RATTAN	SLATHER	THETIS
BUSTER	CULTCH	FLUTED	HOSTEL	MALTHA	PARTLY	RATTER	SLITHY	TINTED
BUSTLE	CULTER	FLUTER	HOTTER	MANTIS	PARTON	RATTLE	SMITHS	TINTIN
BUTTER	CULTUS	FLUTES	HUNTER	MANTLE	PASTEL	RATTON	SMITHY	TIPTOE
BUTTON	CURTAL	FOETAL	HURTLE	MANTRA	PASTIL	RECTAL	SMUTTY	TIPTOP
CACTUS	CURTAX	FOETID	HUSTLE	MANTUA	PASTIS	RECTOR	SNATCH	TITTER
CAFTAN	CURTLY	FOETUS	INSTAL	MAOTAI	PASTON	RECTUM	SNITCH	TITTLE
CAITRA	CURTSY	FOOTER	INSTAR	MARTEL	PASTOR	RECTUS	SNOTTY	TITTUP
CANTAB	CUSTER	FOOTLE	INSTEP	MARTEN	PASTRY	REDTOP	SOFTEN	TOETOE
CANTAL	CUSTOM	FORTHY	INSTIL	MARTHA	PATTEN	RENTAL	SOFTIE	TOLTEC
CANTAR	CUSTOS	FOSTER	IRETON	MARTIN	PATTER	RENTER	SOFTLY	TOMTOM
CANTER	CUTTER	FOUTRE	ISHTAR	MARTYR	PATTON	REPTON	SONTAG	TOOTER
CANTLE	CUTTLE	FRATER	JESTER	MASTER	PECTEN	REUTER	SOOTHE	TOOTHY
CANTON	CUTTOE	FROTHY	JETTON	MASTIC	PECTIN	RHETOR	SORTER	TOOTLE
CANTOR	CYSTIC	FRUTEX	JITTER	MATTED	PENTAD	RHYTHM	SORTES	TOOTSY
CANTUS	DACTYL	FUSTIC	JOSTLE	MATTER	PENTEL	RICTAL	SORTIE	TOTTER
CAPTAN	DAFTIE	FUSTOC	JOTTER	MEATUS	PENTUP	RICTUS	SOUTER	TOTTIE
CAPTOR	DALTON	GAITER	JUSTIN	MELTED	PENTYL	RIOTER	SOWTER	TRITON
CARTEL	DANTON	GANTRY	JUSTLY	MELTON	PEPTIC	ROOTED	SPATHE	TRUTHS
CARTER	DARTER	GARTER	KAFTAN	MENTAL	PESTER	ROOTER	SPITAL	TSETSE
CARTON	DARTLE	GASTER	KANTEN	MENTOR	PESTLE	ROOTLE	SPOTTY	TUFTED
CASTER	DEBTOR	GASTON	KANTHA	MENTUM	PEWTER	ROSTER	SPUTUM	TURTLE
CASTLE	DEFTLY	GENTES	KEATON	MERTON	PHOTON	ROSTOV	STATAL	TWITCH
CASTOR	DENTAL	GENTLE	KELTER	METTLE	PICTOR	ROTTEN	STATED	ULITIS
CASTRO	DEXTER	GENTLY	KELTIC	MILTON	PINTER	ROTTER	STATEN	ULSTER
CATTLE	DIATOM	GENTRY	KELTIE	MINTON	PINTLE	ROUTER	STATES	UNITED
CELTIC	DICTUM	GETTER	KETTLE	MISTER	PISTIL	RUSTAM	STATIC	URETER
CENTER	DIETER	GHETTO	KILTED	MITTEN	PISTOL	RUSTEM	STATOR	VASTLY
CENTRE	DIETER	GIFTED	KILTER	MOATED	PISTON	RUSTIC	STATUE	VECTIS
								VECTOR

VENTIL	ASTUTE	ESCUDO	LIGULE	RHEUMY	URSULA	HEAVED	SUIVEZ	RUNWAY
VENTRE	ATTUNE	EUNUCH	LIGURE	RITUAL	VACUUM	HEAVEN	SURVEY	SEAWAY
VESTAL	AUBURN	EXCUSE	LIQUID	ROBUST	VALUER	HEAVES	SWIVEL	SELWYN
VESTED	AUCUBA	EXEUNT	LIQUOR	ROGUES	VALUTA	HOOVER	SWIVET	SHOWER
VESTRY	AUGURY	EXHUME	LOCULE	ROQUET	VEDUTA	JARVEY	SYLVAN	SKEWED
VIATOR	AUGUST	EXPUGN	LOCUST	ROTULA	VELURE	JEEVES	SYLVIA	SKEWER
VICTIM	AUTUMN	FECULA	LOQUAT	ROTUND	VICUNA	KELVIN	TRAVEL	SLEWED
VICTOR	AVAUNT	FECUND	LUNULE	SALUKI	VISUAL	KNIVES	TRAVIS	SLOWLY
VIRTUE	AVOUCH	FERULA	LUXURY	SALUTE	VOLUME	LARVAE	TRIVET	SNOWED
VORTEX	BAGUIO	FERULE	MACULA	SAMUEL	VOLUTE	LARVAL	TRIVIA	STEWED
WAFTED	BARUCH	FIBULA	MACULE	SATURN	WOBURN	LATVIA	TROVER	STOWER
WAITER	BASUTO	FIGURE	MADURA	SCHUSS	YAKUZA	LEAVEN	TURVES	SUBWAY
WALTER	BEAUNE	FLAUNT	MADURO	SCHUYT	YAOURT	LEAVER	UNEVEN	TAIWAN
WALTON	BEAUTY	FLEURY	MANUAL	SCOUSE	YOGURT	LEAVES	VELVET	TIZWAZ
WANTED	BELUGA	FLOURY	MANUKA	SCRUBS	YORUBA	LOAVES	VERVET	TROWEL
WANTON	BEMUSE	FLOUSH	MANURE	SCRUFF	ALEVIN	LOUVER	WAIVER	VIEWER
WASTED	BENUMB	FROUDE	MAPUTO	SCRUNT	BEAVER	LOUVRE	WEAVER	WEEWEE
WASTEL	BLOUSE	FUTURE	MAQUIS	SECURE	BREVET	MARVEL	WEEVIL	WELWYN
WASTER	BOHUNK	GARUDA	MATURE	SEDUCE	CALVER	NAEVUS	WOLVER	WIGWAM
WATTLE	BOSUNS	GAZUMP	MAZUMA	SEQUEL	CALVIN	NERVAL	AIRWAY	YAHWEH
WELTER	CANUCK	GERUND	MEDUSA	SEQUIN	CANVAS	NERVES	ANSWER	ALEXIA
WHITBY	CANUTE	GREUZE	MINUET	SEXUAL	CANVEY	NERVII	ANYWAY	ALEXIN
WHITED	CARUSO	GROUCH	MINUTE	SHOULD	CARVED	NORVIC	AVOWAL	ALEXIS
WHITEN	CASUAL	GROUND	MISUSE	SHRUNK	CARVEL	OEUVRE	AVOWED	ANOXIA
WHITES	CEDULA	GROUPS	MODULE	SLEUTH	CARVER	OLIVER	BIGWIG	ANOXIC
WINTER	CERUSE	GROUSE	MUTUAL	SLOUCH	CERVIX	OLIVET	BLOWER	ATAXIA
WINTRY	CESURA	GROUTS	NATURE	SLOUGH	CHEVAL	OLIVIA	BLOWUP	ATAXIC
WITTED	CHOUAN	GROUTY	NEBULA	SNOUTY	CHEVET	OUTVIE	BLOWZY	BONXIE
WONTED	CHOUGH	HEAUME	NEBULE	SOLUTE	CHIVES	PARVIS	BOBWIG	DIAXON
WONTON	CLAUDE	HECUBA	NODULE	SPAULD	CHIVVY	PEEVED	BOWWOW	DIOXIN
WORTHY	CLAUSE	ILLUDE	NUCULE	SPOUSE	CLAVIS	PELVIC	BRAWNY	ELIXIR
WORTLE	CLOUDY	IMMUNE	OBTUND	SPRUCE	CLEVER	PELVIS	BREWER	FLAXEN
WRETCH	CLOUGH	IMMURE	OBTUSE	SPRUNG	CLOVEN	PLOVER	BREWIS	HOAXER
WRITER	COBURG	IMPUGN	OCCULT	STRUCK	CLOVER	PRAVDA	BROWNE	JINXED
WRITHE	COLUMN	IMPURE	OCCUPY	STRUNG	CLOVIS	PREVIN	BROWSE	KLAXON
YATTER	COQUET	IMPUTE	ONRUSH	STRUNT	COEVAL	PRIVET	CHOWRY	OREXIS
YESTER	CROUCH	INDUCE	OPPUGN	SUBURB	CONVEX	PROVEN	COBWEB	PINXIT
ZAFTIG	CROUPE	INDUCT	ORDURE	SUTURE	CONVEY	PULVER	CREWEL	PLEXOR
ZOSTER	CROUPY	INFUSE	PADUAN	SYRUPY	CONVOY	PURVEY	DARWIN	PLEXUS
ABDUCT	CROUSE	INGULF	PAPULE	TABULA	CORVÉE	QUAVER	DIMWIT	PRAXIS
ABJURE	CROUTE	INHUME	PARURE	TEGULA	CORVUS	QUIVER	DRAWER	RHEXIS
ABLUSH	CROUTH	INJURE	PENURY	TELUGU	CRAVAT	RENVOI	DROWSE	XERXES
ABOUND	CUPULE	INJURY	PEQUOD	TENURE	CRAVEN	RENVOY	DROWSY	ALIYAH
ABRUPT	CURULE	INRUSH	PERUKE	THOUGH	CULVER	SALVER	EARWAX	ARGYLE
ABSURD	DANUBE	INSULA	PERUSE	THRUSH	CURVED	SALVIA	EARWIG	ARGYLL
ACCUSE	DATURA	INSULT	PIQUET	THRUST	CURVET	SAVVEY	FLAWED	BANYAN
ACQUIT	DEBUNK	INSURE	PLEURA	TIPULA	DELVED	SERVAL	FLOWER	BARYTA
ACTUAL	DEDUCE	IRRUPT	PLOUGH	TITULE	DENVER	SERVER	FROWST	BUNYAN
ADDUCE	DEDUCT	ISEULT	PNEUMA	TOLUIC	DRIVEL	SHAVEN	FROWZY	CANYON
ADDUCT	DEFUSE	ISSUES	PROUST	TOLUOL	DRIVEN	SHAVER	GLOWER	CLAYEY
ADJURE	DELUDE	JAGUAR	PSEUDO	TORULA	DRIVER	SHEVAT	GNAWER	CORYZA
ADJUST	DELUGE	JEJUNE	RADULA	TRAUMA	DROVER	SHIVER	GODWIN	COTYLE
ADSUKI	DELUXE	JESUIT	RAGUSA	TROUGH	DROVES	SHOVEL	GODWIT	CRAYER
AGOUTI	DEMURE	JOCUND	RANULA	TROUPE	ELEVEN	SILVAN	GROWER	CRAYON
ALBUGO	DENUDE	JUJUBE	RAZURE	TROUVÉ	FERVID	SILVER	GROWTH	ENZYME
ALLUDE	DEPUTE	KABUKI	REBUFF	TUBULE	FERVOR	SKIVER	KEYWAY	FRAYED
ALLURE	DEPUTY	KANUCK	REBUKE	TUMULT	FLAVIN	SKIVVY	KOTWAL	GROYNE
AMBUSH	DILUTE	KAPUTT	REDUCE	TYBURN	FLAVOR	SLAVER	LEEWAY	JEKYLL
AMOUNT	DIQUAT	KIKUYU	REFUEL	UDMURT	FRIVOL	SLAVES	LUDWIG	KABYLE
ANNUAL	DISUSE	KORUNA	REFUGE	UNBUSY	GLOVED	SLIVER	MEDWAY	KENYAN
ARGUED	EDMUND	LACUNA	REFUND	UNDULY	GRAVEL	SOLVAY	MIDWAY	LARYNX
ARGUTE	EFFUSE	LAGUNA	REFUSE	UNFURL	GRAVEN	SOLVED	NITWIT	LAWYER
ARMURE	EMBUSY	LAGUNE	REFUTE	UNGULA	GRAVER	SOLVER	NORWAY	LIBYAN
AROUET	EMEUTE	LANUGO	REGULO	UNHURT	GRAVES	SPAVIN	ONEWAY	LLOYDS
AROUND	ENDURE	LAPUTA	REPUGN	UNJUST	GRAVID	STEVEN	OUTWIT	MAGYAR
AROUSE	ENGULF	LEGUME	REPUTE	UNRULY	GROVEL	STOVER	PEEWEE	OOCYTE
ARTURO	ENOUGH	LEMUEL	RESULT	UNSUNG	HALVED		PEEWIT	PAMYAT
ASSUME	ENSURE	LEMURE	RESUME	UNSURE	HALVES		POWWOW	PINYIN
ASSURE	EPAULE	LIGULA	RETURN	UPTURN	HARVEY		PREWAR	PLAYER

□□□□■□

POLYOL	SOZZLE	BANDAR	CARNAL	DIRHAM	GAVIAL	JIMJAM	MAOTAI	OOMPAH
POLYPS	TOLZEY	BANIAN	CARPAL	DISBAR	GEMMAN	JINGAL	MARIAN	ORDEAL
PRAYER	ZIGZAG	BANJAX	CASBAH	DISMAL	GENIAL	JORDAN	MARRAM	ORGEAT
ROSYTH	**6:5**	BANTAM	CASPAR	DISMAY	GERMAN	JOSIAH	MASHAM	ORPHAN
RUNYON		BANYAN	CASUAL	DOLLAR	GEWGAW	JOVIAL	MAYDAY	OSSIAN
SATYRA	ABADAN	BANZAI	CATHAR	DOLMAN	GHAZAL	JUBBAH	MEDIAL	OUTBAR
SAWYER	ABROAD	BAOBAB	CATHAY	DOODAD	GHERAO	JULIAN	MEDIAN	OUTGAS
SLAYER	ACTUAL	BARHAM	CATNAP	DOODAH	GILDAS	JUMBAL	MEDLAR	OUTLAW
SPRYLY	ADONAI	BARMAN	CAUSAL	DORCAS	GILEAD	KAFTAN	MEDWAY	OUTLAY
STAYER	ADRIAN	BARSAC	CAVEAT	DORIAN	GILGAI	KALPAK	MENCAP	OVISAC
SYZYGY	AEGEAN	BATEAU	CAYMAN	DORSAL	GIMBAL	KANSAS	MENIAL	OWLCAR
THEYRE	AERIAL	BATMAN	CEEFAX	DOSSAL	GLOBAL	KASBAH	MENSAL	OXHEAD
TROYES	AFFRAY	BAZAAR	CELIAC	DOWNAY	GOTHAM	KEDDAH	MENTAL	PADUAN
UNDYED	AFGHAN	BEDLAM	CELLAR	DUNBAR	GRAHAM	KENDAL	MERCAT	PALLAH
VOTYAK	AFLOAT	BEDPAN	CERCAL	DUNCAN	GUBBAH	KENSAL	MERMAN	PALLAS
YUMYUM	AIRMAN	BEENAH	CEREAL	DURBAR	GUFFAW	KENYAN	MESCAL	PAMPAS
AMAZED	AIRWAY	BEGGAR	CHAZAN	DURHAM	GUITAR	KEVLAR	MESIAL	PAMYAT
AMAZON	ALEGAR	BEHEAD	CHEVAL	DURIAN	GULLAH	KEYPAD	MICMAC	PARCAE
BALZAC	ALIYAH	BEHRAM	CHINAR	DVORAK	GUNMAN	KEYWAY	MIDDAY	PARIAH
BANZAI	AMORAL	BELIAL	CHITAL	EARWAX	GUSLAR	KHALAT	MIDWAY	PASCAL
BEZZLE	AMTRAK	BEMEAN	CHORAL	ELIJAH	HAEMAL	KHILAT	MINOAN	PATHAN
BLAZER	AMYTAL	BEMOAN	CHOUAN	ENDEAR	HAGGAI	KIDNAP	MISHAP	PAWPAW
BLAZON	ANABAS	BENGAL	CLIMAX	ENGRAM	HALLAL	KIRMAN	MISLAY	PAYDAY
BONZER	ANANAS	BETRAY	COEVAL	ENODAL	HAMMAM	KIRPAN	MISSAL	PEDLAR
BOOZER	ANDEAN	BEULAH	COGNAC	ENSEAL	HANGAR	KITBAG	MITRAL	PELHAM
BORZOI	ANIMAL	BEZOAR	COLLAR	ENTRAP	HANNAH	KITCAT	MOBCAP	PENMAN
BRAZEN	ANNEAL	BHAJAN	COLMAR	ENWRAP	HASSAR	KODIAK	MOIRAI	PENNAE
BRAZIL	ANNUAL	BHARAL	COMBAT	ENZIAN	HEEHAW	KOOLAH	MOLLAH	PENNAL
BUZZER	ANORAK	BHARAT	COMSAT	EPICAL	HELLAS	KOREAN	MONDAY	PENTAD
CHAZAN	ANURAN	BIRNAM	CONFAB	ESCHAR	HEPTAD	KOTWAL	MONIAL	PERHAP
CRAZED	ANYWAY	BISCAY	CONMAN	ESTRAY	HERBAL	KRUMAN	MOOLAH	PHONAL
DANZIG	AORTAL	BOBCAT	CONRAD	FABIAN	HETMAN	KUFIAH	MORGAN	PICKAX
DAZZLE	AOUDAD	BOMBAY	CORRAL	FACIAL	HEYDAY	LABIAL	MORNAY	PIEMAN
DONZEL	APICAL	BONSAI	COSTAR	FAECAL	HITMAN	LABLAB	MORTAL	PILLAR
FIZZED	APPEAL	BORDAR	COTTAR	FANTAN	HOBDAY	LAICAL	MORTAR	PINDAR
FIZZER	APPEAR	BOREAS	COUGAR	FENIAN	HOGGAR	LALLAN	MOSSAD	PINEAL
FIZZLE	APPIAN	BOTHAM	COWMAN	FERIAL	HOOHAH	LAMMAS	MOUTAN	PISGAH
FOOZLE	ARAFAT	BOWMAN	COWPAT	FERMAT	HOOKAH	LANDAU	MULLAH	PITMAN
FRIZZY	ARARAT	BOXCAR	CRAVAT	FESTAL	HOORAH	LARIAT	MURRAM	PLAGAL
FROZEN	ARGHAN	BRAMAH	CRENAL	FEUDAL	HOORAY	LARVAE	MURRAY	PLURAL
FUZZLE	ARREAR	BRIDAL	CRETAN	FILIAL	HOUDAH	LARVAL	MUSCAT	POLLAN
GEEZER	ARRIAN	BROGAN	CRINAL	FINGAL	HOWDAH	LASCAR	MUTUAL	POPLAR
GHAZAL	ASCHAM	BRUMAL	CROTAL	FINIAL	HURRAH	LAWMAN	MYRIAD	PORTAL
GIZZEN	ASCIAN	BRUTAL	CRURAL	FINLAY	HURRAY	LAYMAN	NALLAH	POSTAL
GLAZED	ASHCAN	BUCCAL	CUNEAL	FISCAL	HUSSAR	LEEWAY	NASSAU	PREFAB
GUZZLE	ASHLAR	BUCHAN	CUPMAN	FLORAL	HUZZAH	LEGMAN	NECKAR	PREPAY
HUZZAH	ASHPAN	BULGAR	CURSAL	FOETAL	HYDRAX	LETHAL	NECTAR	PRETAX
JAZZER	ASHTAR	BUNGAY	CURTAL	FOLIAR	HYMNAL	LIBYAN	NERVAL	PREWAR
LIZZIE	ASTRAL	BUNYAN	CURTAX	FORÇAT	HYPHAL	LILIAN	NEURAL	PRIMAL
MAMZER	ASTRAY	BUREAU	CUSHAT	FORMAL	IBADAN	LINEAL	NEWMAN	PULSAR
MIZZEN	ATABAL	BURIAL	CYMBAL	FORMAT	ICECAP	LINEAR	NILGAI	PUNJAB
MIZZLE	ATAMAN	BURLAP	DAEDAL	FORNAX	ICEMAN	LOGJAM	NILGAU	PUNKAH
MOZZLE	ATONAL	BURSAR	DAMMAR	FORRAD	INDIAN	LOOFAH	NINIAN	PURDAH
MUZZLE	ATRIAL	BUSMAN	DECCAN	FORMAT	INGRAM	LOQUAT	NORMAL	PUTEAL
NOZZLE	ATTRAP	BYELAW	DEEJAY	FORRAY	INROAD	LUCIAN	NORMAN	QUASAR
NUZZER	AUGEAN	CAESAR	DEFEAT	FORSAY	INSTAL	LUMBAR	NORWAY	QUIDAM
NUZZLE	AVATAR	CAFTAN	DEFRAG	FRACAS	INSTAR	LUTEAL	NOUGAT	RACIAL
PANZER	AVOWAL	CAIMAN	DEFRAY	FRIDAY	INTRAY	LYDIAN	NOVIAL	RADIAL
PHIZOG	AXEMAN	CALLAS	DELIAN	FRUGAL	IONIAN	MADCAP	NUGGAR	RADIAN
PIAZZA	AZONAL	CANAAN	DEMEAN	FULHAM	IPECAC	MADMAN	NULLAH	RAGBAG
PODZOL	BADMAN	CANNAE	DENIAL	FULMAR	ISAIAH	MADRAS	NUMDAH	RAGLAN
PRIZES	BAGMAN	CANTAB	DENTAL	FUNGAL	ISHTAR	MAENAD	OARLAP	RAGMAN
PUZZLE	BAHRAM	CANTAL	DEODAR	GAGMAN	ISOBAR	MAGYAR	OBITAL	RAMEAU
RAZZIA	BAIKAL	CANVAS	DERHAM	GAJUAR	JACKAL	MAIDAN	OCULAR	RASCAL
RAZZLE	BALAAM	CAPIAS	DERMAL	GAGMAN	JAGUAR	MALIAN	OERLAY	RATBAG
ROZZER	BALKAN	CAPTAN	DEWLAP	GASBAG	JETLAG	MALLAM	OILCAN	RATTAN
SCUZZY	BALLAD	CARDAN	DIANAS	GASMAN	JETSAM	MAMMAL	OILMAN	RECTAL
SIZZLE	BALSAM	CANTAR	DIKTAT	GASPAR	JIBBAH	MANIAC	ONEMAN	REDCAP
SNAZZY	BALZAC	CARFAX	DIQUAT	GATEAU	JIGSAW	MANUAL	ONEWAY	REDCAR

121

REDRAW	SPITAL	TULBAN	GAZEBO	BODACH	FIANCÉ	PALACE	STARCH	CANADA
REGGAE	SPREAD	TURBAN	GRANBY	BODICE	FIASCO	PAPACY	STENCH	CHILDE
REHEAT	SQUEAK	TUSCAN	GRUBBY	BORSCH	FIERCE	PATACA	STITCH	CICADA
RENTAL	SQUEAL	TUSSAH	HECUBA	BOUNCE	FLANCH	PAUNCE	STRICK	CLAUDE
REPEAL	STALAG	TYMBAL	HEREBY	BOUNCY	FLEECE	PAUNCH	STRICT	CLOUDY
REPEAT	STATAL	TYMPAN	IMBIBE	BRANCH	FLEECY	PIERCE	STRUCK	COMEDO
REPLAY	STORAX	UGRIAN	INDABA	BREACH	FLETCH	PIRACY	STUCCO	COMEDY
REREAD	STREAK	UNCIAL	JACOBS	BREECH	FLINCH	PLAICE	SUMACH	CYTODE
RESEAU	STREAM	UNCLAD	JOJOBA	BROACH	FLITCH	PLANCH	SWATCH	DECADE
REVEAL	STYRAX	UNLOAD	JUJUBE	BRONCO	FRANCE	PLEACH	SWITCH	DECIDE
RICRAC	SUBWAY	UNREAD	KARIBA	BROOCH	FRANCK	POLACK	TENACE	DECODE
RICTAL	SUKKAH	UNREAL	KNOBBY	BRUNCH	FRANCO	POLICE	THATCH	DELUDE
RIPSAW	SULTAN	UNSEAM	LAVABO	CALICO	FRENCH	POLICY	THENCE	DENUDE
RITUAL	SUNDAE	UNSEAT	MALIBU	CANUCK	FRESCO	POMACE	THRICE	DERIDE
RODHAM	SUNDAY	UNWRAP	MOOMBA	CHANCE	FRUICT	POUNCE	THWACK	DIRNDL
RUNWAY	SUNHAT	UPBEAT	NASEBY	CHANCY	GLANCE	PRANCE	TIERCE	DIVIDE
RUPIAH	SUNRAY	UPROAR	NEARBY	CHINCH	GLITCH	PREACE	TRANCE	DORADO
RUPIAS	SUNTAN	URINAL	PHOEBE	CHOICE	GREECE	PREACH	TRENCH	EMBODY
RUSTAM	SURTAX	VANDAL	ROKEBY	CHURCH	GROUCH	PRINCE	TRESCO	ENCODE
RYOKAN	SYLVAN	VASSAL	SCABBY	CILICE	GRUTCH	PUMICE	TWITCH	EPERDU
SAGGAR	SYNTAX	VATMAN	SCOOBS	CIVICS	HAUNCH	PUTSCH	UNDECK	ESCUDO
SALAAM	SYRIAN	VEDDAH	SCRIBE	CLENCH	HIJACK	QUAICH	UNLACE	ESPADA
SAMBAL	TAIPAN	VENIAL	SCRUBS	CLINCH	HITECH	QUELCH	UNLOCK	EXPEDE
SAMBAR	TAIWAN	VERBAL	SELLBY	CLOACA	HOOTCH	QUENCH	UNPACK	FACADE
SAMIAN	TAMMAR	VERNAL	SHABBY	CLUNCH	HORACE	QUETCH	UNPICK	FIELDS
SAMPAN	TANNAH	VERSAL	SHAMBA	CLUTCH	HUMECT	QUINCE	URTICA	FOREDO
SANDAL	TARMAC	VESTAL	STRABO	COERCE	IDIOCY	QUITCH	USANCE	FRONDE
SANTAL	TARSAL	VISUAL	STROBE	COMICE	IMPACT	RAUNCH	VARECH	FROUDE
SAPHAR	TARTAN	VIVIAN	STUBBS	CONICS	INDICT	REBECK	VAUNCE	FUMADO
SASHAY	TARTAR	VOTYAK	STUBBY	COPECK	INDUCE	REDACT	VELOCE	GARUDA
SATRAP	TASMAN	VULCAN	THISBE	CRANCH	INDUCT	REDUCE	VENICE	GELADA
SCALAR	TAXMAN	VULGAR	TRILBY	CRATCH	INFECT	REFACE	VESICA	GOURDE
SCARAB	TEABAG	WADHAM	WHITBY	CREACH	INJECT	REFECT	VIVACE	GOURDS
SCREAM	TEHRAN	WAGRAM	YORUBA	CROTCH	INSECT	REJECT	VOMICA	GREEDY
SEAMAN	TELLAR	WALLAH	ABBACY	CROUCH	INTACT	RELICS	WHENCE	GRUNDY
SEAWAY	TEOPAN	WARSAW	ABDUCT	CRUNCH	ITHACA	RELICT	WRENCH	GUARDI
SEESAW	TERNAL	WAYLAY	ABJECT	CRUTCH	JUDICA	RESECT	WRETCH	GUARDS
SENDAL	TERRAE	WEIMAR	ADDICT	CUBICA	KANUCK	ROCOCO	YORICK	GUILDS
SENLAC	TETRAD	WHYDAH	ADDUCE	CULTCH	KIRSCH	ROSACE	ZEBECK	HAIRDO
SEPTAL	THANAH	WIGWAM	ADDUCT	CURACY	KITSCH	ROUNCE	ZURICH	HALIDE
SERDAB	THEBAN	WIRRAL	ADVICE	DEDUCE	KVETCH	SCARCE	ABONDE	HOUNDS
SERIAL	THECAL	WITHAL	AFFECT	DEDUCT	LAUNCE	SCATCH	ABRADE	ILLUDE
SERVAL	THENAR	WOMBAT	AFRICA	DEFACE	LAUNCH	SCONCE	ACCEDE	IMPEDE
SEUMAS	THOMAS	XENIAL	AGENCY	DEFECT	LEGACY	SCORCH	AGENDA	INCEDE
SEURAT	THORAH	YEOMAN	ALCOCK	DEJECT	LORICA	SCOTCH	AIKIDO	INSIDE
SEXTAN	THORAX	YESMAN	ALERCE	DELICE	LUNACY	SCUTCH	ALBEDO	INVADE
SEXUAL	THREAD	ZIGZAG	ALPACA	DELICT	LYRICS	SEANCE	ALLUDE	ISOLDE
SHAMAN	THREAP	ZODIAC	AMERCE	DEPICT	MALICE	SEARCH	AMENDE	JUMADA
SHEVAT	THREAT	ZOPHAR	AMORCE	DETACH	MARACA	SEDUCE	AMENDS	KOMODO
SHIRAZ	THROAT	ZYRIAN	ANGICO	DETECT	MEDICI	SELECT	ARANDA	LAMBDA
SHOFAR	TINPAN	ABDABS	ANTICS	DEVICE	MEDICO	SENECA	ARCADE	LAMEDH
SIGNAL	TIPCAT	AEROBE	APERÇU	DIRECT	MENACE	SILICA	ARCADY	LIBIDO
SILVAN	TITIAN	AKIMBO	APIECE	DRENCH	MEXICO	SKETCH	ARMADA	LIPIDE
SIMIAN	TIZWAZ	AMOEBA	ARIOCH	EFFACE	MOHOCK	SLATCH	ATRIDE	LLOYDS
SINBAD	TOBIAS	ARROBA	ARNICA	EFFECT	MOLECH	SLOUCH	AUBADE	LUANDA
SIRDAR	TOECAP	AUCUBA	ARRACK	EGENCY	MOLOCH	SLUICE	BAHADA	MASADA
SIRKAR	TOERAG	BRUMBY	ASPECT	ELANCE	MONACO	SMIRCH	BARODA	MAUNDY
SIRRAH	TOMCAT	CHUBBY	ATTACH	ELLICE	MONICA	SMOOCH	BEJADE	MELODY
SKYLAB	TOMIAL	CRABBE	ATTACK	ENARCH	MUNICH	SNATCH	BESIDE	MIKADO
SKYMAN	TONGAN	CRABBY	AVOUCH	ENLACE	NAUTCH	SNITCH	BETIDE	MILADY
SLOGAN	TOUCAN	CRAMBO	BARUCH	ENRICH	NEBECK	SOLACE	BLENDE	MONODY
SLOVAK	TOWBAR	CROSBY	BASICS	ENTICE	NOTICE	SONICS	BLONDE	MOULDY
SOCIAL	TRAJAN	CRUMBS	BEDECK	EPARCH	NOUNCE	SOURCE	BLOODY	NEVADA
SOHRAB	TREPAN	DANUBE	BISECT	EROICA	NOVICE	SPEECH	BOARDS	NOBODY
SOLVAY	TRIBAL	DJERBA	BLANCH	ETHICS	NUANCE	SPENCE	BOLIDE	NOMADE
SONTAG	TRICAR	ENROBE	BLANCO	EUNUCH	OBJECT	SPLICE	BOUNDS	NOYADE
SPINAL	TROCAR	EPHEBE	BLEACH	EVINCE	OBTECT	SPRUCE	BRANDY	ONEIDA
SPINAR	TROJAN	FLABBY	BLENCH	EXARCH	OFFICE	STANCE	BROADS	ONSIDE
SPIRAL	TRUMAN	FLAMBÉ	BLOTCH	EXPECT	OPTICS	STANCH	BROODY	OROIDE

OVERDO	AMULET	BASSET	BOUSER	CAREEN	COLTER	CURPEL	DODGEM	ESTEEM
OXHIDE	AMUSED	BATHER	BOWLED	CAREER	COMBED	CURSED	DODGER	ESTHER
PAGODA	ANADEM	BATTEN	BOWLER	CARIES	COMBER	CURVED	DOGGED	ETCHER
PANADA	ANDREW	BATTER	BOWSER	CARMEL	COMPEL	CURVET	DOGGER	ETRIER
PARADE	ANGLED	BAWBEE	BRACER	CARMEN	CONFER	CUSSED	DOLMEN	EUBOEA
PARODY	ANGLER	BAXTER	BRACES	CARNET	CONGEE	CUSSER	DONKEY	EXCEED
PESADE	ANKLET	BEADED	BRAZEN	CARPEL	CONGER	CUSTER	DONNÉE	EXETER
POMADE	ANSWER	BEAKER	BREMEN	CARPER	CONKER	CUTLER	DONZEL	EXOCET
POSADA	ANTHEM	BEARER	BREVET	CARPET	CONNER	CUTLET	DOOFER	EXOGEN
POUNDS	ANTHER	BEATEN	BREWER	CARREL	CONVEX	CUTTER	DOOMED	EYELET
PRAVDA	ANTLER	BEATER	BROKEN	CARTEL	CONVEY	CYGNET	DORMER	FABLED
PSEUDO	APNOEA	BEAVER	BROKER	CARTER	COOKED	CYPHER	DORSET	FABLES
RAPIDS	APOGEE	BECKET	BRUNEI	CARVED	COOKER	DAGGER	DORTER	FACIES
RECEDE	APPLES	BEDDER	BRUNEL	CARVEL	COOLER	DAMNED	DOSSER	FAECES
REMEDY	ARCHED	BEEPER	BUCKED	CARVER	COOPER	DAMPEN	DOTTED	FAGGED
RESEDA	ARCHER	BELIEF	BUCKER	CASHEW	COPIED	DAMPER	DOUCET	FALLEN
RESIDE	ARCHES	BELSEN	BUCKET	CASKET	COPIER	DAMSEL	DOWNER	FALTER
RIYADH	ARGUED	BELTED	BUDGET	CASTER	COPPER	DANCER	DOWSER	FARDEL
ROUNDS	ARMLET	BENDED	BUFFER	CAUDEX	COQUET	DANDER	DOWSET	FARMER
RWANDA	ARNHEM	BENDER	BUFFET	CAUSED	CORBEL	DANGER	DOYLEY	FASCES
SALADE	AROUET	BENNET	BUGGER	CAUSEY	CORKED	DANIEL	DRAGEE	FASTEN
SECEDE	ASHLEY	BERBER	BUGLER	CENSER	CORKER	DAPPER	DRAPER	FATHER
SHANDY	ASLEEP	BERGEN	BULGER	CENTER	CORNEA	DARIEN	DRAWER	FATTEN
SHINDY	ATABEG	BESEEM	BULLER	CERMET	CORNED	DARKEN	DRIVEL	FAUCES
SHODDY	ATTLEE	BESSEL	BULLET	CERTES	CORNEL	DARKEY	DRIVEN	FAUCET
SPEEDO	AUBREY	BESTED	BUMPER	CHAFER	CORNER	DARTER	DRIVER	FAWKES
SPEEDY	AUDLEY	BETHEL	BUNGEE	CHALET	CORNET	DASHED	DRONES	FEEDER
STEADY	AUDREY	BETTER	BUNJEE	CHANEY	CORSET	DAUDET	DROVER	FEELER
STRIDE	AUSPEX	BHAJEE	BUNKER	CHAPEL	CORTES	DAWNEY	DROVES	FELLER
STRODE	AUSTEN	BIASED	BUNSEN	CHASER	CORTEX	DAYBED	DRYDEN	FENCER
STURDY	AUSTER	BICKER	BUNTER	CHEDER	CORTEZ	DEADEN	DUCKED	FENDER
TELEDU	AVOCET	BIDDER	BURDEN	CHENET	CORVÉE	DEAFEN	DUDDER	FENNEL
TEREDO	AVOWED	BIGGER	BURGEE	CHEVET	COSHER	DEALER	DUDEEN	FERRET
TIRADE	AWAKEN	BILLET	BURGER	CHIMER	COSIER	DEARER	DUFFEL	FESTER
TOLEDO	AWOKEN	BINDER	BURIED	CHIMES	COSMEA	DECKED	DUFFER	FETTER
TRENDY	AZALEA	BIOGEN	BURLEY	CHISEL	COSSET	DECKER	DULCET	FETTES
TRIODE	AZORES	BISTER	BURNER	CHIVES	COSTER	DECREE	DUMPER	FIBBED
TUXEDO	AZRAEL	BITTEN	BURNET	CHOKED	COULEE	DECREW	DUNCES	FIBBER
TWEEDS	BACKER	BITTER	BUSHED	CHOKER	COWPER	DEEPEN	DUNDEE	FIDGET
TWEEDY	BACKET	BLAMED	BUSHEL	CHOKEY	COZIER	DEEPER	DUNDER	FILLED
UGANDA	BADGER	BLAZER	BUSKER	CHOLER	CRATER	DEGREE	DUNKER	FILLER
UNMADE	BAILEE	BLIMEY	BUSKET	CHOREA	CRAVEN	DEKKER	DUPLEX	FILLET
UNTIDY	BAILER	BLOWER	BUSTED	CHOREE	CRAYER	DELVED	DUSTED	FILTER
UPSIDE	BAILEY	BOATER	BUSTER	CHOSEN	CRAZED	DENIED	DUSTER	FINDER
VIANDS	BALDER	BOBBER	BUTLER	CINDER	CRENEL	DENIER	DZEREN	FINGER
WEIRDO	BALEEN	BODGER	BUTTER	CIPHER	CREWEL	DENVER	EARNED	FIRMER
XANADU	BALLET	BODIES	BUZZER	CLARET	CRIKEY	DEXTER	EARNER	FISHER
YEZIDI	BANGER	BOILED	CACHET	CLAYEY	CRIMEA	DIADEM	EASIER	FITTED
ZOUNDS	BANKER	BOILER	CADGER	CLEVER	CRIPES	DIAPER	EASTER	FITTER
ABDIEL	BANNED	BOLLEN	CAHIER	CLIMES	CRONET	DIBBER	ECCLES	FIZZED
ACATES	BANNER	BOLTER	CALCED	CLOSED	CRUMEN	DICKER	EDITED	FIZZER
ACUMEN	BANNET	BOMBER	CALKER	CLOSER	CRUSET	DICKEY	EIFFEL	FLAMEN
ADDEEM	BANTER	BONDED	CALLED	CLOSET	CUDGEL	DIESEL	EITHER	FLARES
ADDLED	BARBED	BONDER	CALLER	CLOVEN	CUFFEE	DIETER	ELANET	FLAWED
ADORER	BARBEL	BONNET	CALLET	CLOVER	CUITER	DIFFER	ELATED	FLAXEN
AFFRET	BARBER	BONZER	CALVER	COALER	CULDEE	DIGGER	ELEVEN	FLORET
AFREET	BARBET	BOOKED	CAMBER	COATED	CULLET	DIMMER	ELODEA	FLOWER
AGREED	BARGEE	BOOKER	CAMDEN	COATES	CULMEN	DINNER	ELOPER	FLUTED
AIGLET	BARKER	BOOMER	CAMPED	COBBER	CULTER	DIPPER	ELYSEE	FLUTER
AIRBED	BARLEY	BOOTEE	CAMPER	COBDEN	CULVER	DISHED	EMBLEM	FLUTES
ALFRED	BARNES	BOÖTES	CANCEL	COBWEB	CUMBER	DISHES	ENAMEL	FODDER
ALIPED	BARNET	BOOZER	CANCER	COCKER	CUMMER	DISNEY	ENFREE	FOILED
ALLIED	BARNEY	BORDER	CANKER	CODGER	CUNNER	DISPEL	ENTREE	FOKKER
ALLIER	BARRED	BORNEO	CANNED	COFFEE	CUPPED	DITHER	EOTHEN	FOLDED
ALTHEA	BARREL	BOSKET	CANNEL	COFFER	CUPPER	DJEBEL	EPOPEE	FOLDER
ALUDEL	BARREN	BOSSED	CANTER	COGGER	CURFEW	DOCKED	ERASED	FOOTER
AMAZED	BARTER	BOTHER	CANVEY	COILED	CURIET	DOCKER	ERASER	FORCED
AMBLER	BASHER	BOTLEY	CAPLET	COINER	CURLER	DOCKET	ERODED	FORCES
AMORET	BASKET	BOURÉE	CAPPED	COLLET	CURLEW	DODDER	ESCHEW	FORGED

123

FORGER	GNAWER	HASLET	HOSTEL	JUMPER	LEAVES	MAILER	MORSEL	OPENER
FORGET	GOATEE	HASTEN	HOTBED	JUNKER	LECHER	MALLEE	MORTEM	ORIGEN
FORKED	GOBBET	HATRED	HOTTER	JUNKET	LEDGER	MALLET	MOSLEM	ORKNEY
FORMER	GOBLET	HATTER	HOUSES	KAFFER	LEGGED	MALTED	MOTHER	OSPREY
FOSTER	GOFFER	HAWKED	HOWLER	KAISER	LEGLET	MAMZER	MOTLEY	OSTLER
FOWLER	GOITER	HAWKER	HOYDEN	KANTEN	LEMUEL	MANGER	MOUSER	OSTREA
FRAMED	GOLDEN	HAWSER	HUGHES	KEELER	LENDER	MANNER	MOUSEY	OUNCES
FRATER	GOLFER	HAYLEY	HULLED	KEENER	LENTEL	MARCEL	MOUTER	OUTLET
FRAYED	GOOBER	HEADED	HUMBER	KEEPER	LENTEN	MARKED	MOVIES	OUTSET
FROZEN	GOOLEY	HEADER	HUMMEL	KELPER	LESSEE	MARKER	MUCKER	OXYGEN
FRUTEX	GOPHER	HEALER	HUMMER	KELTER	LESSEN	MARKET	MUDDER	OYSTER
FUHRER	GORGED	HEAPED	HUMPED	KENNEL	LESSER	MARNER	MUFFET	PACKED
FULLER	GORGES	HEARER	HUNGER	KENNET	LESTER	MARTEL	MUGGER	PACKER
FUNDED	GORGET	HEATED	HUNKER	KEPLER	LETTER	MARTEN	MULLER	PACKET
FUNNEL	GOSPEL	HEATER	HUNTER	KERMES	LEYDEN	MARVEL	MULLET	PADDED
FURIES	GOTTEN	HEAVED	HURLEY	KERNEL	LIBBER	MASHED	MUMMER	PAINED
GABLED	GRABEN	HEAVEN	HUSHED	KEYNES	LICHEN	MASHER	MUPPET	PAIRER
GADGET	GRACES	HEAVES	HUXLEY	KHYBER	LIEDER	MASKED	MURDER	PALLET
GAFFER	GRADED	HEBREW	HYADES	KICKER	LIFTED	MASKER	MURIEL	PALMER
GAINER	GRADES	HEEDED	HYPHEN	KIDNEY	LIFTER	MASSED	MUSKEG	PAMPER
GAITER	GRAPES	HEELED	IBIDEM	KILLER	LIGGER	MASSES	MUSKET	PANDER
GALLEN	GRATED	HEIFER	ILKLEY	KILNER	LIMBED	MASTER	MUSSEL	PANTER
GALLET	GRATER	HELLER	IMOGEN	KILTED	LIMBER	MATTED	MUSTER	PANZER
GALLEY	GRAVEL	HELMET	INBRED	KILTER	LIMNER	MATTER	MUTTER	PARCEL
GAMBET	GRAVEN	HELPER	INCHES	KIMMER	LIMPET	MAUSER	MYOGEN	PARGET
GAMMER	GRAVER	HEMPEN	INDEED	KINDER	LINDEN	MAYHEM	NAILED	PARKED
GANDER	GRAVES	HENLEY	INDIES	KIPPER	LINGER	MEAGER	NAILER	PARKER
GANGER	GRIMES	HERDEN	INGRES	KIRBEH	LINKER	MEDLEY	NANSEN	PARLEY
GANGES	GRIPES	HERDER	INKJET	KISLEV	LINNET	MELTED	NANTES	PARPEN
GANNET	GROCER	HERMES	INLIER	KISMET	LINTEL	MEMBER	NAPIER	PARSEC
GAOLER	GROPER	HERPES	INSTEP	KISSEL	LIONEL	MENDEL	NAPLES	PARSEE
GARBED	GROVEL	HERREN	IRONED	KISSER	LIPPED	MENDER	NAPPER	PASSED
GARDEN	GROWER	HICKEY	ISABEL	KITTEN	LISPER	MENDES	NASSER	PASSES
GARGET	GUIDES	HIDDEN	ISOMER	KNIVES	LISTEL	MERCER	NATTER	PASTEL
GARNER	GUINEA	HIGHER	ISRAEL	KOSHER	LISTEN	MERGER	NAUSEA	PATTEN
GARNET	GULLET	HIMMEL	ISSUES	KRAKEN	LISTER	MERSEY	NEAPED	PATTER
GARRET	GULLEY	HINDER	ITCHEN	KRATER	LITTER	MESMER	NEARER	PAUPER
GARTER	GULPER	HINGED	JABBER	KRONER	LOADED	METIER	NEATEN	PAWNEE
GASKET	GUMMED	HINGES	JACKET	KRUGER	LOADER	MICKEY	NECKED	PEAHEN
GASPER	GUNNEL	HIPPED	JAEGER	KUMMEL	LOAFER	MIDDEN	NEEDED	PEAKED
GASSER	GUNNER	HIRSEL	JAGGED	LAAGER	LOAVES	MIDGET	NEPHEW	PECKER
GASTER	GUNTER	HITHER	JAGGER	LACHES	LOCKED	MILDEW	NERVES	PECTEN
GATHER	GURLET	HITLER	JAILER	LACKEY	LOCKER	MILIEU	NETHER	PEDDER
GAUGER	GURNET	HITTER	JAMMED	LADDER	LOCKET	MILLER	NEUTER	PEELED
GEEZER	GURNEY	HOAXER	JARVEY	LADIES	LODGED	MILLET	NIAMEY	PEELER
GEIGER	GUSHER	HOBBES	JASPER	LAFFER	LODGER	MINCER	NICKED	PEEPER
GELLER	GUSSET	HOCKEY	JAZZER	LAMMER	LOGGER	MINDED	NICKEL	PEEVED
GENDER	GUTTER	HODDER	JEEVES	LANCER	LOITER	MINDEL	NICKER	PEEWEE
GENTES	HACKEE	HOGGET	JENNER	LANCET	LONGER	MINDER	NIDGET	PEGLEG
GETTER	HACKER	HOIDEN	JENNET	LANDED	LOOPED	MINUET	NIGGER	PELLET
GEYSER	HAGDEN	HOLDER	JERKER	LANDER	LOOPER	MISLED	NIKKEI	PELMET
GHEBER	HAILER	HOLLER	JERSEY	LAPPER	LOOSEN	MISSED	NIPPER	PENCEL
GIBBER	HALLEY	HOLMES	JESTER	LAPPET	LOOTER	MISSEL	NISSEN	PENSÉE
GIBBET	HALTER	HONIED	JIGGER	LAPSED	LOUDEN	MISTER	NODDED	PENTEL
GIFTED	HALVED	HOODED	JILLET	LARDER	LOUVER	MITRED	NUGGET	PEPPER
GIGLET	HALVES	HOOFED	JINXED	LASHED	LOWKEY	MITTEN	NUMBER	PESTER
GILDED	HAMLET	HOOFER	JITNEY	LASHER	LUBBER	MIZZEN	NUTMEG	PETREL
GILDER	HAMMER	HOOKED	JITTER	LASKET	LUGGER	MOANER	NUTTER	PEWTER
GILLET	HAMPER	HOOKER	JOBBER	LATEEN	LUMBER	MOATED	NUZZER	PHLOEM
GIMLET	HANDEL	HOOKEY	JOCKEY	LATHER	LUSTER	MOCKER	OAKLEY	PHONEY
GIMMER	HANGER	HOOPER	JOGGER	LATTEN	LUTHER	MOIDER	OBITER	PHOOEY
GINGER	HANKER	HOOTER	JOINER	LATTER	LYCHEE	MOLTEN	OCHREA	PICKED
GIRDER	HAPPEN	HOOVER	JOSSER	LAUDER	MADDEN	MONGER	OFFSET	PICKER
GIZZEN	HAPTEN	HOPPER	JOTTER	LAUREL	MADDER	MONKEY	OGADEN	PICKET
GLAZED	HARDEN	HORNED	JUDDER	LAWYER	MAGLEV	MONTEM	OLIVER	PIECES
GLIDER	HARKEN	HORNER	JUDGES	LEADEN	MAGNES	MOPPET	OLIVET	PIGLET
GLOVED	HARMED	HORNET	JUGGER	LEADER	MAGNET	MOREEN	OMELET	PIGPEN
GLOWER	HARVEY	HORSED	JUICER	LEAVEN	MAHLER	MORGEN	ONAGER	PILFER
GLUTEN	HASHED	HOSIER	JULIET	LEAVER	MAIDEN	MORNED	OODLES	PINCER

PINGER	PUPPET	RIMMED	SAWYER	SITREP	STATEN	TATLER	TROVER	WAILER
PINTER	PURLER	RINGED	SCALER	SITTER	STATER	TATTER	TROWEL	WAITER
PIQUET	PURSED	RINGER	SCALES	SKATER	STATES	TAUTEN	TROYES	WAIVER
PISCES	PURSER	RIOTER	SCARED	SKATES	STAYER	TEASEL	TUAREG	WALKER
PISSED	PURVEY	RIPPER	SCARER	SKEWED	STEREO	TEASER	TUCKER	WALLED
PITTED	PUSHER	ROAMER	SCHLEP	SKEWER	STEVEN	TECKEL	TUCKET	WALLER
PITTER	PUSSER	ROARER	SCOLEX	SKIVER	STEWED	TEEPEE	TUFFET	WALLET
PLACED	PUTTEE	ROBBED	SCORER	SLATER	STIPES	TEETER	TUFTED	WALTER
PLACER	PUTTER	ROBBER	SCOTER	SLAVER	STOKER	TEGMEN	TUNNEL	WANDER
PLANET	QUAKER	ROCKER	SCREED	SLAVES	STOKES	TELLER	TUREEN	WANKEL
PLATED	QUAVER	ROCKET	SCREEN	SLAYER	STOLEN	TEMPER	TURKEY	WANTED
PLATEN	QUEBEC	RODNEY	SEABEE	SLEWED	STONED	TENDER	TURNED	WARDEN
PLATER	QUIVER	ROEMER	SEALED	SLICER	STONER	TENNER	TURNER	WARDER
PLATES	QUOTED	ROGUES	SEAMEN	SLIDER	STONES	TERCET	TURRET	WARMER
PLAYER	RABBET	ROLLER	SEAMER	SLIVER	STORER	TERMES	TURVES	WARNER
PLOVER	RABIES	ROMMEL	SEATED	SLOPES	STOREY	TESTER	TUSKER	WARPED
PLUMED	RACHEL	ROMNEY	SECRET	SMILER	STOVER	TESTES	TWICER	WARREN
POCKET	RACKET	RONDEL	SEEDED	SMILES	STOWER	TETHER	TWINED	WASHED
POISED	RAFTER	ROOFER	SEEDER	SMILEY	STREET	THALER	ULSTER	WASHER
POLDER	RAGGED	ROOMER	SEEKER	SMOKER	STUMER	THALES	UMBLES	WASTED
POLLED	RAIDER	ROOTED	SELFED	SMOKEY	STYLET	THAMES	UMBREL	WASTEL
POLLEN	RAISED	ROOTER	SELLER	SNAKED	SUBLET	THANET	UNBRED	WASTER
POLLEX	RAISER	ROQUET	SEMTEX	SNIPER	SUBSET	THEBES	UNDIES	WEAKEN
POMMEL	RAMJET	ROSSER	SENDER	SNIVEL	SUCKEN	THROES	UNDYED	WEAKER
POMPEY	RANCEL	ROSTER	SENNET	SNORER	SUCKER	TICKER	UNEVEN	WEARER
PONDER	RANGER	ROTHER	SENSED	SNOWED	SUCKET	TICKET	UNISEX	WEASEL
PONGEE	RANKED	ROTTEN	SENSES	SOAKED	SUDDEN	TICKEY	UNITED	WEAVER
POOTER	RANKER	ROTTER	SEPTET	SOCCER	SUFFER	TIERED	UNMEET	WEBBED
POPPER	RANTER	ROUGED	SEQUEL	SOCKET	SUITED	TILLER	UNREEL	WEDDED
POPPET	RAPIER	ROUTER	SERIES	SODDEN	SUIVEZ	TIMBER	UNSEEN	WEDGED
PORKER	RAPPED	ROZZER	SERVER	SOFTEN	SULLEN	TINDER	UNUSED	WEEPER
PORTER	RAPPEL	RUBBED	SETTEE	SOILED	SUMMER	TINGED	UPKEEP	WEEWEE
POSSER	RAPPER	RUBBER	SETTER	SOIREE	SUNDER	TINKER	URETER	WELDER
POSSET	RASHER	RUBIES	SÈVRES	SOLDER	SUNDEW	TINNED	USURER	WELLER
POSTER	RASPER	RUCHED	SEXTET	SOLVED	SUNKEN	TINSEL	VALLEY	WELLES
POTEEN	RASTER	RUDDER	SHADED	SOLVER	SUNSET	TINTED	VALUER	WELTER
POTHER	RATHER	RUGGED	SHADES	SOMBER	SUPLEX	TIPPED	VARIED	WESKER
POTTED	RATTER	RUGGER	SHAKEN	SONNET	SUPPER	TIPPER	VARLET	WESLEY
POTTER	READER	RUINED	SHAKER	SOONER	SURFER	TIPPET	VATHEK	WESSEX
POURER	REAMER	RUMMER	SHAKES	SORBET	SURREY	TITFER	VEILED	WETHER
POUTER	REAPER	RUNNEL	SHAPED	SORDES	SURVEY	TITLED	VEINED	WHALER
POWDER	REDDEN	RUNNER	SHARED	SORREL	SUSSEX	TITTER	VELVET	WHALES
POWTER	REDEEM	RUPEES	SHARER	SORTER	SUTLER	TOFFEE	VENDEE	WHITED
PRATER	REDLEG	RUSHED	SHARES	SORTES	SUTTEE	TOGGED	VENDER	WHITEN
PRAYER	REEFER	RUSSET	SHAVEN	SOUPER	SWANEE	TOILET	VENEER	WHITES
PREFER	REELER	RUSTEM	SHAVER	SOUSED	SWEDEN	TOLLED	VERGER	WICKED
PREMED	REFLET	RUTTED	SHEKEL	SOUTER	SWIPES	TOLLER	VERGES	WICKER
PRICED	REFLEX	RUTTER	SHINER	SOVIET	SWIVEL	TOLTEC	VERSED	WICKET
PRICEY	REFUEL	SAANEN	SHIVER	SOWSED	SWIVET	TOLZEY	VERSES	WIDGET
PRIMED	REGLET	SABRES	SHOVEL	SOWTER	SYDNEY	TOOTER	VERSET	WIENER
PRIMER	REGRET	SACHET	SHOWER	SPACED	SYPHER	TOPPER	VERVET	WILDER
PRIVET	REHEEL	SACRED	SHRIEK	SPACER	SYSTEM	TORRES	VESPER	WILLED
PRIZES	RELIEF	SADDEN	SICKEN	SPADES	TABLET	TOSHER	VESSEL	WILLET
PROLEG	RENDER	SALLEE	SICKER	SPICED	TACKET	TOTTER	VESTED	WIMSEY
PROPEL	RENNET	SALLET	SIDNEY	SPICER	TAIPEI	TOUPEE	VIEWER	WINDER
PROPER	RENTER	SALVER	SIFTER	SPIDER	TALKER	TOUPET	VIOLET	WINGED
PROTEA	REOPEN	SAMIEL	SIGNET	SPIKED	TAMPER	TOURER	VISIER	WINGER
PROVEN	REUBEN	SAMLET	SILKEN	SPINET	TANDEM	TOUSER	VIVIEN	WINKER
PRUNER	REUTER	SAMUEL	SILVER	SPLEEN	TANKER	TOWHEE	VIZIER	WINNER
PUCKER	REVIEW	SANDER	SIMMER	SPOKEN	TANNED	TOWNEE	VOICED	WINTER
PUDSEY	RHODES	SANSEI	SIMNEL	SPOKES	TANNER	TOWSER	VOIDED	WISDEN
PUFFED	RHYMER	SAPPER	SIMPER	STAGER	TAPPER	TRACER	VOIDEE	WISHES
PUFFER	RIBBED	SARSEN	SINDER	STAGEY	TAPPET	TRADER	VOIDER	WITHER
PULLET	RICHES	SATEEN	SINGER	STAKES	TARCEL	TRADES	VOLLEY	WITTED
PULLEY	RICKER	SAUCER	SINKER	STAMEN	TARGET	TRALEE	VORTEX	WIZIER
PULVER	RICKEY	SAUGER	SINNER	STAPES	TARSEL	TRAPES	VOSGES	WOLVER
PUMMEL	RIDGED	SAVVEY	SIPPET	STARES	TASSEL	TRAVEL	WACKER	WONDER
PUNNET	RIGGED	SAWDER	SIRREE	STARET	TASSET	TRIBES	WAFTED	WONTED
PUNTER	RIGGER	SAWNEY	SISTER	STATED	TASTER	TRIVET	WAGNER	WOODED

WOODEN	STAFFA	FLEDGE	SMUDGE	CLOTHO	PYRRHO	AGLAIA	BIONIC	COPPIN
WOOFER	STRAFE	FORAGE	SMUDGY	CONCHA	QUICHE	AGNAIL	BIOPIC	COPTIC
WOOKEY	STRIFE	FOREGO	SNAGGY	CONCHY	RANCHO	AGONIC	BIOTIC	CORBIE
WOOLEN	STUFFY	FRIDGE	SNUDGE	CRÈCHE	RHAPHE	ALALIA	BIOTIN	CORRIE
WORKED	TARIFF	FRIGGA	SOCAGE	CROCHE	RHYTHM	ALARIC	BIRDIE	COSMIC
WORKER	THRIFT	FRINGE	SORAGE	CUTCHA	ROUGHY	ALBEIT	BOBBIN	COSSIE
WORSEN	TIPOFF	GARAGE	SPONGE	DAISHO	SADDHU	ALDRIN	BOBWIG	COULIS
WOWSER	TUMEFY	GAVAGE	SPONGY	DELPHI	SAITHE	ALEVIN	BODGIE	COUSIN
WRITER	TYPIFY	GEORGE	SPUNGE	DEPTHS	SANCHO	ALEXIA	BODKIN	COWRIE
XAVIER	UNSAFE	GINKGO	SPURGE	DINGHY	SAPPHO	ALEXIN	BOFFIN	CRASIS
XERXES	UPLIFT	GIORGI	STINGO	DIVEHI	SCATHE	ALEXIS	BONNIE	CREDIT
YABBER	VERIFY	GRANGE	STINGY	DOUCHE	SCYTHE	ALMAIN	BONXIE	CRETIC
YAHWEH	VILIFY	GRINGO	STODGE	DOUGHY	SEETHE	ALOGIA	BOOGIE	CRETIN
YAKKER	WHARFE	GROGGY	STODGY	DRACHM	SEICHE	ALTAIR	BOOKIE	CRISIS
YAMMER	ABREGE	GRUDGE	STOOGE	EARTHY	SHTCHI	AMELIA	BORGIA	CRITIC
YANKEE	AGRÉGÉ	GRUNGE	STREGA	ELISHA	SIDDHA	ANEMIA	BOTHIE	CUBOID
YANKER	ALBUGO	HIDAGE	SWINGE	ELTCHI	SLIGHT	ANEMIC	BOVRIL	CUFFIN
YATTER	ALLEGE	HOMAGE	SYZYGY	FILTHY	SLITHY	ANGLIA	BOWFIN	CULLIS
YEOMEN	AMBAGE	IMPUGN	TELEGA	FLASHY	SLOSHY	ANOXIA	BRAZIL	CUMMIN
YESTER	ARMAGH	INDIGN	TELEGU	FLECHE	SLUSHY	ANOXIC	BREWIS	CUPRIC
YIPPEE	ASSIGN	INDIGO	TELUGU	FLESHY	SMIGHT	ANTLIA	BRIDIE	CURRIE
YONDER	AURIGA	KLUDGE	THINGS	FLIGHT	SMITHS	ANTRIM	BUDGIE	CYANIN
YORKER	AVENGE	KNAGGY	THINGY	FLUSHY	SMITHY	ANUBIS	BULBIL	CYBRID
YUCKER	BARÈGE	LADOGA	THOUGH	FORTHY	SOOTHE	APORIA	BUSKIN	CYCLIC
ZAGREB	BELUGA	LANUGO	TOBAGO	FOUGHT	SORGHO	ARABIA	BYRNIE	CYESIS
ZANDER	BENIGN	LAVAGE	TOWAGE	FRIGHT	SOUGHT	ARABIC	CABBIE	CYMRIC
ZIMMER	BLUDGE	LOUNGE	TRIAGE	FROTHY	SPATHE	ARABIS	CACCIA	CYPRID
ZINGER	BOCAGE	LOVAGE	TROUGH	FURPHY	SULPHA	ARALIA	CADDIE	CYPRIS
ZIPPER	BODEGA	MALAGA	TRUDGE	GANDHI	SWATHE	ARAMIS	CADDIS	CYSTIC
ZITHER	BORAGE	MALIGN	TSONGA	GAUCHE	TAUGHT	ARCHIE	CALAIS	CYTOID
ZONKED	BRIDGE	MANAGE	TWIGGY	GAUCHO	TEETHE	ARCHIL	CALKIN	DACOIT
ZOSTER	CHANGE	MANEGE	TWINGE	GEISHA	TETCHY	ARCTIC	CALLID	DAFTIE
ADRIFT	CHARGE	MENAGE	ULLAGE	GOETHE	TITCHY	ARMPIT	CALVIN	DAHLIA
BEREFT	CHOUGH	METAGE	UNCAGE	GUNGHO	TOOTHY	ASSAIL	CAMAIL	DAIMIO
BOUFFE	CIERGE	MIRAGE	VIRAGO	GURKHA	TOUCHE	ASSOIL	CAPSID	DAMMIT
BRIEFS	CLAGGY	MURAGE	VISAGE	HEIGHT	TOUCHY	ATAXIA	CARLIN	DANZIG
CARAFE	CLERGY	NONAGE	VOLAGE	HONCHO	TRASHY	ATAXIC	CASEIN	DARKIE
CHUFFY	CLOUGH	OBLIGE	VOYAGE	HONSHU	TROCHE	ATOCIA	CASSIA	DARWIN
CLIFFS	COWAGE	OPPUGN	WHINGE	KACCHA	TROPHE	ATOMIC	CASSIO	DEARIE
CODIFY	CRAGGY	ORANGE	AGATHA	KANGHA	TROPHY	ATONIC	CASSIS	DEBRIS
CUTOFF	CREAGH	ORTEGA	ALIGHT	KANTHA	TRUTHS	ATTAIN	CATKIN	DECEIT
DECAFF	CRINGE	OTALGY	APACHE	KNIGHT	TWIGHT	AUNTIE	CATNIP	DEMAIN
FAROFF	CUBAGE	OUTAGE	APATHY	KUCCHA	WEIGHT	AUSSIE	CAVEIN	DENNIS
FLUFFY	DAMAGE	PAPAGO	APHTHA	KWACHA	WHISHT	AUSTIN	CEDRIC	DERAIL
LAYOFF	DÉGAGÉ	PHLEGM	ASADHA	KYUSHU	WORTHY	AZOTIC	CELTIC	DERAIN
MODIFY	DELUGE	PILAGE	AYESHA	LITCHI	WRIGHT	BABBIT	CERVIX	DERMIS
MUNIFY	DESIGN	PLEDGE	BACCHI	LOATHE	WRITHE	BAFFIN	CHEMIC	DERRIS
NIDIFY	DOINGS	PLONGE	BEACHY	LORCHA	ABELIA	BAGNIO	CHERIE	DETAIL
NOTIFY	DOSAGE	PLOUGH	BEEGHA	LOUCHE	ABSEIL	BAGUIO	CHESIL	DETAIN
OSSIFY	DOTAGE	PLUNGE	BERTHA	MALTHA	ABULIA	BAILIE	CHITIN	DEVOID
PACIFY	DREDGE	QUAGGA	BERTHE	MANCHE	ACACIA	BALKIS	CHOPIN	DIACID
PAYOFF	DREGGY	QUAIGH	BITCHY	MANCHU	ACADIA	BALTIC	CITRIC	DIKDIK
PIAFFE	DRONGO	QUANGO	BLIGHT	MARSHY	ACARID	BANDIT	CITRIN	DIMWIT
PILAFF	DRUDGE	RAVAGE	BLITHE	MARTHA	ACEDIA	BARKIS	CLAVIS	DIOXIN
POUFFE	EATAGE	REFUGE	BOLSHY	MONTHS	ACETIC	BARRIE	CLERIC	DIZAIN
PURIFY	EFFIGY	RENEGE	BOUCHE	MUNSHI	ACIDIC	BARRIO	CLINIC	DOBBIN
RAMIFY	ELOIGN	REPUGN	BOUGHT	MURPHY	ACQUIT	BAUCIS	CLONIC	DOMAIN
RAREFY	EMERGE	RESIGN	BRECHT	MURRHA	ADAGIO	BEANIE	CLOVIS	DORRIT
RATIFY	EMULGE	RIVAGE	BRIGHT	NAUGHT	ADJOIN	BEDSIT	COCCID	DROMIO
REBUFF	EMUNGE	SAVAGE	BUDDHA	NAVAHO	ADONIS	BEMOIL	COCHIN	DUBBIN
RECIFE	ENERGY	SCUNGE	BUKSHI	NOUGHT	ADROIT	BERLIN	COFFIN	DUBLIN
RIPOFF	ENGAGE	SEWAGE	BUNCHY	OBECHE	AENEID	BERTIE	COLLIE	DUCKIE
RUNOFF	ENOUGH	SHAGGY	BURKHA	ORACHE	AEOLIC	BESSIE	COMFIT	DUNLIN
SCLAFF	ENRAGE	SILAGE	CATCHY	PATCHY	AEOLIS	BESTIR	COMMIS	DYADIC
SCRUFF	ENSIGN	SLANGY	CAUGHT	PLIGHT	AFFAIR	BEWAIL	COMMIT	EARWIG
SHRIFT	EULOGY	SLEDGE	CHICHI	PONCHO	AFRAID	BIFFIN	COOKIE	ECLAIR
SHROFF	EXPUGN	SLEIGH	CLICHÉ	PSYCHE	AGADIR	BIGGIN	COOLIE	ECURIE
SNIFFY	FLAGGY	SLOUGH	CLOCHE	PSYCHO	AGAMID	BIGWIG	BILLIE	
SPLIFF	FLANGE	SLUDGE	CLOTHE	PUNCHY	AGARIC	BILLIE	COOTIE	

EGERIA	GRAFIN	LACTIC	MUCOID	PELVIC	RENNIN	TAENIA	VIBRIO	MANUKA
ELICIT	GRATIN	LADDIE	MUFFIN	PELVIS	RENOIR	TALKIE	VICTIM	MARKKA
ELIXIR	GRATIS	LANCIA	MURLIN	PENCIL	REPAID	TALLIS	VIOLIN	PERUKE
ELOHIM	GRAVID	LARKIN	MURRIN	PEPTIC	REPAIR	TANKIA	VIRGIL	PLANKS
EMBAIL	HACHIS	LASSIE	MUSLIM	PERKIN	RETAIL	TANNIC	VIRGIN	PLUCKY
EMETIC	HAGGIS	LATVIA	MUSLIN	PERMIT	RETAIN	TANNIN	VISCID	PRANKS
ENJOIN	HALOID	LAURIC	MUZHIK	PÉTAIN	RHEXIS	TAPPIT	WEDGIE	QUIRKY
ENOSIS	HANKIE	LAURIE	MYELIN	PHASIS	RIVLIN	TARDIS	WEEPIE	REBUKE
ENTAIL	HAPTIC	LENTIC	MYOPIA	PHILIP	ROADIE	TARSIA	WEEVIL	REMAKE
EPULIS	HARPIC	LENTIL	MYOPIC	PHOBIA	ROOKIE	TASSIE	WELKIN	RETAKE
EREMIC	HARRIS	LEONID	MYOSIN	PHOBIC	ROSCID	TAWPIE	WELLIE	REVOKE
EROTIC	HAWAII	LESLIE	MYOSIS	PHONIC	RUBRIC	TENNIS	WILLIE	ROTHKO
ESPRIT	HECTIC	LIEBIG	MYSTIC	PHYSIC	RUMKIN	TENPIN	WINNIE	RUBIKS
ETHNIC	HENBIT	LIMBIC	NANKIN	PHYSIO	RUSKIN	TERCIO	WITHIN	SALUKI
EUCLID	HENNIN	LIMPID	NAPKIN	PICNIC	RUSSIA	TERTIA	WOODIE	SAMEKH
EXOTIC	HEREIN	LIQUID	NASTIC	PIDGIN	RUSTIC	TESTIS	WREKIN	SHANKS
EYELID	HERMIT	LITHIA	NEREID	PIERIS	SALMIS	TETTIX	XYLOID	SHEIKH
FABRIC	HERNIA	LIZZIE	NERVII	PINKIE	SALVIA	THALIA	YARDIE	SHIPKA
FARCIN	HEROIC	LOCHIA	NESSIE	PINXIT	SARNIE	THEMIS	YUPPIE	SHRIKE
FASCIA	HEROIN	LOGGIA	NIACIN	PINYIN	SAURIA	THESIS	ZAFTIG	SLACKS
FEERIE	HESTIA	LOONIE	NITRIC	PIPKIN	SAVOIE	THETIC	ZAMBIA	SLEEKY
FERRIS	HISPID	LOURIE	NITWIT	PIPPIN	SCENIC	THETIS	ZENDIK	SLINKY
FERVID	HOGTIE	LUBRIC	NOGGIN	PISTIL	SCIPIO	TIDBIT	ZINNIA	SMACKS
FILLIP	HORRID	LUDWIG	NOOKIE	PLACID	SCORIA	TIEPIN	ZOMBIE	SNEAKY
FIRKIN	HOTAIR	LUTEIN	NORDIC	POETIC	SCOTIA	TIFFIN	NAVAJO	SPARKS
FIZGIG	HOWDIE	MADRID	NORVIC	POMMIE	SEISIN	TIGRIS	ADSUKI	SPARKY
FLAVIN	HUBRIS	MAFFIA	NUBBIN	PONGID	SEPSIS	TILSIT	ALASKA	SPLAKE
FLORID	HUGHIE	MAGGIE	NUDNIK	PONTIC	SEPTIC	TINNIE	BAMAKO	SPOOKY
FLORIN	HUSSIF	MAGPIE	NUNCIO	POPLIN	SEQUIN	TINTIN	BELIKE	STACKS
FOETID	HYBRID	MAJLIS	OBTAIN	POPPIT	SERAIL	TITBIT	BETAKE	STALKS
FORBID	HYBRIS	MANNIN	OGAMIC	PORGIE	SERBIA	TMESIS	BLACKS	STALKY
FORMIC	HYDRIA	MANTIS	OILRIG	PORTIA	SHARIA	TOCSIN	BLINKS	STICKS
FORNIX	HYPNIC	MAQUIS	OLEFIN	POSTIL	SHARIF	TOLUIC	BLOCKS	STICKY
FORPIT	IAMBIC	MARGIN	OLIVIA	POWNIE	SHERIF	TONSIL	BRICKS	STINKO
FOSSIL	IBERIA	MARLIN	ONEDIN	PRAXIS	SIKKIM	TORPID	BROOKE	STINKS
FRIGID	IBIBIO	MARTIN	ONEGIN	PRECIS	SIMKIN	TORRID	BROOKS	STOCKS
FROLIC	ICONIC	MASHIE	OOKPIK	PREFIX	SISKIN	TOTTIE	CHALKY	STOCKY
FULFIL	IMPAIR	MASLIN	ORCHID	PRELIM	SOBEIT	TRAGIC	CHAPKA	STOOKS
FULGID	INLAID	MASSIF	ORCHIS	PREVIN	SOFFIT	TRAVIS	CHEEKY	STRAKE
FUSAIN	INSTIL	MASTIC	ORDAIN	PROBIT	SOFTIE	TRIVIA	CHUKKA	STRIKE
FUSTIC	IRAQIS	MATHIS	OREXIS	PROFIT	SOLEIL	TROPIC	CHUNKY	STROKE
GADOID	IRONIC	MATRIC	ORIGIN	PROLIX	SOPHIA	TUGRIK	CLERKS	SWANKY
GAELIC	ISCHIA	MATRIX	ORPHIC	PROSIT	SORDID	TURBID	CLOAKS	TENGKU
GAIJIN	ISTRIA	MAWKIN	OSIRIS	PRUSIK	SORTIE	TURGID	CRANKY	THANKS
GALLIC	ITALIC	MEALIE	OTITIS	PTERIN	SPADIX	TURNIP	CREAKY	THICKY
GALLIO	JERKIN	MEANIE	OUTBID	PTERIS	SPAVIN	TURPIN	CROAKY	TRICKS
GAMBIA	JESUIT	MEGRIM	OUTFIT	PTOSIS	SPECIE	TUSSIS	CROCKS	TRICKY
GAMBIT	JOPLIN	MEJLIS	OUTLIE	PUBLIC	SPIRIT	TWOBIT	CZAPKA	TROIKA
GARLIC	JOSKIN	MEMOIR	OUTVIE	PUFFIN	SPRAIN	UGARIT	DECOKE	TRUNKS
GAWAIN	JUNKIE	MENDIP	OUTWIT	PULPIT	SQUAIL	ULITIS	DROSKY	UNLIKE
GERBIL	JUSTIN	MENHIR	OXALIC	PUNDIT	STALIN	UMBRIA	EUREKA	UNYOKE
GILLIE	KAFFIR	MERCIA	OXALIS	PUPPIS	STASIS	UMBRIL	EVENKI	UPTAKE
GILPIN	KALMIA	MERKIN	OXTAIL	PURLIN	STATIC	UNCOIL	FLANKS	WHACKO
GIRKIN	KAOLIN	MERLIN	PALAIS	PUTOIS	STERIC	UNFAIR	FLICKS	WHACKY
GIRLIE	KELOID	MERRIE	PALLID	PUTRID	STOGIE	UNGAIN	FLUNKY	WHISKY
GLACIS	KELPIE	MESAIL	PANDIT	PYTHIA	STOLID	UNPAID	FRISKY	YOICKS
GLAMIS	KELTIC	METRIC	PARDIE	RABBIT	STRAIN	UNSAID	GINGKO	AEDILE
GLORIA	KELTIE	MINNIE	PARKIN	RACHIS	STRAIT	UNVEIL	GLINKA	AFIELD
GNOMIC	KELVIN	MISFIT	PARVIS	RAFFIA	STUDIO	URACIL	GREEKS	AIRILY
GOALIE	KEPHIR	MISHIT	PASSIM	RAISIN	STUPID	URANIA	INTAKE	ALKALI
GOBLIN	KERMIS	MISSIS	PASTIL	RANCID	STYMIE	URANIC	INVOKE	ALLELE
GODWIN	KETMIR	MOGGIE	PASTIS	RAPHIA	SUBMIT	URCHIN	JANSKY	ANCILE
GODWIT	KEWPIE	MOHAIR	PATHIC	RAZZIA	SUFFIX	UTOPIA	KABAKA	ANGELA
GOOGIE	KHALIF	MOLLIE	PATOIS	REALIA	SUMMIT	VECTIS	KABUKI	ANGELS
GOOLIE	KHARIF	MORBID	PAYNIM	RECOIL	SUNLIT	VENTIL	KANAKA	ANGOLA
GORGIA	KHILIM	MORRIS	PECTIN	REEKIE	SWABIA	VERDIN	KAZAKH	ANKOLE
GORGIO	KIDDIE	MOSAIC	PEEWIT	REGAIN	SYLVIA	VEREIN	KISHKE	ANNALS
GOSSIP	KILTIE	MOUJIK	PELOID	REJOIN	SYNDIC	VERMIN	LADAKH	ANSELM
GOTHIC	KOOKIE	MOULIN	PELVIS	REMAIN	TACTIC	VERMIS	LUSAKA	APOLLO

APPALL	CEDULA	DOUBLY	GANGLY	JUNGLE	MUESLI	PHYLLO	SAPELE	TATTLE
AQUILA	CHICLE	DOURLY	GARBLE	JUSTLY	MUFFLE	PICKLE	SCILLA	TAUTLY
ARABLE	CHILLI	DUFFLE	GARGLE	KABELE	MUMBLE	PIDDLE	SCILLY	TEGULA
AREOLA	CHILLY	DUMBLY	GENTLE	KABYLE	MURALS	PIFFLE	SCROLL	TEMPLE
AREOLE	CICALA	DUMPLE	GENTLY	KEBELE	MUSCLE	PIMPLE	SCYLLA	TERMLY
ARGYLE	CICELY	DUNELM	GIGGLE	KEENLY	MUTELY	PIMPLY	SEEMLY	THINLY
ARGYLL	CIRCLE	EASILY	GIGOLO	KERALA	MUZZLE	PINTLE	SEMELE	THRALL
ARNOLD	COBALT	ECBOLE	GIRDLE	KETTLE	MYGALE	POBBLE	SENILE	THRILL
AROLLA	COBBLE	EDIBLE	GLADLY	KIBBLE	MYRTLE	POMELO	SETTLE	TICKLE
ATTILA	COCKLE	EERILY	GLIBLY	KIDDLE	MYSELF	POODLE	SEWELL	TICKLY
AUDILE	CODDLE	EMBALE	GOBBLE	KIGALI	NAMELY	POORLY	SHEILA	TIDDLE
AVIDLY	COLDLY	EMBALM	GOGGLE	KINDLE	NAPALM	POPPLE	SHIELD	TIDDLY
AWHILE	COMBLE	ENABLE	GOODLY	KINDLY	NEARLY	PORTLY	SHOULD	TIDILY
AXILLA	COMELY	ENCALM	GOOGLE	KINGLY	NEATLY	POTTLE	SHRILL	TIMELY
AZOLLA	COMPLY	ENFOLD	GOOGLY	KIRTLE	NEBULA	PRIMLY	SICILY	TINGLE
BABBLE	COOLLY	ENGELS	GRILLE	KITTLE	NEBULE	PUDDLE	SICKLE	TINKLE
BAFFLE	CORALS	ENGULF	GRIMLY	LABILE	NEEDLE	PUEBLO	SICKLY	TIPPLE
BAILLY	COSILY	ENROLL	GRISLY	LAMELY	NEPALI	PURELY	SIFFLE	TIPULA
BALDLY	COSTLY	ENSILE	GUGGLE	LASTLY	NEROLI	PURPLE	SIMILE	TITTLE
BANGLE	COTYLE	EPAULE	GURGLE	LATELY	NESTLE	PUZZLE	SIMPLE	TITULE
BARELY	COUPLE	EQUALS	GUTTLE	LAZILY	NETTLE	RABBLE	SIMPLY	TIVOLI
BASALT	CRADLE	EVENLY	GUZZLE	LEWDLY	NEWELL	RADDLE	SINGLE	TODDLE
BATTLE	CRAPLE	EXHALE	HABILE	LIABLE	NIBBLE	RADULA	SINGLY	TOGGLE
BAUBLE	CREOLE	EXTOLL	HACKLE	LIGULA	NICELY	RAFALE	SIPPLE	TOOTLE
BEADLE	CRIBLE	FACILE	HAGGLE	LIGULE	NIELLO	RAFFLE	SIZZLE	TOPPLE
BEAGLE	CRUELS	FAIBLE	HAMBLE	LIKELY	NIGGLE	RAGGLE	SKELLY	TORULA
BECALM	CUDDLE	FAIRLY	HANDLE	LIMPLY	NIGGLY	RAMBLE	SLOWLY	TOUSLE
BEETLE	CUDDLY	FAMILY	HARDLY	LITTLE	NIMBLE	RANKLE	SMALLS	TOWNLY
BEFALL	CUPOLA	FANGLE	HAROLD	LIVELY	NIMBLY	RANULA	SMELLY	TREBLE
BEHALF	CUPULE	FARDLE	HASSLE	LOCALE	NIPPLE	RAPTLY	SMUGLY	TREBLY
BEHELD	CURDLE	FAVELA	HAZILY	LOCULE	NOBBLE	RARELY	SNAILY	TRIFLE
BEHOLD	CURTLY	FECULA	HECKLE	LONELY	NODDLE	RASHLY	SNUGLY	TRIMLY
BEZZLE	CURULE	FEEBLE	HERALD	LORDLY	NODULE	RATTLE	SOFTLY	TRIPLE
BIFOLD	CUTTLE	FEEBLY	HIGHLY	LOUDLY	NOODLE	RAZZLE	SOLELY	TUBULE
BOBBLE	CYBELE	FEMALE	HOBBLE	LOVELL	NOSILY	REALLY	SOMALI	TUILLE
BODILY	DABBLE	FERULA	HOMELY	LOVELY	NOZZLE	RECALL	SORELL	TUMBLE
BOGGLE	DADDLE	FERULE	HOMILY	LOWELL	NUBBLE	REFILL	SORELY	TUMULT
BOLDLY	DAGGLE	FETTLE	HOOPLA	LOYOLA	NUBILE	REGALE	SOUPLE	TUPELO
BOODLE	DANDLE	FIBULA	HOURLY	LUNULE	NUCULE	REGULO	SOURLY	TURTLE
BOOTLE	DANGLE	FICKLE	HUBBLE	MACULA	NUMBLY	RESALE	SOZZLE	TUSSLE
BOTTLE	DAPPLE	FIDDLE	HUCKLE	MACULE	NUZZLE	RESULT	SPAULD	TUVALU
BOUCLÉ	DARGLE	FIDDLY	HUDDLE	MAINLY	OCCULT	REVILE	SPOILS	TWIRLY
BOULLE	DARKLY	FINALE	HUGELY	MANGLE	OPENLY	REVOLT	SPOILT	TYBALT
BOWELS	DARTLE	FINELY	HUMBLE	MANILA	ORACLE	RIBALD	SPRYLY	UNABLE
BRIDLE	DAWDLE	FIPPLE	HURDLE	MANTLE	ORALLY	RIBBLE	SQUALL	UNBOLT
BROLLY	DAZZLE	FIRMLY	HURTLE	MARBLE	ORIOLE	RICHLY	SQUILL	UNDULY
BUBBLE	DEADLY	FIZZLE	HUSTLE	MAYFLY	ORMOLU	RIDDLE	STABLE	UNFOLD
BUBBLY	DEARLY	FLATLY	ICICLE	MEANLY	ORWELL	RIFFLE	STABLY	UNGULA
BUCKLE	DEBILE	FOCSLE	IMPALA	MEASLY	OSWALD	RIPPLE	STALLS	UNHOLY
BUMALO	DECKLE	FOIBLE	IMPALE	MEDDLE	OTELLO	ROOTLE	STAPLE	UNROLL
BUMBLE	DEEPLY	FONDLE	INFOLD	MEEKLY	OUNDLE	ROTULA	STEELE	UNRULY
BUNDLE	DEFILE	FONDLY	INGULF	MERELY	OURALI	ROUBLE	STEELY	UNSOLD
BUNGLE	DEFTLY	FOOTLE	INHALE	METTLE	OVERLY	ROYALS	STIFLE	UNTOLD
BURBLE	DEVILS	FOOZLE	INSOLE	MICKLE	PADDLE	RUBBLE	STOOLS	UNWELL
BURGLE	DEWALI	FOULLY	INSULA	MIDDLE	PAELLA	RUCKLE	STROLL	UPHELD
BUSILY	DIBBLE	FREELY	INSULT	MILDLY	PAMELA	RUDDLE	SUBTLE	UPHILL
BUSTLE	DIDDLE	FRILLS	IRWELL	MINGLE	PAPULE	RUDELY	SUBTLY	UPHOLD
CABALE	DIMPLE	FRILLY	ISEULT	MIZZLE	PAROLE	RUELLE	SUCKLE	URSULA
CACKLE	DINGLE	FUDDLE	ITSELF	MOBILE	PARTLY	RUFFLE	SUPPLE	USABLE
CAGILY	DINGLY	FUMBLE	JABBLE	MODELS	PAYOLA	RUMBLE	SUPPLY	VAINLY
CAJOLE	DIPOLE	FUSELI	JANGLE	MODULE	PEARLS	RUMPLE	SURELY	VASTLY
CALMLY	DIVALI	FUTILE	JEKYLL	MORALE	PEARLY	RUNDLE	TABULA	VERILY
CANDLE	DIWALI	FUZZLE	JEWELS	MORALS	PEBBLE	RUSTLE	TACKLE	VIABLE
CANTLE	DOCILE	GABBLE	JIGGLE	MOSTLY	PEBBLY	SABELE	TAIGLE	VILELY
CASTLE	DODDLE	GADFLY	JINGLE	MOTILE	PEDALO	SADDLE	TAILLE	VIRILE
CATTLE	DONGLE	GAGGLE	JOGGLE	MOTTLE	PEDDLE	SAFELY	TAMALE	VITALS
CAUDLE	DOODLE	GAINLY	JOSTLE	MOZZLE	PEOPLE	SAGELY	TAMELY	VOWELS
CAVELL	DOTTLE	GAMBLE	JUGGLE	MUCKLE	PERILS	SAMPLE	TANGLE	WADDLE
CECILS	DOUBLE	GAMELY	JUMBLE	MUDDLE	PESTLE	SANELY	TARTLY	WAFFLE

WAGGLE	DREAMY	SQUAMA	ASTONE	CORONA	ERRAND	HOSING	MEKONG	PLAINS
WAMBLE	DYNAMO	STEAMY	ASVINA	COSINE	ERRANT	HUMANE	MENINX	PLAINT
WANDLE	ECZEMA	STEMMA	ATHENA	COVENT	ESSENE	HYAENA	MERINO	PLIANT
WANGLE	ENCAMP	STIGMA	ATHENE	COVING	ETHANE	IGUANA	MINING	PLYING
WARBLE	ENIGMA	STORMY	ATHENS	CRANNY	ETHENE	IMMUNE	MODENA	POLAND
WARILY	ENTOMB	TACOMA	ATKINS	CREANT	EUGENE	IMPEND	MOLINE	POLONY
WARMLY	ENZYME	TATAMI	ATTEND	CRIANT	EUXINE	INDENT	MOMENT	POMONA
WATTLE	ESKIMO	TAXEME	ATTONE	CRYING	EVZONE	INFANT	MOPING	PONENT
WAVELL	EXHUME	THERMO	ATTUNE	CYRANO	EXEUNT	INLAND	MOVING	POTENT
WEAKLY	FATIMA	TRAUMA	AVAUNT	CYRENE	EXPAND	INLINE	MOWING	PRYING
WEEKLY	GAZUMP	ULTIMA	AVERNO	DAPHNE	EXPEND	INNING	MURINE	PUISNE
WHEELS	GENOME	ULTIMO	AWNING	DARING	EXTANT	INSANE	MUSANG	PURINE
WHEELY	GLIOMA	VOLUME	BAKING	DATING	EXTEND	INTEND	MUSING	PYRENE
WHOLLY	GLOOMY	WHAMMY	BANANA	DEBUNK	EXTENT	INTENT	MUTANT	PYRONE
WIDELY	GRAMME	XEROMA	BARING	DECANE	FACING	INTONE	MUTINY	QUAINT
WIFELY	GRAMMY	ZEUGMA	BEAUNE	DECANI	FADING	INVENT	NAGANA	QUEENS
WIGGLE	GRIMMS	ZYGOMA	BEGONE	DECANT	FAKING	IODINE	NATANT	RACINE
WIGGLY	HEAUME	AARONS	BEHIND	DECENT	FAMINE	IRVING	NICENE	RACING
WILDLY	INCOME	ABOUND	BELONG	DEDANS	FARAND	ISLAND	NOCENT	RAGING
WIMBLE	INFAME	ABSENT	BERING	DEFEND	FARINA	JACANA	NOVENA	RAKING
WIMPLE	INFAMY	ACCEND	BESANT	DEFINE	FECUND	JACENT	NUTANT	RAPINE
WINKLE	INHUME	ACCENT	BETONY	DEMAND	FELINE	JEJUNE	NYLONS	RARING
WISELY	INTIME	ACHENE	BEYOND	DEMENT	FELONY	JOANNA	OBLONG	RATINE
WOBBLE	JEMIMA	ACHING	BEZANT	DEPEND	FILING	JOCUND	OBTEND	RATING
WOBBLY	JEREMY	ACORNS	BIDENT	DEPONE	FIRING	JOHNNY	OBTUND	RAVINE
WOOLLY	JEROME	ACTING	BIKINI	DETENT	FLAUNT	JURANT	OCEANS	RAVING
WORTLE	LEGUME	ADDEND	BITING	DETENU	FLUENT	KATANA	OCHONE	RECANT
YAFFLE	LEXEME	ADVENE	BLENNY	DINING	FLYING	KETONE	OCTANE	RECENT
YEARLY	LIPOMA	ADVENT	BODONI	DIVINE	FOKINE	KIMONO	OCTANS	REFINE
ABROMA	MADAME	AEGINA	BOEING	DIVING	FOMENT	KORUNA	OCTANT	REFUND
AFLAME	MAXIMS	AGEING	BOHUNK	DJINNI	FORINT	LACING	OENONE	REGENT
ANCOME	MAZUMA	AIDANT	BORANE	DOCENT	FRIAND	LACUNA	OFFEND	REGINA
APLOMB	MIASMA	AILING	BORING	DOESNT	FRIEND	LADING	OFFING	RELENT
ASSUME	OEDEMA	AIRING	BOSUNS	DOLINA	FRYING	LAGUNA	ONDINE	REMAND
ASTHMA	ONCOME	ALBANY	BOTANY	DOLINE	FULANI	LAGUNE	ONIONS	REMIND
AUTUMN	OPTIMA	ALBINO	BOURNE	DOMINO	GALANT	LAMENT	ONLINE	REPENT
BECAME	OPTIME	ALCINA	BOVINE	DOPANT	GALENA	LAMINA	OOLONG	REPINE
BECOME	PANAMA	ALDINE	BOXING	DOTING	GAMINE	LARYNX	ORCINE	RESENT
BELAMY	PARAMO	ALKANE	BRAINS	DOUANE	GAMING	LATENT	ORGANS	RETINA
BENAME	PHASMA	ALKENE	BRAINY	DOZENS	GAPING	LATINA	ORGONE	REWIND
BENUMB	PLASMA	ALMOND	BRAWNY	DOZING	GEMINI	LAYING	ORIANO	RIBAND
BETIME	PLUMMY	ALPINE	BRIAND	DRYING	GERENT	LEGEND	ORIENT	RIDENT
BIGAMY	PNEUMA	ALPINO	BRIONY	DUENNA	GERUND	LEMONY	ORPINE	RIDING
BIREME	PRISMS	ALUMNI	BROWNE	DUGONG	GITANO	LEVANT	ORSINO	RIMINI
BRAHMA	PSALMS	AMMINE	BRYANT	DUMONT	GIVING	LIERNE	OSCINE	RISING
BRAHMS	QUALMS	AMOUNT	BRYONY	DURANT	GOANNA	LIKING	OSTEND	ROBING
BREGMA	RACEME	ANCONA	BUSONI	DURING	GORING	LINING	OUTING	RODENT
BULIMY	REGIME	ANGINA	BUTANE	DYEING	GRAINS	LITANY	PADANG	ROLAND
BYNAME	RENAME	ANOINT	BUTENE	EALING	GRAINY	LIVING	PAEONY	ROMANO
CALIMA	RESUME	ANTONY	BUYING	EAMONN	GRANNY	LOMOND	PALING	ROMANS
CAREME	REVAMP	ANYONE	BYGONE	EARING	GREENE	LOSING	PARANA	ROMANY
CHEMMY	RHEIMS	APHONY	BYLINE	EASING	GREENS	LOVING	PARENT	ROSINA
CHROMA	RHEUMY	APPEND	CANINE	EATING	GRETNA	LUCENT	PATENT	ROTUND
CHROME	SALAMI	ARCANA	CANING	ECHINO	GROUND	LUCINA	PATINA	ROVING
CHROMO	SALOME	ARCANE	CAPONE	EDGING	GROYNE	LUGANO	PAVANE	ROWING
CHUMMY	SCHEMA	ARDENT	CARINA	EDMOND	GUIANA	LUMINA	PAVING	ROXANE
CINEMA	SCHEME	ARGENT	CARING	EDMUND	GUYANA	LUPINE	PAYING	RUBENS
CLAIMS	SCRAMB	AROINT	CASING	EGMONT	HATING	LURING	PEDANT	RULING
CLAMMY	SCRIMP	AROUND	CASINO	EIRANN	HAVANA	LUTINE	PEKING	SABINE
CLEOME	SCUMMY	ARPENT	CEMENT	ELAINE	HAVENT	LYMPNE	PENANG	SALINA
COLUMN	SESAME	ARRANT	CHAINS	ELUANT	HAVING	MAKING	PILING	SALINE
CREAMY	SHAMMY	ARSÈNE	CHOANA	ENDING	HELENA	MALONE	PIMENT	SARONG
CRUMMY	SHIMMY	ARSINE	CLIENT	ENGINE	HERONS	MALONY	PINING	SATINY
DECAMP	SHRIMP	ASCEND	CODING	EOCENE	HEXANE	MANANA	PIPING	SAVANT
DÉCIME	SLUMMY	ASCENT	COGENT	EPPING	HIDING	MARINA	PIRENE	SAVING
DEFAME	SMARMY	ASHINE	COLONY	EQUANT	HIKING	MARINE	PISANO	SAXONY
DENIMS	SMEGMA	ASKING	COMING	EQUINE	HIRING	MATING		SAYING
DHARMA	SODOMY	ASLANT	COOING	ERMINE	HOMING	MATINS		SCRUNT
DODOMA	SOLEMN	ASSENT	COPING	ERNANI	HOMINY	MEDINA		SECANT

SECOND	TISANE	ANYHOW	CARTON	DURION	GOOGOL	LECTOR	NATION	POWWOW
SEEING	TONANT	ARAGON	CASLON	EDISON	GORDON	LEGION	NATRON	PRISON
SELENE	TRANNY	ARCHON	CASTOR	EDITOR	GORGON	LEMNOS	NELSON	PROLOG
SERANG	TRUANT	ASHDOD	CENSOR	ELUTOR	GOUNOD	LENTOR	NESTOR	PROTON
SERENE	TRYING	ASHTON	CEROON	EMPLOY	GRISON	LEPTON	NEURON	PYEDOG
SERINE	TSWANA	ASIMOV	CEYLON	ENAMOR	GRYFON	LESBOS	NEWTON	PYTHON
SEVENS	TUBING	ATHROB	CHADOR	EOZOON	GUENON	LESION	NIGNOG	QUAHOG
SEWING	TUCANA	AUTHOR	CHARON	EPIGON	GUIDON	LESSON	NIMROD	RAGTOP
SHEENY	TUNING	AVALON	CHATON	EPILOG	GUNDOG	LESSOR	NIPPON	RAMROD
SHINNY	TWEENY	BABOON	CHIBOL	ESCROC	HAEMON	LICTOR	NONCOM	RANCOR
SHRANK	TYPING	BALBOA	CHICON	ESCROW	HALLOO	LINGOT	NORROY	RANDOM
SHRINE	TYRANT	BALLOT	CHIGOE	ETALON	HALLOW	LIQUOR	NOTION	RANSOM
SHRINK	TYRONE	BAMBOO	CHIRON	ETHIOP	HANSOM	LISBON	OBERON	RAPTOR
SHRUNK	ULLING	BANDOG	CHITON	ETYMON	HARBOR	LISSOM	OCELOT	RATION
SIDING	UNBEND	BARROW	CITRON	EUSTON	HARLOT	LOLLOP	OCTROI	RATOON
SIENNA	UNBENT	BARTOK	CLAMOR	EXMOOR	HARROW	LONDON	ODDSON	RATTON
SILENE	UNBIND	BARTON	COCOON	FACTOR	HAYBOX	LORIOT	OPTION	REASON
SILENT	UNDINE	BATHOS	COELOM	FAGGOT	HAYDON	LOTION	ORATOR	RECKON
SIMONY	UNDONE	BEACON	COLLOP	FALCON	HAYMOW	LOWBOY	OREGON	RECTOR
SKIING	UNHAND	BECKON	COMMON	FALLOW	HECTOR	LUMMOX	ORISON	REDTOP
SKINNY	UNKIND	BEETON	CONDOM	FANION	HELIOS	LYTTON	OUTTOP	REEBOK
SLOANE	UNSENT	BEFOOL	CONDOR	FARROW	HENSON	MACRON	OVIBOS	REGION
SMYRNA	UNSUNG	BEHOOF	CONVOY	FATHOM	HERIOT	MAGGOT	PALLOR	RENVOI
SOIGNÉ	UNWIND	BELLOC	CORDON	FELLOE	HERMON	MAGNON	PANTON	RENVOY
SOLANO	UPLAND	BELLOW	COSMOS	FELLOW	HESIOD	MAINOR	PAPHOS	REPTON
SOLENT	UPLINK	BENBOW	COTTON	FERVOR	HILTON	MALDON	PARDON	RETOOL
SONANT	URBANE	BENSON	COUPON	FILFOT	HOBNOB	MALLOW	PARLOR	RHETOR
SOWING	URGENT	BESTOW	COWBOY	FIRLOT	HOLLOW	MAMMON	PARROT	RIBBON
SPHENE	URSINE	BETTOR	COWPOX	FLACON	HOOPOE	MANIOC	PARSON	RIPPON
SPHINX	USHANT	BILLOW	CRATON	FLAGON	HORROR	MARMOT	PARTON	ROBSON
SPLENT	VACANT	BISHOP	CRAYON	FLAVOR	HOTPOT	MAROON	PASTON	ROGNON
SPLINT	VAGINA	BLAZON	CREMOR	FOGBOW	HUDSON	MARRON	PASTOR	ROSCOE
SPOONY	VAHINE	BONBON	CRESOL	FOLIOS	HYPNOS	MARROW	PATHOS	ROSTOV
SPRANG	VALENS	BOOBOO	CRONOS	FOLIOT	HYSSOP	MASCOT	PATMOS	RUNYON
SPRING	VALINE	BOOHOO	CROTON	FOLLOW	ICEBOX	MATLOW	PATROL	SAILOR
SPRINT	VICUNA	BORROW	CRUSOE	FORGOT	INCHON	MATRON	PATRON	SALLOW
SPRUNG	VIENNA	BORZOI	CUCKOO	FRAGOR	INDOOR	MEADOW	PATTON	SALMON
SPYING	VIENNE	BOSTON	CURSOR	FRIPON	INFLOW	MELLOW	PAVLOV	SALOON
SQUINT	VIKING	BOTTOM	CUSTOM	FRIVOL	INGROW	MELTON	PELION	SALOOP
STERNE	VISHNU	BOUTON	CUSTOS	FURROW	INKPOT	MEMNON	PENNON	SAMFOO
STRAND	VOLANS	BOWWOW	CUTTOE	FUSION	INTRON	MENTOR	PEPLOS	SAMIOT
STRENE	VOLANT	BRETON	DAEMON	FUSTOC	IRETON	MERLOT	PEQUOD	SAMSON
STRINE	VOLENS	BRITON	DALTON	FYLFOT	ISOPOD	MERROW	PERIOD	SANTON
STRING	VOTING	BUENOS	DAMSON	GABION	JAILOR	MERTON	PERNOD	SARTOR
STRONG	WAKING	BUFFON	DANTON	GALIOT	JAMBOK	METEOR	PERRON	SAVIOR
STRUNG	WAVING	BUNION	DAWSON	GALLON	JAMBON	METHOD	PERSON	SCHMOE
STRUNT	WAXING	BURBOT	DEACON	GALLOP	JAMPOT	MICRON	PETROL	SCHOOL
SUPINE	WERENT	BURROW	DEBTOR	GALLOW	JARGON	MIGNON	PHAROS	SCIROC
SWEENY	WHINNY	BURTON	DEIMOS	GALOOT	JAWBOX	MILTON	PHENOL	SCIRON
SYRINX	WIPING	BUSBOY	DEPLOY	GAMBOL	JERBOA	MINION	PHIZOG	SCROOP
TAHINA	WIRING	BUTTON	DESPOT	GAMMON	JETTON	MINNOW	PHOBOS	SEASON
TAHINI	WOMENS	CACHOU	DIALOG	GANION	JISSOM	MINTON	PHOTON	SECTOR
TAKING	XYLENE	CACOON	DIATOM	GARÇON	JONSON	MIRROR	PICTOR	SELDOM
TALENT	YEMENI	CAHOOT	DIAXON	GARROT	JUNIOR	MONGOL	PIEDOG	SENIOR
TAMANU	YOKING	CALLOP	DIGLOT	GASCON	KANOON	MONROE	PIGEON	SENSOR
TAMINE	ZENANA	CALLOW	DIKKOP	GASTON	KEATON	MOOCOW	PILLOW	SERMON
TAXING	ZONING	CAMION	DIODON	GEASON	KLAXON	MORION	PINION	SEXTON
TECHNO	ABATOR	CANDOR	DIPLOE	GIBBON	KOODOO	MORMON	PISTOL	SHADOW
TENANT	ABLOOM	CANNON	DIPNOI	GIBSON	KOSMOS	MORROW	PISTON	SHALOM
TETANY	ABYDOS	CANNOT	DITTOS	GIDEON	KOUROS	MOSCOW	PLEXOR	SHARON
THORNE	ACAJOU	CANTON	DOBSON	GIGLOT	KOWTOW	MOTION	PODSOL	SHILOH
THORNY	ACTION	CANTOR	DOCTOR	GIRTON	KRATON	MOUTON	PODZOL	SIGNOR
THRENE	ALBION	CANYON	DOLLOP	GLAGOL	KRONOS	MUFLON	POGROM	SIMEON
THRONE	AMADOU	CAPTOR	DONJON	GLAMOR	LAGOON	MUTTON	POIROT	SIMOOM
THRONG	AMAZON	CARBON	DOWSON	GLYCOL	LANDOR	MYELON	POISON	SIMOON
TICINO	AMIDOL	CARBOY	DRAGON	GNOMON	LAPDOG	MYTHOS	POLYOL	SIPHON
TIMING	AMNION	CARNOT	DRALON	GODSON	LAPTOP	NANDOO	POMPOM	SITCOM
TIRANA	ANALOG	CARROT	DROMOS	GOLLOP	LARDON	NARROW	POMPON	SKIDOO
TIRING	ANCHOR	CARSON	DUNLOP	GONION	LATRON	NASION	POTION	SLALOM

SORROW	WALTON	MEROPE	ANGERS	CHOWRY	FLOURY	LUSTRE	REGARD	SUBORN
SPIGOT	WANTON	METOPE	ANGORA	CHYPRE	FLURRY	LUXURY	REMARK	SUBURB
STATOR	WARHOL	OCCUPY	ANKARA	CICERO	FOUTRE	LUZERN	REMORA	SUDARY
STEROL	WATSON	PANOPE	APIARY	COBURG	FRIARY	MADURA	REPORT	SUGARY
STOLON	WEAPON	PARAPH	APPORT	COHERE	FURORE	MADURO	RESORT	SULTRY
STUPOR	WETBOB	PETIPA	ARMORY	COHORT	FUTURE	MAÎTRE	RETARD	SUNDRY
SUCCOR	WHILOM	POLYPS	ARMURE	COMART	GABBRO	MALGRE	RETIRE	SUPERB
SUITOR	WIGEON	PREPPY	ARTERY	CONTRA	GALERE	MALORY	RETORT	SUTURE
SUMMON	WILLOW	PROMPT	ARTURO	COVERT	GALORE	MANTRA	RETURN	TABARD
SYMBOL	WILSON	PYROPE	ASGARD	COWARD	GANTRY	MANURE	REVERE	TAGORE
SYNCOM	WINDOW	RECIPE	ASHORE	CURARE	GAUFRE	MATURE	REVERS	TAMARA
SYPHON	WINNOW	SCAMPI	ASKARI	CURARI	GENERA	MAUGRE	REVERT	TAMARI
TAILOR	WISDOM	SCAMPO	ASMARA	CYBORG	GHARRY	MEAGRE	REVERY	TANTRA
TALBOT	WONTON	SCRAPE	ASPIRE	DATURA	GLAIRE	MEMORY	REWARD	TATERS
TALION	YARROW	SCRAPS	ASSART	DEFORM	GLIÈRE	MESSRS	REWIRE	TAVERN
TALLOT	YELLOW	SCRIPT	ASSERT	DEHORN	GLOIRE	MILORD	REWORD	TAWDRY
TALLOW	ZEALOT	SCULPT	ASSORT	DEIDRE	GOCART	MISÈRE	REWORK	TENDRE
TAMPON	ZIRCON	SERAPE	ASSURE	DEMURE	GOITRE	MISERY	RIVERA	TENURE
TANNOY	ABRUPT	SERAPH	ASTART	DEPART	GOKART	MODERN	ROBERT	TEPHRA
TARROW	ACCEPT	SHARPS	ASTERN	DEPORT	GOVERN	MOZART	ROPERY	THEIRS
TATTOO	ASLOPE	SHERPA	ASWARM	DESCRY	GRIGRI	MYSORE	ROSARY	THEORY
TAUTOG	BICEPS	SKIMPY	ATTIRE	DESERT	HARARE	NAPERY	ROSERY	THEYRE
TEAPOT	CALIPH	SLEEPY	ATTORN	DESIRE	HAVERS	NATURE	ROTARY	THIERS
TEAPOY	CANAPÉ	SLIPPY	AUBURN	DESORB	HAZARD	NITERY	RUBBRA	THWART
TEFLON	CANOPY	SLOPPY	AUGURY	DINERO	HEDERA	NONARY	RUMORS	TIMBRE
TENDON	CHAMPS	SNAPPY	AUMBRY	DISARM	HEGIRA	NOTARY	RUPERT	TISHRI
TENSON	CHEOPS	SNIPPY	AURORA	DIVERS	HEJIRA	OBVERT	SAFARI	TORERO
TENSOR	CHIPPY	STAMPS	AVIARY	DIVERT	HERERO	OCKERS	SAHARA	TOWARD
TERROR	CHIRPY	STEPPE	AYMARA	DIYARI	HETERO	OEUVRE	SALARY	TSHIRT
TEUTON	CHOPPY	STRIPE	BACKRA	DOTARD	HILARY	OILERS	SAMARA	TUBERS
TEVIOT	CLIPPY	STRIPY	BAKERS	DREARY	HOBART	ONAGRA	SARTRE	TUNDRA
THOLOS	CLUMPS	STUMPS	BAKERY	EATERY	HOMBRE	ONWARD	SATIRE	TYBURN
THYMOL	CREEPS	STUMPY	BANTRY	ECHARD	HOWARD	ORDERS	SATORI	UCKERS
TINPOT	CREEPY	SWAMPY	BAYARD	EDWARD	HUNGRY	ORDURE	SATURN	UDMURT
TIPPOO	CRISPY	SYRUPY	BEFORE	EEYORE	IGNORE	ORNERY	SATYRA	ULCERS
TIPTOE	CROPPY	THORPE	BELFRY	EFFORT	IMBARN	ORRERY	SAVORY	UMPIRE
TIPTOP	CROUPE	THRIPS	BESORT	EGBERT	IMMURE	OSBERT	SAYERS	UNBORN
TISSOT	CROUPY	TROMPE	BEURRÉ	ELDERS	IMPART	OSIERY	SBIRRO	UNCORK
TOETOE	CUERPO	TROOPS	BEWARE	ELLERY	IMPORT	OTHERS	SCLERA	UNFURL
TOLUOL	CYNIPS	TROPPO	BICARB	EMBARK	IMPURE	OUTCRY	SCLERE	UNHURT
TOMBOY	DIEPPE	TROUPE	BINARY	EMBERS	INBORN	OXFORD	SCURRY	UNSURE
TOMTOM	DRIPPY	TRUMPS	BISTRE	EMIGRÉ	INFARE	PAHARI	SECURE	UNWARY
TONSOR	DROOPY	TULIPA	BISTRO	EMPIRE	INFIRM	PALTRY	SEMPRE	UPTURN
TORPOR	ECTOPY	UNRIPE	BLEARY	ENCORE	INFORM	PAMIRS	SENORA	UPWARD
TREMOR	ENRAPT	WHOOPS	BOFORS	ENDURE	INHERE	PANFRY	SENTRY	VAGARY
TRICOT	EQUIPE	ABJURE	BOGART	ENFIRE	INJURE	PANTRY	SEVERE	VELCRO
TRIGON	ESCAPE	ABOARD	BOLERO	ENSURE	INJURY	PAPERS	SEVERN	VELURE
TRIPOD	EUROPA	ABSORB	BOWERY	ENTIRE	INSERT	PAPERY	SEVERY	VENERY
TRIPOS	EUROPE	ABSURD	BRIARD	ESCARP	INSURE	PARURE	SHEARS	VENTRE
TRITON	EXCEPT	ACCORD	BUYERS	ESCORT	INTERN	PASTRY	SHEERS	VESTRY
TURBOT	EXEMPT	ACKERS	BYWORD	EUCHRE	INVERT	PENURY	SHERRY	VINERY
TYCOON	FLOPPY	ACTORS	CAFARD	EXEDRA	IZZARD	PETARD	SHIRRA	VIZARD
UNCOOL	FRAPPÉ	ADHERE	CAITRA	EXHORT	INWARD	PETARY	SHUDRA	VOTARY
UNHOOK	FRUMPY	ADJURE	CAMERA	EXPERT	IZZARD	PETERS	SIERRA	WADERS
UNISON	GLUMPS	ADMIRE	CANARD	EXPIRE	JABIRU	PICARD	SKERRY	WARCRY
UNSHOD	GRAMPA	ADSORB	CANARY	EXPIRY	JETHRO	PINERO	SKURRY	WATERS
UPFLOW	GRAMPS	ADVERB	CASTRO	EXPORT	KIAORA	PLEURA	SLURRY	WATERY
UPROOT	GRAPPA	ADVERT	CAVERN	EXSERT	KUMARA	PLIERS	SMEARY	WHERRY
UPSHOT	GRIPPE	AFEARS	CAVORT	EXTERN	KUMERA	POETRY	SOLERA	WINTRY
VECTOR	GROUPS	AFFIRM	CELERY	EXTIRP	LAYARD	POUDRE	SOMBRE	WIPERS
VENDOR	GRUMPH	AFFORD	CENTRE	EXTORT	LEMURE	POWERS	SPHERE	WIVERN
VERNON	GRUMPS	AFTERS	CESARE	FEDORA	LIBERO	PRIORY	SQUARE	WIZARD
VIATOR	GRUMPY	ALBERT	CESURA	FIACRE	LIGURE	QUARRY	SQUIRE	WOBURN
VICTOR	GUELPH	ALLURE	CETERA	FIGARO	LIPARI	RAZURE	SQUIRM	WYVERN
VISION	INCEPT	ALMERY	CHAIRS	FIGURE	LIVERY	REBORE	SQUIRT	YAOURT
VOODOO	IRRUPT	AMHARA	CHAKRA	FILTRÉ	LIZARD	REBORN	STAIRS	YOGURT
WAGGON	JALOPY	AMPERE	CHEERS	FIMBRA	LOUVRE	RECORD	STARRY	ABBESS
WALLOP	JOSEPH	ANCORA	CHEERY	FINERY	LUNARY	REFORM	STEERS	ABLUSH
WALLOW	KAKAPO	ANGARY	CHERRY	FLEURY			STUART	ACCESS

ACCOST	CREASE	FLIMSY	LURIST	QUINSY	UNBUSY	CHITTY	FRUITY	LIGETI
ACCUSE	CREESE	FLOSSY	LUTIST	RACISM	UNEASE	CLARTY	FUGATO	LIGHTS
ACROSS	CREESH	FLOUSH	LYCOSA	RACIST	UNEASY	COMATE	GAIETY	LILITH
ADJUST	CROSSE	FOLKSY	LYRIST	RADISH	UNJUST	COMITY	GAMETE	LIMITS
ADVISE	CROUSE	FOREST	MAOIST	RAGUSA	UNLESS	COOLTH	GARETH	LOCATE
AFRESH	CRUISE	FRAISE	MARISH	RAKISH	UNMASK	COUNTY	GELATE	LOLITA
AGHAST	CUBISM	FROWST	MARIST	RAMOSE	UNREST	COYOTE	GELATO	LORETO
AGUISE	CUBIST	GALOSH	MEDISM	RAPIST	UNWISE	CRAFTY	GHETTO	LUNATE
AGUISH	CUEIST	GANESH	MEDUSA	RAVISH	UPCAST	CRANTS	GHOSTS	LUXATE
AHIMSA	CUISSE	GARISH	MIMOSA	RECAST	UPPISH	CREATE	GIOTTO	MALATE
ALDOSE	CURTSY	GLASSY	MISUSE	RECESS	UTMOST	CRESTA	GIUSTO	MANATI
ALMOST	CYTASE	GLOSSA	MODEST	REFUSE	VADOSE	CRISTA	GOUTTE	MANITO
ALONSO	DALASI	GLOSSY	MODISH	REGEST	VALISE	CROUTE	GRANTA	MAPUTO
AMBUSH	DAMASK	GNEISS	MODIST	REHASH	VANISH	CROUTH	GRANTH	METATE
AMIDST	DANISH	GOLOSH	MOLEST	RELISH	VARESE	CRUFTS	GREATS	MIGHTY
AORIST	DEBASE	GRASSY	MONISM	REMISS	VEDISM	CRUSTA	GREATS	MINUTE
APEPSY	DEFUSE	GREASE	MONIST	REPAST	VENOSE	CRUSTY	GRITTY	MOIETY
APPOSE	DELISH	GREASY	MOPISH	REPOSE	VERISM	CRYPTO	GROTTO	MUCATE
ARGOSY	DEMISE	GRILSE	MORASS	RESIST	WABASH	CUESTA	GROTTY	MUNITE
ARIOSO	DEMIST	GROSSO	MOROSE	REVISE	WHILST	CURATE	GROUTS	MUTATE
ARKOSE	DEPOSE	GROUSE	MOUSSE	RIBOSE	WHIMSY	DAINTY	GROUTY	NEGATE
AROUSE	DESIST	HAMOSE	MULISH	ROBUST	WHOOSH	DAKOTA	GROWTH	NEPETA
ARREST	DETEST	HARASS	MUTISM	ROMISH	WRASSE	DALETH	GUESTS	NICETY
ARTIST	DEVEST	HEARSE	NANISM	RUGOSE	XYLOSE	DEARTH	GUILTY	NIGHTS
ASSESS	DEVISE	HERESY	NEBISH	SADISM	ABATTU	DEBATE	GYRATE	NIGHTY
ASSIST	DICAST	HEXOSE	NEFAST	SADIST	ABLATE	DELATE	HALITE	NILOTE
ATTEST	DIGEST	HOARSE	NEWEST	SALISH	ACUITY	DELETE	HAMATE	NINETY
AUGUST	DISUSE	HOLISM	NIVOSE	SAMOSA	ADNATE	DEMOTE	HAMITE	NOTATE
AUTISM	DIVEST	HOLIST	NODOSE	SCHISM	AERATE	DENOTE	HEALTH	NUDITY
AVERSE	DRESSY	HONEST	NOMISM	SCHIST	AGNATE	DEPUTE	HEARTH	NUMPTY
AVULSE	DRIEST	IFFISH	NOWISE	SCHUSS	AGOUTI	DEPUTY	HEARTS	NUTATE
BANISH	DROPSY	IMBASE	NUDISM	SCOOSH	ALBITE	DEVOTE	HEARTY	OBLATE
BEDASH	DROWSE	IMBOSS	NUDIST	SCORSE	ALECTO	DEWITT	HECATE	ODDITY
BEHEST	DROWSY	IMPISH	OAFISH	SCOUSE	APLITE	DHOOTI	HERETO	OLEATE
BEMUSE	DUMOSE	IMPOSE	OBIISM	SEROSA	ARGUTE	DILATE	HUMITE	OMENTA
BETISE	DURESS	IMPOST	OBLAST	SETOSE	ARISTA	DILUTE	HUMPTY	OMERTA
BIOPSY	DYNAST	INCASE	OBOIST	SEXISM	ARISTO	DIMITY	HYPATE	OOCYTE
BLAISE	ECLOSE	INCEST	OBSESS	SEXIST	ASSETS	DONATE	IGNITE	OOLITE
BLOUSE	EDDISH	INCISE	OBTUSE	SPARSE	ASTUTE	DRAFTY	ILLITE	OPHITE
BLUISH	EFFUSE	INFEST	ODENSE	SPEISS	AUGITE	ECARTÉ	IMPUTE	OPIATE
BOURSE	EFTEST	INFUSE	ODESSA	SPLASH	AVIATE	EFFETE	INCITE	ORBITA
BOYISH	EGOISM	INGEST	OFFISH	SPLOSH	AZERTY	EGESTA	INDITE	ORNATE
BRAISE	EGOIST	INMESH	OGRESS	SPOUSE	BARYTA	EIGHTH	INGATE	OXGATE
BRASSY	EGRESS	INMOST	OLDISH	SQUASH	BASUTO	EIGHTY	INGOTS	PAINTS
BREAST	ELAPSE	INRUSH	ONCOST	SQUISH	BEATTY	ELUATE	INMATE	PAINTY
BROWSE	ELDEST	INSIST	ONRUSH	STRASS	BEAUTY	EMEUTE	INNATE	PAKHTI
BRUISE	ELFISH	INVEST	OPHISM	STRESS	BENITO	ENMITY	INVITE	PAKHTO
BYPASS	ELOISE	JEWESS	OPPOSE	SWOOSH	BERATE	ENSATE	IOLITE	PAKHTU
CAMISE	EMBOSS	JEWISH	ORGASM	SYRISM	BINATE	ENTITY	ISLETS	PALATE
CARESS	EMBUSY	JOCOSE	OSMOSE	TAMISE	BLOTTO	EOLITH	JAUNTY	PARETO
CARUSO	ENCASE	JURIST	OTIOSE	TAOISM	BOGOTA	EQUATE	JUBATE	PARITY
CERISE	ENCASH	KECKSY	OWLISH	TAOIST	BONITO	EQUITY	JUDITH	PASHTO
CERUSE	ENLIST	KETOSE	PAPIST	TEENSY	BORATE	ERMITE	KAPUTT	PASHTU
CHAISE	ENMESH	KHALSA	PARISH	TERESA	BOUNTY	ERSATZ	KARATE	PELOTA
CHASSE	EPRISE	KIBOSH	PERISH	THEISM	BOVATE	ESTATE	KARITE	PESETA
CHEESE	EVULSE	KINASE	PERUSE	THEIST	BREATH	EXCITE	KNOTTY	PETITE
CHEESY	EXCESS	KUMISS	PHRASE	THIRST	BRONTE	EXISTS	KRANTZ	PEYOTE
CHOOSE	EXCISE	KYBOSH	PILOSE	THRASH	CADETS	FAINTS	LANATE	PIGOTT
CHOOSY	EXCUSE	LAISSE	PLEASE	THRESH	CAMOTE	FAULTY	LAPITH	PIGSTY
CHRISM	EXPOSE	LATEST	PLISSÉ	THRIST	CANUTE	FEALTY	LAPUTA	PILATE
CHRIST	FAMISH	LAVISH	POLISH	THRUSH	CAPOTE	FEINTS	LAXITY	PINITE
CIVISM	FAVISM	LAXIST	POTASH	THRUST	CAVITY	FEISTY	LEALTY	PIRATE
CLASSY	FAVOSE	LEGIST	PRAISE	THYRSE	CECITY	FIESTA	LEANTO	PLENTY
CLAUSE	FETISH	LHOTSE	PRIEST	TOLOSA	CERATE	FINITE	LEGATE	PLINTH
CLUMSY	FEWEST	LIAISE	PRISSY	TOOTSY	CHARTA	FIXITY	LEGATO	POINTE
COARSE	FILOSE	LIGASE	PROUST	TOYISH	CHASTE	FLINTY	LENGTH	POINTS
COHOSH	FINEST	LIPASE	PUNISH	TRUISM	CHATTY	FOURTH	LEVITE	POLITE
CORPSE	FINISH	LOCUST	PURIST	TSETSE	CHESTY	FROSTY	LEVITY	POLITY
COURSE	FLENSE	LOWEST	QUEASY	TYPIST	CHINTZ	FRUITS	LIGATE	POTATO

PRESTO	SNOUTY	ALACUS	CHERUB	EYEFUL	LINEUP	PHYLUM	STROUD	ACTIVE
PRETTY	SOLUTE	ALARUM	CHERUP	FABIUS	LINKUP	PICKUP	STROUP	ALCOVE
PRONTO	SONATA	ALLIUM	CHORUS	FACTUM	LITMUS	PILEUM	STYLUS	ARGIVE
PUERTO	SPARTA	AMYCUS	CILIUM	FAMOUS	LOCKUP	PILEUP	SUBDUE	ARRIVE
PUNCTO	SPARTH	ANIMUS	CINQUE	FAROUK	LOLIUM	PILEUS	SUCCUS	BEHAVE
PUPATE	SPILTH	ANTRUM	CIRCUS	FAUNUS	LUMPUR	PLAGUE	SULCUS	BEHOVE
PURITY	SPLITS	ARBOUR	CIRQUE	FAVOUR	LYCEUM	PLAQUE	SULFUR	CHIVVY
PUSHTU	SPORTS	ARDOUR	CIRRUS	FESCUE	MADEUP	PLENUM	TALCUM	CLEAVE
PYRITE	SPORTY	ARMFUL	CITRUS	FITFUL	MAGNUM	PLEXUS	TALMUD	CRUIVE
QUARTO	SPOTTY	ARMOUR	CLAQUE	FITOUT	MAGNUS	PLUTUS	TAMMUZ	DATIVE
QUARTZ	SPRITE	ARNAUT	CLIQUE	FLATUS	MAHOUT	PODIUM	TARGUM	DERIVE
QUINTA	SPRITZ	ARTAUD	CLONUS	FOETUS	MAKEUP	POLLUX	TARSUS	ENDIVE
QUOITS	STILTS	ARTFUL	COCCUS	FOLIUM	MANFUL	POROUS	TAURUS	EVOLVE
QWERTY	STILTY	ARTHUR	COITUS	FONDUE	MANQUÉ	POSEUR	TEACUP	GENEVA
RABATO	STRATA	ASARUM	COLEUS	FRENUM	MANTUA	POSSUM	TEAGUE	GLAIVE
RARITY	SUDATE	ASCIUS	COLOUR	FUNDUS	MARAUD	PRAGUE	TECTUM	GODIVA
REALTY	SURETÉ	ASYLUM	CONCUR	FUNGUS	MARKUP	PRIMUS	TEDIUM	GREAVE
REBATE	SURETY	ATRIUM	CONSUL	FUREUR	MARQUE	PURSUE	TELLUS	GRIEVE
REBITE	SVELTE	AUREUS	CORIUM	FURFUR	MASQUE	PUSHUP	TERGUM	GROOVE
RECITE	SWARTY	AVENUE	CORMUS	GALLUP	MAYBUG	PUTOUT	THOLUS	GROOVY
REFUTE	SWEATY	BACKUP	CORNUA	GALLUS	MAZOUT	QUORUM	THYMUS	MOJAVE
RELATE	SWEETS	BAGFUL	CORNUS	GANGUE	MEATUS	RADIUM	TISSUE	MOTIVE
REMOTE	TAHITI	BANGUI	CORPUS	GENIUS	MEDIUM	RADIUS	TITTUP	MUSIVE
REPUTE	TERETE	BANJUL	CORVUS	GIAOUR	MEDIUS	RAGOUT	TOMIUM	NATIVE
RIALTO	THIRTY	BARIUM	CRATUR	GIDDUP	MELIUS	RAMOUS	TONGUE	OCTAVE
RIGHTO	TIGHTS	BARNUM	CRINUM	GONIUM	MENTUM	RECOUP	TOPHUS	OCTAVO
RIGHTS	TOMATO	BARQUE	CROCUS	GRADUS	MISSUS	RECTUM	TORQUE	OTTAVA
ROSYTH	TONITE	BASQUE	CRONUS	GYPSUM	MOBIUS	RECTUS	TOSSUP	PAREVE
ROTATE	TREATY	BATTUE	CULTUS	HALLUX	MOCKUP	REFLUX	TRAGUS	RELIVE
SAFETY	TRISTE	BAYEUX	CUPFUL	HANGUP	MODIUS	REGIUS	TUMOUR	REMOVE
SAINTS	TRUSTY	BEDAUB	CURIUM	HELIUM	MOPSUS	RESCUE	TURNUP	REVIVE
SALUTE	TWAITE	BEIRUT	CURSUS	HIATUS	MORBUS	RETOUR	TYPHUS	SALIVA
SAMITE	TWENTY	BESSUS	CUSCUS	HICCUP	MORGUE	RÊVEUR	UMLAUT	SATIVE
SANITY	TWISTY	BISQUE	CYCLUS	HIGHUP	MOSQUE	RHESUS	UNIQUE	SCURVY
SAPOTA	UBIETY	BLOWUP	CYDNUS	HIPPUS	MUCOUS	RICTUS	UNPLUG	SHEAVE
SAPOTE	UNDATE	BOOJUM	CYGNUS	HOLDUP	MULTUM	RIGOUR	UNTRUE	SHELVE
SAVATE	UNIATE	BRAQUE	CYPRUS	HONOUR	MURMUR	RISQUÉ	URANUS	SHRIVE
SCAITH	UPDATE	BROGUE	DARIUS	HOOKUP	MUSEUM	ROTGUT	USEFUL	SHROVE
SCANTY	UPPITY	BRUTUS	DELIUS	HORMUZ	NAEVUS	RUCKUS	UTERUS	SKIVVY
SCATTY	UPRATE	BULBUL	DENGUE	HUBBUB	NEBBUK	RUEFUL	VACUUM	SLEAVE
SDEATH	VACATE	BUNKUM	DERGUE	HUMBUG	NEREUS	RUGOUS	VALGUS	SLEEVE
SEBATE	VALETA	BUYOUT	DETOUR	HUMMUS	NERIUM	RUMOUR	VALIUM	SOLIVE
SEDATE	VALUTA	BUZFUZ	DEVOUR	HUMOUR	NESSUS	RUMPUS	VALLUM	STARVE
SEMITE	VANITY	BYSSUS	DEVOUT	HYDRUS	NIMBUS	RUSTUM	VALOUR	STRIVE
SENATE	VEDUTA	CACTUS	DICTUM	HYPNUM	NOBBUT	SACRUM	VAPOUR	STROVE
SHANTY	VELETA	CADMUS	DINKUM	IAMBUS	NOCTUA	SAMBUR	VELLUM	SWERVE
SHASTA	VENITE	CAECUM	DISBUD	ICARUS	NOYOUS	SAPIUM	VELOUR	THEAVE
SHEATH	VERITY	CAIQUE	DISCUS	IMBRUE	OAKNUT	SARGUS	VENDUE	THIEVE
SHEETS	VOLUTE	CALLUP	DISEUR	INDIUM	OBELUS	SAVOUR	VENOUS	THRIVE
SHIFTY	WAPITI	CALLUS	DOLEUR	INFLUX	OBOLUS	SCAPUS	VERDUN	THROVE
SHIITE	WARMTH	CALQUE	DOLIUM	IREFUL	ODIOUS	SCOPUS	VERSUS	TROUVÉ
SHINTO	WEALTH	CAMPUS	DOLOUR	ITERUM	OFFCUT	SCUTUM	VIGOUR	TWELVE
SHINTY	WRAITH	CANGUE	DROGUE	JOSHUA	OLENUS	SEAMUS	VILLUS	VOTIVE
SHIRTY	WREATH	CANTUS	DUGOUT	JOYFUL	OMASUM	SELJUK	VINOUS	ZOUAVE
SHORTS	YEASTY	CARPUS	DUMDUM	JOYOUS	OMNIUM	SEPIUM	VIROUS	ACRAWL
SHTETL	YUKATA	CASQUE	DYBBUK	JULIUS	OPAQUE	SHADUF	VIRTUE	DISOWN
SHUFTI	ZAPATA	CATGUT	EARFUL	JUNCUS	OPTOUT	SHAMUS	VOYEUR	GODOWN
SHUFTY	ZENITH	CATSUP	ECONUT	LABIUM	OSMIUM	SHOGUN	VULGUS	IMPAWN
SIESTA	ZYGOTE	CAUCUS	EFFLUX	LABOUR	OSTIUM	SHROUD	WALNUT	INLAWS
SIGHTS	ABACUS	CAVOUR	EGGCUP	LABRUM	OUTPUT	SINFUL	WALRUS	INTOWN
SLEUTH	ABLAUT	CENSUS	ELBRUS	LANGUR	OUTRUN	SIRIUS	WAMPUM	MALAWI
SMARTY	ACARUS	CENTUM	EMBRUE	LAPSUS	PAIDUP	SLIPUP	WAMPUS	MOHAWK
SMEATH	ACCRUE	CERCUS	ENGLUT	LARRUP	PASQUE	SODIUM	WAYOUT	MOTOWN
SMOOTH	ACINUS	CEREUS	ENNIUS	LASSUS	PEANUT	SOLEUS	WENSUM	OJIBWA
SMUTTY	ACTIUM	CERIUM	EPIRUS	LAWFUL	PENSUM	SOWBUG	WILFUL	OTTAWA
SNEATH	AEGEUS	CESIUM	ERBIUM	LAYOUT	PENTUP	SPROUT	WINDUP	PESHWA
SNIFTY	AEOLUS	CESTUI	EREBUS	LEAGUE	PEPLUM	SPUTUM	WOEFUL	RENOWN
SNOOTY	AIRBUS	CESTUS	EVOLUÉ	LETOUT	PERDUE	STATUE	XENIUM	SCRAWL
SNOTTY	AIRGUN	CHEQUE	EXODUS	LIGNUM	PHLEUM	STATUS	YUMYUM	SCRAWM

SCREWY	IODIZE	ARROBA	CZAPKA	INDABA	MEDINA	REMORA	TERTIA	ZAGREB
SHREWD	IONIZE	ASADHA	DAHLIA	INSULA	MEDUSA	RESEDA	THALIA	ACETIC
SINEWY	KWANZA	ASMARA	DAKOTA	ISCHIA	MERCIA	RETINA	TIPULA	ACIDIC
SPRAWL	NYANZA	ASTHMA	DATURA	ISTRIA	MIASMA	RIVERA	TIRANA	AEOLIC
SQUAWK	PIAZZA	ASVINA	DHARMA	ITHACA	MIMOSA	ROSINA	TOLOSA	AGARIC
STRAWS	RIENZI	ATAXIA	DJERBA	JACANA	MODENA	ROTULA	TORULA	AGONIC
STRAWY	SCHIZO	ATHENA	DODOMA	JEMIMA	MONICA	RUBBRA	TRAUMA	ALARIC
THRAWN	SCUZZY	ATOCIA	DOLINA	JERBOA	MOOMBA	RUSSIA	TRIVIA	ANEMIC
THROWN	SLEAZE	ATTILA	DUENNA	JOANNA	MURRHA	RWANDA	TROIKA	ANOXIC
UPTOWN	SLEAZY	AUCUBA	ECZEMA	JOJOBA	MYOPIA	SAHARA	TSONGA	ARABIC
WIDOWS	SLEEZY	AURIGA	EGERIA	JOSHUA	NAGANA	SALINA	TSWANA	ARCTIC
ANNEXE	SNAZZY	AURORA	EGESTA	JUDICA	NAUSEA	SALIVA	TUCANA	ATAXIC
DELUXE	TWEEZE	AXILLA	ELISHA	JUMADA	NEBULA	SALVIA	TULIPA	ATOMIC
EUTAXY	UFFIZI	AYESHA	ELODEA	KABAKA	NEPETA	SAMARA	TUNDRA	ATONIC
GALAXY	WHEEZE	AYMARA	ENIGMA	KACCHA	NEVADA	SAMOSA	UGANDA	AZOTIC
UNSEXY	WHEEZY	AZALEA	EROICA	KALMIA	NOCTUA	SAPOTA	ULTIMA	BALTIC
ALLEYN	YAKUZA	AZOLLA	ESPADA	KANAKA	NOVENA	SATYRA	UMBRIA	BALZAC
ALWAYS	**6:6**	BACKRA	EUBOEA	KANGHA	NYANZA	SAURIA	UNGULA	BARSAC
ANADYR	ABELIA	BAHADA	EUREKA	KANTHA	OCHREA	SCHEMA	URANIA	BELLOC
ANONYM	ABROMA	BALBOA	EUROPA	KARIBA	ODESSA	SCILLA	URSULA	BIONIC
ARROYO	ABULIA	BANANA	EXEDRA	KATANA	OEDEMA	SCLERA	URTICA	BIOPIC
BILLYO	ACACIA	BARODA	FARINA	KERALA	OJIBWA	SCORIA	UTOPIA	BIOTIC
BOLEYN	ACADIA	BARYTA	FASCIA	KHALSA	OLIVIA	SCOTIA	VAGINA	CEDRIC
BOMBYX	ACEDIA	BEEGHA	FATIMA	KIAORA	OMENTA	SCYLLA	VALETA	CELIAC
BYEBYE	AEGINA	BELUGA	FAVELA	KORUNA	OMERTA	SENECA	VALUTA	CELTIC
COCCYX	AFRICA	BERTHA	FECULA	KUCCHA	ONAGRA	SENORA	VEDUTA	CHEMIC
DACTYL	AGATHA	BODEGA	FEDORA	KUMARA	ONEIDA	SERBIA	VELETA	CITRIC
EMBRYO	AGENDA	BOGOTA	FERULA	KUMERA	OPTIMA	SEROSA	VESICA	CLERIC
EPONYM	AGLAIA	BORGIA	FIBULA	KWACHA	ORBITA	SHAMBA	VICUNA	CLINIC
ERINYS	AHIMSA	BRAHMA	FIESTA	KWANZA	ORTEGA	SHARIA	VIENNA	CLONIC
EVELYN	ALALIA	BREGMA	FIMBRA	LACUNA	OSTREA	SHASTA	VOMICA	COGNAC
GARRYA	ALASKA	BUDDHA	FRIGGA	LADOGA	OTTAVA	SHEILA	XEROMA	COPTIC
KELLYS	ALCINA	BURKHA	GALENA	LAGUNA	OTTAWA	SHERPA	YAKUZA	COSMIC
KIKUYU	ALEXIA	CACCIA	GAMBIA	LAMBDA	PAELLA	SHIPKA	YORUBA	CRETIC
LABRYS	ALOGIA	CAITRA	GARRYA	LAMINA	PAGODA	SHIRRA	YUKATA	CRITIC
MARTYR	ALPACA	CALIMA	GARUDA	LANCIA	PAMELA	SHUDRA	ZAMBIA	CUPRIC
METHYL	ALTHEA	CAMERA	GEISHA	LAPUTA	PANADA	SIDDHA	ZAPATA	CYCLIC
NITRYL	AMELIA	CANADA	GELADA	LATONA	PANAMA	SIENNA	ZENANA	CYMRIC
PAPAYA	AMHARA	CARINA	GENERA	LATVIA	PAPAYA	SIERRA	ZEUGMA	CYSTIC
PENTYL	AMOEBA	CASSIA	GENEVA	LIGULA	PARANA	SIESTA	ZINNIA	DYADIC
PHENYL	ANCONA	CEDULA	GLINKA	LIPOMA	PATACA	SILICA	ZYGOMA	EMETIC
POPEYE	ANCORA	CESURA	GLIOMA	LITHIA	PATINA	SMEGMA	ABSORB	EREMIC
PROPYL	ANEMIA	CETERA	GLORIA	LOCHIA	PAYOLA	SMYRNA	ADSORB	EROTIC
REDEYE	ANGELA	CHAKRA	GLOSSA	LOGGIA	PELOTA	SOLERA	ADVERB	ESCROC
SCHUYT	ANGINA	CHAPKA	GOANNA	LOLITA	PESETA	SONATA	APLOMB	ETHNIC
SELSYN	ANGLIA	CHARTA	GODIVA	LORCHA	PESHWA	SOPHIA	ATHROB	EXOTIC
SELWYN	ANGOLA	CHOANA	GORGIA	LORICA	PETIPA	SPARTA	BAOBAB	FABRIC
TETHYS	ANGORA	CHOREA	GRAMPA	LOYOLA	PHASMA	SQUAMA	BEDAUB	FORMIC
TETRYL	ANKARA	CHROMA	GRANTA	LUANDA	PHOBIA	STAFFA	BENUMB	FROLIC
WELWYN	ANOXIA	CHUKKA	GRAPPA	LUCINA	PIAZZA	STANZA	BICARB	FUSTIC
ZEPHYR	ANTLIA	CICADA	GRETNA	LUMINA	PLASMA	STEMMA	CANTAB	FUSTOC
ABLAZE	APHTHA	CICALA	GUIANA	LUSAKA	PLEURA	STIGMA	CHERUB	GAELIC
AGUIZE	APNOEA	CINEMA	GUINEA	LYCOSA	PNEUMA	STRATA	COBWEB	GALLIC
ASSIZE	APORIA	CLOACA	GURKHA	MACULA	POMONA	STREGA	CONFAB	GARLIC
BELIZE	AQUILA	CONCHA	GUYANA	MADURA	POSADA	SULPHA	DESORB	GNOMIC
BLOWZY	ARABIA	CONTRA	HAVANA	MAFFIA	PRAVDA	SWABIA	ENTOMB	GOTHIC
BREEZE	ARALIA	CORNEA	HECUBA	MALAGA	PROTEA	SYLVIA	HOBNOB	HAPTIC
BREEZY	ARANDA	CORNUA	HEDERA	MALTHA	PYTHIA	TABULA	HUBBUB	HARPIC
BRONZE	ARCANA	CORONA	HEGIRA	MANANA	QUAGGA	TACOMA	LABLAB	HECTIC
CORYZA	AREOLA	CORYZA	HEJIRA	MANILA	QUINTA	TAENIA	PREFAB	HEROIC
FLOOZY	ARISTA	COSMEA	HELENA	MANTRA	RADULA	TAHINA	PUNJAB	HYPNIC
FRANZY	ARMADA	CRESTA	HERNIA	MANTUA	RAFFIA	TAMARA	SCARAB	IAMBIC
FREEZE	ARNICA	CRIMEA	HESTIA	MANUKA	RAGUSA	TANKIA	SCRAMB	ICONIC
FRENZY	AROLLA	CRISTA	HOOPLA	MARACA	RANULA	TANTRA	SERDAB	IPECAC
FRIEZE		CRUSTA	HYAENA	MARINA	RAPHIA	TARSIA	SKYLAB	IRONIC
FRIZZY		CUBICA	HYDRIA	MARKKA	RAZZIA	TEGULA	SOHRAB	ITALIC
FROWZY		CUESTA	IBERIA	MARTHA	REALIA	TELEGA	SUBURB	KELTIC
GLITZY		CUPOLA	IGUANA	MASADA	REGINA	TEPHRA	SUPERB	LACTIC
GREUZE		CUTCHA	IMPALA	MAZUMA		TERESA	WETBOB	LAURIC

LENTIC	ALIPED	CORNED	FRAMED	JAGGED	PARKED	SCREED	UNLOAD	ALBITE
LIMBIC	ALLIED	COWARD	FRAYED	JAMMED	PASSED	SEALED	UNPAID	ALCOVE
LUBRIC	ALMOND	CRAZED	FRIAND	JINXED	PEAKED	SEATED	UNREAD	ALDINE
MANIAC	AMAZED	CUBOID	FRIEND	JOCUND	PEELED	SECOND	UNSAID	ALDOSE
MANIOC	AMUSED	CUPPED	FRIGID	KELOID	PEEVED	SEEDED	UNSHOD	ALERCE
MASTIC	ANGLED	CURSED	FULGID	KEYPAD	PELOID	SELFED	UNSOLD	ALKANE
MATRIC	AOUDAD	CURVED	FUNDED	KILTED	PENTAD	SENSED	UNTOLD	ALKENE
METRIC	APPEND	CUSSED	GABLED	LANDED	PEQUOD	SHADED	UNUSED	ALLEGE
MICMAC	ARCHED	CYBRID	GADOID	LAPSED	PERIOD	SHAPED	UNWIND	ALLELE
MOSAIC	ARGUED	CYPRID	GARBED	LASHED	PERNOD	SHARED	UPHELD	ALLUDE
MYOPIC	ARNOLD	CYTOID	GERUND	LAYARD	PETARD	SHIELD	UPHOLD	ALLURE
MYSTIC	AROUND	DAMNED	GIFTED	LEGEND	PICARD	SHOULD	UPLAND	ALPINE
NASTIC	ARTAUD	DASHED	GILDED	LEGGED	PICKED	SHREWD	UPWARD	AMBAGE
NITRIC	ASCEND	DAYBED	GILEAD	LEONID	PISSED	SHROUD	VARIED	AMENDE
NORDIC	ASGARD	DECKED	GLAZED	LIFTED	PITTED	SINBAD	VEILED	AMERCE
NORVIC	ASHDOD	DEFEND	GLOVED	LIMBED	PLACED	SKEWED	VEINED	AMMINE
OGAMIC	ATTEND	DELVED	GORGED	LIMPED	PLACID	SLEWED	VERSED	AMORCE
ORPHIC	AVOWED	DEMAND	GOUNOD	LIPPED	PLATED	SNAKED	VESTED	AMPERE
OVISAC	BALLAD	DENIED	GRADED	LIQUID	PLUMED	SNOWED	VISCID	ANCILE
OXALIC	BANNED	DEPEND	GRATED	LIZARD	POISED	SOAKED	VIZARD	ANCOME
PARSEC	BARBED	DEVOID	GRAVID	LOADED	POLAND	SOILED	VOICED	ANKOLE
PATHIC	BARRED	DIACID	GROUND	LOCKED	POLLED	SOLVED	VOIDED	ANNEXE
PELVIC	BAYARD	DISBUD	GUMMED	LODGED	PONGID	SORDID	WAFTED	ANYONE
PEPTIC	BEADED	DISHED	HALOID	LOMOND	POTTED	SOUSED	WALLED	APACHE
PHOBIC	BEHEAD	DOCKED	HALVED	LOOPED	PREMED	SOWSED	WANTED	APIECE
PHONIC	BEHELD	DOGGED	HARMED	MADRID	PRICED	SPACED	WARPED	APLITE
PHYSIC	BEHIND	DOODAD	HAROLD	MAENAD	PRIMED	SPAULD	WASHED	APOGEE
PICNIC	BEHOLD	DOOMED	HASHED	MALTED	PUFFED	SPICED	WASTED	APPOSE
POETIC	BELTED	DOTARD	HATRED	MARAUD	PURSED	SPIKED	WEBBED	ARABLE
PONTIC	BENDED	DOTTED	HAWKED	MARKED	PUTRID	SPREAD	WEDDED	ARCADE
PUBLIC	BESTED	DUCKED	HAZARD	MASHED	QUOTED	STATED	WEDGED	ARCANE
QUEBEC	BEYOND	DUSTED	HEADED	MASKED	RAGGED	STEWED	WHITED	ARCHIE
RICRAC	BIASED	EARNED	HEAPED	MASSED	RAISED	STOLID	WICKED	AREOLE
RUBRIC	BIFOLD	ECHARD	HEATED	MATTED	RANKED	STONED	WILLED	ARGIVE
RUSTIC	BLAMED	EDITED	HEAVED	MELTED	RAPPED	STRAND	WINGED	ARGUTE
SCENIC	BOILED	EDMOND	HEEDED	METHOD	RECORD	STROUD	WITTED	ARGYLE
SCIROC	BONDED	EDMUND	HEELED	MILORD	REFUND	STUPID	WIZARD	ARKOSE
SENLAC	BOOKED	EDWARD	HEPTAD	MINDED	REGARD	SUITED	WONTED	ARMURE
SEPTIC	BOSSED	ELATED	HERALD	MISLED	REMAND	TABARD	WOODED	AROUSE
STATIC	BOWLED	ENFOLD	HESIOD	MISSED	REMIND	TALMUD	WORKED	ARRIVE
STERIC	BRIAND	ERASED	HINGED	MITRED	REREAD	TANNED	XYLOID	ARSÈNE
SYNDIC	BRIARD	ERODED	HIPPED	MOATED	RETARD	TETRAD	ZONKED	ARSINE
TACTIC	BUCKED	ERRAND	HISPID	MORBID	REWARD	THREAD	ABJURE	ASHINE
TANNIC	BURIED	EUCLID	HONIED	MORNED	REWIND	TIERED	ABLATE	ASHORE
TARMAC	BUSHED	EXCEED	HOODED	MOSSAD	REWORD	TINGED	ABLAZE	ASLOPE
THETIC	BUSTED	EXPAND	HOOFED	MUCOID	RIBALD	TINNED	ABONDE	ASPIRE
TOLTEC	BYWORD	EXPEND	HOOKED	MYRIAD	RIBAND	TINTED	ABRADE	ASSIZE
TOLUIC	CAFARD	EXTEND	HORNED	NAILED	RIBBED	TIPPED	ABREGE	ASSUME
TRAGIC	CALCED	EYELID	HORRID	NEAPED	RIDGED	TITLED	ACCEDE	ASSURE
TROPIC	CALLED	FABLED	HORSED	NECKED	RIGGED	TOGGED	ACCRUE	ASTONE
URANIC	CALLID	FAGGED	HOTBED	NEEDED	RIMMED	TOLLED	ACCUSE	ASTUTE
ZODIAC	CAMPED	FARAND	HOWARD	NEREID	RINGED	TORPID	ACHENE	ATHENE
ABOARD	CANARD	FECUND	HULLED	NICKED	ROBBED	TORRID	ACTIVE	ATRIDE
ABOUND	CANDID	FERVID	HUMPED	NIMROD	ROLAND	TOWARD	ADDUCE	ATTIRE
ABROAD	CANNED	FIBBED	HUSHED	NODDED	ROLLED	TRIPOD	ADHERE	ATTLEE
ABSURD	CAPPED	FILLED	HYBRID	OBTEND	ROOTED	TUFTED	ADJURE	ATTONE
ACARID	CAPSID	FITTED	IMPEND	OBTUND	ROSCID	TURBID	ADMIRE	ATTUNE
ACCEND	CARVED	FIZZED	INBRED	OFFEND	ROTUND	TURGID	ADNATE	AUBADE
ACCORD	CAUSED	FLAWED	INDEED	ONWARD	ROUGED	TURNED	ADVENE	AUDILE
ADDEND	CHOKED	FLORID	INFOLD	ORCHID	ROUSED	TWINED	ADVICE	AUGITE
ADDLED	CLOSED	FLUTED	INLAID	OSTEND	ROUTED	UNBEND	ADVISE	AUNTIE
AENEID	COATED	FOETID	INLAND	OSWALD	RUBBED	UNBIND	AEDILE	AUSSIE
AFFORD	COCCID	FOILED	INROAD	OUTBID	RUCHED	UNBRED	AERATE	AVENGE
AFIELD	COILED	FOLDED	INTEND	OXFORD	RUGGED	UNCLAD	AEROBE	AVENUE
AFRAID	COMBED	FORBID	INWARD	OXHEAD	RUINED	UNDYED	AFLAME	AVERSE
AGAMID	CONRAD	FORCED	IRONED	PACKED	RUSHED	UNFOLD	AGNATE	AVIATE
AGREED	COOKED	FORGED	ISLAND	PADDED	RUTTED	UNHAND	AGRÉGÉ	AVULSE
AIRBED	COPIED	FORKED	ISOPOD	PAINED	SACRED	UNITED	AGUISE	AWHILE
ALFRED	CORKED	FORRAD	IZZARD	PALLID	SCARED	UNKIND	AGUIZE	BABBLE

BAFFLE	BORATE	CENTRE	CRÈCHE	DELICE	ELOISE	FAVOSE	GIGGLE	HOWDIE
BAILEE	BOTHIE	CERATE	CREESE	DELUDE	ELUATE	FEEBLE	GILLIE	HUBBLE
BAILIE	BOTTLE	CERISE	CREOLE	DELUGE	ELYSEE	FEERIE	GIRDLE	HUCKLE
BANGLE	BOUCHE	CERUSE	CRIBLE	DELUXE	EMBALE	FELINE	GIRLIE	HUDDLE
BARÈGE	BOUCLÉ	CESARE	CRINGE	DEMISE	EMBRUE	FELLOE	GLAIRE	HUGHIE
BARGEE	BOUFFE	CHAISE	CROCHE	DEMOTE	EMERGE	FEMALE	GLAIVE	HUMANE
BARQUE	BOULLE	CHANCE	CROSSE	DEMURE	EMEUTE	FERULE	GLANCE	HUMBLE
BARRIE	BOUNCE	CHANGE	CROUPE	DENGUE	EMIGRÉ	FESCUE	GLIÈRE	HUMITE
BASQUE	BOURÉE	CHARGE	CROUSE	DENOTE	EMPIRE	FETTLE	GLOIRE	HURDLE
BATTLE	BOURNE	CHASSE	CROUTE	DENUDE	EMULGE	FIACRE	GOALIE	HURTLE
BATTUE	BOURSE	CHASTE	CRUISE	DEPONE	EMUNGE	FIANCÉ	GOATEE	HUSTLE
BAUBLE	BOVATE	CHEESE	CRUIVE	DEPOSE	ENABLE	FICKLE	GOBBLE	HYPATE
BAWBEE	BOVINE	CHEQUE	CRUSOE	DEPUTE	ENCASE	FIDDLE	GOETHE	ICICLE
BEADLE	BRAISE	CHERIE	CUBAGE	DERGUE	ENCODE	FIERCE	GOGGLE	IGNITE
BEAGLE	BRAQUE	CHICLE	CUDDLE	DERIDE	ENCORE	FIGURE	GOITRE	IGNORE
BEANIE	BREEZE	CHIGOE	CUFFEE	DERIVE	ENDIVE	FILOSE	GOOGIE	ILLITE
BEAUNE	BRIDGE	CHILDE	CUISSE	DESIRE	ENDURE	FILTRÉ	GOOGLE	ILLUDE
BECAME	BRIDIE	CHOICE	CULDEE	DEVICE	ENFIRE	FINALE	GOOLIE	IMBASE
BECOME	BRIDLE	CHOOSE	CUPULE	DEVISE	ENFREE	FINITE	GOURDE	IMBIBE
BEETLE	BROGUE	CHOREE	CURARE	DEVOTE	ENGAGE	FIPPLE	GOUTTE	IMBRUE
BEFORE	BRONTE	CHROME	CURATE	DIBBLE	ENGINE	FIZZLE	GRAMME	IMMUNE
BEGONE	BRONZE	CHYPRE	CURDLE	DIDDLE	ENLACE	FLAMBÉ	GRANGE	IMMURE
BEHAVE	BROOKE	CIERGE	CURRIE	DIEPPE	ENRAGE	FLANGE	GREASE	IMPALE
BEHOVE	BROWNE	CILICE	CURULE	DILATE	ENROBE	FLECHE	GREAVE	IMPEDE
BEJADE	BROWSE	CINQUE	CUTTLE	DILUTE	ENSATE	FLEDGE	GREECE	IMPOSE
BELIKE	BRUISE	CIRCLE	CUTTOE	DIMPLE	ENSILE	FLEECE	GREENE	IMPURE
BELIZE	BUBBLE	CIRQUE	CYBELE	DINGLE	ENSURE	FLENSE	GREUZE	IMPUTE
BEMUSE	BUCKLE	CLAQUE	CYRENE	DIPLOE	ENTICE	FOCSLE	GRIEVE	INCASE
BENAME	BUDGIE	CLAUDE	CYTASE	DIPOLE	ENTIRE	FOIBLE	GRILLE	INCEDE
BERATE	BUMBLE	CLAUSE	CYTODE	DISUSE	ENTREE	FOKINE	GRILSE	INCISE
BERTHE	BUNDLE	CLEAVE	DABBLE	DIVIDE	ENZYME	FONDLE	GRIPPE	INCITE
BERTIE	BUNGEE	CLEOME	DADDLE	DIVINE	EOCENE	FONDUE	GROOVE	INCOME
BESIDE	BUNGLE	CLICHÉ	DAFTIE	DOCILE	EPAULE	FOOTLE	GROUSE	INDITE
BESSIE	BUNJEE	CLIQUE	DAGGLE	DODDLE	EPHEBE	FOOZLE	GROYNE	INDUCE
BETAKE	BURBLE	CLOCHE	DAMAGE	DOLINE	EPOPEE	FORAGE	GRUDGE	INFAME
BETIDE	BURGEE	CLOTHE	DANDLE	DONATE	EPRISE	FOUTRE	GRUNGE	INFARE
BETIME	BURGLE	COARSE	DANGLE	DONGLE	EQUATE	FRAISE	GUGGLE	INFUSE
BETISE	BUSTLE	COBBLE	DANUBE	DONNÉE	EQUINE	FRANCE	GURGLE	INGATE
BEURRÉ	BUTANE	COCKLE	DAPHNE	DOODLE	EQUIPE	FRAPPÉ	GUTTLE	INHALE
BEWARE	BUTENE	CODDLE	DAPPLE	DOSAGE	ERMINE	FREEZE	GUZZLE	INHERE
BEZZLE	BYEBYE	COERCE	DARGLE	DOTAGE	ERMITE	FRIDGE	GYRATE	INHUME
BHAJEE	BYGONE	COFFEE	DARKIE	DOTTLE	ESCAPE	FRIEZE	HABILE	INJURE
BILLIE	BYLINE	COHERE	DARTLE	DOUANE	ESSENE	FRINGE	HACKEE	INLINE
BINATE	BYNAME	COLLIE	DATIVE	DOUBLE	ESTATE	FRONDE	HACKLE	INMATE
BIRDIE	BYRNIE	COMATE	DAWDLE	DOUCHE	ETHANE	FROUDE	HAGGLE	INNATE
BIREME	CABALE	COMBLE	DAZZLE	DRAGEE	ETHENE	FUDDLE	HALIDE	INSANE
BISQUE	CABBIE	COMICE	DEARIE	DREDGE	EUCHRE	FUMBLE	HALITE	INSIDE
BISTRE	CACKLE	CONGEE	DEBASE	DROGUE	EUGENE	FURORE	HAMATE	INSOLE
BLAISE	CADDIE	COOKIE	DEBATE	DROWSE	EUROPE	FUTILE	HAMBLE	INSURE
BLENDE	CAIQUE	COOLIE	DEBILE	DRUDGE	EUXINE	FUTURE	HAMITE	INTAKE
BLITHE	CAJOLE	COOTIE	DECADE	DUCKIE	EVINCE	FUZZLE	HAMOSE	INTIME
BLONDE	CALQUE	CORBIE	DECANE	DUFFLE	EVOLUÉ	GABBLE	HANDLE	INTONE
BLOUSE	CAMISE	CORPSE	DECIDE	DUMOSE	EVOLVE	GAGGLE	HANKIE	INVADE
BLUDGE	CAMOTE	CORRIE	DÉCIME	DUMPLE	EVULSE	GALERE	HARARE	INVITE
BOBBLE	CANAPÉ	CORVÉE	DECKLE	DUNDEE	EVZONE	GALORE	HASSLE	INVOKE
BOCAGE	CANDLE	COSINE	DECODE	EATAGE	EXCISE	GAMBLE	HEARSE	IODINE
BODGIE	CANGUE	COSSIE	DECOKE	ECARTÉ	EXCITE	GAMETE	HEAUME	IODIZE
BODICE	CANINE	COTYLE	DECREE	ECBOLE	EXCUSE	GAMINE	HECATE	IOLITE
BOGGLE	CANNAE	COULEE	DEDUCE	ECLOSE	EXHALE	GANGUE	HECKLE	IONIZE
BOLIDE	CANTLE	COUPLE	DEFACE	ECURIE	EXHUME	GARAGE	HEXANE	ISOLDE
BONNIE	CANUTE	COURSE	DEFAME	EDIBLE	EXPEDE	GARBLE	HEXOSE	JABBLE
BONXIE	CAPONE	COWAGE	DEFILE	EEYORE	EXPIRE	GARGLE	HIDAGE	JANGLE
BOODLE	CAPOTE	COWRIE	DEFINE	EFFACE	EXPOSE	GAUCHE	HOARSE	JEJUNE
BOOGIE	CARAFE	COYOTE	DEFUSE	EFFETE	FACADE	GAUFRE	HOBBLE	JEROME
BOOKIE	CAREME	CRABBE	DÉGAGÉ	EFFUSE	FACILE	GAVAGE	HOGTIE	JIGGLE
BOOTEE	CASQUE	CRADLE	DEGREE	ELAINE	FAIBLE	GELATE	HOMAGE	JINGLE
BOOTLE	CASTLE	CRAPLE	DEIDRE	ELANCE	FAMINE	GENOME	HOMBRE	JOCOSE
BORAGE	CATTLE	CREASE	DELATE	ELAPSE	FANGLE	GENTLE	HOOPOE	JOGGLE
BORANE	CAUDLE	CREATE	DELETE	ELLICE	FARDLE	GEORGE	HORACE	JOSTLE

Column 1

JUBATE, JUGGLE, JUJUBE, JUMBLE, JUNGLE, JUNKIE, KABELE, KABYLE, KARATE, KARITE, KEBELE, KELPIE, KELTIE, KETONE, KETOSE, KETTLE, KEWPIE, KIBBLE, KIDDIE, KIDDLE, KILTIE, KINASE, KINDLE, KIRTLE, KISHKE, KITTLE, KLUDGE, KOOKIE, LABILE, LADDIE, LAGUNE, LAISSE, LANATE, LARVAE, LASSIE, LAUNCE, LAURIE, LAVAGE, LEAGUE, LEGATE, LEGUME, LEMURE, LESLIE, LESSEE, LEVITE, LEXEME, LHOTSE, LIABLE, LIAISE, LIERNE, LIGASE, LIGATE, LIGULE, LIGURE, LIPASE, LIPIDE, LITTLE, LIZZIE, LOATHE, LOCALE, LOCATE, LOCULE, LOONIE, LOUCHE, LOUNGE, LOURIE, LOUVRE, LOVAGE, LUNATE

Column 2

LUNULE, LUPINE, LUSTRE, LUTINE, LUXATE, LYCHEE, LYMPNE, MACULE, MADAME, MAGGIE, MAGPIE, MAÎTRE, MALATE, MALGRE, MALICE, MALLEE, MALONE, MANAGE, MANCHE, MANEGE, MANGLE, MANQUÉ, MANTLE, MANURE, MARBLE, MARINE, MARQUE, MASHIE, MASQUE, MATURE, MAUGRE, MEAGRE, MEALIE, MEANIE, MEDDLE, MENACE, MENAGE, MEROPE, MERRIE, METAGE, METATE, METOPE, METTLE, MICKLE, MIDDLE, MINGLE, MINNIE, MINUTE, MIRAGE, MISÈRE, MISUSE, MIZZLE, MOBILE, MODULE, MOGGIE, MOJAVE, MOLINE, MOLLIE, MONROE, MORALE, MORGUE, MOROSE, MOSQUE, MOTILE, MOTIVE, MOTTLE, MOUSSE, MOZZLE, MUCATE

Column 3

MUCKLE, MUDDLE, MUFFLE, MUMBLE, MUNITE, MURAGE, MURINE, MUSCLE, MUSIVE, MUTATE, MUZZLE, MYGALE, MYRTLE, MYSORE, NATIVE, NATURE, NEBULE, NEEDLE, NEGATE, NELLIE, NERINE, NESSIE, NESTLE, NETTLE, NIBBLE, NICENE, NIGGLE, NILOTE, NIMBLE, NIPPLE, NIVOSE, NOBBLE, NODDLE, NODOSE, NODULE, NOMADE, NONAGE, NOODLE, NOOKIE, NOTATE, NOTICE, NOUNCE, NOVICE, NOWISE, NOYADE, NOZZLE, NUANCE, NUBBLE, NUBILE, NUCULE, NUTATE, NUZZLE, OBECHE, OBLATE, OBLIGE, OBTUSE, OCHONE, OCTANE, OCTAVE, ODENSE, OENONE, OEUVRE, OFFICE, OLEATE, ONCOME, ONDINE, ONLINE, ONSIDE, OOCYTE

Column 4

OOLITE, OPAQUE, OPHITE, OPIATE, OPPOSE, OPTIME, ORACHE, ORACLE, ORANGE, ORCINE, ORDURE, ORGONE, ORIOLE, ORNATE, OROIDE, ORPINE, OSCINE, OSMOSE, OTIOSE, OUNDLE, OUTAGE, OUTLIE, OUTVIE, OXGATE, OXHIDE, PADDLE, PALACE, PALATE, PANOPE, PARCAE, PARDIE, PAREVE, PAROLE, PARSEE, PARURE, PASQUE, PAUNCE, PAVANE, PAWNEE, PEBBLE, PEDDLE, PEEWEE, PENNAE, PENSÉE, PEOPLE, PERDUE, PERUKE, PERUSE, PESADE, PESTLE, PETITE, PEYOTE, PHOEBE, PHRASE, PIAFFE, PICKLE, PIDDLE, PIERCE, PIFFLE, PILAGE, PILATE, PILOSE, PIMPLE, PINITE, PINKIE, PINTLE, PIRATE

Column 5

PIRENE, PLAGUE, PLAICE, PLAQUE, PLEASE, PLEDGE, PLISSÉ, PLONGE, PLUNGE, POBBLE, POINTE, POLICE, POLITE, POMACE, POMADE, POMMIE, PONGEE, POODLE, POPEYE, POPPLE, PORGIE, POTTLE, POUDRE, POUFFE, POUNCE, POWNIE, PRAGUE, PRAISE, PRANCE, PREACE, PRINCE, PSYCHE, PUDDLE, PUISNE, PUMICE, PUPATE, PURINE, PURPLE, PURSUE, PUTTEE, PUZZLE, PYRENE, PYRITE, PYRONE, PYROPE, QUICHE, QUINCE, RABBLE, RACEME, RACINE, RADDLE, RAFALE, RAFFLE, RAGGLE, RAMBLE, RAMOSE, RANKLE, RAPINE, RATINE, RATTLE, RAVAGE, RAVINE, RAZURE, RAZZLE, REBATE, REBITE, REBORE, REBUKE, RECEDE

Column 6

RECIFE, RECIPE, RECITE, REDEYE, REDUCE, REEKIE, REFACE, REFINE, REFUGE, REFUSE, REFUTE, REGALE, REGGAE, REGIME, RELATE, RELIVE, REMAKE, REMOTE, REMOVE, RENAME, RENEGE, REPINE, REPOSE, REPUTE, RESALE, RESCUE, RESIDE, RESUME, RETAKE, RETIRE, REVERE, REVILE, REVISE, REVIVE, REVOKE, REWIRE, RHAPHE, RIBBLE, RIBOSE, RIDDLE, RIFFLE, RIPPLE, RISQUÉ, RIVAGE, ROADIE, ROOKIE, ROOTLE, ROSACE, ROSCOE, ROTATE, ROUBLE, ROUNCE, ROXANE, RUBBLE, RUCKLE, RUDDLE, RUELLE, RUFFLE, RUGOSE, RUMBLE, RUMPLE, RUNDLE, RUSTLE, SABELE, SABINE, SADDLE, SAITHE, SALADE, SALINE

Column 7

SALLEE, SALOME, SALUTE, SAMITE, SAMPLE, SAPELE, SAPOTE, SARNIE, SARTRE, SATIRE, SATIVE, SAVAGE, SAVATE, SAVOIE, SCARCE, SCATHE, SCHEME, SCHMOE, SCLERE, SCONCE, SCORSE, SCOUSE, SCRAPE, SCRIBE, SCUNGE, SCYTHE, SEABEE, SEANCE, SEBATE, SECEDE, SECURE, SEDATE, SEDUCE, SEETHE, SEICHE, SELENE, SEMELE, SEMITE, SEMPRE, SENATE, SENILE, SERAPE, SERENE, SERINE, SESAME, SETOSE, SETTEE, SETTLE, SEVERE, SEWAGE, SHEAVE, SHELVE, SHIITE, SHRIKE, SHRINE, SHRIVE, SHROVE, SICKLE, SIFFLE, SILAGE, SILENE, SIMILE, SIMPLE, SINGLE, SIPPLE, SIRREE, SIZZLE, SLEAVE, SLEAZE

Column 8

SLEDGE, SLEEVE, SLOANE, SLUDGE, SLUICE, SMUDGE, SNEEZE, SNOOZE, SNUDGE, SOCAGE, SOFTIE, SOIGNÉ, SOIREE, SOLACE, SOLIVE, SOLUTE, SOMBRE, SOOTHE, SORAGE, SORTIE, SOUPLE, SOURCE, SOZZLE, SPARSE, SPATHE, SPENCE, SPHENE, SPHERE, SPLAKE, SPLICE, SPONGE, SPOUSE, SPRITE, SPURGE, SPUNGE, SQUARE, SQUIRE, STABLE, STANCE, STAPLE, STARVE, STATUE, STEELE, STEPPE, STERNE, STIFLE, STODGE, STOGIE, STOOGE, STRAFE, STRAKE, STRENE, STRIDE, STRIFE, STRINE, STRIPE, STRIVE, STRODE, STROKE, STROVE, STYMIE, SUBDUE, SUBTLE, SUCKLE, SUDATE

Column 9

SUNDAE, SUPINE, SUPPLE, SURETÉ, SUTTEE, SUTURE, SVELTE, SWANEE, SWATHE, SWERVE, SWINGE, TACKLE, TAGORE, TAIGLE, TAILLE, TALKIE, TAMALE, TAMINE, TAMISE, TANGLE, TASSIE, TATTLE, TAWPIE, TAXEME, TEAGUE, TEEPEE, TEETHE, TEMPLE, TENACE, TENDRE, TENURE, TERETE, TERRAE, THEAVE, THENCE, THEYRE, THIEVE, THISBE, THORNE, THORPE, THRENE, THRICE, THRIVE, THRONE, THROVE, THYRSE, TICKLE, TIDDLE, TIERCE, TIMBRE, TINGLE, TINKLE, TINNIE, TIPPLE, TIPTOE, TIRADE, TISANE, TISSUE, TITTLE, TITULE, TODDLE, TOETOE, TOFFEE, TOGGLE, TONGUE, TONITE, TOOTLE, TOPPLE, TORQUE

TOTTIE	VENDUE	PAYOFF	FACING	PLYING	AGUISH	EUNUCH	MARISH	SIRRAH
TOUCHE	VENICE	PILAFF	FADING	PROLEG	ALIYAH	EXARCH	MODISH	SKETCH
TOUPEE	VENITE	REBUFF	FAKING	PROLOG	AMBUSH	FAMISH	MOLECH	SLATCH
TOUSLE	VENOSE	RELIEF	FILING	PRYING	ARIOCH	FETISH	MOLLAH	SLEIGH
TOWAGE	VENTRE	RIPOFF	FIRING	PYEDOG	ARMAGH	FINISH	MOLOCH	SLEUTH
TOWHEE	VIABLE	RUNOFF	FIZGIG	QUAHOG	ATTACH	FLANCH	MOOLAH	SLOUCH
TOWNEE	VIENNE	SCLAFF	FLYING	RACING	AVOUCH	FLETCH	MOPISH	SLOUGH
TRALEE	VIRILE	SCRUFF	FRYING	RAGBAG	BANISH	FLINCH	MULISH	SMEATH
TRANCE	VIRTUE	SHADUF	GAMING	RAGING	BARUCH	FLITCH	MULLAH	SMIRCH
TREBLE	VISAGE	SHARIF	GAPING	RAKING	BEDASH	FLOUSH	MUNICH	SMOOCH
TRIAGE	VIVACE	SHERIF	GASBAG	RARING	BEENAH	FOURTH	NALLAH	SMOOTH
TRIFLE	VOIDEE	SHROFF	GIVING	RATBAG	BEULAH	FRENCH	NAUTCH	SNATCH
TRIODE	VOLAGE	SPLIFF	GORING	RATING	BLANCH	GALOSH	NEBISH	SNEATH
TRIPLE	VOLUME	TARIFF	GUNDOG	RAVING	BLEACH	GANESH	NULLAH	SNITCH
TRISTE	VOLUTE	TIPOFF	HATING	REDLEG	BLENCH	GARETH	NUMDAH	SPARTH
TROCHE	VOTIVE	ACHING	HAVING	RIDING	BLOTCH	GARISH	OAFISH	SPEECH
TROMPE	VOYAGE	ACTING	HIDING	RISING	BLUISH	GLITCH	OFFISH	SPILTH
TROPHE	WADDLE	AGEING	HIKING	ROBING	BODACH	GOLOSH	OLDISH	SPLASH
TROUPE	WAFFLE	AILING	HIRING	ROVING	BORSCH	GRANTH	ONRUSH	SPLOSH
TROUVÉ	WAGGLE	AIRING	HOMING	ROWING	BOYISH	GROUCH	OOMPAH	SQUASH
TRUDGE	WAMBLE	ANALOG	HOSING	RULING	BRAMAH	GROWTH	OWLISH	SQUISH
TSETSE	WANDLE	ASKING	HUMBUG	SARONG	BRANCH	GRUMPH	PALLAH	STANCH
TUBULE	WANGLE	ATABEG	INNING	SAVING	BREACH	GRUTCH	PARAPH	STARCH
TUILLE	WARBLE	AWNING	IRVING	SAYING	BREATH	GUBBAH	PARIAH	STENCH
TUMBLE	WATTLE	BAKING	JETLAG	SEEING	BREECH	GUELPH	PARISH	STITCH
TURTLE	WEDGIE	BANDOG	KITBAG	SERANG	BROACH	GULLAH	PAUNCH	SUKKAH
TUSSLE	WEEPIE	BARING	LACING	SEWING	BROOCH	HANNAH	PERISH	SUMACH
TWAITE	WEEWEE	BELONG	LADING	SIDING	BRUNCH	HAUNCH	PISGAH	SWATCH
TWEEZE	WELLIE	BERING	LAPDOG	SKIING	CALIPH	HEALTH	PLANCH	SWITCH
TWELVE	WHARFE	BIGWIG	LAYING	SONTAG	CASBAH	HEARTH	PLEACH	SWOOSH
TWINGE	WHEEZE	BITING	LIEBIG	SOWBUG	CHINCH	HITECH	PLINTH	TANNAH
TYRONE	WHENCE	BOBWIG	LIKING	SOWING	CHOUGH	HOOHAH	PLOUGH	THANAH
ULLAGE	WHINGE	BOEING	LINING	SPRANG	CHURCH	HOOKAH	POLISH	THATCH
UMPIRE	WIGGLE	BORING	LIVING	SPRING	CLENCH	HOORAH	POTASH	THORAH
UNABLE	WILLIE	BOXING	LOSING	SPRUNG	CLINCH	HOOTCH	PREACH	THOUGH
UNCAGE	WIMBLE	BUYING	LOVING	SPYING	CLOUGH	HOUDAH	PUNISH	THRASH
UNDATE	WIMPLE	CANING	LUDWIG	STALAG	CLUNCH	HOWDAH	PUNKAH	THRESH
UNDINE	WINKLE	CARING	LURING	STRING	CLUTCH	HURRAH	PURDAH	THRUSH
UNDONE	WINNIE	CASING	MAKING	STRONG	COHOSH	HUZZAH	PUTSCH	TOYISH
UNEASE	WOBBLE	COBURG	MATING	STRUNG	COOLTH	IFFISH	QUAICH	TRENCH
UNIATE	WOODIE	CODING	MAYBUG	TAKING	CRANCH	IMPISH	QUAIGH	TROUGH
UNIQUE	WORTLE	COMING	MEKONG	TAUTOG	CRATCH	INMESH	QUELCH	TUSSAH
UNLACE	WRASSE	COOING	MINING	TAXING	CREACH	INRUSH	QUENCH	TWITCH
UNLIKE	WRITHE	COPING	MOPING	TEABAG	CREAGH	ISAIAH	QUETCH	UPPISH
UNMADE	XYLENE	COVING	MOVING	THRONG	CREESH	JEWISH	QUITCH	VANISH
UNRIPE	XYLOSE	CRYING	MOWING	TIMING	CROTCH	JIBBAH	RADISH	VARECH
UNSAFE	YAFFLE	CYBORG	MUSANG	TIRING	CROUCH	JOSEPH	RAKISH	VEDDAH
UNSURE	YANKEE	DANZIG	MUSING	TOERAG	CROUTH	JOSIAH	RAUNCH	WABASH
UNTRUE	YARDIE	DARING	MUSKEG	TRYING	CRUNCH	JUBBAH	RAVISH	WALLAH
UNWISE	YIPPEE	DATING	NIGNOG	TUAREG	CRUTCH	JUDITH	REHASH	WARMTH
UNYOKE	YUPPIE	DEFRAG	NUTMEG	TUBING	CULTCH	KASBAH	RELISH	WEALTH
UPDATE	ZOMBIE	DIALOG	OBLONG	TUNING	DALETH	KAZAKH	RIYADH	WHOOSH
UPRATE	ZOUAVE	DINING	OFFING	TYPING	DANISH	KEDDAH	ROMISH	WHYDAH
UPSIDE	ZYGOTE	DIVING	OILRIG	ULLING	DEARTH	KIBOSH	ROSYTH	WRAITH
UPTAKE	BEHALF	DOTING	OOLONG	UNPLUG	DELISH	KIRBEH	RUPIAH	WREATH
URBANE	BEHOOF	DOZING	OULONG	UNSUNG	DETACH	KIRSCH	SALISH	WRENCH
URSINE	BELIEF	DRYING	OUTING	VIKING	DOODAH	KITSCH	SAMEKH	WRETCH
USABLE	CUTOFF	DUGONG	PADANG	VOTING	DRENCH	KOOLAH	SCAITH	YAHWEH
USANCE	DECAFF	DURING	PALING	WAKING	EDDISH	KUFIAH	SCATCH	ZENITH
VACATE	ENGULF	DYEING	PAVING	WAVING	EIGHTH	KVETCH	SCOOSH	ZURICH
VADOSE	FAROFF	EALING	PAYING	WAXING	ELFISH	KYBOSH	SCORCH	ADONAI
VAHINE	HUSSIF	EARING	PEGLEG	WIPING	ELIJAH	LADAKH	SCOTCH	ADSUKI
VALINE	INGULF	EARWIG	PEKING	WIRING	ENARCH	LAMEDH	SCUTCH	AGOUTI
VALISE	ITSELF	EASING	PENANG	YOKING	ENCASH	LAPITH	SDEATH	ALKALI
VARESE	KHALIF	EATING	PHIZOG	ZAFTIG	ENMESH	LAUNCH	SEARCH	ALUMNI
VAUNCE	KHARIF	EDGING	PIEDOG	ZIGZAG	ENOUGH	LAVISH	SERAPH	ASKARI
VELOCE	LAYOFF	ENDING	PILING	ZONING	ENRICH	LENGTH	SHEATH	BACCHI
VELURE	MASSIF	EPILOG	PINING	ABLUSH	EOLITH	LILITH	SHEIKH	BANGUI
VENDEE	MYSELF	EPPING	PIPING	AFRESH	EPARCH	LOOFAH	SHILOH	BANZAI

BIKINI	TAHINI	VATHEK	CARTEL	FENNEL	LETHAL	PORTAL	STROLL	ANSELM
BODONI	TAHITI	VOTYAK	CARVEL	FERIAL	LINEAL	POSTAL	SWIVEL	ANTHEM
BONSAI	TAIPEI	YORICK	CASUAL	FESTAL	LINTEL	POSTIL	SYMBOL	ANTRIM
BORZOI	TAMARI	ZEBECK	CAUSAL	FEUDAL	LISTEL	PRIMAL	TARCEL	ANTRUM
BRUNEI	TATAMI	ZENDIK	CAVELL	FILIAL	LIONEL	PROPEL	TARSAL	ARNHEM
BUKSHI	TISHRI	ABDIEL	CERCAL	FINGAL	LOVELL	PROPYL	TARSEL	ASARUM
BUSONI	TIVOLI	ABSEIL	CEREAL	FINIAL	LOWELL	PUMMEL	TASSEL	ASCHAM
CESTUI	UFFIZI	ACRAWL	CHAPEL	FISCAL	LUTEAL	PUTEAL	TEASEL	ASWARM
CHICHI	WAPITI	ACTUAL	CHESIL	FITFUL	MAMMAL	RACHEL	TECKEL	ASYLUM
CHILLI	YEMENI	AERIAL	CHEVAL	FLORAL	MANFUL	RACIAL	TERNAL	ATRIUM
CURARI	YEZIDI	AGNAIL	CHIBOL	FOETAL	MANUAL	RADIAL	TETRYL	AUTISM
DALASI	ALCOCK	ALUDEL	CHISEL	FORMAL	MARCEL	RANCEL	THECAL	BAHRAM
DECANI	AMTRAK	AMIDOL	CHITAL	FOSSIL	MARTEL	RAPPEL	THRALL	BALAAM
DELPHI	ANORAK	AMORAL	CHORAL	FRIVOL	MARVEL	RASCAL	THRILL	BALSAM
DEWALI	ARRACK	AMYTAL	COEVAL	FRUGAL	MEDIAL	RECALL	THYMOL	BANTAM
DHOOTI	ATTACK	ANIMAL	COMPEL	FULFIL	MENDEL	RECOIL	TINSEL	BARHAM
DIPNOI	BARTOK	ANNEAL	CONSUL	FUNGAL	MENIAL	RECTAL	TOLUOL	BARIUM
DIVALI	BEDECK	ANNUAL	CORBEL	FUNNEL	MENSAL	REFILL	TOMIAL	BARNUM
DIVEHI	BOHUNK	AORTAL	CORNEL	GAMBOL	MENTAL	REFUEL	TONSIL	BECALM
DIWALI	CANUCK	APICAL	CORRAL	GAVIAL	MESAIL	REHEEL	TRAVEL	BEDLAM
DIYARI	COPECK	APPALL	CRENAL	GENIAL	MESCAL	RENTAL	TRIBAL	BEHRAM
DJINNI	DAMASK	APPEAL	CRENEL	GERBIL	MESIAL	REPEAL	TROWEL	BESEEM
ELTCHI	DEBUNK	ARCHIL	CRESOL	GHAZAL	METHYL	RETAIL	TUNNEL	BIRNAM
ERNANI	DIKDIK	ARGYLL	CREWEL	GIMBAL	MINDEL	RETOOL	TYMBAL	BOOJUM
EVENKI	DVORAK	ARMFUL	CRINAL	GLAGOL	MISSAL	REVEAL	UMBREL	BOTHAM
FULANI	DYBBUK	ARTFUL	CROTAL	GLOBAL	MISSEL	RICTAL	UMBRIL	BOTTOM
FUSELI	EMBARK	ASSAIL	CRURAL	GLYCOL	MITRAL	RITUAL	UNCIAL	BUNKUM
GANDHI	FAROUK	ASSOIL	CUDGEL	GOOGOL	MONGOL	ROMMEL	UNCOIL	CAECUM
GEMINI	FRANCK	ASTRAL	CUNEAL	GOSPEL	MONIAL	RONDEL	UNCOOL	CENTUM
GILGAI	HIJACK	ATABAL	CUPFUL	GRAVEL	MORSEL	RUEFUL	UNFURL	CERIUM
GIORGI	JAMBOK	ATONAL	CURPEL	GROVEL	MORTAL	RUNNEL	UNREAL	CESIUM
GRIGRI	KALPAK	ATRIAL	CURSAL	GUNNEL	MURIEL	SAMBAL	UNREEL	CHRISM
GUARDI	KANUCK	AVOWAL	CURTAL	HAEMAL	MUSSEL	SAMIEL	UNROLL	CILIUM
HAGGAI	KODIAK	AZONAL	DACTYL	HALLAL	MUTUAL	SAMUEL	UNVEIL	CIVISM
HAWAII	MOHAWK	AZRAEL	DAEDAL	HANDEL	NERVAL	SANDAL	UNWELL	COELOM
KABUKI	MOHOCK	BAGFUL	DAMSEL	HERBAL	NEURAL	SANTAL	UPHILL	CONDOM
KIGALI	MOUJIK	BAIKAL	DANIEL	HIMMEL	NEWELL	SCHOOL	URACIL	CORIUM
LIGETI	MUZHIK	BANJUL	DENIAL	HIRSEL	NICKEL	SCRAWL	URINAL	CRINUM
LIPARI	NEBBUK	BARBEL	DENTAL	HOSTEL	NITRYL	SCROLL	USEFUL	CUBISM
LITCHI	NEBECK	BARREL	DERAIL	HUMMEL	NORMAL	SENDAL	VANDAL	CURIUM
MALAWI	NUDNIK	BEFALL	DERMAL	HYMNAL	NOVIAL	SEPTAL	VASSAL	CUSTOM
MANATI	OOKPIK	BEFOOL	DETAIL	HYPHAL	OBITAL	SERAIL	VENIAL	DEFORM
MAOTAI	POLACK	BELIAL	DIESEL	INSTAL	ORDEAL	SERIAL	VENTIL	DERHAM
MEDICI	PRUSIK	BEMOIL	DIRNDL	INSTIL	ORWELL	SERVAL	VERBAL	DIADEM
MOIRAI	REBECK	BENGAL	DISMAL	IREFUL	OXTAIL	SEWELL	VERNAL	DIATOM
MUESLI	REEBOK	BESSEL	DISPEL	IRWELL	PARCEL	SEXUAL	VERSAL	DICTUM
MUNSHI	REMARK	BETHEL	DISTAL	ISABEL	PASCAL	SHEKEL	VESSEL	DINKUM
NAGARI	REWORK	BEWAIL	DISTIL	ISRAEL	PASTEL	SHOVEL	VESTAL	DIRHAM
NEPALI	SELJUK	BHARAL	DJEBEL	JACKAL	PASTIL	SHRILL	VIRGIL	DISARM
NEROLI	SHRANK	BOVRIL	DONZEL	JEKYLL	PATROL	SIGNAL	VISUAL	DODGEM
NERVII	SHRIEK	BRAZIL	DORSAL	JINGAL	PENCEL	SIMNEL	WANKEL	DOLIUM
NIKKEI	SHRINK	BRIDAL	DOSSAL	JOVIAL	PENCIL	SINFUL	WARHOL	DRACHM
NILGAI	SHRUNK	BRUMAL	DRIVEL	JOYFUL	PENNAL	SNIVEL	WASTEL	DUMDUM
OCTROI	SLOVAK	BRUNEL	DUFFEL	JUMBAL	PENTEL	SOCIAL	WAVELL	DUNELM
OURALI	SQUAWK	BRUTAL	EARFUL	KENDAL	PENTYL	SOLEIL	WEASEL	DURHAM
PAHARI	SQUEAK	BUCCAL	EIFFEL	KENNEL	PETREL	SORELL	WEEVIL	EGOISM
PAKHTI	STREAK	BULBIL	EMBAIL	KENSAL	PETROL	SORREL	WIRRAL	ELOHIM
RENVOI	STRICK	BULBUL	ENAMEL	KERNEL	PHENOL	SPINAL	WITHAL	EMBALM
RIENZI	STRUCK	BURIAL	ENODAL	KISSEL	PHENYL	SPIRAL	WOEFUL	EMBLEM
RIMINI	THWACK	BUSHEL	ENROLL	KOTWAL	PHONAL	SPITAL	XENIAL	ENCALM
SAFARI	TUGRIK	CAMAIL	ENSEAL	KUMMEL	PINEAL	SPRAWL	ABLOOM	ENGRAM
SALAMI	UNCORK	CANCEL	ENTAIL	LABIAL	PISTIL	SQUAIL	ACTIUM	EPONYM
SALUKI	UNDECK	CANNEL	EPICAL	LAICAL	PISTOL	SQUALL	ADDEEM	ERBIUM
SANSEI	UNHOOK	CANTAL	EXTOLL	LARVAL	PLAGAL	SQUEAL	AFFIRM	ESTEEM
SATORI	UNLOCK	CARMEL	EYEFUL	LAUREL	PLURAL	SQUILL	ALARUM	FACTUM
SCAMPI	UNMASK	CARNAL	FACIAL	LAWFUL	PODSOL	STATAL	ALLIUM	FATHOM
SHTCHI	UNPACK	CARPAL	FAECAL	LEMUEL	PODZOL	STEROL	ANADEM	FAVISM
SHUFTI	UNPICK	CARPEL	FARDEL	LENTEL	POLYOL		ANONYM	FOLIUM
SOMALI	UPLINK	CARREL		LENTIL	POMMEL			FRENUM

FULHAM	PODIUM	YUMYUM	BIFFIN	CITRIN	DUNCAN	GNOMON	JULIAN	MASLIN
GONIUM	POGROM	ABADAN	BIGGIN	CITRON	DUNLIN	GOBLIN	JUSTIN	MATRON
GOTHAM	POMPOM	ACTION	BIOGEN	CLOVEN	DURIAN	GODOWN	KAFTAN	MAWKIN
GRAHAM	POSSUM	ACUMEN	BIOTIN	COBDEN	DURION	GODSON	KANOON	MEDIAN
GYPSUM	PRELIM	ADJOIN	BITTEN	COCHIN	DZEREN	GODWIN	KANTEN	MELTON
HAMMAM	QUIDAM	ADRIAN	BLAZON	COCOON	EAMONN	GOLDEN	KAOLIN	MEMNON
HANSOM	QUORUM	AEGEAN	BOBBIN	COFFIN	EDISON	GONION	KEATON	MERKIN
HELIUM	RACISM	AFGHAN	BODKIN	COLUMN	EIRANN	GORDON	KELVIN	MERLIN
HOLISM	RADIUM	AIRGUN	BOFFIN	COMMON	ELEVEN	GORGON	KENYAN	MERMAN
HYPNUM	RANDOM	AIRMAN	BOLEYN	CONMAN	ELOIGN	GOTTEN	KIRMAN	MERTON
IBIDEM	RANSOM	ALBION	BOLLEN	COPPIN	ENJOIN	GOVERN	KIRPAN	MICRON
INDIUM	RECTUM	ALDRIN	BONBON	CORDON	ENSIGN	GRABEN	KITTEN	MIDDEN
INFIRM	REDEEM	ALEVIN	BOSTON	COTTON	ENZIAN	GRAFIN	KLAXON	MIGNON
INFORM	REFORM	ALEXIN	BOUTON	COUPON	EOTHEN	GRATIN	KOREAN	MILTON
INGRAM	RHYTHM	ALLEYN	BOWFIN	COUSIN	EOZOON	GRAVEN	KRAKEN	MINION
ITERUM	RODHAM	ALMAIN	BOWMAN	COWMAN	EPIGON	GRISON	KRATON	MINOAN
JETSAM	RUSTAM	AMAZON	BRAZEN	CRATON	ETALON	GRYFON	KRUMAN	MINTON
JIMJAM	RUSTEM	AMNION	BREMEN	CRAVEN	ETYMON	GUENON	LAGOON	MITTEN
JISSOM	RUSTUM	ANDEAN	BRETON	CRAYON	EUSTON	GUIDON	LALLAN	MIZZEN
KHILIM	SACRUM	ANURAN	BRITON	CRETAN	EVELYN	GUNMAN	LARDON	MODERN
LABIUM	SADISM	APPIAN	BROGAN	CRETIN	EXOGEN	HAEMON	LARKIN	MOLTEN
LABRUM	SALAAM	ARAGON	BROKEN	CROTON	EXPUGN	HAGDEN	LATEEN	MOREEN
LIGNUM	SALAAM	ARCHON	BUCHAN	CRUMEN	EXTERN	HAPPEN	LATRON	MORGAN
LISSOM	SAPIUM	ARGHAN	BUFFON	CUFFIN	FABIAN	HAPTEN	LATTEN	MORGEN
LOGJAM	SCHISM	ARRIAN	BUNION	CULMEN	FALCON	HARDEN	LAWMAN	MORION
LOLIUM	SCRAWM	ASCIAN	BUNSEN	CUMMIN	FALLEN	HARKEN	LAYMAN	MORMON
LYCEUM	SCREAM	ASHCAN	BUNYAN	CUPMAN	FANION	HASTEN	LEADEN	MOTION
MAGNUM	SCUTUM	ASHPAN	BURDEN	CYANIN	FANTAN	HAYDON	LEAVEN	MOTOWN
MALLAM	SELDOM	ASHTON	BURTON	DAEMON	FARCIN	HEAVEN	LEGION	MOULIN
MARRAM	SEPIUM	ASSIGN	BUSKIN	DALTON	FASTEN	HEMPEN	LEGMAN	MOUTAN
MASHAM	SEXISM	ASTERN	BUSMAN	DAMPEN	FATTEN	HENNIN	LENTEN	MOUTON
MAYHEM	SHALOM	ATAMAN	BUTTON	DAMSON	FENIAN	HENSON	LEPTON	MUFFIN
MEDISM	SIKKIM	ATTAIN	CACOON	DANTON	FINNAN	HERDEN	LESION	MUFLON
MEDIUM	SIMOOM	ATTORN	CAFTAN	DARIEN	FIRKIN	HEREIN	LESSEN	MURLIN
MEGRIM	SITCOM	AUBURN	CAIMAN	DARKEN	FIRMAN	HERMON	LESSON	MURRIN
MENTUM	SLALOM	AUGEAN	CALKIN	DARWIN	FLACON	HEROIN	LEYDEN	MUSLIN
MONISM	SODIUM	AUSTEN	CALVIN	DAWSON	FLAGON	HERREN	LIBYAN	MUTTON
MONTEM	SPUTUM	AUSTIN	CAMDEN	DEACON	FLAMEN	HETMAN	LICHEN	MYELIN
MORTEM	SQUIRM	AUTUMN	CAMION	DEADEN	FLAVIN	HIDDEN	LILIAN	MYELON
MOSLEM	STREAM	AVALON	CANAAN	DEAFEN	FLAXEN	HILTON	LINDEN	MYOGEN
MULTUM	SYNCOM	AWAKEN	CANNON	DECCAN	FLORIN	HITMAN	LISBON	MYOSIN
MURRAM	SYRISM	AWOKEN	CANTON	DEEPEN	FRIPON	HOIDEN	LISTEN	NANKIN
MUSEUM	SYSTEM	AXEMAN	CANYON	DEHORN	FROZEN	HOYDEN	LONDON	NANSEN
MUSLIM	TALCUM	BABOON	CAPTAN	DELIAN	FUSAIN	HUDSON	LOOSEN	NAPKIN
MUTISM	TANDEM	BADMAN	CARBON	DEMAIN	FUSION	HYPHEN	LOTION	NASION
NANISM	TAOISM	BAFFIN	CARDAN	DEMEAN	GABION	IBADAN	LOUDEN	NATION
NAPALM	TARGUM	BAGMAN	CAREEN	DERAIN	GAGMAN	ICEMAN	LUCIAN	NATRON
NERIUM	TECTUM	BALEEN	CARLIN	DESIGN	GAIJIN	IMBARN	LUTEIN	NEATEN
NOMISM	TEDIUM	BALKAN	CARMEN	DETAIN	GALLEN	IMOGEN	LUZERN	NELSON
NONCOM	TERGUM	BANIAN	CARSON	DIAXON	GALLON	IMPAWN	LYDIAN	NEURON
NUDISM	THEISM	BANYAN	CARTON	DIODON	GAMMON	IMPUGN	LYTTON	NEWMAN
OBIISM	TOMIUM	BARMAN	CASEIN	DIOXIN	GANION	INBORN	MACRON	NEWTON
OMASUM	TOMTOM	BARREN	CASLON	DISOWN	GARÇON	INCHON	MADDEN	NIACIN
OMNIUM	TRUISM	BARTON	CATKIN	DIZAIN	GARDEN	INDIAN	MADMAN	NINIAN
OPHISM	UNSEAM	BATMAN	CAVEIN	DOBBIN	GASCON	INDIGN	MAGNON	NIPPON
ORGASM	VACUUM	BATTEN	CAVERN	DOBSON	GASMAN	INTERN	MAIDAN	NISSEN
OSMIUM	VALIUM	BEACON	CAYMAN	DOLMAN	GASTON	INTOWN	MAIDEN	NOGGIN
OSTIUM	VALLUM	BEATEN	CEROON	DOLMEN	GAWAIN	INTRON	MALDON	NORMAN
PASSIM	VEDISM	BECKON	CEYLON	DOMAIN	GEASON	IONIAN	MALIAN	NOTION
PAYNIM	VELLUM	BEDPAN	CHARON	DONJON	GEMMAN	IRETON	MALIGN	NUBBIN
PELHAM	VERISM	BEETON	CHATON	DORIAN	GERMAN	ITCHEN	MAMMON	OBERON
PENSUM	VICTIM	BELSEN	CHAZAN	DOWSON	GIBBON	JAMBON	MANNIN	OBTAIN
PEPLUM	WADHAM	BEMEAN	CHICON	DRAGON	GIBSON	JARGON	MARGIN	ODDSON
PHLEGM	WAGRAM	BEMOAN	CHIRON	DRALON	GIDEON	JERKIN	MARIAN	OGADEN
PHLEUM	WAMPUM	BENIGN	CHITIN	DRIVEN	GILPIN	JETTON	MARLIN	OILCAN
PHLOEM	WENSUM	BENSON	CHITON	DRYDEN	GIRKIN	JONSON	MAROON	OILMAN
PHYLUM	WHILOM	BERGEN	CHOPIN	DUBBIN	GIRTON	JOPLIN	MARRON	OLEFIN
PILEUM	WIGWAM	BERLIN	CHOSEN	DUBLIN	GIZZEN	JORDAN	MARTEN	ONEDIN
PLENUM	XENIUM	BHAJAN	CHOUAN	DUDEEN	GLUTEN	JOSKIN	MARTIN	ONEGIN

ONEMAN	REASON	SOFTEN	UNBORN	BASUTO	HETERO	SBIRRO	HANGUP	ANGLER
OPPUGN	REBORN	SOLEMN	UNEVEN	BENITO	HONCHO	SCAMPO	HICCUP	ANSWER
OPTION	RECKON	SPAVIN	UNGAIN	BILLYO	IBIBIO	SCHIZO	HIGHUP	ANTHER
ORDAIN	REDDEN	SPLEEN	UNISON	BISTRO	INDIGO	SCIPIO	HOLDUP	ANTLER
OREGON	REGAIN	SPOKEN	UNSEEN	BLANCO	JETHRO	SHINTO	HOOKUP	APPEAR
ORIGEN	REGION	SPRAIN	UPTOWN	BLOTTO	KAKAPO	SKIDOO	HYSSOP	ARBOUR
ORIGIN	REJOIN	STALIN	UPTURN	BOLERO	KIMONO	SOLANO	ICECAP	ARCHER
ORISON	REMAIN	STAMEN	URCHIN	BONITO	KOMODO	SORGHO	INSTEP	ARDOUR
ORPHAN	RENNIN	STATEN	VATMAN	BOOBOO	KOODOO	SPEEDO	KIDNAP	ARMOUR
OSSIAN	RENOWN	STEVEN	VERDIN	BOOHOO	LANUGO	STEREO	LAPTOP	ARREAR
OUTRUN	REOPEN	STOLEN	VERDUN	BORNEO	LAVABO	STINGO	LARRUP	ARTHUR
OXYGEN	REPTON	STOLON	VEREIN	BRONCO	LEANTO	STINKO	LINEUP	ASHLAR
PADUAN	REPUGN	STRAIN	VERMIN	BUMALO	LEGATO	STRABO	LINKUP	ASHTAR
PANTON	RESIGN	SUBORN	VERNON	CALICO	LIBERO	STUCCO	LOCKUP	AUSTER
PARDON	RETAIN	SUCKEN	VIOLIN	CARUSO	LIBIDO	STUDIO	LOLLOP	AUTHOR
PARKIN	RETURN	SUDDEN	VIRGIN	CASINO	LORETO	TATTOO	MADCAP	AVATAR
PARPEN	REUBEN	SULLEN	VISION	CASSIO	LUGANO	TECHNO	MADEUP	BACKER
PARSON	RIBBON	SULTAN	VIVIAN	CASTRO	MADURO	TERCIO	MAKEUP	BADGER
PARTON	RIPPON	SUMMON	VIVIEN	CHROMO	MANITO	TEREDO	MARKUP	BAILER
PASTON	RIVLIN	SUNKEN	VULCAN	CICERO	MAPUTO	THERMO	MENCAP	BALDER
PATHAN	ROBSON	SUNTAN	WAGGON	CLOTHO	MEDICO	TICINO	MENDIP	BANDAR
PATRON	ROGNON	SWEDEN	WALTON	COMEDO	MERINO	TIPPOO	MISHAP	BANGER
PATTEN	ROTTEN	SYLVAN	WANTON	CRAMBO	MEXICO	TOBAGO	MOBCAP	BANKER
PATTON	RUMKIN	SYPHON	WARDEN	CRYPTO	MIKADO	TOLEDO	MOCKUP	BANNER
PEAHEN	RUNYON	SYRIAN	WARREN	CUCKOO	MONACO	TOMATO	OARLAP	BANTER
PECTEN	RUSKIN	TAIPAN	WATSON	CUERPO	NANDOO	TORERO	OUTTOP	BARBER
PECTIN	RYOKAN	TAIWAN	WEAKEN	CYRANO	NAVAHO	TRESCO	PAIDUP	BARKER
PELION	SAANEN	TALION	WEAPON	DAIMIO	NAVAJO	TROPPO	PENTUP	BARTER
PENMAN	SADDEN	TAMPON	WELKIN	DAISHO	NIELLO	TUPELO	PERHAP	BASHER
PENNON	SALMON	TANNIN	WELWYN	DINERO	NUNCIO	TUXEDO	PHILIP	BATHER
PERKIN	SALOON	TARTAN	WHITEN	DOMINO	OCTAVO	ULTIMO	PICKUP	BATTER
PERRON	SAMIAN	TASMAN	WIGEON	DORADO	ORIANO	VELCRO	PILEUP	BAXTER
PERSON	SAMPAN	TAUTEN	WILSON	DROMIO	ORSINO	VIBRIO	PUSHUP	BAZAAR
PÉTAIN	SAMSON	TAVERN	WISDEN	DRONGO	OTELLO	VIRAGO	RAGTOP	BEAKER
PHOTON	SANTON	TAXMAN	WITHIN	DYNAMO	OVERDO	VOODOO	RECOUP	BEARER
PIDGIN	SARSEN	TEFLON	WIVERN	ECHINO	PAKHTO	WEIRDO	REDCAP	BEATER
PIEMAN	SATEEN	TEGMEN	WOBURN	EMBRYO	PAPAGO	WHACKO	REDTOP	BEAVER
PIGEON	SATURN	TEHRAN	WONTON	ESCUDO	PARAMO	ASLEEP	REVAMP	BEDDER
PIGPEN	SCIRON	TENDON	WOODEN	ESKIMO	PARETO	ATTRAP	SALOOP	BEEPER
PINION	SCREEN	TENPIN	WOOLEN	FIASCO	PASHTO	BACKUP	SATRAP	BEGGAR
PINYIN	SEAMAN	TENSON	WORSEN	FIGARO	PEDALO	BISHOP	SCHLEP	BENDER
PIPKIN	SEAMEN	TEOPAN	WREKIN	FOREDO	PHYLLO	BLOWUP	SCRIMP	BERBER
PIPPIN	SEASON	TEUTON	WYVERN	FOREGO	PHYSIO	BURLAP	SCROOP	BESTIR
PISTON	SEISIN	THEBAN	YEOMAN	FRANCO	PINERO	CALLOP	SHRIMP	BETTER
PITMAN	SELSYN	THRAWN	YEOMEN	FRESCO	PISANO	CALLUP	SITREP	BETTOR
PLATEN	SELWYN	THROWN	YESMAN	FUGATO	POMELO	CATNAP	SLIPUP	BEZOAR
POISON	SEQUIN	TIEPIN	ZIRCON	FUMADO	PONCHO	CATNIP	STROUP	BICKER
POLLAN	SERMON	TIFFIN	ZYRIAN	GABBRO	POTATO	CATSUP	TEACUP	BIDDER
POLLEN	SEVERN	TINPAN	ADAGIO	GALLIO	PRESTO	CHERUP	THREAP	BIGGER
POMPON	SEXTAN	TINTIN	AIKIDO	GAUCHO	PRONTO	COLLOP	TIPTOP	BINDER
POPLIN	SEXTON	TITIAN	AKIMBO	GAZEBO	PSEUDO	DECAMP	TITTUP	BISTER
POTEEN	SHAKEN	TOCSIN	ALBEDO	GELATO	PSYCHO	DEWLAP	TOECAP	BITTER
POTION	SHAMAN	TONGAN	ALBINO	GHERAO	PUEBLO	DIKKOP	TOSSUP	BLAZER
PREVIN	SHARON	TOUCAN	ALBUGO	GHETTO	PUERTO	DOLLOP	TURNIP	BLOWER
PRISON	SHAVEN	TRAJAN	ALECTO	GIGOLO	PUNCTO	DUNLOP	TURNUP	BOATER
PROTON	SHOGUN	TREPAN	ALONSO	GINGKO	PYRRHO	EGGCUP	UNWRAP	BOBBER
PROVEN	SICKEN	TRIGON	ALPINO	GINKGO	QUANGO	ENCAMP	UPKEEP	BODGER
PTERIN	SILKEN	TRITON	ANGICO	GIOTTO	QUARTO	ENTRAP	WALLOP	BOILER
PUFFIN	SILVAN	TROJAN	APOLLO	GITANO	RABATO	ENWRAP	WINDUP	BOLTER
PURLIN	SIMEON	TRUMAN	ARIOSO	GIUSTO	RANCHO	ESCARP	ABATOR	BOMBER
PYTHON	SIMIAN	TULBAN	ARISTO	GORGIO	REGULO	ETHIOP	ADORER	BONDER
RADIAN	SIMKIN	TURBAN	ARROYO	GRINGO	RIALTO	EXTIRP	AFFAIR	BONZER
RAGLAN	SIMOON	TUREEN	ARTURO	GROSSO	RIGHTO	FILLIP	AGADIR	BOOKER
RAGMAN	SIPHON	TURPIN	AVERNO	GROTTO	ROCOCO	GALLOP	ALEGAR	BOOMER
RAISIN	SISKIN	TUSCAN	BAGNIO	GUNGHO	ROMANO	GALLUP	ALLIER	BOOZER
RATION	SKYMAN	TYBURN	BAGUIO	HAIRDO	ROTHKO	GAZUMP	ALTAIR	BORDAR
RATOON	SLOGAN	TYCOON	BAMAKO	HALLOO	SAMFOO	GIDDUP	AMBLER	BORDER
RATTAN	SLOVEN	TYMPAN	BAMBOO	HERERO	SANCHO	GOLLOP	ANADYR	BOTHER
RATTON	SODDEN	UGRIAN	BARRIO	HERETO	SAPPHO	GOSSIP	ANCHOR	BOUSER

BOWLER	CODGER	DIBBER	FILLER	GUITAR	JAGUAR	LENTOR	MOANER	PILFER
BOWSER	COFFER	DICKER	FILTER	GULPER	JAILER	LESSER	MOCKER	PILLAR
BOXCAR	COGGER	DIETER	FINDER	GUNNER	JAILOR	LESSOR	MOHAIR	PINCER
BRACER	COINER	DIFFER	FINGER	GUNTER	JASPER	LESTER	MOIDER	PINDAR
BREWER	COLLAR	DIGGER	FIRMER	GUSHER	JAZZER	LETTER	MONGER	PINGER
BROKER	COLMAR	DIMMER	FISHER	GUSLAR	JENNER	LIBBER	MORTAR	PINTER
BUCKER	COLTER	DINNER	FITTER	GUTTER	JERKER	LICTOR	MOTHER	PITTER
BUFFER	COMBER	DIPPER	FIZZER	HACKER	JESTER	LIEDER	MOUSER	PLACER
BUGGER	CONCUR	DISBAR	FLAVOR	HAILER	JIGGER	LIFTER	MOUTER	PLATER
BUGLER	CONDOR	DISEUR	FLOWER	HALTER	JITTER	LIGGER	MUCKER	PLAYER
BULGAR	CONFER	DITHER	FLUTER	HAMMER	JOBBER	LIMBER	MUDDER	PLEXOR
BULGER	CONGER	DOCKER	FODDER	HAMPER	JOGGER	LIMNER	MUGGER	PLOVER
BULLER	CONKER	DOCTOR	FOKKER	HANGAR	JOINER	LINEAR	MULLER	POLDER
BUMPER	CONNER	DODDER	FOLDER	HANGER	JOSSER	LINGER	MUMMER	PONDER
BUNKER	COOKER	DODGER	FOLIAR	HANKER	JOTTER	LINKER	MURDER	POOTER
BUNTER	COOLER	DOGGER	FOOTER	HARBOR	JUDDER	LIQUOR	MURMUR	POPLAR
BURGER	COOPER	DOLEUR	FORGER	HASSAR	JUGGER	LISPER	MUSTER	POPPER
BURNER	COPIER	DOLLAR	FORMER	HATTER	JUICER	LISTER	MUTTER	PORKER
BURSAR	COPPER	DOLOUR	FOSTER	HAWKER	JUMPER	LITTER	NAILER	PORTER
BUSKER	CORKER	DOOFER	FOWLER	HAWSER	JUNIOR	LOADER	NAPIER	POSEUR
BUSTER	CORNER	DORMER	FRAGOR	HEADER	JUNKER	LOAFER	NAPPER	POSSER
BUTLER	COSHER	DORTER	FRATER	HEALER	KAFFER	LOCKER	NASSER	POSTER
BUTTER	COSIER	DOSSER	FUHRER	HEARER	KAFFIR	LODGER	NATTER	POTHER
BUZZER	COSTAR	DOWNER	FULLER	HEATER	KAISER	LOGGER	NEARER	POTTER
CADGER	COSTER	DOWSER	FULMAR	HECTOR	KEELER	LOITER	NECKAR	POURER
CAESAR	COTTAR	DRAPER	FUREUR	HEIFER	KEENER	LONGER	NECTAR	POUTER
CAHIER	COUGAR	DRAWER	FURFUR	HELLER	KEEPER	LOOPER	NESTOR	POWDER
CALKER	COWPER	DRIVER	GAFFER	HELPER	KELPER	LOOTER	NETHER	POWTER
CALLER	COZIER	DROVER	GAINER	HERDER	KELTER	LOUVER	NEUTER	PRATER
CALVER	CRATER	DUDDER	GAITER	HIGHER	KEPHIR	LUBBER	NICKER	PRAYER
CAMBER	CRATUR	DUFFER	GAMMER	HINDER	KEPLER	LUGGER	NIGGER	PREFER
CAMPER	CRAYER	DUMPER	GANDER	HITHER	KETMIR	LUMBAR	NIPPER	PREWAR
CANCER	CREMOR	DUNBAR	GANGER	HITLER	KEVLAR	LUMBER	NUGGAR	PRIMER
CANDOR	CUITER	DUNDER	GAOLER	HITTER	KHYBER	LUMPUR	NUMBER	PROPER
CANKER	CULTER	DUNKER	GARNER	HOAXER	KICKER	LUSTER	NUTTER	PRUNER
CANTAR	CULVER	DURBAR	GARTER	HODDER	KILLER	LUTHER	NUZZER	PUCKER
CANTER	CUMBER	DUSTER	GASPAR	HOGGAR	KILNER	MADDER	OBITER	PUFFER
CANTOR	CUMMER	EARNER	GASPER	HOLDER	KILTER	MAGYAR	OCULAR	PULSAR
CAPTOR	CUNNER	EASIER	GASSER	HOLLER	KIMMER	MAHLER	OLIVER	PULVER
CAREER	CUPPER	EASTER	GASTER	HONOUR	KINDER	MAILER	ONAGER	PUNTER
CARPER	CURLER	ECLAIR	GATHER	HOOFER	KIPPER	MAINOR	OPENER	PURLER
CARTER	CURSOR	EDITOR	GAUGER	HOOKER	KISSER	MAMZER	ORATOR	PURSER
CARVER	CUSSER	EITHER	GEEZER	HOOPER	KOSHER	MANGER	OSTLER	PUSHER
CASPAR	CUSTER	ELIXIR	GELLER	HOOTER	KRATER	MANNER	OUTBAR	PUSSER
CASTER	CUTLER	ELOPER	GENDER	HOOVER	KRONER	MARKER	OWLCAR	PUTTER
CASTOR	CUTTER	ELUTOR	GETTER	HOPPER	KRUGER	MARNER	OYSTER	QUAKER
CATHAR	CYPHER	ENAMOR	GEYSER	HORNER	LAAGER	MARTYR	PACKER	QUASAR
CAVOUR	DAGGER	ENDEAR	GHEBER	HORROR	LABOUR	MASHER	PAIRER	QUAVER
CELLAR	DAMMAR	ERASER	GIAOUR	HOSIER	LADDER	MASKER	PALLOR	QUIVER
CENSER	DAMPER	ESCHAR	GIBBER	HOTAIR	LAFFER	MASTER	PALMER	RAFTER
CENSOR	DANCER	ESTHER	GILDER	HOTTER	LAMMER	MATTER	PAMPER	RAIDER
CENTER	DANDER	ETCHER	GIMMER	HOWLER	LANCER	MAUSER	PANDER	RAISER
CHADOR	DANGER	ETRIER	GINGER	HUMBER	LANDER	MEAGER	PANTER	RANCOR
CHAFER	DAPPER	EXETER	GIRDER	HUMMER	LANDOR	MEDLAR	PANZER	RANGER
CHASER	DARTER	EXMOOR	GLAMOR	HUMOUR	LANGUR	MEMBER	PARKER	RANKER
CHEDER	DEALER	FACTOR	GLIDER	HUNGER	LAPPER	MEMOIR	PARLOR	RANTER
CHIMER	DEARER	FALTER	GLOWER	HUNKER	LARDER	MENDER	PASTOR	RAPIER
CHINAR	DEBTOR	FARMER	GNAWER	HUNTER	LASCAR	MENHIR	PATTER	RAPPER
CHOKER	DECKER	FATHER	GOFFER	HUSSAR	LASHER	MENTOR	PAUPER	RAPTOR
CHOLER	DEEPER	FAVOUR	GOITER	IMPAIR	LATHER	MERCER	PECKER	RASHER
CINDER	DEKKER	FEEDER	GOLFER	INDOOR	LATTER	MERGER	PEDDER	RASPER
CIPHER	DENIER	FEELER	GOOBER	INLIER	LAUDER	MESMER	PEDLAR	RASTER
CLAMOR	DENVER	FELLER	GOPHER	INSTAR	LAWYER	METEOR	PEELER	RATHER
CLEVER	DEODAR	FENCER	GRATER	ISHTAR	LEADER	METIER	PEEPER	RATTER
CLOSER	DETOUR	FENDER	GRAVER	ISOBAR	LEAVER	MILLER	PEPPER	READER
CLOVER	DEVOUR	FERVOR	GROCER	ISOMER	LECHER	MINCER	PESTER	REAMER
COALER	DEXTER	FESTER	GROPER	JABBER	LECTOR	MINDER	PEWTER	REAPER
COBBER	DIAPER	FETTER	GROWER	JAEGER	LEDGER	MIRROR	PICKER	RECTOR
COCKER	DIPPER...	FIBBER	GROWER...	JAGGER	LENDER	MISTER	PICTOR	REDCAR

REEFER	SHAKER	TAILOR	VIATOR	ABACUS	BROADS	CROCKS	FAUCES	HINGES
REELER	SHARER	TALKER	VICTOR	ABBESS	BROOKS	CROCUS	FAUNUS	HIPPUS
RENDER	SHAVER	TAMMAR	VIEWER	ABDABS	BRUTUS	CRONOS	FAWKES	HOBBES
RENOIR	SHINER	TAMPER	VIGOUR	ABYDOS	BUENOS	CRONUS	FEINTS	HOLMES
RENTER	SHIVER	TANKER	VISIER	ACARUS	BUYERS	CRUELS	FERRIS	HOUNDS
REPAIR	SHOFAR	TANNER	VIZIER	ACATES	BYPASS	CRUFTS	FETTES	HOUSES
RETOUR	SHOWER	TAPPER	VOIDER	ACCESS	BYSSUS	CRUMBS	FIELDS	HUBRIS
REUTER	SICKER	TARTAR	VOYEUR	ACINUS	CACTUS	CULLIS	FLANKS	HUGHES
RÊVEUR	SIFTER	TASTER	VULGAR	ACKERS	CADDIS	CULTUS	FLARES	HUMMUS
RHETOR	SIGNOR	TATLER	WACKER	ACORNS	CADETS	CURSUS	FLATUS	HYADES
RHYMER	SILVER	TATTER	WAGNER	ACROSS	CADMUS	CUSCUS	FLICKS	HYBRIS
RICKER	SIMMER	TEASER	WAILER	ACTORS	CALAIS	CUSTOS	FLUTES	HYDRUS
RIGGER	SIMPER	TEETER	WAITER	ADONIS	CALLAS	CYCLUS	FOETUS	HYPNOS
RIGOUR	SINDER	TELLAR	WAIVER	AEGEUS	CALLUS	CYDNUS	FOLIOS	IAMBUS
RINGER	SINGER	TELLER	WALKER	AEOLIS	CAMPUS	CYESIS	FORCES	ICARUS
RIOTER	SINKER	TEMPER	WALLER	AEOLUS	CANTUS	CYGNUS	FRACAS	IMBOSS
RIPPER	SINNER	TENDER	WALTER	AFEARS	CANVAS	CYNIPS	FRILLS	INCHES
ROAMER	SIRDAR	TENNER	WANDER	AFTERS	CAPIAS	CYPRIS	FRUITS	INDIES
ROARER	SIRKAR	TENSOR	WARDER	AIRBUS	CARESS	CYPRUS	FUNDUS	INGOTS
ROBBER	SISTER	TERROR	WARMER	ALACUS	CARIES	DARIUS	FUNGUS	INGRES
ROCKER	SITTER	TESTER	WARNER	ALEXIS	CARPUS	DEBRIS	FURIES	INLAWS
ROEMER	SKATER	TETHER	WASHER	ALWAYS	CASSIS	DEDANS	GALLUS	IRAQIS
ROLLER	SKEWER	THALER	WASTER	AMENDS	CAUCUS	DEIMOS	GANGES	ISLETS
ROOFER	SKIVER	THENAR	WEAKER	AMYCUS	CECILS	DELIUS	GENIUS	ISSUES
ROOMER	SLATER	TICKER	WEARER	ANABAS	CENSUS	DENIMS	GENTES	JACOBS
ROOTER	SLAVER	TILLER	WEAVER	ANANAS	CERCUS	DENNIS	GHOSTS	JEEVES
ROSSER	SLAYER	TIMBER	WEEPER	ANGELS	CEREUS	DEPTHS	GILDAS	JEWELS
ROSTER	SLICER	TINDER	WEIMAR	ANGERS	CERTES	DERMIS	GLACIS	JEWESS
ROTHER	SLIDER	TINKER	WELDER	ANIMUS	CESTUS	DERRIS	GLAMIS	JOYOUS
ROTTER	SLIVER	TIPPER	WELLER	ANNALS	CHAINS	DEVILS	GLUMPS	JUDGES
ROUTER	SMILER	TITFER	WELTER	ANTICS	CHAIRS	DIANAS	GNEISS	JULIUS
ROZZER	SMOKER	TITTER	WESKER	ANUBIS	CHAMPS	DIESIS	GORGES	JUNCUS
RUBBER	SNIPER	TOLLER	WETHER	APPLES	CHEERS	DISCUS	GOURDS	KANSAS
RUDDER	SNORER	TONSOR	WHALER	ARABIS	CHEOPS	DISHES	GRACES	KELLYS
RUGGER	SOCCER	TOOTER	WICKER	ARAMIS	CHIMES	DITTOS	GRADES	KERMES
RUMMER	SOLDER	TOPPER	WIENER	ARCHES	CHIVES	DIVERS	GRADUS	KERMIS
RUMOUR	SOLVER	TORPOR	WILDER	ASCIUS	CHORUS	DOINGS	GRAINS	KEYNES
RUNNER	SOMBER	TOSHER	WINDER	ASSESS	CIRCUS	DORCAS	GRAMPS	KNIVES
RUTTER	SOONER	TOTTER	WINGER	ASSETS	CIRRUS	DOZENS	GRAPES	KOSMOS
SAGGAR	SORTER	TOURER	WINKER	ATHENS	CITRUS	DROMOS	GRATIS	KOUROS
SAILOR	SOUPER	TOUSER	WINNER	ATKINS	CIVICS	DRONES	GRAVES	KRONOS
SALVER	SOUTER	TOWBAR	WINTER	AUREUS	CLAIMS	DROVES	GREATS	KUMISS
SAMBAR	SOWTER	TOWSER	WITHER	AZORES	CLAVIS	DUNCES	GREEKS	LABRYS
SAMBUR	SPACER	TRACER	WIZIER	BAKERS	CLERKS	DURESS	GREENS	LACHES
SANDER	SPICER	TRADER	WOLVER	BALKIS	CLIFFS	ECCLES	GRIMES	LADIES
SAPHAR	SPIDER	TREMOR	WONDER	BARKIS	CLIMES	EGRESS	GRIMMS	LAMMAS
SAPPER	SPINAR	TRICAR	WOOFER	BARNES	CLOAKS	ELBRUS	GRIPES	LAPSUS
SARTOR	STAGER	TROCAR	WORKER	BASICS	CLONUS	ELDERS	GROATS	LASSUS
SAUCER	STATER	TROVER	WOWSER	BATHOS	CLOVIS	EMBERS	GROUPS	LAYERS
SAUGER	STATOR	TUCKER	WRITER	BAUCIS	CLUMPS	EMBOSS	GROUTS	LEAVES
SAVIOR	STAYER	TUMOUR	XAVIER	BESSUS	COATES	ENGELS	GRUMPS	LEMNOS
SAVOUR	STOKER	TURNER	YABBER	BICEPS	COCCUS	ENNIUS	GUARDS	LESBOS
SAWDER	STONER	TUSKER	YAKKER	BLACKS	COITUS	ENOSIS	GUESTS	LIGHTS
SAWYER	STORER	TWICER	YAMMER	BLINKS	COLEUS	EPIRUS	GUIDES	LIMITS
SCALAR	STOVER	ULSTER	YANKER	BLOCKS	COMMIS	EPULIS	GUILDS	LITMUS
SCALER	STOWER	UNFAIR	YATTER	BOARDS	CONICS	EQUALS	HACHIS	LLOYDS
SCARER	STUMER	UPROAR	YESTER	BODIES	CORALS	EREBUS	HAGGIS	LOAVES
SCORER	STUPOR	URETER	YONDER	BOFORS	CORMUS	ERINYS	HALVES	LYRICS
SCOTER	SUCCOR	USURER	YORKER	BOÖTES	CORNUS	ETHICS	HARASS	MADRAS
SEAMER	SUCKER	VALOUR	YUCKER	BOREAS	CORPUS	EXCESS	HARRIS	MAGNES
SECTOR	SUFFER	VALUER	ZANDER	BOSUNS	CORTES	EXISTS	HAVERS	MAGNUS
SEEDER	SUITOR	VAPOUR	ZEPHYR	BOUNDS	CORVUS	EXODUS	HEARTS	MAJLIS
SEEKER	SULFUR	VECTOR	ZIMMER	BOWELS	COSMOS	FABIUS	HEAVES	MANTIS
SELLER	SUMMER	VELOUR	ZINGER	BRACES	COULIS	FABLES	HELIOS	MAQUIS
SENDER	SUNDER	VENDER	ZIPPER	BRAHMS	CRANTS	FACIES	HELLAS	MASSES
SENIOR	SUPPER	VENDOR	ZITHER	BRAINS	CRASIS	FAECES	HERMES	MATHIS
SENSOR	SURFER	VENEER	ZOPHAR	BREWIS	CREEPS	FAINTS	HERONS	MATINS
SERVER	SUTLER	VERGER	ZOSTER	BRICKS	CRIPES	FAMOUS	HERPES	MAXIMS
SETTER	SYPHER	VESPER	AARONS	BRIEFS	CRISIS	FASCES	HIATUS	MEATUS

MEDIUS	PELVIS	SALMIS	STRASS	VALGUS	ARARAT	CAHOOT	DESIST	FILLET
MEJLIS	PEPLOS	SARGUS	STRAWS	VECTIS	ARDENT	CALLET	DESPOT	FINEST
MELIUS	PERILS	SAYERS	STRESS	VENOUS	ARGENT	CANNOT	DETECT	FIRLOT
MENDES	PETERS	SCALES	STUBBS	VERGES	ARMLET	CAPLET	DETENT	FITOUT
MESSRS	PHAROS	SCAPUS	STUMPS	VERMIS	ARMPIT	CARNET	DETEST	FLAUNT
MISSIS	PHASIS	SCHUSS	STYLUS	VERSES	ARNAUT	CARNOT	DEVEST	FLIGHT
MISSUS	PHOBOS	SCOOBS	SUCCUS	VERSUS	AROINT	CARPET	DEVOUT	FLORET
MOBIUS	PIECES	SCOPUS	SULCUS	VIANDS	AROUET	CARROT	DEWITT	FLUENT
MODELS	PIERIS	SCRAPS	SWEETS	VILLUS	ARPENT	CASKET	DICAST	FOLIOT
MODIUS	PILEUS	SCRUBS	SWIPES	VINOUS	ARRANT	CATGUT	DIGEST	FOMENT
MONTHS	PISCES	SEAMUS	TALLIS	VIROUS	ARREST	CAUGHT	DIGLOT	FORÇAT
MOPSUS	PLAINS	SENSES	TARDIS	VITALS	ARTIST	CAVEAT	DIKTAT	FOREST
MORALS	PLANKS	SEPSIS	TARSUS	VOLANS	ASCENT	CAVORT	DIMWIT	FORGET
MORASS	PLATES	SERIES	TATERS	VOLENS	ASLANT	CEMENT	DIQUAT	FORGOT
MORBUS	PLEXUS	SEUMAS	TAURUS	VOSGES	ASPECT	CERMET	DIRECT	FORINT
MORRIS	PLIERS	SEVENS	TELLUS	VOWELS	ASSART	CHALET	DIVERT	FORMAT
MOVIES	PLUTUS	SÈVRES	TENNIS	VULGUS	ASSENT	CHENET	DIVEST	FORPIT
MUCOUS	POINTS	SHADES	TERMES	WADERS	ASSERT	CHEVET	DOCENT	FOUGHT
MURALS	POLYPS	SHAKES	TESTES	WALRUS	ASSIST	CHRIST	DOCKET	FRIGHT
MYOSIS	POROUS	SHAMUS	TESTIS	WAMPUS	ASSORT	CLARET	DOESNT	FROWST
MYTHOS	POUNDS	SHANKS	TETHYS	WATERS	ASTART	CLIENT	DOPANT	FRUICT
NAEVUS	POWERS	SHARES	THALES	WELLES	ATTEST	CLOSET	DORRIT	FYLFOT
NANTES	PRANKS	SHARPS	THAMES	WHALES	AUGUST	COBALT	DORSET	GADGET
NAPLES	PRAXIS	SHEARS	THANKS	WHEELS	AVAUNT	COGENT	DOUCET	GALANT
NEREUS	PRECIS	SHEERS	THEBES	WHITES	AVOCET	COHORT	DOWSET	GALIOT
NERVES	PRIMUS	SHEETS	THEIRS	WHOOPS	BABBIT	COLLET	DRIEST	GALLET
NESSUS	PRISMS	SHORTS	THEMIS	WIDOWS	BACKET	COMART	DUGOUT	GALOOT
NIGHTS	PRIZES	SIGHTS	THESIS	WIPERS	BALLET	COMBAT	DULCET	GAMBET
NIMBUS	PSALMS	SIRIUS	THETIS	WISHES	BALLOT	COMFIT	DUMONT	GAMBIT
NOYOUS	PTERIS	SKATES	THIERS	WOMENS	BANDIT	COMMIT	DURANT	GANNET
NYLONS	PTOSIS	SLACKS	THINGS	XERXES	BANNER	COMSAT	DYNAST	GARGET
OBELUS	PUPPIS	SLAVES	THOLOS	YOICKS	BARBET	COQUET	ECONUT	GARNET
OBOLUS	PUTOIS	SLOPES	THOLUS	ZOUNDS	BARNET	CORNET	EFFECT	GARRET
OBSESS	QUALMS	SMACKS	THOMAS	ABDUCT	BASALT	CORSET	EFFORT	GARROT
OCEANS	QUEENS	SMALLS	THRIPS	ABJECT	BASKET	COSSET	EFTEST	GASKET
OCKERS	QUOITS	SMILES	THROES	ABLAUT	BASSET	COVENT	EGBERT	GERENT
OCTANS	RABIES	SMITHS	THYMUS	ABRUPT	BECKET	COVERT	EGMONT	GIBBET
ODIOUS	RACHIS	SOLEUS	TIGHTS	ABSENT	BEDSIT	COWPAT	EGOIST	GIGLET
OGRESS	RADIUS	SONICS	TIGRIS	ACCENT	BEHEST	CRAVAT	ELANET	GIGLOT
OILERS	RAMOUS	SORDES	TMESIS	ACCEPT	BEIRUT	CREANT	ELDEST	GILLET
OLENUS	RAPIDS	SORTES	TOBIAS	ACCOST	BENNET	CREDIT	ELICIT	GIMLET
ONIONS	RECESS	SPADES	TOPHUS	ACQUIT	BEREFT	CRIANT	ELUANT	GOBBET
OODLES	RECTUS	SPARKS	TORRES	ADDICT	BESANT	CRONET	ENGLUT	GOBLET
OPTICS	REGIUS	SPEISS	TRADES	ADDUCT	BESORT	CRUSET	ENLIST	GOCART
ORCHIS	RELICS	SPLITS	TRAGUS	ADJUST	BEZANT	CUBIST	ENRAPT	GODWIT
ORDERS	REMISS	SPOILS	TRAPES	ADRIFT	BHARAT	CUEIST	EQUANT	GOKART
OREXIS	REVERS	SPOKES	TRAVIS	ADROIT	BIDENT	CULLET	ERRANT	GORGET
ORGANS	RHEIMS	SPORTS	TRIBES	ADVENT	BILLET	CURIET	ESCORT	GULLET
OSIRIS	RHESUS	STACKS	TRICKS	ADVERT	BISECT	CURVET	ESPRIT	GURLET
OTHERS	RHEXIS	STAIRS	TRIPOS	AFFECT	BLIGHT	CUSHAT	EXCEPT	GURNET
OTITIS	RHODES	STAKES	TROOPS	AFFRET	BOBCAT	CUTLET	EXEMPT	GUSSET
OUNCES	RICHES	STALKS	TROYES	AFLOAT	BOGART	CYGNET	EXEUNT	HAMLET
OUTGAS	RICTUS	STALLS	TRUMPS	AFREET	BONNET	DACOIT	EXHORT	HARLOT
OVIBOS	RIGHTS	STAMPS	TRUNKS	AGHAST	BOSKET	DAMMIT	EXOCET	HASLET
OXALIS	ROGUES	STAPES	TRUTHS	AIDANT	BOUGHT	DAUDET	EXPECT	HAVENT
PAINTS	ROMANS	STARES	TUBERS	AIGLET	BREAST	DECANT	EXPERT	HEIGHT
PALAIS	ROUNDS	STASIS	TURVES	ALBEIT	BRECHT	DECEIT	EXPORT	HELMET
PALLAS	ROYALS	STATES	TUSSIS	ALBERT	BREVET	DECENT	EXSERT	HENBIT
PAMIRS	RUBENS	STATUS	TWEEDS	ALIGHT	BRIGHT	DEDUCT	EXTANT	HERIOT
PAMPAS	RUBIES	STEERS	TYPHUS	ALMOST	BRYANT	DEFEAT	EXTENT	HERMIT
PAPERS	RUBIKS	STICKS	UCKERS	AMIDST	BUCKET	DEFECT	EXTORT	HOBART
PAPHOS	RUCKUS	STILTS	ULCERS	AMORET	BUDGET	DEJECT	EYELET	HOGGET
PARVIS	RUGOUS	STINKS	ULITIS	AMOUNT	BUFFET	DELICT	FAGGOT	HOLIST
PASSES	RUMORS	STIPES	UMBLES	AMULET	BULLET	DEMENT	FAUCET	HONEST
PASTIS	RUMPUS	STOCKS	UNDIES	ANKLET	BURBOT	DEMIST	FERMAT	HORNET
PATHOS	RUPEES	STOKES	UNLESS	ANOINT	BURNET	DEPART	FEWEST	HOTPOT
PATMOS	RUPIAS	STONES	URANUS	AORIST	BUSKET	DEPICT	FIDGET	HUMECT
PATOIS	SABRES	STOOKS	UTERUS	APPORT	BUYOUT	DEPORT	FILFOT	IMPACT
PEARLS	SAINTS	STOOLS	VALENS	ARAFAT	CACHET	DESERT	FILFOT	IMPART

IMPORT	MAGNET	PANDIT	REPORT	SUBLET	UNSENT	PAVLOV	WILLOW	ANTONY
IMPOST	MAHOUT	PAPIST	RESECT	SUBMIT	UPBEAT	ROSTOV	WINDOW	ANYWAY
INCEPT	MALLET	PARENT	RESENT	SUBSET	UPCAST	ANDREW	WINNOW	APATHY
INCEST	MAOIST	PARGET	RESIST	SUCKET	ANYHOW	BARROW	YARROW	APEPSY
INDENT	MARIST	PARROT	RESORT	SUMMIT	UPLIFT	BELLOW	YELLOW	APHONY
INDICT	MARKET	PATENT	RESULT	SUNHAT	UPROOT	BENBOW	AUSPEX	APIARY
INDUCT	MARMOT	PEANUT	RETORT	SUNLIT	UPSHOT	BESTOW	BANJAX	ARCADY
INFANT	MASCOT	PEDANT	REVERT	SUNSET	URGENT	BILLOW	BAYEUX	ARGOSY
INFECT	MAZOUT	PEEWIT	REVOLT	SWIVET	USHANT	BORROW	BOMBYX	ARMORY
INFEST	MERCAT	PELLET	RIDENT	TABLET	UTMOST	BOWWOW	CARFAX	ARTERY
INGEST	MERLOT	PELMET	ROBERT	TACKET	VACANT	BURROW	CAUDEX	ASHLEY
INJECT	MIDGET	PERMIT	ROBUST	TALBOT	VARLET	BYELAW	CEEFAX	ASTRAY
INKJET	MILLET	PICKET	ROCKET	TALENT	VELVET	CALLOW	CERVIX	AUBREY
INKPOT	MINUET	PIGLET	RODENT	TALLOT	VERSET	CASHEW	CLIMAX	AUDLEY
INMOST	MISFIT	PIGOTT	ROQUET	TAOIST	VERVET	CURFEW	COCCYX	AUDREY
INSECT	MISHIT	PIMENT	ROTGUT	TAPPET	VIOLET	CURLEW	CONVEX	AUGURY
INSERT	MODEST	PINXIT	RUPERT	TAPPIT	VOLANT	DECREW	CORTEX	AUMBRY
INSIST	MODIST	PIQUET	RUSSET	TARGET	WALNUT	ESCHEW	COWPOX	AVIARY
INSULT	MOLEST	PLAINT	SACHET	TASSET	WAYOUT	ESCROW	CURTAX	AVIDLY
INTACT	MOMENT	PLANET	SADIST	TAUGHT	WEIGHT	FALLOW	DUPLEX	AZERTY
INTENT	MONIST	PLIANT	SALLET	TEAPOT	WERENT	FARROW	EARWAX	BAILEY
INVENT	MOPPET	PLIGHT	SAMIOT	TENANT	WHILST	FELLOW	EFFLUX	BAILLY
INVERT	MOZART	POCKET	SAMLET	TERCET	WHISHT	FOGBOW	FORNAX	BAKERY
INVEST	MUFFET	POIROT	SAVANT	TEVIOT	WICKET	FOLLOW	FORNIX	BALDLY
IRRUPT	MULLET	PONENT	SCHIST	THANET	WIDGET	FURROW	FRUTEX	BANTRY
ISEULT	MUPPET	POPPET	SCHUYT	THEIST	WILLET	GALLOW	HALLUX	BARELY
JACENT	MUSCAT	POPPIT	SCRIPT	THIRST	WOMBAT	GEWGAW	HAYBOX	BARLEY
JACKET	MUSKET	POSSET	SCRUNT	THREAT	WRIGHT	GUFFAW	HYDRAX	BARNEY
JAMPOT	MUTANT	POTENT	SCULPT	THRIFT	YAOURT	HALLOW	ICEBOX	BEACHY
JENNET	NATANT	PRIEST	SECANT	THRIST	YOGURT	HARROW	INFLUX	BEATTY
JESUIT	NAUGHT	PRIVET	SECRET	THROAT	ZEALOT	HAYMOW	JAWBOX	BEAUTY
JILLET	NEEDNT	PROBIT	SELECT	THRUST	ABATTU	HEBREW	LARYNX	BELAMY
JULIET	NEFAST	PROFIT	SENNET	THWART	ACAJOU	HEEHAW	LUMMOX	BELFRY
JUNKET	NEWEST	PROMPT	SEPTET	TICKET	AMADOU	HOLLOW	MATRIX	BETONY
JURANT	NIDGET	PROSIT	SEURAT	TIDBIT	APERÇU	INFLOW	MENINX	BETRAY
JURIST	NITWIT	PROUST	SEXIST	TILSIT	BATEAU	INGROW	PICKAX	BIGAMY
KAPUTT	NOBBUT	PULLET	SEXTET	TINPOT	BUREAU	POLLEX	BINARY
KENNET	NOCENT	PULPIT	SHEVAT	TIPCAT	CACHOU	JIGSAW	POLLUX	BIOPSY
KHALAT	NOUGAT	PUNDIT	SHRIFT	TIPPET	DETENU	KOWTOW	PREFIX	BISCAY
KHILAT	NOUGHT	PUNNET	SIGNET	TISSOT	EPERDU	MALLOW	PRETAX	BITCHY
KISMET	NUDIST	PUPPET	SILENT	TITBIT	GATEAU	MARROW	PROLIX	BLEARY
KITCAT	NUGGET	PURIST	SIPPET	TOILET	HONSHU	MATLOW	REFLEX	BLENNY
KNIGHT	NUTANT	PUTOUT	SLIGHT	TOMCAT	JABIRU	MEADOW	REFLUX	BLIMEY
LAMENT	OAKNUT	QUAINT	SMIGHT	TONANT	KIKUYU	MELLOW	SCOLEX	BLOODY
LANCET	OBJECT	RABBET	SOBEIT	TOUPET	KYUSHU	MERROW	SEMTEX	BLOWZY
LAPPET	OBLAST	RABBIT	SOCKET	TRICOT	LANDAU	MILDEW	SPADIX	BODILY
LARIAT	OBOIST	RACIST	SOFFIT	TRIVET	MALIBU	MINNOW	SPHINX	BOLDLY
LASKET	OBTECT	RACKET	SOLENT	TRUANT	MANCHU	MOOCOW	STORAX	BOLSHY
LATENT	OBVERT	RAGOUT	SONANT	TSHIRT	MILIEU	MORROW	STYRAX	BOMBAY
LATEST	OCCULT	RAMJET	SONNET	TUCKET	NASSAU	MOSCOW	SUFFIX	BOTANY
LAXIST	OCELOT	RAPIST	SORBET	TUFFET	NILGAU	NARROW	SUPLEX	BOTLEY
LAYOUT	OCTANT	RECANT	SOUGHT	TUMULT	ORMOLU	NEPHEW	SURTAX	BOUNCY
LEGIST	OFFCUT	RECAST	SOVIET	TURBOT	PAKHTU	OUTLAW	SUSSEX	BOUNTY
LEGLET	OFFSET	RECENT	SPIGOT	TURRET	PASHTU	PAWPAW	SYNTAX	BOWERY
LETOUT	OLIVET	REDACT	SPINET	TWIGHT	PUSHTU	PILLOW	SYRINX	BRAINY
LEVANT	OMELET	REFECT	SPIRIT	TWOBIT	RAMEAU	POWWOW	TETTIX	BRANDY
LIMPET	ONCOST	REFLET	SPLENT	TYBALT	RESEAU	REDRAW	THORAX	BRASSY
LINGOT	OPTOUT	REGENT	SPLINT	TYPIST	SADDHU	REVIEW	UNISEX	BRAWNY
LINNET	ORGEAT	REGEST	SPOILT	TYRANT	TAMANU	RIPSAW	VORTEX	BREEZY
LOCKET	ORIENT	REGLET	SPRINT	UDMURT	TELEDU	SALLOW	WESSEX	BRIONY
LOCUST	OSBERT	REGRET	SPROUT	UGARIT	TELEGU	SEESAW	ABBACY	BROLLY
LOQUAT	OUTFIT	REHEAT	SQUINT	UMLAUT	TELUGU	SHADOW	ACUITY	BROODY
LORIOT	OUTLET	REJECT	SQUIRT	UNBENT	TENGKU	SORROW	AFFRAY	BRUMBY
LOWEST	OUTPUT	RELENT	STRAIT	UNBOLT	TUVALU	SUNDEW	AGENCY	BRYONY
LUCENT	OUTSET	RELICT	STREET	UNHURT	VISHNU	TALLOW	AIRILY	BUBBLY
LURIST	OUTWIT	RENNET	STRICT	UNJUST	XANADU	TARROW	AIRWAY	BULIMY
LUTIST	PACKET	REPAST	STRUNT	UNMEET	ASIMOV	UPFLOW	ALBANY	BUNCHY
LYRIST	PALLET	REPEAT	STUART	UNREST	KISLEV	WALLOW	ALMERY	BUNGAY
MAGGOT	PAMYAT	REPENT	STYLET	UNSEAT	MAGLEV	WARSAW	ANGARY	BURLEY

145

BUSBOY	CREEPY	EXPIRY	GOODLY	KINDLY	MUTINY	PLUMMY	SCILLY	SNIFFY
BUSILY	CRIKEY	FAIRLY	GOOGLY	KINGLY	NAMELY	POETRY	SCREWY	SNIFTY
CAGILY	CRISPY	FAMILY	GOOLEY	KNAGGY	NAPERY	POLICY	SCUMMY	SNIPPY
CALMLY	CROAKY	FAULTY	GRAINY	KNOBBY	NASEBY	POLITY	SCURRY	SNOOTY
CANARY	CROPPY	FEALTY	GRAMMY	KNOTTY	NEARBY	POLONY	SCURVY	SNOTTY
CANOPY	CROSBY	FEEBLY	GRANBY	LACKEY	NEARLY	POMPEY	SCUZZY	SNOUTY
CANVEY	CROUPY	FEISTY	GRANNY	LAMELY	NEATLY	POORLY	SEAWAY	SNUGLY
CARBOY	CRUMMY	FELONY	GRASSY	LASTLY	NIAMEY	PORTLY	SEEMLY	SODOMY
CATCHY	CRUSTY	FIDDLY	GREASY	LATELY	NICELY	PREPAY	SELLBY	SOFTLY
CATHAY	CUDDLY	FILTHY	GREEDY	LAXITY	NICETY	PREPPY	SENTRY	SOLELY
CAUSEY	CURACY	FINELY	GRIMLY	LAZILY	NIDIFY	PRETTY	SEVERY	SOLVAY
CAVITY	CURTLY	FINERY	GRISLY	LEALTY	NIGGLY	PRICEY	SHABBY	SORELY
CECITY	CURTSY	FINLAY	GRITTY	LEEWAY	NIGHTY	PRIMLY	SHAGGY	SOURLY
CELERY	DAINTY	FIRMLY	GROGGY	LEGACY	NIMBLY	PRIORY	SHAMMY	SPARKY
CHALKY	DARKEY	FIXITY	GROOVY	LEMONY	NINETY	PRISSY	SHANDY	SPEEDY
CHANCY	DARKLY	FLABBY	GROTTY	LEVITY	NITERY	PUDSEY	SHANTY	SPONGY
CHANEY	DAWNEY	FLAGGY	GROUTY	LEWDLY	NOBODY	PULLEY	SHEENY	SPOOKY
CHATTY	DEADLY	FLASHY	GRUBBY	LIKELY	NONARY	PUNCHY	SHERRY	SPOONY
CHEEKY	DEARLY	FLATLY	GRUMPY	LIMPLY	NORROY	PURELY	SHIFTY	SPORTY
CHEERY	DEEJAY	FLEECY	GRUNDY	LITANY	NORWAY	PURIFY	SHIMMY	SPOTTY
CHEESY	DEEPLY	FLESHY	GUILTY	LIVELY	NOSILY	PURITY	SHINDY	SPRYLY
CHEMMY	DEFRAY	FLEURY	GULLEY	LIVERY	NOTARY	PURVEY	SHINNY	STABLY
CHERRY	DEFTLY	FLIMSY	GURNEY	LONELY	NOTIFY	QUARRY	SHINTY	STAGEY
CHESTY	DEPLOY	FLINTY	HALLEY	LORDLY	NUDITY	QUEASY	SHIRTY	STALKY
CHILLY	DEPUTY	FLOOZY	HARDLY	LOUDLY	NUMBLY	QUINSY	SHODDY	STARRY
CHIPPY	DESCRY	FLOPPY	HARVEY	LOVELY	NUMPTY	QUIRKY	SHUFTY	STEADY
CHIRPY	DICKEY	FLOSSY	HAYLEY	LOWBOY	OAKLEY	QWERTY	SICILY	STEAMY
CHITTY	DIMITY	FLOURY	HAZILY	LOWKEY	OCCUPY	RAMIFY	SICKLY	STEELY
CHIVVY	DINGHY	FLUFFY	HEARTY	LUNACY	ODDITY	RAPTLY	SIDNEY	STICKY
CHOKEY	DINGLY	FLUNKY	HENLEY	LUNARY	OERLAY	RAREFY	SIMONY	STILTY
CHOOSY	DISMAY	FLURRY	HEREBY	LUXURY	ONEWAY	RARELY	SIMPLY	STINGY
CHOPPY	DISNEY	FLUSHY	HERESY	MAINLY	OPENLY	RARITY	SINEWY	STOCKY
CHOWRY	DONKEY	FOLKSY	HEYDAY	MALONY	ORALLY	RASHLY	SINGLY	STODGY
CHUBBY	DOUBLY	FONDLY	HICKEY	MALORY	ORKNEY	RATIFY	SKELLY	STOREY
CHUFFY	DOUGHY	FORRAY	HIGHLY	MARSHY	ORNERY	REALLY	SKERRY	STORMY
CHUMMY	DOURLY	FORSAY	HILARY	MAUNDY	ORRERY	REALTY	SKIMPY	STRAWY
CHUNKY	DOWNAY	FORTHY	HOBDAY	MAYDAY	OSIERY	REMEDY	SKINNY	STRIPY
CICELY	DOYLEY	FOULLY	HOCKEY	MAYFLY	OSPREY	RENVOY	SKIVVY	STUBBY
CLAGGY	DRAFTY	FRANZY	HOMELY	MEANLY	OSSIFY	REPLAY	SKURRY	STUFFY
CLAMMY	DREAMY	FREELY	HOMILY	MEASLY	OTALGY	REVERY	SLANGY	STUMPY
CLARTY	DREARY	FRENZY	HOMINY	MEDLEY	OUTCRY	RHEUMY	SLEAZY	STURDY
CLASSY	DREGGY	FRIARY	HOOKEY	MEDWAY	OUTLAY	RICHLY	SLEEKY	SUBTLY
CLAYEY	DRESSY	FRIDAY	HOORAY	MEEKLY	OVERLY	RICKEY	SLEEPY	SUBWAY
CLERGY	DRIPPY	FRILLY	HOURLY	MELODY	PACIFY	RODNEY	SLEEZY	SUDARY
CLIPPY	DROOPY	FRISKY	HUGELY	MEMORY	PAEONY	ROKEBY	SLINKY	SUGARY
CLOUDY	DROPSY	FRIZZY	HUMPTY	MERELY	PAINTY	ROMANY	SLIPPY	SULTRY
CLUMSY	DROSKY	FROSTY	HUNGRY	MERSEY	PALTRY	ROMNEY	SLITHY	SUNDAY
CODIFY	DROWSY	FROTHY	HURLEY	MICKEY	PANFRY	ROPERY	SLOPPY	SUNDRY
COLDLY	DUMBLY	FROWZY	HURRAY	MIDDAY	PANTRY	ROSARY	SLOSHY	SUNRAY
COLONY	EARTHY	FRUITY	HUXLEY	MIDWAY	PAPACY	ROSERY	SLOWLY	SUPPLY
COMEDY	EASILY	FRUMPY	IDIOCY	MIGHTY	PAPERY	ROTARY	SLUMMY	SURELY
COMELY	EATERY	FURPHY	ILKLEY	MILADY	PARITY	ROUGHY	SLURRY	SURETY
COMITY	ECTOPY	GADFLY	INFAMY	MILDLY	PARLEY	RUDELY	SLUSHY	SURREY
COMPLY	EERILY	GAIETY	INJURY	MISERY	PARODY	RUNWAY	SMARMY	SURVEY
CONCHY	EFFIGY	GAINLY	INTRAY	MISLAY	PARTLY	SAFELY	SMARTY	SWAMPY
CONVEY	EGENCY	GALAXY	JALOPY	MODIFY	PASTRY	SAFETY	SMEARY	SWANKY
CONVOY	EIGHTY	GALLEY	JANSKY	MOIETY	PATCHY	SAGELY	SMELLY	SWARTY
COOLLY	ELLERY	GAMELY	JARVEY	MONDAY	PAYDAY	SALARY	SMILEY	SWEATY
COSILY	EMBODY	GANGLY	JAUNTY	MONKEY	PEARLY	SANELY	SMITHY	SWEENY
COSTLY	EMBUSY	GANTRY	JEREMY	MONODY	PEBBLY	SANITY	SMOKEY	SYDNEY
COUNTY	EMPLOY	GENTLY	JERSEY	MORNAY	PENURY	SASHAY	SMUDGY	SYRUPY
COWBOY	ENERGY	GENTRY	JITNEY	MOSTLY	PETARY	SATINY	SMUGLY	SYZYGY
CRABBY	ENMITY	GHARRY	JOCKEY	MOTLEY	PHONEY	SAVORY	SMUTTY	TAMELY
CRAFTY	ENTITY	GLADLY	JOHNNY	MOULDY	PHOOEY	SAVVEY	SNAGGY	TANNOY
CRAGGY	EQUITY	GLASSY	JUSTLY	MOUSEY	PIGSTY	SAWNEY	SNAILY	TARTLY
CRANKY	ESTRAY	GLIBLY	KECKSY	MUNIFY	PIMPLY	SAXONY	SNAPPY	TAUTLY
CRANNY	EULOGY	GLITZY	KEENLY	MURPHY	PIRACY	SCABBY	SNAZZY	TAWDRY
CREAKY	EUTAXY	GLOOMY	KEYWAY	MURRAY	PLENTY	SCANTY	SNEAKY	TEAPOY
CREAMY	EVENLY	GLOSSY	KIDNEY	MUTELY	PLUCKY	SCATTY	SNEEZY	TEENSY

TERMLY	TIMELY	TRICKY	TYPIFY	VALLEY	WARCRY	WHIMSY	WOOKEY	SPRITZ
TETANY	TITCHY	TRILBY	UBIETY	VANITY	WARILY	WHINNY	WOOLLY	SUIVEZ
TETCHY	TOLZEY	TRIMLY	UNBUSY	VASTLY	WARMLY	WHISKY	WORTHY	TAMMUZ
THEORY	TOMBOY	TROPHY	UNDULY	VENERY	WATERY	WHITBY	YEARLY	TIZWAZ
THICKY	TOOTHY	TRUSTY	UNEASY	VERIFY	WAYLAY	WHOLLY	YEASTY	
THINGY	TOOTSY	TUMEFY	UNHOLY	VERILY	WEAKLY	WIDELY	BUZFUZ	
THINLY	TOUCHY	TURKEY	UNRULY	VERITY	WEEKLY	WIFELY	CHINTZ	
THIRTY	TOWNLY	TWEEDY	UNSEXY	VESTRY	WESLEY	WIGGLY	CORTEZ	
THORNY	TRANNY	TWEENY	UNTIDY	VILELY	WHACKY	WILDLY	ERSATZ	
TICKEY	TRASHY	TWENTY	UNWARY	VILIFY	WHAMMY	WIMSEY	HORMUZ	
TICKLY	TREATY	TWIGGY	UPPITY	VINERY	WHEELY	WINTRY	KRANTZ	
TIDDLY	TREBLY	TWIRLY	VAGARY	VOLLEY	WHEEZY	WISELY	QUARTZ	
TIDILY	TRENDY	TWISTY	VAINLY	VOTARY	WHERRY	WOBBLY	SHIRAZ	

7:1

AARONIC
ABALONE
ABANDON
ABASHED
ABATTIS
ABAXIAL
ABBASID
ABDOMEN
ABELARD
ABETTOR
ABIDING
ABIDJAN
ABIGAIL
ABILITY
ABIOSIS
ABJOINT
ABLATOR
ABOLISH
ABOUKIR
ABOULIA
ABRAHAM
ABRAXIS
ABREAST
ABRIDGE
ABSCESS
ABSCOND
ABSENCE
ABSINTH
ABSOLVE
ABSTAIN
ABUSIVE
ABYSMAL
ABYSSAL
ACADEME
ACADEMY
ACADIAN
ACARIDA
ACAUDAL
ACCLAIM
ACCOUNT
ACCRETE
ACCRUAL
ACCURSE
ACCUSED
ACCUSER
ACERBIC
ACESTES
ACETATE
ACETONE
ACHAEAN
ACHATES
ACHERON
ACHESON
ACHIEVE
ACHTUNG
ACIDIFY
ACIDITY
ACIFORM
ACOLYTE
ACONITE
ACQUIRE
ACREAGE
ACROBAT
ACRONYM
ACRYLIC
ACTAEON
ACTINAL

ACTINIA	AIRLESS	ALUMNUS	ANIMALS	AQUEOUS	ASSEGAI	AVOIDER
ACTINIC	AIRLIFT	ALVEOLE	ANIMATE	AQUIFER	ASSIEGE	AWESOME
ACTRESS	AIRLINE	ALYSSUM	ANIMIST	AQUILON	ASSISTS	AWFULLY
ACTUARY	AIRLOCK	AMALGAM	ANISEED	AQUINAS	ASSIZES	AWKWARD
ACTUATE	AIRMAIL	AMANITA	ANNATTO	AQUINUS	ASSUAGE	AXILLAR
ACUTELY	AIRPORT	AMATEUR	ANNELID	ARABIAN	ASSUMED	AXOLOTL
ADAMANT	AIRSHIP	AMATORY	ANNOYED	ARABICA	ASSURED	AZIMUTH
ADAMITE	AIRSICK	AMAZING	ANNUITY	ARABIZE	ASSYRIA	AZURITE
ADAPTER	AIRSTOP	AMBAGES	ANNULAR	ARACHNE	ASTARTE	AZYGOUS
ADAPTOR	ALABAMA	AMBIENT	ANNULET	ARAMAIC	ASTILBE	BABBITT
ADAXIAL	ALADDIN	AMBOYNA	ANNULUS	ARBITER	ASTOUND	BABBLER
ADDISON	ALAMODE	AMBROSE	ANODIZE	ARBUTUS	ASTRIDE	BABOOSH
ADDRESS	ALANINE	AMENITY	ANODYNE	ARCADIA	ASUNDER	BABYISH
ADELINE	ALARMED	AMERICA	ANOMALY	ARCHAEA	ATACTIC	BABYLON
ADELPHI	ALASKAN	AMERIGO	ANOSMIA	ARCHAIC	ATAGHAN	BABYSIT
ADENINE	ALBANIA	AMERIND	ANOTHER	ARCHERY	ATARAXY	BACARDI
ADENOID	ALBENIZ	AMHARIC	ANTACID	ARCHIVE	ATAVISM	BACCHIC
ADENOMA	ALBERGO	AMIABLE	ANTARES	ARCHWAY	ATELIER	BACCHUS
ADIPOSE	ALBERTA	AMIABLY	ANTENNA	ARCUATE	ATHEISM	BACILLI
ADJOINT	ALBERTI	AMMETER	ANTHILL	ARDUOUS	ATHEIST	BACKING
ADJOURN	ALBUMEN	AMMONAL	ANTHONY	ARETINO	ATHIRST	BACKLOG
ADJUNCT	ALBUMIN	AMMONIA	ANTHRAX	ARIADNE	ATHLETE	BACKSET
ADMIRAL	ALCALDE	AMNESIA	ANTIBES	ARIDITY	ATHWART	BADNESS
ADMIRED	ALCHEMY	AMNESTY	ANTIGEN	ARIETTA	ATINGLE	BAFFLED
ADMIRER	ALCOHOL	AMOEBIC	ANTIGUA	ARIOSTO	ATISHOO	BAGASSE
ADONAIS	ALCORAN	AMONGST	ANTIOCH	ARIZONA	ATOMIST	BAGEHOT
ADOPTED	ALDABRA	AMORIST	ANTIQUE	ARMBAND	ATOMIZE	BAGGAGE
ADORING	ALDRICH	AMORITE	ANTLERS	ARMHOLE	ATROPHY	BAGHDAD
ADORNED	ALECOST	AMOROSO	ANTONIO	ARMORED	ATROPOS	BAGPIPE
ADRENAL	ALEMBIC	AMOROUS	ANTONYM	ARMORIC	ATTABOY	BAHADUR
ADULATE	ALENÇON	AMPHORA	ANTWERP	ARMOURY	ATTACHE	BAHAMAS
ADVANCE	ALEPINE	AMPLIFY	ANXIETY	ARMREST	ATTAINT	BAHRAIN
ADVERSE	ALEWIFE	AMPOULE	ANXIOUS	AROUSAL	ATTEMPT	BAHREIN
ADVISER	ALFALFA	AMPULLA	ANYBODY	ARRAIGN	ATTICUS	BAILIFF
ADVISOR	ALFONSO	AMTRACK	ANYMORE	ARRANGE	ATTIRED	BAJAZET
AEOLIAN	ALGEBRA	AMUSING	APELIKE	ARRAYED	ATTRACT	BAKLAVA
AERATED	ALGERIA	AMYGDAL	APEPSIA	ARREARS	AUBERGE	BALANCE
AEROBIC	ALGIERS	AMYLASE	APHAGIA	ARRIVAL	AUCTION	BALATON
AEROSOL	ALICANT	AMYLOID	APHASIA	ARRIVED	AUDIBLE	BALCONY
AFFABLE	ALIDADE	AMYLOSE	APHELIA	ARSENAL	AUDIBLY	BALDING
AFFABLY	ALIGNED	ANAEMIA	APHESIS	ARSENIC	AUDITOR	BALDRIC
AFFAIRS	ALIMENT	ANAEMIC	APHONIA	ARTEMIS	AUDUBON	BALDWIN
AFFIXED	ALIMONY	ANAGRAM	APHONIC	ARTEMUS	AUGMENT	BALEFUL
AFFLICT	ALIQUID	ANALOGY	APHOTIC	ARTICLE	AUGUSTA	BALFOUR
AFFRONT	ALIQUOT	ANALYST	APHTHAE	ARTISAN	AUGUSTE	BALLADE
AFGHANI	ALKANET	ANALYZE	APICIUS	ARTISTE	AURALLY	BALLAST
AFRICAN	ALKORAN	ANANIAS	APLASIA	ARTLESS	AUREATE	BALLBOY
AGAINST	ALLEGED	ANARCHY	APOCOPE	ARTWORK	AURELIA	BALLIOL
AGELESS	ALLEGRI	ANATOLE	APOGEAN	ARUNDEL	AUREOLA	BALLOON
AGELONG	ALLEGRO	ANATOMY	APOLOGY	ASCARID	AUREOLE	BALONEY
AGGRADE	ALLENBY	ANCHOVY	APOSTLE	ASCETIC	AURICLE	BAMBINO
AGGRESS	ALLERGY	ANCIENT	APPARAT	ASCITES	AUROCHS	BANANAS
AGILITY	ALLONGE	ANDAMAN	APPAREL	ASCRIBE	AUSLESE	BANBURY
AGISTOR	ALLOWED	ANDANTE	APPEASE	ASEPTIC	AUSTERE	BANDAGE
AGITATE	ALLSTAR	ANDIRON	APPLAUD	ASEXUAL	AUSTRAL	BANDAID
AGITATO	ALMACKS	ANDORRA	APPLIED	ASHAMED	AUSTRIA	BANDBOX
AGONIST	ALMANAC	ANDROID	APPOINT	ASHANTI	AUTARKY	BANDEAU
AGONIZE	ALMONER	ANEMONE	APPOSED	ASHDOWN	AUTOCUE	BANDORE
AGRAPHA	ALPHEUS	ANEROID	APPRIZE	ASHTRAY	AUTOMAT	BANGING
AGRIPPA	ALRIGHT	ANGELIC	APPROVE	ASIATIC	AUTOPSY	BANGKOK
AGROUND	ALSATIA	ANGELUS	APRAXIA	ASININE	AVARICE	BANKING
AIDANCE	ALTERED	ANGEVIN	APRICOT	ASKANCE	AVEBURY	BANKSIA
AILERON	ALTHAEA	ANGIOMA	APROPOS	ASOCIAL	AVENGER	BANNOCK
AILMENT	ALTHING	ANGLING	APSIDAL	ASPASIA	AVERAGE	BANQUET
AIMLESS	ALTHORN	ANGOLAN	APTERAL	ASPERGE	AVESTAN	BANSHEE
AINTREE	ALUMINA	ANGRILY	APTERYX	ASPHALT	AVIATOR	BAPTISM
AIRBASE	ALUMNAE	ANGUISH	APTNESS	ASPIRIN	AVIDITY	BAPTIST
AIRCREW	ALUMNUS	ANGULAR	AQUATIC	ASQUITH	AVIGNON	BAPTIZE
AIRFLOW		ANILINE	AQUAVIT	ASSAULT	AVOCADO	BARBARA

BARBARY	BEGONIA	BIAFRAN	BLOTCHY	BOUNDED	BRITONS	BURMESE	CALORIC
BARENTS	BEGORRA	BIASSED	BLOTTER	BOUNDEN	BRITTLE	BURNELL	CALORIE
BARGAIN	BEGUILE	BIBELOT	BLOUSON	BOUNDER	BRITZKA	BURNHAM	CALTROP
BARKERS	BEHAVED	BICYCLE	BLOWFLY	BOUQUET	BRIXTON	BURNING	CALUMET
BARKING	BEHOOVE	BIDDING	BLOWOUT	BOURBON	BROADEN	BURNISH	CALUMNY
BARMAID	BEIJING	BIFOCAL	BLUBBER	BOURDON	BROADLY	BURNOUS	CALVARY
BARNABY	BEJEWEL	BIGFOOT	BLUFFLY	BOURSIN	BROCADE	BURNOUT	CALYPSO
BARONET	BELABOR	BIGHEAD	BLUNDER	BOUTADE	BROILER	BURSARY	CAMBIUM
BAROQUE	BELARUS	BIGHORN	BLUNTED	BOWDLER	BROKERS	BURSTER	CAMBRAI
BARRACK	BELATED	BIGOTED	BLUNTLY	BOWHEAD	BROMATE	BURUNDI	CAMBRIC
BARRAGE	BELGIAN	BIGOTRY	BLURRED	BOWLING	BROMIDE	BUSHIDO	CAMELOT
BARRIER	BELGIUM	BIGSHOT	BLUSHER	BOWSHOT	BROMINE	BUSHMAN	CAMERON
BARRING	BELIEVE	BILIOUS	BLUSTER	BOXHAUL	BRONCHI	BUSHMEN	CAMILLA
BARYTES	BELINDA	BILLION	BOARDER	BOXROOM	BRONZED	BUSKINS	CAMOGIE
BASCULE	BELISHA	BILLMAN	BOASTER	BOXWOOD	BROTHEL	BUSSING	CAMORRA
BASHFUL	BELLBOY	BILLOWS	BOATING	BOYCOTT	BROTHER	BUSTARD	CAMPANA
BASINET	BELLEEK	BILTONG	BOATMAN	BOYHOOD	BROUGHT	BUSTLER	CAMPARI
BASKING	BELLHOP	BINDERY	BOBSLED	BRACING	BROWNED	BUSTLES	CAMPHOR
BASMATI	BELLINI	BINDING	BOHEMIA	BRACKEN	BROWNIE	BUTANAL	CAMPING
BASSOON	BELLMAN	BIOCIDE	BOHRIUM	BRACKET	BROWSER	BUTANOL	CAMPION
BASTARD	BELLOWS	BIOLOGY	BOILEAU	BRADAWL	BRUISED	BUTCHER	CAMWOOD
BASTIDE	BELOVED	BIOMASS	BOILING	BRADMAN	BRUISER	BUTTERY	CANASTA
BASTION	BEMUSED	BIOTECH	BOLETUS	BRAEMAR	BRUSHER	BUTTONS	CANDACE
BATAVIA	BENARES	BIPLANE	BOLIVAR	BRAHMAN	BRUSQUE	BUZZARD	CANDELA
BATHERS	BENCHER	BIRDMAN	BOLIVIA	BRAHMIN	BRUTISH	BYRONIC	CANDIDA
BATHING	BENDING	BIRETTA	BOLLARD	BRAILLE	BUBBLES	CABARET	CANDIDE
BATHMAT	BENEATH	BISCUIT	BOLOGNA	BRAKING	BUBONIC	CABBAGE	CANDIED
BATHTUB	BENEFIT	BISMUTH	BOLONEY	BRAMBLE	BUCKETS	CABINET	CANDOUR
BATSMAN	BENGALI	BISTORT	BOLSHIE	BRANDED	BUCKEYE	CABLING	CANELLA
BATTELS	BENISON	BITTERN	BOLSHOI	BRANDER	BUCKLER	CABOOSE	CANIDAE
BATTERY	BENNETT	BITTERS	BOLSTER	BRANTUB	BUCKRAM	CACHEXY	CANNERY
BATTING	BENTHAM	BITUMEN	BOMBARD	BRASERO	BUCOLIC	CACIQUE	CANNILY
BAUHAUS	BENTHOS	BIVALVE	BOMBAST	BRAVADO	BUDDING	CADAVER	CANNING
BAUXITE	BENZENE	BIVOUAC	BOMBING	BRAVELY	BUFFALO	CADDISH	CANNOCK
BAYONET	BENZINE	BIZARRE	BONANZA	BRAVERY	BUFFOON	CADENCE	CANNULA
BAZOOKA	BENZOIN	BLABBER	BONDAGE	BRAVURA	BUGABOO	CADENZA	CANONRY
BEACHED	BEOWULF	BLACKEN	BONDMAN	BRAWLER	BUGBEAR	CADMIUM	CANTATA
BEACHES	BEQUEST	BLADDER	BONESET	BRAZIER	BUGGING	CADOGAN	CANTEEN
BEADING	BERCEAU	BLANDLY	BONFIRE	BREADED	BUGGINS	CAEDMON	CANTHUS
BEAMING	BEREAVE	BLANKET	BONKERS	BREADTH	BUGLOSS	CAESIUM	CANTRIP
BEANBAG	BERGSON	BLANKLY	BONNARD	BREAKER	BUILDER	CAESURA	CANTUAR
BEARDED	BERLINE	BLASTED	BOOBOOK	BREATHE	BULBOUS	CAGOULE	CANVASS
BEARHUG	BERMUDA	BLASTER	BOOKIES	BREEDER	BULGHUR	CAHOOTS	CANZONA
BEARING	BERNARD	BLATANT	BOOKING	BRENDAN	BULGING	CAINITE	CANZONE
BEARISH	BERNINI	BLATHER	BOOKISH	BRENNER	BULIMIA	CAIRENE	CAPABLE
BEASTLY	BERSEEM	BLATTER	BOOKLET	BREVITY	BULLACE	CAISSON	CAPABLY
BEATIFY	BERSERK	BLAZERS	BOOKMAN	BREWERY	BULLDOG	CAITIFF	CAPELLA
BEATING	BERTRAM	BLAZING	BOOLEAN	BREWING	BULLETS	CALABAR	CAPITAL
BEATLES	BESEECH	BLEAKLY	BOOMING	BRIBERY	BULLION	CALAMUS	CAPITOL
BEATNIK	BESHREW	BLEEPER	BOORISH	BRICKIE	BULLISH	CALCIFY	CAPORAL
BECAUSE	BESIDES	BLEMISH	BOOSTER	BRIDGES	BULLOCK	CALCINE	CAPRICE
BECKETT	BESIEGE	BLENDER	BOOTLEG	BRIDGET	BULLPEN	CALCITE	CAPSIZE
BEDDING	BESMEAR	BLESSED	BORACIC	BRIDLER	BULRUSH	CALCIUM	CAPSTAN
BEDEVIL	BESPEAK	BLESSES	BORDERS	BRIDLES	BULWARK	CALCULI	CAPSULE
BEDFORD	BESPOKE	BLETHER	BOREDOM	BRIEFLY	BUMBOAT	CALDERA	CAPTAIN
BEDOUIN	BESTIAL	BLIGHTY	BORODIN	BRIGADE	BUMMALO	CALDRON	CAPTION
BEDPOST	BESTREW	BLINDER	BOROUGH	BRIGAND	BUMPKIN	CALECHE	CAPTIVE
BEDROCK	BETHINK	BLINDLY	BORSTAL	BRIGHAM	BUNDOOK	CALENDS	CAPTURE
BEDROOM	BETHUMB	BLINKER	BOSWELL	BRIMFUL	BUNGLER	CALEPIN	CARABID
BEDSIDE	BETIMES	BLISTER	BOTANIC	BRINDLE	BUNTING	CALIBAN	CARACAL
BEDSORE	BETOKEN	BLITHER	BOTARGO	BRINJAL	BUOYANT	CALIBER	CARACAS
BEDTIME	BETROTH	BLITZED	BOTTEGA	BRIOCHE	BURBAGE	CALIBRE	CARACUL
BEEFALO	BETTING	BLOATED	BOTTLED	BRISKET	BURDOCK	CALICHE	CARADOC
BEEHIVE	BETTONG	BLOATER	BOTTLES	BRISKLY	BURETTE	CALLBOX	CARAMBA
BEELINE	BETWEEN	BLOCKED	BOUCLÉE	BRISTLE	BURGEON	CALLBOY	CARAMEL
BEERMAT	BETWIXT	BLOCKER	BOUDOIR	BRISTLY	BURGESS	CALLING	CARAVAN
BEESWAX	BEVERLY	BLOOMER	BOUILLI	BRISTOL	BURGHER	CALLOUS	CARAVEL
BEGGARY	BEWITCH	BLOOPER	BOULDER	BRITAIN	BURGLAR	CALMUCK	CARAWAY
BEGGING	BEZIQUE	BLOSSOM	BOUNCER	BRITISH	BURKINA	CALOMEL	CARBIDE

CARBINE	CATSEYE	CHAPPED	CHIPPED	CLICKER	COLONIC	CONSOLS	COTINGA
CARCASE	CATSPAW	CHAPTER	CHIPPER	CLIMATE	COLORED	CONSORT	COTTAGE
CARCASS	CATTISH	CHARADE	CHIPPIE	CLIMBER	COLOURS	CONSULT	COTTIER
CARDIAC	CATWALK	CHARDIN	CHIRRUP	CLINGER	COLUMBA	CONSUME	COTTONY
CARDOON	CAUSTIC	CHARGED	CHLAMYS	CLINKER	COLUMNS	CONTACT	COUCHÉE
CARDUUS	CAUTERY	CHARGER	CHLORAL	CLIPPED	COMBINE	CONTAIN	COULDNT
CAREERS	CAUTION	CHARGES	CHOCTAW	CLIPPER	COMBING	CONTEMN	COULOMB
CAREFUL	CAVALRY	CHARIOT	CHOKING	CLIPPIE	COMFORT	CONTEND	COULTER
CARGOES	CAVEMAN	CHARITY	CHOLERA	CLIQUEY	COMFREY	CONTENT	COUNCIL
CARIBOU	CAVIARE	CHARLES	CHOOKIE	CLOBBER	COMICAL	CONTEST	COUNSEL
CARIOCA	CAYENNE	CHARLEY	CHOPINE	CLOISON	COMMAND	CONTEXT	COUNTED
CARIOLE	CECILIA	CHARMED	CHOPPER	CLOSELY	COMMEND	CONTORT	COUNTER
CARITAS	CEDILLA	CHARMER	CHORALE	CLOSEUP	COMMENT	CONTOUR	COUNTRY
CARLOAD	CEILIDH	CHARNEL	CHORDAE	CLOSING	COMMODE	CONTROL	COUPLER
CARLYLE	CEILING	CHARPOY	CHORION	CLOSURE	COMMODO	CONVENE	COUPLET
CARMINE	CELADON	CHARRED	CHORIZO	CLOTHED	COMMONS	CONVENT	COUPONS
CARNABY	CELEBES	CHARTER	CHOROID	CLOTHES	COMMUNE	CONVERT	COURAGE
CARNAGE	CELESTA	CHASING	CHORTLE	CLOTURE	COMMUTE	CONVICT	COURBET
CAROLUS	CELESTE	CHASSIS	CHOWDER	CLOUDED	COMPACT	CONVOKE	COURIER
CAROTID	CELLINI	CHASTEN	CHRISOM	CLOYING	COMPANY	COOKERY	COURSER
CAROTIN	CELLIST	CHATEAU	CHRISTY	CLUBMAN	COMPARE	COOKING	COURSES
CAROUSE	CELLULE	CHATHAM	CHRONIC	CLUMBER	COMPASS	COOLANT	COURTLY
CARPORT	CELSIUS	CHATTEL	CHUCKLE	CLUNIAC	COMPERE	COOLING	COUSINS
CARRELL	CEMBALO	CHATTER	CHUFFED	CLUPEID	COMPETE	COONCAN	COUTURE
CARRIED	CENACLE	CHAUCER	CHUKKER	CLUSTER	COMPILE	COPILOT	COVERED
CARRIER	CENSURE	CHAYOTE	CHUNDER	CLUTTER	COMPLEX	COPIOUS	COVERUP
CARRIES	CENTAUR	CHEAPEN	CHUNNEL	COARSEN	COMPORT	COPLAND	COVETED
CARRION	CENTAVO	CHEAPLY	CHUPATI	COASTAL	COMPOSE	COPPERS	COWBANE
CARROLL	CENTRAL	CHEATER	CHUTNEY	COASTER	COMPOST	COPPICE	COWGIRL
CARROTS	CENTRED	CHECKED	CILIATE	COATING	COMPOTE	COPYCAT	COWHAND
CARROTY	CENTRIC	CHECKIN	CIMABUE	COAXIAL	COMPUTE	COPYING	COWHERD
CARSICK	CENTRUM	CHECKUP	CINDERS	COBBLED	COMRADE	COPYIST	COWHIDE
CARTIER	CENTURY	CHEDDAR	CINEMAS	COBBLER	CONAKRY	CORACLE	COWLICK
CARTOON	CEPHEUS	CHEERIO	CINEREA	COCAINE	CONCAVE	CORANTO	COWLING
CARVING	CERAMIC	CHEESED	CIRCLET	COCHLEA	CONCEAL	CORBEAU	COWPOKE
CASCADE	CERTAIN	CHEETAH	CIRCLIP	COCKADE	CONCEDE	CORBETT	COWSHED
CASCARA	CERTIFY	CHEKHOV	CIRCUIT	COCKLES	CONCEIT	CORDATE	COWSLIP
CASEASE	CESSION	CHELSEA	CIRROSE	COCKNEY	CONCEPT	CORDIAL	COXCOMB
CASHBOX	CESSPIT	CHEMISE	CISSOID	COCKPIT	CONCERN	CORDITE	COXLESS
CASHIER	CESTODE	CHEMIST	CISTERN	COCONUT	CONCERT	CORDOBA	COYNESS
CASPIAN	CESTOID	CHEQUER	CITADEL	COCOTTE	CONCISE	CORELLI	CRACKED
CASSATA	CEVICHE	CHERISH	CITHARA	CODEINE	CONCOCT	CORINTH	CRACKER
CASSAVA	CÉZANNE	CHEROOT	CITIZEN	CODICIL	CONCORD	CORKAGE	CRACKLE
CASSOCK	CHABLIS	CHERVIL	CITRINE	CODLING	CONCUSS	CORKING	CRACKLY
CASTILE	CHAFING	CHESTER	CITROEN	COELIAC	CONDEMN	CORNCOB	CRAMMED
CASTING	CHAGALL	CHEVIOT	CITTERN	COERCIVE	CONDOLE	CORNEAL	CRAMMER
CASTLED	CHAGRIN	CHEVRON	CIVILLY	COFFERS	CONDONE	CORNELL	CRAMPED
CASTOFF	CHAINED	CHEWING	CIVVIES	COGENCY	CONDUCT	CORNICE	CRAMPON
CASUALS	CHALDEE	CHIANTI	CLACHAN	COGNATE	CONDUIT	CORNISH	CRANACH
CASUISM	CHALICE	CHIASMA	CLAMBER	COHABIT	CONFESS	CORNROW	CRANIAL
CASUIST	CHALKER	CHICAGO	CLAMOUR	COINAGE	CONFIDE	COROLLA	CRANIUM
CATALAN	CHALONE	CHICANE	CLAMPER	COITION	CONFINE	CORONER	CRANMER
CATALOG	CHAMBER	CHICANO	CLANGER	COLCHIS	CONFIRM	CORONET	CRAPPIE
CATALPA	CHAMBRÉ	CHICKEN	CLAPPER	COLDITZ	CONFORM	CORRECT	CRASHES
CATARRH	CHAMFER	CHICORY	CLARIFY	COLIBRI	CONFUSE	CORRIDA	CRASSUS
CATCALL	CHAMOIS	CHIEFLY	CLARION	COLITIS	CONGEAL	CORRODE	CRAVING
CATCHER	CHAMPAK	CHIFFON	CLARITY	COLLAGE	CONICAL	CORRUPT	CRAWLER
CATCHUP	CHANCEL	CHIGGER	CLASSIC	COLLARD	CONIFER	CORSAGE	CRAZILY
CATECHU	CHANCRE	CHIGNON	CLASTIC	COLLATE	CONJOIN	CORSAIR	CREATED
CATELOG	CHANGED	CHILEAN	CLATTER	COLLECT	CONJURE	CORTEGE	CREATOR
CATERER	CHANGES	CHILLER	CLAVATE	COLLEEN	CONNATE	CORTINA	CREEPER
CATESBY	CHANNEL	CHILLON	CLEANER	COLLEGE	CONNECT	CORUNNA	CREMATE
CATFISH	CHANSON	CHIMERA	CLEANLY	COLLIDE	CONNIVE	CORYDON	CRENATE
CATHEAD	CHANTER	CHIMNEY	CLEANSE	COLLIER	CONNOTE	COSSACK	CRESTED
CATHODE	CHAOTIC	CHINDIT	CLEANUP	COLLOID	CONQUER	COSTARD	CREVICE
CATKINS	CHAPATI	CHINESE	CLEARLY	COLLUDE	CONSENT	COSTING	CREWCUT
CATLIKE	CHAPEAU	CHINOOK	CLEARUP	COLOGNE	CONSIGN	COSTIVE	CREWMAN
CATLING	CHAPLET	CHINTZY	CLEAVER	COLOMBO	CONSIST	COSTUME	CRICKET
CATMINT	CHAPMAN	CHINWAG	CLEMENT	COLONEL	CONSOLE	COTERIE	CRICKEY

CRICOID	CURIOUS	DEADPAN	DEMOTIC	DIDYMUS	DISUSED	DREAMER	EARSHOT
CRIMEAN	CURLING	DEADSET	DENDRON	DIECAST	DITHERY	DREDGER	EARTHEN
CRIMSON	CURRAGH	DEALING	DENIZEN	DIEDRAL	DITTANY	DRESDEN	EARTHLY
CRINKLE	CURRANT	DEANERY	DENMARK	DIEHARD	DITTIES	DRESSED	EASIEST
CRINKLY	CURRENT	DEAREST	DENSELY	DIETARY	DIURNAL	DRESSER	EASTERN
CRINOID	CURRIED	DEATHLY	DENSITY	DIETINE	DIVERGE	DREYFUS	EATABLE
CRIPPLE	CURSIVE	DEBACLE	DENTINE	DIFFUSE	DIVERSE	DRIBBLE	EBBTIDE
CRISPIN	CURSORY	DEBASED	DENTIST	DIGAMMA	DIVIDED	DRIBLET	EBONITE
CRITTER	CURTAIL	DEBATER	DENTURE	DIGGING	DIVINER	DRIFTER	ECBOLIC
CROAKER	CURTAIN	DEBAUCH	DEPLETE	DIGITAL	DIVISOR	DRINKER	ECCRINE
CROATIA	CURTSEY	DEBORAH	DEPLORE	DIGLYPH	DIVORCE	DRIVERS	ECDYSIS
CROCHET	CUSHION	DEBOUCH	DEPOSIT	DIGNIFY	DIVULGE	DRIVING	ECHELON
CROCKET	CUSTARD	DEBRETT	DEPRAVE	DIGNITY	DIZZILY	DRIZZLE	ECHIDNA
CROESUS	CUSTODY	DEBRIEF	DEPRESS	DIGONAL	DNIEPER	DRIZZLY	ECHINUS
CROFTER	CUSTOMS	DEBUSSY	DEPRIVE	DIGRAPH	DOCKING	DROPLET	ECLIPSE
CROOKED	CUTAWAY	DECANAL	DERANGE	DIGRESS	DOCTORS	DROPOUT	ECLOGUE
CROONER	CUTBACK	DECAYED	DERONDA	DILATED	DODDERY	DROPPER	ECOLOGY
CROPPED	CUTICLE	DECEASE	DERRICK	DILATOR	DODGEMS	DROSHKY	ECONOMY
CROPPER	CUTLASS	DECEIVE	DERVISH	DILEMMA	DOESKIN	DROUGHT	ECSTASY
CROQUET	CUTLERY	DECENCY	DERWENT	DILUENT	DOGCART	DRUGGED	ECTASIS
CROQUIS	CUTTERS	DECIBEL	DESCANT	DILUTED	DOGFISH	DRUGGET	ECTOPIA
CROSIER	CUTTING	DECIDED	DESCEND	DIMNESS	DOGFOOD	DRUMLIN	ECUADOR
CROSSED	CUTWORM	DECIDER	DESCENT	DIMPLED	DOGGONE	DRUMMER	EDAPHIC
CROSSLY	CUVETTE	DECIMAL	DESERTS	DINETTE	DOGROSE	DRUNKEN	EDIFICE
CROUTON	CYANIDE	DECLAIM	DESERVE	DINGBAT	DOGWOOD	DRYNESS	EDITION
CROWBAR	CYCLING	DECLARE	DESMOND	DINMONT	DOLEFUL	DUALITY	EDUCATE
CROWDED	CYCLIST	DECLINE	DESPAIR	DIOCESE	DOLLARS	DUBBING	EELPOUT
CROWING	CYCLONE	DECODER	DESPISE	DIOPTER	DOLORES	DUBIETY	EFFECTS
CROZIER	CYCLOPS	DECORUM	DESPITE	DIOPTRE	DOLPHIN	DUBIOUS	EFFENDI
CRUCIAL	CYMBALS	DECREED	DESPOIL	DIORAMA	DOMAINE	DUBNIUM	EFFORCE
CRUCIFY	CYNICAL	DECRYPT	DESPOND	DIORITE	DOMINGO	DUCHESS	EGALITY
CRUDELY	CYNTHIA	DEEPFRY	DESSERT	DIOXIDE	DOMINIC	DUCKING	EGGHEAD
CRUDITY	CYPRESS	DEFACED	DESTINE	DIPLOCK	DONEGAL	DUCTILE	EGLOGUE
CRUELLS	CYPRIOT	DEFAULT	DESTINY	DIPLOMA	DONNISH	DUDGEON	EGOTISM
CRUELLY	CYSTOID	DEFENCE	DESTROY	DIPOLAR	DOODLER	DUKEDOM	EGOTIST
CRUELTY	CYTISUS	DEFENSE	DETAILS	DIPTERA	DOORKEY	DULLARD	EJECTOR
CRUISER	DABBLER	DEFIANT	DETENTE	DIPTYCH	DOORMAN	DUMPISH	ELAMITE
CRUMBLE	DADAISM	DEFICIT	DETRACT	DISABLE	DOORMAT	DUNCIAD	ELASTIC
CRUMBLY	DADAIST	DEFILED	DETRAIN	DISAVOW	DOORWAY	DUNEDIN	ELASTIN
CRUMPET	DAGGERS	DEFINED	DEVALUE	DISBAND	DOPPLER	DUNGEON	ELATION
CRUMPLE	DAGWOOD	DEFLATE	DEVELOP	DISBARK	DORKING	DUNKIRK	ELDERLY
CRUNCHY	DAIMLER	DEFLECT	DEVIANT	DISCARD	DORMANT	DUNNAGE	ELEANOR
CRUPPER	DALILAH	DEFRAUD	DEVIATE	DISCERN	DOROTHY	DUNNOCK	ELECTED
CRUSADE	DAMAGED	DEFROCK	DEVILRY	DISCORD	DOSSIER	DUNSTAN	ELECTOR
CRUSHED	DAMAGES	DEFROST	DEVIOUS	DISCUSS	DOUBLES	DUOPOLY	ELECTRA
CRUSHER	DAMNING	DEFUNCT	DEVISED	DISDAIN	DOUBLET	DURABLE	ELECTRO
CRYPTIC	DAMOSEL	DEGAUSS	DEVISEE	DISEASE	DOUBTER	DURABLY	ELEGANT
CRYPTON	DAMPIER	DEGRADE	DEVOICE	DISGUST	DOUGHTY	DURAMEN	ELEGIAC
CRYSTAL	DAMPING	DEGREES	DEVOLVE	DISJOIN	DOUGLAS	DURRELL	ELEGIST
CSARDAS	DANCING	DEHISCE	DEVOTED	DISLIKE	DOWAGER	DUSTBIN	ELEMENT
CUBICLE	DANTEAN	DEICTIC	DEVOTEE	DISMAST	DOWDILY	DUSTING	ELEVATE
CUCKING	DAPHNID	DEIRDRE	DEWDROP	DISMISS	DOWLAND	DUSTMAN	ELISION
CUCKOLD	DAPHNIS	DEJECTA	DEXTRIN	DISOBEY	DOWSING	DUSTPAN	ELITISM
CUIRASS	DAPPLED	DELAYED	DIABOLO	DISPLAY	DRABBLE	DUTIFUL	ELITIST
CUISINE	DARLING	DELIBES	DIAGRAM	DISPORT	DRACHMA	DVORNIK	ELLIPSE
CULPRIT	DARNING	DELIGHT	DIALECT	DISPOSE	DRACULA	DWELLER	ELOGIUM
CULTURE	DASHING	DELILAH	DIALING	DISPRIN	DRAFTED	DWINDLE	ELUSIVE
CULVERT	DASHPOT	DELIMIT	DIALYSE	DISPUTE	DRAFTEE	DYARCHY	ELUSORY
CUMBRIA	DASTARD	DELIVER	DIAMINE	DISROBE	DRAGGLE	DYNAMIC	ELYSIAN
CUMSHAW	DASYURE	DELOUSE	DIAMOND	DISRUPT	DRAGNET	DYNASTY	ELYSIUM
CUMULUS	DATABLE	DELPHIC	DIAPSID	DISSECT	DRAGOON	EAGERLY	ELYTRON
CUNNING	DAUPHIN	DELTOID	DIARCHY	DISSENT	DRAINED	EARACHE	ELZEVIR
CUPROUS	DAWDLER	DELUDED	DIARIST	DISSTAFF	DRAPERY	EARDRUM	EMANATE
CURABLE	DAYBOOK	DEMERGE	DIBBLER	DISTANT	DRASTIC	EARLDOM	EMBARGO
CURACAO	DAYMARK	DEMERIT	DICKENS	DISTEND	DRAUGHT	EARLIER	EMBASSY
CURATOR	DAYSTAR	DEMESNE	DICTATE	DISTENT	DRAWBAR	EARLOBE	EMBLAZE
CURCUMA	DAYTIME	DEMETER	DICTION	DISTILL	DRAWERS	EARMARK	EMBOLUS
CURDLED	DAZZLED	DEMIGOD	DIDEROT	DISTORT	DRAWING	EARNEST	EMBOWER
CURETTE	DEADEYE	DEMONIC	DIDICOY	DISTURB	DREADED	EARRING	EMBRACE

EMBROIL	ENTROPY	ETTRICK	FACTOID	FELLOWS	FISSILE	FOGLAMP	FRETTED
EMERALD	ENTRUST	EUGENIA	FACTORS	FELSPAR	FISSION	FOLDING	FRIABLE
EMERSON	ENTWINE	EUGENIC	FACTORY	FELUCCA	FISSURE	FOLIAGE	FRIENDS
EMINENT	ENVELOP	EUGENIE	FACTUAL	FEMORAL	FISTFUL	FOLLIES	FRIGATE
EMIRATE	ENVENOM	EULALIE	FACULTY	FENCING	FISTULA	FONDANT	FRILLED
EMOTION	ENVIOUS	EUPEPSY	FADDISH	FENELON	FISTULE	FOOLISH	FRINGED
EMOTIVE	EPAULET	EUPHONY	FADDIST	FENLAND	FITMENT	FOOTAGE	FRISBEE
EMPANEL	EPERGNE	EUSTACE	FAGGOTS	FERMENT	FITNESS	FOOTING	FRISIAN
EMPATHY	EPHEBUS	EUTERPE	FAIENCE	FERMIUM	FITTEST	FOOTMAN	FRISSON
EMPEROR	EPHEDRA	EVACUEE	FAILING	FERROUS	FITTING	FOOTPAD	FRITTER
EMPIRIC	EPHESUS	EVANDER	FAILURE	FERRULE	FIXATED	FOOTSIE	FRIZZLE
EMPLOYS	EPHRAIM	EVASION	FAINTED	FERTILE	FIXEDLY	FOPPISH	FRIZZLY
EMPOWER	EPICARP	EVASIVE	FAINTLY	FERVENT	FIXINGS	FORAMEN	FROEBEL
EMPRESS	EPICENE	EVENING	FAIRING	FERVOUR	FIXTURE	FORBADE	FROGMAN
EMPYEMA	EPICURE	EVENTER	FAIRISH	FESTIVE	FLACCID	FORBEAR	FRONTAL
EMULATE	EPIDOTE	EVEREST	FAIRWAY	FESTOON	FLAGDAY	FORCEPS	FROSTED
EMULSIN	EPIGEAL	EVIDENT	FAJITAS	FETICHE	FLAMING	FOREARM	FROWSTY
ENACTOR	EPIGONE	EXACTLY	FALAFEL	FETLOCK	FLANKER	FOREIGN	FRUMPLE
ENAMOUR	EPIGRAM	EXALTED	FALLACY	FETTERS	FLANNEL	FORELEG	FUCHSIA
ENCHANT	EPISODE	EXAMINE	FALLING	FEVERED	FLAPPED	FOREMAN	FUCHSIN
ENCLASP	EPISTLE	EXAMPLE	FALLOUT	FEYDEAU	FLAPPER	FOREPAW	FUDDLED
ENCLAVE	EPITAPH	EXCERPT	FALSELY	FIANCÉE	FLAREUP	FORESEE	FULCRUM
ENCLOSE	EPITAXY	EXCITED	FALSIES	FIBROID	FLASHER	FOREVER	FULFILL
ENCRUST	EPITHET	EXCLAIM	FALSIFY	FIBROMA	FLATCAR	FORFEIT	FULGENT
ENDEMIC	EPITOME	EXCLUDE	FANATIC	FIBROUS	FLATLET	FORFEND	FULLERS
ENDGAME	EPIZOON	EXCRETA	FANCIED	FICTION	FLATTEN	FORGAVE	FULSOME
ENDLESS	EPSILON	EXCRETE	FANCIER	FIDDLER	FLATTER	FORGERY	FUMETTE
ENDNOTE	EPSTEIN	EXECUTE	FANFARE	FIDELIO	FLAUNCH	FORGIVE	FUNCHAL
ENDOGEN	EQUABLE	EXEGETE	FANGLED	FIDGETS	FLAVOUR	FORGONE	FUNDING
ENDORSE	EQUABLY	EXEMPLA	FANTAIL	FIDGETY	FLEAPIT	FORLORN	FUNERAL
ENDURED	EQUALLY	EXHAUST	FANTASY	FIEFDOM	FLECKED	FORMICA	FUNFAIR
ENDWAYS	EQUATOR	EXHEDRA	FANWORM	FIELDER	FLECKER	FORMING	FUNGOID
ENERGIC	EQUERRY	EXHIBIT	FANWORT	FIFTEEN	FLEDGED	FORMOSA	FUNGOUS
ENFEOFF	EQUINOX	EXIGENT	FANZINE	FIGHTER	FLEEING	FORMULA	FUNNILY
ENFIELD	ERASMUS	EXISTED	FARADAY	FIGLEAF	FLEMING	FORSAKE	FURBISH
ENFORCE	ERASURE	EXITING	FARAWAY	FIGMENT	FLEMISH	FORSTER	FURCATE
ENGAGED	ERECTOR	EXOCARP	FARCEUR	FIGURES	FLEURET	FORTIES	FURIOUS
ENGINED	EREMITE	EXOGAMY	FARMERS	FILARIA	FLEURON	FORTIFY	FURLONG
ENGLAND	ERINYES	EXPANSE	FARMING	FILASSE	FLEXILE	FORTRAN	FURNACE
ENGLISH	ERISKAY	EXPENSE	FARNESE	FILBERT	FLICKER	FORTUNE	FURNISH
ENGORGE	ERITREA	EXPIATE	FARRAGO	FILCHER	FLIGHTY	FORWARD	FURRIER
ENGRAFT	ERODIUM	EXPIRED	FARRIER	FILINGS	FLIPPER	FOSSICK	FURTHER
ENGRAIN	EROSION	EXPLAIN	FARTHER	FILLETS	FLITTER	FOSSULA	FURTIVE
ENGRAVE	EROTICA	EXPLODE	FASCISM	FILLING	FLIVVER	FOULARD	FUSEBOX
ENGROSS	ERRATIC	EXPLOIT	FASCIST	FILMING	FLOATER	FOUNDER	FUSIBLE
ENHANCE	ERRATUM	EXPLORE	FASHION	FIMBRIA	FLODDEN	FOUNDRY	FUSILLI
ENLARGE	ERUDITE	EXPOSED	FASTING	FINAGLE	FLOGGER	FOXHOLE	FUSSILY
ENLIVEN	ESCALOP	EXPOUND	FASTNET	FINALLY	FLOODED	FOXTROT	FUSTIAN
ENNOBLE	ESCAPEE	EXPRESS	FATALLY	FINANCE	FLOOZIE	FRAGILE	FUTTOCK
ENOLOGY	ESCHEAT	EXPUNGE	FATEFUL	FINBACK	FLORIDA	FRAILTY	FUTURES
ENPRINT	ESPARTO	EXTINCT	FATHEAD	FINDING	FLORIST	FRANCIS	GABBLER
ENQUIRE	ESPOUSE	EXTRACT	FATIGUE	FINESSE	FLOTSAM	FRANKLY	GABELLE
ENQUIRY	ESQUIRE	EXTREME	FATNESS	FINFOOT	FLOUNCE	FRANTIC	GABFEST
ENRAGED	ESSENCE	EXTRUDE	FATUITY	FINGERS	FLOWERS	FRAUGHT	GABRIEL
ENSLAVE	ESSENES	EXUDATE	FATUOUS	FINICAL	FLOWERY	FRAZZLE	GADROON
ENSNARE	ESTIVAL	EYEBALL	FAUSTUS	FINICKY	FLOWING	FRECKLE	GADWALL
ENSNARL	ESTOVER	EYEBATH	FAUVISM	FINLAND	FLUENCY	FREEBIE	GAEKWAR
ENSUING	ESTREAT	EYEBROW	FAUVIST	FINNISH	FLUMMOX	FREEDOM	GAGSTER
ENSUITE	ESTUARY	EYEHOLE	FAVELLA	FIRCONE	FLUNKEY	FREEMAN	GAINFUL
ENTEBBE	ETAGÈRE	EYELASH	FAVORED	FIREARM	FLUSHED	FREESIA	GAINSAY
ENTENTE	ETAPLES	EYELESS	FAWNING	FIREBUG	FLUSTER	FREEWAY	GAITERS
ENTERIC	ETCHING	EYELIDS	FEARFUL	FIREDOG	FLUTIST	FREEZER	GALAHAD
ENTERON	ETERNAL	EYESHOT	FEATHER	FIREFLY	FLUTTER	FREIGHT	GALATEA
ENTHRAL	ETESIAN	EYESORE	FEATURE	FIREMAN	FLUVIAL	FRESHEN	GALETTE
ENTHUSE	ETHANOL	EYESPOT	FEBRILE	FIRSTLY	FLYHALF	FRESHER	GALILEE
ENTITLE	ETHICAL	EYEWASH	FEDERAL	FISHERY	FLYLEAF	FRESHET	GALILEO
ENTRAIN	ETHMOID	EZEKIEL	FEEDING	FISHEYE	FLYOVER	FRESHLY	GALIPOT
ENTRANT	ETONIAN	FACETED	FEELING	FISHING	FLYPAST	FRETFUL	GALLANT
ENTREAT	ETRURIA	FACTION	FEIGNED	FISHNET	FOGHORN	FRETSAW	GALLEON

GALLERY	GEORGIC	GODDESS	GREATEN	GUNPLAY	HARDPAN	HELLENE	HOLLAND
GALLING	GERAINT	GODETIA	GREATLY	GUNROOM	HARDTOP	HELLION	HOLMIUM
GALLIUM	GERBERA	GODHEAD	GREAVES	GUNSHOT	HARELIP	HELLISH	HOLSTER
GALLONS	GERMANE	GODLESS	GRECIAN	GUNWALE	HARICOT	HELLUVA	HOMBURG
GALLOWS	GERMANY	GODLIKE	GREENER	GUSHING	HARLECH	HELPFUL	HOMERIC
GALOCHE	GESTALT	GODSEND	GREGORY	GUTLESS	HARMFUL	HELPING	HOMINID
GALOPIN	GESTAPO	GODUNOV	GREMLIN	GUTTATE	HARMONY	HEMLINE	HOMONYM
GALUMPH	GESTATE	GOGGLES	GRENADA	GUYROPE	HARNESS	HEMLOCK	HONESTY
GAMBADO	GESTURE	GOLDING	GRENADE	GUZZLER	HARPIST	HENBANE	HONEYED
GAMBIAN	GETAWAY	GOLDONI	GRENDEL	GWYNETH	HARPOON	HENGIST	HONITON
GAMBLER	GETTING	GOLFING	GREYISH	GYMNAST	HARRIER	HENNAED	HONOURS
GAMBOGE	GHASTLY	GOLIARD	GREYLAG	GYMSLIP	HARRIET	HENPECK	HONOURS
GAMELAN	GHERKIN	GOLIATH	GRIDDLE	HABITAT	HARSHLY	HEPARIN	HOODLUM
GANELON	GHOSTLY	GOMBEEN	GRIFFON	HACHURE	HARVARD	HEPATIC	HOPEFUL
GANGWAY	GIBBONS	GOMORRA	GRIFTER	HACKERY	HARVEST	HEPTANE	HOPKINS
GARBAGE	GIBBOUS	GONDOLA	GRILLED	HACKING	HARWICH	HERBAGE	HOPLITE
GARBLED	GIBLETS	GOODBYE	GRIMACE	HACKLES	HARWOOD	HERBERT	HOPPING
GARBOIL	GIDDILY	GOODIES	GRIMOND	HACKNEY	HASHISH	HERBERY	HOPSACK
GARBURE	GIDDYUP	GOODISH	GRIMSBY	HACKSAW	HASSIUM	HERBIST	HORATIO
GARDENS	GIELGUD	GOODMAN	GRINDER	HADDOCK	HASSOCK	HEREDIA	HORDEUM
GARFISH	GILBERT	GOODWIN	GRISTLE	HADRIAN	HASTATE	HERETIC	HORIZON
GARLAND	GILDING	GOOLIES	GRISTLY	HAFNIUM	HASTILY	HEROINE	HORMONE
GARMENT	GILLRAY	GORDIAN	GRIZZLE	HAGBOLT	HATBAND	HEROISM	HORRIFY
GARNISH	GIMBALS	GORDIUS	GRIZZLY	HAGFISH	HATCHET	HERRICK	HORRORS
GARONNE	GIMBLET	GORILLA	GROCERS	HAGGADA	HATEFUL	HERRIES	HORSING
GAROTTE	GIMMICK	GORSEDD	GROCERY	HAGGARD	HATLESS	HERRING	HOSANNA
GARRICK	GINGHAM	GOSHAWK	GROCKLE	HAGGERY	HATTOCK	HERSELF	HOSIERY
GASCONY	GINSENG	GOSLING	GROGRAM	HAHNIUM	HAUGHTY	HESHVAN	HOSPICE
GASEOUS	GIRAFFE	GOSSIPY	GROINED	HAIRCUT	HAULAGE	HESSIAN	HOSTAGE
GASFIRE	GIRASOL	GOUACHE	GROLIER	HAIRNET	HAULIER	HETAERA	HOSTESS
GASMASK	GIRLISH	GOULASH	GROMMET	HAIRPIN	HAUNTED	HEURISM	HOSTILE
GASOHOL	GIRONDE	GOURMET	GROOVED	HAITIAN	HAUTBOY	HEXAGON	HOTFOOT
GASPING	GISELLE	GRACCHI	GROPIUS	HALBERD	HAWKEYE	HEXAPOD	HOTHEAD
GASTHOF	GIZZARD	GRACILE	GROSSLY	HALBERT	HAYFORK	HEXARCH	HOTLINE
GASTRIC	GLACIAL	GRACKLE	GROTIUS	HALCYON	HAYLOFT	HIBACHI	HOTSHOT
GASTRIN	GLACIER	GRADATE	GROUCHO	HALFWAY	HAYSEED	HICKORY	HOTSPUR
GATEWAY	GLADDEN	GRADELY	GROUCHY	HALFWIT	HAYWARD	HIDALGO	HOUDINI
GATLING	GLAMOUR	GRADUAL	GROUNDS	HALIBUT	HAYWIRE	HIDEOUS	HOUSING
GAUDILY	GLARING	GRAFTER	GROUPER	HALITUS	HAZLETT	HIDEOUT	HOWEVER
GAUGUIN	GLASGOW	GRAINED	GROUPIE	HALLALI	HEADING	HIGGINS	HOWLING
GAUTAMA	GLASSES	GRAINER	GROUSER	HALLMAN	HEADMAN	HIGHEST	HUBBARD
GAVOTTE	GLAZIER	GRAMMAR	GROWING	HALLWAY	HEADSET	HIGHMAN	HULKING
GAWKISH	GLAZING	GRAMPUS	GROWLER	HALOGEN	HEADWAY	HILDING	HUMANLY
GAYNESS	GLEANER	GRANARY	GROWNUP	HALTERE	HEALING	HILLMAN	HUMBLES
GAZELLE	GLEEFUL	GRANDAD	GRUFFLY	HALTING	HEALTHY	HILLMEN	HUMDRUM
GAZETTE	GLENCOE	GRANDEE	GRUMBLE	HALYARD	HEARING	HILLOCK	HUMERUS
GEARBOX	GLENOID	GRANDLY	GRUMMET	HAMMOCK	HEARKEN	HILLTOP	HUMIDOR
GEARING	GLIDING	GRANDMA	GRUYÈRE	HAMSTER	HEARSAY	HIMSELF	HUMMING
GEELONG	GLIMMER	GRANDPA	GRYPHON	HANDBAG	HEARTEN	HINDLEG	HUMMOCK
GEFILTE	GLIMPSE	GRANITA	GUANACO	HANDFUL	HEATHEN	HIPBONE	HUNCHED
GEHENNA	GLISTEN	GRANITE	GUANINE	HANDGUN	HEATHER	HIPSTER	HUNDRED
GELATIN	GLITTER	GRANNIE	GUARANA	HANDILY	HEATING	HIRSUTE	HUNGARY
GELDING	GLOBULE	GRANOLA	GUARANI	HANDLED	HEAVENS	HISPANO	HUNKERS
GEMMATE	GLORIFY	GRANTED	GUARDED	HANDLER	HEAVIER	HISSING	HUNTING
GENERAL	GLOTTAL	GRANTEE	GUBBINS	HANDOUT	HEAVILY	HISTOID	HURDLER
GENERIC	GLOTTIS	GRANULE	GUDGEON	HANDSAW	HEBRAIC	HISTORY	HURDLES
GENESIS	GLOWING	GRAPHIC	GUIDING	HANDSEL	HEBREWS	HITTITE	HURLING
GENETIC	GLUCOSE	GRAPHIS	GUIGNOL	HANDSET	HECKLER	HOARDER	HURRIED
GENISTA	GLUTTON	GRAPNEL	GUILDER	HANGDOG	HECTARE	HOBNAIL	HURTFUL
GENITAL	GLYPTAL	GRAPPLE	GUINEAN	HANGING	HEDGING	HOBSONS	HUSBAND
GENOESE	GLYPTIC	GRATIFY	GUINEAS	HANGMAN	HEEDFUL	HOEDOWN	HUSKILY
GENTEEL	GNARLED	GRATING	GUMBOIL	HANGMEN	HEELTAP	HOGARTH	HUSSARS
GENTIAN	GNATHIC	GRAUPEL	GUMBOOT	HANGOUT	HEIGHTS	HOGBACK	HUSSITE
GENTILE	GNAWING	GRAVITY	GUMDROP	HANOVER	HEINOUS	HOGGING	HUSTLER
GENUINE	GNOCCHI	GRAVLAX	GUMSHOE	HANSARD	HEIRESS	HOGWASH	HYALINE
GEODESY	GNOSTIC	GRAVURE	GUNBOAT	HAPLESS	HELICAL	HOLBEIN	HYALOID
GEOLOGY	GOAHEAD	GRAYISH	GUNFIRE	HAPORTH	HELICON	HOLDALL	HYDATID
GEORDIE	GOBBLER	GRAZING	GUNNERA	HAPPILY	HELIPAD	HOLDING	HYDRANT
GEORGIA	GOBELIN	GREASER	GUNNERY	HARBOUR	HELLCAT	HOLIDAY	HYGIENE

HYMNIST	INCROSS	INVIOUS	JEJUNUM	KATRINE	KNOWALL	LARGESS	LEOTARD
HYMNODY	INCRUST	INVOICE	JELLABA	KATYDID	KNOWHOW	LARGEST	LEPANTO
HYPOGEA	INCUBUS	INVOLVE	JELLIED	KEARTON	KNOWING	LASAGNA	LEPROSY
HYPONYM	INCURVE	INWARDS	JENKINS	KEELING	KNUCKLE	LASAGNE	LEPROUS
HYPOXIA	INDEPTH	IONESCO	JERICHO	KEEPING	KOLKHOZ	LASHING	LESBIAN
IAMBIST	INDEXER	IPOMOEA	JERKILY	KENNEDY	KONTIKI	LASTING	LESOTHO
IBERIAN	INDIANA	IRANIAN	JERSEYS	KENNELS	KOUMISS	LATCHET	LESSING
ICEBERG	INDOORS	IRELAND	JESTING	KENNING	KOWLOON	LATERAL	LETDOWN
ICEFALL	INDULGE	IRIDISE	JEWELER	KENOSIS	KREMLIN	LATERAN	LETTERS
ICEFLOE	INERTIA	IRIDIUM	JEWELRY	KENOTIC	KRISHNA	LATIMER	LETTING
ICELAND	INEXACT	IRKSOME	JEWFISH	KENTISH	KRYPTON	LATRINE	LETTUCE
ICHABOD	INFANCY	IRONING	JEZEBEL	KERATIN	KUBELIK	LATTICE	LEUCINE
ICHNITE	INFARCT	ISADORA	JIMJAMS	KERMESS	KUFIYAH	LATVIAN	LEUCOMA
ICINESS	INFERNO	ISCHIUM	JITTERS	KERNITE	KUMQUAT	LAUNDER	LEVERET
ICTERIC	INFIDEL	ISHMAEL	JITTERY	KEROGEN	KURHAUS	LAUNDRY	LEXICON
ICTERUS	INFIELD	ISLAMIC	JOBBERY	KESTREL	KURSAAL	LAURELS	LIAISON
IDEALLY	INFLAME	ISLANDS	JOBBING	KETCHUP	KYANITE	LAVATER	LIBERAL
IDIOTIC	INFLATE	ISMAILI	JOBLESS	KEYHOLE	LABIATE	LAVOLTA	LIBERIA
IDOLIZE	INFLECT	ISOBASE	JOCASTA	KEYNOTE	LABORED	LAWLESS	LIBERTY
IDYLLIC	INFLICT	ISODORE	JOCULAR	KEYWORD	LABORER	LAWSUIT	LIBRARY
IGNEOUS	INGENUE	ISOGRAM	JOGGING	KHALIFA	LACERTA	LAWYERS	LIBRIUM
IGNOBLE	INGRAIN	ISOHYET	JOGTROT	KHAMSIN	LACEUPS	LAXNESS	LICENCE
IGNORED	INGRATE	ISOLATE	JOHNNIE	KHANATE	LACKING	LAYERED	LICENSE
IKEBANA	INGRESS	ISOMERE	JOHNSON	KHEDIVE	LACONIC	LAYETTE	LICKING
ILIACUS	INGROWN	ISOSPIN	JOINERY	KIBBUTZ	LACQUER	LAYINGS	LIEDOWN
ILLBRED	INHABIT	ISOTONE	JOINING	KICKING	LACTASE	LEACOCK	LIFTOFF
ILLEGAL	INHALER	ISOTOPE	JOINTED	KICKOFF	LACTATE	LEADERS	LIGHTEN
ILLICIT	INHERIT	ISRAELI	JOINTER	KIDNEYS	LACTEAL	LEADING	LIGHTER
ILLNESS	INHIBIT	ISSUANT	JOINTLY	KIELDER	LACTOSE	LEAFLET	LIGHTLY
IMAGERY	INHOUSE	ISTHMUS	JOLLITY	KILDARE	LACUNAE	LEAGUER	LIGNITE
IMAGINE	INHUMAN	ITALIAN	JONQUIL	KILLICK	LADYBUG	LEAKAGE	LIKENED
IMAGING	INITIAL	ITCHING	JOURNAL	KILLING	LAETARE	LEANDER	LILTING
IMAGISM	INJURED	ITEMIZE	JOURNEY	KILLJOY	LAGGARD	LEANING	LIMINAL
IMAGIST	INKLING	ITERATE	JOYLESS	KILOTON	LAGGING	LEAPING	LIMITED
IMHOTEP	INKWELL	IVANHOE	JOYRIDE	KILVERT	LAGONDA	LEARNED	LIMITER
IMITATE	INNARDS	IVORIAN	JUBILEE	KINDRED	LAKSHMI	LEARNER	LIMPKIN
IMMENSE	INNERVE	IVORIEN	JUDAISM	KINESIS	LALIQUE	LEASING	LIMPOPO
IMMERGE	INNINGS	IVRESSE	JUGGINS	KINETIC	LALLANS	LEASOWE	LINACRE
IMMERSE	INQUEST	JACINTH	JUGGLER	KINGCUP	LAMAISM	LEATHER	LINCOLN
IMMORAL	INQUIRE	JACKASS	JUGLANS	KINGDOM	LAMAIST	LEAVING	LINCTUS
IMPASSE	INQUIRY	JACKDAW	JUGULAR	KINGLET	LAMBADA	LEBANON	LINDANE
IMPASTO	INROADS	JACKETS	JUJITSU	KINGPIN	LAMBAST	LECHERY	LINEAGE
IMPAVID	INSCAPE	JACKPOT	JUKEBOX	KINSHIP	LAMBENT	LECTERN	LINEMAN
IMPEACH	INSECTS	JACKSON	JUMBLED	KINSMAN	LAMBERT	LECTURE	LINGUAL
IMPERIL	INSHORE	JACOBIN	JUMBLES	KINTYRE	LAMBETH	LEEWARD	LININGS
IMPETUS	INSIDER	JACOBUS	JUMPING	KIPLING	LAMBING	LEFTIST	LINKAGE
IMPIETY	INSIDES	JACQUES	JUNIPER	KIPPERS	LAMELLA	LEGALLY	LINKING
IMPINGE	INSIGHT	JACUZZI	JUPITER	KISSING	LAMPOON	LEGATEE	LINKMAN
IMPIOUS	INSIPID	JAGGERY	JURYBOX	KITCHEN	LAMPREY	LEGGING	LINNEAN
IMPLANT	INSPECT	JAKARTA	JURYMAN	KITHARA	LANCERS	LEGIBLE	LINOCUT
IMPLIED	INSPIRE	JAMAICA	JUSSIVE	KIWANIS	LANCING	LEGIBLY	LINSANG
IMPLODE	INSTALL	JAMESON	JUSTICE	KLAVIER	LANDING	LEGIONS	LINSEED
IMPLORE	INSTANT	JAMMIES	JUSTIFY	KLEENEX	LANGLEY	LEGLESS	LIONESS
IMPOUND	INSTATE	JAMMING	JUTLAND	KLINKER	LANGTON	LEGPULL	LIONIZE
IMPRESS	INSTEAD	JAMPANI	JUVENAL	KNACKER	LANGUID	LEGROOM	LIPREAD
IMPREST	INSTILL	JANITOR	KADDISH	KNAPPER	LANGUOR	LEGWORK	LIQUEFY
IMPRINT	INSULAR	JANKERS	KAINITE	KNAVERY	LANOLIN	LEISURE	LIQUEUR
IMPROVE	INSULIN	JANUARY	KALENDS	KNEECAP	LANTANA	LEMMATA	LIQUIDS
IMPULSE	INSURER	JAPLISH	KALMUCK	KNEELER	LANTERN	LEMMING	LISSOME
INANITY	INTEGER	JASMINE	KAMERAD	KNEEPAD	LANYARD	LEMPIRA	LISTING
INBOARD	INTENSE	JAVELIN	KAMPALA	KNELLER	LAOCOON	LENDING	LITCHEE
INBUILT	INTERIM	JAVELLE	KAMPONG	KNESSET	LAOTIAN	LENGTHY	LITERAL
INBURST	INTERNE	JAWBONE	KANNADA	KNICKER	LAPPING	LENIENT	LITHELY
INCENSE	INTROIT	JAZZMAN	KARACHI	KNITTED	LAPSANG	LENTIGO	LITHIUM
INCISOR	INTRUDE	JEALOUS	KARAJAN	KNITTER	LAPUTAN	LENTILS	LITOTES
INCLINE	INVADER	JEEPERS	KARAKUL	KNOBBLE	LAPWING	LEONARD	LITURGY
INCLUDE	INVALID	JEEPNEY	KARAOKE	KNOBBLY	LARCENY	LEONINE	LOBELIA
INCOMER	INVEIGH	JEERING	KASHMIR	KNOCKER	LARDOON	LEOPARD	LOBSTER
INCONNU	INVERSE	JEHOVAH	KATORGA	KNOTTED	LARGELY	LEOPOLD	LOCALLY

■□□□□□□

LOCKJAW	MACEDON	MANNING	MATTHEW	MÉTISSE	MISTRAL	MORPHIA	NAHUATL
LOCKNUT	MACHETE	MANNISH	MATTING	METONIC	MITHRAS	MORRELL	NAILBED
LOCKOUT	MACHINE	MANSARD	MATTINS	METONYM	MITOSIS	MORTALS	NAIPAUL
LOCUSTS	MACRAMÉ	MANSION	MATTOCK	METTLED	MITTENS	MORTICE	NAIROBI
LODGING	MADEIRA	MANSIZE	MAUDLIN	MEXICAN	MITZVAH	MORTIFY	NAIVELY
LOFTILY	MADISON	MANTUAN	MAUGHAM	MIASMIC	MIXTURE	MORTISE	NAIVETÉ
LOGBOOK	MADNESS	MANUMIT	MAUNDER	MICHAEL	MOABITE	MOSELLE	NAIVETY
LOGGING	MADONNA	MANXMAN	MAWKISH	MICROBE	MOANING	MOTHERS	NAKEDLY
LOGICAL	MAENADS	MAPPING	MAXILLA	MIDGARD	MOBSTER	MOTTLED	NAMIBIA
LOGWOOD	MAESTRO	MARABOU	MAXIMUM	MIDLAND	MOCKERS	MOUFLON	NANKEEN
LOLLARD	MAFIOSO	MARACAS	MAXWELL	MIDLINE	MOCKERY	MOUILLÉ	NAPHTHA
LOMBARD	MAGENTA	MARANTA	MAYFAIR	MIDMOST	MOCKING	MOULAGE	NAPPING
LONGBOW	MAGGOTY	MARATHA	MAYPOLE	MIDRIFF	MODERNE	MOULDED	NARRATE
LONGING	MAGHREB	MARBLED	MAYWEED	MIDSHIP	MODESTY	MOULDER	NARROWS
LOOKING	MAGICAL	MARBLES	MAZARIN	MIDTERM	MODICUM	MOUNTED	NARTHEX
LOOKOUT	MAGINOT	MARBURG	MAZEPPA	MIDWEEK	MODISTE	MOUNTIE	NARWHAL
LOOMING	MAGNATE	MARCHER	MAZURKA	MIDWEST	MODULAR	MOURNER	NASALLY
LOOSELY	MAGNETO	MARCONI	MEACOCK	MIDWIFE	MODULUS	MOVABLE	NASCENT
LOOTING	MAGNIFY	MARCUSE	MEANDER	MIGRANT	MOELLON	MUDDLED	NASTILY
LORDING	MAGUIRE	MAREMMA	MEANING	MIGRATE	MOFETTE	MUDEJAR	NATCHEZ
LORELEI	MAHATMA	MARENGO	MEASLES	MILEAGE	MOHICAN	MUDFLAP	NATIONS
LOTHAIR	MAHJONG	MARGERY	MEASURE	MILFOIL	MOIDORE	MUDLARK	NATIVES
LOTHIAN	MAHONIA	MARIBOU	MECHLIN	MILITIA	MOISTEN	MUDPACK	NATRIUM
LOTTERY	MAIGRET	MARINER	MECONIC	MILKING	MOITHER	MUEZZIN	NATURAL
LOUNGER	MAILBAG	MARITAL	MEDDLER	MILKMAN	MOLDING	MUFFLED	NAUGHTY
LOURDES	MAILBOX	MARKING	MEDIATE	MILKSOP	MOLIÈRE	MUFFLER	NAVARIN
LOURING	MAILCAR	MARLENE	MEDICAL	MILLAIS	MOLLIFY	MUGGING	NAVARRE
LOUTISH	MAILING	MARLINE	MEDULLA	MILLING	MOLLUSC	MUGWORT	NAVETTE
LOUVRED	MAILMAN	MARLITE	MEERKAT	MILLION	MOLOTOV	MUGWUMP	NEAREST
LOVABLE	MAJESTY	MARLOWE	MEETING	MIMICRY	MOLUCCA	MULATTO	NEARING
LOWBROW	MAJORCA	MARMARA	MEGAERA	MIMULUS	MOMBASA	MULLEIN	NEBBISH
LOWDOWN	MAKINGS	MARMION	MEGARON	MINARET	MOMENTS	MULLION	NEBULAR
LOWLAND	MALACCA	MARMITE	MEGATON	MINCING	MONARCH	MUMMERS	NECKING
LOWPAID	MALACHI	MARQUEE	MEIOSIS	MINDFUL	MONEYED	MUMMERY	NECKLET
LOYALLY	MALAISE	MARQUIS	MEISSEN	MINDSET	MONGREL	MUMMIFY	NECKTIE
LOYALTY	MALARIA	MARRIED	MELANIN	MINERAL	MONILIA	MUNDANE	NECROSE
LOZENGE	MALAYAN	MARRYAT	MELILOT	MINERVA	MONITOR	MUNSTER	NECTARY
LUCARNE	MALEFIC	MARSALA	MELLITE	MINIBUS	MONKISH	MUNTJAC	NEEDFUL
LUCERNE	MALLARD	MARSHAL	MELODIC	MINICAB	MONOCLE	MURAENA	NEEDLES
LUCIDLY	MALLEUS	MARSYAS	MELROSE	MINIMAL	MONOCOT	MURIATE	NEGLECT
LUCIFER	MALLING	MARTENS	MELTING	MINIMAX	MONOLOG	MURILLO	NÉGLIGÉ
LUCKILY	MALMSEY	MARTIAL	MEMBERS	MINIMUM	MONOPLY	MURRAIN	NEGRESS
LUDDITE	MALTASE	MARTIAN	MEMENTO	MINORCA	MONSOON	MUSCOID	NEGRITO
LUDGATE	MALTESE	MARTINI	MEMOIRS	MINSTER	MONSTER	MUSCOVY	NEGROID
LUGGAGE	MALTHUS	MARTLET	MENDING	MINUEND	MONTAGE	MUSETTE	NEITHER
LUGHOLE	MALTOSE	MARTYRS	MENFOLK	MINUTED	MONTAGU	MUSICAL	NEMESIA
LUGSAIL	MAMILLA	MARVELL	MENORAH	MINUTES	MONTANA	MUSKRAT	NEMESIS
LUGWORM	MAMMARY	MARXISM	MENTHOL	MINUTIA	MONTANT	MUSSELS	NEMORAL
LULLABY	MAMMOTH	MARXIST	MENTION	MIOCENE	MONTERO	MUSTANG	NEOLITH
LUMBAGO	MANACLE	MASCARA	MENUHIN	MIRACLE	MONTHLY	MUSTARD	NEOTENY
LUMPISH	MANAGER	MASONIC	MERCERY	MIRADOR	MOODILY	MUTABLE	NEPTUNE
LUMPKIN	MANAGUA	MASONRY	MERCIES	MIRANDA	MOONING	MUTAGEN	NERITIC
LUNATIC	MANAKIN	MASSAGE	MERCURY	MIRIFIC	MOONLIT	MYALGIA	NERVOSA
LUNETTE	MANATEE	MASSEUR	MERITED	MISCAST	MOORHEN	MYANMAR	NERVOUS
LURCHER	MANDALA	MASSINE	MERMAID	MISDEED	MOORING	MYCELLA	NERVURE
LURIDLY	MANDATE	MASSIVE	MERRIER	MISERLY	MOORISH	MYCENAE	NETBALL
LURKING	MANDIOC	MASTERS	MERRILY	MISFIRE	MOPPING	MYCETES	NETSUKE
LUSTFUL	MANGOLD	MASTERY	MESCLUN	MISLEAD	MORAINE	MYELINE	NETTING
LUSTILY	MANHOLE	MASTIFF	MESEEMS	MISPLAY	MORALLY	MYELOID	NETWORK
LUSTRUM	MANHOOD	MASTOID	MESSAGE	MISREAD	MORAVIA	MYELOMA	NEURINE
LUTYENS	MANHUNT	MASURKA	MESSIAH	MISRULE	MORDANT	MYIASIS	NEUROMA
LYCHNIS	MANIHOC	MATADOR	MESSIER	MISSILE	MOREISH	MYNHEER	NEURONE
LYMNAEA	MANIKIN	MATCHED	MESSILY	MISSING	MORELLO	MYRINGA	NEUTRAL
LYNCHET	MANILLA	MATCHET	MESSINA	MISSION	MORESBY	MYSTERY	NEUTRON
LYRICAL	MANIPLE	MATELOT	METALLY	MISSIVE	MORESCO	MYSTIFY	NEVILLE
MACABRE	MANITOU	MATILDA	METAYER	MISSTEP	MORLAND	NABOKOV	NEWBOLT
MACADAM	MANKIND	MATINEE	METHANE	MISTAKE	MORNING	NACELLE	NEWBORN
MACAQUE	MANMADE	MATISSE	METHINK	MISTIME	MOROCCO	NACROUS	NEWBURY
MACBETH	MANNERS	MATTERS	METICAL	MISTOOK	MORONIC	NAGGING	NEWCOME

NEWNESS	NULLITY	OFFBEAT	ORGANUM	OVERARM	PANNAGE	PAYMENT	PERSEID
NEWSBOY	NUMBERS	OFFDUTY	ORGANZA	OVERAWE	PANNIER	PAYROLL	PERSEUS
NEWSMAN	NUMBLES	OFFENCE	ORGIAST	OVERBID	PANNOSE	PEACHUM	PERSIAN
NIAGARA	NUMERAL	OFFENSE	ORIFICE	OVERDUE	PANOPLY	PEACOCK	PERSIST
NIBLICK	NUMERIC	OFFERER	ORIGAMI	OVEREAT	PANTHER	PEANUTS	PERSONA
NICAEAN	NUMMARY	OFFHAND	ORIGINS	OVERFED	PANTIES	PEARLIE	PERSONS
NICOISE	NUNLIKE	OFFICER	ORINOCO	OVERLAP	PANTILE	PEASANT	PERSPEX
NICOSIA	NUNNERY	OFFICES	ORKNEYS	OVERLAY	PANURGE	PEBBLES	PERTAIN
NICTATE	NUPTIAL	OFFLOAD	ORLANDO	OVERLIE	PAPILLA	PECCANT	PERTURB
NIGELLA	NUREYEV	OFFPEAK	ORLEANS	OVERMAN	PAPOOSE	PECCARY	PERTUSE
NIGERIA	NURSERY	OFFSIDE	OROGENY	OVERPAY	PAPRIKA	PECCAVI	PERUSAL
NIGGARD	NURSING	OGREISH	ORONTES	OVERRUN	PAPYRUS	PECKING	PERVADE
NIGHTIE	NURTURE	OILBIRD	OROTUND	OVERSEE	PARABLE	PECKISH	PERVERT
NIGHTLY	NUTCASE	OILCAKE	ORPHEAN	OVERTAX	PARADOR	PECTASE	PESSARY
NINEPIN	NUTLIKE	OILSKIN	ORPHEUS	OVICIDE	PARADOS	PEDDLER	PETIOLE
NINEVEH	NUTMEAT	OKINAWA	ORPHISM	OVIDUCT	PARADOX	PEDICAB	PETRIFY
NIOBEAN	NUTTING	OLDNESS	ORPHREY	OVULATE	PARAGON	PEDICEL	PETROUS
NIOBIUM	NYMPHET	OLDSTER	ORTOLAN	OXALATE	PARAPET	PEDICLE	PETUNIA
NIPPERS	NYNORSK	OLEFINE	ORVIETO	OXBLOOD	PARASOL	PEELING	PFENNIG
NIRVANA	OAKLEAF	OLOROSO	OSBORNE	OXIDASE	PARBOIL	PEEPING	PHAETON
NITRATE	OARFISH	OLYMPIA	OSCULUM	OXIDIZE	PARCHED	PEERAGE	PHALANX
NITRILE	OARLOCK	OLYMPIC	OSMANLI	OXONIAN	PARENTS	PEERESS	PHALLIC
NITRITE	OARSMAN	OLYMPUS	OSMOSIS	PABULUM	PARESIS	PEERING	PHALLUS
NITRODE	OARSMEN	OMENTUM	OSSELET	PACIFIC	PARFAIT	PEEVISH	PHANTOM
NITROUS	OATCAKE	OMICRON	OSSEOUS	PACKAGE	PARINGS	PEGASUS	PHARAOH
NOBBLED	OATMEAL	OMINOUS	OSSICLE	PACKING	PARKING	PELAGIC	PHARYNX
NOBBLER	OBADIAH	OMITTED	OSSUARY	PACKMAN	PARKWAY	PELICAN	PHIDIAS
NOCTUID	OBELISK	OMNIBUS	OSTEOMA	PADDING	PARLOUR	PELORIA	PHILEAS
NODDING	OBESITY	OMPHALE	OSTIOLE	PADDLER	PARLOUS	PELORUS	PHILTER
NODULAR	OBJECTS	ONANISM	OSTRICH	PADDOCK	PARNELL	PELTING	PHILTRE
NOGGING	OBLIGED	ONEIRIC	OTALGIA	PADLOCK	PAROTIC	PENALTY	PHOEBUS
NOISILY	OBLIGOR	ONENESS	OTHELLO	PADRONE	PAROTID	PENANCE	PHOENIX
NOISOME	OBLIQUE	ONEROUS	OTRANTO	PAESTUM	PAROTIS	PENATES	PHONEIN
NOMADIC	OBLOQUY	ONESELF	OTTOMAN	PAGEANT	PARQUET	PENDANT	PHONEME
NOMBRIL	OBSCENE	ONETIME	OUSTITI	PAGEBOY	PARSLEY	PENDING	PHONICS
NOMINAL	OBSCURA	ONGOING	OUTBACK	PAHLAVI	PARSNIP	PENGUIN	PHRASAL
NOMINEE	OBSCURE	ONMIBUS	OUTCAST	PAINFUL	PARTAKE	PENNANT	PHRASER
NONPLUS	OBSEQUY	ONSHORE	OUTCOME	PAINTED	PARTHIA	PENNATE	PHRENIC
NONPROS	OBSERVE	ONSTAGE	OUTCROP	PAINTER	PARTIAL	PENNINE	PHYSICS
NONSTOP	OBTRUDE	ONTARIO	OUTDARE	PAIRING	PARTING	PENSILE	PIANIST
NONSUCH	OBVERSE	ONWARDS	OUTDOOR	PAISLEY	PARTITA	PENSION	PIANOLA
NONSUIT	OBVIATE	OPACITY	OUTFACE	PAJAMAS	PARTNER	PENSIVE	PIASTRE
NOODLES	OBVIOUS	OPALINE	OUTFALL	PALADIN	PARVENU	PENTANE	PIBROCH
NOOLOGY	OCARINA	OPENING	OUTFLOW	PALATAL	PASCHAL	PENTODE	PICADOR
NOONDAY	OCCIPUT	OPERAND	OUTGROW	PALAVER	PASSAGE	PENTOSE	PICARDY
NORFOLK	OCCLUDE	OPERANT	OUTLAST	PALERMO	PASSANT	PEONAGE	PICASSO
NORWICH	OCEANIA	OPERATE	OUTLIER	PALETTE	PASSING	PEPPERS	PICCOLO
NOSEBAG	OCEANIC	OPINION	OUTLINE	PALFREY	PASSION	PEPPERY	PICKAXE
NOSEGAY	OCEANID	OPOSSUM	OUTLIVE	PALINGS	PASSIVE	PEPSINE	PICKING
NOSTRIL	OCELLAR	OPPOSED	OUTLOOK	PALISSY	PASTERN	PERCALE	PICKLED
NOSTRUM	OCELLUS	OPPRESS	OUTPOST	PALLIUM	PASTEUR	PERCENT	PICKLER
NOTABLE	OCTAGON	OPTICAL	OUTPOUR	PALMATE	PASTIES	PERCEPT	PICOTEE
NOTABLY	OCTOBER	OPTIMAL	OUTRAGE	PALMIST	PASTIME	PERCUSS	PICQUET
NOTCHED	OCTOPOD	OPTIMUM	OUTRANK	PALMTOP	PASTURE	PEREIRA	PICTURE
NOTEPAD	OCTOPUS	OPULENT	OUTSHOT	PALMYRA	PATELLA	PERFECT	PIDGEON
NOTHING	OCTUPLE	OPUNTIA	OUTSIDE	PALOMAR	PATHWAY	PERFIDY	PIEBALD
NOTIONS	OCULIST	ORACLES	OUTSIZE	PALOOKA	PATIBLE	PERFORM	PIERCED
NOURISH	ODALISK	ORANGES	OUTSPAN	PALPATE	PATIENT	PERFUME	PIERCER
NOUVEAU	ODDBALL	ORATION	OUTSTAY	PALSIED	PATRIAL	PERFUSE	PIERROT
NOVELLA	ODDMENT	ORATORY	OUTTURN	PALUDAL	PATRICK	PERGOLA	PIETIST
NOVELLO	ODDNESS	ORBITAL	OUTVOTE	PANACEA	PATRIOT	PERHAPS	PIGEONS
NOVELTY	ODONTIC	ORCHARD	OUTWARD	PANACHE	PATTERN	PERIGEE	PIGFISH
NOWHERE	ODORANT	ORCINOL	OUTWEAR	PANCAKE	PAUCITY	PERIWIG	PIGGERY
NOXIOUS	ODOROUS	ORDERED	OUTWORK	PANCRAS	PAULINE	PERJURE	PIGLING
NUCLEAR	ODYSSEY	ORDERLY	OUTWORN	PANDORA	PAUNCHY	PERJURY	PIGMEAT
NUCLEIC	OEDIPUS	ORDINAL	OVARIAN	PANGAEA	PAVIOUR	PERLITE	PIGMENT
NUCLEUS	OERSTED	OREGANO	OVATION	PANGRAM	PAVLOVA	PERMIAN	PIGSKIN
NUCLIDE	OESTRUS	ORESTES	OVERACT	PANICKY	PAYABLE	PERPLEX	PIGTAIL
NULLIFY	OFFBASE	ORGANIC	OVERALL	PANICLE	PAYLOAD	PERRIER	PIGWEED

PIKELET	PLAYPEN	POPOVER	PREMIER	PROPOSE	PUTTING	RAFTING	RECOUNT
PILATUS	PLEADER	POPPING	PREMISE	PROSAIC	PUTTOCK	RAGTIME	RECOVER
PILCHER	PLEASED	POPULAR	PREMISS	PROSODY	PUZZLED	RAGWEED	RECRUIT
PILGRIM	PLEASES	POPULUS	PREMIUM	PROSPER	PUZZLER	RAGWORT	RECTIFY
PILLAGE	PLEATED	PORCIAN	PREPAID	PROTEAN	PYAEMIA	RAILING	RECTORY
PILLBOX	PLEIADE	PORCINE	PREPARE	PROTECT	PYJAMAS	RAILWAY	RECURVE
PILLION	PLENARY	POROSIS	PREPUCE	PROTEGE	PYLORUS	RAIMENT	RECYCLE
PILLORY	PLEROMA	PORTAGE	PREQUEL	PROTEIN	PYRAMID	RAINBOW	REDCOAT
PIMENTO	PLESSOR	PORTEND	PRESAGE	PROTEST	PYRETIC	RAISING	REDDISH
PIMPING	PLEURAL	PORTENT	PRESENT	PROTEUS	PYREXIA	RALEIGH	REDFISH
PINBALL	PLEURON	PORTHOS	PRESIDE	PROTIST	PYRITES	RAMADAN	REDHEAD
PINCERS	PLIABLE	PORTICO	PRESSED	PROUDER	PYROSIS	RAMBLER	REDNECK
PINCHED	PLIANCY	PORTION	PRESUME	PROUDIE	PYRRHIC	RAMEKIN	REDNESS
PINETUM	PLODDER	PORTRAY	PRETEND	PROUDLY	QUADRAT	RAMESES	REDOUBT
PINFISH	PLOSION	POSITIF	PRETEXT	PROVERB	QUAKING	RAMPAGE	REDOUND
PINFOLD	PLOSIVE	POSSESS	PRETZEL	PROVIDE	QUALIFY	RAMPANT	REDPOLL
PINHEAD	PLOTTER	POSTAGE	PREVAIL	PROVING	QUALITY	RAMPART	REDRESS
PINHOLE	PLOWMAN	POSTBAG	PREVENT	PROVISO	QUANTUM	RAMULUS	REDSKIN
PINKEYE	PLUMAGE	POSTBOX	PREVIEW	PROVOKE	QUARREL	RANCHER	REDUCED
PINNACE	PLUMATE	POSTDOC	PREZZIE	PROVOST	QUARTAN	RANCOUR	REDUCER
PINNULA	PLUMBER	POSTERN	PRIAPUS	PROWESS	QUARTER	RANGOON	REDWOOD
PINTADO	PLUMMET	POSTING	PRICKED	PROWLER	QUARTET	RANIDAE	REEKING
PINTAIL	PLUMPER	POSTMAN	PRICKER	PROXIMO	QUARTIC	RANKING	REELECT
PIONEER	PLUMULE	POSTURE	PRICKLE	PRUDENT	QUASSIA	RANSACK	REELING
PIOUSLY	PLUNDER	POSTWAR	PRICKLY	PRUDISH	QUECHUA	RANTING	REENTER
PIPETTE	PLUNGER	POTABLE	PRIESTS	PRURIGO	QUEENLY	RAPHAEL	REENTRY
PIQUANT	PLUTEUS	POTENCY	PRIMACY	PRUSSIC	QUEERER	RAPIDLY	REFEREE
PIRAEUS	PLYWOOD	POTHEEN	PRIMARY	PRYTHEE	QUENTIN	RAPPORT	REFINED
PIRANHA	POACHER	POTHERB	PRIMATE	PSALTER	QUERCUS	RAPTURE	REFINER
PIROGUE	POCHARD	POTHOLE	PRIMEUR	PSYCHIC	QUESTER	RAREBIT	REFLATE
PISCINA	POCHOIR	POTICHE	PRIMING	PTERYLA	QUETZAL	RATAFIA	REFLECT
PISCINE	PODAGRA	POTLACH	PRIMULA	PTOLEMY	QUIBBLE	RATATAT	REFLOAT
PISMIRE	PODESTA	POTLUCK	PRINCES	PTYALIN	QUICHUA	RATCHET	REFRACT
PISTOLE	POETESS	POTOMAC	PRINTED	PUBERAL	QUICKEN	RATIONS	REFRAIN
PITCHED	POINTED	POTOROO	PRINTER	PUBERTY	QUICKER	RATLINE	REFRESH
PITCHER	POINTER	POTSDAM	PRITHEE	PUBLISH	QUICKIE	RATPACK	REFUGEE
PITEOUS	POLARIS	POTSHOT	PRIVACY	PUCCINI	QUICKLY	RATTEEN	REFUSAL
PITFALL	POLEAXE	POTTAGE	PRIVATE	PUCELLE	QUIETEN	RATTLER	REGALIA
PITHEAD	POLECAT	POTTERY	PRIVITY	PUCKISH	QUIETLY	RAUCOUS	REGALLY
PITHILY	POLEMIC	POTTING	PROBAND	PUDDING	QUIETUS	RAUNCHY	REGARDS
PITIFUL	POLENTA	POULENC	PROBATE	PUERILE	QUILTED	RAVAGES	REGATTA
PIVOTAL	POLITIC	POULTRY	PROBITY	PUGWASH	QUILTER	RAVINGS	REGENCY
PIZARRO	POLIZEI	POUNDAL	PROBLEM	PULLMAN	QUINCHE	RAVIOLI	REGIMEN
PIZZAZZ	POLLACK	POUSSIN	PROCEED	PULSATE	QUININE	RAWHIDE	REGNANT
PLACARD	POLLARD	POVERTY	PROCESS	PULSING	QUINONE	RAWNESS	REGRESS
PLACATE	POLLING	POWDERY	PROCTOR	PUMPKIN	QUINTAL	REACTOR	REGROUP
PLACEBO	POLLUTE	POWERED	PROCURE	PUNCHED	QUINTAN	READILY	REGULAR
PLACING	POLONIE	PRAETOR	PRODIGY	PUNCHER	QUINTET	READING	REHOUSE
PLAINLY	POLYGON	PRAIRIE	PRODUCE	PUNGENT	QUITTER	REAGENT	REISSUE
PLANNED	POLYMER	PRALINE	PRODUCT	PUNJABI	QUIXOTE	REALGAR	REJOICE
PLANNER	POLYOMA	PRATTLE	PROFANE	PUNSTER	QUONDAM	REALIGN	RELAPSE
PLANTAR	POLYPOD	PRAYING	PROFESS	PUNTING	QUONSET	REALISM	RELATED
PLANTED	POLYPUS	PREBEND	PROFFER	PURBECK	QUORATE	REALIST	RELAXED
PLANTER	POMEROL	PRECAST	PROFILE	PURCELL	RACCOON	REALITY	RELAYER
PLANURY	POMEROY	PRECEDE	PROFITS	PURITAN	RACEMIC	REALIZE	RELEASE
PLASMIN	POMFRET	PRECEPT	PROFUSE	PURLIEU	RACHIAL	REALTOR	RELIANT
PLASTER	POMMARD	PRECISE	PROGENY	PURLINE	RACHMAN	REARING	RELICTS
PLASTIC	POMPEII	PREDATE	PROGRAM	PURLOIN	RACKETS	REAUMUR	RELIEVE
PLATEAU	POMPOON	PREDIAL	PROJECT	PURPORT	RACKETY	REBECCA	RELIEVO
PLATOON	POMPOUS	PREDICT	PROLONG	PURPOSE	RACKING	REBIRTH	REMAINS
PLATTER	PONIARD	PREDOOM	PROMISE	PURPURA	RACQUET	REBOUND	REMARRY
PLAUDIT	PONTIAC	PREEMPT	PROMOTE	PURSUER	RADDLED	REBUILD	REMBLAI
PLAUTUS	PONTIFF	PREFACE	PRONAOS	PURSUIT	RADIANT	RECEIPT	REMNANT
PLAYBOY	PONTINE	PREFECT	PRONATE	PURVIEW	RADIATE	RECEIVE	REMODEL
PLAYERS	PONTOON	PREHEAT	PRONGED	PUSHING	RADICAL	RECITAL	REMORSE
PLAYFUL	POOFTER	PRELACY	PRONOUN	PUSHKIN	RADICLE	RECLAIM	REMOULD
PLAYING	POOHBAH	PRELATE	PROPANE	PUSTULE	RAEBURN	RECLINE	REMOUNT
PLAYLET	POPCORN	PRELIMS	PROPEND	PUTREFY	RAFFISH	RECLUSE	REMOVAL
PLAYOFF	POPEYED	PRELUDE	PROPHET	PUTTEES	RAFFLES	RECORDS	REMOVED

REMOVER	REVENUE	ROBUSTA	ROWLOCK	SALVAGE	SCALLOP	SEALANT	SETTING
RENEGUE	REVERED	ROCKALL	ROYALLY	SAMARIA	SCALPEL	SEALINK	SETTLED
RENEWAL	REVERIE	ROCKERY	ROYALTY	SAMBUCA	SCALPER	SEALION	SETTLER
REOCCUR	REVERSE	ROCKING	ROZZERS	SAMISEN	SCAMBLE	SEAPORT	SEVENTH
REPAINT	REVISED	ROEBUCK	RUBBERS	SAMNITE	SCAMPER	SEARING	SEVENTY
REPAIRS	REVISER	ROEDEAN	RUBBERY	SAMOOSA	SCANDAL	SEASICK	SEVERAL
REPLACE	REVISIT	ROGUERY	RUBBING	SAMOVAR	SCANNER	SEASIDE	SEVERUS
REPLANT	REVIVAL	ROGUISH	RUBBISH	SAMOYED	SCAPULA	SEATING	SEVILLE
REPLETE	REVIVER	ROISTER	RUBELLA	SAMPLER	SCARIFY	SEATTLE	SEXLESS
REPLEVY	REVOLVE	ROLLERS	RUBEOLA	SAMURAI	SCARING	SEAWALL	SEXTANS
REPLICA	REWRITE	ROLLICK	RUBICON	SANCTUM	SCARLET	SEAWEED	SEXTANT
REPOSAL	REYNARD	ROLLING	RUDERAL	SANCTUS	SCARPER	SECLUDE	SEYMOUR
REPRESS	RHENISH	ROLLMOP	RUDOLPH	SANDALS	SCATTER	SECONAL	SFUMATO
REPRINT	RHENIUM	ROMAINE	RUFFIAN	SANDBAG	SCENERY	SECONDS	SHACKLE
REPROOF	RHIZOID	ROMANCE	RUFFLED	SANDBOX	SCENTED	SECRECY	SHADING
REPROVE	RHIZOME	ROMANIA	RUFFLER	SANDBOY	SCEPTER	SECRETE	SHADOOF
REPTILE	RHODIAN	ROMANOV	RUINOUS	SANDMAN	SCEPTIC	SECRETS	SHADOWY
REPULSE	RHODIUM	ROMANZA	RUMBLER	SANDOWN	SCEPTRE	SECTION	SHAGGED
REPUTED	RHOMBUS	ROMPERS	RUMMAGE	SANDPIT	SCHEMER	SECULAR	SHAKERS
REQUEST	RHONDDA	ROMULUS	RUMORED	SANGRIA	SCHERZO	SEDUCER	SHAKEUP
REQUIEM	RHUBARB	RONDEAU	RUMPLED	SAPIENS	SCHICKS	SEEDBED	SHAKILY
REQUIRE	RHYMING	RONSARD	RUMPOLE	SAPIENT	SCHLEPP	SEEKERS	SHAKING
REQUITE	RIBBING	RONTGEN	RUNAWAY	SAPLING	SCHLOCK	SEEMING	SHALLOT
REREDOS	RIBCAGE	ROOFING	RUNCORN	SAPONIN	SCHLOSS	SEEPAGE	SHALLOW
REROUTE	RIBLESS	ROOFTOP	RUNDOWN	SAPPERS	SCHMUCK	SEETHED	SHAMBLE
RESCIND	RIBWORT	ROOKERY	RUNNERS	SAPPHIC	SCHNELL	SEGMENT	SHAMPOO
RESCUER	RICARDO	ROOKISH	RUNNING	SAPROBE	SCHOLAR	SEISMIC	SHANNON
RESERVE	RICHARD	ROOSTER	RUNNION	SAPWOOD	SCIATIC	SEIZURE	SHAPELY
RESHAPE	RICHTER	ROOTING	RUPTURE	SAQQARA	SCIENCE	SELFISH	SHAPING
RESIANT	RICKETS	RORQUAL	RUSALKA	SARACEN	SCISSOR	SELKIRK	SHARIAH
RESIDUE	RICKETY	ROSACEA	RUSHING	SARCASM	SCLERAL	SELLERS	SHARING
RESOLVE	RICOTTA	ROSALIA	RUSSELL	SARCOMA	SCOFFER	SELLING	SHARPEN
RESOUND	RIDDLED	ROSALIE	RUSSIAN	SARCOUS	SCOLLOP	SELLOFF	SHARPER
RESPECT	RIDDLER	ROSARIO	RUSTLER	SARDANA	SCOOTER	SELLOUT	SHARPLY
RESPIRE	RIDINGS	ROSCIAN	RUTHENE	SARDINE	SCORING	SELTZER	SHASTRI
RESPITE	RIGGING	ROSCIUS	RUTTING	SARGENT	SCORPIO	SELVAGE	SHATTER
RESPOND	RIGHTLY	ROSEATE	RWANDAN	SARMENT	SCOTTIE	SEMINAL	SHAVING
RESPRAY	RIGIDLY	ROSEBUD	SABAEAN	SAROYAN	SCOURER	SEMINAR	SHAWWAL
RESTART	RIGVEDA	ROSEHIP	SABAOTH	SASHIMI	SCOURGE	SEMIPRO	SHEARER
RESTATE	RIMLESS	ROSELLA	SABAYON	SASSABY	SCOWDER	SEMITIC	SHEATHE
RESTFUL	RINGERS	ROSELLE	SABBATH	SASSOON	SCRAGGY	SENATOR	SHEAVES
RESTING	RINGGIT	ROSEOLA	SABRINA	SATANIC	SCRAPER	SENDOFF	SHEBANG
RESTIVE	RINGING	ROSETTA	SACCADE	SATCHEL	SCRAPIE	SENECIO	SHEBEEN
RESTOCK	RINGLET	ROSETTE	SACKBUT	SATIATE	SCRAPPY	SENEGAL	SHELLAC
RESTORE	RIOTERS	ROSSINI	SACKFUL	SATIETY	SCRATCH	SENSATE	SHELLED
RESULTS	RIOTING	ROSTAND	SACKING	SATIRIC	SCRAWNY	SENSORY	SHELLEY
RETAINS	RIOTOUS	ROSTOCK	SADDLER	SATISFY	SCREECH	SENSUAL	SHELTER
RETHINK	RIPCORD	ROSTRAL	SADNESS	SATRAPY	SCREEVE	SEPPUKU	SHELTIE
RETICLE	RIPOSTE	ROSTRUM	SAFFRON	SATSUMA	SCREWED	SEQUELA	SHELVED
RETINAL	RIPPING	ROTATOR	SAGITTA	SAUCILY	SCRIBER	SEQUOIA	SHELVES
RETINUE	RIPTIDE	ROTIFER	SAGOUIN	SAUNTER	SCROOGE	SERAPIS	SHEPPEY
RETIRED	RISIBLE	ROTTING	SAILING	SAURIAN	SCROTAL	SERBIAN	SHERBET
RETIREE	RISKILY	ROTUNDA	SAILORS	SAUROID	SCROTUM	SERCIAL	SHERIFF
RETOUCH	RISOTTO	ROUAULT	SAINTLY	SAUSAGE	SCRUBBY	SERFDOM	SHERMAN
RETRACE	RISSOLE	ROUGHEN	SALABLE	SAVAGES	SCRUFFY	SERINGA	SHIATSU
RETRACT	RIVALRY	ROUGHIE	SALADIN	SAVANNA	SCRUMMY	SERIOUS	SHICKSA
RETRAIN	RIVETED	ROUGHLY	SALAMIS	SAVELOY	SCRUMPY	SERPENS	SHIKARI
RETRAIT	RIVIERA	ROULADE	SALAZAR	SAVINGS	SCRUNCH	SERPENT	SHIMMER
RETREAD	RIVULET	ROULEAU	SALERMO	SAVIOUR	SCRUPLE	SERRIED	SHINDIG
RETREAT	ROADHOG	ROUNDED	SALIENT	SAVOURY	SCUFFLE	SERVANT	SHINGLE
RETRIAL	ROADWAY	ROUNDEL	SALIERI	SAWBILL	SCULLER	SERVICE	SHINGLY
RETSINA	ROAMING	ROUNDER	SALIQUE	SAWDUST	SCUPPER	SERVILE	SHINING
RETURNS	ROARING	ROUNDLY	SALLUST	SAWFISH	SCUTAGE	SERVING	SHINPAD
REUNION	ROASTER	ROUNDUP	SALPINX	SAWMILL	SCUTARI	SESOTHO	SHIPPER
REUNITE	ROBBERS	ROUSING	SALSIFY	SAXHORN	SCUTTER	SESSILE	SHIPTON
REVALUE	ROBBERY	ROUTIER	SALTATE	SCABIES	SCUTTLE	SESSION	SHIRKER
REVELER	ROBERTS	ROUTINE	SALTING	SCAFELL	SEABIRD	SESTINA	SHIRLEY
REVELRY	ROBESON	ROWBOAT	SALTIRE	SCAGLIA	SEAFOOD	SESTINE	SHIVERS
REVENGE	ROBINIA	ROWDILY	SALTPAN	SCALENE	SEAGULL	SETBACK	SHIVERY

SHMOOZE	SIROCCO	SMALLER	SOPRANO	SPLODGE	STARLET	STRATUM	SUFFETE
SHOCKED	SISTERS	SMARTEN	SOPWITH	SPLOTCH	STARLIT	STRATUS	SUFFICE
SHOCKER	SISTINE	SMARTIE	SORCERY	SPLURGE	STARTED	STRAUSS	SUFFOLK
SHOOTER	SITDOWN	SMARTLY	SORDINO	SPOILED	STARTER	STREAKY	SUFFUSE
SHOPPER	SITTING	SMASHED	SORGHUM	SPOILER	STARTLE	STRETCH	SUGARED
SHORTEN	SITUATE	SMASHER	SOROSIS	SPONDEE	STARVED	STREWTH	SUGGEST
SHORTLY	SITWELL	SMATTER	SORROWS	SPONDYL	STATELY	STRIATE	SUICIDE
SHOTGUN	SIXTEEN	SMELTER	SORTING	SPONGER	STATICS	STRIDES	SUKKOTH
SHOUTER	SIZABLE	SMETANA	SOUBISE	SPONSON	STATION	STRIDOR	SULFATE
SHOWBIZ	SIZZLER	SMICKLY	SOUFFLE	SPONSOR	STATIST	STRIGIL	SULKILY
SHOWERS	SJAMBOK	SMIDGIN	SOULFUL	SPOONER	STATURE	STRIKER	SULLAGE
SHOWERY	SKATING	SMILING	SOUNDED	SPORRAN	STATUTE	STRINGS	SULPHUR
SHOWILY	SKELTER	SMITHER	SOUNDER	SPOTTED	STAUNCH	STRINGY	SULTANA
SHOWING	SKEPTIC	SMITTEN	SOUNDLY	SPOTTER	STAYING	STRIPED	SUMATRA
SHOWMAN	SKETCHY	SMOKING	SOURSOP	SPOUSAL	STEALTH	STRIPER	SUMMARY
SHOWOFF	SKIDDAW	SMOLDER	SOUTANE	SPRAINT	STEAMED	STRIPES	SUMMERY
SHRILLY	SKIDPAN	SMOOTHE	SOUTHEY	SPRAYER	STEAMER	STROBIC	SUMMING
SHRIMPS	SKIFFLE	SMOTHER	SOVKHOZ	SPRINGE	STEARIC	STROPHE	SUMMONS
SHRIVEL	SKILFUL	SMUDGED	SOZZLED	SPRINGS	STEARIN	STROPPY	SUNBEAM
SHRIVEN	SKILLED	SMUGGLE	SPACING	SPRINGY	STEEPEN	STRUDEL	SUNBURN
SHRIVER	SKILLET	SNAFFLE	SPADGER	SPROUTS	STEEPLE	STUBBLE	SUNDECK
SHROUDS	SKIMMED	SNAPPER	SPANDAU	SPURREY	STEEPLY	STUBBLY	SUNDIAL
SHUDDER	SKIMMER	SNARLER	SPANDEX	SPURWAY	STEERER	STUDDED	SUNDOWN
SHUFFLE	SKIMMIA	SNARLUP	SPANGLE	SPUTNIK	STELLAR	STUDENT	SUNLAMP
SHUTEYE	SKINFUL	SNEAKER	SPANIEL	SPUTTER	STEMMED	STUDIED	SUNLESS
SHUTTER	SKINNED	SNICKER	SPANISH	SPYHOLE	STENCIL	STUFFED	SUNNILY
SHUTTLE	SKINNER	SNIFFER	SPANKER	SQUADDY	STENGAH	STUMBLE	SUNNITE
SHYLOCK	SKIPPED	SNIFFLE	SPANNER	SQUALID	STENGUN	STUMPED	SUNRISE
SHYNESS	SKIPPER	SNIFTER	SPARING	SQUALLY	STENTOR	STUNNER	SUNROOF
SHYSTER	SKITTER	SNIGGER	SPARKLE	SQUALOR	STEPHEN	STUNTED	SUNSPOT
SIAMESE	SKITTLE	SNIPPET	SPARROW	SQUARED	STEPNEY	STUPEFY	SUNTRAP
SIBLING	SKYBLUE	SNOOKER	SPARTAN	SQUARES	STEPSON	STURMER	SUPPORT
SICKBAY	SKYHIGH	SNOOPER	SPASTIC	SQUASHY	STERILE	STUTTER	SUPPOSE
SICKBED	SKYLARK	SNORING	SPATIAL	SQUEAKY	STERNAL	STYGIAN	SUPREME
SICKERT	SKYLINE	SNORKEL	SPATTER	SQUEERS	STERNLY	STYLING	SUPREMO
SIDDONS	SKYWARD	SNORTER	SPATULA	SQUEEZE	STERNUM	STYLISH	SURCOAT
SIDECAR	SLACKEN	SNORTLE	SPAVINE	SQUELCH	STEROID	STYLIST	SURDITY
SIEMENS	SLACKER	SNOWDON	SPEAKER	SQUIFFY	STETSON	STYLITE	SURFACE
SIEVERT	SLACKLY	SNOWMAN	SPECIAL	SQUILLA	STEVENS	STYLIZE	SURFEIT
SIFTING	SLAMMER	SNUFFLE	SPECIES	SQUINCH	STEWARD	SUAVELY	SURFING
SIGHTED	SLANDER	SNUGGLE	SPECIFY	SQUISHY	STEWING	SUAVITY	SURGEON
SIGNIFY	SLAPPER	SOAKING	SPECKLE	SRAVANA	STICKER	SUBADAR	SURGERY
SIGNING	SLASHED	SOAPBOX	SPECTER	STABILE	STICKLE	SUBAQUA	SURINAM
SIGNORA	SLATTED	SOARING	SPECTRE	STABLES	STIFFEN	SUBATOM	SURMISE
SIGNORI	SLAVERY	SOBERLY	SPELLER	STACHYS	STIFFLY	SUBDUCT	SURNAME
SIKHISM	SLAVISH	SOCAGER	SPENCER	STADDLE	STILTED	SUBDUED	SURPASS
SILENCE	SLAYING	SOCIETY	SPENDER	STADIUM	STILTON	SUBEDAR	SURPLUS
SILESIA	SLEEKLY	SOCKEYE	SPENSER	STAFFER	STINGER	SUBEDIT	SURREAL
SILICON	SLEEPER	SOCKING	SPHENIC	STAGGER	STINKER	SUBFUSC	SURVIVE
SILVERY	SLEEVED	SOCOTRA	SPICATE	STAGING	STIPEND	SUBJECT	SUSANNA
SIMENON	SLEIGHT	SOFABED	SPICULA	STAINED	STIPPLE	SUBJOIN	SUSPECT
SIMILAR	SLENDER	SOJOURN	SPICULE	STAINER	STIRFRY	SUBLIME	SUSPEND
SIMPKIN	SLICKER	SOLANUM	SPIDERS	STALKED	STIRPES	SUBSIDE	SUSTAIN
SIMPLER	SLIDING	SOLDIER	SPIDERY	STALKER	STIRRED	SUBSIDY	SUZETTE
SIMPLEX	SLIMMER	SOLICIT	SPIGNEL	STAMINA	STIRRUP	SUBSIST	SWADDLE
SIMPLON	SLIPPED	SOLIDLY	SPINACH	STAMMER	STOICAL	SUBSOIL	SWAGGER
SIMPSON	SLIPPER	SOLIDUS	SPINATE	STAMPED	STOLLEN	SUBSUME	SWAGMAN
SINATRA	SLIPWAY	SOLOIST	SPINDLE	STAMPER	STOMACH	SUBTEEN	SWAHILI
SINCERE	SLITHER	SOLOMON	SPINDLY	STANDBY	STONILY	SUBTEND	SWALLOW
SINDBAD	SLOBBER	SOLUBLE	SPINNER	STANDIN	STONKER	SUBVERT	SWANSEA
SINGING	SLOGGER	SOLVENT	SPINNEY	STANDUP	STOPGAP	SUBZERO	SWAPPED
SINGLES	SLOPING	SOMALIA	SPINOFF	STANLEY	STOPPED	SUCCEED	SWARTHY
SINGLET	SLOSHED	SOMEHOW	SPINOZA	STANNIC	STOPPER	SUCCESS	SWAYING
SINHALA	SLOTTED	SOMEONE	SPIRITS	STAPLER	STORAGE	SUCCOUR	SWEATED
SINKING	SLOVENE	SOMEWAY	SPITTLE	STARCHY	STORIED	SUCCUMB	SWEATER
SINUATE	SLOWING	SONDAGE	SPLASHY	STARDOM	STORIES	SUCROSE	SWEDISH
SINUOUS	SLUMBER	SOPHISM	SPLAYED	STARETS	STOUTLY	SUCTION	SWEEPER
SIPPING	SLYNESS	SOPHIST	SPLICED	STARING	STRAITS	SUDETEN	SWEETEN
SIRLOIN	SMACKER	SOPPING	SPLICER	STARKLY	STRANGE		SWEETIE

SWEETLY	TANNERY	TENSION	THUMPER	TONTINE	TRANCHE	TROPICS	TWOTIME
SWELTER	TANNING	TENUOUS	THUNDER	TOOLBOX	TRANSIT	TROPISM	TYLOSIS
SWIDDEN	TANTARA	TEQUILA	THYMINE	TOOLING	TRANSOM	TROTSKY	TYMPANO
SWIFTER	TANTIVY	TERBIUM	THYROID	TOOTHED	TRANTER	TROTTER	TYMPANY
SWIFTLY	TANTRUM	TERENCE	THYRSIS	TOOTSIE	TRAPEZE	TROUBLE	TYNWALD
SWIMMER	TAPIOCA	TERMITE	THYSELF	TOPCOAT	TRAPPED	TROUNCE	TYPHOID
SWINDLE	TAPLASH	TERRACE	THYSSEN	TOPIARY	TRAPPER	TROUPER	TYPHOON
SWINGER	TAPPICE	TERRAIN	TIBETAN	TOPICAL	TRAVAIL	TROUSER	TYPICAL
SWINGLE	TAPPING	TERRANE	TICKING	TOPKAPI	TRAWLER	TRUANCY	TYRANNY
SWITHIN	TAPROOM	TERRENE	TICKLER	TOPKNOT	TREACLE	TRUCIAL	TZADDIK
SWIZZLE	TAPROOT	TERRIER	TIDDLER	TOPLESS	TREACLY	TRUCKER	TZARINA
SWOLLEN	TAPSTER	TERRIFY	TIDEWAY	TOPMAST	TREADLE	TRUCKLE	UCCELLO
SYCORAX	TARANTO	TERRINE	TIDINGS	TOPMOST	TREASON	TRUDGEN	UGANDAN
SYCOSIS	TARDILY	TERSELY	TIEPOLO	TOPPING	TREATED	TRUFFLE	UGOLINO
SYMPTOM	TARDIVE	TERSION	TIERCEL	TOPSIDE	TREETOP	TRUMEAU	UKRAINE
SYNAPSE	TARNISH	TERTIAL	TIERCET	TOPSOIL	TREFOIL	TRUMPET	UKULELE
SYNAXIS	TARPEIA	TERTIAN	TIFFANY	TOPSPIN	TREKKER	TRUNDLE	ULEXITE
SYNCOPE	TARQUIN	TESSERA	TIGHTEN	TORCHON	TRELLIS	TRUSTEE	ULULANT
SYNERGY	TARSIER	TESTATE	TIGHTLY	TORMENT	TREMBLE	TRYPSIN	ULULATE
SYNONYM	TARTARE	TESTIFY	TIGRESS	TORNADE	TREMBLY	TSARINA	ULYSSES
SYNOVIA	TARTARY	TESTILY	TIGRISH	TORNADO	TREMOLO	TSARIST	UMBRAGE
SYRINGA	TARTINE	TESTING	TILAPIA	TORONTO	TREPANG	TSIGANE	UMBRIAN
SYRINGE	TASSILI	TESTUDO	TILBURY	TORPEDO	TRESSES	TSIGANY	UMPTEEN
SYSTOLE	TATARIC	TETANUS	TILLAGE	TORPIDS	TRESTLE	TSUNAMI	UNAIDED
TABANID	TATIANA	TEXTILE	TIMBALE	TORREFY	TRIANON	TUATARA	UNAIRED
TABARET	TATTERS	TEXTUAL	TIMBERS	TORRENT	TRIATIC	TUBULAR	UNALIKE
TABASCO	TATTING	TEXTURE	TIMBREL	TORSADE	TRIBUNE	TUBULIN	UNALIVE
TABITHA	TATTLER	THALLUS	TIMELAG	TORSION	TRIBUTE	TUESDAY	UNARMED
TABLEAU	TAURINE	THEATER	TIMEOUT	TORTILE	TRICEPS	TUGBOAT	UNASKED
TABLOID	TAVERNA	THEATRE	TIMIDLY	TORTRIX	TRICKLE	TUITION	UNAWARE
TABORET	TAXABLE	THEORBO	TIMOTHY	TORTURE	TRIDENT	TUMBLER	UNBLOCK
TABULAR	TAXFREE	THEOREM	TIMPANI	TOSSPOT	TRIESTE	TUMBREL	UNBOSOM
TACHISM	TAXICAB	THERAPY	TINFOIL	TOTALLY	TRIFFID	TUMBRIL	UNBOUND
TACITLY	TAXIWAY	THEREBY	TINGLER	TOTEMIC	TRIFLER	TUMULUS	UNBOWED
TACITUS	TBILISI	THEREIN	TINTACK	TOTIENT	TRIFLES	TUNABLE	UNCANNY
TACKLER	TEACAKE	THERESA	TINTERN	TOTTERY	TRIGGER	TUNEFUL	UNCARED
TACTFUL	TEACHER	THERETO	TIPCART	TOUCHED	TRILLED	TUNICLE	UNCINUS
TACTICS	TEALEAF	THERMAL	TIPPING	TOUGHEN	TRILLER	TUNISIA	UNCIVIL
TACTILE	TEARFUL	THERMIC	TIPPLER	TOURING	TRILOGY	TURBARY	UNCLASP
TADPOLE	TEARING	THERMOS	TIPSILY	TOURISM	TRIMMER	TURBINE	UNCLEAN
TAFFETA	TEAROOM	THESEUS	TIPSTER	TOURIST	TRINGLE	TURENNE	UNCLEAR
TAGALOG	TEASHOP	THICKEN	TITANIA	TOWARDS	TRINITY	TURGENT	UNCOUTH
TAGETES	TEASING	THICKET	TITANIC	TOWHEAD	TRINKET	TURKISH	UNCOVER
TAILORS	TEATIME	THICKLY	TITOISM	TOWLINE	TRIPLET	TURMOIL	UNCTION
TAINTED	TEDIOUS	THIEVES	TITOIST	TOWPATH	TRIPLEX	TURNERY	UNCURED
TAKEOFF	TEEMING	THIMBLE	TITRATE	TOWROPE	TRIPODY	TURNING	UNDATED
TAKEOUT	TEENAGE	THINKER	TITULAR	TOXEMIA	TRIPOLI	TURNKEY	UNDERGO
TAKINGS	TEHERAN	THINNER	TOASTED	TOYNBEE	TRIPPER	TURNOUT	UNDOING
TALIPES	TEKTITE	THIRDLY	TOASTER	TOYSHOP	TRIPSIS	TURPETH	UNDRESS
TALIPOT	TELECOM	THIRSTY	TOBACCO	TRACERY	TRIREME	TUSCANY	UNDYING
TALKING	TELFORD	THISTLE	TOCCATA	TRACHEA	TRISECT	TUSSOCK	UNEARTH
TALLBOY	TELLING	THITHER	TODDLER	TRACING	TRISHAW	TUSSORE	UNEQUAL
TALLITH	TELPHER	THOMISM	TOEHOLD	TRACKER	TRISMUS	TUTELAR	UNFADED
TALOOKA	TELSTAR	THOMIST	TOENAIL	TRACTOR	TRISTAN	TWADDLE	UNFIXED
TAMARIN	TEMPERA	THOMSON	TOGGERY	TRADEIN	TRITELY	TWEEDLE	UNFROCK
TAMBOUR	TEMPEST	THOREAU	TOLKIEN	TRADING	TRITIUM	TWEETER	UNGODLY
TAMESIS	TEMPLAR	THORIUM	TOLLMAN	TRADUCE	TRITOMA	TWELFTH	UNGUENT
TAMMANY	TEMPLET	THOUGHT	TOLSTOY	TRAFFIC	TRITONE	TWIDDLE	UNHAPPY
TAMPICO	TEMPTER	THREADS	TOLUENE	TRAGEDY	TRIUMPH	TWIDDLY	UNHEARD
TAMPION	TEMPURA	THRENOS	TOMBOLA	TRAILER	TRIVIAL	TWIGGER	UNHINGE
TANAGER	TENABLE	THRIFTY	TOMFOOL	TRAINED	TRIVIUM	TWINKLE	UNHITCH
TANAGRA	TENANCY	THRISTY	TOMPION	TRAINEE	TROCHEE	TWINSET	UNHORSE
TANBARK	TENANTS	THROATY	TONETIC	TRAINER	TROCHUS	TWISTED	UNICORN
TANCRED	TENDRIL	THROUGH	TONGUES	TRAIPSE	TRODDEN	TWISTER	UNIFORM
TANGENT	TENFOLD	THROWER	TONIGHT	TRAITOR	TROILUS	TWITCHY	UNITARY
TANGIER	TENNIEL	THROWIN	TONNAGE	TRAMCAR	TROLLEY	TWITTER	UNITIES
TANGLED	TENSELY	THRUWAY	TONNEAU	TRAMMEL	TROLLOP	TWOFOLD	UNKEMPT
TANKARD	TENSILE	THUGGEE	TONNISH	TRAMPLE	TROOPER	TWOSOME	UNKNOWN
TANNATE	TENSING	THULIUM	TONSURE	TRAMWAY	TROPHIC	TWOSTEP	UNLADEN

UNLATCH	VACUITY	VIBRANT	WALLABY	WEEKEND	WIMPISH	WRYNOSE	BAFFLED
UNLEASH	VACUOLE	VIBRATE	WALLACE	WEEPING	WINDBAG	WYOMING	BAGASSE
UNLINED	VACUOUS	VIBRATO	WALLEYE	WEIGELA	WINDING	WYSIWYG	BAGEHOT
UNLOOSE	VAGINAL	VICEROY	WALLIES	WEIGHIN	WINDOWS	XANTHOS	BAGGAGE
UNLOVED	VAGRANT	VICINAL	WALLOON	WEIGHTS	WINDROW	XENOPUS	BAGHDAD
UNLUCKY	VAGUELY	VICIOUS	WALPOLE	WEIGHTY	WINDSOR	XERAFIN	BAGPIPE
UNMIXED	VALENCE	VICTORY	WALTZER	WEIRDLY	WINGMAN	XEROSIS	BAHADUR
UNMOVED	VALENCY	VICTUAL	WANGLER	WELCOME	WINNING	XIMENES	BAHAMAS
UNNAMED	VALIANT	VIDIMUS	WANTING	WELDING	WINNOCK	YAHWIST	BAHRAIN
UNNERVE	VALVULE	VIETNAM	WAPPING	WELFARE	WINSOME	YANGTSE	BAHREIN
UNOWNED	VAMOOSE	VIKINGS	WARBECK	WELLIES	WINSTON	YAOUNDE	BAILIFF
UNPAGED	VAMPIRE	VILLAGE	WARBLER	WELLOFF	WIPEOUT	YARDAGE	BAJAZET
UNQUIET	VANADIC	VILLAIN	WARBURG	WENDELL	WIRETAP	YARDARM	BAKLAVA
UNQUOTE	VANDALS	VILLEIN	WARDOUR	WENDISH	WISHFUL	YASHMAK	BALANCE
UNRAVEL	VANDYKE	VILNIUS	WARFARE	WENLOCK	WISHING	YAWNING	BALATON
UNREADY	VANESSA	VINASSE	WARHEAD	WESTERN	WISTFUL	YELLOWS	BALCONY
UNSCREW	VANILLA	VINCENT	WARLIKE	WETBACK	WITCHES	YEREVAN	BALDING
UNSNARL	VANITAS	VINEGAR	WARLING	WETLAND	WITHERS	YEZIDEE	BALDRIC
UNSOUND	VANTAGE	VINTAGE	WARLOCK	WETNESS	WITHOUT	YIDDISH	BALDWIN
UNSTICK	VANUATU	VINTNER	WARLORD	WETSUIT	WITLESS	YOGHURT	BALEFUL
UNSTOCK	VAPOURS	VIOLATE	WARMING	WETTING	WITLOOF	YONKERS	BALFOUR
UNSTUCK	VARIANT	VIOLENT	WARNING	WHACKED	WITNESS	YORKIST	BALLADE
UNTAMED	VARIETY	VIRELAY	WARPATH	WHACKER	WIZENED	YOUNGER	BALLAST
UNTRIED	VARIOLA	VIRGATE	WARRANT	WHALING	WOLFISH	YPSILON	BALLBOY
UNTRUTH	VARIOUS	VIRGULE	WARRING	WHARTON	WOLFRAM	YTTRIUM	BALLIOL
UNTWINE	VARMINT	VIRTUAL	WARRIOR	WHATNOT	WOMANLY	YUCATAN	BALLOON
UNUSUAL	VARNISH	VISCERA	WARSHIP	WHATSIT	WONDERS	ZAIREAN	BALONEY
UNWOUND	VARSITY	VISCOSE	WARTHOG	WHEATEN	WOODCUT	ZAKUSKA	BAMBINO
UPBRAID	VARYING	VISCOUS	WARTIME	WHEEDLE	WOODMAN	ZAMBESI	BANANAS
UPGRADE	VASSAIL	VISIBLE	WARWICK	WHEELED	WOOLLEN	ZAMBIAN	BANBURY
UPRAISE	VATICAN	VISIBLY	WASHDAY	WHEELER	WOOMERA	ZAMORIN	BANDAGE
UPRIGHT	VAUDOIS	VISITOR	WASHERS	WHEELIE	WOOSTER	ZAPOTEC	BANDAID
UPSHOOT	VAUGHAN	VISTULA	WASHING	WHEREAS	WORDILY	ZEALAND	BANDBOX
UPSIDES	VAULTED	VITALLY	WASHOUT	WHEREBY	WORDING	ZEALOUS	BANDEAU
UPSILON	VEDANTA	VITAMIN	WASHTUB	WHEREIN	WORKERS	ZEDOARY	BANDORE
UPSTAGE	VEDETTE	VITIATE	WASPISH	WHETHER	WORKING	ZEMSTVO	BANGING
UPSTART	VEGETAL	VITRAIL	WASSAIL	WHIMPER	WORKMAN	ZEOLITE	BANGKOK
UPSTATE	VEHICLE	VITRIFY	WASTAGE	WHIMSEY	WORKMEN	ZEPHIEL	BANKING
UPSURGE	VELOURS	VITRIOL	WASTING	WHINGER	WORKOUT	ZESTFUL	BANKSIA
UPSWING	VELVETY	VIVALDI	WASTREL	WHIPCAT	WORKSHY	ZETLAND	BANNOCK
UPTIGHT	VENDING	VIVIDLY	WATCHER	WHIPPED	WORKTOP	ZILLION	BANQUET
UPWARDS	VENDOME	VOCALIC	WATERED	WHIPPET	WORLDLY	ZINGARO	BANSHEE
URAEMIA	VENERER	VOCALLY	WATTAGE	WHISKER	WORRIED	ZIONIST	BAPTISM
URALITE	VENISON	VOIVODE	WATTEAU	WHISKEY	WORRIER	ZIZANIA	BAPTIST
URANIAN	VENTOSE	VOLANTE	WATTLES	WHISPER	WORSHIP	ZOFFANY	BAPTIZE
URANISM	VENTRAL	VOLAPUK	WATUTSI	WHISTLE	WORSTED	ZOOLITE	BARBARA
URANITE	VENTURE	VOLCANO	WAVERER	WHITHER	WOTCHER	ZOOLOGY	BARBARY
URANIUM	VERBENA	VOLTAGE	WAXBILL	WHITING	WOULDBE	ZOOTOMY	BARENTS
URETHRA	VERBOSE	VOLTAIC	WAXWING	WHITISH	WOULDNT	ZYGOSIS	BARGAIN
URGENCY	VERDANT	VOLUBLE	WAXWORK	WHITLOW	WOUNDED	ZYMOGEN	BARKERS
URINARY	VERDICT	VOLUBLY	WAYBILL	WHITSUN	WRANGLE	ZYMOSIS	BARKING
URINATE	VERDURE	VOUCHER	WAYLAND	WHITTLE	WRAPPED	ZYMURGY	BARMAID
UROLITH	VERMEER	VOYAGER	WAYMARK	WHOEVER	WRAPPER		BARNABY
URUGUAY	VERMONT	VULGATE	WAYSIDE	WHOOPEE	WRAUGHT	**7:2**	BARONET
USELESS	VERONAL	VULPINE	WAYWARD	WHOOPER	WREATHE	AARONIC	BAROQUE
USUALLY	VERRUCA	VULTURE	WEAKEST	WHOPPER	WRECKED	BABBITT	BARRACK
USURPER	VERSANT	WADDING	WEALDEN	WICKIUP	WRECKER	BABBLER	BARRAGE
UTENSIL	VERSIFY	WAFTING	WEALTHY	WICKLOW	WRESTLE	BABOOSH	BARRIER
UTERINE	VERSION	WAGGISH	WEAPONS	WIDGEON	WRIGGLE	BABYISH	BARRING
UTILITY	VERTIGO	WAGGLER	WEARILY	WIDOWED	WRINGER	BABYLON	BARYTES
UTILIZE	VERULAM	WAGONER	WEARING	WIDOWER	WRINKLE	BABYSIT	BASCULE
UTOPIAN	VERVAIN	WAGTAIL	WEATHER	WIGGING	WRINKLY	BACARDI	BASHFUL
UTRECHT	VESICLE	WAILING	WEAVING	WILDCAT	WRITEUP	BACCHIC	BASINET
UTRICLE	VESPERS	WAITING	WEBBING	WILDING	WRITING	BACCHUS	BASKING
UTRILLO	VESTIGE	WAKEFUL	WEBSITE	WILFRED	WRITTEN	BACILLI	BASMATI
UTTERLY	VETERAN	WALKING	WEBSTER	WILLIAM	WRONGLY	BACKING	BASSOON
UXORIAL	VETIVER	WALKMAN	WEDDING	WILLIES	WROUGHT	BACKLOG	BASTARD
VACANCY	VETTING	WALKOUT	WEDLOCK	WILLING	WRYBILL	BACKSET	BASTIDE
VACCINE	VIADUCT	WALKWAY	WEEKDAY	WILLOWY	WRYNECK	BADNESS	BASTION

BATAVIA	CAMILLA	CARITAS	DADAISM	FALSELY	GAMBLER	HALYARD	JACKSON
BATHERS	CAMOGIE	CARLOAD	DADAIST	FALSIES	GAMBOGE	HAMMOCK	JACOBIN
BATHING	CAMORRA	CARLYLE	DAGGERS	FALSIFY	GAMELAN	HAMSTER	JACOBUS
BATHMAT	CAMPANA	CARMINE	DAGWOOD	FANATIC	GANELON	HANDBAG	JACQUES
BATHTUB	CAMPARI	CARNABY	DAIMLER	FANCIED	GANGWAY	HANDFUL	JACUZZI
BATSMAN	CAMPHOR	CARNAGE	DALILAH	FANCIER	GARBAGE	HANDGUN	JAGGERY
BATTELS	CAMPING	CAROLUS	DAMAGED	FANFARE	GARBLED	HANDILY	JAKARTA
BATTERY	CAMPION	CAROTID	DAMAGES	FANGLED	GARBOIL	HANDLED	JAMAICA
BATTING	CAMWOOD	CAROTIN	DAMNING	FANTAIL	GARBURE	HANDLER	JAMESON
BAUHAUS	CANASTA	CAROUSE	DAMOSEL	FANTASY	GARDENS	HANDOUT	JAMMIES
BAUXITE	CANDACE	CARPORT	DAMPIER	FANWORM	GARFISH	HANDSAW	JAMMING
BAYONET	CANDELA	CARRELL	DAMPING	FANWORT	GARLAND	HANDSEL	JAMPANI
BAZOOKA	CANDIDA	CARRIED	DANCING	FANZINE	GARMENT	HANDSET	JANITOR
CABARET	CANDIDE	CARRIER	DANTEAN	FARADAY	GARNISH	HANGDOG	JANKERS
CABBAGE	CANDIED	CARRIES	DAPHNID	FARAWAY	GARONNE	HANGING	JANUARY
CABINET	CANDOUR	CARRION	DAPHNIS	FARCEUR	GAROTTE	HANGMAN	JAPLISH
CABLING	CANELLA	CARROLL	DAPPLED	FARMERS	GARRICK	HANGMEN	JASMINE
CABOOSE	CANIDAE	CARROTS	DARLING	FARMING	GASCONY	HANGOUT	JAVELIN
CACHEXY	CANNERY	CARROTY	DARNING	FARNESE	GASEOUS	HANOVER	JAVELLE
CACIQUE	CANNILY	CARSICK	DASHING	FARRAGO	GASFIRE	HANSARD	JAWBONE
CADAVER	CANNING	CARTIER	DASHPOT	FARRIER	GASMASK	HAPLESS	JAZZMAN
CADDISH	CANNOCK	CARTOON	DASTARD	FARTHER	GASOHOL	HAPORTH	KADDISH
CADENCE	CANNULA	CARVING	DASYURE	FASCISM	GASPING	HAPPILY	KAINITE
CADENZA	CANONRY	CASCADE	DATABLE	FASCIST	GASTHOF	HARBOUR	KALENDS
CADMIUM	CANTATA	CASCARA	DAUPHIN	FASHION	GASTRIC	HARDPAN	KALMUCK
CADOGAN	CANTEEN	CASEASE	DAWDLER	FASTING	GASTRIN	HARDTOP	KAMERAD
CAEDMON	CANTHUS	CASHBOX	DAYBOOK	FASTNET	GATEWAY	HARELIP	KAMPALA
CAESIUM	CANTRIP	CASHIER	DAYMARK	FATALLY	GATLING	HARICOT	KAMPONG
CAESURA	CANTUAR	CASPIAN	DAYSTAR	FATEFUL	GAUDILY	HARLECH	KANNADA
CAGOULE	CANVASS	CASSATA	DAYTIME	FATHEAD	GAUGUIN	HARMFUL	KARACHI
CAHOOTS	CANZONA	CASSAVA	DAZZLED	FATIGUE	GAUTAMA	HARMONY	KARAJAN
CAINITE	CANZONE	CASSOCK	EAGERLY	FATNESS	GAVOTTE	HARNESS	KARAKUL
CAIRENE	CAPABLE	CASTILE	EARACHE	FATUITY	GAWKISH	HARPIST	KARAOKE
CAISSON	CAPABLY	CASTING	EARDRUM	FATUOUS	GAYNESS	HARPOON	KASHMIR
CAITIFF	CAPELLA	CASTLED	EARLDOM	FAUSTUS	GAZELLE	HARRIER	KATORGA
CALABAR	CAPITAL	CASTOFF	EARLIER	FAUVISM	GAZETTE	HARRIET	KATRINE
CALAMUS	CAPITOL	CASUALS	EARLOBE	FAUVIST	HABITAT	HARSHLY	KATYDID
CALCIFY	CAPORAL	CASUISM	EARMARK	FAVELLA	HACHURE	HARVARD	LABIATE
CALCINE	CAPRICE	CASUIST	EARNEST	FAVORED	HACKERY	HARVEST	LABORED
CALCITE	CAPSIZE	CATALAN	EARRING	FAWNING	HACKING	HARWICH	LABORER
CALCIUM	CAPSTAN	CATALOG	EARSHOT	GABBLER	HACKLES	HARWOOD	LACERTA
CALCULI	CAPSULE	CATALPA	EARTHEN	GABELLE	HACKNEY	HASHISH	LACEUPS
CALDERA	CAPTAIN	CATARRH	EARTHLY	GABFEST	HACKSAW	HASSIUM	LACKING
CALDRON	CAPTION	CATCALL	EASIEST	GABRIEL	HADDOCK	HASSOCK	LACONIC
CALECHE	CAPTIVE	CATCHER	EASTERN	GADROON	HADRIAN	HASTATE	LACQUER
CALENDS	CAPTURE	CATCHUP	EATABLE	GADWALL	HAFNIUM	HASTILY	LACTASE
CALEPIN	CARABID	CATECHU	FACETED	GAEKWAR	HAGBOLT	HATBAND	LACTATE
CALIBAN	CARACAL	CATELOG	FACTION	GAGSTER	HAGFISH	HATCHET	LACTEAL
CALIBER	CARACAS	CATERER	FACTOID	GAINFUL	HAGGADA	HATEFUL	LACTOSE
CALIBRE	CARACUL	CATESBY	FACTORS	GAINSAY	HAGGARD	HATLESS	LACUNAE
CALICHE	CARADOC	CATFISH	FACTORY	GAITERS	HAGGERY	HATTOCK	LADYBUG
CALLBOX	CARAMBA	CATHEAD	FACTUAL	GALAHAD	HAHNIUM	HAUGHTY	LAETARE
CALLBOY	CARAMEL	CATHODE	FACULTY	GALATEA	HAIRCUT	HAULAGE	LAGGARD
CALLING	CARAVAN	CATKINS	FADDISH	GALETTE	HAIRNET	HAULIER	LAGGING
CALLOUS	CARAVEL	CATLIKE	FADDIST	GALILEE	HAIRPIN	HAUNTED	LAGONDA
CALMUCK	CARAWAY	CATLING	FAGGOTS	GALILEO	HAITIAN	HAUTBOY	LAKSHMI
CALOMEL	CARBIDE	CATMINT	FAIENCE	GALIPOT	HALBERD	HAWKEYE	LALIQUE
CALORIC	CARBINE	CATSEYE	FAILING	GALLANT	HALBERT	HAYFORK	LALLANS
CALORIE	CARCASE	CATSPAW	FAILURE	GALLEON	HALCYON	HAYLOFT	LAMAISM
CALTROP	CARCASS	CATTISH	FAINTED	GALLERY	HALFWAY	HAYSEED	LAMAIST
CALUMET	CARDIAC	CATWALK	FAINTLY	GALLING	HALFWIT	HAYWARD	LAMBADA
CALUMNY	CARDOON	CAUSTIC	FAIRING	GALLIUM	HALIBUT	HAYWIRE	LAMBAST
CALVARY	CARDUUS	CAUTERY	FAIRISH	GALLONS	HALIFAX	HAZLETT	LAMBENT
CALYPSO	CAREERS	CAUTION	FAIRWAY	GALLOWS	HALITUS	IAMBIST	LAMBERT
CAMBIUM	CAREFUL	CAVALRY	FAJITAS	GALOCHE	HALLALI	JACINTH	LAMBETH
CAMBRAI	CARGOES	CAVEMAN	FALAFEL	GALOPIN	HALLWAY	JACKASS	LAMBING
CAMBRIC	CARIBOU	CAVIARE	FALLACY	GALUMPH	HALOGEN	JACKDAW	LAMELLA
CAMELOT	CARIOCA	CAYENNE	FALLING	GAMBADO	HALTERE	JACKETS	LAMPOON
CAMERON	CARIOLE	DABBLER	FALLOUT	GAMBIAN	HALTING	JACKPOT	LAMPREY

LANCERS	MAHATMA	MARENGO	NAGGING	PALOMAR	PATHWAY	RATTLER	SARACEN
LANCING	MAHJONG	MARGERY	NAHUATL	PALOOKA	PATIBLE	RAUCOUS	SARCASM
LANDING	MAHONIA	MARIBOU	NAILBED	PALPATE	PATIENT	RAUNCHY	SARCOMA
LANGLEY	MAIGRET	MARINER	NAIPAUL	PALSIED	PATRIAL	RAVAGES	SARCOUS
LANGTON	MAILBAG	MARITAL	NAIROBI	PALUDAL	PATRICK	RAVINGS	SARDANA
LANGUID	MAILBOX	MARKING	NAIVELY	PANACEA	PATRIOT	RAVIOLI	SARDINE
LANGUOR	MAILCAR	MARLENE	NAIVETÉ	PANACHE	PATTERN	RAWHIDE	SARGENT
LANOLIN	MAILING	MARLINE	NAIVETY	PANCAKE	PAUCITY	RAWNESS	SARMENT
LANTANA	MAILMAN	MARLITE	NAKEDLY	PANCRAS	PAULINE	SABAEAN	SAROYAN
LANTERN	MAJESTY	MARLOWE	NAMIBIA	PANDORA	PAUNCHY	SABAOTH	SASHIMI
LANYARD	MAJORCA	MARMARA	NANKEEN	PANGAEA	PAVIOUR	SABAYON	SASSABY
LAOCOON	MAKINGS	MARMION	NAPHTHA	PANGRAM	PAVLOVA	SABBATH	SASSOON
LAOTIAN	MALACCA	MARMITE	NAPPING	PANICKY	PAYABLE	SABRINA	SATANIC
LAPPING	MALACHI	MARQUEE	NARRATE	PANICLE	PAYLOAD	SACCADE	SATCHEL
LAPSANG	MALAISE	MARQUIS	NARROWS	PANNAGE	PAYMENT	SACKBUT	SATIATE
LAPUTAN	MALARIA	MARRIED	NARTHEX	PANNIER	PAYROLL	SACKFUL	SATIETY
LAPWING	MALAYAN	MARRYAT	NARWHAL	PANNOSE	RACCOON	SACKING	SATIRIC
LARCENY	MALEFIC	MARSALA	NASALLY	PANOPLY	RACEMIC	SADDLER	SATISFY
LARDOON	MALLARD	MARSHAL	NASCENT	PANTHER	RACHIAL	SADNESS	SATRAPY
LARGELY	MALLEUS	MARSYAS	NASTILY	PANTIES	RACHMAN	SAFFRON	SATSUMA
LARGESS	MALLING	MARTENS	NATCHEZ	PANTILE	RACKETS	SAGITTA	SAUCILY
LARGEST	MALMSEY	MARTIAL	NATIONS	PANURGE	RACKETY	SAGOUIN	SAUNTER
LASAGNA	MALTASE	MARTIAN	NATIVES	PAPILLA	RACKING	SAILING	SAURIAN
LASAGNE	MALTESE	MARTINI	NATRIUM	PAPOOSE	RACQUET	SAILORS	SAUROID
LASHING	MALTHUS	MARTLET	NATURAL	PAPRIKA	RADDLED	SAINTLY	SAUSAGE
LASTING	MALTOSE	MARTYRS	NAUGHTY	PAPYRUS	RADIANT	SALABLE	SAVAGES
LATCHET	MAMILLA	MARVELL	NAVARIN	PARABLE	RADIATE	SALADIN	SAVANNA
LATERAL	MAMMARY	MARXISM	NAVARRE	PARADOR	RADICAL	SALAMIS	SAVELOY
LATERAN	MAMMOTH	MARXIST	NAVETTE	PARADOS	RADICLE	SALAZAR	SAVINGS
LATIMER	MANACLE	MASCARA	OAKLEAF	PARADOX	RAEBURN	SALERMO	SAVIOUR
LATRINE	MANAGER	MASONIC	OARFISH	PARAGON	RAFFISH	SALIENT	SAVOURY
LATTICE	MANAGUA	MASONRY	OARLOCK	PARAPET	RAFFLES	SALIERI	SAWBILL
LATVIAN	MANAKIN	MASSAGE	OARSMAN	PARASOL	RAFTING	SALIQUE	SAWDUST
LAUNDER	MANATEE	MASSEUR	OARSMEN	PARBOIL	RAGTIME	SALLUST	SAWFISH
LAUNDRY	MANDALA	MASSINE	OATCAKE	PARCHED	RAGWEED	SALPINX	SAWMILL
LAURELS	MANDATE	MASSIVE	OATMEAL	PARENTS	RAGWORT	SALSIFY	SAXHORN
LAVATER	MANDIOC	MASTERS	PABULUM	PARESIS	RAILING	SALTATE	TABANID
LAVOLTA	MANGOLD	MASTERY	PACIFIC	PARFAIT	RAILWAY	SALTING	TABARET
LAWLESS	MANHOLE	MASTIFF	PACKAGE	PARINGS	RAIMENT	SALTIRE	TABASCO
LAWSUIT	MANHOOD	MASTOID	PACKING	PARKING	RAINBOW	SALTPAN	TABITHA
LAWYERS	MANHUNT	MASURKA	PACKMAN	PARKWAY	RAISING	SALVAGE	TABLEAU
LAXNESS	MANIHOC	MATADOR	PADDING	PARLOUR	RALEIGH	SAMARIA	TABLOID
LAYERED	MANIKIN	MATCHED	PADDLER	PARLOUS	RAMADAN	SAMBUCA	TABORET
LAYETTE	MANILLA	MATCHET	PADDOCK	PARNELL	RAMBLER	SAMISEN	TABULAR
LAYINGS	MANIPLE	MATELOT	PADLOCK	PAROTIC	RAMEKIN	SAMNITE	TACHISM
MACABRE	MANITOU	MATILDA	PADRONE	PAROTID	RAMESES	SAMOOSA	TACITLY
MACADAM	MANKIND	MATINEE	PAESTUM	PAROTIS	RAMPAGE	SAMOVAR	TACITUS
MACAQUE	MANMADE	MATISSE	PAGEANT	PARQUET	RAMPANT	SAMOYED	TACKLER
MACBETH	MANNERS	MATTERS	PAGEBOY	PARSLEY	RAMPART	SAMPLER	TACTFUL
MACEDON	MANNING	MATTHEW	PAHLAVI	PARSNIP	RAMULUS	SAMURAI	TACTICS
MACHETE	MANNISH	MATTING	PAINFUL	PARTAKE	RANCHER	SANCTUM	TACTILE
MACHINE	MANSARD	MATTINS	PAINTED	PARTHIA	RANCOUR	SANCTUS	TADPOLE
MACRAMÉ	MANSION	MATTOCK	PAINTER	PARTIAL	RANGOON	SANDALS	TAFFETA
MADEIRA	MANSIZE	MAUDLIN	PAIRING	PARTING	RANIDAE	SANDBAG	TAGALOG
MADISON	MANTUAN	MAUGHAM	PAISLEY	PARTITA	RANKING	SANDBOX	TAGETES
MADNESS	MANUMIT	MAUNDER	PAJAMAS	PARTNER	RANSACK	SANDBOY	TAILORS
MADONNA	MANXMAN	MAWKISH	PALADIN	PARVENU	RANTING	SANDMAN	TAINTED
MAENADS	MAPPING	MAXILLA	PALATAL	PASCHAL	RAPHAEL	SANDOWN	TAKEOFF
MAESTRO	MARABOU	MAXIMUM	PALAVER	PASSAGE	RAPIDLY	SANDPIT	TAKEOUT
MAFIOSO	MARACAS	MAXWELL	PALERMO	PASSANT	RAPPORT	SANGRIA	TAKINGS
MAGENTA	MARANTA	MAYFAIR	PALETTE	PASSING	RAPTURE	SAPIENS	TALIPES
MAGGOTY	MARATHA	MAYPOLE	PALFREY	PASSION	RAREBIT	SAPIENT	TALIPOT
MAGHREB	MARBLED	MAYWEED	PALINGS	PASSIVE	RATAFIA	SAPLING	TALKING
MAGICAL	MARBLES	MAZARIN	PALISSY	PASTERN	RATATAT	SAPONIN	TALLBOY
MAGINOT	MARBURG	MAZEPPA	PALLIUM	PASTEUR	RATCHET	SAPPERS	TALLITH
MAGNATE	MARCHER	MAZURKA	PALMATE	PASTIES	RATIONS	SAPPHIC	TALOOKA
MAGNETO	MARCONI	NABOKOV	PALMIST	PASTIME	RATLINE	SAPROBE	TAMARIN
MAGNIFY	MARCUSE	NACELLE	PALMTOP	PASTURE	RATPACK	SAPWOOD	TAMBOUR
MAGUIRE	MAREMMA	NACROUS	PALMYRA	PATELLA	RATTEEN	SAQQARA	TAMESIS

TAMMANY	VARIANT	WATTEAU	OBSCENE	ICHNITE	SCREEVE	BEACHED	BEOWULF
TAMPICO	VARIETY	WATTLES	OBSCURA	ICINESS	SCREWED	BEACHES	BEQUEST
TAMPION	VARIOLA	WATUTSI	OBSCURE	ICTERIC	SCRIBER	BEADING	BERCEAU
TANAGER	VARIOUS	WAVERER	OBSEQUY	ICTERUS	SCROOGE	BEAMING	BEREAVE
TANAGRA	VARMINT	WAXBILL	OBSERVE	OCARINA	SCROTAL	BEANBAG	BERGSON
TANBARK	VARNISH	WAXWING	OBTRUDE	OCCIPUT	SCROTUM	BEARDED	BERLINE
TANCRED	VARSITY	WAXWORK	OBVERSE	OCCLUDE	SCRUBBY	BEARHUG	BERMUDA
TANGENT	VARYING	WAYBILL	OBVIATE	OCEANIA	SCRUFFY	BEARING	BERNARD
TANGIER	VASSAIL	WAYLAND	OBVIOUS	OCEANIC	SCRUMMY	BEARISH	BERNINI
TANGLED	VATICAN	WAYMARK	TBILISI	OCEANID	SCRUMPY	BEASTLY	BERSEEM
TANKARD	VAUDOIS	WAYSIDE	ACADEME	OCELLAR	SCRUNCH	BEATIFY	BERSERK
TANNATE	VAUGHAN	WAYWARD	ACADEMY	OCELLUS	SCRUPLE	BEATING	BERTRAM
TANNERY	VAULTED	XANTHOS	ACADIAN	OCTAGON	SCUFFLE	BEATLES	BESEECH
TANNING	WADDING	YAHWIST	ACARIDA	OCTOBER	SCULLER	BEATNIK	BESHREW
TANTARA	WAFTING	YANGTSE	ACAUDAL	OCTOPOD	SCUPPER	BECAUSE	BESIDES
TANTIVY	WAGGISH	YAOUNDE	ACCLAIM	OCTOPUS	SCUTAGE	BECKETT	BESIEGE
TANTRUM	WAGGLER	YARDAGE	ACCOUNT	OCTUPLE	SCUTARI	BEDDING	BESMEAR
TAPIOCA	WAGONER	YARDARM	ACCRETE	OCULIST	SCUTTER	BEDEVIL	BESPEAK
TAPLASH	WAGTAIL	YASHMAK	ACCRUAL	SCABIES	SCUTTLE	BEDFORD	BESPOKE
TAPPICE	WAILING	YAWNING	ACCURSE	SCAFELL	UCCELLO	BEDOUIN	BESTIAL
TAPPING	WAITING	ZAIREAN	ACCUSED	SCAGLIA	ADAMANT	BEDPOST	BESTREW
TAPROOM	WAKEFUL	ZAKUSKA	ACCUSER	SCALENE	ADAMITE	BEDROCK	BETHINK
TAPROOT	WALKING	ZAMBESI	ACERBIC	SCALLOP	ADAPTER	BEDROOM	BETHUMB
TAPSTER	WALKMAN	ZAMBIAN	ACESTES	SCALPEL	ADAPTOR	BEDSIDE	BETIMES
TARANTO	WALKOUT	ZAMORIN	ACETATE	SCALPER	ADAXIAL	BEDSORE	BETOKEN
TARDILY	WALKWAY	ZAPOTEC	ACETONE	SCAMBLE	ADDISON	BEDTIME	BETROTH
TARDIVE	WALLABY	ABALONE	ACHAEAN	SCAMPER	ADDRESS	BEEFALO	BETTING
TARNISH	WALLACE	ABANDON	ACHATES	SCANDAL	ADELINE	BEEHIVE	BETTONG
TARPEIA	WALLEYE	ABASHED	ACHERON	SCANNER	ADELPHI	BEELINE	BETWEEN
TARQUIN	WALLIES	ABATTIS	ACHESON	SCAPULA	ADENINE	BEERMAT	BETWIXT
TARSIER	WALLOON	ABAXIAL	ACHIEVE	SCARIFY	ADENOID	BEESWAX	BEVERLY
TARTARE	WALPOLE	ABBASID	ACHTUNG	SCARING	ADENOMA	BEGGARY	BEWITCH
TARTARY	WALTZER	ABDOMEN	ACIDIFY	SCARLET	ADIPOSE	BEGGING	BEZIQUE
TARTINE	WANGLER	ABELARD	ACIDITY	SCARPER	ADJOINT	BEGONIA	CECILIA
TASSILI	WANTING	ABETTOR	ACIFORM	SCATTER	ADJOURN	BEGORRA	CEDILLA
TATARIC	WAPPING	ABIDING	ACOLYTE	SCENERY	ADJUNCT	BEGUILE	CEILIDH
TATIANA	WARBECK	ABIDJAN	ACONITE	SCENTED	ADMIRAL	BEHAVED	CEILING
TATTERS	WARBLER	ABIGAIL	ACQUIRE	SCEPTER	ADMIRED	BEHOOVE	CELADON
TATTING	WARBURG	ABILITY	ACREAGE	SCEPTIC	ADMIRER	BEIJING	CELEBES
TATTLER	WARDOUR	ABIOSIS	ACROBAT	SCEPTRE	ADONAIS	BEJEWEL	CELESTA
TAURINE	WARFARE	ABJOINT	ACRONYM	SCHEMER	ADOPTED	BELABOR	CELESTE
TAVERNA	WARHEAD	ABLATOR	ACRYLIC	SCHERZO	ADORING	BELARUS	CELLINI
TAXABLE	WARLIKE	ABOLISH	ACTAEON	SCHICKS	ADORNED	BELATED	CELLIST
TAXFREE	WARLING	ABOUKIR	ACTINAL	SCHLEPP	ADRENAL	BELGIAN	CELLULE
TAXICAB	WARLOCK	ABOULIA	ACTINIA	SCHLOCK	ADULATE	BELGIUM	CELSIUS
TAXIWAY	WARLORD	ABRAHAM	ACTINIC	SCHLOSS	ADVANCE	BELIEVE	CEMBALO
VACANCY	WARMING	ABRAXIS	ACTRESS	SCHMUCK	ADVERSE	BELINDA	CENACLE
VACCINE	WARNING	ABREAST	ACTUARY	SCHNELL	ADVISER	BELISHA	CENSURE
VACUITY	WARPATH	ABRIDGE	ACTUATE	SCHOLAR	ADVISOR	BELLBOY	CENTAUR
VACUOLE	WARRANT	ABSCESS	ACUTELY	SCIATIC	EDAPHIC	BELLEEK	CENTAVO
VACUOUS	WARRING	ABSCOND	ECBOLIC	SCIENCE	EDIFICE	BELLHOP	CENTRAL
VAGINAL	WARRIOR	ABSENCE	ECCRINE	SCISSOR	EDITION	BELLINI	CENTRED
VAGRANT	WARSHIP	ABSINTH	ECDYSIS	SCLERAL	EDUCATE	BELLMAN	CENTRIC
VAGUELY	WARTHOG	ABSOLVE	ECHELON	SCOFFER	IDEALLY	BELLOWS	CENTRUM
VALENCE	WARTIME	ABSTAIN	ECHIDNA	SCOLLOP	IDIOTIC	BELOVED	CENTURY
VALENCY	WARWICK	ABUSIVE	ECHINUS	SCOOTER	IDOLIZE	BEMUSED	CEPHEUS
VALIANT	WASHDAY	ABYSMAL	ECLIPSE	SCORING	IDYLLIC	BENARES	CERAMIC
VALVULE	WASHERS	ABYSSAL	ECLOGUE	SCORPIO	ODALISK	BENCHER	CERTAIN
VAMOOSE	WASHING	EBBTIDE	ECOLOGY	SCOTTIE	ODDBALL	BENDING	CERTIFY
VAMPIRE	WASHOUT	EBONITE	ECONOMY	SCOURER	ODDMENT	BENEATH	CESSION
VANADIC	WASHTUB	IBERIAN	ECSTASY	SCOURGE	ODDNESS	BENEFIT	CESSPIT
VANDALS	WASPISH	OBADIAH	ECTASIS	SCOWDER	ODONTIC	BENGALI	CESTODE
VANDYKE	WASSAIL	OBELISK	ECTOPIA	SCRAGGY	ODORANT	BENISON	CESTOID
VANESSA	WASTAGE	OBESITY	ECUADOR	SCRAPER	ODOROUS	BENNETT	CEVICHE
VANILLA	WASTING	OBJECTS	ICEBERG	SCRAPIE	ODYSSEY	BENTHAM	CÉZANNE
VANITAS	WASTREL	OBLIGED	ICEFALL	SCRAPPY	AEOLIAN	BENTHOS	DEADEYE
VANTAGE	WATCHER	OBLIGOR	ICEFLOE	SCRATCH	AERATED	BENZENE	DEADPAN
VANUATU	WATERED	OBLIQUE	ICELAND	SCRAWNY	AEROBIC	BENZINE	DEADSET
VAPOURS	WATTAGE	OBLOQUY	ICHABOD	SCREECH	AEROSOL	BENZOIN	DEALING

DEANERY	DENMARK	FERRULE	HEINOUS	KEROGEN	MEASURE	NEITHER	PENSION
DEAREST	DENSELY	FERTILE	HEIRESS	KESTREL	MECHLIN	NEMESIA	PENSIVE
DEATHLY	DENSITY	FERVENT	HELICAL	KETCHUP	MECONIC	NEMESIS	PENTANE
DEBACLE	DENTINE	FERVOUR	HELICON	KEYHOLE	MEDDLER	NEMORAL	PENTODE
DEBASED	DENTIST	FESTIVE	HELIPAD	KEYNOTE	MEDIATE	NEOLITH	PENTOSE
DEBATER	DENTURE	FESTOON	HELLCAT	KEYWORD	MEDICAL	NEOTENY	PEONAGE
DEBAUCH	DEPLETE	FETICHE	HELLENE	LEACOCK	MEDULLA	NEPTUNE	PEPPERS
DEBORAH	DEPLORE	FETLOCK	HELLION	LEADERS	MEERKAT	NERITIC	PEPPERY
DEBOUCH	DEPOSIT	FETTERS	HELLISH	LEADING	MEETING	NERVOSA	PEPSINE
DEBRETT	DEPRAVE	FEVERED	HELLUVA	LEAFLET	MEGAERA	NERVOUS	PERCALE
DEBRIEF	DEPRESS	FEYDEAU	HELPFUL	LEAGUER	MEGARON	NERVURE	PERCENT
DEBUSSY	DEPRIVE	GEARBOX	HELPING	LEAKAGE	MEGATON	NETBALL	PERCEPT
DECANAL	DERANGE	GEARING	HEMLINE	LEANDER	MEIOSIS	NETSUKE	PERCUSS
DECAYED	DERONDA	GEELONG	HEMLOCK	LEANING	MEISSEN	NETTING	PEREIRA
DECEASE	DERRICK	GEFILTE	HENBANE	LEAPING	MELANIN	NETWORK	PERFECT
DECEIVE	DERVISH	GEHENNA	HENGIST	LEARNED	MELILOT	NEURINE	PERFIDY
DECENCY	DERWENT	GELATIN	HENNAED	LEARNER	MELLITE	NEUROMA	PERFORM
DECIBEL	DESCANT	GELDING	HENPECK	LEASING	MELODIC	NEURONE	PERFUME
DECIDED	DESCEND	GEMMATE	HEPARIN	LEASOWE	MELROSE	NEUTRAL	PERFUSE
DECIDER	DESCENT	GENERAL	HEPATIC	LEATHER	MELTING	NEUTRON	PERGOLA
DECIMAL	DESERTS	GENERIC	HEPTANE	LEAVING	MEMBERS	NEVILLE	PERHAPS
DECLAIM	DESERVE	GENESIS	HERBAGE	LEBANON	MEMENTO	NEWBOLT	PERIGEE
DECLARE	DESMOND	GENETIC	HERBERT	LECHERY	MEMOIRS	NEWBORN	PERIWIG
DECLINE	DESPAIR	GENISTA	HERBERY	LECTERN	MENDING	NEWBURY	PERJURE
DECODER	DESPISE	GENITAL	HERBIST	LECTURE	MENFOLK	NEWCOME	PERJURY
DECORUM	DESPITE	GENOESE	HEREDIA	LEEWARD	MENORAH	NEWNESS	PERLITE
DECREED	DESPOIL	GENTEEL	HERETIC	LEFTIST	MENTHOL	NEWSBOY	PERMIAN
DECRYPT	DESPOND	GENTIAN	HEROINE	LEGALLY	MENTION	NEWSMAN	PERPLEX
DEEPFRY	DESSERT	GENTILE	HEROISM	LEGATEE	MENUHIN	OEDIPUS	PERRIER
DEFACED	DESTINE	GENUINE	HERRICK	LEGGING	MERCERY	OERSTED	PERSEID
DEFAULT	DESTINY	GEODESY	HERRIES	LEGIBLE	MERCIES	OESTRUS	PERSEUS
DEFENCE	DESTROY	GEOLOGY	HERRING	LEGIBLY	MERCURY	PEACHUM	PERSIAN
DEFENSE	DETAILS	GEORDIE	HERSELF	LEGIONS	MERITED	PEACOCK	PERSIST
DEFIANT	DETENTE	GEORGIA	HESHVAN	LEGLESS	MERMAID	PEANUTS	PERSONA
DEFICIT	DETRACT	GEORGIC	HESSIAN	LEGPULL	MERRIER	PEARLIE	PERSONS
DEFILED	DETRAIN	GERAINT	HETAERA	LEGROOM	MERRILY	PEASANT	PERSPEX
DEFINED	DEVALUE	GERBERA	HEURISM	LEGWORK	MESCLUN	PEBBLES	PERTAIN
DEFLATE	DEVELOP	GERMANE	HEXAGON	LEISURE	MESEEMS	PECCANT	PERTURB
DEFLECT	DEVIANT	GERMANY	HEXAPOD	LEMMATA	MESSAGE	PECCARY	PERTUSE
DEFRAUD	DEVIATE	GESTALT	HEXARCH	LEMMING	MESSIAH	PECCAVI	PERUSAL
DEFROCK	DEVILRY	GESTAPO	JEALOUS	LEMPIRA	MESSIER	PECKING	PERVADE
DEFROST	DEVIOUS	GESTATE	JEEPERS	LENDING	MESSILY	PECKISH	PERVERT
DEFUNCT	DEVISED	GESTURE	JEEPNEY	LENGTHY	MESSINA	PECTASE	PESSARY
DEGAUSS	DEVISEE	GETAWAY	JEERING	LENIENT	METALLY	PEDDLER	PETIOLE
DEGRADE	DEVOICE	GETTING	JEHOVAH	LENTIGO	METAYER	PEDICAB	PETRIFY
DEGREES	DEVOLVE	HEADING	JEJUNUM	LENTILS	METHANE	PEDICEL	PETROUS
DEHISCE	DEVOTED	HEADMAN	JELLABA	LEONARD	METHINK	PEDICLE	PETUNIA
DEICTIC	DEVOTEE	HEADSET	JELLIED	LEONINE	METICAL	PEELING	REACTOR
DEIRDRE	DEWDROP	HEADWAY	JENKINS	LEOPARD	MÉTISSE	PEEPING	READILY
DEJECTA	DEXTRIN	HEALING	JERICHO	LEOPOLD	METONIC	PEERAGE	READING
DELAYED	EELPOUT	HEALTHY	JERKILY	LEOTARD	METONYM	PEERESS	REAGENT
DELIBES	FEARFUL	HEARING	JERSEYS	LEPANTO	METTLED	PEERING	REALGAR
DELIGHT	FEATHER	HEARKEN	JESTING	LEPROSY	MEXICAN	PEEVISH	REALIGN
DELILAH	FEATURE	HEARSAY	JEWELER	LEPROUS	NEAREST	PEGASUS	REALISM
DELIMIT	FEBRILE	HEARTEN	JEWELRY	LESBIAN	NEARING	PELAGIC	REALIST
DELIVER	FEDERAL	HEATHEN	JEWFISH	LESOTHO	NEBBISH	PELICAN	REALITY
DELOUSE	FEEDING	HEATHER	JEZEBEL	LESSING	NEBULAR	PELORIA	REALIZE
DELPHIC	FEELING	HEATING	KEARTON	LETDOWN	NECKING	PELORUS	REALTOR
DELTOID	FEIGNED	HEAVENS	KEELING	LETTERS	NECKLET	PELTING	REARING
DELUDED	FELLOWS	HEAVIER	KEEPING	LETTING	NECKTIE	PENALTY	REAUMUR
DEMERGE	FELSPAR	HEAVILY	KENNEDY	LETTUCE	NECROSE	PENANCE	REBECCA
DEMERIT	FELUCCA	HEBRAIC	KENNELS	LEUCINE	NECTARY	PENATES	REBIRTH
DEMESNE	FEMORAL	HEBREWS	KENNING	LEUCOMA	NEEDFUL	PENDANT	REBOUND
DEMETER	FENCING	HECKLER	KENOSIS	LEVERET	NEEDLES	PENDING	REBUILD
DEMIGOD	FENELON	HECTARE	KENOTIC	LEXICON	NEGLECT	PENGUIN	RECEIPT
DEMONIC	FENLAND	HEDGING	KENTISH	MEACOCK	NÉGLIGÉ	PENNANT	RECEIVE
DEMOTIC	FERMENT	HEEDFUL	KERATIN	MEANDER	NEGRESS	PENNATE	RECITAL
DENDRON	FERMIUM	HEELTAP	KERMESS	MEANING	NEGRITO	PENNINE	RECLAIM
DENIZEN	FERROUS	HEIGHTS	KERNITE	MEASLES	NEGROID	PENSILE	RECLINE

RECLUSE	REMOVAL	REVELRY	SERCIAL	TERRACE	WEEKEND	AGONIST	CHEAPLY
RECORDS	REMOVED	REVENGE	SERFDOM	TERRAIN	WEEPING	AGONIZE	CHEATER
RECOUNT	REMOVER	REVENUE	SERINGA	TERRANE	WEIGELA	AGRAPHA	CHECKED
RECOVER	RENEGUE	REVERED	SERIOUS	TERRENE	WEIGHIN	AGRIPPA	CHECKIN
RECRUIT	RENEWAL	REVERIE	SERPENS	TERRIER	WEIGHTS	AGROUND	CHECKUP
RECTIFY	REOCCUR	REVERSE	SERPENT	TERRIFY	WEIGHTY	EGALITY	CHEDDAR
RECTORY	REPAINT	REVISED	SERRIED	TERRINE	WEIRDLY	EGGHEAD	CHEERIO
RECURVE	REPAIRS	REVISER	SERVANT	TERSELY	WELCOME	EGLOGUE	CHEESED
RECYCLE	REPLACE	REVISIT	SERVICE	TERSION	WELDING	EGOTISM	CHEETAH
REDCOAT	REPLANT	REVIVAL	SERVILE	TERTIAL	WELFARE	EGOTIST	CHEKHOV
REDDISH	REPLETE	REVIVER	SERVING	TERTIAN	WELLIES	IGNEOUS	CHELSEA
REDFISH	REPLEVY	REVOLVE	SESOTHO	TESSERA	WELLOFF	IGNOBLE	CHEMISE
REDHEAD	REPLICA	REWRITE	SESSILE	TESTATE	WENDELL	IGNORED	CHEMIST
REDNECK	REPOSAL	REYNARD	SESSION	TESTIFY	WENDISH	OGREISH	CHEQUER
REDNESS	REPRESS	SEABIRD	SESTINA	TESTILY	WENLOCK	UGANDAN	CHERISH
REDOUBT	REPRINT	SEAFOOD	SESTINE	TESTING	WESTERN	UGOLINO	CHEROOT
REDOUND	REPROOF	SEAGULL	SETBACK	TESTUDO	WETBACK	CHABLIS	CHERVIL
REDPOLL	REPROVE	SEALANT	SETTING	TETANUS	WETLAND	CHAFING	CHESTER
REDRESS	REPTILE	SEALINK	SETTLED	TEXTILE	WETNESS	CHAGALL	CHEVIOT
REDSKIN	REPULSE	SEALION	SETTLER	TEXTUAL	WETSUIT	CHAGRIN	CHEVRON
REDUCED	REPUTED	SEAPORT	SEVENTH	TEXTURE	WETTING	CHAINED	CHEWING
REDUCER	REQUEST	SEARING	SEVENTY	VEDANTA	XENOPUS	CHALDEE	CHIANTI
REDWOOD	REQUIEM	SEASICK	SEVERAL	VEDETTE	XERAFIN	CHALICE	CHIASMA
REEKING	REQUIRE	SEASIDE	SEVERUS	VEGETAL	XEROSIS	CHALKER	CHICAGO
REELECT	REQUITE	SEATING	SEVILLE	VEHICLE	YELLOWS	CHALONE	CHICANE
REELING	REREDOS	SEATTLE	SEXLESS	VELOURS	YEREVAN	CHAMBER	CHICANO
REENTER	REROUTE	SEAWALL	SEXTANS	VELVETY	YEZIDEE	CHAMBRÉ	CHICKEN
REENTRY	RESCIND	SEAWEED	SEXTANT	VENDING	ZEALAND	CHAMFER	CHICORY
REFEREE	RESCUER	SECLUDE	SEYMOUR	VENDOME	ZEALOUS	CHAMOIS	CHIEFLY
REFINED	RESERVE	SECONAL	TEACAKE	VENERER	ZEDOARY	CHAMPAK	CHIFFON
REFINER	RESHAPE	SECONDS	TEACHER	VENISON	ZEMSTVO	CHANCEL	CHIGGER
REFLATE	RESIANT	SECRECY	TEALEAF	VENTOSE	ZEOLITE	CHANCRE	CHIGNON
REFLECT	RESIDUE	SECRETE	TEARFUL	VENTRAL	ZEPHIEL	CHANGED	CHILEAN
REFLOAT	RESOLVE	SECRETS	TEARING	VENTURE	ZESTFUL	CHANGES	CHILLER
REFRACT	RESOUND	SECTION	TEAROOM	VERBENA	ZETLAND	CHANNEL	CHILLON
REFRAIN	RESPECT	SECULAR	TEASHOP	VERBOSE	AFFABLE	CHANSON	CHIMERA
REFRESH	RESPIRE	SEDUCER	TEASING	VERDANT	AFFABLY	CHANTER	CHIMNEY
REFUGEE	RESPITE	SEEDBED	TEATIME	VERDICT	AFFAIRS	CHAOTIC	CHINDIT
REFUSAL	RESPOND	SEEKERS	TEDIOUS	VERDURE	AFFIXED	CHAPATI	CHINESE
REGALIA	RESPRAY	SEEMING	TEEMING	VERMEER	AFFLICT	CHAPEAU	CHINOOK
REGALLY	RESTART	SEEPAGE	TEENAGE	VERMONT	AFFRONT	CHAPLET	CHINTZY
REGARDS	RESTATE	SEETHED	TEHERAN	VERONAL	AFGHANI	CHAPMAN	CHINWAG
REGATTA	RESTFUL	SEGMENT	TEKTITE	VERRUCA	AFRICAN	CHAPPED	CHIPPED
REGENCY	RESTING	SEISMIC	TELECOM	VERSANT	EFFECTS	CHAPTER	CHIPPER
REGIMEN	RESTIVE	SEIZURE	TELFORD	VERSIFY	EFFENDI	CHARADE	CHIPPIE
REGNANT	RESTOCK	SELFISH	TELLING	VERSION	EFFORCE	CHARDIN	CHIRRUP
REGRESS	RESTORE	SELKIRK	TELPHER	VERTIGO	OFFBASE	CHARGED	CHLAMYS
REGROUP	RESULTS	SELLERS	TELSTAR	VERULAM	OFFBEAT	CHARGER	CHLORAL
REGULAR	RETAINS	SELLING	TEMPERA	VERVAIN	OFFDUTY	CHARGES	CHOCTAW
REHOUSE	RETHINK	SELLOFF	TEMPEST	VESICLE	OFFENCE	CHARIOT	CHOKING
REISSUE	RETICLE	SELLOUT	TEMPLAR	VESPERS	OFFENSE	CHARITY	CHOLERA
REJOICE	RETINAL	SELTZER	TEMPLET	VESTIGE	OFFERER	CHARLES	CHOOKIE
RELAPSE	RETINUE	SELVAGE	TEMPTER	VETERAN	OFFHAND	CHARLEY	CHOPINE
RELATED	RETIRED	SEMINAL	TEMPURA	VETIVER	OFFICER	CHARMED	CHOPPER
RELAXED	RETIREE	SEMINAR	TENABLE	VETTING	OFFICES	CHARMER	CHORALE
RELAYER	RETOUCH	SEMIPRO	TENANCY	WEAKEST	OFFLOAD	CHARNEL	CHORDAE
RELEASE	RETRACE	SEMITIC	TENANTS	WEALDEN	OFFPEAK	CHARPOY	CHORION
RELIANT	RETRACT	SENATOR	TENDRIL	WEALTHY	OFFSIDE	CHARRED	CHORIZO
RELICTS	RETRAIN	SENDOFF	TENFOLD	WEAPONS	PFENNIG	CHARTER	CHOROID
RELIEVE	RETRAIT	SENECIO	TENNIEL	WEARILY	SFUMATO	CHASING	CHORTLE
RELIEVO	RETREAD	SENEGAL	TENSELY	WEARING	AGAINST	CHASSIS	CHOWDER
REMAINS	RETREAT	SENSATE	TENSILE	WEATHER	AGELESS	CHASTEN	CHRISOM
REMARRY	RETRIAL	SENSORY	TENSING	WEAVING	AGELONG	CHATEAU	CHRISTY
REMBLAI	RETSINA	SENSUAL	TENSION	WEBBING	AGGRADE	CHATHAM	CHRONIC
REMNANT	RETURNS	SEPPUKU	TENUOUS	WEBSITE	AGGRESS	CHATTEL	CHUCKLE
REMODEL	REUNION	SEQUELA	TEQUILA	WEBSTER	AGILITY	CHATTER	CHUFFED
REMORSE	REUNITE	SEQUOIA	TERBIUM	WEDDING	AGISTOR	CHAUCER	CHUKKER
REMOULD	REVALUE	SERAPIS	TERENCE	WEDLOCK	AGITATE	CHAYOTE	CHUNDER
REMOUNT	REVELER	SERBIAN	TERMITE	WEEKDAY	AGITATO	CHEAPEN	CHUNNEL

CHUPATI	SHELLAC	THESEUS	WHOOPER	CITROEN	DISLIKE	FINNISH	JIMJAMS
CHUTNEY	SHELLED	THICKEN	WHOPPER	CITTERN	DISMAST	FIRCONE	JITTERS
GHASTLY	SHELLEY	THICKET	AIDANCE	CIVILLY	DISMISS	FIREARM	JITTERY
GHERKIN	SHELTER	THICKLY	AILERON	CIVVIES	DISOBEY	FIREBUG	KIBBUTZ
GHOSTLY	SHELTIE	THIEVES	AILMENT	DIABOLO	DISPLAY	FIREDOG	KICKING
KHALIFA	SHELVED	THIMBLE	AIMLESS	DIAGRAM	DISPORT	FIREFLY	KICKOFF
KHAMSIN	SHELVES	THINKER	AINTREE	DIALECT	DISPOSE	FIREMAN	KIDNEYS
KHANATE	SHEPPEY	THINNER	AIRBASE	DIALING	DISPRIN	FIRSTLY	KIELDER
KHEDIVE	SHERBET	THIRDLY	AIRCREW	DIALYSE	DISPUTE	FISHERY	KILDARE
PHAETON	SHERIFF	THIRSTY	AIRFLOW	DIAMINE	DISROBE	FISHEYE	KILLICK
PHALANX	SHERMAN	THISTLE	AIRLESS	DIAMOND	DISRUPT	FISHING	KILLING
PHALLIC	SHIATSU	THITHER	AIRLIFT	DIAPSID	DISSECT	FISHNET	KILLJOY
PHALLUS	SHICKSA	THOMISM	AIRLINE	DIARCHY	DISSENT	FISSILE	KILOTON
PHANTOM	SHIKARI	THOMIST	AIRLOCK	DIARIST	DISTAFF	FISSION	KILVERT
PHARAOH	SHIMMER	THOMSON	AIRMAIL	DIBBLER	DISTANT	FISSURE	KINDRED
PHARYNX	SHINDIG	THOREAU	AIRPORT	DICKENS	DISTEND	FISTFUL	KINESIS
PHIDIAS	SHINGLE	THORIUM	AIRSHIP	DICTATE	DISTENT	FISTULA	KINETIC
PHILEAS	SHINGLY	THOUGHT	AIRSICK	DICTION	DISTILL	FISTULE	KINGCUP
PHILTER	SHINING	THREADS	AIRSTOP	DIDEROT	DISTORT	FITMENT	KINGDOM
PHILTRE	SHINPAD	THRENOS	BIAFRAN	DIDICOY	DISTURB	FITNESS	KINGLET
PHOEBUS	SHIPPER	THRIFTY	BIASSED	DIDYMUS	DISUSED	FITTEST	KINGPIN
PHOENIX	SHIPTON	THRISTY	BIBELOT	DIECAST	DITHERY	FITTING	KINSHIP
PHONEIN	SHIRKER	THROATY	BICYCLE	DIEDRAL	DITTANY	FIXATED	KINSMAN
PHONEME	SHIRLEY	THROUGH	BIDDING	DIEHARD	DITTIES	FIXEDLY	KINTYRE
PHONICS	SHIVERS	THROWER	BIFOCAL	DIETARY	DIURNAL	FIXINGS	KIPLING
PHRASAL	SHIVERY	THROWIN	BIGFOOT	DIETINE	DIVERGE	FIXTURE	KIPPERS
PHRASER	SHMOOZE	THRUWAY	BIGHEAD	DIFFUSE	DIVERSE	GIBBONS	KISSING
PHRENIC	SHOCKED	THUGGEE	BIGHORN	DIGAMMA	DIVIDED	GIBBOUS	KITCHEN
PHYSICS	SHOCKER	THULIUM	BIGOTED	DIGGING	DIVINER	GIBLETS	KITHARA
RHENISH	SHOOTER	THUMPER	BIGOTRY	DIGITAL	DIVISOR	GIDDILY	KIWANIS
RHENIUM	SHOPPER	THUNDER	BIGSHOT	DIGLYPH	DIVORCE	GIDDYUP	LIAISON
RHIZOID	SHORTEN	THYMINE	BILIOUS	DIGNIFY	DIVULGE	GIELGUD	LIBERAL
RHIZOME	SHORTLY	THYROID	BILLION	DIGNITY	DIZZILY	GILBERT	LIBERIA
RHODIAN	SHOTGUN	THYRSIS	BILLMAN	DIGONAL	FIANCÉE	GILDING	LIBERTY
RHODIUM	SHOUTER	THYSELF	BILLOWS	DIGRAPH	FIBROID	GILLRAY	LIBRARY
RHOMBUS	SHOWBIZ	THYSSEN	BILTONG	DIGRESS	FIBROMA	GIMBALS	LIBRIUM
RHONDDA	SHOWERS	WHACKED	BINDERY	DILATED	FIBROUS	GIMBLET	LICENCE
RHUBARB	SHOWERY	WHACKER	BINDING	DILATOR	FICTION	GIMMICK	LICENSE
RHYMING	SHOWILY	WHALING	BIOCIDE	DILEMMA	FIDDLER	GINGHAM	LICKING
SHACKLE	SHOWING	WHARTON	BIOLOGY	DILUENT	FIDELIO	GINSENG	LIEDOWN
SHADING	SHOWMAN	WHATNOT	BIOMASS	DILUTED	FIDGETS	GIRAFFE	LIFTOFF
SHADOOF	SHOWOFF	WHATSIT	BIOTECH	DIMNESS	FIDGETY	GIRASOL	LIGHTEN
SHADOWY	SHRILLY	WHEATEN	BIPLANE	DIMPLED	FIEFDOM	GIRLISH	LIGHTER
SHAGGED	SHRIMPS	WHEEDLE	BIRDMAN	DINETTE	FIELDER	GIRONDE	LIGHTLY
SHAKERS	SHRIVEL	WHEELED	BIRETTA	DINGBAT	FIFTEEN	GISELLE	LIGNITE
SHAKEUP	SHRIVEN	WHEELER	BISCUIT	DINMONT	FIGHTER	GIZZARD	LIKENED
SHAKILY	SHRIVER	WHEELIE	BISMUTH	DIOCESE	FIGLEAF	HIBACHI	LILTING
SHAKING	SHROUDS	WHEREAS	BISTORT	DIOPTER	FIGMENT	HICKORY	LIMINAL
SHALLOT	SHUDDER	WHEREBY	BITTERN	DIOPTRE	FIGURES	HIDALGO	LIMITED
SHALLOW	SHUFFLE	WHEREIN	BITTERS	DIORAMA	FILARIA	HIDEOUS	LIMITER
SHAMBLE	SHUTEYE	WHETHER	BITUMEN	DIORITE	FILASSE	HIDEOUT	LIMPKIN
SHAMPOO	SHUTTER	WHIMPER	BIVALVE	DIOXIDE	FILBERT	HIGGINS	LIMPOPO
SHANNON	SHUTTLE	WHIMSEY	BIVOUAC	DIPLOCK	FILCHER	HIGHMAN	LINACRE
SHAPELY	SHYLOCK	WHINGER	BIZARRE	DIPLOMA	FILINGS	HIGHEST	LINCOLN
SHAPING	SHYNESS	WHIPCAT	CILIATE	DIPOLAR	FILLETS	HILDING	LINCTUS
SHARIAH	SHYSTER	WHIPPED	CIMABUE	DIPTERA	FILLING	HILLMAN	LINDANE
SHARING	THALLUS	WHIPPET	CINDERS	DIPTYCH	FILMING	HILLMEN	LINEAGE
SHARPEN	THEATER	WHISKER	CINEMAS	DISABLE	FIMBRIA	HILLOCK	LINEMAN
SHARPER	THEATRE	WHISKEY	CINEREA	DISAVOW	FINAGLE	HILLTOP	LINGUAL
SHARPLY	THEORBO	WHISPER	CIRCLET	DISBAND	FINALLY	HIMSELF	LININGS
SHASTRI	THEOREM	WHISTLE	CIRCLIP	DISBARK	FINANCE	HINDLEG	LINKAGE
SHATTER	THERAPY	WHITHER	CIRCUIT	DISCARD	FINBACK	HIPBONE	LINKING
SHAVING	THEREBY	WHITING	CIRROSE	DISCERN	FINDING	HIPSTER	LINKMAN
SHAWWAL	THEREIN	WHITISH	CISSOID	DISCORD	FINESSE	HIRSUTE	LINNEAN
SHEARER	THERESA	WHITLOW	CISTERN	DISCUSS	FINFOOT	HISPANO	LINOCUT
SHEATHE	THERETO	WHITSUN	CITADEL	DISDAIN	FINGERS	HISSING	LINSANG
SHEAVES	THERMAL	WHITTLE	CITHARA	DISEASE	FINICAL	HISTOID	LINSEED
SHEBANG	THERMIC	WHOEVER	CITIZEN	DISGUST	FINICKY	HISTORY	LIONESS
SHEBEEN	THERMOS	WHOOPEE	CITRINE	DISJOIN	FINLAND	HITTITE	LIONIZE

LIPREAD	MISSING	PILATUS	RIPOSTE	TIFFANY	VITRIFY	SKITTLE	ALVEOLE
LIQUEFY	MISSION	PILCHER	RIPPING	TIGHTEN	VITRIOL	SKYBLUE	ALYSSUM
LIQUEUR	MISSIVE	PILGRIM	RIPTIDE	TIGHTLY	VIVALDI	SKYHIGH	BLABBER
LIQUIDS	MISSTEP	PILLAGE	RISIBLE	TIGRESS	VIVIDLY	SKYLARK	BLACKEN
LISSOME	MISTAKE	PILLBOX	RISKILY	TIGRISH	WICKIUP	SKYLINE	BLADDER
LISTING	MISTIME	PILLION	RISOTTO	TILAPIA	WICKLOW	SKYWARD	BLANDLY
LITCHEE	MISTOOK	PILLORY	RISSOLE	TILBURY	WIDGEON	UKRAINE	BLANKET
LITERAL	MISTRAL	PIMENTO	RIVALRY	TILLAGE	WIDOWED	UKULELE	BLANKLY
LITHELY	MITHRAS	PIMPING	RIVETED	TIMBALE	WIDOWER	ALABAMA	BLASTED
LITHIUM	MITOSIS	PINBALL	RIVIERA	TIMBERS	WIGGING	ALADDIN	BLASTER
LITOTES	MITTENS	PINCERS	RIVULET	TIMBREL	WILDCAT	ALAMEIN	BLATANT
LITURGY	MITZVAH	PINCHED	SIAMESE	TIMELAG	WILDING	ALAMODE	BLATHER
MIASMIC	MIXTURE	PINETUM	SIBLING	TIMEOUT	WILFRED	ALANINE	BLATTER
MICHAEL	NIAGARA	PINFISH	SICKBAY	TIMIDLY	WILLIAM	ALARMED	BLAZERS
MICROBE	NIBLICK	PINFOLD	SICKBED	TIMOTHY	WILLIES	ALASKAN	BLAZING
MIDGARD	NICAEAN	PINHEAD	SICKERT	TIMPANI	WILLING	ALBANIA	BLEAKLY
MIDLAND	NICOISE	PINHOLE	SIDDONS	TINFOIL	WILLOWY	ALBENIZ	BLEEPER
MIDLINE	NICOSIA	PINKEYE	SIDECAR	TINGLER	WIMPISH	ALBERGO	BLEMISH
MIDMOST	NICTATE	PINNACE	SIEMENS	TINTACK	WINDBAG	ALBERTA	BLENDER
MIDRIFF	NIGELLA	PINNULA	SIEVERT	TINTERN	WINDING	ALBERTI	BLESSED
MIDSHIP	NIGERIA	PINTADO	SIFTING	TIPCART	WINDOWS	ALBUMEN	BLESSES
MIDTERM	NIGGARD	PINTAIL	SIGHTED	TIPPING	WINDROW	ALBUMIN	BLETHER
MIDWEEK	NIGHTIE	PIONEER	SIGNIFY	TIPPLER	WINDSOR	ALCALDE	BLIGHTY
MIDWEST	NIGHTLY	PIOUSLY	SIGNING	TIPSILY	WINGMAN	ALCHEMY	BLINDER
MIDWIFE	NINEPIN	PIPETTE	SIGNORA	TIPSTER	WINNING	ALCOHOL	BLINDLY
MIGRANT	NINEVEH	PIQUANT	SIGNORI	TITANIA	WINNOCK	ALCORAN	BLINKER
MIGRATE	NIOBEAN	PIRAEUS	SIKHISM	TITANIC	WINSOME	ALDABRA	BLISTER
MILEAGE	NIOBIUM	PIRANHA	SILENCE	TITOISM	WINSTON	ALDRICH	BLITHER
MILFOIL	NIPPERS	PIROGUE	SILESIA	TITOIST	WIPEOUT	ALECOST	BLITZED
MILITIA	NIRVANA	PISCINA	SILICON	TITRATE	WIRETAP	ALEMBIC	BLOATED
MILKING	NITRATE	PISCINE	SILVERY	TITULAR	WISHFUL	ALENÇON	BLOATER
MILKMAN	NITRILE	PISMIRE	SIMENON	VIADUCT	WISHING	ALEPINE	BLOCKED
MILKSOP	NITRITE	PISTOLE	SIMILAR	VIBRANT	WISTFUL	ALEWIFE	BLOCKER
MILLAIS	NITRODE	PITCHED	SIMPKIN	VIBRATE	WITCHES	ALFALFA	BLOOMER
MILLING	NITROUS	PITCHER	SIMPLER	VIBRATO	WITHERS	ALFONSO	BLOOPER
MILLION	OILBIRD	PITEOUS	SIMPLEX	VICEROY	WITHOUT	ALGEBRA	BLOSSOM
MIMICRY	OILCAKE	PITFALL	SIMPLON	VICINAL	WITLESS	ALGERIA	BLOTCHY
MIMULUS	OILSKIN	PITHEAD	SIMPSON	VICIOUS	WITLOOF	ALGIERS	BLOTTER
MINARET	PIANIST	PITHILY	SINATRA	VICTORY	WITNESS	ALICANT	BLOUSON
MINCING	PIANOLA	PITIFUL	SINCERE	VICTUAL	WIZENED	ALIDADE	BLOWFLY
MINDFUL	PIASTRE	PIVOTAL	SINDBAD	VIDIMUS	XIMENES	ALIGNED	BLOWOUT
MINDSET	PIBROCH	PIZARRO	SINGING	VIETNAM	YIDDISH	ALIMENT	BLUBBER
MINERAL	PICADOR	PIZZAZZ	SINGLES	VIKINGS	ZILLION	ALIMONY	BLUFFLY
MINERVA	PICARDY	RIBBING	SINGLET	VILLAGE	ZINGARO	ALIQUID	BLUNDER
MINIBUS	PICASSO	RIBCAGE	SINHALA	VILLAIN	ZIONIST	ALIQUOT	BLUNTED
MINICAB	PICCOLO	RIBLESS	SINKING	VILLEIN	ZIZANIA	ALKANET	BLUNTLY
MINIMAL	PICKAXE	RIBWORT	SINUATE	VILNIUS	EJECTOR	ALKORAN	BLURRED
MINIMAX	PICKING	RICARDO	SINUOUS	VINASSE	SJAMBOK	ALLEGED	BLUSHER
MINIMUM	PICKLED	RICHARD	SIPPING	VINCENT	IKEBANA	ALLEGRI	BLUSTER
MINORCA	PICKLER	RICHTER	SIRLOIN	VINEGAR	OKINAWA	ALLEGRO	CLACHAN
MINSTER	PICOTEE	RICKETS	SIROCCO	VINTAGE	SKATING	ALLENBY	CLAMBER
MINUEND	PICQUET	RICKETY	SISTERS	VINTNER	SKELTER	ALLERGY	CLAMOUR
MINUTED	PICTURE	RICOTTA	SISTINE	VIOLATE	SKEPTIC	ALLONGE	CLAMPER
MINUTES	PIDGEON	RIDDLED	SITDOWN	VIOLENT	SKETCHY	ALLOWED	CLANGER
MINUTIA	PIEBALD	RIDDLER	SITTING	VIRELAY	SKIDDAW	ALLSTAR	CLAPPER
MIOCENE	PIERCED	RIDINGS	SITUATE	VIRGATE	SKIDPAN	ALMACKS	CLARIFY
MIRACLE	PIERCER	RIGGING	SITWELL	VIRGULE	SKIFFLE	ALMANAC	CLARION
MIRADOR	PIERROT	RIGHTLY	SIXTEEN	VIRTUAL	SKILFUL	ALMONER	CLARITY
MIRANDA	PIETIST	RIGIDLY	SIZABLE	VISCERA	SKILLED	ALPHEUS	CLASSIC
MIRIFIC	PIGEONS	RIGVEDA	SIZZLER	VISCOSE	SKILLET	ALREADY	CLASTIC
MISCAST	PIGFISH	RIMLESS	TIBETAN	VISCOUS	SKIMMED	ALRIGHT	CLATTER
MISDEED	PIGGERY	RINGERS	TICKING	VISIBLE	SKIMMER	ALSATIA	CLAVATE
MISERLY	PIGLING	RINGGIT	TICKLER	VISIBLY	SKIMMIA	ALTERED	CLEANER
MISFIRE	PIGMEAT	RINGING	TIDDLER	VISITOR	SKINFUL	ALTHAEA	CLEANLY
MISLEAD	PIGMENT	RINGLET	TIDEWAY	VISTULA	SKINNED	ALTHING	CLEANSE
MISPLAY	PIGSKIN	RIOTERS	TIEPOLO	VITALLY	SKINNER	ALTHORN	CLEANUP
MISREAD	PIGTAIL	RIOTING	TIERCEL	VITAMIN	SKIPPED	ALUMINA	CLEARLY
MISRULE	PIGWEED	RIOTOUS	TIERCET	VITIATE	SKIPPER	ALUMNAE	CLEARUP
MISSILE	PIKELET	RIPCORD	TIERCET	VITRAIL	SKITTER	ALUMNUS	CLEAVER

CLEMENT	FLECKED	ILLNESS	SLAPPER	EMBARGO	SMICKLY	ANTIQUE	GNATHIC
CLICKER	FLECKER	KLAVIER	SLASHED	EMBASSY	SMIDGIN	ANTLERS	GNAWING
CLIMATE	FLEDGED	KLEENEX	SLATTED	EMBLAZE	SMILING	ANTONIO	GNOCCHI
CLIMBER	FLEEING	KLINKER	SLAVERY	EMBOLUS	SMITHER	ANTONYM	GNOSTIC
CLINGER	FLEMING	OLDNESS	SLAVISH	EMBOWER	SMITTEN	ANTWERP	INANITY
CLINKER	FLEMISH	OLDSTER	SLAYING	EMBRACE	SMOKING	ANXIETY	INBOARD
CLIPPED	FLEURET	OLEFINE	SLEEKLY	EMBROIL	SMOLDER	ANXIOUS	INBUILT
CLIPPER	FLEURON	OLOROSO	SLEEPER	EMERALD	SMOOTHE	ANYBODY	INBURST
CLIPPIE	FLEXILE	OLYMPIA	SLEEVED	EMERSON	SMOTHER	ANYMORE	INCENSE
CLIQUEY	FLICKER	OLYMPIC	SLEIGHT	EMINENT	SMUDGED	DNIEPER	INCISOR
CLOBBER	FLIGHTY	OLYMPUS	SLENDER	EMIRATE	SMUGGLE	ENACTOR	INCLINE
CLOISON	FLIPPER	PLACARD	SLICKER	EMOTION	UMBRAGE	ENAMOUR	INCLUDE
CLOSELY	FLITTER	PLACATE	SLIDING	EMOTIVE	UMBRIAN	ENCHANT	INCOMER
CLOSEUP	FLIVVER	PLACEBO	SLIMMER	EMPANEL	UMPTEEN	ENCLASP	INCONNU
CLOSING	FLOATER	PLACING	SLIPPED	EMPATHY	ANAEMIA	ENCLAVE	INCROSS
CLOSURE	FLODDEN	PLAINLY	SLIPPER	EMPEROR	ANAEMIC	ENCLOSE	INCRUST
CLOTHED	FLOGGER	PLANNED	SLIPWAY	EMPIRIC	ANAGRAM	ENCRUST	INCUBUS
CLOTHES	FLOODED	PLANNER	SLITHER	EMPLOYS	ANALOGY	ENCURVE	INCURVE
CLOTURE	FLOOZIE	PLANTAR	SLOBBER	EMPOWER	ANALYST	ENDEMIC	INDEPTH
CLOUDED	FLORIDA	PLANTED	SLOGGER	EMPRESS	ANALYZE	ENDGAME	INDEXER
CLOYING	FLORIST	PLANTER	SLOPING	EMPYEMA	ANANIAS	ENDLESS	INDIANA
CLUBMAN	FLOTSAM	PLANURY	SLOSHED	EMULATE	ANARCHY	ENDNOTE	INDOORS
CLUMBER	FLOUNCE	PLASMIN	SLOTTED	EMULSIN	ANATOLE	ENDOGEN	INDULGE
CLUNIAC	FLOWERS	PLASTER	SLOVENE	IMAGERY	ANATOMY	ENDORSE	INERTIA
CLUPEID	FLOWERY	PLASTIC	SLOWING	IMAGINE	ANCHOVY	ENDURED	INEXACT
CLUSTER	FLOWING	PLATEAU	SLUMBER	IMAGING	ANCIENT	ENDWAYS	INFANCY
CLUTTER	FLUENCY	PLATOON	SLYNESS	IMAGISM	ANDAMAN	ENERGIC	INFARCT
ELAMITE	FLUMMOX	PLATTER	ULEXITE	IMAGIST	ANDANTE	ENFEOFF	INFERNO
ELASTIC	FLUNKEY	PLAUDIT	ULULANT	IMHOTEP	ANDIRON	ENFIELD	INFIDEL
ELASTIN	FLUSHED	PLAUTUS	ULULATE	IMITATE	ANDORRA	ENFORCE	INFIELD
ELATION	FLUSTER	PLAYBOY	ULYSSES	IMMENSE	ANDROID	ENGAGED	INFLAME
ELDERLY	FLUTIST	PLAYERS	AMALGAM	IMMERGE	ANEMONE	ENGINED	INFLATE
ELEANOR	FLUTTER	PLAYFUL	AMANITA	IMMERSE	ANEROID	ENGLAND	INFLECT
ELECTED	FLUVIAL	PLAYING	AMATEUR	IMMORAL	ANGELIC	ENGLISH	INFLICT
ELECTOR	FLYHALF	PLAYLET	AMATORY	IMPASSE	ANGELUS	ENGORGE	INGENUE
ELECTRA	FLYLEAF	PLAYOFF	AMAZING	IMPASTO	ANGEVIN	ENGRAFT	INGRAIN
ELECTRO	FLYOVER	PLAYPEN	AMBAGES	IMPAVID	ANGIOMA	ENGRAIN	INGRATE
ELEGANT	FLYPAST	PLEADER	AMBIENT	IMPEACH	ANGLING	ENGRAVE	INGRESS
ELEGIAC	GLACIAL	PLEASED	AMBOYNA	IMPERIL	ANGOLAN	ENGROSS	INGROWN
ELEGIST	GLACIER	PLEASES	AMBROSE	IMPETUS	ANGRILY	ENHANCE	INHABIT
ELEMENT	GLADDEN	PLEATED	AMENITY	IMPIETY	ANGUISH	ENLARGE	INHALER
ELEVATE	GLAMOUR	PLEIADE	AMERICA	IMPINGE	ANGULAR	ENLIVEN	INHERIT
ELISION	GLARING	PLENARY	AMERIGO	IMPIOUS	ANILINE	ENNOBLE	INHIBIT
ELITISM	GLASGOW	PLEROMA	AMERIND	IMPLANT	ANIMALS	ENOLOGY	INHOUSE
ELITIST	GLASSES	PLESSOR	AMHARIC	IMPLIED	ANIMATE	ENPRINT	INHUMAN
ELLIPSE	GLAZIER	PLEURAL	AMIABLE	IMPLODE	ANIMIST	ENQUIRE	INITIAL
ELOGIUM	GLAZING	PLEURON	AMIABLY	IMPLORE	ANISEED	ENQUIRY	INJURED
ELUSIVE	GLEANER	PLIABLE	AMMETER	IMPOUND	ANNATTO	ENRAGED	INKLING
ELUSORY	GLEEFUL	PLIANCY	AMMONAL	IMPRESS	ANNELID	ENSLAVE	INKWELL
ELYSIAN	GLENCOE	PLODDER	AMMONIA	IMPREST	ANNOYED	ENSNARE	INNARDS
ELYSIUM	GLENOID	PLOSION	AMNESIA	IMPRINT	ANNUITY	ENSNARL	INNERVE
ELYTRON	GLIDING	PLOSIVE	AMNESTY	IMPROVE	ANNULAR	ENSUING	INNINGS
ELZEVIR	GLIMMER	PLOTTER	AMOEBIC	IMPULSE	ANNULET	ENSUITE	INQUEST
FLACCID	GLIMPSE	PLOWMAN	AMONGST	OMENTUM	ANNULUS	ENTEBBE	INQUIRE
FLAGDAY	GLISTEN	PLUMAGE	AMORIST	OMICRON	ANODIZE	ENTENTE	INQUIRY
FLAMING	GLITTER	PLUMATE	AMORITE	OMINOUS	ANODYNE	ENTERIC	INROADS
FLANKER	GLOBULE	PLUMBER	AMOROSO	OMITTED	ANOMALY	ENTERON	INSCAPE
FLANNEL	GLORIFY	PLUMMET	AMOROUS	OMNIBUS	ANOSMIA	ENTHRAL	INSECTS
FLAPPED	GLOTTAL	PLUMPER	AMPHORA	OMPHALE	ANOTHER	ENTHUSE	INSHORE
FLAPPER	GLOTTIS	PLUMULE	AMPLIFY	SMACKER	ANTACID	ENTITLE	INSIDER
FLAREUP	GLOWING	PLUNDER	AMPOULE	SMALLER	ANTARES	ENTRAIN	INSIDES
FLASHER	GLUCOSE	PLUNGER	AMPULLA	SMARTEN	ANTENNA	ENTRANT	INSIGHT
FLATCAR	GLUTTON	PLUTEUS	AMTRACK	SMARTIE	ANTHILL	ENTREAT	INSIPID
FLATLET	GLYPTAL	PLYWOOD	AMUSING	SMARTLY	ANTHONY	ENTROPY	INSPECT
FLATTEN	GLYPTIC	SLACKEN	AMYGDAL	SMASHED	ANTHRAX	ENTRUST	INSPIRE
FLATTER	ILIACUS	SLACKER	AMYLASE	SMASHER	ANTIBES	ENTWINE	INSTALL
FLAUNCH	ILLBRED	SLACKLY	AMYLOID	SMATTER	ANTIGEN	ENVELOP	INSTANT
FLAVOUR	ILLEGAL	SLAMMER	AMYLOSE	SMELTER	ANTIGUA	ENVENOM	INSTATE
FLEAPIT	ILLICIT	SLANDER	EMANATE	SMETANA	ANTIOCH	GNARLED	INSTEAD

INSTILL	SNUGGLE	UNTAMED	BOUTADE	COMMUNE	CONVERT	COURAGE	FOOLISH
INSULAR	UNAIDED	UNTRIED	BOWDLER	COMMUTE	CONVICT	COURBET	FOOTAGE
INSULIN	UNAIRED	UNTRUTH	BOWHEAD	COMPACT	CONVOKE	COURIER	FOOTING
INSURER	UNALIKE	UNTWINE	BOWLING	COMPANY	COOKERY	COURSER	FOOTMAN
INTEGER	UNALIVE	UNUSUAL	BOWSHOT	COMPARE	COOKING	COURSES	FOOTPAD
INTENSE	UNARMED	UNWOUND	BOXHAUL	COMPASS	COOLANT	COURTLY	FOOTSIE
INTERIM	UNASKED	UNWROUND	BOXROOM	COMPERE	COOLING	COUSINS	FOPPISH
INTERNE	UNAWARE	BOARDER	BOXWOOD	COMPETE	COONCAN	COUTURE	FORAMEN
INTROIT	UNBLOCK	BOASTER	BOYCOTT	COMPILE	COPILOT	COVERED	FORBADE
INTRUDE	UNBOSOM	BOATING	BOYHOOD	COMPLEX	COPIOUS	COVERUP	FORBEAR
INVADER	UNBOUND	BOATMAN	COARSEN	COMPORT	COPLAND	COVETED	FORCEPS
INVALID	UNBOWED	BOBSLED	COASTAL	COMPOSE	COPPERS	COWBANE	FOREARM
INVEIGH	UNCANNY	BOHEMIA	COASTER	COMPOST	COPPICE	COWGIRL	FOREIGN
INVERSE	UNCARED	BOHRIUM	COATING	COMPOTE	COPYCAT	COWHAND	FORELEG
INVIOUS	UNCINUS	BOILEAU	COAXIAL	COMPUTE	COPYING	COWHERD	FOREMAN
INVOICE	UNCIVIL	BOILING	COBBLED	COMRADE	COPYIST	COWHIDE	FOREPAW
INVOLVE	UNCLASP	BOLETUS	COBBLER	CONAKRY	ORACLE	COWLICK	FORESEE
INWARDS	UNCLEAN	BOLIVAR	COCAINE	CONCAVE	CORANTO	COWLING	FOREVER
KNACKER	UNCLEAR	BOLIVIA	COCHLEA	CONCEAL	CORBEAU	COWPOKE	FORFEIT
KNAPPER	UNCOUTH	BOLLARD	COCKADE	CONCEDE	CORBETT	COWSHED	FORFEND
KNAVERY	UNCOVER	BOLOGNA	COCKLES	CONCEIT	CORDATE	COWSLIP	FORGAVE
KNEECAP	UNCTION	BOLONEY	COCKNEY	CONCEPT	CORDIAL	COXCOMB	FORGERY
KNEELER	UNCURED	BOLSHIE	COCKPIT	CONCERN	CORDITE	COXLESS	FORGIVE
KNEEPAD	UNDATED	BOLSHOI	COCONUT	CONCERT	CORDOBA	COYNESS	FORGONE
KNELLER	UNDERGO	BOLSTER	COCOTTE	CONCISE	CORELLI	DOCKING	FORLORN
KNESSET	UNDOING	BOMBARD	CODEINE	CONCOCT	CORINTH	DOCTORS	FORMICA
KNICKER	UNDRESS	BOMBAST	CODICIL	CONCORD	CORKAGE	DODDERY	FORMING
KNITTED	UNDYING	BOMBING	CODLING	CONCUSS	CORKING	DODGEMS	FORMOSA
KNITTER	UNEARTH	BONANZA	COELIAC	CONDEMN	CORNCOB	DOESKIN	FORMULA
KNOBBLE	UNEQUAL	BONDAGE	COEXIST	CONDOLE	CORNEAL	DOGCART	FORSAKE
KNOBBLY	UNFADED	BONDMAN	COFFERS	CONDONE	CORNELL	DOGFISH	FORSTER
KNOCKER	UNFIXED	BONESET	COGENCY	CONDUCT	CORNICE	DOGFOOD	FORTIES
KNOTTED	UNFROCK	BONFIRE	COGNATE	CONDUIT	CORNISH	DOGGONE	FORTIFY
KNOWALL	UNGODLY	BONKERS	COHABIT	CONFESS	CORNROW	DOGROSE	FORTRAN
KNOWHOW	UNGUENT	BONNARD	COINAGE	CONFIDE	COROLLA	DOGWOOD	FORTUNE
KNOWING	UNHAPPY	BOOBOOK	COITION	CONFINE	CORONER	DOLEFUL	FORWARD
KNUCKLE	UNHEARD	BOOKIES	COLCHIS	CONFIRM	CORONET	DOLLARS	FOSSICK
ONANISM	UNHINGE	BOOKING	COLDITZ	CONFORM	CORRECT	DOLORES	FOSSULA
ONEIRIC	UNHITCH	BOOKISH	COLIBRI	CONFUSE	CORRIDA	DOLPHIN	FOULARD
ONENESS	UNHORSE	BOOKLET	COLITIS	CONGEAL	CORRODE	DOMAINE	FOUNDER
ONEROUS	UNICORN	BOOKMAN	COLLAGE	CONICAL	CORRUPT	DOMINGO	FOUNDRY
ONESELF	UNIFORM	BOOLEAN	COLLARD	CONIFER	CORSAGE	DOMINIC	FOXHOLE
ONETIME	UNITARY	BOOMING	COLLATE	CONJOIN	CORSAIR	DONEGAL	FOXTROT
ONGOING	UNITIES	BOORISH	COLLECT	CONJURE	CORTEGE	DONNISH	GOAHEAD
ONMIBUS	UNKEMPT	BOOSTER	COLLEEN	CONNATE	CORTINA	DOODLER	GOBBLER
ONSHORE	UNKNOWN	BOOTLEG	COLLEGE	CONNECT	CORUNNA	DOORKEY	GOBELIN
ONSTAGE	UNLADEN	BORACIC	COLLIDE	CONNIVE	CORYDON	DOORMAN	GODDESS
ONTARIO	UNLATCH	BORDERS	COLLIER	CONNOTE	COSSACK	DOORMAT	GODETIA
ONWARDS	UNLEASH	BOREDOM	COLLOID	CONQUER	COSTARD	DOORWAY	GODHEAD
SNAFFLE	UNLINED	BOROCIN	COLLUDE	CONSENT	COSTING	DOPPLER	GODLESS
SNAPPER	UNLOOSE	BORSTAL	COLOGNE	CONSIGN	COSTIVE	DORKING	GODLIKE
SNARLER	UNLOVED	BOSWELL	COLOMBO	CONSIST	COSTUME	DORMANT	GODSEND
SNARLUP	UNLUCKY	BOTANIC	COLONEL	CONSOLE	COTERIE	DOROTHY	GODUNOV
SNEAKER	UNMIXED	BOTARGO	COLONIC	CONSOLS	COTINGA	DOSSIER	GOGGLES
SNICKER	UNMOVED	BOTTEGA	COLORED	CONSORT	COTTAGE	DOUBLES	GOLDING
SNIFFER	UNNAMED	BOTTLED	COLOURS	CONSULT	COTTIER	DOUBLET	GOLDONI
SNIFFLE	UNNERVE	BOTTLES	COLUMBA	CONSUME	COTTONY	DOUBTER	GOLFING
SNIFTER	UNOWNED	BOUCLÉE	COLUMNS	CONTACT	COUCHÉE	DOUGHTY	GOLIARD
SNIGGER	UNPAGED	BOUDOIR	COMBINE	CONTAIN	COULDNT	DOUGLAS	GOLIATH
SNIPPET	UNQUIET	BOUILLI	COMBING	CONTEMN	COULOMB	DOWAGER	GOMBEEN
SNOOKER	UNQUOTE	BOULDER	COMFORT	CONTEND	COULTER	DOWDILY	GOMORRA
SNOOPER	UNRAVEL	BOUNCER	COMFREY	CONTENT	COUNCIL	DOWLAND	GONDOLA
SNORING	UNREADY	BOUNDED	COMICAL	CONTEST	COUNSEL	DOWSING	GOODBYE
SNORKEL	UNSCREW	BOUNDEN	COMMAND	CONTEXT	COUNTED	FOGHORN	GOODIES
SNORTER	UNSNARL	BOUNDER	COMMEND	CONTORT	COUNTER	FOGLAMP	GOODISH
SNORTLE	UNSOUND	BOUQUET	COMMENT	CONTOUR	COUNTRY	FOLDING	GOODMAN
SNOWDON	UNSTICK	BOURBON	COMMODE	CONTROL	COUPLER	FOLIAGE	GOODWIN
SNOWMAN	UNSTOCK	BOURDON	COMMODO	CONVENE	COUPLET	FOLLIES	GOOLIES
SNUFFLE	UNSTUCK	BOURSIN	COMMONS	CONVENT	COUPONS	FONDANT	GORDIAN

GORDIUS	JOHNSON	MOFETTE	NOBBLER	POMPOUS	ROCKERY	ROYALTY	TONNISH
GORILLA	JOINERY	MOHICAN	NOCTUID	PONIARD	ROCKING	ROZZERS	TONSURE
GORSEDD	JOINING	MOIDORE	NODDING	PONTIAC	ROEBUCK	SOAKING	TONTINE
GOSHAWK	JOINTED	MOISTEN	NODULAR	PONTIFF	ROEDEAN	SOAPBOX	TOOLBOX
GOSLING	JOINTER	MOITHER	NOGGING	PONTINE	ROGUERY	SOARING	TOOLING
GOSSIPY	JOINTLY	MOLDING	NOISILY	PONTOON	ROGUISH	SOBERLY	TOOTHED
GOUACHE	JOLLITY	MOLIÈRE	NOISOME	POOFTER	ROISTER	SOCAGER	TOOTSIE
GOULASH	JONQUIL	MOLLIFY	NOMADIC	POOHBAH	ROLLERS	SOCIETY	TOPCOAT
GOURMET	JOURNAL	MOLLUSC	NOMBRIL	POPCORN	ROLLICK	SOCKEYE	TOPIARY
HOARDER	JOURNEY	MOLOTOV	NOMINAL	POPEYED	ROLLING	SOCKING	TOPICAL
HOBNAIL	JOYLESS	MOLUCCA	NOMINEE	POPOVER	ROLLMOP	SOCOTRA	TOPKAPI
HOBSONS	JOYRIDE	MOMBASA	NONPLUS	POPPING	ROMAINE	SOFABED	TOPKNOT
HOEDOWN	KOLKHOZ	MOMENTS	NONPROS	POPULAR	ROMANCE	SOJOURN	TOPLESS
HOGARTH	KONTIKI	MONARCH	NONSTOP	POPULUS	ROMANIA	SOLANUM	TOPMAST
HOGBACK	KOUMISS	MONEYED	NONSUCH	PORCIAN	ROMANOV	SOLDIER	TOPMOST
HOGGING	KOWLOON	MONGREL	NONSUIT	PORCINE	ROMANZA	SOLICIT	TOPPING
HOGWASH	LOBELIA	MONILIA	NOODLES	POROSIS	ROMULUS	SOLIDLY	TOPSIDE
HOLBEIN	LOBSTER	MONITOR	NOOLOGY	PORTAGE	RONDEAU	SOLIDUS	TOPSOIL
HOLDALL	LOCALLY	MONKISH	NOONDAY	PORTEND	RONSARD	SOLOIST	TOPSPIN
HOLDING	LOCKJAW	MONOCLE	NORFOLK	PORTENT	RONTGEN	SOLOMON	TORCHON
HOLIDAY	LOCKNUT	MONOCOT	NORWICH	PORTHOS	ROOFING	SOLUBLE	TORMENT
HOLLAND	LOCKOUT	MONOLOG	NOSEBAG	PORTICO	ROOFTOP	SOLVENT	TORNADE
HOLMIUM	LOCUSTS	MONOPLY	NOSEGAY	PORTION	ROOKERY	SOMALIA	TORNADO
HOLSTER	LODGING	MONSOON	NOSTRIL	PORTRAY	ROOKISH	SOMEHOW	TORONTO
HOMBURG	LOFTILY	MONSTER	NOSTRUM	POSITIF	ROOSTER	SOMEONE	TORPEDO
HOMERIC	LOGBOOK	MONTAGE	NOTABLE	POSSESS	ROOTING	SOMEWAY	TORPIDS
HOMINID	LOGGING	MONTAGU	NOTABLY	POSTAGE	RORQUAL	SONDAGE	TORREFY
HOMONYM	LOGICAL	MONTANA	NOTCHED	POSTBAG	ROSACEA	SOPHISM	TORRENT
HONESTY	LOGWOOD	MONTANT	NOTEPAD	POSTBOX	ROSALIA	SOPHIST	TORSADE
HONEYED	LOLLARD	MONTERO	NOTHING	POSTDOC	ROSALIE	SOPPING	TORSION
HONITON	LOMBARD	MONTHLY	NOTIONS	POSTERN	ROSARIO	SOPRANO	TORTILE
HONOURS	LONGBOW	MOODILY	NOURISH	POSTING	ROSCIAN	SOPWITH	TORTRIX
HOODLUM	LONGING	MOONING	NOUVEAU	POSTMAN	ROSCIUS	SORCERY	TORTURE
HOPEFUL	LOOKING	MOONLIT	NOVELLA	POSTURE	ROSEATE	SORDINO	TOSSPOT
HOPKINS	LOOKOUT	MOORHEN	NOVELLO	POSTWAR	ROSEBUD	SORGHUM	TOTALLY
HOPLITE	LOOMING	MOORING	NOVELTY	POTABLE	ROSEHIP	SOROSIS	TOTEMIC
HOPPING	LOOSELY	MOORISH	NOWHERE	POTENCY	ROSELLA	SORROWS	TOTIENT
HOPSACK	LOOTING	MOPPING	NOXIOUS	POTHEEN	ROSELLE	SORTING	TOTTERY
HORATIO	LORDING	MORAINE	POACHER	POTHERB	ROSEOLA	SOUBISE	TOUCHED
HORDEUM	LORELEI	MORALLY	POCHARD	POTHOLE	ROSETTA	SOUFFLE	TOUGHEN
HORIZON	LOTHAIR	MORAVIA	POCHOIR	POTICHE	ROSETTE	SOULFUL	TOURING
HORMONE	LOTHIAN	MORDANT	PODAGRA	POTLACH	ROSSINI	SOUNDED	TOURISM
HORRIFY	LOTTERY	MOREISH	PODESTA	POTLUCK	ROSTAND	SOUNDER	TOURIST
HORRORS	LOUNGER	MORELLO	POETESS	POTOMAC	ROSTOCK	SOUNDLY	TOWARDS
HORSING	LOURDES	MORESBY	POINTED	POTOROO	ROSTRAL	SOURSOP	TOWHEAD
HOSANNA	LOURING	MORESCO	POINTER	POTSDAM	ROSTRUM	SOUTANE	TOWLINE
HOSIERY	LOUTISH	MORLAND	POLARIS	POTSHOT	ROTATOR	SOUTHEY	TOWPATH
HOSPICE	LOUVRED	MORNING	POLEAXE	POTTAGE	ROTIFER	SOVKHOZ	TOWROPE
HOSTAGE	LOVABLE	MOROCCO	POLECAT	POTTERY	ROTTING	SOZZLED	TOXEMIA
HOSTESS	LOWBROW	MORONIC	POLEMIC	POTTING	ROTUNDA	TOASTED	TOYNBEE
HOSTILE	LOWDOWN	MORPHIA	POLENTA	POULENC	ROUAULT	TOASTER	TOYSHOP
HOTFOOT	LOWLAND	MORRELL	POLITIC	POULTRY	ROUGHEN	TOBACCO	VOCALIC
HOTHEAD	LOWPAID	MORTALS	POLIZEI	POUNDAL	ROUGHIE	TOCCATA	VOCALLY
HOTLINE	LOYALLY	MORTICE	POLLACK	POUSSIN	ROUGHLY	TODDLER	VOIVODE
HOTSHOT	LOYALTY	MORTIFY	POLLARD	POVERTY	ROULADE	TOEHOLD	VOLANTE
HOTSPUR	LOZENGE	MORTISE	POLLING	POWDERY	ROULEAU	TOENAIL	VOLAPUK
HOUDINI	MOABITE	MOSELLE	POLLUTE	POWERED	ROUNDED	TOGGERY	VOLCANO
HOUSING	MOANING	MOTHERS	POLONIE	ROADHOG	ROUNDEL	TOLKIEN	VOLTAGE
HOWEVER	MOBSTER	MOTTLED	POLYGON	ROADWAY	ROUNDER	TOLLMAN	VOLTAIC
HOWLING	MOCKERS	MOUFLON	POLYMER	ROAMING	ROUNDLY	TOLSTOY	VOLUBLE
IONESCO	MOCKERY	MOUILLÉ	POLYOMA	ROARING	ROUNDUP	TOLUENE	VOLUBLY
JOBBERY	MOCKING	MOULAGE	POLYPOD	ROASTER	ROUSING	TOMBOLA	VOUCHER
JOBBING	MODERNE	MOULDED	POLYPUS	ROBBERS	ROUTIER	TOMFOOL	VOYAGER
JOBLESS	MODESTY	MOULDER	POMEROL	ROBBERY	ROUTINE	TOMPION	WOLFISH
JOCASTA	MODICUM	MOUNTED	POMEROY	ROBERTS	ROWBOAT	TONETIC	WOLFRAM
JOCULAR	MODISTE	MOUNTIE	POMFRET	ROBESON	ROWDILY	TONGUES	WOMANLY
JOGGING	MODULAR	MOURNER	POMMARD	ROBINIA	ROWLOCK	TONIGHT	WONDERS
JOGTROT	MODULUS	MOVABLE	POMPEII	ROBUSTA	ROYALLY	TONNAGE	WOODCUT
JOHNNIE	MOELLON	NOBBLED	POMPOON	ROCKALL	ROYALLY	TONNEAU	WOODMAN

WOOLLEN	EPICURE	SPINDLY	SQUARED	BRASERO	CRAMPED	CRYPTIC	FREEWAY
WOOMERA	EPIDOTE	SPINNER	SQUARES	BRAVADO	CRAMPON	CRYPTON	FREEZER
WOOSTER	EPIGEAL	SPINNEY	SQUASHY	BRAVELY	CRANACH	CRYSTAL	FREIGHT
WORDILY	EPIGONE	SPINOFF	SQUEAKY	BRAVERY	CRANIAL	DRABBLE	FRESHEN
WORDING	EPIGRAM	SPINOZA	SQUEERS	BRAVURA	CRANIUM	DRACHMA	FRESHER
WORKERS	EPISODE	SPIRITS	SQUEEZE	BRAWLER	CRANMER	DRACULA	FRESHET
WORKING	EPISTLE	SPITTLE	SQUELCH	BRAZIER	CRAPPIE	DRAFTED	FRESHLY
WORKMAN	EPITAPH	SPLASHY	SQUIFFY	BREADED	CRASHES	DRAFTEE	FRETFUL
WORKMEN	EPITAXY	SPLAYED	SQUILLA	BREADTH	CRASSUS	DRAGGLE	FRETSAW
WORKOUT	EPITHET	SPLICED	SQUINCH	BREAKER	CRAVING	DRAGNET	FRETTED
WORKSHY	EPITOME	SPLICER	SQUISHY	BREATHE	CRAWLER	DRAGOON	FRIABLE
WORKTOP	EPIZOON	SPLODGE	ARABIAN	BREEDER	CRAZILY	DRAINED	FRIENDS
WORLDLY	EPSILON	SPLOTCH	ARABICA	BRENDAN	CREATED	DRAPERY	FRIGATE
WORRIED	EPSTEIN	SPLURGE	ARABIZE	BRENNER	CREATOR	DRASTIC	FRILLED
WORRIER	IPOMOEA	SPOILED	ARACHNE	BREVITY	CREEPER	DRAUGHT	FRINGED
WORSHIP	OPACITY	SPOILER	ARAMAIC	BREWERY	CREMATE	DRAWBAR	FRISBEE
WORSTED	OPALINE	SPONDEE	ARBITER	BREWING	CRENATE	DRAWERS	FRISIAN
WOTCHER	OPENING	SPONDYL	ARBUTUS	BRIBERY	CRESTED	DRAWING	FRISSON
WOULDBE	OPERAND	SPONGER	ARCADIA	BRICKIE	CREVICE	DREADED	FRITTER
WOULDNT	OPERANT	SPONSON	ARCHAEA	BRIDGES	CREWCUT	DREAMER	FRIZZLE
WOUNDED	OPERATE	SPONSOR	ARCHAIC	BRIDGET	CREWMAN	DREDGER	FRIZZLY
YOGHURT	OPINION	SPOONER	ARCHERY	BRIDLER	CRICKET	DRESDEN	FROEBEL
YONKERS	OPOSSUM	SPORRAN	ARCHIVE	BRIDLES	CRICKEY	DRESSED	FROGMAN
YORKIST	OPPOSED	SPOTTED	ARCHWAY	BRIEFLY	CRICOID	DRESSER	FRONTAL
YOUNGER	OPPRESS	SPOTTER	ARCUATE	BRIGADE	CRIMEAN	DREYFUS	FROSTED
ZOFFANY	OPTICAL	SPOUSAL	ARDUOUS	BRIGAND	CRIMSON	DRIBBLE	FROWSTY
ZOOLITE	OPTIMAL	SPRAINT	ARETINO	BRIGHAM	CRINKLE	DRIBLET	FRUMPLE
ZOOLOGY	OPTIMUM	SPRAYER	ARIADNE	BRIMFUL	CRINKLY	DRIFTER	GRACCHI
ZOOTOMY	OPULENT	SPRINGE	ARIDITY	BRINDLE	CRINOID	DRINKER	GRACILE
APELIKE	OPUNTIA	SPRINGS	ARIETTA	BRINJAL	CRIPPLE	DRIVERS	GRACKLE
APEPSIA	SPACING	SPRINGY	ARIOSTO	BRIOCHE	CRISPIN	DRIVING	GRADATE
APHAGIA	SPADGER	SPROUTS	ARIZONA	BRISKET	CRITTER	DRIZZLE	GRADELY
APHASIA	SPANDAU	SPURREY	ARMBAND	BRISKLY	CROAKER	DRIZZLY	GRADUAL
APHELIA	SPANDEX	SPURWAY	ARMHOLE	BRISTLE	CROATIA	DROPLET	GRAFTER
APHESIS	SPANGLE	SPUTNIK	ARMORED	BRISTLY	CROCHET	DROPOUT	GRAINED
APHONIA	SPANIEL	SPUTTER	ARMORIC	BRISTOL	CROCKET	DROPPER	GRAINER
APHONIC	SPANISH	SPYHOLE	ARMOURY	BRITAIN	CROESUS	DROSHKY	GRAMMAR
APHOTIC	SPANKER	UPBRAID	ARMREST	BRITISH	CROFTER	DROUGHT	GRAMPUS
APHTHAE	SPANNER	UPGRADE	AROUSAL	BRITONS	CROOKED	DRUGGED	GRANARY
APICIUS	SPARING	UPRAISE	ARRAIGN	BRITTLE	CROONER	DRUGGET	GRANDAD
APLASIA	SPARKLE	UPRIGHT	ARRANGE	BRITZKA	CROPPED	DRUMLIN	GRANDEE
APOCOPE	SPARROW	UPSHOOT	ARRAYED	BRIXTON	CROPPER	DRUMMER	GRANDLY
APOGEAN	SPARTAN	UPSIDES	ARREARS	BROADEN	CROQUET	DRUNKEN	GRANDMA
APOLOGY	SPASTIC	UPSILON	ARRIVAL	BROADLY	CROQUIS	DRYNESS	GRANDPA
APOSTLE	SPATIAL	UPSTAGE	ARRIVED	BROCADE	CROSIER	ERASMUS	GRANITA
APPARAT	SPATTER	UPSTART	ARSENAL	BROILER	CROSSED	ERASURE	GRANITE
APPAREL	SPATULA	UPSTATE	ARSENIC	BROKERS	CROSSLY	ERECTOR	GRANNIE
APPEASE	SPAVINE	UPSURGE	ARTEMIS	BROMATE	CROUTON	EREMITE	GRANOLA
APPLAUD	SPEAKER	UPSWING	ARTEMUS	BROMIDE	CROWBAR	ERINYES	GRANTED
APPLIED	SPECIAL	UPTIGHT	ARTICLE	BROMINE	CROWDED	ERISKAY	GRANTEE
APPOINT	SPECIES	UPWARDS	ARTISAN	BRONCHI	CROWING	ERITREA	GRANULE
APPOSED	SPECIFY	YPSILON	ARTISTE	BRONZED	CROZIER	ERODIUM	GRAPHIC
APPRIZE	SPECKLE	AQUATIC	ARTLESS	BROTHEL	CRUCIAL	EROSION	GRAPHIS
APPROVE	SPECTER	AQUAVIT	ARTWORK	BROTHER	CRUCIFY	EROTICA	GRAPNEL
APRAXIA	SPECTRE	AQUEOUS	ARUNDEL	BROUGHT	CRUDELY	ERRATIC	GRAPPLE
APRICOT	SPELLER	AQUIFER	BRACING	BROWNED	CRUDITY	ERRATUM	GRATIFY
APROPOS	SPENCER	AQUILON	BRACKEN	BROWNIE	CRUELLS	ERUDITE	GRATING
APSIDAL	SPENDER	AQUINAS	BRACKET	BROWSER	CRUELLY	FRAGILE	GRAUPEL
APTERAL	SPENSER	AQUINUS	BRADAWL	BRUISED	CRUELTY	FRAILTY	GRAVITY
APTERYX	SPHENIC	EQUABLE	BRADMAN	BRUISER	CRUISER	FRANCIS	GRAVLAX
APTNESS	SPICATE	EQUABLY	BRAEMAR	BRUSHER	CRUMBLE	FRANKLY	GRAVURE
EPAULET	SPICULA	EQUALLY	BRAHMAN	BRUSQUE	CRUMBLY	FRANTIC	GRAYISH
EPERGNE	SPICULE	EQUATOR	BRAHMIN	BRUTISH	CRUMPET	FRAUGHT	GRAZING
EPHEBUS	SPIDERS	EQUERRY	BRAILLE	CRACKED	CRUMPLE	FRAZZLE	GREASER
EPHEDRA	SPIDERY	EQUINOX	BRAKING	CRACKER	CRUNCHY	FRECKLE	GREATEN
EPHESUS	SPIGNEL	SQUADDY	BRAMBLE	CRACKLE	CRUPPER	FREEBIE	GREATLY
EPHRAIM	SPINACH	SQUALID	BRANDED	CRACKLY	CRUSADE	FREEDOM	GREAVES
EPICARP	SPINATE	SQUALLY	BRANDER	CRAMMED	CRUSHED	FREEMAN	GRECIAN
EPICENE	SPINDLE	SQUALOR	BRANTUB	CRAMMER	CRUSHER	FREESIA	GREENER

GREGORY	ORIFICE	PRIMULA	TRACING	TRISHAW	ASCARID	OSSEOUS	STAINED
GREMLIN	ORIGAMI	PRINCES	TRACKER	TRISMUS	ASCETIC	OSSICLE	STAINER
GRENADA	ORIGINS	PRINTED	TRACTOR	TRISTAN	ASCITES	OSSUARY	STALKED
GRENADE	ORINOCO	PRINTER	TRADEIN	TRITELY	ASCRIBE	OSTEOMA	STALKER
GRENDEL	ORKNEYS	PRITHEE	TRADING	TRITIUM	ASEPTIC	OSTIOLE	STAMINA
GREYISH	ORLANDO	PRIVACY	TRADUCE	TRITOMA	ASEXUAL	OSTRICH	STAMMER
GREYLAG	ORLEANS	PRIVATE	TRAFFIC	TRITONE	ASHAMED	PSALTER	STAMPED
GRIDDLE	OROGENY	PRIVITY	TRAGEDY	TRIUMPH	ASHANTI	PSYCHIC	STAMPER
GRIFFON	ORONTES	PROBAND	TRAILER	TRIVIAL	ASHDOWN	TSARINA	STANDBY
GRIFTER	OROTUND	PROBATE	TRAINED	TRIVIUM	ASHTRAY	TSARIST	STANDIN
GRILLED	ORPHEAN	PROBITY	TRAINEE	TROCHEE	ASIATIC	TSIGANE	STANDUP
GRIMACE	ORPHEUS	PROBLEM	TRAINER	TROCHUS	ASININE	TSIGANY	STANLEY
GRIMOND	ORPHISM	PROCEED	TRAIPSE	TRODDEN	ASKANCE	TSUNAMI	STANNIC
GRIMSBY	ORPHREY	PROCESS	TRAITOR	TROILUS	ASOCIAL	USELESS	STAPLER
GRINDER	ORTOLAN	PROCTOR	TRAMCAR	TROLLEY	ASPASIA	USUALLY	STARCHY
GRISTLE	ORVIETO	PROCURE	TRAMMEL	TROLLOP	ASPERGE	USURPER	STARDOM
GRISTLY	PRAETOR	PRODIGY	TRAMPLE	TROOPER	ASPHALT	ATACTIC	STARETS
GRIZZLE	PRAIRIE	PRODUCE	TRAMWAY	TROPHIC	ASPIRIN	ATAGHAN	STARING
GRIZZLY	PRALINE	PRODUCT	TRANCHE	TROPICS	ASQUITH	ATARAXY	STARKLY
GROCERS	PRATTLE	PROFANE	TRANSIT	TROPISM	ASSAULT	ATAVISM	STARLET
GROCERY	PRAYING	PROFESS	TRANSOM	TROTSKY	ASSEGAI	ATELIER	STARLIT
GROCKLE	PREBEND	PROFFER	TRANTER	TROTTER	ASSIEGE	ATHEISM	STARTED
GROGRAM	PRECAST	PROFILE	TRAPEZE	TROUBLE	ASSISTS	ATHEIST	STARTER
GROINED	PRECEDE	PROFITS	TRAPPED	TROUNCE	ASSIZES	ATHIRST	STARTLE
GROLIER	PRECEPT	PROFUSE	TRAPPER	TROUPER	ASSUAGE	ATHLETE	STARVED
GROMMET	PRECISE	PROGENY	TRAVAIL	TROUSER	ASSUMED	ATHWART	STATELY
GROOVED	PREDATE	PROGRAM	TRAWLER	TRUANCY	ASSURED	ATINGLE	STATICS
GROPIUS	PREDIAL	PROJECT	TREACLE	TRUCIAL	ASSYRIA	ATISHOO	STATION
GROSSLY	PREDICT	PROLONG	TREACLY	TRUCKER	ASTARTE	ATOMIST	STATIST
GROTIUS	PREDOOM	PROMISE	TREADLE	TRUCKLE	ASTILBE	ATOMIZE	STATURE
GROUCHO	PREEMPT	PROMOTE	TREASON	TRUDGEN	ASTOUND	ATROPHY	STATUTE
GROUCHY	PREFACE	PRONAOS	TREATED	TRUFFLE	ASTRIDE	ATROPOS	STAUNCH
GROUNDS	PREFECT	PRONATE	TREETOP	TRUMEAU	ASUNDER	ATTABOY	STAYING
GROUPER	PREHEAT	PRONGED	TREFOIL	TRUMPET	CSARDAS	ATTACHE	STEALTH
GROUPIE	PRELACY	PRONOUN	TREKKER	TRUNDLE	ESCALOP	ATTAINT	STEAMED
GROUSER	PRELATE	PROPANE	TRELLIS	TRUSTEE	ESCAPEE	ATTEMPT	STEAMER
GROWING	PRELIMS	PROPEND	TREMBLE	TRYPSIN	ESCHEAT	ATTICUS	STEARIC
GROWLER	PRELUDE	PROPHET	TREMBLY	URAEMIA	ESPARTO	ATTIRED	STEARIN
GROWNUP	PREMIER	PROPOSE	TREMOLO	URALITE	ESPOUSE	ATTRACT	STEEPEN
GRUFFLY	PREMISE	PROSAIC	TREPANG	URANIAN	ESQUIRE	ETAGÈRE	STEEPLE
GRUMBLE	PREMISS	PROSODY	TRESSES	URANISM	ESSENCE	ETAPLES	STEEPLY
GRUMMET	PREMIUM	PROSPER	TRESTLE	URANITE	ESSENES	ETCHING	STEERER
GRUYÈRE	PREPAID	PROTEAN	TRIANON	URANIUM	ESTIVAL	ETERNAL	STELLAR
GRYPHON	PREPARE	PROTECT	TRIATIC	URETHRA	ESTOVER	ETESIAN	STEMMED
IRANIAN	PREPUCE	PROTEGE	TRIBUNE	URGENCY	ESTREAT	ETHANOL	STENCIL
IRELAND	PREQUEL	PROTEIN	TRIBUTE	URINARY	ESTUARY	ETHICAL	STENGAH
IRIDISE	PRESAGE	PROTEST	TRICEPS	URINATE	ISADORA	ETHMOID	STENGUN
IRIDIUM	PRESENT	PROTEUS	TRICKLE	UROLITH	ISCHIUM	ETONIAN	STENTOR
IRKSOME	PRESIDE	PROTIST	TRIDENT	URUGUAY	ISHMAEL	ETRURIA	STEPHEN
IRONING	PRESSED	PROUDER	TRIESTE	WRANGLE	ISLAMIC	ETTRICK	STEPNEY
KREMLIN	PRESUME	PROUDIE	TRIFFID	WRAPPED	ISLANDS	ITALIAN	STEPSON
KRISHNA	PRETEND	PROUDLY	TRIFLER	WRAPPER	ISMAILI	ITCHING	STERILE
KRYPTON	PRETEXT	PROVERB	TRIFLES	WRAUGHT	ISOBASE	ITEMIZE	STERNAL
ORACLES	PRETZEL	PROVIDE	TRIGGER	WREATHE	ISODORE	ITERATE	STERNLY
ORANGES	PREVAIL	PROVING	TRILLED	WRECKED	ISOGRAM	OTALGIA	STERNUM
ORATION	PREVENT	PROVISO	TRILLER	WRECKER	ISOHYET	OTHELLO	STEROID
ORATORY	PREVIEW	PROVOKE	TRILOGY	WRESTLE	ISOLATE	OTRANTO	STETSON
ORBITAL	PREZZIE	PROVOST	TRIMMER	WRIGGLE	ISOMERE	OTTOMAN	STEVENS
ORCHARD	PRIAPUS	PROWESS	TRINGLE	WRINGER	ISOSPIN	PTERYLA	STEWARD
ORCINOL	PRICKED	PROWLER	TRINITY	WRINKLE	ISOTONE	PTOLEMY	STEWING
ORDERED	PRICKER	PROXIMO	TRINKET	WRINKLY	ISOTOPE	PTYALIN	STICKER
ORDERLY	PRICKLE	PRUDENT	TRIPLET	WRITEUP	ISRAELI	STABILE	STICKLE
ORDINAL	PRICKLY	PRUDISH	TRIPLEX	WRITING	ISSUANT	STABLES	STIFFEN
OREGANO	PRIESTS	PRURIGO	TRIPODY	WRITTEN	ISTHMUS	STACHYS	STIFFLY
ORESTES	PRIMACY	PRUSSIC	TRIPOLI	WRONGLY	OSBORNE	STADDLE	STILTED
ORGANIC	PRIMARY	PRYTHEE	TRIPPER	WROUGHT	OSCULUM	STADIUM	STILTON
ORGANUM	PRIMATE	SRAVANA	TRIPSIS	WRYBILL	OSMANLI	STAFFER	STINGER
ORGANZA	PRIMEUR	TRACERY	TRIREME	WRYNECK	OSMOSIS	STAGGER	STINKER
ORGIAST	PRIMING	TRACHEA	TRISECT	WRYNOSE	OSSELET	STAGING	STIPEND

STIPPLE	AUBERGE	BURNELL	DUBIOUS	GUARANI	JUVENAL	NULLITY	PURITAN
STIRFRY	AUCTION	BURNHAM	DUBNIUM	GUARDED	KUBELIK	NUMBERS	PURLIEU
STIRPES	AUDIBLE	BURNING	DUCHESS	GUBBINS	KUFIYAH	NUMBLES	PURLINE
STIRRED	AUDIBLY	BURNISH	DUCKING	GUDGEON	KUMQUAT	NUMERAL	PURLOIN
STIRRUP	AUDITOR	BURNOUS	DUCTILE	GUIDING	KURHAUS	NUMERIC	PURPORT
STOICAL	AUDUBON	BURNOUT	DUDGEON	GUIGNOL	KURSAAL	NUMMARY	PURPOSE
STOLLEN	AUGMENT	BURSARY	DUKEDOM	GUILDER	LUCARNE	NUNLIKE	PURPURA
STOMACH	AUGUSTA	BURSTER	DULLARD	GUINEAN	LUCERNE	NUNNERY	PURSUER
STONILY	AUGUSTE	BURUNDI	DUMPISH	GUINEAS	LUCIDLY	NUPTIAL	PURSUIT
STONKER	AURALLY	BUSHIDO	DUNCIAD	GUMBOIL	LUCIFER	NUREYEV	PURVIEW
STOPGAP	AUREATE	BUSHMAN	DUNEDIN	GUMBOOT	LUCKILY	NURSERY	PUSHING
STOPPED	AURELIA	BUSHMEN	DUNGEON	GUMDROP	LUDDITE	NURSING	PUSHKIN
STOPPER	AUREOLA	BUSKINS	DUNKIRK	GUMSHOE	LUDGATE	NURTURE	PUSTULE
STORAGE	AUREOLE	BUSSING	DUNNAGE	GUNBOAT	LUGGAGE	NUTCASE	PUTREFY
STORIED	AURICLE	BUSTARD	DUNNOCK	GUNFIRE	LUGHOLE	NUTLIKE	PUTTEES
STORIES	AUROCHS	BUSTLER	DUNSTAN	GUNNERA	LUGSAIL	NUTMEAT	PUTTING
STOUTLY	AUSLESE	BUSTLES	DUOPOLY	GUNNERY	LUGWORM	NUTTING	PUTTOCK
STRAITS	AUSTERE	BUTANAL	DURABLE	GUNPLAY	LULLABY	OUSTITI	PUZZLED
STRANGE	AUSTRAL	BUTANOL	DURABLY	GUNROOM	LUMBAGO	OUTBACK	PUZZLER
STRATUM	AUSTRIA	BUTCHER	DURAMEN	GUNSHOT	LUMPISH	OUTCAST	QUADRAT
STRATUS	AUTARKY	BUTTERY	DURRELL	GUNWALE	LUMPKIN	OUTCOME	QUAKING
STRAUSS	AUTOCUE	BUTTONS	DUSTBIN	GUSHING	LUNATIC	OUTCROP	QUALIFY
STREAKY	AUTOMAT	BUZZARD	DUSTING	GUTLESS	LUNETTE	OUTDARE	QUALITY
STRETCH	AUTOPSY	CUBICLE	DUSTMAN	GUTTATE	LURCHER	OUTDOOR	QUANTUM
STREWTH	BUBBLES	CUCKING	DUSTPAN	GUYROPE	LURIDLY	OUTFACE	QUARREL
STRIATE	BUBONIC	CUCKOLD	DUTIFUL	GUZZLER	LURKING	OUTFALL	QUARTAN
STRIDES	BUCKETS	CUIRASS	EUGENIA	HUBBARD	LUSTFUL	OUTFLOW	QUARTER
STRIDOR	BUCKEYE	CUISINE	EUGENIC	HULKING	LUSTILY	OUTGROW	QUARTET
STRIGIL	BUCKLER	CULPRIT	EUGENIE	HUMANLY	LUSTRUM	OUTLAST	QUARTIC
STRIKER	BUCKRAM	CULTURE	EULALIE	HUMBLES	LUTYENS	OUTLIER	QUASSIA
STRINGS	BUCOLIC	CULVERT	EUPEPSY	HUMDRUM	MUDDLED	OUTLINE	QUECHUA
STRINGY	BUDDING	CUMBRIA	EUPHONY	HUMERUS	MUDEJAR	OUTLIVE	QUEENLY
STRIPED	BUFFALO	CUMSHAW	EUSTACE	HUMIDOR	MUDFLAP	OUTLOOK	QUEERER
STRIPER	BUFFOON	CUMULUS	EUTERPE	HUMMING	MUDLARK	OUTPOST	QUENTIN
STRIPES	BUGABOO	CUNNING	FUCHSIA	HUMMOCK	MUDPACK	OUTPOUR	QUERCUS
STROBIC	BUGBEAR	CUPROUS	FUCHSIN	HUNCHED	MUEZZIN	OUTRAGE	QUESTER
STROPHE	BUGGING	CURABLE	FUDDLED	HUNDRED	MUFFLED	OUTRANK	QUETZAL
STROPPY	BUGGINS	CURACAO	FULCRUM	HUNGARY	MUFFLER	OUTSHOT	QUIBBLE
STRUDEL	BUGLOSS	CURATOR	FULFILL	HUNKERS	MUGGING	OUTSIDE	QUICHUA
STUBBLE	BUILDER	CURCUMA	FULGENT	HUNTING	MUGWORT	OUTSIZE	QUICKEN
STUBBLY	BULBOUS	CURDLED	FULLERS	HURDLER	MUGWUMP	OUTSPAN	QUICKER
STUDDED	BULGHUR	CURETTE	FULSOME	HURDLES	MULATTO	OUTSTAY	QUICKIE
STUDENT	BULGING	CURIOUS	FUMETTE	HURLING	MULLEIN	OUTTURN	QUICKLY
STUDIED	BULIMIA	CURLING	FUNCHAL	HURRIED	MULLION	OUTVOTE	QUIETEN
STUFFED	BULLACE	CURRAGH	FUNDING	HURTFUL	MUMMERS	OUTWARD	QUIETLY
STUMBLE	BULLDOG	CURRANT	FUNERAL	HUSBAND	MUMMERY	OUTWEAR	QUIETUS
STUMPED	BULLETS	CURRENT	FUNFAIR	HUSKILY	MUMMIFY	OUTWORK	QUILTED
STUNNER	BULLION	CURRIED	FUNGOID	HUSSARS	MUNDANE	OUTWORN	QUILTER
STUNTED	BULLISH	CURSIVE	FUNGOUS	HUSSITE	MUNSTER	PUBERAL	QUINCHE
STUPEFY	BULLOCK	CURSORY	FUNNILY	HUSTLER	MUNTJAC	PUBERTY	QUININE
STURMER	BULLPEN	CURTAIL	FURBISH	JUBILEE	MURAENA	PUBLISH	QUINONE
STUTTER	BULRUSH	CURTAIN	FURCATE	JUDAISM	MURIATE	PUCCINI	QUINTAL
STYGIAN	BULWARK	CURTSEY	FURIOUS	JUGGINS	MURILLO	PUCELLE	QUINTAN
STYLING	BUMBOAT	CUSHION	FURLONG	JUGGLER	MURRAIN	PUCKISH	QUINTET
STYLISH	BUMMALO	CUSTARD	FURNACE	JUGLANS	MUSCOID	PUDDING	QUITTER
STYLIST	BUMPKIN	CUSTODY	FURNISH	JUGULAR	MUSCOVY	PUERILE	QUIXOTE
STYLITE	BUNDOOK	CUSTOMS	FURRIER	JUJITSU	MUSETTE	PUGWASH	QUONDAM
STYLIZE	BUNGLER	CUTAWAY	FURTHER	JUKEBOX	MUSICAL	PULLMAN	QUONSET
STYPTIC	BUNTING	CUTBACK	FURTIVE	JUMBLED	MUSKRAT	PULSATE	QUORATE
UTENSIL	BUOYANT	CUTICLE	FUSEBOX	JUMBLES	MUSSELS	PULSING	RUBBERS
UTERINE	BURBAGE	CUTLASS	FUSIBLE	JUMPING	MUSTANG	PUMPKIN	RUBBERY
UTILITY	BURDOCK	CUTLERY	FUSILLI	JUNIPER	MUSTARD	PUNCHED	RUBBING
UTILIZE	BURETTE	CUTTERS	FUSSILY	JUPITER	MUTABLE	PUNCHER	RUBBISH
UTOPIAN	BURGEON	CUTTING	FUSTIAN	JURYBOX	MUTAGEN	PUNGENT	RUBELLA
UTRECHT	BURGESS	CUTWORM	FUTTOCK	JURYMAN	NUCLEAR	PUNJABI	RUBEOLA
UTRICLE	BURGHER	CUVETTE	FUTURES	JUSSIVE	NUCLEIC	PUNSTER	RUBICON
UTRILLO	BURGLAR	DUALITY	GUANACO	JUSTICE	NUCLEUS	PUNTING	RUDERAL
UTTERLY	BURKINA	DUBBING	GUANINE	JUSTIFY	NUCLIDE	PURBECK	RUDOLPH
YTTRIUM	BURMESE	DUBIETY	GUARANA	JUTLAND	NULLIFY	PURCELL	RUFFIAN

RUFFLED	SUNBEAM	AVARICE	SWIFTER	OXIDIZE	PYRITES	ANALYST	BRAZIER
RUFFLER	SUNBURN	AVEBURY	SWIFTLY	OXONIAN	PYROSIS	ANALYZE	CHABLIS
RUINOUS	SUNDECK	AVENGER	SWIMMER	UXORIAL	PYRRHIC	ANANIAS	CHAFING
RUMBLER	SUNDIAL	AVERAGE	SWINDLE	BYRONIC	SYCORAX	ANATOLE	CHAGALL
RUMMAGE	SUNDOWN	AVESTAN	SWINGER	CYANIDE	SYCOSIS	ANATOMY	CHAGRIN
RUMORED	SUNLAMP	AVIATOR	SWINGLE	CYCLING	SYMPTOM	ARABIAN	CHAINED
RUMPLED	SUNLESS	AVIDITY	SWITHIN	CYCLIST	SYNAPSE	ARABICA	CHALDEE
RUMPOLE	SUNNILY	AVIGNON	SWIZZLE	CYCLONE	SYNAXIS	ARABIZE	CHALICE
RUNAWAY	SUNNITE	AVOCADO	SWOLLEN	CYCLOPS	SYNCOPE	ARACHNE	CHALKER
RUNCORN	SUNRISE	AVOIDER	TWADDLE	CYMBALS	SYNERGY	ARAMAIC	CHALONE
RUNDOWN	SUNROOF	DVORNIK	TWEEDLE	CYNICAL	SYNONYM	ATACTIC	CHAMBER
RUNNERS	SUNSPOT	EVACUEE	TWEETER	CYNTHIA	SYNOVIA	ATAGHAN	CHAMBRÉ
RUNNING	SUNTRAP	EVANDER	TWELFTH	CYPRESS	SYRINGA	ATARAXY	CHAMFER
RUNNION	SUPPORT	EVASION	TWIDDLE	CYPRIOT	SYRINGE	ATAVISM	CHAMOIS
RUPTURE	SUPPOSE	EVASIVE	TWIDDLY	CYSTOID	SYSTOLE	AVARICE	CHAMPAK
RUSALKA	SUPREME	EVENING	TWIGGER	CYTISUS	TYLOSIS	BEACHED	CHANCEL
RUSHING	SUPREMO	EVENTER	TWINKLE	DYARCHY	TYMPANO	BEACHES	CHANCRE
RUSSELL	SURCOAT	EVEREST	TWINSET	DYNAMIC	TYMPANY	BEADING	CHANGED
RUSSIAN	SURDITY	EVIDENT	TWISTED	DYNASTY	TYNWALD	BEAMING	CHANGES
RUSTLER	SURFACE	IVANHOE	TWISTER	EYEBALL	TYPHOID	BEANBAG	CHANNEL
RUTHENE	SURFEIT	IVORIAN	TWITCHY	EYEBATH	TYPHOON	BEARDED	CHANSON
RUTTING	SURFING	IVORIEN	TWITTER	EYEBROW	TYPICAL	BEARHUG	CHANTER
SUAVELY	SURGEON	IVRESSE	TWOFOLD	EYEHOLE	TYRANNY	BEARING	CHAOTIC
SUAVITY	SURGERY	OVARIAN	TWOSOME	EYELASH	WYOMING	BEARISH	CHAPATI
SUBADAR	SURINAM	OVATION	TWOSTEP	EYELESS	WYSIWYG	BEASTLY	CHAPEAU
SUBAQUA	SURMISE	OVERACT	TWOTIME	EYELIDS	ZYGOSIS	BEATIFY	CHAPLET
SUBATOM	SURNAME	OVERALL	AXILLAR	EYESHOT	ZYMOGEN	BEATING	CHAPMAN
SUBDUCT	SURPASS	OVERARM	AXOLOTL	EYESORE	ZYMOSIS	BEATLES	CHAPPED
SUBDUED	SURPLUS	OVERAWE	EXACTLY	EYESPOT	ZYMURGY	BEATNIK	CHAPTER
SUBEDAR	SURREAL	OVERBID	EXALTED	EYEWASH	AZIMUTH	BIAFRAN	CHARADE
SUBEDIT	SURVIVE	OVERDUE	EXAMINE	GYMNAST	AZURITE	BIASSED	CHARDIN
SUBFUSC	SUSANNA	OVEREAT	EXAMPLE	GYMSLIP	AZYGOUS	BLABBER	CHARGED
SUBJECT	SUSPECT	OVERFED	EXCERPT	HYALINE	EZEKIEL	BLACKEN	CHARGER
SUBJOIN	SUSPEND	OVERLAP	EXCITED	HYALOID	TZADDIK	BLADDER	CHARGES
SUBLIME	SUSTAIN	OVERLAY	EXCLAIM	HYDATID	TZARINA	BLANDLY	CHARIOT
SUBSIDE	SUZETTE	OVERLIE	EXCLUDE	HYDRANT		BLANKET	CHARITY
SUBSIDY	TUATARA	OVERMAN	EXCRETA	HYDRATE	**7:3**	BLANKLY	CHARLES
SUBSIST	TUBULAR	OVERPAY	EXCRETE	HYGIENE	ABALONE	BLASTED	CHARLEY
SUBSOIL	TUBULIN	OVERRUN	EXECUTE	HYMNIST	ABANDON	BLASTER	CHARMED
SUBSUME	TUESDAY	OVERSEE	EXEGETE	HYMNODY	ABASHED	BLATANT	CHARMER
SUBTEEN	TUGBOAT	OVERTAX	EXEMPLA	HYPOGEA	ABATTIS	BLATHER	CHARNEL
SUBTEND	TUITION	OVICIDE	EXHAUST	HYPONYM	ABAXIAL	BLATTER	CHARPOY
SUBVERT	TUMBLER	OVIDUCT	EXHEDRA	HYPOXIA	ACADEME	BLAZERS	CHARRED
SUBZERO	TUMBREL	OVULATE	EXHIBIT	KYANITE	ACADEMY	BLAZING	CHARTER
SUCCEED	TUMBRIL	AWESOME	EXIGENT	LYCHNIS	ACADIAN	BOARDER	CHASING
SUCCESS	TUMULUS	AWFULLY	EXISTED	LYMNAEA	ACARIDA	BOASTER	CHASSIS
SUCCOUR	TUNABLE	AWKWARD	EXITING	LYNCHET	ACAUDAL	BOATING	CHASTEN
SUCCUMB	TUNEFUL	DWELLER	EXOCARP	LYRICAL	ADAMANT	BOATMAN	CHATEAU
SUCROSE	TUNICLE	DWINDLE	EXOGAMY	MYALGIA	ADAMITE	BRACING	CHATHAM
SUCTION	TUNISIA	GWYNETH	EXPANSE	MYANMAR	ADAPTER	BRACKEN	CHATTEL
SUDETEN	TURBARY	RWANDAN	EXPENSE	MYCELLA	ADAPTOR	BRACKET	CHATTER
SUFFETE	TURBINE	SWADDLE	EXPIATE	MYCENAE	ADAXIAL	BRADAWL	CHAUCER
SUFFICE	TURENNE	SWAGGER	EXPIRED	MYCETES	AGAINST	BRADMAN	CHAYOTE
SUFFOLK	TURGENT	SWAGMAN	EXPLAIN	MYELINE	ALABAMA	BRAEMAR	CLACHAN
SUFFUSE	TURKISH	SWAHILI	EXPLODE	MYELOID	ALADDIN	BRAHMAN	CLAMBER
SUGARED	TURMOIL	SWALLOW	EXPLOIT	MYELOMA	ALAMEIN	BRAHMIN	CLAMOUR
SUGGEST	TURNERY	SWANSEA	EXPLORE	MYIASIS	ALAMODE	BRAILLE	CLAMPER
SUICIDE	TURNING	SWAPPED	EXPOSED	MYNHEER	ALANINE	BRAKING	CLANGER
SUKKOTH	TURNKEY	SWARTHY	EXPOUND	MYRINGA	ALARMED	BRAMBLE	CLAPPER
SULFATE	TURNOUT	SWAYING	EXPRESS	MYSTERY	ALASKAN	BRANDED	CLARIFY
SULKILY	TURPETH	SWEATED	EXPUNGE	MYSTIFY	AMALGAM	BRANDER	CLARION
SULLAGE	TUSCANY	SWEATER	EXTINCT	NYMPHET	AMANITA	BRANTUB	CLARITY
SULPHUR	TUSSOCK	SWEDISH	EXTRACT	NYNORSK	AMATEUR	BRASERO	CLASSIC
SULTANA	TUSSORE	SWEEPER	EXTREME	PYAEMIA	AMATORY	BRAVADO	CLASTIC
SUMATRA	TUTELAR	SWEETEN	EXTRUDE	PYJAMAS	AMAZING	BRAVELY	CLATTER
SUMMARY	VULGATE	SWEETIE	EXUDATE	PYLORUS	ANAEMIA	BRAVERY	CLAVATE
SUMMERY	VULPINE	SWEETLY	OXALATE	PYRAMID	ANAEMIC	BRAVURA	COARSEN
SUMMING	VULTURE	SWELTER	OXBLOOD	PYRETIC	ANAGRAM	BRAWLER	COASTAL
SUMMONS	YUCATAN	SWIDDEN	OXIDASE	PYREXIA	ANALOGY	BRAWLER	COASTER

COATING	ETAPLES	GRANITE	LEANING	PLAUTUS	SEAPORT	SPANKER	TEAROOM
COAXIAL	EVACUEE	GRANNIE	LEAPING	PLAYBOY	SEARING	SPANNER	TEASHOP
CRACKED	EVANDER	GRANOLA	LEARNED	PLAYERS	SEASICK	SPARING	TEASING
CRACKER	EVASION	GRANTED	LEARNER	PLAYFUL	SEASIDE	SPARKLE	TEATIME
CRACKLE	EVASIVE	GRANTEE	LEASING	PLAYING	SEATING	SPARROW	THALLUS
CRACKLY	EXACTLY	GRANULE	LEASOWE	PLAYLET	SEATTLE	SPARTAN	TOASTED
CRAMMED	EXALTED	GRAPHIC	LEATHER	PLAYOFF	SEAWALL	SPASTIC	TOASTER
CRAMMER	EXAMINE	GRAPHIS	LEAVING	PLAYPEN	SEAWEED	SPATIAL	TRACERY
CRAMPED	EXAMPLE	GRAPNEL	LIAISON	POACHER	SHACKLE	SPATTER	TRACHEA
CRAMPON	FEARFUL	GRAPPLE	MEACOCK	PRAETOR	SHADING	SPATULA	TRACING
CRANACH	FEATHER	GRATIFY	MEANDER	PRAIRIE	SHADOOF	SPAVINE	TRACKER
CRANIAL	FEATURE	GRATING	MEANING	PRALINE	SHADOWY	SRAVANA	TRACTOR
CRANIUM	FIANCÉE	GRAUPEL	MEASLES	PRATTLE	SHAGGED	STABILE	TRADEIN
CRANMER	FLACCID	GRAVITY	MEASURE	PRAYING	SHAKERS	STABLES	TRADING
CRAPPIE	FLAGDAY	GRAVLAX	MIASMIC	PSALTER	SHAKEUP	STACHYS	TRADUCE
CRASHES	FLAMING	GRAVURE	MOABITE	PYAEMIA	SHAKILY	STADDLE	TRAFFIC
CRASSUS	FLANKER	GRAYISH	MOANING	QUADRAT	SHAKING	STADIUM	TRAGEDY
CRAVING	FLANNEL	GRAZING	MYALGIA	QUAKING	SHALLOT	STAFFER	TRAILER
CRAWLER	FLAPPED	GUANACO	MYANMAR	QUALIFY	SHALLOW	STAGGER	TRAINED
CRAZILY	FLAPPER	GUANINE	NEAREST	QUALITY	SHAMBLE	STAGING	TRAINEE
CSARDAS	FLAREUP	GUARANA	NEARING	QUANTUM	SHAMPOO	STAINED	TRAINER
CYANIDE	FLASHER	GUARANI	NIAGARA	QUARREL	SHANNON	STAINER	TRAIPSE
DEADEYE	FLATCAR	GUARDED	OBADIAH	QUARTAN	SHAPELY	STALKED	TRAITOR
DEADPAN	FLATLET	HEADING	OCARINA	QUARTER	SHAPING	STALKER	TRAMCAR
DEADSET	FLATTEN	HEADMAN	ODALISK	QUARTET	SHARIAH	STAMINA	TRAMMEL
DEALING	FLATTER	HEADSET	ONANISM	QUARTIC	SHARING	STAMMER	TRAMPLE
DEANERY	FLAUNCH	HEADWAY	OPACITY	QUASSIA	SHARPEN	STAMPED	TRAMWAY
DEAREST	FLAVOUR	HEALING	OPALINE	REACTOR	SHARPER	STAMPER	TRANCHE
DEATHLY	FRAGILE	HEALTHY	ORACLES	READILY	SHARPLY	STANDBY	TRANSIT
DIABOLO	FRAILTY	HEARING	ORANGES	READING	SHASTRI	STANDIN	TRANSOM
DIAGRAM	FRANCIS	HEARKEN	ORATION	REAGENT	SHATTER	STANDUP	TRANTER
DIALECT	FRANKLY	HEARSAY	ORATORY	REALGAR	SHAVING	STANLEY	TRAPEZE
DIALING	FRANTIC	HEARTEN	OTALGIA	REALIGN	SHAWWAL	STANNIC	TRAPPED
DIALYSE	FRAUGHT	HEATHEN	OVARIAN	REALISM	SIAMESE	STAPLER	TRAPPER
DIAMINE	FRAZZLE	HEATHER	OVATION	REALIST	SJAMBOK	STARCHY	TRAVAIL
DIAMOND	GEARBOX	HEATING	OXALATE	REALITY	SKATING	STARDOM	TRAWLER
DIAPSID	GEARING	HEAVENS	PEACHUM	REALIZE	SLACKEN	STARETS	TSARINA
DIARCHY	GHASTLY	HEAVIER	PEACOCK	REALTOR	SLACKER	STARING	TSARIST
DIARIST	GLACIAL	HEAVILY	PEANUTS	REARING	SLACKLY	STARKLY	TUATARA
DRABBLE	GLACIER	HOARDER	PEARLIE	REAUMUR	SLAMMER	STARLET	TWADDLE
DRACHMA	GLADDEN	HYALINE	PEASANT	ROADHOG	SLANDER	STARLIT	TZADDIK
DRACULA	GLAMOUR	HYALOID	PHAETON	ROADWAY	SLAPPER	STARTED	TZARINA
DRAFTED	GLARING	IMAGERY	PHALANX	ROAMING	SLASHED	STARTER	UGANDAN
DRAFTEE	GLASGOW	IMAGINE	PHALLIC	ROARING	SLATTED	STARTLE	UNAIDED
DRAGGLE	GLASSES	IMAGING	PHALLUS	ROASTER	SLAVERY	STARVED	UNAIRED
DRAGNET	GLAZIER	IMAGISM	PHANTOM	RWANDAN	SLAVISH	STATELY	UNALIKE
DRAGOON	GLAZING	IMAGIST	PHARAOH	SCABIES	SLAYING	STATICS	UNALIVE
DRAINED	GNARLED	INANITY	PHARYNX	SCAFELL	SMACKER	STATION	UNARMED
DRAPERY	GNATHIC	IRANIAN	PIANIST	SCAGLIA	SMALLER	STATIST	UNASKED
DRASTIC	GNAWING	ISADORA	PIANOLA	SCALENE	SMARTEN	STATURE	UNAWARE
DRAUGHT	GOAHEAD	ITALIAN	PIASTRE	SCALLOP	SMARTIE	STATUTE	URAEMIA
DRAWBAR	GRACCHI	IVANHOE	PLACARD	SCALPEL	SMARTLY	STAUNCH	URALITE
DRAWERS	GRACILE	JEALOUS	PLACATE	SCALPER	SMASHED	STAYING	URANIAN
DRAWING	GRACKLE	KEARTON	PLACEBO	SCAMBLE	SMASHER	SUAVELY	URANISM
DUALITY	GRADATE	KHALIFA	PLACING	SCAMPER	SMATTER	SUAVITY	URANITE
DYARCHY	GRADELY	KHAMSIN	PLAINLY	SCANDAL	SNAFFLE	SWADDLE	URANIUM
EDAPHIC	GRADUAL	KHANATE	PLANNED	SCANNER	SNAPPER	SWAGGER	VIADUCT
EGALITY	GRAFTER	KLAVIER	PLANNER	SCAPULA	SNARLER	SWAGMAN	WEAKEST
ELAMITE	GRAINED	KNACKER	PLANTAR	SCARIFY	SNARLUP	SWAHILI	WEALDEN
ELASTIC	GRAINER	KNAPPER	PLANTED	SCARING	SOAKING	SWALLOW	WEALTHY
ELASTIN	GRAMMAR	KNAVERY	PLANTER	SCARLET	SOAPBOX	SWANSEA	WEAPONS
ELATION	GRAMPUS	KYANITE	PLANURY	SCARPER	SOARING	SWAPPED	WEARILY
EMANATE	GRANARY	LEACOCK	PLASMIN	SCATTER	SPACING	SWARTHY	WEARING
ENACTOR	GRANDAD	LEADERS	PLASTER	SEABIRD	SPADGER	SWAYING	WEATHER
ENAMOUR	GRANDEE	LEADING	PLASTIC	SEAFOOD	SPANDAU	TEACAKE	WEAVING
EPAULET	GRANDLY	LEAFLET	PLATEAU	SEAGULL	SPANDEX	TEACHER	WHACKED
ERASMUS	GRANDMA	LEAGUER	PLATOON	SEALANT	SPANGLE	TEALEAF	WHACKER
ERASURE	GRANDPA	LEAKAGE	PLATTER	SEALINK	SPANIEL	TEARFUL	WHALING
ETAGÈRE	GRANITA	LEANDER	PLAUDIT	SEALION	SPANISH	TEARING	WHARTON

WHATNOT	GABBLER	RUBBING	ANCIENT	ECCRINE	LACTOSE	PICARDY	SUCCUMB
WHATSIT	GABELLE	RUBBISH	ARCADIA	ENCHANT	LACUNAE	PICASSO	SUCROSE
WRANGLE	GABFEST	RUBELLA	ARCHAEA	ENCLASP	LECHERY	PICCOLO	SUCTION
WRAPPED	GABRIEL	RUBEOLA	ARCHAIC	ENCLAVE	LECTERN	PICKAXE	SYCORAX
WRAPPER	GIBBONS	RUBICON	ARCHERY	ENCLOSE	LECTURE	PICKING	SYCOSIS
WRAUGHT	GIBBOUS	SABAEAN	ARCHIVE	ENCRUST	LICENCE	PICKLED	TACHISM
ZEALAND	GIBLETS	SABAOTH	ARCHWAY	ESCALOP	LICENSE	PICKLER	TACITLY
ZEALOUS	GOBBLER	SABAYON	ARCUATE	ESCAPEE	LICKING	PICOTEE	TACITUS
ABBASID	GOBELIN	SABBATH	ASCARID	ESCHEAT	LOCALLY	PICQUET	TACKLER
ALBANIA	GUBBINS	SABRINA	ASCETIC	ETCHING	LOCKJAW	PICTURE	TACTFUL
ALBENIZ	HABITAT	SIBLING	ASCITES	EXCERPT	LOCKNUT	POCHARD	TACTICS
ALBERGO	HEBRAIC	SOBERLY	ASCRIBE	EXCITED	LOCKOUT	POCHOIR	TACTILE
ALBERTA	HEBREWS	SUBADAR	AUCTION	EXCLAIM	LOCUSTS	PUCCINI	TICKING
ALBERTI	HIBACHI	SUBAQUA	BACARDI	EXCLUDE	LUCARNE	PUCELLE	TICKLER
ALBUMEN	HOBNAIL	SUBATOM	BACCHIC	EXCRETA	LUCERNE	PUCKISH	TOCCATA
ALBUMIN	HOBSONS	SUBDUCT	BACCHUS	EXCRETE	LUCIDLY	RACCOON	UCCELLO
AMBAGES	HUBBARD	SUBDUED	BACILLI	FACETED	LUCIFER	RACEMIC	UNCANNY
AMBIENT	INBOARD	SUBEDAR	BACKING	FACTION	LUCKILY	RACHIAL	UNCARED
AMBOYNA	INBUILT	SUBEDIT	BACKLOG	FACTOID	LYCHNIS	RACHMAN	UNCINUS
AMBROSE	INBURST	SUBFUSC	BACKSET	FACTORS	MACABRE	RACKETS	UNCIVIL
ARBITER	JOBBERY	SUBJECT	BECAUSE	FACTORY	MACADAM	RACKETY	UNCLASP
ARBUTUS	JOBBING	SUBJOIN	BECKETT	FACTUAL	MACAQUE	RACKING	UNCLEAN
AUBERGE	JOBLESS	SUBLIME	BICYCLE	FACULTY	MACBETH	RACQUET	UNCLEAR
BABBITT	JUBILEE	SUBSIDE	BUCKETS	FICTION	MACEDON	RECEIPT	UNCOUTH
BABBLER	KIBBUTZ	SUBSIDY	BUCKEYE	FUCHSIA	MACHETE	RECEIVE	UNCOVER
BABOOSH	KUBELIK	SUBSIST	BUCKLER	FUCHSIN	MACHINE	RECITAL	UNCTION
BABYISH	LABIATE	SUBSOIL	BUCKRAM	HACHURE	MACRAMÉ	RECLAIM	UNCURED
BABYLON	LABORED	SUBSUME	BUCOLIC	HACKERY	MECHLIN	RECLINE	VACANCY
BABYSIT	LABORER	SUBTEEN	CACHEXY	HACKING	MECONIC	RECLUSE	VACCINE
BIBELOT	LEBANON	SUBTEND	CACIQUE	HACKLES	MICHAEL	RECORDS	VACUITY
BOBSLED	LIBERAL	SUBVERT	CECILIA	HACKNEY	MICROBE	RECOUNT	VACUOLE
BUBBLES	LIBERIA	SUBZERO	COCAINE	HACKSAW	MOCKERS	RECOVER	VACUOUS
BUBONIC	LIBERTY	TABANID	COCHLEA	HECKLER	MOCKERY	RECRUIT	VICEROY
CABARET	LIBRARY	TABARET	COCKADE	HECTARE	MOCKING	RECTIFY	VICINAL
CABBAGE	LIBRIUM	TABASCO	COCKLES	HICKORY	MYCELLA	RECTORY	VICIOUS
CABINET	LOBELIA	TABITHA	COCKNEY	INCENSE	MYCENAE	RECURVE	VICTORY
CABLING	LOBSTER	TABLEAU	COCKPIT	INCISOR	MYCETES	RECYCLE	VICTUAL
CABOOSE	MOBSTER	TABLOID	COCONUT	INCLINE	NACELLE	RICARDO	VOCALIC
COBBLED	NABOKOV	TABORET	COCOTTE	INCLUDE	NACROUS	RICHARD	VOCALLY
COBBLER	NEBBISH	TABULAR	CUCKING	INCOMER	NECKING	RICHTER	WICKIUP
CUBICLE	NEBULAR	TIBETAN	CUCKOLD	INCONNU	NECKLET	RICKETS	WICKLOW
DABBLER	NIBLICK	TOBACCO	CYCLING	INCROSS	NECKTIE	RICKETY	YUCATAN
DEBACLE	NOBBLED	TUBULAR	CYCLIST	INCRUST	NECROSE	RICOTTA	ABDOMEN
DEBASED	NOBBLER	TUBULIN	CYCLONE	INCUBUS	NECTARY	ROCKALL	ADDISON
DEBATER	ORBITAL	UMBRAGE	CYCLOPS	INCURVE	NICAEAN	ROCKERY	ADDRESS
DEBAUCH	OSBORNE	UMBRIAN	DECANAL	ISCHIUM	NICOISE	ROCKING	AIDANCE
DEBORAH	OXBLOOD	UNBLOCK	DECAYED	ITCHING	NICOSIA	SACCADE	ALDABRA
DEBOUCH	PABULUM	UNBOSOM	DECEASE	JACINTH	NICTATE	SACKBUT	ALDRICH
DEBRETT	PEBBLES	UNBOUND	DECEIVE	JACKASS	NOCTUID	SACKFUL	ANDAMAN
DEBRIEF	PIBROCH	UNBOWED	DECENCY	JACKDAW	NUCLEAR	SACKING	ANDANTE
DEBUSSY	PUBERAL	UPBRAID	DECIBEL	JACKETS	NUCLEIC	SECLUDE	ANDIRON
DIBBLER	PUBERTY	VIBRANT	DECIDED	JACKPOT	NUCLEUS	SECONAL	ANDORRA
DUBBING	PUBLISH	VIBRATE	DECIDER	JACKSON	NUCLIDE	SECONDS	ANDROID
DUBIETY	REBECCA	VIBRATO	DECIMAL	JACOBIN	OCCIPUT	SECRECY	ARDUOUS
DUBIOUS	REBIRTH	WEBBING	DECLAIM	JACOBUS	OCCLUDE	SECRETE	AUDIBLE
DUBNIUM	REBOUND	WEBSITE	DECLARE	JACQUES	ORCHARD	SECRETS	AUDIBLY
EBBTIDE	REBUILD	WEBSTER	DECLINE	JACUZZI	ORCINOL	SECTION	AUDITOR
ECBOLIC	RIBBING	ACCLAIM	DECODER	JOCASTA	OSCULUM	SECULAR	AUDUBON
EMBARGO	RIBCAGE	ACCOUNT	DECORUM	JOCULAR	PACIFIC	SICKBAY	BADNESS
EMBASSY	RIBLESS	ACCRETE	DECREED	KICKING	PACKAGE	SICKBED	BEDDING
EMBLAZE	RIBWORT	ACCRUAL	DECRYPT	KICKOFF	PACKING	SICKERT	BEDEVIL
EMBOLUS	ROBBERS	ACCURSE	DICKENS	LACERTA	PACKMAN	SOCAGER	BEDFORD
EMBOWER	ROBBERY	ACCUSED	DICTATE	LACEUPS	PECCANT	SOCIETY	BEDOUIN
EMBRACE	ROBERTS	ACCUSER	DICTION	LACKING	PECCARY	SOCKEYE	BEDPOST
EMBROIL	ROBESON	ALCALDE	DOCKING	LACONIC	PECCAVI	SOCKING	BEDROCK
FEBRILE	ROBINIA	ALCHEMY	DOCTORS	LACQUER	PECKING	SOCOTRA	BEDROOM
FIBROID	ROBUSTA	ALCOHOL	DUCHESS	LACTASE	PECKISH	SUCCEED	BEDSIDE
FIBROMA	RUBBERS	ALCORAN	DUCKING	LACTATE	PECTASE	SUCCESS	BEDSORE
FIBROUS	RUBBERY	ANCHOVY	DUCTILE	LACTEAL	PICADOR	SUCCOUR	BEDTIME

177

BIDDING	LUDDITE	REDRESS	AVENGER	CREWMAN	FREEDOM	MEETING	PRECAST
BUDDING	LUDGATE	REDSKIN	AVERAGE	DEEPFRY	FREEMAN	MOELLON	PRECEDE
CADAVER	MADEIRA	REDUCED	AVESTAN	DIECAST	FREESIA	MUEZZIN	PRECEPT
CADDISH	MADISON	REDUCER	AWESOME	DIEDRAL	FREEWAY	MYELINE	PRECISE
CADENCE	MADNESS	REDWOOD	BEEFALO	DIEHARD	FREEZER	MYELOID	PREDATE
CADENZA	MADONNA	RIDDLED	BEEHIVE	DIETARY	FREIGHT	MYELOMA	PREDIAL
CADMIUM	MEDDLER	RIDDLER	BEELINE	DIETINE	FRESHEN	NEEDFUL	PREDICT
CADOGAN	MEDIATE	RIDINGS	BEERMAT	DOESKIN	FRESHER	NEEDLES	PREDOOM
CEDILLA	MEDICAL	RUDERAL	BEESWAX	DREADED	FRESHET	OBELISK	PREEMPT
CODEINE	MEDULLA	RUDOLPH	BLEAKLY	DREAMER	FRESHLY	OBESITY	PREFACE
CODICIL	MIDGARD	SADDLER	BLEEPER	DREDGER	FRETFUL	OCEANIA	PREFECT
CODLING	MIDLAND	SADNESS	BLEMISH	DRESDEN	FRETSAW	OCEANIC	PREHEAT
DADAISM	MIDLINE	SEDUCER	BLENDER	DRESSED	FRETTED	OCEANID	PRELACY
DADAIST	MIDMOST	SIDDONS	BLESSED	DRESSER	GAEKWAR	OCELLAR	PRELATE
DIDEROT	MIDRIFF	SIDECAR	BLESSES	DREYFUS	GEELONG	OCELLUS	PRELIMS
DIDICOY	MIDSHIP	SUDETEN	BLETHER	DWELLER	GHERKIN	OLEFINE	PRELUDE
DIDYMUS	MIDTERM	TADPOLE	BREADED	EJECTOR	GIELGUD	OMENTUM	PREMIER
DODDERY	MIDWEEK	TEDIOUS	BREADTH	ELEANOR	GLEANER	ONEIRIC	PREMISE
DODGEMS	MIDWEST	TIDDLER	BREAKER	ELECTED	GLEEFUL	ONENESS	PREMISS
DUDGEON	MIDWIFE	TIDEWAY	BREATHE	ELECTOR	GLENCOE	ONEROUS	PREMIUM
ECDYSIS	MODERNE	TIDINGS	BREEDER	ELECTRA	GLENOID	ONESELF	PREPAID
ELDERLY	MODESTY	TODDLER	BRENDAN	ELECTRO	GREASER	ONETIME	PREPARE
ENDEMIC	MODICUM	UNDATED	BRENNER	ELEGANT	GREATEN	OPENING	PREPUCE
ENDGAME	MODISTE	UNDERGO	BREVITY	ELEGIAC	GREATLY	OPERAND	PREQUEL
ENDLESS	MODULAR	UNDOING	BREWERY	ELEGIST	GREAVES	OPERANT	PRESAGE
ENDNOTE	MODULUS	UNDRESS	BREWING	ELEMENT	GRECIAN	OPERATE	PRESENT
ENDOGEN	MUDDLED	UNDYING	CAEDMON	ELEVATE	GREENER	OREGANO	PRESIDE
ENDORSE	MUDEJAR	VEDANTA	CAESIUM	EMERALD	GREGORY	ORESTES	PRESSED
ENDURED	MUDFLAP	VEDETTE	CAESURA	EMERSON	GREMLIN	OVERACT	PRESSOR
ENDWAYS	MUDLARK	VIDIMUS	CHEAPEN	ENERGIC	GRENADA	OVERALL	PRESUME
FADDISH	MUDPACK	WADDING	CHEAPLY	EPERGNE	GRENADE	OVERARM	PRETEND
FADDIST	NODDING	WEDDING	CHEATER	ERECTOR	GRENDEL	OVERAWE	PRETEXT
FEDERAL	NODULAR	WEDLOCK	CHECKED	EREMITE	GREYISH	OVERBID	PRETZEL
FIDDLER	ODDBALL	WIDGEON	CHECKIN	ETERNAL	GREYLAG	OVERDUE	PREVAIL
FIDELIO	ODDMENT	WIDOWED	CHECKUP	ETESIAN	HEEDFUL	OVEREAT	PREVENT
FIDGETS	ODDNESS	WIDOWER	CHEDDAR	EVENING	HEELTAP	OVERFED	PREVIEW
FIDGETY	OEDIPUS	YIDDISH	CHEERIO	EVENTER	HOEDOWN	OVERLAP	PREZZIE
FUDDLED	OLDNESS	ZEDOARY	CHEESED	EVEREST	IBERIAN	OVERLAY	PTERYLA
GADROON	OLDSTER	ABELARD	CHEETAH	EXECUTE	ICEBERG	OVERLIE	PUERILE
GADWALL	ORDERED	ABETTOR	CHEKHOV	EXEGETE	ICEFALL	OVERMAN	QUECHUA
GIDDILY	ORDERLY	ACERBIC	CHELSEA	EXEMPLA	ICEFLOE	OVERPAY	QUEENLY
GIDDYUP	ORDINAL	ACESTES	CHEMISE	EYEBALL	ICELAND	OVERRUN	QUEERER
GODDESS	PADDING	ACETATE	CHEMIST	EYEBATH	IDEALLY	OVERSEE	QUENTIN
GODETIA	PADDLER	ACETONE	CHEQUER	EYEBROW	IKEBANA	OVERTAX	QUERCUS
GODHEAD	PADDOCK	ADELINE	CHERISH	EYEHOLE	INERTIA	PAESTUM	QUESTER
GODLESS	PADLOCK	ADELPHI	CHEROOT	EYELASH	INEXACT	PEELING	QUETZAL
GODLIKE	PADRONE	ADENINE	CHERVIL	EYELESS	IRELAND	PEEPING	RAEBURN
GODSEND	PEDDLER	ADENOID	CHESTER	EYELIDS	ITEMIZE	PEERAGE	REEKING
GODUNOV	PEDICAB	ADENOMA	CHEVIOT	EYESHOT	ITERATE	PEERESS	REELECT
GUDGEON	PEDICEL	AGELESS	CHEVRON	EYESORE	JEEPERS	PEERING	REELING
HADDOCK	PEDICLE	AGELONG	CHEWING	EYESPOT	JEEPNEY	PEEVISH	REENTER
HADRIAN	PIDGEON	ALECOST	CLEANER	EYEWASH	JEERING	PFENNIG	REENTRY
HEDGING	PODAGRA	ALEMBIC	CLEANLY	EZEKIEL	KEELING	PIEBALD	RHENISH
HIDALGO	PODESTA	ALENÇON	CLEANSE	FEEDING	KEEPING	PIERCED	RHENIUM
HIDEOUS	PUDDING	ALEPINE	CLEANUP	FEELING	KHEDIVE	PIERCER	ROEBUCK
HIDEOUT	RADDLED	ALEWIFE	CLEARLY	FIEFDOM	KIELDER	PIERROT	ROEDEAN
HYDATID	RADIANT	AMENITY	CLEARUP	FIELDER	KLEENEX	PIETIST	SCENERY
HYDRANT	RADIATE	AMERICA	CLEAVER	FLEAPIT	KNEECAP	PLEADER	SCENTED
HYDRATE	RADICAL	AMERIGO	CLEMENT	FLECKED	KNEELER	PLEASED	SCEPTER
INDEPTH	RADICLE	AMERIND	COELIAC	FLECKER	KNEEPAD	PLEASES	SCEPTIC
INDEXER	REDCOAT	ANEMONE	COEXIST	FLEDGED	KNELLER	PLEATED	SCEPTRE
INDIANA	REDDISH	ANEROID	CREATED	FLEEING	KNESSET	PLEIADE	SEEDBED
INDOORS	REDFISH	APELIKE	CREATOR	FLEMING	KREMLIN	PLENARY	SEEKERS
INDULGE	REDHEAD	APEPSIA	CREEPER	FLEMISH	LAETARE	PLEROMA	SEEMING
JUDAISM	REDNECK	ARETINO	CREMATE	FLEURET	LEEWARD	PLESSOR	SEEPAGE
KADDISH	REDNESS	ASEPTIC	CRENATE	FLEURON	LIEDOWN	PLEURAL	SEETHED
KIDNEYS	REDOUBT	ASEXUAL	CRESTED	FLEXILE	MAENADS	PLEURON	SHEARER
LADYBUG	REDOUND	ATELIER	CREVICE	FRECKLE	MAESTRO	POETESS	SHEATHE
LODGING	REDPOLL	AVEBURY	CREWCUT	FREEBIE	MEERKAT	PREBEND	SHEAVES
							SHEBANG

SHEBEEN	SWEETLY	AFFLICT	REFLATE	DEGAUSS	LEGALLY	RAGTIME	ASHDOWN
SHELLAC	SWELTER	AFFRONT	REFLECT	DEGRADE	LEGATEE	RAGWEED	ASHTRAY
SHELLED	TEEMING	ALFALFA	REFLOAT	DEGREES	LEGGING	RAGWORT	ATHEISM
SHELLEY	TEENAGE	ALFONSO	REFRACT	DIGAMMA	LEGIBLE	REGALIA	ATHEIST
SHELTER	THEATER	AWFULLY	REFRAIN	DIGGING	LEGIBLY	REGALLY	ATHIRST
SHELTIE	THEATRE	BAFFLED	REFRESH	DIGITAL	LEGIONS	REGARDS	ATHLETE
SHELVED	THEORBO	BIFOCAL	REFUGEE	DIGLYPH	LEGLESS	REGATTA	ATHWART
SHELVES	THEOREM	BUFFALO	REFUSAL	DIGNIFY	LEGPULL	REGENCY	BAHADUR
SHEPPEY	THERAPY	BUFFOON	RUFFIAN	DIGNITY	LEGROOM	REGIMEN	BAHAMAS
SHERBET	THEREBY	COFFERS	RUFFLED	DIGONAL	LEGWORK	REGNANT	BAHRAIN
SHERIFF	THEREIN	DEFACED	RUFFLER	DIGRAPH	LIGHTEN	REGRESS	BAHREIN
SHERMAN	THERESA	DEFAULT	SAFFRON	DIGRESS	LIGHTER	REGROUP	BEHAVED
SIEMENS	THERETO	DEFENCE	SIFTING	DOGCART	LIGHTLY	REGULAR	BEHOOVE
SIEVERT	THERMAL	DEFENSE	SOFABED	DOGFISH	LIGNITE	RIGGING	BOHEMIA
SKELTER	THERMIC	DEFIANT	SUFFETE	DOGFOOD	LOGBOOK	RIGHTLY	BOHRIUM
SKEPTIC	THERMOS	DEFICIT	SUFFICE	DOGGONE	LOGGING	RIGIDLY	CAHOOTS
SKETCHY	THESEUS	DEFILED	SUFFOLK	DOGROSE	LOGICAL	RIGVEDA	COHABIT
SLEEKLY	TIEPOLO	DEFINED	SUFFUSE	DOGWOOD	LOGWOOD	ROGUERY	DEHISCE
SLEEPER	TIERCEL	DEFLATE	TAFFETA	EAGERLY	LUGGAGE	ROGUISH	ECHELON
SLEEVED	TIERCET	DEFLECT	TIFFANY	EGGHEAD	LUGHOLE	SAGITTA	ECHIDNA
SLEIGHT	TOEHOLD	DEFRAUD	UNFADED	ENGAGED	LUGSAIL	SAGOUIN	ECHINUS
SLENDER	TOENAIL	DEFROCK	UNFIXED	ENGINED	LUGWORM	SEGMENT	ENHANCE
SMELTER	TREACLE	DEFROST	UNFROCK	ENGLAND	MAGENTA	SIGHTED	EPHEBUS
SMETANA	TREACLY	DEFUNCT	WAFTING	ENGLISH	MAGGOTY	SIGNIFY	EPHEDRA
SNEAKER	TREADLE	DIFFUSE	ZOFFANY	ENGORGE	MAGHREB	SIGNING	EPHESUS
SPEAKER	TREASON	EFFECTS	AFGHANI	ENGRAFT	MAGICAL	SIGNORA	EPHRAIM
SPECIAL	TREATED	EFFENDI	AGGRADE	ENGRAIN	MAGINOT	SIGNORI	ETHANOL
SPECIES	TREETOP	EFFORCE	AGGRESS	ENGRAVE	MAGNATE	SUGARED	ETHICAL
SPECIFY	TREFOIL	ENFEOFF	ALGEBRA	ENGROSS	MAGNETO	SUGGEST	ETHMOID
SPECKLE	TREKKER	ENFIELD	ALGERIA	EUGENIA	MAGNIFY	TAGALOG	EXHAUST
SPECTER	TRELLIS	ENFORCE	ALGIERS	EUGENIC	MEGAERA	TAGETES	EXHEDRA
SPECTRE	TREMBLE	FIFTEEN	ANGELIC	EUGENIE	MEGARON	TIGHTEN	EXHIBIT
SPELLER	TREMBLY	GEFILTE	ANGELUS	FAGGOTS	MEGATON	TIGHTLY	GEHENNA
SPENCER	TREMOLO	HAFNIUM	ANGEVIN	FIGHTER	MIGRANT	TIGRESS	HAHNIUM
SPENDER	TREPANG	INFANCY	ANGIOMA	FIGLEAF	MIGRATE	TIGRISH	ICHABOD
SPENSER	TRESSES	INFARCT	ANGLING	FIGMENT	MUGGING	TOGGERY	ICHNITE
STEALTH	TRESTLE	INFERNO	ANGOLAN	FIGURES	MUGWORT	TUGBOAT	IMHOTEP
STEAMED	TUESDAY	INFIDEL	ANGRILY	FOGHORN	MUGWUMP	UNGODLY	INHABIT
STEAMER	TWEEDLE	INFIELD	ANGUISH	FOGLAMP	NAGGING	UNGUENT	INHALER
STEARIC	TWEETER	INFLAME	ANGULAR	GAGSTER	NEGLECT	UPGRADE	INHERIT
STEARIN	TWELFTH	INFLATE	AUGMENT	GOGGLES	NÉGLIGÉ	URGENCY	INHIBIT
STEEPEN	ULEXITE	INFLECT	AUGUSTA	HAGBOLT	NEGRESS	VAGINAL	INHOUSE
STEEPLE	UNEARTH	INFLICT	AUGUSTE	HAGFISH	NEGRITO	VAGRANT	INHUMAN
STEEPLY	UNEQUAL	KUFIYAH	BAGASSE	HAGGADA	NEGROID	VAGUELY	ISHMAEL
STEERER	URETHRA	LEFTIST	BAGEHOT	HAGGARD	NIGELLA	VEGETAL	JEHOVAH
STELLAR	USELESS	LIFTOFF	BAGGAGE	HAGGERY	NIGERIA	WAGGISH	JOHNNIE
STEMMED	UTENSIL	LOFTILY	BAGHDAD	HIGGINS	NIGGARD	WAGGLER	JOHNSON
STENCIL	UTERINE	MAFIOSO	BAGPIPE	HIGHEST	NIGHTIE	WAGONER	MAHATMA
STENGAH	VIETNAM	MOFETTE	BEGGARY	HIGHMAN	NIGHTLY	WAGTAIL	MAHJONG
STENGUN	WEEKDAY	MUFFLED	BEGGING	HOGARTH	NOGGING	WIGGING	MAHONIA
STENTOR	WEEKEND	MUFFLER	BEGONIA	HOGBACK	ONGOING	YOGHURT	MOHICAN
STEPHEN	WEEPING	OFFBASE	BEGORRA	HOGGING	ORGANIC	ZYGOSIS	NAHUATL
STEPNEY	WHEATEN	OFFBEAT	BEGUILE	HOGWASH	ORGANUM	ACHAEAN	OTHELLO
STEPSON	WHEEDLE	OFFDUTY	BIGFOOT	HYGIENE	ORGANZA	ACHATES	PAHLAVI
STERILE	WHEELED	OFFENCE	BIGHEAD	INGENUE	ORGIAST	ACHERON	REHOUSE
STERNAL	WHEELER	OFFENSE	BIGHORN	INGRAIN	PAGEANT	ACHESON	SCHEMER
STERNLY	WHEELIE	OFFERER	BIGOTED	INGRATE	PAGEBOY	ACHIEVE	SCHERZO
STERNUM	WHEREAS	OFFHAND	BIGOTRY	INGRESS	PEGASUS	ACHTUNG	SCHICKS
STEROID	WHEREBY	OFFICER	BIGSHOT	INGROWN	PIGEONS	AMHARIC	SCHLEPP
STETSON	WHEREIN	OFFICES	BUGABOO	JAGGERY	PIGFISH	APHAGIA	SCHLOCK
STEVENS	WHETHER	OFFLOAD	BUGBEAR	JOGGING	PIGGERY	APHASIA	SCHLOSS
STEWARD	WREATHE	OFFPEAK	BUGGING	JOGTROT	PIGLING	APHELIA	SCHMUCK
STEWING	WRECKED	OFFSIDE	BUGGINS	JUGGINS	PIGMEAT	APHESIS	SCHNELL
SWEATED	WRECKER	RAFFISH	BUGLOSS	JUGGLER	PIGMENT	APHONIA	SCHOLAR
SWEATER	WRESTLE	RAFFLES	CAGOULE	JUGLANS	PIGSKIN	APHONIC	SPHENIC
SWEDISH	AFFABLE	RAFTING	COGENCY	JUGULAR	PIGTAIL	APHOTIC	TEHERAN
SWEEPER	AFFABLY	REFEREE	COGNATE	LAGGARD	PIGWEED	APHTHAE	UNHAPPY
SWEETEN	AFFAIRS	REFINED	DAGGERS	LAGGING	PUGWASH	ASHAMED	UNHEARD
SWEETIE	AFFIXED	REFINER	DAGWOOD	LAGONDA		ASHANTI	UNHINGE

UNHITCH	BRINJAL	DAIMLER	GLIDING	OKINAWA	REISSUE	SPINATE	TRIPOLI
UNHORSE	BRIOCHE	DEICTIC	GLIMMER	OMICRON	RHIZOID	SPINDLE	TRIPPER
VEHICLE	BRISKET	DEIRDRE	GLIMPSE	OMINOUS	RHIZOME	SPINDLY	TRIPSIS
YAHWIST	BRISKLY	DNIEPER	GLISTEN	OMITTED	ROISTER	SPINNER	TRIREME
ABIDING	BRISTLE	DRIBBLE	GLITTER	OPINION	RUINOUS	SPINNEY	TRISECT
ABIDJAN	BRISTLY	DRIBLET	GRIDDLE	ORIFICE	SAILING	SPINOFF	TRISHAW
ABIGAIL	BRISTOL	DRIFTER	GRIFFON	ORIGAMI	SAILORS	SPINOZA	TRISMUS
ABILITY	BRITAIN	DRINKER	GRIFTER	ORIGINS	SAINTLY	SPIRITS	TRISTAN
ABIOSIS	BRITISH	DRIVERS	GRILLED	ORINOCO	SCIATIC	SPITTLE	TRITELY
ACIDIFY	BRITONS	DRIVING	GRIMACE	OVICIDE	SCIENCE	STICKER	TRITIUM
ACIDITY	BRITTLE	DRIZZLE	GRIMOND	OVIDUCT	SCISSOR	STICKLE	TRITOMA
ACIFORM	BRITZKA	DRIZZLY	GRIMSBY	OXIDASE	SEISMIC	STIFFEN	TRITONE
ADIPOSE	BRIXTON	DWINDLE	GRINDER	OXIDIZE	SEIZURE	STIFFLY	TRIUMPH
AGILITY	BUILDER	EDIFICE	GRISTLE	PAINFUL	SHIATSU	STILTED	TRIVIAL
AGISTOR	CAINITE	EDITION	GRISTLY	PAINTED	SHICKSA	STILTON	TRIVIUM
AGITATE	CAIRENE	ELISION	GRIZZLE	PAINTER	SHIKARI	STINGER	TSIGANE
AGITATO	CAISSON	ELITISM	GRIZZLY	PAIRING	SHIMMER	STINKER	TSIGANY
ALICANT	CAITIFF	ELITIST	GUIDING	PAISLEY	SHINDIG	STIPEND	TUITION
ALIDADE	CEILIDH	EMINENT	GUIGNOL	PHIDIAS	SHINGLE	STIPPLE	TWIDDLE
ALIGNED	CEILING	EMIRATE	GUILDER	PHILEAS	SHINGLY	STIRFRY	TWIDDLY
ALIMENT	CHIANTI	EPICARP	GUINEAN	PHILTER	SHINING	STIRPES	TWIGGER
ALIMONY	CHIASMA	EPICENE	GUINEAS	PHILTRE	SHINPAD	STIRRED	TWINKLE
ALIQUID	CHICAGO	EPICURE	HAIRCUT	PLIABLE	SHIPPER	STIRRUP	TWINSET
ALIQUOT	CHICANE	EPIDOTE	HAIRNET	PLIANCY	SHIPTON	SUICIDE	TWISTED
AMIABLE	CHICANO	EPIGEAL	HAIRPIN	POINTED	SHIRKER	SWIDDEN	TWISTER
AMIABLY	CHICKEN	EPIGONE	HAITIAN	POINTER	SHIRLEY	SWIFTER	TWITCHY
ANILINE	CHICORY	EPIGRAM	HEIGHTS	PRIAPUS	SHIVERS	SWIFTLY	TWITTER
ANIMALS	CHIEFLY	EPISODE	HEINOUS	PRICKED	SHIVERY	SWIMMER	UNICORN
ANIMATE	CHIFFON	EPISTLE	HEIRESS	PRICKER	SKIDDAW	SWINDLE	UNIFORM
ANIMIST	CHIGGER	EPITAPH	ICINESS	PRICKLE	SKIDPAN	SWINGER	UNITARY
ANISEED	CHIGNON	EPITAXY	IDIOTIC	PRICKLY	SKIFFLE	SWINGLE	UNITIES
APICIUS	CHILEAN	EPITHET	ILIACUS	PRIESTS	SKILFUL	SWITHIN	URINARY
ARIADNE	CHILLER	EPITOME	IMITATE	PRIMACY	SKILLED	SWIZZLE	URINATE
ARIDITY	CHILLON	EPIZOON	INITIAL	PRIMARY	SKILLET	TAILORS	UTILITY
ARIETTA	CHIMERA	ERINYES	IRIDISE	PRIMATE	SKIMMED	TAINTED	UTILIZE
ARIOSTO	CHIMNEY	ERISKAY	IRIDIUM	PRIMEUR	SKIMMER	TBILISI	VOIVODE
ARIZONA	CHINDIT	ERITREA	JOINERY	PRIMING	SKIMMIA	THICKEN	WAILING
ASIATIC	CHINESE	EVIDENT	JOINING	PRIMULA	SKINFUL	THICKET	WAITING
ASININE	CHINOOK	EXIGENT	JOINTED	PRINCES	SKINNED	THICKLY	WEIGELA
ATINGLE	CHINTZY	EXISTED	JOINTER	PRINTED	SKINNER	THIEVES	WEIGHIN
ATISHOO	CHINWAG	EXITING	JOINTLY	PRINTER	SKIPPED	THIMBLE	WEIGHTS
AVIATOR	CHIPPED	FAIENCE	KAINITE	PRITHEE	SKIPPER	THINKER	WEIGHTY
AVIDITY	CHIPPER	FAILING	KLINKER	PRIVACY	SKITTER	THINNER	WEIRDLY
AVIGNON	CHIPPIE	FAILURE	KNICKER	PRIVATE	SKITTLE	THIRDLY	WHIMPER
AXILLAR	CHIRRUP	FAINTED	KNITTED	PRIVITY	SLICKER	THIRSTY	WHIMSEY
AZIMUTH	CLICKER	FAINTLY	KNITTER	QUIBBLE	SLIDING	THISTLE	WHINGER
BAILIFF	CLIMATE	FAIRING	KRISHNA	QUICHUA	SLIMMER	THITHER	WHIPCAT
BEIJING	CLIMBER	FAIRISH	LEISURE	QUICKEN	SLIPPED	TRIANON	WHIPLOW
BLIGHTY	CLINGER	FAIRWAY	MAIGRET	QUICKER	SLIPPER	TRIATIC	WHIPPET
BLINDER	CLINKER	FEIGNED	MAILBAG	QUICKIE	SLIPWAY	TRIBUNE	WHISKER
BLINDLY	CLIPPED	FLICKER	MAILBOX	QUICKLY	SLITHER	TRIBUTE	WHISKEY
BLINKER	CLIPPER	FLIGHTY	MAILCAR	QUIETEN	SMICKLY	TRICEPS	WHISPER
BLISTER	CLIPPIE	FLIPPER	MAILING	QUIETLY	SMIDGIN	TRICKLE	WHISTLE
BLITHER	CLIQUEY	FLITTER	MAILMAN	QUIETUS	SMILING	TRIDENT	WHITHER
BLITZED	COINAGE	FLIVVER	MEIOSIS	QUILTED	SMITHER	TRIESTE	WHITING
BOILEAU	COITION	FRIABLE	MEISSEN	QUILTER	SMITTEN	TRIFFID	WHITISH
BOILING	CRICKET	FRIENDS	MOIDORE	QUINCHE	SNICKER	TRIFLER	WHITLOW
BRIBERY	CRICKEY	FRIGATE	MOISTEN	QUININE	SNIFFER	TRIFLES	WHITSUN
BRICKIE	CRICOID	FRILLED	MOITHER	QUINONE	SNIFFLE	TRIGGER	WHITTLE
BRIDGES	CRIMEAN	FRINGED	MYIASIS	QUINTAL	SNIFTER	TRILLED	WRIGGLE
BRIDGET	CRIMSON	FRISBEE	NAILBED	QUINTAN	SNIGGER	TRILLER	WRINGER
BRIDLER	CRINKLE	FRISIAN	NAIPAUL	QUINTET	SNIPPET	TRILOGY	WRINKLE
BRIDLES	CRINKLY	FRISSON	NAIROBI	QUITTER	SPICATE	TRIMMER	WRINKLY
BRIEFLY	CRINOID	FRITTER	NAIVELY	QUIXOTE	SPICULA	TRINGLE	WRITEUP
BRIGADE	CRIPPLE	FRIZZLE	NAIVETÉ	RAILING	SPICULE	TRINITY	WRITING
BRIGAND	CRISPIN	FRIZZLY	NAIVETY	RAILWAY	SPIDERS	TRINKET	WRITTEN
BRIGHAM	CRITTER	GAINFUL	NEITHER	RAIMENT	SPIDERY	TRIPLET	ZAIREAN
BRIMFUL	CUIRASS	GAINSAY	NOISILY	RAINBOW	SPIGNEL	TRIPLEX	ABJOINT
BRINDLE	CUISINE	GAITERS	NOISOME	RAISING	SPINACH	TRIPODY	ADJOINT

ADJOURN	BALLOON	CALUMET	FALAFEL	HELLCAT	MILLAIS	POLYPUS	TALIPES
ADJUNCT	BALONEY	CALUMNY	FALLACY	HELLENE	MILLING	PULLMAN	TALIPOT
BAJAZET	BELABOR	CALVARY	FALLING	HELLION	MILLION	PULSATE	TALKING
BEJEWEL	BELARUS	CALYPSO	FALLOUT	HELLISH	MOLDING	PULSING	TALLBOY
DEJECTA	BELATED	CELADON	FALSELY	HELLUVA	MOLLIFY	PYLORUS	TALLITH
FAJITAS	BELGIAN	CELEBES	FALSIES	HELPFUL	MOLLUSC	RALEIGH	TALOOKA
INJURED	BELGIUM	CELESTA	FALSIFY	HELPING	MOLIÈRE	RELAPSE	TELECOM
JEJUNUM	BELIEVE	CELESTE	FELLOWS	HILDING	MOLOTOV	RELATED	TELFORD
JUJITSU	BELINDA	CELLINI	FELSPAR	HILLMAN	MOLUCCA	RELAXED	TELLING
MAJESTY	BELISHA	CELLIST	FELUCCA	HILLMEN	MULATTO	RELAYER	TELPHER
MAJORCA	BELLBOY	CELLULE	FILARIA	HILLOCK	MULLEIN	RELEASE	TELSTAR
OBJECTS	BELLEEK	CELSIUS	FILASSE	HILLTOP	MULLION	RELIANT	TILAPIA
PAJAMAS	BELLHOP	CHLAMYS	FILBERT	HOLBEIN	NULLIFY	RELICTS	TILBURY
PYJAMAS	BELLINI	CHLORAL	FILCHER	HOLDALL	NULLITY	RELIEVE	TILLAGE
REJOICE	BELLMAN	CILIATE	FILINGS	HOLDING	OBLIGED	RELIEVO	TOLKIEN
SOJOURN	BELLOWS	COLCHIS	FILLETS	HOLIDAY	OBLIGOR	ROLLERS	TOLLMAN
ALKANET	BELOVED	COLDITZ	FILLING	HOLLAND	OBLIQUE	ROLLICK	TOLSTOY
ALKORAN	BILIOUS	COLIBRI	FILMING	HOLMIUM	OBLOQUY	ROLLING	TOLUENE
ASKANCE	BILLION	COLITIS	FOLDING	HOLSTER	OILBIRD	ROLLMOP	TYLOSIS
AWKWARD	BILLMAN	COLLAGE	FOLIAGE	HULKING	OILCAKE	SALABLE	UNLADEN
BAKLAVA	BILLOWS	COLLARD	FOLLIES	ILLBRED	OILSKIN	SALADIN	UNLATCH
DUKEDOM	BILTONG	COLLATE	FULCRUM	ILLEGAL	ORLANDO	SALAMIS	UNLEASH
INKLING	BOLETUS	COLLECT	FULFILL	ILLICIT	ORLEANS	SALAZAR	UNLINED
INKWELL	BOLIVAR	COLLEEN	FULGENT	ILLNESS	PALADIN	SALERMO	UNLOOSE
IRKSOME	BOLIVIA	COLLEGE	FULLERS	ISLAMIC	PALATAL	SALIENT	UNLOVED
JAKARTA	BOLLARD	COLLIDE	FULSOME	ISLANDS	PALAVER	SALIERI	UNLUCKY
JUKEBOX	BOLOGNA	COLLIER	GALAHAD	JELLABA	PALERMO	SALIQUE	VALENCE
LAKSHMI	BOLONEY	COLLOID	GALATEA	JELLIED	PALETTE	SALLUST	VALENCY
LIKENED	BOLSHIE	COLLUDE	GALETTE	JOLLITY	PALFREY	SALPINX	VALIANT
MAKINGS	BOLSHOI	COLOGNE	GALILEE	KALENDS	PALINGS	SALSIFY	VALVULE
NAKEDLY	BOLSTER	COLOMBO	GALILEO	KALMUCK	PALISSY	SALTATE	VELOURS
OAKLEAF	BULBOUS	COLONEL	GALIPOT	KILDARE	PALLIUM	SALTING	VELVETY
ORKNEYS	BULGHUR	COLONIC	GALLANT	KILLICK	PALMATE	SALTIRE	VILLAGE
PIKELET	BULGING	COLORED	GALLEON	KILLING	PALMIST	SALTPAN	VILLAIN
SIKHISM	BULIMIA	COLOURS	GALLERY	KILLJOY	PALMTOP	SALVAGE	VILLEIN
SUKKOTH	BULLACE	COLUMBA	GALLING	KILOTON	PALMYRA	SCLERAL	VILNIUS
TAKEOFF	BULLDOG	COLUMNS	GALLIUM	KILVERT	PALOMAR	SELFISH	VOLANTE
TAKEOUT	BULLETS	CULPRIT	GALLONS	KOLKHOZ	PALOOKA	SELKIRK	VOLAPUK
TAKINGS	BULLION	CULTURE	GALLOWS	LALIQUE	PALPATE	SELLERS	VOLCANO
TEKTITE	BULLISH	CULVERT	GALOCHE	LALLANS	PALUDAL	SELLING	VOLTAGE
UNKEMPT	BULLOCK	DALILAH	GALOPIN	LILTING	PELAGIC	SELLOFF	VOLTAIC
UNKNOWN	BULLPEN	DELAYED	GALUMPH	LOLLARD	PELICAN	SELLOUT	VOLUBLE
VIKINGS	BULRUSH	DELIBES	GELATIN	LULLABY	PELORUS	SELTZER	VOLUBLY
WAKEFUL	BULWARK	DELIGHT	GELDING	MALACCA	PELTING	SELVAGE	VULGATE
ZAKUSKA	CALABAR	DELILAH	GILBERT	MALACHI	PILATUS	SILENCE	VULPINE
ABLATOR	CALAMUS	DELIMIT	GILDING	MALAISE	PILCHER	SILESIA	VULTURE
AILERON	CALCIFY	DELIVER	GILLRAY	MALARIA	PILGRIM	SILICON	WALKING
AILMENT	CALCINE	DELOUSE	GOLDING	MALAYAN	PILLAGE	SILVERY	WALKMAN
ALLEGED	CALCITE	DELPHIC	GOLDONI	MALEFIC	PILLBOX	SOLANUM	WALKOUT
ALLEGRI	CALCIUM	DELTOID	GOLFING	MALLARD	PILLION	SOLDIER	WALKWAY
ALLEGRO	CALCULI	DELUDED	GOLIARD	MALLEUS	PILLORY	SOLICIT	WALLABY
ALLENBY	CALDERA	DILATED	GOLIATH	MALLING	POLARIS	SOLIDLY	WALLACE
ALLERGY	CALDRON	DILATOR	HALBERD	MALMSEY	POLEAXE	SOLIDUS	WALLEYE
ALLONGE	CALECHE	DILEMMA	HALBERT	MALTASE	POLECAT	SOLOIST	WALLIES
ALLOWED	CALENDS	DILUENT	HALCYON	MALTESE	POLEMIC	SOLOMON	WALLOON
ALLSTAR	CALEPIN	DILUTED	HALFWAY	MALTHUS	POLENTA	SOLUBLE	WALPOLE
APLASIA	CALIBAN	DOLEFUL	HALFWIT	MALTOSE	POLITIC	SOLVENT	WALTZER
BALANCE	CALIBER	DOLLARS	HALIBUT	MELANIN	POLIZEI	SPLASHY	WELCOME
BALATON	CALIBRE	DOLORES	HALIFAX	MELILOT	POLLACK	SPLAYED	WELDING
BALCONY	CALICHE	DOLPHIN	HALITUS	MELLITE	POLLARD	SPLICED	WELFARE
BALDING	CALLBOX	DULLARD	HALLALI	MELODIC	POLLING	SPLICER	WELLIES
BALDRIC	CALLBOY	ECLIPSE	HALLWAY	MELROSE	POLLUTE	SPLODGE	WELLOFF
BALDWIN	CALLING	ECLOGUE	HALOGEN	MELTING	POLONIE	SPLOTCH	WILDCAT
BALEFUL	CALLOUS	EELPOUT	HALTERE	MILEAGE	POLYGON	SPLURGE	WILDING
BALFOUR	CALMUCK	EGLOGUE	HALTING	MILFOIL	POLYMER	SULFATE	WILFRED
BALLADE	CALOMEL	ELLIPSE	HALYARD	MILITIA	POLYOMA	SULKILY	WILLIAM
BALLAST	CALORIC	ENLARGE	HELICAL	MILKING	POLYPOD	SULLAGE	WILLIES
BALLBOY	CALORIE	ENLIVEN	HELICON	MILKMAN		SULPHUR	WILLING
BALLIOL	CALTROP	EULALIE	HELIPAD	MILKSOP		SULTANA	WILLOWY

WOLFISH	COMPUTE	JAMAICA	POMEROL	SUMMONS	BENARES	CONCOCT	DUNNAGE
WOLFRAM	COMRADE	JAMESON	POMEROY	SYMPTOM	BENCHER	CONCORD	DUNNOCK
YELLOWS	CUMBRIA	JAMMIES	POMFRET	TAMARIN	BENDING	CONCUSS	DUNSTAN
ZILLION	CUMSHAW	JAMMING	POMMARD	TAMBOUR	BENEATH	CONDEMN	DYNAMIC
ADMIRAL	CUMULUS	JAMPANI	POMPEII	TAMESIS	BENEFIT	CONDOLE	DYNASTY
ADMIRED	CYMBALS	JIMJAMS	POMPOON	TAMMANY	BENGALI	CONDONE	ENNOBLE
ADMIRER	DAMAGED	JUMBLED	POMPOUS	TAMPICO	BENISON	CONDUCT	FANATIC
AIMLESS	DAMAGES	JUMBLES	PUMPKIN	TAMPION	BENNETT	CONDUIT	FANCIED
ALMACKS	DAMNING	JUMPING	RAMADAN	TEMPERA	BENTHAM	CONFESS	FANCIER
ALMANAC	DAMOSEL	KAMERAD	RAMBLER	TEMPEST	BENTHOS	CONFIDE	FANFARE
ALMONER	DAMPIER	KAMPALA	RAMEKIN	TEMPLAR	BENZENE	CONFINE	FANGLED
AMMETER	DAMPING	KAMPONG	RAMESES	TEMPLET	BENZINE	CONFIRM	FANTAIL
AMMONAL	DEMERGE	KUMQUAT	RAMPAGE	TEMPTER	BENZOIN	CONFORM	FANTASY
AMMONIA	DEMERIT	LAMAISM	RAMPANT	TEMPURA	BINDERY	CONFUSE	FANWORM
ARMBAND	DEMESNE	LAMAIST	RAMPART	TIMBALE	BINDING	CONGEAL	FANWORT
ARMHOLE	DEMETER	LAMBADA	RAMULUS	TIMBERS	BONANZA	CONICAL	FANZINE
ARMORED	DEMIGOD	LAMBAST	REMAINS	TIMBREL	BONDAGE	CONIFER	FENCING
ARMORIC	DEMONIC	LAMBENT	REMARRY	TIMELAG	BONDMAN	CONJOIN	FENELON
ARMOURY	DEMOTIC	LAMBERT	REMBLAI	TIMEOUT	BONESET	CONJURE	FENLAND
ARMREST	DIMNESS	LAMBETH	REMNANT	TIMIDLY	BONFIRE	CONNATE	FINAGLE
BAMBINO	DIMPLED	LAMBING	REMODEL	TIMOTHY	BONKERS	CONNECT	FINALLY
BEMUSED	DOMAINE	LAMELLA	REMORSE	TIMPANI	BONNARD	CONNIVE	FINANCE
BOMBARD	DOMINGO	LAMPOON	REMOULD	TOMBOLA	BUNDOOK	CONNOTE	FINBACK
BOMBAST	DOMINIC	LAMPREY	REMOUNT	TOMFOOL	BUNGLER	CONQUER	FINDING
BOMBING	DUMPISH	LEMMATA	REMOVAL	TOMPION	BUNTING	CONSENT	FINESSE
BUMBOAT	FEMORAL	LEMMING	REMOVED	TUMBLER	CANASTA	CONSIGN	FINFOOT
BUMMALO	FIMBRIA	LEMPIRA	REMOVER	TUMBREL	CANDACE	CONSIST	FINGERS
BUMPKIN	FUMETTE	LIMINAL	RIMLESS	TUMBRIL	CANDELA	CONSOLE	FINICAL
CAMBIUM	GAMBADO	LIMITED	ROMAINE	TUMULUS	CANDIDA	CONSOLS	FINICKY
CAMBRAI	GAMBIAN	LIMITER	ROMANCE	TYMPANO	CANDIDE	CONSORT	FINLAND
CAMBRIC	GAMBLER	LIMPKIN	ROMANIA	TYMPANY	CANDIED	CONSULT	FINNISH
CAMELOT	GAMBOGE	LIMPOPO	ROMANOV	UNMIXED	CANDOUR	CONSUME	FONDANT
CAMERON	GAMELAN	LOMBARD	ROMANZA	UNMOVED	CANELLA	CONTACT	FUNCHAL
CAMILLA	GEMMATE	LUMBAGO	ROMPERS	VAMOOSE	CANIDAE	CONTAIN	FUNDING
CAMOGIE	GIMBALS	LUMPISH	ROMULUS	VAMPIRE	CANNERY	CONTEMN	FUNERAL
CAMORRA	GIMBLET	LUMPKIN	RUMBLER	WIMPISH	CANNILY	CONTEND	FUNFAIR
CAMPANA	GIMMICK	LYMNAEA	RUMMAGE	WOMANLY	CANNING	CONTENT	FUNGOID
CAMPARI	GOMBEEN	MAMILLA	RUMORED	XIMENES	CANNOCK	CONTEST	FUNGOUS
CAMPHOR	GOMORRA	MAMMARY	RUMPLED	ZAMBESI	CANNULA	CONTEXT	FUNNILY
CAMPING	GUMBOIL	MAMMOTH	RUMPOLE	ZAMBIAN	CANONRY	CONTORT	GANELON
CAMPION	GUMBOOT	MEMBERS	SAMARIA	ZAMORIN	CANTATA	CONTOUR	GANGWAY
CAMWOOD	GUMDROP	MEMENTO	SAMBUCA	ZEMSTVO	CANTEEN	CONTROL	GENERAL
CEMBALO	GUMSHOE	MEMOIRS	SAMISEN	ZYMOGEN	CANTHUS	CONVENE	GENERIC
CIMABUE	GYMNAST	MIMICRY	SAMNITE	ZYMOSIS	CANTRIP	CONVENT	GENESIS
COMBINE	GYMSLIP	MIMULUS	SAMOOSA	ZYMURGY	CANTUAR	CONVERT	GENETIC
COMBING	HAMMOCK	MOMBASA	SAMOVAR	AINTREE	CANVASS	CONVICT	GENISTA
COMFORT	HAMSTER	MOMENTS	SAMOYED	AMNESIA	CANZONA	CONVOKE	GENITAL
COMFREY	HEMLINE	MUMMERS	SAMPLER	AMNESTY	CANZONE	CUNNING	GENOESE
COMICAL	HEMLOCK	MUMMERY	SAMURAI	ANNATTO	CENACLE	CYNICAL	GENTEEL
COMMAND	HIMSELF	MUMMIFY	SEMINAL	ANNELID	CENSURE	CYNTHIA	GENTIAN
COMMEND	HOMBURG	NAMIBIA	SEMINAR	ANNOYED	CENTAUR	DANCING	GENTILE
COMMENT	HOMERIC	NEMESIA	SEMIPRO	ANNUITY	CENTAVO	DANTEAN	GENUINE
COMMODE	HOMINID	NEMESIS	SEMITIC	ANNULAR	CENTRAL	DENDRON	GINGHAM
COMMODO	HOMONYM	NEMORAL	SHMOOZE	ANNULET	CENTRED	DENIZEN	GINSENG
COMMONS	HUMANLY	NOMADIC	SIMENON	ANNULUS	CENTRIC	DENMARK	GONDOLA
COMMUNE	HUMBLES	NOMBRIL	SIMILAR	BANANAS	CENTRUM	DENSELY	GUNBOAT
COMMUTE	HUMDRUM	NOMINAL	SIMPKIN	BANBURY	CENTURY	DENSITY	GUNFIRE
COMPACT	HUMERUS	NOMINEE	SIMPLER	BANDAGE	CINDERS	DENTINE	GUNNERA
COMPANY	HUMIDOR	NUMBERS	SIMPLEX	BANDAID	CINEMAS	DENTIST	GUNNERY
COMPARE	HUMMING	NUMBLES	SIMPLON	BANDBOX	CINEREA	DENTURE	GUNPLAY
COMPASS	HUMMOCK	NUMERAL	SIMPSON	BANDEAU	CONAKRY	DINETTE	GUNROOM
COMPERE	HYMNIST	NUMERIC	SOMALIA	BANDORE	CONCAVE	DINGBAT	GUNSHOT
COMPETE	HYMNODY	NUMMARY	SOMEHOW	BANGING	CONCEAL	DINMONT	GUNWALE
COMPILE	IAMBIST	NYMPHET	SOMEONE	BANGKOK	CONCEDE	DONEGAL	HANDBAG
COMPLEX	IMMENSE	ONMIBUS	SOMEWAY	BANKING	CONCEIT	DONNISH	HANDFUL
COMPORT	IMMERGE	OSMANLI	SUMATRA	BANKSIA	CONCEPT	DUNCIAD	HANDGUN
COMPOSE	IMMERSE	OSMOSIS	SUMMARY	BANNOCK	CONCERN	DUNEDIN	HANDILY
COMPOST	IMMORAL	PIMENTO	SUMMERY	BANQUET	CONCERT	DUNGEON	HANDLED
COMPOTE	ISMAILI	PIMPING	SUMMING	BANSHEE	CONCISE	DUNKIRK	HANDLER

HANDOUT	LENIENT	MINSTER	PENTODE	SINGLES	UNNERVE	AROUSAL	CLOSING
HANDSAW	LENTIGO	MINUEND	PENTOSE	SINGLET	VANADIC	ASOCIAL	CLOSURE
HANDSEL	LENTILS	MINUTED	PINBALL	SINHALA	VANDALS	ATOMIST	CLOTHED
HANDSET	LINACRE	MINUTES	PINCERS	SINKING	VANDYKE	ATOMIZE	CLOTHES
HANGDOG	LINCOLN	MINUTIA	PINCHED	SINUATE	VANESSA	AVOCADO	CLOTURE
HANGING	LINCTUS	MONARCH	PINETUM	SINUOUS	VANILLA	AVOIDER	CLOUDED
HANGMAN	LINDANE	MONEYED	PINFISH	SONDAGE	VANITAS	AXOLOTL	CLOYING
HANGMEN	LINEAGE	MONGREL	PINFOLD	SUNBEAM	VANTAGE	BEOWULF	COOKERY
HANGOUT	LINEMAN	MONILIA	PINHEAD	SUNBURN	VANUATU	BIOCIDE	COOKING
HANOVER	LINGUAL	MONITOR	PINHOLE	SUNDECK	VENDING	BIOLOGY	COOLANT
HANSARD	LININGS	MONKISH	PINKEYE	SUNDIAL	VENDOME	BIOMASS	COOLING
HENBANE	LINKAGE	MONOCLE	PINNACE	SUNDOWN	VENERER	BIOTECH	COONCAN
HENGIST	LINKING	MONOCOT	PINNULA	SUNLAMP	VENISON	BLOATED	CROAKER
HENNAED	LINKMAN	MONOLOG	PINTADO	SUNLESS	VENTOSE	BLOATER	CROATIA
HENPECK	LINNEAN	MONOPLY	PINTAIL	SUNNILY	VENTRAL	BLOCKED	CROCHET
HINDLEG	LINOCUT	MONSOON	PONIARD	SUNNITE	VENTURE	BLOCKER	CROCKET
HONESTY	LINSANG	MONSTER	PONTIAC	SUNRISE	VINASSE	BLOOMER	CROESUS
HONEYED	LINSEED	MONTAGE	PONTIFF	SUNROOF	VINCENT	BLOOPER	CROFTER
HONITON	LONGBOW	MONTAGU	PONTINE	SUNSPOT	VINEGAR	BLOSSOM	CROOKED
HONOURS	LONGING	MONTANA	PONTOON	SUNTRAP	VINTAGE	BLOTCHY	CROONER
HUNCHED	LUNATIC	MONTANT	PUNCHED	SYNAPSE	VINTNER	BLOTTER	CROPPED
HUNDRED	LUNETTE	MONTERO	PUNCHER	SYNAXIS	WANGLER	BLOUSON	CROPPER
HUNGARY	LYNCHET	MONTHLY	PUNGENT	SYNCOPE	WANTING	BLOWFLY	CROQUET
HUNKERS	MANACLE	MUNDANE	PUNJABI	SYNERGY	WENDELL	BLOWOUT	CROQUIS
HUNTING	MANAGER	MUNSTER	PUNSTER	SYNONYM	WENDISH	BOOBOOK	CROSIER
IGNEOUS	MANAGUA	MUNTJAC	PUNTING	SYNOVIA	WENLOCK	BOOKIES	CROSSED
IGNOBLE	MANAKIN	MYNHEER	RANCHER	TANAGER	WINDBAG	BOOKING	CROSSLY
IGNORED	MANATEE	NANKEEN	RANCOUR	TANAGRA	WINDING	BOOKISH	CROUTON
INNARDS	MANDALA	NINEPIN	RANGOON	TANBARK	WINDOWS	BOOKLET	CROWBAR
INNERVE	MANDATE	NINEVEH	RANIDAE	TANCRED	WINDROW	BOOKMAN	CROWDED
INNINGS	MANDIOC	NONPLUS	RANKING	TANGENT	WINDSOR	BOOLEAN	CROWING
IONESCO	MANGOLD	NONPROS	RANSACK	TANGIER	WINGMAN	BOOMING	CROZIER
JANITOR	MANHOLE	NONSTOP	RANTING	TANGLED	WINNING	BOORISH	DIOCESE
JANKERS	MANHOOD	NONSUCH	RENEGUE	TANKARD	WINNOCK	BOOSTER	DIOPTER
JANUARY	MANHUNT	NONSUIT	RENEWAL	TANNATE	WINSOME	BOOTLEG	DIOPTRE
JENKINS	MANIHOC	NUNLIKE	RINGERS	TANNERY	WINSTON	BROADEN	DIORAMA
JONQUIL	MANIKIN	NUNNERY	RINGGIT	TANNING	WONDERS	BROADLY	DIORITE
JUNIPER	MANILLA	NYNORSK	RINGING	TANTARA	XANTHOS	BROCADE	DIOXIDE
KANNADA	MANIPLE	OMNIBUS	RINGLET	TANTIVY	XENOPUS	BROILER	DOODLER
KENNEDY	MANITOU	PANACEA	RONDEAU	TANTRUM	YANGTSE	BROKERS	DOORKEY
KENNELS	MANKIND	PANACHE	RONSARD	TENABLE	YONKERS	BROMATE	DOORMAN
KENNING	MANMADE	PANCAKE	RONTGEN	TENANCY	ZINGARO	BROMIDE	DOORMAT
KENOSIS	MANNERS	PANCRAS	RUNAWAY	TENANTS	ABOLISH	BROMINE	DOORWAY
KENOTIC	MANNING	PANDORA	RUNCORN	TENDRIL	ABOUKIR	BRONCHI	DROPLET
KENTISH	MANNISH	PANGAEA	RUNDOWN	TENFOLD	ABOULIA	BRONZED	DROPPER
KINDRED	MANSARD	PANGRAM	RUNNERS	TENNIEL	ACOLYTE	BROTHEL	DROSHKY
KINESIS	MANSION	PANICKY	RUNNING	TENSELY	ACONITE	BROTHER	DROUGHT
KINETIC	MANSIZE	PANICLE	RUNNION	TENSILE	ADONAIS	BROUGHT	DUOPOLY
KINGCUP	MANTUAN	PANNAGE	SANCTUM	TENSING	ADOPTED	BROWNED	DVORNIK
KINGDOM	MANUMIT	PANNIER	SANCTUS	TENSION	ADORING	BROWNIE	EBONITE
KINGLET	MANXMAN	PANNOSE	SANDALS	TENUOUS	ADORNED	BROWSER	ECOLOGY
KINGPIN	MENDING	PANOPLY	SANDBAG	TINFOIL	AEOLIAN	BUOYANT	ECONOMY
KINSHIP	MENFOLK	PANTHER	SANDBOX	TINGLER	AGONIST	CHOCTAW	EGOTISM
KINSMAN	MENORAH	PANTIES	SANDBOY	TINTACK	AGONIZE	CHOKING	EGOTIST
KINTYRE	MENTHOL	PANTILE	SANDMAN	TINTERN	AMOEBIC	CHOLERA	ELOGIUM
KONTIKI	MENTION	PANURGE	SANDOWN	TONETIC	AMONGST	CHOOKIE	EMOTION
LANCERS	MENUHIN	PENALTY	SANDPIT	TONGUES	AMORIST	CHOPINE	EMOTIVE
LANCING	MINARET	PENANCE	SANGRIA	TONIGHT	AMORITE	CHOPPER	ENOLOGY
LANDING	MINCING	PENATES	SENATOR	TONNAGE	AMOROSO	CHORALE	ERODIUM
LANGLEY	MINDFUL	PENDANT	SENDOFF	TONNEAU	AMOROUS	CHORDAE	EROSION
LANGTON	MINDSET	PENDING	SENECIO	TONNISH	ANODIZE	CHORION	EROTICA
LANGUID	MINERAL	PENGUIN	SENEGAL	TONSURE	ANODYNE	CHORIZO	ETONIAN
LANGUOR	MINERVA	PENNANT	SENSATE	TONTINE	ANOMALY	CHOROID	EXOCARP
LANOLIN	MINIBUS	PENNATE	SENSORY	TUNABLE	ANOSMIA	CHORTLE	EXOGAMY
LANTANA	MINICAB	PENNINE	SENSUAL	TUNEFUL	ANOTHER	CHOWDER	FLOATER
LANTERN	MINIMAL	PENSILE	SINATRA	TUNICLE	APOCOPE	CLOBBER	FLODDEN
LANYARD	MINIMAX	PENSION	SINCERE	TUNISIA	APOGEAN	CLOISON	FLOGGER
LENDING	MINIMUM	PENSIVE	SINDBAD	TYNWALD	APOLOGY	CLOSELY	FLOGGED
LENGTHY	MINORCA	PENTANE	SINGING	UNNAMED	APOSTLE	CLOSEUP	FLOODED

FLOOZIE	ISOTONE	PROCTOR	SCORPIO	THOUGHT	BAPTIST	FOPPISH	PIPETTE
FLORIDA	ISOTOPE	PROCURE	SCOTTIE	TOOLBOX	BAPTIZE	HAPLESS	POPCORN
FLORIST	IVORIAN	PRODIGY	SCOURER	TOOLING	BIPLANE	HAPORTH	POPEYED
FLOTSAM	IVORIEN	PRODUCE	SCOURGE	TOOTHED	CAPABLE	HAPPILY	POPOVER
FLOUNCE	KNOBBLE	PRODUCT	SCOWDER	TOOTSIE	CAPABLY	HEPARIN	POPPING
FLOWERS	KNOBBLY	PROFANE	SHOCKED	TROCHEE	CAPELLA	HEPATIC	POPULAR
FLOWERY	KNOCKER	PROFESS	SHOCKER	TROCHUS	CAPITAL	HEPTANE	POPULUS
FLOWING	KNOTTED	PROFFER	SHOOTER	TRODDEN	CAPITOL	HIPBONE	RAPHAEL
FOOLISH	KNOWALL	PROFILE	SHOPPER	TROILUS	CAPORAL	HIPSTER	RAPIDLY
FOOTAGE	KNOWHOW	PROFITS	SHORTEN	TROLLEY	CAPRICE	HOPEFUL	RAPPORT
FOOTING	KNOWING	PROFUSE	SHORTLY	TROLLOP	CAPSIZE	HOPKINS	RAPTURE
FOOTMAN	LAOCOON	PROGENY	SHOTGUN	TROOPER	CAPSTAN	HOPLITE	REPAINT
FOOTPAD	LAOTIAN	PROGRAM	SHOUTER	TROPHIC	CAPSULE	HOPPING	REPAIRS
FOOTSIE	LEONARD	PROJECT	SHOWBIZ	TROPICS	CAPTAIN	HOPSACK	REPLACE
FROEBEL	LEONINE	PROLONG	SHOWERS	TROPISM	CAPTION	HYPOGEA	REPLANT
FROGMAN	LEOPARD	PROMISE	SHOWERY	TROTSKY	CAPTIVE	HYPONYM	REPLETE
FRONTAL	LEOPOLD	PROMOTE	SHOWILY	TROTTER	CAPTURE	HYPOXIA	REPLEVY
FROSTED	LEOTARD	PRONAOS	SHOWING	TROUBLE	CEPHEUS	IMPASSE	REPLICA
FROWSTY	LIONESS	PRONATE	SHOWMAN	TROUNCE	COPILOT	IMPASTO	REPOSAL
GEODESY	LIONIZE	PRONGED	SHOWOFF	TROUPER	COPIOUS	IMPAVID	REPRESS
GEOLOGY	LOOKING	PRONOUN	SLOBBER	TROUSER	COPLAND	IMPEACH	REPRINT
GEORDIE	LOOKOUT	PROPANE	SLOGGER	TWOFOLD	COPPERS	IMPERIL	REPROOF
GEORGIA	LOOMING	PROPEND	SLOPING	TWOSOME	COPPICE	IMPETUS	REPROVE
GEORGIC	LOOSELY	PROPHET	SLOSHED	TWOSTEP	COPYCAT	IMPIETY	REPTILE
GHOSTLY	LOOTING	PROPOSE	SLOTTED	TWOTIME	COPYING	IMPINGE	REPULSE
GLOBULE	MIOCENE	PROSAIC	SLOVENE	UGOLINO	COPYIST	IMPIOUS	REPUTED
GLORIFY	MOODILY	PROSODY	SLOWING	UNOWNED	CUPROUS	IMPLANT	RIPCORD
GLOTTAL	MOONING	PROSPER	SMOKING	UROLITH	CYPRESS	IMPLIED	RIPOSTE
GLOTTIS	MOONLIT	PROTEAN	SMOLDER	UTOPIAN	CYPRIOT	IMPLODE	RIPPING
GLOWING	MOORHEN	PROTECT	SMOOTHE	UXORIAL	DAPHNID	IMPLORE	RIPTIDE
GNOCCHI	MOORING	PROTEGE	SMOTHER	VIOLATE	DAPHNIS	IMPOUND	RUPTURE
GNOSTIC	MOORISH	PROTEIN	SNOOKER	VIOLENT	DAPPLED	IMPREST	SAPIENS
GOODBYE	NEOLITH	PROTEST	SNOOPER	WHOEVER	DEPLETE	IMPRINT	SAPIENT
GOODIES	NEOTENY	PROTEUS	SNORING	WHOOPEE	DEPLORE	IMPROVE	SAPLING
GOODISH	NIOBEAN	PROTIST	SNORKEL	WHOOPER	DEPOSIT	IMPULSE	SAPONIN
GOODMAN	NIOBIUM	PROUDER	SNORTER	WHOPPER	DEPRAVE	JAPLISH	SAPPERS
GOODWIN	NOODLES	PROUDIE	SNORTLE	WOODCUT	DEPRESS	JUPITER	SAPPHIC
GOOLIES	NOOLOGY	PROUDLY	SNOWDON	WOODMAN	DEPRIVE	KIPLING	SAPROBE
GROCERS	NOONDAY	PROVERB	SNOWMAN	WOOLLEN	DIPLOCK	KIPPERS	SAPWOOD
GROCERY	ODONTIC	PROVIDE	SPOILED	WOOMERA	DIPLOMA	LAPPING	SEPPUKU
GROCKLE	ODORANT	PROVING	SPOILER	WOOSTER	DIPOLAR	LAPSANG	SIPPING
GROGRAM	ODOROUS	PROVISO	SPONDEE	WRONGLY	DIPTERA	LAPUTAN	SOPHISM
GROINED	OLOROSO	PROVOKE	SPONDYL	WROUGHT	DIPTYCH	LAPWING	SOPHIST
GROLIER	OPOSSUM	PROVOST	SPONGER	WYOMING	DOPPLER	LEPANTO	SOPPING
GROMMET	OROGENY	PTOLEMY	SPONSON	YAOUNDE	EMPANEL	LEPROSY	SOPRANO
GROOVED	ORONTES	QUONDAM	SPONSOR	ZEOLITE	EMPATHY	LEPROUS	SOPWITH
GROPIUS	OROTUND	QUONSET	SPOONER	ZIONIST	EMPEROR	LIPREAD	SUPPORT
GROSSLY	OXONIAN	QUORATE	SPORRAN	ZOOLITE	EMPIRIC	MAPPING	SUPPOSE
GROTIUS	PEONAGE	REOCCUR	SPOTTED	ZOOLOGY	EMPLOYS	MOPPING	SUPREME
GROUCHO	PHOEBUS	RHODIAN	SPOTTER	ZOOTOMY	EMPOWER	NAPHTHA	SUPREMO
GROUCHY	PHOENIX	RHODIUM	SPOUSAL	ALPHEUS	EMPRESS	NAPPING	TAPIOCA
GROUNDS	PHONEIN	RHOMBUS	STOICAL	AMPHORA	EMPYEMA	NEPTUNE	TAPLASH
GROUPER	PHONEME	RHONDDA	STOLLEN	AMPLIFY	ENPRINT	NIPPERS	TAPPICE
GROUPIE	PHONICS	RIOTERS	STOMACH	AMPOULE	ESPARTO	NUPTIAL	TAPPING
GROUSER	PIONEER	RIOTING	STONILY	AMPULLA	ESPOUSE	OMPHALE	TAPROOM
GROWING	PIOUSLY	RIOTOUS	STONKER	APPARAT	EUPEPSY	OPPOSED	TAPROOT
GROWLER	PLODDER	ROOFING	STOPGAP	APPAREL	EUPHONY	OPPRESS	TAPSTER
GROWNUP	PLOSION	ROOFTOP	STOPPED	APPEASE	EXPANSE	ORPHEAN	TIPCART
HOODLUM	PLOSIVE	ROOKERY	STOPPER	APPLAUD	EXPENSE	ORPHEUS	TIPPING
IDOLIZE	PLOTTER	ROOKISH	STORAGE	APPLIED	EXPIATE	ORPHISM	TIPPLER
IPOMOEA	PLOWMAN	ROOSTER	STORIED	APPOINT	EXPIRED	ORPHREY	TIPSILY
IRONING	POOFTER	ROOTING	STORIES	APPOSED	EXPLAIN	PAPILLA	TIPSTER
ISOBASE	POOHBAH	SCOFFER	STOUTLY	APPRIZE	EXPLODE	PAPOOSE	TOPCOAT
ISODORE	PROBAND	SCOLLOP	SWOLLEN	APPROVE	EXPLOIT	PAPRIKA	TOPIARY
ISOGRAM	PROBATE	SCOOTER	THOMISM	ASPASIA	EXPLORE	PAPYRUS	TOPICAL
ISOHYET	PROBITY	SCORING	THOMIST	ASPERGE	EXPOSED	PEPPERS	TOPKAPI
ISOLATE	PROBLEM	SCORING	THOMSON	ASPHALT	EXPOUND	PEPPERY	TOPKNOT
ISOMERE	PROCEED	SCOFFER	THOREAU	ASPIRIN	EXPRESS	PEPPERY	TOPLESS
ISOSPIN	PROCESS	SCORING	THORIUM	BAPTISM	EXPUNGE	PEPSINE	TOPMAST

TOPMOST	APRAXIA	BYRONIC	CORNCOB	FARMING	GERAINT	KERNITE	MORDANT
TOPPING	APRICOT	CARABID	CORNEAL	FARNESE	GERBERA	KEROGEN	MOREISH
TOPSIDE	APROPOS	CARACAL	CORNELL	FARRAGO	GERMANE	KURHAUS	MORELLO
TOPSOIL	ARRAIGN	CARACAS	CORNICE	FARRIER	GERMANY	KURSAAL	MORESBY
TOPSPIN	ARRANGE	CARACUL	CORNISH	FARTHER	GIRAFFE	LARCENY	MORESCO
TYPHOID	ARRAYED	CARADOC	CORNROW	FERMENT	GIRASOL	LARDOON	MORLAND
TYPHOON	ARREARS	CARAMBA	COROLLA	FERMIUM	GIRLISH	LARGELY	MORNING
TYPICAL	ARRIVAL	CARAMEL	CORONER	FERROUS	GIRONDE	LARGESS	MOROCCO
UMPTEEN	ARRIVED	CARAVAN	CORONET	FERRULE	GORDIAN	LARGEST	MORONIC
UNPAGED	ATROPHY	CARAVEL	CORRECT	FERTILE	GORDIUS	LORDING	MORPHIA
VAPOURS	ATROPOS	CARAWAY	CORRIDA	FERVENT	GORILLA	LORELEI	MORRELL
WAPPING	AURALLY	CARBIDE	CORRODE	FERVOUR	GORSEDD	LURCHER	MORTALS
WIPEOUT	AUREATE	CARBINE	CORRUPT	FIRCONE	HARBOUR	LURIDLY	MORTICE
ZAPOTEC	AURELIA	CARCASE	CORSAGE	FIREARM	HARDPAN	LURKING	MORTIFY
ZEPHIEL	AUREOLA	CARCASS	CORSAIR	FIREBUG	HARDTOP	LYRICAL	MORTISE
ACQUIRE	AUREOLE	CARDIAC	CORTEGE	FIREDOG	HARELIP	MARABOU	MURAENA
ASQUITH	AURICLE	CARDOON	CORTINA	FIREFLY	HARICOT	MARACAS	MURIATE
BEQUEST	AUROCHS	CARDUUS	CORUNNA	FIREMAN	HARLECH	MARANTA	MURILLO
ENQUIRE	BARBARA	CAREERS	CORYDON	FIRSTLY	HARNESS	MARATHA	MURRAIN
ENQUIRY	BARBARY	CAREFUL	CURABLE	FORAMEN	HARPIST	MARBLED	MYRINGA
ESQUIRE	BARENTS	CARGOES	CURACAO	FORBADE	HARPOON	MARBLES	NARRATE
INQUEST	BARGAIN	CARIBOU	CURATOR	FORBEAR	HARRIER	MARBURG	NARROWS
INQUIRE	BARKERS	CARIOCA	CURCUMA	FORCEPS	HARRIET	MARCHER	NARTHEX
INQUIRY	BARKING	CARIOLE	CURDLED	FOREARM	HARSHLY	MARCONI	NARWHAL
LIQUEFY	BARMAID	CARITAS	CURETTE	FOREIGN	HARVARD	MARCUSE	NERITIC
LIQUEUR	BARNABY	CARLOAD	CURIOUS	FORELEG	HARVEST	MAREMMA	NERVOSA
LIQUIDS	BARONET	CARLYLE	CURLING	FOREMAN	HARWICH	MARENGO	NERVOUS
PIQUANT	BAROQUE	CARMINE	CURRAGH	FOREPAW	HARWOOD	MARGERY	NERVURE
REQUEST	BARRACK	CARNABY	CURRANT	FORESEE	HERBAGE	MARIBOU	NIRVANA
REQUIEM	BARRAGE	CARNAGE	CURRENT	FOREVER	HERBERT	MARINER	NORFOLK
REQUIRE	BARRIER	CAROLUS	CURRIED	FORFEIT	HERBERY	MARITAL	NORWICH
REQUITE	BARRING	CAROTID	CURSIVE	FORFEND	HERBIST	MARKING	NUREYEV
SAQQARA	BARYTES	CAROTIN	CURSORY	FORGAVE	HEREDIA	MARLENE	NURSERY
SEQUELA	BERCEAU	CAROUSE	CURTAIL	FORGERY	HERETIC	MARLINE	NURSING
SEQUOIA	BEREAVE	CARPORT	CURTAIN	FORGIVE	HEROINE	MARLITE	NURTURE
TEQUILA	BERGSON	CARRELL	CURTSEY	FORGONE	HEROISM	MARLOWE	OARFISH
UNQUIET	BERLINE	CARRIED	DARLING	FORLORN	HERRICK	MARMARA	OARLOCK
UNQUOTE	BERMUDA	CARRIER	DARNING	FORMICA	HERRIES	MARMION	OARSMAN
AARONIC	BERNARD	CARRION	DERANGE	FORMING	HERRING	MARMITE	OARSMEN
ABRAHAM	BERNINI	CARROLL	DERONDA	FORMOSA	HERSELF	MARQUEE	OERSTED
ABRAXIS	BERSEEM	CARROTS	DERRICK	FORMULA	HIRSUTE	MARQUIS	OGREISH
ABREAST	BERSERK	CARROTY	DERVISH	FORSAKE	HORATIO	MARRIED	OTRANTO
ABRIDGE	BERTRAM	CARSICK	DERWENT	FORSTER	HORDEUM	MARRYAT	PARABLE
ACREAGE	BIRDMAN	CARTIER	DORKING	FORTIES	HORIZON	MARSALA	PARADOR
ACROBAT	BIRETTA	CARTOON	DORMANT	FORTIFY	HORMONE	MARSHAL	PARADOS
ACRONYM	BORACIC	CARVING	DOROTHY	FORTRAN	HORRIFY	MARSYAS	PARADOX
ACRYLIC	BORDERS	CERAMIC	DURABLE	FORTUNE	HORRORS	MARTENS	PARAGON
ADRENAL	BOREDOM	CERTAIN	DURABLY	FORWARD	HORSING	MARTIAL	PARAPET
AERATED	BORODIN	CERTIFY	DURAMEN	FURBISH	HURDLER	MARTIAN	PARASOL
AEROBIC	BOROUGH	CHRISOM	DURRELL	FURCATE	HURDLES	MARTINI	PARBOIL
AEROSOL	BORSTAL	CHRISTY	EARACHE	FURIOUS	HURLING	MARTLET	PARCHED
AFRICAN	BURBAGE	CHRONIC	EARDRUM	FURLONG	HURRIED	MARTYRS	PARENTS
AGRAPHA	BURDOCK	CIRCLET	EARLDOM	FURNACE	HURTFUL	MARVELL	PARESIS
AGRIPPA	BURETTE	CIRCLIP	EARLIER	FURNISH	INROADS	MARXISM	PARFAIT
AGROUND	BURGEON	CIRCUIT	EARLOBE	FURRIER	ISRAELI	MARXIST	PARINGS
AIRBASE	BURGESS	CIRROSE	EARMARK	FURTHER	IVRESSE	MERCERY	PARKING
AIRCREW	BURGHER	CORACLE	EARNEST	FURTIVE	JERICHO	MERCIES	PARKWAY
AIRFLOW	BURGLAR	CORANTO	EARRING	GARBAGE	JERKILY	MERCURY	PARLOUR
AIRLESS	BURKINA	CORBEAU	EARSHOT	GARBLED	JERSEYS	MERITED	PARLOUS
AIRLIFT	BURMESE	CORBETT	EARTHEN	GARBOIL	JURYBOX	MERMAID	PARNELL
AIRLINE	BURNELL	CORDATE	EARTHLY	GARBURE	JURYMAN	MERRIER	PAROTIC
AIRLOCK	BURNHAM	CORDIAL	ENRAGED	GARDENS	KARACHI	MERRILY	PAROTID
AIRMAIL	BURNING	CORDITE	ERRATIC	GARFISH	KARAJAN	MIRACLE	PAROTIS
AIRPORT	BURNISH	CORDOBA	ERRATUM	GARLAND	KARAKUL	MIRADOR	PARQUET
AIRSHIP	BURNOUS	CORELLI	ETRURIA	GARMENT	KARAOKE	MIRANDA	PARSLEY
AIRSICK	BURNOUT	CORINTH	FARADAY	GARNISH	KERATIN	MIRIFIC	PARSNIP
AIRSTOP	BURSARY	CORKAGE	FARAWAY	GARONNE	KERMESS	MORAINE	PARTAKE
ALREADY	BURSTER	CORKING	FARCEUR	GAROTTE		MORALLY	PARTHIA
ALRIGHT	BURUNDI		FARMERS	GARRICK		MORAVIA	PARTIAL

PARTING	PYROSIS	STRATUM	TORCHON	WARLOCK	BESMEAR	DISAVOW	FUSEBOX
PARTITA	PYRRHIC	STRATUS	TORMENT	WARLORD	BESPEAK	DISBAND	FUSIBLE
PARTNER	RAREBIT	STRAUSS	TORNADE	WARMING	BESPOKE	DISBARK	FUSILLI
PARVENU	REREDOS	STREAKY	TORNADO	WARNING	BESTIAL	DISCARD	FUSSILY
PERCALE	REROUTE	STRETCH	TORONTO	WARPATH	BESTREW	DISCERN	FUSTIAN
PERCENT	RORQUAL	STREWTH	TORPEDO	WARRANT	BISCUIT	DISCORD	GASCONY
PERCEPT	SARACEN	STRIATE	TORPIDS	WARRING	BISMUTH	DISCUSS	GASEOUS
PERCUSS	SARCASM	STRIDES	TORREFY	WARRIOR	BISTORT	DISDAIN	GASFIRE
PEREIRA	SARCOMA	STRIDOR	TORRENT	WARSHIP	BOSWELL	DISEASE	GASMASK
PERFECT	SARCOUS	STRIGIL	TORSADE	WARTHOG	BUSHIDO	DISGUST	GASOHOL
PERFIDY	SARDANA	STRIKER	TORSION	WARTIME	BUSHMAN	DISJOIN	GASPING
PERFORM	SARDINE	STRINGS	TORTILE	WARWICK	BUSHMEN	DISLIKE	GASTHOF
PERFUME	SARGENT	STRINGY	TORTRIX	WIRETAP	BUSKINS	DISMAST	GASTRIC
PERFUSE	SARMENT	STRIPED	TORTURE	WORDILY	BUSSING	DISMISS	GASTRIN
PERGOLA	SAROYAN	STRIPER	TURBARY	WORDING	BUSTARD	DISOBEY	GESTALT
PERHAPS	SCRAGGY	STRIPES	TURBINE	WORKERS	BUSTLER	DISPLAY	GESTAPO
PERIGEE	SCRAPER	STROBIC	TURENNE	WORKING	BUSTLES	DISPORT	GESTATE
PERIWIG	SCRAPIE	STROPHE	TURGENT	WORKMAN	CASCADE	DISPOSE	GESTURE
PERJURE	SCRAPPY	STROPPY	TURKISH	WORKMEN	CASCARA	DISPRIN	GISELLE
PERJURY	SCRATCH	STRUDEL	TURMOIL	WORKOUT	CASEASE	DISPUTE	GOSHAWK
PERLITE	SCRAWNY	SURCOAT	TURNERY	WORKSHY	CASHBOX	DISROBE	GOSLING
PERMIAN	SCREECH	SURDITY	TURNING	WORKTOP	CASHIER	DISRUPT	GOSSIPY
PERPLEX	SCREEVE	SURFACE	TURNKEY	WORLDLY	CASPIAN	DISSECT	GUSHING
PERRIER	SCREWED	SURFEIT	TURNOUT	WORRIED	CASSATA	DISSENT	HASHISH
PERSEID	SCRIBER	SURFING	TURPETH	WORRIER	CASSAVA	DISTAFF	HASSIUM
PERSEUS	SCROOGE	SURGEON	TYRANNY	WORSHIP	CASSOCK	DISTANT	HASSOCK
PERSIAN	SCROTAL	SURGERY	UKRAINE	WORSTED	CASTILE	DISTEND	HASTATE
PERSIST	SCROTUM	SURINAM	UNRAVEL	XERAFIN	CASTING	DISTENT	HASTILY
PERSONA	SCRUBBY	SURMISE	UNREADY	XEROSIS	CASTLED	DISTILL	HESHVAN
PERSONS	SCRUFFY	SURNAME	UPRAISE	YARDAGE	CASTOFF	DISTORT	HESSIAN
PERSPEX	SCRUMMY	SURPASS	UPRIGHT	YARDARM	CASUALS	DISTURB	HISPANO
PERTAIN	SCRUMPY	SURPLUS	UTRECHT	YEREVAN	CASUISM	DISUSED	HISSING
PERTURB	SCRUNCH	SURREAL	UTRICLE	YORKIST	CASUIST	DOSSIER	HISTOID
PERTUSE	SCRUPLE	SURVIVE	UTRILLO	ABSCESS	CESSION	DUSTBIN	HISTORY
PERUSAL	SERAPIS	SYRINGA	VARIANT	ABSCOND	CESSPIT	DUSTING	HOSANNA
PERVADE	SERBIAN	SYRINGE	VARIETY	ABSENCE	CESTODE	DUSTMAN	HOSIERY
PERVERT	SERCIAL	TARANTO	VARIOLA	ABSINTH	CESTOID	DUSTPAN	HOSPICE
PHRASAL	SERFDOM	TARDILY	VARIOUS	ABSOLVE	CISSOID	EASIEST	HOSTAGE
PHRASER	SERINGA	TARDIVE	VARMINT	ABSTAIN	CISTERN	EASTERN	HOSTESS
PHRENIC	SERIOUS	TARNISH	VARNISH	ALSATIA	COSSACK	ECSTASY	HOSTILE
PIRAEUS	SERPENS	TARPEIA	VARSITY	APSIDAL	COSTARD	ENSLAVE	HUSBAND
PIRANHA	SERPENT	TARQUIN	VARYING	ARSENAL	COSTING	ENSNARE	HUSKILY
PIROGUE	SERRIED	TARSIER	VERBENA	ARSENIC	COSTIVE	ENSNARL	HUSSARS
PORCIAN	SERVANT	TARTARE	VERBOSE	ASSAULT	COSTUME	ENSUING	HUSSITE
PORCINE	SERVICE	TARTARY	VERDANT	ASSEGAI	CUSHION	ENSUITE	HUSTLER
POROSIS	SERVILE	TARTINE	VERDICT	ASSIEGE	CUSTARD	EPSILON	INSCAPE
PORTAGE	SERVING	TERBIUM	VERDURE	ASSISTS	CUSTODY	EPSTEIN	INSECTS
PORTEND	SHRILLY	TERENCE	VERMEER	ASSIZES	CUSTOMS	ESSENCE	INSHORE
PORTENT	SHRIMPS	TERMITE	VERMONT	ASSUAGE	CYSTOID	ESSENES	INSIDER
PORTHOS	SHRIVEL	TERRACE	VERONAL	ASSUMED	DASHING	EUSTACE	INSIDES
PORTICO	SHRIVEN	TERRAIN	VERRUCA	ASSURED	DASHPOT	FASCISM	INSIGHT
PORTION	SHRIVER	TERRANE	VERSANT	ASSYRIA	DASTARD	FASCIST	INSIPID
PORTRAY	SHROUDS	TERRENE	VERSIFY	AUSLESE	DASYURE	FASHION	INSPECT
PURBECK	SIRLOIN	TERRIER	VERSION	AUSTERE	DESCANT	FASTING	INSPIRE
PURCELL	SIROCCO	TERRIFY	VERTIGO	AUSTRAL	DESCEND	FASTNET	INSTALL
PURITAN	SORCERY	TERRINE	VERULAM	AUSTRIA	DESCENT	FESTIVE	INSTANT
PURLIEU	SORDINO	TERSELY	VERVAIN	BASCULE	DESERTS	FESTOON	INSTATE
PURLINE	SORGHUM	TERSION	VIRELAY	BASHFUL	DESERVE	FISHERY	INSTEAD
PURLOIN	SOROSIS	TERTIAL	VIRGATE	BASINET	DESMOND	FISHEYE	INSTILL
PURPORT	SORROWS	TERTIAN	VIRGULE	BASKING	DESPAIR	FISHING	INSULAR
PURPOSE	SORTING	THREADS	VIRTUAL	BASMATI	DESPISE	FISHNET	INSULIN
PURPURA	SPRAINT	THRENOS	WARBECK	BASSOON	DESPITE	FISSILE	INSURER
PURSUER	SPRAYER	THRIFTY	WARBLER	BASTARD	DESPOIL	FISSION	ISSUANT
PURSUIT	SPRINGE	THRISTY	WARBURG	BASTIDE	DESPOND	FISSURE	JASMINE
PURVIEW	SPRINGS	THROATY	WARDOUR	BASTION	DESSERT	FISTFUL	JESTING
PYRAMID	SPRINGY	THROUGH	WARFARE	BESEECH	DESTINE	FISTULA	JUSSIVE
PYRETIC	SPROUTS	THROWER	WARHEAD	BESHREW	DESTINY	FISTULE	JUSTICE
PYREXIA	STRAITS	THROWIN	WARLIKE	BESIDES	DESTROY	FOSSICK	JUSTIFY
PYRITES	STRANGE	THRUWAY	WARLING	BESIEGE	DISABLE	FOSSULA	KASHMIR

KESTREL	OBSCURA	ROSALIE	VISIBLE	ATTRACT	CUTAWAY	HATLESS	MITHRAS
KISSING	OBSCURE	ROSARIO	VISIBLY	AUTARKY	CUTBACK	HATTOCK	MITOSIS
LASAGNA	OBSEQUY	ROSCIAN	VISITOR	AUTOCUE	CUTICLE	HETAERA	MITTENS
LASAGNE	OBSERVE	ROSCIUS	VISTULA	AUTOMAT	CUTLASS	HITTITE	MITZVAH
LASHING	OESTRUS	ROSEATE	WASHDAY	AUTOPSY	CUTLERY	HOTFOOT	MOTHERS
LASTING	ONSHORE	ROSEBUD	WASHERS	BATAVIA	CUTTERS	HOTHEAD	MOTTLED
LESBIAN	ONSTAGE	ROSEHIP	WASHING	BATHERS	CUTTING	HOTLINE	MUTABLE
LESOTHO	OSSELET	ROSELLA	WASHOUT	BATHING	CUTWORM	HOTSHOT	MUTAGEN
LESSING	OSSEOUS	ROSELLE	WASHTUB	BATHMAT	CYTISUS	HOTSPUR	NATCHEZ
LISSOME	OSSICLE	ROSEOLA	WASPISH	BATHTUB	DATABLE	ICTERIC	NATIONS
LISTING	OSSUARY	ROSETTA	WASSAIL	BATSMAN	DETAILS	ICTERUS	NATIVES
LUSTFUL	OUSTITI	ROSETTE	WASTAGE	BATTELS	DETENTE	INTEGER	NATRIUM
LUSTILY	PASCHAL	ROSSINI	WASTING	BATTERY	DETRACT	INTENSE	NATURAL
LUSTRUM	PASSAGE	ROSTAND	WASTREL	BATTING	DETRAIN	INTERIM	NETBALL
MASCARA	PASSANT	ROSTOCK	WESTERN	BETHINK	DITHERY	INTERNE	NETSUKE
MASONIC	PASSING	ROSTRAL	WISHFUL	BETHUMB	DITTANY	INTROIT	NETTING
MASONRY	PASSION	ROSTRUM	WISHING	BETIMES	DITTIES	INTRUDE	NETWORK
MASSAGE	PASSIVE	RUSALKA	WISTFUL	BETOKEN	DUTIFUL	ISTHMUS	NITRATE
MASSEUR	PASTERN	RUSHING	WYSIWYG	BETROTH	EATABLE	JITTERS	NITRILE
MASSINE	PASTEUR	RUSSELL	YASHMAK	BETTING	ECTASIS	JITTERY	NITRITE
MASSIVE	PASTIES	RUSSIAN	YPSILON	BETTONG	ECTOPIA	JUTLAND	NITRODE
MASTERS	PASTIME	RUSTLER	ZESTFUL	BETWEEN	ENTEBBE	KATORGA	NITROUS
MASTERY	PASTURE	SASHIMI	ACTAEON	BETWIXT	ENTENTE	KATRINE	NOTABLE
MASTIFF	PESSARY	SASSABY	ACTINAL	BITTERN	ENTERIC	KATYDID	NOTABLY
MASTOID	PISCINA	SASSOON	ACTINIA	BITTERS	ENTERON	KETCHUP	NOTCHED
MASURKA	PISCINE	SESOTHO	ACTINIC	BITUMEN	ENTHRAL	KITCHEN	NOTEPAD
MESCLUN	PISMIRE	SESSILE	ACTRESS	BOTANIC	ENTHUSE	KITHARA	NOTHING
MESEEMS	PISTOLE	SESSION	ACTUARY	BOTARGO	ENTITLE	LATCHET	NOTIONS
MESSAGE	POSITIF	SESTINA	ACTUATE	BOTTEGA	ENTRAIN	LATERAL	NUTCASE
MESSIAH	POSSESS	SESTINE	ALTERED	BOTTLED	ENTRANT	LATERAN	NUTLIKE
MESSIER	POSTAGE	SISTERS	ALTHAEA	BOTTLES	ENTREAT	LATIMER	NUTMEAT
MESSILY	POSTBAG	SISTINE	ALTHING	BUTANAL	ENTROPY	LATRINE	NUTTING
MESSINA	POSTBOX	SUSANNA	ALTHORN	BUTANOL	ENTRUST	LATTICE	OATCAKE
MISCAST	POSTDOC	SUSPECT	AMTRACK	BUTCHER	ENTWINE	LATVIAN	OATMEAL
MISDEED	POSTERN	SUSPEND	ANTACID	BUTTERY	ESTIVAL	LETDOWN	OBTRUDE
MISERLY	POSTING	SUSTAIN	ANTARES	BUTTONS	ESTOVER	LETTERS	OCTAGON
MISFIRE	POSTMAN	SYSTOLE	ANTENNA	CATALAN	ESTREAT	LETTING	OCTOBER
MISLEAD	POSTURE	TASSILI	ANTHILL	CATALOG	ESTUARY	LETTUCE	OCTOPOD
MISPLAY	POSTWAR	TESSERA	ANTHONY	CATALPA	ETTRICK	LITCHEE	OCTOPUS
MISREAD	PUSHING	TESTATE	ANTHRAX	CATARRH	EUTERPE	LITERAL	OCTUPLE
MISRULE	PUSHKIN	TESTIFY	ANTIBES	CATCALL	EXTINCT	LITHELY	ONTARIO
MISSILE	PUSTULE	TESTILY	ANTIGEN	CATCHER	EXTRACT	LITHIUM	OPTICAL
MISSING	RESCIND	TESTING	ANTIGUA	CATCHUP	EXTREME	LITOTES	OPTIMAL
MISSION	RESCUER	TESTUDO	ANTIOCH	CATECHU	EXTRUDE	LITURGY	OPTIMUM
MISSIVE	RESERVE	TOSSPOT	ANTIQUE	CATELOG	FATALLY	LOTHAIR	ORTOLAN
MISSTEP	RESHAPE	TUSCANY	ANTLERS	CATERER	FATEFUL	LOTHIAN	OSTEOMA
MISTAKE	RESIANT	TUSSOCK	ANTONIO	CATESBY	FATHEAD	LOTTERY	OSTIOLE
MISTIME	RESIDUE	TUSSORE	ANTONYM	CATFISH	FATIGUE	LUTYENS	OSTRICH
MISTOOK	RESOLVE	UNSCREW	ANTWERP	CATHEAD	FATNESS	MATADOR	OTTOMAN
MISTRAL	RESOUND	UNSNARL	APTERAL	CATHODE	FATUITY	MATCHED	OUTBACK
MOSELLE	RESPECT	UNSOUND	APTERYX	CATKINS	FATUOUS	MATCHET	OUTCAST
MUSCOID	RESPIRE	UNSTICK	APTNESS	CATLIKE	FETICHE	MATELOT	OUTCOME
MUSCOVY	RESPITE	UNSTOCK	ARTEMIS	CATLING	FETLOCK	MATILDA	OUTCROP
MUSETTE	RESPOND	UNSTUCK	ARTEMUS	CATMINT	FETTERS	MATINEE	OUTDARE
MUSICAL	RESPRAY	UPSHOOT	ARTICLE	CATSEYE	FITMENT	MATISSE	OUTDOOR
MUSKRAT	RESTART	UPSIDES	ARTISAN	CATSPAW	FITNESS	MATTERS	OUTFACE
MUSSELS	RESTATE	UPSILON	ARTISTE	CATTISH	FITTEST	MATTHEW	OUTFALL
MUSTANG	RESTFUL	UPSTAGE	ARTLESS	CATWALK	FITTING	MATTING	OUTFLOW
MUSTARD	RESTING	UPSTART	ARTWORK	CITADEL	FUTTOCK	MATTINS	OUTGROW
MYSTERY	RESTIVE	UPSTATE	ASTARTE	CITHARA	FUTURES	MATTOCK	OUTLAST
MYSTIFY	RESTOCK	UPSURGE	ASTILBE	CITIZEN	GATEWAY	METALLY	OUTLIER
NASALLY	RESTORE	UPSWING	ASTOUND	CITRINE	GATLING	METAYER	OUTLINE
NASCENT	RESULTS	VASSAIL	ASTRIDE	CITROEN	GETAWAY	METHANE	OUTLIVE
NASTILY	RISIBLE	VESICLE	ATTABOY	CITRONE	GETTING	METHINK	OUTLOOK
NOSEBAG	RISKILY	VESPERS	ATTACHE	CITTERN	GUTLESS	METICAL	OUTPOST
NOSEGAY	RISOTTO	VESTIGE	ATTACHE	COTERIE	GUTTATE	MÉTISSE	OUTPOUR
NOSTRIL	RISSOLE	VISCERA	ATTEMPT	COTINGA	HATBAND	METONIC	OUTRAGE
NOSTRUM	ROSACEA	VISCOSE	ATTICUS	COTTAGE	HATCHET	METONYM	OUTRANK
OBSCENE	ROSALIA	VISCOUS	ATTIRED	COTTIER	HATEFUL	METTLED	OUTSHOT

187

OUTSIDE	RETREAT	WETTING	CLUSTER	FLUMMOX	PAULINE	SOUTHEY	ADVANCE
OUTSIZE	RETRIAL	WITCHES	CLUTTER	FLUNKEY	PAUNCHY	SPURREY	ADVERSE
OUTSPAN	RETSINA	WITHERS	COUCHÉE	FLUSHED	PLUMAGE	SPURWAY	ADVISER
OUTSTAY	RETURNS	WITHOUT	COULDNT	FLUSTER	PLUMATE	SPUTNIK	ADVISOR
OUTTURN	ROTATOR	WITLESS	COULOMB	FLUTIST	PLUMBER	SPUTTER	ALVEOLE
OUTVOTE	ROTIFER	WITLOOF	COULTER	FLUTTER	PLUMMET	SQUADDY	BEVERLY
OUTWARD	ROTTING	WITNESS	COUNCIL	FLUVIAL	PLUMPER	SQUALID	BIVALVE
OUTWEAR	ROTUNDA	WOTCHER	COUNSEL	FOULARD	PLUMULE	SQUALLY	BIVOUAC
OUTWORK	RUTHENE	YTTRIUM	COUNTED	FOUNDER	PLUNDER	SQUALOR	CAVALRY
OUTWORN	RUTTING	ZETLAND	COUNTER	FOUNDRY	PLUNGER	SQUARED	CAVEMAN
PATELLA	SATANIC	ABUSIVE	COUNTRY	FRUMPLE	PLUTEUS	SQUARES	CAVIARE
PATHWAY	SATCHEL	ACUTELY	COUPLER	GAUDILY	POULENC	SQUASHY	CEVICHE
PATIBLE	SATIATE	ADULATE	COUPLET	GAUGUIN	POULTRY	SQUEAKY	CIVILLY
PATIENT	SATIETY	ALUMINA	COUPONS	GAUTAMA	POUNDAL	SQUEERS	CIVVIES
PATRIAL	SATIRIC	ALUMNAE	COURAGE	GLUCOSE	POUSSIN	SQUEEZE	COVERED
PATRICK	SATISFY	ALUMNUS	COURBET	GLUTTON	PRUDENT	SQUIFFY	COVERUP
PATRIOT	SATRAPY	AMUSING	COURIER	GOUACHE	PRUDISH	SQUILLA	COVETED
PATTERN	SATSUMA	AQUATIC	COURSER	GOULASH	PRURIGO	SQUINCH	CUVETTE
PETIOLE	SETBACK	AQUAVIT	COURSES	GOURMET	PRUSSIC	SQUISHY	DEVALUE
PETRIFY	SETTING	AQUEOUS	COURTLY	GRUFFLY	RAUCOUS	STUBBLE	DEVELOP
PETROUS	SETTLED	AQUIFER	COUSINS	GRUMBLE	RAUNCHY	STUBBLY	DEVIANT
PETUNIA	SETTLER	AQUILON	COUTURE	GRUMMET	REUNION	STUDDED	DEVIATE
PITCHED	SITDOWN	AQUINAS	CRUCIAL	GRUYÈRE	REUNITE	STUDENT	DEVILRY
PITCHER	SITTING	AQUINUS	CRUCIFY	HAUGHTY	RHUBARB	STUDIED	DEVIOUS
PITEOUS	SITUATE	ARUNDEL	CRUDELY	HAULAGE	ROUAULT	STUFFED	DEVISED
PITFALL	SITWELL	ASUNDER	CRUDITY	HAULIER	ROUGHEN	STUMBLE	DEVISEE
PITHEAD	TATARIC	AZURITE	CRUELLS	HAUNTED	ROUGHIE	STUMPED	DEVOICE
PITHILY	TATIANA	BAUHAUS	CRUELLY	HAUTBOY	ROUGHLY	STUNNER	DEVOLVE
PITIFUL	TATTERS	BAUXITE	CRUELTY	HEURISM	ROULADE	STUNTED	DEVOTED
POTABLE	TATTING	BLUBBER	CRUISER	HOUDINI	ROULEAU	STUPEFY	DEVOTEE
POTENCY	TATTLER	BLUFFLY	CRUMBLE	HOUSING	ROUNDED	STURMER	DIVERGE
POTHEEN	TETANUS	BLUNDER	CRUMBLY	JOURNAL	ROUNDEL	STUTTER	DIVERSE
POTHERB	TITANIA	BLUNTED	CRUMPET	JOURNEY	ROUNDER	TAURINE	DIVIDED
POTHOLE	TITANIC	BLUNTLY	CRUMPLE	KNUCKLE	ROUNDLY	THUGGEE	DIVINER
POTICHE	TITOISM	BLURRED	CRUNCHY	KOUMISS	ROUNDUP	THULIUM	DIVISOR
POTLACH	TITOIST	BLUSHER	CRUPPER	LAUNDER	ROUSING	THUMPER	DIVORCE
POTLUCK	TITRATE	BLUSTER	CRUSADE	LAUNDRY	ROUTIER	THUNDER	DIVULGE
POTOMAC	TITULAR	BOUCLÉE	CRUSHED	LAURELS	ROUTINE	TOUCHED	ENVELOP
POTOROO	TOTALLY	BOUDOIR	CRUSHER	LEUCINE	SAUCILY	TOUGHEN	ENVENOM
POTSDAM	TOTEMIC	BOUILLI	DAUPHIN	LEUCOMA	SAUNTER	TOURING	ENVIOUS
POTSHOT	TOTIENT	BOULDER	DIURNAL	LOUNGER	SAURIAN	TOURISM	FAVELLA
POTTAGE	TOTTERY	BOUNCER	DOUBLES	LOURDES	SAUROID	TOURIST	FAVORED
POTTERY	TUTELAR	BOUNDED	DOUBLET	LOURING	SAUSAGE	TRUANCY	FEVERED
POTTING	UNTAMED	BOUNDEN	DOUBTER	LOUTISH	SCUFFLE	TRUCIAL	GAVOTTE
PUTREFY	UNTRIED	BOUNDER	DOUGHTY	LOUVRED	SCULLER	TRUCKER	INVADER
PUTTEES	UNTRUTH	BOUQUET	DOUGLAS	MAUDLIN	SCUPPER	TRUCKLE	INVALID
PUTTING	UNTWINE	BOURBON	DRUGGED	MAUGHAM	SCUTAGE	TRUDGEN	INVEIGH
PUTTOCK	UPTIGHT	BOURDON	DRUGGET	MAUNDER	SCUTARI	TRUFFLE	INVERSE
RATAFIA	UTTERLY	BOURSIN	DRUMLIN	MOUFLON	SCUTTER	TRUMEAU	INVIOUS
RATATAT	VATICAN	BOUTADE	DRUMMER	MOUILLÉ	SCUTTLE	TRUMPET	INVOICE
RATCHET	VETERAN	BRUISED	DRUNKEN	MOULAGE	SFUMATO	TRUNDLE	INVOLVE
RATIONS	VETIVER	BRUISER	ECUADOR	MOULDED	SHUDDER	TRUSTEE	JAVELIN
RATLINE	VETTING	BRUSHER	EDUCATE	MOULDER	SHUFFLE	TSUNAMI	JAVELLE
RATPACK	VITALLY	BRUSQUE	ELUSIVE	MOUNTED	SHUTEYE	UKULELE	JUVENAL
RATTEEN	VITAMIN	BRUTISH	ELUSORY	MOUNTIE	SHUTTER	ULULANT	LAVATER
RATTLER	VITIATE	CAUSTIC	EMULATE	MOURNER	SHUTTLE	ULULATE	LAVOLTA
RETAINS	VITRAIL	CAUTERY	EMULSIN	NAUGHTY	SLUMBER	UNUSUAL	LEVERET
RETHINK	VITRIFY	CAUTION	EQUABLE	NEURINE	SMUDGED	URUGUAY	LOVABLE
RETICLE	VITRIOL	CHUCKLE	EQUABLY	NEUROMA	SMUGGLE	USUALLY	MOVABLE
RETINAL	WATCHER	CHUFFED	EQUALLY	NEURONE	SNUFFLE	USURPER	NAVARIN
RETINUE	WATERED	CHUKKER	EQUATOR	NEUTRAL	SNUGGLE	VAUDOIS	NAVARRE
RETIRED	WATTAGE	CHUNDER	EQUERRY	NEUTRON	SOUBISE	VAUGHAN	NAVETTE
RETIREE	WATTEAU	CHUNNEL	EQUINOX	NOURISH	SOUFFLE	VAULTED	NEVILLE
RETOUCH	WATTLES	CHUPATI	ERUDITE	NOUVEAU	SOULFUL	VOUCHER	NOVELLA
RETRACE	WATUTSI	CHUTNEY	EXUDATE	OCULIST	SOUNDED	WOULDBE	NOVELLO
RETRACT	WETBACK	CLUBMAN	FAUSTUS	OPULENT	SOUNDER	WOULDNT	NOVELTY
RETRAIN	WETLAND	CLUMBER	FAUVISM	OPUNTIA	SOUNDLY	WOUNDED	OBVERSE
RETRAIT	WETNESS	CLUNIAC	FAUVIST	OVULATE	SOURSOP	WOUNDED	OBVIATE
RETREAD	WETSUIT	CLUPEID	FLUENCY	PAUCITY	SOUTANE	YOUNGER	OBVIOUS

ORVIETO	JAWBONE	SEXLESS	MAYFAIR	JAZZMAN	ASPASIA	CHEAPLY	ENHANCE
PAVIOUR	JEWELER	SEXTANS	MAYPOLE	JEZEBEL	ASSAULT	CHEATER	ENLARGE
PAVLOVA	JEWELRY	SEXTANT	MAYWEED	LOZENGE	ASTARTE	CHIANTI	ENRAGED
PIVOTAL	JEWFISH	SIXTEEN	ODYSSEY	MAZARIN	ATTABOY	CHIASMA	EQUABLE
POVERTY	KIWANIS	TAXABLE	OLYMPIA	MAZEPPA	ATTACHE	CHLAMYS	EQUABLY
RAVAGES	KOWLOON	TAXFREE	OLYMPIC	MAZURKA	ATTAINT	CIMABUE	EQUALLY
RAVINGS	LAWLESS	TAXICAB	OLYMPUS	PIZARRO	AURALLY	CITADEL	EQUATOR
RAVIOLI	LAWSUIT	TAXIWAY	PAYABLE	PIZZAZZ	AUTARKY	CLEANER	ERRATIC
REVALUE	LAWYERS	TEXTILE	PAYLOAD	PUZZLED	AVIATOR	CLEANLY	ERRATUM
REVELER	LOWBROW	TEXTUAL	PAYMENT	PUZZLER	BACARDI	CLEANSE	ESCALOP
REVELRY	LOWDOWN	TEXTURE	PAYROLL	ROZZERS	BAGASSE	CLEANUP	ESCAPEE
REVENGE	LOWLAND	TOXEMIA	PHYSICS	SIZABLE	BAHADUR	CLEARLY	ESPARTO
REVENUE	LOWPAID	WAXBILL	PLYWOOD	SIZZLER	BAHAMAS	CLEARUP	ETHANOL
REVERED	MAWKISH	WAXWING	PRYTHEE	SOZZLED	BAJAZET	CLEAVER	EULALIE
REVERIE	NEWBOLT	WAXWORK	PSYCHIC	SUZETTE	BALANCE	COCAINE	EXHAUST
REVERSE	NEWBORN	ABYSMAL	PTYALIN	WIZENED	BALATON	COHABIT	EXPANSE
REVISED	NEWBURY	ABYSSAL	REYNARD	YEZIDEE	BANANAS	CONAKRY	FALAFEL
REVISER	NEWCOME	ALYSSUM	RHYMING	ZIZANIA	BATAVIA	CORACLE	FANATIC
REVISIT	NEWNESS	AMYGDAL	ROYALLY	**7:4**	BECAUSE	CORANTO	FARADAY
REVIVAL	NEWSBOY	AMYLASE	ROYALTY	ABBASID	BEHAVED	CREATED	FARAWAY
REVIVER	NEWSMAN	AMYLOID	SEYMOUR	ABLATOR	BELABOR	CREATOR	FATALLY
REVOLVE	NOWHERE	AMYLOSE	SHYLOCK	ABRAHAM	BELARUS	CROAKER	FILARIA
RIVALRY	ONWARDS	ANYBODY	SHYNESS	ABRAXIS	BELATED	CROATIA	FILASSE
RIVETED	POWDERY	ANYMORE	SHYSTER	ACHAEAN	BENARES	CURABLE	FINAGLE
RIVIERA	POWERED	AZYGOUS	SKYBLUE	ACHATES	BIVALVE	CURACAO	FINALLY
RIVULET	RAWHIDE	BAYONET	SKYHIGH	ACTAEON	BIZARRE	CURATOR	FINANCE
SAVAGES	RAWNESS	BOYCOTT	SKYLARK	ADVANCE	BLEAKLY	CUTAWAY	FIXATED
SAVANNA	REWRITE	BOYHOOD	SKYLINE	AERATED	BLOATED	DADAISM	FLEAPIT
SAVELOY	ROWBOAT	CAYENNE	SKYWARD	AFFABLE	BLOATER	DADAIST	FLOATER
SAVINGS	ROWDILY	COYNESS	SLYNESS	AFFABLY	BONANZA	DAMAGED	FORAMEN
SAVIOUR	ROWLOCK	CRYPTIC	SPYHOLE	AFFAIRS	BORACIC	DAMAGES	FRIABLE
SAVOURY	SAWBILL	CRYPTON	STYGIAN	AGRAPHA	BOTANIC	DATABLE	GALAHAD
SEVENTH	SAWDUST	CRYSTAL	STYLING	AIDANCE	BOTARGO	DEBACLE	GALATEA
SEVENTY	SAWFISH	DAYBOOK	STYLISH	ALBANIA	BREADED	DEBASED	GELATIN
SEVERAL	SAWMILL	DAYMARK	STYLIST	ALCALDE	BREADTH	DEBATER	GERAINT
SEVERUS	TOWARDS	DAYSTAR	STYLITE	ALDABRA	BREAKER	DEBAUCH	GETAWAY
SEVILLE	TOWHEAD	DAYTIME	STYLIZE	ALFALFA	BREATHE	DECANAL	GIRAFFE
SOVKHOZ	TOWLINE	DRYNESS	STYPTIC	ALKANET	BROADEN	DECAYED	GIRASOL
TAVERNA	TOWPATH	ELYSIAN	THYMINE	ALMACKS	BROADLY	DEFACED	GLEANER
VIVALDI	TOWROPE	ELYSIUM	THYROID	ALMANAC	BUGABOO	DEFAULT	GOUACHE
VIVIDLY	UNWOUND	ELYTRON	THYRSIS	ALSATIA	BUTANAL	DEGAUSS	GREASER
WAVERER	UPWARDS	FEYDEAU	THYSELF	AMBAGES	BUTANOL	DERANGE	GREATEN
BEWITCH	YAWNING	FLYHALF	THYSSEN	AMHARIC	CABARET	DETAILS	GREATLY
BOWDLER	ANXIETY	FLYLEAF	TOYNBEE	AMIABLE	CADAVER	DEVALUE	GREAVES
BOWHEAD	ANXIOUS	FLYOVER	TOYSHOP	AMIABLY	CALABAR	DIGAMMA	HEPARIN
BOWLING	BOXHAUL	FLYPAST	TRYPSIN	ANDAMAN	CALAMUS	DILATED	HEPATIC
BOWSHOT	BOXROOM	GAYNESS	ULYSSES	ANDANTE	CANASTA	DILATOR	HETAERA
COWBANE	BOXWOOD	GLYPTAL	VOYAGER	ANNATTO	CAPABLE	DISABLE	HEXAGON
COWGIRL	COXCOMB	GLYPTIC	WAYBILL	ANTACID	CAPABLY	DISAVOW	HEXAPOD
COWHAND	COXLESS	GRYPHON	WAYLAND	ANTARES	CARABID	DOMAINE	HEXARCH
COWHERD	DEXTRIN	GUYROPE	WAYMARK	APHAGIA	CARACAL	DOWAGER	HIBACHI
COWHIDE	FIXATED	GWYNETH	WAYSIDE	APHASIA	CARACAS	DREADED	HIDALGO
COWLICK	FIXEDLY	HAYFORK	WAYWARD	APLASIA	CARACUL	DREAMER	HOGARTH
COWLING	FIXINGS	HAYLOFT	WRYBILL	APPARAT	CARADOC	DURABLE	HORATIO
COWPOKE	FIXTURE	HAYSEED	WRYNECK	APPAREL	CARAMBA	DURABLY	HOSANNA
COWSHED	FOXHOLE	HAYWARD	WRYNOSE	APRAXIA	CARAMEL	DURAMEN	HUMANLY
COWSLIP	FOXTROT	HAYWIRE	BAZOOKA	AQUATIC	CARAVAN	DYNAMIC	HYDATID
DAWDLER	HEXAGON	IDYLLIC	BEZIQUE	AQUAVIT	CARAVEL	DYNASTY	ICHABOD
DEWDROP	HEXAPOD	JOYLESS	BIZARRE	ARCADIA	CARAWAY	EARACHE	IDEALLY
DOWAGER	HEXARCH	JOYRIDE	BUZZARD	ARIADNE	CATALAN	EATABLE	ILIACUS
DOWDILY	LAXNESS	KEYHOLE	CÉZANNE	ARRAIGN	CATALOG	ECTASIS	IMPASSE
DOWLAND	LEXICON	KEYNOTE	DAZZLED	ARRANGE	CATALPA	ECUADOR	IMPASTO
DOWSING	MAXILLA	KEYWORD	DIZZILY	ARRAYED	CATARRH	ELEANOR	IMPAVID
FAWNING	MAXIMUM	KRYPTON	ELZEVIR	ASCARID	CAVALRY	EMBARGO	INFANCY
GAWKISH	MAXWELL	LAYERED	GAZELLE	ASHAMED	CELADON	EMBASSY	INFARCT
HAWKEYE	MEXICAN	LAYETTE	GAZETTE	ASHANTI	CENACLE	EMPANEL	INHABIT
HOWEVER	MIXTURE	LAYINGS	GIZZARD	ASIATIC	CERAMIC	EMPATHY	INHALER
HOWLING	NOXIOUS	LOYALLY	GUZZLER	ASKANCE	CÉZANNE	ENGAGED	INNARDS
INWARDS	SAXHORN	LOYALTY	HAZLETT		CHEAPEN		INVADER

189

INVALID	MUTABLE	REGARDS	SQUALOR	UPRAISE	DIABOLO	KIBBUTZ	SETBACK
INWARDS	MUTAGEN	REGATTA	SQUARED	UPWARDS	DIBBLER	KNOBBLE	SHEBANG
ISLAMIC	MYIASIS	RELAPSE	SQUARES	USUALLY	DISBAND	KNOBBLY	SHEBEEN
ISLANDS	NASALLY	RELATED	SQUASHY	VACANCY	DISBARK	LAMBADA	SKYBLUE
ISMAILI	NAVARIN	RELAXED	STEALTH	VANADIC	DOUBLES	LAMBAST	SLOBBER
ISRAELI	NAVARRE	RELAYER	STEAMED	VEDANTA	DOUBLET	LAMBENT	SOUBISE
JAKARTA	NICAEAN	REMAINS	STEAMER	VINASSE	DOUBTER	LAMBERT	STABILE
JAMAICA	NOMADIC	REMARRY	STEARIC	VITALLY	DRABBLE	LAMBETH	STABLES
JOCASTA	NOTABLE	REPAINT	STEARIN	VITAMIN	DRIBBLE	LAMBING	STUBBLE
JUDAISM	NOTABLY	REPAIRS	STRAITS	VIVALDI	DRIBLET	LESBIAN	STUBBLY
KARACHI	OCEANIA	RETAINS	STRANGE	VOCALIC	DUBBING	LOGBOOK	SUNBEAM
KARAJAN	OCEANIC	REVALUE	STRATUM	VOCALLY	EYEBALL	LOMBARD	SUNBURN
KARAKUL	OCEANID	RICARDO	STRATUS	VOLANTE	EYEBATH	LOWBROW	TAMBOUR
KARAOKE	OCTAGON	RIVALRY	STRAUSS	VOLAPUK	EYEBROW	LUMBAGO	TANBARK
KERATIN	ONTARIO	ROMAINE	SUBADAR	VOYAGER	FILBERT	MACBETH	TERBIUM
KIWANIS	ONWARDS	ROMANCE	SUBAQUA	WHEATEN	FIMBRIA	MARBLED	TILBURY
LAMAISM	ORGANIC	ROMANIA	SUBATOM	WOMANLY	FINBACK	MARBLES	TIMBALE
LAMAIST	ORGANUM	ROMANOV	SUGARED	WREATHE	FORBADE	MARBURG	TIMBERS
LASAGNA	ORGANZA	ROMANZA	SUMATRA	XERAFIN	FORBEAR	MEMBERS	TIMBREL
LASAGNE	ORLANDO	ROSACEA	SUSANNA	YUCATAN	FURBISH	MOABITE	TOMBOLA
LAVATER	OSMANLI	ROSALIA	SWEATED	ZIZANIA	GABBLER	MOMBASA	TRIBUNE
LEBANON	OTRANTO	ROSALIE	SWEATER	AIRBASE	GAMBADO	NEBBISH	TRIBUTE
LEGALLY	PAJAMAS	ROSARIO	SYNAPSE	ALABAMA	GAMBIAN	NETBALL	TUGBOAT
LEGATEE	PALADIN	ROTATOR	SYNAXIS	ANYBODY	GAMBLER	NEWBOLT	TUMBLER
LEPANTO	PALATAL	ROUAULT	TABANID	ARABIAN	GAMBOGE	NEWBORN	TUMBREL
LINACRE	PALAVER	ROYALLY	TABARET	ARABICA	GARBAGE	NEWBURY	TUMBRIL
LOCALLY	PANACEA	ROYALTY	TABASCO	ARABIZE	GARBLED	NIOBEAN	TURBARY
LOVABLE	PANACHE	RUNAWAY	TAGALOG	ARMBAND	GARBOIL	NIOBIUM	TURBINE
LOYALLY	PARABLE	RUSALKA	TAMARIN	AVEBURY	GARBURE	NOBBLED	VERBENA
LOYALTY	PARADOR	SABAEAN	TANAGER	BABBITT	GERBERA	NOBBLER	VERBOSE
LUCARNE	PARADOS	SABAOTH	TANAGRA	BABBLER	GIBBONS	NOMBRIL	WARBECK
LUNATIC	PARADOX	SABAYON	TARANTO	BAMBINO	GIBBOUS	NUMBERS	WARBLER
MACABRE	PARAGON	SALABLE	TATARIC	BANBURY	GILBERT	NUMBLES	WARBURG
MACADAM	PARAPET	SALADIN	TAXABLE	BARBARA	GIMBALS	ODDBALL	WAXBILL
MACAQUE	PARASOL	SALAMIS	TENABLE	BARBARY	GIMBLET	OFFBASE	WAYBILL
MAHATMA	PAYABLE	SALAZAR	TENANCY	BLABBER	GLOBULE	OFFBEAT	WEBBING
MALACCA	PEGASUS	SAMARIA	TENANTS	BLUBBER	GOBBLER	OILBIRD	WETBACK
MALACHI	PELAGIC	SARACEN	TETANUS	BOMBARD	GOMBEEN	OUTBACK	WRYBILL
MALAISE	PENALTY	SATANIC	THEATER	BOMBAST	GUBBINS	PARBOIL	ZAMBESI
MALARIA	PENANCE	SAVAGES	THEATRE	BOMBING	GUMBOIL	PEBBLES	ZAMBIAN
MALAYAN	PENATES	SAVANNA	TILAPIA	BOOBOOK	GUMBOOT	PIEBALD	ABSCESS
MANACLE	PHRASAL	SCIATIC	TITANIA	BRIBERY	GUNBOAT	PINBALL	ABSCOND
MANAGER	PHRASER	SCRAGGY	TITANIC	BUBBLES	HAGBOLT	PREBEND	AIRCREW
MANAGUA	PICADOR	SCRAPER	TOBACCO	BUGBEAR	HALBERD	PROBAND	ALECOST
MANAKIN	PICARDY	SCRAPIE	TOTALLY	BULBOUS	HALBERT	PROBATE	ALICANT
MANATEE	PICASSO	SCRAPPY	TOWARDS	BUMBOAT	HARBOUR	PROBITY	APICIUS
MARABOU	PILATUS	SCRATCH	TREACLE	BURBAGE	HATBAND	PROBLEM	APOCOPE
MARACAS	PIRAEUS	SCRAWNY	TREACLY	CABBAGE	HENBANE	PURBECK	ARACHNE
MARANTA	PIRANHA	SENATOR	TREADLE	CAMBIUM	HERBAGE	QUIBBLE	ASOCIAL
MARATHA	PIZARRO	SERAPIS	TREASON	CAMBRAI	HERBERT	RAEBURN	ATACTIC
MATADOR	PLEADER	SHEARER	TREATED	CAMBRIC	HERBERY	RAMBLER	AVOCADO
MAZARIN	PLEASED	SHEATHE	TRIANON	CARBIDE	HERBIST	REMBLAI	BACCHIC
MEGAERA	PLEASES	SHEAVES	TRIATIC	CARBINE	HIPBONE	RHUBARB	BACCHUS
MEGARON	PLEATED	SHIATSU	TRUANCY	CEMBALO	HOGBACK	RIBBING	BALCONY
MEGATON	PLIABLE	SINATRA	TUNABLE	CHABLIS	HOLBEIN	ROBBERS	BASCULE
MELANIN	PLIANCY	SIZABLE	TYRANNY	CLOBBER	HOMBURG	ROBBERY	BEACHED
METALLY	PODAGRA	SNEAKER	UKRAINE	CLUBMAN	HUBBARD	ROEBUCK	BEACHES
METAYER	POLARIS	SOCAGER	UNCANNY	COBBLED	HUMBLES	ROWBOAT	BENCHER
MINARET	POTABLE	SOFABED	UNCARED	COBBLER	HUSBAND	RUBBERS	BERCEAU
MIRACLE	PRIAPUS	SOLANUM	UNDATED	COMBINE	IAMBIST	RUBBERY	BIOCIDE
MIRADOR	PTYALIN	SOMALIA	UNEARTH	COMBING	ICEBERG	RUBBING	BISCUIT
MIRANDA	PYJAMAS	SPEAKER	UNFADED	CORBEAU	IKEBANA	RUBBISH	BLACKEN
MONARCH	PYRAMID	SPLASHY	UNHAPPY	CORBETT	ILLBRED	RUMBLER	BLOCKED
MORAINE	RAMADAN	SPLAYED	UNLADEN	COWBANE	ISOBASE	SABBATH	BLOCKER
MORALLY	RATAFIA	SPRAINT	UNLATCH	CUMBRIA	JAWBONE	SAMBUCA	BOUCLÉE
MORAVIA	RATATAT	SPRAYER	UNNAMED	CUTBACK	JOBBERY	SAWBILL	BOYCOTT
MOVABLE	RAVAGES	SQUADDY	UNPAGED	CYMBALS	JOBBING	SCABIES	BRACING
MULATTO	REGALIA	SQUALID	UNRAVEL	DABBLER	JUMBLED	SEABIRD	BRACKEN
MURAENA	REGALLY	SQUALLY	UNTAMED	DAYBOOK	JUMBLES	SERBIAN	BRACKET

BRICKIE	DRACULA	MARCHER	PRICKLE	SUCCOUR	BEDDING	FEEDING	ISODORE
BROCADE	DUNCIAD	MARCONI	PRICKLY	SUCCUMB	BENDING	FEYDEAU	KADDISH
BUTCHER	EDUCATE	MARCUSE	PROCEED	SUICIDE	BIDDING	FIDDLER	KHEDIVE
CALCIFY	EJECTOR	MASCARA	PROCESS	SURCOAT	BINDERY	FINDING	KILDARE
CALCINE	ELECTED	MATCHED	PROCTOR	SYNCOPE	BINDING	FLEDGED	KINDRED
CALCITE	ELECTOR	MATCHET	PROCURE	TANCRED	BIRDMAN	FLODDEN	LANDING
CALCIUM	ELECTRA	MEACOCK	PSYCHIC	TEACAKE	BLADDER	FLODDEN	LARDOON
CALCULI	ELECTRO	MERCERY	PUCCINI	TEACHER	BONDAGE	FOLDING	LEADERS
CARCASE	ENACTOR	MERCIES	PUNCHED	THICKEN	BONDMAN	FONDANT	LEADING
CARCASS	EPICARP	MERCURY	PUNCHER	THICKET	BORDERS	FUDDLED	LEADING
CASCADE	EPICENE	MESCLUN	PURCELL	THICKLY	BOUDOIR	FUNDING	LENDING
CASCARA	EPICURE	MINCING	QUECHUA	TIPCART	BOWDLER	GARDENS	LETDOWN
CATCALL	ERECTOR	MIOCENE	QUICHUA	TOCCATA	BRADAWL	GAUDILY	LIEDOWN
CATCHER	EVACUEE	MISCAST	QUICKEN	TOPCOAT	BRADMAN	GELDING	LINDANE
CATCHUP	EXACTLY	MUSCOID	QUICKER	TORCHON	BRIDGES	GEODESY	LORDING
CHECKED	EXECUTE	MUSCOVY	QUICKIE	TOUCHED	BRIDGET	GIDDILY	LOWDOWN
CHECKIN	EXOCARP	NASCENT	QUICKLY	TRACERY	BRIDLER	GIDDYUP	LUDDITE
CHECKUP	FANCIED	NATCHEZ	RACCOON	TRACHEA	BRIDLES	GILDING	MANDALA
CHICAGO	FANCIER	NEWCOME	RANCHER	TRACING	BUDDING	GLADDEN	MANDATE
CHICANE	FARCEUR	NOTCHED	RANCOUR	TRACKER	BUNDOOK	GLIDING	MANDIOC
CHICANO	FASCISM	NUTCASE	RATCHET	TRACTOR	BURDOCK	GODDESS	MAUDLIN
CHICKEN	FASCIST	OATCAKE	RAUCOUS	TRICEPS	CADDISH	GOLDING	MEDDLER
CHICORY	FENCING	OBSCENE	REACTOR	TRICKLE	CAEDMON	GOLDONI	MENDING
CHOCTAW	FILCHER	OBSCURA	REDCOAT	TROCHEE	CALDERA	GONDOLA	MINDFUL
CHUCKLE	FIRCONE	OBSCURE	REOCCUR	TROCHUS	CALDRON	GOODBYE	MINDSET
CIRCLET	FLACCID	OILCAKE	RESCIND	TRUCIAL	CANDACE	GOODIES	MISDEED
CIRCLIP	FLECKED	OMICRON	RESCUER	TRUCKER	CANDELA	GOODISH	MOIDORE
CIRCUIT	FLECKER	OPACITY	RIBCAGE	TRUCKLE	CANDIDA	GOODMAN	MOLDING
CLACHAN	FLICKER	ORACLES	RIPCORD	TUSCANY	CANDIDE	GOODWIN	MOODILY
CLICKER	FORCEPS	OUTCAST	ROSCIAN	UNICORN	CANDIED	GORDIAN	MORDANT
COLCHIS	FRECKLE	OUTCOME	ROSCIUS	UNSCREW	CANDOUR	GORDIUS	MUDDLED
CONCAVE	FULCRUM	OUTCROP	RUNCORN	VACCINE	CARDIAC	GRADATE	MUNDANE
CONCEAL	FUNCHAL	OVICIDE	SACCADE	VINCENT	CARDOON	GRADELY	NEEDFUL
CONCEDE	FURCATE	PANCAKE	SANCTUM	VISCERA	CARDUUS	GRADUAL	NEEDLES
CONCEIT	GASCONY	PANCRAS	SANCTUS	VISCOSE	CHEDDAR	GRIDDLE	NODDING
CONCEPT	GLACIAL	PARCHED	SARCASM	VISCOUS	CINDERS	GUIDING	NOODLES
CONCERN	GLACIER	PASCHAL	SARCOMA	VOLCANO	COLDITZ	GUMDROP	OBADIAH
CONCERT	GLUCOSE	PAUCITY	SARCOUS	VOUCHER	CONDEMN	HADDOCK	OFFDUTY
CONCISE	GNOCCHI	PEACHUM	SATCHEL	WATCHER	CONDOLE	HANDBAG	OUTDARE
CONCOCT	GRACCHI	PEACOCK	SAUCILY	WELCOME	CONDONE	HANDFUL	OUTDOOR
CONCORD	GRACILE	PECCANT	SERCIAL	WHACKED	CONDUCT	HANDGUN	OVIDUCT
CONCUSS	GRACKLE	PECCARY	SHACKLE	WHACKER	CONDUIT	HANDILY	OXIDASE
COUCHÉE	GRECIAN	PECCAVI	SHICKSA	WITCHES	CORDATE	HANDLED	OXIDIZE
COXCOMB	GROCERS	PERCALE	SHOCKED	WOTCHER	CORDIAL	HANDLER	PADDING
CRACKED	GROCERY	PERCENT	SHOCKER	WRECKED	CORDITE	HANDOUT	PADDLER
CRACKER	GROCKLE	PERCEPT	SHOCKER	WRECKER	CORDOBA	HANDSAW	PADDOCK
CRACKLE	HALCYON	PERCUSS	SINCERE	ABIDING	CRUDELY	HANDSEL	PANDORA
CRACKLY	HATCHET	PICCOLO	SLACKEN	ABIDJAN	CRUDITY	HANDSET	PEDDLER
CRICKET	HUNCHED	PILCHER	SLACKER	ACADEME	CURDLED	HARDPAN	PENDANT
CRICKEY	INSCAPE	PINCERS	SLACKLY	ACADEMY	DAWDLER	HARDTOP	PENDING
CRICOID	KETCHUP	PINCHED	SLICKER	ACADIAN	DEADEYE	HEADING	PHIDIAS
CROCHET	KITCHEN	PINCHED	SMACKER	ACIDIFY	DEADMAN	HEADMAN	PLODDER
CROCKET	KNACKER	PISCINA	SMICKLY	ACIDITY	DEADPAN	HEADSET	POWDERY
CRUCIAL	KNICKER	PISCINE	SNICKER	ALADDIN	DEADSET	HEADWAY	PREDATE
CRUCIFY	KNOCKER	PITCHED	SORCERY	ALIDADE	DENDRON	HEEDFUL	PREDIAL
CURCUMA	KNUCKLE	PITCHER	SPACING	ANODIZE	DEWDROP	HILDING	PREDICT
DANCING	LANCERS	PLACARD	SPECIAL	ANODYNE	DIEDRAL	HINDLEG	PREDOOM
DEICTIC	LANCING	PLACATE	SPECIES	ARIDITY	DISDAIN	HOEDOWN	PRODIGY
DESCANT	LAOCOON	PLACEBO	SPECIFY	ASHDOWN	DODDERY	HOLDALL	PRODUCE
DESCEND	LARCENY	PLACING	SPECKLE	AVIDITY	DOODLER	HOLDING	PRODUCT
DESCENT	LATCHET	POACHER	SPECTER	BALDING	DOWDILY	HOODLUM	PRUDENT
DIECAST	LEACOCK	POPCORN	SPECTRE	BALDRIC	DREDGER	HORDEUM	PRUDISH
DIOCESE	LEUCINE	PORCIAN	SPICATE	BALDWIN	EARDRUM	HOUDINI	PUDDING
DISCARD	LEUCOMA	PORCINE	SPICULA	BANDAGE	EPIDOTE	HUMDRUM	QUADRAT
DISCERN	LINCOLN	PRECAST	SPICULE	BANDAID	ERODIUM	HUNDRED	RADDLED
DISCORD	LINCTUS	PRECEDE	STACHYS	BANDBOX	ERUDITE	HURDLER	READILY
DISCUSS	LITCHEE	PRECEPT	STICKER	BANDEAU	EVIDENT	HURDLES	READING
DOGCART	LURCHER	PRECISE	STICKLE	BANDORE	EXUDATE	IRIDISE	REDDISH
DRACHMA	LYNCHET	PRICKED	SUCCEED	BEADING	FADDISH	IRIDIUM	RHODIAN
		PRICKER	SUCCESS		FADDIST	ISADORA	RHODIUM

RIDDLED	VANDYKE	ARREARS	COVERUP	FEVERED	INCENSE	MISERLY	POLECAT
RIDDLER	VAUDOIS	ARSENAL	COVETED	FIDELIO	INDEPTH	MODERNE	POLEMIC
ROADHOG	VENDING	ARSENIC	CREEPER	FINESSE	INDEXER	MODESTY	POLENTA
ROADWAY	VENDOME	ARTEMIS	CROESUS	FIREARM	INFERNO	MOFETTE	POMEROL
ROEDEAN	VERDANT	ARTEMUS	CRUELLS	FIREBUG	INGENUE	MOMENTS	POMEROY
RONDEAU	VERDICT	ASCETIC	CRUELLY	FIREDOG	INHERIT	MONEYED	POPEYED
ROWDILY	VERDURE	ASPERGE	CRUELTY	FIREFLY	INNERVE	MOREISH	POTENCY
RUNDOWN	VIADUCT	ASSEGAI	CURETTE	FIREMAN	INSECTS	MORELLO	POVERTY
SADDLER	WADDING	ATHEISM	CUVETTE	FIXEDLY	INTEGER	MORESBY	POWERED
SANDALS	WARDOUR	ATHEIST	DECEASE	FLEEING	INTENSE	MORESCO	PRAETOR
SANDBAG	WEDDING	ATTEMPT	DECEIVE	FLUENCY	INTERIM	MOSELLE	PREEMPT
SANDBOX	WELDING	AUBERGE	DECENCY	FOREARM	INTERNE	MUDEJAR	PRIESTS
SANDBOY	WENDELL	AUREATE	DEFENCE	FOREIGN	INVEIGH	MUSETTE	PUBERAL
SANDMAN	WENDISH	AURELIA	DEFENSE	FORELEG	INVERSE	MYCELLA	PUBERTY
SANDOWN	WILDCAT	AUREOLA	DEJECTA	FOREMAN	IONESCO	MYCENAE	PUCELLE
SANDPIT	WILDING	AUREOLE	DEMERGE	FOREPAW	IVRESSE	MYCETES	PYAEMIA
SARDANA	WINDBAG	BAGEHOT	DEMERIT	FORESEE	JAMESON	NACELLE	PYRETIC
SARDINE	WINDING	BALEFUL	DEMESNE	FOREVER	JAVELIN	NAKEDLY	PYREXIA
SAWDUST	WINDOWS	BARENTS	DEMETER	FREEBIE	JAVELLE	NAVETTE	QUEENLY
SEEDBED	WINDROW	BEDEVIL	DESERTS	FREEDOM	JEZEBEL	NEMESIA	QUEERER
SENDOFF	WINDSOR	BEJEWEL	DESERVE	FREEMAN	JEWELER	NEMESIS	QUIETEN
SHADING	WONDERS	BENEATH	DETENTE	FREESIA	JEWELRY	NIGELLA	QUIETLY
SHADOOF	WOODCUT	BENEFIT	DEVELOP	FREEWAY	JEZEBEL	NIGERIA	QUIETUS
SHADOWY	WOODMAN	BEREAVE	DIDEROT	FREEZER	JUKEBOX	NINEPIN	RACEMIC
SHUDDER	WORDILY	BESEECH	DILEMMA	FRIENDS	JUVENAL	NINEVEH	RALEIGH
SIDDONS	WORDING	BEVERLY	DINETTE	FROEBEL	KALENDS	NOSEBAG	RAMEKIN
SINDBAD	YARDAGE	BIBELOT	DISEASE	FUMETTE	KAMERAD	NOSEGAY	RAMESES
SITDOWN	YARDARM	BIRETTA	DIVERGE	FUNERAL	KINESIS	NOTEPAD	RAREBIT
SKIDDAW	YIDDISH	BLEEPER	DIVERSE	FUSEBOX	KINETIC	NOVELLA	REBECCA
SKIDPAN	ABREAST	BOHEMIA	DNIEPER	GABELLE	KLEENEX	NOVELLO	RECEIPT
SLIDING	ABSENCE	BOLETUS	DOLEFUL	GALETTE	KNEECAP	NOVELTY	RECEIVE
SMIDGIN	ACHERON	BONESET	DONEGAL	GAMELAN	KNEELER	NUMERAL	REFEREE
SMUDGED	ACHESON	BOREDOM	DUKEDOM	GANELON	KNEEPAD	NUMERIC	REGENCY
SOLDIER	ACREAGE	BRAEMAR	DUNEDIN	GASEOUS	KUBELIK	NUREYEV	RELEASE
SONDAGE	ADRENAL	BREEDER	EAGERLY	GATEWAY	LACERTA	OBJECTS	RENEGUE
SORDINO	ADVERSE	BRIEFLY	ECHELON	GAZELLE	LACEUPS	OBSEQUY	RENEWAL
SPADGER	AILERON	BURETTE	EFFECTS	GAZETTE	LAMELLA	OBSERVE	REREDOS
SPIDERS	ALBENIZ	CADENCE	EFFENDI	GEHENNA	LATERAL	OBVERSE	RESERVE
SPIDERY	ALBERGO	CADENZA	ELDERLY	GENERAL	LATERAN	OFFENCE	REVELER
STADDLE	ALBERTA	CALECHE	ELZEVIR	GENERIC	LAYERED	OFFENSE	REVELRY
STADIUM	ALBERTI	CALENDS	EMPEROR	GENESIS	LAYETTE	OFFERER	REVENGE
STUDDED	ALGEBRA	CALEPIN	ENDEMIC	GENETIC	LEVERET	OGREISH	REVENUE
STUDENT	ALGERIA	CAMELOT	ENFEOFF	GISELLE	LIBERAL	ORDERED	REVERED
STUDIED	ALLEGED	CAMERON	ENTEBBE	GLEEFUL	LIBERIA	ORDERLY	REVERIE
SUBDUCT	ALLEGRI	CANELLA	ENTENTE	GOBELIN	LIBERTY	ORLEANS	REVERSE
SUBDUED	ALLEGRO	CAPELLA	ENTERIC	GODETIA	LICENCE	OSSELET	RIVETED
SUNDECK	ALLENBY	CAREERS	ENTERON	GREENER	LICENSE	OSSEOUS	ROBERTS
SUNDIAL	ALLERGY	CAREFUL	ENVELOP	HARELIP	LIKENED	OSTEOMA	ROBESON
SUNDOWN	ALREADY	CASEASE	ENVENOM	HATEFUL	LINEAGE	OTHELLO	ROSEATE
SURDITY	ALTERED	CATECHU	EPHEBUS	HEREDIA	LINEMAN	PAGEANT	ROSEBUD
SWADDLE	ALVEOLE	CATELOG	EPHEDRA	HERETIC	LITERAL	PAGEBOY	ROSEHIP
SWEDISH	AMMETER	CATERER	EPHESUS	HIDEOUS	LOBELIA	PALERMO	ROSELLA
SWIDDEN	AMNESIA	CATESBY	EQUERRY	HIDEOUT	LORELEI	PALETTE	ROSELLE
TARDILY	AMNESTY	CAVEMAN	ESSENCE	HOMERIC	LOZENGE	PARENTS	ROSEOLA
TARDIVE	AMOEBIC	CAYENNE	ESSENES	HONESTY	LUCERNE	PARESIS	ROSETTA
TENDRIL	ANAEMIA	CELEBES	EUGENIA	HONEYED	LUNETTE	PATELLA	ROSETTE
TIDDLER	ANAEMIC	CELESTA	EUGENIC	HOPEFUL	MACEDON	PEREIRA	RUBELLA
TODDLER	ANGELIC	CELESTE	EUGENIE	HOWEVER	MADEIRA	PHAETON	RUBEOLA
TRADEIN	ANGELUS	CHEERIO	EUPEPSY	HUMERUS	MAGENTA	PHOEBUS	RUDERAL
TRADING	ANGEVIN	CHEESED	EUTERPE	ICTERIC	MAJESTY	PHOENIX	SALERMO
TRADUCE	ANNELID	CHEETAH	EXCERPT	ICTERUS	MALEFIC	PHRENIC	SAVELOY
TRIDENT	ANTENNA	CHIEFLY	EXHEDRA	IGNEOUS	MAREMMA	PIGEONS	SCHEMER
TRODDEN	APHELIA	CINEMAS	EXPENSE	ILLEGAL	MARENGO	PIKELET	SCHERZO
TRUDGEN	APHESIS	CINEREA	FACETED	IMMENSE	MATELOT	PIMENTO	SCIENCE
TWADDLE	APPEASE	CODEINE	FAIENCE	IMMERGE	MAZEPPA	PINETUM	SCLERAL
TWIDDLE	APTERAL	COGENCY	FATEFUL	IMMERSE	MEMENTO	PIPETTE	SCREECH
TWIDDLY	APTERYX	CORELLI	FAVELLA	IMPEACH	MESEEMS	PITEOUS	SCREEVE
TZADDIK	AQUEOUS	COTERIE	FEDERAL	IMPERIL	MILEAGE	PODESTA	SCREWED
VANDALS	ARIETTA	COVERED	FENELON	IMPETUS	MINERVA	POLEAXE	SENECIO

SENEGAL	URAEMIA	GASFIRE	SKIFFLE	BUNGLER	HAGGERY	PIGGERY	AFGHANI
SEVENTH	URGENCY	GOLFING	SNAFFLE	BURGEON	HANGDOG	PILGRIM	ALCHEMY
SEVENTY	UTRECHT	GRAFTER	SNIFFER	BURGESS	HANGING	PROGENY	ALPHEUS
SEVERAL	UTTERLY	GRIFFON	SNIFFLE	BURGHER	HANGMAN	PROGRAM	ALTHAEA
SEVERUS	VALENCE	GRIFTER	SNIFTER	BURGLAR	HANGMEN	PUNGENT	ALTHING
SIDECAR	VALENCY	GRUFFLY	SNUFFLE	CARGOES	HANGOUT	RANGOON	ALTHORN
SILENCE	VANESSA	GUNFIRE	SOUFFLE	CHAGALL	HAUGHTY	REAGENT	AMPHORA
SILESIA	VEDETTE	HAGFISH	STAFFER	CHAGRIN	HEDGING	RIGGING	ANCHOVY
SIMENON	VEGETAL	HALFWAY	STIFFEN	CHIGGER	HEIGHTS	RINGERS	ANTHILL
SLEEKLY	VENERER	HALFWIT	STIFFLY	CHIGNON	HENGIST	RINGGIT	ANTHONY
SLEEPER	VETERAN	HAYFORK	STUFFED	CONGEAL	HIGGINS	RINGING	ANTHRAX
SLEEVED	VICEROY	HOTFOOT	SUBFUSC	COWGIRL	HOGGING	RINGLET	ARCHAEA
SOBERLY	VINEGAR	ICEFALL	SUFFETE	DAGGERS	HUNGARY	ROUGHEN	ARCHAIC
SOMEHOW	VIRELAY	ICEFLOE	SUFFICE	DIAGRAM	IMAGERY	ROUGHIE	ARCHERY
SOMEONE	WAKEFUL	JEWFISH	SUFFOLK	DIGGING	IMAGINE	ROUGHLY	ARCHIVE
SOMEWAY	WATERED	LEAFLET	SUFFUSE	DINGBAT	IMAGING	SANGRIA	ARCHWAY
SPHENIC	WAVERER	MAYFAIR	SULFATE	DISGUST	IMAGISM	SARGENT	ARMHOLE
SQUEAKY	WHEEDLE	MENFOLK	SURFACE	DODGEMS	IMAGIST	SCAGLIA	ASPHALT
SQUEERS	WHEELED	MILFOIL	SURFEIT	DOGGONE	ISOGRAM	SEAGULL	BAGHDAD
SQUEEZE	WHEELER	MISFIRE	SURFING	DOUGHTY	JAGGERY	SHAGGED	BASHFUL
SQUELCH	WHEELIE	MOUFLON	SWIFTER	DOUGLAS	JOGGING	SINGING	BATHERS
STEEPEN	WHOEVER	MUDFLAP	SWIFTLY	DRAGGLE	JUGGINS	SINGLES	BATHING
STEEPLE	WIPEOUT	MUFFLED	TAFFETA	DRAGNET	JUGGLER	SINGLET	BATHMAT
STEEPLY	WIRETAP	MUFFLER	TAXFREE	DRAGOON	KINGCUP	SLOGGER	BATHTUB
STEERER	WIZENED	NORFOLK	TELFORD	DRUGGED	KINGDOM	SMUGGLE	BAUHAUS
STREAKY	XIMENES	OARFISH	TENFOLD	DRUGGET	KINGLET	SNIGGER	BEEHIVE
STRETCH	YEREVAN	OLEFINE	TIFFANY	DUDGEON	KINGPIN	SNUGGLE	BESHREW
STREWTH	ACIFORM	ORIFICE	TINFOIL	DUNGEON	LAGGARD	SORGHUM	BETHINK
SUBEDAR	AIRFLOW	OUTFACE	TOMFOOL	ELEGANT	LAGGING	SPIGNEL	BETHUMB
SUBEDIT	BAFFLED	OUTFALL	TRAFFIC	ELEGIAC	LANGLEY	STAGGER	BIGHEAD
SUDETEN	BALFOUR	OUTFLOW	TREFOIL	ELEGIST	LANGTON	STAGING	BIGHORN
SUZETTE	BEDFORD	PALFREY	TRIFFID	ELOGIUM	LANGUID	STYGIAN	BOWHEAD
SWEEPER	BEEFALO	PARFAIT	TRIFLER	ENDGAME	LANGUOR	SUGGEST	BOXHAUL
SWEETEN	BIAFRAN	PERFECT	TRIFLES	EPIGEAL	LARGELY	SURGEON	BOYHOOD
SWEETIE	BIGFOOT	PERFIDY	TRUFFLE	EPIGONE	LARGESS	SURGERY	BRAHMAN
SWEETLY	BLUFFLY	PERFORM	TWOFOLD	EPIGRAM	LARGEST	SWAGGER	BRAHMIN
SYNERGY	BONFIRE	PERFUME	UNIFORM	ETAGÈRE	LEAGUER	SWAGMAN	BUSHIDO
TAGETES	BUFFALO	PERFUSE	WARFARE	EXEGETE	LEGGING	TANGENT	BUSHMAN
TAKEOFF	BUFFOON	PIGFISH	WELFARE	EXIGENT	LENGTHY	TANGIER	BUSHMEN
TAKEOUT	CATFISH	PINFISH	WILFRED	EXOGAMY	LINGUAL	TANGLED	CACHEXY
TAMESIS	CHAFING	PINFOLD	WOLFISH	FAGGOTS	LODGING	THUGGEE	CASHBOX
TAVERNA	CHIFFON	PITFALL	WOLFRAM	FANGLED	LOGGING	TINGLER	CASHIER
TEHERAN	CHUFFED	POMFRET	ZOFFANY	FEIGNED	LONGBOW	TOGGERY	CATHEAD
TELECOM	COFFERS	POOFTER	ABIGAIL	FIDGETS	LONGING	TONGUES	CATHODE
TERENCE	COMFORT	PREFACE	ALIGNED	FIDGETY	LUDGATE	TOUGHEN	CEPHEUS
THIEVES	COMFREY	PREFECT	AMYGDAL	FINGERS	LUGGAGE	TRAGEDY	CITHARA
THREADS	CONFESS	PROFANE	ANAGRAM	FLAGDAY	MAGGOTY	TRIGGER	COCHLEA
THRENOS	CONFIDE	PROFESS	APOGEAN	FLIGHTY	MAIGRET	TSIGANE	COWHAND
TIBETAN	CONFINE	PROFFER	ATAGHAN	FLOGGER	MANGOLD	TSIGANY	COWHERD
TIDEWAY	CONFIRM	PROFILE	AVIGNON	FORGAVE	MARGERY	TURGENT	COWHIDE
TIMELAG	CONFORM	PROFITS	AZYGOUS	FORGIVE	MAUGHAM	URUGUAY	CUSHION
TIMEOUT	CONFUSE	PROFUSE	BAGGAGE	FORGONE	MIDGARD	VAUGHAN	DAPHNID
TONETIC	CROFTER	RAFFISH	BANGING	FRAGILE	MONGREL	VIRGATE	DAPHNIS
TOTEMIC	DIFFUSE	RAFFLES	BANGKOK	FRIGATE	MUGGING	VIRGULE	DASHING
TOXEMIA	DOGFISH	REDFISH	BARGAIN	FROGMAN	NAGGING	VULGATE	DASHPOT
TREETOP	DOGFOOD	ROOFING	BEGGARY	FULGENT	NAUGHTY	WAGGISH	DIEHARD
TRIESTE	DRAFTED	ROOFTOP	BEGGING	FUNGOID	NIAGARA	WAGGLER	DITHERY
TUNEFUL	DRAFTEE	RUFFIAN	BELGIAN	FUNGOUS	NIGGARD	WANGLER	DUCHESS
TURENNE	DRIFTER	RUFFLED	BELGIUM	GANGWAY	NOGGING	WEIGELA	EGGHEAD
TUTELAR	EDIFICE	RUFFLER	BENGALI	GAUGUIN	OREGANO	WEIGHIN	ENCHANT
TWEEDLE	FANFARE	SAFFRON	BERGSON	GINGHAM	ORIGAMI	WEIGHTS	ENTHRAL
TWEETER	FIEFDOM	SAWFISH	BLIGHTY	GOGGLES	ORIGINS	WEIGHTY	ENTHUSE
UCCELLO	FINFOOT	SCAFELL	BRIGADE	GREGORY	OROGENY	WIDGEON	ESCHEAT
UNDERGO	FORFEIT	SCOFFER	BRIGAND	GROGRAM	OUTGROW	WIGGING	ETCHING
UNHEARD	FORFEND	SCUFFLE	BRIGHAM	GUDGEON	PANGAEA	WINGMAN	EUPHONY
UNKEMPT	FULFILL	SEAFOOD	BUGGING	GUIGNOL	PANGRAM	WRIGGLE	EYEHOLE
UNLEASH	FUNFAIR	SELFISH	BUGGINS	HAGGADA	PENGUIN	YANGTSE	FASHION
UNNERVE	GABFEST	SERFDOM	BULGHUR	HAGGARD	PERGOLA	ZINGARO	FATHEAD
UNREADY	GARFISH	SHUFFLE	BULGING	HAGGARD	PIDGEON		FIGHTER

FISHERY	PITHEAD	AGRIPPA	CAPITOL	ECLIPSE	INSIGHT	MONITOR	RANIDAE
FISHEYE	PITHILY	ALGIERS	CARIBOU	ELLIPSE	INSIPID	MOUILLÉ	RAPIDLY
FISHING	POCHARD	ALRIGHT	CARIOCA	EMPIRIC	INVIOUS	MURIATE	RATIONS
FISHNET	POCHOIR	AMBIENT	CARIOLE	ENFIELD	JACINTH	MURILLO	RAVINGS
FLYHALF	POOHBAH	ANCIENT	CARITAS	ENGINED	JANITOR	MUSICAL	RAVIOLI
FOGHORN	POTHEEN	ANDIRON	CAVIARE	ENLIVEN	JERICHO	MYRINGA	REBIRTH
FOXHOLE	POTHERB	ANGIOMA	CECILIA	ENTITLE	JUBILEE	NAMIBIA	RECITAL
FUCHSIA	POTHOLE	ANTIBES	CEDILLA	ENVIOUS	JUJITSU	NATIONS	REFINED
FUCHSIN	PREHEAT	ANTIGEN	CEVICHE	EPSILON	JUNIPER	NATIVES	REFINER
GOAHEAD	PUSHING	ANTIGUA	CHAINED	EQUINOX	JUPITER	NERITIC	REGIMEN
GODHEAD	PUSHKIN	ANTIOCH	CHRISOM	ESTIVAL	KUFIYAH	NEVILLE	RELIANT
GOSHAWK	RACHIAL	ANTIQUE	CHRISTY	ETHICAL	LABIATE	NOMINAL	RELICTS
GUSHING	RACHMAN	ANXIETY	CILIATE	EXCITED	LALIQUE	NOMINEE	RELIEVE
HACHURE	RAPHAEL	ANXIOUS	CITIZEN	EXHIBIT	LATIMER	NOTIONS	RELIEVO
HASHISH	RAWHIDE	APRICOT	CIVILLY	EXPIATE	LAYINGS	NOXIOUS	RESIANT
HESHVAN	REDHEAD	APSIDAL	CLOISON	EXPIRED	LEGIBLE	OBLIGED	RESIDUE
HIGHEST	RESHAPE	AQUIFER	CODICIL	EXTINCT	LEGIBLY	OBLIGOR	RETICLE
HIGHMAN	RETHINK	AQUILON	COLIBRI	FAJITAS	LEGIONS	OBLIQUE	RETINAL
HOTHEAD	RICHARD	AQUINAS	COLITIS	FATIGUE	LENIENT	OBVIATE	RETINUE
INSHORE	RICHTER	AQUINUS	COMICAL	FETICHE	LEXICON	OBVIOUS	RETIRED
ISCHIUM	RIGHTLY	ARBITER	CONICAL	FILINGS	LIAISON	OCCIPUT	RETIREE
ISOHYET	RUSHING	ARRIVAL	CONIFER	FINICAL	LIMINAL	OEDIPUS	REVISED
ISTHMUS	RUTHENE	ARRIVED	COPILOT	FINICKY	LIMITED	OFFICER	REVISER
ITCHING	SASHIMI	ARTICLE	COPIOUS	FIXINGS	LIMITER	OFFICES	REVISIT
KASHMIR	SAXHORN	ARTISAN	CORINTH	FOLIAGE	LININGS	OMNIBUS	REVIVAL
KEYHOLE	SIGHTED	ARTISTE	COTINGA	FRAILTY	LOGICAL	ONEIRIC	REVIVER
KITHARA	SIKHISM	ASCITES	CRUISER	FREIGHT	LUCIDLY	ONMIBUS	RIDINGS
KURHAUS	SINHALA	ASPIRIN	CUBICLE	FURIOUS	LUCIFER	OPTICAL	RIGIDLY
LASHING	SKYHIGH	ASSIEGE	CURIOUS	FUSIBLE	LURIDLY	OPTIMAL	RISIBLE
LECHERY	SOPHISM	ASSISTS	CUTICLE	FUSILLI	LYRICAL	OPTIMUM	RIVIERA
LIGHTEN	SOPHIST	ASSIZES	CYNICAL	GALILEE	MADISON	ORBITAL	ROBINIA
LIGHTER	SPYHOLE	ASTILBE	CYTISUS	GALILEO	MAFIOSO	ORCINOL	ROTIFER
LIGHTLY	SWAHILI	ATHIRST	DALILAH	GALIPOT	MAGICAL	ORDINAL	RUBICON
LITHELY	TACHISM	ATTICUS	DECIBEL	GEFILTE	MAGINOT	ORGIAST	SAGITTA
LITHIUM	TIGHTEN	ATTIRED	DECIDED	GENISTA	MAKINGS	ORVIETO	SALIENT
LOTHAIR	TIGHTLY	AUDIBLE	DECIDER	GENITAL	MAMILLA	OSSICLE	SALIERI
LOTHIAN	TOEHOLD	AUDIBLY	DECIMAL	GOLIARD	MANIHOC	OSTIOLE	SALIQUE
LUGHOLE	TOWAHEAD	AUDITOR	DEFIANT	GOLIATH	MANIKIN	PACIFIC	SAMISEN
LYCHNIS	TYPHOID	AURICLE	DEFICIT	GORILLA	MANILLA	PALINGS	SAPIENS
MACHETE	TYPHOON	AVOIDER	DEFILED	GRAINED	MANIPLE	PALISSY	SAPIENT
MACHINE	UPSHOOT	BACILLI	DEFINED	GRAINER	MANITOU	PANICKY	SATIATE
MAGHREB	WARHEAD	BASINET	DEHISCE	GROINED	MARIBOU	PANICLE	SATIETY
MANHOLE	WASHDAY	BELIEVE	DELIBES	HABITAT	MARINER	PAPILLA	SATIRIC
MANHOOD	WASHERS	BELINDA	DELIGHT	HALIBUT	MARITAL	PARINGS	SATISFY
MANHUNT	WASHING	BELISHA	DELILAH	HALIFAX	MATILDA	PATIBLE	SAVINGS
MECHLIN	WASHOUT	BENISON	DELIMIT	HALITUS	MATINEE	PATIENT	SAVIOUR
METHANE	WASHTUB	BESIDES	DELIVER	HARICOT	MATISSE	PAVIOUR	SCHICKS
METHINK	WISHFUL	BESIEGE	DEMIGOD	HELICAL	MAXILLA	PEDICAB	SCRIBER
MICHAEL	WISHING	BETIMES	DENIZEN	HELICON	MAXIMUM	PEDICEL	SEMINAL
MITHRAS	WITHERS	BEWITCH	DEVIANT	HELIPAD	MEDIATE	PEDICLE	SEMINAR
MOTHERS	WITHOUT	BEZIQUE	DEVIATE	HOLIDAY	MEDICAL	PELICAN	SEMIPRO
MYNHEER	YASHMAK	BILIOUS	DEVILRY	HOMINID	MELILOT	PERIGEE	SEMITIC
NAPHTHA	YOGHURT	BOLIVAR	DEVIOUS	HONITON	MERITED	PERIWIG	SERINGA
NIGHTIE	ZEPHIEL	BOLIVIA	DEVISED	HORIZON	METICAL	PETIOLE	SERIOUS
NIGHTLY	ABRIDGE	BOUILLI	DEVISEE	HOSIERY	MÉTISSE	PITIFUL	SEVILLE
NOTHING	ABSINTH	BRAILLE	DIDICOY	HUMIDOR	MEXICAN	PLAINLY	SHRILLY
NOWHERE	ACHIEVE	BROILER	DIGITAL	HYGIENE	MILITIA	PLEIADE	SHRIMPS
OFFHAND	ACTINAL	BRUISED	DIVIDED	ILLICIT	MIMICRY	POLITIC	SHRIVEL
OMPHALE	ACTINIA	BRUISER	DIVINER	IMPIETY	MINIBUS	POLIZEI	SHRIVEN
ONSHORE	ACTINIC	BULIMIA	DIVISOR	IMPINGE	MINICAB	PONIARD	SHRIVER
ORCHARD	ADDISON	CABINET	DOMINGO	IMPIOUS	MINIMAL	POSITIF	SILICON
ORPHEAN	ADMIRAL	CACIQUE	DOMINIC	INCISOR	MINIMAX	POTICHE	SIMILAR
ORPHEUS	ADMIRED	CALIBAN	DRAINED	INDIANA	MINIMUM	PRAIRIE	SLEIGHT
ORPHISM	ADMIRER	CALIBER	DUBIETY	INFIDEL	MIRIFIC	PURITAN	SOCIETY
ORPHREY	ADVISER	CALIBRE	DUBIOUS	INFIELD	MODICUM	PYRITES	SOLICIT
PATHWAY	ADVISOR	CALICHE	DUTIFUL	INHIBIT	MODISTE	RADIANT	SOLIDLY
PERHAPS	AFFIXED	CAMILLA	EASIEST	INNINGS	MOHICAN	RADIATE	SOLIDUS
PINHEAD	AFRICAN	CANIDAE	ECHIDNA	INSIDER	MOLIÈRE	RADICAL	SPLICED
PINHOLE	AGAINST	CAPITAL	ECHINUS	INSIDES	MONILIA	RADICLE	SPLICER

SPOILED	VAGINAL	COOKING	PECKING	YONKERS	BUILDER	DIALING	GATLING
SPOILER	VALIANT	CORKAGE	PECKISH	YORKIST	BULLACE	DIALYSE	GEELONG
SPRINGE	VANILLA	CORKING	PICKAXE	ABALONE	BULLDOG	DIGLYPH	GEOLOGY
SPRINGS	VANITAS	CUCKING	PICKING	ABELARD	BULLETS	DIPLOCK	GIBLETS
SPRINGY	VARIANT	CUCKOLD	PICKLED	ABILITY	BULLION	DIPLOMA	GIELGUD
SQUIFFY	VARIETY	DICKENS	PICKLER	ABOLISH	BULLISH	DISLIKE	GILLRAY
SQUILLA	VARIOLA	DOCKING	PINKEYE	ACCLAIM	BULLOCK	DOLLARS	GIRLISH
SQUINCH	VARIOUS	DORKING	PUCKISH	ACOLYTE	BULLPEN	DOWLAND	GODLESS
SQUISHY	VATICAN	DUCKING	QUAKING	ADELINE	CABLING	DUALITY	GODLIKE
STAINED	VEHICLE	DUNKIRK	RACKETS	ADELPHI	CALLBOX	DULLARD	GOOLIES
STAINER	VENISON	EZEKIEL	RACKETY	ADULATE	CALLBOY	DWELLER	GOSLING
STOICAL	VESICLE	GAEKWAR	RACKING	AEOLIAN	CALLING	EARLDOM	GOULASH
STRIATE	VETIVER	GAWKISH	RANKING	AFFLICT	CALLOUS	EARLIER	GRILLED
STRIDES	VICINAL	HACKERY	REEKING	AGELESS	CARLOAD	EARLOBE	GROLIER
STRIDOR	VICIOUS	HACKING	RICKETS	AGELONG	CARLYLE	ECOLOGY	GUILDER
STRIGIL	VIDIMUS	HACKLES	RICKETY	AGILITY	CATLIKE	EGALITY	GUTLESS
STRIKER	VIKINGS	HACKNEY	RISKILY	AIMLESS	CATLING	EMBLAZE	HALLALI
STRINGS	VISIBLE	HACKSAW	ROCKALL	AIRLESS	CEILIDH	EMPLOYS	HALLWAY
STRINGY	VISIBLY	HAWKEYE	ROCKERY	AIRLIFT	CEILING	EMULATE	HAPLESS
STRIPED	VISITOR	HECKLER	ROCKING	AIRLINE	CELLINI	EMULSIN	HARLECH
STRIPER	VITIATE	HICKORY	ROOKERY	AIRLOCK	CELLIST	ENCLASP	HATLESS
STRIPES	VIVIDLY	HOPKINS	ROOKISH	AMALGAM	CELLULE	ENCLAVE	HAULAGE
SURINAM	WYSIWYG	HULKING	SACKBUT	AMPLIFY	CHALDEE	ENCLOSE	HAULIER
SYRINGA	YEZIDEE	HUNKERS	SACKFUL	AMYLASE	CHALICE	ENDLESS	HAYLOFT
SYRINGE	YPSILON	HUSKILY	SACKING	AMYLOID	CHALKER	ENGLAND	HAZLETT
TABITHA	BEIJING	JACKASS	SEEKERS	AMYLOSE	CHALONE	ENGLISH	HEALING
TACITLY	CONJOIN	JACKDAW	SELKIRK	ANALOGY	CHELSEA	ENOLOGY	HEALTHY
TACITUS	CONJURE	JACKETS	SHAKERS	ANALYST	CHILEAN	ENSLAVE	HEELTAP
TAKINGS	DISJOIN	JACKPOT	SHAKEUP	ANALYZE	CHILLER	EXALTED	HELLCAT
TALIPES	JIMJAMS	JACKSON	SHAKILY	ANGLING	CHILLON	EXCLAIM	HELLENE
TALIPOT	MAHJONG	JANKERS	SHAKING	ANILINE	CHOLERA	EXCLUDE	HELLION
TAPIOCA	PERJURE	JENKINS	SHIKARI	ANTLERS	CODLING	EXPLAIN	HELLISH
TATIANA	PERJURY	JERKILY	SICKBAY	APELIKE	COELIAC	EXPLODE	HELLUVA
TAXICAB	PROJECT	KICKING	SICKBED	APOLOGY	COLLAGE	EXPLOIT	HEMLINE
TAXIWAY	PUNJABI	KICKOFF	SICKERT	APPLAUD	COLLARD	EXPLORE	HEMLOCK
TEDIOUS	SUBJECT	KOLKHOZ	SINKING	APPLIED	COLLATE	EYELASH	HILLMAN
THRIFTY	SUBJOIN	LACKING	SMOKING	ARTLESS	COLLECT	EYELESS	HILLMEN
THRISTY	BACKING	LEAKAGE	SOAKING	ATELIER	COLLEEN	EYELIDS	HILLOCK
TIDINGS	BACKLOG	LICKING	SOCKEYE	ATHLETE	COLLEGE	FAILING	HILLTOP
TIMIDLY	BACKSET	LINKAGE	SOCKING	AUSLESE	COLLIDE	FAILURE	HOLLAND
TONIGHT	BANKING	LINKING	SOVKHOZ	AXILLAR	COLLIER	FALLACY	HOPLITE
TOPIARY	BANKSIA	LINKMAN	SUKKOTH	AXOLOTL	COLLOID	FALLING	HOTLINE
TOPICAL	BARKERS	LOCKJAW	SULKILY	BAILIFF	COLLUDE	FALLOUT	HOWLING
TOTIENT	BARKING	LOCKNUT	TACKLER	BAKLAVA	COOLANT	FEELING	HURLING
TRAILER	BASKING	LOCKOUT	TALKING	BALLADE	COOLING	FELLOWS	HYALINE
TRAINED	BECKETT	LOOKING	TANKARD	BALLAST	COPLAND	FENLAND	HYALOID
TRAINEE	BONKERS	LOOKOUT	TICKING	BALLBOY	COULDNT	FETLOCK	ICELAND
TRAINER	BOOKIES	LUCKILY	TICKLER	BALLIOL	COULOMB	FIELDER	IDOLIZE
TRAIPSE	BOOKING	LURKING	TOLKIEN	BALLOON	COULTER	FIGLEAF	IDYLLIC
TRAITOR	BOOKISH	MANKIND	TOPKAPI	BEELINE	COWLICK	FILLETS	IMPLANT
TROILUS	BOOKLET	MARKING	TOPKNOT	BELLBOY	COWLING	FILLING	IMPLIED
TUNICLE	BOOKMAN	MAWKISH	TREKKER	BELLEEK	COXLESS	FINLAND	IMPLODE
TUNISIA	BRAKING	MILKING	TURKISH	BELLHOP	CURLING	FLYLEAF	IMPLORE
TYPICAL	BROKERS	MILKMAN	WALKING	BELLINI	CUTLASS	FOGLAMP	INCLINE
UNAIDED	BUCKETS	MILKSOP	WALKMAN	BELLMAN	CUTLERY	FOLLIES	INCLUDE
UNAIRED	BUCKEYE	MOCKERS	WALKOUT	BELLOWS	CYCLING	FOOLISH	INFLAME
UNCINUS	BUCKLER	MOCKERY	WALKWAY	BERLINE	CYCLIST	FORLORN	INFLATE
UNCIVIL	BUCKRAM	MOCKING	WEAKEST	BILLION	CYCLONE	FOULARD	INFLECT
UNFIXED	BURKINA	MONKISH	WEEKDAY	BILLMAN	CYCLOPS	FRILLED	INFLICT
UNHINGE	BUSKINS	MUSKRAT	WEEKEND	BILLOWS	DARLING	FULLERS	INKLING
UNHITCH	CATKINS	NANKEEN	WICKIUP	BIOLOGY	DEALING	FURLONG	IRELAND
UNLINED	CHEKHOV	NECKING	WICKLOW	BIPLANE	DECLAIM	GALLANT	ISOLATE
UNMIXED	CHOKING	NECKLET	WORKERS	BOILEAU	DECLARE	GALLEON	ITALIAN
UPRIGHT	CHUKKER	NECKTIE	WORKING	BOILING	DECLINE	GALLERY	JAPLISH
UPSIDES	COCKADE	PACKAGE	WORKMAN	BOLLARD	DEFLATE	GALLING	JEALOUS
UPSILON	COCKLES	PACKING	WORKMEN	BOOLEAN	DEFLECT	GALLIUM	JELLABA
UPTIGHT	COCKNEY	PACKMAN	WORKOUT	BOULDER	DEPLETE	GALLONS	JELLIED
UTRICLE	COCKPIT	PARKING	WORKSHY	BOWLING	DEPLORE	GALLOWS	JOBLESS
UTRILLO	COOKERY	PARKWAY	WORKTOP	BUGLOSS	DIALECT	GARLAND	JOLLITY

JOYLESS	OCELLAR	REALITY	SOULFUL	WALLIES	BROMINE	FITMENT	PALMATE
JUGLANS	OCELLUS	REALIZE	SPELLER	WALLOON	BUMMALO	FLAMING	PALMIST
JUTLAND	OCULIST	REALTOR	STALKED	WARLIKE	BURMESE	FLEMING	PALMTOP
KEELING	ODALISK	RECLAIM	STALKER	WARLING	CADMIUM	FLEMISH	PALMYRA
KHALIFA	OFFLOAD	RECLINE	STELLAR	WARLOCK	CALMUCK	FLUMMOX	PAYMENT
KIELDER	OPALINE	RECLUSE	STILTED	WARLORD	CARMINE	FORMICA	PERMIAN
KILLICK	OPULENT	REELECT	STILTON	WAYLAND	CATMINT	FORMING	PIGMEAT
KILLING	OTALGIA	REELING	STOLLEN	WEALDEN	CHAMBER	FORMOSA	PIGMENT
KILLJOY	OUTLAST	REFLATE	STYLING	WEALTHY	CHAMBRÉ	FORMULA	PISMIRE
KIPLING	OUTLIER	REFLECT	STYLISH	WEDLOCK	CHAMFER	FRUMPLE	PLUMAGE
KNELLER	OUTLINE	REFLOAT	STYLIST	WELLIES	CHAMOIS	GARMENT	PLUMATE
KOWLOON	OUTLIVE	REPLACE	STYLITE	WELLOFF	CHAMPAK	GASMASK	PLUMBER
LALLANS	OUTLOOK	REPLANT	STYLIZE	WENLOCK	CHEMISE	GEMMATE	PLUMMET
LAWLESS	OVULATE	REPLETE	SUBLIME	WETLAND	CHEMIST	GERMANE	PLUMPER
LEGLESS	OXALATE	REPLEVY	SULLAGE	WHALING	CHIMERA	GERMANY	PLUMULE
LOLLARD	OXBLOOD	REPLICA	SUNLAMP	WILLIAM	CHIMNEY	GIMMICK	POMMARD
LOWLAND	PADLOCK	RIBLESS	SUNLESS	WILLIES	CLAMBER	GLAMOUR	PREMIER
LULLABY	PAHLAVI	RIMLESS	SWALLOW	WILLING	CLAMOUR	GLIMMER	PREMISE
MAILBAG	PALLIUM	ROLLERS	SWELTER	WILLOWY	CLAMPER	GLIMPSE	PREMISS
MAILBOX	PARLOUR	ROLLICK	SWOLLEN	WITLESS	CLEMENT	GRAMMAR	PREMIUM
MAILCAR	PARLOUS	ROLLING	TABLEAU	WITLOOF	CLIMATE	GRAMPUS	PRIMACY
MAILING	PAULINE	ROLLMOP	TABLOID	WOOLLEN	CLIMBER	GREMLIN	PRIMARY
MAILMAN	PAVLOVA	ROULADE	TAILORS	WORLDLY	CLUMBER	GRIMACE	PRIMATE
MALLARD	PAYLOAD	ROULEAU	TALLBOY	WOULDBE	COMMAND	GRIMOND	PRIMEUR
MALLEUS	PEELING	ROWLOCK	TALLITH	WOULDNT	COMMEND	GRIMSBY	PRIMING
MALLING	PERLITE	SAILING	TAPLASH	YELLOWS	COMMENT	GROMMET	PRIMULA
MARLENE	PHALANX	SAILORS	TBILISI	ZEALAND	COMMODE	GRUMBLE	PROMISE
MARLINE	PHALLIC	SALLUST	TEALEAF	ZEALOUS	COMMODO	GRUMMET	PROMOTE
MARLITE	PHALLUS	SAPLING	TELLING	ZEOLITE	COMMONS	HAMMOCK	RAIMENT
MARLOWE	PHILEAS	SCALENE	THALLUS	ZETLAND	COMMUNE	HARMFUL	RHOMBUS
MELLITE	PHILTER	SCALLOP	THULIUM	ZILLION	COMMUTE	HARMONY	RHYMING
MIDLAND	PHILTRE	SCALPEL	TILLAGE	ZOOLITE	CRAMMED	HOLMIUM	ROAMING
MIDLINE	PIGLING	SCALPER	TOLLMAN	ZOOLOGY	CRAMMER	HORMONE	RUMMAGE
MILLAIS	PILLAGE	SCHLEPP	TOOLBOX	ADAMANT	CRAMPED	HUMMING	SARMENT
MILLING	PILLBOX	SCHLOCK	TOOLING	ADAMITE	CRAMPON	HUMMOCK	SAWMILL
MILLION	PILLION	SCHLOSS	TOPLESS	AILMENT	CREMATE	IPOMOEA	SCAMBLE
MISLEAD	PILLORY	SCOLLOP	TOWLINE	AIRMAIL	CRIMEAN	ISHMAEL	SCAMPER
MOELLON	POLLACK	SCULLER	TRELLIS	ALAMEIN	CRIMSON	ISOMERE	SCHMUCK
MOLLIFY	POLLARD	SEALANT	TRILLED	ALAMODE	CRUMBLE	ITEMIZE	SEEMING
MOLLUSC	POLLING	SEALINK	TRILLER	ALEMBIC	CRUMBLY	JAMMIES	SEGMENT
MORLAND	POLLUTE	SEALION	TRILOGY	ALIMENT	CRUMPET	JAMMING	SEYMOUR
MOULAGE	POTLACH	SECLUDE	TROLLEY	ALIMONY	CRUMPLE	JASMINE	SFUMATO
MOULDED	POTLUCK	SELLERS	TROLLOP	ALUMINA	DAIMLER	KALMUCK	SHAMBLE
MOULDER	POULENC	SELLING	TWELFTH	ALUMNAE	DAYMARK	KERMESS	SHAMPOO
MUDLARK	POULTRY	SELLOFF	UGOLINO	ALUMNUS	DENMARK	KHAMSIN	SHIMMER
MULLEIN	PRALINE	SELLOUT	UKULELE	ANEMONE	DESMOND	KOUMISS	SIAMESE
MULLION	PRELACY	SEXLESS	ULULANT	ANIMALS	DIAMINE	KREMLIN	SIEMENS
MYALGIA	PRELATE	SHALLOT	ULULATE	ANIMATE	DIAMOND	LEMMATA	SJAMBOK
MYELINE	PRELIMS	SHALLOW	UNALIKE	ANIMIST	DINMONT	LEMMING	SKIMMED
MYELOID	PRELUDE	SHELLAC	UNALIVE	ANOMALY	DISMAST	LOOMING	SKIMMER
MYELOMA	PROLONG	SHELLED	UNBLOCK	ANYMORE	DISMISS	MALMSEY	SKIMMIA
NAILBED	PSALTER	SHELLEY	UNCLASP	ARAMAIC	DORMANT	MAMMARY	SLAMMER
NEGLECT	PTOLEMY	SHELTER	UNCLEAN	ATOMIST	DRUMLIN	MAMMOTH	SLIMMER
NÉGLIGÉ	PUBLISH	SHELTIE	UNCLEAR	ATOMIZE	DRUMMER	MANMADE	SLUMBER
NEOLITH	PULLMAN	SHELVED	URALITE	AUGMENT	EARMARK	MARMARA	STAMINA
NIBLICK	PURLIEU	SHELVES	UROLITH	AZIMUTH	ELAMITE	MARMION	STAMMER
NOOLOGY	PURLINE	SHYLOCK	USELESS	BARMAID	ELEMENT	MARMITE	STAMPED
NUCLEAR	PURLOIN	SIBLING	UTILITY	BASMATI	ENAMOUR	MERMAID	STAMPER
NUCLEIC	QUALIFY	SIRLOIN	UTILIZE	BEAMING	EREMITE	MIDMOST	STEMMED
NUCLEUS	QUALITY	SKELTER	VAULTED	BERMUDA	ETHMOID	MUMMERS	STOMACH
NUCLIDE	QUILTED	SKILFUL	VILLAGE	BESMEAR	EXAMINE	MUMMERY	STUMBLE
NULLIFY	QUILTER	SKILLED	VILLAIN	BIOMASS	EXAMPLE	MUMMIFY	STUMPED
NULLITY	RAILING	SKILLET	VILLEIN	BISMUTH	EXEMPLA	NUMMARY	SUMMARY
NUNLIKE	RAILWAY	SKYLARK	VIOLATE	BLEMISH	FARMERS	NUTMEAT	SUMMERY
NUTLIKE	RATLINE	SKYLINE	VIOLENT	BOOMING	FARMING	OATMEAL	SUMMING
OAKLEAF	REALGAR	SMALLER	WAILING	BRAMBLE	FERMENT	ODDMENT	SUMMONS
OARLOCK	REALIGN	SMELTER	WALLABY	BRIMFUL	FERMIUM	OLYMPIA	SURMISE
OBELISK	REALISM	SMILING	WALLACE	BROMATE	FIGMENT	OLYMPIC	SWIMMER
OCCLUDE	REALIST	SMOLDER	WALLEYE	BROMIDE	FILMING	OLYMPUS	TAMMANY

TEEMING	BOUNCER	CRINKLE	GRANOLA	MANNING	PRONAOS	SPANDEX	TSUNAMI
TERMITE	BOUNDED	CRINKLY	GRANTED	MANNISH	PRONATE	SPANGLE	TURNERY
THIMBLE	BOUNDEN	CRINOID	GRANTEE	MAUNDER	PRONGED	SPANIEL	TURNING
THOMISM	BOUNDER	CRUNCHY	GRANULE	MEANDER	PRONOUN	SPANISH	TURNKEY
THOMIST	BRANDED	CUNNING	GRENADA	MEANING	QUANTUM	SPANKER	TURNOUT
THOMSON	BRANDER	CYANIDE	GRENADE	MOANING	QUENTIN	SPANNER	TWINKLE
THUMPER	BRANTUB	DAMNING	GRENDEL	MOONING	QUINCHE	SPENCER	TWINSET
THYMINE	BRENDAN	DARNING	GRINDER	MOONLIT	QUININE	SPENDER	UGANDAN
TOPMAST	BRENNER	DEANERY	GUANACO	MORNING	QUINONE	SPENSER	UNKNOWN
TOPMOST	BRINDLE	DIGNIFY	GUANINE	MOUNTED	QUINTAL	SPINACH	UNSNARL
TORMENT	BRINJAL	DIGNITY	GUINEAN	MOUNTIE	QUINTAN	SPINATE	URANIAN
TRAMCAR	BRONCHI	DIMNESS	GUINEAS	MYANMAR	QUINTET	SPINDLE	URANISM
TRAMMEL	BRONZED	DONNISH	GUNNERA	NEWNESS	QUONDAM	SPINDLY	URANITE
TRAMPLE	BURNELL	DRINKER	GUNNERY	NOONDAY	QUONSET	SPINNER	URANIUM
TRAMWAY	BURNHAM	DRUNKEN	GWYNETH	NUNNERY	RAINBOW	SPINNEY	URINARY
TREMBLE	BURNING	DRYNESS	GYMNAST	ODDNESS	RAUNCHY	SPINOFF	URINATE
TREMBLY	BURNISH	DUBNIUM	HAFNIUM	ODONTIC	RAWNESS	SPINOZA	UTENSIL
TREMOLO	BURNOUS	DUNNAGE	HAHNIUM	OKINAWA	REDNECK	SPONDEE	VARNISH
TRIMMER	BURNOUT	DUNNOCK	HARNESS	OLDNESS	REDNESS	SPONDYL	VILNIUS
TRUMEAU	CAINITE	DWINDLE	HAUNTED	OMENTUM	REENTER	SPONGER	WARNING
TRUMPET	CANNERY	EARNEST	HEINOUS	OMINOUS	REENTRY	SPONSON	WETNESS
TURMOIL	CANNILY	EBONITE	HENNAED	ONANISM	REGNANT	SPONSOR	WHINGER
VARMINT	CANNING	ECONOMY	HOBNAIL	ONENESS	REMNANT	STANDBY	WINNING
VERMEER	CANNOCK	EMANATE	HYMNIST	OPENING	REUNION	STANDIN	WINNOCK
VERMONT	CANNULA	EMINENT	HYMNODY	OPINION	REUNITE	STANDUP	WITNESS
WARMING	CARNABY	ENDNOTE	ICHNITE	OPUNTIA	REYNARD	STANLEY	WOUNDED
WAYMARK	CARNAGE	ENSNARE	ICINESS	ORANGES	RHENISH	STANNIC	WRANGLE
WHIMPER	CHANCEL	ENSNARL	ILLNESS	ORINOCO	RHENIUM	STENCIL	WRINGER
WHIMSEY	CHANCRE	ERINYES	INANITY	ORKNEYS	RHONDDA	STENGAH	WRINKLE
WOOMERA	CHANGED	ETONIAN	IRANIAN	ORONTES	ROUNDED	STENGUN	WRINKLY
WYOMING	CHANGES	EVANDER	IRONING	OXONIAN	ROUNDEL	STENTOR	WRONGLY
ABANDON	CHANNEL	EVENING	IVANHOE	PAINFUL	ROUNDER	STINGER	WRYNECK
ACONITE	CHANSON	EVENTER	JOHNNIE	PAINTED	ROUNDLY	STINKER	WRYNOSE
ADENINE	CHANTER	FAINTED	JOHNSON	PAINTER	ROUNDUP	STONILY	YAWNING
ADENOID	CHINDIT	FAINTLY	JOINERY	PANNAGE	RUINOUS	STONKER	YOUNGER
ADENOMA	CHINESE	FARNESE	JOINING	PANNIER	RUNNERS	STUNNER	ZIONIST
ADONAIS	CHINOOK	FATNESS	JOINTED	PANNOSE	RUNNING	STUNTED	AARONIC
AGONIST	CHINTZY	FAWNING	JOINTER	PARNELL	RUNNION	SUNNILY	ABDOMEN
AGONIZE	CHINWAG	FIANCÉE	JOINTLY	PAUNCHY	RWANDAN	SUNNITE	ABIOSIS
ALANINE	CHUNDER	FINNISH	KAINITE	PEANUTS	SADNESS	SURNAME	ABJOINT
ALENÇON	CHUNNEL	FITNESS	KANNADA	PENNANT	SAINTLY	SWANSEA	ABSOLVE
AMANITA	CLANGER	FLANKER	KENNEDY	PENNATE	SAMNITE	SWINDLE	ACCOUNT
AMENITY	CLINGER	FLANNEL	KENNELS	PENNINE	SAUNTER	SWINGER	ACROBAT
AMONGST	CLINKER	FLUNKEY	KENNING	PEONAGE	SCANDAL	SWINGLE	ACRONYM
ANANIAS	CLUNIAC	FOUNDER	KERNITE	PFENNIG	SCANNER	TAINTED	ADJOINT
APTNESS	COGNATE	FOUNDRY	KEYNOTE	PHANTOM	SCENERY	TANNATE	ADJOURN
ARUNDEL	COINAGE	FRANCIS	KHANATE	PHONEIN	SCENTED	TANNERY	AEROBIC
ASININE	CONNATE	FRANKLY	KIDNEYS	PHONEME	SCHNELL	TANNING	AEROSOL
ASUNDER	CONNECT	FRANTIC	KLINKER	PHONICS	SHANNON	TARNISH	AGROUND
ATINGLE	CONNIVE	FRINGED	KYANITE	PIANIST	SHINDIG	TEENAGE	ALCOHOL
AVENGER	CONNOTE	FRONTAL	LAUNDER	PIANOLA	SHINGLE	TENNIEL	ALCORAN
BADNESS	COONCAN	FUNNILY	LAUNDRY	PINNACE	SHINGLY	THINKER	ALFONSO
BANNOCK	CORNCOB	FURNACE	LAXNESS	PINNULA	SHINING	THINNER	ALKORAN
BARNABY	CORNEAL	FURNISH	LEANDER	PIONEER	SHINPAD	THUNDER	ALLONGE
BEANBAG	CORNELL	GAINFUL	LEANING	PLANNED	SHYNESS	TOENAIL	ALLOWED
BENNETT	CORNICE	GAINSAY	LEONARD	PLANNER	SIGNIFY	TONNAGE	ALMONER
BERNARD	CORNISH	GARNISH	LEONINE	PLANTAR	SIGNING	TONNEAU	AMBOYNA
BERNINI	CORNROW	GAYNESS	LIGNITE	PLANTED	SIGNORA	TONNISH	AMMONAL
BLANDLY	COUNCIL	GLENCOE	LINNEAN	PLANTER	SIGNORI	TORNADE	AMMONIA
BLANKET	COUNSEL	GLENOID	LIONESS	PLANURY	SKINFUL	TORNADO	AMPOULE
BLANKLY	COUNTED	GRANARY	LIONIZE	PLENARY	SKINNED	TOYNBEE	ANDORRA
BLENDER	COUNTER	GRANDAD	LOUNGER	PLUNDER	SKINNER	TRANCHE	ANGOLAN
BLINDER	COUNTRY	GRANDEE	LYMNAEA	PLUNGER	SLANDER	TRANSIT	ANNOYED
BLINDLY	COYNESS	GRANDLY	MADNESS	POINTED	SLENDER	TRANSOM	ANTONIO
BLINKER	CRANACH	GRANDMA	MAENADS	POINTER	SLYNESS	TRANTER	ANTONYM
BLUNDER	CRANIAL	GRANDPA	MAGNATE	POUNDAL	SOUNDED	TRINGLE	APHONIA
BLUNTED	CRANIUM	GRANITA	MAGNETO	PRINCES	SOUNDER	TRINITY	APHONIC
BLUNTLY	CRANMER	GRANITE	MAGNIFY	PRINTED	SOUNDLY	TRINKET	APHOTIC
BONNARD	CRENATE	GRANNIE	MANNERS	PRINTER	SPANDAU	TRUNDLE	APPOINT

APPOSED	CROOKED	IMPOUND	PELORIA	STROBIC	CARPORT	DROPLET	OFFPEAK
APROPOS	CROONER	INBOARD	PELORUS	STROPHE	CASPIAN	DROPOUT	OUTPOST
ARIOSTO	DAMOSEL	INCOMER	PICOTEE	STROPPY	CHAPATI	DROPPER	OUTPOUR
ARMORED	DEBORAH	INCONNU	PIROGUE	SYCORAX	CHAPEAU	DUMPISH	PALPATE
ARMORIC	DEBOUCH	INDOORS	PIVOTAL	SYCOSIS	CHAPLET	DUOPOLY	PEEPING
ARMOURY	DECODER	INHOUSE	POLONIE	SYNONYM	CHAPMAN	EDAPHIC	PEPPERS
ASTOUND	DECORUM	INROADS	POPOVER	SYNOVIA	CHAPPED	EELPOUT	PEPPERY
ATROPHY	DELOUSE	INVOICE	POROSIS	TABORET	CHAPTER	ETAPLES	PERPLEX
ATROPOS	DEMONIC	INVOLVE	POTOMAC	TALOOKA	CHIPPED	FLAPPED	PIMPING
AUROCHS	DEMOTIC	JACOBIN	POTOROO	THEORBO	CHIPPER	FLAPPER	POMPEII
AUTOCUE	DEPOSIT	JACOBUS	PYLORUS	THEOREM	CHIPPIE	FLIPPER	POMPOON
AUTOMAT	DERONDA	JEHOVAH	PYROSIS	THROATY	CHOPINE	FLYPAST	POMPOUS
AUTOPSY	DEVOICE	KATORGA	REBOUND	THROUGH	CHOPPER	FOPPISH	POPPING
BABOOSH	DEVOLVE	KENOSIS	RECORDS	THROWER	CHUPATI	GASPING	PREPAID
BALONEY	DEVOTED	KENOTIC	RECOUNT	THROWIN	CLAPPER	GLYPTAL	PREPARE
BARONET	DEVOTEE	KEROGEN	RECOVER	TIMOTHY	CLIPPED	GLYPTIC	PREPUCE
BAROQUE	DIGONAL	KILOTON	REDOUBT	TITOISM	CLIPPER	GRAPHIC	PROPANE
BAYONET	DIPOLAR	LABORED	REDOUND	TITOIST	CLIPPIE	GRAPHIS	PROPEND
BAZOOKA	DISOBEY	LABORER	REHOUSE	TORONTO	CLUPEID	GRAPNEL	PROPHET
BEDOUIN	DIVORCE	LACONIC	REJOICE	TROOPER	COMPACT	GRAPPLE	PROPOSE
BEGONIA	DOLORES	LAGONDA	REMODEL	TYLOSIS	COMPANY	GROPIUS	PUMPKIN
BEGORRA	DOROTHY	LANOLIN	REMORSE	UNBOSOM	COMPARE	GRYPHON	PURPORT
BEHOOVE	ECBOLIC	LAVOLTA	REMOULD	UNBOUND	COMPASS	GUNPLAY	PURPOSE
BELOVED	ECLOGUE	LESOTHO	REMOUNT	UNBOWED	COMPERE	HAPPILY	PURPURA
BETOKEN	ECTOPIA	LINOCUT	REMOVAL	UNCOUTH	COMPETE	HARPIST	RAMPAGE
BIFOCAL	EFFORCE	LITOTES	REMOVED	UNCOVER	COMPILE	HARPOON	RAMPANT
BIGOTED	EGLOGUE	MADONNA	REMOVER	UNDOING	COMPLEX	HELPFUL	RAMPART
BIGOTRY	EMBOLUS	MAHONIA	REPOSAL	UNGODLY	COMPORT	HELPING	RAPPORT
BIVOUAC	EMBOWER	MAJORCA	REROUTE	UNHORSE	COMPOSE	HENPECK	RATPACK
BLOOMER	EMPOWER	MASONIC	RESOLVE	UNLOOSE	COMPOST	HISPANO	REDPOLL
BLOOPER	ENDOGEN	MASONRY	RESOUND	UNLOVED	COMPOTE	HOPPING	RESPECT
BOLOGNA	ENDORSE	MECONIC	RETOUCH	UNMOVED	COMPUTE	HOSPICE	RESPIRE
BOLONEY	ENFORCE	MEIOSIS	REVOLVE	UNSOUND	COPPERS	INSPECT	RESPITE
BORODIN	ENGORGE	MELODIC	RICOTTA	UNWOUND	COPPICE	INSPIRE	RESPOND
BOROUGH	ENNOBLE	MEMOIRS	RIPOSTE	VAMOOSE	COUPLER	JAMPANI	RESPRAY
BRIOCHE	ESPOUSE	MENORAH	RISOTTO	VAPOURS	COUPLET	JEEPERS	RIPPING
BUBONIC	ESTOVER	METONIC	RUDOLPH	VELOURS	COUPONS	JEEPNEY	ROMPERS
BUCOLIC	EXPOSED	METONYM	RUMORED	VERONAL	COWPOKE	JUMPING	RUMPLED
BYRONIC	EXPOUND	MINORCA	SAGOUIN	WAGONER	CRAPPIE	KAMPALA	RUMPOLE
CABOOSE	FAVORED	MITOSIS	SAMOOSA	WHOOPEE	CRIPPLE	KAMPONG	SALPINX
CADOGAN	FEMORAL	MOLOTOV	SAMOVAR	WHOOPER	CROPPED	KEEPING	SAMPLER
CAGOULE	FLOODED	MONOCLE	SAMOYED	WIDOWED	CROPPER	KIPPERS	SAPPERS
CAHOOTS	FLOOZIE	MONOCOT	SAPONIN	WIDOWER	CRUPPER	KNAPPER	SAPPHIC
CALOMEL	FLYOVER	MONOLOG	SAROYAN	XENOPUS	CRYPTIC	KRYPTON	SCAPULA
CALORIC	GALOCHE	MONOPLY	SAVOURY	XEROSIS	CRYPTON	LAMPOON	SCEPTER
CALORIE	GALOPIN	MOROCCO	SCHOLAR	ZAMORIN	CULPRIT	LAMPREY	SCEPTIC
CAMOGIE	GARONNE	MORONIC	SCOOTER	ZAPOTEC	DAMPIER	LAPPING	SCEPTRE
CAMORRA	GAROTTE	NABOKOV	SCROOGE	ZEDOARY	DAMPING	LEAPING	SCUPPER
CANONRY	GASOHOL	NEMORAL	SCROTAL	ZYGOSIS	DAPPLED	LEGPULL	SEAPORT
CAPORAL	GAVOTTE	NICOISE	SCROTUM	ZYMOGEN	DAUPHIN	LEMPIRA	SEEPAGE
CAROLUS	GENOESE	NICOSIA	SECONAL	ZYMOSIS	DEEPFRY	LEOPARD	SEPPUKU
CAROTID	GIRONDE	NYNORSK	SECONDS	ADAPTER	DELPHIC	LEOPOLD	SERPENS
CAROTIN	GOMORRA	OBLOQUY	SESOTHO	ADAPTOR	DESPAIR	LIMPKIN	SERPENT
CAROUSE	GROOVED	OCTOBER	SHMOOZE	ADIPOSE	DESPISE	LIMPOPO	SHAPELY
CHAOTIC	HALOGEN	OCTOPOD	SHOOTER	ADOPTED	DESPITE	LOWPAID	SHAPING
CHLORAL	HANOVER	OCTOPUS	SHROUDS	AIRPORT	DESPOIL	LUMPISH	SHEPPEY
CHOOKIE	HAPORTH	ONGOING	SIROCCO	ALEPINE	DESPOND	LUMPKIN	SHIPPER
CHRONIC	HEROINE	OPPOSED	SMOOTHE	APEPSIA	DIAPSID	MAPPING	SHIPTON
COCONUT	HEROISM	ORTOLAN	SNOOKER	ASEPTIC	DIMPLED	MAYPOLE	SHOPPER
COCOTTE	HOMONYM	OSBORNE	SNOOPER	BAGPIPE	DIOPTER	MISPLAY	SIMPKIN
COLOGNE	HONOURS	OSMOSIS	SOCOTRA	BEDPOST	DIOPTRE	MOPPING	SIMPLER
COLOMBO	HYPOGEA	OTTOMAN	SOJOURN	BESPEAK	DISPLAY	MORPHIA	SIMPLEX
COLONEL	HYPONYM	PALOMAR	SOLOIST	BESPOKE	DISPORT	MUDPACK	SIMPLON
COLONIC	HYPOXIA	PALOOKA	SOLOMON	BUMPKIN	DISPOSE	NAIPAUL	SIMPSON
COLORED	IDIOTIC	PANOPLY	SOROSIS	CAMPANA	DISPRIN	NAPPING	SIPPING
COLOURS	IGNOBLE	PAPOOSE	SPLODGE	CAMPARI	DISPUTE	NIPPERS	SKEPTIC
COROLLA	IGNORED	PAROTIC	SPLOTCH	CAMPHOR	DOLPHIN	NONPLUS	SKIPPED
CORONER	IMHOTEP	PAROTID	SPOONER	CAMPING	DOPPLER	NONPROS	SKIPPER
CORONET	IMMORAL	PAROTIS	SPROUTS	CAMPION	DRAPERY	NYMPHET	SLAPPER

SLIPPED	VESPERS	ATARAXY	COARSEN	ENPRINT	HOARDER	NEGRITO	QUARTER
SLIPPER	VULPINE	ATTRACT	COMRADE	ENTRAIN	HORRIFY	NEGROID	QUARTET
SLIPWAY	WALPOLE	AVARICE	CORRECT	ENTRANT	HORRORS	NEURINE	QUARTIC
SLOPING	WAPPING	AVERAGE	CORRIDA	ENTREAT	HURRIED	NEUROMA	QUERCUS
SNAPPER	WARPATH	AZURITE	CORRODE	ENTROPY	HYDRANT	NEURONE	QUORATE
SNIPPET	WASPISH	BAHRAIN	CORRUPT	ENTRUST	HYDRATE	NITRATE	REARING
SOAPBOX	WEAPONS	BAHREIN	COURAGE	EPERGNE	IBERIAN	NITRILE	RECRUIT
SOPPING	WEEPING	BARRACK	COURBET	EPHRAIM	IMPRESS	NITRITE	REDRESS
STAPLER	WHIPCAT	BARRAGE	COURIER	ESTREAT	IMPREST	NITRODE	REFRACT
STEPHEN	WHIPPED	BARRIER	COURSER	ETERNAL	IMPRINT	NITROUS	REFRAIN
STEPNEY	WHIPPET	BARRING	COURSES	ETTRICK	IMPROVE	NOURISH	REFRESH
STEPSON	WHOPPER	BEARDED	COURTLY	EVEREST	INCROSS	OBTRUDE	REGRESS
STIPEND	WIMPISH	BEARHUG	CSARDAS	EXCRETA	INCRUST	OCARINA	REGROUP
STIPPLE	WRAPPED	BEARING	CUIRASS	EXCRETE	INERTIA	ODORANT	REPRESS
STOPGAP	WRAPPER	BEARISH	CUPROUS	EXPRESS	INGRAIN	ODOROUS	REPRINT
STOPPED	ALIQUID	BEDROCK	CURRAGH	EXTRACT	INGRATE	OLOROSO	REPROOF
STOPPER	ALIQUOT	BEDROOM	CURRANT	EXTREME	INGRESS	ONEROUS	REPROVE
STUPEFY	BANQUET	BEERMAT	CURRENT	EXTRUDE	INGROWN	OPERAND	RETRACE
STYPTIC	BOUQUET	BETROTH	CURRIED	FAIRING	INTROIT	OPERANT	RETRACT
SULPHUR	CHEQUER	BLURRED	CYPRESS	FAIRISH	INTRUDE	OPERATE	RETRAIN
SUPPORT	CLIQUEY	BOARDER	CYPRIOT	FAIRWAY	ITERATE	OPPRESS	RETRAIT
SUPPOSE	CONQUER	BOHRIUM	DEAREST	FARRAGO	IVORIAN	OSTRICH	RETREAD
SURPASS	CROQUET	BOORISH	DEBRETT	FARRIER	IVORIEN	OUTRAGE	RETREAT
SURPLUS	CROQUIS	BOURBON	DEBRIEF	FEARFUL	JEERING	OUTRANK	RETRIAL
SUSPECT	JACQUES	BOURDON	DECREED	FEBRILE	JOURNAL	OVARIAN	REWRITE
SUSPEND	JONQUIL	BOURSIN	DECRYPT	FERROUS	JOURNEY	OVERACT	ROARING
SWAPPED	KUMQUAT	BOXROOM	DEFRAUD	FERRULE	JOYRIDE	OVERALL	SABRINA
SYMPTOM	LACQUER	BULRUSH	DEFROCK	FIBROID	KATRINE	OVERARM	SAPROBE
TADPOLE	MARQUEE	CAIRENE	DEFROST	FIBROMA	KEARTON	OVERAWE	SATRAPY
TAMPICO	MARQUIS	CAPRICE	DEGRADE	FIBROUS	LATRINE	OVERBID	SAURIAN
TAMPION	PARQUET	CARRELL	DEGREES	FLAREUP	LAURELS	OVERDUE	SAUROID
TAPPICE	PICQUET	CARRIED	DEIRDRE	FLORIDA	LEARNED	OVEREAT	SCARIFY
TAPPING	PREQUEL	CARRIER	DEPRAVE	FLORIST	LEARNER	OVERFED	SCARING
TARPEIA	RACQUET	CARRIES	DEPRESS	FURRIER	LEGROOM	OVERLAP	SCARLET
TELPHER	RORQUAL	CARRION	DEPRIVE	GABRIEL	LEPROSY	OVERLAY	SCARPER
TEMPERA	SAQQARA	CARROLL	DERRICK	GADROON	LEPROUS	OVERLIE	SCORING
TEMPEST	TARQUIN	CARROTS	DETRACT	GARRICK	LIBRARY	OVERMAN	SCORPIO
TEMPLAR	UNEQUAL	CARROTY	DETRAIN	GEARBOX	LIBRIUM	OVERPAY	SEARING
TEMPLET	ACARIDA	CHARADE	DIARCHY	GEARING	LIPREAD	OVERRUN	SECRECY
TEMPTER	ACCRETE	CHARDIN	DIARIST	GEORDIE	LOURDES	OVERSEE	SECRETE
TEMPURA	ACCRUAL	CHARGED	DIGRAPH	GEORGIA	LOURING	OVERTAX	SECRETS
TIEPOLO	ACERBIC	CHARGER	DIGRESS	GEORGIC	MACRAMÉ	PADRONE	SERRIED
TIMPANI	ACTRESS	CHARGES	DIORAMA	GHERKIN	MARRIED	PAIRING	SHARIAH
TIPPING	ADDRESS	CHARIOT	DIORITE	GLARING	MARRYAT	PAPRIKA	SHARING
TIPPLER	ADORING	CHARITY	DISROBE	GLORIFY	MEERKAT	PATRIAL	SHARPEN
TOMPION	ADORNED	CHARLES	DISRUPT	GNARLED	MELROSE	PATRICK	SHARPER
TOPPING	AFFRONT	CHARLEY	DIURNAL	GOURMET	MERRIER	PATRIOT	SHARPLY
TORPEDO	AGGRADE	CHARMED	DOGROSE	GUARANA	MERRILY	PAYROLL	SHERBET
TORPIDS	AGGRESS	CHARMER	DOORKEY	GUARANI	MICROBE	PEARLIE	SHERIFF
TOWPATH	ALARMED	CHARNEL	DOORMAN	GUARDED	MIDRIFF	PEERAGE	SHERMAN
TRAPEZE	ALDRICH	CHARPOY	DOORMAT	GUNROOM	MIGRANT	PEERESS	SHIRKER
TRAPPED	AMBROSE	CHARRED	DOORWAY	GUYROPE	MIGRATE	PEERING	SHIRLEY
TRAPPER	AMERICA	CHARTER	DURRELL	HADRIAN	MISREAD	PERRIER	SHORTEN
TREPANG	AMERIGO	CHERISH	DVORNIK	HAIRCUT	MISRULE	PETRIFY	SHORTLY
TRIPLET	AMERIND	CHEROOT	DYARCHY	HAIRNET	MOORHEN	PETROUS	SMARTEN
TRIPLEX	AMORIST	CHERVIL	EARRING	HAIRPIN	MOORING	PHARAOH	SMARTIE
TRIPODY	AMORITE	CHIRRUP	ECCRINE	HARRIER	MOORISH	PHARYNX	SMARTLY
TRIPOLI	AMOROSO	CHORALE	EMBRACE	HARRIET	MORRELL	PIBROCH	SNARLER
TRIPPER	AMOROUS	CHORDAE	EMBROIL	HEARING	MOURNER	PIERCED	SNARLUP
TRIPSIS	AMTRACK	CHORION	EMERALD	HEARKEN	MURRAIN	PIERCER	SNORING
TROPHIC	ANARCHY	CHORIZO	EMERSON	HEARSAY	NACROUS	PIERROT	SNORKEL
TROPICS	ANDROID	CHOROID	EMIRATE	HEARTEN	NAIROBI	PLEROMA	SNORTER
TROPISM	ANEROID	CHORTLE	EMPRESS	HEBRAIC	NARRATE	PRURIGO	SNORTLE
TRYPSIN	ANGRILY	CIRROSE	ENCRUST	HEBREWS	NARROWS	PTERYLA	SOARING
TURPETH	APPRIZE	CITRINE	ENERGIC	HEIRESS	NATRIUM	PUERILE	SOPRANO
TYMPANO	APPROVE	CITROEN	ENGRAFT	HERRICK	NEAREST	PUTREFY	SORROWS
TYMPANY	ARMREST	CLARIFY	ENGRAIN	HERRIES	NEARING	PYRRHIC	SOURSOP
UTOPIAN	ASCRIBE	CLARION	ENGRAVE	HERRING	NECROSE	QUARREL	SPARING
VAMPIRE	ASTRIDE	CLARITY	ENGROSS	HEURISM	NEGRESS	QUARTAN	SPARKLE

SPARROW	TORREFY	BEESWAX	CONSULT	FLUSHED	LEISURE	PALSIED	SCISSOR
SPARTAN	TORRENT	BERSEEM	CONSUME	FLUSTER	LESSING	PARSLEY	SEASICK
SPIRITS	TOURING	BERSERK	CORSAGE	FORSAKE	LINSANG	PARSNIP	SEASIDE
SPORRAN	TOURISM	BIASSED	CORSAIR	FORSTER	LINSEED	PASSAGE	SEISMIC
SPURREY	TOURIST	BIGSHOT	COSSACK	FOSSICK	LISSOME	PASSANT	SENSATE
SPURWAY	TOWROPE	BLASTED	COUSINS	FOSSULA	LOBSTER	PASSING	SENSORY
STARCHY	TRIREME	BLASTER	COWSHED	FRESHEN	LOOSELY	PASSION	SENSUAL
STARDOM	TSARINA	BLESSED	COWSLIP	FRESHER	LUGSAIL	PASSIVE	SESSILE
STARETS	TSARIST	BLESSES	CRASHES	FRESHET	MAESTRO	PEASANT	SESSION
STARING	TZARINA	BLISTER	CRASSUS	FRESHLY	MANSARD	PENSILE	SHASTRI
STARKLY	UMBRAGE	BLOSSOM	CRESTED	FRISBEE	MANSION	PENSION	SHYSTER
STARLET	UMBRIAN	BLUSHER	CRISPIN	FRISIAN	MANSIZE	PENSIVE	SLASHED
STARLIT	UNARMED	BLUSTER	CROSIER	FRISSON	MARSALA	PEPSINE	SLOSHED
STARTED	UNDRESS	BOASTER	CROSSED	FROSTED	MARSHAL	PERSEID	SMASHED
STARTER	UNFROCK	BOBSLED	CROSSLY	FULSOME	MARSYAS	PERSEUS	SMASHER
STARTLE	UNTRIED	BOLSHIE	CRUSADE	FUSSILY	MASSAGE	PERSIAN	SPASTIC
STARVED	UNTRUTH	BOLSHOI	CRUSHED	GAGSTER	MASSEUR	PERSIST	SUBSIDE
STERILE	UPBRAID	BOLSTER	CRUSHER	GHASTLY	MASSINE	PERSONA	SUBSIDY
STERNAL	UPGRADE	BOOSTER	CRYSTAL	GHOSTLY	MASSIVE	PERSONS	SUBSIST
STERNLY	USURPER	BORSTAL	CUISINE	GINSENG	MEASLES	PERSPEX	SUBSOIL
STERNUM	UTERINE	BOWSHOT	CUMSHAW	GLASGOW	MEASURE	PESSARY	SUBSUME
STEROID	UXORIAL	BRASERO	CURSIVE	GLASSES	MEISSEN	PHYSICS	SUNSPOT
STIRFRY	VAGRANT	BRISKET	CURSORY	GLISTEN	MESSAGE	PIASTRE	TAPSTER
STIRPES	VERRUCA	BRISKLY	DAYSTAR	GNOSTIC	MESSIAH	PIGSKIN	TARSIER
STIRRED	VIBRANT	BRISTLE	DENSELY	GODSEND	MESSIER	PLASMIN	TASSILI
STIRRUP	VIBRATE	BRISTLY	DENSITY	GORSEDD	MESSILY	PLASTER	TEASHOP
STORAGE	VIBRATO	BRISTOL	DESSERT	GOSSIPY	MESSINA	PLASTIC	TEASING
STORIED	VITRAIL	BRUSHER	DISSECT	GRISTLE	MIASMIC	PLESSOR	TELSTAR
STORIES	VITRIFY	BRUSQUE	DISSENT	GRISTLY	MIDSHIP	PLOSION	TENSELY
STURMER	VITRIOL	BURSARY	DOESKIN	GROSSLY	MINSTER	PLOSIVE	TENSILE
SUCROSE	WARRANT	BURSTER	DOSSIER	GUMSHOE	MISSILE	POSSESS	TENSING
SUNRISE	WARRING	BUSSING	DOWSING	GUNSHOT	MISSING	POTSDAM	TENSION
SUNROOF	WARRIOR	CAESIUM	DRASTIC	GYMSLIP	MISSION	POTSHOT	TERSELY
SUPREME	WEARILY	CAESURA	DRESDEN	HAMSTER	MISSIVE	POUSSIN	TERSION
SUPREMO	WEARING	CAISSON	DRESSED	HANSARD	MISSTEP	PRESAGE	TESSERA
SURREAL	WEIRDLY	CAPSIZE	DRESSER	HARSHLY	MOBSTER	PRESENT	THESEUS
SWARTHY	WHARTON	CAPSTAN	DROSHKY	HASSIUM	MOISTEN	PRESIDE	THISTLE
TAPROOM	WHEREAS	CAPSULE	DUNSTAN	HASSOCK	MONSOON	PRESSED	THYSELF
TAPROOT	WHEREBY	CARSICK	EARSHOT	HAYSEED	MONSTER	PRESUME	THYSSEN
TAURINE	WHEREIN	CASSATA	ELASTIC	HERSELF	MUNSTER	PROSAIC	TIPSILY
TEARFUL	WORRIED	CASSAVA	ELASTIN	HESSIAN	MUSSELS	PROSODY	TIPSTER
TEARING	WORRIER	CASSOCK	ELISION	HIMSELF	NETSUKE	PROSPER	TOASTED
TEAROOM	YTTRIUM	CATSEYE	ELUSIVE	HIPSTER	NEWSBOY	PRUSSIC	TOASTER
TERRACE	ZAIREAN	CATSPAW	ELUSORY	HIRSUTE	NEWSMAN	PULSATE	TOLSTOY
TERRAIN	ABASHED	CAUSTIC	ELYSIAN	HISSING	NOISILY	PULSING	TONSURE
TERRANE	ABUSIVE	CELSIUS	ELYSIUM	HOBSONS	NOISOME	PUNSTER	TOPSIDE
TERRENE	ABYSMAL	CENSURE	EPISODE	HOLSTER	NONSTOP	PURSUER	TOPSOIL
TERRIER	ABYSSAL	CESSION	EPISTLE	HOPSACK	NONSUCH	PURSUIT	TOPSPIN
TERRIFY	ACESTES	CESSPIT	ERASMUS	HORSING	NONSUIT	QUASSIA	TORSADE
TERRINE	AGISTOR	CHASING	ERASURE	HOTSHOT	NURSERY	QUESTER	TORSION
THERAPY	AIRSHIP	CHASSIS	ERISKAY	HOTSPUR	NURSING	RAISING	TOSSPOT
THEREBY	AIRSICK	CHASTEN	EROSION	HOUSING	OARSMAN	RANSACK	TOYSHOP
THEREIN	AIRSTOP	CHESTER	ETESIAN	HUSSARS	OARSMEN	REDSKIN	TRESSES
THERESA	ALASKAN	CISSOID	EVASION	HUSSITE	OBESITY	REISSUE	TRESTLE
THERETO	ALLSTAR	CLASSIC	EVASIVE	IRKSOME	ODYSSEY	RETSINA	TRISECT
THERMAL	ALYSSUM	CLASTIC	EXISTED	ISOSPIN	OERSTED	RISSOLE	TRISHAW
THERMIC	AMUSING	CLOSELY	EYESHOT	JERSEYS	OFFSIDE	ROASTER	TRISMUS
THERMOS	ANISEED	CLOSEUP	EYESORE	JUSSIVE	OILSKIN	ROISTER	TRISTAN
THIRDLY	ANOSMIA	CLOSING	EYESPOT	KINSHIP	OLDSTER	RONSARD	TRUSTEE
THIRSTY	APOSTLE	CLOSURE	FALSELY	KINSMAN	ONESELF	ROOSTER	TUESDAY
THOREAU	ATISHOO	CLUSTER	FALSIES	KISSING	OPOSSUM	ROSSINI	TUSSOCK
THORIUM	AVESTAN	COASTAL	FALSIFY	KNESSET	ORESTES	ROUSING	TUSSORE
THYROID	AWESOME	COASTER	FAUSTUS	KRISHNA	OUTSHOT	RUSSELL	TWISTED
THYRSIS	BANSHEE	CONSENT	FELSPAR	KURSAAL	OUTSIDE	RUSSIAN	TWISTER
TIERCEL	BASSOON	CONSIGN	FIRSTLY	LAKSHMI	OUTSIZE	SALSIFY	TWOSOME
TIERCET	BATSMAN	CONSIST	FISSILE	LAPSANG	OUTSPAN	SASSABY	TWOSTEP
TIGRESS	BEASTLY	CONSOLE	FISSION	LAWSUIT	OUTSTAY	SASSOON	ULYSSES
TIGRISH	BEDSIDE	CONSOLS	FISSURE	LEASING	PAESTUM	SATSUMA	UNASKED
TITRATE	BEDSORE	CONSORT	FLASHER	LEASOWE	PAISLEY	SAUSAGE	UNUSUAL

VARSITY	BITTERS	CLOTHED	DUSTMAN	FRETTED	KNOTTED	MONTERO	PLATTER
VASSAIL	BLATANT	CLOTHES	DUSTPAN	FRITTER	KONTIKI	MONTHLY	PLOTTER
VERSANT	BLATHER	CLOTURE	EARTHEN	FURTHER	LACTASE	MORTALS	PLUTEUS
VERSIFY	BLATTER	CLUTTER	EARTHLY	FURTIVE	LACTATE	MORTICE	POETESS
VERSION	BLETHER	COATING	EASTERN	FUSTIAN	LACTEAL	MORTIFY	PONTIAC
WARSHIP	BLITHER	COITION	EBBTIDE	FUTTOCK	LACTOSE	MORTISE	PONTIFF
WASSAIL	BLITZED	CONTACT	ECSTASY	GAITERS	LAETARE	MOTTLED	PONTINE
WAYSIDE	BLOTCHY	CONTAIN	EDITION	GASTHOF	LANTANA	MUNTJAC	PONTOON
WEBSITE	BLOTTER	CONTEMN	EGOTISM	GASTRIC	LANTERN	MUSTANG	PORTAGE
WEBSTER	BOATING	CONTEND	EGOTIST	GASTRIN	LAOTIAN	MUSTARD	PORTEND
WETSUIT	BOATMAN	CONTENT	ELATION	GAUTAMA	LASTING	MYSTERY	PORTENT
WHISKER	BOOTLEG	CONTEST	ELITISM	GENTEEL	LATTICE	MYSTIFY	PORTHOS
WHISKEY	BOTTEGA	CONTEXT	ELITIST	GENTIAN	LEATHER	NARTHEX	PORTICO
WHISPER	BOTTLED	CONTORT	ELYTRON	GENTILE	LECTERN	NASTILY	PORTION
WHISTLE	BOTTLES	CONTOUR	EMOTION	GESTALT	LECTURE	NECTARY	PORTRAY
WINSOME	BOUTADE	CONTROL	EMOTIVE	GESTAPO	LEFTIST	NEITHER	POSTAGE
WINSTON	BRITAIN	CORTEGE	EPITAPH	GESTATE	LENTIGO	NEOTENY	POSTBAG
WOOSTER	BRITISH	CORTINA	EPITAXY	GESTURE	LENTILS	NEPTUNE	POSTBOX
WORSHIP	BRITONS	COSTARD	EPITHET	GETTING	LEOTARD	NETTING	POSTDOC
WORSTED	BRITTLE	COSTING	EPITOME	GLITTER	LETTERS	NEUTRAL	POSTERN
WRESTLE	BRITZKA	COSTIVE	EPSTEIN	GLOTTAL	LETTING	NEUTRON	POSTING
ZEMSTVO	BROTHEL	COSTUME	ERITREA	GLOTTIS	LETTUCE	NICTATE	POSTMAN
ABATTIS	BROTHER	COTTAGE	EROTICA	GLUTTON	LIFTOFF	NOCTUID	POSTURE
ABETTOR	BRUTISH	COTTIER	EUSTACE	GNATHIC	LILTING	NOSTRIL	POSTWAR
ABSTAIN	BUNTING	COTTONY	EXITING	GRATIFY	LISTING	NOSTRUM	POTTAGE
ACETATE	BUSTARD	COUTURE	FACTION	GRATING	LOFTILY	NUPTIAL	POTTERY
ACETONE	BUSTLER	CRITTER	FACTOID	GROTIUS	LOOTING	NURTURE	POTTING
ACHTUNG	BUSTLES	CULTURE	FACTORS	GUTTATE	LOTTERY	NUTTING	PRATTLE
ACUTELY	BUTTERY	CURTAIL	FACTORY	HAITIAN	LOUTISH	OESTRUS	PRETEND
AGITATE	BUTTONS	CURTAIN	FACTUAL	HALTERE	LUSTFUL	OMITTED	PRETEXT
AGITATO	CAITIFF	CURTSEY	FANTAIL	HALTING	LUSTILY	ONETIME	PRETZEL
AINTREE	CALTROP	CUSTARD	FANTASY	HASTATE	LUSTRUM	ONSTAGE	PRITHEE
AMATEUR	CANTATA	CUSTODY	FARTHER	HASTILY	MALTASE	ORATION	PROTEAN
AMATORY	CANTEEN	CUSTOMS	FASTING	HATTOCK	MALTESE	ORATORY	PROTECT
ANATOLE	CANTHUS	CUTTERS	FASTNET	HAUTBOY	MALTHUS	OROTUND	PROTEGE
ANATOMY	CANTRIP	CUTTING	FEATHER	HEATHEN	MALTOSE	OUSTITI	PROTEIN
ANOTHER	CANTUAR	CYNTHIA	FEATURE	HEATHER	MANTUAN	OUTTURN	PROTEST
APHTHAE	CAPTAIN	CYSTOID	FERTILE	HEATING	MARTENS	OVATION	PROTEUS
ARETINO	CAPTION	DANTEAN	FESTIVE	HECTARE	MARTIAL	PANTHER	PROTIST
ASHTRAY	CAPTIVE	DASTARD	FESTOON	HEPTANE	MARTIAN	PANTIES	PRYTHEE
AUCTION	CAPTURE	DAYTIME	FETTERS	HISTOID	MARTINI	PANTILE	PUNTING
AUSTERE	CARTIER	DEATHLY	FICTION	HISTORY	MARTLET	PARTAKE	PUSTULE
AUSTRAL	CARTOON	DELTOID	FIFTEEN	HITTITE	MARTYRS	PARTHIA	PUTTEES
AUSTRIA	CASTILE	DENTINE	FISTFUL	HOSTAGE	MASTERS	PARTIAL	PUTTING
BAPTISM	CASTING	DENTIST	FISTULA	HOSTESS	MASTERY	PARTING	PUTTOCK
BAPTIST	CASTLED	DENTURE	FISTULE	HOSTILE	MASTIFF	PARTITA	QUETZAL
BAPTIZE	CASTOFF	DESTINE	FITTEST	HUNTING	MASTOID	PARTNER	QUITTER
BASTARD	CATTISH	DESTINY	FITTING	HURTFUL	MATTERS	PASTERN	RAFTING
BASTIDE	CAUTERY	DESTROY	FIXTURE	HUSTLER	MATTHEW	PASTEUR	RAGTIME
BASTION	CAUTION	DEXTRIN	FLATCAR	IMITATE	MATTING	PASTIES	RANTING
BATTELS	CENTAUR	DICTATE	FLATLET	INITIAL	MATTINS	PASTIME	RAPTURE
BATTERY	CENTAVO	DICTION	FLATTEN	INSTALL	MATTOCK	PASTURE	RATTEEN
BATTING	CENTRAL	DIETARY	FLATTER	INSTANT	MEETING	PATTERN	RATTLER
BEATIFY	CENTRED	DIETINE	FLITTER	INSTATE	MELTING	PECTASE	RECTIFY
BEATING	CENTRIC	DIPTERA	FLOTSAM	INSTEAD	MENTHOL	PELTING	RECTORY
BEATLES	CENTRUM	DIPTYCH	FLUTIST	INSTILL	MENTION	PENTANE	REPTILE
BEATNIK	CENTURY	DISTAFF	FLUTTER	ISOTONE	METTLED	PENTODE	RESTART
BEDTIME	CERTAIN	DISTANT	FOOTAGE	ISOTOPE	MIDTERM	PENTOSE	RESTATE
BENTHAM	CERTIFY	DISTEND	FOOTING	JESTING	MISTAKE	PERTAIN	RESTFUL
BENTHOS	CESTODE	DISTENT	FOOTMAN	JITTERS	MISTIME	PERTURB	RESTING
BERTRAM	CESTOID	DISTILL	FOOTPAD	JITTERY	MISTOOK	PERTUSE	RESTIVE
BESTIAL	CHATEAU	DISTORT	FOOTSIE	JOGTROT	MISTRAL	PICTURE	RESTOCK
BESTREW	CHATHAM	DISTURB	FORTIES	JUSTICE	MITTENS	PIETIST	RESTORE
BETTING	CHATTEL	DITTANY	FORTIFY	JUSTIFY	MIXTURE	PIGTAIL	RIOTERS
BETTONG	CHATTER	DITTIES	FORTRAN	KENTISH	MOITHER	PINTADO	RIOTING
BILTONG	CHUTNEY	DOCTORS	FORTUNE	KESTREL	MONTAGE	PINTAIL	RIOTOUS
BIOTECH	CISTERN	DUCTILE	FOXTROT	KINTYRE	MONTAGU	PISTOLE	RIPTIDE
BISTORT	CITTERN	DUSTBIN	FRETFUL	KNITTED	MONTANA	PLATEAU	RONTGEN
BITTERN	CLATTER	DUSTING	FRETSAW	KNITTER	MONTANT	PLATOON	ROOTING

ROSTAND	STATURE	VENTOSE	ARDUOUS	IMPULSE	REDUCER	VOLUBLY	PREVIEW
ROSTOCK	STATUTE	VENTRAL	AROUSAL	INBUILT	REFUGEE	WATUTSI	PRIVACY
ROSTRAL	STETSON	VENTURE	ASQUITH	INBURST	REFUSAL	WRAUGHT	PRIVATE
ROSTRUM	STUTTER	VERTIGO	ASSUAGE	INCUBUS	REGULAR	WROUGHT	PRIVITY
ROTTING	SUBTEEN	VESTIGE	ASSUMED	INCURVE	REPULSE	YAOUNDE	PROVERB
ROUTIER	SUBTEND	VETTING	ASSURED	INDULGE	REPUTED	ZAKUSKA	PROVIDE
ROUTINE	SUCTION	VICTORY	AUDUBON	INHUMAN	REQUEST	ZYMURGY	PROVING
RUPTURE	SULTANA	VICTUAL	AUGUSTA	INJURED	REQUIEM	ATAVISM	PROVISO
RUSTLER	SUNTRAP	VIETNAM	AUGUSTE	INQUEST	REQUIRE	BRAVADO	PROVOKE
RUTTING	SUSTAIN	VINTAGE	AWFULLY	INQUIRE	REQUITE	BRAVELY	PROVOST
SALTATE	SWITHIN	VINTNER	BEGUILE	INQUIRY	RESULTS	BRAVERY	PURVIEW
SALTING	SYSTOLE	VIRTUAL	BEMUSED	INSULAR	RETURNS	BRAVURA	RIGVEDA
SALTIRE	TACTFUL	VISTULA	BEQUEST	INSULIN	RIVULET	BREVITY	SALVAGE
SALTPAN	TACTICS	VOLTAGE	BITUMEN	INSURER	ROBUSTA	CALVARY	SELVAGE
SCATTER	TACTILE	VOLTAIC	BLOUSON	ISSUANT	ROGUERY	CANVASS	SERVANT
SCOTTIE	TANTARA	VULTURE	BROUGHT	JACUZZI	ROGUISH	CARVING	SERVICE
SCUTAGE	TANTIVY	WAFTING	BURUNDI	JANUARY	ROMULUS	CHEVIOT	SERVILE
SCUTARI	TANTRUM	WAGTAIL	CALUMET	JEJUNUM	ROTUNDA	CHEVRON	SERVING
SCUTTER	TARTARE	WAITING	CALUMNY	JOCULAR	SAMURAI	CIVVIES	SHAVING
SCUTTLE	TARTARY	WALTZER	CASUALS	JUGULAR	SCOURER	CLAVATE	SHIVERS
SEATING	TARTINE	WANTING	CASUISM	LACUNAE	SCOURGE	CONVENE	SHIVERY
SEATTLE	TATTERS	WARTHOG	CASUIST	LAPUTAN	SCRUBBY	CONVENT	SIEVERT
SECTION	TATTING	WARTIME	CHAUCER	LIQUEFY	SCRUFFY	CONVERT	SILVERY
SEETHED	TATTLER	WASTAGE	CLOUDED	LIQUEUR	SCRUMMY	CONVICT	SLAVERY
SELTZER	TEATIME	WASTING	COLUMBA	LIQUIDS	SCRUMPY	CONVOKE	SLAVISH
SESTINA	TEKTITE	WASTREL	COLUMNS	LITURGY	SCRUNCH	CRAVING	SLOVENE
SESTINE	TERTIAL	WATTAGE	CORUNNA	LOCUSTS	SCRUPLE	CREVICE	SOLVENT
SETTING	TERTIAN	WATTEAU	CROUTON	MAGUIRE	SECULAR	CULVERT	SPAVINE
SETTLED	TESTATE	WATTLES	CUMULUS	MANUMIT	SEDUCER	DERVISH	SRAVANA
SETTLER	TESTIFY	WEATHER	DEBUSSY	MASURKA	SEQUELA	DRIVERS	STEVENS
SEXTANS	TESTILY	WESTERN	DEFUNCT	MAZURKA	SEQUOIA	DRIVING	SUAVELY
SEXTANT	TESTING	WETTING	DELUDED	MEDULLA	SHOUTER	ELEVATE	SUAVITY
SHATTER	TESTUDO	WHATNOT	DILUENT	MENUHIN	SINUATE	FAUVISM	SUBVERT
SHOTGUN	TEXTILE	WHATSIT	DILUTED	MIMULUS	SINUOUS	FAUVIST	SURVIVE
SHUTEYE	TEXTUAL	WHETHER	DISUSED	MINUEND	SITUATE	FERVENT	TRAVAIL
SHUTTER	TEXTURE	WHITHER	DIVULGE	MINUTED	SOLUBLE	FERVOUR	TRIVIAL
SHUTTLE	THITHER	WHITING	DRAUGHT	MINUTES	SPLURGE	FLAVOUR	TRIVIUM
SIFTING	TINTACK	WHITISH	DROUGHT	MINUTIA	SPOUSAL	FLIVVER	VALVULE
SISTERS	TINTERN	WHITLOW	ENDURED	MODULAR	STAUNCH	FLUVIAL	VELVETY
SISTINE	TONTINE	WHITSUN	ENQUIRE	MODULUS	STOUTLY	GRAVITY	VERVAIN
SITTING	TOOTHED	WHITTLE	ENQUIRY	MOLUCCA	STRUDEL	GRAVLAX	VOIVODE
SIXTEEN	TOOTSIE	WISTFUL	ENSUING	NAHUATL	TABULAR	GRAVURE	WEAVING
SKATING	TORTILE	WRITEUP	ENSUITE	NATURAL	TENUOUS	HARVARD	ALEWIFE
SKETCHY	TORTRIX	WRITING	EPAULET	NEBULAR	TEQUILA	HARVEST	ANTWERP
SKITTER	TORTURE	WRITTEN	ESQUIRE	NODULAR	THOUGHT	HEAVENS	ARTWORK
SKITTLE	TOTTERY	XANTHOS	ESTUARY	OCTUPLE	THRUWAY	HEAVIER	ATHWART
SLATTED	TRITELY	ZESTFUL	ETRURIA	OSCULUM	TITULAR	HEAVILY	AWKWARD
SLITHER	TRITIUM	ZOOTOMY	EXPUNGE	OSSUARY	TOLUENE	KILVERT	BEOWULF
SLOTTED	TRITOMA	ABOUKIR	FACULTY	PABULUM	TRIUMPH	KLAVIER	BETWEEN
SMATTER	TRITONE	ABOULIA	FATUITY	PALUDAL	TROUBLE	KNAVERY	BETWIXT
SMETANA	TROTSKY	ACAUDAL	FATUOUS	PANURGE	TROUNCE	LATVIAN	BLOWFLY
SMITHER	TROTTER	ACCURSE	FELUCCA	PERUSAL	TROUPER	LEAVING	BLOWOUT
SMITTEN	TUATARA	ACCUSED	FIGURES	PETUNIA	TROUSER	LOUVRED	BOSWELL
SMOTHER	TUITION	ACCUSER	FLAUNCH	PIOUSLY	TUBULAR	MARVELL	BOXWOOD
SORTING	TWITCHY	ACQUIRE	FLEURET	PIQUANT	TUBULIN	NAIVELY	BRAWLER
SOUTANE	TWITTER	ACTUARY	FLEURON	PLAUDIT	TUMULUS	NAIVETÉ	BREWERY
SOUTHEY	TWOTIME	ACTUATE	FLOUNCE	PLAUTUS	UNCURED	NAIVETY	BREWING
SPATIAL	UMPTEEN	ADJUNCT	FRAUGHT	PLEURAL	UNGUENT	NERVOSA	BROWNED
SPATTER	UNCTION	ALBUMEN	FUTURES	PLEURON	UNLUCKY	NERVOUS	BROWNIE
SPATULA	UNITARY	ALBUMIN	GALUMPH	POPULAR	UNQUIET	NERVURE	BROWSER
SPITTLE	UNITIES	AMPULLA	GENUINE	POPULUS	UNQUOTE	NIRVANA	BULWARK
SPOTTED	UNSTICK	ANGUISH	GODUNOV	PROUDER	UPSURGE	NOUVEAU	CAMWOOD
SPOTTER	UNSTOCK	ANGULAR	GRAUPEL	PROUDIE	OUTVOTE	OUTVOTE	CATWALK
SPUTNIK	UNSTUCK	ANNUITY	GROUCHO	PROUDLY	VACUITY	PARVENU	CHEWING
SPUTTER	UPSTAGE	ANNULAR	GROUCHY	RAMULUS	VACUOLE	PEEVISH	CHOWDER
STATELY	UPSTART	ANNULET	GROUNDS	REAUMUR	VACUOUS	PERVADE	CRAWLER
STATICS	UPSTATE	ANNULUS	GROUPER	REBUILD	VAGUELY	PERVERT	CREWCUT
STATION	URETHRA	ARBUTUS	GROUPIE	RECURVE	VANUATU	PREVAIL	CREWMAN
STATIST	VANTAGE	ARCUATE	GROUSER	REDUCED	VOLUBLE	PREVENT	CROWBAR

CROWDED	SHAWWAL	JURYMAN	SWIZZLE	BEREAVE	COLLARD	DOGCART	FRIGATE
CROWING	SHOWBIZ	KATYDID		BERNARD	COLLATE	DOLLARS	FUNFAIR
CUTWORM	SHOWERS	LADYBUG	**7:5**	BIOMASS	COMMAND	DORMANT	FURCATE
DAGWOOD	SHOWERY	LANYARD	ABELARD	BIPLANE	COMPACT	DOWLAND	FURNACE
DERWENT	SHOWILY	LAWYERS	ABIGAIL	BLATANT	COMPANY	DULLARD	GADWALL
DOGWOOD	SHOWING	LUTYENS	ABREAST	BOLLARD	COMPARE	DUNNAGE	GALLANT
DRAWBAR	SHOWMAN	PAPYRUS	ABSTAIN	BOMBARD	COMPASS	EARMARK	GAMBADO
DRAWERS	SHOWOFF	PLAYBOY	ACCLAIM	BOMBAST	COMRADE	ECSTASY	GARBAGE
DRAWING	SITWELL	PLAYERS	ACETATE	BONDAGE	CONCAVE	EDUCATE	GARLAND
ENDWAYS	SKYWARD	PLAYFUL	ACREAGE	BONNARD	CONNATE	ELEGANT	GASMASK
ENTWINE	SLOWING	PLAYING	ACTUARY	BOUTADE	CONTACT	ELEVATE	GAUTAMA
EYEWASH	SNOWDON	PLAYLET	ACTUATE	BOXHAUL	CONTAIN	EMANATE	GEMMATE
FANWORM	SNOWMAN	PLAYOFF	ADAMANT	BRADAWL	COOLANT	EMBLAZE	GERMANE
FANWORT	SOPWITH	PLAYPEN	ADONAIS	BRAVADO	COPLAND	EMBRACE	GERMANY
FLOWERS	STEWARD	POLYGON	ADULATE	BRIGADE	CORDATE	EMERALD	GESTALT
FLOWERY	STEWING	POLYMER	AFGHANI	BRIGAND	CORKAGE	EMIRATE	GESTAPO
FLOWING	TRAWLER	POLYOMA	AGGRADE	BRITAIN	CORSAGE	EMULATE	GESTATE
FORWARD	TYNWALD	POLYPOD	AGITATE	BROCADE	CORSAIR	ENCHANT	GIMBALS
FROWSTY	UNAWARE	POLYPUS	AGITATO	BROMATE	COSSACK	ENCLASP	GIZZARD
GADWALL	UNOWNED	PRAYING	AIRBASE	BUFFALO	COSTARD	ENCLAVE	GOLIARD
GLOWING	UNTWINE	RECYCLE	AIRMAIL	BULLACE	COTTAGE	ENDGAME	GOLIATH
GNAWING	UPSWING	SLAYING	ALABAMA	BULWARK	COURAGE	ENDWAYS	GOSHAWK
GROWING	WARWICK	STAYING	ALICANT	BUMMALO	COWBANE	ENGLAND	GOULASH
GROWLER	WAXWING	SWAYING	ALIDADE	BUOYANT	COWHAND	ENGRAFT	GRADATE
GROWNUP	WAXWORK	UNDYING	ALREADY	BURBAGE	CRANACH	ENGRAIN	GRANARY
GUNWALE	WAYWARD	VARYING	ALTHAEA	BURSARY	CREMATE	ENGRAVE	GRENADA
HARWICH	YAHWIST	AMAZING	AMTRACK	BUSTARD	CRENATE	ENSLAVE	GRENADE
HARWOOD	ABAXIAL	ARIZONA	AMYLASE	BUZZARD	CRUSADE	ENSNARE	GRIMACE
HAYWARD	ADAXIAL	BENZENE	ANIMALS	CABBAGE	CUIRASS	ENSNARL	GUANACO
HAYWIRE	ASEXUAL	BENZINE	ANIMATE	CALVARY	CURRAGH	ENTRAIN	GUARANA
HOGWASH	BAUXITE	BENZOIN	ANOMALY	CAMPANA	CURRANT	ENTRANT	GUARANI
INKWELL	BRIXTON	BLAZERS	APPEASE	CAMPARI	CURTAIL	EPHRAIM	GUNWALE
KEYWORD	COAXIAL	BLAZING	APPLAUD	CANDACE	CURTAIN	EPICARP	GUTTATE
KNOWALL	COEXIST	BRAZIER	ARAMAIC	CANTATA	CUSTARD	EPITAPH	GYMNAST
KNOWHOW	DIOXIDE	BUZZARD	ARCHAEA	CANVASS	CUTBACK	EPITAXY	HAGGADA
KNOWING	FLEXILE	CANZONA	ARCHAIC	CAPTAIN	CUTLASS	ESTUARY	HAGGARD
LAPWING	INEXACT	CANZONE	ARCUATE	CARCASE	CYMBALS	EUSTACE	HALLALI
LEEWARD	MANXMAN	CRAZILY	ARMBAND	CARCASS	DASTARD	EXCLAIM	HALYARD
LEGWORK	MARXISM	CROZIER	ARREARS	CARNABY	DAYMARK	EXOCARP	HANSARD
LOGWOOD	MARXIST	DAZZLED	ASPHALT	CARNAGE	DECEASE	EXOGAMY	HARVARD
LUGWORM	PROXIMO	DIZZILY	ASSUAGE	CASCADE	DECLAIM	EXPIATE	HASTATE
MAXWELL	QUIXOTE	DRIZZLE	ATARAXY	CASCARA	DECLARE	EXPLAIN	HATBAND
MAYWEED	ULEXITE	DRIZZLY	ATHWART	CASEASE	DEFIANT	EXTRACT	HAULAGE
MIDWEEK	ACRYLIC	EPIZOON	ATTRACT	CASSATA	DEFLATE	EXUDATE	HAYWARD
MIDWEST	ASSYRIA	FANZINE	AUREATE	CASSAVA	DEFRAUD	EYEBALL	HEBRAIC
MIDWIFE	BABYISH	FRAZZLE	AVERAGE	CASUALS	DEGRADE	EYEBATH	HECTARE
MUGWORT	BABYLON	FRIZZLE	AVOCADO	CATCALL	DEPRAVE	EYELASH	HENBANE
MUGWUMP	BABYSIT	FRIZZLY	AWKWARD	CATWALK	DESCANT	EYEWASH	HENNAED
NARWHAL	BARYTES	GIZZARD	BAGGAGE	CAVIARE	DESPAIR	FALLACY	HEPTANE
NETWORK	BICYCLE	GLAZIER	BAHRAIN	CEMBALO	DETRACT	FANFARE	HERBAGE
NORWICH	BUOYANT	GLAZING	BAKLAVA	CENTAUR	DETRAIN	FANTAIL	HISPANO
OUTWARD	CALYPSO	GRAZING	BALLADE	CENTAVO	DEVIANT	FANTASY	HOBNAIL
OUTWEAR	CHAYOTE	GRIZZLE	BALLAST	CERTAIN	DEVIATE	FARRAGO	HOGBACK
OUTWORK	CLOYING	GRIZZLY	BANDAGE	CHAGALL	DICTATE	FENLAND	HOGWASH
OUTWORN	COPYCAT	GUZZLER	BANDAID	CHAPATI	DIECAST	FINBACK	HOLDALL
PIGWEED	COPYING	JAZZMAN	BARBARA	CHARADE	DIEHARD	FINLAND	HOLLAND
PLOWMAN	COPYIST	MITZVAH	BARBARY	CHICAGO	DIETARY	FIREARM	HOPSACK
PLYWOOD	CORYDON	MUEZZIN	BARGAIN	CHICANE	DIGRAPH	FLYHALF	HOSTAGE
PROWESS	DASYURE	PIZZAZZ	BARMAID	CHICANO	DIORAMA	FLYPAST	HUBBARD
PROWLER	DIDYMUS	PREZZIE	BARNABY	CHORALE	DISBAND	FOGLAMP	HUNGARY
PUGWASH	DREYFUS	PUZZLED	BARRACK	CHUPATI	DISBARK	FOLIAGE	HUSBAND
RAGWEED	ECDYSIS	PUZZLER	BARRAGE	CILIATE	DISCARD	FONDANT	HUSSARS
RAGWORT	EMPYEMA	RHIZOID	BASMATI	CITHARA	DISDAIN	FOOTAGE	HYDRANT
REDWOOD	GRAYISH	RHIZOME	BASTARD	CLAVATE	DISEASE	FORBADE	HYDRATE
RIBWORT	GREYISH	ROZZERS	BAUHAUS	CLIMATE	DISMAST	FOREARM	ICEFALL
SAPWOOD	GREYLAG	SEIZURE	BEEFALO	COCKADE	DISTAFF	FORGAVE	ICELAND
SCOWDER	GRUYÈRE	SIZZLER	BEGGARY	COGNATE	DISTANT	FORSAKE	IKEBANA
SEAWALL	HALYARD	SOZZLED	BENEATH	COINAGE	DITTANY	FORWARD	IMITATE
SEAWEED	JURYBOX	SUBZERO	BENGALI	COLLAGE	DITTANY	FOULARD	IMPEACH

203

IMPLANT	MAGNATE	ORGIAST	POLLACK	SABBATH	THERAPY	VOLTAGE	CLUMBER
INBOARD	MALLARD	ORIGAMI	POLLARD	SACCADE	THREADS	VOLTAIC	COHABIT
INDIANA	MALTASE	ORLEANS	POMMARD	SALTATE	THROATY	VULGATE	COLIBRI
INEXACT	MAMMARY	OSSUARY	PONIARD	SALVAGE	TIFFANY	WAGTAIL	COURBET
INFLAME	MANDALA	OUTBACK	PORTAGE	SANDALS	TILLAGE	WALLABY	CROWBAR
INFLATE	MANDATE	OUTCAST	POSTAGE	SAQQARA	TIMBALE	WALLACE	CRUMBLE
INGRAIN	MANMADE	OUTDARE	POTLACH	SARCASM	TIMPANI	WARFARE	CRUMBLY
INGRATE	MANSARD	OUTFACE	POTTAGE	SARDANA	TINTACK	WARPATH	CURABLE
INROADS	MARMARA	OUTFALL	PRECAST	SASSABY	TIPCART	WARRANT	DATABLE
INSCAPE	MARSALA	OUTLAST	PREDATE	SATIATE	TITRATE	WASSAIL	DECIBEL
INSTALL	MASCARA	OUTRAGE	PREFACE	SATRAPY	TOCCATA	WASTAGE	DELIBES
INSTANT	MASSAGE	OUTRANK	PRELACY	SAUSAGE	TOENAIL	WATTAGE	DINGBAT
INSTATE	MAYFAIR	OUTWARD	PRELATE	SCUTAGE	TONNAGE	WAYLAND	DISABLE
IRELAND	MEDIATE	OVERACT	PREPAID	SCUTARI	TOPIARY	WAYMARK	DISOBEY
ISHMAEL	MERMAID	OVERALL	PREPARE	SEALANT	TOPKAPI	WAYWARD	DRABBLE
ISOBASE	MESSAGE	OVERARM	PRESAGE	SEAWALL	TOPMAST	WELFARE	DRAWBAR
ISOLATE	METHANE	OVERAWE	PREVAIL	SEEPAGE	TORNADE	WETBACK	DRIBBLE
ISSUANT	MICHAEL	OVULATE	PRIMACY	SELVAGE	TORNADO	WETLAND	DURABLE
ITERATE	MIDGARD	OXALATE	PRIMARY	SENSATE	TORSADE	YARDAGE	DURABLY
JACKASS	MIDLAND	OXIDASE	PRIMATE	SERVANT	TOWPATH	YARDARM	DUSTBIN
JAMPANI	MIGRANT	PACKAGE	PRIVACY	SETBACK	TRAVAIL	ZEALAND	EATABLE
JANUARY	MIGRATE	PAGEANT	PRIVATE	SEXTANS	TREPANG	ZEDOARY	ENNOBLE
JELLABA	MILEAGE	PAHLAVI	PROBAND	SEXTANT	TSIGANE	ZETLAND	ENTEBBE
JIMJAMS	MILLAIS	PALMATE	PROBATE	SFUMATO	TSIGANY	ZINGARO	EPHEBUS
JUGLANS	MISCAST	PALPATE	PROFANE	SHEBANG	TSUNAMI	ZOFFANY	EQUABLE
JUTLAND	MISTAKE	PANCAKE	PRONAOS	SHIKARI	TUATARA	ACERBIC	EQUABLY
KAMPALA	MOMBASA	PANGAEA	PRONATE	SINHALA	TURBARY	ACROBAT	EXHIBIT
KANNADA	MONTAGE	PANNAGE	PROPANE	SINUATE	TUSCANY	AEROBIC	FIREBUG
KHANATE	MONTAGU	PARFAIT	PROSAIC	SITUATE	TYMPANO	AFFABLE	FREEBIE
KILDARE	MONTANA	PARTAKE	PUGWASH	SKYLARK	TYMPANY	AFFABLY	FRIABLE
KITHARA	MONTANT	PASSAGE	PULSATE	SKYWARD	TYNWALD	ALDABRA	FRISBEE
KNOWALL	MORDANT	PASSANT	PUNJABI	SMETANA	ULULANT	ALEMBIC	FROEBEL
KURHAUS	MORLAND	PEASANT	QUORATE	SONDAGE	ULULATE	ALGEBRA	FUSEBOX
KURSAAL	MORTALS	PECCANT	RADIANT	SOPRANO	UMBRAGE	AMIABLE	FUSIBLE
LABIATE	MOULAGE	PECCARY	RADIATE	SOUTANE	UNAWARE	AMIABLY	GEARBOX
LACTASE	MUDLARK	PECCAVI	RAMPAGE	SPICATE	UNCLASP	AMOEBIC	GOODBYE
LACTATE	MUDPACK	PECTASE	RAMPANT	SPINACH	UNHEARD	ANTIBES	GRUMBLE
LAETARE	MUNDANE	PEERAGE	RAMPART	SPINATE	UNITARY	ATTABOY	HALIBUT
LAGGARD	MURIATE	PENDANT	RANSACK	SQUEAKY	UNLEASH	AUDIBLE	HANDBAG
LALLANS	MURRAIN	PENNANT	RAPHAEL	SRAVANA	UNREADY	AUDIBLY	HAUTBOY
LAMBADA	MUSTANG	PENNATE	RATPACK	STEWARD	UNSNARL	AUDUBON	ICHABOD
LAMBAST	MUSTARD	PENTANE	RECLAIM	STOMACH	UPBRAID	BALLBOY	IGNOBLE
LANTANA	NAHUATL	PEONAGE	REFLATE	STORAGE	UPGRADE	BANDBOX	INCUBUS
LANYARD	NAIPAUL	PERCALE	REFRACT	STREAKY	UPSTAGE	BEANBAG	INHABIT
LAPSANG	NARRATE	PERHAPS	REFRAIN	STRIATE	UPSTART	BELABOR	INHIBIT
LEAKAGE	NECTARY	PERTAIN	REGNANT	SULFATE	UPSTATE	BELLBOY	JACOBIN
LEEWARD	NETBALL	PERVADE	RELEASE	SULLAGE	URINARY	BLABBER	JACOBUS
LEMMATA	NIAGARA	PESSARY	RELIANT	SULTANA	URINATE	BLUBBER	JEZEBEL
LEONARD	NICTATE	PHALANX	REMNANT	SUMMARY	VAGRANT	BOURBON	JUKEBOX
LEOPARD	NIGGARD	PHARAOH	REPLACE	SUNLAMP	VALIANT	BRAMBLE	JURYBOX
LEOTARD	NIRVANA	PICKAXE	REPLANT	SURFACE	VANDALS	BUGABOO	KNOBBLE
LIBRARY	NITRATE	PIEBALD	RESHAPE	SURNAME	VANTAGE	CALABAR	KNOBBLY
LINDANE	NUMMARY	PIGTAIL	RESIANT	SURPASS	VANUATU	CALIBAN	LADYBUG
LINEAGE	NUTCASE	PILLAGE	RESTART	SUSTAIN	VARIANT	CALIBER	LEGIBLE
LINKAGE	OATCAKE	PINBALL	RESTATE	TAMMANY	VASSAIL	CALIBRE	LEGIBLY
LINSANG	OBVIATE	PINNACE	RETRACE	TANBARK	VERDANT	CALLBOX	LONGBOW
LOLLARD	ODDBALL	PINTADO	RETRACT	TANKARD	VERSANT	CALLBOY	LOVABLE
LOMBARD	ODORANT	PINTAIL	RETRAIN	TANNATE	VERVAIN	CAPABLE	MACABRE
LOTHAIR	OFFBASE	PIQUANT	RETRAIT	TANTARA	VIBRANT	CAPABLY	MAILBAG
LOWLAND	OFFHAND	PITFALL	REYNARD	TAPLASH	VIBRATE	CARABID	MAILBOX
LOWPAID	OILCAKE	PIZZAZZ	RHUBARB	TARTARE	VIBRATO	CARIBOU	MARABOU
LUDGATE	OKINAWA	PLACARD	RIBCAGE	TARTARY	VILLAGE	CASHBOX	MARIBOU
LUGGAGE	OMPHALE	PLACATE	RICHARD	TATIANA	VILLAIN	CELEBES	MINIBUS
LUGSAIL	ONSTAGE	PLEIADE	ROCKALL	TEACAKE	VINTAGE	CHAMBER	MOVABLE
LULLABY	OPERAND	PLENARY	RONSARD	TEENAGE	VIOLATE	CHAMBRÉ	MUTABLE
LUMBAGO	OPERANT	PLUMAGE	ROSEATE	TERRACE	VIRGATE	CIMABUE	NAILBED
LYMNAEA	OPERATE	PLUMATE	ROSTAND	TERRAIN	VITIATE	CLAMBER	NAMIBIA
MACRAMÉ	ORCHARD	POCHARD	ROULADE	TERRANE	VITRAIL	CLIMBER	NEWSBOY
MAENADS	OREGANO	POLEAXE	RUMMAGE	TESTATE	VOLCANO	CLOBBER	NOSEBAG

NOTABLE	ANARCHY	HELICON	SEDUCER	BRENDAN	INSIDES	SOUNDED	AILMENT
NOTABLY	ANTACID	HELLCAT	SENECIO	BRINDLE	INVADER	SOUNDER	AIMLESS
OCTOBER	APRICOT	HIBACHI	SIDECAR	BROADEN	JACKDAW	SOUNDLY	AIRLESS
OMNIBUS	ARTICLE	ILIACUS	SILICON	BROADLY	KATYDID	SPANDAU	ALAMEIN
ONMIBUS	ATTACHE	ILLICIT	SIROCCO	BUILDER	KIELDER	SPANDEX	ALCHEMY
OVERBID	ATTICUS	INSECTS	SKETCHY	BULLDOG	KINGDOM	SPENDER	ALGIERS
PAGEBOY	AURICLE	JERICHO	SOLICIT	CANIDAE	LAUNDER	SPINDLE	ALIMENT
PARABLE	AUROCHS	KARACHI	SPENCER	CARADOC	LAUNDRY	SPINDLY	ALPHEUS
PATIBLE	AUTOCUE	KINGCUP	SPLICED	CELADON	LEANDER	SPLODGE	AMATEUR
PAYABLE	BICYCLE	KNEECAP	SPLICER	CHALDEE	LOURDES	SPONDEE	AMBIENT
PHOEBUS	BIFOCAL	LEXICON	STARCHY	CHARDIN	LUCIDLY	SPONDYL	ANCIENT
PILLBOX	BLOTCHY	LINACRE	STENCIL	CHEDDAR	LURIDLY	SQUADDY	ANISEED
PLAYBOY	BORACIC	LINOCUT	STOICAL	CHINDIT	MACADAM	STADDLE	ANTLERS
PLIABLE	BOUNCER	LOGICAL	TAXICAB	CHORDAE	MACEDON	STANDBY	ANTWERP
PLUMBER	BRIOCHE	LYRICAL	TELECOM	CHOWDER	MATADOR	STANDIN	ANXIETY
POOHBAH	BRONCHI	MAGICAL	TIERCEL	CHUNDER	MAUNDER	STANDUP	APOGEAN
POSTBAG	CALECHE	MAILCAR	TIERCET	CITADEL	MEANDER	STARDOM	APTNESS
POSTBOX	CALICHE	MALACCA	TOBACCO	CLOUDED	MELODIC	STRIDES	ARCHERY
POTABLE	CARACAL	MALACHI	TOPICAL	CORYDON	MIRADOR	STRIDOR	ARMREST
QUIBBLE	CARACAS	MANACLE	TRAMCAR	COULDNT	MOULDED	STRUDEL	ARTLESS
RAINBOW	CARACUL	MARACAS	TRANCHE	CROWDED	MOULDER	STUDDED	ASSIEGE
RAREBIT	CATECHU	MEDICAL	TREACLE	CSARDAS	NAKEDLY	SUBADAR	ATHLETE
RHOMBUS	CENACLE	METICAL	TREACLY	DECIDED	NOMADIC	SUBEDAR	AUGMENT
RISIBLE	CEVICHE	MEXICAN	TUNICLE	DECIDER	NOONDAY	SUBEDIT	AUSLESE
ROSEBUD	CHANCEL	MIMICRY	TWITCHY	DECODER	OVERDUE	SWADDLE	AUSTERE
SACKBUT	CHANCRE	MINICAB	TYPICAL	DEIRDRE	PALADIN	SWIDDEN	BADNESS
SALABLE	CHAUCER	MIRACLE	UNLUCKY	DELUDED	PALUDAL	SWINDLE	BAHREIN
SANDBAG	CODICIL	MODICUM	UTRECHT	DIVIDED	PARADOR	THIRDLY	BANDEAU
SANDBOX	COMICAL	MOHICAN	UTRICLE	DREADED	PARADOS	THUNDER	BARKERS
SANDBOY	CONICAL	MOLUCCA	VATICAN	DRESDEN	PARADOX	TIMIDLY	BATHERS
SCAMBLE	COONCAN	MONOCLE	VEHICLE	DUKEDOM	PICADOR	TREADLE	BATTELS
SCRIBER	COPYCAT	MONOCOT	VESICLE	DUNEDIN	PLAUDIT	TRODDEN	BATTERY
SCRUBBY	CORACLE	MOROCCO	WHIPCAT	DWINDLE	PLEADER	TRUNDLE	BECKETT
SEEDBED	CORNCOB	MUSICAL	WILDCAT	EARLDOM	PLODDER	TUESDAY	BELIEVE
SHAMBLE	COUNCIL	OBJECTS	WOODCUT	ECHIDNA	PLUNDER	TWADDLE	BELLEEK
SHERBET	CREWCUT	OFFICER	ABANDON	ECUADOR	POSTDOC	TWEEDLE	BENNETT
SHOWBIZ	CRUNCHY	OFFICES	ABRIDGE	EPHEDRA	POTSDAM	TWIDDLE	BENZENE
SICKBAY	CUBICLE	OPTICAL	ACAUDAL	EVANDER	POUNDAL	TWIDDLY	BEQUEST
SICKBED	CURACAO	OSSICLE	ALADDIN	EXHEDRA	PROUDER	TZADDIK	BERCEAU
SINDBAD	CUTICLE	PANACEA	AMYGDAL	FARADAY	PROUDIE	UGANDAN	BERSEEM
SIZABLE	CYNICAL	PANACHE	APSIDAL	FIEFDOM	PROUDLY	UNAIDED	BERSERK
SJAMBOK	DEBACLE	PANICKY	ARCADIA	FIELDER	QUONDAM	UNFADED	BESEECH
SLOBBER	DEFACED	PANICLE	ARIADNE	FIREDOG	RAMADAN	UNGODLY	BESIEGE
SLUMBER	DEFICIT	PAUNCHY	ARUNDEL	FIXEDLY	RANIDAE	UNLADEN	BESMEAR
SOAPBOX	DEJECTA	PEDICAB	ASUNDER	FLAGDAY	RAPIDLY	UPSIDES	BESPEAK
SOFABED	DIARCHY	PEDICEL	AVOIDER	FLODDEN	REMODEL	VANADIC	BETWEEN
SOLUBLE	DIDICOY	PEDICLE	BAGHDAD	FLOODED	REREDOS	VIVIDLY	BIGHEAD
STROBIC	DYARCHY	PELICAN	BAHADUR	FOUNDER	RESIDUE	WASHDAY	BINDERY
STUBBLE	EARACHE	PIERCED	BEARDED	FOUNDRY	RHONDDA	WEALDEN	BIOTECH
STUBBLY	EFFECTS	PIERCER	BESIDES	FREEDOM	RIGIDLY	WEEKDAY	BITTERN
STUMBLE	ETHICAL	POLECAT	BLADDER	GEORDIE	ROUNDED	WEIRDLY	BITTERS
TALLBOY	FELUCCA	POTICHE	BLANDLY	GLADDEN	ROUNDEL	WHEEDLE	BLAZERS
TAXABLE	FETICHE	PRINCES	BLENDER	GRANDAD	ROUNDER	WORLDLY	BOILEAU
TENABLE	FIANCÉE	QUERCUS	BLINDER	GRANDEE	ROUNDLY	WOULDBE	BONKERS
THIMBLE	FINICAL	QUINCHE	BLINDLY	GRANDLY	ROUNDUP	WOULDNT	BOOLEAN
TOOLBOX	FINICKY	RADICAL	BLUNDER	GRANDMA	RWANDAN	WOUNDED	BORDERS
TOYNBEE	FLACCID	RADICLE	BOARDER	GRANDPA	SALADIN	YEZIDEE	BOSWELL
TREMBLE	FLATCAR	RAUNCHY	BOREDOM	GRENDEL	SCANDAL	ABSCESS	BOTTEGA
TREMBLY	FRANCIS	REBECCA	BORODIN	GRIDDLE	SCOWDER	ACADEME	BOWHEAD
TROUBLE	GALOCHE	RECYCLE	BOULDER	GRINDER	SERFDOM	ACADEMY	BRASERO
TUNABLE	GLENCOE	REDUCED	BOUNDED	GUARDED	SHINDIG	ACCRETE	BRAVELY
VISIBLE	GNOCCHI	REDUCER	BOUNDEN	GUILDER	SHUDDER	ACHAEAN	BRAVERY
VISIBLY	GOUACHE	RELICTS	BOUNDER	HANGDOG	SKIDDAW	ACHIEVE	BREWERY
VOLUBLE	GRACCHI	REOCCUR	BOURDON	HEREDIA	SLANDER	ACTAEON	BRIBERY
VOLUBLY	GROUCHO	RETICLE	BRANDED	HOARDER	SLENDER	ACTRESS	BROKERS
WINDBAG	GROUCHY	ROSACEA	BRANDER	HOLIDAY	SMOLDER	ACUTELY	BUCKETS
AFRICAN	HAIRCUT	RUBICON	BREADED	HUMIDOR	SNOWDON	ADDRESS	BUCKEYE
ALENÇON	HARICOT	SARACEN	BREADTH	INFIDEL	SOLIDLY	AGELESS	BUGBEAR
ALMACKS	HELICAL	SCHICKS	BREEDER	INSIDER	SOLIDUS	AGGRESS	BULLETS

BURGEON	CRUDELY	EXPRESS	HACKERY	LANCERS	NAIVELY	PIRAEUS	RESPECT
BURGESS	CULVERT	EXTREME	HAGGERY	LANTERN	NAIVETÉ	PITHEAD	RETREAD
BURMESE	CURRENT	EYELESS	HALBERD	LARCENY	NAIVETY	PLACEBO	RETREAT
BURNELL	CUTLERY	FALSELY	HALBERT	LARGELY	NANKEEN	PLATEAU	RIBLESS
BUTTERY	CUTTERS	FARCEUR	HALTERE	LARGESS	NASCENT	PLAYERS	RICKETS
CACHEXY	CYPRESS	FARMERS	HAPLESS	LARGEST	NEAREST	PLUTEUS	RICKETY
CAIRENE	DAGGERS	FARNESE	HARLECH	LAURELS	NEGLECT	POETESS	RIGVEDA
CALDERA	DANTEAN	FATHEAD	HARNESS	LAWLESS	NEGRESS	POMPEII	RIMLESS
CANDELA	DEADEYE	FATNESS	HARVEST	LAWYERS	NEOTENY	PORTEND	RINGERS
CANNERY	DEANERY	FERMENT	HATLESS	LAXNESS	NEWNESS	PORTENT	RIOTERS
CANTEEN	DEAREST	FERVENT	HAWKEYE	LEADERS	NICAEAN	POSSESS	RIVIERA
CAREERS	DEBRETT	FETTERS	HAYSEED	LECHERY	NIOBEAN	POSTERN	ROBBERS
CARRELL	DECREED	FEYDEAU	HAZLETT	LECTERN	NIPPERS	POTHEEN	ROBBERY
CATHEAD	DEFLECT	FIDGETS	HEAVENS	LEGLESS	NOUVEAU	POTHERB	ROCKERY
CATSEYE	DEGREES	FIDGETY	HEBREWS	LENIENT	NOWHERE	POTTERY	ROEDEAN
CAUTERY	DENSELY	FIFTEEN	HEIRESS	LETTERS	NUCLEAR	POWDERY	ROGUERY
CEPHEUS	DEPLETE	FIGLEAF	HELLENE	LINNEAN	NUCLEIC	PREBEND	ROLLERS
CHAPEAU	DEPRESS	FIGMENT	HENPECK	LINSEED	NUCLEUS	PRECEDE	ROMPERS
CHATEAU	DERWENT	FILBERT	HERBERT	LIONESS	NUMBERS	PRECEPT	RONDEAU
CHILEAN	DESCEND	FILLETS	HERBERY	LIPREAD	NUNNERY	PREFECT	ROOKERY
CHIMERA	DESCENT	FINGERS	HERSELF	LIQUEFY	NURSERY	PREHEAT	ROULEAU
CHINESE	DESSERT	FISHERY	HETAERA	LIQUEUR	NUTMEAT	PRESENT	ROZZERS
CHOLERA	DIALECT	FISHEYE	HIGHEST	LITHELY	OAKLEAF	PRETEND	RUBBERS
CINDERS	DICKENS	FITMENT	HIMSELF	LOOSELY	OATMEAL	PRETEXT	RUBBERY
CISTERN	DIGRESS	FITNESS	HOLBEIN	LOTTERY	OBSCENE	PREVENT	RUNNERS
CITTERN	DILUENT	FITTEST	HORDEUM	LUTYENS	ODDMENT	PRIMEUR	RUSSELL
CLEMENT	DIMNESS	FLAREUP	HOSIERY	MACBETH	ODDNESS	PROCEED	RUTHENE
CLOSELY	DIOCESE	FLOWERS	HOSTESS	MACHETE	OFFBEAT	PROCESS	SABAEAN
CLOSEUP	DIPTERA	FLOWERY	HOTHEAD	MADNESS	OFFPEAK	PROFESS	SADNESS
CLUPEID	DISCERN	FLYLEAF	HUNKERS	MAGNETO	OLDNESS	PROGENY	SALIENT
COFFERS	DISSECT	FORBEAR	HYGIENE	MALLEUS	ONENESS	PROJECT	SALIERI
COLLECT	DISSENT	FORCEPS	ICEBERG	MALTESE	ONESELF	PROPEND	SAPIENS
COLLEEN	DISTEND	FORFEIT	ICINESS	MANNERS	OPPRESS	PROTEAN	SAPIENT
COLLEGE	DISTENT	FORFEND	ILLNESS	MARGERY	OPULENT	PROTECT	SAPPERS
COMMEND	DITHERY	FORGERY	IMAGERY	MARLENE	ORKNEYS	PROTEGE	SARGENT
COMMENT	DODDERY	FULGENT	IMPIETY	MARTENS	OROGENY	PROTEIN	SARMENT
COMPERE	DODGEMS	FULLERS	IMPRESS	MARVELL	ORPHEAN	PROTEST	SATIETY
COMPETE	DRAPERY	GABFEST	IMPREST	MASSEUR	ORPHEUS	PROTEUS	SCAFELL
CONCEAL	DRAWERS	GAITERS	INFIELD	MASTERS	ORVIETO	PROVERB	SCALENE
CONCEDE	DRIVERS	GALLEON	INFLECT	MASTERY	OUTWEAR	PROWESS	SCENERY
CONCEIT	DRYNESS	GALLERY	INGRESS	MATTERS	OVEREAT	PRUDENT	SCHLEPP
CONCEPT	DUBIETY	GARDENS	INKWELL	MAXWELL	PARNELL	PTOLEMY	SCHNELL
CONCERN	DUCHESS	GARMENT	INQUEST	MAYWEED	PASTERN	PUNGENT	SCREECH
CONCERT	DUDGEON	GAYNESS	INSPECT	MEGAERA	PASTEUR	PURBECK	SCREEVE
CONDEMN	DUNGEON	GENOESE	INSTEAD	MEMBERS	PATIENT	PURCELL	SEAWEED
CONFESS	DURRELL	GENTEEL	ISOMERE	MERCERY	PATTERN	PUTREFY	SECRECY
CONGEAL	EARNEST	GEODESY	ISRAELI	MESEEMS	PAYMENT	PUTTEES	SECRETE
CONNECT	EASIEST	GERBERA	JACKETS	MIDTERM	PEERESS	RACKETS	SECRETS
CONSENT	EASTERN	GIBLETS	JAGGERY	MIDWEEK	PEPPERS	RACKETY	SEEKERS
CONTEMN	EGGHEAD	GILBERT	JANKERS	MIDWEST	PEPPERY	RAGWEED	SEGMENT
CONTEND	ELEMENT	GINSENG	JEEPERS	MINUEND	PERCENT	RAIMENT	SELLERS
CONTENT	EMINENT	GOAHEAD	JERSEYS	MIOCENE	PERCEPT	RATTEEN	SEQUELA
CONTEST	EMPRESS	GODDESS	JITTERS	MISDEED	PERFECT	RAWNESS	SERPENS
CONTEXT	EMPYEMA	GODHEAD	JITTERY	MISLEAD	PERSEID	REAGENT	SERPENT
CONVENE	ENDLESS	GODLESS	JOBBERY	MISREAD	PERSEUS	REDHEAD	SEXLESS
CONVENT	ENFIELD	GODSEND	JOBLESS	MITTENS	PERVERT	REDNECK	SHAKERS
CONVERT	ENTREAT	GOMBEEN	JOINERY	MOCKERS	PHILEAS	REDNESS	SHAKEUP
COOKERY	EPICENE	GORSEDD	JOYLESS	MOCKERY	PHONEIN	REDRESS	SHAPELY
COPPERS	EPIGEAL	GRADELY	KENNEDY	MOLIÈRE	PHONEME	REELECT	SHEBEEN
CORBEAU	EPSTEIN	GROCERS	KENNELS	MONTERO	PIDGEON	REFLECT	SHIVERS
CORBETT	ESCHEAT	GROCERY	KERMESS	MORRELL	PIGGERY	REFRESH	SHIVERY
CORNEAL	ESTREAT	GRUYÈRE	KIDNEYS	MOTHERS	PIGMEAT	REGRESS	SHOWERS
CORNELL	ETAGÈRE	GUDGEON	KILVERT	MULLEIN	PIGMENT	RELIEVE	SHOWERY
CORRECT	EVEREST	GUINEAN	KIPPERS	MUMMERS	PIGWEED	RELIEVO	SHUTEYE
CORTEGE	EVIDENT	GUINEAS	KNAVERY	MUMMERY	PINCERS	REPLETE	SHYNESS
COWHERD	EXCRETA	GUNNERA	LACTEAL	MURAENA	PINHEAD	REPLEVY	SIAMESE
COXLESS	EXCRETE	GUNNERY	LAMBENT	MUSSELS	PINKEYE	REPRESS	SICKERT
COYNESS	EXEGETE	GUTLESS	LAMBERT	MYNHEER	PIONEER	REQUEST	SIEMENS
CRIMEAN	EXIGENT	GWYNETH	LAMBETH	MYSTERY	PIONEER	REQUEST	SIEVERT

SILVERY	TONNEAU	BLOWFLY	TEARFUL	GLASGOW	TRINGLE	CRUSHER	MIDSHIP
SINCERE	TOPLESS	BLUFFLY	THRIFTY	HALOGEN	TRUDGEN	CUMSHAW	MOITHER
SISTERS	TORMENT	BRIEFLY	TRAFFIC	HANDGUN	TWIGGER	CYNTHIA	MONTHLY
SITWELL	TORPEDO	BRIMFUL	TRIFFID	HEXAGON	UNPAGED	DAUPHIN	MOORHEN
SIXTEEN	TORREFY	CAREFUL	TRUFFLE	HYPOGEA	UPRIGHT	DEATHLY	MORPHIA
SLAVERY	TORRENT	CHAMFER	TUNEFUL	ILLEGAL	UPTIGHT	DELPHIC	NARTHEX
SLOVENE	TOTIENT	CHIEFLY	TWELFTH	INSIGHT	VINEGAR	DOLPHIN	NARWHAL
SLYNESS	TOTTERY	CHIFFON	WAKEFUL	INTEGER	VOYAGER	DOUGHTY	NATCHEZ
SOCIETY	TOWHEAD	CHUFFED	WISHFUL	KEROGEN	WHINGER	DRACHMA	NAUGHTY
SOCKEYE	TRACERY	CONIFER	WISTFUL	LASAGNA	WRANGLE	DROSHKY	NEITHER
SOLVENT	TRADEIN	DEEPFRY	XERAFIN	LASAGNE	WRAUGHT	EARSHOT	NOTCHED
SORCERY	TRAGEDY	DOLEFUL	ZESTFUL	LOUNGER	WRIGGLE	EARTHEN	NYMPHET
SPIDERS	TRAPEZE	DREYFUS	ALLEGED	MANAGER	WRINGER	EARTHLY	OUTSHOT
SPIDERY	TRICEPS	DUTIFUL	ALLEGRI	MANAGUA	WRONGLY	EDAPHIC	PANTHER
SQUEERS	TRIDENT	FALAFEL	ALLEGRO	MUTAGEN	WROUGHT	EPITHET	PARCHED
SQUEEZE	TRIREME	FATEFUL	ALRIGHT	MYALGIA	YOUNGER	EYESHOT	PARTHIA
STARETS	TRISECT	FEARFUL	AMALGAM	NOSEGAY	ZYMOGEN	FARTHER	PASCHAL
STATELY	TRITELY	FIREFLY	AMBAGES	OBLIGED	ABASHED	FEATHER	PEACHUM
STEVENS	TRUMEAU	FISTFUL	AMONGST	OBLIGOR	ABRAHAM	FILCHER	PILCHER
STIPEND	TURGENT	FRETFUL	ANTIGEN	OCTAGON	AIRSHIP	FLASHER	PINCHED
STUDENT	TURNERY	GAINFUL	ANTIGUA	ORANGES	ALCOHOL	FLIGHTY	PITCHED
STUPEFY	TURPETH	GIRAFFE	APHAGIA	OTALGIA	ANOTHER	FLUSHED	PITCHER
SUAVELY	UKULELE	GLEEFUL	ASSEGAI	PARAGON	APHTHAE	FRESHEN	POACHER
SUBJECT	UMPTEEN	GRIFFON	ATINGLE	PELAGIC	ARACHNE	FRESHER	PORTHOS
SUBTEEN	UNCLEAN	GRUFFLY	AVENGER	PERIGEE	ATAGHAN	FRESHET	POTSHOT
SUBTEND	UNCLEAR	HALIFAX	BOLOGNA	PIROGUE	ATISHOO	FRESHLY	PRITHEE
SUBVERT	UNDRESS	HANDFUL	BRIDGES	PLUNGER	BACCHIC	FUNCHAL	PROPHET
SUBZERO	UNGUENT	HARMFUL	BRIDGET	PODAGRA	BACCHUS	FURTHER	PRYTHEE
SUCCEED	USELESS	HATEFUL	BROUGHT	POLYGON	BAGEHOT	GALAHAD	PSYCHIC
SUCCESS	VAGUELY	HEEDFUL	CADOGAN	PRONGED	BANSHEE	GASOHOL	PUNCHED
SUFFETE	VARIETY	HELPFUL	CAMOGIE	RAVAGES	BEACHED	GASTHOF	PUNCHER
SUGGEST	VELVETY	HOPEFUL	CHANGED	REALGAR	BEACHES	GINGHAM	PYRRHIC
SUMMERY	VERBENA	HURTFUL	CHANGES	REFUGEE	BEARHUG	GNATHIC	QUECHUA
SUNBEAM	VERMEER	LUCIFER	CHARGED	RENEGUE	BELLHOP	GRAPHIC	QUICHUA
SUNDECK	VESPERS	LUSTFUL	CHARGER	RINGGIT	BENCHER	GRAPHIS	RANCHER
SUNLESS	VILLEIN	MALEFIC	CHARGES	RONTGEN	BENTHAM	GRYPHON	RATCHET
SUPREME	VINCENT	MINDFUL	CHIGGER	SAVAGES	BENTHOS	GUMSHOE	ROADHOG
SUPREMO	VIOLENT	MIRIFIC	CLANGER	SCRAGGY	BIGSHOT	GUNSHOT	ROSEHIP
SURFEIT	VISCERA	NEEDFUL	CLINGER	SENEGAL	BLATHER	HARSHLY	ROUGHEN
SURGEON	WALLEYE	OVERFED	COLOGNE	SHAGGED	BLETHER	HATCHET	ROUGHIE
SURGERY	WARBECK	PACIFIC	DAMAGED	SHINGLE	BLIGHTY	HAUGHTY	ROUGHLY
SURREAL	WARHEAD	PAINFUL	DAMAGES	SHINGLY	BLITHER	HEATHEN	SAPPHIC
SUSPECT	WASHERS	PITIFUL	DELIGHT	SHOTGUN	BLUSHER	HEATHER	SATCHEL
SUSPEND	WATTEAU	PLAYFUL	DEMIGOD	SLEIGHT	BOLSHIE	HEIGHTS	SEETHED
TABLEAU	WEAKEST	PROFFER	DONEGAL	SLOGGER	BOLSHOI	HOTSHOT	SLASHED
TAFFETA	WEEKEND	RATAFIA	DOWAGER	SMIDGIN	BOWSHOT	HUNCHED	SLITHER
TANGENT	WEIGELA	RESTFUL	DRAGGLE	SMUDGED	BRIGHAM	IVANHOE	SLOSHED
TANNERY	WENDELL	ROTIFER	DRAUGHT	SMUGGLE	BROTHEL	KETCHUP	SMASHED
TARPEIA	WESTERN	SACKFUL	DREDGER	SNIGGER	BROTHER	KINSHIP	SMASHER
TATTERS	WETNESS	SCOFFER	DROUGHT	SNUGGLE	BRUSHER	KITCHEN	SMITHER
TEALEAF	WHEREAS	SCRUFFY	DRUGGED	SOCAGER	BULGHUR	KNOWHOW	SMOTHER
TEMPERA	WHEREBY	SCUFFLE	DRUGGET	SPADGER	BURGHER	KOLKHOZ	SOMEHOW
TEMPEST	WHEREIN	SHUFFLE	ECLOGUE	SPANGLE	BURNHAM	KRISHNA	SORGHUM
TENSELY	WIDGEON	SKIFFLE	EGLOGUE	SPONGER	BUTCHER	LAKSHMI	SOUTHEY
TERRENE	WITHERS	SKILFUL	ENDOGEN	STAGGER	CAMPHOR	LATCHET	SOVKHOZ
TERSELY	WITLESS	SKINFUL	ENERGIC	STENGAH	CANTHUS	LEATHER	STACHYS
TESSERA	WITNESS	SNAFFLE	ENGAGED	STENGUN	CATCHER	LITCHEE	STEPHEN
THEREBY	WONDERS	SNIFFER	ENRAGED	STINGER	CATCHUP	LURCHER	SULPHUR
THEREIN	WOOMERA	SNIFFLE	EPERGNE	STOPGAP	CHATHAM	LYNCHET	SWITHIN
THERESA	WORKERS	SNUFFLE	FATIGUE	STRIGIL	CHEKHOV	MALTHUS	TEACHER
THERETO	WRITEUP	SOUFFLE	FINAGLE	SWAGGER	CLACHAN	MANIHOC	TEASHOP
THESEUS	WRYNECK	SOULFUL	FLEDGED	SWINGER	CLOTHED	MARCHER	TELPHER
THOREAU	YONKERS	SQUIFFY	FLOGGER	SWINGLE	CLOTHES	MARSHAL	THITHER
THYSELF	ZAIREAN	STAFFER	FRAUGHT	TANAGER	COLCHIS	MATCHED	TOOTHED
TIGRESS	ZAMBESI	STIFFEN	FREIGHT	TANAGRA	COUCHÉE	MATCHET	TORCHON
TIMBERS	AQUIFER	STIFFLY	FRINGED	THOUGHT	COWSHED	MATTHEW	TOUCHED
TINTERN	BALEFUL	STIRFRY	GEORGIA	THUGGEE	CRASHES	MAUGHAM	TOUGHEN
TOGGERY	BASHFUL	STUFFED	GEORGIC	TONIGHT	CROCHET	MENTHOL	TOYSHOP
TOLUENE	BENEFIT	TACTFUL	GIELGUD	TRIGGER	CRUSHED	MENUHIN	TRACHEA

TRISHAW	ANNUITY	BELLINI	CAPTION	CONCISE	DEPRIVE	ENQUIRY	FOLDING
TROCHEE	ANODIZE	BENDING	CAPTIVE	CONFIDE	DERRICK	ENSUING	FOLLIES
TROCHUS	ANTHILL	BENZINE	CARBIDE	CONFINE	DERVISH	ENSUITE	FOOLISH
TROPHIC	APELIKE	BERLINE	CARBINE	CONFIRM	DESPISE	ENTWINE	FOOTING
URETHRA	APICIUS	BERNINI	CARDIAC	CONNIVE	DESPITE	EREMITE	FOPPISH
VAUGHAN	APPLIED	BESTIAL	CARMINE	CONSIGN	DESTINE	ERODIUM	FOREIGN
VOUCHER	APPOINT	BETHINK	CARRIED	CONSIST	DESTINY	EROSION	FORGIVE
WARSHIP	APPRIZE	BETTING	CARRIER	CONVICT	DETAILS	EROTICA	FORMICA
WARTHOG	ARABIAN	BETWIXT	CARRIES	COOKING	DEVOICE	ERUDITE	FORMING
WATCHER	ARABICA	BIDDING	CARRION	COOLING	DIALING	ESQUIRE	FORTIES
WEATHER	ARABIZE	BILLION	CARSICK	COPPICE	DIAMINE	ETCHING	FORTIFY
WEIGHIN	ARCHIVE	BINDING	CARTIER	COPYING	DIARIST	ETESIAN	FOSSICK
WEIGHTS	ARETINO	BIOCIDE	CARVING	COPYIST	DICTION	ETONIAN	FRAGILE
WEIGHTY	ARIDITY	BLAZING	CASHIER	CORDIAL	DIETINE	ETTRICK	FRISIAN
WHETHER	ARRAIGN	BLEMISH	CASPIAN	CORDITE	DIGGING	EVASION	FULFILL
WHITHER	ASCRIBE	BOATING	CASTILE	CORKING	DIGNIFY	EVASIVE	FUNDING
WITCHES	ASININE	BOHRIUM	CASTING	CORNICE	DIGNITY	EVENING	FUNNILY
WORSHIP	ASOCIAL	BOILING	CASUISM	CORNISH	DIORITE	EXAMINE	FURBISH
WOTCHER	ASQUITH	BOMBING	CASUIST	CORRIDA	DIOXIDE	EXITING	FURNISH
XANTHOS	ASTRIDE	BONFIRE	CATFISH	CORTINA	DISLIKE	EYELIDS	FURRIER
ABAXIAL	ATAVISM	BOOKIES	CATKINS	COSTING	DISMISS	EZEKIEL	FURTIVE
ABIDING	ATELIER	BOOKING	CATLIKE	COSTIVE	DISTILL	FACTION	FUSSILY
ABILITY	ATHEISM	BOOKISH	CATLING	COTTIER	DITTIES	FADDISH	FUSTIAN
ABJOINT	ATHEIST	BOOMING	CATMINT	COURIER	DIZZILY	FADDIST	GABRIEL
ABOLISH	ATOMIST	BOORISH	CATTISH	COUSINS	DOCKING	FAILING	GALLING
ABUSIVE	ATOMIZE	BOWLING	CAUTION	COWGIRL	DOGFISH	FAIRING	GALLIUM
ACADIAN	ATTAINT	BRACING	CEILIDH	COWHIDE	DONNISH	FAIRISH	GAMBIAN
ACARIDA	AUCTION	BRAKING	CEILING	COWLICK	DOMAINE	FALLING	GARFISH
ACIDIFY	AVARICE	BRAZIER	CELLINI	COWLING	DORKING	FALSIES	GARNISH
ACIDITY	AVIDITY	BREVITY	CELLIST	CRANIAL	DOSSIER	FALSIFY	GARRICK
ACONITE	AZURITE	BREWING	CELSIUS	CRANIUM	DOWDILY	FANCIED	GASFIRE
ACQUIRE	BABBITT	BRITISH	CERTIFY	CRAVING	DOWSING	FANCIER	GASPING
ADAMITE	BABYISH	BROMIDE	CESSION	CRAZILY	DRAWING	FANZINE	GATLING
ADAXIAL	BACKING	BROMINE	CHAFING	CREVICE	DRIVING	FARMING	GAUDILY
ADELINE	BAGPIPE	BRUTISH	CHALICE	CROSIER	DUALITY	FARRIER	GAWKISH
ADENINE	BAILIFF	BUDDING	CHARIOT	CROWING	DUBBING	FASCISM	GEARING
ADJOINT	BALDING	BUGGING	CHARITY	CROZIER	DUBNIUM	FASCIST	GELDING
ADORING	BALLIOL	BUGGINS	CHASING	CRUCIAL	DUCKING	FASHION	GENTIAN
AEOLIAN	BAMBINO	BULGING	CHEMISE	CRUCIFY	DUCTILE	FASTING	GENTILE
AFFAIRS	BANGING	BULLION	CHEMIST	CRUDITY	DUMPISH	FATUITY	GENUINE
AFFLICT	BANKING	BULLISH	CHERISH	CUCKING	DUNCIAD	FAUVISM	GERAINT
AGILITY	BAPTISM	BUNTING	CHEVIOT	CUISINE	DUNKIRK	FAUVIST	GETTING
AGONIST	BAPTIST	BURKINA	CHEWING	CUNNING	DUSTING	FAWNING	GIDDILY
AGONIZE	BAPTIZE	BURNING	CHOKING	CURLING	EARLIER	FEBRILE	GILDING
AIRLIFT	BARKING	BURNISH	CHOPINE	CURRIED	EARRING	FEEDING	GIMMICK
AIRLINE	BARRIER	BUSHIDO	CHORION	CURSIVE	EBBTIDE	FEELING	GIRLISH
AIRSICK	BARRING	BUSKINS	CHORIZO	CUSHION	EBONITE	FENCING	GLACIAL
ALANINE	BASKING	BUSSING	CITRINE	CUTTING	ECCRINE	FERMIUM	GLACIER
ALDRICH	BASTIDE	CABLING	CIVVIES	CYANIDE	EDIFICE	FERTILE	GLARING
ALEPINE	BASTION	CADDISH	CLARIFY	CYCLING	EDITION	FESTIVE	GLAZIER
ALEWIFE	BATHING	CADMIUM	CLARION	CYCLIST	EGALITY	FICTION	GLAZING
ALTHING	BATTING	CAESIUM	CLARITY	CYPRIOT	EGOTISM	FILLING	GLIDING
ALUMINA	BAUXITE	CAINITE	CLOSING	DADAISM	EGOTIST	FILMING	GLORIFY
AMANITA	BEADING	CAITIFF	CLOYING	DADAIST	ELAMITE	FINDING	GLOWING
AMAZING	BEAMING	CALCIFY	CLUNIAC	DAMNING	ELATION	FINNISH	GNAWING
AMENITY	BEARING	CALCINE	COATING	DAMPIER	ELEGIAC	FISHING	GODLIKE
AMERICA	BEARISH	CALCITE	COAXIAL	DAMPING	ELEGIST	FISSILE	GOLDING
AMERIGO	BEATIFY	CALCIUM	COCAINE	DANCING	ELISION	FISSION	GOLFING
AMERIND	BEATING	CALLING	CODEINE	DARLING	ELITISM	FITTING	GOODIES
AMORIST	BEDDING	CAMBIUM	CODLING	DARNING	ELITIST	FLAMING	GOODISH
AMORITE	BEDSIDE	CAMPING	COELIAC	DASHING	ELOGIUM	FLEEING	GOOLIES
AMPLIFY	BEDTIME	CAMPION	COEXIST	DAYTIME	ELUSIVE	FLEMING	GORDIAN
AMUSING	BEEHIVE	CANDIDA	COITION	DEALING	ELYSIAN	FLEMISH	GORDIUS
ANANIAS	BEELINE	CANDIDE	COLDITZ	DEBRIEF	ELYSIUM	FLEXILE	GOSLING
ANGLING	BEGGING	CANDIED	COLLIDE	DECEIVE	EMOTION	FLORIDA	GOSSIPY
ANGRILY	BEGUILE	CANNILY	COLLIER	DECLINE	EMOTIVE	FLORIST	GRACILE
ANGUISH	BEIJING	CANNING	COMBINE	DENSITY	ENGLISH	FLOWING	GRANITA
ANILINE	BELGIAN	CAPRICE	COMBING	DENTINE	ENPRINT	FLUTIST	GRANITE
ANIMIST	BELGIUM	CAPSIZE	COMPILE	DENTIST	ENQUIRE	FLUVIAL	GRATIFY

GRATING	HOUDINI	KATRINE	LOUTISH	MOLLIFY	ORIGINS	PINFISH	RALEIGH
GRAVITY	HOUSING	KEELING	LUCKILY	MONKISH	ORPHISM	PISCINA	RANKING
GRAYISH	HOWLING	KEEPING	LUDDITE	MOODILY	OSTRICH	PISCINE	RANTING
GRAZING	HULKING	KENNING	LUMPISH	MOONING	OUSTITI	PISMIRE	RATLINE
GRECIAN	HUMMING	KENTISH	LURKING	MOORING	OUTLIER	PITHILY	RAWHIDE
GREYISH	HUNTING	KERNITE	LUSTILY	MOORISH	OUTLINE	PLACING	READILY
GROLIER	HURLING	KHALIFA	MACHINE	MOPPING	OUTLIVE	PLAYING	READING
GROPIUS	HURRIED	KHEDIVE	MADEIRA	MORAINE	OUTSIDE	PLOSION	REALIGN
GROTIUS	HUSKILY	KICKING	MAGNIFY	MOREISH	OUTSIZE	PLOSIVE	REALISM
GROWING	HUSSITE	KILLICK	MAGUIRE	MORNING	OVARIAN	POLLING	REALIST
GUANINE	HYALINE	KILLING	MAILING	MORTICE	OVATION	PONTIAC	REALITY
GUBBINS	HYMNIST	KIPLING	MALAISE	MORTIFY	OVICIDE	PONTIFF	REALIZE
GUIDING	IAMBIST	KISSING	MALLING	MORTISE	OXIDIZE	PONTINE	REARING
GUNFIRE	IBERIAN	KLAVIER	MANDIOC	MUGGING	OXONIAN	POPPING	REBUILD
GUSHING	ICHNITE	KNOWING	MANKIND	MULLION	PACKING	PORCIAN	RECEIPT
HACKING	IDOLIZE	KONTIKI	MANNING	MUMMIFY	PADDING	PORCINE	RECEIVE
HADRIAN	IMAGINE	KOUMISS	MANNISH	MYELINE	PAIRING	PORTICO	RECLINE
HAFNIUM	IMAGING	KYANITE	MANSION	MYSTIFY	PALLIUM	PORTION	RECTIFY
HAGFISH	IMAGISM	LACKING	MANSIZE	NAGGING	PALMIST	POSTING	REDDISH
HAHNIUM	IMAGIST	LAGGING	MAPPING	NAPPING	PALSIED	POTTING	REDFISH
HAITIAN	IMPLIED	LAMAISM	MARKING	NASTILY	PANNIER	PRALINE	REEKING
HALTING	IMPRINT	LAMAIST	MARLINE	NEARING	PANTILE	PRAYING	REELING
HANDILY	INANITY	LAMBING	MARLITE	NEBBISH	PAPRIKA	PRECISE	REJOICE
HANGING	INBUILT	LANCING	MARMION	NECKING	PARKING	PREDIAL	REMAINS
HAPPILY	INCLINE	LANDING	MARMITE	NÉGLIGÉ	PARTIAL	PREDICT	REPAINT
HARPIST	INFLICT	LAOTIAN	MARRIED	NEGRITO	PARTING	PRELIMS	REPAIRS
HARRIER	INITIAL	LAPPING	MARTIAL	NEOLITH	PARTITA	PREMIER	REPLICA
HARRIET	INKLING	LAPWING	MARTIAN	NETTING	PASSING	PREMISE	REPRINT
HARWICH	INQUIRE	LASHING	MARTINI	NEURINE	PASSION	PREMISS	REPTILE
HASHISH	INQUIRY	LASTING	MARXISM	NIBLICK	PASSIVE	PREMIUM	REQUIEM
HASSIUM	INSPIRE	LATRINE	MARXIST	NICOISE	PASTIES	PRESIDE	REQUIRE
HASTILY	INSTILL	LATTICE	MASSINE	NIOBIUM	PASTIME	PREVIEW	REQUITE
HAULIER	INVEIGH	LATVIAN	MASSIVE	NITRILE	PATRIAL	PRIMING	RESCIND
HAYWIRE	INVOICE	LEADING	MASTIFF	NITRITE	PATRICK	PRIVITY	RESPIRE
HEADING	IRANIAN	LEANING	MATTING	NODDING	PATRIOT	PROBITY	RESPITE
HEALING	IRIDISE	LEAPING	MATTINS	NOGGING	PAUCITY	PRODIGY	RESTING
HEARING	IRIDIUM	LEASING	MAWKISH	NOISILY	PAULINE	PROFILE	RESTIVE
HEATING	IRONING	LEAVING	MEANING	NORWICH	PECKING	PROMISE	RETAINS
HEAVIER	ISCHIUM	LEFTIST	MEETING	NOTHING	PECKISH	PROTIST	RETHINK
HEAVILY	ISMAILI	LEGGING	MELLITE	NOURISH	PEELING	PROVIDE	RETRIAL
HEDGING	ITALIAN	LEMMING	MELTING	NUCLIDE	PEEPING	PROVING	RETSINA
HELLION	ITCHING	LEMPIRA	MEMOIRS	NULLIFY	PEERING	PROVISO	REUNION
HELLISH	ITEMIZE	LENDING	MENDING	NULLITY	PEEVISH	PROXIMO	REUNITE
HELPING	IVORIAN	LENTIGO	MENTION	NUNLIKE	PELTING	PRUDISH	REWRITE
HEMLINE	IVORIEN	LENTILS	MERCIES	NUPTIAL	PENDING	PRURIGO	RHENISH
HENGIST	JAMAICA	LEONINE	MERRIER	NURSING	PENNINE	PUBLISH	RHENIUM
HERBIST	JAMMIES	LESBIAN	MERRILY	NUTLIKE	PENSILE	PUCCINI	RHODIAN
HEROINE	JAMMING	LESSING	MESSIAH	NUTTING	PENSION	PUCKISH	RHODIUM
HEROISM	JAPLISH	LETTING	MESSIER	OARFISH	PENSIVE	PUDDING	RHYMING
HERRICK	JASMINE	LEUCINE	MESSILY	OBADIAH	PEREIRA	PULSING	RIBBING
HERRIES	JEERING	LIBRIUM	MESSINA	OBELISK	PERFIDY	PUNTING	RIGGING
HERRING	JELLIED	LICKING	METHINK	OBESITY	PERLITE	PURLIEU	RINGING
HESSIAN	JENKINS	LIGNITE	MIDLINE	OCARINA	PERMIAN	PURLINE	RIOTING
HEURISM	JERKILY	LILTING	MIDRIFF	OCULIST	PERRIER	PURVIEW	RIPPING
HIGGINS	JESTING	LINKING	MIDWIFE	ODALISK	PERSIAN	PUSHING	RIPTIDE
HILDING	JEWFISH	LIONIZE	MILKING	OFFSIDE	PERSIST	PUTTING	RISKILY
HISSING	JOBBING	LIQUIDS	MILLING	OGREISH	PETRIFY	QUAKING	ROAMING
HITTITE	JOGGING	LISTING	MILLION	OILBIRD	PHIDIAS	QUALIFY	ROARING
HOGGING	JOINING	LITHIUM	MINCING	OLEFINE	PHONICS	QUALITY	ROCKING
HOLDING	JOLLITY	LODGING	MISFIRE	ONANISM	PHYSICS	QUININE	ROGUISH
HOLMIUM	JOYRIDE	LOFTILY	MISSILE	ONETIME	PIANIST	RACHIAL	ROLLICK
HOPKINS	JUDAISM	LOGGING	MISSING	ONGOING	PICKING	RACKING	ROLLING
HOPLITE	JUGGINS	LONGING	MISSION	OPACITY	PIETIST	RAFFISH	ROMAINE
HOPPING	JUMPING	LOOKING	MISSIVE	OPALINE	PIGFISH	RAFTING	ROOFING
HORRIFY	JUSSIVE	LOOMING	MISTIME	OPENING	PIGLING	RAGTIME	ROOKISH
HORSING	JUSTICE	LOOTING	MOABITE	OPINION	PILLION	RAILING	ROOTING
HOSPICE	JUSTIFY	LORDING	MOANING	ORATION	PIMPING	RAISING	ROSCIAN
HOSTILE	KADDISH	LOTHIAN	MOCKING	ORIFICE			ROSCIUS
HOTLINE	KAINITE	LOURING	MOLDING				ROSSINI

ROTTING	SIGNIFY	SUCTION	TITOISM	VERSIFY	YORKIST	GROCKLE	UNASKED
ROUSING	SIGNING	SUFFICE	TITOIST	VERSION	YTTRIUM	HEARKEN	WHACKED
ROUTIER	SIKHISM	SUICIDE	TOLKIEN	VERTIGO	ZAMBIAN	KARAKUL	WHACKER
ROUTINE	SINGING	SULKILY	TOMPION	VESTIGE	ZEOLITE	KLINKER	WHISKER
ROWDILY	SINKING	SUMMING	TONNISH	VETTING	ZEPHIEL	KNACKER	WHISKEY
RUBBING	SIPPING	SUNDIAL	TONTINE	VILNIUS	ZILLION	KNICKER	WRECKED
RUBBISH	SISTINE	SUNNILY	TOOLING	VITRIFY	ZIONIST	KNOCKER	WRECKER
RUFFIAN	SITTING	SUNNITE	TOPPING	VITRIOL	ZOOLITE	KNUCKLE	WRINKLE
RUNNING	SKATING	SUNRISE	TOPSIDE	VULPINE	ABIDJAN	LIMPKIN	WRINKLY
RUNNION	SKYHIGH	SURDITY	TORPIDS	WADDING	BRINJAL	LUMPKIN	ABOULIA
RUSHING	SKYLINE	SURFING	TORSION	WAFTING	KARAJAN	MANAKIN	ABSOLVE
RUSSIAN	SLAVISH	SURMISE	TORTILE	WAGGISH	KILLJOY	MANIKIN	ACRYLIC
RUTTING	SLAYING	SURVIVE	TOURING	WAILING	LOCKJAW	MEERKAT	AIRFLOW
SABRINA	SLIDING	SWAHILI	TOURISM	WAITING	MUDEJAR	NABOKOV	ALCALDE
SACKING	SLOPING	SWAYING	TOURIST	WALKING	MUNTJAC	OILSKIN	ALFALFA
SAILING	SLOWING	SWEDISH	TOWLINE	WALLIES	ABOUKIR	PIGSKIN	AMPULLA
SALPINX	SMILING	TACHISM	TRACING	WANTING	ALASKAN	PRICKED	ANGELIC
SALSIFY	SMOKING	TACTICS	TRADING	WAPPING	BANGKOK	PRICKER	ANGELUS
SALTING	SNORING	TACTILE	TRINITY	WARLIKE	BETOKEN	PRICKLE	ANGOLAN
SALTIRE	SOAKING	TALKING	TRITIUM	WARLING	BLACKEN	PRICKLY	ANGULAR
SAMNITE	SOARING	TALLITH	TRIVIAL	WARMING	BLANKET	PUMPKIN	ANNELID
SAPLING	SOCKING	TAMPICO	TRIVIUM	WARNING	BLANKLY	PUSHKIN	ANNULAR
SARDINE	SOLDIER	TAMPION	TROPICS	WARRING	BLEAKLY	QUICKEN	ANNULET
SASHIMI	SOLOIST	TANGIER	TROPISM	WARRIOR	BLINKER	QUICKER	ANNULUS
SAUCILY	SOPHISM	TANNING	TRUCIAL	WARTIME	BLOCKED	QUICKIE	APHELIA
SAURIAN	SOPHIST	TANTIVY	TSARINA	WARWICK	BLOCKER	QUICKLY	AQUILON
SAWBILL	SOPPING	TAPPICE	TSARIST	WASHING	BRACKEN	RAMEKIN	ASTILBE
SAWFISH	SOPWITH	TAPPING	TUITION	WASPISH	BRACKET	REDSKIN	AURALLY
SAWMILL	SORDINO	TARDILY	TURBINE	WASTING	BREAKER	SHACKLE	AURELIA
SCABIES	SORTING	TARDIVE	TURKISH	WAXBILL	BRICKIE	SHICKSA	AWFULLY
SCARIFY	SOUBISE	TARNISH	TURNING	WAXWING	BRISKET	SHIRKER	AXILLAR
SCARING	SPACING	TARSIER	TWOTIME	WAYBILL	BRISKLY	SHOCKED	BABBLER
SCORING	SPANIEL	TARTINE	TZARINA	WAYSIDE	BUMPKIN	SHOCKER	BABYLON
SEABIRD	SPANISH	TASSILI	UGOLINO	WEARILY	CHALKER	SIMPKIN	BACILLI
SEALINK	SPARING	TATTING	UKRAINE	WEARING	CHECKED	SLACKEN	BACKLOG
SEALION	SPATIAL	TAURINE	ULEXITE	WEAVING	CHECKIN	SLACKER	BAFFLED
SEARING	SPAVINE	TBILISI	UMBRIAN	WEBBING	CHECKUP	SLACKLY	BEATLES
SEASICK	SPECIAL	TEARING	UNALIKE	WEBSITE	CHICKEN	SLEEKLY	BIBELOT
SEASIDE	SPECIES	TEASING	UNALIVE	WEDDING	CHOOKIE	SLICKER	BIVALVE
SEATING	SPECIFY	TEATIME	UNCTION	WEEPING	CHUCKLE	SMACKER	BOBSLED
SECTION	SPIRITS	TEEMING	UNDOING	WELDING	CHUKKER	SMICKLY	BOOKLET
SEEMING	SPRAINT	TEKTITE	UNDYING	WELLIES	CLICKER	SNEAKER	BOOTLEG
SELFISH	STABILE	TELLING	UNITIES	WENDISH	CLINKER	SNICKER	BOTTLED
SELKIRK	STADIUM	TENNIEL	UNQUIET	WETTING	CONAKRY	SNOOKER	BOTTLES
SELLING	STAGING	TENSILE	UNSTICK	WHALING	CRACKED	SNORKEL	BOUCLÉE
SERBIAN	STAMINA	TENSING	UNTRIED	WHITING	CRACKER	SPANKER	BOUILLI
SERCIAL	STARING	TENSION	UNTWINE	WHITISH	CRACKLE	SPARKLE	BOWDLER
SERRIED	STATICS	TEQUILA	UPRAISE	WICKIUP	CRACKLY	SPEAKER	BRAILLE
SERVICE	STATION	TERBIUM	UPSWING	WIGGING	CRICKET	SPECKLE	BRAWLER
SERVILE	STATIST	TERMITE	URALITE	WILDING	CRICKEY	STALKED	BRIDLER
SERVING	STAYING	TERRIER	URANIAN	WILLIAM	CRINKLE	STALKER	BRIDLES
SESSILE	STERILE	TERRIFY	URANISM	WILLIES	CRINKLY	STARKLY	BROILER
SESSION	STEWING	TERRINE	URANITE	WILLING	CROAKER	STICKER	BUBBLES
SESTINA	STONILY	TERSION	URANIUM	WIMPISH	CROCKET	STICKLE	BUCKLER
SESTINE	STORIED	TERTIAL	UROLITH	WINDING	CROOKED	STINKER	BUCOLIC
SETTING	STORIES	TERTIAN	UTERINE	WINNING	DOESKIN	STONKER	BUNGLER
SHADING	STRAITS	TESTIFY	UTILITY	WISHING	DOORKEY	STRIKER	BURGLAR
SHAKILY	STUDIED	TESTILY	UTILIZE	WOLFISH	DRINKER	THICKEN	BUSTLER
SHAKING	STYGIAN	TESTING	UTOPIAN	WORDILY	DRUNKEN	THICKET	BUSTLES
SHAPING	STYLING	TEXTILE	UXORIAL	WORDING	ERISKAY	THICKLY	CAMELOT
SHARIAH	STYLISH	THOMISM	VACCINE	WORKING	FLANKER	THINKER	CAMILLA
SHARING	STYLIST	THOMIST	VACUITY	WORRIED	FLECKED	TRACKER	CANELLA
SHAVING	STYLITE	THORIUM	VAMPIRE	WORRIER	FLECKER	TREKKER	CAPELLA
SHERIFF	STYLIZE	THULIUM	VARMINT	WRITING	FLICKER	TRICKLE	CAROLUS
SHINING	SUAVITY	THYMINE	VARNISH	WRYBILL	FLUNKEY	TRINKET	CASTLED
SHOWILY	SUBLIME	TICKING	VARSITY	WYOMING	FRANKLY	TRUCKER	CATALAN
SHOWING	SUBSIDE	TIGRISH	VARYING	YAHWIST	FRECKLE	TRUCKLE	CATALOG
SIBLING	SUBSIDY	TIPPING	VENDING	YAWNING	GHERKIN	TURNKEY	CATALPA
SIFTING	SUBSIST	TIPSILY	VERDICT	YIDDISH	GRACKLE	TWINKLE	CATELOG

CAVALRY	FENELON	KNELLER	ORACLES	RUSTLER	TODDLER	BOOKMAN	JURYMAN
CECILIA	FIDDLER	KREMLIN	ORTOLAN	SADDLER	TOTALLY	BRADMAN	KASHMIR
CEDILLA	FIDELIO	KUBELIK	OSCULUM	SAMPLER	TRAILER	BRAEMAR	KINSMAN
CHABLIS	FINALLY	LAMELLA	OSSELET	SAVELOY	TRAWLER	BRAHMAN	LATIMER
CHAPLET	FLATLET	LANGLEY	OTHELLO	SCAGLIA	TRELLIS	BRAHMIN	LINEMAN
CHARLES	FORELEG	LANOLIN	OUTFLOW	SCALLOP	TRIFLER	BULIMIA	LINKMAN
CHARLEY	FRAILTY	LAVOLTA	OVERLAP	SCARLET	TRIFLES	BUSHMAN	MAILMAN
CHILLER	FRILLED	LEAFLET	OVERLAY	SCHOLAR	TRILLED	BUSHMEN	MANUMIT
CHILLON	FUDDLED	LEGALLY	OVERLIE	SCOLLOP	TRILLER	CAEDMON	MANXMAN
CIRCLET	FUSILLI	LOBELIA	PABULUM	SCULLER	TRIPLET	CALAMUS	MAREMMA
CIRCLIP	GABBLER	LOCALLY	PADDLER	SECULAR	TRIPLEX	CALOMEL	MAXIMUM
CIVILLY	GABELLE	LORELEI	PAISLEY	SETTLED	TROILUS	CALUMET	MIASMIC
COBBLED	GALILEE	LOYALLY	PAPILLA	SETTLER	TROLLEY	CALUMNY	MILKMAN
COBBLER	GALILEO	LOYALTY	PARSLEY	SEVILLE	TROLLOP	CARAMBA	MINIMAL
COCHLEA	GAMBLER	MAMILLA	PATELLA	SHALLOT	TUBULAR	CARAMEL	MINIMAX
COCKLES	GAMELAN	MANILLA	PEARLIE	SHALLOW	TUBULIN	CAVEMAN	MINIMUM
COMPLEX	GANELON	MARBLED	PEBBLES	SHELLAC	TUMBLER	CERAMIC	MYANMAR
COPILOT	GARBLED	MARBLES	PEDDLER	SHELLED	TUMULUS	CHAPMAN	NEWSMAN
CORELLI	GAZELLE	MARTLET	PENALTY	SHELLEY	TUTELAR	CHARMED	OARSMAN
COROLLA	GEFILTE	MATELOT	PERPLEX	SHIRLEY	UCCELLO	CHARMER	OARSMEN
COUPLER	GIMBLET	MATILDA	PHALLIC	SHRILLY	UPSILON	CHLAMYS	OPTIMAL
COUPLET	GISELLE	MAUDLIN	PHALLUS	SIMILAR	USUALLY	CINEMAS	OPTIMUM
COWSLIP	GNARLED	MAXILLA	PICKLED	SIMPLER	UTRILLO	CLUBMAN	OTTOMAN
CRAWLER	GOBBLER	MEASLES	PICKLER	SIMPLEX	VANILLA	COLOMBO	OVERMAN
CRUELLS	GOBELIN	MECHLIN	PIKELET	SIMPLON	VERULAM	COLUMBA	PACKMAN
CRUELLY	GOGGLES	MEDDLER	PLAYLET	SINGLES	VIRELAY	COLUMNS	PAJAMAS
CRUELTY	GORILLA	MEDULLA	POPULAR	SINGLET	VITALLY	CRAMMED	PALOMAR
CUMULUS	GRAVLAX	MELILOT	POPULUS	SIZZLER	VIVALDI	CRAMMER	PLASMIN
CURDLED	GREMLIN	MESCLUN	PROBLEM	SKILLED	VOCALIC	CRANMER	PLOWMAN
DABBLER	GREYLAG	METALLY	PROWLER	SKILLET	VOCALLY	CREWMAN	PLUMMET
DAIMLER	GRILLED	METTLED	PTYALIN	SKYBLUE	WAGGLER	DECIMAL	POLEMIC
DALILAH	GROWLER	MIMULUS	PUCELLE	SMALLER	WANGLER	DELIMIT	POLYMER
DAPPLED	GUNPLAY	MISPLAY	PUZZLED	SNARLER	WARBLER	DIDYMUS	POSTMAN
DAWDLER	GUZZLER	MODULAR	PUZZLER	SNARLUP	WATTLES	DIGAMMA	POTOMAC
DAZZLED	GYMSLIP	MODULUS	RADDLED	SOMALIA	WHEELED	DILEMMA	PREEMPT
DEFILED	HACKLES	MOELLON	RAFFLES	SOZZLED	WHEELER	DOORMAN	PULLMAN
DELILAH	HANDLED	MONILIA	RAMBLER	SPELLER	WHEELIE	DOORMAT	PYAEMIA
DEVALUE	HANDLER	MONOLOG	RAMULUS	SPOILED	WHITLOW	DREAMER	PYJAMAS
DEVELOP	HARELIP	MOONLIT	RATTLER	SPOILER	WICKLOW	DRUMMER	PYRAMID
DEVILRY	HECKLER	MORALLY	REGALIA	SQUALID	WOOLLEN	DURAMEN	RACEMIC
DEVOLVE	HIDALGO	MORELLO	REGALLY	SQUALLY	YPSILON	DUSTMAN	RACHMAN
DIBBLER	HINDLEG	MOSELLE	REGULAR	SQUALOR	ABDOMEN	DYNAMIC	REAUMUR
DIMPLED	HOODLUM	MOTTLED	REMBLAI	SQUELCH	ABYSMAL	ENDEMIC	REGIMEN
DIPOLAR	HUMBLES	MOUFLON	REPULSE	SQUILLA	ALARMED	ERASMUS	ROLLMOP
DISPLAY	HURDLER	MOUILLÉ	RESOLVE	STABLES	ALBUMEN	FIREMAN	SALAMIS
DIVULGE	HURDLES	MUDDLED	RESULTS	STANLEY	ALBUMIN	FLUMMOX	SANDMAN
DOODLER	HUSTLER	MUDFLAP	REVALUE	STAPLER	ANAEMIA	FOOTMAN	SCHEMER
DOPPLER	ICEFLOE	MUFFLED	REVELER	STARLET	ANAEMIC	FORAMEN	SCRUMMY
DOUBLES	IDEALLY	MUFFLER	REVELRY	STARLIT	ANDAMAN	FOREMAN	SCRUMPY
DOUBLET	IDYLLIC	MURILLO	REVOLVE	STEALTH	ANOSMIA	FREEMAN	SEISMIC
DOUGLAS	IMPULSE	MYCELLA	RIDDLED	STELLAR	ARTEMIS	FROGMAN	SHERMAN
DRIBLET	INDULGE	NACELLE	RIDDLER	STOLLEN	ARTEMUS	GALUMPH	SHIMMER
DROPLET	INHALER	NASALLY	RINGLET	SURPLUS	ASHAMED	GLIMMER	SHOWMAN
DRUMLIN	INSULAR	NEBULAR	RIVALRY	SWALLOW	ASSUMED	GOODMAN	SHRIMPS
DWELLER	INSULIN	NECKLET	RIVULET	SWOLLEN	ATTEMPT	GOURMET	SKIMMED
ECBOLIC	INVALID	NEEDLES	ROMULUS	TABULAR	AUTOMAT	GRAMMAR	SKIMMER
ECHELON	INVOLVE	NEVILLE	ROSALIA	TACKLER	BAHAMAS	GROMMET	SKIMMIA
EMBOLUS	JAVELIN	NIGELLA	ROSALIE	TAGALOG	BATHMAT	GRUMMET	SLAMMER
ENVELOP	JAVELLE	NOBBLED	ROSELLA	TANGLED	BATSMAN	HANGMAN	SLIMMER
EPAULET	JEWELER	NOBBLER	ROSELLE	TATTLER	BEERMAT	HANGMEN	SNOWMAN
EPSILON	JEWELRY	NODULAR	ROYALLY	TEMPLAR	BELLMAN	HEADMAN	SOLOMON
EQUALLY	JOCULAR	NONPLUS	ROYALTY	TEMPLET	BETIMES	HIGHMAN	STAMMER
ESCALOP	JUBILEE	NOODLES	RUBELLA	THALLUS	BILLMAN	HILLMAN	STEAMED
ETAPLES	JUGGLER	NOVELLA	RUDOLPH	TICKLER	BIRDMAN	HILLMEN	STEAMER
EULALIE	JUGULAR	NOVELLO	RUFFLED	TIDDLER	BITUMEN	INCOMER	STEMMED
FACULTY	JUMBLED	NOVELTY	RUFFLER	TIMELAG	BLOOMER	INHUMAN	STURMER
FANGLED	JUMBLES	NUMBLES	RUMBLER	TINGLER	BOATMAN	ISLAMIC	SWAGMAN
FATALLY	KINGLET	OCELLAR	RUMPLED	TIPPLER	BOHEMIA	ISTHMUS	SWIMMER
FAVELLA	KNEELER	OCELLUS	RUSALKA	TITULAR	BONDMAN	JAZZMAN	THERMAL

THERMIC	BEATNIK	EMPANEL	LACONIC	POLENTA	TARANTO	ANATOMY	CABOOSE
THERMOS	BEGONIA	ENGINED	LACUNAE	POLONIE	TENANCY	ANCHOVY	CAHOOTS
TOLLMAN	BELINDA	ENHANCE	LAGONDA	POTENCY	TENANTS	ANDROID	CALLOUS
TOTEMIC	BOLONEY	ENTENTE	LAYINGS	QUEENLY	TERENCE	ANEMONE	CAMWOOD
TOXEMIA	BONANZA	ENVENOM	LEARNED	RAVINGS	TETANUS	ANEROID	CANDOUR
TRAMMEL	BOTANIC	EQUINOX	LEARNER	REFINED	THINNER	ANGIOMA	CANNOCK
TRIMMER	BRENNER	ESSENCE	LEBANON	REFINER	THRENOS	ANTHONY	CANZONA
TRISMUS	BROWNED	ESSENES	LEPANTO	REGENCY	TIDINGS	ANTIOCH	CANZONE
TRIUMPH	BROWNIE	ETERNAL	LICENCE	RETINAL	TITANIA	ANXIOUS	CARDOON
UNARMED	BUBONIC	ETHANOL	LICENSE	RETINUE	TITANIC	ANYBODY	CARGOES
UNKEMPT	BURUNDI	EUGENIA	LIKENED	REVENGE	TOPKNOT	ANYMORE	CARIOCA
UNNAMED	BUTANAL	EUGENIC	LIMINAL	REVENUE	TORONTO	APOCOPE	CARIOLE
UNTAMED	BUTANOL	EUGENIE	LININGS	RIDINGS	TRAINED	APOLOGY	CARLOAD
URAEMIA	BYRONIC	EXPANSE	LOCKNUT	ROBINIA	TRAINEE	APPROVE	CARPORT
VIDIMUS	CABINET	EXPENSE	LOZENGE	ROMANCE	TRAINER	AQUEOUS	CARROLL
VITAMIN	CADENCE	EXPUNGE	LYCHNIS	ROMANIA	TRIANON	ARDUOUS	CARROTS
WALKMAN	CADENZA	EXTINCT	MADONNA	ROMANOV	TROUNCE	ARIZONA	CARROTY
WINGMAN	CALENDS	FAIENCE	MAGENTA	ROMANZA	TRUANCY	ARMHOLE	CARTOON
WOODMAN	CANONRY	FASTNET	MAGINOT	ROTUNDA	TURENNE	ARTWORK	CASSOCK
WORKMAN	CAYENNE	FEIGNED	MAHONIA	SAPONIN	TYRANNY	ASHDOWN	CASTOFF
WORKMEN	CÉZANNE	FILINGS	MAKINGS	SATANIC	UNCANNY	AUREOLA	CATHODE
YASHMAK	CHAINED	FISHNET	MARANTA	SAVANNA	UNCINUS	AUREOLE	CESTODE
AARONIC	CHANNEL	FIXINGS	MARENGO	SAVINGS	UNHINGE	AWESOME	CESTOID
ABSENCE	CHARNEL	FLANNEL	MARINER	SCANNER	UNLINED	AXOLOTL	CHALONE
ABSINTH	CHIANTI	FLAUNCH	MASONIC	SCIENCE	UNOWNED	AZYGOUS	CHAMOIS
ACRONYM	CHIGNON	FLOUNCE	MASONRY	SCRUNCH	URGENCY	BABOOSH	CHAYOTE
ACTINAL	CHIMNEY	FLUENCY	MATINEE	SECONAL	VACANCY	BALCONY	CHEROOT
ACTINIA	CHRONIC	FRIENDS	MECONIC	SECONDS	VAGINAL	BALFOUR	CHICORY
ACTINIC	CHUNNEL	GARONNE	MELANIN	SEMINAL	VALENCE	BALLOON	CHINOOK
ADJUNCT	CHUTNEY	GEHENNA	MEMENTO	SEMINAR	VALENCY	BANDORE	CHOROID
ADORNED	CLEANER	GIRONDE	METONIC	SERINGA	VEDANTA	BANNOCK	CIRROSE
ADRENAL	CLEANLY	GODUNOV	METONYM	SEVENTH	VERONAL	BASSOON	CISSOID
ADVANCE	CLEANSE	GLEANER	MIRANDA	SEVENTY	VICINAL	BAZOOKA	CITROEN
AGAINST	CLEANUP	GRAINED	MOMENTS	SHANNON	VIETNAM	BEDFORD	CLAMOUR
AIDANCE	COCKNEY	GRAINER	MORONIC	SILENCE	VIKINGS	BEDPOST	COLLOID
ALBANIA	COCONUT	GRANNIE	MOURNER	SIMENON	VINTNER	BEDROCK	COMFORT
ALBENIZ	COGENCY	GRAPNEL	MYCENAE	SKINNED	VOLANTE	BEDROOM	COMMODE
ALFONSO	COLONEL	GREENER	MYRINGA	SKINNER	WAGONER	BEDSORE	COMMODO
ALIGNED	COLONIC	GROINED	NOMINAL	SOLANUM	WHATNOT	BEHOOVE	COMMONS
ALKANET	CORANTO	GROUNDS	NOMINEE	SPANNER	WIZENED	BELLOWS	COMPORT
ALLENBY	CORINTH	GROWNUP	OCEANIA	SPHENIC	WOMANLY	BENZOIN	COMPOSE
ALLONGE	CORONER	GUIGNOL	OCEANIC	SPIGNEL	XIMENES	BESPOKE	COMPOST
ALMANAC	CORONET	HACKNEY	OCEANID	SPINNER	YAOUNDE	BETROTH	COMPOTE
ALMONER	CORUNNA	HAIRNET	OFFENCE	SPINNEY	ZIZANIA	BETTONG	CONCOCT
ALUMNAE	COTINGA	HOMINID	OFFENSE	SPOONER	ABALONE	BIGFOOT	CONCORD
ALUMNUS	CROONER	HOMONYM	ORCINOL	SPRINGE	ABSCOND	BIGHORN	CONDOLE
AMMONAL	DAPHNID	HOSANNA	ORDINAL	SPRINGS	ACETONE	BILIOUS	CONDONE
AMMONIA	DAPHNIS	HUMANLY	ORGANIC	SPRINGY	ACIFORM	BILLOWS	CONFORM
ANDANTE	DECANAL	HYPONYM	ORGANUM	SPUTNIK	ADENOID	BILTONG	CONJOIN
ANTENNA	DECENCY	IMMENSE	ORGANZA	SQUINCH	ADENOMA	BIOLOGY	CONNOTE
ANTONIO	DEFENCE	IMPINGE	ORLANDO	STAINED	ADIPOSE	BISTORT	CONSOLE
ANTONYM	DEFENSE	INCENSE	OSMANLI	STAINER	AFFRONT	BLOWOUT	CONSOLS
APHONIA	DEFINED	INCONNU	OTRANTO	STANNIC	AGELONG	BOOBOOK	CONSORT
APHONIC	DEFUNCT	INFANCY	PALINGS	STAUNCH	AIRLOCK	BOUDOIR	CONTORT
AQUINAS	DEMONIC	INGENUE	PARENTS	STEPNEY	AIRPORT	BOXROOM	CONTOUR
AQUINAS	DERANGE	INNINGS	PARINGS	STERNAL	ALAMODE	BOXWOOD	CONVOKE
ARRANGE	DERONDA	INTENSE	PARSNIP	STERNLY	ALECOST	BOYCOTT	COPIOUS
ARSENAL	DETENTE	ISLANDS	PARTNER	STERNUM	ALIMONY	BOYHOOD	CORDOBA
ARSENIC	DIGONAL	JACINTH	PENANCE	STRANGE	ALTHORN	BRITONS	CORRODE
ASHANTI	DIURNAL	JEEPNEY	PETUNIA	STRINGS	ALVEOLE	BUFFOON	COTTONY
ASKANCE	DIVINER	JEJUNUM	PFENNIG	STRINGY	AMATORY	BUGLOSS	COULOMB
AVIGNON	DOMINGO	JOHNNIE	PHOENIX	STUNNER	AMBROSE	BULBOUS	COUPONS
BALANCE	DOMINIC	JOURNAL	PHRENIC	SURINAM	AMOROSO	BULLOCK	COWPOKE
BALONEY	DRAGNET	JOURNEY	PIMENTO	SUSANNA	AMOROUS	BUMBOAT	COXCOMB
BANANAS	DRAINED	JUVENAL	PIRANHA	SYNONYM	AMPHORA	BUNDOOK	CRICOID
BARENTS	DVORNIK	KALENDS	PLAINLY	SYRINGA	AMYLOID	BURDOCK	CRINOID
BARONET	ECHINUS	KIWANIS	PLANNED	SYRINGE	AMYLOSE	BURNOUS	CUCKOLD
BASINET	EFFENDI	KLEENEX	PLANNER	TABANID	ANALOGY	BURNOUT	CUPROUS
BAYONET	ELEANOR		PLIANCY	TAKINGS	ANATOLE	BUTTONS	CURIOUS

CURSORY	FALLOUT	HIPBONE	MANHOLE	PANNOSE	RESTOCK	SURCOAT	WALKOUT
CUSTODY	FANWORM	HISTOID	MANHOOD	PAPOOSE	RESTORE	SYNCOPE	WALLOON
CUSTOMS	FANWORT	HISTORY	MARCONI	PARBOIL	RHIZOID	SYSTOLE	WALPOLE
CUTWORM	FATUOUS	HOBSONS	MARLOWE	PARLOUR	RHIZOME	TABLOID	WARDOUR
CYCLONE	FELLOWS	HOEDOWN	MASTOID	PARLOUS	RIBWORT	TADPOLE	WARLOCK
CYCLOPS	FERROUS	HORMONE	MATTOCK	PAVIOUR	RIOTOUS	TAILORS	WARLORD
CYSTOID	FERVOUR	HORRORS	MAYPOLE	PAVLOVA	RIPCORD	TAKEOFF	WASHOUT
DAGWOOD	FESTOON	HOTFOOT	MEACOCK	PAYLOAD	RISSOLE	TAKEOUT	WAXWORK
DAYBOOK	FETLOCK	HUMMOCK	MELROSE	PAYROLL	ROSEOLA	TALOOKA	WEAPONS
DEFROCK	FIBROID	HYALOID	MENFOLK	PEACOCK	ROSTOCK	TAMBOUR	WEDLOCK
DEFROST	FIBROMA	HYMNODY	MICROBE	PENTODE	ROWBOAT	TAPIOCA	WELCOME
DELTOID	FIBROUS	IGNEOUS	MIDMOST	PENTOSE	ROWLOCK	TAPROOM	WELLOFF
DEPLORE	FINFOOT	IMPIOUS	MILFOIL	PERFORM	RUBEOLA	TAPROOT	WENLOCK
DESMOND	FIRCONE	IMPLODE	MISTOOK	PERGOLA	RUINOUS	TEAROOM	WILLOWY
DESPOIL	FLAVOUR	IMPLORE	MOIDORE	PERSONA	RUMPOLE	TEDIOUS	WINDOWS
DESPOND	FOGHORN	IMPROVE	MONSOON	PERSONS	RUNCORN	TELFORD	WINNOCK
DEVIOUS	FORGONE	INCROSS	MUGWORT	PETIOLE	RUNDOWN	TENFOLD	WINSOME
DIABOLO	FORLORN	INDOORS	MUSCOID	PETROUS	SABAOTH	TENUOUS	WIPEOUT
DIAMOND	FORMOSA	INGROWN	MUSCOVY	PIANOLA	SAILORS	THYROID	WITHOUT
DINMONT	FOXHOLE	INSHORE	MYELOID	PIBROCH	SAMOOSA	TIEPOLO	WITLOOF
DIPLOCK	FULSOME	INTROIT	MYELOMA	PICCOLO	SANDOWN	TIMEOUT	WORKOUT
DIPLOMA	FUNGOID	INVIOUS	NACROUS	PIGEONS	SAPROBE	TINFOIL	WRYNOSE
DISCORD	FUNGOUS	IPOMOEA	NAIROBI	PILLORY	SAPWOOD	TOEHOLD	YELLOWS
DISJOIN	FURIOUS	IRKSOME	NARROWS	PINFOLD	SARCOMA	TOMBOLA	ZEALOUS
DISPORT	FURLONG	ISADORA	NATIONS	PINHOLE	SARCOUS	TOMFOOL	ZOOLOGY
DISPOSE	FUTTOCK	ISODORE	NECROSE	PISTOLE	SASSOON	TOPCOAT	ZOOTOMY
DISROBE	GADROON	ISOTONE	NEGROID	PITEOUS	SAUROID	TOPMOST	ADELPHI
DISTORT	GALLONS	ISOTOPE	NERVOSA	PLATOON	SAVIOUR	TOPSOIL	AGRAPHA
DOCTORS	GALLOWS	JAWBONE	NERVOUS	PLAYOFF	SAXHORN	TOWROPE	AGRIPPA
DOGFOOD	GAMBOGE	JEALOUS	NETWORK	PLEROMA	SCHLOCK	TREFOIL	APROPOS
DOGGONE	GARBOIL	KAMPONG	NEUROMA	PLYWOOD	SCHLOSS	TREMOLO	ATROPHY
DOGROSE	GASCONY	KARAOKE	NEURONE	POCHOIR	SCROOGE	TRILOGY	ATROPOS
DOGWOOD	GASEOUS	KEYHOLE	NEWBOLT	POLYOMA	SEAFOOD	TRIPODY	AUTOPSY
DRAGOON	GEELONG	KEYNOTE	NEWBORN	POMPOON	SEAPORT	TRIPOLI	BLEEPER
DROPOUT	GEOLOGY	KEYWORD	NEWCOME	POMPOUS	SELLOFF	TRITOMA	BLOOPER
DUBIOUS	GIBBONS	KICKOFF	NITRODE	PONTOON	SELLOUT	TRITONE	BULLPEN
DUNNOCK	GIBBOUS	KOWLOON	NITROUS	POPCORN	SENDOFF	TUGBOAT	CALEPIN
DUOPOLY	GLAMOUR	LACTOSE	NOISOME	POTHOLE	SENSORY	TURMOIL	CALYPSO
EARLOBE	GLENOID	LAMPOON	NOOLOGY	PREDOOM	SEQUOIA	TURNOUT	CATSPAW
ECOLOGY	GLUCOSE	LAOCOON	NORFOLK	PROLONG	SERIOUS	TUSSOCK	CESSPIT
ECONOMY	GOLDONI	LARDOON	NOTIONS	PROMOTE	SEYMOUR	TUSSORE	CHAMPAK
EELPOUT	GONDOLA	LEACOCK	NOXIOUS	PRONOUN	SHADOOF	TWOFOLD	CHAPPED
ELUSORY	GRANOLA	LEASOWE	OARLOCK	PROPOSE	SHADOWY	TWOSOME	CHARPOY
EMBROIL	GREGORY	LEGIONS	OBVIOUS	PROSODY	SHMOOZE	TYPHOID	CHEAPEN
EMPLOYS	GRIMOND	LEGROOM	ODOROUS	PROVOKE	SHOWOFF	TYPHOON	CHEAPLY
ENAMOUR	GUMBOIL	LEGWORK	OFFLOAD	PROVOST	SHYLOCK	UNBLOCK	CHIPPED
ENCLOSE	GUMBOOT	LEOPOLD	OLOROSO	PURLOIN	SIDDONS	UNFROCK	CHIPPER
ENDNOTE	GUNBOAT	LEPROSY	OMINOUS	PURPORT	SIGNORA	UNICORN	CHIPPIE
ENFEOFF	GUNROOM	LEPROUS	ONEROUS	PURPOSE	SIGNORI	UNIFORM	CHOPPER
ENGROSS	GUYROPE	LETDOWN	ONSHORE	PUTTOCK	SINUOUS	UNKNOWN	CLAMPER
ENOLOGY	HADDOCK	LEUCOMA	ORATORY	QUINONE	SIRLOIN	UNLOOSE	CLAPPER
ENTROPY	HAGBOLT	LIEDOWN	ORINOCO	QUIXOTE	SITDOWN	UNQUOTE	CLIPPED
ENVIOUS	HAMMOCK	LIFTOFF	OSSEOUS	RACCOON	SOMEONE	UNSTOCK	CLIPPER
EPIDOTE	HANDOUT	LIMPOPO	OSTEOMA	RAGWORT	SORROWS	UPSHOOT	CLIPPIE
EPIGONE	HANGOUT	LINCOLN	OSTIOLE	RANCOUR	SPINOFF	VACUOLE	COCKPIT
EPISODE	HARBOUR	LISSOME	OUTCOME	RANGOON	SPINOZA	VACUOUS	CRAMPED
EPITOME	HARMONY	LOCKOUT	OUTDOOR	RAPPORT	SPYHOLE	VAMOOSE	CRAMPON
EPIZOON	HARPOON	LOGBOOK	OUTLOOK	RATIONS	STEROID	VARIOLA	CRAPPIE
ETHMOID	HARWOOD	LOGWOOD	OUTPOST	RAUCOUS	SUBJOIN	VARIOUS	CREEPER
EUPHONY	HASSOCK	LOOKOUT	OUTPOUR	RAVIOLI	SUBSOIL	VAUDOIS	CRIPPLE
EXPLODE	HATTOCK	LOWDOWN	OUTVOTE	RECTORY	SUCCOUR	VENDOME	CRISPIN
EXPLOIT	HAYFORK	LUGHOLE	OUTWORK	REDCOAT	SUCROSE	VENTOSE	CROPPED
EXPLORE	HAYLOFT	LUGWORM	OUTWORN	REDPOLL	SUFFOLK	VERBOSE	CROPPER
EYEHOLE	HEINOUS	MAFIOSO	OXBLOOD	REDWOOD	SUKKOTH	VERMONT	CRUMPET
EYESORE	HEMLOCK	MAGGOTY	PADDOCK	REFLOAT	SUMMONS	VICIOUS	CRUMPLE
FACTOID	HICKORY	MAHJONG	PADLOCK	REGROUP	SUNDOWN	VICTORY	CRUPPER
FACTORS	HIDEOUS	MALTOSE	PADRONE	REPROOF	SUNROOF	VISCOSE	DASHPOT
FACTORY	HIDEOUT	MAMMOTH	PALOOKA	REPROVE	SUPPORT	VISCOUS	DEADPAN
FAGGOTS	HILLOCK	MANGOLD	PANDORA	RESPOND	SUPPOSE	VOIVODE	DNIEPER

DROPPER	SCARPER	WHOPPER	BLURRED	ENTERIC	KINDRED	PALFREY	SQUARED
DUSTPAN	SCORPIO	WRAPPED	BOTARGO	ENTERON	LABORED	PANCRAS	SQUARES
ECLIPSE	SCRAPER	WRAPPER	BUCKRAM	ENTHRAL	LABORER	PANGRAM	STEARIC
ECTOPIA	SCRAPIE	XENOPUS	CABARET	EPIGRAM	LACERTA	PANURGE	STEARIN
ELLIPSE	SCRAPPY	ANTIQUE	CALDRON	EQUERRY	LAMPREY	PAPYRUS	STEERER
ESCAPEE	SCRUPLE	BAROQUE	CALORIC	ERITREA	LATERAL	PELORIA	STIRRED
EUPEPSY	SCUPPER	BEZIQUE	CALORIE	ESPARTO	LATERAN	PELORUS	STIRRUP
EXAMPLE	SEMIPRO	BRUSQUE	CALTROP	ETRURIA	LAYERED	PICARDY	SUGARED
EXEMPLA	SERAPIS	CACIQUE	CAMBRAI	EUTERPE	LEVERET	PIERROT	SUNTRAP
EYESPOT	SHAMPOO	LALIQUE	CAMBRIC	EXCERPT	LIBERAL	PILGRIM	SYCORAX
FELSPAR	SHARPEN	MACAQUE	CAMERON	EXPIRED	LIBERIA	PIZARRO	SYNERGY
FLAPPED	SHARPER	OBLIQUE	CAMORRA	EYEBROW	LIBERTY	PLEURAL	TABARET
FLAPPER	SHARPLY	OBLOQUY	CANTRIP	FAVORED	LITERAL	PLEURON	TABORET
FLEAPIT	SHEPPEY	OBSEQUY	CAPORAL	FEDERAL	LITURGY	POLARIS	TAMARIN
FLIPPER	SHINPAD	SALIQUE	CATARRH	FEMORAL	LOUVRED	POMEROL	TANCRED
FOOTPAD	SHIPPER	SUBAQUA	CATERER	FEVERED	LOWBROW	POMEROY	TANTRUM
FOREPAW	SHOPPER	ACCURSE	CENTRAL	FIGURES	LUCARNE	POMFRET	TATARIC
FRUMPLE	SKIDPAN	ACHERON	CENTRED	FILARIA	LUCERNE	PORTRAY	TAVERNA
GALIPOT	SKIPPED	ADMIRAL	CENTRIC	FIMBRIA	LUSTRUM	POTOROO	TAXFREE
GALOPIN	SKIPPER	ADMIRED	CENTRUM	FLEURET	MAGHREB	POVERTY	TEHERAN
GLIMPSE	SLAPPER	ADMIRER	CHAGRIN	FLEURON	MAIGRET	POWERED	TENDRIL
GRAMPUS	SLEEPER	ADVERSE	CHARRED	FORTRAN	MAJORCA	PRAIRIE	THEORBO
GRAPPLE	SLIPPED	AILERON	CHEERIO	FOXTROT	MALARIA	PROGRAM	THEOREM
GRAUPEL	SLIPPER	AINTREE	CHEVRON	FULCRUM	MASURKA	PUBERAL	TIMBREL
GROUPER	SNAPPER	AIRCREW	CHIRRUP	FUNERAL	MAZARIN	PUBERTY	TORTRIX
GROUPIE	SNIPPET	ALBERGO	CHLORAL	FUTURES	MAZURKA	PYLORUS	TOWARDS
HAIRPIN	SNOOPER	ALBERTA	CINEREA	GASTRIC	MEGARON	QUADRAT	TUMBREL
HARDPAN	STAMPED	ALBERTI	CLEARLY	GASTRIN	MENORAH	QUARREL	TUMBRIL
HELIPAD	STAMPER	ALCORAN	CLEARUP	GENERAL	MINARET	QUEERER	UNAIRED
HEXAPOD	STEEPEN	ALGERIA	COLORED	GENERIC	MINERAL	REBIRTH	UNCARED
HOTSPUR	STEEPLE	ALKORAN	COMFREY	GILLRAY	MINERVA	RECORDS	UNCURED
INDEPTH	STEEPLY	ALLERGY	CONTROL	GOMORRA	MINORCA	RECURVE	UNDERGO
INSIPID	STIPPLE	ALTERED	CORNROW	GROGRAM	MISERLY	REFEREE	UNEARTH
ISOSPIN	STIRPES	AMHARIC	COTERIE	GUMDROP	MISTRAL	REGARDS	UNHORSE
JACKPOT	STOPPED	ANAGRAM	COVERED	HAPORTH	MITHRAS	REMARRY	UNNERVE
JUNIPER	STOPPER	ANDIRON	COVERUP	HEPARIN	MODERNE	REMORSE	UNSCREW
KINGPIN	STRIPED	ANDORRA	CULPRIT	HEXARCH	MONARCH	RESERVE	UPSURGE
KNAPPER	STRIPER	ANTARES	CUMBRIA	HOGARTH	MONGREL	RESPRAY	UPWARDS
KNEEPAD	STRIPES	ANTHRAX	DEBORAH	HOMERIC	MUSKRAT	RETIRED	UTTERLY
MANIPLE	STROPHE	APPARAT	DECORUM	HUMDRUM	NATURAL	RETIREE	VENERER
MAZEPPA	STROPPY	APPAREL	DEMERGE	HUMERUS	NAVARIN	RETURNS	VENTRAL
MONOPLY	STUMPED	APTERAL	DEMERIT	HUNDRED	NAVARRE	REVERED	VETERAN
NINEPIN	SUNSPOT	APTERYX	DENDRON	ICTERIC	NEMORAL	REVERIE	VICEROY
NOTEPAD	SWAPPED	ARMORED	DESERTS	ICTERUS	NEUTRAL	REVERSE	WASTREL
OCCIPUT	SWEEPER	ARMORIC	DESERVE	IGNORED	NEUTRON	RICARDO	WATERED
OCTOPOD	SYNAPSE	ASCARID	DESTROY	ILLBRED	NIGERIA	ROBERTS	WAVERER
OCTOPUS	TALIPES	ASHTRAY	DEWDROP	IMMERGE	NOMBRIL	ROSARIO	WILFRED
OCTUPLE	TALIPOT	ASPERGE	DEXTRIN	IMMERSE	NONPROS	ROSTRAL	WINDROW
OEDIPUS	THUMPER	ASPIRIN	DIAGRAM	IMMORAL	NOSTRIL	ROSTRUM	WOLFRAM
OLYMPIA	TILAPIA	ASSURED	DIDEROT	IMPERIL	NOSTRUM	RUDERAL	ZAMORIN
OLYMPIC	TOPSPIN	ASSYRIA	DIEDRAL	INBURST	NUMERAL	RUMORED	ZYMURGY
OLYMPUS	TOSSPOT	ASTARTE	DISPRIN	INCURVE	NUMERIC	SAFFRON	ABBASID
OUTSPAN	TRAIPSE	ATHIRST	DIVERGE	INFARCT	NYNORSK	SALERMO	ABIOSIS
OVERPAY	TRAMPLE	ATTIRED	DIVERSE	INFERNO	OBSERVE	SAMARIA	ABYSSAL
PANOPLY	TRAPPED	AUBERGE	DIVORCE	INHERIT	OBVERSE	SAMURAI	ACCUSED
PARAPET	TRAPPER	AUSTRAL	DOLORES	INJURED	OESTRUS	SANGRIA	ACCUSER
PERSPEX	TRIPPER	AUSTRIA	EAGERLY	INNARDS	OFFERER	SATIRIC	ACHESON
PLAYPEN	TROOPER	AUTARKY	EARDRUM	INNERVE	OMICRON	SCHERZO	ADDISON
PLUMPER	TROUPER	BACARDI	EFFORCE	INSURER	ONEIRIC	SCLERAL	ADVISER
POLYPOD	TRUMPET	BALDRIC	ELDERLY	INTERIM	ONTARIO	SCOURER	ADVISOR
POLYPUS	UNHAPPY	BEGORRA	ELYTRON	INTERNE	ONWARDS	SCOURGE	AEROSOL
PRIAPUS	USURPER	BELARUS	EMBARGO	INVERSE	ORDERED	SEVERAL	ALYSSUM
PROSPER	VOLAPUK	BENARES	EMPEROR	INWARDS	ORDERLY	SEVERUS	AMNESIA
RELAPSE	WHIMPER	BERTRAM	EMPIRIC	ISOGRAM	ORPHREY	SHEARER	AMNESTY
SALTPAN	WHIPPED	BESHREW	ENDORSE	JAKARTA	OSBORNE	SOBERLY	APEPSIA
SANDPIT	WHIPPET	BESTREW	ENDURED	JOGTROT	OUTCROP	SPARROW	APHASIA
SCALPEL	WHISPER	BEVERLY	ENFORCE	KAMERAD	OUTGROW	SPLURGE	APHESIS
SCALPER	WHOOPEE	BIAFRAN	ENGORGE	KATORGA	OVERRUN	SPORRAN	APLASIA
SCAMPER	WHOOPER	BIZARRE	ENLARGE	KESTREL	PALERMO	SPURREY	APPOSED

ARIOSTO	EMBASSY	OVERSEE	TYLOSIS	BRANTUB	DIOPTRE	GODETIA	MILITIA
AROUSAL	EMERSON	PALISSY	ULYSSES	BREATHE	DOROTHY	GRAFTER	MINSTER
ARTISAN	EMULSIN	PARASOL	UNBOSOM	BRISTLE	DOUBTER	GRANTED	MINUTED
ARTISTE	EPHESUS	PARESIS	UTENSIL	BRISTLY	DRAFTED	GRANTEE	MINUTES
ASPASIA	EXPOSED	PEGASUS	VANESSA	BRISTOL	DRAFTEE	GREATEN	MINUTIA
ASSISTS	FILASSE	PERUSAL	VENISON	BRITTLE	DRASTIC	GREATLY	MISSTEP
AUGUSTA	FINESSE	PHRASAL	VINASSE	BRIXTON	DRIFTER	GRIFTER	MOBSTER
AUGUSTE	FLOTSAM	PHRASER	WHATSIT	BURETTE	DUNSTAN	GRISTLE	MOFETTE
BABYSIT	FOOTSIE	PICASSO	WHIMSEY	BURSTER	EJECTOR	GRISTLY	MOISTEN
BACKSET	FORESEE	PIOUSLY	WHITSUN	CAPITAL	ELASTIC	HABITAT	MOLOTOV
BAGASSE	FREESIA	PLEASED	WINDSOR	CAPITOL	ELASTIN	HALITUS	MONITOR
BANKSIA	FRETSAW	PLEASES	WORKSHY	CAPSTAN	ELECTED	HAMSTER	MONSTER
BELISHA	FRISSON	PLESSOR	XEROSIS	CARITAS	ELECTOR	HARDTOP	MOUNTED
BEMUSED	FROWSTY	PODESTA	ZAKUSKA	CAROTID	ELECTRA	HAUNTED	MOUNTIE
BENISON	FUCHSIA	POROSIS	ZYGOSIS	CAROTIN	ELECTRO	HEALTHY	MULATTO
BERGSON	FUCHSIN	POUSSIN	ZYMOSIS	CAUSTIC	EMPATHY	HEARTEN	MUNSTER
BIASSED	GAINSAY	PRESSED	ABATTIS	CHANTER	ENACTOR	HEELTAP	MUSETTE
BLESSED	GENESIS	PRIESTS	ABETTOR	CHAOTIC	ENTITLE	HEPATIC	MYCETES
BLESSES	GENISTA	PRUSSIC	ABLATOR	CHAPTER	EPISTLE	HERETIC	NAPHTHA
BLOSSOM	GIRASOL	PYROSIS	ACESTES	CHARTER	EQUATOR	HILLTOP	NAVETTE
BLOUSON	GLASSES	QUASSIA	ACHATES	CHASTEN	ERECTOR	HIPSTER	NECKTIE
BONESET	GREASER	QUONSET	ADAPTER	CHATTEL	ERRATIC	HOLSTER	NERITIC
BOURSIN	GRIMSBY	RAMESES	ADAPTOR	CHATTER	ERRATUM	HONITON	NIGHTIE
BROWSER	GROSSLY	REFUSAL	ADOPTED	CHEATER	EVENTER	HORATIO	NIGHTLY
BRUISED	GROUSER	REISSUE	AERATED	CHEETAH	EXACTLY	HYDATID	NONSTOP
BRUISER	HACKSAW	REPOSAL	AGISTOR	CHESTER	EXALTED	IDIOTIC	ODONTIC
CAISSON	HANDSAW	REVISED	AIRSTOP	CHINTZY	EXCITED	IMHOTEP	OERSTED
CANASTA	HANDSEL	REVISER	ALLSTAR	CHOCTAW	EXISTED	IMPETUS	OLDSTER
CATESBY	HANDSET	REVISIT	ALSATIA	CHORTLE	FACETED	INERTIA	OMENTUM
CELESTA	HEADSET	RIPOSTE	AMMETER	CLASTIC	FAINTED	JANITOR	OMITTED
CELESTE	HEARSAY	ROBESON	ANNATTO	CLATTER	FAINTLY	JOINTED	OPUNTIA
CHANSON	HONESTY	ROBUSTA	APHOTIC	CLUSTER	FAJITAS	JOINTER	ORBITAL
CHASSIS	IMPASSE	SAMISEN	APOSTLE	CLUTTER	FANATIC	JOINTLY	ORESTES
CHEESED	IMPASTO	SATISFY	AQUATIC	COASTAL	FAUSTUS	JUJITSU	ORONTES
CHELSEA	INCISOR	SCISSOR	ARBITER	COASTER	FIGHTER	JUPITER	OUTSTAY
CHIASMA	IONESCO	SILESIA	ARBUTUS	COCOTTE	FIRSTLY	KEARTON	OVERTAX
CHRISOM	IVRESSE	SIMPSON	ARIETTA	COLITIS	FIXATED	KENOTIC	PAESTUM
CHRISTY	JACKSON	SOROSIS	ASCETIC	COULTER	FLATTEN	KERATIN	PAINTED
CLASSIC	JAMESON	SOURSOP	ASCITES	COUNTED	FLATTER	KILOTON	PAINTER
CLOISON	JOCASTA	SPENSER	ASEPTIC	COUNTER	FLITTER	KINETIC	PALATAL
COARSEN	JOHNSON	SPLASHY	ASIATIC	COUNTRY	FLOATER	KNITTED	PALETTE
COUNSEL	KENOSIS	SPONSON	ATACTIC	COURTLY	FLUSTER	KNITTER	PALMTOP
COURSER	KHAMSIN	SPONSOR	AUDITOR	COVETED	FLUTTER	KNOTTED	PAROTIC
COURSES	KINESIS	SPOUSAL	AVESTAN	CREATED	FORSTER	KRYPTON	PAROTID
CRASSUS	KNESSET	SQUASHY	AVIATOR	CREATOR	FRANTIC	LANGTON	PAROTIS
CRIMSON	LIAISON	SQUISHY	BALATON	CRESTED	FRETTED	LAPUTAN	PENATES
CROESUS	LOCUSTS	STEPSON	BARYTES	CRITTER	FRITTER	LAVATER	PHAETON
CROSSED	MADISON	STETSON	BATHTUB	CROATIA	FRONTAL	LAYETTE	PHANTOM
CROSSLY	MAJESTY	SWANSEA	BEASTLY	CROFTER	FROSTED	LEGATEE	PHILTER
CRUISER	MALMSEY	SYCOSIS	BELATED	CROUTON	FUMETTE	LENGTHY	PHILTRE
CURTSEY	MATISSE	TABASCO	BEWITCH	CRYPTIC	GAGSTER	LESOTHO	PIASTRE
CYTISUS	MEIOSIS	TAMESIS	BIGOTED	CRYPTON	GALATEA	LIGHTEN	PICOTEE
DAMOSEL	MEISSEN	THIRSTY	BIGOTRY	CRYSTAL	GALETTE	LIGHTER	PILATUS
DEADSET	MÉTISSE	THOMSON	BIRETTA	CURATOR	GAROTTE	LIGHTLY	PINETUM
DEBASED	MILKSOP	THRISTY	BLASTED	CURETTE	GAVOTTE	LIMITED	PIPETTE
DEBUSSY	MINDSET	THYRSIS	BLASTER	CUVETTE	GAZETTE	LIMITER	PIVOTAL
DEHISCE	MITOSIS	THYSSEN	BLATTER	DAYSTAR	GELATIN	LINCTUS	PLANTAR
DEMESNE	MODESTY	TOOTSIE	BLISTER	DEBATER	GENETIC	LITOTES	PLANTED
DEPOSIT	MODISTE	TRANSIT	BLOATED	DEICTIC	GENITAL	LOBSTER	PLANTER
DEVISED	MORESBY	TRANSOM	BLOATER	DEMETER	GHASTLY	LUNATIC	PLASTER
DEVISEE	MORESCO	TREASON	BLOTTER	DEMOTIC	GHOSTLY	LUNETTE	PLASTIC
DIAPSID	MYIASIS	TRESSES	BLUNTED	DEVOTED	GLISTEN	MAESTRO	PLATTER
DISUSED	NEMESIA	TRIESTE	BLUNTLY	DEVOTEE	GLITTER	MAHATMA	PLAUTUS
DIVISOR	NEMESIS	TRIPSIS	BLUSTER	DIGITAL	GLOTTAL	MANATEE	PLEATED
DRESSED	NICOSIA	TROTSKY	BOASTER	DILATED	GLOTTIS	MANITOU	PLOTTER
DRESSER	ODYSSEY	TROUSER	BOLETUS	DILATOR	GLUTTON	MARATHA	POINTED
DYNASTY	OPOSSUM	TRYPSIN	BOLSTER	DILUTED	GLYPTAL	MARITAL	POINTER
ECDYSIS	OPPOSED	TUNISIA	BOOSTER	DINETTE	GLYPTIC	MEGATON	POLITIC
ECTASIS	OSMOSIS	TWINSET	BORSTAL	DIOPTER	GNOSTIC	MERITED	POOFTER

POSITIF	SENATOR	SWIFTER	ADJOURN	DELOUSE	MARQUEE	RESCUER	VULTURE
POULTRY	SESOTHO	SWIFTLY	AGROUND	DENTURE	MARQUIS	RESOUND	WARBURG
PRAETOR	SHASTRI	SYMPTOM	ALIQUID	DIFFUSE	MEASURE	RETOUCH	WETSUIT
PRATTLE	SHATTER	TABITHA	ALIQUOT	DISCUSS	MERCURY	ROEBUCK	YOGHURT
PRINTED	SHEATHE	TACITLY	AMPOULE	DISGUST	MISRULE	RORQUAL	ANGEVIN
PRINTER	SHELTER	TACITUS	ARMOURY	DISPUTE	MIXTURE	ROUAULT	AQUAVIT
PROCTOR	SHELTIE	TAGETES	ASEXUAL	DISRUPT	MOLLUSC	RUPTURE	ARRIVAL
PSALTER	SHIATSU	TAINTED	ASSAULT	DISTURB	MUGWUMP	SAGOUIN	ARRIVED
PUNSTER	SHIPTON	TAPSTER	ASTOUND	DRACULA	NEPTUNE	SALLUST	BATAVIA
PURITAN	SHOOTER	TELSTAR	AVEBURY	ENCRUST	NERVURE	SAMBUCA	BEDEVIL
PYRETIC	SHORTEN	TEMPTER	AZIMUTH	ENTHUSE	NETSUKE	SATSUMA	BEHAVED
PYRITES	SHORTLY	THEATER	BANBURY	ENTRUST	NEWBURY	SAVOURY	BELOVED
QUANTUM	SHOUTER	THEATRE	BANQUET	EPICURE	NOCTUID	SAWDUST	BOLIVAR
QUARTAN	SHUTTER	THISTLE	BASCULE	ERASURE	NONSUCH	SCAPULA	BOLIVIA
QUARTER	SHUTTLE	TIBETAN	BECAUSE	ESPOUSE	NONSUIT	SECLUDE	CADAVER
QUARTET	SHYSTER	TIGHTEN	BEDOUIN	EVACUEE	NURTURE	SEIZURE	CARAVAN
QUARTIC	SIGHTED	TIGHTLY	BEOWULF	EXCLUDE	OBSCURA	SENSUAL	CARAVEL
QUENTIN	SINATRA	TIMOTHY	BERMUDA	EXECUTE	OBSCURE	SEPPUKU	CHERVIL
QUESTER	SKELTER	TIPSTER	BETHUMB	EXHAUST	OBTRUDE	SHROUDS	CLEAVER
QUIETEN	SKEPTIC	TOASTED	BISCUIT	EXPOUND	OCCLUDE	SOJOURN	DELIVER
QUIETLY	SKITTER	TOASTER	BISMUTH	EXTRUDE	OFFDUTY	SPATULA	DISAVOW
QUIETUS	SKITTLE	TOLSTOY	BIVOUAC	FACTUAL	OROTUND	SPICULA	ELZEVIR
QUILTED	SLATTED	TONETIC	BOROUGH	FAILURE	OUTTURN	SPICULE	ENLIVEN
QUILTER	SLOTTED	TRACTOR	BOUQUET	FEATURE	OVIDUCT	SPROUTS	ESTIVAL
QUINTAL	SMARTEN	TRAITOR	BRAVURA	FERRULE	PARQUET	STATURE	ESTOVER
QUINTAN	SMARTIE	TRANTER	BULRUSH	FISSURE	PASTURE	STATUTE	FLIVVER
QUINTET	SMARTLY	TREATED	CAESURA	FISTULA	PEANUTS	STRAUSS	FLYOVER
QUITTER	SMATTER	TREETOP	CAGOULE	FISTULE	PENGUIN	SUBDUCT	FOREVER
RATATAT	SMELTER	TRESTLE	CALCULI	FIXTURE	PERCUSS	SUBDUED	GREAVES
REACTOR	SMITTEN	TRIATIC	CALMUCK	FORMULA	PERFUME	SUBFUSC	GROOVED
REALTOR	SMOOTHE	TRISTAN	CANNULA	FORTUNE	PERFUSE	SUBSUME	HANOVER
RECITAL	SNIFTER	TROTTER	CANTUAR	FOSSULA	PERJURE	SUCCUMB	HESHVAN
REENTER	SNORTER	TRUSTEE	CAPSULE	GARBURE	PERJURY	SUFFUSE	HOWEVER
REENTRY	SNORTLE	TWEETER	CAPTURE	GAUGUIN	PERTURB	SUNBURN	IMPAVID
REGATTA	SOCOTRA	TWISTED	CARDUUS	GESTURE	PERTUSE	TARQUIN	JEHOVAH
RELATED	SPARTAN	TWISTER	CAROUSE	GLOBULE	PICQUET	TEMPURA	MITZVAH
REPUTED	SPASTIC	TWITTER	CELLULE	GRADUAL	PICTURE	TESTUDO	MORAVIA
RICHTER	SPATTER	TWOSTEP	CENSURE	GRANULE	PINNULA	TEXTUAL	NATIVES
RICOTTA	SPECTER	UNDATED	CENTURY	GRAVURE	PLANURY	TEXTURE	NINEVEH
RIGHTLY	SPECTRE	UNHITCH	CHEQUER	HACHURE	PLUMULE	THROUGH	PALAVER
RISOTTO	SPITTLE	UNLATCH	CIRCUIT	HELLUVA	POLLUTE	TILBURY	POPOVER
RIVETED	SPLOTCH	VANITAS	CLIQUEY	HIRSUTE	POSTURE	TONGUES	RECOVER
ROASTER	SPOTTED	VAULTED	CLOSURE	HOMBURG	POTLUCK	TONSURE	REMOVAL
ROISTER	SPOTTER	VEDETTE	CLOTURE	HONOURS	PRELUDE	TORTURE	REMOVED
ROOFTOP	SPUTTER	VEGETAL	COLLUDE	IMPOUND	PREPUCE	TRADUCE	REMOVER
ROOSTER	STARTED	VISITOR	COLOURS	INCLUDE	PREQUEL	TRIBUNE	REVIVAL
ROSETTA	STARTER	WASHTUB	COMMUNE	INCRUST	PRESUME	TRIBUTE	REVIVER
ROSETTE	STARTLE	WATUTSI	COMMUTE	INHOUSE	PRIMULA	UNBOUND	SAMOVAR
ROTATOR	STENTOR	WEALTHY	COMPUTE	INTRUDE	PROCURE	UNCOUTH	SHEAVES
SAGITTA	STILTED	WEBSTER	CONCUSS	JACQUES	PRODUCE	UNEQUAL	SHELVED
SAINTLY	STILTON	WHARTON	CONDUCT	JONQUIL	PRODUCT	UNSOUND	SHELVES
SANCTUM	STOUTLY	WHEATEN	CONDUIT	KALMUCK	PROFUSE	UNSTUCK	SHRIVEL
SANCTUS	STRATUM	WHISTLE	CONFUSE	KIBBUTZ	PURPURA	UNTRUTH	SHRIVEN
SAUNTER	STRATUS	WHITTLE	CONJURE	KUMQUAT	PURSUER	UNUSUAL	SHRIVER
SCATTER	STRETCH	WINSTON	CONQUER	LACEUPS	PURSUIT	UNWOUND	SLEEVED
SCENTED	STUNTED	WIRETAP	CONSULT	LACQUER	PUSTULE	URUGUAY	STARVED
SCEPTER	STUTTER	WOOSTER	CONSUME	LANGUID	RACQUET	VALVULE	SYNOVIA
SCEPTIC	STYPTIC	WORKTOP	CORRUPT	LANGUOR	RAEBURN	VAPOURS	THIEVES
SCEPTRE	SUBATOM	WORSTED	COSTUME	LAWSUIT	RAPTURE	VELOURS	UNCIVIL
SCIATIC	SUDETEN	WREATHE	COUTURE	LEAGUER	REBOUND	VENTURE	UNCOVER
SCOOTER	SUMATRA	WRESTLE	CROQUET	LECTURE	RECLUSE	VERDURE	UNLOVED
SCOTTIE	SUZETTE	WRITTEN	CROQUIS	LEGPULL	RECOUNT	VERRUCA	UNMOVED
SCRATCH	SWARTHY	YANGTSE	CULTURE	LEISURE	RECRUIT	VETIVER	UNRAVEL
SCROTAL	SWEATED	YUCATAN	CURCUMA	LETTUCE	REDOUBT	VIADUCT	VETIVER
SCROTUM	SWEATER	ZAPOTEC	DASYURE	LINGUAL	REDOUND	VICTUAL	WHOEVER
SCUTTER	SWEETEN	ZEMSTVO	DEBAUCH	MANHUNT	REHOUSE	VIRGULE	YEREVAN
SCUTTLE	SWEETIE	ACCOUNT	DEBOUCH	MANTUAN	REMOULD	VIRTUAL	ALLOWED
SEATTLE	SWEETLY	ACCRUAL	DEFAULT	MARBURG	REMOUNT	VISTULA	ARCHWAY
SEMITIC	SWELTER	ACHTUNG	DEGAUSS	MARCUSE	REROUTE		BALDWIN

BEESWAX	DIPTYCH	AEOLIAN	BOWHEAD	CRYSTAL	FOREPAW	INHUMAN	MINIMAL
BEJEWEL	ERINYES	AFRICAN	BRADMAN	CSARDAS	FORTRAN	INITIAL	MINIMAX
CARAWAY	GIDDYUP	ALASKAN	BRAEMAR	CUMSHAW	FREEMAN	INSTEAD	MISLEAD
CHINWAG	HALCYON	ALCORAN	BRAHMAN	CURACAO	FREEWAY	INSULAR	MISPLAY
CUTAWAY	HONEYED	ALKORAN	BRENDAN	CUTAWAY	FRETSAW	IRANIAN	MISREAD
DOORWAY	ISOHYET	ALLSTAR	BRIGHAM	CYNICAL	FRISIAN	ISOGRAM	MISTRAL
EMBOWER	KINTYRE	ALMANAC	BRINJAL	DALILAH	FROGMAN	ITALIAN	MITHRAS
EMPOWER	KUFIYAH	ALUMNAE	BUCKRAM	DANTEAN	FRONTAL	IVORIAN	MITZVAH
FAIRWAY	MALAYAN	AMALGAM	BUGBEAR	DAYSTAR	FUNCHAL	JACKDAW	MODULAR
FARAWAY	MARRYAT	AMMONAL	BUMBOAT	DEADPAN	FUNERAL	JAZZMAN	MOHICAN
FREEWAY	MARSYAS	AMYGDAL	BURGLAR	DEBORAH	FUSTIAN	JEHOVAH	MUDEJAR
GAEKWAR	MARTYRS	ANAGRAM	BURNHAM	DECANAL	GAEKWAR	JOCULAR	MUDFLAP
GANGWAY	METAYER	ANANIAS	BUSHMAN	DECIMAL	GAINSAY	JOURNAL	MUNTJAC
GATEWAY	MONEYED	ANDAMAN	BUTANAL	DELILAH	GALAHAD	JUGULAR	MUSICAL
GETAWAY	NUREYEV	ANGOLAN	CADOGAN	DIAGRAM	GAMBIAN	JURYMAN	MUSKRAT
GOODWIN	PALMYRA	ANGULAR	CALABAR	DIEDRAL	GAMELAN	JUVENAL	MYANMAR
HALFWAY	PHARYNX	ANNULAR	CALIBAN	DIGITAL	GANGWAY	KAMERAD	MYCENAE
HALFWIT	POPEYED	ANTHRAX	CAMBRAI	DIGONAL	GATEWAY	KARAJAN	NARWHAL
HALLWAY	PTERYLA	APHTHAE	CANIDAE	DINGBAT	GENERAL	KINSMAN	NATURAL
HEADWAY	RELAYER	APOGEAN	CANTUAR	DIPOLAR	GENITAL	KNEECAP	NEBULAR
PARKWAY	SABAYON	APPARAT	CAPITAL	DISPLAY	GENTIAN	KNEEPAD	NEMORAL
PATHWAY	SAMOYED	APSIDAL	CAPORAL	DIURNAL	GETAWAY	KUFIYAH	NEUTRAL
PERIWIG	SAROYAN	APTERAL	CAPSTAN	DONEGAL	GILLRAY	KUMQUAT	NEWSMAN
POSTWAR	SPLAYED	AQUINAS	CARACAL	DOORMAN	GINGHAM	KURSAAL	NICAEAN
RAILWAY	SPRAYER	ARABIAN	CARACAS	DOORMAT	GLACIAL	LACTEAL	NIOBEAN
RENEWAL	VANDYKE	ARCHWAY	CARAVAN	DOORWAY	GLOTTAL	LACUNAE	NODULAR
ROADWAY	ASSIZES	AROUSAL	CARAWAY	DOUGLAS	GLYPTAL	LAOTIAN	NOMINAL
RUNAWAY	BAJAZET	ARRIVAL	CARDIAC	DRAWBAR	GOAHEAD	LAPUTAN	NOONDAY
SCRAWNY	BLITZED	ARSENAL	CARITAS	DUNCIAD	GODHEAD	LATERAL	NOSEBAG
SCREWED	BRITZKA	ARTISAN	CARLOAD	DUNSTAN	GOODMAN	LATERAN	NOSEGAY
SHAWWAL	BRONZED	ASEXUAL	CASPIAN	DUSTMAN	GORDIAN	LATVIAN	NOTEPAD
SLIPWAY	CITIZEN	ASHTRAY	CATALAN	DUSTPAN	GRADUAL	LESBIAN	NOUVEAU
SOMEWAY	DENIZEN	ASOCIAL	CATHEAD	EGGHEAD	GRAMMAR	LIBERAL	NUCLEAR
SPURWAY	DRIZZLE	ASSEGAI	CATSPAW	ELEGIAC	GRANDAD	LIMINAL	NUMERAL
STREWTH	DRIZZLY	ATAGHAN	CAVEMAN	ELYSIAN	GRAVLAX	LINEMAN	NUPTIAL
TAXIWAY	FLOOZIE	AUSTRAL	CENTRAL	ENTHRAL	GRECIAN	LINGUAL	NUTMEAT
THROWER	FRAZZLE	AUTOMAT	CHAMPAK	ENTREAT	GREYLAG	LINKMAN	OAKLEAF
THROWIN	FREEZER	AVESTAN	CHAPEAU	EPIGEAL	GROGRAM	LINNEAN	OARSMAN
THRUWAY	FRIZZLE	AXILLAR	CHAPMAN	EPIGRAM	GUINEAN	LIPREAD	OATMEAL
TIDEWAY	FRIZZLY	BAGHDAD	CHATEAU	ERISKAY	GUINEAS	LITERAL	OBADIAH
TRAMWAY	GRIZZLE	BAHAMAS	CHATHAM	ESCHEAT	GUNBOAT	LOCKJAW	OCELLAR
UNBOWED	GRIZZLY	BANANAS	CHEDDAR	ESTIVAL	GUNPLAY	LOGICAL	OFFBEAT
WALKWAY	HORIZON	BANDEAU	CHEETAH	ESTREAT	HABITAT	LOTHIAN	OFFLOAD
WIDOWED	JACUZZI	BATHMAT	CHILEAN	ETERNAL	HACKSAW	LYRICAL	OFFPEAK
WIDOWER	MUEZZIN	BATSMAN	CHINWAG	ETESIAN	HADRIAN	MACADAM	OPTICAL
WYSIWYG	POLIZEI	BEANBAG	CHLORAL	ETHICAL	HAITIAN	MAGICAL	OPTIMAL
ABRAXIS	PRETZEL	BEERMAT	CHOCTAW	ETONIAN	HALFWAY	MAILBAG	ORBITAL
AFFIXED	PREZZIE	BEESWAX	CHORDAE	FACTUAL	HALIFAX	MAILCAR	ORDINAL
APRAXIA	QUETZAL	BELGIAN	CINEMAS	FAIRWAY	HALLWAY	MAILMAN	ORPHEAN
HYPOXIA	SALAZAR	BELLMAN	CLACHAN	FAJITAS	HANDBAG	MALAYAN	ORTOLAN
INDEXER	SELTZER	BENTHAM	CLUBMAN	FARADAY	HANDSAW	MANTUAN	OTTOMAN
PYREXIA	SWIZZLE	BERCEAU	CLUNIAC	FARAWAY	HANGMAN	MANXMAN	OUTSPAN
RELAXED	WALTZER	BERTRAM	COASTAL	FATHEAD	HARDPAN	MARACAS	OUTSTAY
SYNAXIS	**7:6**	BESMEAR	COAXIAL	FEDERAL	HEADMAN	MARITAL	OUTWEAR
UNFIXED		BESPEAK	COELIAC	FELSPAR	HEADWAY	MARRYAT	OVARIAN
UNMIXED	ABAXIAL	BESTIAL	COMICAL	FEMORAL	HEARSAY	MARSHAL	OVEREAT
ACOLYTE	ABIDJAN	BIAFRAN	CONCEAL	FEYDEAU	HEELTAP	MARSYAS	OVERLAP
AMBOYNA	ABRAHAM	BIFOCAL	CONGEAL	FIGLEAF	HELICAL	MARTIAL	OVERLAY
ANALYST	ABYSMAL	BIGHEAD	CONICAL	FINICAL	HELIPAD	MARTIAN	OVERMAN
ANALYZE	ABYSSAL	BILLMAN	COONCAN	FIREMAN	HELLCAT	MAUGHAM	OVERPAY
ANNOYED	ACADIAN	BIRDMAN	COPYCAT	FLAGDAY	HESHVAN	MEDICAL	OVERTAX
ANODYNE	ACAUDAL	BIVOUAC	CORBEAU	FLATCAR	HESSIAN	MEERKAT	OXONIAN
ARRAYED	ACCRUAL	BOATMAN	CORDIAL	FLOTSAM	HIGHMAN	MENORAH	PACKMAN
CARLYLE	ACHAEAN	BOILEAU	CORNEAL	FLUVIAL	HILLMAN	MESSIAH	PAJAMAS
DECAYED	ACROBAT	BOLIVAR	CRANIAL	FLYLEAF	HOLIDAY	METICAL	PALATAL
DECRYPT	ACTINAL	BONDMAN	CREWMAN	FOOTMAN	HOTHEAD	MEXICAN	PALOMAR
DELAYED	ADAXIAL	BOOKMAN	CRIMEAN	FOOTPAD	IBERIAN	MILKMAN	PALUDAL
DIALYSE	ADMIRAL	BOOLEAN	CROWBAR	FORBEAR	ILLEGAL	MINERAL	PANCRAS
DIGLYPH	ADRENAL	BORSTAL	CRUCIAL	FOREMAN	IMMORAL	MINICAB	PANGRAM

PARKWAY	RETREAT	SUNBEAM	WALKWAY	BEDROCK	FORMICA	PERFECT	SUFFICE
PARTIAL	RETRIAL	SUNDIAL	WARHEAD	BESEECH	FOSSICK	PHONICS	SUNDECK
PASCHAL	REVIVAL	SUNTRAP	WASHDAY	BEWITCH	FURNACE	PHYSICS	SURFACE
PATHWAY	RHODIAN	SURCOAT	WATTEAU	BIOTECH	FUTTOCK	PIBROCH	SUSPECT
PATRIAL	ROADWAY	SURINAM	WEEKDAY	BULLACE	GARRICK	PINNACE	TABASCO
PAYLOAD	ROEDEAN	SURREAL	WHEREAS	BULLOCK	GIMMICK	PLIANCY	TACTICS
PEDICAB	RONDEAU	SWAGMAN	WHIPCAT	BURDOCK	GRIMACE	POLLACK	TAMPICO
PELICAN	RORQUAL	SYCORAX	WILDCAT	CADENCE	GUANACO	PORTICO	TAPIOCA
PERMIAN	ROSCIAN	TABLEAU	WILLIAM	CALMUCK	HADDOCK	POTENCY	TAPPICE
PERSIAN	ROSTRAL	TABULAR	WINDBAG	CANDACE	HAMMOCK	POTLACH	TENANCY
PERUSAL	ROULEAU	TAXICAB	WINGMAN	CANNOCK	HARLECH	POTLUCK	TERENCE
PHIDIAS	ROWBOAT	TAXIWAY	WIRETAP	CAPRICE	HARWICH	PREDICT	TERRACE
PHILEAS	RUDERAL	TEALEAF	WOLFRAM	CARIOCA	HASSOCK	PREFACE	TINTACK
PHRASAL	RUFFIAN	TEHERAN	WOODMAN	CARSICK	HATTOCK	PREFECT	TOBACCO
PIGMEAT	RUNAWAY	TELSTAR	WORKMAN	CASSOCK	HEMLOCK	PRELACY	TRADUCE
PINHEAD	RUSSIAN	TEMPLAR	YASHMAK	CHALICE	HENPECK	PREPUCE	TRISECT
PITHEAD	RWANDAN	TERTIAL	YEREVAN	COGENCY	HERRICK	PRIMACY	TROPICS
PIVOTAL	SABAEAN	TERTIAN	YUCATAN	COLLECT	HEXARCH	PRIVACY	TROUNCE
PLANTAR	SALAZAR	TEXTUAL	ZAIREAN	COMPACT	HILLOCK	PRODUCE	TRUANCY
PLATEAU	SALTPAN	THERMAL	ZAMBIAN	CONCOCT	HOGBACK	PRODUCT	TUSSOCK
PLEURAL	SAMOVAR	THOREAU	ALLENBY	CONDUCT	HOPSACK	PROJECT	UNBLOCK
PLOWMAN	SAMURAI	THRUWAY	ASCRIBE	CONNECT	HOSPICE	PROTECT	UNFROCK
POLECAT	SANDBAG	TIBETAN	ASTILBE	CONTACT	HUMMOCK	PURBECK	UNHITCH
PONTIAC	SANDMAN	TIDEWAY	BARNABY	CONVICT	IMPEACH	PUTTOCK	UNLATCH
POOHBAH	SAROYAN	TIMELAG	CARAMBA	COPPICE	INEXACT	RANSACK	UNSTICK
POPULAR	SAURIAN	TITULAR	CARNABY	CORNICE	INFANCY	RATPACK	UNSTOCK
PORCIAN	SCANDAL	TOLLMAN	CATESBY	CORRECT	INFARCT	REBECCA	UNSTUCK
PORTRAY	SCHOLAR	TONNEAU	COLOMBO	COSSACK	INFLECT	REDNECK	URGENCY
POSTBAG	SCLERAL	TOPCOAT	COLUMBA	COWLICK	INFLICT	REELECT	VACANCY
POSTMAN	SCROTAL	TOPICAL	CORDOBA	CRANACH	INSPECT	REFLECT	VALENCE
POSTWAR	SECONAL	TOWHEAD	DISROBE	CREVICE	INVOICE	REFRACT	VALENCY
POTOMAC	SECULAR	TRAMCAR	EARLOBE	CUTBACK	IONESCO	REGENCY	VERDICT
POTSDAM	SEMINAL	TRAMWAY	ENTEBBE	DEBAUCH	JAMAICA	REJOICE	VERRUCA
POUNDAL	SEMINAR	TRISHAW	GRIMSBY	DEBOUCH	JUSTICE	REPLACE	VIADUCT
PREDIAL	SENEGAL	TRISTAN	JELLABA	DECENCY	KALMUCK	REPLICA	WALLACE
PREHEAT	SENSUAL	TRIVIAL	LULLABY	DEFENCE	KILLICK	RESPECT	WARBECK
PROGRAM	SERBIAN	TRUCIAL	MICROBE	DEFLECT	LATTICE	RESTOCK	WARLOCK
PROTEAN	SERCIAL	TRUMEAU	MORESBY	DEFROCK	LEACOCK	RETOUCH	WARWICK
PUBERAL	SEVERAL	TUBULAR	NAIROBI	DEFUNCT	LETTUCE	RETRACE	WEDLOCK
PULLMAN	SHARIAH	TUESDAY	PLACEBO	DEHISCE	LICENCE	RETRACT	WENLOCK
PURITAN	SHAWWAL	TUGBOAT	PUNJABI	DERRICK	MAJORCA	ROEBUCK	WETBACK
PYJAMAS	SHELLAC	TUTELAR	REDOUBT	DETRACT	MALACCA	ROLLICK	WINNOCK
QUADRAT	SHERMAN	TYPICAL	SAPROBE	DEVOICE	MATTOCK	ROMANCE	WRYNECK
QUARTAN	SHINPAD	UGANDAN	SASSABY	DIALECT	MEACOCK	ROSTOCK	ACARIDA
QUETZAL	SHOWMAN	UMBRIAN	SCRUBBY	DIPLOCK	MINORCA	ROWLOCK	AGGRADE
QUINTAL	SICKBAY	UNCLEAN	STANDBY	DIPTYCH	MOLUCCA	SAMBUCA	ALAMODE
QUINTAN	SIDECAR	UNCLEAR	THEORBO	DISSECT	MONARCH	SCHLOCK	ALCALDE
QUONDAM	SIMILAR	UNEQUAL	THEREBY	DIVORCE	MORESCO	SCHMUCK	ALIDADE
RACHIAL	SINDBAD	UNUSUAL	WALLABY	DUNNOCK	MOROCCO	SCIENCE	ALREADY
RACHMAN	SKIDDAW	URANIAN	WHEREBY	EDIFICE	MORTICE	SCRATCH	ANYBODY
RADICAL	SKIDPAN	URUGUAY	WOULDBE	EFFORCE	MUDPACK	SCREECH	ASTRIDE
RAILWAY	SLIPWAY	UTOPIAN	ABSENCE	EMBRACE	NEGLECT	SCRUNCH	AVOCADO
RAMADAN	SNOWMAN	UXORIAL	ADJUNCT	ENFORCE	NIBLICK	SEASICK	BACARDI
RANIDAE	SOMEWAY	VAGINAL	ADVANCE	ENHANCE	NONSUCH	SECRECY	BALLADE
RATATAT	SPANDAU	VANITAS	AFFLICT	EROTICA	NORWICH	SERVICE	BASTIDE
REALGAR	SPARTAN	VATICAN	AIDANCE	ESSENCE	OARLOCK	SETBACK	BEDSIDE
RECITAL	SPATIAL	VAUGHAN	AIRLOCK	ETTRICK	OFFENCE	SHYLOCK	BELINDA
REDCOAT	SPECIAL	VEGETAL	AIRSICK	EUSTACE	ORIFICE	SILENCE	BERMUDA
REDHEAD	SPORRAN	VENTRAL	ALDRICH	EXTINCT	ORINOCO	SIROCCO	BIOCIDE
REFLOAT	SPOUSAL	VERONAL	AMERICA	EXTRACT	OSTRICH	SPINACH	BOUTADE
REFUSAL	SPURWAY	VERULAM	AMTRACK	FAIENCE	OUTBACK	SPLOTCH	BRAVADO
REGULAR	STELLAR	VETERAN	ANTIOCH	FALLACY	OUTFACE	SQUELCH	BRIGADE
REMBLAI	STENGAH	VICINAL	ARABICA	FELUCCA	OVERACT	SQUINCH	BROCADE
REMOVAL	STERNAL	VICTUAL	ASKANCE	FETLOCK	OVIDUCT	STATICS	BROMIDE
RENEWAL	STOICAL	VIETNAM	ATTRACT	FINANCE	PADDOCK	STAUNCH	BURUNDI
REPOSAL	STOPGAP	VINEGAR	AVARICE	FINBACK	PADLOCK	STOMACH	BUSHIDO
RESPRAY	STYGIAN	VIRELAY	BALANCE	FLAUNCH	PATRICK	STRETCH	CALENDS
RETINAL	SUBADAR	VIRTUAL	BANNOCK	FLOUNCE	PEACOCK	SUBDUCT	CANDIDA
RETREAD	SUBEDAR	WALKMAN	BARRACK	FLUENCY	PENANCE	SUBJECT	CANDIDE

CARBIDE	PERFIDY	ALTERED	BLASTED	BRUISED	CHICKEN	COVERED	DEVOTED
CASCADE	PERVADE	ALTHAEA	BLASTER	BRUISER	CHIGGER	COVETED	DEVOTEE
CATHODE	PICARDY	AMBAGES	BLATHER	BRUSHER	CHILLER	COWSHED	DIBBLER
CEILIDH	PINTADO	AMMETER	BLATTER	BUBBLES	CHIMNEY	CRACKED	DILATED
CESTODE	PLEIADE	ANISEED	BLEEPER	BUCKLER	CHIPPED	CRACKER	DILATER
CHARADE	PRECEDE	ANNOYED	BLENDER	BUILDER	CHIPPER	CRAMMED	DILUTED
COCKADE	PRELUDE	ANNULET	BLESSED	BULLPEN	CHOPPER	CRAMMER	DIMPLED
COLLIDE	PRESIDE	ANOTHER	BLESSES	BUNGLER	CHOWDER	CRAMPED	DIOPTER
COLLUDE	PROSODY	ANTARES	BLETHER	BURGHER	CHUFFED	CRANMER	DISOBEY
COMMODE	PROVIDE	ANTIBES	BLINDER	BURSTER	CHUKKER	CRASHES	DISUSED
COMMODO	RAWHIDE	ANTIGEN	BLINKER	BUSHMEN	CHUNDER	CRAWLER	DITTIES
COMRADE	RECORDS	APPAREL	BLISTER	BUSTLER	CHUNNEL	CREATED	DIVIDED
CONCEDE	REGARDS	APPLIED	BLITHER	BUSTLES	CHUTNEY	CREEPER	DIVINER
CONFIDE	RHONDDA	APPOSED	BLITZED	BUTCHER	CINEREA	CRESTED	DNIEPER
CORRIDA	RICARDO	AQUIFER	BLOATED	CABARET	CIRCLET	CRICKET	DOLORES
CORRODE	RIGVEDA	ARBITER	BLOATER	CABINET	CITADEL	CRICKEY	DOODLER
COWHIDE	RIPTIDE	ARCHAEA	BLOCKED	CADAVER	CITIZEN	CRITTER	DOORKEY
CRUSADE	ROTUNDA	ARMORED	BLOCKER	CALIBER	CITROEN	CROAKER	DOPPLER
CUSTODY	ROULADE	ARRAYED	BLOOMER	CALOMEL	CIVVIES	CROCHET	DOSSIER
CYANIDE	SACCADE	ARRIVED	BLOOPER	CALUMET	CLAMBER	CROCKET	DOUBLES
DEGRADE	SEASIDE	ARUNDEL	BLOTTER	CANDIED	CLAMPER	CROCKET	DOUBLET
DERONDA	SECLUDE	ASCITES	BLUBBER	CANTEEN	CLANGER	CROFTER	DOUBTER
DIOXIDE	SECONDS	ASHAMED	BLUNDER	CARAMEL	CLAPPER	CROOKED	DOWAGER
EBBTIDE	SHROUDS	ASSIZES	BLUNTED	CARAVEL	CLATTER	CROONER	DRAFTED
EFFENDI	SQUADDY	ASSUMED	BLURRED	CARGOES	CLEANER	CROPPED	DRAFTEE
EPISODE	SUBSIDE	ASSURED	BLUSHER	CARRIED	CLEAVER	CROPPER	DRAGNET
EXCLUDE	SUBSIDY	ASUNDER	BLUSTER	CARRIER	CLICKER	CROQUET	DRAINED
EXPLODE	SUICIDE	ATELIER	BOARDER	CARRIES	CLIMBER	CROSIER	DREADED
EXTRUDE	TESTUDO	ATTIRED	BOASTER	CARTIER	CLINGER	CROSSED	DREAMER
EYELIDS	THREADS	AVENGER	BOBSLED	CASHIER	CLINKER	CROWDED	DREDGER
FLORIDA	TOPSIDE	AVOIDER	BOLONEY	CASTLED	CLIPPED	CRUISER	DRESDEN
FORBADE	TORNADE	BABBLER	BOLSTER	CATCHER	CLIPPER	CRUMPET	DRESSED
FRIENDS	TORNADO	BACKSET	BONESET	CATERER	CLIQUEY	CRUPPER	DRESSER
GAMBADO	TORPEDO	BAFFLED	BOOKIES	CELEBES	CLOBBER	CRUSHED	DRIBLET
GIRONDE	TORPIDS	BAJAZET	BOOKLET	CENTRED	CLOTHED	CRUSHER	DRIFTER
GORSEDD	TORSADE	BALONEY	BOOSTER	CHAINED	CLOTHES	CURDLED	DRINKER
GRENADA	TOWARDS	BANQUET	BOOTLEG	CHALDEE	CLOUDED	CURRIED	DROPLET
GRENADE	TRAGEDY	BANSHEE	BOTTLED	CHALKER	CLUMBER	CURTSEY	DROPPER
GROUNDS	TRIPODY	BARONET	BOTTLES	CHAMBER	CLUSTER	DABBLER	DRUGGED
HAGGADA	UNREADY	BARRIER	BOUCLÉE	CHAMFER	CLUTTER	DAIMLER	DRUGGET
HYMNODY	UPGRADE	BARYTES	BOULDER	CHANCEL	COARSEN	DAMAGED	DRUMMER
IMPLODE	UPWARDS	BASINET	BOUNCER	CHANGED	COASTER	DAMAGES	DRUNKEN
INCLUDE	VIVALDI	BAYONET	BOUNDED	CHANGES	COBBLED	DAMOSEL	DURAMEN
INNARDS	VOIVODE	BEACHED	BOUNDEN	CHANNEL	COBBLER	DAMPIER	DWELLER
INROADS	WAYSIDE	BEACHES	BOUNDER	CHANTER	COCHLEA	DAPPLED	EARLIER
INTRUDE	YAOUNDE	BEARDED	BOUQUET	CHAPLET	COCKLES	DAWDLER	EARTHEN
INWARDS	ABASHED	BEATLES	BOWDLER	CHAPPED	COCKNEY	DAZZLED	ELECTED
ISLANDS	ABDOMEN	BEHAVED	BRACKEN	CHAPTER	COLLEEN	DEADSET	EMBOWER
JOYRIDE	ACCUSED	BEJEWEL	BRACKET	CHARGED	COLLIER	DEBASED	EMPANEL
KALENDS	ACCUSER	BELATED	BRANDED	CHARGER	COLONEL	DEBATER	EMPOWER
KANNADA	ACESTES	BELLEEK	BRANDER	CHARGES	COLORED	DEBRIEF	ENDOGEN
KENNEDY	ACHATES	BELOVED	BRAWLER	CHARLES	COMFREY	DECAYED	ENDURED
LAGONDA	ADAPTER	BEMUSED	BRAZIER	CHARLEY	COMPLEX	DECIBEL	ENGAGED
LAMBADA	ADMIRED	BENARES	BREADED	CHARMED	CONIFER	DECIDED	ENGINED
LIQUIDS	ADMIRER	BENCHER	BREAKER	CHARMER	CONQUER	DECIDER	ENLIVEN
MAENADS	ADOPTED	BERSEEM	BREEDER	CHARNEL	CORONER	DECODER	ENRAGED
MANMADE	ADORNED	BESHREW	BRENNER	CHARRED	CORONET	DECREED	EPAULET
MATILDA	ADVISER	BESIDES	BRIDGES	CHARTER	COTTIER	DEFACED	EPITHET
MIRANDA	AERATED	BESTREW	BRIDGET	CHASTEN	COUCHÉE	DEFILED	ERINYES
NITRODE	AFFIXED	BETIMES	BRIDLER	CHATTEL	COULTER	DEFINED	ERITREA
NUCLIDE	AINTREE	BETOKEN	BRIDLES	CHATTER	COUNSEL	DEGREES	ESCAPEE
OBTRUDE	AIRCREW	BETWEEN	BRISKET	CHAUCER	COUNTED	DELAYED	ESSENES
OCCLUDE	ALARMED	BIASSED	BROADEN	CHEAPEN	COUNTER	DELIBES	ESTOVER
OFFSIDE	ALBUMEN	BIGOTED	BROILER	CHEATER	COUPLER	DELIVER	ETAPLES
ONWARDS	ALIGNED	BITUMEN	BRONZED	CHECKED	COUPLET	DELUDED	EVACUEE
ORLANDO	ALKANET	BLABBER	BROTHEL	CHEESED	COURBET	DEMETER	EVANDER
OUTSIDE	ALLEGED	BLACKEN	BROTHER	CHELSEA	COURIER	DENIZEN	EVENTER
OVICIDE	ALLOWED	BLADDER	BROWNED	CHEQUER	COURSER	DEVISED	EXALTED
PENTODE	ALMONER	BLANKET	BROWSER	CHESTER	COURSES	DEVISEE	EXISTED

EXPIRED	FROSTED	HARRIET	KLEENEX	MERCIES	OUTLIER	POOFTER	REGIMEN
EXPOSED	FUDDLED	HATCHET	KLINKER	MERITED	OVERFED	POPEYED	RELATED
EZEKIEL	FURRIER	HAULIER	KNACKER	MERRIER	OVERSEE	POPOVER	RELAXED
FACETED	FURTHER	HAUNTED	KNAPPER	MESSIER	PADDLER	POTHEEN	RELAYER
FAINTED	FUTURES	HAYSEED	KNEELER	METAYER	PAINTED	POWERED	REMODEL
FALAFEL	GABBLER	HEADSET	KNELLER	METTLED	PAINTER	PREMIER	REMOVED
FALSIES	GABRIEL	HEARKEN	KNESSET	MICHAEL	PAISLEY	PREQUEL	REMOVER
FANCIED	GAGSTER	HEARTEN	KNICKER	MIDWEEK	PALAVER	PRESSED	REPUTED
FANCIER	GALATEA	HEATHEN	KNITTED	MINARET	PALFREY	PRETZEL	REQUIEM
FANGLED	GALILEE	HEATHER	KNITTER	MINDSET	PALSIED	PREVIEW	RESCUER
FARRIER	GALILEO	HEAVIER	KNOCKER	MINSTER	PANACEA	PRICKED	RETIRED
FARTHER	GAMBLER	HECKLER	KNOTTED	MINUTED	PANGAEA	PRICKER	RETIREE
FASTNET	GARBLED	HENNAED	LABORED	MINUTES	PANNIER	PRINCES	REVELER
FAVORED	GENTEEL	HERRIES	LABORER	MISDEED	PANTHER	PRINTED	REVERED
FEATHER	GIMBLET	HILLMEN	LACQUER	MISSTEP	PANTIES	PRINTER	REVISED
FEIGNED	GLACIER	HINDLEG	LAMPREY	MOBSTER	PARAPET	PRITHEE	REVISER
FEVERED	GLADDEN	HIPSTER	LANGLEY	MOISTEN	PARCHED	PROBLEM	REVIVER
FIANCÉE	GLASSES	HOARDER	LATCHET	MOITHER	PARQUET	PROCEED	RICHTER
FIDDLER	GLAZIER	HOLSTER	LATIMER	MONEYED	PARSLEY	PROFFER	RIDDLED
FIELDER	GLEANER	HONEYED	LAUNDER	MONGREL	PARTNER	PRONGED	RIDDLER
FIFTEEN	GLIMMER	HOWEVER	LAVATER	MONSTER	PASTIES	PROPHET	RINGLET
FIGHTER	GLISTEN	HUMBLES	LAYERED	MOORHEN	PEBBLES	PROSPER	RIVETED
FIGURES	GLITTER	HUNCHED	LEAFLET	MOTTLED	PEDDLER	PROUDER	RIVULET
FILCHER	GNARLED	HUNDRED	LEAGUER	MOULDED	PEDICEL	PROWLER	ROASTER
FISHNET	GOBBLER	HURDLER	LEANDER	MOULDER	PENATES	PRYTHEE	ROISTER
FIXATED	GOGGLES	HURDLES	LEARNED	MOUNTED	PERIGEE	PSALTER	RONTGEN
FLANKER	GOMBEEN	HURRIED	LEARNER	MOURNER	PERPLEX	PUNCHED	ROOSTER
FLANNEL	GOODIES	HUSTLER	LEATHER	MUDDLED	PERRIER	PUNCHER	ROSACEA
FLAPPED	GOOLIES	HYPOGEA	LEGATEE	MUFFLED	PERSPEX	PUNSTER	ROTIFER
FLAPPER	GOURMET	IGNORED	LEVERET	MUFFLER	PHILTER	PURLIEU	ROUGHEN
FLASHER	GRAFTER	ILLBRED	LIGHTEN	MUNSTER	PHRASER	PURSUER	ROUNDED
FLATLET	GRAINED	IMHOTEP	LIGHTER	MUTAGEN	PICKLED	PURVIEW	ROUNDEL
FLATTEN	GRAINER	IMPLIED	LIKENED	MYCETES	PICKLER	PUTTEES	ROUNDER
FLATTER	GRANDEE	INCOMER	LIMITED	MYNHEER	PICOTEE	PUZZLED	ROUTIER
FLECKED	GRANTED	INDEXER	LIMITER	NAILBED	PICQUET	PUZZLER	RUFFLED
FLECKER	GRANTEE	INFIDEL	LINSEED	NANKEEN	PIERCED	PYRITES	RUFFLER
FLEDGED	GRAPNEL	INHALER	LITCHEE	NARTHEX	PIERCER	QUARREL	RUMBLER
FLEURET	GRAUPEL	INJURED	LITOTES	NATCHEZ	PIGWEED	QUARTER	RUMORED
FLICKER	GREASER	INSIDER	LOBSTER	NATIVES	PIKELET	QUARTET	RUMPLED
FLIPPER	GREATEN	INSIDES	LORELEI	NECKLET	PILCHER	QUEERER	RUSTLER
FLITTER	GREAVES	INSURER	LOUNGER	NEEDLES	PINCHED	QUESTER	SADDLER
FLIVVER	GREENER	INTEGER	LOURDES	NEITHER	PIONEER	QUICKEN	SAMISEN
FLOATER	GRENDEL	INVADER	LOUVRED	NINEVEH	PITCHED	QUICKER	SAMOYED
FLODDEN	GRIFTER	IPOMOEA	LUCIFER	NOBBLED	PITCHER	QUIETEN	SAMPLER
FLOGGER	GRILLED	ISHMAEL	LURCHER	NOBBLER	PLANNED	QUILTED	SARACEN
FLOODED	GRINDER	ISOHYET	LYMNAEA	NOMINEE	PLANNER	QUILTER	SATCHEL
FLUNKEY	GROINED	IVORIEN	LYNCHET	NOODLES	PLANTED	QUINTET	SAUNTER
FLUSHED	GROLIER	JACQUES	MAGHREB	NOTCHED	PLANTER	QUITTER	SAVAGES
FLUSTER	GROMMET	JAMMIES	MAIGRET	NUMBLES	PLASTER	QUONSET	SCABIES
FLUTTER	GROOVED	JEEPNEY	MALMSEY	NUREYEV	PLATTER	RACQUET	SCALPEL
FLYOVER	GROUPER	JELLIED	MANAGER	NYMPHET	PLAYLET	RADDLED	SCALPER
FOLLIES	GROUSER	JEWELER	MANATEE	OARSMEN	PLAYPEN	RAFFLES	SCAMPER
FORAMEN	GROWLER	JEZEBEL	MARBLED	OBLIGED	PLEADER	RAGWEED	SCANNER
FORELEG	GRUMMET	JOINTED	MARBLES	OCTOBER	PLEASED	RAMBLER	SCARLET
FORESEE	GUARDED	JOINTER	MARCHER	ODYSSEY	PLEASES	RAMESES	SCARPER
FOREVER	GUILDER	JOURNEY	MARINER	OERSTED	PLEATED	RANCHER	SCATTER
FORSTER	GUZZLER	JUBILEE	MARQUEE	OFFERER	PLODDER	RAPHAEL	SCENTED
FORTIES	HACKLES	JUGGLER	MARRIED	OFFICER	PLOTTER	RATCHET	SCEPTER
FOUNDER	HACKNEY	JUMBLED	MARTLET	OFFICES	PLUMBER	RATTEEN	SCHEMER
FREEZER	HAIRNET	JUMBLES	MATCHED	OLDSTER	PLUMMET	RATTLER	SCOFFER
FRESHEN	HALOGEN	JUNIPER	MATCHET	OMITTED	PLUMPER	RAVAGES	SCOOTER
FRESHER	HAMSTER	JUPITER	MATINEE	OPPOSED	PLUNDER	RECOVER	SCOURER
FRESHET	HANDLED	KEROGEN	MATTHEW	ORACLES	PLUNGER	REDUCED	SCOWDER
FRETTED	HANDLER	KESTREL	MAUNDER	ORANGES	POACHER	REDUCER	SCRAPER
FRILLED	HANDSEL	KIELDER	MAYWEED	ORDERED	POINTED	REENTER	SCREWED
FRINGED	HANDSET	KINDRED	MEANDER	ORESTES	POINTER	REFEREE	SCRIBER
FRISBEE	HANGMEN	KINGLET	MEASLES	ORONTES	POLIZEI	REFINED	SCULLER
FRITTER	HANOVER	KITCHEN	MEDDLER	ORPHREY	POLYMER	REFINER	SCUPPER
FROEBEL	HARRIER	KLAVIER	MEISSEN	OSSELET	POMFRET	REFUGEE	SCUTTER

220

SEAWEED	SLIPPER	STABLES	TABORET	TRIMMER	WATCHER	ENGRAFT	BOROUGH
SEDUCER	SLITHER	STAFFER	TACKLER	TRINKET	WATERED	FALSIFY	BOTARGO
SEEDBED	SLOBBER	STAGGER	TAGETES	TRIPLET	WATTLES	FORTIFY	BOTTEGA
SEETHED	SLOGGER	STAINED	TAINTED	TRIPLEX	WAVERER	GIRAFFE	BURBAGE
SELTZER	SLOSHED	STAINER	TALIPES	TRIPPER	WEALDEN	GLORIFY	CABBAGE
SERRIED	SLOTTED	STALKED	TANAGER	TROCHEE	WEATHER	GRATIFY	CARNAGE
SETTLED	SLUMBER	STALKER	TANCRED	TRODDEN	WEBSTER	HAYLOFT	CHICAGO
SETTLER	SMACKER	STAMMER	TANGIER	TROLLEY	WELLIES	HORRIFY	COINAGE
SHAGGED	SMALLER	STAMPED	TANGLED	TROOPER	WHACKED	JUSTIFY	COLLAGE
SHARPEN	SMARTEN	STAMPER	TAPSTER	TROTTER	WHACKER	KHALIFA	COLLEGE
SHARPER	SMASHED	STANLEY	TARSIER	TROUPER	WHEATEN	KICKOFF	CONSIGN
SHATTER	SMASHER	STAPLER	TATTLER	TROUSER	WHEELED	LIFTOFF	CORKAGE
SHEARER	SMATTER	STARLET	TAXFREE	TRUCKER	WHEELER	LIQUEFY	CORSAGE
SHEAVES	SMELTER	STARTED	TEACHER	TRUDGEN	WHETHER	MAGNIFY	CORTEGE
SHEBEEN	SMITHER	STARTER	TELPHER	TRUMPET	WHIMPER	MASTIFF	COTINGA
SHELLED	SMITTEN	STARVED	TEMPLET	TRUSTEE	WHIMSEY	MIDRIFF	COTTAGE
SHELLEY	SMOLDER	STEAMED	TEMPTER	TUMBLER	WHINGER	MIDWIFE	COURAGE
SHELTER	SMOTHER	STEAMER	TENNIEL	TUMBREL	WHIPPED	MOLLIFY	CURRAGH
SHELVED	SMUDGED	STEEPEN	TERRIER	TURNKEY	WHIPPET	MORTIFY	DEMERGE
SHELVES	SNAPPER	STEERER	THEATER	TWEETER	WHISKER	MUMMIFY	DERANGE
SHEPPEY	SNARLER	STEMMED	THEOREM	TWIGGER	WHISKEY	MYSTIFY	DIVERGE
SHERBET	SNEAKER	STEPHEN	THICKEN	TWINSET	WHISPER	NULLIFY	DIVULGE
SHIMMER	SNICKER	STEPNEY	THICKET	TWISTED	WHITHER	PETRIFY	DOMINGO
SHIPPER	SNIFFER	STICKER	THIEVES	TWISTER	WHOEVER	PLAYOFF	DUNNAGE
SHIRKER	SNIFTER	STIFFEN	THINKER	TWITTER	WHOOPEE	PONTIFF	ECOLOGY
SHIRLEY	SNIGGER	STILTED	THINNER	TWOSTEP	WHOOPER	PUTREFY	EMBARGO
SHOCKED	SNIPPET	STINGER	THITHER	ULYSSES	WHOPPER	QUALIFY	ENGORGE
SHOCKER	SNOOKER	STINKER	THROWER	UMPTEEN	WIDOWED	RECTIFY	ENLARGE
SHOOTER	SNOOPER	STIRPES	THUGGEE	UNAIDED	WIDOWER	SALSIFY	ENOLOGY
SHOPPER	SNORKEL	STIRRED	THUMPER	UNAIRED	WILFRED	SATISFY	EXPUNGE
SHORTEN	SNORTER	STOLLEN	THUNDER	UNARMED	WILLIES	SCARIFY	FARRAGO
SHOUTER	SOCAGER	STONKER	THYSSEN	UNASKED	WITCHES	SCRUFFY	FILINGS
SHRIVEL	SOFABED	STOPPED	TICKLER	UNBOWED	WIZENED	SELLOFF	FIXINGS
SHRIVEN	SOLDIER	STOPPER	TIDDLER	UNCARED	WOOLLEN	SENDOFF	FOLIAGE
SHRIVER	SOUNDED	STORIED	TIERCEL	UNCOVER	WOOSTER	SHERIFF	FOOTAGE
SHUDDER	SOUNDER	STORIES	TIERCET	UNCURED	WORKMEN	SHOWOFF	FOREIGN
SHUTTER	SOUTHEY	STRIDES	TIGHTEN	UNDATED	WORRIED	SIGNIFY	GAMBOGE
SHYSTER	SOZZLED	STRIKER	TIMBREL	UNFADED	WORRIER	SPECIFY	GARBAGE
SICKBED	SPADGER	STRIPED	TINGLER	UNFIXED	WORSTED	SPINOFF	GEOLOGY
SIGHTED	SPANDEX	STRIPER	TIPPLER	UNITIES	WOTCHER	SQUIFFY	HAULAGE
SIMPLER	SPANIEL	STRIPES	TIPSTER	UNLADEN	WOUNDED	STUPEFY	HERBAGE
SIMPLEX	SPANKER	STRUDEL	TOASTED	UNLINED	WRAPPED	TAKEOFF	HIDALGO
SINGLES	SPANNER	STUDDED	TOASTER	UNLOVED	WRAPPER	TERRIFY	HOSTAGE
SINGLET	SPATTER	STUDIED	TODDLER	UNMIXED	WRECKED	TESTIFY	IMMERGE
SIXTEEN	SPEAKER	STUFFED	TOLKIEN	UNMOVED	WRECKER	TORREFY	IMPINGE
SIZZLER	SPECIES	STUMPED	TONGUES	UNNAMED	WRINGER	VERSIFY	INDULGE
SKELTER	SPECTER	STUNNER	TOOTHED	UNOWNED	WRITTEN	VITRIFY	INNINGS
SKILLED	SPELLER	STUNTED	TOUCHED	UNPAGED	XIMENES	WELLOFF	INVEIGH
SKILLET	SPENCER	STURMER	TOUGHEN	UNQUIET	YEZIDEE	ABRIDGE	KATORGA
SKIMMED	SPENDER	STUTTER	TOYNBEE	UNRAVEL	YOUNGER	ACREAGE	LAYINGS
SKIMMER	SPENSER	SUBDUED	TRACHEA	UNSCREW	ZAPOTEC	ALBERGO	LEAKAGE
SKINNED	SPIGNEL	SUBTEEN	TRACKER	UNTAMED	ZEPHIEL	ALLERGY	LENTIGO
SKINNER	SPINNER	SUCCEED	TRAILER	UNTRIED	ZYMOGEN	ALLONGE	LINEAGE
SKIPPED	SPINNEY	SUDETEN	TRAINED	UPSIDES	ACIDIFY	AMERIGO	LININGS
SKIPPER	SPLAYED	SUGARED	TRAINEE	USURPER	AIRLIFT	ANALOGY	LINKAGE
SKITTER	SPLICED	SWAGGER	TRAINER	VAULTED	ALEWIFE	APOLOGY	LITURGY
SLACKEN	SPLICER	SWANSEA	TRAMMEL	VENERER	ALFALFA	ARRAIGN	LOZENGE
SLACKER	SPOILED	SWAPPED	TRANTER	VERMEER	AMPLIFY	ARRANGE	LUGGAGE
SLAMMER	SPOILER	SWEATED	TRAPPED	VETIVER	BAILIFF	ASPERGE	LUMBAGO
SLANDER	SPONDEE	SWEATER	TRAPPER	VINTNER	BEATIFY	ASSIEGE	MAKINGS
SLAPPER	SPONGER	SWEEPER	TRAWLER	VOUCHER	CAITIFF	ASSUAGE	MARENGO
SLASHED	SPOONER	SWEETEN	TREATED	VOYAGER	CALCIFY	AUBERGE	MASSAGE
SLATTED	SPOTTED	SWELTER	TREKKER	WAGGLER	CASTOFF	AVERAGE	MESSAGE
SLEEPER	SPOTTER	SWIDDEN	TRESSES	WAGONER	CERTIFY	BAGGAGE	MILEAGE
SLEEVED	SPRAYER	SWIFTER	TRIFLER	WALLIES	CLARIFY	BANDAGE	MONTAGE
SLENDER	SPURREY	SWIMMER	TRIFLES	WALTZER	CRUCIFY	BARRAGE	MONTAGU
SLICKER	SPUTTER	SWINGER	TRIGGER	WANGLER	DIGNIFY	BESIEGE	MOULAGE
SLIMMER	SQUARED	SWOLLEN	TRILLED	WARBLER	DISTAFF	BIOLOGY	MYRINGA
SLIPPED	SQUARES	TABARET	TRILLER	WASTREL	ENFEOFF	BONDAGE	NÉGLIGÉ

NOOLOGY	VILLAGE	SWARTHY	AQUAVIT	CHABLIS	DISPRIN	GEORGIA	KUBELIK
ONSTAGE	VINTAGE	TABITHA	ARAMAIC	CHAGRIN	DOESKIN	GEORGIC	LACONIC
OUTRAGE	VOLTAGE	THOUGHT	ARCADIA	CHAMOIS	DOLPHIN	GHERKIN	LANGUID
PACKAGE	WASTAGE	TIMOTHY	ARCHAIC	CHAOTIC	DOMINIC	GLENOID	LANOLIN
PALINGS	WATTAGE	TONIGHT	ARMORIC	CHARDIN	DRASTIC	GLOTTIS	LAWSUIT
PANNAGE	YARDAGE	TRANCHE	ARSENIC	CHASSIS	DRUMLIN	GLYPTIC	LIBERIA
PANURGE	ZOOLOGY	TWITCHY	ARTEMIS	CHECKIN	DUNEDIN	GNATHIC	LIMPKIN
PARINGS	ZYMURGY	UPRIGHT	ASCARID	CHEERIO	DUSTBIN	GNOSTIC	LOBELIA
PASSAGE	ADELPHI	UPTIGHT	ASCETIC	CHERVIL	DVORNIK	GOBELIN	LOTHAIR
PEERAGE	AGRAPHA	UTRECHT	ASEPTIC	CHINDIT	DYNAMIC	GODETIA	LOWPAID
PEONAGE	ALRIGHT	WEALTHY	ASIATIC	CHIPPIE	ECBOLIC	GOODWIN	LUGSAIL
PILLAGE	ANARCHY	WORKSHY	ASPASIA	CHOOKIE	ECDYSIS	GRANNIE	LUMPKIN
PLUMAGE	ATROPHY	WRAUGHT	ASPIRIN	CHOROID	ECTASIS	GRAPHIC	LUNATIC
PORTAGE	ATTACHE	WREATHE	ASSYRIA	CHRONIC	ECTOPIA	GRAPHIS	LYCHNIS
POSTAGE	AUROCHS	WROUGHT	ATACTIC	CIRCLIP	EDAPHIC	GREMLIN	MAHONIA
POTTAGE	BELISHA	AARONIC	AURELIA	CIRCUIT	ELASTIC	GROUPIE	MALARIA
PRESAGE	BLOTCHY	ABATTIS	AUSTRIA	CISSOID	ELASTIN	GUMBOIL	MALEFIC
PRODIGY	BREATHE	ABBASID	BABYSIT	CLASSIC	ELZEVIR	GYMSLIP	MANAKIN
PROTEGE	BRIOCHE	ABIGAIL	BACCHIC	CLASTIC	EMBROIL	HAIRPIN	MANIKIN
PRURIGO	BRONCHI	ABIOSIS	BAHRAIN	CLIPPIE	EMPIRIC	HALFWIT	MANUMIT
RALEIGH	BROUGHT	ABOUKIR	BAHREIN	CLUPEID	EMULSIN	HARELIP	MARQUIS
RAMPAGE	CALECHE	ABOULIA	BALDRIC	COCKPIT	ENDEMIC	HEBRAIC	MASONIC
RAVINGS	CALICHE	ABRAXIS	BALDWIN	CODICIL	ENERGIC	HEPARIN	MASTOID
REALIGN	CATECHU	ABSTAIN	BANDAID	COHABIT	ENGRAIN	HEPATIC	MAUDLIN
REVENGE	CEVICHE	ACCLAIM	BANKSIA	COLCHIS	ENTERIC	HEREDIA	MAYFAIR
RIBCAGE	CRUNCHY	ACERBIC	BARGAIN	COLITIS	ENTRAIN	HERETIC	MAZARIN
RIDINGS	DELIGHT	ACRYLIC	BARMAID	COLLOID	EPHRAIM	HISTOID	MECHLIN
RUMMAGE	DIARCHY	ACTINIA	BATAVIA	COLONIC	EPSTEIN	HOBNAIL	MECONIC
SALVAGE	DOROTHY	ACTINIC	BEATNIK	CONCEIT	ERRATIC	HOLBEIN	MEIOSIS
SAUSAGE	DRAUGHT	ADENOID	BEDEVIL	CONDUIT	ETHMOID	HOMERIC	MELANIN
SAVINGS	DROUGHT	ADONAIS	BEDOUIN	CONJOIN	ETRURIA	HOMINID	MELODIC
SCOURGE	DYARCHY	AEROBIC	BEGONIA	CONTAIN	EUGENIA	HORATIO	MENUHIN
SCRAGGY	EARACHE	AIRMAIL	BENEFIT	CORSAIR	EUGENIC	HYALOID	MERMAID
SCROOGE	EMPATHY	AIRSHIP	BENZOIN	COTERIE	EUGENIE	HYDATID	METONIC
SCUTAGE	FETICHE	ALADDIN	BISCUIT	COUNCIL	EULALIE	HYPOXIA	MIASMIC
SEEPAGE	FRAUGHT	ALAMEIN	BOHEMIA	COWSLIP	EXCLAIM	ICTERIC	MIDSHIP
SELVAGE	FREIGHT	ALBANIA	BOLIVIA	CRAPPIE	EXHIBIT	IDIOTIC	MILFOIL
SERINGA	GALOCHE	ALBENIZ	BOLSHIE	CRICOID	EXPLAIN	IDYLLIC	MILITIA
SKYHIGH	GNOCCHI	ALBUMIN	BORACIC	CRINOID	EXPLOIT	ILLICIT	MILLAIS
SONDAGE	GOUACHE	ALEMBIC	BORODIN	CRISPIN	FACTOID	IMPAVID	MINUTIA
SPLODGE	GRACCHI	ALGERIA	BOTANIC	CROATIA	FANATIC	IMPERIL	MIRIFIC
SPLURGE	GROUCHO	ALIQUID	BOUDOIR	CROQUIS	FANTAIL	INERTIA	MITOSIS
SPRINGE	GROUCHY	ALSATIA	BOURSIN	CRYPTIC	FIBROID	INGRAIN	MONILIA
SPRINGS	HEALTHY	AMHARIC	BRAHMIN	CULPRIT	FIDELIO	INHABIT	MOONLIT
SPRINGY	HIBACHI	AMMONIA	BRICKIE	CUMBRIA	FILARIA	INHERIT	MORAVIA
STORAGE	INSIGHT	AMNESIA	BRITAIN	CURTAIL	FIMBRIA	INHIBIT	MORONIC
STRANGE	JERICHO	AMOEBIC	BROWNIE	CURTAIN	FLACCID	INSIPID	MORPHIA
STRINGS	KARACHI	AMYLOID	BUBONIC	CYNTHIA	FLEAPIT	INSULIN	MOUNTIE
STRINGY	LENGTHY	ANAEMIA	BUCOLIC	CYSTOID	FLOOZIE	INTERIM	MUEZZIN
SULLAGE	LESOTHO	ANAEMIC	BULIMIA	DAPHNID	FOOTSIE	INTROIT	MULLEIN
SYNERGY	MALACHI	ANDROID	BUMPKIN	DAPHNIS	FORFEIT	INVALID	MURRAIN
SYRINGA	MARATHA	ANEROID	BYRONIC	DAUPHIN	FRANCIS	ISLAMIC	MUSCOID
SYRINGE	NAPHTHA	ANGELIC	CALEPIN	DECLAIM	FRANTIC	ISOSPIN	MYALGIA
TAKINGS	PANACHE	ANGEVIN	CALORIC	DEFICIT	FREEBIE	JACOBIN	MYELOID
TEENAGE	PAUNCHY	ANNELID	CALORIE	DEICTIC	FREESIA	JAVELIN	MYIASIS
THROUGH	PIRANHA	ANOSMIA	CAMBRIC	DELIMIT	FUCHSIA	JOHNNIE	NAMIBIA
TIDINGS	POTICHE	ANTACID	CAMOGIE	DELPHIC	FUCHSIN	JONQUIL	NAVARIN
TILLAGE	QUINCHE	ANTONIO	CANTRIP	DELTOID	FUNFAIR	KASHMIR	NECKTIE
TONNAGE	RAUNCHY	APEPSIA	CAPTAIN	DEMERIT	FUNGOID	KATYDID	NEGROID
TRILOGY	SESOTHO	APHAGIA	CARABID	DEMONIC	GALOPIN	KENOSIS	NEMESIA
UMBRAGE	SHEATHE	APHASIA	CAROTID	DEMOTIC	GARBOIL	KENOTIC	NEMESIS
UNDERGO	SKETCHY	APHELIA	CAROTIN	DEPOSIT	GASTRIC	KERATIN	NERITIC
UNHINGE	SLEIGHT	APHESIS	CAUSTIC	DESPAIR	GASTRIN	KHAMSIN	NICOSIA
UPSTAGE	SMOOTHE	APHONIA	CECILIA	DESPOIL	GAUGUIN	KINESIS	NIGERIA
UPSURGE	SPLASHY	APHONIC	CENTRIC	DETRAIN	GELATIN	KINETIC	NIGHTIE
VANTAGE	SQUASHY	APHOTIC	CERAMIC	DEXTRIN	GENERIC	KINGPIN	NINEPIN
VERTIGO	SQUISHY	APLASIA	CERTAIN	DIAPSID	GENESIS	KINSHIP	NOCTUID
VESTIGE	STARCHY	APRAXIA	CESSPIT	DISDAIN	GENETIC	KIWANIS	NOMADIC
VIKINGS	STROPHE	AQUATIC	CESTOID	DISJOIN	GEORDIE	KREMLIN	NOMBRIL

NONSUIT	PURLOIN	SOROSIS	UNCIVIL	VANDYKE	CAPABLY	DRIZZLY	GLOBULE
NOSTRIL	PURSUIT	SPASTIC	UPBRAID	WARLIKE	CAPELLA	DUCTILE	GONDOLA
NUCLEIC	PUSHKIN	SPHENIC	URAEMIA	ZAKUSKA	CAPSULE	DUOPOLY	GORILLA
NUMERIC	PYAEMIA	SPUTNIK	UTENSIL	ACUTELY	CARIOLE	DURABLE	GRACILE
OCEANIA	PYRAMID	SQUALID	VANADIC	AFFABLE	CARLYLE	DURABLY	GRACKLE
OCEANIC	PYRETIC	STANDIN	VASSAIL	AFFABLY	CARRELL	DURRELL	GRADELY
OCEANID	PYREXIA	STANNIC	VAUDOIS	ALVEOLE	CARROLL	DWINDLE	GRANDLY
ODONTIC	PYROSIS	STARLIT	VERVAIN	AMIABLE	CASTILE	EAGERLY	GRANOLA
OILSKIN	PYRRHIC	STEARIC	VILLAIN	AMIABLY	CASUALS	EARTHLY	GRANULE
OLYMPIA	QUARTIC	STEARIN	VILLEIN	AMPOULE	CATCALL	EATABLE	GRAPPLE
OLYMPIC	QUASSIA	STENCIL	VITAMIN	AMPULLA	CATWALK	ELDERLY	GREATLY
ONEIRIC	QUENTIN	STEROID	VITRAIL	ANATOLE	CEDILLA	EMERALD	GRIDDLE
ONTARIO	QUICKIE	STRIGIL	VOCALIC	ANGRILY	CELLULE	ENFIELD	GRISTLE
OPUNTIA	RACEMIC	STROBIC	VOLTAIC	ANIMALS	CEMBALO	ENNOBLE	GRISTLY
ORGANIC	RAMEKIN	STYPTIC	WAGTAIL	ANOMALY	CENACLE	ENTITLE	GRIZZLE
OSMOSIS	RAREBIT	SUBEDIT	WARSHIP	ANTHILL	CHAGALL	EPISTLE	GRIZZLY
OTALGIA	RATAFIA	SUBJOIN	WASSAIL	APOSTLE	CHEAPLY	EQUABLE	GROCKLE
OVERBID	RECLAIM	SUBSOIL	WEIGHIN	ARMHOLE	CHIEFLY	EQUABLY	GROSSLY
OVERLIE	RECRUIT	SURFEIT	WETSUIT	ARTICLE	CHORALE	EQUALLY	GRUFFLY
PACIFIC	REDSKIN	SUSTAIN	WHATSIT	ASPHALT	CHORTLE	EXACTLY	GRUMBLE
PALADIN	REFRAIN	SWEETIE	WHEELIE	ASSAULT	CHUCKLE	EXAMPLE	GUNWALE
PARBOIL	REGALIA	SWITHIN	WHEREIN	ATINGLE	CIVILLY	EXEMPLA	HAGBOLT
PARESIS	RETRAIN	SYCOSIS	WORSHIP	AUDIBLE	CLEANLY	EYEBALL	HALLALI
PARFAIT	RETRAIT	SYNAXIS	XERAFIN	AUDIBLY	CLEARLY	EYEHOLE	HANDILY
PAROTIC	REVERIE	SYNOVIA	XEROSIS	AURALLY	CLOSELY	FAINTLY	HAPPILY
PAROTID	REVISIT	TABANID	ZAMORIN	AUREOLA	COMPILE	FALSELY	HARSHLY
PAROTIS	RHIZOID	TABLOID	ZIZANIA	AUREOLE	CONDOLE	FATALLY	HASTILY
PARSNIP	RINGGIT	TAMARIN	ZYGOSIS	AURICLE	CONSOLE	FAVELLA	HEAVILY
PARTHIA	ROBINIA	TAMESIS	ZYMOSIS	AWFULLY	CONSOLS	FEBRILE	HERSELF
PEARLIE	ROMANIA	TARPEIA	ALMACKS	BACILLI	CONSULT	FERRULE	HIMSELF
PELAGIC	ROSALIA	TARQUIN	APELIKE	BASCULE	CORACLE	FERTILE	HOLDALL
PELORIA	ROSALIE	TATARIC	AUTARKY	BATTELS	CORELLI	FINAGLE	HOSTILE
PENGUIN	ROSARIO	TENDRIL	BAZOOKA	BEASTLY	CORNELL	FINALLY	HUMANLY
PERIWIG	ROSEHIP	TERRAIN	BESPOKE	BEEFALO	COROLLA	FIREFLY	HUSKILY
PERSEID	ROUGHIE	THEREIN	BRITZKA	BEGUILE	COURTLY	FIRSTLY	ICEFALL
PERTAIN	SAGOUIN	THERMIC	CATLIKE	BENGALI	CRACKLE	FISSILE	IDEALLY
PETUNIA	SALADIN	THROWIN	CONVOKE	BEOWULF	CRACKLY	FISTULA	IGNOBLE
PFENNIG	SALAMIS	THYROID	COWPOKE	BEVERLY	CRAZILY	FISTULE	INBUILT
PHALLIC	SAMARIA	THYRSIS	DISLIKE	BICYCLE	CRINKLE	FIXEDLY	INFIELD
PHOENIX	SANDPIT	TILAPIA	DROSHKY	BLANDLY	CRINKLY	FLEXILE	INKWELL
PHONEIN	SANGRIA	TINFOIL	FINICKY	BLANKLY	CRIPPLE	FLYHALF	INSTALL
PHRENIC	SAPONIN	TITANIA	FORSAKE	BLEAKLY	CROSSLY	FORMULA	INSTILL
PIGSKIN	SAPPHIC	TITANIC	GODLIKE	BLINDLY	CRUDELY	FOSSULA	ISMAILI
PIGTAIL	SATANIC	TOENAIL	KARAOKE	BLOWFLY	CRUELLS	FOXHOLE	ISRAELI
PILGRIM	SATIRIC	TONETIC	KONTIKI	BLUFFLY	CRUELLY	FRAGILE	JAVELLE
PINTAIL	SAUROID	TOOTSIE	MASURKA	BLUNTLY	CRUMBLE	FRANKLY	JERKILY
PLASMIN	SCAGLIA	TOPSOIL	MAZURKA	BOSWELL	CRUMBLY	FRAZZLE	JOINTLY
PLASTIC	SCEPTIC	TOPSPIN	MISTAKE	BOUILLI	CRUMPLE	FRECKLE	KAMPALA
PLAUDIT	SCIATIC	TORTRIX	NETSUKE	BRAILLE	CUBICLE	FRESHLY	KENNELS
POCHOIR	SCORPIO	TOTEMIC	NUNLIKE	BRAMBLE	CUCKOLD	FRIABLE	KEYHOLE
POLARIS	SCOTTIE	TOXEMIA	NUTLIKE	BRAVELY	CURABLE	FRIZZLE	KNOBBLE
POLEMIC	SCRAPIE	TRADEIN	OATCAKE	BRIEFLY	CUTICLE	FRIZZLY	KNOBBLY
POLITIC	SEISMIC	TRAFFIC	OILCAKE	BRINDLE	CYMBALS	FRUMPLE	KNOWALL
POLONIE	SEMITIC	TRANSIT	PALOOKA	BRISKLY	DATABLE	FULFILL	KNUCKLE
POMPEII	SENECIO	TRAVAIL	PANCAKE	BRISTLE	DEATHLY	FUNNILY	LAMELLA
POROSIS	SEQUOIA	TREFOIL	PANICKY	BRISTLY	DEBACLE	FUSIBLE	LARGELY
POSITIF	SERAPIS	TRELLIS	PAPRIKA	BRITTLE	DEFAULT	FUSILLI	LAURELS
POUSSIN	SHELTIE	TRIATIC	PARTAKE	BROADLY	DENSELY	FUSSILY	LEGALLY
PRAIRIE	SHINDIG	TRIFFID	PROVOKE	BUFFALO	DETAILS	GABELLE	LEGIBLE
PREPAID	SHOWBIZ	TRIPSIS	RUSALKA	BUMMALO	DIABOLO	GADWALL	LEGIBLY
PREVAIL	SILESIA	TROPHIC	SCHICKS	BURNELL	DISABLE	GAUDILY	LEGPULL
PREZZIE	SIMPKIN	TRYPSIN	SEPPUKU	CAGOULE	DISTILL	GAZELLE	LENTILS
PROSAIC	SIRLOIN	TUBULIN	SQUEAKY	CALCULI	DIZZILY	GENTILE	LEOPOLD
PROTEIN	SKEPTIC	TUMBRIL	STREAKY	CAMILLA	DOWDILY	GESTALT	LIGHTLY
PROUDIE	SKIMMIA	TUNISIA	TALOOKA	CANDELA	DRABBLE	GHASTLY	LINCOLN
PRUSSIC	SMARTIE	TURMOIL	TEACAKE	CANELLA	DRACULA	GHOSTLY	LITHELY
PSYCHIC	SMIDGIN	TYLOSIS	TROTSKY	CANNILY	DRAGGLE	GIDDILY	LOCALLY
PTYALIN	SOLICIT	TYPHOID	UNALIKE	CANNULA	DRIBBLE	GIMBALS	LOFTILY
PUMPKIN	SOMALIA	TZADDIK	UNLUCKY	CAPABLE	DRIZZLE	GISELLE	LOOSELY

LOVABLE	OUTFALL	ROUGHLY	SPYHOLE	TRINGLE	BETHUMB	SUPREME	BASKING
LOYALLY	OVERALL	ROUNDLY	SQUALLY	TRIPOLI	CHIASMA	SUPREMO	BATHING
LUCIDLY	PANICLE	ROWDILY	SQUILLA	TRITELY	CONDEMN	SURNAME	BATTING
LUCKILY	PANOPLY	ROYALLY	STABILE	TROUBLE	CONSUME	TEATIME	BEADING
LUGHOLE	PANTILE	RUBELLA	STADDLE	TRUCKLE	CONTEMN	TRIREME	BEAMING
LURIDLY	PAPILLA	RUBEOLA	STARKLY	TRUFFLE	COSTUME	TRITOMA	BEARING
LUSTILY	PARABLE	RUMPOLE	STARTLE	TRUNDLE	COULOMB	TSUNAMI	BEATING
MAMILLA	PARNELL	RUSSELL	STATELY	TUNABLE	COXCOMB	TWOSOME	BEDDING
MANACLE	PATELLA	SAINTLY	STEEPLE	TUNICLE	CURCUMA	TWOTIME	BEELINE
MANDALA	PATIBLE	SALABLE	STEEPLY	TWADDLE	CUSTOMS	VENDOME	BEGGING
MANGOLD	PAYABLE	SANDALS	STERILE	TWEEDLE	DAYTIME	WARTIME	BEIJING
MANHOLE	PAYROLL	SAUCILY	STERNLY	TWIDDLE	DIGAMMA	WELCOME	BELLINI
MANILLA	PEDICLE	SAWBILL	STICKLE	TWIDDLY	DILEMMA	WINSOME	BENDING
MANIPLE	PENSILE	SAWMILL	STIFFLY	TWINKLE	DIORAMA	ZOOTOMY	BENZENE
MARSALA	PERCALE	SCAFELL	STIPPLE	TWOFOLD	DIPLOMA	ABALONE	BENZINE
MARVELL	PERGOLA	SCAMBLE	STONILY	TYNWALD	DODGEMS	ABIDING	BERLINE
MAXILLA	PETIOLE	SCAPULA	STOUTLY	UCCELLO	DRACHMA	ABJOINT	BERNINI
MAXWELL	PIANOLA	SCHNELL	STUBBLE	UKULELE	ECONOMY	ABSCOND	BETHINK
MAYPOLE	PICCOLO	SCRUPLE	STUBBLY	UNGODLY	EMPYEMA	ACCOUNT	BETTING
MEDULLA	PIEBALD	SCUFFLE	STUMBLE	USUALLY	ENDGAME	ACETONE	BETTONG
MENFOLK	PINBALL	SCUTTLE	SUAVELY	UTRICLE	EPITOME	ACHTUNG	BIDDING
MERRILY	PINFOLD	SEAGULL	SUFFOLK	UTRILLO	EXOGAMY	ADAMANT	BILTONG
MESSILY	PINHOLE	SEATTLE	SULKILY	UTTERLY	EXTREME	ADELINE	BINDING
METALLY	PINNULA	SEQUELA	SUNNILY	VACUOLE	FIBROMA	ADENINE	BIPLANE
MIRACLE	PIOUSLY	SERVILE	SWADDLE	VAGUELY	FOGLAMP	ADJOINT	BLATANT
MISERLY	PISTOLE	SESSILE	SWAHILI	VALVULE	FULSOME	ADORING	BLAZING
MISRULE	PITFALL	SEVILLE	SWEETLY	VANDALS	GAUTAMA	AFFRONT	BOATING
MISSILE	PITHILY	SHACKLE	SWIFTLY	VANILLA	GRANDMA	AFGHANI	BOILING
MONOCLE	PLAINLY	SHAKILY	SWINDLE	VARIOLA	INFLAME	AGELONG	BOLOGNA
MONOPLY	PLIABLE	SHAMBLE	SWINGLE	VEHICLE	IRKSOME	AGROUND	BOMBING
MONTHLY	PLUMULE	SHAPELY	SWIZZLE	VESICLE	JIMJAMS	AILMENT	BOOKING
MOODILY	POTABLE	SHARPLY	SYSTOLE	VIRGULE	LAKSHMI	AIRLINE	BOOMING
MORALLY	POTHOLE	SHINGLE	TACITLY	VISIBLE	LEUCOMA	ALANINE	BOWLING
MORELLO	PRATTLE	SHINGLY	TACTILE	VISIBLY	LISSOME	ALEPINE	BRACING
MORRELL	PRICKLE	SHORTLY	TADPOLE	VISTULA	MACRAMÉ	ALICANT	BRAKING
MORTALS	PRICKLY	SHOWILY	TARDILY	VITALLY	MAHATMA	ALIMENT	BREWING
MOSELLE	PRIMULA	SHRILLY	TASSILI	VIVIDLY	MAREMMA	ALIMONY	BRIGAND
MOUILLÉ	PROFILE	SHUFFLE	TAXABLE	VOCALLY	MESEEMS	ALTHING	BRITONS
MOVABLE	PROUDLY	SHUTTLE	TENABLE	VOLUBLE	MISTIME	ALUMINA	BROMINE
MURILLO	PTERYLA	SINHALA	TENFOLD	VOLUBLY	MUGWUMP	AMAZING	BUDDING
MUSSELS	PUCELLE	SITWELL	TENSELY	WALPOLE	MYELOMA	AMBIENT	BUGGING
MUTABLE	PUERILE	SIZABLE	TENSILE	WAXBILL	NEUROMA	AMBOYNA	BUGGINS
MYCELLA	PURCELL	SKIFFLE	TEQUILA	WAYBILL	NOISOME	AMERIND	BULGING
NACELLE	PUSTULE	SKITTLE	TERSELY	WEARILY	ONETIME	AMUSING	BUNTING
NAIVELY	QUEENLY	SLACKLY	TESTILY	WEIGELA	ORIGAMI	ANCIENT	BUOYANT
NAKEDLY	QUIBBLE	SLEEKLY	TEXTILE	WEIRDLY	OSTEOMA	ANEMONE	BURKINA
NASALLY	QUICKLY	SMARTLY	THICKLY	WENDELL	OUTCOME	ANGLING	BURNING
NASTILY	QUIETLY	SMICKLY	THIMBLE	WHEEDLE	PALERMO	ANILINE	BUSKINS
NETBALL	RADICLE	SMUGGLE	THIRDLY	WHISTLE	PASTIME	ANODYNE	BUSSING
NEVILLE	RAPIDLY	SNAFFLE	THISTLE	WHITTLE	PERFUME	ANTENNA	BUTTONS
NEWBOLT	RAVIOLI	SNIFFLE	THYSELF	WOMANLY	PHONEME	ANTHONY	CABLING
NIGELLA	READILY	SNORTLE	TIEPOLO	WORDILY	PLEROMA	APPOINT	CAIRENE
NIGHTLY	REBUILD	SNUFFLE	TIGHTLY	WORLDLY	POLYOMA	ARACHNE	CALCINE
NITRILE	RECYCLE	SNUGGLE	TIMBALE	WRANGLE	PRELIMS	ARETINO	CALLING
NOISILY	REDPOLL	SOBERLY	TIMIDLY	WRESTLE	PRESUME	ARIADNE	CALUMNY
NORFOLK	REGALLY	SOLIDLY	TIPSILY	WRIGGLE	PROXIMO	ARIZONA	CAMPANA
NOTABLE	REMOULD	SOLUBLE	TOEHOLD	WRINKLE	PTOLEMY	ARMBAND	CAMPING
NOTABLY	REPTILE	SOUFFLE	TOMBOLA	WRINKLY	RAGTIME	ASININE	CANNING
NOVELLA	RETICLE	SOUNDLY	TORTILE	WRONGLY	RHIZOME	ASTOUND	CANZONA
NOVELLO	RIGHTLY	SPANGLE	TOTALLY	WRYBILL	SALERMO	ATTAINT	CANZONE
OCTUPLE	RIGIDLY	SPARKLE	TRAMPLE	ACADEME	SARCOMA	AUGMENT	CARBINE
ODDBALL	RISIBLE	SPATULA	TREACLE	ACADEMY	SASHIMI	BACKING	CARMINE
OMPHALE	RISKILY	SPECKLE	TREACLY	ADENOMA	SATSUMA	BALCONY	CARVING
ONESELF	RISSOLE	SPICULA	TREADLE	ALABAMA	SCRUMMY	BALDING	CASTING
ORDERLY	ROCKALL	SPICULE	TREMBLE	ALCHEMY	SUBLIME	BAMBINO	CATKINS
OSMANLI	ROSELLA	SPINDLE	TREMBLY	ANATOMY	SUBSUME	BANGING	CATLING
OSSICLE	ROSELLE	SPINDLY	TREMOLO	ANGIOMA	SUCCUMB	BANKING	CATMINT
OSTIOLE	ROSEOLA	SPITTLE	TRESTLE	AWESOME	SUNLAMP	BARKING	CAYENNE
OTHELLO	ROUAULT	SPITTLE	TRICKLE	BEDTIME	SUNLAMP	BARRING	CEILING

CELLINI	DECLINE	FEEDING	GUIDING	JEERING	LURKING	NOTHING	PORTEND
CÉZANNE	DEFIANT	FEELING	GUSHING	JENKINS	LUTYENS	NOTIONS	PORTENT
CHAFING	DEMESNE	FENCING	HACKING	JESTING	MACHINE	NURSING	POSTING
CHALONE	DENTINE	FENLAND	HALTING	JOBBING	MADONNA	NUTTING	POTTING
CHASING	DERWENT	FERMENT	HANGING	JOGGING	MAHJONG	OBSCENE	POULENC
CHEWING	DESCANT	FERVENT	HARMONY	JOINING	MAILING	OCARINA	PRALINE
CHICANE	DESCEND	FIGMENT	HATBAND	JUGGINS	MALLING	ODDMENT	PRAYING
CHICANO	DESCENT	FILLING	HEADING	JUGLANS	MANHUNT	ODORANT	PREBEND
CHOKING	DESMOND	FILMING	HEALING	JUMPING	MANKIND	OFFHAND	PRESENT
CHOPINE	DESPOND	FINDING	HEARING	JUTLAND	MANNING	OLEFINE	PRETEND
CITRINE	DESTINE	FINLAND	HEATING	KAMPONG	MAPPING	ONGOING	PREVENT
CLEMENT	DESTINY	FIRCONE	HEAVENS	KATRINE	MARCONI	OPALINE	PRIMING
CLOSING	DEVIANT	FISHING	HEDGING	KEELING	MARKING	OPENING	PROBAND
CLOYING	DIALING	FITMENT	HELLENE	KEEPING	MARLENE	OPERAND	PROFANE
COATING	DIAMINE	FITTING	HELPING	KENNING	MARLINE	OPERANT	PROGENY
COCAINE	DIAMOND	FLAMING	HEMLINE	KICKING	MARTENS	OPULENT	PROLONG
CODEINE	DICKENS	FLEEING	HENBANE	KILLING	MARTINI	OREGANO	PROPANE
CODLING	DIETINE	FLEMING	HEPTANE	KIPLING	MASSINE	ORIGINS	PROPEND
COLOGNE	DIGGING	FLOWING	HEROINE	KISSING	MATTING	ORLEANS	PROVING
COLUMNS	DILUENT	FOLDING	HERRING	KNOWING	MATTINS	OROGENY	PRUDENT
COMBINE	DINMONT	FONDANT	HIGGINS	KRISHNA	MEANING	OROTUND	PUCCINI
COMBING	DISBAND	FOOTING	HILDING	LACKING	MEETING	OSBORNE	PUDDING
COMMAND	DISSENT	FORFEND	HIPBONE	LAGGING	MELTING	OUTLINE	PULSING
COMMEND	DISTANT	FORGONE	HISPANO	LALLANS	MENDING	OUTRANK	PUNGENT
COMMENT	DISTEND	FORMING	HISSING	LAMBENT	MESSINA	PACKING	PUNTING
COMMONS	DISTENT	FORTUNE	HOBSONS	LAMBING	METHANE	PADDING	PURLINE
COMMUNE	DITTANY	FULGENT	HOGGING	LANCING	METHINK	PADRONE	PUSHING
COMPANY	DOCKING	FUNDING	HOLDING	LANDING	MIDLAND	PAGEANT	PUTTING
CONDONE	DOGGONE	FURLONG	HOLLAND	LANTANA	MIDLINE	PAIRING	QUAKING
CONFINE	DOMAINE	GALLANT	HOPKINS	LAPPING	MIGRANT	PARKING	QUININE
CONSENT	DORKING	GALLING	HOPPING	LAPSANG	MILKING	PARTING	QUINONE
CONTEND	DORMANT	GALLONS	HORMONE	LAPWING	MILLING	PARVENU	RACKING
CONTENT	DOWLAND	GARDENS	HORSING	LARCENY	MINCING	PASSANT	RADIANT
CONVENE	DOWSING	GARLAND	HOSANNA	LASAGNA	MINUEND	PASSING	RAFTING
CONVENT	DRAWING	GARMENT	HOTLINE	LASAGNE	MIOCENE	PATIENT	RAILING
COOKING	DRIVING	GARONNE	HOUDINI	LASHING	MISSING	PAULINE	RAIMENT
COOLANT	DUBBING	GASCONY	HOUSING	LASTING	MITTENS	PAYMENT	RAISING
COOLING	DUCKING	GASPING	HOWLING	LATRINE	MOANING	PEASANT	RAMPANT
COPLAND	DUSTING	GATLING	HULKING	LEADING	MOCKING	PECCANT	RANKING
COPYING	EARRING	GEARING	HUMMING	LEANING	MODERNE	PECKING	RANTING
CORKING	ECCRINE	GEELONG	HUNTING	LEAPING	MOLDING	PEELING	RATIONS
CORTINA	ECHIDNA	GEHENNA	HURLING	LEASING	MONTANA	PEEPING	RATLINE
CORUNNA	ELEGANT	GELDING	HUSBAND	LEAVING	MONTANT	PEERING	READING
COSTING	ELEMENT	GENUINE	HYALINE	LEGGING	MOONING	PELTING	REAGENT
COTTONY	EMINENT	GERAINT	HYDRANT	LEGIONS	MOORING	PENDANT	REARING
COULDNT	ENCHANT	GERMANE	HYGIENE	LEMMING	MOPPING	PENDING	REBOUND
COUPONS	ENGLAND	GERMANY	ICELAND	LENDING	MORAINE	PENNANT	RECLINE
COUSINS	ENPRINT	GETTING	IKEBANA	LENIENT	MORDANT	PENNINE	RECOUNT
COWBANE	ENSUING	GIBBONS	IMAGINE	LEONINE	MORLAND	PENTANE	REDOUND
COWHAND	ENTRANT	GILDING	IMAGING	LESSING	MORNING	PEPSINE	REEKING
COWLING	ENTWINE	GINSENG	IMPLANT	LETTING	MUGGING	PERCENT	REELING
CRAVING	EPERGNE	GLARING	IMPOUND	LEUCINE	MUNDANE	PERSONA	REGNANT
CROWING	EPICENE	GLAZING	IMPRINT	LICKING	MURAENA	PERSONS	RELIANT
CUCKING	EPIGONE	GLIDING	INCLINE	LILTING	MUSTANG	PHALANX	REMAINS
CUISINE	ETCHING	GLOWING	INCONNU	LINDANE	MYELINE	PHARYNX	REMNANT
CUNNING	EUPHONY	GNAWING	INDIANA	LINKING	NAGGING	PICKING	REMOUNT
CURLING	EVENING	GODSEND	INFERNO	LINSANG	NAPPING	PIGEONS	REPAINT
CURRANT	EVIDENT	GOLDING	INKLING	LISTING	NASCENT	PIGLING	REPLANT
CURRENT	EXAMINE	GOLDONI	INSTANT	LODGING	NATIONS	PIGMENT	REPRINT
CUTTING	EXIGENT	GOLFING	INTERNE	LOGGING	NEARING	PIMPING	RESCIND
CYCLING	EXITING	GOSLING	IRELAND	LONGING	NECKING	PIQUANT	RESIANT
CYCLONE	EXPOUND	GRATING	IRONING	LOOKING	NEOTENY	PISCINA	RESOUND
DAMNING	FAILING	GRAZING	ISOTONE	LOOMING	NEPTUNE	PISCINE	RESPOND
DAMPING	FAIRING	GRIMOND	ISSUANT	LOOTING	NETTING	PLACING	RESTING
DANCING	FALLING	GROWING	ITCHING	LORDING	NEURINE	PLAYING	RETAINS
DARLING	FANZINE	GUANINE	JAMMING	LOURING	NEURONE	POLLING	RETHINK
DARNING	FARMING	GUARANA	JAMPANI	LOWLAND	NIRVANA	PONTINE	RETSINA
DASHING	FASTING	GUARANI	JASMINE	LUCARNE	NODDING	POPPING	RETURNS
DEALING	FAWNING	GUBBINS	JAWBONE	LUCERNE	NOGGING	PORCINE	RHYMING

RIBBING	SINGING	TIFFANY	WARNING	BALLOON	CHILLON	EYESPOT	KINGDOM
RIGGING	SINKING	TIMPANI	WARRANT	BANDBOX	CHINOOK	FACTION	KNOWHOW
RINGING	SIPPING	TIPPING	WARRING	BANGKOK	CHORION	FASHION	KOLKHOZ
RIOTING	SISTINE	TOLUENE	WASHING	BASSOON	CHRISOM	FENELON	KOWLOON
RIPPING	SITTING	TONTINE	WASTING	BASTION	CLARION	FESTOON	KRYPTON
ROAMING	SKATING	TOOLING	WAXWING	BEDROOM	CLOISON	FICTION	LAMPOON
ROARING	SKYLINE	TOPPING	WAYLAND	BELABOR	COITION	FIEFDOM	LANGTON
ROCKING	SLAYING	TORMENT	WEAPONS	BELLBOY	CONTROL	FINFOOT	LANGUOR
ROLLING	SLIDING	TORRENT	WEARING	BELLHOP	COPILOT	FIREDOG	LAOCOON
ROMAINE	SLOPING	TOTIENT	WEAVING	BENISON	CORNCOB	FISSION	LARDOON
ROOFING	SLOVENE	TOURING	WEBBING	BENTHOS	CORNROW	FLEURON	LEBANON
ROOTING	SLOWING	TOWLINE	WEDDING	BERGSON	CORYDON	FLUMMOX	LEGROOM
ROSSINI	SMETANA	TRACING	WEEKEND	BIBELOT	CRAMPON	FOXTROT	LEXICON
ROSTAND	SMILING	TRADING	WEEPING	BIGFOOT	CREATOR	FREEDOM	LIAISON
ROTTING	SMOKING	TREPANG	WELDING	BIGSHOT	CRIMSON	FRISSON	LOGBOOK
ROUSING	SNORING	TRIBUNE	WETLAND	BILLION	CROUTON	FUSEBOX	LOGWOOD
ROUTINE	SOAKING	TRIDENT	WETTING	BLOSSOM	CRYPTON	GADROON	LONGBOW
RUBBING	SOARING	TRITONE	WHALING	BLOUSON	CURATOR	GALIPOT	LOWBROW
RUNNING	SOCKING	TSARINA	WHITING	BOLSHOI	CUSHION	GALLEON	MACEDON
RUSHING	SOLVENT	TSIGANE	WIGGING	BOOBOOK	CYPRIOT	GANELON	MADISON
RUTHENE	SOMEONE	TSIGANY	WILDING	BOREDOM	DAGWOOD	GASOHOL	MAGINOT
RUTTING	SOPPING	TURBINE	WILLING	BOURBON	DASHPOT	GASTHOF	MAILBOX
SABRINA	SOPRANO	TURENNE	WINDING	BOURDON	DAYBOOK	GEARBOX	MANDIOC
SACKING	SORDINO	TURGENT	WINNING	BOWSHOT	DEMIGOD	GIRASOL	MANHOOD
SAILING	SORTING	TURNING	WISHING	BOXROOM	DENDRON	GLASGOW	MANIHOC
SALIENT	SOUTANE	TUSCANY	WORDING	BOXWOOD	DESTROY	GLENCOE	MANITOU
SALPINX	SPACING	TYMPANO	WORKING	BOYHOOD	DEVELOP	GLUTTON	MANSION
SALTING	SPARING	TYMPANY	WOULDNT	BRISTOL	DEWDROP	GODUNOV	MARABOU
SAPIENS	SPAVINE	TYRANNY	WRITING	BRIXTON	DICTION	GRIFFON	MARIBOU
SAPIENT	SPRAINT	TZARINA	WYOMING	BUFFOON	DIDEROT	GRYPHON	MARMION
SAPLING	SRAVANA	UGOLINO	YAWNING	BUGABOO	DIDICOY	GUDGEON	MATADOR
SARDANA	STAGING	UKRAINE	ZEALAND	BULLDOG	DILATOR	GUIGNOL	MATELOT
SARDINE	STAMINA	ULULANT	ZETLAND	BULLION	DISAVOW	GUMBOOT	MEGARON
SARGENT	STARING	UNBOUND	ZOFFANY	BUNDOOK	DIVISOR	GUMDROP	MEGATON
SARMENT	STAYING	UNCANNY	ABANDON	BURGEON	DOGFOOD	GUMSHOE	MELILOT
SAVANNA	STEVENS	UNDOING	ABETTOR	BUTANOL	DOGWOOD	GUNROOM	MENTHOL
SCALENE	STEWING	UNDYING	ABLATOR	CAEDMON	DRAGOON	GUNSHOT	MENTION
SCARING	STIPEND	UNGUENT	ACHERON	CAISSON	DUDGEON	HALCYON	MILKSOP
SCORING	STUDENT	UNSOUND	ACHESON	CALDRON	DUKEDOM	HANGDOG	MILLION
SCRAWNY	STYLING	UNTWINE	ACTAEON	CALLBOX	DUNGEON	HARDTOP	MIRADOR
SEALANT	SUBTEND	UNWOUND	ADAPTOR	CALLBOY	EARLDOM	HARICOT	MISSION
SEALINK	SULTANA	UPSWING	ADDISON	CALTROP	EARSHOT	HARPOON	MISTOOK
SEARING	SUMMING	UTERINE	ADVISOR	CAMELOT	ECHELON	HARWOOD	MOELLON
SEATING	SUMMONS	VACCINE	AEROSOL	CAMERON	ECUADOR	HAUTBOY	MOLOTOV
SEEMING	SURFING	VAGRANT	AGISTOR	CAMPHOR	EDITION	HELICON	MONITOR
SEGMENT	SUSANNA	VALIANT	AILERON	CAMPION	EJECTOR	HELLION	MONOCOT
SELLING	SUSPEND	VARIANT	AIRFLOW	CAMWOOD	ELATION	HEXAGON	MONOLOG
SERPENS	SWAYING	VARMINT	AIRSTOP	CAPITOL	ELEANOR	HEXAPOD	MONSOON
SERPENT	TALKING	VARYING	ALCOHOL	CAPTION	ELECTOR	HILLTOP	MOUFLON
SERVANT	TAMMANY	VENDING	ALENÇON	CARADOC	ELISION	HONITON	MULLION
SERVING	TANGENT	VERBENA	ALIQUOT	CARDOON	ELYTRON	HORIZON	NABOKOV
SESTINA	TANNING	VERDANT	ANDIRON	CARIBOU	EMERSON	HOTFOOT	NEUTRON
SESTINE	TAPPING	VERMONT	APRICOT	CARRION	EMOTION	HOTSHOT	NEWSBOY
SETTING	TARTINE	VERSANT	APROPOS	CARTOON	EMPEROR	HUMIDOR	NONPROS
SEXTANS	TATIANA	VETTING	AQUILON	CASHBOX	ENACTOR	ICEFLOE	NONSTOP
SEXTANT	TATTING	VIBRANT	ATISHOO	CATALOG	ENTERON	ICHABOD	OBLIGOR
SHADING	TAURINE	VINCENT	ATROPOS	CATELOG	ENVELOP	INCISOR	OCTAGON
SHAKING	TAVERNA	VIOLENT	ATTABOY	CAUTION	ENVENOM	IVANHOE	OCTOPOD
SHAPING	TEARING	VOLCANO	AUCTION	CELADON	EPIZOON	JACKPOT	OMICRON
SHARING	TEASING	VULPINE	AUDITOR	CESSION	EPSILON	JACKSON	OPINION
SHAVING	TEEMING	WADDING	AUDUBON	CHANSON	EQUATOR	JAMESON	ORATION
SHEBANG	TELLING	WAFTING	AVIATOR	CHARIOT	EQUINOX	JANITOR	ORCINOL
SHINING	TENSING	WAILING	AVIGNON	CHARPOY	ERECTOR	JOGTROT	OUTCROP
SHOWING	TERRANE	WAITING	BABYLON	CHEKHOV	EROSION	JOHNSON	OUTDOOR
SIBLING	TERRENE	WALKING	BACKLOG	CHEROOT	ESCALOP	JUKEBOX	OUTFLOW
SIDDONS	TERRINE	WANTING	BAGEHOT	CHEVIOT	ETHANOL	JURYBOX	OUTGROW
SIEMENS	TESTING	WAPPING	BALATON	CHEVRON	EVASION	KEARTON	OUTLOOK
SIFTING	THYMINE	WARLING	BALLBOY	CHIFFON	EYEBROW	KILLJOY	OUTSHOT
SIGNING	TICKING	WARMING	BALLIOL	CHIGNON	EYESHOT	KILOTON	OVATION

OXBLOOD	SEALION	TROLLOP	THERAPY	BURSARY	DEANERY	FOREARM	JEWELRY
PAGEBOY	SECTION	TUITION	TOPKAPI	BUSTARD	DECLARE	FORGERY	JITTERS
PALMTOP	SENATOR	TYPHOON	TOWROPE	BUTTERY	DEEPFRY	FORLORN	JITTERY
PARADOR	SERFDOM	UNBOSOM	TRICEPS	BUZZARD	DEIRDRE	FORWARD	JOBBERY
PARADOS	SESSION	UNCTION	TRIUMPH	CAESURA	DENMARK	FOULARD	JOINERY
PARADOX	SHADOOF	UPSHOOT	UNHAPPY	CALDERA	DENTURE	FOUNDRY	KEYWORD
PARAGON	SHALLOT	UPSILON	UNKEMPT	CALIBRE	DEPLORE	FULLERS	KILDARE
PARASOL	SHALLOW	VENISON	ABELARD	CALVARY	DESSERT	GAITERS	KILVERT
PASSION	SHAMPOO	VERSION	ACIFORM	CAMORRA	DEVILRY	GALLERY	KINTYRE
PATRIOT	SHANNON	VICEROY	ACQUIRE	CAMPARI	DIEHARD	GARBURE	KIPPERS
PENSION	SHIPTON	VISITOR	ACTUARY	CANNERY	DIETARY	GASFIRE	KITHARA
PHAETON	SILICON	VITRIOL	ADJOURN	CANONRY	DIOPTRE	GERBERA	KNAVERY
PHANTOM	SIMENON	WALLOON	AFFAIRS	CAPTURE	DIPTERA	GESTURE	LAETARE
PHARAOH	SIMPLON	WARRIOR	AIRPORT	CAREERS	DISBARK	GILBERT	LAGGARD
PICADOR	SIMPSON	WARTHOG	ALDABRA	CARPORT	DISCARD	GIZZARD	LAMBERT
PIDGEON	SJAMBOK	WHARTON	ALGEBRA	CASCARA	DISCERN	GOLIARD	LANCERS
PIERROT	SNOWDON	WHATNOT	ALGIERS	CATARRH	DISCORD	GOMORRA	LANTERN
PILLBOX	SOAPBOX	WHITLOW	ALLEGRI	CAUTERY	DISPORT	GRANARY	LANYARD
PILLION	SOLOMON	WICKLOW	ALLEGRO	CAVALRY	DISTORT	GRAVURE	LAUNDRY
PLATOON	SOMEHOW	WIDGEON	ALTHORN	CAVIARE	DISTURB	GREGORY	LAWYERS
PLAYBOY	SOURSOP	WINDROW	AMATORY	CENSURE	DITHERY	GROCERS	LEADERS
PLESSOR	SOVKHOZ	WINDSOR	AMPHORA	CENTURY	DOCTORS	GROCERY	LECHERY
PLEURON	SPARROW	WINSTON	ANDORRA	CHAMBRÉ	DODDERY	GRUYÈRE	LECTERN
PLOSION	SPONSON	WITLOOF	ANTLERS	CHANCRE	DOGCART	GUNFIRE	LECTURE
PLYWOOD	SPONSOR	WORKTOP	ANTWERP	CHICORY	DOLLARS	GUNNERA	LEEWARD
POLYGON	SQUALOR	XANTHOS	ANYMORE	CHIMERA	DRAPERY	GUNNERY	LEGWORK
POLYPOD	STARDOM	YPSILON	ARCHERY	CHOLERA	DRAWERS	HACHURE	LEISURE
POMEROL	STATION	ZILLION	ARMOURY	CINDERS	DRIVERS	HACKERY	LEMPIRA
POMEROY	STENTOR	AGRIPPA	ARREARS	CISTERN	DULLARD	HAGGARD	LEONARD
POMPOON	STEPSON	APOCOPE	ARTWORK	CITHARA	DUNKIRK	HAGGERY	LEOPARD
PONTOON	STETSON	ATTEMPT	ATHWART	CITTERN	EARMARK	HALBERD	LEOTARD
PORTHOS	STILTON	BAGPIPE	AUSTERE	CLOSURE	EASTERN	HALBERT	LETTERS
PORTION	STRIDOR	CATALPA	AVEBURY	CLOTURE	ELECTRA	HALTERE	LIBRARY
POSTBOX	SUBATOM	CONCEPT	AWKWARD	COFFERS	ELECTRO	HALYARD	LINACRE
POSTDOC	SUCTION	CORRUPT	BANBURY	COLIBRI	ELUSORY	HANSARD	LOLLARD
POTOROO	SUNROOF	CYCLOPS	BANDORE	COLLARD	ENQUIRE	HARVARD	LOMBARD
POTSHOT	SUNSPOT	DECRYPT	BARBARA	COLOURS	ENQUIRY	HAYFORK	LOTTERY
PRAETOR	SURGEON	DIGLYPH	BARBARY	COMFORT	ENSNARE	HAYWARD	LUGWORM
PREDOOM	SWALLOW	DIGRAPH	BARKERS	COMPARE	ENSNARL	HAYWIRE	MACABRE
PROCTOR	SYMPTOM	DISRUPT	BASTARD	COMPERE	EPHEDRA	HECTARE	MADEIRA
PRONAOS	TAGALOG	ENTROPY	BATHERS	COMPORT	EPICARP	HERBERT	MAESTRO
RACCOON	TALIPOT	EPITAPH	BATTERY	CONAKRY	EPICURE	HERBERY	MAGUIRE
RAINBOW	TALLBOY	EUTERPE	BEDFORD	CONCERN	EQUERRY	HETAERA	MALLARD
RANGOON	TAMPION	EXCERPT	BEDSORE	CONCERT	ERASURE	HICKORY	MAMMARY
REACTOR	TAPROOM	FORCEPS	BEGGARY	CONCORD	ESQUIRE	HISTORY	MANNERS
REALTOR	TAPROOT	GALUMPH	BEGORRA	CONFIRM	ESTUARY	HOMBURG	MANSARD
REDWOOD	TEAROOM	GESTAPO	BERNARD	CONFORM	ETAGÈRE	HONOURS	MARBURG
REPROOF	TEASHOP	GOSSIPY	BERSERK	CONJURE	EXHEDRA	HORRORS	MARGERY
REREDOS	TELECOM	GRANDPA	BIGHORN	CONSORT	EXOCARP	HOSIERY	MARMARA
REUNION	TENSION	GUYROPE	BIGOTRY	CONTORT	EXPLORE	HUBBARD	MARTYRS
ROADHOG	TERSION	INSCAPE	BINDERY	CONVERT	EYESORE	HUNGARY	MASCARA
ROBESON	THERMOS	ISOTOPE	BISTORT	COOKERY	FACTORS	HUNKERS	MASONRY
ROLLMOP	THOMSON	LACEUPS	BITTERN	COPPERS	FACTORY	HUSSARS	MASTERS
ROMANOV	THRENOS	LIMPOPO	BITTERS	COSTARD	FAILURE	ICEBERG	MASTERY
ROOFTOP	TOLSTOY	MAZEPPA	BIZARRE	COUNTRY	FANFARE	IMAGERY	MATTERS
ROTATOR	TOMFOOL	PERCEPT	BLAZERS	COUTURE	FANWORM	IMPLORE	MEASURE
RUBICON	TOMPION	PERHAPS	BOLLARD	COWGIRL	FANWORT	INBOARD	MEGAERA
RUNNION	TOOLBOX	PRECEPT	BOMBARD	COWHERD	FARMERS	INDOORS	MEMBERS
SABAYON	TOPKNOT	PREEMPT	BONFIRE	CULTURE	FEATURE	INQUIRE	MEMOIRS
SAFFRON	TORCHON	RECEIPT	BONKERS	CULVERT	FETTERS	INQUIRY	MERCERY
SANDBOX	TORSION	RESHAPE	BONNARD	CURSORY	FILBERT	INSHORE	MERCURY
SANDBOY	TOSSPOT	RUDOLPH	BORDERS	CUSTARD	FINGERS	INSPIRE	MIDGARD
SAPWOOD	TOYSHOP	SATRAPY	BRASERO	CUTLERY	FIREARM	ISADORA	MIDTERM
SASSOON	TRACTOR	SCHLEPP	BRAVERY	CUTTERS	FISHERY	ISODORE	MIMICRY
SAVELOY	TRAITOR	SCRAPPY	BRAVURA	CUTWORM	FISSURE	ISOMERE	MISFIRE
SCALLOP	TRANSOM	SCRUMPY	BREWERY	DAGGERS	FIXTURE	JAGGERY	MIXTURE
SCISSOR	TREASON	SHRIMPS	BRIBERY	DASTARD	FLOWERS	JANKERS	MOCKERS
SCOLLOP	TREETOP	STROPPY	BROKERS	DASYURE	FLOWERY	JANUARY	MOCKERY
SEAFOOD	TRIANON	SYNCOPE	BULWARK	DAYMARK	FOGHORN	JEEPERS	MOIDORE

MOLIÈRE	POPCORN	SHASTRI	UNSNARL	BABYISH	DENTIST	FITTEST	JACKASS
MONTERO	POSTERN	SHIKARI	UPSTART	BADNESS	DEPRESS	FLEMISH	JAPLISH
MOTHERS	POSTURE	SHIVERS	URETHRA	BAGASSE	DERVISH	FLORIST	JEWFISH
MUDLARK	POTHERB	SHIVERY	URINARY	BALLAST	DESPISE	FLUTIST	JOBLESS
MUGWORT	POTTERY	SHOWERS	VAMPIRE	BAPTISM	DIALYSE	FLYPAST	JOYLESS
MUMMERS	POULTRY	SHOWERY	VAPOURS	BAPTIST	DIARIST	FOOLISH	JUDAISM
MUMMERY	POWDERY	SICKERT	VELOURS	BEARISH	DIECAST	FOPPISH	JUJITSU
MUSTARD	PREPARE	SIEVERT	VENTURE	BECAUSE	DIFFUSE	FORMOSA	KADDISH
MYSTERY	PRIMARY	SIGNORA	VERDURE	BEDPOST	DIGRESS	FURBISH	KENTISH
NAVARRE	PROCURE	SIGNORI	VESPERS	BEQUEST	DIMNESS	FURNISH	KERMESS
NECTARY	PROVERB	SILVERY	VICTORY	BIOMASS	DIOCESE	GABFEST	KOUMISS
NERVURE	PURPORT	SINATRA	VISCERA	BLEMISH	DISCUSS	GARFISH	LACTASE
NETWORK	PURPURA	SINCERE	VULTURE	BOMBAST	DISEASE	GARNISH	LACTOSE
NEWBORN	RAEBURN	SISTERS	WARBURG	BOOKISH	DISGUST	GASMASK	LAMAISM
NEWBURY	RAGWORT	SKYLARK	WARFARE	BOORISH	DISMAST	GAWKISH	LAMAIST
NIAGARA	RAMPART	SKYWARD	WARLORD	BRITISH	DISMISS	GAYNESS	LAMBAST
NIGGARD	RAPPORT	SLAVERY	WASHERS	BRUTISH	DISPOSE	GENOESE	LARGESS
NIPPERS	RAPTURE	SOCOTRA	WAXWORK	BUGLOSS	DIVERSE	GEODESY	LARGEST
NOWHERE	RECTORY	SOJOURN	WAYMARK	BULLISH	DOGFISH	GIRLISH	LAWLESS
NUMBERS	REENTRY	SORCERY	WAYWARD	BULRUSH	DOGROSE	GLIMPSE	LAXNESS
NUMMARY	REMARRY	SPECTRE	WELFARE	BURGESS	DONNISH	GLUCOSE	LEFTIST
NUNNERY	REPAIRS	SPIDERS	WESTERN	BURMESE	DRYNESS	GODDESS	LEGLESS
NURSERY	REQUIRE	SPIDERY	WITHERS	BURNISH	DUCHESS	GODLESS	LEPROSY
NURTURE	RESPIRE	SQUEERS	WONDERS	CABOOSE	DUMPISH	GOODISH	LICENSE
OBSCURA	RESTART	STATURE	WOOMERA	CADDISH	EARNEST	GOULASH	LIONESS
OBSCURE	RESTORE	STEWARD	WORKERS	CALYPSO	EASIEST	GRAYISH	LOUTISH
OILBIRD	REVELRY	STIRFRY	YARDARM	CANVASS	ECLIPSE	GREYISH	LUMPISH
ONSHORE	REYNARD	SUBVERT	YOGHURT	CARCASE	ECSTASY	GUTLESS	MADNESS
ORATORY	RHUBARB	SUBZERO	YONKERS	CARCASS	EGOTISM	GYMNAST	MAFIOSO
ORCHARD	RIBWORT	SUMATRA	ZEDOARY	CAROUSE	EGOTIST	HAGFISH	MALAISE
OSSUARY	RICHARD	SUMMARY	ZINGARO	CASEASE	ELEGIST	HAPLESS	MALTASE
OUTDARE	RINGERS	SUMMERY	ABOLISH	CASUISM	ELITISM	HARNESS	MALTESE
OUTTURN	RIOTERS	SUNBURN	ABREAST	CASUIST	ELITIST	HARPIST	MALTOSE
OUTWARD	RIPCORD	SUPPORT	ABSCESS	CATFISH	ELLIPSE	HARVEST	MANNISH
OUTWORK	RIVALRY	SURGERY	ACCURSE	CATTISH	EMBASSY	HASHISH	MARCUSE
OUTWORN	RIVIERA	TAILORS	ACTRESS	CELLIST	EMPRESS	HATLESS	MARXISM
OVERARM	ROBBERS	TANAGRA	ADDRESS	CHEMISE	ENCLASP	HEIRESS	MARXIST
PALMYRA	ROBBERY	TANBARK	ADIPOSE	CHEMIST	ENCLOSE	HELLISH	MATISSE
PANDORA	ROCKERY	TANKARD	ADVERSE	CHERISH	ENCRUST	HENGIST	MAWKISH
PASTERN	ROGUERY	TANNERY	AGAINST	CHINESE	ENDLESS	HERBIST	MELROSE
PASTURE	ROLLERS	TANTARA	AGELESS	CIRROSE	ENDORSE	HEROISM	MÉTISSE
PATTERN	ROMPERS	TARTARE	AGGRESS	CLEANSE	ENGLISH	HIGHEST	MIDMOST
PECCARY	RONSARD	TARTARY	AGONIST	COEXIST	ENGROSS	HOGWASH	MIDWEST
PEPPERS	ROOKERY	TATTERS	AIMLESS	COMPASS	ENTHUSE	HOSTESS	MISCAST
PEPPERY	ROZZERS	TELFORD	AIRBASE	COMPOSE	ENTRUST	HYMNIST	MOLLUSC
PEREIRA	RUBBERS	TEMPERA	AIRLESS	COMPOST	ESPOUSE	IAMBIST	MOMBASA
PERFORM	RUBBERY	TEMPURA	ALECOST	CONCISE	EUPEPSY	ICINESS	MONKISH
PERJURE	RUNCORN	TESSERA	ALFONSO	CONCUSS	EVEREST	ILLNESS	MOORISH
PERJURY	RUNNERS	TEXTURE	AMBROSE	CONFESS	EXHAUST	IMAGISM	MOREISH
PERTURB	RUPTURE	THEATRE	AMONGST	CONFUSE	EXPANSE	IMAGIST	MORTISE
PERVERT	SAILORS	TILBURY	AMORIST	CONSIST	EXPENSE	IMMENSE	NEAREST
PESSARY	SALIERI	TIMBERS	AMOROSO	CONTEST	EXPRESS	IMMERSE	NEBBISH
PHILTRE	SALTIRE	TINTERN	AMYLASE	COPYIST	EYELASH	IMPASSE	NECROSE
PIASTRE	SAPPERS	TIPCART	AMYLOSE	CORNISH	EYELESS	IMPRESS	NEGRESS
PICTURE	SAQQARA	TOGGERY	ANALYST	COXLESS	EYEWASH	IMPREST	NERVOSA
PIGGERY	SAVOURY	TONSURE	ANGUISH	COYNESS	FADDISH	IMPULSE	NEWNESS
PILLORY	SAXHORN	TOPIARY	ANIMIST	CUIRASS	FADDIST	INBURST	NICOISE
PINCERS	SCENERY	TORTURE	APPEASE	CUTLASS	FAIRISH	INCENSE	NOURISH
PISMIRE	SCEPTRE	TOTTERY	APTNESS	CYCLIST	FANTASY	INCROSS	NUTCASE
PIZARRO	SCUTARI	TRACERY	ARMREST	CYPRESS	FARNESE	INCRUST	NYNORSK
PLACARD	SEABIRD	TUATARA	ARTLESS	DADAISM	FASCISM	INGRESS	OARFISH
PLANURY	SEAPORT	TURBARY	ATAVISM	DADAIST	FASCIST	INHOUSE	OBELISK
PLAYERS	SEEKERS	TURNERY	ATHEISM	DEAREST	FATNESS	INHUSE	OBVERSE
PLENARY	SEIZURE	TUSSORE	ATHEIST	DEBUSSY	FAUVISM	INQUEST	OCULIST
POCHARD	SELKIRK	UNAWARE	ATHIRST	DECEASE	FAUVIST	INTENSE	ODALISK
PODAGRA	SELLERS	UNHEARD	ATOMIST	DEFENSE	FILASSE	INVERSE	ODDNESS
POLLARD	SEMIPRO	UNICORN	AUSLESE	DEFROST	FINESSE	IRIDISE	OFFBASE
POMMARD	SENSORY	UNIFORM	AUTOPSY	DEGAUSS	FINNISH	ISOBASE	OFFENSE
PONIARD	SHAKERS	UNITARY	BABOOSH	DELOUSE	FITNESS	IVRESSE	OGREISH

OLDNESS	RHENISH	UNLEASH	AZIMUTH	DEVIATE	HONESTY	NARRATE	RESULTS
OLOROSO	RIBLESS	UNLOOSE	AZURITE	DICTATE	HOPLITE	NAUGHTY	REUNITE
ONANISM	RIMLESS	UPRAISE	BABBITT	DIGNITY	HUSSITE	NAVETTE	REWRITE
ONENESS	ROGUISH	URANISM	BARENTS	DINETTE	HYDRATE	NEGRITO	RICKETS
OPPRESS	ROOKISH	USELESS	BASMATI	DIORITE	ICHNITE	NEOLITH	RICKETY
ORGIAST	RUBBISH	VAMOOSE	BAUXITE	DISPUTE	IMITATE	NICTATE	RICOTTA
ORPHISM	SADNESS	VANESSA	BECKETT	DOUGHTY	IMPASTO	NITRATE	RIPOSTE
OUTCAST	SALLUST	VARNISH	BENEATH	DUALITY	IMPIETY	NITRITE	RISOTTO
OUTLAST	SAMOOSA	VENTOSE	BENNETT	DUBIETY	INANITY	NOVELTY	ROBERTS
OUTPOST	SARCASM	VERBOSE	BETROTH	DYNASTY	INDEPTH	NULLITY	ROBUSTA
OXIDASE	SAWDUST	VINASSE	BIRETTA	EBONITE	INFLATE	OBESITY	ROSEATE
PALISSY	SAWFISH	VISCOSE	BISMUTH	EDUCATE	INGRATE	OBJECTS	ROSETTA
PALMIST	SCHLOSS	WAGGISH	BLIGHTY	EFFECTS	INSECTS	OBVIATE	ROSETTE
PANNOSE	SELFISH	WASPISH	BOYCOTT	EGALITY	INSTATE	OFFDUTY	ROYALTY
PAPOOSE	SEXLESS	WATUTSI	BREADTH	ELAMITE	ISOLATE	OPACITY	SABAOTH
PECKISH	SHIATSU	WEAKEST	BREVITY	ELEVATE	ITERATE	OPERATE	SABBATH
PECTASE	SHICKSA	WENDISH	BROMATE	EMANATE	JACINTH	ORVIETO	SAGITTA
PEERESS	SHYNESS	WETNESS	BUCKETS	EMIRATE	JACKETS	OTRANTO	SALTATE
PEEVISH	SIAMESE	WHITISH	BULLETS	EMULATE	JAKARTA	OUSTITI	SAMNITE
PENTOSE	SIKHISM	WIMPISH	BURETTE	ENDNOTE	JOCASTA	OUTVOTE	SATIATE
PERCUSS	SLAVISH	WITLESS	CAHOOTS	ENSUITE	JOLLITY	OVULATE	SATIETY
PERFUSE	SLYNESS	WITNESS	CAINITE	ENTENTE	KAINITE	OXALATE	SECRETE
PERSIST	SOLOIST	WOLFISH	CALCITE	EPIDOTE	KERNITE	PALETTE	SECRETS
PERTUSE	SOPHISM	WRYNOSE	CANASTA	EREMITE	KEYNOTE	PALMATE	SENSATE
PIANIST	SOPHIST	YAHWIST	CANTATA	ERUDITE	KHANATE	PALPATE	SEVENTH
PICASSO	SOUBISE	YANGTSE	CARROTS	ESPARTO	KIBBUTZ	PARENTS	SEVENTY
PIETIST	SPANISH	YIDDISH	CARROTY	EXCRETA	KYANITE	PARTITA	SFUMATO
PIGFISH	STATIST	YORKIST	CASSATA	EXCRETE	LABIATE	PAUCITY	SINUATE
PINFISH	STRAUSS	ZAMBESI	CELESTA	EXECUTE	LACERTA	PEANUTS	SITUATE
POETESS	STYLISH	ZIONIST	CELESTE	EXEGETE	LACTATE	PENALTY	SOCIETY
POSSESS	STYLIST	ABILITY	CHAPATI	EXPIATE	LAMBETH	PENNATE	SOPWITH
PRECAST	SUBFUSC	ABSINTH	CHARITY	EXUDATE	LAVOLTA	PERLITE	SPICATE
PRECISE	SUBSIST	ACCRETE	CHAYOTE	EYEBATH	LAYETTE	PIMENTO	SPINATE
PREMISE	SUCCESS	ACETATE	CHIANTI	FACULTY	LEMMATA	PIPETTE	SPIRITS
PREMISS	SUCROSE	ACIDITY	CHRISTY	FAGGOTS	LEPANTO	PLACATE	SPROUTS
PROCESS	SUFFUSE	ACOLYTE	CHUPATI	FATUITY	LIBERTY	PLUMATE	STARETS
PROFESS	SUGGEST	ACONITE	CILIATE	FIDGETS	LIGNITE	PODESTA	STATUTE
PROFUSE	SUNLESS	ACTUATE	CLARITY	FIDGETY	LOCUSTS	POLENTA	STEALTH
PROMISE	SUNRISE	ADAMITE	CLAVATE	FILLETS	LOYALTY	POLLUTE	STRAITS
PROPOSE	SUPPOSE	ADULATE	CLIMATE	FLIGHTY	LUDDITE	POVERTY	STREWTH
PROTEST	SURMISE	AGILITY	COCOTTE	FRAILTY	LUDGATE	PREDATE	STRIATE
PROTIST	SURPASS	AGITATE	COGNATE	FRIGATE	LUNETTE	PRELATE	STYLITE
PROVISO	SWEDISH	AGITATO	COLDITZ	FROWSTY	MACBETH	PRIESTS	SUAVITY
PROVOST	SYNAPSE	ALBERTA	COLLATE	FUMETTE	MACHETE	PRIMATE	SUFFETE
PROWESS	TACHISM	ALBERTI	COMMUTE	FURCATE	MAGENTA	PRIVATE	SUKKOTH
PRUDISH	TAPLASH	AMANITA	COMPETE	GALETTE	MAGGOTY	PRIVITY	SULFATE
PUBLISH	TARNISH	AMENITY	COMPOTE	GAROTTE	MAGNATE	PROBATE	SUNNITE
PUCKISH	TBILISI	AMNESTY	COMPUTE	GAVOTTE	MAGNETO	PROBITY	SURDITY
PUGWASH	TEMPEST	AMORITE	CONNATE	GAZETTE	MAJESTY	PROFITS	SUZETTE
PURPOSE	THERESA	ANDANTE	CONNOTE	GEFILTE	MAMMOTH	PROMOTE	TAFFETA
RAFFISH	THOMISM	ANIMATE	CORANTO	GEMMATE	MANDATE	PRONATE	TALLITH
RAWNESS	THOMIST	ANNATTO	CORBETT	GENISTA	MARANTA	PUBERTY	TANNATE
REALISM	TIGRESS	ANNUITY	CORDATE	GESTATE	MARLITE	PULSATE	TARANTO
REALIST	TIGRISH	ANXIETY	CORDITE	GIBLETS	MARMITE	QUALITY	TEKTITE
RECLUSE	TITOISM	ARCUATE	CORINTH	GOLIATH	MEDIATE	QUIXOTE	TENANTS
REDDISH	TITOIST	ARIDITY	CREMATE	GRADATE	MELLITE	QUORATE	TERMITE
REDFISH	TONNISH	ARIETTA	CRENATE	GRANITA	MEMENTO	RACKETS	TESTATE
REDNESS	TOPLESS	ARIOSTO	CRUDITY	GRANITE	MIGRATE	RACKETY	THERETO
REDRESS	TOPMAST	ARTISTE	CRUELTY	GRAVITY	MOABITE	RADIATE	THIRSTY
REFRESH	TOPMOST	ASHANTI	CURETTE	GUTTATE	MODESTY	REALITY	THRIFTY
REGRESS	TOURISM	ASQUITH	CUVETTE	GWYNETH	MODISTE	REBIRTH	THRISTY
REHOUSE	TOURIST	ASSISTS	DEBRETT	HAPORTH	MOFETTE	REFLATE	THROATY
RELAPSE	TRAIPSE	ASTARTE	DEFLATE	HASTATE	MOMENTS	REGATTA	TITRATE
RELEASE	TROPISM	ATHLETE	DEJECTA	HAUGHTY	MULATTO	RELICTS	TOCCATA
REMORSE	TSARIST	AUGUSTA	DENSITY	HAZLETT	MURIATE	REPLETE	TORONTO
REPRESS	TURKISH	AUGUSTE	DEPLETE	HEIGHTS	MUSETTE	REQUITE	TOWPATH
REPULSE	UNCLASP	AUREATE	DESERTS	HIRSUTE	NAHUATL	REROUTE	TRIBUTE
REQUEST	UNDRESS	AVIDITY	DESPITE	HITTITE	NAIVETÉ	RESPITE	TRIESTE
REVERSE	UNHORSE	AXOLOTL	DETENTE	HOGARTH	NAIVETY	RESTATE	TRINITY

229

TURPETH	BOLETUS	ERASMUS	IRIDIUM	OUTPOUR	SANCTUS	WIPEOUT	REPROVE
TWELFTH	BOXHAUL	ERODIUM	ISCHIUM	OVERDUE	SARCOUS	WISHFUL	RESERVE
ULEXITE	BRANTUB	ERRATUM	ISTHMUS	OVERRUN	SAVIOUR	WISTFUL	RESOLVE
ULULATE	BRIMFUL	FALLOUT	JACOBUS	PABULUM	SCROTUM	WITHOUT	RESTIVE
UNCOUTH	BRUSQUE	FARCEUR	JEALOUS	PAESTUM	SELLOUT	WOODCUT	REVOLVE
UNEARTH	BULBOUS	FATEFUL	JEJUNUM	PAINFUL	SERIOUS	WORKOUT	SCREEVE
UNQUOTE	BULGHUR	FATIGUE	KARAKUL	PALLIUM	SEVERUS	WRITEUP	SURVIVE
UNTRUTH	BURNOUS	FATUOUS	KETCHUP	PAPYRUS	SEYMOUR	XENOPUS	TANTIVY
UPSTATE	BURNOUT	FAUSTUS	KINGCUP	PARLOUR	SHAKEUP	YTTRIUM	TARDIVE
URALITE	CACIQUE	FEARFUL	KURHAUS	PARLOUS	SHOTGUN	ZEALOUS	UNALIVE
URANITE	CADMIUM	FERMIUM	LADYBUG	PASTEUR	SINUOUS	ZESTFUL	UNNERVE
URINATE	CAESIUM	FERROUS	LALIQUE	PAVIOUR	SKILFUL	ABSOLVE	ZEMSTVO
UROLITH	CALAMUS	FERVOUR	LEPROUS	PEACHUM	SKINFUL	ABUSIVE	ASHDOWN
UTILITY	CALCIUM	FIBROUS	LIBRIUM	PEGASUS	SKYBLUE	ACHIEVE	BELLOWS
VACUITY	CALLOUS	FIREBUG	LINCTUS	PELORUS	SNARLUP	ANCHOVY	BILLOWS
VANUATU	CAMBIUM	FISTFUL	LINOCUT	PERSEUS	SOLANUM	APPROVE	BRADAWL
VARIETY	CANDOUR	FLAREUP	LIQUEUR	PETROUS	SOLIDUS	ARCHIVE	FELLOWS
VARSITY	CANTHUS	FLAVOUR	LITHIUM	PHALLUS	SORGHUM	BAKLAVA	GALLOWS
VEDANTA	CARACUL	FRETFUL	LOCKNUT	PHOEBUS	SOULFUL	BEEHIVE	GOSHAWK
VEDETTE	CARDUUS	FULCRUM	LOCKOUT	PILATUS	STADIUM	BEHOOVE	HEBREWS
VELVETY	CAREFUL	FUNGOUS	LOOKOUT	PINETUM	STANDUP	BELIEVE	HOEDOWN
VIBRATE	CAROLUS	FURIOUS	LUSTFUL	PIRAEUS	STENGUN	BEREAVE	INGROWN
VIBRATO	CATCHUP	GAINFUL	LUSTRUM	PIROGUE	STERNUM	BIVALVE	LEASOWE
VIOLATE	CELSIUS	GALLIUM	MACAQUE	PITEOUS	STIRRUP	CAPTIVE	LETDOWN
VIRGATE	CENTAUR	GASEOUS	MALLEUS	PITIFUL	STRATUM	CASSAVA	LIEDOWN
VITIATE	CENTRUM	GIBBOUS	MALTHUS	PLAUTUS	STRATUS	CENTAVO	LOWDOWN
VOLANTE	CEPHEUS	GIDDYUP	MANAGUA	PLAYFUL	SUBAQUA	CONCAVE	MARLOWE
VULGATE	CHECKUP	GIELGUD	MASSEUR	PLUTEUS	SUCCOUR	CONNIVE	NARROWS
WARPATH	CHIRRUP	GLAMOUR	MAXIMUM	POLYPUS	SULPHUR	COSTIVE	OKINAWA
WEBSITE	CIMABUE	GLEEFUL	MESCLUN	POMPOUS	SURPLUS	CURSIVE	OVERAWE
WEIGHTS	CLAMOUR	GORDIUS	MIMULUS	POPULUS	TACITUS	DECEIVE	RUNDOWN
WEIGHTY	CLEANUP	GRAMPUS	MINDFUL	PREMIUM	TACTFUL	DEPRAVE	SANDOWN
ZEOLITE	CLEARUP	GROPIUS	MINIBUS	PRIAPUS	TAKEOUT	DEPRIVE	SHADOWY
ZOOLITE	CLOSEUP	GROTIUS	MINIMUM	PRIMEUR	TAMBOUR	DESERVE	SITDOWN
ALPHEUS	COCONUT	GROWNUP	MODICUM	PRONOUN	TANTRUM	DEVOLVE	SORROWS
ALUMNUS	CONTOUR	HAFNIUM	MODULUS	PROTEUS	TEARFUL	ELUSIVE	SUNDOWN
ALYSSUM	COPIOUS	HAHNIUM	NACROUS	PYLORUS	TEDIOUS	EMOTIVE	UNKNOWN
AMATEUR	COVERUP	HAIRCUT	NAIPAUL	QUANTUM	TENUOUS	ENCLAVE	WILLOWY
AMOROUS	CRANIUM	HALIBUT	NATRIUM	QUECHUA	TERBIUM	ENGRAVE	WINDOWS
ANGELUS	CRASSUS	HALITUS	NEEDFUL	QUERCUS	TETANUS	ENSLAVE	YELLOWS
ANNULUS	CREWCUT	HANDFUL	NERVOUS	QUICHUA	THALLUS	EVASIVE	ATARAXY
ANTIGUA	CROESUS	HANDGUN	NIOBIUM	QUIETUS	THESEUS	FESTIVE	BETWIXT
ANTIQUE	CUMULUS	HANDOUT	NITROUS	RAMULUS	THORIUM	FORGAVE	CACHEXY
ANXIOUS	CUPROUS	HANGOUT	NONPLUS	RANCOUR	THULIUM	FORGIVE	CONTEXT
APICIUS	CURIOUS	HARBOUR	NOSTRUM	RAUCOUS	TIMEOUT	FURTIVE	EPITAXY
APPLAUD	CYTISUS	HARMFUL	NOXIOUS	REAUMUR	TRISMUS	HELLUVA	PICKAXE
AQUEOUS	DECORUM	HASSIUM	NUCLEUS	REGROUP	TRITIUM	IMPROVE	POLEAXE
AQUINUS	DEFRAUD	HATEFUL	OBLIQUE	REISSUE	TRIVIUM	INCURVE	PRETEXT
ARBUTUS	DEVALUE	HEEDFUL	OBLOQUY	RENEGUE	TROCHUS	INNERVE	ACRONYM
ARDUOUS	DEVIOUS	HEINOUS	OBSEQUY	REOCCUR	TROILUS	INVOLVE	ANTONYM
ARTEMUS	DIDYMUS	HELPFUL	OBVIOUS	RESIDUE	TUMULUS	JUSSIVE	APTERYX
ATTICUS	DOLEFUL	HIDEOUS	OCCIPUT	RESTFUL	TUNEFUL	KHEDIVE	BUCKEYE
AUTOCUE	DREYFUS	HIDEOUT	OCELLUS	RETINUE	TURNOUT	MASSIVE	CATSEYE
AZYGOUS	DROPOUT	HOLMIUM	OCTOPUS	REVALUE	UNCINUS	MINERVA	CHLAMYS
BACCHUS	DUBIOUS	HOODLUM	ODOROUS	REVENUE	URANIUM	MISSIVE	DEADEYE
BAHADUR	DUBNIUM	HOPEFUL	OEDIPUS	RHENIUM	VACUOUS	MUSCOVY	EMPLOYS
BALEFUL	DUTIFUL	HORDEUM	OESTRUS	RHODIUM	VARIOUS	OBSERVE	ENDWAYS
BALFOUR	EARDRUM	HOTSPUR	OLYMPUS	RHOMBUS	VICIOUS	OUTLIVE	FISHEYE
BAROQUE	ECHINUS	HUMDRUM	OMENTUM	RIOTOUS	VIDIMUS	PAHLAVI	GOODBYE
BASHFUL	ECLOGUE	HUMERUS	OMINOUS	ROMULUS	VILNIUS	PASSIVE	HAWKEYE
BATHTUB	EELPOUT	HURTFUL	OMNIBUS	ROSCIUS	VISCOUS	PAVLOVA	HOMONYM
BAUHAUS	EGLOGUE	ICTERUS	ONEROUS	ROSEBUD	VOLAPUK	PECCAVI	HYPONYM
BEARHUG	ELOGIUM	IGNEOUS	ONMIBUS	ROSTRUM	WAKEFUL	PENSIVE	JERSEYS
BELARUS	ELYSIUM	ILIACUS	OPOSSUM	ROUNDUP	WALKOUT	PLOSIVE	KIDNEYS
BELGIUM	EMBOLUS	IMPETUS	OPTIMUM	RUINOUS	WARDOUR	RECEIVE	METONYM
BEZIQUE	ENAMOUR	IMPIOUS	ORGANUM	SACKBUT	WASHOUT	RECURVE	ORKNEYS
BILIOUS	ENVIOUS	INCUBUS	ORPHEUS	SACKFUL	WASHTUB	RELIEVE	PINKEYE
BLOWOUT	EPHEBUS	INGENUE	OSCULUM	SALIQUE	WHITSUN	RELIEVO	SHUTEYE
BOHRIUM	EPHESUS	INVIOUS	OSSEOUS	SANCTUM	WICKIUP	REPLEVY	SOCKEYE

SPONDYL	APHASIA	CORRIDA	IPOMOEA	NEMESIA	ROSETTA	URAEMIA	CHRONIC
STACHYS	APHELIA	CORTINA	ISADORA	NERVOSA	ROTUNDA	URETHRA	CLASSIC
SYNONYM	APHONIA	CORUNNA	JAKARTA	NEUROMA	RUBELLA	URAEMIA	CLASTIC
WALLEYE	APLASIA	COTINGA	JAMAICA	NIAGARA	RUBEOLA	VANESSA	CLUNIAC
WYSIWYG	APRAXIA	CROATIA	JELLABA	NICOSIA	RUSALKA	VANILLA	COELIAC
AGONIZE	ARABICA	CUMBRIA	JOCASTA	NIGELLA	SABRINA	VARIOLA	COLONIC
ANALYZE	ARCADIA	CURCUMA	KAMPALA	NIGERIA	SAGITTA	VEDANTA	CRYPTIC
ANODIZE	ARCHAEA	CYNTHIA	KANNADA	NIRVANA	SAMARIA	VERBENA	DEICTIC
APPRIZE	ARIETTA	DEJECTA	KATORGA	NOVELLA	SAMBUCA	VERRUCA	DELPHIC
ARABIZE	ARIZONA	DERONDA	KHALIFA	OBSCURA	SAMOOSA	VISCERA	DEMONIC
ATOMIZE	ASPASIA	DIGAMMA	KITHARA	OCARINA	SANGRIA	VISTULA	DEMOTIC
BAPTIZE	ASSYRIA	DILEMMA	KRISHNA	OCEANIA	SAQQARA	WEIGELA	DOMINIC
BONANZA	AUGUSTA	DIORAMA	LACERTA	OKINAWA	SARCOMA	WOOMERA	DRASTIC
CADENZA	AURELIA	DIPLOMA	LAGONDA	OLYMPIA	SARDANA	ZAKUSKA	DYNAMIC
CAPSIZE	AUREOLA	DIPTERA	LAMBADA	OPUNTIA	SATSUMA	ZIZANIA	ECBOLIC
CHINTZY	AUSTRIA	DRACHMA	LAMELLA	ORGANZA	SAVANNA	BATHTUB	EDAPHIC
CHORIZO	BAKLAVA	DRACULA	LANTANA	OSTEOMA	SCAGLIA	BETHUMB	ELASTIC
EMBLAZE	BANKSIA	ECHIDNA	LASAGNA	OTALGIA	SCAPULA	BRANTUB	ELEGIAC
IDOLIZE	BARBARA	ECTOPIA	LAVOLTA	PALMYRA	SEQUELA	CORNCOB	EMPIRIC
ITEMIZE	BATAVIA	ELECTRA	LEMMATA	PALOOKA	SEQUOIA	COULOMB	ENDEMIC
JACUZZI	BAZOOKA	EMPYEMA	LEMPIRA	PANACEA	SERINGA	COXCOMB	ENERGIC
LIONIZE	BEGONIA	EPHEDRA	LEUCOMA	PANDORA	SESTINA	DISTURB	ENTERIC
MANSIZE	BEGORRA	ERITREA	LIBERIA	PANGAEA	SHICKSA	MAGHREB	ERRATIC
ORGANZA	BELINDA	EROTICA	LOBELIA	PAPILLA	SIGNORA	MINICAB	EUGENIC
OUTSIZE	BELISHA	ETRURIA	LYMNAEA	PAPRIKA	SILESIA	PEDICAB	FANATIC
OXIDIZE	BERMUDA	EUGENIA	MADEIRA	PARTHIA	SINATRA	PERTURB	FRANTIC
PIZZAZZ	BIRETTA	EXCRETA	MADONNA	PARTITA	SINHALA	POTHERB	GASTRIC
REALIZE	BOHEMIA	EXEMPLA	MAGENTA	PATELLA	SKIMMIA	PROVERB	GENERIC
ROMANZA	BOLIVIA	EXHEDRA	MAHATMA	PAVLOVA	SMETANA	RHUBARB	GENETIC
SCHERZO	BOLOGNA	FAVELLA	MAHONIA	PELORIA	SOCOTRA	SUCCUMB	GEORGIC
SHMOOZE	BONANZA	FELUCCA	MAJORCA	PEREIRA	SOMALIA	TAXICAB	GLYPTIC
SPINOZA	BOTTEGA	FIBROMA	MALACCA	PERGOLA	SPATULA	WASHTUB	GNATHIC
SQUEEZE	BRAVURA	FILARIA	MALARIA	PERSONA	SPICULA	AARONIC	GNOSTIC
STYLIZE	BRITZKA	FIMBRIA	MAMILLA	PETUNIA	SPINOZA	ACERBIC	GRAPHIC
TRAPEZE	BULIMIA	FISTULA	MANAGUA	PIANOLA	SQUILLA	ACRYLIC	HEBRAIC
UTILIZE	BURKINA	FLORIDA	MANDALA	PINNULA	SRAVANA	ACTINIC	HEPATIC
	CADENZA	FORMICA	MANILLA	PIRANHA	STAMINA	AEROBIC	HERETIC
7:7	CAESURA	FORMOSA	MARANTA	PISCINA	SUBAQUA	ALEMBIC	HOMERIC
ABOULIA	CALDERA	FORMULA	MARATHA	PLEROMA	SULTANA	ALMANAC	ICTERIC
ACARIDA	CAMILLA	FOSSULA	MAREMMA	PODAGRA	SUMATRA	AMHARIC	IDIOTIC
ACTINIA	CAMORRA	FREESIA	MARMARA	PODESTA	SUSANNA	AMOEBIC	IDYLLIC
ADENOMA	CAMPANA	FUCHSIA	MARSALA	POLENTA	SWANSEA	ANAEMIC	ISLAMIC
AGRAPHA	CANASTA	GALATEA	MASCARA	POLYOMA	SYNOVIA	ANGELIC	KENOTIC
AGRIPPA	CANDELA	GAUTAMA	MASURKA	PRIMULA	SYRINGA	APHONIC	KINETIC
ALABAMA	CANDIDA	GEHENNA	MATILDA	PTERYLA	TABITHA	APHOTIC	LACONIC
ALBANIA	CANELLA	GENISTA	MAXILLA	PURPURA	TAFFETA	AQUATIC	LUNATIC
ALBERTA	CANNULA	GEORGIA	MAZEPPA	PYAEMIA	TALOOKA	ARAMAIC	MALEFIC
ALDABRA	CANTATA	GERBERA	MAZURKA	PYREXIA	TANAGRA	ARCHAIC	MANDIOC
ALFALFA	CANZONA	GODETIA	MEDULLA	QUASSIA	TANTARA	ARMORIC	MANIHOC
ALGEBRA	CAPELLA	GOMORRA	MEGAERA	QUECHUA	TAPIOCA	ARSENIC	MASONIC
ALGERIA	CARAMBA	GONDOLA	MESSINA	QUICHUA	TARPEIA	ASCETIC	MECONIC
ALSATIA	CARIOCA	GORILLA	MILITIA	RATAFIA	TATIANA	ASEPTIC	MELODIC
ALTHAEA	CASCARA	GRANDMA	MINERVA	REBECCA	TAVERNA	ASIATIC	METONIC
ALUMINA	CASSATA	GRANDPA	MINORCA	REGALIA	TEMPERA	ATACTIC	MIASMIC
AMANITA	CASSAVA	GRANITA	MINUTIA	REGATTA	TEMPURA	BACCHIC	MIRIFIC
AMBOYNA	CATALPA	GRANOLA	MIRANDA	REPLICA	TEQUILA	BALDRIC	MOLLUSC
AMERICA	CECILIA	GRENADA	MOLUCCA	RETSINA	TESSERA	BIVOUAC	MORONIC
AMMONIA	CEDILLA	GUARANA	MOMBASA	RHONDDA	THERESA	BORACIC	MUNTJAC
AMNESIA	CELESTA	GUNNERA	MONILIA	RICOTTA	TILAPIA	BOTANIC	NERITIC
AMPHORA	CHELSEA	HAGGADA	MONTANA	RIGVEDA	TITANIA	BUBONIC	NOMADIC
AMPULLA	CHIASMA	HELLUVA	MORAVIA	RIVIERA	TOCCATA	BUCOLIC	NUCLEIC
ANAEMIA	CHIMERA	HEREDIA	MORPHIA	ROBINIA	TOMBOLA	BYRONIC	NUMERIC
ANDORRA	CHOLERA	HETAERA	MURAENA	ROBUSTA	TOXEMIA	CALORIC	OCEANIC
ANGIOMA	CINEREA	HOSANNA	MYALGIA	ROMANIA	TRACHEA	CAMBRIC	ODONTIC
ANOSMIA	CITHARA	HYPOGEA	MYCELLA	ROMANZA	TRITOMA	CARADOC	OLYMPIC
ANTENNA	COCHLEA	HYPOXIA	MYELOMA	ROSACEA	TSARINA	CARDIAC	ONEIRIC
ANTIGUA	COLUMBA	IKEBANA	MYRINGA	ROSALIA	TUATARA	CAUSTIC	ORGANIC
APEPSIA	CORDOBA	INDIANA	NAMIBIA	ROSELLA	TUNISIA	CENTRIC	PACIFIC
APHAGIA	COROLLA	INERTIA	NAPHTHA	ROSEOLA	TZARINA	CERAMIC	PAROTIC

PELAGIC	ANNOYED	CHARGED	DIAMOND	GARLAND	LABORED	ORDERED	REVERED
PHALLIC	ANTACID	CHARMED	DIAPSID	GIELGUD	LAGGARD	OROTUND	REVISED
PHRENIC	APPLAUD	CHARRED	DIEHARD	GIZZARD	LANGUID	OUTWARD	REYNARD
PLASTIC	APPLIED	CHECKED	DILATED	GLENOID	LANYARD	OVERBID	RHIZOID
POLEMIC	APPOSED	CHEESED	DILUTED	GNARLED	LAYERED	OVERFED	RICHARD
POLITIC	ARMBAND	CHIPPED	DIMPLED	GOAHEAD	LEARNED	OXBLOOD	RIDDLED
PONTIAC	ARMORED	CHOROID	DISBAND	GODHEAD	LEEWARD	PAINTED	RIPCORD
POSTDOC	ARRAYED	CHUFFED	DISCARD	GODSEND	LEONARD	PALSIED	RIVETED
POTOMAC	ARRIVED	CISSOID	DISCORD	GOLIARD	LEOPARD	PARCHED	RONSARD
POULENC	ASCARID	CLIPPED	DISTEND	GORSEDD	LEOPOLD	PAROTID	ROSEBUD
PROSAIC	ASHAMED	CLOTHED	DISUSED	GRAINED	LEOTARD	PAYLOAD	ROSTAND
PRUSSIC	ASSUMED	CLOUDED	DIVIDED	GRANDAD	LIKENED	PERSEID	ROUNDED
PSYCHIC	ASSURED	CLUPEID	DOGFOOD	GRANTED	LIMITED	PICKLED	RUFFLED
PYRETIC	ASTOUND	COBBLED	DOGWOOD	GRILLED	LINSEED	PIEBALD	RUMORED
PYRRHIC	ATTIRED	COLLARD	DOWLAND	GRIMOND	LIPREAD	PIERCED	RUMPLED
QUARTIC	AWKWARD	COLLOID	DRAFTED	GROINED	LOGWOOD	PIGWEED	SAMOYED
RACEMIC	BAFFLED	COLORED	DRAINED	GROOVED	LOLLARD	PINCHED	SAPWOOD
SAPPHIC	BAGHDAD	COMMAND	DREADED	GUARDED	LOMBARD	PINFOLD	SAUROID
SATANIC	BANDAID	COMMEND	DRESSED	HAGGARD	LOUVRED	PINHEAD	SCENTED
SATIRIC	BARMAID	CONCORD	DRUGGED	HALBERD	LOWLAND	PITCHED	SCREWED
SCEPTIC	BASTARD	CONTEND	DULLARD	HALYARD	LOWPAID	PITHEAD	SEABIRD
SCIATIC	BEACHED	COPLAND	DUNCIAD	HANDLED	MALLARD	PLACARD	SEAFOOD
SEISMIC	BEARDED	COSTARD	EGGHEAD	HANSARD	MANGOLD	PLANNED	SEAWEED
SEMITIC	BEDFORD	COUNTED	ELECTED	HARVARD	MANHOOD	PLANTED	SEEDBED
SHELLAC	BEHAVED	COVERED	EMERALD	HARWOOD	MANKIND	PLEASED	SEETHED
SKEPTIC	BELATED	COVETED	ENDURED	HATBAND	MANSARD	PLEATED	SERRIED
SPASTIC	BELOVED	COWHAND	ENFIELD	HAUNTED	MARBLED	PLYWOOD	SETTLED
SPHENIC	BEMUSED	COWHERD	ENGAGED	HAYSEED	MARRIED	POCHARD	SHAGGED
STANNIC	BERNARD	COWSHED	ENGINED	HAYWARD	MASTOID	POINTED	SHELLED
STEARIC	BIASSED	CRACKED	ENGLAND	HELIPAD	MATCHED	POLLARD	SHELVED
STROBIC	BIGHEAD	CRAMMED	ENRAGED	HENNAED	MAYWEED	POLYPOD	SHINPAD
STYPTIC	BIGOTED	CRAMPED	ETHMOID	HEXAPOD	MERITED	POMMARD	SHOCKED
SUBFUSC	BLASTED	CREATED	EXALTED	HISTOID	MERMAID	PONIARD	SICKBED
TATARIC	BLESSED	CRESTED	EXCITED	HOLLAND	METTLED	POPEYED	SIGHTED
THERMIC	BLITZED	CRICOID	EXISTED	HOMINID	MIDGARD	PORTEND	SINDBAD
TITANIC	BLOATED	CRINOID	EXPIRED	HONEYED	MIDLAND	POWERED	SKILLED
TONETIC	BLOCKED	CROOKED	EXPOSED	HOTHEAD	MINUEND	PREBEND	SKIMMED
TOTEMIC	BLUNTED	CROPPED	EXPOUND	HUBBARD	MINUTED	PREPAID	SKINNED
TRAFFIC	BLURRED	CROSSED	FACETED	HUNCHED	MISDEED	PRESSED	SKIPPED
TRIATIC	BOBSLED	CROWDED	FACTOID	HUNDRED	MISLEAD	PRETEND	SKYWARD
TROPHIC	BOLLARD	CRUSHED	FAINTED	HURRIED	MISREAD	PRICKED	SLASHED
VANADIC	BOMBARD	CUCKOLD	FANCIED	HUSBAND	MONEYED	PRINTED	SLATTED
VOCALIC	BONNARD	CURDLED	FANGLED	HYALOID	MORLAND	PROBAND	SLEEVED
VOLTAIC	BOTTLED	CURRIED	FATHEAD	HYDATID	MOTTLED	PROCEED	SLIPPED
ZAPOTEC	BOUNDED	CUSTARD	FAVORED	ICELAND	MOULDED	PRONGED	SLOSHED
ABASHED	BOWHEAD	CYSTOID	FEIGNED	ICHABOD	MOUNTED	PROPEND	SLOTTED
ABBASID	BOXWOOD	DAGWOOD	FENLAND	IGNORED	MUDDLED	PUNCHED	SMASHED
ABELARD	BOYHOOD	DAMAGED	FEVERED	ILLBRED	MUFFLED	PUZZLED	SMUDGED
ABSCOND	BRANDED	DAPHNID	FIBROID	IMPAVID	MUSCOID	PYRAMID	SOFABED
ACCUSED	BREADED	DAPPLED	FINLAND	IMPLIED	MUSTARD	QUILTED	SOUNDED
ADENOID	BRIGAND	DASTARD	FIXATED	IMPOUND	MYELOID	RADDLED	SOZZLED
ADMIRED	BRONZED	DAZZLED	FLACCID	INBOARD	NAILBED	RAGWEED	SPLAYED
ADOPTED	BROWNED	DEBASED	FLAPPED	INFIELD	NEGROID	REBOUND	SPLICED
ADORNED	BRUISED	DECAYED	FLECKED	INJURED	NIGGARD	REBUILD	SPOILED
AERATED	BUSTARD	DECIDED	FLEDGED	INSIPID	NOBBLED	REDHEAD	SPOTTED
AFFIXED	BUZZARD	DECREED	FLOODED	INSTEAD	NOCTUID	REDOUND	SQUALID
AGROUND	CAMWOOD	DEFACED	FLUSHED	INVALID	NOTCHED	REDUCED	SQUARED
ALARMED	CANDIED	DEFILED	FOOTPAD	IRELAND	NOTEPAD	REDWOOD	STAINED
ALIGNED	CARABID	DEFINED	FORFEND	JELLIED	OBLIGED	REFINED	STALKED
ALIQUID	CARLOAD	DEFRAUD	FORWARD	JOINTED	OCEANID	RELATED	STAMPED
ALLEGED	CAROTID	DELAYED	FOULARD	JUMBLED	OCTOPOD	RELAXED	STARTED
ALLOWED	CARRIED	DELTOID	FRETTED	JUTLAND	OERSTED	REMOULD	STARVED
ALTERED	CASTLED	DELUDED	FRILLED	KAMERAD	OFFHAND	REMOVED	STEAMED
AMERIND	CATHEAD	DEMIGOD	FRINGED	KATYDID	OFFLOAD	REPUTED	STEMMED
AMYLOID	CENTRED	DESCEND	FROSTED	KEYWORD	OILBIRD	RESCIND	STEROID
ANDROID	CESTOID	DESMOND	FUDDLED	KINDRED	OMITTED	RESOUND	STEWARD
ANEROID	CHAINED	DESPOND	FUNGOID	KNEEPAD	OPERAND	RESPOND	STILTED
ANISEED	CHANGED	DEVISED	GALAHAD	KNITTED	OPPOSED	RETIRED	STIPEND
ANNELID	CHAPPED	DEVOTED	GARBLED	KNOTTED	ORCHARD	RETREAD	STIRRED

STOPPED	WETLAND	ANYMORE	BERLINE	CATHODE	CONFINE	DEPLETE	EMULATE
STORIED	WHACKED	APELIKE	BESIEGE	CATLIKE	CONFUSE	DEPLORE	ENCLAVE
STRIPED	WHEELED	APHTHAE	BESPOKE	CATSEYE	CONJURE	DEPRAVE	ENCLOSE
STUDDED	WHIPPED	APOCOPE	BEZIQUE	CAVIARE	CONNATE	DEPRIVE	ENDGAME
STUDIED	WIDOWED	APOSTLE	BICYCLE	CAYENNE	CONNIVE	DERANGE	ENDNOTE
STUFFED	WILFRED	APPEASE	BIOCIDE	CELESTE	CONNOTE	DESERVE	ENDORSE
STUMPED	WIZENED	APPRIZE	BIPLANE	CELLULE	CONSOLE	DESPISE	ENFORCE
STUNTED	WORRIED	APPROVE	BIVALVE	CENACLE	CONSUME	DESPITE	ENGORGE
SUBDUED	WORSTED	ARABIZE	BIZARRE	CENSURE	CONVENE	DESTINE	ENGRAVE
SUBTEND	WOUNDED	ARACHNE	BOLSHIE	CESTODE	CONVOKE	DETENTE	ENHANCE
SUCCEED	WRAPPED	ARCHIVE	BONDAGE	CEVICHE	COPPICE	DEVALUE	ENLARGE
SUGARED	WRECKED	ARCUATE	BONFIRE	CÉZANNE	CORACLE	DEVIATE	ENNOBLE
SUSPEND	ZEALAND	ARIADNE	BOUCLÉE	CHALDEE	CORDATE	DEVISEE	ENQUIRE
SWAPPED	ZETLAND	ARMHOLE	BOUTADE	CHALICE	CORDITE	DEVOICE	ENSLAVE
SWEATED	ABALONE	ARRANGE	BRAILLE	CHALONE	CORKAGE	DEVOLVE	ENSNARE
TABANID	ABRIDGE	ARTICLE	BRAMBLE	CHAMBRÉ	CORNICE	DEVOTEE	ENSUITE
TABLOID	ABSENCE	ARTISTE	BREATHE	CHANCRE	CORRODE	DIALYSE	ENTEBBE
TAINTED	ABSOLVE	ASCRIBE	BRICKIE	CHARADE	CORSAGE	DIAMINE	ENTENTE
TANCRED	ABUSIVE	ASININE	BRIGADE	CHAYOTE	CORTEGE	DICTATE	ENTHUSE
TANGLED	ACADEME	ASKANCE	BRINDLE	CHEMISE	COSTIVE	DIETINE	ENTITLE
TANKARD	ACCRETE	ASPERGE	BRIOCHE	CHICANE	COSTUME	DINETTE	ENTWINE
TELFORD	ACCURSE	ASSIEGE	BRISTLE	CHINESE	COTERIE	DIOCESE	EPERGNE
TENFOLD	ACETATE	ASSUAGE	BRITTLE	CHIPPIE	COTTAGE	DIOPTRE	EPICENE
THYROID	ACETONE	ASTARTE	BROCADE	CHOOKIE	COUCHÉE	DIORITE	EPICURE
TOASTED	ACHIEVE	ASTILBE	BROMATE	CHOPINE	COURAGE	DIOXIDE	EPIDOTE
TOEHOLD	ACOLYTE	ASTRIDE	BROMIDE	CHORALE	COUTURE	DIPHONE	EPIGONE
TOOTHED	ACONITE	ATHLETE	BROMINE	CHORDAE	COWBANE	DISABLE	EPISODE
TOUCHED	ACQUIRE	ATINGLE	BROWNIE	CHORTLE	COWHIDE	DISEASE	EPISTLE
TOWHEAD	ACREAGE	ATOMIZE	BRUSQUE	CHUCKLE	COWPOKE	DISLIKE	EPITOME
TRAINED	ACTUATE	ATTACHE	BUCKEYE	CILIATE	CRACKLE	DISPOSE	EQUABLE
TRAPPED	ADAMITE	AUBERGE	BULLACE	CIMABUE	CRAPPIE	DISPUTE	ERASURE
TREATED	ADELINE	AUDIBLE	BURBAGE	CIRROSE	CREMATE	DISROBE	EREMITE
TRIFFID	ADENINE	AUGUSTE	BURETTE	CITRINE	CRENATE	DIVERGE	ERUDITE
TRILLED	ADIPOSE	AUREATE	BURMESE	CLAVATE	CREVICE	DIVERSE	ESCAPEE
TWISTED	ADULATE	AUREOLE	CABBAGE	CLEANSE	CRINKLE	DIVORCE	ESPOUSE
TWOFOLD	ADVANCE	AURICLE	CABOOSE	CLIMATE	CRIPPLE	DIVULGE	ESQUIRE
TYNWALD	ADVERSE	AUSLESE	CACIQUE	CLIPPIE	CRUMBLE	DOGGONE	ESSENCE
TYPHOID	AFFABLE	AUSTERE	CADENCE	CLOSURE	CRUMPLE	DOGROSE	ETAGÈRE
UNAIDED	AGGRADE	AUTOCUE	CAGOULE	CLOTURE	CRUSADE	DOMAINE	EUGENIE
UNAIRED	AGITATE	AVARICE	CAINITE	COCAINE	CUBICLE	DRABBLE	EULALIE
UNARMED	AGONIZE	AVERAGE	CAIRENE	COCKADE	CUISINE	DRAFTEE	EUSTACE
UNASKED	AIDANCE	AWESOME	CALCINE	COCOTTE	CULTURE	DRAGGLE	EUTERPE
UNBOUND	AINTREE	AZURITE	CALCITE	CODEINE	CURABLE	DRIBBLE	EVACUEE
UNBOWED	AIRBASE	BAGASSE	CALECHE	COGNATE	CURETTE	DRIZZLE	EVASIVE
UNCARED	AIRLINE	BAGGAGE	CALIBRE	COINAGE	CURSIVE	DUCTILE	EXAMINE
UNCURED	ALAMODE	BAGPIPE	CALICHE	COLLAGE	CUTICLE	DUNNAGE	EXAMPLE
UNDATED	ALANINE	BALANCE	CALORIE	COLLATE	CUVETTE	DURABLE	EXCLUDE
UNFADED	ALCALDE	BALLADE	CAMOGIE	COLLEGE	CYANIDE	DWINDLE	EXCRETE
UNFIXED	ALEPINE	BANDAGE	CANDACE	COLLIDE	CYCLONE	EARACHE	EXECUTE
UNHEARD	ALEWIFE	BANDORE	CANDIDE	COLLUDE	DASYURE	EARLOBE	EXEGETE
UNLINED	ALIDADE	BANSHEE	CANIDAE	COLOGNE	DATABLE	EATABLE	EXPANSE
UNLOVED	ALLONGE	BAPTIZE	CANZONE	COMBINE	DAYTIME	EBBTIDE	EXPENSE
UNMIXED	ALUMNAE	BAROQUE	CAPABLE	COMMODE	DEADEYE	EBONITE	EXPIATE
UNMOVED	ALVEOLE	BARRAGE	CAPRICE	COMMUNE	DEBACLE	ECCRINE	EXPLODE
UNNAMED	AMBROSE	BASCULE	CAPSIZE	COMMUTE	DECEASE	ECLIPSE	EXPLORE
UNOWNED	AMIABLE	BASTIDE	CAPSULE	COMPARE	DECEIVE	ECLOGUE	EXPUNGE
UNPAGED	AMORITE	BAUXITE	CAPTIVE	COMPERE	DECLARE	EDIFICE	EXTREME
UNSOUND	AMPOULE	BECAUSE	CAPTURE	COMPETE	DECLINE	EDUCATE	EXTRUDE
UNTAMED	AMYLASE	BEDSIDE	CARBIDE	COMPILE	DEFENCE	EFFORCE	EXUDATE
UNTRIED	AMYLOSE	BEDSORE	CARBINE	COMPOSE	DEFENSE	EGLOGUE	EYEHOLE
UNWOUND	ANALYZE	BEDTIME	CARCASE	COMPOTE	DEFLATE	ELAMITE	EYESORE
UPBRAID	ANATOLE	BEEHIVE	CARIOLE	COMPUTE	DEGRADE	ELEVATE	FAIENCE
VAULTED	ANDANTE	BEELINE	CARLYLE	COMRADE	DEHISCE	ELLIPSE	FAILURE
WARHEAD	ANEMONE	BEGUILE	CARMINE	CONCAVE	DEIRDRE	ELUSIVE	FANFARE
WARLORD	ANILINE	BEHOOVE	CARNAGE	CONCISE	DELOUSE	EMANATE	FANZINE
WATERED	ANIMATE	BELIEVE	CAROUSE	CONCEDE	DEMERGE	EMBLAZE	FARNESE
WAYLAND	ANODIZE	BENZENE	CASCADE	CONDOLE	DEMESNE	EMBRACE	FATIGUE
WAYWARD	ANODYNE	BENZINE	CASEASE	CONDONE	DENTINE	EMIRATE	FEATURE
WEEKEND	ANTIQUE	BEREAVE	CASTILE	CONFIDE	DENTURE	EMOTIVE	FEBRILE

FERRULE	GLENCOE	IMPLODE	LAYETTE	MIDWIFE	OBSERVE	PENSILE	PRIVATE
FERTILE	GLIMPSE	IMPLORE	LEAKAGE	MIGRATE	OBTRUDE	PENSIVE	PROBATE
FESTIVE	GLOBULE	IMPROVE	LEASOWE	MILEAGE	OBVERSE	PENTANE	PROCURE
FETICHE	GLUCOSE	IMPULSE	LECTURE	MIOCENE	OBVIATE	PENTODE	PRODUCE
FIANCÉE	GODLIKE	INCENSE	LEGATEE	MIRACLE	OCCLUDE	PENTOSE	PROFANE
FILASSE	GOODBYE	INCLINE	LEGIBLE	MISFIRE	OCTUPLE	PEONAGE	PROFILE
FINAGLE	GOUACHE	INCLUDE	LEISURE	MISRULE	OFFBASE	PEPSINE	PROFUSE
FINANCE	GRACILE	INCURVE	LEONINE	MISSILE	OFFENCE	PERCALE	PROMISE
FINESSE	GRACKLE	INDULGE	LETTUCE	MISSIVE	OFFENSE	PERFUME	PROMOTE
FIRCONE	GRADATE	INFLAME	LEUCINE	MISTAKE	OFFSIDE	PERFUSE	PRONATE
FISHEYE	GRANDEE	INFLATE	LICENCE	MISTIME	OILCAKE	PERIGEE	PROPANE
FISSILE	GRANITE	INGENUE	LICENSE	MIXTURE	OLEFINE	PERJURE	PROPOSE
FISSURE	GRANNIE	INGRATE	LIGNITE	MOABITE	OMPHALE	PERLITE	PROTEGE
FISTULE	GRANTEE	INHOUSE	LINACRE	MODERNE	ONETIME	PERTUSE	PROUDIE
FIXTURE	GRANULE	INNERVE	LINDANE	MODISTE	ONSHORE	PERVADE	PROVIDE
FLEXILE	GRAPPLE	INQUIRE	LINEAGE	MOFETTE	ONSTAGE	PETIOLE	PROVOKE
FLOOZIE	GRAVURE	INSCAPE	LINKAGE	MOIDORE	OPALINE	PHILTRE	PRYTHEE
FLOUNCE	GRENADE	INSHORE	LIONIZE	MOLIÈRE	OPERATE	PHONEME	PUCELLE
FOLIAGE	GRIDDLE	INSPIRE	LISSOME	MONOCLE	ORIFICE	PIASTRE	PUERILE
FOOTAGE	GRIMACE	INSTATE	LITCHEE	MONTAGE	OSBORNE	PICKAXE	PULSATE
FOOTSIE	GRISTLE	INTENSE	LOVABLE	MORAINE	OSSICLE	PICOTEE	PURLINE
FORBADE	GRIZZLE	INTERNE	LOZENGE	MORTICE	OSTIOLE	PICTURE	PURPOSE
FORESEE	GROCKLE	INTRUDE	LUCARNE	MORTISE	OUTCOME	PILLAGE	PUSTULE
FORGAVE	GROUPIE	INVERSE	LUCERNE	MOSELLE	OUTDARE	PINHOLE	QUIBBLE
FORGIVE	GRUMBLE	INVOICE	LUDDITE	MOUILLÉ	OUTFACE	PINKEYE	QUICKIE
FORGONE	GRUYÈRE	INVOLVE	LUDGATE	MOULAGE	OUTLINE	PINNACE	QUINCHE
FORSAKE	GUANINE	IRIDISE	LUGGAGE	MOUNTIE	OUTLIVE	PIPETTE	QUININE
FORTUNE	GUMSHOE	IRKSOME	LUGHOLE	MOVABLE	OUTRAGE	PIROGUE	QUINONE
FOXHOLE	GUNFIRE	ISOBASE	LUNETTE	MUNDANE	OUTSIDE	PISCINE	QUIXOTE
FRAGILE	GUNWALE	ISODORE	MACABRE	MURIATE	OUTSIZE	PISMIRE	QUORATE
FRAZZLE	GUTTATE	ISOLATE	MACAQUE	MUSETTE	OUTVOTE	PISTOLE	RADIATE
FRECKLE	GUYROPE	ISOMERE	MACHETE	MUTABLE	OVERAWE	PLACATE	RADICLE
FREEBIE	HACHURE	ISOTONE	MACRAMÉ	MYCENAE	OVERDUE	PLEIADE	RAGTIME
FRIABLE	HALTERE	ISOTOPE	MAGNATE	MYELINE	OVERLIE	PLIABLE	RAMPAGE
FRIGATE	HASTATE	ITEMIZE	MAGUIRE	NACELLE	OVERSEE	PLOSIVE	RANIDAE
FRISBEE	HAULAGE	ITERATE	MALAISE	NAIVETÉ	OVICIDE	PLUMAGE	RAPTURE
FRIZZLE	HAWKEYE	IVANHOE	MALTASE	NARRATE	OVULATE	PLUMATE	RATLINE
FRUMPLE	HAYWIRE	IVRESSE	MALTESE	NAVARRE	OXALATE	PLUMULE	RAWHIDE
FULSOME	HECTARE	JASMINE	MALTOSE	NAVETTE	OXIDASE	POLEAXE	REALIZE
FUMETTE	HELLENE	JAVELLE	MANACLE	NECKTIE	OXIDIZE	POLLUTE	RECEIVE
FURCATE	HEMLINE	JAWBONE	MANATEE	NECROSE	PACKAGE	POLONIE	RECLINE
FURNACE	HENBANE	JOHNNIE	MANDATE	NÉGLIGÉ	PADRONE	PONTINE	RECLUSE
FURTIVE	HEPTANE	JOYRIDE	MANHOLE	NEPTUNE	PALETTE	PORCINE	RECURVE
FUSIBLE	HERBAGE	JUBILEE	MANIPLE	NERVURE	PALMATE	PORTAGE	RECYCLE
GABELLE	HEROINE	JUSSIVE	MANMADE	NETSUKE	PALPATE	POSTAGE	REFEREE
GALETTE	HIPBONE	JUSTICE	MANSIZE	NEURINE	PANACHE	POSTURE	REFLATE
GALILEE	HIRSUTE	KAINITE	MARCUSE	NEURONE	PANCAKE	POTABLE	REFUGEE
GALOCHE	HITTITE	KARAOKE	MARLENE	NEVILLE	PANICLE	POTHOLE	REHOUSE
GAMBOGE	HOPLITE	KATRINE	MARLINE	NEWCOME	PANNAGE	POTICHE	REISSUE
GARBAGE	HORMONE	KERNITE	MARLITE	NICOISE	PANNOSE	POTTAGE	REJOICE
GARBURE	HOSPICE	KEYHOLE	MARLOWE	NICTATE	PANTILE	PRAIRIE	RELAPSE
GARONNE	HOSTAGE	KEYNOTE	MARMITE	NIGHTIE	PANURGE	PRALINE	RELEASE
GAROTTE	HOSTILE	KHANATE	MARQUEE	NITRATE	PAPOOSE	PRATTLE	RELIEVE
GASFIRE	HOTLINE	KHEDIVE	MASSAGE	NITRILE	PARABLE	PRECEDE	REMORSE
GAVOTTE	HUSSITE	KILDARE	MASSINE	NITRITE	PARTAKE	PRECISE	RENEGUE
GAZELLE	HYALINE	KINTYRE	MASSIVE	NITRODE	PARTAGE	PREDATE	REPLACE
GAZETTE	HYDRATE	KNOBBLE	MATINEE	NOISOME	PASSIVE	PREFACE	REPLETE
GEFILTE	HYGIENE	KNUCKLE	MATISSE	NOMINEE	PASTIME	PRELATE	REPROVE
GEMMATE	ICEFLOE	KYANITE	MAYPOLE	NOTABLE	PASTURE	PRELUDE	REPTILE
GENOESE	ICHNITE	LABIATE	MEASURE	NOWHERE	PATIBLE	PREMISE	REPULSE
GENTILE	IDOLIZE	LACTASE	MEDIATE	NUCLIDE	PAULINE	PREPARE	REQUIRE
GENUINE	IGNOBLE	LACTATE	MELLITE	NUNLIKE	PAYABLE	PREPUCE	REQUITE
GEORDIE	IMAGINE	LACTOSE	MELROSE	NURTURE	PEARLIE	PRESAGE	REROUTE
GERMANE	IMITATE	LACUNAE	MESSAGE	NUTCASE	PECTASE	PRESIDE	RESERVE
GESTATE	IMMENSE	LAETARE	METHANE	NUTLIKE	PEDICLE	PRESUME	RESHAPE
GESTURE	IMMERGE	LALIQUE	MÉTISSE	OATCAKE	PEERAGE	PREZZIE	RESIDUE
GIRAFFE	IMMERSE	LASAGNE	MICROBE	OBLIQUE	PENANCE	PRICKLE	RESOLVE
GIRONDE	IMPASSE	LATRINE	MIDLINE	OBSCENE	PENNATE	PRIMATE	RESPIRE
GISELLE	IMPINGE	LATTICE	MIDWIFE	OBSCURE	PENNINE	PRITHEE	RESPITE

RESTATE	SESTINE	STYLITE	TORNADE	VACUOLE	DISTAFF	BOOTLEG	FALLING
RESTIVE	SEVILLE	STYLIZE	TORSADE	VALENCE	ENFEOFF	BOWLING	FARMING
RESTORE	SHACKLE	SUBLIME	TORTILE	VALVULE	FIGLEAF	BRACING	FASTING
RETICLE	SHAMBLE	SUBSIDE	TORTURE	VAMOOSE	FLYHALF	BRAKING	FAWNING
RETINUE	SHEATHE	SUBSUME	TOWLINE	VAMPIRE	FLYLEAF	BREWING	FEEDING
RETIREE	SHELTIE	SUCROSE	TOWROPE	VANDYKE	GASTHOF	BUDDING	FEELING
RETRACE	SHINGLE	SUFFETE	TOYNBEE	VANTAGE	HERSELF	BUGGING	FENCING
REUNITE	SHMOOZE	SUFFICE	TRADUCE	VEDETTE	HIMSELF	BULGING	FILLING
REVALUE	SHUFFLE	SUFFUSE	TRAINEE	VEHICLE	KICKOFF	BULLDOG	FILMING
REVENGE	SHUTEYE	SUICIDE	TRAIPSE	VENDOME	LIFTOFF	BUNTING	FINDING
REVENUE	SHUTTLE	SULFATE	TRAMPLE	VENTOSE	MASTIFF	BURNING	FIREBUG
REVERIE	SIAMESE	SULLAGE	TRANCHE	VENTURE	MIDRIFF	BUSSING	FIREDOG
REVERSE	SILENCE	SUNNITE	TRAPEZE	VERBOSE	OAKLEAF	CABLING	FISHING
REVOLVE	SINCERE	SUNRISE	TREACLE	VERDURE	ONESELF	CALLING	FITTING
REWRITE	SINUATE	SUPPOSE	TREADLE	VESICLE	PLAYOFF	CAMPING	FLAMING
RHIZOME	SISTINE	SUPREME	TREMBLE	VESTIGE	PONTIFF	CANNING	FLEEING
RIBCAGE	SITUATE	SURFACE	TRESTLE	VIBRATE	POSITIF	CARVING	FLEMING
RIPOSTE	SIZABLE	SURMISE	TRIBUNE	VILLAGE	REPROOF	CASTING	FLOWING
RIPTIDE	SKIFFLE	SURNAME	TRIBUTE	VINASSE	SELLOFF	CATALOG	FOLDING
RISIBLE	SKITTLE	SURVIVE	TRICKLE	VINTAGE	SENDOFF	CATELOG	FOOTING
RISSOLE	SKYBLUE	SUZETTE	TRIESTE	VIOLATE	SHADOOF	CATLING	FORELEG
ROMAINE	SKYLINE	SWADDLE	TRINGLE	VIRGATE	SHERIFF	CEILING	FORMING
ROMANCE	SLOVENE	SWEETIE	TRIREME	VIRGULE	SHOWOFF	CHAFING	FUNDING
ROSALIE	SMARTIE	SWINDLE	TRITONE	VISCOSE	SPINOFF	CHASING	FURLONG
ROSEATE	SMOOTHE	SWINGLE	TROCHEE	VISIBLE	SUNROOF	CHEWING	GALLING
ROSELLE	SMUGGLE	SWIZZLE	TROUBLE	VITIATE	TAKEOFF	CHINWAG	GASPING
ROSETTE	SNAFFLE	SYNAPSE	TROUNCE	VOIVODE	TEALEAF	CHOKING	GATLING
ROUGHIE	SNIFFLE	SYNCOPE	TRUCKLE	VOLANTE	THYSELF	CLOSING	GEARING
ROULADE	SNORTLE	SYRINGE	TRUFFLE	VOLTAGE	WELLOFF	CLOYING	GEELONG
ROUTINE	SNUFFLE	SYSTOLE	TRUNDLE	VOLUBLE	WITLOOF	COATING	GELDING
RUMMAGE	SNUGGLE	TACTILE	TRUSTEE	VULGATE	ABIDING	CODLING	GETTING
RUMPOLE	SOCKEYE	TADPOLE	TSIGANE	VULPINE	ACHTUNG	COMBING	GILDING
RUPTURE	SOLUBLE	TANNATE	TUNABLE	VULTURE	ADORING	COOKING	GINSENG
RUTHENE	SOMEONE	TAPPICE	TUNICLE	WALLACE	AGELONG	COOLING	GLARING
SACCADE	SONDAGE	TARDIVE	TURBINE	WALLEYE	ALTHING	COPYING	GLAZING
SALABLE	SOUBISE	TARTARE	TURENNE	WALPOLE	AMAZING	CORKING	GLIDING
SALIQUE	SOUFFLE	TARTINE	TUSSORE	WARFARE	AMUSING	COSTING	GLOWING
SALTATE	SOUTANE	TAURINE	TWADDLE	WARLIKE	ANGLING	COWLING	GNAWING
SALTIRE	SPANGLE	TAXABLE	TWEEDLE	WARTIME	BACKING	CRAVING	GOLDING
SALVAGE	SPARKLE	TAXFREE	TWIDDLE	WASTAGE	BACKLOG	CROWING	GOLFING
SAMNITE	SPAVINE	TEACAKE	TWINKLE	WATTAGE	BALDING	CUCKING	GOSLING
SAPROBE	SPECKLE	TEATIME	TWOSOME	WAYSIDE	BANGING	CUNNING	GRATING
SARDINE	SPECTRE	TEENAGE	TWOTIME	WEBSITE	BANKING	CURLING	GRAZING
SATIATE	SPICATE	TEKTITE	UKRAINE	WELCOME	BARKING	CUTTING	GREYLAG
SAUSAGE	SPICULE	TENABLE	UKULELE	WELFARE	BARRING	CYCLING	GROWING
SCALENE	SPINATE	TENSILE	ULEXITE	WHEEDLE	BASKING	DAMNING	GUIDING
SCAMBLE	SPINDLE	TERENCE	ULULATE	WHEELIE	BATHING	DAMPING	GUSHING
SCEPTRE	SPITTLE	TERMITE	UMBRAGE	WHISTLE	BATTING	DANCING	HACKING
SCIENCE	SPLODGE	TERRACE	UNALIKE	WHITTLE	BEADING	DARLING	HALTING
SCOTTIE	SPLURGE	TERRANE	UNALIVE	WHOOPEE	BEAMING	DARNING	HANDBAG
SCOURGE	SPONDEE	TERRENE	UNAWARE	WINSOME	BEANBAG	DASHING	HANGDOG
SCRAPIE	SPRINGE	TERRINE	UNHINGE	WOULDBE	BEARHUG	DEALING	HANGING
SCREEVE	SPYHOLE	TESTATE	UNHORSE	WRANGLE	BEARING	DIALING	HEADING
SCROOGE	SQUEEZE	TEXTILE	UNLOOSE	WREATHE	BEATING	DIGGING	HEALING
SCRUPLE	STABILE	TEXTURE	UNNERVE	WRESTLE	BEDDING	DOCKING	HEARING
SCUFFLE	STADDLE	THEATRE	UNQUOTE	WRIGGLE	BEGGING	DORKING	HEATING
SCUTAGE	STARTLE	THIMBLE	UNTWINE	WRINKLE	BEIJING	DOWSING	HEDGING
SCUTTLE	STATURE	THISTLE	UPGRADE	WRYNOSE	BENDING	DRAWING	HELPING
SEASIDE	STATUTE	THUGGEE	UPRAISE	YANGTSE	BETTING	DRIVING	HERRING
SEATTLE	STEEPLE	THYMINE	UPSTAGE	YAOUNDE	BETTONG	DUBBING	HILDING
SECLUDE	STERILE	TILLAGE	UPSTATE	YARDAGE	BIDDING	DUCKING	HINDLEG
SECRETE	STICKLE	TIMBALE	UPSURGE	YEZIDEE	BILTONG	DUSTING	HISSING
SEEPAGE	STIPPLE	TITRATE	URALITE	ZEOLITE	BINDING	EARRING	HOGGING
SEIZURE	STORAGE	TOLUENE	URANITE	ZOOLITE	BLAZING	ENSUING	HOLDING
SELVAGE	STRANGE	TONNAGE	URINATE	BAILIFF	BOATING	ETCHING	HOMBURG
SENSATE	STRIATE	TONSURE	UTERINE	BEOWULF	BOILING	EVENING	HOPPING
SERVICE	STROPHE	TONTINE	UTILIZE	CAITIFF	BOMBING	EXITING	HORSING
SERVILE	STUBBLE	TOOTSIE	UTRICLE	CASTOFF	BOOKING	FAILING	HOUSING
SESSILE	STUMBLE	TOPSIDE	VACCINE	DEBRIEF	BOOMING	FAIRING	HOWLING

HULKING	MEANING	RANKING	SPARING	WORKING	GARFISH	REDFISH	BASMATI
HUMMING	MEETING	RANTING	STAGING	WRITING	GARNISH	REFRESH	BELLINI
HUNTING	MELTING	READING	STARING	WYOMING	GAWKISH	RETOUCH	BENGALI
HURLING	MENDING	REARING	STAYING	WYSIWYG	GIRLISH	RHENISH	BERNINI
ICEBERG	MILKING	REEKING	STEWING	YAWNING	GOLIATH	ROGUISH	BOLSHOI
IMAGING	MILLING	REELING	STYLING	ABOLISH	GOODISH	ROOKISH	BOUILLI
INKLING	MINCING	RESTING	SUMMING	ABSINTH	GOULASH	RUBBISH	BRONCHI
IRONING	MISSING	RHYMING	SURFING	ALDRICH	GRAYISH	RUDOLPH	BURUNDI
ITCHING	MOANING	RIBBING	SWAYING	ANGUISH	GREYISH	SABAOTH	CALCULI
JAMMING	MOCKING	RIGGING	TAGALOG	ANTIOCH	GWYNETH	SABBATH	CAMBRAI
JEERING	MOLDING	RINGING	TALKING	ASQUITH	HAGFISH	SAWFISH	CAMPARI
JESTING	MONOLOG	RIOTING	TANNING	AZIMUTH	HAPORTH	SCRATCH	CELLINI
JOBBING	MOONING	RIPPING	TAPPING	BABOOSH	HARLECH	SCREECH	CHAPATI
JOGGING	MOORING	ROADHOG	TATTING	BABYISH	HARWICH	SCRUNCH	CHIANTI
JOINING	MOPPING	ROAMING	TEARING	BEARISH	HASHISH	SELFISH	CHUPATI
JUMPING	MORNING	ROARING	TEASING	BENEATH	HELLISH	SEVENTH	COLIBRI
KAMPONG	MUGGING	ROCKING	TEEMING	BESEECH	HEXARCH	SHARIAH	CORELLI
KEELING	MUSTANG	ROLLING	TELLING	BETROTH	HOGARTH	SKYHIGH	EFFENDI
KEEPING	NAGGING	ROOFING	TENSING	BEWITCH	HOGWASH	SLAVISH	FUSILLI
KENNING	NAPPING	ROOTING	TESTING	BIOTECH	IMPEACH	SOPWITH	GNOCCHI
KICKING	NEARING	ROTTING	TICKING	BISMUTH	INDEPTH	SPANISH	GOLDONI
KILLING	NECKING	ROUSING	TIMELAG	BLEMISH	INVEIGH	SPINACH	GRACCHI
KIPLING	NETTING	RUBBING	TIPPING	BOOKISH	JACINTH	SPLOTCH	GUARANI
KISSING	NODDING	RUNNING	TOOLING	BOORISH	JAPLISH	SQUELCH	HALLALI
KNOWING	NOGGING	RUSHING	TOPPING	BOROUGH	JEHOVAH	SQUINCH	HIBACHI
LACKING	NOSEBAG	RUTTING	TOURING	BREADTH	JEWFISH	STAUNCH	HOUDINI
LADYBUG	NOTHING	SACKING	TRACING	BRITISH	KADDISH	STEALTH	ISMAILI
LAGGING	NURSING	SAILING	TRADING	BRUTISH	KENTISH	STENGAH	ISRAELI
LAMBING	NUTTING	SALTING	TREPANG	BULLISH	KUFIYAH	STOMACH	JACUZZI
LANCING	ONGOING	SANDBAG	TURNING	BULRUSH	LAMBETH	STRETCH	JAMPANI
LANDING	OPENING	SAPLING	UNDOING	BURNISH	LOUTISH	STREWTH	KARACHI
LAPPING	PACKING	SCARING	UNDYING	CADDISH	LUMPISH	STYLISH	KONTIKI
LAPSANG	PADDING	SCORING	UPSWING	CATARRH	MACBETH	SUKKOTH	LAKSHMI
LAPWING	PAIRING	SEARING	VARYING	CATFISH	MAMMOTH	SWEDISH	LORELEI
LASHING	PARKING	SEATING	VENDING	CATTISH	MANNISH	TALLITH	MALACHI
LASTING	PARTING	SEEMING	VETTING	CEILIDH	MAWKISH	TAPLASH	MARCONI
LEADING	PASSING	SELLING	WADDING	CHEETAH	MENORAH	TARNISH	MARTINI
LEANING	PECKING	SERVING	WAFTING	CHERISH	MESSIAH	THROUGH	NAIROBI
LEAPING	PEELING	SETTING	WAILING	CORINTH	MITZVAH	TIGRISH	ORIGAMI
LEASING	PEEPING	SHADING	WAITING	CORNISH	MONARCH	TONNISH	OSMANLI
LEAVING	PEERING	SHAKING	WALKING	CRANACH	MONKISH	TOWPATH	OUSTITI
LEGGING	PELTING	SHAPING	WANTING	CURRAGH	MOORISH	TRIUMPH	PAHLAVI
LEMMING	PENDING	SHARING	WAPPING	DALILAH	MOREISH	TURKISH	PECCAVI
LENDING	PERIWIG	SHAVING	WARBURG	DEBAUCH	NEBBISH	TURPETH	POLIZEI
LESSING	PFENNIG	SHEBANG	WARLING	DEBORAH	NEOLITH	TWELFTH	POMPEII
LETTING	PICKING	SHINDIG	WARMING	DEBOUCH	NINEVEH	UNCOUTH	PUCCINI
LICKING	PIGLING	SHINING	WARNING	DELILAH	NONSUCH	UNEARTH	PUNJABI
LILTING	PIMPING	SHOWING	WARRING	DERVISH	NORWICH	UNHITCH	RAVIOLI
LINKING	PLACING	SIBLING	WARTHOG	DIGLYPH	NOURISH	UNLATCH	REMBLAI
LINSANG	PLAYING	SIFTING	WASHING	DIGRAPH	OARFISH	UNLEASH	ROSSINI
LISTING	POLLING	SIGNING	WASTING	DIPTYCH	OBADIAH	UNTRUTH	SALIERI
LODGING	POPPING	SINGING	WAXWING	DOGFISH	OGREISH	UROLITH	SAMURAI
LOGGING	POSTBAG	SINKING	WEARING	DONNISH	OSTRICH	VARNISH	SASHIMI
LONGING	POSTING	SIPPING	WEAVING	DUMPISH	PECKISH	WAGGISH	SCUTARI
LOOKING	POTTING	SITTING	WEBBING	ENGLISH	PEEVISH	WARPATH	SHASTRI
LOOMING	PRAYING	SKATING	WEDDING	EPITAPH	PHARAOH	WASPISH	SHIKARI
LOOTING	PRIMING	SLAYING	WEEPING	EYEBATH	PIBROCH	WENDISH	SIGNORI
LORDING	PROLONG	SLIDING	WELDING	EYELASH	PIGFISH	WHITISH	SWAHILI
LOURING	PROVING	SLOPING	WETTING	EYEWASH	PINFISH	WIMPISH	TASSILI
LURKING	PUDDING	SLOWING	WHALING	FADDISH	POOHBAH	WOLFISH	TBILISI
MAHJONG	PULSING	SMILING	WHITING	FAIRISH	POTLACH	YIDDISH	TIMPANI
MAILBAG	PUNTING	SMOKING	WIGGING	FINNISH	PRUDISH	ADELPHI	TOPKAPI
MAILING	PUSHING	SNORING	WILDING	FLAUNCH	PUBLISH	AFGHANI	TRIPOLI
MALLING	PUTTING	SOAKING	WILLING	FLEMISH	PUCKISH	ALBERTI	TSUNAMI
MANNING	QUAKING	SOARING	WINDBAG	FOOLISH	PUGWASH	ALLEGRI	VIVALDI
MAPPING	RACKING	SOCKING	WINDING	FOPPISH	RAFFISH	ASHANTI	WATUTSI
MARBURG	RAFTING	SOPPING	WINNING	FURBISH	RALEIGH	ASSEGAI	ZAMBESI
MARKING	RAILING	SORTING	WISHING	FURNISH	REBIRTH	BACARDI	AIRLOCK
MATTING	RAISING	SPACING	WORDING	GALUMPH	REDDISH	BACILLI	AIRSICK

AMTRACK	MISTOOK	ACAUDAL	CONGEAL	GRADUAL	NEMORAL	SACKFUL	UXORIAL
ARTWORK	MUDLARK	ACCRUAL	CONICAL	GRAPNEL	NETBALL	SATCHEL	VAGINAL
BANGKOK	MUDPACK	ACTINAL	CONTROL	GRAUPEL	NEUTRAL	SAWBILL	VASSAIL
BANNOCK	NETWORK	ADAXIAL	CORDIAL	GRENDEL	NOMBRIL	SAWMILL	VEGETAL
BARRACK	NIBLICK	ADMIRAL	CORNEAL	GUIGNOL	NOMINAL	SCAFELL	VENTRAL
BEATNIK	NORFOLK	ADRENAL	CORNELL	GUMBOIL	NOSTRIL	SCALPEL	VERONAL
BEDROCK	NYNORSK	AEROSOL	COUNCIL	HANDFUL	NUMERAL	SCANDAL	VICINAL
BELLEEK	OARLOCK	AIRMAIL	COUNSEL	HANDSEL	NUPTIAL	SCHNELL	VICTUAL
BERSERK	OBELISK	ALCOHOL	COWGIRL	HARMFUL	OATMEAL	SCLERAL	VIRTUAL
BESPEAK	ODALISK	AMMONAL	CRANIAL	HATEFUL	ODDBALL	SCROTAL	VITRAIL
BETHINK	OFFPEAK	AMYGDAL	CRUCIAL	HEEDFUL	OPTICAL	SEAGULL	VITRIOL
BOOBOOK	OUTBACK	ANTHILL	CRYSTAL	HELICAL	OPTIMAL	SEAWALL	WAGTAIL
BULLOCK	OUTLOOK	APPAREL	CURTAIL	HELPFUL	ORBITAL	SECONAL	WAKEFUL
BULWARK	OUTRANK	APSIDAL	CYNICAL	HOBNAIL	ORCINOL	SEMINAL	WASSAIL
BUNDOOK	OUTWORK	APTERAL	DAMOSEL	HOLDALL	ORDINAL	SENEGAL	WASTREL
BURDOCK	PADDOCK	AROUSAL	DECANAL	HOPEFUL	OUTFALL	SENSUAL	WAXBILL
CALMUCK	PADLOCK	ARRIVAL	DECIBEL	HURTFUL	OVERALL	SERCIAL	WAYBILL
CANNOCK	PATRICK	ARSENAL	DECIMAL	ICEFALL	PAINFUL	SEVERAL	WENDELL
CARSICK	PEACOCK	ARUNDEL	DESPOIL	ILLEGAL	PALATAL	SHAWWAL	WISHFUL
CASSOCK	POLLACK	ASEXUAL	DIEDRAL	IMMORAL	PALUDAL	SHRIVEL	WISTFUL
CATWALK	POTLUCK	ASOCIAL	DIGITAL	IMPERIL	PARASOL	SITWELL	WRYBILL
CHAMPAK	PURBECK	AUSTRAL	DIGONAL	INFIDEL	PARBOIL	SKILFUL	ZEPHIEL
CHINOOK	PUTTOCK	AXOLOTL	DISTILL	INITIAL	PARNELL	SKINFUL	ZESTFUL
COSSACK	RANSACK	BALEFUL	DIURNAL	INKWELL	PARTIAL	SNORKEL	ABRAHAM
COWLICK	RATPACK	BALLIOL	DOLEFUL	INSTALL	PASCHAL	SOULFUL	ACCLAIM
CUTBACK	REDNECK	BASHFUL	DONEGAL	INSTILL	PATRIAL	SPANIEL	ACIFORM
DAYBOOK	RESTOCK	BEDEVIL	DURRELL	ISHMAEL	PAYROLL	SPATIAL	ACRONYM
DAYMARK	RETHINK	BEJEWEL	DUTIFUL	JEZEBEL	PEDICEL	SPECIAL	ALYSSUM
DEFROCK	ROEBUCK	BESTIAL	EMBROIL	JONQUIL	PERUSAL	SPIGNEL	AMALGAM
DENMARK	ROLLICK	BIFOCAL	EMPANEL	JOURNAL	PHRASAL	SPONDYL	ANAGRAM
DERRICK	ROSTOCK	BORSTAL	ENSNARL	JUVENAL	PIGTAIL	SPOUSAL	ANTONYM
DIPLOCK	ROWLOCK	BOSWELL	ENTHRAL	KARAKUL	PINBALL	STENCIL	ATAVISM
DISBARK	SCHLOCK	BOXHAUL	EPIGEAL	KESTREL	PINTAIL	STERNAL	ATHEISM
DUNKIRK	SCHMUCK	BRADAWL	ESTIVAL	KNOWALL	PITFALL	STOICAL	BAPTISM
DUNNOCK	SEALINK	BRIMFUL	ETERNAL	KURSAAL	PITIFUL	STRIGIL	BEDROOM
DVORNIK	SEASICK	BRINJAL	ETHANOL	LACTEAL	PIVOTAL	STRUDEL	BELGIUM
EARMARK	SELKIRK	BRISTOL	ETHICAL	LATERAL	PLAYFUL	SUBSOIL	BENTHAM
ETTRICK	SETBACK	BROTHEL	EYEBALL	LEGPULL	PLEURAL	SUNDIAL	BERSEEM
FETLOCK	SHYLOCK	BURNELL	EZEKIEL	LIBERAL	POMEROL	SURREAL	BERTRAM
FINBACK	SJAMBOK	BUTANAL	FACTUAL	LIMINAL	POUNDAL	TACTFUL	BLOSSOM
FOSSICK	SKYLARK	BUTANOL	FALAFEL	LINGUAL	PREDIAL	TEARFUL	BOHRIUM
FUTTOCK	SPUTNIK	CALOMEL	FANTAIL	LITERAL	PREQUEL	TENDRIL	BOREDOM
GARRICK	SUFFOLK	CAPITAL	FATEFUL	LOGICAL	PRETZEL	TENNIEL	BOXROOM
GASMASK	SUNDECK	CAPITOL	FEARFUL	LUGSAIL	PREVAIL	TERTIAL	BRIGHAM
GIMMICK	TANBARK	CAPORAL	FEDERAL	LUSTFUL	PUBERAL	TEXTUAL	BUCKRAM
GOSHAWK	TINTACK	CARACAL	FEMORAL	LYRICAL	PURCELL	THERMAL	BURNHAM
HADDOCK	TUSSOCK	CARACUL	FINICAL	MAGICAL	QUARREL	TIERCEL	CADMIUM
HAMMOCK	TZADDIK	CARAMEL	FISTFUL	MARITAL	QUETZAL	TIMBREL	CAESIUM
HASSOCK	UNBLOCK	CARAVEL	FLANNEL	MARSHAL	QUINTAL	TINFOIL	CALCIUM
HATTOCK	UNFROCK	CAREFUL	FLUVIAL	MARTIAL	RACHIAL	TOENAIL	CAMBIUM
HAYFORK	UNSTICK	CARRELL	FRETFUL	MARVELL	RADICAL	TOMFOOL	CASUISM
HEMLOCK	UNSTOCK	CARROLL	FROEBEL	MAXWELL	RAPHAEL	TOPICAL	CENTRUM
HENPECK	UNSTUCK	CATCALL	FRONTAL	MEDICAL	RECITAL	TOPSOIL	CHATHAM
HERRICK	VOLAPUK	CENTRAL	FULFILL	MENTHOL	REDPOLL	TRAMMEL	CHRISOM
HILLOCK	WARBECK	CHAGALL	FUNCHAL	METICAL	REFUSAL	TRAVAIL	CONFIRM
HOGBACK	WARLOCK	CHANCEL	FUNERAL	MICHAEL	REMODEL	TREFOIL	CONFORM
HOPSACK	WARWICK	CHANNEL	GABRIEL	MILFOIL	REMOVAL	TRIVIAL	CRANIUM
HUMMOCK	WAXWORK	CHARNEL	GADWALL	MINDFUL	RENEWAL	TRUCIAL	CUTWORM
KALMUCK	WAYMARK	CHATTEL	GAINFUL	MINERAL	REPOSAL	TUMBREL	DADAISM
KILLICK	WEDLOCK	CHERVIL	GARBOIL	MINIMAL	RESTFUL	TUMBRIL	DECLAIM
KUBELIK	WENLOCK	CHLORAL	GASOHOL	MISTRAL	RETINAL	TUNEFUL	DECORUM
LEACOCK	WETBACK	CHUNNEL	GENERAL	MONGREL	RETRIAL	TURMOIL	DIAGRAM
LEGWORK	WINNOCK	CITADEL	GENITAL	MORRELL	REVIVAL	TYPICAL	DUBNIUM
LOGBOOK	WRYNECK	COASTAL	GENTEEL	MUSICAL	ROCKALL	UNCIVIL	DUKEDOM
MATTOCK	YASHMAK	COAXIAL	GIRASOL	NAHUATL	RORQUAL	UNEQUAL	EARDRUM
MEACOCK	ABAXIAL	CODICIL	GLACIAL	NAIPAUL	ROSTRAL	UNRAVEL	EARLDOM
MENFOLK	ABIGAIL	COLONEL	GLEEFUL	NARWHAL	ROUNDEL	UNSNARL	EGOTISM
METHINK	ABYSMAL	COMICAL	GLOTTAL	NATURAL	RUDERAL	UNUSUAL	ELITISM
MIDWEEK	ABYSSAL	CONCEAL	GLYPTAL	NEEDFUL	RUSSELL	UTENSIL	ELOGIUM

ELYSIUM	PEACHUM	ACTAEON	BRADMAN	COONCAN	FIREMAN	HOLBEIN	MAUDLIN
ENVENOM	PERFORM	ADDISON	BRAHMAN	CORYDON	FISSION	HONITON	MAZARIN
EPHRAIM	PHANTOM	ADJOURN	BRAHMIN	CRAMPON	FLATTEN	HORIZON	MECHLIN
EPIGRAM	PILGRIM	AEOLIAN	BRENDAN	CREWMAN	FLEURON	IBERIAN	MEGARON
ERODIUM	PINETUM	AFRICAN	BRITAIN	CRIMEAN	FLODDEN	INGRAIN	MEGATON
ERRATUM	POTSDAM	AILERON	BRIXTON	CRIMSON	FOGHORN	INGROWN	MEISSEN
EXCLAIM	PREDOOM	ALADDIN	BROADEN	CRISPIN	FOOTMAN	INHUMAN	MELANIN
FANWORM	PREMIUM	ALAMEIN	BUFFOON	CROUTON	FORAMEN	INSULIN	MENTION
FASCISM	PROBLEM	ALASKAN	BULLION	CRYPTON	FOREIGN	IRANIAN	MENUHIN
FAUVISM	PROGRAM	ALBUMEN	BULLPEN	CURTAIN	FOREMAN	ISOSPIN	MESCLUN
FERMIUM	QUANTUM	ALBUMIN	BUMPKIN	CUSHION	FORLORN	ITALIAN	MEXICAN
FIEFDOM	QUONDAM	ALCORAN	BURGEON	DANTEAN	FORTRAN	IVORIAN	MILKMAN
FIREARM	REALISM	ALENÇON	BUSHMAN	DAUPHIN	FREEMAN	IVORIEN	MILLION
FLOTSAM	RECLAIM	ALKORAN	BUSHMEN	DEADPAN	FRESHEN	JACKSON	MISSION
FOREARM	REQUIEM	ALTHORN	CADOGAN	DENDRON	FRISIAN	JACOBIN	MOELLON
FREEDOM	RHENIUM	ANDAMAN	CAEDMON	DENIZEN	FRISSON	JAMESON	MOHICAN
FULCRUM	RHODIUM	ANDIRON	CAISSON	DETRAIN	FROGMAN	JAVELIN	MOISTEN
GALLIUM	ROSTRUM	ANGEVIN	CALDRON	DEXTRIN	FUCHSIN	JAZZMAN	MONSOON
GINGHAM	SANCTUM	ANGOLAN	CALEPIN	DICTION	FUSTIAN	JOHNSON	MOORHEN
GROGRAM	SARCASM	ANTIGEN	CALIBAN	DISCERN	GADROON	JURYMAN	MOUFLON
GUNROOM	SCROTUM	APOGEAN	CAMERON	DISDAIN	GALLEON	KARAJAN	MUEZZIN
HAFNIUM	SERFDOM	AQUILON	CAMPION	DISJOIN	GALOPIN	KEARTON	MULLEIN
HAHNIUM	SIKHISM	ARABIAN	CANTEEN	DISPRIN	GAMBIAN	KERATIN	MULLION
HASSIUM	SOLANUM	ARRAIGN	CAPSTAN	DOESKIN	GAMELAN	KEROGEN	MURRAIN
HEROISM	SOPHISM	ARTISAN	CAPTAIN	DOLPHIN	GANELON	KHAMSIN	MUTAGEN
HEURISM	SORGHUM	ASHDOWN	CAPTION	DOORMAN	GASTRIN	KILOTON	NANKEEN
HOLMIUM	STADIUM	ASPIRIN	CARAVAN	DRAGOON	GAUGUIN	KINGPIN	NAVARIN
HOMONYM	STARDOM	ATAGHAN	CARDOON	DRESDEN	GELATIN	KINSMAN	NEUTRON
HOODLUM	STERNUM	AUCTION	CAROTIN	DRUMLIN	GENTIAN	KITCHEN	NEWBORN
HORDEUM	STRATUM	AUDUBON	CARRION	DRUNKEN	GHERKIN	KOWLOON	NEWSMAN
HUMDRUM	SUBATOM	AVESTAN	CARTOON	DUDGEON	GLADDEN	KREMLIN	NICAEAN
HYPONYM	SUNBEAM	AVIGNON	CASPIAN	DUNEDIN	GLISTEN	KRYPTON	NINEPIN
IMAGISM	SURINAM	BABYLON	CATALAN	DUNGEON	GLUTTON	LAMPOON	NIOBEAN
INTERIM	SYMPTOM	BAHRAIN	CAUTION	DURAMEN	GOBELIN	LANGTON	OARSMAN
IRIDIUM	SYNONYM	BAHREIN	CAVEMAN	DUSTBIN	GOMBEEN	LANOLIN	OARSMEN
ISCHIUM	TACHISM	BALATON	CELADON	DUSTMAN	GOODMAN	LANTERN	OCTAGON
ISOGRAM	TANTRUM	BALDWIN	CERTAIN	DUSTPAN	GOODWIN	LAOCOON	OILSKIN
JEJUNUM	TAPROOM	BALLOON	CESSION	EARTHEN	GORDIAN	LAOTIAN	OMICRON
JUDAISM	TEAROOM	BARGAIN	CHAGRIN	EASTERN	GREATEN	LAPUTAN	OPINION
KINGDOM	TELECOM	BASSOON	CHANSON	ECHELON	GRECIAN	LARDOON	ORATION
LAMAISM	TERBIUM	BASTION	CHAPMAN	EDITION	GREMLIN	LATERAN	ORPHEAN
LEGROOM	THEOREM	BATSMAN	CHARDIN	ELASTIN	GRIFFON	LATVIAN	ORTOLAN
LIBRIUM	THOMISM	BEDOUIN	CHASTEN	ELATION	GRYPHON	LEBANON	OTTOMAN
LITHIUM	THORIUM	BELGIAN	CHEAPEN	ELISION	GUDGEON	LECTERN	OUTSPAN
LUGWORM	THULIUM	BELLMAN	CHECKIN	ELYSIAN	GUINEAN	LESBIAN	OUTTURN
LUSTRUM	TITOISM	BENISON	CHEVRON	ELYTRON	HADRIAN	LETDOWN	OUTWORN
MACADAM	TOURISM	BENZOIN	CHICKEN	EMERSON	HAIRPIN	LEXICON	OVARIAN
MARXISM	TRANSOM	BERGSON	CHIFFON	EMOTION	HAITIAN	LIAISON	OVATION
MAUGHAM	TRITIUM	BETOKEN	CHIGNON	EMULSIN	HALCYON	LIEDOWN	OVERMAN
MAXIMUM	TRIVIUM	BETWEEN	CHILEAN	ENDOGEN	HALOGEN	LIGHTEN	OVERRUN
METONYM	TROPISM	BIAFRAN	CHILLON	ENGRAIN	HANDGUN	LIMPKIN	OXONIAN
MIDTERM	UNBOSOM	BIGHORN	CHORION	ENLIVEN	HANGMAN	LINCOLN	PACKMAN
MINIMUM	UNIFORM	BILLION	CISTERN	ENTERON	HANGMEN	LINEMAN	PALADIN
MODICUM	URANISM	BILLMAN	CITIZEN	ENTRAIN	HARDPAN	LINKMAN	PARAGON
NATRIUM	URANIUM	BIRDMAN	CITROEN	EPIZOON	HARPOON	LINNEAN	PASSION
NIOBIUM	VERULAM	BITTERN	CITTERN	EPSILON	HEADMAN	LOTHIAN	PASTERN
NOSTRUM	VIETNAM	BITUMEN	CLACHAN	EPSTEIN	HEARKEN	LOWDOWN	PATTERN
OMENTUM	WILLIAM	BLACKEN	CLARION	EROSION	HEARTEN	LUMPKIN	PELICAN
ONANISM	WOLFRAM	BLOUSON	CLOISON	ETESIAN	HEATHEN	MACEDON	PENGUIN
OPOSSUM	YARDARM	BOATMAN	CLUBMAN	ETONIAN	HELICON	MADISON	PENSION
OPTIMUM	YTTRIUM	BONDMAN	COARSEN	EVASION	HELLION	MAILMAN	PERMIAN
ORGANUM	ABANDON	BOOKMAN	COITION	EXPLAIN	HEPARIN	MALAYAN	PERSIAN
ORPHISM	ABDOMEN	BOOLEAN	COLLEEN	FACTION	HESHVAN	MANAKIN	PERTAIN
OSCULUM	ABIDJAN	BORODIN	CONCERN	FASHION	HESSIAN	MANIKIN	PHAETON
OVERARM	ABSTAIN	BOUNDEN	CONDEMN	FENELON	HEXAGON	MANSION	PHONEIN
PABULUM	ACADIAN	BOURBON	CONJOIN	FESTOON	HIGHMAN	MANTUAN	PIDGEON
PAESTUM	ACHAEAN	BOURDON	CONSIGN	FICTION	HILLMAN	MANXMAN	PIGSKIN
PALLIUM	ACHERON	BOURSIN	CONTAIN	FIFTEEN	HILLMEN	MARMION	PILLION
PANGRAM	ACHESON	BRACKEN	CONTEMN		HOEDOWN	MARTIAN	PLASMIN

PLATOON	SAXHORN	THOMSON	AGITATO	OLOROSO	CLEANUP	ADAPTER	BROTHER
PLAYPEN	SEALION	THROWIN	ALBERGO	ONTARIO	CLEARUP	ADAPTOR	BROWSER
PLEURON	SECTION	THYSSEN	ALFONSO	OREGANO	CLOSEUP	ADMIRER	BRUISER
PLOSION	SERBIAN	TIBETAN	ALLEGRO	ORINOCO	COVERUP	ADVISER	BRUSHER
PLOWMAN	SESSION	TIGHTEN	AMERIGO	ORLANDO	COWSLIP	ADVISOR	BUCKLER
POLYGON	SHANNON	TINTERN	AMOROSO	ORVIETO	DEVELOP	AGISTOR	BUGBEAR
POMPOON	SHARPEN	TOLKIEN	ANNATTO	OTHELLO	DEWDROP	ALLSTAR	BUILDER
PONTOON	SHEBEEN	TOLLMAN	ANTONIO	OTRANTO	ENCLASP	ALMONER	BULGHUR
POPCORN	SHERMAN	TOMPION	ARETINO	PALERMO	ENVELOP	AMATEUR	BUNGLER
PORCIAN	SHIPTON	TOPSPIN	ARIOSTO	PICASSO	EPICARP	AMMETER	BURGHER
PORTION	SHORTEN	TORCHON	ATISHOO	PICCOLO	ESCALOP	ANGULAR	BURGLAR
POSTERN	SHOTGUN	TORSION	AVOCADO	PIMENTO	EXOCARP	ANNULAR	BURSTER
POSTMAN	SHOWMAN	TOUGHEN	BAMBINO	PINTADO	FLAREUP	ANOTHER	BUSTLER
POTHEEN	SHRIVEN	TRADEIN	BEEFALO	PIZARRO	FOGLAMP	AQUIFER	BUTCHER
POUSSIN	SILICON	TREASON	BOTARGO	PLACEBO	GIDDYUP	ARBITER	CADAVER
PRONOUN	SIMENON	TRIANON	BRASERO	PORTICO	GROWNUP	ASUNDER	CALABAR
PROTEAN	SIMPKIN	TRISTAN	BRAVADO	POTOROO	GUMDROP	ATELIER	CALIBER
PROTEIN	SIMPLON	TRODDEN	BUFFALO	PROVISO	GYMSLIP	AUDITOR	CAMPHOR
PTYALIN	SIMPSON	TRUDGEN	BUGABOO	PROXIMO	HARDTOP	AVENGER	CANDOUR
PULLMAN	SIRLOIN	TRYPSIN	BUMMALO	PRURIGO	HARELIP	AVIATOR	CANTUAR
PUMPKIN	SITDOWN	TUBULIN	BUSHIDO	RELIEVO	HEELTAP	AVOIDER	CARRIER
PURITAN	SIXTEEN	TUITION	CALYPSO	RICARDO	HILLTOP	AXILLAR	CARTIER
PURLOIN	SKIDPAN	TYPHOON	CEMBALO	RISOTTO	IMHOTEP	BABBLER	CASHIER
PUSHKIN	SLACKEN	UGANDAN	CENTAVO	ROSARIO	KETCHUP	BAHADUR	CATCHER
QUARTAN	SMARTEN	UMBRIAN	CHEERIO	SALERMO	KINGCUP	BALFOUR	CATERER
QUENTIN	SMIDGIN	UMPTEEN	CHICAGO	SCHERZO	KINSHIP	BARRIER	CENTAUR
QUICKEN	SMITTEN	UNCLEAN	CHICANO	SCORPIO	KNEECAP	BELABOR	CHALKER
QUIETEN	SNOWDON	UNCTION	CHORIZO	SEMIPRO	MIDSHIP	BENCHER	CHAMBER
QUINTAN	SNOWMAN	UNICORN	COLOMBO	SENECIO	MILKSOP	BESMEAR	CHAMFER
RACCOON	SOJOURN	UNKNOWN	COMMODO	SESOTHO	MISSTEP	BLABBER	CHANTER
RACHMAN	SOLOMON	UNLADEN	CORANTO	SFUMATO	MUDFLAP	BLADDER	CHAPTER
RAEBURN	SPARTAN	UPSILON	CURACAO	SHAMPOO	MUGWUMP	BLASTER	CHARGER
RAMADAN	SPONSON	URANIAN	DIABOLO	SIROCCO	NONSTOP	BLATHER	CHARMER
RAMEKIN	SPORRAN	UTOPIAN	DOMINGO	SOPRANO	OUTCROP	BLATTER	CHARTER
RANGOON	STANDIN	VATICAN	ELECTRO	SORDINO	OVERLAP	BLEEPER	CHATTER
RATTEEN	STATION	VAUGHAN	EMBARGO	SUBZERO	PALMTOP	BLENDER	CHAUCER
REALIGN	STEARIN	VENISON	ESPARTO	SUPREMO	PARSNIP	BLETHER	CHEATER
REDSKIN	STEEPEN	VERSION	FARRAGO	TABASCO	REGROUP	BLINDER	CHEDDAR
REFRAIN	STENGUN	VERVAIN	FIDELIO	TAMPICO	ROLLMOP	BLINKER	CHEQUER
REGIMEN	STEPHEN	VETERAN	GALILEO	TARANTO	ROOFTOP	BLISTER	CHESTER
RETRAIN	STEPSON	VILLAIN	GAMBADO	TESTUDO	ROSEHIP	BLITHER	CHIGGER
REUNION	STETSON	VILLEIN	GESTAPO	THEORBO	ROUNDUP	BLOATER	CHILLER
RHODIAN	STIFFEN	VITAMIN	GROUCHO	THERETO	SCALLOP	BLOCKER	CHIPPER
ROBESON	STILTON	WALKMAN	GUANACO	TIEPOLO	SCHLEPP	BLOOMER	CHOPPER
ROEDEAN	STOLLEN	WALLOON	HIDALGO	TOBACCO	SCOLLOP	BLOOPER	CHOWDER
RONTGEN	STYGIAN	WEALDEN	HISPANO	TORNADO	SHAKEUP	BLOTTER	CHUKKER
ROSCIAN	SUBJOIN	WEIGHIN	HORATIO	TORONTO	SNARLUP	BLUBBER	CHUNDER
ROUGHEN	SUBTEEN	WESTERN	IMPASTO	TORPEDO	SOURSOP	BLUNDER	CLAMBER
RUBICON	SUCTION	WHARTON	INFERNO	TREMOLO	STANDUP	BLUSHER	CLAMOUR
RUFFIAN	SUDETEN	WHEATEN	IONESCO	TYMPANO	STIRRUP	BLUSTER	CLAMPER
RUNCORN	SUNBURN	WHEREIN	JERICHO	UCCELLO	STOPGAP	BOARDER	CLANGER
RUNDOWN	SUNDOWN	WHITSUN	LENTIGO	UGOLINO	SUNLAMP	BOASTER	CLAPPER
RUNNION	SURGEON	WIDGEON	LEPANTO	UNDERGO	SUNTRAP	BOLIVAR	CLATTER
RUSSIAN	SUSTAIN	WINGMAN	LESOTHO	UTRILLO	TEASHOP	BOLSTER	CLEANER
RWANDAN	SWAGMAN	WINSTON	LIMPOPO	VERTIGO	TOYSHOP	BOOSTER	CLEAVER
SABAEAN	SWEETEN	WOODMAN	LUMBAGO	VIBRATO	TREETOP	BOUDOIR	CLICKER
SABAYON	SWIDDEN	WOOLLEN	MAESTRO	VOLCANO	TROLLOP	BOULDER	CLIMBER
SAFFRON	SWITHIN	WORKMAN	MAFIOSO	ZEMSTVO	TWOSTEP	BOUNCER	CLINGER
SAGOUIN	SWOLLEN	WORKMEN	MAGNETO	ZINGARO	UNCLASP	BOUNDER	CLINKER
SALADIN	TAMARIN	WRITTEN	MARENGO	AIRSHIP	WARSHIP	BOWDLER	CLIPPER
SALTPAN	TAMPION	XERAFIN	MEMENTO	AIRSTOP	WICKIUP	BRAEMAR	CLOBBER
SAMISEN	TARQUIN	YEREVAN	MONTERO	ANTWERP	WIRETAP	BRANDER	CLUMBER
SANDMAN	TEHERAN	YPSILON	MORELLO	BELLHOP	WORKTOP	BRAWLER	CLUSTER
SANDOWN	TENSION	YUCATAN	MORESCO	CALTROP	WORSHIP	BRAZIER	CLUTTER
SAPONIN	TERRAIN	ZAIREAN	MOROCCO	CANTRIP	WRITEUP	BREAKER	COASTER
SARACEN	TERSION	ZAMBIAN	MULATTO	CATCHUP	ABETTOR	BREEDER	COBBLER
SAROYAN	TERTIAN	ZAMORIN	MURILLO	CHECKUP	ABLATOR	BRENNER	COLLIER
SASSOON	THEREIN	ZILLION	NEGRITO	CHIRRUP	ABOUKIR	BRIDLER	CONIFER
SAURIAN	THICKEN	ZYMOGEN	NOVELLO	CIRCLIP	ACCUSER	BROILER	CONQUER

CONTOUR	ENAMOUR	HANOVER	MEANDER	POCHOIR	SCARPER	SNEAKER	TANGIER
CORONER	EQUATOR	HARBOUR	MEDDLER	POINTER	SCATTER	SNICKER	TAPSTER
CORSAIR	ERECTOR	HARRIER	MERRIER	POLYMER	SCEPTER	SNIFFER	TARSIER
COTTIER	ESTOVER	HAULIER	MESSIER	POOFTER	SCHEMER	SNIFTER	TATTLER
COULTER	EVANDER	HEATHER	METAYER	POPOVER	SCHOLAR	SNIGGER	TEACHER
COUNTER	EVENTER	HEAVIER	MINSTER	POPULAR	SCISSOR	SNOOKER	TELPHER
COUPLER	FANCIER	HECKLER	MIRADOR	POSTWAR	SCOFFER	SNOOPER	TELSTAR
COURIER	FARCEUR	HIPSTER	MOBSTER	PRAETOR	SCOOTER	SNORTER	TEMPLAR
COURSER	FARRIER	HOARDER	MODULAR	PREMIER	SCOURER	SOCAGER	TEMPTER
CRACKER	FARTHER	HOLSTER	MOITHER	PRICKER	SCOWDER	SOLDIER	TERRIER
CRAMMER	FEATHER	HOTSPUR	MONITOR	PRIMEUR	SCRAPER	SOUNDER	THEATER
CRANMER	FELSPAR	HOWEVER	MONSTER	PRIMUS	SCRIBER	SPADGER	THINKER
CRANMER	FELSPAR	HOWEVER	MONSTER	PRINTER	SCRIBER	SPADGER	THINKER
CRAWLER	FERVOUR	HUMIDOR	MOULDER	PROCTOR	SCULLER	SPANKER	THINNER
CREATOR	FIDDLER	HURDLER	MOURNER	PROFFER	SCUPPER	SPANNER	THITHER
CREEPER	FIELDER	HUSTLER	MUDEJAR	PROSPER	SCUTTER	SPATTER	THROWER
CRITTER	FIGHTER	INCISOR	MUFFLER	PROUDER	SECULAR	SPEAKER	THUMPER
CROAKER	FILCHER	INCOMER	MUNSTER	PROWLER	SEDUCER	SPECTER	THUNDER
CROFTER	FLANKER	INDEXER	MYANMAR	PSALTER	SELTZER	SPELLER	TICKLER
CROONER	FLAPPER	INHALER	MYNHEER	PUNCHER	SEMINAR	SPENCER	TIDDLER
CROPPER	FLASHER	INSIDER	NEBULAR	PUNSTER	SENATOR	SPENDER	TINGLER
CROSIER	FLATCAR	INSULAR	NEITHER	PURSUER	SETTLER	SPENSER	TIPPLER
CROWBAR	FLATTER	INSURER	NOBBLER	PUZZLER	SEYMOUR	SPINNER	TIPSTER
CROZIER	FLAVOUR	INTEGER	NODULAR	QUARTER	SHARPER	SPLICER	TITULAR
CRUISER	FLECKER	INVADER	NUCLEAR	QUEERER	SHATTER	SPOILER	TOASTER
CRUPPER	FLICKER	JANITOR	OBLIGOR	QUESTER	SHEARER	SPONGER	TODDLER
CRUSHER	FLIPPER	JEWELER	OCELLAR	QUICKER	SHELTER	SPONSOR	TRACKER
CURATOR	FLITTER	JOCULAR	OCTOBER	QUILTER	SHIMMER	SPOONER	TRACTOR
DABBLER	FLIVVER	JOINTER	OFFERER	QUITTER	SHIPPER	SPOTTER	TRAILER
DAIMLER	FLOATER	JUGGLER	OFFICER	RAMBLER	SHIRKER	SPRAYER	TRAINER
DAMPIER	FLOGGER	JUGULAR	OLDSTER	RANCHER	SHOCKER	SPUTTER	TRAITOR
DAWDLER	FLUSTER	JUNIPER	OUTDOOR	RANCOUR	SHOOTER	SQUALOR	TRAMCAR
DAYSTAR	FLUTTER	JUPITER	OUTLIER	RATTLER	SHOPPER	STAFFER	TRANTER
DEBATER	FLYOVER	KASHMIR	OUTPOUR	REACTOR	SHOUTER	STAGGER	TRAPPER
DECIDER	FORBEAR	KIELDER	OUTWEAR	REALGAR	SHRIVER	STAINER	TRAWLER
DECODER	FOREVER	KLAVIER	PADDLER	REALTOR	SHUDDER	STALKER	TREKKER
DELIVER	FORSTER	KLINKER	PAINTER	REAUMUR	SHUTTER	STAMMER	TRIFLER
DEMETER	FOUNDER	KNACKER	PALAVER	RECOVER	SHYSTER	STAMPER	TRIGGER
DESPAIR	FREEZER	KNAPPER	PALOMAR	REDUCER	SIDECAR	STAPLER	TRILLER
DIBBLER	FRESHER	KNEELER	PANNIER	REENTER	SIMILAR	STARTER	TRIMMER
DILATOR	FRITTER	KNELLER	PANTHER	REFINER	SIMPLER	STEAMER	TRIPPER
DIOPTER	FUNFAIR	KNICKER	PARADOR	REGULAR	SIZZLER	STEERER	TROOPER
DIPOLAR	FURRIER	KNITTER	PARLOUR	RELAYER	SKELTER	STELLAR	TROTTER
DIVINER	FURTHER	KNOCKER	PARTNER	REMOVER	SKIMMER	STENTOR	TROUPER
DIVISOR	GABBLER	LABORER	PASTEUR	REOCCUR	SKINNER	STICKER	TROUSER
DNIEPER	GAEKWAR	LACQUER	PAVIOUR	RESCUER	SKIPPER	STINGER	TRUCKER
DOODLER	GAGSTER	LANGUOR	PEDDLER	REVELER	SKITTER	STINKER	TUBULAR
DOPPLER	GAMBLER	LATIMER	PERRIER	REVISER	SLACKER	STONKER	TUMBLER
DOSSIER	GLACIER	LAUNDER	PHILTER	REVIVER	SLAMMER	STOPPER	TUTELAR
DOUBTER	GLAMOUR	LAVATER	PHRASER	RICHTER	SLANDER	STRIDOR	TWEETER
DOWAGER	GLAZIER	LEAGUER	PICADOR	RIDDLER	SLAPPER	STRIKER	TWIGGER
DRAWBAR	GLEANER	LEANDER	PICKLER	ROASTER	SLEEPER	STRIPER	TWISTER
DREAMER	GLIMMER	LEARNER	PIERCER	ROISTER	SLENDER	STUNNER	TWITTER
DREDGER	GLITTER	LEATHER	PILCHER	ROOSTER	SLICKER	STURMER	UNCLEAR
DRESSER	GOBBLER	LIGHTER	PIONEER	ROTATOR	SLIMMER	STUTTER	UNCOVER
DRIFTER	GRAFTER	LIMITER	PITCHER	ROTIFER	SLIPPER	SUBADAR	USURPER
DRINKER	GRAINER	LIQUEUR	PLANNER	ROUNDER	SLITHER	SUBEDAR	VENERER
DROPPER	GRAMMAR	LOBSTER	PLANTAR	ROUTIER	SLOBBER	SUCCOUR	VERMEER
DRUMMER	GREASER	LOTHAIR	PLANTER	RUFFLER	SLOGGER	SULPHUR	VETIVER
DWELLER	GREENER	LOUNGER	PLASTER	RUMBLER	SLUMBER	SWAGGER	VINEGAR
EARLIER	GRIFTER	LUCIFER	PLATTER	RUSTLER	SMACKER	SWEATER	VINTNER
ECUADOR	GRINDER	LURCHER	PLEADER	SADDLER	SMALLER	SWEEPER	VISITOR
EJECTOR	GROLIER	MAILCAR	PLESSOR	SALAZAR	SMASHER	SWELTER	VOUCHER
ELEANOR	GROUPER	MANAGER	PLODDER	SAMOVAR	SMATTER	SWIFTER	VOYAGER
ELECTOR	GROUSER	MARCHER	PLOTTER	SAMPLER	SMELTER	SWIMMER	WAGGLER
ELZEVIR	GROWLER	MARINER	PLUMBER	SAUNTER	SMITHER	SWINGER	WAGONER
EMBOWER	GUILDER	MASSEUR	PLUMPER	SAVIOUR	SMOLDER	TABULAR	WALTZER
EMPEROR	GUZZLER	MATADOR	PLUNDER	SCALPER	SMOTHER	TACKLER	WANGLER
EMPOWER	HAMSTER	MAUNDER	PLUNGER	SCAMPER	SNAPPER	TAMBOUR	WARBLER
ENACTOR	HANDLER	MAYFAIR	POACHER	SCANNER	SNARLER	TANAGER	WARDOUR

240

WARRIOR	ATROPOS	CHAMOIS	DREYFUS	GOGGLES	JITTERS	MODULUS	PEERESS
WATCHER	ATTICUS	CHANGES	DRIVERS	GOODIES	JOBLESS	MOMENTS	PEGASUS
WAVERER	AUROCHS	CHARGES	DRYNESS	GOOLIES	JOYLESS	MORTALS	PELORUS
WEATHER	AZYGOUS	CHARLES	DUBIOUS	GORDIUS	JUGGINS	MOTHERS	PENATES
WEBSTER	BACCHUS	CHASSIS	DUCHESS	GRAMPUS	JUGLANS	MUMMERS	PEPPERS
WHACKER	BADNESS	CHLAMYS	ECDYSIS	GRAPHIS	JUMBLES	MUSSELS	PERCUSS
WHEELER	BAHAMAS	CINDERS	ECHINUS	GREAVES	KALENDS	MYCETES	PERHAPS
WHETHER	BANANAS	CINEMAS	ECTASIS	GROCERS	KENNELS	MYIASIS	PERSEUS
WHIMPER	BARENTS	CIVVIES	EFFECTS	GROPIUS	KENOSIS	NACROUS	PERSONS
WHINGER	BARKERS	CLOTHES	EMBOLUS	GROTIUS	KERMESS	NARROWS	PETROUS
WHISKER	BARYTES	COCKLES	EMPLOYS	GROUNDS	KIDNEYS	NATIONS	PHALLUS
WHISPER	BATHERS	COFFERS	EMPRESS	GUBBINS	KINESIS	NATIVES	PHIDIAS
WHITHER	BATTELS	COLCHIS	ENDLESS	GUINEAS	KIPPERS	NEEDLES	PHILEAS
WHOEVER	BAUHAUS	COLITIS	ENDWAYS	GUTLESS	KIWANIS	NEGRESS	PHOEBUS
WHOOPER	BEACHES	COLOURS	ENGROSS	HACKLES	KOUMISS	NEMESIS	PHONICS
WHOPPER	BEATLES	COLUMNS	ENVIOUS	HALITUS	KURHAUS	NERVOUS	PHYSICS
WIDOWER	BELARUS	COMMONS	EPHEBUS	HAPLESS	LACEUPS	NEWNESS	PIGEONS
WINDSOR	BELLOWS	COMPASS	EPHESUS	HARNESS	LALLANS	NIPPERS	PILATUS
WOOSTER	BENARES	CONCUSS	ERASMUS	HATLESS	LANCERS	NITROUS	PINCERS
WORRIER	BENTHOS	CONFESS	ERINYES	HEAVENS	LARGESS	NONPLUS	PIRAEUS
WOTCHER	BESIDES	CONSOLS	ESSENES	HEBREWS	LAURELS	NONPROS	PITEOUS
WRAPPER	BETIMES	COPIOUS	ETAPLES	HEIGHTS	LAWLESS	NOODLES	PLAUTUS
WRECKER	BILIOUS	COPPERS	EXPRESS	HEINOUS	LAWYERS	NOTIONS	PLAYERS
WRINGER	BILLOWS	COUPONS	EYELESS	HEIRESS	LAXNESS	NOXIOUS	PLEASES
YOUNGER	BIOMASS	COURSES	EYELIDS	HERRIES	LAYINGS	NUCLEUS	PLUTEUS
ABATTIS	BITTERS	COUSINS	FACTORS	HIDEOUS	LEADERS	NUMBERS	POETESS
ABIOSIS	BLAZERS	COXLESS	FAGGOTS	HIGGINS	LEGIONS	NUMBLES	POLARIS
ABRAXIS	BLESSES	COYNESS	FAJITAS	HOBSONS	LEGLESS	OBJECTS	POLYPUS
ABSCESS	BOLETUS	CRASHES	FALSIES	HONOURS	LENTILS	OBVIOUS	POMPOUS
ACESTES	BONKERS	CRASSUS	FARMERS	HOPKINS	LEPROUS	OCELLUS	POPULUS
ACHATES	BOOKIES	CROESUS	FATNESS	HORRORS	LETTERS	OCTOPUS	POROSIS
ACTRESS	BORDERS	CROQUIS	FATUOUS	HOSTESS	LINCTUS	ODDNESS	PORTHOS
ADDRESS	BOTTLES	CRUELLS	FAUSTUS	HUMBLES	LININGS	ODOROUS	POSSESS
ADONAIS	BRIDGES	CSARDAS	FELLOWS	HUMERUS	LIONESS	OEDIPUS	PRELIMS
AFFAIRS	BRIDLES	CUIRASS	FERROUS	HUNKERS	LIQUIDS	OESTRUS	PREMISS
AGELESS	BRITONS	CUMULUS	FETTERS	HURDLES	LITOTES	OFFICES	PRIAPUS
AGGRESS	BROKERS	CUPROUS	FIBROUS	HUSSARS	LOCUSTS	OLDNESS	PRIESTS
AIMLESS	BUBBLES	CURIOUS	FIDGETS	ICINESS	LOURDES	OLYMPUS	PRINCES
AIRLESS	BUCKETS	CUSTOMS	FIGURES	ICTERUS	LUTYENS	OMINOUS	PROCESS
ALGIERS	BUGGINS	CUTLASS	FILINGS	IGNEOUS	LYCHNIS	OMNIBUS	PROFESS
ALMACKS	BUGLOSS	CUTTERS	FILLETS	ILIACUS	MADNESS	ONENESS	PROFITS
ALPHEUS	BULBOUS	CYCLOPS	FINGERS	ILLNESS	MAENADS	ONEROUS	PRONAOS
ALUMNUS	BULLETS	CYMBALS	FITNESS	IMPETUS	MAKINGS	ONMIBUS	PROTEUS
AMBAGES	BURGESS	CYPRESS	FIXINGS	IMPIOUS	MALLEUS	ONWARDS	PROWESS
AMOROUS	BURNOUS	CYTISUS	FLOWERS	IMPRESS	MALTHUS	OPPRESS	PUTTEES
ANANIAS	BUSKINS	DAGGERS	FOLLIES	INCROSS	MANNERS	ORACLES	PYJAMAS
ANGELUS	BUSTLES	DAMAGES	FORCEPS	INCUBUS	MARACAS	ORANGES	PYLORUS
ANIMALS	BUTTONS	DAPHNIS	FORTIES	INDOORS	MARBLES	ORESTES	PYRITES
ANNULUS	CAHOOTS	DEGAUSS	FRANCIS	INGRESS	MARQUIS	ORIGINS	PYROSIS
ANTARES	CALAMUS	DEGREES	FRIENDS	INNARDS	MARSYAS	ORKNEYS	QUERCUS
ANTIBES	CALENDS	DELIBES	FULLERS	INNINGS	MARTENS	ORLEANS	QUIETUS
ANTLERS	CALLOUS	DEPRESS	FUNGOUS	INROADS	MARTYRS	ORONTES	RACKETS
ANXIOUS	CANTHUS	DESERTS	FURIOUS	INSECTS	MASTERS	ORPHEUS	RAFFLES
APHESIS	CANVASS	DETAILS	FUTURES	INSIDES	MATTERS	OSMOSIS	RAMESES
APICIUS	CARACAS	DEVIOUS	GAITERS	INVIOUS	MATTINS	OSSEOUS	RAMULUS
APROPOS	CARCASS	DICKENS	GALLONS	INWARDS	MEASLES	PAJAMAS	RATIONS
APTNESS	CARDUUS	DIDYMUS	GALLOWS	ISLANDS	MEIOSIS	PALINGS	RAUCOUS
AQUEOUS	CAREERS	DIGRESS	GARDENS	ISTHMUS	MEMBERS	PANCRAS	RAVAGES
AQUINAS	CARGOES	DIMNESS	GASEOUS	JACKASS	MEMOIRS	PANTIES	RAVINGS
AQUINUS	CARITAS	DISCUSS	GAYNESS	JACKETS	MERCIES	PAPYRUS	RAWNESS
ARBUTUS	CAROLUS	DISMISS	GENESIS	JACOBUS	MESEEMS	PARADOS	RECORDS
ARDUOUS	CARRIES	DITTIES	GIBBONS	JACQUES	MILLAIS	PARENTS	REDNESS
ARREARS	CARROTS	DOCTORS	GIBBOUS	JAMMIES	MIMULUS	PARESIS	REDRESS
ARTEMIS	CASUALS	DODGEMS	GIBLETS	JANKERS	MINIBUS	PARINGS	REGARDS
ARTEMUS	CATKINS	DOLLARS	GIMBALS	JEALOUS	MINUTES	PARLOUS	REGRESS
ARTLESS	CELEBES	DOLORES	GLASSES	JEEPERS	MITHRAS	PAROTIS	RELICTS
ASCITES	CELSIUS	DOUBLES	GLOTTIS	JENKINS	MITOSIS	PASTIES	REMAINS
ASSISTS	CEPHEUS	DOUGLAS	GODDESS	JERSEYS	MITTENS	PEANUTS	REPAIRS
ASSIZES	CHABLIS	DRAWERS	GODLESS	JIMJAMS	MOCKERS	PEBBLES	REPRESS

REREDOS	STABLES	VAUDOIS	ATHWART	COLLECT	DETRACT	FIGMENT	INBURST
RESULTS	STACHYS	VELOURS	ATOMIST	COMFORT	DEVIANT	FILBERT	INCRUST
RETAINS	STARETS	VESPERS	ATTAINT	COMMENT	DIALECT	FINFOOT	INEXACT
RETURNS	STATICS	VICIOUS	ATTEMPT	COMPACT	DIARIST	FISHNET	INFARCT
RHOMBUS	STEVENS	VIDIMUS	ATTRACT	COMPORT	DIDEROT	FITMENT	INFLECT
RIBLESS	STIRPES	VIKINGS	AUGMENT	COMPOST	DIECAST	FITTEST	INFLICT
RICKETS	STORIES	VILNIUS	AUTOMAT	CONCEIT	DILUENT	FLATLET	INHABIT
RIDINGS	STRAITS	VISCOUS	BABBITT	CONCEPT	DINGBAT	FLEAPIT	INHERIT
RIMLESS	STRATUS	WALLIES	BABYSIT	CONCERT	DINMONT	FLEURET	INHIBIT
RINGERS	STRAUSS	WASHERS	BACKSET	CONCOCT	DISGUST	FLORIST	INQUEST
RIOTERS	STRIDES	WATTLES	BAGEHOT	CONDUCT	DISMAST	FLUTIST	INSIGHT
RIOTOUS	STRINGS	WEAPONS	BAJAZET	CONDUIT	DISPORT	FLYPAST	INSPECT
ROBBERS	STRIPES	WEIGHTS	BALLAST	CONNECT	DISRUPT	FONDANT	INSTANT
ROBERTS	SUCCESS	WELLIES	BANQUET	CONSENT	DISSECT	FORFEIT	INTROIT
ROLLERS	SUMMONS	WETNESS	BAPTIST	CONSIST	DISSENT	FOXTROT	ISOHYET
ROMPERS	SUNLESS	WHEREAS	BARONET	CONSORT	DISTANT	FRAUGHT	ISSUANT
ROMULUS	SURPASS	WILLIES	BASINET	CONSULT	DISTENT	FREIGHT	JACKPOT
ROSCIUS	SURPLUS	WINDOWS	BATHMAT	CONTACT	DISTORT	FRESHET	JOGTROT
ROZZERS	SYCOSIS	WITCHES	BAYONET	CONTENT	DOGCART	FULGENT	KILVERT
RUBBERS	SYNAXIS	WITHERS	BECKETT	CONTEST	DOORMAT	GABFEST	KINGLET
RUINOUS	TACITUS	WITLESS	BEDPOST	CONTEXT	DORMANT	GALIPOT	KNESSET
RUNNERS	TACTICS	WITNESS	BEERMAT	CONTORT	DOUBLET	GALLANT	KUMQUAT
SADNESS	TAGETES	WONDERS	BENEFIT	CONVENT	DRAGNET	GARMENT	LAMAIST
SAILORS	TAILORS	WORKERS	BENNETT	CONVERT	DRAUGHT	GERAINT	LAMBAST
SALAMIS	TAKINGS	XANTHOS	BEQUEST	CONVICT	DRIBLET	GESTALT	LAMBENT
SANCTUS	TALIPES	XENOPUS	BETWIXT	COOLANT	DROPLET	GILBERT	LAMBERT
SANDALS	TAMESIS	XEROSIS	BIBELOT	COPILOT	DROPOUT	GIMBLET	LARGEST
SAPIENS	TATTERS	XIMENES	BIGFOOT	COPYCAT	DROUGHT	GOURMET	LATCHET
SAPPERS	TEDIOUS	YELLOWS	BIGSHOT	COPYIST	DRUGGET	GROMMET	LAWSUIT
SARCOUS	TENANTS	YONKERS	BISCUIT	CORBETT	EARNEST	GRUMMET	LEAFLET
SAVAGES	TENUOUS	ZEALOUS	BISTORT	CORONET	EARSHOT	GUMBOOT	LEFTIST
SAVINGS	TETANUS	ZYGOSIS	BLANKET	CORRECT	EASIEST	GUNBOAT	LENIENT
SCABIES	THALLUS	ZYMOSIS	BLATANT	CORRUPT	EELPOUT	GUNSHOT	LEVERET
SCHICKS	THERMOS	ABJOINT	BLOWOUT	COULDNT	EGOTIST	GYMNAST	LINOCUT
SCHLOSS	THESEUS	ABREAST	BOMBAST	COUPLET	ELEGANT	HABITAT	LOCKNUT
SECONDS	THIEVES	ACCOUNT	BONESET	COURBET	ELEGIST	HAGBOLT	LOCKOUT
SECRETS	THREADS	ACROBAT	BOOKLET	CREWCUT	ELEMENT	HAIRCUT	LOOKOUT
SEEKERS	THRENOS	ADAMANT	BOUQUET	CRICKET	ELITIST	HAIRNET	LYNCHET
SELLERS	THYRSIS	ADJOINT	BOWSHOT	CROCHET	EMINENT	HALBERT	MAGINOT
SERAPIS	TIDINGS	ADJUNCT	BOYCOTT	CROCKET	ENCHANT	HALFWIT	MAIGRET
SERIOUS	TIGRESS	AFFLICT	BRACKET	CROQUET	ENCRUST	HALIBUT	MANHUNT
SERPENS	TIMBERS	AFFRONT	BRIDGET	CRUMPET	ENGRAFT	HANDOUT	MANUMIT
SEVERUS	TONGUES	AGAINST	BRISKET	CULPRIT	ENPRINT	HANDSET	MARRYAT
SEXLESS	TOPLESS	AGONIST	BROUGHT	CULVERT	ENTRANT	HANGOUT	MARTLET
SEXTANS	TORPIDS	AILMENT	BUMBOAT	CURRANT	ENTREAT	HARICOT	MARXIST
SHAKERS	TOWARDS	AIRLIFT	BUOYANT	CURRENT	ENTRUST	HARPIST	MATCHET
SHEAVES	TRELLIS	AIRPORT	BURNOUT	CYCLIST	EPAULET	HARRIET	MATELOT
SHELVES	TRESSES	ALECOST	CABARET	CYPRIOT	EPITHET	HARVEST	MEERKAT
SHIVERS	TRICEPS	ALICANT	CABINET	DADAIST	ESCHEAT	HATCHET	MELILOT
SHOWERS	TRIFLES	ALIMENT	CALUMET	DASHPOT	ESTREAT	HAYLOFT	MIDMOST
SHRIMPS	TRIPSIS	ALIQUOT	CAMELOT	DEADSET	EVEREST	HAZLETT	MIDWEST
SHROUDS	TRISMUS	ALKANET	CARPORT	DEAREST	EVIDENT	HEADSET	MIGRANT
SHYNESS	TROCHUS	ALRIGHT	CASUIST	DEBRETT	EXCERPT	HELLCAT	MINARET
SIDDONS	TROILUS	AMBIENT	CATMINT	DECRYPT	EXHAUST	HENGIST	MINDSET
SIEMENS	TROPICS	AMONGST	CELLIST	DEFAULT	EXHIBIT	HERBERT	MISCAST
SINGLES	TUMULUS	AMORIST	CESSPIT	DEFIANT	EXIGENT	HERBIST	MONOCOT
SINUOUS	TYLOSIS	ANALYST	CHAPLET	DEFICIT	EXPLOIT	HIDEOUT	MONTANT
SISTERS	ULYSSES	ANCIENT	CHARIOT	DEFLECT	EXTINCT	HIGHEST	MOONLIT
SLYNESS	UNCINUS	ANIMIST	CHEMIST	DEFROST	EXTRACT	HOTFOOT	MORDANT
SOLIDUS	UNDRESS	ANNULET	CHEROOT	DEFUNCT	EYESHOT	HOTSHOT	MUGWORT
SOROSIS	UNITIES	APPARAT	CHEVIOT	DELIGHT	EYESPOT	HYDRANT	MUSKRAT
SORROWS	UPSIDES	APPOINT	CHINDIT	DELIMIT	FADDIST	HYMNIST	NASCENT
SPECIES	UPWARDS	APRICOT	CIRCLET	DEMERIT	FALLOUT	IAMBIST	NEAREST
SPIDERS	USELESS	AQUAVIT	CIRCUIT	DENTIST	FANWORT	ILLICIT	NECKLET
SPIRITS	VACUOUS	ARMREST	CLEMENT	DEPOSIT	FASCIST	IMAGIST	NEGLECT
SPRINGS	VANDALS	ASPHALT	COCKPIT	DERWENT	FASTNET	IMPLANT	NEWBOLT
SPROUTS	VANITAS	ASSAULT	COCONUT	DESCANT	FAUVIST	IMPREST	NONSUIT
SQUARES	VAPOURS	ATHEIST	COEXIST	DESCENT	FERMENT	IMPRINT	NUTMEAT
SQUEERS	VARIOUS	ATHIRST	COHABIT	DESSERT	FERVENT	INBUILT	NYMPHET

OCCIPUT	QUADRAT	SNIPPET	VARIANT	BESHREW	TORTRIX	BLUNTLY	CURTSEY
OCULIST	QUARTET	SOLICIT	VARMINT	BESTREW	TRIPLEX	BOLONEY	CUSTODY
ODDMENT	QUINTET	SOLOIST	VERDANT	CATSPAW	ABILITY	BRAVELY	CUTAWAY
ODORANT	QUONSET	SOLVENT	VERDICT	CHOCTAW	ACADEMY	BRAVERY	CUTLERY
OFFBEAT	RACQUET	SOPHIST	VERMONT	CORNROW	ACIDIFY	BREVITY	DEANERY
OPERANT	RADIANT	SPRAINT	VERSANT	CUMSHAW	ACIDITY	BREWERY	DEATHLY
OPULENT	RAGWORT	STARLET	VIADUCT	DISAVOW	ACTUARY	BRIBERY	DEBUSSY
ORGIAST	RAIMENT	STARLIT	VIBRANT	EYEBROW	ACUTELY	BRIEFLY	DECENCY
OSSELET	RAMPANT	STATIST	VINCENT	FOREPAW	AFFABLY	BRISKLY	DEEPFRY
OUTCAST	RAMPART	STUDENT	VIOLENT	FRETSAW	AGILITY	BRISTLY	DENSELY
OUTLAST	RAPPORT	STYLIST	WALKOUT	GLASGOW	ALCHEMY	BROADLY	DENSITY
OUTPOST	RAREBIT	SUBDUCT	WARRANT	HACKSAW	ALIMONY	BURSARY	DESTINY
OUTSHOT	RATATAT	SUBEDIT	WASHOUT	HANDSAW	ALLENBY	BUTTERY	DESTROY
OVERACT	RATCHET	SUBJECT	WEAKEST	JACKDAW	ALLERGY	CACHEXY	DEVILRY
OVEREAT	REAGENT	SUBSIST	WETSUIT	KNOWHOW	ALREADY	CALCIFY	DIARCHY
OVIDUCT	REALIST	SUBVERT	WHATNOT	LOCKJAW	AMATORY	CALLBOY	DIDICOY
PAGEANT	RECEIPT	SUGGEST	WHATSIT	LONGBOW	AMENITY	CALUMNY	DIETARY
PALMIST	RECOUNT	SUNSPOT	WHIPCAT	LOWBROW	AMIABLY	CALVARY	DIGNIFY
PARAPET	RECRUIT	SUPPORT	WHIPPET	MATTHEW	AMNESTY	CANNERY	DIGNITY
PARFAIT	REDCOAT	SURCOAT	WILDCAT	OUTFLOW	AMPLIFY	CANNILY	DISOBEY
PARQUET	REDOUBT	SURFEIT	WIPEOUT	OUTGROW	ANALOGY	CANONRY	DISPLAY
PASSANT	REELECT	SUSPECT	WITHOUT	PREVIEW	ANARCHY	CAPABLY	DITHERY
PATIENT	REFLECT	TABARET	WOODCUT	PURVIEW	ANATOMY	CARAWAY	DITTANY
PATRIOT	REFLOAT	TABORET	WORKOUT	RAINBOW	ANCHOVY	CARNABY	DIZZILY
PAYMENT	REFRACT	TAKEOUT	WOULDNT	SHALLOW	ANGRILY	CARROTY	DODDERY
PEASANT	REGNANT	TALIPOT	WRAUGHT	SKIDDAW	ANNUITY	CATESBY	DOORKEY
PECCANT	RELIANT	TANGENT	WROUGHT	SOMEHOW	ANOMALY	CAUTERY	DOORWAY
PENDANT	REMNANT	TAPROOT	YAHWIST	SPARROW	ANTHONY	CAVALRY	DOROTHY
PENNANT	REMOUNT	TEMPEST	YOGHURT	SWALLOW	ANXIETY	CENTURY	DOUGHTY
PERCENT	REPAINT	TEMPLET	YORKIST	TRISHAW	ANYBODY	CERTIFY	DOWDILY
PERCEPT	REPLANT	THICKET	ZIONIST	UNSCREW	APOLOGY	CHARITY	DRAPERY
PERFECT	REPRINT	THOMIST	BANDEAU	WHITLOW	ARCHERY	CHARLEY	DRIZZLY
PERSIST	REQUEST	THOUGHT	BERCEAU	WICKLOW	ARCHWAY	CHARPOY	DROSHKY
PERVERT	RESIANT	TIERCET	BOILEAU	WINDROW	ARIDITY	CHEAPLY	DUALITY
PIANIST	RESPECT	TIMEOUT	CARIBOU	ANTHRAX	ARMOURY	CHICORY	DUBIETY
PICQUET	RESTART	TIPCART	CATECHU	APTERYX	ASHTRAY	CHIEFLY	DUOPOLY
PIERROT	RETRACT	TITOIST	CHAPEAU	BANDBOX	ATARAXY	CHIMNEY	DURABLY
PIETIST	RETRAIT	TONIGHT	CHATEAU	BEESWAX	ATROPHY	CHINTZY	DYARCHY
PIGMEAT	RETREAT	TOPCOAT	CORBEAU	CALLBOX	ATTABOY	CHRISTY	DYNASTY
PIGMENT	REVISIT	TOPKNOT	FEYDEAU	CASHBOX	AUDIBLY	CHUTNEY	EAGERLY
PIKELET	RIBWORT	TOPMAST	INCONNU	COMPLEX	AURALLY	CIVILLY	EARTHLY
PIQUANT	RINGGIT	TOPMOST	JUJITSU	EQUINOX	AUTARKY	CLARIFY	ECOLOGY
PLAUDIT	RINGLET	TORMENT	MANITOU	FLUMMOX	AUTOPSY	CLARITY	ECONOMY
PLAYLET	RIVULET	TORRENT	MARABOU	FUSEBOX	AVEBURY	CLEANLY	ECSTASY
PLUMMET	ROUAULT	TOSSPOT	MARIBOU	GEARBOX	AVIDITY	CLEARLY	EGALITY
POLECAT	ROWBOAT	TOTIENT	MONTAGU	GRAVLAX	AWFULLY	CLIQUEY	ELDERLY
POMFRET	SACKBUT	TOURIST	NOUVEAU	HALIFAX	BALCONY	CLOSELY	ELUSORY
PORTENT	SALIENT	TRANSIT	PARVENU	JUKEBOX	BALLBOY	COCKNEY	EMBASSY
POTSHOT	SALLUST	TRIDENT	PLATEAU	JURYBOX	BALONEY	COGENCY	EMPATHY
PRECAST	SANDPIT	TRINKET	PURLIEU	KLEENEX	BANBURY	COMFREY	ENOLOGY
PRECEPT	SAPIENT	TRIPLET	RONDEAU	MAILBOX	BARBARY	COMPANY	ENQUIRY
PREDICT	SARGENT	TRISECT	ROULEAU	MINIMAX	BARNABY	CONAKRY	ENTROPY
PREEMPT	SARMENT	TRUMPET	SEPPUKU	NARTHEX	BATTERY	COOKERY	EPITAXY
PREFECT	SAWDUST	TSARIST	SHIATSU	OVERTAX	BEASTLY	COTTONY	EQUABLY
PREHEAT	SCARLET	TUGBOAT	SPANDAU	PARADOX	BEATIFY	COUNTRY	EQUALLY
PRESENT	SEALANT	TURGENT	TABLEAU	PERPLEX	BEGGARY	COURTLY	EQUERRY
PRETEXT	SEAPORT	TURNOUT	THOREAU	PERSPEX	BELLBOY	CRACKLY	ERISKAY
PREVENT	SEGMENT	TWINSET	TONNEAU	PHALANX	BEVERLY	CRAZILY	ESTUARY
PRODUCT	SELLOUT	ULULANT	TRUMEAU	PHARYNX	BIGOTRY	CRICKEY	EUPEPSY
PROJECT	SERPENT	UNGUENT	VANUATU	PHOENIX	BINDERY	CRINKLY	EUPHONY
PROPHET	SERVANT	UNKEMPT	WATTEAU	PILLBOX	BIOLOGY	CROSSLY	EXACTLY
PROTECT	SEXTANT	UNQUIET	CHEKHOV	POSTBOX	BLANDLY	CRUCIFY	EXOGAMY
PROTEST	SHALLOT	UPRIGHT	GODUNOV	SALPINX	BLANKLY	CRUDELY	FACTORY
PROTIST	SHERBET	UPSHOOT	MOLOTOV	SANDBOX	BLEAKLY	CRUDITY	FACULTY
PROVOST	SICKERT	UPSTART	NABOKOV	SIMPLEX	BLIGHTY	CRUELLY	FAINTLY
PRUDENT	SIEVERT	UPTIGHT	NUREYEV	SOAPBOX	BLINDLY	CRUELTY	FAIRWAY
PUNGENT	SINGLET	UTRECHT	ROMANOV	SPANDEX	BLOTCHY	CRUMBLY	FALLACY
PURPORT	SKILLET	VAGRANT	AIRCREW	SYCORAX	BLOWFLY	CRUNCHY	FALSELY
PURSUIT	SLEIGHT	VALIANT	AIRFLOW	TOOLBOX	BLUFFLY	CURSORY	FALSIFY

FANTASY	HALFWAY	LOFTILY	OBLOQUY	QUALITY	SHEPPEY	SURDITY	TYRANNY
FARADAY	HALLWAY	LOOSELY	OBSEQUY	QUEENLY	SHINGLY	SURGERY	UNCANNY
FARAWAY	HANDILY	LOTTERY	ODYSSEY	QUICKLY	SHIRLEY	SWARTHY	UNGODLY
FATALLY	HAPPILY	LOYALLY	OFFDUTY	QUIETLY	SHIVERY	SWEETLY	UNHAPPY
FATUITY	HARMONY	LOYALTY	OPACITY	RACKETY	SHORTLY	SWIFTLY	UNITARY
FIDGETY	HARSHLY	LUCIDLY	ORATORY	RAILWAY	SHOWERY	SYNERGY	UNLUCKY
FINALLY	HASTILY	LUCKILY	ORDERLY	RAPIDLY	SHOWILY	TACITLY	UNREADY
FINICKY	HAUGHTY	LULLABY	OROGENY	RAUNCHY	SHRILLY	TALLBOY	URGENCY
FIREFLY	HAUTBOY	LURIDLY	ORPHREY	READILY	SICKBAY	TAMMANY	URINARY
FIRSTLY	HEADWAY	LUSTILY	OSSUARY	REALITY	SIGNIFY	TANNERY	URUGUAY
FISHERY	HEALTHY	MAGGOTY	OUTSTAY	RECTIFY	SILVERY	TANTIVY	USUALLY
FIXEDLY	HEARSAY	MAGNIFY	OVERLAY	RECTORY	SKETCHY	TARDILY	UTILITY
FLAGDAY	HEAVILY	MAJESTY	OVERPAY	REENTRY	SLACKLY	TARTARY	UTTERLY
FLIGHTY	HERBERY	MALMSEY	PAGEBOY	REGALLY	SLAVERY	TAXIWAY	VACANCY
FLOWERY	HICKORY	MAMMARY	PAISLEY	REGENCY	SLEEKLY	TENANCY	VACUITY
FLUENCY	HISTORY	MARGERY	PALFREY	REMARRY	SLIPWAY	TENSELY	VAGUELY
FLUNKEY	HOLIDAY	MASONRY	PALISSY	REPLEVY	SMARTLY	TERRIFY	VALENCY
FORGERY	HONESTY	MASTERY	PANICKY	RESPRAY	SMICKLY	TERSELY	VARIETY
FORTIFY	HORRIFY	MERCERY	PANOPLY	REVELRY	SOBERLY	TESTIFY	VARSITY
FOUNDRY	HOSIERY	MERCURY	PARKWAY	RICKETY	SOCIETY	TESTILY	VELVETY
FRAILTY	HUMANLY	MERRILY	PARSLEY	RIGHTLY	SOLIDLY	THERAPY	VERSIFY
FRANKLY	HUNGARY	MESSILY	PATHWAY	RIGIDLY	SOMEWAY	THEREBY	VICEROY
FREEWAY	HUSKILY	METALLY	PAUCITY	RISKILY	SORCERY	THICKLY	VICTORY
FRESHLY	HYMNODY	MIMICRY	PAUNCHY	RIVALRY	SOUNDLY	THIRDLY	VIRELAY
FRIZZLY	IDEALLY	MISERLY	PECCARY	ROADWAY	SOUTHEY	THIRSTY	VISIBLY
FROWSTY	IMAGERY	MISPLAY	PENALTY	ROBBERY	SPECIFY	THRIFTY	VITALLY
FUNNILY	IMPIETY	MOCKERY	PEPPERY	ROCKERY	SPIDERY	THRISTY	VITRIFY
FUSSILY	INANITY	MODESTY	PERFIDY	ROGUERY	SPINDLY	THROATY	VIVIDLY
GAINSAY	INFANCY	MOLLIFY	PERJURY	ROOKERY	SPINNEY	THRUWAY	VOCALLY
GALLERY	INQUIRY	MONOPLY	PESSARY	ROUGHLY	SPLASHY	TIDEWAY	VOLUBLY
GANGWAY	JAGGERY	MONTHLY	PETRIFY	ROUNDLY	SPRINGY	TIFFANY	WALKWAY
GASCONY	JANUARY	MOODILY	PICARDY	ROWDILY	SPURREY	TIGHTLY	WALLABY
GATEWAY	JEEPNEY	MORALLY	PIGGERY	ROYALLY	SPURWAY	TILBURY	WASHDAY
GAUDILY	JERKILY	MORESBY	PILLORY	ROYALTY	SQUADDY	TIMIDLY	WEALTHY
GEODESY	JEWELRY	MORTIFY	PIOUSLY	RUBBERY	SQUALLY	TIMOTHY	WEARILY
GEOLOGY	JITTERY	MUMMERY	PITHILY	RUNAWAY	SQUASHY	TIPSILY	WEEKDAY
GERMANY	JOBBERY	MUMMIFY	PLAINLY	SAINTLY	SQUEAKY	TOGGERY	WEIGHTY
GETAWAY	JOINERY	MUSCOVY	PLANURY	SALSIFY	SQUIFFY	TOLSTOY	WEIRDLY
GHASTLY	JOINTLY	MYSTERY	PLAYBOY	SANDBOY	SQUISHY	TOPIARY	WHEREBY
GHOSTLY	JOLLITY	MYSTIFY	PLENARY	SASSABY	STANDBY	TORREFY	WHIMSEY
GIDDILY	JOURNEY	NAIVELY	PLIANCY	SATIETY	STANLEY	TOTALLY	WHISKEY
GILLRAY	JUSTIFY	NAIVETY	POMEROY	SATISFY	STARCHY	TOTTERY	WILLOWY
GLORIFY	KENNEDY	NAKEDLY	PORTRAY	SATRAPY	STARKLY	TRACERY	WOMANLY
GOSSIPY	KILLJOY	NASALLY	POTENCY	SAUCILY	STATELY	TRAGEDY	WORDILY
GRADELY	KNAVERY	NASTILY	POTTERY	SAVELOY	STEEPLY	TRAMWAY	WORKSHY
GRANARY	KNOBBLY	NAUGHTY	POULTRY	SAVOURY	STEPNEY	TREACLY	WORLDLY
GRANDLY	LAMPREY	NECTARY	POVERTY	SCARIFY	STERNLY	TREMBLY	WRINKLY
GRATIFY	LANGLEY	NEOTENY	POWDERY	SCENERY	STIFFLY	TRILOGY	WRONGLY
GRAVITY	LARCENY	NEWBURY	PRELACY	SCRAGGY	STIRFRY	TRINITY	ZEDOARY
GREATLY	LARGELY	NEWSBOY	PRICKLY	SCRAPPY	STONILY	TRIPODY	ZOFFANY
GREGORY	LAUNDRY	NIGHTLY	PRIMACY	SCRAWNY	STOUTLY	TRITELY	ZOOLOGY
GRIMSBY	LECHERY	NOISILY	PRIMARY	SCRUBBY	STREAKY	TROLLEY	ZOOTOMY
GRISTLY	LEGALLY	NOOLOGY	PRIVACY	SCRUFFY	STRINGY	TROTSKY	ZYMURGY
GRIZZLY	LEGIBLY	NOONDAY	PRIVITY	SCRUMMY	STROPPY	TRUANCY	ALBENIZ
GROCERY	LENGTHY	NOSEGAY	PROBITY	SCRUMPY	STUBBLY	TSIGANY	COLDITZ
GROSSLY	LEPROSY	NOTABLY	PRODIGY	SECRECY	STUPEFY	TUESDAY	KIBBUTZ
GROUCHY	LIBERTY	NOVELTY	PROGENY	SENSORY	SUAVELY	TURBARY	KOLKHOZ
GRUFFLY	LIBRARY	NULLIFY	PROSODY	SEVENTY	SUAVITY	TURNERY	NATCHEZ
GUNNERY	LIGHTLY	NULLITY	PROUDLY	SHADOWY	SUBSIDY	TURNKEY	PIZZAZZ
GUNPLAY	LIQUEFY	NUMMARY	PTOLEMY	SHAKILY	SULKILY	TUSCANY	SHOWBIZ
HACKERY	LITHELY	NUNNERY	PUBERTY	SHAPELY	SUMMARY	TWIDDLY	SOVKHOZ
HACKNEY	LITURGY	NURSERY	PUTREFY	SHARPLY	SUMMERY	TWITCHY	
HAGGERY	LOCALLY	OBESITY	QUALIFY	SHELLEY	SUNNILY	TYMPANY	

8:1

	ACQUIRER	AGRARIAN	ALMIGHTY	ANGSTROM	AQUARIUS	ASSEMBLY
AARDVARK	ACRIMONY	AGREEING	ALOPECIA	ANGUILLA	AQUATINT	ASSESSOR
AASVOGEL	ACROMION	AGRICOLA	ALPHABET	ANIMATED	AQUEDUCT	ASSIGNEE
ABATTOIR	ACROSTIC	AGRIMONY	ALPINIST	ANISETTE	AQUILINE	ASSORTED
ABBASIDE	ACTINIDE	AGRONOMY	ALSATIAN	ANNALIST	ARACHNID	ASSUMING
ABDICATE	ACTINIUM	AIGRETTE	ALTHOUGH	ANNAMITE	ARALDITE	ASSYRIAN
ABDUCENS	ACTIVATE	AIGUILLE	ALTITUDE	ANNEALER	ARAMAEAN	ASTATINE
ABDUCTED	ACTIVELY	AIRBORNE	ALTRUISM	ANNELIDA	ARAMANTH	ASTERISK
ABDUCTOR	ACTIVISM	AIRBRAKE	ALTRUIST	ANNOTATE	ARBALEST	ASTEROID
ABERDEEN	ACTIVIST	AIRCRAFT	ALUMINUM	ANNOUNCE	ARBOREAL	ASTHENIA
ABERRANT	ACTIVITY	AIREDALE	ALVEOLUS	ANNOYING	ARCADIAN	ASTONISH
ABESSIVE	ACTUALLY	AIRFIELD	AMANDINE	ANNUALLY	ARCHAISM	ASTUTELY
ABEYANCE	ADDENDUM	AIRINESS	AMARANTH	ANOREXIA	ARCHDUKE	ASUNCION
ABINGDON	ADDICTED	AIRLINER	AMARETTO	ANOREXIC	ARCHIVES	ATALANTA
ABJECTLY	ADDITION	AIRPLANE	AMATEURS	ANSERINE	ARCTURUS	ATARAXIA
ABLATION	ADDITIVE	AIRSCREW	AMBIANCE	ANTECEDE	ARDENNES	ATARAXIC
ABLATIVE	ADELAIDE	AIRSPEED	AMBIENCE	ANTEDATE	ARDENTLY	ATHANASY
ABLUTION	ADENITIS	AIRSTRIP	AMBITION	ANTELOPE	ARETHUSA	ATHELING
ABNEGATE	ADENOIDS	AIRTIGHT	AMBROSIA	ANTENNAE	ARGESTES	ATHENIAN
ABNORMAL	ADEQUACY	AIRWAVES	AMBULANT	ANTEPOST	ARGININE	ATHEROMA
ABOMASUM	ADEQUATE	AKKADIAN	AMBULATE	ANTERIOR	ARGONAUT	ATHETISE
ABORTION	ADESSIVE	ALACRITY	AMBUSHED	ANTEROOM	ARGUABLE	ATHETOID
ABORTIVE	ADHERENT	ALARMING	AMENABLE	ANTIBODY	ARGUABLY	ATHLETIC
ABRASION	ADHESION	ALARMIST	AMERICAN	ANTIDOTE	ARGUMENT	ATLANTIC
ABRASIVE	ADHESIVE	ALBACORE	AMERICAS	ANTIHERO	ARKANSAS	ATLANTIS
ABRIDGED	ADJACENT	ALBANIAN	AMETHYST	ANTILLES	ARMAGNAC	ATOMIZER
ABROGATE	ADJUSTER	ALBERICH	AMICABLE	ANTILOPE	ARMALITE	ATROCITY
ABRUPTLY	ADJUSTOR	ALBINONI	AMICABLY	ANTIMERE	ARMAMENT	ATTACHED
ABSCISSA	ADJUTAGE	ALBURNUM	AMMONIAC	ANTIMONY	ARMATURE	ATTACKER
ABSENTEE	ADJUTANT	ALCATRAZ	AMMONITE	ANTIPHON	ARMCHAIR	ATTENDER
ABSINTHE	ADJUVANT	ALCESTIS	AMMONOID	ANTIPOPE	ARMENIAN	ATTESTOR
ABSOLUTE	ADMIRING	ALCHEMIC	AMORETTI	ANYPLACE	ARMORIAL	ATTITUDE
ABSOLVED	ADMONISH	ALDEHYDE	AMORETTO	ANYTHING	ARMORICA	ATTORNEY
ABSORBED	ADOPTION	ALDERMAN	AMORTIZE	ANYWHERE	ARMOURED	ATYPICAL
ABSORBER	ADOPTIVE	ALDERNEY	AMPERAGE	AOTEAROA	AROMATIC	AUBUSSON
ABSTRACT	ADORABLE	ALEATORY	AMPUTATE	APERIENT	ARPEGGIO	AUCASSIN
ABSTRUSE	ADRIATIC	ALEHOUSE	AMRITSAR	APERITIF	ARQUEBUS	AUDACITY
ABSURDLY	ADROITLY	ALEMAINE	AMUNDSEN	APERTURE	ARRANGER	AUDIENCE
ABUNDANT	ADULATOR	ALEUTIAN	AMUSETTE	APHELION	ARRESTED	AUDITION
ABUTILON	ADULTERY	ALFRESCO	AMYGDALA	APHORISM	ARRESTER	AUDITORY
ABUTMENT	ADVANCED	ALGERIAN	ANABASIS	APIARIST	ARROGANT	AUGUSTUS
ACADEMIA	ADVANCER	ALGERINE	ANABATIC	APNEUSIS	ARROGATE	AURELIAN
ACADEMIC	ADVISORY	ALGOLOGY	ANACONDA	APOLLYON	ARSONIST	AURICULA
ACANTHUS	ADVOCACY	ALGORISM	ANACREON	APOLOGIA	ARTEFACT	AUSPICES
ACAPULCO	ADVOCATE	ALHAMBRA	ANAGLYPH	APOLOGUE	ARTERIAL	AUSTRIAN
ACCENTED	AEGROTAT	ALICANTE	ANALECTA	APOPHYGE	ARTESIAN	AUTARCHY
ACCENTOR	AEROBICS	ALIENATE	ANALEMMA	APOPLEXY	ARTFULLY	AUTISTIC
ACCEPTED	AERODYNE	ALIENISM	ANALOGUE	APOSTASY	ARTICLED	AUTOBAHN
ACCEPTOR	AEROFLOT	ALIENIST	ANALYSER	APOSTATE	ARTICLES	AUTOCRAT
ACCIDENT	AEROFOIL	ALIQUANT	ANALYSIS	APOSTLES	ARTIFACT	AUTOGAMY
ACCOLADE	AEROGRAM	ALKALIFY	ANALYTIC	APOTHEGM	ARTIFICE	AUTOGIRO
ACCOUNTS	AEROLITH	ALKALINE	ANAPAEST	APPALLED	ARTISTIC	AUTOGYRO
ACCREDIT	AERONAUT	ALKALOID	ANAPHASE	APPANAGE	ARTISTRY	AUTOMATE
ACCURACY	AEROSTAT	ALLEGORY	ANARCHIC	APPARENT	ASBESTOS	AUTONOMY
ACCURATE	AESTHETE	ALLELUIA	ANATHEMA	APPELLANT	ASCIDIAN	AUTOTYPE
ACCURSED	AFFECTED	ALLERGEN	ANATOLIA	APPENDIX	ASCIDIUM	AUTUMNAL
ACCUSING	AFFERENT	ALLERGIC	ANATOMIC	APPETITE	ASCOCARP	AVAILING
ACCUSTOM	AFFINITY	ALLEYWAY	ANCESTOR	APPLAUSE	ASCORBIC	AVENTINE
ACENTRIC	AFFLATUS	ALLIANCE	ANCESTRY	APPLETON	ASMODEUS	AVERSION
ACERBATE	AFFLUENT	ALLOCATE	ANCHISES	APPLIQUÉ	ASPERGES	AVIATION
ACERBITY	AFFUSION	ALLOGAMY	ANCHORET	APPOSITE	ASPERITY	AVICENNA
ACHIEVED	AGACERIE	ALLOPATH	ANDERSON	APPRAISE	ASPERMIA	AVIFAUNA
ACHIEVER	AGGRIEVE	ALLOWING	ANDORRAN	APPRISED	ASPHODEL	AVOGADRO
ACHILLES	AGITATED	ALLSPICE	ANDREWES	APPROACH	ASPHYXIA	AVULSION
ACIDHEAD	AGITATOR	ALLURING	ANECDOTE	APPROVAL	ASPIRANT	AYRSHIRE
ACOUSTIC	AGITPROP	ALLUSION	ANEURYSM	APPROVED	ASPIRATE	BAATHIST
ACQUAINT	AGNATION	ALLUSIVE	ANGELICA	APTITUDE	ASPIRING	BABBLING
ACQUIRED	AGNOSTIC	ALLUVIAL	ANGLESEY	AQUALUNG	ASSASSIN	BABUSHKA
	AGONIZED	ALLUVIUM	ANGLICAN	AQUARIUM	ASSEMBLE	BABYHOOD

BACCARAT	BARBICAN	BEGORRAH	BIOSCOPE	BONEYARD	BRIGHTEN	BUSULFAN
BACCHANT	BARBIZON	BEGRUDGE	BIRDCAGE	BONHOMIE	BRIGHTLY	BUSYBODY
BACHELOR	BARDOLPH	BEHAVIOR	BIRDSEED	BONIFACE	BRIGHTON	BUTCHERS
BACILLUS	BAREBACK	BEHEMOTH	BIRTHDAY	BONSPIEL	BRIMMING	BUTCHERY
BACKACHE	BAREFOOT	BEHOLDEN	BISCAYAN	BOOKABLE	BRINDISI	BUTTERED
BACKBITE	BARENESS	BEHOLDER	BISEXUAL	BOOKCASE	BRINDLED	BUTTOCKS
BACKBONE	BARGELLO	BELABOUR	BISMARCK	BOOKMARK	BRINGING	BUTTRESS
BACKCHAT	BARGEMAN	BELGRADE	BITTERLY	BOOKROOM	BRISLING	BUZZWORD
BACKCOMB	BARITONE	BELIEVER	BLACKBOY	BOOKSHOP	BRISTLED	CABERNET
BACKDATE	BARNABAS	BELITTLE	BLACKCAP	BOOKWORK	BRISTLES	CABLECAR
BACKDROP	BARNACLE	BELLPUSH	BLACKFLY	BOOKWORM	BROADWAY	CABLEWAY
BACKFIRE	BARNARDS	BELLYFUL	BLACKING	BOOTLESS	BROCCOLI	CABOCHON
BACKHAND	BARNYARD	BELPAESE	BLACKISH	BOOTNECK	BROCHURE	CABOODLE
BACKLASH	BARONESS	BENEDICK	BLACKLEG	BORACITE	BROILING	CABOTAGE
BACKLESS	BARONETS	BENEDICT	BLACKOUT	BORDEAUX	BROMELIA	CABRIOLE
BACKPACK	BARONIAL	BENEFICE	BLANDISH	BORDELLO	BROMPTON	CACHALOT
BACKROOM	BARRACKS	BENEFITS	BLASTOFF	BORDERER	BRONCHUS	CACHEPOT
BACKSIDE	BARRATRY	BENENDEN	BLASTULA	BORECOLE	BROODING	CACHEXIA
BACKSPIN	BARRETTE	BENGHAZI	BLEACHER	BOREHOLE	BROUGHAM	CADASTRE
BACKSTOP	BARTERED	BENJAMIN	BLEEDING	BORODINO	BROUHAHA	CADILLAC
BACKWARD	BASEBALL	BEQUEATH	BLENDING	BORROWED	BROWBEAT	CADUCEUS
BACKYARD	BASEBORN	BERBERIS	BLENHEIM	BORROWER	BROWNING	CAERLEON
BACTERIA	BASELESS	BERCEUSE	BLESSING	BORSTALL	BROWNISH	CAFFEINE
BACTRIAN	BASELINE	BEREAVED	BLIGHTER	BOSWORTH	BROWSING	CAGINESS
BADINAGE	BASEMENT	BERGAMOT	BLINDING	BOTANIST	BRUCKNER	CAJOLERY
BADLANDS	BASENESS	BERGENIA	BLINKERS	BOTHERED	BRUISING	CAKEHOLE
BAEDEKER	BASIDIUM	BERGERAC	BLINKING	BOTHWELL	BRUMAIRE	CAKEWALK
BAFFLING	BASILICA	BERIBERI	BLISSFUL	BOTSWANA	BRUNETTE	CALABASH
BAGHEERA	BASILISK	BERKELEY	BLITHELY	BOTTLING	BRUSSELS	CALAMINE
BAGPIPES	BASINFUL	BERTRAND	BLIZZARD	BOTTOMRY	BRUTALLY	CALAMITY
BAGUETTE	BASKETRY	BESIEGED	BLOCKADE	BOTULISM	BRYOZOAN	CALCEATE
BAHAMIAN	BASSINET	BESMIRCH	BLOCKAGE	BOUFFANT	BUBBLING	CALCRETE
BAHRAINI	BASSWOOD	BESOTTED	BLOOMERS	BOUNCING	BUCKBEAN	CALCULUS
BAILMENT	BASTILLE	BESOUGHT	BLOOMING	BOUNDARY	BUCKFAST	CALCUTTA
BAKELITE	BATAVIAN	BESPOKEN	BLOTCHED	BOUTIQUE	BUCKLING	CALDERON
BALANCED	BATHETIC	BESSEMER	BLOWFISH	BOUZOUKI	BUCKSHEE	CALENDAR
BALDNESS	BATHROBE	BESTIARY	BLOWHOLE	BOWSPRIT	BUCKSHOT	CALENDER
BALDRICK	BATHROOM	BESTOWER	BLOWLAMP	BRABAZON	BUCKSKIN	CALFSKIN
BALEARIC	BATTERED	BESTRIDE	BLOWPIPE	BRACELET	BUDAPEST	CALIGULA
BALINESE	BAUDRICK	BETATRON	BLUDGEON	BRACHIAL	BUDDHISM	CALIPERS
BALLCOCK	BAVARIAN	BETHESDA	BLUEBACK	BRACKETS	BUDDHIST	CALLGIRL
BALLGIRL	BAYBERRY	BETJEMAN	BLUEBELL	BRACKISH	BUDDLEIA	CALLIOPE
BALLISTA	BAYREUTH	BETRAYAL	BLUECOAT	BRADBURY	BUGGERED	CALLIPER
BALLOCKS	BEAKLESS	BETRAYER	BLUENOSE	BRADSHAW	BUILDING	CALLISTO
BALLPARK	BEANPOLE	BEVERAGE	BLURRING	BRAGANZA	BULGARIA	CALMNESS
BALLROOM	BEARABLE	BEWILDER	BLUSHING	BRAGGART	BULKHEAD	CALOTYPE
BALLYHOO	BEARINGS	BIANNUAL	BLUSTERY	BRAGGING	BULLDOZE	CALTHROP
BALMORAL	BEARSKIN	BIATHLON	BOADICEA	BRAMANTE	BULLETIN	CALVADOS
BALUSTER	BEATIFIC	BIBLICAL	BOARDING	BRANCHED	BULLFROG	CAMARGUE
BANALITY	BEAUFORT	BIBULOUS	BOASTFUL	BRANDADE	BULLHORN	CAMBERED
BANDANNA	BEAUMONT	BICONVEX	BOASTING	BRANDISH	BULLRING	CAMBODIA
BANDEROL	BEAUTIFY	BICUSPID	BOATBILL	BRANDNEW	BULLYRAG	CAMBRIAN
BANDITTI	BECALMED	BIENNIAL	BOATLOAD	BRASILIA	BUMBLING	CAMELLIA
BANDSMAN	BECHAMEL	BIFOCALS	BOBBYPIN	BRASSARD	BUMMAREE	CAMEROON
BANISTER	BECOMING	BIGAMIST	BOBOLINK	BRASSICA	BUNFIGHT	CAMISOLE
BANKBOOK	BEDABBLE	BIGAMOUS	BODLEIAN	BRATPACK	BUNGALOW	CAMOMILE
BANKNOTE	BEDCOVER	BIGARADE	BODYLINE	BREACHES	BUNGLING	CAMPAIGN
BANKROLL	BEDMAKER	BIGNONIA	BODYWORK	BREAKING	BUOYANCY	CAMPBELL
BANKRUPT	BEDSTEAD	BILBERRY	BOEOTIAN	BREAKOUT	BURBERRY	CAMPSITE
BANLIEUE	BEDSTRAW	BILLFOLD	BOGEYMAN	BREATHER	BURDENED	CAMPTOWN
BANNERET	BEERBOHM	BILLHOOK	BOHEMIAN	BREECHES	BURGLARY	CAMSHAFT
BANTLING	BEESWING	BILLYBOY	BOLDNESS	BREEDING	BURGRAVE	CAMSTONE
BAPTISED	BEETLING	BILLYCAN	BOLIVIAN	BREEZILY	BURGUNDY	CANADIAN
BARABBAS	BEETROOT	BILOBATE	BOLLOCKS	BRETHREN	BURNTOUT	CANAILLE
BARATHEA	BEFRIEND	BINDWEED	BOLTHOLE	BREVIARY	BURROWER	CANALISE
BARBADOS	BEFUDDLE	BINNACLE	BONDSMAN	BRIBABLE	BURSITIS	CANARIES
BARBARIC	BEGETTER	BINOMIAL	BONEFISH	BRICKBAT	BURSTING	CANBERRA
BARBECUE	BEGGARLY	BIOGRAPH	BONEHEAD	BRIDGING	BUSINESS	CANDIDLY
BARBERRY	BEGINNER	BIOMETRY	BONELESS	BRIEFING	BUSTLING	CANISTER

CANNABIS	CATATONY	CHARLADY	CICATRIX	CLOWNISH	COMBINED	CONVULSE
CANNIBAL	CATCHING	CHARLOCK	CICERONE	CLUBBING	COMEBACK	COOKBOOK
CANOEING	CATECHOL	CHARMING	CICISBEO	CLUBFOOT	COMEDIAN	COOKWARE
CANOEIST	CATEGORY	CHARTISM	CILIATED	CLUELESS	COMEDOWN	COOLNESS
CANONESS	CATERING	CHARTIST	CINCHONA	CLUMSILY	COMMANDO	COPULATE
CANONIZE	CATHEDRA	CHARTRES	CINERAMA	COACHING	COMMENCE	COPYBOOK
CANOODLE	CATHETER	CHASSEUR	CINEREAL	COACHMAN	COMMERCE	COPYHOLD
CANTICLE	CATHOLIC	CHASTISE	CINGULUM	COALESCE	COMMONER	COQUETRY
CANTORIS	CATHOUSE	CHASTITY	CINNABAR	COALHOLE	COMMONLY	COQUETTE
CAPACITY	CATILINE	CHASUBLE	CINNAMON	COALMINE	COMMUNAL	CORDOVAN
CAPERING	CATSMEAT	CHATTELS	CIRCINUS	COALPORT	COMMUTER	CORDUROY
CAPITALS	CATTLEYA	CHEATERS	CIRCUITY	COARSELY	COMPARED	CORDWAIN
CAPRIOLE	CATULLUS	CHEATING	CIRCULAR	COATRACK	COMPILER	CORIOLIS
CAPSICUM	CAUDILLO	CHECKERS	CISTERNA	COATTAIL	COMPLAIN	CORMORAN
CAPSIZED	CAULDRON	CHECKING	CITATION	COAUTHOR	COMPLETE	CORNETTO
CAPSTONE	CAUSEWAY	CHECKOUT	CIVILIAN	COBBLERS	COMPLINE	CORNHILL
CAPTIOUS	CAUTIOUS	CHEEKILY	CIVILITY	COBWEBBY	COMPOSED	CORNICHE
CAPUCHIN	CAVALIER	CHEERFUL	CIVILIZE	COCACOLA	COMPOSER	CORNMEAL
CAPYBARA	CAVATINA	CHEERILY	CLADDING	COCCIDAE	COMPOUND	CORNWALL
CARABINE	CELANESE	CHEERING	CLAIMANT	COCHLEAR	COMPRESS	CORONARY
CARACOLE	CELERIAC	CHEMICAL	CLAMBAKE	COCKATOO	COMPRISE	CORONOID
CARAPACE	CELERITY	CHENILLE	CLANGING	COCKAYNE	COMPUTER	CORPORAL
CARBOLIC	CELIBACY	CHEQUERS	CLANGOUR	COCKBOAT	CONCEIVE	CORRAGIO
CARBONIC	CELIBATE	CHEROKEE	CLANNISH	COCKCROW	CONCERTO	CORRIDOR
CARCAJOU	CELLARER	CHERUBIC	CLANSMAN	COCKEREL	CONCHOID	CORRODED
CARCANET	CELLULAR	CHERUBIM	CLAPPERS	COCKEYED	CONCLAVE	CORSELET
CARDAMOM	CEMENTUM	CHERWELL	CLAPPING	COCKTAIL	CONCLUDE	CORSICAN
CARDIGAN	CEMETERY	CHESHIRE	CLAPTRAP	CODPIECE	CONCORDE	CORUNDUM
CARDINAL	CENOBITE	CHESSMAN	CLARENCE	COERCION	CONCRETE	CORVETTE
CAREFREE	CENOTAPH	CHESSMEN	CLARINET	COERCIVE	CONDENSE	COSINESS
CARELESS	CENOZOIC	CHESTNUT	CLASHING	COGITATE	CONFETTI	COSMETIC
CAREWORN	CENTAURY	CHEVIOTS	CLASPING	COGNOMEN	CONFINED	COSTMARY
CARILLON	CENTERED	CHEYENNE	CLASSICS	COGWHEEL	CONFINES	COTOPAXI
CARJACOU	CENTRIST	CHIASMUS	CLASSIFY	COHERENT	CONFLATE	COTSWOLD
CARNAUBA	CENTRODE	CHICHEWA	CLAUDIUS	COHESION	CONFLICT	COTTAGER
CARNEGIE	CEPHALIN	CHICKENS	CLAVECIN	COHESIVE	CONFOUND	COUCHANT
CARNIVAL	CERAMICS	CHICKPEA	CLAVICLE	COIFFEUR	CONFRONT	COUCHING
CAROLINA	CERASTES	CHILDERS	CLAWBACK	COIFFURE	CONFUSED	COUGHING
CAROLINE	CERATOID	CHILDISH	CLAYMORE	COINCIDE	CONGRATS	COUNTESS
CAROTENE	CERBERUS	CHILDREN	CLEANERS	COLANDER	CONGRESS	COUNTIES
CAROUSAL	CEREBRAL	CHILIAST	CLEANING	COLDBOOT	CONJUGAL	COUNTING
CAROUSEL	CEREBRUM	CHILLADA	CLEANSED	COLDNESS	CONJURER	COUPERIN
CARRAWAY	CEREMENT	CHILLING	CLEANSER	COLESLAW	CONJUROR	COUPLING
CARRIAGE	CEREMONY	CHILTERN	CLEARCUT	COLIFORM	CONQUEST	COURTESY
CARRIOLE	CERULEAN	CHIMAERA	CLEARING	COLISEUM	CONSERVE	COUSCOUS
CARRYALL	CERVELAT	CHINAMAN	CLEARWAY	COLLAGEN	CONSIDER	COVALENT
CARRYCOT	CERVICAL	CHINDITS	CLEAVAGE	COLLAPSE	CONSOMMÉ	COVENANT
CARRYING	CESSPOOL	CHIPMUNK	CLEAVERS	COLLARED	CONSPIRE	COVENTRY
CARTHAGE	CETACEAN	CHITCHAT	CLEMATIS	COLLATOR	CONSTANT	COVERAGE
CARTLOAD	CHACONNE	CHIVALRY	CLEMENCY	COLLECTS	CONSTRUE	COVERING
CARUCATE	CHADBAND	CHLORATE	CLERICAL	COLLEGES	CONSULAR	COVERLET
CARYATID	CHAINSAW	CHLORIDE	CLERIHEW	COLLIERS	CONSUMED	COVETOUS
CASANOVA	CHAIRMAN	CHLORINE	CLEVERLY	COLLIERY	CONSUMER	COWARDLY
CASEMATE	CHALDEAN	CHOIRBOY	CLIFFORD	COLLOQUY	CONTANGO	COWBERRY
CASEMENT	CHALDRON	CHOLERIC	CLIMATIC	COLOMBIA	CONTEMPT	COXSWAIN
CASHMERE	CHAMBERS	CHOOSING	CLIMBING	COLONIAL	CONTENTS	COYSTRIL
CASSETTE	CHAMPERS	CHOPPING	CLINCHER	COLONIST	CONTINUE	COZINESS
CASTANET	CHAMPION	CHORDATA	CLINGING	COLONIZE	CONTINUO	CRACKERS
CASTAWAY	CHANCERY	CHORDATE	CLINICAL	COLOPHON	CONTRACT	CRACKING
CASTOFFS	CHANDLER	CHORIAMB	CLINKERS	COLORADO	CONTRARY	CRACKPOT
CASTRATE	CHANGING	CHRISTEN	CLIPPERS	COLORANT	CONTRAST	CRAFTILY
CASTRATO	CHANTAGE	CHRISTIE	CLIPPING	COLORFUL	CONTRITE	CRAMOISY
CASUALLY	CHANTREY	CHRISTOM	CLIQUISH	COLORING	CONTRIVE	CRANEFLY
CASUALTY	CHAPATTI	CHROMITE	CLITORIS	COLOSSAL	CONTROLS	CRATCHIT
CATACOMB	CHAPERON	CHROMIUM	CLIVEDEN	COLOSSUS	CONVENER	CRAVATES
CATALYST	CHAPLAIN	CHUMMAGE	CLODPOLL	COLOURED	CONVERGE	CRAWFISH
CATAMITE	CHARCOAL	CHURLISH	CLOISTER	COLUMBAN	CONVERSE	CRAWLING
CATAPULT	CHARGING	CHUTZPAH	CLOTHIER	COLUMBUS	CONVEYOR	CRAYFISH
CATARACT	CHARISMA	CIBORIUM	CLOTHING	COMATOSE	CONVINCE	CREAMERY

CREATION	CUTPRICE	DECIMATE	DESCRIBE	DIMINISH	DISUNITY	DOWNTURN
CREATIVE	CUTPURSE	DECIPHER	DESELECT	DINGBATS	DIURETIC	DOWNWARD
CREATURE	CUTWATER	DECISION	DESERTED	DINOSAUR	DIVIDEND	DOXOLOGY
CREDIBLE	CYANOGEN	DECISIVE	DESERTER	DIOCESAN	DIVIDERS	DRACAENA
CREDIBLY	CYANOSIS	DECKHAND	DESERVED	DIOGENES	DIVINITY	DRACONIC
CREDITOR	CYCLADES	DECLUTCH	DESIGNER	DIONYSUS	DIVISION	DRAGOONS
CREOSOTE	CYCLAMEN	DECORATE	DESIROUS	DIOPTRIC	DIVISIVE	DRAGSTER
CREPITUS	CYCLICAL	DECOROUS	DESOLATE	DIPHENYL	DIVORCED	DRAINAGE
CRESCENT	CYCLOSIS	DECOUPLE	DESPATCH	DIPLOMAT	DIVORCEE	DRAINING
CRETONNE	CYLINDER	DECREASE	DESPOTIC	DIPSTICK	DJELLABA	DRAMATIC
CREVASSE	CYNICISM	DECREPIT	DESTINED	DIPTERAL	DJIBOUTI	DRAUGHTS
CRIBBAGE	CYNOSURE	DECRETAL	DESTRUCT	DIRECTLY	DOCILITY	DRAUGHTY
CRICHTON	CYRENIAC	DEDICATE	DETACHED	DIRECTOR	DOCKLAND	DRAWBACK
CRIMINAL	CYRILLIC	DEEPNESS	DETAILED	DISABLED	DOCKSIDE	DREADFUL
CRINGING	CYSTITIS	DEERSKIN	DETAINEE	DISABUSE	DOCKYARD	DREAMILY
CRIPPLED	CYTOLOGY	DEFEATED	DETAINER	DISAGREE	DOCTORAL	DREAMING
CRISPIAN	CYTOSINE	DEFECATE	DETECTOR	DISALLOW	DOCTORED	DREARILY
CRITICAL	CZAREVNA	DEFECTOR	DETHRONE	DISARRAY	DOCTRINE	DRESSAGE
CRITIQUE	DABCHICK	DEFENDER	DETONATE	DISASTER	DOCUMENT	DRESSING
CROATIAN	DAEDALUS	DEFIANCE	DETOXIFY	DISBURSE	DOGBERRY	DRIBLETS
CROCKERY	DAFFODIL	DEFILADE	DETRITUS	DISCIPLE	DOGGEDLY	DRIFTING
CROCKETT	DAINTIES	DEFINITE	DEUTERON	DISCLAIM	DOGGEREL	DRINKING
CROMLECH	DAINTILY	DEFLOWER	DEVIANCE	DISCLOSE	DOGHOUSE	DRIPPING
CROMWELL	DAIQUIRI	DEFORMED	DEVILISH	DISCOLOR	DOGMATIC	DRIVEWAY
CRONYISM	DAIRYMAN	DEFREEZE	DEVILLED	DISCOUNT	DOGSBODY	DROOPING
CROONING	DALMATIC	DEFTNESS	DEVONIAN	DISCOVER	DOGSTAIL	DROPHEAD
CROSSBAR	DAMASCUS	DEGRADED	DEVOTION	DISCREET	DOGTOOTH	DROPPING
CROSSING	DAMNABLE	DEJECTED	DEWBERRY	DISCRETE	DOGWATCH	DROPSHOT
CROSSLET	DAMOCLES	DELAWARE	DEWEYED	DISEASED	DOLDRUMS	DROWNING
CROTCHET	DAMPNESS	DELEGATE	DEXTROSE	DISFAVOR	DOLOMITE	DROWSILY
CROUPIER	DANAIDES	DELETION	DEXTROUS	DISGORGE	DOLOROUS	DRUBBING
CROWFOOT	DANDRUFF	DELICACY	DIABETES	DISGRACE	DOMESDAY	DRUDGERY
CROWNING	DANEGELD	DELICATE	DIABETIC	DISGUISE	DOMESTIC	DRUGGIST
CRUCIATE	DANKNESS	DELIRIUM	DIABOLIC	DISHEVEL	DOMICILE	DRUMBEAT
CRUCIBLE	DARKENED	DELIVERY	DIAGNOSE	DISHONOR	DOMINANT	DRUMHEAD
CRUCIFER	DARKNESS	DELUSION	DIAGONAL	DISINTER	DOMINATE	DRUMLINE
CRUCIFIX	DARKROOM	DEMEANOR	DIALLING	DISJUNCT	DOMINEER	DRUMMING
CRUMHORN	DARTMOOR	DEMENTED	DIALOGUE	DISKETTE	DOMINION	DRUNKARD
CRUMMOCK	DASHWOOD	DEMENTIA	DIALYSIS	DISLIKED	DOMINOES	DRYCLEAN
CRUNCHIE	DATABASE	DEMERARA	DIAMANTE	DISLODGE	DONATION	DRYGOODS
CRUSADER	DATELESS	DEMERSAL	DIAMETER	DISLOYAL	DONATIST	DRYSTONE
CRUSHING	DATELINE	DEMIJOHN	DIAMONDS	DISMALLY	DOOLALLY	DUBONNET
CRUTCHED	DAUGHTER	DEMISTER	DIANTHUS	DISMAYED	DOOMSDAY	DUCHESSE
CRUZEIRO	DAUNTING	DEMIURGE	DIAPASON	DISMOUNT	DOORBELL	DUCKBILL
CRYOLITE	DAVIDSON	DEMOCRAT	DIAPHONE	DISORDER	DOORKNOB	DUCKLING
CRYSTALS	DAYBREAK	DEMOLISH	DIARESIS	DISPATCH	DOORPOST	DUCKWEED
CUCUMBER	DAYDREAM	DEMONIAC	DIARRHEA	DISPENSE	DOORSILL	DUELLIST
CUCURBIT	DAYLIGHT	DEMOTION	DIASPORA	DISPERSE	DOORSTEP	DULCIMER
CULINARY	DAZZLING	DEMURELY	DIASTASE	DISPIRIT	DOPAMINE	DULCINEA
CULLINAN	DEADBEAT	DEMURRAL	DIASTOLE	DISPLACE	DORMOUSE	DULLNESS
CULLODEN	DEADENED	DENARIUS	DIATONIC	DISPOSAL	DOTTEREL	DUMBBELL
CULOTTES	DEADENER	DENATURE	DIATRIBE	DISPOSED	DOUBLETS	DUMBNESS
CULPABLE	DEADHEAD	DENDRITE	DIAZEPAM	DISPROVE	DOUBLOON	DUMFOUND
CULTURAL	DEADLINE	DENDROID	DICTATES	DISPUTED	DOUBTFUL	DUMPLING
CULTURED	DEADLOCK	DENOUNCE	DICTATOR	DISQUIET	DOUBTING	DUNGHILL
CULVERIN	DEADWOOD	DENTICLE	DICYCLIC	DISRAELI	DOUGHBOY	DUODENAL
CUPBOARD	DEAFNESS	DENTURES	DIDACTIC	DISSOLVE	DOUGHNUT	DUODENUM
CUPIDITY	DEALINGS	DEPARTED	DIDDICOY	DISSUADE	DOVECOTE	DURABLES
CURATIVE	DEATHBED	DEPILATE	DIEHARDS	DISTANCE	DOVETAIL	DURATION
CURLICUE	DEBILITY	DEPORTEE	DIELDRIN	DISTASTE	DOWNBEAT	DUTCHMAN
CURRENCY	DEBONAIR	DEPRAVED	DIERESIS	DISTINCT	DOWNCAST	DUTIABLE
CURRICLE	DECADENT	DEPRIVED	DIFFRACT	DISTRACT	DOWNFALL	DUTYFREE
CURSITOR	DECANTER	DEPUTIZE	DIGGINGS	DISTRAIN	DOWNHILL	DWARFISH
CURTAINS	DECAYING	DERANGED	DIGITIZE	DISTRAIT	DOWNLOAD	DWARFISM
CURTNESS	DECEASED	DERELICT	DIGIZINE	DISTRESS	DOWNPLAY	DWELLING
CUSPIDOR	DECEIVER	DERISION	DILATION	DISTRICT	DOWNPOUR	DYNAMICS
CUSTOMER	DECEMBER	DERISIVE	DILATORY	DISTRUST	DOWNSIDE	DYNAMISM
CUTENESS	DECEMVIR	DERISORY	DILIGENT	DISUNION	DOWNSIZE	DYNAMITE
CUTHBERT	DECENTLY	DEROGATE	DILUTION	DISUNITE	DOWNTOWN	DYNASTIC

DYNATRON	EMBEDDED	ENSHROUD	ESPOUSAL	EXCHANGE	FANDANGO	FILAMENT
DYSLEXIA	EMBEZZLE	ENSIFORM	ESPRESSO	EXCISION	FANLIGHT	FILARIUM
DYSLEXIC	EMBITTER	ENSILAGE	ESSAYIST	EXCITING	FANTASIA	FILENAME
DZONGKHA	EMBLAZON	ENTANGLE	ESSONITE	EXECRATE	FARCICAL	FILIGREE
EARLIEST	EMBODIED	ENTHALPY	ESTANCIA	EXECUTED	FAREWELL	FILIPINO
EARNINGS	EMBOLDEN	ENTHRALL	ESTEEMED	EXECUTOR	FARMHAND	FILTHILY
EARPHONE	EMBOLISM	ENTHRONE	ESTHETIC	EXEGESIS	FARMLAND	FILTRATE
EARPIECE	EMBOSSED	ENTICING	ESTIMATE	EXEGETIC	FARMYARD	FINALIST
EASEMENT	EMBRACED	ENTIRELY	ESTIVATE	EXEMPLAR	FAROUCHE	FINALITY
EASINESS	EMBRACES	ENTIRETY	ESTONIAN	EXERCISE	FARRIERY	FINALIZE
EASTERLY	EMERGENT	ENTITLED	ESTOPPEL	EXERTION	FARTHEST	FINDINGS
EASTLAKE	EMERGING	ENTRAILS	ESTOVERS	EXHUMATE	FARTHING	FINESPUN
EASTWARD	EMERITUS	ENTRANCE	ESTRAGON	EXIGENCY	FASCICLE	FINISHED
EATABLES	EMERSION	ENTREATY	ESTROGEN	EXIGUITY	FASTBACK	FINISHER
ECHINATE	EMIGRANT	ENTRENCH	ETCETERA	EXIGUOUS	FASTENER	FIREARMS
ECHINOPS	EMIGRATE	ENTREPOT	ETERNITY	EXISTENT	FASTNESS	FIREBACK
ECLECTIC	EMINENCE	ENTRYISM	ETHEREAL	EXISTING	FATALISM	FIREBALL
ECLOSION	EMINENCY	ENVELOPE	ETHERIFY	EXOCRINE	FATALIST	FIREBIRD
ECOFREAK	EMIRATES	ENVIABLE	ETHERISE	EXOERGIC	FATALITY	FIREBOLT
ECONOMIC	EMISSARY	ENVIRONS	ETHIOPIA	EXORCISM	FATHERLY	FIREDAMP
ECSTASIS	EMISSION	ENVISAGE	ETHNARCH	EXORCIST	FATIGUED	FIRESIDE
ECSTATIC	EMMANUEL	ENVISION	ETHOLOGY	EXORCIZE	FATIGUES	FIRESTEP
ECTODERM	EMOTICON	EOHIPPUS	ETHYLENE	EXORDIUM	FATSTOCK	FIRETRAP
EDENTATE	EMPHASIS	EPHEMERA	ETIOLATE	EXPANDED	FAULKNER	FIREWEED
EDGEHILL	EMPHATIC	EPHESIAN	ETRURIAN	EXPECTED	FAVORITE	FIREWOOD
EDGEWAYS	EMPLOYED	EPICURUS	ETRUSCAN	EXPEDITE	FAVOURED	FIREWORK
EDGEWISE	EMPLOYEE	EPIDEMIC	EUCYCLIC	EXPENDED	FEARLESS	FIRMNESS
EDUCATED	EMPLOYER	EPIDURAL	EUDOXIAN	EXPENSES	FEARSOME	FIRMWARE
EDUCATOR	EMPORIUM	EPIGAMIC	EUGENICS	EXPLICIT	FEASIBLE	FISHBONE
EERINESS	EMPYREAL	EPIGRAPH	EULOGIST	EXPLODED	FEASIBLY	FISHCAKE
EFFERENT	EMPYREAN	EPILEPSY	EULOGIUM	EXPLORER	FEATHERS	FISHHOOK
EFFICACY	EMULATOR	EPILOGUE	EULOGIZE	EXPONENT	FEATHERY	FISHMEAL
EFFLUENT	EMULGENT	EPIPHANY	EUPEPSIA	EXPORTER	FEATURED	FISHPOND
EFFLUVIA	EMULSIFY	EPIPHYTE	EUPHONIA	EXPOSURE	FEATURES	FISHWIFE
EFFUSION	EMULSION	EPIPLOON	EUPHONIC	EXPRESSO	FEBRUARY	FISSIPED
EFFUSIVE	ENCAENIA	EPISODIC	EUPHORIA	EXTENDED	FECKLESS	FITFULLY
EGGPLANT	ENCAMPED	EPISTYLE	EUPHORIC	EXTENSOR	FECULENT	FIXATION
EGGSHELL	ENCIRCLE	EPITASIS	EUPHUISM	EXTERIOR	FEDAYEEN	FIXATIVE
EGGTIMER	ENCLOSED	EPITHEMA	EURASIAN	EXTERNAL	FEDERACY	FLAGGING
EGOISTIC	ENCLOTHE	EQUALITY	EUROLAND	EXTERNAT	FEDERATE	FLAGPOLE
EGOMANIA	ENCOMIUM	EQUALIZE	EUROPEAN	EXTRADOS	FEEDBACK	FLAGRANT
EGYPTIAN	ENCROACH	EQUATION	EUROPIUM	EXULTANT	FEELGOOD	FLAGSHIP
EIDECTIC	ENCUMBER	EQUIPAGE	EUROSTAR	EXULTING	FEELINGS	FLAMENCO
EIGHTEEN	ENDANGER	EQUITANT	EURYDICE	EYEGLASS	FELDSPAR	FLAMEOUT
EINSTEIN	ENDEAVOR	EQUULEUS	EUSTATIC	EYELINER	FELICITY	FLAMINGO
EJECTION	ENDOCARP	ERADIATE	EUTROPHY	EYEPIECE	FELLAHIN	FLANDERS
ELDORADO	ENDODERM	ERECTILE	EUTROPIC	EYESHADE	FEMININE	FLANNELS
ELDRITCH	ENDOGAMY	ERECTING	EVACUANT	EYESIGHT	FEMINISM	FLAPJACK
ELECTION	ENDURING	ERECTION	EVACUATE	EYETOOTH	FEMINIST	FLAPPING
ELECTIVE	ENDYMION	ERGOTISE	EVALUATE	FABULOUS	FEMINITY	FLASHGUN
ELECTORS	ENERGIZE	ERGOTISM	EVANESCE	FACEACHE	FENCIBLE	FLASHILY
ELECTRIC	ENERVATE	ERIDANUS	EVENNESS	FACELESS	FENESTRA	FLASHING
ELECTRON	ENFEEBLE	ERIKSSON	EVENSONG	FACELIFT	FEROCITY	FLATBOAT
ELECTRUM	ENFILADE	ERUCTATE	EVENTFUL	FACILITY	FERRYMAN	FLATFISH
ELEGANCE	ENGAGING	ERUPTION	EVENTIDE	FACTIOUS	FESTIVAL	FLATFOOT
ELEMENTS	ENGENDER	ERUPTURE	EVENTUAL	FACTOTUM	FETCHING	FLATMATE
ELEPHANT	ENGINEER	ERYTHEMA	EVERMORE	FAINITES	FETTLING	FLATPICK
ELEVATED	ENGRAVER	ESCALADE	EVERYDAY	FAINTING	FEVERFEW	FLATTERY
ELEVATOR	ENIWETOK	ESCALATE	EVERYMAN	FAIRNESS	FEVERISH	FLATWARE
ELEVENTH	ENKINDLE	ESCALOPE	EVERYONE	FAITHFUL	FIBROSIS	FLATWORM
ELIGIBLE	ENLARGED	ESCAPADE	EVICTION	FALCONRY	FIDDLING	FLAUBERT
ELKHOUND	ENLARGER	ESCAPISM	EVIDENCE	FALKLAND	FIDELITY	FLAUTIST
ELLIPSIS	ENMESHED	ESCAPIST	EVILDOER	FALLIBLE	FIDUCIAL	FLAVORED
ELLIPTIC	ENORMITY	ESCARGOT	EWIGKEIT	FALSETTO	FIELDING	FLAWLESS
ELONGATE	ENORMOUS	ESCORIAL	EXACTING	FAMILIAR	FIENDISH	FLAXSEED
ELOQUENT	ENRICHED	ESCULENT	EXACTION	FAMISHED	FIERCELY	FLEABITE
ELSINORE	ENSCONCE	ESOTERIC	EXAMINEE	FAMOUSLY	FIFTIETH	FLEETING
EMACIATE	ENSEMBLE	ESPALIER	EXAMINER	FANCIFUL	FIGHTING	FLEISHIG
EMBATTLE	ENSHRINE	ESPECIAL	EXCAVATE	FANCYMAN	FIGURINE	FLEXIBLE

FLEXIBLY	FORENSIC	FRISKILY	GANGRENE	GIRASOLE	GRANDEUR	GUYANESE
FLIMSILY	FORESAIL	FRONDEUR	GANGSTER	GIRLHOOD	GRANDKID	GYMKHANA
FLINDERS	FORESHIP	FRONTAGE	GANISTER	GIRONDIN	GRANDSON	GYRATION
FLIPPANT	FORESKIN	FRONTIER	GANYMEDE	GIVEAWAY	GRANULAR	GYRATORY
FLIPPERS	FORESTAY	FRONTMAN	GAOLBIRD	GLABELLA	GRANULES	GYROSTAT
FLIPPING	FORESTER	FROSTILY	GARAMOND	GLABROUS	GRAPHEME	HABAKKUK
FLIRTING	FORESTRY	FROSTING	GARDENER	GLADNESS	GRAPHICS	HABANERA
FLOATING	FORETELL	FRUCTIFY	GARDENIA	GLADSOME	GRAPHITE	HABITUAL
FLOGGING	FOREWARN	FRUCTOSE	GARDYLOO	GLANCING	GRASPING	HABSBURG
FLOODING	FOREWORD	FRUGALLY	GARGANEY	GLANDERS	GRATEFUL	HACIENDA
FLOODLIT	FORFEITS	FRUITFUL	GARGOYLE	GLASNOST	GRATINEE	HAGGADAH
FLOORING	FORKLIFT	FRUITING	GARISHLY	GLASSFUL	GRATUITY	HAIRBAND
FLORENCE	FORKTAIL	FRUITION	GARLICKY	GLAUCOMA	GRAVAMEN	HAIRLESS
FLOTILLA	FORMALIN	FRUMENTY	GARMENTS	GLAUCOUS	GRAVELLY	HAIRLIKE
FLOUNCED	FORMALLY	FRUMPISH	GARRIGUE	GLEAMING	GRAVITAS	HAIRLINE
FLOUNDER	FORMERLY	FUCHSITE	GARRISON	GLEESOME	GRAYLING	HAIRWORM
FLOURISH	FORMLESS	FUGITIVE	GARROTTE	GLISSADE	GREATEST	HALFFULL
FLUENTLY	FORMOSAN	FUGLEMAN	GASOLIER	GLOAMING	GREEDILY	HALFHOUR
FLUIDITY	FORMWORK	FULLBACK	GASOLINE	GLOATING	GREENBAG	HALFMAST
FLUMMERY	FORSAKEN	FULLNESS	GASTRULA	GLOBALLY	GREENERY	HALFTERM
FLUORIDE	FORSLACK	FULLPAGE	GASWORKS	GLOBULAR	GREENFLY	HALFTIME
FLUORINE	FORSOOTH	FULLSIZE	GATEFOLD	GLOBULIN	GREENING	HALFYEAR
FLUORITE	FORSWEAR	FULLTIME	GATEPOST	GLOOMILY	GREENISH	HALLIARD
FLUSHING	FORTIETH	FUMAROLE	GATHERED	GLORIANA	GREENOCK	HALLMARK
FLYBLOWN	FORTRESS	FUMBLING	GAUNTLET	GLORIOLE	GREETING	HALLOWED
FLYDRIVE	FORTUITY	FUMIGATE	GAZPACHO	GLORIOUS	GRENACHE	HAMARTIA
FLYSHEET	FORWARDS	FUMITORY	GAZUNDER	GLOSSARY	GRIDIRON	HAMILTON
FLYWHEEL	FOULNESS	FUNCTION	GELASTIC	GLOSSEME	GRIDLOCK	HAMMERED
FOGBOUND	FOUNDING	FUNERARY	GELATINE	GLOXINIA	GRIEVOUS	HANDBALL
FOGLIGHT	FOUNTAIN	FUNEREAL	GEMINATE	GLUMPISH	GRILLING	HANDBILL
FOLDEROL	FOURFOLD	FUNGIBLE	GEMOLOGY	GLUTAEUS	GRIMALDI	HANDBOOK
FOLKLORE	FOURPART	FURBELOW	GENDARME	GLUTTONY	GRIMNESS	HANDCART
FOLKSONG	FOURSOME	FURLOUGH	GENERATE	GLYCERIN	GRINDING	HANDCLAP
FOLLICLE	FOURTEEN	FURROWED	GENEROUS	GLYCOGEN	GRIPPING	HANDCUFF
FOLLOWED	FOXGLOVE	FURTHEST	GENETICS	GNASHING	GRISELDA	HANDGRIP
FOLLOWER	FOXHOUND	FURUNCLE	GENETRIX	GOALPOST	GRISETTE	HANDHELD
FOLLOWUP	FRABJOUS	FUSAROLE	GENIALLY	GOATSKIN	GRIZZLED	HANDICAP
FONDLING	FRACTION	FUSELAGE	GENITALS	GOBSMACK	GROGGILY	HANDMADE
FONDNESS	FRACTURE	FUSEWIRE	GENITIVE	GODCHILD	GROOMING	HANDMAID
FOOLSCAP	FRAGMENT	FUSIFORM	GENOCIDE	GOIDELIC	GROSBEAK	HANDOVER
FOOTBALL	FRAGRANT	FUSILIER	GENTRIFY	GOLDFISH	GROSCHEN	HANDRAIL
FOOTFALL	FRANCIUM	FUTILITY	GEODESIC	GOLDMINE	GROUNDED	HANDSOME
FOOTHOLD	FRANKISH	FUTURISM	GEODETIC	GOLFBALL	GROUPING	HANDYMAN
FOOTLING	FRANKLIN	FUTURIST	GEOMANCY	GOLFCLUB	GROUTING	HANGINGS
FOOTNOTE	FRAULEIN	GABONESE	GEOMETER	GOLGOTHA	GROWLING	HANGNAIL
FOOTPATH	FRAXINUS	GABORONE	GEOMETRY	GOLLIWOG	GRUDGING	HANGOVER
FOOTREST	FRAZZLED	GADABOUT	GEOPHONE	GONDWANA	GRUESOME	HANNIBAL
FOOTSORE	FREAKISH	GADARENE	GEORGIAN	GONFALON	GRUMBLER	HANUKKAH
FOOTSTEP	FRECKLED	GADGETRY	GEOTAXIS	GOODNESS	GRUMPILY	HAPSBURG
FOOTWEAR	FRECKLES	GADOGADO	GERANIUM	GOODSIRE	GUAIACUM	HARANGUE
FOOTWORK	FREEHAND	GADZOOKS	GERMAINE	GOODWIFE	GUARDIAN	HARASSED
FORCEFUL	FREEHOLD	GAILLARD	GERMANIC	GOODWILL	GUERIDON	HARDBACK
FORCIBLE	FREEPOST	GALACTIC	GERMINAL	GOODWOOD	GUERILLA	HARDCORE
FORCIBLY	FREETOWN	GALBANUM	GERONIMO	GOODYEAR	GUERNSEY	HARDENED
FOREBEAR	FREEZING	GALILEAN	GERTRUDE	GOOFBALL	GUIANIAN	HARDHACK
FOREBODE	FREMITUS	GALLERIA	GESTURES	GOOSEGOG	GUIDANCE	HARDLINE
FORECAST	FRENETIC	GALLIARD	GHANAIAN	GORGEOUS	GUILTILY	HARDNESS
FOREDECK	FRENULUM	GALLIPOT	GHOULISH	GORMLESS	GUJARATI	HARDSHIP
FOREDOOM	FRENZIED	GALLOPER	GIACONDA	GOSSAMER	GULFWEED	HARDTACK
FOREFOOT	FREQUENT	GALLOWAY	GIANTESS	GOURMAND	GULLIBLE	HARDWARE
FOREGONE	FRESHEST	GALLUMPH	GIGABYTE	GOVERNOR	GULLIVER	HARDWOOD
FOREHAND	FRESHMAN	GALOSHES	GIGANTIC	GRACEFUL	GUMMOSIS	HAREBELL
FOREHEAD	FRETWORK	GALVANIC	GIGAWATT	GRACIOUS	GUMPTION	HARFLEUR
FORELAND	FREUDIAN	GAMBLING	GIGLAMPS	GRADIENT	GUNMETAL	HARMLESS
FORELOCK	FRICTION	GAMEBIRD	GIMCRACK	GRADUATE	GUNPOINT	HARMONIC
FOREMILK	FRIENDLY	GAMENESS	GINGERLY	GRAFFITI	GUNSMITH	HARRIDAN
FOREMOST	FRIGHTEN	GANGLAND	GINGIVAL	GRAINING	GURDWARA	HARRISON
FORENAME	FRIGIDLY	GANGLING	GIOCONDA	GRAMERCY	GUSSETED	HARTFORD
FORENOON	FRIPPERY	GANGLION	GIOVANNI	GRANDDAD	GUTTURAL	HARUSPEX

HASTINGS	HEMIPODE	HOLOZOIC	HUNTRESS	IMPUDENT	INSECURE	ISOLATED
HATCHERY	HENCHMAN	HOLYHEAD	HUNTSMAN	IMPUNITY	INSIGNIA	ISOSTASY
HATCHING	HENEQUEN	HOLYROOD	HURDLING	IMPURIFY	INSOLENT	ISOTHERE
HATCHWAY	HENHOUSE	HOMELAND	HUSHHUSH	IMPURITY	INSOMNIA	ISOTHERM
HATHAWAY	HEPATICA	HOMELESS	HUSTINGS	INACTION	INSPIRED	ISTANBUL
HATTERAS	HEPTAGON	HOMEMADE	HYACINTH	INACTIVE	INSPIRIT	ISTHMIAN
HAUNCHES	HEPTARCH	HOMEPAGE	HYDATOID	INASMUCH	INSTANCE	IVOIRIEN
HAUNTING	HERACLES	HOMESICK	HYDROGEN	INCENSED	INSTINCT	JACKAROO
HAVDALAH	HERACLID	HOMESPUN	HYDROXYL	INCHOATE	INSTRUCT	JACKBOOT
HAVILDAR	HERALDIC	HOMEWARD	HYGIENIC	INCIDENT	INSULATE	JACKETED
HAWAIIAN	HERALDRY	HOMEWORK	HYPERION	INCISION	INTAGLIO	JACOBEAN
HAWFINCH	HERCULES	HOMICIDE	HYPNOSIS	INCISIVE	INTEGRAL	JACOBITE
HAWTHORN	HERDSMAN	HONDURAN	HYPNOTIC	INCLINED	INTELSAT	JACQUARD
HAYFEVER	HEREDITY	HONDURAS	HYPOGEAL	INCLUDED	INTENDED	JAILBIRD
HAYFIELD	HEREFORD	HONESTLY	HYSTERIA	INCOMING	INTENTLY	JALOUSIE
HAYMAKER	HEREWARD	HONEYDEW	HYSTERIC	INCREASE	INTERACT	JAMAICAN
HAYSTACK	HEREWITH	HONEYPOT	ICEBLINK	INCUBATE	INTERCOM	JAMBOREE
HAZELNUT	HERITAGE	HONGKONG	ICEFIELD	INDEBTED	INTEREST	JANGLING
HAZINESS	HERMETIC	HONOLULU	ICEHOUSE	INDECENT	INTERIOR	JAPANESE
HEADACHE	HERMIONE	HONORARY	IDEALISM	INDENTED	INTERMIT	JAPONICA
HEADBAND	HERPETIC	HOODWINK	IDEALIST	INDEXING	INTERNAL	JAUNDICE
HEADGEAR	HERSCHEL	HOOKWORM	IDEALIZE	INDIAMAN	INTERNEE	JAUNTILY
HEADHUNT	HESITANT	HOOLIGAN	IDENTIFY	INDICANT	INTERNET	JEALOUSY
HEADLAMP	HESITATE	HOPELESS	IDENTITY	INDICATE	INTERPOL	JEANETTE
HEADLAND	HETAIRIA	HOPFIELD	IDEOGRAM	INDIGENT	INTERVAL	JEBUSITE
HEADLESS	HEXAGRAM	HORATIAN	IDEOLOGY	INDIRECT	INTIFADA	JEFFREYS
HEADLINE	HEYTHROP	HORATIUS	IDIOGRAM	INDOLENT	INTIMACY	JEHOVAHS
HEADLONG	HIAWATHA	HORLICKS	IDLENESS	INDUCIVE	INTIMATE	JELLICOE
HEADMARK	HIBERNIA	HORMONAL	IDOLATER	INDUCTOR	INTRADOS	JEOPARDY
HEADMOST	HIBISCUS	HORNBEAM	IDOLATRY	INDUSTRY	INTRENCH	JEPHTHAH
HEADREST	HICCOUGH	HORNBILL	IGNITION	INEDIBLE	INTREPID	JEREBOAM
HEADROOM	HIDEAWAY	HORNBOOK	IGNOMINY	INEQUITY	INTRIGUE	JEREMIAD
HEADSHIP	HIDROSIS	HORNFELS	IGNORANT	INEXPERT	INTRUDER	JEREMIAH
HEADWIND	HIERARCH	HORNPIPE	ILLFATED	INFAMOUS	INUNDATE	JEROBOAM
HEADWORD	HIERATIC	HORNPOUT	ILLINOIS	INFANTRY	INVASION	JERRYCAN
HEARTIES	HIGHBALL	HORNTAIL	ILLUMINE	INFECTED	INVASIVE	JETTISON
HEARTILY	HIGHBORN	HOROLOGY	ILLUSION	INFERIOR	INVEIGLE	JEWELLED
HEATEDLY	HIGHBROW	HORRIBLE	ILLUSIVE	INFERNAL	INVENTED	JEWELLER
HEATSPOT	HIGHGATE	HORRIBLY	ILLUSORY	INFESTED	INVENTOR	JIGGERED
HEATWAVE	HIGHLAND	HORRIFIC	IMAGINED	INFINITE	INVERTED	JIMCRACK
HEAVENLY	HIGHNESS	HORSEBOX	IMBECILE	INFINITY	INVERTER	JINGOISM
HEBETUDE	HIGHRISE	HORSEFLY	IMITATOR	INFLAMED	INVESTOR	JINGOIST
HEBRAISM	HIGHROAD	HORSEMAN	IMMANENT	INFLATED	INVITING	JODHPURS
HEBRIDES	HIJACKER	HORSEMEN	IMMANUEL	INFLIGHT	INVOLUTE	JOHANNES
HECATOMB	HILARITY	HOSEPIPE	IMMATURE	INFLUENT	INVOLVED	JOHNSONS
HECKLING	HILLSIDE	HOSPITAL	IMMERSED	INFORMAL	INWARDLY	JOINTURE
HEDGEHOG	HINDMOST	HOSTELRY	IMMINENT	INFORMED	IOLANTHE	JOKINGLY
HEDGEROW	HINDUISM	HOTELIER	IMMOBILE	INFORMER	IRISCOPE	JONATHAN
HEDONISM	HINDWARD	HOTHOUSE	IMMODEST	INFRARED	IRISHISM	JONCANOE
HEDONIST	HIPSTERS	HOTPLATE	IMMOLATE	INFRINGE	IRISHMAN	JONGLEUR
HEEDLESS	HIRAGANA	HOUSEMAN	IMMORTAL	INFUSION	IRISHMEN	JORROCKS
HEELBALL	HIRELING	HOVERFLY	IMMUNITY	INGROWTH	IRONCLAD	JOTTINGS
HEELTAPS	HISPANIC	HOWDYEDO	IMMUNIZE	INGUINAL	IRONICAL	JOVIALLY
HEGEMONY	HISTORIC	HOWITZER	IMPACTED	INHALANT	IRONSIDE	JOYFULLY
HEIGHTEN	HITHERTO	HUCKSTER	IMPAIRED	INHERENT	IRONWARE	JOYSTICK
HEIRLESS	HOARDING	HUMANELY	IMPELLED	INHUMANE	IRONWOOD	JUBILANT
HEIRLOOM	HOARSELY	HUMANISM	IMPERIAL	INIMICAL	IRONWORK	JUBILATE
HELIPORT	HOBBLING	HUMANIST	IMPETIGO	INIQUITY	IROQUOIS	JUDGMENT
HELLADIC	HOGMANAY	HUMANITY	IMPLICIT	INITIATE	IRRIGATE	JUDICIAL
HELLBENT	HOGSHEAD	HUMANIZE	IMPOLITE	INJECTOR	IRRITANT	JUGGLING
HELLENIC	HOKKAIDO	HUMIDIFY	IMPORTER	INKSTAIN	IRRITATE	JULIENNE
HELLFIRE	HOLDFAST	HUMIDITY	IMPOSING	INNOCENT	ISABELLA	JUMPSUIT
HELMETED	HOLDINGS	HUMILITY	IMPOSTER	INNOVATE	ISABELLE	JUNCTION
HELMSMAN	HOLIDAYS	HUMORIST	IMPOSTOR	INNUENDO	ISLANDER	JUNCTURE
HELPLESS	HOLINESS	HUMOROUS	IMPOTENT	INOCULUM	ISOBARIC	JURASSIC
HELPLINE	HOLISTIC	HUMPBACK	IMPRISON	INQUIRER	ISOCLINE	JURATORY
HELPMATE	HOLLOWAY	HUMPHREY	IMPROPER	INSANELY	ISOGENIC	JUSTNESS
HELSINKI	HOLOCENE	HUNDREDS	IMPROVED	INSANITY	ISOGLOSS	JUVENILE
HELVETIA	HOLOGRAM	HUNGRILY	IMPROVER	INSCRIBE	ISOGONAL	JYAISTHA

KACHAHRI	KRUMHORN	LAVENGRO	LIKEABLE	LOOPHOLE	MAHARAJA	MARCELLA
KALAHARI	KUFFIYEH	LAVISHLY	LIKENESS	LOOSEBOX	MAHARANI	MARCELLO
KAMIKAZE	KYPHOSIS	LAWCOURT	LIKEWISE	LOPSIDED	MAHJONGG	MARGARET
KANGAROO	LABOURED	LAWFULLY	LILONGWE	LORDOSIS	MAHOGANY	MARGINAL
KARTTIKA	LABOURER	LAWMAKER	LIMACINE	LORDSHIP	MAIDENLY	MARGRAVE
KATAKANA	LABRADOR	LAWRENCE	LIMBLESS	LORRAINE	MAIEUTIC	MARIACHI
KATMANDU	LABURNUM	LAXATIVE	LIMERICK	LOTHARIO	MAILBOAT	MARIANAS
KATTEGAT	LACERATE	LAYABOUT	LIMITING	LOUDNESS	MAILSHOT	MARIGOLD
KAZACHOK	LACEWING	LAZINESS	LIMONITE	LOUVERED	MAINLAND	MARINADE
KEDGEREE	LACINATE	LEACHING	LIMPNESS	LOVEBIRD	MAINLINE	MARINATE
KEELHAUL	LACKADAY	LEADSMAN	LINCHPIN	LOVELACE	MAINMAST	MARITIME
KEENNESS	LACKLAND	LEAFLESS	LINCOLNS	LOVELESS	MAINSAIL	MARJORAM
KEEPSAKE	LACONIAN	LEAPFROG	LINESMAN	LOVELORN	MAINSTAY	MARKDOWN
KENTUCKY	LACROSSE	LEARNING	LINGERIE	LOVESICK	MAINTAIN	MARKEDLY
KERCHIEF	LADRONES	LEATHERY	LINGUIST	LOVINGLY	MAINYARD	MARKSMAN
KERMESSE	LADYBIRD	LEAVENED	LINIMENT	LOWCLASS	MAJESTIC	MARMOSET
KEROSENE	LADYFISH	LEAVINGS	LINNAEAN	LOWERING	MAJOLICA	MARONITE
KESTEVEN	LADYLIKE	LEBANESE	LINNAEUS	LOWLANDS	MAJORITY	MAROQUIN
KEYBOARD	LADYSHIP	LECITHIN	LINOLEUM	LOWLYING	MALAGASY	MARQUESA
KEYSTONE	LAIDBACK	LECTRICE	LINOTYPE	LOYALIST	MALAKOFF	MARQUESS
KHARTOUM	LAKELAND	LECTURER	LIPSTICK	LUCIDITY	MALAMUTE	MARQUISE
KIBITZER	LAKESIDE	LECTURES	LISTENER	LUCKLESS	MALARIAL	MARRIAGE
KICKBACK	LAMASERY	LEFTHAND	LISTERIA	LUKEWARM	MALARKEY	MARSHALL
KICKSHAW	LAMBSKIN	LEFTOVER	LISTLESS	LULWORTH	MALAWIAN	MARTELLO
KIDGLOVE	LAMENESS	LEFTWARD	LITERACY	LUMINARY	MALAYSIA	MARTINET
KILKENNY	LAMENTED	LEFTWING	LITERARY	LUMINOUS	MALDIVES	MARTYRED
KILLDEER	LAMINATE	LEGALISM	LITERATE	LUMPFISH	MALGRADO	MARYLAND
KILOBYTE	LAMPPOST	LEGALITY	LITERATI	LUNCHBOX	MALINGER	MARZIPAN
KILOGRAM	LANCELET	LEGALIZE	LITIGANT	LUNCHEON	MALLARMÉ	MASCARON
KILOVOLT	LANCELOT	LEGATION	LITIGATE	LUNGFISH	MALLEATE	MASSACRE
KILOWATT	LANDFALL	LEGGINGS	LITTORAL	LUNGWORT	MALLORCA	MASSENET
KINDLING	LANDFILL	LEINSTER	LIVELONG	LUPERCAL	MALODOUR	MASSEUSE
KINDNESS	LANDLADY	LEISURED	LIVERIED	LUSCIOUS	MALTREAT	MASSICOT
KINETICS	LANDLOCK	LEMONADE	LIVERISH	LUSHNESS	MALVASIA	MASTERLY
KINGPOST	LANDLORD	LENGTHEN	LIVEWARE	LUSTRINE	MALVOLIO	MASTHEAD
KINGSHIP	LANDMARK	LENIENCY	LIVIDITY	LUSTROUS	MAMELUKE	MASTODON
KINGSIZE	LANDMASS	LEONARDO	LOADSTAR	LUTENIST	MANAGING	MATABELE
KINGSLEY	LANDMINE	LEONIDAS	LOANWORD	LUTETIUM	MANCIPLE	MATAMORE
KINGSTON	LANDRACE	LETHARGY	LOATHING	LUTHERAN	MANDAMUS	MATCHBOX
KINKAJOU	LANDSEER	LETTERED	LOBBYIST	LYNCHING	MANDARIN	MATCHING
KINSFOLK	LANDSLIP	LEUKEMIA	LOBELINE	LYREBIRD	MANDATED	MATERIAL
KINSHASA	LANDWARD	LEVELLER	LOBOTOMY	LYRICISM	MANDIBLE	MATERNAL
KIPPERED	LANGLAND	LEVERAGE	LOCALITY	LYRICIST	MANDIOCA	MATHURIN
KITEMARK	LANGLAUF	LEVITATE	LOCALIZE	LYSANDER	MANDOLIN	MATRONLY
KLONDIKE	LANGUAGE	LEWDNESS	LOCATION	LYSERGIC	MANDRAKE	MATTRESS
KNACKERS	LANGUISH	LEWISITE	LOCATIVE	MACARONI	MANDRILL	MATURATE
KNAPSACK	LANOLINE	LIBATION	LOCKABLE	MACAROON	MANEUVER	MATURITY
KNAPWEED	LANSBURY	LIBELOUS	LOCOWEED	MACASSAR	MANFULLY	MAVERICK
KNEEDEEP	LAPIDARY	LIBERATE	LODESTAR	MACAULAY	MANGONEL	MAXIMIZE
KNEEHIGH	LAPIDATE	LIBERIAN	LODGINGS	MACERATE	MANGROVE	MAYORESS
KNICKERS	LARGESSE	LIBRETTO	LOGISTIC	MACHEATH	MANIACAL	MAZARINE
KNIGHTLY	LARKSPUR	LICENSED	LOGOTYPE	MACHINES	MANICURE	MCKINLEY
KNITTING	LAROUSSE	LICENSEE	LOITERER	MACHISMO	MANIFEST	MEALTIME
KNITWEAR	LASHINGS	LICORICE	LOLLIPOP	MACKEREL	MANIFOLD	MEALYBUG
KNOBLESS	LATCHKEY	LIEGEMAN	LOMBARDY	MACMAHON	MANITOBA	MEANNESS
KNOCKERS	LATENESS	LIENTERY	LONDONER	MACREADY	MANNERED	MEANTIME
KNOCKING	LATERITE	LIFEBELT	LONESOME	MACULATE	MANNERLY	MEASURED
KNOCKOUT	LATINIST	LIFEBOAT	LONGBOAT	MADHOUSE	MANNIKIN	MEATLESS
KNOTWEED	LATITUDE	LIFEBUOY	LONGHAND	MADRIGAL	MANORIAL	MECHANIC
KNOTWORK	LATTERLY	LIFELESS	LONGHAUL	MADWOMAN	MANPOWER	MEDALIST
KOHLRABI	LAUDABLE	LIFELIKE	LONGHORN	MAECENAS	MANTILLA	MEDDLING
KOLINSKY	LAUDABLY	LIFELINE	LONGLAND	MAESTOSO	MANTISSA	MEDIATOR
KOMSOMOL	LAUDANUM	LIFELONG	LONGSHIP	MAGAZINE	MANTLING	MEDICATE
KORRIGAN	LAUGHING	LIFESPAN	LONGSTAY	MAGELLAN	MANUALLY	MEDICINE
KOURMISS	LAUGHTER	LIFETIME	LONGSTOP	MAGICIAN	MAQUETTE	MEDIEVAL
KOUSKOUS	LAUREATE	LIGAMENT	LONGTERM	MAGISTER	MARABOUT	MEDIOCRE
KRAKATOA	LAURENCE	LIGATURE	LONGTIME	MAGNESIA	MARASMUS	MEDITATE
KREPLACH	LAVATORY	LIGHTING	LONICERA	MAGNETIC	MARATHON	MEEKNESS
KROMESKY	LAVENDER	LIGNEOUS	LONSDALE	MAGNOLIA	MARAUDER	MEGABYTE

MEGALITH	MILITATE	MOLESTER	MOTORWAY	NAUPLIUS	NOBELIUM	OCCIDENT
MEGAPODE	MILKLESS	MOLLUSCS	MOUFFLON	NAUSEATE	NOBILITY	OCCUPANT
MEGAVOLT	MILKMAID	MOLUCCAS	MOUNTAIN	NAUSEOUS	NOBLEMAN	OCCUPIED
MEGAWATT	MILKWEED	MOULDING	MOUNTING	NAUTICAL	NOCTURNE	OCCUPIER
MELAMINE	MILKWORT	MOMENTUM	MOURNFUL	NAUTILUS	NOISETTE	OCTAROON
MELANITE	MILLIBAR	MONADISM	MOURNING	NAVARINO	NOMARCHY	OCTONARY
MELANOMA	MILLINER	MONANDRY	MOUSSAKA	NAVIGATE	NOMINATE	ODDMENTS
MELCHIOR	MILLIONS	MONARCHY	MOUTHFUL	NAZARENE	NOMOGRAM	ODIOUSLY
MELEAGER	MILLPOND	MONASTIC	MOVEABLE	NDJAMENA	NONESUCH	ODOMETER
MELTDOWN	MILLRACE	MONAURAL	MOVEMENT	NEARNESS	NONSENSE	ODYSSEUS
MEMBRANE	MINAMATA	MONDRIAN	MUCHNESS	NEATHERD	NONSTICK	OEDIPEAN
MEMORIAL	MINATORY	MONETARY	MUCILAGE	NEATNESS	NOONTIME	OEILLADE
MEMORIAM	MINCEPIE	MONETISE	MUDFLATS	NEBRASKA	NORMALLY	OENOLOGY
MEMORIZE	MINDANAO	MONEYBOX	MUDGUARD	NEBULOUS	NORMANDY	OENOPHIL
MEMSAHIB	MINDLESS	MONGOLIA	MUDSTONE	NECKBAND	NORSEMAN	OFFBREAK
MENACING	MINEHEAD	MONGOOSE	MUHAMMAD	NECKLACE	NORSEMEN	OFFCOLOR
MENANDER	MINIMIZE	MONICKER	MUHARRAM	NECKLINE	NORTHERN	OFFENDED
MENELAUS	MINISTER	MONKFISH	MULBERRY	NECKWEAR	NORTHING	OFFENDER
MENHADEN	MINISTRY	MONMOUTH	MULETEER	NECROSIS	NOSEBAND	OFFERING
MENISCUS	MINORESS	MONOACID	MULEWORT	NEEDLESS	NOSEDIVE	OFFICERS
MENSURAL	MINORITE	MONOGAMY	MULLIGAN	NEGATION	NOSOLOGY	OFFICIAL
MENSWEAR	MINORITY	MONOGRAM	MULTIPLE	NEGATIVE	NOSTRILS	OFFPRINT
MENTALLY	MINOTAUR	MONOGYNY	MULTIPLY	NEGLIGEE	NOSTROMO	OFFSHOOT
MERCALLI	MINSTREL	MONOHULL	MUMBLING	NEGRILLO	NOTARIAL	OFFSHORE
MERCATOR	MINUTELY	MONOLITH	MUNCHKIN	NEHEMIAH	NOTATION	OFFSIDER
MERCEDES	MINUTIAE	MONOPOLE	MUNIMENT	NEIGHBOR	NOTEBOOK	OFFSTAGE
MERCHANT	MIREPOIX	MONOPOLY	MURDERER	NEMATODE	NOTECASE	OILCLOTH
MERCIFUL	MIRLITON	MONORAIL	MURRHINE	NEMATOID	NOTIONAL	OILFIELD
MEREDITH	MIRRORED	MONOTONY	MUSCADET	NEMBUTAL	NOVELIST	OILINESS
MERIDIAN	MIRTHFUL	MONOTYPE	MUSCATEL	NENUPHAR	NOVEMBER	OILSKINS
MERINGUE	MISAPPLY	MONOXIDE	MUSCULAR	NEOMYCIN	NOWADAYS	OILSLICK
MERISTEM	MISCARRY	MONROVIA	MUSHROOM	NEOPHYTE	NUCLEATE	OINTMENT
MESCALIN	MISCHIEF	MONSTERA	MUSICIAN	NEPALESE	NUCLEOLE	OKLAHOMA
MESMERIC	MISCOUNT	MONTCALM	MUSQUASH	NEPENTHE	NUFFIELD	OLDSTYLE
MESODERM	MISERERE	MONTEITH	MUSTACHE	NEPHRITE	NUGATORY	OLDWORLD
MESOLITE	MISGUIDE	MONUMENT	MUTATION	NEPIONIC	NUISANCE	OLEACEAE
MESOZOIC	MISHMASH	MOONBEAM	MUTCHKIN	NEPOTISM	NUMBNESS	OLEANDER
MESSAGER	MISJUDGE	MOORCOCK	MUTILATE	NESCIENT	NUMERACY	OLEASTER
MESSIDOR	MISMATCH	MOORINGS	MUTINEER	NESTLING	NUMERALS	OLIGARCH
MESSMATE	MISNOMER	MOORLAND	MUTINOUS	NEURITIS	NUMERATE	OLIPHANT
MESSUAGE	MISOGYNY	MOQUETTE	MUTUALLY	NEUROSIS	NUMEROUS	OLYMPIAD
METABOLA	MISPLACE	MORALIST	MYCELIUM	NEUROTIC	NUMINOUS	OLYMPIAN
MÉTAIRIE	MISPRINT	MORALITY	MYCOLOGY	NEUTRINO	NUPTIALS	OLYMPICS
METALLED	MISQUOTE	MORALIZE	MYELITIS	NEWCOMER	NURSLING	OMDURMAN
METALLIC	MISSOURI	MORAVIAN	MYOBLAST	NEWFOUND	NUTHATCH	OMELETTE
METAPHOR	MISSPELL	MORBIDLY	MYOSOTIS	NEWHAVEN	NUTHOUSE	OMISSION
METEORIC	MISSPENT	MORBILLI	MYRIAPOD	NEWSCAST	NUTRIENT	OMNIFORM
METHANOL	MISTAKEN	MOREOVER	MYRMIDON	NEWSHAWK	NUTSHELL	OMNIVORE
METHODIC	MISTREAT	MOREPORK	MYSTICAL	NEWSPEAK	OBDURACY	OMPHALOS
METONYMY	MISTRESS	MORESQUE	MYSTIQUE	NEWSREEL	OBDURATE	ONCOLOGY
METRICAL	MISTRUST	MORIBUND	MYTHICAL	NEWSROOM	OBEDIENT	ONCOMING
METRITIS	MITIGATE	MOROCCAN	NAGASAKI	NIBELUNG	OBITUARY	ONESIDED
MEUNIÈRE	MNEMONIC	MOROSELY	NAMELESS	NICENESS	OBJECTOR	ONETRACK
MICHIGAN	MOBILITY	MORPHEME	NAMESAKE	NICHOLAS	OBLATION	ONLOOKER
MICRODOT	MOBILIZE	MORPHEUS	NAMIBIAN	NICKNACK	OBLIGATE	ONSCREEN
MIDBRAIN	MOCCASIN	MORPHINE	NAPOLEON	NICKNAME	OBLIGING	ONTOLOGY
MIDDLING	MODELING	MORRISON	NARCOSES	NICOTINE	OBLIVION	OOPHORON
MIDFIELD	MODELLER	MORTALLY	NARCOSIS	NIDATION	OBSCURED	OPENCAST
MIDLANDS	MODERATE	MORTGAGE	NARCOTIC	NIGERIAN	OBSERVED	OPENDOOR
MIDNIGHT	MODERATO	MORTIMER	NARGILEH	NIGERIEN	OBSERVER	OPENNESS
MIDPOINT	MODESTLY	MORTUARY	NARRATOR	NIGGLING	OBSESSED	OPENPLAN
MIGHTILY	MODIFIER	MOSQUITO	NARROWLY	NIGHTCAP	OBSIDIAN	OPENWORK
MIGNONNE	MODULATE	MOTHBALL	NATALITY	NIGHTJAR	OBSOLETE	OPERABLE
MIGRAINE	MOHAMMED	MOTHERLY	NATIONAL	NIHILISM	OBSTACLE	OPERATIC
MILANESE	MOISTURE	MOTIVATE	NATIVITY	NIHILIST	OBSTRUCT	OPERATOR
MILDEWED	MOLASSES	MOTORCAR	NATTERED	NIJINSKY	OBTAINED	OPERETTA
MILDNESS	MOLECULE	MOTORING	NATURISM	NINEPINS	OBTUSELY	OPHIDIAN
MILITANT	MOLEHILL	MOTORIST	NATURIST	NINETEEN	OCCAMIST	OPOPANAX
MILITARY	MOLESKIN	MOTORMAN	NATURIST	NITROGEN	OCCASION	OPPONENT

OPPOSING	OVERFILL	PALUDISM	PATENTED	PERICLES	PILLAGER	PLIOCENE
OPPOSITE	OVERFLOW	PAMPERED	PATENTEE	PERIDERM	PILLARED	PLOTINUS
OPTICIAN	OVERFULL	PAMPHLET	PATENTLY	PERILOUS	PILOTAGE	PLOUGHED
OPTIMATE	OVERHAND	PANATELA	PATERNAL	PERILUNE	PILSENER	PLUCKILY
OPTIMISM	OVERHANG	PANCREAS	PATHETIC	PERIODIC	PILTDOWN	PLUCKING
OPTIMIST	OVERHAUL	PANDANUS	PATHOGEN	PERIPETY	PIMIENTO	PLUGHOLE
OPTIONAL	OVERHEAD	PANDANUS	PATIENCE	PERISHED	PINAFORE	PLUMBAGO
OPULENCE	OVERHEAR	PANDEMIC	PATULOUS	PERISHER	PINDARIC	PLUMBING
OPUSCULE	OVERHEAT	PANDOWDY	PAULINUS	PERJURED	PINEWOOD	PLUNGING
ORANGERY	OVERKILL	PANEGYRY	PAVEMENT	PERJURER	PINNACLE	PLUTARCH
ORATORIO	OVERLAID	PANELING	PAVILION	PERMEATE	PINNIPED	PLYMOUTH
ORCADIAN	OVERLAND	PANELLED	PAWNSHOP	PEROXIDE	PINOCHLE	POCHETTE
ORCHITIS	OVERLEAF	PANGLOSS	PAYCHECK	PERSHING	PINPOINT	POCKMARK
ORDERING	OVERLOAD	PANGOLIN	PEACEFUL	PERSONAL	PINPRICK	PODARGUS
ORDINAND	OVERLOOK	PANNICLE	PEARLING	PERSPIRE	PINTABLE	POETICAL
ORDINARY	OVERLORD	PANNIKIN	PEARMAIN	PERSUADE	PINWHEEL	POIGNANT
ORDINATE	OVERMUCH	PANORAMA	PECORINO	PERSUANT	PIPELINE	POISONER
ORDNANCE	OVERPASS	PANPIPES	PECTORAL	PERTNESS	PIPERINE	POITIERS
ORESTEIA	OVERPLAY	PANTALON	PECULATE	PERUVIAN	PIQUANCY	POKEWEED
ORGANDIE	OVERRATE	PANTHEON	PECULIAR	PERVERSE	PIRANESI	POLARIZE
ORGANISM	OVERRIDE	PAPILLON	PEDAGOGY	PERVIOUS	PIROZHKI	POLISHED
ORGANIST	OVERRIPE	PARABOLA	PEDANTIC	PETANQUE	PISCATOR	POLISHER
ORGANIZE	OVERRULE	PARADIGM	PEDANTRY	PETERLOO	PISIFORM	POLITELY
ORIENTAL	OVERSEAS	PARAFFIN	PEDDLING	PETITION	PISSHEAD	POLITICO
ORIGINAL	OVERSEER	PARAGUAY	PEDERAST	PETRARCH	PITCAIRN	POLITICS
ORNAMENT	OVERSHOE	PARAKEET	PEDESTAL	PETULANT	PITHLESS	POLLIWOG
ORPHANED	OVERSHOT	PARALLAX	PEDICURE	PEVENSEY	PITIABLE	POLLSTER
ORPIMENT	OVERSIZE	PARALLEL	PEDIGREE	PHALANGE	PITILESS	POLLUTED
ORTHODOX	OVERSOLD	PARALYZE	PEDIMENT	PHALGUNA	PITTANCE	POLLUTER
OSCULATE	OVERSTAY	PARAMOUR	PEDUNCLE	PHANTASM	PIZZERIA	POLONIUM
OSTERLEY	OVERSTEP	PARANOIA	PEEKABOO	PHARISEE	PLACABLE	POLTROON
OTOSCOPE	OVERTAKE	PARANOID	PEELINGS	PHARMACY	PLACEMAT	POLYANNA
OTTAVINO	OVERTIME	PARAQUAT	PEEPHOLE	PHEASANT	PLACEMEN	POLYARCH
OUISTITI	OVERTONE	PARASHAH	PEEPSHOW	PHENOLIC	PLACENTA	POLYCARP
OUTBOARD	OVERTURE	PARASITE	PEERLESS	PHILEMON	PLACIDLY	POLYGAMY
OUTBREAK	OVERTURN	PARDONER	PEIGNOIR	PHILIPPI	PLANCHET	POLYGLOT
OUTBURST	OVERVIEW	PARENTAL	PEKINESE	PHILLIPS	PLANGENT	POLYGYNY
OUTCLASS	OVERWORK	PARIETAL	PELAGIUS	PHILOMEL	PLANKING	POLYMATH
OUTDATED	OXBRIDGE	PARISIAN	PELLAGRA	PHLEGMON	PLANKTON	POLYSEME
OUTDOORS	OXPECKER	PARKLAND	PELLETED	PHONETIC	PLANNING	POLYSEMY
OUTFIELD	OXYMORON	PARLANCE	PELLICLE	PHORMIUM	PLANTAIN	POMANDER
OUTFLANK	OXYTOCIN	PARMESAN	PELLMELL	PHOSGENE	PLASTRON	PONSONBY
OUTGOING	PABULOUS	PARODIST	PELLUCID	PHOTOFIT	PLATANUS	PONTIFEX
OUTHOUSE	PACHINKO	PAROLLES	PEMBROKE	PHOTOPSY	PLATEFUL	PONYTAIL
OUTLYING	PACIFIER	PAROUSIA	PEMMICAN	PHREATIC	PLATELET	POOLROOM
OUTMATCH	PACIFISM	PAROXYSM	PENALIZE	PHRYGIAN	PLATFORM	POORNESS
OUTMODED	PACIFIST	PARSIFAL	PENCHANT	PHTHISIC	PLATINUM	POPINJAY
OUTREACH	PACKAGED	PARTERRE	PENDULUM	PHTHISIS	PLATONIC	POPPADOM
OUTREMER	PADDLING	PARTHIAN	PENELOPE	PHYLLOME	PLATYPUS	POPSICLE
OUTRIDER	PAGANINI	PARTICLE	PENITENT	PHYSALIA	PLAUDITS	POPULACE
OUTRIGHT	PAGINATE	PARTISAN	PENKNIFE	PHYSICAL	PLAYBACK	POPULATE
OUTSHINE	PAINLESS	PARTTIME	PENNINES	PHYSIQUE	PLAYBILL	POPULIST
OUTSIDER	PAINTING	PASHMINA	PENOLOGY	PICAROON	PLAYFAIR	POPULOUS
OUTSMART	PAKISTAN	PASSABLE	PENTACLE	PICKINGS	PLAYGIRL	POROSITY
OUTSTRIP	PALATIAL	PASSABLY	PENTAGON	PICKLOCK	PLAYMATE	PORPHYRA
OUTWARDS	PALATINE	PASSBOOK	PENTARCH	PICKMEUP	PLAYROOM	PORPHYRY
OUTWEIGH	PALEFACE	PASSERBY	PENUMBRA	PICKWICK	PLAYSUIT	PORPOISE
OVARITIS	PALENESS	PASSIBLE	PENZANCE	PICTURES	PLAYTIME	PORRIDGE
OVENBIRD	PALGRAVE	PASSOVER	PEPERONI	PIDDLING	PLEADING	PORTABLE
OVENWARE	PALIMONY	PASSPORT	PERACUTE	PIECHART	PLEASANT	PORTHOLE
OVERALLS	PALINODE	PASSWORD	PERCEIVE	PIECRUST	PLEASING	PORTIÈRE
OVERBOOK	PALISADE	PASTICHE	PERCEVAL	PIERCING	PLEASURE	PORTLAND
OVERCAST	PALLADIO	PASTILLE	PERCIVAL	PIERETTE	PLEBEIAN	PORTRAIT
OVERCOAT	PALLIATE	PASTORAL	PERFECTA	PIERIDES	PLECTRUM	PORTUGAL
OVERCOME	PALMATED	PASTRAMI	PERFECTO	PIGSWILL	PLEIADES	POSEIDON
OVERDONE	PALMETTO	PASTURES	PERFORCE	PILASTER	PLEONASM	POSITION
OVERDOSE	PALMITIN	PATAGIUM	PERFUMED	PILCHARD	PLETHORA	POSITIVE
OVERDRAW	PALPABLE	PATCHILY	PERIANTH	PILFERER	PLEURISY	POSITRON
OVERFEED	PALPABLY	PATELLAR	PERICARP	PILGRIMS	PLIMSOLL	POSOLOGY

POSSIBLE	PROBABLY	PUISSANT	RAGSTONE	REDEPLOY	REPRIEVE	RIGHTFUL
POSSIBLY	PROCAINE	PULITZER	RAILHEAD	REDESIGN	REPRISAL	RIGHTIST
POSTCARD	PROCEEDS	PULLDOWN	RAILINGS	REDIRECT	REPROACH	RIGIDITY
POSTCODE	PROCLAIM	PULLOVER	RAILLERY	REDLIGHT	REPUBLIC	RIGOROUS
POSTDATE	PROCURER	PUNCTUAL	RAILROAD	REDOLENT	REQUIRED	RINGDOVE
POSTMARK	PRODIGAL	PUNCTURE	RAINBIRD	REDOUBLE	RESEARCH	RINGHALS
POSTPAID	PRODROME	PUNGENCY	RAINCOAT	REDSHANK	RESEMBLE	RINGSIDE
POSTPONE	PRODUCER	PUNISHED	RAINDROP	REDSHIFT	RESERVED	RINGTAIL
POTATOES	PRODUCES	PUNITIVE	RAINFALL	REDSTART	RESETTLE	RINGWALL
POTBELLY	PRODUCTS	PURBLIND	RAINWEAR	REEDLING	RESIDENT	RINGWORM
POTBOUND	PROFORMA	PURCHASE	RAISONNÉ	REEDSMAN	RESIDUAL	RIPARIAN
POTEMKIN	PROFOUND	PURIFIED	RAMBLING	REEMPLOY	RESIDUUM	RIPENESS
POTHOLER	PROFUSER	PURIFIER	RAMBUTAN	REFERRAL	RESIGNED	RIPPLING
POTLATCH	PROGERIA	PURLIEUS	RAMEQUIN	REFINERY	RESINOUS	RISSOLES
POTSHERD	PROGRADE	PURPLISH	RAMPARTS	REFORMED	RESISTOR	RITUALLY
POTSTONE	PROGRESS	PURSLANE	RANDOMLY	REFORMER	RESOLUTE	RIVALISE
POULAINE	PROHIBIT	PURULENT	RANELAGH	REFRINGE	RESOLVED	RIVERAIN
POULTICE	PROLAPSE	PURVEYOR	RANKNESS	REFUGIUM	RESONANT	RIVERINE
POUNDAGE	PROLIFIC	PUSHBIKE	RAPACITY	REGAINED	RESONATE	RIVETING
POWDERED	PROLOGUE	PUSHCART	RAPECAKE	REGICIDE	RESOURCE	ROADSHOW
POWERFUL	PROMISED	PUSHDOWN	RAPIDITY	REGIMENT	RESPECTS	ROADSIDE
PRACTICE	PROMOTER	PUSHOVER	RAREFIED	REGIONAL	RESPIGHI	ROADSTER
PRACTISE	PROMPTER	PUSSYCAT	RASCALLY	REGISTER	RESPONSE	ROASTING
PRAIRIAL	PROMPTLY	PUSTULAR	RASHNESS	REGISTRY	RESTLESS	ROBINSON
PRANDIAL	PRONATOR	PUTATIVE	RASPUTIN	REGULATE	RESTORER	ROBOTICS
PRATFALL	PROPERLY	PUZZLING	RASSELAS	REHEARSE	RESTRAIN	ROBUSTLY
PRATTLER	PROPERTY	PYELITIS	RATEABLE	REIGNING	RESTRICT	ROCHDALE
PREACHER	PROPHASE	PYORRHEA	RATIONAL	REINDEER	RESTROOM	ROCKETRY
PREAMBLE	PROPHECY	PYRAMIDS	RATTIGAN	REINSURE	RETAILER	RODERICK
PRECINCT	PROPHESY	PYRENEES	RATTLING	REINVEST	RETAINER	ROENTGEN
PRECIOUS	PROPOLIS	PYRIFORM	RAVENOUS	REJOINED	RETARDED	ROGATION
PRECLUDE	PROPOSAL	QUADRANT	REACTION	REKINDLE	RETICENT	ROLLCALL
PRECURSE	PROPOSED	QUADRATE	REACTIVE	RELATING	RETICULE	ROLYPOLY
PREDATOR	PROPOSER	QUADRIGA	READABLE	RELATION	RETIRING	ROMANCER
PREDELLA	PROPOUND	QUADROON	READIEST	RELATIVE	RETRENCH	ROMANIAN
PREGNANT	PROROGUE	QUAESTOR	READJUST	RELAXING	RETRIEVE	ROMANSCH
PREJUDGE	PROSPECT	QUAGMIRE	REAFFIRM	RELAYING	REUSABLE	ROMANTIC
PREMIERE	PROSPERO	QUAINTLY	REALTIME	RELEASED	REVANCHE	ROOFLESS
PREMISES	PROSTATE	QUANDARY	REAPPEAR	RELEGATE	REVEALED	ROOFTOPS
PREMOLAR	PROTEASE	QUANTIFY	REARMOST	RELEVANT	REVEILLE	ROOMMATE
PRENATAL	PROTÉGÉE	QUANTITY	REARWARD	RELIABLE	REVELLER	ROOTLESS
PREPARED	PROTOCOL	QUARTERS	REASONED	RELIABLY	REVEREND	ROSALIND
PRESENCE	PROTOZOA	QUARTIER	REASSERT	RELIANCE	REVERENT	ROSALINE
PRESERVE	PROTRUDE	QUARTILE	REASSESS	RELIEVED	REVERSAL	ROSAMOND
PRESSING	PROVABLE	QUATORZE	REASSIGN	RELIGION	REVERSED	ROSEFISH
PRESSMAN	PROVERBS	QUATRAIN	REASSUME	RELOCATE	REVIEWER	ROSEMARY
PRESSURE	PROVIDED	QUAYSIDE	REASSURE	REMEDIAL	REVISION	ROSEROOT
PRESTIGE	PROVIDER	QUENELLE	REAWAKEN	REMEMBER	REVIVIFY	ROSEWOOD
PRETENCE	PROVINCE	QUESTION	REBUTTAL	REMINDER	REVIVING	ROSINESS
PRETENSE	PROXIMAL	QUIBBLER	RECEDING	REMITTAL	REVOLVER	ROSSETTI
PRETORIA	PRUDENCE	QUICKSET	RECEIPTS	REMNANTS	REYNOLDS	ROTATION
PRETTILY	PRUNELLA	QUIETUDE	RECEIVED	REMOTELY	RHAPSODY	ROTATORY
PREVIOUS	PRURIENT	QUILTING	RECEIVER	REMOUNTS	RHEOSTAT	ROTENONE
PRIAPISM	PRUSSIAN	QUINCUNX	RECENTLY	RENEGADE	RHETORIC	ROUGHAGE
PRIESTLY	PSALMIST	QUINTAIN	RECEPTOR	RENMINBI	RHOMBOID	ROULETTE
PRIGGISH	PSALMODY	QUIRINAL	RECESSED	RENOUNCE	RHONCHUS	ROUNDERS
PRIMEVAL	PSALTERY	QUISLING	RECHARGE	RENOVATE	RHYTHMIC	ROUSSEAU
PRIMNESS	PSEUDERY	QUIXOTIC	RECKLESS	RENOWNED	RIBALDRY	ROYALIST
PRIMROSE	PTEROPOD	QUOTABLE	RECKONER	REORIENT	RIBSTONE	RUBAIYAT
PRINCELY	PTOMAINE	QUOTIENT	RECORDER	REPAIRER	RICHNESS	RUBBISHY
PRINCESS	PTYALISM	RABELAIS	RECOURSE	REPARTEE	RICKSHAW	RUBICUND
PRINTING	PUBLICAN	RACHITIS	RECOVERY	REPAYING	RICOCHET	RUBIDIUM
PRINTOUT	PUBLICLY	RACIALLY	RECREATE	REPEATED	RIDDANCE	RUCKSACK
PRIORESS	PUCKERED	RACINESS	RECRUITS	REPEATER	RIDGEWAY	RUCTIONS
PRIORITY	PUDENDUM	RACKRENT	RECUSANT	REPHRASE	RIDICULE	RUDENESS
PRISONER	PUFFBALL	RACLETTE	REDACTOR	REPLEVIN	RIESLING	RUDIMENT
PRISTINE	PUGILISM	RADIANCE	REDBRICK	REPORTED	RIFFRAFF	RUEFULLY
PRIVATES	PUGILIST	RADIATOR	REDEEMER	REPORTER	RIFLEMAN	RUGGEDLY
PROBABLE	PUGNOSED	RAGNARÖK	REDEFINE	REPOUSSÉ	RIGATONI	RULEBOOK

RUMBLING	SATURATE	SCRAWLED	SEMITONE	SHINGLES	SIMPLIFY	SLUGFEST
RUMINANT	SATURDAY	SCREAMER	SEMOLINA	SHIPMATE	SIMULATE	SLUGGARD
RUMINATE	SATURNIA	SCREENED	SENGREEN	SHIPMENT	SINAPISM	SLUGGISH
RUMOURED	SAUCEPAN	SCREWTOP	SENILITY	SHIPPING	SINCLAIR	SLUMMING
RUNABOUT	SAUROPOD	SCRIABIN	SENORITA	SHIPWORM	SINECURE	SLURRING
RUNCIBLE	SAUSAGES	SCRIBBLE	SENSIBLE	SHIPYARD	SINFONIA	SLUTTISH
RUNNERUP	SAVAGELY	SCRIBBLY	SENSIBLY	SHIVERED	SINGSONG	SLYBOOTS
RUSHMORE	SAVAGERY	SCRIPTUM	SENSUOUS	SHOCKING	SINGULAR	SMALLEST
RUSTLESS	SAVANNAH	SCROFULA	SENTENCE	SHODDILY	SINISTER	SMALLPOX
RUSTLING	SAVOURED	SCROUNGE	SENTIENT	SHOEBILL	SINKHOLE	SMARTEST
RUTABAGA	SAVOYARD	SCRUBBER	SENTINEL	SHOEHORN	SIRENIAN	SMASHING
RUTHLESS	SAWBONES	SCRUPLES	SEPARATE	SHOELACE	SISTERLY	SMELTING
RYEGRASS	SAWHORSE	SCRUTINY	SEQUENCE	SHOELESS	SISYPHUS	SMIDGEON
SABOTAGE	SAXATILE	SCULLERY	SERAFILE	SHOETREE	SITTELLA	SMOCKING
SABOTEUR	SAYONARA	SCULLION	SERAGLIO	SHOOTING	SITUATED	SMOLLETT
SACRISTY	SCABBARD	SCULPTOR	SERAPHIC	SHOOTOUT	SIXPENCE	SMOOTHER
SADDLERY	SCABIOUS	SCYBALUM	SERAPHIM	SHOPPING	SIXTIETH	SMOOTHLY
SADDLING	SCABROUS	SEABOARD	SERENADE	SHOPTALK	SIZEABLE	SMOULDER
SADDUCEE	SCAFFOLD	SEABORNE	SERENATA	SHORTAGE	SIZZLING	SMUGGLED
SADISTIC	SCALDING	SEAFARER	SERENELY	SHOULDER	SKELETAL	SMUGGLER
SAGACITY	SCALENUS	SEAFLOOR	SERENITY	SHOUTING	SKELETON	SMUGNESS
SAGENESS	SCALLION	SEAFORTH	SERGEANT	SHOWBOAT	SKEWBALD	SNACKBAR
SAILBOAT	SCANDIUM	SEAFRONT	SERIATIM	SHOWCASE	SKIBOOTS	SNAPPILY
SAINFOIN	SCANNING	SEAGOING	SERJEANT	SHOWDOWN	SKIDDING	SNAPSHOT
SALACITY	SCANSION	SEALSKIN	SEROLOGY	SHOWGIRL	SKILLFUL	SNATCHER
SALARIED	SCANTIES	SEALYHAM	SEROTYPE	SHOWROOM	SKILLING	SNEAKERS
SALEABLE	SCANTILY	SEAMLESS	SERRATED	SHRAPNEL	SKILLION	SNEAKING
SALEROOM	SCAPHOID	SEAMSTER	SERVICES	SHREDDER	SKINDEEP	SNEERING
SALESMAN	SCAPULAR	SEAPLANE	SERVIENT	SHREWDLY	SKINHEAD	SNEEZING
SALINGER	SCARCELY	SEARCHER	SERVITOR	SHREWISH	SKINWORK	SNIFFLER
SALINITY	SCARCITY	SEASCAPE	SEVERELY	SHROUDED	SKIPJACK	SNOBBERY
SALIVARY	SCARFACE	SEASHELL	SEVEREST	SHRUNKEN	SKIPPING	SNOBBISH
SALIVATE	SCATHING	SEASHORE	SEVERITY	SHUTDOWN	SKIRMISH	SNOOTILY
SALTBUSH	SCAVENGE	SEASONAL	SEWERAGE	SHUTTERS	SKIRTING	SNORTING
SALTLICK	SCENARIO	SEASONED	SEXOLOGY	SIBERIAN	SKITTISH	SNOWBALL
SALTNESS	SCHAPSKA	SEAWARDS	SEXUALLY	SIBILANT	SKITTLES	SNOWDROP
SALUTARY	SCHEDULE	SECLUDED	SHABBILY	SICILIAN	SKULKING	SNOWFALL
SALUTORY	SCHEMING	SECONDER	SHACKLES	SICKLIST	SKULLCAP	SNOWLINE
SALVADOR	SCHILLER	SECONDLY	SHADRACH	SICKNESS	SKYLIGHT	SNUFFBOX
SAMARIUM	SCHIZOID	SECRETLY	SHAGBARK	SICKROOM	SKYPILOT	SOAKAWAY
SAMENESS	SCHMALTZ	SECURELY	SHAGREEN	SIDEKICK	SLANGING	SOAPBARK
SAMIZDAT	SCHMOOZE	SECURITY	SHAKEOUT	SIDELINE	SLANTING	SOAPSUDS
SAMPHIRE	SCHNAPPS	SEDATELY	SHALLOWS	SIDELONG	SLAPBANG	SOBERING
SANCTIFY	SCHOONER	SEDATION	SHAMBLES	SIDEREAL	SLAPDASH	SOBRIETY
SANCTION	SCHUBERT	SEDATIVE	SHAMEFUL	SIDERITE	SLAPJACK	SOCALLED
SANCTITY	SCHUMANN	SEDIMENT	SHAMROCK	SIDESHOW	SLATTERN	SOCIABLE
SANDARAC	SCIATICA	SEDITION	SHANGAAN	SIDESLIP	SLEEPERS	SOCIALLY
SANDBANK	SCIENCES	SEDULOUS	SHANGHAI	SIDESMAN	SLEEPILY	SOCRATES
SANDWICH	SCILICET	SEEDLESS	SHANTUNG	SIDESTEP	SLEEPING	SOCRATIC
SANGLIER	SCIMITAR	SEEDLING	SHAREOUT	SIDEWALK	SLIGHTED	SODALITE
SANGUINE	SCIROCCO	SEEDSMAN	SHAVUOTH	SIDEWARD	SLIGHTLY	SODALITY
SANITARY	SCISSION	SEETHING	SHEARMAN	SIDEWAYS	SLIMNESS	SOFTBACK
SANITIZE	SCISSORS	SEIGNIOR	SHEEPDOG	SIGHTING	SLIPOVER	SOFTBALL
SANSERIF	SCOFFING	SELASSIE	SHEEPISH	SIGHTSEE	SLIPPERS	SOFTENER
SANSKRIT	SCOLDING	SELBORNE	SHEIKDOM	SIGNALER	SLIPPERY	SOFTNESS
SANTIAGO	SCORCHED	SELECTED	SHELDUCK	SIGNALLY	SLIPPING	SOFTWARE
SAPONITE	SCORCHER	SELECTOR	SHELVING	SIGNORIA	SLIPSHOD	SOFTWOOD
SAPPHIRE	SCORNFUL	SELENITE	SHEPHERD	SIGNPOST	SLIPSLOP	SOLARIUM
SAPPHIST	SCORPION	SELENIUM	SHERATON	SILENCER	SLOBBERY	SOLDIERS
SARABAND	SCORPIUS	SELEUCID	SHERIDAN	SILENTLY	SLOPPILY	SOLDIERY
SARATOGA	SCOTLAND	SELFHELP	SHERLOCK	SILESIAN	SLOTHFUL	SOLECISM
SARDINIA	SCOTSMAN	SELFLESS	SHERWOOD	SILICATE	SLOVAKIA	SOLEMNLY
SARDONIC	SCOTTISH	SELFMADE	SHETLAND	SILICONE	SLOVENIA	SOLENOID
SARDONYX	SCOURING	SELFPITY	SHIELING	SILICULA	SLOVENLY	SOLIDIFY
SARGASSO	SCOWLING	SELFSAME	SHIFTING	SILKTAIL	SLOWDOWN	SOLIDITY
SASSANID	SCRABBLE	SELVEDGE	SHIGELLA	SILKWORM	SLOWNESS	SOLITARY
SATIATED	SCRAMBLE	SEMESTER	SHIITAKE	SILOXANE	SLOWPOKE	SOLITUDE
SATIRIST	SCRAPPLE	SEMINARY	SHILLING	SILURIAN	SLOWWORM	SOLSTICE
SATIRIZE	SCRATCHY	SEMIOTIC	SHINBONE	SIMONIAC	SLUGABED	SOLUTION

SOLVABLE	SPINNING	STALLION	STOPOVER	SUBTOTAL	SWEARING	TAPESTRY
SOLVENCY	SPINSTER	STALWART	STOPPAGE	SUBTRACT	SWEATING	TAPEWORM
SOMBRELY	SPINTEXT	STAMENED	STOPPING	SUBURBAN	SWEEPING	TAPHOUSE
SOMBRERO	SPIRACLE	STAMPEDE	STOREMAN	SUBURBIA	SWEETSOP	TARBOOSH
SOMEBODY	SPIRALLY	STANDARD	STOREYED	SUCCEEDS	SWELLING	TARRAGON
SOMERSET	SPIRELET	STANDING	STORMING	SUCCINCT	SWERVING	TARTARIC
SOMETIME	SPIRITED	STANDISH	STORMONT	SUCCUBUS	SWILLING	TARTARUS
SOMEWHAT	SPIRITUS	STANDOFF	STOWAWAY	SUCHLIKE	SWIMMING	TARTNESS
SONATINA	SPITEFUL	STANHOPE	STRABISM	SUCKLING	SWIMSUIT	TARTRATE
SONGBIRD	SPITFIRE	STANNARY	STRACHEY	SUDAMENT	SWINDLER	TARTUFFE
SONGSTER	SPITHEAD	STANNITE	STRADDLE	SUDAMINA	SWINEPOX	TASHKENT
SONOGRAM	SPITTING	STAPELIA	STRAGGLE	SUDANESE	SWINGING	TASMANIA
SONOROUS	SPITTOON	STAPHYLE	STRAGGLY	SUDARIUM	SWIRLING	TASTEFUL
SOOTHING	SPLASHER	STARCHED	STRAIGHT	SUDDENLY	SYBARITE	TATTERED
SOOTHSAY	SPLATTER	STARDUST	STRAINED	SUFFERER	SYCAMORE	TAUTNESS
SORBONNE	SPLENDID	STARFISH	STRAINER	SUFFRAGE	SYLLABIC	TAVERNER
SORCERER	SPLENDOR	STARGAZE	STRAITEN	SUICIDAL	SYLLABLE	TAXATION
SORDIDLY	SPLINTER	STARKERS	STRANDED	SUITABLE	SYLLABUB	TAXONOMY
SORENESS	SPLITTER	STARLESS	STRANGER	SUITABLY	SYLLABUS	TAXPAYER
SORORITY	SPLUTTER	STARLING	STRANGLE	SUITCASE	SYLVANER	TAYBERRY
SOUCHONG	SPOILAGE	STAROSTA	STRAPPED	SUKIYAKI	SYLVATIC	TEACHERS
SOULLESS	SPOILING	STARTERS	STRAPPER	SULFURIC	SYMBIONT	TEACHING
SOUNDING	SPOLIATE	STARTING	STRATEGY	SULLENLY	SYMBOLIC	TEACLOTH
SOURCING	SPOONFUL	STARVING	STRATIFY	SULLIVAN	SYMMETRY	TEAKWOOD
SOURNESS	SPORADIC	STATUARY	STREAKED	SULPHATE	SYMPATHY	TEAMMATE
SOURPUSS	SPORTING	STAYSAIL	STREAKER	SULPHIDE	SYMPHONY	TEAMSTER
SOURWOOD	SPORTIVE	STEADILY	STREAMER	SUMERIAN	SYMPTOMS	TEAMWORK
SOUTHEND	SPOTLESS	STEALING	STRENGTH	SUMMITRY	SYNCLINE	TEARABLE
SOUTHERN	SPOTTING	STEALTHY	STRESSED	SUNBATHE	SYNDROME	TEARAWAY
SOUTHPAW	SPRAINED	STEAPSIN	STRETCHY	SUNBURNT	SYNOPSIS	TEARDROP
SOUVENIR	SPRAWLED	STEATITE	STRIATED	SUNBURST	SYNOPTIC	TEASPOON
SPACEMAN	SPREADER	STEATOMA	STRIATUM	SUNCREAM	SYNTEXIS	TECTONIC
SPACIOUS	SPRINGER	STEENBOK	STRICKEN	SUNDANCE	SYPHILIS	TEENAGER
SPADEFUL	SPRINKLE	STEERAGE	STRICKLE	SUNDRIED	SYRACUSE	TEESHIRT
SPANDREL	SPRINTER	STEERING	STRICTLY	SUNDRIES	SYRINGES	TEETHING
SPANGLED	SPRITELY	STEINWAY	STRIDENT	SUNGLASS	SYSTEMIC	TEETOTAL
SPANIARD	SPRITZER	STELLATE	STRIKING	SUNLIGHT	TABBYCAT	TEFILLIN
SPANKING	SPROCKET	STENDHAL	STRINGED	SUNSHADE	TABLEMAT	TEGUMENT
SPANNING	SPRUCELY	STENOSED	STRINGER	SUNSHINE	TABULATE	TELECAST
SPARAXIS	SPRYNESS	STENOSIS	STRIPPED	SUPERBLY	TACITURN	TELECOMS
SPARKING	SPURIOUS	STEPHENS	STRIPPER	SUPERBUG	TACTICAL	TELEFILM
SPARKLER	SPURNING	STERLING	STRIVING	SUPERIOR	TACTLESS	TELEGONY
SPARRING	SPYGLASS	STICCATO	STROLLER	SUPERMAN	TAFFRAIL	TELEGRAM
SPARSELY	SQUABBLE	STICKILY	STRONGLY	SUPERNAL	TAHITIAN	TELEMARK
SPARSITY	SQUADDIE	STICKING	STRUGGLE	SUPERTAX	TAILBACK	TELETHON
SPARTANS	SQUADRON	STICKLER	STRUMPET	SUPPLANT	TAILGATE	TELEVISE
SPAVINED	SQUAMATA	STIFLING	STUBBORN	SUPPLIER	TAILLESS	TELLTALE
SPAWNING	SQUAMOUS	STIGMATA	STUCCOED	SUPPLIES	TAILPIPE	TELLURIC
SPEAKERS	SQUANDER	STILETTO	STUDENTS	SUPPOSED	TAILSKID	TEMERITY
SPEAKING	SQUARELY	STILWELL	STUDIOUS	SUPPRESS	TAILSPIN	TEMPERED
SPECIFIC	SQUATTER	STIMULUS	STUFFILY	SURENESS	TAKEAWAY	TEMPLATE
SPECIMEN	SQUEAKER	STINGING	STUFFING	SURFBOAT	TAKEHOME	TEMPORAL
SPECIOUS	SQUEALER	STINGRAY	STULTIFY	SURGICAL	TAKEOVER	TEMPTING
SPECKLED	SQUEEGEE	STINKING	STUNNING	SURICATE	TALENTED	TENACITY
SPECTRAL	SQUEEZER	STINKPOT	STUPIDLY	SURMOUNT	TALISMAN	TENDENCY
SPECTRUM	SQUIGGLE	STIRLING	STURDILY	SURPLICE	TAMANDUA	TENDERLY
SPECULUM	SQUIRREL	STIRRING	STURGEON	SURPRISE	TAMARACK	TENEBRAE
SPEEDILY	STABBING	STOCCATA	STYLIZED	SURROUND	TAMARIND	TENEBRIO
SPEEDWAY	STABLING	STOCKADE	SUBHUMAN	SURVEYOR	TAMARISK	TENEMENT
SPELLING	STACCATO	STOCKCAR	SUBJECTS	SURVIVAL	TAMENESS	TENESMUS
SPELLMAN	STAFFING	STOCKING	SUBLEASE	SURVIVOR	TAMWORTH	TENNYSON
SPENDING	STAFFORD	STOCKIST	SUBMERGE	SUSPENSE	TANDOORI	TENTACLE
SPHAGNUM	STAGGERS	STOCKMAN	SUBPOENA	SUZERAIN	TANGIBLE	TEQUILLA
SPHENOID	STAGHORN	STOCKPOT	SUBSHRUB	SVENGALI	TANGIBLY	TERATOMA
SPICCATO	STAGNANT	STOICISM	SUBSONIC	SWADDLER	TANTALUM	TERIYAKI
SPIFFING	STAGNATE	STOKESAY	SUBTENSE	SWANSKIN	TANTALUS	TERMINAL
SPILLAGE	STAIRWAY	STOLIDLY	SUBTITLE	SWANSONG	TANZANIA	TERMINUS
SPILLWAY	STAKEOUT	STONEFLY	SUBTLETY	SWARMING	TAPENADE	TERRACED
SPINIFEX	STALKING	STOPCOCK	SUBTOPIA	SWASTIKA	TAPERING	TERRAPIN

TERRIBLE	TICKTACK	TRACTION	TROUSERS	UNBURDEN	UNRIFLED	VALVULAR
TERRIBLY	TICKTOCK	TRADEOFF	TRUCKING	UNBUTTON	UNSALTED	VANADIUM
TERRIFIC	TIDEMARK	TRAILING	TRUCKLED	UNCARING	UNSAVORY	VANADOUS
TERTIARY	TIDINESS	TRAINING	TRUENESS	UNCHASTE	UNSEALED	VANBRUGH
TERYLENE	TIEBREAK	TRAITORS	TRUMPERY	UNCIFORM	UNSEEDED	VANGUARD
TESTATOR	TIGHTWAD	TRAMLINE	TRUNCATE	UNCLOVEN	UNSEEMLY	VANISHED
TESTATUM	TIMBERED	TRANQUIL	TRUNNION	UNCOMBED	UNSETTLE	VANQUISH
TESTICLE	TIMELESS	TRANSACT	TRUSTFUL	UNCOMMON	UNSHAKEN	VAPORIZE
TETCHILY	TIMIDITY	TRANSECT	TRUSTING	UNCOOKED	UNSIGNED	VAPOROUS
TETRAGON	TIMOROUS	TRANSEPT	TRUTHFUL	UNCOUPLE	UNSOCIAL	VARIABLE
TETRAPOD	TINCTURE	TRANSFER	TSAREVNA	UNCTUOUS	UNSOLVED	VARIANCE
TETRARCH	TINGLING	TRANSFIX	TUBELESS	UNCURBED	UNSPOILT	VARICOSE
TEUTONIC	TINNITUS	TRANSHIP	TUBENOSE	UNDERAGE	UNSPOKEN	VARIETAL
TEXTBOOK	TINSELLY	TRANSKEI	TUBERCLE	UNDERARM	UNSTABLE	VARIFORM
TEXTURED	TINSMITH	TRANSMIT	TUBEROSE	UNDERBID	UNSTATED	VARIORUM
THAILAND	TINTAGEL	TRAPDOOR	TUBEROUS	UNDERCUT	UNSTEADY	VASCULAR
THALAMUS	TIPSTAFF	TRAPPIST	TUNGSTEN	UNDERDOG	UNSUITED	VASTNESS
THALLIUM	TIRAMISU	TRASHCAN	TUNGSTIC	UNDERFED	UNTANGLE	VAULTING
THANATOS	TIRELESS	TRAVELER	TUNGUSIC	UNDERFUR	UNTAPPED	VAUXHALL
THANKFUL	TIRESIAS	TRAVERSE	TUNICATE	UNDERLAY	UNTHREAD	VEGETATE
THATAWAY	TIRESOME	TRAVESTY	TUNISIAN	UNDERLIE	UNTIDILY	VEHEMENT
THATCHED	TITANESS	TREASURE	TUPAMARO	UNDERPIN	UNTILLED	VELLEITY
THATCHER	TITANISM	TREASURY	TUPPENNY	UNDERRUN	UNTIMELY	VELOCITY
THEATRIC	TITANITE	TREATISE	TURANDOT	UNDERSEA	UNTOWARD	VENALITY
THEBAINE	TITANIUM	TREELESS	TURBANED	UNDERTOW	UNUNBIUM	VENDETTA
THEMATIC	TITICACA	TREELINE	TURBOJET	UNDULANT	UNUSABLE	VENERATE
THEOCRAT	TITIVATE	TREETOPS	TURGENEV	UNDULATE	UNVARIED	VENEREAL
THEOLOGY	TITMOUSE	TREMBLER	TURGIDLY	UNEARNED	UNVERSED	VENETIAN
THEORIST	TOADFLAX	TREMBLES	TURKOMAN	UNEASILY	UNVOICED	VENGEFUL
THEORIZE	TOBOGGAN	TRENCHER	TURMERIC	UNENDING	UNWANTED	VENOMOUS
THESPIAN	TOGETHER	TRESPASS	TURNBACK	UNERRING	UNWEANED	VENTURED
THIAMINE	TOILSOME	TRIANGLE	TURNCOAT	UNEVENLY	UNWIELDY	VERACITY
THICKSET	TOISEACH	TRIASSIC	TURNCOCK	UNFADING	UNWONTED	VERANDAH
THIEVERY	TOLBOOTH	TRIBUNAL	TURNOVER	UNFASTEN	UNWORTHY	VERBALLY
THIEVING	TOLERANT	TRICHOID	TURNPIKE	UNFETTER	UPCOMING	VERBATIM
THIEVISH	TOLERATE	TRICKERY	TURNSPIT	UNFILLED	UPHEAVAL	VERBIAGE
THINGAMY	TOLLGATE	TRICYCLE	TURRETED	UNFORCED	UPHOLDER	VERDERER
THINKING	TOMAHAWK	TRIFLING	TUSITALA	UNFREEZE	UPMARKET	VERJUICE
THINNESS	TOMATOES	TRIGLYPH	TUTELAGE	UNGAINLY	UPPERCUT	VERLAINE
THINNING	TOMENTUM	TRIGRAPH	TUTELARY	UNGULATE	UPRIGHTS	VERMOUTH
THIOUREA	TOMORROW	TRILEMMA	TUTORIAL	UNHARMED	UPRISING	VERONESE
THIRTEEN	TONALITY	TRILLING	TWEEZERS	UNHEATED	UPSTAIRS	VERONICA
THOLEPIN	TONELESS	TRILLION	TWELVEMO	UNHEROIC	UPSTREAM	VERSICLE
THOMPSON	TONSURED	TRILLIUM	TWILIGHT	UNHINGED	UPTURNED	VERTEBRA
THORACIC	TOPCLASS	TRIMARAN	TWIRLING	UNICYCLE	URBANITY	VERTICAL
THOROUGH	TOPHEAVY	TRIMMING	TWISTING	UNIFYING	URBANIZE	VESPERAL
THOUGHTS	TOPLEVEL	TRIMNESS	TWITCHER	UNIONISM	URETHANE	VESPUCCI
THOUSAND	TOPNOTCH	TRINCULO	TWOPENNY	UNIONIST	URGENTLY	VESTIARY
THRACIAN	TOPOLOGY	TRINIDAD	TWOPIECE	UNIONIZE	URSULINE	VESTMENT
THRALDOM	TOREADOR	TRIPLING	TYMPANUM	UNIPOLAR	USEFULLY	VESUVIUS
THRASHER	TORTILLA	TRIPTANE	TYPECAST	UNIQUELY	USUFRUCT	VEXATION
THREATEN	TORTOISE	TRIPTYCH	TYPEFACE	UNITEDLY	USURIOUS	VEXILLUM
THRENODY	TORTUOUS	TRISTICH	TYROLEAN	UNIVALVE	UTENSILS	VIATICUM
THRESHER	TORTURED	TRISTRAM	TYROSINE	UNIVERSE	UXORIOUS	VIBRANCY
THRILLER	TORTURER	TRITICAL	TZATZIKI	UNJUSTLY	VACANTLY	VIBRATOR
THROMBIN	TOTALITY	TRITICUM	UBIQUITY	UNKINDLY	VACATION	VIBURNUM
THROMBUS	TOTALIZE	TRIUNITY	UDOMETER	UNLAWFUL	VAGABOND	VICARAGE
THROTTLE	TOUCHING	TROCHAIC	UGLINESS	UNLEADED	VAGARIES	VICARIAL
THRUSTER	TOULOUSE	TROCHLEA	ULCERATE	UNLIKELY	VAGRANCY	VICINITY
THUMPING	TOVARICH	TROLLOPE	ULCEROUS	UNLISTED	VAISAKHA	VICTORIA
THUNDERY	TOWELING	TROMBONE	ULTERIOR	UNLOADED	VALENCIA	VICTUALS
THURIBLE	TOWERING	TROOPING	ULTIMATE	UNLOCKED	VALERIAN	VIETCONG
THURIFER	TOWNSHIP	TROPICAL	UMBRELLA	UNLOVELY	VALETING	VIGILANT
THURSDAY	TOWNSMAN	TROTLINE	UNABATED	UNMANNED	VALHALLA	VIGNETTE
TIBERIAS	TOXAEMIA	TROTTERS	UNAWARES	UNMARKED	VALIDATE	VIGOROUS
TIBERIUS	TOXICITY	TROTTOIR	UNBEATEN	UNNERVED	VALIDITY	VILENESS
TICKLING	TOXOCARA	TROUBLED	UNBIASED	UNPERSON	VALKYRIE	VILLAGER
TICKLISH	TRACHOMA	TROUBLES	UNBIDDEN	UNPLACED	VALLETTA	VILLAINY
TICKSEED	TRACKING	TROUNCER	UNBROKEN	UNREASON	VALUABLE	VINCIBLE

VINCULUM	WARPAINT	WILDFOWL	WRANGLER	BACCHANT	BARBIZON	CALENDAR
VINDALOO	WARPLANE	WILDLIFE	WRAPPING	BACHELOR	BARDOLPH	CALENDER
VINEGARY	WARRANTY	WILDNESS	WRATHFUL	BACILLUS	BAREBACK	CALFSKIN
VINEYARD	WASHABLE	WILFULLY	WREATHED	BACKACHE	BAREFOOT	CALIGULA
VIOLATOR	WASHBOWL	WILINESS	WRECKAGE	BACKBITE	BARENESS	CALIPERS
VIOLENCE	WASHDOWN	WILLIAMS	WRESTLER	BACKBONE	BARGELLO	CALLGIRL
VIPERISH	WASHROOM	WINDBURN	WRETCHED	BACKCHAT	BARGEMAN	CALLIOPE
VIPEROUS	WASTEFUL	WINDFALL	WRINGING	BACKCOMB	BARITONE	CALLIPER
VIREMENT	WATCHDOG	WINDGALL	WRINKLED	BACKDATE	BARNABAS	CALLISTO
VIRGINAL	WATCHFUL	WINDHOEK	WRISTLET	BACKDROP	BARNACLE	CALMNESS
VIRGINIA	WATCHING	WINDINGS	WRITEOFF	BACKFIRE	BARNARDS	CALOTYPE
VIRILITY	WATCHMAN	WINDLASS	WRITHING	BACKHAND	BARNYARD	CALTHROP
VIROLOGY	WATERBUG	WINDLESS	WRITINGS	BACKLASH	BARONESS	CALVADOS
VIRTUOSI	WATERING	WINDMILL	WRONGFUL	BACKLESS	BARONETS	CAMARGUE
VIRTUOSO	WATERLOO	WINDPIPE	WYCLIFFE	BACKPACK	BARONIAL	CAMBERED
VIRTUOUS	WATERMAN	WINDSOCK	XANTHOMA	BACKROOM	BARRACKS	CAMBODIA
VIRULENT	WATERSKI	WINDWARD	XANTIPPE	BACKSIDE	BARRATRY	CAMBRIAN
VISCERAL	WATERWAY	WINGLESS	XENOGAMY	BACKSPIN	BARRETTE	CAMELLIA
VISCOUNT	WAVEBAND	WINGSPAN	XENOLITH	BACKSTOP	BARTERED	CAMEROON
VISELIKE	WAVERING	WINIFRED	XENOPHON	BACKWARD	BASEBALL	CAMISOLE
VISIGOTH	WAVERLEY	WINNINGS	XERAPHIM	BACKYARD	BASEBORN	CAMOMILE
VISITANT	WAXWORKS	WINNIPEG	YACHTING	BACTERIA	BASELESS	CAMPAIGN
VISITING	WAYFARER	WIRELESS	YAKITORI	BACTRIAN	BASELINE	CAMPBELL
VISUALLY	WEAKFISH	WIREWORM	YARMULKA	BADINAGE	BASEMENT	CAMPSITE
VITALISM	WEAKLING	WISEACRE	YATAGHAN	BADLANDS	BASENESS	CAMPTOWN
VITALITY	WEAKNESS	WISHBONE	YEARBOOK	BAEDEKER	BASIDIUM	CAMSHAFT
VITALIZE	WEAPONRY	WISTERIA	YEARLING	BAFFLING	BASILICA	CAMSTONE
VITAMINS	WEARABLE	WITCHERY	YEARLONG	BAGHEERA	BASILISK	CANADIAN
VITELLUS	WEDGWOOD	WITCHING	YEARNING	BAGPIPES	BASINFUL	CANAILLE
VITILIGO	WEIGHING	WITHDRAW	YEOMANRY	BAGUETTE	BASKETRY	CANALISE
VITREOUS	WELLBRED	WITHERED	YERSINIA	BAHAMIAN	BASSINET	CANARIES
VIVACITY	WELLNIGH	WITHHOLD	YIELDING	BAHRAINI	BASSWOOD	CANBERRA
VIVARIUM	WELLPAID	WIZARDRY	YODELLER	BAILMENT	BASTILLE	CANDIDLY
VOCALIST	WELSHMAN	WOBBLING	YOGHOURT	BAKELITE	BATAVIAN	CANISTER
VOCALIZE	WEREWOLF	WOEFULLY	YOKOHAMA	BALANCED	BATHETIC	CANNABIS
VOCATION	WESLEYAN	WOLFBANE	YOSEMITE	BALDNESS	BATHROBE	CANNIBAL
VOCATIVE	WESTERLY	WOLSELEY	YOUNGEST	BALDRICK	BATHROOM	CANOEING
VOIDANCE	WESTWARD	WOMANISH	YOURSELF	BALEARIC	BATTERED	CANOEIST
VOLATILE	WETLANDS	WOMANIZE	YOUTHFUL	BALINESE	BAUDRICK	CANONESS
VOLCANIC	WHACKING	WONDROUS	YUGOSLAV	BALLCOCK	BAVARIAN	CANONIZE
VOLITION	WHARFAGE	WOODBINE	YULETIDE	BALLGIRL	BAYBERRY	CANOODLE
VOLPLANE	WHATEVER	WOODCOCK	ZAKOUSKI	BALLISTA	BAYREUTH	CANTICLE
VOLSCIAN	WHEATEAR	WOODENLY	ZAMINDAR	BALLOCKS	CABERNET	CANTORIS
VOLTAIRE	WHEEZILY	WOODLAND	ZARZUELA	BALLPARK	CABLECAR	CAPACITY
VOMITING	WHEEZING	WOODRUFF	ZASTRUGA	BALLROOM	CABLEWAY	CAPERING
VOMITORY	WHENEVER	WOODSHED	ZEDEKIAH	BALLYHOO	CABOCHON	CAPITALS
VORACITY	WHEREVER	WOODSMAN	ZEPHYRUS	BALMORAL	CABOODLE	CAPRIOLE
VORTICAL	WHIMBREL	WOODWARD	ZEPPELIN	BALUSTER	CABOTAGE	CAPSICUM
VOWELIZE	WHINCHAT	WOODWIND	ZIBELINE	BANALITY	CABRIOLE	CAPSIZED
VOYAGEUR	WHIPCORD	WOODWORK	ZIGGURAT	BANDANNA	CACHALOT	CAPSTONE
VULGARLY	WHIPHAND	WOODWORM	ZIMBABWE	BANDEROL	CACHEPOT	CAPTIOUS
WAGGONER	WHIPJACK	WOOLLENS	ZIRCONIA	BANDITTI	CACHEXIA	CAPUCHIN
WAINSCOT	WHIPLASH	WOOLPACK	ZODIACAL	BANDSMAN	CADASTRE	CAPYBARA
WAITRESS	WHIPPING	WOOLSACK	ZOETROPE	BANISTER	CADILLAC	CARABINE
WALKOVER	WHIRLING	WORDBOOK	ZOONOSIS	BANKBOOK	CADUCEUS	CARACOLE
WALKYRIE	WHISKERS	WORDLESS	ZOOPHYTE	BANKNOTE	CAERLEON	CARAPACE
WALLSEND	WHISKERY	WORKABLE	ZOOSPERM	BANKROLL	CAFFEINE	CARBOLIC
WALLWORT	WHISTLER	WORKADAY	ZOOSPORE	BANKRUPT	CAGINESS	CARBONIC
WALTZING	WHITECAP	WORKBOOK	ZUCCHINI	BANLIEUE	CAJOLERY	CARCAJOU
WAMBLING	WHITEHOT	WORKINGS	ZWIEBACK	BANNERET	CAKEHOLE	CARCANET
WANDERER	WHITENER	WORKLOAD	**8:2**	BANTLING	CAKEWALK	CARDAMOM
WARDRESS	WHITLING	WORKMATE	AARDVARK	BAPTISED	CALABASH	CARDIGAN
WARDROBE	WHODUNIT	WORKROOM	AASVOGEL	BARABBAS	CALAMINE	CARDINAL
WARDROOM	WHOOPING	WORKSHOP	BAATHIST	BARATHEA	CALAMITY	CAREFREE
WARDSHIP	WHOPPING	WORMCAST	BABBLING	BARBADOS	CALCEATE	CARELESS
WARFARIN	WICKEDLY	WORMWOOD	BABUSHKA	BARBARIC	CALCRETE	CAREWORN
WARHORSE	WIDENING	WORRYING	BABYHOOD	BARBECUE	CALCULUS	CARILLON
WARINESS	WILDFELL	WORTHIES	BACCARAT	BARBERRY	CALCUTTA	CARJACOU
WARMBOOT	WILDFIRE	WORTHILY		BARBICAN	CALDERON	CARNAUBA

CARNEGIE	DARKENED	FAVORITE	HALFTIME	JACKBOOT	LAPIDATE	MAJOLICA
CARNIVAL	DARKNESS	FAVOURED	HALFYEAR	JACKETED	LARGESSE	MAJORITY
CAROLINA	DARKROOM	GABONESE	HALLIARD	JACOBEAN	LARKSPUR	MALAGASY
CAROLINE	DARTMOOR	GABORONE	HALLMARK	JACOBITE	LAROUSSE	MALAKOFF
CAROTENE	DASHWOOD	GADABOUT	HALLOWED	JACQUARD	LASHINGS	MALAMUTE
CAROUSAL	DATABASE	GADARENE	HAMARTIA	JAILBIRD	LATCHKEY	MALARIAL
CAROUSEL	DATELESS	GADGETRY	HAMILTON	JALOUSIE	LATENESS	MALARKEY
CARRAWAY	DATELINE	GADOGADO	HAMMERED	JAMAICAN	LATERITE	MALAWIAN
CARRIAGE	DAUGHTER	GADZOOKS	HANDBALL	JAMBOREE	LATINIST	MALAYSIA
CARRIOLE	DAUNTING	GAILLARD	HANDBILL	JANGLING	LATITUDE	MALDIVES
CARRYALL	DAVIDSON	GALACTIC	HANDBOOK	JAPANESE	LATTERLY	MALGRADO
CARRYCOT	DAYBREAK	GALBANUM	HANDCART	JAPONICA	LAUDABLE	MALINGER
CARRYING	DAYDREAM	GALILEAN	HANDCLAP	JAUNDICE	LAUDABLY	MALLARMÉ
CARTHAGE	DAYLIGHT	GALLERIA	HANDCUFF	JAUNTILY	LAUDANUM	MALLEATE
CARTLOAD	DAZZLING	GALLIARD	HANDGRIP	KACHAHRI	LAUGHING	MALLORCA
CARUCATE	EARLIEST	GALLIPOT	HANDHELD	KALAHARI	LAUGHTER	MALODOUR
CARYATID	EARNINGS	GALLOPER	HANDICAP	KAMIKAZE	LAUREATE	MALTREAT
CASANOVA	EARPHONE	GALLOWAY	HANDMADE	KANGAROO	LAURENCE	MALVASIA
CASEMATE	EARPIECE	GALLUMPH	HANDMAID	KARTTIKA	LAVATORY	MALVOLIO
CASEMENT	EASEMENT	GALOSHES	HANDOVER	KATAKANA	LAVENDER	MAMELUKE
CASHMERE	EASINESS	GALVANIC	HANDRAIL	KATMANDU	LAVENGRO	MANAGING
CASSETTE	EASTERLY	GAMBLING	HANDSOME	KATTEGAT	LAVISHLY	MANCIPLE
CASTANET	EASTLAKE	GAMEBIRD	HANDYMAN	KAZACHOK	LAWCOURT	MANDAMUS
CASTAWAY	EASTWARD	GAMENESS	HANGINGS	LABOURED	LAWFULLY	MANDARIN
CASTOFFS	EATABLES	GANGLAND	HANGNAIL	LABOURER	LAWMAKER	MANDATED
CASTRATE	FABULOUS	GANGLING	HANGOVER	LABRADOR	LAWRENCE	MANDIBLE
CASTRATO	FACEACHE	GANGLION	HANNIBAL	LABURNUM	LAXATIVE	MANDIOCA
CASUALLY	FACELESS	GANGRENE	HANUKKAH	LACERATE	LAYABOUT	MANDOLIN
CASUALTY	FACELIFT	GANGSTER	HAPSBURG	LACEWING	LAZINESS	MANDRAKE
CATACOMB	FACILITY	GANISTER	HARANGUE	LACINATE	MACARONI	MANDRILL
CATALYST	FACTIOUS	GANYMEDE	HARASSED	LACKADAY	MACAROON	MANEUVER
CATAMITE	FACTOTUM	GAOLBIRD	HARDBACK	LACKLAND	MACASSAR	MANFULLY
CATAPULT	FAINITES	GARAMOND	HARDCORE	LACONIAN	MACAULAY	MANGONEL
CATARACT	FAINTING	GARDENER	HARDENED	LACROSSE	MACERATE	MANGROVE
CATATONY	FAIRNESS	GARDENIA	HARDHACK	LADRONES	MACHEATH	MANIACAL
CATCHING	FAITHFUL	GARDYLOO	HARDLINE	LADYBIRD	MACHINES	MANICURE
CATECHOL	FALCONRY	GARGANEY	HARDNESS	LADYFISH	MACHISMO	MANIFEST
CATEGORY	FALKLAND	GARGOYLE	HARDSHIP	LADYLIKE	MACKEREL	MANIFOLD
CATERING	FALLIBLE	GARISHLY	HARDTACK	LADYSHIP	MACMAHON	MANITOBA
CATHEDRA	FALSETTO	GARLICKY	HARDWARE	LAIDBACK	MACREADY	MANNERED
CATHETER	FAMILIAR	GARMENTS	HAREBELL	LAKELAND	MACULATE	MANNERLY
CATHOLIC	FAMISHED	GARRIGUE	HARFLEUR	LAKESIDE	MADHOUSE	MANNIKIN
CATHOUSE	FAMOUSLY	GARRISON	HARMLESS	LAMASERY	MADRIGAL	MANORIAL
CATILINE	FANCIFUL	GARROTTE	HARMONIC	LAMBSKIN	MADWOMAN	MANPOWER
CATSMEAT	FANCYMAN	GASOLIER	HARRIDAN	LAMENESS	MAECENAS	MANTILLA
CATTLEYA	FANDANGO	GASOLINE	HARRISON	LAMENTED	MAESTOSO	MANTISSA
CATULLUS	FANLIGHT	GASTRULA	HARTFORD	LAMINATE	MAGAZINE	MANTLING
CAUDILLO	FANTASIA	GASWORKS	HARUSPEX	LAMPPOST	MAGELLAN	MANUALLY
CAULDRON	FARCICAL	GATEFOLD	HASTINGS	LANCELET	MAGICIAN	MAQUETTE
CAUSEWAY	FAREWELL	GATEPOST	HATCHERY	LANCELOT	MAGISTER	MARABOUT
CAUTIOUS	FARMHAND	GATHERED	HATCHING	LANDFALL	MAGNESIA	MARASMUS
CAVALIER	FARMLAND	GAUNTLET	HATCHWAY	LANDFILL	MAGNETIC	MARATHON
CAVATINA	FARMYARD	GAZPACHO	HATHAWAY	LANDLADY	MAGNOLIA	MARAUDER
DABCHICK	FAROUCHE	GAZUNDER	HABAKKUK	LANDLOCK	MAHARAJA	MARCELLA
DAEDALUS	FARRIERY	HABANERA	HAUNCHES	LANDLORD	MAHARANI	MARCELLO
DAFFODIL	FARTHEST	HABITUAL	HAUNTING	LANDMARK	MAHJONGG	MARGARET
DAINTIES	FARTHING	HABSBURG	HAVDALAH	LANDMASS	MAHOGANY	MARGINAL
DAINTILY	FASCICLE	HACIENDA	HAVILDAR	LANDMINE	MAIDENLY	MARGRAVE
DAIQUIRI	FASTBACK	HAGGADAH	HAWAIIAN	LANDRACE	MAIEUTIC	MARIACHI
DAIRYMAN	FASTENER	HAGGADAH	HAWFINCH	LANDSEER	MAILBOAT	MARIANAS
DALMATIC	FASTNESS	HAIRBAND	HAWTHORN	LANDSLIP	MAILSHOT	MARIGOLD
DAMASCUS	FATALISM	HAIRLESS	HAYFEVER	LANDWARD	MAINLAND	MARINADE
DAMNABLE	FATALIST	HAIRLIKE	HAYFIELD	LANGLAND	MAINLINE	MARINATE
DAMOCLES	FATALITY	HAIRLINE	HAYMAKER	LANGLAUF	MAINMAST	MARITIME
DAMPNESS	FATHERLY	HAIRWORM	HAYSTACK	LANGUAGE	MAINSAIL	MARJORAM
DANAIDES	FATIGUED	HALFFULL	HAZELNUT	LANGUISH	MAINSTAY	MARKDOWN
DANDRUFF	FATIGUES	HALFHOUR	HAZINESS	LANOLINE	MAINTAIN	MARKEDLY
DANEGELD	FATSTOCK	HALFMAST	JACKAROO	LANSBURY	MAINYARD	MARKSMAN
DANKNESS	FAULKNER	HALFTERM	JACKBOOT	LAPIDARY	MAJESTIC	MARMOSET

260

MARONITE	PAINLESS	PARTTIME	RATTLING	SAWBONES	VALKYRIE	ZAKOUSKI
MAROQUIN	PAINTING	PASHMINA	RAVENOUS	SAWHORSE	VALLETTA	ZAMINDAR
MARQUESA	PAKISTAN	PASSABLE	SABOTAGE	SAXATILE	VALUABLE	ZARZUELA
MARQUESS	PALATIAL	PASSABLY	SABOTEUR	SAYONARA	VALVULAR	ZASTRUGA
MARQUISE	PALATINE	PASSBOOK	SACRISTY	TABBYCAT	VANADIUM	ABATTOIR
MARRIAGE	PALEFACE	PASSERBY	SADDLERY	TABLEMAT	VANADOUS	ABBASIDE
MARSHALL	PALENESS	PASSIBLE	SADDLING	TABULATE	VANBRUGH	ABDICATE
MARTELLO	PALGRAVE	PASSOVER	SADDUCEE	TACITURN	VANGUARD	ABDUCENS
MARTINET	PALIMONY	PASSPORT	SADISTIC	TACTICAL	VANISHED	ABDUCTED
MARTYRED	PALINODE	PASSWORD	SAGACITY	TACTLESS	VANQUISH	ABDUCTOR
MARYLAND	PALISADE	PASTICHE	SAGENESS	TAFFRAIL	VAPORIZE	ABERDEEN
MARZIPAN	PALLADIO	PASTILLE	SAILBOAT	TAHITIAN	VAPOROUS	ABERRANT
MASCARON	PALLIATE	PASTORAL	SAINFOIN	TAILBACK	VARIABLE	ABESSIVE
MASSACRE	PALMATED	PASTRAMI	SALACITY	TAILGATE	VARIANCE	ABEYANCE
MASSENET	PALMETTO	PASTURES	SALARIED	TAILLESS	VARICOSE	ABINGDON
MASSEUSE	PALMITIN	PATAGIUM	SALEABLE	TAILPIPE	VARIETAL	ABJECTLY
MASSICOT	PALPABLE	PATCHILY	SALEROOM	TAILSKID	VARIFORM	ABLATION
MASTERLY	PALPABLY	PATELLAR	SALESMAN	TAILSPIN	VARIORUM	ABLATIVE
MASTHEAD	PALUDISM	PATENTED	SALINGER	TAKEAWAY	VASCULAR	ABLUTION
MASTODON	PAMPERED	PATENTEE	SALINITY	TAKEHOME	VASTNESS	ABNEGATE
MATABELE	PAMPHLET	PATENTLY	SALIVARY	TAKEOVER	VAULTING	ABNORMAL
MATAMORE	PANATELA	PATERNAL	SALIVATE	TALENTED	VAUXHALL	ABOMASUM
MATCHBOX	PANCREAS	PATHETIC	SALTBUSH	TALISMAN	WAGGONER	ABORTION
MATCHING	PANDANUS	PATHOGEN	SALTLICK	TAMANDUA	WAINSCOT	ABORTIVE
MATERIAL	PANDARUS	PATIENCE	SALTNESS	TAMARACK	WAITRESS	ABRASION
MATERNAL	PANDEMIC	PATULOUS	SALUTARY	TAMARIND	WALKOVER	ABRASIVE
MATHURIN	PANDOWDY	PAULINUS	SALUTORY	TAMARISK	WALKYRIE	ABRIDGED
MATRONLY	PANEGYRY	PAVEMENT	SALVADOR	TAMENESS	WALLSEND	ABROGATE
MATTRESS	PANELING	PAVILION	SAMARIUM	TAMWORTH	WALLWORT	ABRUPTLY
MATURATE	PANELLED	PAWNSHOP	SAMENESS	TANDOORI	WALTZING	ABSCISSA
MATURITY	PANGLOSS	PAYCHECK	SAMIZDAT	TANGIBLE	WAMBLING	ABSENTEE
MAVERICK	PANGOLIN	RABELAIS	SAMPHIRE	TANGIBLY	WANDERER	ABSINTHE
MAXIMIZE	PANNICLE	RACHITIS	SANCTIFY	TANTALUM	WARDRESS	ABSOLUTE
MAYORESS	PANNIKIN	RACIALLY	SANCTION	TANTALUS	WARDROBE	ABSOLVED
MAZARINE	PANORAMA	RACINESS	SANCTITY	TANZANIA	WARDROOM	ABSORBED
NAGASAKI	PANPIPES	RACKRENT	SANDARAC	TAPENADE	WARDSHIP	ABSORBER
NAMELESS	PANTALON	RACLETTE	SANDBANK	TAPERING	WARFARIN	ABSTRACT
NAMESAKE	PANTHEON	RADIANCE	SANDWICH	TAPESTRY	WARHORSE	ABSTRUSE
NAMIBIAN	PAPILLON	RADIATOR	SANGLIER	TAPEWORM	WARINESS	ABSURDLY
NAPOLEON	PARABOLA	RAGNARÖK	SANGUINE	TAPHOUSE	WARMBOOT	ABUNDANT
NARCOSES	PARADIGM	RAGSTONE	SANITARY	TARBOOSH	WARPAINT	ABUTILON
NARCOSIS	PARAFFIN	RAILHEAD	SANITIZE	TARRAGON	WARPLANE	ABUTMENT
NARCOTIC	PARAGUAY	RAILINGS	SANSERIF	TARTARIC	WARRANTY	OBDURACY
NARGILEH	PARAKEET	RAILLERY	SANSKRIT	TARTARUS	WASHABLE	OBDURATE
NARRATOR	PARALLAX	RAILROAD	SANTIAGO	TARTNESS	WASHBOWL	OBEDIENT
NARROWLY	PARALLEL	RAINBIRD	SAPONITE	TARTRATE	WASHDOWN	OBITUARY
NATALITY	PARALYZE	RAINCOAT	SAPPHIRE	TARTUFFE	WASHROOM	OBJECTOR
NATIONAL	PARAMOUR	RAINDROP	SAPPHIST	TASHKENT	WASTEFUL	OBLATION
NATIVITY	PARANOIA	RAINFALL	SARABAND	TASMANIA	WATCHDOG	OBLIGATE
NATTERED	PARANOID	RAINWEAR	SARATOGA	TASTEFUL	WATCHFUL	OBLIGING
NATURISM	PARAQUAT	RAISONNÉ	SARDINIA	TATTERED	WATCHING	OBLIVION
NATURIST	PARASHAH	RAMBLING	SARDONIC	TAUTNESS	WATCHMAN	OBSCURED
NAUPLIUS	PARASITE	RAMBUTAN	SARDONYX	TAVERNER	WATERBUG	OBSERVED
NAUSEATE	PARDONER	RAMEQUIN	SARGASSO	TAXATION	WATERING	OBSERVER
NAUSEOUS	PARENTAL	RAMPARTS	SASSANID	TAXONOMY	WATERLOO	OBSESSED
NAUTICAL	PARIETAL	RANDOMLY	SATIATED	TAXPAYER	WATERMAN	OBSIDIAN
NAUTILUS	PARISIAN	RANELAGH	SATIRIST	TAYBERRY	WATERSKI	OBSOLETE
NAVARINO	PARKLAND	RANKNESS	SATIRIZE	VACANTLY	WATERWAY	OBSTACLE
NAVIGATE	PARLANCE	RAPACITY	SATURATE	VACATION	WAVEBAND	OBSTRUCT
NAZARENE	PARMESAN	RAPECAKE	SATURDAY	VAGABOND	WAVERING	OBTAINED
PABULOUS	PARODIST	RAPIDITY	SATURNIA	VAGARIES	WAVERLEY	OBTUSELY
PACHINKO	PAROLLES	RAREFIED	SAUCEPAN	VAGRANCY	WAXWORKS	UBIQUITY
PACIFIER	PAROUSIA	RASCALLY	SAUROPOD	VAISAKHA	WAYFARER	ACADEMIA
PACIFISM	PAROXYSM	RASHNESS	SAUSAGES	VALENCIA	XANTHOMA	ACADEMIC
PACIFIST	PARSIFAL	RASPUTIN	SAVAGELY	VALERIAN	XANTIPPE	ACANTHUS
PACKAGED	PARTERRE	RASSELAS	SAVAGERY	VALETING	YACHTING	ACAPULCO
PADDLING	PARTHIAN	RATEABLE	SAVANNAH	VALHALLA	YAKITORI	ACCENTED
PAGANINI	PARTICLE	RATIONAL	SAVOURED	VALIDATE	YARMULKA	ACCENTOR
PAGINATE	PARTISAN	RATTIGAN	SAVOYARD	VALIDITY	YATAGHAN	ACCEPTED

ACCEPTOR	SCARFACE	ADJUSTER	BEERBOHM	CENTRIST	DELIRIUM	FEARSOME
ACCIDENT	SCATHING	ADJUSTOR	BEESWING	CENTRODE	DELIVERY	FEASIBLE
ACCOLADE	SCAVENGE	ADJUTAGE	BEETLING	CEPHALIN	DELUSION	FEASIBLY
ACCOUNTS	SCENARIO	ADJUTANT	BEETROOT	CERAMICS	DEMEANOR	FEATHERS
ACCREDIT	SCHAPSKA	ADJUVANT	BEFRIEND	CERASTES	DEMENTED	FEATHERY
ACCURACY	SCHEDULE	ADMIRING	BEFUDDLE	CERATOID	DEMENTIA	FEATURED
ACCURATE	SCHEMING	ADMONISH	BEGETTER	CERBERUS	DEMERARA	FEATURES
ACCURSED	SCHILLER	ADOPTION	BEGGARLY	CEREBRAL	DEMERSAL	FEBRUARY
ACCUSING	SCHIZOID	ADOPTIVE	BEGINNER	CEREBRUM	DEMIJOHN	FECKLESS
ACCUSTOM	SCHMALTZ	ADORABLE	BEGORRAH	CEREMENT	DEMISTER	FECULENT
ACENTRIC	SCHMOOZE	ADRIATIC	BEGRUDGE	CEREMONY	DEMIURGE	FEDAYEEN
ACERBATE	SCHNAPPS	ADROITLY	BEHAVIOR	CERULEAN	DEMOCRAT	FEDERACY
ACERBITY	SCHOONER	ADULATOR	BEHEMOTH	CERVELAT	DEMOLISH	FEDERATE
ACHIEVED	SCHUBERT	ADULTERY	BEHOLDEN	CERVICAL	DEMONIAC	FEEDBACK
ACHIEVER	SCHUMANN	ADVANCED	BEHOLDER	CESSPOOL	DEMOTION	FEELGOOD
ACHILLES	SCIATICA	ADVANCER	BELABOUR	CETACEAN	DEMURELY	FEELINGS
ACIDHEAD	SCIENCES	ADVISORY	BELGRADE	DEADBEAT	DEMURRAL	FELDSPAR
ACOUSTIC	SCILICET	ADVOCACY	BELIEVER	DEADENED	DENARIUS	FELICITY
ACQUAINT	SCIMITAR	ADVOCATE	BELITTLE	DEADENER	DENATURE	FELLAHIN
ACQUIRED	SCIROCCO	EDENTATE	BELLPUSH	DEADHEAD	DENDRITE	FEMININE
ACQUIRER	SCISSION	EDGEHILL	BELLYFUL	DEADLINE	DENDROID	FEMINISM
ACRIMONY	SCISSORS	EDGEWAYS	BELPAESE	DEADLOCK	DENOUNCE	FEMINIST
ACROMION	SCOFFING	EDGEWISE	BENEDICK	DEADWOOD	DENTICLE	FEMINITY
ACROSTIC	SCOLDING	EDUCATED	BENEDICT	DEAFNESS	DENTURES	FENCIBLE
ACTINIDE	SCORCHED	EDUCATOR	BENEFICE	DEALINGS	DEPARTED	FENESTRA
ACTINIUM	SCORCHER	IDEALISM	BENEFITS	DEATHBED	DEPILATE	FEROCITY
ACTIVATE	SCORNFUL	IDEALIST	BENENDEN	DEBILITY	DEPORTEE	FERRYMAN
ACTIVELY	SCORPION	IDEALIZE	BENGHAZI	DEBONAIR	DEPRAVED	FESTIVAL
ACTIVISM	SCORPIUS	IDENTIFY	BENJAMIN	DECADENT	DEPRIVED	FETCHING
ACTIVIST	SCOTLAND	IDENTITY	BEQUEATH	DECANTER	DEPUTIZE	FETTLING
ACTIVITY	SCOTSMAN	IDEOGRAM	BERBERIS	DECAYING	DERANGED	FEVERFEW
ACTUALLY	SCOTTISH	IDEOLOGY	BERCEUSE	DECEASED	DERELICT	FEVERISH
ECHINATE	SCOURING	IDIOGRAM	BEREAVED	DECEIVER	DERISION	GELASTIC
ECHINOPS	SCOWLING	IDLENESS	BERGAMOT	DECEMBER	DERISIVE	GELATINE
ECLECTIC	SCRABBLE	IDOLATER	BERGENIA	DECEMVIR	DERISORY	GEMINATE
ECLOSION	SCRAMBLE	IDOLATRY	BERGERAC	DECENTLY	DEROGATE	GEMOLOGY
ECOFREAK	SCRAPPLE	NDJAMENA	BERIBERI	DECIMATE	DESCRIBE	GENDARME
ECONOMIC	SCRATCHY	ODDMENTS	BERKELEY	DECIPHER	DESELECT	GENERATE
ECSTASIS	SCRAWLED	ODIOUSLY	BERTRAND	DECISION	DESERTED	GENEROUS
ECSTATIC	SCREAMER	ODOMETER	BESIEGED	DECISIVE	DESERTER	GENETICS
ECTODERM	SCREENED	ODYSSEUS	BESMIRCH	DECKHAND	DESERVED	GENETRIX
ICEBLINK	SCREWTOP	UDOMETER	BESOTTED	DECLUTCH	DESIGNER	GENIALLY
ICEFIELD	SCRIABIN	AEGROTAT	BESOUGHT	DECORATE	DESIROUS	GENITALS
ICEHOUSE	SCRIBBLE	AEROBICS	BESPOKEN	DECOROUS	DESOLATE	GENITIVE
MCKINLEY	SCRIBBLY	AERODYNE	BESSEMER	DECOUPLE	DESPATCH	GENOCIDE
OCCAMIST	SCRIPTUM	AEROFLOT	BESTIARY	DECREASE	DESPOTIC	GENTRIFY
OCCASION	SCROFULA	AEROFOIL	BESTOWER	DECREPIT	DESTINED	GEODESIC
OCCIDENT	SCROUNGE	AEROGRAM	BESTRIDE	DECRETAL	DESTRUCT	GEODETIC
OCCUPANT	SCRUBBER	AEROLITH	BETATRON	DEDICATE	DETACHED	GEOMANCY
OCCUPIED	SCRUPLES	AERONAUT	BETHESDA	DEEPNESS	DETAILED	GEOMETER
OCCUPIER	SCRUTINY	AEROSTAT	BETJEMAN	DEERSKIN	DETAINEE	GEOMETRY
OCTAROON	SCULLERY	AESTHETE	BETRAYAL	DEFEATED	DETAINER	GEOPHONE
OCTONARY	SCULLION	BEAKLESS	BETRAYER	DEFECATE	DETECTOR	GEORGIAN
SCABBARD	SCULPTOR	BEANPOLE	BEVERAGE	DEFECTOR	DETHRONE	GEOTAXIS
SCABIOUS	SCYBALUM	BEARABLE	BEWILDER	DEFENDER	DETONATE	GERANIUM
SCABROUS	ADDENDUM	BEARINGS	CELANESE	DEFIANCE	DETOXIFY	GERMAINE
SCAFFOLD	ADDICTED	BEARSKIN	CELERIAC	DEFILADE	DETRITUS	GERMANIC
SCALDING	ADDITION	BEATIFIC	CELERITY	DEFINITE	DEUTERON	GERMINAL
SCALENUS	ADDITIVE	BEAUFORT	CELIBACY	DEFLOWER	DEVIANCE	GERONIMO
SCALLION	ADELAIDE	BEAUMONT	CELIBATE	DEFORMED	DEVILISH	GERTRUDE
SCANDIUM	ADENITIS	BEAUTIFY	CELLARER	DEFREEZE	DEVILLED	GESTURES
SCANNING	ADENOIDS	BECALMED	CELLULAR	DEFTNESS	DEVONIAN	HEADACHE
SCANSION	ADEQUACY	BECHAMEL	CEMENTUM	DEGRADED	DEVOTION	HEADBAND
SCANTIES	ADEQUATE	BECOMING	CEMETERY	DEJECTED	DEWBERRY	HEADGEAR
SCANTILY	ADESSIVE	BEDABBLE	CENOBITE	DELAWARE	DEWYEYED	HEADHUNT
SCAPHOID	ADHERENT	BEDCOVER	CENOTAPH	DELEGATE	DEXTROSE	HEADLAMP
SCAPULAR	ADHESION	BEDMAKER	CENOZOIC	DELETION	DEXTROUS	HEADLAND
SCARCELY	ADHESIVE	BEDSTEAD	CENTAURY	DELICACY	EERINESS	HEADLESS
SCARCITY	ADJACENT	BEDSTRAW	CENTERED	DELICATE	FEARLESS	HEADLINE

HEADLONG	JEALOUSY	MEATLESS	NEBULOUS	PELLICLE	REASSIGN	RELIGION
HEADMARK	JEANETTE	MECHANIC	NECKBAND	PELLMELL	REASSUME	RELOCATE
HEADMOST	JEBUSITE	MEDALIST	NECKLACE	PELLUCID	REASSURE	REMEDIAL
HEADREST	JEFFREYS	MEDDLING	NECKLINE	PEMBROKE	REAWAKEN	REMEMBER
HEADROOM	JEHOVAHS	MEDIATOR	NECKWEAR	PEMMICAN	REBUTTAL	REMINDER
HEADSHIP	JELLICOE	MEDICATE	NECROSIS	PENALIZE	RECEDING	REMITTAL
HEADWIND	JEOPARDY	MEDICINE	NEEDLESS	PENCHANT	RECEIPTS	REMNANTS
HEADWORD	JEPHTHAH	MEDIEVAL	NEGATION	PENDULUM	RECEIVED	REMOTELY
HEARTIES	JEREBOAM	MEDIOCRE	NEGATIVE	PENELOPE	RECEIVER	REMOUNTS
HEARTILY	JEREMIAD	MEDITATE	NEGLIGEE	PENITENT	RECENTLY	RENEGADE
HEATEDLY	JEREMIAH	MEEKNESS	NEGRILLO	PENKNIFE	RECEPTOR	RENMINBI
HEATSPOT	JEROBOAM	MEGABYTE	NEHEMIAH	PENNINES	RECESSED	RENOUNCE
HEATWAVE	JERRYCAN	MEGALITH	NEIGHBOR	PENOLOGY	RECHARGE	RENOVATE
HEAVENLY	JETTISON	MEGAPODE	NEMATODE	PENTACLE	RECKLESS	RENOWNED
HEBETUDE	JEWELLED	MEGAVOLT	NEMATOID	PENTAGON	RECKONER	REORIENT
HEBRAISM	JEWELLER	MEGAWATT	NEMBUTAL	PENTARCH	RECORDER	REPAIRER
HEBRIDES	KEDGEREE	MELAMINE	NENUPHAR	PENUMBRA	RECOURSE	REPARTEE
HECATOMB	KEELHAUL	MELANITE	NEOMYCIN	PENZANCE	RECOVERY	REPAYING
HECKLING	KEENNESS	MELANOMA	NEOPHYTE	PEPERONI	RECREATE	REPEATED
HEDGEHOG	KEEPSAKE	MELCHIOR	NEPALESE	PERACUTE	RECRUITS	REPEATER
HEDGEROW	KENTUCKY	MELEAGER	NEPENTHE	PERCEIVE	RECUSANT	REPHRASE
HEDONISM	KERCHIEF	MELTDOWN	NEPHRITE	PERCEVAL	REDACTOR	REPLEVIN
HEDONIST	KERMESSE	MEMBRANE	NEPIONIC	PERCIVAL	REDBRICK	REPORTED
HEEDLESS	KEROSENE	MEMORIAL	NEPOTISM	PERFECTA	REDEEMER	REPORTER
HEELBALL	KESTEVEN	MEMORIAM	NESCIENT	PERFECTO	REDEFINE	REPOUSSÉ
HEELTAPS	KEYBOARD	MEMORIZE	NESTLING	PERFORCE	REDEPLOY	REPRIEVE
HEGEMONY	KEYSTONE	MEMSAHIB	NEURITIS	PERFUMED	REDESIGN	REPRISAL
HEIGHTEN	LEACHING	MENACING	NEUROSIS	PERIANTH	REDIRECT	REPROACH
HEIRLESS	LEADSMAN	MENANDER	NEUROTIC	PERICARP	REDLIGHT	REPUBLIC
HEIRLOOM	LEAFLESS	MENELAUS	NEUTRINO	PERICLES	REDOLENT	REQUIRED
HELIPORT	LEAPFROG	MENHADEN	NEWCOMER	PERIDERM	REDOUBLE	RESEARCH
HELLADIC	LEARNING	MENISCUS	NEWFOUND	PERILOUS	REDSHANK	RESEMBLE
HELLBENT	LEATHERY	MENSURAL	NEWHAVEN	PERILUNE	REDSHIFT	RESERVED
HELLENIC	LEAVENED	MENSWEAR	NEWSCAST	PERIODIC	REDSTART	RESETTLE
HELLFIRE	LEAVINGS	MENTALLY	NEWSHAWK	PERIPETY	REEDLING	RESIDENT
HELMETED	LEBANESE	MERCALLI	NEWSPEAK	PERISHED	REEDSMAN	RESIDUAL
HELMSMAN	LECITHIN	MERCATOR	NEWSREEL	PERISHER	REEMPLOY	RESIDUUM
HELPLESS	LECTRICE	MERCEDES	NEWSROOM	PERJURED	REFERRAL	RESIGNED
HELPLINE	LECTURER	MERCHANT	OEDIPEAN	PERJURER	REFINERY	RESINOUS
HELPMATE	LECTURES	MERCIFUL	OEILLADE	PERMEATE	REFORMED	RESISTOR
HELSINKI	LEFTHAND	MEREDITH	OENOLOGY	PEROXIDE	REFORMER	RESOLUTE
HELVETIA	LEFTOVER	MERIDIAN	OENOPHIL	PERSHING	REFRINGE	RESOLVED
HEMIPODE	LEFTWARD	MERINGUE	PEACEFUL	PERSONAL	REFUGIUM	RESONANT
HENCHMAN	LEFTWING	MERISTEM	PEARLING	PERSPIRE	REGAINED	RESONATE
HENEQUEN	LEGALISM	MESCALIN	PEARMAIN	PERSUADE	REGICIDE	RESOURCE
HENHOUSE	LEGALITY	MESMERIC	PECORINO	PERSUANT	REGIMENT	RESPECTS
HEPATICA	LEGALIZE	MESODERM	PECTORAL	PERTNESS	REGIONAL	RESPIGHI
HEPTAGON	LEGATION	MESOLITE	PECULATE	PERUVIAN	REGISTER	RESPONSE
HEPTARCH	LEGGINGS	MESOZOIC	PECULIAR	PERVERSE	REGISTRY	RESTLESS
HERACLES	LEINSTER	MESSAGER	PEDAGOGY	PERVIOUS	REGULATE	RESTORER
HERACLID	LEISURED	MESSIDOR	PEDANTIC	PETANQUE	REHEARSE	RESTRAIN
HERALDIC	LEMONADE	MESSMATE	PEDANTRY	PETERLOO	REIGNING	RESTRICT
HERALDRY	LENGTHEN	MESSUAGE	PEDDLING	PETITION	REINDEER	RESTROOM
HERCULES	LENIENCY	METABOLA	PEDERAST	PETRARCH	REINSURE	RETAILER
HERDSMAN	LEONARDO	MÉTAIRIE	PEDESTAL	PETULANT	REINVEST	RETAINER
HEREDITY	LEONIDAS	METALLED	PEDICURE	PEVENSEY	REJOINED	RETARDED
HEREFORD	LETHARGY	METALLIC	PEDIGREE	REACTION	REKINDLE	RETICENT
HEREWARD	LETTERED	METAPHOR	PEDIMENT	REACTIVE	RELATING	RETICULE
HEREWITH	LEUKEMIA	METEORIC	PEDUNCLE	READABLE	RELATION	RETIRING
HERITAGE	LEVELLER	METHANOL	PEEKABOO	READIEST	RELATIVE	RETRENCH
HERMETIC	LEVERAGE	METHODIC	PEELINGS	READJUST	RELAXING	RETRIEVE
HERMIONE	LEVITATE	METONYMY	PEEPHOLE	REAFFIRM	RELAYING	REUSABLE
HERPETIC	LEWDNESS	METRICAL	PEEPSHOW	REALTIME	RELEASED	REVANCHE
HERSCHEL	LEWISITE	METRITIS	PEERLESS	REAPPEAR	RELEGATE	REVEALED
HESITANT	MEALTIME	MEUNIÈRE	PEIGNOIR	REARMOST	RELEVANT	REVEILLE
HESITATE	MEALYBUG	NEARNESS	PEKINESE	REARWARD	RELIABLE	REVELLER
HETAIRIA	MEANNESS	NEATHERD	PELAGIUS	REASONED	RELIABLY	REVEREND
HEXAGRAM	MEANTIME	NEATNESS	PELLAGRA	REASSERT	RELIANCE	REVERENT
HEYTHROP	MEASURED	NEBRASKA	PELLETED	REASSESS	RELIEVED	REVERSAL

REVERSED	SENTINEL	TERATOMA	WETLANDS	CHAMPION	CHORDATA	SHERLOCK
REVIEWER	SEPARATE	TERIYAKI	XENOGAMY	CHANCERY	CHORDATE	SHERWOOD
REVISION	SEQUENCE	TERMINAL	XENOLITH	CHANDLER	CHORIAMB	SHETLAND
REVIVIFY	SERAFILE	TERMINUS	XENOPHON	CHANGING	CHRISTEN	SHIELING
REVIVING	SERAGLIO	TERRACED	XERAPHIM	CHANTAGE	CHRISTIE	SHIFTING
REVOLVER	SERAPHIC	TERRAPIN	YEARBOOK	CHANTREY	CHRISTOM	SHIGELLA
REYNOLDS	SERAPHIM	TERRIBLE	YEARLING	CHAPATTI	CHROMITE	SHIITAKE
SEABOARD	SERENADE	TERRIBLY	YEARLONG	CHAPERON	CHROMIUM	SHILLING
SEABORNE	SERENATA	TERRIFIC	YEARNING	CHAPLAIN	CHUMMAGE	SHINBONE
SEAFARER	SERENELY	TERTIARY	YEOMANRY	CHARCOAL	CHURLISH	SHINGLES
SEAFLOOR	SERENITY	TERYLENE	YERSINIA	CHARGING	CHUTZPAH	SHIPMATE
SEAFORTH	SERGEANT	TESTATOR	ZEDEKIAH	CHARISMA	GHANAIAN	SHIPMENT
SEAFRONT	SERIATIM	TESTATUM	ZEPHYRUS	CHARLADY	GHOULISH	SHIPPING
SEAGOING	SERJEANT	TESTICLE	ZEPPELIN	CHARLOCK	KHARTOUM	SHIPWORM
SEALSKIN	SEROLOGY	TETCHILY	AFFECTED	CHARMING	PHALANGE	SHIPYARD
SEALYHAM	SEROTYPE	TETRAGON	AFFERENT	CHARTISM	PHALGUNA	SHIVERED
SEAMLESS	SERRATED	TETRAPOD	AFFINITY	CHARTIST	PHANTASM	SHOCKING
SEAMSTER	SERVICES	TETRARCH	AFFLATUS	CHARTRES	PHARISEE	SHODDILY
SEAPLANE	SERVIENT	TEUTONIC	AFFLUENT	CHASSEUR	PHARMACY	SHOEBILL
SEARCHER	SERVITOR	TEXTBOOK	AFFUSION	CHASTISE	PHEASANT	SHOEHORN
SEASCAPE	SEVERELY	TEXTURED	EFFERENT	CHASTITY	PHENOLIC	SHOELACE
SEASHELL	SEVEREST	VEGETATE	EFFICACY	CHASUBLE	PHILEMON	SHOELESS
SEASHORE	SEVERITY	VEHEMENT	EFFLUENT	CHATTELS	PHILIPPI	SHOETREE
SEASONAL	SEWERAGE	VELLEITY	EFFLUVIA	CHEATERS	PHILLIPS	SHOOTING
SEASONED	SEXOLOGY	VELOCITY	EFFUSION	CHEATING	PHILOMEL	SHOOTOUT
SEAWARDS	SEXUALLY	VENALITY	EFFUSIVE	CHECKERS	PHLEGMON	SHOPPING
SECLUDED	TEACHERS	VENDETTA	OFFBREAK	CHECKING	PHONETIC	SHOPTALK
SECONDER	TEACHING	VENERATE	OFFCOLOR	CHECKOUT	PHORMIUM	SHORTAGE
SECONDLY	TEACLOTH	VENEREAL	OFFENDED	CHEEKILY	PHOSGENE	SHOULDER
SECRETLY	TEAKWOOD	VENETIAN	OFFENDER	CHEERFUL	PHOTOFIT	SHOUTING
SECURELY	TEAMMATE	VENGEFUL	OFFERING	CHEERILY	PHOTOPSY	SHOWBOAT
SECURITY	TEAMSTER	VENOMOUS	OFFICERS	CHEERING	PHREATIC	SHOWCASE
SEDATELY	TEAMWORK	VENTURED	OFFICIAL	CHEMICAL	PHRYGIAN	SHOWDOWN
SEDATION	TEARABLE	VERACITY	OFFPRINT	CHENILLE	PHTHISIC	SHOWGIRL
SEDATIVE	TEARAWAY	VERANDAH	OFFSHOOT	CHEQUERS	PHTHISIS	SHOWROOM
SEDIMENT	TEARDROP	VERBALLY	OFFSHORE	CHEROKEE	PHYLLOME	SHRAPNEL
SEDITION	TEASPOON	VERBATIM	OFFSIDER	CHERUBIC	PHYSALIA	SHREDDER
SEDULOUS	TECTONIC	VERBIAGE	OFFSTAGE	CHERUBIM	PHYSICAL	SHREWDLY
SEEDLESS	TEENAGER	VERDERER	AGACERIE	CHERWELL	PHYSIQUE	SHREWISH
SEEDLING	TEESHIRT	VERJUICE	AGGRIEVE	CHESHIRE	RHAPSODY	SHROUDED
SEEDSMAN	TEETHING	VERLAINE	AGITATED	CHESSMAN	RHEOSTAT	SHRUNKEN
SEETHING	TEETOTAL	VERMOUTH	AGITATOR	CHESSMEN	RHETORIC	SHUTDOWN
SEIGNIOR	TEFILLIN	VERONESE	AGITPROP	CHESTNUT	RHOMBOID	SHUTTERS
SELASSIE	TEGUMENT	VERONICA	AGNATION	CHEVIOTS	RHONCHUS	THAILAND
SELBORNE	TELECAST	VERSICLE	AGNOSTIC	CHEYENNE	RHYTHMIC	THALAMUS
SELECTED	TELECOMS	VERTEBRA	AGONIZED	CHIASMUS	SHABBILY	THALLIUM
SELECTOR	TELEFILM	VERTICAL	AGRARIAN	CHICHEWA	SHACKLES	THANATOS
SELENITE	TELEGONY	VESPERAL	AGREEING	CHICKENS	SHADRACH	THANKFUL
SELENIUM	TELEGRAM	VESPUCCI	AGRICOLA	CHICKPEA	SHAGBARK	THATAWAY
SELEUCID	TELEMARK	VESTIARY	AGRIMONY	CHILDERS	SHAGREEN	THATCHED
SELFHELP	TELETHON	VESTMENT	AGRONOMY	CHILDISH	SHAKEOUT	THATCHER
SELFLESS	TELEVISE	VESUVIUS	EGGPLANT	CHILDREN	SHALLOWS	THEATRIC
SELFMADE	TELLTALE	VEXATION	EGGSHELL	CHILIAST	SHAMBLES	THEBAINE
SELFPITY	TELLURIC	VEXILLUM	EGGTIMER	CHILLADA	SHAMEFUL	THEMATIC
SELFSAME	TEMERITY	WEAKFISH	EGOISTIC	CHILLING	SHAMROCK	THEOCRAT
SELVEDGE	TEMPERED	WEAKLING	EGOMANIA	CHILTERN	SHANGAAN	THEOLOGY
SEMESTER	TEMPLATE	WEAKNESS	EGYPTIAN	CHIMAERA	SHANGHAI	THEORIST
SEMINARY	TEMPORAL	WEAPONRY	IGNITION	CHINAMAN	SHANTUNG	THEORIZE
SEMIOTIC	TEMPTING	WEARABLE	IGNOMINY	CHINDITS	SHAREOUT	THESPIAN
SEMITONE	TENACITY	WEDGWOOD	IGNORANT	CHIPMUNK	SHAVUOTH	THIAMINE
SEMOLINA	TENDENCY	WEIGHING	UGLINESS	CHITCHAT	SHEARMAN	THICKSET
SENGREEN	TENDERLY	WELLBRED	CHACONNE	CHIVALRY	SHEEPDOG	THIEVERY
SENILITY	TENEBRAE	WELLNIGH	CHADBAND	CHLORATE	SHEEPISH	THIEVING
SENORITA	TENEBRIO	WELLPAID	CHAINSAW	CHLORIDE	SHEIKDOM	THIEVISH
SENSIBLE	TENEMENT	WELSHMAN	CHAIRMAN	CHLORINE	SHELDUCK	THINGAMY
SENSIBLY	TENESMUS	WEREWOLF	CHALDEAN	CHOIRBOY	SHELVING	THINKING
SENSUOUS	TENNYSON	WESLEYAN	CHALDRON	CHOLERIC	SHEPHERD	THINNESS
SENTENCE	TENTACLE	WESTERLY	CHAMBERS	CHOOSING	SHERATON	THINNING
SENTIENT	TEQUILLA	WESTWARD	CHAMPERS	CHOPPING	SHERIDAN	THIOUREA

THIRTEEN	BICUSPID	DICYCLIC	DISRAELI	FISHWIFE	KINGSTON	MIDFIELD
THOLEPIN	BIENNIAL	DIDACTIC	DISSOLVE	FISSIPED	KINKAJOU	MIDLANDS
THOMPSON	BIFOCALS	DIDDICOY	DISSUADE	FITFULLY	KINSFOLK	MIDNIGHT
THORACIC	BIGAMIST	DIEHARDS	DISTANCE	FIXATION	KINSHASA	MIDPOINT
THOROUGH	BIGAMOUS	DIELDRIN	DISTASTE	FIXATIVE	KIPPERED	MIGHTILY
THOUGHTS	BIGARADE	DIERESIS	DISTINCT	GIACONDA	KITEMARK	MIGNONNE
THOUSAND	BIGNONIA	DIFFRACT	DISTRACT	GIANTESS	LIBATION	MIGRAINE
THRACIAN	BILBERRY	DIGGINGS	DISTRAIN	GIGABYTE	LIBELOUS	MILANESE
THRALDOM	BILLFOLD	DIGITIZE	DISTRAIT	GIGANTIC	LIBERATE	MILDEWED
THRASHER	BILLHOOK	DIGIZINE	DISTRESS	GIGAWATT	LIBERIAN	MILDNESS
THREATEN	BILLYBOY	DILATION	DISTRICT	GIGLAMPS	LIBRETTO	MILITANT
THRENODY	BILLYCAN	DILATORY	DISTRUST	GIMCRACK	LICENSED	MILITARY
THRESHER	BILOBATE	DILIGENT	DISUNION	GINGERLY	LICENSEE	MILITATE
THRILLER	BINDWEED	DILUTION	DISUNITE	GINGIVAL	LICORICE	MILKLESS
THROMBIN	BINNACLE	DIMINISH	DISUNITY	GIOCONDA	LIEGEMAN	MILKMAID
THROMBUS	BINOMIAL	DINGBATS	DIURETIC	GIOVANNI	LIENTERY	MILKWEED
THROTTLE	BIOGRAPH	DINOSAUR	DIVIDEND	GIRASOLE	LIFEBELT	MILKWORT
THRUSTER	BIOMETRY	DIOCESAN	DIVIDERS	GIRLHOOD	LIFEBOAT	MILLIBAR
THUMPING	BIOSCOPE	DIOGENES	DIVINITY	GIRONDIN	LIFEBUOY	MILLINER
THUNDERY	BIRDCAGE	DIONYSUS	DIVISION	GIVEAWAY	LIFELESS	MILLIONS
THURIBLE	BIRDSEED	DIOPTRIC	DIVISIVE	HIAWATHA	LIFELIKE	MILLPOND
THURIFER	BIRTHDAY	DIPHENYL	DIVORCED	HIBERNIA	LIFELINE	MILLRACE
THURSDAY	BISCAYAN	DIPLOMAT	DIVORCEE	HIBISCUS	LIFELONG	MINAMATA
WHACKING	BISEXUAL	DIPSTICK	EIDECTIC	HICCOUGH	LIFESPAN	MINATORY
WHARFAGE	BISMARCK	DIPTERAL	EIGHTEEN	HIDEAWAY	LIFETIME	MINCEPIE
WHATEVER	BITTERLY	DIRECTLY	EINSTEIN	HIDROSIS	LIGAMENT	MINDANAO
WHEATEAR	CIBORIUM	DIRECTOR	FIBROSIS	HIERARCH	LIGATURE	MINDLESS
WHEEZILY	CICATRIX	DISABLED	FIDDLING	HIERATIC	LIGHTING	MINEHEAD
WHEEZING	CICERONE	DISABUSE	FIDELITY	HIGHBALL	LIGNEOUS	MINIMIZE
WHENEVER	CICISBEO	DISAGREE	FIDUCIAL	HIGHBORN	LIKEABLE	MINISTER
WHEREVER	CILIATED	DISALLOW	FIELDING	HIGHBROW	LIKENESS	MINISTRY
WHIMBREL	CINCHONA	DISARRAY	FIENDISH	HIGHGATE	LIKEWISE	MINORESS
WHINCHAT	CINERAMA	DISASTER	FIERCELY	HIGHLAND	LILONGWE	MINORITE
WHIPCORD	CINEREAL	DISBURSE	FIFTIETH	HIGHNESS	LIMACINE	MINORITY
WHIPHAND	CINGULUM	DISCIPLE	FIGHTING	HIGHRISE	LIMBLESS	MINOTAUR
WHIPJACK	CINNABAR	DISCLAIM	FIGURINE	HIGHROAD	LIMERICK	MINSTREL
WHIPLASH	CINNAMON	DISCLOSE	FILAMENT	HIJACKER	LIMITING	MINUTELY
WHIPPING	CIRCINUS	DISCOLOR	FILARIUM	HILARITY	LIMONITE	MINUTIAE
WHIRLING	CIRCUITY	DISCOUNT	FILENAME	HILLSIDE	LIMPNESS	MIREPOIX
WHISKERS	CIRCULAR	DISCOVER	FILIGREE	HINDMOST	LINCHPIN	MIRLITON
WHISKERY	CISTERNA	DISCREET	FILIPINO	HINDUISM	LINCOLNS	MIRRORED
WHISTLER	CITATION	DISCRETE	FILTHILY	HINDWARD	LINESMAN	MIRTHFUL
WHITECAP	CIVILIAN	DISEASED	FILTRATE	HIPSTERS	LINGERIE	MISAPPLY
WHITEHOT	CIVILITY	DISFAVOR	FINALIST	HIRAGANA	LINGUIST	MISCARRY
WHITENER	CIVILIZE	DISGORGE	FINALITY	HIRELING	LINIMENT	MISCHIEF
WHITLING	DIABETES	DISGRACE	FINALIZE	HISPANIC	LINNAEAN	MISCOUNT
WHODUNIT	DIABETIC	DISGUISE	FINDINGS	HISTORIC	LINNAEUS	MISERERE
WHOOPING	DIABOLIC	DISHEVEL	FINESPUN	HITHERTO	LINOLEUM	MISGUIDE
WHOPPING	DIAGNOSE	DISHONOR	FINISHED	JIGGERED	LINOTYPE	MISHMASH
AIGRETTE	DIAGONAL	DISINTER	FINISHER	JIMCRACK	LIPSTICK	MISJUDGE
AIGUILLE	DIALLING	DISJUNCT	FIREARMS	JINGOISM	LISTENER	MISMATCH
AIRBORNE	DIALOGUE	DISKETTE	FIREBACK	JINGOIST	LISTERIA	MISNOMER
AIRBRAKE	DIALYSIS	DISLIKED	FIREBALL	KIBITZER	LISTLESS	MISOGYNY
AIRCRAFT	DIAMANTE	DISLODGE	FIREBIRD	KICKBACK	LITERACY	MISPLACE
AIREDALE	DIAMETER	DISLOYAL	FIREBOLT	KICKSHAW	LITERARY	MISPRINT
AIRFIELD	DIAMONDS	DISMALLY	FIREDAMP	KIDGLOVE	LITERATE	MISQUOTE
AIRINESS	DIANTHUS	DISMAYED	FIRESIDE	KILKENNY	LITERATI	MISSOURI
AIRLINER	DIAPASON	DISMOUNT	FIRESTEP	KILLDEER	LITIGANT	MISSPELL
AIRPLANE	DIAPHONE	DISORDER	FIRETRAP	KILOBYTE	LITIGATE	MISSPENT
AIRSCREW	DIARESIS	DISPATCH	FIREWEED	KILOGRAM	LITTORAL	MISTAKEN
AIRSPEED	DIARRHEA	DISPENSE	FIREWOOD	KILOVOLT	LIVELONG	MISTREAT
AIRSTRIP	DIASPORA	DISPERSE	FIREWORK	KILOWATT	LIVERIED	MISTRESS
AIRTIGHT	DIASTASE	DISPIRIT	FIRMNESS	KINDLING	LIVERISH	MISTRUST
AIRWAVES	DIASTOLE	DISPLACE	FIRMWARE	KINDNESS	LIVEWARE	MITIGATE
BIANNUAL	DIATONIC	DISPOSAL	FISHBONE	KINETICS	LIVIDITY	NIBELUNG
BIATHLON	DIATRIBE	DISPOSED	FISHCAKE	KINGPOST	MICHIGAN	NICENESS
BIBLICAL	DIAZEPAM	DISPROVE	FISHHOOK	KINGSHIP	MICRODOT	NICHOLAS
BIBULOUS	DICTATES	DISPUTED	FISHMEAL	KINGSIZE	MIDBRAIN	NICKNACK
BICONVEX	DICTATOR	DISQUIET	FISHPOND	KINGSLEY	MIDDLING	NICKNAME

NICOTINE	RICKSHAW	SINGSONG	VIPERISH	DJELLABA	ALLURING	CLASSICS
NIDATION	RICOCHET	SINGULAR	VIPEROUS	DJIBOUTI	ALLUSION	CLASSIFY
NIGERIAN	RIDDANCE	SINISTER	VIREMENT	EJECTION	ALLUSIVE	CLAUDIUS
NIGERIEN	RIDGEWAY	SINKHOLE	VIRGINAL	AKKADIAN	ALLUVIAL	CLAVECIN
NIGGLING	RIDICULE	SIRENIAN	VIRGINIA	OKLAHOMA	ALLUVIUM	CLAVICLE
NIGHTCAP	RIESLING	SISTERLY	VIRILITY	SKELETAL	ALMIGHTY	CLAWBACK
NIGHTJAR	RIFFRAFF	SISYPHUS	VIROLOGY	SKELETON	ALOPECIA	CLAYMORE
NIHILISM	RIFLEMAN	SITTELLA	VIRTUOSI	SKEWBALD	ALPHABET	CLEANERS
NIHILIST	RIGATONI	SITUATED	VIRTUOSO	SKIBOOTS	ALPINIST	CLEANING
NIJINSKY	RIGHTFUL	SIXPENCE	VIRTUOUS	SKIDDING	ALSATIAN	CLEANSED
NINEPINS	RIGHTIST	SIXTIETH	VIRULENT	SKILLFUL	ALTHOUGH	CLEANSER
NINETEEN	RIGIDITY	SIZEABLE	VISCERAL	SKILLING	ALTITUDE	CLEARCUT
NITROGEN	RIGOROUS	SIZZLING	VISCOUNT	SKILLION	ALTRUISM	CLEARING
OILCLOTH	RINGDOVE	TIBERIAS	VISELIKE	SKINDEEP	ALTRUIST	CLEARWAY
OILFIELD	RINGHALS	TIBERIUS	VISIGOTH	SKINHEAD	ALUMINUM	CLEAVAGE
OILINESS	RINGSIDE	TICKLING	VISITANT	SKINWORK	ALVEOLUS	CLEAVERS
OILSKINS	RINGTAIL	TICKLISH	VISITING	SKIPJACK	BLACKBOY	CLEMATIS
OILSLICK	RINGWALL	TICKSEED	VISUALLY	SKIPPING	BLACKCAP	CLEMENCY
OINTMENT	RINGWORM	TICKTACK	VITALISM	SKIRMISH	BLACKFLY	CLERICAL
PICAROON	RIPARIAN	TICKTOCK	VITALITY	SKIRTING	BLACKING	CLERIHEW
PICKINGS	RIPENESS	TIDEMARK	VITALIZE	SKITTISH	BLACKISH	CLEVERLY
PICKLOCK	RIPPLING	TIDINESS	VITAMINS	SKITTLES	BLACKLEG	CLIFFORD
PICKMEUP	RISSOLES	TIEBREAK	VITELLUS	SKULKING	BLACKOUT	CLIMATIC
PICKWICK	RITUALLY	TIGHTWAD	VITILIGO	SKULLCAP	BLANDISH	CLIMBING
PICTURES	RIVALISE	TIMBERED	VITREOUS	SKYLIGHT	BLASTOFF	CLINCHER
PIDDLING	RIVERAIN	TIMELESS	VIVACITY	SKYPILOT	BLASTULA	CLINGING
PIECHART	RIVERINE	TIMIDITY	VIVARIUM	ALACRITY	BLEACHER	CLINICAL
PIECRUST	RIVETING	TIMOROUS	WICKEDLY	ALARMING	BLEEDING	CLINKERS
PIERCING	SIBERIAN	TINCTURE	WIDENING	ALARMIST	BLENDING	CLIPPERS
PIERETTE	SIBILANT	TINGLING	WILDFELL	ALBACORE	BLENHEIM	CLIPPING
PIERIDES	SICILIAN	TINNITUS	WILDFIRE	ALBANIAN	BLESSING	CLIQUISH
PIGSWILL	SICKLIST	TINSELLY	WILDFOWL	ALBERICH	BLIGHTER	CLITORIS
PILASTER	SICKNESS	TINSMITH	WILDLIFE	ALBINONI	BLINDING	CLIVEDEN
PILCHARD	SICKROOM	TINTAGEL	WILDNESS	ALBURNUM	BLINKERS	CLODPOLL
PILFERER	SIDEKICK	TIPSTAFF	WILFULLY	ALCATRAZ	BLINKING	CLOISTER
PILGRIMS	SIDELINE	TIRAMISU	WILINESS	ALCESTIS	BLISSFUL	CLOTHIER
PILLAGER	SIDELONG	TIRELESS	WILLIAMS	ALCHEMIC	BLITHELY	CLOTHING
PILLARED	SIDEREAL	TIRESIAS	WINDBURN	ALDEHYDE	BLIZZARD	CLOWNISH
PILOTAGE	SIDERITE	TIRESOME	WINDFALL	ALDERMAN	BLOCKADE	CLUBBING
PILSENER	SIDESHOW	TITANESS	WINDGALL	ALDERNEY	BLOCKAGE	CLUBFOOT
PILTDOWN	SIDESLIP	TITANISM	WINDHOEK	ALEATORY	BLOOMERS	CLUELESS
PIMIENTO	SIDESMAN	TITANITE	WINDINGS	ALEHOUSE	BLOOMING	CLUMSILY
PINAFORE	SIDESTEP	TITANIUM	WINDLASS	ALEMAINE	BLOTCHED	ELDORADO
PINDARIC	SIDEWALK	TITICACA	WINDLESS	ALEUTIAN	BLOWFISH	ELDRITCH
PINEWOOD	SIDEWARD	TITIVATE	WINDMILL	ALFRESCO	BLOWHOLE	ELECTION
PINNACLE	SIDEWAYS	TITMOUSE	WINDPIPE	ALGERIAN	BLOWLAMP	ELECTIVE
PINNIPED	SIGHTING	VIATICUM	WINDSOCK	ALGERINE	BLOWPIPE	ELECTORS
PINOCHLE	SIGHTSEE	VIBRANCY	WINDWARD	ALGOLOGY	BLUDGEON	ELECTRIC
PINPOINT	SIGNALER	VIBRATOR	WINGLESS	ALGORISM	BLUEBACK	ELECTRON
PINPRICK	SIGNALLY	VIBURNUM	WINGSPAN	ALHAMBRA	BLUEBELL	ELECTRUM
PINTABLE	SIGNORIA	VICARAGE	WINIFRED	ALICANTE	BLUECOAT	ELEGANCE
PINWHEEL	SIGNPOST	VICARIAL	WINNINGS	ALIENATE	BLUENOSE	ELEMENTS
PIPELINE	SILENCER	VICINITY	WINNIPEG	ALIENISM	BLURRING	ELEPHANT
PIPERINE	SILENTLY	VICTORIA	WIRELESS	ALIENIST	BLUSHING	ELEVATED
PIQUANCY	SILESIAN	VICTUALS	WIREWORM	ALIQUANT	BLUSTERY	ELEVATOR
PIRANESI	SILICATE	VIETCONG	WISEACRE	ALKALIFY	CLADDING	ELEVENTH
PIROZHKI	SILICONE	VIGILANT	WISHBONE	ALKALINE	CLAIMANT	ELIGIBLE
PISCATOR	SILICULA	VIGNETTE	WISTERIA	ALKALOID	CLAMBAKE	ELKHOUND
PISIFORM	SILKTAIL	VIGOROUS	WITCHERY	ALLEGORY	CLANGING	ELLIPSIS
PISSHEAD	SILKWORM	VILENESS	WITCHING	ALLELUIA	CLANGOUR	ELLIPTIC
PITCAIRN	SILOXANE	VILLAGER	WITHDRAW	ALLERGEN	CLANNISH	ELONGATE
PITHLESS	SILURIAN	VILLAINY	WITHERED	ALLERGIC	CLANSMAN	ELOQUENT
PITIABLE	SIMONIAC	VINCIBLE	WITHHOLD	ALLEYWAY	CLAPPERS	ELSINORE
PITILESS	SIMPLIFY	VINCULUM	WIZARDRY	ALLIANCE	CLAPPING	FLAGGING
PITTANCE	SIMULATE	VINDALOO	YIELDING	ALLOCATE	CLAPTRAP	FLAGPOLE
PIZZERIA	SINAPISM	VINEGARY	ZIBELINE	ALLOGAMY	CLARENCE	FLAGRANT
RIBALDRY	SINCLAIR	VINEYARD	ZIGGURAT	ALLOPATH	CLARINET	FLAGSHIP
RIBSTONE	SINECURE	VIOLATOR	ZIMBABWE	ALLOWING	CLASHING	FLAMENCO
RICHNESS	SINFONIA	VIOLENCE	ZIRCONIA	ALLSPICE	CLASPING	FLAMEOUT

FLAMINGO	GLOBULAR	PLIMSOLL	AMMONIAC	IMPOLITE	ANNAMITE	ENTHRONE
FLANDERS	GLOBULIN	PLIOCENE	AMMONITE	IMPORTER	ANNEALER	ENTICING
FLANNELS	GLOOMILY	PLOTINUS	AMMONOID	IMPOSING	ANNELIDA	ENTIRELY
FLAPJACK	GLORIANA	PLOUGHED	AMORETTI	IMPOSTER	ANNOTATE	ENTIRETY
FLAPPING	GLORIOLE	PLUCKILY	AMORETTO	IMPOSTOR	ANNOUNCE	ENTITLED
FLASHGUN	GLORIOUS	PLUCKING	AMORTIZE	IMPOTENT	ANNOYING	ENTRAILS
FLASHILY	GLOSSARY	PLUGHOLE	AMPERAGE	IMPRISON	ANNUALLY	ENTRANCE
FLASHING	GLOSSEME	PLUMBAGO	AMPUTATE	IMPROPER	ANOREXIA	ENTREATY
FLATBOAT	GLOXINIA	PLUMBING	AMRITSAR	IMPROVED	ANOREXIC	ENTRENCH
FLATFISH	GLUMPISH	PLUNGING	AMUNDSEN	IMPROVER	ANSERINE	ENTREPOT
FLATFOOT	GLUTAEUS	PLUTARCH	AMUSETTE	IMPUDENT	ANTECEDE	ENTRYISM
FLATMATE	GLUTTONY	PLYMOUTH	AMYGDALA	IMPUNITY	ANTEDATE	ENVELOPE
FLATPICK	GLYCERIN	SLANGING	EMACIATE	IMPURIFY	ANTELOPE	ENVIABLE
FLATTERY	GLYCOGEN	SLANTING	EMBATTLE	IMPURITY	ANTENNAE	ENVIRONS
FLATWARE	ILLFATED	SLAPBANG	EMBEDDED	OMDURMAN	ANTEPOST	ENVISAGE
FLATWORM	ILLINOIS	SLAPDASH	EMBEZZLE	OMELETTE	ANTERIOR	ENVISION
FLAUBERT	ILLUMINE	SLAPJACK	EMBITTER	OMISSION	ANTEROOM	GNASHING
FLAUTIST	ILLUSION	SLATTERN	EMBLAZON	OMNIFORM	ANTIBODY	INACTION
FLAVORED	ILLUSIVE	SLEEPERS	EMBODIED	OMNIVORE	ANTIDOTE	INACTIVE
FLAWLESS	ILLUSORY	SLEEPILY	EMBOLDEN	OMPHALOS	ANTIHERO	INASMUCH
FLAXSEED	KLONDIKE	SLEEPING	EMBOLISM	SMALLEST	ANTILLES	INCENSED
FLEABITE	OLDSTYLE	SLIGHTED	EMBOSSED	SMALLPOX	ANTILOPE	INCHOATE
FLEETING	OLDWORLD	SLIGHTLY	EMBRACED	SMARTEST	ANTIMERE	INCIDENT
FLEISHIG	OLEACEAE	SLIMNESS	EMBRACES	SMASHING	ANTIMONY	INCISION
FLEXIBLE	OLEANDER	SLIPOVER	EMERGENT	SMELTING	ANTIPHON	INCISIVE
FLEXIBLY	OLEASTER	SLIPPERS	EMERGING	SMIDGEON	ANTIPOPE	INCLINED
FLIMSILY	OLIGARCH	SLIPPERY	EMERITUS	SMOCKING	ANYPLACE	INCLUDED
FLINDERS	OLIPHANT	SLIPPING	EMERSION	SMOLLETT	ANYTHING	INCOMING
FLIPPANT	OLYMPIAD	SLIPSHOD	EMIGRANT	SMOOTHER	ANYWHERE	INCREASE
FLIPPERS	OLYMPIAN	SLIPSLOP	EMIGRATE	SMOOTHLY	ENCAENIA	INCUBATE
FLIPPING	OLYMPICS	SLOBBERY	EMINENCE	SMOULDER	ENCAMPED	INDEBTED
FLIRTING	PLACABLE	SLOPPILY	EMINENCY	SMUGGLED	ENCIRCLE	INDECENT
FLOATING	PLACEMAT	SLOTHFUL	EMIRATES	SMUGGLER	ENCLOSED	INDENTED
FLOGGING	PLACEMEN	SLOVAKIA	EMISSARY	SMUGNESS	ENCLOTHE	INDEXING
FLOODING	PLACENTA	SLOVENIA	EMISSION	UMBRELLA	ENCOMIUM	INDIAMAN
FLOODLIT	PLACIDLY	SLOVENLY	EMMANUEL	ANABASIS	ENCROACH	INDICANT
FLOORING	PLANCHET	SLOWDOWN	EMOTICON	ANABATIC	ENCUMBER	INDICATE
FLORENCE	PLANGENT	SLOWNESS	EMPHASIS	ANACONDA	ENDANGER	INDIGENT
FLOTILLA	PLANKING	SLOWPOKE	EMPHATIC	ANACREON	ENDEAVOR	INDIRECT
FLOUNCED	PLANKTON	SLOWWORM	EMPLOYED	ANAGLYPH	ENDOCARP	INDOLENT
FLOUNDER	PLANNING	SLUGABED	EMPLOYEE	ANALECTA	ENDODERM	INDUCIVE
FLOURISH	PLANTAIN	SLUGFEST	EMPLOYER	ANALEMMA	ENDOGAMY	INDUCTOR
FLUENTLY	PLASTRON	SLUGGARD	EMPORIUM	ANALOGUE	ENDURING	INDUSTRY
FLUIDITY	PLATANUS	SLUGGISH	EMPYREAL	ANALYSER	ENDYMION	INEDIBLE
FLUMMERY	PLATEFUL	SLUMMING	EMPYREAN	ANALYSIS	ENERGIZE	INEQUITY
FLUORIDE	PLATELET	SLURRING	EMULATOR	ANALYTIC	ENERVATE	INEXPERT
FLUORINE	PLATFORM	SLUTTISH	EMULGENT	ANAPAEST	ENFEEBLE	INFAMOUS
FLUORITE	PLATINUM	SLYBOOTS	EMULSIFY	ANAPHASE	ENFILADE	INFANTRY
FLUSHING	PLATONIC	ULCERATE	EMULSION	ANARCHIC	ENGAGING	INFECTED
FLYBLOWN	PLATYPUS	ULCEROUS	IMAGINED	ANATHEMA	ENGENDER	INFERIOR
FLYDRIVE	PLAUDITS	ULTERIOR	IMBECILE	ANATOLIA	ENGINEER	INFERNAL
FLYSHEET	PLAYBACK	ULTIMATE	IMITATOR	ANATOMIC	ENGRAVER	INFESTED
FLYWHEEL	PLAYBILL	AMANDINE	IMMANENT	ANCESTOR	ENIWETOK	INFINITE
GLABELLA	PLAYFAIR	AMARANTH	IMMANUEL	ANCESTRY	ENKINDLE	INFINITY
GLABROUS	PLAYGIRL	AMARETTO	IMMATURE	ANCHISES	ENLARGED	INFLAMED
GLADNESS	PLAYMATE	AMATEURS	IMMERSED	ANCHORET	ENLARGER	INFLATED
GLADSOME	PLAYROOM	AMBIANCE	IMMINENT	ANDERSON	ENMESHED	INFLIGHT
GLANCING	PLAYSUIT	AMBIENCE	IMMOBILE	ANDORRAN	ENORMITY	INFLUENT
GLANDERS	PLAYTIME	AMBITION	IMMODEST	ANDREWES	ENORMOUS	INFORMAL
GLASNOST	PLEADING	AMBROSIA	IMMOLATE	ANECDOTE	ENRICHED	INFORMED
GLASSFUL	PLEASANT	AMBULANT	IMMORTAL	ANEURYSM	ENSCONCE	INFORMER
GLAUCOMA	PLEASING	AMBULATE	IMMUNITY	ANGELICA	ENSEMBLE	INFRARED
GLAUCOUS	PLEASURE	AMBUSHED	IMMUNIZE	ANGLESEY	ENSHRINE	INFRINGE
GLEAMING	PLEBEIAN	AMERICAN	IMPACTED	ANGLICAN	ENSHROUD	INFUSION
GLEESOME	PLECTRUM	AMERICAS	IMPAIRED	ANGSTROM	ENSIFORM	INGROWTH
GLISSADE	PLEIADES	AMETHYST	IMPELLED	ANGUILLA	ENSILAGE	INGUINAL
GLOAMING	PLEONASM	AMICABLE	IMPERIAL	ANIMATED	ENTANGLE	INHALANT
GLOATING	PLETHORA	AMICABLY	IMPETIGO	ANISETTE	ENTHALPY	INHERENT
GLOBALLY	PLEURISY		IMPLICIT	ANNALIST	ENTHRALL	INHUMANE

INIMICAL	KNOCKERS	UNFADING	UNWONTED	COATRACK	COMPILER	CORIOLIS
INIQUITY	KNOCKING	UNFASTEN	UNWORTHY	COATTAIL	COMPLAIN	CORMORAN
INITIATE	KNOCKOUT	UNFETTER	AOTEAROA	COAUTHOR	COMPLETE	CORNETTO
INJECTOR	KNOTWEED	UNFILLED	BOADICEA	COBBLERS	COMPLINE	CORNHILL
INKSTAIN	KNOTWORK	UNFORCED	BOARDING	COBWEBBY	COMPOSED	CORNICHE
INNOCENT	MNEMONIC	UNFREEZE	BOASTFUL	COCACOLA	COMPOSER	CORNMEAL
INNOVATE	ONCOLOGY	UNGAINLY	BOASTING	COCCIDAE	COMPOUND	CORNWALL
INNUENDO	ONCOMING	UNGULATE	BOATBILL	COCHLEAR	COMPRESS	CORONARY
INOCULUM	ONESIDED	UNHARMED	BOATLOAD	COCKATOO	COMPRISE	CORONOID
INQUIRER	ONETRACK	UNHEATED	BOBBYPIN	COCKAYNE	COMPUTER	CORPORAL
INSANELY	ONLOOKER	UNHEROIC	BOBOLINK	COCKBOAT	CONCEIVE	CORRAGIO
INSANITY	ONSCREEN	UNHINGED	BODLEIAN	COCKCROW	CONCERTO	CORRIDOR
INSCRIBE	ONTOLOGY	UNICYCLE	BODYLINE	COCKEREL	CONCHOID	CORRODED
INSECURE	SNACKBAR	UNIFYING	BODYWORK	COCKEYED	CONCLAVE	CORSELET
INSIGNIA	SNAPPILY	UNIONISM	BOEOTIAN	COCKTAIL	CONCLUDE	CORSICAN
INSOLENT	SNAPSHOT	UNIONIST	BOGEYMAN	CODPIECE	CONCORDE	CORUNDUM
INSOMNIA	SNATCHER	UNIONIZE	BOHEMIAN	COERCION	CONCRETE	CORVETTE
INSPIRED	SNEAKERS	UNIPOLAR	BOLDNESS	COERCIVE	CONDENSE	COSINESS
INSPIRIT	SNEAKING	UNIQUELY	BOLIVIAN	COGITATE	CONFETTI	COSMETIC
INSTANCE	SNEERING	UNITEDLY	BOLLOCKS	COGNOMEN	CONFINED	COSTMARY
INSTINCT	SNEEZING	UNIVALVE	BOLTHOLE	COGWHEEL	CONFINES	COTOPAXI
INSTRUCT	SNIFFLER	UNIVERSE	BONDSMAN	COHERENT	CONFLATE	COTSWOLD
INSULATE	SNOBBERY	UNJUSTLY	BONEFISH	COHESION	CONFLICT	COTTAGER
INTAGLIO	SNOBBISH	UNKINDLY	BONEHEAD	COHESIVE	CONFOUND	COUCHANT
INTEGRAL	SNOOTILY	UNLAWFUL	BONELESS	COIFFEUR	CONFRONT	COUCHING
INTELSAT	SNORTING	UNLEADED	BONEYARD	COIFFURE	CONFUSED	COUGHING
INTENDED	SNOWBALL	UNLIKELY	BONHOMIE	COINCIDE	CONGRATS	COUNTESS
INTENTLY	SNOWDROP	UNLISTED	BONIFACE	COLANDER	CONGRESS	COUNTIES
INTERACT	SNOWFALL	UNLOADED	BONSPIEL	COLDBOOT	CONJUGAL	COUNTING
INTERCOM	SNOWLINE	UNLOCKED	BOOKABLE	COLDNESS	CONJURER	COUPERIN
INTEREST	SNUFFBOX	UNLOVELY	BOOKCASE	COLESLAW	CONJUROR	COUPLING
INTERIOR	UNABATED	UNMANNED	BOOKMARK	COLIFORM	CONQUEST	COURTESY
INTERMIT	UNAWARES	UNMARKED	BOOKROOM	COLISEUM	CONSERVE	COUSCOUS
INTERNAL	UNBEATEN	UNNERVED	BOOKSHOP	COLLAGEN	CONSIDER	COVALENT
INTERNEE	UNBIASED	UNPERSON	BOOKWORK	COLLAPSE	CONSOMMÉ	COVENANT
INTERNET	UNBIDDEN	UNPLACED	BOOKWORM	COLLARED	CONSPIRE	COVENTRY
INTERPOL	UNBROKEN	UNREASON	BOOTLESS	COLLATOR	CONSTANT	COVERAGE
INTERVAL	UNBURDEN	UNRIFLED	BOOTNECK	COLLECTS	CONSTRUE	COVERING
INTIFADA	UNBUTTON	UNSALTED	BORACITE	COLLEGES	CONSULAR	COVERLET
INTIMACY	UNCARING	UNSAVORY	BORDEAUX	COLLIERS	CONSUMED	COVETOUS
INTIMATE	UNCHASTE	UNSEALED	BORDELLO	COLLIERY	CONSUMER	COWARDLY
INTRADOS	UNCIFORM	UNSEEDED	BORDERER	COLLOQUY	CONTANGO	COWBERRY
INTRENCH	UNCLOVEN	UNSEEMLY	BORECOLE	COLOMBIA	CONTEMPT	COXSWAIN
INTREPID	UNCOMBED	UNSETTLE	BOREHOLE	COLONIAL	CONTENTS	COYSTRIL
INTRIGUE	UNCOMMON	UNSHAKEN	BORODINO	COLONIST	CONTINUE	COZINESS
INTRUDER	UNCOOKED	UNSIGNED	BORROWED	COLONIZE	CONTINUO	DOCILITY
INUNDATE	UNCOUPLE	UNSOCIAL	BORROWER	COLOPHON	CONTRACT	DOCKLAND
INVASION	UNCTUOUS	UNSOLVED	BORSTALL	COLORADO	CONTRARY	DOCKSIDE
INVASIVE	UNCURBED	UNSPOILT	BOSWORTH	COLORANT	CONTRAST	DOCKYARD
INVEIGLE	UNDERAGE	UNSPOKEN	BOTANIST	COLORFUL	CONTRITE	DOCTORAL
INVENTED	UNDERARM	UNSTABLE	BOTHERED	COLORING	CONTRIVE	DOCTORED
INVENTOR	UNDERBID	UNSTATED	BOTHWELL	COLOSSAL	CONTROLS	DOCTRINE
INVERTED	UNDERCUT	UNSTEADY	BOTSWANA	COLOSSUS	CONVENER	DOCUMENT
INVERTER	UNDERDOG	UNSUITED	BOTTLING	COLOURED	CONVERGE	DOGBERRY
INVESTOR	UNDERFED	UNTANGLE	BOTTOMRY	COLUMBAN	CONVERSE	DOGGEDLY
INVITING	UNDERFUR	UNTAPPED	BOTULISM	COLUMBUS	CONVEYOR	DOGGEREL
INVOLUTE	UNDERLAY	UNTHREAD	BOUFFANT	COMATOSE	CONVINCE	DOGHOUSE
INVOLVED	UNDERLIE	UNTIDILY	BOUNCING	COMBINED	CONVULSE	DOGMATIC
INWARDLY	UNDERPIN	UNTILLED	BOUNDARY	COMEBACK	COOKBOOK	DOGSBODY
KNACKERS	UNDERRUN	UNTIMELY	BOUTIQUE	COMEDIAN	COOKWARE	DOGSTAIL
KNAPSACK	UNDERSEA	UNTOWARD	BOUZOUKI	COMEDOWN	COOLNESS	DOGTOOTH
KNAPWEED	UNDERTOW	UNUNBIUM	BOWSPRIT	COMMANDO	COPULATE	DOGWATCH
KNEEDEEP	UNDULANT	UNUSABLE	COACHING	COMMENCE	COPYBOOK	DOLDRUMS
KNEEHIGH	UNDULATE	UNVARIED	COACHMAN	COMMERCE	COPYHOLD	DOLOMITE
KNICKERS	UNEARNED	UNVERSED	COALESCE	COMMONER	COQUETRY	DOLOROUS
KNIGHTLY	UNEASILY	UNVOICED	COALHOLE	COMMONLY	COQUETTE	DOMESDAY
KNITTING	UNENDING	UNWANTED	COALMINE	COMMUNAL	CORDOVAN	DOMESTIC
KNITWEAR	UNERRING	UNWEANED	COALPORT	COMMUTER	CORDUROY	DOMICILE
KNOBLESS	UNEVENLY	UNWIELDY	COARSELY	COMPARED	CORDWAIN	DOMINANT

DOMINATE	FOREFOOT	GOSSAMER	HOWDYEDO	LOVINGLY	MOREPORK	POIGNANT	
DOMINEER	FOREGONE	GOURMAND	HOWITZER	LOWCLASS	MORESQUE	POISONER	
DOMINION	FOREHAND	GOVERNOR	IOLANTHE	LOWERING	MORIBUND	POITIERS	
DOMINOES	FOREHEAD	HOARDING	JODHPURS	LOWLANDS	MOROCCAN	POKEWEED	
DONATION	FORELAND	HOARSELY	JOHANNES	LOWLYING	MOROSELY	POLARIZE	
DONATIST	FORELOCK	HOBBLING	JOHNSONS	LOYALIST	MORPHEME	POLISHED	
DOOLALLY	FOREMILK	HOGMANAY	JOINTURE	MOBILITY	MORPHEUS	POLISHER	
DOOMSDAY	FOREMOST	HOGSHEAD	JOKINGLY	MOBILIZE	MORPHINE	POLITELY	
DOORBELL	FORENAME	HOKKAIDO	JONATHAN	MOCCASIN	MORRISON	POLITICO	
DOORKNOB	FORENOON	HOLDFAST	JONCANOE	MODELING	MORTALLY	POLITICS	
DOORPOST	FORENSIC	HOLDINGS	JONGLEUR	MODELLER	MORTGAGE	POLLIWOG	
DOORSILL	FORESAIL	HOLIDAYS	JORROCKS	MODERATE	MORTIMER	POLLSTER	
DOORSTEP	FORESHIP	HOLINESS	JOTTINGS	MODERATO	MORTUARY	POLLUTED	
DOPAMINE	FORESKIN	HOLISTIC	JOVIALLY	MODESTLY	MOSQUITO	POLLUTER	
DORMOUSE	FORESTAY	HOLLOWAY	JOYFULLY	MODIFIER	MOTHBALL	POLONIUM	
DOTTEREL	FORESTER	HOLOCENE	JOYSTICK	MODULATE	MOTHERLY	POLTROON	
DOUBLETS	FORESTRY	HOLOGRAM	KOHLRABI	MOHAMMED	MOTIVATE	POLYANNA	
DOUBLOON	FORETELL	HOLOZOIC	KOLINSKY	MOISTURE	MOTORCAR	POLYARCH	
DOUBTFUL	FOREWARN	HOLYHEAD	KOMSOMOL	MOLASSES	MOTORING	POLYCARP	
DOUBTING	FOREWORD	HOLYROOD	KORRIGAN	MOLECULE	MOTORIST	POLYGAMY	
DOUGHBOY	FORFEITS	HOMELAND	KOURMISS	MOLEHILL	MOTORIZE	POLYGLOT	
DOUGHNUT	FORKLIFT	HOMELESS	KOUSKOUS	MOLESKIN	MOTORMAN	POLYGYNY	
DOVECOTE	FORKTAIL	HOMEMADE	LOADSTAR	MOLESTER	MOTORWAY	POLYMATH	
DOVETAIL	FORMALIN	HOMEPAGE	LOANWORD	MOLLUSCS	MOUFFLON	POLYSEME	
DOWNBEAT	FORMALLY	HOMESICK	LOATHING	MOLUCCAS	MOULDING	POLYSEMY	
DOWNCAST	FORMERLY	HOMESPUN	LOBBYIST	MOMENTUM	MOUNTAIN	POMANDER	
DOWNFALL	FORMLESS	HOMEWARD	LOBELINE	MONADISM	MOUNTING	PONSONBY	
DOWNHILL	FORMOSAN	HOMEWORK	LOBOTOMY	MONANDRY	MOURNFUL	PONTIFEX	
DOWNLOAD	FORMWORK	HOMICIDE	LOCALITY	MONARCHY	MOURNING	PONYTAIL	
DOWNPLAY	FORSAKEN	HONDURAN	LOCALIZE	MONASTIC	MOUSSAKA	POOLROOM	
DOWNPOUR	FORSLACK	HONDURAS	LOCATION	MONAURAL	MOUTHFUL	POORNESS	
DOWNSIDE	FORSOOTH	HONESTLY	LOCATIVE	MONDRIAN	MOVEABLE	POPINJAY	
DOWNSIZE	FORSWEAR	HONEYDEW	LOCKABLE	MONETARY	MOVEMENT	POPPADOM	
DOWNTOWN	FORTIETH	HONEYPOT	LOCOWEED	MONETISE	NOBELIUM	POPSICLE	
DOWNTURN	FORTRESS	HONGKONG	LODESTAR	MONEYBOX	NOBILITY	POPULACE	
DOWNWARD	FORTUITY	HONOLULU	LODGINGS	MONGOLIA	NOBLEMAN	POPULATE	
DOXOLOGY	FORWARDS	HONORARY	LOGISTIC	MONGOOSE	NOCTURNE	POPULIST	
EOHIPPUS	FOULNESS	HOODWINK	LOGOTYPE	MONICKER	NOISETTE	POPULOUS	
FOGBOUND	FOUNDING	HOOKWORM	LOITERER	MONKFISH	NOMARCHY	POROSITY	
FOGLIGHT	FOUNTAIN	HOOLIGAN	LOLLIPOP	MONMOUTH	NOMINATE	PORPHYRA	
FOLDEROL	FOURFOLD	HOPELESS	LOMBARDY	MONOACID	NOMOGRAM	PORPHYRY	
FOLKLORE	FOURPART	HOPFIELD	LONDONER	MONOGAMY	NONESUCH	PORPOISE	
FOLKSONG	FOURSOME	HORATIAN	LONESOME	MONOGRAM	NONSENSE	PORRIDGE	
FOLLICLE	FOURTEEN	HORATIUS	LONGBOAT	MONOGYNY	NONSTICK	PORTABLE	
FOLLOWED	FOXGLOVE	HORLICKS	LONGHAND	MONOHULL	NOONTIME	PORTHOLE	
FOLLOWER	FOXHOUND	HORMONAL	LONGHAUL	MONOLITH	NORMALLY	PORTIÈRE	
FOLLOWUP	GOALPOST	HORNBEAM	LONGHORN	MONOPOLE	NORMANDY	PORTLAND	
FONDLING	GOATSKIN	HORNBILL	LONGLAND	MONOPOLY	NORSEMAN	PORTRAIT	
FONDNESS	GOBSMACK	HORNBOOK	LONGSHIP	MONORAIL	NORSEMEN	PORTUGAL	
FOOLSCAP	GODCHILD	HORNFELS	LONGSTAY	MONOTONY	NORTHERN	POSEIDON	
FOOTBALL	GOIDELIC	HORNPIPE	LONGSTOP	MONOTYPE	NORTHING	POSITION	
FOOTFALL	GOLDFISH	HORNPOUT	LONGTERM	MONOXIDE	NOSEBAND	POSITIVE	
FOOTHOLD	GOLDMINE	HORNTAIL	LONGTIME	MONROVIA	NOSEDIVE	POSITRON	
FOOTLING	GOLFBALL	HOROLOGY	LONICERA	MONSTERA	NOSOLOGY	POSOLOGY	
FOOTNOTE	GOLFCLUB	HORRIBLE	LONSDALE	MONTCALM	NOSTRILS	POSSIBLE	
FOOTPATH	GOLGOTHA	HORRIBLY	LOOPHOLE	MONTEITH	NOSTROMO	POSSIBLY	
FOOTREST	GOLLIWOG	HORRIFIC	LOOSEBOX	MONUMENT	NOTARIAL	POSTCARD	
FOOTSORE	GONDWANA	HORSEBOX	LOPSIDED	MOONBEAM	NOTATION	POSTCODE	
FOOTSTEP	GONFALON	HORSEFLY	LORDOSIS	MOORCOCK	NOTEBOOK	POSTDATE	
FOOTWEAR	GOODNESS	HORSEMAN	LORDSHIP	MOORINGS	NOTECASE	POSTMARK	
FOOTWORK	GOODSIRE	HORSEMEN	LORRAINE	MOORLAND	NOTIONAL	POSTPAID	
FORCEFUL	GOODWIFE	HOSEPIPE	LOTHARIO	MOQUETTE	NOVELIST	POSTPONE	
FORCIBLE	GOODWILL	HOSPITAL	LOUDNESS	MORALIST	NOVEMBER	POTATOES	
FORCIBLY	GOODWOOD	HOSTELRY	LOUVERED	MORALITY	NOWADAYS	POTBELLY	
FOREBEAR	GOODYEAR	HOTELIER	LOVEBIRD	MORALIZE	OOPHORON	POTBOUND	
FOREBODE	GOOFBALL	HOTHOUSE	LOVELACE	MORAVIAN	POCHETTE	POTEMKIN	
FORECAST	GOOSEGOG	HOTPLATE	LOVELESS	MORBIDLY	POCKMARK	POTHOLER	
FOREDECK	GORGEOUS	HOUSEMAN	LOVELORN	MORBILLI	PODARGUS	POTLATCH	
FOREDOOM	GORMLESS	HOVERFLY	LOVESICK	MOREOVER	POETICAL	POTSHERD	

POTSTONE	SOLIDIFY	TOWELING	ZOONOSIS	OPTIMIST	SPOTLESS	ARGUABLE
POULAINE	SOLIDITY	TOWERING	ZOOPHYTE	OPTIONAL	SPOTTING	ARGUABLY
POULTICE	SOLITARY	TOWNSHIP	ZOOSPERM	OPULENCE	SPRAINED	ARGUMENT
POUNDAGE	SOLITUDE	TOWNSMAN	ZOOSPORE	OPUSCULE	SPRAWLED	ARKANSAS
POWDERED	SOLSTICE	TOXAEMIA	APERIENT	SPACEMAN	SPREADER	ARMAGNAC
POWERFUL	SOLUTION	TOXICITY	APERITIF	SPACIOUS	SPRINGER	ARMALITE
ROADSHOW	SOLVABLE	TOXOCARA	APERTURE	SPADEFUL	SPRINKLE	ARMAMENT
ROADSIDE	SOLVENCY	VOCALIST	APHELION	SPANDREL	SPRINTER	ARMATURE
ROADSTER	SOMBRELY	VOCALIZE	APHORISM	SPANGLED	SPRITELY	ARMCHAIR
ROASTING	SOMBRERO	VOCATION	APIARIST	SPANIARD	SPRITZER	ARMENIAN
ROBINSON	SOMEBODY	VOCATIVE	APNEUSIS	SPANKING	SPROCKET	ARMORIAL
ROBOTICS	SOMERSET	VOIDANCE	APOLLYON	SPANNING	SPRUCELY	ARMORICA
ROBUSTLY	SOMETIME	VOLATILE	APOLOGIA	SPARAXIS	SPRYNESS	ARMOURED
ROCHDALE	SOMEWHAT	VOLCANIC	APOLOGUE	SPARKING	SPURIOUS	AROMATIC
ROCKETRY	SONATINA	VOLITION	APOPHYGE	SPARKLER	SPURNING	ARPEGGIO
RODERICK	SONGBIRD	VOLPLANE	APOPLEXY	SPARRING	SPYGLASS	ARQUEBUS
ROENTGEN	SONGSTER	VOLSCIAN	APOSTASY	SPARSELY	UPCOMING	ARRANGER
ROGATION	SONOGRAM	VOLTAIRE	APOSTATE	SPARSITY	UPHEAVAL	ARRESTED
ROLLCALL	SONOROUS	VOMITING	APOSTLES	SPARTANS	UPHOLDER	ARRESTER
ROLYPOLY	SOOTHING	VOMITORY	APOTHEGM	SPAVINED	UPMARKET	ARROGANT
ROMANCER	SOOTHSAY	VORACITY	APPALLED	SPAWNING	UPPERCUT	ARROGATE
ROMANIAN	SORBONNE	VORTICAL	APPANAGE	SPEAKERS	UPPRIGHTS	ARSONIST
ROMANSCH	SORCERER	VOWELIZE	APPARENT	SPEAKING	UPRISING	ARTEFACT
ROMANTIC	SORDIDLY	VOYAGEUR	APPELANT	SPECIFIC	UPSTAIRS	ARTERIAL
ROOFLESS	SORENESS	WOBBLING	APPENDIX	SPECIMEN	UPSTREAM	ARTESIAN
ROOFTOPS	SORORITY	WOEFULLY	APPETITE	SPECIOUS	UPTURNED	ARTFULLY
ROOMMATE	SOUCHONG	WOLFBANE	APPLAUSE	SPECKLED	AQUALUNG	ARTICLED
ROOTLESS	SOULLESS	WOLSELEY	APPLETON	SPECTRAL	AQUARIUM	ARTICLES
ROSALIND	SOUNDING	WOMANISH	APPLIQUÉ	SPECTRUM	AQUARIUS	ARTIFACT
ROSALINE	SOURCING	WOMANIZE	APPOSITE	SPECULUM	AQUATINT	ARTIFICE
ROSAMOND	SOURNESS	WONDROUS	APPRAISE	SPEEDILY	AQUEDUCT	ARTISTIC
ROSEFISH	SOURPUSS	WOODBINE	APPRISED	SPEEDWAY	AQUILINE	ARTISTRY
ROSEMARY	SOURWOOD	WOODCOCK	APPROACH	SPELLING	EQUALITY	BRABAZON
ROSEROOT	SOUTHEND	WOODENLY	APPROVAL	SPELLMAN	EQUALIZE	BRACELET
ROSEWOOD	SOUTHERN	WOODLAND	APPROVED	SPENDING	EQUATION	BRACHIAL
ROSINESS	SOUTHPAW	WOODRUFF	APTITUDE	SPHAGNUM	EQUIPAGE	BRACKETS
ROSSETTI	SOUVENIR	WOODSHED	EPHEMERA	SPHENOID	EQUITANT	BRACKISH
ROTATION	TOADFLAX	WOODSMAN	EPHESIAN	SPICCATO	EQUULEUS	BRADBURY
ROTATORY	TOBOGGAN	WOODWARD	EPICURUS	SPIFFING	SQUABBLE	BRADSHAW
ROTENONE	TOGETHER	WOODWIND	EPIDEMIC	SPILLAGE	SQUADDIE	BRAGANZA
ROUGHAGE	TOILSOME	WOODWORK	EPIDURAL	SPILLWAY	SQUADRON	BRAGGART
ROULETTE	TOISEACH	WOODWORM	EPIGAMIC	SPINIFEX	SQUAMATA	BRAGGING
ROUNDERS	TOLBOOTH	WOOLLENS	EPIGRAPH	SPINNING	SQUAMOUS	BRAMANTE
ROUSSEAU	TOLERANT	WOOLPACK	EPILEPSY	SPINSTER	SQUANDER	BRANCHED
ROYALIST	TOLERATE	WOOLSACK	EPILOGUE	SPINTEXT	SQUARELY	BRANDADE
SOAKAWAY	TOLLGATE	WORDBOOK	EPIPHANY	SPIRACLE	SQUATTER	BRANDISH
SOAPBARK	TOMAHAWK	WORDLESS	EPIPHYTE	SPIRALLY	SQUEAKER	BRANDNEW
SOAPSUDS	TOMATOES	WORKABLE	EPIPLOON	SPIRELET	SQUEALER	BRASILIA
SOBERING	TOMENTUM	WORKADAY	EPISODIC	SPIRITED	SQUEEGEE	BRASSARD
SOBRIETY	TOMORROW	WORKBOOK	EPISTYLE	SPIRITUS	SQUEEZER	BRASSICA
SOCALLED	TONALITY	WORKINGS	EPITASIS	SPITEFUL	SQUIGGLE	BRATPACK
SOCIABLE	TONELESS	WORKLOAD	EPITHEMA	SPITFIRE	SQUIRREL	BREACHES
SOCIALLY	TONSURED	WORKMATE	OPENCAST	SPITHEAD	ARACHNID	BREAKING
SOCRATES	TOPCLASS	WORKROOM	OPENDOOR	SPITTING	ARALDITE	BREAKOUT
SOCRATIC	TOPHEAVY	WORKSHOP	OPENNESS	SPITTOON	ARAMAEAN	BREATHER
SODALITE	TOPLEVEL	WORMCAST	OPENPLAN	SPLASHER	ARAMANTH	BREECHES
SODALITY	TOPNOTCH	WORMWOOD	OPENWORK	SPLATTER	ARBALEST	BREEDING
SOFTBACK	TOPOLOGY	WORRYING	OPERABLE	SPLENDID	ARBOREAL	BREEZILY
SOFTBALL	TOREADOR	WORTHIES	OPERATIC	SPLENDOR	ARCADIAN	BRETHREN
SOFTENER	TORTILLA	WORTHILY	OPERATOR	SPLINTER	ARCHAISM	BREVIARY
SOFTNESS	TORTOISE	YODELLER	OPERETTA	SPLITTER	ARCHDUKE	BRIBABLE
SOFTWARE	TORTUOUS	YOGHOURT	OPHIDIAN	SPLUTTER	ARCHIVES	BRICKBAT
SOFTWOOD	TORTURED	YOKOHAMA	OPOPANAX	SPOILAGE	ARCTURUS	BRIDGING
SOLARIUM	TORTURER	YOSEMITE	OPPONENT	SPOILING	ARDENNES	BRIEFING
SOLDIERS	TOTALITY	YOUNGEST	OPPOSING	SPOLIATE	ARDENTLY	BRIGHTEN
SOLDIERY	TOTALIZE	YOURSELF	OPPOSITE	SPOONFUL	ARETHUSA	BRIGHTLY
SOLECISM	TOUCHING	YOUTHFUL	OPTICIAN	SPORADIC	ARGESTES	BRIGHTON
SOLEMNLY	TOULOUSE	ZODIACAL	OPTIMATE	SPORTING	ARGININE	BRIMMING
SOLENOID	TOVARICH	ZOETROPE	OPTIMISM	SPORTIVE	ARGONAUT	BRINDISI

BRINDLED	CROWFOOT	FRAGRANT	GREEDILY	ORTHODOX	PROMISED	TRIBUNAL
BRINGING	CROWNING	FRANCIUM	GREENBAG	PRACTICE	PROMOTER	TRICHOID
BRISLING	CRUCIATE	FRANKISH	GREENERY	PRACTISE	PROMPTER	TRICKERY
BRISTLED	CRUCIBLE	FRANKLIN	GREENFLY	PRAIRIAL	PROMPTLY	TRICYCLE
BRISTLES	CRUCIFER	FRAULEIN	GREENING	PRANDIAL	PRONATOR	TRIFLING
BROADWAY	CRUCIFIX	FRAXINUS	GREENISH	PRATFALL	PROPERLY	TRIGLYPH
BROCCOLI	CRUMHORN	FRAZZLED	GREENOCK	PRATTLER	PROPERTY	TRIGRAPH
BROCHURE	CRUMMOCK	FREAKISH	GREETING	PREACHER	PROPHASE	TRILEMMA
BROILING	CRUNCHIE	FRECKLED	GRENACHE	PREAMBLE	PROPHECY	TRILLING
BROMELIA	CRUSADER	FRECKLES	GRIDIRON	PRECINCT	PROPHESY	TRILLION
BROMPTON	CRUSHING	FREEHAND	GRIDLOCK	PRECIOUS	PROPOLIS	TRILLIUM
BRONCHUS	CRUTCHED	FREEHOLD	GRIEVOUS	PRECLUDE	PROPOSAL	TRIMARAN
BROODING	CRUZEIRO	FREEPOST	GRILLING	PRECURSE	PROPOSED	TRIMMING
BROUGHAM	CRYOLITE	FREETOWN	GRIMALDI	PREDATOR	PROPOSER	TRIMNESS
BROUHAHA	CRYSTALS	FREEZING	GRIMNESS	PREDELLA	PROPOUND	TRINCULO
BROWBEAT	DRACAENA	FREMITUS	GRINDING	PREGNANT	PROROGUE	TRINIDAD
BROWNING	DRACONIC	FRENETIC	GRIPPING	PREJUDGE	PROSPECT	TRIPLING
BROWNISH	DRAGOONS	FRENULUM	GRISELDA	PREMIERE	PROSPERO	TRIPTANE
BROWSING	DRAGSTER	FRENZIED	GRISETTE	PREMISES	PROSTATE	TRIPTYCH
BRUCKNER	DRAINAGE	FREQUENT	GRIZZLED	PREMOLAR	PROTEASE	TRISTICH
BRUISING	DRAINING	FRESHEST	GROGGILY	PRENATAL	PROTÉGÉE	TRISTRAM
BRUMAIRE	DRAMATIC	FRESHMAN	GROOMING	PREPARED	PROTOCOL	TRITICAL
BRUNETTE	DRAUGHTS	FRETWORK	GROSBEAK	PRESENCE	PROTOZOA	TRITICUM
BRUSSELS	DRAUGHTY	FREUDIAN	GROSCHEN	PRESERVE	PROTRUDE	TRIUNITY
BRUTALLY	DRAWBACK	FRICTION	GROUNDED	PRESSING	PROVABLE	TROCHAIC
BRYOZOAN	DREADFUL	FRIENDLY	GROUPING	PRESSMAN	PROVERBS	TROCHLEA
CRACKERS	DREAMILY	FRIGHTEN	GROUTING	PRESSURE	PROVIDED	TROLLOPE
CRACKING	DREAMING	FRIGIDLY	GROWLING	PRESTIGE	PROVIDER	TROMBONE
CRACKPOT	DREARILY	FRIPPERY	GRUDGING	PRETENCE	PROVINCE	TROOPING
CRAFTILY	DRESSAGE	FRISKILY	GRUESOME	PRETENSE	PROXIMAL	TROPICAL
CRAMOISY	DRESSING	FRONDEUR	GRUMBLER	PRETORIA	PRUDENCE	TROTLINE
CRANEFLY	DRIBLETS	FRONTAGE	GRUMPILY	PRETTILY	PRUNELLA	TROTTERS
CRATCHIT	DRIFTING	FRONTIER	IRISCOPE	PREVIOUS	PRURIENT	TROTTOIR
CRAVATES	DRINKING	FRONTMAN	IRISHISM	PRIAPISM	PRUSSIAN	TROUBLED
CRAWFISH	DRIPPING	FROSTILY	IRISHMAN	PRIESTLY	TRACHOMA	TROUBLES
CRAWLING	DRIVEWAY	FROSTING	IRISHMEN	PRIGGISH	TRACKING	TROUNCER
CRAYFISH	DROOPING	FRUCTIFY	IRONCLAD	PRIMEVAL	TRACTION	TROUSERS
CREAMERY	DROPHEAD	FRUCTOSE	IRONICAL	PRIMNESS	TRADEOFF	TRUCKING
CREATION	DROPPING	FRUGALLY	IRONSIDE	PRIMROSE	TRAILING	TRUCKLED
CREATIVE	DROPSHOT	FRUITFUL	IRONWARE	PRINCELY	TRAINING	TRUENESS
CREATURE	DROWNING	FRUITING	IRONWOOD	PRINCESS	TRAITORS	TRUMPERY
CREDIBLE	DROWSILY	FRUITION	IRONWORK	PRINTING	TRAMLINE	TRUNCATE
CREDIBLY	DRUBBING	FRUMENTY	IROQUOIS	PRINTOUT	TRANQUIL	TRUNNION
CREDITOR	DRUDGERY	FRUMPISH	IRRIGATE	PRIORESS	TRANSACT	TRUSTFUL
CREOSOTE	DRUGGIST	GRACEFUL	IRRITANT	PRIORITY	TRANSECT	TRUSTING
CREPITUS	DRUMBEAT	GRACIOUS	IRRITATE	PRISONER	TRANSEPT	TRUTHFUL
CRESCENT	DRUMHEAD	GRADIENT	KRAKATOA	PRISTINE	TRANSFER	URBANITY
CRETONNE	DRUMLINE	GRADUATE	KREPLACH	PRIVATES	TRANSFIX	URBANIZE
CREVASSE	DRUMMING	GRAFFITI	KROMESKY	PROBABLE	TRANSHIP	URETHANE
CRIBBAGE	DRUNKARD	GRAINING	KRUMHORN	PROBABLY	TRANSKEI	URGENTLY
CRICHTON	DRYCLEAN	GRAMERCY	ORANGERY	PROCAINE	TRANSMIT	URSULINE
CRIMINAL	DRYGOODS	GRANDDAD	ORATORIO	PROCEEDS	TRAPDOOR	WRANGLER
CRINGING	DRYSTONE	GRANDEUR	ORCADIAN	PROCLAIM	TRAPPIST	WRAPPING
CRIPPLED	ERADIATE	GRANDKID	ORCHITIS	PROCURER	TRASHCAN	WRATHFUL
CRISPIAN	ERECTILE	GRANDSON	ORDERING	PRODIGAL	TRAVELER	WREATHED
CRITICAL	ERECTING	GRANULAR	ORDINAND	PRODROME	TRAVERSE	WRECKAGE
CRITIQUE	ERECTION	GRANULES	ORDINARY	PRODUCER	TRAVESTY	WRESTLER
CROATIAN	ERGOTISE	GRAPHEME	ORDINATE	PRODUCES	TREASURE	WRETCHED
CROCKERY	ERGOTISM	GRAPHICS	ORDNANCE	PRODUCTS	TREASURY	WRINGING
CROCKETT	ERIDANUS	GRAPHITE	ORESTEIA	PROFORMA	TREATISE	WRINKLED
CROMLECH	ERIKSSON	GRASPING	ORGANDIE	PROFOUND	TREELESS	WRISTLET
CROMWELL	ERUCTATE	GRATEFUL	ORGANISM	PROFUSER	TREELINE	WRITEOFF
CRONYISM	ERUPTION	GRATINEE	ORGANIST	PROGERIA	TREETOPS	WRITHING
CROONING	ERUPTURE	GRATUITY	ORGANIZE	PROGRADE	TREMBLER	WRITINGS
CROSSBAR	ERYTHEMA	GRAVAMEN	ORIENTAL	PROGRESS	TREMBLES	WRONGFUL
CROSSING	FRABJOUS	GRAVELLY	ORIGINAL	PROHIBIT	TRENCHER	ASBESTOS
CROSSLET	FRACTION	GRAVITAS	ORNAMENT	PROLAPSE	TRESPASS	ASCIDIAN
CROTCHET	FRACTURE	GRAYLING	ORPHANED	PROLIFIC	TRIANGLE	ASCIDIUM
CROUPIER	FRAGMENT	GREATEST	ORPIMENT	PROLOGUE	TRIASSIC	ASCOCARP

271

ASCORBIC	PSALTERY	STARCHED	STRAIGHT	BUCKBEAN	CUTPURSE	FUSILIER
ASMODEUS	PSEUDERY	STARDUST	STRAINED	BUCKFAST	CUTWATER	FUTILITY
ASPERGES	TSAREVNA	STARFISH	STRAINER	BUCKLING	DUBONNET	FUTURISM
ASPERITY	USEFULLY	STARGAZE	STRAITEN	BUCKSHEE	DUCHESSE	FUTURIST
ASPERMIA	USUFRUCT	STARKERS	STRANDED	BUCKSHOT	DUCKBILL	GUAIACUM
ASPHODEL	USURIOUS	STARLESS	STRANGER	BUCKSKIN	DUCKLING	GUARDIAN
ASPHYXIA	ATALANTA	STARLING	STRANGLE	BUDAPEST	DUCKWEED	GUERIDON
ASPIRANT	ATARAXIA	STAROSTA	STRAPPED	BUDDHISM	DUELLIST	GUERILLA
ASPIRATE	ATARAXIC	STARTERS	STRAPPER	BUDDHIST	DULCIMER	GUERNSEY
ASPIRING	ATHANASY	STARTING	STRATEGY	BUDDLEIA	DULCINEA	GUIANIAN
ASSASSIN	ATHELING	STARVING	STRATIFY	BUGGERED	DULLNESS	GUIDANCE
ASSEMBLE	ATHENIAN	STATUARY	STREAKED	BUILDING	DUMBBELL	GUILTILY
ASSEMBLY	ATHEROMA	STAYSAIL	STREAKER	BULGARIA	DUMBNESS	GUJARATI
ASSESSOR	ATHETISE	STEADILY	STREAMER	BULKHEAD	DUMFOUND	GULFWEED
ASSIGNEE	ATHETOID	STEALING	STRENGTH	BULLDOZE	DUMPLING	GULLIBLE
ASSORTED	ATHLETIC	STEALTHY	STRESSED	BULLETIN	DUNGHILL	GULLIVER
ASSUMING	ATLANTIC	STEAPSIN	STRETCHY	BULLFROG	DUODENAL	GUMMOSIS
ASSYRIAN	ATLANTIS	STEATITE	STRIATED	BULLHORN	DUODENUM	GUMPTION
ASTATINE	ATOMIZER	STEATOMA	STRIATUM	BULLRING	DURABLES	GUNMETAL
ASTERISK	ATROCITY	STEENBOK	STRICKEN	BULLYRAG	DURATION	GUNPOINT
ASTEROID	ATTACHED	STEERAGE	STRICKLE	BUMBLING	DUTCHMAN	GUNSMITH
ASTHENIA	ATTACKER	STEERING	STRICTLY	BUMMAREE	DUTIABLE	GURDWARA
ASTONISH	ATTENDER	STEINWAY	STRIDENT	BUNFIGHT	DUTYFREE	GUSSETED
ASTUTELY	ATTESTOR	STELLATE	STRIKING	BUNGALOW	EUCYCLIC	GUTTURAL
ASUNCION	ATTITUDE	STENDHAL	STRINGED	BUNGLING	EUDOXIAN	GUYANESE
ESCALADE	ATTORNEY	STENOSED	STRINGER	BUOYANCY	EUGENICS	HUCKSTER
ESCALATE	ATYPICAL	STENOSIS	STRIPPED	BURBERRY	EULOGIST	HUMANELY
ESCALOPE	ETCETERA	STEPHENS	STRIPPER	BURDENED	EULOGIUM	HUMANISM
ESCAPADE	ETERNITY	STERLING	STRIVING	BURGLARY	EULOGIZE	HUMANIST
ESCAPISM	ETHEREAL	STICCATO	STROLLER	BURGRAVE	EUPEPSIA	HUMANITY
ESCAPIST	ETHERIFY	STICKILY	STRONGLY	BURGUNDY	EUPHONIA	HUMANIZE
ESCARGOT	ETHERISE	STICKING	STRUGGLE	BURNTOUT	EUPHONIC	HUMIDIFY
ESCORIAL	ETHIOPIA	STICKLER	STRUMPET	BURROWER	EUPHORIA	HUMIDITY
ESCULENT	ETHNARCH	STIFLING	STUBBORN	BURSITIS	EUPHORIC	HUMILITY
ESOTERIC	ETHOLOGY	STIGMATA	STUCCOED	BURSTING	EUPHUISM	HUMORIST
ESPALIER	ETHYLENE	STILETTO	STUDENTS	BUSINESS	EURASIAN	HUMOROUS
ESPECIAL	ETIOLATE	STILWELL	STUDIOUS	BUSTLING	EUROLAND	HUMPBACK
ESPOUSAL	ETRURIAN	STIMULUS	STUFFILY	BUSULFAN	EUROPEAN	HUMPHREY
ESPRESSO	ETRUSCAN	STINGING	STUFFING	BUSYBODY	EUROPIUM	HUNDREDS
ESSAYIST	OTOSCOPE	STINGRAY	STULTIFY	BUTCHERS	EUROSTAR	HUNGRILY
ESSONITE	OTTAVINO	STINKING	STUNNING	BUTCHERY	EURYDICE	HUNTRESS
ESTANCIA	PTEROPOD	STINKPOT	STUPIDLY	BUTTERED	EUSTATIC	HUNTSMAN
ESTEEMED	PTOMAINE	STIRLING	STURDILY	BUTTOCKS	EUTROPHY	HURDLING
ESTHETIC	PTYALISM	STIRRING	STURGEON	BUTTRESS	EUTROPIC	HUSHHUSH
ESTIMATE	STABBING	STOCCATA	STYLIZED	BUZZWORD	FUCHSITE	HUSTINGS
ESTIVATE	STABLING	STOCKADE	UTENSILS	CUCUMBER	FUGITIVE	JUBILANT
ESTONIAN	STACCATO	STOCKCAR	AUBUSSON	CUCURBIT	FUGLEMAN	JUBILATE
ESTOPPEL	STAFFING	STOCKING	AUCASSIN	CULINARY	FULLBACK	JUDGMENT
ESTOVERS	STAFFORD	STOCKIST	AUDACITY	CULLINAN	FULLNESS	JUDICIAL
ESTRAGON	STAGGERS	STOCKMAN	AUDIENCE	CULLODEN	FULLPAGE	JUGGLING
ESTROGEN	STAGHORN	STOCKPOT	AUDITION	CULOTTES	FULLSIZE	JULIENNE
ISABELLA	STAGNANT	STOICISM	AUDITORY	CULPABLE	FULLTIME	JUMPSUIT
ISABELLE	STAGNATE	STOKESAY	AUGUSTUS	CULTURAL	FUMAROLE	JUNCTION
ISLANDER	STAIRWAY	STOLIDLY	AURELIAN	CULTURED	FUMBLING	JUNCTURE
ISOBARIC	STAKEOUT	STONEFLY	AURICULA	CULVERIN	FUMIGATE	JURASSIC
ISOCLINE	STALKING	STOPCOCK	AUSPICES	CUPBOARD	FUMITORY	JURATORY
ISOGENIC	STALLION	STOPOVER	AUSTRIAN	CUPIDITY	FUNCTION	JUSTNESS
ISOGLOSS	STALWART	STOPPAGE	AUTARCHY	CURATIVE	FUNERARY	JUVENILE
ISOGONAL	STAMENED	STOPPING	AUTISTIC	CURLICUE	FUNEREAL	KUFFIYEH
ISOLATED	STAMPEDE	STOREMAN	AUTOBAHN	CURRENCY	FUNGIBLE	LUCIDITY
ISOSTASY	STANDARD	STOREYED	AUTOCRAT	CURRICLE	FURBELOW	LUCKLESS
ISOTHERE	STANDING	STORMING	AUTOGAMY	CURSITOR	FURLOUGH	LUKEWARM
ISOTHERM	STANDISH	STORMONT	AUTOGIRO	CURTAINS	FURROWED	LULWORTH
ISTANBUL	STANDOFF	STOWAWAY	AUTOGYRO	CURTNESS	FURTHEST	LUMINARY
ISTHMIAN	STANHOPE	STRABISM	AUTOMATE	CUSPIDOR	FURUNCLE	LUMINOUS
OSCULATE	STANNARY	STRACHEY	AUTONOMY	CUSTOMER	FUSAROLE	LUMPFISH
OSTERLEY	STANNITE	STRADDLE	AUTOTYPE	CUTENESS	FUSELAGE	LUNCHBOX
PSALMIST	STAPELIA	STRAGGLE	AUTUMNAL	CUTHBERT	FUSEWIRE	LUNCHEON
PSALMODY	STAPHYLE	STRAGGLY	BUBBLING	CUTPRICE	FUSIFORM	LUNGFISH

LUNGWORT	OUTMATCH	QUINTAIN	SUNBURNT	AVENTINE	OVERTONE	EXPENSES
LUPERCAL	OUTMODED	QUIRINAL	SUNBURST	AVERSION	OVERTURE	EXPLICIT
LUSCIOUS	OUTREACH	QUISLING	SUNCREAM	AVIATION	OVERTURN	EXPLODED
LUSHNESS	OUTREMER	QUIXOTIC	SUNDANCE	AVICENNA	OVERVIEW	EXPLORER
LUSTRINE	OUTRIDER	QUOTABLE	SUNDRIED	AVIFAUNA	OVERWORK	EXPONENT
LUSTROUS	OUTRIGHT	QUOTIENT	SUNDRIES	AVOGADRO	SVENGALI	EXPORTER
LUTENIST	OUTSHINE	RUBAIYAT	SUNGLASS	AVULSION	DWARFISH	EXPOSURE
LUTETIUM	OUTSIDER	RUBBISHY	SUNLIGHT	EVACUANT	DWARFISM	EXPRESSO
LUTHERAN	OUTSMART	RUBICUND	SUNSHADE	EVACUATE	DWELLING	EXTENDED
MUCHNESS	OUTSTRIP	RUBIDIUM	SUNSHINE	EVALUATE	EWIGKEIT	EXTENSOR
MUCILAGE	OUTWARDS	RUCKSACK	SUPERBLY	EVANESCE	SWADDLER	EXTERIOR
MUDFLATS	OUTWEIGH	RUCTIONS	SUPERBUG	EVENNESS	SWANSKIN	EXTERNAL
MUDGUARD	PUBLICAN	RUDENESS	SUPERIOR	EVENSONG	SWANSONG	EXTERNAT
MUDSTONE	PUBLICLY	RUDIMENT	SUPERMAN	EVENTFUL	SWARMING	EXTRADOS
MUHAMMAD	PUCKERED	RUEFULLY	SUPERNAL	EVENTIDE	SWASTIKA	EXULTANT
MUHARRAM	PUDENDUM	RUGGEDLY	SUPERTAX	EVENTUAL	SWEARING	EXULTING
MULBERRY	PUFFBALL	RULEBOOK	SUPPLANT	EVERMORE	SWEATING	OXBRIDGE
MULETEER	PUGILISM	RUMBLING	SUPPLIER	EVERYDAY	SWEEPING	OXPECKER
MULEWORT	PUGILIST	RUMINANT	SUPPLIES	EVERYMAN	SWEETSOP	OXYMORON
MULLIGAN	PUGNOSED	RUMINATE	SUPPOSED	EVERYONE	SWELLING	OXYTOCIN
MULTIPLE	PUISSANT	RUMOURED	SUPPRESS	EVICTION	SWERVING	UXORIOUS
MULTIPLY	PULITZER	RUNABOUT	SURENESS	EVIDENCE	SWILLING	AYRSHIRE
MUMBLING	PULLDOWN	RUNCIBLE	SURFBOAT	EVILDOER	SWIMMING	CYANOGEN
MUNCHKIN	PULLOVER	RUNNERUP	SURGICAL	IVOIRIEN	SWIMSUIT	CYANOSIS
MUNIMENT	PUNCTUAL	RUSHMORE	SURICATE	OVARITIS	SWINDLER	CYCLADES
MURDERER	PUNCTURE	RUSTLESS	SURMOUNT	OVENBIRD	SWINEPOX	CYCLAMEN
MURRHINE	PUNGENCY	RUSTLING	SURPLICE	OVENWARE	SWINGING	CYCLICAL
MUSCADET	PUNISHED	RUTABAGA	SURPRISE	OVERALLS	SWIRLING	CYCLOSIS
MUSCATEL	PUNITIVE	RUTHLESS	SURROUND	OVERBOOK	TWEEZERS	CYLINDER
MUSCULAR	PURBLIND	SUBHUMAN	SURVEYOR	OVERCAST	TWELVEMO	CYNICISM
MUSHROOM	PURCHASE	SUBJECTS	SURVIVAL	OVERCOAT	TWILIGHT	CYNOSURE
MUSICIAN	PURIFIED	SUBLEASE	SURVIVOR	OVERCOME	TWIRLING	CYRENIAC
MUSQUASH	PURIFIER	SUBMERGE	SUSPENSE	OVERDONE	TWISTING	CYRILLIC
MUSTACHE	PURLIEUS	SUBPOENA	SUZERAIN	OVERDOSE	TWITCHER	CYSTITIS
MUTATION	PURPLISH	SUBSHRUB	TUBELESS	OVERDRAW	TWOPENNY	CYTOLOGY
MUTCHKIN	PURSLANE	SUBSONIC	TUBENOSE	OVERFEED	TWOPIECE	CYTOSINE
MUTILATE	PURULENT	SUBTENSE	TUBERCLE	OVERFILL	ZWIEBACK	DYNAMICS
MUTINEER	PURVEYOR	SUBTITLE	TUBEROSE	OVERFLOW	EXACTING	DYNAMISM
MUTINOUS	PUSHBIKE	SUBTLETY	TUBEROUS	OVERFULL	EXACTION	DYNAMITE
MUTUALLY	PUSHCART	SUBTOPIA	TUNGSTEN	OVERHAND	EXAMINEE	DYNASTIC
NUCLEATE	PUSHDOWN	SUBTOTAL	TUNGSTIC	OVERHANG	EXAMINER	DYNATRON
NUCLEOLE	PUSHOVER	SUBTRACT	TUNGUSIC	OVERHAUL	EXCAVATE	DYSLEXIA
NUFFIELD	PUSSYCAT	SUBURBAN	TUNICATE	OVERHEAD	EXCHANGE	DYSLEXIC
NUGATORY	PUSTULAR	SUBURBIA	TUNISIAN	OVERHEAR	EXCISION	EYEGLASS
NUISANCE	PUTATIVE	SUCCEEDS	TUPAMARO	OVERHEAT	EXCITING	EYELINER
NUMBNESS	PUZZLING	SUCCINCT	TUPPENNY	OVERKILL	EXECRATE	EYEPIECE
NUMERACY	QUADRANT	SUCCUBUS	TURANDOT	OVERLAID	EXECUTED	EYESHADE
NUMERALS	QUADRATE	SUCHLIKE	TURBANED	OVERLAND	EXECUTOR	EYESIGHT
NUMERATE	QUADRIGA	SUCKLING	TURBOJET	OVERLEAF	EXEGESIS	EYETOOTH
NUMEROUS	QUADROON	SUDAMENT	TURGENEV	OVERLOAD	EXEGETIC	GYMKHANA
NUMINOUS	QUAESTOR	SUDAMINA	TURGIDLY	OVERLOOK	EXEMPLAR	GYRATION
NUPTIALS	QUAGMIRE	SUDANESE	TURKOMAN	OVERLORD	EXERCISE	GYRATORY
NURSLING	QUAINTLY	SUDARIUM	TURMERIC	OVERMUCH	EXERTION	GYROSTAT
NUTHATCH	QUANDARY	SUDDENLY	TURNBACK	OVERPASS	EXHUMATE	HYACINTH
NUTHOUSE	QUANTIFY	SUFFERER	TURNCOAT	OVERPLAY	EXIGENCY	HYDATOID
NUTRIENT	QUANTITY	SUFFRAGE	TURNCOCK	OVERRATE	EXIGUITY	HYDROGEN
NUTSHELL	QUARTERS	SUICIDAL	TURNOVER	OVERRIDE	EXIGUOUS	HYDROXYL
OUISTITI	QUARTIER	SUITABLE	TURNPIKE	OVERRIPE	EXISTENT	HYGIENIC
OUTBOARD	QUARTILE	SUITABLY	TURNSPIT	OVERRULE	EXISTING	HYPERION
OUTBREAK	QUATORZE	SUITCASE	TURRETED	OVERSEAS	EXOCRINE	HYPNOSIS
OUTBURST	QUATRAIN	SUKIYAKI	TUSITALA	OVERSEER	EXOERGIC	HYPNOTIC
OUTCLASS	QUAYSIDE	SULFURIC	TUTELAGE	OVERSHOE	EXORCISM	HYPOGEAL
OUTDATED	QUENELLE	SULLENLY	TUTELARY	OVERSHOT	EXORCIST	HYSTERIA
OUTDOORS	QUESTION	SULLIVAN	TUTORIAL	OVERSIZE	EXORCIZE	HYSTERIC
OUTFIELD	QUIBBLER	SULPHATE	VULGARLY	OVERSOLD	EXORDIUM	JYAISTHA
OUTFLANK	QUICKSET	SULPHIDE	YUGOSLAV	OVERSTAY	EXPANDED	KYPHOSIS
OUTGOING	QUIETUDE	SUMERIAN	YULETIDE	OVERSTEP	EXPECTED	LYNCHING
OUTHOUSE	QUILTING	SUMMITRY	ZUCCHINI	OVERTAKE	EXPEDITE	LYREBIRD
OUTLYING	QUINCUNX	SUNBATHE	AVAILING	OVERTIME	EXPENDED	LYRICISM

LYRICIST
LYSANDER
LYSERGIC
MYCELIUM
MYCOLOGY
MYELITIS
MYOBLAST
MYOSOTIS
MYRIAPOD
MYRMIDON
MYSTICAL
MYSTIQUE
MYTHICAL
PYELITIS
PYORRHEA
PYRAMIDS
PYRENEES
PYRIFORM
RYEGRASS
SYBARITE
SYCAMORE
SYLLABIC
SYLLABLE
SYLLABUB
SYLLABUS
SYLVANER
SYLVATIC
SYMBIONT
SYMBOLIC
SYMMETRY
SYMPATHY
SYMPHONY
SYMPTOMS
SYNCLINE
SYNDROME
SYNOPSIS
SYNOPTIC
SYNTEXIS
SYPHILIS
SYRACUSE
SYRINGES
SYSTEMIC
TYMPANUM
TYPECAST
TYPEFACE
TYROLEAN
TYROSINE
WYCLIFFE
CZAREVNA
DZONGKHA
TZATZIKI

8:3

ABATTOIR
ACADEMIA
ACADEMIC
ACANTHUS
ACAPULCO
AGACERIE
ALACRITY
ALARMING
ALARMIST
AMANDINE
AMARANTH
AMARETTO
AMATEURS
ANABASIS
ANABATIC
ANACONDA

ANACREON
ANAGLYPH
ANALECTA
ANALEMMA
ANALOGUE
ANALYSER
ANALYSIS
ANALYTIC
ANAPAEST
ANAPHASE
ANARCHIC
ANATHEMA
ANATOLIA
ANATOMIC
ARACHNID
ARALDITE
ARAMAEAN
ARAMANTH
ATALANTA
ATARAXIA
ATARAXIC
AVAILING
BAATHIST
BEAKLESS
BEANPOLE
BEARABLE
BEARINGS
BEARSKIN
BEATIFIC
BEAUFORT
BEAUMONT
BEAUTIFY
BIANNUAL
BIATHLON
BLACKBOY
BLACKCAP
BLACKFLY
BLACKING
BLACKISH
BLACKLEG
BLACKOUT
BLANDISH
BLASTOFF
BLASTULA
BOADICEA
BOARDING
BOASTFUL
BOASTING
BOATBILL
BOATLOAD
BRABAZON
BRACELET
BRACHIAL
BRACKETS
BRACKISH
BRADBURY
BRADSHAW
BRAGANZA
BRAGGART
BRAGGING
BRAMANTE
BRANCHED
BRANDADE
BRANDISH
BRANDNEW
BRASILIA
BRASSARD
BRASSICA
BRATPACK

CHACONNE
CHADBAND
CHAINSAW
CHAIRMAN
CHALDEAN
CHALDRON
CHAMBERS
CHAMPERS
CHAMPION
CHANCERY
CHANDLER
CHANGING
CHANTAGE
CHANTREY
CHAPATTI
CHAPERON
CHAPLAIN
CHARCOAL
CHARGING
CHARISMA
CHARLADY
CHARLOCK
CHARMING
CHARTISM
CHARTIST
CHARTRES
CHASSEUR
CHASTISE
CHASTITY
CHASUBLE
CHATTELS
CLADDING
CLAIMANT
CLAMBAKE
CLANGING
CLANGOUR
CLANNISH
CLANSMAN
CLAPPERS
CLAPPING
CLAPTRAP
CLARENCE
CLARINET
CLASHING
CLASPING
CLASSICS
CLASSIFY
CLAUDIUS
CLAVECIN
CLAVICLE
CLAWBACK
CLAYMORE
COACHING
COACHMAN
COALESCE
COALHOLE
COALMINE
COALPORT
COARSELY
COATRACK
COATTAIL
COAUTHOR
CRACKERS
CRACKING
CRACKPOT
CRAFTILY
CRAMOISY
CRANEFLY
CRATCHIT

CRAVATES
CRAWFISH
CRAWLING
CRAYFISH
CYANOGEN
CYANOSIS
CZAREVNA
DEADBEAT
DEADENED
DEADENER
DEADHEAD
DEADLINE
DEADLOCK
DEADWOOD
DEAFNESS
DEALINGS
DEATHBED
DIABETES
DIABETIC
DIABOLIC
DIAGNOSE
DIAGONAL
DIALLING
DIALOGUE
DIALYSIS
DIAMANTE
DIAMETER
DIAMONDS
DIANTHUS
DIAPASON
DIAPHONE
DIARESIS
DIARRHEA
DIASPORA
DIASTASE
DIASTOLE
DIATONIC
DIATRIBE
DIAZEPAM
DRACAENA
DRACONIC
DRAGOONS
DRAGSTER
DRAINAGE
DRAINING
DRAMATIC
DRAUGHTS
DRAUGHTY
DRAWBACK
DWARFISH
DWARFISM
EMACIATE
ERADIATE
EVACUANT
EVACUATE
EVALUATE
EVANESCE
EXACTING
EXACTION
EXAMINEE
EXAMINER
FEARLESS
FEARSOME
FEASIBLE
FEASIBLY
FEATHERS
FEATHERY
FEATURED
FEATURES

FLAGGING
FLAGPOLE
FLAGRANT
FLAGSHIP
FLAMENCO
FLAMEOUT
FLANDERS
FLANNELS
FLAPJACK
FLAPPING
FLASHGUN
FLASHILY
FLASHING
FLATBOAT
FLATFISH
FLATFOOT
FLATMATE
FLATPICK
FLATTERY
FLATWARE
FLATWORM
FLAUBERT
FLAUTIST
FLAVORED
FLAWLESS
FLAXSEED
FRABJOUS
FRACTION
FRACTURE
FRAGMENT
FRAGRANT
FRANCIUM
FRANKISH
FRANKLIN
FRAULEIN
FRAXINUS
FRAZZLED
GHANAIAN
GIACONDA
GIANTESS
GLABELLA
GLABROUS
GLADNESS
GLADSOME
GLANCING
GLANDERS
GLASNOST
GLASSFUL
GLAUCOMA
GLAUCOUS
GNASHING
GOALPOST
GOATSKIN
GRACEFUL
GRACIOUS
GRADIENT
GRADUATE
GRAFFITI
GRAINING
GRAMERCY
GRANDDAD
GRANDEUR
GRANDKID
GRANDSON
GRANULAR
GRANULES
GRAPHEME
GRAPHICS

GRAPHITE
GRASPING
GRATEFUL
GRATINEE
GRATUITY
GRAVAMEN
GRAVELLY
GRAVITAS
GRAYLING
GUAIACUM
GUARDIAN
HEADACHE
HEADBAND
HEADGEAR
HEADHUNT
HEADLAMP
HEADLAND
HEADLESS
HEADLINE
HEADLONG
HEADMARK
HEADMOST
HEADREST
HEADROOM
HEADSHIP
HEADWIND
HEADWORD
HEARTIES
HEARTILY
HEATEDLY
HEATSPOT
HEATWAVE
HEAVENLY
HIAWATHA
HOARDING
HOARSELY
HYACINTH
IMAGINED
INACTION
INACTIVE
INASMUCH
ISABELLA
ISABELLE
JEALOUSY
JEANETTE
JYAISTHA
KHARTOUM
KNACKERS
KNAPSACK
KNAPWEED
KRAKATOA
LEACHING
LEADSMAN
LEAFLESS
LEAPFROG
LEARNING
LEATHERY
LEAVENED
LEAVINGS
LOADSTAR
LOANWORD
LOATHING
MEALTIME
MEALYBUG
MEANNESS
MEANTIME
MEASURED
MEATLESS
NEARNESS

NEATHERD
NEATNESS
ORANGERY
ORATORIO
OVARITIS
PEACEFUL
PEARLING
PEARMAIN
PHALANGE
PHALGUNA
PHANTASM
PHARISEE
PHARMACY
PLACABLE
PLACEMAT
PLACEMEN
PLACENTA
PLACIDLY
PLANCHET
PLANGENT
PLANKING
PLANKTON
PLANNING
PLANTAIN
PLASTRON
PLATANUS
PLATEFUL
PLATELET
PLATFORM
PLATINUM
PLATONIC
PLATYPUS
PLAUDITS
PLAYBACK
PLAYBILL
PLAYFAIR
PLAYGIRL
PLAYMATE
PLAYROOM
PLAYSUIT
PLAYTIME
PRACTICE
PRACTISE
PRAIRIAL
PRANDIAL
PRATFALL
PRATTLER
PSALMIST
PSALMODY
PSALTERY
QUADRANT
QUADRATE
QUADRIGA
QUADROON
QUAESTOR
QUAGMIRE
QUAINTLY
QUANDARY
QUANTIFY
QUANTITY
QUARTERS
QUARTIER
QUARTILE
QUATORZE
QUATRAIN
QUAYSIDE
REACTION
REACTIVE
READABLE

READIEST	SHANTUNG	STAROSTA	WRATHFUL	HIBISCUS	TIBERIUS	BACKSPIN
READJUST	SHAREOUT	STARTERS	YEARBOOK	HOBBLING	TOBOGGAN	BACKSTOP
REAFFIRM	SHAVUOTH	STARTING	YEARLING	IMBECILE	TUBELESS	BACKWARD
REALTIME	SLANGING	STARVING	YEARLONG	JEBUSITE	TUBENOSE	BACKYARD
REAPPEAR	SLANTING	STATUARY	YEARNING	JUBILANT	TUBERCLE	BACTERIA
REARMOST	SLAPBANG	STAYSAIL	ABBASIDE	JUBILATE	TUBEROSE	BACTRIAN
REARWARD	SLAPDASH	SWADDLER	ALBACORE	KIBITZER	TUBEROUS	BECALMED
REASONED	SLAPJACK	SWANSKIN	ALBANIAN	LABOURED	UMBRELLA	BECHAMEL
REASSERT	SLATTERN	SWANSONG	ALBERICH	LABOURER	UNBEATEN	BECOMING
REASSESS	SMALLEST	SWARMING	ALBINONI	LABRADOR	UNBIASED	BICONVEX
REASSIGN	SMALLPOX	SWASTIKA	ALBURNUM	LABURNUM	UNBIDDEN	BICUSPID
REASSUME	SMARTEST	TEACHERS	AMBIANCE	LEBANESE	UNBROKEN	BUCKBEAN
REASSURE	SMASHING	TEACHING	AMBIENCE	LIBATION	UNBURDEN	BUCKFAST
REAWAKEN	SNACKBAR	TEACLOTH	AMBITION	LIBELOUS	UNBUTTON	BUCKLING
RHAPSODY	SNAPPILY	TEAKWOOD	AMBROSIA	LIBERATE	URBANITY	BUCKSHEE
ROADSHOW	SNAPSHOT	TEAMMATE	AMBULANT	LIBERIAN	URBANIZE	BUCKSHOT
ROADSIDE	SNATCHER	TEAMSTER	AMBULATE	LIBRETTO	VIBRANCY	BUCKSKIN
ROADSTER	SOAKAWAY	TEAMWORK	AMBUSHED	LOBBYIST	VIBRATOR	CACHALOT
ROASTING	SOAPBARK	TEARABLE	ARBALEST	LOBELINE	VIBURNUM	CACHEPOT
SCABBARD	SOAPSUDS	TEARAWAY	ARBOREAL	LOBOTOMY	WOBBLING	CACHEXIA
SCABIOUS	SPACEMAN	TEARDROP	ASBESTOS	MOBILITY	ZIBELINE	CICATRIX
SCABROUS	SPACIOUS	TEASPOON	AUBUSSON	MOBILIZE	ACCENTED	CICERONE
SCAFFOLD	SPADEFUL	THAILAND	BABBLING	NEBRASKA	ACCENTOR	CICISBEO
SCALDING	SPANDREL	THALAMUS	BABUSHKA	NEBULOUS	ACCEPTED	COCACOLA
SCALENUS	SPANGLED	THALLIUM	BABYHOOD	NIBELUNG	ACCEPTOR	COCCIDAE
SCALLION	SPANIARD	THANATOS	BIBLICAL	NOBELIUM	ACCIDENT	COCHLEAR
SCANDIUM	SPANKING	THANKFUL	BIBULOUS	NOBILITY	ACCOLADE	COCKATOO
SCANNING	SPANNING	THATAWAY	BOBBYPIN	NOBLEMAN	ACCOUNTS	COCKAYNE
SCANSION	SPARAXIS	THATCHED	BOBOLINK	OXBRIDGE	ACCREDIT	COCKBOAT
SCANTIES	SPARKING	THATCHER	BUBBLING	PABULOUS	ACCURACY	COCKCROW
SCANTILY	SPARKLER	TOADFLAX	CABERNET	PUBLICAN	ACCURATE	COCKEREL
SCAPHOID	SPARRING	TRACHOMA	CABLECAR	PUBLICLY	ACCURSED	COCKEYED
SCAPULAR	SPARSELY	TRACKING	CABLEWAY	RABELAIS	ACCUSING	COCKTAIL
SCARCELY	SPARSITY	TRACTION	CABOCHON	REBUTTAL	ACCUSTOM	CUCUMBER
SCARCITY	SPARTANS	TRADEOFF	CABOODLE	RIBALDRY	ALCATRAZ	CUCURBIT
SCARFACE	SPAVINED	TRAILING	CABOTAGE	RIBSTONE	ALCESTIS	CYCLADES
SCATHING	SPAWNING	TRAINING	CABRIOLE	ROBINSON	ALCHEMIC	CYCLAMEN
SCAVENGE	STABBING	TRAITORS	CIBORIUM	ROBOTICS	ANCESTOR	CYCLICAL
SEABOARD	STABLING	TRAMLINE	COBBLERS	ROBUSTLY	ANCESTRY	CYCLOSIS
SEABORNE	STACCATO	TRANQUIL	COBWEBBY	RUBAIYAT	ANCHISES	DECADENT
SEAFARER	STAFFING	TRANSACT	DABCHICK	RUBBISHY	ANCHORET	DECANTER
SEAFLOOR	STAFFORD	TRANSECT	DEBILITY	RUBICUND	ARCADIAN	DECAYING
SEAFORTH	STAGGERS	TRANSEPT	DEBONAIR	RUBIDIUM	ARCHAISM	DECEASED
SEAFRONT	STAGHORN	TRANSFER	DUBONNET	SABOTAGE	ARCHDUKE	DECEIVER
SEAGOING	STAGNANT	TRANSFIX	EMBATTLE	SABOTEUR	ARCHIVES	DECEMBER
SEALSKIN	STAGNATE	TRANSHIP	EMBEDDED	SIBERIAN	ARCTURUS	DECEMVIR
SEALYHAM	STAIRWAY	TRANSKEI	EMBEZZLE	SIBILANT	ASCIDIAN	DECENTLY
SEAMLESS	STAKEOUT	TRANSMIT	EMBITTER	SOBERING	ASCIDIUM	DECIMATE
SEAMSTER	STALKING	TRAPDOOR	EMBLAZON	SOBRIETY	ASCOCARP	DECIPHER
SEAPLANE	STALLION	TRAPPIST	EMBODIED	SUBHUMAN	ASCORBIC	DECISION
SEARCHER	STALWART	TRASHCAN	EMBOLDEN	SUBJECTS	AUCASSIN	DECISIVE
SEASCAPE	STAMENED	TRAVELER	EMBOLISM	SUBLEASE	BACCARAT	DECKHAND
SEASHELL	STAMPEDE	TRAVERSE	EMBOSSED	SUBMERGE	BACCHANT	DECLUTCH
SEASHORE	STANDARD	TRAVESTY	EMBRACED	SUBPOENA	BACHELOR	DECORATE
SEASONAL	STANDING	TSAREVNA	EMBRACES	SUBSHRUB	BACILLUS	DECOROUS
SEASONED	STANDISH	TZATZIKI	FABULOUS	SUBSONIC	BACKACHE	DECOUPLE
SEAWARDS	STANDOFF	UNABATED	FEBRUARY	SUBTENSE	BACKBITE	DECREASE
SHABBILY	STANHOPE	UNAWARES	FIBROSIS	SUBTITLE	BACKBONE	DECREPIT
SHACKLES	STANNARY	VIATICUM	GABONESE	SUBTLETY	BACKCHAT	DECRETAL
SHADRACH	STANNITE	WEAKFISH	GABORONE	SUBTOPIA	BACKCOMB	DICTATES
SHAGBARK	STAPELIA	WEAKLING	GOBSMACK	SUBTOTAL	BACKDATE	DICTATOR
SHAGREEN	STAPHYLE	WEAKNESS	HABAKKUK	SUBTRACT	BACKDROP	DICYCLIC
SHAKEOUT	STARCHED	WEAPONRY	HABANERA	SUBURBAN	BACKFIRE	DOCILITY
SHALLOWS	STARDUST	WEARABLE	HABITUAL	SUBURBIA	BACKHAND	DOCKLAND
SHAMBLES	STARFISH	WHACKING	HABSBURG	SYBARITE	BACKLASH	DOCKSIDE
SHAMEFUL	STARGAZE	WHARFAGE	HEBETUDE	TABBYCAT	BACKLESS	DOCKYARD
SHAMROCK	STARKERS	WHATEVER	HEBRAISM	TABLEMAT	BACKPACK	DOCTORAL
SHANGAAN	STARLESS	WRANGLER	HEBRIDES	TABULATE	BACKROOM	DOCTORED
SHANGHAI	STARLING	WRAPPING	HIBERNIA	TIBERIAS	BACKSIDE	DOCTRINE

DOCUMENT	LECTRICE	PICKLOCK	UNCHASTE	ENDANGER	MIDNIGHT	SEDULOUS
DUCHESSE	LECTURER	PICKMEUP	UNCIFORM	ENDEAVOR	MIDPOINT	SIDEKICK
DUCKBILL	LECTURES	PICKWICK	UNCLOVEN	ENDOCARP	MODELING	SIDELINE
DUCKLING	LICENSED	PICTURES	UNCOMBED	ENDODERM	MODELLER	SIDELONG
DUCKWEED	LICENSEE	POCHETTE	UNCOMMON	ENDOGAMY	MODERATE	SIDEREAL
ENCAENIA	LICORICE	POCKMARK	UNCOOKED	ENDURING	MODERATO	SIDERITE
ENCAMPED	LOCALITY	PUCKERED	UNCOUPLE	ENDYMION	MODESTLY	SIDESHOW
ENCIRCLE	LOCALIZE	RACHITIS	UNCTUOUS	EUDOXIAN	MODIFIER	SIDESLIP
ENCLOSED	LOCATION	RACIALLY	UNCURBED	FEDAYEEN	MODULATE	SIDESMAN
ENCLOTHE	LOCATIVE	RACINESS	UPCOMING	FEDERACY	MUDFLATS	SIDESTEP
ENCOMIUM	LOCKABLE	RACKRENT	VACANTLY	FEDERATE	MUDGUARD	SIDEWALK
ENCROACH	LOCOWEED	RACLETTE	VACATION	FIDDLING	MUDSTONE	SIDEWARD
ENCUMBER	LUCIDITY	RECEDING	VICARAGE	FIDELITY	NIDATION	SIDEWAYS
ESCALADE	LUCKLESS	RECEIPTS	VICARIAL	FIDUCIAL	OBDURACY	SODALITE
ESCALATE	MACARONI	RECEIVED	VICINITY	GADABOUT	OBDURATE	SODALITY
ESCALOPE	MACAROON	RECEIVER	VICTORIA	GADARENE	ODDMENTS	SUDAMENT
ESCAPADE	MACASSAR	RECENTLY	VICTUALS	GADGETRY	OEDIPEAN	SUDAMINA
ESCAPISM	MACAULAY	RECEPTOR	VOCALIST	GADOGADO	OLDSTYLE	SUDANESE
ESCAPIST	MACERATE	RECESSED	VOCALIZE	GADZOOKS	OLDWORLD	SUDARIUM
ESCARGOT	MACHEATH	RECHARGE	VOCATION	GODCHILD	OMDURMAN	SUDDENLY
ESCORIAL	MACHINES	RECKLESS	VOCATIVE	HEDGEHOG	ORDERING	TIDEMARK
ESCULENT	MACHISMO	RECKONER	WICKEDLY	HEDGEROW	ORDINAND	TIDINESS
ETCETERA	MACKEREL	RECORDER	WYCLIFFE	HEDONISM	ORDINARY	UNDERAGE
EUCYCLIC	MACMAHON	RECOURSE	YACHTING	HEDONIST	ORDINATE	UNDERARM
EXCAVATE	MACREADY	RECOVERY	ZUCCHINI	HIDEAWAY	ORDNANCE	UNDERBID
EXCHANGE	MACULATE	RECREATE	ABDICATE	HIDROSIS	PADDLING	UNDERCUT
EXCISION	MECHANIC	RECRUITS	ABDUCENS	HYDATOID	PEDAGOGY	UNDERDOG
EXCITING	MICHIGAN	RECUSANT	ABDUCTED	HYDROGEN	PEDANTIC	UNDERFED
FACEACHE	MICRODOT	RICHNESS	ABDUCTOR	HYDROXYL	PEDANTRY	UNDERFUR
FACELESS	MOCCASIN	RICKSHAW	ADDENDUM	INDEBTED	PEDDLING	UNDERLAY
FACELIFT	MUCHNESS	RICOCHET	ADDICTED	INDECENT	PEDERAST	UNDERLIE
FACILITY	MUCILAGE	ROCHDALE	ADDITION	INDENTED	PEDESTAL	UNDERPIN
FACTIOUS	MYCELIUM	ROCKETRY	ADDITIVE	INDEXING	PEDICURE	UNDERRUN
FACTOTUM	MYCOLOGY	RUCKSACK	ALDEHYDE	INDIAMAN	PEDIGREE	UNDERSEA
FECKLESS	NECKBAND	RUCTIONS	ALDERMAN	INDICANT	PEDIMENT	UNDERTOW
FECULENT	NECKLACE	SACRISTY	ALDERNEY	INDICATE	PEDUNCLE	UNDULANT
FUCHSITE	NECKLINE	SECLUDED	ANDERSON	INDIGENT	PIDDLING	UNDULATE
HACIENDA	NECKWEAR	SECONDER	ANDORRAN	INDIRECT	PODARGUS	WEDGWOOD
HECATOMB	NECROSIS	SECONDLY	ANDREWES	INDOLENT	PUDENDUM	WIDENING
HECKLING	NICENESS	SECRETLY	ARDENNES	INDUCIVE	RADIANCE	YODELLER
HICCOUGH	NICHOLAS	SECURELY	ARDENTLY	INDUCTOR	RADIATOR	ZEDEKIAH
HUCKSTER	NICKNACK	SECURITY	AUDACITY	INDUSTRY	REDACTOR	ZODIACAL
INCENSED	NICKNAME	SICILIAN	AUDIENCE	JODHPURS	REDBRICK	ABERDEEN
INCHOATE	NICOTINE	SICKLIST	AUDITION	JUDGMENT	REDEEMER	ABERRANT
INCIDENT	NOCTURNE	SICKNESS	AUDITORY	JUDICIAL	REDEFINE	ABESSIVE
INCISION	NUCLEATE	SICKROOM	BADINAGE	KEDGEREE	REDEPLOY	ABEYANCE
INCISIVE	NUCLEOLE	SOCALLED	BADLANDS	KIDGLOVE	REDESIGN	ACENTRIC
INCLINED	OCCAMIST	SOCIABLE	BEDABBLE	LADRONES	REDIRECT	ACERBATE
INCLUDED	OCCASION	SOCIALLY	BEDCOVER	LADYBIRD	REDLIGHT	ACERBITY
INCOMING	OCCIDENT	SOCRATES	BEDMAKER	LADYFISH	REDOLENT	ADELAIDE
INCREASE	OCCUPANT	SOCRATIC	BEDSTEAD	LADYLIKE	REDOUBLE	ADENITIS
INCUBATE	OCCUPIED	SUCCEEDS	BEDSTRAW	LADYSHIP	REDSHANK	ADENOIDS
JACKAROO	OCCUPIER	SUCCINCT	BODLEIAN	LODESTAR	REDSHIFT	ADEQUACY
JACKBOOT	ONCOLOGY	SUCCUBUS	BODYLINE	LODGINGS	REDSTART	ADEQUATE
JACKETED	ONCOMING	SUCHLIKE	BODYWORK	MADHOUSE	RIDDANCE	ADESSIVE
JACOBEAN	ORCADIAN	SUCKLING	BUDAPEST	MADRIGAL	RIDGEWAY	ALEATORY
JACOBITE	ORCHITIS	SYCAMORE	BUDDHISM	MADWOMAN	RIDICULE	ALEHOUSE
JACQUARD	OSCULATE	TACITURN	BUDDHIST	MEDALIST	RODERICK	ALEMAINE
KACHAHRI	PACHINKO	TACTICAL	BUDDLEIA	MEDDLING	RUDENESS	ALEUTIAN
KICKBACK	PACIFIER	TACTLESS	CADASTRE	MEDIATOR	RUDIMENT	AMENABLE
KICKSHAW	PACIFISM	TECTONIC	CADILLAC	MEDICATE	SADDLERY	AMERICAN
LACERATE	PACIFIST	TICKLING	CADUCEUS	MEDICINE	SADDLING	AMERICAS
LACEWING	PACKAGED	TICKLISH	CODPIECE	MEDIEVAL	SADDUCEE	AMETHYST
LACINATE	PECORINO	TICKSEED	DEDICATE	MEDIOCRE	SADISTIC	ANECDOTE
LACKADAY	PECTORAL	TICKTACK	DIDACTIC	MEDITATE	SEDATELY	ANEURYSM
LACKLAND	PECULATE	TICKTOCK	DIDDICOY	MIDBRAIN	SEDATION	APERIENT
LACONIAN	PECULIAR	ULCERATE	EIDECTIC	MIDDLING	SEDATIVE	APERITIF
LACROSSE	PICAROON	ULCEROUS	ELDORADO	MIDFIELD	SEDIMENT	APERTURE
LECITHIN	PICKINGS	UNCARING	ELDRITCH	MIDLANDS	SEDITION	ARETHUSA

AVENTINE	CREOSOTE	FEELINGS	MEEKNESS	OVERWORK	SHEARMAN	THEORIST
AVERSION	CREPITUS	FIELDING	MNEMONIC	PEEKABOO	SHEEPDOG	THEORIZE
BAEDEKER	CRESCENT	FIENDISH	MYELITIS	PEELINGS	SHEEPISH	THESPIAN
BEERBOHM	CRETONNE	FIERCELY	NEEDLESS	PEEPHOLE	SHEIKDOM	TIEBREAK
BEESWING	CREVASSE	FLEABITE	OBEDIENT	PEEPSHOW	SHELDUCK	TREASURE
BEETLING	DAEDALUS	FLEETING	OLEACEAE	PEERLESS	SHELVING	TREASURY
BEETROOT	DEEPNESS	FLEISHIG	OLEANDER	PHEASANT	SHEPHERD	TREATISE
BIENNIAL	DEERSKIN	FLEXIBLE	OLEASTER	PHENOLIC	SHERATON	TREELESS
BLEACHER	DIEHARDS	FLEXIBLY	OMELETTE	PIECHART	SHERIDAN	TREELINE
BLEEDING	DIELDRIN	FREAKISH	ONESIDED	PIECRUST	SHERLOCK	TREETOPS
BLENDING	DIERESIS	FRECKLED	ONETRACK	PIERCING	SHERWOOD	TREMBLER
BLENHEIM	DJELLABA	FRECKLES	OPENCAST	PIERETTE	SHETLAND	TREMBLES
BLESSING	DREADFUL	FREEHAND	OPENDOOR	PIERIDES	SKELETAL	TRENCHER
BOEOTIAN	DREAMILY	FREEHOLD	OPENNESS	PLEADING	SKELETON	TRESPASS
BREACHES	DREAMING	FREEPOST	OPENPLAN	PLEASANT	SKEWBALD	TWEEZERS
BREAKING	DREARILY	FREETOWN	OPENWORK	PLEASING	SLEEPERS	TWELVEMO
BREAKOUT	DRESSAGE	FREEZING	OPERABLE	PLEASURE	SLEEPILY	UNEARNED
BREATHER	DRESSING	FREMITUS	OPERATIC	PLEBEIAN	SLEEPING	UNEASILY
BREECHES	DUELLIST	FRENETIC	OPERATOR	PLECTRUM	SMELTING	UNENDING
BREEDING	DWELLING	FRENULUM	OPERETTA	PLEIADES	SNEAKERS	UNERRING
BREEZILY	EDENTATE	FRENZIED	ORESTEIA	PLEONASM	SNEAKING	UNEVENLY
BRETHREN	EJECTION	FREQUENT	OVENBIRD	PLETHORA	SNEERING	URETHANE
BREVIARY	ELECTION	FRESHEST	OVENWARE	PLEURISY	SNEEZING	USEFULLY
CAERLEON	ELECTIVE	FRESHMAN	OVERALLS	POETICAL	SPEAKERS	UTENSILS
CHEATERS	ELECTORS	FRETWORK	OVERBOOK	PREACHER	SPEAKING	VIETCONG
CHEATING	ELECTRIC	FREUDIAN	OVERCAST	PREAMBLE	SPECIFIC	WHEATEAR
CHECKERS	ELECTRON	GLEAMING	OVERCOAT	PRECINCT	SPECIMEN	WHEEZILY
CHECKING	ELECTRUM	GLEESOME	OVERCOME	PRECIOUS	SPECIOUS	WHEEZING
CHECKOUT	ELEGANCE	GREATEST	OVERDONE	PRECLUDE	SPECKLED	WHENEVER
CHEEKILY	ELEMENTS	GREEDILY	OVERDOSE	PRECURSE	SPECTRAL	WHEREVER
CHEERFUL	ELEPHANT	GREENBAG	OVERDRAW	PREDATOR	SPECTRUM	WOEFULLY
CHEERILY	ELEVATED	GREENERY	OVERFEED	PREDELLA	SPECULUM	WREATHED
CHEERING	ELEVATOR	GREENFLY	OVERFILL	PREGNANT	SPEEDILY	WRECKAGE
CHEMICAL	ELEVENTH	GREENING	OVERFLOW	PREJUDGE	SPEEDWAY	WRESTLER
CHENILLE	EMERGENT	GREENISH	OVERFULL	PREMIERE	SPELLING	WRETCHED
CHEQUERS	EMERGING	GREENOCK	OVERHAND	PREMISES	SPELLMAN	YIELDING
CHEROKEE	EMERITUS	GREETING	OVERHANG	PREMOLAR	SPENDING	ZOETROPE
CHERUBIC	EMERSION	GRENACHE	OVERHAUL	PRENATAL	STEADILY	AFFECTED
CHERUBIM	ENERGIZE	GUERIDON	OVERHEAD	PREPARED	STEALING	AFFERENT
CHERWELL	ENERVATE	GUERILLA	OVERHEAR	PRESENCE	STEALTHY	AFFINITY
CHESHIRE	ERECTILE	GUERNSEY	OVERHEAT	PRESERVE	STEAPSIN	AFFLATUS
CHESSMAN	ERECTING	HEADLESS	OVERKILL	PRESSING	STEATITE	AFFLUENT
CHESSMEN	ERECTION	HEELBALL	OVERLAID	PRESSMAN	STEATOMA	AFFUSION
CHESTNUT	ETERNITY	HEELTAPS	OVERLAND	PRESSURE	STEENBOK	ALFRESCO
CHEVIOTS	EVENNESS	HIERARCH	OVERLEAF	PRESTIGE	STEERAGE	BAFFLING
CHEYENNE	EVENSONG	HIERATIC	OVERLOAD	PRETENCE	STEERING	BEFRIEND
CLEANERS	EVENTFUL	ICEBLINK	OVERLOOK	PRETENSE	STEINWAY	BEFUDDLE
CLEANING	EVENTIDE	ICEFIELD	OVERLORD	PRETORIA	STELLATE	BIFOCALS
CLEANSED	EVENTUAL	ICEHOUSE	OVERMUCH	PRETTILY	STENDHAL	CAFFEINE
CLEANSER	EVERMORE	IDEALISM	OVERPASS	PREVIOUS	STENOSED	DAFFODIL
CLEARCUT	EVERYDAY	IDEALIST	OVERPLAY	PSEUDERY	STENOSIS	DEFEATED
CLEARING	EVERYMAN	IDEALIZE	OVERRATE	PTEROPOD	STEPHENS	DEFECATE
CLEARWAY	EVERYONE	IDENTIFY	OVERRIDE	PYELITIS	STERLING	DEFECTOR
CLEAVAGE	EXECRATE	IDENTITY	OVERRIPE	QUENELLE	SVENGALI	DEFENDER
CLEAVERS	EXECUTED	IDEOGRAM	OVERRULE	QUESTION	SWEARING	DEFIANCE
CLEMATIS	EXECUTOR	IDEOLOGY	OVERSEAS	REEDLING	SWEATING	DEFILADE
CLEMENCY	EXEGESIS	INEDIBLE	OVERSEER	REEDSMAN	SWEEPING	DEFINITE
CLERICAL	EXEGETIC	INEQUITY	OVERSHOE	REEMPLOY	SWEETSOP	DEFLOWER
CLERIHEW	EXEMPLAR	INEXPERT	OVERSHOT	RHEOSTAT	SWELLING	DEFORMED
CLEVERLY	EXERCISE	KEELHAUL	OVERSIZE	RHETORIC	SWERVING	DEFREEZE
COERCION	EXERTION	KEENNESS	OVERSOLD	RIESLING	TEENAGER	DEFTNESS
COERCIVE	EYEGLASS	KEEPSAKE	OVERSTAY	ROENTGEN	TEESHIRT	DIFFRACT
CREAMERY	EYELINER	KNEEDEEP	OVERSTEP	RUEFULLY	TEETHING	EFFERENT
CREATION	EYEPIECE	KNEEHIGH	OVERTAKE	RYEGRASS	TEETOTAL	EFFICACY
CREATIVE	EYESHADE	KREPLACH	OVERTIME	SCENARIO	THEATRIC	EFFLUENT
CREATURE	EYESIGHT	LIEGEMAN	OVERTONE	SEEDLESS	THEBAINE	EFFLUVIA
CREDIBLE	EYETOOTH	LIENTERY	OVERTURE	SEEDLING	THEMATIC	EFFUSION
CREDIBLY	FEEDBACK	MAECENAS	OVERTURN	SEEDSMAN	THEOCRAT	EFFUSIVE
CREDITOR	FEELGOOD	MAESTOSO	OVERVIEW	SEETHING	THEOLOGY	ENFEEBLE

ENFILADE	UNFETTER	FIGHTING	PAGINATE	COHERENT	ANISETTE	DAINTILY
FIFTIETH	UNFILLED	FIGURINE	PIGSWILL	COHESION	APIARIST	DAIQUIRI
INFAMOUS	UNFORCED	FOGBOUND	PUGILISM	COHESIVE	AVIATION	DAIRYMAN
INFANTRY	UNFREEZE	FOGLIGHT	PUGILIST	ECHINATE	AVICENNA	DJIBOUTI
INFECTED	AEGROTAT	FUGITIVE	PUGNOSED	ECHINOPS	AVIFAUNA	DRIBLETS
INFERIOR	AGGRIEVE	FUGLEMAN	RAGNARÖK	EOHIPPUS	BAILMENT	DRIFTING
INFERNAL	AIGRETTE	GIGABYTE	RAGSTONE	EPHEMERA	BLIGHTER	DRINKING
INFESTED	AIGUILLE	GIGANTIC	REGAINED	EPHESIAN	BLINDING	DRIPPING
INFINITE	ALGERIAN	GIGAWATT	REGICIDE	ETHEREAL	BLINKERS	DRIVEWAY
INFINITY	ALGERINE	GIGLAMPS	REGIMENT	ETHERIFY	BLINKING	ELIGIBLE
INFLAMED	ALGOLOGY	HAGGADAH	REGIONAL	ETHERISE	BLISSFUL	EMIGRANT
INFLATED	ALGORISM	HEGEMONY	REGISTER	ETHIOPIA	BLITHELY	EMIGRATE
INFLIGHT	ANGELICA	HIGHBALL	REGISTRY	ETHNARCH	BLIZZARD	EMINENCE
INFLUENT	ANGLESEY	HIGHBORN	REGULATE	ETHOLOGY	BRIBABLE	EMINENCY
INFORMAL	ANGLICAN	HIGHBROW	RIGATONI	ETHYLENE	BRICKBAT	EMIRATES
INFORMED	ANGSTROM	HIGHGATE	RIGHTFUL	EXHUMATE	BRIDGING	EMISSARY
INFORMER	ANGUILLA	HIGHLAND	RIGHTIST	INHALANT	BRIEFING	EMISSION
INFRARED	ARGESTES	HIGHNESS	RIGIDITY	INHERENT	BRIGHTEN	ENIWETOK
INFRINGE	ARGININE	HIGHRISE	RIGOROUS	INHUMANE	BRIGHTLY	EPICURUS
INFUSION	ARGONAUT	HIGHROAD	ROGATION	JEHOVAHS	BRIGHTON	EPIDEMIC
JEFFREYS	ARGUABLE	HOGMANAY	RUGGEDLY	JOHANNES	BRIMMING	EPIDURAL
KUFFIYEH	ARGUABLY	HOGSHEAD	SAGACITY	JOHNSONS	BRINDISI	EPIGAMIC
LEFTHAND	ARGUMENT	HYGIENIC	SAGENESS	KOHLRABI	BRINDLED	EPIGRAPH
LEFTOVER	AUGUSTUS	INGROWTH	SIGHTING	MAHARAJA	BRINGING	EPILEPSY
LEFTWARD	BAGHEERA	INGUINAL	SIGHTSEE	MAHARANI	BRISLING	EPILOGUE
LEFTWING	BAGPIPES	JIGGERED	SIGNALER	MAHJONGG	BRISTLED	EPIPHANY
LIFEBELT	BAGUETTE	JUGGLING	SIGNALLY	MAHOGANY	BRISTLES	EPIPHYTE
LIFEBOAT	BEGETTER	LEGALISM	SIGNORIA	MOHAMMED	BUILDING	EPIPLOON
LIFEBUOY	BEGGARLY	LEGALITY	SIGNPOST	MUHAMMAD	CHIASMUS	EPISODIC
LIFELESS	BEGINNER	LEGALIZE	TEGUMENT	MUHARRAM	CHICHEWA	EPISTYLE
LIFELIKE	BEGORRAH	LEGATION	TIGHTWAD	NEHEMIAH	CHICKENS	EPITASIS
LIFELINE	BEGRUDGE	LEGGINGS	TOGETHER	NIHILISM	CHICKPEA	EPITHEMA
LIFELONG	BIGAMIST	LIGAMENT	UNGAINLY	NIHILIST	CHILDERS	ERIDANUS
LIFESPAN	BIGAMOUS	LIGATURE	UNGULATE	OPHIDIAN	CHILDISH	ERIKSSON
LIFETIME	BIGARADE	LIGHTING	URGENTLY	REHEARSE	CHILDREN	ETIOLATE
NUFFIELD	BIGNONIA	LIGNEOUS	VAGABOND	SCHAPSKA	CHILIAST	EVICTION
OFFBREAK	BOGEYMAN	LOGISTIC	VAGARIES	SCHEDULE	CHILLADA	EVIDENCE
OFFCOLOR	BUGGERED	LOGOTYPE	VAGRANCY	SCHEMING	CHILLING	EVILDOER
OFFENDED	CAGINESS	MAGAZINE	VEGETATE	SCHILLER	CHILTERN	EWIGKEIT
OFFENDER	COGITATE	MAGELLAN	VIGILANT	SCHIZOID	CHIMAERA	EXIGENCY
OFFERING	COGNOMEN	MAGICIAN	VIGNETTE	SCHMALTZ	CHINAMAN	EXIGUITY
OFFICERS	COGWHEEL	MAGISTER	VIGOROUS	SCHMOOZE	CHINDITS	EXIGUOUS
OFFICIAL	DEGRADED	MAGNESIA	WAGGONER	SCHNAPPS	CHIPMUNK	EXISTENT
OFFPRINT	DIGGINGS	MAGNETIC	YOGHOURT	SCHOONER	CHITCHAT	EXISTING
OFFSHOOT	DIGITIZE	MAGNOLIA	YUGOSLAV	SCHUBERT	CHIVALRY	FAINITES
OFFSHORE	DIGIZINE	MEGABYTE	ZIGGURAT	SCHUMANN	CLIFFORD	FAINTING
OFFSIDER	DOGBERRY	MEGALITH	ACHIEVED	SPHAGNUM	CLIMATIC	FAIRNESS
OFFSTAGE	DOGGEDLY	MEGAPODE	ACHIEVER	SPHENOID	CLIMBING	FAITHFUL
PUFFBALL	DOGGEREL	MEGAVOLT	ACHILLES	TAHITIAN	CLINCHER	FLIMSILY
REFERRAL	DOGHOUSE	MEGAWATT	ADHERENT	UNHARMED	CLINGING	FLINDERS
REFINERY	DOGMATIC	MIGHTILY	ADHESION	UNHEATED	CLINICAL	FLIPPANT
REFORMED	DOGSBODY	MIGNONNE	ADHESIVE	UNHEROIC	CLINKERS	FLIPPERS
REFORMER	DOGSTAIL	MIGRAINE	ALHAMBRA	UNHINGED	CLIPPERS	FLIPPING
REFRINGE	DOGTOOTH	NAGASAKI	APHELION	UPHEAVAL	CLIPPING	FLIRTING
REFUGIUM	DOGWATCH	NEGATION	APHORISM	UPHOLDER	CLIQUISH	FRICTION
RIFFRAFF	EDGEHILL	NEGATIVE	ATHANASY	VEHEMENT	CLITORIS	FRIENDLY
RIFLEMAN	EDGEWAYS	NEGLIGEE	ATHELING	ABINGDON	CLIVEDEN	FRIGHTEN
SOFTBACK	EDGEWISE	NEGRILLO	ATHENIAN	ACIDHEAD	COIFFEUR	FRIGIDLY
SOFTBALL	EGGPLANT	NIGERIAN	ATHEROMA	AGITATED	COIFFURE	FRIPPERY
SOFTENER	EGGSHELL	NIGERIEN	ATHETISE	AGITATOR	COINCIDE	FRISKILY
SOFTNESS	EGGTIMER	NIGGLING	ATHETOID	AGITPROP	CRIBBAGE	GAILLARD
SOFTWARE	EIGHTEEN	NIGHTCAP	ATHLETIC	ALICANTE	CRICHTON	GLISSADE
SOFTWOOD	ENGAGING	NIGHTJAR	BAHAMIAN	ALIENATE	CRIMINAL	GOIDELIC
SUFFERER	ENGENDER	NUGATORY	BAHRAINI	ALIENISM	CRINGING	GRIDIRON
SUFFRAGE	ENGINEER	ORGANDIE	BEHAVIOR	ALIENIST	CRIPPLED	GRIDLOCK
TAFFRAIL	ENGRAVER	ORGANISM	BEHEMOTH	ALIQUANT	CRISPIAN	GRIEVOUS
TEFILLIN	ERGOTISE	ORGANIST	BEHOLDEN	AMICABLE	CRITICAL	GRILLING
UNFADING	ERGOTISM	ORGANIZE	BEHOLDER	AMICABLY	CRITIQUE	GRIMALDI
UNFASTEN	EUGENICS	PAGANINI	BOHEMIAN	ANIMATED	DAINTIES	GRIMNESS

GRINDING	POISONER	SKINDEEP	TAILSPIN	WHISKERY	ALLELUIA	CALLGIRL
GRIPPING	POITIERS	SKINHEAD	THIAMINE	WHISTLER	ALLERGEN	CALLIOPE
GRISELDA	PRIAPISM	SKINWORK	THICKSET	WHITECAP	ALLERGIC	CALLIPER
GRISETTE	PRIESTLY	SKIPJACK	THIEVERY	WHITEHOT	ALLEYWAY	CALLISTO
GRIZZLED	PRIGGISH	SKIPPING	THIEVING	WHITENER	ALLIANCE	CALMNESS
GUIANIAN	PRIMEVAL	SKIRMISH	THIEVISH	WHITLING	ALLOCATE	CALOTYPE
GUIDANCE	PRIMNESS	SKIRTING	THINGAMY	WRINGING	ALLOGAMY	CALTHROP
GUILTILY	PRIMROSE	SKITTISH	THINKING	WRINKLED	ALLOPATH	CALVADOS
HAIRBAND	PRINCELY	SKITTLES	THINNESS	WRISTLET	ALLOWING	CELANESE
HAIRLESS	PRINCESS	SLIGHTED	THINNING	WRITEOFF	ALLSPICE	CELERIAC
HAIRLIKE	PRINTING	SLIGHTLY	THIOUREA	WRITHING	ALLURING	CELERITY
HAIRLINE	PRINTOUT	SLIMNESS	THIRTEEN	WRITINGS	ALLUSION	CELIBACY
HAIRWORM	PRIORESS	SLIPOVER	TOILSOME	ZWIEBACK	ALLUSIVE	CELIBATE
HEIGHTEN	PRIORITY	SLIPPERS	TOISEACH	ABJECTLY	ALLUVIAL	CELLARER
HEIRLESS	PRISONER	SLIPPERY	TRIANGLE	ADJACENT	ALLUVIUM	CELLULAR
HEIRLOOM	PRISTINE	SLIPPING	TRIASSIC	ADJUSTER	BALANCED	CHLORATE
IDIOGRAM	PRIVATES	SLIPSHOD	TRIBUNAL	ADJUSTOR	BALDNESS	CHLORIDE
IMITATOR	PUISSANT	SLIPSLOP	TRICHOID	ADJUTAGE	BALDRICK	CHLORINE
INIMICAL	QUIBBLER	SMIDGEON	TRICKERY	ADJUTANT	BALEARIC	CILIATED
INIQUITY	QUICKSET	SNIFFLER	TRICYCLE	ADJUVANT	BALINESE	COLANDER
INITIATE	QUIETUDE	SPICCATO	TRIFLING	CAJOLERY	BALLCOCK	COLDBOOT
IRISCOPE	QUILTING	SPIFFING	TRIGLYPH	DEJECTED	BALLGAME	COLDNESS
IRISHISM	QUINCUNX	SPILLAGE	TRIGRAPH	GUJARATI	BALLGIRL	COLESLAW
IRISHMAN	QUINTAIN	SPILLWAY	TRILEMMA	HIJACKER	BALLISTA	COLIFORM
IRISHMEN	QUIRINAL	SPINIFEX	TRILLING	INJECTOR	BALLOCKS	COLISEUM
JAILBIRD	QUISLING	SPINNING	TRILLION	MAJESTIC	BALLOONS	COLLAGEN
JOINTURE	QUIXOTIC	SPINSTER	TRILLIUM	MAJOLICA	BALLPARK	COLLAPSE
KNICKERS	RAILHEAD	SPINTEXT	TRIMARAN	MAJORITY	BALLROOM	COLLARED
KNIGHTLY	RAILINGS	SPIRACLE	TRIMMING	NDJAMENA	BALLYHOO	COLLATOR
KNITTING	RAILLERY	SPIRALLY	TRIMNESS	NIJINSKY	BALMORAL	COLLECTS
KNITWEAR	RAILROAD	SPIRELET	TRINCULO	OBJECTOR	BALUSTER	COLLEGES
LAIDBACK	RAINBIRD	SPIRITED	TRINIDAD	REJOINED	BELABOUR	COLLIERS
LEINSTER	RAINCOAT	SPIRITUS	TRIPLING	UNJUSTLY	BELGRADE	COLLIERY
LEISURED	RAINDROP	SPITEFUL	TRIPTANE	AKKADIAN	BELIEVER	COLLOQUY
LOITERER	RAINFALL	SPITFIRE	TRIPTYCH	ALKALIFY	BELITTLE	COLOMBIA
MAIDENLY	RAINWEAR	SPITHEAD	TRISTICH	ALKALINE	BELLPUSH	COLONIAL
MAIEUTIC	RAISONNÉ	SPITTING	TRISTRAM	ALKALOID	BELLYFUL	COLONIST
MAILBOAT	REIGNING	SPITTOON	TRITICAL	ARKANSAS	BELPAESE	COLONIZE
MAILSHOT	REINDEER	STICCATO	TRITICUM	BAKELITE	BILBERRY	COLOPHON
MAINLAND	REINSURE	STICKILY	TRIUNITY	CAKEHOLE	BILLFOLD	COLORADO
MAINLINE	REINVEST	STICKING	TWILIGHT	CAKEWALK	BILLHOOK	COLORANT
MAINMAST	SAILBOAT	STICKLER	TWIRLING	ELKHOUND	BILLYBOY	COLORFUL
MAINSAIL	SAINFOIN	STIFLING	TWISTING	ENKINDLE	BILLYCAN	COLORING
MAINSTAY	SCIATICA	STIGMATA	TWITCHER	HOKKAIDO	BILOBATE	COLOSSAL
MAINTAIN	SCIENCES	STILETTO	UBIQUITY	INKSTAIN	BOLDNESS	COLOSSUS
MAINYARD	SCILICET	STILWELL	UNICYCLE	JOKINGLY	BOLIVIAN	COLOURED
MOISTURE	SCIMITAR	STIMULUS	UNIFYING	LAKELAND	BOLLOCKS	COLUMBAN
NEIGHBOR	SCIROCCO	STINGING	UNIONISM	LAKESIDE	BOLTHOLE	COLUMBUS
NOISETTE	SCISSION	STINGRAY	UNIONIST	LIKEABLE	BULGARIA	CULINARY
NUISANCE	SCISSORS	STINKING	UNIONIZE	LIKENESS	BULKHEAD	CULLINAN
OBITUARY	SEIGNIOR	STINKPOT	UNIPOLAR	LIKEWISE	BULLDOZE	CULLODEN
ODIOUSLY	SHIELING	STIRLING	UNIQUELY	LUKEWARM	BULLETIN	CULOTTES
OEILLADE	SHIFTING	STIRRING	UNITEDLY	MCKINLEY	BULLFROG	CULPABLE
OLIGARCH	SHIGELLA	SUICIDAL	UNIVALVE	PAKISTAN	BULLHORN	CULTURAL
OLIPHANT	SHIITAKE	SUITABLE	UNIVERSE	PEKINESE	BULLRING	CULTURED
OMISSION	SHILLING	SUITABLY	VAISAKHA	POKEWEED	BULLYRAG	CULVERIN
ORIENTAL	SHINBONE	SUITCASE	VOIDANCE	REKINDLE	CALABASH	CYLINDER
ORIGINAL	SHINGLES	SWILLING	WAINSCOT	SUKIYAKI	CALAMINE	DALMATIC
OUISTITI	SHIPMATE	SWIMMING	WAITRESS	TAKEAWAY	CALAMITY	DELAWARE
PAINLESS	SHIPMENT	SWIMSUIT	WEIGHING	TAKEHOME	CALCEATE	DELEGATE
PAINTING	SHIPPING	SWINDLER	WHIMBREL	TAKEOVER	CALCRETE	DELETION
PEIGNOIR	SHIPWORM	SWINEPOX	WHINCHAT	UNKINDLY	CALCULUS	DELICACY
PHILEMON	SHIPYARD	SWINGING	WHIPCORD	YAKITORI	CALCUTTA	DELICATE
PHILIPPI	SHIVERED	SWIRLING	WHIPHAND	YOKOHAMA	CALDERON	DELIRIUM
PHILLIPS	SKIBOOTS	TAILBACK	WHIPJACK	ZAKOUSKI	CALENDAR	DELIVERY
PHILOMEL	SKIDDING	TAILGATE	WHIPLASH	ABLATION	CALENDER	DELUSION
PLIMSOLL	SKILLFUL	TAILLESS	WHIPPING	ABLATIVE	CALFSKIN	DILATION
PLIOCENE	SKILLING	TAILPIPE	WHIRLING	ABLUTION	CALIGULA	DILATORY
POIGNANT	SKILLION	TAILSKID	WHISKERS	ALLEGORY	CALIPERS	DILIGENT

DILUTION	HALFYEAR	MELAMINE	PILCHARD	SELENIUM	UNLIKELY	CAMELLIA
DOLDRUMS	HALLIARD	MELANITE	PILFERER	SELEUCID	UNLISTED	CAMEROON
DOLOMITE	HALLMARK	MELANOMA	PILGRIMS	SELFHELP	UNLOADED	CAMISOLE
DOLOROUS	HALLOWED	MELCHIOR	PILLAGER	SELFLESS	UNLOCKED	CAMOMILE
DULCIMER	HELIPORT	MELEAGER	PILLARED	SELFMADE	UNLOVELY	CAMPAIGN
DULCINEA	HELLADIC	MELTDOWN	PILOTAGE	SELFPITY	VALENCIA	CAMPBELL
DULLNESS	HELLBENT	MILANESE	PILSENER	SELFSAME	VALERIAN	CAMPSITE
ECLECTIC	HELLENIC	MILDEWED	PILTDOWN	SELVEDGE	VALETING	CAMPTOWN
ECLOSION	HELLFIRE	MILDNESS	POLARIZE	SILENCER	VALHALLA	CAMSHAFT
ELLIPSIS	HELMETED	MILITANT	POLISHED	SILENTLY	VALIDATE	CAMSTONE
ELLIPTIC	HELMSMAN	MILITARY	POLISHER	SILESIAN	VALIDITY	CEMENTUM
ENLARGED	HELPLESS	MILITATE	POLITELY	SILICATE	VALKYRIE	CEMETERY
ENLARGER	HELPLINE	MILKLESS	POLITICO	SILICONE	VALLETTA	COMATOSE
EULOGIST	HELPMATE	MILKMAID	POLITICS	SILICULA	VALUABLE	COMBINED
EULOGIUM	HELSINKI	MILKWEED	POLLIWOG	SILKTAIL	VALVULAR	COMEBACK
EULOGIZE	HELVETIA	MILKWORT	POLLSTER	SILKWORM	VELLEITY	COMEDIAN
FALCONRY	HILARITY	MILLIBAR	POLLUTED	SILOXANE	VELOCITY	COMEDOWN
FALKLAND	HILLSIDE	MILLINER	POLLUTER	SILURIAN	VILENESS	COMMANDO
FALLIBLE	HOLDFAST	MILLIONS	POLONIUM	SOLARIUM	VILLAGER	COMMENCE
FALSETTO	HOLDINGS	MILLPOND	POLTROON	SOLDIERS	VILLAINY	COMMERCE
FELDSPAR	HOLIDAYS	MILLRACE	POLYANNA	SOLDIERY	VOLATILE	COMMONER
FELICITY	HOLINESS	MOLASSES	POLYARCH	SOLECISM	VOLCANIC	COMMONLY
FELLAHIN	HOLISTIC	MOLECULE	POLYCARP	SOLEMNLY	VOLITION	COMMUNAL
FILAMENT	HOLLOWAY	MOLEHILL	POLYGAMY	SOLENOID	VOLPLANE	COMMUTER
FILARIUM	HOLOCENE	MOLESKIN	POLYGLOT	SOLIDIFY	VOLSCIAN	COMPARED
FILENAME	HOLOGRAM	MOLESTER	POLYGYNY	SOLIDITY	VOLTAIRE	COMPILER
FILIGREE	HOLOZOIC	MOLLUSCS	POLYMATH	SOLITARY	VULGARLY	COMPLAIN
FILIPINO	HOLYHEAD	MOLUCCAS	POLYSEME	SOLITUDE	WALKOVER	COMPLETE
FILTHILY	HOLYROOD	MULBERRY	POLYSEMY	SOLSTICE	WALKYRIE	COMPLINE
FILTRATE	IDLENESS	MULETEER	PULITZER	SOLUTION	WALLSEND	COMPOSED
FOLDEROL	ILLFATED	MULEWORT	PULLDOWN	SOLVABLE	WALLWORT	COMPOSER
FOLKLORE	ILLINOIS	MULLIGAN	PULLOVER	SOLVENCY	WALTZING	COMPOUND
FOLKSONG	ILLUMINE	MULTIPLE	RELATING	SPLASHER	WELLBRED	COMPRESS
FOLLICLE	ILLUSION	MULTIPLY	RELATION	SPLATTER	WELLNIGH	COMPRISE
FOLLOWED	ILLUSIVE	OBLATION	RELATIVE	SPLENDID	WELLPAID	COMPUTER
FOLLOWER	ILLUSORY	OBLIGATE	RELAXING	SPLENDOR	WELSHMAN	DAMASCUS
FOLLOWUP	IOLANTHE	OBLIGING	RELAYING	SPLINTER	WILDFELL	DAMNABLE
FULLBACK	ISLANDER	OBLIVION	RELEASED	SPLITTER	WILDFIRE	DAMOCLES
FULLNESS	JALOUSIE	OILCLOTH	RELEGATE	SPLUTTER	WILDFOWL	DAMPNESS
FULLPAGE	JELLICOE	OILFIELD	RELEVANT	SULFURIC	WILDLIFE	DEMEANOR
FULLSIZE	JULIENNE	OILINESS	RELIABLE	SULLENLY	WILDNESS	DEMENTED
FULLTIME	KALAHARI	OILSKINS	RELIABLY	SULLIVAN	WILFULLY	DEMENTIA
GALACTIC	KILKENNY	OILSLICK	RELIANCE	SULPHATE	WILINESS	DEMERARA
GALBANUM	KILLDEER	OKLAHOMA	RELIEVED	SULPHIDE	WILLIAMS	DEMERSAL
GALILEAN	KILOBYTE	ONLOOKER	RELIGION	SYLLABIC	WOLFBANE	DEMIJOHN
GALLERIA	KILOGRAM	PALATIAL	RELOCATE	SYLLABLE	WOLSELEY	DEMISTER
GALLIARD	KILOVOLT	PALATINE	ROLLCALL	SYLLABUB	YULETIDE	DEMIURGE
GALLIPOT	KILOWATT	PALEFACE	ROLYPOLY	SYLLABUS	ADMIRING	DEMOCRAT
GALLOPER	KOLINSKY	PALENESS	RULEBOOK	SYLVANER	ADMONISH	DEMOLISH
GALLOWAY	LILONGWE	PALGRAVE	SALACITY	SYLVATIC	ALMIGHTY	DEMONIAC
GALLUMPH	LOLLIPOP	PALIMONY	SALARIED	TALENTED	AMMONIAC	DEMOTION
GALOSHES	LULWORTH	PALINODE	SALEABLE	TALISMAN	AMMONITE	DEMURELY
GALVANIC	MALAGASY	PALISADE	SALEROOM	TELECAST	AMMONOID	DEMURRAL
GELASTIC	MALAKOFF	PALLADIO	SALESMAN	TELECOMS	ARMAGNAC	DIMINISH
GELATINE	MALAMUTE	PALLIATE	SALINGER	TELEFILM	ARMALITE	DOMESDAY
GOLDFISH	MALARIAL	PALMATED	SALINITY	TELEGONY	ARMAMENT	DOMESTIC
GOLDMINE	MALARKEY	PALMETTO	SALIVARY	TELEGRAM	ARMATURE	DOMICILE
GOLFBALL	MALAWIAN	PALMITIN	SALIVATE	TELEMARK	ARMCHAIR	DOMINANT
GOLFCLUB	MALAYSIA	PALPABLE	SALTBUSH	TELETHON	ARMENIAN	DOMINATE
GOLGOTHA	MALDIVES	PALPABLY	SALTLICK	TELEVISE	ARMORIAL	DOMINEER
GOLLIWOG	MALGRADO	PALUDISM	SALTNESS	TELLTALE	ARMORICA	DOMINION
GULFWEED	MALINGER	PELAGIUS	SALUTARY	TELLURIC	ARMOURED	DOMINOES
GULLIBLE	MALLARMÉ	PELLAGRA	SALUTORY	TOLBOOTH	ASMODEUS	DUMBBELL
GULLIVER	MALLEATE	PELLICLE	SALVADOR	TOLERANT	BUMBLING	DUMBNESS
HALFFULL	MALLORCA	PELLETED	SELASSIE	TOLERATE	BUMMAREE	DUMFOUND
HALFHOUR	MALODOUR	PELLMELL	SELBORNE	TOLLGATE	CAMARGUE	DUMPLING
HALFMAST	MALTREAT	PELLUCID	SELECTED	UGLINESS	CAMBERED	EMMANUEL
HALFTERM	MALVASIA	PHLEGMON	SELECTOR	UNLAWFUL	CAMBODIA	ENMESHED
HALFTIME	MALVOLIO	PILASTER	SELENITE	UNLEADED	CAMBRIAN	FAMILIAR

FAMISHED	LIMBLESS	SOMBRELY	BANTLING	CONJUGAL	FONDNESS	IGNORANT
FAMOUSLY	LIMERICK	SOMBRERO	BENEDICK	CONJURER	FUNCTION	INNOCENT
FEMININE	LIMITING	SOMEBODY	BENEDICT	CONJUROR	FUNERARY	INNOVATE
FEMINISM	LIMONITE	SOMERSET	BENEFICE	CONQUEST	FUNEREAL	INNUENDO
FEMINIST	LIMPNESS	SOMETIME	BENEFITS	CONSERVE	FUNGIBLE	JANGLING
FEMINITY	LOMBARDY	SOMEWHAT	BENENDEN	CONSIDER	GANGLAND	JINGOISM
FUMAROLE	LUMINARY	SUMERIAN	BENGHAZI	CONSOMMÉ	GANGLING	JINGOIST
FUMBLING	LUMINOUS	SUMMITRY	BENJAMIN	CONSPIRE	GANGLION	JONATHAN
FUMIGATE	LUMPFISH	SYMBIONT	BINDWEED	CONSTANT	GANGRENE	JONCANOE
FUMITORY	MAMELUKE	SYMBOLIC	BINNACLE	CONSTRUE	GANGSTER	JONGLEUR
GAMBLING	MEMBRANE	SYMMETRY	BINOMIAL	CONSULAR	GANISTER	JUNCTION
GAMEBIRD	MEMORIAL	SYMPATHY	BONDSMAN	CONSUMED	GANYMEDE	JUNCTURE
GAMENESS	MEMORIAM	SYMPHONY	BONEFISH	CONSUMER	GENDARME	KANGAROO
GEMINATE	MEMORIZE	SYMPTOMS	BONEHEAD	CONTANGO	GENERATE	KENTUCKY
GEMOLOGY	MEMSAHIB	TAMANDUA	BONELESS	CONTEMPT	GENEROUS	KINDLING
GIMCRACK	MOMENTUM	TAMARACK	BONEYARD	CONTENTS	GENETICS	KINDNESS
GUMMOSIS	MUMBLING	TAMARIND	BONHOMIE	CONTINUE	GENETRIX	KINETICS
GUMPTION	NAMELESS	TAMARISK	BONIFACE	CONTINUO	GENIALLY	KINGPOST
GYMKHANA	NAMESAKE	TAMENESS	BONSPIEL	CONTRACT	GENITALS	KINGSHIP
HAMARTIA	NAMIBIAN	TAMWORTH	BUNFIGHT	CONTRARY	GENITIVE	KINGSIZE
HAMILTON	NEMATODE	TEMERITY	BUNGALOW	CONTRAST	GENOCIDE	KINGSLEY
HAMMERED	NEMATOID	TEMPERED	BUNGLING	CONTRITE	GENTRIFY	KINGSTON
HEMIPODE	NEMBUTAL	TEMPLATE	CANADIAN	CONTRIVE	GINGERLY	KINKAJOU
HOMELAND	NOMARCHY	TEMPORAL	CANAILLE	CONTROLS	GINGIVAL	KINSFOLK
HOMELESS	NOMINATE	TEMPTING	CANALISE	CONVENER	GONDWANA	KINSHASA
HOMEMADE	NOMOGRAM	TIMBERED	CANARIES	CONVERGE	GONFALON	LANCELET
HOMEPAGE	NUMBNESS	TIMELESS	CANBERRA	CONVERSE	GUNMETAL	LANCELOT
HOMESICK	NUMERACY	TIMIDITY	CANDIDLY	CONVEYOR	GUNPOINT	LANDFALL
HOMESPUN	NUMERALS	TIMOROUS	CANISTER	CONVINCE	GUNSMITH	LANDFILL
HOMEWARD	NUMERATE	TOMAHAWK	CANNABIS	CONVULSE	HANDBALL	LANDLADY
HOMEWORK	NUMEROUS	TOMATOES	CANNIBAL	CYNICISM	HANDBILL	LANDLOCK
HOMICIDE	NUMINOUS	TOMENTUM	CANOEING	CYNOSURE	HANDBOOK	LANDLORD
HUMANELY	PAMPERED	TOMORROW	CANOEIST	DANAIDES	HANDCART	LANDMARK
HUMANISM	PAMPHLET	TYMPANUM	CANONESS	DANDRUFF	HANDCLAP	LANDMASS
HUMANIST	PEMBROKE	UNMANNED	CANONIZE	DANEGELD	HANDCUFF	LANDMINE
HUMANITY	PEMMICAN	UNMARKED	CANOODLE	DANKNESS	HANDGRIP	LANDRACE
HUMANIZE	PIMIENTO	UPMARKET	CANTICLE	DENARIUS	HANDHELD	LANDSEER
HUMIDIFY	POMANDER	VOMITING	CANTORIS	DENATURE	HANDICAP	LANDSLIP
HUMIDITY	RAMBLING	VOMITORY	CENOBITE	DENDRITE	HANDMADE	LANDWARD
HUMILITY	RAMBUTAN	WAMBLING	CENOTAPH	DENDROID	HANDMAID	LANGLAND
HUMORIST	RAMEQUIN	WOMANISH	CENOZOIC	DENOUNCE	HANDOVER	LANGLAUF
HUMOROUS	RAMPARTS	WOMANIZE	CENTAURY	DENTICLE	HANDRAIL	LANGUAGE
HUMPBACK	REMEDIAL	ZAMINDAR	CENTERED	DENTURES	HANDSOME	LANGUISH
HUMPHREY	REMEMBER	ZIMBABWE	CENTRIST	DINGBATS	HANDYMAN	LANOLINE
IMMANENT	REMINDER	ABNEGATE	CENTRODE	DINOSAUR	HANGINGS	LANSBURY
IMMANUEL	REMITTAL	ABNORMAL	CINCHONA	DONATION	HANGNAIL	LENGTHEN
IMMATURE	REMNANTS	AGNATION	CINERAMA	DONATIST	HANGOVER	LENIENCY
IMMERSED	REMOTELY	AGNOSTIC	CINEREAL	DUNGHILL	HANNIBAL	LINCHPIN
IMMINENT	REMOUNTS	ANNALIST	CINGULUM	DYNAMICS	HANUKKAH	LINCOLNS
IMMOBILE	ROMANCER	ANNAMITE	CINNABAR	DYNAMISM	HENCHMAN	LINESMAN
IMMODEST	ROMANIAN	ANNEALER	CINNAMON	DYNAMITE	HENEQUEN	LINGERIE
IMMOLATE	ROMANSCH	ANNELIDA	CONCEIVE	DYNASTIC	HENHOUSE	LINGUIST
IMMORTAL	ROMANTIC	ANNOTATE	CONCERTO	DYNATRON	HINDMOST	LINIMENT
IMMUNITY	RUMBLING	ANNOUNCE	CONCHOID	EINSTEIN	HINDUISM	LINNAEAN
IMMUNIZE	RUMINANT	ANNOYING	CONCLAVE	FANCIFUL	HINDWARD	LINNAEUS
JAMAICAN	RUMINATE	ANNUALLY	CONCLUDE	FANCYMAN	HONDURAN	LINOLEUM
JAMBOREE	RUMOURED	APNEUSIS	CONCORDE	FANDANGO	HONDURAS	LINOTYPE
JIMCRACK	SAMARIUM	BANALITY	CONCRETE	FANLIGHT	HONESTLY	LONDONER
JUMPSUIT	SAMENESS	BANDANNA	CONDENSE	FANTASIA	HONEYDEW	LONESOME
KAMIKAZE	SAMIZDAT	BANDEROL	CONFETTI	FENCIBLE	HONEYPOT	LONGBOAT
KOMSOMOL	SAMPHIRE	BANDITTI	CONFINED	FENESTRA	HONGKONG	LONGHAND
LAMASERY	SEMESTER	BANDSMAN	CONFINES	FINALIST	HONOLULU	LONGHAUL
LAMBSKIN	SEMINARY	BANISTER	CONFLATE	FINALITY	HONORARY	LONGHORN
LAMENESS	SEMIOTIC	BANKBOOK	CONFLICT	FINALIZE	HUNDREDS	LONGLAND
LAMENTED	SEMITONE	BANKNOTE	CONFOUND	FINDINGS	HUNGRILY	LONGSHIP
LAMINATE	SEMOLINA	BANKROLL	CONFRONT	FINESPUN	HUNTRESS	LONGSTAY
LAMPPOST	SIMONIAC	BANKRUPT	CONFUSED	FINISHED	HUNTSMAN	LONGSTOP
LEMONADE	SIMPLIFY	BANLIEUE	CONGRATS	FINISHER	IGNITION	LONGTERM
LIMACINE	SIMULATE	BANNERET	CONGRESS	FONDLING	IGNOMINY	LONGTIME

LONICERA	MONGOOSE	PINNIPED	SUNCREAM	WINDLESS	BRONCHUS	EXOERGIC
LONSDALE	MONICKER	PINOCHLE	SUNDANCE	WINDMILL	BROODING	EXORCISM
LUNCHBOX	MONKFISH	PINPOINT	SUNDRIED	WINDPIPE	BROUGHAM	EXORCIST
LUNCHEON	MONMOUTH	PINPRICK	SUNDRIES	WINDSOCK	BROUHAHA	EXORCIZE
LUNGFISH	MONOACID	PINTABLE	SUNGLASS	WINDWARD	BROWBEAT	EXORDIUM
LUNGWORT	MONOGAMY	PINWHEEL	SUNLIGHT	WINGLESS	BROWNING	FLOATING
LYNCHING	MONOGRAM	PONSONBY	SUNSHADE	WINGSPAN	BROWNISH	FLOGGING
MANAGING	MONOGYNY	PONTIFEX	SUNSHINE	WINIFRED	BROWSING	FLOODING
MANCIPLE	MONOHULL	PONYTAIL	SYNCLINE	WINNINGS	BUOYANCY	FLOODLIT
MANDAMUS	MONOLITH	PUNCTUAL	SYNDROME	WINNIPEG	CHOIRBOY	FLOORING
MANDARIN	MONOPOLE	PUNCTURE	SYNOPSIS	WONDROUS	CHOLERIC	FLORENCE
MANDATED	MONOPOLY	PUNGENCY	SYNOPTIC	XANTHOMA	CHOOSING	FLOTILLA
MANDIBLE	MONORAIL	PUNISHED	SYNTEXIS	XANTIPPE	CHOPPING	FLOUNCED
MANDIOCA	MONOTONY	PUNITIVE	TANDOORI	XENOGAMY	CHORDATA	FLOUNDER
MANDOLIN	MONOTYPE	RANDOMLY	TANGIBLE	XENOLITH	CHORDATE	FLOURISH
MANDRAKE	MONOXIDE	RANELAGH	TANGIBLY	XENOPHON	CHORIAMB	FOOLSCAP
MANDRILL	MONROVIA	RANKNESS	TANTALUM	ABOMASUM	CLODPOLL	FOOTBALL
MANEUVER	MONSTERA	RENEGADE	TANTALUS	ABORTION	CLOISTER	FOOTFALL
MANFULLY	MONTCALM	RENMINBI	TANZANIA	ABORTIVE	CLOTHIER	FOOTHOLD
MANGONEL	MONTEITH	RENOUNCE	TENACITY	ACOUSTIC	CLOTHING	FOOTLING
MANGROVE	MONUMENT	RENOVATE	TENDENCY	ADOPTION	CLOWNISH	FOOTNOTE
MANIACAL	MUNCHKIN	RENOWNED	TENDERLY	ADOPTIVE	COOKBOOK	FOOTPATH
MANICURE	MUNIMENT	RINGDOVE	TENEBRAE	ADORABLE	COOKWARE	FOOTREST
MANIFEST	NENUPHAR	RINGHALS	TENEBRIO	AGONIZED	COOLNESS	FOOTSORE
MANIFOLD	NINEPINS	RINGSIDE	TENEMENT	ALOPECIA	CROATIAN	FOOTSTEP
MANITOBA	NINETEEN	RINGTAIL	TENESMUS	AMORETTI	CROCKERY	FOOTWEAR
MANNERED	NONESUCH	RINGWALL	TENNYSON	AMORETTO	CROCKETT	FOOTWORK
MANNERLY	NONSENSE	RINGWORM	TENTACLE	AMORTIZE	CROMLECH	FRONDEUR
MANNIKIN	NONSTICK	RUNABOUT	TINCTURE	ANOREXIA	CROMWELL	FRONTAGE
MANORIAL	OENOLOGY	RUNCIBLE	TINGLING	ANOREXIC	CRONYISM	FRONTIER
MANPOWER	OENOPHIL	RUNNERUP	TINNITUS	APOLLYON	CROONING	FRONTMAN
MANTILLA	OINTMENT	SANCTIFY	TINSELLY	APOLOGIA	CROSSBAR	FROSTILY
MANTISSA	OMNIFORM	SANCTION	TINSMITH	APOLOGUE	CROSSING	FROSTING
MANTLING	OMNIVORE	SANCTITY	TINTAGEL	APOPHYGE	CROSSLET	GAOLBIRD
MANUALLY	ORNAMENT	SANDARAC	TONALITY	APOPLEXY	CROTCHET	GEODESIC
MENACING	PANATELA	SANDBANK	TONELESS	APOSTASY	CROUPIER	GEODETIC
MENANDER	PANCREAS	SANDWICH	TONSURED	APOSTATE	CROWFOOT	GEOMANCY
MENELAUS	PANDANUS	SANGLIER	TUNGSTEN	APOSTLES	CROWNING	GEOMETER
MENHADEN	PANDARUS	SANGUINE	TUNGSTIC	APOTHEGM	DIOCESAN	GEOMETRY
MENISCUS	PANDEMIC	SANITARY	TUNGUSIC	AROMATIC	DIOGENES	GEOPHONE
MENSURAL	PANDOWDY	SANITIZE	TUNICATE	ATOMIZER	DIONYSUS	GEORGIAN
MENSWEAR	PANEGYRY	SANSERIF	TUNISIAN	AVOGADRO	DIOPTRIC	GEOTAXIS
MENTALLY	PANELING	SANSKRIT	UNNERVED	BIOGRAPH	DOOLALLY	GHOULISH
MINAMATA	PANELLED	SANTIAGO	VANADIUM	BIOMETRY	DOOMSDAY	GIOCONDA
MINATORY	PANGLOSS	SENGREEN	VANADOUS	BIOSCOPE	DOORBELL	GIOVANNI
MINCEPIE	PANGOLIN	SENILITY	VANBRUGH	BLOCKADE	DOORKNOB	GLOAMING
MINDANAO	PANICLE	SENORITA	VANGUARD	BLOCKAGE	DOORPOST	GLOATING
MINDLESS	PANNIKIN	SENSIBLE	VANISHED	BLOOMERS	DOORSILL	GLOBALLY
MINEHEAD	PANORAMA	SENSIBLY	VANQUISH	BLOOMING	DOORSTEP	GLOBULAR
MINIMIZE	PANPIPES	SENSUOUS	VENALITY	BLOTCHED	DROOPING	GLOBULIN
MINISTER	PANTALON	SENTENCE	VENDETTA	BLOWFISH	DROPHEAD	GLOOMILY
MINISTRY	PANTHEON	SENTIENT	VENERATE	BLOWHOLE	DROPPING	GLORIANA
MINORESS	PENALIZE	SENTINEL	VENEREAL	BLOWLAMP	DROPSHOT	GLORIOLE
MINORITE	PENCHANT	SINAPISM	VENETIAN	BLOWPIPE	DROWNING	GLORIOUS
MINORITY	PENDULUM	SINCLAIR	VENGEFUL	BOOKABLE	DROWSILY	GLOSSARY
MINOTAUR	PENELOPE	SINECURE	VENOMOUS	BOOKCASE	DUODENAL	GLOSSEME
MINSTREL	PENITENT	SINFONIA	VENTURED	BOOKMARK	DUODENUM	GLOXINIA
MINUTELY	PENKNIFE	SINGSONG	VINCIBLE	BOOKROOM	DZONGKHA	GOODNESS
MINUTIAE	PENNINES	SINGULAR	VINCULUM	BOOKSHOP	ECOFREAK	GOODSIRE
MONADISM	PENOLOGY	SINISTER	VINDALOO	BOOKWORK	ECONOMIC	GOODWIFE
MONANDRY	PENTACLE	SINKHOLE	VINEGARY	BOOKWORM	EGOISTIC	GOODWILL
MONARCHY	PENTAGON	SONATINA	VINEYARD	BOOTLESS	EGOMANIA	GOODWOOD
MONASTIC	PENTARCH	SONGBIRD	WANDERER	BOOTNECK	ELONGATE	GOODYEAR
MONAURAL	PENUMBRA	SONGSTER	WINDBURN	BROADWAY	ELOQUENT	GOOFBALL
MONDRIAN	PENZANCE	SONOGRAM	WINDFALL	BROCCOLI	EMOTICON	GOOSEGOG
MONETARY	PINAFORE	SONOROUS	WINDGALL	BROCHURE	ENORMITY	GROGGILY
MONETISE	PINDARIC	SUNBATHE	WINDHOEK	BROILING	ENORMOUS	GROOMING
MONEYBOX	PINEWOOD	SUNBURNT	WINDINGS	BROMELIA	ESOTERIC	GROSBEAK
MONGOLIA	PINNACLE	SUNBURST	WINDLASS	BROMPTON	EXOCRINE	GROSCHEN

GROUNDED	PRODUCER	SHOEHORN	STOWAWAY	ASPERGES	HEPTARCH	REPAYING
GROUPING	PRODUCES	SHOELACE	THOLEPIN	ASPERITY	HIPSTERS	REPEATED
GROUTING	PRODUCTS	SHOELESS	THOMPSON	ASPERMIA	HOPELESS	REPEATER
GROWLING	PROFORMA	SHOETREE	THORACIC	ASPHODEL	HOPFIELD	REPHRASE
HOODWINK	PROFOUND	SHOOTING	THOROUGH	ASPHYXIA	HYPERION	REPLEVIN
HOOKWORM	PROFUSER	SHOOTOUT	THOUGHTS	ASPIRANT	HYPNOSIS	REPORTED
HOOLIGAN	PROGERIA	SHOPPING	THOUSAND	ASPIRATE	HYPNOTIC	REPORTER
IDOLATER	PROGRADE	SHOPTALK	TROCHAIC	ASPIRING	HYPOGEAL	REPOUSSÉ
IDOLATRY	PROGRESS	SHORTAGE	TROCHLEA	BAPTISED	IMPACTED	REPRIEVE
INOCULUM	PROHIBIT	SHOULDER	TROLLOPE	CAPACITY	IMPAIRED	REPRISAL
IRONCLAD	PROLAPSE	SHOUTING	TROMBONE	CAPERING	IMPELLED	REPROACH
IRONICAL	PROLIFIC	SHOWBOAT	TROOPING	CAPITALS	IMPERIAL	REPUBLIC
IRONSIDE	PROLOGUE	SHOWCASE	TROPICAL	CAPRIOLE	IMPETIGO	RIPARIAN
IRONWARE	PROMISED	SHOWDOWN	TROTLINE	CAPSICUM	IMPLICIT	RIPENESS
IRONWOOD	PROMOTER	SHOWGIRL	TROTTERS	CAPSIZED	IMPOLITE	RIPPLING
IRONWORK	PROMPTER	SHOWROOM	TROTTOIR	CAPSTONE	IMPORTER	SAPONITE
IROQUOIS	PROMPTLY	SLOBBERY	TROUBLED	CAPTIOUS	IMPOSING	SAPPHIRE
ISOBARIC	PRONATOR	SLOPPILY	TROUBLES	CAPUCHIN	IMPOSTER	SAPPHIST
ISOCLINE	PROPERLY	SLOTHFUL	TROUNCER	CAPYBARA	IMPOSTOR	SEPARATE
ISOGENIC	PROPERTY	SLOVAKIA	TROUSERS	CEPHALIN	IMPOTENT	SUPERBLY
ISOGLOSS	PROPHASE	SLOVENIA	TWOPENNY	COPULATE	IMPRISON	SUPERBUG
ISOGONAL	PROPHECY	SLOVENLY	TWOPIECE	COPYBOOK	IMPROPER	SUPERIOR
ISOLATED	PROPHESY	SLOWDOWN	UDOMETER	COPYHOLD	IMPROVED	SUPERMAN
ISOSTASY	PROPOLIS	SLOWNESS	UXORIOUS	CUPBOARD	IMPROVER	SUPERNAL
ISOTHERE	PROPOSAL	SLOWPOKE	VIOLATOR	CUPIDITY	IMPUDENT	SUPERTAX
ISOTHERM	PROPOSED	SLOWWORM	VIOLENCE	DEPARTED	IMPUNITY	SUPPLANT
IVOIRIEN	PROPOSER	SMOCKING	WHODUNIT	DEPILATE	IMPURIFY	SUPPLIER
JEOPARDY	PROPOUND	SMOLLETT	WHOOPING	DEPORTEE	IMPURITY	SUPPLIES
KLONDIKE	PROROGUE	SMOOTHER	WHOPPING	DEPRAVED	JAPANESE	SUPPOSED
KNOBLESS	PROSPECT	SMOOTHLY	WOODBINE	DEPRIVED	JAPONICA	SUPPRESS
KNOCKERS	PROSPERO	SMOULDER	WOODCOCK	DEPUTIZE	JEPHTHAH	SYPHILIS
KNOCKING	PROSTATE	SNOBBERY	WOODENLY	DIPHENYL	KIPPERED	TAPENADE
KNOCKOUT	PROTEASE	SNOBBISH	WOODLAND	DIPLOMAT	KYPHOSIS	TAPERING
KNOTWEED	PROTÉGÉE	SNOOTILY	WOODRUFF	DIPSTICK	LAPIDARY	TAPESTRY
KNOTWORK	PROTOCOL	SNORTING	WOODSHED	DIPTERAL	LAPIDATE	TAPEWORM
KROMESKY	PROTOZOA	SNOWBALL	WOODSMAN	DOPAMINE	LIPSTICK	TAPHOUSE
LEONARDO	PROTRUDE	SNOWDROP	WOODWARD	EMPHASIS	LOPSIDED	TIPSTAFF
LEONIDAS	PROVABLE	SNOWFALL	WOODWIND	EMPHATIC	LUPERCAL	TOPCLASS
LOOPHOLE	PROVERBS	SNOWLINE	WOODWORK	EMPLOYED	NAPOLEON	TOPHEAVY
LOOSEBOX	PROVIDED	SOOTHING	WOODWORM	EMPLOYEE	NEPALESE	TOPLEVEL
MOONBEAM	PROVIDER	SOOTHSAY	WOOLLENS	EMPLOYER	NEPENTHE	TOPNOTCH
MOORCOCK	PROVINCE	SPOILAGE	WOOLPACK	EMPORIUM	NEPHRITE	TOPOLOGY
MOORINGS	PROXIMAL	SPOILING	WOOLSACK	EMPYREAL	NEPIONIC	TUPAMARO
MOORLAND	PTOMAINE	SPOLIATE	WRONGFUL	EMPYREAN	NEPOTISM	TUPPENNY
MYOBLAST	PYORRHEA	SPOONFUL	YEOMANRY	ESPALIER	NUPTIALS	TYPECAST
MYOSOTIS	QUOTABLE	SPORADIC	ZOONOSIS	ESPECIAL	OMPHALOS	TYPEFACE
NEOMYCIN	QUOTIENT	SPORTING	ZOOPHYTE	ESPOUSAL	OOPHORON	UNPERSON
NEOPHYTE	REORIENT	SPORTIVE	ZOOSPERM	ESPRESSO	OPPONENT	UNPLACED
NOONTIME	RHOMBOID	SPOTLESS	ZOOSPORE	EUPEPSIA	OPPOSING	UPPERCUT
ODOMETER	RHONCHUS	SPOTTING	ALPHABET	EUPHONIA	OPPOSITE	VAPORIZE
OPOPANAX	ROOFLESS	STOCCATA	ALPINIST	EUPHONIC	ORPHANED	VAPOROUS
OTOSCOPE	ROOFTOPS	STOCKADE	AMPERAGE	EUPHORIA	ORPIMENT	VIPERISH
PHONETIC	ROOMMATE	STOCKCAR	AMPUTATE	EUPHORIC	OXPECKER	VIPEROUS
PHORMIUM	ROOTLESS	STOCKING	APPALLED	EUPHUISM	PAPILLON	ZEPHYRUS
PHOSGENE	SCOFFING	STOCKIST	APPANAGE	EXPANDED	PEPERONI	ZEPPELIN
PHOTOFIT	SCOLDING	STOCKMAN	APPARENT	EXPECTED	PIPELINE	ACQUAINT
PHOTOPSY	SCORCHED	STOCKPOT	APPELANT	EXPEDITE	PIPERINE	ACQUIRED
PLOTINUS	SCORCHER	STOICISM	APPENDIX	EXPENDED	POPINJAY	ACQUIRER
PLOUGHED	SCORNFUL	STOKESAY	APPETITE	EXPENSES	POPPADOM	ARQUEBUS
POOLROOM	SCORPION	STOLIDLY	APPLAUSE	EXPLICIT	POPSICLE	BEQUEATH
POORNESS	SCORPIUS	STONEFLY	APPLETON	EXPLODED	POPULACE	COQUETRY
PROBABLE	SCOTLAND	STOPCOCK	APPLIQUÉ	EXPLORER	POPULATE	COQUETTE
PROBABLY	SCOTSMAN	STOPOVER	APPOSITE	EXPONENT	POPULIST	INQUIRER
PROCAINE	SCOTTISH	STOPPAGE	APPRAISE	EXPORTER	POPULOUS	MAQUETTE
PROCEEDS	SCOURING	STOPPING	APPRISED	EXPOSURE	RAPACITY	MOQUETTE
PROCLAIM	SCOWLING	STOREMAN	APPROACH	EXPRESSO	RAPECAKE	PIQUANCY
PROCURER	SHOCKING	STOREYED	APPROVAL	HAPSBURG	RAPIDITY	REQUIRED
PRODIGAL	SHODDILY	STORMING	APPROVED	HEPATICA	REPAIRER	SEQUENCE
PRODROME	SHOEBILL	STORMONT	ARPEGGIO	HEPTAGON	REPARTEE	TEQUILLA

AARDVARK	BARRACKS	CERASTES	ETRUSCAN	FORSAKEN	HEREWITH	MARKDOWN
ABRASION	BARRATRY	CERATOID	EURASIAN	FORSLACK	HERITAGE	MARKEDLY
ABRASIVE	BARRETTE	CERBERUS	EUROLAND	FORSOOTH	HERMETIC	MARKSMAN
ABRIDGED	BARTERED	CEREBRAL	EUROPEAN	FORSWEAR	HERMIONE	MARMOSET
ABROGATE	BERBERIS	CEREBRUM	EUROPIUM	FORTIETH	HERPETIC	MARONITE
ABRUPTLY	BERCEUSE	CEREMENT	EUROSTAR	FORTRESS	HERSCHEL	MAROQUIN
ACRIMONY	BEREAVED	CEREMONY	EURYDICE	FORTUITY	HIRAGANA	MARQUESA
ACROMION	BERGAMOT	CERULEAN	FARCICAL	FORWARDS	HIRELING	MARQUESS
ACROSTIC	BERGENIA	CERVELAT	FAREWELL	FURBELOW	HORATIAN	MARQUISE
ADRIATIC	BERGERAC	CERVICAL	FARMHAND	FURLOUGH	HORATIUS	MARRIAGE
ADROITLY	BERIBERI	CHRISTEN	FARMLAND	FURROWED	HORLICKS	MARSHALL
AEROBICS	BERKELEY	CHRISTIE	FARMYARD	FURTHEST	HORMONAL	MARTELLO
AERODYNE	BERTRAND	CHRISTOM	FAROUCHE	FURUNCLE	HORNBEAM	MARTINET
AEROFLOT	BIRDCAGE	CHROMITE	FARRIERY	GARAMOND	HORNBILL	MARTYRED
AEROFOIL	BIRDSEED	CHROMIUM	FARTHEST	GARDENER	HORNBOOK	MARYLAND
AEROGRAM	BIRTHDAY	CIRCINUS	FARTHING	GARDENIA	HORNFELS	MARZIPAN
AEROLITH	BORACITE	CIRCUITY	FEROCITY	GARDYLOO	HORNPIPE	MERCALLI
AERONAUT	BORDEAUX	CIRCULAR	FERRYMAN	GARGANEY	HORNPOUT	MERCATOR
AEROSTAT	BORDELLO	CORDOVAN	FIREARMS	GARGOYLE	HORNTAIL	MERCEDES
AGRARIAN	BORDERER	CORDUROY	FIREBACK	GARISHLY	HOROLOGY	MERCHANT
AGREEING	BORECOLE	CORDWAIN	FIREBALL	GARLICKY	HORRIBLE	MERCIFUL
AGRICOLA	BOREHOLE	CORIOLIS	FIREBIRD	GARMENTS	HORRIBLY	MEREDITH
AGRIMONY	BORODINO	CORMORAN	FIREBOLT	GARRIGUE	HORRIFIC	MERIDIAN
AGRONOMY	BORROWED	CORNETTO	FIREDAMP	GARRISON	HORSEBOX	MERINGUE
AIRBORNE	BORROWER	CORNHILL	FIRESIDE	GARROTTE	HORSEFLY	MERISTEM
AIRBRAKE	BORSTALL	CORNICHE	FIRESTEP	GERANIUM	HORSEMAN	MIREPOIX
AIRCRAFT	BURBERRY	CORNMEAL	FIRETRAP	GERMAINE	HORSEMEN	MIRLITON
AIREDALE	BURDENED	CORNWALL	FIREWEED	GERMANIC	HURDLING	MIRRORED
AIRFIELD	BURGLARY	CORONARY	FIREWOOD	GERMINAL	IRRIGATE	MIRTHFUL
AIRINESS	BURGRAVE	CORONOID	FIREWORK	GERONIMO	IRRITANT	MORALIST
AIRLINER	BURGUNDY	CORPORAL	FIRMNESS	GERTRUDE	IRRITATE	MORALITY
AIRPLANE	BURNTOUT	CORRAGIO	FIRMWARE	GIRASOLE	JEREBOAM	MORALIZE
AIRSCREW	BURROWER	CORRIDOR	FORCEFUL	GIRLHOOD	JEREMIAD	MORAVIAN
AIRSPEED	BURSITIS	CORRODED	FORCIBLE	GIRONDIN	JEREMIAH	MORBIDLY
AIRSTRIP	BURSTING	CORSELET	FORCIBLY	GORGEOUS	JEROBOAM	MORBILLI
AIRTIGHT	CARABINE	CORSICAN	FOREBEAR	GORMLESS	JERRYCAN	MOREOVER
AIRWAVES	CARACOLE	CORUNDUM	FOREBODE	GURDWARA	JORROCKS	MOREPORK
AMRITSAR	CARAPACE	CORVETTE	FORECAST	GYRATION	JURASSIC	MORESQUE
ARRANGER	CARBOLIC	CURATIVE	FOREDECK	GYRATORY	JURATORY	MORIBUND
ARRESTED	CARBONIC	CURLICUE	FOREDOOM	GYROSTAT	KARTTIKA	MOROCCAN
ARRESTER	CARCAJOU	CURRENCY	FOREFOOT	HARANGUE	KERCHIEF	MOROSELY
ARROGANT	CARCANET	CURRICLE	FOREGONE	HARASSED	KERMESSE	MORPHEME
ARROGATE	CARDAMOM	CURSITOR	FOREHAND	HARDBACK	KEROSENE	MORPHEUS
ATROCITY	CARDIGAN	CURTAINS	FOREHEAD	HARDCORE	KORRIGAN	MORPHINE
AURELIAN	CARDINAL	CURTNESS	FORELAND	HARDENED	LARGESSE	MORRISON
AURICULA	CAREFREE	CYRENIAC	FORELOCK	HARDHACK	LARKSPUR	MORTALLY
AYRSHIRE	CARELESS	CYRILLIC	FOREMILK	HARDLINE	LAROUSSE	MORTGAGE
BARABBAS	CAREWORN	DARKENED	FOREMOST	HARDNESS	LORDOSIS	MORTIMER
BARATHEA	CARILLON	DARKNESS	FORENAME	HARDSHIP	LORDSHIP	MORTUARY
BARBADOS	CARJACOU	DARKROOM	FORENOON	HARDTACK	LORRAINE	MURDERER
BARBARIC	CARNAUBA	DARTMOOR	FORENSIC	HARDWARE	LYREBIRD	MURRHINE
BARBECUE	CARNEGIE	DERANGED	FORESAIL	HARDWOOD	LYRICISM	MYRIAPOD
BARBERRY	CARNIVAL	DERELICT	FORESHIP	HAREBELL	LYRICIST	MYRMIDON
BARBICAN	CAROLINA	DERISION	FORESKIN	HARFLEUR	MARABOUT	NARCOSES
BARBIZON	CAROLINE	DERISIVE	FORESTAY	HARMLESS	MARASMUS	NARCOSIS
BARDOLPH	CAROTENE	DERISORY	FORESTER	HARMONIC	MARATHON	NARCOTIC
BAREBACK	CAROUSAL	DEROGATE	FORESTRY	HARRIDAN	MARAUDER	NARGILEH
BAREFOOT	CAROUSEL	DIRECTLY	FORETELL	HARRISON	MARCELLA	NARRATOR
BARENESS	CARRAWAY	DIRECTOR	FOREWARN	HARTFORD	MARCELLO	NARROWLY
BARGELLO	CARRIAGE	DORMOUSE	FOREWORD	HARUSPEX	MARGARET	NORMALLY
BARGEMAN	CARRIOLE	DURABLES	FORFEITS	HERACLES	MARGINAL	NORMANDY
BARITONE	CARRYALL	DURATION	FORKLIFT	HERACLID	MARGRAVE	NORSEMAN
BARNABAS	CARRYCOT	EARLIEST	FORKTAIL	HERALDIC	MARIACHI	NORSEMEN
BARNACLE	CARRYING	EARNINGS	FORMALIN	HERALDRY	MARIANAS	NORTHERN
BARNARDS	CARTHAGE	EARPHONE	FORMALLY	HERCULES	MARIGOLD	NORTHING
BARNYARD	CARTLOAD	EARPIECE	FORMERLY	HERDSMAN	MARINADE	NURSLING
BARONESS	CARUCATE	EERINESS	FORMLESS	HEREDITY	MARINATE	PARABOLA
BARONETS	CARYATID	ENRICHED	FORMOSAN	HEREFORD	MARITIME	PARADIGM
BARONIAL	CERAMICS	ETRURIAN	FORMWORK	HEREWARD	MARJORAM	PARAFFIN

PARAGUAY	PORTHOLE	SORORITY	TARTUFFE	VERONICA	ASSORTED	DISABLED
PARAKEET	PORTIÈRE	SPRAINED	TERATOMA	VERSICLE	ASSUMING	DISABUSE
PARALLAX	PORTLAND	SPRAWLED	TERIYAKI	VERTEBRA	ASSYRIAN	DISAGREE
PARALLEL	PORTRAIT	SPREADER	TERMINAL	VERTICAL	AUSPICES	DISALLOW
PARALYZE	PORTUGAL	SPRINGER	TERMINUS	VIREMENT	AUSTRIAN	DISARRAY
PARAMOUR	PURBLIND	SPRINKLE	TERRACED	VIRGINAL	BASEBALL	DISASTER
PARANOIA	PURCHASE	SPRINTER	TERRAPIN	VIRGINIA	BASEBORN	DISBURSE
PARANOID	PURIFIED	SPRITELY	TERRIBLE	VIRILITY	BASELESS	DISCIPLE
PARAQUAT	PURIFIER	SPRITZER	TERRIBLY	VIROLOGY	BASELINE	DISCLAIM
PARASHAH	PURLIEUS	SPROCKET	TERRIFIC	VIRTUOSI	BASEMENT	DISCLOSE
PARASITE	PURPLISH	SPRUCELY	TERTIARY	VIRTUOSO	BASENESS	DISCOLOR
PARDONER	PURSLANE	SPRYNESS	TERYLENE	VIRTUOUS	BASIDIUM	DISCOUNT
PARENTAL	PURULENT	STRABISM	THRACIAN	VIRULENT	BASILICA	DISCOVER
PARIETAL	PURVEYOR	STRACHEY	THRALDOM	VORACITY	BASILISK	DISCREET
PARISIAN	PYRAMIDS	STRADDLE	THRASHER	VORTICAL	BASINFUL	DISCRETE
PARKLAND	PYRENEES	STRAGGLE	THREATEN	WARDRESS	BASKETRY	DISEASED
PARLANCE	PYRIFORM	STRAGGLY	THRENODY	WARDROBE	BASSINET	DISFAVOR
PARMESAN	RAREFIED	STRAIGHT	THRESHER	WARDROOM	BASSWOOD	DISGORGE
PARODIST	SARABAND	STRAINED	THRILLER	WARDSHIP	BASTILLE	DISGRACE
PAROLLES	SARATOGA	STRAINER	THROMBIN	WARFARIN	BESIEGED	DISGUISE
PAROUSIA	SARDINIA	STRAITEN	THROMBUS	WARHORSE	BESMIRCH	DISHEVEL
PAROXYSM	SARDONIC	STRANDED	THROTTLE	WARINESS	BESOTTED	DISHONOR
PARSIFAL	SARDONYX	STRANGER	THRUSTER	WARMBOOT	BESOUGHT	DISINTER
PARTERRE	SARGASSO	STRANGLE	TIRAMISU	WARPAINT	BESPOKEN	DISJUNCT
PARTHIAN	SCRABBLE	STRAPPED	TIRELESS	WARPLANE	BESSEMER	DISKETTE
PARTICLE	SCRAMBLE	STRAPPER	TIRESIAS	WARRANTY	BESTIARY	DISLIKED
PARTISAN	SCRAPPLE	STRATEGY	TIRESOME	WEREWOLF	BESTOWER	DISLODGE
PARTTIME	SCRATCHY	STRATIFY	TOREADOR	WIRELESS	BESTRIDE	DISLOYAL
PERACUTE	SCRAWLED	STREAKED	TORTILLA	WIREWORM	BISCAYAN	DISMALLY
PERCEIVE	SCREAMER	STREAKER	TORTOISE	WORDBOOK	BISEXUAL	DISMAYED
PERCEVAL	SCREENED	STREAMER	TORTUOUS	WORDLESS	BISMARCK	DISMOUNT
PERCIVAL	SCREWTOP	STRENGTH	TORTURED	WORKABLE	BOSWORTH	DISORDER
PERFECTA	SCRIABIN	STRESSED	TORTURER	WORKADAY	BUSINESS	DISPATCH
PERFECTO	SCRIBBLE	STRETCHY	TURANDOT	WORKBOOK	BUSTLING	DISPENSE
PERFORCE	SCRIBBLY	STRIATED	TURBANED	WORKINGS	BUSULFAN	DISPERSE
PERFUMED	SCRIPTUM	STRIATUM	TURBOJET	WORKLOAD	BUSYBODY	DISPIRIT
PERIANTH	SCROFULA	STRICKEN	TURGENEV	WORKMATE	CASANOVA	DISPLACE
PERICARP	SCROUNGE	STRICKLE	TURGIDLY	WORKROOM	CASEMATE	DISPOSAL
PERICLES	SCRUBBER	STRICTLY	TURKOMAN	WORKSHOP	CASEMENT	DISPOSED
PERIDERM	SCRUPLES	STRIDENT	TURMERIC	WORMCAST	CASHMERE	DISPROVE
PERILOUS	SCRUTINY	STRIKING	TURNBACK	WORMWOOD	CASSETTE	DISPUTED
PERILUNE	SERAFILE	STRINGED	TURNCOAT	WORRYING	CASTANET	DISQUIET
PERIODIC	SERAGLIO	STRINGER	TURNCOCK	WORTHIES	CASTAWAY	DISRAELI
PERIPETY	SERAPHIC	STRIPPED	TURNOVER	WORTHILY	CASTOFFS	DISSOLVE
PERISHED	SERAPHIM	STRIPPER	TURNPIKE	XERAPHIM	CASTRATE	DISSUADE
PERISHER	SERENADE	STRIVING	TURNSPIT	YARMULKA	CASTRATO	DISTANCE
PERJURED	SERENATA	STROLLER	TURRETED	YERSINIA	CASUALLY	DISTASTE
PERJURER	SERENELY	STRONGLY	TYROLEAN	ZARZUELA	CASUALTY	DISTINCT
PERMEATE	SERENITY	STRUGGLE	TYROSINE	ZIRCONIA	CESSPOOL	DISTRACT
PEROXIDE	SERGEANT	STRUMPET	UNREASON	AASVOGEL	CISTERNA	DISTRAIN
PERSHING	SERIATIM	SURENESS	UNRIFLED	ABSCISSA	COSINESS	DISTRAIT
PERSONAL	SERJEANT	SURFBOAT	UPRIGHTS	ABSENTEE	COSMETIC	DISTRESS
PERSPIRE	SEROLOGY	SURGICAL	UPRISING	ABSINTHE	COSTMARY	DISTRICT
PERSUADE	SEROTYPE	SURICATE	VARIABLE	ABSOLUTE	CUSPIDOR	DISTRUST
PERSUANT	SERRATED	SURMOUNT	VARIANCE	ABSOLVED	CUSTOMER	DISUNION
PERTNESS	SERVICES	SURPLICE	VARICOSE	ABSORBED	CYSTITIS	DISUNITE
PERUVIAN	SERVIENT	SURPRISE	VARIETAL	ABSORBER	DASHWOOD	DISUNITY
PERVERSE	SERVITOR	SURROUND	VARIFORM	ABSTRACT	DESCRIBE	DYSLEXIA
PERVIOUS	SHRAPNEL	SURVEYOR	VARIORUM	ABSTRUSE	DESELECT	DYSLEXIC
PHREATIC	SHREDDER	SURVIVAL	VERACITY	ABSURDLY	DESERTED	EASEMENT
PHRYGIAN	SHREWDLY	SURVIVOR	VERANDAH	AESTHETE	DESERTER	EASINESS
PIRANESI	SHREWISH	SYRACUSE	VERBALLY	ALSATIAN	DESERVED	EASTERLY
PIROZHKI	SHROUDED	SYRINGES	VERBATIM	ANSERINE	DESIGNER	EASTLAKE
POROSITY	SHRUNKEN	TARBOOSH	VERBIAGE	ARSONIST	DESIROUS	EASTWARD
PORPHYRA	SIRENIAN	TARRAGON	VERDERER	ASSASSIN	DESOLATE	ECSTASIS
PORPHYRY	SORBONNE	TARTARIC	VERJUICE	ASSEMBLE	DESPATCH	ECSTATIC
PORPOISE	SORCERER	TARTARUS	VERLAINE	ASSEMBLY	DESPOTIC	ELSINORE
PORRIDGE	SORDIDLY	TARTNESS	VERMOUTH	ASSESSOR	DESTINED	ENSCONCE
PORTABLE	SORENESS	TARTRATE	VERONESE	ASSIGNEE	DESTRUCT	ENSEMBLE

ENSHRINE	MASSACRE	PASSOVER	RUSTLING	ALTRUISM	BOTTOMRY	ESTANCIA
ENSHROUD	MASSENET	PASSPORT	SASSANID	ALTRUIST	BOTULISM	ESTEEMED
ENSIFORM	MASSEUSE	PASSWORD	SISTERLY	ANTECEDE	BUTCHERS	ESTHETIC
ENSILAGE	MASSICOT	PASTICHE	SISYPHUS	ANTEDATE	BUTCHERY	ESTIMATE
ESSAYIST	MASTERLY	PASTILLE	SUSPENSE	ANTELOPE	BUTTERED	ESTIVATE
ESSONITE	MASTHEAD	PASTORAL	SYSTEMIC	ANTENNAE	BUTTOCKS	ESTONIAN
EUSTATIC	MASTODON	PASTRAMI	TASHKENT	ANTEPOST	BUTTRESS	ESTOPPEL
FASCICLE	MESCALIN	PASTURES	TASMANIA	ANTERIOR	CATACOMB	ESTOVERS
FASTBACK	MESMERIC	PISCATOR	TASTEFUL	ANTEROOM	CATALYST	ESTRAGON
FASTENER	MESODERM	PISIFORM	TESTATOR	ANTIBODY	CATAMITE	ESTROGEN
FASTNESS	MESOLITE	PISSHEAD	TESTATUM	ANTIDOTE	CATAPULT	EUTROPHY
FESTIVAL	MESOZOIC	POSEIDON	TESTICLE	ANTIHERO	CATARACT	EUTROPIC
FISHBONE	MESSAGER	POSITION	TUSITALA	ANTILLES	CATATONY	EXTENDED
FISHCAKE	MESSIDOR	POSITIVE	UNSALTED	ANTILOPE	CATCHING	EXTENSOR
FISHHOOK	MESSMATE	POSITRON	UNSAVORY	ANTIMERE	CATECHOL	EXTERIOR
FISHMEAL	MESSUAGE	POSOLOGY	UNSEALED	ANTIMONY	CATEGORY	EXTERNAL
FISHPOND	MISAPPLY	POSSIBLE	UNSEEDED	ANTIPHON	CATERING	EXTERNAT
FISHWIFE	MISCARRY	POSSIBLY	UNSEEMLY	ANTIPOPE	CATHEDRA	EXTRADOS
FISSIPED	MISCHIEF	POSTCARD	UNSETTLE	AOTEAROA	CATHETER	FATALISM
FUSAROLE	MISCOUNT	POSTCODE	UNSHAKEN	APTITUDE	CATHOLIC	FATALIST
FUSELAGE	MISERERE	POSTDATE	UNSIGNED	ARTEFACT	CATHOUSE	FATALITY
FUSEWIRE	MISGUIDE	POSTMARK	UNSOCIAL	ARTERIAL	CATILINE	FATHERLY
FUSIFORM	MISHMASH	POSTPAID	UNSOLVED	ARTESIAN	CATSMEAT	FATIGUED
FUSILIER	MISJUDGE	POSTPONE	UNSPOILT	ARTFULLY	CATTLEYA	FATIGUES
GASOLIER	MISMATCH	PUSHBIKE	UNSPOKEN	ARTICLED	CATULLUS	FATSTOCK
GASOLINE	MISNOMER	PUSHCART	UNSTABLE	ARTICLES	CETACEAN	FETCHING
GASTRULA	MISOGYNY	PUSHDOWN	UNSTATED	ARTIFACT	CITATION	FETTLING
GASWORKS	MISPLACE	PUSHOVER	UNSTEADY	ARTIFICE	COTOPAXI	FITFULLY
GESTURES	MISPRINT	PUSSYCAT	UNSUITED	ARTISTIC	COTSWOLD	FUTILITY
GOSSAMER	MISQUOTE	PUSTULAR	UPSTAIRS	ARTISTRY	COTTAGER	FUTURISM
GUSSETED	MISSOURI	RASCALLY	UPSTREAM	ASTATINE	CUTENESS	FUTURIST
HASTINGS	MISSPELL	RASHNESS	URSULINE	ASTERISK	CUTHBERT	GATEFOLD
HESITANT	MISSPENT	RASPUTIN	VASCULAR	ASTEROID	CUTPRICE	GATEPOST
HESITATE	MISTAKEN	RASSELAS	VASTNESS	ASTHENIA	CUTPURSE	GATHERED
HISPANIC	MISTREAT	RESEARCH	VESPERAL	ASTONISH	CUTWATER	GUTTURAL
HISTORIC	MISTRESS	RESEMBLE	VESPUCCI	ASTUTELY	CYTOLOGY	HATCHERY
HOSEPIPE	MISTRUST	RESERVED	VESTIARY	ATTACHED	CYTOSINE	HATCHING
HOSPITAL	MOSQUITO	RESETTLE	VESTMENT	ATTACKER	DATABASE	HATCHWAY
HOSTELRY	MUSCADET	RESIDENT	VESUVIUS	ATTENDER	DATELESS	HATHAWAY
HUSHHUSH	MUSCATEL	RESIDUAL	VISCERAL	ATTESTOR	DATELINE	HATTERAS
HUSTINGS	MUSCULAR	RESIDUUM	VISCOUNT	ATTITUDE	DETACHED	HETAIRIA
HYSTERIA	MUSHROOM	RESIGNED	VISELIKE	ATTORNEY	DETAILED	HITHERTO
HYSTERIC	MUSICIAN	RESINOUS	VISIGOTH	AUTARCHY	DETAINEE	HOTELIER
INSANELY	MUSQUASH	RESISTOR	VISITANT	AUTISTIC	DETAINER	HOTHOUSE
INSANITY	MUSTACHE	RESOLUTE	VISITING	AUTOBAHN	DETECTOR	HOTPLATE
INSCRIBE	MYSTICAL	RESOLVED	VISUALLY	AUTOCRAT	DETHRONE	INTAGLIO
INSECURE	MYSTIQUE	RESONANT	WASHABLE	AUTOGAMY	DETONATE	INTEGRAL
INSIGNIA	NESCIENT	RESONATE	WASHBOWL	AUTOGIRO	DETOXIFY	INTELSAT
INSOLENT	NESTLING	RESOURCE	WASHDOWN	AUTOGYRO	DETRITUS	INTENDED
INSOMNIA	NOSEBAND	RESPECTS	WASHROOM	AUTOMATE	DOTTEREL	INTENTLY
INSPIRED	NOSEDIVE	RESPIGHI	WASTEFUL	AUTONOMY	DUTCHMAN	INTERACT
INSPIRIT	NOSOLOGY	RESPONSE	WESLEYAN	AUTOTYPE	DUTIABLE	INTERCOM
INSTANCE	NOSTRILS	RESTLESS	WESTERLY	AUTUMNAL	DUTYFREE	INTEREST
INSTINCT	NOSTROMO	RESTORER	WESTWARD	BATAVIAN	EATABLES	INTERIOR
INSTRUCT	OBSCURED	RESTRAIN	WISEACRE	BATHETIC	ECTODERM	INTERMIT
INSULATE	OBSERVED	RESTRICT	WISHBONE	BATHROBE	ENTANGLE	INTERNAL
JUSTNESS	OBSERVER	RESTROOM	WISTERIA	BATHROOM	ENTHALPY	INTERNEE
KESTEVEN	OBSESSED	RISSOLES	YOSEMITE	BATTERED	ENTHRALL	INTERNET
LASHINGS	OBSIDIAN	ROSALIND	ZASTRUGA	BETATRON	ENTHRONE	INTERPOL
LISTENER	OBSOLETE	ROSALINE	ACTINIDE	BETHESDA	ENTICING	INTERVAL
LISTERIA	OBSTACLE	ROSAMOND	ACTINIUM	BETJEMAN	ENTIRELY	INTIFADA
LISTLESS	OBSTRUCT	ROSEFISH	ACTIVATE	BETRAYAL	ENTIRETY	INTIMACY
LUSCIOUS	ONSCREEN	ROSEMARY	ACTIVELY	BETRAYER	ENTITLED	INTIMATE
LUSHNESS	PASHMINA	ROSEROOT	ACTIVISM	BITTERLY	ENTRAILS	INTRADOS
LUSTRINE	PASSABLE	ROSEWOOD	ACTIVIST	BOTANIST	ENTRANCE	INTRENCH
LUSTROUS	PASSABLY	ROSINESS	ACTIVITY	BOTHERED	ENTREATY	INTREPID
LYSANDER	PASSBOOK	ROSSETTI	ACTUALLY	BOTHWELL	ENTRENCH	INTRIGUE
LYSERGIC	PASSERBY	RUSHMORE	ALTHOUGH	BOTSWANA	ENTREPOT	INTRUDER
MASCARON	PASSIBLE	RUSTLESS	ALTITUDE	BOTTLING	ENTRYISM	ISTANBUL

ISTHMIAN	NATURISM	PITILESS	VITILIGO	COUNTESS	FRUCTOSE	PRUSSIAN
JETTISON	NATURIST	PITTANCE	VITREOUS	COUNTIES	FRUGALLY	REUSABLE
JOTTINGS	NITROGEN	POTATOES	WATCHDOG	COUNTING	FRUITFUL	ROUGHAGE
KATAKANA	NOTARIAL	POTBELLY	WATCHFUL	COUPERIN	FRUITING	ROULETTE
KATMANDU	NOTATION	POTBOUND	WATCHING	COUPLING	FRUITION	ROUNDERS
KATTEGAT	NOTEBOOK	POTEMKIN	WATCHMAN	COURTESY	FRUMENTY	ROUSSEAU
KITEMARK	NOTECASE	POTHOLER	WATERBUG	COUSCOUS	FRUMPISH	SAUCEPAN
LATCHKEY	NOTIONAL	POTLATCH	WATERING	CRUCIATE	GAUNTLET	SAUROPOD
LATENESS	NUTHATCH	POTSHERD	WATERLOO	CRUCIBLE	GLUMPISH	SAUSAGES
LATERITE	NUTHOUSE	POTSTONE	WATERMAN	CRUCIFER	GLUTAEUS	SCULLERY
LATINIST	NUTRIENT	PUTATIVE	WATERSKI	CRUCIFIX	GLUTTONY	SCULLION
LATITUDE	NUTSHELL	RATEABLE	WATERWAY	CRUMHORN	GOURMAND	SCULPTOR
LATTERLY	OBTAINED	RATIONAL	WETLANDS	CRUMMOCK	GRUDGING	SHUTDOWN
LETHARGY	OBTUSELY	RATTIGAN	WITCHERY	CRUNCHIE	GRUESOME	SHUTTERS
LETTERED	OCTAROON	RATTLING	WITCHING	CRUSADER	GRUMBLER	SKULKING
LITERACY	OCTONARY	RETAILER	WITHDRAW	CRUSHING	GRUMPILY	SKULLCAP
LITERARY	ONTOLOGY	RETAINER	WITHERED	CRUTCHED	HAUNCHES	SLUGABED
LITERATE	OPTICIAN	RETARDED	WITHHOLD	CRUZEIRO	HAUNTING	SLUGFEST
LITERATI	OPTIMATE	RETICENT	YATAGHAN	DAUGHTER	HOUSEMAN	SLUGGARD
LITIGANT	OPTIMISM	RETICULE	ABUNDANT	DAUNTING	INUNDATE	SLUGGISH
LITIGATE	OPTIMIST	RETIRING	ABUTILON	DEUTERON	JAUNDICE	SLUMMING
LITTORAL	OPTIONAL	RETRENCH	ABUTMENT	DIURETIC	JAUNTILY	SLURRING
LOTHARIO	ORTHODOX	RETRIEVE	ADULATOR	DOUBLETS	KOURMISS	SLUTTISH
LUTENIST	OSTERLEY	RITUALLY	ADULTERY	DOUBLOON	KOUSKOUS	SMUGGLED
LUTETIUM	OTTAVINO	ROTATION	ALUMINUM	DOUBTFUL	KRUMHORN	SMUGGLER
LUTHERAN	OUTBOARD	ROTATORY	AMUNDSEN	DOUBTING	LAUDABLE	SMUGNESS
MATABELE	OUTBREAK	ROTENONE	AMUSETTE	DOUGHBOY	LAUDABLY	SNUFFBOX
MATAMORE	OUTBURST	RUTABAGA	AQUALUNG	DOUGHNUT	LAUDANUM	SOUCHONG
MATCHBOX	OUTCLASS	RUTHLESS	AQUARIUM	DRUBBING	LAUGHING	SOULLESS
MATCHING	OUTDATED	SATIATED	AQUARIUS	DRUDGERY	LAUGHTER	SOUNDING
MATERIAL	OUTDOORS	SATIRIST	AQUATINT	DRUGGIST	LAUREATE	SOURCING
MATERNAL	OUTFIELD	SATIRIZE	AQUEDUCT	DRUMBEAT	LAURENCE	SOURNESS
MATHURIN	OUTFLANK	SATURATE	AQUILINE	DRUMHEAD	LEUKEMIA	SOURPUSS
MATRONLY	OUTGOING	SATURDAY	ASUNCION	DRUMLINE	LOUDNESS	SOURWOOD
MATTRESS	OUTHOUSE	SATURNIA	AVULSION	DRUMMING	LOUVERED	SOUTHEND
MATURATE	OUTLYING	SITTELLA	BAUDRICK	DRUNKARD	MEUNIÈRE	SOUTHERN
MATURITY	OUTMATCH	SITUATED	BLUDGEON	EDUCATED	MOUFFLON	SOUTHPAW
METABOLA	OUTMODED	TATTERED	BLUEBACK	EDUCATOR	MOULDING	SOUVENIR
MÉTAIRIE	OUTREACH	TETCHILY	BLUEBELL	EMULATOR	MOUNTAIN	SPURIOUS
METALLED	OUTREMER	TETRAGON	BLUECOAT	EMULGENT	MOUNTING	SPURNING
METALLIC	OUTRIDER	TETRAPOD	BLUENOSE	EMULSIFY	MOURNFUL	SQUABBLE
METAPHOR	OUTRIGHT	TETRARCH	BLURRING	EMULSION	MOURNING	SQUADDIE
METEORIC	OUTSHINE	TITANESS	BLUSHING	EQUALITY	MOUSSAKA	SQUADRON
METHANOL	OUTSIDER	TITANISM	BLUSTERY	EQUALIZE	MOUTHFUL	SQUAMATA
METHODIC	OUTSMART	TITANITE	BOUFFANT	EQUATION	NAUPLIUS	SQUAMOUS
METONYMY	OUTSTRIP	TITANIUM	BOUNCING	EQUIPAGE	NAUSEATE	SQUANDER
METRICAL	OUTWARDS	TITICACA	BOUNDARY	EQUITANT	NAUSEOUS	SQUARELY
METRITIS	OUTWEIGH	TITIVATE	BOUTIQUE	EQUULEUS	NAUTICAL	SQUATTER
MITIGATE	PATAGIUM	TITMOUSE	BOUZOUKI	ERUCTATE	NAUTILUS	SQUEAKER
MOTHBALL	PATCHILY	TOTALITY	BRUCKNER	ERUPTION	NEURITIS	SQUEALER
MOTHERLY	PATELLAR	TOTALIZE	BRUISING	ERUPTURE	NEUROSIS	SQUEEGEE
MOTIVATE	PATENTED	TUTELAGE	BRUMAIRE	EXULTANT	NEUROTIC	SQUEEZER
MOTORCAR	PATENTEE	TUTELARY	BRUNETTE	EXULTING	NEUTRINO	SQUIGGLE
MOTORING	PATENTLY	TUTORIAL	BRUSSELS	FAULKNER	OPULENCE	SQUIRREL
MOTORIST	PATERNAL	ULTERIOR	BRUTALLY	FLUENTLY	OPUSCULE	STUBBORN
MOTORIZE	PATHETIC	ULTIMATE	CAUDILLO	FLUIDITY	PAULINUS	STUCCOED
MOTORMAN	PATHOGEN	UNTANGLE	CAULDRON	FLUMMERY	PLUCKILY	STUDENTS
MOTORWAY	PATIENCE	UNTAPPED	CAUSEWAY	FLUORIDE	PLUCKING	STUDIOUS
MUTATION	PATULOUS	UNTHREAD	CAUTIOUS	FLUORINE	PLUGHOLE	STUFFILY
MUTCHKIN	PETANQUE	UNTIDILY	CHUMMAGE	FLUORITE	PLUMBAGO	STUFFING
MUTILATE	PETERLOO	UNTILLED	CHURLISH	FLUSHING	PLUMBING	STULTIFY
MUTINEER	PETITION	UNTIMELY	CHUTZPAH	FOULNESS	PLUNGING	STUNNING
MUTINOUS	PETRARCH	UNTOWARD	CLUBBING	FOUNDING	PLUTARCH	STUPIDLY
MUTUALLY	PETULANT	UPTURNED	CLUBFOOT	FOUNTAIN	POULAINE	STURDILY
MYTHICAL	PHTHISIC	VITALISM	CLUELESS	FOURFOLD	POULTICE	STURGEON
NATALITY	PHTHISIS	VITALITY	CLUMSILY	FOURPART	POUNDAGE	TAUTNESS
NATIONAL	PITCAIRN	VITALIZE	COUCHANT	FOURSOME	PRUDENCE	TEUTONIC
NATIVITY	PITHLESS	VITAMINS	COUCHING	FOURTEEN	PRUNELLA	THUMPING
NATTERED	PITIABLE	VITELLUS	COUGHING	FRUCTIFY	PRURIENT	THUNDERY

287

THURIBLE	HAVDALAH	SEVERITY	UNWONTED	OLYMPIAD	APPARENT	CAVATINA
THURIFER	HAVILDAR	TAVERNER	UNWORTHY	OLYMPIAN	AQUALUNG	CELANESE
THURSDAY	HOVERFLY	TOVARICH	VOWELIZE	OLYMPICS	AQUARIUM	CERAMICS
TOUCHING	INVASION	UNVARIED	COXSWAIN	OXYMORON	AQUARIUS	CERASTES
TOULOUSE	INVASIVE	UNVERSED	DEXTROSE	OXYTOCIN	AQUATINT	CERATOID
TRUCKING	INVEIGLE	UNVOICED	DEXTROUS	PAYCHECK	ARBALEST	CETACEAN
TRUCKLED	INVENTED	VIVACITY	DOXOLOGY	PHYLLOME	ARCADIAN	CHEATERS
TRUENESS	INVENTOR	VIVARIUM	FIXATION	PHYSALIA	ARKANSAS	CHEATING
TRUMPERY	INVERTED	WAVEBAND	FIXATIVE	PHYSICAL	ARMAGNAC	CHIASMUS
TRUNCATE	INVERTER	WAVERING	FOXGLOVE	PHYSIQUE	ARMALITE	CICATRIX
TRUNNION	INVESTOR	WAVERLEY	FOXHOUND	PLYMOUTH	ARMAMENT	CITATION
TRUSTFUL	INVITING	BEWILDER	HEXAGRAM	PTYALISM	ARMATURE	CLEANERS
TRUSTING	INVOLUTE	BOWSPRIT	LAXATIVE	REYNOLDS	ARRANGER	CLEANING
TRUTHFUL	INVOLVED	COWARDLY	MAXIMIZE	RHYTHMIC	ASSASSIN	CLEANSED
UNUNBIUM	JOVIALLY	COWBERRY	SAXATILE	ROYALIST	ASTATINE	CLEANSER
UNUSABLE	JUVENILE	DEWBERRY	SEXOLOGY	SAYONARA	ATHANASY	CLEARCUT
USUFRUCT	LAVATORY	DEWYEYED	SEXUALLY	SCYBALUM	ATLANTIC	CLEARING
USURIOUS	LAVENDER	DOWNBEAT	SIXPENCE	SKYLIGHT	ATLANTIS	CLEARWAY
VAULTING	LAVENGRO	DOWNCAST	SIXTIETH	SKYPILOT	ATTACHED	CLEAVAGE
VAUXHALL	LAVISHLY	DOWNFALL	TAXATION	SLYBOOTS	ATTACKER	CLEAVERS
YOUNGEST	LEVELLER	DOWNHILL	TAXONOMY	SPYGLASS	AUCASSIN	COCACOLA
YOURSELF	LEVERAGE	DOWNLOAD	TAXPAYER	STYLIZED	AUDACITY	COLANDER
YOUTHFUL	LEVITATE	DOWNPLAY	TEXTBOOK	TAYBERRY	AUTARCHY	COMATOSE
ADVANCED	LIVELONG	DOWNPOUR	TEXTURED	VOYAGEUR	AVIATION	COVALENT
ADVANCER	LIVERIED	DOWNSIDE	TOXAEMIA	WAYFARER	BAHAMIAN	COWARDLY
ADVISORY	LIVERISH	DOWNSIZE	TOXICITY	BUZZWORD	BALANCED	CREAMERY
ADVOCACY	LIVEWARE	DOWNTOWN	TOXOCARA	COZINESS	BANALITY	CREATION
ADVOCATE	LIVIDITY	DOWNTURN	VEXATION	DAZZLING	BARABBAS	CREATIVE
ALVEOLUS	LOVEBIRD	DOWNWARD	VEXILLUM	GAZPACHO	BARATHEA	CREATURE
BAVARIAN	LOVELACE	HAWAIIAN	WAXWORKS	GAZUNDER	BATAVIAN	CROATIAN
BEVERAGE	LOVELESS	HAWFINCH	AMYGDALA	HAZELNUT	BAVARIAN	CURATIVE
CAVALIER	LOVELORN	HAWTHORN	ANYPLACE	HAZINESS	BECALMED	DAMASCUS
CAVATINA	LOVESICK	HOWDYEDO	ANYTHING	KAZACHOK	BEDABBLE	DANAIDES
CIVILIAN	LOVINGLY	HOWITZER	ANYWHERE	LAZINESS	BEHAVIOR	DATABASE
CIVILITY	MAVERICK	INWARDLY	ATYPICAL	MAZARINE	BELABOUR	DECADENT
CIVILIZE	MOVEABLE	JEWELLED	BAYBERRY	NAZARENE	BETATRON	DECANTER
COVALENT	MOVEMENT	JEWELLER	BAYREUTH	PIZZERIA	BIGAMIST	DECAYING
COVENANT	NAVARINO	LAWCOURT	BRYOZOAN	PUZZLING	BIGAMOUS	DELAWARE
COVENTRY	NAVIGATE	LAWFULLY	COYSTRIL	SIZEABLE	BIGARADE	DENARIUS
COVERAGE	NOVELIST	LAWMAKER	CRYOLITE	SIZZLING	BLEACHER	DENATURE
COVERING	NOVEMBER	LAWRENCE	CRYSTALS	SUZERAIN	BORACITE	DEPARTED
COVERLET	PAVEMENT	LEWDNESS	DAYBREAK	WIZARDRY	BOTANIST	DERANGED
COVETOUS	PAVILION	LEWISITE	DAYDREAM	**8:4**	BREACHES	DETACHED
DAVIDSON	PEVENSEY	LOWCLASS	DAYLIGHT		BREAKING	DETAILED
DEVIANCE	RAVENOUS	LOWERING	DRYCLEAN	ABBASIDE	BREAKOUT	DETAINEE
DEVILISH	REVANCHE	LOWLANDS	DRYGOODS	ABLATION	BREATHER	DETAINER
DEVILLED	REVEALED	LOWLYING	DRYSTONE	ABLATIVE	BROADWAY	DIDACTIC
DEVONIAN	REVEILLE	NEWCOMER	EGYPTIAN	ABRASION	BUDAPEST	DILATION
DEVOTION	REVELLER	NEWFOUND	ERYTHEMA	ABRASIVE	CADASTRE	DILATORY
DIVIDEND	REVEREND	NEWHAVEN	FLYBLOWN	ADJACENT	CALABASH	DISABLED
DIVIDERS	REVERENT	NEWSCAST	FLYDRIVE	ADVANCED	CALAMINE	DISABUSE
DIVINITY	REVERSAL	NEWSHAWK	FLYSHEET	ADVANCER	CALAMITY	DISAGREE
DIVISION	REVERSED	NEWSPEAK	FLYWHEEL	AGNATION	CAMARGUE	DISALLOW
DIVISIVE	REVIEWER	NEWSREEL	GLYCERIN	AGRARIAN	CANADIAN	DISARRAY
DIVORCED	REVISION	NEWSROOM	GLYCOGEN	AKKADIAN	CANAILLE	DISASTER
DIVORCEE	REVIVIFY	NOWADAYS	GUYANESE	ALBACORE	CANALISE	DONATION
DOVECOTE	REVIVING	PAWNSHOP	HAYFEVER	ALBANIAN	CANARIES	DONATIST
DOVETAIL	REVOLVER	POWDERED	HAYFIELD	ALCATRAZ	CAPACITY	DOPAMINE
ENVELOPE	RIVALISE	POWERFUL	HAYMAKER	ALEATORY	CARABINE	DREADFUL
ENVIABLE	RIVERAIN	SAWBONES	HAYSTACK	ALHAMBRA	CARACOLE	DREAMILY
ENVIRONS	RIVERINE	SAWHORSE	HEYTHROP	ALKALIFY	CARAPACE	DREAMING
ENVISAGE	RIVETING	SEWERAGE	JOYFULLY	ALKALINE	CASANOVA	DREARILY
ENVISION	SAVAGELY	TOWELING	JOYSTICK	ALKALOID	CATACOMB	DURABLES
FAVORITE	SAVAGERY	TOWERING	KEYBOARD	ALSATIAN	CATALYST	DURATION
FAVOURED	SAVANNAH	TOWNSHIP	KEYSTONE	ANNALIST	CATAMITE	DYNAMICS
FEVERFEW	SAVOURED	TOWNSMAN	LAYABOUT	ANNAMITE	CATAPULT	DYNAMISM
FEVERISH	SAVOYARD	UNWANTED	LOYALIST	APIARIST	CATARACT	DYNAMITE
GIVEAWAY	SEVERELY	UNWEANED	MAYORESS	APPALLED	CATATONY	DYNASTIC
GOVERNOR	SEVEREST	UNWIELDY	ODYSSEUS	APPANAGE	CAVALIER	DYNATRON

EATABLES	HEPATICA	MACAULAY	OBLATION	REPAIRER	SQUADDIE	UNCARING
EMBATTLE	HERACLES	MAGAZINE	OBTAINED	REPARTEE	SQUADRON	UNEARNED
EMMANUEL	HERACLID	MAHARAJA	OCCAMIST	REPAYING	SQUAMATA	UNEASILY
ENCAENIA	HERALDIC	MAHARANI	OCCASION	RETAILER	SQUAMOUS	UNFADING
ENCAMPED	HERALDRY	MALAGASY	OCTAROON	RETAINER	SQUANDER	UNFASTEN
ENDANGER	HETAIRIA	MALAKOFF	OKLAHOMA	RETARDED	SQUARELY	UNGAINLY
ENGAGING	HEXAGRAM	MALAMUTE	OLEACEAE	REVANCHE	SQUATTER	UNHARMED
ENLARGED	HIJACKER	MALARIAL	OLEANDER	RIBALDRY	STEADILY	UNLAWFUL
ENLARGER	HILARITY	MALARKEY	OLEASTER	RIGATONI	STEALING	UNMANNED
ENTANGLE	HIRAGANA	MALAWIAN	ORCADIAN	RIPARIAN	STEALTHY	UNMARKED
EQUALITY	HORATIAN	MALAYSIA	ORGANDIE	RIVALISE	STEAPSIN	UNSALTED
EQUALIZE	HORATIUS	MANAGING	ORGANISM	ROGATION	STEATITE	UNSAVORY
EQUATION	HUMANELY	MARABOUT	ORGANIST	ROMANCER	STEATOMA	UNTANGLE
ESCALADE	HUMANISM	MARASMUS	ORGANIZE	ROMANIAN	STRABISM	UNTAPPED
ESCALATE	HUMANIST	MARATHON	ORNAMENT	ROMANSCH	STRACHEY	UNVARIED
ESCALOPE	HUMANITY	MARAUDER	OTTAVINO	ROMANTIC	STRADDLE	UNWANTED
ESCAPADE	HUMANIZE	MATABELE	PAGANINI	ROSALIND	STRAGGLE	UPMARKET
ESCAPISM	HYDATOID	MATAMORE	PALATIAL	ROSALINE	STRAGGLY	URBANITY
ESCAPIST	IDEALISM	MAZARINE	PALATINE	ROSAMOND	STRAIGHT	URBANIZE
ESCARGOT	IDEALIST	MEDALIST	PANATELA	ROTATION	STRAINED	VACANTLY
ESPALIER	IDEALIZE	MEGABYTE	PARABOLA	ROTATORY	STRAINER	VACATION
ESSAYIST	IMMANENT	MEGALITH	PARADIGM	ROYALIST	STRAITEN	VAGABOND
ESTANCIA	IMMANUEL	MEGAPODE	PARAFFIN	RUBAIYAT	STRANDED	VAGARIES
EURASIAN	IMMATURE	MEGAVOLT	PARAGUAY	RUNABOUT	STRANGER	VANADIUM
EXCAVATE	IMPACTED	MEGAWATT	PARAKEET	RUTABAGA	STRANGLE	VANADOUS
EXPANDED	IMPAIRED	MELAMINE	PARALLAX	SAGACITY	STRAPPED	VENALITY
FATALISM	INFAMOUS	MELANITE	PARALLEL	SALACITY	STRAPPER	VERACITY
FATALIST	INFANTRY	MELANOMA	PARALYZE	SALARIED	STRATEGY	VERANDAH
FATALITY	INHALANT	MENACING	PARAMOUR	SAMARIUM	STRATIFY	VEXATION
FEDAYEEN	INSANELY	MENANDER	PARANOIA	SARABAND	SUDAMENT	VICARAGE
FILAMENT	INSANITY	METABOLA	PARANOID	SARATOGA	SUDAMINA	VICARIAL
FILARIUM	INTAGLIO	MÉTAIRIE	PARAQUAT	SAVAGELY	SUDANESE	VITALISM
FINALIST	INVASION	METALLED	PARASHAH	SAVAGERY	SUDARIUM	VITALITY
FINALITY	INVASIVE	METALLIC	PARASITE	SAVANNAH	SWEARING	VITALIZE
FINALIZE	INWARDLY	METAPHOR	PATAGIUM	SAXATILE	SWEATING	VITAMINS
FIXATION	IOLANTHE	MILANESE	PEDAGOGY	SCHAPSKA	SYBARITE	VIVACITY
FIXATIVE	ISLANDER	MINAMATA	PEDANTIC	SCIATICA	SYCAMORE	VIVARIUM
FLEABITE	ISTANBUL	MINATORY	PEDANTRY	SCRABBLE	SYRACUSE	VOCALIST
FLOATING	JAMAICAN	MISAPPLY	PELAGIUS	SCRAMBLE	TAMANDUA	VOCALIZE
FREAKISH	JAPANESE	MOHAMMED	PENALIZE	SCRAPPLE	TAMARACK	VOCATION
FUMAROLE	JOHANNES	MOLASSES	PERACUTE	SCRATCHY	TAMARIND	VOCATIVE
FUSAROLE	JONATHAN	MONADISM	PETANQUE	SCRAWLED	TAMARISK	VOLATILE
GADABOUT	JURASSIC	MONANDRY	PHEASANT	SEDATELY	TAXATION	VORACITY
GADARENE	JURATORY	MONARCHY	PICAROON	SEDATION	TENACITY	VOYAGEUR
GALACTIC	KALAHARI	MONASTIC	PILASTER	SEDATIVE	TERATOMA	WHEATEAR
GARAMOND	KATAKANA	MONAURAL	PINAFORE	SELASSIE	THEATRIC	WIZARDRY
GELASTIC	KAZACHOK	MORALIST	PIRANESI	SEPARATE	THIAMINE	WOMANISH
GELATINE	LAMASERY	MORALITY	PLEADING	SERAFILE	THRACIAN	WOMANIZE
GERANIUM	LAVATORY	MORALIZE	PLEASANT	SERAGLIO	THRALDOM	WREATHED
GIGABYTE	LAXATIVE	MORAVIAN	PLEASING	SERAPHIC	THRASHER	XERAPHIM
GIGANTIC	LAYABOUT	MUHAMMAD	PLEASURE	SERAPHIM	TIRAMISU	YATAGHAN
GIGAWATT	LEBANESE	MUHARRAM	PODARGUS	SHEARMAN	TITANESS	AIRBORNE
GIRASOLE	LEGALISM	MUTATION	POLARIZE	SHRAPNEL	TITANISM	AIRBRAKE
GLEAMING	LEGALITY	NAGASAKI	POMANDER	SINAPISM	TITANITE	ANABASIS
GLOAMING	LEGALIZE	NATALITY	POTATOES	SNEAKERS	TITANIUM	ANABATIC
GLOATING	LEGATION	NAVARINO	PREACHER	SNEAKING	TOMAHAWK	BABBLING
GREATEST	LIBATION	NAZARENE	PREAMBLE	SOCALLED	TOMATOES	BARBADOS
GUIANIAN	LIGAMENT	NDJAMENA	PRIAPISM	SODALITE	TONALITY	BARBARIC
GUJARATI	LIGATURE	NEGATION	PTYALISM	SODALITY	TOTALITY	BARBECUE
GUYANESE	LIMACINE	NEGATIVE	PUTATIVE	SOLARIUM	TOTALIZE	BARBERRY
GYRATION	LOCALITY	NEMATODE	PYRAMIDS	SONATINA	TOVARICH	BARBICAN
GYRATORY	LOCALIZE	NEMATOID	RAPACITY	SPEAKERS	TOXAEMIA	BARBIZON
HABAKKUK	LOCATION	NEPALESE	REDACTOR	SPEAKING	TREASURE	BAYBERRY
HABANERA	LOCATIVE	NIDATION	REGAINED	SPHAGNUM	TREASURY	BERBERIS
HAMARTIA	LOYALIST	NOMARCHY	RELATING	SPLASHER	TREATISE	BILBERRY
HARANGUE	LYSANDER	NOTARIAL	RELATION	SPLATTER	TRIANGLE	BOBBYPIN
HARASSED	MACARONI	NOTATION	RELATIVE	SPRAINED	TRIASSIC	BRABAZON
HAWAIIAN	MACAROON	NOWADAYS	RELAXING	SPRAWLED	TUPAMARO	BRIBABLE
HECATOMB	MACASSAR	NUGATORY	RELAYING	SQUABBLE	TURANDOT	BUBBLING

BUMBLING	PEMBROKE	BACCARAT	DISCLOSE	HYACINTH	PERCIVAL	SUICIDAL
BURBERRY	PLEBEIAN	BACCHANT	DISCOLOR	INACTION	PIECHART	SUNCREAM
CAMBERED	POTBELLY	BEDCOVER	DISCOUNT	INACTIVE	PIECRUST	SYNCLINE
CAMBODIA	POTBOUND	BERCEUSE	DISCOVER	INOCULUM	PILCHARD	TEACHERS
CAMBRIAN	PROBABLE	BISCAYAN	DISCREET	INSCRIBE	PISCATOR	TEACHING
CANBERRA	PROBABLY	BLACKBOY	DISCRETE	ISOCLINE	PITCAIRN	TEACLOTH
CARBOLIC	PURBLIND	BLACKCAP	DRACAENA	JIMCRACK	PLACABLE	TETCHILY
CARBONIC	QUIBBLER	BLACKFLY	DRACONIC	JONCANOE	PLACEMAT	THICKSET
CERBERUS	RAMBLING	BLACKING	DRYCLEAN	JUNCTION	PLACEMEN	TINCTURE
CLUBBING	RAMBUTAN	BLACKISH	DULCIMER	JUNCTURE	PLACENTA	TOPCLASS
CLUBFOOT	REDBRICK	BLACKLEG	DULCINEA	KERCHIEF	PLACIDLY	TOUCHING
COBBLERS	RUBBISHY	BLACKOUT	DUTCHMAN	KNACKERS	PLECTRUM	TRACHOMA
COMBINED	RUMBLING	BLOCKADE	EDUCATED	KNICKERS	PLUCKILY	TRACKING
COWBERRY	SAWBONES	BLOCKAGE	EDUCATOR	KNOCKERS	PLUCKING	TRACTION
CRIBBAGE	SCABBARD	BRACELET	EJECTION	KNOCKING	PRACTICE	TRICHOID
CUPBOARD	SCABIOUS	BRACHIAL	ELECTION	KNOCKOUT	PRACTISE	TRICKERY
DAYBREAK	SCABROUS	BRACKETS	ELECTIVE	LANCELET	PRECINCT	TRICYCLE
DEWBERRY	SCYBALUM	BRACKISH	ELECTORS	LANCELOT	PRECIOUS	TROCHAIC
DIABETES	SEABOARD	BRICKBAT	ELECTRIC	LATCHKEY	PRECLUDE	TROCHLEA
DIABETIC	SEABORNE	BROCCOLI	ELECTRON	LAWCOURT	PRECURSE	TRUCKING
DIABOLIC	SELBORNE	BROCHURE	ELECTRUM	LEACHING	PROCAINE	TRUCKLED
DISBURSE	SHABBILY	BRUCKNER	EMACIATE	LINCHPIN	PROCEEDS	UNICYCLE
DJIBOUTI	SKIBOOTS	BUTCHERS	ENSCONCE	LINCOLNS	PROCLAIM	VASCULAR
DOGBERRY	SLOBBERY	BUTCHERY	EPICURUS	LOWCLASS	PROCURER	VINCIBLE
DOUBLETS	SLYBOOTS	CALCEATE	ERECTILE	LUNCHBOX	PUNCTUAL	VINCULUM
DOUBLOON	SNOBBERY	CALCRETE	ERECTING	LUNCHEON	PUNCTURE	VISCERAL
DOUBTFUL	SNOBBISH	CALCULUS	ERECTION	LUSCIOUS	PURCHASE	VISCOUNT
DOUBTING	SOMBRELY	CALCUTTA	ERUCTATE	LYNCHING	QUICKSET	VOLCANIC
DRIBLETS	SOMBRERO	CARCAJOU	EVACUANT	MAECENAS	RASCALLY	WATCHDOG
DRUBBING	SORBONNE	CARCANET	EVACUATE	MANCIPLE	REACTION	WATCHFUL
DUMBBELL	STABBING	CATCHING	EVICTION	MARCELLA	REACTIVE	WATCHING
DUMBNESS	STABLING	CHACONNE	EXACTING	MARCELLO	RUNCIBLE	WATCHMAN
FLYBLOWN	STUBBORN	CHECKERS	EXACTION	MASCARON	SANCTIFY	WHACKING
FOGBOUND	SUNBATHE	CHECKING	EXECRATE	MATCHBOX	SANCTION	WITCHERY
FRABJOUS	SUNBURNT	CHECKOUT	EXECUTED	MATCHING	SANCTITY	WITCHING
FUMBLING	SUNBURST	CHICHEWA	EXECUTOR	MELCHIOR	SAUCEPAN	WRECKAGE
FURBELOW	SYMBIONT	CHICKENS	EXOCRINE	MERCALLI	SHACKLES	ZIRCONIA
GALBANUM	SYMBOLIC	CHICKPEA	FALCONRY	MERCATOR	SHOCKING	ZUCCHINI
GAMBLING	TABBYCAT	CINCHONA	FANCIFUL	MERCEDES	SINCLAIR	AARDVARK
GLABELLA	TARBOOSH	CIRCINUS	FANCYMAN	MERCHANT	SMOCKING	ACADEMIA
GLABROUS	TAYBERRY	CIRCUITY	FARCICAL	MERCIFUL	SNACKBAR	ACADEMIC
GLOBALLY	THEBAINE	CIRCULAR	FASCICLE	MESCALIN	SORCERER	ACIDHEAD
GLOBULAR	TIEBREAK	COACHING	FENCIBLE	MINCEPIE	SOUCHONG	BAEDEKER
GLOBULIN	TIMBERED	COACHMAN	FETCHING	MISCARRY	SPACEMAN	BALDNESS
HOBBLING	TOLBOOTH	COCCIDAE	FORCEFUL	MISCHIEF	SPACIOUS	BALDRICK
ICEBLINK	TRIBUNAL	CONCEIVE	FORCIBLE	MISCOUNT	SPECIFIC	BANDANNA
ISABELLA	TURBANED	CONCERTO	FORCIBLY	MOCCASIN	SPECIMEN	BANDEROL
ISABELLE	TURBOJET	CONCHOID	FRACTION	MUNCHKIN	SPECIOUS	BANDITTI
ISOBARIC	UNABATED	CONCLAVE	FRACTURE	MUSCADET	SPECKLED	BANDSMAN
JAMBOREE	VANBRUGH	CONCLUDE	FRECKLED	MUSCATEL	SPECTRAL	BARDOLPH
KEYBOARD	VERBALLY	CONCORDE	FRECKLES	MUSCULAR	SPECTRUM	BAUDRICK
KNOBLESS	VERBATIM	CONCRETE	FRICTION	MUTCHKIN	SPECULUM	BINDWEED
LAMBSKIN	VERBIAGE	COUCHANT	FRUCTIFY	NARCOSES	SPICCATO	BIRDCAGE
LIMBLESS	WAMBLING	COUCHING	FRUCTOSE	NARCOSIS	STACCATO	BIRDSEED
LOBBYIST	WOBBLING	CRACKERS	FUNCTION	NARCOTIC	STICCATO	BLUDGEON
LOMBARDY	ZIMBABWE	CRACKING	GIACONDA	NESCIENT	STICKILY	BOADICEA
MEMBRANE	ABSCISSA	CRACKPOT	GIMCRACK	NEWCOMER	STICKING	BOLDNESS
MIDBRAIN	AGACERIE	CRICHTON	GIOCONDA	OBSCURED	STICKLER	BONDSMAN
MORBIDLY	AIRCRAFT	CROCKERY	GLYCERIN	OFFCOLOR	STOCCATA	BORDEAUX
MORBILLI	ALACRITY	CROCKETT	GLYCOGEN	OILCLOTH	STOCKADE	BORDELLO
MULBERRY	ALICANTE	CRUCIATE	GODCHILD	ONSCREEN	STOCKCAR	BORDERER
MUMBLING	AMICABLE	CRUCIBLE	GRACEFUL	OUTCLASS	STOCKING	BRADBURY
MYOBLAST	AMICABLY	CRUCIFER	GRACIOUS	PANCREAS	STOCKIST	BRADSHAW
NEMBUTAL	ANACONDA	CRUCIFIX	HATCHERY	PATCHILY	STOCKMAN	BRIDGING
NUMBNESS	ANACREON	DABCHICK	HATCHING	PAYCHECK	STOCKPOT	BUDDHISM
OFFBREAK	ANECDOTE	DESCRIBE	HATCHWAY	PEACEFUL	STUCCOED	BUDDHIST
OUTBOARD	ARACHNID	DIOCESAN	HENCHMAN	PENCHANT	SUCCEEDS	BUDDLEIA
OUTBREAK	ARMCHAIR	DISCIPLE	HERCULES	PERCEIVE	SUCCINCT	BURDENED
OUTBURST	AVICENNA	DISCLAIM	HICCOUGH	PERCEVAL	SUCCUBUS	CALDERON

CANDIDLY	GRIDLOCK	LANDMASS	ROADSIDE	WOODWARD	ASBESTOS	CATEGORY
CARDAMOM	GRUDGING	LANDMINE	ROADSTER	WOODWIND	ASPERGES	CATERING
CARDIGAN	GUIDANCE	LANDRACE	SADDLERY	WOODWORK	ASPERITY	CELERIAC
CARDINAL	GURDWARA	LANDSEER	SADDLING	WOODWORM	ASPERMIA	CELERITY
CAUDILLO	HANDBALL	LANDSLIP	SADDUCEE	WORDBOOK	ASSEMBLE	CEMENTUM
CHADBAND	HANDBILL	LANDWARD	SANDARAC	WORDLESS	ASSEMBLY	CEMETERY
CLADDING	HANDBOOK	LAUDABLE	SANDBANK	ABJECTLY	ASSESSOR	CEREBRAL
CLODPOLL	HANDCART	LAUDABLY	SANDWICH	ABNEGATE	ASTERISK	CEREBRUM
COLDBOOT	HANDCLAP	LAUDANUM	SARDINIA	ABSENTEE	ASTEROID	CEREMENT
COLDNESS	HANDCUFF	LEADSMAN	SARDONIC	ACCENTED	ATHELING	CEREMONY
CONDENSE	HANDGRIP	LEWDNESS	SARDONYX	ACCENTOR	ATHENIAN	CHEEKILY
CORDOVAN	HANDHELD	LOADSTAR	SEEDLESS	ACCEPTED	ATHEROMA	CHEERFUL
CORDUROY	HANDICAP	LONDONER	SEEDLING	ACCEPTOR	ATHETISE	CHEERILY
CORDWAIN	HANDMADE	LORDOSIS	SEEDSMAN	ADDENDUM	ATHETOID	CHEERING
CREDIBLE	HANDMAID	LORDSHIP	SHADRACH	ADHERENT	ATTENDER	CICERONE
CREDIBLY	HANDOVER	LOUDNESS	SHODDILY	ADHESION	ATTESTOR	CINERAMA
CREDITOR	HANDRAIL	MAIDENLY	SKIDDING	ADHESIVE	AURELIAN	CINEREAL
DAEDALUS	HANDSOME	MALDIVES	SMIDGEON	AFFECTED	BAKELITE	CLUELESS
DANDRUFF	HANDYMAN	MANDAMUS	SOLDIERS	AFFERENT	BALEARIC	COHERENT
DAYDREAM	HARDBACK	MANDARIN	SOLDIERY	AGREEING	BAREBACK	COHESION
DEADBEAT	HARDCORE	MANDATED	SORDIDLY	AIREDALE	BAREFOOT	COHESIVE
DEADENED	HARDENED	MANDIBLE	SPADEFUL	ALBERICH	BARENESS	COLESLAW
DEADENER	HARDHACK	MANDIOCA	STUDENTS	ALCESTIS	BASEBALL	COMEBACK
DEADHEAD	HARDLINE	MANDOLIN	STUDIOUS	ALDEHYDE	BASEBORN	COMEDIAN
DEADLINE	HARDNESS	MANDRAKE	SUDDENLY	ALDERMAN	BASELESS	COMEDOWN
DEADLOCK	HARDSHIP	MANDRILL	SUNDANCE	ALDERNEY	BASELINE	COVENANT
DEADWOOD	HARDTACK	MEDDLING	SUNDRIED	ALGERIAN	BASEMENT	COVENTRY
DENDRITE	HARDWARE	MIDDLING	SUNDRIES	ALGERINE	BASENESS	COVERAGE
DENDROID	HARDWOOD	MILDEWED	SWADDLER	ALIENATE	BEGETTER	COVERING
DIDDICOY	HAVDALAH	MILDNESS	SYNDROME	ALIENISM	BEHEMOTH	COVERLET
DOLDRUMS	HEADACHE	MINDANAO	TANDOORI	ALIENIST	BENEDICK	COVETOUS
DRUDGERY	HEADBAND	MINDLESS	TENDENCY	ALLEGORY	BENEDICT	CUTENESS
DUODENAL	HEADGEAR	MONDRIAN	TENDERLY	ALLELUIA	BENEFICE	CYRENIAC
DUODENUM	HEADHUNT	MURDERER	TOADFLAX	ALLERGEN	BENEFITS	DANEGELD
EPIDEMIC	HEADLAMP	NEEDLESS	TRADEOFF	ALLERGIC	BENENDEN	DATELESS
EPIDURAL	HEADLAND	OBEDIENT	VENDETTA	ALLEYWAY	BEREAVED	DATELINE
ERADIATE	HEADLESS	OUTDATED	VERDERER	ALVEOLUS	BEVERAGE	DECEASED
ERIDANUS	HEADLINE	OUTDOORS	VINDALOO	AMPERAGE	BISEXUAL	DECEIVER
EVIDENCE	HEADLONG	PADDLING	VOIDANCE	ANCESTOR	BLEEDING	DECEMBER
FANDANGO	HEADMARK	PANDANUS	WANDERER	ANCESTRY	BLUEBACK	DECEMVIR
FEEDBACK	HEADMOST	PANDARUS	WARDRESS	ANDERSON	BLUEBELL	DECENTLY
FELDSPAR	HEADREST	PANDEMIC	WARDROBE	ANGELICA	BLUECOAT	DEFEATED
FIDDLING	HEADROOM	PANDOWDY	WARDROOM	ANNEALER	BLUENOSE	DEFECATE
FINDINGS	HEADSHIP	PARDONER	WARDSHIP	ANNELIDA	BOGEYMAN	DEFECTOR
FLYDRIVE	HEADWIND	PEDDLING	WHODUNIT	ANSERINE	BOHEMIAN	DEFENDER
FOLDEROL	HEADWORD	PENDULUM	WILDFELL	ANTECEDE	BONEFISH	DEJECTED
FONDLING	HEEDLESS	PIDDLING	WILDFIRE	ANTEDATE	BONEHEAD	DELEGATE
FONDNESS	HERDSMAN	PINDARIC	WILDFOWL	ANTELOPE	BONELESS	DELETION
GARDENER	HINDMOST	POWDERED	WILDLIFE	ANTENNAE	BONEYARD	DEMEANOR
GARDENIA	HINDUISM	PREDATOR	WILDNESS	ANTEPOST	BORECOLE	DEMENTED
GARDYLOO	HINDWARD	PREDELLA	WINDBURN	ANTERIOR	BOREHOLE	DEMENTIA
GENDARME	HOLDFAST	PRODIGAL	WINDFALL	ANTEROOM	BREECHES	DEMERARA
GEODESIC	HOLDINGS	PRODROME	WINDGALL	AOTEAROA	BREEDING	DEMERSAL
GEODETIC	HONDURAN	PRODUCER	WINDHOEK	APHELION	BREEZILY	DERELICT
GLADNESS	HONDURAS	PRODUCES	WINDINGS	APNEUSIS	BRIEFING	DESELECT
GLADSOME	HOODWINK	PRODUCTS	WINDLASS	APPELANT	CABERNET	DESERTED
GOIDELIC	HOWDYEDO	PRUDENCE	WINDLESS	APPENDIX	CAKEHOLE	DESERTER
GOLDFISH	HUNDREDS	QUADRANT	WINDMILL	APPETITE	CAKEWALK	DESERVED
GOLDMINE	HURDLING	QUADRATE	WINDPIPE	AQUEDUCT	CALENDAR	DETECTOR
GONDWANA	INEDIBLE	QUADRIGA	WINDSOCK	ARDENNES	CALENDER	DIRECTLY
GOODNESS	KINDLING	QUADROON	WINDWARD	ARDENTLY	CAMELLIA	DIRECTOR
GOODSIRE	KINDNESS	RANDOMLY	WONDROUS	ARGESTES	CAMEROON	DISEASED
GOODWIFE	LAIDBACK	READABLE	WOODBINE	ARMENIAN	CAPERING	DOMESDAY
GOODWILL	LANDFALL	READIEST	WOODCOCK	ARPEGGIO	CAREFREE	DOMESTIC
GOODWOOD	LANDFILL	READJUST	WOODENLY	ARRESTED	CARELESS	DOVECOTE
GOODYEAR	LANDLADY	REEDLING	WOODLAND	ARRESTER	CAREWORN	DOVETAIL
GRADIENT	LANDLOCK	REEDSMAN	WOODRUFF	ARTEFACT	CASEMATE	EASEMENT
GRADUATE	LANDLORD	RIDDANCE	WOODSHED	ARTERIAL	CASEMENT	ECLECTIC
GRIDIRON	LANDMARK	ROADSHOW	WOODSMAN	ARTESIAN	CATECHOL	EDGEHILL

EDGEWAYS	FOREMILK	HOSEPIPE	LIFEBELT	MOVEABLE	QUIETUDE	SERENADE
EDGEWISE	FOREMOST	HOTELIER	LIFEBOAT	MOVEMENT	RABELAIS	SERENATA
EFFERENT	FORENAME	HOVERFLY	LIFEBUOY	MULETEER	RAMEQUIN	SERENELY
EIDECTIC	FORENOON	HYPERION	LIFELESS	MULEWORT	RANELAGH	SERENITY
EMBEDDED	FORENSIC	IDLENESS	LIFELIKE	MYCELIUM	RAPECAKE	SEVERELY
EMBEZZLE	FORESAIL	IMBECILE	LIFELINE	NAMELESS	RAREFIED	SEVEREST
ENDEAVOR	FORESHIP	IMMERSED	LIFELONG	NAMESAKE	RATEABLE	SEVERITY
ENFEEBLE	FORESKIN	IMPELLED	LIFESPAN	NEHEMIAH	RAVENOUS	SEWERAGE
ENGENDER	FORESTAY	IMPERIAL	LIFETIME	NEPENTHE	RECEDING	SHEEPDOG
ENMESHED	FORESTER	IMPETIGO	LIKEABLE	NIBELUNG	RECEIPTS	SHEEPISH
ENSEMBLE	FORESTRY	INCENSED	LIKENESS	NICENESS	RECEIVED	SHIELING
ENVELOPE	FORETELL	INDEBTED	LIKEWISE	NIGERIAN	RECEIVER	SHOEBILL
EPHEMERA	FOREWARN	INDECENT	LIMERICK	NIGERIEN	RECENTLY	SHOEHORN
EPHESIAN	FOREWORD	INDENTED	LINESMAN	NINEPINS	RECEPTOR	SHOELACE
ESPECIAL	FREEHAND	INDEXING	LITERACY	NINETEEN	RECESSED	SHOELESS
ESTEEMED	FREEHOLD	INFECTED	LITERARY	NOBELIUM	REDEEMER	SHOETREE
ETCETERA	FREEPOST	INFERIOR	LITERATE	NONESUCH	REDEFINE	SHREDDER
ETHEREAL	FREETOWN	INFERNAL	LITERATI	NOSEBAND	REDEPLOY	SHREWDLY
ETHERIFY	FREEZING	INFESTED	LIVELONG	NOSEDIVE	REDESIGN	SHREWISH
ETHERISE	FRIENDLY	INHERENT	LIVERIED	NOTEBOOK	REFERRAL	SIBERIAN
EUGENICS	FUNERARY	INJECTOR	LIVERISH	NOTECASE	REHEARSE	SIDEKICK
EUPEPSIA	FUNEREAL	INSECURE	LIVEWARE	NOVELIST	RELEASED	SIDELINE
EXOERGIC	FUSELAGE	INTEGRAL	LOBELINE	NOVEMBER	RELEGATE	SIDELONG
EXPECTED	FUSEWIRE	INTELSAT	LODESTAR	NUMERACY	RELEVANT	SIDEREAL
EXPEDITE	GAMEBIRD	INTENDED	LONESOME	NUMERALS	REMEDIAL	SIDERITE
EXPENDED	GAMENESS	INTENTLY	LOVEBIRD	NUMERATE	REMEMBER	SIDESHOW
EXPENSES	GATEFOLD	INTERACT	LOVELACE	NUMEROUS	RENEGADE	SIDESLIP
EXTENDED	GATEPOST	INTERCOM	LOVELESS	OBJECTOR	REPEATED	SIDESMAN
EXTENSOR	GENERATE	INTEREST	LOVELORN	OBSERVED	REPEATER	SIDESTEP
EXTERIOR	GENEROUS	INTERIOR	LOVESICK	OBSERVER	RESEARCH	SIDEWALK
EXTERNAL	GENETICS	INTERMIT	LOWERING	OBSESSED	RESEMBLE	SIDEWARD
EXTERNAT	GENETRIX	INTERNAL	LUKEWARM	OFFENDED	RESERVED	SIDEWAYS
FACEACHE	GIVEAWAY	INTERNEE	LUPERCAL	OFFENDER	RESETTLE	SILENCER
FACELESS	GLEESOME	INTERNET	LUTENIST	OFFERING	REVEALED	SILENTLY
FACELIFT	GOVERNOR	INTERPOL	LUTETIUM	ORDERING	REVEILLE	SILESIAN
FAREWELL	GREEDILY	INTERVAL	LYREBIRD	ORIENTAL	REVELLER	SINECURE
FEDERACY	GREENBAG	INVEIGLE	LYSERGIC	OSTERLEY	REVEREND	SIRENIAN
FEDERATE	GREENERY	INVENTED	MACERATE	OXPECKER	REVERENT	SIZEABLE
FENESTRA	GREENFLY	INVENTOR	MAGELLAN	PALEFACE	REVERSAL	SLEEPERS
FEVERFEW	GREENING	INVERTED	MAIEUTIC	PALENESS	REVERSED	SLEEPILY
FEVERISH	GREENISH	INVERTER	MAJESTIC	PANEGYRY	RIPENESS	SLEEPING
FIDELITY	GREENOCK	INVESTOR	MAMELUKE	PANELING	RIVERAIN	SNEERING
FILENAME	GREETING	JEREBOAM	MANEUVER	PANELLED	RIVERINE	SNEEZING
FINESPUN	GRIEVOUS	JEREMIAD	MATERIAL	PARENTAL	RIVETING	SOBERING
FIREARMS	GRUESOME	JEREMIAH	MATERNAL	PATELLAR	RODERICK	SOLECISM
FIREBACK	HAREBELL	JEWELLED	MAVERICK	PATENTED	ROSEFISH	SOLEMNLY
FIREBALL	HAZELNUT	JEWELLER	MELEAGER	PATENTEE	ROSEMARY	SOLENOID
FIREBIRD	HEBETUDE	JUVENILE	MENELAUS	PATENTLY	ROSEROOT	SOMEBODY
FIREBOLT	HEGEMONY	KINETICS	MEREDITH	PATERNAL	ROSEWOOD	SOMERSET
FIREDAMP	HENEQUEN	KITEMARK	METEORIC	PAVEMENT	ROTENONE	SOMETIME
FIRESIDE	HEREDITY	KNEEDEEP	MINEHEAD	PEDERAST	RUDENESS	SOMEWHAT
FIRESTEP	HEREFORD	KNEEHIGH	MIREPOIX	PEDESTAL	RULEBOOK	SORENESS
FIRETRAP	HEREWARD	LACERATE	MISERERE	PENELOPE	SAGENESS	SPEEDILY
FIREWEED	HEREWITH	LACEWING	MODELING	PEPERONI	SALEABLE	SPEEDWAY
FIREWOOD	HIBERNIA	LAKELAND	MODELLER	PETERLOO	SALEROOM	SPHENOID
FIREWORK	HIDEAWAY	LAKESIDE	MODERATE	PEVENSEY	SALESMAN	SPLENDID
FLEETING	HIRELING	LAMENESS	MODERATO	PHLEGMON	SAMENESS	SPLENDOR
FLUENTLY	HOMELAND	LAMENTED	MODESTLY	PINEWOOD	SCHEDULE	SPREADER
FOREBEAR	HOMELESS	LATENESS	MOLECULE	PIPELINE	SCHEMING	SQUEAKER
FOREBODE	HOMEMADE	LATERITE	MOLEHILL	PIPERINE	SCIENCES	SQUEALER
FORECAST	HOMEPAGE	LAVENDER	MOLESKIN	POKEWEED	SCREAMER	SQUEEGEE
FOREDECK	HOMESICK	LAVENGRO	MOLESTER	POSEIDON	SCREENED	SQUEEZER
FOREDOOM	HOMESPUN	LEVELLER	MOMENTUM	POTEMKIN	SCREWTOP	STEENBOK
FOREFOOT	HOMEWARD	LEVERAGE	MONETARY	POWERFUL	SELECTED	STEERAGE
FOREGONE	HOMEWORK	LIBELOUS	MONETISE	PRIESTLY	SELECTOR	STEERING
FOREHAND	HONESTLY	LIBERATE	MONEYBOX	PUDENDUM	SELENITE	STREAKED
FOREHEAD	HONEYDEW	LIBERIAN	MOREOVER	PYRENEES	SELENIUM	STREAKER
FORELAND	HONEYPOT	LICENSED	MOREPORK	QUAESTOR	SELEUCID	STREAMER
FORELOCK	HOPELESS	LICENSEE	MORESQUE	QUAESTOR	SEMESTER	STRENGTH

STRESSED	TYPECAST	YOSEMITE	PERFORCE	BUNGLING	HEDGEROW	PILGRIMS
STRETCHY	TYPEFACE	YULETIDE	PERFUMED	BURGLARY	HEIGHTEN	PLUGHOLE
SUMERIAN	ULCERATE	ZEDEKIAH	PILFERER	BURGRAVE	HONGKONG	POIGNANT
SUPERBLY	ULCEROUS	ZIBELINE	PROFORMA	BURGUNDY	HUNGRILY	PREGNANT
SUPERBUG	ULTERIOR	ZWIEBACK	PROFOUND	CINGULUM	IMAGINED	PRIGGISH
SUPERIOR	UNBEATEN	AIRFIELD	PROFUSER	CONGRATS	ISOGENIC	PROGERIA
SUPERMAN	UNDERAGE	ARTFULLY	PUFFBALL	CONGRESS	ISOGLOSS	PROGRADE
SUPERNAL	UNDERARM	AVIFAUNA	REAFFIRM	COUGHING	ISOGONAL	PROGRESS
SUPERTAX	UNDERBID	BAFFLING	RIFFRAFF	DAUGHTER	JANGLING	PUNGENCY
SURENESS	UNDERCUT	BOUFFANT	ROOFLESS	DIAGNOSE	JIGGERED	QUAGMIRE
SUZERAIN	UNDERDOG	BUNFIGHT	ROOFTOPS	DIAGONAL	JINGOISM	REIGNING
SWEEPING	UNDERFED	CAFFEINE	RUEFULLY	DIGGINGS	JINGOIST	RIDGEWAY
SWEETSOP	UNDERFUR	CALFSKIN	SCAFFOLD	DINGBATS	JONGLEUR	RINGDOVE
TAKEAWAY	UNDERLAY	CLIFFORD	SCOFFING	DIOGENES	JUDGMENT	RINGHALS
TAKEHOME	UNDERLIE	COIFFEUR	SEAFARER	DISGORGE	JUGGLING	RINGSIDE
TAKEOVER	UNDERPIN	COIFFURE	SEAFLOOR	DOGGEDLY	KANGAROO	RINGTAIL
TALENTED	UNDERRUN	CONFETTI	SEAFORTH	DOGGEREL	KEDGEREE	RINGWALL
TAMENESS	UNDERSEA	CONFINED	SEAFRONT	DOUGHBOY	KIDGLOVE	RINGWORM
TAPENADE	UNDERTOW	CONFINES	SELFHELP	DOUGHNUT	KINGPOST	ROUGHAGE
TAPERING	UNFETTER	CONFLATE	SELFLESS	DRAGOONS	KINGSHIP	RUGGEDLY
TAPESTRY	UNHEATED	CONFLICT	SELFMADE	DRAGSTER	KINGSIZE	RYEGRASS
TAPEWORM	UNHEROIC	CONFOUND	SELFPITY	DRUGGIST	KINGSLEY	SANGLIER
TAVERNER	UNLEADED	CONFRONT	SELFSAME	DRYGOODS	KINGSTON	SANGUINE
TELECAST	UNNERVED	CONFUSED	SHIFTING	DUNGHILL	KNIGHTLY	SARGASSO
TELECOMS	UNPERSON	CRAFTILY	SINFONIA	ELEGANCE	LANGLAND	SEAGOING
TELEFILM	UNREASON	DAFFODIL	SNIFFLER	ELIGIBLE	LANGLAUF	SEIGNIOR
TELEGONY	UNSEALED	DEAFNESS	SNUFFBOX	EMIGRANT	LANGUAGE	SENGREEN
TELEGRAM	UNSEEDED	DIFFRACT	SPIFFING	EMIGRATE	LANGUISH	SERGEANT
TELEMARK	UNSEEMLY	DISFAVOR	STAFFING	EPIGAMIC	LARGESSE	SHAGBARK
TELETHON	UNSETTLE	DRIFTING	STAFFORD	EPIGRAPH	LAUGHING	SHAGREEN
TELEVISE	UNVERSED	DUMFOUND	STIFLING	EWIGKEIT	LAUGHTER	SHIGELLA
TEMERITY	UNWEANED	ECOFREAK	STUFFILY	EXEGESIS	LEGGINGS	SINGSONG
TENEBRAE	UPHEAVAL	FITFULLY	STUFFING	EXEGETIC	LENGTHEN	SINGULAR
TENEBRIO	UPPERCUT	FORFEITS	SUFFERER	EXIGENCY	LIEGEMAN	SLIGHTED
TENEMENT	URGENTLY	GOLFBALL	SUFFRAGE	EXIGUITY	LINGERIE	SLIGHTLY
TENESMUS	VALENCIA	GOLFCLUB	SULFURIC	EXIGUOUS	LINGUIST	SLUGABED
THIEVERY	VALERIAN	GONFALON	SURFBOAT	EYEGLASS	LODGINGS	SLUGFEST
THIEVING	VALETING	GOOFBALL	TAFFRAIL	FLAGGING	LONGBOAT	SLUGGARD
THIEVISH	VEGETATE	GRAFFITI	TRIFLING	FLAGPOLE	LONGHAND	SLUGGISH
THREATEN	VEHEMENT	GULFWEED	UNIFYING	FLAGRANT	LONGHAUL	SMUGGLED
THRENODY	VENERATE	HALFFULL	USEFULLY	FLAGSHIP	LONGHORN	SMUGGLER
THRESHER	VENEREAL	HALFHOUR	USUFRUCT	FLOGGING	LONGLAND	SMUGNESS
TIBERIAS	VENETIAN	HALFMAST	WARFARIN	FOXGLOVE	LONGSHIP	SONGBIRD
TIBERIUS	VILENESS	HALFTERM	WAYFARER	FRAGMENT	LONGSTAY	SONGSTER
TIDEMARK	VINEGARY	HALFTIME	WILFULLY	FRAGRANT	LONGSTOP	SPYGLASS
TIMELESS	VINEYARD	HALFYEAR	WOEFULLY	FRIGHTEN	LONGTERM	STAGGERS
TIRELESS	VIPERISH	HARFLEUR	WOLFBANE	FRIGIDLY	LONGTIME	STAGHORN
TIRESIAS	VIPEROUS	HAWFINCH	AMYGDALA	FRUGALLY	LUNGFISH	STAGNANT
TIRESOME	VIREMENT	HAYFEVER	ANAGLYPH	FUNGIBLE	LUNGWORT	STAGNATE
TOGETHER	VISELIKE	HAYFIELD	AVOGADRO	GADGETRY	MALGRADO	STIGMATA
TOLERANT	VITELLUS	HOPFIELD	BARGELLO	GANGLAND	MANGONEL	SUNGLASS
TOLERATE	VOWELIZE	ICEFIELD	BARGEMAN	GANGLING	MANGROVE	SURGICAL
TOMENTUM	WATERBUG	ILLFATED	BEGGARLY	GANGLION	MARGARET	TANGIBLE
TONELESS	WATERING	JEFFREYS	BELGRADE	GANGRENE	MARGINAL	TANGIBLY
TOREADOR	WATERLOO	JOYFULLY	BENGHAZI	GANGSTER	MARGRAVE	TINGLING
TOWELING	WATERMAN	KUFFIYEH	BERGAMOT	GARGANEY	MISGUIDE	TRIGLYPH
TOWERING	WATERSKI	LAWFULLY	BERGENIA	GARGOYLE	MONGOLIA	TRIGRAPH
TREELESS	WATERWAY	LEAFLESS	BERGERAC	GINGERLY	MONGOOSE	TUNGSTEN
TREELINE	WAVEBAND	MANFULLY	BLIGHTER	GINGIVAL	MUDGUARD	TUNGSTIC
TREETOPS	WAVERING	MIDFIELD	BRAGANZA	GOLGOTHA	NARGILEH	TUNGUSIC
TRUENESS	WAVERLEY	MOUFFLON	BRAGGART	GORGEOUS	NEIGHBOR	TURGENEV
TUBELESS	WEREWOLF	MUDFLATS	BRAGGING	GROGGILY	NIGGLING	TURGIDLY
TUBENOSE	WHEEZILY	NEWFOUND	BRIGHTEN	HAGGADAH	OLIGARCH	VANGUARD
TUBERCLE	WHEEZING	NUFFIELD	BRIGHTLY	HANGINGS	ORIGINAL	VENGEFUL
TUBEROSE	WIDENING	OILFIELD	BRIGHTON	HANGNAIL	OUTGOING	VIRGINAL
TUBEROUS	WIRELESS	OUTFIELD	BUGGERED	HANGOVER	PALGRAVE	VIRGINIA
TUTELAGE	WIREWORM	OUTFLANK	BULGARIA	HEDGEHOG	PANGLOSS	VULGARLY
TUTELARY	WISEACRE	PERFECTA	BUNGALOW		PANGOLIN	WAGGONER
TWEEZERS	YODELLER	PERFECTO			PEIGNOIR	WEDGWOOD

WEIGHING	FOXHOUND	PUSHBIKE	ALTITUDE	CHOIRBOY	ECHINATE	HAVILDAR
WINGLESS	FUCHSITE	PUSHCART	AMBIANCE	CHRISTEN	ECHINOPS	HAZINESS
WINGSPAN	GATHERED	PUSHDOWN	AMBIENCE	CHRISTIE	EERINESS	HELIPORT
ZIGGURAT	HATHAWAY	PUSHOVER	AMBITION	CHRISTOM	EFFICACY	HEMIPODE
ALCHEMIC	HENHOUSE	RACHITIS	AMRITSAR	CICISBEO	EGOISTIC	HERITAGE
ALEHOUSE	HIGHBALL	RASHNESS	ANTIBODY	CILIATED	ELLIPSIS	HESITANT
ALPHABET	HIGHBORN	RECHARGE	ANTIDOTE	CIVILIAN	ELLIPTIC	HESITATE
ALTHOUGH	HIGHBROW	REPHRASE	ANTIHERO	CIVILITY	ELSINORE	HIBISCUS
ANCHISES	HIGHGATE	RICHNESS	ANTILLES	CIVILIZE	EMBITTER	HOLIDAYS
ANCHORET	HIGHLAND	RIGHTFUL	ANTILOPE	CLAIMANT	ENCIRCLE	HOLINESS
ARCHAISM	HIGHNESS	RIGHTIST	ANTIMERE	CLOISTER	ENFILADE	HOLISTIC
ARCHDUKE	HIGHRISE	ROCHDALE	ANTIMONY	COGITATE	ENGINEER	HOMICIDE
ARCHIVES	HIGHROAD	RUSHMORE	ANTIPHON	COLIFORM	ENKINDLE	HOWITZER
ASPHODEL	HITHERTO	RUTHLESS	ANTIPOPE	COLISEUM	ENRICHED	HUMIDIFY
ASPHYXIA	HOTHOUSE	SAWHORSE	APTITUDE	CORIOLIS	ENSIFORM	HUMIDITY
ASTHENIA	HUSHHUSH	SIGHTING	AQUILINE	COSINESS	ENSILAGE	HUMILITY
BACHELOR	ICEHOUSE	SIGHTSEE	ARGININE	COZINESS	ENTICING	HYGIENIC
BAGHEERA	INCHOATE	SUBHUMAN	ARTICLED	CULINARY	ENTIRELY	IGNITION
BATHETIC	ISTHMIAN	SUCHLIKE	ARTICLES	CUPIDITY	ENTIRETY	ILLINOIS
BATHROBE	JEPHTHAH	SYPHILIS	ARTIFACT	CYLINDER	ENTITLED	IMMINENT
BATHROOM	JODHPURS	TAPHOUSE	ARTIFICE	CYNICISM	ENVIABLE	INCIDENT
BECHAMEL	KACHAHRI	TASHKENT	ARTISTIC	CYRILLIC	ENVIRONS	INCISION
BETHESDA	KYPHOSIS	TIGHTWAD	ARTISTRY	DAVIDSON	ENVISAGE	INCISIVE
BONHOMIE	LASHINGS	TOPHEAVY	ASCIDIAN	DEBILITY	ENVISION	INDIAMAN
BOTHERED	LETHARGY	UNCHASTE	ASCIDIUM	DECIMATE	EOHIPPUS	INDICANT
BOTHWELL	LIGHTING	UNSHAKEN	ASPIRANT	DECIPHER	EQUIPAGE	INDICATE
CACHALOT	LOTHARIO	UNTHREAD	ASPIRATE	DECISION	EQUITANT	INDIGENT
CACHEPOT	LUSHNESS	VALHALLA	ASPIRING	DECISIVE	ESTIMATE	INDIRECT
CACHEXIA	LUTHERAN	WARHORSE	ASSIGNEE	DEDICATE	ESTIVATE	INFINITE
CASHMERE	MACHEATH	WASHABLE	ATTITUDE	DEFIANCE	ETHIOPIA	INFINITY
CATHEDRA	MACHINES	WASHBOWL	AUDIENCE	DEFILADE	EXCISION	INSIGNIA
CATHETER	MACHISMO	WASHDOWN	AUDITION	DEFINITE	EXCITING	INTIFADA
CATHOLIC	MADHOUSE	WASHROOM	AUDITORY	DELICACY	FACILITY	INTIMACY
CATHOUSE	MATHURIN	WISHBONE	AURICULA	DELICATE	FAMILIAR	INTIMATE
CEPHALIN	MECHANIC	WITHDRAW	AUTISTIC	DELIRIUM	FAMISHED	INVITING
COCHLEAR	MENHADEN	WITHERED	AVAILING	DELIVERY	FATIGUED	IRRIGATE
CUTHBERT	METHANOL	WITHHOLD	BACILLUS	DEMIJOHN	FATIGUES	IRRITANT
DASHWOOD	METHODIC	YACHTING	BADINAGE	DEMISTER	FELICITY	IRRITATE
DETHRONE	MICHIGAN	YOGHOURT	BALINESE	DEMIURGE	FEMININE	IVOIRIEN
DIEHARDS	MIGHTILY	ZEPHYRUS	BANISTER	DEPILATE	FEMINISM	JOKINGLY
DIPHENYL	MISHMASH	ABDICATE	BARITONE	DERISION	FEMINIST	JOVIALLY
DISHEVEL	MOTHBALL	ABRIDGED	BASIDIUM	DERISIVE	FEMINITY	JUBILANT
DISHONOR	MOTHERLY	ABSINTHE	BASILICA	DERISORY	FILIGREE	JUBILATE
DOGHOUSE	MUCHNESS	ACCIDENT	BASILISK	DESIGNER	FILIPINO	JUDICIAL
DUCHESSE	MUSHROOM	ACHIEVED	BASINFUL	DESIROUS	FINISHED	JULIENNE
EIGHTEEN	MYTHICAL	ACHIEVER	BEGINNER	DEVIANCE	FINISHER	JYAISTHA
ELKHOUND	NEPHRITE	ACHILLES	BELIEVER	DEVILISH	FLEISHIG	KAMIKAZE
EMPHASIS	NEWHAVEN	ACRIMONY	BELITTLE	DEVILLED	FLUIDITY	KIBITZER
EMPHATIC	NICHOLAS	ACTINIDE	BERIBERI	DIGITIZE	FRUITFUL	KOLINSKY
ENSHRINE	NIGHTCAP	ACTINIUM	BESIEGED	DIGIZINE	FRUITING	LACINATE
ENSHROUD	NIGHTJAR	ACTIVATE	BEWILDER	DILIGENT	FRUITION	LAMINATE
ENTHALPY	NUTHATCH	ACTIVELY	BOLIVIAN	DIMINISH	FUGITIVE	LAPIDARY
ENTHRALL	NUTHOUSE	ACTIVISM	BONIFACE	DISINTER	FUMIGATE	LAPIDATE
ENTHRONE	OMPHALOS	ACTIVIST	BROILING	DIVIDEND	FUMITORY	LATINIST
ESTHETIC	OOPHORON	ACTIVITY	BRUISING	DIVIDERS	FUSIFORM	LATITUDE
EUPHONIA	ORCHITIS	ADDICTED	BUSINESS	DIVINITY	FUSILIER	LAVISHLY
EUPHONIC	ORPHANED	ADDITION	CADILLAC	DIVISION	FUTILITY	LAZINESS
EUPHORIA	ORTHODOX	ADDITIVE	CAGINESS	DIVISIVE	GALILEAN	LECITHIN
EUPHORIC	OUTHOUSE	ADMIRING	CALIGULA	DOCILITY	GANISTER	LENIENCY
EUPHUISM	PACHINKO	ADRIATIC	CALIPERS	DOMICILE	GARISHLY	LEVITATE
EXCHANGE	PASHMINA	ADVISORY	CAMISOLE	DOMINANT	GEMINATE	LEWISITE
FATHERLY	PATHETIC	AFFINITY	CANISTER	DOMINATE	GENIALLY	LIMITING
FIGHTING	PATHOGEN	AGRICOLA	CAPITALS	DOMINEER	GENITALS	LINIMENT
FISHBONE	PHTHISIC	AGRIMONY	CARILLON	DOMINION	GENITIVE	LITIGANT
FISHCAKE	PHTHISIS	AIRINESS	CATILINE	DOMINOES	GRAINING	LITIGATE
FISHHOOK	PITHLESS	ALBINONI	CELIBACY	DRAINAGE	GUAIACUM	LIVIDITY
FISHMEAL	POCHETTE	ALLIANCE	CELIBATE	DRAINING	HABITUAL	LOGISTIC
FISHPOND	POTHOLER	ALMIGHTY	CHAINSAW	DUTIABLE	HACIENDA	LONICERA
FISHWIFE	PROHIBIT	ALPINIST	CHAIRMAN	EASINESS	HAMILTON	LOVINGLY

LUCIDITY	OFFICERS	RACINESS	SICILIAN	UNSIGNED	BANKROLL	MARKSMAN
LUMINARY	OFFICIAL	RADIANCE	SILICATE	UNTIDILY	BANKRUPT	MEEKNESS
LUMINOUS	OILINESS	RADIATOR	SILICONE	UNTILLED	BASKETRY	MILKLESS
LYRICISM	OMNIFORM	RAPIDITY	SILICULA	UNTIMELY	BEAKLESS	MILKMAID
LYRICIST	OMNIVORE	RATIONAL	SINISTER	UNWIELDY	BERKELEY	MILKWEED
MAGICIAN	OPHIDIAN	REDIRECT	SOCIABLE	UPRIGHTS	BOOKABLE	MILKWORT
MAGISTER	OPTICIAN	REFINERY	SOCIALLY	UPRISING	BOOKCASE	MONKFISH
MALINGER	OPTIMATE	REGICIDE	SOLIDIFY	VALIDATE	BOOKMARK	NECKBAND
MANIACAL	OPTIMISM	REGIMENT	SOLIDITY	VALIDITY	BOOKROOM	NECKLACE
MANICURE	OPTIMIST	REGIONAL	SOLITARY	VANISHED	BOOKSHOP	NECKLINE
MANIFEST	OPTIONAL	REGISTER	SOLITUDE	VARIABLE	BOOKWORK	NECKWEAR
MANIFOLD	ORDINAND	REGISTRY	SPLINTER	VARIANCE	BOOKWORM	NICKNACK
MANITOBA	ORDINARY	REKINDLE	SPLITTER	VARICOSE	BUCKBEAN	NICKNAME
MARIACHI	ORDINATE	RELIABLE	SPOILAGE	VARIETAL	BUCKFAST	PACKAGED
MARIANAS	ORPIMENT	RELIABLY	SPOILING	VARIFORM	BUCKLING	PARKLAND
MARIGOLD	PACIFIER	RELIANCE	SPRINGER	VARIORUM	BUCKSHEE	PEEKABOO
MARINADE	PACIFISM	RELIEVED	SPRINKLE	VEXILLUM	BUCKSHOT	PENKNIFE
MARINATE	PACIFIST	RELIGION	SPRINTER	VICINITY	BUCKSKIN	PICKINGS
MARITIME	PAGINATE	REMINDER	SPRITELY	VIGILANT	BULKHEAD	PICKLOCK
MAXIMIZE	PAKISTAN	REMITTAL	SPRITZER	VIRILITY	COCKATOO	PICKMEUP
MCKINLEY	PALIMONY	RESIDENT	SQUIGGLE	VISIGOTH	COCKAYNE	PICKWICK
MEDIATOR	PALINODE	RESIDUAL	SQUIRREL	VISITANT	COCKBOAT	POCKMARK
MEDICATE	PALISADE	RESIDUUM	STAIRWAY	VISITING	COCKCROW	PUCKERED
MEDICINE	PAPILLON	RESIGNED	STEINWAY	VITILIGO	COCKEREL	RACKRENT
MEDIEVAL	PARIETAL	RESINOUS	STOICISM	VOLITION	COCKEYED	RANKNESS
MEDIOCRE	PARISIAN	RESISTOR	STRIATED	VOMITING	COCKTAIL	RECKLESS
MEDITATE	PATIENCE	RETICENT	STRIATUM	VOMITORY	COOKBOOK	RECKONER
MENISCUS	PAVILION	RETICULE	STRICKEN	WARINESS	COOKWARE	RICKSHAW
MERIDIAN	PEDICURE	RETIRING	STRICKLE	WILINESS	DANKNESS	ROCKETRY
MERINGUE	PEDIGREE	REVIEWER	STRICTLY	WINIFRED	DARKENED	RUCKSACK
MERISTEM	PEDIMENT	REVISION	STRIDENT	YAKITORI	DARKNESS	SHAKEOUT
MILITANT	PEKINESE	REVIVIFY	STRIKING	ZAMINDAR	DARKROOM	SICKLIST
MILITARY	PENITENT	REVIVING	STRINGED	ZODIACAL	DECKHAND	SICKNESS
MILITATE	PERIANTH	RIDICULE	STRINGER	BENJAMIN	DISKETTE	SICKROOM
MINIMIZE	PERICARP	RIGIDITY	STRIPPED	BETJEMAN	DOCKLAND	SILKTAIL
MINISTER	PERICLES	ROBINSON	STRIPPER	CARJACOU	DOCKSIDE	SILKWORM
MINISTRY	PERIDERM	ROSINESS	STRIVING	CONJUGAL	DOCKYARD	SINKHOLE
MITIGATE	PERILOUS	RUBICUND	SUKIYAKI	CONJURER	DUCKBILL	SOAKAWAY
MOBILITY	PERILUNE	RUBIDIUM	SURICATE	CONJUROR	DUCKLING	STAKEOUT
MOBILIZE	PERIODIC	RUDIMENT	SYRINGES	DISJUNCT	DUCKWEED	STOKESAY
MODIFIER	PERIPETY	RUMINANT	TACITURN	MAHJONGG	ERIKSSON	SUCKLING
MONICKER	PERISHED	RUMINATE	TAHITIAN	MARJORAM	FALKLAND	TEAKWOOD
MORIBUND	PERISHER	SADISTIC	TALISMAN	MISJUDGE	FECKLESS	TICKLING
MOTIVATE	PETITION	SALINGER	TEFILLIN	PERJURED	FOLKLORE	TICKLISH
MUCILAGE	PIMIENTO	SALINITY	TERIYAKI	PERJURER	FOLKSONG	TICKSEED
MUNIMENT	PISIFORM	SALIVARY	THAILAND	PREJUDGE	FORKLIFT	TICKTACK
MUSICIAN	PITIABLE	SALIVATE	THRILLER	SERJEANT	FORKTAIL	TICKTOCK
MUTILATE	PITILESS	SAMIZDAT	TIDINESS	SUBJECTS	GYMKHANA	TURKOMAN
MUTINEER	PLEIADES	SANITARY	TIMIDITY	VERJUICE	HECKLING	VALKYRIE
MUTINOUS	POLISHED	SANITIZE	TITICACA	BACKACHE	HOKKAIDO	WALKOVER
MYRIAPOD	POLISHER	SATIATED	TITIVATE	BACKBITE	HOOKWORM	WALKYRIE
NAMIBIAN	POLITELY	SATIRIST	TOXICITY	BACKBONE	HUCKSTER	WEAKFISH
NATIONAL	POLITICO	SATIRIZE	TRAILING	BACKCHAT	JACKAROO	WEAKLING
NATIVITY	POLITICS	SCHILLER	TRAINING	BACKCOMB	JACKBOOT	WEAKNESS
NAVIGATE	POPINJAY	SCHIZOID	TRAITORS	BACKDATE	JACKETED	WICKEDLY
NEPIONIC	POSITION	SCRIABIN	TUNICATE	BACKDROP	KICKBACK	WORKABLE
NIHILISM	POSITIVE	SCRIBBLE	TUNISIAN	BACKFIRE	KICKSHAW	WORKADAY
NIHILIST	POSITRON	SCRIBBLY	TUSITALA	BACKHAND	KILKENNY	WORKBOOK
NIJINSKY	PRAIRIAL	SCRIPTUM	UGLINESS	BACKLASH	KINKAJOU	WORKINGS
NOBILITY	PUGILISM	SEDIMENT	ULTIMATE	BACKLESS	KRAKATOA	WORKLOAD
NOMINATE	PUGILIST	SEDITION	UNBIASED	BACKPACK	LACKADAY	WORKMATE
NOTIONAL	PULITZER	SEMINARY	UNBIDDEN	BACKROOM	LACKLAND	WORKROOM
NUMINOUS	PUNISHED	SEMIOTIC	UNCIFORM	BACKSIDE	LARKSPUR	WORKSHOP
OBLIGATE	PUNITIVE	SEMITONE	UNFILLED	BACKSPIN	LEUKEMIA	ADELAIDE
OBLIGING	PURIFIED	SENILITY	UNHINGED	BACKSTOP	LOCKABLE	ADULATOR
OBLIVION	PURIFIER	SERIATIM	UNKINDLY	BACKWARD	LUCKLESS	ADULTERY
OBSIDIAN	PYRIFORM	SHEIKDOM	UNLIKELY	BACKYARD	MACKEREL	AFFLATUS
OCCIDENT	QUAINTLY	SHIITAKE	UNLISTED	BANKBOOK	MARKDOWN	AFFLUENT
OEDIPEAN	RACIALLY	SIBILANT	UNRIFLED	BANKNOTE	MARKEDLY	AIRLINER

ANALECTA	COLLARED	FOOLSCAP	MILLPOND	SCALLION	TRILLIUM	CRIMINAL
ANALEMMA	COLLATOR	FOULNESS	MILLRACE	SCILICET	TROLLOPE	CROMLECH
ANALOGUE	COLLECTS	FUGLEMAN	MIRLITON	SCOLDING	TWELVEMO	CROMWELL
ANALYSER	COLLEGES	FULLBACK	MOLLUSCS	SCULLERY	TWILIGHT	CRUMHORN
ANALYSIS	COLLIERS	FULLNESS	MOULDING	SCULLION	UNCLOVEN	CRUMMOCK
ANALYTIC	COLLIERY	FULLPAGE	MULLIGAN	SCULPTOR	UNPLACED	DALMATIC
ANGLESEY	COLLOQUY	FULLSIZE	MYELITIS	SEALSKIN	VALLETTA	DIAMANTE
ANGLICAN	COOLNESS	FULLTIME	NEGLIGEE	SEALYHAM	VAULTING	DIAMETER
APOLLYON	CULLINAN	FURLOUGH	NOBLEMAN	SECLUDED	VELLEITY	DIAMONDS
APOLOGIA	CULLODEN	GAILLARD	NUCLEATE	SHALLOWS	VERLAINE	DISMALLY
APOLOGUE	CURLICUE	GALLERIA	NUCLEOLE	SHELDUCK	VILLAGER	DISMAYED
APPLAUSE	CYCLADES	GALLIARD	OEILLADE	SHELVING	VILLAINY	DISMOUNT
APPLETON	CYCLAMEN	GALLIPOT	OMELETTE	SHILLING	VIOLATOR	DOGMATIC
APPLIQUÉ	CYCLICAL	GALLOPER	OPULENCE	SKELETAL	VIOLENCE	DOOMSDAY
ARALDITE	CYCLOSIS	GALLOWAY	OUTLYING	SKELETON	WALLSEND	DORMOUSE
ATALANTA	DAYLIGHT	GALLUMPH	PALLADIO	SKILLFUL	WALLWORT	DRAMATIC
ATHLETIC	DEALINGS	GAOLBIRD	PALLIATE	SKILLING	WELLBRED	DRUMBEAT
AVULSION	DECLUTCH	GARLICKY	PARLANCE	SKILLION	WELLNIGH	DRUMHEAD
BADLANDS	DEFLOWER	GIGLAMPS	PAULINUS	SKULKING	WELLPAID	DRUMLINE
BAILMENT	DIALLING	GIRLHOOD	PEELINGS	SKULLCAP	WESLEYAN	DRUMMING
BALLCOCK	DIALOGUE	GOALPOST	PELLAGRA	SKYLIGHT	WETLANDS	EGOMANIA
BALLGIRL	DIALYSIS	GOLLIWOG	PELLETED	SMALLEST	WILLIAMS	ELEMENTS
BALLISTA	DIELDRIN	GRILLING	PELLICLE	SMALLPOX	WOOLLENS	EXAMINEE
BALLOCKS	DIPLOMAT	GUILTILY	PELLMELL	SMELTING	WOOLPACK	EXAMINER
BALLPARK	DISLIKED	GULLIBLE	PELLUCID	SMOLLETT	WOOLSACK	EXEMPLAR
BALLROOM	DISLODGE	GULLIVER	PHALANGE	SOULLESS	WYCLIFFE	FARMHAND
BALLYHOO	DISLOYAL	HALLIARD	PHALGUNA	SPELLING	YIELDING	FARMLAND
BANLIEUE	DJELLABA	HALLMARK	PHILEMON	SPELLMAN	ABOMASUM	FARMYARD
BELLPUSH	DOOLALLY	HALLOWED	PHILIPPI	SPILLAGE	ALEMAINE	FIRMNESS
BELLYFUL	DUELLIST	HEELBALL	PHILLIPS	SPILLWAY	ALUMINUM	FIRMWARE
BIBLICAL	DULLNESS	HEELTAPS	PHILOMEL	SPOLIATE	ANIMATED	FLAMENCO
BILLFOLD	DWELLING	HELLADIC	PHYLLOME	STALKING	ARAMAEAN	FLAMEOUT
BILLHOOK	DYSLEXIA	HELLBENT	PILLAGER	STALLION	ARAMANTH	FLAMINGO
BILLYBOY	DYSLEXIC	HELLENIC	PILLARED	STALWART	AROMATIC	FLIMSILY
BILLYCAN	EARLIEST	HELLFIRE	POLLIWOG	STELLATE	ATOMIZER	FLUMMERY
BODLEIAN	EFFLUENT	HILLSIDE	POLLSTER	STILETTO	BALMORAL	FORMALIN
BOLLOCKS	EFFLUVIA	HOLLOWAY	POLLUTED	STILWELL	BEDMAKER	FORMALLY
BUILDING	EMBLAZON	HOOLIGAN	POLLUTER	STOLIDLY	BESMIRCH	FORMERLY
BULLDOZE	EMPLOYED	HORLICKS	POOLROOM	STULTIFY	BIOMETRY	FORMLESS
BULLETIN	EMPLOYEE	IDOLATER	POTLATCH	STYLIZED	BISMARCK	FORMOSAN
BULLFROG	EMPLOYER	IDOLATRY	POULAINE	SUBLEASE	BRAMANTE	FORMWORK
BULLHORN	EMULATOR	IMPLICIT	POULTICE	SULLENLY	BRIMMING	FREMITUS
BULLRING	EMULGENT	INCLINED	PROLAPSE	SULLIVAN	BROMELIA	FRUMENTY
BULLYRAG	EMULSIFY	INCLUDED	PROLIFIC	SUNLIGHT	BROMPTON	FRUMPISH
CABLECAR	EMULSION	INFLAMED	PROLOGUE	SWELLING	BRUMAIRE	GARMENTS
CABLEWAY	ENCLOSED	INFLATED	PSALMIST	SWILLING	BUMMAREE	GEOMANCY
CALLGIRL	ENCLOTHE	INFLIGHT	PSALMODY	SYLLABIC	CALMNESS	GEOMETER
CALLIOPE	EPILEPSY	INFLUENT	PSALTERY	SYLLABLE	CHAMBERS	GEOMETRY
CALLIPER	EPILOGUE	ISOLATED	PUBLICAN	SYLLABUB	CHAMPERS	GERMAINE
CALLISTO	EVALUATE	JAILBIRD	PUBLICLY	SYLLABUS	CHAMPION	GERMANIC
CAULDRON	EVILDOER	JEALOUSY	PULLDOWN	TABLEMAT	CHEMICAL	GERMINAL
CELLARER	EXPLICIT	JELLICOE	PULLOVER	TAILBACK	CHIMAERA	GLUMPISH
CELLULAR	EXPLODED	KEELHAUL	PURLIEUS	TAILGATE	CHUMMAGE	GORMLESS
CHALDEAN	EXPLORER	KILLDEER	PYELITIS	TAILLESS	CLAMBAKE	GRAMERCY
CHALDRON	EXULTANT	KOHLRABI	QUILTING	TAILPIPE	CLEMATIS	GRIMALDI
CHILDERS	EXULTING	LOLLIPOP	RACLETTE	TAILSKID	CLEMENCY	GRIMNESS
CHILDISH	EYELINER	LOWLANDS	RAILHEAD	TAILSPIN	CLIMATIC	GRUMBLER
CHILDREN	FALLIBLE	LOWLYING	RAILINGS	TELLTALE	CLIMBING	GRUMPILY
CHILIAST	FANLIGHT	MAILBOAT	RAILLERY	TELLURIC	CLUMSILY	GUMMOSIS
CHILLADA	FAULKNER	MAILSHOT	RAILROAD	THALAMUS	COMMANDO	GUNMETAL
CHILLING	FEELGOOD	MALLARMÉ	REALTIME	THALLIUM	COMMENCE	HAMMERED
CHILTERN	FEELINGS	MALLEATE	REDLIGHT	THOLEPIN	COMMERCE	HARMLESS
CHOLERIC	FELLAHIN	MALLORCA	REPLEVIN	TOILSOME	COMMONER	HARMONIC
COALESCE	FIELDING	MEALTIME	RIFLEMAN	TOLLGATE	COMMONLY	HAYMAKER
COALHOLE	FOGLIGHT	MEALYBUG	ROLLCALL	TOPLEVEL	COMMUNAL	HELMETED
COALMINE	FOLLICLE	MIDLANDS	ROULETTE	TOULOUSE	COMMUTER	HELMSMAN
COALPORT	FOLLOWED	MILLIBAR	SAILBOAT	TRILEMMA	CORMORAN	HERMETIC
COLLAGEN	FOLLOWER	MILLINER	SCALDING	TRILLING	COSMETIC	HERMIONE
COLLAPSE	FOLLOWUP	MILLIONS	SCALENUS	TRILLION	CRAMOISY	HOGMANAY

HORMONAL	TASMANIA	CARNAUBA	EVENTIDE	MAGNESIA	RAINDROP	THANATOS
INIMICAL	TEAMMATE	CARNEGIE	EVENTUAL	MAGNETIC	RAINFALL	THANKFUL
KATMANDU	TEAMSTER	CARNIVAL	FAINITES	MAGNOLIA	RAINWEAR	THINGAMY
KERMESSE	TEAMWORK	CHANCERY	FAINTING	MAINLAND	REINDEER	THINKING
KROMESKY	TERMINAL	CHANDLER	FIENDISH	MAINLINE	REINSURE	THINNESS
KRUMHORN	TERMINUS	CHANGING	FLANDERS	MAINMAST	REINVEST	THINNING
LAWMAKER	THEMATIC	CHANTAGE	FLANNELS	MAINSAIL	REMNANTS	THUNDERY
MACMAHON	THOMPSON	CHANTREY	FLINDERS	MAINSTAY	REYNOLDS	TINNITUS
MARMOSET	THUMPING	CHENILLE	FOUNDING	MAINTAIN	RHONCHUS	TOPNOTCH
MESMERIC	TITMOUSE	CHINAMAN	FOUNTAIN	MAINYARD	ROENTGEN	TOWNSHIP
MISMATCH	TRAMLINE	CHINDITS	FRANCIUM	MANNERED	ROUNDERS	TOWNSMAN
MNEMONIC	TREMBLER	CINNABAR	FRANKISH	MANNERLY	RUNNERUP	TRANQUIL
MONMOUTH	TREMBLES	CINNAMON	FRANKLIN	MANNIKIN	SAINFOIN	TRANSACT
MYRMIDON	TRIMARAN	CLANGING	FRENETIC	MEANNESS	SCANDIUM	TRANSECT
NEOMYCIN	TRIMMING	CLANGOUR	FRENULUM	MEANTIME	SCANNING	TRANSEPT
NORMALLY	TRIMNESS	CLANNISH	FRENZIED	MEUNIÈRE	SCANSION	TRANSFER
NORMANDY	TROMBONE	CLANSMAN	FRONDEUR	MIDNIGHT	SCANTIES	TRANSFIX
ODDMENTS	TRUMPERY	CLINCHER	FRONTAGE	MIGNONNE	SCANTILY	TRANSHIP
ODOMETER	TURMERIC	CLINGING	FRONTIER	MISNOMER	SCENARIO	TRANSKEI
OLYMPIAD	UDOMETER	CLINICAL	FRONTMAN	MOONBEAM	SCHNAPPS	TRANSMIT
OLYMPIAN	VERMOUTH	CLINKERS	GAUNTLET	MOUNTAIN	SHANGAAN	TRENCHER
OLYMPICS	WARMBOOT	COGNOMEN	GHANAIAN	MOUNTING	SHANGHAI	TRINCULO
OUTMATCH	WHIMBREL	COINCIDE	GIANTESS	NOONTIME	SHANTUNG	TRINIDAD
OUTMODED	WORMCAST	CORNETTO	GLANCING	OPENCAST	SHINBONE	TRUNCATE
OXYMORON	WORMWOOD	CORNHILL	GLANDERS	OPENDOOR	SHINGLES	TRUNNION
PALMATED	YARMULKA	CORNICHE	GRANDDAD	OPENNESS	SIGNALER	TURNBACK
PALMETTO	YEOMANRY	CORNMEAL	GRANDEUR	OPENPLAN	SIGNALLY	TURNCOAT
PALMITIN	ABINGDON	CORNWALL	GRANDKID	OPENWORK	SIGNORIA	TURNCOCK
PARMESAN	ABUNDANT	COUNTESS	GRANDSON	ORANGERY	SIGNPOST	TURNOVER
PEMMICAN	ACANTHUS	COUNTIES	GRANULAR	ORDNANCE	SKINDEEP	TURNPIKE
PERMEATE	ACENTRIC	COUNTING	GRANULES	OVENBIRD	SKINHEAD	TURNSPIT
PLIMSOLL	ADENITIS	CRANEFLY	GRENACHE	OVENWARE	SKINWORK	UNENDING
PLUMBAGO	ADENOIDS	CRINGING	GRINDING	PAINLESS	SLANGING	UNUNBIUM
PLUMBING	AGONIZED	CRONYISM	HANNIBAL	PAINTING	SLANTING	UTENSILS
PLYMOUTH	AMANDINE	CRUNCHIE	HAUNCHES	PANNICLE	SOUNDING	VIGNETTE
PREMIERE	AMENABLE	CYANOGEN	HAUNTING	PANNIKIN	SPANDREL	WAINSCOT
PREMISES	AMUNDSEN	CYANOSIS	HORNBEAM	PAWNSHOP	SPANGLED	WHENEVER
PREMOLAR	ASUNCION	DAINTIES	HORNBILL	PENNINES	SPANIARD	WHINCHAT
PRIMEVAL	AVENTINE	DAINTILY	HORNBOOK	PHANTASM	SPANKING	WINNINGS
PRIMNESS	BANNERET	DAMNABLE	HORNFELS	PHENOLIC	SPANNING	WINNIPEG
PRIMROSE	BARNABAS	DAUNTING	HORNPIPE	PHONETIC	SPENDING	WRANGLER
PROMISED	BARNACLE	DIANTHUS	HORNPOUT	PINNACLE	SPINIFEX	WRINGING
PROMOTER	BARNARDS	DIONYSUS	HORNTAIL	PINNIPED	SPINNING	WRINKLED
PROMPTER	BARNYARD	DOWNBEAT	HYPNOSIS	PLANCHET	SPINSTER	WRONGFUL
PROMPTLY	BEANPOLE	DOWNCAST	HYPNOTIC	PLANGENT	SPINTEXT	YOUNGEST
PTOMAINE	BIANNUAL	DOWNFALL	IDENTIFY	PLANKING	STANDARD	ZOONOSIS
REEMPLOY	BIENNIAL	DOWNHILL	IDENTITY	PLANKTON	STANDING	ABNORMAL
RENMINBI	BIGNONIA	DOWNLOAD	INUNDATE	PLANNING	STANDISH	ABROGATE
RHOMBOID	BINNACLE	DOWNPLAY	IRONCLAD	PLANTAIN	STANDOFF	ABSOLUTE
ROOMMATE	BLANDISH	DOWNPOUR	IRONICAL	PLUNGING	STANHOPE	ABSOLVED
SCHMALTZ	BLENDING	DOWNSIDE	IRONSIDE	POUNDAGE	STANNARY	ABSORBED
SCHMOOZE	BLENHEIM	DOWNSIZE	IRONWARE	PRANDIAL	STANNITE	ABSORBER
SCIMITAR	BLINDING	DOWNTOWN	IRONWOOD	PRENATAL	STENDHAL	ACCOLADE
SEAMLESS	BLINKERS	DOWNTURN	IRONWORK	PRINCELY	STENOSED	ACCOUNTS
SEAMSTER	BLINKING	DOWNWARD	JAUNDICE	PRINCESS	STENOSIS	ACROMION
SHAMBLES	BOUNCING	DRINKING	JAUNTILY	PRINTING	STINGING	ACROSTIC
SHAMEFUL	BOUNDARY	DRUNKARD	JEANETTE	PRINTOUT	STINGRAY	ADMONISH
SHAMROCK	BRANCHED	DZONGKHA	JOHNSONS	PRONATOR	STINKING	ADROITLY
SLIMNESS	BRANDADE	EARNINGS	JOINTURE	PRUNELLA	STINKPOT	ADVOCACY
SLUMMING	BRANDISH	ECONOMIC	KEENNESS	PUGNOSED	STONEFLY	ADVOCATE
STAMENED	BRANDNEW	EDENTATE	KLONDIKE	QUANDARY	STUNNING	AEROBICS
STAMPEDE	BRINDISI	ELONGATE	LEINSTER	QUANTIFY	SVENGALI	AERODYNE
STIMULUS	BRINDLED	EMINENCE	LEONARDO	QUANTITY	SWANSKIN	AEROFLOT
SUBMERGE	BRINGING	EMINENCY	LEONIDAS	QUENELLE	SWANSONG	AEROFOIL
SUMMITRY	BRONCHUS	ETHNARCH	LIENTERY	QUINCUNX	SWINDLER	AEROGRAM
SURMOUNT	BRUNETTE	EVANESCE	LIGNEOUS	QUINTAIN	SWINEPOX	AEROLITH
SWIMMING	BURNTOUT	EVENNESS	LINNAEAN	RAGNARÖK	SWINGING	AERONAUT
SWIMSUIT	CANNABIS	EVENSONG	LINNAEUS	RAINBIRD	TEENAGER	AEROSTAT
SYMMETRY	CANNIBAL	EVENTFUL	LOANWORD	RAINCOAT	TENNYSON	AGNOSTIC

□□□■□□□□

AGRONOMY	CANOODLE	EMBOLDEN	IMMOBILE	MONOGYNY	REPOUSSÉ	UNIONIST
ALGOLOGY	CAROLINA	EMBOLISM	IMMODEST	MONOHULL	RESOLUTE	UNIONIZE
ALGORISM	CAROLINE	EMBOSSED	IMMOLATE	MONOLITH	RESOLVED	UNLOADED
ALLOCATE	CAROTENE	EMPORIUM	IMMORTAL	MONOPOLE	RESONANT	UNLOCKED
ALLOGAMY	CAROUSAL	ENCOMIUM	IMPOLITE	MONOPOLY	RESONATE	UNLOVELY
ALLOPATH	CAROUSEL	ENDOCARP	IMPORTER	MONORAIL	RESOURCE	UNSOCIAL
ALLOWING	CENOBITE	ENDODERM	IMPOSING	MONOTONY	REVOLVER	UNSOLVED
AMMONIAC	CENOTAPH	ENDOGAMY	IMPOSTER	MONOTYPE	RHEOSTAT	UNTOWARD
AMMONITE	CENOZOIC	ERGOTISE	IMPOSTOR	MONOXIDE	RICOCHET	UNVOICED
AMMONOID	CHLORATE	ERGOTISM	IMPOTENT	MOROCCAN	RIGOROUS	UNWONTED
ANDORRAN	CHLORIDE	ESCORIAL	INCOMING	MOROSELY	ROBOTICS	UNWORTHY
ANNOTATE	CHLORINE	ESPOUSAL	INDOLENT	MOTORCAR	RUMOURED	UPCOMING
ANNOUNCE	CHOOSING	ESSONITE	INFORMAL	MOTORING	SABOTAGE	UPHOLDER
ANNOYING	CHROMITE	ESTONIAN	INFORMED	MOTORIST	SABOTEUR	VAPORIZE
APHORISM	CHROMIUM	ESTOPPEL	INFORMER	MOTORIZE	SAPONITE	VAPOROUS
APPOSITE	CIBORIUM	ESTOVERS	INNOCENT	MOTORMAN	SAVOURED	VELOCITY
ARBOREAL	COLOMBIA	ETHOLOGY	INNOVATE	MOTORWAY	SAVOYARD	VENOMOUS
ARGONAUT	COLONIAL	ETIOLATE	INSOLENT	MYCOLOGY	SAYONARA	VERONESE
ARMORIAL	COLONIST	EUDOXIAN	INSOMNIA	NAPOLEON	SCHOONER	VERONICA
ARMORICA	COLONIZE	EULOGIST	INVOLUTE	NEPOTISM	SCROFULA	VIGOROUS
ARMOURED	COLOPHON	EULOGIUM	INVOLVED	NICOTINE	SCROUNGE	VIROLOGY
ARROGANT	COLORADO	EULOGIZE	JACOBEAN	NOMOGRAM	SECONDER	WHOOPING
ARROGATE	COLORANT	EUROLAND	JACOBITE	NOSOLOGY	SECONDLY	XENOGAMY
ARSONIST	COLORFUL	EUROPEAN	JALOUSIE	OBSOLETE	SEMOLINA	XENOLITH
ASCOCARP	COLORING	EUROPIUM	JAPONICA	OCTONARY	SENORITA	XENOPHON
ASCORBIC	COLOSSAL	EUROSTAR	JEHOVAHS	ODIOUSLY	SEROLOGY	YOKOHAMA
ASMODEUS	COLOSSUS	EXPONENT	JEROBOAM	OENOLOGY	SEROTYPE	YUGOSLAV
ASSORTED	COLOURED	EXPORTER	KEROSENE	OENOPHIL	SEXOLOGY	ZAKOUSKI
ASTONISH	CORONARY	EXPOSURE	KILOBYTE	ONCOLOGY	SHOOTING	ACAPULCO
ATROCITY	CORONOID	FAMOUSLY	KILOGRAM	ONCOMING	SHOOTOUT	ADOPTION
ATTORNEY	COTOPAXI	FAROUCHE	KILOVOLT	ONLOOKER	SHROUDED	ADOPTIVE
AUTOBAHN	CREOSOTE	FAVORITE	KILOWATT	ONTOLOGY	SILOXANE	AIRPLANE
AUTOCRAT	CROONING	FAVOURED	LABOURED	OPPONENT	SIMONIAC	ALOPECIA
AUTOGAMY	CRYOLITE	FEROCITY	LABOURER	OPPOSING	SMOOTHER	ANAPAEST
AUTOGIRO	CULOTTES	FLOODING	LACONIAN	OPPOSITE	SMOOTHLY	ANAPHASE
AUTOGYRO	CYNOSURE	FLOODLIT	LANOLINE	PANORAMA	SNOOTILY	ANYPLACE
AUTOMATE	CYTOLOGY	FLOORING	LAROUSSE	PARODIST	SONOGRAM	APOPHYGE
AUTONOMY	CYTOSINE	FLUORIDE	LEMONADE	PAROLLES	SONOROUS	APOPLEXY
AUTOTYPE	DAMOCLES	FLUORINE	LICORICE	PAROUSIA	SORORITY	ATYPICAL
BARONESS	DEBONAIR	FLUORITE	LILONGWE	PAROXYSM	SPOONFUL	AUSPICES
BARONETS	DECORATE	GABONESE	LIMONITE	PECORINO	SPROCKET	BAGPIPES
BARONIAL	DECOROUS	GABORONE	LINOLEUM	PENOLOGY	STROLLER	BELPAESE
BECOMING	DECOUPLE	GADOGADO	LINOTYPE	PEROXIDE	STRONGLY	BESPOKEN
BEGORRAH	DEFORMED	GALOSHES	LOBOTOMY	PILOTAGE	SYNOPSIS	CAMPAIGN
BEHOLDEN	DEMOCRAT	GASOLIER	LOCOWEED	PINOCHLE	SYNOPTIC	CAMPBELL
BEHOLDER	DEMOLISH	GASOLINE	LOGOTYPE	PIROZHKI	TAXONOMY	CAMPSITE
BESOTTED	DEMONIAC	GEMOLOGY	MAHOGANY	PLEONASM	THEOCRAT	CAMPTOWN
BESOUGHT	DEMOTION	GENOCIDE	MAJOLICA	PLIOCENE	THEOLOGY	CHAPATTI
BICONVEX	DENOUNCE	GERONIMO	MAJORITY	POLONIUM	THEORIST	CHAPERON
BIFOCALS	DEPORTEE	GIRONDIN	MALODOUR	POROSITY	THEORIZE	CHAPLAIN
BILOBATE	DEROGATE	GLOOMILY	MANORIAL	POSOLOGY	THIOUREA	CHIPMUNK
BINOMIAL	DESOLATE	GROOMING	MARONITE	PRIORESS	THROMBIN	CHOPPING
BLOOMERS	DETONATE	GYROSTAT	MAROQUIN	PRIORITY	THROMBUS	CLAPPERS
BLOOMING	DETOXIFY	HEDONISM	MAYORESS	RECORDER	THROTTLE	CLAPPING
BOBOLINK	DEVONIAN	HEDONIST	MEMORIAL	RECOURSE	TIMOROUS	CLAPTRAP
BOEOTIAN	DEVOTION	HOLOCENE	MEMORIAM	RECOVERY	TOBOGGAN	CLIPPERS
BORODINO	DINOSAUR	HOLOGRAM	MEMORIZE	REDOLENT	TOMORROW	CLIPPING
BROODING	DISORDER	HOLOZOIC	MESODERM	REDOUBLE	TOPOLOGY	CODPIECE
BRYOZOAN	DIVORCED	HONOLULU	MESOLITE	REFORMED	TOXOCARA	COMPARED
CABOCHON	DIVORCEE	HONORARY	MESOZOIC	REFORMER	TROOPING	COMPILER
CABOODLE	DOLOMITE	HOROLOGY	METONYMY	REJOINED	TUTORIAL	COMPLAIN
CABOTAGE	DOLOROUS	HUMORIST	MINORESS	RELOCATE	TYROLEAN	COMPLETE
CAJOLERY	DOXOLOGY	HUMOROUS	MINORITE	REMOTELY	TYROSINE	COMPLINE
CALOTYPE	DROOPING	HYPOGEAL	MINORITY	REMOUNTS	UNCOMBED	COMPOSED
CAMOMILE	DUBONNET	IDEOGRAM	MINOTAUR	RENOUNCE	UNCOMMON	COMPOSER
CANOEING	ECLOSION	IDEOLOGY	MISOGYNY	RENOVATE	UNCOOKED	COMPOUND
CANOEIST	ECTODERM	IDIOGRAM	MONOACID	RENOWNED	UNCOUPLE	COMPRESS
CANONESS	ELDORADO	IGNOMINY	MONOGAMY	REPORTED	UNFORCED	COMPRISE
CANONIZE	EMBODIED	IGNORANT	MONOGRAM	REPORTER	UNIONISM	COMPUTER

CORPORAL	KIPPERED	SIXPENCE	WHOPPING	BARRETTE	DIURETIC	GUARDIAN
COUPERIN	KNAPSACK	SKIPJACK	WRAPPING	BAYREUTH	DOORBELL	GUERIDON
COUPLING	KNAPWEED	SKIPPING	ZEPPELIN	BEARABLE	DOORKNOB	GUERILLA
CREPITUS	KREPLACH	SKYPILOT	ZOOPHYTE	BEARINGS	DOORPOST	GUERNSEY
CRIPPLED	LAMPPOST	SLAPBANG	ADEQUACY	BEARSKIN	DOORSILL	HAIRBAND
CULPABLE	LEAPFROG	SLAPDASH	ADEQUATE	BEERBOHM	DOORSTEP	HAIRLESS
CUSPIDOR	LIMPNESS	SLAPJACK	ALIQUANT	BEFRIEND	DWARFISH	HAIRLIKE
CUTPRICE	LOOPHOLE	SLIPOVER	CHEQUERS	BEGRUDGE	DWARFISM	HAIRLINE
CUTPURSE	LUMPFISH	SLIPPERS	CLIQUISH	BETRAYAL	ELDRITCH	HAIRWORM
DAMPNESS	MANPOWER	SLIPPERY	CONQUEST	BETRAYER	EMBRACED	HARRIDAN
DEEPNESS	MIDPOINT	SLIPPING	DAIQUIRI	BLURRING	EMBRACES	HARRISON
DESPATCH	MISPLACE	SLIPSHOD	DISQUIET	BOARDING	EMERGENT	HEARTIES
DESPOTIC	MISPRINT	SLIPSLOP	ELOQUENT	BORROWED	EMERGING	HEARTILY
DIAPASON	MORPHEME	SLOPPILY	FREQUENT	BORROWER	EMERITUS	HEBRAISM
DIAPHONE	MORPHEUS	SNAPPILY	INEQUITY	BURROWER	EMERSION	HEBRIDES
DIOPTRIC	MORPHINE	SNAPSHOT	INIQUITY	CABRIOLE	EMIRATES	HEIRLESS
DISPATCH	NAUPLIUS	SOAPBARK	IROQUOIS	CAERLEON	ENCROACH	HEIRLOOM
DISPENSE	NEOPHYTE	SOAPSUDS	JACQUARD	CAPRIOLE	ENERGIZE	HIDROSIS
DISPERSE	OFFPRINT	STAPELIA	MARQUESA	CARRAWAY	ENERVATE	HIERARCH
DISPIRIT	OLIPHANT	STAPHYLE	MARQUESS	CARRIAGE	ENGRAVER	HIERATIC
DISPLACE	OPOPANAX	STEPHENS	MARQUISE	CARRIOLE	ENORMITY	HOARDING
DISPOSAL	PALPABLE	STOPCOCK	MISQUOTE	CARRYALL	ENORMOUS	HOARSELY
DISPOSED	PALPABLY	STOPOVER	MOSQUITO	CARRYCOT	ENTRAILS	HORRIBLE
DISPROVE	PAMPERED	STOPPAGE	MUSQUASH	CARRYING	ENTRANCE	HORRIBLY
DISPUTED	PAMPHLET	STOPPING	UBIQUITY	CHARCOAL	ENTREATY	HORRIFIC
DRIPPING	PANPIPES	STUPIDLY	UNIQUELY	CHARGING	ENTRENCH	HYDROGEN
DROPHEAD	PEEPHOLE	SUBPOENA	VANQUISH	CHARISMA	ENTREPOT	HYDROXYL
DROPPING	PEEPSHOW	SULPHATE	ABERDEEN	CHARLADY	ENTRYISM	IMPRISON
DROPSHOT	PINPOINT	SULPHIDE	ABERRANT	CHARLOCK	ESPRESSO	IMPROPER
DUMPLING	PINPRICK	SUPPLANT	ABORTION	CHARMING	ESTRAGON	IMPROVED
EARPHONE	POPPADOM	SUPPLIER	ABORTIVE	CHARTISM	ESTROGEN	IMPROVER
EARPIECE	PORPHYRA	SUPPLIES	ACCREDIT	CHARTIST	ETERNITY	INCREASE
EGGPLANT	PORPHYRY	SUPPOSED	ACERBATE	CHARTRES	EUTROPHY	INFRARED
EGYPTIAN	PORPOISE	SUPPRESS	ACERBITY	CHEROKEE	EUTROPIC	INFRINGE
ELEPHANT	PREPARED	SURPLICE	ADORABLE	CHERUBIC	EVERMORE	INGROWTH
EPIPHANY	PROPERLY	SURPRISE	AEGROTAT	CHERUBIM	EVERYDAY	INTRADOS
EPIPHYTE	PROPERTY	SUSPENSE	AGGRIEVE	CHERWELL	EVERYMAN	INTRENCH
EPIPLOON	PROPHASE	SYMPATHY	AIGRETTE	CHORDATA	EVERYONE	INTREPID
ERUPTION	PROPHECY	SYMPHONY	ALARMING	CHORDATE	EXERCISE	INTRIGUE
ERUPTURE	PROPHESY	SYMPTOMS	ALARMIST	CHORIAMB	EXERTION	INTRUDER
EYEPIECE	PROPOLIS	TAXPAYER	ALFRESCO	CHURLISH	EXORCISM	JERRYCAN
FLAPJACK	PROPOSAL	TEMPERED	ALTRUISM	CLARENCE	EXORCIST	JORROCKS
FLAPPING	PROPOSED	TEMPLATE	ALTRUIST	CLARINET	EXORCIZE	KHARTOUM
FLIPPANT	PROPOSER	TEMPORAL	AMARANTH	CLERICAL	EXORDIUM	KORRIGAN
FLIPPERS	PROPOUND	TEMPTING	AMARETTO	CLERIHEW	EXPRESSO	KOURMISS
FLIPPING	PURPLISH	TRAPDOOR	AMBROSIA	COARSELY	EXTRADOS	LABRADOR
FRIPPERY	RAMPARTS	TRAPPIST	AMERICAN	COERCION	FAIRNESS	LACROSSE
GAZPACHO	RASPUTIN	TRIPLING	AMERICAS	COERCIVE	FARRIERY	LADRONES
GEOPHONE	REAPPEAR	TRIPTANE	AMORETTI	CORRAGIO	FEARLESS	LAUREATE
GRAPHEME	RESPECTS	TRIPTYCH	AMORETTO	CORRIDOR	FEARSOME	LAURENCE
GRAPHICS	RESPIGHI	TROPICAL	AMORTIZE	CORRODED	FEBRUARY	LAWRENCE
GRAPHITE	RESPONSE	TUPPENNY	ANARCHIC	COURTESY	FERRYMAN	LEARNING
GRIPPING	RHAPSODY	TWOPENNY	ANDREWES	CURRENCY	FIBROSIS	LIBRETTO
GUMPTION	RIPPLING	TWOPIECE	ANOREXIA	CURRICLE	FIERCELY	LORRAINE
GUNPOINT	SAMPHIRE	TYMPANUM	ANOREXIC	CZAREVNA	FLIRTING	MACREADY
HELPLESS	SAPPHIRE	UNIPOLAR	APERIENT	DAIRYMAN	FLORENCE	MADRIGAL
HELPLINE	SAPPHIST	UNSPOILT	APERITIF	DECREASE	FOURFOLD	MARRIAGE
HELPMATE	SCAPHOID	UNSPOKEN	APERTURE	DECREPIT	FOURPART	MATRONLY
HERPETIC	SCAPULAR	VESPERAL	APPRAISE	DECRETAL	FOURSOME	METRICAL
HISPANIC	SEAPLANE	VESPUCCI	APPRISED	DEERSKIN	FOURTEEN	METRITIS
HOSPITAL	SHEPHERD	VOLPLANE	APPROACH	DEFREEZE	FURROWED	MICRODOT
HOTPLATE	SHIPMATE	WARPAINT	APPROVAL	DEGRADED	GARRIGUE	MIGRAINE
HUMPBACK	SHIPMENT	WARPLANE	APPROVED	DEPRAVED	GARRISON	MIRRORED
HUMPHREY	SHIPPING	WEAPONRY	ATARAXIA	DEPRIVED	GARROTTE	MONROVIA
INSPIRED	SHIPWORM	WHIPCORD	ATARAXIC	DETRITUS	GEORGIAN	MOORCOCK
INSPIRIT	SHIPYARD	WHIPHAND	AVERSION	DIARESIS	GLORIANA	MOORINGS
JEOPARDY	SHOPPING	WHIPJACK	BAHRAINI	DIARRHEA	GLORIOLE	MOORLAND
JUMPSUIT	SHOPTALK	WHIPLASH	BARRACKS	DIERESIS	GLORIOUS	MORRISON
KEEPSAKE	SIMPLIFY	WHIPPING	BARRATRY	DISRAELI	GOURMAND	MOURNFUL

MOURNING	OXBRIDGE	SPARSITY	WHARFAGE	CLASSICS	GLOSSARY	NEWSCAST
MURRHINE	PEARLING	SPARTANS	WHEREVER	CLASSIFY	GLOSSEME	NEWSHAWK
NARRATOR	PEARMAIN	SPIRACLE	WHIRLING	CONSERVE	GNASHING	NEWSPEAK
NARROWLY	PEERLESS	SPIRALLY	WORRYING	CONSIDER	GOBSMACK	NEWSREEL
NEARNESS	PETRARCH	SPIRELET	YEARBOOK	CONSOMMÉ	GOOSEGOG	NEWSROOM
NEBRASKA	PHARISEE	SPIRITED	YEARLING	CONSPIRE	GOSSAMER	NOISETTE
NECROSIS	PHARMACY	SPIRITUS	YEARLONG	CONSTANT	GRASPING	NONSENSE
NEGRILLO	PHORMIUM	SPORADIC	YEARNING	CONSTRUE	GRISELDA	NONSTICK
NEURITIS	PIERCING	SPORTING	YOURSELF	CONSULAR	GRISETTE	NORSEMAN
NEUROSIS	PIERETTE	SPORTIVE	ABESSIVE	CONSUMED	GROSBEAK	NORSEMEN
NEUROTIC	PIERIDES	SPURIOUS	ADESSIVE	CONSUMER	GROSCHEN	NUISANCE
NITROGEN	POORNESS	SPURNING	AIRSCREW	CORSELET	GUNSMITH	NURSLING
NUTRIENT	PORRIDGE	STARCHED	AIRSPEED	CORSICAN	GUSSETED	NUTSHELL
OPERABLE	PROROGUE	STARDUST	AIRSTRIP	COTSWOLD	HABSBURG	ODYSSEUS
OPERATIC	PRURIENT	STARFISH	ALLSPICE	COUSCOUS	HAPSBURG	OFFSHOOT
OPERATOR	PTEROPOD	STARGAZE	AMUSETTE	COXSWAIN	HAYSTACK	OFFSHORE
OPERETTA	PYORRHEA	STARKERS	ANGSTROM	COYSTRIL	HELSINKI	OFFSIDER
OUTREACH	QUARTERS	STARLESS	ANISETTE	CRESCENT	HERSCHEL	OFFSTAGE
OUTREMER	QUARTIER	STARLING	APOSTASY	CRISPIAN	HIPSTERS	OILSKINS
OUTRIDER	QUARTILE	STAROSTA	APOSTATE	CROSSBAR	HOGSHEAD	OILSLICK
OUTRIGHT	QUIRINAL	STARTERS	APOSTLES	CROSSING	HORSEBOX	OLDSTYLE
OVARITIS	REARMOST	STARTING	AYRSHIRE	CROSSLET	HORSEFLY	OMISSION
OVERALLS	REARWARD	STARVING	BASSINET	CRUSADER	HORSEMAN	ONESIDED
OVERBOOK	RECREATE	STERLING	BASSWOOD	CRUSHING	HORSEMEN	OPUSCULE
OVERCAST	RECRUITS	STIRLING	BEDSTEAD	CRYSTALS	HOUSEMAN	ORESTEIA
OVERCOAT	REFRINGE	STIRRING	BEDSTRAW	CURSITOR	INASMUCH	OTOSCOPE
OVERCOME	REORIENT	STOREMAN	BEESWING	DIASPORA	INKSTAIN	OUISTITI
OVERDONE	REPRIEVE	STOREYED	BESSEMER	DIASTASE	IRISCOPE	OUTSHINE
OVERDOSE	REPRISAL	STORMING	BIOSCOPE	DIASTOLE	IRISHISM	OUTSIDER
OVERDRAW	REPROACH	STORMONT	BLASTOFF	DIPSTICK	IRISHMAN	OUTSMART
OVERFEED	RETRENCH	STURDILY	BLASTULA	DISSOLVE	IRISHMEN	OUTSTRIP
OVERFILL	RETRIEVE	STURGEON	BLESSING	DISSUADE	ISOSTASY	PARSIFAL
OVERFLOW	SACRISTY	SURROUND	BLISSFUL	DOGSBODY	JOYSTICK	PASSABLE
OVERFULL	SAUROPOD	SWARMING	BLUSHING	DOGSTAIL	KEYSTONE	PASSABLY
OVERHAND	SCARCELY	SWERVING	BLUSTERY	DRESSAGE	KINSFOLK	PASSBOOK
OVERHANG	SCARCITY	SWIRLING	BOASTFUL	DRESSING	KINSHASA	PASSERBY
OVERHAUL	SCARFACE	TARRAGON	BOASTING	DRYSTONE	KOMSOMOL	PASSIBLE
OVERHEAD	SCIROCCO	TEARABLE	BONSPIEL	EGGSHELL	KOUSKOUS	PASSOVER
OVERHEAR	SCORCHED	TEARAWAY	BORSTALL	EINSTEIN	LANSBURY	PASSPORT
OVERHEAT	SCORCHER	TEARDROP	BOTSWANA	EMISSARY	LEISURED	PASSWORD
OVERKILL	SCORNFUL	TERRACED	BOWSPRIT	EMISSION	LIPSTICK	PERSHING
OVERLAID	SCORPION	TERRAPIN	BRASILIA	EPISODIC	LONSDALE	PERSONAL
OVERLAND	SCORPIUS	TERRIBLE	BRASSARD	EPISTYLE	LOOSEBOX	PERSPIRE
OVERLEAF	SEARCHER	TERRIBLY	BRASSICA	EXISTENT	LOPSIDED	PERSUADE
OVERLOAD	SECRETLY	TERRIFIC	BRISLING	EXISTING	MAESTOSO	PERSUANT
OVERLOOK	SERRATED	TETRAGON	BRISTLED	EYESHADE	MARSHALL	PHOSGENE
OVERLORD	SHAREOUT	TETRAPOD	BRISTLES	EYESIGHT	MASSACRE	PHYSALIA
OVERMUCH	SHERATON	TETRARCH	BRUSSELS	FALSETTO	MASSENET	PHYSICAL
OVERPASS	SHERIDAN	THIRTEEN	BURSITIS	FATSTOCK	MASSEUSE	PHYSIQUE
OVERPLAY	SHERLOCK	THORACIC	BURSTING	FEASIBLE	MASSICOT	PIGSWILL
OVERRATE	SHERWOOD	THOROUGH	CAMSHAFT	FEASIBLY	MEASURED	PILSENER
OVERRIDE	SHORTAGE	THURIBLE	CAMSTONE	FISSIPED	MEMSAHIB	PISSHEAD
OVERRIPE	SKIRMISH	THURIFER	CAPSICUM	FLASHGUN	MENSURAL	PLASTRON
OVERRULE	SKIRTING	THURSDAY	CAPSIZED	FLASHILY	MENSWEAR	POISONER
OVERSEAS	SLURRING	TSAREVNA	CAPSTONE	FLASHING	MESSAGER	PONSONBY
OVERSEER	SMARTEST	TURRETED	CASSETTE	FLUSHING	MESSIDOR	POPSICLE
OVERSHOE	SNORTING	TWIRLING	CATSMEAT	FLYSHEET	MESSMATE	POSSIBLE
OVERSHOT	SOBRIETY	UMBRELLA	CAUSEWAY	FORSAKEN	MESSUAGE	POSSIBLY
OVERSIZE	SOCRATES	UNBROKEN	CESSPOOL	FORSLACK	MINSTREL	POTSHERD
OVERSOLD	SOCRATIC	UNERRING	CHASSEUR	FORSOOTH	MISSOURI	POTSTONE
OVERSTAY	SOURCING	UNFREEZE	CHASTISE	FORSWEAR	MISSPELL	PRESENCE
OVERSTEP	SOURNESS	USURIOUS	CHASTITY	FRESHEST	MISSPENT	PRESERVE
OVERTAKE	SOURPUSS	UXORIOUS	CHASUBLE	FRESHMAN	MOISTURE	PRESSING
OVERTIME	SOURWOOD	VAGRANCY	CHESHIRE	FRISKILY	MONSTERA	PRESSMAN
OVERTONE	SPARAXIS	VIBRANCY	CHESSMAN	FROSTILY	MOUSSAKA	PRESSURE
OVERTURE	SPARKING	VIBRATOR	CHESSMEN	FROSTING	MUDSTONE	PRESTIGE
OVERTURN	SPARKLER	VITREOUS	CHESTNUT	GLASNOST	MYOSOTIS	PRISONER
OVERVIEW	SPARRING	WARRANTY	CLASHING	GLASSFUL	NAUSEATE	PRISTINE
OVERWORK	SPARSELY	WEARABLE	CLASPING	GLISSADE	NAUSEOUS	PROSPECT

PROSPERO	WHISKERY	CASTANET	DOCTORAL	GRATEFUL	MELTDOWN	PLETHORA
PROSTATE	WHISTLER	CASTAWAY	DOCTORED	GRATINEE	MENTALLY	PLOTINUS
PRUSSIAN	WOLSELEY	CASTOFFS	DOCTRINE	GRATUITY	MIRTHFUL	PLUTARCH
PUISSANT	WRESTLER	CASTRATE	DOGTOOTH	GUTTURAL	MISTAKEN	POETICAL
PURSLANE	WRISTLET	CASTRATO	DOTTEREL	HARTFORD	MISTREAT	POITIERS
PUSSYCAT	YERSINIA	CATTLEYA	EASTERLY	HASTINGS	MISTRESS	POLTROON
QUESTION	ZOOSPERM	CAUTIOUS	EASTLAKE	HATTERAS	MISTRUST	PONTIFEX
QUISLING	ZOOSPORE	CENTAURY	EASTWARD	HAWTHORN	MONTCALM	PORTABLE
RAGSTONE	ABATTOIR	CENTERED	ECSTASIS	HEATEDLY	MONTEITH	PORTHOLE
RAISONNÉ	ABSTRACT	CENTRIST	ECSTATIC	HEATSPOT	MORTALLY	PORTIÈRE
RASSELAS	ABSTRUSE	CENTRODE	EGGTIMER	HEATWAVE	MORTGAGE	PORTLAND
REASONED	ABUTILON	CHATTELS	EMOTICON	HEPTAGON	MORTIMER	PORTRAIT
REASSERT	ABUTMENT	CHITCHAT	EPITASIS	HEPTARCH	MORTUARY	PORTUGAL
REASSESS	AESTHETE	CHUTZPAH	EPITHEMA	HEYTHROP	MOUTHFUL	POSTCARD
REASSIGN	AGITATED	CISTERNA	ERYTHEMA	HISTORIC	MULTIPLE	POSTCODE
REASSUME	AGITATOR	CLITORIS	ESOTERIC	HOSTELRY	MULTIPLY	POSTDATE
REASSURE	AGITPROP	CLOTHIER	EUSTATIC	HUNTRESS	MUSTACHE	POSTMARK
REDSHANK	AIRTIGHT	CLOTHING	EYETOOTH	HUNTSMAN	MYSTICAL	POSTPAID
REDSHIFT	AMATEURS	COATRACK	FACTIOUS	HUSTINGS	MYSTIQUE	POSTPONE
REDSTART	AMETHYST	COATTAIL	FACTOTUM	HYSTERIA	NATTERED	PRATFALL
REUSABLE	ANATHEMA	CONTANGO	FAITHFUL	HYSTERIC	NAUTICAL	PRATTLER
RIBSTONE	ANATOLIA	CONTEMPT	FANTASIA	IMITATOR	NAUTILUS	PRETENCE
RIESLING	ANATOMIC	CONTENTS	FARTHEST	INITIATE	NEATHERD	PRETENSE
RISSOLES	ANYTHING	CONTINUE	FARTHING	INSTANCE	NEATNESS	PRETORIA
ROASTING	APOTHEGM	CONTINUO	FASTBACK	INSTINCT	NESTLING	PRETTILY
ROSSETTI	ARCTURUS	CONTRACT	FASTENER	INSTRUCT	NEUTRINO	PROTEASE
ROUSSEAU	ARETHUSA	CONTRARY	FASTNESS	ISOTHERE	NOCTURNE	PROTÉGÉE
SANSERIF	AUSTRIAN	CONTRAST	FEATHERS	ISOTHERM	NORTHERN	PROTOCOL
SANSKRIT	BAATHIST	CONTRITE	FEATHERY	JETTISON	NORTHING	PROTOZOA
SASSANID	BACTERIA	CONTRIVE	FEATURED	JOTTINGS	NOSTRILS	PROTRUDE
SAUSAGES	BACTRIAN	CONTROLS	FEATURES	JUSTNESS	NOSTROMO	PUSTULAR
SCISSION	BANTLING	COSTMARY	FESTIVAL	KARTTIKA	NUPTIALS	QUATORZE
SCISSORS	BAPTISED	COTTAGER	FETTLING	KATTEGAT	OBITUARY	QUATRAIN
SEASCAPE	BARTERED	CRATCHIT	FIFTIETH	KENTUCKY	OBSTACLE	QUOTABLE
SEASHELL	BASTILLE	CRETONNE	FILTHILY	KESTEVEN	OBSTRUCT	QUOTIENT
SEASHORE	BATTERED	CRITICAL	FILTRATE	KNITTING	OINTMENT	RATTIGAN
SEASONAL	BEATIFIC	CRITIQUE	FLATBOAT	KNITWEAR	ONETRACK	RATTLING
SEASONED	BEETLING	CROTCHET	FLATFISH	KNOTWEED	ORATORIO	RESTLESS
SENSIBLE	BEETROOT	CRUTCHED	FLATFOOT	KNOTWORK	OXYTOCIN	RESTORER
SENSIBLY	BERTRAND	CULTURAL	FLATMATE	LATTERLY	PANTALON	RESTRAIN
SENSUOUS	BESTIARY	CULTURED	FLATPICK	LEATHERY	PANTHEON	RESTRICT
SMASHING	BESTOWER	CURTAINS	FLATTERY	LECTRICE	PARTERRE	RESTROOM
SOLSTICE	BESTRIDE	CURTNESS	FLATWARE	LECTURER	PARTHIAN	RHETORIC
SUBSHRUB	BIATHLON	CUSTOMER	FLATWORM	LECTURES	PARTICLE	RHYTHMIC
SUBSONIC	BIRTHDAY	CYSTITIS	FLOTILLA	LEFTHAND	PARTISAN	ROOTLESS
SUNSHADE	BITTERLY	DARTMOOR	FOOTBALL	LEFTOVER	PARTTIME	RUCTIONS
SUNSHINE	BLITHELY	DEATHBED	FOOTFALL	LEFTWARD	PASTICHE	RUSTLESS
SWASTIKA	BLOTCHED	DEFTNESS	FOOTHOLD	LEFTWING	PASTILLE	RUSTLING
TEASPOON	BOATBILL	DENTICLE	FOOTLING	LETTERED	PASTORAL	SALTBUSH
TEESHIRT	BOATLOAD	DENTURES	FOOTNOTE	LISTENER	PASTRAMI	SALTLICK
THESPIAN	BOLTHOLE	DESTINED	FOOTPATH	LISTERIA	PASTURES	SALTNESS
TINSELLY	BOOTLESS	DESTRUCT	FOOTREST	LISTLESS	PECTORAL	SANTIAGO
TINSMITH	BOOTNECK	DEUTERON	FOOTSORE	LITTORAL	PENTACLE	SCATHING
TIPSTAFF	BOTTLING	DEXTROSE	FOOTSTEP	LOATHING	PENTAGON	SCOTLAND
TOISEACH	BOTTOMRY	DEXTROUS	FOOTWEAR	LOITERER	PENTARCH	SCOTSMAN
TONSURED	BOUTIQUE	DIATONIC	FOOTWORK	LUSTRINE	PERTNESS	SCOTTISH
TRASHCAN	BRATPACK	DIATRIBE	FORTIETH	LUSTROUS	PHOTOFIT	SEETHING
TRESPASS	BRETHREN	DICTATES	FORTRESS	MALTREAT	PHOTOPSY	SENTENCE
TRISTICH	BRUTALLY	DICTATOR	FORTUITY	MANTILLA	PICTURES	SENTIENT
TRISTRAM	BUSTLING	DIPTERAL	FRETWORK	MANTISSA	PILTDOWN	SENTINEL
TRUSTFUL	BUTTERED	DISTANCE	FURTHEST	MANTLING	PINTABLE	SHETLAND
TRUSTING	BUTTOCKS	DISTASTE	GASTRULA	MARTELLO	PITTANCE	SHUTDOWN
TWISTING	BUTTRESS	DISTINCT	GENTRIFY	MARTINET	PLATANUS	SHUTTERS
UNUSABLE	CALTHROP	DISTRACT	GEOTAXIS	MARTYRED	PLATEFUL	SISTERLY
VAISAKHA	CANTICLE	DISTRAIN	GERTRUDE	MASTERLY	PLATELET	SITTELLA
VERSICLE	CANTORIS	DISTRAIT	GESTURES	MASTHEAD	PLATFORM	SIXTIETH
VOLSCIAN	CAPTIOUS	DISTRESS	GLUTAEUS	MASTODON	PLATINUM	SKITTISH
WELSHMAN	CARTHAGE	DISTRICT	GLUTTONY	MATTRESS	PLATONIC	SKITTLES
WHISKERS	CARTLOAD	DISTRUST	GOATSKIN	MEATLESS	PLATYPUS	SLATTERN

SLOTHFUL	TROTTOIR	ADJUTANT	DRAUGHTY	NEBULOUS	TEQUILLA	PROVIDER
SLUTTISH	TRUTHFUL	ADJUVANT	EFFUSION	NENUPHAR	THOUGHTS	PROVINCE
SNATCHER	TWITCHER	AFFUSION	EFFUSIVE	OBDURACY	THOUSAND	PURVEYOR
SOFTBACK	TZATZIKI	AIGUILLE	ENCUMBER	OBDURATE	THRUSTER	SALVADOR
SOFTBALL	UNCTUOUS	ALBURNUM	ENDURING	OBTUSELY	TRIUNITY	SCAVENGE
SOFTENER	UNITEDLY	ALEUTIAN	EQUULEUS	OCCUPANT	TROUBLED	SELVEDGE
SOFTNESS	UNSTABLE	ALLURING	ESCULENT	OCCUPIED	TROUBLES	SERVICES
SOFTWARE	UNSTATED	ALLUSION	ETRURIAN	OCCUPIER	TROUNCER	SERVIENT
SOFTWOOD	UNSTEADY	ALLUSIVE	ETRUSCAN	OMDURMAN	TROUSERS	SERVITOR
SOOTHING	UPSTAIRS	ALLUVIAL	EXHUMATE	OSCULATE	UNBURDEN	SHAVUOTH
SOOTHSAY	UPSTREAM	ALLUVIUM	FABULOUS	PABULOUS	UNBUTTON	SHIVERED
SOUTHEND	URETHANE	AMBULANT	FECULENT	PALUDISM	UNCURBED	SLOVAKIA
SOUTHERN	VASTNESS	AMBULATE	FIDUCIAL	PATULOUS	UNDULANT	SLOVENIA
SOUTHPAW	VENTURED	AMBUSHED	FIGURINE	PECULATE	UNDULATE	SLOVENLY
SPITEFUL	VERTEBRA	AMPUTATE	FLAUBERT	PECULIAR	UNGULATE	SOLVABLE
SPITFIRE	VERTICAL	ANEURYSM	FLAUTIST	PEDUNCLE	UNJUSTLY	SOLVENCY
SPITHEAD	VESTIARY	ANGUILLA	FLOUNCED	PENUMBRA	UNSUITED	SOUVENIR
SPITTING	VESTMENT	ANNUALLY	FLOUNDER	PERUVIAN	UPTURNED	SPAVINED
SPITTOON	VIATICUM	ARGUABLE	FLOURISH	PETULANT	URSULINE	SURVEYOR
SPOTLESS	VICTORIA	ARGUABLY	FRAULEIN	PIQUANCY	VALUABLE	SURVIVAL
SPOTTING	VICTUALS	ARGUMENT	FREUDIAN	PLAUDITS	VESUVIUS	SURVIVOR
STATUARY	VIETCONG	ARQUEBUS	FURUNCLE	PLEURISY	VIBURNUM	SYLVANER
SUBTENSE	VIRTUOSI	ASSUMING	FUTURISM	PLOUGHED	VIRULENT	SYLVATIC
SUBTITLE	VIRTUOSO	ASTUTELY	FUTURIST	POPULACE	VISUALLY	TRAVELER
SUBTLETY	VIRTUOUS	AUBUSSON	GAZUNDER	POPULATE	AASVOGEL	TRAVERSE
SUBTOPIA	VOLTAIRE	AUGUSTUS	GHOULISH	POPULIST	BREVIARY	TRAVESTY
SUBTOTAL	VORTICAL	AUTUMNAL	GLAUCOMA	POPULOUS	CALVADOS	UNEVENLY
SUBTRACT	WAITRESS	BABUSHKA	GLAUCOUS	PSEUDERY	CERVELAT	UNIVALVE
SUITABLE	WALTZING	BAGUETTE	GROUNDED	PURULENT	CERVICAL	UNIVERSE
SUITABLY	WASTEFUL	BALUSTER	GROUPING	REBUTTAL	CHEVIOTS	VALVULAR
SUITCASE	WESTERLY	BEAUFORT	GROUTING	RECUSANT	CHIVALRY	AIRWAVES
SYNTEXIS	WESTWARD	BEAUMONT	HANUKKAH	REFUGIUM	CLAVECIN	ANYWHERE
SYSTEMIC	WHATEVER	BEAUTIFY	HARUSPEX	REGULATE	CLAVICLE	BLOWFISH
TACTICAL	WHITECAP	BEFUDDLE	ILLUMINE	REPUBLIC	CLEVERLY	BLOWHOLE
TACTLESS	WHITEHOT	BEQUEATH	ILLUSION	REQUIRED	CLIVEDEN	BLOWLAMP
TANTALUM	WHITENER	BIBULOUS	ILLUSIVE	RITUALLY	CONVENER	BLOWPIPE
TANTALUS	WHITLING	BICUSPID	ILLUSORY	ROBUSTLY	CONVERGE	BOSWORTH
TARTARIC	WISTERIA	BOTULISM	IMMUNITY	SALUTARY	CONVERSE	BROWBEAT
TARTARUS	WORTHIES	BROUGHAM	IMMUNIZE	SALUTORY	CONVEYOR	BROWNING
TARTNESS	WORTHILY	BROUHAHA	IMPUDENT	SATURATE	CONVINCE	BROWNISH
TARTRATE	WRATHFUL	BUSULFAN	IMPUNITY	SATURDAY	CONVULSE	BROWSING
TARTUFFE	WRETCHED	CADUCEUS	IMPURIFY	SATURNIA	CORVETTE	CLAWBACK
TASTEFUL	WRITEOFF	CAPUCHIN	IMPURITY	SCHUBERT	CRAVATES	CLOWNISH
TATTERED	WRITHING	CARUCATE	INCUBATE	SCHUMANN	CREVASSE	COBWEBBY
TAUTNESS	WRITINGS	CASUALLY	INDUCIVE	SCOURING	CULVERIN	COGWHEEL
TECTONIC	XANTHOMA	CASUALTY	INDUCTOR	SCRUBBER	DRIVEWAY	CRAWFISH
TEETHING	XANTIPPE	CATULLUS	INDUSTRY	SCRUPLES	ELEVATED	CRAWLING
TEETOTAL	YOUTHFUL	CERULEAN	INFUSION	SCRUTINY	ELEVATOR	CROWFOOT
TENTACLE	ZASTRUGA	CLAUDIUS	INGUINAL	SECURELY	ELEVENTH	CROWNING
TERTIARY	ZOETROPE	COAUTHOR	INHUMANE	SECURITY	FLAVORED	CUTWATER
TESTATOR	ABDUCENS	COLUMBAN	INNUENDO	SEDULOUS	GALVANIC	DOGWATCH
TESTATUM	ABDUCTED	COLUMBUS	INQUIRER	SEQUENCE	GIOVANNI	DRAWBACK
TESTICLE	ABDUCTOR	COPULATE	INSULATE	SEXUALLY	GRAVAMEN	DROWNING
TEUTONIC	ABLUTION	COQUETRY	JEBUSITE	SHOULDER	GRAVELLY	DROWSILY
TEXTBOOK	ABRUPTLY	COQUETTE	LABURNUM	SHOUTING	GRAVITAS	ENIWETOK
TEXTURED	ABSURDLY	CORUNDUM	MACULATE	SHRUNKEN	HEAVENLY	FLAWLESS
THATAWAY	ACCURACY	CROUPIER	MANUALLY	SILURIAN	HELVETIA	FLYWHEEL
THATCHED	ACCURATE	CUCUMBER	MAQUETTE	SIMULATE	LEAVENED	FORWARDS
THATCHER	ACCURSED	CUCURBIT	MATURATE	SITUATED	LEAVINGS	GASWORKS
TINTAGEL	ACCUSING	DELUSION	MATURITY	SMOULDER	LOUVERED	GROWLING
TORTILLA	ACCUSTOM	DEMURELY	MINUTELY	SOLUTION	MALVASIA	HIAWATHA
TORTOISE	ACOUSTIC	DEMURRAL	MINUTIAE	SPLUTTER	MALVOLIO	LULWORTH
TORTUOUS	ACQUAINT	DEPUTIZE	MODULATE	SPRUCELY	PERVERSE	MADWOMAN
TORTURED	ACQUIRED	DILUTION	MOLUCCAS	STRUGGLE	PERVIOUS	OLDWORLD
TORTURER	ACQUIRER	DISUNION	MONUMENT	STRUMPET	PREVIOUS	OUTWARDS
TRITICAL	ACTUALLY	DISUNITE	MOQUETTE	SUBURBAN	PRIVATES	OUTWEIGH
TRITICUM	ADJUSTER	DISUNITY	MUTUALLY	SUBURBIA	PROVABLE	PINWHEEL
TROTLINE	ADJUSTOR	DOCUMENT	NATURISM	TABULATE	PROVERBS	REAWAKEN
TROTTERS	ADJUTAGE	DRAUGHTS	NATURIST	TEGUMENT	PROVIDED	SCOWLING

SEAWARDS	PLAYTIME	ARGUABLY	CLEMATIS	ENTRAILS	INTRADOS	NEWHAVEN
SHOWBOAT	POLYANNA	AROMATIC	CLIMATIC	ENTRANCE	ISOBARIC	NORMALLY
SHOWCASE	POLYARCH	ATALANTA	COCKATOO	ENVIABLE	ISOLATED	NORMANDY
SHOWDOWN	POLYCARP	ATARAXIA	COCKAYNE	EPIGAMIC	JACKAROO	NUISANCE
SHOWGIRL	POLYGAMY	ATARAXIC	COLLAGEN	EPITASIS	JEOPARDY	NUTHATCH
SHOWROOM	POLYGLOT	AVIFAUNA	COLLAPSE	ERIDANUS	JONCANOE	OBSTACLE
SKEWBALD	POLYGYNY	AVOGADRO	COLLARED	ESTRAGON	JOVIALLY	OLIGARCH
SLOWDOWN	POLYMATH	BACCARAT	COLLATOR	ETHNARCH	KACHAHRI	OMPHALOS
SLOWNESS	POLYSEME	BACKACHE	COMMANDO	EUSTATIC	KANGAROO	OPERABLE
SLOWPOKE	POLYSEMY	BADLANDS	COMPARED	EXCHANGE	KATMANDU	OPERATIC
SLOWWORM	PONYTAIL	BAHRAINI	CONTANGO	EXTRADOS	KINKAJOU	OPERATOR
SNOWBALL	QUAYSIDE	BALEARIC	CORRAGIO	FACEACHE	KRAKATOA	OPOPANAX
SNOWDROP	ROLYPOLY	BANDANNA	COTTAGER	FANDANGO	LABRADOR	ORDNANCE
SNOWFALL	SISYPHUS	BARBADOS	CRAVATES	FANTASIA	LACKADAY	ORPHANED
SNOWLINE	SPRYNESS	BARBARIC	CREVASSE	FELLAHIN	LAUDABLE	OUTDATED
SPAWNING	STAYSAIL	BARNABAS	CRUSADER	FIREARMS	LAUDABLY	OUTMATCH
STOWAWAY	TERYLENE	BARNACLE	CULPABLE	FORMALIN	LAUDANUM	OUTWARDS
TAMWORTH	BLIZZARD	BARNARDS	CURTAINS	FORMALLY	LAWMAKER	OVERALLS
UNAWARES	BOUZOUKI	BARRACKS	CUTWATER	FORSAKEN	LEONARDO	PACKAGED
WAXWORKS	BUZZWORD	BARRATRY	CYCLADES	FORWARDS	LETHARGY	PALLADIO
FLAXSEED	CRUZEIRO	BEARABLE	CYCLAMEN	FRUGALLY	LIKEABLE	PALMATED
FLEXIBLE	DAZZLING	BECHAMEL	DAEDALUS	GALBANUM	LINNAEAN	PALPABLE
FLEXIBLY	DIAZEPAM	BEDMAKER	DALMATIC	GALVANIC	LINNAEUS	PALPABLY
FRAXINUS	FRAZZLED	BEGGARLY	DAMNABLE	GARGANEY	LOCKABLE	PANDANUS
GLOXINIA	GADZOOKS	BELPAESE	DECEASED	GAZPACHO	LOMBARDY	PANDARUS
INEXPERT	GRIZZLED	BENJAMIN	DEFEATED	GENDARME	LORRAINE	PANTALON
PROXIMAL	MARZIPAN	BEREAVED	DEFIANCE	GENIALLY	LOTHARIO	PARLANCE
QUIXOTIC	PENZANCE	BERGAMOT	DEGRADED	GEOMANCY	LOWLANDS	PASSABLE
VAUXHALL	PIZZERIA	BETRAYAL	DEMEANOR	GEOTAXIS	MACMAHON	PASSABLY
ABEYANCE	PUZZLING	BETRAYER	DEPRAVED	GERMAINE	MALLARMÉ	PEEKABOO
ASSYRIAN	SIZZLING	BINNACLE	DESPATCH	GERMANIC	MALVASIA	PELLAGRA
BABYHOOD	TANZANIA	BISCAYAN	DEVIANCE	GHANAIAN	MANDAMUS	PENTACLE
BODYLINE	ZARZUELA	BISMARCK	DIAMANTE	GIGLAMPS	MANDARIN	PENTAGON
BODYWORK	**8:5**	BOOKABLE	DIAPASON	GIOVANNI	MANDATED	PENTARCH
BUOYANCY	ABEYANCE	BRABAZON	DICTATES	GIVEAWAY	MANIACAL	PENZANCE
BUSYBODY	ABOMASUM	BRAGANZA	DICTATOR	GLOBALLY	MANUALLY	PERIANTH
CAPYBARA	ACQUAINT	BRAMANTE	DIEHARDS	GLUTAEUS	MARGARET	PETRARCH
CARYATID	ACTUALLY	BRIBABLE	DISEASED	GONFALON	MARIACHI	PHALANGE
CHEYENNE	ADELAIDE	BRUMAIRE	DISFAVOR	GOSSAMER	MARIANAS	PHREATIC
CLAYMORE	ADORABLE	BRUTALLY	DISMALLY	GRAVAMEN	MASCARON	PHYSALIA
COPYBOOK	ADRIATIC	BULGARIA	DISMAYED	GRENACHE	MASSACRE	PILLAGER
COPYHOLD	ADULATOR	BUMMAREE	DISPATCH	GRIMALDI	MECHANIC	PILLARED
CRAYFISH	AFFLATUS	BUNGALOW	DISRAELI	GUAIACUM	MEDIATOR	PINDARIC
DEWYEYED	AGITATED	BUOYANCY	DISTANCE	GUIDANCE	MELEAGER	PINNACLE
DICYCLIC	AGITATOR	CACHALOT	DISTASTE	HAGGADAH	MEMSAHIB	PINTABLE
DUTYFREE	AIRWAVES	CALVADOS	DOGMATIC	HATHAWAY	MENHADEN	PIQUANCY
EMPYREAL	ALEMAINE	CAMPAIGN	DOGWATCH	HAVDALAH	MENTALLY	PISCATOR
EMPYREAN	ALICANTE	CANNABIS	DOOLALLY	HAYMAKER	MERCALLI	PITCAIRN
ENDYMION	ALLIANCE	CARCAJOU	DRACAENA	HEADACHE	MERCATOR	PITIABLE
ETHYLENE	ALPHABET	CARCANET	DRAMATIC	HEBRAISM	MESCALIN	PITTANCE
EUCYCLIC	AMARANTH	CARDAMOM	DUTIABLE	HELLADIC	MESSAGER	PLACABLE
EURYDICE	AMBIANCE	CARJACOU	ECSTASIS	HEPTAGON	METHANOL	PLATANUS
GANYMEDE	AMENABLE	CARNAUBA	ECSTATIC	HEPTARCH	MIDLANDS	PLEIADES
GRAYLING	AMICABLE	CARRAWAY	EDUCATED	HIAWATHA	MIGRAINE	PLUTARCH
HOLYHEAD	AMICABLY	CARYATID	EDUCATOR	HIDEAWAY	MINDANAO	POLYANNA
HOLYROOD	ANABASIS	CASTANET	EGOMANIA	HIERARCH	MISCARRY	POLYARCH
LADYBIRD	ANABATIC	CASTAWAY	ELEGANCE	HIERATIC	MISMATCH	POPPADOM
LADYFISH	ANAPAEST	CASUALLY	ELEVATED	HISPANIC	MISTAKEN	PORTABLE
LADYLIKE	ANIMATED	CASUALTY	ELEVATOR	HOGMANAY	MOCCASIN	POTLATCH
LADYSHIP	ANNEALER	CELLARER	EMBLAZON	HOKKAIDO	MONOACID	POULAINE
MARYLAND	ANNUALLY	CENTAURY	EMBRACED	IDOLATER	MORTALLY	PREDATOR
PHRYGIAN	AOTEAROA	CEPHALIN	EMBRACES	IDOLATRY	MOVEABLE	PRENATAL
PLAYBACK	APPLAUSE	CHAPATTI	EMIRATES	ILLFATED	MUSCADET	PREPARED
PLAYBILL	APPRAISE	CHIMAERA	EMPHASIS	IMITATOR	MUSCATEL	PRIVATES
PLAYFAIR	ARAMAEAN	CHINAMAN	EMPHATIC	INDIAMAN	MUSTACHE	PROBABLE
PLAYGIRL	ARAMANTH	CHIVALRY	EMULATOR	INFLAMED	MUTUALLY	PROBABLY
PLAYMATE	ARCHAISM	CILIATED	ENDEAVOR	INFLATED	MYRIAPOD	PROCAINE
PLAYROOM	ARGUABLE	CINNABAR	ENGRAVER	INFRARED	NARRATOR	PROLAPSE
PLAYSUIT		CINNAMON	ENTHALPY	INSTANCE	NEBRASKA	PRONATOR

PROVABLE	STRIATUM	VERBALLY	COOKBOOK	KILOBYTE	STRABISM	BREECHES
PTOMAINE	SUITABLE	VERBATIM	COPYBOOK	LADYBIRD	STUBBORN	BROCCOLI
QUOTABLE	SUITABLY	VERLAINE	CRIBBAGE	LAIDBACK	SURFBOAT	BRONCHUS
RACIALLY	SUNBATHE	VIBRANCY	CUTHBERT	LANSBURY	TAILBACK	CABOCHON
RADIANCE	SUNDANCE	VIBRATOR	DATABASE	LAYABOUT	TENEBRAE	CADUCEUS
RADIATOR	SYLLABIC	VILLAGER	DEADBEAT	LIFEBELT	TENEBRIO	CAPACITY
RAGNARÖK	SYLLABLE	VILLAINY	DINGBATS	LIFEBOAT	TEXTBOOK	CAPUCHIN
RAMPARTS	SYLLABUB	VINDALOO	DISABLED	LIFEBUOY	TREMBLER	CARACOLE
RASCALLY	SYLLABUS	VIOLATOR	DISABUSE	LONGBOAT	TREMBLES	CARUCATE
RATEABLE	SYLVANER	VISUALLY	DOGSBODY	LOVEBIRD	TROMBONE	CATACOMB
READABLE	SYLVATIC	VOIDANCE	DOORBELL	LYREBIRD	TROUBLED	CATECHOL
REAWAKEN	SYMPATHY	VOLCANIC	DOWNBEAT	MAILBOAT	TROUBLES	CETACEAN
RECHARGE	TAKEAWAY	VOLTAIRE	DRAWBACK	MARABOUT	TURNBACK	CHANCERY
REHEARSE	TANTALUM	VULGARLY	DRUBBING	MATABELE	UNUNBIUM	CHARCOAL
RELEASED	TANTALUS	WARFARIN	DRUMBEAT	MEGABYTE	VAGABOND	CHITCHAT
RELIABLE	TANZANIA	WARPAINT	DUCKBILL	METABOLA	WARMBOOT	CLINCHER
RELIABLY	TARRAGON	WARRANTY	DUMBBELL	MOONBEAM	WASHBOWL	COCACOLA
RELIANCE	TARTARIC	WASHABLE	DURABLES	MORIBUND	WAVEBAND	COCKCROW
REMNANTS	TARTARUS	WAYFARER	EATABLES	MOTHBALL	WELLBRED	COERCION
REPEATED	TASMANIA	WEARABLE	FASTBACK	NAMIBIAN	WHIMBREL	COERCIVE
REPEATER	TAXPAYER	WETLANDS	FEEDBACK	NECKBAND	WINDBURN	COINCIDE
RESEARCH	TEARABLE	WISEACRE	FIREBACK	NOSEBAND	WISHBONE	COUSCOUS
REUSABLE	TEARAWAY	WORKABLE	FIREBALL	NOTEBOOK	WOLFBANE	CRATCHIT
REVEALED	TEENAGER	WORKADAY	FIREBIRD	OVENBIRD	WOODBINE	CRESCENT
RIDDANCE	TENTACLE	YEOMANRY	FIREBOLT	OVERBOOK	WORDBOOK	CROTCHET
RITUALLY	TERRACED	ZIMBABWE	FISHBONE	PARABOLA	WORKBOOK	CRUNCHIE
SALEABLE	TERRAPIN	ZODIACAL	FLATBOAT	PASSBOOK	YEARBOOK	CRUTCHED
SALVADOR	TESTATOR	ACERBATE	FLAUBERT	PLAYBACK	ZWIEBACK	CYNICISM
SANDARAC	TESTATUM	ACERBITY	FLEABITE	PLAYBILL	ABDICATE	DAMOCLES
SARGASSO	TETRAGON	AEROBICS	FOOTBALL	PLUMBAGO	ABDUCENS	DEDICATE
SASSANID	TETRAPOD	ANTIBODY	FOREBEAR	PLUMBING	ABDUCTED	DEFECATE
SATIATED	TETRARCH	AUTOBAHN	FOREBODE	PUFFBALL	ABDUCTOR	DEFECTOR
SAUSAGES	THALAMUS	BACKBITE	FULLBACK	PUSHBIKE	ABJECTLY	DEJECTED
SCENARIO	THANATOS	BACKBONE	GADABOUT	QUIBBLER	ADDICTED	DELICACY
SCHMALTZ	THATAWAY	BANKBOOK	GAMEBIRD	RAINBIRD	ADJACENT	DELICATE
SCHNAPPS	THEBAINE	BARABBAS	GAOLBIRD	REPUBLIC	ADVOCACY	DEMOCRAT
SCREAMER	THEMATIC	BAREBACK	GIGABYTE	RHOMBOID	ADVOCATE	DETACHED
SCRIABIN	THORACIC	BASEBALL	GOLFBALL	RULEBOOK	AFFECTED	DETECTOR
SCYBALUM	THREATEN	BASEBORN	GOOFBALL	RUNABOUT	AGRICOLA	DICYCLIC
SEAFARER	TINTAGEL	BEDABBLE	GROSBEAK	RUTABAGA	AIRSCREW	DIDACTIC
SEAWARDS	TOREADOR	BEERBOHM	GRUMBLER	SAILBOAT	ALBACORE	DIRECTLY
SERIATIM	TRIMARAN	BELABOUR	HABSBURG	SALTBUSH	ALLOCATE	DIRECTOR
SERRATED	TURBANED	BERIBERI	HAIRBAND	SARABAND	ANARCHIC	DOMICILE
SEXUALLY	TYMPANUM	BILOBATE	HANDBALL	SCABBARD	ANTECEDE	DOVECOTE
SHERATON	UNABATED	BLUEBACK	HANDBILL	SCHUBERT	ARTICLED	DOWNCAST
SIGNALER	UNAWARES	BLUEBELL	HANDBOOK	SCRABBLE	ARTICLES	ECLECTIC
SIGNALLY	UNBEATEN	BOATBILL	HAPSBURG	SCRIBBLE	ASCOCARP	EFFICACY
SITUATED	UNBIASED	BRADBURY	HARDBACK	SCRIBBLY	ASUNCION	EIDECTIC
SIZEABLE	UNCHASTE	BROWBEAT	HAREBELL	SCRUBBER	ATROCITY	ENDOCARP
SLOVAKIA	UNHEATED	BUCKBEAN	HEADBAND	SHABBILY	ATTACHED	ENRICHED
SLUGABED	UNIVALVE	BUSYBODY	HEELBALL	SHAGBARK	ATTACKER	ENTICING
SOAKAWAY	UNLEADED	CALABASH	HELLBENT	SHAMBLES	AUDACITY	ESPECIAL
SOCIABLE	UNLOADED	CAMPBELL	HIGHBALL	SHINBONE	AURICULA	EUCYCLIC
SOCIALLY	UNPLACED	CAPYBARA	HIGHBORN	SHOEBILL	AUTOCRAT	EXERCISE
SOCRATES	UNREASON	CARABINE	HIGHBROW	SHOWBOAT	BACKCHAT	EXORCISM
SOCRATIC	UNSEALED	CELIBACY	HORNBEAM	SKEWBALD	BACKCOMB	EXORCIST
SOLVABLE	UNSHAKEN	CELIBATE	HORNBILL	SLAPBANG	BALLCOCK	EXORCIZE
SPARAXIS	UNSTABLE	CENOBITE	HORNBOOK	SLOBBERY	BIFOCALS	EXPECTED
SPIRACLE	UNSTATED	CEREBRAL	HUMPBACK	SNOBBERY	BIOSCOPE	FELICITY
SPIRALLY	UNUSABLE	CEREBRUM	IMMOBILE	SNOBBISH	BIRDCAGE	FEROCITY
SPORADIC	UNWEANED	CHADBAND	INCUBATE	SNOWBALL	BLEACHER	FIDUCIAL
SPREADER	UPHEAVAL	CHAMBERS	INDEBTED	SOAPBARK	BLOTCHED	FIERCELY
SQUEAKER	UPSTAIRS	CLAMBAKE	JACKBOOT	SOFTBACK	BLUECOAT	FISHCAKE
SQUEALER	VAGRANCY	CLAWBACK	JACOBEAN	SOFTBALL	BOOKCASE	FORECAST
STOWAWAY	VAISAKHA	CLIMBING	JACOBITE	SOMEBODY	BORACITE	FRANCIUM
STREAKED	VALHALLA	CLUBBING	JAILBIRD	SONGBIRD	BORECOLE	GALACTIC
STREAKER	VALUABLE	COCKBOAT	JEREBOAM	SQUABBLE	BOUNCING	GENOCIDE
STREAMER	VARIABLE	COLDBOOT	JEROBOAM	STABBING	BRANCHED	GLANCING
STRIATED	VARIANCE	COMEBACK	KICKBACK	STABBING	BREACHES	GLAUCOMA

GLAUCOUS	POSTCODE	TURNCOCK	CHORDATA	NOWADAYS	SWADDLER	BERGENIA
GOLFCLUB	PREACHER	TWITCHER	CHORDATE	OBSIDIAN	SWINDLER	BERGERAC
GROSCHEN	PRINCELY	TYPECAST	CLADDING	OCCIDENT	TEARDROP	BERKELEY
HANDCART	PRINCESS	UNLOCKED	CLAUDIUS	OPENDOOR	THUNDERY	BESIEGED
HANDCLAP	PUSHCART	UNSOCIAL	COMEDIAN	OPHIDIAN	TIMIDITY	BESSEMER
HANDCUFF	QUINCUNX	VARICOSE	COMEDOWN	ORCADIAN	TRAPDOOR	BETHESDA
HARDCORE	RAINCOAT	VELOCITY	CUPIDITY	OVERDONE	UNBIDDEN	BETJEMAN
HAUNCHES	RAPACITY	VERACITY	DAVIDSON	OVERDOSE	UNENDING	BILBERRY
HERACLES	RAPECAKE	VIETCONG	DECADENT	OVERDRAW	UNFADING	BIOMETRY
HERACLID	REDACTOR	VIVACITY	DIELDRIN	PALUDISM	UNTIDILY	BITTERLY
HERSCHEL	REGICIDE	VOLSCIAN	DIVIDEND	PARADIGM	VALIDATE	BODLEIAN
HIJACKER	RELOCATE	VORACITY	DIVIDERS	PARODIST	VALIDITY	BORDEAUX
HOLOCENE	RETICENT	WHINCHAT	DREADFUL	PERIDERM	VANADIUM	BORDELLO
HOMICIDE	RETICULE	WHIPCORD	ECTODERM	PILTDOWN	VANADOUS	BORDERER
IMBECILE	RHONCHUS	WOODCOCK	EMBEDDED	PLAUDITS	WASHDOWN	BOTHERED
IMPACTED	RICOCHET	WORMCAST	EMBODIED	PLEADING	WITHDRAW	BRACELET
INDECENT	RIDICULE	WRETCHED	ENDODERM	POSTDATE	YIELDING	BROMELIA
INDICANT	ROLLCALL	ABERDEEN	EURYDICE	POUNDAGE	ACADEMIA	BRUNETTE
INDICATE	RUBICUND	ABRIDGED	EVILDOER	PRANDIAL	ACADEMIC	BUGGERED
INDUCIVE	SAGACITY	ABUNDANT	EXORDIUM	PSEUDERY	ACCREDIT	BULLETIN
INDUCTOR	SALACITY	ACCIDENT	EXPEDITE	PULLDOWN	ACHIEVED	BURBERRY
INFECTED	SCARCELY	AERODYNE	FIELDING	PUSHDOWN	ACHIEVER	BURDENED
INJECTOR	SCARCITY	AIREDALE	FIENDISH	QUANDARY	AGACERIE	BUTTERED
INNOCENT	SCORCHED	AKKADIAN	FIREDAMP	RAINDROP	AGREEING	CABLECAR
INSECURE	SCORCHER	AMANDINE	FLANDERS	RAPIDITY	AIGRETTE	CABLEWAY
IRISCOPE	SEARCHER	AMUNDSEN	FLINDERS	RECEDING	ALCHEMIC	CACHEPOT
IRONCLAD	SEASCAPE	AMYGDALA	FLOODING	REINDEER	ALFRESCO	CACHEXIA
JUDICIAL	SELECTED	ANECDOTE	FLOODLIT	REMEDIAL	ALOPECIA	CAFFEINE
KAZACHOK	SELECTOR	ANTEDATE	FLUIDITY	RESIDENT	AMARETTO	CALCEATE
LIMACINE	SHOWCASE	ANTIDOTE	FOREDECK	RESIDUAL	AMATEURS	CALDERON
LONICERA	SILICATE	AQUEDUCT	FOREDOOM	RESIDUUM	AMBIENCE	CAMBERED
LYRICISM	SILICONE	ARALDITE	FOUNDING	RIGIDITY	AMORETTI	CANBERRA
LYRICIST	SILICULA	ARCADIAN	FREUDIAN	RINGDOVE	AMORETTO	CANOEING
MAGICIAN	SINECURE	ARCHDUKE	FRONDEUR	ROCHDALE	AMUSETTE	CANOEIST
MANICURE	SNATCHER	ASCIDIAN	GLANDERS	ROUNDERS	ANALECTA	CARNEGIE
MEDICATE	SOLECISM	ASCIDIUM	GRANDDAD	RUBIDIUM	ANALEMMA	CASSETTE
MEDICINE	SOURCING	ASMODEUS	GRANDEUR	SCALDING	ANDREWES	CATHEDRA
MENACING	SPICCATO	BACKDATE	GRANDKID	SCANDIUM	ANGLESEY	CATHETER
MOLECULE	SPROCKET	BACKDROP	GRANDSON	SCHEDULE	ANISETTE	CAUSEWAY
MOLUCCAS	SPRUCELY	BASIDIUM	GREEDILY	SCOLDING	ANOREXIA	CENTERED
MONICKER	STACCATO	BEFUDDLE	GRINDING	SHELDUCK	ANOREXIC	CERBERUS
MONTCALM	STARCHED	BENEDICK	GUARDIAN	SHODDILY	APPLETON	CERVELAT
MOORCOCK	STICCATO	BENEDICT	HEREDITY	SHOWDOWN	ARQUEBUS	CHAPERON
MOROCCAN	STOCCATA	BLANDISH	HOARDING	SHREDDER	ASTHENIA	CHEYENNE
MUSICIAN	STOICISM	BLEEDING	HOLIDAYS	SHUTDOWN	ATHLETIC	CHOLERIC
NEWSCAST	STOPCOCK	BLENDING	HUMIDIFY	SKIDDING	AUDIENCE	CISTERNA
NOTECASE	STRACHEY	BLINDING	HUMIDITY	SKINDEEP	AVICENNA	CLARENCE
OBJECTOR	STRICKEN	BOARDING	IMMODEST	SLAPDASH	BACHELOR	CLAVECIN
OFFICERS	STRICKLE	BORODINO	IMPUDENT	SLOWDOWN	BACTERIA	CLEMENCY
OFFICIAL	STRICTLY	BOUNDARY	INCIDENT	SNOWDROP	BAEDEKER	CLEVERLY
OLEACEAE	STUCCOED	BRANDADE	INUNDATE	SOLIDIFY	BAGHEERA	CLIVEDEN
OPENCAST	SUITCASE	BRANDISH	JAUNDICE	SOLIDITY	BAGUETTE	COALESCE
OPTICIAN	SURICATE	BRANDNEW	KILLDEER	SOUNDING	BANDEROL	COBWEBBY
OPUSCULE	SYRACUSE	BREEDING	KLONDIKE	SPANDREL	BANNERET	COCKEREL
OTOSCOPE	TELECAST	BRINDISI	KNEEDEEP	SPEEDILY	BARBECUE	COCKEYED
OVERCAST	TELECOMS	BRINDLED	LAPIDARY	SPEEDWAY	BARBERRY	COLLECTS
OVERCOAT	TENACITY	BROADWAY	LAPIDATE	SPENDING	BARGELLO	COLLEGES
OVERCOME	THATCHED	BROODING	LIVIDITY	SQUADDIE	BARGEMAN	COMMENCE
OXPECKER	THATCHER	BUILDING	LONSDALE	SQUADRON	BARRETTE	COMMERCE
PEDICURE	THEOCRAT	BULLDOZE	LUCIDITY	STANDARD	BARTERED	CONCEIVE
PERACUTE	THRACIAN	CANADIAN	MALODOUR	STANDING	BASKETRY	CONCERTO
PERICARP	TITICACA	CAULDRON	MARKDOWN	STANDISH	BATHETIC	CONDENSE
PERICLES	TOXICITY	CHALDEAN	MELTDOWN	STANDOFF	BATTERED	CONFETTI
PIERCING	TOXOCARA	CHALDRON	MEREDITH	STARDUST	BAYBERRY	CONSERVE
PINOCHLE	TRENCHER	CHANDLER	MERIDIAN	STEADILY	BAYREUTH	CONTEMPT
PLANCHET	TRINCULO	CHILDERS	MESODERM	STENDHAL	BELIEVER	CONTENTS
PLIOCENE	TRUNCATE	CHILDISH	MONADISM	STRADDLE	BEQUEATH	CONVENER
POLYCARP	TUNICATE	CHILDREN	MOULDING	STRIDENT	BERBERIS	CONVERGE
POSTCARD	TURNCOAT	CHINDITS	NOSEDIVE	STURDILY	BERCEUSE	CONVERSE

CONVEYOR	EXEGETIC	ISABELLA	NORSEMAN	REPLEVIN	TATTERED	BEAUFORT
COQUETRY	EXIGENCY	ISABELLE	NORSEMEN	RESPECTS	TAYBERRY	BENEFICE
COQUETTE	EXPRESSO	ISOGENIC	NUCLEATE	RETRENCH	TEMPERED	BENEFITS
CORNETTO	FALSETTO	JACKETED	NUCLEOLE	REVIEWER	TENDENCY	BILLFOLD
CORSELET	FASTENER	JEANETTE	ODDMENTS	RIDGEWAY	TENDERLY	BLOWFISH
CORVETTE	FATHERLY	JIGGERED	ODOMETER	RIFLEMAN	THOLEPIN	BONEFISH
COSMETIC	FLAMENCO	JULIENNE	OMELETTE	ROCKETRY	TIMBERED	BONIFACE
COUPERIN	FLAMEOUT	KATTEGAT	OPERETTA	ROSSETTI	TINSELLY	BOUFFANT
COWBERRY	FLORENCE	KEDGEREE	OPULENCE	ROULETTE	TOISEACH	BRIEFING
CRANEFLY	FOLDEROL	KERMESSE	OUTREACH	RUGGEDLY	TOPHEAVY	BUCKFAST
CRUZEIRO	FORCEFUL	KESTEVEN	OUTREMER	RUNNERUP	TOPLEVEL	BULLFROG
CULVERIN	FORFEITS	KILKENNY	OUTWEIGH	SANSERIF	TOXAEMIA	CAREFREE
CURRENCY	FORMERLY	KIPPERED	PALMETTO	SAUCEPAN	TRADEOFF	CLIFFORD
CZAREVNA	FRENETIC	KROMESKY	PANDEMIC	SCALENUS	TRAVELER	CLUBFOOT
DARKENED	FRUMENTY	LANCELET	PARIETAL	SCAVENGE	TRAVERSE	COIFFEUR
DEADENED	FUGLEMAN	LANCELOT	PARMESAN	SCREENED	TRAVESTY	COIFFURE
DEADENER	FURBELOW	LARGESSE	PARTERRE	SECRETLY	TRILEMMA	COLIFORM
DECREASE	GADGETRY	LATTERLY	PASSERBY	SELVEDGE	TSAREVNA	CRAWFISH
DECREPIT	GALLERIA	LAUREATE	PATHETIC	SENTENCE	TUPPENNY	CRAYFISH
DECRETAL	GARDENER	LAURENCE	PATIENCE	SEQUENCE	TURGENEV	CROWFOOT
DEFREEZE	GARDENIA	LAWRENCE	PEACEFUL	SERGEANT	TURMERIC	DOWNFALL
DEUTERON	GARMENTS	LEAVENED	PELLETED	SERJEANT	TURRETED	DUTYFREE
DEWBERRY	GATHERED	LENIENCY	PERCEIVE	SHAKEOUT	TWOPENNY	DWARFISH
DEWYEYED	GEODESIC	LETTERED	PERCEVAL	SHAMEFUL	UDOMETER	DWARFISM
DIABETES	GEODETIC	LEUKEMIA	PERFECTA	SHAREOUT	UMBRELLA	ENSIFORM
DIABETIC	GEOMETER	LIBRETTO	PERFECTO	SHIGELLA	UNEVENLY	FLATFISH
DIAMETER	GEOMETRY	LIEGEMAN	PERMEATE	SHIVERED	UNFREEZE	FLATFOOT
DIARESIS	GINGERLY	LIGNEOUS	PERVERSE	SISTERLY	UNITEDLY	FOOTFALL
DIAZEPAM	GLABELLA	LINGERIE	PHILEMON	SITTELLA	UNIVERSE	FOREFOOT
DIERESIS	GLYCERIN	LISTENER	PHONETIC	SIXPENCE	UNSEEDED	FOURFOLD
DIOCESAN	GOIDELIC	LISTERIA	PIERETTE	SKELETAL	UNSEEMLY	FUSIFORM
DIOGENES	GOOSEGOG	LOITERER	PILFERER	SKELETON	UNSTEADY	GATEFOLD
DIPHENYL	GORGEOUS	LOOSEBOX	PILSENER	SLOVENIA	UNWIELDY	GOLDFISH
DIPTERAL	GRACEFUL	LOUVERED	PIMIENTO	SLOVENLY	VALLETTA	GRAFFITI
DISHEVEL	GRAMERCY	LUTHERAN	PIZZERIA	SOFTENER	VARIETAL	HALFFULL
DISKETTE	GRATEFUL	MACHEATH	PLACEMAT	SOLVENCY	VELLEITY	HARTFORD
DISPENSE	GRAVELLY	MACKEREL	PLACEMEN	SORCERER	VENDETTA	HELLFIRE
DISPERSE	GRISELDA	MACREADY	PLACENTA	SOUVENIR	VENGEFUL	HEREFORD
DIURETIC	GRISETTE	MAECENAS	PLATEFUL	SPACEMAN	VERDERER	HOLDFAST
DOGBERRY	GUNMETAL	MAGNESIA	PLATELET	SPADEFUL	VERTEBRA	HORNFELS
DOGGEDLY	GUSSETED	MAGNETIC	PLEBEIAN	SPIRELET	VESPERAL	INTIFADA
DOGGEREL	HACIENDA	MAIDENLY	POCHETTE	SPITEFUL	VIGNETTE	KINSFOLK
DOTTEREL	HAMMERED	MALLEATE	POTBELLY	SQUEEGEE	VIOLENCE	LADYFISH
DRIVEWAY	HARDENED	MANNERED	POWDERED	SQUEEZER	VISCERAL	LANDFALL
DUCHESSE	HATTERAS	MANNERLY	PREDELLA	STAKEOUT	VITREOUS	LANDFILL
DUODENAL	HAYFEVER	MAQUETTE	PRESENCE	STAMENED	WANDERER	LEAPFROG
DUODENUM	HEATEDLY	MARCELLA	PRESERVE	STAPELIA	WASTEFUL	LUMPFISH
DYSLEXIA	HEAVENLY	MARCELLO	PRETENCE	STILETTO	WESLEYAN	LUNGFISH
DYSLEXIC	HEDGEHOG	MARKEDLY	PRETENSE	STOKESAY	WESTERLY	MANIFEST
EASTERLY	HEDGEROW	MARTELLO	PRIMEVAL	STONEFLY	WHATEVER	MANIFOLD
ELEMENTS	HELLENIC	MASSENET	PROCEEDS	STOREMAN	WHENEVER	MODIFIER
ELEVENTH	HELMETED	MASSEUSE	PROGERIA	STOREYED	WHEREVER	MONKFISH
EMINENCE	HELVETIA	MASTERLY	PROPERLY	STUDENTS	WHITECAP	MOUFFLON
EMINENCY	HERMETIC	MEDIEVAL	PROPERTY	SUBJECTS	WHITEHOT	OMNIFORM
ENCAENIA	HERPETIC	MERCEDES	PROTEASE	SUBLEASE	WHITENER	OVERFEED
ENFEEBLE	HITHERTO	MESMERIC	PROTÉGÉE	SUBMERGE	WICKEDLY	OVERFILL
ENIWETOK	HORSEBOX	MILDEWED	PROVERBS	SUBTENSE	WISTERIA	OVERFLOW
ENTREATY	HORSEFLY	MINCEPIE	PRUDENCE	SUCCEEDS	WITHERED	OVERFULL
ENTRENCH	HORSEMAN	MONTEITH	PRUNELLA	SUDDENLY	WOLSELEY	PACIFIER
ENTREPOT	HORSEMEN	MOQUETTE	PUCKERED	SUFFERER	WOODENLY	PACIFISM
EPIDEMIC	HOSTELRY	MOTHERLY	PUNGENCY	SULLENLY	WRITEOFF	PACIFIST
EPILEPSY	HOUSEMAN	MULBERRY	PURVEYOR	SURVEYOR	ZEPPELIN	PALEFACE
ESOTERIC	HYGIENIC	MURDERER	QUENELLE	SUSPENSE	AEROFLOT	PARAFFIN
ESPRESSO	HYSTERIA	NATTERED	RACLETTE	SWINEPOX	AEROFOIL	PINAFORE
ESTEEMED	HYSTERIC	NAUSEATE	RASSELAS	SYMMETRY	ARTEFACT	PISIFORM
ESTHETIC	INCREASE	NAUSEOUS	RECREATE	SYNTEXIS	ARTIFACT	PLATFORM
EVANESCE	INNUENDO	NOBLEMAN	REDEEMER	SYSTEMIC	ARTIFICE	PLAYFAIR
EVIDENCE	INTRENCH	NOISETTE	RELIEVED	TABLEMAT	BACKFIRE	PRATFALL
EXEGESIS	INTREPID	NONSENSE	RELIEVED	TASTEFUL	BAREFOOT	PURIFIED

PURIFIER	DELEGATE	PELAGIUS	ANATHEMA	DOUGHBOY	KEELHAUL	PLETHORA
PYRIFORM	DEROGATE	PHALGUNA	ANTIHERO	DOUGHNUT	KERCHIEF	PLUGHOLE
RAINFALL	DESIGNER	PHLEGMON	ANYTHING	DOWNHILL	KINSHASA	PORPHYRA
RAREFIED	DILIGENT	PHOSGENE	ANYWHERE	DROPHEAD	KNEEHIGH	PORPHYRY
REAFFIRM	DISAGREE	PHRYGIAN	APOPHYGE	DRUMHEAD	KNIGHTLY	PORTHOLE
REDEFINE	DRAUGHTS	PLANGENT	APOTHEGM	DUNGHILL	KRUMHORN	POTSHERD
ROSEFISH	DRAUGHTY	PLAYGIRL	ARACHNID	DUTCHMAN	LATCHKEY	PROPHASE
SAINFOIN	DRUDGERY	PLOUGHED	ARETHUSA	EARPHONE	LAUGHING	PROPHECY
SCAFFOLD	DRUGGIST	PLUNGING	ARMCHAIR	EDGEHILL	LAUGHTER	PROPHESY
SCARFACE	DZONGKHA	POLYGAMY	AYRSHIRE	EGGSHELL	LEACHING	PURCHASE
SCOFFING	ELONGATE	POLYGLOT	BAATHIST	ELEPHANT	LEATHERY	RAILHEAD
SCROFULA	EMERGENT	POLYGYNY	BABYHOOD	EPIPHANY	LEFTHAND	REDSHANK
SERAFILE	EMERGING	PRIGGISH	BACCHANT	EPIPHYTE	LINCHPIN	REDSHIFT
SLUGFEST	EMULGENT	REFUGIUM	BACKHAND	EPITHEMA	LOATHING	RHYTHMIC
SNIFFLER	ENDOGAMY	RELEGATE	BENGHAZI	ERYTHEMA	LONGHAND	RINGHALS
SNOWFALL	ENERGIZE	RELIGION	BIATHLON	EYESHADE	LONGHAUL	ROUGHAGE
SNUFFBOX	ENGAGING	RENEGADE	BILLHOOK	FAITHFUL	LONGHORN	SAMPHIRE
SPIFFING	EULOGIST	RESIGNED	BIRTHDAY	FARMHAND	LOOPHOLE	SAPPHIRE
SPITFIRE	EULOGIUM	SAVAGELY	BLENHEIM	FARTHEST	LUNCHBOX	SAPPHIST
STAFFING	EULOGIZE	SAVAGERY	BLIGHTER	FARTHING	LUNCHEON	SCAPHOID
STAFFORD	FATIGUED	SERAGLIO	BLITHELY	FEATHERS	LYNCHING	SCATHING
STARFISH	FATIGUES	SHANGAAN	BLOWHOLE	FEATHERY	MARSHALL	SEASHELL
STUFFILY	FEELGOOD	SHANGHAI	BLUSHING	FETCHING	MASTHEAD	SEASHORE
STUFFING	FILIGREE	SHINGLES	BOLTHOLE	FILTHILY	MATCHBOX	SEETHING
TELEFILM	FLAGGING	SHOWGIRL	BONEHEAD	FISHHOOK	MATCHING	SELFHELP
TOADFLAX	FLOGGING	SLANGING	BOREHOLE	FLASHGUN	MELCHIOR	SHEPHERD
TYPEFACE	FOREGONE	SLUGGARD	BRACHIAL	FLASHILY	MERCHANT	SHOEHORN
UNCIFORM	FUMIGATE	SLUGGISH	BRETHREN	FLASHING	MINEHEAD	SINKHOLE
UNRIFLED	GADOGADO	SMIDGEON	BRIGHTEN	FLUSHING	MIRTHFUL	SKINHEAD
VARIFORM	GEORGIAN	SMUGGLED	BRIGHTLY	FLYSHEET	MISCHIEF	SLIGHTED
WEAKFISH	GROGGILY	SMUGGLER	BRIGHTON	FLYWHEEL	MOLEHILL	SLIGHTLY
WHARFAGE	GRUDGING	SONOGRAM	BROCHURE	FOOTHOLD	MONOHULL	SLOTHFUL
WILDFELL	HANDGRIP	SPANGLED	BROUHAHA	FOREHAND	MORPHEME	SMASHING
WILDFIRE	HEADGEAR	SPHAGNUM	BUDDHISM	FOREHEAD	MORPHEUS	SOOTHING
WILDFOWL	HEXAGRAM	SQUIGGLE	BUDDHIST	FREEHAND	MORPHINE	SOOTHSAY
WINDFALL	HIGHGATE	STAGGERS	BULKHEAD	FREEHOLD	MOUTHFUL	SOUCHONG
WINIFRED	HIRAGANA	STARGAZE	BULLHORN	FRESHEST	MUNCHKIN	SOUTHEND
ABINGDON	HOLOGRAM	STINGING	BUTCHERS	FRESHMAN	MURRHINE	SOUTHERN
ABNEGATE	HYPOGEAL	STINGRAY	BUTCHERY	FRIGHTEN	MUTCHKIN	SOUTHPAW
ABROGATE	IDEOGRAM	STRAGGLE	CAKEHOLE	FURTHEST	NEATHERD	SPITHEAD
AEROGRAM	IDIOGRAM	STRAGGLY	CALTHROP	GEOPHONE	NEIGHBOR	STAGHORN
ALLEGORY	INDIGENT	STRUGGLE	CAMSHAFT	GIRLHOOD	NEOPHYTE	STANHOPE
ALLOGAMY	INSIGNIA	STURGEON	CARTHAGE	GNASHING	NEWSHAWK	STAPHYLE
ALMIGHTY	INTAGLIO	SVENGALI	CATCHING	GODCHILD	NORTHERN	STEPHENS
ARMAGNAC	INTEGRAL	SWINGING	CHESHIRE	GRAPHEME	NORTHING	SUBSHRUB
ARPEGGIO	IRRIGATE	TAILGATE	CHICHEWA	GRAPHICS	NUTSHELL	SULPHATE
ARROGANT	KILOGRAM	TELEGONY	CINCHONA	GRAPHITE	OFFSHOOT	SULPHIDE
ARROGATE	LITIGANT	TELEGRAM	CLASHING	GYMKHANA	OFFSHORE	SUNSHADE
ASSIGNEE	LITIGATE	THINGAMY	CLOTHIER	HALFHOUR	OKLAHOMA	SUNSHINE
AUTOGAMY	MAHOGANY	THOUGHTS	CLOTHING	HANDHELD	OLIPHANT	SYMPHONY
AUTOGIRO	MALAGASY	TOBOGGAN	COACHING	HARDHACK	OUTSHINE	TAKEHOME
AUTOGYRO	MANAGING	TOLLGATE	COACHMAN	HATCHERY	OVERHAND	TEACHERS
BALLGIRL	MARIGOLD	UNSIGNED	COALHOLE	HATCHING	OVERHANG	TEACHING
BLUDGEON	MISOGYNY	UPRIGHTS	COGWHEEL	HATCHWAY	OVERHAUL	TEESHIRT
BRAGGART	MITIGATE	VINEGARY	CONCHOID	HAWTHORN	OVERHEAD	TEETHING
BRAGGING	MONOGAMY	VISIGOTH	COPYHOLD	HEADHUNT	OVERHEAR	TETCHILY
BRIDGING	MONOGRAM	VOYAGEUR	CORNHILL	HEIGHTEN	OVERHEAT	TOMAHAWK
BRINGING	MONOGYNY	WINDGALL	COUCHANT	HENCHMAN	PAMPHLET	TOUCHING
BROUGHAM	MORTGAGE	WRANGLER	COUCHING	HEYTHROP	PANTHEON	TRACHOMA
CALIGULA	NAVIGATE	WRINGING	COUGHING	HOGSHEAD	PARTHIAN	TRASHCAN
CALLGIRL	NOMOGRAM	WRONGFUL	CRICHTON	HOLYHEAD	PATCHILY	TRICHOID
CATEGORY	OBLIGATE	XENOGAMY	CRUMHORN	HUMPHREY	PAYCHECK	TROCHAIC
CHANGING	OBLIGING	YATAGHAN	CRUSHING	HUSHHUSH	PEEPHOLE	TROCHLEA
CHARGING	ORANGERY	YOUNGEST	DABCHICK	IRISHISM	PENCHANT	TRUTHFUL
CLANGING	PANEGYRY	ACIDHEAD	DAUGHTER	IRISHMAN	PERSHING	URETHANE
CLANGOUR	PARAGUAY	AESTHETE	DEADHEAD	IRISHMEN	PIECHART	VAUXHALL
CLINGING	PATAGIUM	ALDEHYDE	DEATHBED	ISOTHERE	PILCHARD	WATCHDOG
CRINGING	PEDAGOGY	AMETHYST	DECKHAND	ISOTHERM	PINWHEEL	WATCHFUL
DANEGELD	PEDIGREE	ANAPHASE	DIAPHONE	KALAHARI	PISSHEAD	WATCHING

WATCHMAN	CANDIDLY	DETAINER	GRATINEE	MANDIBLE	PASTICHE	RETAILER
WEIGHING	CANNIBAL	DETRITUS	GRAVITAS	MANDIOCA	PASTILLE	RETAINER
WELSHMAN	CANTICLE	DIDDICOY	GRIDIRON	MANNIKIN	PAULINUS	RETRIEVE
WHIPHAND	CAPRIOLE	DIGGINGS	GUERIDON	MANTILLA	PEELINGS	REVEILLE
WINDHOEK	CAPSICUM	DISCIPLE	GUERILLA	MANTISSA	PELLICLE	RUBAIYAT
WITCHERY	CAPSIZED	DISLIKED	GULLIBLE	MARGINAL	PEMMICAN	RUBBISHY
WITCHING	CAPTIOUS	DISPIRIT	GULLIVER	MARRIAGE	PENNINES	RUCTIONS
WITHHOLD	CARDIGAN	DISTINCT	HALLIARD	MARTINET	PERCIVAL	RUNCIBLE
WORTHIES	CARDINAL	DULCIMER	HANDICAP	MARZIPAN	PERVIOUS	SACRISTY
WORTHILY	CARNIVAL	DULCINEA	HANGINGS	MASSICOT	PHARISEE	SANTIAGO
WRATHFUL	CARRIAGE	EARLIEST	HANNIBAL	MERCIFUL	PHILIPPI	SARDINIA
WRITHING	CARRIOLE	EARNINGS	HARRIDAN	MESSIDOR	PHTHISIC	SCABIOUS
XANTHOMA	CAUDILLO	EARPIECE	HARRISON	MÉTAIRIE	PHTHISIS	SCILICET
YOKOHAMA	CAUTIOUS	EGGTIMER	HASTINGS	METRICAL	PHYSICAL	SCIMITAR
YOUTHFUL	CERVICAL	ELDRITCH	HAWAIIAN	METRITIS	PHYSIQUE	SENSIBLE
ZOOPHYTE	CHARISMA	ELIGIBLE	HAWFINCH	MEUNIÈRE	PICKINGS	SENSIBLY
ZUCCHINI	CHEMICAL	EMACIATE	HAYFIELD	MICHIGAN	PIERIDES	SENTIENT
ABSCISSA	CHENILLE	EMERITUS	HEBRIDES	MIDFIELD	PINNIPED	SENTINEL
ABUTILON	CHEVIOTS	EMOTICON	HELSINKI	MIDNIGHT	PLACIDLY	SERVICES
ACQUIRED	CHILIAST	ERADIATE	HERMIONE	MILLIBAR	PLATINUM	SERVIENT
ACQUIRER	CHORIAMB	EXAMINEE	HETAIRIA	MILLINER	PLOTINUS	SERVITOR
ADENITIS	CIRCINUS	EXAMINER	HOLDINGS	MILLIONS	POETICAL	SHERIDAN
ADROITLY	CLARINET	EXPLICIT	HOOLIGAN	MIRLITON	POITIERS	SIXTIETH
AGGRIEVE	CLAVICLE	EYELINER	HOPFIELD	MOORINGS	POLLIWOG	SKYLIGHT
AGONIZED	CLERICAL	EYEPIECE	HORLICKS	MORBIDLY	PONTIFEX	SKYPILOT
AIGUILLE	CLERIHEW	EYESIGHT	HORRIBLE	MORBILLI	POPSICLE	SOBRIETY
AIRFIELD	CLINICAL	FACTIOUS	HORRIBLY	MORRISON	PORRIDGE	SOLDIERS
AIRLINER	COCCIDAE	FAINITES	HORRIFIC	MORTIMER	PORTIÈRE	SOLDIERY
AIRTIGHT	CODPIECE	FALLIBLE	HOSPITAL	MULLIGAN	POSEIDON	SORDIDLY
ALUMINUM	COLLIERS	FANCIFUL	HUSTINGS	MULTIPLE	POSSIBLE	SPACIOUS
AMERICAN	COLLIERY	FANLIGHT	HYACINTH	MULTIPLY	POSSIBLY	SPANIARD
AMERICAS	COMBINED	FARCICAL	ICEFIELD	MYELITIS	PRECINCT	SPAVINED
ANCHISES	COMPILER	FARRIERY	IMAGINED	MYRMIDON	PRECIOUS	SPECIFIC
ANGLICAN	CONFINED	FASCICLE	IMPAIRED	MYSTICAL	PREMIERE	SPECIMEN
ANGUILLA	CONFINES	FEASIBLE	IMPLICIT	MYSTIQUE	PREMISES	SPECIOUS
APERIENT	CONSIDER	FEASIBLY	IMPRISON	MYTHICAL	PREVIOUS	SPINIFEX
APERITIF	CONTINUE	FEELINGS	INCLINED	NARGILEH	PRODIGAL	SPIRITED
APPLIQUÉ	CONTINUO	FENCIBLE	INEDIBLE	NAUTICAL	PROHIBIT	SPIRITUS
APPRISED	CONVINCE	FESTIVAL	INFLIGHT	NAUTILUS	PROLIFIC	SPOLIATE
ARCHIVES	CORNICHE	FIFTIETH	INFRINGE	NEGLIGEE	PROMISED	SPRAINED
ATOMIZER	CORRIDOR	FINDINGS	INGUINAL	NEGRILLO	PROVIDED	SPURIOUS
ATYPICAL	CORSICAN	FISSIPED	INIMICAL	NESCIENT	PROVIDER	STOLIDLY
AUSPICES	CREDIBLE	FLAMINGO	INITIATE	NEURITIS	PROVINCE	STRAIGHT
BAGPIPES	CREDIBLY	FLEXIBLE	INQUIRER	NUFFIELD	PROXIMAL	STRAINED
BALLISTA	CREDITOR	FLEXIBLY	INSPIRED	NUPTIALS	PRURIENT	STRAINER
BANDITTI	CREPITUS	FLOTILLA	INSPIRIT	NUTRIENT	PUBLICAN	STRAITEN
BANLIEUE	CRIMINAL	FOGLIGHT	INSTINCT	OBEDIENT	PUBLICLY	STUDIOUS
BAPTISED	CRITICAL	FOLLICLE	INTRIGUE	OBTAINED	PURLIEUS	STUPIDLY
BARBICAN	CRITIQUE	FORCIBLE	INVEIGLE	OFFSIDER	PYELITIS	STYLIZED
BARBIZON	CRUCIATE	FORCIBLY	IRONICAL	OILFIELD	QUIRINAL	SUBTITLE
BASSINET	CRUCIBLE	FORTIETH	JAMAICAN	ONESIDED	QUOTIENT	SUCCINCT
BASTILLE	CRUCIFER	FRAXINUS	JELLICOE	ORCHITIS	RACHITIS	SUICIDAL
BEARINGS	CRUCIFIX	FREMITUS	JETTISON	ORIGINAL	RAILINGS	SULLIVAN
BEATIFIC	CULLINAN	FRIGIDLY	JOTTINGS	OUTFIELD	RATTIGAN	SUMMITRY
BEFRIEND	CURLICUE	FUNGIBLE	KORRIGAN	OUTRIDER	READIEST	SUNLIGHT
BESMIRCH	CURRICLE	GALLIARD	KUFFIYEH	OUTRIGHT	RECEIPTS	SURGICAL
BESTIARY	CURSITOR	GALLIPOT	LASHINGS	OUTSIDER	RECEIVED	SURVIVAL
BIBLICAL	CUSPIDOR	GARLICKY	LEAVINGS	OVARITIS	RECEIVER	SURVIVOR
BOADICEA	CYCLICAL	GARRIGUE	LEGGINGS	OXBRIDGE	REDLIGHT	SYMBIONT
BOUTIQUE	CYSTITIS	GARRISON	LEONIDAS	PACHINKO	REFRINGE	SYPHILIS
BRASILIA	DANAIDES	GERMINAL	LODGINGS	PALLIATE	REGAINED	TACTICAL
BREVIARY	DAYLIGHT	GINGIVAL	LOLLIPOP	PALMITIN	REJOINED	TANGIBLE
BUNFIGHT	DEALINGS	GLORIANA	LOPSIDED	PANNICLE	RENMINBI	TANGIBLY
BURSITIS	DECEIVER	GLORIOLE	LUSCIOUS	PANNIKIN	REORIENT	TEQUILA
CABRIOLE	DENTICLE	GLORIOUS	MACHINES	PANPIPES	REPAIRER	TERMINAL
CALLIOPE	DEPRIVED	GLOXINIA	MACHISMO	PARSIFAL	REPRIEVE	TERMINUS
CALLIPER	DESTINED	GOLLIWOG	MADRIGAL	PARTICLE	REPRISAL	TERRIBLE
CALLISTO	DETAILED	GRACIOUS	MALDIVES	PARTISAN	REQUIRED	TERRIBLY
CANAILLE	DETAINEE	GRADIENT	MANCIPLE	PASSIBLE	RESPIGHI	TERRIFIC

TERTIARY	CRACKPOT	TRICKERY	BOTULISM	DISALLOW	FRAULEIN	ISOCLINE
TESTICLE	CROCKERY	TRUCKING	BRISLING	DISCLAIM	FUMBLING	ISOGLOSS
THURIBLE	CROCKETT	TRUCKLED	BROILING	DISCLOSE	FUSELAGE	JANGLING
THURIFER	DOORKNOB	UNLIKELY	BUBBLING	DISPLACE	FUSILIER	JEWELLED
TINNITUS	DRINKING	WHACKING	BUCKLING	DJELLABA	FUTILITY	JEWELLER
TORTILLA	DRUNKARD	WHISKERS	BUDDLEIA	DOCILITY	GAILLARD	JONGLEUR
TRINIDAD	EWIGKEIT	WHISKERY	BUMBLING	DOCKLAND	GALILEAN	JUBILANT
TRITICAL	FAULKNER	WRECKAGE	BUNGLING	DOUBLETS	GAMBLING	JUBILATE
TRITICUM	FRANKISH	WRINKLED	BURGLARY	DOUBLOON	GANGLAND	JUGGLING
TROPICAL	FRANKLIN	ZEDEKIAH	BUSTLING	DOWNLOAD	GANGLING	KIDGLOVE
TURGIDLY	FREAKISH	ABSOLUTE	BUSULFAN	DOXOLOGY	GANGLION	KINDLING
TWILIGHT	FRECKLED	ABSOLVED	CADILLAC	DRIBLETS	GASOLIER	KNOBLESS
TWOPIECE	FRECKLES	ACCOLADE	CAERLEON	DRUMLINE	GASOLINE	KREPLACH
UNGAINLY	FRISKILY	ACHILLES	CAJOLERY	DRYCLEAN	GEMOLOGY	LACKLAND
UNSUITED	HABAKKUK	AEROLITH	CAMELLIA	DUCKLING	GHOULISH	LADYLIKE
UNVOICED	HANUKKAH	AIRPLANE	CANALISE	DUELLIST	GORMLESS	LAKELAND
USURIOUS	HONGKONG	ALGOLOGY	CARELESS	DUMPLING	GRAYLING	LANDLADY
UXORIOUS	KAMIKAZE	ALKALIFY	CARILLON	DWELLING	GRIDLOCK	LANDLOCK
VERBIAGE	KATAKANA	ALKALINE	CAROLINA	EASTLAKE	GRILLING	LANDLORD
VERSICLE	KNACKERS	ALKALOID	CAROLINE	EGGPLANT	GROWLING	LANGLAND
VERTICAL	KNICKERS	ALLELUIA	CARTLOAD	EMBOLDEN	HAIRLESS	LANGLAUF
VESTIARY	KNOCKERS	AMBULANT	CATALYST	EMBOLISM	HAIRLIKE	LANOLINE
VIATICUM	KNOCKING	AMBULATE	CATILINE	ENFILADE	HAIRLINE	LEAFLESS
VINCIBLE	KNOCKOUT	ANAGLYPH	CATTLEYA	ENSILAGE	HAMILTON	LEGALISM
VIRGINAL	KOUSKOUS	ANGELICA	CATULLUS	ENVELOPE	HARDLINE	LEGALITY
VIRGINIA	MALAKOFF	ANNALIST	CAVALIER	EPIPLOON	HARFLEUR	LEGALIZE
VORTICAL	OILSKINS	ANNELIDA	CERULEAN	EQUALITY	HARMLESS	LEVELLER
WILLIAMS	OVERKILL	ANTELOPE	CHAPLAIN	EQUALIZE	HAVILDAR	LIBELOUS
WINDINGS	PARAKEET	ANTILLES	CHARLADY	EQUULEUS	HAZELNUT	LIFELESS
WINNINGS	PLANKING	ANTILOPE	CHARLOCK	ESCALADE	HEADLAMP	LIFELIKE
WINNIPEG	PLANKTON	ANYPLACE	CHILLADA	ESCALATE	HEADLAND	LIFELINE
WORKINGS	PLUCKILY	APHELION	CHILLING	ESCALOPE	HEADLESS	LIFELONG
WRITINGS	PLUCKING	APOLLYON	CHURLISH	ESCULENT	HEADLINE	LIMBLESS
WYCLIFFE	QUICKSET	APOPLEXY	CIVILIAN	ESPALIER	HEADLONG	LINOLEUM
XANTIPPE	SANSKRIT	APPALLED	CIVILITY	ETHOLOGY	HECKLING	LISTLESS
YERSINIA	SHACKLES	APPELANT	CIVILIZE	ETHYLENE	HEEDLESS	LIVELONG
DEMIJOHN	SHEIKDOM	AQUALUNG	CLUELESS	ETIOLATE	HEIRLESS	LOBELINE
FLAPJACK	SHOCKING	AQUILINE	COBBLERS	EUROLAND	HEIRLOOM	LOCALITY
FRABJOUS	SIDEKICK	ARBALEST	COCHLEAR	EYEGLASS	HELPLESS	LOCALIZE
READJUST	SKULKING	ARMALITE	COMPLAIN	FABULOUS	HELPLINE	LONGLAND
SKIPJACK	SMOCKING	ARMALITE	COMPLETE	FACELESS	HERALDIC	LOVELACE
SLAPJACK	SNACKBAR	AURELIAN	COMPLINE	FACELIFT	HERALDRY	LOVELESS
WHIPJACK	SNEAKERS	AVAILING	CONCLAVE	FACILITY	HIGHLAND	LOVELORN
BLACKBOY	SNEAKING	BABBLING	CONCLUDE	FALKLAND	HIRELING	LOWCLASS
BLACKCAP	SPANKING	BACILLUS	CONFLATE	FAMILIAR	HOBBLING	LOYALIST
BLACKFLY	SPARKING	BACKLASH	CONFLICT	FARMLAND	HOMELAND	LUCKLESS
BLACKING	SPARKLER	BACKLESS	COPULATE	FATALISM	HOMELESS	MACULATE
BLACKISH	SPEAKERS	BAFFLING	COUPLING	FATALIST	HONOLULU	MAGELLAN
BLACKLEG	SPEAKING	BAKELITE	COVALENT	FATALITY	HOPELESS	MAINLAND
BLACKOUT	SPECKLED	BANALITY	CRAWLING	FEARLESS	HOROLOGY	MAINLINE
BLINKERS	STALKING	BANTLING	CROMLECH	FECKLESS	HOTELIER	MAJOLICA
BLINKING	STARKERS	BASELESS	CRYOLITE	FECULENT	HOTPLATE	MAMELUKE
BLOCKADE	STICKILY	BASELINE	CYRILLIC	FETTLING	HUMILITY	MANTLING
BLOCKAGE	STICKING	BASILICA	CYTOLOGY	FIDDLING	HURDLING	MARYLAND
BRACKETS	STICKLER	BASILISK	DATELESS	FIDELITY	ICEBLINK	MEATLESS
BRACKISH	STINKING	BEAKLESS	DATELINE	FINALIST	IDEALISM	MEDALIST
BREAKING	STINKPOT	BECALMED	DAZZLING	FINALITY	IDEALIST	MEDDLING
BREAKOUT	STOCKADE	BEETLING	DEADLINE	FINALIZE	IDEALIZE	MEGALITH
BRICKBAT	STOCKCAR	BEHOLDEN	DEADLOCK	FLAWLESS	IDEOLOGY	MENELAUS
BRUCKNER	STOCKING	BEHOLDER	DEBILITY	FLYBLOWN	IMMOLATE	MESOLITE
CHECKERS	STOCKIST	BEWILDER	DEFILADE	FOLKLORE	IMPELLED	METALLED
CHECKING	STOCKMAN	BIBULOUS	DEMOLISH	FONDLING	IMPOLITE	METALLIC
CHECKOUT	STOCKPOT	BLOWLAMP	DEPILATE	FOOTLING	INDOLENT	MIDDLING
CHEEKILY	STRIKING	BOATLOAD	DERELICT	FORELAND	INHALANT	MILKLESS
CHICKENS	TASHKENT	BOBOLINK	DESELECT	FORELOCK	INSOLENT	MINDLESS
CHICKPEA	THANKFUL	BODYLINE	DESOLATE	FORKLIFT	INSULATE	MISPLACE
CLINKERS	THICKSET	BONELESS	DEVILISH	FORMLESS	INTELSAT	MOBILITY
CRACKERS	THINKING	BOOTLESS	DEVILLED	FORSLACK	INVOLUTE	MOBILIZE
CRACKING	TRACKING	BOTTLING	DIALLING	FOXGLOVE	INVOLVED	MODELING

MODELLER	PENALIZE	SEAPLANE	SYNCLINE	WEAKLING	COLOMBIA	ISTHMIAN
MODULATE	PENELOPE	SEDULOUS	TABULATE	WHIPLASH	COLUMBAN	JEREMIAD
MONOLITH	PENOLOGY	SEEDLESS	TACTLESS	WHIRLING	COLUMBUS	JEREMIAH
MOORLAND	PERILOUS	SEEDLING	TAILLESS	WHITLING	CORNMEAL	JUDGMENT
MORALIST	PERILUNE	SELFLESS	TEACLOTH	WILDLIFE	COSTMARY	KITEMARK
MORALITY	PETULANT	SEMOLINA	TEFILLIN	WINDLASS	CREAMERY	KOURMISS
MORALIZE	PHILLIPS	SENILITY	TEMPLATE	WINDLESS	CRUMMOCK	LANDMARK
MUCILAGE	PHYLLOME	SEROLOGY	TERYLENE	WINGLESS	CUCUMBER	LANDMASS
MUDFLATS	PICKLOCK	SEXOLOGY	THAILAND	WIRELESS	DARTMOOR	LANDMINE
MUMBLING	PIDDLING	SHALLOWS	THALLIUM	WOBBLING	DECEMBER	LIGAMENT
MUTILATE	PIPELINE	SHERLOCK	THEOLOGY	WOODLAND	DECEMVIR	LINIMENT
MYCELIUM	PITHLESS	SHETLAND	THRALDOM	WOOLLENS	DECIMATE	MAINMAST
MYCOLOGY	PITILESS	SHIELING	THRILLER	WORDLESS	DOCUMENT	MALAMUTE
MYOBLAST	POPULACE	SHILLING	TICKLING	WORKLOAD	DOLOMITE	MATAMORE
NAMELESS	POPULATE	SHOELACE	TICKLISH	XENOLITH	DOPAMINE	MAXIMIZE
NAPOLEON	POPULIST	SHOELESS	TIMELESS	YEARLING	DREAMILY	MELAMINE
NATALITY	POPULOUS	SHOULDER	TINGLING	YEARLONG	DREAMING	MESSMATE
NAUPLIUS	PORTLAND	SIBILANT	TIRELESS	YODELLER	DRUMMING	MILKMAID
NEBULOUS	POSOLOGY	SICILIAN	TONALITY	ZIBELINE	DYNAMICS	MINAMATA
NECKLACE	PRECLUDE	SICKLIST	TONELESS	ABUTMENT	DYNAMISM	MINIMIZE
NECKLINE	PROCLAIM	SIDELINE	TOPCLASS	ACRIMONY	DYNAMITE	MISHMASH
NEEDLESS	PTYALISM	SIDELONG	TOPOLOGY	ACROMION	EASEMENT	MOHAMMED
NEPALESE	PUGILISM	SIMPLIFY	TOTALITY	AGRIMONY	ENCAMPED	MONUMENT
NESTLING	PUGILIST	SIMULATE	TOTALIZE	ALARMING	ENCOMIUM	MOVEMENT
NIBELUNG	PURBLIND	SINCLAIR	TOWELING	ALARMIST	ENCUMBER	MUHAMMAD
NIGGLING	PURPLISH	SIZZLING	TRAILING	ALHAMBRA	ENDYMION	MUNIMENT
NIHILISM	PURSLANE	SKILLFUL	TRAMLINE	ANNAMITE	ENORMITY	NDJAMENA
NIHILIST	PURULENT	SKILLING	TREELESS	ANTIMERE	ENORMOUS	NEHEMIAH
NOBELIUM	PUZZLING	SKILLION	TREELINE	ANTIMONY	ENSEMBLE	NOVEMBER
NOBILITY	QUISLING	SKULLCAP	TRIFLING	ARGUMENT	EPHEMERA	OCCAMIST
NOSOLOGY	RABELAIS	SMALLEST	TRIGLYPH	ARMAMENT	ESTIMATE	OINTMENT
NOVELIST	RAILLERY	SMALLPOX	TRILLING	ASSEMBLE	EVERMORE	ONCOMING
NURSLING	RAMBLING	SMOLLETT	TRILLION	ASSEMBLY	EXHUMATE	OPTIMATE
OBSOLETE	RANELAGH	SMOULDER	TRILLIUM	ASSUMING	FILAMENT	OPTIMISM
OEILLADE	RATTLING	SNOWLINE	TRIPLING	AUTOMATE	FISHMEAL	OPTIMIST
OENOLOGY	RECKLESS	SOCALLED	TROLLOPE	AUTUMNAL	FLATMATE	ORNAMENT
OILCLOTH	REDOLENT	SODALITE	TROTLINE	BAHAMIAN	FLUMMERY	ORPIMENT
OILSLICK	REEDLING	SODALITY	TUBELESS	BAILMENT	FOREMILK	OUTSMART
ONCOLOGY	REGULATE	SOULLESS	TUTELAGE	BASEMENT	FOREMOST	OVERMUCH
ONTOLOGY	RESOLUTE	SPELLING	TUTELARY	BEAUMONT	FRAGMENT	PALIMONY
OSCULATE	RESOLVED	SPELLMAN	TWIRLING	BECOMING	GANYMEDE	PARAMOUR
OUTCLASS	RESTLESS	SPILLAGE	TYROLEAN	BEHEMOTH	GARAMOND	PASHMINA
OUTFLANK	REVELLER	SPILLWAY	UNDULANT	BIGAMIST	GLEAMING	PAVEMENT
OVERLAID	REVOLVER	SPOILAGE	UNDULATE	BIGAMOUS	GLOAMING	PEARMAIN
OVERLAND	RIBALDRY	SPOILING	UNFILLED	BINOMIAL	GLOOMILY	PEDIMENT
OVERLEAF	RIESLING	SPOTLESS	UNGULATE	BLOOMERS	GOBSMACK	PELLMELL
OVERLOAD	RIPPLING	SPYGLASS	UNSALTED	BLOOMING	GOLDMINE	PENUMBRA
OVERLOOK	RIVALISE	STABLING	UNSOLVED	BOHEMIAN	GOURMAND	PHARMACY
OVERLORD	ROOFLESS	STALLION	UNTILLED	BOOKMARK	GROOMING	PHORMIUM
PABULOUS	ROOTLESS	STARLESS	UPHOLDER	BRIMMING	GUNSMITH	PICKMEUP
PADDLING	ROSALIND	STARLING	URSULINE	CALAMINE	HALFMAST	PLAYMATE
PAINLESS	ROSALINE	STEALING	VENALITY	CALAMITY	HALLMARK	POCKMARK
PANELING	ROYALIST	STEALTHY	VEXILLUM	CAMOMILE	HANDMADE	POLYMATH
PANELLED	RUMBLING	STELLATE	VIGILANT	CASEMATE	HANDMAID	POSTMARK
PANGLOSS	RUSTLESS	STERLING	VIRILITY	CASEMENT	HEADMARK	POTEMKIN
PAPILLON	RUSTLING	STIFLING	VIROLOGY	CASHMERE	HEADMOST	PREAMBLE
PARALLAX	RUTHLESS	STIRLING	VIRULENT	CATAMITE	HEGEMONY	PSALMIST
PARALLEL	SADDLERY	STROLLER	VISELIKE	CATSMEAT	HELPMATE	PSALMODY
PARALYZE	SADDLING	SUBTLETY	VITALISM	CERAMICS	HINDMOST	PYRAMIDS
PARKLAND	SALTLICK	SUCHLIKE	VITALITY	CEREMENT	HOMEMADE	QUAGMIRE
PAROLLES	SANGLIER	SUCKLING	VITALIZE	CEREMONY	IGNOMINY	REARMOST
PATELLAR	SCALLION	SUNGLASS	VITELLUS	CHARMING	ILLUMINE	REGIMENT
PATULOUS	SCHILLER	SUPPLANT	VITILIGO	CHIPMUNK	INASMUCH	REMEMBER
PAVILION	SCOTLAND	SUPPLIER	VOCALIST	CHROMITE	INCOMING	RESEMBLE
PEARLING	SCOWLING	SUPPLIES	VOCALIZE	CHROMIUM	INFAMOUS	ROOMMATE
PECULATE	SCULLERY	SURPLICE	VOLPLANE	CHUMMAGE	INHUMANE	ROSAMOND
PECULIAR	SCULLION	SWELLING	VOWELIZE	CLAIMANT	INSOMNIA	ROSEMARY
PEDDLING	SEAFLOOR	SWILLING	WAMBLING	CLAYMORE	INTIMACY	RUDIMENT
PEERLESS	SEAMLESS	SWIRLING	WARPLANE	COALMINE	INTIMATE	RUSHMORE

SCHEMING	ANTENNAE	COZINESS	FEMINISM	INSANITY	NICKNACK	ROMANCER
SCHUMANN	APPANAGE	CROONING	FEMINIST	INTENDED	NICKNAME	ROMANIAN
SCRAMBLE	APPENDIX	CROWNING	FEMINITY	INTENTLY	NIJINSKY	ROMANSCH
SEDIMENT	ARDENNES	CULINARY	FILENAME	INVENTED	NOMINATE	ROMANTIC
SELFMADE	ARDENTLY	CURTNESS	FIRMNESS	INVENTOR	NUMBNESS	ROSINESS
SHIPMATE	ARGININE	CUTENESS	FLANNELS	IOLANTHE	NUMINOUS	ROTENONE
SHIPMENT	ARGONAUT	CYLINDER	FLOUNCED	ISLANDER	OCTONARY	RUDENESS
SKIRMISH	ARKANSAS	CYRENIAC	FLOUNDER	ISTANBUL	OFFENDED	RUMINANT
SLUMMING	ARMENIAN	DAMPNESS	FLUENTLY	JAPANESE	OFFENDER	RUMINATE
SOLEMNLY	ARRANGER	DANKNESS	FONDNESS	JAPONICA	OILINESS	SAGENESS
SQUAMATA	ARSONIST	DARKNESS	FOOTNOTE	JOHANNES	OLEANDER	SALINGER
SQUAMOUS	ASTONISH	DEAFNESS	FORENAME	JOKINGLY	OPENNESS	SALINITY
STIGMATA	ATHANASY	DEBONAIR	FORENOON	JUSTNESS	OPPONENT	SALTNESS
STORMING	ATHENIAN	DECANTER	FORENSIC	JUVENILE	ORDINAND	SAMENESS
STORMONT	ATLANTIC	DECENTLY	FOULNESS	KEENNESS	ORDINARY	SAPONITE
STRUMPET	ATLANTIS	DEEPNESS	FRIENDLY	KINDNESS	ORDINATE	SAVANNAH
SUDAMENT	ATTENDER	DEFENDER	FULLNESS	KOLINSKY	ORGANDIE	SAYONARA
SUDAMINA	AUTONOMY	DEFINITE	FURUNCLE	LACINATE	ORGANISM	SCANNING
SWARMING	BADINAGE	DEFTNESS	GABONESE	LACONIAN	ORGANIST	SCIENCES
SWIMMING	BALANCED	DEMENTED	GAMENESS	LAMENESS	ORGANIZE	SCORNFUL
SYCAMORE	BALDNESS	DEMENTIA	GAZUNDER	LAMENTED	ORIENTAL	SECONDER
TEAMMATE	BALINESE	DEMONIAC	GEMINATE	LAMINATE	PAGANINI	SECONDLY
TEGUMENT	BANKNOTE	DERANGED	GERANIUM	LATENESS	PAGINATE	SEIGNIOR
TELEMARK	BARENESS	DETONATE	GERONIMO	LATINIST	PALENESS	SELENITE
TENEMENT	BARONESS	DEVONIAN	GIGANTIC	LAVENDER	PALINODE	SELENIUM
THIAMINE	BARONETS	DIAGNOSE	GIRONDIN	LAVENGRO	PARANOIA	SEMINARY
THROMBIN	BARONIAL	DIMINISH	GLADNESS	LAZINESS	PARANOID	SERENADE
THROMBUS	BASENESS	DISINTER	GLASNOST	LEARNING	PARENTAL	SERENATA
TIDEMARK	BASINFUL	DISUNION	GOODNESS	LEBANESE	PATENTED	SERENELY
TINSMITH	BEGINNER	DISUNITE	GRAINING	LEMONADE	PATENTEE	SERENITY
TIRAMISU	BENENDEN	DISUNITY	GREENBAG	LEWDNESS	PATENTLY	SHRUNKEN
TRIMMING	BIANNUAL	DIVINITY	GREENERY	LICENSED	PEDANTIC	SICKNESS
TUPAMARO	BICONVEX	DOMINANT	GREENFLY	LICENSEE	PEDANTRY	SILENCER
ULTIMATE	BIENNIAL	DOMINATE	GREENING	LIKENESS	PEDUNCLE	SILENTLY
UNCOMBED	BLUENOSE	DOMINEER	GREENISH	LILONGWE	PEIGNOIR	SIMONIAC
UNCOMMON	BOLDNESS	DOMINION	GREENOCK	LIMONITE	PEKINESE	SIRENIAN
UNTIMELY	BOOTNECK	DOMINOES	GRIMNESS	LIMPNESS	PENKNIFE	SLIMNESS
UPCOMING	BOTANIST	DRAINAGE	GROUNDED	LOUDNESS	PERTNESS	SLOWNESS
VEHEMENT	BROWNING	DRAINING	GUERNSEY	LOVINGLY	PETANQUE	SMUGNESS
VENOMOUS	BROWNISH	DROWNING	GUIANIAN	LUMINARY	PEVENSEY	SOFTNESS
VESTMENT	BUSINESS	DUBONNET	GUYANESE	LUMINOUS	PIRANESI	SOLENOID
VIREMENT	CAGINESS	DULLNESS	HABANERA	LUSHNESS	PLANNING	SORENESS
VITAMINS	CALENDAR	DUMBNESS	HANGNAIL	LUTENIST	PLEONASM	SOURNESS
WINDMILL	CALENDER	EASINESS	HARANGUE	LYSANDER	POIGNANT	SPANNING
WORKMATE	CALMNESS	ECHINATE	HARDNESS	MALINGER	POLONIUM	SPAWNING
YOSEMITE	CANONESS	ECHINOPS	HAZINESS	MARINADE	POMANDER	SPHENOID
ABSENTEE	CANONIZE	EERINESS	HEDONISM	MARINATE	POORNESS	SPINNING
ABSINTHE	CASANOVA	ELSINORE	HEDONIST	MARONITE	POPINJAY	SPLENDID
ACCENTED	CELANESE	EMMANUEL	HIGHNESS	MCKINLEY	PREGNANT	SPLENDOR
ACCENTOR	CEMENTUM	ENDANGER	HOLINESS	MEANNESS	PRIMNESS	SPLINTER
ACTINIDE	CHAINSAW	ENGENDER	HUMANELY	MEEKNESS	PUDENDUM	SPOONFUL
ACTINIUM	CLANNISH	ENGINEER	HUMANISM	MELANITE	PYRENEES	SPRINGER
ADDENDUM	CLEANERS	ENKINDLE	HUMANIST	MELANOMA	QUAINTLY	SPRINKLE
ADMONISH	CLEANING	ENTANGLE	HUMANITY	MENANDER	RACINESS	SPRINTER
ADVANCED	CLEANSED	ESSONITE	HUMANIZE	MERINGUE	RANKNESS	SPRYNESS
ADVANCER	CLEANSER	ESTANCIA	IDLENESS	METONYMY	RASHNESS	SPURNING
AERONAUT	CLOWNISH	ESTONIAN	ILLINOIS	MILANESE	RAVENOUS	SQUANDER
AFFINITY	COLANDER	ETERNITY	IMMANENT	MILDNESS	RECENTLY	STAGNANT
AGRONOMY	COLDNESS	EUGENICS	IMMANUEL	MOMENTUM	REFINERY	STAGNATE
AIRINESS	COLONIAL	EVENNESS	IMMINENT	MONANDRY	REIGNING	STANNARY
ALBANIAN	COLONIST	EXPANDED	IMMUNITY	MOURNFUL	REKINDLE	STANNITE
ALBINONI	COLONIZE	EXPENDED	IMMUNIZE	MOURNING	REMINDER	STEENBOK
ALIENATE	COOLNESS	EXPENSES	IMPUNITY	MUCHNESS	RESINOUS	STEINWAY
ALIENISM	CORONARY	EXPONENT	INCENSED	MUTINEER	RESONANT	STRANDED
ALIENIST	CORONOID	EXTENDED	INDENTED	MUTINOUS	RESONATE	STRANGER
ALPINIST	CORUNDUM	EXTENSOR	INFANTRY	NEARNESS	REVANCHE	STRANGLE
AMMONIAC	COSINESS	FAIRNESS	INFINITE	NEATNESS	RICHNESS	STRENGTH
AMMONITE	COVENANT	FASTNESS	INFINITY	NEPENTHE	RIPENESS	STRINGED
AMMONOID	COVENTRY	FEMININE	INSANELY	NICENESS	ROBINSON	STRINGER

STRONGLY	ANACONDA	DIATONIC	GUNPOINT	MYOSOTIS	PULLOVER	UNCLOVEN
STUNNING	ANALOGUE	DIPLOMAT	HALLOWED	NARCOSES	PUSHOVER	UNCOOKED
SUDANESE	ANATOLIA	DISCOLOR	HANDOVER	NARCOSIS	QUATORZE	UNIPOLAR
SURENESS	ANATOMIC	DISCOUNT	HANGOVER	NARCOTIC	QUIXOTIC	UNSPOILT
SYRINGES	ANCHORET	DISCOVER	HARMONIC	NARROWLY	RAISONNÉ	UNSPOKEN
TALENTED	APOLOGIA	DISGORGE	HENHOUSE	NATIONAL	RANDOMLY	VARIORUM
TAMANDUA	APOLOGUE	DISHONOR	HICCOUGH	NECROSIS	RATIONAL	VERMOUTH
TAMENESS	APPROACH	DISLODGE	HIDROSIS	NEPIONIC	REASONED	VICTORIA
TAPENADE	APPROVAL	DISLOYAL	HISTORIC	NEUROSIS	RECKONER	VISCOUNT
TARTNESS	APPROVED	DISMOUNT	HOLLOWAY	NEUROTIC	REGIONAL	WAGGONER
TAUTNESS	ASPHODEL	DISPOSAL	HORMONAL	NEWCOMER	REPROACH	WALKOVER
TAXONOMY	BALLOCKS	DISPOSED	HOTHOUSE	NEWFOUND	RESPONSE	WARHORSE
THINNESS	BALMORAL	DISSOLVE	HYDROGEN	NICHOLAS	RESTORER	WAXWORKS
THINNING	BARDOLPH	DJIBOUTI	HYDROXYL	NITROGEN	REYNOLDS	WEAPONRY
THRENODY	BEDCOVER	DOCTORAL	HYPNOSIS	NOTIONAL	RHETORIC	YOGHOURT
TIDINESS	BESPOKEN	DOCTORED	HYPNOTIC	NUTHOUSE	RISSOLES	ZIRCONIA
TITANESS	BESTOWER	DOGHOUSE	ICEHOUSE	OFFCOLOR	SARDONIC	ZOONOSIS
TITANISM	BIGNONIA	DOGTOOTH	IMPROPER	OLDWORLD	SARDONYX	ABRUPTLY
TITANITE	BOLLOCKS	DORMOUSE	IMPROVED	ONLOOKER	SAUROPOD	ACCEPTED
TITANIUM	BONHOMIE	DRACONIC	IMPROVER	OOPHORON	SAWBONES	ACCEPTOR
TOMENTUM	BORROWED	DRAGOONS	INCHOATE	OPTIONAL	SAWHORSE	AGITPROP
TRAINING	BORROWER	DRYGOODS	INGROWTH	ORATORIO	SCHMOOZE	AIRSPEED
TRIANGLE	BOSWORTH	DUMFOUND	ISOGONAL	ORTHODOX	SCHOONER	ALLOPATH
TRIMNESS	BOTTOMRY	ECONOMIC	JAMBOREE	OUTBOARD	SCIROCCO	ALLSPICE
TRIUNITY	BOUZOUKI	ELKHOUND	JEALOUSY	OUTDOORS	SEABOARD	ANTEPOST
TROUNCER	BURROWER	EMPLOYED	JINGOISM	OUTGOING	SEABORNE	ANTIPHON
TRUENESS	BUTTOCKS	EMPLOYEE	JINGOIST	OUTHOUSE	SEAFORTH	ANTIPOPE
TRUNNION	CABOODLE	EMPLOYER	JORROCKS	OUTMODED	SEAGOING	BACKPACK
TUBENOSE	CAMBODIA	ENCLOSED	KEYBOARD	OXYMORON	SEASONAL	BALLPARK
TURANDOT	CANOODLE	ENCLOTHE	KOMSOMOL	OXYTOCIN	SEASONED	BEANPOLE
UGLINESS	CANTORIS	ENCROACH	KYPHOSIS	PANDOWDY	SELBORNE	BELLPUSH
UNHINGED	CARBOLIC	ENSCONCE	LACROSSE	PANGOLIN	SEMIOTIC	BLOWPIPE
UNIONISM	CARBONIC	EPILOGUE	LADRONES	PARDONER	SIGNORIA	BONSPIEL
UNIONIST	CASTOFFS	EPISODIC	LAWCOURT	PASSOVER	SINFONIA	BOWSPRIT
UNIONIZE	CATHOLIC	ESTROGEN	LEFTOVER	PASTORAL	SKIBOOTS	BRATPACK
UNKINDLY	CATHOUSE	ETHIOPIA	LINCOLNS	PATHOGEN	SLIPOVER	BROMPTON
UNMANNED	CHACONNE	EUPHONIA	LITTORAL	PECTORAL	SLYBOOTS	BUDAPEST
UNTANGLE	CHEROKEE	EUPHONIC	LONDONER	PERFORCE	SORBONNE	CALIPERS
UNWANTED	CLITORIS	EUPHORIA	LORDOSIS	PERIODIC	STAROSTA	CARAPACE
UNWONTED	COGNOMEN	EUPHORIC	LULWORTH	PERSONAL	STENOSED	CATAPULT
URBANITY	COLLOQUY	EUTROPHY	MADHOUSE	PHENOLIC	STENOSIS	CESSPOOL
URBANIZE	COMMONER	EUTROPIC	MADWOMAN	PHILOMEL	STOPOVER	CHAMPERS
URGENTLY	COMMONLY	EXPLODED	MAGNOLIA	PHOTOFIT	SUBPOENA	CHAMPION
VACANTLY	COMPOSED	EXPLORER	MAHJONGG	PHOTOPSY	SUBSONIC	CHOPPING
VALENCIA	COMPOSER	EYETOOTH	MALLORCA	PINPOINT	SUBTOPIA	CLAPPERS
VASTNESS	COMPOUND	FACTOTUM	MALVOLIO	PLATONIC	SUBTOTAL	CLAPPING
VERANDAH	CONCORDE	FALCONRY	MANDOLIN	PLYMOUTH	SUPPOSED	CLASPING
VERONESE	CONFOUND	FIBROSIS	MANGONEL	POISONER	SURMOUNT	CLIPPERS
VERONICA	CONSOMMÉ	FLAVORED	MANPOWER	PONSONBY	SURROUND	CLIPPING
VICINITY	CORDOVAN	FOGBOUND	MARJORAM	PORPOISE	SYMBOLIC	CLODPOLL
VILENESS	CORIOLIS	FOLLOWED	MARMOSET	POTBOUND	TAKEOVER	COALPORT
WARINESS	CORMORAN	FOLLOWER	MASTODON	POTHOLER	TAMWORTH	COLOPHON
WEAKNESS	CORPORAL	FOLLOWUP	MATRONLY	PREMOLAR	TANDOORI	CONSPIRE
WELLNIGH	CORRODED	FORMOSAN	MEDIOCRE	PRETORIA	TAPHOUSE	COTOPAXI
WIDENING	CRAMOISY	FORSOOTH	METEORIC	PRISONER	TARBOOSH	CRIPPLED
WILDNESS	CRETONNE	FOXHOUND	METHODIC	PROFORMA	TECTONIC	CRISPIAN
WILINESS	CULLODEN	FURLOUGH	MICRODOT	PROFOUND	TEETOTAL	CROUPIER
WOMANISH	CUPBOARD	FURROWED	MIDPOINT	PROLOGUE	TEMPORAL	DECIPHER
WOMANIZE	CUSTOMER	GADZOOKS	MIGNONNE	PROMOTER	TEUTONIC	DIASPORA
YEARNING	CYANOGEN	GALLOPER	MIRRORED	PROPOLIS	THOROUGH	DOORPOST
ZAMINDAR	CYANOSIS	GALLOWAY	MISCOUNT	PROPOSAL	TITMOUSE	DOWNPLAY
AASVOGEL	CYCLOSIS	GARGOYLE	MISNOMER	PROPOSED	TOLBOOTH	DOWNPOUR
ADENOIDS	DAFFODIL	GARROTTE	MISSOURI	PROPOSER	TOPNOTCH	DRIPPING
AEGROTAT	DEFLOWER	GASWORKS	MNEMONIC	PROPOUND	TORTOISE	DROOPING
AIRBORNE	DESPOTIC	GIACONDA	MONGOLIA	PROROGUE	TOULOUSE	DROPPING
ALEHOUSE	DIABOLIC	GIOCONDA	MONGOOSE	PROTOCOL	TURBOJET	ELLIPSIS
ALTHOUGH	DIAGONAL	GLYCOGEN	MONMOUTH	PROTOZOA	TURKOMAN	ELLIPTIC
ALVEOLUS	DIALOGUE	GOLGOTHA	MONROVIA	PTEROPOD	TURNOVER	EOHIPPUS
AMBROSIA	DIAMONDS	GUMMOSIS	MOREOVER	PUGNOSED	UNBROKEN	EQUIPAGE

ESCAPADE	PROMPTER	ZOOSPERM	BALLROOM	COVERING	ENTIRETY	IGNORANT
ESCAPISM	PROMPTLY	ZOOSPORE	BANKROLL	COVERLET	ENVIRONS	IMMERSED
ESCAPIST	PROSPECT	HENEQUEN	BANKRUPT	COWARDLY	EPIGRAPH	IMMORTAL
ESTOPPEL	PROSPERO	MAROQUIN	BATHROBE	CUCURBIT	ESCARGOT	IMPERIAL
EUPEPSIA	REAPPEAR	PARAQUAT	BATHROOM	CUTPRICE	ESCORIAL	IMPORTER
EUROPEAN	RECEPTOR	RAMEQUIN	BAUDRICK	DANDRUFF	ETHEREAL	IMPURIFY
EUROPIUM	REDEPLOY	TRANQUIL	BAVARIAN	DARKROOM	ETHERIFY	IMPURITY
EXEMPLAR	REEMPLOY	ABERRANT	BEETROOT	DAYBREAK	ETHERISE	INDIRECT
FILIPINO	ROLYPOLY	ABNORMAL	BEGORRAH	DAYDREAM	ETRURIAN	INFERIOR
FISHPOND	SCHAPSKA	ABSORBED	BELGRADE	DECORATE	EXECRATE	INFERNAL
FLAGPOLE	SCORPION	ABSORBER	BERTRAND	DECOROUS	EXOCRINE	INFORMAL
FLAPPING	SCORPIUS	ABSTRACT	BESTRIDE	DEFORMED	EXOERGIC	INFORMED
FLATPICK	SCRAPPLE	ABSTRUSE	BEVERAGE	DELIRIUM	EXPORTER	INFORMER
FLIPPANT	SCRIPTUM	ABSURDLY	BIGARADE	DEMERARA	EXTERIOR	INHERENT
FLIPPERS	SCRUPLES	ACCURACY	BIOGRAPH	DEMERSAL	EXTERNAL	INSCRIBE
FLIPPING	SCULPTOR	ACCURATE	BLURRING	DEMURELY	EXTERNAT	INSTRUCT
FOOTPATH	SELFPITY	ACCURSED	BOOKROOM	DEMURRAL	FAVORITE	INTERACT
FOURPART	SERAPHIC	ADHERENT	BULLRING	DENARIUS	FEDERACY	INTERCOM
FREEPOST	SERAPHIM	ADMIRING	BURGRAVE	DENDRITE	FEDERATE	INTEREST
FRIPPERY	SHEEPDOG	AFFERENT	BUTTRESS	DENDROID	FEVERFEW	INTERIOR
FRUMPISH	SHEEPISH	AGRARIAN	CABERNET	DEPARTED	FEVERISH	INTERMIT
FULLPAGE	SHIPPING	AIRBRAKE	CALCRETE	DEPORTEE	FIGURINE	INTERNAL
GATEPOST	SHOPPING	AIRCRAFT	CAMARGUE	DESCRIBE	FILARIUM	INTERNEE
GLUMPISH	SHRAPNEL	ALACRITY	CAMBRIAN	DESERTED	FILTRATE	INTERNET
GOALPOST	SIGNPOST	ALBERICH	CAMEROON	DESERTER	FLAGRANT	INTERPOL
GRASPING	SINAPISM	ALBURNUM	CANARIES	DESERVED	FLOORING	INTERVAL
GRIPPING	SISYPHUS	ALDERMAN	CAPERING	DESIROUS	FLOURISH	INVERTED
GROUPING	SKIPPING	ALDERNEY	CASTRATE	DESTRUCT	FLUORIDE	INVERTER
GRUMPILY	SLEEPERS	ALGERIAN	CASTRATO	DETHRONE	FLUORINE	INWARDLY
HELIPORT	SLEEPILY	ALGERINE	CATARACT	DEXTROSE	FLUORITE	IVOIRIEN
HEMIPODE	SLEEPING	ALGORISM	CATERING	DEXTROUS	FLYDRIVE	JEFFREYS
HOMEPAGE	SLIPPERS	ALLERGEN	CELERIAC	DIARRHEA	FOOTREST	JIMCRACK
HORNPIPE	SLIPPERY	ALLERGIC	CELERITY	DIATRIBE	FORTRESS	KOHLRABI
HORNPOUT	SLIPPING	ALLURING	CENTRIST	DIFFRACT	FRAGRANT	LABURNUM
HOSEPIPE	SLOPPILY	AMPERAGE	CENTRODE	DISARRAY	FUMAROLE	LACERATE
INEXPERT	SLOWPOKE	ANACREON	CHAIRMAN	DISCREET	FUNERARY	LANDRACE
JODHPURS	SNAPPILY	ANDERSON	CHEERFUL	DISCRETE	FUNEREAL	LATERITE
KINGPOST	SOURPUSS	ANDORRAN	CHEERILY	DISGRACE	FUSAROLE	LECTRICE
LAMPPOST	STAMPEDE	ANEURYSM	CHEERING	DISORDER	FUTURISM	LEVERAGE
MEGAPODE	STEAPSIN	ANSERINE	CHLORATE	DISPROVE	FUTURIST	LIBERATE
METAPHOR	STOPPAGE	ANTERIOR	CHLORIDE	DISTRACT	GABORONE	LIBERIAN
MILLPOND	STOPPING	ANTEROOM	CHLORINE	DISTRAIN	GADARENE	LICORICE
MIREPOIX	STRAPPED	APHORISM	CHOIRBOY	DISTRAIT	GANGRENE	LIMERICK
MISAPPLY	STRAPPER	APIARIST	CIBORIUM	DISTRESS	GASTRULA	LITERACY
MISSPELL	STRIPPED	APPARENT	CICERONE	DISTRICT	GENERATE	LITERARY
MISSPENT	STRIPPER	AQUARIUM	CINERAMA	DISTRUST	GENEROUS	LITERATE
MONOPOLE	SWEEPING	AQUARIUS	CINEREAL	DIVORCED	GENTRIFY	LITERATI
MONOPOLY	SYNOPSIS	ARBOREAL	CLEARCUT	DIVORCEE	GERTRUDE	LIVERIED
MOREPORK	SYNOPTIC	ARMORIAL	CLEARING	DOCTRINE	GIMCRACK	LIVERISH
NENUPHAR	TAILPIPE	ARMORICA	CLEARWAY	DOLDRUMS	GLABROUS	LOWERING
NEWSPEAK	TEASPOON	ARTERIAL	COATRACK	DOLOROUS	GOVERNOR	LUPERCAL
NINEPINS	THESPIAN	ASCORBIC	COHERENT	DREARILY	GUJARATI	LUSTRINE
OCCUPANT	THOMPSON	ASPERGES	COLORADO	ECOFREAK	HAMARTIA	LUSTROUS
OCCUPIED	THUMPING	ASPERITY	COLORANT	EFFERENT	HANDRAIL	LYSERGIC
OCCUPIER	TRAPPIST	ASPERMIA	COLORFUL	ELDORADO	HEADREST	MACARONI
OEDIPEAN	TRESPASS	ASPIRANT	COLORING	EMIGRANT	HEADROOM	MACAROON
OENOPHIL	TROOPING	ASPIRATE	COMPRESS	EMIGRATE	HIBERNIA	MACERATE
OLYMPIAD	TRUMPERY	ASPIRING	COMPRISE	EMPORIUM	HIGHRISE	MAHARAJA
OLYMPIAN	TURNPIKE	ASSORTED	CONCRETE	EMPYREAL	HIGHROAD	MAHARANI
OLYMPICS	UNTAPPED	ASSYRIAN	CONFRONT	EMPYREAN	HILARITY	MAJORITY
OPENPLAN	WELLPAID	ASTERISK	CONGRATS	ENCIRCLE	HOLYROOD	MALARIAL
OVERPASS	WHIPPING	ASTEROID	CONGRESS	ENDURING	HONORARY	MALARKEY
OVERPLAY	WHOOPING	ATHEROMA	CONTRACT	ENLARGED	HOVERFLY	MALGRADO
PASSPORT	WHOPPING	ATTORNEY	CONTRARY	ENLARGER	HUMORIST	MALTREAT
PERIPETY	WINDPIPE	AUSTRIAN	CONTRAST	ENSHRINE	HUMOROUS	MANDRAKE
PERSPIRE	WOOLPACK	AUTARCHY	CONTRITE	ENSHROUD	HUNDREDS	MANDRILL
POSTPAID	WRAPPING	BACKROOM	CONTRIVE	ENTHRALL	HUNGRILY	MANGROVE
POSTPONE	XENOPHON	BACTRIAN	CONTROLS	ENTHRONE	HUNTRESS	MANORIAL
PRIAPISM	XERAPHIM	BALDRICK	COVERAGE	ENTIRELY	HYPERION	MARGRAVE

MATERIAL	OVERRIDE	RYEGRASS	TAMARACK	VIGOROUS	BANISTER	DOWNSIDE
MATERNAL	OVERRIPE	SALARIED	TAMARIND	VIPERISH	BEARSKIN	DOWNSIZE
MATTRESS	OVERRULE	SALEROOM	TAMARISK	VIPEROUS	BICUSPID	DRAGSTER
MATURATE	PALGRAVE	SAMARIUM	TAPERING	VIVARIUM	BIRDSEED	DRESSAGE
MATURITY	PANCREAS	SATIRIST	TARTRATE	WAITRESS	BLESSING	DRESSING
MAVERICK	PANORAMA	SATIRIZE	TAVERNER	WARDRESS	BLISSFUL	DROPSHOT
MAYORESS	PASTRAMI	SATURATE	TEMERITY	WARDROBE	BONDSMAN	DROWSILY
MAZARINE	PATERNAL	SATURDAY	THEORIST	WARDROOM	BOOKSHOP	DYNASTIC
MEMBRANE	PECORINO	SATURNIA	THEORIZE	WASHROOM	BRADSHAW	ECLOSION
MEMORIAL	PEDERAST	SCABROUS	TIBERIAS	WATERBUG	BRASSARD	EFFUSION
MEMORIAM	PEMBROKE	SCOURING	TIBERIUS	WATERING	BRASSICA	EFFUSIVE
MEMORIZE	PEPERONI	SEAFRONT	TIEBREAK	WATERLOO	BROWSING	EGOISTIC
MIDBRAIN	PETERLOO	SECURELY	TIMOROUS	WATERMAN	BRUISING	EMBOSSED
MILLRACE	PICAROON	SECURITY	TOLERANT	WATERSKI	BRUSSELS	EMERSION
MINORESS	PIECRUST	SENGREEN	TOLERATE	WATERWAY	BUCKSHEE	EMISSARY
MINORITE	PILGRIMS	SENORITA	TOMORROW	WAVERING	BUCKSHOT	EMISSION
MINORITY	PINPRICK	SEPARATE	TOVARICH	WAVERLEY	BUCKSKIN	EMULSIFY
MISERERE	PIPERINE	SEVERELY	TOWERING	WIZARDRY	CADASTRE	EMULSION
MISPRINT	PLAYROOM	SEVEREST	TRIGRAPH	WONDROUS	CALFSKIN	ENMESHED
MISTREAT	PLEURISY	SEVERITY	TUBERCLE	WOODRUFF	CAMISOLE	ENVISAGE
MISTRESS	PODARGUS	SEWERAGE	TUBEROSE	WORKROOM	CAMPSITE	ENVISION
MISTRUST	POLARIZE	SHADRACH	TUBEROUS	ZASTRUGA	CANISTER	EPHESIAN
MODERATE	POLTROON	SHAGREEN	TUTORIAL	ZOETROPE	CERASTES	ERIKSSON
MODERATO	POOLROOM	SHAMROCK	ULCERATE	ABBASIDE	CHASSEUR	ETRUSCAN
MONARCHY	PORTRAIT	SHEARMAN	ULCEROUS	ABESSIVE	CHESSMAN	EURASIAN
MONDRIAN	POWERFUL	SHOWROOM	ULTERIOR	ABRASION	CHESSMEN	EUROSTAR
MONORAIL	PRAIRIAL	SIBERIAN	UNBURDEN	ABRASIVE	CHIASMUS	EVENSONG
MOTORCAR	PRIMROSE	SICKROOM	UNCARING	ACCUSING	CHOOSING	EXCISION
MOTORING	PRIORESS	SIDEREAL	UNCURBED	ACCUSTOM	CHRISTEN	EXPOSURE
MOTORIST	PRIORITY	SIDERITE	UNDERAGE	ACOUSTIC	CHRISTIE	FAMISHED
MOTORIZE	PRODROME	SILURIAN	UNDERARM	ACROSTIC	CHRISTOM	FEARSOME
MOTORMAN	PROGRADE	SLURRING	UNDERBID	ADESSIVE	CICISBEO	FELDSPAR
MOTORWAY	PROGRESS	SNEERING	UNDERCUT	ADHESION	CLANSMAN	FENESTRA
MUHARRAM	PROTRUDE	SOBERING	UNDERDOG	ADHESIVE	CLASSICS	FINESPUN
MUSHROOM	PYORRHEA	SOLARIUM	UNDERFED	ADJUSTER	CLASSIFY	FINISHED
NATURISM	QUADRANT	SOMBRELY	UNDERFUR	ADJUSTOR	CLOISTER	FINISHER
NATURIST	QUADRATE	SOMBRERO	UNDERLAY	ADVISORY	CLUMSILY	FIRESIDE
NAVARINO	QUADRIGA	SOMERSET	UNDERLIE	AEROSTAT	COARSELY	FIRESTEP
NAZARENE	QUADROON	SONOROUS	UNDERPIN	AFFUSION	COHESION	FLAGSHIP
NEPHRITE	QUATRAIN	SORORITY	UNDERRUN	AGNOSTIC	COHESIVE	FLAXSEED
NEUTRINO	RACKRENT	SPARRING	UNDERSEA	ALCESTIS	COLESLAW	FLEISHIG
NEWSREEL	RAILROAD	SQUARELY	UNDERTOW	ALLUSION	COLISEUM	FLIMSILY
NEWSROOM	RECORDER	SQUIRREL	UNEARNED	ALLUSIVE	COLOSSAL	FOLKSONG
NIGERIAN	REDBRICK	STAIRWAY	UNERRING	AMBUSHED	COLOSSUS	FOOLSCAP
NIGERIEN	REDIRECT	STEERAGE	UNFORCED	ANCESTOR	CREOSOTE	FOOTSORE
NOMARCHY	REFERRAL	STEERING	UNHARMED	ANCESTRY	CROSSBAR	FOOTSTEP
NOSTRILS	REFORMED	STIRRING	UNHEROIC	APPOSITE	CROSSING	FORESAIL
NOSTROMO	REFORMER	SUBTRACT	UNMARKED	ARGESTES	CROSSLET	FORESHIP
NOTARIAL	REPARTEE	SUBURBAN	UNNERVED	ARRESTED	CYNOSURE	FORESKIN
NUMERACY	REPHRASE	SUBURBIA	UNPERSON	ARRESTER	CYTOSINE	FORESTAY
NUMERALS	REPORTED	SUDARIUM	UNTHREAD	ARTESIAN	DAMASCUS	FORESTER
NUMERATE	REPORTER	SUFFRAGE	UNVARIED	ARTISTIC	DECISION	FORESTRY
NUMEROUS	RESERVED	SUMERIAN	UNVERSED	ARTISTRY	DECISIVE	FOURSOME
OBDURACY	RESTRAIN	SUNCREAM	UNWORTHY	ASBESTOS	DEERSKIN	FUCHSITE
OBDURATE	RESTRICT	SUNDRIED	UPMARKET	ASSASSIN	DELUSION	FULLSIZE
OBSERVED	RESTROOM	SUNDRIES	UPPERCUT	ASSESSOR	DEMISTER	GALOSHES
OBSERVER	RETARDED	SUPERBLY	UPSTREAM	ATTESTOR	DERISION	GANGSTER
OBSTRUCT	RETIRING	SUPERBUG	UPTURNED	AUBUSSON	DERISIVE	GANISTER
OCTAROON	REVEREND	SUPERIOR	USUFRUCT	AUCASSIN	DERISORY	GARISHLY
OFFBREAK	REVERENT	SUPERMAN	VAGARIES	AUGUSTUS	DINOSAUR	GELASTIC
OFFERING	REVERSAL	SUPERNAL	VALERIAN	AUTISTIC	DISASTER	GIRASOLE
OFFPRINT	REVERSED	SUPERTAX	VANBRUGH	AVERSION	DIVISION	GLADSOME
OMDURMAN	RIFFRAFF	SUPPRESS	VAPORIZE	AVULSION	DIVISIVE	GLASSFUL
ONETRACK	RIGOROUS	SURPRISE	VAPOROUS	BABUSHKA	DOCKSIDE	GLASSFUL
ONSCREEN	RIPARIAN	SUZERAIN	VENERATE	BACKSIDE	DOMESDAY	GLEESOME
ORDERING	RIVERAIN	SWEARING	VENEREAL	BACKSPIN	DOMESTIC	GLISSADE
OSTERLEY	RIVERINE	SYBARITE	VIBURNUM	BACKSTOP	DOOMSDAY	GLOSSARY
OUTBREAK	RODERICK	SYNDROME	VICARAGE	BALUSTER	DOORSILL	GLOSSEME
OVERRATE	ROSEROOT	TAFFRAIL	VICARIAL	BANDSMAN	DOORSTEP	GOODSIRE

GRUESOME	MACASSAR	QUAESTOR	THURSDAY	ANNOTATE	COCKTAIL	ERGOTISM
GYROSTAT	MAGISTER	QUAYSIDE	TICKSEED	APERTURE	COGITATE	ERUCTATE
HANDSOME	MAILSHOT	REASSERT	TIRESIAS	APOSTASY	COMATOSE	ERUPTION
HARASSED	MAINSAIL	REASSESS	TIRESOME	APOSTATE	CONSTANT	ERUPTURE
HARDSHIP	MAINSTAY	REASSIGN	TOILSOME	APOSTLES	CONSTRUE	ETCETERA
HARUSPEX	MAJESTIC	REASSUME	TOWNSHIP	APPETITE	COUNTESS	EVENTFUL
HEADSHIP	MARASMUS	REASSURE	TOWNSMAN	APTITUDE	COUNTIES	EVENTIDE
HEATSPOT	MARKSMAN	RECESSED	TRANSACT	AQUATINT	COUNTING	EVENTUAL
HELMSMAN	MENISCUS	RECUSANT	TRANSECT	ARMATURE	COURTESY	EVICTION
HERDSMAN	MERISTEM	REDESIGN	TRANSEPT	ASTATINE	COVETOUS	EXACTING
HIBISCUS	MINISTER	REEDSMAN	TRANSFER	ASTUTELY	COYSTRIL	EXACTION
HILLSIDE	MINISTRY	REGISTER	TRANSFIX	ATHETISE	CRAFTILY	EXCITING
HOARSELY	MODESTLY	REGISTRY	TRANSHIP	ATHETOID	CREATION	EXERTION
HOLISTIC	MOLASSES	REINSURE	TRANSKEI	ATTITUDE	CREATIVE	EXISTENT
HOMESICK	MOLESKIN	RESISTOR	TRANSMIT	AUDITION	CREATURE	EXISTING
HOMESPUN	MOLESTER	REVISION	TREASURE	AUDITORY	CROATIAN	EXULTANT
HONESTLY	MONASTIC	RHAPSODY	TREASURY	AUTOTYPE	CRYSTALS	EXULTING
HUCKSTER	MORESQUE	RHEOSTAT	TRIASSIC	AVENTINE	CULOTTES	FAINTING
HUNTSMAN	MOROSELY	RICKSHAW	TROUSERS	AVIATION	CURATIVE	FATSTOCK
ILLUSION	MOUSSAKA	RINGSIDE	TUNGSTEN	BARATHEA	DAINTIES	FIGHTING
ILLUSIVE	NAGASAKI	ROADSHOW	TUNGSTIC	BARITONE	DAINTILY	FIRETRAP
ILLUSORY	NAMESAKE	ROADSIDE	TUNISIAN	BEAUTIFY	DAUNTING	FIXATION
IMPOSING	NONESUCH	ROADSTER	TURNSPIT	BEDSTEAD	DELETION	FIXATIVE
IMPOSTER	OBSESSED	ROBUSTLY	TYROSINE	BEDSTRAW	DEMOTION	FLATTERY
IMPOSTOR	OBTUSELY	ROUSSEAU	UNEASILY	BEGETTER	DENATURE	FLAUTIST
INCISION	OCCASION	RUCKSACK	UNFASTEN	BELITTLE	DEPUTIZE	FLEETING
INCISIVE	ODYSSEUS	SADISTIC	UNJUSTLY	BESOTTED	DEVOTION	FLIRTING
INDUSTRY	OLEASTER	SALESMAN	UNLISTED	BETATRON	DIANTHUS	FLOATING
INFESTED	OMISSION	SCANSION	UPRISING	BLASTOFF	DIASTASE	FORETELL
INFUSION	OPPOSING	SCISSION	UTENSILS	BLASTULA	DIASTOLE	FORKTAIL
INVASION	OPPOSITE	SCISSORS	VANISHED	BLUSTERY	DIGITIZE	FOUNTAIN
INVASIVE	OVERSEAS	SCOTSMAN	WAINSCOT	BOASTFUL	DILATION	FOURTEEN
INVESTOR	OVERSEER	SEALSKIN	WALLSEND	BOASTING	DILATORY	FRACTION
IRONSIDE	OVERSHOE	SEAMSTER	WARDSHIP	BOEOTIAN	DILUTION	FRACTURE
JEBUSITE	OVERSHOT	SEEDSMAN	WINDSOCK	BORSTALL	DIOPTRIC	FREETOWN
JOHNSONS	OVERSIZE	SELASSIE	WINGSPAN	BREATHER	DIPSTICK	FRICTION
JUMPSUIT	OVERSOLD	SELFSAME	WOODSHED	BRISTLED	DOGSTAIL	FRONTAGE
JURASSIC	OVERSTAY	SEMESTER	WOODSMAN	BRISTLES	DONATION	FRONTIER
JYAISTHA	OVERSTEP	SIDESHOW	WOOLSACK	BURNTOUT	DONATIST	FRONTMAN
KEEPSAKE	PAKISTAN	SIDESLIP	WORKSHOP	BURSTING	DOUBTFUL	FROSTILY
KEROSENE	PALISADE	SIDESMAN	YOURSELF	CABOTAGE	DOUBTING	FROSTING
KICKSHAW	PARASHAH	SIDESTEP	YUGOSLAV	CALOTYPE	DOVETAIL	FRUCTIFY
KINGSHIP	PARASITE	SILESIAN	ABATTOIR	CAMPTOWN	DOWNTOWN	FRUCTOSE
KINGSIZE	PARISIAN	SINGSONG	ABLATION	CAMSTONE	DOWNTURN	FRUITFUL
KINGSLEY	PAWNSHOP	SINISTER	ABLATIVE	CAPITALS	DRIFTING	FRUITING
KINGSTON	PEDESTAL	SLIPSHOD	ABLUTION	CAPSTONE	DRYSTONE	FRUITION
KNAPSACK	PEEPSHOW	SLIPSLOP	ABORTION	CAROTENE	DURATION	FUGITIVE
LADYSHIP	PERISHED	SNAPSHOT	ABORTIVE	CATATONY	DYNATRON	FULLTIME
LAKESIDE	PERISHER	SOAPSUDS	ACANTHUS	CAVATINA	EDENTATE	FUMITORY
LAMASERY	PHEASANT	SONGSTER	ACENTRIC	CEMETERY	EGYPTIAN	FUNCTION
LAMBSKIN	PILASTER	SPARSELY	ADDITION	CENOTAPH	EIGHTEEN	GAUNTLET
LANDSEER	PLAYSUIT	SPARSITY	ADDITIVE	CERATOID	EINSTEIN	GELATINE
LANDSLIP	PLEASANT	SPINSTER	ADJUTAGE	CHANTAGE	EJECTION	GENETICS
LARKSPUR	PLEASING	SPLASHER	ADJUTANT	CHANTREY	ELECTION	GENETRIX
LAVISHLY	PLEASURE	STAYSAIL	ADOPTION	CHARTISM	ELECTIVE	GENITALS
LEADSMAN	PLIMSOLL	STRESSED	ADOPTIVE	CHARTIST	ELECTORS	GENITIVE
LEINSTER	POLISHED	SWANSKIN	ADULTERY	CHARTRES	ELECTRIC	GIANTESS
LEWISITE	POLISHER	SWANSONG	AGNATION	CHASTISE	ELECTRON	GLOATING
LIFESPAN	POLLSTER	SWIMSUIT	AIRSTRIP	CHASTITY	ELECTRUM	GLUTTONY
LINESMAN	POLYSEME	TAILSKID	ALCATRAZ	CHATTELS	EMBATTLE	GREATEST
LOADSTAR	POLYSEMY	TAILSPIN	ALEATORY	CHEATERS	EMBITTER	GREETING
LODESTAR	POROSITY	TALISMAN	ALEUTIAN	CHEATING	ENTITLED	GROUTING
LOGISTIC	PRESSING	TAPESTRY	ALSATIAN	CHESTNUT	EPISTYLE	GUILTILY
LONESOME	PRESSMAN	TEAMSTER	ALTITUDE	CHILTERN	EQUATION	GUMPTION
LONGSHIP	PRESSURE	TENESMUS	AMBITION	CICATRIX	EQUITANT	GYRATION
LONGSTAY	PRIESTLY	THOUSAND	AMORTIZE	CITATION	ERECTILE	GYRATORY
LONGSTOP	PRUSSIAN	THRASHER	AMPUTATE	CLAPTRAP	ERECTING	HABITUAL
LORDSHIP	PUISSANT	THRESHER	AMRITSAR	COATTAIL	ERECTION	HALFTERM
LOVESICK	PUNISHED	THRUSTER	ANGSTROM	COAUTHOR	ERGOTISE	HALFTIME

HARDTACK	MANITOBA	POSITIVE	SCRATCHY	TELETHON	CALCULUS	GLOBULIN
HAUNTING	MARATHON	POSITRON	SCRUTINY	TELLTALE	CALCUTTA	GRADUATE
HAYSTACK	MARITIME	POTATOES	SEDATELY	TEMPTING	CAROUSAL	GRANULAR
HEARTIES	MEALTIME	POTSTONE	SEDATION	TERATOMA	CAROUSEL	GRANULES
HEARTILY	MEANTIME	POULTICE	SEDATIVE	THEATRIC	CELLULAR	GRATUITY
HEBETUDE	MEDITATE	PRACTICE	SEDITION	THIRTEEN	CHASUBLE	GUTTURAL
HECATOMB	MIGHTILY	PRACTISE	SEMITONE	THROTTLE	CHEQUERS	HERCULES
HEELTAPS	MILITANT	PRATTLER	SEROTYPE	TICKTACK	CHERUBIC	HINDUISM
HEPATICA	MILITARY	PRESTIGE	SHANTUNG	TICKTOCK	CHERUBIM	HONDURAN
HERITAGE	MILITATE	PRETTILY	SHIFTING	TIGHTWAD	CINGULUM	HONDURAS
HESITANT	MINATORY	PRINTING	SHIITAKE	TINCTURE	CIRCUITY	INCLUDED
HESITATE	MINOTAUR	PRINTOUT	SHOETREE	TIPSTAFF	CIRCULAR	INEQUITY
HIPSTERS	MINSTREL	PRISTINE	SHOOTING	TOGETHER	CLIQUISH	INFLUENT
HORATIAN	MINUTELY	PROSTATE	SHOOTOUT	TOMATOES	COLOURED	INIQUITY
HORATIUS	MINUTIAE	PSALTERY	SHOPTALK	TRACTION	COMMUNAL	INOCULUM
HORNTAIL	MOISTURE	PULITZER	SHORTAGE	TRAITORS	COMMUTER	INTRUDER
HOWITZER	MONETARY	PUNCTUAL	SHOUTING	TREATISE	COMPUTER	IROQUOIS
HYDATOID	MONETISE	PUNCTURE	SHUTTERS	TREETOPS	CONFUSED	JACQUARD
IDENTIFY	MONOTONY	PUNITIVE	SIGHTING	TRIPTANE	CONJUGAL	JALOUSIE
IDENTITY	MONOTYPE	PUTATIVE	SIGHTSEE	TRIPTYCH	CONJURER	JOYFULLY
IGNITION	MONSTERA	QUANTIFY	SILKTAIL	TRISTICH	CONJUROR	KENTUCKY
IMMATURE	MOUNTAIN	QUANTITY	SKIRTING	TRISTRAM	CONQUEST	LABOURED
IMPETIGO	MOUNTING	QUARTERS	SKITTISH	TROTTERS	CONSULAR	LABOURER
IMPOTENT	MUDSTONE	QUARTIER	SKITTLES	TROTTOIR	CONSUMED	LANGUAGE
INACTION	MULETEER	QUARTILE	SLANTING	TRUSTFUL	CONSUMER	LANGUISH
INACTIVE	MUTATION	QUESTION	SLATTERN	TRUSTING	CONVULSE	LAROUSSE
INKSTAIN	NEGATION	QUIETUDE	SLUTTISH	TUSITALA	CORDUROY	LAWFULLY
INVITING	NEGATIVE	QUILTING	SMARTEST	TWISTING	CULTURAL	LECTURER
IRRITANT	NEMATODE	QUINTAIN	SMELTING	UNBUTTON	CULTURED	LECTURES
IRRITATE	NEMATOID	RAGSTONE	SMOOTHER	UNFETTER	CUTPURSE	LEISURED
ISOSTASY	NEPOTISM	REACTION	SMOOTHLY	UNSETTLE	DAIQUIRI	LINGUIST
JAUNTILY	NICOTINE	REACTIVE	SNOOTILY	VACATION	DECLUTCH	MACAULAY
JEPHTHAH	NIDATION	REALTIME	SNORTING	VALETING	DECOUPLE	MAIEUTIC
JOINTURE	NIGHTCAP	REBUTTAL	SOLITARY	VAULTING	DEMIURGE	MANEUVER
JONATHAN	NIGHTJAR	REDSTART	SOLITUDE	VEGETATE	DENOUNCE	MANFULLY
JOYSTICK	NINETEEN	RELATING	SOLSTICE	VENETIAN	DENTURES	MARAUDER
JUNCTION	NONSTICK	RELATION	SOLUTION	VEXATION	DISBURSE	MARQUESA
JUNCTURE	NOONTIME	RELATIVE	SOMETIME	VISITANT	DISGUISE	MARQUESS
JURATORY	NOTATION	REMITTAL	SONATINA	VISITING	DISJUNCT	MARQUISE
KARTTIKA	NUGATORY	REMOTELY	SPARTANS	VOCATION	DISPUTED	MATHURIN
KEYSTONE	OBLATION	RESETTLE	SPECTRAL	VOCATIVE	DISQUIET	MEASURED
KHARTOUM	OFFSTAGE	RIBSTONE	SPECTRUM	VOLATILE	DISSUADE	MENSURAL
KIBITZER	OLDSTYLE	RIGATONI	SPINTEXT	VOLITION	EFFLUENT	MESSUAGE
KINETICS	ORESTEIA	RIGHTFUL	SPITTING	VOMITING	EFFLUVIA	MISGUIDE
KNITTING	OUISTITI	RIGHTIST	SPITTOON	VOMITORY	ELOQUENT	MISJUDGE
LATITUDE	OUTSTRIP	RINGTAIL	SPLATTER	WHEATEAR	EPICURUS	MISQUOTE
LAVATORY	OVERTAKE	RIVETING	SPLITTER	WHISTLER	EPIDURAL	MOLLUSCS
LAXATIVE	OVERTIME	ROASTING	SPLUTTER	WREATHED	ESPOUSAL	MONAURAL
LECITHIN	OVERTONE	ROBOTICS	SPORTING	WRESTLER	EUPHUISM	MORTUARY
LEGATION	OVERTURE	ROENTGEN	SPORTIVE	WRISTLET	EVACUANT	MOSQUITO
LENGTHEN	OVERTURN	ROGATION	SPOTTING	YACHTING	EVACUATE	MUDGUARD
LEVITATE	PAINTING	ROOFTOPS	SPRITELY	YAKITORI	EVALUATE	MUSCULAR
LIBATION	PALATIAL	ROTATION	SPRITZER	YULETIDE	EXECUTED	MUSQUASH
LIENTERY	PALATINE	ROTATORY	SQUATTER	ACAPULCO	EXECUTOR	NEMBUTAL
LIFETIME	PANATELA	SABOTAGE	STARTERS	ACCOUNTS	EXIGUITY	NOCTURNE
LIGATURE	PARTTIME	SABOTEUR	STARTING	ADEQUACY	EXIGUOUS	OBITUARY
LIGHTING	PENITENT	SALUTARY	STEATITE	ADEQUATE	FAMOUSLY	OBSCURED
LIMITING	PETITION	SALUTORY	STEATOMA	AFFLUENT	FAROUCHE	ODIOUSLY
LINOTYPE	PHANTASM	SANCTIFY	STRATEGY	ALIQUANT	FAVOURED	OUTBURST
LIPSTICK	PILOTAGE	SANCTION	STRATIFY	ALTRUISM	FEATURED	PAROUSIA
LOBOTOMY	PLANTAIN	SANCTITY	STRETCHY	ALTRUIST	FEATURES	PASTURES
LOCATION	PLASTRON	SANITARY	STULTIFY	ANNOUNCE	FEBRUARY	PELLUCID
LOCATIVE	PLAYTIME	SANITIZE	SWASTIKA	APNEUSIS	FITFULLY	PENDULUM
LOGOTYPE	PLECTRUM	SARATOGA	SWEATING	ARCTURUS	FORTUITY	PERFUMED
LONGTERM	POLITELY	SAXATILE	SWEETSOP	ARMOURED	FRENULUM	PERJURED
LONGTIME	POLITICO	SCANTIES	SYMPTOMS	ARTFULLY	FREQUENT	PERJURER
LUTETIUM	POLITICS	SCANTILY	TACITURN	BEGRUDGE	GALLUMPH	PERSUADE
MAESTOSO	PONYTAIL	SCIATICA	TAHITIAN	BESOUGHT	GESTURES	PERSUANT
MAINTAIN	POSITION	SCOTTISH	TAXATION	BURGUNDY	GLOBULAR	PICTURES

POLLUTED
POLLUTER
PORTUGAL
PRECURSE
PREJUDGE
PROCURER
PRODUCER
PRODUCES
PRODUCTS
PROFUSER
PUSTULAR
RAMBUTAN
RASPUTIN
RECOURSE
RECRUITS
REDOUBLE
REMOUNTS
RENOUNCE
REPOUSSÉ
RESOURCE
RUEFULLY
RUMOURED
SADDUCEE
SANGUINE
SAVOURED
SCAPULAR
SCROUNGE
SECLUDED
SELEUCID
SENSUOUS
SHAVUOTH
SHROUDED
SINGULAR
SPECULUM
STATUARY
STIMULUS
SUBHUMAN
SUCCUBUS
SULFURIC
SUNBURNT
SUNBURST
TARTUFFE
TELLURIC
TEXTURED
THIOUREA
TONSURED
TORTUOUS
TORTURED
TORTURER
TRIBUNAL
TUNGUSIC
UBIQUITY
UNCOUPLE
UNCTUOUS
UNIQUELY
USEFULLY
VALVULAR
VANGUARD
VANQUISH
VASCULAR
VENTURED
VERJUICE
VESPUCCI
VICTUALS
VINCULUM
VIRTUOSI
VIRTUOSO
VIRTUOUS
WHODUNIT

WILFULLY
WOEFULLY
YARMULKA
ZAKOUSKI
ZARZUELA
ZIGGURAT
AARDVARK
ACTIVATE
ACTIVELY
ACTIVISM
ACTIVIST
ACTIVITY
ADJUVANT
ALLUVIAL
ALLUVIUM
BATAVIAN
BEHAVIOR
BOLIVIAN
CLEAVAGE
CLEAVERS
DELIVERY
ENERVATE
ESTIVATE
ESTOVERS
EXCAVATE
GRIEVOUS
INNOVATE
JEHOVAHS
KILOVOLT
MEGAVOLT
MORAVIAN
MOTIVATE
NATIVITY
OBLIVION
OMNIVORE
OTTAVINO
OVERVIEW
PERUVIAN
RECOVERY
REINVEST
RELEVANT
RENOVATE
REVIVIFY
REVIVING
SALIVARY
SALIVATE
SHELVING
STARVING
STRIVING
SWERVING
TELEVISE
THIEVERY
THIEVING
THIEVISH
TITIVATE
TWELVEMO
UNLOVELY
UNSAVORY
VESUVIUS
ALLOWING
BACKWARD
BASSWOOD
BEESWING
BINDWEED
BODYWORK
BOOKWORK
BOOKWORM
BOTHWELL
BOTSWANA

BUZZWORD
CAKEWALK
CAREWORN
CHERWELL
COOKWARE
CORDWAIN
CORNWALL
COTSWOLD
COXSWAIN
CROMWELL
DASHWOOD
DEADWOOD
DELAWARE
DOWNWARD
DUCKWEED
EASTWARD
EDGEWAYS
EDGEWISE
FAREWELL
FIREWEED
FIREWOOD
FIREWORK
FIRMWARE
FISHWIFE
FLATWARE
FLATWORM
FOOTWEAR
FOOTWORK
FOREWARN
FOREWORD
FORMWORK
FORSWEAR
FRETWORK
FUSEWIRE
GIGAWATT
GONDWANA
GOODWIFE
GOODWILL
GOODWOOD
GULFWEED
GURDWARA
HAIRWORM
HARDWARE
HARDWOOD
HEADWIND
HEADWORD
HEATWAVE
HEREWARD
HEREWITH
HINDWARD
HOMEWARD
HOMEWORK
HOODWINK
HOOKWORM
IRONWARE
IRONWOOD
IRONWORK
KILOWATT
KNAPWEED
KNITWEAR
KNOTWEED
KNOTWORK
LACEWING
LANDWARD
LEFTWARD
LEFTWING
LIKEWISE
LIVEWARE
LOANWORD

LOCOWEED
LUKEWARM
LUNGWORT
MALAWIAN
MEGAWATT
MENSWEAR
MILKWEED
MILKWORT
MULEWORT
NECKWEAR
OPENWORK
OVENWARE
OVERWORK
PASSWORD
PICKWICK
PIGSWILL
PINEWOOD
POKEWEED
RAINWEAR
REARWARD
RENOWNED
RINGWALL
RINGWORM
ROSEWOOD
SANDWICH
SCRAWLED
SCREWTOP
SHERWOOD
SHIPWORM
SHREWDLY
SHREWISH
SIDEWALK
SIDEWARD
SIDEWAYS
SILKWORM
SKINWORK
SLOWWORM
SOFTWARE
SOFTWOOD
SOMEWHAT
SOURWOOD
SPRAWLED
STALWART
STILWELL
TAPEWORM
TEAKWOOD
TEAMWORK
UNLAWFUL
UNTOWARD
WALLWORT
WEDGWOOD
WEREWOLF
WESTWARD
WINDWARD
WIREWORM
WOODWARD
WOODWIND
WOODWORK
WOODWORM
WORMWOOD
BISEXUAL
DETOXIFY
EUDOXIAN
INDEXING
MONOXIDE
PAROXYSM
PEROXIDE
RELAXING
SILOXANE

ALLEYWAY
ANALYSER
ANALYSIS
ANALYTIC
ANNOYING
ASPHYXIA
BACKYARD
BALLYHOO
BARNYARD
BELLYFUL
BILLYBOY
BILLYCAN
BOBBYPIN
BOGEYMAN
BONEYARD
BULLYRAG
CARRYALL
CARRYCOT
CARRYING
CRONYISM
DAIRYMAN
DECAYING
DIALYSIS
DIONYSUS
DOCKYARD
ENTRYISM
ESSAYIST
EVERYDAY
EVERYMAN
EVERYONE
FANCYMAN
FARMYARD
FEDAYEEN
FERRYMAN
GARDYLOO
GOODYEAR
HALFYEAR
HANDYMAN
HONEYDEW
HONEYPOT
HOWDYEDO
JERRYCAN
LOBBYIST
LOWLYING
MAINYARD
MALAYSIA
MARTYRED
MEALYBUG
MONEYBOX
NEOMYCIN
OUTLYING
PLATYPUS
PUSSYCAT
RELAYING
REPAYING
SAVOYARD
SEALYHAM
SHIPYARD
SUKIYAKI
TABBYCAT
TENNYSON
TERIYAKI
TRICYCLE
UNICYCLE
UNIFYING
VALKYRIE
VINEYARD
WALKYRIE
WORRYING

ZEPHYRUS
BLIZZARD
BREEZILY
BRYOZOAN
CENOZOIC
CHUTZPAH
DIGIZINE
EMBEZZLE
FRAZZLED
FREEZING
FRENZIED
GRIZZLED
HOLOZOIC
MAGAZINE
MESOZOIC
PIROZHKI
SAMIZDAT
SCHIZOID
SNEEZING
TWEEZERS
TZATZIKI
WALTZING
WHEEZILY
WHEEZING

8:6

AARDVARK
ABDICATE
ABERRANT
ABNEGATE
ABROGATE
ABSTRACT
ABUNDANT
ACCOLADE
ACCURACY
ACCURATE
ACERBATE
ACTIVATE
ADEQUACY
ADEQUATE
ADJUTAGE
ADJUTANT
ADJUVANT
ADVOCACY
ADVOCATE
AERONAUT
AIRBRAKE
AIRCRAFT
AIREDALE
AIRPLANE
ALIENATE
ALIQUANT
ALLOCATE
ALLOGAMY
ALLOPATH
AMBULANT
AMBULATE
AMPERAGE
AMPUTATE
AMYGDALA
ANAPHASE
ANNOTATE
ANTEDATE
ANYPLACE
APOSTASY
APOSTATE
APPANAGE
APPELANT
APPROACH

ARGONAUT
ARMCHAIR
ARROGANT
ARROGATE
ARTEFACT
ARTIFACT
ASCOCARP
ASPIRANT
ASPIRATE
ATHANASY
AUTOBAHN
AUTOGAMY
AUTOMATE
BACCHANT
BACKDATE
BACKHAND
BACKLASH
BACKPACK
BACKWARD
BACKYARD
BADINAGE
BALLPARK
BAREBACK
BARNYARD
BASEBALL
BELGRADE
BENGHAZI
BEQUEATH
BERTRAND
BESTIARY
BEVERAGE
BIFOCALS
BIGARADE
BILOBATE
BIOGRAPH
BIRDCAGE
BLIZZARD
BLOCKADE
BLOCKAGE
BLOWLAMP
BLUEBACK
BONEYARD
BONIFACE
BOOKCASE
BOOKMARK
BORDEAUX
BORSTALL
BOTSWANA
BOUFFANT
BOUNDARY
BRAGGART
BRANDADE
BRASSARD
BRATPACK
BREVIARY
BROUHAHA
BUCKFAST
BURGLARY
BURGRAVE
CABOTAGE
CAKEWALK
CALABASH
CALCEATE
CAMSHAFT
CAPITALS
CAPYBARA
CARAPACE
CARRIAGE
CARRYALL

CARTHAGE	DEMERARA	EXCAVATE	HAIRBAND	JUBILATE	MARGRAVE	OCCUPANT
CARUCATE	DEPILATE	EXECRATE	HALFMAST	KALAHARI	MARINADE	OCTONARY
CASEMATE	DEROGATE	EXHUMATE	HALLIARD	KAMIKAZE	MARINATE	OEILLADE
CASTRATE	DESOLATE	EXULTANT	HALLMARK	KATAKANA	MARRIAGE	OFFSTAGE
CASTRATO	DETONATE	EYEGLASS	HANDBALL	KEELHAUL	MARSHALL	OLIPHANT
CATARACT	DIASTASE	EYESHADE	HANDCART	KEEPSAKE	MARYLAND	ONETRACK
CELIBACY	DIFFRACT	FALKLAND	HANDMADE	KEYBOARD	MATURATE	OPENCAST
CELIBATE	DINGBATS	FARMHAND	HANDMAID	KICKBACK	MEDICATE	OPTIMATE
CENOTAPH	DINOSAUR	FARMLAND	HANDRAIL	KILOWATT	MEDITATE	ORDINAND
CHADBAND	DISCLAIM	FARMYARD	HANGNAIL	KINSHASA	MEGAWATT	ORDINARY
CHANTAGE	DISGRACE	FASTBACK	HARDBACK	KITEMARK	MEMBRANE	ORDINATE
CHAPLAIN	DISPLACE	FEBRUARY	HARDHACK	KNAPSACK	MENELAUS	OSCULATE
CHARLADY	DISSUADE	FEDERACY	HARDTACK	KOHLRABI	MERCHANT	OUTBOARD
CHILIAST	DISTRACT	FEDERATE	HARDWARE	KREPLACH	MESSMATE	OUTCLASS
CHILLADA	DISTRAIN	FEEDBACK	HAYSTACK	LACERATE	MESSUAGE	OUTFLANK
CHLORATE	DISTRAIT	FILENAME	HEADBAND	LACINATE	MIDBRAIN	OUTREACH
CHORDATA	DJELLABA	FILTRATE	HEADLAMP	LACKLAND	MILITANT	OUTSMART
CHORDATE	DOCKLAND	FIREBACK	HEADLAND	LAIDBACK	MILITARY	OVENWARE
CHORIAMB	DOCKYARD	FIREBALL	HEADMARK	LAKELAND	MILITATE	OVERCAST
CHUMMAGE	DOGSTAIL	FIREDAMP	HEATWAVE	LAMINATE	MILKMAID	OVERHAND
CINERAMA	DOMINANT	FIRMWARE	HEELBALL	LANDFALL	MILLRACE	OVERHANG
CLAIMANT	DOMINATE	FISHCAKE	HEELTAPS	LANDLADY	MINAMATA	OVERHAUL
CLAMBAKE	DOVETAIL	FLAGRANT	HELPMATE	LANDMARK	MINOTAUR	OVERLAID
CLAWBACK	DOWNCAST	FLAPJACK	HEREWARD	LANDMASS	MISHMASH	OVERLAND
CLEAVAGE	DOWNFALL	FLATMATE	HERITAGE	LANDRACE	MISPLACE	OVERPASS
COATRACK	DOWNWARD	FLATWARE	HESITANT	LANDWARD	MITIGATE	OVERRATE
COATTAIL	DRAINAGE	FLIPPANT	HESITATE	LANGLAND	MODERATE	OVERTAKE
COCKTAIL	DRAWBACK	FOOTBALL	HIGHBALL	LANGLAUF	MODERATO	PAGINATE
COGITATE	DRESSAGE	FOOTFALL	HIGHGATE	LANGUAGE	MODULATE	PALEFACE
COLORADO	DRUNKARD	FOOTPATH	HIGHLAND	LAPIDARY	MONETARY	PALGRAVE
COLORANT	EASTLAKE	FORECAST	HINDWARD	LAPIDATE	MONOGAMY	PALISADE
COMEBACK	EASTWARD	FOREHAND	HIRAGANA	LAUREATE	MONORAIL	PALLIATE
COMPLAIN	ECHINATE	FORELAND	HOLDFAST	LEFTHAND	MONTCALM	PANORAMA
CONCLAVE	EDENTATE	FORENAME	HOLIDAYS	LEFTWARD	MOORLAND	PARKLAND
CONFLATE	EDGEWAYS	FORESAIL	HOMELAND	LEMONADE	MORTGAGE	PASTRAMI
CONGRATS	EFFICACY	FOREWARN	HOMEMADE	LEVERAGE	MORTUARY	PEARMAIN
CONSTANT	EGGPLANT	FORKTAIL	HOMEPAGE	LEVITATE	MOTHBALL	PECULATE
CONTRACT	ELDORADO	FORSLACK	HOMEWARD	LIBERATE	MOTIVATE	PEDERAST
CONTRARY	ELEPHANT	FOUNTAIN	HONORARY	LITERACY	MOUNTAIN	PENCHANT
CONTRAST	ELONGATE	FOURPART	HORNTAIL	LITERARY	MOUSSAKA	PERICARP
COOKWARE	EMACIATE	FRAGRANT	HOTPLATE	LITERATE	MUCILAGE	PERMEATE
COPULATE	EMIGRANT	FREEHAND	HUMPBACK	LITERATI	MUDFLATS	PERSUADE
CORDWAIN	EMIGRATE	FRONTAGE	IGNORANT	LITIGANT	MUDGUARD	PERSUANT
CORNWALL	EMISSARY	FULLBACK	IMMOLATE	LITIGATE	MUSQUASH	PETULANT
CORONARY	ENCROACH	FULLPAGE	INCHOATE	LIVEWARE	MUTILATE	PHANTASM
COSTMARY	ENDOCARP	FUMIGATE	INCREASE	LONGHAND	MYOBLAST	PHARMACY
COTOPAXI	ENDOGAMY	FUNERARY	INCUBATE	LONGHAUL	NAGASAKI	PHEASANT
COUCHANT	ENERVATE	FUSELAGE	INDICANT	LONGLAND	NAMESAKE	PIECHART
COVENANT	ENFILADE	GADOGADO	INDICATE	LONSDALE	NAUSEATE	PILCHARD
COVERAGE	ENSILAGE	GAILLARD	INHALANT	LOVELACE	NAVIGATE	PILOTAGE
COXSWAIN	ENTHRALL	GALLIARD	INHUMANE	LOWCLASS	NECKBAND	PLANTAIN
CRIBBAGE	ENTREATY	GANGLAND	INITIATE	LUKEWARM	NECKLACE	PLAYBACK
CRUCIATE	ENVISAGE	GEMINATE	INKSTAIN	LUMINARY	NEWSCAST	PLAYFAIR
CRYSTALS	EPIGRAPH	GENERATE	INNOVATE	MACERATE	NEWSHAWK	PLAYMATE
CULINARY	EPIPHANY	GENITALS	INSULATE	MACHEATH	NICKNACK	PLEASANT
CUPBOARD	EQUIPAGE	GIGAWATT	INTERACT	MACREADY	NICKNAME	PLEONASM
DATABASE	EQUITANT	GIMCRACK	INTIFADA	MACULATE	NOMINATE	PLUMBAGO
DEBONAIR	ERADIATE	GLISSADE	INTIMACY	MAHARAJA	NOSEBAND	POCKMARK
DECIMATE	ERUCTATE	GLORIANA	INTIMATE	MAHARANI	NOTECASE	POIGNANT
DECKHAND	ESCALADE	GLOSSARY	INUNDATE	MAHOGANY	NOWADAYS	POLYCARP
DECORATE	ESCALATE	GOBSMACK	IRONWARE	MAINLAND	NUCLEATE	POLYGAMY
DECREASE	ESCAPADE	GOLFBALL	IRRIGATE	MAINMAST	NUMERACY	POLYMATH
DEDICATE	ESTIMATE	GONDWANA	IRRITANT	MAINSAIL	NUMERALS	PONYTAIL
DEFECATE	ESTIVATE	GOOFBALL	IRRITATE	MAINTAIN	NUMERATE	POPULACE
DEFILADE	ETIOLATE	GOURMAND	ISOSTASY	MAINYARD	NUPTIALS	POPULATE
DELAWARE	EUROLAND	GRADUATE	JACQUARD	MALAGASY	OBDURACY	PORTLAND
DELEGATE	EVACUANT	GUJARATI	JEHOVAHS	MALGRADO	OBDURATE	PORTRAIT
DELICACY	EVACUATE	GURDWARA	JIMCRACK	MALLEATE	OBITUARY	POSTCARD
DELICATE	EVALUATE	GYMKHANA	JUBILANT	MANDRAKE	OBLIGATE	POSTDATE

POSTMARK	SCOTLAND	STOPPAGE	VAUXHALL	COLUMBAN	QUOTABLE	AUTARCHY
POSTPAID	SEABOARD	SUBLEASE	VEGETATE	COLUMBUS	RATEABLE	BACKACHE
POUNDAGE	SEAPLANE	SUBTRACT	VENERATE	CREDIBLE	READABLE	BALANCED
PRATFALL	SEASCAPE	SUFFRAGE	VERBIAGE	CREDIBLY	REDOUBLE	BALLOCKS
PREGNANT	SELFMADE	SUITCASE	VESTIARY	CROSSBAR	RELIABLE	BARBECUE
PROCLAIM	SELFSAME	SUKIYAKI	VICARAGE	CRUCIBLE	RELIABLY	BARBICAN
PROGRADE	SEMINARY	SULPHATE	VICTUALS	CUCUMBER	REMEMBER	BARNACLE
PROPHASE	SEPARATE	SUNGLASS	VIGILANT	CUCURBIT	RESEMBLE	BARRACKS
PROSTATE	SERENADE	SUNSHADE	VINEGARY	CULPABLE	REUSABLE	BIBLICAL
PROTEASE	SERENATA	SUPPLANT	VINEYARD	DAMNABLE	RUNCIBLE	BILLYCAN
PUFFBALL	SERGEANT	SURICATE	VISITANT	DEATHBED	SALEABLE	BINNACLE
PUISSANT	SERJEANT	SUZERAIN	VOLPLANE	DECEMBER	SCRABBLE	BLACKCAP
PURCHASE	SEWERAGE	SVENGALI	WARPLANE	DOUGHBOY	SCRAMBLE	BOADICEA
PURSLANE	SHADRACH	TABULATE	WAVEBAND	DUTIABLE	SCRIABIN	BOLLOCKS
PUSHCART	SHAGBARK	TAFFRAIL	WELLPAID	ELIGIBLE	SCRIBBLE	BUTTOCKS
QUADRANT	SHANGAAN	TAILBACK	WESTWARD	ENCUMBER	SCRIBBLY	CABLECAR
QUADRATE	SHETLAND	TAILGATE	WHARFAGE	ENFEEBLE	SCRUBBER	CANTICLE
QUANDARY	SHIITAKE	TAMARACK	WHIPHAND	ENSEMBLE	SENSIBLE	CAPSICUM
QUATRAIN	SHIPMATE	TAPENADE	WHIPJACK	ENVIABLE	SENSIBLY	CARJACOU
QUINTAIN	SHIPYARD	TARTRATE	WHIPLASH	FALLIBLE	SIZEABLE	CARRYCOT
RABELAIS	SHOELACE	TEAMMATE	WILLIAMS	FEASIBLE	SLUGABED	CERVICAL
RAINFALL	SHOPTALK	TELECAST	WINDFALL	FEASIBLY	SNACKBAR	CHEMICAL
RANELAGH	SHORTAGE	TELEMARK	WINDGALL	FENCIBLE	SNUFFBOX	CLAVECIN
RAPECAKE	SHOWCASE	TELLTALE	WINDLASS	FLEXIBLE	SOCIABLE	CLAVICLE
REARWARD	SIBILANT	TEMPLATE	WINDWARD	FLEXIBLY	SOLVABLE	CLEARCUT
RECREATE	SIDEWALK	TERIYAKI	WOLFBANE	FORCIBLE	SQUABBLE	CLERICAL
RECUSANT	SIDEWARD	TERTIARY	WOODLAND	FORCIBLY	STEENBOK	CLINICAL
REDSHANK	SIDEWAYS	THAILAND	WOODWARD	FUNGIBLE	SUBURBAN	COLLECTS
REDSTART	SILICATE	THINGAMY	WOOLPACK	GREENBAG	SUBURBIA	CORNICHE
REGULATE	SILKTAIL	THOUSAND	WOOLSACK	GULLIBLE	SUCCUBUS	CORSICAN
RELEGATE	SILOXANE	TICKTACK	WORKMATE	HANNIBAL	SUITABLE	CRITICAL
RELEVANT	SIMULATE	TIDEMARK	WORMCAST	HORRIBLE	SUITABLY	CURLICUE
RELOCATE	SINCLAIR	TIPSTAFF	WRECKAGE	HORRIBLY	SUPERBLY	CURRICLE
RENEGADE	SKEWBALD	TITICACA	XENOGAMY	HORSEBOX	SUPERBUG	CYCLICAL
RENOVATE	SKIPJACK	TITIVATE	YOKOHAMA	INEDIBLE	SYLLABIC	DAMASCUS
REPHRASE	SLAPBANG	TOISEACH	ZWIEBACK	ISTANBUL	SYLLABLE	DENTICLE
REPROACH	SLAPDASH	TOLERANT	ABSORBED	LAUDABLE	SYLLABUB	DIDDICOY
RESONANT	SLAPJACK	TOLERATE	ABSORBER	LAUDABLY	SYLLABUS	DIVORCED
RESONATE	SLUGGARD	TOLLGATE	ADORABLE	LIKEABLE	TANGIBLE	DIVORCEE
RESTRAIN	SNOWBALL	TOMAHAWK	ALHAMBRA	LOCKABLE	TANGIBLY	EMBRACED
RIFFRAFF	SNOWFALL	TOPCLASS	ALPHABET	LOOSEBOX	TEARABLE	EMBRACES
RINGHALS	SOAPBARK	TOPHEAVY	AMENABLE	LUNCHBOX	TERRIBLE	EMOTICON
RINGTAIL	SOFTBACK	TOXOCARA	AMICABLE	MANDIBLE	TERRIBLY	ENCIRCLE
RINGWALL	SOFTBALL	TRANSACT	AMICABLY	MATCHBOX	THROMBIN	ESTANCIA
RIVERAIN	SOFTWARE	TRESPASS	ARGUABLE	MEALYBUG	THROMBUS	ETRUSCAN
ROCHDALE	SOLITARY	TRIGRAPH	ARGUABLY	MILLIBAR	THURIBLE	EXPLICIT
ROLLCALL	SPANIARD	TRIPTANE	ARQUEBUS	MONEYBOX	UNCOMBED	FACEACHE
ROOMMATE	SPARTANS	TROCHAIC	ASCORBIC	MOVEABLE	UNCURBED	FARCICAL
ROSEMARY	SPICCATO	TRUNCATE	ASSEMBLE	NEIGHBOR	UNDERBID	FAROUCHE
ROUGHAGE	SPILLAGE	TUNICATE	ASSEMBLY	NOVEMBER	UNSTABLE	FASCICLE
RUCKSACK	SPOILAGE	TUPAMARO	BARABBAS	OPERABLE	UNUSABLE	FLOUNCED
RUMINANT	SPOLIATE	TURNBACK	BARNABAS	PALPABLE	VALUABLE	FOLLICLE
RUMINATE	SPYGLASS	TUSITALA	BEARABLE	PALPABLY	VARIABLE	FOOLSCAP
RUTABAGA	SQUAMATA	TUTELAGE	BEDABBLE	PASSABLE	VERTEBRA	FURUNCLE
RYEGRASS	STACCATO	TUTELARY	BILLYBOY	PASSABLY	VINCIBLE	GARLICKY
SABOTAGE	STAGNANT	TYPECAST	BLACKBOY	PASSIBLE	WASHABLE	GAZPACHO
SALIVARY	STAGNATE	TYPEFACE	BOOKABLE	PEEKABOO	WATERBUG	GRENACHE
SALIVATE	STALWART	ULCERATE	BRIBABLE	PENUMBRA	WEARABLE	GUAIACUM
SALUTARY	STANDARD	ULTIMATE	BRICKBAT	PINTABLE	WORKABLE	HANDICAP
SANDBANK	STANNARY	UNDERAGE	CANNABIS	PITIABLE	ZIMBABWE	HEADACHE
SANITARY	STARGAZE	UNDERARM	CANNIBAL	PLACABLE	ADVANCED	HIBISCUS
SANTIAGO	STATUARY	UNDULANT	CHASUBLE	PORTABLE	ADVANCER	HORLICKS
SARABAND	STAYSAIL	UNDULATE	CHERUBIC	POSSIBLE	ALOPECIA	IMPLICIT
SATURATE	STEERAGE	UNGULATE	CHERUBIM	POSSIBLY	AMERICAN	INIMICAL
SAVOYARD	STELLATE	UNSTEADY	CHOIRBOY	PREAMBLE	AMERICAS	INTERCOM
SAYONARA	STICCATO	UNTOWARD	CICISBEO	PROBABLE	ANALECTA	IRONICAL
SCABBARD	STIGMATA	URETHANE	CINNABAR	PROBABLY	ANGLICAN	JAMAICAN
SCARFACE	STOCCATA	VALIDATE	COBWEBBY	PROHIBIT	ATYPICAL	JELLICOE
SCHUMANN	STOCKADE	VANGUARD	COLOMBIA	PROVABLE	AUSPICES	JERRYCAN

JORROCKS	TRICYCLE	EMBOLDEN	POMANDER	ADHERENT	BUTCHERY	CRESCENT
KENTUCKY	TRITICAL	ENGENDER	POPPADOM	ADJACENT	BUTTRESS	CROCKERY
LUPERCAL	TRITICUM	ENKINDLE	PORRIDGE	ADULTERY	CADUCEUS	CROCKETT
MANIACAL	TROPICAL	EPISODIC	POSEIDON	AESTHETE	CAERLEON	CROMLECH
MARIACHI	TROUNCER	EVERYDAY	PREJUDGE	AFFERENT	CAGINESS	CROMWELL
MASSACRE	TUBERCLE	EXPANDED	PROVIDED	AFFLUENT	CAJOLERY	CURTNESS
MASSICOT	UNDERCUT	EXPENDED	PROVIDER	AGGRIEVE	CALCRETE	CUTENESS
MEDIOCRE	UNFORCED	EXPLODED	PUDENDUM	AIRFIELD	CALIPERS	CUTHBERT
MENISCUS	UNICYCLE	EXTENDED	RECORDER	AIRINESS	CALMNESS	DAMPNESS
METRICAL	UNPLACED	EXTRADOS	REKINDLE	AIRSPEED	CAMPBELL	DANEGELD
MOLUCCAS	UNVOICED	FLOUNDER	REMINDER	ANACREON	CANONESS	DANKNESS
MONARCHY	UPPERCUT	FRIENDLY	RETARDED	ANAPAEST	CARELESS	DARKNESS
MONOACID	VALENCIA	FRIGIDLY	RIBALDRY	ANATHEMA	CAROTENE	DATELESS
MOROCCAN	VERSICLE	GAZUNDER	RUGGEDLY	ANTECEDE	CASEMENT	DAYBREAK
MOTORCAR	VERTICAL	GIRONDIN	SALVADOR	ANTIHERO	CASHMERE	DAYDREAM
MUSTACHE	VESPUCCI	GRANDDAD	SAMIZDAT	ANTIMERE	CATSMEAT	DEADBEAT
MYSTICAL	VIATICUM	GROUNDED	SATURDAY	ANYWHERE	CATTLEYA	DEADHEAD
MYTHICAL	VORTICAL	GUERIDON	SECLUDED	APERIENT	CELANESE	DEAFNESS
NAUTICAL	WAINSCOT	HAGGADAH	SECONDER	APOPLEXY	CEMETERY	DECADENT
NEOMYCIN	WHITECAP	HARRIDAN	SECONDLY	APOTHEGM	CEREMENT	DEEPNESS
NIGHTCAP	WISEACRE	HAVILDAR	SELVEDGE	APPARENT	CERULEAN	DEFREEZE
NOMARCHY	ZODIACAL	HEATEDLY	SHEEPDOG	ARAMAEAN	CETACEAN	DEFTNESS
OBSTACLE	ABINGDON	HEBRIDES	SHEIKDOM	ARBALEST	CHALDEAN	DELIVERY
OXYTOCIN	ABSURDLY	HELLADIC	SHERIDAN	ARBOREAL	CHAMBERS	DEMURELY
PANNICLE	ACCREDIT	HERALDIC	SHOULDER	ARGUMENT	CHAMPERS	DESELECT
PARTICLE	ADDENDUM	HERALDRY	SHREDDER	ARMAMENT	CHANCERY	DILIGENT
PASTICHE	APPENDIX	HONEYDEW	SHREWDLY	ASMODEUS	CHASSEUR	DISCREET
PEDUNCLE	ASPHODEL	INCLUDED	SHROUDED	ASTUTELY	CHATTELS	DISCRETE
PELLICLE	ATTENDER	INTENDED	SMOULDER	BACKLESS	CHEATERS	DISRAELI
PELLUCID	AVOGADRO	INTRADOS	SORDIDLY	BAGHEERA	CHECKERS	DISTRESS
PEMMICAN	BARBADOS	INTRUDER	SPLENDID	BAILMENT	CHEQUERS	DIVIDEND
PENTACLE	BEFUDDLE	INWARDLY	SPLENDOR	BALDNESS	CHERWELL	DIVIDERS
PERFECTA	BEGRUDGE	ISLANDER	SPORADIC	BALINESE	CHICHEWA	DOCUMENT
PERFECTO	BEHOLDEN	LABRADOR	SPREADER	BANLIEUE	CHICKENS	DOMINEER
PHYSICAL	BEHOLDER	LACKADAY	SQUADDIE	BARENESS	CHILDERS	DOORBELL
PINNACLE	BENENDEN	LAVENDER	SQUANDER	BARONESS	CHILTERN	DOUBLETS
POETICAL	BEWILDER	LEONIDAS	STOLIDLY	BARONETS	CHIMAERA	DOWNBEAT
POPSICLE	BIRTHDAY	LOPSIDED	STRADDLE	BASELESS	CINEREAL	DRACAENA
PRODUCER	CABOODLE	LYSANDER	STRANDED	BASEMENT	CLAPPERS	DRIBLETS
PRODUCES	CALENDAR	MARAUDER	STUPIDLY	BASENESS	CLEANERS	DROPHEAD
PRODUCTS	CALENDER	MARKEDLY	SUICIDAL	BEAKLESS	CLEAVERS	DRUDGERY
PROTOCOL	CALVADOS	MASTODON	TAMANDUA	BEDSTEAD	CLINKERS	DRUMBEAT
PUBLICAN	CAMBODIA	MENANDER	THRALDOM	BEFRIEND	CLIPPERS	DRUMHEAD
PUBLICLY	CANDIDLY	MENHADEN	THURSDAY	BELPAESE	CLUELESS	DRYCLEAN
PUSSYCAT	CANOODLE	MERCEDES	TOREADOR	BERIBERI	COARSELY	DUCKWEED
RESPECTS	CATHEDRA	MESSIDOR	TRINIDAD	BINDWEED	COBBLERS	DULLNESS
REVANCHE	CLIVEDEN	METHODIC	TURANDOT	BIRDSEED	COCHLEAR	DUMBBELL
ROMANCER	COCCIDAE	MICRODOT	TURGIDLY	BLENHEIM	CODPIECE	DUMBNESS
SADDUCEE	COLANDER	MISJUDGE	UNBIDDEN	BLINKERS	COGWHEEL	EARLIEST
SCIENCES	CONSIDER	MONANDRY	UNBURDEN	BLITHELY	COHERENT	EARPIECE
SCILICET	CORRIDOR	MORBIDLY	UNDERDOG	BLOOMERS	COIFFEUR	EASEMENT
SCIROCCO	CORRODED	MUSCADET	UNITEDLY	BLUDGEON	COLDNESS	EASINESS
SCRATCHY	CORUNDUM	MYRMIDON	UNKINDLY	BLUEBELL	COLISEUM	ECOFREAK
SELEUCID	COWARDLY	OFFENDED	UNLEADED	BLUSTERY	COLLIERS	ECTODERM
SERVICES	CRUSADER	OFFENDER	UNLOADED	BOLDNESS	COLLIERY	EERINESS
SILENCER	CULLODEN	OFFSIDER	UNSEEDED	BONEHEAD	COMPLETE	EFFERENT
SKULLCAP	CUSPIDOR	OLEANDER	UPHOLDER	BONELESS	COMPRESS	EFFLUENT
SPIRACLE	CYCLADES	ONESIDED	VERANDAH	BOOTLESS	CONCRETE	EGGSHELL
STOCKCAR	CYLINDER	ORGANDIE	WATCHDOG	BOOTNECK	CONGRESS	EIGHTEEN
STRETCHY	DAFFODIL	ORTHODOX	WICKEDLY	BOTHWELL	CONQUEST	EINSTEIN
SUBJECTS	DANAIDES	OUTMODED	WIZARDRY	BRACKETS	COOLNESS	ELOQUENT
SURGICAL	DEFENDER	OUTRIDER	WORKADAY	BROWBEAT	CORNMEAL	EMERGENT
TABBYCAT	DEGRADED	OUTSIDER	ZAMINDAR	BRUSSELS	COSINESS	EMPYREAL
TACTICAL	DISLODGE	OXBRIDGE	ABDUCENS	BUCKBEAN	COUNTESS	EMPYREAN
TENTACLE	DISORDER	PALLADIO	ABERDEEN	BUDAPEST	COURTESY	EMULGENT
TERRACED	DOGGEDLY	PERIODIC	ABUTMENT	BUDDLEIA	COVALENT	ENDODERM
TESTICLE	DOMESDAY	PIERIDES	ACCIDENT	BULKHEAD	COZINESS	ENGINEER
THORACIC	DOOMSDAY	PLACIDLY	ACIDHEAD	BUSINESS	CRACKERS	ENTIRELY
TRASHCAN	EMBEDDED	PLEIADES	ACTIVELY	BUTCHERS	CREAMERY	ENTIRETY

EPHEMERA	GAMENESS	INFLUENT	MIDFIELD	OVERHEAT	REDIRECT	SMARTEST
EPITHEMA	GANGRENE	INHERENT	MILANESE	OVERLEAF	REDOLENT	SMIDGEON
EQUULEUS	GANYMEDE	INNOCENT	MILDNESS	OVERSEAS	REFINERY	SMOLLETT
ERYTHEMA	GIANTESS	INSANELY	MILKLESS	OVERSEER	REGIMENT	SMUGNESS
ESCULENT	GLADNESS	INSOLENT	MILKWEED	PAINLESS	REINDEER	SNEAKERS
ESTOVERS	GLANDERS	INTEREST	MINDLESS	PALENESS	REINVEST	SNOBBERY
ETCETERA	GLOSSEME	ISOTHERE	MINEHEAD	PANATELA	REMOTELY	SOBRIETY
ETHEREAL	GLUTAEUS	ISOTHERM	MINORESS	PANCREAS	REORIENT	SOFTNESS
ETHYLENE	GOODNESS	JACOBEAN	MINUTELY	PANTHEON	REPRIEVE	SOLDIERS
EUROPEAN	GOODYEAR	JAPANESE	MISERERE	PARAKEET	RESIDENT	SOLDIERY
EVENNESS	GORMLESS	JEFFREYS	MISSPELL	PAVEMENT	RESTLESS	SOMBRELY
EWIGKEIT	GRADIENT	JONGLEUR	MISSPENT	PAYCHECK	RETICENT	SOMBRERO
EXISTENT	GRANDEUR	JUDGMENT	MISTREAT	PEDIMENT	RETRIEVE	SORENESS
EXPONENT	GRAPHEME	JUSTNESS	MISTRESS	PEERLESS	REVEREND	SOULLESS
EYEPIECE	GREATEST	KEENNESS	MONSTERA	PEKINESE	REVERENT	SOURNESS
FACELESS	GREENERY	KEROSENE	MONUMENT	PELLMELL	RICHNESS	SOUTHEND
FAIRNESS	GRIMNESS	KILLDEER	MOONBEAM	PENITENT	RIPENESS	SOUTHERN
FAREWELL	GROSBEAK	KINDNESS	MOROSELY	PERIDERM	ROOFLESS	SPARSELY
FARRIERY	GULFWEED	KNACKERS	MORPHEME	PERIPETY	ROOTLESS	SPEAKERS
FARTHEST	GUYANESE	KNAPWEED	MORPHEUS	PERTNESS	ROSINESS	SPINTEXT
FASTNESS	HABANERA	KNEEDEEP	MOVEMENT	PHOSGENE	ROUNDERS	SPITHEAD
FEARLESS	HAIRLESS	KNICKERS	MUCHNESS	PICKMEUP	ROUSSEAU	SPOTLESS
FEATHERS	HALFTERM	KNITWEAR	MULETEER	PINWHEEL	RUDENESS	SPRITELY
FEATHERY	HALFYEAR	KNOBLESS	MUNIMENT	PIRANESI	RUDIMENT	SPRUCELY
FECKLESS	HANDHELD	KNOCKERS	MUTINEER	PISSHEAD	RUSTLESS	SPRYNESS
FECULENT	HARDNESS	KNOTWEED	NAMELESS	PITHLESS	RUTHLESS	SQUARELY
FEDAYEEN	HAREBELL	LAMASERY	NAPOLEON	PITILESS	SABOTEUR	STAGGERS
FIERCELY	HARFLEUR	LAMENESS	NAZARENE	PLANGENT	SADDLERY	STAMPEDE
FIFTIETH	HARMLESS	LANDSEER	NDJAMENA	PLIOCENE	SAGENESS	STARKERS
FILAMENT	HATCHERY	LATENESS	NEARNESS	POITIERS	SALTNESS	STARLESS
FIREWEED	HAYFIELD	LAZINESS	NEATHERD	POKEWEED	SAMENESS	STARTERS
FIRMNESS	HAZINESS	LEAFLESS	NEATNESS	POLITELY	SAVAGELY	STEPHENS
FISHMEAL	HEADGEAR	LEATHERY	NECKWEAR	POLYSEME	SAVAGERY	STILWELL
FLANDERS	HEADLESS	LEBANESE	NEEDLESS	POLYSEMY	SCARCELY	STRATEGY
FLANNELS	HEADREST	LEWDNESS	NEPALESE	POORNESS	SCHUBERT	STRIDENT
FLATTERY	HEEDLESS	LIENTERY	NESCIENT	PORTIÈRE	SCULLERY	STURGEON
FLAUBERT	HEIRLESS	LIFEBELT	NEWSPEAK	POTSHERD	SEAMLESS	SUBPOENA
FLAWLESS	HELLBENT	LIFELESS	NEWSREEL	PREMIERE	SEASHELL	SUBTLETY
FLAXSEED	HELPLESS	LIGAMENT	NICENESS	PRIMNESS	SECURELY	SUCCEEDS
FLINDERS	HIGHNESS	LIKENESS	NINETEEN	PRINCELY	SEDATELY	SUDAMENT
FLIPPERS	HIPSTERS	LIMBLESS	NORTHERN	PRINCESS	SEDIMENT	SUDANESE
FLUMMERY	HOARSELY	LIMPNESS	NUFFIELD	PRIORESS	SEEDLESS	SUNCREAM
FLYSHEET	HOGSHEAD	LINIMENT	NUMBNESS	PROCEEDS	SELFHELP	SUPPRESS
FLYWHEEL	HOLINESS	LINNAEAN	NUTRIENT	PROGRESS	SELFLESS	SURENESS
FONDNESS	HOLOCENE	LINNAEUS	NUTSHELL	PROPHECY	SENGREEN	TACTLESS
FOOTREST	HOLYHEAD	LINOLEUM	OBEDIENT	PROPHESY	SENTIENT	TAILLESS
FOOTWEAR	HOMELESS	LISTLESS	OBSOLETE	PROSPECT	SERENELY	TAMENESS
FOREBEAR	HOPELESS	LOCOWEED	OBTUSELY	PROSPERO	SERVIENT	TARTNESS
FOREDECK	HOPFIELD	LONGTERM	OCCIDENT	PRURIENT	SEVERELY	TASHKENT
FOREHEAD	HORNBEAM	LONICERA	ODYSSEUS	PSALTERY	SEVEREST	TAUTNESS
FORETELL	HORNFELS	LOUDNESS	OEDIPEAN	PSEUDERY	SHAGREEN	TEACHERS
FORMLESS	HOWDYEDO	LOVELESS	OFFBREAK	PURLIEUS	SHEPHERD	TEGUMENT
FORSWEAR	HUMANELY	LUCKLESS	OFFICERS	PURULENT	SHIPMENT	TENEMENT
FORTIETH	HUNDREDS	LUNCHEON	OILFIELD	PYRENEES	SHOELESS	TERYLENE
FORTRESS	HUNTRESS	LUSHNESS	OILINESS	QUARTERS	SHUTTERS	THIEVERY
FOULNESS	HYPOGEAL	MALTREAT	OINTMENT	QUOTIENT	SICKNESS	THINNESS
FOURTEEN	ICEFIELD	MANIFEST	OLEACEAE	RACINESS	SIDEREAL	THIRTEEN
FRAGMENT	IDLENESS	MARQUESA	ONSCREEN	RACKRENT	SIXTIETH	THUNDERY
FRAULEIN	IMMANENT	MARQUESS	OPENNESS	RAILHEAD	SKINDEEP	TICKSEED
FREQUENT	IMMINENT	MASTHEAD	OPPONENT	RAILLERY	SKINHEAD	TIDINESS
FRESHEST	IMMODEST	MATABELE	ORANGERY	RAINWEAR	SLATTERN	TIEBREAK
FRIPPERY	IMPOTENT	MATTRESS	ORESTEIA	RANKNESS	SLEEPERS	TIMELESS
FRONDEUR	IMPUDENT	MAYORESS	ORNAMENT	RASHNESS	SLIMNESS	TIRELESS
FULLNESS	INCIDENT	MEANNESS	ORPIMENT	READIEST	SLIPPERS	TITANESS
FUNEREAL	INDECENT	MEATLESS	OUTBREAK	REAPPEAR	SLIPPERY	TONELESS
FURTHEST	INDIGENT	MEEKNESS	OUTFIELD	REASSERT	SLOBBERY	TRANSECT
GABONESE	INDIRECT	MENSWEAR	OVERFEED	REASSESS	SLOWNESS	TRANSEPT
GADARENE	INDOLENT	MESODERM	OVERHEAD	RECKLESS	SLUGFEST	TREELESS
GALILEAN	INEXPERT	MEUNIÈRE	OVERHEAR	RECOVERY	SMALLEST	TRICKERY

TRIMNESS	GLASSFUL	CORRAGIO	STRAGGLY	FLEISHIG	THATCHED	ALIENISM
TROTTERS	GRACEFUL	COTTAGER	STRAIGHT	FORESHIP	THATCHER	ALIENIST
TROUSERS	GRATEFUL	CYANOGEN	STRANGER	GALOSHES	THOUGHTS	ALKALIFY
TRUENESS	GREENFLY	DAYLIGHT	STRANGLE	GARISHLY	THRASHER	ALKALINE
TRUMPERY	HORRIFIC	DERANGED	STRENGTH	GROSCHEN	THRESHER	ALLOWING
TUBELESS	HORSEFLY	DIALOGUE	STRINGED	HARDSHIP	TOGETHER	ALLSPICE
TWEEZERS	HOVERFLY	ENDANGER	STRINGER	HAUNCHES	TOWNSHIP	ALLURING
TWELVEMO	MERCIFUL	ENLARGED	STRONGLY	HEADSHIP	TRANSHIP	ALLUSION
TWOPIECE	MIRTHFUL	ENLARGER	STRUGGLE	HEDGEHOG	TRENCHER	ALLUSIVE
TYROLEAN	MOURNFUL	ENTANGLE	SUNLIGHT	HERSCHEL	TWITCHER	ALLUVIAL
UGLINESS	MOUTHFUL	EPILOGUE	SYRINGES	JEPHTHAH	UPRIGHTS	ALLUVIUM
UNFREEZE	PARAFFIN	ESCARGOT	TARRAGON	JONATHAN	VANISHED	ALPINIST
UNIQUELY	PARSIFAL	ESTRAGON	TEENAGER	KACHAHRI	WARDSHIP	ALSATIAN
UNLIKELY	PEACEFUL	ESTROGEN	TETRAGON	KAZACHOK	WHINCHAT	ALTRUISM
UNLOVELY	PHOTOFIT	EXOERGIC	TINTAGEL	KICKSHAW	WHITEHOT	ALTRUIST
UNTHREAD	PLATEFUL	EYESIGHT	TOBOGGAN	KINGSHIP	WOODSHED	AMANDINE
UNTIMELY	PONTIFEX	FANLIGHT	TRIANGLE	LADYSHIP	WORKSHOP	AMBITION
UPSTREAM	POWERFUL	FLASHGUN	TWILIGHT	LAVISHLY	WREATHED	AMMONIAC
VASTNESS	PROLIFIC	FOGLIGHT	UNHINGED	LECITHIN	WRETCHED	AMMONITE
VEHEMENT	RIGHTFUL	GARRIGUE	UNTANGLE	LENGTHEN	XENOPHON	AMORTIZE
VENEREAL	SCORNFUL	GLYCOGEN	VILLAGER	LONGSHIP	XERAPHIM	ANGELICA
VERONESE	SHAMEFUL	GOOSEGOG	ACANTHUS	LORDSHIP	YATAGHAN	ANNALIST
VESTMENT	SKILLFUL	HARANGUE	ALMIGHTY	MACMAHON	ABBASIDE	ANNAMITE
VILENESS	SLOTHFUL	HEPTAGON	AMBUSHED	MAILSHOT	ABESSIVE	ANNELIDA
VIREMENT	SPADEFUL	HOOLIGAN	ANARCHIC	MARATHON	ABLATION	ANNOYING
VIRULENT	SPECIFIC	HYDROGEN	ANTIPHON	MEMSAHIB	ABLATIVE	ANSERINE
VOYAGEUR	SPINIFEX	INFLIGHT	ATTACHED	METAPHOR	ABLUTION	ANTERIOR
WAITRESS	SPITEFUL	INTRIGUE	BABUSHKA	NENUPHAR	ABORTION	ANYTHING
WALLSEND	SPOONFUL	INVEIGLE	BACKCHAT	OENOPHIL	ABORTIVE	APHELION
WARDRESS	STONEFLY	JOKINGLY	BALLYHOO	OVERSHOE	ABRASION	APHORISM
WARINESS	TARTUFFE	KATTEGAT	BARATHEA	OVERSHOT	ABRASIVE	APIARIST
WEAKNESS	TASTEFUL	KORRIGAN	BLEACHER	PARASHAH	ACCUSING	APPETITE
WHEATEAR	TERRIFIC	LAVENGRO	BLOTCHED	PAWNSHOP	ACERBITY	APPOSITE
WHISKERS	THANKFUL	LILONGWE	BOOKSHOP	PEEPSHOW	ACQUAINT	APPRAISE
WHISKERY	THURIFER	LOVINGLY	BRADSHAW	PERISHED	ACROMION	AQUARIUM
WILDFELL	TRANSFER	LYSERGIC	BRANCHED	PERISHER	ACTINIDE	AQUARIUS
WILDNESS	TRANSFIX	MADRIGAL	BREACHES	PINOCHLE	ACTINIUM	AQUATINT
WILINESS	TRUSTFUL	MALINGER	BREATHER	PIROZHKI	ACTIVISM	AQUILINE
WINDLESS	TRUTHFUL	MELEAGER	BREECHES	PLANCHET	ACTIVIST	ARALDITE
WINGLESS	UNDERFED	MERINGUE	BRONCHUS	PLOUGHED	ACTIVITY	ARCADIAN
WIRELESS	UNDERFUR	MESSAGER	BROUGHAM	POLISHED	ADDITION	ARCHAISM
WITCHERY	UNLAWFUL	MICHIGAN	BUCKSHEE	POLISHER	ADDITIVE	ARGININE
WOOLLENS	VENGEFUL	MIDNIGHT	BUCKSHOT	PREACHER	ADELAIDE	ARMALITE
WORDLESS	WASTEFUL	MULLIGAN	CABOCHON	PUNISHED	ADENOIDS	ARMENIAN
YOUNGEST	WATCHFUL	NEGLIGEE	CAPUCHIN	PYORRHEA	ADESSIVE	ARMORIAL
YOURSELF	WRATHFUL	NITROGEN	CATECHOL	RHONCHUS	ADHESION	ARMORICA
ZARZUELA	WRONGFUL	OUTRIGHT	CHITCHAT	RICKSHAW	ADHESIVE	ARSONIST
ZOOSPERM	WYCLIFFE	PACKAGED	CLERIHEW	RICOCHET	ADMIRING	ARTERIAL
BASINFUL	YOUTHFUL	PATHOGEN	CLINCHER	ROADSHOW	ADMONISH	ARTESIAN
BEATIFIC	AASVOGEL	PELLAGRA	COAUTHOR	SCORCHED	ADOPTION	ARTIFICE
BELLYFUL	ABRIDGED	PENTAGON	COLOPHON	SCORCHER	ADOPTIVE	ASCIDIAN
BLACKFLY	AIRTIGHT	PILLAGER	CRATCHIT	SEALYHAM	AEROBICS	ASCIDIUM
BLISSFUL	ALLERGEN	PODARGUS	CROTCHET	SEARCHER	AEROLITH	ASPERITY
BOASTFUL	ALLERGIC	PORTUGAL	CRUNCHIE	SERAPHIC	AFFINITY	ASPIRING
BUSULFAN'	ANALOGUE	PRODIGAL	CRUTCHED	SERAPHIM	AFFUSION	ASSUMING
CASTOFFS	APOLOGIA	PROLOGUE	DECIPHER	SHANGHAI	AGNATION	ASSYRIAN
CHEERFUL	APOLOGUE	PROROGUE	DETACHED	SIDESHOW	AGRARIAN	ASTATINE
COLORFUL	ARPEGGIO	PROTÉGÉE	DIANTHUS	SISYPHUS	AGREEING	ASTERISK
CRANEFLY	ARRANGER	RATTIGAN	DIARRHEA	SLIPSHOD	AKKADIAN	ASTONISH
CRUCIFER	ASPERGES	REDLIGHT	DRAUGHTS	SMOOTHER	ALACRITY	ASUNCION
CRUCIFIX	BESIEGED	RESPIGHI	DRAUGHTY	SMOOTHLY	ALARMING	ATHELING
DOUBTFUL	BESOUGHT	ROENTGEN	DROPSHOT	SNAPSHOT	ALARMIST	ATHENIAN
DREADFUL	BUNFIGHT	SALINGER	ENMESHED	SNATCHER	ALBANIAN	ATHETISE
EVENTFUL	CAMARGUE	SAUSAGES	ENRICHED	SOMEWHAT	ALBERICH	ATROCITY
FAITHFUL	CARDIGAN	SKYLIGHT	FAMISHED	SPLASHER	ALEMAINE	AUDACITY
FANCIFUL	CARNEGIE	SPRINGER	FELLAHIN	STARCHED	ALEUTIAN	AUDITION
FEVERFEW	COLLAGEN	SQUEEGEE	FINISHED	STENDHAL	ALGERIAN	AURELIAN
FORCEFUL	COLLEGES	SQUIGGLE	FINISHER	STRACHEY	ALGERINE	AUSTRIAN
FRUITFUL	CONJUGAL	STRAGGLE	FLAGSHIP	TELETHON	ALGORISM	AUTOGIRO

AVAILING	BOTULISM	CHARTIST	COUPLING	DISUNION	ENGAGING	FEMINITY
AVENTINE	BOUNCING	CHASTISE	COVERING	DISUNITE	ENORMITY	FEROCITY
AVERSION	BRACHIAL	CHASTITY	CRACKING	DISUNITY	ENSHRINE	FETCHING
AVIATION	BRACKISH	CHEATING	CRAFTILY	DIVINITY	ENTICING	FETTLING
AVULSION	BRAGGING	CHECKING	CRAMOISY	DIVISION	ENTRAILS	FEVERISH
AYRSHIRE	BRANDISH	CHEEKILY	CRAWFISH	DIVISIVE	ENTRYISM	FIDDLING
BAATHIST	BRASSICA	CHEERILY	CRAWLING	DOCILITY	ENVISION	FIDELITY
BABBLING	BREAKING	CHEERING	CRAYFISH	DOCKSIDE	EPHESIAN	FIDUCIAL
BACKBITE	BREEDING	CHESHIRE	CREATION	DOCTRINE	EQUALITY	FIELDING
BACKFIRE	BREEZILY	CHILDISH	CREATIVE	DOLOMITE	EQUALIZE	FIENDISH
BACKSIDE	BRIDGING	CHILLING	CRINGING	DOMICILE	EQUATION	FIGHTING
BACTRIAN	BRIEFING	CHINDITS	CRISPIAN	DOMINION	ERECTILE	FIGURINE
BAFFLING	BRIMMING	CHLORIDE	CROATIAN	DONATION	ERECTING	FILARIUM
BAHAMIAN	BRINDISI	CHLORINE	CRONYISM	DONATIST	ERECTION	FILIPINO
BAHRAINI	BRINGING	CHOOSING	CROONING	DOORSILL	ERGOTISE	FILTHILY
BAKELITE	BRISLING	CHOPPING	CROSSING	DOPAMINE	ERGOTISM	FINALIST
BALDRICK	BROILING	CHROMITE	CROUPIER	DOUBTING	ERUPTION	FINALITY
BALLGIRL	BROODING	CHROMIUM	CROWNING	DOWNHILL	ESCAPISM	FINALIZE
BANALITY	BROWNING	CHURLISH	CRUSHING	DOWNSIDE	ESCAPIST	FIREBIRD
BANTLING	BROWNISH	CIBORIUM	CRUZEIRO	DOWNSIZE	ESCORIAL	FIRESIDE
BARONIAL	BROWSING	CIRCUITY	CRYOLITE	DRAINING	ESPALIER	FISHWIFE
BASELINE	BRUISING	CITATION	CUPIDITY	DREAMILY	ESPECIAL	FIXATION
BASIDIUM	BRUMAIRE	CIVILIAN	CURATIVE	DREAMING	ESSAYIST	FIXATIVE
BASILICA	BUBBLING	CIVILITY	CURTAINS	DREARILY	ESSONITE	FLAGGING
BASILISK	BUCKLING	CIVILIZE	CUTPRICE	DRESSING	ESTONIAN	FLAPPING
BATAVIAN	BUDDHISM	CLADDING	CYNICISM	DRIFTING	ETERNITY	FLASHILY
BAUDRICK	BUDDHIST	CLANGING	CYRENIAC	DRINKING	ETHERIFY	FLASHING
BAVARIAN	BUILDING	CLANNISH	CYTOSINE	DRIPPING	ETHERISE	FLATFISH
BEAUTIFY	BULLRING	CLAPPING	DABCHICK	DROOPING	ETRURIAN	FLATPICK
BECOMING	BUMBLING	CLASHING	DAINTIES	DROPPING	EUDOXIAN	FLAUTIST
BEESWING	BUNGLING	CLASPING	DAINTILY	DROWNING	EUGENICS	FLEABITE
BEETLING	BURSTING	CLASSICS	DAIQUIRI	DROWSILY	EULOGIST	FLEETING
BEHAVIOR	BUSTLING	CLASSIFY	DATELINE	DRUBBING	EULOGIUM	FLIMSILY
BENEDICK	CAFFEINE	CLAUDIUS	DAUNTING	DRUGGIST	EULOGIZE	FLIPPING
BENEDICT	CALAMINE	CLEANING	DAZZLING	DRUMLINE	EUPHUISM	FLIRTING
BENEFICE	CALAMITY	CLEARING	DEADLINE	DRUMMING	EURASIAN	FLOATING
BENEFITS	CALLGIRL	CLIMBING	DEBILITY	DUCKBILL	EUROPIUM	FLOGGING
BESTRIDE	CAMBRIAN	CLINGING	DECAYING	DUCKLING	EURYDICE	FLOODING
BIENNIAL	CAMOMILE	CLIPPING	DECISION	DUELLIST	EVENTIDE	FLOORING
BIGAMIST	CAMPAIGN	CLIQUISH	DECISIVE	DUMPLING	EVICTION	FLOURISH
BINOMIAL	CAMPSITE	CLOTHIER	DEFINITE	DUNGHILL	EXACTING	FLUIDITY
BLACKING	CANADIAN	CLOTHING	DELETION	DURATION	EXACTION	FLUORIDE
BLACKISH	CANALISE	CLOWNISH	DELIRIUM	DWARFISH	EXCISION	FLUORINE
BLANDISH	CANARIES	CLUBBING	DELUSION	DWARFISM	EXCITING	FLUORITE
BLEEDING	CANOEING	CLUMSILY	DEMOLISH	DWELLING	EXERCISE	FLUSHING
BLENDING	CANOEIST	COACHING	DEMONIAC	DYNAMICS	EXERTION	FLYDRIVE
BLESSING	CANONIZE	COALMINE	DEMOTION	DYNAMISM	EXIGUITY	FONDLING
BLINDING	CAPACITY	COERCION	DENARIUS	DYNAMITE	EXISTING	FOOTLING
BLINKING	CAPERING	COERCIVE	DENDRITE	ECLOSION	EXOCRINE	FOREMILK
BLOOMING	CARABINE	COHESION	DEPUTIZE	EDGEHILL	EXORCISM	FORFEITS
BLOWFISH	CAROLINA	COHESIVE	DERELICT	EDGEWISE	EXORCIST	FORKLIFT
BLOWPIPE	CAROLINE	COINCIDE	DERISION	EFFUSION	EXORCIZE	FORTUITY
BLURRING	CARRYING	COLONIAL	DERISIVE	EFFUSIVE	EXORDIUM	FOUNDING
BLUSHING	CATAMITE	COLONIST	DESCRIBE	EGYPTIAN	EXPEDITE	FRACTION
BOARDING	CATCHING	COLONIZE	DETOXIFY	EJECTION	EXTERIOR	FRANCIUM
BOASTING	CATERING	COLORING	DEVILISH	ELECTION	EXULTING	FRANKISH
BOATBILL	CATILINE	COMEDIAN	DEVONIAN	ELECTIVE	FACELIFT	FREAKISH
BOBOLINK	CAVALIER	COMPLINE	DEVOTION	EMBODIED	FACILITY	FREEZING
BODLEIAN	CAVATINA	COMPRISE	DIALLING	EMBOLISM	FAINTING	FRENZIED
BODYLINE	CELERIAC	CONCEIVE	DIATRIBE	EMERGING	FAMILIAR	FREUDIAN
BOEOTIAN	CELERITY	CONFLICT	DIGITIZE	EMERSION	FARTHING	FRICTION
BOHEMIAN	CENOBITE	CONSPIRE	DIGIZINE	EMISSION	FATALISM	FRISKILY
BOLIVIAN	CENTRIST	CONTRITE	DILATION	EMPORIUM	FATALIST	FRONTIER
BONEFISH	CERAMICS	CONTRIVE	DILUTION	EMULSIFY	FATALITY	FROSTILY
BONSPIEL	CHAMPION	CORNHILL	DIMINISH	EMULSION	FAVORITE	FROSTING
BORACITE	CHANGING	COUCHING	DIPSTICK	ENCOMIUM	FELICITY	FRUCTIFY
BORODINO	CHARGING	COUGHING	DISGUISE	ENDURING	FEMININE	FRUITING
BOTANIST	CHARMING	COUNTIES	DISQUIET	ENDYMION	FEMINISM	FRUITION
BOTTLING	CHARTISM	COUNTING	DISTRICT	ENERGIZE	FEMINIST	FRUMPISH

FUCHSITE	GYRATION	IMPUNITY	LECTRICE	MEANTIME	NEUTRINO	PALATIAL
FUGITIVE	HAIRLIKE	IMPURIFY	LEFTWING	MEDALIST	NICOTINE	PALATINE
FULLSIZE	HAIRLINE	IMPURITY	LEGALISM	MEDDLING	NIDATION	PALUDISM
FULLTIME	HALFTIME	INACTION	LEGALITY	MEDICINE	NIGERIAN	PANELING
FUMBLING	HANDBILL	INACTIVE	LEGALIZE	MEGALITH	NIGERIEN	PARADIGM
FUNCTION	HARDLINE	INCISION	LEGATION	MELAMINE	NIGGLING	PARASITE
FUSEWIRE	HATCHING	INCISIVE	LEWISITE	MELANITE	NIHILISM	PARISIAN
FUSILIER	HAUNTING	INCOMING	LIBATION	MELCHIOR	NIHILIST	PARODIST
FUTILITY	HAWAIIAN	INDEXING	LIBERIAN	MEMORIAL	NINEPINS	PARTHIAN
FUTURISM	HEADLINE	INDUCIVE	LICORICE	MEMORIAM	NOBELIUM	PARTTIME
FUTURIST	HEADWIND	INEQUITY	LIFELIKE	MEMORIZE	NOBILITY	PASHMINA
GAMBLING	HEARTIES	INFERIOR	LIFELINE	MENACING	NONSTICK	PATAGIUM
GAMEBIRD	HEARTILY	INFINITE	LIFETIME	MEREDITH	NOONTIME	PATCHILY
GANGLING	HEBRAISM	INFINITY	LIGHTING	MERIDIAN	NORTHING	PAVILION
GANGLION	HECKLING	INFUSION	LIKEWISE	MESOLITE	NOSEDIVE	PEARLING
GAOLBIRD	HEDONISM	INIQUITY	LIMACINE	MIDDLING	NOSTRILS	PECORINO
GASOLIER	HEDONIST	INSANITY	LIMERICK	MIDPOINT	NOTARIAL	PECULIAR
GASOLINE	HELLFIRE	INSCRIBE	LIMITING	MIGHTILY	NOTATION	PEDDLING
GELATINE	HELPLINE	INTERIOR	LIMONITE	MIGRAINE	NOVELIST	PELAGIUS
GENETICS	HEPATICA	INVASION	LINGUIST	MINIMIZE	NURSLING	PENALIZE
GENITIVE	HEREDITY	INVASIVE	LIPSTICK	MINORITE	OBLATION	PENKNIFE
GENOCIDE	HEREWITH	INVITING	LIVERIED	MINORITY	OBLIGING	PERCEIVE
GENTRIFY	HIGHRISE	IRISHISM	LIVERISH	MINUTIAE	OBLIVION	PEROXIDE
GEORGIAN	HILARITY	IRONSIDE	LIVIDITY	MISCHIEF	OBSIDIAN	PERSHING
GERANIUM	HILLSIDE	ISOCLINE	LOATHING	MISGUIDE	OCCAMIST	PERSPIRE
GERMAINE	HINDUISM	ISTHMIAN	LOBBYIST	MISPRINT	OCCASION	PERUVIAN
GERONIMO	HIRELING	IVOIRIEN	LOBELINE	MOBILITY	OCCUPIED	PETITION
GHANAIAN	HOARDING	JACOBITE	LOCALITY	MOBILIZE	OCCUPIER	PHILLIPS
GHOULISH	HOBBLING	JAILBIRD	LOCALIZE	MODELING	OFFERING	PHORMIUM
GLANCING	HOKKAIDO	JANGLING	LOCATION	MODIFIER	OFFICIAL	PHRYGIAN
GLEAMING	HOMESICK	JAPONICA	LOCATIVE	MOLEHILL	OFFPRINT	PICKWICK
GLOAMING	HOMICIDE	JAUNDICE	LONGTIME	MONADISM	OILSKINS	PIDDLING
GLOATING	HOODWINK	JAUNTILY	LORRAINE	MONDRIAN	OILSLICK	PIERCING
GLOOMILY	HORATIAN	JEBUSITE	LOVEBIRD	MONETISE	OLYMPIAD	PIGSWILL
GLUMPISH	HORATIUS	JEREMIAD	LOVESICK	MONKFISH	OLYMPIAN	PILGRIMS
GNASHING	HORNBILL	JEREMIAH	LOWERING	MONOLITH	OLYMPICS	PINPOINT
GODCHILD	HORNPIPE	JINGOISM	LOWLYING	MONOXIDE	OMISSION	PINPRICK
GOLDFISH	HOSEPIPE	JINGOIST	LOYALIST	MONTEITH	ONCOMING	PIPELINE
GOLDMINE	HOTELIER	JOYSTICK	LUCIDITY	MORALIST	OPHIDIAN	PIPERINE
GOODSIRE	HUMANISM	JUDICIAL	LUMPFISH	MORALITY	OPPOSING	PITCAIRN
GOODWIFE	HUMANIST	JUGGLING	LUNGFISH	MORALIZE	OPPOSITE	PLANKING
GOODWILL	HUMANITY	JUNCTION	LUSTRINE	MORAVIAN	OPTICIAN	PLANNING
GRAFFITI	HUMANIZE	JUVENILE	LUTENIST	MORPHINE	OPTIMISM	PLAUDITS
GRAINING	HUMIDIFY	KARTTIKA	LUTETIUM	MOSQUITO	OPTIMIST	PLAYBILL
GRAPHICS	HUMIDITY	KERCHIEF	LYNCHING	MOTORING	ORCADIAN	PLAYGIRL
GRAPHITE	HUMILITY	KINDLING	LYREBIRD	MOTORIST	ORDERING	PLAYTIME
GRASPING	HUMORIST	KINETICS	LYRICISM	MOTORIZE	ORGANISM	PLEADING
GRATUITY	HUNGRILY	KINGSIZE	LYRICIST	MOULDING	ORGANIST	PLEASING
GRAYLING	HURDLING	KLONDIKE	MAGAZINE	MOUNTING	ORGANIZE	PLEBEIAN
GREEDILY	HYPERION	KNEEHIGH	MAGICIAN	MOURNING	OTTAVINO	PLEURISY
GREENING	ICEBLINK	KNITTING	MAINLINE	MUMBLING	OUISTITI	PLUCKILY
GREENISH	IDEALISM	KNOCKING	MAJOLICA	MURRHINE	OUTGOING	PLUCKING
GREETING	IDEALIST	KOURMISS	MAJORITY	MUSICIAN	OUTLYING	PLUMBING
GRILLING	IDEALIZE	LACEWING	MALARIAL	MUTATION	OUTSHINE	PLUNGING
GRINDING	IDENTIFY	LACONIAN	MALAWIAN	MYCELIUM	OUTWEIGH	POLARIZE
GRIPPING	IDENTITY	LADYBIRD	MANAGING	NAMIBIAN	OVENBIRD	POLITICO
GROGGILY	IGNITION	LADYFISH	MANDRILL	NATALITY	OVERFILL	POLITICS
GROOMING	IGNOMINY	LADYLIKE	MANORIAL	NATIVITY	OVERKILL	POLONIUM
GROUPING	ILLUMINE	LAKESIDE	MANTLING	NATURISM	OVERRIDE	POPULIST
GROUTING	ILLUSION	LANDFILL	MARITIME	NATURIST	OVERRIPE	POROSITY
GROWLING	ILLUSIVE	LANDMINE	MARONITE	NAUPLIUS	OVERSIZE	PORPOISE
GRUDGING	IMBECILE	LANGUISH	MARQUISE	NAVARINO	OVERTIME	POSITION
GRUMPILY	IMMOBILE	LANOLINE	MATCHING	NECKLINE	OVERVIEW	POSITIVE
GUARDIAN	IMMUNITY	LATERITE	MATERIAL	NEGATION	PACIFIER	POULAINE
GUIANIAN	IMMUNIZE	LATINIST	MATURITY	NEGATIVE	PACIFISM	POULTICE
GUILTILY	IMPERIAL	LAUGHING	MAVERICK	NEHEMIAH	PACIFIST	PRACTICE
GUMPTION	IMPETIGO	LAXATIVE	MAXIMIZE	NEPHRITE	PADDLING	PRACTISE
GUNPOINT	IMPOLITE	LEACHING	MAZARINE	NEPOTISM	PAGANINI	PRAIRIAL
GUNSMITH	IMPOSING	LEARNING	MEALTIME	NESTLING	PAINTING	PRANDIAL

PRESSING	RIGHTIST	SEEDLING	SNOWLINE	STUFFILY	TITANITE	VAPORIZE
PRESTIGE	RIGIDITY	SEETHING	SOBERING	STUFFING	TITANIUM	VAULTING
PRETTILY	RINGSIDE	SEIGNIOR	SODALITE	STULTIFY	TONALITY	VELLEITY
PRIAPISM	RIPARIAN	SELENITE	SODALITY	STUNNING	TORTOISE	VELOCITY
PRIGGISH	RIPPLING	SELENIUM	SOLARIUM	STURDILY	TOTALITY	VENALITY
PRINTING	RIVALISE	SELFPITY	SOLECISM	SUCHLIKE	TOTALIZE	VENETIAN
PRIORITY	RIVERINE	SEMOLINA	SOLIDIFY	SUCKLING	TOUCHING	VERACITY
PRISTINE	RIVETING	SENILITY	SOLIDITY	SUDAMINA	TOVARICH	VERJUICE
PROCAINE	ROADSIDE	SENORITA	SOLSTICE	SUDARIUM	TOWELING	VERLAINE
PRUSSIAN	ROASTING	SERAFILE	SOLUTION	SULPHIDE	TOWERING	VERONICA
PSALMIST	ROBOTICS	SERENITY	SOMETIME	SUMERIAN	TOXICITY	VESUVIUS
PTOMAINE	RODERICK	SEVERITY	SONATINA	SUNDRIED	TRACKING	VEXATION
PTYALISM	ROGATION	SHABBILY	SONGBIRD	SUNDRIES	TRACTION	VICARIAL
PUGILISM	ROMANIAN	SHEEPISH	SOOTHING	SUNSHINE	TRAILING	VICINITY
PUGILIST	ROSALIND	SHELVING	SORORITY	SUPERIOR	TRAINING	VILLAINY
PUNITIVE	ROSALINE	SHIELING	SOUNDING	SUPPLIER	TRAMLINE	VIPERISH
PURBLIND	ROSEFISH	SHIFTING	SOURCING	SUPPLIES	TRAPPIST	VIRILITY
PURIFIED	ROTATION	SHILLING	SPANKING	SURPLICE	TREATISE	VISELIKE
PURIFIER	ROYALIST	SHIPPING	SPANNING	SURPRISE	TREELINE	VISITING
PURPLISH	RUBIDIUM	SHOCKING	SPARKING	SWARMING	TRIFLING	VITALISM
PUSHBIKE	RUMBLING	SHODDILY	SPARRING	SWASTIKA	TRILLING	VITALITY
PUTATIVE	RUSTLING	SHOEBILL	SPARSITY	SWEARING	TRILLION	VITALIZE
PUZZLING	SADDLING	SHOOTING	SPAWNING	SWEATING	TRILLIUM	VITAMINS
PYRAMIDS	SAGACITY	SHOPPING	SPEAKING	SWEEPING	TRIMMING	VITILIGO
QUADRIGA	SALACITY	SHOUTING	SPEEDILY	SWELLING	TRIPLING	VIVACITY
QUAGMIRE	SALARIED	SHOWGIRL	SPELLING	SWERVING	TRISTICH	VIVARIUM
QUANTIFY	SALINITY	SHREWISH	SPENDING	SWILLING	TRIUNITY	VOCALIST
QUANTITY	SALTLICK	SIBERIAN	SPIFFING	SWIMMING	TROOPING	VOCALIZE
QUARTIER	SAMARIUM	SICILIAN	SPINNING	SWINGING	TROTLINE	VOCATION
QUARTILE	SAMPHIRE	SICKLIST	SPITFIRE	SWIRLING	TRUCKING	VOCATIVE
QUAYSIDE	SANCTIFY	SIDEKICK	SPITTING	SYBARITE	TRUNNION	VOLATILE
QUESTION	SANCTION	SIDELINE	SPOILING	SYNCLINE	TRUSTING	VOLITION
QUILTING	SANCTITY	SIDERITE	SPORTING	TAHITIAN	TUNISIAN	VOLSCIAN
QUISLING	SANDWICH	SIGHTING	SPORTIVE	TAILPIPE	TURNPIKE	VOLTAIRE
RAINBIRD	SANGLIER	SILESIAN	SPOTTING	TAMARIND	TUTORIAL	VOMITING
RAMBLING	SANGUINE	SILURIAN	SPURNING	TAMARISK	TWIRLING	VORACITY
RAPACITY	SANITIZE	SIMONIAC	STABBING	TAPERING	TWISTING	VOWELIZE
RAPIDITY	SAPONITE	SIMPLIFY	STABLING	TAXATION	TYROSINE	WALTZING
RAREFIED	SAPPHIRE	SINAPISM	STAFFING	TEACHING	TZATZIKI	WAMBLING
RATTLING	SAPPHIST	SIRENIAN	STALKING	TEESHIRT	UBIQUITY	WARPAINT
REACTION	SATIRIST	SIZZLING	STALLION	TEETHING	ULTERIOR	WATCHING
REACTIVE	SATIRIZE	SKIDDING	STANDING	TELEFILM	UNCARING	WATERING
REAFFIRM	SAXATILE	SKILLING	STANDISH	TELEVISE	UNEASILY	WAVERING
REALTIME	SCALDING	SKILLION	STANNITE	TEMERITY	UNENDING	WEAKFISH
REASSIGN	SCALLION	SKIPPING	STARFISH	TEMPTING	UNERRING	WEAKLING
RECEDING	SCANDIUM	SKIRMISH	STARLING	TENACITY	UNFADING	WEIGHING
RECRUITS	SCANNING	SKIRTING	STARTING	TETCHILY	UNFYING	WELLNIGH
REDBRICK	SCANSION	SKITTISH	STARVING	THALLIUM	UNIONISM	WHACKING
REDEFINE	SCANTIES	SKULKING	STEADILY	THEBAINE	UNIONIST	WHEEZILY
REDESIGN	SCANTILY	SLANGING	STEALING	THEORIST	UNIONIZE	WHEEZING
REDSHIFT	SCARCITY	SLANTING	STEATITE	THEORIZE	UNSOCIAL	WHIPPING
REEDLING	SCATHING	SLEEPILY	STEERING	THESPIAN	UNSPOILT	WHIRLING
REFUGIUM	SCHEMING	SLEEPING	STERLING	THIAMINE	UNTIDILY	WHITLING
REGICIDE	SCIATICA	SLIPPING	STICKILY	THIEVING	UNUNBIUM	WHOOPING
REIGNING	SCISSION	SLOPPILY	STICKING	THIEVISH	UNVARIED	WHOPPING
RELATING	SCOFFING	SLUGGISH	STIFLING	THINKING	UPCOMING	WIDENING
RELATION	SCOLDING	SLUMMING	STINGING	THINNING	UPRISING	WILDFIRE
RELATIVE	SCORPION	SLURRING	STINKING	THRACIAN	UPSTAIRS	WILDLIFE
RELAXING	SCORPIUS	SLUTTISH	STIRLING	THUMPING	URBANITY	WINDMILL
RELAYING	SCOTTISH	SMASHING	STIRRING	TIBERIAS	URBANIZE	WINDPIPE
RELIGION	SCOURING	SMELTING	STOCKING	TIBERIUS	URSULINE	WITCHING
REMEDIAL	SCOWLING	SMOCKING	STOCKIST	TICKLING	UTENSILS	WOBBLING
REPAYING	SCRUTINY	SNAPPILY	STOICISM	TICKLISH	VACATION	WOMANISH
RESTRICT	SCULLION	SNEAKING	STOPPING	TIMIDITY	VAGARIES	WOMANIZE
RETIRING	SEAGOING	SNEERING	STORMING	TINGLING	VALERIAN	WOODBINE
REVISION	SECURITY	SNEEZING	STRABISM	TINSMITH	VALETING	WOODWIND
REVIVIFY	SEDATION	SNOBBISH	STRATIFY	TIRAMISU	VALIDITY	WORRYING
REVIVING	SEDATIVE	SNOOTILY	STRIKING	TIRESIAS	VANADIUM	WORTHIES
RIESLING	SEDITION	SNORTING	STRIVING	TITANISM	VANQUISH	WORTHILY

WRAPPING	UNSHAKEN	DAMOCLES	LEVELLER	REEMPLOY	UNFILLED	DIPLOMAT
WRINGING	UNSPOKEN	DETAILED	LINCOLNS	REPUBLIC	UNIPOLAR	DULCIMER
WRITHING	UPMARKET	DEVILLED	MACAULAY	RETAILER	UNIVALVE	DUTCHMAN
XENOLITH	VAISAKHA	DIABOLIC	MAGELLAN	REVEALED	UNRIFLED	ECONOMIC
YACHTING	ABUTILON	DICYCLIC	MAGNOLIA	REVEILLE	UNSEALED	EGGTIMER
YEARLING	ACAPULCO	DISABLED	MALVOLIO	REVELLER	UNTILLED	EPIDEMIC
YEARNING	ACHILLES	DISALLOW	MANDOLIN	REYNOLDS	UNWIELDY	EPIGAMIC
YIELDING	ACTUALLY	DISCOLOR	MANFULLY	RISSOLES	USEFULLY	ESTEEMED
.YOSEMITE	AEROFLOT	DISMALLY	MANTILLA	RITUALLY	VALHALLA	EVERYMAN
YULETIDE	AIGUILLE	DISSOLVE	MANUALLY	RUEFULLY	VALVULAR	FANCYMAN
ZEDEKIAH	ALVEOLUS	DOOLALLY	MARCELLA	SCAPULAR	VASCULAR	FERRYMAN
ZIBELINE	ANATOLIA	DOWNPLAY	MARCELLO	SCHILLER	VERBALLY	FRESHMAN
ZUCCHINI	ANGUILLA	DURABLES	MARTELLO	SCHMALTZ	VEXILLUM	FRONTMAN
CARCAJOU	ANNEALER	EATABLES	MCKINLEY	SCRAWLED	VINCULUM	FUGLEMAN
KINKAJOU	ANNUALLY	ENTHALPY	MENTALLY	SCRUPLES	VINDALOO	GALLUMPH
NIGHTJAR	ANTILLES	ENTITLED	MERCALLI	SCYBALUM	VISUALLY	GIGLAMPS
POPINJAY	APOSTLES	EUCYCLIC	MESCALIN	SERAGLIO	VITELLUS	GOSSAMER
TURBOJET	APPALLED	EXEMPLAR	METALLED	SEXUALLY	WATERLOO	GRAVAMEN
ATTACKER	ARTFULLY	FITFULLY	METALLIC	SHACKLES	WAVERLEY	HANDYMAN
BAEDEKER	ARTICLED	FLOODLIT	MODELLER	SHAMBLES	WHISTLER	HELMSMAN
BEARSKIN	ARTICLES	FLOTILLA	MONGOLIA	SHIGELLA	WILFULLY	HENCHMAN
BEDMAKER	BACHELOR	FORMALIN	MORBILLI	SHINGLES	WOEFULLY	HERDSMAN
BESPOKEN	BACILLUS	FORMALLY	MORTALLY	SIDESLIP	WOLSELEY	HORSEMAN
BUCKSKIN	BARDOLPH	FRANKLIN	MOUFFLON	SIGNALER	WRANGLER	HORSEMEN
CALFSKIN	BARGELLO	FRAZZLED	MUSCULAR	SIGNALLY	WRESTLER	HOUSEMAN
CHEROKEE	BASTILLE	FRECKLED	MUTUALLY	SINGULAR	WRINKLED	HUNTSMAN
DEERSKIN	BERKELEY	FRECKLES	NARGILEH	SITTELLA	WRISTLET	INDIAMAN
DISLIKED	BIATHLON	FRENULUM	NAUTILUS	SKITTLES	YARMULKA	INFLAMED
DZONGKHA	BLACKLEG	FRUGALLY	NEGRILLO	SKYPILOT	YODELLER	INFORMAL
FORESKIN	BORDELLO	FURBELOW	NICHOLAS	SLIPSLOP	YUGOSLAV	INFORMED
FORSAKEN	BRACELET	GARDYLOO	NORMALLY	SMUGGLED	ZEPPELIN	INFORMER
GOATSKIN	BRASILIA	GAUNTLET	OFFCOLOR	SMUGGLER	ABNORMAL	INTERMIT
GRANDKID	BRINDLED	GENIALLY	OMPHALOS	SNIFFLER	ACADEMIA	IRISHMAN
HABAKKUK	BRISTLED	GLABELLA	OPENPLAN	SOCALLED	ACADEMIC	IRISHMEN
HANUKKAH	BRISTLES	GLOBALLY	OSTERLEY	SOCIALLY	ALCHEMIC	KOMSOMOL
HAYMAKER	BROMELIA	GLOBULAR	OVERALLS	SPANGLED	ALDERMAN	LEADSMAN
HIJACKER	BRUTALLY	GLOBULIN	OVERFLOW	SPARKLER	ANALEMMA	LEUKEMIA
LAMBSKIN	BUNGALOW	GOIDELIC	OVERPLAY	SPECKLED	ANATOMIC	LIEGEMAN
LATCHKEY	CACHALOT	GOLFCLUB	PAMPHLET	SPECULUM	ASPERMIA	LINESMAN
LAWMAKER	CADILLAC	GONFALON	PANELLED	SPIRALLY	BANDSMAN	MADWOMAN
MALARKEY	CALCULUS	GRANULAR	PANGOLIN	SPIRELET	BARGEMAN	MANDAMUS
MANNIKIN	CAMELLIA	GRANULES	PANTALON	SPRAWLED	BECALMED	MARASMUS
MISTAKEN	CANAILLE	GRAVELLY	PAPILLON	SQUEALER	BECHAMEL	MARKSMAN
MOLESKIN	CARBOLIC	GRIMALDI	PARALLAX	STAPELIA	BENJAMIN	MISNOMER
MONICKER	CARILLON	GRISELDA	PARALLEL	STICKLER	BERGAMOT	MOHAMMED
MUNCHKIN	CASUALLY	GRIZZLED	PAROLLES	STIMULUS	BESSEMER	MORTIMER
MUTCHKIN	CASUALTY	GRUMBLER	PASTILLE	STROLLER	BETJEMAN	MOTORMAN
ONLOOKER	CATHOLIC	GUERILLA	PATELLAR	SWADDLER	BOGEYMAN	MUHAMMAD
OXPECKER	CATULLUS	HANDCLAP	PENDULUM	SWINDLER	BONDSMAN	NEWCOMER
PANNIKIN	CAUDILLO	HAVDALAH	PERICLES	SYMBOLIC	BONHOMIE	NOBLEMAN
POTEMKIN	CELLULAR	HERACLES	PETERLOO	SYPHILIS	BOTTOMRY	NORSEMAN
REAWAKEN	CEPHALIN	HERACLID	PHENOLIC	TANTALUM	CARDAMOM	NORSEMEN
SEALSKIN	CERVELAT	HERCULES	PHYSALIA	TANTALUS	CHAIRMAN	OMDURMAN
SHRUNKEN	CHANDLER	HOSTELRY	PLATELET	TEFILLIN	CHESSMAN	OUTREMER
SLOVAKIA	CHENILLE	IMPELLED	POLYGLOT	TEQUILLA	CHESSMEN	PANDEMIC
SPRINKLE	CHIVALRY	INOCULUM	POTBELLY	THRILLER	CHIASMUS	PERFUMED
SPROCKET	CINGULUM	INTAGLIO	POTHOLER	TINSELLY	CHINAMAN	PHILEMON
SQUEAKER	CIRCULAR	IRONCLAD	PRATTLER	TOADFLAX	CINNAMON	PHILOMEL
STREAKED	COLESLAW	ISABELLA	PREDELLA	TORTILLA	CLANSMAN	PHLEGMON
STREAKER	COMPILER	ISABELLE	PREMOLAR	TRAVELER	COACHMAN	PLACEMAT
STRICKEN	CONSULAR	JEWELLED	PROPOLIS	TREMBLER	COGNOMEN	PLACEMEN
STRICKLE	CONVULSE	JEWELLER	PRUNELLA	TREMBLES	CONSOMMÉ	PRESSMAN
SWANSKIN	CORIOLIS	JOVIALLY	PUSTULAR	TROCHLEA	CONSUMED	PROXIMAL
TAILSKID	CORSELET	JOYFULLY	QUENELLE	TROUBLED	CONSUMER	RANDOMLY
TRANSKEI	COVERLET	KINGSLEY	QUIBBLER	TROUBLES	CONTEMPT	REDEEMER
UNBROKEN	CRIPPLED	LANCELET	RACIALLY	TRUCKLED	CUSTOMER	REEDSMAN
UNCOOKED	CROSSLET	LANCELOT	RASCALLY	UMBRELLA	CYCLAMEN	REFORMED
UNLOCKED	CYRILLIC	LANDSLIP	RASSELAS	UNDERLAY	DAIRYMAN	REFORMER
UNMARKED	DAEDALUS	LAWFULLY	REDEPLOY	UNDERLIE	DEFORMED	RHYTHMIC

RIFLEMAN	BURDENED	EMINENCE	INSOMNIA	PEELINGS	SLOVENIA	ADVISORY
SALESMAN	BURGUNDY	EMINENCY	INSTANCE	PENNINES	SLOVENLY	AEROFOIL
SCOTSMAN	CABERNET	ENCAENIA	INSTINCT	PENZANCE	SOFTENER	AGRICOLA
SCREAMER	CARBONIC	ENSCONCE	INTERNAL	PERIANTH	SOLEMNLY	AGRIMONY
SEEDSMAN	CARCANET	ENTRANCE	INTERNEE	PERSONAL	SOLVENCY	AGRONOMY
SHEARMAN	CARDINAL	ENTRENCH	INTERNET	PHALANGE	SORBONNE	ALBACORE
SIDESMAN	CASTANET	ERIDANUS	INTRENCH	PICKINGS	SOUVENIR	ALBINONI
SPACEMAN	CHACONNE	EUPHONIA	ISOGENIC	PILSENER	SPAVINED	ALEATORY
SPECIMEN	CHESTNUT	EUPHONIC	ISOGONAL	PIMIENTO	SPHAGNUM	ALGOLOGY
SPELLMAN	CHEYENNE	EVIDENCE	JOHANNES	PIQUANCY	SPRAINED	ALKALOID
STOCKMAN	CIRCINUS	EXAMINEE	JONCANOE	PITTANCE	STAMENED	ALLEGORY
STOREMAN	CLARENCE	EXAMINER	JOTTINGS	PLACENTA	STRAINED	AMMONOID
STREAMER	CLARINET	EXCHANGE	JULIENNE	PLATANUS	STRAINER	ANECDOTE
SUBHUMAN	CLEMENCY	EXIGENCY	KATMANDU	PLATINUM	STUDENTS	ANTELOPE
SUPERMAN	COMBINED	EXTERNAL	KILKENNY	PLATONIC	SUBSONIC	ANTEPOST
SYSTEMIC	COMMANDO	EXTERNAT	LABURNUM	PLOTINUS	SUBTENSE	ANTEROOM
TABLEMAT	COMMENCE	EYELINER	LADRONES	POISONER	SUCCINCT	ANTIBODY
TALISMAN	COMMONER	FALCONRY	LASHINGS	POLYANNA	SUDDENLY	ANTIDOTE
TENESMUS	COMMONLY	FANDANGO	LAUDANUM	PONSONBY	SULLENLY	ANTILOPE
THALAMUS	COMMUNAL	FASTENER	LAURENCE	PRECINCT	SUNDANCE	ANTIMONY
TOWNSMAN	CONDENSE	FAULKNER	LAWRENCE	PRESENCE	SUPERNAL	ANTIPOPE
TOXAEMIA	CONFINED	FEELINGS	LEAVENED	PRETENCE	SUSPENSE	ASTEROID
TRANSMIT	CONFINES	FINDINGS	LEAVINGS	PRETENSE	SYLVANER	ATHEROMA
TRILEMMA	CONTANGO	FLAMENCO	LEGGINGS	PRISONER	TANZANIA	ATHETOID
TURKOMAN	CONTENTS	FLAMINGO	LENIENCY	PROVINCE	TASMANIA	AUDITORY
UNCOMMON	CONTINUE	FLORENCE	LISTENER	PRUDENCE	TAVERNER	AUTONOMY
UNHARMED	CONTINUO	FRAXINUS	LODGINGS	PUNGENCY	TECTONIC	BABYHOOD
UNSEEMLY	CONVENER	FRUMENTY	LONDONER	QUIRINAL	TENDENCY	BACKBONE
WATCHMAN	CONVINCE	GALBANUM	LOWLANDS	RADIANCE	TERMINAL	BACKCOMB
WATERMAN	CRETONNE	GALVANIC	MACHINES	RAILINGS	TERMINUS	BACKROOM
WELSHMAN	CRIMINAL	GARDENER	MAECENAS	RAISONNÉ	TEUTONIC	BALLCOCK
WOODSMAN	CULLINAN	GARDENIA	MAHJONGG	RATIONAL	TRIBUNAL	BALLROOM
ABEYANCE	CURRENCY	GARGANEY	MAIDENLY	REASONED	TUPPENNY	BANKBOOK
ACCOUNTS	DARKENED	GARMENTS	MANGONEL	RECKONER	TURBANED	BANKNOTE
AIRLINER	DEADENED	GEOMANCY	MARGINAL	REFRINGE	TURGENEV	BANKROLL
ALBURNUM	DEADENER	GERMANIC	MARIANAS	REGAINED	TWOPENNY	BAREFOOT
ALDERNEY	DEALINGS	GERMINAL	MARTINET	REGIONAL	TYMPANUM	BARITONE
ALICANTE	DEFIANCE	GIACONDA	MASSENET	REJOINED	UNEARNED	BASEBORN
ALLIANCE	DEMEANOR	GIOCONDA	MATERNAL	RELIANCE	UNEVENLY	BASSWOOD
ALUMINUM	DENOUNCE	GIOVANNI	MATRONLY	REMNANTS	UNGAINLY	BATHROBE
AMARANTH	DESIGNER	GLOXINIA	MECHANIC	REMOUNTS	UNMANNED	BATHROOM
AMBIANCE	DESTINED	GOVERNOR	METHANOL	RENMINBI	UNSIGNED	BEANPOLE
AMBIENCE	DETAINEE	GRATINEE	MIDLANDS	RENOUNCE	UNWEANED	BEAUFORT
ANACONDA	DETAINER	GUIDANCE	MIGNONNE	RENOWNED	UPTURNED	BEAUMONT
ANNOUNCE	DEVIANCE	HACIENDA	MILLINER	RESIGNED	VAGRANCY	BEERBOHM
ANTENNAE	DIAGONAL	HANGINGS	MINDANAO	RESPONSE	VARIANCE	BEETROOT
ARACHNID	DIAMANTE	HARDENED	MNEMONIC	RETAINER	VIBRANCY	BEHEMOTH
ARAMANTH	DIAMONDS	HARMONIC	MOORINGS	RETRENCH	VIBURNUM	BELABOUR
ARDENNES	DIATONIC	HASTINGS	NATIONAL	RIDDANCE	VIOLENCE	BIBULOUS
ARMAGNAC	DIGGINGS	HAWFINCH	NEPIONIC	SARDINIA	VIRGINAL	BIGAMOUS
ASSIGNEE	DIOGENES	HAZELNUT	NONSENSE	SARDONIC	VIRGINIA	BILLFOLD
ASTHENIA	DIPHENYL	HEAVENLY	NORMANDY	SARDONYX	VOIDANCE	BILLHOOK
ATALANTA	DISHONOR	HELLENIC	NOTIONAL	SASSANID	VOLCANIC	BIOSCOPE
ATTORNEY	DISJUNCT	HELSINKI	NUISANCE	SATURNIA	WAGGONER	BLACKOUT
AUDIENCE	DISPENSE	HIBERNIA	OBTAINED	SAVANNAH	WARRANTY	BLASTOFF
AUTUMNAL	DISTANCE	HISPANIC	ODDMENTS	SAWBONES	WEAPONRY	BLOWHOLE
AVICENNA	DISTINCT	HOGMANAY	OPOPANAX	SCALENUS	WETLANDS	BLUECOAT
BADLANDS	DOORKNOB	HOLDINGS	OPTIONAL	SCAVENGE	WHITENER	BLUENOSE
BANDANNA	DOUGHNUT	HORMONAL	OPULENCE	SCHOONER	WHODUNIT	BOATLOAD
BASSINET	DRACONIC	HUSTINGS	ORDNANCE	SCREENED	WINDINGS	BODYWORK
BEARINGS	DUBONNET	HYACINTH	ORIGINAL	SCROUNGE	WINNINGS	BOLTHOLE
BEGINNER	DULCINEA	HYGIENIC	ORPHANED	SEASONAL	WOODENLY	BOOKROOM
BERGENIA	DUODENAL	IMAGINED	PACHINKO	SEASONED	WORKINGS	BOOKWORK
BIGNONIA	DUODENUM	INCLINED	PANDANUS	SENTENCE	WRITINGS	BOOKWORM
BRAGANZA	EARNINGS	INFERNAL	PARDONER	SENTINEL	YEOMANRY	BORECOLE
BRAMANTE	EGOMANIA	INFRINGE	PARLANCE	SEQUENCE	YERSINIA	BOREHOLE
BRANDNEW	ELEGANCE	INGUINAL	PATERNAL	SHRAPNEL	ZIRCONIA	BREAKOUT
BRUCKNER	ELEMENTS	INNUENDO	PATIENCE	SINFONIA	ABATTOIR	BROCCOLI
BUOYANCY	ELEVENTH	INSIGNIA	PAULINUS	SIXPENCE	ACRIMONY	BRYOZOAN

BULLDOZE	DEMIJOHN	FOOTWORK	HEMIPODE	MANIFOLD	PANGLOSS	ROTENONE
BULLHORN	DENDROID	FOREBODE	HEREFORD	MANITOBA	PARABOLA	RUCTIONS
BURNTOUT	DERISORY	FOREDOOM	HERMIONE	MARABOUT	PARAMOUR	RULEBOOK
BUSYBODY	DESIROUS	FOREFOOT	HIGHBORN	MARIGOLD	PARANOIA	RUNABOUT
BUZZWORD	DETHRONE	FOREGONE	HIGHROAD	MARKDOWN	PARANOID	RUSHMORE
CABRIOLE	DEXTROSE	FORELOCK	HINDMOST	MATAMORE	PASSBOOK	SAILBOAT
CAKEHOLE	DEXTROUS	FOREMOST	HOLOZOIC	MEGAPODE	PASSPORT	SAINFOIN
CALLIOPE	DIAGNOSE	FORENOON	HOLYROOD	MEGAVOLT	PASSWORD	SALEROOM
CAMEROON	DIAPHONE	FOREWORD	HOMEWORK	MELANOMA	PATULOUS	SALUTORY
CAMISOLE	DIASPORA	FORMWORK	HONGKONG	MELTDOWN	PEDAGOGY	SARATOGA
CAMPTOWN	DIASTOLE	FORSOOTH	HOOKWORM	MESOZOIC	PEEPHOLE	SCABIOUS
CAMSTONE	DILATORY	FOURFOLD	HORNBOOK	METABOLA	PEIGNOIR	SCABROUS
CAPRIOLE	DISCLOSE	FOURSOME	HORNPOUT	MILKWORT	PEMBROKE	SCAFFOLD
CAPSTONE	DISPROVE	FOXGLOVE	HOROLOGY	MILLIONS	PENELOPE	SCAPHOID
CAPTIOUS	DOGSBODY	FRABJOUS	HUMOROUS	MILLPOND	PENOLOGY	SCHIZOID
CARACOLE	DOGTOOTH	FREEHOLD	HYDATOID	MINATORY	PEPERONI	SCHMOOZE
CAREWORN	DOLOROUS	FREEPOST	IDEOLOGY	MIREPOIX	PERILOUS	SCISSORS
CARRIOLE	DOMINOES	FREETOWN	ILLINOIS	MISQUOTE	PERVIOUS	SEAFLOOR
CARTLOAD	DOORPOST	FRETWORK	ILLUSORY	MONGOOSE	PHYLLOME	SEAFRONT
CASANOVA	DOUBLOON	FRUCTOSE	INFAMOUS	MONOPOLE	PICAROON	SEASHORE
CATACOMB	DOVECOTE	FUMAROLE	IRISCOPE	MONOPOLY	PICKLOCK	SEDULOUS
CATATONY	DOWNLOAD	FUMITORY	IRONWOOD	MONOTONY	PILTDOWN	SEMITONE
CATEGORY	DOWNPOUR	FUSAROLE	IRONWORK	MOORCOCK	PINAFORE	SENSUOUS
CAUTIOUS	DOWNTOWN	FUSIFORM	IROQUOIS	MOREPORK	PINEWOOD	SEROLOGY
CENOZOIC	DOXOLOGY	GABORONE	ISOGLOSS	MUDSTONE	PISIFORM	SEXOLOGY
CENTRODE	DRAGOONS	GADABOUT	JACKBOOT	MULEWORT	PLATFORM	SHAKEOUT
CERATOID	DRYGOODS	GADZOOKS	JEREBOAM	MUSHROOM	PLAYROOM	SHALLOWS
CEREMONY	DRYSTONE	GARAMOND	JEROBOAM	MUTINOUS	PLETHORA	SHAMROCK
CESSPOOL	EARPHONE	GATEFOLD	JOHNSONS	MYCOLOGY	PLIMSOLL	SHAREOUT
CHARCOAL	ECHINOPS	GATEPOST	JURATORY	NAUSEOUS	PLUGHOLE	SHAVUOTH
CHARLOCK	ELECTORS	GEMOLOGY	KEYSTONE	NEBULOUS	POLTROON	SHERLOCK
CHECKOUT	ELSINORE	GENEROUS	KHARTOUM	NEMATODE	POOLROOM	SHERWOOD
CHEVIOTS	ENORMOUS	GEOPHONE	KIDGLOVE	NEMATOID	POPULOUS	SHINBONE
CICERONE	ENSHROUD	GIRASOLE	KILOVOLT	NEWSROOM	PORTHOLE	SHIPWORM
CINCHONA	ENSIFORM	GIRLHOOD	KINGPOST	NOSOLOGY	POSOLOGY	SHOEHORN
CLANGOUR	ENTHRONE	GLABROUS	KINSFOLK	NOSTROMO	POSTCODE	SHOOTOUT
CLAYMORE	ENVELOPE	GLADSOME	KNOCKOUT	NOTEBOOK	POSTPONE	SHOWBOAT
CLIFFORD	ENVIRONS	GLASNOST	KNOTWORK	NUCLEOLE	POTATOES	SHOWDOWN
CLODPOLL	EPIPLOON	GLAUCOMA	KOUSKOUS	NUGATORY	POTSTONE	SHOWROOM
CLUBFOOT	ESCALOPE	GLAUCOUS	KRUMHORN	NUMEROUS	PRECIOUS	SHUTDOWN
COALHOLE	ETHOLOGY	GLEESOME	LAMPPOST	NUMINOUS	PREVIOUS	SICKROOM
COALPORT	EVENSONG	GLORIOLE	LANDLOCK	OCTAROON	PRIMROSE	SIDELONG
COCACOLA	EVERMORE	GLORIOUS	LANDLORD	OENOLOGY	PRINTOUT	SIGNPOST
COCKBOAT	EVERYONE	GLUTTONY	LAVATORY	OFFSHOOT	PRODROME	SILICONE
COLDBOOT	EVILDOER	GOALPOST	LAYABOUT	OFFSHORE	PSALMODY	SILKWORM
COLIFORM	EXIGUOUS	GOODWOOD	LIBELOUS	OILCLOTH	PULLDOWN	SINGSONG
COMATOSE	EYETOOTH	GORGEOUS	LIFEBOAT	OKLAHOMA	PUSHDOWN	SINKHOLE
COMEDOWN	FABULOUS	GRACIOUS	LIFELONG	OMNIFORM	PYRIFORM	SKIBOOTS
CONCHOID	FACTIOUS	GREENOCK	LIGNEOUS	OMNIVORE	QUADROON	SKINWORK
CONFRONT	FATSTOCK	GRIDLOCK	LIVELONG	ONCOLOGY	RAGSTONE	SLOWDOWN
CONTROLS	FEARSOME	GRIEVOUS	LOANWORD	ONTOLOGY	RAILROAD	SLOWPOKE
COOKBOOK	FEELGOOD	GRUESOME	LOBOTOMY	OPENDOOR	RAINCOAT	SLOWWORM
COPYBOOK	FIREBOLT	GYRATORY	LONESOME	OPENWORK	RAVENOUS	SLYBOOTS
COPYHOLD	FIREWOOD	HAIRWORM	LONGBOAT	OTOSCOPE	REARMOST	SOFTWOOD
CORONOID	FIREWORK	HALFHOUR	LONGHORN	OUTDOORS	RESINOUS	SOLENOID
COTSWOLD	FISHBONE	HANDBOOK	LOOPHOLE	OVERBOOK	RESTROOM	SOMEBODY
COUSCOUS	FISHHOOK	HANDSOME	LOVELORN	OVERCOAT	RHAPSODY	SONOROUS
COVETOUS	FISHPOND	HARDCORE	LUMINOUS	OVERCOME	RHOMBOID	SOUCHONG
CREOSOTE	FLAGPOLE	HARDWOOD	LUNGWORT	OVERDONE	RIBSTONE	SOURWOOD
CROWFOOT	FLAMEOUT	HARTFORD	LUSCIOUS	OVERDOSE	RIGATONI	SPACIOUS
CRUMHORN	FLATBOAT	HAWTHORN	LUSTROUS	OVERLOAD	RIGOROUS	SPECIOUS
CRUMMOCK	FLATFOOT	HEADLONG	MACARONI	OVERLOOK	RINGDOVE	SPHENOID
CYTOLOGY	FLATWORM	HEADMOST	MACAROON	OVERLORD	RINGWORM	SPITTOON
DARKROOM	FLYBLOWN	HEADROOM	MAESTOSO	OVERSOLD	ROLYPOLY	SPURIOUS
DARTMOOR	FOLKLORE	HEADWORD	MAILBOAT	OVERTONE	ROOFTOPS	SQUAMOUS
DASHWOOD	FOLKSONG	HECATOMB	MALAKOFF	OVERWORK	ROSAMOND	STAFFORD
DEADLOCK	FOOTHOLD	HEGEMONY	MALODOUR	PABULOUS	ROSEROOT	STAGHORN
DEADWOOD	FOOTNOTE	HEIRLOOM	MANDIOCA	PALIMONY	ROSEWOOD	STAKEOUT
DECOROUS	FOOTSORE	HELIPORT	MANGROVE	PALINODE	ROTATORY	STANDOFF

STANHOPE	VIRTUOSO	INTERPOL	ARCTURUS	CONJURER	GRAMERCY	MEASURED
STEATOMA	VIRTUOUS	INTREPID	ARMOURED	CONJUROR	GRIDIRON	MENSURAL
STOPCOCK	VISIGOTH	LARKSPUR	AUTOCRAT	CONSERVE	GUTTURAL	MESMERIC
STORMONT	VITREOUS	LIFESPAN	BACCARAT	CONSTRUE	HAMMERED	MÉTAIRIE
STUBBORN	VOMITORY	LINCHPIN	BACKDROP	CONVERGE	HANDGRIP	METEORIC
STUCCOED	WALLWORT	LOLLIPOP	BACTERIA	CONVERSE	HATTERAS	MINSTREL
STUDIOUS	WARDROBE	MANCIPLE	BALEARIC	CORDUROY	HEDGEROW	MIRRORED
SURFBOAT	WARDROOM	MARZIPAN	BALMORAL	CORMORAN	HEPTARCH	MISCARRY
SWANSONG	WARMBOOT	MINCEPIE	BANDEROL	CORPORAL	HETAIRIA	MONAURAL
SYCAMORE	WASHBOWL	MISAPPLY	BANNERET	COUPERIN	HEXAGRAM	MONOGRAM
SYMBIONT	WASHDOWN	MULTIPLE	BARBARIC	COWBERRY	HEYTHROP	MOTHERLY
SYMPHONY	WASHROOM	MULTIPLY	BARBERRY	COYSTRIL	HIERARCH	MUHARRAM
SYMPTOMS	WEDGWOOD	MYRIAPOD	BARNARDS	CULTURAL	HIGHBROW	MULBERRY
SYNDROME	WEREWOLF	PANPIPES	BARTERED	CULTURED	HISTORIC	MURDERER
TAKEHOME	WHIPCORD	PHILIPPI	BATTERED	CULVERIN	HITHERTO	NATTERED
TANDOORI	WILDFOWL	PHOTOPSY	BAYBERRY	CUTPURSE	HOLOGRAM	NOCTURNE
TAPEWORM	WINDHOEK	PINNIPED	BEDSTRAW	DEMIURGE	HONDURAN	NOMOGRAM
TARBOOSH	WINDSOCK	PLATYPUS	BEGGARLY	DEMOCRAT	HONDURAS	OBSCURED
TAXONOMY	WIREWORM	PROLAPSE	BEGORRAH	DEMURRAL	HUMPHREY	OLDWORLD
TEACLOTH	WISHBONE	PTEROPOD	BERBERIS	DENTURES	HYSTERIA	OLIGARCH
TEAKWOOD	WITHHOLD	RECEIPTS	BERGERAC	DEUTERON	HYSTERIC	OOPHORON
TEAMWORK	WONDROUS	SAUCEPAN	BESMIRCH	DEWBERRY	IDEOGRAM	ORATORIO
TEASPOON	WOODCOCK	SAUROPOD	BETATRON	DIEHARDS	IDIOGRAM	OUTBURST
TELECOMS	WOODWORM	SCHNAPPS	BILBERRY	DIELDRIN	IMPAIRED	OUTSTRIP
TELEGONY	WOODWORK	SCRAPPLE	BISMARCK	DIOPTRIC	INFRARED	OUTWARDS
TERATOMA	WORDBOOK	SMALLPOX	BITTERLY	DIPTERAL	INQUIRER	OVERDRAW
TEXTBOOK	WORKBOOK	SOUTHPAW	BORDERER	DISAGREE	INSPIRED	OXYMORON
THEOLOGY	WORKLOAD	STINKPOT	BOSWORTH	DISARRAY	INSPIRIT	PAMPERED
THRENODY	WORKROOM	STOCKPOT	BOTHERED	DISBURSE	INTEGRAL	PANDARUS
TICKTOCK	WORMWOOD	STRAPPED	BOWSPRIT	DISGORGE	ISOBARIC	PARTERRE
TIMOROUS	WRITEOFF	STRAPPER	BRETHREN	DISPERSE	JACKAROO	PASSERBY
TIRESOME	XANTHOMA	STRIPPED	BUGGERED	DISPIRIT	JAMBOREE	PASTORAL
TOILSOME	YAKITORI	STRIPPER	BULGARIA	DOCTORAL	JEOPARDY	PASTURES
TOLBOOTH	YEARBOOK	STRUMPET	BULLFROG	DOCTORED	JIGGERED	PECTORAL
TOMATOES	YEARLONG	SUBTOPIA	BULLYRAG	DOGBERRY	KANGAROO	PEDIGREE
TOPOLOGY	ZOETROPE	SWINEPOX	BUMMAREE	DOGGEREL	KEDGEREE	PENTARCH
TORTUOUS	ZOOSPORE	TAILSPIN	BURBERRY	DOTTEREL	KILOGRAM	PERFORCE
TRACHOMA	BACKSPIN	TERRAPIN	BUTTERED	DUTYFREE	KIPPERED	PERJURED
TRADEOFF	BAGPIPES	TETRAPOD	CALDERON	DYNATRON	LABOURED	PERJURER
TRAITORS	BICUSPID	THOLEPIN	CALTHROP	EASTERLY	LABOURER	PERVERSE
TRAPDOOR	BOBBYPIN	TURNSPIT	CAMBERED	ELECTRIC	LATTERLY	PETRARCH
TREETOPS	CACHEPOT	UNCOUPLE	CANBERRA	ELECTRON	LEAPFROG	PICTURES
TRICHOID	CALLIPER	UNDERPIN	CANTORIS	ELECTRUM	LECTURER	PILFERER
TROLLOPE	CHICKPEA	UNTAPPED	CAREFREE	EPICURUS	LECTURES	PILLARED
TROMBONE	CHUTZPAH	WINGSPAN	CAULDRON	EPIDURAL	LEISURED	PINDARIC
TROTTOIR	COLLAPSE	WINNIPEG	CELLARER	ESOTERIC	LEONARDO	PIZZERIA
TUBENOSE	CRACKPOT	XANTIPPE	CENTERED	ETHNARCH	LETHARGY	PLASTRON
TUBEROSE	DECOUPLE	APPLIQUÉ	CERBERUS	EUPHORIA	LETTERED	PLECTRUM
TUBEROUS	DECREPIT	BOUTIQUE	CEREBRAL	EUPHORIC	LINGERIE	PLUTARCH
TURNCOAT	DIAZEPAM	COLLOQUY	CEREBRUM	EXPLORER	LISTERIA	POLYARCH
TURNCOCK	DISCIPLE	CRITIQUE	CHALDRON	FATHERLY	LITTORAL	POSITRON
ULCEROUS	ENCAMPED	MORESQUE	CHANTREY	FAVOURED	LOITERER	POWDERED
UNCIFORM	ENTREPOT	MYSTIQUE	CHAPERON	FEATURED	LOMBARDY	PRECURSE
UNCTUOUS	EOHIPPUS	PETANQUE	CHARTRES	FEATURES	LOTHARIO	PREPARED
UNHEROIC	EPILEPSY	PHYSIQUE	CHILDREN	FILIGREE	LOUVERED	PRESERVE
UNSAVORY	ESTOPPEL	ACENTRIC	CHOLERIC	FIREARMS	LULWORTH	PRETORIA
USURIOUS	ETHIOPIA	ACQUIRED	CICATRIX	FIRETRAP	LUTHERAN	PROCURER
UXORIOUS	EUTROPHY	ACQUIRER	CISTERNA	FLAVORED	MACKEREL	PROFORMA
VAGABOND	EUTROPIC	AEROGRAM	CLAPTRAP	FOLDEROL	MALLARMÉ	PROGERIA
VANADOUS	FELDSPAR	AGACERIE	CLEVERLY	FORMERLY	MALLORCA	PROPERLY
VAPOROUS	FINESPUN	AGITPROP	CLITORIS	FORWARDS	MANDARIN	PROPERTY
VARICOSE	FISSIPED	AIRBORNE	COCKCROW	GALLERIA	MANNERED	PROVERBS
VARIFORM	GALLIPOT	AIRSCREW	COCKEREL	GASWORKS	MANNERLY	PUCKERED
VENOMOUS	GALLOPER	AIRSTRIP	COLLARED	GATHERED	MARGARET	QUATORZE
VIETCONG	HARUSPEX	ALCATRAZ	COLOURED	GENDARME	MARJORAM	RAGNARÖK
VIGOROUS	HEATSPOT	ANCHORET	COMMERCE	GENETRIX	MARTYRED	RAINDROP
VIPEROUS	HOMESPUN	ANDORRAN	COMPARED	GESTURES	MASCARON	RAMPARTS
VIROLOGY	HONEYPOT	ANGSTROM	CONCERTO	GINGERLY	MASTERLY	RECHARGE
VIRTUOSI	IMPROPER	AOTEAROA	CONCORDE	GLYCERIN	MATHURIN	RECOURSE

329

REFERRAL	UNIVERSE	DIERESIS	NEUROSIS	ACCUSTOM	CANISTER	DOMESTIC
REHEARSE	VALKYRIE	DIOCESAN	NIJINSKY	ACOUSTIC	CARYATID	DOORSTEP
REPAIRER	VARIORUM	DIONYSUS	OBSESSED	ACROSTIC	CASSETTE	DRAGSTER
REQUIRED	VENTURED	DISEASED	ODIOUSLY	ADDICTED	CATHETER	DRAMATIC
RESEARCH	VERDERER	DISPOSAL	PARMESAN	ADENITIS	CEMENTUM	DYNASTIC
RESOURCE	VESPERAL	DISPOSED	PAROUSIA	ADJUSTER	CERASTES	ECLECTIC
RESTORER	VICTORIA	DISTASTE	PARTISAN	ADJUSTOR	CHAPATTI	ECSTATIC
RHETORIC	VISCERAL	DUCHESSE	PEVENSEY	ADRIATIC	CHRISTEN	EDUCATED
RUMOURED	VULGARLY	ECSTASIS	PHARISEE	ADROITLY	CHRISTIE	EDUCATOR
RUNNERUP	WALKYRIE	ELLIPSIS	PHTHISIC	ADULATOR	CHRISTOM	EGOISTIC
SANDARAC	WANDERER	EMBOSSED	PHTHISIS	AEGROTAT	CILIATED	EIDECTIC
SANSERIF	WARFARIN	EMPHASIS	PREMISES	AEROSTAT	CLEMATIS	ELDRITCH
SANSKRIT	WARHORSE	ENCLOSED	PROFUSER	AFFECTED	CLIMATIC	ELEVATED
SAVOURED	WAXWORKS	EPITASIS	PROMISED	AFFLATUS	CLOISTER	ELEVATOR
SAWHORSE	WAYFARER	ERIKSSON	PROPOSAL	AGITATED	COCKATOO	ELLIPTIC
SCENARIO	WELLBRED	ESPOUSAL	PROPOSED	AGITATOR	COLLATOR	EMBATTLE
SEABORNE	WESTERLY	ESPRESSO	PROPOSER	AGNOSTIC	COMMUTER	EMBITTER
SEAFARER	WHIMBREL	EUPEPSIA	PUGNOSED	AIGRETTE	COMPUTER	EMERITUS
SEAFORTH	WINIFRED	EVANESCE	QUICKSET	ALCESTIS	CONFETTI	EMIRATES
SEAWARDS	WISTERIA	EXEGESIS	RECESSED	AMARETTO	COQUETRY	EMPHATIC
SELBORNE	WITHDRAW	EXPENSES	RELEASED	AMORETTI	COQUETTE	EMULATOR
SHIVERED	WITHERED	EXPRESSO	REPOUSSÉ	AMORETTO	CORNETTO	ENCLOTHE
SHOETREE	ZEPHYRUS	EXTENSOR	REPRISAL	AMUSETTE	CORVETTE	ENIWETOK
SIGNORIA	ZIGGURAT	FAMOUSLY	REVERSAL	ANABATIC	COSMETIC	ESTHETIC
SISTERLY	ABOMASUM	FANTASIA	REVERSED	ANALYTIC	COVENTRY	EUROSTAR
SNOWDROP	ABSCISSA	FIBROSIS	ROBINSON	ANCESTOR	CRAVATES	EUSTATIC
SONOGRAM	ACCURSED	FORENSIC	ROMANSCH	ANCESTRY	CREDITOR	EXECUTED
SORCERER	ALFRESCO	FORMOSAN	RUBBISHY	ANIMATED	CREPITUS	EXECUTOR
SPANDREL	AMBROSIA	GARRISON	SACRISTY	ANISETTE	CRICHTON	EXEGETIC
SPECTRAL	AMRITSAR	GEODESIC	SARGASSO	APERITIF	CULOTTES	EXPECTED
SPECTRUM	AMUNDSEN	GRANDSON	SCHAPSKA	APPLETON	CURSITOR	EXPORTER
SQUADRON	ANABASIS	GUERNSEY	SELASSIE	ARDENTLY	CUTWATER	FACTOTUM
SQUIRREL	ANALYSER	GUMMOSIS	SIGHTSEE	ARGESTES	CYSTITIS	FAINITES
STINGRAY	ANALYSIS	HARASSED	SOMERSET	AROMATIC	DALMATIC	FALSETTO
SUBMERGE	ANCHISES	HARRISON	SOOTHSAY	ARRESTED	DAUGHTER	FENESTRA
SUBSHRUB	ANDERSON	HIDROSIS	STAROSTA	ARRESTER	DECANTER	FIRESTEP
SUFFERER	ANGLESEY	HYPNOSIS	STEAPSIN	ARTISTIC	DECENTLY	FLUENTLY
SULFURIC	APNEUSIS	IMMERSED	STENOSED	ARTISTRY	DECLUTCH	FOOTSTEP
SUNBURNT	APPRISED	IMPRISON	STENOSIS	ASBESTOS	DECRETAL	FORESTAY
SUNBURST	ARKANSAS	INCENSED	STOKESAY	ASSORTED	DEFEATED	FORESTER
TAMWORTH	ASSASSIN	INTELSAT	STRESSED	ATHLETIC	DEFECTOR	FORESTRY
TARTARIC	ASSESSOR	JALOUSIE	SUPPOSED	ATLANTIC	DEJECTED	FREMITUS
TARTARUS	AUBUSSON	JETTISON	SWEETSOP	ATLANTIS	DEMENTED	FRENETIC
TATTERED	AUCASSIN	JURASSIC	SYNOPSIS	ATTESTOR	DEMENTIA	FRIGHTEN
TAYBERRY	BALLISTA	KERMESSE	TENNYSON	AUGUSTUS	DEMISTER	GADGETRY
TEARDROP	BAPTISED	KOLINSKY	THICKSET	AUTISTIC	DEPARTED	GALACTIC
TELEGRAM	BETHESDA	KROMESKY	THOMPSON	BACKSTOP	DEPORTEE	GANGSTER
TELLURIC	CALLISTO	KYPHOSIS	TRAVESTY	BAGUETTE	DESERTED	GANISTER
TEMPERED	CAROUSAL	LACROSSE	TRIASSIC	BALUSTER	DESERTER	GARROTTE
TEMPORAL	CAROUSEL	LARGESSE	TUNGUSIC	BANDITTI	DESPATCH	GELASTIC
TENDERLY	CHAINSAW	LAROUSSE	UNBIASED	BANISTER	DESPOTIC	GEODETIC
TENEBRAE	CHARISMA	LICENSED	UNCHASTE	BARRATRY	DETECTOR	GEOMETER
TENEBRIO	CLEANSED	LICENSEE	UNDERSEA	BARRETTE	DETRITUS	GEOMETRY
TETRARCH	CLEANSER	LORDOSIS	UNPERSON	BASKETRY	DIABETES	GIGANTIC
TEXTURED	COALESCE	MACASSAR	UNREASON	BATHETIC	DIABETIC	GOLGOTHA
THEATRIC	COLOSSAL	MACHISMO	UNVERSED	BEGETTER	DIAMETER	GRAVITAS
THEOCRAT	COLOSSUS	MAGNESIA	WATERSKI	BELITTLE	DICTATES	GRISETTE
THIOUREA	COMPOSED	MALAYSIA	ZAKOUSKI	BESOTTED	DICTATOR	GUNMETAL
TIMBERED	COMPOSER	MALVASIA	ZOONOSIS	BIOMETRY	DIDACTIC	GUSSETED
TOMORROW	CONFUSED	MANTISSA	ABDUCTED	BLIGHTER	DIRECTLY	GYROSTAT
TONSURED	CREVASSE	MARMOSET	ABDUCTOR	BRIGHTEN	DIRECTOR	HAMARTIA
TORTURED	CYANOSIS	MOCCASIN	ABJECTLY	BRIGHTLY	DISASTER	HAMILTON
TORTURER	CYCLOSIS	MOLASSES	ABRUPTLY	BRIGHTON	DISINTER	HEIGHTEN
TRAVERSE	DAVIDSON	MOLLUSCS	ABSENTEE	BROMPTON	DISKETTE	HELMETED
TRIMARAN	DECEASED	MORRISON	ABSINTHE	BRUNETTE	DISPATCH	HELVETIA
TRISTRAM	DEMERSAL	NARCOSES	ACCENTED	BULLETIN	DISPUTED	HERMETIC
TURMERIC	DIALYSIS	NARCOSIS	ACCENTOR	BURSITIS	DIURETIC	HERPETIC
UNAWARES	DIAPASON	NEBRASKA	ACCEPTED	CADASTRE	DOGMATIC	HIAWATHA
UNDERRUN	DIARESIS	NECROSIS	ACCEPTOR	CALCUTTA	DOGWATCH	HIERATIC

HOLISTIC	NARCOTIC	REGISTRY	TEAMSTER	CALIGULA	MALAMUTE	SWIMSUIT
HONESTLY	NARRATOR	REMITTAL	TEETOTAL	CARNAUBA	MAMELUKE	SYRACUSE
HOSPITAL	NEMBUTAL	REPARTEE	TESTATOR	CATAPULT	MANICURE	TACITURN
HUCKSTER	NEPENTHE	REPEATED	TESTATUM	CATHOUSE	MAROQUIN	TAPHOUSE
HYPNOTIC	NEURITIS	REPEATER	THANATOS	CENTAURY	MASSEUSE	THOROUGH
IDOLATER	NEUROTIC	REPORTED	THEMATIC	CHIPMUNK	MISCOUNT	TINCTURE
IDOLATRY	NOISETTE	REPORTER	THREATEN	COIFFURE	MISSOURI	TITMOUSE
ILLFATED	NUTHATCH	RESETTLE	THROTTLE	COMPOUND	MISTRUST	TOULOUSE
IMITATOR	OBJECTOR	RESISTOR	THRUSTER	CONCLUDE	MOISTURE	TRANQUIL
IMMORTAL	ODOMETER	RHEOSTAT	TINNITUS	CONFOUND	MOLECULE	TREASURE
IMPACTED	OLEASTER	ROADSTER	TOMENTUM	CREATURE	MONMOUTH	TREASURY
IMPORTER	OMELETTE	ROBUSTLY	TOPNOTCH	CYNOSURE	MONOHULL	TRINCULO
IMPOSTER	OPERATIC	ROCKETRY	TUNGSTEN	DANDRUFF	MORIBUND	USUFRUCT
IMPOSTOR	OPERATOR	ROMANTIC	TUNGSTIC	DENATURE	NEWFOUND	VANBRUGH
INDEBTED	OPERETTA	ROSSETTI	TURRETED	DESTRUCT	NIBELUNG	VERMOUTH
INDENTED	ORCHITIS	ROULETTE	UDOMETER	DISABUSE	NONESUCH	VISCOUNT
INDUCTOR	ORIENTAL	SADISTIC	UNABATED	DISCOUNT	NUTHOUSE	WINDBURN
INDUSTRY	OUTDATED	SATIATED	UNBEATEN	DISMOUNT	OBSTRUCT	WOODRUFF
INFANTRY	OUTMATCH	SCIMITAR	UNBUTTON	DISTRUST	OPUSCULE	YOGHOURT
INFECTED	OVARITIS	SCREWTOP	UNDERTOW	DJIBOUTI	OUTHOUSE	ZASTRUGA
INFESTED	OVERSTAY	SCRIPTUM	UNFASTEN	DOGHOUSE	OVERFULL	ABSOLVED
INFLATED	OVERSTEP	SCULPTOR	UNFETTER	DOLDRUMS	OVERMUCH	ACHIEVED
INJECTOR	PAKISTAN	SEAMSTER	UNHEATED	DORMOUSE	OVERRULE	ACHIEVER
INTENTLY	PALMATED	SECRETLY	UNJUSTLY	DOWNTURN	OVERTURE	AIRWAVES
INVENTED	PALMETTO	SELECTED	UNLISTED	DUMFOUND	OVERTURN	APPROVAL
INVENTOR	PALMITIN	SELECTOR	UNSALTED	ELKHOUND	PARAGUAY	APPROVED
INVERTED	PARENTAL	SEMESTER	UNSETTLE	EMMANUEL	PARAQUAT	ARCHIVES
INVERTER	PARIETAL	SEMIOTIC	UNSTATED	ERUPTURE	PEDICURE	BEDCOVER
INVESTOR	PATENTED	SERIATIM	UNSUITED	EVENTUAL	PERACUTE	BELIEVER
IOLANTHE	PATENTEE	SERRATED	UNWANTED	EXPOSURE	PERILUNE	BEREAVED
ISOLATED	PATENTLY	SERVITOR	UNWONTED	FATIGUED	PHALGUNA	BICONVEX
JACKETED	PATHETIC	SHERATON	UNWORTHY	FATIGUES	PIECRUST	CARNIVAL
JEANETTE	PEDANTIC	SIDESTEP	URGENTLY	FOGBOUND	PLAYSUIT	CORDOVAN
JYAISTHA	PEDANTRY	SILENTLY	VACANTLY	FOXHOUND	PLEASURE	CZAREVNA
KINGSTON	PEDESTAL	SINISTER	VALLETTA	FRACTURE	PLYMOUTH	DECEIVER
KNIGHTLY	PELLETED	SITUATED	VARIETAL	FURLOUGH	POTBOUND	DECEMVIR
KRAKATOA	PHONETIC	SKELETAL	VENDETTA	GASTRULA	PRECLUDE	DEPRAVED
LAMENTED	PHREATIC	SKELETON	VERBATIM	GERTRUDE	PRESSURE	DEPRIVED
LAUGHTER	PIERETTE	SLIGHTED	VIBRATOR	HABITUAL	PROFOUND	DESERVED
LEINSTER	PILASTER	SLIGHTLY	VIGNETTE	HABSBURG	PROPOUND	DISCOVER
LIBRETTO	PISCATOR	SOCRATES	VIOLATOR	HALFFULL	PROTRUDE	DISFAVOR
LOADSTAR	PLANKTON	SOCRATIC	ABSOLUTE	HANDCUFF	PUNCTUAL	DISHEVEL
LODESTAR	POCHETTE	SONGSTER	ABSTRUSE	HAPSBURG	PUNCTURE	EFFLUVIA
LOGISTIC	POLLSTER	SPINSTER	ALEHOUSE	HEADHUNT	QUIETUDE	ENDEAVOR
LONGSTAY	POLLUTED	SPIRITED	ALLELUIA	HEBETUDE	QUINCUNX	ENGRAVER
LONGSTOP	POLLUTER	SPIRITUS	ALTHOUGH	HENEQUEN	RAMEQUIN	FESTIVAL
MAGISTER	POTLATCH	SPLATTER	ALTITUDE	HENHOUSE	READJUST	GINGIVAL
MAGNETIC	PREDATOR	SPLINTER	AMATEURS	HICCOUGH	REASSUME	GULLIVER
MAIEUTIC	PRENATAL	SPLITTER	APERTURE	HONOLULU	REASSURE	HANDOVER
MAINSTAY	PRIESTLY	SPLUTTER	APPLAUSE	HOTHOUSE	REINSURE	HANGOVER
MAJESTIC	PRIVATES	SPRINTER	APTITUDE	HUSHHUSH	RESIDUAL	HAYFEVER
MANDATED	PROMOTER	SQUATTER	AQUALUNG	ICEHOUSE	RESIDUUM	IMPROVED
MAQUETTE	PROMPTER	STEALTHY	AQUEDUCT	IMMANUEL	RESOLUTE	IMPROVER
MEDIATOR	PROMPTLY	STILETTO	ARCHDUKE	IMMATURE	RETICULE	INTERVAL
MERCATOR	PRONATOR	STRAITEN	ARETHUSA	INASMUCH	RIDICULE	INVOLVED
MERISTEM	PYELITIS	STRIATED	ARMATURE	INSECURE	RUBICUND	KESTEVEN
METRITIS	QUAESTOR	STRIATUM	ATTITUDE	INSTRUCT	SALTBUSH	LEFTOVER
MINISTER	QUAINTLY	STRICTLY	AURICULA	INVOLUTE	SCHEDULE	MALDIVES
MINISTRY	QUIXOTIC	SUBTITLE	AVIFAUNA	JEALOUSY	SCROFULA	MANEUVER
MIRLITON	RACHITIS	SUBTOTAL	BANKRUPT	JODHPURS	SHANTUNG	MEDIEVAL
MISMATCH	RACLETTE	SUMMITRY	BAYREUTH	JOINTURE	SHELDUCK	MONROVIA
MODESTLY	RADIATOR	SUNBATHE	BELLPUSH	JUMPSUIT	SILICULA	MOREOVER
MOLESTER	RAMBUTAN	SUPERTAX	BERCEUSE	JUNCTURE	SINECURE	NEWHAVEN
MOMENTUM	RASPUTIN	SYLVATIC	BIANNUAL	LANSBURY	SINECURE	OBSERVED
MONASTIC	REBUTTAL	SYMMETRY	BISEXUAL	LATITUDE	SOAPSUDS	OBSERVER
MOQUETTE	RECENTLY	SYMPATHY	BLASTULA	LAWCOURT	SOLITUDE	PASSOVER
MUSCATEL	RECEPTOR	SYNOPTIC	BOUZOUKI	LIFEBUOY	SOURPUSS	PERCEVAL
MYELITIS	REDACTOR	TALENTED	BRADBURY	LIGATURE	STARDUST	PERCIVAL
MYOSOTIS	REGISTER	TAPESTRY	BROCHURE	MADHOUSE	SURMOUNT	PRIMEVAL

PULLOVER	THATAWAY	ZOOPHYTE	BAVARIAN	CINNABAR	EMPYREAN	HARRIDAN
PUSHOVER	TIGHTWAD	AGONIZED	BEDSTEAD	CIRCULAR	EPHESIAN	HATCHWAY
RECEIVED	WATERWAY	ATOMIZER	BEDSTRAW	CIVILIAN	EPIDURAL	HATHAWAY
RECEIVER	ANOREXIA	BARBIZON	BEGORRAH	CLANSMAN	ESCORIAL	HATTERAS
RELIEVED	ANOREXIC	BRABAZON	BERGERAC	CLAPTRAP	ESPECIAL	HAVDALAH
REPLEVIN	ASPHYXIA	CAPSIZED	BETJEMAN	CLEARWAY	ESPOUSAL	HAVILDAR
RESERVED	ATARAXIA	EMBEZZLE	BETRAYAL	CLERICAL	ESTONIAN	HAWAIIAN
RESOLVED	ATARAXIC	EMBLAZON	BIANNUAL	CLINICAL	ETHEREAL	HEADGEAR
REVOLVER	CACHEXIA	HOWITZER	BIBLICAL	COACHMAN	ETRURIAN	HELMSMAN
SLIPOVER	DYSLEXIA	KIBITZER	BIENNIAL	COCCIDAE	ETRUSCAN	HENCHMAN
STOPOVER	DYSLEXIC	PROTOZOA	BILLYCAN	COCHLEAR	EUDOXIAN	HERDSMAN
SULLIVAN	GEOTAXIS	PULITZER	BINOMIAL	COCKBOAT	EURASIAN	HEXAGRAM
SURVIVAL	HYDROXYL	SPRITZER	BIRTHDAY	COLESLAW	EUROPEAN	HIDEAWAY
SURVIVOR	SPARAXIS	SQUEEZER	BISCAYAN	COLONIAL	EUROSTAR	HIGHROAD
TAKEOVER	SYNTEXIS	STYLIZED	BISEXUAL	COLOSSAL	EVENTUAL	HOGMANAY
TOPLEVEL	AERODYNE		BLACKCAP	COLUMBAN	EVERYDAY	HOGSHEAD
TSAREVNA	ALDEHYDE	**8:7**	BLUECOAT	COMEDIAN	EVERYMAN	HOLLOWAY
TURNOVER	AMETHYST	ABNORMAL	BOATLOAD	COMMUNAL	EXEMPLAR	HOLOGRAM
UNCLOVEN	ANAGLYPH	ACIDHEAD	BODLEIAN	CONJUGAL	EXTERNAL	HOLYHEAD
UNNERVED	ANEURYSM	AEGROTAT	BOEOTIAN	CONSULAR	EXTERNAT	HONDURAN
UNSOLVED	APOLLYON	AEROGRAM	BOGEYMAN	CORDOVAN	FAMILIAR	HONDURAS
UPHEAVAL	APOPHYGE	AEROSTAT	BOHEMIAN	CORMORAN	FANCYMAN	HOOLIGAN
WALKOVER	AUTOGYRO	AGRARIAN	BOLIVIAN	CORNMEAL	FARCICAL	HORATIAN
WHATEVER	AUTOTYPE	AKKADIAN	BONDSMAN	CORPORAL	FELDSPAR	HORMONAL
WHENEVER	BETRAYAL	ALBANIAN	BONEHEAD	CORSICAN	FERRYMAN	HORNBEAM
WHEREVER	BETRAYER	ALCATRAZ	BRACHIAL	CRIMINAL	FESTIVAL	HORSEMAN
ALLEYWAY	BISCAYAN	ALDERMAN	BRADSHAW	CRISPIAN	FIDUCIAL	HOSPITAL
ANDREWES	CALOTYPE	ALEUTIAN	BRICKBAT	CRITICAL	FIRETRAP	HOUSEMAN
BESTOWER	CATALYST	ALGERIAN	BROADWAY	CROATIAN	FISHMEAL	HUNTSMAN
BORROWED	COCKAYNE	ALLEYWAY	BROUGHAM	CROSSBAR	FLATBOAT	HYPOGEAL
BORROWER	COCKEYED	ALLUVIAL	BROWBEAT	CULLINAN	FOOLSCAP	IDEOGRAM
BROADWAY	CONVEYOR	ALSATIAN	BRYOZOAN	CULTURAL	FOOTWEAR	IDIOGRAM
BURROWER	DEWEYED	AMERICAN	BUCKBEAN	CYCLICAL	FOREBEAR	IMMORTAL
CABLEWAY	DISLOYAL	AMERICAS	BULKHEAD	CYRENIAC	FOREHEAD	IMPERIAL
CARRAWAY	DISMAYED	AMMONIAC	BULLYRAG	DAIRYMAN	FORESTAY	INDIAMAN
CASTAWAY	EMPLOYED	AMRITSAR	BUSULFAN	DAYBREAK	FORMOSAN	INFERNAL
CAUSEWAY	EMPLOYEE	ANDORRAN	CABLECAR	DAYDREAM	FORSWEAR	INFORMAL
CLEARWAY	EMPLOYER	ANGLICAN	CABLEWAY	DEADBEAT	FRESHMAN	INGUINAL
DEFLOWER	EPIPHYTE	ANTENNAE	CADILLAC	DEADHEAD	FREUDIAN	INIMICAL
DRIVEWAY	EPISTYLE	APPROVAL	CALENDAR	DECRETAL	FRONTMAN	INTEGRAL
FOLLOWED	GARGOYLE	ARAMAEAN	CAMBRIAN	DEMERSAL	FUGLEMAN	INTELSAT
FOLLOWER	GIGABYTE	ARBOREAL	CANADIAN	DEMOCRAT	FUNEREAL	INTERNAL
FOLLOWUP	KILOBYTE	ARCADIAN	CANNIBAL	DEMONIAC	GALILEAN	INTERVAL
FURROWED	KUFFIYEH	ARKANSAS	CARDIGAN	DEMURRAL	GALLOWAY	IRISHMAN
GALLOWAY	LINOTYPE	ARMAGNAC	CARDINAL	DEVONIAN	GEORGIAN	IRONCLAD
GIVEAWAY	LOGOTYPE	ARMENIAN	CARNIVAL	DIAGONAL	GERMINAL	IRONICAL
GOLLIWOG	MEGABYTE	ARMORIAL	CAROUSAL	DIAZEPAM	GHANAIAN	ISOGONAL
HALLOWED	METONYMY	ARTERIAL	CARRAWAY	DIOCESAN	GINGIVAL	ISTHMIAN
HATCHWAY	MISOGYNY	ARTESIAN	CARTLOAD	DIPLOMAT	GIVEAWAY	JACOBEAN
HATHAWAY	MONOGYNY	ASCIDIAN	CASTAWAY	DIPTERAL	GLOBULAR	JAMAICAN
HIDEAWAY	MONOTYPE	ASSYRIAN	CATSMEAT	DISARRAY	GOODYEAR	JEPHTHAH
HOLLOWAY	NEOPHYTE	ATHENIAN	CAUSEWAY	DISLOYAL	GRANDDAD	JEREBOAM
INGROWTH	OLDSTYLE	ATYPICAL	CELERIAC	DISPOSAL	GRANULAR	JEREMIAD
MANPOWER	PANEGYRY	AURELIAN	CELLULAR	DOCTORAL	GRAVITAS	JEREMIAH
MILDEWED	PARALYZE	AUSTRIAN	CEREBRAL	DOMESDAY	GREENBAG	JEROBOAM
MOTORWAY	PAROXYSM	AUTOCRAT	CERULEAN	DOOMSDAY	GROSBEAK	JERRYCAN
NARROWLY	POLYGYNY	AUTUMNAL	CERVELAT	DOWNBEAT	GUARDIAN	JONATHAN
PANDOWDY	PORPHYRA	BACCARAT	CERVICAL	DOWNLOAD	GUIANIAN	JUDICIAL
POLLIWOG	PORPHYRY	BACKCHAT	CETACEAN	DOWNPLAY	GUNMETAL	KATTEGAT
REVIEWER	PURVEYOR	BACTRIAN	CHAINSAW	DRIVEWAY	GUTTURAL	KICKSHAW
RIDGEWAY	RUBAIYAT	BAHAMIAN	CHAIRMAN	DROPHEAD	GYROSTAT	KILOGRAM
SOAKAWAY	SEROTYPE	BALMORAL	CHALDEAN	DRUMBEAT	HABITUAL	KNITWEAR
SPEEDWAY	STAPHYLE	BANDSMAN	CHARCOAL	DRUMHEAD	HAGGADAH	KORRIGAN
SPILLWAY	STOREYED	BARABBAS	CHEMICAL	DRYCLEAN	HALFYEAR	LACKADAY
STAIRWAY	SURVEYOR	BARBICAN	CHESSMAN	DUODENAL	HANDCLAP	LACONIAN
STEINWAY	TAXPAYER	BARGEMAN	CHINAMAN	DUTCHMAN	HANDICAP	LEADSMAN
STOWAWAY	TRIGLYPH	BARNABAS	CHITCHAT	ECOFREAK	HANDYMAN	LEONIDAS
TAKEAWAY	TRIPTYCH	BARONIAL	CHUTZPAH	EGYPTIAN	HANNIBAL	LIBERIAN
TEARAWAY	WESLEYAN	BATAVIAN	CINEREAL	EMPYREAL	HANUKKAH	LIEGEMAN

LIFEBOAT	NENUPHAR	POPINJAY	SIRENIAN	TUNISIAN	AMBIANCE	DISTINCT
LIFESPAN	NEWSPEAK	PORTUGAL	SKELETAL	TURKOMAN	AMBIENCE	DISTRACT
LINESMAN	NICHOLAS	PRAIRIAL	SKINHEAD	TURNCOAT	ANGELICA	DISTRICT
LINNAEAN	NIGERIAN	PRANDIAL	SKULLCAP	TUTORIAL	ANNOUNCE	DOGWATCH
LITTORAL	NIGHTCAP	PREMOLAR	SNACKBAR	TYROLEAN	ANYPLACE	DRAWBACK
LOADSTAR	NIGHTJAR	PRENATAL	SOAKAWAY	UNDERLAY	APPROACH	DYNAMICS
LODESTAR	NOBLEMAN	PRESSMAN	SOMEWHAT	UNIPOLAR	AQUEDUCT	EARPIECE
LONGBOAT	NOMOGRAM	PRIMEVAL	SONOGRAM	UNSOCIAL	ARMORICA	EFFICACY
LONGSTAY	NORSEMAN	PRODIGAL	SOOTHSAY	UNTHREAD	ARTEFACT	ELDRITCH
LUPERCAL	NOTARIAL	PROPOSAL	SOUTHPAW	UPHEAVAL	ARTIFACT	ELEGANCE
LUTHERAN	NOTIONAL	PROXIMAL	SPACEMAN	UPSTREAM	ARTIFICE	EMINENCE
MACASSAR	OBSIDIAN	PRUSSIAN	SPECTRAL	VALERIAN	AUDIENCE	EMINENCY
MACAULAY	OEDIPEAN	PUBLICAN	SPEEDWAY	VALVULAR	BACKPACK	ENCROACH
MADRIGAL	OFFBREAK	PUNCTUAL	SPELLMAN	VARIETAL	BALDRICK	ENSCONCE
MADWOMAN	OFFICIAL	PUSSYCAT	SPILLWAY	VASCULAR	BALLCOCK	ENTRANCE
MAECENAS	OLEACEAE	PUSTULAR	SPITHEAD	VENEREAL	BAREBACK	ENTRENCH
MAGELLAN	OLYMPIAD	QUIRINAL	STAIRWAY	VENETIAN	BASILICA	ETHNARCH
MAGICIAN	OLYMPIAN	RAILHEAD	STEINWAY	VERANDAH	BAUDRICK	EUGENICS
MAILBOAT	OMDURMAN	RAILROAD	STENDHAL	VERTICAL	BENEDICK	EURYDICE
MAINSTAY	OPENPLAN	RAINCOAT	STINGRAY	VESPERAL	BENEDICT	EVANESCE
MALARIAL	OPHIDIAN	RAINWEAR	STOCKCAR	VICARIAL	BENEFICE	EVIDENCE
MALAWIAN	OPOPANAX	RAMBUTAN	STOCKMAN	VIRGINAL	BESMIRCH	EXIGENCY
MALTREAT	OPTICIAN	RASSELAS	STOKESAY	VISCERAL	BISMARCK	EYEPIECE
MANIACAL	OPTIONAL	RATIONAL	STOREMAN	VOLSCIAN	BLUEBACK	FASTBACK
MANORIAL	ORCADIAN	RATTIGAN	STOWAWAY	VORTICAL	BONIFACE	FATSTOCK
MARGINAL	ORIENTAL	REAPPEAR	SUBHUMAN	WATCHMAN	BOOTNECK	FEDERACY
MARIANAS	ORIGINAL	REBUTTAL	SUBTOTAL	WATERMAN	BRASSICA	FEEDBACK
MARJORAM	OUTBREAK	REEDSMAN	SUBURBAN	WATERWAY	BRATPACK	FIREBACK
MARKSMAN	OVERCOAT	REFERRAL	SUICIDAL	WELSHMAN	BUOYANCY	FLAMENCO
MARZIPAN	OVERDRAW	REGIONAL	SULLIVAN	WESLEYAN	CARAPACE	FLAPJACK
MASTHEAD	OVERHEAD	REMEDIAL	SUMERIAN	WHEATEAR	CATARACT	FLATPICK
MATERIAL	OVERHEAR	REMITTAL	SUNCREAM	WHINCHAT	CELIBACY	FLORENCE
MATERNAL	OVERHEAT	REPRISAL	SUPERMAN	WHITECAP	CERAMICS	FOREDECK
MEDIEVAL	OVERLEAF	RESIDUAL	SUPERNAL	WINGSPAN	CHARLOCK	FORELOCK
MEMORIAL	OVERLOAD	REVERSAL	SUPERTAX	WITHDRAW	CLARENCE	FORSLACK
MEMORIAM	OVERPLAY	RHEOSTAT	SURFBOAT	WOODSMAN	CLASSICS	FULLBACK
MENSURAL	OVERSEAS	RICKSHAW	SURGICAL	WORKADAY	CLAWBACK	GENETICS
MENSWEAR	OVERSTAY	RIDGEWAY	SURVIVAL	WORKLOAD	CLEMENCY	GEOMANCY
MERIDIAN	PAKISTAN	RIFLEMAN	TABBYCAT	YATAGHAN	COALESCE	GIMCRACK
METRICAL	PALATIAL	RIPARIAN	TABLEMAT	YUGOSLAV	COATRACK	GOBSMACK
MICHIGAN	PANCREAS	ROMANIAN	TACTICAL	ZAMINDAR	CODPIECE	GRAMERCY
MILLIBAR	PARAGUAY	ROUSSEAU	TAHITIAN	ZEDEKIAH	COMEBACK	GRAPHICS
MINDANAO	PARALLAX	RUBAIYAT	TAKEAWAY	ZIGGURAT	COMMENCE	GREENOCK
MINEHEAD	PARAQUAT	SAILBOAT	TALISMAN	ZODIACAL	COMMERCE	GRIDLOCK
MINUTIAE	PARASHAH	SALESMAN	TEARAWAY	BATHROBE	CONFLICT	GUIDANCE
MISTREAT	PARENTAL	SAMIZDAT	TEETOTAL	CARNAUBA	CONTRACT	HARDBACK
MOLUCCAS	PARIETAL	SANDARAC	TELEGRAM	COBWEBBY	CONVINCE	HARDHACK
MONAURAL	PARISIAN	SATURDAY	TEMPORAL	DESCRIBE	CROMLECH	HARDTACK
MONDRIAN	PARMESAN	SAUCEPAN	TENEBRAE	DIATRIBE	CRUMMOCK	HAWFINCH
MONOGRAM	PARSIFAL	SAVANNAH	TERMINAL	DJELLABA	CURRENCY	HAYSTACK
MOONBEAM	PARTHIAN	SCAPULAR	THATAWAY	INSCRIBE	CUTPRICE	HEPATICA
MORAVIAN	PARTISAN	SCIMITAR	THEOCRAT	KOHLRABI	DABCHICK	HEPTARCH
MOROCCAN	PASTORAL	SCOTSMAN	THESPIAN	MANITOBA	DEADLOCK	HIERARCH
MOTORCAR	PATELLAR	SEALYHAM	THRACIAN	PASSERBY	DECLUTCH	HOMESICK
MOTORMAN	PATERNAL	SEASONAL	THURSDAY	PONSONBY	DEFIANCE	HUMPBACK
MOTORWAY	PECTORAL	SEEDSMAN	TIBERIAS	PROVERBS	DELICACY	INASMUCH
MUHAMMAD	PECULIAR	SHANGAAN	TIEBREAK	RENMINBI	DENOUNCE	INDIRECT
MUHARRAM	PEDESTAL	SHANGHAI	TIGHTWAD	WARDROBE	DERELICT	INSTANCE
MULLIGAN	PEMMICAN	SHEARMAN	TIRESIAS	ABEYANCE	DESELECT	INSTINCT
MUSCULAR	PERCEVAL	SHERIDAN	TOADFLAX	ABSTRACT	DESPATCH	INSTRUCT
MUSICIAN	PERCIVAL	SHOWBOAT	TOBOGGAN	ACAPULCO	DESTRUCT	INTERACT
MYSTICAL	PERSONAL	SIBERIAN	TOWNSMAN	ACCURACY	DEVIANCE	INTIMACY
MYTHICAL	PERUVIAN	SICILIAN	TRASHCAN	ADEQUACY	DIFFRACT	INTRENCH
NAMIBIAN	PHRYGIAN	SIDEREAL	TRIBUNAL	ADVOCACY	DIPSTICK	JAPONICA
NATIONAL	PHYSICAL	SIDESMAN	TRIMARAN	AEROBICS	DISGRACE	JAUNDICE
NAUTICAL	PISSHEAD	SILESIAN	TRINIDAD	ALBERICH	DISJUNCT	JIMCRACK
NECKWEAR	PLACEMAT	SILURIAN	TRISTRAM	ALFRESCO	DISPATCH	JOYSTICK
NEHEMIAH	PLEBEIAN	SIMONIAC	TRITICAL	ALLIANCE	DISPLACE	KICKBACK
NEMBUTAL	POETICAL	SINGULAR	TROPICAL	ALLSPICE	DISTANCE	KINETICS

KNAPSACK	PROSPECT	VOIDANCE	HEBETUDE	AASVOGEL	BAPTISED	CENTERED
KREPLACH	PROVINCE	WHIPJACK	HEMIPODE	ABDUCTED	BARATHEA	CERASTES
LAIDBACK	PRUDENCE	WINDSOCK	HILLSIDE	ABERDEEN	BARTERED	CHANDLER
LANDLOCK	PUNGENCY	WOODCOCK	HOKKAIDO	ABRIDGED	BASSINET	CHANTREY
LANDRACE	RADIANCE	WOOLPACK	HOMEMADE	ABSENTEE	BATTERED	CHARTRES
LAURENCE	REDBRICK	WOOLSACK	HOMICIDE	ABSOLVED	BECALMED	CHEROKEE
LAWRENCE	REDIRECT	ZWIEBACK	HOWDYEDO	ABSORBED	BECHAMEL	CHESSMEN
LECTRICE	RELIANCE	ABBASIDE	HUNDREDS	ABSORBER	BEDCOVER	CHICKPEA
LENIENCY	RENOUNCE	ACCOLADE	INNUENDO	ACCENTED	BEDMAKER	CHILDREN
LICORICE	REPROACH	ACTINIDE	INTIFADA	ACCEPTED	BEGETTER	CHRISTEN
LIMERICK	RESEARCH	ADELAIDE	IRONSIDE	ACCURSED	BEGINNER	CICISBEO
LIPSTICK	RESOURCE	ADENOIDS	JEOPARDY	ACHIEVED	BEHOLDEN	CILIATED
LITERACY	RESTRICT	ALDEHYDE	KATMANDU	ACHIEVER	BEHOLDER	CLARINET
LOVELACE	RETRENCH	ALTITUDE	LAKESIDE	ACHILLES	BELIEVER	CLEANSED
LOVESICK	RIDDANCE	ANACONDA	LANDLADY	ACQUIRED	BENENDEN	CLEANSER
MAJOLICA	ROBOTICS	ANNELIDA	LATITUDE	ACQUIRER	BEREAVED	CLERIHEW
MALLORCA	RODERICK	ANTECEDE	LEMONADE	ADDICTED	BERKELEY	CLINCHER
MANDIOCA	ROMANSCH	ANTIBODY	LEONARDO	ADJUSTER	BESIEGED	CLIVEDEN
MAVERICK	RUCKSACK	APTITUDE	LOMBARDY	ADVANCED	BESOTTED	CLOISTER
MILLRACE	SALTLICK	ATTITUDE	LOWLANDS	ADVANCER	BESPOKEN	CLOTHIER
MISMATCH	SANDWICH	BACKSIDE	MACREADY	AFFECTED	BESSEMER	COCKEREL
MISPLACE	SCARFACE	BADLANDS	MALGRADO	AGITATED	BESTOWER	COCKEYED
MOLLUSCS	SCIATICA	BARNARDS	MARINADE	AGONIZED	BETRAYER	COGNOMEN
MOORCOCK	SCIROCCO	BELGRADE	MEGAPODE	AIRLINER	BEWILDER	COGWHEEL
NECKLACE	SENTENCE	BESTRIDE	MIDLANDS	AIRSCREW	BICONVEX	COLANDER
NICKNACK	SEQUENCE	BETHESDA	MISGUIDE	AIRSPEED	BINDWEED	COLLAGEN
NONESUCH	SHADRACH	BIGARADE	MONOXIDE	AIRWAVES	BIRDSEED	COLLARED
NONSTICK	SHAMROCK	BLOCKADE	NEMATODE	ALDERNEY	BLACKLEG	COLLEGES
NUISANCE	SHELDUCK	BRANDADE	NORMANDY	ALLERGEN	BLEACHER	COLOURED
NUMERACY	SHERLOCK	BURGUNDY	OEILLADE	ALPHABET	BLIGHTER	COMBINED
NUTHATCH	SHOELACE	BUSYBODY	OUTWARDS	AMBUSHED	BLOTCHED	COMMONER
OBDURACY	SIDEKICK	CENTRODE	OVERRIDE	AMUNDSEN	BOADICEA	COMMUTER
OBSTRUCT	SIXPENCE	CHARLADY	PALINODE	ANALYSER	BONSPIEL	COMPARED
OILSLICK	SKIPJACK	CHILLADA	PALISADE	ANCHISES	BORDERER	COMPILER
OLIGARCH	SLAPJACK	CHLORIDE	PANDOWDY	ANCHORET	BORROWED	COMPOSED
OLYMPICS	SOFTBACK	COINCIDE	PEROXIDE	ANDREWES	BORROWER	COMPOSER
ONETRACK	SOLSTICE	COLORADO	PERSUADE	ANGLESEY	BOTHERED	COMPUTER
OPULENCE	SOLVENCY	COMMANDO	POSTCODE	ANIMATED	BRACELET	CONFINED
ORDNANCE	STOPCOCK	CONCLUDE	PRECLUDE	ANNEALER	BRANCHED	CONFINES
OUTMATCH	SUBTRACT	CONCORDE	PROCEEDS	ANTILLES	BRANDNEW	CONFUSED
OUTREACH	SUCCINCT	DEFILADE	PROGRADE	APOSTLES	BREACHES	CONJURER
OVERMUCH	SUNDANCE	DIAMONDS	PROTRUDE	APPALLED	BREATHER	CONSIDER
PALEFACE	SURPLICE	DIEHARDS	PSALMODY	APPRISED	BREECHES	CONSUMED
PARLANCE	TAILBACK	DISSUADE	PYRAMIDS	APPROVED	BRETHREN	CONSUMER
PATIENCE	TAMARACK	DOCKSIDE	QUAYSIDE	ARCHIVES	BRIGHTEN	CONVENER
PAYCHECK	TENDENCY	DOGSBODY	QUIETUDE	ARDENNES	BRINDLED	CORRODED
PENTARCH	TETRARCH	DOWNSIDE	REGICIDE	ARGESTES	BRISTLED	CORSELET
PENZANCE	TICKTACK	DRYGOODS	RENEGADE	ARMOURED	BRISTLES	COTTAGER
PERFORCE	TICKTOCK	ELDORADO	REYNOLDS	ARRANGER	BRUCKNER	COUNTIES
PETRARCH	TITICACA	ENFILADE	RHAPSODY	ARRESTED	BUCKSHEE	COVERLET
PHARMACY	TOISEACH	ESCALADE	RINGSIDE	ARRESTER	BUGGERED	CRAVATES
PICKLOCK	TOPNOTCH	ESCAPADE	ROADSIDE	ARTICLED	BUMMAREE	CRIPPLED
PICKWICK	TOVARICH	EVENTIDE	SEAWARDS	ARTICLES	BURDENED	CROSSLET
PINPRICK	TRANSACT	EYESHADE	SELFMADE	ASPERGES	BURROWER	CROTCHET
PIQUANCY	TRANSECT	FIRESIDE	SERENADE	ASPHODEL	BUTTERED	CROUPIER
PITTANCE	TRIPTYCH	FLUORIDE	SOAPSUDS	ASSIGNEE	CABERNET	CRUCIFER
PLAYBACK	TRISTICH	FOREBODE	SOLITUDE	ASSORTED	CALENDER	CRUSADER
PLUTARCH	TURNBACK	FORWARDS	SOMEBODY	ATOMIZER	CALLIPER	CRUTCHED
POLITICO	TURNCOCK	GADOGADO	STAMPEDE	ATTACHED	CAMBERED	CUCUMBER
POLITICS	TWOPIECE	GANYMEDE	STOCKADE	ATTACKER	CANARIES	CULLODEN
POLYARCH	TYPEFACE	GENOCIDE	SUCCEEDS	ATTENDER	CANISTER	CULOTTES
POPULACE	USUFRUCT	GERTRUDE	SULPHIDE	ATTORNEY	CAPSIZED	CULTURED
POTLATCH	VAGRANCY	GIACONDA	SUNSHADE	AUSPICES	CARCANET	CUSTOMER
POULTICE	VARIANCE	GIOCONDA	TAPENADE	BAEDEKER	CAREFREE	CUTWATER
PRACTICE	VERJUICE	GLISSADE	THRENODY	BAGPIPES	CAROUSEL	CYANOGEN
PRECINCT	VERONICA	GRIMALDI	UNSTEADY	BALANCED	CASTANET	CYCLADES
PRESENCE	VESPUCCI	GRISELDA	UNWIELDY	BALUSTER	CATHETER	CYCLAMEN
PRETENCE	VIBRANCY	HACIENDA	WETLANDS	BANISTER	CAVALIER	CYLINDER
PROPHECY	VIOLENCE	HANDMADE	YULETIDE	BANNERET	CELLARER	DAINTIES

DAMOCLES	DURABLES	FLYSHEET	IMAGINED	LEISURED	NIGERIEN	PINWHEEL
DANAIDES	DUTYFREE	FLYWHEEL	IMMANUEL	LENGTHEN	NINETEEN	PLACEMEN
DARKENED	EATABLES	FOLLOWED	IMMERSED	LETTERED	NITROGEN	PLANCHET
DAUGHTER	EDUCATED	FOLLOWER	IMPACTED	LEVELLER	NORSEMEN	PLATELET
DEADENED	EGGTIMER	FOOTSTEP	IMPAIRED	LICENSED	NOVEMBER	PLEIADES
DEADENER	EIGHTEEN	FORESTER	IMPELLED	LICENSEE	OBSCURED	PLOUGHED
DEATHBED	ELEVATED	FORSAKEN	IMPORTER	LISTENER	OBSERVED	POISONER
DECANTER	EMBEDDED	FOURTEEN	IMPOSTER	LIVERIED	OBSERVER	POKEWEED
DECEASED	EMBITTER	FRAZZLED	IMPROPER	LOCOWEED	OBSESSED	POLISHED
DECEIVER	EMBODIED	FRECKLED	IMPROVED	LOITERER	OBTAINED	POLISHER
DECEMBER	EMBOLDEN	FRECKLES	IMPROVER	LONDONER	OCCUPIED	POLLSTER
DECIPHER	EMBOSSED	FRENZIED	INCENSED	LOPSIDED	OCCUPIER	POLLUTED
DEFEATED	EMBRACED	FRIGHTEN	INCLINED	LOUVERED	ODOMETER	POLLUTER
DEFENDER	EMBRACES	FRONTIER	INCLUDED	LYSANDER	OFFENDED	POMANDER
DEFLOWER	EMIRATES	FURROWED	INDEBTED	MACHINES	OFFENDER	PONTIFEX
DEFORMED	EMMANUEL	FUSILIER	INDENTED	MACKEREL	OFFSIDER	POTATOES
DEGRADED	EMPLOYED	GALLOPER	INFECTED	MAGISTER	OLEANDER	POTHOLER
DEJECTED	EMPLOYEE	GALOSHES	INFESTED	MALARKEY	OLEASTER	POWDERED
DEMENTED	EMPLOYER	GANGSTER	INFLAMED	MALDIVES	ONESIDED	PRATTLER
DEMISTER	ENCAMPED	GANISTER	INFLATED	MALINGER	ONLOOKER	PREACHER
DENTURES	ENCLOSED	GARDENER	INFORMED	MANDATED	ONSCREEN	PREMISES
DEPARTED	ENCUMBER	GARGANEY	INFORMER	MANEUVER	ORPHANED	PREPARED
DEPORTEE	ENDANGER	GASOLIER	INFRARED	MANGONEL	OSTERLEY	PRISONER
DEPRAVED	ENGENDER	GATHERED	INQUIRER	MANNERED	OUTDATED	PRIVATES
DEPRIVED	ENGINEER	GAUNTLET	INSPIRED	MANPOWER	OUTMODED	PROCURER
DERANGED	ENGRAVER	GAZUNDER	INTENDED	MARAUDER	OUTREMER	PRODUCER
DESERTED	ENLARGED	GEOMETER	INTERNEE	MARGARET	OUTRIDER	PRODUCES
DESERTER	ENLARGER	GESTURES	INTERNET	MARMOSET	OUTSIDER	PROFUSER
DESERVED	ENMESHED	GLYCOGEN	INTRUDER	MARTINET	OVERFEED	PROMISED
DESIGNER	ENRICHED	GOSSAMER	INVENTED	MARTYRED	OVERSEER	PROMOTER
DESTINED	ENTITLED	GRANULES	INVERTED	MASSENET	OVERSTEP	PROMPTER
DETACHED	ESPALIER	GRATINEE	INVERTER	MCKINLEY	OVERVIEW	PROPOSED
DETAILED	ESTEEMED	GRAVAMEN	INVOLVED	MEASURED	OXPECKER	PROPOSER
DETAINEE	ESTOPPEL	GRIZZLED	IRISHMEN	MELEAGER	PACIFIER	PROTÉGÉE
DETAINER	ESTROGEN	GROSCHEN	ISLANDER	MENANDER	PACKAGED	PROVIDED
DEVILLED	EVILDOER	GROUNDED	ISOLATED	MENHADEN	PALMATED	PROVIDER
DEWYEYED	EXAMINEE	GRUMBLER	IVOIRIEN	MERCEDES	PAMPERED	PUCKERED
DIABETES	EXAMINER	GUERNSEY	JACKETED	MERISTEM	PAMPHLET	PUGNOSED
DIAMETER	EXECUTED	GULFWEED	JAMBOREE	MESSAGER	PANELLED	PULITZER
DIARRHEA	EXPANDED	GULLIVER	JEWELLED	METALLED	PANPIPES	PULLOVER
DICTATES	EXPECTED	GUSSETED	JEWELLER	MILDEWED	PARAKEET	PUNISHED
DIOGENES	EXPENDED	HALLOWED	JIGGERED	MILKWEED	PARALLEL	PURIFIED
DISABLED	EXPENSES	HAMMERED	JOHANNES	MILLINER	PARDONER	PURIFIER
DISAGREE	EXPLODED	HANDOVER	KEDGEREE	MINISTER	PAROLLES	PUSHOVER
DISASTER	EXPLORER	HANGOVER	KERCHIEF	MINSTREL	PASSOVER	PYORRHEA
DISCOVER	EXPORTER	HARASSED	KESTEVEN	MIRRORED	PASTURES	PYRENEES
DISCREET	EXTENDED	HARDENED	KIBITZER	MISCHIEF	PATENTED	QUARTIER
DISEASED	EYELINER	HARUSPEX	KILLDEER	MISNOMER	PATENTEE	QUIBBLER
DISHEVEL	FAINITES	HAUNCHES	KINGSLEY	MISTAKEN	PATHOGEN	QUICKSET
DISINTER	FAMISHED	HAYFEVER	KIPPERED	MODELLER	PEDIGREE	RAREFIED
DISLIKED	FASTENER	HAYMAKER	KNAPWEED	MODIFIER	PELLETED	REASONED
DISMAYED	FATIGUED	HEARTIES	KNEEDEEP	MOHAMMED	PENNINES	REAWAKEN
DISORDER	FATIGUES	HEBRIDES	KNOTWEED	MOLASSES	PERFUMED	RECEIVED
DISPOSED	FAULKNER	HEIGHTEN	KUFFIYEH	MOLESTER	PERICLES	RECEIVER
DISPUTED	FAVOURED	HELMETED	LABOURED	MONICKER	PERISHED	RECESSED
DISQUIET	FEATURED	HENEQUEN	LABOURER	MOREOVER	PERISHER	RECKONER
DIVORCED	FEATURES	HERACLES	LADRONES	MORTIMER	PERJURED	RECORDER
DIVORCEE	FEDAYEEN	HERCULES	LAMENTED	MULETEER	PERJURER	REDEEMER
DOCTORED	FEVERFEW	HERSCHEL	LANCELET	MURDERER	PEVENSEY	REFORMED
DOGGEREL	FILIGREE	HIJACKER	LANDSEER	MUSCADET	PHARISEE	REFORMER
DOMINEER	FINISHED	HONEYDEW	LATCHKEY	MUSCATEL	PHILOMEL	REGAINED
DOMINOES	FINISHER	HORSEMEN	LAUGHTER	MUTINEER	PICTURES	REGISTER
DOORSTEP	FIRESTEP	HOTELIER	LAVENDER	NARCOSES	PIERIDES	REINDEER
DOTTEREL	FIREWEED	HOWITZER	LAWMAKER	NARGILEH	PILASTER	REJOINED
DRAGSTER	FISSIPED	HUCKSTER	LEAVENED	NATTERED	PILFERER	RELEASED
DUBONNET	FLAVORED	HUMPHREY	LECTURER	NEGLIGEE	PILLAGER	RELIEVED
DUCKWEED	FLAXSEED	HYDROGEN	LECTURES	NEWCOMER	PILLARED	REMEMBER
DULCIMER	FLOUNCED	IDOLATER	LEFTOVER	NEWHAVEN	PILSENER	REMINDER
DULCINEA	FLOUNDER	ILLFATED	LEINSTER	NEWSREEL	PINNIPED	RENOWNED

REPAIRER	SIGHTSEE	STRIATED	UNABATED	WINNIPEG	CHANTAGE	PENOLOGY
REPARTEE	SIGNALER	STRICKEN	UNAWARES	WITHERED	CHUMMAGE	PHALANGE
REPEATED	SILENCER	STRINGED	UNBEATEN	WOLSELEY	CLEAVAGE	PICKINGS
REPEATER	SINISTER	STRINGER	UNBIASED	WOODSHED	CONTANGO	PILOTAGE
REPORTED	SITUATED	STRIPPED	UNBIDDEN	WORTHIES	CONVERGE	PLUMBAGO
REPORTER	SKINDEEP	STRIPPER	UNBROKEN	WRANGLER	COVERAGE	PORRIDGE
REQUIRED	SKITTLES	STROLLER	UNBURDEN	WREATHED	CRIBBAGE	POSOLOGY
RESERVED	SLIGHTED	STRUMPET	UNCLOVEN	WRESTLER	CYTOLOGY	POUNDAGE
RESIGNED	SLIPOVER	STUCCOED	UNCOMBED	WRETCHED	DEALINGS	PREJUDGE
RESOLVED	SLUGABED	STYLIZED	UNCOOKED	WRINKLED	DEMIURGE	PRESTIGE
RESTORER	SMOOTHER	SUFFERER	UNCURBED	WRISTLET	DIGGINGS	QUADRIGA
RETAILER	SMOULDER	SUNDRIED	UNDERFED	YODELLER	DISGORGE	RAILINGS
RETAINER	SMUGGLED	SUNDRIES	UNDERSEA	AIRCRAFT	DISLODGE	RANELAGH
RETARDED	SMUGGLER	SUPPLIER	UNEARNED	ALKALIFY	DOXOLOGY	REASSIGN
REVEALED	SNATCHER	SUPPLIES	UNFASTEN	BEAUTIFY	DRAINAGE	RECHARGE
REVELLER	SNIFFLER	SUPPOSED	UNFETTER	BLASTOFF	DRESSAGE	REDESIGN
REVERSED	SOCALLED	SWADDLER	UNFILLED	CAMSHAFT	EARNINGS	REFRINGE
REVIEWER	SOCRATES	SWINDLER	UNFORCED	CASTOFFS	ENSILAGE	ROUGHAGE
REVOLVER	SOFTENER	SYLVANER	UNHARMED	CLASSIFY	ENVISAGE	RUTABAGA
RICOCHET	SOMERSET	SYRINGES	UNHEATED	DANDRUFF	EQUIPAGE	SABOTAGE
RISSOLES	SONGSTER	TAKEOVER	UNHINGED	DETOXIFY	ETHOLOGY	SANTIAGO
ROADSTER	SORCERER	TALENTED	UNLEADED	EMULSIFY	EXCHANGE	SARATOGA
ROENTGEN	SPANDREL	TATTERED	UNLISTED	ETHERIFY	FANDANGO	SCAVENGE
ROMANCER	SPANGLED	TAVERNER	UNLOADED	FACELIFT	FEELINGS	SCROUNGE
RUMOURED	SPARKLER	TAXPAYER	UNLOCKED	FISHWIFE	FINDINGS	SELVEDGE
SADDUCEE	SPAVINED	TEAMSTER	UNMANNED	FORKLIFT	FLAMINGO	SEROLOGY
SALARIED	SPECIMEN	TEENAGER	UNMARKED	FRUCTIFY	FRONTAGE	SEWERAGE
SALINGER	SPECKLED	TEMPERED	UNNERVED	GENTRIFY	FULLPAGE	SEXOLOGY
SANGLIER	SPINIFEX	TERRACED	UNPLACED	GOODWIFE	FURLOUGH	SHORTAGE
SATIATED	SPINSTER	TEXTURED	UNRIFLED	HANDCUFF	FUSELAGE	SPILLAGE
SAUSAGES	SPIRELET	THATCHED	UNSALTED	HUMIDIFY	GEMOLOGY	SPOILAGE
SAVOURED	SPIRITED	THATCHER	UNSEALED	IDENTIFY	HANGINGS	STEERAGE
SAWBONES	SPLASHER	THICKSET	UNSEEDED	IMPURIFY	HASTINGS	STOPPAGE
SCANTIES	SPLATTER	THIOUREA	UNSHAKEN	MALAKOFF	HERITAGE	STRATEGY
SCHILLER	SPLINTER	THIRTEEN	UNSIGNED	PENKNIFE	HICCOUGH	SUBMERGE
SCHOONER	SPLITTER	THRASHER	UNSOLVED	QUANTIFY	HOLDINGS	SUFFRAGE
SCIENCES	SPLUTTER	THREATEN	UNSPOKEN	REDSHIFT	HOMEPAGE	THEOLOGY
SCILICET	SPRAINED	THRESHER	UNSTATED	REVIVIFY	HOROLOGY	THOROUGH
SCORCHED	SPRAWLED	THRILLER	UNSUITED	RIFFRAFF	HUSTINGS	TOPOLOGY
SCORCHER	SPREADER	THRUSTER	UNTAPPED	SANCTIFY	IDEOLOGY	TUTELAGE
SCRAWLED	SPRINGER	THURIFER	UNTILLED	SIMPLIFY	IMPETIGO	UNDERAGE
SCREAMER	SPRINTER	TICKSEED	UNVARIED	SOLIDIFY	INFRINGE	VANBRUGH
SCREENED	SPRITZER	TIMBERED	UNVERSED	STANDOFF	JOTTINGS	VERBIAGE
SCRUBBER	SPROCKET	TINTAGEL	UNVOICED	STRATIFY	KNEEHIGH	VICARAGE
SCRUPLES	SQUANDER	TOGETHER	UNWANTED	STULTIFY	LANGUAGE	VIROLOGY
SEAFARER	SQUATTER	TOMATOES	UNWEANED	TARTUFFE	LASHINGS	VITILIGO
SEAMSTER	SQUEAKER	TONSURED	UNWONTED	TIPSTAFF	LEAVINGS	WELLNIGH
SEARCHER	SQUEALER	TOPLEVEL	UPHOLDER	TRADEOFF	LEGGINGS	WHARFAGE
SEASONED	SQUEEGEE	TORTURED	UPMARKET	WILDLIFE	LETHARGY	WINDINGS
SECLUDED	SQUEEZER	TORTURER	UPTURNED	WOODRUFF	LEVERAGE	WINNINGS
SECONDER	SQUIRREL	TRANSFER	VAGARIES	WRITEOFF	LODGINGS	WORKINGS
SELECTED	STAMENED	TRANSKEI	VANISHED	WYCLIFFE	MAHJONGG	WRECKAGE
SEMESTER	STARCHED	TRAVELER	VENTURED	ADJUTAGE	MARRIAGE	WRITINGS
SENGREEN	STENOSED	TREMBLER	VERDERER	ALGOLOGY	MESSUAGE	ZASTRUGA
SENTINEL	STICKLER	TREMBLES	VILLAGER	ALTHOUGH	MISJUDGE	ABSINTHE
SERRATED	STOPOVER	TRENCHER	WAGGONER	AMPERAGE	MOORINGS	AIRTIGHT
SERVICES	STOREYED	TROCHLEA	WALKOVER	APOPHYGE	MORTGAGE	AUTARCHY
SHACKLES	STRACHEY	TROUBLED	WANDERER	APOTHEGM	MUCILAGE	AUTOBAHN
SHAGREEN	STRAINED	TROUBLES	WAVERLEY	APPANAGE	MYCOLOGY	BACKACHE
SHAMBLES	STRAINER	TROUNCER	WAYFARER	BADINAGE	NOSOLOGY	BEERBOHM
SHINGLES	STRAITEN	TRUCKLED	WELLBRED	BEARINGS	OENOLOGY	BESOUGHT
SHIVERED	STRANDED	TUNGSTEN	WHATEVER	BEGRUDGE	OFFSTAGE	BROUHAHA
SHOETREE	STRANGER	TURBANED	WHENEVER	BEVERAGE	ONCOLOGY	BUNFIGHT
SHOULDER	STRAPPED	TURBOJET	WHEREVER	BIRDCAGE	ONTOLOGY	CORNICHE
SHRAPNEL	STRAPPER	TURGENEV	WHIMBREL	BLOCKAGE	OUTWEIGH	DAYLIGHT
SHREDDER	STREAKED	TURNOVER	WHISTLER	CABOTAGE	OXBRIDGE	DEMIJOHN
SHROUDED	STREAKER	TURRETED	WHITENER	CAMPAIGN	PARADIGM	DZONGKHA
SHRUNKEN	STREAMER	TWITCHER	WINDHOEK	CARRIAGE	PEDAGOGY	ENCLOTHE
SIDESTEP	STRESSED	UDOMETER	WINIFRED	CARTHAGE	PEELINGS	EUTROPHY

EYESIGHT	APOLOGIA	COATTAIL	ENCAENIA	HERALDIC	MESOZOIC	PLAYSUIT
FACEACHE	APPENDIX	COCKTAIL	EPIDEMIC	HERMETIC	MÉTAIRIE	PONYTAIL
FANLIGHT	ARACHNID	COLOMBIA	EPIGAMIC	HERPETIC	METALLIC	PORTRAIT
FAROUCHE	ARMCHAIR	COMPLAIN	EPISODIC	HETAIRIA	METEORIC	POSTPAID
FOGLIGHT	AROMATIC	CONCHOID	EPITASIS	HIBERNIA	METHODIC	POTEMKIN
GAZPACHO	ARPEGGIO	CORDWAIN	ESOTERIC	HIDROSIS	METRITIS	PRETORIA
GOLGOTHA	ARTISTIC	CORIOLIS	ESTANCIA	HIERATIC	MIDBRAIN	PROCLAIM
GRENACHE	ASCORBIC	CORONOID	ESTHETIC	HISPANIC	MILKMAID	PROGERIA
HEADACHE	ASPERMIA	CORRAGIO	ETHIOPIA	HISTORIC	MINCEPIE	PROHIBIT
HIAWATHA	ASPHYXIA	COSMETIC	EUCYCLIC	HOLISTIC	MIREPOIX	PROLIFIC
INFLIGHT	ASSASSIN	COUPERIN	EUPEPSIA	HOLOZOIC	MNEMONIC	PROPOLIS
IOLANTHE	ASTEROID	COXSWAIN	EUPHONIA	HORNTAIL	MOCCASIN	PYELITIS
JEHOVAHS	ASTHENIA	COYSTRIL	EUPHONIC	HORRIFIC	MOLESKIN	QUATRAIN
JYAISTHA	ATARAXIA	CRATCHIT	EUPHORIA	HYDATOID	MONASTIC	QUINTAIN
MARIACHI	ATARAXIC	CRUCIFIX	EUPHORIC	HYGIENIC	MONGOLIA	QUIXOTIC
MIDNIGHT	ATHETOID	CRUNCHIE	EUSTATIC	HYPNOSIS	MONOACID	RABELAIS
MONARCHY	ATHLETIC	CUCURBIT	EUTROPIC	HYPNOTIC	MONORAIL	RACHITIS
MUSTACHE	ATLANTIC	CULVERIN	EWIGKEIT	HYSTERIA	MONROVIA	RAMEQUIN
NEPENTHE	ATLANTIS	CYANOSIS	EXEGESIS	HYSTERIC	MOUNTAIN	RASPUTIN
NOMARCHY	AUCASSIN	CYCLOSIS	EXEGETIC	ILLINOIS	MUNCHKIN	REPLEVIN
OUTRIGHT	AUTISTIC	CYRILLIC	EXOERGIC	IMPLICIT	MUTCHKIN	REPUBLIC
PASTICHE	BACKSPIN	CYSTITIS	EXPLICIT	INKSTAIN	MYELITIS	RESTRAIN
REDLIGHT	BACTERIA	DAFFODIL	FANTASIA	INSIGNIA	MYOSOTIS	RHETORIC
RESPIGHI	BALEARIC	DALMATIC	FELLAHIN	INSOMNIA	NARCOSIS	RHOMBOID
REVANCHE	BARBARIC	DEBONAIR	FIBROSIS	INSPIRIT	NARCOTIC	RHYTHMIC
RUBBISHY	BATHETIC	DECEMVIR	FLAGSHIP	INTAGLIO	NECROSIS	RINGTAIL
SCRATCHY	BEARSKIN	DECREPIT	FLEISHIG	INTERMIT	NEMATOID	RIVERAIN
SKYLIGHT	BEATIFIC	DEERSKIN	FLOODLIT	INTREPID	NEOMYCIN	ROMANTIC
STEALTHY	BENJAMIN	DEMENTIA	FORENSIC	IROQUOIS	NEPIONIC	SADISTIC
STRAIGHT	BERBERIS	DENDROID	FORESAIL	ISOBARIC	NEURITIS	SAINFOIN
STRETCHY	BERGENIA	DESPOTIC	FORESHIP	ISOGENIC	NEUROSIS	SANSERIF
SUNBATHE	BICUSPID	DIABETIC	FORESKIN	JALOUSIE	NEUROTIC	SANSKRIT
SUNLIGHT	BIGNONIA	DIABOLIC	FORKTAIL	JUMPSUIT	OENOPHIL	SARDINIA
SYMPATHY	BLENHEIM	DIALYSIS	FORMALIN	JURASSIC	OPERATIC	SARDONIC
TWILIGHT	BOBBYPIN	DIARESIS	FOUNTAIN	KINGSHIP	ORATORIO	SASSANID
UNWORTHY	BONHOMIE	DIATONIC	FRANKLIN	KYPHOSIS	ORCHITIS	SATURNIA
VAISAKHA	BOWSPRIT	DICYCLIC	FRAULEIN	LADYSHIP	ORESTEIA	SCAPHOID
ABATTOIR	BRASILIA	DIDACTIC	FRENETIC	LAMBSKIN	ORGANDIE	SCENARIO
ACADEMIA	BROMELIA	DIELDRIN	GALACTIC	LANDSLIP	OUTSTRIP	SCHIZOID
ACADEMIC	BUCKSKIN	DIERESIS	GALLERIA	LECITHIN	OVARITIS	SCRIABIN
ACCREDIT	BUDDLEIA	DIOPTRIC	GALVANIC	LEUKEMIA	OVERLAID	SEALSKIN
ACENTRIC	BULGARIA	DISCLAIM	GARDENIA	LINCHPIN	OXYTOCIN	SELASSIE
ACOUSTIC	BULLETIN	DISPIRIT	GELASTIC	LINGERIE	PALLADIO	SELEUCID
ACROSTIC	BURSITIS	DISTRAIN	GENETRIX	LISTERIA	PALMITIN	SEMIOTIC
ADENITIS	CACHEXIA	DISTRAIT	GEODESIC	LOGISTIC	PANDEMIC	SERAGLIO
ADRIATIC	CALFSKIN	DIURETIC	GEODETIC	LONGSHIP	PANGOLIN	SERAPHIC
AEROFOIL	CAMBODIA	DOGMATIC	GEOTAXIS	LORDOSIS	PANNIKIN	SERAPHIM
AGACERIE	CAMELLIA	DOGSTAIL	GERMANIC	LORDSHIP	PARAFFIN	SERIATIM
AGNOSTIC	CANNABIS	DOMESTIC	GIGANTIC	LOTHARIO	PARANOIA	SIDESLIP
AIRSTRIP	CANTORIS	DOVETAIL	GIRONDIN	LYSERGIC	PARANOID	SIGNORIA
ALCESTIS	CAPUCHIN	DRACONIC	GLOBULIN	MAGNESIA	PAROUSIA	SILKTAIL
ALCHEMIC	CARBOLIC	DRAMATIC	GLOXINIA	MAGNETIC	PATHETIC	SINCLAIR
ALKALOID	CARBONIC	DYNASTIC	GLYCERIN	MAGNOLIA	PEARMAIN	SINFONIA
ALLELUIA	CARNEGIE	DYSLEXIA	GOATSKIN	MAIEUTIC	PEDANTIC	SLOVAKIA
ALLERGIC	CARYATID	DYSLEXIC	GOIDELIC	MAINSAIL	PEIGNOIR	SLOVENIA
ALOPECIA	CATHOLIC	ECLECTIC	GRANDKID	MAINTAIN	PELLUCID	SOCRATIC
AMBROSIA	CENOZOIC	ECONOMIC	GUMMOSIS	MAJESTIC	PERIODIC	SOLENOID
AMMONOID	CEPHALIN	ECSTASIS	HAMARTIA	MALAYSIA	PHENOLIC	SOUVENIR
ANABASIS	CERATOID	ECSTATIC	HANDGRIP	MALVASIA	PHONETIC	SPARAXIS
ANABATIC	CHAPLAIN	EFFLUVIA	HANDMAID	MALVOLIO	PHOTOFIT	SPECIFIC
ANALYSIS	CHERUBIC	EGOISTIC	HANDRAIL	MANDARIN	PHREATIC	SPHENOID
ANALYTIC	CHERUBIM	EGOMANIA	HANGNAIL	MANDOLIN	PHTHISIC	SPLENDID
ANARCHIC	CHOLERIC	EIDECTIC	HARDSHIP	MANNIKIN	PHTHISIS	SPORADIC
ANATOLIA	CHRISTIE	EINSTEIN	HEADSHIP	MAROQUIN	PHYSALIA	SQUADDIE
ANATOMIC	CICATRIX	ELECTRIC	HELLADIC	MATHURIN	PINDARIC	STAPELIA
ANOREXIA	CLAVECIN	ELLIPSIS	HELLENIC	MECHANIC	PIZZERIA	STAYSAIL
ANOREXIC	CLEMATIS	ELLIPTIC	HELLENIC	MEMSAHIB	PLANTAIN	STEAPSIN
APERITIF	CLIMATIC	EMPHASIS	HELVETIA	MESCALIN	PLATONIC	STENOSIS
APNEUSIS	CLITORIS	EMPHATIC	HERACLID	MESMERIC	PLAYFAIR	SUBSONIC

SUBTOPIA	ARCHDUKE	ARDENTLY	CLEVERLY	FATHERLY	HEATEDLY	MIDFIELD
SUBURBIA	BABUSHKA	ARGUABLE	CLODPOLL	FEASIBLE	HEAVENLY	MIGHTILY
SULFURIC	BALLOCKS	ARGUABLY	CLUMSILY	FEASIBLY	HEELBALL	MINUTELY
SUZERAIN	BARRACKS	ARTFULLY	COALHOLE	FENCIBLE	HIGHBALL	MISAPPLY
SWANSKIN	BOLLOCKS	ASSEMBLE	COARSELY	FIERCELY	HOARSELY	MISSPELL
SWIMSUIT	BOUZOUKI	ASSEMBLY	COCACOLA	FILTHILY	HONESTLY	MODESTLY
SYLLABIC	BUTTOCKS	ASTUTELY	COMMONLY	FIREBALL	HONOLULU	MOLECULE
SYLVATIC	CLAMBAKE	AURICULA	CONTROLS	FIREBOLT	HOPFIELD	MOLEHILL
SYMBOLIC	EASTLAKE	BANKROLL	COPYHOLD	FITFULLY	HORNBILL	MONOHULL
SYNOPSIS	FISHCAKE	BARGELLO	CORNHILL	FLAGPOLE	HORNFELS	MONOPOLE
SYNOPTIC	GADZOOKS	BARNACLE	CORNWALL	FLANNELS	HORRIBLE	MONOPOLY
SYNTEXIS	GARLICKY	BASEBALL	COTSWOLD	FLASHILY	HORRIBLY	MONTCALM
SYPHILIS	GASWORKS	BASTILLE	COWARDLY	FLEXIBLE	HORSEFLY	MORBIDLY
SYSTEMIC	HAIRLIKE	BEANPOLE	CRAFTILY	FLEXIBLY	HOVERFLY	MORBILLI
TAFFRAIL	HELSINKI	BEARABLE	CRANEFLY	FLIMSILY	HUMANELY	MOROSELY
TAILSKID	HORLICKS	BEDABBLE	CREDIBLE	FLOTILLA	HUNGRILY	MORTALLY
TAILSPIN	JORROCKS	BEFUDDLE	CREDIBLY	FLUENTLY	ICEFIELD	MOTHBALL
TANZANIA	KARTTIKA	BEGGARLY	CROMWELL	FOLLICLE	IMBECILE	MOTHERLY
TARTARIC	KEEPSAKE	BELITTLE	CRUCIBLE	FOOTBALL	IMMOBILE	MOVEABLE
TASMANIA	KENTUCKY	BIFOCALS	CRYSTALS	FOOTFALL	INEDIBLE	MULTIPLE
TECTONIC	KLONDIKE	BILLFOLD	CULPABLE	FOOTHOLD	INSANELY	MULTIPLY
TEFILLIN	KOLINSKY	BINNACLE	CURRICLE	FORCIBLE	INTENTLY	MUTUALLY
TELLURIC	KROMESKY	BITTERLY	DAINTILY	FORCIBLY	INVEIGLE	NARROWLY
TENEBRIO	LADYLIKE	BLACKFLY	DAMNABLE	FOREMILK	INWARDLY	NEGRILLO
TERRAPIN	LIFELIKE	BLASTULA	DANEGELD	FORETELL	ISABELLA	NORMALLY
TERRIFIC	MAMELUKE	BLITHELY	DECENTLY	FORMALLY	ISABELLE	NOSTRILS
TEUTONIC	MANDRAKE	BLOWHOLE	DECOUPLE	FORMERLY	JAUNTILY	NUCLEOLE
THEATRIC	MOUSSAKA	BLUEBELL	DEMURELY	FOURFOLD	JOKINGLY	NUFFIELD
THEMATIC	NAGASAKI	BOATBILL	DENTICLE	FREEHOLD	JOVIALLY	NUMERALS
THOLEPIN	NAMESAKE	BOLTHOLE	DIASTOLE	FRIENDLY	JOYFULLY	NUPTIALS
THORACIC	NEBRASKA	BOOKABLE	DIRECTLY	FRIGIDLY	JUVENILE	NUTSHELL
THROMBIN	NIJINSKY	BORDELLO	DISCIPLE	FRISKILY	KILOVOLT	OBSTACLE
TOWNSHIP	OVERTAKE	BORECOLE	DISMALLY	FROSTILY	KINSFOLK	OBTUSELY
TOXAEMIA	PACHINKO	BOREHOLE	DISRAELI	FRUGALLY	KNIGHTLY	ODIOUSLY
TRANQUIL	PEMBROKE	BORSTALL	DOGGEDLY	FUMAROLE	LANDFALL	OILFIELD
TRANSFIX	PIROZHKI	BOTHWELL	DOMICILE	FUNGIBLE	LANDFILL	OLDSTYLE
TRANSHIP	PUSHBIKE	BREEZILY	DOOLALLY	FURUNCLE	LATTERLY	OLDWORLD
TRANSMIT	RAPECAKE	BRIBABLE	DOORBELL	FUSAROLE	LAUDABLE	OPERABLE
TRIASSIC	SCHAPSKA	BRIGHTLY	DOORSILL	GARGOYLE	LAUDABLY	OPUSCULE
TRICHOID	SHIITAKE	BROCCOLI	DOWNFALL	GARISHLY	LAVISHLY	OUTFIELD
TROCHAIC	SLOWPOKE	BRUSSELS	DOWNHILL	GASTRULA	LAWFULLY	OVERALLS
TROTTOIR	SUCHLIKE	BRUTALLY	DREAMILY	GATEFOLD	LIFEBELT	OVERFILL
TUNGSTEN	SUKIYAKI	CABOODLE	DREARILY	GENIALLY	LIKEABLE	OVERFULL
TUNGUSIC	SWASTIKA	CABRIOLE	DROWSILY	GENITALS	LOCKABLE	OVERKILL
TURMERIC	TERIYAKI	CAKEHOLE	DUCKBILL	GINGERLY	LONSDALE	OVERRULE
TURNSPIT	TURNPIKE	CAKEWALK	DUMBBELL	GIRASOLE	LOOPHOLE	OVERSOLD
UNDERBID	TZATZIKI	CALIGULA	DUNGHILL	GLABELLA	LOVINGLY	PALPABLE
UNDERLIE	VISELIKE	CAMISOLE	DUTIABLE	GLOBALLY	MAIDENLY	PALPABLY
UNDERPIN	WATERSKI	CAMOMILE	EASTERLY	GLOOMILY	MANCIPLE	PANATELA
UNHEROIC	WAXWORKS	CAMPBELL	EDGEHILL	GLORIOLE	MANDIBLE	PANNICLE
VALENCIA	YARMULKA	CANAILLE	EGGSHELL	GODCHILD	MANDRILL	PARABOLA
VALKYRIE	ZAKOUSKI	CANDIDLY	ELIGIBLE	GOLFBALL	MANFULLY	PARTICLE
VERBATIM	ABJECTLY	CANOODLE	EMBATTLE	GOODWILL	MANIFOLD	PASSABLE
VICTORIA	ABRUPTLY	CANTICLE	EMBEZZLE	GOOFBALL	MANNERLY	PASSABLY
VIRGINIA	ABSURDLY	CAPITALS	ENCIRCLE	GRAVELLY	MANTILLA	PASSIBLE
VOLCANIC	ACTIVELY	CAPRIOLE	ENFEEBLE	GREEDILY	MANUALLY	PASTILLE
WALKYRIE	ACTUALLY	CARACOLE	ENKINDLE	GREENFLY	MARCELLA	PATCHILY
WARDSHIP	ADORABLE	CARRIOLE	ENSEMBLE	GROGGILY	MARCELLO	PATENTLY
WARFARIN	ADROITLY	CARRYALL	ENTANGLE	GRUMPILY	MARIGOLD	PEDUNCLE
WELLPAID	AGRICOLA	CASUALLY	ENTHRALL	GUERILLA	MARKEDLY	PEEPHOLE
WHODUNIT	AIGUILLE	CATAPULT	ENTIRELY	GUILTILY	MARSHALL	PELLICLE
WISTERIA	AIREDALE	CAUDILLO	ENTRAILS	GULLIBLE	MARTELLO	PELLMELL
XERAPHIM	AIRFIELD	CHASUBLE	ENVIABLE	HALFFULL	MASTERLY	PENTACLE
YERSINIA	AMENABLE	CHATTELS	EPISTYLE	HANDBALL	MATABELE	PIGSWILL
ZEPPELIN	AMICABLE	CHEEKILY	ERECTILE	HANDBILL	MATRONLY	PINNACLE
ZIRCONIA	AMICABLY	CHEERILY	FALLIBLE	HANDHELD	MEGAVOLT	PINOCHLE
ZOONOSIS	AMYGDALA	CHENILLE	FAMOUSLY	HAREBELL	MENTALLY	PINTABLE
MAHARAJA	ANGUILLA	CHERWELL	FAREWELL	HAYFIELD	MERCALLI	PITIABLE
AIRBRAKE	ANNUALLY	CLAVICLE	FASCICLE	HEARTILY	METABOLA	PLACABLE

PLACIDLY	SCRIBBLY	STUFFILY	WEARABLE	NOSTROMO	ANYTHING	BUBBLING
PLAYBILL	SCROFULA	STUPIDLY	WEREWOLF	OKLAHOMA	APERIENT	BUCKLING
PLIMSOLL	SEASHELL	STURDILY	WESTERLY	OVERCOME	APPARENT	BUILDING
PLUCKILY	SECONDLY	SUBTITLE	WHEEZILY	OVERTIME	APPELANT	BULLRING
PLUGHOLE	SECRETLY	SUDDENLY	WICKEDLY	PANORAMA	APPELLANT	BUMBLING
POLITELY	SECURELY	SUITABLE	WILDFELL	PARTTIME	AQUALUNG	BUNGLING
POPSICLE	SEDATELY	SUITABLY	WILFULLY	PASTRAMI	AQUATINT	BURSTING
PORTABLE	SELFHELP	SULLENLY	WINDFALL	PHYLLOME	AQUILINE	BUSTLING
PORTHOLE	SENSIBLE	SUPERBLY	WINDGALL	PILGRIMS	ARGININE	CAFFEINE
POSSIBLE	SENSIBLY	SVENGALI	WINDMILL	PLAYTIME	ARGUMENT	CALAMINE
POSSIBLY	SERAFILE	SYLLABLE	WITHHOLD	POLYGAMY	ARMAMENT	CAMSTONE
POTBELLY	SERENELY	TANGIBLE	WOEFULLY	POLYSEME	ARROGANT	CANOEING
PRATFALL	SEVERELY	TANGIBLY	WOODENLY	POLYSEMY	ASPIRANT	CAPERING
PREAMBLE	SEXUALLY	TEARABLE	WORKABLE	PRODROME	ASPIRING	CAPSTONE
PREDELLA	SHABBILY	TELEFILM	WORTHILY	PROFORMA	ASSUMING	CARABINE
PRETTILY	SHIGELLA	TELLTALE	YOURSELF	REALTIME	ASTATINE	CAROLINA
PRIESTLY	SHODDILY	TENDERLY	ZARZUELA	REASSUME	ATHELING	CAROLINE
PRINCELY	SHOEBILL	TENTACLE	AGRONOMY	SELFSAME	AVAILING	CAROTENE
PROBABLE	SHOPTALK	TEQUILLA	ALLOGAMY	SOMETIME	AVENTINE	CARRYING
PROBABLY	SHREWDLY	TERRIBLE	ANALEMMA	STEATOMA	AVICENNA	CASEMENT
PROMPTLY	SIDEWALK	TERRIBLY	ANATHEMA	SYMPTOMS	AVIFAUNA	CASTANOY
PROPERLY	SIGNALLY	TESTICLE	ATHEROMA	SYNDROME	BABBLING	CATATONY
PROVABLE	SILENTLY	TETCHILY	AUTOGAMY	TAKEHOME	BACCHANT	CATCHING
PRUNELLA	SILICULA	THROTTLE	AUTONOMY	TAXONOMY	BACKBONE	CATERING
PUBLICLY	SINKHOLE	THURIBLE	BACKCOMB	TELECOMS	BACKHAND	CATILINE
PUFFBALL	SISTERLY	TINSELLY	BLOWLAMP	TERATOMA	BAFFLING	CAVATINA
QUAINTLY	SITTELLA	TORTILLA	CATACOMB	THINGAMY	BAHRAINI	CEREMENT
QUARTILE	SIZEABLE	TRIANGLE	CHARISMA	TIRESOME	BAILMENT	CEREMONY
QUENELLE	SKEWBALD	TRICYCLE	CHORIAMB	TOILSOME	BANDANNA	CHACONNE
QUOTABLE	SLEEPILY	TRINCULO	CINERAMA	TRACHOMA	BANTLING	CHADBAND
RACIALLY	SLIGHTLY	TUBERCLE	CONSOMMÉ	TRILEMMA	BARITONE	CHANGING
RAINFALL	SLOPPILY	TURGIDLY	DOLDRUMS	TWELVEMO	BASELINE	CHARGING
RANDOMLY	SLOVENLY	TUSITALA	ENDOGAMY	WILLIAMS	BASEMENT	CHARMING
RASCALLY	SMOOTHLY	UMBRELLA	EPITHEMA	XANTHOMA	BEAUMONT	CHEATING
RATEABLE	SNAPPILY	UNCOUPLE	ERYTHEMA	XENOGAMY	BECOMING	CHECKING
READABLE	SNOOTILY	UNEASILY	FEARSOME	YOKOHAMA	BEESWING	CHEERING
RECENTLY	SNOWBALL	UNEVENLY	FILENAME	ABDUCENS	BEETLING	CHEYENNE
REDOUBLE	SNOWFALL	UNGAINLY	FIREARMS	ABERRANT	BEFRIEND	CHICKENS
REKINDLE	SOCIABLE	UNICYCLE	FIREDAMP	ABUNDANT	BERTRAND	CHILLING
RELIABLE	SOCIALLY	UNIQUELY	FORENAME	ABUTMENT	BLACKING	CHIPMUNK
RELIABLY	SOFTBALL	UNITEDLY	FOURSOME	ACCIDENT	BLEEDING	CHLORINE
REMOTELY	SOLEMNLY	UNJUSTLY	FULLTIME	ACCUSING	BLENDING	CHOOSING
RESEMBLE	SOLVABLE	UNKINDLY	GENDARME	ACQUAINT	BLESSING	CHOPPING
RESETTLE	SOMBRELY	UNLIKELY	GERONIMO	ACRIMONY	BLINDING	CICERONE
RETICULE	SORDIDLY	UNLOVELY	GLADSOME	ADHERENT	BLINKING	CINCHONA
REUSABLE	SPARSELY	UNSEEMLY	GLAUCOMA	ADJACENT	BLOOMING	CISTERNA
REVEILLE	SPEEDILY	UNSETTLE	GLEESOME	ADJUTANT	BLURRING	CLADDING
RIDICULE	SPIRACLE	UNSPOILT	GLOSSEME	ADJUVANT	BLUSHING	CLAIMANT
RINGHALS	SPIRALLY	UNSTABLE	GRAPHEME	ADMIRING	BOARDING	CLANGING
RINGWALL	SPRINKLE	UNTANGLE	GRUESOME	AERODYNE	BOASTING	CLAPPING
RITUALLY	SPRITELY	UNTIDILY	HALFTIME	AFFERENT	BOBOLINK	CLASHING
ROBUSTLY	SPRUCELY	UNTIMELY	HANDSOME	AFFLUENT	BODYLINE	CLASPING
ROCHDALE	SQUABBLE	UNUSABLE	HEADLAMP	AGREEING	BORODINO	CLEANING
ROLLCALL	SQUARELY	URGENTLY	HECATOMB	AGRIMONY	BOTSWANA	CLEARING
ROLYPOLY	SQUIGGLE	USEFULLY	LIFETIME	AIRBORNE	BOTTLING	CLIMBING
RUEFULLY	STAPHYLE	UTENSILS	LOBOTOMY	AIRPLANE	BOUFFANT	CLINGING
RUGGEDLY	STEADILY	VACANTLY	LONESOME	ALARMING	BOUNCING	CLIPPING
RUNCIBLE	STICKILY	VALHALLA	LONGTIME	ALBINONI	BRAGGING	CLOTHING
SALEABLE	STILWELL	VALUABLE	MACHISMO	ALEMAINE	BREAKING	CLUBBING
SAVAGELY	STOLIDLY	VARIABLE	MALLARMÉ	ALGERINE	BREEDING	COACHING
SAXATILE	STONEFLY	VAUXHALL	MARITIME	ALIQUANT	BRIDGING	COALMINE
SCAFFOLD	STRADDLE	VERBALLY	MEALTIME	ALKALINE	BRIEFING	COCKAYNE
SCANTILY	STRAGGLE	VERSICLE	MEANTIME	ALLOWING	BRIMMING	COHERENT
SCARCELY	STRAGGLY	VICTUALS	MELANOMA	ALLURING	BRINGING	COLORANT
SCHEDULE	STRANGLE	VINCIBLE	METONYMY	AMANDINE	BRISLING	COLORING
SCRABBLE	STRICKLE	VISUALLY	MONOGAMY	AMBULANT	BROILING	COMPLINE
SCRAMBLE	STRICTLY	VOLATILE	MORPHEME	ANNOYING	BROODING	COMPOUND
SCRAPPLE	STRONGLY	VULGARLY	NICKNAME	ANSERINE	BROWNING	CONFOUND
SCRIBBLE	STRUGGLE	WASHABLE	NOONTIME	ANTIMONY	BROWSING	CONFRONT
						CONSTANT

COUCHANT	EMERGING	FREEZING	HURDLING	MACARONI	OINTMENT	PROCAINE
COUCHING	EMIGRANT	FREQUENT	ICEBLINK	MAGAZINE	OLIPHANT	PROFOUND
COUGHING	EMULGENT	FROSTING	IGNOMINY	MAHARANI	ONCOMING	PROPOUND
COUNTING	ENDURING	FRUITING	IGNORANT	MAHOGANY	OPPONENT	PRURIENT
COUPLING	ENGAGING	FUMBLING	ILLUMINE	MAINLAND	OPPOSING	PTOMAINE
COVALENT	ENSHRINE	GABORONE	IMMANENT	MAINLINE	ORDERING	PUISSANT
COVENANT	ENTHRONE	GADARENE	IMMINENT	MANAGING	ORDINAND	PURBLIND
COVERING	ENTICING	GAMBLING	IMPOSING	MANTLING	ORNAMENT	PURSLANE
CRACKING	ENVIRONS	GANGLAND	IMPOTENT	MARYLAND	ORPIMENT	PURULENT
CRAWLING	EPIPHANY	GANGLING	IMPUDENT	MATCHING	OTTAVINO	PUZZLING
CRESCENT	EQUITANT	GANGRENE	INCIDENT	MAZARINE	OUTFLANK	QUADRANT
CRETONNE	ERECTING	GARAMOND	INCOMING	MEDDLING	OUTGOING	QUILTING
CRINGING	ESCULENT	GASOLINE	INDECENT	MEDICINE	OUTLYING	QUINCUNX
CROONING	ETHYLENE	GELATINE	INDEXING	MELAMINE	OUTSHINE	QUISLING
CROSSING	EUROLAND	GEOPHONE	INDICANT	MEMBRANE	OVERDONE	QUOTIENT
CROWNING	EVACUANT	GERMAINE	INDIGENT	MENACING	OVERHAND	RACKRENT
CRUSHING	EVENSONG	GIOVANNI	INDOLENT	MERCHANT	OVERHANG	RAGSTONE
CURTAINS	EVERYONE	GLANCING	INFLUENT	MIDDLING	OVERLAND	RAISONNÉ
CYTOSINE	EXACTING	GLEAMING	INHALANT	MIDPOINT	OVERTONE	RAMBLING
CZAREVNA	EXCITING	GLOAMING	INHERENT	MIGNONNE	PADDLING	RATTLING
DATELINE	EXISTENT	GLOATING	INHUMANE	MIGRAINE	PAGANINI	RECEDING
DAUNTING	EXISTING	GLORIANA	INNOCENT	MILITANT	PAINTING	RECUSANT
DAZZLING	EXOCRINE	GLUTTONY	INSOLENT	MILLIONS	PALATINE	REDEFINE
DEADLINE	EXPONENT	GNASHING	INVITING	MILLPOND	PALIMONY	REDOLENT
DECADENT	EXULTANT	GOLDMINE	IRRITANT	MISCOUNT	PANELING	REDSHANK
DECAYING	EXULTING	GONDWANA	ISOCLINE	MISOGYNY	PARKLAND	REEDLING
DECKHAND	FAINTING	GOURMAND	JANGLING	MISPRINT	PASHMINA	REGIMENT
DETHRONE	FALKLAND	GRADIENT	JOHNSONS	MISSPENT	PAVEMENT	REIGNING
DIALLING	FARMHAND	GRAINING	JUBILANT	MODELING	PEARLING	RELATING
DIAPHONE	FARMLAND	GRASPING	JUDGMENT	MONOGYNY	PECORINO	RELAXING
DIGIZINE	FARTHING	GRAYLING	JUGGLING	MONOTONY	PEDDLING	RELAYING
DILIGENT	FECULENT	GREENING	JULIENNE	MONUMENT	PEDIMENT	RELEVANT
DISCOUNT	FEMININE	GREETING	KATAKANA	MOORLAND	PENCHANT	REORIENT
DISMOUNT	FETCHING	GRILLING	KEROSENE	MORIBUND	PENITENT	REPAYING
DIVIDEND	FETTLING	GRINDING	KEYSTONE	MORPHINE	PEPERONI	RESIDENT
DOCKLAND	FIDDLING	GRIPPING	KILKENNY	MOTORING	PERILUNE	RESONANT
DOCTRINE	FIELDING	GROOMING	KINDLING	MOULDING	PERSHING	RETICENT
DOCUMENT	FIGHTING	GROUPING	KNITTING	MOUNTING	PERSUANT	RETIRING
DOMINANT	FIGURINE	GROUTING	KNOCKING	MOURNING	PETULANT	REVEREND
DOPAMINE	FILAMENT	GROWLING	LACEWING	MOVEMENT	PHALGUNA	REVERENT
DOUBTING	FILIPINO	GRUDGING	LACKLAND	MUDSTONE	PHEASANT	REVIVING
DRACAENA	FISHBONE	GUNPOINT	LAKELAND	MUMBLING	PHOSGENE	RIBSTONE
DRAGOONS	FISHPOND	GYMKHANA	LANDMINE	MUNIMENT	PIDDLING	RIESLING
DRAINING	FLAGGING	HAIRBAND	LANGLAND	MURRHINE	PIERCING	RIGATONI
DREAMING	FLAGRANT	HAIRLINE	LANOLINE	NAVARINO	PINPOINT	RIGATONI
DRESSING	FLAPPING	HARDLINE	LAUGHING	NAZARENE	PIPELINE	RIPPLING
DRIFTING	FLASHING	HATCHING	LEACHING	NDJAMENA	PIPERINE	RIVERINE
DRINKING	FLEETING	HAUNTING	LEARNING	NECKBAND	PLANGENT	RIVETING
DRIPPING	FLIPPANT	HEADBAND	LEFTHAND	NECKLINE	PLANKING	ROASTING
DROOPING	FLIPPING	HEADHUNT	LEFTWING	NESCIENT	PLANNING	ROSALIND
DROPPING	FLIRTING	HEADLAND	LIFELINE	NESTLING	PLEADING	ROSALINE
DROWNING	FLOATING	HEADLINE	LIFELONG	NEUTRINO	PLEASANT	ROSAMOND
DRUBBING	FLOGGING	HEADLONG	LIGAMENT	NEWFOUND	PLEASING	ROTENONE
DRUMLINE	FLOODING	HEADWIND	LIGHTING	NIBELUNG	PLIOCENE	RUBICUND
DRUMMING	FLOORING	HECKLING	LIMACINE	NICOTINE	PLUCKING	RUCTIONS
DRYSTONE	FLUORINE	HEGEMONY	LIMITING	NIGGLING	PLUMBING	RUDIMENT
DUCKLING	FLUSHING	HELLBENT	LINCOLNS	NINEPINS	PLUNGING	RUMBLING
DUMFOUND	FOGBOUND	HELPLINE	LINIMENT	NOCTURNE	POIGNANT	RUMINANT
DUMPLING	FOLKSONG	HERMIONE	LITIGANT	NORTHING	POLYANNA	RUSTLING
DWELLING	FONDLING	HESITANT	LIVELONG	NOSEBAND	POLYGYNY	SADDLING
EARPHONE	FOOTLING	HIGHLAND	LOATHING	NURSLING	PORTLAND	SANDBANK
EASEMENT	FOREGONE	HIRAGANA	LOBELINE	NUTRIENT	POSTPONE	SANGUINE
EFFERENT	FOREHAND	HIRELING	LONGHAND	OBEDIENT	POTBOUND	SARABAND
EFFLUENT	FORELAND	HOARDING	LONGLAND	OBLIGING	POTSTONE	SCALDING
EGGPLANT	FOUNDING	HOBBLING	LORRAINE	OCCIDENT	POULAINE	SCANNING
ELEPHANT	FOXHOUND	HOLOCENE	LOWERING	OCCUPANT	PREGNANT	SCATHING
ELKHOUND	FRAGMENT	HOMELAND	LOWLYING	OFFERING	PRESSING	SCHEMING
ELOQUENT	FRAGRANT	HONGKONG	LUSTRINE	OFFPRINT	PRINTING	SCHUMANN
EMERGENT	FREEHAND	HOODWINK	LYNCHING	OILSKINS	PRISTINE	SCOFFING
						SCOLDING

SCOTLAND	SPARKING	TEETHING	WALTZING	APHELION	COCKCROW	ENIWETOK
SCOURING	SPARRING	TEGUMENT	WAMBLING	APOLLYON	COERCION	ENTREPOT
SCOWLING	SPARTANS	TELEGONY	WARPAINT	APPLETON	COHESION	ENVISION
SCRUTINY	SPAWNING	TEMPTING	WARPLANE	ASBESTOS	COLDBOOT	EPIPLOON
SEABORNE	SPEAKING	TENEMENT	WATCHING	ASSESSOR	COLLATOR	EQUATION
SEAFRONT	SPELLING	TERYLENE	WATERING	ASUNCION	COLOPHON	ERECTION
SEAGOING	SPENDING	THAILAND	WAVEBAND	ATTESTOR	CONJUROR	ERIKSSON
SEAPLANE	SPIFFING	THEBAINE	WAVERING	AUBUSSON	CONVEYOR	ERUPTION
SEDIMENT	SPINNING	THIAMINE	WEAKLING	AUDITION	COOKBOOK	ESCARGOT
SEEDLING	SPITTING	THIEVING	WEIGHING	AVERSION	COPYBOOK	ESTRAGON
SEETHING	SPOILING	THINKING	WHACKING	AVIATION	CORDUROY	EVICTION
SELBORNE	SPORTING	THINNING	WHEEZING	AVULSION	CORRIDOR	EXACTION
SEMITONE	SPOTTING	THOUSAND	WHIPHAND	BABYHOOD	CRACKPOT	EXCISION
SEMOLINA	SPURNING	THUMPING	WHIPPING	BACHELOR	CREATION	EXECUTOR
SENTIENT	STABBING	TICKLING	WHIRLING	BACKDROP	CREDITOR	EXERTION
SERGEANT	STABLING	TINGLING	WHITLING	BACKROOM	CRICHTON	EXTENSOR
SERJEANT	STAFFING	TOLERANT	WHOOPING	BACKSTOP	CROWFOOT	EXTERIOR
SERVIENT	STAGNANT	TOUCHING	WHOPPING	BALLROOM	CURSITOR	EXTRADOS
SHANTUNG	STALKING	TOWELING	WIDENING	BALLYHOO	CUSPIDOR	FEELGOOD
SHELVING	STANDING	TOWERING	WISHBONE	BANDEROL	DARKROOM	FIREWOOD
SHETLAND	STARLING	TRACKING	WITCHING	BANKBOOK	DARTMOOR	FISHHOOK
SHIELING	STARTING	TRAILING	WOBBLING	BARBADOS	DASHWOOD	FIXATION
SHIFTING	STARVING	TRAINING	WOLFBANE	BARBIZON	DAVIDSON	FLATFOOT
SHILLING	STEALING	TRAMLINE	WOODBINE	BAREFOOT	DEADWOOD	FOLDEROL
SHINBONE	STEERING	TREELINE	WOODLAND	BASSWOOD	DECISION	FOREDOOM
SHIPMENT	STEPHENS	TRIFLING	WOODWIND	BATHROOM	DEFECTOR	FOREFOOT
SHIPPING	STERLING	TRILLING	WOOLLENS	BEETROOT	DELETION	FORENOON
SHOCKING	STICKING	TRIMMING	WORRYING	BEHAVIOR	DELUSION	FRACTION
SHOOTING	STIFLING	TRIPLING	WRAPPING	BERGAMOT	DEMEANOR	FRICTION
SHOPPING	STINGING	TRIPTANE	WRINGING	BETATRON	DEMOTION	FRUITION
SHOUTING	STINKING	TROMBONE	WRITHING	BIATHLON	DERISION	FUNCTION
SIBILANT	STIRLING	TROOPING	YACHTING	BILLHOOK	DETECTOR	FURBELOW
SIDELINE	STIRRING	TROTLINE	YEARLING	BILLYBOY	DEUTERON	GALLIPOT
SIDELONG	STOCKING	TRUCKING	YEARLONG	BLACKBOY	DEVOTION	GANGLION
SIGHTING	STOPPING	TRUSTING	YEARNING	BLUDGEON	DIAPASON	GARDYLOO
SILICONE	STORMING	TSAREVNA	YIELDING	BOOKROOM	DICTATOR	GARRISON
SILOXANE	STORMONT	TUPPENNY	ZIBELINE	BOOKSHOP	DIDDICOY	GIRLHOOD
SINGSONG	STRIDENT	TWIRLING	ZUCCHINI	BRABAZON	DILATION	GOLLIWOG
SIZZLING	STRIKING	TWISTING	ABDUCTOR	BRIGHTON	DILUTION	GONFALON
SKIDDING	STRIVING	TWOPENNY	ABINGDON	BROMPTON	DIRECTOR	GOODWOOD
SKILLING	STUFFING	TYROSINE	ABLATION	BUCKSHOT	DISALLOW	GOOSEGOG
SKIPPING	STUNNING	UNCARING	ABLUTION	BULLFROG	DISCOLOR	GOVERNOR
SKIRTING	SUBPOENA	UNDULANT	ABORTION	BUNGALOW	DISFAVOR	GRANDSON
SKULKING	SUCKLING	UNENDING	ABRASION	CABOCHON	DISHONOR	GRIDIRON
SLANGING	SUDAMENT	UNERRING	ABUTILON	CACHALOT	DISUNION	GUERIDON
SLANTING	SUDAMINA	UNFADING	ACCENTOR	CACHEPOT	DIVISION	GUMPTION
SLAPBANG	SUNBURNT	UNIFYING	ACCEPTOR	CAERLEON	DOMINION	GYRATION
SLEEPING	SUNSHINE	UPCOMING	ACCUSTOM	CALDERON	DONATION	HAMILTON
SLIPPING	SUPPLANT	UPRISING	ACROMION	CALTHROP	DOORKNOB	HANDBOOK
SLUMMING	SURMOUNT	URETHANE	ADDITION	CALVADOS	DOUBLOON	HARDWOOD
SLURRING	SURROUND	URSULINE	ADHESION	CAMEROON	DOUGHBOY	HARRISON
SMASHING	SWANSONG	VAGABOND	ADJUSTOR	CARCAJOU	DROPSHOT	HEADROOM
SMELTING	SWARMING	VALETING	ADOPTION	CARDAMOM	DURATION	HEATSPOT
SMOCKING	SWEARING	VAULTING	ADULATOR	CARILLON	DYNATRON	HEDGEHOG
SNEAKING	SWEATING	VEHEMENT	AEROFLOT	CARJACOU	ECLOSION	HEDGEROW
SNEERING	SWEEPING	VERLAINE	AFFUSION	CARRYCOT	EDUCATOR	HEIRLOOM
SNEEZING	SWELLING	VESTMENT	AGITATOR	CATECHOL	EFFUSION	HEPTAGON
SNORTING	SWERVING	VIETCONG	AGITPROP	CAULDRON	EJECTION	HEYTHROP
SNOWLINE	SWILLING	VIGILANT	AGNATION	CESSPOOL	ELECTION	HIGHBROW
SOBERING	SWIMMING	VILLAINY	ALLUSION	CHALDRON	ELECTRON	HOLYROOD
SONATINA	SWINGING	VIREMENT	AMBITION	CHAMPION	ELEVATOR	HONEYPOT
SOOTHING	SWIRLING	VIRULENT	ANACREON	CHAPERON	EMBLAZON	HORNBOOK
SORBONNE	SYMBIONT	VISCOUNT	ANCESTOR	CHOIRBOY	EMERSION	HORSEBOX
SOUCHONG	SYMPHONY	VISITANT	ANDERSON	CHRISTOM	EMISSION	HYPERION
SOUNDING	SYNCLINE	VISITING	ANGSTROM	CINNAMON	EMOTICON	IGNITION
SOURCING	TAMARIND	VITAMINS	ANTERIOR	CITATION	EMULATOR	ILLUSION
SOUTHEND	TAPERING	VOLPLANE	ANTEROOM	CLUBFOOT	EMULSION	IMITATOR
SPANKING	TASHKENT	VOMITING	ANTIPHON	COAUTHOR	ENDEAVOR	IMPOSTOR
SPANNING	TEACHING	WALLSEND	AOTEAROA	COCKATOO	ENDYMION	IMPRISON

INACTION	OBJECTOR	ROBINSON	THRALDOM	PHILLIPS	BRUMAIRE	DILATORY
INCISION	OBLATION	ROGATION	TOMORROW	ROOFTOPS	BULLHORN	DIVIDERS
INDUCTOR	OBLIVION	ROSEROOT	TOREADOR	SCHNAPPS	BURBERRY	DOCKYARD
INFERIOR	OCCASION	ROSEWOOD	TRACTION	SEASCAPE	BURGLARY	DOGBERRY
INFUSION	OCTAROON	ROTATION	TRAPDOOR	SEROTYPE	BUTCHERS	DOWNTURN
INJECTOR	OFFCOLOR	RULEBOOK	TRILLION	STANHOPE	BUTCHERY	DOWNWARD
INTERCOM	OFFSHOOT	SALEROOM	TRUNNION	TAILPIPE	BUZZWORD	DRUDGERY
INTERIOR	OMISSION	SALVADOR	TURANDOT	TRANSEPT	CADASTRE	DRUNKARD
INTERPOL	OMPHALOS	SANCTION	ULTERIOR	TREETOPS	CAJOLERY	EASTWARD
INTRADOS	OOPHORON	SAUROPOD	UNBUTTON	TRIGLYPH	CALIPERS	ECTODERM
INVASION	OPENDOOR	SCALLION	UNCOMMON	TRIGRAPH	CALLGIRL	ELECTORS
INVENTOR	OPERATOR	SCANSION	UNDERDOG	TROLLOPE	CANBERRA	ELSINORE
INVESTOR	ORTHODOX	SCISSION	UNDERTOW	WINDPIPE	CAPYBARA	EMISSARY
IRONWOOD	OVERBOOK	SCORPION	UNPERSON	XANTIPPE	CAREWORN	ENDOCARP
JACKAROO	OVERFLOW	SCREWTOP	UNREASON	ZOETROPE	CASHMERE	ENDODERM
JACKBOOT	OVERLOOK	SCULLION	VACATION	AARDVARK	CATEGORY	ENSIFORM
JELLICOE	OVERSHOE	SCULPTOR	VEXATION	ADULTERY	CATHEDRA	EPHEMERA
JETTISON	OVERSHOT	SEAFLOOR	VIBRATOR	ADVISORY	CEMETERY	ERUPTURE
JONCANOE	OXYMORON	SEDATION	VINDALOO	ALBACORE	CENTAURY	ESTOVERS
JUNCTION	PANTALON	SEDITION	VIOLATOR	ALEATORY	CHAMBERS	ETCETERA
KANGAROO	PANTHEON	SEIGNIOR	VOCATION	ALHAMBRA	CHAMPERS	EVERMORE
KAZACHOK	PAPILLON	SELECTOR	VOLITION	ALLEGORY	CHANCERY	EXPOSURE
KINGSTON	PASSBOOK	SERVITOR	WAINSCOT	AMATEURS	CHEATERS	FALCONRY
KINKAJOU	PAVILION	SHEEPDOG	WARDROOM	ANCESTRY	CHECKERS	FARMYARD
KOMSOMOL	PAWNSHOP	SHEIKDOM	WARMBOOT	ANTIHERO	CHEQUERS	FARRIERY
KRAKATOA	PEEKABOO	SHERATON	WASHROOM	ANTIMERE	CHESHIRE	FEATHERS
LABRADOR	PEEPSHOW	SHERWOOD	WATCHDOG	ANYWHERE	CHILDERS	FEATHERY
LANCELOT	PENTAGON	SHOWROOM	WATERLOO	APERTURE	CHILTERN	FEBRUARY
LEAPFROG	PETERLOO	SICKROOM	WEDGWOOD	ARMATURE	CHIMAERA	FENESTRA
LEGATION	PETITION	SIDESHOW	WHITEHOT	ARTISTRY	CHIVALRY	FIREBIRD
LIBATION	PHILEMON	SKELETON	WORDBOOK	ASCOCARP	CLAPPERS	FIREWORK
LIFEBUOY	PHLEGMON	SKILLION	WORKBOOK	AUDITORY	CLAYMORE	FIRMWARE
LOCATION	PICAROON	SKYPILOT	WORKROOM	AUTOGIRO	CLEANERS	FLANDERS
LOLLIPOP	PINEWOOD	SLIPSHOD	WORKSHOP	AUTOGYRO	CLEAVERS	FLATTERY
LONGSTOP	PISCATOR	SLIPSLOP	WORMWOOD	AVOGADRO	CLIFFORD	FLATWARE
LOOSEBOX	PLANKTON	SMALLPOX	XENOPHON	AYRSHIRE	CLINKERS	FLATWORM
LUNCHBOX	PLASTRON	SMIDGEON	YEARBOOK	BACKFIRE	CLIPPERS	FLAUBERT
LUNCHEON	PLAYROOM	SNAPSHOT	ANAGLYPH	BACKWARD	COALPORT	FLINDERS
MACAROON	POLLIWOG	SNOWDROP	ANTELOPE	BACKYARD	COBBLERS	FLIPPERS
MACMAHON	POLTROON	SNUFFBOX	ANTILOPE	BAGHEERA	COIFFURE	FLUMMERY
MAILSHOT	POLYGLOT	SOFTWOOD	ANTIPOPE	BALLGIRL	COLIFORM	FOLKLORE
MARATHON	POOLROOM	SOLUTION	AUTOTYPE	BALLPARK	COLLIERS	FOOTSORE
MASCARON	POPPADOM	SOURWOOD	BANKRUPT	BARBERRY	COLLIERY	FOOTWORK
MASSICOT	POSEIDON	SPITTOON	BARDOLPH	BARNYARD	CONSPIRE	FORESTRY
MASTODON	POSITION	SPLENDOR	BIOGRAPH	BARRATRY	CONTRARY	FOREWARN
MATCHBOX	POSITRON	SQUADRON	BIOSCOPE	BASEBORN	COOKWARE	FOREWORD
MEDIATOR	PREDATOR	STALLION	BLOWPIPE	BASKETRY	COQUETRY	FORMWORK
MELCHIOR	PRONATOR	STEENBOK	CALLIOPE	BAYBERRY	CORONARY	FOURPART
MERCATOR	PROTOCOL	STINKPOT	CALOTYPE	BEAUFORT	COSTMARY	FRACTURE
MESSIDOR	PROTOZOA	STOCKPOT	CENOTAPH	BERIBERI	COVENTRY	FRETWORK
METAPHOR	PTEROPOD	STURGEON	CONTEMPT	BESTIARY	COWBERRY	FRIPPERY
METHANOL	PURVEYOR	SUPERIOR	ECHINOPS	BILBERRY	CRACKERS	FUMITORY
MICRODOT	QUADROON	SURVEYOR	ENTHALPY	BIOMETRY	CREAMERY	FUNERARY
MIRLITON	QUAESTOR	SURVIVOR	ENVELOPE	BLINKERS	CREATURE	FUSEWIRE
MONEYBOX	QUESTION	SWEETSOP	EPIGRAPH	BLIZZARD	CROCKERY	FUSIFORM
MORRISON	RADIATOR	SWINEPOX	ESCALOPE	BLOOMERS	CRUMHORN	GADGETRY
MOUFFLON	RAGNARÖK	TARRAGON	GALLUMPH	BLUSTERY	CRUZEIRO	GAILLARD
MUSHROOM	RAINDROP	TAXATION	GIGLAMPS	BODYWORK	CULINARY	GALLIARD
MUTATION	REACTION	TEAKWOOD	HEELTAPS	BONEYARD	CUPBOARD	GAMEBIRD
MYRIAPOD	RECEPTOR	TEARDROP	HORNPIPE	BOOKMARK	CUTHBERT	GAOLBIRD
MYRMIDON	REDACTOR	TEASPOON	HOSEPIPE	BOOKWORK	CYNOSURE	GEOMETRY
NAPOLEON	REDEPLOY	TELETHON	IRISCOPE	BOOKWORM	DAIQUIRI	GLANDERS
NARRATOR	REEMPLOY	TENNYSON	LINOTYPE	BOTTOMRY	DELAWARE	GLOSSARY
NEGATION	RELATION	TESTATOR	LOGOTYPE	BOUNDARY	DELIVERY	GOODSIRE
NEIGHBOR	RELIGION	TETRAGON	MONOTYPE	BRADBURY	DEMERARA	GREENERY
NEWSROOM	RESISTOR	TETRAPOD	OTOSCOPE	BRAGGART	DENATURE	GURDWARA
NIDATION	RESTROOM	TEXTBOOK	OVERRIPE	BRASSARD	DERISORY	GYRATORY
NOTATION	REVISION	THANATOS	PENELOPE	BREVIARY	DEWBERRY	HABANERA
NOTEBOOK	ROADSHOW	THOMPSON	PHILIPPI	BROCHURE	DIASPORA	HABSBURG

HAIRWORM	LONGHORN	PLATFORM	SKINWORK	VINEYARD	BELPAESE	CUTPURSE
HALFTERM	LONGTERM	PLAYGIRL	SLATTERN	VOLTAIRE	BERCEUSE	CYNICISM
HALLIARD	LONICERA	PLEASURE	SLEEPERS	VOMITORY	BIGAMIST	DAMPNESS
HALLMARK	LOVEBIRD	PLETHORA	SLIPPERS	WALLWORT	BLACKISH	DANKNESS
HANDCART	LOVELORN	POCKMARK	SLIPPERY	WEAPONRY	BLANDISH	DARKNESS
HAPSBURG	LUKEWARM	POITIERS	SLOBBERY	WESTWARD	BLOWFISH	DATABASE
HARDCORE	LUMINARY	POLYCARP	SLOWWORM	WHIPCORD	BLUENOSE	DATELESS
HARDWARE	LUNGWORT	PORPHYRA	SLUGGARD	WHISKERS	BOLDNESS	DEAFNESS
HARTFORD	LYREBIRD	PORPHYRY	SNEAKERS	WHISKERY	BONEFISH	DECREASE
HATCHERY	MAINYARD	PORTIÈRE	SNOBBERY	WILDFIRE	BONELESS	DEEPNESS
HAWTHORN	MANICURE	POSTCARD	SOAPBARK	WINDBURN	BOOKCASE	DEFTNESS
HEADMARK	MASSACRE	POSTMARK	SOFTWARE	WINDWARD	BOOTLESS	DEMOLISH
HEADWORD	MATAMORE	POTSHERD	SOLDIERS	WIREWORM	BOTANIST	DEVILISH
HELIPORT	MEDIOCRE	PREMIERE	SOLDIERY	WISEACRE	BOTULISM	DEXTROSE
HELLFIRE	MESODERM	PRESSURE	SOLITARY	WITCHERY	BRACKISH	DIAGNOSE
HERALDRY	MEUNIÈRE	PROSPERO	SOMBRERO	WIZARDRY	BRANDISH	DIASTASE
HEREFORD	MILITARY	PSALTERY	SONGBIRD	WOODWARD	BRINDISI	DIMINISH
HEREWARD	MILKWORT	PSEUDERY	SOUTHERN	WOODWORK	BROWNISH	DISABUSE
HIGHBORN	MINATORY	PUNCTURE	SPANIARD	WOODWORM	BUCKFAST	DISBURSE
HINDWARD	MINISTRY	PUSHCART	SPEAKERS	YAKITORI	BUDAPEST	DISCLOSE
HIPSTERS	MISCARRY	PYRIFORM	SPITFIRE	YEOMANRY	BUDDHISM	DISGUISE
HOMEWARD	MISERERE	QUAGMIRE	STAFFORD	YOGHOURT	BUDDHIST	DISPENSE
HOMEWORK	MISSOURI	QUANDARY	STAGGERS	ZOOSPERM	BUSINESS	DISPERSE
HONORARY	MOISTURE	QUARTERS	STAGHORN	ZOOSPORE	BUTTRESS	DISTRESS
HOOKWORM	MONANDRY	RAILLERY	STALWART	ABSCISSA	CAGINESS	DISTRUST
HOSTELRY	MONETARY	RAINBIRD	STANDARD	ABSTRUSE	CALABASH	DOGHOUSE
IDOLATRY	MONSTERA	REAFFIRM	STANNARY	ACTIVISM	CALMNESS	DONATIST
ILLUSORY	MOREPORK	REARWARD	STARKERS	ACTIVIST	CANALISE	DOORPOST
IMMATURE	MORTUARY	REASSERT	STARTERS	ADMONISH	CANOEIST	DORMOUSE
INDUSTRY	MUDGUARD	REASSURE	STATUARY	AIRINESS	CANONESS	DOWNCAST
INEXPERT	MULBERRY	RECOVERY	STUBBORN	ALARMIST	CARELESS	DRUGGIST
INFANTRY	MULEWORT	REDSTART	SUMMITRY	ALEHOUSE	CATALYST	DUCHESSE
INSECURE	NEATHERD	REFINERY	SYCAMORE	ALGORISM	CATHOUSE	DUELLIST
IRONWARE	NORTHERN	REGISTRY	SYMMETRY	ALIENISM	CELANESE	DULLNESS
IRONWORK	NUGATORY	REINSURE	TACITURN	ALIENIST	CENTRIST	DUMBNESS
ISOTHERE	OBITUARY	RIBALDRY	TANDOORI	ALPINIST	CHARTISM	DWARFISH
ISOTHERM	OCTONARY	RINGWORM	TAPESTRY	ALTRUISM	CHARTIST	DWARFISM
JACQUARD	OFFICERS	ROCKETRY	TAPEWORM	ALTRUIST	CHASTISE	DYNAMISM
JAILBIRD	OFFSHORE	ROSEMARY	TAYBERRY	AMETHYST	CHILDISH	EARLIEST
JODHPURS	OMNIFORM	ROTATORY	TEACHERS	ANAPAEST	CHILIAST	EASINESS
JOINTURE	OMNIVORE	ROUNDERS	TEAMWORK	ANAPHASE	CHURLISH	EDGEWISE
JUNCTURE	OPENWORK	RUSHMORE	TEESHIRT	ANEURYSM	CLANNISH	EERINESS
JURATORY	ORANGERY	SADDLERY	TELEMARK	ANNALIST	CLIQUISH	EMBOLISM
KACHAHRI	ORDINARY	SALIVARY	TERTIARY	ANTEPOST	CLOWNISH	ENTRYISM
KALAHARI	OUTBOARD	SALUTARY	THIEVERY	APHORISM	CLUELESS	EPILEPSY
KEYBOARD	OUTDOORS	SALUTORY	THUNDERY	APIARIST	COLDNESS	ERGOTISE
KITEMARK	OUTSMART	SAMPHIRE	TIDEMARK	APOSTASY	COLLAPSE	ERGOTISM
KNACKERS	OVENBIRD	SANITARY	TINCTURE	APPLAUSE	COLONIST	ESCAPISM
KNICKERS	OVENWARE	SAPPHIRE	TOXOCARA	APPRAISE	COMATOSE	ESCAPIST
KNOCKERS	OVERLORD	SAVAGERY	TRAITORS	ARBALEST	COMPRESS	ESPRESSO
KNOTWORK	OVERTURE	SAVOYARD	TREASURE	ARCHAISM	COMPRISE	ESSAYIST
KRUMHORN	OVERTURN	SAYONARA	TREASURY	ARETHUSA	CONDENSE	ETHERISE
LADYBIRD	OVERWORK	SCABBARD	TRICKERY	ARSONIST	CONGRESS	EULOGIST
LAMASERY	PANEGYRY	SCHUBERT	TROTTERS	ASTERISK	CONQUEST	EUPHUISM
LANDLORD	PARTERRE	SCISSORS	TROUSERS	ASTONISH	CONTRAST	EVENNESS
LANDMARK	PASSPORT	SCULLERY	TRUMPERY	ATHANASY	CONVERSE	EXERCISE
LANDWARD	PASSWORD	SEABOARD	TUPAMARO	ATHETISE	CONVULSE	EXORCISM
LANSBURY	PEDANTRY	SEASHORE	TUTELARY	BAATHIST	COOLNESS	EXORCIST
LAPIDARY	PEDICURE	SEMINARY	TWEEZERS	BACKLASH	COSINESS	EXPRESSO
LAVATORY	PELLAGRA	SHAGBARK	UNCIFORM	BACKLESS	COUNTESS	EYEGLASS
LAVENGRO	PENUMBRA	SHEPHERD	UNDERARM	BALDNESS	COURTESY	FACELESS
LAWCOURT	PERICARP	SHIPWORM	UNSAVORY	BALINESE	COZINESS	FAIRNESS
LEATHERY	PERIDERM	SHIPYARD	UNTOWARD	BARENESS	CRAMOISY	FARTHEST
LEFTWARD	PERSPIRE	SHOEHORN	UPSTAIRS	BARONESS	CRAWFISH	FASTNESS
LIENTERY	PIECHART	SHOWGIRL	VANGUARD	BASELESS	CRAYFISH	FATALISM
LIGATURE	PILCHARD	SHUTTERS	VARIFORM	BASENESS	CREVASSE	FATALIST
LITERARY	PINAFORE	SIDEWARD	VERTEBRA	BASILISK	CRONYISM	FEARLESS
LIVEWARE	PISIFORM	SILKWORM	VESTIARY	BEAKLESS	CURTNESS	FECKLESS
LOANWORD	PITCAIRN	SINECURE	VINEGARY	BELLPUSH	CUTENESS	FEMINISM

FEMINIST	HUNTRESS	MATTRESS	PIECRUST	SEVEREST	TONELESS	AMARETTO
FEVERISH	HUSHHUSH	MAYORESS	PIRANESI	SHEEPISH	TOPCLASS	AMBULATE
FIENDISH	ICEHOUSE	MEANNESS	PITHLESS	SHOELESS	TORTOISE	AMMONITE
FINALIST	IDEALISM	MEATLESS	PITILESS	SHOWCASE	TOULOUSE	AMORETTI
FIRMNESS	IDEALIST	MEDALIST	PLEONASM	SHREWISH	TRAPPIST	AMORETTO
FLATFISH	IDLENESS	MEEKNESS	PLEURISY	SICKLIST	TRAVERSE	AMPUTATE
FLAUTIST	IMMODEST	MILANESE	POORNESS	SICKNESS	TREATISE	AMUSETTE
FLAWLESS	INCREASE	MILDNESS	POPULIST	SIGNPOST	TREELESS	ANALECTA
FLOURISH	INTEREST	MILKLESS	PORPOISE	SINAPISM	TRESPASS	ANECDOTE
FONDNESS	IRISHISM	MINDLESS	PRACTISE	SKIRMISH	TRIMNESS	ANISETTE
FOOTREST	ISOGLOSS	MINORESS	PRECURSE	SKITTISH	TRUENESS	ANNAMITE
FORECAST	ISOSTASY	MISHMASH	PRETENSE	SLAPDASH	TUBELESS	ANNOTATE
FOREMOST	JAPANESE	MISTRESS	PRIAPISM	SLIMNESS	TUBENOSE	ANTEDATE
FORMLESS	JEALOUSY	MISTRUST	PRIGGISH	SLOWNESS	TUBEROSE	ANTIDOTE
FORTRESS	JINGOISM	MONADISM	PRIMNESS	SLUGFEST	TYPECAST	APOSTATE
FOULNESS	JINGOIST	MONETISE	PRIMROSE	SLUGGISH	UGLINESS	APPETITE
FRANKISH	JUSTNESS	MONGOOSE	PRINCESS	SLUTTISH	UNIONISM	APPOSITE
FREAKISH	KEENNESS	MONKFISH	PRIORESS	SMALLEST	UNIONIST	ARALDITE
FREEPOST	KERMESSE	MORALIST	PROGRESS	SMARTEST	UNIVERSE	ARAMANTH
FRESHEST	KINDNESS	MOTORIST	PROLAPSE	SMUGNESS	VANQUISH	ARMALITE
FRUCTOSE	KINGPOST	MUCHNESS	PROPHASE	SNOBBISH	VARICOSE	ARROGATE
FRUMPISH	KINSHASA	MUSQUASH	PROPHESY	SOFTNESS	VASTNESS	ASPERITY
FULLNESS	KNOBLESS	MYOBLAST	PROTEASE	SOLECISM	VERONESE	ASPIRATE
FURTHEST	KOURMISS	NAMELESS	PSALMIST	SORENESS	VILENESS	ATALANTA
FUTURISM	LACROSSE	NATURISM	PTYALISM	SOULLESS	VIPERISH	ATROCITY
FUTURIST	LADYFISH	NATURIST	PUGILISM	SOURNESS	VIRTUOSI	AUDACITY
GABONESE	LAMENESS	NEARNESS	PUGILIST	SOURPUSS	VIRTUOSO	AUTOMATE
GAMENESS	LAMPPOST	NEATNESS	PURCHASE	SPOTLESS	VITALISM	BACKBITE
GATEPOST	LANDMASS	NEEDLESS	PURPLISH	SPRYNESS	VOCALIST	BACKDATE
GHOULISH	LANGUISH	NEPALESE	RACINESS	STANDISH	WAITRESS	BAGUETTE
GIANTESS	LARGESSE	NEPOTISM	RANKNESS	STARDUST	WARDRESS	BAKELITE
GLADNESS	LAROUSSE	NEWSCAST	RASHNESS	STARFISH	WARHORSE	BALLISTA
GLASNOST	LATENESS	NICENESS	READIEST	STARLESS	WARINESS	BANALITY
GLUMPISH	LATINIST	NIHILISM	READJUST	STOCKIST	WEAKFISH	BANDITTI
GOALPOST	LAZINESS	NIHILIST	REARMOST	STOICISM	WEAKNESS	BANKNOTE
GOLDFISH	LEAFLESS	NONSENSE	REASSESS	STRABISM	WHIPLASH	BARONETS
GOODNESS	LEBANESE	NOTECASE	RECKLESS	SUBLEASE	WILDNESS	BARRETTE
GORMLESS	LEGALISM	NOVELIST	RECOURSE	SUBTENSE	WILINESS	BAYREUTH
GREATEST	LEWDNESS	NUMBNESS	REHEARSE	SUDANESE	WINDLASS	BEHEMOTH
GREENISH	LIFELESS	NUTHOUSE	REINVEST	SUITCASE	WINDLESS	BENEFITS
GRIMNESS	LIKENESS	OCCAMIST	REPHRASE	SUNBURST	WINGLESS	BEQUEATH
GUYANESE	LIKEWISE	OILINESS	REPOUSSÉ	SUNGLASS	WIRELESS	BILOBATE
HAIRLESS	LIMBLESS	OPENCAST	RESPONSE	SUPPRESS	WOMANISH	BORACITE
HALFMAST	LIMPNESS	OPENNESS	RESTLESS	SURENESS	WORDLESS	BOSWORTH
HARDNESS	LINGUIST	OPTIMISM	RICHNESS	SURPRISE	WORMCAST	BRACKETS
HARMLESS	LISTLESS	OPTIMIST	RIGHTIST	SUSPENSE	YOUNGEST	BRAMANTE
HAZINESS	LIVERISH	ORGANISM	RIVALISE	SYRACUSE	ABDICATE	BRUNETTE
HEADLESS	LOBBYIST	ORGANIST	ROOFLESS	TACTLESS	ABNEGATE	CALAMITY
HEADMOST	LOUDNESS	OUTBURST	ROOTLESS	TAILLESS	ABROGATE	CALCEATE
HEADREST	LOVELESS	OUTCLASS	ROSEFISH	TAMARISK	ABSOLUTE	CALCRETE
HEBRAISM	LOWCLASS	OUTHOUSE	ROSINESS	TAMENESS	ACCOUNTS	CALCUTTA
HEDONISM	LOYALIST	OVERCAST	ROYALIST	TAPHOUSE	ACCURATE	CALLISTO
HEDONIST	LUCKLESS	OVERDOSE	RUDENESS	TARBOOSH	ACERBATE	CAMPSITE
HEEDLESS	LUMPFISH	OVERPASS	RUSTLESS	TARTNESS	ACERBITY	CAPACITY
HEIRLESS	LUNGFISH	PACIFISM	RUTHLESS	TAUTNESS	ACTIVATE	CARUCATE
HELPLESS	LUSHNESS	PACIFIST	RYEGRASS	TELECAST	ACTIVITY	CASEMATE
HENHOUSE	LUTENIST	PAINLESS	SAGENESS	TELEVISE	ADEQUATE	CASSETTE
HIGHNESS	LYRICISM	PALENESS	SALTBUSH	THEORIST	ADVOCATE	CASTRATE
HIGHRISE	LYRICIST	PALUDISM	SALTNESS	THIEVISH	AEROLITH	CASTRATO
HINDMOST	MADHOUSE	PANGLOSS	SAMENESS	THINNESS	AFFINITY	CASUALTY
HINDUISM	MAESTOSO	PARODIST	SAPPHIST	TICKLISH	AIGRETTE	CATAMITE
HOLDFAST	MALAGASY	PEDERAST	SARGASSO	TIDINESS	ALACRITY	CELERITY
HOLINESS	MANIFEST	PEERLESS	SATIRIST	TIMELESS	ALICANTE	CELIBATE
HOMELESS	MANTISSA	PEKINESE	SAWHORSE	TIRAMISU	ALIENATE	CENOBITE
HOPELESS	MARQUESA	PERTNESS	SCOTTISH	TIRELESS	ALLOCATE	CHAPATTI
HOTHOUSE	MARQUESS	PERVERSE	SEAMLESS	TITANESS	ALLOPATH	CHASTITY
HUMANISM	MARQUISE	PHANTASM	SEEDLESS	TITANISM	ALMIGHTY	CHEVIOTS
HUMANIST	MASSEUSE	PHOTOPSY	SELFLESS	TITMOUSE	AMARANTH	CHINDITS
HUMORIST						CHLORATE

CHORDATA	ERADIATE	IMMUNITY	MINORITY	RAMPARTS	STUDENTS	ALUMINUM
CHORDATE	ERUCTATE	IMPOLITE	MISQUOTE	RAPACITY	SUBJECTS	ALVEOLUS
CHROMITE	ESCALATE	IMPUNITY	MITIGATE	RAPIDITY	SUBTLETY	ANALOGUE
CIRCUITY	ESSONITE	IMPURITY	MOBILITY	RECEIPTS	SULPHATE	APOLOGUE
CIVILITY	ESTIMATE	INCHOATE	MODERATE	RECREATE	SURICATE	APPLIQUÉ
COGITATE	ESTIVATE	INCUBATE	MODERATO	RECRUITS	SYBARITE	AQUARIUM
COLLECTS	ETERNITY	INDICATE	MODULATE	REGULATE	TABULATE	AQUARIUS
COMPLETE	ETIOLATE	INEQUITY	MONMOUTH	RELEGATE	TAILGATE	ARCTURUS
CONCERTO	EVACUATE	INFINITE	MONOLITH	RELOCATE	TAMWORTH	ARGONAUT
CONCRETE	EVALUATE	INFINITY	MONTEITH	REMNANTS	TARTRATE	ARQUEBUS
CONFETTI	EXCAVATE	INGROWTH	MOQUETTE	REMOUNTS	TEACLOTH	ASCIDIUM
CONFLATE	EXECRATE	INNOVATE	MORALITY	RENOVATE	TEAMMATE	ASMODEUS
CONGRATS	EXHUMATE	INIQUITY	MOSQUITO	RESOLUTE	TEMERITY	AUGUSTUS
CONTENTS	EXIGUITY	INITIATE	MOTIVATE	RESONATE	TEMPLATE	BACILLUS
CONTRITE	EXPEDITE	INNOVATE	MUDFLATS	RESPECTS	TENACITY	BANLIEUE
COPULATE	EYETOOTH	INSANITY	MUTILATE	RIGIDITY	THOUGHTS	BARBECUE
COQUETTE	FACILITY	INSULATE	NATALITY	ROOMMATE	TIMIDITY	BASIDIUM
CORNETTO	FALSETTO	INTIMATE	NATIVITY	ROSSETTI	TINSMITH	BASINFUL
CORVETTE	FATALITY	INUNDATE	NAUSEATE	ROULETTE	TITANITE	BELABOUR
CREOSOTE	FAVORITE	INVOLUTE	NAVIGATE	RUMINATE	TITIVATE	BELLYFUL
CROCKETT	FEDERATE	IRRIGATE	NEOPHYTE	SACRISTY	TOLBOOTH	BIBULOUS
CRUCIATE	FELICITY	IRRITATE	NEPHRITE	SAGACITY	TOLERATE	BIGAMOUS
CRYOLITE	FEMINITY	JACOBITE	NOBILITY	SALACITY	TOLLGATE	BLACKOUT
CUPIDITY	FEROCITY	JEANETTE	NOISETTE	SALINITY	TONALITY	BLISSFUL
DEBILITY	FIDELITY	JEBUSITE	NOMINATE	SALIVATE	TOTALITY	BOASTFUL
DECIMATE	FIFTIETH	JUBILATE	NUCLEATE	SANCTITY	TOXICITY	BORDEAUX
DECORATE	FILTRATE	KILOBYTE	NUMERATE	SAPONITE	TRAVESTY	BOUTIQUE
DEDICATE	FINALITY	KILOWATT	OBDURATE	SATURATE	TRIUNITY	BREAKOUT
DEFECATE	FLATMATE	LACERATE	OBLIGATE	SCARCITY	TRUNCATE	BRONCHUS
DEFINITE	FLEABITE	LACINATE	OBSOLETE	SCHMALTZ	TUNICATE	BURNTOUT
DELEGATE	FLUIDITY	LAMINATE	ODDMENTS	SEAFORTH	UBIQUITY	CADUCEUS
DELICATE	FLUORITE	LAPIDATE	OILCLOTH	SECURITY	ULCERATE	CALCULUS
DENDRITE	FOOTNOTE	LATERITE	OMELETTE	SELENITE	ULTIMATE	CAMARGUE
DEPILATE	FOOTPATH	LAUREATE	OPERETTA	SELFPITY	UNCHASTE	CAPSICUM
DEROGATE	FORFEITS	LEGALITY	OPPOSITE	SENILITY	UNDULATE	CAPTIOUS
DESOLATE	FORSOOTH	LEVITATE	OPTIMATE	SENORITA	UNGULATE	CATULLUS
DETONATE	FORTIETH	LEWISITE	ORDINATE	SEPARATE	UPRIGHTS	CAUTIOUS
DIAMANTE	FORTUITY	LIBERATE	OSCULATE	SERENATA	URBANITY	CEMENTUM
DINGBATS	FRUMENTY	LIBRETTO	OUISTITI	SERENITY	VALIDATE	CERBERUS
DISCRETE	FUCHSITE	LIMONITE	OVERRATE	SEVERITY	VALIDITY	CEREBRUM
DISKETTE	FUMIGATE	LITERATE	PAGINATE	SHAVUOTH	VALLETTA	CHASSEUR
DISTASTE	FUTILITY	LITERATI	PALLIATE	SHIPMATE	VEGETATE	CHECKOUT
DISUNITE	GARMENTS	LITIGATE	PALMETTO	SIDERITE	VELLEITY	CHEERFUL
DISUNITY	GARROTTE	LIVIDITY	PARASITE	SILICATE	VELOCITY	CHESTNUT
DIVINITY	GEMINATE	LOCALITY	PECULATE	SIMULATE	VENALITY	CHIASMUS
DJIBOUTI	GENERATE	LUCIDITY	PERACUTE	SIXTIETH	VENDETTA	CHROMIUM
DOCILITY	GIGABYTE	LULWORTH	PERFECTA	SKIBOOTS	VENERATE	CIBORIUM
DOGTOOTH	GIGAWATT	MACERATE	PERFECTO	SLYBOOTS	VERACITY	CINGULUM
DOLOMITE	GRADUATE	MACHEATH	PERIANTH	SMOLLETT	VERMOUTH	CIRCINUS
DOMINATE	GRAFFITI	MACULATE	PERIPETY	SOBRIETY	VICINITY	CLANGOUR
DOUBLETS	GRAPHITE	MAJORITY	PERMEATE	SODALITE	VIGNETTE	CLAUDIUS
DOVECOTE	GRATUITY	MALAMUTE	PIERETTE	SODALITY	VIRILITY	CLEARCUT
DRAUGHTS	GRISETTE	MALLEATE	PIMIENTO	SOLIDITY	VISIGOTH	COIFFEUR
DRAUGHTY	GUJARATI	MAQUETTE	PLACENTA	SORORITY	VITALITY	COLISEUM
DRIBLETS	GUNSMITH	MARINATE	PLAUDITS	SPARSITY	VIVACITY	COLLOQUY
DYNAMITE	HELPMATE	MARONITE	PLAYMATE	SPICCATO	VORACITY	COLORFUL
ECHINATE	HEREDITY	MATURATE	PLYMOUTH	SPOLIATE	WARRANTY	COLOSSUS
EDENTATE	HEREWITH	MATURITY	POCHETTE	SQUAMATA	WORKMATE	COLUMBUS
ELEMENTS	HESITATE	MEDICATE	POLYMATH	STACCATO	XENOLITH	CONSTRUE
ELEVENTH	HIGHGATE	MEDITATE	POPULATE	STAGNATE	YOSEMITE	CONTINUE
ELONGATE	HILARITY	MEGABYTE	POROSITY	STANNITE	ZOOPHYTE	CONTINUO
EMACIATE	HITHERTO	MEGALITH	POSTDATE	STAROSTA	ABOMASUM	CORUNDUM
EMIGRATE	HOTPLATE	MEGAWATT	PRIORITY	STEATITE	ACANTHUS	COUSCOUS
ENERVATE	HUMANITY	MELANITE	PRODUCTS	STELLATE	ACTINIUM	COVETOUS
ENORMITY	HUMIDITY	MEREDITH	PROPERTY	STICCATO	ADDENDUM	CREPITUS
ENTIRETY	HUMILITY	MESOLITE	PROSTATE	STIGMATA	AERONAUT	CRITIQUE
ENTREATY	HYACINTH	MESSMATE	QUADRATE	STILETTO	AFFLATUS	CURLICUE
EPIPHYTE	IDENTITY	MILITATE	QUANTITY	STOCCATA	ALBURNUM	DAEDALUS
EQUALITY	IMMOLATE	MINORITE	RACLETTE	STRENGTH	ALLUVIUM	DAMASCUS

DECOROUS	HALFHOUR	PENDULUM	STRIATUM	ABLATIVE	NEWSHAWK	URBANIZE
DELIRIUM	HARANGUE	PERILOUS	STUDIOUS	ABORTIVE	PILTDOWN	VAPORIZE
DENARIUS	HARFLEUR	PERVIOUS	SUBSHRUB	ABRASIVE	PULLDOWN	VITALIZE
DESIROUS	HAZELNUT	PETANQUE	SUCCUBUS	ADDITIVE	PUSHDOWN	VOCALIZE
DETRITUS	HIBISCUS	PHORMIUM	SUDARIUM	ADESSIVE	SHALLOWS	VOWELIZE
DEXTROUS	HOMESPUN	PHYSIQUE	SUPERBUG	ADHESIVE	SHOWDOWN	WOMANIZE
DIALOGUE	HORATIUS	PICKMEUP	SYLLABUB	ADOPTIVE	SHUTDOWN	**8:8**
DIANTHUS	HORNPOUT	PLATANUS	SYLLABUS	AGGRIEVE	SLOWDOWN	ABSCISSA
DINOSAUR	HUMOROUS	PLATEFUL	TAMANDUA	ALLUSIVE	TOMAHAWK	ACADEMIA
DIONYSUS	INFAMOUS	PLATINUM	TANTALUM	BURGRAVE	WASHBOWL	AGRICOLA
DOLOROUS	INOCULUM	PLATYPUS	TANTALUS	CASANOVA	WASHDOWN	ALHAMBRA
DOUBTFUL	INTRIGUE	PLECTRUM	TARTARUS	COERCIVE	WILDFOWL	ALLELUIA
DOUGHNUT	ISTANBUL	PLOTINUS	TASTEFUL	COHESIVE	ZIMBABWE	ALOPECIA
DOWNPOUR	JONGLEUR	PODARGUS	TENESMUS	CONCEIVE	APOPLEXY	AMBROSIA
DREADFUL	KEELHAUL	POLONIUM	TERMINUS	CONCLAVE	COTOPAXI	AMYGDALA
DUODENUM	KHARTOUM	POPULOUS	TESTATUM	CONSERVE	SPINTEXT	ANACONDA
ELECTRUM	KNOCKOUT	POWERFUL	THALAMUS	CONTRIVE	CATTLEYA	ANALECTA
EMERITUS	KOUSKOUS	PRECIOUS	THALLIUM	CREATIVE	DIPHENYL	ANALEMMA
EMPORIUM	LABURNUM	PREVIOUS	THANKFUL	CURATIVE	EDGEWAYS	ANATHEMA
ENCOMIUM	LANGLAUF	PRINTOUT	THROMBUS	DECISIVE	HOLIDAYS	ANATOLIA
ENORMOUS	LARKSPUR	PROLOGUE	TIBERIUS	DERISIVE	HYDROXYL	ANGELICA
ENSHROUD	LAUDANUM	PROROGUE	TIMOROUS	DISPROVE	JEFFREYS	ANGUILLA
EOHIPPUS	LAYABOUT	PUDENDUM	TINNITUS	DISSOLVE	NOWADAYS	ANNELIDA
EPICURUS	LIBELOUS	PURLIEUS	TITANIUM	DIVISIVE	SARDONYX	ANOREXIA
EPILOGUE	LIGNEOUS	RAVENOUS	TOMENTUM	EFFUSIVE	SIDEWAYS	AOTEAROA
EQUULEUS	LINNAEUS	REFUGIUM	TORTUOUS	ELECTIVE	AMORTIZE	APOLOGIA
ERIDANUS	LINOLEUM	RESIDUUM	TRILLIUM	FIXATIVE	BENGHAZI	ARETHUSA
EULOGIUM	LONGHAUL	RESINOUS	TRITICUM	FLYDRIVE	BRAGANZA	ARMORICA
EUROPIUM	LUMINOUS	RHONCHUS	TRUSTFUL	FOXGLOVE	BULLDOZE	ASPERMIA
EVENTFUL	LUSCIOUS	RIGHTFUL	TRUTHFUL	FUGITIVE	CANONIZE	ASPHYXIA
EXIGUOUS	LUSTROUS	RIGOROUS	TUBEROUS	GENITIVE	CIVILIZE	ASTHENIA
EXORDIUM	LUTETIUM	RUBIDIUM	TYMPANUM	HEATWAVE	COLONIZE	ATALANTA
FABULOUS	MALODOUR	RUNABOUT	ULCEROUS	ILLUSIVE	DEFREEZE	ATARAXIA
FACTIOUS	MANDAMUS	RUNNERUP	UNCTUOUS	INACTIVE	DEPUTIZE	ATHEROMA
FACTOTUM	MARABOUT	SABOTEUR	UNDERCUT	INCISIVE	DIGITIZE	AURICULA
FAITHFUL	MARASMUS	SAMARIUM	UNDERFUR	INDUCIVE	DOWNSIZE	AVICENNA
FANCIFUL	MEALYBUG	SCABIOUS	UNDERRUN	INVASIVE	ENERGIZE	AVIFAUNA
FILARIUM	MENELAUS	SCABROUS	UNLAWFUL	KIDGLOVE	EQUALIZE	BABUSHKA
FINESPUN	MENISCUS	SCALENUS	UNUNBIUM	LAXATIVE	EULOGIZE	BACTERIA
FLAMEOUT	MERCIFUL	SCANDIUM	UPPERCUT	LOCATIVE	EXORCIZE	BAGHEERA
FLASHGUN	MERINGUE	SCORNFUL	USURIOUS	MANGROVE	FINALIZE	BALLISTA
FOLLOWUP	MINOTAUR	SCORPIUS	UXORIOUS	MARGRAVE	FULLSIZE	BANDANNA
FORCEFUL	MIRTHFUL	SCRIPTUM	VANADIUM	NEGATIVE	HUMANIZE	BARATHEA
FRABJOUS	MOMENTUM	SCYBALUM	VANADOUS	NOSEDIVE	IDEALIZE	BASILICA
FRANCIUM	MORESQUE	SEDULOUS	VAPOROUS	PALGRAVE	IMMUNIZE	BERGENIA
FRAXINUS	MORPHEUS	SELENIUM	VARIORUM	PERCEIVE	KAMIKAZE	BETHESDA
FREMITUS	MOURNFUL	SENSUOUS	VENGEFUL	POSITIVE	KINGSIZE	BIGNONIA
FRENULUM	MOUTHFUL	SHAKEOUT	VENOMOUS	PRESERVE	LEGALIZE	BLASTULA
FRONDEUR	MUTINOUS	SHAMEFUL	VESUVIUS	PUNITIVE	LOCALIZE	BOADICEA
FRUITFUL	MYCELIUM	SHAREOUT	VEXILLUM	PUTATIVE	MAXIMIZE	BOTSWANA
GADABOUT	MYSTIQUE	SHOOTOUT	VIATICUM	REACTIVE	MEMORIZE	BRAGANZA
GALBANUM	NAUPLIUS	SISYPHUS	VIBURNUM	RELATIVE	MINIMIZE	BRASILIA
GARRIGUE	NAUSEOUS	SKILLFUL	VIGOROUS	REPRIEVE	MOBILIZE	BRASSICA
GENEROUS	NAUTILUS	SLOTHFUL	VINCULUM	RETRIEVE	MORALIZE	BROMELIA
GERANIUM	NEBULOUS	SOLARIUM	VIPEROUS	RINGDOVE	MOTORIZE	BROUHAHA
GLABROUS	NOBELIUM	SONOROUS	VIRTUOUS	SEDATIVE	ORGANIZE	BUDDLEIA
GLASSFUL	NUMEROUS	SPACIOUS	VITELLUS	SPORTIVE	OVERSIZE	BULGARIA
GLAUCOUS	NUMINOUS	SPADEFUL	VITREOUS	TOPHEAVY	PARALYZE	CACHEXIA
GLORIOUS	ODYSSEUS	SPECIOUS	VIVARIUM	UNIVALVE	PENALIZE	CALCUTTA
GLUTAEUS	OVERHAUL	SPECTRUM	VOYAGEUR	VOCATIVE	POLARIZE	CALIGULA
GOLFCLUB	PABULOUS	SPECULUM	WASTEFUL	CAMPTOWN	QUATORZE	CAMBODIA
GORGEOUS	PANDANUS	SPHAGNUM	WATCHFUL	CHICHEWA	SANITIZE	CAMELLIA
GRACEFUL	PANDARUS	SPIRITUS	WATERBUG	COMEDOWN	SATIRIZE	CANBERRA
GRACIOUS	PARAMOUR	SPITEFUL	WONDROUS	DOWNTOWN	SCHMOOZE	CAPYBARA
GRANDEUR	PATAGIUM	SPOONFUL	WRATHFUL	FLYBLOWN	STARGAZE	CARNAUBA
GRATEFUL	PATULOUS	SPURIOUS	WRONGFUL	FREETOWN	THEORIZE	CAROLINA
GRIEVOUS	PAULINUS	SQUAMOUS	YOUTHFUL	LILONGWE	TOTALIZE	CASANOVA
GUAIACUM	PEACEFUL	STAKEOUT	ZEPHYRUS	MARKDOWN	UNFREEZE	CATHEDRA
HABAKKUK	PELAGIUS	STIMULUS	ABESSIVE	MELTDOWN	UNIONIZE	

CATTLEYA	KARTTIKA	SILICULA	ANABATIC	GALVANIC	SYLLABIC	BICUSPID
CAVATINA	KATAKANA	SINFONIA	ANALYTIC	GELASTIC	SYLVATIC	BILLFOLD
CHARISMA	KINSHASA	SITTELLA	ANARCHIC	GEODESIC	SYMBOLIC	BINDWEED
CHICHEWA	KRAKATOA	SLOVAKIA	ANATOMIC	GEODETIC	SYNOPTIC	BIRDSEED
CHICKPEA	LEUKEMIA	SLOVENIA	ANOREXIC	GERMANIC	SYSTEMIC	BLIZZARD
CHILLADA	LISTERIA	SONATINA	ARMAGNAC	GIGANTIC	TARTARIC	BLOTCHED
CHIMAERA	LONICERA	SQUAMATA	AROMATIC	GOIDELIC	TECTONIC	BOATLOAD
CHORDATA	MAGNESIA	STAPELIA	ARTISTIC	HARMONIC	TELLURIC	BONEHEAD
CINCHONA	MAGNOLIA	STAROSTA	ASCORBIC	HELLADIC	TERRIFIC	BONEYARD
CINERAMA	MAHARAJA	STEATOMA	ATARAXIC	HELLENIC	TEUTONIC	BORROWED
CISTERNA	MAJOLICA	STIGMATA	ATHLETIC	HERALDIC	THEATRIC	BOTHERED
COCACOLA	MALAYSIA	STOCCATA	ATLANTIC	HERMETIC	THEMATIC	BRANCHED
COLOMBIA	MALLORCA	SUBPOENA	AUTISTIC	HERPETIC	THORACIC	BRASSARD
CZAREVNA	MALVASIA	SUBTOPIA	BALEARIC	HIERATIC	TRIASSIC	BRINDLED
DEMENTIA	MANDIOCA	SUBURBIA	BARBARIC	HISPANIC	TROCHAIC	BRISTLED
DEMERARA	MANITOBA	SUDAMINA	BATHETIC	HISTORIC	TUNGSTIC	BUGGERED
DIARRHEA	MANTILLA	SWASTIKA	BEATIFIC	HOLISTIC	TUNGUSIC	BULKHEAD
DIASPORA	MANTISSA	TAMANDUA	BERGERAC	HOLOZOIC	TURMERIC	BURDENED
DJELLABA	MARCELLA	TANZANIA	CADILLAC	HORRIFIC	UNHEROIC	BUTTERED
DRACAENA	MARQUESA	TASMANIA	CARBOLIC	HYGIENIC	VOLCANIC	BUZZWORD
DULCINEA	MELANOMA	TEQUILLA	CARBONIC	HYPNOTIC	ABDUCTED	CAMBERED
DYSLEXIA	METABOLA	TERATOMA	CATHOLIC	HYSTERIC	ABRIDGED	CAPSIZED
DZONGKHA	MINAMATA	THIOUREA	CELERIAC	ISOBARIC	ABSOLVED	CARTLOAD
EFFLUVIA	MONGOLIA	TITICACA	CENOZOIC	ISOGENIC	ABSORBED	CARYATID
EGOMANIA	MONROVIA	TORTILLA	CHERUBIC	JURASSIC	ACCENTED	CENTERED
ENCAENIA	MONSTERA	TOXAEMIA	CHOLERIC	LOGISTIC	ACCEPTED	CERATOID
EPHEMERA	MOUSSAKA	TOXOCARA	CLIMATIC	LYSERGIC	ACCURSED	CHADBAND
EPITHEMA	NDJAMENA	TRACHOMA	COSMETIC	MAGNETIC	ACHIEVED	CILIATED
ERYTHEMA	NEBRASKA	TRILEMMA	CYRENIAC	MAIEUTIC	ACIDHEAD	CLEANSED
ESTANCIA	OKLAHOMA	TROCHLEA	CYRILLIC	MAJESTIC	ACQUIRED	CLIFFORD
ETCETERA	OPERETTA	TSAREVNA	DALMATIC	MECHANIC	ADDICTED	COCKEYED
ETHIOPIA	ORESTEIA	TUSITALA	DEMONIAC	MESMERIC	ADVANCED	COLLARED
EUPEPSIA	PANATELA	UMBRELLA	DESPOTIC	MESOZOIC	AFFECTED	COLOURED
EUPHONIA	PANORAMA	UNDERSEA	DIABETIC	METALLIC	AGITATED	COMBINED
EUPHORIA	PARABOLA	VAISAKHA	DIABOLIC	METEORIC	AGONIZED	COMPARED
FANTASIA	PARANOIA	VALENCIA	DIATONIC	METHODIC	AIRFIELD	COMPOSED
FENESTRA	PAROUSIA	VALHALLA	DICYCLIC	MNEMONIC	AIRSPEED	COMPOUND
FLOTILLA	PASHMINA	VALLETTA	DIDACTIC	MONASTIC	ALKALOID	CONCHOID
GALLERIA	PELLAGRA	VENDETTA	DIOPTRIC	NARCOTIC	AMBUSHED	CONFINED
GARDENIA	PENUMBRA	VERONICA	DIURETIC	NEPIONIC	AMMONOID	CONFOUND
GASTRULA	PERFECTA	VERTEBRA	DOGMATIC	NEUROTIC	ANIMATED	CONFUSED
GIACONDA	PHALGUNA	VICTORIA	DOMESTIC	OPERATIC	APPALLED	CONSUMED
GIOCONDA	PHYSALIA	VIRGINIA	DRACONIC	PANDEMIC	APPRISED	COPYHOLD
GLABELLA	PIZZERIA	WISTERIA	DRAMATIC	PATHETIC	APPROVED	CORONOID
GLAUCOMA	PLACENTA	XANTHOMA	DYNASTIC	PEDANTIC	ARACHNID	CORRODED
GLORIANA	PLETHORA	YARMULKA	DYSLEXIC	PERIODIC	ARMOURED	COTSWOLD
GLOXINIA	POLYANNA	YERSINIA	ECLECTIC	PHENOLIC	ARRESTED	CRIPPLED
GOLGOTHA	PORPHYRA	YOKOHAMA	ECONOMIC	PHONETIC	ARTICLED	CRUTCHED
GONDWANA	PREDELLA	ZARZUELA	ECSTATIC	PHREATIC	ASSORTED	CULTURED
GRISELDA	PRETORIA	ZASTRUGA	EGOISTIC	PHTHISIC	ASTEROID	CUPBOARD
GUERILLA	PROFORMA	ZIRCONIA	EIDECTIC	PINDARIC	ATHETOID	DANEGELD
GURDWARA	PROGERIA	BACKCOMB	ELECTRIC	PLATONIC	ATTACHED	DARKENED
GYMKHANA	PROTOZOA	CATACOMB	ELLIPTIC	PROLIFIC	BABYHOOD	DASHWOOD
HABANERA	PRUNELLA	CHORIAMB	EMPHATIC	QUIXOTIC	BACKHAND	DEADENED
HACIENDA	PYORRHEA	DOORKNOB	EPIDEMIC	REPUBLIC	BACKWARD	DEADHEAD
HAMARTIA	QUADRIGA	GOLFCLUB	EPIGAMIC	RHETORIC	BACKYARD	DEADWOOD
HELVETIA	RUTABAGA	HECATOMB	EPISODIC	RHYTHMIC	BALANCED	DEATHBED
HEPATICA	SARATOGA	MEMSAHIB	ESOTERIC	ROMANTIC	BAPTISED	DECEASED
HETAIRIA	SARDINIA	SUBSHRUB	ESTHETIC	SADISTIC	BARNYARD	DECKHAND
HIAWATHA	SATURNIA	SYLLABUB	EUCYCLIC	SANDARAC	BARTERED	DEFEATED
HIBERNIA	SAYONARA	ACADEMIC	EUPHONIC	SARDINE	BASSWOOD	DEFORMED
HIRAGANA	SCHAPSKA	ACENTRIC	EUPHORIC	SEMIOTIC	BATTERED	DEGRADED
HYSTERIA	SCIATICA	ACOUSTIC	EUSTATIC	SERAPHIC	BECALMED	DEJECTED
INSIGNIA	SCROFULA	ACROSTIC	EUTROPIC	SIMONIAC	BEDSTEAD	DEMENTED
INSOMNIA	SEMOLINA	ADRIATIC	EXEGETIC	SOCRATIC	BEFRIEND	DENDROID
INTIFADA	SENORITA	AGNOSTIC	EXOERGIC	SPECIFIC	BEREAVED	DEPARTED
ISABELLA	SERENATA	ALCHEMIC	FORENSIC	SPORADIC	BERTRAND	DEPRAVED
JAPONICA	SHIGELLA	ALLERGIC	FRENETIC	SUBSONIC	BESIEGED	DEPRIVED
JYAISTHA	SIGNORIA	AMMONIAC	GALACTIC	SULFURIC	BESOTTED	DERANGED

DESERTED	FOOTHOLD	INCLINED	MIRRORED	PROFOUND	SITUATED	UNCOOKED
DESERVED	FOREHAND	INCLUDED	MOHAMMED	PROMISED	SKEWBALD	UNCURBED
DESTINED	FOREHEAD	INDEBTED	MONOACID	PROPOSED	SKINHEAD	UNDERBID
DETACHED	FORELAND	INDENTED	MOORLAND	PROPOUND	SLIGHTED	UNDERFED
DETAILED	FOREWORD	INFECTED	MORIBUND	PROVIDED	SLIPSHOD	UNEARNED
DEVILLED	FOURFOLD	INFESTED	MUDGUARD	PTEROPOD	SLUGABED	UNFILLED
DEWYEYED	FOXHOUND	INFLAMED	MUHAMMAD	PUCKERED	SLUGGARD	UNFORCED
DISABLED	FRAZZLED	INFLATED	MYRIAPOD	PUGNOSED	SMUGGLED	UNHARMED
DISEASED	FRECKLED	INFORMED	NATTERED	PUNISHED	SOCALLED	UNHEATED
DISLIKED	FREEHAND	INFRARED	NEATHERD	PURBLIND	SOFTWOOD	UNHINGED
DISMAYED	FREEHOLD	INSPIRED	NECKBAND	PURIFIED	SOLENOID	UNLEADED
DISPOSED	FRENZIED	INTENDED	NEMATOID	RAILHEAD	SONGBIRD	UNLISTED
DISPUTED	FURROWED	INVENTED	NEWFOUND	RAILROAD	SOURWOOD	UNLOADED
DIVIDEND	GAILLARD	INVERTED	NOSEBAND	RAINBIRD	SOUTHEND	UNLOCKED
DIVORCED	GALLIARD	INVOLVED	NUFFIELD	RAREFIED	SPANGLED	UNMANNED
DOCKLAND	GAMEBIRD	IRONCLAD	OBSCURED	REARWARD	SPANIARD	UNMARKED
DOCKYARD	GANGLAND	IRONWOOD	OBSERVED	REASONED	SPAVINED	UNNERVED
DOCTORED	GAOLBIRD	ISOLATED	OBSESSED	RECEIVED	SPECKLED	UNPLACED
DOWNLOAD	GARAMOND	JACKETED	OBTAINED	RECESSED	SPHENOID	UNRIFLED
DOWNWARD	GATEFOLD	JACQUARD	OCCUPIED	REFORMED	SPIRITED	UNSALTED
DROPHEAD	GATHERED	JAILBIRD	OFFENDED	REGAINED	SPITHEAD	UNSEALED
DRUMHEAD	GIRLHOOD	JEREMIAD	OILFIELD	REJOINED	SPLENDID	UNSEEDED
DRUNKARD	GODCHILD	JEWELLED	OLDWORLD	RELEASED	SPRAINED	UNSIGNED
DUCKWEED	GOODWOOD	JIGGERED	OLYMPIAD	RELIEVED	SPRAWLED	UNSOLVED
DUMFOUND	GOURMAND	KEYBOARD	ONESIDED	RENOWNED	STAFFORD	UNSTATED
EASTWARD	GRANDDAD	KIPPERED	ORDINAND	REPEATED	STAMENED	UNSUITED
EDUCATED	GRANDKID	KNAPWEED	ORPHANED	REPORTED	STANDARD	UNTAPPED
ELEVATED	GRIZZLED	KNOTWEED	OUTBOARD	REQUIRED	STARCHED	UNTHREAD
ELKHOUND	GROUNDED	LABOURED	OUTDATED	RESERVED	STENOSED	UNTILLED
EMBEDDED	GULFWEED	LACKLAND	OUTFIELD	RESIGNED	STOREYED	UNTOWARD
EMBODIED	GUSSETED	LADYBIRD	OUTMODED	RESOLVED	STRAINED	UNVARIED
EMBOSSED	HAIRBAND	LAKELAND	OVENBIRD	RETARDED	STRANDED	UNVERSED
EMBRACED	HALLIARD	LAMENTED	OVERFEED	REVEALED	STRAPPED	UNVOICED
EMPLOYED	HALLOWED	LANDLORD	OVERHAND	REVEREND	STREAKED	UNWANTED
ENCAMPED	HAMMERED	LANDWARD	OVERHEAD	REVERSED	STRESSED	UNWEANED
ENCLOSED	HANDHELD	LANGLAND	OVERLAID	RHOMBOID	STRIATED	UNWONTED
ENLARGED	HANDMAID	LEAVENED	OVERLAND	ROSALIND	STRINGED	UPTURNED
ENMESHED	HARASSED	LEFTHAND	OVERLOAD	ROSAMOND	STRIPPED	VAGABOND
ENRICHED	HARDENED	LEFTWARD	OVERLORD	ROSEWOOD	STUCCOED	VANGUARD
ENSHROUD	HARDWOOD	LEISURED	OVERSOLD	RUBICUND	STYLIZED	VANISHED
ENTITLED	HARTFORD	LETTERED	PACKAGED	RUMOURED	SUNDRIED	VENTURED
ESTEEMED	HAYFIELD	LICENSED	PALMATED	SALARIED	SUPPOSED	VINEYARD
EUROLAND	HEADBAND	LIVERIED	PAMPERED	SARABAND	SURROUND	WALLSEND
EXECUTED	HEADLAND	LOANWORD	PANELLED	SASSANID	TAILSKID	WAVEBAND
EXPANDED	HEADWIND	LOCOWEED	PARANOID	SATIATED	TALENTED	WEDGWOOD
EXPECTED	HEADWORD	LONGHAND	PARKLAND	SAUROPOD	TAMARIND	WELLBRED
EXPENDED	HELMETED	LONGLAND	PASSWORD	SAVOURED	TEAKWOOD	WELLPAID
EXPLODED	HERACLID	LOPSIDED	PATENTED	SAVOYARD	TEMPERED	WESTWARD
EXTENDED	HEREFORD	LOUVERED	PELLETED	SCABBARD	TERRACED	WHIPCORD
FALKLAND	HEREWARD	LOVEBIRD	PELLUCID	SCAFFOLD	TETRAPOD	WHIPHAND
FAMISHED	HIGHLAND	LYREBIRD	PERFUMED	SCAPHOID	TEXTURED	WINDWARD
FARMHAND	HIGHROAD	MAINLAND	PERISHED	SCHIZOID	THAILAND	WINIFRED
FARMLAND	HINDWARD	MAINYARD	PERJURED	SCORCHED	THATCHED	WITHERED
FARMYARD	HOGSHEAD	MANDATED	PILCHARD	SCOTLAND	THOUSAND	WITHHOLD
FATIGUED	HOLYHEAD	MANIFOLD	PILLARED	SCRAWLED	TICKSEED	WOODLAND
FAVOURED	HOLYROOD	MANNERED	PINEWOOD	SCREENED	TIGHTWAD	WOODSHED
FEATURED	HOMELAND	MARIGOLD	PINNIPED	SEABOARD	TIMBERED	WOODWARD
FEELGOOD	HOMEWARD	MARTYRED	PISSHEAD	SEASONED	TONSURED	WOODWIND
FINISHED	HOPFIELD	MARYLAND	PLOUGHED	SECLUDED	TORTURED	WORKLOAD
FIREBIRD	HYDATOID	MASTHEAD	POKEWEED	SELECTED	TRICHOID	WORMWOOD
FIREWEED	ICEFIELD	MEASURED	POLISHED	SELEUCID	TRINIDAD	WREATHED
FIREWOOD	ILLFATED	METALLED	POLLUTED	SERRATED	TROUBLED	WRETCHED
FISHPOND	IMAGINED	MIDFIELD	PORTLAND	SHEPHERD	TRUCKLED	WRINKLED
FISSIPED	IMMERSED	MILDEWED	POSTCARD	SHERWOOD	TURBANED	ABBASIDE
FLAVORED	IMPACTED	MILKMAID	POSTPAID	SHETLAND	TURRETED	ABDICATE
FLAXSEED	IMPAIRED	MILKWEED	POTBOUND	SHIPYARD	UNABATED	ABESSIVE
FLOUNCED	IMPELLED	MILLPOND	POTSHERD	SHIVERED	UNBIASED	ABEYANCE
FOGBOUND	IMPROVED	MINEHEAD	POWDERED	SHROUDED	UNCOMBED	ABLATIVE
FOLLOWED	INCENSED		PREPARED	SIDEWARD		ABNEGATE

ABORTIVE	ANTIMERE	BIOSCOPE	CELIBATE	CREATURE	DISGORGE	ENVISAGE
ABRASIVE	ANTIPOPE	BIRDCAGE	CENOBITE	CREDIBLE	DISGRACE	EPILOGUE
ABROGATE	ANYPLACE	BLOCKADE	CENTRODE	CREOSOTE	DISGUISE	EPIPHYTE
ABSENTEE	ANYWHERE	BLOCKAGE	CHACONNE	CRETONNE	DISKETTE	EPISTYLE
ABSINTHE	APERTURE	BLOWHOLE	CHANTAGE	CREVASSE	DISLODGE	EQUALIZE
ABSOLUTE	APOLOGUE	BLOWPIPE	CHASTISE	CRIBBAGE	DISPENSE	EQUIPAGE
ABSTRUSE	APOPHYGE	BLUENOSE	CHASUBLE	CRITIQUE	DISPERSE	ERADIATE
ACCOLADE	APOSTATE	BODYLINE	CHENILLE	CRUCIATE	DISPLACE	ERECTILE
ACCURATE	APPANAGE	BOLTHOLE	CHEROKEE	CRUCIBLE	DISPROVE	ERGOTISE
ACERBATE	APPETITE	BONHOMIE	CHESHIRE	CRUNCHIE	DISSOLVE	ERUCTATE
ACTINIDE	APPLAUSE	BONIFACE	CHEYENNE	CRYOLITE	DISSUADE	ERUPTURE
ACTIVATE	APPLIQUÉ	BOOKABLE	CHLORATE	CULPABLE	DISTANCE	ESCALADE
ADDITIVE	APPOSITE	BOOKCASE	CHLORIDE	CURATIVE	DISTASTE	ESCALATE
ADELAIDE	APPRAISE	BORACITE	CHLORINE	CURLICUE	DISUNITE	ESCALOPE
ADEQUATE	APTITUDE	BORECOLE	CHORDATE	CURRICLE	DIVISIVE	ESCAPADE
ADESSIVE	AQUILINE	BOREHOLE	CHRISTIE	CUTPRICE	DIVORCEE	ESSONITE
ADHESIVE	ARALDITE	BOUTIQUE	CHROMITE	CUTPURSE	DOCKSIDE	ESTIMATE
ADJUTAGE	ARCHDUKE	BRAMANTE	CHUMMAGE	CYNOSURE	DOCTRINE	ESTIVATE
ADOPTIVE	ARGININE	BRANDADE	CICERONE	CYTOSINE	DOGHOUSE	ETHERISE
ADORABLE	ARGUABLE	BRIBABLE	CIVILIZE	DAMNABLE	DOLOMITE	ETHYLENE
ADVOCATE	ARMALITE	BROCHURE	CLAMBAKE	DATABASE	DOMICILE	ETIOLATE
AERODYNE	ARMATURE	BRUMAIRE	CLARENCE	DATELINE	DOMINATE	EULOGIZE
AESTHETE	ARROGATE	BRUNETTE	CLAVICLE	DEADLINE	DOPAMINE	EURYDICE
AGACERIE	ARTIFICE	BUCKSHEE	CLAYMORE	DECIMATE	DORMOUSE	EVACUATE
AGGRIEVE	ASPIRATE	BULLDOZE	CLEAVAGE	DECISIVE	DOVECOTE	EVALUATE
AIGRETTE	ASSEMBLE	BUMMAREE	COALESCE	DECORATE	DOWNSIDE	EVANESCE
AIGUILLE	ASSIGNEE	BURGRAVE	COALHOLE	DECOUPLE	DOWNSIZE	EVENTIDE
AIRBORNE	ASTATINE	CABOODLE	COALMINE	DECREASE	DRAINAGE	EVERMORE
AIRBRAKE	ATHETISE	CABOTAGE	COCCIDAE	DEDICATE	DRESSAGE	EVERYONE
AIREDALE	ATTITUDE	CABRIOLE	COCKAYNE	DEFECATE	DRUMLINE	EVIDENCE
AIRPLANE	AUDIENCE	CADASTRE	CODPIECE	DEFIANCE	DRYSTONE	EXAMINEE
ALBACORE	AUTOMATE	CAFFEINE	COERCIVE	DEFILADE	DUCHESSE	EXCAVATE
ALDEHYDE	AUTOTYPE	CAKEHOLE	COGITATE	DEFINITE	DUTIABLE	EXCHANGE
ALEHOUSE	AVENTINE	CALAMINE	COHESIVE	DEFREEZE	DUTYFREE	EXECRATE
ALEMAINE	AYRSHIRE	CALCEATE	COIFFURE	DELAWARE	DYNAMITE	EXERCISE
ALGERINE	BACKACHE	CALCRETE	COINCIDE	DELEGATE	EARPHONE	EXHUMATE
ALICANTE	BACKBITE	CALLIOPE	COLLAPSE	DELICATE	EARPIECE	EXOCRINE
ALIENATE	BACKBONE	CALOTYPE	COLONIZE	DEMIURGE	EASTLAKE	EXORCIZE
ALKALINE	BACKDATE	CAMARGUE	COMATOSE	DENATURE	ECHINATE	EXPEDITE
ALLIANCE	BACKFIRE	CAMISOLE	COMMENCE	DENDRITE	EDENTATE	EXPOSURE
ALLOCATE	BACKSIDE	CAMOMILE	COMMERCE	DENOUNCE	EDGEWISE	EYEPIECE
ALLSPICE	BADINAGE	CAMPSITE	COMPLETE	DENTICLE	EFFUSIVE	EYESHADE
ALLUSIVE	BAGUETTE	CAMSTONE	COMPLINE	DEPILATE	ELECTIVE	FACEACHE
ALTITUDE	BAKELITE	CANAILLE	COMPRISE	DEPORTEE	ELEGANCE	FALLIBLE
AMANDINE	BALINESE	CANALISE	CONCEIVE	DEPUTIZE	ELIGIBLE	FAROUCHE
AMBIANCE	BANKNOTE	CANONIZE	CONCLAVE	DERISIVE	ELONGATE	FASCICLE
AMBIENCE	BANLIEUE	CANOODLE	CONCLUDE	DEROGATE	ELSINORE	FAVORITE
AMBULATE	BARBECUE	CANTICLE	CONCORDE	DESCRIBE	EMACIATE	FEARSOME
AMENABLE	BARITONE	CAPRIOLE	CONCRETE	DESOLATE	EMBATTLE	FEASIBLE
AMICABLE	BARNACLE	CAPSTONE	CONDENSE	DETAINEE	EMBEZZLE	FEDERATE
AMMONITE	BARRETTE	CARABINE	CONFLATE	DETHRONE	EMIGRATE	FEMININE
AMORTIZE	BASELINE	CARACOLE	CONSERVE	DETONATE	EMINENCE	FENCIBLE
AMPERAGE	BASTILLE	CARAPACE	CONSOMMÉ	DEVIANCE	EMPLOYEE	FIGURINE
AMPUTATE	BATHROBE	CAREFREE	CONSPIRE	DEXTROSE	ENCIRCLE	FILENAME
AMUSETTE	BEANPOLE	CARNEGIE	CONSTRUE	DIAGNOSE	ENCLOTHE	FILIGREE
ANALOGUE	BEARABLE	CAROLINE	CONTINUE	DIALOGUE	ENERGIZE	FILTRATE
ANAPHASE	BEDABBLE	CAROTENE	CONTRITE	DIAMANTE	ENERVATE	FINALIZE
ANECDOTE	BEFUDDLE	CARRIAGE	CONTRIVE	DIAPHONE	ENFEEBLE	FIRESIDE
ANISETTE	BEGRUDGE	CARRIOLE	CONVERGE	DIASTASE	ENFILADE	FIRMWARE
ANNAMITE	BELGRADE	CARTHAGE	CONVERSE	DIASTOLE	ENKINDLE	FISHBONE
ANNOTATE	BELITTLE	CARUCATE	CONVINCE	DIATRIBE	ENSCONCE	FISHCAKE
ANNOUNCE	BELPAESE	CASEMATE	CONVULSE	DIGITIZE	ENSEMBLE	FISHWIFE
ANSERINE	BENEFICE	CASHMERE	COOKWARE	DIGIZINE	ENSHRINE	FIXATIVE
ANTECEDE	BERCEUSE	CASSETTE	COPULATE	DISABUSE	ENSILAGE	FLAGPOLE
ANTEDATE	BESTRIDE	CASTRATE	COQUETTE	DISAGREE	ENTANGLE	FLATMATE
ANTELOPE	BEVERAGE	CATAMITE	CORNICHE	DISBURSE	ENTHRONE	FLATWARE
ANTENNAE	BIGARADE	CATHOUSE	CORVETTE	DISCIPLE	ENTRANCE	FLEABITE
ANTIDOTE	BILOBATE	CATILINE	COVERAGE	DISCLOSE	ENVELOPE	FLEXIBLE
ANTILOPE	BINNACLE	CELANESE	CREATIVE	DISCRETE	ENVIABLE	FLORENCE

FLUORIDE	HALFTIME	IRONWARE	LINGERIE	MINCEPIE	OFFSTAGE	PERFORCE
FLUORINE	HANDMADE	IRRIGATE	LINOTYPE	MINIMIZE	OLDSTYLE	PERILUNE
FLUORITE	HANDSOME	IRRITATE	LITERATE	MINORITE	OLEACEAE	PERMEATE
FLYDRIVE	HARANGUE	ISABELLE	LITIGATE	MINUTIAE	OMELETTE	PEROXIDE
FOLKLORE	HARDCORE	ISOCLINE	LIVEWARE	MISERERE	OMNIVORE	PERSPIRE
FOLLICLE	HARDLINE	ISOTHERE	LOBELINE	MISGUIDE	OPERABLE	PERSUADE
FOOTNOTE	HARDWARE	JACOBITE	LOCALIZE	MISJUDGE	OPPOSITE	PERVERSE
FOOTSORE	HEADACHE	JALOUSIE	LOCATIVE	MISPLACE	OPTIMATE	PETANQUE
FORCIBLE	HEADLINE	JAMBOREE	LOCKABLE	MISQUOTE	OPULENCE	PHALANGE
FOREBODE	HEATWAVE	JAPANESE	LOGOTYPE	MITIGATE	OPUSCULE	PHARISEE
FOREGONE	HEBETUDE	JAUNDICE	LONESOME	MOBILIZE	ORDINATE	PHOSGENE
FORENAME	HELLFIRE	JEANETTE	LONGTIME	MODERATE	ORDNANCE	PHYLLOME
FOURSOME	HELPLINE	JEBUSITE	LONSDALE	MODULATE	ORGANDIE	PHYSIQUE
FOXGLOVE	HELPMATE	JELLICOE	LOOPHOLE	MOISTURE	ORGANIZE	PIERETTE
FRACTURE	HEMIPODE	JOINTURE	LORRAINE	MOLECULE	OSCULATE	PILOTAGE
FRONTAGE	HENHOUSE	JONCANOE	LOVELACE	MONETISE	OTOSCOPE	PINAFORE
FRUCTOSE	HERITAGE	JUBILATE	LUSTRINE	MONGOOSE	OUTHOUSE	PINNACLE
FUCHSITE	HERMIONE	JULIENNE	MACERATE	MONOPOLE	OUTSHINE	PINOCHLE
FUGITIVE	HESITATE	JUNCTURE	MACULATE	MONOTYPE	OVENWARE	PINTABLE
FULLPAGE	HIGHGATE	JUVENILE	MADHOUSE	MONOXIDE	OVERCOME	PIPELINE
FULLSIZE	HIGHRISE	KAMIKAZE	MAGAZINE	MOQUETTE	OVERDONE	PIPERINE
FULLTIME	HILLSIDE	KEDGEREE	MAINLINE	MORALIZE	OVERDOSE	PITIABLE
FUMAROLE	HOLOCENE	KEEPSAKE	MALAMUTE	MORESQUE	OVERRATE	PITTANCE
FUMIGATE	HOMEMADE	KERMESSE	MALLARMÉ	MORPHEME	OVERRIDE	PLACABLE
FUNGIBLE	HOMEPAGE	KEROSENE	MALLEATE	MORPHINE	OVERRIPE	PLAYMATE
FURUNCLE	HOMICIDE	KEYSTONE	MAMELUKE	MORTGAGE	OVERRULE	PLAYTIME
FUSAROLE	HORNPIPE	KIDGLOVE	MANCIPLE	MOTIVATE	OVERSHOE	PLEASURE
FUSELAGE	HORRIBLE	KILOBYTE	MANDIBLE	MOTORIZE	OVERSIZE	PLIOCENE
FUSEWIRE	HOSEPIPE	KINGSIZE	MANDRAKE	MOVEABLE	OVERTAKE	PLUGHOLE
GABONESE	HOTHOUSE	KLONDIKE	MANGROVE	MUCILAGE	OVERTIME	POCHETTE
GABORONE	HOTPLATE	LACERATE	MANICURE	MUDSTONE	OVERTONE	POLARIZE
GADARENE	HUMANIZE	LACINATE	MAQUETTE	MULTIPLE	OVERTURE	POLYSEME
GANGRENE	ICEHOUSE	LACROSSE	MARGRAVE	MURRHINE	OXBRIDGE	POPSICLE
GANYMEDE	IDEALIZE	LADYLIKE	MARINADE	MUSTACHE	PAGINATE	POPULACE
GARGOYLE	ILLUMINE	LAKESIDE	MARINATE	MUTILATE	PALATINE	POPULATE
GARRIGUE	ILLUSIVE	LAMINATE	MARITIME	MYSTIQUE	PALEFACE	PORPOISE
GARROTTE	IMBECILE	LANDMINE	MARONITE	NAMESAKE	PALGRAVE	PORRIDGE
GASOLINE	IMMATURE	LANDRACE	MARQUISE	NAUSEATE	PALINODE	PORTABLE
GELATINE	IMMOBILE	LANGUAGE	MARRIAGE	NAVIGATE	PALISADE	PORTHOLE
GEMINATE	IMMOLATE	LANOLINE	MASSACRE	NAZARENE	PALLIATE	PORTIÈRE
GENDARME	IMMUNIZE	LAPIDATE	MASSEUSE	NECKLACE	PALPABLE	POSITIVE
GENERATE	IMPOLITE	LARGESSE	MATABELE	NECKLINE	PANNICLE	POSSIBLE
GENITIVE	INACTIVE	LAROUSSE	MATAMORE	NEGATIVE	PARALYZE	POSTCODE
GENOCIDE	INCHOATE	LATERITE	MATURATE	NEGLIGEE	PARASITE	POSTDATE
GEOPHONE	INCISIVE	LATITUDE	MAXIMIZE	NEMATODE	PARLANCE	POSTPONE
GERMAINE	INCREASE	LAUDABLE	MAZARINE	NEOPHYTE	PARTERRE	POTSTONE
GERTRUDE	INCUBATE	LAUREATE	MEALTIME	NEPALESE	PARTICLE	POULAINE
GIGABYTE	INDICATE	LAURENCE	MEANTIME	NEPENTHE	PARTTIME	POULTICE
GIRASOLE	INDUCIVE	LAWRENCE	MEDICATE	NEPHRITE	PASSABLE	POUNDAGE
GLADSOME	INEDIBLE	LAXATIVE	MEDICINE	NICKNAME	PASSIBLE	PRACTICE
GLEESOME	INFINITE	LEBANESE	MEDIOCRE	NICOTINE	PASTICHE	PRACTISE
GLISSADE	INFRINGE	LECTRICE	MEDITATE	NOCTURNE	PASTILLE	PREAMBLE
GLORIOLE	INHUMANE	LEGALIZE	MEGABYTE	NOISETTE	PATENTEE	PRECLUDE
GLOSSEME	INITIATE	LEMONADE	MEGAPODE	NOMINATE	PATIENCE	PRECURSE
GOLDMINE	INNOVATE	LEVERAGE	MELAMINE	NONSENSE	PECULATE	PREJUDGE
GOODSIRE	INSCRIBE	LEVITATE	MELANITE	NOONTIME	PEDICURE	PREMIERE
GOODWIFE	INSECURE	LEWISITE	MEMBRANE	NOSEDIVE	PEDIGREE	PRESENCE
GRADUATE	INSTANCE	LIBERATE	MEMORIZE	NOTECASE	PEDUNCLE	PRESERVE
GRAPHEME	INSULATE	LICENSEE	MERINGUE	NUCLEATE	PEEPHOLE	PRESSURE
GRAPHITE	INTERNEE	LICORICE	MESOLITE	NUCLEOLE	PEKINESE	PRESTIGE
GRATINEE	INTIMATE	LIFELIKE	MESSMATE	NUISANCE	PELLICLE	PRETENCE
GRENACHE	INTRIGUE	LIFELINE	MESSUAGE	NUMERATE	PEMBROKE	PRETENSE
GRISETTE	INUNDATE	LIFETIME	MÉTAIRIE	NUTHOUSE	PENALIZE	PRIMROSE
GRUESOME	INVASIVE	LIGATURE	MEUNIERE	OBDURATE	PENELOPE	PRISTINE
GUIDANCE	INVEIGLE	LIKEABLE	MIGNONNE	OBLIGATE	PENKNIFE	PROBABLE
GULLIBLE	INVOLUTE	LIKEWISE	MIGRAINE	OBSOLETE	PENTACLE	PROCAINE
GUYANESE	IOLANTHE	LILONGWE	MILANESE	OBSTACLE	PENZANCE	PRODROME
HAIRLIKE	IRISCOPE	LIMACINE	MILITATE	OEILLADE	PERACUTE	PROGRADE
HAIRLINE	IRONSIDE	LIMONITE	MILLRACE	OFFSHORE	PERCEIVE	PROLAPSE

PROLOGUE	REVEILLE	SIGHTSEE	SYNDROME	UNIVALVE	MALAKOFF	CAPERING
PROPHASE	RIBSTONE	SILICATE	SYRACUSE	UNIVERSE	MISCHIEF	CARRYING
PROROGUE	RIDDANCE	SILICONE	TABULATE	UNSETTLE	OVERLEAF	CATCHING
PROSTATE	RIDICULE	SILOXANE	TAILGATE	UNSTABLE	RIFFRAFF	CATERING
PROTEASE	RINGDOVE	SIMULATE	TAILPIPE	UNTANGLE	SANSERIF	CHANGING
PROTÉGÉE	RINGSIDE	SINECURE	TAKEHOME	UNUSABLE	STANDOFF	CHARGING
PROTRUDE	RIVALISE	SINKHOLE	TANGIBLE	URBANIZE	TIPSTAFF	CHARMING
PROVABLE	RIVERINE	SIXPENCE	TAPENADE	URETHANE	TRADEOFF	CHEATING
PROVINCE	ROADSIDE	SIZEABLE	TAPHOUSE	URSULINE	WEREWOLF	CHECKING
PRUDENCE	ROCHDALE	SLOWPOKE	TARTRATE	VALIDATE	WOODRUFF	CHEERING
PTOMAINE	ROOMMATE	SNOWLINE	TARTUFFE	VALKYRIE	WRITEOFF	CHILLING
PUNCTURE	ROSALINE	SOCIABLE	TEAMMATE	VALUABLE	YOURSELF	CHOOSING
PUNITIVE	ROTENONE	SODALITE	TEARABLE	VAPORIZE	ACCUSING	CHOPPING
PURCHASE	ROUGHAGE	SOFTWARE	TELEVISE	VARIABLE	ADMIRING	CLADDING
PURSLANE	ROULETTE	SOLITUDE	TELLTALE	VARIANCE	AGREEING	CLANGING
PUSHBIKE	RUMINATE	SOLSTICE	TEMPLATE	VARICOSE	ALARMING	CLAPPING
PUTATIVE	RUNCIBLE	SOLVABLE	TENEBRAE	VEGETATE	ALLOWING	CLASHING
QUADRATE	RUSHMORE	SOMETIME	TENTACLE	VENERATE	ALLURING	CLASPING
QUAGMIRE	SABOTAGE	SORBONNE	TERRIBLE	VERBIAGE	ANNOYING	CLEANING
QUARTILE	SADDUCEE	SPILLAGE	TERYLENE	VERJUICE	ANYTHING	CLEARING
QUATORZE	SALEABLE	SPIRACLE	TESTICLE	VERLAINE	AQUALUNG	CLIMBING
QUAYSIDE	SALIVATE	SPITFIRE	THEBAINE	VERONESE	ASPIRING	CLINGING
QUENELLE	SAMPHIRE	SPOILAGE	THEORIZE	VERSICLE	ASSUMING	CLIPPING
QUIETUDE	SANGUINE	SPOLIATE	THIAMINE	VICARAGE	ATHELING	CLOTHING
QUOTABLE	SANITIZE	SPORTIVE	THROTTLE	VIGNETTE	AVAILING	CLUBBING
RACLETTE	SAPONITE	SPRINKLE	THURIBLE	VINCIBLE	BABBLING	COACHING
RADIANCE	SAPPHIRE	SQUABBLE	TINCTURE	VIOLENCE	BAFFLING	COLORING
RAGSTONE	SATIRIZE	SQUADDIE	TIRESOME	VISELIKE	BANTLING	COUCHING
RAISONNÉ	SATURATE	SQUEEGEE	TITANITE	VITALIZE	BECOMING	COUGHING
RAPECAKE	SAWHORSE	SQUIGGLE	TITIVATE	VOCALIZE	BEESWING	COUNTING
RATEABLE	SAXATILE	STAGNATE	TITMOUSE	VOCATIVE	BEETLING	COUPLING
REACTIVE	SCARFACE	STAMPEDE	TOILSOME	VOIDANCE	BLACKING	COVERING
READABLE	SCAVENGE	STANHOPE	TOLERATE	VOLATILE	BLACKLEG	CRACKING
REALTIME	SCHEDULE	STANNITE	TOLLGATE	VOLPLANE	BLEEDING	CRAWLING
REASSUME	SCHMOOZE	STAPHYLE	TORTOISE	VOLTAIRE	BLENDING	CRINGING
REASSURE	SCRABBLE	STARGAZE	TOTALIZE	VOWELIZE	BLESSING	CROONING
RECHARGE	SCRAMBLE	STEATITE	TOULOUSE	WALKYRIE	BLINDING	CROSSING
RECOURSE	SCRAPPLE	STEERAGE	TRAMLINE	WARDROBE	BLINKING	CROWNING
RECREATE	SCRIBBLE	STELLATE	TRAVERSE	WARHORSE	BLOOMING	CRUSHING
REDEFINE	SCROUNGE	STOCKADE	TREASURE	WARPLANE	BLURRING	DAUNTING
REDOUBLE	SEABORNE	STOPPAGE	TREATISE	WASHABLE	BLUSHING	DAZZLING
REFRINGE	SEAPLANE	STRADDLE	TREELINE	WEARABLE	BOARDING	DECAYING
REGICIDE	SEASCAPE	STRAGGLE	TRIANGLE	WHARFAGE	BOASTING	DIALLING
REGULATE	SEASHORE	STRANGLE	TRICYCLE	WILDFIRE	BOTTLING	DOUBTING
REHEARSE	SEDATIVE	STRICKLE	TRIPTANE	WILDLIFE	BOUNCING	DRAINING
REINSURE	SELASSIE	STRUGGLE	TROLLOPE	WINDPIPE	BRAGGING	DREAMING
REKINDLE	SELBORNE	SUBLEASE	TROMBONE	WISEACRE	BREAKING	DRESSING
RELATIVE	SELENITE	SUBMERGE	TROTLINE	WISHBONE	BREEDING	DRIFTING
RELEGATE	SELFMADE	SUBTENSE	TRUNCATE	WOLFBANE	BRIDGING	DRINKING
RELIABLE	SELFSAME	SUBTITLE	TUBENOSE	WOMANIZE	BRIEFING	DRIPPING
RELIANCE	SELVEDGE	SUCHLIKE	TUBERCLE	WOODBINE	BRIMMING	DROOPING
RELOCATE	SEMITONE	SUDANESE	TUBEROSE	WORKABLE	BRINGING	DROPPING
RENEGADE	SENSIBLE	SUFFRAGE	TUNICATE	WORKMATE	BRISLING	DROWNING
RENOUNCE	SENTENCE	SUITABLE	TURNPIKE	WRECKAGE	BROILING	DRUBBING
RENOVATE	SEPARATE	SUITCASE	TUTELAGE	WYCLIFFE	BROODING	DRUMMING
REPARTEE	SEQUENCE	SULPHATE	TWOPIECE	XANTIPPE	BROWNING	DUCKLING
REPHRASE	SERAFILE	SULPHIDE	TYPEFACE	YOSEMITE	BROWSING	DUMPLING
REPOUSSÉ	SERENADE	SUNBATHE	TYROSINE	YULETIDE	BRUISING	DWELLING
REPRIEVE	SEROTYPE	SUNDANCE	ULCERATE	ZIBELINE	BUBBLING	EMERGING
RESEMBLE	SEWERAGE	SUNSHADE	ULTIMATE	ZIMBABWE	BUCKLING	ENDURING
RESETTLE	SHIITAKE	SUNSHINE	UNCHASTE	ZOETROPE	BUILDING	ENGAGING
RESOLUTE	SHINBONE	SURICATE	UNCOUPLE	ZOOPHYTE	BULLFROG	ENTICING
RESONATE	SHIPMATE	SURPLICE	UNDERAGE	ZOOSPORE	BULLRING	ERECTING
RESOURCE	SHOELACE	SURPRISE	UNDERLIE	APERITIF	BULLYRAG	EVENSONG
RESPONSE	SHOETREE	SUSPENSE	UNDULATE	BLASTOFF	BUMBLING	EXACTING
RETICULE	SHORTAGE	SYBARITE	UNFREEZE	DANDRUFF	BUNGLING	EXCITING
RETRIEVE	SHOWCASE	SYCAMORE	UNGULATE	HANDCUFF	BURSTING	EXISTING
REUSABLE	SIDELINE	SYLLABLE	UNICYCLE	KERCHIEF	BUSTLING	EXULTING
REVANCHE	SIDERITE	SYNCLINE	UNIONIZE	LANGLAUF	CANOEING	FAINTING

FARTHING	KNOCKING	RELAXING	SPENDING	TWISTING	BROWNISH	LUNGFISH
FETCHING	LACEWING	RELAYING	SPIFFING	UNCARING	CALABASH	MACHEATH
FETTLING	LAUGHING	REPAYING	SPINNING	UNDERDOG	CENOTAPH	MEGALITH
FIDDLING	LEACHING	RETIRING	SPITTING	UNENDING	CHILDISH	MEREDITH
FIELDING	LEAPFROG	REVIVING	SPOILING	UNERRING	CHURLISH	MISHMASH
FIGHTING	LEARNING	RIESLING	SPORTING	UNFADING	CHUTZPAH	MISMATCH
FLAGGING	LEFTWING	RIPPLING	SPOTTING	UNIFYING	CLANNISH	MONKFISH
FLAPPING	LIFELONG	RIVETING	SPURNING	UPCOMING	CLIQUISH	MONMOUTH
FLASHING	LIGHTING	ROASTING	STABBING	UPRISING	CLOWNISH	MONOLITH
FLEETING	LIMITING	RUMBLING	STABLING	VALETING	CRAWFISH	MONTEITH
FLEISHIG	LIVELONG	RUSTLING	STAFFING	VAULTING	CRAYFISH	MUSQUASH
FLIPPING	LOATHING	SADDLING	STALKING	VIETCONG	CROMLECH	NARGILEH
FLIRTING	LOWERING	SCALDING	STANDING	VISITING	DECLUTCH	NEHEMIAH
FLOATING	LOWLYING	SCANNING	STARLING	VOMITING	DEMOLISH	NONESUCH
FLOGGING	LYNCHING	SCATHING	STARTING	WALTZING	DESPATCH	NUTHATCH
FLOODING	MAHJONGG	SCHEMING	STARVING	WAMBLING	DEVILISH	OILCLOTH
FLOORING	MANAGING	SCOFFING	STEALING	WATCHDOG	DIMINISH	OLIGARCH
FLUSHING	MANTLING	SCOLDING	STEERING	WATCHING	DISPATCH	OUTMATCH
FOLKSONG	MATCHING	SCOURING	STERLING	WATERBUG	DOGTOOTH	OUTREACH
FONDLING	MEALYBUG	SCOWLING	STICKING	WATERING	DOGWATCH	OUTWEIGH
FOOTLING	MEDDLING	SEAGOING	STIFLING	WAVERING	DWARFISH	OVERMUCH
FOUNDING	MENACING	SEEDLING	STINGING	WEAKLING	ELDRITCH	PARASHAH
FREEZING	MIDDLING	SEETHING	STINKING	WEIGHING	ELEVENTH	PENTARCH
FROSTING	MODELING	SHANTUNG	STIRLING	WHACKING	ENCROACH	PERIANTH
FRUITING	MOTORING	SHEEPDOG	STIRRING	WHEEZING	ENTRENCH	PETRARCH
FUMBLING	MOULDING	SHELVING	STOCKING	WHIPPING	EPIGRAPH	PLUTARCH
GAMBLING	MOUNTING	SHIELING	STOPPING	WHIRLING	ETHNARCH	PLYMOUTH
GANGLING	MOURNING	SHIFTING	STORMING	WHITLING	EYETOOTH	POLYARCH
GLANCING	MUMBLING	SHILLING	STRIKING	WHOOPING	FEVERISH	POLYMATH
GLEAMING	NESTLING	SHIPPING	STRIVING	WHOPPING	FIENDISH	POTLATCH
GLOAMING	NIBELUNG	SHOCKING	STUFFING	WIDENING	FIFTIETH	PRIGGISH
GLOATING	NIGGLING	SHOOTING	STUNNING	WINNIPEG	FLATFISH	PURPLISH
GNASHING	NORTHING	SHOPPING	SUCKLING	WITCHING	FLOURISH	RANELAGH
GOLLIWOG	NURSLING	SHOUTING	SUPERBUG	WOBBLING	FOOTPATH	REPROACH
GOOSEGOG	OBLIGING	SIDELONG	SWANSONG	WORRYING	FORSOOTH	RESEARCH
GRAINING	OFFERING	SIGHTING	SWARMING	WRAPPING	FORTIETH	RETRENCH
GRASPING	ONCOMING	SINGSONG	SWEARING	WRINGING	FRANKISH	ROMANSCH
GRAYLING	OPPOSING	SIZZLING	SWEATING	WRITHING	FREAKISH	ROSEFISH
GREENBAG	ORDERING	SKIDDING	SWEEPING	YACHTING	FRUMPISH	SALTBUSH
GREENING	OUTGOING	SKILLING	SWELLING	YEARLING	FURLOUGH	SANDWICH
GREETING	OUTLYING	SKIPPING	SWERVING	YEARLONG	GALLUMPH	SAVANNAH
GRILLING	OVERHANG	SKIRTING	SWILLING	YEARNING	GHOULISH	SCOTTISH
GRINDING	PADDLING	SKULKING	SWIMMING	YIELDING	GLUMPISH	SEAFORTH
GRIPPING	PAINTING	SLANGING	SWINGING	ADMONISH	GOLDFISH	SHADRACH
GROOMING	PANELING	SLANTING	SWIRLING	AEROLITH	GREENISH	SHAVUOTH
GROUPING	PEARLING	SLAPBANG	TAPERING	ALBERICH	GUNSMITH	SHEEPISH
GROUTING	PEDDLING	SLEEPING	TEACHING	ALLOPATH	HAGGADAH	SHREWISH
GROWLING	PERSHING	SLIPPING	TEETHING	ALTHOUGH	HANUKKAH	SIXTIETH
GRUDGING	PIDDLING	SLUMMING	TEMPTING	AMARANTH	HAVDALAH	SKIRMISH
HABSBURG	PIERCING	SLURRING	THIEVING	ANAGLYPH	HAWFINCH	SKITTISH
HAPSBURG	PLANKING	SMASHING	THINKING	APPROACH	HEPTARCH	SLAPDASH
HATCHING	PLANNING	SMELTING	THINNING	ARAMANTH	HEREWITH	SLUGGISH
HAUNTING	PLEADING	SMOCKING	THUMPING	ASTONISH	HICCOUGH	SLUTTISH
HEADLONG	PLEASING	SNEAKING	TICKLING	BACKLASH	HIERARCH	SNOBBISH
HECKLING	PLUCKING	SNEERING	TINGLING	BARDOLPH	HUSHHUSH	STANDISH
HEDGEHOG	PLUMBING	SNEEZING	TOUCHING	BAYREUTH	HYACINTH	STARFISH
HIRELING	PLUNGING	SNORTING	TOWELING	BEGORRAH	INASMUCH	STRENGTH
HOARDING	POLLIWOG	SOBERING	TOWERING	BEHEMOTH	INGROWTH	TAMWORTH
HOBBLING	PRESSING	SOOTHING	TRACKING	BELLPUSH	INTRENCH	TARBOOSH
HONGKONG	PRINTING	SOUCHONG	TRAILING	BEQUEATH	JEPHTHAH	TEACLOTH
HURDLING	PUZZLING	SOUNDING	TRAINING	BESMIRCH	JEREMIAH	TETRARCH
IMPOSING	QUILTING	SOURCING	TRIFLING	BIOGRAPH	KNEEHIGH	THIEVISH
INCOMING	QUISLING	SPANKING	TRILLING	BLACKISH	KREPLACH	THOROUGH
INDEXING	RAMBLING	SPANNING	TRIMMING	BLANDISH	KUFFIYEH	TICKLISH
INVITING	RATTLING	SPARKING	TRIPLING	BLOWFISH	LADYFISH	TINSMITH
JANGLING	RECEDING	SPARRING	TROOPING	BONEFISH	LANGUISH	TOISEACH
JUGGLING	REEDLING	SPAWNING	TRUCKING	BOSWORTH	LIVERISH	TOLBOOTH
KINDLING	REIGNING	SPEAKING	TRUSTING	BRACKISH	LULWORTH	TOPNOTCH
KNITTING	RELATING	SPELLING	TWIRLING	BRANDISH	LUMPFISH	TOVARICH

TRIGLYPH	ZAKOUSKI	HOODWINK	TEAMWORK	CHEMICAL	FIDUCIAL	MANORIAL
TRIGRAPH	ZUCCHINI	HORNBOOK	TELEMARK	CHERWELL	FIREBALL	MARGINAL
TRIPTYCH	AARDVARK	HUMPBACK	TEXTBOOK	CINEREAL	FISHMEAL	MARSHALL
TRISTICH	ASTERISK	ICEBLINK	TICKTACK	CLERICAL	FLYWHEEL	MATERIAL
VANBRUGH	BACKPACK	IRONWORK	TICKTOCK	CLINICAL	FOLDEROL	MATERNAL
VANQUISH	BALDRICK	JIMCRACK	TIDEMARK	CLODPOLL	FOOTBALL	MEDIEVAL
VERANDAH	BALLCOCK	JOYSTICK	TIEBREAK	COATTAIL	FOOTFALL	MEMORIAL
VERMOUTH	BALLPARK	KAZACHOK	TOMAHAWK	COCKEREL	FORCEFUL	MENSURAL
VIPERISH	BANKBOOK	KICKBACK	TURNBACK	COCKTAIL	FORESAIL	MERCIFUL
VISIGOTH	BAREBACK	KINSFOLK	TURNCOCK	COGWHEEL	FORETELL	METHANOL
WEAKFISH	BASILISK	KITEMARK	WHIPJACK	COLONIAL	FORKTAIL	METRICAL
WELLNIGH	BAUDRICK	KNAPSACK	WINDHOEK	COLORFUL	FRUITFUL	MINSTREL
WHIPLASH	BENEDICK	KNOTWORK	WINDSOCK	COLOSSAL	FUNEREAL	MIRTHFUL
WOMANISH	BILLHOOK	LAIDBACK	WOODCOCK	COMMUNAL	GERMINAL	MISSPELL
XENOLITH	BISMARCK	LANDLOCK	WOODWORK	CONJUGAL	GINGIVAL	MOLEHILL
ZEDEKIAH	BLUEBACK	LANDMARK	WOOLPACK	CORNHILL	GLASSFUL	MONAURAL
ALBINONI	BOBOLINK	LIMERICK	WOOLSACK	CORNMEAL	GOLFBALL	MONOHULL
AMORETTI	BODYWORK	LIPSTICK	WORDBOOK	CORNWALL	GOODWILL	MONORAIL
BAHRAINI	BOOKMARK	LOVESICK	WORKBOOK	CORPORAL	GOOFBALL	MOTHBALL
BANDITTI	BOOKWORM	MAVERICK	YEARBOOK	COYSTRIL	GRACEFUL	MOURNFUL
BENGHAZI	BOOTNECK	MOORCOCK	ZWIEBACK	CRIMINAL	GRATEFUL	MOUTHFUL
BERIBERI	BRATPACK	MOREPORK	AASVOGEL	CRITICAL	GUNMETAL	MUSCATEL
BOUZOUKI	CAKEWALK	NEWSHAWK	ABNORMAL	CROMWELL	GUTTURAL	MYSTICAL
BRINDISI	CHARLOCK	NEWSPEAK	AEROFOIL	CULTURAL	HABITUAL	MYTHICAL
BROCCOLI	CHIPMUNK	NICKNACK	ALLUVIAL	CYCLICAL	HALFFULL	NATIONAL
CHAPATTI	CLAWBACK	NONSTICK	APPROVAL	DAFFODIL	HANDBALL	NAUTICAL
CONFETTI	COATRACK	NOTEBOOK	ARBOREAL	DECRETAL	HANDBILL	NEMBUTAL
COTOPAXI	COMEBACK	OFFBREAK	ARMORIAL	DEMERSAL	HANDRAIL	NEWSREEL
DAIQUIRI	COOKBOOK	OILSLICK	ARTERIAL	DEMURRAL	HANGNAIL	NOTARIAL
DISRAELI	COPYBOOK	ONETRACK	ASPHODEL	DIAGONAL	HANNIBAL	NOTIONAL
DJIBOUTI	CRUMMOCK	OPENWORK	ATYPICAL	DIPHENYL	HAREBELL	NUTSHELL
GIOVANNI	DABCHICK	OUTBREAK	AUTUMNAL	DIPTERAL	HEELBALL	OENOPHIL
GRAFFITI	DAYBREAK	OUTFLANK	BALLGIRL	DISHEVEL	HERSCHEL	OFFICIAL
GRIMALDI	DEADLOCK	OVERBOOK	BALMORAL	DISLOYAL	HIGHBALL	OPTIONAL
GUJARATI	DIPSTICK	OVERLOOK	BANDEROL	DISPOSAL	HORMONAL	ORIENTAL
HELSINKI	DRAWBACK	OVERWORK	BANKROLL	DOCTORAL	HORNBILL	ORIGINAL
KACHAHRI	ECOFREAK	PASSBOOK	BARONIAL	DOGGEREL	HORNTAIL	OVERFILL
KALAHARI	ENIWETOK	PAYCHECK	BASEBALL	DOGSTAIL	HOSPITAL	OVERFULL
KOHLRABI	FASTBACK	PICKLOCK	BASINFUL	DOORBELL	HYDROXYL	OVERHAUL
LITERATI	FATSTOCK	PICKWICK	BECHAMEL	DOORSILL	HYPOGEAL	OVERKILL
MACARONI	FEEDBACK	PINPRICK	BELLYFUL	DOTTEREL	IMMANUEL	PALATIAL
MAHARANI	FIREBACK	PLAYBACK	BETRAYAL	DOUBTFUL	IMMORTAL	PARALLEL
MARIACHI	FIREWORK	POCKMARK	BIANNUAL	DOVETAIL	IMPERIAL	PARENTAL
MERCALLI	FISHHOOK	POSTMARK	BIBLICAL	DOWNFALL	INFERNAL	PARIETAL
MISSOURI	FLAPJACK	RAGNARÖK	BIENNIAL	DOWNHILL	INFORMAL	PARSIFAL
MORBILLI	FLATPACK	REDBRICK	BINOMIAL	DREADFUL	INGUINAL	PASTORAL
NAGASAKI	FOOTWORK	REDSHANK	BISEXUAL	DUCKBILL	INIMICAL	PATERNAL
OUISTITI	FOREDECK	RODERICK	BLISSFUL	DUMBBELL	INTEGRAL	PEACEFUL
PAGANINI	FORELOCK	RUCKSACK	BLUEBELL	DUNGHILL	INTERNAL	PECTORAL
PASTRAMI	FOREMILK	RULEBOOK	BOASTFUL	DUODENAL	INTERPOL	PEDESTAL
PEPERONI	FORMWORK	SALTLICK	BOATBILL	EDGEHILL	INTERVAL	PELLMELL
PHILIPPI	FORSLACK	SANDBANK	BONSPIEL	EGGSHELL	IRONICAL	PERCEVAL
PIRANESI	FRETWORK	SHAGBARK	BORSTALL	EMMANUEL	ISOGONAL	PERCIVAL
PIROZHKI	FULLBACK	SHAMROCK	BOTHWELL	EMPYREAL	ISTANBUL	PERSONAL
RENMINBI	GIMCRACK	SHELDUCK	BRACHIAL	ENTHRALL	JUDICIAL	PHILOMEL
RESPIGHI	GOBSMACK	SHERLOCK	CALLGIRL	EPIDURAL	KEELHAUL	PHYSICAL
RIGATONI	GREENOCK	SHOPTALK	CAMPBELL	ESCORIAL	KOMSOMOL	PIGSWILL
ROSSETTI	GRIDLOCK	SIDEKICK	CANNIBAL	ESPECIAL	LANDFALL	PINWHEEL
SHANGHAI	GROSBEAK	SIDEWALK	CARDINAL	ESPOUSAL	LANDFILL	PLATEFUL
SUKIYAKI	HABAKKUK	SKINWORK	CARNIVAL	ESTOPPEL	LITTORAL	PLAYBILL
SVENGALI	HALLMARK	SKIPJACK	CAROUSAL	ETHEREAL	LONGHAUL	PLAYGIRL
TANDOORI	HANDBOOK	SLAPJACK	CAROUSEL	EVENTFUL	LUPERCAL	PLIMSOLL
TERIYAKI	HARDBACK	SOAPBARK	CARRYALL	EVENTUAL	MACKEREL	POETICAL
TRANSKEI	HARDHACK	SOFTBACK	CATECHOL	EXTERNAL	MADRIGAL	PONYTAIL
TZATZIKI	HARDTACK	STEENBOK	CEREBRAL	FAITHFUL	MAINSAIL	PORTUGAL
VESPUCCI	HAYSTACK	STOPCOCK	CERVICAL	FANCIFUL	MALARIAL	POWERFUL
VIRTUOSI	HEADMARK	TAILBACK	CESSPOOL	FARCICAL	MANDRILL	PRAIRIAL
WATERSKI	HOMESICK	TAMARACK	CHARCOAL	FAREWELL	MANGONEL	PRANDIAL
YAKITORI	HOMEWORK	TAMARISK	CHEERFUL	FESTIVAL	MANIACAL	PRATFALL

PRENATAL	UNLAWFUL	CORUNDUM	LUTETIUM	SOLARIUM	AMBITION	CAERLEON
PRIMEVAL	UNSOCIAL	CRONYISM	LYRICISM	SOLECISM	AMERICAN	CALDERON
PRODIGAL	UPHEAVAL	CYNICISM	MARJORAM	SONOGRAM	AMUNDSEN	CALFSKIN
PROPOSAL	VARIETAL	DARKROOM	MEMORIAM	SPECTRUM	ANACREON	CAMBRIAN
PROTOCOL	VAUXHALL	DAYDREAM	MERISTEM	SPECULUM	ANDERSON	CAMEROON
PROXIMAL	VENEREAL	DELIRIUM	MESODERM	SPHAGNUM	ANDORRAN	CAMPAIGN
PUFFBALL	VENGEFUL	DIAZEPAM	MOMENTUM	STOICISM	ANGLICAN	CAMPTOWN
PUNCTUAL	VERTICAL	DISCLAIM	MONADISM	STRABISM	ANTIPHON	CANADIAN
QUIRINAL	VESPERAL	DUODENUM	MONOGRAM	STRIATUM	APHELION	CAPUCHIN
RAINFALL	VICARIAL	DWARFISM	MONTCALM	SUDARIUM	APOLLYON	CARDIGAN
RATIONAL	VIRGINAL	DYNAMISM	MOONBEAM	SUNCREAM	APPLETON	CAREWORN
REBUTTAL	VISCERAL	ECTODERM	MUHARRAM	TANTALUM	ARAMAEAN	CARILLON
REFERRAL	VORTICAL	ELECTRUM	MUSHROOM	TAPEWORM	ARCADIAN	CAULDRON
REGIONAL	WASHBOWL	EMBOLISM	MYCELIUM	TELEFILM	ARMENIAN	CEPHALIN
REMEDIAL	WASTEFUL	EMPORIUM	NATURISM	TELEGRAM	ARTESIAN	CERULEAN
REMITTAL	WATCHFUL	ENCOMIUM	NEPOTISM	TESTATUM	ASCIDIAN	CETACEAN
REPRISAL	WHIMBREL	ENDODERM	NEWSROOM	THALLIUM	ASSASSIN	CHAIRMAN
RESIDUAL	WILDFELL	ENSIFORM	NIHILISM	THRALDOM	ASSYRIAN	CHALDEAN
REVERSAL	WILDFOWL	ENTRYISM	NOBELIUM	TITANISM	ASUNCION	CHALDRON
RIGHTFUL	WINDFALL	ERGOTISM	NOMOGRAM	TITANIUM	ATHENIAN	CHAMPION
RINGTAIL	WINDGALL	ESCAPISM	OMNIFORM	TOMENTUM	AUBUSSON	CHAPERON
RINGWALL	WINDMILL	EULOGIUM	OPTIMISM	TRILLIUM	AUCASSIN	CHAPLAIN
ROLLCALL	WRATHFUL	EUPHUISM	ORGANISM	TRISTRAM	AUDITION	CHESSMAN
SCORNFUL	WRONGFUL	EUROPIUM	PACIFISM	TRITICUM	AURELIAN	CHESSMEN
SEASHELL	YOUTHFUL	EXORCISM	PALUDISM	TYMPANUM	AUSTRIAN	CHILDREN
SEASONAL	ZODIACAL	EXORDIUM	PARADIGM	UNCIFORM	AUTOBAHN	CHILTERN
SENTINEL	ABOMASUM	FACTOTUM	PAROXYSM	UNDERARM	AVERSION	CHINAMAN
SHAMEFUL	ACCUSTOM	FATALISM	PATAGIUM	UNIONISM	AVIATION	CHRISTEN
SHOEBILL	ACTINIUM	FEMINISM	PENDULUM	UNUNBIUM	AVULSION	CINNAMON
SHOWGIRL	ACTIVISM	FILARIUM	PERIDERM	UPSTREAM	BACKSPIN	CITATION
SHRAPNEL	ADDENDUM	FLATWORM	PHANTASM	VANADIUM	BACTRIAN	CIVILIAN
SIDEREAL	AEROGRAM	FOREDOOM	PHORMIUM	VARIFORM	BAHAMIAN	CLANSMAN
SILKTAIL	ALBURNUM	FRANCIUM	PISIFORM	VARIORUM	BANDSMAN	CLAVECIN
SKELETAL	ALGORISM	FRENULUM	PLATFORM	VERBATIM	BARBICAN	CLIVEDEN
SKILLFUL	ALIENISM	FUSIFORM	PLATINUM	VEXILLUM	BARBIZON	COACHMAN
SLOTHFUL	ALLUVIUM	FUTURISM	PLAYROOM	VIATICUM	BARGEMAN	COERCION
SNOWBALL	ALTRUISM	GALBANUM	PLECTRUM	VIBURNUM	BASEBORN	COGNOMEN
SNOWFALL	ALUMINUM	GERANIUM	PLEONASM	VINCULUM	BATAVIAN	COHESION
SOFTBALL	ANEURYSM	GUAIACUM	POLONIUM	VITALISM	BAVARIAN	COLLAGEN
SPADEFUL	ANGSTROM	HAIRWORM	POOLROOM	VIVARIUM	BEARSKIN	COLOPHON
SPANDREL	ANTEROOM	HALFTERM	POPPADOM	WARDROOM	BEHOLDEN	COLUMBAN
SPECTRAL	APHORISM	HEADROOM	PRIAPISM	WASHROOM	BENENDEN	COMEDIAN
SPITEFUL	APOTHEGM	HEBRAISM	PROCLAIM	WIREWORM	BENJAMIN	COMEDOWN
SPOONFUL	AQUARIUM	HEDONISM	PTYALISM	WOODWORM	BESPOKEN	COMPLAIN
SQUIRREL	ARCHAISM	HEIRLOOM	PUDENDUM	WORKROOM	BETATRON	CORDOVAN
STAYSAIL	ASCIDIUM	HEXAGRAM	PUGILISM	XERAPHIM	BETJEMAN	CORDWAIN
STENDHAL	BACKROOM	HINDUISM	PYRIFORM	ZOOSPERM	BIATHLON	CORMORAN
STILWELL	BALLROOM	HOLOGRAM	REAFFIRM	ABERDEEN	BILLYCAN	CORSICAN
SUBTOTAL	BASIDIUM	HOOKWORM	REFUGIUM	ABINGDON	BISCAYAN	COUPERIN
SUICIDAL	BATHROOM	HORNBEAM	RESIDUUM	ABLATION	BLUDGEON	COXSWAIN
SUPERNAL	BEERBOHM	HUMANISM	RESTROOM	ABLUTION	BOBBYPIN	CREATION
SURGICAL	BLENHEIM	IDEALISM	RINGWORM	ABORTION	BODLEIAN	CRICHTON
SURVIVAL	BOOKROOM	IDEOGRAM	RUBIDIUM	ABRASION	BOEOTIAN	CRISPIAN
TACTICAL	BOOKWORM	IDIOGRAM	SALEROOM	ABUTILON	BOGEYMAN	CROATIAN
TAFFRAIL	BOTULISM	INOCULUM	SAMARIUM	ACROMION	BOHEMIAN	CRUMHORN
TASTEFUL	BROUGHAM	INTERCOM	SCANDIUM	ADDITION	BOLIVIAN	CULLINAN
TEETOTAL	BUDDHISM	IRISHISM	SCRIPTUM	ADHESION	BONDSMAN	CULLODEN
TEMPORAL	CAPSICUM	ISOTHERM	SCYBALUM	ADOPTION	BRABAZON	CULVERIN
TERMINAL	CARDAMOM	JEREBOAM	SEALYHAM	AFFUSION	BRETHREN	CYANOGEN
THANKFUL	CEMENTUM	JEROBOAM	SELENIUM	AGNATION	BRIGHTEN	CYCLAMEN
TINTAGEL	CEREBRUM	JINGOISM	SERAPHIM	AGRARIAN	BRIGHTON	DAIRYMAN
TOPLEVEL	CHARTISM	KHARTOUM	SERIATIM	AKKADIAN	BROMPTON	DAVIDSON
TRANQUIL	CHERUBIM	KILOGRAM	SHEIKDOM	ALBANIAN	BRYOZOAN	DECISION
TRIBUNAL	CHRISTOM	LABURNUM	SHIPWORM	ALDERMAN	BUCKBEAN	DEERSKIN
TRITICAL	CHROMIUM	LAUDANUM	SHOWROOM	ALEUTIAN	BUCKSKIN	DELETION
TROPICAL	CIBORIUM	LEGALISM	SICKROOM	ALGERIAN	BULLETIN	DELUSION
TRUSTFUL	CINGULUM	LINOLEUM	SILKWORM	ALLERGEN	BULLHORN	DEMIJOHN
TRUTHFUL	COLIFORM	LONGTERM	SINAPISM	ALLUSION	BUSULFAN	DEMOTION
TUTORIAL	COLISEUM	LUKEWARM	SLOWWORM	ALSATIAN	CABOCHON	DERISION

DEUTERON	FORSAKEN	ISTHMIAN	MUTCHKIN	POTEMKIN	SOLUTION	VENETIAN
DEVONIAN	FOUNTAIN	IVOIRIEN	MYRMIDON	PRESSMAN	SOUTHERN	VEXATION
DEVOTION	FOURTEEN	JACOBEAN	NAMIBIAN	PRUSSIAN	SPACEMAN	VOCATION
DIAPASON	FRACTION	JAMAICAN	NAPOLEON	PUBLICAN	SPECIMEN	VOLITION
DIELDRIN	FRANKLIN	JERRYCAN	NEGATION	PULLDOWN	SPELLMAN	VOLSCIAN
DILATION	FRAULEIN	JETTISON	NEOMYCIN	PUSHDOWN	SPITTOON	WARFARIN
DILUTION	FREETOWN	JONATHAN	NEWHAVEN	QUADROON	SQUADRON	WASHDOWN
DIOCESAN	FRESHMAN	JUNCTION	NIDATION	QUATRAIN	STAGHORN	WATCHMAN
DISTRAIN	FREUDIAN	KESTEVEN	NIGERIAN	QUATRAIN	STALLION	WATERMAN
DISUNION	FRICTION	KINGSTON	NIGERIEN	QUESTION	STEAPSIN	WELSHMAN
DIVISION	FRIGHTEN	KORRIGAN	NINETEEN	QUINTAIN	STOCKMAN	WESLEYAN
DOMINION	FRONTMAN	KRUMHORN	NITROGEN	RAMBUTAN	STOREMAN	WINDBURN
DONATION	FRUITION	LACONIAN	NOBLEMAN	RAMEQUIN	STRAITEN	WINGSPAN
DOUBLOON	FUGLEMAN	LAMBSKIN	NORSEMAN	RASPUTIN	STRICKEN	WOODSMAN
DOWNTOWN	FUNCTION	LEADSMAN	NORSEMEN	RATTIGAN	STUBBORN	XENOPHON
DOWNTURN	GALILEAN	LECITHIN	NORTHERN	REACTION	STURGEON	YATAGHAN
DRYCLEAN	GANGLION	LEGATION	NOTATION	REASSIGN	SUBHUMAN	ZEPPELIN
DURATION	GARRISON	LENGTHEN	OBLATION	REAWAKEN	SUBURBAN	ACAPULCO
DUTCHMAN	GEORGIAN	LIBATION	OBLIVION	REDESIGN	SULLIVAN	ALFRESCO
DYNATRON	GHANAIAN	LIBERIAN	OBSIDIAN	RELATION	SUMERIAN	AMARETTO
ECLOSION	GIRONDIN	LIEGEMAN	OCCASION	RELIGION	SUPERMAN	AMORETTO
EFFUSION	GLOBULIN	LIFESPAN	OCTAROON	REPLEVIN	SUZERAIN	ANTIHERO
EGYPTIAN	GLYCERIN	LINCHPIN	OEDIPEAN	RESTRAIN	SWANSKIN	ARPEGGIO
EIGHTEEN	GLYCOGEN	LINESMAN	OLYMPIAN	REVISION	TACITURN	AUTOGIRO
EINSTEIN	GOATSKIN	LINNAEAN	OMDURMAN	RIFLEMAN	TAHITIAN	AUTOGYRO
EJECTION	GONFALON	LOCATION	OMISSION	RIPARIAN	TAILSPIN	AVOGADRO
ELECTION	GRANDSON	LONGHORN	ONSCREEN	RIVERAIN	TALISMAN	BALLYHOO
ELECTRON	GRAVAMEN	LOVELORN	OOPHORON	ROBINSON	TARRAGON	BARGELLO
EMBLAZON	GRIDIRON	LUNCHEON	OPENPLAN	ROENTGEN	TAXATION	BORDELLO
EMBOLDEN	GROSCHEN	LUTHERAN	OPHIDIAN	ROGATION	TEASPOON	BORODINO
EMERSION	GUARDIAN	MACAROON	OPTICIAN	ROMANIAN	TEFILLIN	CALLISTO
EMISSION	GUERIDON	MACMAHON	ORCADIAN	ROTATION	TELETHON	CASTRATO
EMOTICON	GUIANIAN	MADWOMAN	OVERTURN	SAINFOIN	TENNYSON	CAUDILLO
EMPYREAN	GUMPTION	MAGELLAN	OXYMORON	SALESMAN	TERRAPIN	CICISBEO
EMULSION	GYRATION	MAGICIAN	OXYTOCIN	SANCTION	TETRAGON	COCKATOO
ENDYMION	HAMILTON	MAINTAIN	PAKISTAN	SAUCEPAN	THESPIAN	COLORADO
ENVISION	HANDYMAN	MALAWIAN	PALMITIN	SCALLION	THIRTEEN	COMMANDO
EPHESIAN	HARRIDAN	MANDARIN	PANGOLIN	SCANSION	THOLEPIN	CONCERTO
EPIPLOON	HARRISON	MANDOLIN	PANNIKIN	SCHUMANN	THOMPSON	CONTANGO
EQUATION	HAWAIIAN	MANNIKIN	PANTALON	SCISSION	THRACIAN	CONTINUO
ERECTION	HAWTHORN	MARATHON	PANTHEON	SCORPION	THREATEN	CORNETTO
ERIKSSON	HEIGHTEN	MARKDOWN	PAPILLON	SCOTSMAN	THROMBIN	CORRAGIO
ERUPTION	HELMSMAN	MARKSMAN	PARAFFIN	SCRIABIN	TOBOGGAN	CRUZEIRO
ESTONIAN	HENCHMAN	MAROQUIN	PARISIAN	SCULLION	TOWNSMAN	ELDORADO
ESTRAGON	HENEQUEN	MARZIPAN	PARMESAN	SEALSKIN	TRACTION	ESPRESSO
ESTROGEN	HEPTAGON	MASCARON	PARTHIAN	SEDATION	TRASHCAN	EXPRESSO
ETRURIAN	HERDSMAN	MASTODON	PARTISAN	SEDITION	TRILLION	FALSETTO
ETRUSCAN	HIGHBORN	MATHURIN	PATHOGEN	SEEDSMAN	TRIMARAN	FANDANGO
EUDOXIAN	HOMESPUN	MELTDOWN	PAVILION	SENGREEN	TRUNNION	FILIPINO
EURASIAN	HONDURAN	MENHADEN	PEARMAIN	SHAGREEN	TUNGSTEN	FLAMENCO
EUROPEAN	HOOLIGAN	MERIDIAN	PEMMICAN	SHANGAAN	TUNISIAN	FLAMINGO
EVERYMAN	HORATIAN	MESCALIN	PENTAGON	SHEARMAN	TURKOMAN	GADOGADO
EVICTION	HORSEMAN	MICHIGAN	PERUVIAN	SHERATON	TYROLEAN	GARDYLOO
EXACTION	HORSEMEN	MIDBRAIN	PETITION	SHERIDAN	UNBEATEN	GAZPACHO
EXCISION	HOUSEMAN	MIRLITON	PHILEMON	SHOEHORN	UNBIDDEN	GERONIMO
EXERTION	HUNTSMAN	MISTAKEN	PHLEGMON	SHOWDOWN	UNBROKEN	HITHERTO
FANCYMAN	HYDROGEN	MOCCASIN	PHRYGIAN	SHRUNKEN	UNBURDEN	HOKKAIDO
FEDAYEEN	HYPERION	MOLESKIN	PICAROON	SHUTDOWN	UNBUTTON	HOWDYEDO
FELLAHIN	IGNITION	MONDRIAN	PILTDOWN	SIBERIAN	UNCLOVEN	IMPETIGO
FERRYMAN	ILLUSION	MORAVIAN	PITCAIRN	SICILIAN	UNCOMMON	INNUENDO
FINESPUN	IMPRISON	MOROCCAN	PLACEMEN	SIDESMAN	UNDERPIN	INTAGLIO
FIXATION	INACTION	MORRISON	PLANKTON	SILESIAN	UNDERRUN	JACKAROO
FLASHGUN	INCISION	MOTORMAN	PLANTAIN	SILURIAN	UNFASTEN	KANGAROO
FLYBLOWN	INDIAMAN	MOUFFLON	PLASTRON	SIRENIAN	UNPERSON	LAVENGRO
FORENOON	INFUSION	MOUNTAIN	PLEBEIAN	SKELETON	UNREASON	LEONARDO
FORESKIN	INKSTAIN	MULLIGAN	POLTROON	SKILLION	UNSHAKEN	LIBRETTO
FOREWARN	INVASION	MUNCHKIN	POSEIDON	SLATTERN	UNSPOKEN	LOTHARIO
FORMALIN	IRISHMAN	MUSICIAN	POSITION	SLOWDOWN	VACATION	MACHISMO
FORMOSAN	IRISHMEN	MUTATION	POSITRON	SMIDGEON	VALERIAN	MAESTOSO

MALGRADO	KINGSHIP	BELIEVER	DEFECTOR	GLOBULAR	MELCHIOR	POTHOLER
MALVOLIO	KNEEDEEP	BESSEMER	DEFENDER	GOODYEAR	MELEAGER	PRATTLER
MARCELLO	LADYSHIP	BESTOWER	DEFLOWER	GOSSAMER	MENANDER	PREACHER
MARTELLO	LANDSLIP	BETRAYER	DEMEANOR	GOVERNOR	MENSWEAR	PREDATOR
MINDANAO	LOLLIPOP	BEWILDER	DEMISTER	GRANDEUR	MERCATOR	PREMOLAR
MODERATO	LONGSHIP	BLEACHER	DESERTER	GRANULAR	MESSAGER	PRISONER
MOSQUITO	LONGSTOP	BLIGHTER	DESIGNER	GRUMBLER	MESSIDOR	PROCURER
NAVARINO	LORDSHIP	BORDERER	DETAINER	GULLIVER	METAPHOR	PRODUCER
NEGRILLO	NIGHTCAP	BORROWER	DETECTOR	HALFHOUR	MILLIBAR	PROFUSER
NEUTRINO	OUTSTRIP	BREATHER	DIAMETER	HALFYEAR	MILLINER	PROMOTER
NOSTROMO	OVERSTEP	BRUCKNER	DICTATOR	HANDOVER	MINISTER	PROMPTER
ORATORIO	PAWNSHOP	BURROWER	DINOSAUR	HANGOVER	MINOTAUR	PRONATOR
OTTAVINO	PERICARP	CABLECAR	DIRECTOR	HARFLEUR	MISNOMER	PROPOSER
PACHINKO	PICKMEUP	CALENDAR	DISASTER	HAVILDAR	MODELLER	PROVIDER
PALLADIO	POLYCARP	CALENDER	DISCOLOR	HAYFEVER	MODIFIER	PULITZER
PALMETTO	RAINDROP	CALLIPER	DISCOVER	HAYMAKER	MOLESTER	PULLOVER
PECORINO	RUNNERUP	CANISTER	DISFAVOR	HEADGEAR	MONICKER	PURIFIER
PEEKABOO	SCREWTOP	CATHETER	DISHONOR	HIJACKER	MOREOVER	PURVEYOR
PERFECTO	SELFHELP	CAVALIER	DISINTER	HOTELIER	MORTIMER	PUSHOVER
PETERLOO	SIDESLIP	CELLARER	DISORDER	HOWITZER	MOTORCAR	PUSTULAR
PIMIENTO	SIDESTEP	CELLULAR	DOMINEER	HUCKSTER	MULETEER	QUAESTOR
PLUMBAGO	SKINDEEP	CHANDLER	DOWNPOUR	IDOLATER	MURDERER	QUARTIER
POLITICO	SKULLCAP	CHASSEUR	DRAGSTER	IMITATOR	MUSCULAR	QUIBBLER
PROSPERO	SLIPSLOP	CINNABAR	DULCIMER	IMPORTER	MUTINEER	RADIATOR
SANTIAGO	SNOWDROP	CIRCULAR	EDUCATOR	IMPOSTER	NARRATOR	RAINWEAR
SARGASSO	SWEETSOP	CLANGOUR	EGGTIMER	IMPOSTOR	NECKWEAR	REAPPEAR
SCENARIO	TEARDROP	CLEANSER	ELEVATOR	IMPROPER	NEIGHBOR	RECEIVER
SCIROCCO	TOWNSHIP	CLINCHER	EMBITTER	IMPROVER	NENUPHAR	RECEPTOR
SERAGLIO	TRANSHIP	CLOISTER	EMPLOYER	INDUCTOR	NEWCOMER	RECKONER
SOMBRERO	WARDSHIP	CLOTHIER	EMULATOR	INFERIOR	NIGHTJAR	RECORDER
SPICCATO	WHITECAP	COAUTHOR	ENCUMBER	INFORMER	NOVEMBER	REDACTOR
STACCATO	WORKSHOP	COCHLEAR	ENDANGER	INJECTOR	OBJECTOR	REDEEMER
STICCATO	ABATTOIR	COIFFEUR	ENDEAVOR	INQUIRER	OBSERVER	REFORMER
STILETTO	ABDUCTOR	COLANDER	ENGENDER	INTERIOR	OCCUPIER	REGISTER
TENEBRIO	ABSORBER	COLLATOR	ENGINEER	INTRUDER	ODOMETER	REINDEER
TRINCULO	ACCENTOR	COMMONER	ENGRAVER	INVENTOR	OFFCOLOR	REMEMBER
TUPAMARO	ACCEPTOR	COMMUTER	ENLARGER	INVERTER	OFFENDER	REMINDER
TWELVEMO	ACHIEVER	COMPILER	ESPALIER	INVESTOR	OFFSIDER	REPAIRER
VINDALOO	ACQUIRER	COMPOSER	EUROSTAR	ISLANDER	OLEANDER	REPEATER
VIRTUOSO	ADJUSTER	COMPUTER	EVILDOER	JEWELLER	OLEASTER	REPORTER
VITILIGO	ADJUSTOR	CONJURER	EXAMINER	JONGLEUR	ONLOOKER	RESISTOR
WATERLOO	ADULATOR	CONJUROR	EXECUTOR	KIBITZER	OPENDOOR	RESTORER
AGITPROP	ADVANCER	CONSIDER	EXEMPLAR	KILLDEER	OPERATOR	RETAILER
AIRSTRIP	AGITATOR	CONSULAR	EXPLORER	KNITWEAR	OUTREMER	RETAINER
ASCOCARP	AIRLINER	CONSUMER	EXPORTER	LABOURER	OUTRIDER	REVELLER
BACKDROP	AMRITSAR	CONVENER	EXTENSOR	LABRADOR	OUTSIDER	REVIEWER
BACKSTOP	ANALYSER	CONVEYOR	EXTERIOR	LANDSEER	OVERHEAR	REVOLVER
BLACKCAP	ANCESTOR	CORRIDOR	EYELINER	LARKSPUR	OVERSEER	ROADSTER
BLOWLAMP	ANNEALER	COTTAGER	FAMILIAR	LAUGHTER	OXPECKER	ROMANCER
BOOKSHOP	ANTERIOR	CREDITOR	FASTENER	LAVENDER	PACIFIER	SABOTEUR
CALTHROP	ARMCHAIR	CROSSBAR	FAULKNER	LAWMAKER	PARAMOUR	SALINGER
CLAPTRAP	ARRANGER	CROUPIER	FELDSPAR	LECTURER	PARDONER	SALVADOR
DOORSTEP	ARRESTER	CRUCIFER	FINISHER	LEFTOVER	PASSOVER	SANGLIER
ENDOCARP	ASSESSOR	CRUSADER	FLOUNDER	LEINSTER	PATELLAR	SCAPULAR
FIREDAMP	ATOMIZER	CUCUMBER	FOLLOWER	LEVELLER	PECULIAR	SCHILLER
FIRESTEP	ATTACKER	CURSITOR	FOOTWEAR	LISTENER	PEIGNOIR	SCHOONER
FIRETRAP	ATTENDER	CUSPIDOR	FOREBEAR	LOADSTAR	PERISHER	SCIMITAR
FLAGSHIP	ATTESTOR	CUSTOMER	FORESTER	LODESTAR	PERJURER	SCORCHER
FOLLOWUP	BACHELOR	CUTWATER	FORSWEAR	LOITERER	PILASTER	SCREAMER
FOOLSCAP	BAEDEKER	CYLINDER	FRONDEUR	LONDONER	PILFERER	SCRUBBER
FOOTSTEP	BALUSTER	DARTMOOR	FRONTIER	LYSANDER	PILLAGER	SCULPTOR
FORESHIP	BANISTER	DAUGHTER	FUSILIER	MACASSAR	PILSENER	SEAFARER
HANDCLAP	BEDCOVER	DEADENER	GALLOPER	MAGISTER	PISCATOR	SEAFLOOR
HANDGRIP	BEDMAKER	DEBONAIR	GANGSTER	MALINGER	PLAYFAIR	SEAMSTER
HANDICAP	BEGETTER	DECANTER	GANISTER	MALODOUR	POISONER	SEARCHER
HARDSHIP	BEGINNER	DECEIVER	GARDENER	MANEUVER	POLISHER	SECONDER
HEADLAMP	BEHAVIOR	DECEMBER	GASOLIER	MANPOWER	POLLSTER	SEIGNIOR
HEADSHIP	BEHOLDER	DECEMVIR	GAZUNDER	MARAUDER	POLLUTER	SELECTOR
HEYTHROP	BELABOUR	DECIPHER	GEOMETER	MEDIATOR	POMANDER	SEMESTER

SERVITOR	TORTURER	ATLANTIS	CHEVIOTS	DIALYSIS	FIREARMS	HOLINESS
SHOULDER	TRANSFER	AUGUSTUS	CHIASMUS	DIAMONDS	FIRMNESS	HOMELESS
SHREDDER	TRAPDOOR	AUSPICES	CHICKENS	DIANTHUS	FLANDERS	HONDURAS
SIGNALER	TRAVELER	BACILLUS	CHILDERS	DIARESIS	FLANNELS	HOPELESS
SILENCER	TREMBLER	BACKLESS	CHINDITS	DICTATES	FLAWLESS	HORATIUS
SINCLAIR	TRENCHER	BADLANDS	CIRCINUS	DIEHARDS	FLINDERS	HORLICKS
SINGULAR	TROTTOIR	BAGPIPES	CLAPPERS	DIERESIS	FLIPPERS	HORNFELS
SINISTER	TROUNCER	BALDNESS	CLASSICS	DIGGINGS	FONDNESS	HUMOROUS
SLIPOVER	TURNOVER	BALLOCKS	CLAUDIUS	DINGBATS	FORFEITS	HUNDREDS
SMOOTHER	TWITCHER	BARABBAS	CLEANERS	DIOGENES	FORMLESS	HUNTRESS
SMOULDER	UDOMETER	BARBADOS	CLEAVERS	DIONYSUS	FORTRESS	HUSTINGS
SMUGGLER	ULTERIOR	BARENESS	CLEMATIS	DISTRESS	FORWARDS	HYPNOSIS
SNACKBAR	UNDERFUR	BARNABAS	CLINKERS	DIVIDERS	FOULNESS	IDLENESS
SNATCHER	UNFETTER	BARNARDS	CLIPPERS	DOLDRUMS	FRABJOUS	ILLINOIS
SNIFFLER	UNIPOLAR	BARONESS	CLITORIS	DOLOROUS	FRAXINUS	INFAMOUS
SOFTENER	UPHOLDER	BARONETS	CLUELESS	DOMINOES	FRECKLES	INTRADOS
SONGSTER	VALVULAR	BARRACKS	COBBLERS	DOUBLETS	FREMITUS	IROQUOIS
SORCERER	VASCULAR	BASELESS	COLDNESS	DRAGOONS	FULLNESS	ISOGLOSS
SOUVENIR	VERDERER	BASENESS	COLLECTS	DRAUGHTS	GADZOOKS	JEFFREYS
SPARKLER	VIBRATOR	BEAKLESS	COLLEGES	DRIBLETS	GALOSHES	JEHOVAHS
SPINSTER	VILLAGER	BEARINGS	COLLIERS	DRYGOODS	GAMENESS	JODHPURS
SPLASHER	VIOLATOR	BENEFITS	COLOSSUS	DULLNESS	GARMENTS	JOHANNES
SPLATTER	VOYAGEUR	BERBERIS	COLUMBUS	DUMBNESS	GASWORKS	JOHNSONS
SPLENDOR	WAGGONER	BIBULOUS	COMPRESS	DURABLES	GENEROUS	JORROCKS
SPLINTER	WALKOVER	BIFOCALS	CONFINES	DYNAMICS	GENETICS	JOTTINGS
SPLITTER	WANDERER	BIGAMOUS	CONGRATS	EARNINGS	GENITALS	JUSTNESS
SPLUTTER	WAYFARER	BLINKERS	CONGRESS	EASINESS	GEOTAXIS	KEENNESS
SPREADER	WHATEVER	BLOOMERS	CONTENTS	EATABLES	GESTURES	KINDNESS
SPRINGER	WHEATEAR	BOLDNESS	CONTROLS	ECHINOPS	GIANTESS	KINETICS
SPRINTER	WHENEVER	BOLLOCKS	COOLNESS	ECSTASIS	GIGLAMPS	KNACKERS
SPRITZER	WHEREVER	BONELESS	CORIOLIS	EDGEWAYS	GLABROUS	KNICKERS
SQUANDER	WHISTLER	BOOTLESS	COSINESS	EERINESS	GLADNESS	KNOBLESS
SQUATTER	WHITENER	BRACKETS	COUNTESS	ELECTORS	GLANDERS	KNOCKERS
SQUEAKER	WRANGLER	BREACHES	COUNTIES	ELEMENTS	GLAUCOUS	KOURMISS
SQUEALER	WRESTLER	BREECHES	COUSCOUS	ELLIPSIS	GLORIOUS	KOUSKOUS
SQUEEZER	YODELLER	BRISTLES	COVETOUS	EMBRACES	GLUTAEUS	KYPHOSIS
STICKLER	ZAMINDAR	BRONCHUS	COZINESS	EMERITUS	GOODNESS	LADRONES
STOCKCAR	ABDUCENS	BRUSSELS	CRACKERS	EMIRATES	GORGEOUS	LAMENESS
STOPOVER	ACANTHUS	BURSITIS	CRAVATES	EMPHASIS	GORMLESS	LANDMASS
STRAINER	ACCOUNTS	BUSINESS	CREPITUS	ENORMOUS	GRACIOUS	LASHINGS
STRANGER	ACHILLES	BUTCHERS	CRYSTALS	ENTRAILS	GRANULES	LATENESS
STRAPPER	ADENITIS	BUTTOCKS	CULOTTES	ENVIRONS	GRAPHICS	LAZINESS
STREAKER	ADENOIDS	BUTTRESS	CURTAINS	EOHIPPUS	GRAVITAS	LEAFLESS
STREAMER	AEROBICS	CADUCEUS	CURTNESS	EPICURUS	GRIEVOUS	LEAVINGS
STRINGER	AFFLATUS	CAGINESS	CUTENESS	EPITASIS	GRIMNESS	LECTURES
STRIPPER	AIRINESS	CALCULUS	CYANOSIS	EQUULEUS	GUMMOSIS	LEGGINGS
STROLLER	AIRWAVES	CALIPERS	CYCLADES	ERIDANUS	HAIRLESS	LEONIDAS
SUFFERER	ALCESTIS	CALMNESS	CYCLOSIS	ESTOVERS	HANGINGS	LEWDNESS
SUPERIOR	ALVEOLUS	CALVADOS	CYSTITIS	EUGENICS	HARDNESS	LIBELOUS
SUPPLIER	AMATEURS	CANARIES	DAEDALUS	EVENNESS	HARMLESS	LIFELESS
SURVEYOR	AMERICAS	CANNABIS	DAINTIES	EXEGESIS	HASTINGS	LIGNEOUS
SURVIVOR	ANABASIS	CANONESS	DAMASCUS	EXIGUOUS	HATTERAS	LIKENESS
SWADDLER	ANALYSIS	CANTORIS	DAMOCLES	EXPENSES	HAUNCHES	LIMBLESS
SWINDLER	ANCHISES	CAPITALS	DAMPNESS	EXTRADOS	HAZINESS	LIMPNESS
SYLVANER	ANDREWES	CAPTIOUS	DANAIDES	EYEGLASS	HEADLESS	LINCOLNS
TAKEOVER	ANTILLES	CARELESS	DANKNESS	FABULOUS	HEARTIES	LINNAEUS
TAVERNER	APNEUSIS	CASTOFFS	DARKNESS	FACELESS	HEBRIDES	LISTLESS
TAXPAYER	APOSTLES	CATULLUS	DATELESS	FACTIOUS	HEEDLESS	LODGINGS
TEAMSTER	AQUARIUS	CAUTIOUS	DEAFNESS	FAINITES	HEELTAPS	LORDOSIS
TEENAGER	ARCHIVES	CERAMICS	DEALINGS	FAIRNESS	HEIRLESS	LOUDNESS
TESTATOR	ARCTURUS	CERASTES	DECOROUS	FASTNESS	HELPLESS	LOVELESS
THATCHER	ARDENNES	CERBERUS	DEEPNESS	FATIGUES	HERACLES	LOWCLASS
THRASHER	ARGESTES	CHAMBERS	DEFTNESS	FEARLESS	HERCULES	LOWLANDS
THRESHER	ARKANSAS	CHAMPERS	DENARIUS	FEATHERS	HIBISCUS	LUCKLESS
THRILLER	ARQUEBUS	CHARTRES	DENTURES	FEATURES	HIDROSIS	LUMINOUS
THRUSTER	ARTICLES	CHATTELS	DESIROUS	FECKLESS	HIGHNESS	LUSCIOUS
THURIFER	ASBESTOS	CHEATERS	DETRITUS	FEELINGS	HIPSTERS	LUSHNESS
TOGETHER	ASMODEUS	CHECKERS	DEXTROUS	FIBROSIS	HOLDINGS	LUSTROUS
TOREADOR	ASPERGES	CHEQUERS	DIABETES	FINDINGS	HOLIDAYS	MACHINES

MAECENAS	OVERPASS	RECEIPTS	SONOROUS	TREELESS	ADJUTANT	BUNFIGHT
MALDIVES	OVERSEAS	RECKLESS	SORENESS	TREETOPS	ADJUVANT	BURNTOUT
MANDAMUS	PABULOUS	RECRUITS	SOULLESS	TREMBLES	AEGROTAT	CABERNET
MARASMUS	PAINLESS	REMNANTS	SOURNESS	TRESPASS	AEROFLOT	CACHALOT
MARIANAS	PALENESS	REMOUNTS	SOURPUSS	TRIMNESS	AERONAUT	CACHEPOT
MARQUESS	PANCREAS	RESINOUS	SPACIOUS	TROTTERS	AEROSTAT	CAMSHAFT
MATTRESS	PANDANUS	RESPECTS	SPARAXIS	TROUBLES	AFFERENT	CANOEIST
MAYORESS	PANDARUS	RESTLESS	SPARTANS	TROUSERS	AFFLUENT	CARCANET
MEANNESS	PANGLOSS	REYNOLDS	SPEAKERS	TRUENESS	AIRCRAFT	CARRYCOT
MEATLESS	PAROLLES	RHONCHUS	SPECIOUS	TUBELESS	AIRTIGHT	CASEMENT
MEEKNESS	PASTURES	RICHNESS	SPIRITUS	TUBEROUS	ALARMIST	CASTANET
MENELAUS	PATULOUS	RIGOROUS	SPOTLESS	TWEEZERS	ALIENIST	CATALYST
MENISCUS	PAULINUS	RINGHALS	SPRYNESS	UGLINESS	ALIQUANT	CATAPULT
MERCEDES	PEELINGS	RIPENESS	SPURIOUS	ULCEROUS	ALPHABET	CATARACT
METRITIS	PEERLESS	RISSOLES	SPYGLASS	UNAWARES	ALPINIST	CATSMEAT
MIDLANDS	PELAGIUS	ROBOTICS	SQUAMOUS	UNCTUOUS	ALTRUIST	CENTRIST
MILDNESS	PENNINES	ROOFLESS	STAGGERS	UPRIGHTS	AMBULANT	CEREMENT
MILKLESS	PERICLES	ROOFTOPS	STARKERS	UPSTAIRS	AMETHYST	CERVELAT
MILLIONS	PERILOUS	ROOTLESS	STARLESS	USURIOUS	ANAPAEST	CHARTIST
MINDLESS	PERTNESS	ROSINESS	STARTERS	UTENSILS	ANCHORET	CHECKOUT
MINORESS	PERVIOUS	ROUNDERS	STENOSIS	UXORIOUS	ANNALIST	CHESTNUT
MISTRESS	PHILLIPS	RUCTIONS	STEPHENS	VAGARIES	ANTEPOST	CHILIAST
MOLASSES	PHTHISIS	RUDENESS	STIMULUS	VANADOUS	APERIENT	CHITCHAT
MOLLUSCS	PICKINGS	RUSTLESS	STUDENTS	VAPOROUS	APIARIST	CLAIMANT
MOLUCCAS	PICTURES	RUTHLESS	STUDIOUS	VASTNESS	APPARENT	CLARINET
MOORINGS	PIERIDES	RYEGRASS	SUBJECTS	VENOMOUS	APPELANT	CLEARCUT
MORPHEUS	PILGRIMS	SAGENESS	SUCCEEDS	VESUVIUS	AQUATINT	CLUBFOOT
MUCHNESS	PITHLESS	SALTNESS	SUCCUBUS	VICTUALS	AQUEDUCT	COALPORT
MUDFLATS	PITILESS	SAMENESS	SUNDRIES	VIGOROUS	ARBALEST	COCKBOAT
MUTINOUS	PLATANUS	SAUSAGES	SUNGLASS	VILENESS	ARGONAUT	COHERENT
MYELITIS	PLATYPUS	SAWBONES	SUPPLIES	VIPEROUS	ARGUMENT	COLDBOOT
MYOSOTIS	PLAUDITS	SCABIOUS	SUPPRESS	VIRTUOUS	ARMAMENT	COLONIST
NAMELESS	PLEIADES	SCABROUS	SURENESS	VITAMINS	ARROGANT	COLORANT
NARCOSES	PLOTINUS	SCALENUS	SYLLABUS	VITELLUS	ARSONIST	CONFLICT
NARCOSIS	PODARGUS	SCANTIES	SYMPTOMS	VITREOUS	ARTEFACT	CONFRONT
NAUPLIUS	POITIERS	SCHNAPPS	SYNOPSIS	WAITRESS	ARTIFACT	CONQUEST
NAUSEOUS	POLITICS	SCIENCES	SYNTEXIS	WARDRESS	ASPIRANT	CONSTANT
NAUTILUS	POORNESS	SCISSORS	SYPHILIS	WARINESS	AUTOCRAT	CONTEMPT
NEARNESS	POPULOUS	SCORPIUS	SYRINGES	WAXWORKS	BAATHIST	CONTRACT
NEATNESS	POTATOES	SCRUPLES	TACTLESS	WEAKNESS	BACCARAT	CONTRAST
NEBULOUS	PRECIOUS	SEAMLESS	TAILLESS	WETLANDS	BACCHANT	CORSELET
NECROSIS	PREMISES	SEAWARDS	TAMENESS	WHISKERS	BACKCHAT	COUCHANT
NEEDLESS	PREVIOUS	SEDULOUS	TANTALUS	WILDNESS	BAILMENT	COVALENT
NEURITIS	PRIMNESS	SEEDLESS	TARTARUS	WILINESS	BANKRUPT	COVENANT
NEUROSIS	PRINCESS	SELFLESS	TARTNESS	WILLIAMS	BANNERET	COVERLET
NICENESS	PRIORESS	SENSUOUS	TAUTNESS	WINDINGS	BAREFOOT	CRACKPOT
NICHOLAS	PRIVATES	SERVICES	TEACHERS	WINDLASS	BASEMENT	CRATCHIT
NINEPINS	PROCEEDS	SHACKLES	TELECOMS	WINDLESS	BASSINET	CRESCENT
NOSTRILS	PRODUCES	SHALLOWS	TENESMUS	WINGLESS	BEAUFORT	CROCKETT
NOWADAYS	PRODUCTS	SHAMBLES	TERMINUS	WINNINGS	BEAUMONT	CROSSLET
NUMBNESS	PROGRESS	SHINGLES	THALAMUS	WIRELESS	BEETROOT	CROTCHET
NUMERALS	PROPOLIS	SHOELESS	THANATOS	WONDROUS	BENEDICT	CROWFOOT
NUMEROUS	PROVERBS	SHUTTERS	THINNESS	WOOLLENS	BERGAMOT	CUCURBIT
NUMINOUS	PURLIEUS	SICKNESS	THOUGHTS	WORDLESS	BESOUGHT	CUTHBERT
NUPTIALS	PYELITIS	SIDEWAYS	THROMBUS	WORKINGS	BIGAMIST	DAYLIGHT
ODDMENTS	PYRAMIDS	SISYPHUS	TIBERIAS	WORTHIES	BLACKOUT	DEADBEAT
ODYSSEUS	PYRENEES	SKIBOOTS	TIBERIUS	WRITINGS	BLUECOAT	DECADENT
OFFICERS	QUARTERS	SKITTLES	TIDINESS	ZEPHYRUS	BOTANIST	DECREPIT
OILINESS	RABELAIS	SLEEPERS	TIMELESS	ZOONOSIS	BOUFFANT	DEMOCRAT
OILSKINS	RACHITIS	SLIMNESS	TIMOROUS	ABERRANT	BOWSPRIT	DERELICT
OLYMPICS	RACINESS	SLIPPERS	TINNITUS	ABSTRACT	BRACELET	DESELECT
OMPHALOS	RAILINGS	SLOWNESS	TIRELESS	ABUNDANT	BRAGGART	DESTRUCT
OPENNESS	RAMPARTS	SLYBOOTS	TIRESIAS	ABUTMENT	BREAKOUT	DIFFRACT
ORCHITIS	RANKNESS	SMUGNESS	TITANESS	ACCIDENT	BRICKBAT	DILIGENT
OUTCLASS	RASHNESS	SNEAKERS	TOMATOES	ACCREDIT	BROWBEAT	DIPLOMAT
OUTDOORS	RASSELAS	SOAPSUDS	TONELESS	ACQUAINT	BUCKFAST	DISCOUNT
OUTWARDS	RAVENOUS	SOCRATES	TOPCLASS	ACTIVIST	BUCKSHOT	DISCREET
OVARITIS	REASSESS	SOFTNESS	TORTUOUS	ADHERENT	BUDAPEST	DISJUNCT
OVERALLS		SOLDIERS	TRAITORS	ADJACENT	BUDDHIST	DISMOUNT

DISPIRIT	FOURPART	JUDGMENT	OFFPRINT	REDOLENT	SUNBURNT	BRANDNEW
DISQUIET	FRAGMENT	JUMPSUIT	OFFSHOOT	REDSHIFT	SUNBURST	BUNGALOW
DISTINCT	FRAGRANT	KATTEGAT	OINTMENT	REDSTART	SUNLIGHT	CHAINSAW
DISTRACT	FREEPOST	KILOVOLT	OLIPHANT	REGIMENT	SUPPLANT	CLERIHEW
DISTRAIT	FREQUENT	KILOWATT	OPENCAST	REINVEST	SURFBOAT	COCKCROW
DISTRICT	FRESHEST	KINGPOST	OPPONENT	RELEVANT	SURMOUNT	COLESLAW
DISTRUST	FURTHEST	KNOCKOUT	OPTIMIST	REORIENT	SWIMSUIT	DISALLOW
DOCUMENT	FUTURIST	LAMPPOST	ORGANIST	RESIDENT	SYMBIONT	FEVERFEW
DOMINANT	GADABOUT	LANCELET	ORNAMENT	RESONANT	TABBYCAT	FURBELOW
DONATIST	GALLIPOT	LANCELOT	ORPIMENT	RESTRICT	TABLEMAT	HEDGEROW
DOORPOST	GATEPOST	LATINIST	OUTBURST	RETICENT	TASHKENT	HIGHBROW
DOUGHNUT	GAUNTLET	LAWCOURT	OUTRIGHT	REVERENT	TEESHIRT	HONEYDEW
DOWNBEAT	GIGAWATT	LAYABOUT	OUTSMART	RHEOSTAT	TEGUMENT	KICKSHAW
DOWNCAST	GLASNOST	LIFEBELT	OVERCAST	RICOCHET	TELECAST	OVERDRAW
DROPSHOT	GOALPOST	LIFEBOAT	OVERCOAT	RIGHTIST	TENEMENT	OVERFLOW
DRUGGIST	GRADIENT	LIGAMENT	OVERHEAT	ROSEROOT	THEOCRAT	OVERVIEW
DRUMBEAT	GREATEST	LINGUIST	OVERSHOT	ROYALIST	THEORIST	PEEPSHOW
DUBONNET	GUNPOINT	LINIMENT	PACIFIST	RUBAIYAT	THICKSET	RICKSHAW
DUELLIST	GYROSTAT	LITIGANT	PAMPHLET	RUDIMENT	TOLERANT	ROADSHOW
EARLIEST	HALFMAST	LOBBYIST	PARAKEET	RUMINANT	TRANSACT	SIDESHOW
EASEMENT	HANDCART	LONGBOAT	PARAQUAT	RUNABOUT	TRANSECT	SOUTHPAW
EFFERENT	HAZELNUT	LOYALIST	PARODIST	SAILBOAT	TRANSEPT	TOMORROW
EFFLUENT	HEADHUNT	LUNGWORT	PASSPORT	SAMIZDAT	TRANSMIT	UNDERTOW
EGGPLANT	HEADMOST	LUTENIST	PAVEMENT	SANSKRIT	TRAPPIST	WITHDRAW
ELEPHANT	HEADREST	LYRICIST	PEDERAST	SAPPHIST	TURANDOT	APPENDIX
ELOQUENT	HEATSPOT	MAILBOAT	PEDIMENT	SATIRIST	TURBOJET	BICONVEX
EMERGENT	HEDONIST	MAILSHOT	PENCHANT	SCHUBERT	TURNCOAT	BORDEAUX
EMIGRANT	HELIPORT	MAINMAST	PENITENT	SCILICET	TURNSPIT	CICATRIX
EMULGENT	HELLBENT	MALTREAT	PERSUANT	SEAFRONT	TWILIGHT	CRUCIFIX
ENTREPOT	HESITANT	MANIFEST	PETULANT	SEDIMENT	TYPECAST	GENETRIX
EQUITANT	HINDMOST	MARABOUT	PHEASANT	SENTIENT	UNDERCUT	HARUSPEX
ESCAPIST	HOLDFAST	MARGARET	PHOTOFIT	SERGEANT	UNDULANT	HORSEBOX
ESCARGOT	HONEYPOT	MARMOSET	PIECHART	SERJEANT	UNIONIST	LOOSEBOX
ESCULENT	HORNPOUT	MARTINET	PIECRUST	SERVIENT	UNSPOILT	LUNCHBOX
ESSAYIST	HUMANIST	MASSENET	PINPOINT	SEVEREST	UPMARKET	MATCHBOX
EULOGIST	HUMORIST	MASSICOT	PLACEMAT	SHAKEOUT	UPPERCUT	MIREPOIX
EVACUANT	IDEALIST	MEDALIST	PLANCHET	SHAREOUT	USUFRUCT	MONEYBOX
EWIGKEIT	IGNORANT	MEGAVOLT	PLANGENT	SHIPMENT	VEHEMENT	OPOPANAX
EXISTENT	IMMANENT	MEGAWATT	PLATELET	SHOOTOUT	VESTMENT	ORTHODOX
EXORCIST	IMMINENT	MERCHANT	PLAYSUIT	SHOWBOAT	VIGILANT	PARALLAX
EXPLICIT	IMMODEST	MICRODOT	PLEASANT	SIBILANT	VIREMENT	PONTIFEX
EXPONENT	IMPLICIT	MIDNIGHT	POIGNANT	SICKLIST	VIRULENT	QUINCUNX
EXTERNAT	IMPOTENT	MIDPOINT	POLYGLOT	SIGNPOST	VISCOUNT	SARDONYX
EXULTANT	IMPUDENT	MILITANT	POPULIST	SKYLIGHT	VISITANT	SMALLPOX
EYESIGHT	INCIDENT	MILKWORT	PORTRAIT	SKYPILOT	VOCALIST	SNUFFBOX
FACELIFT	INDECENT	MISCOUNT	PRECINCT	SLUGFEST	WAINSCOT	SPINIFEX
FANLIGHT	INDICANT	MISPRINT	PREGNANT	SMALLEST	WALLWORT	SUPERTAX
FARTHEST	INDIGENT	MISSPENT	PRINTOUT	SMARTEST	WARMBOOT	SWINEPOX
FATALIST	INDIRECT	MISTREAT	PROHIBIT	SMOLLETT	WARPAINT	TOADFLAX
FECULENT	INDOLENT	MISTRUST	PROSPECT	SNAPSHOT	WHINCHAT	TRANSFIX
FEMINIST	INEXPERT	MONUMENT	PRURIENT	SOMERSET	WHITEHOT	ABJECTLY
FILAMENT	INFLIGHT	MORALIST	PSALMIST	SOMEWHAT	WHODUNIT	ABRUPTLY
FINALIST	INFLUENT	MOTORIST	PUGILIST	SPINTEXT	WORMCAST	ABSURDLY
FIREBOLT	INHALANT	MOVEMENT	PUISSANT	SPIRELET	WRISTLET	ACCURACY
FLAGRANT	INHERENT	MULEWORT	PURULENT	SPROCKET	YOGHOURT	ACERBITY
FLAMEOUT	INNOCENT	MUNIMENT	PUSHCART	STAGNANT	YOUNGEST	ACRIMONY
FLATBOAT	INSOLENT	MUSCADET	PUSSYCAT	STAKEOUT	ZIGGURAT	ACTIVELY
FLATFOOT	INSPIRIT	MYOBLAST	QUADRANT	STALWART	CARCAJOU	ACTIVITY
FLAUBERT	INSTINCT	NATURIST	QUICKSET	STARDUST	CARJACOU	ACTUALLY
FLAUTIST	INSTRUCT	NESCIENT	QUOTIENT	STINKPOT	HONOLULU	ADEQUACY
FLIPPANT	INTELSAT	NEWSCAST	RACKRENT	STOCKIST	KATMANDU	ADROITLY
FLOODLIT	INTERACT	NIHILIST	RAINCOAT	STOCKPOT	KINKAJOU	ADULTERY
FLYSHEET	INTEREST	NOVELIST	READIEST	STORMONT	ROUSSEAU	ADVISORY
FOGLIGHT	INTERMIT	NUTRIENT	READJUST	STRAIGHT	TIRAMISU	ADVOCACY
FOOTREST	INTERNET	OBEDIENT	REARMOST	STRIDENT	TURGENEV	AFFINITY
FORECAST	IRRITANT	OBSTRUCT	REASSERT	STRUMPET	YUGOSLAV	AGRIMONY
FOREFOOT	JACKBOOT	OCCAMIST	RECUSANT	SUBTRACT	AIRSCREW	AGRONOMY
FOREMOST	JINGOIST	OCCIDENT	REDIRECT	SUCCINCT	BEDSTRAW	ALACRITY
FORKLIFT	JUBILANT	OCCUPANT	REDLIGHT	SUDAMENT	BRADSHAW	ALDERNEY

ALEATORY	CASUALLY	DOMESDAY	FRUCTIFY	IMPURIFY	MENTALLY	PHARMACY
ALGOLOGY	CASUALTY	DOOLALLY	FRUGALLY	IMPURITY	METONYMY	PHOTOPSY
ALKALIFY	CATATONY	DOOMSDAY	FRUMENTY	INDUSTRY	MIGHTILY	PIQUANCY
ALLEGORY	CATEGORY	DOUGHBOY	FUMITORY	INEQUITY	MILITARY	PLACIDLY
ALLEYWAY	CAUSEWAY	DOWNPLAY	FUNERARY	INFANTRY	MINATORY	PLEURISY
ALLOGAMY	CELERITY	DOXOLOGY	FUTILITY	INFINITY	MINISTRY	PLUCKILY
ALMIGHTY	CELIBACY	DRAUGHTY	GADGETRY	INIQUITY	MINORITY	POLITELY
AMICABLY	CEMETERY	DREAMILY	GALLOWAY	INSANELY	MINUTELY	POLYGAMY
ANCESTRY	CENTAURY	DREARILY	GARGANEY	INSANITY	MISAPPLY	POLYGYNY
ANGLESEY	CEREMONY	DRIVEWAY	GARISHLY	INTENTLY	MISCARRY	POLYSEMY
ANNUALLY	CHANCERY	DROWSILY	GARLICKY	INTIMACY	MISOGYNY	PONSONBY
ANTIBODY	CHANTREY	DRUDGERY	GEMOLOGY	INWARDLY	MOBILITY	POPINJAY
ANTIMONY	CHARLADY	EASTERLY	GENIALLY	ISOSTASY	MODESTLY	POROSITY
APOPLEXY	CHASTITY	EFFICACY	GENTRIFY	JAUNTILY	MONANDRY	PORPHYRY
APOSTASY	CHEEKILY	EMINENCY	GEOMANCY	JEALOUSY	MONARCHY	POSOLOGY
ARDENTLY	CHEERILY	EMISSARY	GEOMETRY	JEOPARDY	MONETARY	POSSIBLY
ARGUABLY	CHIVALRY	EMULSIFY	GINGERLY	JOKINGLY	MONOGAMY	POTBELLY
ARTFULLY	CHOIRBOY	ENDOGAMY	GIVEAWAY	JOVIALLY	MONOGYNY	PRETTILY
ARTISTRY	CIRCUITY	ENORMITY	GLOBALLY	JOYFULLY	MONOPOLY	PRIESTLY
ASPERITY	CIVILITY	ENTHALPY	GLOOMILY	JURATORY	MONOTONY	PRINCELY
ASSEMBLY	CLASSIFY	ENTIRELY	GLOSSARY	KENTUCKY	MORALITY	PRIORITY
ASTUTELY	CLEARWAY	ENTIRETY	GLUTTONY	KILKENNY	MORBIDLY	PROBABLY
ATHANASY	CLEMENCY	ENTREATY	GRAMERCY	KINGSLEY	MOROSELY	PROMPTLY
ATROCITY	CLEVERLY	EPILEPSY	GRATUITY	KNIGHTLY	MORTALLY	PROPERLY
ATTORNEY	CLUMSILY	EPIPHANY	GRAVELLY	KOLINSKY	MORTUARY	PROPERTY
AUDACITY	COARSELY	EQUALITY	GREEDILY	KROMESKY	MOTHERLY	PROPHECY
AUDITORY	COBWEBBY	ETERNITY	GREENERY	LACKADAY	MOTORWAY	PROPHESY
AUTARCHY	COLLIERY	ETHERIFY	GREENFLY	LAMASERY	MULBERRY	PSALMODY
AUTOGAMY	COLLOQUY	ETHOLOGY	GROGGILY	LANDLADY	MULTIPLY	PSALTERY
AUTONOMY	COMMONLY	EUTROPHY	GRUMPILY	LANSBURY	MUTUALLY	PSEUDERY
BANALITY	CONTRARY	EVERYDAY	GUERNSEY	LAPIDARY	MYCOLOGY	PUBLICLY
BARBERRY	COQUETRY	EXIGENCY	GUILTILY	LATCHKEY	NARROWLY	PUNGENCY
BARRATRY	CORDUROY	EXIGUITY	GYRATORY	LATTERLY	NATALITY	QUAINTLY
BASKETRY	CORONARY	FACILITY	HATCHERY	LAUDABLY	NATIVITY	QUANDARY
BAYBERRY	COSTMARY	FALCONRY	HATCHWAY	LAVATORY	NIJINSKY	QUANTIFY
BEAUTIFY	COURTESY	FAMOUSLY	HATHAWAY	LAVISHLY	NOBILITY	QUANTITY
BEGGARLY	COVENTRY	FARRIERY	HEARTILY	LAWFULLY	NOMARCHY	RACIALLY
BERKELEY	COWARDLY	FATALITY	HEATEDLY	LEATHERY	NORMALLY	RAILLERY
BESTIARY	COWBERRY	FATHERLY	HEAVENLY	LEGALITY	NORMANDY	RANDOMLY
BILBERRY	CRAFTILY	FEASIBLY	HEGEMONY	LENIENCY	NOSOLOGY	RAPACITY
BILLYBOY	CRAMOISY	FEATHERY	HERALDRY	LETHARGY	NUGATORY	RAPIDITY
BIOMETRY	CRANEFLY	FEBRUARY	HEREDITY	LIENTERY	NUMERACY	RASCALLY
BIRTHDAY	CREAMERY	FEDERACY	HIDEAWAY	LIFEBUOY	OBDURACY	RECENTLY
BITTERLY	CREDIBLY	FELICITY	HILARITY	LITERACY	OBITUARY	RECOVERY
BLACKBOY	CROCKERY	FEMINITY	HOARSELY	LITERARY	OBTUSELY	REDEPLOY
BLACKFLY	CULINARY	FEROCITY	HOGMANAY	LIVIDITY	OCTONARY	REEMPLOY
BLITHELY	CUPIDITY	FIDELITY	HOLLOWAY	LOBOTOMY	ODIOUSLY	REFINERY
BLUSTERY	CURRENCY	FIERCELY	HONESTLY	LOCALITY	OENOLOGY	REGISTRY
BOTTOMRY	CYTOLOGY	FILTHILY	HONORARY	LOMBARDY	ONCOLOGY	RELIABLY
BOUNDARY	DAINTILY	FINALITY	HOROLOGY	LONGSTAY	ONTOLOGY	REMOTELY
BRADBURY	DEBILITY	FITFULLY	HORRIBLY	LOVINGLY	ORANGERY	REVIVIFY
BREEZILY	DECENTLY	FLASHILY	HORSEFLY	LUCIDITY	ORDINARY	RHAPSODY
BREVIARY	DELICACY	FLATTERY	HOSTELRY	LUMINARY	OSTERLEY	RIBALDRY
BRIGHTLY	DELIVERY	FLEXIBLY	HOVERFLY	MACAULAY	OVERPLAY	RIDGEWAY
BROADWAY	DEMURELY	FLIMSILY	HUMANELY	MACREADY	OVERSTAY	RIGIDITY
BRUTALLY	DERISORY	FLUENTLY	HUMANITY	MAHOGANY	PALIMONY	RITUALLY
BUOYANCY	DETOXIFY	FLUIDITY	HUMIDIFY	MAIDENLY	PALPABLY	ROBUSTLY
BURBERRY	DEWBERRY	FLUMMERY	HUMIDITY	MAINSTAY	PANDOWDY	ROCKETRY
BURGLARY	DIDDICOY	FORCIBLY	HUMILITY	MAJORITY	PANEGYRY	ROLYPOLY
BURGUNDY	DILATORY	FORESTAY	HUMPHREY	MALAGASY	PARAGUAY	ROSEMARY
BUSYBODY	DIRECTLY	FORESTRY	HUNGRILY	MALARKEY	PASSABLY	ROTATORY
BUTCHERY	DISARRAY	FORMALLY	IDENTIFY	MANFULLY	PASSERBY	RUBBISHY
CABLEWAY	DISMALLY	FORMERLY	IDENTITY	MANNERLY	PATCHILY	RUEFULLY
CAJOLERY	DISUNITY	FORTUITY	IDEOLOGY	MANUALLY	PATENTLY	RUGGEDLY
CALAMITY	DIVINITY	FRIENDLY	IDOLATRY	MARKEDLY	PEDAGOGY	SACRISTY
CANDIDLY	DOCILITY	FRIGIDLY	IGNOMINY	MASTERLY	PEDANTRY	SADDLERY
CAPACITY	DOGBERRY	FRIPPERY	ILLUSORY	MATRONLY	PENOLOGY	SAGACITY
CARRAWAY	DOGGEDLY	FRISKILY	IMMUNITY	MATURITY	PERIPETY	SALACITY
CASTAWAY	DOGSBODY	FROSTILY	IMPUNITY	MCKINLEY	PEVENSEY	SALINITY

SALIVARY	SEXOLOGY	SOMEBODY	STRICTLY	THEOLOGY	UNKINDLY	VIVACITY
SALUTARY	SEXUALLY	SOOTHSAY	STRONGLY	THIEVERY	UNLIKELY	VOMITORY
SALUTORY	SHABBILY	SORDIDLY	STUFFILY	THINGAMY	UNLOVELY	VORACITY
SANCTIFY	SHODDILY	SORORITY	STULTIFY	THRENODY	UNSAVORY	VULGARLY
SANCTITY	SHREWDLY	SPARSELY	STUPIDLY	THUNDERY	UNSEEMLY	WARRANTY
SANITARY	SIGNALLY	SPARSITY	STURDILY	THURSDAY	UNSTEADY	WATERWAY
SATURDAY	SILENTLY	SPEEDILY	SUBTLETY	TIMIDITY	UNTIDILY	WAVERLEY
SAVAGELY	SIMPLIFY	SPEEDWAY	SUDDENLY	TINSELLY	UNTIMELY	WEAPONRY
SAVAGERY	SISTERLY	SPILLWAY	SUITABLY	TONALITY	UNWIELDY	WESTERLY
SCANTILY	SLEEPILY	SPIRALLY	SULLENLY	TOPHEAVY	UNWORTHY	WHEEZILY
SCARCELY	SLIGHTLY	SPRITELY	SUMMITRY	TOPOLOGY	URBANITY	WHISKERY
SCARCITY	SLIPPERY	SPRUCELY	SUPERBLY	TOTALITY	URGENTLY	WICKEDLY
SCRATCHY	SLOBBERY	SQUARELY	SYMMETRY	TOXICITY	USEFULLY	WILFULLY
SCRIBBLY	SLOPPILY	STAIRWAY	SYMPATHY	TRAVESTY	VACANTLY	WITCHERY
SCRUTINY	SLOVENLY	STANNARY	SYMPHONY	TREASURY	VAGRANCY	WIZARDRY
SCULLERY	SMOOTHLY	STATUARY	TAKEAWAY	TRICKERY	VALIDITY	WOEFULLY
SECONDLY	SNAPPILY	STEADILY	TANGIBLY	TRIUNITY	VELLEITY	WOLSELEY
SECRETLY	SNOBBERY	STEALTHY	TAPESTRY	TRUMPERY	VELOCITY	WOODENLY
SECURELY	SNOOTILY	STEINWAY	TAXONOMY	TUPPENNY	VENALITY	WORKADAY
SECURITY	SOAKAWAY	STICKILY	TAYBERRY	TURGIDLY	VERACITY	WORTHILY
SEDATELY	SOBRIETY	STINGRAY	TEARAWAY	TUTELARY	VERBALLY	XENOGAMY
SELFPITY	SOCIALLY	STOKESAY	TELEGONY	TWOPENNY	VESTIARY	YEOMANRY
SEMINARY	SODALITY	STOLIDLY	TEMERITY	UBIQUITY	VIBRANCY	ALCATRAZ
SENILITY	SOLDIERY	STONEFLY	TENACITY	UNDERLAY	VICINITY	SCHMALTZ
SENSIBLY	SOLEMNLY	STOWAWAY	TENDENCY	UNEASILY	VILLAINY	
SERENELY	SOLIDIFY	STRACHEY	TENDERLY	UNEVENLY	VINEGARY	
SERENITY	SOLIDITY	STRAGGLY	TERRIBLY	UNGAINLY	VIRILITY	
SEROLOGY	SOLITARY	STRATEGY	TERTIARY	UNIQUELY	VIROLOGY	
SEVERELY	SOLVENCY	STRATIFY	TETCHILY	UNITEDLY	VISUALLY	
SEVERITY	SOMBRELY	STRETCHY	THATAWAY	UNJUSTLY	VITALITY	

9:1

ABANDONED	ADMIRABLY	AIRCOOLED	AMOROUSLY	ANTHOLOGY	ARCHIVOLT	ASYMMETRY	
ABANDONEE	ADMIRALTY	AIRSTREAM	AMORPHOUS	ANTICLINE	ARCTOGAEA	ASYNDETON	
ABASEMENT	ADMISSION	AITCHBONE	AMPERSAND	ANTIGONUS	ARDUOUSLY	ASYNERGIA	
ABATEMENT	ADMITTING	ALABASTER	AMPHIBIAN	ANTIHELIX	AREOPAGUS	ATAHUALPA	
ABDOMINAL	ADMIXTURE	ALBATROSS	AMPLIFIER	ANTINOVEL	ARGENTINA	ATAVISTIC	
ABDUCTION	ADMONITOR	ALBERTINE	AMPLITUDE	ANTIPASTO	ARGENTINE	ATHEISTIC	
ABERNETHY	ADORATION	ALCHEMIST	AMSTERDAM	ANTIPATHY	ARISTOTLE	ATHELSTAN	
ABERRANCE	ADORNMENT	ALCOHOLIC	AMUSEMENT	ANTIPHONY	ARKWRIGHT	ATHENAEUM	
ABHORRENT	ADRENALIN	ALDEBARAN	AMUSINGLY	ANTIPODES	ARLINGTON	ATHLETICS	
ABLUTIONS	ADULATION	ALERTNESS	AMYGDALUS	ANTIQUARY	ARMADILLO	ATONALITY	
ABOLITION	ADULTERER	ALEURITIS	ANABOLISM	ANTIQUITY	ARMAMENTS	ATONEMENT	
ABOMINATE	ADULTHOOD	ALEXANDER	ANABRANCH	ANTISERUM	ARMISTICE	ATROCIOUS	
ABORIGINE	ADUMBRATE	ALEXANDRA	ANAEROBIC	ANTITOXIC	ARMSTRONG	ATTACKING	
ABOUNDING	ADVANTAGE	ALGEBRAIC	ANAGLYPTA	ANTITOXIN	ARQUEBUSE	ATTAINDER	
ABOUTFACE	ADVECTION	ALGORITHM	ANALEPTIC	ANTIVENIN	ARRESTING	ATTEMPTED	
ABOUTTURN	ADVENTIST	ALICYCLIC	ANALGESIA	ANTONINUS	ARRIVISTE	ATTENDANT	
ABSCONDER	ADVENTIVE	ALIGNMENT	ANALGESIC	ANXIOUSLY	ARROGANCE	ATTENTION	
ABSORBENT	ADVENTURE	ALIPHATIC	ANALOGOUS	APARTHEID	ARROWHEAD	ATTENTIVE	
ABSORBING	ADVERBIAL	ALLANTOID	ANAPLASIA	APARTMENT	ARROWROOT	ATTENUATE	
ABSTAINER	ADVERSARY	ALLANTOIS	ANAPLASTY	APATHETIC	ARSENICAL	ATTITUDES	
ABSTINENT	ADVERSELY	ALLEGEDLY	ANARCHIST	APENNINES	ARTEMISIA	ATTRIBUTE	
ABSURDITY	ADVERSITY	ALLEGIANT	ANASTASIA	APERIODIC	ARTERIOLE	ATTRITION	
ABUNDANCE	ADVERTISE	ALLEMANDE	ANATOLIAN	APERITIVE	ARTHRITIC	ATTUITION	
ABYSMALLY	ADVISABLE	ALLEVIATE	ANATOMIST	APHERESIS	ARTHRITIS	AUBERGINE	
ACADEMIST	ADVISEDLY	ALLIGATOR	ANATOMIZE	APHRODITE	ARTHROPOD	AUBRIETIA	
ACARIASIS	ADVOCATED	ALLOCARPY	ANCESTRAL	APOCRYPHA	ARTHROSIS	AUCTORIAL	
ACCENTUAL	AEPYORNIS	ALLOGRAFT	ANCHORAGE	APOENZYME	ARTHURIAN	AUDACIOUS	
ACCESSION	AERODROME	ALLOGRAPH	ANCHORITE	APOLLONUS	ARTICHOKE	AUGUSTINE	
ACCESSORY	AEROPLANE	ALLOPATHY	ANCHORMAN	APOLOGIST	ARTICULAR	AURICULAR	
ACCIDENTS	AEROSPACE	ALLOTMENT	ANCILLARY	APOLOGIZE	ARTIFICER	AUSTERITY	
ACCLIMATE	AEROTAXIS	ALLOWABLE	ANCIPITAL	APOPHATIC	ARTILLERY	AUSTRALIA	
ACCLIVITY	AESCHYLUS	ALLOWANCE	ANDANTINO	APOPHYSIS	ASCENDANT	AUTEURISM	
ACCOMPANY	AESTHETIC	ALMANDINE	ANDROCLES	APOSTOLIC	ASCENDING	AUTHENTIC	
ACCORDANT	AFFECTING	ALONGSIDE	ANDROMEDA	APPALLING	ASCENSION	AUTHORESS	
ACCORDING	AFFECTION	ALOOFNESS	ANECDOTAL	APPARATUS	ASCERTAIN	AUTHORITY	
ACCORDION	AFFIDAVIT	ALPENGLOW	ANECDOTES	APPARITOR	ASCLEPIUS	AUTHORIZE	
ACCRETION	AFFILIATE	ALPENHORN	ANGELFISH	APPEALING	ASHKENAZI	AUTOCLAVE	
ACETAMIDE	AFFLICTED	ALTERABLE	ANGIOGRAM	APPENDAGE	ASHMOLEAN	AUTOCRACY	
ACETYLENE	AFFLUENCE	ALTERCATE	ANGLICISM	APPERTAIN	ASPARAGUS	AUTOCROSS	
ACIDULATE	AFFRICATE	ALTERNATE	ANGOSTURA	APPETIZER	ASPARTAME	AUTOGRAPH	
ACIDULOUS	AFLATOXIN	ALTIMETER	ANGUISHED	APPLEJACK	ASPERSION	AUTOLATRY	
ACONCAGUA	AFORESAID	ALTIPLANO	ANHYDRIDE	APPLIANCE	ASPIRATOR	AUTOLYCUS	
ACOUSTICS	AFRIKAANS	ALTISSIMO	ANHYDRITE	APPLICANT	ASPLENIUM	AUTOLYSIS	
ACQUIESCE	AFRIKANER	ALUMINIUM	ANHYDROUS	APPOINTED	ASSAILANT	AUTOMAKER	
ACQUITTAL	AFTERCARE	ALVEOLATE	ANIMALISM	APPOINTEE	ASSERTING	AUTOMATED	
ACROBATIC	AFTERDAMP	AMARANTIN	ANIMALITY	APPORTION	ASSERTION	AUTOMATIC	
ACROPETAL	AFTERGLOW	AMARYLLIS	ANIMATION	APPRAISAL	ASSERTIVE	AUTOMATON	
ACROPHONY	AFTERMATH	AMAUROSIS	ANIMISTIC	APPREHEND	ASSIDUITY	AUTONOMIC	
ACROPOLIS	AFTERMOST	AMAZEMENT	ANIMOSITY	APPROVING	ASSIDUOUS	AUTOPILOT	
ACTUALITY	AFTERNOON	AMAZONITE	ANISOGAMY	AQUAPLANE	ASSISTANT	AUTOROUTE	
ACTUARIAL	AFTERWORD	AMBERGRIS	ANKYLOSIS	AQUARELLE	ASSOCIATE	AUTOSCOPY	
ACUMINATE	AGALACTIC	AMBIGUITY	ANNAPOLIS	AQUILEGIA	ASSONANCE	AUXILIARY	
ACUTENESS	AGAMEMNON	AMBIGUOUS	ANNAPURNA	ARABESQUE	ASSUETUDE	AUXOTROPH	
ACYCLOVIR	AGGRAVATE	AMBITIOUS	ANNOTATED	ARABICIZE	ASSURANCE	AVAILABLE	
ADAPTABLE	AGGREGATE	AMBLYOPIA	ANNOTATOR	ARABINOSE	ASSUREDLY	AVALANCHE	
ADDERWORT	AGGRESSOR	AMBROSIAL	ANNOUNCER	ARACHNOID	ASTHMATIC	AVOCATION	
ADDICTION	AGGRIEVED	AMBROSIAN	ANNOYANCE	ARAGONITE	ASTOUNDED	AVOIDABLE	
ADDICTIVE	AGINCOURT	AMBROTYPE	ANNULMENT	ARAUCARIA	ASTRAGALS	AVOIDANCE	
ADDRESSED	AGITATION	AMBULANCE	ANOINTING	ARBITRAGE	ASTRAKHAN	AVUNCULAR	
ADDRESSEE	AGONIZING	AMBUSCADE	ANOMALOUS	ARBITRARY	ASTRODOME	AWAKENING	
ADENOIDAL	AGREEABLE	AMELAKITE	ANONYMITY	ARBITRATE	ASTROLABE	AWARENESS	
ADEPTNESS	AGREEABLY	AMENDMENT	ANONYMOUS	ARBORETUM	ASTROLOGY	AWESTRUCK	
ADHERENCE	AGREEMENT	AMENHOTEP	ANOPHELES	ARCHANGEL	ASTRONAUT	AWKWARDLY	
ADJECTIVE	AGUECHEEK	AMERICANO	ANSCHLUSS	ARCHETYPE	ASTRONOMY	AXIOMATIC	
ADJOINING	AHASUERUS	AMERICIUM	ANSWERING	ARCHIBALD	ASTROPHEL	AXMINSTER	
ADMIRABLE	AIMLESSLY	AMIANTHUS	ANTARCTIC	ARCHITECT	ASTROTURF	AYATOLLAH	
	AINSWORTH	AMIDSHIPS	ANTENATAL	ARCHIVIST	ASTUCIOUS	AYCKBOURN	

AYLESBURY	BARRICADE	BICYCLIST	BLUNDERER	BREADLINE	BUTTERFLY	CAPITULUM
BACHARACH	BARRISTER	BIFURCATE	BLUNTNESS	BREAKABLE	BUTTERNUT	CAPORETTO
BACKBENCH	BARTENDER	BIGHEADED	BLUSTERER	BREAKAGES	BYPRODUCT	CAPRICCIO
BACKBITER	BARTHOLDI	BILATERAL	BOANERGES	BREAKAWAY	BYSTANDER	CAPRICORN
BACKBOARD	BARTHOLIN	BILINGUAL	BOARDROOM	BREAKDOWN	BYZANTINE	CAPTAINCY
BACKCLOTH	BARYSCOPE	BILIRUBIN	BOARDWALK	BREAKEVEN	CABALLERO	CAPTIVATE
BACKPEDAL	BASEBOARD	BILLABONG	BOATHOUSE	BREAKFAST	CABLEGRAM	CAPTIVITY
BACKSHISH	BASECOURT	BILLBOARD	BOATSWAIN	BREAKNECK	CABRIOLET	CARACALLA
BACKSLIDE	BASHFULLY	BILLIARDS	BOBSLEIGH	BREATHING	CACHAEMIA	CARAMBOLA
BACKSPACE	BASICALLY	BILLOWING	BOCCACCIO	BREECHING	CACHECTIC	CARBAMATE
BACKSTAGE	BASILICAL	BILLYCOCK	BODYGUARD	BRICKWORK	CACOPHONY	CARBAMIDE
BACKSWORD	BASILICON	BIMONTHLY	BOLECTION	BRICKYARD	CADASTRAL	CARBONADE
BACKTRACK	BASKETFUL	BINOCULAR	BOLIVIANO	BRIDEWELL	CAESAREAN	CARBONADO
BACKWARDS	BASTINADE	BIOGRAPHY	BOLOGNESE	BRIDLEWAY	CAFETERIA	CARBONARI
BACKWATER	BASTINADO	BIOLOGIST	BOLSHEVIK	BRIEFCASE	CAFETIERE	CARBONATE
BACKWOODS	BATHTOWEL	BIOSPHERE	BOMBARDON	BRIEFNESS	CAGOULARD	CARBONIZE
BACTERIAL	BATTALION	BIPARTITE	BOMBASINE	BRIGADIER	CAIRNGORM	CARBUNCLE
BACTERIUM	BATTLEAXE	BIRDBRAIN	BOMBASTIC	BRIGADOON	CAKESTAND	CARCINOMA
BADMINTON	BEACHHEAD	BIRDTABLE	BOMBSHELL	BRILLIANT	CALABOOSE	CARDBOARD
BAGATELLE	BEACHWEAR	BIRTHMARK	BONAPARTE	BRIMSTONE	CALABRESE	CAREERIST
BAINMARIE	BEANFEAST	BIRTHRATE	BONDSTONE	BRIQUETTE	CALCANEUM	CAREFULLY
BAKEHOUSE	BEARDLESS	BIRTHWORT	BOOBIALLA	BRISKNESS	CALCANEUS	CARETAKER
BAKSHEESH	BEARDSLEY	BISECTION	BOOBYTRAP	BRISTLING	CALCINATE	CARIBBEAN
BALACLAVA	BEATITUDE	BISHOPRIC	BOOKLOVER	BRITANNIA	CALCULATE	CARMELITE
BALALAIKA	BEAUTEOUS	BIZARRELY	BOOKMAKER	BRITANNIC	CALDARIUM	CARNATION
BALDAQUIN	BEAUTIFUL	BLACKBALL	BOOKSHELF	BRITSCHKA	CALEDONIA	CARNELIAN
BALEFULLY	BECHSTEIN	BLACKBIRD	BOOKSTALL	BROADCAST	CALEMBOUR	CARNIVORE
BALLADEER	BECQUEREL	BLACKBUCK	BOOKSTAND	BROADLOOM	CALENDULA	CARPACCIO
BALLADIST	BEDFELLOW	BLACKDAMP	BOOKSTORE	BROADSIDE	CALENTURE	CARPENTER
BALLERINA	BEDJACKET	BLACKFACE	BOOMERANG	BROKERAGE	CALIBRATE	CARPENTRY
BALLISTIC	BEDRAGGLE	BLACKFOOT	BOONDOCKS	BROMINATE	CALLIPERS	CARPETING
BALLPOINT	BEDRIDDEN	BLACKHEAD	BOOTBLACK	BRONCHIAL	CALLOSITY	CARTESIAN
BALTHAZAR	BEDSITTER	BLACKJACK	BOOTLACES	BROTHERLY	CALLOUSLY	CARTHORSE
BALTIMORE	BEDSPREAD	BLACKLEAD	BORDEREAU	BROUGHTON	CALORIFIC	CARTILAGE
BAMBOOZLE	BEEFEATER	BLACKLIST	BORDERING	BRUMMAGEM	CALPURNIA	CARTOGRAM
BANDALORE	BEEFSTEAK	BLACKMAIL	BORNAGAIN	BRUNHILDE	CALVANISM	CARTOUCHE
BANDICOOT	BEEKEEPER	BLACKMORE	BORROWING	BRUSHWOOD	CALVINIST	CARTRIDGE
BANDOLEER	BEELZEBUB	BLACKNESS	BOSPHORUS	BRUSQUELY	CALVITIES	CARTTRACK
BANDOLERO	BEESTINGS	BLACKWOOD	BOSSANOVA	BRUTALISM	CAMBODIAN	CARTULARY
BANDOLIER	BEETHOVEN	BLAMELESS	BOSSINESS	BRUTALITY	CAMBRIDGE	CARTWHEEL
BANDOLINE	BEGINNING	BLANDNESS	BOSTONIAN	BRUTALIZE	CAMBUSCAN	CARYOPSIS
BANDSTAND	BEHAVIOUR	BLASPHEME	BOTANICAL	BUBBLEGUM	CAMCORDER	CASHPOINT
BANDWAGON	BELATEDLY	BLASPHEMY	BOTSWANAN	BUCCANEER	CAMEMBERT	CASSANDRA
BANEBERRY	BELEAGUER	BLATANTLY	BOTTLEFUL	BUCENTAUR	CAMERAMAN	CASSATION
BANISTERS	BELIEVING	BLEACHERS	BOULEVARD	BUCHAREST	CAMPANILE	CASSEROLE
BANQUETTE	BELLICOSE	BLESSINGS	BOUNDLESS	BUCKETFUL	CAMPANULA	CASSONADE
BANTERING	BELLYACHE	BLINDFOLD	BOUNTEOUS	BUCKTEETH	CANALETTO	CASSOULET
BAPTISMAL	BELLYFLOP	BLINDNESS	BOUNTIFUL	BUCKTHORN	CANAVERAL	CASSOWARY
BARAGOUIN	BELONGING	BLINDSPOT	BOURGEOIS	BUCKWHEAT	CANCEROUS	CASTANETS
BARBARIAN	BELVEDERE	BLINDWORM	BOXWALLAH	BUDGETARY	CANDIDACY	CASTELLAN
BARBARISM	BENBECULA	BLINKERED	BOYFRIEND	BUFFETING	CANDIDATE	CASTIGATE
BARBARITY	BENCHMARK	BLISTERED	BRACTEOLE	BULGARIAN	CANDLELIT	CASTILIAN
BARBARIZE	BENIGHTED	BLOATWARE	BRADLAUGH	BULKINESS	CANDLEMAS	CASTRATED
BARBAROUS	BERGAMASK	BLOCKHEAD	BRAINCASE	BULLDOZER	CANDYTUFT	CASUARINA
BARBITONE	BERGANDER	BLOODBATH	BRAINLESS	BULLFIGHT	CANNELURE	CASUISTIC
BARBOTINE	BERGOMASK	BLOODLESS	BRAINWASH	BULLFINCH	CANNONADE	CASUISTRY
BARCELONA	BERKELIUM	BLOODROOT	BRAINWAVE	BUMBLEBEE	CANONICAL	CATACLYSM
BAREBONES	BERNSTEIN	BLOODSHED	BRAMBLING	BUMPTIOUS	CANTABILE	CATACOMBS
BAREFACED	BERSERKER	BLOODSHOT	BRANCHING	BUNDESTAG	CANTHARIS	CATALEPSY
BARMBRACK	BERYLLIUM	BLOODWORM	BRANDIRON	BURKINABE	CANTHARUS	CATALOGUE
BARMECIDE	BESPANGLE	BLOWTORCH	BRASENOSE	BURLESQUE	CANTONESE	CATALYSIS
BARNABITE	BETHLEHEM	BLUEBEARD	BRASSERIE	BURLINESS	CANVASSER	CATALYTIC
BARNACLES	BETROTHAL	BLUEBERRY	BRASSICAS	BURROUGHS	CAPACIOUS	CATAMARAN
BARNSTORM	BETROTHED	BLUEPRINT	BRASSIERE	BURROWING	CAPACITOR	CATAMOUNT
BAROMETER	BETTERTON	BLUESHIFT	BRASSWARE	BURUNDIAN	CAPARISON	CATAPLASM
BARONETCY	BEVERIDGE	BLUESTONE	BRATWURST	BUTTERBUR	CAPILLARY	CATAPLEXY
BARRACUDA	BICONCAVE	BLUFFNESS	BRAZILIAN	BUTTERCUP	CAPITULAR	CATARRHAL

CATATONIA	CHALUMEAU	CHLOROSIS	COARCTATE	COMMANDER	CONJURING	CORPUSCLE
CATATONIC	CHAMELEON	CHOCOLATE	COASTLINE	COMMENSAL	CONNECTED	CORRECTED
CATCHCROP	CHAMFRAIN	CHOLELITH	COCHINEAL	COMMISSAR	CONNECTOR	CORRECTLY
CATCHMENT	CHAMINADE	CHONDRITE	COCKAIGNE	COMMITTAL	CONNEXION	CORRECTOR
CATCHPOLE	CHAMOMILE	CHONDROID	COCKATIEL	COMMITTED	CONNOTATE	CORREGGIO
CATCHPOLL	CHAMPAGNE	CHORISTER	COCKFIGHT	COMMITTEE	CONNUBIAL	CORRELATE
CATCHWORD	CHAMPAIGN	CHRISTIAN	COCKROACH	COMMODITY	CONQUEROR	CORROSION
CATECHISM	CHAMPERTY	CHRISTMAS	COCKSCOMB	COMMODORE	CONSCIOUS	CORROSIVE
CATECHIZE	CHAMPLAIN	CHROMATIC	COCKSFOOT	COMMOTION	CONSCRIPT	CORRUGATE
CATERWAUL	CHAMPLEVÉ	CHRONICLE	COCKSWAIN	COMMUNION	CONSENSUS	CORRUPTER
CATHARSIS	CHANCROID	CHRYSALIS	COCUSWOOD	COMMUNISM	CONSIGNEE	CORTISONE
CATHARTIC	CHANTEUSE	CHURCHILL	COELOSTAT	COMMUNIST	CONSIGNOR	CORUSCATE
CATHEDRAL	CHANTILLY	CHURCHMAN	COEMPTION	COMMUNITY	CONSOCIES	COSMETICS
CATHEPSIN	CHAPARRAL	CHURIDARS	COENOBITE	COMMUTATE	CONSONANT	COSMOGONY
CATHERINE	CHAPERONE	CIGARETTE	COENOBIUM	COMPACTLY	CONSTABLE	COSMOLOGY
CATSKILLS	CHARABANC	CILIOLATE	COFFERDAM	COMPANIES	CONSTANCE	COSMONAUT
CATTLEMAN	CHARACTER	CIMMERIAN	COFFINITE	COMPANION	CONSTANCY	COSTUMIER
CATTLEPEN	CHARGEFUL	CINEMATIC	COGNITION	COMPELLED	CONSTRICT	COTANGENT
CAUCASIAN	CHARIVARI	CINEPHILE	COGNITIVE	COMPETENT	CONSTRUCT	COTHURNUS
CAUCASOID	CHARLATAN	CINERARIA	COGNIZANT	COMPETING	CONSULATE	COTYLEDON
CAUSATION	CHARLOTTE	CINEREOUS	COHERENCE	COMPLAINT	CONSUMING	COUCHETTE
CAUTERIZE	CHAROLAIS	CIPOLLINO	COINTREAU	COMPLIANT	CONTAGION	COUNSELOR
CAVALCADE	CHARTERED	CIRCADIAN	COLCHICUM	COMPONENT	CONTAINER	COUNTDOWN
CAVENDISH	CHARTREUX	CIRCINATE	COLERIDGE	COMPOSING	CONTEMPER	COUNTLESS
CAVERNOUS	CHARWOMAN	CIRCULATE	COLLAPSAR	COMPOSITE	CONTENDER	COUNTRIES
CAVORTING	CHARYBDIS	CIRRHOSIS	COLLATION	COMPOSURE	CONTENTED	COURGETTE
CEANOTHUS	CHASTENED	CIVILISED	COLLEAGUE	COMPOTIER	CONTINENT	COURTELLE
CEASEFIRE	CHATTERER	CIVILIZED	COLLECTED	COMPUTING	CONTINUAL	COURTEOUS
CEASELESS	CHAUFFEUR	CLAMOROUS	COLLECTOR	CONCAVITY	CONTINUUM	COURTESAN
CEDARWOOD	CHAVENDER	CLAMPDOWN	COLLEGIAN	CONCEALED	CONTRALTO	COURTROOM
CELANDINE	CHAWBACON	CLAPBOARD	COLLIGATE	CONCEITED	CONTRIVED	COURTSHIP
CELEBRANT	CHEAPJACK	CLARENDON	COLLIMATE	CONCERNED	CONTRIVER	COURTYARD
CELEBRATE	CHEAPNESS	CLARIFIER	COLLISION	CONCERTED	CONTUMACY	COUTURIER
CELEBRITY	CHEAPSIDE	CLASSICAL	COLLOCATE	CONCIERGE	CONTUMELY	COVALENCY
CELESTIAL	CHECKBOOK	CLASSLESS	COLLODION	CONCISELY	CONTUSION	COVELLITE
CELLARIST	CHECKLIST	CLASSMATE	COLLOIDAL	CONCISION	CONUNDRUM	COVERDALE
CELLULITE	CHECKMATE	CLASSROOM	COLLOTYPE	CONCLUDED	CONVECTOR	COVERTURE
CELLULOID	CHECKROOM	CLEANNESS	COLLUSION	CONCORDAT	CONVERTED	COWARDICE
CELLULOSE	CHEEKBONE	CLEANSING	COLLUSIVE	CONCOURSE	CONVERTER	COXSACKIE
CENTAURUS	CHEERLESS	CLEARANCE	COLLYRIUM	CONCUBINE	CONVINCED	CRACKDOWN
CENTENARY	CHEMISTRY	CLEARNESS	COLOCYNTH	CONCUSSED	CONVIVIAL	CRACKLING
CENTERING	CHEONGSAM	CLEARWING	COLOMBIAN	CONDEMNED	COOKHOUSE	CRACKSMAN
CENTIGRAM	CHEQUERED	CLEOPATRA	COLOMBIER	CONDENSER	COOPERATE	CRACOVIAN
CENTIPEDE	CHERISHED	CLEPSYDRA	COLONNADE	CONDIMENT	COPIOUSLY	CRAFTSMAN
CENTRALLY	CHERNOZEM	CLERGYMAN	COLOPHONY	CONDITION	COPROLITE	CRANBERRY
CENTREING	CHERUBINI	CLEVELAND	COLORLESS	CONDUCIVE	COPYRIGHT	CRANBORNE
CENTURION	CHEVALIER	CLIENTELE	COLOSSEUM	CONDUCTOR	CORALLINE	CRAPULENT
CERATITIS	CHICANERY	CLIMACTIC	COLOSTOMY	CONDUCTUS	CORDIALLY	CRAPULOUS
CERATODUS	CHICKADEE	CLINGFILM	COLOSTRUM	CONDYLOMA	CORDUROYS	CRASHLAND
CEREBRATE	CHICKWEED	CLINICIAN	COLOURFUL	CONFESSED	CORDYLINE	CRAZINESS
CERECLOTH	CHIEFTAIN	CLIPBOARD	COLOURING	CONFESSOR	CORIANDER	CREDULITY
CEROMANCY	CHIHUAHUA	CLOAKROOM	COLOURIST	CONFIDANT	CORKSCREW	CREDULOUS
CERTAINLY	CHILBLAIN	CLOCKWISE	COLTSFOOT	CONFIDENT	CORMORANT	CREMATION
CERTAINTY	CHILDCARE	CLOCKWORK	COLUMBARY	CONFIRMED	CORNBRASH	CREMATORY
CERTIFIED	CHILDHOOD	CLOISONNÉ	COLUMBATE	CONFITEOR	CORNCRAKE	CRENATION
CERTITUDE	CHILDLESS	CLOSENESS	COLUMBIAN	CONFLATED	CORNEILLE	CREPITATE
CERUSSITE	CHILDLIKE	CLOUDLESS	COLUMBINE	CONFORMAL	CORNELIAN	CREPOLINE
CERVANTES	CHILOPODA	CLUBHOUSE	COLUMBITE	CONFUCIUS	CORNERMAN	CRESCELLE
CESSATION	CHINATOWN	CLUSTERED	COLUMBIUM	CONFUSING	CORNETIST	CRESCENDO
CEVAPCICI	CHINOVNIK	COACHLOAD	COLUMELLA	CONFUSION	CORNFIELD	CRETINOUS
CEYLONESE	CHINSTRAP	COADJUTOR	COLUMNIST	CONGENIAL	CORNFLOUR	CRIBELLUM
CHABAZITE	CHIPBOARD	COAGULANT	COMBATANT	CONGERIES	CORNSTALK	CRICKETER
CHAFFINCH	CHIPOLATA	COAGULATE	COMBATIVE	CONGESTED	COROLLARY	CRIMINATE
CHAIRLIFT	CHIPPINGS	COALESCED	COMFORTER	CONGOLESE	CORPORATE	CRINOLINE
CHALAZION	CHIROPODY	COALFIELD	COMICALLY	CONGRUENT	CORPOREAL	CRIPPLING
CHALIAPIN	CHISELLER	COALITION	COMINFORM	CONGRUOUS	CORPOSANT	CRISPNESS
CHALLENGE	CHLAMYDES	COALMINER	COMINTERN	CONJUGATE	CORPULENT	CRITERION

CRITICISM	DAEDALIAN	DECURSIVE	DESICCATE	DIGITALIN	DISSENTER	DRAWKNIFE
CRITICIZE	DAIRYMAID	DECUSSATE	DESIGNATE	DIGITALIS	DISSIDENT	DREAMLAND
CROCKFORD	DALLIANCE	DEDICATED	DESIGNING	DIGNIFIED	DISSIPATE	DREAMLESS
CROCODILE	DALMATIAN	DEDUCTION	DESIPIENT	DIGNITARY	DISSOLUTE	DRIFTWOOD
CROISSANT	DALTONISM	DEDUCTIVE	DESIRABLE	DILIGENCE	DISSOLVED	DRINKABLE
CROOKBACK	DAMASCENE	DEERHOUND	DESPERADO	DIMENSION	DISSONANT	DRIPSTONE
CROOKEDLY	DAMBUSTER	DEFALCATE	DESPERATE	DINGINESS	DISTANTLY	DROMEDARY
CROQUETTE	DAMNATION	DEFAULTER	DESPOTISM	DINNERSET	DISTEMPER	DROPPINGS
CROSSBEAM	DAMNEDEST	DEFEATISM	DESTITUTE	DIOCLETES	DISTENDED	DROPSICAL
CROSSBILL	DAMSELFLY	DEFEATIST	DESTROYED	DIONYSIAN	DISTILLER	DRUGSTORE
CROSSBRED	DANDELION	DEFECTION	DESTROYER	DIONYSIUS	DISTORTED	DRUMSTICK
CROSSEYED	DANDIFIED	DEFECTIVE	DESUETUDE	DIPHTHONG	DISTRAINT	DRUNKENLY
CROSSFIRE	DANDYPRAT	DEFENDANT	DESULTORY	DIPLOMACY	DISTURBED	DRYASDUST
CROSSOVER	DANGEROUS	DEFENDERS	DETECTION	DIRECTION	DISUNITED	DUBIOUSLY
CROSSWALK	DANTHONIA	DEFENSIVE	DETECTIVE	DIRECTIVE	DITHERING	DUBROVNIK
CROSSWIND	DAREDEVIL	DEFERENCE	DETENTION	DIRECTORS	DITHYRAMB	DUCKBOARD
CROSSWISE	DARTAGNAN	DEFERMENT	DETERGENT	DIRECTORY	DIVERGENT	DUIKERBOK
CROSSWORD	DARTBOARD	DEFICIENT	DETERMINE	DIRIGIBLE	DIVERGING	DULCINIST
CROTCHETY	DARTMOUTH	DEFINABLE	DETERRENT	DIRTINESS	DIVERSIFY	DUMBARTON
CROUSTADE	DARWINIAN	DEFLATION	DETONATOR	DISABLING	DIVERSION	DUMBFOUND
CROWNLIKE	DASHBOARD	DEFLECTOR	DETRACTOR	DISAFFIRM	DIVERSITY	DUNDREARY
CROWSBILL	DASHWHEEL	DEFOLIANT	DETRIMENT	DISAPPEAR	DIVERTING	DUNGAREES
CROWSFOOT	DASTARDLY	DEFOLIATE	DETRITION	DISARMING	DIVIDENDS	DUNGENESS
CRUCIALLY	DAUNTLESS	DEFORMITY	DEUCALION	DISBELIEF	DIVISIBLE	DUNGEONER
CRUCIFORM	DAVENPORT	DEGRADING	DEUTERIUM	DISBURDEN	DIXIELAND	DUNSINANE
CRUDENESS	DAYSPRING	DEHYDRATE	DEVASTATE	DISCARDED	DIZYGOTIC	DUNSTABLE
CRUMBLING	DEACONESS	DEJECTION	DEVELOPED	DISCHARGE	DIZZINESS	DUODECIMO
CRUSTACEA	DEADLIGHT	DELACROIX	DEVELOPER	DISCLOSED	DJELLABAH	DUPLICAND
CRYOGENIC	DEAFENING	DELICIOUS	DEVIATION	DISCOLOUR	DOCTORATE	DUPLICATE
CRYOMETER	DEAMINATE	DELIGHTED	DEVILFISH	DISCOMFIT	DOCTRINAL	DUPLICITY
CRYPTOGAM	DEATHBLOW	DELINEATE	DEVILMENT	DISCOURSE	DOCUMENTS	DUTIFULLY
CTESIPHON	DEATHLESS	DELIRIOUS	DEVIOUSLY	DISCOVERT	DODDIPOLL	DWINDLING
CUBBYHOLE	DEATHTRAP	DELIVERER	DEVONPORT	DISCOVERY	DOGMATISM	DYNAMITED
CUCHULAIN	DEBATABLE	DELPHINUS	DEXTERITY	DISCREDIT	DOGMATIZE	DYSENTERY
CUFFLINKS	DEBAUCHED	DEMAGOGUE	DEXTEROUS	DISEMBARK	DOLEFULLY	DYSPEPSIA
CULMINATE	DEBAUCHEE	DEMANDING	DEXTRORSE	DISENGAGE	DOLOMITES	DYSPEPTIC
CULTIVATE	DEBENTURE	DEMARCATE	DIABLERIE	DISENTOMB	DOLOMITIC	DYSPHAGIA
CUNCTATOR	DEBUTANTE	DEMEANING	DIACRITIC	DISFAVOUR	DOMICILED	DYSPRAXIA
CUNEIFORM	DECACHORD	DEMEANOUR	DIAERESIS	DISFIGURE	DOMINANCE	DYSTROPHY
CUPRESSUS	DECADENCE	DEMETRIUS	DIAGNOSIS	DISGRACED	DOMINICAL	EAGERNESS
CURETTAGE	DECALITRE	DEMITASSE	DIALECTAL	DISGUISED	DOMINICAN	EAGLEWOOD
CURFUFFLE	DECALOGUE	DEMOCRACY	DIALECTIC	DISGUSTED	DONATELLO	EALDORMAN
CURIOSITY	DECAMERON	DEMULCENT	DIALOGITE	DISHCLOTH	DONCASTER	EARNESTLY
CURIOUSLY	DECASTYLE	DEMURRAGE	DIAMETRIC	DISHONEST	DONIZETTI	EARTHFLAX
CURRENTLY	DECATHLON	DENIGRATE	DIANDROUS	DISHONOUR	DOODLEBUG	EARTHLING
CURRYCOMB	DECEITFUL	DENSENESS	DIANETICS	DISHWATER	DOORFRAME	EARTHWORK
CURSORILY	DECEMVIRI	DENTISTRY	DIANOETIC	DISINFECT	DORMITION	EARTHWORM
CURTILAGE	DECENNIAL	DENTITION	DIAPHRAGM	DISLOCATE	DORMITORY	EASTBOUND
CURVATURE	DECEPTION	DEODORANT	DIAPHYSIS	DISMANTLE	DOSIMETER	EASTERNER
CURVEBALL	DECEPTIVE	DEODORIZE	DIARRHOEA	DISMEMBER	DOSSHOUSE	EASTLINGS
CUSPIDORE	DECESSION	DEOXIDISE	DIASTASIS	DISMISSAL	DOTHEBOYS	EASTWARDS
CUSTODIAL	DECIDEDLY	DEPARTURE	DIATHERMY	DISOBLIGE	DOUBTLESS	EASYGOING
CUSTODIAN	DECIDUOUS	DEPASTURE	DIATHESIS	DISORIENT	DOUKHOBOR	EAVESDROP
CUSTOMARY	DECILLION	DEPENDANT	DIATOMITE	DISPARAGE	DOWELLING	EBRILLADE
CUSTOMIZE	DECKCHAIR	DEPENDENT	DIAZEUXIS	DISPARATE	DOWNGRADE	EBULLIENT
CUTANEOUS	DECLARING	DEPENDING	DICHOTOMY	DISPARITY	DOWNRIGHT	ECARDINES
CUTTHROAT	DECLINING	DEPICTION	DICTATION	DISPENSER	DOWNSTAGE	ECCENTRIC
CYCLAMATE	DECLIVITY	DEPOSITOR	DIDACTICS	DISPERSAL	DOWNTREND	ECHEVERIA
CYCLOLITH	DECOCTION	DEPRAVITY	DIETETICS	DISPERSED	DOWNWARDS	ECHIDNINE
CYCLORAMA	DECOLLATE	DEPRECATE	DIETICIAN	DISPLACED	DRACONIAN	ECLAMPSIA
CYCLOTRON	DECOMPOSE	DEPREDATE	DIFFERENT	DISPLAYED	DRAFTSMAN	ECOLOGIST
CYMBELINE	DECONTROL	DEPRESSED	DIFFICULT	DISPLEASE	DRAGONFLY	ECONOMICS
CYMBIDIUM	DECORATED	DERRINGER	DIFFIDENT	DISPUTANT	DRAINPIPE	ECONOMIST
CYNEGETIC	DECORATOR	DESCARTES	DIFFUSION	DISREGARD	DRAMATICS	ECONOMIZE
CYNICALLY	DECRETALS	DESECRATE	DIGASTRIC	DISREPAIR	DRAMATIST	ECOSPHERE
CYTOKININ	DECRETORY	DESERTION	DIGESTION	DISREPUTE	DRAMATIZE	ECOSSAISE
DACHSHUND	DECUMBENT	DESERVING	DIGESTIVE	DISSEMBLE	DRAVIDIAN	ECOSYSTEM

ECTOMORPH	EMBROCATE	ENHYDRITE	EQUIPMENT	EVANGELIC	EXPERTISE	FANTASIZE	
ECTOPLASM	EMBROGLIO	ENIGMATIC	EQUIPOISE	EVAPORATE	EXPIATION	FANTASTIC	
ECTOTHERM	EMBROIDER	ENJOYABLE	EQUISETUM	EVASIVELY	EXPIATORY	FARANDOLE	
ECTROPION	EMBROILED	ENJOYMENT	EQUITABLE	EVENTUATE	EXPISCATE	FARMHOUSE	
EDDINGTON	EMBRYONIC	ENLIGHTEN	EQUITABLY	EVERGLADE	EXPLETIVE	FARMSTEAD	
EDDYSTONE	EMERGENCE	ENLIVENED	EQUIVOCAL	EVERGREEN	EXPLICATE	FASCINATE	
EDELWEISS	EMERGENCY	ENNERDALE	EQUIVOQUE	EVERYBODY	EXPLOITER	FASHIONED	
EDGEWORTH	EMINENTLY	ENQUIRIES	ERADICATE	EVIDENTLY	EXPLOSION	FASTENING	
EDINBURGH	EMMERDALE	ENQUIRING	ERGATANER	EVITERNAL	EXPLOSIVE	FASTTRACK	
EDITORIAL	EMOLLIATE	ENRAPTURE	ERIOMETER	EVOCATION	EXPORTING	FATIDICAL	
EDUCATION	EMOLLIENT	ENROLMENT	ERISTICAL	EVOCATIVE	EXPOSITOR	FATISCENT	
EDUCATIVE	EMOLUMENT	ENSCONCED	EROGENOUS	EVOCATORY	EXPRESSED	FATTENING	
EDWARDIAN	EMOTIONAL	ENSHEATHE	EROSTRATE	EVOLUTION	EXPRESSLY	FATUOUSLY	
EFFECTIVE	EMPAESTIC	ENSORCELL	EROTICISM	EXACTMENT	EXPULSION	FAULCHION	
EFFECTUAL	EMPANOPLY	ENSTATITE	ERPINGHAM	EXACTNESS	EXPURGATE	FAULTLESS	
EFFICIENT	EMPENNAGE	ENTELECHY	ERRONEOUS	EXANIMATE	EXQUISITE	FAVORABLE	
EFFINGHAM	EMPHASIZE	ENTERITIS	ERSTWHILE	EXANTHEMA	EXSICCATE	FAVORABLY	
EFFLUENCE	EMPHLYSIS	ENTERTAIN	ERUCIFORM	EXARATION	EXTEMPORE	FAVOURITE	
EFFLUVIUM	EMPHYSEMA	ENTHYMEME	ERUDITION	EXCALIBUR	EXTENSILE	FEARFULLY	
EFFULGENT	EMPIRICAL	ENTOPHYTE	ERYTHRITE	EXCAMBION	EXTENSION	FEATHERED	
EGAREMENT	EMPLECTON	ENTOURAGE	ESCALATOR	EXCAVATOR	EXTENSIVE	FEBRIFUGE	
EGLANTINE	EMPLOYEES	ENTRAMMEL	ESCOPETTE	EXCELLENT	EXTENUATE	FECUNDITY	
EGREGIOUS	EMPTINESS	ENTRANCED	ESCULENTS	EXCELSIOR	EXTIRPATE	FEDUCIARY	
EGRESSION	EMULATION	ENTRECHAT	ESEMPLASY	EXCEPTION	EXTORTION	FEEDSTUFF	
EIDERDOWN	ENACTMENT	ENTRECÔTE	ESMERALDA	EXCESSIVE	EXTRACTOR	FEMINEITY	
EIDOGRAPH	ENAMELLED	ENTREMETS	ESOPHAGUS	EXCHEQUER	EXTRADITE	FENCIBLES	
EIGHTIETH	ENAMOURED	ENTROPION	ESPAGNOLE	EXCIPIENT	EXTREMELY	FENUGREEK	
EIGHTSOME	ENCANTHIS	ENTROPIUM	ESPERANCE	EXCISEMAN	EXTREMISM	FERACIOUS	
EJACULATE	ENCAUSTIC	ENUCLEATE	ESPERANTO	EXCITABLE	EXTREMIST	FERDINAND	
ELABORATE	ENCELADUS	ENUMERATE	ESPIONAGE	EXCLAIMED	EXTREMITY	FERINGHEE	
ELAEOLITE	ENCHANTED	ENUNCIATE	ESPLANADE	EXCLUDING	EXTRICATE	FERMENTED	
ELASTOMER	ENCHANTER	ENVERMEIL	ESQUILINE	EXCLUSION	EXTRINSIC	FEROCIOUS	
ELATERIUM	ENCHEASON	EPARCHATE	ESSENTIAL	EXCLUSIVE	EXTROVERT	FERROTYPE	
ELBOWROOM	ENCHILADA	EPAULETTE	ESTABLISH	EXCORIATE	EXTRUSION	FERRYBOAT	
ELECTORAL	ENCHORIAL	EPEDAPHIC	ESTAFETTE	EXCREMENT	EXUBERANT	FERTILITY	
ELECTRESS	ENCIRCLED	EPEOLATRY	ESTAMINET	EXCULPATE	EXUDATION	FERTILIZE	
ELECTRIFY	ENCLOSURE	EPHEDRINE	ESTHETICS	EXCURSION	EYEBRIGHT	FERVENTLY	
ELECTRODE	ENCOLPION	EPHEMERAL	ESTIMABLE	EXCUSABLE	EYELETEER	FESTINATE	
ELECTUARY	ENCOLPIUM	EPHEMERIS	ESTRANGED	EXCUSABLY	EYEOPENER	FESTIVITY	
ELEGANTLY	ENCOMPASS	EPHEMERON	ESTRAPADE	EXECRABLE	EYESHADOW	FEUDALISM	
ELEMENTAL	ENCOUNTER	EPHESIANS	ESTRELDID	EXECRABLY	EYESPLICE	FEUDATORY	
ELEVATION	ENCOURAGE	EPHIALTES	ETCETERAS	EXECUTANT	EYESTRAIN	FEUILLANT	
ELEVENSES	ENCRATITE	EPICEDIUM	ETERNALLY	EXECUTION	FABACEOUS	FIBROLINE	
ELIMINATE	ENCUMBENT	EPICENTRE	ETHANOATE	EXECUTIVE	FABRICATE	FIBROLITE	
ELIZABETH	ENDEARING	EPICLESIS	ETHELBERT	EXECUTRIX	FABULINUS	FICTIONAL	
ELKOSHITE	ENDEAVOUR	EPICUREAN	ETHEREOUS	EXEMPLARY	FACECLOTH	FIDUCIARY	
ELLESMERE	ENDECAGON	EPICYCLIC	ETHIOPIAN	EXEMPLIFY	FACETIOUS	FIELDFARE	
ELLINGTON	ENDEICTIC	EPIDERMIS	ETHNOLOGY	EXEMPTION	FACSIMILE	FIELDSMAN	
ELOCUTION	ENDLESSLY	EPIGAEOUS	ETIOLATED	EXEQUATUR	FACTIONAL	FIELDWORK	
ELONGATED	ENDOCRINE	EPIGENOUS	ETIQUETTE	EXERCISED	FACTORIAL	FIFTEENTH	
ELOPEMENT	ENDOERGIC	EPILATION	ETYMOLOGY	EXERCISES	FACTORISE	FIGURANTE	
ELOQUENCE	ENDOMORPH	EPILEPTIC	EUCHARIST	EXHAUSTED	FACTUALLY	FILICALES	
ELSEWHERE	ENDOSPERM	EPINASTIC	EUCHLORIC	EXHIBITOR	FACUNDITY	FILIGRAIN	
ELUCIDATE	ENDOWMENT	EPINICION	EUCLIDEAN	EXISTENCE	FAINTNESS	FILLIPEEN	
ELUTRIATE	ENDPAPERS	EPINIKION	EUDAEMONY	EXODERMIS	FAIRYLAND	FILLISTER	
EMACIATED	ENDURABLE	EPIPHRAGM	EUHEMERUS	EXOGENOUS	FAIRYTALE	FILMMAKER	
EMANATION	ENDURANCE	EPIPHYSIS	EUMENIDES	EXONERATE	FAITHLESS	FILMSTRIP	
EMBARRASS	ENERGETIC	EPIPHYTIC	EUMYCETES	EXORATION	FALANGIST	FILOPLUME	
EMBASSADE	ENERGUMEN	EPIPOLISM	EUPHEMISM	EXOSPHERE	FALDSTOOL	FILOSELLE	
EMBASSAGE	ENERINITE	EPISCOPAL	EUPHONIUM	EXOSTOSIS	FALERNIAN	FILTERING	
EMBATTLED	ENGARLAND	EPISTAXIS	EUPHORBIA	EXPANSION	FALKLANDS	FILTERTIP	
EMBELLISH	ENGINEERS	EPISTOLER	EUPHRATES	EXPANSIVE	FALLOPIAN	FINANCIAL	
EMBEZZLER	ENGRAINED	EPITHESIS	EURHYTHMY	EXPATIATE	FALSEHOOD	FINANCIER	
EMBRACERY	ENGRAVING	EPITOMIZE	EURIPIDES	EXPECTANT	FALSENESS	FINGERING	
EMBRACING	ENGRENAGE	EPONYMOUS	EUSKARIAN	EXPECTING	FAMAGUSTA	FINGERTIP	
EMBRANGLE	ENGROSSED	EPULATION	EUTROPHIC	EXPEDIENT	FANATICAL	FINICKING	
EMBRASURE	ENGROSSER	EQUALIZER	EVAGATION	EXPENSIVE	FANDANGLE	FINICKITY	

366

FINISHING	FOLKETING	FRACTIOUS	FURNITURE	GENETICAL	GOBETWEEN	GREENSAND
FINLANDIA	FOLKWEAVE	FRAGILITY	FURTIVELY	GENEVIEVE	GODDESSES	GREENWEED
FIORITURA	FOLLOWING	FRAGMENTS	FUSILLADE	GENIALITY	GODFATHER	GREENWICH
FIREBRAND	FOMALHAUT	FRAGONARD	FUSSINESS	GENITALIA	GODLINESS	GREENWOOD
FIREBREAK	FOODSTORE	FRAGRANCE	FUSTIGATE	GENTEELLY	GODMOTHER	GREENYARD
FIREDRAKE	FOODSTUFF	FRAGRANCY	FUSTINESS	GENTILITY	GODOLPHIN	GREETINGS
FIREGUARD	FOOLHARDY	FRAMBOISE	FUZZINESS	GENTLEMAN	GODPARENT	GREGARINE
FIRELIGHT	FOOLISHLY	FRAMEWORK	GABARDINE	GENTLEMEN	GOLDCREST	GREGORIAN
FIREPLACE	FOOLPROOF	FRANCESCA	GABERDINE	GENUFLECT	GOLDFIELD	GRENADIER
FIREPROOF	FOOTBRAKE	FRANCHISE	GABIONADE	GENUINELY	GOLDFINCH	GRENADINE
FIRESTONE	FOOTHILLS	FRANCOLIN	GAELTACHT	GEODESIST	GOLDSINNY	GRENVILLE
FIREWATER	FOOTLOOSE	FRANGLAIS	GAINFULLY	GEOGRAPHY	GOLDSMITH	GREYBEARD
FIREWORKS	FOOTPLATE	FRANKNESS	GAINSAYER	GEOLOGIST	GOMPHOSIS	GREYHOUND
FIRMAMENT	FOOTPRINT	FRATCHETY	GALACTOSE	GEOMETRIC	GONDOLIER	GREYWACKE
FIRSTEVER	FOOTSTALL	FRATERNAL	GALANTINE	GEOMETRID	GONGORISM	GRIEVANCE
FIRSTHAND	FOOTSTOOL	FREDERICK	GALAPAGOS	GEORGETTE	GONIATITE	GRIMALKIN
FIRSTRATE	FORASMUCH	FREEBOARD	GALATIANS	GERFALCON	GOODNIGHT	GRIMINESS
FISHERMAN	FORBIDDEN	FREELANCE	GALDRAGON	GERIATRIC	GOONHILLY	GRINGOLET
FISHGUARD	FORCEMEAT	FREEMASON	GALENGALE	GERMANCER	GOOSANDER	GRISAILLE
FISHPLATE	FOREANENT	FREEPHONE	GALINGALE	GERMANDER	GOOSEFOOT	GROCERIES
FLABELLUM	FOREBEARS	FREESTONE	GALIONGEE	GERMANITE	GOOSEHERD	GROSGRAIN
FLAGELLIN	FOREBRAIN	FREESTYLE	GALLABEAH	GERMANIUM	GOOSENECK	GROSVENOR
FLAGELLUM	FORECLOSE	FREEWHEEL	GALLANTLY	GERMICIDE	GOOSESTEP	GROTESQUE
FLAGEOLET	FORECOURT	FREIGHTER	GALLANTRY	GERMINATE	GOSLARITE	GROUNDHOG
FLAGITATE	FOREFRONT	FRENCHMAN	GALLICISM	GERUNDIVE	GOSPELLER	GROUNDING
FLAGRANCE	FOREGOING	FRENCHMEN	GALLINULE	GESSAMINE	GOSSAMERY	GROUNDNUT
FLAGSTAFF	FOREIGNER	FREQUENCY	GALLIPOLI	GESTATION	GOSSYPINE	GROUNDSEL
FLAGSTONE	FORESHORE	FRESHENER	GALLIVANT	GIBBERISH	GOSSYPIUM	GRUBBINOL
FLAMMABLE	FORESIGHT	FRESHNESS	GALLOPADE	GIBEONITE	GOTHAMITE	GRUELLING
FLAMSTEED	FORESPEAK	FRETFULLY	GALLSTONE	GIBRALTAR	GOVERNESS	GRUFFNESS
FLASHBACK	FORESPEND	FRICASSEE	GALLYCROW	GIDDINESS	GOVERNING	GRUMBLING
FLASHBULB	FORESTAGE	FRIESLAND	GALRAVAGE	GIGAHERTZ	GRACELESS	GUACAMOLE
FLASHCUBE	FORESTALL	FRIGATOON	GALVANISM	GIGANTISM	GRADATION	GUARANTEE
FLATTENED	FORESTERS	FRIGHTFUL	GALVANIZE	GILGAMESH	GRADGRIND	GUARANTOR
FLATTENER	FORETASTE	FRIGIDITY	GANGPLANK	GINGERADE	GRADUALLY	GUARDRAIL
FLATTERED	FOREWOMAN	FRITHBORH	GARDENING	GINGLYMUS	GRADUATED	GUARDROOM
FLATTERER	FORFEITED	FRIVOLITY	GARDEROBE	GINORMOUS	GRAMPIANS	GUARDSMAN
FLATULENT	FORFICATE	FRIVOLOUS	GARGANTUA	GIRANDOLE	GRANDIOSE	GUATEMALA
FLAVORING	FORGATHER	FRIZZANTE	GARGARISM	GIRONDIST	GRANDNESS	GUERRILLA
FLAVOURED	FORGETFUL	FROBISHER	GARIBALDI	GLABELLAR	GRANDSIRE	GUESSWORK
FLECHETTE	FORGETIVE	FROGMARCH	GARNISHEE	GLADIATOR	GRANULATE	GUIDEBOOK
FLEDGLING	FORGIVING	FROGMOUTH	GARNITURE	GLADIOLUS	GRANULITE	GUIDELINE
FLEETWOOD	FORGOTTEN	FROGSPAWN	GARRULITY	GLADSTONE	GRANULOSE	GUILDHALL
FLESHLESS	FORJASKIT	FROISSART	GARRULOUS	GLAIREOUS	GRAPESHOT	GUILELESS
FLESHPOTS	FORJESKIT	FROSTBITE	GARRYOWEN	GLAMORIZE	GRAPETREE	GUILLEMOT
FLEXITIME	FORLORNLY	FRUCTIDOR	GASCONADE	GLAMOROUS	GRAPEVINE	GUILLOCHE
FLINTLOCK	FORMALIST	FRUGALITY	GASHOLDER	GLANDULAR	GRAPHICAL	GUILTLESS
FLIPPANCY	FORMALITY	FRUITCAKE	GASOMETER	GLASSWARE	GRAPPLING	GUINEVERE
FLOODGATE	FORMALIZE	FRUITERER	GASPEREAU	GLASSWORT	GRASSLAND	GUITARIST
FLOORSHOW	FORMATION	FRUITLESS	GATECRASH	GLEANINGS	GRATICULE	GUJARATHI
FLOPHOUSE	FORMATIVE	FRUSTRATE	GATESHEAD	GLEEFULLY	GRATITUDE	GUMSHIELD
FLORESTAN	FORMULATE	FUGACIOUS	GATHERING	GLENDOWER	GRAVADLAX	GUNCOTTON
FLORIMELL	FORNICATE	FUGGINESS	GAUDEAMUS	GLENGARRY	GRAVESEND	GUNPOWDER
FLOTATION	FORSYTHIA	FULLBLOWN	GAUDINESS	GLENLIVET	GRAVESIDE	GUSTATION
FLOURMILL	FORTALICE	FULLERENE	GAULEITER	GLISSANDO	GRAVEYARD	GUTENBERG
FLOWCHART	FORTHWINK	FULLGROWN	GAUNTNESS	GLOMERATE	GRAVITATE	GUTTERING
FLOWERBED	FORTHWITH	FULLSCALE	GAVELKIND	GLOMERULE	GREASEGUN	GYMNASIUM
FLOWERING	FORTILAGE	FULMINANT	GAWKINESS	GLORIFIED	GREATCOAT	GYMNASTIC
FLOWERPOT	FORTITUDE	FULMINATE	GAZETTEER	GLORYHOLE	GREATNESS	GYNOECIUM
FLOWSTONE	FORTNIGHT	FUNDAMENT	GEARLEVER	GLUCINIUM	GREENAWAY	GYROMANCY
FLUCTUATE	FORTUNATE	FUNGIBLES	GEARSHIFT	GLUCOSIDE	GREENBACK	GYROPLANE
FLUORSPAR	FORWANDER	FUNGICIDE	GEARSTICK	GLUTAMINE	GREENFEED	GYROSCOPE
FLUSTERED	FOSSILISE	FUNICULAR	GEARWHEEL	GLUTINOUS	GREENGAGE	HABERDINE
FLYWEIGHT	FOSSORIAL	FUNICULUS	GELIGNITE	GLYCERIDE	GREENHEAD	HABERGEON
FOGGINESS	FOUNDLING	FURACIOUS	GENEALOGY	GLYCERINE	GREENHORN	HABITABLE
FOGRAMITE	FOURPENCE	FURIOUSLY	GENERALLY	GMELINITE	GREENMAIL	HABITUATE
FOLIOLOSE	FOURWHEEL	FURNIMENT	GENERATOR	GOALMOUTH	GREENROOM	HACKAMORE

HACKBERRY	HARPOONER	HERBALIST	HOBGOBLIN	HUCKABACK	ILLIBERAL	INAMORATA
HACKNEYED	HARQUEBUS	HERBARIUM	HOBNAILED	HUMANKIND	ILLICITLY	INAMORATO
HACQUETON	HARROGATE	HERBICIDE	HOCCAMORE	HUMANMADE	ILLOGICAL	INANIMATE
HADROSAUR	HARROWING	HERBIVORE	HODIERNAL	HUMDINGER	IMAGELESS	INANITION
HAECCEITY	HARSHNESS	HERBORIST	HODMANDOD	HUMILIATE	IMAGINARY	INAUDIBLE
HAEMALOMA	HARTSHORN	HERCULEAN	HODOGRAPH	HUMONGOUS	IMBALANCE	INAUDIBLY
HAEMATITE	HARVESTER	HEREAFTER	HODOMETER	HUMUNGOUS	IMBRANGLE	INAUGURAL
HAILSTONE	HASHEMITE	HERETICAL	HOLDERBAT	HUNCHBACK	IMBRICATE	INCAPABLE
HAILSTORM	HASTENING	HERITABLE	HOLINSHED	HUNDREDTH	IMBROCATE	INCARDINE
HAIRBRUSH	HASTINESS	HERMANDAD	HOLLERITH	HUNGARIAN	IMBROGLIO	INCARNATE
HAIRPIECE	HATCHBACK	HERMITAGE	HOLLYHOCK	HUNKYDORY	IMITATION	INCAUTION
HAIRSTYLE	HATCHMENT	HERODOTUS	HOLLYWOOD	HURRICANE	IMITATIVE	INCENTIVE
HALFBAKED	HAUGHTILY	HERONSHAW	HOLOCAUST	HURRICANO	IMMANACLE	INCEPTION
HALFDOZEN	HAUTMONDE	HERPESTES	HOLOGRAPH	HURRIEDLY	IMMANENCE	INCEPTIVE
HALFEMPTY	HAVERSACK	HESITANCE	HOLOPHOTE	HUSBANDLY	IMMANENCY	INCESSANT
HALFPENNY	HAWCUBITE	HESITANCY	HOLYSTONE	HUSBANDRY	IMMEDIACY	INCIDENCE
HALFSTAFF	HAWKSBILL	HESPERIAN	HOMEBOUND	HUSKINESS	IMMEDIATE	INCIPIENT
HALITOSIS	HAWSEHOLE	HESSONITE	HOMEGROWN	HUTTERITE	IMMELMANN	INCITATUS
HALLOWEEN	HAWTHORNE	HESTERNAL	HOMEOPATH	HYDRANGEA	IMMENSELY	INCLEMENT
HALLOWMAS	HAYMAKING	HESYCHASM	HOMEOWNER	HYDRAULIC	IMMENSITY	INCLUDING
HALLSTATT	HAYMARKET	HESYCHAST	HOMESTEAD	HYDRAZINE	IMMERSION	INCLUSION
HALOBIONT	HAYRADDIN	HETERODOX	HOMEWARDS	HYDROFOIL	IMMIGRANT	INCLUSIVE
HALOPHILE	HAZARDOUS	HETEROSIS	HOMICIDAL	HYDROPULT	IMMIGRATE	INCOGNITO
HALOTHANE	HAZELWORT	HEURISTIC	HOMOGRAFT	HYDROSTAT	IMMINENCE	INCOMINGS
HAMADRYAD	HEADBOARD	HEXAGONAL	HOMOGRAPH	HYGIENIST	IMMODESTY	INCOMMODE
HAMBURGER	HEADCLOTH	HEXAMERON	HOMOPHONE	HYLOBATES	IMMORALLY	INCONDITE
HAMFATTER	HEADDRESS	HEXAMETER	HOMOPTERA	HYPALLAGE	IMMORTALS	INCORRECT
HAMFISTED	HEADFIRST	HEXASTICH	HONEYCOMB	HYPERBOLA	IMMOVABLE	INCREASED
HAMMERING	HEADINESS	HEXATEUCH	HONEYMOON	HYPERBOLE	IMMOVABLY	INCREMENT
HAMMURABI	HEADLIGHT	HEYPRESTO	HONKYTONK	HYPERLINK	IMMUNISER	INCUBATOR
HAMPSHIRE	HEADLINED	HIBERNATE	HONORABLE	HYPEROPIA	IMMUTABLE	INCULCATE
HAMPSTEAD	HEADPIECE	HIBERNIAN	HONORIFIC	HYPHENATE	IMMUTABLY	INCULPATE
HAMSTRING	HEADSCARF	HIDEBOUND	HOOLACHAN	HYPINOSIS	IMPACTION	INCUMBENT
HAMSTRUNG	HEADSTALL	HIDEOUSLY	HOPEFULLY	HYPNOTISM	IMPAIRTIAL	INCURABLE
HANDBRAKE	HEADSTONE	HIERARCHY	HOPLOLOGY	HYPNOTIST	IMPARTIAL	INCURABLY
HANDCUFFS	HEALTHILY	HIGHCLASS	HOPSCOTCH	HYPNOTIZE	IMPASSION	INCURIOUS
HANDINESS	HEARDSMAN	HIGHFLYER	HORDEOLUM	HYPOBLAST	IMPASSIVE	INCURSION
HANDIWORK	HEARTACHE	HIGHLANDS	HOREHOUND	HYPOCAUST	IMPATIENT	INDECENCY
HANDPIECE	HEARTBEAT	HIGHLIGHT	HORNSTONE	HYPOCRISY	IMPEACHER	INDECORUM
HANDSHAKE	HEARTBURN	HIGHSPEED	HOROSCOPE	HYPOCRITE	IMPEDANCE	INDELIBLE
HANDSPIKE	HEARTFELT	HIJACKING	HORRIFIED	HYSTERICS	IMPELLING	INDELIBLY
HANDSTAND	HEARTHRUG	HILARIOUS	HORSEBACK	IBUPROFEN	IMPENDING	INDEMNIFY
HANKERING	HEARTLAND	HILLBILLY	HORSEHAIR	ICELANDER	IMPERATOR	INDEMNITY
HANSEATIC	HEARTLESS	HIMALAYAN	HORSELESS	ICELANDIC	IMPERFECT	INDENTURE
HAPHAZARD	HEARTWOOD	HIMALAYAS	HORSEPLAY	ICHNEUMON	IMPERIOUS	INDICATES
HAPPENING	HEATHLAND	HIMYARITE	HORSESHOE	ICHNOLITE	IMPETUOUS	INDICATOR
HAPPINESS	HEAVINESS	HINDBRAIN	HORSETAIL	ICTERIDAE	IMPLEMENT	INDICTION
HARBINGER	HEAVISIDE	HINDEMITH	HORSEWHIP	IDEALOGUE	IMPLICATE	INDIGENCE
HARDANGER	HEAVYDUTY	HINDRANCE	HORTATIVE	IDENTICAL	IMPLUVIUM	INDIGNANT
HARDBOARD	HEBRIDEAN	HINDSIGHT	HORTATORY	IDENTIKIT	IMPOLITIC	INDIGNITY
HARDCOVER	HECOGENIN	HINGELESS	HOSPITIUM	IDEOGRAPH	IMPORTANT	INDOLENCE
HARDIHOOD	HECTOGRAM	HIPPOCRAS	HOSTILITY	IDEOPATHY	IMPORTUNE	INDONESIA
HARDINESS	HECTORING	HIPPODAME	HOTHEADED	IDIOBLAST	IMPOSTURE	INDRAUGHT
HARDLINER	HEDERATED	HIPPOLYTA	HOTTENTOT	IDIOGRAPH	IMPOTENCE	INDUCTION
HARDSHELL	HEDYPHANE	HIPPOLYTE	HOURGLASS	IDIOMATIC	IMPOUNDER	INDUCTIVE
HARESTANE	HELLEBORE	HIRUNDINE	HOURSTONE	IDIOPHONE	IMPRECATE	INDULGENT
HARIGALDS	HELPFULLY	HISTAMINE	HOUSEBOAT	IDIOPLASM	IMPRECISE	INDWELLER
HARIOLATE	HELVELLYN	HISTIDINE	HOUSECOAT	IDIOTICON	IMPRESSED	INEBRIATE
HARLEQUIN	HEMINGWAY	HISTOGRAM	HOUSEHOLD	IGNESCENT	IMPROBITY	INEFFABLE
HARLESTON	HEMIPTERA	HISTOLOGY	HOUSELEEK	IGNORAMUS	IMPROMPTU	INELEGANT
HARMALINE	HEMISTICH	HISTORIAN	HOUSEMAID	IGNORANCE	IMPROVING	INERTNESS
HARMATTAN	HEMITROPE	HITCHCOCK	HOUSEROOM	IGUANODON	IMPROVISE	INERUDITE
HARMONICA	HEMSTITCH	HITCHHIKE	HOUSEWIFE	ILCHESTER	IMPRUDENT	INFANTILE
HARMONIST	HENDIADYS	HOARFROST	HOUSEWORK	ILLEGALLY	IMPSONITE	INFATUATE
HARMONIUM	HENPECKED	HOARHOUND	HOUYHNHNM	ILLEGIBLE	IMPUDENCE	INFECTING
HARMONIZE	HEPATICAL	HOARSTONE	HOWTOWDIE	ILLEGIBLY	IMPULSION	INFECTION
HARMOTOME	HEPATITIS	HOBBINOLL	HOYDENISH	ILLGOTTEN	IMPULSIVE	INFERENCE

INFERTILE	INSWINGER	IRONSIDES	JOBSEEKER	KNOBSTICK	LATECOMER	LIGHTFACE
INFIELDER	INTEGRATE	IRONSTONE	JOBSWORTH	KNOCKDOWN	LATENIGHT	LIGHTFOOT
INFIRMARY	INTEGRITY	IRONWORKS	JOCKSTRAP	KNOTGRASS	LATERALLY	LIGHTLESS
INFIRMITY	INTELLECT	IRRADIANT	JOCKTELEG	KNOWINGLY	LATESCENT	LIGHTNESS
INFLATION	INTENDANT	IRRADIATE	JOCULARLY	KNOWLEDGE	LATHYRISM	LIGHTNING
INFLEXION	INTENDING	IRRAWADDY	JOHANNINE	KOMINFORM	LATICLAVE	LIGHTSHIP
INFLUENCE	INTENSELY	IRREGULAR	JORDANIAN	KONIMETER	LATRATION	LIGHTSOME
INFLUENZA	INTENSIFY	IRRITABLE	JOSEPHINE	KONISCOPE	LATTERDAY	LILYWHITE
INFORMANT	INTENSITY	IRRITABLY	JOSEPHSON	KROPOTKIN	LAUDATION	LIMBURGER
INFURIATE	INTENSIVE	IRRITATED	JOUISANCE	KRUMMHORN	LAUDATORY	LIMEHOUSE
INGENIOUS	INTENTION	IRRUPTION	JOVIALITY	LABORIOUS	LAUGHABLE	LIMELIGHT
INGENUITY	INTERBRED	IRVINGISM	JUBILANCE	LABOURITE	LAUNCELOT	LIMESTONE
INGENUOUS	INTERCEDE	ISALLOBAR	JUDGEMENT	LABYRINTH	LAUNCHING	LIMITLESS
INGESTION	INTERCEPT	ISCHAEMIC	JUDICIARY	LACCOLITE	LAUNDRESS	LIMOUSINE
INGLENOOK	INTERCITY	ISINGLASS	JUDICIOUS	LACERATED	LAVOISIER	LIMPIDITY
INGRAINED	INTERDICT	ISLAMABAD	JUICINESS	LACHRYMAL	LAWMAKING	LINDBERGH
INGROWING	INTERFACE	ISOCLINAL	JUNEBERRY	LACINIATE	LAWMONGER	LINEAMENT
INHERITED	INTERFERE	ISOCRATES	JUNKETING	LACKBEARD	LAWNMOWER	LINEOLATE
INHERITOR	INTERJECT	ISODORIAN	JURIDICAL	LACONICAL	LAZARETTO	LINGERING
INHIBITED	INTERLACE	ISOLATION	JUSTIFIED	LACTATION	LAZYBONES	LINGFIELD
INHIBITOR	INTERLARD	ISOMERASE	JUSTINIAN	LADYSMITH	LAZZARONE	LINKLATER
INHUMANLY	INTERLOCK	ISOMETRIC	JUVENILIA	LAEVULOSE	LEAFMOULD	LINTSTOCK
INITIALLY	INTERLOPE	ISOPROPYL	JUXTAPOSE	LAFAYETTE	LEAFSTALK	LIONHEART
INITIATED	INTERLUDE	ISOSCELES	KABELJOUW	LAGNIAPPE	LEAKPROOF	LIPPITUDE
INITIATOR	INTERMENT	ISOTACTIC	KALSOMINE	LAGOMORPH	LEASEBACK	LIQUEFIED
INJECTION	INTERNODE	ISOTROPIC	KARABINER	LAKEFRONT	LEASEHOLD	LIQUIDATE
INJURIOUS	INTERPLAY	ISRAELITE	KARAKORAM	LAMARTINE	LEASTWAYS	LIQUIDITY
INJUSTICE	INTERPOSE	ITALICIZE	KARYOTYPE	LAMASERAI	LEASTWISE	LIQUIDIZE
INNERMOST	INTERPRET	ITERATION	KENTIGERN	LAMBSWOOL	LECANORAM	LIQUORICE
INNISFAIL	INTERRUPT	ITINERANT	KENTLEDGE	LAMINATED	LECHEROUS	LIQUORISH
INNISFREE	INTERSECT	ITINERARY	KEPLARIAN	LAMINITIS	LEFTOVERS	LISTENING
INNKEEPER	INTERVENE	ITINERATE	KERATITIS	LAMPADARY	LEFTWARDS	LITERALLY
INNOCENCE	INTERVIEW	JACARANDA	KERBSTONE	LAMPADION	LEGENDARY	LITHOCYST
INNOCUOUS	INTESTATE	JACKFRUIT	KERFUFFLE	LAMPBLACK	LEGIONARY	LITHOPONE
INNOVATOR	INTESTINE	JACKKNIFE	KERMESITE	LAMPLIGHT	LEGISLATE	LITHUANIA
INOCULATE	INTRICACY	JACKSCREW	KEYHOLDER	LAMPSHADE	LEHRJAHRE	LITIGIOUS
INOPINATE	INTRICATE	JACKSNIPE	KEYSTROKE	LANCASTER	LEICESTER	LITURGICS
INORGANIC	INTRIGUED	JACKSTRAW	KHALIFATE	LANCEWOOD	LEISURELY	LIVERPOOL
INPATIENT	INTRIGUER	JACQUERIE	KHANSAMAH	LANCINATE	LEITMOTIF	LIVERWORT
INQUILINE	INTRINSIC	JAGGANATH	KICKSHAWS	LANDAULET	LEITMOTIV	LIVERYMAN
INQUINATE	INTRODUCE	JAMBALAYA	KIDNAPPED	LANDDROST	LENGTHILY	LIVESTOCK
INQUIRING	INTROITUS	JAMPACKED	KIDNAPPER	LANDGRAVE	LENIENTLY	LIVRAISON
INQUORATE	INTROVERT	JANISSARY	KIESERITE	LANDLOPER	LENINGRAD	LJUBLJANA
INSCRIBED	INTRUSION	JANSENISM	KILDERKIN	LANDOWNER	LEPROSERY	LOADSTONE
INSELBERG	INTRUSIVE	JANSENIST	KILLARNEY	LANDSCAPE	LESTRIGON	LOAMSHIRE
INSENSATE	INTUITION	JARGONIZE	KILOCYCLE	LANDSLIDE	LETHARGIC	LOATHSOME
INSERTION	INTUITIVE	JARLSBERG	KILOHERTZ	LANDSMAAL	LETTERBOX	LOBLOLLYS
INSHALLAH	INTUMESCE	JAUNDICED	KILOMETER	LANDSTURM	LETTERING	LOBSCOUSE
INSIDIOUS	INUMBRATE	JAWBATION	KILOMETRE	LANDWARDS	LEUCOCYTE	LOCALIZED
INSINCERE	INUNCTION	JAYWALKER	KINGMAKER	LANGOUSTE	LEUCOTOME	LOCELLATE
INSINUATE	INUSITATE	JEALOUSLY	KINGSIZED	LANGRIDGE	LEUKAEMIA	LOCHINVAR
INSIPIENT	INVECTIVE	JELLYFISH	KINKCOUGH	LANGSPIEL	LEVANTINE	LOCKSMITH
INSISTENT	INVENTION	JENNETING	KINSWOMAN	LANGUAGES	LEVERAGED	LODESTONE
INSOLENCE	INVENTIVE	JEPHTHAHS	KINTLEDGE	LANGUEDOC	LEVIATHAN	LODGEMENT
INSOLUBLE	INVENTORY	JEQUIRITY	KISSINGER	LANGUETTE	LEVITICUS	LOFTINESS
INSOLVENT	INVERNESS	JERAHMEEL	KISWAHILI	LANGUIDLY	LIABILITY	LOGARITHM
INSOMNIAC	INVERSION	JERKINESS	KITCHENER	LANKINESS	LIBELLOUS	LOGICALLY
INSPECTOR	INVERTASE	JERKWATER	KITTENISH	LANTHANUM	LIBERALLY	LOGISTICS
INSPIRING	INVIDIOUS	JERUSALEM	KITTIWAKE	LAODICEAN	LIBERATED	LOGOGRIPH
INSTANTER	INVIOLATE	JESSAMINE	KLEMPERER	LAPLANDER	LIBERATOR	LOGOTHETE
INSTANTLY	INVISIBLE	JESSERANT	KLENDUSIC	LAPSTREAK	LIBERTIES	LOHENGRIN
INSTIGATE	INVOICING	JETSTREAM	KLINOSTAT	LARGENESS	LIBERTINE	LOINCLOTH
INSTITUTE	INVOLUCRE	JEWELLERY	KNACKERED	LARGHETTO	LIBRARIAN	LOITERING
INSULATOR	IODOPHILE	JIGGUMBOB	KNAPSCULL	LARGITION	LICKERISH	LOMBARDIC
INSULTING	IPHIGENIA	JITTERBUG	KNAPSKULL	LASERWORT	LIENTERIC	LONDONESE
INSURANCE	IPRINDOLE	JOBCENTRE	KNEECORDS	LASSITUDE	LIFEGUARD	LONGCHAMP
INSURGENT	IRASCIBLE	JOBERNOWL	KNIPHOFIA	LASTDITCH	LIFESTYLE	LONGEDFOR

LONGEVITY	MADRESSAH	MARQUESAS	MELANESIA	MICROCYTE	MISONEIST	MOONLIGHT
LONGICORN	MADRILENE	MARQUETRY	MELANOSIS	MICROFILM	MISPICKEL	MOONRAKER
LONGINGLY	MAELSTROM	MARROWFAT	MELANOTIC	MICROINCH	MISPLACED	MOONSHINE
LONGITUDE	MAGDALENE	MARSHLAND	MELBOURNE	MICROLITE	MISSHAPEN	MOONSTONE
LONGLIVED	MAGDEBURG	MARSUPIAL	MELIORATE	MICROLITH	MISSIONER	MORATORIA
LONGRANGE	MAGICALLY	MARSUPIUM	MELODIOUS	MICROMOLE	MISSTROKE	MORATORIO
LONGSHORE	MAGNALIUM	MARTINEAU	MELODRAMA	MICROTOME	MISTEMPER	MORBIDITY
LOOKALIKE	MAGNESIUM	MARTINMAS	MELONLIKE	MICROTONE	MISTIGRIS	MORECAMBE
LOOSEHEAD	MAGNETISM	MARTYRDOM	MELPOMENE	MICROVOLT	MISTINESS	MORGANITE
LOOSELEAF	MAGNETIZE	MARVELOUS	MEMORABLE	MICROWATT	MISTLETOE	MORMONISM
LOOSENESS	MAGNETRON	MASCULINE	MEMORITER	MICROWAVE	MITHRAISM	MORTALITY
LOQUACITY	MAGNIFIER	MASEFIELD	MENADIONE	MIDDLEMAN	MITRAILLE	MORTGAGEE
LORGNETTE	MAGNITUDE	MASOCHISM	MENAGERIE	MIDDLESEX	MNEMOSYNE	MORTGAGOR
LOUDMOUTH	MAHARAJAH	MASOCHIST	MENDACITY	MIDDLETON	MOBOCRACY	MORTICIAN
LOUISIANA	MAHARANEE	MASSINGER	MENDELISM	MIDDLINGS	MOCCASINS	MORTIFIED
LOUSEWORT	MAHARISHI	MASSIVELY	MENDICANT	MIDHEAVEN	MOCKERNUT	MORTSTONE
LOWLANDER	MAINFRAME	MASSORETE	MENIPPEAN	MIDIANITE	MODELLING	MOSCHATEL
LOWLIGHTS	MAINTENON	MASSYMORE	MENNONITE	MIDINETTE	MODERATOR	MOSKONFYT
LOWLINESS	MAJORDOMO	MASTERFUL	MENOMINEE	MIDRASHIM	MODERNISM	MOTHBALLS
LUBAVITCH	MAJORETTE	MASTERMAN	MENOPAUSE	MIDSTREAM	MODERNIST	MOTHEATEN
LUBRICANT	MAJUSCULE	MASTICATE	MENSHEVIK	MIDSUMMER	MODERNITY	MOTHERING
LUBRICATE	MAKESHIFT	MATAGOURI	MENSTRUAL	MIDWIFERY	MODERNIZE	MOTOCROSS
LUCIFERIN	MALACHITE	MATCHBOOK	MENSTRUUM	MIDWINTER	MODESTINE	MOTORBIKE
LUCRATIVE	MALATHION	MATCHLESS	MENTALITY	MIGRATION	MODILLION	MOTORBOAT
LUCRETIUS	MALAYSIAN	MATCHLOCK	MENTATION	MIGRATORY	MOGADISHU	MOTORCADE
LUCTATION	MALEBOLGE	MATCHWOOD	MENTICIDE	MILESTONE	MOISTNESS	MOTORISTS
LUCUBRATE	MALENGINE	MATELASSE	MENTIONED	MILITANCY	MOLECULAR	MOURNIVAL
LUDICROUS	MALFORMED	MATERNITY	MENUISIER	MILKSHAKE	MOLESKINS	MOUSEHOLE
LUMBERING	MALICIOUS	MATHURINE	MEPACRINE	MILLAMANT	MOLLITIES	MOUSELIKE
LUMBRICUS	MALIGNANT	MATRIARCH	MERCAPTAN	MILLENIAL	MOLLYMAWK	MOUSETRAP
LUMINAIRE	MALIGNITY	MATRICIDE	MERCENARY	MILLEPEDE	MOMENTARY	MOUSTACHE
LUMINANCE	MALLANDER	MATRIMONY	MERCERIZE	MILLEPORE	MOMENTOUS	MOUTHLESS
LUNCHTIME	MALLEABLE	MATTAMORE	MERCILESS	MILLIGRAM	MONACTINE	MOUTHWASH
LURIDNESS	MALLEMUCK	MATUTINAL	MERCURIAL	MILLINERY	MONASTERY	MOYGASHEL
LUSTIHOOD	MALLENDER	MAULSTICK	MERESWINE	MILLIONTH	MONASTRAL	MRIDAMGAM
LUSTINESS	MALLEOLUS	MAURITIAN	MERGANSER	MILLIPEDE	MONATOMIC	MRIDANGAM
LUTESCENT	MAMMALIAN	MAURITIUS	MEROCRINE	MILLIVOLT	MONERGISM	MUCHLOVED
LUXEMBURG	MANDATARY	MAUSOLEUM	MERRIMENT	MILLIWATT	MONEYWORT	MUCKENDER
LUXURIANT	MANDATORY	MAVOURNIN	MESENTERY	MILLSTONE	MONGOLIAN	MUCORALES
LUXURIATE	MANDICATE	MAXILLARY	MESMERISM	MILOMETER	MONGOLISM	MUDDINESS
LUXURIOUS	MANDOLINE	MAYFLOWER	MESMERIZE	MINACIOUS	MONKSHOOD	MUFFETTEE
LYMESWOLD	MANDUCATE	MAYORALTY	MESOBLAST	MINCEMEAT	MONOCEROS	MUGGLETON
LYMPHATIC	MANGANATE	MEANDRIAN	MESOMORPH	MINEFIELD	MONOCHORD	MUGLARITE
LYRICALLY	MANGANESE	MEANWHILE	MESSALINA	MINELAYER	MONOCOQUE	MUJAHIDIN
LYSIMETER	MANGETOUT	MEASURING	MESSENGER	MINIATURE	MONOCULAR	MULTIFORM
MACADAMIA	MANGOUSTE	MEATBALLS	MESSIANIC	MINISKIRT	MONODRAMA	MULTIPLEX
MACARONIC	MANHANDLE	MECHANICS	METABASIS	MINKSTONE	MONOGRAPH	MULTITUDE
MACARTHUR	MANHATTAN	MECHANISM	METABOLIC	MINNESOTA	MONOLAYER	MUMCHANCE
MACCABEES	MANIFESTO	MECHANIZE	METALLOID	MINUSCULE	MONOLOGUE	MUMPSIMUS
MACDONALD	MANLINESS	MEDALLION	METALWORK	MINUTEMAN	MONOMACHY	MUNDUNGUS
MACEDOINE	MANNEQUIN	MEDALLIST	METAPELET	MIRABELLE	MONOMANIA	MUNICIPAL
MACEDONIA	MANNERING	MEDIAEVAL	METAPHASE	MIRTHLESS	MONOMETER	MUNIMENTS
MACHINATE	MANNERISM	MEDIATION	METEORITE	MISBEHAVE	MONOPLANE	MUNITIONS
MACHINERY	MANOEUVRE	MEDICALLY	METEOROID	MISCHANCE	MONOSTICH	MURDERESS
MACHINING	MANOMETER	MEDICATED	METHADONE	MISCREANT	MONOTROCH	MURDEROUS
MACHINIST	MANSFIELD	MEDICINAL	METHEGLIN	MISDIRECT	MONOXYLON	MURKINESS
MACKENZIE	MANUBRIUM	MEDITATOR	METHODISM	MISERABLE	MONSIGNOR	MURMURING
MACQUARIE	MAPPEMOND	MEDMENHAM	METHODIST	MISERABLY	MONSTROUS	MUSCADINE
MACROCOSM	MARAUDING	MEDRESSEH	METHOXIDE	MISFALLEN	MONTACUTE	MUSCARINE
MACROLOGY	MARCASITE	MEGACYCLE	METRICATE	MISFIRING	MONTAIGNE	MUSCOVADO
MACTATION	MARCHPANE	MEGAHERTZ	METROLAND	MISGIVING	MONTANISM	MUSCOVITE
MADARIAGA	MARGARINE	MEGAPHONE	METRONOME	MISGUIDED	MONTANIST	MUSHINESS
MADAROSIS	MARIJUANA	MEGASCOPE	MEZZANINE	MISHANDLE	MONTESPAN	MUSHROOMS
MADDENING	MARKETEER	MEGASPORE	MEZZOTINT	MISINFORM	MONTEZUMA	MUSICALLY
MADELEINE	MARKETING	MEHITABEL	MICKLETON	MISLOCATE	MONTICULE	MUSICHALL
MADRASSAH	MARMALADE	MEKOMETER	MICROCHIP	MISMANAGE	MONZONITE	MUSKETEER
MADREPORE	MARMOREAL	MELAMPODE	MICROCOSM	MISOCLERE	MOODINESS	MUSKETOON

■□□□□□□□□

MUSKOGEAN	NEUROGLIA	NOSEBLEED	OCEANIDES	ORATORIAN	OVERDRAFT	PALMATION
MUSSITATE	NEUROLOGY	NOSTALGIA	OCHLOCRAT	ORBICULAR	OVERDRAWN	PALMISTRY
MUSSOLINI	NEUTRALLY	NOSTALGIC	OCKHAMIST	ORCHESTRA	OVERDRESS	PALMITATE
MUSSULMAN	NEVERMORE	NOSTOLOGY	OCTACHORD	ORDINAIRE	OVERDRIVE	PALOVERDE
MUSTINESS	NEWCASTLE	NOTARIKON	OCTAGONAL	ORDINANCE	OVEREXERT	PALPATION
MUTILATED	NEWLYWEDS	NOTCHBACK	OCTASTICH	ORGANELLE	OVERGROWN	PALPEBRAL
MUTOSCOPE	NEWMARKET	NOTEPAPER	OCTILLION	ORGANICAL	OVERHASTY	PALPITATE
MUTTERING	NEWSAGENT	NOTOCHORD	OCTOBRIST	ORGANISED	OVERHEADS	PALSGRAVE
MUTUALISM	NEWSFLASH	NOTONECTA	OCTOPLOID	ORGANISER	OVERJOYED	PALUDRINE
MUZZINESS	NEWSHOUND	NOTORIETY	OCULIFORM	ORGANIZED	OVERLYING	PANATELLA
MYOFIBRIL	NEWSPAPER	NOTORIOUS	ODALISQUE	ORGANIZER	OVERNIGHT	PANCHAYAT
MYOGLOBIN	NEWSPRINT	NOVELETTE	ODDJOBMAN	ORGANZINE	OVERPAINT	PANDATION
MYRMECOID	NEWSSHEET	NOVICIATE	ODELSTING	ORGIASTIC	OVERPOISE	PANDEMIAN
MYSTERIES	NEWSSTALL	NOVITIATE	ODOURLESS	ORGILLOUS	OVERPOWER	PANDURATE
MYSTICISM	NEWSSTAND	NOVOCAINE	OESTROGEN	ORICALCHE	OVERPRINT	PANEGOISM
MYTHOLOGY	NIAISERIE	NOVODAMUS	OFFCHANCE	ORIENTATE	OVERRATED	PANEGYRIC
NABATHEAN	NICARAGUA	NUCLEOLUS	OFFCOLOUR	ORIFLAMME	OVERREACH	PANELLING
NAKEDNESS	NICCOLITE	NUMBSKULL	OFFENBACH	ORIGENIST	OVERREACT	PANELLIST
NAMEPLATE	NICKNEVEN	NUMERAIRE	OFFENDING	ORIGINATE	OVERRIDER	PANETTONE
NANTUCKET	NICODEMUS	NUMERATOR	OFFENSIVE	ORMANDINE	OVERSHADE	PANHANDLE
NAPIERIAN	NICTITATE	NUMERICAL	OFFERTORY	OROBANCHE	OVERSHOES	PANNIKELL
NARCISSUS	NIDDERING	NUMMULITE	OFFICIALS	OROGRAPHY	OVERSHOOT	PANORAMIC
NARGHILLY	NIDERLING	NUNCUPATE	OFFICIANT	ORPHANAGE	OVERSIGHT	PANTAGAMY
NARRATION	NIEBELUNG	NUREMBERG	OFFICIATE	ORPHARION	OVERSIZED	PANTALEON
NARRATIVE	NIETZSCHE	NURSEMAID	OFFICIOUS	ORPINGTON	OVERSLEEP	PANTALOON
NARROWING	NIGGARDLY	NUTJOBBER	OFFSEASON	ORTANIQUE	OVERSPEND	PANTHEISM
NASEBERRY	NIGHTCLUB	NUTRIMENT	OFFSPRING	ORTHODOXY	OVERSPILL	PANTHENOL
NASHVILLE	NIGHTFALL	NUTRITION	OILTANKER	ORTHOLOGY	OVERSTATE	PANTOFFLE
NASTINESS	NIGHTFIRE	NUTRITIVE	OKEYDOKEY	ORTHOPTER	OVERSTEER	PANTOMIME
NATHANIEL	NIGHTGLOW	NYSTAGMUS	OLECRANON	ORTHOTONE	OVERTHROW	PANTOUFLE
NATHELESS	NIGHTGOWN	OARSWOMAN	OLENELLUS	OSCILLATE	OVERTONES	PAPARAZZI
NATHEMORE	NIGHTHAWK	OASTHOUSE	OLEOGRAPH	OSTENSIVE	OVERTRUMP	PAPARAZZO
NATROLITE	NIGHTMARE	OBBLIGATO	OLEORESIN	OSTEODERM	OVERVALUE	PAPERBACK
NATURALLY	NIGHTSPOT	OBCORDATE	OLFACTORY	OSTEOPATH	OVERWEIGH	PAPERCLIP
NAUGHTILY	NIGHTTIME	OBEDIENCE	OLIGARCHY	OSTRACISE	OVERWHELM	PAPERWORK
NAUMACHIA	NIGHTWORK	OBEISANCE	OLIGOCENE	OSTRACISM	OVIPAROUS	PAPILLOTE
NAUSEATED	NIGRITUDE	OBFUSCATE	OLIVENITE	OSTRACIZE	OVULATION	PARABASIS
NAVIGABLE	NIGROSINE	OBJECTIFY	OMBUDSMAN	OSTROGOTH	OWLEGLASS	PARABLAST
NAVIGATOR	NINEPENCE	OBJECTION	OMINOUSLY	OTHERWISE	OWNERSHIP	PARABOLIC
NEBBISHER	NINETIETH	OBJECTIVE	OMNIRANGE	OTTERBURN	OXIDATION	PARACHUTE
NECESSARY	NIPCHEESE	OBJURGATE	OMOPHAGIC	OTTRELITE	OXYGENATE	PARACLETE
NECESSITY	NIPPERKIN	OBLIQUELY	ONCOMETER	OUBLIETTE	OZOCERITE	PARACUSIS
NECKVERSE	NITHSDALE	OBLIVIOUS	ONOMASTIC	OUDENARDE	OZOKERITE	PARAGOGUE
NECTARINE	NOBLENESS	OBNOXIOUS	ONSLAUGHT	OUGHTNESS	PACEMAKER	PARAGRAPH
NEFANDOUS	NOCTURNAL	OBREPTION	ONTHESPOT	OUROBOROS	PACHYDERM	PARALYSIS
NEFARIOUS	NOISELESS	OBSCENELY	ONTOGENCY	OUROBORUS	PACKAGING	PARALYTIC
NEFERTITI	NOISINESS	OBSCENITY	OPENENDED	OURSELVES	PADEMELON	PARAMEDIC
NEGLECTED	NOLLEKENS	OBSCURELY	OPENHEART	OUTERMOST	PAGEANTRY	PARAMETER
NEGLIGENT	NOMINALLY	OBSCURITY	OPERATING	OUTFITTER	PAGLIACCI	PARAMOUNT
NEGOTIATE	NOMINATOR	OBSECRATE	OPERATION	OUTGOINGS	PAILLASSE	PARANOIAC
NEGRITUDE	NOMOCRACY	OBSEQUIES	OPERATIVE	OUTGROWTH	PAILLETTE	PARANYMPH
NEIGHBOUR	NOMOTHETE	OBSERVANT	OPERCULUM	OUTNUMBER	PAINFULLY	PARASCENE
NEODYMIUM	NONENTITY	OBSESSION	OPHIUCHUS	OUTOFTOWN	PAINTWORK	PARASCEVE
NEOLITHIC	NONILLION	OBSESSIVE	OPOBALSAM	OUTRIGGER	PAKISTANI	PARASITIC
NEOLOGISM	NONPAREIL	OBSTETRIC	OPODELDOC	OUTROOPER	PALAESTRA	PARATAXIS
NEPHALISM	NONPROFIT	OBSTINACY	OPPENHEIM	OUTSIDERS	PALAFITTE	PARATHION
NEPHALIST	NONSMOKER	OBSTINATE	OPPONENTS	OUTSKIRTS	PALAMPORE	PARATROOP
NEPHELINE	NOOSPHERE	OBTAINING	OPPORTUNE	OUTSPOKEN	PALANKEEN	PARBUCKLE
NEPHRITIC	NORMALACY	OBTRUSION	OPPRESSED	OUTSPREAD	PALANQUIN	PARCHEESI
NEPHRITIS	NORMALITY	OBTRUSIVE	OPPRESSOR	OUTTHRUST	PALATABLE	PARCHMENT
NEPTUNIUM	NORMALIZE	OBVENTION	OPSIMATHY	OUTWARDLY	PALEMPORE	PARDALOTE
NERITIDAE	NORMATIVE	OBVIOUSLY	OPTICALLY	OUTWORKER	PALEOLITH	PAREGORIC
NERVOUSLY	NORTHEAST	OCCIPITAL	OPTOMETRY	OVENPROOF	PALESTINE	PARENTAGE
NESCIENCE	NORTHERLY	OCCLUSION	OPTOPHONE	OVERBLOWN	PALINURUS	PARENTING
NEUCHATEL	NORTHWARD	OCCULTIST	OPULENTLY	OVERBOARD	PALLADIAN	PARFLECHE
NEURALGIA	NORTHWEST	OCCUPANCY	ORANGEADE	OVERCLOUD	PALLADIUM	PARHELION
NEURALGIC	NORWEGIAN	OCCUPYING	ORANGEMAN	OVERCROWD	PALLIASSE	PARHYPATE

PARNASITE	PEIRASTIC	PERSECUTE	PHRENITIS	PLASTIQUE	PONDEROSA	PRECURSOR
PARNASSUS	PEKINGESE	PERSEVERE	PHTHALATE	PLATITUDE	PONDEROUS	PREDATORY
PAROCHIAL	PELLAGRIN	PERSIMMON	PHYCOLOGY	PLATONIST	PONTLEVIS	PREDICANT
PAROCHINE	PELLITORY	PERSONAGE	PHYLLOPOD	PLAUSIBLE	POORHOUSE	PREDICATE
PAROTITIS	PELMANISM	PERSONATE	PHYLOGENY	PLAUSIBLY	POPLITEAL	PREDICTOR
PARRICIDE	PEMPHIGUS	PERSONIFY	PHYSICIAN	PLAUSTRAL	POPPERING	PREDIKANT
PARSIMONY	PENDENNIS	PERSONNEL	PHYSICIST	PLAYFULLY	POPPYCOCK	PREDILECT
PARSONAGE	PENDLETON	PERSUADED	PHYTOLITE	PLAYGROUP	POPULARLY	PREFATORY
PARTAKING	PENDRAGON	PERTINENT	PHYTOTRON	PLAYHOUSE	POPULATED	PREFERRED
PARTHENON	PENDULATE	PERTURBED	PIACEVOLE	PLAYTHING	PORBEAGLE	PREFIGURE
PARTHOLON	PENDULOUS	PERTUSATE	PICKABACK	PLEASANCE	PORCELAIN	PREGNANCY
PARTIALLY	PENETRATE	PERTUSSIS	PICKETING	PLEIOCENE	PORCUPINE	PREHALLUX
PARTICLES	PENFRIEND	PERVASION	PICKTHANK	PLENITUDE	PORIFERAN	PREJUDICE
PARTITION	PENILLION	PERVASIVE	PICNICKER	PLENTEOUS	PORPOISES	PRELECTOR
PARTRIDGE	PENINSULA	PERVERTED	PICOFARAD	PLENTIFUL	PORPORATE	PRELUSORY
PARTTIMER	PENISTONE	PESSIMISM	PICTOGRAM	PLETHORIC	PORRINGER	PREMATURE
PASSAMENT	PENITENCE	PESSIMIST	PICTORIAL	PLIMSOLLS	PORTERAGE	PREMONISH
PASSENGER	PENNILESS	PESTICIDE	PIECEMEAL	PLOUGHMAN	PORTFOLIO	PREMOTION
PASSEPIED	PENNYWORT	PESTILENT	PIECEWORK	PLUMBEOUS	PORTRAYAL	PREOCCUPY
PASSERINE	PENPUSHER	PETAURIST	PIEPOWDER	PLUMBLINE	PORTREEVE	PREORDAIN
PASSIVELY	PENSIONER	PETERSHAM	PIERGLASS	PLUMDAMAS	PORTULACA	PREPOLLEX
PASSIVITY	PENSIVELY	PETHIDINE	PIGGYBACK	PLUMPNESS	POSSESSED	PRESBYTER
PASTERNAK	PENSTEMON	PETILLANT	PIGGYBANK	PLUNDERER	POSSESSOR	PRESCIENT
PASTICCIO	PENTAGRAM	PETRIFIED	PIGHEADED	PLURALISM	POSSIBLES	PRESCRIBE
PASTORALE	PENTECOST	PETROLEUM	PIGNERATE	PLURALITY	POSTCARDS	PRESCUTUM
PASTURAGE	PENTHOUSE	PETROLOGY	PIKESTAFF	PLUTOCRAT	POSTERIOR	PRESENTED
PATCHOULI	PENTOSANE	PETTICOAT	PILASTERS	PLUTONIUM	POSTERITY	PRESENTER
PATCHOULY	PENURIOUS	PETTINESS	PILFERAGE	PNEUMATIC	POSTHOUSE	PRESENTLY
PATCHWORK	PEPPERONI	PETTITOES	PILFERING	PNEUMONIA	POSTILION	PRESERVED
PATERCOVE	PEPPERPOT	PETULANCE	PILLICOCK	POCKETFUL	POSTNATAL	PRESERVER
PATERNITY	PERAEOPOD	PHACOLITE	PIMPERNEL	POCKMANKY	POSTPONED	PRESERVES
PATHOGENY	PERCALINE	PHAGOCYTE	PINCHBECK	POETASTER	POSTULANT	PRESHRUNK
PATHOLOGY	PERCHANCE	PHALANGER	PINCHCOCK	POETICIZE	POSTULATE	PRESIDENT
PATHTRAIN	PERCHERON	PHALAROPE	PINEAPPLE	POIGNANCY	POSTWOMAN	PRESIDIAL
PATIENTLY	PERCOLATE	PHANARIOT	PINHOOKER	POINTEDLY	POTASSIUM	PRESIDIUM
PATRIARCH	PERDITION	PHANSIGAR	PINKERTON	POINTLESS	POTBOILER	PRESSGANG
PATRICIAN	PEREGRINE	PHANTASMA	PINOCCHIO	POINTSMAN	POTENTATE	PRETENDER
PATRICIDE	PERENNIAL	PHARAMOND	PINSTRIPE	POISONING	POTENTIAL	PRETERITE
PATRIMONY	PERFECTLY	PHARISAIC	PIPEDREAM	POISONOUS	POTHOLING	PRETERMIT
PATRIOTIC	PERFERVID	PHARSALIA	PIPESTONE	POKERWORK	POTHUNTER	PREVALENT
PATROCLUS	PERFORANS	PHELLOGEN	PIPSQUEAK	POLEMARCH	POTPOURRI	PREVERNAL
PATROLMAN	PERFORATE	PHENACITE	PIQUANTLY	POLEMICAL	POTTINGAR	PRICELESS
PATRONAGE	PERFORMED	PHENAKISM	PIRATICAL	POLIANITE	POUJADIST	PRIESTESS
PATRONESS	PERFORMER	PHENYTOIN	PIROUETTE	POLICEMAN	POULTERER	PRIESTLEY
PATRONIZE	PERFUMERY	PHEROMONE	PISTACHIO	POLITBURO	POWELLITE	PRIMAEVAL
PATTERNED	PERGAMENE	PHIGALIAN	PISTAREEN	POLITESSE	POWERBOAT	PRIMARILY
PAULOWNIA	PERGUNNAH	PHILANDER	PISTOLEER	POLITICAL	POWERLESS	PRIMAVERA
PAUSANIAS	PERIAKTOS	PHILATELY	PITCHFORK	POLITIQUE	PRACTICAL	PRIMIPARA
PAWKINESS	PERIANDER	PHILIPPIC	PITCHPINE	POLLINATE	PRACTISED	PRIMITIAE
PAYCHEQUE	PERIBOLOS	PHILISTER	PITCHPOLE	POLLUTANT	PRACTOLOL	PRIMITIVE
PAYMASTER	PERICLASE	PHILLABEG	PITCHPOLL	POLLUTION	PRAGMATIC	PRIMULINE
PEACEABLE	PERICUTIN	PHILLIBEG	PITIFULLY	POLONAISE	PRANKSTER	PRINCETON
PEACEABLY	PERIMETER	PHILOLOGY	PITUITARY	POLVERINE	PREBENDAL	PRINCIPAL
PEACETIME	PERIMORPH	PHITONIUM	PITUITRIN	POLYANDRY	PRECATORY	PRINCIPLE
PEARLWORT	PERIODATE	PHLEBITIS	PIXILATED	POLYESTER	PRECEDENT	PRINTABLE
PEASANTRY	PERIPATUS	PHONECARD	PIZZICATO	POLYGONAL	PRECEDING	PRISMATIC
PEASEWEEP	PERIPHERY	PHONETICS	PLACATORY	POLYGRAPH	PRECENTOR	PRIVATEER
PECKSNIFF	PERISCIAN	PHONOGRAM	PLACEMENT	POLYMORPH	PRECEPTOR	PRIVATELY
PECULATOR	PERISCOPE	PHONOLITE	PLACIDITY	POLYNESIA	PRECIEUSE	PRIVATION
PECUNIARY	PERISHING	PHONOLOGY	PLAINNESS	POLYPHASE	PRECINCTS	PRIVATIZE
PEDAGOGUE	PERISTOME	PHOSPHATE	PLAINSMAN	POLYPHONE	PRECIPICE	PRIVILEGE
PEDERASTY	PERISTYLE	PHOSPHENE	PLAINSONG	POLYPHONY	PRECISELY	PROACTIVE
PEDICULAR	PERMANENT	PHOTOCOPY	PLAINTIFF	POLYTHENE	PRECISIAN	PROBABLES
PEDIGREES	PERMEABLE	PHOTOGENE	PLAINTIVE	POMOERIUM	PRECISION	PROBATION
PEDOMETER	PERMITTED	PHOTOSTAT	PLANETARY	POMPADOUR	PRECISIVE	PROBOSCIS
PEEVISHLY	PERPETUAL	PHOTOTUBE	PLASTERED	POMPHOLYX	PRECOCITY	PROCACITY
PEGMATITE	PERPLEXED	PHRENETIC	PLASTERER	POMPOSITY	PRECONISE	PROCEDURE

PROCERITY	PROVISION	QUALIFIED	RASPATORY	REDUCIBLE	REPELLENT	RETICULUM
PROCESSOR	PROVOKING	QUALIFIER	RASPBERRY	REDUCTION	REPELLING	RETINITIS
PROCLITIC	PROVOLONE	QUANTICAL	RATEPAYER	REDUNDANT	REPENTANT	RETORSION
PROCOELUS	PROXIMATE	QUANTOCKS	RATHERIPE	REEDINESS	REPERCUSS	RETORTION
PROCONSUL	PROXIMITY	QUARENDEN	RATHERISH	REEXAMINE	REPERTORY	RETRACTOR
PROCREATE	PRUDENTLY	QUARTERLY	RATIONALE	REFECTION	REPLACING	RETRIEVAL
PRODROMAL	PRURIENCE	QUARTETTE	RATIONING	REFECTORY	REPLENISH	RETRIEVER
PRODROMUS	PRYTANEUM	QUASIMODO	RATTLEBAG	REFERENCE	REPLETION	RETROCEDE
PROENZYME	PSEUDAXIS	QUAVERING	RAUCOUSLY	REFERRING	REPLETIVE	RETROFLEX
PROFANELY	PSEUDONYM	QUEERNESS	RAVISHING	REFINANCE	REPLICANT	RETROVERT
PROFANITY	PSORIASIS	QUENNELLE	RAZORBILL	REFLATION	REPLICATE	RETURNING
PROFESSED	PSYCHICAL	QUERCETIN	REACHABLE	REFLECTOR	REPORTAGE	REVEALING
PROFESSOR	PSYCHOSIS	QUERCETUS	REACTANCE	REFLEXION	REPORTING	REVELLING
PROFITEER	PSYCHOTIC	QUERIMONY	READDRESS	REFLEXIVE	REPOSSESS	REVERENCE
PROFUSELY	PTARMIGAN	QUERULOUS	READINESS	REFORMIST	REPREHEND	REVERSING
PROFUSION	PTERIDIUM	QUICKLIME	READYEARN	REFRACTOR	REPRESENT	REVERSION
PROGNOSIS	PTEROSAUR	QUICKNESS	READYMADE	REFRESHER	REPRESSED	REVETMENT
PROGRAMME	PUBLICIST	QUICKSAND	REALISTIC	REFULGENT	REPRESSOR	REVICTUAL
PROJECTED	PUBLICITY	QUICKSTEP	REALITIES	REFURBISH	REPRIMAND	REVOLTING
PROJECTOR	PUBLICIZE	QUIESCENT	REANIMATE	REFUSENIK	REPROBATE	REVOLVING
PROKARYON	PUBLISHED	QUIETNESS	REARGUARD	REGARDANT	REPROCESS	REVULSION
PROKOFIEV	PUBLISHER	QUILLWORT	REARHORSE	REGARDFUL	REPRODUCE	REWARDING
PROLACTIN	PUCELLAGE	QUINQUINA	REARMOUSE	REGARDING	REPROVING	REWORKING
PROLAMINE	PUERILITY	QUINTETTE	REARRANGE	REGISSEUR	REPTATION	REYKJAVIK
PROLEPSIS	PUERPERAL	QUINTROON	REARWARDS	REGISTRAR	REPTILIAN	RHAPSODIC
PROLIXITY	PUFFINESS	QUINTUPLE	REASONING	REGRETFUL	REPUDIATE	RHEOTAXIS
PROLONGED	PUGNACITY	QUITTANCE	REBELLION	REGUERDON	REPUGNANT	RHEUMATIC
PROLUSION	PUISSANCE	QUIVERFUL	REBOATION	REGULARLY	REPULSION	RHODESIAN
PROMACHOS	PULLULATE	QUIVERING	RECALLING	REGULATOR	REPULSIVE	RHODOLITE
PROMENADE	PULMONARY	QUIZZICAL	RECAPTURE	REHEARSAL	REPUTABLE	RHODOPSIN
PROMINENT	PULMONATE	QUODLIBET	RECEIVING	REICHSRAT	REPUTEDLY	RHYMESTER
PROMISING	PULPITEER	QUOTATION	RECEPTION	REICHSTAG	REQUISITE	RIBBONISM
PROMOTION	PULSATION	QUOTIDIAN	RECEPTIVE	REIMBURSE	REREMOUSE	RICERCARE
PROMPTING	PULVERIZE	QUOTITION	RECESSION	REINFORCE	RESENTFUL	RICHELIEU
PROMUSCIS	PUMMELLED	RACCABOUT	RECESSIVE	REINSTATE	RESERPINE	RIDERHOOD
PRONGHORN	PUNCHLINE	RACCAHOUT	RECIPIENT	REISTAFEL	RESERVIST	RIDERLESS
PRONOUNCE	PUNCTILIO	RACEHORSE	RECKONING	REITERATE	RESERVOIR	RIDGEBACK
PROOFREAD	PUNCTUATE	RACETRACK	RECLAIMED	REJECTION	RESHUFFLE	RIDGELING
PROPAGATE	PUNGENTLY	RACIALISM	RECLAIMER	REJOICING	RESIDENCE	RIDGEPOLE
PROPELLED	PUNISHING	RACIALIST	RECOGNIZE	REJOINDER	RESIDENCY	RIGHTEOUS
PROPELLER	PUPILLAGE	RACKETEER	RECOLLECT	RELATIONS	RESIDUARY	RIGHTHAND
PROPERDIN	PUPPETEER	RACKSTRAW	RECOMMEND	RELEVANCE	RESILIENT	RIGHTNESS
PROPHETIC	PURCHASER	RACONTEUR	RECONCILE	RELIGEUSE	RESISTANT	RIGHTWING
PROPIONIC	PURDONIUM	RADCLIFFE	RECONDITE	RELIGIOSO	RESNATRON	RIGMAROLE
PROPONENT	PURGATIVE	RADDLEMAN	RECONVENE	RELIGIOUS	RESONANCE	RIGOLETTO
PROPRIETY	PURGATORY	RADIANTLY	RECORDING	RELIQUARY	RESONATOR	RILLETTES
PROPTOSIS	PURIFYING	RADIATING	RECORDIST	RELIQUIAE	RESORTING	RINGFENCE
PROPYLENE	PURITANIC	RADIATION	RECOVERED	RELUCTANT	RESOURCES	RINGSIDER
PROROGATE	PURPOSELY	RADICALLY	RECTANGLE	REMAINDER	RESPECTED	RIOTOUSLY
PROSCRIBE	PURSUANCE	RADICCHIO	RECTIFIER	REMAINING	RESPECTER	RIPIENIST
PROSECUTE	PURULENCE	RADIOGRAM	RECTITUDE	REMBRANDT	RESSALDAR	RISKINESS
PROSELYTE	PUSHCHAIR	RADIOLOGY	RECTORIAL	REMINISCE	RESTIFORM	RIVERSIDE
PROSIMIAN	PUSSYFOOT	RAFFINOSE	RECUMBENT	REMISSION	RESTITUTE	ROADBLOCK
PROSTRATE	PYGMALION	RAINCHECK	RECURRENT	REMONTANT	RESTRAINT	ROADHOUSE
PROTAMINE	PYONGYANG	RAINGAUGE	RECURRING	REMOULADE	RESULTANT	ROADSTEAD
PROTECTOR	PYRAMIDAL	RAINSTORM	RECURSIVE	REMOVABLE	RESULTING	ROADWORKS
PROTESTER	PYRETHRUM	RAINWATER	RECUSANCE	RENASCENT	RESURFACE	ROBERTSON
PROTHESIS	PYROMANCY	RAMILLIES	REDBREAST	RENCONTRE	RESURGENT	ROCAMBOLE
PROTHORAX	PYROMANIA	RANCIDITY	REDDENDUM	RENDERING	RESURRECT	ROISTERER
PROTOSTAR	PYRRHONIC	RANCOROUS	REDEEMING	RENDITION	RETAILING	ROOSEVELT
PROTOTYPE	PYTHONESS	RANDINESS	REDHANDED	RENEWABLE	RETAINING	ROOTSTOCK
PROUDHORN	QUADRATIC	RANGELAND	REDHEADED	RENFIERST	RETALIATE	ROQUEFORT
PROUSTITE	QUADRATUS	RANTIPOLE	REDINGOTE	RENOVATOR	RETENTION	RORSCHACH
PROVEDORE	QUADRILLE	RAPACIOUS	REDIVIVUS	RENTALLER	RETENTIVE	ROSCOMMON
PROVENDER	QUADRUPED	RAPTORIAL	REDLETTER	REPAYABLE	RETIARIUS	ROSEWATER
PROVIDENT	QUADRUPLE	RAPTUROUS	REDOLENCE	REPAYMENT	RETICENCE	ROSINANTE
PROVIDING	QUAILPIPE	RASKOLNIK	REDSTREAK	REPECHAGE	RETICULAR	ROSMARINE

ROSMINIAN	SALANGANE	SCALDFISH	SCRAPBOOK	SEMBLANCE	SHARESMAN	SICCATIVE
ROSTELLUM	SALERATUS	SCALEABLE	SCRAPINGS	SEMEIOTIC	SHARKSKIN	SICILIANO
ROTAPLANE	SALESGIRL	SCALLAWAG	SCRAPPING	SEMIBREVE	SHARPENER	SICKENING
ROTTERDAM	SALESLADY	SCALLIONS	SCRATCHED	SEMICOLON	SHARPNESS	SIDEBOARD
ROTUNDATE	SALICETUM	SCALLOPED	SCRATCHES	SEMIFINAL	SHASHLICK	SIDEBURNS
ROTUNDITY	SALLYPORT	SCALLYWAG	SCREENING	SEMIFLUID	SHATTERED	SIDELIGHT
ROUGHCAST	SALLYPOST	SCAMBLING	SCREWBALL	SEMIGLOSS	SHAVELING	SIDEROSIS
ROUGHNECK	SALOPETTE	SCANSORES	SCREWEDUP	SEMIOLOGY	SHEARLING	SIDESWIPE
ROUGHNESS	SALTINESS	SCANTLING	SCREWPINE	SEMIOTICS	SHECHINAH	SIDETRACK
ROUGHSHOD	SALTPETER	SCAPEGOAT	SCREWTAPE	SEMIRAMIS	SHECHITAH	SIDEWARDS
ROUMANIAN	SALTPETRE	SCAPOLITE	SCRIMMAGE	SEMIVOWEL	SHEEPFOLD	SIEGFRIED
ROUMANSCH	SALTWATER	SCARECROW	SCRIMPING	SENESCENT	SHEEPMEAT	SIGHTLESS
ROUNCEVAL	SALTWORKS	SCARIFIER	SCRIMSHAW	SENESCHAL	SHEEPSKIN	SIGHTSEER
ROUNCIVAL	SALUBRITY	SCARLATTI	SCRIPTURE	SENIORITY	SHEERLEGS	SIGNALLER
ROUNDBACK	SALVARSAN	SCATTERED	SCRIVENER	SENSATION	SHEERNESS	SIGNALMAN
ROUNDELAY	SALVATION	SCAVENGER	SCRODDLED	SENSELESS	SHEFFIELD	SIGNATORY
ROUNDFISH	SAMARITAN	SCELERATE	SCROUNGER	SENSILLUM	SHEIKHDOM	SIGNATURE
ROUNDHAND	SANCTUARY	SCENTLESS	SCRUBBING	SENSITIVE	SHELDDUCK	SIGNBOARD
ROUNDHEAD	SANDALLED	SCEPTICAL	SCRUFFILY	SENSITIZE	SHELDRAKE	SILICOSIS
ROUNDSMAN	SANDARACH	SCHEELITE	SCRUMMAGE	SENSORIUM	SHELLBACK	SILLINESS
ROUSSETTE	SANDHURST	SCHEHITAH	SCRUMPING	SENSUALLY	SHELLFISH	SILTSTONE
ROUTINELY	SANDPAPER	SCHELLING	SCRUTATOR	SENTIENCE	SHELLSUIT	SILURIDAE
ROWDINESS	SANDPIPER	SCHEMATIC	SCUDDALER	SENTIMENT	SHELTERED	SILVEREYE
ROXBURGHE	SANDSTONE	SCHIAVONE	SCULPTING	SEPARABLE	SHEMOZZLE	SIMEONITE
ROZINANTE	SANDSTORM	SCHILLING	SCULPTURE	SEPARATED	SHENSTONE	SIMILARLY
RUBBERIZE	SANGFROID	SCHLEMIEL	SCUNCHEON	SEPARATOR	SHEPHERDS	SIMPLETON
RUBICELLE	SANHEDRIM	SCHLEMIHL	SCURRIOUR	SEPHARDIM	SHETLANDS	SIMPLISTE
RUDBECKIA	SANHEDRIN	SCHLENTER	SCYTHEMAN	SEPIOLITE	SHEWBREAD	SIMULATED
RUDDIGORE	SANHEDRON	SCHLIEREN	SDEIGNFUL	SEPTEMBER	SHIELDING	SIMULATOR
RUDDLEMAN	SANNYASIN	SCHMALTZY	SEABOTTLE	SEPTIMOLE	SHIFTLESS	SIMULCAST
RUDIMENTS	SANTAYANA	SCHMIEDER	SEAFARING	SEPULCHER	SHIFTWORK	SINCERELY
RUFESCENT	SANTONICA	SCHMUTTER	SEANNACHY	SEPULCHRE	SHILLABER	SINCERITY
RUFFIANLY	SAPODILLA	SCHNAPPER	SEARCHING	SEPULTURE	SHINTOISM	SINGALESE
RUGGELACH	SAPSUCKER	SCHNAUZER	SEASONING	SEQUENCER	SHIPOWNER	SINGAPORE
RUINATION	SARBACANE	SCHNECKEN	SEAWORTHY	SEQUESTER	SHIPSHAPE	SINGLESEX
RUINOUSLY	SARCASTIC	SCHNITTKE	SEBACEOUS	SEQUINNED	SHIPWRECK	SINGLETON
RUNAROUND	SARMENTUM	SCHNITZEL	SEBASTIAN	SERAPHINE	SHIVERING	SINGSPIEL
RUNCINATE	SARTORIAL	SCHNORKEL	SECATEURS	SERASKIER	SHOEMAKER	SINGULTUS
RUNESTAVE	SARTORIUS	SCHNORRER	SECESSION	SERBONIAN	SHOESHINE	SINKANSEN
RUNNYMEDE	SASKATOON	SCHNOZZLE	SECLUSION	SERENADER	SHOLOKHOV	SINUOSITY
RUSHLIGHT	SASQUATCH	SCHOLARCH	SECONDARY	SERENGETI	SHOPFLOOR	SINUSITIS
RUSTICATE	SASSAFRAS	SCHOLARLY	SECRETARY	SERIALIST	SHOPFRONT	SIPHUNCLE
RUSTINESS	SASSENACH	SCHOLIAST	SECRETION	SERIALIZE	SHOREBIRD	SIRBONIAN
RUTHENIAN	SASSOLITE	SCHOOLBOY	SECRETIVE	SERIATION	SHORTCAKE	SISSERARY
RUTHENIUM	SATELLITE	SCHOOLING	SECTARIAN	SERIGRAPH	SHORTFALL	SISYPHEAN
SABBATIAN	SATIATION	SCHOOLMAN	SECTIONAL	SERIOUSLY	SHORTHAND	SITUATION
SABLEFISH	SATINWOOD	SCIAMACHY	SECTORIAL	SERMONIZE	SHORTHAUL	SIXTEENMO
SACCHARIN	SATIRICAL	SCIARIDAE	SEDENTARY	SERRATION	SHORTHOLD	SIXTEENTH
SACKCLOTH	SATISFIED	SCIENTISM	SEDGEMOOR	SERREFILE	SHORTHORN	SKEDADDLE
SACKERSON	SATURATED	SCIENTIST	SEDITIOUS	SERVICING	SHORTLIST	SKEPTICAL
SACRAMENT	SATURNIAN	SCINTILLA	SEDUCTION	SERVIETTE	SHORTNESS	SKETCHILY
SACRARIUM	SATURNINE	SCIOMANCY	SEDUCTIVE	SERVILELY	SHORTSTAY	SKETCHMAP
SACRIFICE	SATURNISM	SCISSORER	SEEMINGLY	SERVILITY	SHORTSTOP	SKETCHPAD
SACRILEGE	SATYRIDAE	SCLAUNDER	SEGMENTED	SERVITUDE	SHORTTERM	SKEWWHIFF
SACRISTAN	SATYRINAE	SCLEROSIS	SEGREGATE	SETACEOUS	SHOVELFUL	SKIAMACHY
SADDENING	SAUCEBOAT	SCLEROTAL	SELACHION	SEVENTEEN	SHOVELLER	SKILFULLY
SADDLEBAG	SAUCINESS	SCOLECITE	SELECTING	SEVERALLY	SHOWINESS	SKINDIVER
SAFEGUARD	SAUCISSON	SCOLIOSIS	SELECTION	SEVERANCE	SHOWPIECE	SKINFLINT
SAFFLOWER	SAUTERNES	SCOLIOTIC	SELECTIVE	SEXUALITY	SHRIMPING	SKINTIGHT
SAGACIOUS	SAUVIGNON	SCONCHEON	SELFISHLY	SFORZANDO	SHRINKAGE	SKYJACKER
SAGAPENUM	SAVERNAKE	SCORBUTIC	SELJUKIAN	SHADINESS	SHRINKING	SLABSTONE
SAGEBRUSH	SAXIFRAGE	SCORBUTUS	SELLOTAPE	SHAKEDOWN	SHRUBBERY	SLACKNESS
SAGITTARY	SAXITOXIN	SCORCHING	SEMANTEME	SHAKINESS	SHUBUNKIN	SLAMMAKIN
SAILCLOTH	SAXOPHONE	SCORODITE	SEMANTICS	SHAMEFAST	SHUFFLING	SLANTWISE
SAINTFOIN	SCABLANDS	SCOTCHMAN	SEMANTIDE	SHAMELESS	SHUTTERED	SLAPHAPPY
SAINTHOOD	SCAGLIOLA	SCOUNDREL	SEMANTRON	SHAMIANAH	SIBILANCE	SLAPSTICK
SALACIOUS	SCALARIUM	SCRAMBLER	SEMAPHORE	SHAPELESS	SIBYLLINE	SLAUGHTER

SLAVISHLY	SOPHISTER	SPICINESS	STANDARDS	STOCKINET	STUPEFIED	SUPERVISE
SLEEKLESS	SOPHISTIC	SPIDERWEB	STANDERBY	STOCKINGS	STUPIDITY	SUPINATOR
SLEEPLESS	SOPHISTRY	SPIKENARD	STANDGALE	STOCKPILE	STYLISHLY	SUPPLIANT
SLEEPWALK	SOPHOCLES	SPILLICAN	STANDPIPE	STOCKROOM	STYLISTIC	SUPPLICAT
SLIGHTEST	SOPHOMORE	SPILLIKIN	STANNATOR	STOCKWORK	STYLOBATE	SUPPORTER
SLIMINESS	SOPORIFIC	SPINDRIER	STARBOARD	STOCKYARD	SUBALTERN	SUPPOSING
SLINGBACK	SOPPINESS	SPINDRIFT	STARGAZER	STOICALLY	SUBCELLAR	SUPPURATE
SLINGSHOT	SORCERESS	SPINELESS	STARKNESS	STOKEHOLD	SUBCORTEX	SUPREMACY
SLIVOVICA	SORROWFUL	SPINNAKER	STARLIGHT	STOLIDITY	SUBDIVIDE	SUPREMELY
SLIVOVITZ	SORTILEGE	SPINNERET	STARSTONE	STOMACHIC	SUBDOLOUS	SUQUAMISH
SLOUGHING	SOSTENUTO	SPIRITISM	STARTLING	STONEBOAT	SUBEDITOR	SURCHARGE
SLOVENIAN	SOTTISIER	SPIRITOUS	STATEHOOD	STONECHAT	SUBENTIRE	SURCINGLE
SLOWCOACH	SOUBRETTE	SPIRITUAL	STATELESS	STONECROP	SUBFOSSIL	SURFBOARD
SLUGHORNE	SOUFRIERE	SPLAYFOOT	STATEMENT	STONEHAND	SUBJACENT	SURFEITED
SLUMBERER	SOULFULLY	SPLENDOUR	STATEROOM	STONELESS	SUBJUGATE	SURLINESS
SMALLNESS	SOUNDBITE	SPLENETIC	STATESIDE	STONEWALL	SUBLIMATE	SURMULLET
SMALLTIME	SOUNDLESS	SPLENITIS	STATESMAN	STONEWARE	SUBLIMELY	SURPRISED
SMARTNESS	SOUNDNESS	SPLINTERS	STATEWIDE	STONEWORK	SUBMARINE	SURQUEDRY
SMOKEFREE	SOURDOUGH	SPLITTING	STATIONED	STONEWORT	SUBMERGED	SURREJOIN
SMOKELESS	SOUTENEUR	SPODUMENE	STATIONER	STONKERED	SUBNORMAL	SURRENDER
SMUGGLING	SOUTHDOWN	SPOFFORTH	STATISTIC	STOOLBALL	SUBROGATE	SURROGATE
SNAILFISH	SOUTHEAST	SPOILSMAN	STATOCYST	STOPLIGHT	SUBSCRIBE	SURVEYING
SNAKEWEED	SOUTHERLY	SPOKESMAN	STATOLITH	STOREROOM	SUBSCRIPT	SURVIVING
SNEERWELL	SOUTHWARD	SPONGEBAG	STATUETTE	STORIATED	SUBSIDIZE	SUSCITATE
SNOWBOUND	SOUTHWARK	SPONSORED	STATUTORY	STORNAWAY	SUBSTANCE	SUSPECTED
SNOWDONIA	SOUTHWEST	SPOONBILL	STAUNCHLY	STORYBOOK	SUBSTRATA	SUSPENDED
SNOWDRIFT	SOUVLAKIA	SPOONFEED	STAVANGER	STORYLINE	SUBSTRATE	SUSPENDER
SNOWFLAKE	SOUWESTER	SPOROCARP	STEADFAST	STOUTNESS	SUBTENANT	SUSPENSOR
SNOWSHOES	SOVENANCE	SPORTSMAN	STEAMBOAT	STOVEPIPE	SUBTITLED	SUSPICION
SNOWSTORM	SOVEREIGN	SPORTSMEN	STEAMSHIP	STOWNLINS	SUCCEEDED	SUSTAINED
SNOWWHITE	SPACELESS	SPOTLIGHT	STEELHEAD	STRAGGLER	SUCCENTOR	SWADDLING
SOAPBERRY	SPACESHIP	SPRAICKLE	STEELYARD	STRAINING	SUCCESSOR	SWAGGERER
SOAPSTONE	SPACESUIT	SPRAUCHLE	STEENBRAS	STRANGELY	SUCCINATE	SWANIMOTE
SOBERNESS	SPADASSIN	SPREADING	STEENKIRK	STRANGLER	SUCCOTASH	SWANSDOWN
SOBRIQUET	SPAGHETTI	SPRECHERY	STEEPNESS	STRANGLES	SUCCUBINE	SWEATBAND
SOCIALISM	SPARINGLY	SPRIGHTLY	STEERSMAN	STRANGURY	SUCCULENT	SWEEPINGS
SOCIALIST	SPARKLERS	SPRINGALD	STEGNOSIS	STRAPHANG	SUCCURSAL	SWEETENER
SOCIALITE	SPARKLING	SPRINGBOK	STEGNOTIC	STRAPLESS	SUDORIFIC	SWEETMEAT
SOCIALIZE	SPARTACUS	SPRINGLET	STEGOSAUR	STRAPPADO	SUETONIUS	SWEETNESS
SOCIOLECT	SPASMODIC	SPRINKLER	STEINBECK	STRAPPING	SUFFERING	SWEETSHOP
SOCIOLOGY	SPATIALLY	SPRITEFUL	STEINBOCK	STRATAGEM	SUFFOCATE	SWIFTNESS
SOFTCOVER	SPATTERED	SPRITSAIL	STENOPAIC	STRATEGIC	SUFFRAGAN	SWIMMERET
SOFTENING	SPATULATE	SPUNCULID	STERADIAN	STREAMING	SUFFUSION	SWINBURNE
SOGGINESS	SPEAKEASY	SQUADRONE	STERCORAL	STREETAGE	SUGARCANE	SWINEHERD
SOLDERING	SPEARHEAD	SQUALIDLY	STERILITY	STREETCAR	SULFUROUS	SWINGEING
SOLDIERLY	SPEARMINT	SQUATTERS	STERILIZE	STRENUOUS	SULKINESS	SWORDFISH
SOLEMNITY	SPEARSIDE	SQUEAMISH	STERNFAST	STRESSFUL	SULPHONIC	SWORDPLAY
SOLEMNIZE	SPEARWORT	SQUINANCY	STERNNESS	STRETCHED	SULPHURIC	SWORDSMAN
SOLFEGGIO	SPECIALLY	SQUINTING	STEVEDORE	STRETCHER	SULTANATE	SWOTHLING
SOLFERINO	SPECIALTY	SQUIREAGE	STEVENSON	STRIATION	SUMMARILY	SYBARITIC
SOLFIDIAN	SPECIFICS	SQUIRMING	STIFFENER	STRICTURE	SUMMARIZE	SYCOPHANT
SOLICITOR	SPECIFIED	STABILITY	STIFFNESS	STRIDENCY	SUMMATION	SYLLABARY
SOLILOQUY	SPECIMENS	STABILIZE	STIGMATIC	STRINGENT	SUMPTUARY	SYLLABLES
SOLIPSISM	SPECTACLE	STABLEBOY	STILLBORN	STRINGOPS	SUMPTUOUS	SYLLEPSIS
SOLITAIRE	SPECTATOR	STABLELAD	STILLNESS	STRIPLING	SUNBATHER	SYLLOGISM
SOLLICKER	SPECULATE	STABLEMAN	STILLROOM	STROBILUS	SUNDOWNER	SYLPHLIKE
SOMASCOPE	SPEECHIFY	STAGEHAND	STILTBIRD	STROLLING	SUNFLOWER	SYLVANITE
SOMEPLACE	SPEEDBOAT	STAGGERED	STIMULANT	STROMBOLI	SUNSCREEN	SYMBIOSIS
SOMETHING	SPEEDWELL	STAGIRITE	STIMULATE	STRONGARM	SUNSTROKE	SYMBIOTIC
SOMETIMES	SPELDRING	STAGYRITE	STINGAREE	STRONGYLE	SUNTANNED	SYMBOLISM
SOMEWHERE	SPELLBIND	STAINLESS	STINKBIRD	STRONTIUM	SUPERCOOL	SYMBOLIST
SOMMELIER	SPELUNKER	STAIRCASE	STINKHORN	STROSSERS	SUPERETTE	SYMBOLIZE
SOMNOLENT	SPHACELUS	STALEMATE	STINKWOOD	STRUCTURE	SUPERFINE	SYMMETRIC
SONGSMITH	SPHENDONE	STALENESS	STIPULATE	STRUMITIS	SUPERNOVA	SYMPHONIC
SONNETEER	SPHERICAL	STALWORTH	STIRABOUT	STRUTTING	SUPERSEDE	SYMPHYSIS
SONOMETER	SPHINCTER	STAMMERER	STOCKFISH	STUMBLING	SUPERSTAR	SYMPODIUM
SOOTERKIN	SPICILEGE	STANCHION	STOCKHOLM	STUMPWORK	SUPERVENE	SYMPOSIUM

SYNAGOGUE	TAXIMETER	TESTIMONY	TICHBORNE	TOXOPHILY	TRIBUTARY	TURNTABLE
SYNANGIUM	TAYASSUID	TETRAGRAM	TICTACTOE	TRACEABLE	TRICERION	TURPITUDE
SYNCHYSIS	TEACHABLE	TETRALOGY	TIERCERON	TRACHINUS	TRICKLESS	TURQUOISE
SYNCOMIUM	TEAKETTLE	TETRARCHY	TIGHTENER	TRACKLESS	TRICKSTER	TUTIORISM
SYNCOPATE	TEARFULLY	TETTEROUS	TIGHTHEAD	TRACKSUIT	TRICLINIC	TWAYBLADE
SYNDICATE	TEARSHEET	THACKERAY	TIGHTNESS	TRACTABLE	TRICOLOUR	TWENTIETH
SYNEDRION	TECHNICAL	THALASSIC	TIGHTROPE	TRADEMARK	TRICUSPID	TWINKLING
SYNERGIST	TECHNIQUE	THANATISM	TIMENOGUY	TRADESMAN	TRIDYMITE	TYMPANIST
SYNIZESIS	TECTIFORM	THANKLESS	TIMEPIECE	TRADEWIND	TRIENNIAL	TYPICALLY
SYNOECETE	TECTONICS	THATCHING	TIMESHARE	TRADITION	TRIERARCH	TYRANNIZE
SYNOVITIS	TECTORIAL	THAUMATIN	TIMETABLE	TRAFALGAR	TRIETERIC	TYRANNOUS
SYNTACTIC	TEDIOSITY	THECODONT	TIMOCRACY	TRAGEDIAN	TRIFORIUM	UKRAINIAN
SYNTHESIS	TEDIOUSLY	THELEMITE	TIMPANIST	TRAGELAPH	TRIHEDRON	ULIGINOUS
SYNTHETIC	TEESWATER	THELONIUS	TINGUAITE	TRAINABLE	TRILITHON	ULLSWATER
SYPHILOMA	TEIRESIAS	THEOBROMA	TIPPERARY	TRAMLINES	TRILOBITE	ULTIMATUM
SYRIACISM	TEKNONYMY	THEOCRACY	TIPSINESS	TRANSCEND	TRIMESTER	ULTRONEUS
SYRPHIDAE	TELEGRAPH	THEOSOPHY	TIPULIDAE	TRANSEUNT	TRIMMINGS	UMBILICAL
TABANIDAE	TELEOLOGY	THERALITE	TIREDNESS	TRANSFORM	TRINKETER	UMBILICUS
TABASHEER	TELEPATHY	THERAPIST	TISIPHONE	TRANSFUSE	TRIPITAKA	UMBRATILE
TABBOULEH	TELEPHONE	THEREFORE	TITHEBARN	TRANSHUME	TRIPMETER	UMPTEENTH
TABELLION	TELEPHONY	THEREUPON	TITILLATE	TRANSIENT	TRISAGION	UNABASHED
TABLATURE	TELEPHOTO	THERMIDOR	TITRATION	TRANSLATE	TRITENESS	UNADOPTED
TABLELAND	TELESALES	THERSITES	TITTLEBAT	TRANSMUTE	TRITICALE	UNALLOYED
TABLEWARE	TELESCOPE	THESAURUS	TOADSTONE	TRANSPIRE	TRITURATE	UNALTERED
TABULATOR	TELESTICH	THICKHEAD	TOADSTOOL	TRANSPORT	TRIUMPHAL	UNANIMITY
TACAMAHAC	TELLINGLY	THICKNESS	TOASTRACK	TRANSPOSE	TRIVIALLY	UNANIMOUS
TACHILITE	TELLURIAN	THIGHBONE	TOBERMORY	TRANSSHIP	TROCHILIC	UNASHAMED
TACHYLITE	TELLURION	THINGUMMY	TOCCATINA	TRANSVAAL	TROCHILUS	UNBALANCE
TACHYLYTE	TELLURIUM	THINKABLE	TOLERABLE	TRAPEZIAL	TROMPETTE	UNBEKNOWN
TACKINESS	TELOPHASE	THINNINGS	TOLERABLY	TRAPEZIST	TRONDHEIM	UNBENDING
TACTFULLY	TEMPERATE	THIRDSMAN	TOLERANCE	TRAPEZIUM	TROOPSHIP	UNBIASSED
TACTICIAN	TEMPORARY	THIRSTILY	TOLERATED	TRAPEZIUS	TROOSTITE	UNBOUNDED
TAHSILDAR	TEMPORIZE	THIRSTING	TOLLHOUSE	TRAPEZOID	TROPAELIN	UNBRIDLED
TAILBOARD	TEMPTRESS	THIRTIETH	TOLPUDDLE	TRAPPINGS	TROPARION	UNCEASING
TAILLEFER	TEMULENCE	THORNBACK	TOMBSTONE	TRASIMENE	TROSSACHS	UNCERTAIN
TAILLIGHT	TENACIOUS	THORNBILL	TOMENTOSE	TRATTORIA	TROUBADOR	UNCHANGED
TAILPIECE	TENACULUM	THORNDYKE	TONBRIDGE	TRAUMATIC	TROUSSEAU	UNCHARGED
TAILPLANE	TENAILLON	THORNLESS	TONOMETER	TRAVELERS	TRUCKLOAD	UNCHECKED
TALKATIVE	TENDERIZE	THOUSANDS	TONOPLAST	TRAVELING	TRUCULENT	UNCHRISOM
TALMUDIST	TENEBROSE	THRALLDOM	TOOTHACHE	TRAVELLER	TRUEPENNY	UNCLAIMED
TAMERLANE	TENEMENTS	THRASHING	TOOTHCOMB	TREACHERY	TRUMPEDUP	UNCLOTHED
TAMOXIFEN	TENNESSEE	THRASONIC	TOOTHLESS	TREADMILL	TRUMPETER	UNCLOUDED
TANGERINE	TENSENESS	THREADFIN	TOOTHPICK	TREASURER	TRUNCATED	UNCONCERN
TANTALITE	TENTATIVE	THREEFOLD	TOOTHSOME	TREATMENT	TRUNCHEON	UNCONFINE
TANTALIZE	TENTORIUM	THREESOME	TOPDRAWER	TREBIZOND	TRUNKFISH	UNCORRECT
TANTARARA	TENUOUSLY	THRENETIC	TOPIARIST	TREBUCHET	TRUTINATE	UNCOUPLED
TANZANIAN	TEPHILLIN	THREONINE	TOPICALLY	TREDRILLE	TRYPHOEUS	UNCOURTLY
TAOISEACH	TERAHERTZ	THRESHOLD	TORBANITE	TREETRUNK	TSAREVICH	UNCOVERED
TAPDANCER	TEREBINTH	THRIFTILY	TORMENTER	TREGEAGLE	TUBBINESS	UNCROSSED
TARANTASS	TERMAGANT	THRILLANT	TORMENTIL	TREGETOUR	TUILERIES	UNCROWNED
TARANTULA	TERMAGENT	THRILLING	TORMENTOR	TREILLAGE	TUILLETTE	UNDAMAGED
TARAXACUM	TERMINATE	THROATILY	TORMENTUM	TREMATODE	TULIPWOOD	UNDAUNTED
TARDINESS	TERPINEOL	THROBBING	TORTELIER	TREMBLING	TUMESCENT	UNDECIDED
TARGETEER	TERRACING	THRONGING	TOSCANINI	TREMOLITE	TUMMYACHE	UNDEFILED
TARMACKED	TERRARIUM	THROWAWAY	TOTALIZER	TREMULANT	TUNGSTATE	UNDEFINED
TARNATION	TERRICOLE	THROWBACK	TOTAQUINE	TREMULATE	TUNGSTOUS	UNDERBITE
TARPAULIN	TERRIFIED	THROWDOWN	TOTTENHAM	TREMULOUS	TURBIDITY	UNDERBRED
TARRAGONA	TERRITORY	THROWSTER	TOUCHDOWN	TRENCHANT	TURBINATE	UNDERCAST
TARTAREAN	TERRORISM	THUMBLING	TOUCHLINE	TRETINOIN	TURBOPROP	UNDERCOAT
TASMANIAN	TERRORIST	THUMBNAIL	TOUCHWOOD	TREVELYAN	TURBULENT	UNDERDONE
TASSELLED	TERRORIZE	THUMBTACK	TOUGHNESS	TRIANGLED	TURCOPOLE	UNDERFEED
TASTELESS	TERSENESS	THUNDERER	TOURNEDOS	TRIATHLON	TURMAGENT	UNDERFELT
TAUCHNITZ	TESTAMENT	THYESTEAN	TOVARISCH	TRIBALISM	TURNABOUT	UNDERFLOW
TAUTOLOGY	TESTATRIX	THYLACINE	TOWCESTER	TRIBESMAN	TURNBULLS	UNDERFOOT
TAVERNERS	TESTDRIVE	THYRATRON	TOWELLING	TRIBESMEN	TURNROUND	UNDERGRAD
TAVISTOCK	TESTICLES	THYRISTOR	TOWNSFOLK	TRIBOLOGY	TURNSTILE	UNDERHAND
TAXIDERMY	TESTIFIER	THYROXINE	TOXIGENIC	TRIBUNATE	TURNSTONE	UNDERHUNG

■□□□□□□□□

UNDERLINE	UNSETTLED	VARIATION	VICTORIAN	WAGONLOAD	WELTGEIST	WISCONSIN
UNDERLING	UNSHACKLE	VARICELLA	VICTORINE	WAHABIITE	WENCESLAS	WISECRACK
UNDERMINE	UNSHEATHE	VARIEGATE	VIDELICET	WAISTBAND	WESTBOUND	WISTFULLY
UNDERMOST	UNSIGHTLY	VARIOLATE	VIDEODISC	WAISTCOAT	WESTERNER	WITCHETTY
UNDERPAID	UNSINNING	VARIOUSLY	VIDEODISK	WAISTLINE	WESTWARDS	WITHDRAWN
UNDERPASS	UNSKILLED	VARISCITE	VIDEOTAPE	WAITERAGE	WHALEBOAT	WITHERING
UNDERRATE	UNSPARING	VASECTOMY	VIENTIANE	WALDENSES	WHALEBONE	WITHERITE
UNDERSEAL	UNSPOILED	VEGETABLE	VIEWPOINT	WALDFLUTE	WHALEMEAT	WITHSTAND
UNDERSELL	UNSULLIED	VEGETATOR	VIGESIMAL	WALDGRAVE	WHEATGERM	WITHYWIND
UNDERSIDE	UNTENABLE	VEHEMENCE	VIGILANCE	WALKABOUT	WHEATMEAL	WITNESSED
UNDERSIGN	UNTIMEOUS	VEHICULAR	VIGILANTE	WALLABIES	WHEELBASE	WITTICISM
UNDERSONG	UNTOUCHED	VEILLEUSE	VINDICATE	WALLBOARD	WHEREFORE	WITTINGLY
UNDERTAKE	UNTRAINED	VELASQUEZ	VIOLATION	WALLOPING	WHEREUPON	WOBBEGONG
UNDERTONE	UNTREATED	VELDSKOEN	VIOLENTLY	WALLOWING	WHERRYMAN	WODEHOUSE
UNDERWALK	UNTRODDEN	VELLENAGE	VIOLINIST	WALLPAPER	WHETSTONE	WOEBEGONE
UNDERWEAR	UNTUTORED	VELLICATE	VIPASSANA	WALLYDRAG	WHICHEVER	WOLFHOUND
UNDERWENT	UNTYPICAL	VELODROME	VIRGINALS	WALPURGIS	WHIMSICAL	WOLLASTON
UNDERWOOD	UNUNUNIUM	VELVETEEN	VIRGINIAN	WAMBENGER	WHINSTONE	WOLVERINE
UNDILUTED	UNUSUALLY	VENERABLE	VIRGINITY	WANCHANCY	WHIPROUND	WOMANHOOD
UNDIVIDED	UNVARYING	VENEREOUS	VIRGINIUM	WANDERING	WHIPSNADE	WOMANISER
UNDOUBTED	UNWATERED	VENEZUELA	VIRGULATE	WANWORTHY	WHIRLIGIG	WOMANIZER
UNDRESSED	UNWELCOME	VENGEANCE	VIRTUALLY	WAPENTAKE	WHIRLPOOL	WOMANKIND
UNEARTHLY	UNWILLING	VENIALITY	VIRULENCE	WAPINSHAW	WHIRLWIND	WOMENFOLK
UNEATABLE	UNWITTING	VENTIFACT	VISAGISTE	WAREHOUSE	WHISTLING	WONDERFUL
UNEQUALED	UNWORRIED	VENTILATE	VISCOSITY	WARMONGER	WHITAKERS	WOODBORER
UNETHICAL	UNWRITTEN	VENTRICLE	VISIONARY	WARTCRESS	WHITEBAIT	WOODCHUCK
UNEXPOSED	UPAITHRIC	VENUSBERG	VISUALIZE	WASHBASIN	WHITEDAMP	WOODCRAFT
UNFAILING	UPANISHAD	VERACIOUS	VITASCOPE	WASHBOARD	WHITEFISH	WOODENTOP
UNFEELING	UPCOUNTRY	VERATRINE	VITELLIUS	WASHCLOTH	WHITEHALL	WOODHOUSE
UNFITTING	UPHOLSTER	VERBALIZE	VITIATION	WASHERMAN	WHITEHEAD	WOODLANDS
UNFLEDGED	UPLIFTING	VERBASCUM	VITRIOLIC	WASHSTAND	WHITENESS	WOODLOUSE
UNFOUNDED	UPPERCASE	VERBERATE	VITRUVIAN	WASPISHLY	WHITENING	WOODSHOCK
UNGUARDED	UPPERMOST	VERBOSITY	VIVACIOUS	WASSERMAN	WHITEWALL	WOOLINESS
UNHAPPILY	UPSETTING	VERDIGRIS	VIVIDNESS	WASTELAND	WHITEWASH	WOOMERANG
UNHEALTHY	URANISCUS	VERIDICAL	VOICELESS	WASTWATER	WHITEWING	WORCESTER
UNHEEDING	UREDINIAL	VERITABLE	VOLAGEOUS	WATCHWORD	WHITEWOOD	WORDINESS
UNHELPFUL	URICONIAN	VERKAMPTE	VOLATILE	WATERBABY	WHITTAWER	WORDSMITH
UNHOPEFUL	URINATION	VERMIFORM	VOLCANISM	WATERBUTT	WHITWORTH	WORKFORCE
UNIFORMED	UROKINASE	VERMIFUGE	VOLGOGRAD	WATERFALL	WHIZZBANG	WORKHORSE
UNIFORMLY	URTICARIA	VERMILION	VOLKSRAAD	WATERFORD	WHODUNNIT	WORKHOUSE
UNINJURED	URUGUAYAN	VERMINOUS	VOLTIGEUR	WATERFOWL	WHOLEFOOD	WORKPLACE
UNINVITED	USHERETTE	VERNATION	VOLTINISM	WATERGATE	WHOLEMEAL	WORKSPACE
UNISEXUAL	UTICENSIS	VERSATILE	VOLTMETER	WATERHOLE	WHOLENESS	WORLDWIDE
UNITARIAN	UTTERANCE	VERSIFIER	VOLTURNUS	WATERLESS	WHOLESALE	WORMEATEN
UNIVALENT	UTTERLESS	VERSIONAL	VOLUCRINE	WATERLILY	WHOLESOME	WORRISOME
UNIVERSAL	UTTERMOST	VERTEBRAE	VOLUNTARY	WATERLINE	WHOSOEVER	WORTHLESS
UNKNOWING	UVAROVITE	VERTEBRAL	VOLUNTEER	WATERMARK	WHUNSTANE	WRANGLERS
UNLEARNED	VACCINATE	VERTIPORT	VOODOOISM	WATERMILL	WIDOWHOOD	WREAKLESS
UNLIMITED	VACILLATE	VERTUMNUS	VORACIOUS	WATERSHED	WILDGEESE	WRECKFISH
UNLUCKILY	VAGINITIS	VESICULAR	VORTICISM	WATERSIDE	WILLEMITE	WRESTLING
UNMARRIED	VAGUENESS	VESPASIAN	VORTIGERN	WATERWEED	WILLESDEN	WRONGDOER
UNMATCHED	VAINGLORY	VESTIBULE	VOUCHSAFE	WAVELLITE	WILLFULLY	WRONGFOOT
UNMINDFUL	VALDENSES	VESTIGIAL	VULCANIAN	WAYZGOOSE	WILLINGLY	WULFENITE
UNMUSICAL	VALENTINE	VESTITURE	VULCANIST	WEAKENING	WILLOWING	WURLITZER
UNNATURAL	VALIANTLY	VESTMENTS	VULCANITE	WEARINESS	WILLPOWER	WUTHERING
UNNERVING	VALUATION	VEXATIONS	VULCANIZE	WEARISOME	WIMBLEDON	WYANDOTTE
UNNOTICED	VALUELESS	VEXATIOUS	VULGARIAN	WEBFOOTED	WINCANTON	XANTHIPPE
UNOPPOSED	VALVASSOR	VEXILLARY	VULGARISM	WEDGEWOOD	WINCOPIPE	XENOMANIA
UNPOPULAR	VANCOUVER	VIABILITY	VULGARITY	WEDNESDAY	WINDBREAK	XENOPHOBE
UNPRECISE	VANDALISM	VIBRATILE	VULPINITE	WEIGHTING	WINDCHILL	XEROPHYTE
UNREFINED	VANDALIZE	VIBRATION	VULTURINE	WEIRDNESS	WINDFALLS	XEROSTOMA
UNRELATED	VANISHING	VIBRATORY	WAFERTHIN	WELCOMING	WINDHOVER	XYLOPHONE
UNRUFFLED	VANTBRASS	VICARIOUS	WAGENBOOM	WELDSTADT	WINDSCALE	YACHTSMAN
UNSAVOURY	VAPORETTO	VICEREGAL	WAGHALTER	WELLBEING	WINDSWEPT	YACHTSMEN
UNSCATHED	VAPORIFIC	VICEREINE	WAGNERIAN	WELLBUILT	WINEBERRY	YARDSTICK
UNSECURED	VAPORIZER	VICIOUSLY	WAGNERITE	WELLKNOWN	WINEGLASS	YELLOWISH
UNSELFISH	VARANGIAN	VICTIMIZE	WAGONETTE	WELSUMMER	WINNEBAGO	YESTERDAY

YESTEREVE	BANISTERS	CALLOSITY	CARTESIAN	DALTONISM	FASHIONED	HABITUATE
YGGDRASIL	BANQUETTE	CALLOUSLY	CARTHORSE	DAMASCENE	FASTENING	HACKAMORE
YOHIMBINE	BANTERING	CALORIFIC	CARTILAGE	DAMBUSTER	FASTTRACK	HACKBERRY
YORKSHIRE	BAPTISMAL	CALPURNIA	CARTOGRAM	DAMNATION	FATIDICAL	HACKNEYED
YOUNGSTER	BARAGOUIN	CALVANISM	CARTOUCHE	DAMNEDEST	FATISCENT	HACQUETON
YTTERBIUM	BARBARIAN	CALVINIST	CARTRIDGE	DAMSELFLY	FATTENING	HADROSAUR
ZEALANDER	BARBARISM	CALVITIES	CARTULARY	DANDELION	FATUOUSLY	HAECCEITY
ZECHARIAH	BARBARITY	CAMBODIAN	CARTWHEEL	DANDIFIED	FAULCHION	HAEMALOMA
ZEITGEIST	BARBARIZE	CAMBRIDGE	CARYOPSIS	DANDYPRAT	FAULTLESS	HAEMATITE
ZENOCRATE	BARBAROUS	CAMBUSCAN	CASHPOINT	DANGEROUS	FAVORABLE	HAILSTONE
ZEPHANIAH	BARBITONE	CAMCORDER	CASSANDRA	DANTHONIA	FAVORABLY	HAILSTORM
ZIBELLINE	BARBOTINE	CAMEMBERT	CASSATION	DAREDEVIL	FAVOURITE	HAIRBRUSH
ZINFANDEL	BARCELONA	CAMERAMAN	CASSEROLE	DARTAGNAN	GABARDINE	HAIRPIECE
ZINKENITE	BAREBONES	CAMPANILE	CASSONADE	DARTBOARD	GABERDINE	HAIRSTYLE
ZIRCONIUM	BAREFACED	CAMPANULA	CASSOULET	DARTMOUTH	GABIONADE	HALFBAKED
ZOOLOGIST	BARMBRACK	CANALETTO	CASSOWARY	DARWINIAN	GAELTACHT	HALFDOZEN
ZOOMANTIC	BARMECIDE	CANAVERAL	CASTANETS	DASHBOARD	GAINFULLY	HALFEMPTY
ZOOSCOPIC	BARNABITE	CANCEROUS	CASTELLAN	DASHWHEEL	GAINSAYER	HALFPENNY
ZOROASTER	BARNACLES	CANDIDACY	CASTIGATE	DASTARDLY	GALACTOSE	HALFSTAFF
ZUCCHETTO	BARNSTORM	CANDIDATE	CASTILIAN	DAUNTLESS	GALANTINE	HALITOSIS
ZYGOMATIC	BAROMETER	CANDLELIT	CASTRATED	DAVENPORT	GALAPAGOS	HALLOWEEN
ZYGOSPORE	BARONETCY	CANDLEMAS	CASUARINA	DAYSPRING	GALATIANS	HALLOWMAS
ZYMOMETER	BARRACUDA	CANDYTUFT	CASUISTIC	EAGERNESS	GALDRAGON	HALLSTATT
9:2	BARRICADE	CANNELURE	CASUISTRY	EAGLEWOOD	GALENGALE	HALOBIONT
BACHARACH	BARRISTER	CANNONADE	CATACLYSM	EALDORMAN	GALINGALE	HALOPHILE
BACKBENCH	BARTENDER	CANONICAL	CATACOMBS	EARNESTLY	GALIONGEE	HALOTHANE
BACKBITER	BARTHOLDI	CANTABILE	CATALEPSY	EARTHFLAX	GALLABEAH	HAMADRYAD
BACKBOARD	BARTHOLIN	CANTHARIS	CATALOGUE	EARTHLING	GALLANTLY	HAMBURGER
BACKCLOTH	BARYSCOPE	CANTHARUS	CATALYSIS	EARTHWORK	GALLANTRY	HAMFATTER
BACKPEDAL	BASEBOARD	CANTONESE	CATALYTIC	EARTHWORM	GALLICISM	HAMFISTED
BACKSHISH	BASECOURT	CANVASSER	CATAMARAN	EASTBOUND	GALLINULE	HAMMERING
BACKSLIDE	BASHFULLY	CAPACIOUS	CATAMOUNT	EASTERNER	GALLIPOLI	HAMMURABI
BACKSPACE	BASICALLY	CAPACITOR	CATAPLASM	EASTLINGS	GALLIVANT	HAMPSHIRE
BACKSTAGE	BASILICAL	CAPARISON	CATAPLEXY	EASTWARDS	GALLOPADE	HAMPSTEAD
BACKSWORD	BASILICON	CAPILLARY	CATARRHAL	EASYGOING	GALLSTONE	HAMSTRING
BACKTRACK	BASKETFUL	CAPITULAR	CATATONIA	EAVESDROP	GALLYCROW	HAMSTRUNG
BACKWARDS	BASTINADE	CAPITULUM	CATATONIC	FABACEOUS	GALRAVAGE	HANDBRAKE
BACKWATER	BASTINADO	CAPORETTO	CATCHCROP	FABRICATE	GALVANISM	HANDCUFFS
BACKWOODS	BATHTOWEL	CAPRICCIO	CATCHMENT	FABULINUS	GALVANIZE	HANDINESS
BACTERIAL	BATTALION	CAPRICORN	CATCHPOLE	FACECLOTH	GANGPLANK	HANDIWORK
BACTERIUM	BATTLEAXE	CAPTAINCY	CATCHPOLL	FACETIOUS	GARDENING	HANDPIECE
BADMINTON	CABALLERO	CAPTIVATE	CATCHWORD	FACSIMILE	GARDEROBE	HANDSHAKE
BAGATELLE	CABLEGRAM	CAPTIVITY	CATECHISM	FACTIONAL	GARGANTUA	HANDSPIKE
BAINMARIE	CABRIOLET	CARACALLA	CATECHIZE	FACTORIAL	GARGARISM	HANDSTAND
BAKEHOUSE	CACHAEMIA	CARAMBOLA	CATERWAUL	FACTORISE	GARIBALDI	HANKERING
BAKSHEESH	CACHECTIC	CARBAMATE	CATHARSIS	FACTUALLY	GARNISHEE	HANSEATIC
BALACLAVA	CACOPHONY	CARBAMIDE	CATHARTIC	FACUNDITY	GARNITURE	HAPHAZARD
BALALAIKA	CADASTRAL	CARBONADE	CATHEDRAL	FAINTNESS	GARRULITY	HAPPENING
BALDAQUIN	CAESAREAN	CARBONADO	CATHEPSIN	FAIRYLAND	GARRULOUS	HAPPINESS
BALEFULLY	CAFETERIA	CARBONARI	CATHERINE	FAIRYTALE	GARRYOWEN	HARBINGER
BALLADEER	CAFETIERE	CARBONATE	CATSKILLS	FAITHLESS	GASCONADE	HARDANGER
BALLADIST	CAGOULARD	CARBONIZE	CATTLEMAN	FALANGIST	GASHOLDER	HARDBOARD
BALLERINA	CAIRNGORM	CARBUNCLE	CATTLEPEN	FALDSTOOL	GASOMETER	HARDCOVER
BALLISTIC	CAKESTAND	CARCINOMA	CAUCASIAN	FALERNIAN	GASPEREAU	HARDIHOOD
BALLPOINT	CALABOOSE	CARDBOARD	CAUCASOID	FALKLANDS	GATECRASH	HARDINESS
BALTHAZAR	CALABRESE	CAREERIST	CAUSATION	FALLOPIAN	GATESHEAD	HARDLINER
BALTIMORE	CALCANEUM	CAREFULLY	CAUTERIZE	FALSEHOOD	GATHERING	HARDSHELL
BAMBOOZLE	CALCANEUS	CARETAKER	CAVALCADE	FALSENESS	GAUDEAMUS	HARESTANE
BANDALORE	CALCINATE	CARIBBEAN	CAVENDISH	FAMAGUSTA	GAUDINESS	HARIGALDS
BANDICOOT	CALCULATE	CARMELITE	CAVERNOUS	FANATICAL	GAULEITER	HARIOLATE
BANDOLEER	CALDARIUM	CARNATION	CAVORTING	FANDANGLE	GAUNTNESS	HARLEQUIN
BANDOLERO	CALEDONIA	CARNELIAN	DACHSHUND	FANTASIZE	GAVELKIND	HARLESTON
BANDOLIER	CALEMBOUR	CARNIVORE	DAEDALIAN	FANTASTIC	GAWKINESS	HARMALINE
BANDOLINE	CALENDULA	CARPACCIO	DAIRYMAID	FARANDOLE	GAZETTEER	HARMATTAN
BANDSTAND	CALENTURE	CARPENTER	DALLIANCE	FARMHOUSE	HABERDINE	HARMONICA
BANDWAGON	CALIBRATE	CARPENTRY	DALMATIAN	FARMSTEAD	HABERGEON	HARMONIST
BANEBERRY	CALLIPERS	CARPETING		FASCINATE	HABITABLE	HARMONIUM

HARMONIZE	LAMBSWOOL	MACHINATE	MANNERISM	NASEBERRY	PANTOMIME	PATCHWORK
HARMOTOME	LAMINATED	MACHINERY	MANOEUVRE	NASHVILLE	PANTOUFLE	PATERCOVE
HARPOONER	LAMINITIS	MACHINING	MANOMETER	NASTINESS	PAPARAZZI	PATERNITY
HARQUEBUS	LAMPADION	MACHINIST	MANSFIELD	NATHANIEL	PAPARAZZO	PATHOGENY
HARROGATE	LAMPBLACK	MACKENZIE	MANUBRIUM	NATHELESS	PAPERBACK	PATHOLOGY
HARROWING	LAMPLIGHT	MACQUARIE	MAPPEMOND	NATHEMORE	PAPERCLIP	PATHTRAIN
HARSHNESS	LAMPSHADE	MACROCOSM	MARAUDING	NATROLITE	PAPERWORK	PATIENTLY
HARTSHORN	LANCASTER	MACROLOGY	MARCASITE	NATURALLY	PAPILLOTE	PATRIARCH
HARVESTER	LANCEWOOD	MACTATION	MARCHPANE	NAUGHTILY	PARABASIS	PATRICIAN
HASHEMITE	LANCINATE	MADARIAGA	MARGARINE	NAUMACHIA	PARABLAST	PATRICIDE
HASTENING	LANDAULET	MADAROSIS	MARIJUANA	NAUSEATED	PARABOLIC	PATRIMONY
HASTINESS	LANDDROST	MADDENING	MARKETEER	NAVIGABLE	PARACHUTE	PATRIOTIC
HATCHBACK	LANDGRAVE	MADELEINE	MARKETING	NAVIGATOR	PARACLETE	PATROCLUS
HATCHMENT	LANDLOPER	MADRASSAH	MARMALADE	OARSWOMAN	PARACUSIS	PATROLMAN
HAUGHTILY	LANDOWNER	MADREPORE	MARMOREAL	OASTHOUSE	PARAGOGUE	PATRONAGE
HAUTMONDE	LANDSCAPE	MADRESSAH	MARQUESAS	PACEMAKER	PARAGRAPH	PATRONESS
HAVERSACK	LANDSLIDE	MADRILENE	MARQUETRY	PACHYDERM	PARALYSIS	PATRONIZE
HAWCUBITE	LANDSMAAL	MAELSTROM	MARROWFAT	PACKAGING	PARALYTIC	PATTERNED
HAWKSBILL	LANDSTURM	MAGDALENE	MARSHLAND	PADEMELON	PARAMEDIC	PAULOWNIA
HAWSEHOLE	LANDWARDS	MAGDEBURG	MARSUPIAL	PAGEANTRY	PARAMETER	PAUSANIAS
HAWTHORNE	LANGOUSTE	MAGICALLY	MARSUPIUM	PAGLIACCI	PARAMOUNT	PAWKINESS
HAYMAKING	LANGRIDGE	MAGNALIUM	MARTINEAU	PAILLASSE	PARANOIAC	PAYCHEQUE
HAYMARKET	LANGSPIEL	MAGNESIUM	MARTINMAS	PAILLETTE	PARANYMPH	PAYMASTER
HAYRADDIN	LANGUAGES	MAGNETISM	MARTYRDOM	PAINFULLY	PARASCENE	RACCABOUT
HAZARDOUS	LANGUEDOC	MAGNETIZE	MARVELOUS	PAINTWORK	PARASCEVE	RACCAHOUT
HAZELWORT	LANGUETTE	MAGNETRON	MASCULINE	PAKISTANI	PARASITIC	RACEHORSE
JACARANDA	LANGUIDLY	MAGNIFIER	MASEFIELD	PALAESTRA	PARATAXIS	RACETRACK
JACKFRUIT	LANKINESS	MAGNITUDE	MASOCHISM	PALAFITTE	PARATHION	RACIALISM
JACKKNIFE	LANTHANUM	MAHARAJAH	MASOCHIST	PALAMPORE	PARATROOP	RACIALIST
JACKSCREW	LAODICEAN	MAHARANEE	MASSINGER	PALANKEEN	PARBUCKLE	RACKETEER
JACKSNIPE	LAPLANDER	MAHARISHI	MASSIVELY	PALANQUIN	PARCHEESI	RACKSTRAW
JACKSTRAW	LAPSTREAK	MAINFRAME	MASSORETE	PALATABLE	PARCHMENT	RACONTEUR
JACQUERIE	LARGENESS	MAINTENON	MASSYMORE	PALEMPORE	PARDALOTE	RADCLIFFE
JAGGANATH	LARGHETTO	MAJORDOMO	MASTERFUL	PALEOLITH	PAREGORIC	RADDLEMAN
JAMBALAYA	LARGITION	MAJORETTE	MASTERMAN	PALESTINE	PARENTAGE	RADIANTLY
JAMPACKED	LASERWORT	MAJUSCULE	MASTICATE	PALINURUS	PARENTING	RADIATING
JANISSARY	LASSITUDE	MAKESHIFT	MATAGOURI	PALLADIAN	PARFLECHE	RADIATION
JANSENISM	LASTDITCH	MALACHITE	MATCHBOOK	PALLADIUM	PARHELION	RADICALLY
JANSENIST	LATECOMER	MALATHION	MATCHLESS	PALLIASSE	PARHYPATE	RADICCHIO
JARGONIZE	LATENIGHT	MALAYSIAN	MATCHLOCK	PALMATION	PARNASITE	RADIOGRAM
JARLSBERG	LATERALLY	MALEBOLGE	MATCHWOOD	PALMISTRY	PARNASSUS	RADIOLOGY
JAUNDICED	LATESCENT	MALENGINE	MATELASSE	PALMITATE	PAROCHIAL	RAFFINOSE
JAWBATION	LATHYRISM	MALFORMED	MATERNITY	PALOVERDE	PAROCHINE	RAINCHECK
JAYWALKER	LATICLAVE	MALICIOUS	MATHURINE	PALPATION	PAROTITIS	RAINGAUGE
KABELJOUW	LATRATION	MALIGNANT	MATRIARCH	PALPEBRAL	PARRICIDE	RAINSTORM
KALSOMINE	LATTERDAY	MALIGNITY	MATRICIDE	PALPITATE	PARSIMONY	RAINWATER
KARABINER	LAUDATION	MALLANDER	MATRIMONY	PALSGRAVE	PARSONAGE	RAMILLIES
KARAKORAM	LAUDATORY	MALLEABLE	MATTAMORE	PALUDRINE	PARTAKING	RANCIDITY
KARYOTYPE	LAUGHABLE	MALLEMUCK	MATUTINAL	PANATELLA	PARTHENON	RANCOROUS
LABORIOUS	LAUNCELOT	MALLENDER	MAULSTICK	PANCHAYAT	PARTHOLON	RANDINESS
LABOURITE	LAUNCHING	MALLEOLUS	MAURITIAN	PANDATION	PARTIALLY	RANGELAND
LABYRINTH	LAUNDRESS	MAMMALIAN	MAURITIUS	PANDEMIAN	PARTICLES	RANTIPOLE
LACCOLITE	LAVOISIER	MANDATARY	MAUSOLEUM	PANDURATE	PARTITION	RAPACIOUS
LACERATED	LAWMAKING	MANDATORY	MAVOURNIN	PANEGOISM	PARTRIDGE	RAPTORIAL
LACHRYMAL	LAWMONGER	MANDICATE	MAXILLARY	PANEGYRIC	PARTTIMER	RAPTUROUS
LACINIATE	LAWNMOWER	MANDOLINE	MAYFLOWER	PANELLING	PASSAMENT	RASKOLNIK
LACKBEARD	LAZARETTO	MANDUCATE	MAYORALTY	PANELLIST	PASSENGER	RASPATORY
LACONICAL	LAZYBONES	MANGANATE	NABATHEAN	PANETTONE	PASSEPIED	RASPBERRY
LACTATION	LAZZARONE	MANGANESE	NAKEDNESS	PANHANDLE	PASSERINE	RATEPAYER
LADYSMITH	MACADAMIA	MANGETOUT	NAMEPLATE	PANNIKELL	PASSIVELY	RATHERIPE
LAEVULOSE	MACARONIC	MANGOUSTE	NANTUCKET	PANORAMIC	PASSIVITY	RATHERISH
LAFAYETTE	MACARTHUR	MANHANDLE	NAPIERIAN	PANTAGAMY	PASTERNAK	RATIONALE
LAGNIAPPE	MACCABEES	MANHATTAN	NARCISSUS	PANTALEON	PASTICCIO	RATIONING
LAGOMORPH	MACDONALD	MANIFESTO	NARGHILLY	PANTALOON	PASTORALE	RATTLEBAG
LAKEFRONT	MACEDOINE	MANLINESS	NARRATION	PANTHEISM	PASTURAGE	RAUCOUSLY
LAMARTINE	MACEDONIA	MANNEQUIN	NARRATIVE	PANTHENOL	PATCHOULI	RAVISHING
LAMASERAI	MACEDONIA	MANNERING	NARROWING	PANTOFFLE	PATCHOULY	RAZORBILL

SABBATIAN	SATIATION	TAVISTOCK	WASHSTAND	OBSCENELY	ICTERIDAE	SCIENTISM
SABLEFISH	SATINWOOD	TAXIDERMY	WASPISHLY	OBSCENITY	OCCIPITAL	SCIENTIST
SACCHARIN	SATIRICAL	TAXIMETER	WASSERMAN	OBSCURELY	OCCLUSION	SCINTILLA
SACKCLOTH	SATISFIED	TAYASSUID	WASTELAND	OBSCURITY	OCCULTIST	SCIOMANCY
SACKERSON	SATURATED	VACCINATE	WASTWATER	OBSECRATE	OCCUPANCY	SCISSORER
SACRAMENT	SATURNIAN	VACILLATE	WATCHWORD	OBSEQUIES	OCCUPYING	SCLAUNDER
SACRARIUM	SATURNINE	VAGINITIS	WATERBABY	OBSERVANT	OCEANIDES	SCLEROSIS
SACRIFICE	SATURNISM	VAGUENESS	WATERBUTT	OBSESSION	OCHLOCRAT	SCLEROTAL
SACRILEGE	SATYRIDAE	VAINGLORY	WATERFALL	OBSESSIVE	OCKHAMIST	SCOLECITE
SACRISTAN	SATYRINAE	VALDENSES	WATERFORD	OBSTETRIC	OCTACHORD	SCOLIOSIS
SADDENING	SAUCEBOAT	VALENTINE	WATERFOWL	OBSTINACY	OCTAGONAL	SCOLIOTIC
SADDLEBAG	SAUCINESS	VALIANTLY	WATERGATE	OBSTINATE	OCTASTICH	SCONCHEON
SAFEGUARD	SAUCISSON	VALUATION	WATERHOLE	OBTAINING	OCTILLION	SCORBUTIC
SAFFLOWER	SAUTERNES	VALUELESS	WATERLESS	OBTRUSION	OCTOBRIST	SCORBUTUS
SAGACIOUS	SAUVIGNON	VALVASSOR	WATERLILY	OBTRUSIVE	OCTOPLOID	SCORCHING
SAGAPENUM	SAVERNAKE	VANCOUVER	WATERLINE	OBVENTION	OCULIFORM	SCORODITE
SAGEBRUSH	SAXIFRAGE	VANDALISM	WATERMARK	OBVIOUSLY	SCABLANDS	SCOTCHMAN
SAGITTARY	SAXITOXIN	VANDALIZE	WATERMILL	ACADEMIST	SCAGLIOLA	SCOUNDREL
SAILCLOTH	SAXOPHONE	VANISHING	WATERSHED	ACARIASIS	SCALARIUM	SCRAMBLER
SAINTFOIN	TABANIDAE	VANTBRASS	WATERSIDE	ACCENTUAL	SCALDFISH	SCRAPBOOK
SAINTHOOD	TABASHEER	VAPORETTO	WATERWEED	ACCESSION	SCALEABLE	SCRAPINGS
SALACIOUS	TABBOULEH	VAPORIFIC	WAVELLITE	ACCESSORY	SCALLAWAG	SCRAPPING
SALANGANE	TABELLION	VAPORIZER	WAYZGOOSE	ACCIDENTS	SCALLIONS	SCRATCHED
SALERATUS	TABLATURE	VARANGIAN	XANTHIPPE	ACCLIMATE	SCALLOPED	SCRATCHES
SALESGIRL	TABLELAND	VARIATION	YACHTSMAN	ACCLIVITY	SCALLYWAG	SCREENING
SALESLADY	TABLEWARE	VARICELLA	YACHTSMEN	ACCOMPANY	SCAMBLING	SCREWBALL
SALICETUM	TABULATOR	VARIEGATE	YARDSTICK	ACCORDANT	SCANSORES	SCREWEDUP
SALLYPORT	TACAMAHAC	VARIOLATE	ABANDONED	ACCORDING	SCANTLING	SCREWPINE
SALLYPOST	TACHILITE	VARIOUSLY	ABANDONEE	ACCORDION	SCAPEGOAT	SCREWTAPE
SALOPETTE	TACHYLITE	VARISCITE	ABASEMENT	ACCRETION	SCAPOLITE	SCRIMMAGE
SALTINESS	TACHYLYTE	VASECTOMY	ABATEMENT	ACETAMIDE	SCARECROW	SCRIMPING
SALTPETER	TACKINESS	WAFERTHIN	ABDOMINAL	ACETYLENE	SCARIFIER	SCRIMSHAW
SALTPETRE	TACTFULLY	WAGENBOOM	ABDUCTION	ACIDULATE	SCARLATTI	SCRIPTURE
SALTWATER	TACTICIAN	WAGHALTER	ABERNETHY	ACIDULOUS	SCATTERED	SCRIVENER
SALTWORKS	TAHSILDAR	WAGNERIAN	ABERRANCE	ACONCAGUA	SCAVENGER	SCRODDLED
SALUBRITY	TAILBOARD	WAGNERITE	ABHORRENT	ACOUSTICS	SCELERATE	SCROUNGER
SALVARSAN	TAILLEFER	WAGONETTE	ABLUTIONS	ACQUIESCE	SCENTLESS	SCRUBBING
SALVATION	TAILLIGHT	WAGONLOAD	ABOLITION	ACQUITTAL	SCEPTICAL	SCRUFFILY
SAMARITAN	TAILPIECE	WAHABIITE	ABOMINATE	ACROBATIC	SCHEELITE	SCRUMMAGE
SANCTUARY	TAILPLANE	WAISTBAND	ABORIGINE	ACROPETAL	SCHEHITAH	SCRUMPING
SANDALLED	TALKATIVE	WAISTCOAT	ABOUNDING	ACROPHONY	SCHELLING	SCRUTATOR
SANDARACH	TALMUDIST	WAISTLINE	ABOUTFACE	ACROPOLIS	SCHEMATIC	SCUDDALER
SANDHURST	TAMERLANE	WAITERAGE	ABOUTTURN	ACTUALITY	SCHIAVONE	SCULPTING
SANDPAPER	TAMOXIFEN	WALDENSES	ABSCONDER	ACTUARIAL	SCHILLING	SCULPTURE
SANDPIPER	TANGERINE	WALDFLUTE	ABSORBENT	ACUMINATE	SCHLEMIEL	SCUNCHEON
SANDSTONE	TANTALITE	WALDGRAVE	ABSORBING	ACUTENESS	SCHLEMIHL	SCURRIOUR
SANDSTORM	TANTALIZE	WALKABOUT	ABSTAINER	ACYCLOVIR	SCHLENTER	SCYTHEMAN
SANGFROID	TANTARARA	WALLABIES	ABSTINENT	ECARDINES	SCHLIEREN	ADAPTABLE
SANHEDRIM	TANZANIAN	WALLBOARD	ABSURDITY	ECCENTRIC	SCHMALTZY	ADDERWORT
SANHEDRIN	TAOISEACH	WALLOPING	ABUNDANCE	ECHEVERIA	SCHMIEDER	ADDICTION
SANHEDRON	TAPDANCER	WALLOWING	ABYSMALLY	ECHIDNINE	SCHMUTTER	ADDICTIVE
SANNYASIN	TARANTASS	WALLPAPER	EBRILLADE	ECLAMPSIA	SCHNAPPER	ADDRESSED
SANTAYANA	TARANTULA	WALLYDRAG	EBULLIENT	ECOLOGIST	SCHNAUZER	ADDRESSEE
SANTONICA	TARAXACUM	WALPURGIS	IBUPROFEN	ECONOMICS	SCHNECKEN	ADENOIDAL
SAPODILLA	TARDINESS	WAMBENGER	OBBLIGATO	ECONOMIST	SCHNITTKE	ADEPTNESS
SAPSUCKER	TARGETEER	WANCHANCY	OBCORDATE	ECONOMIZE	SCHNITZEL	ADHERENCE
SARBACANE	TARMACKED	WANDERING	OBEDIENCE	ECOSPHERE	SCHNORKEL	ADJECTIVE
SARCASTIC	TARNATION	WANWORTHY	OBEISANCE	ECOSSAISE	SCHNORRER	ADJOINING
SARMENTUM	TARPAULIN	WAPENTAKE	OBFUSCATE	ECOSYSTEM	SCHNOZZLE	ADMIRABLE
SARTORIAL	TARRAGONA	WAPINSHAW	OBJECTIFY	ECTOMORPH	SCHOLARCH	ADMIRABLY
SARTORIUS	TARTAREAN	WAREHOUSE	OBJECTION	ECTOPLASM	SCHOLARLY	ADMIRALTY
SASKATOON	TASMANIAN	WARMONGER	OBJECTIVE	ECTOTHERM	SCHOLIAST	ADMISSION
SASQUATCH	TASSELLED	WARTCRESS	OBJURGATE	ECTROPION	SCHOOLBOY	ADMITTING
SASSAFRAS	TASTELESS	WASHBASIN	OBLIQUELY	ICELANDER	SCHOOLING	ADMIXTURE
SASSENACH	TAUCHNITZ	WASHBOARD	OBLIVIOUS	ICELANDIC	SCHOOLMAN	ADMONITOR
SASSOLITE	TAUTOLOGY	WASHCLOTH	OBNOXIOUS	ICHNEUMON	SCIAMACHY	ADORATION
SATELLITE	TAVERNERS	WASHERMAN	OBREPTION	ICHNOLITE	SCIARIDAE	ADORNMENT

380

ADRENALIN	BEEFSTEAK	DEADLIGHT	DELACROIX	DEVELOPER	GESTATION	HEURISTIC
ADULATION	BEEKEEPER	DEAFENING	DELICIOUS	DEVIATION	HEADBOARD	HEXAGONAL
ADULTERER	BEELZEBUB	DEAMINATE	DELIGHTED	DEVILFISH	HEADCLOTH	HEXAMERON
ADULTHOOD	BEESTINGS	DEATHBLOW	DELINEATE	DEVILMENT	HEADDRESS	HEXAMETER
ADUMBRATE	BEETHOVEN	DEATHLESS	DELIRIOUS	DEVIOUSLY	HEADFIRST	HEXASTICH
ADVANTAGE	BEHAVIOUR	DEATHTRAP	DELIVERER	DEVONPORT	HEADINESS	HEXATEUCH
ADVECTION	BELATEDLY	DEBATABLE	DELPHINUS	DEXTERITY	HEADLIGHT	HEYPRESTO
ADVENTIST	BELEAGUER	DEBAUCHED	DEMAGOGUE	DEXTEROUS	HEADLINED	JEALOUSLY
ADVENTIVE	BELIEVING	DEBAUCHEE	DEMANDING	DEXTRORSE	HEADPIECE	JELLYFISH
ADVENTURE	BELLICOSE	DEBENTURE	DEMARCATE	FEARFULLY	HEADSCARF	JENNETING
ADVERBIAL	BELLYACHE	DEBUTANTE	DEMEANING	FEATHERED	HEADSTALL	JEPHTHAHS
ADVERSARY	BELLYFLOP	DECACHORD	DEMEANOUR	FEBRIFUGE	HEADSTONE	JEQUIRITY
ADVERSELY	BELONGING	DECADENCE	DEMETRIUS	FECUNDITY	HEALTHILY	JERAHMEEL
ADVERSITY	BELVEDERE	DECALITRE	DEMITASSE	FEDUCIARY	HEARDSMAN	JERKINESS
ADVERTISE	BENBECULA	DECALOGUE	DEMOCRACY	FEEDSTUFF	HEARTACHE	JERKWATER
ADVISABLE	BENCHMARK	DECAMERON	DEMULCENT	FEMINEITY	HEARTBEAT	JERUSALEM
ADVISEDLY	BENIGHTED	DECASTYLE	DEMURRAGE	FENCIBLES	HEARTBURN	JESSAMINE
ADVOCATED	BERGAMASK	DECATHLON	DENIGRATE	FENUGREEK	HEARTFELT	JESSERANT
EDDINGTON	BERGANDER	DECEITFUL	DENSENESS	FERACIOUS	HEARTHRUG	JETSTREAM
EDDYSTONE	BERGOMASK	DECEMVIRI	DENTISTRY	FERDINAND	HEARTLAND	JEWELLERY
EDELWEISS	BERKELIUM	DECENNIAL	DENTITION	FERINGHEE	HEARTLESS	KENTIGERN
EDGEWORTH	BERNSTEIN	DECEPTION	DEODORANT	FERMENTED	HEARTWOOD	KENTLEDGE
EDINBURGH	BERSERKER	DECEPTIVE	DEODORIZE	FEROCIOUS	HEATHLAND	KEPLARIAN
EDITORIAL	BERYLLIUM	DECESSION	DEOXIDISE	FERROTYPE	HEAVINESS	KERATITIS
EDUCATION	BESPANGLE	DECIDEDLY	DEPARTURE	FERRYBOAT	HEAVISIDE	KERBSTONE
EDUCATIVE	BETHLEHEM	DECIDUOUS	DEPASTURE	FERTILITY	HEAVYDUTY	KERFUFFLE
EDWARDIAN	BETROTHAL	DECILLION	DEPENDANT	FERTILIZE	HEBRIDEAN	KERMESITE
IDEALOGUE	BETROTHED	DECKCHAIR	DEPENDENT	FERVENTLY	HECOGENIN	KEYHOLDER
IDENTICAL	BETTERTON	DECLARING	DEPENDING	FESTINATE	HECTOGRAM	KEYSTROKE
IDENTIKIT	BEVERIDGE	DECLINING	DEPICTION	FESTIVITY	HECTORING	LEAFMOULD
IDEOGRAPH	CEANOTHUS	DECLIVITY	DEPOSITOR	FEUDALISM	HEDERATED	LEAFSTALK
IDEOPATHY	CEASEFIRE	DECOCTION	DEPRAVITY	FEUDATORY	HEDYPHANE	LEAKPROOF
IDIOBLAST	CEASELESS	DECOLLATE	DEPRECATE	FEUILLANT	HELLEBORE	LEASEBACK
IDIOGRAPH	CEDARWOOD	DECOMPOSE	DEPREDATE	GEARLEVER	HELPFULLY	LEASEHOLD
IDIOMATIC	CELANDINE	DECONTROL	DEPRESSED	GEARSHIFT	HELVELLYN	LEASTWAYS
IDIOPHONE	CELEBRANT	DECORATED	DERRINGER	GEARSTICK	HEMINGWAY	LEASTWISE
IDIOPLASM	CELEBRATE	DECORATOR	DESCARTES	GEARWHEEL	HEMIPTERA	LECANORAM
IDIOTICON	CELEBRITY	DECRETALS	DESECRATE	GELIGNITE	HEMISTICH	LECHEROUS
ODALISQUE	CELESTIAL	DECRETORY	DESERTION	GENEALOGY	HEMITROPE	LEFTOVERS
ODDJOBMAN	CELLARIST	DECUMBENT	DESERVING	GENERALLY	HEMSTITCH	LEFTWARDS
ODELSTING	CELLULITE	DECURSIVE	DESICCATE	GENERATOR	HENDIADYS	LEGENDARY
ODOURLESS	CELLULOID	DECUSSATE	DESIGNATE	GENETICAL	HENPECKED	LEGIONARY
SDEIGNFUL	CELLULOSE	DEDICATED	DESIGNING	GENEVIEVE	HEPATICAL	LEGISLATE
AEPYORNIS	CENTAURUS	DEDUCTION	DESIPIENT	GENIALITY	HEPATITIS	LEHRJAHRE
AERODROME	CENTENARY	DEDUCTIVE	DESIRABLE	GENITALIA	HERBALIST	LEICESTER
AEROPLANE	CENTERING	DEERHOUND	DESPERADO	GENTEELLY	HERBARIUM	LEISURELY
AEROSPACE	CENTIGRAM	DEFALCATE	DESPERATE	GENTILITY	HERBICIDE	LEITMOTIF
AEROTAXIS	CENTIPEDE	DEFAULTER	DESPOTISM	GENTLEMAN	HERBIVORE	LEITMOTIV
AESCHYLUS	CENTRALLY	DEFEATISM	DESTITUTE	GENTLEMEN	HERBORIST	LENGTHILY
AESTHETIC	CENTREING	DEFEATIST	DESTROYED	GENUFLECT	HERCULEAN	LENIENTLY
BEACHHEAD	CENTURION	DEFECTION	DESTROYER	GENUINELY	HEREAFTER	LENINGRAD
BEACHWEAR	CERATITIS	DEFECTIVE	DESUETUDE	GEODESIST	HERETICAL	LEPROSERY
BEANFEAST	CERATODUS	DEFENDANT	DESULTORY	GEOGRAPHY	HERITABLE	LESTRIGON
BEARDLESS	CEREBRATE	DEFENDERS	DETECTION	GEOLOGIST	HERMANDAD	LETHARGIC
BEARDSLEY	CERECLOTH	DEFENSIVE	DETECTIVE	GEOMETRIC	HERMITAGE	LETTERBOX
BEATITUDE	CEROMANCY	DEFERENCE	DETENTION	GEOMETRID	HERODOTUS	LETTERING
BEAUTEOUS	CERTAINLY	DEFERMENT	DETERGENT	GEORGETTE	HERONSHAW	LEUCOCYTE
BEAUTIFUL	CERTAINTY	DEFICIENT	DETERMINE	GERFALCON	HERPESTES	LEUCOTOME
BECHSTEIN	CERTIFIED	DEFINABLE	DETERRENT	GERIATRIC	HESITANCE	LEUKAEMIA
BECQUEREL	CERTITUDE	DEFLATION	DETONATOR	GERMANCER	HESITANCY	LEVANTINE
BEDFELLOW	CERUSSITE	DEFLECTOR	DETRACTOR	GERMANDER	HESPERIAN	LEVERAGED
BEDJACKET	CERVANTES	DEFOLIANT	DETRIMENT	GERMANITE	HESSONITE	LEVIATHAN
BEDRAGGLE	CESSATION	DEFOLIATE	DETRITION	GERMANIUM	HESTERNAL	LEVITICUS
BEDRIDDEN	CEVAPCICI	DEFORMITY	DEUCALION	GERMICIDE	HESYCHASM	MEANDRIAN
BEDSITTER	CEYLONESE	DEGRADING	DEUTERIUM	GERMINATE	HESYCHAST	MEANWHILE
BEDSPREAD	DEACONESS	DEHYDRATE	DEVASTATE	GERUNDIVE	HETERODOX	MEASURING
BEEFEATER		DEJECTION	DEVELOPED	GESSAMINE	HETEROSIS	MEATBALLS

MECHANICS	METABASIS	PEASEWEEP	PERIPHERY	RECLAIMED	REJECTION	RESHUFFLE
MECHANISM	METABOLIC	PECKSNIFF	PERISCIAN	RECLAIMER	REJOICING	RESIDENCE
MECHANIZE	METALLOID	PECULATOR	PERISCOPE	RECOGNIZE	REJOINDER	RESIDENCY
MEDALLION	METALWORK	PECUNIARY	PERISHING	RECOLLECT	RELATIONS	RESIDUARY
MEDALLIST	METAPELET	PEDAGOGUE	PERISTOME	RECOMMEND	RELEVANCE	RESILIENT
MEDIAEVAL	METAPHASE	PEDERASTY	PERISTYLE	RECONCILE	RELIGEUSE	RESISTANT
MEDIATION	METEORITE	PEDICULAR	PERMANENT	RECONDITE	RELIGIOSO	RESNATRON
MEDICALLY	METEOROID	PEDIGREES	PERMEABLE	RECONVENE	RELIGIOUS	RESONANCE
MEDICATED	METHADONE	PEDOMETER	PERMITTED	RECORDING	RELIQUARY	RESONATOR
MEDICINAL	METHEGLIN	PEEVISHLY	PERPETUAL	RECORDIST	RELIQUIAE	RESORTING
MEDITATOR	METHODISM	PEGMATITE	PERPLEXED	RECOVERED	RELUCTANT	RESOURCES
MEDMENHAM	METHODIST	PEIRASTIC	PERSECUTE	RECTANGLE	REMAINDER	RESPECTED
MEDRESSEH	METHOXIDE	PEKINGESE	PERSEVERE	RECTIFIER	REMAINING	RESPECTER
MEGACYCLE	METRICATE	PELLAGRIN	PERSIMMON	RECTITUDE	REMBRANDT	RESSALDAR
MEGAHERTZ	METROLAND	PELLITORY	PERSONAGE	RECTORIAL	REMINISCE	RESTIFORM
MEGAPHONE	METRONOME	PELMANISM	PERSONATE	RECUMBENT	REMISSION	RESTITUTE
MEGASCOPE	MEZZANINE	PEMPHIGUS	PERSONIFY	RECURRENT	REMONTANT	RESTRAINT
MEGASPORE	MEZZOTINT	PENDENNIS	PERSONNEL	RECURRING	REMOULADE	RESULTANT
MEHITABEL	NEBBISHER	PENDLETON	PERSUADED	RECURSIVE	REMOVABLE	RESULTING
MEKOMETER	NECESSARY	PENDRAGON	PERTINENT	RECUSANCE	RENASCENT	RESURFACE
MELAMPODE	NECESSITY	PENDULATE	PERTURBED	REDBREAST	RENCONTRE	RESURGENT
MELANESIA	NECKVERSE	PENDULOUS	PERTUSATE	REDDENDUM	RENDERING	RESURRECT
MELANOSIS	NECTARINE	PENETRATE	PERTUSSIS	REDEEMING	RENDITION	RETAILING
MELANOTIC	NEFANDOUS	PENFRIEND	PERVASION	REDHANDED	RENEWABLE	RETAINING
MELBOURNE	NEFARIOUS	PENILLION	PERVASIVE	REDHEADED	RENFIERST	RETALIATE
MELIORATE	NEFERTITI	PENINSULA	PERVERTED	REDINGOTE	RENOVATOR	RETENTION
MELODIOUS	NEGLECTED	PENISTONE	PESSIMISM	REDIVIVUS	RENTALLER	RETENTIVE
MELODRAMA	NEGLIGENT	PENNILESS	PESSIMIST	REDLETTER	REPAYABLE	RETIARIUS
MELONLIKE	NEGOTIATE	PENNYWORT	PESTICIDE	REDOLENCE	REPAYMENT	RETICENCE
MELPOMENE	NEGRITUDE	PENPUSHER	PESTILENT	REDSTREAK	REPECHAGE	RETICULAR
MEMORABLE	NEIGHBOUR	PENSIONER	PETAURIST	REDUCIBLE	REPELLENT	RETICULUM
MEMORITER	NEODYMIUM	PENSIVELY	PETERSHAM	REDUCTION	REPELLING	RETINITIS
MENADIONE	NEOLITHIC	PENSTEMON	PETHIDINE	REDUNDANT	REPENTANT	RETORSION
MENAGERIE	NEOLOGISM	PENTAGRAM	PETILLANT	REEDINESS	REPERCUSS	RETORTION
MENDACITY	NEPHALISM	PENTECOST	PETRIFIED	REEXAMINE	REPERTORY	RETRACTOR
MENDELISM	NEPHALIST	PENTHOUSE	PETROLEUM	REFECTION	REPLACING	RETRIEVAL
MENDICANT	NEPHELINE	PENTOSANE	PETROLOGY	REFECTORY	REPLENISH	RETRIEVER
MENIPPEAN	NEPHRITIC	PENURIOUS	PETTICOAT	REFERENCE	REPLETION	RETROCEDE
MENNONITE	NEPHRITIS	PEPPERONI	PETTINESS	REFERRING	REPLETIVE	RETROFLEX
MENOMINEE	NEPTUNIUM	PEPPERPOT	PETTITOES	REFINANCE	REPLICANT	RETROVERT
MENOPAUSE	NERITIDAE	PERAEOPOD	PETULANCE	REFLATION	REPLICATE	RETURNING
MENSHEVIK	NERVOUSLY	PERCALINE	REACHABLE	REFLECTOR	REPORTAGE	REVEALING
MENSTRUAL	NESCIENCE	PERCALINE	REACTANCE	REFLEXION	REPORTING	REVELLING
MENSTRUUM	NEUCHATEL	PERCHANCE	READDRESS	REFLEXIVE	REPOSSESS	REVERENCE
MENTALITY	NEURALGIA	PERCHERON	READINESS	REFORMIST	REPREHEND	REVERSING
MENTATION	NEURALGIC	PERCOLATE	READYEARN	REFRACTOR	REPRESENT	REVERSION
MENTICIDE	NEUROGLIA	PERDITION	READYMADE	REFRESHER	REPRESSED	REVETMENT
MENTIONED	NEUROLOGY	PEREGRINE	REALISTIC	REFULGENT	REPRESSOR	REVICTUAL
MENUISIER	NEUTRALLY	PERENNIAL	REALITIES	REFURBISH	REPRIMAND	REVOLTING
MEPACRINE	NEVERMORE	PERFECTLY	REANIMATE	REFUSENIK	REPROBATE	REVOLVING
MERCAPTAN	NEWCASTLE	PERFERVID	REARGUARD	REGARDANT	REPROCESS	REVULSION
MERCENARY	NEWLYWEDS	PERFORANS	REARHORSE	REGARDFUL	REPRODUCE	REWARDING
MERCERIZE	NEWMARKET	PERFORATE	REARMOUSE	REGARDING	REPROVING	REWORKING
MERCILESS	NEWSAGENT	PERFORMED	REARRANGE	REGISSEUR	REPTATION	REYKJAVIK
MERCURIAL	NEWSFLASH	PERFORMER	REARWARDS	REGISTRAR	REPTILIAN	SEABOTTLE
MERESWINE	NEWSHOUND	PERFUMERY	REASONING	REGRETFUL	REPUDIATE	SEAFARING
MERGANSER	NEWSPAPER	PERGAMENE	REBELLION	REGUERDON	REPUGNANT	SEANNACHY
MEROCRINE	NEWSPRINT	PERGUNNAH	REBOATION	REGULARLY	REPULSION	SEARCHING
MERRIMENT	NEWSSHEET	PERIAKTOS	RECALLING	REGULATOR	REPULSIVE	SEASONING
MESENTERY	NEWSSTALL	PERIANDER	RECAPTURE	REHEARSAL	REPUTABLE	SEAWORTHY
MESMERISM	NEWSSTAND	PERIBOLOS	RECEIVING	REICHSRAT	REPUTEDLY	SEBACEOUS
MESMERIZE	OESTROGEN	PERICLASE	RECEPTION	REICHSTAG	REQUISITE	SEBASTIAN
MESOBLAST	PEACEABLE	PERICUTIN	RECEPTIVE	REIMBURSE	REREMOUSE	SECATEURS
MESOMORPH	PEACEABLY	PERIMETER	RECESSION	REINFORCE	RESENTFUL	SECESSION
MESSALINA	PEACETIME	PERIMORPH	RECESSIVE	REINSTATE	RESERPINE	SECLUSION
MESSENGER	PEARLWORT	PERIODATE	RECIPIENT	REISTAFEL	RESERVIST	SECONDARY
MESSIANIC	PEASANTRY	PERIPATUS	RECKONING	REITERATE	RESERVOIR	SECRETARY

SECRETION	SERIALIZE	TERPINEOL	VESTMENTS	OFFICIANT	CHEAPNESS	PHILANDER
SECRETIVE	SERIATION	TERRACING	VEXATIONS	OFFICIATE	CHEAPSIDE	PHILATELY
SECTARIAN	SERIGRAPH	TERRARIUM	VEXATIOUS	OFFICIOUS	CHECKBOOK	PHILIPPIC
SECTIONAL	SERIOUSLY	TERRICOLE	VEXILLARY	OFFSEASON	CHECKLIST	PHILISTER
SECTORIAL	SERMONIZE	TERRIFIED	WEAKENING	OFFSPRING	CHECKMATE	PHILLABEG
SEDENTARY	SERRATION	TERRITORY	WEARINESS	SFORZANDO	CHECKROOM	PHILLIBEG
SEDGEMOOR	SERREFILE	TERRORISM	WEARISOME	AGALACTIC	CHEEKBONE	PHILOLOGY
SEDITIOUS	SERVICING	TERRORIST	WEBFOOTED	AGAMEMNON	CHEERLESS	PHITONIUM
SEDUCTION	SERVIETTE	TERRORIZE	WEDGEWOOD	AGGRAVATE	CHEMISTRY	PHLEBITIS
SEDUCTIVE	SERVILELY	TERSENESS	WEDNESDAY	AGGREGATE	CHEONGSAM	PHONECARD
SEEMINGLY	SERVILITY	TESTAMENT	WEIGHTING	AGGRESSOR	CHEQUERED	PHONETICS
SEGMENTED	SERVITUDE	TESTATRIX	WEIRDNESS	AGGRIEVED	CHERISHED	PHONOGRAM
SEGREGATE	SETACEOUS	TESTDRIVE	WELCOMING	AGINCOURT	CHERNOZEM	PHONOLITE
SELACHION	SEVENTEEN	TESTICLES	WELDSTADT	AGITATION	CHERUBINI	PHONOLOGY
SELECTING	SEVERALLY	TESTIFIER	WELLBEING	AGONIZING	CHEVALIER	PHOSPHATE
SELECTION	SEVERANCE	TESTIMONY	WELLBUILT	AGREEABLE	CHICANERY	PHOSPHENE
SELECTIVE	SEXUALITY	TETRAGRAM	WELLKNOWN	AGREEABLY	CHICKADEE	PHOTOCOPY
SELFISHLY	TEACHABLE	TETRALOGY	WELSUMMER	AGREEMENT	CHICKWEED	PHOTOGENE
SELJUKIAN	TEAKETTLE	TETRARCHY	WELTGEIST	AGUECHEEK	CHIEFTAIN	PHOTOSTAT
SELLOTAPE	TEARFULLY	TETTEROUS	WENCESLAS	EGAREMENT	CHIHUAHUA	PHOTOTUBE
SEMANTEME	TEARSHEET	VEGETABLE	WESTBOUND	EGLANTINE	CHILBLAIN	PHRENETIC
SEMANTICS	TECHNICAL	VEGETATOR	WESTERNER	EGREGIOUS	CHILDCARE	PHRENITIS
SEMANTIDE	TECHNIQUE	VEHEMENCE	WESTWARDS	EGRESSION	CHILDHOOD	PHTHALATE
SEMANTRON	TECTIFORM	VEHICULAR	XENOMANIA	IGNESCENT	CHILDLESS	PHYCOLOGY
SEMAPHORE	TECTONICS	VEILLEUSE	XENOPHOBE	IGNORAMUS	CHILDLIKE	PHYLLOPOD
SEMBLANCE	TECTORIAL	VELASQUEZ	XEROPHYTE	IGNORANCE	CHILOPODA	PHYLOGENY
SEMEIOTIC	TEDIOSITY	VELDSKOEN	XEROSTOMA	IGUANODON	CHINATOWN	PHYSICIAN
SEMIBREVE	TEDIOUSLY	VELLENAGE	YELLOWISH	YGGDRASIL	CHINOVNIK	PHYSICIST
SEMICOLON	TEESWATER	VELLICATE	YESTERDAY	AHASUERUS	CHINSTRAP	PHYTOLITE
SEMIFINAL	TEIRESIAS	VELODROME	YESTEREVE	CHABAZITE	CHIPBOARD	PHYTOTRON
SEMIFLUID	TEKNONYMY	VELVETEEN	ZEALANDER	CHAFFINCH	CHIPOLATA	RHAPSODIC
SEMIGLOSS	TELEGRAPH	VENERABLE	ZECHARIAH	CHAIRLIFT	CHIPPINGS	RHEOTAXIS
SEMIOLOGY	TELEOLOGY	VENEREOUS	ZEITGEIST	CHALAZION	CHIROPODY	RHEUMATIC
SEMIOTICS	TELEPATHY	VENEZUELA	ZENOCRATE	CHALIAPIN	CHISELLER	RHODESIAN
SEMIRAMIS	TELEPHONE	VENGEANCE	ZEPHANIAH	CHALLENGE	CHLAMYDES	RHODOLITE
SEMIVOWEL	TELEPHONY	VENIALITY	AFFECTING	CHALUMEAU	CHLOROSIS	RHODOPSIN
SENESCENT	TELEPHOTO	VENTIFACT	AFFECTION	CHAMELEON	CHOCOLATE	RHYMESTER
SENESCHAL	TELESALES	VENTILATE	AFFIDAVIT	CHAMFRAIN	CHOLELITH	SHADINESS
SENIORITY	TELESCOPE	VENTRICLE	AFFILIATE	CHAMINADE	CHONDRITE	SHAKEDOWN
SENSATION	TELESTICH	VENUSBERG	AFFLICTED	CHAMOMILE	CHONDROID	SHAKINESS
SENSELESS	TELLINGLY	VERACIOUS	AFFLUENCE	CHAMPAGNE	CHORISTER	SHAMEFAST
SENSILLUM	TELLURIAN	VERATRINE	AFFRICATE	CHAMPAIGN	CHRISTIAN	SHAMELESS
SENSITIVE	TELLURION	VERBALIZE	AFLATOXIN	CHAMPERTY	CHRISTMAS	SHAMIANAH
SENSITIZE	TELLURIUM	VERBASCUM	AFORESAID	CHAMPLAIN	CHROMATIC	SHAPELESS
SENSORIUM	TELOPHASE	VERBERATE	AFRIKAANS	CHAMPLEVÉ	CHRONICLE	SHARESMAN
SENSUALLY	TEMPERATE	VERBOSITY	AFRIKANER	CHANCROID	CHRYSALIS	SHARKSKIN
SENTIENCE	TEMPORARY	VERDIGRIS	AFTERCARE	CHANTEUSE	CHURCHILL	SHARPENER
SENTIMENT	TEMPORIZE	VERIDICAL	AFTERDAMP	CHANTILLY	CHURCHMAN	SHARPNESS
SEPARABLE	TEMPTRESS	VERITABLE	AFTERGLOW	CHAPARRAL	CHURIDARS	SHASHLICK
SEPARATED	TEMULENCE	VERKAMPTE	AFTERMATH	CHAPERONE	KHALIFATE	SHATTERED
SEPARATOR	TENACIOUS	VERMIFORM	AFTERMOST	CHARABANC	KHANSAMAH	SHAVELING
SEPHARDIM	TENACULUM	VERMIFUGE	AFTERNOON	CHARACTER	PHACOLITE	SHEARLING
SEPIOLITE	TENAILLON	VERMILION	AFTERWORD	CHARGEFUL	PHAGOCYTE	SHECHINAH
SEPTEMBER	TENDERIZE	VERMINOUS	EFFECTIVE	CHARIVARI	PHALANGER	SHECHITAH
SEPTIMOLE	TENEBROSE	VERNATION	EFFECTUAL	CHARLATAN	PHALAROPE	SHEEPFOLD
SEPULCHER	TENEMENTS	VERSATILE	EFFICIENT	CHARLOTTE	PHANARIOT	SHEEPMEAT
SEPULCHRE	TENNESSEE	VERSIFIER	EFFINGHAM	CHAROLAIS	PHANSIGAR	SHEEPSKIN
SEPULTURE	TENSENESS	VERSIONAL	EFFLUENCE	CHARTERED	PHANTASMA	SHEERLEGS
SEQUENCER	TENTATIVE	VERTEBRAE	EFFLUVIUM	CHARTREUX	PHARAMOND	SHEERNESS
SEQUESTER	TENTORIUM	VERTEBRAL	EFFULGENT	CHARWOMAN	PHARISAIC	SHEFFIELD
SEQUINNED	TENUOUSLY	VERTIPORT	OFFCHANCE	CHARYBDIS	PHARSALIA	SHEIKHDOM
SERAPHINE	TEPHILLIN	VERTUMNUS	OFFCOLOUR	CHASTENED	PHELLOGEN	SHELDDUCK
SERASKIER	TERAHERTZ	VESICULAR	OFFENBACH	CHATTERER	PHENACITE	SHELDRAKE
SERBONIAN	TEREBINTH	VESPASIAN	OFFENDING	CHAUFFEUR	PHENAKISM	SHELLBACK
SERENADER	TERMAGANT	VESTIBULE	OFFENSIVE	CHAVENDER	PHENYTOIN	SHELLFISH
SERENGETI	TERMAGENT	VESTIGIAL	OFFERTORY	CHAWBACON	PHEROMONE	SHELLSUIT
SERIALIST	TERMINATE	VESTITURE	OFFICIALS	CHEAPJACK	PHIGALIAN	SHELTERED

SHEMOZZLE	THIRDSMAN	WHITEWOOD	DIANOETIC	DISINFECT	FILOPLUME	HIRUNDINE
SHENSTONE	THIRSTILY	WHITTAWER	DIAPHRAGM	DISLOCATE	FILOSELLE	HISTAMINE
SHEPHERDS	THIRSTING	WHITWORTH	DIAPHYSIS	DISMANTLE	FILTERING	HISTIDINE
SHETLANDS	THIRTIETH	WHIZZBANG	DIARRHOEA	DISMEMBER	FILTERTIP	HISTOGRAM
SHEWBREAD	THORNBACK	WHODUNNIT	DIASTASIS	DISMISSAL	FINANCIAL	HISTOLOGY
SHIELDING	THORNBILL	WHOLEFOOD	DIATHERMY	DISOBLIGE	FINANCIER	HISTORIAN
SHIFTLESS	THORNDYKE	WHOLEMEAL	DIATHESIS	DISORIENT	FINGERING	HITCHCOCK
SHIFTWORK	THORNLESS	WHOLENESS	DIATOMITE	DISPARAGE	FINGERTIP	HITCHHIKE
SHILLABER	THOUSANDS	WHOLESALE	DIAZEUXIS	DISPARATE	FINICKING	JIGGUMBOB
SHINTOISM	THRALLDOM	WHOLESOME	DICHOTOMY	DISPARITY	FINICKITY	JITTERBUG
SHIPOWNER	THRASHING	WHOSOEVER	DICTATION	DISPENSER	FINISHING	KICKSHAWS
SHIPSHAPE	THRASONIC	WHUNSTANE	DIDACTICS	DISPERSAL	FINLANDIA	KIDNAPPED
SHIPWRECK	THREADFIN	AIMLESSLY	DIETETICS	DISPERSED	FIORITURA	KIDNAPPER
SHIVERING	THREEFOLD	AINSWORTH	DIETICIAN	DISPLACED	FIREBRAND	KIESERITE
SHOEMAKER	THREESOME	AIRCOOLED	DIFFERENT	DISPLAYED	FIREBREAK	KILDERKIN
SHOESHINE	THRENETIC	AIRSTREAM	DIFFICULT	DISPLEASE	FIREDRAKE	KILLARNEY
SHOLOKHOV	THREONINE	AITCHBONE	DIFFIDENT	DISPUTANT	FIREGUARD	KILOCYCLE
SHOPFLOOR	THRESHOLD	BICONCAVE	DIFFUSION	DISREGARD	FIRELIGHT	KILOHERTZ
SHOPFRONT	THRIFTILY	BICYCLIST	DIGASTRIC	DISREPAIR	FIREPLACE	KILOMETER
SHOREBIRD	THRILLANT	BIFURCATE	DIGESTION	DISREPUTE	FIREPROOF	KILOMETRE
SHORTCAKE	THRILLING	BIGHEADED	DIGESTIVE	DISSEMBLE	FIRESTONE	KINGMAKER
SHORTFALL	THROATILY	BILATERAL	DIGITALIN	DISSENTER	FIREWATER	KINGSIZED
SHORTHAND	THROBBING	BILINGUAL	DIGITALIS	DISSIDENT	FIREWORKS	KINKCOUGH
SHORTHAUL	THRONGING	BILIRUBIN	DIGNIFIED	DISSIPATE	FIRMAMENT	KINSWOMAN
SHORTHOLD	THROWAWAY	BILLABONG	DIGNITARY	DISSOLUTE	FIRSTEVER	KINTLEDGE
SHORTHORN	THROWBACK	BILLBOARD	DILIGENCE	DISSOLVED	FIRSTHAND	KISSINGER
SHORTLIST	THROWDOWN	BILLIARDS	DIMENSION	DISSONANT	FIRSTRATE	KISWAHILI
SHORTNESS	THROWSTER	BILLOWING	DINGINESS	DISTANTLY	FISHERMAN	KITCHENER
SHORTSTAY	THUMBLING	BILLYCOCK	DINNERSET	DISTEMPER	FISHGUARD	KITTENISH
SHORTSTOP	THUMBNAIL	BIMONTHLY	DIOCLETES	DISTENDED	FISHPLATE	KITTIWAKE
SHORTTERM	THUMBTACK	BINOCULAR	DIONYSIAN	DISTILLER	GIBBERISH	LIABILITY
SHOVELFUL	THUNDERER	BIOGRAPHY	DIONYSIUS	DISTORTED	GIBEONITE	LIBELLOUS
SHOVELLER	THYESTEAN	BIOLOGIST	DIPHTHONG	DISTRAINT	GIBRALTAR	LIBERALLY
SHOWINESS	THYLACINE	BIOSPHERE	DIPLOMACY	DISTURBED	GIDDINESS	LIBERATED
SHOWPIECE	THYRATRON	BIPARTITE	DIRECTION	DISUNITED	GIGAHERTZ	LIBERATOR
SHRIMPING	THYRISTOR	BIRDBRAIN	DIRECTIVE	DITHERING	GIGANTISM	LIBERTIES
SHRINKAGE	THYROXINE	BIRDTABLE	DIRECTORS	DITHYRAMB	GILGAMESH	LIBERTINE
SHRINKING	WHALEBOAT	BIRTHMARK	DIRECTORY	DIVERGENT	GINGERADE	LIBRARIAN
SHRUBBERY	WHALEBONE	BIRTHRATE	DIRIGIBLE	DIVERGING	GINGLYMUS	LICKERISH
SHUBUNKIN	WHALEMEAT	BIRTHWORT	DIRTINESS	DIVERSIFY	GINORMOUS	LIENTERIC
SHUFFLING	WHEATGERM	BISECTION	DISABLING	DIVERSION	GIRANDOLE	LIFEGUARD
SHUTTERED	WHEATMEAL	BISHOPRIC	DISAFFIRM	DIVERSITY	GIRONDIST	LIFESTYLE
THACKERAY	WHEELBASE	BIZARRELY	DISAPPEAR	DIVERTING	HIBERNATE	LIGHTFACE
THALASSIC	WHEREFORE	CIGARETTE	DISARMING	DIVIDENDS	HIBERNIAN	LIGHTFOOT
THANATISM	WHEREUPON	CILIOLATE	DISBELIEF	DIVISIBLE	HIDEBOUND	LIGHTLESS
THANKLESS	WHERRYMAN	CIMMERIAN	DISBURDEN	DIXIELAND	HIDEOUSLY	LIGHTNESS
THATCHING	WHETSTONE	CINEMATIC	DISCARDED	DIZYGOTIC	HIERARCHY	LIGHTNING
THAUMATIN	WHICHEVER	CINEPHILE	DISCHARGE	DIZZINESS	HIGHCLASS	LIGHTSHIP
THECODONT	WHIMSICAL	CINERARIA	DISCLOSED	EIDERDOWN	HIGHFLYER	LIGHTSOME
THELEMITE	WHINSTONE	CINEREOUS	DISCOLOUR	EIDOGRAPH	HIGHLANDS	LILYWHITE
THELONIUS	WHIPROUND	CIPOLLINO	DISCOMFIT	EIGHTIETH	HIGHLIGHT	LIMBURGER
THEOBROMA	WHIPSNADE	CIRCADIAN	DISCOURSE	EIGHTSOME	HIGHSPEED	LIMEHOUSE
THEOCRACY	WHIRLIGIG	CIRCINATE	DISCOVERT	FIBROLINE	HIJACKING	LIMELIGHT
THEOSOPHY	WHIRLPOOL	CIRCULATE	DISCOVERY	FIBROLITE	HILARIOUS	LIMESTONE
THERALITE	WHIRLWIND	CIRRHOSIS	DISCREDIT	FICTIONAL	HILLBILLY	LIMITLESS
THERAPIST	WHISTLING	CIVILISED	DISEMBARK	FIDUCIARY	HIMALAYAN	LIMOUSINE
THEREFORE	WHITAKERS	CIVILIZED	DISENGAGE	FIELDFARE	HIMALAYAS	LIMPIDITY
THEREUPON	WHITEBAIT	DIABLERIE	DISENTOMB	FIELDSMAN	HIMYARITE	LINDBERGH
THERMIDOR	WHITEDAMP	DIACRITIC	DISFAVOUR	FIELDWORK	HINDBRAIN	LINEAMENT
THERSITES	WHITEFISH	DIAERESIS	DISFIGURE	FIFTEENTH	HINDEMITH	LINEOLATE
THESAURUS	WHITEHALL	DIAGNOSIS	DISGRACED	FIGURANTE	HINDRANCE	LINGERING
THICKHEAD	WHITEHEAD	DIALECTAL	DISGUISED	FILICALES	HINDSIGHT	LINGFIELD
THICKNESS	WHITENESS	DIALECTIC	DISGUSTED	FILIGRAIN	HINGELESS	LINKLATER
THIGHBONE	WHITENING	DIALOGITE	DISHCLOTH	FILLIPEEN	HIPPOCRAS	LINTSTOCK
THINGUMMY	WHITEWALL	DIAMETRIC	DISHONEST	FILLISTER	HIPPODAME	LIONHEART
THINKABLE	WHITEWASH	DIANDROUS	DISHONOUR	FILMMAKER	HIPPOLYTA	LIPPITUDE
THINNINGS	WHITEWING	DIANETICS	DISHWATER	FILMSTRIP	HIPPOLYTE	LIQUEFIED

LIQUIDATE	MINNESOTA	PICTOGRAM	SIDEBOARD	TITTLEBAT	WITCHETTY	ALTIMETER
LIQUIDITY	MINUSCULE	PICTORIAL	SIDEBURNS	VIABILITY	WITHDRAWN	ALTIPLANO
LIQUIDIZE	MINUTEMAN	PIECEMEAL	SIDELIGHT	VIBRATILE	WITHERING	ALTISSIMO
LIQUORICE	MIRABELLE	PIECEWORK	SIDEROSIS	VIBRATION	WITHERITE	ALUMINIUM
LIQUORISH	MIRTHLESS	PIEPOWDER	SIDESWIPE	VIBRATORY	WITHSTAND	ALVEOLATE
LISTENING	MISBEHAVE	PIERGLASS	SIDETRACK	VICARIOUS	WITHYWIND	BLACKBALL
LITERALLY	MISCHANCE	PIGGYBACK	SIDEWARDS	VICEREGAL	WITNESSED	BLACKBIRD
LITHOCYST	MISCREANT	PIGGYBANK	SIEGFRIED	VICEREINE	WITTICISM	BLACKBUCK
LITHOPONE	MISDIRECT	PIGHEADED	SIGHTLESS	VICIOUSLY	WITTINGLY	BLACKDAMP
LITHUANIA	MISERABLE	PIGNERATE	SIGHTSEER	VICTIMIZE	ZIBELLINE	BLACKFACE
LITIGIOUS	MISERABLY	PIKESTAFF	SIGNALLER	VICTORIAN	ZINFANDEL	BLACKFOOT
LITURGICS	MISFALLEN	PILASTERS	SIGNALMAN	VICTORINE	ZINKENITE	BLACKHEAD
LIVERPOOL	MISFIRING	PILFERAGE	SIGNATORY	VIDELICET	ZIRCONIUM	BLACKJACK
LIVERWORT	MISGIVING	PILFERING	SIGNATURE	VIDEODISC	DJELLABAH	BLACKLEAD
LIVERYMAN	MISGUIDED	PILLICOCK	SIGNBOARD	VIDEODISK	EJACULATE	BLACKLIST
LIVESTOCK	MISHANDLE	PIMPERNEL	SILICOSIS	VIDEOTAPE	LJUBLJANA	BLACKMAIL
LIVRAISON	MISINFORM	PINCHBECK	SILLINESS	VIENTIANE	OKEYDOKEY	BLACKMORE
MICKLETON	MISLOCATE	PINCHCOCK	SILTSTONE	VIEWPOINT	SKEDADDLE	BLACKNESS
MICROCHIP	MISMANAGE	PINEAPPLE	SILURIDAE	VIGESIMAL	SKEPTICAL	BLACKWOOD
MICROCOSM	MISOCLERE	PINHOOKER	SILVEREYE	VIGILANCE	SKETCHILY	BLAMELESS
MICROCYTE	MISONEIST	PINKERTON	SIMEONITE	VIGILANTE	SKETCHMAP	BLANDNESS
MICROFILM	MISPICKEL	PINOCCHIO	SIMILARLY	VINDICATE	SKETCHPAD	BLASPHEME
MICROINCH	MISPLACED	PINSTRIPE	SIMPLETON	VIOLATION	SKEWWHIFF	BLASPHEMY
MICROLITE	MISSHAPEN	PIPEDREAM	SIMPLISTE	VIOLENTLY	SKIAMACHY	BLATANTLY
MICROLITH	MISSIONER	PIPESTONE	SIMULATED	VIOLINIST	SKILFULLY	BLEACHERS
MICROMOLE	MISSTROKE	PIPSQUEAK	SIMULATOR	VIPASSANA	SKINDIVER	BLESSINGS
MICROTOME	MISTEMPER	PIQUANTLY	SIMULCAST	VIRGINALS	SKINFLINT	BLINDFOLD
MICROTONE	MISTIGRIS	PIRATICAL	SINCERELY	VIRGINIAN	SKINTIGHT	BLINDNESS
MICROVOLT	MISTINESS	PIROUETTE	SINCERITY	VIRGINITY	SKYJACKER	BLINDSPOT
MICROWATT	MISTLETOE	PISTACHIO	SINGALESE	VIRGINIUM	UKRAINIAN	BLINDWORM
MICROWAVE	MITHRAISM	PISTAREEN	SINGAPORE	VIRGULATE	ALABASTER	BLINKERED
MIDDLEMAN	MITRAILLE	PISTOLEER	SINGLESEX	VIRTUALLY	ALBATROSS	BLISTERED
MIDDLESEX	NIAISERIE	PITCHFORK	SINGLETON	VIRULENCE	ALBERTINE	BLOATWARE
MIDDLETON	NICARAGUA	PITCHPINE	SINGSPIEL	VISAGISTE	ALCHEMIST	BLOCKHEAD
MIDDLINGS	NICCOLITE	PITCHPOLE	SINGULTUS	VISCOSITY	ALCOHOLIC	BLOODBATH
MIDHEAVEN	NICKNEVEN	PITCHPOLL	SINKANSEN	VISIONARY	ALDEBARAN	BLOODLESS
MIDIANITE	NICODEMUS	PITIFULLY	SINUOSITY	VISUALIZE	ALERTNESS	BLOODROOT
MIDINETTE	NICTITATE	PITUITARY	SINUSITIS	VITASCOPE	ALEURITIS	BLOODSHED
MIDRASHIM	NIDDERING	PITUITRIN	SIPHUNCLE	VITELLIUS	ALEXANDER	BLOODSHOT
MIDSTREAM	NIDERLING	PIXILATED	SIRBONIAN	VITIATION	ALEXANDRA	BLOODWORM
MIDSUMMER	NIEBELUNG	PIZZICATO	SISSERARY	VITRIOLIC	ALGEBRAIC	BLOWTORCH
MIDWIFERY	NIETZSCHE	RIBBONISM	SISYPHEAN	VITRUVIAN	ALGORITHM	BLUEBEARD
MIDWINTER	NIGGARDLY	RICERCARE	SITUATION	VIVACIOUS	ALICYCLIC	BLUEBERRY
MIGRATION	NIGHTCLUB	RICHELIEU	SIXTEENMO	VIVIDNESS	ALIGNMENT	BLUEPRINT
MIGRATORY	NIGHTFALL	RIDERHOOD	SIXTEENTH	WIDOWHOOD	ALIPHATIC	BLUESHIFT
MILESTONE	NIGHTFIRE	RIDERLESS	TICHBORNE	WILDGEESE	ALLANTOID	BLUESTONE
MILITANCY	NIGHTGLOW	RIDGEBACK	TICTACTOE	WILLEMITE	ALLANTOIS	BLUFFNESS
MILKSHAKE	NIGHTGOWN	RIDGELING	TIERCERON	WILLESDEN	ALLEGEDLY	BLUNDERER
MILLAMANT	NIGHTHAWK	RIDGEPOLE	TIGHTENER	WILLFULLY	ALLEGIANT	BLUNTNESS
MILLENIAL	NIGHTMARE	RIGHTEOUS	TIGHTHEAD	WILLINGLY	ALLEMANDE	BLUSTERER
MILLEPEDE	NIGHTSPOT	RIGHTHAND	TIGHTNESS	WILLOWING	ALLEVIATE	CLAMOROUS
MILLEPORE	NIGHTTIME	RIGHTNESS	TIGHTROPE	WILLPOWER	ALLIGATOR	CLAMPDOWN
MILLIGRAM	NIGHTWORK	RIGHTWING	TIMENOGUY	WIMBLEDON	ALLOCARPY	CLAPBOARD
MILLINERY	NIGRITUDE	RIGMAROLE	TIMEPIECE	WINCANTON	ALLOGRAFT	CLARENDON
MILLIONTH	NIGROSINE	RIGOLETTO	TIMESHARE	WINCOPIPE	ALLOGRAPH	CLARIFIER
MILLIPEDE	NINEPENCE	RILLETTES	TIMETABLE	WINDBREAK	ALLOPATHY	CLASSICAL
MILLIVOLT	NINETIETH	RINGFENCE	TIMOCRACY	WINDCHILL	ALLOTMENT	CLASSLESS
MILLIWATT	NIPCHEESE	RINGSIDER	TIMPANIST	WINDFALLS	ALLOWABLE	CLASSMATE
MILLSTONE	NIPPERKIN	RIOTOUSLY	TINGUAITE	WINDHOVER	ALLOWANCE	CLASSROOM
MILOMETER	NITHSDALE	RIPIENIST	TIPPERARY	WINDSCALE	ALMANDINE	CLEANNESS
MINACIOUS	OILTANKER	RISKINESS	TIPSINESS	WINDSWEPT	ALONGSIDE	CLEANSING
MINCEMEAT	PIACEVOLE	RIVERSIDE	TIPULIDAE	WINEBERRY	ALOOFNESS	CLEARANCE
MINEFIELD	PICKABACK	SIBILANCE	TIREDNESS	WINEGLASS	ALPENGLOW	CLEARNESS
MINELAYER	PICKETING	SIBYLLINE	TISIPHONE	WINNEBAGO	ALPENHORN	CLEARWING
MINIATURE	PICKTHANK	SICCATIVE	TITHEBARN	WISCONSIN	ALTERABLE	CLEOPATRA
MINISKIRT	PICNICKER	SICILIANO	TITILLATE	WISECRACK	ALTERCATE	CLEPSYDRA
MINKSTONE	PICOFARAD	SICKENING	TITRATION	WISTFULLY	ALTERNATE	CLERGYMAN

CLEVELAND	FLIPPANCY	PLAINSONG	AMBITIOUS	IMBROGLIO	UMBILICAL	ANTIPATHY
CLIENTELE	FLOODGATE	PLAINTIFF	AMBLYOPIA	IMITATION	UMBILICUS	ANTIPHONY
CLIMACTIC	FLOORSHOW	PLAINTIVE	AMBROSIAL	IMITATIVE	UMBRATILE	ANTIPODES
CLINGFILM	FLOPHOUSE	PLANETARY	AMBROSIAN	IMMANACLE	UMPTEENTH	ANTIQUARY
CLINICIAN	FLORESTAN	PLASTERED	AMBROTYPE	IMMANENCE	ANABOLISM	ANTIQUITY
CLIPBOARD	FLORIMELL	PLASTERER	AMBULANCE	IMMANENCY	ANABRANCH	ANTISERUM
CLOAKROOM	FLOTATION	PLASTIQUE	AMBUSCADE	IMMEDIACY	ANAEROBIC	ANTITOXIC
CLOCKWISE	FLOURMILL	PLATITUDE	AMELAKITE	IMMEDIATE	ANAGLYPTA	ANTITOXIN
CLOCKWORK	FLOWCHART	PLATONIST	AMENDMENT	IMMELMANN	ANALEPTIC	ANTIVENIN
CLOISONNÉ	FLOWERBED	PLAUSIBLE	AMENHOTEP	IMMENSELY	ANALGESIA	ANTONINUS
CLOSENESS	FLOWERING	PLAUSIBLY	AMERICANO	IMMENSITY	ANALGESIC	ANXIOUSLY
CLOUDLESS	FLOWERPOT	PLAUSTRAL	AMERICIUM	IMMERSION	ANALOGOUS	ENACTMENT
CLUBHOUSE	FLOWSTONE	PLAYFULLY	AMIANTHUS	IMMIGRANT	ANAPLASIA	ENAMELLED
CLUSTERED	FLUCTUATE	PLAYGROUP	AMIDSHIPS	IMMIGRATE	ANAPLASTY	ENAMOURED
ELABORATE	FLUORSPAR	PLAYHOUSE	AMOROUSLY	IMMINENCE	ANARCHIST	ENCANTHIS
ELAEOLITE	FLUSTERED	PLAYTHING	AMORPHOUS	IMMODESTY	ANASTASIA	ENCAUSTIC
ELASTOMER	FLYWEIGHT	PLEASANCE	AMPERSAND	IMMORALLY	ANATOLIAN	ENCELADUS
ELATERIUM	GLABELLAR	PLEIOCENE	AMPHIBIAN	IMMORTALS	ANATOMIST	ENCHANTED
ELBOWROOM	GLADIATOR	PLENITUDE	AMPLIFIER	IMMOVABLE	ANATOMIZE	ENCHANTER
ELECTORAL	GLADIOLUS	PLENTEOUS	AMPLITUDE	IMMOVABLY	ANCESTRAL	ENCHEASON
ELECTRESS	GLADSTONE	PLENTIFUL	AMSTERDAM	IMMUNISER	ANCHORAGE	ENCHILADA
ELECTRIFY	GLAIREOUS	PLETHORIC	AMUSEMENT	IMMUTABLE	ANCHORITE	ENCHORIAL
ELECTRODE	GLAMORIZE	PLIMSOLLS	AMUSINGLY	IMMUTABLY	ANCHORMAN	ENCIRCLED
ELECTUARY	GLAMOROUS	PLOUGHMAN	AMYGDALUS	IMPACTION	ANCILLARY	ENCLOSURE
ELEGANTLY	GLANDULAR	PLUMBEOUS	EMACIATED	IMPARTIAL	ANCIPITAL	ENCOLPION
ELEMENTAL	GLASSWARE	PLUMBLINE	EMANATION	IMPASSION	ANDANTINO	ENCOLPIUM
ELEVATION	GLASSWORT	PLUMDAMAS	EMBARRASS	IMPASSIVE	ANDROCLES	ENCOMPASS
ELEVENSES	GLEANINGS	PLUMPNESS	EMBASSAGE	IMPATIENT	ANDROMEDA	ENCOUNTER
ELIMINATE	GLEEFULLY	PLUNDERER	EMBATTLED	IMPEACHER	ANECDOTAL	ENCOURAGE
ELIZABETH	GLENDOWER	PLURALISM	EMBELLISH	IMPEDANCE	ANECDOTES	ENCRATITE
ELKOSHITE	GLENGARRY	PLURALITY	EMBEZZLER	IMPELLING	ANGELFISH	ENCUMBENT
ELLESMERE	GLENLIVET	PLUTOCRAT	EMBRACERY	IMPENDING	ANGIOGRAM	ENDEARING
ELLINGTON	GLISSANDO	PLUTONIUM	EMBRACING	IMPERATOR	ANGLICISM	ENDEAVOUR
ELOCUTION	GLOMERATE	SLABSTONE	EMBRANGLE	IMPERFECT	ANGOSTURA	ENDECAGON
ELONGATED	GLOMERULE	SLACKNESS	EMBRASURE	IMPERIOUS	ANGUISHED	ENDEICTIC
ELOPEMENT	GLORIFIED	SLAMMAKIN	EMBROCATE	IMPETUOUS	ANHYDRIDE	ENDLESSLY
ELOQUENCE	GLORYHOLE	SLANTWISE	EMBROGLIO	IMPLEMENT	ANHYDRITE	ENDOCRINE
ELSEWHERE	GLUCINIUM	SLAPHAPPY	EMBROIDER	IMPLICATE	ANHYDROUS	ENDOERGIC
ELUCIDATE	GLUCOSIDE	SLAPSTICK	EMBROILED	IMPLUVIUM	ANIMALISM	ENDOMORPH
ELUTRIATE	GLUTAMINE	SLAUGHTER	EMBRYONIC	IMPOLITIC	ANIMALITY	ENDOSPERM
FLABELLUM	GLUTINOUS	SLAVISHLY	EMERGENCE	IMPORTANT	ANIMATION	ENDOWMENT
FLAGELLIN	GLYCERIDE	SLEEKNESS	EMERGENCY	IMPORTUNE	ANIMISTIC	ENDPAPERS
FLAGELLUM	GLYCERINE	SLEEPLESS	EMINENTLY	IMPOSTURE	ANIMOSITY	ENDURABLE
FLAGEOLET	ILCHESTER	SLEEPWALK	EMMERDALE	IMPOTENCE	ANISOGAMY	ENDURANCE
FLAGITATE	ILLEGALLY	SLIGHTEST	EMOLLIATE	IMPOUNDER	ANKYLOSIS	ENERGETIC
FLAGRANCE	ILLEGIBLE	SLIMINESS	EMOLLIENT	IMPRECATE	ANNAPOLIS	ENERGUMEN
FLAGSTAFF	ILLEGIBLY	SLINGBACK	EMOLUMENT	IMPRECISE	ANNAPURNA	ENERINITE
FLAGSTONE	ILLGOTTEN	SLINGSHOT	EMOTIONAL	IMPRESSED	ANNOTATED	ENGARLAND
FLAMMABLE	ILLIBERAL	SLIVOVICA	EMPAESTIC	IMPROBITY	ANNOTATOR	ENGINEERS
FLAMSTEED	ILLICITLY	SLIVOVITZ	EMPANOPLY	IMPROMPTU	ANNOUNCER	ENGRAINED
FLASHBACK	ILLOGICAL	SLOUGHING	EMPENNAGE	IMPROVING	ANNOYANCE	ENGRAVING
FLASHBULB	KLEMPERER	SLOVENIAN	EMPHASIZE	IMPROVISE	ANNULMENT	ENGRENAGE
FLASHCUBE	KLENDUSIC	SLOWCOACH	EMPHLYSIS	IMPRUDENT	ANOINTING	ENGROSSED
FLATTENED	KLINOSTAT	SLUGHORNE	EMPHYSEMA	IMPSONITE	ANOMALOUS	ENGROSSER
FLATTENER	OLECRANON	SLUMBERER	EMPIRICAL	IMPUDENCE	ANONYMITY	ENHYDRITE
FLATTERED	OLENELLUS	ULIGINOUS	EMPLECTON	IMPULSION	ANONYMOUS	ENIGMATIC
FLATTERER	OLEOGRAPH	ULLSWATER	EMPLOYEES	IMPULSIVE	ANOPHELES	ENJOYABLE
FLATULENT	OLEORESIN	ULTIMATUM	EMPTINESS	OMBUDSMAN	ANSCHLUSS	ENJOYMENT
FLAVORING	OLFACTORY	ULTRONEUS	EMULATION	OMINOUSLY	ANSWERING	ENLIGHTEN
FLAVOURED	OLIGARCHY	AMARANTIN	GMELINITE	OMNIRANGE	ANTARCTIC	ENLIVENED
FLECHETTE	OLIGOCENE	AMARYLLIS	IMAGELESS	OMOPHAGIC	ANTENATAL	ENNERDALE
FLEDGLING	OLIVENITE	AMAUROSIS	IMAGINARY	SMALLNESS	ANTICLINE	ENQUIRIES
FLEETWOOD	PLACATORY	AMAZEMENT	IMBALANCE	SMALLTIME	ANTIGONUS	ENQUIRING
FLESHLESS	PLACEMENT	AMAZONITE	IMBRANGLE	SMARTNESS	ANTIHELIX	ENRAPTURE
FLESHPOTS	PLACIDITY	AMBERGRIS	IMBRICATE	SMOKEFREE	ANTINOVEL	ENROLMENT
FLEXITIME	PLAINNESS	AMBIGUITY	IMBROCATE	SMOKELESS	ANTIPASTO	ENSCONCED
FLINTLOCK	PLAINSMAN	AMBIGUOUS		SMUGGLING		ENSHEATHE

ENSORCELL	INDIGENCE	INSHALLAH	INTUMESCE	UNCONFINE	UNITARIAN	BONDSTONE
ENSTATITE	INDIGNANT	INSIDIOUS	INUMBRATE	UNCORRECT	UNIVALENT	BOOBIALLA
ENTELECHY	INDIGNITY	INSINCERE	INUNCTION	UNCOUPLED	UNIVERSAL	BOOBYTRAP
ENTERITIS	INDOLENCE	INSINUATE	INUSITATE	UNCOURTLY	UNKNOWING	BOOKLOVER
ENTERTAIN	INDONESIA	INSIPIENT	INVECTIVE	UNCOVERED	UNLEARNED	BOOKMAKER
ENTHYMEME	INDRAUGHT	INSISTENT	INVENTION	UNCROSSED	UNLIMITED	BOOKSHELF
ENTOPHYTE	INDUCTION	INSOLENCE	INVENTIVE	UNCROWNED	UNLUCKILY	BOOKSTALL
ENTOURAGE	INDUCTIVE	INSOLUBLE	INVENTORY	UNDAMAGED	UNMARRIED	BOOKSTAND
ENTRAMMEL	INDULGENT	INSOLVENT	INVERNESS	UNDAUNTED	UNMATCHED	BOOKSTORE
ENTRANCED	INDWELLER	INSOMNIAC	INVERSION	UNDECIDED	UNMINDFUL	BOOMERANG
ENTRECHAT	INEBRIATE	INSPECTOR	INVERTASE	UNDEFILED	UNMUSICAL	BOONDOCKS
ENTRECÔTE	INEFFABLE	INSPIRING	INVIDIOUS	UNDEFINED	UNNATURAL	BOOTBLACK
ENTREMETS	INELEGANT	INSTANTER	INVIOLATE	UNDERBITE	UNNERVING	BOOTLACES
ENTROPION	INERTNESS	INSTANTLY	INVISIBLE	UNDERBRED	UNNOTICED	BORDEREAU
ENTROPIUM	INERUDITE	INSTIGATE	INVOICING	UNDERCAST	UNOPPOSED	BORDERING
ENUCLEATE	INFANTILE	INSTITUTE	INVOLUCRE	UNDERCOAT	UNPOPULAR	BORNAGAIN
ENUMERATE	INFATUATE	INSULATOR	KNACKERED	UNDERDONE	UNPRECISE	BORROWING
ENUNCIATE	INFECTING	INSULTING	KNAPSCULL	UNDERFEED	UNREFINED	BOSPHORUS
ENVERMEIL	INFECTION	INSURANCE	KNAPSKULL	UNDERFELT	UNRELATED	BOSSANOVA
INABILITY	INFERENCE	INSURGENT	KNEECORDS	UNDERFLOW	UNRUFFLED	BOSSINESS
INAMORATA	INFERTILE	INSWINGER	KNIPHOFIA	UNDERFOOT	UNSAVOURY	BOSTONIAN
INAMORATO	INFIELDER	INTEGRATE	KNOBSTICK	UNDERGRAD	UNSCATHED	BOTANICAL
INANIMATE	INFIRMARY	INTEGRITY	KNOCKDOWN	UNDERHAND	UNSECURED	BOTSWANAN
INANITION	INFIRMITY	INTELLECT	KNOTGRASS	UNDERHUNG	UNSELFISH	BOTTLEFUL
INAUDIBLE	INFLATION	INTENDANT	KNOWINGLY	UNDERLINE	UNSETTLED	BOULEVARD
INAUDIBLY	INFLEXION	INTENDING	KNOWLEDGE	UNDERLING	UNSHACKLE	BOUNDLESS
INAUGURAL	INFLUENCE	INTENSELY	MNEMOSYNE	UNDERMINE	UNSHEATHE	BOUNTEOUS
INCAPABLE	INFLUENZA	INTENSIFY	ONCOMETER	UNDERMOST	UNSIGHTLY	BOUNTIFUL
INCARDINE	INFORMANT	INTENSITY	ONOMASTIC	UNDERPAID	UNSINNING	BOURGEOIS
INCARNATE	INFURIATE	INTENSIVE	ONSLAUGHT	UNDERPASS	UNSKILLED	BOXWALLAH
INCAUTION	INGENIOUS	INTENTION	ONTHESPOT	UNDERRATE	UNSPARING	BOYFRIEND
INCENTIVE	INGENUITY	INTERBRED	ONTOGENCY	UNDERSEAL	UNSPOILED	COACHLOAD
INCEPTION	INGENUOUS	INTERCEDE	PNEUMATIC	UNDERSELL	UNSULLIED	COADJUTOR
INCEPTIVE	INGESTION	INTERCEPT	PNEUMONIA	UNDERSIDE	UNTENABLE	COAGULANT
INCESSANT	INGLENOOK	INTERCITY	SNAILFISH	UNDERSIGN	UNTIMEOUS	COAGULATE
INCIDENCE	INGRAINED	INTERDICT	SNAKEWEED	UNDERSONG	UNTOUCHED	COALESCED
INCIPIENT	INGROWING	INTERFACE	SNEERWELL	UNDERTAKE	UNTRAINED	COALFIELD
INCITATUS	INHERITED	INTERFERE	SNOWBOUND	UNDERTONE	UNTREATED	COALITION
INCLEMENT	INHERITOR	INTERJECT	SNOWDONIA	UNDERWALK	UNTRODDEN	COALMINER
INCLUDING	INHIBITED	INTERLACE	SNOWDRIFT	UNDERWEAR	UNTUTORED	COARCTATE
INCLUSION	INHIBITOR	INTERLARD	SNOWFLAKE	UNDERWENT	UNTYPICAL	COASTLINE
INCLUSIVE	INHUMANLY	INTERLOCK	SNOWSHOES	UNDERWOOD	UNUNUNIUM	COCHINEAL
INCOGNITO	INITIALLY	INTERLOPE	SNOWSTORM	UNDILUTED	UNUSUALLY	COCKAIGNE
INCOMINGS	INITIATED	INTERLUDE	SNOWWHITE	UNDIVIDED	UNVARYING	COCKATIEL
INCOMMODE	INITIATOR	INTERMENT	UNABASHED	UNDOUBTED	UNWATERED	COCKFIGHT
INCONDITE	INJECTION	INTERNODE	UNADOPTED	UNDRESSED	UNWELCOME	COCKROACH
INCORRECT	INJURIOUS	INTERPLAY	UNALLOYED	UNEARTHLY	UNWILLING	COCKSCOMB
INCREASED	INJUSTICE	INTERPOSE	UNALTERED	UNEATABLE	UNWITTING	COCKSFOOT
INCREMENT	INNERMOST	INTERPRET	UNANIMITY	UNEQUALED	UNWORRIED	COCKSWAIN
INCUBATOR	INNISFAIL	INTERRUPT	UNANIMOUS	UNETHICAL	UNWRITTEN	COCUSWOOD
INCULCATE	INNISFREE	INTERSECT	UNASHAMED	UNEXPOSED	BOANERGES	COELOSTAT
INCULPATE	INNKEEPER	INTERVENE	UNBALANCE	UNFAILING	BOARDROOM	COEMPTION
INCUMBENT	INNOCENCE	INTERVIEW	UNBEKNOWN	UNFEELING	BOARDWALK	COENOBITE
INCURABLE	INNOCUOUS	INTESTATE	UNBENDING	UNFITTING	BOATHOUSE	COENOBIUM
INCURABLY	INNOVATOR	INTESTINE	UNBIASSED	UNFLEDGED	BOATSWAIN	COFFERDAM
INCURIOUS	INOCULATE	INTRICACY	UNBOUNDED	UNFOUNDED	BOBSLEIGH	COFFINITE
INCURSION	INOPINATE	INTRICATE	UNBRIDLED	UNGUARDED	BOCCACCIO	COGNITION
INDECENCY	INORGANIC	INTRIGUED	UNCEASING	UNHAPPILY	BODYGUARD	COGNITIVE
INDECORUM	INPATIENT	INTRIGUER	UNCERTAIN	UNHEALTHY	BOLECTION	COGNIZANT
INDELIBLE	INQUILINE	INTRINSIC	UNCHANGED	UNHEEDING	BOLIVIANO	COHERENCE
INDELIBLY	INQUINATE	INTRODUCE	UNCHARGED	UNHELPFUL	BOLOGNESE	COINTREAU
INDEMNIFY	INQUIRING	INTROITUS	UNCHECKED	UNHOPEFUL	BOLSHEVIK	COLCHICUM
INDEMNITY	INQUORATE	INTROVERT	UNCHRISOM	UNIFORMED	BOMBARDON	COLERIDGE
INDENTURE	INSCRIBED	INTRUSION	UNCLAIMED	UNIFORMLY	BOMBASINE	COLLAPSAR
INDICATES	INSELBERG	INTRUSIVE	UNCLOTHED	UNINJURED	BOMBASTIC	COLLATION
INDICATOR	INSENSATE	INTUITION	UNCLOUDED	UNINVITED	BOMBSHELL	COLLEAGUE
INDICTION	INSERTION	INTUITIVE	UNCONCERN	UNISEXUAL	BONAPARTE	COLLECTED

COLLECTOR	CONCAVITY	CONTINUUM	COURTESAN	FORECLOSE	GOOSENECK	HOTTENTOT
COLLEGIAN	CONCEALED	CONTRALTO	COURTROOM	FORECOURT	GOOSESTEP	HOURGLASS
COLLIGATE	CONCEITED	CONTRIVED	COURTSHIP	FOREFRONT	GOSLARITE	HOURSTONE
COLLIMATE	CONCERNED	CONTRIVER	COURTYARD	FOREGOING	GOSPELLER	HOUSEBOAT
COLLISION	CONCERTED	CONTUMACY	COUTURIER	FOREIGNER	GOSSAMERY	HOUSECOAT
COLLOCATE	CONCIERGE	CONTUMELY	COVALENCY	FORESHORE	GOSSYPINE	HOUSEHOLD
COLLODION	CONCISELY	CONTUSION	COVELLITE	FORESIGHT	GOSSYPIUM	HOUSELEEK
COLLOIDAL	CONCISION	CONUNDRUM	COVERDALE	FORESPEAK	GOTHAMITE	HOUSEMAID
COLLOTYPE	CONCLUDED	CONVECTOR	COVERTURE	FORESPEND	GOVERNESS	HOUSEROOM
COLLUSION	CONCORDAT	CONVERTED	COWARDICE	FORESTAGE	GOVERNING	HOUSEWIFE
COLLUSIVE	CONCOURSE	CONVERTER	COXSACKIE	FORESTALL	HOARFROST	HOUSEWORK
COLLYRIUM	CONCUBINE	CONVINCED	DOCTORATE	FORESTERS	HOARHOUND	HOUYHNHNM
COLOCYNTH	CONCUSSED	CONVIVIAL	DOCTRINAL	FORETASTE	HOARSTONE	HOWTOWDIE
COLOMBIAN	CONDEMNED	COOKHOUSE	DOCUMENTS	FOREWOMAN	HOBBINOLL	HOYDENISH
COLOMBIER	CONDENSER	COOPERATE	DODDIPOLL	FORFEITED	HOBGOBLIN	IODOPHILE
COLONNADE	CONDIMENT	COPIOUSLY	DOGMATISM	FORFICATE	HOBNAILED	JOBCENTRE
COLOPHONY	CONDITION	COPROLITE	DOGMATIZE	FORGATHER	HOCCAMORE	JOBERNOWL
COLORLESS	CONDUCIVE	COPYRIGHT	DOLEFULLY	FORGETFUL	HODIERNAL	JOBSEEKER
COLOSSEUM	CONDUCTOR	CORALLINE	DOLOMITES	FORGETIVE	HODMANDOD	JOBSWORTH
COLOSTOMY	CONDUCTUS	CORDIALLY	DOLOMITIC	FORGIVING	HODOGRAPH	JOCKSTRAP
COLOSTRUM	CONDYLOMA	CORDUROYS	DOMICILED	FORGOTTEN	HODOMETER	JOCKTELEG
COLOURFUL	CONFESSED	CORDYLINE	DOMINANCE	FORJASKIT	HOLDERBAT	JOCULARLY
COLOURING	CONFESSOR	CORIANDER	DOMINICAL	FORJESKIT	HOLINSHED	JOHANNINE
COLOURIST	CONFIDANT	CORKSCREW	DOMINICAN	FORLORNLY	HOLLERITH	JORDANIAN
COLTSFOOT	CONFIDENT	CORMORANT	DONATELLO	FORMALIST	HOLLYHOCK	JOSEPHINE
COLUMBARY	CONFIRMED	CORNBRASH	DONCASTER	FORMALITY	HOLLYWOOD	JOSEPHSON
COLUMBATE	CONFITEOR	CORNCRAKE	DONIZETTI	FORMALIZE	HOLOCAUST	JOUISANCE
COLUMBIAN	CONFLATED	CORNEILLE	DOODLEBUG	FORMATION	HOLOGRAPH	JOVIALITY
COLUMBINE	CONFORMAL	CORNELIAN	DOORFRAME	FORMATIVE	HOLOPHOTE	KOMINFORM
COLUMBITE	CONFUCIUS	CORNERMAN	DORMITION	FORMULATE	HOLYSTONE	KONIMETER
COLUMBIUM	CONFUSING	CORNETIST	DORMITORY	FORNICATE	HOMEBOUND	KONISCOPE
COLUMELLA	CONFUSION	CORNFIELD	DOSIMETER	FORSYTHIA	HOMEGROWN	LOADSTONE
COLUMNIST	CONGENIAL	CORNFLOUR	DOSSHOUSE	FORTALICE	HOMEOPATH	LOAMSHIRE
COMBATANT	CONGERIES	CORNSTALK	DOTHEBOYS	FORTHWINK	HOMEOWNER	LOATHSOME
COMBATIVE	CONGESTED	COROLLARY	DOUBTLESS	FORTHWITH	HOMESTEAD	LOBLOLLYS
COMFORTER	CONGOLESE	CORPORATE	DOUKHOBOR	FORTILAGE	HOMEWARDS	LOBSCOUSE
COMICALLY	CONGRUENT	CORPOREAL	DOWELLING	FORTITUDE	HOMICIDAL	LOCALIZED
COMINFORM	CONGRUOUS	CORPOSANT	DOWNGRADE	FORTNIGHT	HOMOGRAFT	LOCELLATE
COMINTERN	CONJUGATE	CORPULENT	DOWNRIGHT	FORTUNATE	HOMOGRAPH	LOCHINVAR
COMMANDER	CONJURING	CORPUSCLE	DOWNSTAGE	FORWANDER	HOMOPHONE	LOCKSMITH
COMMENSAL	CONNECTED	CORRECTED	DOWNTREND	FOSSILISE	HOMOPTERA	LODESTONE
COMMISSAR	CONNECTOR	CORRECTLY	DOWNWARDS	FOSSORIAL	HONEYCOMB	LODGEMENT
COMMITTAL	CONNEXION	CORRECTOR	FOGGINESS	FOUNDLING	HONEYMOON	LOFTINESS
COMMITTED	CONNOTATE	CORREGGIO	FOGRAMITE	FOURPENCE	HONKYTONK	LOGARITHM
COMMITTEE	CONNUBIAL	CORRELATE	FOLIOLOSE	FOURWHEEL	HONORABLE	LOGICALLY
COMMODITY	CONQUEROR	CORROSION	FOLKETING	GOALMOUTH	HONORIFIC	LOGISTICS
COMMODORE	CONSCIOUS	CORROSIVE	FOLKWEAVE	GOBETWEEN	HOOLACHAN	LOGOGRIPH
COMMOTION	CONSCRIPT	CORRUGATE	FOLLOWING	GODDESSES	HOPEFULLY	LOGOTHETE
COMMUNION	CONSENSUS	CORRUPTER	FOMALHAUT	GODFATHER	HOPLOLOGY	LOHENGRIN
COMMUNISM	CONSIGNEE	CORTISONE	FOODSTORE	GODLINESS	HOPSCOTCH	LOINCLOTH
COMMUNIST	CONSIGNOR	CORUSCATE	FOODSTUFF	GODMOTHER	HORDEOLUM	LOITERING
COMMUNITY	CONSOCIES	COSMETICS	FOOLHARDY	GODOLPHIN	HOREHOUND	LOMBARDIC
COMMUTATE	CONSONANT	COSMOGONY	FOOLISHLY	GODPARENT	HORNSTONE	LONDONESE
COMPACTLY	CONSTABLE	COSMOLOGY	FOOLPROOF	GOLDCREST	HOROSCOPE	LONGCHAMP
COMPANIES	CONSTANCE	COSMONAUT	FOOTBRAKE	GOLDFIELD	HORRIFIED	LONGEDFOR
COMPANION	CONSTANCY	COSTUMIER	FOOTHILLS	GOLDFINCH	HORSEBACK	LONGEVITY
COMPELLED	CONSTRICT	COTANGENT	FOOTLOOSE	GOLDSINNY	HORSEHAIR	LONGICORN
COMPETENT	CONSTRUCT	COTHURNUS	FOOTPLATE	GOLDSMITH	HORSELESS	LONGINGLY
COMPETING	CONSULATE	COTYLEDON	FOOTPRINT	GOMPHOSIS	HORSEPLAY	LONGITUDE
COMPLAINT	CONSUMING	COUCHETTE	FOOTSTALL	GONDOLIER	HORSESHOE	LONGLIVED
COMPLIANT	CONTAGION	COUNSELOR	FOOTSTOOL	GONGORISM	HORSETAIL	LONGRANGE
COMPONENT	CONTAINER	COUNTDOWN	FORASMUCH	GONIATITE	HORSEWHIP	LONGSHORE
COMPOSING	CONTEMPER	COUNTLESS	FORBIDDEN	GOODNIGHT	HORTATIVE	LOOKALIKE
COMPOSITE	CONTENDER	COUNTRIES	FORCEMEAT	GOONHILLY	HORTATORY	LOOSEHEAD
COMPOSURE	CONTENTED	COURGETTE	FOREANENT	GOOSANDER	HOSPITIUM	LOOSELEAF
COMPOTIER	CONTINENT	COURTELLE	FOREBEARS	GOOSEFOOT	HOSTILITY	LOOSENESS
COMPUTING	CONTINUAL	COURTEOUS	FOREBRAIN	GOOSEHERD	HOTHEADED	LOQUACITY

LORGNETTE	MORBIDITY	NOVODAMUS	POSTILION	SOCIOLECT	TOLLHOUSE	WOODCHUCK	
LOUDMOUTH	MORECAMBE	POCKETFUL	POSTNATAL	SOCIOLOGY	TOLPUDDLE	WOODCRAFT	
LOUISIANA	MORGANITE	POCKMANKY	POSTPONED	SOFTCOVER	TOMBSTONE	WOODENTOP	
LOUSEWORT	MORMONISM	POETASTER	POSTULANT	SOFTENING	TOMENTOSE	WOODHOUSE	
LOWLANDER	MORTALITY	POETICIZE	POSTULATE	SOGGINESS	TONBRIDGE	WOODLANDS	
LOWLIGHTS	MORTGAGEE	POIGNANCY	POSTWOMAN	SOLDERING	TONOMETER	WOODLOUSE	
LOWLINESS	MORTGAGOR	POINTEDLY	POTASSIUM	SOLDIERLY	TONOPLAST	WOODSHOCK	
MOBOCRACY	MORTICIAN	POINTLESS	POTBOILER	SOLEMNITY	TOOTHACHE	WOOLINESS	
MOCCASINS	MORTIFIED	POINTSMAN	POTENTATE	SOLEMNIZE	TOOTHCOMB	WOOMERANG	
MOCKERNUT	MORTSTONE	POISONING	POTENTIAL	SOLFEGGIO	TOOTHLESS	WORCESTER	
MODELLING	MOSCHATEL	POISONOUS	POTHOLING	SOLFERINO	TOOTHPICK	WORDINESS	
MODERATOR	MOSKONFYT	POKERWORK	POTHUNTER	SOLFIDIAN	TOOTHSOME	WORDSMITH	
MODERNISM	MOTHBALLS	POLEMARCH	POTPOURRI	SOLICITOR	TOPDRAWER	WORKFORCE	
MODERNIST	MOTHEATEN	POLEMICAL	POTTINGAR	SOLILOQUY	TOPIARIST	WORKHORSE	
MODERNITY	MOTHERING	POLIANITE	POUJADIST	SOLIPSISM	TOPICALLY	WORKHOUSE	
MODERNIZE	MOTOCROSS	POLICEMAN	POULTERER	SOLITAIRE	TORBANITE	WORKPLACE	
MODESTINE	MOTORBIKE	POLITBURO	POWELLITE	SOLLICKER	TORMENTER	WORKSPACE	
MODILLION	MOTORBOAT	POLITESSE	POWERBOAT	SOMASCOPE	TORMENTIL	WORLDWIDE	
MOGADISHU	MOTORCADE	POLITICAL	POWERLESS	SOMEPLACE	TORMENTOR	WORMEATEN	
MOISTNESS	MOTORISTS	POLITIQUE	ROADBLOCK	SOMETHING	TORMENTUM	WORRISOME	
MOLECULAR	MOURNIVAL	POLLINATE	ROADHOUSE	SOMETIMES	TORTELIER	WORTHLESS	
MOLESKINS	MOUSEHOLE	POLLUTANT	ROADSTEAD	SOMEWHERE	TOSCANINI	YOHIMBINE	
MOLLITIES	MOUSELIKE	POLLUTION	ROADWORKS	SOMMELIER	TOTALIZER	YORKSHIRE	
MOLLYMAWK	MOUSETRAP	POLONAISE	ROBERTSON	SOMNOLENT	TOTAQUINE	YOUNGSTER	
MOMENTARY	MOUSTACHE	POLVERINE	ROCAMBOLE	SONGSMITH	TOTTENHAM	ZOOLOGIST	
MOMENTOUS	MOUTHLESS	POLYANDRY	ROISTERER	SONNETEER	TOUCHDOWN	ZOOMANTIC	
MONACTINE	MOUTHWASH	POLYESTER	ROOSEVELT	SONOMETER	TOUCHLINE	ZOOSCOPIC	
MONASTERY	MOYGASHEL	POLYGONAL	ROOTSTOCK	SOOTERKIN	TOUCHWOOD	ZOROASTER	
MONASTRAL	NOBLENESS	POLYGRAPH	ROQUEFORT	SOPHISTER	TOUGHNESS	APARTHEID	
MONATOMIC	NOCTURNAL	POLYMORPH	RORSCHACH	SOPHISTIC	TOURNEDOS	APARTMENT	
MONERGISM	NOISELESS	POLYNESIA	ROSCOMMON	SOPHISTRY	TOVARISCH	APATHETIC	
MONEYWORT	NOISINESS	POLYPHASE	ROSEWATER	SOPHOCLES	TOWCESTER	APENNINES	
MONGOLIAN	NOLLEKENS	POLYPHONE	ROSINANTE	SOPHOMORE	TOWELLING	APERIODIC	
MONGOLISM	NOMINALLY	POLYPHONY	ROSMARINE	SOPORIFIC	TOWNSFOLK	APERITIVE	
MONKSHOOD	NOMINATOR	POLYTHENE	ROSMINIAN	SOPPINESS	TOXIGENIC	APHERESIS	
MONOCEROS	NOMOCRACY	POMOERIUM	ROSTELLUM	SORCERESS	TOXOPHILY	APHRODITE	
MONOCHORD	NOMOTHETE	POMPADOUR	ROTAPLANE	SORROWFUL	VOICELESS	APOCRYPHA	
MONOCOQUE	NONENTITY	POMPHOLYX	ROTTERDAM	SORTILEGE	VOLAGEOUS	APOENZYME	
MONOCULAR	NONILLION	POMPOSITY	ROTUNDATE	SOSTENUTO	VOLATIBLE	APOLLONUS	
MONODRAMA	NONPAREIL	PONDEROSA	ROTUNDITY	SOTTISIER	VOLCANISM	APOLOGIST	
MONOGRAPH	NONPROFIT	PONDEROUS	ROUGHCAST	SOUBRETTE	VOLGOGRAD	APOLOGIZE	
MONOLAYER	NONSMOKER	PONTLEVIS	ROUGHNECK	SOUFRIERE	VOLKSRAAD	APOPHATIC	
MONOLOGUE	NOOSPHERE	POORHOUSE	ROUGHNESS	SOULFULLY	VOLTIGEUR	APOPHYSIS	
MONOMACHY	NORMALACY	POPLITEAL	ROUGHSHOD	SOUNDBITE	VOLTINISM	APOSTOLIC	
MONOMANIA	NORMALITY	POPPERING	ROUMANIAN	SOUNDLESS	VOLTMETER	APPALLING	
MONOMETER	NORMALIZE	POPPYCOCK	ROUMANSCH	SOUNDNESS	VOLTURNUS	APPARATUS	
MONOPLANE	NORMATIVE	POPULARLY	ROUNCEVAL	SOURDOUGH	VOLUCRINE	APPARITOR	
MONOSTICH	NORTHEAST	POPULATED	ROUNCIVAL	SOUTENEUR	VOLUNTARY	APPEALING	
MONOTROCH	NORTHERLY	PORBEAGLE	ROUNDBACK	SOUTHDOWN	VOLUNTEER	APPENDAGE	
MONOXYLON	NORTHWARD	PORCELAIN	ROUNDELAY	SOUTHEAST	VOODOOISM	APPERTAIN	
MONSIGNOR	NORTHWEST	PORCUPINE	ROUNDFISH	SOUTHERLY	VORACIOUS	APPETIZER	
MONSTROUS	NORWEGIAN	PORIFERAN	ROUNDHAND	SOUTHWARD	VORTICISM	APPLEJACK	
MONTACUTE	NOSEBLEED	PORPOISES	ROUNDHEAD	SOUTHWARK	VORTIGERN	APPLIANCE	
MONTAIGNE	NOSTALGIA	PORPORATE	ROUNDSMAN	SOUTHWEST	VOUCHSAFE	APPLICANT	
MONTANISM	NOSTALGIC	PORRINGER	ROUSSETTE	SOUVLAKIA	WOBBEGONG	APPOINTED	
MONTANIST	NOSTOLOGY	PORTERAGE	ROUTINELY	SOUWESTER	WODEHOUSE	APPOINTEE	
MONTESPAN	NOTARIKON	PORTFOLIO	ROWDINESS	SOVENANCE	WOEBEGONE	APPORTION	
MONTEZUMA	NOTCHBACK	PORTRAYAL	ROXBURGHE	SOVEREIGN	WOLFHOUND	APPRAISAL	
MONTICULE	NOTEPAPER	PORTREEVE	ROZINANTE	TOADSTONE	WOLLASTON	APPREHEND	
MONZONITE	NOTOCHORD	PORTULACA	SOAPBERRY	TOADSTOOL	WOLVERINE	APPROVING	
MOODINESS	NOTONECTA	POSSESSED	SOAPSTONE	TOASTRACK	WOMANHOOD	EPARCHATE	
MOONLIGHT	NOTORIETY	POSSESSOR	SOBERNESS	TOBERMORY	WOMANISER	EPAULETTE	
MOONRAKER	NOTORIOUS	POSSIBLES	SOBRIQUET	TOCCATINA	WOMANIZER	EPEDAPHIC	
MOONSHINE	NOVELETTE	POSTCARDS	SOCIALISM	TOLERABLE	WOMENFOLK	EPEOLATRY	
MOONSTONE	NOVICIATE	POSTERIOR	SOCIALIST	TOLERABLY	WONDERFUL	EPHEDRINE	
MORATORIA	NOVITIATE	POSTERITY	SOCIALITE	TOLERANCE	WOODBORER	EPHEMERAL	
MORATORIO	NOVOCAINE	POSTHOUSE	SOCIALIZE	TOLERATED	WOODBORER	EPHEMERIS	

EPHEMERON	SPECIALTY	UPPERMOST	BRACTEOLE	CRAZINESS	DRUMSTICK	GRACELESS
EPHESIANS	SPECIFICS	UPSETTING	BRADLAUGH	CREDULITY	DRUNKENLY	GRADATION
EPHIALTES	SPECIFIED	AQUAPLANE	BRAINCASE	CREDULOUS	DRYASDUST	GRADGRIND
EPICEDIUM	SPECIMENS	AQUARELLE	BRAINLESS	CREMATION	ERADICATE	GRADUALLY
EPICENTRE	SPECTACLE	AQUILEGIA	BRAINWASH	CREMATORY	ERGATANER	GRADUATED
EPICLESIS	SPECTATOR	EQUALIZER	BRAINWAVE	CRENATION	ERIOMETER	GRAMPIANS
EPICUREAN	SPECULATE	EQUIPMENT	BRAMBLING	CREPITATE	ERISTICAL	GRANDIOSE
EPICYCLIC	SPEECHIFY	EQUIPOISE	BRANCHING	CREPOLINE	EROGENOUS	GRANDNESS
EPIDERMIS	SPEEDBOAT	EQUISETUM	BRANDIRON	CRESCELLE	EROSTRATE	GRANDSIRE
EPIGAEOUS	SPEEDWELL	EQUITABLE	BRASENOSE	CRESCENDO	EROTICISM	GRANULATE
EPIGENOUS	SPELDRING	EQUITABLY	BRASSERIE	CRETINOUS	ERPINGHAM	GRANULITE
EPILATION	SPELLBIND	EQUIVOCAL	BRASSICAS	CRIBELLUM	ERRONEOUS	GRANULOSE
EPILEPTIC	SPELUNKER	EQUIVOQUE	BRASSIERE	CRICKETER	ERSTWHILE	GRAPESHOT
EPINASTIC	SPHACELUS	SQUADRONE	BRASSWARE	CRIMINATE	ERUCIFORM	GRAPETREE
EPINICION	SPHENDONE	SQUALIDLY	BRATWURST	CRINOLINE	ERUDITION	GRAPEVINE
EPINIKION	SPHERICAL	SQUATTERS	BRAZILIAN	CRIPPLING	ERYTHRITE	GRAPHICAL
EPIPHRAGM	SPHINCTER	SQUEAMISH	BREADLINE	CRISPNESS	FRACTIOUS	GRAPPLING
EPIPHYSIS	SPICILEGE	SQUINANCY	BREAKABLE	CRITERION	FRAGILITY	GRASSLAND
EPIPHYTIC	SPICINESS	SQUINTING	BREAKAGES	CRITICISM	FRAGMENTS	GRATICULE
EPIPOLISM	SPIDERWEB	SQUIREAGE	BREAKAWAY	CRITICIZE	FRAGONARD	GRATITUDE
EPISCOPAL	SPIKENARD	SQUIRMING	BREAKDOWN	CROCKFORD	FRAGRANCE	GRAVADLAX
EPISTAXIS	SPILLICAN	ARABESQUE	BREAKEVEN	CROCODILE	FRAGRANCY	GRAVESEND
EPISTOLER	SPILLIKIN	ARABICIZE	BREAKFAST	CROISSANT	FRAMBOISE	GRAVESIDE
EPITHESIS	SPINDRIER	ARABINOSE	BREAKNECK	CROOKBACK	FRAMEWORK	GRAVEYARD
EPITOMIZE	SPINDRIFT	ARACHNOID	BREATHING	CROOKEDLY	FRANCESCA	GRAVITATE
EPONYMOUS	SPINELESS	ARAGONITE	BREECHING	CROQUETTE	FRANCHISE	GREASEGUN
EPULATION	SPINNAKER	ARAUCARIA	BRICKWORK	CROSSBEAM	FRANCOLIN	GREATCOAT
IPHIGENIA	SPINNERET	ARBITRAGE	BRICKYARD	CROSSBILL	FRANGLAIS	GREATNESS
IPRINDOLE	SPIRITISM	ARBITRARY	BRIDEWELL	CROSSBRED	FRANKNESS	GREENAWAY
OPENENDED	SPIRITOUS	ARBITRATE	BRIDLEWAY	CROSSEYED	FRATCHETY	GREENBACK
OPENHEART	SPIRITUAL	ARBORETUM	BRIEFCASE	CROSSFIRE	FRATERNAL	GREENFEED
OPERATING	SPLAYFOOT	ARCHANGEL	BRIEFNESS	CROSSOVER	FREDERICK	GREENGAGE
OPERATION	SPLENDOUR	ARCHETYPE	BRIGADIER	CROSSWALK	FREEBOARD	GREENHEAD
OPERATIVE	SPLENETIC	ARCHIBALD	BRIGADOON	CROSSWIND	FREELANCE	GREENHORN
OPERCULUM	SPLENITIS	ARCHITECT	BRILLIANT	CROSSWISE	FREEMASON	GREENMAIL
OPHIUCHUS	SPLINTERS	ARCHIVIST	BRIMSTONE	CROSSWORD	FREEPHONE	GREENROOM
OPOBALSAM	SPLITTING	ARCHIVOLT	BRIQUETTE	CROTCHETY	FREESTONE	GREENSAND
OPODELDOC	SPODUMENE	ARCTOGAEA	BRISKNESS	CROUSTADE	FREESTYLE	GREENWEED
OPPENHEIM	SPOFFORTH	ARDUOUSLY	BRISTLING	CROWNLIKE	FREEWHEEL	GREENWICH
OPPONENTS	SPOILSMAN	AREOPAGUS	BRITANNIA	CROWSBILL	FREIGHTER	GREENWOOD
OPPORTUNE	SPOKESMAN	ARGENTINA	BRITANNIC	CROWSFOOT	FRENCHMAN	GREENYARD
OPPRESSED	SPONGEBAG	ARGENTINE	BRITSCHKA	CRUCIALLY	FRENCHMEN	GREETINGS
OPPRESSOR	SPONSORED	ARISTOTLE	BROADCAST	CRUCIFORM	FREQUENCY	GREGARINE
OPSIMATHY	SPOONBILL	ARKWRIGHT	BROADLOOM	CRUDENESS	FRESHENER	GREGORIAN
OPTICALLY	SPOONFEED	ARLINGTON	BROADSIDE	CRUMBLING	FRESHNESS	GRENADIER
OPTOMETRY	SPOROCARP	ARMADILLO	BROKERAGE	CRUSTACEA	FRETFULLY	GRENADINE
OPTOPHONE	SPORTSMAN	ARMAMENTS	BROMINATE	CRYOGENIC	FRICASSEE	GRENVILLE
OPULENTLY	SPORTSMEN	ARMISTICE	BRONCHIAL	CRYOMETER	FRIESLAND	GREYBEARD
SPACELESS	SPOTLIGHT	ARMSTRONG	BROTHERLY	CRYPTOGAM	FRIGATOON	GREYHOUND
SPACESHIP	SPRAICKLE	ARQUEBUSE	BROUGHTON	DRACONIAN	FRIGHTFUL	GREYWACKE
SPACESUIT	SPRAUCHLE	ARRESTING	BRUMMAGEM	DRAFTSMAN	FRIGIDITY	GRIEVANCE
SPADASSIN	SPREADING	ARRIVISTE	BRUNHILDE	DRAGONFLY	FRITHBORH	GRIMALKIN
SPAGHETTI	SPRECHERY	ARROGANCE	BRUSHWOOD	DRAINPIPE	FRIVOLITY	GRIMINESS
SPARINGLY	SPRIGHTLY	ARROWHEAD	BRUSQUELY	DRAMATICS	FRIVOLOUS	GRINGOLET
SPARKLERS	SPRINGALD	ARROWROOT	BRUTALISM	DRAMATIST	FRIZZANTE	GRISAILLE
SPARKLING	SPRINGBOK	ARSENICAL	BRUTALITY	DRAMATIZE	FROBISHER	GROCERIES
SPARTACUS	SPRINGLET	ARTEMISIA	BRUTALIZE	DRAVIDIAN	FROGMARCH	GROSGRAIN
SPASMODIC	SPRINKLER	ARTERIOLE	CRACKDOWN	DRAWKNIFE	FROGMOUTH	GROSVENOR
SPATIALLY	SPRITEFUL	ARTHRITIC	CRACKLING	DREAMLAND	FROGSPAWN	GROTESQUE
SPATTERED	SPRITSAIL	ARTHRITIS	CRACKSMAN	DREAMLESS	FROISSART	GROUNDHOG
SPATULATE	SPUNCULID	ARTHROPOD	CRACOVIAN	DRIFTWOOD	FROSTBITE	GROUNDING
SPEAKEASY	UPAITHRIC	ARTHROSIS	CRAFTSMAN	DRINKABLE	FRUCTIDOR	GROUNDNUT
SPEARHEAD	UPANISHAD	ARTHURIAN	CRANBERRY	DRIPSTONE	FRUGALITY	GROUNDSEL
SPEARMINT	UPCOUNTRY	ARTICHOKE	CRANBORNE	DROMEDARY	FRUITCAKE	GRUBBINOL
SPEARSIDE	UPHOLSTER	ARTICULAR	CRAPULENT	DROPPINGS	FRUITERER	GRUELLING
SPEARWORT	UPLIFTING	ARTIFICER	CRAPULOUS	DROPSICAL	FRUITLESS	GRUFFNESS
SPECIALLY	UPPERCASE	ARTILLERY	CRASHLAND	DRUGSTORE	FRUSTRATE	GRUMBLING

IRASCIBLE	PRECOCITY	PROCACITY	PROVIDENT	TRETINOIN	WRONGDOER	ISOCRATES
IRONSIDES	PRECONISE	PROCEDURE	PROVIDING	TREVELYAN	WRONGFOOT	ISODORIAN
IRONSTONE	PRECURSOR	PROCERITY	PROVISION	TRIANGLED	ASCENDANT	ISOLATION
IRONWORKS	PREDATORY	PROCESSOR	PROVOKING	TRIATHLON	ASCENDING	ISOMERASE
IRRADIANT	PREDICANT	PROCLITIC	PROVOLONE	TRIBALISM	ASCENSION	ISOMETRIC
IRRADIATE	PREDICATE	PROCOELUS	PROXIMATE	TRIBESMAN	ASCERTAIN	ISOPROPYL
IRRAWADDY	PREDICTOR	PROCONSUL	PROXIMITY	TRIBESMEN	ASCLEPIUS	ISOSCELES
IRREGULAR	PREDIKANT	PROCREATE	PRUDENTLY	TRIBOLOGY	ASHKENAZI	ISOTACTIC
IRRITABLE	PREDILECT	PRODROMAL	PRURIENCE	TRIBUNATE	ASHMOLEAN	ISOTROPIC
IRRITABLY	PREFATORY	PRODROMUS	PRYTANEUM	TRIBUTARY	ASPARAGUS	ISRAELITE
IRRITATED	PREFERRED	PROENZYME	TRACEABLE	TRICERION	ASPARTAME	OSCILLATE
IRRUPTION	PREFIGURE	PROFANELY	TRACHINUS	TRICKLESS	ASPERSION	OSTENSIVE
IRVINGISM	PREGNANCY	PROFANITY	TRACKLESS	TRICKSTER	ASPIRATOR	OSTEODERM
KROPOTKIN	PREHALLUX	PROFESSED	TRACKSUIT	TRICLINIC	ASPLENIUM	OSTEOPATH
KRUMMHORN	PREJUDICE	PROFESSOR	TRACTABLE	TRICOLOUR	ASSAILANT	OSTRACISE
MRIDAMGAM	PRELECTOR	PROFITEER	TRADEMARK	TRICUSPID	ASSERTING	OSTRACISM
MRIDANGAM	PRELUSORY	PROFUSELY	TRADESMAN	TRIDYMITE	ASSERTION	OSTRACIZE
ORANGEADE	PREMATURE	PROFUSION	TRADEWIND	TRIENNIAL	ASSERTIVE	OSTROGOTH
ORANGEMAN	PREMONISH	PROGNOSIS	TRADITION	TRIERARCH	ASSIDUITY	PSEUDAXIS
ORATORIAN	PREMOTION	PROGRAMME	TRAFALGAR	TRIETERIC	ASSIDUOUS	PSEUDONYM
ORBICULAR	PREOCCUPY	PROJECTED	TRAGEDIAN	TRIFORIUM	ASSISTANT	PSORIASIS
ORCHESTRA	PREORDAIN	PROJECTOR	TRAGELAPH	TRIHEDRON	ASSOCIATE	PSYCHICAL
ORDINAIRE	PREPOLLEX	PROKARYON	TRAINABLE	TRILITHON	ASSONANCE	PSYCHOSIS
ORDINANCE	PRESBYTER	PROKOFIEV	TRAMLINES	TRILOBITE	ASSUETUDE	PSYCHOTIC
ORGANELLE	PRESCIENT	PROLACTIN	TRANSCEND	TRIMESTER	ASSURANCE	TSAREVICH
ORGANICAL	PRESCRIBE	PROLAMINE	TRANSEUNT	TRIMMINGS	ASSUREDLY	USHERETTE
ORGANISED	PRESCUTUM	PROLEPSIS	TRANSFORM	TRINKETER	ASTHMATIC	ATAHUALPA
ORGANISER	PRESENTED	PROLIXITY	TRANSFUSE	TRIPITAKA	ASTOUNDED	ATAVISTIC
ORGANIZED	PRESENTER	PROLONGED	TRANSHUME	TRIPMETER	ASTRAGALS	ATHEISTIC
ORGANIZER	PRESENTLY	PROLUSION	TRANSIENT	TRISAGION	ASTRAKHAN	ATHELSTAN
ORGANZINE	PRESERVED	PROMACHOS	TRANSLATE	TRITENESS	ASTRODOME	ATHENAEUM
ORGIASTIC	PRESERVER	PROMENADE	TRANSMUTE	TRITICALE	ASTROLABE	ATHLETICS
ORGILLOUS	PRESERVES	PROMINENT	TRANSPIRE	TRITURATE	ASTROLOGY	ATONALITY
ORICALCHE	PRESHRUNK	PROMISING	TRANSPORT	TRIUMPHAL	ASTRONAUT	ATONEMENT
ORIENTATE	PRESIDENT	PROMOTION	TRANSPOSE	TRIVIALLY	ASTRONOMY	ATROCIOUS
ORIFLAMME	PRESIDIAL	PROMPTING	TRANSSHIP	TROCHILIC	ASTROPHEL	ATTACKING
ORIGENIST	PRESIDIUM	PROMUSCIS	TRANSVAAL	TROCHLEAS	ASTROTURF	ATTAINDER
ORIGINATE	PRESSGANG	PRONGHORN	TRAPEZIAL	TROMPETTE	ASTUCIOUS	ATTEMPTED
ORMANDINE	PRETENDER	PRONOUNCE	TRAPEZIST	TRONDHEIM	ASYMMETRY	ATTENDANT
OROBANCHE	PRETERITE	PROOFREAD	TRAPEZIUM	TROOPSHIP	ASYNDETON	ATTENTION
OROGRAPHY	PRETERMIT	PROPAGATE	TRAPEZIUS	TROOSTITE	ASYNERGIA	ATTENTIVE
ORPHANAGE	PREVALENT	PROPELLED	TRAPEZOID	TROPAELIN	ESCALATOR	ATTENUATE
ORPHARION	PREVERNAL	PROPELLER	TRAPPINGS	TROPARION	ESCOPETTE	ATTITUDES
ORPINGTON	PRICELESS	PROPERDIN	TRASIMENE	TROSSACHS	ESCULENTS	ATTRIBUTE
ORTANIQUE	PRIESTESS	PROPHETIC	TRATTORIA	TROUBADOR	ESEMPLASY	ATTRITION
ORTHODOXY	PRIESTLEY	PROPIONIC	TRAUMATIC	TROUSSEAU	ESMERALDA	ATTUITION
ORTHOLOGY	PRIMAEVAL	PROPONENT	TRAVELERS	TRUCKLOAD	ESOPHAGUS	CTESIPHON
ORTHOPTER	PRIMARILY	PROPRIETY	TRAVELING	TRUCULENT	ESPAGNOLE	ETCETERAS
ORTHOTONE	PRIMAVERA	PROPTOSIS	TRAVELLER	TRUEPENNY	ESPERANCE	ETERNALLY
PRACTICAL	PRIMIPARA	PROPYLENE	TREACHERY	TRUMPEDUP	ESPERANTO	ETHANOATE
PRACTISED	PRIMITIAE	PROROGATE	TREADMILL	TRUMPETER	ESPIONAGE	ETHELBERT
PRACTOLOL	PRIMITIVE	PROSCRIBE	TREASURER	TRUNCATED	ESPLANADE	ETHEREOUS
PRAGMATIC	PRIMULINE	PROSECUTE	TREATMENT	TRUNCHEON	ESQUILINE	ETHIOPIAN
PRANKSTER	PRINCETON	PROSELYTE	TREBIZOND	TRUNKFISH	ESSENTIAL	ETHNOLOGY
PREBENDAL	PRINCIPAL	PROSIMIAN	TREBUCHET	TRUTINATE	ESTABLISH	ETIOLATED
PRECATORY	PRINCIPLE	PROSTRATE	TREDRILLE	TRYPHOEUS	ESTAFETTE	ETIQUETTE
PRECEDENT	PRINTABLE	PROTAMINE	TREETRUNK	URANISCUS	ESTAMINET	ETYMOLOGY
PRECEDING	PRISMATIC	PROTECTOR	TREGEAGLE	UREDINIAL	ESTHETICS	ITALICIZE
PRECENTOR	PRIVATEER	PROTESTER	TREGETOUR	URICONIAN	ESTIMABLE	ITERATION
PRECEPTOR	PRIVATELY	PROTHESIS	TREILLAGE	URINATION	ESTRANGED	ITINERANT
PRECIEUSE	PRIVATION	PROTHORAX	TREMATODE	UROKINASE	ESTRAPADE	ITINERARY
PRECINCTS	PRIVATIZE	PROTOSTAR	TREMBLING	URTICARIA	ESTRELDID	ITINERATE
PRECIPICE	PRIVILEGE	PROTOTYPE	TREMOLITE	URUGUAYAN	ISALLOBAR	OTHERWISE
PRECISELY	PROACTIVE	PROUDHORN	TREMULANT	WRANGLERS	ISCHAEMIC	OTTERBURN
PRECISIAN	PROBABLES	PROUSTITE	TREMULATE	WREAKLESS	ISINGLASS	OTTRELITE
PRECISION	PROBATION	PROVEDORE	TREMULOUS	WRECKFISH	ISLAMABAD	PTARMIGAN
PRECISIVE	PROBOSCIS	PROVENDER	TRENCHANT	WRESTLING	ISOCLINAL	PTERIDIUM

PTEROSAUR	STIFFENER	STRICTURE	BULGARIAN	EUMYCETES	HUNKYDORY	MUSHINESS
STABILITY	STIFFNESS	STRIDENCY	BULKINESS	EUPHEMISM	HURRICANE	MUSHROOMS
STABILIZE	STIGMATIC	STRINGENT	BULLDOZER	EUPHONIUM	HURRICANO	MUSICALLY
STABLEBOY	STILLBORN	STRINGOPS	BULLFIGHT	EUPHORBIA	HURRIEDLY	MUSICHALL
STABLELAD	STILLNESS	STRIPLING	BULLFINCH	EUPHRATES	HUSBANDLY	MUSKETEER
STABLEMAN	STILLROOM	STROBILUS	BUMBLEBEE	EURHYTHMY	HUSBANDRY	MUSKETOON
STAGEHAND	STILTBIRD	STROLLING	BUMPTIOUS	EURIPIDES	HUSKINESS	MUSKOGEAN
STAGGERED	STIMULANT	STROMBOLI	BUNDESTAG	EUSKARIAN	HUTTERITE	MUSSITATE
STAGIRITE	STIMULATE	STRONGARM	BURKINABE	EUTROPHIC	JUBILANCE	MUSSOLINI
STAGYRITE	STINGAREE	STRONGYLE	BURLESQUE	FUGACIOUS	JUDGEMENT	MUSSULMAN
STAINLESS	STINGBIRD	STRONTIUM	BURLINESS	FUGGINESS	JUDICIARY	MUSTINESS
STAIRCASE	STINKBIRD	STROSSERS	BURROUGHS	FULLBLOWN	JUDICIOUS	MUTILATED
STALEMATE	STINKHORN	STRUCTURE	BURROWING	FULLERENE	JUICINESS	MUTOSCOPE
STALENESS	STINKWOOD	STRUMITIS	BURUNDIAN	FULLGROWN	JUNEBERRY	MUTTERING
STALWORTH	STIPULATE	STRUTTING	BUTTERBUR	FULLSCALE	JUNKETING	MUTUALISM
STAMMERER	STIRABOUT	STUMBLING	BUTTERCUP	FULMINANT	JURIDICAL	MUZZINESS
STANCHION	STOCKFISH	STUMPWORK	BUTTERFLY	FULMINATE	JUSTIFIED	NUCLEOLUS
STANDARDS	STOCKHOLM	STUPEFIED	BUTTERNUT	FUNDAMENT	JUSTINIAN	NUMBSKULL
STANDERBY	STOCKINET	STUPIDITY	CUBBYHOLE	FUNGIBLES	JUVENILIA	NUMERAIRE
STANDGALE	STOCKINGS	STYLISHLY	CUCHULAIN	FUNGICIDE	JUXTAPOSE	NUMERATOR
STANDPIPE	STOCKPILE	STYLISTIC	CUFFLINKS	FUNICULAR	LUBAVITCH	NUMERICAL
STANNATOR	STOCKROOM	STYLOBATE	CULMINATE	FUNICULUS	LUBRICANT	NUMMULITE
STARBOARD	STOCKWORK	UTICENSIS	CULTIVATE	FURACIOUS	LUBRICATE	NUNCUPATE
STARGAZER	STOCKYARD	UTTERANCE	CUNCTATOR	FURIOUSLY	LUCIFERIN	NUREMBERG
STARKNESS	STOICALLY	UTTERLESS	CUNEIFORM	FURNIMENT	LUCRATIVE	NURSEMAID
STARLIGHT	STOKEHOLD	UTTERMOST	CUPRESSUS	FURNITURE	LUCRETIUS	NUTJOBBER
STARSTONE	STOLIDITY	YTTERBIUM	CURETTAGE	FURTIVELY	LUCTATION	NUTRIMENT
STARTLING	STOMACHIC	AUBERGINE	CURFUFFLE	FUSILLADE	LUCUBRATE	NUTRITION
STATEHOOD	STONEBOAT	AUBRIETIA	CURIOSITY	FUSSINESS	LUDICROUS	NUTRITIVE
STATELESS	STONECHAT	AUCTORIAL	CURIOUSLY	FUSTIGATE	LUMBERING	OUBLIETTE
STATEMENT	STONECROP	AUDACIOUS	CURRENTLY	FUSTINESS	LUMBRICUS	OUDENARDE
STATEROOM	STONEHAND	AUGUSTINE	CURRYCOMB	FUZZINESS	LUMINAIRE	OUGHTNESS
STATESIDE	STONELESS	AURICULAR	CURSORILY	GUACAMOLE	LUMINANCE	OUROBOROS
STATESMAN	STONEWALL	AUSTERITY	CURTILAGE	GUARANTEE	LUNCHTIME	OUROBORUS
STATEWIDE	STONEWARE	AUSTRALIA	CURVATURE	GUARANTOR	LURIDNESS	OURSELVES
STATIONED	STONEWORK	AUTEURISM	CURVEBALL	GUARDRAIL	LUSTIHOOD	OUTERMOST
STATIONER	STONEWORT	AUTHENTIC	CUSPIDORE	GUARDROOM	LUSTINESS	OUTFITTER
STATISTIC	STONKERED	AUTHORESS	CUSTODIAL	GUARDSMAN	LUTESCENT	OUTGOINGS
STATOCYST	STOOLBALL	AUTHORITY	CUSTODIAN	GUATEMALA	LUXEMBURG	OUTGROWTH
STATOLITH	STOPLIGHT	AUTHORIZE	CUSTOMARY	GUERRILLA	LUXURIANT	OUTNUMBER
STATUETTE	STOREROOM	AUTOCLAVE	CUSTOMIZE	GUESSWORK	LUXURIATE	OUTOFTOWN
STATUTORY	STORIATED	AUTOCRACY	CUTANEOUS	GUIDEBOOK	LUXURIOUS	OUTRIGGER
STAUNCHLY	STORNAWAY	AUTOCROSS	CUTTHROAT	GUIDELINE	MUCHLOVED	OUTROOPER
STAVANGER	STORYBOOK	AUTOGRAPH	DUBIOUSLY	GUILDHALL	MUCKENDER	OUTSIDERS
STEADFAST	STORYLINE	AUTOLATRY	DUBROVNIK	GUILELESS	MUCORALES	OUTSKIRTS
STEAMBOAT	STOUTNESS	AUTOLYCUS	DUCKBOARD	GUILLEMOT	MUDDINESS	OUTSPOKEN
STEAMSHIP	STOVEPIPE	AUTOLYSIS	DUIKERBOK	GUILLOCHE	MUFFETTEE	OUTSPREAD
STEELHEAD	STOWNLINS	AUTOMAKER	DULCINIST	GUILTLESS	MUGGLETON	OUTTHRUST
STEELYARD	STRAGGLER	AUTOMATED	DUMBARTON	GUINEVERE	MUGLARITE	OUTWARDLY
STEENBRAS	STRAINING	AUTOMATIC	DUMBFOUND	GUITARIST	MUJAHIDIN	OUTWORKER
STEENKIRK	STRANGELY	AUTOMATON	DUNDREARY	GUJARATHI	MULTIFORM	PUBLICIST
STEEPNESS	STRANGLER	AUTONOMIC	DUNGAREES	GUMSHIELD	MULTIPLEX	PUBLICITY
STEERSMAN	STRANGLES	AUTOPILOT	DUNGENESS	GUNCOTTON	MULTITUDE	PUBLICIZE
STEGNOSIS	STRANGURY	AUTOROUTE	DUNGEONER	GUNPOWDER	MUMCHANCE	PUBLISHED
STEGNOTIC	STRAPHANG	AUTOSCOPY	DUNSINANE	GUSTATION	MUMPSIMUS	PUBLISHER
STEGOSAUR	STRAPLESS	AUXILIARY	DUNSTABLE	GUTENBERG	MUNDUNGUS	PUCELLAGE
STEINBECK	STRAPPADO	AUXOTROPH	DUODECIMO	GUTTERING	MUNICIPAL	PUERILITY
STEINBOCK	STRAPPING	BUBBLEGUM	DUPLICAND	HUCKABACK	MUNIMENTS	PUERPERAL
STENOPAIC	STRATAGEM	BUCCANEER	DUPLICATE	HUMANKIND	MUNITIONS	PUFFINESS
STERADIAN	STRATEGIC	BUCENTAUR	DUPLICITY	HUMANMADE	MURDERESS	PUGNACITY
STERCORAL	STREAMING	BUCHAREST	DUTIFULLY	HUMDINGER	MURDEROUS	PUISSANCE
STERILITY	STREETAGE	BUCKETFUL	EUCHARIST	HUMILIATE	MURKINESS	PULLULATE
STERILIZE	STREETCAR	BUCKTEETH	EUCHLORIC	HUMONGOUS	MURMURING	PULMONARY
STERNFAST	STRENUOUS	BUCKTHORN	EUCLIDEAN	HUMUNGOUS	MUSCADINE	PULMONATE
STERNNESS	STRESSFUL	BUCKWHEAT	EUDAEMONY	HUNCHBACK	MUSCARINE	PULPITEER
STEVEDORE	STRETCHED	BUDGETARY	EUHEMERUS	HUNDREDTH	MUSCOVADO	PULSATION
STEVENSON	STRETCHER	BUFFETING	EUMENIDES	HUNGARIAN	MUSCOVITE	PULVERIZE

PUMMELLED	RUGGELACH	SUPERCOOL	VULPINITE	OVULATION	EXEMPTION	CYCLOTRON
PUNCHLINE	RUINATION	SUPERETTE	VULTURINE	UVAROVITE	EXEQUATUR	CYMBELINE
PUNCTILIO	RUINOUSLY	SUPERFINE	WULFENITE	AWAKENING	EXERCISED	CYMBIDIUM
PUNCTUATE	RUNAROUND	SUPERNOVA	WURLITZER	AWARENESS	EXERCISES	CYNEGETIC
PUNGENTLY	RUNCINATE	SUPERSEDE	WUTHERING	AWESTRUCK	EXHAUSTED	CYNICALLY
PUNISHING	RUNESTAVE	SUPERSTAR	ZUCCHETTO	AWKWARDLY	EXHIBITOR	CYTOKININ
PUPILLAGE	RUNNYMEDE	SUPERVENE	AVAILABLE	DWINDLING	EXISTENCE	DYNAMITED
PUPPETEER	RUSHLIGHT	SUPERVISE	AVALANCHE	OWLEGLASS	EXODERMIS	DYSENTERY
PURCHASER	RUSTICATE	SUPINATOR	AVOCATION	OWNERSHIP	EXOGENOUS	DYSPEPSIA
PURDONIUM	RUSTINESS	SUPPLIANT	AVOIDABLE	SWADDLING	EXONERATE	DYSPEPTIC
PURGATIVE	RUTHENIAN	SUPPLICAT	AVOIDANCE	SWAGGERER	EXORATION	DYSPHAGIA
PURGATORY	RUTHENIUM	SUPPORTER	AVUNCULAR	SWANIMOTE	EXOSPHERE	DYSPRAXIA
PURIFYING	SUBALTERN	SUPPOSING	EVAGATION	SWANSDOWN	EXOSTOSIS	DYSTROPHY
PURITANIC	SUBCELLAR	SUPPURATE	EVANGELIC	SWEATBAND	EXPANSION	EYEBRIGHT
PURPOSELY	SUBCORTEX	SUPREMACY	EVAPORATE	SWEEPINGS	EXPANSIVE	EYELETEER
PURSUANCE	SUBDIVIDE	SUPREMELY	EVASIVELY	SWEETENER	EXPATIATE	EYEOPENER
PURULENCE	SUBDOLOUS	SUQUAMISH	EVENTUATE	SWEETMEAT	EXPECTANT	EYESHADOW
PUSHCHAIR	SUBEDITOR	SURCHARGE	EVERGLADE	SWEETNESS	EXPECTING	EYESPLICE
PUSSYFOOT	SUBENTIRE	SURCINGLE	EVERGREEN	SWEETSHOP	EXPEDIENT	EYESTRAIN
QUADRATIC	SUBFOSSIL	SURFBOARD	EVERYBODY	SWIFTNESS	EXPENSIVE	GYMNASIUM
QUADRATUS	SUBJACENT	SURFEITED	EVIDENTLY	SWIMMERET	EXPERTISE	GYMNASTIC
QUADRILLE	SUBJUGATE	SURLINESS	EVITERNAL	SWINBURNE	EXPIATION	GYNOECIUM
QUADRUPED	SUBLIMATE	SURMULLET	EVOCATION	SWINEHERD	EXPIATORY	GYROMANCY
QUADRUPLE	SUBLIMELY	SURPRISED	EVOCATIVE	SWINGEING	EXPISCATE	GYROPLANE
QUAILPIPE	SUBMARINE	SURQUEDRY	EVOCATORY	SWORDFISH	EXPLETIVE	GYROSCOPE
QUALIFIED	SUBMERGED	SURREJOIN	EVOLUTION	SWORDPLAY	EXPLICATE	HYDRANGEA
QUALIFIER	SUBNORMAL	SURRENDER	OVENPROOF	SWORDSMAN	EXPLOITER	HYDRAULIC
QUANTICAL	SUBROGATE	SURROGATE	OVERBLOWN	SWOTHLING	EXPLOSION	HYDRAZINE
QUANTOCKS	SUBSCRIBE	SURVEYING	OVERBOARD	TWAYBLADE	EXPLOSIVE	HYDROFOIL
QUARENDEN	SUBSCRIPT	SURVIVING	OVERCLOUD	TWENTIETH	EXPORTING	HYDROPULT
QUARTERLY	SUBSIDIZE	SUSCITATE	OVERCROWD	TWINKLING	EXPOSITOR	HYDROSTAT
QUARTETTE	SUBSTANCE	SUSPECTED	OVERDRAFT	AXIOMATIC	EXPRESSED	HYGIENIST
QUASIMODO	SUBSTRATA	SUSPENDED	OVERDRAWN	AXMINSTER	EXPRESSLY	HYLOBATES
QUAVERING	SUBSTRATE	SUSPENDER	OVERDRESS	EXACTMENT	EXPULSION	HYPALLAGE
QUEERNESS	SUBTENANT	SUSPENSOR	OVERDRIVE	EXACTNESS	EXPURGATE	HYPERBOLA
QUENNELLE	SUBTITLED	SUSPICION	OVEREXERT	EXANIMATE	EXQUISITE	HYPERBOLE
QUERCETIN	SUCCEEDED	SUSTAINED	OVERGROWN	EXANTHEMA	EXSICCATE	HYPERLINK
QUERCETUS	SUCCENTOR	TUBBINESS	OVERHASTY	EXARATION	EXTEMPORE	HYPEROPIA
QUERIMONY	SUCCESSOR	TUILERIES	OVERHEADS	EXCALIBUR	EXTENSILE	HYPHENATE
QUERULOUS	SUCCINATE	TUILLETTE	OVERJOYED	EXCAMBION	EXTENSION	HYPINOSIS
QUICKLIME	SUCCOTASH	TULIPWOOD	OVERLYING	EXCAVATOR	EXTENSIVE	HYPNOTISM
QUICKNESS	SUCCUBINE	TUMESCENT	OVERNIGHT	EXCELLENT	EXTENUATE	HYPNOTIST
QUICKSAND	SUCCULENT	TUMMYACHE	OVERPAINT	EXCELSIOR	EXTIRPATE	HYPNOTIZE
QUICKSTEP	SUCCURSAL	TUNGSTATE	OVERPOISE	EXCEPTION	EXTORTION	HYPOBLAST
QUIESCENT	SUDORIFIC	TUNGSTOUS	OVERPOWER	EXCESSIVE	EXTRACTOR	HYPOCAUST
QUIETNESS	SUETONIUS	TURBIDITY	OVERPRINT	EXCHEQUER	EXTRADITE	HYPOCRISY
QUILLWORT	SUFFERING	TURBINATE	OVERRATED	EXCIPIENT	EXTREMELY	HYPOCRITE
QUINQUINA	SUFFOCATE	TURBOPROP	OVERREACH	EXCISEMAN	EXTREMISM	HYSTERICS
QUINTETTE	SUFFRAGAN	TURBULENT	OVERREACT	EXCITABLE	EXTREMIST	LYMESWOLD
QUINTROON	SUFFUSION	TURCOPOLE	OVERRIDER	EXCLAIMED	EXTREMITY	LYMPHATIC
QUINTUPLE	SUGARCANE	TURMAGENT	OVERSHADE	EXCLUDING	EXTRICATE	LYRICALLY
QUITTANCE	SULFUROUS	TURNABOUT	OVERSHOES	EXCLUSION	EXTRINSIC	LYSIMETER
QUIVERFUL	SULKINESS	TURNBULLS	OVERSHOOT	EXCLUSIVE	EXTROVERT	MYOFIBRIL
QUIVERING	SULPHONIC	TURNROUND	OVERSIGHT	EXCORIATE	EXTRUSION	MYOGLOBIN
QUIZZICAL	SULPHURIC	TURNSTILE	OVERSIZED	EXCREMENT	EXUBERANT	MYRMECOID
QUODLIBET	SULTANATE	TURNSTONE	OVERSLEEP	EXCULPATE	EXUDATION	MYSTERIES
QUOTATION	SUMMARILY	TURNTABLE	OVERSPEND	EXCURSION	OXIDATION	MYSTICISM
QUOTIDIAN	SUMMARIZE	TURPITUDE	OVERSPILL	EXCUSABLE	OXYGENATE	MYTHOLOGY
QUOTITION	SUMMATION	TURQUOISE	OVERSTATE	EXCUSABLY	AYATOLLAH	NYSTAGMUS
RUBBERIZE	SUMPTUARY	TUTIORISM	OVERSTEER	EXECRABLE	AYCKBOURN	PYGMALION
RUBICELLE	SUMPTUOUS	VULCANIAN	OVERTHROW	EXECRABLY	AYLESBURY	PYONGYANG
RUDBECKIA	SUNBATHER	VULCANIST	OVERTONES	EXECUTANT	BYPRODUCT	PYRAMIDAL
RUDDIGORE	SUNDOWNER	VULCANITE	OVERTRUMP	EXECUTION	BYSTANDER	PYRETHRUM
RUDDLEMAN	SUNFLOWER	VULCANIZE	OVERVALUE	EXECUTIVE	BYZANTINE	PYROMANCY
RUDIMENTS	SUNSCREEN	VULGARIAN	OVERWEIGH	EXECUTRIX	CYCLAMATE	PYROMANIA
RUFESCENT	SUNSTROKE	VULGARISM	OVERWHELM	EXEMPLARY	CYCLOLITH	PYRRHONIC
RUFFIANLY	SUNTANNED	VULGARITY	OVIPAROUS	EXEMPLIFY	CYCLORAMA	PYTHONESS

SYBARITIC	ANALEPTIC	BRANDIRON	CRACKDOWN	EXANIMATE	GRAPESHOT	LEAFMOULD
SYCOPHANT	ANALGESIA	BRASENOSE	CRACKLING	EXANTHEMA	GRAPETREE	LEAFSTALK
SYLLABARY	ANALGESIC	BRASSERIE	CRACKSMAN	EXARATION	GRAPEVINE	LEAKPROOF
SYLLABLES	ANALOGOUS	BRASSICAS	CRACOVIAN	FEARFULLY	GRAPHICAL	LEASEBACK
SYLLEPSIS	ANAPLASIA	BRASSIERE	CRAFTSMAN	FEATHERED	GRAPPLING	LEASEHOLD
SYLLOGISM	ANAPLASTY	BRASSWARE	CRANBERRY	FLABELLUM	GRASSLAND	LEASTWAYS
SYLPHLIKE	ANARCHIST	BRATWURST	CRANBORNE	FLAGELLIN	GRATICULE	LEASTWISE
SYLVANITE	ANASTASIA	BRAZILIAN	CRAPULENT	FLAGELLUM	GRATITUDE	LIABILITY
SYMBIOSIS	ANATOLIAN	CEANOTHUS	CRAPULOUS	FLAGEOLET	GRAVADLAX	LOADSTONE
SYMBIOTIC	ANATOMIST	CEASEFIRE	CRASHLAND	FLAGITATE	GRAVESEND	LOAMSHIRE
SYMBOLISM	ANATOMIZE	CEASELESS	CRAZINESS	FLAGRANCE	GRAVESIDE	LOATHSOME
SYMBOLIST	APARTHEID	CHABAZITE	DEACONESS	FLAGSTAFF	GRAVEYARD	MEANDRIAN
SYMBOLIZE	APARTMENT	CHAFFINCH	DEADLIGHT	FLAGSTONE	GRAVITATE	MEANWHILE
SYMMETRIC	APATHETIC	CHAIRLIFT	DEAFENING	FLAMMABLE	GUACAMOLE	MEASURING
SYMPHONIC	ARABESQUE	CHALAZION	DEAMINATE	FLAMSTEED	GUARANTEE	MEATBALLS
SYMPHYSIS	ARABICIZE	CHALIAPIN	DEATHBLOW	FLASHBACK	GUARANTOR	NIAISERIE
SYMPODIUM	ARABINOSE	CHALLENGE	DEATHLESS	FLASHBULB	GUARDRAIL	ODALISQUE
SYMPOSIUM	ARACHNOID	CHALUMEAU	DEATHTRAP	FLASHCUBE	GUARDROOM	ORANGEADE
SYNAGOGUE	ARAGONITE	CHAMELEON	DIABLERIE	FLATTENED	GUARDSMAN	ORANGEMAN
SYNANGIUM	ARAUCARIA	CHAMFRAIN	DIACRITIC	FLATTENER	GUATEMALA	ORATORIAN
SYNCHYSIS	ATAHUALPA	CHAMINADE	DIAERESIS	FLATTERED	HEADBOARD	PEACEABLE
SYNCOMIUM	ATAVISTIC	CHAMOMILE	DIAGNOSIS	FLATTERER	HEADCLOTH	PEACEABLY
SYNCOPATE	AVAILABLE	CHAMPAGNE	DIALECTAL	FLATULENT	HEADDRESS	PEACETIME
SYNDICATE	AVALANCHE	CHAMPAIGN	DIALECTIC	FLAVORING	HEADFIRST	PEARLWORT
SYNEDRION	AWAKENING	CHAMPERTY	DIALOGITE	FLAVOURED	HEADINESS	PEASANTRY
SYNERGIST	AWARENESS	CHAMPLAIN	DIAMETRIC	FRACTIOUS	HEADLIGHT	PEASEWEEP
SYNIZESIS	AYATOLLAH	CHAMPLEVÉ	DIANDROUS	FRAGILITY	HEADLINED	PHACOLITE
SYNOECETE	BEACHHEAD	CHANCROID	DIANETICS	FRAGMENTS	HEADPIECE	PHAGOCYTE
SYNOVITIS	BEACHWEAR	CHANTEUSE	DIANOETIC	FRAGONARD	HEADSCARF	PHALANGER
SYNTACTIC	BEANFEAST	CHANTILLY	DIAPHRAGM	FRAGRANCE	HEADSTALL	PHALAROPE
SYNTHESIS	BEARDLESS	CHAPARRAL	DIAPHYSIS	FRAGRANCY	HEADSTONE	PHANARIOT
SYNTHETIC	BEARDSLEY	CHAPERONE	DIARRHOEA	FRAMBOISE	HEALTHILY	PHANSIGAR
SYPHILOMA	BEATITUDE	CHARABANC	DIASTASIS	FRAMEWORK	HEARDSMAN	PHANTASMA
SYRIACISM	BEAUTEOUS	CHARACTER	DIATHERMY	FRANCESCA	HEARTACHE	PHARAMOND
SYRPHIDAE	BEAUTIFUL	CHARGEFUL	DIATHESIS	FRANCHISE	HEARTBEAT	PHARISAIC
TYMPANIST	BLACKBALL	CHARIVARI	DIATOMITE	FRANCOLIN	HEARTBURN	PHARSALIA
TYPICALLY	BLACKBIRD	CHARLATAN	DIAZEUXIS	FRANGLAIS	HEARTFELT	PIACEVOLE
TYRANNIZE	BLACKBUCK	CHARLOTTE	DRACONIAN	FRANKNESS	HEARTHRUG	PLACATORY
TYRANNOUS	BLACKDAMP	CHAROLAIS	DRAFTSMAN	FRATCHETY	HEARTLAND	PLACEMENT
WYANDOTTE	BLACKFACE	CHARTERED	DRAGONFLY	FRATERNAL	HEARTLESS	PLACIDITY
XYLOPHONE	BLACKFOOT	CHARTREUX	DRAINPIPE	GEARLEVER	HEARTWOOD	PLAINNESS
ZYGOMATIC	BLACKHEAD	CHARWOMAN	DRAMATICS	GEARSHIFT	HEATHLAND	PLAINSMAN
ZYGOSPORE	BLACKJACK	CHARYBDIS	DRAMATIST	GEARSTICK	HEAVINESS	PLAINSONG
ZYMOMETER	BLACKLEAD	CHASTENED	DRAMATIZE	GEARWHEEL	HEAVISIDE	PLAINTIFF
OZOCERITE	BLACKLIST	CHATTERER	DRAVIDIAN	GLABELLAR	HEAVYDUTY	PLAINTIVE
OZOKERITE	BLACKMAIL	CHAUFFEUR	DRAWKNIFE	GLADIATOR	HOARFROST	PLANETARY
9:3	BLACKMORE	CHAVENDER	ECARDINES	GLADIOLUS	HOARHOUND	PLASTERED
ABANDONED	BLACKNESS	CHAWBACON	EGAREMENT	GLADSTONE	HOARSTONE	PLASTERER
ABANDONEE	BLACKWOOD	CLAMOROUS	EJACULATE	GLAIREOUS	IMAGELESS	PLASTIQUE
ABASEMENT	BLAMELESS	CLAMPDOWN	ELABORATE	GLAMORIZE	IMAGINARY	PLATITUDE
ABATEMENT	BLANDNESS	CLAPBOARD	ELAEOLITE	GLAMOROUS	INABILITY	PLATONIST
ACADEMIST	BLASPHEME	CLARENDON	ELASTOMER	GLANDULAR	INAMORATA	PLAUSIBLE
ACARIASIS	BLASPHEMY	CLARIFIER	ELATERIUM	GLASSWARE	INAMORATO	PLAUSIBLY
ADAPTABLE	BLATANTLY	CLASSICAL	EMACIATED	GLASSWORT	INANIMATE	PLAUSTRAL
AGALACTIC	BOANERGES	CLASSLESS	EMANATION	GOALMOUTH	INANITION	PLAYFULLY
AGAMEMNON	BOARDROOM	CLASSMATE	ENACTMENT	GRACELESS	INAUDIBLE	PLAYGROUP
AHASUERUS	BOARDWALK	CLASSROOM	ENAMELLED	GRADATION	INAUDIBLY	PLAYHOUSE
ALABASTER	BOATHOUSE	COACHLOAD	ENAMOURED	GRADGRIND	INAUGURAL	PLAYTHING
AMARANTIN	BOATSWAIN	COADJUTOR	EPARCHATE	GRADUALLY	IRASCIBLE	PRACTICAL
AMARYLLIS	BRACTEOLE	COAGULANT	EPAULETTE	GRADUATED	ISALLOBAR	PRACTISED
AMAUROSIS	BRADLAUGH	COAGULATE	ERADICATE	GRAMPIANS	ITALICIZE	PRACTOLOL
AMAZEMENT	BRAINCASE	COALESCED	EVAGATION	GRANDIOSE	JEALOUSLY	PRAGMATIC
AMAZONITE	BRAINWASH	COALFIELD	EVANGELIC	GRANDNESS	KHALIFATE	PRANKSTER
ANABOLISM	BRAINWAVE	COALITION	EVAPORATE	GRANDSIRE	KHANSAMAH	PTARMIGAN
ANABRANCH	BRAMBLING	COALMINER	EVASIVELY	GRANULATE	KNACKERED	QUADRATIC
ANAEROBIC	BRANCHING	COARCTATE	EXACTMENT	GRANULITE	KNAPSCULL	QUADRATUS
ANAGLYPTA		COASTLINE	EXACTNESS	GRANULOSE	KNAPSKULL	QUADRILLE

QUADRUPED	SHARPNESS	STATIONER	UNADOPTED	FABACEOUS	RUBICELLE	ACCORDING
QUADRUPLE	SHASHLICK	STATISTIC	UNALLOYED	FABRICATE	SABBATIAN	ACCORDION
QUAILPIPE	SHATTERED	STATOCYST	UNALTERED	FABULINUS	SABLEFISH	ACCRETION
QUALIFIED	SHAVELING	STATOLITH	UNANIMITY	FEBRIFUGE	SEBACEOUS	ALCHEMIST
QUALIFIER	SLABSTONE	STATUETTE	UNANIMOUS	FIBROLINE	SEBASTIAN	ALCOHOLIC
QUANTICAL	SLACKNESS	STATUTORY	UNASHAMED	FIBROLITE	SIBILANCE	ANCESTRAL
QUANTOCKS	SLAMMAKIN	STAUNCHLY	UPAITHRIC	GABARDINE	SIBYLLINE	ANCHORAGE
QUARENDEN	SLANTWISE	STAVANGER	UPANISHAD	GABERDINE	SOBERNESS	ANCHORITE
QUARTERLY	SLAPHAPPY	SWADDLING	URANISCUS	GABIONADE	SOBRIQUET	ANCHORMAN
QUARTETTE	SLAPSTICK	SWAGGERER	UVAROVITE	GIBBERISH	SUBALTERN	ANCILLARY
QUASIMODO	SLAUGHTER	SWANIMOTE	VIABILITY	GIBEONITE	SUBCELLAR	ANCIPITAL
QUAVERING	SLAVISHLY	SWANSDOWN	WEAKENING	GIBRALTAR	SUBCORTEX	ARCHANGEL
REACHABLE	SMALLNESS	TEACHABLE	WEARINESS	GOBETWEEN	SUBDIVIDE	ARCHETYPE
REACTANCE	SMALLTIME	TEAKETTLE	WEARISOME	HABERDINE	SUBDOLOUS	ARCHIBALD
READDRESS	SMARTNESS	TEARFULLY	WHALEBOAT	HABERGEON	SUBEDITOR	ARCHITECT
READINESS	SNAILFISH	TEARSHEET	WHALEBONE	HABITABLE	SUBENTIRE	ARCHIVIST
READYEARN	SNAKEWEED	THACKERAY	WHALEMEAT	HABITUATE	SUBFOSSIL	ARCHIVOLT
READYMADE	SOAPBERRY	THALASSIC	WRANGLERS	HEBRIDEAN	SUBJACENT	ARCTOGAEA
REALISTIC	SOAPSTONE	THANATISM	WYANDOTTE	HIBERNATE	SUBJUGATE	ASCENDANT
REALITIES	SPACELESS	THANKLESS	ZEALANDER	HIBERNIAN	SUBLIMATE	ASCENDING
REANIMATE	SPACESHIP	THATCHING	ALBATROSS	HOBBINOLL	SUBLIMELY	ASCENSION
REARGUARD	SPACESUIT	THAUMATIN	ALBERTINE	HOBGOBLIN	SUBMARINE	ASCERTAIN
REARHORSE	SPADASSIN	TOADSTONE	AMBERGRIS	HOBNAILED	SUBMERGED	ASCLEPIUS
REARMOUSE	SPAGHETTI	TOADSTOOL	AMBIGUITY	IMBALANCE	SUBNORMAL	AUCTORIAL
REARRANGE	SPARINGLY	TOASTRACK	AMBIGUOUS	IMBRANGLE	SUBROGATE	AYCKBOURN
REARWARDS	SPARKLERS	TRACEABLE	AMBITIOUS	IMBRICATE	SUBSCRIBE	BACHARACH
REASONING	SPARKLING	TRACHINUS	AMBLYOPIA	IMBROCATE	SUBSCRIPT	BACKBENCH
RHAPSODIC	SPARTACUS	TRACKLESS	AMBROSIAL	IMBROGLIO	SUBSIDIZE	BACKBITER
ROADBLOCK	SPASMODIC	TRACKSUIT	AMBROSIAN	JOBCENTRE	SUBSTANCE	BACKBOARD
ROADHOUSE	SPATIALLY	TRACTABLE	AMBROTYPE	JOBERNOWL	SUBSTRATA	BACKCLOTH
ROADSTEAD	SPATTERED	TRADEMARK	AMBULANCE	JOBSEEKER	SUBSTRATE	BACKPEDAL
ROADWORKS	SPATULATE	TRADESMAN	AMBUSCADE	JOBSWORTH	SUBTENANT	BACKSHISH
SCABLANDS	STABILITY	TRADEWIND	ARBITRAGE	JUBILANCE	SUBTITLED	BACKSLIDE
SCAGLIOLA	STABILIZE	TRADITION	ARBITRARY	KABELJOUW	SYBARITIC	BACKSPACE
SCALARIUM	STABLEBOY	TRAFALGAR	ARBITRATE	LABORIOUS	TABANIDAE	BACKSTAGE
SCALDFISH	STABLELAD	TRAGEDIAN	ARBORETUM	LABOURITE	TABASHEER	BACKSWORD
SCALEABLE	STABLEMAN	TRAGELAPH	AUBERGINE	LABYRINTH	TABBOULEH	BACKTRACK
SCALLAWAG	STAGEHAND	TRAINABLE	AUBRIETIA	LIBELLOUS	TABELLION	BACKWARDS
SCALLIONS	STAGGERED	TRAMLINES	BOBSLEIGH	LIBERALLY	TABLATURE	BACKWATER
SCALLOPED	STAGIRITE	TRANSCEND	BUBBLEGUM	LIBERATED	TABLELAND	BACKWOODS
SCALLYWAG	STAGYRITE	TRANSEUNT	CABALLERO	LIBERATOR	TABLEWARE	BACTERIAL
SCAMBLING	STAINLESS	TRANSFORM	CABLEGRAM	LIBERTIES	TABULATOR	BACTERIUM
SCANSORES	STAIRCASE	TRANSFUSE	CABRIOLET	LIBERTINE	TOBERMORY	BECHSTEIN
SCANTLING	STALEMATE	TRANSHUME	CUBBYHOLE	LIBRARIAN	TUBBINESS	BECQUEREL
SCAPEGOAT	STALENESS	TRANSIENT	DEBATABLE	LOBLOLLYS	UMBILICAL	BICONCAVE
SCAPOLITE	STALWORTH	TRANSLATE	DEBAUCHED	LOBSCOUSE	UMBILICUS	BICYCLIST
SCARECROW	STAMMERER	TRANSMUTE	DEBAUCHEE	LUBAVITCH	UMBRATILE	BOCCACCIO
SCARIFIER	STANCHION	TRANSPIRE	DEBENTURE	LUBRICANT	UNBALANCE	BUCCANEER
SCARLATTI	STANDARDS	TRANSPORT	DEBUTANTE	LUBRICATE	UNBEKNOWN	BUCENTAUR
SCATTERED	STANDERBY	TRANSPOSE	DUBIOUSLY	MOBOCRACY	UNBENDING	BUCHAREST
SCAVENGER	STANDGALE	TRANSSHIP	DUBROVNIK	NABATHEAN	UNBIASSED	BUCKETFUL
SEABOTTLE	STANDPIPE	TRANSVAAL	ELBOWROOM	NEBBISHER	UNBOUNDED	BUCKTEETH
SEAFARING	STANNATOR	TRAPEZIAL	EMBARRASS	NOBLENESS	UNBRIDLED	BUCKTHORN
SEANNACHY	STARBOARD	TRAPEZIST	EMBASSADE	OBBLIGATO	VIBRATILE	BUCKWHEAT
SEARCHING	STARGAZER	TRAPEZIUM	EMBASSAGE	OMBUDSMAN	VIBRATION	CACHAEMIA
SEASONING	STARKNESS	TRAPEZIUS	EMBATTLED	ORBICULAR	VIBRATORY	CACHECTIC
SEAWORTHY	STARLIGHT	TRAPEZOID	EMBELLISH	OUBLIETTE	WEBFOOTED	CACOPHONY
SHADINESS	STARSTONE	TRAPPINGS	EMBEZZLER	PUBLICIST	WOBBEGONG	COCHINEAL
SHAKEDOWN	STARTLING	TRASIMENE	EMBRACERY	PUBLICITY	ZIBELLINE	COCKAIGNE
SHAKINESS	STATEHOOD	TRATTORIA	EMBRACING	PUBLICIZE	ACCENTUAL	COCKATIEL
SHAMEFAST	STATELESS	TRAUMATIC	EMBRANGLE	PUBLISHED	ACCESSION	COCKFIGHT
SHAMELESS	STATEMENT	TRAVELERS	EMBRASURE	PUBLISHER	ACCESSORY	COCKROACH
SHAMIANAH	STATEROOM	TRAVELING	EMBROCATE	REBELLION	ACCIDENTS	COCKSCOMB
SHAPELESS	STATESIDE	TRAVELLER	EMBROGLIO	REBOATION	ACCLIMATE	COCKSFOOT
SHARESMAN	STATESMAN	TSAREVICH	EMBROIDER	RIBBONISM	ACCLIVITY	COCKSWAIN
SHARKSKIN	STATEWIDE	TWAYBLADE	EMBROILED	ROBERTSON	ACCOMPANY	COCUSWOOD
SHARPENER	STATIONED	UNABASHED	EMBRYONIC	RUBBERIZE	ACCORDANT	CUCHULAIN

CYCLAMATE	EXCALIBUR	INCURABLE	MICROWAVE	RECONVENE	UNCEASING	ENDEICTIC
CYCLOLITH	EXCAMBION	INCURABLY	MOCCASINS	RECORDING	UNCERTAIN	ENDLESSLY
CYCLORAMA	EXCAVATOR	INCURIOUS	MOCKERNUT	RECORDIST	UNCHANGED	ENDOCRINE
CYCLOTRON	EXCELLENT	INCURSION	MUCHLOVED	RECOVERED	UNCHARGED	ENDOERGIC
DACHSHUND	EXCELSIOR	ISCHAEMIC	MUCKENDER	RECTANGLE	UNCHECKED	ENDOMORPH
DECACHORD	EXCEPTION	JACARANDA	MUCORALES	RECTIFIER	UNCHRISOM	ENDOSPERM
DECADENCE	EXCESSIVE	JACKFRUIT	NECESSARY	RECTITUDE	UNCLAIMED	ENDOWMENT
DECALITRE	EXCHEQUER	JACKKNIFE	NECESSITY	RECTORIAL	UNCLOTHED	ENDPAPERS
DECALOGUE	EXCIPIENT	JACKSCREW	NECKVERSE	RECUMBENT	UNCLOUDED	ENDURABLE
DECAMERON	EXCISEMAN	JACKSNIPE	NECTARINE	RECURRENT	UNCONCERN	ENDURANCE
DECASTYLE	EXCITABLE	JACKSTRAW	NICARAGUA	RECURRING	UNCONFINE	EUDAEMONY
DECATHLON	EXCLAIMED	JACQUERIE	NICCOLITE	RECURSIVE	UNCORRECT	FEDUCIARY
DECEITFUL	EXCLUDING	JOCKSTRAP	NICKNEVEN	RECUSANCE	UNCOUPLED	FIDUCIARY
DECEMVIRI	EXCLUSION	JOCKTELEG	NICODEMUS	RICERCARE	UNCOURTLY	GIDDINESS
DECENNIAL	EXCLUSIVE	JOCULARLY	NICTITATE	RICHELIEU	UNCOVERED	GODDESSES
DECEPTION	EXCORIATE	KICKSHAWS	NOCTURNAL	ROCAMBOLE	UNCROSSED	GODFATHER
DECEPTIVE	EXCREMENT	LACCOLITE	NUCLEOLUS	SACCHARIN	UNCROWNED	GODLINESS
DECESSION	EXCULPATE	LACERATED	OBCORDATE	SACKCLOTH	UPCOUNTRY	GODMOTHER
DECIDEDLY	EXCURSION	LACHRYMAL	OCCIPITAL	SACKERSON	VACCINATE	GODOLPHIN
DECIDUOUS	EXCUSABLE	LACINIATE	OCCLUSION	SACRAMENT	VACILLATE	GODPARENT
DECILLION	EXCUSABLY	LACKBEARD	OCCULTIST	SACRARIUM	VICARIOUS	HADROSAUR
DECKCHAIR	FACECLOTH	LACONICAL	OCCUPANCY	SACRIFICE	VICEREGAL	HEDERATED
DECLARING	FACETIOUS	LACTATION	OCCUPYING	SACRILEGE	VICEREINE	HEDYPHANE
DECLINING	FACSIMILE	LECANORAM	ONCOMETER	SACRISTAN	VICIOUSLY	HIDEBOUND
DECLIVITY	FACTIONAL	LECHEROUS	ORCHESTRA	SECATEURS	VICTIMIZE	HIDEOUSLY
DECOCTION	FACTORIAL	LICKERISH	OSCILLATE	SECESSION	VICTORIAN	HODIERNAL
DECOLLATE	FACTORISE	LOCALIZED	PACEMAKER	SECLUSION	VICTORINE	HODMANDOD
DECOMPOSE	FACTUALLY	LOCELLATE	PACHYDERM	SECONDARY	YACHTSMAN	HODOGRAPH
DECONTROL	FACUNDITY	LOCHINVAR	PACKAGING	SECRETARY	YACHTSMEN	HODOMETER
DECORATED	FECUNDITY	LOCKSMITH	PECKSNIFF	SECRETION	ZECHARIAH	HYDRANGEA
DECORATOR	FICTIONAL	LUCIFERIN	PECULATOR	SECRETIVE	ZUCCHETTO	HYDRAULIC
DECRETALS	HACKAMORE	LUCRATIVE	PECUNIARY	SECTARIAN	ABDOMINAL	HYDRAZINE
DECRETORY	HACKBERRY	LUCRETIUS	PICKABACK	SECTIONAL	ABDUCTION	HYDROFOIL
DECUMBENT	HACKNEYED	LUCTATION	PICKETING	SECTORIAL	ADDERWORT	HYDROPULT
DECURSIVE	HACQUETON	LUCUBRATE	PICKTHANK	SICCATIVE	ADDICTION	HYDROSTAT
DECUSSATE	HECOGENIN	MACADAMIA	PICNICKER	SICILIANO	ADDICTIVE	INDECENCY
DICHOTOMY	HECTOGRAM	MACARONIC	PICOFARAD	SICKENING	ADDRESSED	INDECORUM
DICTATION	HECTORING	MACARTHUR	PICTOGRAM	SOCIALISM	ADDRESSEE	INDELIBLE
DOCTORATE	HOCCAMORE	MACCABEES	PICTORIAL	SOCIALIST	ALDEBARAN	INDELIBLY
DOCTRINAL	HUCKABACK	MACDONALD	POCKETFUL	SOCIALITE	ANDANTINO	INDEMNIFY
DOCUMENTS	ILCHESTER	MACEDOINE	POCKMANKY	SOCIALIZE	ANDROCLES	INDEMNITY
DUCKBOARD	INCAPABLE	MACEDONIA	PUCELLAGE	SOCIOLECT	ANDROMEDA	INDENTURE
ECCENTRIC	INCARDINE	MACHINATE	RACCABOUT	SOCIOLOGY	ARDUOUSLY	INDICATES
ENCANTHIS	INCARNATE	MACHINERY	RACCAHOUT	SUCCEEDED	AUDACIOUS	INDICATOR
ENCAUSTIC	INCAUTION	MACHINING	RACEHORSE	SUCCENTOR	BADMINTON	INDICTION
ENCELADUS	INCENTIVE	MACHINIST	RACETRACK	SUCCESSOR	BEDFELLOW	INDIGENCE
ENCHANTED	INCEPTION	MACKENZIE	RACIALISM	SUCCINATE	BEDJACKET	INDIGNANT
ENCHANTER	INCEPTIVE	MACQUARIE	RACIALIST	SUCCOTASH	BEDRAGGLE	INDIGNITY
ENCHEASON	INCESSANT	MACROCOSM	RACKETEER	SUCCUBINE	BEDRIDDEN	INDOLENCE
ENCHILADA	INCIDENCE	MACROLOGY	RACKSTRAW	SUCCULENT	BEDSITTER	INDONESIA
ENCHORIAL	INCIPIENT	MACTATION	RACONTEUR	SUCCURSAL	BEDSPREAD	INDRAUGHT
ENCIRCLED	INCITATUS	MECHANICS	RECALLING	SYCOPHANT	BODYGUARD	INDUCTION
ENCLOSURE	INCLEMENT	MECHANISM	RECAPTURE	TACAMAHAC	BUDGETARY	INDUCTIVE
ENCOLPION	INCLUDING	MECHANIZE	RECEIVING	TACHILITE	CADASTRAL	INDULGENT
ENCOLPIUM	INCLUSION	MICKLETON	RECEPTION	TACHYLITE	CEDARWOOD	INDWELLER
ENCOMPASS	INCLUSIVE	MICROCHIP	RECEPTIVE	TACHYLYTE	DEDICATED	IODOPHILE
ENCOUNTER	INCOGNITO	MICROCOSM	RECESSION	TACKINESS	DEDUCTION	JUDGEMENT
ENCOURAGE	INCOMINGS	MICROCYTE	RECESSIVE	TACTFULLY	DEDUCTIVE	JUDICIARY
ENCRATITE	INCOMMODE	MICROFILM	RECIPIENT	TACTICIAN	DIDACTICS	JUDICIOUS
ENCUMBENT	INCONDITE	MICROINCH	RECKONING	TECHNICAL	DODDIPOLL	KIDNAPPED
ESCALATOR	INCORRECT	MICROLITE	RECLAIMED	TECHNIQUE	EDDINGTON	KIDNAPPER
ESCOPETTE	INCREASED	MICROLITH	RECLAIMER	TECTIFORM	EDDYSTONE	LADYSMITH
ESCULENTS	INCREMENT	MICROMOLE	RECOGNIZE	TECTONICS	EIDERDOWN	LODESTONE
ETCETERAS	INCUBATOR	MICROTOME	RECOLLECT	TECTORIAL	EIDOGRAPH	LODGEMENT
EUCHARIST	INCULCATE	MICROTONE	RECOMMEND	TICHBORNE	ENDEARING	LUDICROUS
EUCHLORIC	INCULPATE	MICROVOLT	RECONCILE	TICTACTOE	ENDEAVOUR	MADARIAGA
EUCLIDEAN	INCUMBENT	MICROWATT	RECONDITE	TOCCATINA	ENDECAGON	MADAROSIS

MADDENING	REDSTREAK	UNDOUBTED	CLEANNESS	EYELETEER	HIERARCHY	OVERSIZED
MADELEINE	REDUCIBLE	UNDRESSED	CLEANSING	EYEOPENER	ICELANDER	OVERSLEEP
MADRASSAH	REDUCTION	VIDELICET	CLEARANCE	EYESHADOW	ICELANDIC	OVERSPEND
MADREPORE	REDUNDANT	VIDEODISC	CLEARNESS	EYESPLICE	IDEALOGUE	OVERSPILL
MADRESSAH	RIDERHOOD	VIDEODISK	CLEARWING	EYESTRAIN	IDENTICAL	OVERSTATE
MADRILENE	RIDERLESS	VIDEOTAPE	CLEOPATRA	FEEDSTUFF	IDENTIKIT	OVERSTEER
MEDALLION	RIDGEBACK	WEDGEWOOD	CLEPSYDRA	FIELDFARE	IDEOGRAPH	OVERTHROW
MEDALLIST	RIDGELING	WEDNESDAY	CLERGYMAN	FIELDSMAN	IDEOPATHY	OVERTONES
MEDIAEVAL	RIDGEPOLE	WIDOWHOOD	CLEVELAND	FIELDWORK	INEBRIATE	OVERTRUMP
MEDIATION	RUDBECKIA	WODEHOUSE	COELOSTAT	FLECHETTE	INEFFABLE	OVERVALUE
MEDICALLY	RUDDIGORE	ABERNETHY	COEMPTION	FLEDGLING	INELEGANT	OVERWEIGH
MEDICATED	RUDDLEMAN	ABERRANCE	COENOBITE	FLEETWOOD	INERTNESS	OVERWHELM
MEDICINAL	RUDIMENTS	ACETAMIDE	COENOBIUM	FLESHLESS	INERUDITE	PEEVISHLY
MEDITATOR	SADDENING	ACETYLENE	CREDULITY	FLESHPOTS	ITERATION	PHELLOGEN
MEDMENHAM	SADDLEBAG	ADENOIDAL	CREDULOUS	FLEXITIME	KIESERITE	PHENACITE
MEDRESSEH	SEDENTARY	ADEPTNESS	CREMATION	FREDERICK	KLEMPERER	PHENAKISM
MIDDLEMAN	SEDGEMOOR	ALERTNESS	CREMATORY	FREEBOARD	KLENDUSIC	PHENYTOIN
MIDDLESEX	SEDITIOUS	ALEURITIS	CRENATION	FREELANCE	KNEECORDS	PHEROMONE
MIDDLETON	SEDUCTION	ALEXANDER	CREPITATE	FREEMASON	LAEVULOSE	PIECEMEAL
MIDDLINGS	SEDUCTIVE	ALEXANDRA	CREPOLINE	FREEPHONE	LIENTERIC	PIECEWORK
MIDHEAVEN	SIDEBOARD	AMELAKITE	CRESCELLE	FREESTONE	MAELSTROM	PIEPOWDER
MIDIANITE	SIDEBURNS	AMENDMENT	CRESCENDO	FREESTYLE	MNEMOSYNE	PIERGLASS
MIDINETTE	SIDELIGHT	AMENHOTEP	CRETINOUS	FREEWHEEL	NIEBELUNG	PLEASANCE
MIDRASHIM	SIDEROSIS	AMERICANO	CTESIPHON	FREIGHTER	NIETZSCHE	PLEIOCENE
MIDSTREAM	SIDESWIPE	AMERICIUM	DAEDALIAN	FRENCHMAN	OBEDIENCE	PLENITUDE
MIDSUMMER	SIDETRACK	ANECDOTAL	DEERHOUND	FRENCHMEN	OBEISANCE	PLENTEOUS
MIDWIFERY	SIDEWARDS	ANECDOTES	DIETETICS	FREQUENCY	OCEANIDES	PLENTIFUL
MIDWINTER	SUDORIFIC	APENNINES	DIETICIAN	FRESHENER	ODELSTING	PLETHORIC
MODELLING	TEDIOSITY	APERIODIC	DJELLABAH	FRESHNESS	OKEYDOKEY	PNEUMATIC
MODERATOR	TEDIOUSLY	APERITIVE	DREAMLAND	FRETFULLY	OLECRANON	PNEUMONIA
MODERNISM	UNDAMAGED	AREOPAGUS	DREAMLESS	GAELTACHT	OLENELLUS	POETASTER
MODERNIST	UNDAUNTED	AWESTRUCK	EDELWEISS	GLEANINGS	OLEOGRAPH	POETICIZE
MODERNITY	UNDECIDED	BEEFEATER	ELECTORAL	GLEEFULLY	OLEORESIN	PREBENDAL
MODERNIZE	UNDEFILED	BEEFSTEAK	ELECTRESS	GLENDOWER	OPENENDED	PRECATORY
MODESTINE	UNDEFINED	BEEKEEPER	ELECTRIFY	GLENGARRY	OPENHEART	PRECEDENT
MODILLION	UNDERBITE	BEELZEBUB	ELECTRODE	GLENLIVET	OPERATING	PRECEDING
MUDDINESS	UNDERBRED	BEESTINGS	ELECTUARY	GMELINITE	OPERATION	PRECENTOR
NIDDERING	UNDERCAST	BEETHOVEN	ELEGANTLY	GREASEGUN	OPERATIVE	PRECEPTOR
NIDERLING	UNDERCOAT	BLEACHERS	ELEMENTAL	GREATCOAT	OPERCULUM	PRECIEUSE
ODDJOBMAN	UNDERDONE	BLESSINGS	ELEVATION	GREATNESS	OVENPROOF	PRECINCTS
ORDINAIRE	UNDERFEED	BREADLINE	ELEVENSES	GREENAWAY	OVERBLOWN	PRECIPICE
ORDINANCE	UNDERFELT	BREAKABLE	EMERGENCE	GREENBACK	OVERBOARD	PRECISELY
OUDENARDE	UNDERFLOW	BREAKAGES	EMERGENCY	GREENFEED	OVERCLOUD	PRECISIAN
PADEMELON	UNDERFOOT	BREAKAWAY	ENERGETIC	GREENGAGE	OVERCROWD	PRECISION
PEDAGOGUE	UNDERGRAD	BREAKDOWN	ENERGUMEN	GREENHEAD	OVERDRAFT	PRECISIVE
PEDERASTY	UNDERHAND	BREAKEVEN	ENERINITE	GREENHORN	OVERDRAWN	PRECOCITY
PEDICULAR	UNDERHUNG	BREAKFAST	EPEDAPHIC	GREENMAIL	OVERDRESS	PRECONISE
PEDIGREES	UNDERLINE	BREAKNECK	EPEOLATRY	GREENROOM	OVERDRIVE	PRECURSOR
PEDOMETER	UNDERLING	BREATHING	ESEMPLASY	GREENSAND	OVEREXERT	PREDATORY
RADCLIFFE	UNDERMINE	BREECHING	ETERNALLY	GREENWEED	OVERGROWN	PREDICANT
RADDLEMAN	UNDERMOST	CAESAREAN	EVENTUATE	GREENWICH	OVERHASTY	PREDICATE
RADIANTLY	UNDERPAID	CHEAPJACK	EVERGLADE	GREENWOOD	OVERHEADS	PREDICTOR
RADIATING	UNDERPASS	CHEAPNESS	EVERGREEN	GREENYARD	OVERJOYED	PREDIKANT
RADIATION	UNDERRATE	CHEAPSIDE	EVERYBODY	GREETINGS	OVERLYING	PREDILECT
RADICALLY	UNDERSEAL	CHECKBOOK	EXECRABLE	GREGARINE	OVERNIGHT	PREFATORY
RADICCHIO	UNDERSELL	CHECKLIST	EXECRABLY	GREGORIAN	OVERPAINT	PREFERRED
RADIOGRAM	UNDERSIDE	CHECKMATE	EXECUTANT	GRENADIER	OVERPOISE	PREFIGURE
RADIOLOGY	UNDERSIGN	CHECKROOM	EXECUTION	GRENADINE	OVERPOWER	PREGNANCY
REDBREAST	UNDERSONG	CHEEKBONE	EXECUTIVE	GRENVILLE	OVERPRINT	PREHALLUX
REDDENDUM	UNDERTAKE	CHEERLESS	EXECUTRIX	GREYBEARD	OVERRATED	PREJUDICE
REDEEMING	UNDERTONE	CHEMISTRY	EXEMPLARY	GREYHOUND	OVERREACH	PRELECTOR
REDHANDED	UNDERWALK	CHEONGSAM	EXEMPLIFY	GREYWACKE	OVERREACT	PRELUSORY
REDHEADED	UNDERWEAR	CHEQUERED	EXEMPTION	GUERRILLA	OVERRIDER	PREMATURE
REDINGOTE	UNDERWENT	CHERISHED	EXEQUATUR	GUESSWORK	OVERSHADE	PREMONISH
REDIVIVUS	UNDERWOOD	CHERNOZEM	EXERCISED	HAECCEITY	OVERSHOES	PREMOTION
REDLETTER	UNDILUTED	CHERUBINI	EXERCISES	HAEMALOMA	OVERSHOOT	PREOCCUPY
REDOLENCE	UNDIVIDED	CHEVALIER	EYEBRIGHT	HAEMATITE	OVERSIGHT	PREORDAIN

PREPOLLEX	SKETCHMAP	THERMIDOR	DEFERENCE	REFLATION	ENGRENAGE	NIGGARDLY
PRESBYTER	SKETCHPAD	THERSITES	DEFERMENT	REFLECTOR	ENGROSSED	NIGHTCLUB
PRESCIENT	SKEWWHIFF	THESAURUS	DEFICIENT	REFLEXION	ENGROSSER	NIGHTFALL
PRESCRIBE	SLEEKNESS	TIERCERON	DEFINABLE	REFLEXIVE	ERGATANER	NIGHTFIRE
PRESCUTUM	SLEEPLESS	TREACHERY	DEFLATION	REFORMIST	FIGURANTE	NIGHTGLOW
PRESENTED	SLEEPWALK	TREADMILL	DEFLECTOR	REFRACTOR	FOGGINESS	NIGHTGOWN
PRESENTER	SNEERWELL	TREASURER	DEFOLIANT	REFRESHER	FOGRAMITE	NIGHTHAWK
PRESENTLY	SPEAKEASY	TREATMENT	DEFOLIATE	REFULGENT	FUGACIOUS	NIGHTMARE
PRESERVED	SPEARHEAD	TREBIZOND	DEFORMITY	REFURBISH	FUGGINESS	NIGHTSPOT
PRESERVER	SPEARMINT	TREBUCHET	DIFFERENT	REFUSENIK	GIGAHERTZ	NIGHTTIME
PRESERVES	SPEARSIDE	TREDRILLE	DIFFICULT	RUFESCENT	GIGANTISM	NIGHTWORK
PRESHRUNK	SPEARWORT	TREETRUNK	DIFFIDENT	RUFFIANLY	HIGHCLASS	NIGRITUDE
PRESIDENT	SPECIALLY	TREGEAGLE	DIFFUSION	SAFEGUARD	HIGHFLYER	NIGROSINE
PRESIDIAL	SPECIALTY	TREGETOUR	EFFECTIVE	SAFFLOWER	HIGHLANDS	ORGANELLE
PRESIDIUM	SPECIFICS	TREILLAGE	EFFECTUAL	SOFTCOVER	HIGHLIGHT	ORGANICAL
PRESSGANG	SPECIFIED	TREMATODE	EFFICIENT	SOFTENING	HIGHSPEED	ORGANISED
PRETENDER	SPECIMENS	TREMBLING	EFFINGHAM	SUFFERING	HYGIENIST	ORGANISER
PRETERITE	SPECTACLE	TREMOLITE	EFFLUENCE	SUFFOCATE	INGENIOUS	ORGANIZED
PRETERMIT	SPECTATOR	TREMULANT	EFFLUVIUM	SUFFRAGAN	INGENUITY	ORGANIZER
PREVALENT	SPECULATE	TREMULATE	EFFULGENT	SUFFUSION	INGENUOUS	ORGANZINE
PREVERNAL	SPEECHIFY	TREMULOUS	FIFTEENTH	UNFAILING	INGESTION	ORGIASTIC
PSEUDAXIS	SPEEDBOAT	TRENCHANT	INFANTILE	UNFEELING	INGLENOOK	ORGILLOUS
PSEUDONYM	SPEEDWELL	TRETINOIN	INFATUATE	UNFITTING	INGRAINED	OUGHTNESS
PTERIDIUM	SPELDRING	TREVELYAN	INFECTING	UNFLEDGED	INGROWING	PAGEANTRY
PTEROSAUR	SPELLBIND	TWENTIETH	INFECTION	UNFOUNDED	JAGGANATH	PAGLIACCI
PUERILITY	SPELUNKER	UNEARTHLY	INFERENCE	WAFERTHIN	JIGGUMBOB	PEGMATITE
PUERPERAL	STEADFAST	UNEATABLE	INFERTILE	AGGRAVATE	LAGNIAPPE	PIGGYBACK
QUEERNESS	STEAMBOAT	UNEQUALED	INFIELDER	AGGREGATE	LAGOMORPH	PIGGYBANK
QUENNELLE	STEAMSHIP	UNETHICAL	INFIRMARY	AGGRESSOR	LEGENDARY	PIGHEADED
QUERCETIN	STEELHEAD	UNEXPOSED	INFIRMITY	AGGRIEVED	LEGIONARY	PIGNERATE
QUERCETUS	STEELYARD	UREDINIAL	INFLATION	ALGEBRAIC	LEGISLATE	PUGNACITY
QUERIMONY	STEENBRAS	VIENTIANE	INFLEXION	ALGORITHM	LIGHTFACE	PYGMALION
QUERULOUS	STEENKIRK	VIEWPOINT	INFLUENCE	ANGELFISH	LIGHTFOOT	REGARDANT
REEDINESS	STEEPNESS	WHEATGERM	INFLUENZA	ANGIOGRAM	LIGHTLESS	REGARDFUL
REEXAMINE	STEERSMAN	WHEATMEAL	INFORMANT	ANGLICISM	LIGHTNESS	REGARDING
RHEOTAXIS	STEGNOSIS	WHEELBASE	INFURIATE	ANGOSTURA	LIGHTNING	REGISSEUR
RHEUMATIC	STEGNOTIC	WHEREFORE	LAFAYETTE	ANGUISHED	LIGHTSHIP	REGISTRAR
SCELERATE	STEGOSAUR	WHEREUPON	LEFTOVERS	ARGENTINA	LIGHTSOME	REGRETFUL
SCENTLESS	STEINBECK	WHERRYMAN	LEFTWARDS	ARGENTINE	LOGARITHM	REGUERDON
SCEPTICAL	STEINBOCK	WHETSTONE	LIFEGUARD	AUGUSTINE	LOGICALLY	REGULARLY
SDEIGNFUL	STENOPAIC	WOEBEGONE	LIFESTYLE	BAGATELLE	LOGISTICS	REGULATOR
SEEMINGLY	STERADIAN	WREAKLESS	LOFTINESS	BEGINNING	LOGOGRIPH	RIGHTEOUS
SHEARLING	STERCORAL	WRECKFISH	MUFFETTEE	BIGHEADED	LOGOTHETE	RIGHTHAND
SHECHINAH	STERILITY	WRESTLING	NEFANDOUS	CAGOULARD	MAGDALENE	RIGHTNESS
SHECHITAH	STERILIZE	AFFECTING	NEFARIOUS	CIGARETTE	MAGDEBURG	RIGHTWING
SHEEPFOLD	STERNFAST	AFFECTION	NEFERTITI	COGNITION	MAGICALLY	RIGMAROLE
SHEEPMEAT	STERNNESS	AFFIDAVIT	OBFUSCATE	COGNITIVE	MAGNALIUM	RIGOLETTO
SHEEPSKIN	STEVEDORE	AFFILIATE	OFFCHANCE	COGNIZANT	MAGNESIUM	RUGGELACH
SHEERLEGS	STEVENSON	AFFLICTED	OFFCOLOUR	DEGRADING	MAGNETISM	SAGACIOUS
SHEERNESS	SUETONIUS	AFFLUENCE	OFFENBACH	DIGASTRIC	MAGNETIZE	SAGAPENUM
SHEFFIELD	SWEATBAND	AFFRICATE	OFFENDING	DIGESTION	MAGNETRON	SAGEBRUSH
SHEIKHDOM	SWEEPINGS	BIFURCATE	OFFENSIVE	DIGESTIVE	MAGNIFIER	SAGITTARY
SHELDDUCK	SWEETENER	BUFFETING	OFFERTORY	DIGITALIN	MAGNITUDE	SEGMENTED
SHELDRAKE	SWEETMEAT	CAFETERIA	OFFICIALS	DIGITALIS	MEGACYCLE	SEGREGATE
SHELLBACK	SWEETNESS	CAFETIERE	OFFICIANT	DIGNIFIED	MEGAHERTZ	SIGHTLESS
SHELLFISH	SWEETSHOP	COFFERDAM	OFFICIATE	DIGNITARY	MEGAPHONE	SIGHTSEER
SHELLSUIT	TEESWATER	COFFINITE	OFFICIOUS	DOGMATISM	MEGASCOPE	SIGNALLER
SHELTERED	THECODONT	CUFFLINKS	OFFSEASON	DOGMATIZE	MEGASPORE	SIGNALMAN
SHEMOZZLE	THELEMITE	DEFALCATE	OFFSPRING	EAGERNESS	MIGRATION	SIGNATORY
SHENSTONE	THELONIUS	DEFAULTER	OLFACTORY	EAGLEWOOD	MIGRATORY	SIGNATURE
SHEPHERDS	THEOBROMA	DEFEATISM	PUFFINESS	EDGEWORTH	MOGADISHU	SIGNBOARD
SHETLANDS	THEOCRACY	DEFEATIST	RAFFINOSE	EIGHTIETH	MUGGLETON	SOGGINESS
SHEWBREAD	THEOSOPHY	DEFECTION	REFECTION	EIGHTSOME	MUGLARITE	SUGARCANE
SIEGFRIED	THERALITE	DEFECTIVE	REFECTORY	ENGARLAND	NEGLECTED	TIGHTENER
SKEDADDLE	THERAPIST	DEFENDANT	REFERENCE	ENGINEERS	NEGLIGENT	TIGHTHEAD
SKEPTICAL	THEREFORE	DEFENDERS	REFERRING	ENGRAINED	NEGOTIATE	TIGHTNESS
SKETCHILY	THEREUPON	DEFENSIVE	REFINANCE	ENGRAVING	NEGRITUDE	TIGHTROPE

UNGUARDED	OTHERWISE	BLINKERED	EPICLESIS	IDIOPHONE	PRIMIPARA	SKINTIGHT
VAGINITIS	REHEARSAL	BLISTERED	EPICUREAN	IDIOPLASM	PRIMITIAE	SLIGHTEST
VAGUENESS	SCHEELITE	BRICKWORK	EPICYCLIC	IDIOTICON	PRIMITIVE	SLIMINESS
VEGETABLE	SCHEHITAH	BRICKYARD	EPIDERMIS	IMITATION	PRIMULINE	SLINGBACK
VEGETATOR	SCHELLING	BRIDEWELL	EPIGAEOUS	IMITATIVE	PRINCETON	SLINGSHOT
VIGESIMAL	SCHEMATIC	BRIDLEWAY	EPIGENOUS	INITIALLY	PRINCIPAL	SLIVOVICA
VIGILANCE	SCHIAVONE	BRIEFCASE	EPILATION	INITIATED	PRINCIPLE	SLIVOVITZ
VIGILANTE	SCHILLING	BRIEFNESS	EPILEPTIC	INITIATOR	PRINTABLE	SPICILEGE
WAGENBOOM	SCHLEMIEL	BRIGADIER	EPINASTIC	ISINGLASS	PRISMATIC	SPICINESS
WAGHALTER	SCHLEMIHL	BRIGADOON	EPINICION	ITINERANT	PRIVATEER	SPIDERWEB
WAGNERIAN	SCHLENTER	BRILLIANT	EPINIKION	ITINERARY	PRIVATELY	SPIKENARD
WAGNERITE	SCHLIEREN	BRIMSTONE	EPIPHRAGM	ITINERATE	PRIVATION	SPILLICAN
WAGONETTE	SCHMALTZY	BRIQUETTE	EPIPHYSIS	JUICINESS	PRIVATIZE	SPILLIKIN
WAGONLOAD	SCHMIEDER	BRISKNESS	EPIPHYTIC	KLINOSTAT	PRIVILEGE	SPINDRIER
YGGDRASIL	SCHMUTTER	BRISTLING	EPIPOLISM	KNIPHOFIA	PUISSANCE	SPINDRIFT
ZYGOMATIC	SCHNAPPER	BRITANNIA	EPISCOPAL	LEICESTER	QUICKLIME	SPINELESS
ZYGOSPORE	SCHNAUZER	BRITANNIC	EPISTAXIS	LEISURELY	QUICKNESS	SPINNAKER
ABHORRENT	SCHNECKEN	BRITSCHKA	EPISTOLER	LEITMOTIF	QUICKSAND	SPINNERET
ADHERENCE	SCHNITTKE	CAIRNGORM	EPITHESIS	LEITMOTIV	QUICKSTEP	SPIRITISM
ANHYDRIDE	SCHNITZEL	CHICANERY	EPITOMIZE	LOINCLOTH	QUIESCENT	SPIRITOUS
ANHYDRITE	SCHNORKEL	CHICKADEE	ERIOMETER	LOITERING	QUIETNESS	SPIRITUAL
ANHYDROUS	SCHNORRER	CHICKWEED	ERISTICAL	MAINFRAME	QUILLWORT	STIFFENER
APHERESIS	SCHNOZZLE	CHIEFTAIN	ETIOLATED	MAINTENON	QUINQUINA	STIFFNESS
APHRODITE	SCHOLARCH	CHIHUAHUA	ETIQUETTE	MOISTNESS	QUINTETTE	STIGMATIC
ASHKENAZI	SCHOLARLY	CHILBLAIN	EVIDENTLY	MRIDAMGAM	QUINTROON	STILLBORN
ASHMOLEAN	SCHOLIAST	CHILDCARE	EVITERNAL	MRIDANGAM	QUINTUPLE	STILLNESS
ATHEISTIC	SCHOOLBOY	CHILDHOOD	EXISTENCE	NEIGHBOUR	QUITTANCE	STILLROOM
ATHELSTAN	SCHOOLING	CHILDLESS	FAINTNESS	NOISELESS	QUIVERFUL	STILTBIRD
ATHENAEUM	SCHOOLMAN	CHILDLIKE	FAIRYLAND	NOISINESS	QUIVERING	STIMULANT
ATHLETICS	SPHACELUS	CHILOPODA	FAIRYTALE	OLIGARCHY	QUIZZICAL	STIMULATE
BEHAVIOUR	SPHENDONE	CHINATOWN	FAITHLESS	OLIGOCENE	RAINCHECK	STINGAREE
COHERENCE	SPHERICAL	CHINOVNIK	FLINTLOCK	OLIVENITE	RAINGAUGE	STINKBIRD
DEHYDRATE	SPHINCTER	CHINSTRAP	FLIPPANCY	OMINOUSLY	RAINSTORM	STINKHORN
ECHEVERIA	TAHSILDAR	CHIPBOARD	FRICASSEE	ORICALCHE	RAINWATER	STINKWOOD
ECHIDNINE	UNHAPPILY	CHIPOLATA	FRIESLAND	ORIENTATE	REICHSRAT	STIPULATE
ENHYDRITE	UNHEALTHY	CHIPPINGS	FRIGATOON	ORIFLAMME	REICHSTAG	STIRABOUT
EPHEDRINE	UNHEEDING	CHIROPODY	FRIGHTFUL	ORIGENIST	REIMBURSE	SWIFTNESS
EPHEMERAL	UNHELPFUL	CHISELLER	FRIGIDITY	ORIGINATE	REINFORCE	SWIMMERET
EPHEMERIS	UNHOPEFUL	CLIENTELE	FRITHBORH	OVIPAROUS	REINSTATE	SWINBURNE
EPHEMERON	UPHOLSTER	CLIMACTIC	FRIVOLITY	OXIDATION	REISTAFEL	SWINEHERD
EPHESIANS	USHERETTE	CLINGFILM	FRIVOLOUS	PAILLASSE	REITERATE	SWINGEING
EPHIALTES	VEHEMENCE	CLINICIAN	FRIZZANTE	PAILLETTE	ROISTERER	TAILBOARD
ETHANOATE	VEHICULAR	CLIPBOARD	GAINFULLY	PAINFULLY	RUINATION	TAILLEFER
ETHELBERT	WAHABIITE	COINTREAU	GAINSAYER	PAINTWORK	RUINOUSLY	TAILLIGHT
ETHEREOUS	YOHIMBINE	CRIBELLUM	GLISSANDO	PEIRASTIC	SAILCLOTH	TAILPIECE
ETHIOPIAN	ACIDULATE	CRICKETER	GRIEVANCE	PHIGALIAN	SAINTFOIN	TAILPLANE
ETHNOLOGY	ACIDULOUS	CRIMINATE	GRIMALKIN	PHILANDER	SAINTHOOD	TEIRESIAS
EUHEMERUS	AGINCOURT	CRINOLINE	GRIMINESS	PHILATELY	SCIAMACHY	THICKHEAD
EXHAUSTED	AGITATION	CRIPPLING	GRINGOLET	PHILIPPIC	SCIARIDAE	THICKNESS
EXHIBITOR	ALICYCLIC	CRISPNESS	GRISAILLE	PHILISTER	SCIENTISM	THIGHBONE
ICHNEUMON	ALIGNMENT	CRITERION	GUIDEBOOK	PHILLABEG	SCIENTIST	THINGUMMY
ICHNOLITE	ALIPHATIC	CRITICISM	GUIDELINE	PHILLIBEG	SCINTILLA	THINKABLE
INHERITED	AMIANTHUS	CRITICIZE	GUILDHALL	PHILOLOGY	SCIOMANCY	THINNINGS
INHERITOR	AMIDSHIPS	DAIRYMAID	GUILELESS	PHITONIUM	SCISSORER	THIRDSMAN
INHIBITED	ANIMALISM	DRIFTWOOD	GUILLEMOT	PLIMSOLLS	SHIELDING	THIRSTILY
INHIBITOR	ANIMALITY	DRINKABLE	GUILLOCHE	POIGNANCY	SHIFTLESS	THIRSTING
INHUMANLY	ANIMATION	DRIPSTONE	GUILTLESS	POINTEDLY	SHIFTWORK	THIRTIETH
IPHIGENIA	ANIMISTIC	DUIKERBOK	GUINEVERE	POINTLESS	SHILLABER	TRIANGLED
JOHANNINE	ANIMOSITY	DWINDLING	GUITARIST	POINTSMAN	SHINTOISM	TRIATHLON
LEHRJAHRE	ANISOGAMY	EDINBURGH	HAILSTONE	POISONING	SHIPOWNER	TRIBALISM
LOHENGRIN	ARISTOTLE	EDITORIAL	HAILSTORM	POISONOUS	SHIPSHAPE	TRIBESMAN
MAHARAJAH	AXIOMATIC	ELIMINATE	HAIRBRUSH	PRICELESS	SHIPWRECK	TRIBESMEN
MAHARANEE	BAINMARIE	ELIZABETH	HAIRPIECE	PRIESTESS	SHIVERING	TRIBOLOGY
MAHARISHI	BLINDFOLD	EMINENTLY	HAIRSTYLE	PRIESTLEY	SKIAMACHY	TRIBUNATE
MEHITABEL	BLINDNESS	ENIGMATIC	IDIOBLAST	PRIMAEVAL	SKILFULLY	TRIBUTARY
OCHLOCRAT	BLINDSPOT	EPICEDIUM	IDIOGRAPH	PRIMARILY	SKINDIVER	TRICERION
OPHIUCHUS	BLINDWORM	EPICENTRE	IDIOMATIC	PRIMAVERA	SKINFLINT	TRICKLESS

TRICKSTER	WHITEWOOD	BALLADIST	COLLEAGUE	FILIGRAIN	HOLLYHOCK	MULTIFORM
TRICLINIC	WHITTAWER	BALLERINA	COLLECTED	FILLIPEEN	HOLLYWOOD	MULTIPLEX
TRICOLOUR	WHITWORTH	BALLISTIC	COLLECTOR	FILLISTER	HOLOCAUST	MULTITUDE
TRICUSPID	WHIZZBANG	BALLPOINT	COLLEGIAN	FILMMAKER	HOLOGRAPH	NOLLEKENS
TRIDYMITE	ZEITGEIST	BALTHAZAR	COLLIGATE	FILMSTRIP	HOLOPHOTE	OBLIQUELY
TRIENNIAL	ADJECTIVE	BALTIMORE	COLLIMATE	FILOPLUME	HOLYSTONE	OBLIVIOUS
TRIERARCH	ADJOINING	BELATEDLY	COLLISION	FILOSELLE	HYLOBATES	OILTANKER
TRIETERIC	DEJECTION	BELEAGUER	COLLOCATE	FILTERING	ILLEGALLY	OWLEGLASS
TRIFORIUM	ENJOYABLE	BELIEVING	COLLODION	FILTERTIP	ILLEGIBLE	PALAESTRA
TRIHEDRON	ENJOYMENT	BELLICOSE	COLLOIDAL	FILTERTIP	ILLEGIBLY	PALAFITTE
TRILITHON	GUJARATHI	BELLYACHE	COLLOTYPE	FOLIOLOSE	ILLGOTTEN	PALAMPORE
TRILOBITE	HIJACKING	BELLYFLOP	COLLUSION	FOLKETING	ILLIBERAL	PALANKEEN
TRIMESTER	INJECTION	BELONGING	COLLUSIVE	FOLKWEAVE	ILLICITLY	PALANQUIN
TRIMMINGS	INJURIOUS	BELVEDERE	COLLYRIUM	FOLLOWING	ILLOGICAL	PALATABLE
TRINKETER	INJUSTICE	BILATERAL	COLOCYNTH	FULLBLOWN	ISLAMABAD	PALEMPORE
TRIPITAKA	MAJORDOMO	BILINGUAL	COLOMBIAN	FULLERENE	JELLYFISH	PALEOLITH
TRIPMETER	MAJORETTE	BILIRUBIN	COLOMBIER	FULLGROWN	KALSOMINE	PALESTINE
TRISAGION	MAJUSCULE	BILLABONG	COLONNADE	FULLSCALE	KILDERKIN	PALINURUS
TRITENESS	MUJAHIDIN	BILLBOARD	COLOPHONY	FULMINANT	KILLARNEY	PALLADIAN
TRITICALE	OBJECTIFY	BILLIARDS	COLORLESS	FULMINATE	KILOCYCLE	PALLADIUM
TRITURATE	OBJECTION	BILLOWING	COLOSSEUM	GALACTOSE	KILOHERTZ	PALLIASSE
TRIUMPHAL	OBJECTIVE	BILLYCOCK	COLOSTOMY	GALANTINE	KILOMETER	PALMATION
TRIVIALLY	OBJURGATE	BOLECTION	COLOSTRUM	GALAPAGOS	KILOMETRE	PALMISTRY
TUILERIES	REJECTION	BOLIVIANO	COLOURFUL	GALATIANS	LILYWHITE	PALMITATE
TUILLETTE	REJOICING	BOLOGNESE	COLOURING	GALDRAGON	MALACHITE	PALOVERDE
TWINKLING	REJOINDER	BOLSHEVIK	COLOURIST	GALENGALE	MALATHION	PALPATION
ULIGINOUS	ANKYLOSIS	BULGARIAN	COLTSFOOT	GALINGALE	MALAYSIAN	PALPEBRAL
UNIFORMED	ARKWRIGHT	BULKINESS	COLUMBARY	GALIONGEE	MALEBOLGE	PALPITATE
UNIFORMLY	AWKWARDLY	BULLDOZER	COLUMBATE	GALLABEAH	MALENGINE	PALSGRAVE
UNINJURED	BAKEHOUSE	BULLFIGHT	COLUMBIAN	GALLANTLY	MALFORMED	PALUDRINE
UNINVITED	BAKSHEESH	BULLFINCH	COLUMBINE	GALLANTRY	MALICIOUS	PELLAGRIN
UNISEXUAL	CAKESTAND	CALABOOSE	COLUMBITE	GALLICISM	MALIGNANT	PELLITORY
UNITARIAN	ELKOSHITE	CALABRESE	COLUMBIUM	GALLINULE	MALIGNITY	PELMANISM
UNIVALENT	LAKEFRONT	CALCANEUM	COLUMELLA	GALLIPOLI	MALLANDER	PHLEBITIS
UNIVERSAL	MAKESHIFT	CALCANEUS	COLUMNIST	GALLIVANT	MALLEABLE	PILASTERS
URICONIAN	MEKOMETER	CALCINATE	CULMINATE	GALLOPADE	MALLEMUCK	PILFERAGE
URINATION	NAKEDNESS	CALCULATE	CULTIVATE	GALLSTONE	MALLENDER	PILFERING
UTICENSIS	OCKHAMIST	CALDARIUM	DALLIANCE	GALLYCROW	MALLEOLUS	PILLICOCK
VAINGLORY	PAKISTANI	CALEDONIA	DALMATIAN	GALRAVAGE	MELAMPODE	POLEMARCH
VEILLEUSE	PEKINGESE	CALEMBOUR	DALTONISM	GALVANISM	MELANESIA	POLEMICAL
VOICELESS	PIKESTAFF	CALENDULA	DELACROIX	GALVANIZE	MELANOSIS	POLIANITE
WAISTBAND	POKERWORK	CALENTURE	DELICIOUS	GELIGNITE	MELANOTIC	POLICEMAN
WAISTCOAT	TEKNONYMY	CALIBRATE	DELIGHTED	GILGAMESH	MELBOURNE	POLITBURO
WAISTLINE	UNKNOWING	CALLIPERS	DELINEATE	GOLDCREST	MELIORATE	POLITESSE
WAITERAGE	ABLUTIONS	CALLOSITY	DELIRIOUS	GOLDFIELD	MELODIOUS	POLITICAL
WEIGHTING	AFLATOXIN	CALLOUSLY	DELIVERER	GOLDFINCH	MELODRAMA	POLITIQUE
WEIRDNESS	ALLANTOID	CALORIFIC	DELPHINUS	GOLDSINNY	MELONLIKE	POLLINATE
WHICHEVER	ALLANTOIS	CALPURNIA	DILIGENCE	GOLDSMITH	MELPOMENE	POLLUTANT
WHIMSICAL	ALLEGEDLY	CALVANISM	DOLEFULLY	HALFBAKED	MILESTONE	POLLUTION
WHINSTONE	ALLEGIANT	CALVINIST	DOLOMITES	HALFDOZEN	MILITANCY	POLONAISE
WHIPROUND	ALLEMANDE	CALVITIES	DOLOMITIC	HALFEMPTY	MILKSHAKE	POLVERINE
WHIPSNADE	ALLEVIATE	CELANDINE	DULCINIST	HALFPENNY	MILLAMANT	POLYANDRY
WHIRLIGIG	ALLIGATOR	CELEBRANT	EALDORMAN	HALFSTAFF	MILLENIAL	POLYESTER
WHIRLPOOL	ALLOCARPY	CELEBRATE	ECLAMPSIA	HALITOSIS	MILLEPEDE	POLYGONAL
WHIRLWIND	ALLOGRAFT	CELEBRITY	EGLANTINE	HALLOWEEN	MILLEPORE	POLYGRAPH
WHISTLING	ALLOGRAPH	CELESTIAL	ELLESMERE	HALLOWMAS	MILLIGRAM	POLYMORPH
WHITAKERS	ALLOPATHY	CELLARIST	ELLINGTON	HALLSTATT	MILLINERY	POLYNESIA
WHITEBAIT	ALLOTMENT	CELLULITE	ENLIGHTEN	HALOBIONT	MILLIONTH	POLYPHASE
WHITEDAMP	ALLOWABLE	CELLULOID	ENLIVENED	HALOPHILE	MILLIPEDE	POLYPHONE
WHITEFISH	ALLOWANCE	CELLULOSE	FALANGIST	HALOTHANE	MILLIVOLT	POLYPHONY
WHITEHALL	ARLINGTON	CHLAMYDES	FALDSTOOL	HELLEBORE	MILLIWATT	POLYTHENE
WHITEHEAD	AYLESBURY	CHLOROSIS	FALERNIAN	HELPFULLY	MILLSTONE	PULLULATE
WHITENESS	BALACLAVA	CILIOLATE	FALKLANDS	HELVELLYN	MILOMETER	PULMONARY
WHITENING	BALALAIKA	COLCHICUM	FALLOPIAN	HILARIOUS	MOLECULAR	PULMONATE
WHITEWALL	BALDAQUIN	COLERIDGE	FALSEHOOD	HILLBILLY	MOLESKINS	PULPITEER
WHITEWASH	BALEFULLY	COLLAPSAR	FALSENESS	HOLDERBAT	MOLLITIES	PULSATION
WHITEWING	BALLADEER	COLLATION	FILICALES	HOLINSHED	MOLLYMAWK	PULVERIZE

RELATIONS	SYLLOGISM	WALKABOUT	COMMISSAR	HAMPSHIRE	LIMOUSINE	SOMASCOPE
RELEVANCE	SYLPHLIKE	WALLABIES	COMMITTAL	HAMPSTEAD	LIMPIDITY	SOMEPLACE
RELIGEUSE	SYLVANITE	WALLBOARD	COMMITTED	HAMSTRING	LOMBARDIC	SOMETHING
RELIGIOSO	TALKATIVE	WALLOPING	COMMITTEE	HAMSTRUNG	LUMBERING	SOMETIMES
RELIGIOUS	TALMUDIST	WALLOWING	COMMODITY	HEMINGWAY	LUMBRICUS	SOMEWHERE
RELIQUARY	TELEGRAPH	WALLPAPER	COMMODORE	HEMIPTERA	LUMINAIRE	SOMMELIER
RELIQUIAE	TELEOLOGY	WALLYDRAG	COMMOTION	HEMISTICH	LUMINANCE	SOMNOLENT
RELUCTANT	TELEPATHY	WALPURGIS	COMMUNION	HEMITROPE	LYMESWOLD	SUMMARILY
RILLETTES	TELEPHONE	WELCOMING	COMMUNISM	HEMSTITCH	LYMPHATIC	SUMMARIZE
SALACIOUS	TELEPHONY	WELDSTADT	COMMUNIST	HIMALAYAN	MAMMALIAN	SUMMATION
SALANGANE	TELEPHOTO	WELLBEING	COMMUNITY	HIMALAYAS	MEMORABLE	SUMPTUARY
SALERATUS	TELESALES	WELLBUILT	COMMUTATE	HIMYARITE	MEMORITER	SUMPTUOUS
SALESGIRL	TELESCOPE	WELLKNOWN	COMPACTLY	HOMEBOUND	MOMENTARY	SYMBIOSIS
SALESLADY	TELESTICH	WELSUMMER	COMPANIES	HOMEGROWN	MOMENTOUS	SYMBIOTIC
SALICETUM	TELLINGLY	WELTGEIST	COMPANION	HOMEOPATH	MUMCHANCE	SYMBOLISM
SALLYPORT	TELLURIAN	WILDGEESE	COMPELLED	HOMEOWNER	MUMPSIMUS	SYMBOLIST
SALLYPOST	TELLURION	WILLEMITE	COMPETENT	HOMESTEAD	NAMEPLATE	SYMBOLIZE
SALOPETTE	TELLURIUM	WILLESDEN	COMPETING	HOMEWARDS	NOMINALLY	SYMMETRIC
SALTINESS	TELOPHASE	WILLFULLY	COMPLAINT	HOMICIDAL	NOMINATOR	SYMPHONIC
SALTPETER	TOLERABLE	WILLINGLY	COMPLIANT	HOMOGRAFT	NOMOCRACY	SYMPHYSIS
SALTPETRE	TOLERABLY	WILLOWING	COMPONENT	HOMOGRAPH	NOMOTHETE	SYMPODIUM
SALTWATER	TOLERANCE	WILLPOWER	COMPOSING	HOMOPHONE	NUMBSKULL	SYMPOSIUM
SALTWORKS	TOLERATED	WOLFHOUND	COMPOSITE	HOMOPTERA	NUMERAIRE	TAMERLANE
SALUBRITY	TOLLHOUSE	WOLLASTON	COMPOSURE	HUMANKIND	NUMERATOR	TAMOXIFEN
SALVARSAN	TOLPUDDLE	WOLVERINE	COMPOTIER	HUMANMADE	NUMERICAL	TEMPERATE
SALVATION	TULIPWOOD	WULFENITE	COMPUTING	HUMDINGER	NUMMULITE	TEMPORARY
SCLAUNDER	ULLSWATER	XYLOPHONE	CYMBELINE	HUMILIATE	ORMANDINE	TEMPORIZE
SCLEROSIS	UNLEARNED	YELLOWISH	CYMBIDIUM	HUMONGOUS	PEMPHIGUS	TEMPTRESS
SCLEROTAL	UNLIMITED	ADMIRABLE	DAMASCENE	HUMUNGOUS	PIMPERNEL	TEMULENCE
SELACHION	UNLUCKILY	ADMIRABLY	DAMBUSTER	IMMANACLE	POMOERIUM	TIMENOGUY
SELECTING	UPLIFTING	ADMIRALTY	DAMNATION	IMMANENCE	POMPADOUR	TIMEPIECE
SELECTION	VALDENSES	ADMISSION	DAMNEDEST	IMMANENCY	POMPHOLYX	TIMESHARE
SELECTIVE	VALENTINE	ADMITTING	DAMSELFLY	IMMEDIACY	POMPOSITY	TIMETABLE
SELFISHLY	VALIANTLY	ADMIXTURE	DEMAGOGUE	IMMEDIATE	PUMMELLED	TIMOCRACY
SELJUKIAN	VALUATION	ADMONITOR	DEMANDING	IMMELMANN	RAMILLIES	TIMPANIST
SELLOTAPE	VALUELESS	AIMLESSLY	DEMARCATE	IMMENSELY	REMAINDER	TOMBSTONE
SILICOSIS	VALVASSOR	ALMANDINE	DEMEANING	IMMENSITY	REMAINING	TOMENTOSE
SILLINESS	VELASQUEZ	ARMADILLO	DEMEANOUR	IMMERSION	REMBRANDT	TUMESCENT
SILTSTONE	VELDSKOEN	ARMAMENTS	DEMETRIUS	IMMIGRANT	REMINISCE	TUMMYACHE
SILURIDAE	VELLENAGE	ARMISTICE	DEMITASSE	IMMIGRATE	REMISSION	TYMPANIST
SILVEREYE	VELLICATE	ARMSTRONG	DEMOCRACY	IMMINENCE	REMONTANT	UNMARRIED
SOLDERING	VELODROME	AXMINSTER	DEMULCENT	IMMODESTY	REMOULADE	UNMATCHED
SOLDIERLY	VELVETEEN	BAMBOOZLE	DEMURRAGE	IMMORALLY	REMOVABLE	UNMINDFUL
SOLEMNITY	VOLAGEOUS	BIMONTHLY	DIMENSION	IMMORTALS	SAMARITAN	UNMUSICAL
SOLEMNIZE	VOLATIBLE	BOMBARDON	DOMICILED	IMMOVABLE	SEMANTEME	WAMBENGER
SOLFEGGIO	VOLCANISM	BOMBASINE	DOMINANCE	IMMOVABLY	SEMANTICS	WIMBLEDON
SOLFERINO	VOLGOGRAD	BOMBASTIC	DOMINICAL	IMMUNISER	SEMANTIDE	WOMANHOOD
SOLFIDIAN	VOLKSRAAD	BOMBSHELL	DOMINICAN	IMMUTABLE	SEMANTRON	WOMANISER
SOLICITOR	VOLTIGEUR	BUMBLEBEE	DUMBARTON	IMMUTABLY	SEMAPHORE	WOMANIZER
SOLILOQUY	VOLTINISM	BUMPTIOUS	DUMBFOUND	JAMBALAYA	SEMBLANCE	WOMANKIND
SOLIPSISM	VOLTMETER	CAMBODIAN	EMMERDALE	JAMPACKED	SEMEIOTIC	WOMENFOLK
SOLITAIRE	VOLTURNUS	CAMBRIDGE	ESMERALDA	KOMINFORM	SEMIBREVE	ZYMOMETER
SOLLICKER	VOLUCRINE	CAMBUSCAN	EUMENIDES	LAMARTINE	SEMICOLON	AINSWORTH
SPLAYFOOT	VOLUNTARY	CAMCORDER	EUMYCETES	LAMASERAI	SEMIFINAL	ANNAPOLIS
SPLENDOUR	VOLUNTEER	CAMEMBERT	FAMAGUSTA	LAMBSWOOL	SEMIFLUID	ANNAPURNA
SPLENETIC	VULCANIAN	CAMERAMAN	FEMINEITY	LAMINATED	SEMIGLOSS	ANNOTATED
SPLENITIS	VULCANIST	CAMPANILE	FOMALHAUT	LAMINITIS	SEMIOLOGY	ANNOTATOR
SPLINTERS	VULCANITE	CAMPANULA	GOMPHOSIS	LAMPADARY	SEMIOTICS	ANNOUNCER
SPLITTING	VULCANIZE	CIMMERIAN	GUMSHIELD	LAMPADION	SEMIRAMIS	ANNOYANCE
SULFUROUS	VULGARIAN	COMBATANT	GYMNASIUM	LAMPBLACK	SEMIVOWEL	ANNULMENT
SULKINESS	VULGARISM	COMBATIVE	GYMNASTIC	LAMPLIGHT	SIMEONITE	BANDALORE
SULPHONIC	VULGARITY	COMFORTER	HAMADRYAD	LAMPSHADE	SIMILARLY	BANDICOOT
SULPHURIC	VULPINITE	COMICALLY	HAMBURGER	LIMBURGER	SIMPLETON	BANDOLEER
SULTANATE	VULTURINE	COMINFORM	HAMFATTER	LIMEHOUSE	SIMPLISTE	BANDOLERO
SYLLABARY	WALDENSES	COMINTERN	HAMFISTED	LIMELIGHT	SIMULATED	BANDOLIER
SYLLABLES	WALDFLUTE	COMMANDER	HAMMERING	LIMESTONE	SIMULATOR	BANDOLINE
SYLLEPSIS	WALDGRAVE	COMMENSAL	HAMMURABI	LIMITLESS	SIMULCAST	BANDSTAND

BANDWAGON	CONFLATED	DINNERSET	HINDEMITH	LINGFIELD	MONGOLIAN	PENDRAGON
BANEBERRY	CONFORMAL	DONATELLO	HINDRANCE	LINKLATER	MONGOLISM	PENDULATE
BANISTERS	CONFUCIUS	DONCASTER	HINDSIGHT	LINTSTOCK	MONKSHOOD	PENDULOUS
BANQUETTE	CONFUSING	DONIZETTI	HINGELESS	LONDONESE	MONOCEROS	PENETRATE
BANTERING	CONFUSION	DUNDREARY	HONEYCOMB	LONGCHAMP	MONOCHORD	PENFRIEND
BENBECULA	CONGENIAL	DUNGAREES	HONEYMOON	LONGEDFOR	MONOCOQUE	PENILLION
BENCHMARK	CONGERIES	DUNGENESS	HONKYTONK	LONGEVITY	MONOCULAR	PENINSULA
BENIGHTED	CONGESTED	DUNGEONER	HONORABLE	LONGICORN	MONODRAMA	PENISTONE
BINOCULAR	CONGOLESE	DUNSINANE	HONORIFIC	LONGINGLY	MONOGRAPH	PENITENCE
BONAPARTE	CONGRUENT	DUNSTABLE	HUNCHBACK	LONGITUDE	MONOLAYER	PENNILESS
BONDSTONE	CONGRUOUS	DYNAMITED	HUNDREDTH	LONGLIVED	MONOLOGUE	PENNYWORT
BUNDESTAG	CONJUGATE	ENNERDALE	HUNGARIAN	LONGRANGE	MONOMACHY	PENPUSHER
CANALETTO	CONJURING	FANATICAL	HUNKYDORY	LONGSHORE	MONOMANIA	PENSIONER
CANAVERAL	CONNECTED	FANDANGLE	IGNESCENT	LUNCHTIME	MONOMETER	PENSIVELY
CANCEROUS	CONNECTOR	FANTASIZE	IGNORAMUS	MANDATARY	MONOPLANE	PENSTEMON
CANDIDACY	CONNEXION	FANTASTIC	IGNORANCE	MANDATORY	MONOSTICH	PENTAGRAM
CANDIDATE	CONNOTATE	FENCIBLES	INNERMOST	MANDICATE	MONOTROCH	PENTECOST
CANDLELIT	CONNUBIAL	FENUGREEK	INNISFAIL	MANDOLINE	MONOXYLON	PENTHOUSE
CANDLEMAS	CONQUEROR	FINANCIAL	INNISFREE	MANDUCATE	MONSIGNOR	PENTOSANE
CANDYTUFT	CONSCIOUS	FINANCIER	INNKEEPER	MANGANATE	MONSTROUS	PENURIOUS
CANNELURE	CONSCRIPT	FINGERING	INNOCENCE	MANGANESE	MONTACUTE	PINCHBECK
CANNONADE	CONSENSUS	FINGERTIP	INNOCUOUS	MANGETOUT	MONTAIGNE	PINCHCOCK
CANONICAL	CONSIGNEE	FINICKING	INNOVATOR	MANGOUSTE	MONTANISM	PINEAPPLE
CANTABILE	CONSIGNOR	FINICKITY	JANISSARY	MANHANDLE	MONTANIST	PINHOOKER
CANTHARIS	CONSOCIES	FINISHING	JANSENISM	MANHATTAN	MONTESPAN	PINKERTON
CANTHARUS	CONSONANT	FINLANDIA	JANSENIST	MANIFESTO	MONTEZUMA	PINOCCHIO
CANTONESE	CONSTABLE	FUNDAMENT	JENNETING	MANLINESS	MONTICULE	PINSTRIPE
CANVASSER	CONSTANCE	FUNGIBLES	JUNEBERRY	MANNEQUIN	MONZONITE	PONDEROSA
CENTAURUS	CONSTANCY	FUNGICIDE	JUNKETING	MANNERING	MUNDUNGUS	PONDEROUS
CENTENARY	CONSTRICT	FUNICULAR	KENTIGERN	MANNERISM	MUNICIPAL	PONTLEVIS
CENTERING	CONSTRUCT	FUNICULUS	KENTLEDGE	MANOEUVRE	MUNIMENTS	PUNCHLINE
CENTIGRAM	CONSULATE	GANGPLANK	KINGMAKER	MANOMETER	MUNITIONS	PUNCTILIO
CENTIPEDE	CONSUMING	GENEALOGY	KINGSIZED	MANSFIELD	NANTUCKET	PUNCTUATE
CENTRALLY	CONTAGION	GENERALLY	KINKCOUGH	MANUBRIUM	NINEPENCE	PUNGENTLY
CENTREING	CONTAINER	GENERATOR	KINSWOMAN	MENADIONE	NINETIETH	PUNISHING
CENTURION	CONTEMPER	GENETICAL	KINTLEDGE	MENAGERIE	NONENTITY	RANCIDITY
CINEMATIC	CONTENDER	GENEVIEVE	KONIMETER	MENDACITY	NONILLION	RANCOROUS
CINEPHILE	CONTENTED	GENIALITY	KONISCOPE	MENDELISM	NONPAREIL	RANDINESS
CINERARIA	CONTINENT	GENITALIA	LANCASTER	MENDICANT	NONPROFIT	RANGELAND
CINEREOUS	CONTINUAL	GENTEELLY	LANCEWOOD	MENIPPEAN	NONSMOKER	RANTIPOLE
CONCAVITY	CONTINUUM	GENTILITY	LANCINATE	MENNONITE	NUNCUPATE	RENASCENT
CONCEALED	CONTRALTO	GENTLEMAN	LANDAULET	MENOMINEE	OBNOXIOUS	RENCONTRE
CONCEITED	CONTRIVED	GENTLEMEN	LANDDROST	MENOPAUSE	OMNIRANGE	RENDERING
CONCERNED	CONTRIVER	GENUFLECT	LANDGRAVE	MENSHEVIK	OWNERSHIP	RENDITION
CONCERTED	CONTUMACY	GENUINELY	LANDLOPER	MENSTRUAL	PANATELLA	RENEWABLE
CONCIERGE	CONTUMELY	GINGERADE	LANDOWNER	MENSTRUUM	PANCHAYAT	RENFIERST
CONCISELY	CONTUSION	GINGLYMUS	LANDSCAPE	MENTALITY	PANDATION	RENOVATOR
CONCISION	CONUNDRUM	GINORMOUS	LANDSLIDE	MENTATION	PANDEMIAN	RENTALLER
CONCLUDED	CONVECTOR	GONDOLIER	LANDSMAAL	MENTICIDE	PANDURATE	RINGFENCE
CONCORDAT	CONVERTED	GONGORISM	LANDSTURM	MENTIONED	PANEGOISM	RINGSIDER
CONCOURSE	CONVERTER	GONIATITE	LANDWARDS	MENUISIER	PANEGYRIC	RUNAROUND
CONCUBINE	CONVINCED	GUNCOTTON	LANGOUSTE	MINACIOUS	PANELLING	RUNCINATE
CONCUSSED	CONVIVIAL	GUNPOWDER	LANGRIDGE	MINCEMEAT	PANELLIST	RUNESTAVE
CONDEMNED	CUNCTATOR	GYNOECIUM	LANGSPIEL	MINEFIELD	PANETTONE	RUNNYMEDE
CONDENSER	CUNEIFORM	HANDBRAKE	LANGUAGES	MINELAYER	PANHANDLE	SANCTUARY
CONDIMENT	CYNEGETIC	HANDCUFFS	LANGUEDOC	MINIATURE	PANNIKELL	SANDALLED
CONDITION	CYNICALLY	HANDINESS	LANGUETTE	MINISKIRT	PANORAMIC	SANDARACH
CONDUCIVE	DANDELION	HANDIWORK	LANGUIDLY	MINKSTONE	PANTAGAMY	SANDHURST
CONDUCTOR	DANDIFIED	HANDPIECE	LANKINESS	MINNESOTA	PANTALEON	SANDPAPER
CONDUCTUS	DANDYPRAT	HANDSHAKE	LANTHANUM	MINUSCULE	PANTALOON	SANDPIPER
CONDYLOMA	DANGEROUS	HANDSPIKE	LENGTHILY	MINUTEMAN	PANTHEISM	SANDSTONE
CONFESSED	DANTHONIA	HANDSTAND	LENIENTLY	MONACTINE	PANTHENOL	SANDSTORM
CONFESSOR	DENIGRATE	HANKERING	LENINGRAD	MONASTERY	PANTOFFLE	SANGFROID
CONFIDANT	DENSENESS	HANSEATIC	LINDBERGH	MONASTRAL	PANTOMIME	SANHEDRIM
CONFIDENT	DENTISTRY	HENDIADYS	LINEAMENT	MONATOMIC	PANTOUFLE	SANHEDRIN
CONFIRMED	DENTITION	HENPECKED	LINEOLATE	MONERGISM	PENDENNIS	SANHEDRON
CONFITEOR	DINGINESS	HINDBRAIN	LINGERING	MONEYWORT	PENDLETON	SANNYASIN

SANTAYANA	TONOPLAST	APOLOGIST	CROSSWALK	FOOLISHLY	LOOSELEAF	PROLONGED
SANTONICA	TUNGSTATE	APOLOGIZE	CROSSWIND	FOOLPROOF	LOOSENESS	PROLUSION
SENESCENT	TUNGSTOUS	APOPHATIC	CROSSWISE	FOOTBRAKE	MOODINESS	PROMACHOS
SENESCHAL	UNNATURAL	APOPHYSIS	CROSSWORD	FOOTHILLS	MOONLIGHT	PROMENADE
SENIORITY	UNNERVING	APOSTOLIC	CROTCHETY	FOOTLOOSE	MOONRAKER	PROMINENT
SENSATION	UNNOTICED	ATONALITY	CROUSTADE	FOOTPLATE	MOONSHINE	PROMISING
SENSELESS	VANCOUVER	ATONEMENT	CROWNLIKE	FOOTPRINT	MOONSTONE	PROMOTION
SENSILLUM	VANDALISM	AVOCATION	CROWSBILL	FOOTSTALL	MYOFIBRIL	PROMPTING
SENSITIVE	VANDALIZE	AVOIDABLE	CROWSFOOT	FOOTSTOOL	MYOGLOBIN	PROMUSCIS
SENSITIZE	VANISHING	AVOIDANCE	DEODORANT	FROBISHER	NEODYMIUM	PRONGHORN
SENSORIUM	VANTBRASS	BIOGRAPHY	DEODORIZE	FROGMARCH	NEOLITHIC	PRONOUNCE
SENSUALLY	VENERABLE	BIOLOGIST	DEOXIDISE	FROGMOUTH	NEOLOGISM	PROOFREAD
SENTIENCE	VENEREOUS	BIOSPHERE	DIOCLETES	FROGSPAWN	NOOSPHERE	PROPAGATE
SENTIMENT	VENEZUELA	BLOATWARE	DIONYSIAN	FROISSART	ODOURLESS	PROPELLED
SINCERELY	VENGEANCE	BLOCKHEAD	DIONYSIUS	FROSTBITE	OMOPHAGIC	PROPELLER
SINCERITY	VENIALITY	BLOODBATH	DOODLEBUG	GEODESIST	ONOMASTIC	PROPERDIN
SINGALESE	VENTIFACT	BLOODLESS	DOORFRAME	GEOGRAPHY	OPOBALSAM	PROPHETIC
SINGAPORE	VENTILATE	BLOODROOT	DROMEDARY	GEOLOGIST	OPODELDOC	PROPIONIC
SINGLESEX	VENTRICLE	BLOODSHED	DROPPINGS	GEOMETRIC	OROBANCHE	PROPONENT
SINGLETON	VENUSBERG	BLOODSHOT	DROPSICAL	GEOMETRID	OROGRAPHY	PROPRIETY
SINGSPIEL	VINDICATE	BLOODWORM	DUODECIMO	GEORGETTE	OZOCERITE	PROPTOSIS
SINGULTUS	WANCHANCY	BLOWTORCH	ECOLOGIST	GLOMERATE	OZOKERITE	PROPYLENE
SINKANSEN	WANDERING	BOOBIALLA	ECONOMICS	GLOMERULE	PHONECARD	PROROGATE
SINUOSITY	WANWORTHY	BOOBYTRAP	ECONOMIST	GLORIFIED	PHONETICS	PROSCRIBE
SINUSITIS	WENCESLAS	BOOKLOVER	ECONOMIZE	GLORYHOLE	PHONOGRAM	PROSECUTE
SONGSMITH	WINCANTON	BOOKMAKER	ECOSPHERE	GOODNIGHT	PHONOLITE	PROSELYTE
SONNETEER	WINCOPIPE	BOOKSHELF	ECOSSAISE	GOONHILLY	PHONOLOGY	PROSIMIAN
SONOMETER	WINDBREAK	BOOKSTALL	ECOSYSTEM	GOOSANDER	PHOSPHATE	PROSTRATE
SUNBATHER	WINDCHILL	BOOKSTAND	ELOCUTION	GOOSEFOOT	PHOSPHENE	PROTAMINE
SUNDOWNER	WINDFALLS	BOOKSTORE	ELONGATED	GOOSEHERD	PHOTOCOPY	PROTECTOR
SUNFLOWER	WINDHOVER	BOOMERANG	ELOPEMENT	GOOSENECK	PHOTOGENE	PROTESTER
SUNSCREEN	WINDSCALE	BOONDOCKS	ELOQUENCE	GOOSESTEP	PHOTOSTAT	PROTHESIS
SUNSTROKE	WINDSWEPT	BOOTBLACK	EMOLLIATE	GROCERIES	PHOTOTUBE	PROTHORAX
SUNTANNED	WINEBERRY	BOOTLACES	EMOLLIENT	GROSGRAIN	PLOUGHMAN	PROTOSTAR
SYNAGOGUE	WINEGLASS	BROADCAST	EMOLUMENT	GROSVENOR	POORHOUSE	PROTOTYPE
SYNANGIUM	WINNEBAGO	BROADLOOM	EMOTIONAL	GROTESQUE	PROACTIVE	PROUDHORN
SYNCHYSIS	WONDERFUL	BROADSIDE	EPONYMOUS	GROUNDHOG	PROBABLES	PROUSTITE
SYNCOMIUM	XANTHIPPE	BROKERAGE	EROGENOUS	GROUNDING	PROBATION	PROVEDORE
SYNCOPATE	XENOMANIA	BROMINATE	EROSTRATE	GROUNDNUT	PROBOSCIS	PROVENDER
SYNDICATE	XENOPHOBE	BRONCHIAL	EROTICISM	GROUNDSEL	PROCACITY	PROVIDENT
SYNEDRION	ZENOCRATE	BROTHERLY	ESOPHAGUS	HOOLACHAN	PROCEDURE	PROVIDING
SYNERGIST	ZINFANDEL	BROUGHTON	EVOCATION	INOCULATE	PROCERITY	PROVISION
SYNIZESIS	ZINKENITE	CHOCOLATE	EVOCATIVE	INOPINATE	PROCESSOR	PROVOKING
SYNOECETE	ABOLITION	CHOLELITH	EVOCATORY	INORGANIC	PROCLITIC	PROVOLONE
SYNOVITIS	ABOMINATE	CHONDRITE	EVOLUTION	IRONSIDES	PROCOELUS	PROXIMATE
SYNTACTIC	ABORIGINE	CHONDROID	EXODERMIS	IRONSTONE	PROCONSUL	PROXIMITY
SYNTHESIS	ABOUNDING	CHORISTER	EXOGENOUS	IRONWORKS	PROCREATE	PSORIASIS
SYNTHETIC	ABOUTFACE	CLOAKROOM	EXONERATE	ISOCLINAL	PRODROMAL	PYONGYANG
TANGERINE	ABOUTTURN	CLOCKWISE	EXORATION	ISOCRATES	PRODROMUS	QUODLIBET
TANTALITE	ACONCAGUA	CLOCKWORK	EXOSPHERE	ISODORIAN	PROENZYME	QUOTATION
TANTALIZE	ACOUSTICS	CLOISONNÉ	EXOSTOSIS	ISOLATION	PROFANELY	QUOTIDIAN
TANTARARA	ADORATION	CLOSENESS	FIORITURA	ISOMERASE	PROFANITY	QUOTITION
TANZANIAN	ADORNMENT	CLOUDLESS	FLOODGATE	ISOMETRIC	PROFESSED	RHODESIAN
TENACIOUS	AFORESAID	COOKHOUSE	FLOORSHOW	ISOPROPYL	PROFESSOR	RHODOLITE
TENACULUM	AGONIZING	COOPERATE	FLOPHOUSE	ISOSCELES	PROFITEER	RHODOPSIN
TENAILLON	ALONGSIDE	CROCKFORD	FLORESTAN	ISOTACTIC	PROFUSELY	RIOTOUSLY
TENDERIZE	ALOOFNESS	CROCODILE	FLORIMELL	ISOTROPIC	PROFUSION	ROOSEVELT
TENEBROSE	AMOROUSLY	CROISSANT	FLOTATION	KNOBSTICK	PROGNOSIS	ROOTSTOCK
TENEMENTS	AMORPHOUS	CROOKBACK	FLOURMILL	KNOCKDOWN	PROGRAMME	SCOLECITE
TENNESSEE	ANOINTING	CROOKEDLY	FLOWCHART	KNOTGRASS	PROJECTED	SCOLIOSIS
TENSENESS	ANOMALOUS	CROQUETTE	FLOWERBED	KNOWINGLY	PROJECTOR	SCOLIOTIC
TENTATIVE	ANONYMITY	CROSSBEAM	FLOWERING	KNOWLEDGE	PROKARYON	SCONCHEON
TENTORIUM	ANONYMOUS	CROSSBILL	FLOWERPOT	KROPOTKIN	PROKOFIEV	SCORBUTIC
TENUOUSLY	ANOPHELES	CROSSBRED	FLOWSTONE	LAODICEAN	PROLACTIN	SCORBUTUS
TINGUAITE	APOCRYPHA	CROSSEYED	FOODSTORE	LIONHEART	PROLAMINE	SCORCHING
TONBRIDGE	APOENZYME	CROSSFIRE	FOODSTUFF	LOOKALIKE	PROLEPSIS	SCORODITE
TONOMETER	APOLLONUS	CROSSOVER	FOOLHARDY	LOOSEHEAD	PROLIXITY	SCOTCHMAN

SCOUNDREL	STONEWORK	AEPYORNIS	EMPHASIZE	IMPASSION	PIPESTONE	SUPERCOOL
SFORZANDO	STONEWORT	ALPENGLOW	EMPHLYSIS	IMPASSIVE	PIPSQUEAK	SUPERETTE
SHOEMAKER	STONKERED	ALPENHORN	EMPHYSEMA	IMPATIENT	POPLITEAL	SUPERFINE
SHOESHINE	STOOLBALL	AMPERSAND	EMPIRICAL	IMPEACHER	POPPERING	SUPERNOVA
SHOLOKHOV	STOPLIGHT	AMPHIBIAN	EMPLECTON	IMPEDANCE	POPPYCOCK	SUPERSEDE
SHOPFLOOR	STOREROOM	AMPLIFIER	EMPLOYEES	IMPELLING	POPULARLY	SUPERSTAR
SHOPFRONT	STORIATED	AMPLITUDE	EMPTINESS	IMPENDING	POPULATED	SUPERVENE
SHOREBIRD	STORNAWAY	APPALLING	ERPINGHAM	IMPERATOR	PUPILLAGE	SUPERVISE
SHORTCAKE	STORYBOOK	APPARATUS	ESPAGNOLE	IMPERFECT	PUPPETEER	SUPINATOR
SHORTFALL	STORYLINE	APPARITOR	ESPERANCE	IMPERIOUS	RAPACIOUS	SUPPLIANT
SHORTHAND	STOUTNESS	APPEALING	ESPERANTO	IMPETUOUS	RAPTORIAL	SUPPLICAT
SHORTHAUL	STOVEPIPE	APPENDAGE	ESPIONAGE	IMPLEMENT	RAPTUROUS	SUPPORTER
SHORTHOLD	STOWNLINS	APPERTAIN	ESPLANADE	IMPLICATE	REPAYABLE	SUPPOSING
SHORTHORN	SWORDFISH	APPETIZER	EUPHEMISM	IMPLUVIUM	REPAYMENT	SUPPURATE
SHORTLIST	SWORDPLAY	APPLEJACK	EUPHONIUM	IMPOLITIC	REPECHAGE	SUPREMACY
SHORTNESS	SWORDSMAN	APPLIANCE	EUPHORBIA	IMPORTANT	REPELLENT	SUPREMELY
SHORTSTAY	SWOTHLING	APPLICANT	EUPHRATES	IMPORTUNE	REPELLING	SYPHILOMA
SHORTSTOP	TAOISEACH	APPOINTED	EXPANSION	IMPOSTURE	REPENTANT	TAPDANCER
SHORTTERM	THORNBACK	APPOINTEE	EXPANSIVE	IMPOTENCE	REPERCUSS	TEPHILLIN
SHOVELFUL	THORNBILL	APPORTION	EXPATIATE	IMPOUNDER	REPERTORY	TIPPERARY
SHOVELLER	THORNDYKE	APPRAISAL	EXPECTANT	IMPRECATE	REPLACING	TIPSINESS
SHOWINESS	THORNLESS	APPREHEND	EXPECTING	IMPRECISE	REPLENISH	TIPULIDAE
SHOWPIECE	THOUSANDS	APPROVING	EXPEDIENT	IMPRESSED	REPLETION	TOPDRAWER
SLOUGHING	TOOTHACHE	ASPARAGUS	EXPENSIVE	IMPROBITY	REPLETIVE	TOPIARIST
SLOVENIAN	TOOTHCOMB	ASPARTAME	EXPERTISE	IMPROMPTU	REPLICANT	TOPICALLY
SLOWCOACH	TOOTHLESS	ASPERSION	EXPIATION	IMPROVING	REPLICATE	TYPICALLY
SMOKEFREE	TOOTHPICK	ASPIRATOR	EXPIATORY	IMPROVISE	REPORTAGE	UMPTEENTH
SMOKELESS	TOOTHSOME	ASPLENIUM	EXPISCATE	IMPRUDENT	REPORTING	UNPOPULAR
SNOWBOUND	TROCHILIC	BAPTISMAL	EXPLETIVE	IMPSONITE	REPOSSESS	UNPRECISE
SNOWDONIA	TROCHILUS	BIPARTITE	EXPLICATE	IMPUDENCE	REPREHEND	UPPERCASE
SNOWDRIFT	TROMPETTE	BYPRODUCT	EXPLOITER	IMPULSION	REPRESENT	UPPERMOST
SNOWFLAKE	TRONDHEIM	CAPACIOUS	EXPLOSION	IMPULSIVE	REPRESSED	VAPORETTO
SNOWSHOES	TROOPSHIP	CAPACITOR	EXPLOSIVE	INPATIENT	REPRESSOR	VAPORIFIC
SNOWSTORM	TROOSTITE	CAPARISON	EXPORTING	JEPHTHAHS	REPRIMAND	VAPORIZER
SNOWWHITE	TROPAELIN	CAPILLARY	EXPOSITOR	KEPLARIAN	REPROBATE	VIPASSANA
SOOTERKIN	TROPARION	CAPITULAR	EXPRESSED	LAPLANDER	REPROCESS	WAPENTAKE
SPODUMENE	TROSSACHS	CAPITULUM	EXPRESSLY	LAPSTREAK	REPRODUCE	WAPINSHAW
SPOFFORTH	TROUBADOR	CAPORETTO	EXPULSION	LEPROSORY	REPROVING	ZEPHANIAH
SPOILSMAN	TROUSSEAU	CAPRICCIO	EXPURGATE	LIPPITUDE	REPTATION	ACQUIESCE
SPOKESMAN	UNOPPOSED	CAPRICORN	HAPHAZARD	MAPPEMOND	REPTILIAN	ACQUITTAL
SPONGEBAG	UROKINASE	CAPTAINCY	HAPPENING	MEPACRINE	REPUDIATE	ARQUEBUSE
SPONSORED	VIOLATION	CAPTIVATE	HAPPINESS	NAPIERIAN	REPUGNANT	ENQUIRIES
SPOONBILL	VIOLENTLY	CAPTIVITY	HEPATICAL	NEPHALISM	REPULSION	ENQUIRING
SPOONFEED	VIOLINIST	CIPOLLINO	HEPATITIS	NEPHALIST	REPULSIVE	ESQUILINE
SPOROCARP	VOODOOISM	COPIOUSLY	HIPPOCRAS	NEPHELINE	REPUTABLE	EXQUISITE
SPORTSMAN	WHODUNNIT	COPROLITE	HIPPODAME	NEPHRITIC	REPUTEDLY	INQUILINE
SPORTSMEN	WHOLEFOOD	COPYRIGHT	HIPPOLYTA	NEPHRITIS	RIPIENIST	INQUINATE
SPOTLIGHT	WHOLEMEAL	CUPRESSUS	HIPPOLYTE	NEPTUNIUM	SAPODILLA	INQUIRING
STOCKFISH	WHOLENESS	DEPARTURE	HOPEFULLY	NIPCHEESE	SAPSUCKER	INQUORATE
STOCKHOLM	WHOLESALE	DEPASTURE	HOPLOLOGY	NIPPERKIN	SEPARABLE	JEQUIRITY
STOCKINET	WHOLESOME	DEPENDANT	HOPSCOTCH	OPPENHEIM	SEPARATED	LIQUEFIED
STOCKINGS	WHOSOEVER	DEPENDENT	HYPALLAGE	OPPONENTS	SEPARATOR	LIQUIDATE
STOCKPILE	WOODBORER	DEPENDING	HYPERBOLA	OPPORTUNE	SEPHARDIM	LIQUIDITY
STOCKROOM	WOODCHUCK	DEPICTION	HYPERBOLE	OPPRESSED	SEPIOLITE	LIQUIDIZE
STOCKWORK	WOODCRAFT	DEPOSITOR	HYPERLINK	OPPRESSOR	SEPTEMBER	LIQUORICE
STOCKYARD	WOODENTOP	DEPRAVITY	HYPEROPIA	ORPHANAGE	SEPTIMOLE	LIQUORISH
STOICALLY	WOODHOUSE	DEPRECATE	HYPHENATE	ORPHARION	SEPULCHER	LOQUACITY
STOKEHOLD	WOODLANDS	DEPREDATE	HYPINOSIS	ORPINGTON	SEPULCHRE	PIQUANTLY
STOLIDITY	WOODLOUSE	DEPRESSED	HYPNOTISM	PAPARAZZI	SEPULTURE	REQUISITE
STOMACHIC	WOODSHOCK	DIPHTHONG	HYPNOTIST	PAPARAZZO	SIPHUNCLE	ROQUEFORT
STONEBOAT	WOOLINESS	DIPLOMACY	HYPNOTIZE	PAPERBACK	SOPHISTER	SEQUENCER
STONECHAT	WOOMERANG	DUPLICAND	HYPOBLAST	PAPERCLIP	SOPHISTIC	SEQUESTER
STONECROP	WRONGDOER	DUPLICATE	HYPOCAUST	PAPERWORK	SOPHISTRY	SEQUINNED
STONEHAND	WRONGFOOT	DUPLICITY	HYPOCRISY	PAPILLOTE	SOPHOCLES	SUQUAMISH
STONELESS	ZOOLOGIST	EMPAESTIC	HYPOCRITE	PEPPERONI	SOPHOMORE	ACROBATIC
STONEWALL	ZOOMANTIC	EMPANOPLY	IMPACTION	PEPPERPOT	SOPORIFIC	ACROPETAL
STONEWARE	ZOOSCOPIC	EMPENNAGE	IMPARTIAL	PIPEDREAM	SOPPINESS	ACROPHONY

ACROPOLIS	CARACALLA	CORNFIELD	FERTILITY	FURTIVELY	HORDEOLUM	MERCAPTAN
ADRENALIN	CARAMBOLA	CORNFLOUR	FERTILIZE	GARDENING	HOREHOUND	MERCENARY
AERODROME	CARBAMATE	CORNSTALK	FERVENTLY	GARDEROBE	HORNSTONE	MERCERIZE
AEROPLANE	CARBAMIDE	COROLLARY	FIREBRAND	GARGANTUA	HOROSCOPE	MERCILESS
AEROSPACE	CARBONADE	CORPORATE	FIREBREAK	GARGARISM	HORRIFIED	MERCURIAL
AEROTAXIS	CARBONADO	CORPOREAL	FIREDRAKE	GARIBALDI	HORSEBACK	MERESWINE
AFRIKAANS	CARBONARI	CORPOSANT	FIREGUARD	GARNISHEE	HORSEHAIR	MERGANSER
AFRIKANER	CARBONATE	CORPULENT	FIRELIGHT	GARNITURE	HORSELESS	MEROCRINE
AGREEABLE	CARBONIZE	CORPUSCLE	FIREPLACE	GARRULITY	HORSEPLAY	MERRIMENT
AGREEABLY	CARBUNCLE	CORRECTED	FIREPROOF	GARRULOUS	HORSESHOE	MIRABELLE
AGREEMENT	CARCINOMA	CORRECTLY	FIRESTONE	GARRYOWEN	HORSETAIL	MIRTHLESS
AIRCOOLED	CARDBOARD	CORRECTOR	FIREWATER	GERFALCON	HORSEWHIP	MORATORIA
AIRSTREAM	CAREERIST	CORREGGIO	FIREWORKS	GERIATRIC	HORTATIVE	MORATORIO
ARRESTING	CAREFULLY	CORRELATE	FIRMAMENT	GERMANCER	HORTATORY	MORBIDITY
ARRIVISTE	CARETAKER	CORROSION	FIRSTEVER	GERMANITE	HURRICANE	MORECAMBE
ARROGANCE	CARIBBEAN	CORROSIVE	FIRSTHAND	GERMANIUM	HURRICANO	MORGANITE
ARROWHEAD	CARMELITE	CORRUGATE	FIRSTRATE	GERMICIDE	HURRIEDLY	MORMONISM
ARROWROOT	CARNATION	CORRUPTER	FORASMUCH	GERMINATE	IPRINDOLE	MORTALITY
ATROCIOUS	CARNELIAN	CORTISONE	FORBIDDEN	GERUNDIVE	IRRADIANT	MORTGAGEE
AURICULAR	CARNIVORE	CORUSCATE	FORCEMEAT	GIRANDOLE	IRRADIATE	MORTGAGOR
BARAGOUIN	CARPACCIO	CURETTAGE	FOREANENT	GIRONDIST	IRRAWADDY	MORTICIAN
BARBARIAN	CARPENTER	CURFUFFLE	FOREBEARS	GYROMANCY	IRREGULAR	MORTIFIED
BARBARISM	CARPENTRY	CURIOSITY	FOREBRAIN	GYROPLANE	IRRITABLE	MORTSTONE
BARBARITY	CARPETING	CURIOUSLY	FORECLOSE	GYROSCOPE	IRRITABLY	MURDERESS
BARBARIZE	CARTESIAN	CURRENTLY	FORECOURT	HARBINGER	IRRITATED	MURDEROUS
BARBAROUS	CARTHORSE	CURRYCOMB	FOREFRONT	HARDANGER	IRRUPTION	MURKINESS
BARBITONE	CARTILAGE	CURSORILY	FOREGOING	HARDBOARD	ISRAELITE	MURMURING
BARBOTINE	CARTOGRAM	CURTILAGE	FOREIGNER	HARDCOVER	JARGONIZE	MYRMECOID
BARCELONA	CARTOUCHE	CURVATURE	FORESHORE	HARDIHOOD	JERAHMEEL	NARCISSUS
BAREBONES	CARTRIDGE	CURVEBALL	FORESIGHT	HARDINESS	JERKINESS	NARGHILLY
BAREFACED	CARTTRACK	DAREDEVIL	FORESPEAK	HARDLINER	JERKWATER	NARRATION
BARMBRACK	CARTULARY	DARTAGNAN	FORESPEND	HARDSHELL	JERUSALEM	NARRATIVE
BARMECIDE	CARTWHEEL	DARTBOARD	FORESTAGE	HARESTANE	JORDANIAN	NARROWING
BARNABITE	CARYOPSIS	DARTMOUTH	FORESTALL	HARIGALDS	JURIDICAL	NERITIDAE
BARNACLES	CERATITIS	DARWINIAN	FORESTERS	HARIOLATE	KARABINER	NERVOUSLY
BARNSTORM	CERATODUS	DERRINGER	FORETASTE	HARLEQUIN	KARAKORAM	NORMALACY
BAROMETER	CEREBRATE	DIRECTION	FOREWOMAN	HARLESTON	KARYOTYPE	NORMALITY
BARONETCY	CERECLOTH	DIRECTIVE	FORFEITED	HARMALINE	KERATITIS	NORMALIZE
BARRACUDA	CEROMANCY	DIRECTORS	FORFICATE	HARMATTAN	KERBSTONE	NORMATIVE
BARRICADE	CERTAINLY	DIRECTORY	FORGATHER	HARMONICA	KERFUFFLE	NORTHEAST
BARRISTER	CERTAINTY	DIRIGIBLE	FORGETFUL	HARMONIST	KERMESITE	NORTHERLY
BARTENDER	CERTIFIED	DIRTINESS	FORGETIVE	HARMONIUM	LARGENESS	NORTHWARD
BARTHOLDI	CERTITUDE	DORMITION	FORGIVING	HARMONIZE	LARGHETTO	NORTHWEST
BARTHOLIN	CERUSSITE	DORMITORY	FORGOTTEN	HARMOTOME	LARGITION	NORWEGIAN
BARYSCOPE	CERVANTES	EARNESTLY	FORJASKIT	HARPOONER	LORGNETTE	NUREMBERG
BERGAMASK	CHRISTIAN	EARTHFLAX	FORJESKIT	HARQUEBUS	LURIDNESS	NURSEMAID
BERGANDER	CHRISTMAS	EARTHLING	FORLORNLY	HARROGATE	LYRICALLY	OARSWOMAN
BERGOMASK	CHROMATIC	EARTHWORK	FORMALIST	HARROWING	MARAUDING	OBREPTION
BERKELIUM	CHRONICLE	EARTHWORM	FORMALITY	HARSHNESS	MARCASITE	OUROBOROS
BERNSTEIN	CHRYSALIS	EBRILLADE	FORMALIZE	HARTSHORN	MARCHPANE	OUROBORUS
BERSERKER	CIRCADIAN	EGREGIOUS	FORMATION	HARVESTER	MARGARINE	OURSELVES
BERYLLIUM	CIRCINATE	EGRESSION	FORMATIVE	HERBALIST	MARIJUANA	PARABASIS
BIRDBRAIN	CIRCULATE	ENRAPTURE	FORMULATE	HERBARIUM	MARKETEER	PARABLAST
BIRDTABLE	CIRRHOSIS	ENROLMENT	FORNICATE	HERBICIDE	MARKETING	PARABOLIC
BIRTHMARK	CORALLINE	ERRONEOUS	FORSYTHIA	HERBIVORE	MARMALADE	PARACHUTE
BIRTHRATE	CORDIALLY	EURHYTHMY	FORTALICE	HERBORIST	MARMOREAL	PARACLETE
BIRTHWORT	CORDUROYS	EURIPIDES	FORTHWINK	HERCULEAN	MARQUESAS	PARACUSIS
BORDEREAU	CORDYLINE	FARANDOLE	FORTHWITH	HEREAFTER	MARQUETRY	PARAGOGUE
BORDERING	CORIANDER	FARMHOUSE	FORTILAGE	HERETICAL	MARROWFAT	PARAGRAPH
BORNAGAIN	CORKSCREW	FARMSTEAD	FORTITUDE	HERITABLE	MARSHLAND	PARALYSIS
BORROWING	CORMORANT	FERACIOUS	FORTNIGHT	HERMANDAD	MARSUPIAL	PARALYTIC
BURKINABE	CORNBRASH	FERDINAND	FORTUNATE	HERMITAGE	MARSUPIUM	PARAMEDIC
BURLESQUE	CORNCRAKE	FERINGHEE	FORWANDER	HERODOTUS	MARTINEAU	PARAMETER
BURLINESS	CORNEILLE	FERMENTED	FURACIOUS	HERONSHAW	MARTINMAS	PARAMOUNT
BURROUGHS	CORNELIAN	FEROCIOUS	FURIOUSLY	HERPESTES	MARTYRDOM	PARANOIAC
BURROWING	CORNERMAN	FERROTYPE	FURNIMENT	HERBIVORE...		
BURUNDIAN	CORNETIST	FERRYBOAT	FURNITURE	HIRUNDINE	MARVELOUS	PARASCENE

PARASCEVE	PERPLEXED	SCRIPTURE	STRIDENCY	THROBBING	VIRTUALLY	BOSSINESS
PARASITIC	PERSECUTE	SCRIVENER	STRINGENT	THRONGING	VIRULENCE	BOSTONIAN
PARATAXIS	PERSEVERE	SCRODDLED	STRINGOPS	THROWAWAY	VORACIOUS	BYSTANDER
PARATHION	PERSIMMON	SCROUNGER	STRIPLING	THROWBACK	VORTICISM	CASHPOINT
PARATROOP	PERSONAGE	SCRUBBING	STROBILUS	THROWDOWN	VORTIGERN	CASSANDRA
PARBUCKLE	PERSONATE	SCRUFFILY	STROLLING	THROWSTER	WAREHOUSE	CASSATION
PARCHEESI	PERSONIFY	SCRUMMAGE	STROMBOLI	TIREDNESS	WARMONGER	CASSEROLE
PARCHMENT	PERSONNEL	SCRUMPING	STRONGARM	TORBANITE	WARTCRESS	CASSONADE
PARDALOTE	PERSUADED	SCRUTATOR	STRONGYLE	TORMENTER	WORCESTER	CASSOULET
PAREGORIC	PERTINENT	SERAPHINE	STRONTIUM	TORMENTIL	WORDINESS	CASSOWARY
PARENTAGE	PERTURBED	SERASKIER	STROSSERS	TORMENTOR	WORDSMITH	CASTANETS
PARENTING	PERTUSATE	SERBONIAN	STRUCTURE	TORMENTUM	WORKFORCE	CASTELLAN
PARFLECHE	PERTUSSIS	SERENADER	STRUMITIS	TORTELIER	WORKHORSE	CASTIGATE
PARHELION	PERVASION	SERENGETI	STRUTTING	TURBIDITY	WORKHOUSE	CASTILIAN
PARHYPATE	PERVASIVE	SERIALIST	SURCHARGE	TURBINATE	WORKPLACE	CASTRATED
PARNASITE	PERVERTED	SERIALIZE	SURCINGLE	TURBOPROP	WORKSPACE	CASUARINA
PARNASSUS	PHRENETIC	SERIATION	SURFBOARD	TURBULENT	WORLDWIDE	CASUISTIC
PAROCHIAL	PHRENITIS	SERIGRAPH	SURFEITED	TURCOPOLE	WORMEATEN	CASUISTRY
PAROCHINE	PIRATICAL	SERIOUSLY	SURLINESS	TURMAGENT	WORRISOME	CESSATION
PAROTITIS	PIROUETTE	SERMONIZE	SURMULLET	TURNABOUT	WORTHLESS	COSMETICS
PARRICIDE	PORBEAGLE	SERRATION	SURPRISED	TURNBULLS	WURLITZER	COSMOGONY
PARSIMONY	PORCELAIN	SERREFILE	SURQUEDRY	TURNROUND	XEROPHYTE	COSMOLOGY
PARSONAGE	PORCUPINE	SERVICING	SURREJOIN	TURNSTILE	XEROSTOMA	COSMONAUT
PARTAKING	PORIFERAN	SERVIETTE	SURRENDER	TURNSTONE	YARDSTICK	COSTUMIER
PARTHENON	PORPOISES	SERVILELY	SURROGATE	TURNTABLE	YORKSHIRE	CUSPIDORE
PARTHOLON	PORPORATE	SERVILITY	SURVEYING	TURPITUDE	ZIRCONIUM	CUSTODIAL
PARTIALLY	PORRINGER	SERVITUDE	SURVIVING	TURQUOISE	ZOROASTER	CUSTODIAN
PARTICLES	PORTERAGE	SHRIMPING	SYRIACISM	TYRANNIZE	ABSCONDER	CUSTOMARY
PARTITION	PORTFOLIO	SHRINKAGE	SYRPHIDAE	TYRANNOUS	ABSORBENT	CUSTOMIZE
PARTRIDGE	PORTRAYAL	SHRINKING	TARANTASS	UKRAINIAN	ABSORBING	DASHBOARD
PARTTIMER	PORTREEVE	SHRUBBERY	TARANTULA	UNREFINED	ABSTAINER	DASHWHEEL
PERAEOPOD	PORTULACA	SIRBONIAN	TARAXACUM	UNRELATED	ABSTINENT	DASTARDLY
PERCALINE	PURCHASER	SORCERESS	TARDINESS	UNRUFFLED	ABSURDITY	DESCARTES
PERCHANCE	PURDONIUM	SORROWFUL	TARGETEER	VARANGIAN	AESCHYLUS	DESECRATE
PERCHERON	PURGATIVE	SORTILEGE	TARMACKED	VARIATION	AESTHETIC	DESERTION
PERCOLATE	PURGATORY	SPRAICKLE	TARNATION	VARICELLA	AMSTERDAM	DESERVING
PERDITION	PURIFYING	SPRAUCHLE	TARPAULIN	VARIEGATE	ANSCHLUSS	DESICCATE
PEREGRINE	PURITANIC	SPREADING	TARRAGONA	VARIOLATE	ANSWERING	DESIGNATE
PERENNIAL	PURPOSELY	SPRECHERY	TARTAREAN	VARIOUSLY	ARSENICAL	DESIGNING
PERFECTLY	PURSUANCE	SPRIGHTLY	TERAHERTZ	VARISCITE	ASSAILANT	DESIPIENT
PERFERVID	PURULENCE	SPRINGALD	TEREBINTH	VERACIOUS	ASSERTING	DESIRABLE
PERFORANS	PYRAMIDAL	SPRINGBOK	TERMAGANT	VERATRINE	ASSERTION	DESPERADO
PERFORATE	PYRETHRUM	SPRINGLET	TERMAGENT	VERBALIZE	ASSERTIVE	DESPERATE
PERFORMED	PYROMANCY	SPRINKLER	TERMINATE	VERBASCUM	ASSIDUITY	DESPOTISM
PERFORMER	PYROMANIA	SPRITEFUL	TERPINEOL	VERBERATE	ASSIDUOUS	DESTITUTE
PERFUMERY	PYRRHONIC	SPRITSAIL	TERRACING	VERBOSITY	ASSISTANT	DESTROYED
PERGAMENE	REREMOUSE	STRAGGLER	TERRARIUM	VERDIGRIS	ASSOCIATE	DESTROYER
PERGUNNAH	RORSCHACH	STRAINING	TERRICOLE	VERIDICAL	ASSONANCE	DESUETUDE
PERIAKTOS	SARBACANE	STRANGELY	TERRIFIED	VERITABLE	ASSUETUDE	DESULTORY
PERIANDER	SARCASTIC	STRANGLER	TERRITORY	VERKAMPTE	ASSURANCE	DISABLING
PERIBOLOS	SARMENTUM	STRANGLES	TERRORISM	VERMIFORM	ASSUREDLY	DISAFFIRM
PERICLASE	SARTORIAL	STRANGURY	TERRORIST	VERMIFUGE	AUSTERITY	DISAPPEAR
PERICUTIN	SARTORIUS	STRAPHANG	TERRORIZE	VERMILION	AUSTRALIA	DISARMING
PERIMETER	SCRAMBLER	STRAPLESS	TERSENESS	VERMINOUS	BASEBOARD	DISBELIEF
PERIMORPH	SCRAPBOOK	STRAPPADO	THRALLDOM	VERNATION	BASECOURT	DISBURDEN
PERIODATE	SCRAPINGS	STRAPPING	THRASHING	VERSATILE	BASHFULLY	DISCARDED
PERIPATUS	SCRAPPING	STRATAGEM	THRASONIC	VERSIFIER	BASICALLY	DISCHARGE
PERIPHERY	SCRATCHED	STRATEGIC	THREADFIN	VERSIONAL	BASILICAL	DISCLOSED
PERISCIAN	SCRATCHES	STREAMING	THREEFOLD	VERTEBRAE	BASILICON	DISCOLOUR
PERISCOPE	SCREENING	STREETAGE	THREESOME	VERTEBRAL	BASKETFUL	DISCOMFIT
PERISHING	SCREWBALL	STREETCAR	THRENETIC	VERTIPORT	BASTINADE	DISCOURSE
PERISTOME	SCREWEDUP	STRENUOUS	THREONINE	VERTUMNUS	BASTINADO	DISCOVERT
PERISTYLE	SCREWPINE	STRESSFUL	THRESHOLD	VIRGINALS	BESPANGLE	DISCOVERY
PERMANENT	SCREWTAPE	STRETCHED	THRIFTILY	VIRGINIAN	BISECTION	DISCREDIT
PERMEABLE	SCRIMMAGE	STRETCHER	THRILLANT	VIRGINITY	BISHOPRIC	DISEMBARK
PERMITTED	SCRIMPING	STRIATION	THRILLING	VIRGINIUM	BOSPHORUS	DISENGAGE
PERPETUAL	SCRIMSHAW	STRICTURE	THROATILY	VIRGULATE	BOSSANOVA	DISENTOMB

DISFAVOUR	FASHIONED	INSULATOR	MUSCADINE	POSTNATAL	TESTICLES	ANTIGONUS
DISFIGURE	FASTENING	INSULTING	MUSCARINE	POSTPONED	TESTIFIER	ANTIHELIX
DISGRACED	FASTTRACK	INSURANCE	MUSCOVADO	POSTULANT	TESTIMONY	ANTINOVEL
DISGUISED	FESTINATE	INSURGENT	MUSCOVITE	POSTULATE	TISIPHONE	ANTIPASTO
DISGUSTED	FESTIVITY	INSWINGER	MUSHINESS	POSTWOMAN	TOSCANINI	ANTIPATHY
DISHCLOTH	FISHERMAN	JESSAMINE	MUSHROOMS	PUSHCHAIR	UNSAVOURY	ANTIPHONY
DISHONEST	FISHGUARD	JESSERANT	MUSICALLY	PUSSYFOOT	UNSCATHED	ANTIPODES
DISHONOUR	FISHPLATE	JOSEPHINE	MUSICHALL	RASKOLNIK	UNSECURED	ANTIQUARY
DISHWATER	FOSSILISE	JOSEPHSON	MUSKETEER	RASPATORY	UNSELFISH	ANTIQUITY
DISINFECT	FOSSORIAL	JUSTIFIED	MUSKETOON	RASPBERRY	UNSETTLED	ANTISERUM
DISLOCATE	FUSILLADE	JUSTINIAN	MUSKOGEAN	RESENTFUL	UNSHACKLE	ANTITOXIC
DISMANTLE	FUSSINESS	KISSINGER	MUSSITATE	RESERPINE	UNSHEATHE	ANTITOXIN
DISMEMBER	FUSTIGATE	KISWAHILI	MUSSOLINI	RESERVIST	UNSIGHTLY	ANTIVENIN
DISMISSAL	FUSTINESS	LASERWORT	MUSSULMAN	RESERVOIR	UNSINNING	ANTONINUS
DISOBLIGE	GASCONADE	LASSITUDE	MUSTINESS	RESHUFFLE	UNSKILLED	ARTEMISIA
DISORIENT	GASHOLDER	LASTDITCH	MYSTERIES	RESIDENCE	UNSPARING	ARTERIOLE
DISPARAGE	GASOMETER	LESTRIGON	MYSTICISM	RESIDENCY	UNSPOILED	ARTHRITIC
DISPARATE	GASPEREAU	LISTENING	NASEBERRY	RESIDUARY	UNSULLIED	ARTHRITIS
DISPARITY	GESSAMINE	LUSTIHOOD	NASHVILLE	RESILIENT	UPSETTING	ARTHROPOD
DISPENSER	GESTATION	LUSTINESS	NASTINESS	RESISTANT	VASECTOMY	ARTHROSIS
DISPERSAL	GOSLARITE	LYSIMETER	NESCIENCE	RESNATRON	VESICULAR	ARTHURIAN
DISPERSED	GOSPELLER	MASCULINE	NOSEBLEED	RESONANCE	VESPASIAN	ARTICHOKE
DISPLACED	GOSSAMERY	MASEFIELD	NOSTALGIA	RESONATOR	VESTIBULE	ARTICULAR
DISPLAYED	GOSSYPINE	MASOCHISM	NOSTALGIC	RESORTING	VESTIGIAL	ARTIFICER
DISPLEASE	GOSSYPIUM	MASOCHIST	NOSTOLOGY	RESOURCES	VESTITURE	ARTILLERY
DISPUTANT	GUSTATION	MASSINGER	NYSTAGMUS	RESPECTED	VESTMENTS	ASTHMATIC
DISREGARD	HASHEMITE	MASSIVELY	OASTHOUSE	RESPECTER	VISAGISTE	ASTOUNDED
DISREPAIR	HASTENING	MASSORETE	OBSCENELY	RESSALDAR	VISCOSITY	ASTRAGALS
DISREPUTE	HASTINESS	MASSYMORE	OBSCENITY	RESTIFORM	VISIONARY	ASTRAKHAN
DISSEMBLE	HESITANCE	MASTERFUL	OBSCURELY	RESTITUTE	VISUALIZE	ASTRODOME
DISSENTER	HESITANCY	MASTERMAN	OBSCURITY	RESTRAINT	WASHBASIN	ASTROLABE
DISSIDENT	HESPERIAN	MASTICATE	OBSECRATE	RESULTANT	WASHBOARD	ASTROLOGY
DISSIPATE	HESSONITE	MESENTERY	OBSEQUIES	RESULTING	WASHCLOTH	ASTRONAUT
DISSOLUTE	HESTERNAL	MESMERISM	OBSERVANT	RESURFACE	WASHERMAN	ASTRONOMY
DISSOLVED	HESYCHASM	MESMERIZE	OBSESSION	RESURGENT	WASHSTAND	ASTROPHEL
DISSONANT	HESYCHAST	MESOBLAST	OBSESSIVE	RESURRECT	WASPISHLY	ASTROTURF
DISTANTLY	HISTAMINE	MESOMORPH	OBSTETRIC	RISKINESS	WASSERMAN	ASTUCIOUS
DISTEMPER	HISTIDINE	MESSALINA	OBSTINACY	ROSCOMMON	WASTELAND	ATTACKING
DISTENDED	HISTOGRAM	MESSENGER	OBSTINATE	ROSEWATER	WASTWATER	ATTAINDER
DISTILLER	HISTOLOGY	MESSIANIC	OESTROGEN	ROSINANTE	WESTBOUND	ATTEMPTED
DISTORTED	HISTORIAN	MISBEHAVE	ONSLAUGHT	ROSMARINE	WESTERNER	ATTENDANT
DISTRAINT	HOSPITIUM	MISCHANCE	OPSIMATHY	ROSMINIAN	WESTWARDS	ATTENTION
DISTURBED	HOSTILITY	MISCREANT	PASSAMENT	ROSTELLUM	WISCONSIN	ATTENTIVE
DISUNITED	HUSBANDLY	MISDIRECT	PASSENGER	RUSHLIGHT	WISECRACK	ATTENUATE
DOSIMETER	HUSBANDRY	MISERABLE	PASSEPIED	RUSTICATE	WISTFULLY	ATTITUDES
DOSSHOUSE	HUSKINESS	MISERABLY	PASSERINE	RUSTINESS	YESTERDAY	ATTRIBUTE
DYSENTERY	HYSTERICS	MISFALLEN	PASSIVELY	SASKATOON	YESTEREVE	ATTRITION
DYSPEPSIA	INSCRIBED	MISFIRING	PASSIVITY	SASQUATCH	ACTUALITY	ATTUITION
DYSPEPTIC	INSELBERG	MISGIVING	PASTERNAK	SASSAFRAS	ACTUARIAL	AUTEURISM
DYSPHAGIA	INSENSATE	MISGUIDED	PASTICCIO	SASSENACH	AFTERCARE	AUTHENTIC
DYSPRAXIA	INSERTION	MISHANDLE	PASTORALE	SASSOLITE	AFTERDAMP	AUTHORESS
DYSTROPHY	INSHALLAH	MISINFORM	PASTURAGE	SISSERARY	AFTERGLOW	AUTHORITY
EASTBOUND	INSIDIOUS	MISLOCATE	PESSIMISM	SISYPHEAN	AFTERMATH	AUTHORIZE
EASTERNER	INSINCERE	MISMANAGE	PESSIMIST	SOSTENUTO	AFTERMOST	AUTOCLAVE
EASTLINGS	INSINUATE	MISOCLERE	PESTICIDE	SUSCITATE	AFTERNOON	AUTOCRACY
EASTWARDS	INSIPIENT	MISONEIST	PESTILENT	SUSPECTED	AFTERWORD	AUTOCROSS
EASYGOING	INSISTENT	MISPICKEL	PISTACHIO	SUSPENDED	AITCHBONE	AUTOGRAPH
ELSEWHERE	INSOLENCE	MISPLACED	PISTAREEN	SUSPENDER	ALTERABLE	AUTOLATRY
ENSCONCED	INSOLUBLE	MISSHAPEN	PISTOLEER	SUSPENSOR	ALTERCATE	AUTOLYCUS
ENSHEATHE	INSOLVENT	MISSIONER	POSSESSED	SUSPICION	ALTERNATE	AUTOLYSIS
ENSORCELL	INSOMNIAC	MISSTROKE	POSSESSOR	SUSTAINED	ALTIMETER	AUTOMAKER
ENSTATITE	INSPECTOR	MISTEMPER	POSSIBLES	TASMANIAN	ALTIPLANO	AUTOMATED
ERSTWHILE	INSPIRING	MISTIGRIS	POSTCARDS	TASSELLED	ALTISSIMO	AUTOMATIC
ESSENTIAL	INSTANTER	MISTINESS	POSTERIOR	TASTELESS	ANTARCTIC	AUTOMATON
EUSKARIAN	INSTANTLY	MISTLETOE	POSTERITY	TESTAMENT	ANTENATAL	AUTONOMIC
EXSICCATE	INSTIGATE	MOSCHATEL	POSTHOUSE	TESTATRIX	ANTHOLOGY	AUTOPILOT
FASCINATE	INSTITUTE	MOSKONFYT	POSTILION	TESTDRIVE	ANTICLINE	AUTOROUTE

AUTOSCOPY	ECTROPION	INTENSITY	MATCHWOOD	ONTOGENCY	PITCHPOLE	TOTALIZER
BATHTOWEL	ENTELECHY	INTENSIVE	MATELASSE	OPTICALLY	PITCHPOLL	TOTAQUINE
BATTALION	ENTERITIS	INTENTION	MATERNITY	OPTOMETRY	PITIFULLY	TOTTENHAM
BATTLEAXE	ENTERTAIN	INTERBRED	MATHURINE	OPTOPHONE	PITUITARY	TUTIORISM
BETHLEHEM	ENTHYMEME	INTERCEDE	MATRIARCH	ORTANIQUE	PITUITRIN	ULTIMATUM
BETROTHAL	ENTOPHYTE	INTERCEPT	MATRICIDE	ORTHODOXY	POTASSIUM	ULTRONEUS
BETROTHED	ENTOURAGE	INTERCITY	MATRIMONY	ORTHOLOGY	POTBOILER	UNTENABLE
BETTERTON	ENTRAMMEL	INTERDICT	MATTAMORE	ORTHOPTER	POTENTATE	UNTIMEOUS
BOTANICAL	ENTRANCED	INTERFACE	MATUTINAL	ORTHOTONE	POTENTIAL	UNTOUCHED
BOTSWANAN	ENTRECHAT	INTERFERE	METABASIS	OSTENSIVE	POTHOLING	UNTRAINED
BOTTLEFUL	ENTRECÔTE	INTERJECT	METABOLIC	OSTEODERM	POTHUNTER	UNTREATED
BUTTERBUR	ENTREMETS	INTERLACE	METALLOID	OSTEOPATH	POTPOURRI	UNTRODDEN
BUTTERCUP	ENTROPION	INTERLARD	METALWORK	OSTRACISE	POTTINGAR	UNTUTORED
BUTTERFLY	ENTROPIUM	INTERLOCK	METAPELET	OSTRACISM	PYTHONESS	UNTYPICAL
BUTTERNUT	ESTABLISH	INTERLOPE	METAPHASE	OSTRACIZE	RATEPAYER	URTICARIA
CATACLYSM	ESTAFETTE	INTERLUDE	METEORITE	OSTROGOTH	RATHERIPE	UTTERANCE
CATACOMBS	ESTAMINET	INTERMENT	METEOROID	OTTERBURN	RATHERISH	UTTERLESS
CATALEPSY	ESTHETICS	INTERNODE	METHADONE	OTTRELITE	RATIONALE	UTTERMOST
CATALOGUE	ESTIMABLE	INTERPLAY	METHEGLIN	OUTERMOST	RATIONING	VITASCOPE
CATALYSIS	ESTRANGED	INTERPOSE	METHODISM	OUTFITTER	RATTLEBAG	VITELLIUS
CATALYTIC	ESTRAPADE	INTERPRET	METHODIST	OUTGOINGS	RETAILING	VITIATION
CATAMARAN	ESTRELDID	INTERRUPT	METHOXIDE	OUTGROWTH	RETAINING	VITRIOLIC
CATAMOUNT	EUTROPHIC	INTERSECT	METRICATE	OUTNUMBER	RETALIATE	VITRUVIAN
CATAPLASM	EXTEMPORE	INTERVENE	METROLAND	OUTOFTOWN	RETENTION	WATCHWORD
CATAPLEXY	EXTENSILE	INTERVIEW	METRONOME	OUTRIGGER	RETENTIVE	WATERBABY
CATARRHAL	EXTENSION	INTESTATE	MITHRAISM	OUTROOPER	RETIARIUS	WATERBUTT
CATATONIA	EXTENSIVE	INTESTINE	MITRAILLE	OUTSIDERS	RETICENCE	WATERFALL
CATATONIC	EXTENUATE	INTRICACY	MOTHBALLS	OUTSKIRTS	RETICULAR	WATERFORD
CATCHCROP	EXTIRPATE	INTRICATE	MOTHEATEN	OUTSPOKEN	RETICULUM	WATERFOWL
CATCHMENT	EXTORTION	INTRIGUED	MOTHERING	OUTSPREAD	RETINITIS	WATERGATE
CATCHPOLE	EXTRACTOR	INTRIGUER	MOTOCROSS	OUTTHRUST	RETORSION	WATERHOLE
CATCHPOLL	EXTRADITE	INTRINSIC	MOTORBIKE	OUTWARDLY	RETORTION	WATERLESS
CATCHWORD	EXTREMELY	INTRODUCE	MOTORBOAT	OUTWORKER	RETRACTOR	WATERLILY
CATECHISM	EXTREMISM	INTROITUS	MOTORCADE	PATCHOULI	RETRIEVAL	WATERLINE
CATECHIZE	EXTREMIST	INTROVERT	MOTORISTS	PATCHOULY	RETRIEVER	WATERMARK
CATERWAUL	EXTREMITY	INTRUSION	MUTILATED	PATCHWORK	RETROCEDE	WATERMILL
CATHARSIS	EXTRICATE	INTRUSIVE	MUTOSCOPE	PATERCOVE	RETROFLEX	WATERSHED
CATHARTIC	EXTRINSIC	INTUITION	MUTTERING	PATERNITY	RETROVERT	WATERSIDE
CATHEDRAL	EXTROVERT	INTUITIVE	MUTUALISM	PATHOGENY	RETURNING	WATERWEED
CATHEPSIN	EXTRUSION	INTUMESCE	MYTHOLOGY	PATHOLOGY	ROTAPLANE	WITCHETTY
CATHERINE	FATIDICAL	JETSTREAM	NATHANIEL	PATHTRAIN	ROTTERDAM	WITHDRAWN
CATSKILLS	FATISCENT	JITTERBUG	NATHELESS	PATIENTLY	ROTUNDATE	WITHERING
CATTLEMAN	FATTENING	KITCHENER	NATHEMORE	PATRIARCH	ROTUNDITY	WITHERITE
CATTLEPEN	FATUOUSLY	KITTENISH	NATROLITE	PATRICIAN	RUTHENIAN	WITHSTAND
COTANGENT	GATECRASH	KITTIWAKE	NATURALLY	PATRICIDE	RUTHENIUM	WITHYWIND
COTHURNUS	GATESHEAD	LATECOMER	NITHSDALE	PATRIMONY	SATELLITE	WITNESSED
COTYLEDON	GATHERING	LATENIGHT	NOTARIKON	PATRIOTIC	SATIATION	WITTICISM
CUTANEOUS	GOTHAMITE	LATERALLY	NOTCHBACK	PATROCLUS	SATINWOOD	WITTINGLY
CUTTHROAT	GUTENBERG	LATESCENT	NOTEPAPER	PATROLMAN	SATIRICAL	WUTHERING
CYTOKININ	GUTTERING	LATHYRISM	NOTOCHORD	PATRONAGE	SATISFIED	YTTERBIUM
DETECTION	HATCHBACK	LATICLAVE	NOTONECTA	PATRONESS	SATURATED	ABUNDANCE
DETECTIVE	HATCHMENT	LATRATION	NOTORIETY	PATRONIZE	SATURNIAN	ACUMINATE
DETENTION	HETERODOX	LATTERDAY	NOTORIOUS	PETAURIST	SATURNINE	ACUTENESS
DETERGENT	HETEROSIS	LETHARGIC	NUTJOBBER	PETERSHAM	SATURNISM	ADULATION
DETERMINE	HITCHCOCK	LETTERBOX	NUTRIMENT	PETHIDINE	SATYRIDAE	ADULTERER
DETERRENT	HITCHHIKE	LETTERING	NUTRITION	PETILLANT	SATYRINAE	ADULTHOOD
DETONATOR	HOTHEADED	LITERALLY	NUTRITIVE	PETRIFIED	SETACEOUS	ADUMBRATE
DETRACTOR	HOTTENTOT	LITHOCYST	OBTAINING	PETROLEUM	SITUATION	AGUECHEEK
DETRIMENT	HUTTERITE	LITHOPONE	OBTRUSION	PETROLOGY	SOTTISIER	ALUMINIUM
DETRITION	ICTERIDAE	LITHUANIA	OBTRUSIVE	PETTICOAT	TETRAGRAM	AMUSEMENT
DITHERING	INTEGRATE	LITIGIOUS	OCTACHORD	PETTINESS	TETRALOGY	AMUSINGLY
DITHYRAMB	INTEGRITY	LITURGICS	OCTAGONAL	PETTITOES	TETRARCHY	AQUAPLANE
DOTHEBOYS	INTELLECT	LUTESCENT	OCTASTICH	PETULANCE	TETTEROUS	AQUARELLE
DUTIFULLY	INTENDANT	MATAGOURI	OCTILLION	PHTHALATE	TITHEBARN	AQUILEGIA
ECTOMORPH	INTENDING	MATCHBOOK	OCTOBRIST	PITCHFORK	TITILLATE	AVUNCULAR
ECTOPLASM	INTENSELY	MATCHLESS	OCTOPLOID	PITCHPINE	TITRATION	BLUEBEARD
ECTOTHERM	INTENSIFY	MATCHLOCK	ONTHESPOT	PITCHPINE	TITTLEBAT	BLUEBERRY

BLUEPRINT	EQUISETUM	LEUCOTOME	SCULPTING	ADVENTIST	LEVERAGED	NEWLYWEDS
BLUESHIFT	EQUITABLE	LEUKAEMIA	SCULPTURE	ADVENTIVE	LEVIATHAN	NEWMARKET
BLUESTONE	EQUITABLY	LJUBLJANA	SCUNCHEON	ADVENTURE	LEVITICUS	NEWSAGENT
BLUFFNESS	EQUIVOCAL	LOUDMOUTH	SCURRIOUR	ADVERBIAL	LIVERPOOL	NEWSFLASH
BLUNDERER	EQUIVOQUE	LOUISIANA	SHUBUNKIN	ADVERSARY	LIVERWORT	NEWSHOUND
BLUNTNESS	ERUCIFORM	LOUSEWORT	SHUFFLING	ADVERSELY	LIVERYMAN	NEWSPAPER
BLUSTERER	ERUDITION	MAULSTICK	SHUTTERED	ADVERSITY	LIVESTOCK	NEWSPRINT
BOULEVARD	EXUBERANT	MAURITIAN	SLUGHORNE	ADVERTISE	LIVRAISON	NEWSSHEET
BOUNDLESS	EXUDATION	MAURITIUS	SLUMBERER	ADVISABLE	MAVOURNIN	NEWSSTALL
BOUNTEOUS	FAULCHION	MAUSOLEUM	SMUGGLING	ADVISEDLY	NAVIGABLE	NEWSSTAND
BOUNTIFUL	FAULTLESS	MOURNIVAL	SOUBRETTE	ADVOCATED	NAVIGATOR	PAWKINESS
BOURGEOIS	FEUDALISM	MOUSEHOLE	SOUFRIERE	ALVEOLATE	NEVERMORE	POWELLITE
BRUMMAGEM	FEUDATORY	MOUSELIKE	SOULFULLY	BEVERIDGE	NOVELETTE	POWERBOAT
BRUNHILDE	FEUILLANT	MOUSETRAP	SOUNDBITE	CAVALCADE	NOVICIATE	POWERLESS
BRUSHWOOD	FLUCTUATE	MOUSTACHE	SOUNDLESS	CAVENDISH	NOVITIATE	REWARDING
BRUSQUELY	FLUORSPAR	MOUTHLESS	SOUNDNESS	CAVERNOUS	NOVOCAINE	REWORKING
BRUTALISM	FLUSTERED	MOUTHWASH	SOURDOUGH	CAVORTING	NOVODAMUS	ROWDINESS
BRUTALITY	FOUNDLING	NAUGHTILY	SOUTENEUR	CEVAPCICI	OBVENTION	TOWCESTER
BRUTALIZE	FOURPENCE	NAUMACHIA	SOUTHDOWN	CIVILISED	OBVIOUSLY	TOWELLING
CAUCASIAN	FOURWHEEL	NAUSEATED	SOUTHEAST	CIVILIZED	RAVISHING	TOWNSFOLK
CAUCASOID	FRUCTIDOR	NEUCHATEL	SOUTHERLY	COVALENCY	REVEALING	UNWATERED
CAUSATION	FRUGALITY	NEURALGIA	SOUTHWARD	COVELLITE	REVELLING	UNWELCOME
CAUTERIZE	FRUITCAKE	NEURALGIC	SOUTHWARK	COVERDALE	REVERENCE	UNWILLING
CHURCHILL	FRUITEEER	NEUROGLIA	SOUTHWEST	COVERTURE	REVERSING	UNWITTING
CHURCHMAN	FRUITLESS	NEUROLOGY	SOUVLAKIA	DAVENPORT	REVERSION	UNWORRIED
CHURIDARS	FRUSTRATE	NEUTRALLY	SOUWESTER	DEVASTATE	REVETMENT	UNWRITTEN
CLUBHOUSE	GAUDEAMUS	OCULIFORM	SPUNCULID	DEVELOPED	REVICTUAL	ANXIOUSLY
CLUSTERED	GAUDINESS	OPULENTLY	SQUADRONE	DEVELOPER	REVOLTING	AUXILIARY
COUCHETTE	GAULEITER	OVULATION	SQUALIDLY	DEVIATION	REVOLVING	AUXOTROPH
COUNSELOR	GAUNTNESS	PAULOWNIA	SQUATTERS	DEVILFISH	REVULSION	BOXWALLAH
COUNTDOWN	GLUCINIUM	PAUSANIAS	SQUEAMISH	DEVILMENT	RIVERSIDE	COXSACKIE
COUNTLESS	GLUCOSIDE	PLUMBEOUS	SQUINANCY	DEVIOUSLY	SAVERNAKE	DEXTERITY
COUNTRIES	GLUTAMINE	PLUMBLINE	SQUINTING	DEVONPORT	SEVENTEEN	DEXTEROUS
COURGETTE	GLUTINOUS	PLUMDAMAS	SQUIREAGE	DIVERGENT	SEVERALLY	DEXTRORSE
COURTELLE	GRUBBINOL	PLUMPNESS	SQUIRMING	DIVERGING	SEVERANCE	DIXIELAND
COURTEOUS	GRUELLING	PLUNDERER	STUMBLING	DIVERSIFY	SOVENANCE	HEXAGONAL
COURTESAN	GRUFFNESS	PLURALISM	STUMPWORK	DIVERSION	SOVEREIGN	HEXAMERON
COURTROOM	GRUMBLING	PLURALITY	STUPEFIED	DIVERSITY	TAVERNERS	HEXAMETER
COURTSHIP	HAUGHTILY	PLUTOCRAT	STUPIDITY	DIVERTING	TAVISTOCK	HEXASTICH
COURTYARD	HAUTMONDE	PLUTONIUM	TAUCHNITZ	DIVIDENDS	TOVARISCH	HEXATEUCH
COUTURIER	HEURISTIC	POUJADIST	TAUTOLOGY	DIVISIBLE	UNVARYING	JUXTAPOSE
CRUCIALLY	HOURGLASS	POULTERER	THUMBLING	EAVESDROP	VIVACIOUS	LUXEMBURG
CRUCIFORM	HOURSTONE	PRUDENTLY	THUMBNAIL	ENVERMEIL	VIVIDNESS	LUXURIANT
CRUDENESS	HOUSEBOAT	PRURIENCE	THUMBTACK	FAVORABLE	WAVELLITE	LUXURIATE
CRUMBLING	HOUSECOAT	RAUCOUSLY	THUNDERER	FAVORABLY	COWARDICE	LUXURIOUS
CRUSTACEA	HOUSEHOLD	ROUGHCAST	TOUCHDOWN	FAVOURITE	DOWELLING	MAXILLARY
DAUNTLESS	HOUSELEEK	ROUGHNECK	TOUCHLINE	GAVELKIND	DOWNGRADE	PIXILATED
DEUCALION	HOUSEMAID	ROUGHNESS	TOUCHWOOD	GOVERNESS	DOWNRIGHT	ROXBURGHE
DEUTERIUM	HOUSEROOM	ROUGHSHOD	TOUGHNESS	GOVERNING	DOWNSTAGE	SAXIFRAGE
DOUBTLESS	HOUSEWIFE	ROUMANIAN	TOURNEDOS	HAVERSACK	DOWNTREND	SAXITOXIN
DOUKHOBOR	HOUSEWORK	ROUMANSCH	TRUCKLOAD	INVECTIVE	DOWNWARDS	SAXOPHONE
DRUGSTORE	HOUYHNHNM	ROUNCEVAL	TRUCULENT	INVENTION	EDWARDIAN	SEXUALITY
DRUMSTICK	IBUPROFEN	ROUNCIVAL	TRUEPENNY	INVENTIVE	GAWKINESS	SIXTEENMO
DRUNKENLY	IGUANODON	ROUNDBACK	TRUMPEDUP	INVENTORY	HAWCUBITE	SIXTEENTH
EBULLIENT	INUMBRATE	ROUNDELAY	TRUMPETER	INVERNESS	HAWKSBILL	TAXIDERMY
EDUCATION	INUNCTION	ROUNDFISH	TRUNCATED	INVERSION	HAWSEHOLE	TAXIMETER
EDUCATIVE	INUSITATE	ROUNDHAND	TRUNCHEON	INVERTASE	HAWTHORNE	TOXIGENIC
ELUCIDATE	JAUNDICED	ROUNDHEAD	TRUNKFISH	INVIDIOUS	HOWTOWDIE	TOXOPHILY
ELUTRIATE	JOUISANCE	ROUNDSMAN	TRUTINATE	INVIOLATE	JAWBATION	VEXATIONS
EMULATION	KRUMMHORN	ROUSSETTE	UNUNUNIUM	INVISIBLE	JEWELLERY	VEXATIOUS
ENUCLEATE	LAUDATION	ROUTINELY	UNUSUALLY	INVOICING	LAWMAKING	VEXILLARY
ENUMERATE	LAUDATORY	SAUCEBOAT	URUGUAYAN	INVOLUCRE	LAWMONGER	ABYSMALLY
ENUNCIATE	LAUGHABLE	SAUCINESS	VOUCHSAFE	IRVINGISM	LAWNMOWER	ACYCLOVIR
EPULATION	LAUNCELOT	SAUCISSON	WHUNSTANE	JOVIALITY	LOWLANDER	AMYGDALUS
EQUALIZER	LAUNCHING	SAUTERNES	YOUNGSTER	JUVENILIA	LOWLIGHTS	ASYMMETRY
EQUIPMENT	LAUNDRESS	SAUVIGNON	ADVANTAGE	LAVOISIER	LOWLINESS	ASYNDETON
EQUIPOISE	LEUCOCYTE	SCUDDALER	ADVECTION	LEVANTINE	NEWCASTLE	ASYNERGIA

BOYFRIEND	RAZORBILL	CATALOGUE	EMBASSADE	IGUANODON	METALWORK	PIRATICAL
CEYLONESE	ROZINANTE	CATALYSIS	EMBASSAGE	IMBALANCE	METAPELET	PLEASANCE
CRYOGENIC	**9:4**	CATALYTIC	EMBATTLED	IMMANACLE	METAPHASE	POTASSIUM
CRYOMETER	ADVANTAGE	CATAMARAN	EMPAESTIC	IMMANENCE	MINACIOUS	PROACTIVE
CRYPTOGAM	AFLATOXIN	CATAMOUNT	EMPANOPLY	IMMANENCY	MIRABELLE	PYRAMIDAL
DAYSPRING	ALBATROSS	CATAPLASM	ENCANTHIS	IMPACTION	MOGADISHU	RAPACIOUS
DRYASDUST	ALLANTOID	CATAPLEXY	ENCAUSTIC	IMPARTIAL	MONACTINE	RECALLING
ERYTHRITE	ALLANTOIS	CATARRHAL	ENGARLAND	IMPASSION	MONASTERY	RECAPTURE
ETYMOLOGY	ALMANDINE	CATATONIA	ENRAPTURE	IMPASSIVE	MONASTRAL	REGARDANT
FLYWEIGHT	AMIANTHUS	CATATONIC	EQUALIZER	IMPATIENT	MONATOMIC	REGARDFUL
GLYCERIDE	ANDANTINO	CAVALCADE	ERGATANER	INCAPABLE	MORATORIA	REGARDING
GLYCERINE	ANNAPOLIS	CEDARWOOD	ESCALATOR	INCARDINE	MORATORIO	RELATIONS
HAYMAKING	ANNAPURNA	CELANDINE	ESPAGNOLE	INCARNATE	MUJAHIDIN	REMAINDER
HAYMARKET	ANTARCTIC	CERATITIS	ESTABLISH	INCAUTION	NABATHEAN	REMAINING
HAYRADDIN	APPALLING	CERATODUS	ESTAFETTE	INFANTILE	NEFANDOUS	RENASCENT
HEYPRESTO	APPARATUS	CEVAPCICI	ESTAMINET	INFATUATE	NEFARIOUS	REPAYABLE
HOYDENISH	APPARITOR	CHEAPJACK	ETHANOATE	INPATIENT	NICARAGUA	REPAYMENT
JAYWALKER	AQUAPLANE	CHEAPNESS	EUDAEMONY	IRRADIANT	NOTARIKON	RETAILING
KEYHOLDER	AQUARELLE	CHEAPSIDE	EXCALIBUR	IRRADIATE	OBTAINING	RETAINING
KEYSTROKE	ARMADILLO	CHLAMYDES	EXCAMBION	IRRAWADDY	OCEANIDES	RETALIATE
MAYFLOWER	ARMAMENTS	CIGARETTE	EXCAVATOR	ISLAMABAD	OCTACHORD	REWARDING
MAYORALTY	ASPARAGUS	CLEANNESS	EXHAUSTED	ISRAELITE	OCTAGONAL	ROCAMBOLE
MOYGASHEL	ASPARTAME	CLEANSING	EXPANSION	JACARANDA	OCTASTICH	ROTAPLANE
OXYGENATE	ASSAILANT	CLEARANCE	EXPANSIVE	JERAHMEEL	OLFACTORY	RUNAROUND
PAYCHEQUE	ATTACKING	CLEARNESS	EXPATIATE	JOHANNINE	ORGANELLE	SAGACIOUS
PAYMASTER	ATTAINDER	CLEARWING	FABACEOUS	KARABINER	ORGANICAL	SAGAPENUM
PHYCOLOGY	AUDACIOUS	CLOAKROOM	FALANGIST	KARAKORAM	ORGANISED	SALACIOUS
PHYLLOPOD	BAGATELLE	CORALLINE	FAMAGUSTA	KERATITIS	ORGANISER	SALANGANE
PHYLOGENY	BALACLAVA	COTANGENT	FANATICAL	LAFAYETTE	ORGANIZED	SAMARITAN
PHYSICIAN	BALALAIKA	COVALENCY	FARANDOLE	LAMARTINE	ORGANIZER	SCIAMACHY
PHYSICIST	BARAGOUIN	COWARDICE	FERACIOUS	LAMASERAI	ORGANZINE	SCIARIDAE
PHYTOLITE	BEHAVIOUR	CUTANEOUS	FINANCIAL	LAZARETTO	ORMANDINE	SCLAUNDER
PHYTOTRON	BELATEDLY	DAMASCENE	FINANCIER	LECANORAM	ORTANIQUE	SCRAMBLER
PRYTANEUM	BILATERAL	DEBATABLE	FOMALHAUT	LEVANTINE	PALAESTRA	SCRAPBOOK
PSYCHICAL	BIPARTITE	DEBAUCHED	FORASMUCH	LOCALIZED	PALAFITTE	SCRAPINGS
PSYCHOSIS	BIZARRELY	DEBAUCHEE	FUGACIOUS	LOGARITHM	PALAMPORE	SCRAPPING
PSYCHOTIC	BLEACHERS	DECACHORD	FURACIOUS	LUBAVITCH	PALANKEEN	SCRATCHED
REYKJAVIK	BLOATWARE	DECADENCE	GABARDINE	MACADAMIA	PALANQUIN	SCRATCHES
RHYMESTER	BONAPARTE	DECALITRE	GALACTOSE	MACARONIC	PALATABLE	SEBACEOUS
SCYTHEMAN	BOTANICAL	DECALOGUE	GALANTINE	MACARTHUR	PANATELLA	SEBASTIAN
SKYJACKER	BREADLINE	DECAMERON	GALAPAGOS	MADARIAGA	PAPARAZZI	SECATEURS
STYLISHLY	BREAKABLE	DECASTYLE	GALATIANS	MADAROSIS	PAPARAZZO	SELACHION
STYLISTIC	BREAKAGES	DECATHLON	GIGAHERTZ	MAHARAJAH	PARABASIS	SEMANTEME
STYLOBATE	BREAKAWAY	DEFALCATE	GIGANTISM	MAHARANEE	PARABLAST	SEMANTICS
TAYASSUID	BREAKDOWN	DEFAULTER	GIRANDOLE	MAHARISHI	PARABOLIC	SEMANTIDE
THYESTEAN	BREAKEVEN	DELACROIX	GLEANINGS	MALACHITE	PARACHUTE	SEMANTRON
THYLACINE	BREAKFAST	DEMAGOGUE	GREASEGUN	MALATHION	PARACLETE	SEMAPHORE
THYRATRON	BREAKNECK	DEMANDING	GREATCOAT	MALAYSIAN	PARACUSIS	SEPARABLE
THYRISTOR	BREATHING	DEMARCATE	GREATNESS	MARAUDING	PARAGOGUE	SEPARATED
THYROXINE	BROADCAST	DEPARTURE	GUJARATHI	MATAGOURI	PARAGRAPH	SEPARATOR
TRYPHOEUS	BROADLOOM	DEPASTURE	HAMADRYAD	MEDALLION	PARALYSIS	SERAPHINE
WAYZGOOSE	BROADSIDE	DEVASTATE	HAZARDOUS	MEDALLIST	PARALYTIC	SERASKIER
BIZARRELY	BYZANTINE	DIDACTICS	HEPATICAL	MEGACYCLE	PARAMEDIC	SETACEOUS
BYZANTINE	CABALLERO	DIGASTRIC	HEPATITIS	MEGAHERTZ	PARAMETER	SHEARLING
DIZYGOTIC	CADASTRAL	DISABLING	HEXAGONAL	MEGAPHONE	PARAMOUNT	SKIAMACHY
DIZZINESS	CALABOOSE	DISAFFIRM	HEXAMERON	MEGASCOPE	PARANOIAC	SOMASCOPE
FUZZINESS	CALABRESE	DISAPPEAR	HEXAMETER	MEGASPORE	PARANYMPH	SPEAKEASY
GAZETTEER	CANALETTO	DISARMING	HEXASTICH	MELAMPODE	PARASCENE	SPEARHEAD
HAZARDOUS	CANAVERAL	DONATELLO	HEXATEUCH	MELANESIA	PARASCEVE	SPEARMINT
HAZELWORT	CAPACIOUS	DREAMLAND	HIJACKING	MELANOSIS	PARASITIC	SPEARSIDE
LAZARETTO	CAPACITOR	DREAMLESS	HILARIOUS	MELANOTIC	PARATAXIS	SPEARWORT
LAZYBONES	CAPARISON	DRYASDUST	HIMALAYAN	MENADIONE	PARATHION	SPHACELUS
LAZZARONE	CARACALLA	DYNAMITED	HIMALAYAS	MENAGERIE	PARATROOP	SPLAYFOOT
MEZZANINE	CARAMBOLA	ECLAMPSIA	HUMANKIND	MEPACRINE	PEDAGOGUE	SPRAICKLE
MEZZOTINT	CATACLYSM	EDWARDIAN	HUMANMADE	METABASIS	PERAEOPOD	SPRAUCHLE
MUZZINESS	CATACOMBS	EGLANTINE	HYPALLAGE	METABOLIC	PETAURIST	SQUADRONE
PIZZICATO	CATALEPSY	EMBARRASS	IDEALOGUE	METALLOID	PILASTERS	SQUALIDLY

SQUATTERS	VICARIOUS	EYEBRIGHT	SYMBIOSIS	BUCCANEER	DISCREDIT	KITCHENER
STEADFAST	VIPASSANA	FLABELLUM	SYMBIOTIC	CALCANEUM	DONCASTER	KNACKERED
STEAMBOAT	VISAGISTE	FORBIDDEN	SYMBOLISM	CALCANEUS	DRACONIAN	KNOCKDOWN
STEAMSHIP	VITASCOPE	FROBISHER	SYMBOLIST	CALCINATE	DULCINIST	LACCOLITE
STRAGGLER	VIVACIOUS	GIBBERISH	SYMBOLIZE	CALCULATE	EDUCATION	LANCASTER
STRAINING	VOLAGEOUS	GLABELLAR	TABBOULEH	CAMCORDER	EDUCATIVE	LANCEWOOD
STRANGELY	VOLATILE	GRUBBINOL	TOMBSTONE	CANCEROUS	EJACULATE	LANCINATE
STRANGLER	VORACIOUS	HAMBURGER	TONBRIDGE	CARCINOMA	ELECTORAL	LEICESTER
STRANGLES	WAHABIITE	HARBINGER	TORBANITE	CATCHCROP	ELECTRESS	LEUCOCYTE
STRANGURY	WHEATGERM	HERBALIST	TREBIZOND	CATCHMENT	ELECTRIFY	LEUCOTOME
STRAPHANG	WHEATMEAL	HERBARIUM	TREBUCHET	CATCHPOLE	ELECTRODE	LUNCHTIME
STRAPLESS	WOMANHOOD	HERBICIDE	TRIBALISM	CATCHPOLL	ELECTUARY	MACCABEES
STRAPPADO	WOMANISER	HERBIVORE	TRIBESMAN	CATCHWORD	ELOCUTION	MARCASITE
STRAPPING	WOMANIZER	HERBORIST	TRIBESMEN	CAUCASIAN	ELUCIDATE	MARCHPANE
STRATAGEM	WOMANKIND	HOBBINOLL	TRIBOLOGY	CAUCASOID	EMACIATED	MASCULINE
STRATEGIC	WREAKLESS	HUSBANDLY	TRIBUNATE	CHECKBOOK	ENACTMENT	MATCHBOOK
SUBALTERN	ALABASTER	HUSBANDRY	TRIBUTARY	CHECKLIST	ENSCONCED	MATCHLESS
SUGARCANE	ANABOLISM	INABILITY	TUBBINESS	CHECKMATE	ENUCLEATE	MATCHLOCK
SWEATBAND	ANABRANCH	INEBRIATE	TURBIDITY	CHECKROOM	EPICEDIUM	MATCHWOOD
SYBARITIC	ARABESQUE	JAMBALAYA	TURBINATE	CHICANERY	EPICENTRE	MERCAPTAN
SYNAGOGUE	ARABICIZE	JAWBATION	TURBOPROP	CHICKADEE	EPICLESIS	MERCENARY
SYNANGIUM	ARABINOSE	KERBSTONE	TURBULENT	CHICKWEED	EPICUREAN	MERCERIZE
TABANIDAE	BAMBOOZLE	KNOBSTICK	UNABASHED	CHOCOLATE	EPICYCLIC	MERCILESS
TABASHEER	BARBARIAN	LAMBSWOOL	VERBALIZE	CIRCADIAN	ERUCIFORM	MERCURIAL
TACAMAHAC	BARBARISM	LIABILITY	VERBASCUM	CIRCINATE	EVOCATION	MINCEMEAT
TARANTASS	BARBARITY	LIMBURGER	VERBERATE	CIRCULATE	EVOCATIVE	MISCHANCE
TARANTULA	BARBARIZE	LJUBLJANA	VERBOSITY	CLOCKWISE	EVOCATORY	MISCREANT
TARAXACUM	BARBAROUS	LOMBARDIC	VIABILITY	CLOCKWORK	EXACTMENT	MOCCASINS
TAYASSUID	BARBITONE	LUMBERING	WAMBENGER	COACHLOAD	EXACTNESS	MOSCHATEL
TENACIOUS	BARBOTINE	LUMBRICUS	WIMBLEDON	COLCHICUM	EXECRABLE	MUMCHANCE
TENACULUM	BENBECULA	MELBOURNE	WOBBEGONG	CONCAVITY	EXECRABLY	MUSCADINE
TENAILLON	BOMBARDON	MISBEHAVE	WOEBEGONE	CONCEALED	EXECUTANT	MUSCARINE
TERAHERTZ	BOMBASINE	MORBIDITY	ABSCONDER	CONCEITED	EXECUTION	MUSCOVADO
THRALLDOM	BOMBASTIC	NEBBISHER	ACYCLOVIR	CONCERNED	EXECUTIVE	MUSCOVITE
THRASHING	BOMBSHELL	NIEBELUNG	AESCHYLUS	CONCERTED	EXECUTRIX	NARCISSUS
THRASONIC	BOOBIALLA	NUMBSKULL	AIRCOOLED	CONCIERGE	FASCINATE	NESCIENCE
TOTALIZER	BOOBYTRAP	OPOBALSAM	AITCHBONE	CONCISELY	FENCIBLES	NEUCHATEL
TOTAQUINE	BUBBLEGUM	OROBANCHE	ALICYCLIC	CONCISION	FLECHETTE	NEWCASTLE
TOVARISCH	BUMBLEBEE	PARBUCKLE	ANECDOTAL	CONCLUDED	FLUCTUATE	NICCOLITE
TREACHERY	CAMBODIAN	PORBEAGLE	ANECDOTES	CONCORDAT	FORCEMEAT	NICCHEESE
TREADMILL	CAMBRIDGE	POTBOILER	ANSCHLUSS	CONCOURSE	FRACTIOUS	NOTCHBACK
TREASURER	CAMBUSCAN	PREBENDAL	APOCRYPHA	CONCUBINE	FRICASSEE	NUNCUPATE
TREATMENT	CARBAMATE	PROBABLES	ARACHNOID	CONCUSSED	FRUCTIDOR	OBSCENELY
TRIANGLED	CARBAMIDE	PROBATION	AVOCATION	COUCHETTE	GASCONADE	OBSCENITY
TRIATHLON	CARBONADE	PROBOSCIS	BARCELONA	CRACKDOWN	GLUCINIUM	OBSCURELY
TYRANNIZE	CARBONADO	REDBREAST	BEACHHEAD	CRACKLING	GLUCOSIDE	OBSCURITY
TYRANNOUS	CARBONARI	REMBRANDT	BEACHWEAR	CRACKSMAN	GLYCERIDE	OFFCHANCE
UKRAINIAN	CARBONATE	RIBBONISM	BENCHMARK	CRACOVIAN	GLYCERINE	OFFCOLOUR
UNBALANCE	CARBONIZE	ROXBURGHE	BLACKBALL	CRICKETER	GRACELESS	OLECRANON
UNDAMAGED	CARBUNCLE	RUBBERIZE	BLACKBIRD	CROCKFORD	GROCERIES	ORICALCHE
UNDAUNTED	CHABAZITE	RUDBECKIA	BLACKBUCK	CROCODILE	GUACAMOLE	OZOCERITE
UNEARTHLY	CLUBHOUSE	SABBATIAN	BLACKDAMP	CRUCIALLY	GUNCOTTON	PANCHAYAT
UNEATABLE	COMBATANT	SARBACANE	BLACKFACE	CRUCIFORM	HAECCEITY	PARCHEESI
UNFAILING	COMBATIVE	SCABLANDS	BLACKFOOT	CUNCTATOR	HATCHBACK	PARCHMENT
UNHAPPILY	CRIBELLUM	SEABOTTLE	BLACKHEAD	DEACONESS	HATCHMENT	PATCHOULI
UNMARRIED	CUBBYHOLE	SEMBLANCE	BLACKJACK	DESCARTES	HAWCUBITE	PATCHOULY
UNMATCHED	CYMBELINE	SERBONIAN	BLACKLEAD	DEUCALION	HERCULEAN	PATCHWORK
UNNATURAL	CYMBIDIUM	SHUBUNKIN	BLACKLIST	DIACRITIC	HITCHCOCK	PAYCHEQUE
UNSAVOURY	DAMBUSTER	SIRBONIAN	BLACKMAIL	DIOCLETES	HITCHHIKE	PEACEABLE
UNVARYING	DIABLERIE	SLABSTONE	BLACKMORE	DISCARDED	HOCCAMORE	PEACEABLY
UNWATERED	DISBELIEF	SOUBRETTE	BLACKNESS	DISCHARGE	HUNCHBACK	PEACETIME
VARANGIAN	DISBURDEN	STABILITY	BLACKWOOD	DISCLOSED	INOCULATE	PERCALINE
VELASQUEZ	DOUBTLESS	STABILIZE	BLOCKHEAD	DISCOLOUR	INSCRIBED	PERCHANCE
VERACIOUS	DUMBARTON	STABLEBOY	BOCCACCIO	DISCOMFIT	ISOCLINAL	PERCHERON
VERATRINE	DUMBFOUND	STABLELAD	BRACTEOLE	DISCOURSE	ISOCRATES	PERCOLATE
VEXATIONS	ELABORATE	STABLEMAN	BRICKWORK	DISCOVERT	JOBCENTRE	PHACOLITE
VEXATIOUS	EXUBERANT	SUNBATHER	BRICKYARD	DISCOVERY	JUICINESS	PHYCOLOGY

PIACEVOLE	SARCASTIC	TRICKSTER	CONDIMENT	HANDCUFFS	MIDDLEMAN	SANDALLED
PIECEMEAL	SAUCEBOAT	TRICLINIC	CONDITION	HANDINESS	MIDDLESEX	SANDARACH
PIECEWORK	SAUCINESS	TRICOLOUR	CONDUCIVE	HANDIWORK	MIDDLETON	SANDHURST
PINCHBECK	SAUCISSON	TRICUSPID	CONDUCTOR	HANDPIECE	MIDDLINGS	SANDPAPER
PINCHCOCK	SHECHINAH	TROCHILIC	CONDUCTUS	HANDSHAKE	MISDIRECT	SANDPIPER
PITCHFORK	SHECHITAH	TROCHILUS	CONDYLOMA	HANDSPIKE	MOODINESS	SANDSTONE
PITCHPINE	SICCATIVE	TRUCKLOAD	CORDIALLY	HANDSTAND	MRIDAMGAM	SANDSTORM
PITCHPOLE	SINCERELY	TRUCULENT	CORDUROYS	HARDANGER	MRIDANGAM	SCUDDALER
PITCHPOLL	SINCERITY	TURCOPOLE	CORDYLINE	HARDBOARD	MUDDINESS	SHADINESS
PLACATORY	SLACKNESS	UNSCATHED	CREDULITY	HARDCOVER	MUNDUNGUS	SKEDADDLE
PLACEMENT	SORCERESS	URICONIAN	CREDULOUS	HARDIHOOD	MURDERESS	SOLDERING
PLACIDITY	SPACELESS	UTICENSIS	CRUDENESS	HARDINESS	MURDEROUS	SOLDIERLY
PORCELAIN	SPACESHIP	VACCINATE	DAEDALIAN	HARDLINER	NEODYMIUM	SPADASSIN
PORCUPINE	SPACESUIT	VANCOUVER	DANDELION	HARDSHELL	NIDDERING	SPIDERWEB
PRACTICAL	SPECIALLY	VISCOSITY	DANDIFIED	HEADBOARD	OBEDIENCE	SPODUMENE
PRACTISED	SPECIALTY	VOICELESS	DANDYPRAT	HEADCLOTH	OPODELDOC	SUBDIVIDE
PRACTOLOL	SPECIFICS	VOLCANISM	DEADLIGHT	HEADDRESS	OXIDATION	SUBDOLOUS
PRECATORY	SPECIFIED	VOUCHSAFE	DEODORANT	HEADFIRST	PANDATION	SUNDOWNER
PRECEDENT	SPECIMENS	VULCANIAN	DEODORIZE	HEADINESS	PANDEMIAN	SWADDLING
PRECEDING	SPECTACLE	VULCANIST	DODDIPOLL	HEADLIGHT	PANDURATE	SYNDICATE
PRECENTOR	SPECTATOR	VULCANITE	DOODLEBUG	HEADLINED	PARDALOTE	TAPDANCER
PRECEPTOR	SPECULATE	VULCANIZE	DUNDREARY	HEADPIECE	PENDENNIS	TARDINESS
PRECIEUSE	SPICILEGE	WANCHANCY	DUODECIMO	HEADSCARF	PENDLETON	TENDERIZE
PRECINCTS	SPICINESS	WATCHWORD	EALDORMAN	HEADSTALL	PENDRAGON	TOADSTONE
PRECIPICE	STOCKFISH	WELCOMING	EPEDAPHIC	HEADSTONE	PENDULATE	TOADSTOOL
PRECISELY	STOCKHOLM	WENCESLAS	EPIDERMIS	HENDIADYS	PENDULOUS	TOPDRAWER
PRECISIAN	STOCKINET	WHICHEVER	ERADICATE	HINDBRAIN	PERDITION	TRADEMARK
PRECISION	STOCKINGS	WINCANTON	ERUDITION	HINDEMITH	PONDEROSA	TRADESMAN
PRECISIVE	STOCKPILE	WINCOPIPE	EVIDENTLY	HINDRANCE	PONDEROUS	TRADEWIND
PRECOCITY	STOCKROOM	WISCONSIN	EXODERMIS	HINDSIGHT	PREDATORY	TRADITION
PRECONISE	STOCKWORK	WITCHETTY	EXUDATION	HOLDERBAT	PREDICANT	TREDRILLE
PRECURSOR	STOCKYARD	WORCESTER	FALDSTOOL	HORDEOLUM	PREDICATE	TRIDYMITE
PRICELESS	SUBCELLAR	WRECKFISH	FANDANGLE	HOYDENISH	PREDICTOR	UNADOPTED
PROCACITY	SUBCORTEX	ZIRCONIUM	FEEDSTUFF	HUMDINGER	PREDIKANT	UREDINIAL
PROCEDURE	SUCCEEDED	ZUCCHETTO	FERDINAND	HUNDREDTH	PREDILECT	VALDENSES
PROCERITY	SUCCENTOR	ACADEMIST	FEUDALISM	ISODORIAN	PRODROMAL	VANDALISM
PROCESSOR	SUCCESSOR	ACIDULATE	FEUDATORY	JORDANIAN	PRODROMUS	VANDALIZE
PROCLITIC	SUCCINATE	ACIDULOUS	FLEDGLING	KILDERKIN	PRUDENTLY	VELDSKOEN
PROCOELUS	SUCCOTASH	AMIDSHIPS	FOODSTORE	LANDAULET	PURDONIUM	VERDIGRIS
PROCONSUL	SUCCUBINE	BALDAQUIN	FOODSTUFF	LANDDROST	QUADRATIC	VINDICATE
PROCREATE	SUCCULENT	BANDALORE	FREDERICK	LANDGRAVE	QUADRATUS	VOODOOISM
PSYCHICAL	SUCCURSAL	BANDICOOT	FUNDAMENT	LANDLOPER	QUADRILLE	WALDENSES
PSYCHOSIS	SURCHARGE	BANDOLEER	GALDRAGON	LANDOWNER	QUADRUPED	WALDFLUTE
PSYCHOTIC	SURCINGLE	BANDOLERO	GARDENING	LANDSCAPE	QUADRUPLE	WALDGRAVE
PUNCHLINE	SUSCITATE	BANDOLIER	GARDEROBE	LANDSLIDE	QUODLIBET	WANDERING
PUNCTILIO	SYNCHYSIS	BANDOLINE	GAUDEAMUS	LANDSMAAL	RADDLEMAN	WELDSTADT
PUNCTUATE	SYNCOMIUM	BANDSTAND	GAUDINESS	LANDSTURM	RANDINESS	WHODUNNIT
PURCHASER	SYNCOPATE	BANDWAGON	GEODESIST	LANDWARDS	READDRESS	WILDGEESE
QUICKLIME	TAUCHNITZ	BIRDBRAIN	GIDDINESS	LAODICEAN	READINESS	WINDBREAK
QUICKNESS	TEACHABLE	BIRDTABLE	GLADIATOR	LAUDATION	READYEARN	WINDCHILL
QUICKSAND	THACKERAY	BONDSTONE	GLADIOLUS	LAUDATORY	READYMADE	WINDFALLS
QUICKSTEP	THECODONT	BORDEREAU	GLADSTONE	LINDBERGH	REDDENDUM	WINDHOVER
RACCABOUT	THICKHEAD	BORDERING	GODDESSES	LOADSTONE	REEDINESS	WINDSCALE
RACCAHOUT	THICKNESS	BRADLAUGH	GOLDCREST	LONDONESE	RENDERING	WINDSWEPT
RADCLIFFE	TOCCATINA	BRIDEWELL	GOLDFIELD	LOUDMOUTH	RENDITION	WONDERFUL
RANCIDITY	TOSCANINI	BRIDLEWAY	GOLDFINCH	MACDONALD	RHODESIAN	WOODBORER
RANCOROUS	TOUCHDOWN	BUNDESTAG	GOLDSINNY	MADDENING	RHODOLITE	WOODCHUCK
RAUCOUSLY	TOUCHLINE	CALDARIUM	GOLDSMITH	MAGDALENE	RHODOPSIN	WOODCRAFT
REACHABLE	TOUCHWOOD	CANDIDACY	GONDOLIER	MAGDEBURG	ROADBLOCK	WOODENTOP
REACTANCE	TOWCESTER	CANDIDATE	GOODNIGHT	MANDATARY	ROADHOUSE	WOODHOUSE
REICHSRAT	TRACEABLE	CANDLELIT	GRADATION	MANDATORY	ROADSTEAD	WOODLANDS
REICHSTAG	TRACHINUS	CANDLEMAS	GRADGRIND	MANDICATE	ROADWORKS	WOODLOUSE
RENCONTRE	TRACKLESS	CANDYTUFT	GRADUALLY	MANDOLINE	ROWDINESS	WOODSHOCK
ROSCOMMON	TRACKSUIT	CARDBOARD	GRADUATED	MANDUCATE	RUDDIGORE	WORDINESS
RUNCINATE	TRACTABLE	COADJUTOR	GUIDEBOOK	MENDACITY	RUDDLEMAN	WORDSMITH
SACCHARIN	TRICERION	CONDEMNED	GUIDELINE	MENDELISM	SADDENING	YARDSTICK
SANCTUARY	TRICKLESS	CONDENSER	HANDBRAKE	MENDICANT	SADDLEBAG	YGGDRASIL

ACCENTUAL	ASSERTIVE	COVERTURE	EGREGIOUS	FOREFRONT	HOMEBOUND	INTENSIVE
ACCESSION	ATHEISTIC	CUNEIFORM	EGRESSION	FOREGOING	HOMEGROWN	INTENTION
ACCESSORY	ATHELSTAN	CURETTAGE	EIDERDOWN	FOREIGNER	HOMEOPATH	INTERBRED
ADDERWORT	ATHENAEUM	CYNEGETIC	ELAEOLITE	FORESHORE	HOMEOWNER	INTERCEDE
ADHERENCE	ATTEMPTED	DAREDEVIL	ELLESMERE	FORESIGHT	HOMESTEAD	INTERCEPT
ADJECTIVE	ATTENDANT	DAVENPORT	ELSEWHERE	FORESPEAK	HOMEWARDS	INTERCITY
ADRENALIN	ATTENTION	DEBENTURE	EMBELLISH	FORESPEND	HONEYCOMB	INTERDICT
ADVECTION	ATTENTIVE	DECEITFUL	EMBEZZLER	FORESTAGE	HONEYMOON	INTERFACE
ADVENTIST	ATTENUATE	DECEMVIRI	EMMERDALE	FORESTALL	HOPEFULLY	INTERFERE
ADVENTIVE	AUBERGINE	DECENNIAL	EMPENNAGE	FORESTERS	HOREHOUND	INTERJECT
ADVENTURE	AUTEURISM	DECEPTION	ENCELADUS	FORETASTE	HYPERBOLA	INTERLACE
ADVERBIAL	AYLESBURY	DECEPTIVE	ENDEARING	FOREWOMAN	HYPERBOLE	INTERLARD
ADVERSARY	BAKEHOUSE	DECESSION	ENDEAVOUR	FREEBOARD	HYPERLINK	INTERLOCK
ADVERSELY	BALEFULLY	DEFEATISM	ENDECAGON	FREELANCE	HYPEROPIA	INTERLOPE
ADVERSITY	BANEBERRY	DEFEATIST	ENDEICTIC	FREEMASON	ICTERIDAE	INTERLUDE
ADVERTISE	BAREBONES	DEFECTION	ENNERDALE	FREEPHONE	IGNESCENT	INTERMENT
AFFECTING	BAREFACED	DEFECTIVE	ENTELECHY	FREESTONE	ILLEGALLY	INTERNODE
AFFECTION	BASEBOARD	DEFENDANT	ENTERITIS	FREESTYLE	ILLEGIBLE	INTERPLAY
AFTERCARE	BASECOURT	DEFENDERS	ENTERTAIN	FREEWHEEL	ILLEGIBLY	INTERPOSE
AFTERDAMP	BELEAGUER	DEFENSIVE	ENVERMEIL	FRIESLAND	IMMEDIACY	INTERPRET
AFTERGLOW	BEVERIDGE	DEFERENCE	EPHEDRINE	GABERDINE	IMMEDIATE	INTERRUPT
AFTERMATH	BISECTION	DEFERMENT	EPHEMERAL	GALENGALE	IMMELMANN	INTERSECT
AFTERMOST	BLUEBEARD	DEJECTION	EPHEMERIS	GATECRASH	IMMENSELY	INTERVENE
AFTERNOON	BLUEBERRY	DEMEANING	EPHEMERON	GATESHEAD	IMMENSITY	INTERVIEW
AFTERWORD	BLUEPRINT	DEMEANOUR	EPHESIANS	GAVELKIND	IMMERSION	INTESTATE
AGREEABLE	BLUESHIFT	DEMETRIUS	ESMERALDA	GAZETTEER	IMPEACHER	INTESTINE
AGREEABLY	BLUESTONE	DEPENDANT	ESPERANCE	GENEALOGY	IMPEDANCE	INVECTIVE
AGREEMENT	BOLECTION	DEPENDENT	ESPERANTO	GENERALLY	IMPELLING	INVENTION
AGUECHEEK	BREECHING	DEPENDING	ESSENTIAL	GENERATOR	IMPENDING	INVENTIVE
ALBERTINE	BRIEFCASE	DESECRATE	ETCETERAS	GENETICAL	IMPERATOR	INVENTORY
ALDEBARAN	BRIEFNESS	DESERTION	ETHELBERT	GENEVIEVE	IMPERFECT	INVERNESS
ALGEBRAIC	BUCENTAUR	DESERVING	ETHEREOUS	GIBEONITE	IMPERIOUS	INVERSION
ALLEGEDLY	CAFETERIA	DETECTION	EUHEMERUS	GLEEFULLY	IMPETUOUS	INVERTASE
ALLEGIANT	CAFETIERE	DETECTIVE	EUMENIDES	GOBETWEEN	INCENTIVE	IRREGULAR
ALLEMANDE	CAKESTAND	DETENTION	EXCELLENT	GOVERNESS	INCEPTION	JEWELLERY
ALLEVIATE	CALEDONIA	DETERGENT	EXCELSIOR	GOVERNING	INCEPTIVE	JOBERNOWL
ALPENGLOW	CALEMBOUR	DETERMINE	EXCEPTION	GREENAWAY	INCESSANT	JOSEPHINE
ALPENHORN	CALENDULA	DETERRENT	EXCESSIVE	GREENBACK	INDECENCY	JOSEPHSON
ALTERABLE	CALENTURE	DEVELOPED	EXPECTANT	GREENFEED	INDECORUM	JUNEBERRY
ALTERCATE	CAMEMBERT	DEVELOPER	EXPECTING	GREENGAGE	INDELIBLE	JUVENILIA
ALTERNATE	CAMERAMAN	DIAERESIS	EXPEDIENT	GREENHEAD	INDELIBLY	KABELJOUW
ALVEOLATE	CAREERIST	DIGESTION	EXPENSIVE	GREENHORN	INDEMNIFY	KNEECORDS
AMBERGRIS	CAREFULLY	DIGESTIVE	EXPERTISE	GREENMAIL	INDEMNITY	LACERATED
AMPERSAND	CARETAKER	DIMENSION	EXTEMPORE	GREENROOM	INDENTURE	LAKEFRONT
ANAEROBIC	CATECHISM	DIRECTION	EXTENSILE	GREENSAND	INFECTING	LASERWORT
ANCESTRAL	CATECHIZE	DIRECTIVE	EXTENSION	GREENWEED	INFECTION	LATECOMER
ANGELFISH	CATERWAUL	DIRECTORS	EXTENSIVE	GREENWICH	INFERENCE	LATENIGHT
ANTENATAL	CAVENDISH	DIRECTORY	EXTENUATE	GREENWOOD	INFERTILE	LATERALLY
APHERESIS	CAVERNOUS	DISEMBARK	FACECLOTH	GREENYARD	INGENIOUS	LATESCENT
APOENZYME	CELEBRANT	DISENGAGE	FACETIOUS	GREETINGS	INGENUITY	LEGENDARY
APPEALING	CELEBRATE	DISENTOMB	FALERNIAN	GRIEVANCE	INGENUOUS	LEVERAGED
APPENDAGE	CELEBRITY	DIVERGENT	FIREBRAND	GRUELLING	INGESTION	LIBELLOUS
APPERTAIN	CELESTIAL	DIVERGING	FIREBREAK	GUTENBERG	INHERITED	LIBERALLY
APPETIZER	CEREBRATE	DIVERSIFY	FIREDRAKE	HABERDINE	INHERITOR	LIBERATED
ARGENTINA	CERECLOTH	DIVERSION	FIREGUARD	HABERGEON	INJECTION	LIBERATOR
ARGENTINE	CHEEKBONE	DIVERSITY	FIRELIGHT	HARESTANE	INNERMOST	LIBERTIES
ARRESTING	CHEERLESS	DIVERTING	FIREPLACE	HAVERSACK	INSELBERG	LIBERTINE
ARSENICAL	CHIEFTAIN	DOLEFULLY	FIREPROOF	HAZELWORT	INSENSATE	LIFEGUARD
ARTEMISIA	CINEMATIC	DOWELLING	FIRESTONE	HEDERATED	INSERTION	LIFESTYLE
ARTERIOLE	CINEPHILE	DYSENTERY	FIREWATER	HEREAFTER	INTEGRATE	LIMEHOUSE
ASCENDANT	CINERARIA	EAGERNESS	FIREWORKS	HERETICAL	INTEGRITY	LIMELIGHT
ASCENDING	CINEREOUS	EAVESDROP	FLEETWOOD	HETERODOX	INTELLECT	LIMESTONE
ASCENSION	CLIENTELE	ECCENTRIC	FOREANENT	HETEROSIS	INTENDANT	LINEAMENT
ASCERTAIN	COHERENCE	ECHEVERIA	FOREBEARS	HIBERNATE	INTENDING	LINEOLATE
ASPERSION	COLERIDGE	EDGEWORTH	FOREBRAIN	HIBERNIAN	INTENSELY	LITERALLY
ASSERTING	COVELLITE	EFFECTIVE	FORECLOSE	HIDEBOUND	INTENSIFY	LIVERPOOL
ASSERTION	COVERDALE	EFFECTUAL	FORECOURT	HIDEOUSLY	INTENSITY	LIVERWORT

LIVERYMAN	OBVENTION	RECEIVING	SENESCENT	SUPERSTAR	UNDERHAND	WATERLESS
LIVESTOCK	OFFENBACH	RECEPTION	SENESCHAL	SUPERVENE	UNDERHUNG	WATERLILY
LOCELLATE	OFFENDING	RECEPTIVE	SERENADER	SUPERVISE	UNDERLINE	WATERLINE
LODESTONE	OFFENSIVE	RECESSION	SERENGETI	SWEEPINGS	UNDERLING	WATERMARK
LOHENGRIN	OFFERTORY	RECESSIVE	SEVENTEEN	SWEETENER	UNDERMINE	WATERMILL
LUTESCENT	OPPENHEIM	REDEEMING	SEVERALLY	SWEETMEAT	UNDERMOST	WATERSHED
LUXEMBURG	ORIENTATE	REFECTION	SEVERANCE	SWEETNESS	UNDERPAID	WATERSIDE
LYMESWOLD	OSTENSIVE	REFECTORY	SHEEPFOLD	SWEETSHOP	UNDERPASS	WATERWEED
MACEDOINE	OSTEODERM	REFERENCE	SHEEPMEAT	SYNEDRION	UNDERRATE	WAVELLITE
MACEDONIA	OSTEOPATH	REFERRING	SHEEPSKIN	SYNERGIST	UNDERSEAL	WHEELBASE
MADELEINE	OTHERWISE	REHEARSAL	SHEERLEGS	TABELLION	UNDERSELL	WINEBERRY
MAKESHIFT	OTTERBURN	REJECTION	SHEERNESS	TAMERLANE	UNDERSIDE	WINEGLASS
MALEBOLGE	OUDENARDE	RELEVANCE	SHIELDING	TAVERNERS	UNDERSIGN	WISECRACK
MALENGINE	OUTERMOST	RENEWABLE	SHOEMAKER	TELEGRAPH	UNDERSONG	WODEHOUSE
MASEFIELD	OWLEGLASS	REPECHAGE	SHOESHINE	TELEOLOGY	UNDERTAKE	WOMENFOLK
MATELASSE	OWNERSHIP	REPELLENT	SIDEBOARD	TELEPATHY	UNDERTONE	YTTERBIUM
MATERNITY	PACEMAKER	REPELLING	SIDEBURNS	TELEPHONE	UNDERWALK	ZIBELLINE
MERESWINE	PADEMELON	REPENTANT	SIDELIGHT	TELEPHONY	UNDERWEAR	BEDFELLOW
MESENTERY	PAGEANTRY	REPERCUSS	SIDEROSIS	TELEPHOTO	UNDERWENT	BEEFEATER
METEORITE	PALEMPORE	REPERTORY	SIDESWIPE	TELESALES	UNDERWOOD	BEEFSTEAK
METEOROID	PALEOLITH	REREMOUSE	SIDETRACK	TELESCOPE	UNFEELING	BLUFFNESS
MILESTONE	PALESTINE	RESENTFUL	SIDEWARDS	TELESTICH	UNHEALTHY	BOYFRIEND
MINEFIELD	PANEGOISM	RESERPINE	SIMEONITE	TENEBROSE	UNHEEDING	BUFFETING
MINELAYER	PANEGYRIC	RESERVIST	SLEEKNESS	TENEMENTS	UNHELPFUL	CHAFFINCH
MISERABLE	PANELLING	RESERVOIR	SLEEPLESS	TEREBINTH	UNLEARNED	COFFERDAM
MISERABLY	PANELLIST	RETENTION	SLEEPWALK	THREADFIN	UNNERVING	COFFINITE
MODELLING	PANETTONE	RETENTIVE	SNEERWELL	THREEFOLD	UNREFINED	COMFORTER
MODERATOR	PAPERBACK	REVEALING	SOBERNESS	THREESOME	UNRELATED	CONFESSED
MODERNISM	PAPERCLIP	REVELLING	SOLEMNITY	THRENETIC	UNSECURED	CONFESSOR
MODERNIST	PAPERWORK	REVERENCE	SOLEMNIZE	THREONINE	UNSELFISH	CONFIDANT
MODERNITY	PAREGORIC	REVERSING	SOMEPLACE	THRESHOLD	UNSETTLED	CONFIDENT
MODERNIZE	PARENTAGE	REVERSION	SOMETHING	THYESTEAN	UNTENABLE	CONFIRMED
MODESTINE	PARENTING	REVETMENT	SOMETIMES	TIMENOGUY	UNWELCOME	CONFITEOR
MOLECULAR	PATERCOVE	RICERCARE	SOMEWHERE	TIMEPIECE	UPPERCASE	CONFLATED
MOLESKINS	PATERNITY	RIDERHOOD	SOVENANCE	TIMESHARE	UPPERMOST	CONFORMAL
MOMENTARY	PEDERASTY	RIDERLESS	SOVEREIGN	TIMETABLE	UPSETTING	CONFUCIUS
MOMENTOUS	PENETRATE	RIVERSIDE	SPEECHIFY	TIREDNESS	USHERETTE	CONFUSING
MONERGISM	PEREGRINE	ROBERTSON	SPEEDBOAT	TOBERMORY	UTTERANCE	CONFUSION
MONEYWORT	PERENNIAL	ROSEWATER	SPEEDWELL	TOLERABLE	UTTERLESS	CRAFTSMAN
MORECAMBE	PETERSHAM	RUFESCENT	SPHENDONE	TOLERABLY	UTTERMOST	CUFFLINKS
NAKEDNESS	PHLEBITIS	RUNESTAVE	SPHERICAL	TOLERANCE	VALENTINE	CURFUFFLE
NAMEPLATE	PHRENETIC	SAFEGUARD	SPLENDOUR	TOLERATED	VASECTOMY	DEAFENING
NASEBERRY	PHRENITIS	SAGEBRUSH	SPLENETIC	TOMENTOSE	VEGETABLE	DIFFERENT
NECESSARY	PIKESTAFF	SALERATUS	SPLENITIS	TOWELLING	VEGETATOR	DIFFICULT
NECESSITY	PINEAPPLE	SALESGIRL	SPREADING	TREETRUNK	VEHEMENCE	DIFFIDENT
NEFERTITI	PIPEDREAM	SALESLADY	SPRECHERY	TRIENNIAL	VENERABLE	DIFFUSION
NEVERMORE	PIPESTONE	SATELLITE	SQUEAMISH	TRIERARCH	VENEREOUS	DISFAVOUR
NIDERLING	POKERWORK	SAVERNAKE	STEELHEAD	TRIETERIC	VENEZUELA	DISFIGURE
NINEPENCE	POLEMARCH	SCHEELITE	STEELYARD	TRUEPENNY	VICEREGAL	DRAFTSMAN
NINETIETH	POLEMICAL	SCHEHITAH	STEENBRAS	TUMESCENT	VICEREINE	DRIFTWOOD
NONENTITY	POTENTATE	SCHELLING	STEENKIRK	UNBEKNOWN	VIDELICET	FORFEITED
NOSEBLEED	POTENTIAL	SCHEMATIC	STEEPNESS	UNBENDING	VIDEODISC	FORFICATE
NOTEPAPER	POWELLITE	SCIENTISM	STEERSMAN	UNCEASING	VIDEODISK	GERFALCON
NOVELETTE	POWERBOAT	SCIENTIST	STREAMING	UNCERTAIN	VIDEOTAPE	GODFATHER
NUMERAIRE	POWERLESS	SCLEROSIS	STREETAGE	UNDECIDED	VIGESIMAL	GRUFFNESS
NUMERATOR	PRIESTESS	SCLEROTAL	STREETCAR	UNDEFILED	VITELLIUS	HALFBAKED
NUMERICAL	PRIESTLEY	SCREENING	STRENUOUS	UNDEFINED	WAFERTHIN	HALFDOZEN
NUREMBERG	PROENZYME	SCREWBALL	STRESSFUL	UNDERBITE	WAGENBOOM	HALFEMPTY
OBJECTIFY	PUCELLAGE	SCREWEDUP	STRETCHED	UNDERBRED	WAPENTAKE	HALFPENNY
OBJECTION	PYRETHRUM	SCREWPINE	STRETCHER	UNDERCAST	WAREHOUSE	HAMFATTER
OBJECTIVE	QUEERNESS	SCREWTAPE	SUBEDITOR	UNDERCOAT	WATERBABY	HAMFISTED
OBREPTION	QUIESCENT	SECESSION	SUBENTIRE	UNDERDONE	WATERBUTT	INEFFABLE
OBSECRATE	QUIETNESS	SEDENTARY	SUPERCOOL	UNDERFEED	WATERFALL	KERFUFFLE
OBSEQUIES	RACEHORSE	SELECTING	SUPERETTE	UNDERFELT	WATERFORD	LEAFMOULD
OBSERVANT	RACETRACK	SELECTION	SUPERFINE	UNDERFLOW	WATERFOWL	LEAFSTALK
OBSESSION	RATEPAYER	SELECTIVE	SUPERNOVA	UNDERFOOT	WATERGATE	MALFORMED
OBSESSIVE	REBELLION	SEMEIOTIC	SUPERSEDE	UNDERGRAD	WATERHOLE	MALFORMED

MAYFLOWER	ARAGONITE	GARGARISM	ORIGINATE	URUGUAYAN	DOTHEBOYS	MECHANIZE
MISFALLEN	BERGAMASK	GEOGRAPHY	OROGRAPHY	VENGEANCE	EIGHTIETH	METHADONE
MISFIRING	BERGANDER	GILGAMESH	OUTGOINGS	VIRGINALS	EIGHTSOME	METHEGLIN
MUFFETTEE	BERGOMASK	GINGERADE	OUTGROWTH	VIRGINIAN	EMPHASIZE	METHODISM
MYOFIBRIL	BIOGRAPHY	GINGLYMUS	OXYGENATE	VIRGINITY	EMPHLYSIS	METHODIST
ORIFLAMME	BRIGADIER	GONGORISM	PERGAMENE	VIRGINIUM	EMPHYSEMA	METHOXIDE
OUTFITTER	BRIGADOON	GREGARINE	PERGUNNAH	VIRGULATE	ENCHANTED	MIDHEAVEN
PARFLECHE	BUDGETARY	GREGORIAN	PHAGOCYTE	VOLGOGRAD	ENCHANTER	MISHANDLE
PENFRIEND	BULGARIAN	HAUGHTILY	PHIGALIAN	VULGARIAN	ENCHEASON	MITHRAISM
PERFECTLY	COAGULANT	HINGELESS	PIGGYBACK	VULGARISM	ENCHILADA	MOTHBALLS
PERFERVID	COAGULATE	HOBGOBLIN	PIGGYBANK	VULGARITY	ENCHORIAL	MOTHEATEN
PERFORANS	CONGENIAL	HUNGARIAN	POIGNANCY	WEDGEWOOD	ENSHEATHE	MOTHERING
PERFORATE	CONGERIES	ILLGOTTEN	PRAGMATIC	WEIGHTING	ENTHYMEME	MUCHLOVED
PERFORMED	CONGESTED	IMAGELESS	PREGNANCY	ALCHEMIST	ESTHETICS	MUSHINESS
PERFORMER	CONGOLESE	IMAGINARY	PROGNOSIS	AMPHIBIAN	EUCHARIST	MUSHROOMS
PERFUMERY	CONGRUENT	JAGGANATH	PROGRAMME	ANCHORAGE	EUCHLORIC	MYTHOLOGY
PILFERAGE	CONGRUOUS	JARGONIZE	PUNGENTLY	ANCHORITE	EUPHEMISM	NASHVILLE
PILFERING	DANGEROUS	JIGGUMBOB	PURGATIVE	ANCHORMAN	EUPHONIUM	NATHANIEL
PREFATORY	DIAGNOSIS	JUDGEMENT	PURGATORY	ANTHOLOGY	EUPHORBIA	NATHELESS
PREFERRED	DINGINESS	KINGMAKER	RANGELAND	ARCHANGEL	EUPHRATES	NATHEMORE
PREFIGURE	DISGRACED	KINGSIZED	RIDGEBACK	ARCHETYPE	EURHYTHMY	NEPHALISM
PROFANELY	DISGUISED	LANGOUSTE	RIDGELING	ARCHIBALD	EXCHEQUER	NEPHALIST
PROFANITY	DISGUSTED	LANGRIDGE	RIDGEPOLE	ARCHITECT	FASHIONED	NEPHELINE
PROFESSED	DRAGONFLY	LANGSPIEL	RINGFENCE	ARCHIVIST	FISHERMAN	NEPHRITIC
PROFESSOR	DRUGSTORE	LANGUAGES	RINGSIDER	ARCHIVOLT	FISHGUARD	NEPHRITIS
PROFITEER	DUNGAREES	LANGUEDOC	ROUGHCAST	ARTHRITIC	FISHPLATE	NIGHTCLUB
PROFUSELY	DUNGENESS	LANGUETTE	ROUGHNECK	ARTHRITIS	GASHOLDER	NIGHTFALL
PROFUSION	DUNGEONER	LANGUIDLY	ROUGHNESS	ARTHROPOD	GATHERING	NIGHTFIRE
PUFFINESS	ELEGANTLY	LARGENESS	ROUGHSHOD	ARTHROSIS	GOTHAMITE	NIGHTGLOW
RAFFINOSE	ENIGMATIC	LARGHETTO	RUGGELACH	ARTHURIAN	HAPHAZARD	NIGHTGOWN
RENFIERST	EPIGAEOUS	LARGITION	SANGFROID	ASTHMATIC	HASHEMITE	NIGHTHAWK
RUFFIANLY	EPIGENOUS	LAUGHABLE	SCAGLIOLA	ATAHUALPA	HIGHCLASS	NIGHTMARE
SAFFLOWER	EROGENOUS	LENGTHILY	SEDGEMOOR	AUTHENTIC	HIGHFLYER	NIGHTSPOT
SEAFARING	EVAGATION	LINGERING	SIEGFRIED	AUTHORESS	HIGHLANDS	NIGHTTIME
SELFISHLY	EXOGENOUS	LINGFIELD	SINGALESE	AUTHORITY	HIGHLIGHT	NIGHTWORK
SHEFFIELD	FINGERING	LODGEMENT	SINGAPORE	AUTHORIZE	HIGHSPEED	NITHSDALE
SHIFTLESS	FINGERTIP	LONGCHAMP	SINGLESEX	BACHARACH	HOTHEADED	OCKHAMIST
SHIFTWORK	FLAGELLIN	LONGEDFOR	SINGLETON	BASHFULLY	HYPHENATE	ONTHESPOT
SHUFFLING	FLAGELLUM	LONGEVITY	SINGSPIEL	BATHTOWEL	ILCHESTER	ORCHESTRA
SOLFEGGIO	FLAGEOLET	LONGICORN	SINGULTUS	BECHSTEIN	INSHALLAH	ORPHANAGE
SOLFERINO	FLAGITATE	LONGINGLY	SLIGHTEST	BETHLEHEM	ISCHAEMIC	ORPHARION
SOLFIDIAN	FLAGRANCE	LONGITUDE	SLUGHORNE	BIGHEADED	JEPHTHAHS	ORTHODOXY
SOUFRIERE	FLAGSTAFF	LONGLIVED	SMUGGLING	BISHOPRIC	KEYHOLDER	ORTHOLOGY
SPOFFORTH	FLAGSTONE	LONGRANGE	SOGGINESS	BUCHAREST	LACHRYMAL	ORTHOPTER
STIFFENER	FOGGINESS	LONGSHORE	SONGSMITH	CACHAEMIA	LATHYRISM	ORTHOTONE
STIFFNESS	FORGATHER	LORGNETTE	SPAGHETTI	CACHECTIC	LECHEROUS	OUGHTNESS
SUBFOSSIL	FORGETFUL	MANGANATE	STAGEHAND	CASHPOINT	LETHARGIC	PACHYDERM
SUFFERING	FORGETIVE	MANGANESE	STAGGERED	CATHARSIS	LIGHTFACE	PANHANDLE
SUFFOCATE	FORGIVING	MANGETOUT	STAGIRITE	CATHARTIC	LIGHTFOOT	PARHELION
SUFFRAGAN	FORGOTTEN	MANGOUSTE	STAGYRITE	CATHEDRAL	LIGHTLESS	PARHYPATE
SUFFUSION	FRAGILITY	MARGARINE	STEGNOSIS	CATHEPSIN	LIGHTNESS	PATHOGENY
SULFUROUS	FRAGMENTS	MERGANSER	STEGNOTIC	CATHERINE	LIGHTNING	PATHOLOGY
SUNFLOWER	FRAGONARD	MISGIVING	STEGOSAUR	CHIHUAHUA	LIGHTSHIP	PATHTRAIN
SURFBOARD	FRAGRANCE	MISGUIDED	STIGMATIC	COCHINEAL	LIGHTSOME	PETHIDINE
SURFEITED	FRAGRANCY	MONGOLIAN	SWAGGERER	COTHURNUS	LITHOCYST	PHTHALATE
SWIFTNESS	FRIGATOON	MONGOLISM	TANGERINE	CUCHULAIN	LITHOPONE	PIGHEADED
TRAFALGAR	FRIGHTFUL	MORGANITE	TARGETEER	DACHSHUND	LITHUANIA	PINHOOKER
TRIFORIUM	FRIGIDITY	MOYGASHEL	THIGHBONE	DASHBOARD	LOCHINVAR	POTHOLING
UNIFORMED	FROGMARCH	MUGGLETON	TINGUAITE	DASHWHEEL	MACHINATE	POTHUNTER
UNIFORMLY	FROGMOUTH	MYOGLOBIN	TOUGHNESS	DICHOTOMY	MACHINERY	PREHALLUX
WEBFOOTED	FROGSPAWN	NARGHILLY	TRAGEDIAN	DIPHTHONG	MACHINING	PUSHCHAIR
WOLFHOUND	FRUGALITY	NAUGHTILY	TRAGELAPH	DISHCLOTH	MACHINIST	PYTHONESS
WULFENITE	FUGGINESS	NEIGHBOUR	TREGEAGLE	DISHONEST	MANHANDLE	RATHERIPE
ZINFANDEL	FUNGIBLES	NIGGARDLY	TREGETOUR	DISHONOUR	MANHATTAN	RATHERISH
ALIGNMENT	FUNGICIDE	OLIGARCHY	TUNGSTATE	DISHWATER	MATHURINE	REDHANDED
AMYGDALUS	GANGPLANK	OLIGOCENE	TUNGSTOUS	DITHERING	MECHANICS	REDHEADED
ANAGLYPTA	GARGANTUA	ORIGENIST	ULIGINOUS	DITHYRAMB	MECHANISM	RESHUFFLE

RICHELIEU	AFFIDAVIT	CAPILLARY	ENCIRCLED	HESITANCY	LUCIFERIN	PAKISTANI
RIGHTEOUS	AFFILIATE	CAPITULAR	ENGINEERS	HODIERNAL	LUDICROUS	PALINURUS
RIGHTHAND	AFRIKAANS	CAPITULUM	ENLIGHTEN	HOLINSHED	LUMINAIRE	PAPILLOTE
RIGHTNESS	AFRIKANER	CARIBBEAN	ENLIVENED	HOMICIDAL	LUMINANCE	PATIENTLY
RIGHTWING	ALLIGATOR	CHAIRLIFT	EPHIALTES	HUMILIATE	LURIDNESS	PEDICULAR
RUSHLIGHT	ALTIMETER	CHRISTIAN	EQUIPMENT	HYGIENIST	LYRICALLY	PEDIGREES
RUTHENIAN	ALTIPLANO	CHRISTMAS	EQUIPOISE	HYPINOSIS	LYSIMETER	PEKINGESE
RUTHENIUM	ALTISSIMO	CILIOLATE	EQUISETUM	ILLIBERAL	MAGICALLY	PENILLION
SANHEDRIM	AMBIGUITY	CIVILISED	EQUITABLE	ILLICITLY	MALICIOUS	PENINSULA
SANHEDRIN	AMBIGUOUS	CIVILIZED	EQUITABLY	IMMIGRANT	MALIGNANT	PENISTONE
SANHEDRON	AMBITIOUS	CLOISONNÉ	EQUIVOCAL	IMMIGRATE	MALIGNITY	PENITENCE
SEPHARDIM	ANCILLARY	COMICALLY	EQUIVOQUE	IMMINENCE	MANIFESTO	PERIAKTOS
SIGHTLESS	ANCIPITAL	COMINFORM	ERPINGHAM	INCIDENCE	MARIJUANA	PERIANDER
SIGHTSEER	ANGIOGRAM	COMINTERN	ESPIONAGE	INCIPIENT	MAXILLARY	PERIBOLOS
SIPHUNCLE	ANOINTING	COPIOUSLY	ESTIMABLE	INCITATUS	MEDIAEVAL	PERICLASE
SOPHISTER	ANTICLINE	CORIANDER	ETHIOPIAN	INDICATES	MEDIATION	PERICUTIN
SOPHISTIC	ANTIGONUS	CROISSANT	EURIPIDES	INDICATOR	MEDICALLY	PERIMETER
SOPHISTRY	ANTIHELIX	CURIOSITY	EXCIPIENT	INDICTION	MEDICATED	PERIMORPH
SOPHOCLES	ANTINOVEL	CURIOUSLY	EXCISEMAN	INDIGENCE	MEDICINAL	PERIODATE
SOPHOMORE	ANTIPASTO	CYNICALLY	EXCITABLE	INDIGNANT	MEDITATOR	PERIPATUS
SYPHILOMA	ANTIPATHY	DECIDEDLY	EXHIBITOR	INDIGNITY	MEHITABEL	PERIPHERY
TACHILITE	ANTIPHONY	DECIDUOUS	EXPIATION	INFIELDER	MELIORATE	PERISCIAN
TACHYLITE	ANTIPODES	DECILLION	EXPIATORY	INFIRMARY	MENIPPEAN	PERISCOPE
TACHYLYTE	ANTIQUARY	DEDICATED	EXPISCATE	INFIRMITY	MIDIANITE	PERISHING
TECHNICAL	ANTIQUITY	DEFICIENT	EXSICCATE	INHIBITED	MIDINETTE	PERISTOME
TECHNIQUE	ANTISERUM	DEFINABLE	EXTIRPATE	INHIBITOR	MILITANCY	PERISTYLE
TEPHILLIN	ANTITOXIC	DELICIOUS	FATIDICAL	INNISFAIL	MINIATURE	PETILLANT
TICHBORNE	ANTITOXIN	DELIGHTED	FATISCENT	INNISFREE	MINISKIRT	PITIFULLY
TIGHTENER	ANTIVENIN	DELINEATE	FEMINEITY	INSIDIOUS	MISINFORM	PIXILATED
TIGHTHEAD	ANXIOUSLY	DELIRIOUS	FERINGHEE	INSINCERE	MODILLION	PLAINNESS
TIGHTNESS	AQUILEGIA	DELIVERER	FEUILLANT	INSINUATE	MUNICIPAL	PLAINSMAN
TIGHTROPE	ARBITRAGE	DEMITASSE	FILICALES	INSIPIENT	MUNIMENTS	PLAINSONG
TITHEBARN	ARBITRARY	DENIGRATE	FILIGRAIN	INSISTENT	MUNITIONS	PLAINTIFF
TRIHEDRON	ARBITRATE	DEPICTION	FINICKING	INVIDIOUS	MUSICALLY	PLAINTIVE
UNCHANGED	ARLINGTON	DESICCATE	FINICKITY	INVIOLATE	MUSICHALL	PLEIOCENE
UNCHARGED	ARMISTICE	DESIGNATE	FINISHING	INVISIBLE	MUTILATED	POLIANITE
UNCHECKED	ARRIVISTE	DESIGNING	FOLIOLOSE	IPHIGENIA	NAPIERIAN	POLICEMAN
UNCHRISOM	ARTICHOKE	DESIPIENT	FREIGHTER	IPRINDOLE	NAVIGABLE	POLITBURO
UNSHACKLE	ARTICULAR	DESIRABLE	FROISSART	IRRITABLE	NAVIGATOR	POLITESSE
UNSHEATHE	ARTIFICER	DEVIATION	FRUITCAKE	IRRITABLY	NERITIDAE	POLITICAL
WAGHALTER	ARTILLERY	DEVILFISH	FRUITERER	IRRITATED	NIAISERIE	POLITIQUE
WASHBASIN	ASPIRATOR	DEVILMENT	FRUITLESS	IRVINGISM	NOMINALLY	PORIFERAN
WASHBOARD	ASSIDUITY	DEVIOUSLY	FUNICULAR	JANISSARY	NOMINATOR	PUNISHING
WASHCLOTH	ASSIDUOUS	DIGITALIN	FUNICULUS	JOUISANCE	NONILLION	PUPILLAGE
WASHERMAN	ASSISTANT	DIGITALIS	FURIOUSLY	JOVIALITY	NOVICIATE	PURIFYING
WASHSTAND	ATTITUDES	DILIGENCE	FUSILLADE	JUBILANCE	NOVITIATE	PURITANIC
WITHDRAWN	AURICULAR	DIRIGIBLE	GABIONADE	JUDICIARY	OBEISANCE	QUAILPIPE
WITHERING	AUXILIARY	DISINFECT	GALINGALE	JUDICIOUS	OBLIQUELY	RACIALISM
WITHERITE	AVAILABLE	DIVIDENDS	GALIONGEE	JURIDICAL	OBLIVIOUS	RACIALIST
WITHSTAND	AVOIDABLE	DIVISIBLE	GARIBALDI	KOMINFORM	OBVIOUSLY	RADIANTLY
WITHYWIND	AVOIDANCE	DIXIELAND	GELIGNITE	KONIMETER	OCCIPITAL	RADIATING
WUTHERING	AXMINSTER	DOMICILED	GENIALITY	KONISCOPE	OCTILLION	RADIATION
YACHTSMAN	BANISTERS	DOMINANCE	GENITALIA	LACINIATE	OFFICIALS	RADICALLY
YACHTSMEN	BASICALLY	DOMINICAL	GERIATRIC	LAMINATED	OFFICIANT	RADICCHIO
ZECHARIAH	BASILICAL	DOMINICAN	GLAIREOUS	LAMINITIS	OFFICIATE	RADIOGRAM
ZEPHANIAH	BASILICON	DONIZETTI	GONIATITE	LATICLAVE	OFFICIOUS	RADIOLOGY
ACCIDENTS	BEGINNING	DOSIMETER	HABITABLE	LEGIONARY	OMNIRANGE	RAMILLIES
ADDICTION	BELIEVING	DRAINPIPE	HABITUATE	LEGISLATE	OPHIUCHUS	RATIONALE
ADDICTIVE	BENIGHTED	DUBIOUSLY	HALITOSIS	LENIENTLY	OPSIMATHY	RATIONING
ADMIRABLE	BILINGUAL	DUTIFULLY	HARIGALDS	LENINGRAD	OPTICALLY	RAVISHING
ADMIRABLY	BILIRUBIN	EBRILLADE	HARIOLATE	LEVIATHAN	ORBICULAR	RECIPIENT
ADMIRALTY	BOLIVIANO	ECHIDNINE	HEMINGWAY	LEVITICUS	ORDINAIRE	REDINGOTE
ADMISSION	BRAINCASE	EDDINGTON	HEMIPTERA	LIMITLESS	ORDINANCE	REDIVIVUS
ADMITTING	BRAINLESS	EFFICIENT	HEMISTICH	LITIGIOUS	ORGIASTIC	REFINANCE
ADMIXTURE	BRAINWASH	EFFINGHAM	HEMITROPE	LOGICALLY	ORGILLOUS	REGISSEUR
ADVISABLE	BRAINWAVE	ELLINGTON	HERITABLE	LOGISTICS	ORPINGTON	REGISTRAR
ADVISEDLY	CALIBRATE	EMPIRICAL	HESITANCE	LOUISIANA	OSCILLATE	RELIGEUSE

RELIGIOSO	SOCIALIZE	UNWILLING	BOOKSTALL	MUCKENDER	AMPLIFIER	COLLECTED
RELIGIOUS	SOCIOLECT	UNWITTING	BOOKSTAND	MURKINESS	AMPLITUDE	COLLECTOR
RELIQUARY	SOCIOLOGY	UPAITHRIC	BOOKSTORE	MUSKETEER	ANALEPTIC	COLLEGIAN
RELIQUIAE	SOLICITOR	UPLIFTING	BROKERAGE	MUSKETOON	ANALGESIA	COLLIGATE
REMINISCE	SOLILOQUY	URTICARIA	BUCKETFUL	MUSKOGEAN	ANALGESIC	COLLIMATE
REMISSION	SOLIPSISM	VACILLATE	BUCKTEETH	NECKVERSE	ANALOGOUS	COLLISION
RESIDENCE	SOLITAIRE	VAGINITIS	BUCKTHORN	NICKNEVEN	ANGLICISM	COLLOCATE
RESIDENCY	SPHINCTER	VALIANTLY	BUCKWHEAT	OZOKERITE	APOLLONUS	COLLODION
RESIDUARY	SPLINTERS	VANISHING	BULKINESS	PACKAGING	APOLOGIST	COLLOIDAL
RESILIENT	SPLITTING	VARIATION	BURKINABE	PAWKINESS	APOLOGIZE	COLLOTYPE
RESISTANT	SPOILSMAN	VARICELLA	COCKAIGNE	PECKSNIFF	APPLEJACK	COLLUSION
RETIARIUS	SPRIGHTLY	VARIEGATE	COCKATIEL	PICKABACK	APPLIANCE	COLLUSIVE
RETICENCE	SPRINGALD	VARIOLATE	COCKFIGHT	PICKETING	APPLICANT	COLLYRIUM
RETICULAR	SPRINGBOK	VARIOUSLY	COCKROACH	PICKTHANK	ASCLEPIUS	CYCLAMATE
RETICULUM	SPRINGLET	VARISCITE	COCKSCOMB	PINKERTON	ASPLENIUM	CYCLOLITH
RETINITIS	SPRINKLER	VEHICULAR	COCKSFOOT	POCKETFUL	ATHLETICS	CYCLORAMA
REVICTUAL	SPRITEFUL	VENIALITY	COCKSWAIN	POCKMANKY	AVALANCHE	CYCLOTRON
RIPIENIST	SPRITSAIL	VERIDICAL	COOKHOUSE	PROKARYON	BALLADEER	DALLIANCE
ROSINANTE	SQUINANCY	VERITABLE	CORKSCREW	PROKOFIEV	BALLADIST	DECLARING
ROZINANTE	SQUINTING	VESICULAR	DECKCHAIR	RACKETEER	BALLERINA	DECLINING
RUBICELLE	SQUIREAGE	VEXILLARY	DOUKHOBOR	RACKSTRAW	BALLISTIC	DECLIVITY
RUDIMENTS	SQUIRMING	VICIOUSLY	DUCKBOARD	RASKOLNIK	BALLPOINT	DEFLATION
SAGITTARY	STAINLESS	VIGILANCE	DUIKERBOK	RECKONING	BEELZEBUB	DEFLECTOR
SALICETUM	STAIRCASE	VIGILANTE	EUSKARIAN	REYKJAVIK	BELLICOSE	DIALECTAL
SATIATION	STEINBECK	VISIONARY	FALKLANDS	RISKINESS	BELLYACHE	DIALECTIC
SATINWOOD	STEINBOCK	VITIATION	FOLKETING	SACKCLOTH	BELLYFLOP	DIALOGITE
SATIRICAL	STOICALLY	VIVIDNESS	FOLKWEAVE	SACKERSON	BILLABONG	DIPLOMACY
SATISFIED	STRIATION	WAPINSHAW	GAWKINESS	SASKATOON	BILLBOARD	DISLOCATE
SAXIFRAGE	STRICTURE	YOHIMBINE	HACKAMORE	SHAKEDOWN	BILLIARDS	DJELLABAH
SAXITOXIN	STRIDENCY	BEDJACKET	HACKBERRY	SHAKINESS	BILLOWING	DUPLICAND
SCHIAVONE	STRINGENT	CONJUGATE	HACKNEYED	SICKENING	BILLYCOCK	DUPLICATE
SCHILLING	STRINGOPS	CONJURING	HANKERING	SINKANSEN	BIOLOGIST	DUPLICITY
SCRIMMAGE	STRIPLING	FORJASKIT	HAWKSBILL	SMOKEFREE	BOULEVARD	EAGLEWOOD
SCRIMPING	SUPINATOR	FORJESKIT	HONKYTONK	SMOKELESS	BRILLIANT	EBULLIENT
SCRIMSHAW	SYNIZESIS	NUTJOBBER	HUCKABACK	SNAKEWEED	BULLDOZER	ECOLOGIST
SCRIPTURE	SYRIACISM	ODDJOBMAN	HUNKYDORY	SPIKENARD	BULLFIGHT	EDELWEISS
SCRIVENER	TAOISEACH	POUJADIST	HUSKINESS	SPOKESMAN	BULLFINCH	EFFLUENCE
SDEIGNFUL	TAVISTOCK	PREJUDICE	INNKEEPER	STOKEHOLD	BURLESQUE	EFFLUVIUM
SEDITIOUS	TAXIDERMY	PROJECTED	JACKFRUIT	SULKINESS	BURLINESS	EMOLLIATE
SEMIBREVE	TAXIMETER	PROJECTOR	JACKKNIFE	TACKINESS	CABLEGRAM	EMOLLIENT
SEMICOLON	TEDIOSITY	SELJUKIAN	JACKSCREW	TALKATIVE	CALLIPERS	EMOLUMENT
SEMIFINAL	TEDIOUSLY	SKYJACKER	JACKSNIPE	TEAKETTLE	CALLOSITY	EMPLECTON
SEMIFLUID	THRIFTILY	SUBJACENT	JACKSTRAW	UNSKILLED	CALLOUSLY	EMPLOYEES
SEMIGLOSS	THRILLANT	SUBJUGATE	JERKINESS	UROKINASE	CELLARIST	EMULATION
SEMIOLOGY	THRILLING	ASHKENAZI	JERKWATER	VERKAMPTE	CELLULITE	ENCLOSURE
SEMIOTICS	TISIPHONE	AWAKENING	JOCKSTRAP	VOLKSRAAD	CELLULOID	ENDLESSLY
SEMIRAMIS	TITILLATE	AYCKBOURN	JOCKTELEG	WALKABOUT	CELLULOSE	EPILATION
SEMIVOWEL	TOPIARIST	BACKBENCH	JUNKETING	WEAKENING	CEYLONESE	EPILEPTIC
SENIORITY	TOPICALLY	BACKBITER	KICKSHAWS	WORKFORCE	CHALAZION	EPULATION
SEPIOLITE	TOXIGENIC	BACKBOARD	KINKCOUGH	WORKHORSE	CHALIAPIN	ESPLANADE
SERIALIST	TRAINABLE	BACKCLOTH	LACKBEARD	WORKHOUSE	CHALLENGE	EUCLIDEAN
SERIALIZE	TREILLAGE	BACKPEDAL	LANKINESS	WORKPLACE	CHALUMEAU	EVOLUTION
SERIATION	TULIPWOOD	BACKSHISH	LEAKPROOF	WORKSPACE	CHILBLAIN	EXCLAIMED
SERIGRAPH	TUTIORISM	BACKSLIDE	LEUKAEMIA	YORKSHIRE	CHILDCARE	EXCLUDING
SERIOUSLY	TYPICALLY	BACKSPACE	LICKERISH	ZINKENITE	CHILDHOOD	EXCLUSION
SHEIKHDOM	ULTIMATUM	BACKSTAGE	LINKLATER	ABOLITION	CHILDLESS	EXCLUSIVE
SHRIMPING	UMBILICAL	BACKSWORD	LOCKSMITH	ACCLIMATE	CHILDLIKE	EXPLETIVE
SHRINKAGE	UMBILICUS	BACKTRACK	LOOKALIKE	ACCLIVITY	CHILOPODA	EXPLICATE
SHRINKING	UNBIASSED	BACKWARDS	MACKENZIE	ADULATION	CHOLELITH	EXPLOITER
SIBILANCE	UNDILUTED	BACKWATER	MARKETEER	ADULTERER	COALESCED	EXPLOSION
SICILIANO	UNDIVIDED	BACKWOODS	MARKETING	ADULTHOOD	COALFIELD	EXPLOSIVE
SILICOSIS	UNFITTING	BASKETFUL	MICKLETON	AFFLICTED	COALITION	EYELETEER
SIMILARLY	UNLIMITED	BEEKEEPER	MILKSHAKE	AFFLUENCE	COALMINER	FALLOPIAN
SNAILFISH	UNMINDFUL	BERKELIUM	MINKSTONE	AGALACTIC	COELOSTAT	FAULCHION
SOCIALISM	UNSIGHTLY	BOOKLOVER	MOCKERNUT	AIMLESSLY	COLLAPSAR	FAULTLESS
SOCIALIST	UNSINNING	BOOKMAKER	MONKSHOOD	AMBLYOPIA	COLLATION	FIELDFARE
SOCIALITE	UNTIMEOUS	BOOKSHELF	MOSKONFYT	AMELAKITE	COLLEAGUE	FIELDSMAN

FIELDWORK	ITALICIZE	PHILIPPIC	SECLUSION	VELLENAGE	CHEMISTRY	FORMATIVE
FILLIPEEN	JARLSBERG	PHILISTER	SELLOTAPE	VELLICATE	CIMMERIAN	FORMULATE
FILLISTER	JEALOUSLY	PHILLABEG	SHELDDUCK	VIOLATION	CLAMOROUS	FRAMBOISE
FINLANDIA	JELLYFISH	PHILLIBEG	SHELDRAKE	VIOLENTLY	CLAMPDOWN	FRAMEWORK
FOLLOWING	KEPLARIAN	PHILOLOGY	SHELLBACK	VIOLINIST	CLIMACTIC	FULMINANT
FOOLHARDY	KHALIFATE	PHYLLOPOD	SHELLFISH	WALLABIES	COEMPTION	FULMINATE
FOOLISHLY	KILLARNEY	PHYLOGENY	SHELLSUIT	WALLBOARD	COMMANDER	GEOMETRIC
FOOLPROOF	LAPLANDER	PILLICOCK	SHELTERED	WALLOPING	COMMENSAL	GEOMETRID
FORLORNLY	LOBLOLLYS	POLLINATE	SHILLABER	WALLOWING	COMMISSAR	GERMANCER
FULLBLOWN	LOWLANDER	POLLUTANT	SHOLOKHOV	WALLPAPER	COMMITTAL	GERMANDER
FULLERENE	LOWLIGHTS	POLLUTION	SILLINESS	WALLYDRAG	COMMITTED	GERMANITE
FULLGROWN	LOWLINESS	POPLITEAL	SKILFULLY	WELLBEING	COMMITTEE	GERMANIUM
FULLSCALE	MAELSTROM	POULTERER	SMALLNESS	WELLBUILT	COMMODITY	GERMICIDE
GAELTACHT	MALLANDER	PRELECTOR	SMALLTIME	WELLKNOWN	COMMODORE	GERMINATE
GALLABEAH	MALLEABLE	PRELUSORY	SOLLICKER	WHALEBOAT	COMMOTION	GLAMORIZE
GALLANTLY	MALLEMUCK	PROLACTIN	SOULFULLY	WHALEBONE	COMMUNION	GLAMOROUS
GALLANTRY	MALLENDER	PROLAMINE	SPELDRING	WHALEMEAT	COMMUNISM	GLOMERATE
GALLICISM	MALLEOLUS	PROLEPSIS	SPELLBIND	WHOLEFOOD	COMMUNIST	GLOMERULE
GALLINULE	MANLINESS	PROLIXITY	SPELUNKER	WHOLEMEAL	COMMUNITY	GODMOTHER
GALLIPOLI	MAULSTICK	PROLONGED	SPILLICAN	WHOLENESS	COMMUTATE	GRAMPIANS
GALLIVANT	MILLAMANT	PROLUSION	SPILLIKIN	WHOLESALE	CORMORANT	GRIMALKIN
GALLOPADE	MILLENIAL	PUBLICIST	STALEMATE	WHOLESOME	COSMETICS	GRIMINESS
GALLSTONE	MILLEPEDE	PUBLICITY	STALENESS	WILLEMITE	COSMOGONY	GRUMBLING
GALLYCROW	MILLEPORE	PUBLICIZE	STALWORTH	WILLESDEN	COSMOLOGY	HAEMALGINA
GAULEITER	MILLIGRAM	PUBLISHED	STILLBORN	WILLFULLY	COSMONAUT	HAEMATITE
GEOLOGIST	MILLINERY	PUBLISHER	STILLNESS	WILLINGLY	CREMATION	HAMMERING
GMELINITE	MILLIONTH	PULLULATE	STILLROOM	WILLOWING	CREMATORY	HAMMURABI
GOALMOUTH	MILLIPEDE	QUALIFIED	STILTBIRD	WILLPOWER	CRIMINATE	HARMALINE
GODLINESS	MILLIVOLT	QUALIFIER	STOLIDITY	WOLLASTON	CRUMBLING	HARMATTAN
GOSLARITE	MILLIWATT	QUILLWORT	STYLISHLY	WOOLINESS	CULMINATE	HARMONICA
GUILDHALL	MILLSTONE	REALISTIC	STYLISTIC	WORLDWIDE	DALMATIAN	HARMONIST
GUILELESS	MISLOCATE	REALITIES	STYLOBATE	WURLITZER	DEAMINATE	HARMONIUM
GUILLEMOT	MOLLITIES	RECLAIMED	SUBLIMATE	YELLOWISH	DIAMETRIC	HARMONIZE
GUILLOCHE	MOLLYMAWK	RECLAIMER	SUBLIMELY	ZEALANDER	DISMANTLE	HARMOTOME
GUILTLESS	MUGLARITE	REDLETTER	SURLINESS	ZOOLOGIST	DISMEMBER	HAYMAKING
HAILSTONE	NEGLECTED	REFLATION	SYLLABARY	ABOMINATE	DISMISSAL	HAYMARKET
HAILSTORM	NEGLIGENT	REFLECTOR	SYLLABLES	ACUMINATE	DOGMATISM	HERMANDAD
HALLOWEEN	NEOLITHIC	REFLEXION	SYLLEPSIS	ADUMBRATE	DOGMATIZE	HERMITAGE
HALLOWMAS	NEOLOGISM	REFLEXIVE	SYLLOGISM	AGAMEMNON	DORMITION	HODMANDOD
HALLSTATT	NEWLYWEDS	REPLACING	TABLATURE	ALUMINIUM	DORMITORY	INAMORATA
HARLEQUIN	NOBLENESS	REPLENISH	TABLELAND	ANIMALISM	DRAMATICS	INAMORATO
HARLESTON	NOLLEKENS	REPLETION	TABLEWARE	ANIMALITY	DRAMATIST	INUMBRATE
HEALTHILY	NUCLEOLUS	REPLETIVE	TAILBOARD	ANIMATION	DRAMATIZE	ISOMERASE
HELLEBORE	OBBLIGATO	REPLICANT	TAILLEFER	ANIMISTIC	DROMEDARY	ISOMETRIC
HILLBILLY	OCCLUSION	REPLICATE	TAILLIGHT	ANIMOSITY	DRUMSTICK	KERMESITE
HOLLERITH	OCHLOCRAT	RILLETTES	TAILPIECE	ANOMALOUS	ELEMENTAL	KLEMPERER
HOLLYHOCK	OCULIFORM	SABLEFISH	TAILPLANE	ASHMOLEAN	ELIMINATE	KRUMMHORN
HOLLYWOOD	ODALISQUE	SAILCLOTH	TELLINGLY	ASYMMETRY	ENAMELLED	LAWMAKING
HOOLACHAN	ODELSTING	SALLYPORT	TELLURIAN	BADMINTON	ENAMOURED	LAWMONGER
HOPLOLOGY	ONSLAUGHT	SALLYPOST	TELLURION	BARMBRACK	ENUMERATE	LOAMSHIRE
ICELANDER	OPULENTLY	SCALARIUM	TELLURIUM	BARMECIDE	ESEMPLASY	MAMMALIAN
ICELANDIC	OUBLIETTE	SCALDFISH	THALASSIC	BLAMELESS	ETYMOLOGY	MARMALADE
IMPLEMENT	OVULATION	SCALEABLE	THELEMITE	BOOMERANG	EXEMPLARY	MARMOREAL
IMPLICATE	PAGLIACCI	SCALLAWAG	THELONIUS	BRAMBLING	EXEMPLIFY	MEDMENHAM
IMPLUVIUM	PAILLASSE	SCALLIONS	THYLACINE	BRIMSTONE	EXEMPTION	MESMERISM
INCLEMENT	PAILLETTE	SCALLOPED	TOLLHOUSE	BROMINATE	FARMHOUSE	MESMERIZE
INCLUDING	PALLADIAN	SCALLYWAG	TRILITHON	BRUMMAGEM	FARMSTEAD	MISMANAGE
INCLUSION	PALLADIUM	SCELERATE	TRILOBITE	CARMELITE	FERMENTED	MNEMOSYNE
INCLUSIVE	PALLIASSE	SCHLEMIEL	TUILERIES	CHAMELEON	FILMMAKER	MORMONISM
INELEGANT	PAULOWNIA	SCHLEMIHL	TUILLETTE	CHAMFRAIN	FILMSTRIP	MURMURING
INFLATION	PELLAGRIN	SCHLENTER	UNALLOYED	CHAMINADE	FIRMAMENT	MYRMECOID
INFLEXION	PELLITORY	SCHLIEREN	UNALTERED	CHAMOMILE	FLAMMABLE	NAUMACHIA
INFLUENCE	PHALANGER	SCOLECITE	UNCLAIMED	CHAMPAGNE	FLAMSTEED	NEWMARKET
INFLUENZA	PHALAROPE	SCOLIOSIS	UNCLOTHED	CHAMPAIGN	FORMALIST	NORMALACY
INGLENOOK	PHELLOGEN	SCOLIOTIC	UNCLOUDED	CHAMPERTY	FORMALITY	NORMALITY
ISALLOBAR	PHILANDER	SCULPTING	UNFLEDGED	CHAMPLAIN	FORMALIZE	NORMALIZE
ISOLATION	PHILATELY	SCULPTURE	VEILLEUSE	CHAMPLEVÉ	FORMATION	NORMATIVE

NUMMULITE	SUBMERGED	BLANDNESS	DIANOETIC	GYMNASIUM	PARNASITE	SCHNAUZER
ONOMASTIC	SUMMARILY	BLINDFOLD	DIGNIFIED	GYMNASTIC	PARNASSUS	SCHNECKEN
PALMATION	SUMMARIZE	BLINDNESS	DIGNITARY	HOBNAILED	PENNILESS	SCHNITTKE
PALMISTRY	SUMMATION	BLINDSPOT	DINNERSET	HORNSTONE	PENNYWORT	SCHNITZEL
PALMITATE	SURMULLET	BLINDWORM	DIONYSIAN	HYPNOTISM	PHANARIOT	SCHNORKEL
PAYMASTER	SWIMMERET	BLINKERED	DIONYSIUS	HYPNOTIST	PHANSIGAR	SCHNORRER
PEGMATITE	SYMMETRIC	BLUNDERER	DOWNGRADE	HYPNOTIZE	PHANTASMA	SCHNOZZLE
PELMANISM	TALMUDIST	BLUNTNESS	DOWNRIGHT	ICHNEUMON	PHENACITE	SCINTILLA
PERMANENT	TARMACKED	BOANERGES	DOWNSTAGE	ICHNOLITE	PHENAKISM	SCONCHEON
PERMEABLE	TASMANIAN	BOONDOCKS	DOWNTREND	IDENTICAL	PHENYTOIN	SCUNCHEON
PERMITTED	TERMAGANT	BORNAGAIN	DOWNWARDS	IDENTIKIT	PHONECARD	SEANNACHY
PLIMSOLLS	TERMAGENT	BOUNDLESS	DRINKABLE	INANIMATE	PHONETICS	SHENSTONE
PLUMBEOUS	TERMINATE	BOUNTEOUS	DRUNKENLY	INANITION	PHONOGRAM	SHINTOISM
PLUMBLINE	THUMBLING	BOUNTIFUL	DWINDLING	INUNCTION	PHONOLITE	SIGNALLER
PLUMDAMAS	THUMBNAIL	BRANCHING	EARNESTLY	IRONSIDES	PHONOLOGY	SIGNALMAN
PLUMPNESS	THUMBTACK	BRANDIRON	ECONOMICS	IRONSTONE	PICNICKER	SIGNATORY
PREMATURE	TORMENTER	BRONCHIAL	ECONOMIST	IRONWORKS	PIGNERATE	SIGNATURE
PREMONISH	TORMENTIL	BRUNHILDE	ECONOMIZE	ISINGLASS	PLANETARY	SIGNBOARD
PREMOTION	TORMENTOR	CANNELURE	EDINBURGH	ITINERANT	PLENITUDE	SKINDIVER
PRIMAEVAL	TORMENTUM	CANNONADE	ELONGATED	ITINERARY	PLENTEOUS	SKINFLINT
PRIMARILY	TRAMLINES	CARNATION	EMANATION	ITINERATE	PLENTIFUL	SKINTIGHT
PRIMAVERA	TREMATODE	CARNELIAN	EMINENTLY	JAUNDICED	PLUNDERER	SLANTWISE
PRIMIPARA	TREMBLING	CARNIVORE	ENUNCIATE	JENNETING	POINTEDLY	SLINGBACK
PRIMITIAE	TREMOLITE	CEANOTHUS	EPINASTIC	KHANSAMAH	POINTLESS	SLINGSHOT
PRIMITIVE	TREMULANT	CHANCROID	EPINICION	KIDNAPPED	POINTSMAN	SOMNOLENT
PRIMULINE	TREMULATE	CHANTEUSE	EPINIKION	KIDNAPPER	PRANKSTER	SONNETEER
PROMACHOS	TREMULOUS	CHANTILLY	EPONYMOUS	KLENDUSIC	PRINCETON	SOUNDBITE
PROMENADE	TRIMESTER	CHINATOWN	ETHNOLOGY	KLINOSTAT	PRINCIPAL	SOUNDLESS
PROMINENT	TRIMMINGS	CHINOVNIK	EVANGELIC	LAGNIAPPE	PRINCIPLE	SOUNDNESS
PROMISING	TROMPETTE	CHINSTRAP	EVENTUATE	LAUNCELOT	PRINTABLE	SPINDRIER
PROMOTION	TRUMPEDUP	CHONDRITE	EXANIMATE	LAUNCHING	PRONGHORN	SPINDRIFT
PROMPTING	TRUMPETER	CHONDROID	EXANTHEMA	LAUNDRESS	PRONOUNCE	SPINELESS
PROMUSCIS	TUMMYACHE	CLINGFILM	EXONERATE	LAWNMOWER	PUGNACITY	SPINNAKER
PULMONARY	TURMAGENT	CLINICIAN	FAINTNESS	LIENTERIC	PYONGYANG	SPINNERET
PULMONATE	VERMIFORM	COENOBITE	FLINTLOCK	LIONHEART	QUANTICAL	SPONGEBAG
PUMMELLED	VERMIFUGE	COENOBIUM	FORNICATE	LOINCLOTH	QUANTOCKS	SPONSORED
PYGMALION	VERMILION	COGNITION	FOUNDLING	MAGNALIUM	QUENNELLE	SPUNCULID
REIMBURSE	VERMINOUS	COGNITIVE	FRANCESCA	MAGNESIUM	QUINQUINA	STANCHION
RHYMESTER	WARMONGER	COGNIZANT	FRANCHISE	MAGNETISM	QUINTETTE	STANDARDS
RIGMAROLE	WHIMSICAL	COINTREAU	FRANCOLIN	MAGNETIZE	QUINTROON	STANDERBY
ROSMARINE	WOOMERANG	CONNECTED	FRANGLAIS	MAGNETRON	QUINTUPLE	STANDGALE
ROSMINIAN	WORMEATEN	CONNECTOR	FRANKNESS	MAGNIFIER	RAINCHECK	STANNATOR
ROUMANIAN	ZOOMANTIC	CONNEXION	FRENCHMAN	MAGNITUDE	RAINGAUGE	STENOPAIC
ROUMANSCH	ABANDONED	CONNOTATE	FRENCHMEN	MAINFRAME	RAINSTORM	STINGAREE
SARMENTUM	ABANDONEE	CONNUBIAL	FURNIMENT	MAINTENON	RAINWATER	STINKBIRD
SCAMBLING	ABUNDANCE	CORNBRASH	FURNITURE	MANNEQUIN	REANIMATE	STINKHORN
SCHMALTZY	ACONCAGUA	CORNCRAKE	GAINFULLY	MANNERING	REINFORCE	STINKWOOD
SCHMIEDER	ADENOIDAL	CORNEILLE	GAINSAYER	MANNERISM	REINSTATE	STONEBOAT
SCHMUTTER	AGINCOURT	CORNELIAN	GARNISHEE	MEANDRIAN	RESNATRON	STONECHAT
SEEMINGLY	AGONIZING	CORNERMAN	GARNITURE	MEANWHILE	ROUNCEVAL	STONECROP
SEGMENTED	ALONGSIDE	CORNETIST	GAUNTNESS	MENNONITE	ROUNCIVAL	STONEHAND
SERMONIZE	AMENDMENT	CORNFIELD	GLANDULAR	MINNESOTA	ROUNDBACK	STONELESS
SHAMEFAST	AMENHOTEP	CORNFLOUR	GLENDOWER	MOONLIGHT	ROUNDELAY	STONEWALL
SHAMELESS	ANONYMITY	CORNSTALK	GLENGARRY	MOONRAKER	ROUNDFISH	STONEWARE
SHAMIANAH	ANONYMOUS	COUNSELOR	GLENLIVET	MOONSHINE	ROUNDHAND	STONEWORK
SHEMOZZLE	APENNINES	COUNTDOWN	GOONHILLY	MOONSTONE	ROUNDHEAD	STONEWORT
SLAMMAKIN	ASYNDETON	COUNTLESS	GRANDIOSE	OLENELLUS	ROUNDSMAN	STONKERED
SLIMINESS	ASYNERGIA	COUNTRIES	GRANDNESS	OMINOUSLY	RUINATION	SUBNORMAL
SLUMBERER	ATONALITY	CRANBERRY	GRANDSIRE	OPENENDED	RUINOUSLY	SWANIMOTE
SOMMELIER	ATONEMENT	CRANBORNE	GRANULATE	OPENHEART	RUNNYMEDE	SWANSDOWN
STAMMERER	AVUNCULAR	CRENATION	GRANULITE	ORANGEADE	SAINTFOIN	SWINBURNE
STIMULANT	BAINMARIE	CRINOLINE	GRANULOSE	ORANGEMAN	SAINTHOOD	SWINEHERD
STIMULATE	BARNABITE	DAMNATION	GRENADIER	OUTNUMBER	SANNYASIN	SWINGEING
STOMACHIC	BARNACLES	DAMNEDEST	GRENADINE	OVENPROOF	SCANSORES	TARNATION
STUMBLING	BARNSTORM	DAUNTLESS	GRENVILLE	PAINFULLY	SCANTLING	TEKNONYMY
STUMPWORK	BEANFEAST	DIANDROUS	GRINGOLET	PAINTWORK	SCENTLESS	TENNESSEE
SUBMARINE	BERNSTEIN	DIANETICS	GUINEVERE	PANNIKELL	SCHNAPPER	TENNESSEE

THANATISM	ACROPETAL	BOLOGNESE	ENROLMENT	IMMORALLY	MONODRAMA	RECONVENE
THANKLESS	ACROPHONY	CACOPHONY	ENSORCELL	IMMORTALS	MONOGRAPH	RECORDING
THINGUMMY	ACROPOLIS	CAGOULARD	ENTOPHYTE	IMMOVABLE	MONOLAYER	RECORDIST
THINKABLE	ADJOINING	CALORIFIC	ENTOURAGE	IMMOVABLY	MONOLOGUE	RECOVERED
THINNINGS	ADMONITOR	CANONICAL	EPEOLATRY	IMPOLITIC	MONOMACHY	REDOLENCE
THUNDERER	ADVOCATED	CAPORETTO	ERIOMETER	IMPORTANT	MONOMANIA	REFORMIST
TOWNSFOLK	AERODROME	CAVORTING	ERRONEOUS	IMPORTUNE	MONOMETER	REJOICING
TRANSCEND	AEROPLANE	CEROMANCY	ESCOPETTE	IMPOSTURE	MONOPLANE	REJOINDER
TRANSEUNT	AEROSPACE	CHEONGSAM	ETIOLATED	IMPOTENCE	MONOSTICH	REMONTANT
TRANSFORM	AEROTAXIS	CHLOROSIS	EXCORIATE	IMPOUNDER	MONOTROCH	REMOULADE
TRANSFUSE	ALCOHOLIC	CHROMATIC	EXPORTING	INCOGNITO	MONOXYLON	REMOVABLE
TRANSHUME	ALGORITHM	CHRONICLE	EXPOSITOR	INCOMINGS	MOTOCROSS	RENOVATOR
TRANSIENT	ALLOCARPY	CIPOLLINO	EXTORTION	INCOMMODE	MOTORBIKE	REPORTAGE
TRANSLATE	ALLOGRAFT	CLEOPATRA	EYEOPENER	INCONDITE	MOTORBOAT	REPORTING
TRANSMUTE	ALLOGRAPH	COLOCYNTH	FAVORABLE	INCORRECT	MOTORCADE	REPOSSESS
TRANSPIRE	ALLOPATHY	COLOMBIAN	FAVORABLY	INDOLENCE	MOTORISTS	RESONANCE
TRANSPORT	ALLOTMENT	COLOMBIER	FAVOURITE	INDONESIA	MUCORALES	RESONATOR
TRANSPOSE	ALLOWABLE	COLONNADE	FEROCIOUS	INFORMANT	MUTOSCOPE	RESORTING
TRANSSHIP	ALLOWANCE	COLOPHONY	FILOPLUME	INNOCENCE	NEGOTIATE	RESOURCES
TRANSVAAL	ALOOFNESS	COLORLESS	FILOSELLE	INNOCUOUS	NICODEMUS	RETORSION
TRENCHANT	ANGOSTURA	COLOSSEUM	FLOODGATE	INNOVATOR	NOMOCRACY	RETORTION
TRINKETER	ANNOTATED	COLOSTOMY	FLOORSHOW	INSOLENCE	NOMOTHETE	REVOLTING
TRONDHEIM	ANNOTATOR	COLOSTRUM	FLUORSPAR	INSOLUBLE	NOTOCHORD	REVOLVING
TRUNCATED	ANNOUNCER	COLOURFUL	GASOMETER	INSOLVENT	NOTONECTA	REWORKING
TRUNCHEON	ANNOYANCE	COLOURING	GINORMOUS	INSOMNIAC	NOTORIETY	RHEOTAXIS
TRUNKFISH	ANTONINUS	COLOURIST	GIRONDIST	INVOICING	NOTORIOUS	RIGOLETTO
TURNABOUT	APPOINTED	COROLLARY	GODOLPHIN	INVOLUCRE	NOVOCAINE	SALOPETTE
TURNBULLS	APPOINTEE	CROOKBACK	GYNOECIUM	IODOPHILE	NOVODAMUS	SAPODILLA
TURNROUND	APPORTION	CROOKEDLY	GYROMANCY	KILOCYCLE	OBCORDATE	SAXOPHONE
TURNSTILE	ARBORETUM	CRYOGENIC	GYROPLANE	KILOHERTZ	OBNOXIOUS	SCHOLARCH
TURNSTONE	AREOPAGUS	CRYOMETER	GYROSCOPE	KILOMETER	OCTOBRIST	SCHOLARLY
TURNTABLE	ARROGANCE	CYTOKININ	HALOBIONT	KILOMETRE	OCTOPLOID	SCHOLIAST
TWENTIETH	ARROWHEAD	DECOCTION	HALOPHILE	LABORIOUS	OLEOGRAPH	SCHOOLBOY
TWINKLING	ARROWROOT	DECOLLATE	HALOTHANE	LABOURITE	OLEORESIN	SCHOOLING
UNANIMITY	ASSOCIATE	DECOMPOSE	HECOGENIN	LACONICAL	ONCOMETER	SCHOOLMAN
UNANIMOUS	ASSONANCE	DECONTROL	HERODOTUS	LAGOMORPH	ONTOGENCY	SCIOMANCY
UNINJURED	ASTOUNDED	DECORATED	HERONSHAW	LAVOISIER	OPPONENTS	SCRODDLED
UNINVITED	ATROCIOUS	DECORATOR	HODOGRAPH	LIMOUSINE	OPPORTUNE	SCROUNGER
UNKNOWING	AUTOCLAVE	DEFOLIANT	HODOMETER	LOGOGRIPH	OPTOMETRY	SECONDARY
UNUNUNIUM	AUTOCRACY	DEFOLIATE	HOLOCAUST	LOGOTHETE	OPTOPHONE	SONOMETER
UPANISHAD	AUTOCROSS	DEFORMITY	HOLOGRAPH	MAJORDOMO	OUROBOROS	SOPORIFIC
URANISCUS	AUTOGRAPH	DEMOCRACY	HOLOPHOTE	MAJORETTE	OUROBORUS	SPOONBILL
URINATION	AUTOLATRY	DEPOSITOR	HOMOGRAFT	MANOEUVRE	OUTOFTOWN	SPOONFEED
VAINGLORY	AUTOLYCUS	DETONATOR	HOMOGRAPH	MANOMETER	PALOVERDE	STOOLBALL
VERNATION	AUTOLYSIS	DEVONPORT	HOMOPHONE	MASOCHISM	PANORAMIC	STROBILUS
VIENTIANE	AUTOMAKER	DISOBLIGE	HOMOPTERA	MASOCHIST	PAROCHIAL	STROLLING
WAGNERIAN	AUTOMATED	DISORIENT	HONORABLE	MAVOURNIN	PAROCHINE	STROMBOLI
WAGNERITE	AUTOMATIC	DOLOMITES	HONORIFIC	MAYORALTY	PAROTITIS	STRONGARM
WEDNESDAY	AUTOMATON	DOLOMITIC	HOROSCOPE	MEKOMETER	PEDOMETER	STRONGYLE
WHINSTONE	AUTONOMIC	ECTOMORPH	HUMONGOUS	MELODIOUS	PICOFARAD	STRONTIUM
WHUNSTANE	AUTOPILOT	ECTOPLASM	HYLOBATES	MELODRAMA	PINOCCHIO	STROSSERS
WINNEBAGO	AUTOROUTE	ECTOTHERM	HYPOBLAST	MELONLIKE	PIROUETTE	SUDORIFIC
WITNESSED	AUTOSCOPY	EIDOGRAPH	HYPOCAUST	MEMORABLE	POLONAISE	SYCOPHANT
WRANGLERS	AUXOTROPH	ELBOWROOM	HYPOCRISY	MEMORITER	POMOERIUM	SYNOECETE
WRONGDOER	AXIOMATIC	ELKOSHITE	HYPOCRITE	MENOMINEE	PREOCCUPY	SYNOVITIS
WRONGFOOT	BAROMETER	ENCOLPION	IDEOGRAPH	MENOPAUSE	PREORDAIN	TAMOXIFEN
WYANDOTTE	BARONETCY	ENCOLPIUM	IDEOPATHY	MEROCRINE	PROOFREAD	TELOPHASE
YOUNGSTER	BELONGING	ENCOMPASS	IDIOBLAST	MESOBLAST	PYROMANCY	THEOBROMA
ABDOMINAL	BICONCAVE	ENCOUNTER	IDIOGRAPH	MESOMORPH	PYROMANIA	THEOCRACY
ABHORRENT	BIMONTHLY	ENCOURAGE	IDIOMATIC	MILOMETER	RACONTEUR	THEOSOPHY
ABSORBENT	BINOCULAR	ENDOCRINE	IDIOPHONE	MISOCLERE	RAZORBILL	THROATILY
ABSORBING	BLOODBATH	ENDOERGIC	IDIOPLASM	MISONEIST	REBOATION	THROBBING
ACCOMPANY	BLOODLESS	ENDOMORPH	IDIOTICON	MOBOCRACY	RECOGNIZE	THRONGING
ACCORDANT	BLOODROOT	ENDOSPERM	IGNORAMUS	MONOCEROS	RECOLLECT	THROWAWAY
ACCORDING	BLOODSHED	ENDOWMENT	IGNORANCE	MONOCHORD	RECOMMEND	THROWBACK
ACCORDION	BLOODSHOT	ENJOYABLE	ILLOGICAL	MONOCOQUE	RECONCILE	THROWDOWN
ACROBATIC	BLOODWORM	ENJOYMENT	IMMODESTY	MONOCULAR	RECONDITE	THROWSTER

TIMOCRACY	COMPANION	GUNPOWDER	PROPERDIN	TRAPEZIAL	ANARCHIST	COARCTATE
TONOMETER	COMPELLED	HAMPSHIRE	PROPHETIC	TRAPEZIST	ANDROCLES	COPROLITE
TONOPLAST	COMPETENT	HAMPSTEAD	PROPIONIC	TRAPEZIUM	ANDROMEDA	CORRECTED
TOXOPHILY	COMPETING	HAPPENING	PROPONENT	TRAPEZIUS	APARTHEID	CORRECTLY
TROOPSHIP	COMPLAINT	HAPPINESS	PROPRIETY	TRAPEZOID	APARTMENT	CORRECTOR
TROOSTITE	COMPLIANT	HARPOONER	PROPTOSIS	TRAPPINGS	APERIODIC	CORREGGIO
UNBOUNDED	COMPONENT	HELPFULLY	PROPYLENE	TRIPITAKA	APERITIVE	CORRELATE
UNCONCERN	COMPOSING	HENPECKED	PULPITEER	TRIPMETER	APHRODITE	CORROSION
UNCONFINE	COMPOSITE	HERPESTES	PUPPETEER	TROPAELIN	APPRAISAL	CORROSIVE
UNCORRECT	COMPOSURE	HESPERIAN	PURPOSELY	TROPARION	APPREHEND	CORRUGATE
UNCOUPLED	COMPOTIER	HEYPRESTO	RASPATORY	TRYPHOEUS	APPROVING	CORRUPTER
UNCOURTLY	COMPUTING	HIPPOCRAS	RASPBERRY	TURPITUDE	ASTRAGALS	COURGETTE
UNCOVERED	COOPERATE	HIPPODAME	RESPECTED	TYMPANIST	ASTRAKHAN	COURTELLE
UNDOUBTED	CORPORATE	HIPPOLYTA	RESPECTER	UNOPPOSED	ASTRODOME	COURTEOUS
UNFOUNDED	CORPOREAL	HIPPOLYTE	RHAPSODIC	UNSPARING	ASTROLABE	COURTESAN
UNHOPEFUL	CORPOSANT	HOSPITIUM	SCAPEGOAT	UNSPOILED	ASTROLOGY	COURTROOM
UNNOTICED	CORPULENT	IBUPROFEN	SCAPOLITE	VESPASIAN	ASTRONAUT	COURTSHIP
UNPOPULAR	CORPUSCLE	INOPINATE	SCEPTICAL	VULPINITE	ASTRONOMY	COURTYARD
UNTOUCHED	CRAPULENT	INSPECTOR	SHAPELESS	WALPURGIS	ASTROPHEL	CUPRESSUS
UNWORRIED	CRAPULOUS	INSPIRING	SHEPHERDS	WASPISHLY	ASTROTURF	CURRENTLY
UPCOUNTRY	CREPITATE	ISOPROPYL	SHIPOWNER	WHIPROUND	ATTRIBUTE	CURRYCOMB
UPHOLSTER	CREPOLINE	JAMPACKED	SHIPSHAPE	WHIPSNADE	ATTRITION	DAIRYMAID
VAPOROTIC	CRIPPLING	KNAPSCULL	SHIPWRECK	BANQUETTE	AUBRIETIA	DECRETALS
VAPORIFIC	CRYPTOGAM	KNAPSKULL	SHOPFLOOR	BECQUEREL	AWARENESS	DECRETORY
VAPORIZER	CUSPIDORE	KNIPHOFIA	SHOPFRONT	BRIQUETTE	BARRACUDA	DEERHOUND
VELODROME	DELPHINUS	KROPOTKIN	SIMPLETON	CHEQUERED	BARRICADE	DEGRADING
WAGONETTE	DESPERADO	LAMPADARY	SIMPLISTE	CONQUEROR	BARRISTER	DEPRAVITY
WAGONLOAD	DESPERATE	LAMPADION	SKEPTICAL	CROQUETTE	BEARDLESS	DEPRECATE
WIDOWHOOD	DESPOTISM	LAMPBLACK	SLAPHAPPY	ELOQUENCE	BEARDSLEY	DEPREDATE
XENOMANIA	DIAPHRAGM	LAMPLIGHT	SLAPSTICK	ETIQUETTE	BEDRAGGLE	DEPRESSED
XENOPHOBE	DIAPHYSIS	LAMPSHADE	SOAPBERRY	EXEQUATUR	BEDRIDDEN	DERRINGER
XEROPHYTE	DISPARAGE	LIMPIDITY	SOAPSTONE	FREQUENCY	BETROTHAL	DETRACTOR
XEROSTOMA	DISPARATE	LIPPITUDE	SOPPINESS	HACQUETON	BETROTHED	DETRIMENT
XYLOPHONE	DISPARITY	LYMPHATIC	STIPULATE	HARQUEBUS	BOARDROOM	DETRITION
ZENOCRATE	DISPENSER	MAPPEMOND	STOPLIGHT	JACQUERIE	BOARDWALK	DIARRHOEA
ZOROASTER	DISPERSAL	MELPOMENE	STUPEFIED	MACQUARIE	BORROWING	DISREGARD
ZYGOMATIC	DISPERSED	MISPICKEL	STUPIDITY	MARQUESAS	BOURGEOIS	DISREPAIR
ZYGOSPORE	DISPLACED	MISPLACED	SULPHONIC	MARQUETRY	BURROUGHS	DISREPUTE
ZYMOMETER	DISPLAYED	MUMPSIMUS	SULPHURIC	SASQUATCH	BURROWING	DOORFRAME
ADAPTABLE	DISPLEASE	NIPPERKIN	SUMPTUARY	SURQUEDRY	BYPRODUCT	DUBROVNIK
ADEPTNESS	DISPUTANT	NONPAREIL	SUMPTUOUS	TURQUOISE	CABRIOLET	ECARDINES
ALIPHATIC	DRIPSTONE	NONPROFIT	SUPPLIANT	UNEQUALED	CAIRNGORM	ECTROPION
ANAPLASIA	DROPPINGS	OMOPHAGIC	SUPPLICAT	ABERNETHY	CAPRICCIO	EGAREMENT
ANAPLASTY	DROPSICAL	OVIPAROUS	SUPPORTER	ABERRANCE	CAPRICORN	EMBRACERY
ANOPHELES	DYSPEPSIA	PALPATION	SUPPOSING	ABORIGINE	CHARABANC	EMBRACING
APOPHATIC	DYSPEPTIC	PALPEBRAL	SUPPURATE	ACARIASIS	CHARACTER	EMBRANGLE
APOPHYSIS	DYSPHAGIA	PALPITATE	SURPRISED	ACCRETION	CHARGEFUL	EMBRASURE
BESPANGLE	DYSPRAXIA	PEMPHIGUS	SUSPECTED	ADDRESSED	CHARIVARI	EMBROCATE
BOSPHORUS	ELOPEMENT	PENPUSHER	SUSPENDED	ADDRESSEE	CHARLATAN	EMBROGLIO
BUMPTIOUS	ENDPAPERS	PEPPERONI	SUSPENDER	ADORATION	CHARLOTTE	EMBROIDER
CALPURNIA	EPIPHRAGM	PEPPERPOT	SUSPENSOR	ADORNMENT	CHAROLAIS	EMBROILED
CAMPANILE	EPIPHYSIS	PERPETUAL	SUSPICION	AFFRICATE	CHARTERED	EMBRYONIC
CAMPANULA	EPIPHYTIC	PERPLEXED	SYLPHLIKE	AFORESAID	CHARTREUX	EMERGENCE
CARPACCIO	EPIPOLISM	PIEPOWDER	SYMPHONIC	AGGRAVATE	CHARWOMAN	EMERGENCY
CARPENTER	ESOPHAGUS	PIMPERNEL	SYMPHYSIS	AGGREGATE	CHARYBDIS	ENCRATITE
CARPENTRY	EVAPORATE	POMPADOUR	SYMPODIUM	AGGRESSOR	CHERISHED	ENERGETIC
CARPETING	FLIPPANCY	POMPHOLYX	SYMPOSIUM	AGGRIEVED	CHERNOZEM	ENERGUMEN
CHAPARRAL	FLOPHOUSE	POMPOSITY	SYRPHIDAE	ALERTNESS	CHERUBINI	ENERINITE
CHAPERONE	GASPEREAU	POPPERING	TARPAULIN	AMARANTIN	CHIROPODY	ENGRAINED
CHIPBOARD	GODPARENT	POPPYCOCK	TEMPERATE	AMARYLLIS	CHORISTER	ENGRAVING
CHIPOLATA	GOMPHOSIS	PORPOISES	TEMPORARY	AMBROSIAL	CHURCHILL	ENGRENAGE
CHIPPINGS	GOSPELLER	PORPORATE	TEMPORIZE	AMBROSIAN	CHURCHMAN	ENGROSSED
CLAPBOARD	GRAPESHOT	POTPOURRI	TEMPTRESS	AMBROTYPE	CHURIDARS	ENGROSSER
CLEPSYDRA	GRAPETREE	PREPOLLEX	TERPINEOL	AMERICANO	CIRRHOSIS	ENTRAMMEL
CLIPBOARD	GRAPEVINE	PROPAGATE	TIMPANIST	AMERICIUM	CLARENDON	ENTRANCED
COMPACTLY	GRAPHICAL	PROPELLED	TIPPERARY	AMOROUSLY	CLARIFIER	ENTRECHAT
COMPANIES	GRAPPLING	PROPELLER	TOLPUDDLE	AMORPHOUS	CLERGYMAN	ENTRECÔTE

ENTREMETS	HARROWING	LUCRATIVE	OVERBOARD	PTERIDIUM	SHORTLIST	THIRDSMAN
ENTROPION	HAYRADDIN	LUCRETIUS	OVERCLOUD	PTEROSAUR	SHORTNESS	THIRSTILY
ENTROPIUM	HEARDSMAN	MACROCOSM	OVERCROWD	PUERILITY	SHORTSTAY	THIRSTING
EPARCHATE	HEARTACHE	MACROLOGY	OVERDRAFT	PUERPERAL	SHORTSTOP	THIRTIETH
ESTRANGED	HEARTBEAT	MADRASSAH	OVERDRAWN	PYRRHONIC	SHORTTERM	THORNBACK
ESTRAPADE	HEARTBURN	MADREPORE	OVERDRESS	QUARENDEN	SMARTNESS	THORNBILL
ESTRELDID	HEARTFELT	MADRESSAH	OVERDRIVE	QUARTERLY	SOBRIQUET	THORNDYKE
ETERNALLY	HEARTHRUG	MADRILENE	OVEREXERT	QUARTETTE	SORROWFUL	THORNLESS
EUTROPHIC	HEARTLAND	MARROWFAT	OVERGROWN	QUERCETIN	SOURDOUGH	THYRATRON
EVERGLADE	HEARTLESS	MATRIARCH	OVERHASTY	QUERCETUS	SPARINGLY	THYRISTOR
EVERGREEN	HEARTWOOD	MATRICIDE	OVERHEADS	QUERIMONY	SPARKLERS	THYROXINE
EVERYBODY	HEBRIDEAN	MATRIMONY	OVERJOYED	QUERULOUS	SPARKLING	TIERCERON
EXARATION	HEURISTIC	MAURITIAN	OVERLYING	REARGUARD	SPARTACUS	TITRATION
EXCREMENT	HIERARCHY	MAURITIUS	OVERNIGHT	REARHORSE	SPIRITISM	TOURNEDOS
EXERCISED	HOARFROST	MEDRESSEH	OVERPAINT	REARMOUSE	SPIRITOUS	TSAREVICH
EXERCISES	HOARHOUND	MERRIMENT	OVERPOISE	REARRANGE	SPIRITUAL	ULTRONEUS
EXORATION	HOARSTONE	METRICATE	OVERPOWER	REARWARDS	SPOROCARP	UMBRATILE
EXPRESSED	HORRIFIED	METROLAND	OVERPRINT	REFRACTOR	SPORTSMAN	UNBRIDLED
EXPRESSLY	HOURGLASS	METRONOME	OVERRATED	REFRESHER	SPORTSMEN	UNCROSSED
EXTRACTOR	HOURSTONE	MICROCHIP	OVERREACH	REGRETFUL	STARBOARD	UNCROWNED
EXTRADITE	HURRICANE	MICROCOSM	OVERREACT	REPREHEND	STARGAZER	UNDRESSED
EXTREMELY	HURRICANO	MICROCYTE	OVERRIDER	REPRESENT	STARKNESS	UNPRECISE
EXTREMISM	HURRIEDLY	MICROFILM	OVERSHADE	REPRESSED	STARLIGHT	UNTRAINED
EXTREMIST	HYDRANGEA	MICROINCH	OVERSHOES	REPRESSOR	STARSTONE	UNTREATED
EXTREMITY	HYDRAULIC	MICROLITE	OVERSHOOT	REPRIMAND	STARTLING	UNTRODDEN
EXTRICATE	HYDRAZINE	MICROLITH	OVERSIGHT	REPROBATE	STERADIAN	UNWRITTEN
EXTRINSIC	HYDROFOIL	MICROMOLE	OVERSIZED	REPROCESS	STERCORAL	UVAROVITE
EXTROVERT	HYDROPULT	MICROTOME	OVERSLEEP	REPRODUCE	STERILITY	VIBRATILE
EXTRUSION	HYDROSTAT	MICROTONE	OVERSPEND	REPROVING	STERILIZE	VIBRATION
FABRICATE	IMBRANGLE	MICROVOLT	OVERSPILL	RETRACTOR	STERNFAST	VIBRATORY
FAIRYLAND	IMBRICATE	MICROWATT	OVERSTATE	RETRIEVAL	STERNNESS	VITRIOLIC
FAIRYTALE	IMBROCATE	MICROWAVE	OVERSTEER	RETRIEVER	STIRABOUT	VITRUVIAN
FEARFULLY	IMBROGLIO	MIDRASHIM	OVERTHROW	RETROCEDE	STOREROOM	WEARINESS
FEBRIFUGE	IMPRECATE	MIGRATION	OVERTONES	RETROFLEX	STORIATED	WEARISOME
FERROTYPE	IMPRECISE	MIGRATORY	OVERTRUMP	RETROVERT	STORNAWAY	WEIRDNESS
FERRYBOAT	IMPRESSED	MITRAILLE	OVERVALUE	SACRAMENT	STORYBOOK	WHEREFORE
FIBROLINE	IMPROBITY	MOURNIVAL	OVERWEIGH	SACRARIUM	STORYLINE	WHEREUPON
FIBROLITE	IMPROMPTU	NARRATION	OVERWHELM	SACRIFICE	SUBROGATE	WHERRYMAN
FIORITURA	IMPROVING	NARRATIVE	PARRICIDE	SACRILEGE	SUPREMACY	WHIRLIGIG
FLORESTAN	IMPROVISE	NARROWING	PATRIARCH	SACRISTAN	SUPREMELY	WHIRLPOOL
FLORIMELL	IMPRUDENT	NATROLITE	PATRICIAN	SCARECROW	SURREJOIN	WHIRLWIND
FOGRAMITE	INCREASED	NEGRITUDE	PATRICIDE	SCARIFIER	SURRENDER	WORRISOME
FOURPENCE	INCREMENT	NEURALGIA	PATRIMONY	SCARLATTI	SURROGATE	ABASEMENT
FOURWHEEL	INDRAUGHT	NEURALGIC	PATRIOTIC	SCORBUTIC	SWORDFISH	ABYSMALLY
GALRAVAGE	INERTNESS	NEUROGLIA	PATROCLUS	SCORBUTUS	SWORDPLAY	AHASUERUS
GARRULITY	INERUDITE	NEUROLOGY	PATROLMAN	SCORCHING	SWORDSMAN	AINSWORTH
GARRULOUS	INGRAINED	NIGRITUDE	PATRONAGE	SCORODITE	TARRAGONA	AIRSTREAM
GARRYOWEN	INGROWING	NIGROSINE	PATRONESS	SCURRIOUR	TEARFULLY	AMUSEMENT
GEARLEVER	INORGANIC	NUTRIMENT	PATRONIZE	SEARCHING	TEARSHEET	AMUSINGLY
GEARSHIFT	INTRICACY	NUTRITION	PEARLWORT	SECRETARY	TEIRESIAS	ANASTASIA
GEARSTICK	INTRICATE	NUTRITIVE	PEIRASTIC	SECRETION	TERRACING	ANISOGAMY
GEARWHEEL	INTRIGUED	OBTRUSION	PETRIFIED	SECRETIVE	TERRARIUM	APOSTOLIC
GEORGETTE	INTRIGUER	OBTRUSIVE	PETROLEUM	SEGREGATE	TERRICOLE	ARISTOTLE
GIBRALTAR	INTRINSIC	OPERATING	PETROLOGY	SERRATION	TERRIFIED	ARMSTRONG
GLORIFIED	INTRODUCE	OPERATION	PHARAMOND	SERREFILE	TERRITORY	AWESTRUCK
GLORYHOLE	INTROITUS	OPERATIVE	PHARISAIC	SFORZANDO	TERRORISM	BAKSHEESH
GUARANTEE	INTROVERT	OPERCULUM	PHARSALIA	SHARESMAN	TERRORIST	BEDSITTER
GUARANTOR	INTRUSION	OPPRESSED	PHEROMONE	SHARKSKIN	TERRORIZE	BEDSPREAD
GUARDRAIL	INTRUSIVE	OPPRESSOR	PIERGLASS	SHARPENER	TETRAGRAM	BEESTINGS
GUARDROOM	ITERATION	OSTRACISE	PLURALISM	SHARPNESS	TETRALOGY	BERSERKER
GUARDSMAN	LATRATION	OSTRACISM	PLURALITY	SHOREBIRD	TETRARCHY	BIOSPHERE
GUERRILLA	LEHRJAHRE	OSTRACIZE	POORHOUSE	SHORTCAKE	THERALITE	BLASPHEME
HADROSAUR	LEPROSERY	OSTROGOTH	PORRINGER	SHORTFALL	THERAPIST	BLASPHEMY
HAIRBRUSH	LIBRARIAN	OTTRELITE	PROROGATE	SHORTHAND	THEREFORE	BLESSINGS
HAIRPIECE	LIVRAISON	OUTRIGGER	PRURIENCE	SHORTHAUL	THEREUPON	BLISTERED
HAIRSTYLE	LUBRICANT	OUTROOPER	PSORIASIS	SHORTHOLD	THERMIDOR	BLUSTERER
HARROGATE	LUBRICATE	OVERBLOWN	PTARMIGAN	SHORTHORN	THERSITES	BOBSLEIGH

BOLSHEVIK	DAYSPRING	HAMSTRING	MIDSTREAM	PIPSQUEAK	TAHSILDAR	BOOTBLACK
BOSSANOVA	DENSENESS	HAMSTRUNG	MIDSUMMER	PLASTERED	TASSELLED	BOOTLACES
BOSSINESS	DIASTASIS	HANSEATIC	MISSHAPEN	PLASTERER	TEESWATER	BOSTONIAN
BOTSWANAN	DISSEMBLE	HARSHNESS	MISSIONER	PLASTIQUE	TENSENESS	BOTTLEFUL
BRASENOSE	DISSENTER	HAWSEHOLE	MISSTROKE	POISONING	TERSENESS	BRATWURST
BRASSERIE	DISSIDENT	HEMSTITCH	MOISTNESS	POISONOUS	THESAURUS	BRITANNIA
BRASSICAS	DISSIPATE	HESSONITE	MONSIGNOR	POSSESSED	TIPSINESS	BRITANNIC
BRASSIERE	DISSOLUTE	HOPSCOTCH	MONSTROUS	POSSESSOR	TOASTRACK	BRITSCHKA
BRASSWARE	DISSOLVED	HORSEBACK	MOUSEHOLE	POSSIBLES	TRASIMENE	BROTHERLY
BRISKNESS	DISSONANT	HORSEHAIR	MOUSELIKE	PRESBYTER	TRISAGION	BRUTALISM
BRISTLING	DOSSHOUSE	HORSELESS	MOUSETRAP	PRESCIENT	TROSSACHS	BRUTALITY
BRUSHWOOD	DUNSINANE	HORSEPLAY	MOUSTACHE	PRESCRIBE	ULLSWATER	BRUTALIZE
BRUSQUELY	DUNSTABLE	HORSESHOE	MUSSITATE	PRESCUTUM	UNASHAMED	BUTTERBUR
CAESAREAN	ECOSPHERE	HORSETAIL	MUSSOLINI	PRESENTED	UNISEXUAL	BUTTERCUP
CASSANDRA	ECOSSAISE	HORSEWHIP	MUSSULMAN	PRESENTER	UNUSUALLY	BUTTERFLY
CASSATION	ECOSYSTEM	HOUSEBOAT	NAUSEATED	PRESENTLY	VERSATILE	BUTTERNUT
CASSEROLE	ELASTOMER	HOUSECOAT	NEWSAGENT	PRESERVED	VERSIFIER	BYSTANDER
CASSONADE	EPISCOPAL	HOUSEHOLD	NEWSFLASH	PRESERVER	VERSIONAL	CANTABILE
CASSOULET	EPISTAXIS	HOUSELEEK	NEWSHOUND	PRESERVES	WAISTBAND	CANTHARIS
CASSOWARY	EPISTOLER	HOUSEMAID	NEWSPAPER	PRESHRUNK	WAISTCOAT	CANTHARUS
CATSKILLS	ERISTICAL	HOUSEROOM	NEWSPRINT	PRESIDENT	WAISTLINE	CANTONESE
CAUSATION	EROSTRATE	HOUSEWIFE	NEWSSHEET	PRESIDIAL	WASSERMAN	CAPTAINCY
CEASEFIRE	EVASIVELY	HOUSEWORK	NEWSSTALL	PRESIDIUM	WELSUMMER	CAPTIVATE
CEASELESS	EXISTENCE	IMPSONITE	NEWSSTAND	PRESSGANG	WHISTLING	CAPTIVITY
CESSATION	EXOSPHERE	INUSITATE	NOISELESS	PRISMATIC	WHOSOEVER	CARTESIAN
CHASTENED	EXOSTOSIS	IRASCIBLE	NOISINESS	PROSCRIBE	WRESTLING	CARTHORSE
CHISELLER	EYESHADOW	ISOSCELES	NONSMOKER	PROSECUTE	ZOOSCOPIC	CARTILAGE
CLASSICAL	EYESPLICE	JANSENISM	NOOSPHERE	PROSELYTE	ABATEMENT	CARTOGRAM
CLASSLESS	EYESTRAIN	JANSENIST	NURSEMAID	PROSIMIAN	ABSTAINER	CARTOUCHE
CLASSMATE	FACSIMILE	JESSAMINE	OARSWOMAN	PROSTRATE	ABSTINENT	CARTRIDGE
CLASSROOM	FALSEHOOD	JESSERANT	OFFSEASON	PUISSANCE	ACETAMIDE	CARTTRACK
CLOSENESS	FALSENESS	JETSTREAM	OFFSPRING	PULSATION	ACETYLENE	CARTULARY
CLUSTERED	FIRSTEVER	JOBSEEKER	OURSELVES	PURSUANCE	ACUTENESS	CARTWHEEL
COASTLINE	FIRSTHAND	JOBSWORTH	OUTSIDERS	PUSSYFOOT	AESTHETIC	CASTANETS
CONSCIOUS	FIRSTRATE	KALSOMINE	OUTSKIRTS	QUASIMODO	AGITATION	CASTELLAN
CONSCRIPT	FLASHBACK	KEYSTROKE	OUTSPOKEN	REASONING	AMSTERDAM	CASTIGATE
CONSENSUS	FLASHBULB	KIESERITE	OUTSPREAD	REDSTREAK	ANATOLIAN	CASTILIAN
CONSIGNEE	FLASHCUBE	KINSWOMAN	PALSGRAVE	REISTAFEL	ANATOMIST	CASTRATED
CONSIGNOR	FLESHLESS	KISSINGER	PARSIMONY	RESSALDAR	ANATOMIZE	CATTLEMAN
CONSOCIES	FLESHPOTS	LAPSTREAK	PARSONAGE	ROISTERER	APATHETIC	CATTLEPEN
CONSONANT	FLUSTERED	LASSITUDE	PASSAMENT	ROOSEVELT	ARCTOGAEA	CAUTERIZE
CONSTABLE	FORSYTHIA	LEASEBACK	PASSENGER	RORSCHACH	AUCTORIAL	CENTAURUS
CONSTANCE	FOSSILISE	LEASEHOLD	PASSEPIED	ROUSSETTE	AUSTERITY	CENTENARY
CONSTANCY	FOSSORIAL	LEASTWAYS	PASSERINE	SAPSUCKER	AUSTRALIA	CENTERING
CONSTRICT	FRESHENER	LEASTWISE	PASSIVELY	SASSAFRAS	AYATOLLAH	CENTIGRAM
CONSTRUCT	FRESHNESS	LEISURELY	PASSIVITY	SASSENACH	BACTERIAL	CENTIPEDE
CONSULATE	FROSTBITE	LOBSCOUSE	PAUSANIAS	SASSOLITE	BACTERIUM	CENTRALLY
CONSUMING	FRUSTRATE	LOOSEHEAD	PEASANTRY	SCISSORER	BALTHAZAR	CENTREING
COXSACKIE	FUSSINESS	LOOSELEAF	PEASEWEEP	SEASONING	BALTIMORE	CENTURION
CRASHLAND	GESSAMINE	LOOSENESS	PENSIONER	SENSATION	BANTERING	CERTAINLY
CRESCELLE	GLASSWARE	LOUSEWORT	PENSIVELY	SENSELESS	BAPTISMAL	CERTAINTY
CRESCENDO	GLASSWORT	MANSFIELD	PENSTEMON	SENSILLUM	BARTENDER	CERTIFIED
CRISPNESS	GLISSANDO	MARSHLAND	PERSECUTE	SENSITIVE	BARTHOLDI	CERTITUDE
CROSSBEAM	GOOSANDER	MARSUPIAL	PERSEVERE	SENSITIZE	BARTHOLIN	CHATTERER
CROSSBILL	GOOSEFOOT	MARSUPIUM	PERSIMMON	SENSORIUM	BASTINADE	COLTSFOOT
CROSSBRED	GOOSEHERD	MASSINGER	PERSONAGE	SENSUALLY	BASTINADO	CONTAGION
CROSSEYED	GOOSENECK	MASSIVELY	PERSONATE	SHASHLICK	BATTALION	CONTAINER
CROSSFIRE	GOOSESTEP	MASSORETE	PERSONIFY	SISSERARY	BATTLEAXE	CONTEMPER
CROSSOVER	GOSSAMERY	MASSYMORE	PERSONNEL	SPASMODIC	BEATITUDE	CONTENDER
CROSSWALK	GOSSYPINE	MAUSOLEUM	PERSUADED	SUBSCRIBE	BEETHOVEN	CONTENTED
CROSSWIND	GOSSYPIUM	MEASURING	PESSIMISM	SUBSCRIPT	BETTERTON	CONTINENT
CROSSWISE	GRASSLAND	MENSHEVIK	PESSIMIST	SUBSIDIZE	BIRTHMARK	CONTINUAL
CROSSWORD	GRISAILLE	MENSTRUAL	PHOSPHATE	SUBSTANCE	BIRTHRATE	CONTINUUM
CRUSTACEA	GROSGRAIN	MENSTRUUM	PHOSPHENE	SUBSTRATA	BIRTHWORT	CONTRALTO
CTESIPHON	GROSVENOR	MESSALINA	PHYSICIAN	SUBSTRATE	BLATANTLY	CONTRIVED
CURSORILY	GUESSWORK	MESSENGER	PHYSICIST	SUNSCREEN	BOATHOUSE	CONTRIVER
DAMSELFLY	GUMSHIELD	MESSIANIC	PINSTRIPE	SUNSTROKE	BOATSWAIN	CONTUMACY

CONTUMELY	EPITOMIZE	HASTINESS	MEATBALLS	PARTIALLY	PROTOSTAR	SOUTHERLY
CONTUSION	EROTICISM	HAUTMONDE	MENTALITY	PARTICLES	PROTOTYPE	SOUTHWARD
CORTISONE	ERSTWHILE	HAWTHORNE	MENTATION	PARTITION	PRYTANEUM	SOUTHWARK
COSTUMIER	ERYTHRITE	HEATHLAND	MENTICIDE	PARTRIDGE	QUITTANCE	SOUTHWEST
COUTURIER	EVITERNAL	HECTOGRAM	MENTIONED	PARTTIMER	QUOTATION	SPATIALLY
CRETINOUS	FACTIONAL	HECTORING	MIRTHLESS	PASTERNAK	QUOTIDIAN	SPATTERED
CRITERION	FACTORIAL	HESTERNAL	MISTEMPER	PASTICCIO	QUOTITION	SPATULATE
CRITICISM	FACTORISE	HISTAMINE	MISTIGRIS	PASTORALE	RANTIPOLE	SPOTLIGHT
CRITICIZE	FACTUALLY	HISTIDINE	MISTINESS	PASTURAGE	RAPTORIAL	STATEHOOD
CROTCHETY	FAITHLESS	HISTOGRAM	MISTLETOE	PATTERNED	RAPTUROUS	STATELESS
CULTIVATE	FANTASIZE	HISTOLOGY	MONTACUTE	PENTAGRAM	RATTLEBAG	STATEMENT
CURTILAGE	FANTASTIC	HISTORIAN	MONTAIGNE	PENTECOST	RECTANGLE	STATEROOM
CUSTODIAL	FASTENING	HORTATIVE	MONTANISM	PENTHOUSE	RECTIFIER	STATESIDE
CUSTODIAN	FASTTRACK	HORTATORY	MONTANIST	PENTOSANE	RECTITUDE	STATESMAN
CUSTOMARY	FATTENING	HOSTILITY	MONTESPAN	PERTINENT	RECTORIAL	STATEWIDE
CUSTOMIZE	FEATHERED	HOTTENTOT	MONTEZUMA	PERTUSATE	REITERATE	STATIONED
CUTTHROAT	FERTILITY	HOWTOWDIE	MONTICULE	PERTUSSIS	RENTALLER	STATIONER
DALTONISM	FERTILIZE	HUTTERITE	MORTALITY	PERVASATE	REPTATION	STATISTIC
DANTHONIA	FESTINATE	HYSTERICS	MORTGAGEE	PESTICIDE	REPTILIAN	STATOCYST
DARTAGNAN	FESTIVITY	IMITATION	MORTGAGOR	PESTILENT	RESTIFORM	STATOLITH
DARTBOARD	FICTIONAL	IMITATIVE	MORTICIAN	PETTICOAT	RESTITUTE	STATUETTE
DARTMOUTH	FIFTEENTH	INITIALLY	MORTIFIED	PETTINESS	RESTRAINT	STATUTORY
DASTARDLY	FILTERING	INITIATED	MORTSTONE	PETTITOES	RIOTOUSLY	SUBTENANT
DEATHBLOW	FILTERTIP	INITIATOR	MOUTHLESS	PHITONIUM	ROOTSTOCK	SUBTITLED
DEATHLESS	FLATTENED	INSTANTER	MOUTHWASH	PHOTOCOPY	ROSTELLUM	SUETONIUS
DEATHTRAP	FLATTENER	INSTANTLY	MULTIFORM	PHOTOGENE	ROTTERDAM	SULTANATE
DENTISTRY	FLATTERED	INSTIGATE	MULTIPLEX	PHOTOSTAT	ROUTINELY	SUNTANNED
DENTITION	FLATTERER	INSTITUTE	MULTITUDE	PHOTOTUBE	RUSTICATE	SUSTAINED
DESTITUTE	FLATULENT	ISOTACTIC	MUSTINESS	PHYTOLITE	RUSTINESS	SWOTHLING
DESTROYED	FLOTATION	ISOTROPIC	MUTTERING	PHYTOTRON	SALTINESS	SYNTACTIC
DESTROYER	FOOTBRAKE	JITTERBUG	MYSTERIES	PICTOGRAM	SALTPETER	SYNTHESIS
DEUTERIUM	FOOTHILLS	JUSTIFIED	MYSTICISM	PICTORIAL	SALTPETRE	SYNTHETIC
DEXTERITY	FOOTLOOSE	JUSTINIAN	NANTUCKET	PISTACHIO	SALTWATER	TACTFULLY
DEXTEROUS	FOOTPLATE	JUXTAPOSE	NASTINESS	PISTAREEN	SALTWORKS	TACTICIAN
DEXTRORSE	FOOTPRINT	KENTIGERN	NECTARINE	PISTOLEER	SANTAYANA	TANTALITE
DIATHERMY	FOOTSTALL	KENTLEDGE	NEPTUNIUM	PLATITUDE	SANTONICA	TANTALIZE
DIATHESIS	FOOTSTOOL	KINTLEDGE	NEUTRALLY	PLATONIST	SARTORIAL	TANTARARA
DIATOMITE	FORTALICE	KITTENISH	NICTITATE	PLETHORIC	SARTORIUS	TARTAREAN
DICTATION	FORTHWINK	KITTIWAKE	NIETZSCHE	PLUTOCRAT	SAUTERNES	TASTELESS
DIETETICS	FORTHWITH	KNOTGRASS	NOCTURNAL	PLUTONIUM	SCATTERED	TAUTOLOGY
DIETICIAN	FORTILAGE	LACTATION	NORTHEAST	POETASTER	SCOTCHMAN	TECTIFORM
DIRTINESS	FORTITUDE	LANTHANUM	NORTHERLY	POETICIZE	SCYTHEMAN	TECTONICS
DISTANTLY	FORTNIGHT	LASTDITCH	NORTHWARD	PONTLEVIS	SECTARIAN	TECTORIAL
DISTEMPER	FORTUNATE	LATTERDAY	NORTHWEST	PORTERAGE	SECTIONAL	TENTATIVE
DISTENDED	FRATCHETY	LEFTOVERS	NOSTALGIA	PORTFOLIO	SECTORIAL	TENTORIUM
DISTILLER	FRATERNAL	LEFTWARDS	NOSTALGIC	PORTRAYAL	SENTIENCE	TESTAMENT
DISTORTED	FRETFULLY	LEITMOTIF	NOSTOLOGY	PORTREEVE	SENTIMENT	TESTATRIX
DISTRAINT	FRITHBORH	LEITMOTIV	NYSTAGMUS	PORTULACA	SEPTEMBER	TESTDRIVE
DISTURBED	FURTIVELY	LESTRIGON	OASTHOUSE	POSTCARDS	SEPTIMOLE	TESTICLES
DOCTORATE	FUSTIGATE	LETTERBOX	OBSTETRIC	POSTERIOR	SHATTERED	TESTIFIER
DOCTRINAL	FUSTINESS	LETTERING	OBSTINACY	POSTERITY	SHETLANDS	TESTIMONY
DYSTROPHY	GENTEELLY	LINTSTOCK	OBSTINATE	POSTHOUSE	SHUTTERED	TETTEROUS
EARTHFLAX	GENTILITY	LISTENING	OESTROGEN	POSTILION	SILTSTONE	THATCHING
EARTHLING	GENTLEMAN	LOATHSOME	OILTANKER	POSTNATAL	SIXTEENMO	TICTACTOE
EARTHWORK	GENTLEMEN	LOFTINESS	ORATORIAN	POSTPONED	SIXTEENTH	TITTLEBAT
EARTHWORM	GESTATION	LOITERING	OUTTHRUST	POSTULANT	SKETCHILY	TOOTHACHE
EASTBOUND	GLUTAMINE	LUCTATION	PANTAGAMY	POSTULATE	SKETCHMAP	TOOTHCOMB
EASTERNER	GLUTINOUS	LUSTIHOOD	PANTALEON	POSTWOMAN	SKETCHPAD	TOOTHLESS
EASTLINGS	GRATICULE	LUSTINESS	PANTALOON	POTTINGAR	SOFTCOVER	TOOTHPICK
EASTWARDS	GRATITUDE	MACTATION	PANTHEISM	PRETENDER	SOFTENING	TOOTHSOME
EDITORIAL	GROTESQUE	MARTINEAU	PANTHENOL	PRETERITE	SOOTERKIN	TORTELIER
ELATERIUM	GUATEMALA	MARTINMAS	PANTOFFLE	PRETERMIT	SORTILEGE	TOTTENHAM
ELUTRIATE	GUITARIST	MARTYRDOM	PANTOMIME	PROTAMINE	SOSTENUTO	TRATTORIA
EMOTIONAL	GUSTATION	MASTERFUL	PANTOUFLE	PROTECTOR	SOTTISIER	TRETINOIN
EMPTINESS	GUTTERING	MASTERMAN	PARTAKING	PROTESTER	SOUTENEUR	TRITENESS
ENSTATITE	HARTSHORN	MASTICATE	PARTHENON	PROTHESIS	SOUTHDOWN	TRITICALE
EPITHESIS	HASTENING	MATTAMORE	PARTHOLON	PROTHORAX	SOUTHEAST	TRITURATE

TRUTINATE	ACTUALITY	EXQUISITE	LUXURIANT	REVULSION	BELVEDERE	SERVICING
UMPTEENTH	ACTUARIAL	FABULINUS	LUXURIATE	RHEUMATIC	CALVANISM	SERVIETTE
UNETHICAL	ALEURITIS	FACUNDITY	LUXURIOUS	ROQUEFORT	CALVINIST	SERVILELY
UNITARIAN	AMAUROSIS	FATUOUSLY	MAJUSCULE	ROTUNDATE	CALVITIES	SERVILITY
VANTBRASS	AMBULANCE	FECUNDITY	MANUBRIUM	ROTUNDITY	CANVASSER	SERVITUDE
VENTIFACT	AMBUSCADE	FEDUCIARY	MATUTINAL	SALUBRITY	CERVANTES	SHAVELING
VENTILATE	ANGUISHED	FENUGREEK	MENUISIER	SATURATED	CHAVENDER	SHIVERING
VENTRICLE	ANNULMENT	FIDUCIARY	MINUSCULE	SATURNIAN	CHEVALIER	SHOVELFUL
VERTEBRAE	ARAUCARIA	FIGURANTE	MINUTEMAN	SATURNINE	CLEVELAND	SHOVELLER
VERTEBRAL	ARDUOUSLY	FLOURMILL	MUTUALISM	SATURNISM	CONVECTOR	SILVEREYE
VERTIPORT	ARQUEBUSE	GENUFLECT	NATURALLY	SCOUNDREL	CONVERTED	SLAVISHLY
VERTUMNUS	ASSUETUDE	GENUINELY	OBFUSCATE	SCRUBBING	CONVERTER	SLIVOVICA
VESTIBULE	ASSURANCE	GERUNDIVE	OBJURGATE	SCRUFFILY	CONVINCED	SLIVOVITZ
VESTIGIAL	ASSUREDLY	GROUNDHOG	OCCULTIST	SCRUMMAGE	CONVIVIAL	SLOVENIAN
VESTITURE	ASTUCIOUS	GROUNDING	OCCUPANCY	SCRUMPING	CURVATURE	SOUVLAKIA
VESTMENTS	ATTUITION	GROUNDNUT	OCCUPYING	SCRUTATOR	CURVEBALL	STAVANGER
VICTIMIZE	AUGUSTINE	GROUNDSEL	ODOURLESS	SEDUCTION	DRAVIDIAN	STEVEDORE
VICTORIAN	BEAUTEOUS	HIRUNDINE	OMBUDSMAN	SEDUCTIVE	ELEVATION	STEVENSON
VICTORINE	BEAUTIFUL	HUMUNGOUS	PALUDRINE	SEPULCHER	ELEVENSES	STOVEPIPE
VIRTUALLY	BIFURCATE	IMMUNISER	PECULATOR	SEPULCHRE	FERVENTLY	SURVEYING
VOLTIGEUR	BROUGHTON	IMMUTABLE	PECUNIARY	SEPULTURE	FLAVORING	SURVIVING
VOLTINISM	BURUNDIAN	IMMUTABLY	PENURIOUS	SEQUENCER	FLAVOURED	SYLVANITE
VOLTMETER	CASUARINA	IMPUDENCE	PETULANCE	SEQUESTER	FRIVOLITY	TRAVELERS
VOLTURNUS	CASUISTIC	IMPULSION	PIQUANTLY	SEQUINNED	FRIVOLOUS	TRAVELING
VORTICISM	CASUISTRY	IMPULSIVE	PITUITARY	SEXUALITY	GALVANISM	TRAVELLER
VORTIGERN	CERUSSITE	INAUDIBLE	PITUITRIN	SHRUBBERY	GALVANIZE	TREVELYAN
VULTURINE	CHAUFFEUR	INAUDIBLY	PLAUSIBLE	SILURIDAE	GRAVADLAX	TRIVIALLY
WAITERAGE	CLOUDLESS	INAUGURAL	PLAUSIBLY	SIMULATED	GRAVESEND	UNIVALENT
WARTCRESS	COCUSWOOD	INCUBATOR	PLAUSTRAL	SIMULATOR	GRAVESIDE	UNIVERSAL
WASTELAND	COLUMBARY	INCULCATE	PLOUGHMAN	SIMULCAST	GRAVEYARD	VALVASSOR
WASTWATER	COLUMBATE	INCULPATE	PNEUMATIC	SINUOSITY	GRAVITATE	VELVETEEN
WELTGEIST	COLUMBIAN	INCUMBENT	PNEUMONIA	SINUSITIS	HARVESTER	WOLVERINE
WESTBOUND	COLUMBINE	INCURABLE	POPULARLY	SITUATION	HEAVINESS	ANSWERING
WESTERNER	COLUMBITE	INCURABLY	POPULATED	SLAUGHTER	HEAVISIDE	ARKWRIGHT
WESTWARDS	COLUMBIUM	INCURIOUS	PROUDHORN	SLOUGHING	HEAVYDUTY	AWKWARDLY
WHETSTONE	COLUMELLA	INCURSION	PROUSTITE	STAUNCHLY	HELVELLYN	BLOWTORCH
WHITAKERS	COLUMNIST	INDUCTION	PSEUDAXIS	STOUTNESS	LAEVULOSE	BOXWALLAH
WHITEBAIT	CONUNDRUM	INDUCTIVE	PSEUDONYM	STRUCTURE	MARVELOUS	CHAWBACON
WHITEDAMP	CORUSCATE	INDULGENT	PURULENCE	STRUMITIS	NERVOUSLY	CROWNLIKE
WHITEFISH	CROUSTADE	INFURIATE	RECUMBENT	STRUTTING	OLIVENITE	CROWSBILL
WHITEHALL	DEBUTANTE	INHUMANLY	RECURRENT	SUQUAMISH	PEEVISHLY	CROWSFOOT
WHITEHEAD	DECUMBENT	INJURIOUS	RECURRING	TABULATOR	PERVASION	DARWINIAN
WHITENESS	DECURSIVE	INJUSTICE	RECURSIVE	TEMULENCE	PERVASIVE	DRAWKNIFE
WHITENING	DECUSSATE	INQUILINE	RECUSANCE	TENUOUSLY	PERVERTED	FLOWCHART
WHITEWALL	DEDUCTION	INQUINATE	REDUCIBLE	THAUMATIN	POLVERINE	FLOWERBED
WHITEWASH	DEDUCTIVE	INQUIRING	REDUCTION	THOUSANDS	PREVALENT	FLOWERING
WHITEWING	DEMULCENT	INQUORATE	REDUNDANT	TIPULIDAE	PREVERNAL	FLOWERPOT
WHITEWOOD	DEMURRAGE	INSULATOR	REFULGENT	TRAUMATIC	PRIVATEER	FLOWSTONE
WHITTAWER	DESUETUDE	INSULTING	REFURBISH	TRIUMPHAL	PRIVATELY	FLYWEIGHT
WHITWORTH	DESULTORY	INSURANCE	REFUSENIK	TROUBADOR	PRIVATION	FORWANDER
WISTFULLY	DISUNITED	INSURGENT	REGUERDON	TROUSSEAU	PRIVATIZE	INDWELLER
WITTICISM	DOCUMENTS	INTUITION	REGULARLY	UNGUARDED	PRIVILEGE	INSWINGER
WITTINGLY	EFFULGENT	INTUITIVE	REGULATOR	UNLUCKILY	PROVEDORE	JAYWALKER
WORTHLESS	ENCUMBENT	INTUMESCE	RELUCTANT	UNMUSICAL	PROVENDER	KISWAHILI
XANTHIPPE	ENDURABLE	IRRUPTION	REPUDIATE	UNRUFFLED	PROVIDENT	KNOWINGLY
YESTERDAY	ENDURANCE	JEQUIRITY	REPUGNANT	UNSULLIED	PROVIDING	KNOWLEDGE
YESTEREVE	ENQUIRIES	JERUSALEM	REPULSION	UNTUTORED	PROVISION	MIDWIFERY
ZEITGEIST	ENQUIRING	JOCULARLY	REPULSIVE	VAGUENESS	PROVOKING	MIDWINTER
ABDUCTION	EPAULETTE	LIQUEFIED	REPUTABLE	VALUATION	PROVOLONE	NORWEGIAN
ABLUTIONS	ESCULENTS	LIQUIDATE	REPUTEDLY	VALUELESS	PULVERIZE	OUTWARDLY
ABOUNDING	ESQUILINE	LIQUIDITY	REQUISITE	VENUSBERG	QUAVERING	OUTWORKER
ABOUTFACE	EXCULPATE	LIQUIDIZE	RESULTANT	VIRULENCE	QUIVERFUL	SEAWORTHY
ABOUTTURN	EXCURSION	LIQUORICE	RESULTING	VISUALIZE	QUIVERING	SHEWBREAD
ABSURDITY	EXCUSABLE	LIQUORISH	RESURFACE	VOLUCRINE	SALVARSAN	SHOWINESS
ACOUSTICS	EXCUSABLY	LITURGICS	RESURGENT	VOLUNTARY	SALVATION	SHOWPIECE
ACQUIESCE	EXPULSION	LOQUACITY	RESURRECT	VOLUNTEER	SAUVIGNON	SKEWWHIFF
ACQUITTAL	EXPURGATE	LUCUBRATE	RETURNING	ATAVISTIC	SCAVENGER	SLOWCOACH

SNOWBOUND	SATYRIDAE	BEDJACKET	COCKATIEL	ENDEARING	GERMANDER	INFLATION
SNOWDONIA	SATYRINAE	BEDRAGGLE	COLLAPSAR	ENDEAVOUR	GERMANITE	INGRAINED
SNOWDRIFT	SIBYLLINE	BELEAGUER	COLLATION	ENDPAPERS	GERMANIUM	INSHALLAH
SNOWFLAKE	SISYPHEAN	BERGAMASK	COMBATANT	ENGRAINED	GESSAMINE	INSTANTER
SNOWSHOES	TWAYBLADE	BERGANDER	COMBATIVE	ENGRAVING	GESTATION	INSTANTLY
SNOWSTORM	UNTYPICAL	BESPANGLE	COMMANDER	ENSTATITE	GIBRALTAR	ISCHAEMIC
SNOWWHITE	AMAZEMENT	BILLABONG	COMPACTLY	ENTRAMMEL	GILGAMESH	ISOLATION
SOUWESTER	AMAZONITE	BLATANTLY	COMPANIES	ENTRANCED	GLUTAMINE	ISOTACTIC
STOWNLINS	BRAZILIAN	BOCCACCIO	COMPANION	EPEDAPHIC	GODFATHER	ITERATION
VIEWPOINT	CRAZINESS	BOMBARDON	CONCAVITY	EPHIALTES	GODPARENT	JAGGANATH
WANWORTHY	DIAZEUXIS	BOMBASINE	CONTAGION	EPIGAEOUS	GONIATITE	JAMBALAYA
ALEXANDER	DIZZINESS	BOMBASTIC	CONTAINER	EPILATION	GOOSANDER	JAMPACKED
ALEXANDRA	ELIZABETH	BORNAGAIN	CORIANDER	EPINASTIC	GOSLARITE	JAWBATION
DEOXIDISE	FRIZZANTE	BOSSANOVA	COXSACKIE	EPULATION	GOSSAMERY	JAYWALKER
FLEXITIME	FUZZINESS	BOXWALLAH	CREMATION	ESPLANADE	GOTHAMITE	JESSAMINE
PROXIMATE	LAZZARONE	BRIGADIER	CREMATORY	ESTRANGED	GRADATION	JORDANIAN
PROXIMITY	MEZZANINE	BRIGADOON	CRENATION	ESTRAPADE	GRAVADLAX	JOVIALITY
REEXAMINE	MEZZOTINT	BRITANNIA	CURVATURE	EUCHARIST	GREGARINE	JUXTAPOSE
UNEXPOSED	MONZONITE	BRITANNIC	CYCLAMATE	EUSKARIAN	GRENADIER	KEPLARIAN
AEPYORNIS	MUZZINESS	BRUTALISM	DAEDALIAN	EVAGATION	GRENADINE	KIDNAPPED
ANHYDRIDE	PIZZICATO	BRUTALITY	DALMATIAN	EVOCATION	GRIMALKIN	KIDNAPPER
ANHYDRITE	QUIZZICAL	BRUTALIZE	DAMNATION	EVOCATIVE	GRISAILLE	KILLARNEY
ANHYDROUS	TANZANIAN	BUCCANEER	DARTAGNAN	EVOCATORY	GUACAMOLE	KISWAHILI
ANKYLOSIS	WAYZGOOSE	BUCHAREST	DASTARDLY	EXARATION	GUARANTEE	LACTATION
BARYSCOPE	WHIZZBANG	BULGARIAN	DECLARING	EXCLAIMED	GUARANTOR	LAMPADARY
BERYLLIUM	**9:5**	BYSTANDER	DEFEATISM	EXORATION	GUITARIST	LAMPADION
BICYCLIST	ABSTAINER	CACHAEMIA	DEFEATIST	EXPIATION	GUSTATION	LANCASTER
BODYGUARD	ACETAMIDE	CAESAREAN	DEFLATION	EXPIATORY	GYMNASIUM	LANDAULET
CARYOPSIS	ACTUALITY	CALCANEUM	DEGRADING	EXTRACTOR	GYMNASTIC	LAPLANDER
CHRYSALIS	ACTUARIAL	CALCANEUS	DEMEANING	EXTRADITE	HACKAMORE	LATRATION
COPYRIGHT	ADORATION	CALDARIUM	DEMEANOUR	EXUDATION	HAEMALOMA	LAUDATION
COTYLEDON	ADULATION	CALVANISM	DEPRAVITY	FANDANGLE	HAEMATITE	LAUDATORY
DEHYDRATE	AGALACTIC	CAMPANILE	DESCARTES	FANTASIZE	HAMFATTER	LAWMAKING
DIZYGOTIC	AGGRAVATE	CAMPANULA	DETRACTOR	FANTASTIC	HAPHAZARD	LAZZARONE
EASYGOING	AGITATION	CANTABILE	DEUCALION	FEUDALISM	HARDANGER	LETHARGIC
EDDYSTONE	ALABASTER	CANVASSER	DEVIATION	FEUDATORY	HARMALINE	LEUKAEMIA
ENHYDRITE	ALEXANDER	CAPTAINCY	DICTATION	FINLANDIA	HARMATTAN	LEVIATHAN
EUMYCETES	ALEXANDRA	CARBAMATE	DISCARDED	FIRMAMENT	HAYMAKING	LIBRARIAN
GREYBEARD	AMARANTIN	CARBAMIDE	DISFAVOUR	FLOTATION	HAYMARKET	LINEAMENT
GREYHOUND	AMELAKITE	CARNATION	DISMANTLE	FOGRAMITE	HAYRADDIN	LIVRAISON
GREYWACKE	ANIMALISM	CARPACCIO	DISPARAGE	FOREANENT	HERBALIST	LOMBARDIC
HEDYPHANE	ANIMALITY	CASSANDRA	DISPARATE	FORGATHER	HERBARIUM	LOOKALIKE
HESYCHASM	ANIMATION	CASSATION	DISPARITY	FORJASKIT	HEREAFTER	LOQUACITY
HESYCHAST	ANOMALOUS	CASTANETS	DISTANTLY	FORMALISM	HERMANDAD	LOWLANDER
HIMYARITE	APPEALING	CASUARINA	DOGMATISM	FORMALITY	HIERARCHY	LUCRATIVE
HOLYSTONE	APPRAISAL	CATHARSIS	DOGMATIZE	FORMALIZE	HIMYARITE	LUCTATION
HOUYHNHNM	ARCHANGEL	CATHARTIC	DONCASTER	FORMATION	HISTAMINE	MACCABEES
KARYOTYPE	ASTRAGALS	CAUCASIAN	DRAMATICS	FORMATIVE	HOBNAILED	MACTATION
LABYRINTH	ASTRAKHAN	CAUCASOID	DRAMATIST	FORTALICE	HOCCAMORE	MADRASSAH
LADYSMITH	ATONALITY	CAUSATION	DRAMATIZE	FORWANDER	HODMANDOD	MAGDALENE
LAZYBONES	AVALANCHE	CELLARIST	DUMBARTON	FRICASSEE	HOOLACHAN	MAGNALIUM
LILYWHITE	AVOCATION	CENTAURUS	DUNGAREES	FRIGATOON	HORTATIVE	MALLANDER
OKEYDOKEY	AWKWARDLY	CERTAINLY	EDUCATION	FRUGALITY	HORTATORY	MAMMALIAN
PLAYFULLY	BACHARACH	CERTAINTY	EDUCATIVE	FUNDAMENT	HUCKABACK	MANDATARY
PLAYGROUP	BALDAQUIN	CERVANTES	ELEGANTLY	GALLABEAH	HUNGARIAN	MANDATORY
PLAYHOUSE	BALLADEER	CESSATION	ELEVATION	GALLANTLY	HUSBANDLY	MANGANATE
PLAYTHING	BALLADIST	CHABAZITE	ELIZABETH	GALLANTRY	HUSBANDRY	MANGANESE
POLYANDRY	BANDALORE	CHALAZION	EMANATION	GALRAVAGE	HYDRANGEA	MANHANDLE
POLYESTER	BARBARIAN	CHAPARRAL	EMBRACERY	GALVANISM	HYDRAULIC	MANHATTAN
POLYGONAL	BARBARISM	CHARABANC	EMBRACING	GALVANIZE	HYDRAZINE	MARCASITE
POLYGRAPH	BARBARITY	CHARACTER	EMBRANGLE	GARGANTUA	ICELANDER	MARGARINE
POLYMORPH	BARBARIZE	CHEVALIER	EMBRASURE	GARGARISM	ICELANDIC	MARMALADE
POLYNESIA	BARBAROUS	CHICANERY	EMPHASIZE	GENEALOGY	IMBRANGLE	MATTAMORE
POLYPHASE	BARNABITE	CHINATOWN	EMULATION	GENIALITY	IMITATION	MECHANICS
POLYPHONE	BARNACLES	CIRCADIAN	ENCHANTED	GERFALCON	IMITATIVE	MECHANISM
POLYPHONY	BARRACUDA	CLIMACTIC	ENCHANTER	GERIATRIC	IMPEACHER	MECHANIZE
POLYTHENE	BATTALION	COCKAIGNE	ENCRATITE	GERMANCER	INDRAUGHT	MEDIAEVAL

MEDIATION	ORPHARION	PREVALENT	SASSAFRAS	TASMANIAN	VIBRATION	EDINBURGH
MENDACITY	OSTRACISE	PRIMAEVAL	SATIATION	TENTATIVE	VIBRATORY	ESTABLISH
MENTALITY	OSTRACISM	PRIMARILY	SCALARIUM	TERMAGANT	VIOLATION	EXHIBITOR
MENTATION	OSTRACIZE	PRIMAVERA	SCHIAVONE	TERMAGENT	VISUALIZE	FIREBRAND
MERCAPTAN	OUTWARDLY	PRIVATEER	SCHMALTZY	TERRACING	VITIATION	FIREBREAK
MERGANSER	OVIPAROUS	PRIVATELY	SCHNAPPER	TERRARIUM	VOLCANISM	FOOTBRAKE
MESSALINA	OVULATION	PRIVATION	SCHNAUZER	TESTAMENT	VULCANIAN	FOREBEARS
METHADONE	OXIDATION	PRIVATIZE	SEAFARING	TESTATRIX	VULCANIST	FOREBRAIN
MEZZANINE	PACKAGING	PROBABLES	SECTARIAN	TETRAGRAM	VULCANITE	FRAMBOISE
MIDIANITE	PAGEANTRY	PROBATION	SENSATION	TETRALOGY	VULCANIZE	FREEBOARD
MIDRASHIM	PALLADIAN	PROCACITY	SEPHARDIM	TETRARCHY	VULGARIAN	FULLBLOWN
MIGRATION	PALLADIUM	PROFANELY	SERIALIST	THALASSIC	VULGARISM	GARIBALDI
MIGRATORY	PALMATION	PROFANITY	SERIALIZE	THANATISM	VULGARITY	GREYBEARD
MILLAMANT	PALPATION	PROKARYON	SERIATION	THERALITE	WAGHALTER	GRUBBINOL
MINIATURE	PANDATION	PROLACTIN	SERRATION	THERAPIST	WALKABOUT	GRUMBLING
MISFALLEN	PANHANDLE	PROLAMINE	SEXUALITY	THESAURUS	WALLABIES	HACKBERRY
MISHANDLE	PANTAGAMY	PROMACHOS	SICCATIVE	THREADFIN	WHITAKERS	HAIRBRUSH
MISMANAGE	PANTALEON	PROPAGATE	SIGNALLER	THROATILY	WINCANTON	HALFBAKED
MITRAILLE	PANTALOON	PROTAMINE	SIGNALMAN	THYLACINE	WOLLASTON	HALOBIONT
MOCCASINS	PARDALOTE	PRYTANEUM	SIGNATORY	THYRATRON	ZEALANDER	HANDBRAKE
MONTACUTE	PARNASITE	PUGNACITY	SIGNATURE	TICTACTOE	ZECHARIAH	HARDBOARD
MONTAIGNE	PARNASSUS	PULSATION	SINGALESE	TIMPANIST	ZEPHANIAH	HEADBOARD
MONTANISM	PARTAKING	PURGATIVE	SINGAPORE	TITRATION	ZINFANDEL	HIDEBOUND
MONTANIST	PASSAMENT	PURGATORY	SINKANSEN	TOCCATINA	ZOOMANTIC	HILLBILLY
MORGANITE	PAUSANIAS	PYGMALION	SITUATION	TOPIARIST	ZOROASTER	HINDBRAIN
MORTALITY	PAYMASTER	QUOTATION	SKEDADDLE	TORBANITE	ACROBATIC	HOMEBOUND
MOYGASHEL	PEASANTRY	RACCABOUT	SKYJACKER	TOSCANINI	ADUMBRATE	HYLOBATES
MRIDAMGAM	PEGMATITE	RACCAHOUT	SOCIALISM	TRAFALGAR	ALDEBARAN	HYPOBLAST
MRIDANGAM	PEIRASTIC	RACIALISM	SOCIALIST	TREMATODE	ALGEBRAIC	IDIOBLAST
MUGLARITE	PELLAGRIN	RACIALIST	SOCIALITE	TRIBALISM	AYCKBOURN	ILLIBERAL
MUSCADINE	PELMANISM	RADIANTLY	SOCIALIZE	TRISAGION	BACKBENCH	INCUBATOR
MUSCARINE	PENTAGRAM	RADIATING	SPADASSIN	TROPAELIN	BACKBITER	INHIBITED
MUTUALISM	PERCALINE	RADIATION	SPREADING	TROPARION	BACKBOARD	INHIBITOR
NARRATION	PERGAMENE	RASPATORY	SQUEAMISH	TURMAGENT	BANEBERRY	INUMBRATE
NARRATIVE	PERIAKTOS	REBOATION	STAVANGER	TURNABOUT	BAREBONES	JUNEBERRY
NATHANIEL	PERIANDER	RECLAIMED	STERADIAN	TYMPANIST	BARMBRACK	KARABINER
NAUMACHIA	PERMANENT	RECLAIMER	STIRABOUT	UMBRATILE	BASEBOARD	LACKBEARD
NECTARINE	PERVASION	RECTANGLE	STOMACHIC	UNABASHED	BILLBOARD	LAMPBLACK
NEPHALISM	PERVASIVE	REDHANDED	STREAMING	UNBIASSED	BIRDBRAIN	LAZYBONES
NEPHALIST	PHALANGER	REEXAMINE	STRIATION	UNCEASING	BLUEBEARD	LINDBERGH
NEURALGIA	PHALAROPE	REFLATION	SUBJACENT	UNCHANGED	BLUEBERRY	LUCUBRATE
NEURALGIC	PHANARIOT	REFRACTOR	SUBMARINE	UNCHARGED	BOOTBLACK	MALEBOLGE
NEWCASTLE	PHARAMOND	REHEARSAL	SULTANATE	UNCLAIMED	BRAMBLING	MANUBRIUM
NEWMARKET	PHENACITE	RENTALLER	SUMMARILY	UNGUARDED	CALABOOSE	MEATBALLS
NEWSAGENT	PHENAKISM	REPLACING	SUMMARIZE	UNHEALTHY	CALABRESE	MESOBLAST
NIGGARDLY	PHIGALIAN	REPTATION	SUMMATION	UNITARIAN	CALIBRATE	METABASIS
NONPAREIL	PHILANDER	RESNATRON	SUNBATHER	UNIVALENT	CARDBOARD	METABOLIC
NORMALACY	PHILATELY	RESSALDAR	SUNTANNED	UNLEARNED	CARIBBEAN	MIRABELLE
NORMALITY	PHTHALATE	RETIARIUS	SUQUAMISH	UNSCATHED	CELEBRANT	MOTHBALLS
NORMALIZE	PICKABACK	RETRACTOR	SUSTAINED	UNSHACKLE	CELEBRATE	NASEBERRY
NORMATIVE	PINEAPPLE	REVEALING	SYLLABARY	UNSPARING	CELEBRITY	NOSEBLEED
NOSTALGIA	PIQUANTLY	RIGMAROLE	SYLLABLES	UNTRAINED	CEREBRATE	OCTOBRIST
NOSTALGIC	PISTACHIO	ROSMARINE	SYLVANITE	URINATION	CHAWBACON	OUROBOROS
NYSTAGMUS	PISTAREEN	ROUMANIAN	SYNTACTIC	VALIANTLY	CHILBLAIN	OUROBORUS
OCKHAMIST	PLACATORY	ROUMANSCH	SYRIACISM	VALUATION	CHIPBOARD	OVERBLOWN
OILTANKER	PLURALISM	RUINATION	TABLATURE	VALVASSOR	CLAPBOARD	OVERBOARD
OLIGARCHY	PLURALITY	SABBATIAN	TALKATIVE	VANDALISM	CLIPBOARD	PARABASIS
ONOMASTIC	POETASTER	SACRAMENT	TANTALITE	VANDALIZE	CORNBRASH	PARABLAST
ONSLAUGHT	POLIANITE	SACRARIUM	TANTALIZE	VARIATION	CRANBERRY	PARABOLIC
OPERATING	POLYANDRY	SALVARSAN	TANTARARA	VENIALITY	CRANBORNE	PERIBOLOS
OPERATION	POMPADOUR	SALVATION	TANZANIAN	VERBALIZE	CRUMBLING	PHLEBITIS
OPERATIVE	POUJADIST	SANDALLED	TAPDANCER	VERBASCUM	DARTBOARD	PLUMBEOUS
OPOBALSAM	PRECATORY	SANDARACH	TARMACKED	VERKAMPTE	DASHBOARD	PLUMBLINE
ORGIASTIC	PREDATORY	SANTAYANA	TARNATION	VERNATION	DISABLING	PRESBYTER
ORICALCHE	PREFATORY	SARBACANE	TARPAULIN	VERSATILE	DISOBLIGE	RASPBERRY
OROBANCHE	PREHALLUX	SARCASTIC	TARRAGONA	VESPASIAN	DUCKBOARD	REIMBURSE
ORPHANAGE	PREMATURE	SASKATOON	TARTAREAN	VIBRATILE	EASTBOUND	ROADBLOCK

SAGEBRUSH	AUTOCLAVE	ENUNCIATE	JUDICIARY	PINOCCHIO	STRICTURE	BLOODSHOT
SALUBRITY	AUTOCRACY	EPARCHATE	JUDICIOUS	POLICEMAN	STRUCTURE	BLOODWORM
SCAMBLING	AUTOCROSS	EPISCOPAL	KILOCYCLE	POSTCARDS	SUBSCRIBE	BLUNDERER
SCORBUTIC	AVUNCULAR	EUMYCETES	KINKCOUGH	PREOCCUPY	SUBSCRIPT	BOARDROOM
SCORBUTUS	BACKCLOTH	EXERCISED	KNEECORDS	PRESCIENT	SUNSCREEN	BOARDWALK
SCRUBBING	BALACLAVA	EXERCISES	LATECOMER	PRESCRIBE	TENACIOUS	BOONDOCKS
SEMIBREVE	BASECOURT	EXPECTANT	LATICLAVE	PRESCUTUM	TENACULUM	BOUNDLESS
SHEWBREAD	BASICALLY	EXPECTING	LAUNCELOT	PRINCETON	THATCHING	BRANDIRON
SHRUBBERY	BICYCLIST	EXSICCATE	LAUNCHING	PRINCIPAL	THEOCRACY	BREADLINE
SIDEBOARD	BINOCULAR	FABACEOUS	LOBSCOUSE	PRINCIPLE	TIERCERON	BROADCAST
SIDEBURNS	BISECTION	FACECLOTH	LOGICALLY	PROACTIVE	TIMOCRACY	BROADLOOM
SIGNBOARD	BLEACHERS	FAULCHION	LOINCLOTH	PROSCRIBE	TOPICALLY	BROADSIDE
SLUMBERER	BOLECTION	FEDUCIARY	LONGCHAMP	PUSHCHAIR	TREACHERY	BULLDOZER
SNOWBOUND	BRANCHING	FERACIOUS	LUDICROUS	QUERCETIN	TRENCHANT	CALEDONIA
SOAPBERRY	BREECHING	FEROCIOUS	LYRICALLY	QUERCETUS	TRUNCATED	CHILDCARE
STARBOARD	BRONCHIAL	FIDUCIARY	MAGICALLY	RADICALLY	TRUNCHEON	CHILDHOOD
STROBILUS	CAPACIOUS	FILICALES	MALACHITE	RADICCHIO	TYPICALLY	CHILDLESS
STUMBLING	CAPACITOR	FINICKING	MALICIOUS	RAINCHECK	UNDECIDED	CHILDLIKE
SURFBOARD	CARACALLA	FINICKITY	MASOCHISM	RAPACIOUS	UNLUCKILY	CHONDRITE
SWINBURNE	CATACLYSM	FLOWCHART	MASOCHIST	REDUCIBLE	UNSECURED	CHONDROID
TAILBOARD	CATACOMBS	FORECLOSE	MEDICALLY	REDUCTION	URTICARIA	CLOUDLESS
TENEBROSE	CATECHISM	FORECOURT	MEDICATED	REFECTION	VARICELLA	DAREDEVIL
TEREBINTH	CATECHIZE	FRANCESCA	MEDICINAL	REFECTORY	VASECTOMY	DECADENCE
THEOBROMA	CERECLOTH	FRANCHISE	MEGACYCLE	REJECTION	VEHICULAR	DECIDEDLY
THROBBING	CHANCROID	FRANCOLIN	MEPACRINE	RELUCTANT	VERACIOUS	DECIDUOUS
THUMBLING	CHURCHILL	FRATCHETY	MEROCRINE	REPECHAGE	VESICULAR	DEHYDRATE
THUMBNAIL	CHURCHMAN	FRENCHMAN	MINACIOUS	RETICENCE	VIVACIOUS	DIANDROUS
THUMBTACK	COARCTATE	FRENCHMEN	MISOCLERE	RETICULAR	VOLUCRINE	DIVIDENDS
TICHBORNE	COLOCYNTH	FUGACIOUS	MOBOCRACY	RETICULUM	VORACIOUS	DWINDLING
TREMBLING	COMICALLY	FUNICULAR	MOLECULAR	REVICTUAL	WARTCRESS	ECARDINES
TROUBADOR	CONSCIOUS	FUNICULUS	MONACTINE	RORSCHACH	WASHCLOTH	ECHIDNINE
TURNBULLS	CONSCRIPT	FURACIOUS	MONOCEROS	ROUNCEVAL	WINDCHILL	ENHYDRITE
TWAYBLADE	CORNCRAKE	GALACTOSE	MONOCHORD	ROUNCIVAL	WISECRACK	EPHEDRINE
VANTBRASS	CRESCELLE	GATECRASH	MONOCOQUE	RUBICELLE	WOODCHUCK	EXPEDIENT
WAHABIITE	CRESCENDO	GOLDCREST	MONOCULAR	SACKCLOTH	WOODCRAFT	FATIDICAL
WALLBOARD	CROTCHETY	HAECCEITY	MORECAMBE	SAGACIOUS	ZENOCRATE	FIELDFARE
WASHBASIN	CYNICALLY	HANDCUFFS	MOTOCROSS	SAILCLOTH	ZOOSCOPIC	FIELDSMAN
WASHBOARD	DECACHORD	HARDCOVER	MUNICIPAL	SALACIOUS	ABANDONED	FIELDWORK
WELLBEING	DECKCHAIR	HEADCLOTH	MUSICALLY	SALICETUM	ABANDONEE	FIREDRAKE
WELLBUILT	DECOCTION	HESYCHASM	MUSICHALL	SCONCHEON	ABUNDANCE	FLOODGATE
WESTBOUND	DEDICATED	HESYCHAST	NOMOCRACY	SCORCHING	ACCIDENTS	FOUNDLING
WINDBREAK	DEDUCTION	HIGHCLASS	NOTOCHORD	SCOTCHMAN	AERODROME	GLANDULAR
WINEBERRY	DEDUCTIVE	HIJACKING	NOVICIATE	SCUNCHEON	AFFIDAVIT	GLENDOWER
WOODBORER	DEFECTION	HOLOCAUST	NOVOCAINE	SEARCHING	AMENDMENT	GRANDIOSE
ABDUCTION	DEFECTIVE	HOMICIDAL	OBJECTIFY	SEBACEOUS	AMYGDALUS	GRANDNESS
ACONCAGUA	DEFICIENT	HOPSCOTCH	OBJECTION	SEDUCTION	ANECDOTAL	GRANDSIRE
ADDICTION	DEJECTION	HYPOCAUST	OBJECTIVE	SEDUCTIVE	ANECDOTES	GUARDRAIL
ADDICTIVE	DELACROIX	HYPOCRISY	OBSECRATE	SELACHIAN	ANHYDRIDE	GUARDROOM
ADJECTIVE	DELICIOUS	HYPOCRITE	OCTACHORD	SELECTING	ANHYDRITE	GUARDSMAN
ADVECTION	DEMOCRACY	ILLICITLY	OFFICIALS	SELECTION	ANHYDROUS	GUILDHALL
ADVOCATED	DEPICTION	IMPACTION	OFFICIANT	SELECTIVE	ARMADILLO	HALFDOZEN
AFFECTING	DESECRATE	INDECENCY	OFFICIATE	SEMICOLON	ASSIDUITY	HAMADRYAD
AFFECTION	DESICCATE	INDECORUM	OFFICIOUS	SETACEOUS	ASSIDUOUS	HEADDRESS
AGINCOURT	DETECTION	INDICATES	OLFACTORY	SILICOSIS	ASYNDETON	HEARDSMAN
AGUECHEEK	DETECTIVE	INDICATOR	OPERCULUM	SKETCHILY	AVOIDABLE	HERODOTUS
ALLOCARPY	DIDACTICS	INDICTION	OPTICALLY	SKETCHMAP	AVOIDANCE	IMMEDIACY
ANARCHIST	DIRECTION	INDUCTION	ORBICULAR	SKETCHPAD	BEARDLESS	IMMEDIATE
ANTICLINE	DIRECTIVE	INDUCTIVE	OVERCLOUD	SLOWCOACH	BEARDSLEY	IMMODESTY
ARAUCARIA	DIRECTORS	INFECTING	OVERCROWD	SOFTCOVER	BLANDNESS	IMPEDANCE
ARTICHOKE	DIRECTORY	INFECTION	PARACHUTE	SOLICITOR	BLINDFOLD	IMPUDENCE
ARTICULAR	DISHCLOTH	INJECTION	PARACLETE	SPEECHIFY	BLINDNESS	INAUDIBLE
ASSOCIATE	DOMICILED	INNOCENCE	PARACUSIS	SPHACELUS	BLINDSPOT	INAUDIBLY
ASTUCIOUS	EFFECTIVE	INNOCUOUS	PAROCHIAL	SPRECHERY	BLINDWORM	INCIDENCE
ATROCIOUS	EFFECTUAL	INUNCTION	PAROCHINE	SPUNCULID	BLOODBATH	INSIDIOUS
ATTACKING	EFFICIENT	INVECTIVE	PEDICULAR	STANCHION	BLOODLESS	INVIDIOUS
AUDACIOUS	ENDECAGON	IRASCIBLE	PERICLASE	STERCORAL	BLOODROOT	IRRADIANT
AURICULAR	ENDOCRINE	ISOSCELES	PERICUTIN	STOICALLY	BLOODSHED	IRRADIATE

JAUNDICED	STRIDENCY	BEEFEATER	CONCEALED	DISPENSER	FALSEHOOD	GUINEVERE
JURIDICAL	SUBEDITOR	BEEKEEPER	CONCEITED	DISPERSAL	FALSENESS	GUTTERING
KLENDUSIC	SWADDLING	BELIEVING	CONCERNED	DISPERSED	FASTENING	GYNOECIUM
LANDDROST	SWORDFISH	BELVEDERE	CONCERTED	DISREGARD	FATTENING	HALFEMPTY
LASTDITCH	SWORDPLAY	BENBECULA	CONDEMNED	DISREPAIR	FERMENTED	HAMMERING
LAUNDRESS	SWORDSMAN	BERKELIUM	CONDENSER	DISREPUTE	FERVENTLY	HANKERING
LURIDNESS	SYNEDRION	BERSERKER	CONFESSED	DISSEMBLE	FIFTEENTH	HANSEATIC
MACADAMIA	TAXIDERMY	BETTERTON	CONFESSOR	DISSENTER	FILTERING	HAPPENING
MACEDOINE	TESTDRIVE	BIGHEADED	CONGENIAL	DISTEMPER	FILTERTIP	HARLEQUIN
MACEDONIA	THIRDSMAN	BLAMELESS	CONGERIES	DISTENDED	FINGERING	HARLESTON
MEANDRIAN	THUNDERER	BOANERGES	CONGESTED	DITHERING	FINGERTIP	HARVESTER
MELODIOUS	TIREDNESS	BOOMERANG	CONNECTED	DIXIELAND	FISHERMAN	HASHEMITE
MELODRAMA	TREADMILL	BORDEREAU	CONNECTOR	DOTHEBOYS	FLABELLUM	HASTENING
MENADIONE	TRONDHEIM	BORDERERY	CONNEXION	DROMEDARY	FLAGELLIN	HAWSEHOLE
MOGADISHU	VELODROME	BOULEVARD	CONSENSUS	DUIKERBOK	FLAGELLUM	HELLEBORE
MONODRAMA	VERIDICAL	BRASENOSE	CONTEMPER	DUNGENESS	FLAGEOLET	HELVELLYN
NAKEDNESS	VIVIDNESS	BRIDEWELL	CONTENDER	DUNGEONER	FLORESTAN	HENPECKED
NICODEMUS	WEIRDNESS	BROKERAGE	CONTENTED	DUODECIMO	FLOWERBED	HERPESTES
NOVODAMUS	WITHDRAWN	BUCKETFUL	CONVECTOR	DYSPEPSIA	FLOWERING	HESPERIAN
OKEYDOKEY	WORLDWIDE	BUDGETARY	CONVERTED	DYSPEPTIC	FLOWERPOT	HESTERNAL
OMBUDSMAN	WYANDOTTE	BUFFETING	CONVERTER	EAGLEWOOD	FLYWEIGHT	HINDEMITH
OVERDRAFT	ABASEMENT	BUNDESTAG	COOPERATE	EARNESTLY	FOLKETING	HINGELESS
OVERDRAWN	ABATEMENT	BURLESQUE	CORNEILLE	EASTERNER	FORCEMEAT	HODIERNAL
OVERDRESS	ACADEMIST	BUTTERBUR	CORNELIAN	EGAREMENT	FORFEITED	HOLDERBAT
OVERDRIVE	ACCRETION	BUTTERCUP	CORNERMAN	ELATERIUM	FORGETFUL	HOLLERITH
PALUDRINE	ACUTENESS	BUTTERFLY	CORNETIST	ELEMENTAL	FORGETIVE	HORDEOLUM
PIPEDREAM	ADDRESSED	BUTTERNUT	CORRECTED	ELEVENSES	FORJESKIT	HORSEBACK
PLUMDAMAS	ADDRESSEE	CABLEGRAM	CORRECTLY	ELOPEMENT	FRAMEWORK	HORSEHAIR
PLUNDERER	AFORESAID	CACHECTIC	CORRECTOR	EMINENTLY	FRATERNAL	HORSELESS
PROUDHORN	AGAMEMNON	CANCEROUS	CORREGGIO	EMPAESTIC	FREDERICK	HORSEPLAY
PSEUDAXIS	AGGREGATE	CANNELURE	CORRELATE	EMPLECTON	FULLERENE	HORSESHOE
PSEUDONYM	AGGRESSOR	CAREERIST	COSMETICS	ENAMELLED	GARDENING	HORSETAIL
READDRESS	AGREEABLE	CARMELITE	CRIBELLUM	ENCHEASON	GARDEROBE	HORSEWHIP
REPUDIATE	AGREEABLY	CARNELIAN	CRITERION	ENDLESSLY	GASPEREAU	HOTHEADED
RESIDENCE	AGREEMENT	CARPENTER	CRUDENESS	ENDOERGIC	GATHERING	HOTTENTOT
RESIDENCY	AIMLESSLY	CARPENTRY	CUPRESSUS	ENGRENAGE	GAUDEAMUS	HOUSEBOAT
RESIDUARY	ALCHEMIST	CARPETING	CURRENTLY	ENSHEATHE	GAULEITER	HOUSECOAT
ROUNDBACK	AMAZEMENT	CARTESIAN	CURVEBALL	ENTRECHAT	GENTEELLY	HOUSEHOLD
ROUNDELAY	AMSTERDAM	CASSEROLE	CYMBELINE	ENTRECÔTE	GEODESIST	HOUSELEEK
ROUNDFISH	AMUSEMENT	CASTELLAN	DAMNEDEST	ENTREMETS	GEOMETRIC	HOUSEMAID
ROUNDHAND	ANALEPTIC	CATHEDRAL	DAMSELFLY	ENUMERATE	GEOMETRID	HOUSEROOM
ROUNDHEAD	ANSWERING	CATHEPSIN	DANDELION	EPICEDIUM	GIBBERISH	HOUSEWIFE
ROUNDSMAN	APPLEJACK	CATHERINE	DANGEROUS	EPICENTRE	GINGERADE	HOUSEWORK
SAPODILLA	APPREHEND	CAUTERIZE	DEAFENING	EPIDERMIS	GLABELLAR	HOYDENISH
SCALDFISH	ARABESQUE	CEASEFIRE	DECRETALS	EPIGENOUS	GLOMERATE	HUTTERITE
SCRODDLED	ARCHETYPE	CEASELESS	DECRETORY	EPILEPTIC	GLOMERULE	HYGIENIST
SCUDDALER	ARQUEBUSE	CENTENARY	DEFLECTOR	EROGENOUS	GLYCERIDE	HYPHENATE
SHELDDUCK	ASCLEPIUS	CENTERING	DENSENESS	ESTHETICS	GLYCERINE	HYSTERICS
SHELDRAKE	ASHKENAZI	CHAMELEON	DEPRECATE	ESTRELDID	GODDESSES	ICHNEUMON
SKINDIVER	ASPLENIUM	CHAPERONE	DEPREDATE	EUDAEMONY	GOOSEFOOT	ILCHESTER
SNOWDONIA	ASSUETUDE	CHAVENDER	DEPRESSED	EUPHEMISM	GOOSEHERD	IMAGELESS
SNOWDRIFT	ASYNERGIA	CHISELLER	DESPERADO	EVIDENTLY	GOOSENECK	IMPLEMENT
SOUNDBITE	ATHLETICS	CHOLELITH	DESPERATE	EVITERNAL	GOOSESTEP	IMPRECATE
SOUNDLESS	ATONEMENT	CIMMERIAN	DESUETUDE	EXCHEQUER	GOSPELLER	IMPRECISE
SOUNDNESS	AUSTERITY	CLARENDON	DEUTERIUM	EXCREMENT	GRACELESS	IMPRESSED
SOURDOUGH	AUTHENTIC	CLEVELAND	DEXTERITY	EXODERMIS	GRAPESHOT	INCLEMENT
SPEEDBOAT	AWAKENING	CLOSENESS	DEXTEROUS	EXOGENOUS	GRAPETREE	INCREASED
SPEEDWELL	AWARENESS	COALESCED	DIALECTAL	EXONERATE	GRAPEVINE	INCREMENT
SPELDRING	BACTERIAL	COFFERDAM	DIALECTIC	EXPLETIVE	GRAVESEND	INDWELLER
SPINDRIER	BACTERIUM	COLLEAGUE	DIAMETRIC	EXPRESSED	GRAVESIDE	INELEGANT
SPINDRIFT	BALLERINA	COLLECTED	DIANETICS	EXPRESSLY	GRAVEYARD	INFIELDER
SQUADRONE	BANTERING	COLLECTOR	DIAZEUXIS	EXTREMELY	GROCERIES	INFLEXION
STANDARDS	BARCELONA	COLLEGIAN	DIETETICS	EXTREMISM	GROTESQUE	INGLENOOK
STANDERBY	BARMECIDE	COMMENSAL	DIFFERENT	EXTREMIST	GUATEMALA	INNKEEPER
STANDGALE	BARTENDER	COMPELLED	DINNERSET	EXTREMITY	GUIDEBOOK	INSPECTOR
STANDPIPE	BASKETFUL	COMPETENT	DISBELIEF	EXUBERANT	GUIDELINE	ISOMERASE
STEADFAST	BEDFELLOW	COMPETING	DISMEMBER	EYELETEER	GUILELESS	ISOMETRIC

ISRAELITE	MENDELISM	PALAESTRA	PRETENDER	ROSTELLUM	SOOTERKIN	TEIRESIAS
ITINERANT	MERCENARY	PALPEBRAL	PRETERITE	ROTTERDAM	SORCERESS	TEMPERATE
ITINERARY	MERCERIZE	PANDEMIAN	PRETERMIT	RUBBERIZE	SOSTENUTO	TENDERIZE
ITINERATE	MESMERISM	PARHELION	PREVERNAL	RUDBECKIA	SOUTENEUR	TENNESSEE
JANSENISM	MESMERIZE	PASSENGER	PRICELESS	RUGGELACH	SOUWESTER	TENSENESS
JANSENIST	MESSENGER	PASSEPIED	PROCEDURE	RUTHENIAN	SPACELESS	TERSENESS
JENNETING	METHEGLIN	PASSERINE	PROCERITY	RUTHENIUM	SPACESHIP	TETTEROUS
JESSERANT	MIDHEAVEN	PASTERNAK	PROCESSOR	SABLEFISH	SPACESUIT	THELEMITE
JITTERBUG	MILLENIAL	PATIENTLY	PROFESSED	SACKERSON	SPIDERWEB	THEREFORE
JOBCENTRE	MILLEPEDE	PATTERNED	PROFESSOR	SADDENING	SPIKENARD	THEREUPON
JOBSEEKER	MILLEPORE	PEACEABLE	PROJECTED	SANHEDRIM	SPINELESS	THREEFOLD
JUDGEMENT	MINCEMEAT	PEACEABLY	PROJECTOR	SANHEDRIN	SPOKESMAN	THREESOME
JUNKETING	MINNESOTA	PEACETIME	PROLEPSIS	SANHEDRON	STAGEHAND	TIPPERARY
KERMESITE	MISBEHAVE	PEASEWEEP	PROMENADE	SARMENTUM	STALEMATE	TITHEBARN
KIESERITE	MISTEMPER	PENDENNIS	PROPELLED	SASSENACH	STALENESS	TORMENTER
KILDERKIN	MOCKERNUT	PENTECOST	PROPELLER	SAUCEBOAT	STATEHOOD	TORMENTIL
KITTENISH	MONTESPAN	PEPPERONI	PROPERDIN	SAUTERNES	STATELESS	TORMENTOR
LANCEWOOD	MONTEZUMA	PEPPERPOT	PROSECUTE	SCALEABLE	STATEMENT	TORMENTUM
LARGENESS	MOTHEATEN	PERAEOPOD	PROSELYTE	SCAPEGOAT	STATEROOM	TORTELIER
LATTERDAY	MOTHERING	PERFECTLY	PROTECTOR	SCARECROW	STATESIDE	TOTTENHAM
LEASEBACK	MOUSEHOLE	PERFERVID	PROTESTER	SCAVENGER	STATESMAN	TOWCESTER
LEASEHOLD	MOUSELIKE	PERMEABLE	PROVEDORE	SCELERATE	STATEWIDE	TRACEABLE
LECHEROUS	MOUSETRAP	PERPETUAL	PROVENDER	SCHEELITE	STEVEDORE	TRADEMARK
LEICESTER	MUCKENDER	PERSECUTE	PRUDENTLY	SCHLEMIEL	STEVENSON	TRADESMAN
LENIENTLY	MUFFETTEE	PERSEVERE	PULVERIZE	SCHLEMIHL	STOKEHOLD	TRADEWIND
LETTERBOX	MURDERESS	PERVERTED	PUMMELLED	SCHLENTER	STONEBOAT	TRAGEDIAN
LETTERING	MURDEROUS	PHONECARD	PUNGENTLY	SCHNECKEN	STONECHAT	TRAGELAPH
LICKERISH	MUSKETEER	PHONETICS	PUPPETEER	SCOLECITE	STONECROP	TRAPEZIAL
LINGERING	MUSKETOON	PIACEVOLE	QUARENDEN	SCREENING	STONEHAND	TRAPEZIST
LIQUEFIED	MUTTERING	PICKETING	QUAVERING	SECRETARY	STONELESS	TRAPEZIUM
LISTENING	MYRMECOID	PIECEMEAL	QUIVERFUL	SECRETION	STONEWALL	TRAPEZIUS
LODGEMENT	MYSTERIES	PIECEWORK	QUIVERING	SECRETIVE	STONEWARE	TRAPEZOID
LOITERING	NAPIERIAN	PIGHEADED	RACKETEER	SEDGEMOOR	STONEWORK	TRAVELERS
LONGEDFOR	NATHELESS	PIGNERATE	RANGELAND	SEGMENTED	STONEWORT	TRAVELING
LONGEVITY	NATHEMORE	PILFERAGE	RATHERIPE	SEGREGATE	STOREROOM	TRAVELLER
LOOSEHEAD	NAUSEATED	PILFERING	RATHERISH	SENSELESS	STOVEPIPE	TREGEAGLE
LOOSELEAF	NEGLECTED	PIMPERNEL	REDDENDUM	SEPTEMBER	STREETAGE	TREGETOUR
LOOSENESS	NEPHELINE	PINKERTON	REDEEMING	SEQUENCER	STREETCAR	TREVELYAN
LOUSEWORT	NIDDERING	PLACEMENT	REDHEADED	SEQUESTER	STUPEFIED	TRIBESMAN
LUCRETIUS	NIEBELUNG	PLANETARY	REDLETTER	SERREFILE	SUBCELLAR	TRIBESMEN
LUMBERING	NIPPERKIN	POCKETFUL	REFLECTOR	SHAKEDOWN	SUBMERGED	TRICERION
MACKENZIE	NOBLENESS	POLVERINE	REFLEXION	SHAMEFAST	SUBTENANT	TRIHEDRON
MADDENING	NOISELESS	POLYESTER	REFLEXIVE	SHAMELESS	SUCCEEDED	TRIMESTER
MADREPORE	NOLLEKENS	POMOERIUM	REFRESHER	SHAPELESS	SUCCENTOR	TRITENESS
MADRESSAH	NORWEGIAN	PONDEROSA	REGRETFUL	SHARESMAN	SUCCESSOR	TSAREVICH
MAGDEBURG	NUCLEOLUS	PONDEROUS	REGUERDON	SHAVELING	SUFFERING	TUILERIES
MAGNESIUM	NURSEMAID	POPPERING	REITERATE	SHIVERING	SUPREMACY	UMPTEENTH
MAGNETISM	OBSCENELY	PORBEAGLE	RENDERING	SHOREBIRD	SUPREMELY	UNCHECKED
MAGNETIZE	OBSCENITY	PORCELAIN	REPLENISH	SHOVELFUL	SURFEITED	UNDRESSED
MAGNETRON	OBSTETRIC	PORTERAGE	REPLETION	SHOVELLER	SURREJOIN	UNFEELING
MALLEABLE	OFFSEASON	POSSESSED	REPLETIVE	SICKENING	SURRENDER	UNFLEDGED
MALLEMUCK	OLENELLUS	POSSESSOR	REPREHEND	SILVEREYE	SURVEYING	UNHEEDING
MALLENDER	OLIVENITE	POSTERIOR	REPRESENT	SINCERELY	SUSPECTED	UNISEXUAL
MALLEOLUS	ONTHESPOT	POSTERITY	REPRESSED	SINCERITY	SUSPENDED	UNIVERSAL
MANGETOUT	OPENENDED	PREBENDAL	REPRESSOR	SISSERARY	SUSPENDER	UNPRECISE
MANNEQUIN	OPODELDOC	PRECEDENT	RESPECTED	SIXTEENMO	SUSPENSOR	UNSHEATHE
MANNERING	OPPRESSED	PRECEDING	RESPECTER	SIXTEENTH	SWINEHERD	UNTREATED
MANNERISM	OPPRESSOR	PRECENTOR	RHODESIAN	SLOVENIAN	SYLLEPSIS	UTICENSIS
MANOEUVRE	OPULENTLY	PRECEPTOR	RHYMESTER	SMOKEFREE	SYMMETRIC	VAGUENESS
MAPPEMOND	ORCHESTRA	PREFERRED	RICHELIEU	SMOKELESS	SYNOECETE	VALDENSES
MARKETEER	ORIGENIST	PRELECTOR	RIDGEBACK	SNAKEWEED	TABLELAND	VALUELESS
MARKETING	OTTRELITE	PRESENTED	RIDGELING	SOFTENING	TABLEWARE	VARIEGATE
MARVELOUS	OURSELVES	PRESENTER	RIDGEPOLE	SOLDERING	TANGERINE	VELLENAGE
MASTERFUL	OVEREXERT	PRESENTLY	RILLETTES	SOLFEGGIO	TARGETEER	VELVETEEN
MASTERMAN	OXYGENATE	PRESERVED	RIPIENIST	SOLFERINO	TASSELLED	VENGEANCE
MEDMENHAM	OZOCERITE	PRESERVER	ROOSEVELT	SOMMELIER	TASTELESS	VERBERATE
MEDRESSEH	OZOKERITE	PRESERVES	ROQUEFORT	SONNETEER	TEAKETTLE	VERTEBRAE

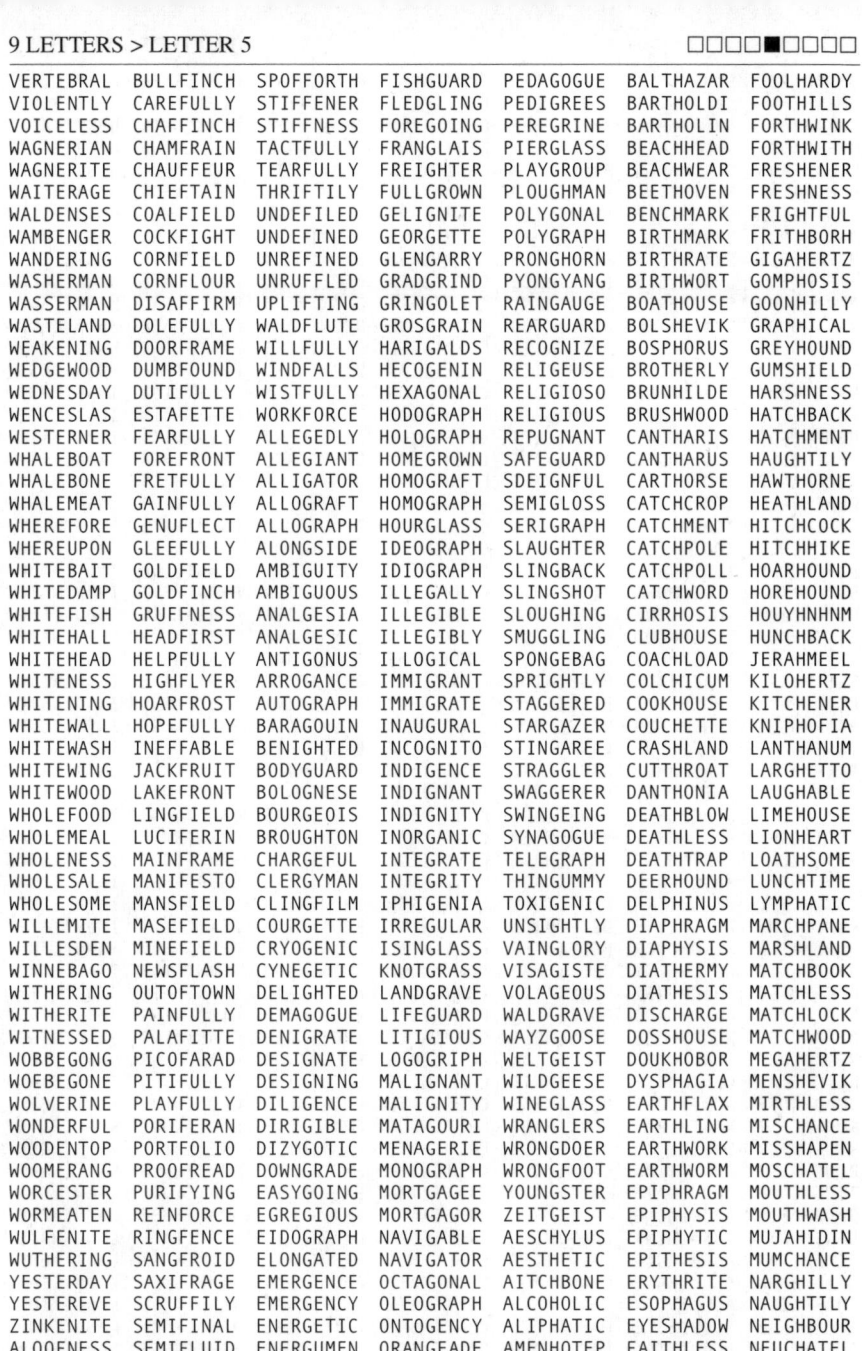

VERTEBRAL	BULLFINCH	SPOFFORTH	FISHGUARD	PEDAGOGUE	BALTHAZAR	FOOLHARDY
VIOLENTLY	CAREFULLY	STIFFENER	FLEDGLING	PEDIGREES	BARTHOLDI	FOOTHILLS
VOICELESS	CHAFFINCH	STIFFNESS	FOREGOING	PEREGRINE	BARTHOLIN	FORTHWINK
WAGNERIAN	CHAMFRAIN	TACTFULLY	FRANGLAIS	PIERGLASS	BEACHHEAD	FORTHWITH
WAGNERITE	CHAUFFEUR	TEARFULLY	FREIGHTER	PLAYGROUP	BEACHWEAR	FRESHENER
WAITERAGE	CHIEFTAIN	THRIFTILY	FULLGROWN	PLOUGHMAN	BEETHOVEN	FRESHNESS
WALDENSES	COALFIELD	UNDEFILED	GELIGNITE	POLYGONAL	BENCHMARK	FRIGHTFUL
WAMBENGER	COCKFIGHT	UNDEFINED	GEORGETTE	POLYGRAPH	BIRTHMARK	FRITHBORH
WANDERING	CORNFIELD	UNREFINED	GLENGARRY	PRONGHORN	BIRTHRATE	GIGAHERTZ
WASHERMAN	CORNFLOUR	UNRUFFLED	GRADGRIND	PYONGYANG	BIRTHWORT	GOMPHOSIS
WASSERMAN	DISAFFIRM	UPLIFTING	GRINGOLET	RAINGAUGE	BOATHOUSE	GOONHILLY
WASTELAND	DOLEFULLY	WALDFLUTE	GROSGRAIN	REARGUARD	BOLSHEVIK	GRAPHICAL
WEAKENING	DOORFRAME	WILLFULLY	HARIGALDS	RECOGNIZE	BOSPHORUS	GREYHOUND
WEDGEWOOD	DUMBFOUND	WINDFALLS	HECOGENIN	RELIGEUSE	BROTHERLY	GUMSHIELD
WEDNESDAY	DUTIFULLY	WISTFULLY	HEXAGONAL	RELIGIOSO	BRUNHILDE	HARSHNESS
WENCESLAS	ESTAFETTE	WORKFORCE	HODOGRAPH	RELIGIOUS	BRUSHWOOD	HATCHBACK
WESTERNER	FEARFULLY	ALLEGEDLY	HOLOGRAPH	REPUGNANT	CANTHARIS	HATCHMENT
WHALEBOAT	FOREFRONT	ALLEGIANT	HOMEGROWN	SAFEGUARD	CANTHARUS	HAUGHTILY
WHALEBONE	FRETFULLY	ALLIGATOR	HOMOGRAFT	SDEIGNFUL	CARTHORSE	HAWTHORNE
WHALEMEAT	GAINFULLY	ALLOGRAFT	HOMOGRAPH	SEMIGLOSS	CATCHCROP	HEATHLAND
WHEREFORE	GENUFLECT	ALLOGRAPH	HOURGLASS	SERIGRAPH	CATCHMENT	HITCHCOCK
WHEREUPON	GLEEFULLY	ALONGSIDE	IDEOGRAPH	SLAUGHTER	CATCHPOLE	HITCHHIKE
WHITEBAIT	GOLDFIELD	AMBIGUITY	IDIOGRAPH	SLINGBACK	CATCHPOLL	HOARHOUND
WHITEDAMP	GOLDFINCH	AMBIGUOUS	ILLEGALLY	SLINGSHOT	CATCHWORD	HOREHOUND
WHITEFISH	GRUFFNESS	ANALGESIA	ILLEGIBLE	SLOUGHING	CIRRHOSIS	HOUYHNHNM
WHITEHALL	HEADFIRST	ANALGESIC	ILLEGIBLY	SMUGGLING	CLUBHOUSE	HUNCHBACK
WHITEHEAD	HELPFULLY	ANTIGONUS	ILLOGICAL	SPONGEBAG	COACHLOAD	JERAHMEEL
WHITENESS	HIGHFLYER	ARROGANCE	IMMIGRANT	SPRIGHTLY	COLCHICUM	KILOHERTZ
WHITENING	HOARFROST	AUTOGRAPH	IMMIGRATE	STAGGERED	COOKHOUSE	KITCHENER
WHITEWALL	HOPEFULLY	BARAGOUIN	INAUGURAL	STARGAZER	COUCHETTE	KNIPHOFIA
WHITEWASH	INEFFABLE	BENIGHTED	INCOGNITO	STINGAREE	CRASHLAND	LANTHANUM
WHITEWING	JACKFRUIT	BODYGUARD	INDIGENCE	STRAGGLER	CUTTHROAT	LARGHETTO
WHITEWOOD	LAKEFRONT	BOLOGNESE	INDIGNANT	SWAGGERER	DANTHONIA	LAUGHABLE
WHOLEFOOD	LINGFIELD	BOURGEOIS	INDIGNITY	SWINGEING	DEATHBLOW	LIMEHOUSE
WHOLEMEAL	LUCIFERIN	BROUGHTON	INORGANIC	SYNAGOGUE	DEATHLESS	LIONHEART
WHOLENESS	MAINFRAME	CHARGEFUL	INTEGRATE	TELEGRAPH	DEATHTRAP	LOATHSOME
WHOLESALE	MANIFESTO	CLERGYMAN	INTEGRITY	THINGUMMY	DEERHOUND	LUNCHTIME
WHOLESOME	MANSFIELD	CLINGFILM	IPHIGENIA	TOXIGENIC	DELPHINUS	LYMPHATIC
WILLEMITE	MASEFIELD	COURGETTE	IRREGULAR	UNSIGHTLY	DIAPHRAGM	MARCHPANE
WILLESDEN	MINEFIELD	CRYOGENIC	ISINGLASS	VAINGLORY	DIAPHYSIS	MARSHLAND
WINNEBAGO	NEWSFLASH	CYNEGETIC	KNOTGRASS	VISAGISTE	DIATHERMY	MATCHBOOK
WITHERING	OUTOFTOWN	DELIGHTED	LANDGRAVE	VOLAGEOUS	DIATHESIS	MATCHLESS
WITHERITE	PAINFULLY	DEMAGOGUE	LIFEGUARD	WALDGRAVE	DISCHARGE	MATCHLOCK
WITNESSED	PALAFITTE	DENIGRATE	LITIGIOUS	WAYZGOOSE	DOSSHOUSE	MATCHWOOD
WOBBEGONG	PICOFARAD	DESIGNATE	LOGOGRIPH	WELTGEIST	DOUKHOBOR	MEGAHERTZ
WOEBEGONE	PITIFULLY	DESIGNING	MALIGNANT	WILDGEESE	DYSPHAGIA	MENSHEVIK
WOLVERINE	PLAYFULLY	DILIGENCE	MALIGNITY	WINEGLASS	EARTHFLAX	MIRTHLESS
WONDERFUL	PORIFERAN	DIRIGIBLE	MATAGOURI	WRANGLERS	EARTHLING	MISCHANCE
WOODENTOP	PORTFOLIO	DIZYGOTIC	MENAGERIE	WRONGDOER	EARTHWORK	MISSHAPEN
WOOMERANG	PROOFREAD	DOWNGRADE	MONOGRAPH	WRONGFOOT	EARTHWORM	MOSCHATEL
WORCESTER	PURIFYING	EASYGOING	MORTGAGEE	YOUNGSTER	EPIPHRAGM	MOUTHLESS
WORMEATEN	REINFORCE	EGREGIOUS	MORTGAGOR	ZEITGEIST	EPIPHYSIS	MOUTHWASH
WULFENITE	RINGFENCE	EIDOGRAPH	NAVIGABLE	AESCHYLUS	EPIPHYTIC	MUJAHIDIN
WUTHERING	SANGFROID	ELONGATED	NAVIGATOR	AESTHETIC	EPITHESIS	MUMCHANCE
YESTERDAY	SAXIFRAGE	EMERGENCE	OCTAGONAL	AITCHBONE	ERYTHRITE	NARGHILLY
YESTEREVE	SCRUFFILY	EMERGENCY	OLEOGRAPH	ALCOHOLIC	ESOPHAGUS	NAUGHTILY
ZINKENITE	SEMIFINAL	ENERGETIC	ONTOGENY	ALIPHATIC	EYESHADOW	NEIGHBOUR
ALOOFNESS	SEMIFLUID	ENERGUMEN	ORANGEADE	AMENHOTEP	FAITHLESS	NEUCHATEL
ARTIFICER	SHEFFIELD	ENLIGHTEN	ORANGEMAN	ANOPHELES	FARMHOUSE	NEWSHOUND
BALEFULLY	SHOPFLOOR	ESPAGNOLE	OVERGROWN	ANSCHLUSS	FEATHERED	NIPCHEESE
BAREFACED	SHOPFRONT	EVANGELIC	OWLEGLASS	ANTIHELIX	FLASHBACK	NORTHEAST
BASHFULLY	SHUFFLING	EVERGLADE	PALSGRAVE	APATHETIC	FLASHBULB	NORTHERLY
BEANFEAST	SIEGFRIED	EVERGREEN	PANEGOISM	APOPHATIC	FLASHCUBE	NORTHWARD
BLUFFNESS	SKILFULLY	FAMAGUSTA	PANEGYRIC	APOPHYSIS	FLECHETTE	NORTHWEST
BRIEFCASE	SKINFLINT	FENUGREEK	PARAGOGUE	ARACHNOID	FLESHLESS	NOTCHBACK
BRIEFNESS	SNOWFLAKE	FILIGRAIN	PARAGRAPH	BAKEHOUSE	FLESHPOTS	OASTHOUSE
BULLFIGHT	SOULFULLY	FIREGUARD	PAREGORIC	BAKSHEESH	FLOPHOUSE	OFFCHANCE

OMOPHAGIC	SOUTHWEST	AMPHIBIAN	CENTIGRAM	DENTISTRY	FILLISTER	HERBICIDE
OPENHEART	SPAGHETTI	AMPLIFIER	CENTIPEDE	DENTITION	FIORITURA	HERBIVORE
OUTTHRUST	SULPHONIC	AMPLITUDE	CERTIFIED	DEOXIDISE	FLAGITATE	HERMITAGE
OVERHASTY	SULPHURIC	AMUSINGLY	CERTITUDE	DERRINGER	FLEXITIME	HEURISTIC
OVERHEADS	SURCHARGE	ANGLICISM	CHALIAPIN	DESTITUTE	FLORIMELL	HISTIDINE
PANCHAYAT	SWOTHLING	ANGUISHED	CHAMINADE	DETRIMENT	FOGGINESS	HOBBINOLL
PANTHEISM	SYLPHLIKE	ANIMISTIC	CHARIVARI	DETRITION	FOOLISHLY	HORRIFIED
PANTHENOL	SYMPHONIC	APERIODIC	CHEMISTRY	DIETICIAN	FORBIDDEN	HOSPITIUM
PARCHEESI	SYMPHYSIS	APERITIVE	CHERISHED	DIFFICULT	FOREIGNER	HOSTILITY
PARCHMENT	SYNCHYSIS	APPLIANCE	CHORISTER	DIFFIDENT	FORFICATE	HUMDINGER
PARTHENON	SYNTHESIS	APPLICANT	CHURIDARS	DIGNIFIED	FORGIVING	HURRICANE
PARTHOLON	SYNTHETIC	APPOINTED	CIRCINATE	DIGNITARY	FORNICATE	HURRICANO
PATCHOULI	SYRPHIDAE	APPOINTEE	CLARIFIER	DINGINESS	FORTILAGE	HURRIEDLY
PATCHOULY	TAUCHNITZ	ARABICIZE	CLINICIAN	DIRTINESS	FORTITUDE	HUSKINESS
PATCHWORK	TEACHABLE	ARABINOSE	COALITION	DISFIGURE	FOSSILISE	IMAGINARY
PAYCHEQUE	TERAHERTZ	ARCHIBALD	COCHINEAL	DISMISSAL	FRAGILITY	IMBRICATE
PEMPHIGUS	THIGHBONE	ARCHITECT	COFFINITE	DISSIDENT	FRIGIDITY	IMPLICATE
PENTHOUSE	TOLLHOUSE	ARCHIVIST	COGNITION	DISSIPATE	FROBISHER	INABILITY
PERCHANCE	TOOTHACHE	ARCHIVOLT	COGNITIVE	DISTILLER	FUGGINESS	INANIMATE
PERCHERON	TOOTHCOMB	ASSAILANT	COGNIZANT	DIZZINESS	FULMINANT	INANITION
PINCHBECK	TOOTHLESS	ATAVISTIC	COLLIGATE	DODDIPOLL	FULMINATE	INITIALLY
PINCHCOCK	TOOTHPICK	ATHEISTIC	COLLIMATE	DORMITION	FUNGIBLES	INITIATED
PITCHFORK	TOOTHSOME	ATTAINDER	COLLISION	DORMITORY	FUNGICIDE	INITIATOR
PITCHPINE	TOUCHDOWN	ATTRIBUTE	COMMISSAR	DRAVIDIAN	FURNIMENT	INOPINATE
PITCHPOLE	TOUCHLINE	ATTRITION	COMMITTAL	DULCINIST	FURNITURE	INQUILINE
PITCHPOLL	TOUCHWOOD	ATTUITION	COMMITTED	DUNSINANE	FURTIVELY	INQUINATE
PLAYHOUSE	TOUGHNESS	AUBRIETIA	COMMITTEE	DUPLICAND	FUSSINESS	INQUIRING
PLETHORIC	TRACHINUS	BADMINTON	CONCIERGE	DUPLICATE	FUSTIGATE	INSPIRING
POMPHOLYX	TROCHILIC	BALLISTIC	CONCISELY	DUPLICITY	FUSTINESS	INSTIGATE
POORHOUSE	TROCHILUS	BALTIMORE	CONCISION	ELIMINATE	FUZZINESS	INSTITUTE
POSTHOUSE	TRYPHOEUS	BANDICOOT	CONDIMENT	ELUCIDATE	GALLICISM	INSWINGER
PRESHRUNK	UNASHAMED	BAPTISMAL	CONDITION	EMACIATED	GALLINULE	INTRICACY
PROPHETIC	UNETHICAL	BARBITONE	CONFIDANT	EMOTIONAL	GALLIPOLI	INTRICATE
PROTHESIS	VOUCHSAFE	BARRICADE	CONFIDENT	EMPTINESS	GALLIVANT	INTRIGUED
PROTHORAX	WANCHANCY	BARRISTER	CONFIRMED	ENCHILADA	GARNISHEE	INTRIGUER
PSYCHICAL	WAREHOUSE	BASTINADE	CONFITEOR	ENDEICTIC	GARNITURE	INTRINSIC
PSYCHOSIS	WATCHWORD	BASTINADO	CONSIGNEE	ENERINITE	GAUDINESS	INTUITION
PSYCHOTIC	WEIGHTING	BEATITUDE	CONSIGNOR	ENQUIRIES	GAWKINESS	INTUITIVE
PUNCHLINE	WHICHEVER	BEDRIDDEN	CONTINENT	ENQUIRING	GENTILITY	INUSITATE
PURCHASER	WINDHOVER	BEDSITTER	CONTINUAL	EPINICION	GENUINELY	INVOICING
PYRRHONIC	WITCHETTY	BELLICOSE	CONTINUUM	EPINIKION	GERMICIDE	ITALICIZE
RACEHORSE	WODEHOUSE	BILLIARDS	CONVINCED	ERADICATE	GERMINATE	JEQUIRITY
REACHABLE	WOLFHOUND	BOOBIALLA	CONVIVIAL	EROTICISM	GIDDINESS	JERKINESS
REARHORSE	WOODHOUSE	BOSSINESS	CORDIALLY	ERUCIFORM	GLADIATOR	JUICINESS
REICHSRAT	WORKHORSE	BRAZILIAN	CORTISONE	ERUDITION	GLADIOLUS	JUSTIFIED
REICHSTAG	WORKHOUSE	BROMINATE	CRAZINESS	ESQUILINE	GLORIFIED	JUSTINIAN
ROADHOUSE	WORTHLESS	BULKINESS	CREPITATE	EUCLIDEAN	GLUCINIUM	KENTIGERN
ROUGHCAST	XANTHIPPE	BURKINABE	CRETINOUS	EVASIVELY	GLUTINOUS	KHALIFATE
ROUGHNECK	ZUCCHETTO	BURLINESS	CRIMINATE	EXANIMATE	GMELINITE	KISSINGER
ROUGHNESS	ABOLITION	CABRIOLET	CRITICISM	EXPLICATE	GODLINESS	KITTIWAKE
ROUGHSHOD	ABOMINATE	CALCINATE	CRITICIZE	EXQUISITE	GRATICULE	KNOWINGLY
SACCHARIN	ABORIGINE	CALLIPERS	CRUCIALLY	EXTRICATE	GRATITUDE	LAGNIAPPE
SANDHURST	ABSTINENT	CALVINIST	CRUCIFORM	EXTRINSIC	GRAVITATE	LANCINATE
SCHEHITAH	ACARIASIS	CALVITIES	CTESIPHON	FABRICATE	GRIMINESS	LANKINESS
SCYTHEMAN	ACCLIMATE	CANDIDACY	CULMINATE	FACSIMILE	HAMFISTED	LAODICEAN
SHASHLICK	ACCLIVITY	CANDIDATE	CULTIVATE	FACTIONAL	HANDINESS	LARGITION
SHECHINAH	ACQUIESCE	CAPRICCIO	CUNEIFORM	FASCINATE	HANDIWORK	LASSITUDE
SHECHITAH	ACQUITTAL	CAPRICORN	CURTILAGE	FASHIONED	HAPPINESS	LAVOISIER
SHEPHERDS	ACUMINATE	CAPTIVATE	CUSPIDORE	FEBRIFUGE	HARBINGER	LIABILITY
SLAPHAPPY	ADJOINING	CAPTIVITY	CYMBIDIUM	FENCIBLES	HARDIHOOD	LIMPIDITY
SLIGHTEST	AFFLICTED	CARCINOMA	DALLIANCE	FERDINAND	HARDINESS	LIPPITUDE
SLUGHORNE	AFFRICATE	CARNIVORE	DANDIFIED	FERTILITY	HASTINESS	LIQUIDATE
SOUTHDOWN	AGGRIEVED	CARTILAGE	DARWINIAN	FERTILIZE	HEADINESS	LIQUIDITY
SOUTHEAST	AGONIZING	CASTIGATE	DEAMINATE	FESTINATE	HEAVINESS	LIQUIDIZE
SOUTHERLY	ALUMINIUM	CASTILIAN	DECEITFUL	FESTIVITY	HEAVISIDE	LOCHINVAR
SOUTHWARD	AMERICANO	CASUISTIC	DECLINING	FICTIONAL	HEBRIDEAN	LOFTINESS
SOUTHWARK	AMERICIUM	CASUISTRY	DECLIVITY	FILLIPEEN	HENDIADYS	LONGICORN

LONGINGLY	MYSTICISM	PHYSICIAN	RANDINESS	SHAKINESS	TELLINGLY	WASPISHLY
LONGITUDE	NARCISSUS	PHYSICIST	RANTIPOLE	SHAMIANAH	TENAILLON	WEARINESS
LOWLIGHTS	NASTINESS	PICNICKER	READINESS	SHOWINESS	TEPHILLIN	WEARISOME
LOWLINESS	NEBBISHER	PILLICOCK	REALISTIC	SILLINESS	TERMINATE	WILLINGLY
LUBRICANT	NEGLIGENT	PITUITARY	REALITIES	SLAVISHLY	TERPINEOL	WITTICISM
LUBRICATE	NEGRITUDE	PITUITRIN	REANIMATE	SLIMINESS	TERRICOLE	WITTINGLY
LUSTIHOOD	NEOLITHIC	PIZZICATO	RECEIVING	SOBRIQUET	TERRIFIED	WOOLINESS
LUSTINESS	NESCIENCE	PLACIDITY	RECTIFIER	SOGGINESS	TERRITORY	WORDINESS
MACHINATE	NICTITATE	PLATITUDE	RECTITUDE	SOLDIERLY	TESTICLES	WORRISOME
MACHINERY	NIGRITUDE	PLENITUDE	REEDINESS	SOLFIDIAN	TESTIFIER	WURLITZER
MACHINING	NOISINESS	POETICIZE	REJOICING	SOLLICKER	TESTIMONY	COADJUTOR
MACHINIST	NUTRIMENT	POLLINATE	REJOINDER	SOPHISTER	THYRISTOR	LEHRJAHRE
MADRILENE	NUTRITION	POPLITEAL	REMAINDER	SOPHISTIC	TIPSINESS	MARIJUANA
MAGNIFIER	NUTRITIVE	PORRINGER	REMAINING	SOPHISTRY	TRADITION	OVERJOYED
MAGNITUDE	OBBLIGATO	POSSIBLES	RENDITION	SOPPINESS	TRASIMENE	REYKJAVIK
MANDICATE	OBEDIENCE	POSTILION	RENFIERST	SORTILEGE	TREBIZOND	UNINJURED
MANLINESS	OBSTINACY	POTTINGAR	REPLICANT	SOTTISIER	TRETINOIN	AFRIKAANS
MARTINEAU	OBSTINATE	PRECIEUSE	REPLICATE	SPARINGLY	TRILITHON	AFRIKANER
MARTINMAS	OBTAINING	PRECINCTS	REPRIMAND	SPATIALLY	TRIPITAKA	BLACKBALL
MASSINGER	OCULIFORM	PRECIPICE	REPTILIAN	SPECIALLY	TRITICALE	BLACKBIRD
MASSIVELY	ODALISQUE	PRECISELY	REQUISITE	SPECIALTY	TRIVIALLY	BLACKBUCK
MASTICATE	ORIGINATE	PRECISIAN	RESTIFORM	SPECIFICS	TRUTINATE	BLACKDAMP
MATRIARCH	OUBLIETTE	PRECISION	RESTITUTE	SPECIFIED	TUBBINESS	BLACKFACE
MATRICIDE	OUTFITTER	PRECISIVE	RETAILING	SPECIMENS	TURBIDITY	BLACKFOOT
MATRIMONY	OUTRIGGER	PREDICANT	RETAINING	SPICILEGE	TURBINATE	BLACKHEAD
MAURITIAN	OUTSIDERS	PREDICATE	RETRIEVAL	SPICINESS	TURPITUDE	BLACKJACK
MAURITIUS	PAGLIACCI	PREDICTOR	RETRIEVER	SPIRITISM	UKRAINIAN	BLACKLEAD
MENDICANT	PALLIASSE	PREDIKANT	RISKINESS	SPIRITOUS	ULIGINOUS	BLACKLIST
MENTICIDE	PALMISTRY	PREDILECT	ROSMINIAN	SPIRITUAL	UNANIMITY	BLACKMAIL
MENTIONED	PALMITATE	PREFIGURE	ROUTINELY	SPRAICKLE	UNANIMOUS	BLACKMORE
MENUISIER	PALPITATE	PRESIDENT	ROWDINESS	STABILITY	UNBRIDLED	BLACKNESS
MERCILESS	PANNIKELL	PRESIDIAL	RUDDIGORE	STABILIZE	UNFAILING	BLACKWOOD
MERRIMENT	PARRICIDE	PRESIDIUM	RUFFIANLY	STAGIRITE	UNSKILLED	BLINKERED
MESSIANIC	PARSIMONY	PRIMIPARA	RUNCINATE	STATIONED	UNWRITTEN	BLOCKHEAD
METRICATE	PARTIALLY	PRIMITIAE	RUSTICATE	STATIONER	UPANISHAD	BREAKABLE
MIDWIFERY	PARTICLES	PRIMITIVE	RUSTINESS	STATISTIC	URANISCUS	BREAKAGES
MIDWINTER	PARTITION	PRIVILEGE	SACRIFICE	STERILITY	UREDINIAL	BREAKAWAY
MILLIGRAM	PASSIVELY	PROFITEER	SACRILEGE	STERILIZE	UROKINASE	BREAKDOWN
MILLINERY	PASSIVITY	PROLIXITY	SACRISTAN	STOLIDITY	VACCINATE	BREAKEVEN
MILLIONTH	PASTICCIO	PROMINENT	SALTINESS	STORIATED	VELLICATE	BREAKFAST
MILLIPEDE	PATRIARCH	PROMISING	SAUCINESS	STRAINING	VENTIFACT	BREAKNECK
MILLIVOLT	PATRICIAN	PROPIONIC	SAUCISSON	STUPIDITY	VENTILATE	BRICKWORK
MILLIWATT	PATRICIDE	PROSIMIAN	SAUVIGNON	STYLISHLY	VERDIGRIS	BRICKYARD
MISDIRECT	PATRIMONY	PROVIDENT	SCARIFIER	STYLISTIC	VERMIFORM	BRISKNESS
MISFIRING	PATRIOTIC	PROVIDING	SCHLIEREN	SUBDIVIDE	VERMIFUGE	CATSKILLS
MISGIVING	PAWKINESS	PROVISION	SCHMIEDER	SUBLIMATE	VERMILION	CHECKBOOK
MISPICKEL	PEEVISHLY	PROXIMATE	SCHNITTKE	SUBLIMELY	VERMINOUS	CHECKLIST
MISSIONER	PELLITORY	PROXIMITY	SCHNITZEL	SUBSIDIZE	VERSIFIER	CHECKMATE
MISTIGRIS	PENNILESS	PRURIENCE	SCOLIOSIS	SUBTITLED	VERSIONAL	CHECKROOM
MISTINESS	PENSIONER	PSORIASIS	SCOLIOTIC	SUCCINATE	VERTIPORT	CHEEKBONE
MOLLITIES	PENSIVELY	PTERIDIUM	SECTIONAL	SULKINESS	VESTIBULE	CHICKADEE
MONSIGNOR	PERDITION	PUBLICIST	SEEMINGLY	SURCINGLE	VESTIGIAL	CHICKWEED
MONTICULE	PERMITTED	PUBLICITY	SELFISHLY	SURLINESS	VESTITURE	CLOAKROOM
MOODINESS	PERSIMMON	PUBLICIZE	SEMEIOTIC	SURVIVING	VIABILITY	CLOCKWISE
MORBIDITY	PERTINENT	PUBLISHED	SENSILLUM	SUSCITATE	VICTIMIZE	CLOCKWORK
MORTICIAN	PESSIMISM	PUBLISHER	SENSITIVE	SUSPICION	VINDICATE	CRACKDOWN
MORTIFIED	PESSIMIST	PUERILITY	SENSITIZE	SWANIMOTE	VIOLINIST	CRACKLING
MUDDINESS	PESTICIDE	PUFFINESS	SENTIENCE	SYMBIOSIS	VIRGINALS	CRACKSMAN
MULTIFORM	PESTILENT	PULPITEER	SENTIMENT	SYMBIOTIC	VIRGINIAN	CRICKETER
MULTIPLEX	PETHIDINE	QUALIFIED	SEPTIMOLE	SYNDICATE	VIRGINITY	CROCKFORD
MULTITUDE	PETRIFIED	QUALIFIER	SEQUINNED	SYPHILOMA	VIRGINIUM	CROOKBACK
MURKINESS	PETTICOAT	QUASIMODO	SERVICING	TACHILITE	VIRGINIUM	CROOKEDLY
MUSHINESS	PETTINESS	QUERIMONY	SERVIETTE	TACKINESS	VOLTIGEUR	CYTOKININ
MUSSITATE	PETTITOES	QUOTIDIAN	SERVILELY	TACTICIAN	VOLTINISM	DRAWKNIFE
MUSTINESS	PHARISAIC	QUOTITION	SERVILITY	TAHSILDAR	VORTICISM	DRINKABLE
MUZZINESS	PHILIPPIC	RAFFINOSE	SERVITUDE	TARDINESS	VORTIGERN	DRUNKENLY
MYOFIBRIL	PHILISTER	RANCIDITY	SHADINESS	TECTIFORM	VULPINITE	FRANKNESS

JACKKNIFE	BALALAIKA	EBRILLADE	INDULGENT	PARFLECHE	SEPULCHRE	UNBALANCE
KARAKORAM	BASILICAL	EBULLIENT	INSELBERG	PEARLWORT	SEPULTURE	UNDILUTED
KNACKERED	BASILICON	EFFULGENT	INSOLENCE	PECULATOR	SHELLBACK	UNHELPFUL
KNOCKDOWN	BATTLEAXE	EMBELLISH	INSOLUBLE	PENDLETON	SHELLFISH	UNRELATED
OUTSKIRTS	BERYLLIUM	EMOLLIATE	INSOLVENT	PENILLION	SHELLSUIT	UNSELFISH
PRANKSTER	BETHLEHEM	EMOLLIENT	INSULATOR	PERPLEXED	SHETLANDS	UNSULLIED
QUICKLIME	BOBSLEIGH	EMPHLYSIS	INSULTING	PETILLANT	SHIELDING	UNWELCOME
QUICKNESS	BOOKLOVER	ENCELADUS	INTELLECT	PETULANCE	SHILLABER	UNWILLING
QUICKSAND	BOOTLACES	ENCOLPION	INVOLUCRE	PHELLOGEN	SIBILANCE	UPHOLSTER
QUICKSTEP	BOTTLEFUL	ENCOLPIUM	ISALLOBAR	PHILLABEG	SIBYLLINE	VACILLATE
SHARKSKIN	BRADLAUGH	ENROLMENT	ISOCLINAL	PHILLIBEG	SICILIANO	VEILLEUSE
SHEIKHDOM	BRIDLEWAY	ENTELECHY	JEWELLERY	PHYLLOPOD	SIDELIGHT	VEXILLARY
SLACKNESS	BRILLIANT	ENUCLEATE	JOCULARLY	PIXILATED	SIMILARLY	VIDELICET
SLEEKNESS	BUBBLEGUM	EPAULETTE	JUBILANCE	PONTLEVIS	SIMPLETON	VIGILANCE
SPARKLERS	BUMBLEBEE	EPEOLATRY	KABELJOUW	POPULARLY	SIMPLISTE	VIGILANTE
SPARKLING	CABALLERO	EPICLESIS	KENTLEDGE	POPULATED	SIMULATED	VIRULENCE
SPEAKEASY	CANALETTO	EQUALIZER	KINTLEDGE	POWELLITE	SIMULATOR	VITELLIUS
STARKNESS	CANDLELIT	ESCALATOR	KNOWLEDGE	PROCLITIC	SIMULCAST	WAVELLITE
STINKBIRD	CANDLEMAS	ESCULENTS	LAMPLIGHT	PUCELLAGE	SINGLESEX	WHEELBASE
STINKHORN	CAPILLARY	ETHELBERT	LANDLOPER	PUPILLAGE	SINGLETON	WHIRLIGIG
STINKWOOD	CATALEPSY	ETIOLATED	LIBELLOUS	PURULENCE	SMALLNESS	WHIRLPOOL
STOCKFISH	CATALOGUE	EUCHLORIC	LIMELIGHT	QUAILPIPE	SMALLTIME	WHIRLWIND
STOCKHOLM	CATALYSIS	EXCALIBUR	LINKLATER	QUILLWORT	SNAILFISH	WIMBLEDON
STOCKINET	CATALYTIC	EXCELLENT	LJUBLJANA	QUODLIBET	SOLILOQUY	WOODLANDS
STOCKINGS	CATTLEMAN	EXCELSIOR	LOCALIZED	RADCLIFFE	SOUVLAKIA	WOODLOUSE
STOCKPILE	CATTLEPEN	EXCULPATE	LOCELLATE	RADDLEMAN	SPELLBIND	ZIBELLINE
STOCKROOM	CAVALCADE	EXPULSION	LONGLIVED	RAMILLIES	SPILLICAN	ABDOMINAL
STOCKWORK	CHALLENGE	FABULINUS	MADELEINE	RATTLEBAG	SPILLIKIN	ABYSMALLY
STOCKYARD	CHARLATAN	FALKLANDS	MATELASSE	REBELLION	SPOILSMAN	ACCOMPANY
STONKERED	CHARLOTTE	FEUILLANT	MAXILLARY	RECALLING	SPOTLIGHT	ALLEMANDE
THACKERAY	CIPOLLINO	FIRELIGHT	MAYFLOWER	RECOLLECT	SQUALIDLY	ALTIMETER
THANKLESS	CIVILISED	FOMALHAUT	MEDALLION	REDOLENCE	STABLEBOY	ARMAMENTS
THICKHEAD	CIVILIZED	FOOTLOOSE	MEDALLIST	REFULGENT	STABLELAD	ARTEMISIA
THICKNESS	COMPLAINT	FREELANCE	METALLOID	REGULARLY	STABLEMAN	ASTHMATIC
THINKABLE	COMPLIANT	FUSILLADE	METALWORK	REGULATOR	STARLIGHT	ASYMMETRY
TRACKLESS	CONCLUDED	GAVELKIND	MICKLETON	REPELLENT	STEELHEAD	ATTEMPTED
TRACKSUIT	CONFLATED	GEARLEVER	MIDDLEMAN	REPELLING	STEELYARD	AUTOMAKER
TRICKLESS	CORALLINE	GENTLEMAN	MIDDLESEX	REPULSION	STILLBORN	AUTOMATED
TRICKSTER	COROLLARY	GENTLEMEN	MIDDLETON	REPULSIVE	STILLNESS	AUTOMATIC
TRINKETER	COTYLEDON	GINGLYMUS	MIDDLINGS	RESILIENT	STILLROOM	AUTOMATON
TRUCKLOAD	COVALENCY	GLENLIVET	MINELAYER	RESULTANT	STOOLBALL	AXIOMATIC
TRUNKFISH	COVELLITE	GODOLPHIN	MISPLACED	RESULTING	STOPLIGHT	BAINMARIE
TWINKLING	CUFFLINKS	GRUELLING	MISTLETOE	RETALIATE	STROLLING	BAROMETER
UNBEKNOWN	DEADLIGHT	GUILLEMOT	MODELLING	REVELLING	SUBALTERN	BOOKMAKER
WELLKNOWN	DECALITRE	GUILLOCHE	MODILLION	REVOLTING	SUNFLOWER	BRUMMAGEM
WREAKLESS	DECALOGUE	HARDLINER	MONOLAYER	REVOLVING	SUPPLIANT	CALEMBOUR
WRECKFISH	DECILLION	HAZELWORT	MONOLOGUE	REVULSION	SUPPLICAT	CAMEMBERT
ACYCLOVIR	DECOLLATE	HEADLIGHT	MOONLIGHT	RIGOLETTO	TABELLION	CARAMBOLA
AFFILIATE	DEFALCATE	HEADLINED	MUCHLOVED	RUDDLEMAN	TABULATOR	CATAMARAN
AMBULANCE	DEFOLIANT	HIGHLANDS	MUGGLETON	RUSHLIGHT	TAILLEFER	CATAMOUNT
ANAGLYPTA	DEFOLIATE	HIGHLIGHT	MUTILATED	SADDLEBAG	TAILLIGHT	CEROMANCY
ANAPLASIA	DEMULCENT	HIMALAYAN	MYOGLOBIN	SAFFLOWER	TEMULENCE	CHLAMYDES
ANAPLASTY	DESULTORY	HIMALAYAS	NONILLION	SATELLITE	THRALLDOM	CHROMATIC
ANCILLARY	DEVELOPED	HUMILIATE	NOVELETTE	SCABLANDS	THRILLANT	CINEMATIC
ANGELFISH	DEVELOPER	HYPALLAGE	OCCULTIST	SCAGLIOLA	THRILLING	COALMINER
ANKYLOSIS	DEVILFISH	IDEALOGUE	OCTILLION	SCALLAWAG	TIPULIDAE	COLOMBIAN
ANNULMENT	DEVILMENT	IMBALANCE	ORGILLOUS	SCALLIONS	TITILLATE	COLOMBIER
APOLLONUS	DIABLERIE	IMMELMANN	ORIFLAMME	SCALLOPED	TITTLEBAT	COLUMBARY
APPALLING	DIOCLETES	IMPELLING	OSCILLATE	SCALLYWAG	TOTALIZER	COLUMBATE
AQUILEGIA	DISCLOSED	IMPOLITIC	OVERLYING	SCARLATTI	TOWELLING	COLUMBIAN
ARTILLERY	DISPLACED	IMPULSION	PAILLASSE	SCHELLING	TRAMLINES	COLUMBINE
ATHELSTAN	DISPLAYED	IMPULSIVE	PAILLETTE	SCHILLING	TREILLAGE	COLUMBITE
AUTOLATRY	DISPLEASE	INCULCATE	PANELLING	SCHOLARCH	TRICLINIC	COLUMBIUM
AUTOLYCUS	DJELLABAH	INCULPATE	PANELLIST	SCHOLARLY	TUILLETTE	COLUMELLA
AUTOLYSIS	DOODLEBUG	INDELIBLE	PAPILLOTE	SCHOLIAST	UMBILICAL	COLUMNIST
AUXILIARY	DOWELLING	INDELIBLY	PARALYSIS	SEMBLANCE	UMBILICUS	CRYOMETER
AVAILABLE	EASTLINGS	INDOLENCE	PARALYTIC	SEPULCHER	UNALLOYED	DARTMOUTH

DECAMERON	MESOMORPH	THAUMATIN	BRAINWASH	EXPANSIVE	INGENUITY	ORIENTATE
DECEMVIRI	MILOMETER	THERMIDOR	BRAINWAVE	EXPENSIVE	INGENUOUS	ORMANDINE
DECOMPOSE	MONOMACHY	TONOMETER	BUCENTAUR	EXTENSILE	INSENSATE	ORPINGTON
DECUMBENT	MONOMANIA	TRAUMATIC	BURUNDIAN	EXTENSION	INSINCERE	ORTANIQUE
DISEMBARK	MONOMETER	TRIMMINGS	BYZANTINE	EXTENSIVE	INSINUATE	OSTENSIVE
DOCUMENTS	MUNIMENTS	TRIPMETER	CAIRNGORM	EXTENUATE	INTENDANT	OUDENARDE
DOLOMITES	NONSMOKER	TRIUMPHAL	CALENDULA	FACUNDITY	INTENDING	OVERNIGHT
DOLOMITIC	NUREMBERG	ULTIMATUM	CALENTURE	FALANGIST	INTENSELY	PALANKEEN
DOSIMETER	ONCOMETER	UNDAMAGED	CANONICAL	FARANDOLE	INTENSIFY	PALANQUIN
DREAMLAND	OPSIMATHY	UNLIMITED	CAVENDISH	FECUNDITY	INTENSITY	PALINURUS
DREAMLESS	OPTOMETRY	UNTIMEOUS	CELANDINE	FEMINEITY	INTENSIVE	PARANOIAC
DYNAMITED	PACEMAKER	VEHEMENCE	CHEONGSAM	FERINGHEE	INTENTION	PARANYMPH
ECLAMPSIA	PADEMELON	VESTMENTS	CHERNOZEM	FINANCIAL	INVENTION	PARENTAGE
ECTOMORPH	PALAMPORE	VOLTMETER	CHRONICLE	FINANCIER	INVENTIVE	PARENTING
ENCOMPASS	PALEMPORE	XENOMANIA	CLEANNESS	FORTNIGHT	INVENTORY	PECUNIARY
ENCUMBENT	PARAMEDIC	YOHIMBINE	CLEANSING	GALANTINE	IPRINDOLE	PEKINGESE
ENDOMORPH	PARAMETER	ZYGOMATIC	CLIENTELE	GALENGALE	IRVINGISM	PENINSULA
ENIGMATIC	PARAMOUNT	ZYMOMETER	COLONNADE	GALINGALE	JOHANNINE	PERENNIAL
EPHEMERAL	PEDOMETER	ABERNETHY	COMINFORM	GERUNDIVE	JUVENILIA	PHRENETIC
EPHEMERIS	PERIMETER	ABOUNDING	COMINTERN	GIGANTISM	KOMINFORM	PHRENITIS
EPHEMERON	PERIMORPH	ACCENTUAL	CONUNDRUM	GIRANDOLE	LACINIATE	PLAINNESS
ERIOMETER	PNEUMATIC	ADMONITOR	COTANGENT	GIRONDIST	LACONICAL	PLAINSMAN
ESTAMINET	PNEUMONIA	ADORNMENT	CROWNLIKE	GLEANINGS	LAMINATED	PLAINSONG
ESTIMABLE	POCKMANKY	ADRENALIN	CUTANEOUS	GOODNIGHT	LAMINITIS	PLAINTIFF
EUHEMERUS	POLEMARCH	ADVANTAGE	DAVENPORT	GREENAWAY	LATENIGHT	PLAINTIVE
EXCAMBION	POLEMICAL	ADVENTIST	DEBENTURE	GREENBACK	LECANORAM	POIGNANCY
EXTEMPORE	POLYMORPH	ADVENTIVE	DECENNIAL	GREENFEED	LEGENDARY	POLONAISE
FILMMAKER	PRAGMATIC	ADVENTURE	DECONTROL	GREENGAGE	LENINGRAD	POLYNESIA
FLAMMABLE	PRISMATIC	ALIGNMENT	DEFENDANT	GREENHEAD	LEVANTINE	POSTNATAL
FRAGMENTS	PTARMIGAN	ALLANTOID	DEFENDERS	GREENHORN	LOHENGRIN	POTENTATE
FREEMASON	PYRAMIDAL	ALLANTOIS	DEFENSIVE	GREENMAIL	LORGNETTE	POTENTIAL
FROGMARCH	PYROMANCY	ALMANDINE	DEFINABLE	GREENROOM	LUMINAIRE	PREGNANCY
FROGMOUTH	PYROMANIA	ALPENGLOW	DELINEATE	GREENSAND	LUMINANCE	PROENZYME
GASOMETER	REARMOUSE	ALPENHORN	DEMANDING	GREENWEED	MALENGINE	PROGNOSIS
GOALMOUTH	RECOMMEND	AMIANTHUS	DEPENDANT	GREENWICH	MELANESIA	QUENNELLE
GYROMANCY	RECUMBENT	ANDANTINO	DEPENDENT	GREENWOOD	MELANOSIS	RACONTEUR
HAUTMONDE	REREMOUSE	ANOINTING	DEPENDING	GREENYARD	MELANOTIC	RECONCILE
HEXAMERON	RHEUMATIC	ANTENATAL	DETENTION	GROUNDHOG	MELONLIKE	RECONDITE
HEXAMETER	ROCAMBOLE	ANTINOVEL	DETONATOR	GROUNDING	MESENTERY	RECONVENE
HODOMETER	RUDIMENTS	ANTONINUS	DEVONPORT	GROUNDNUT	MIDINETTE	REDINGOTE
IDIOMATIC	SCHEMATIC	APENNINES	DIAGNOSIS	GROUNDSEL	MISINFORM	REDUNDANT
INCOMINGS	SCIAMACHY	APOENZYME	DIMENSION	GUTENBERG	MISONEIST	REFINANCE
INCOMMODE	SCIOMANCY	APPENDAGE	DISENGAGE	HACKNEYED	MOMENTARY	REMINISCE
INCUMBENT	SCRAMBLER	ARGENTINA	DISENTOMB	HEMINGWAY	MOMENTOUS	REMONTANT
INDEMNIFY	SCRIMMAGE	ARGENTINE	DISINFECT	HERONSHAW	MOURNIVAL	REPENTANT
INDEMNITY	SCRIMPING	ARLINGTON	DISUNITED	HIRUNDINE	NEFANDOUS	RESENTFUL
INHUMANLY	SCRIMSHAW	ARSENICAL	DOMINANCE	HOLINSHED	NICKNEVEN	RESONANCE
INSOMNIAC	SCRUMMAGE	ASCENDANT	DOMINICAL	HUMANKIND	NOMINALLY	RESONATOR
INTUMESCE	SCRUMPING	ASCENDING	DOMINICAN	HUMANMADE	NOMINATOR	RETENTION
ISLAMABAD	SHOEMAKER	ASCENSION	DRAINPIPE	HUMONGOUS	NONENTITY	RETENTIVE
KILOMETER	SHRIMPING	ASSONANCE	DYSENTERY	HUMUNGOUS	NOTONECTA	RETINITIS
KILOMETRE	SKIAMACHY	ATHENAEUM	ECCENTRIC	HYPINOSIS	OBVENTION	ROSINANTE
KINGMAKER	SLAMMAKIN	ATTENDANT	EDDINGTON	IGUANODON	OCEANIDES	ROTUNDATE
KONIMETER	SOLEMNITY	ATTENTION	EFFINGHAM	IMMANACLE	OFFENBACH	ROTUNDITY
KRUMMHORN	SOLEMNIZE	ATTENTIVE	EGLANTINE	IMMANENCE	OFFENDING	ROZINANTE
LAGOMORPH	SONOMETER	ATTENUATE	ELLINGTON	IMMANENCY	OFFENSIVE	SALANGANE
LAWNMOWER	SPASMODIC	AUTONOMIC	EMPANOPLY	IMMENSELY	OPPENHEIM	SATINWOOD
LEAFMOULD	STAMMERER	AXMINSTER	EMPENNAGE	IMMENSITY	OPPONENTS	SCIENTISM
LEITMOTIF	STEAMBOAT	BARONETCY	ENCANTHIS	IMMINENCE	ORDINAIRE	SCIENTIST
LEITMOTIV	STEAMSHIP	BEGINNING	ENGINEERS	IMMUNISER	ORDINANCE	SCOUNDREL
LOUDMOUTH	STIGMATIC	BELONGING	ERPINGHAM	IMPENDING	ORGANELLE	SEANNACHY
LUXEMBURG	STROMBOLI	BICONCAVE	ERRONEOUS	INCENTIVE	ORGANICAL	SECONDARY
LYSIMETER	STRUMITIS	BILINGUAL	ESSENTIAL	INCONDITE	ORGANISED	SEDENTARY
MANOMETER	SWIMMERET	BIMONTHLY	ETERNALLY	INDENTURE	ORGANISER	SEMANTEME
MEKOMETER	TACAMAHAC	BOTANICAL	ETHANOATE	INDONESIA	ORGANIZED	SEMANTICS
MELAMPODE	TAXIMETER	BRAINCASE	EUMENIDES	INFANTILE	ORGANIZER	SEMANTIDE
MENOMINEE	TENEMENTS	BRAINLESS	EXPANSION	INGENIOUS	ORGANZINE	SEMANTRON

SERENADER	TYRANNOUS	BAMBOOZLE	CONSONANT	EMPLOYEES	HARROGATE	MACROCOSM
SERENGETI	UNBENDING	BANDOLEER	COPIOUSLY	ENAMOURED	HARROWING	MACROLOGY
SEVENTEEN	UNCONCERN	BANDOLERO	COPROLITE	ENCHORIAL	HECTOGRAM	MALFORMED
SHRINKAGE	UNCONFINE	BANDOLIER	CORMORANT	ENCLOSURE	HECTORING	MANDOLINE
SHRINKING	UNMINDFUL	BANDOLINE	CORPORATE	ENGROSSED	HERBORIST	MANGOUSTE
SOVENANCE	UNSINNING	BARBOTINE	CORPOREAL	ENGROSSER	HESSONITE	MARMOREAL
SPHENDONE	UNTENABLE	BERGOMASK	CORPOSANT	ENSCONCED	HIDEOUSLY	MARROWFAT
SPHINCTER	VAGINITIS	BETROTHAL	CORROSION	ENTROPION	HIPPOCRAS	MASSORETE
SPINNAKER	VALENTINE	BETROTHED	CORROSIVE	ENTROPIUM	HIPPODAME	MAUSOLEUM
SPINNERET	VARANGIAN	BILLOWING	COSMOGONY	EPIPOLISM	HIPPOLYTA	MELBOURNE
SPLENDOUR	VOLUNTARY	BIOLOGIST	COSMOLOGY	EPITOMIZE	HIPPOLYTE	MELIORATE
SPLENETIC	VOLUNTEER	BISHOPRIC	COSMONAUT	ESPIONAGE	HISTOGRAM	MELPOMENE
SPLENITIS	WAGENBOOM	BORROWING	CRACOVIAN	ETHIOPIAN	HISTOLOGY	MENNONITE
SPLINTERS	WAGONETTE	BOSTONIAN	CREPOLINE	ETHNOLOGY	HISTORIAN	METEORITE
SPOONBILL	WAGONLOAD	BURROUGHS	CRINOLINE	ETYMOLOGY	HOBGOBLIN	METEOROID
SPOONFEED	WAPENTAKE	BURROWING	CROCODILE	EUPHONIUM	HOMEOPATH	METHODISM
SPRINGALD	WAPINSHAW	BYPRODUCT	CURIOSITY	EUPHORBIA	HOMEOWNER	METHODIST
SPRINGBOK	WOMANHOOD	CALLOSITY	CURIOUSLY	EUTROPHIC	HOPLOLOGY	METHOXIDE
SPRINGLET	WOMANISER	CALLOUSLY	CURSORILY	EVAPORATE	HOWTOWDIE	METROLAND
SPRINKLER	WOMANIZER	CAMBODIAN	CUSTODIAL	EXPLOITER	HYDROFOIL	METRONOME
SQUINANCY	WOMANKIND	CAMCORDER	CUSTODIAN	EXPLOSION	HYDROPULT	MEZZOTINT
SQUINTING	WOMENFOLK	CANNONADE	CUSTOMARY	EXPLOSIVE	HYDROSTAT	MICROCHIP
STAINLESS	ABSCONDER	CANTONESE	CUSTOMIZE	EXTROVERT	HYPNOTISM	MICROCOSM
STANNATOR	ADENOIDAL	CARBONADE	CYCLOLITH	FACTORIAL	HYPNOTIST	MICROCYTE
STAUNCHLY	AEPYORNIS	CARBONADO	CYCLORAMA	FACTORISE	HYPNOTIZE	MICROFILM
STEENBRAS	AIRCOOLED	CARBONARI	CYCLOTRON	FALLOPIAN	ICHNOLITE	MICROINCH
STEENKIRK	ALVEOLATE	CARBONATE	DALTONISM	FATUOUSLY	ILLGOTTEN	MICROLITE
STEGNOSIS	AMAZONITE	CARBONIZE	DEACONESS	FERROTYPE	IMBROCATE	MICROLITH
STEGNOTIC	AMBROSIAL	CARTOGRAM	DEODORANT	FIBROLINE	IMBROGLIO	MICROMOLE
STEINBECK	AMBROSIAN	CARTOUCHE	DEODORIZE	FIBROLITE	IMPROBITY	MICROTOME
STEINBOCK	AMBROTYPE	CARYOPSIS	DESPOTISM	FLAVORING	IMPROMPTU	MICROTONE
STERNFAST	AMOROUSLY	CASSONADE	DEVIOUSLY	FLAVOURED	IMPROVING	MICROVOLT
STERNNESS	ANABOLISM	CASSOULET	DIALOGITE	FOLIOLOSE	IMPROVISE	MICROWATT
STORNAWAY	ANALOGOUS	CASSOWARY	DIANOETIC	FOLLOWING	IMPSONITE	MICROWAVE
STOWNLINS	ANATOLIAN	CEANOTHUS	DIATOMITE	FORGOTTEN	INAMORATA	MISLOCATE
STRANGELY	ANATOMIST	CEYLONESE	DICHOTOMY	FORLORNLY	INAMORATO	MNEMOSYNE
STRANGLER	ANATOMIZE	CHAMOMILE	DIPLOMACY	FOSSORIAL	INGROWING	MONGOLIAN
STRANGLES	ANCHORAGE	CHAROLAIS	DISCOLOUR	FRAGONARD	INQUORATE	MONGOLISM
STRANGURY	ANCHORITE	CHILOPODA	DISCOMFIT	FRIVOLITY	INTRODUCE	MONZONITE
STRENUOUS	ANCHORMAN	CHINOVNIK	DISCOURSE	FRIVOLOUS	INTROITUS	MORMONISM
STRINGENT	ANDROCLES	CHIPOLATA	DISCOVERT	FURIOUSLY	INTROVERT	MOSKONFYT
STRINGOPS	ANDROMEDA	CHIROPODY	DISCOVERY	GABIONADE	INVIOLATE	MUSCOVADO
STRONGARM	ANGIOGRAM	CHOCOLATE	DISHONEST	GALIONGEE	ISODORIAN	MUSCOVITE
STRONGYLE	ANIMOSITY	CILIOLATE	DISHONOUR	GALLOPADE	JARGONIZE	MUSKOGEAN
STRONTIUM	ANISOGAMY	CLAMOROUS	DISLOCATE	GASCONADE	JEALOUSLY	MUSSOLINI
SUBENTIRE	ANTHOLOGY	COELOSTAT	DISSOLUTE	GASHOLDER	KALSOMINE	MYTHOLOGY
SUPINATOR	ANXIOUSLY	COENOBITE	DISSOLVED	GEOLOGIST	KARYOTYPE	NARROWING
SYNANGIUM	APHRODITE	COENOBIUM	DISSONANT	GIBEONITE	KEYHOLDER	NATROLITE
TABANIDAE	APOLOGIST	COLLOCATE	DISTORTED	GLAMORIZE	KLINOSTAT	NEOLOGISM
TARANTASS	APOLOGIZE	COLLODION	DOCTORATE	GLAMOROUS	KROPOTKIN	NERVOUSLY
TARANTULA	APPROVING	COLLOIDAL	DRACONIAN	GLUCOSIDE	LACCOLITE	NEUROGLIA
TECHNICAL	ARAGONITE	COLLOTYPE	DRAGONFLY	GODMOTHER	LANDOWNER	NEUROLOGY
TECHNIQUE	ARCTOGAEA	COMFORTER	DUBIOUSLY	GONDOLIER	LANGOUSTE	NICCOLITE
THINNINGS	ARDUOUSLY	COMMODITY	DUBROVNIK	GONGORISM	LAWMONGER	NIGROSINE
THORNBACK	ASHMOLEAN	COMMODORE	EALDORMAN	GREGORIAN	LEFTOVERS	NOSTOLOGY
THORNBILL	ASTRODOME	COMMOTION	ECOLOGIST	GUNCOTTON	LEGIONARY	NUTJOBBER
THORNDYKE	ASTROLABE	COMPONENT	ECONOMICS	GUNPOWDER	LEPROSERY	OBVIOUSLY
THORNLESS	ASTROLOGY	COMPOSING	ECONOMIST	HADROSAUR	LEUCOCYTE	OCHLOCRAT
THRENETIC	ASTRONAUT	COMPOSITE	ECONOMIZE	HALLOWEEN	LEUCOTOME	ODDJOBMAN
THRONGING	ASTRONOMY	COMPOSURE	ECTROPION	HALLOWMAS	LINEOLATE	OFFCOLOUR
TIMENOGUY	ASTROPHEL	COMPOTIER	EDITORIAL	HARIOLATE	LIQUORICE	OLIGOCENE
TOMENTOSE	ASTROTURF	CONCORDAT	ELABORATE	HARMONICA	LIQUORISH	OMINOUSLY
TOURNEDOS	AUCTORIAL	CONCOURSE	ELAEOLITE	HARMONIST	LITHOCYST	ORATORIAN
TRAINABLE	AUTHORESS	CONFORMAL	EMBROCATE	HARMONIUM	LITHOPONE	ORTHODOXY
TRIANGLED	AUTHORITY	CONGOLESE	EMBROGLIO	HARMONIZE	LOBLOLLYS	ORTHOLOGY
TRIENNIAL	AUTHORIZE	CONNOTATE	EMBROIDER	HARMOTOME	LONDONESE	ORTHOPTER
TYRANNIZE	AYATOLLAH	CONSOCIES	EMBROILED	HARPOONER	MACDONALD	ORTHOTONE

436

OSTEODERM	PRECONISE	SENIORITY	TRICOLOUR	BLASPHEME	HEADPIECE	SANDPAPER
OSTEOPATH	PREMONISH	SENSORIUM	TRIFORIUM	BLASPHEMY	HEDYPHANE	SANDPIPER
OSTROGOTH	PREMOTION	SEPIOLITE	TRILOBITE	BLUEPRINT	HEMIPTERA	SAXOPHONE
OUTGOINGS	PREPOLLEX	SERBONIAN	TURBOPROP	BONAPARTE	HOLOPHOTE	SCRAPBOOK
OUTROOPER	PROBOSCIS	SERIOUSLY	TURCOPOLE	CACOPHONY	HOMOPHONE	SCRAPINGS
OUTWORKER	PROCOELUS	SERMONIZE	TUTIORISM	CASHPOINT	HOMOPTERA	SCRAPPING
PALEOLITH	PROCONSUL	SHEMOZZLE	ULTRONEUS	CATAPLASM	IDEOPATHY	SCRIPTURE
PANTOFFLE	PROKOFIEV	SHIPOWNER	UNADOPTED	CATAPLEXY	IDIOPHONE	SCULPTING
PANTOMIME	PROLONGED	SHOLOKHOV	UNCLOTHED	CEVAPCICI	IDIOPLASM	SCULPTURE
PANTOUFLE	PROMOTION	SIMEONITE	UNCLOUDED	CHAMPAGNE	INCAPABLE	SEMAPHORE
PARSONAGE	PRONOUNCE	SINUOSITY	UNCROSSED	CHAMPAIGN	INCEPTION	SERAPHINE
PASTORALE	PROPONENT	SIRBONIAN	UNCROWNED	CHAMPERTY	INCEPTIVE	SHARPENER
PATHOGENY	PROROGATE	SLIVOVICA	UNIFORMED	CHAMPLAIN	INCIPIENT	SHARPNESS
PATHOLOGY	PROTOSTAR	SLIVOVITZ	UNIFORMLY	CHAMPLEVÉ	INSIPIENT	SHEEPFOLD
PATROCLUS	PROTOTYPE	SOCIOLECT	UNKNOWING	CHEAPJACK	IODOPHILE	SHEEPMEAT
PATROLMAN	PROVOKING	SOCIOLOGY	UNSPOILED	CHEAPNESS	IRRUPTION	SHEEPSKIN
PATRONAGE	PROVOLONE	SOMNOLENT	UNTRODDEN	CHEAPSIDE	JOSEPHINE	SHOWPIECE
PATRONESS	PTEROSAUR	SOPHOCLES	URICONIAN	CHIPPINGS	JOSEPHSON	SISYPHEAN
PATRONIZE	PULMONARY	SOPHOMORE	UVAROVITE	CINEPHILE	KLEMPERER	SLEEPLESS
PAULOWNIA	PULMONATE	SORROWFUL	VANCOUVER	CLAMPDOWN	LEAKPROOF	SLEEPWALK
PENTOSANE	PURDONIUM	SPOROCARP	VARIOLATE	CLEOPATRA	MEGAPHONE	SOLIPSISM
PERCOLATE	PURPOSELY	STATOCYST	VARIOUSLY	COEMPTION	MENIPPEAN	SOMEPLACE
PERFORANS	PYTHONESS	STATOLITH	VERBOSITY	COLOPHONY	MENOPAUSE	STEEPNESS
PERFORATE	RADIOGRAM	STEGOSAUR	VICIOUSLY	CRIPPLING	METAPELET	STRAPHANG
PERFORMED	RADIOLOGY	STENOPAIC	VICTORIAN	CRISPNESS	METAPHASE	STRAPLESS
PERFORMER	RANCOROUS	STYLOBATE	VICTORINE	DAYSPRING	MONOPLANE	STRAPPADO
PERIODATE	RAPTORIAL	SUBCORTEX	VIDEODISC	DECEPTION	NAMEPLATE	STRAPPING
PERSONAGE	RASKOLNIK	SUBDOLOUS	VIDEODISK	DECEPTIVE	NEWSPAPER	STRIPLING
PERSONATE	RATIONALE	SUBFOSSIL	VIDEOTAPE	DESIPIENT	NEWSPRINT	STUMPWORK
PERSONIFY	RATIONING	SUBNORMAL	VISCOSITY	DISAPPEAR	NINEPENCE	SWEEPINGS
PERSONNEL	RAUCOUSLY	SUBROGATE	VISIONARY	DROPPINGS	NOOSPHERE	SYCOPHANT
PETROLEUM	REASONING	SUCCOTASH	VOLGOGRAD	ECOSPHERE	NOTEPAPER	TAILPIECE
PETROLOGY	RECKONING	SUETONIUS	VOODOOISM	ECTOPLASM	OBREPTION	TAILPLANE
PHACOLITE	RECTORIAL	SUFFOCATE	WALLOPING	ENRAPTURE	OCCIPITAL	TELEPATHY
PHAGOCYTE	RENCONTRE	SUNDOWNER	WALLOWING	ENTOPHYTE	OCCUPANCY	TELEPHONE
PHEROMONE	REPROBATE	SUPPORTER	WANWORTHY	EQUIPMENT	OCCUPYING	TELEPHONY
PHILOLOGY	REPROCESS	SUPPOSING	WARMONGER	EQUIPOISE	OCTOPLOID	TELEPHOTO
PHITONIUM	REPRODUCE	SURROGATE	WEBFOOTED	ESCOPETTE	OFFSPRING	TELOPHASE
PHONOGRAM	REPROVING	SYLLOGISM	WELCOMING	ESEMPLASY	OPTOPHONE	TIMEPIECE
PHONOLITE	RETROCEDE	SYMBOLISM	WHOSOEVER	EURIPIDES	OUTSPOKEN	TISIPHONE
PHONOLOGY	RETROFLEX	SYMBOLIST	WILLOWING	EXCEPTION	OUTSPREAD	TONOPLAST
PHOTOCOPY	RETROVERT	SYMBOLIZE	WINCOPIPE	EXCIPIENT	OVENPROOF	TOXOPHILY
PHOTOGENE	RHODOLITE	SYMPODIUM	WISCONSIN	EXEMPLARY	OVERPAINT	TRAPPINGS
PHOTOSTAT	RHODOPSIN	SYMPOSIUM	YELLOWISH	EXEMPLIFY	OVERPOISE	TROMPETTE
PHOTOTUBE	RIBBONISM	SYNCOMIUM	ZIRCONIUM	EXEMPTION	OVERPOWER	TROOPSHIP
PHYCOLOGY	RIOTOUSLY	SYNCOPATE	ZOOLOGIST	EXOSPHERE	OVERPRINT	TRUEPENNY
PHYLOGENY	ROSCOMMON	TABBOULEH	ACROPETAL	EYEOPENER	PERIPATUS	TRUMPEDUP
PHYTOLITE	RUINOUSLY	TAUTOLOGY	ACROPHONY	EYESPLICE	PERIPHERY	TRUMPETER
PHYTOTRON	SANTONICA	TECTONICS	ACROPOLIS	FILOPLUME	PHOSPHATE	TULIPWOOD
PICTOGRAM	SARTORIAL	TECTORIAL	AEROPLANE	FIREPLACE	PHOSPHENE	UNEXPOSED
PICTORIAL	SARTORIUS	TEDIOSITY	ALLOPATHY	FIREPROOF	PLUMPNESS	UNHAPPILY
PIEPOWDER	SASSOLITE	TEDIOUSLY	ALTIPLANO	FISHPLATE	POLYPHASE	UNHOPEFUL
PINHOOKER	SCAPOLITE	TEKNONYMY	AMORPHOUS	FLIPPANCY	POLYPHONE	UNOPPOSED
PISTOLEER	SCHNORKEL	TELEOLOGY	ANCIPITAL	FOOLPROOF	POLYPHONY	UNPOPULAR
PLATONIST	SCHNORRER	TEMPORARY	ANNAPOLIS	FOOTPLATE	POSTPONED	UNTYPICAL
PLEIOCENE	SCHNOZZLE	TEMPORIZE	ANNAPURNA	FOOTPRINT	PROMPTING	VIEWPOINT
PLUTOCRAT	SCHOOLBOY	TENTORIUM	ANTIPASTO	FOURPENCE	PUERPERAL	WALLPAPER
PLUTONIUM	SCHOOLING	TENUOUSLY	ANTIPATHY	FREEPHONE	RATEPAYER	WILLPOWER
POISONING	SCHOOLMAN	TERRORISM	ANTIPHONY	GALAPAGOS	RECAPTURE	WORKPLACE
POISONOUS	SCORODITE	TERRORIST	ANTIPODES	GANGPLANK	RECEPTION	XENOPHOBE
POMPOSITY	SEABOTTLE	TERRORIZE	AQUAPLANE	GRAMPIANS	RECEPTIVE	XEROPHYTE
PORPOISES	SEASONING	THECODONT	AREOPAGUS	GRAPPLING	RECIPIENT	XYLOPHONE
PORPORATE	SEAWORTHY	THELONIUS	AUTOPILOT	GYROPLANE	ROTAPLANE	ANTIQUARY
POTBOILER	SECTORIAL	THREONINE	BACKPEDAL	HAIRPIECE	SAGAPENUM	ANTIQUITY
POTHOLING	SELLOTAPE	THYROXINE	BALLPOINT	HALFPENNY	SALOPETTE	BRUSQUELY
POTPOURRI	SEMIOLOGY	TREMOLITE	BEDSPREAD	HALOPHILE	SALTPETER	OBLIQUELY
PRECOCITY	SEMIOTICS	TRIBOLOGY	BIOSPHERE	HANDPIECE	SALTPETRE	OBSEQUIES

PIPSQUEAK	AUSTRALIA	DISARMING	GUERRILLA	INTERLOPE	MODERNIZE	PRODROMUS
QUINQUINA	AUTOROUTE	DISCREDIT	GUJARATHI	INTERLUDE	MONERGISM	PROGRAMME
RELIQUARY	BEVERIDGE	DISGRACED	HABERDINE	INTERMENT	MOONRAKER	PROPRIETY
RELIQUIAE	BIFURCATE	DISORIENT	HABERGEON	INTERNODE	MOTORBIKE	QUADRATIC
TOTAQUINE	BILIRUBIN	DISTRAINT	HAVERSACK	INTERPLAY	MOTORBOAT	QUADRATUS
ABERRANCE	BIOGRAPHY	DIVERGENT	HAZARDOUS	INTERPOSE	MOTORCADE	QUADRILLE
ABHORRENT	BIPARTITE	DIVERGING	HEDERATED	INTERPRET	MOTORISTS	QUADRUPED
ABSORBENT	BIZARRELY	DIVERSIFY	HETERODOX	INTERRUPT	MUCORALES	QUADRUPLE
ABSORBING	BOYFRIEND	DIVERSION	HETEROSIS	INTERSECT	MUSHROOMS	QUEERNESS
ABSURDITY	CALORIFIC	DIVERSITY	HEYPRESTO	INTERVENE	NATURALLY	RAZORBILL
ACCORDANT	CAMBRIDGE	DIVERTING	HIBERNATE	INTERVIEW	NEFARIOUS	REARRANGE
ACCORDING	CAMERAMAN	DOCTRINAL	HIBERNIAN	INVERNESS	NEFERTITI	RECORDING
ACCORDION	CAPARISON	DOWNRIGHT	HILARIOUS	INVERSION	NEPHRITIC	RECORDIST
ADDERWORT	CAPORETTO	DUNDREARY	HINDRANCE	INVERTASE	NEPHRITIS	RECURRENT
ADHERENCE	CARTRIDGE	DYSPRAXIA	HONORABLE	ISOCRATES	NEUTRALLY	RECURRING
ADMIRABLE	CASTRATED	DYSTROPHY	HONORIFIC	ISOPROPYL	NEVERMORE	RECURSIVE
ADMIRABLY	CATARRHAL	EAGERNESS	HUNDREDTH	ISOTROPIC	NICARAGUA	REDBREAST
ADMIRALTY	CATERWAUL	EDWARDIAN	HYPERBOLA	JACARANDA	NIDERLING	REFERENCE
ADVERBIAL	CAVERNOUS	EIDERDOWN	HYPERBOLE	JOBERNOWL	NONPROFIT	REFERRING
ADVERSARY	CAVORTING	ELUTRIATE	HYPERLINK	LABORIOUS	NOTARIKON	REFORMIST
ADVERSELY	CEDARWOOD	EMBARRASS	HYPEROPIA	LABYRINTH	NOTORIETY	REFURBISH
ADVERSITY	CENTRALLY	EMMERDALE	IBUPROFEN	LACERATED	NOTORIOUS	REGARDANT
ADVERTISE	CENTREING	EMPIRICAL	ICTERIDAE	LACHRYMAL	NUMERAIRE	REGARDFUL
AFTERCARE	CHAIRLIFT	ENCIRCLED	IGNORAMUS	LAMARTINE	NUMERATOR	REGARDING
AFTERDAMP	CHEERLESS	ENDURABLE	IGNORANCE	LANGRIDGE	NUMERICAL	REMBRANDT
AFTERGLOW	CHLOROSIS	ENDURANCE	IMMERSION	LASERWORT	OBCORDATE	REPERCUSS
AFTERMATH	CIGARETTE	ENGARLAND	IMMORALLY	LATERALLY	OBJURGATE	REPERTORY
AFTERMOST	CINERARIA	ENNERDALE	IMMORTALS	LAZARETTO	OBSERVANT	REPORTAGE
AFTERNOON	CINEREOUS	ENSORCELL	IMPARTIAL	LESTRIGON	ODOURLESS	REPORTING
AFTERWORD	CLEARANCE	ENTERITIS	IMPERATOR	LEVERAGED	OESTROGEN	RESERPINE
ALBERTINE	CLEARNESS	ENTERTAIN	IMPERFECT	LIBERALLY	OFFERTORY	RESERVIST
ALEURITIS	CLEARWING	ENVERMEIL	IMPERIOUS	LIBERATED	OLECRANON	RESERVOIR
ALGORITHM	COCKROACH	ESMERALDA	IMPORTANT	LIBERATOR	OLEORESIN	RESORTING
ALTERABLE	COHERENCE	ESPERANCE	IMPORTUNE	LIBERTIES	OMNIRANGE	RESTRAINT
ALTERCATE	COLERIDGE	ESPERANTO	INCARDINE	LIBERTINE	OPPORTUNE	RESURFACE
ALTERNATE	COLORLESS	ETHEREOUS	INCARNATE	LITERALLY	OROGRAPHY	RESURGENT
AMAUROSIS	CONGRUENT	EUPHRATES	INCORRECT	LITURGICS	OTHERWISE	RESURRECT
AMBERGRIS	CONGRUOUS	EXCORIATE	INCURABLE	LIVERPOOL	OTTERBURN	RETORSION
AMPERSAND	CONTRALTO	EXCURSION	INCURABLY	LIVERWORT	OUTERMOST	RETORTION
ANABRANCH	CONTRIVED	EXECRABLE	INCURIOUS	LIVERYMAN	OUTGROWTH	RETURNING
ANAEROBIC	CONTRIVER	EXECRABLY	INCURSION	LOGARITHM	OVERRATED	REVERENCE
ANTARCTIC	COPYRIGHT	EXPERTISE	INEBRIATE	LONGRANGE	OVERREACH	REVERSING
APHERESIS	COVERDALE	EXPORTING	INFERENCE	LUMBRICUS	OVERREACT	REVERSION
APOCRYPHA	COVERTURE	EXPURGATE	INFERTILE	LUXURIANT	OVERRIDER	REWARDING
APPARATUS	COWARDICE	EXTIRPATE	INFIRMARY	LUXURIATE	OWNERSHIP	REWORKING
APPARITOR	DECORATED	EXTORTION	INFIRMITY	LUXURIOUS	PANORAMIC	RICERCARE
APPERTAIN	DECORATOR	EYEBRIGHT	INFORMANT	MACARONIC	PAPARAZZI	RIDERHOOD
APPORTION	DECURSIVE	FALERNIAN	INFURIATE	MACARTHUR	PAPARAZZO	RIDERLESS
AQUARELLE	DEFERENCE	FAVORABLE	INHERITED	MADARIAGA	PAPERBACK	RIVERSIDE
ARBORETUM	DEFERMENT	FAVORABLY	INHERITOR	MADAROSIS	PAPERCLIP	ROBERTSON
ARKWRIGHT	DEFORMITY	FIGURANTE	INJURIOUS	MAHARAJAH	PAPERWORK	RUNAROUND
ARTERIOLE	DELIRIOUS	FLAGRANCE	INNERMOST	MAHARANEE	PARTRIDGE	SALERATUS
ARTHRITIC	DEMARCATE	FLOORSHOW	INSCRIBED	MAHARISHI	PATERCOVE	SAMARITAN
ARTHRITIS	DEMURRAGE	FLOURMILL	INSERTION	MAJORDOMO	PATERNITY	SATIRICAL
ARTHROPOD	DEPARTURE	FLUORSPAR	INSURANCE	MAJORETTE	PEDERASTY	SATURATED
ARTHROSIS	DESERTION	FRAGRANCE	INSURGENT	MATERNITY	PENDRAGON	SATURNIAN
ASCERTAIN	DESERVING	FRAGRANCY	INTERBRED	MAYORALTY	PENFRIEND	SATURNINE
ASPARAGUS	DESIRABLE	GABARDINE	INTERCEDE	MEMORABLE	PENURIOUS	SATURNISM
ASPARTAME	DESTROYED	GABERDINE	INTERCEPT	MEMORITER	PETERSHAM	SATYRIDAE
ASPERSION	DESTROYER	GALDRAGON	INTERCITY	MISCREANT	POKERWORK	SATYRINAE
ASPIRATOR	DETERGENT	GENERALLY	INTERDICT	MISERABLE	PORTRAYAL	SAVERNAKE
ASSERTING	DETERMINE	GENERATOR	INTERFACE	MISERABLY	PORTREEVE	SCIARIDAE
ASSERTION	DETERRENT	GEOGRAPHY	INTERFERE	MITHRAISM	POWERBOAT	SCLEROSIS
ASSERTIVE	DEXTRORSE	GINORMOUS	INTERJECT	MODERATOR	POWERLESS	SCLEROTAL
ASSURANCE	DIACRITIC	GLAIREOUS	INTERLACE	MODERNISM	PREORDAIN	SCURRIOUR
ASSUREDLY	DIAERESIS	GOVERNESS	INTERLARD	MODERNIST	PROCREATE	SEMIRAMIS
AUBERGINE	DIARRHOEA	GOVERNING	INTERLOCK	MODERNITY	PRODROMAL	SEPARABLE

SEPARATED	UNDERLING	ANCESTRAL	CROSSEYED	FORESTALL	JACKSTRAW	NEWSSTAND
SEPARATOR	UNDERMINE	ANGOSTURA	CROSSFIRE	FORESTERS	JANISSARY	NIAISERIE
SEVERALLY	UNDERMOST	ANTISERUM	CROSSOVER	FREESTONE	JARLSBERG	NITHSDALE
SEVERANCE	UNDERPAID	ARMISTICE	CROSSWALK	FREESTYLE	JERUSALEM	NUMBSKULL
SHEARLING	UNDERPASS	ARRESTING	CROSSWIND	FRIESLAND	JOCKSTRAP	OBEISANCE
SHEERLEGS	UNDERRATE	ASSISTANT	CROSSWISE	FROGSPAWN	JOUISANCE	OBFUSCATE
SHEERNESS	UNDERSEAL	AUGUSTINE	CROSSWORD	FROISSART	KERBSTONE	OBSESSION
SIDEROSIS	UNDERSELL	AUTOSCOPY	CROUSTADE	FULLSCALE	KHANSAMAH	OBSESSIVE
SILURIDAE	UNDERSIDE	AYLESBURY	CROWSBILL	GAINSAYER	KICKSHAWS	OCTASTICH
SNEERWELL	UNDERSIGN	BACKSHISH	CROWSFOOT	GALLSTONE	KINGSIZED	ODELSTING
SOBERNESS	UNDERSONG	BACKSLIDE	DACHSHUND	GATESHEAD	KNAPSCULL	OVERSHADE
SOPORIFIC	UNDERTAKE	BACKSPACE	DAMASCENE	GEARSHIFT	KNAPSKULL	OVERSHOES
SOUBRETTE	UNDERTONE	BACKSTAGE	DECASTYLE	GEARSTICK	KNOBSTICK	OVERSHOOT
SOUFRIERE	UNDERWALK	BACKSWORD	DECESSION	GLADSTONE	KONISCOPE	OVERSIGHT
SOVEREIGN	UNDERWEAR	BANDSTAND	DECUSSATE	GLASSWARE	LADYSMITH	OVERSIZED
SPEARHEAD	UNDERWENT	BANISTERS	DEPASTURE	GLASSWORT	LAMASERAI	OVERSLEEP
SPEARMINT	UNDERWOOD	BARNSTORM	DEPOSITOR	GLISSANDO	LAMBSWOOL	OVERSPEND
SPEARSIDE	UNEARTHLY	BARYSCOPE	DEVASTATE	GOLDSINNY	LAMPSHADE	OVERSPILL
SPEARWORT	UNMARRIED	BECHSTEIN	DIGASTRIC	GOLDSMITH	LANDSCAPE	OVERSTATE
SPHERICAL	UNNERVING	BEEFSTEAK	DIGESTION	GRASSLAND	LANDSLIDE	OVERSTEER
SQUIREAGE	UNVARYING	BERNSTEIN	DIGESTIVE	GREASEGUN	LANDSMAAL	PAKISTANI
SQUIRMING	UNWORRIED	BLESSINGS	DIVISIBLE	GUESSWORK	LANDSTURM	PALESTINE
STAIRCASE	UPPERCASE	BLUESHIFT	DOWNSTAGE	GYROSCOPE	LANGSPIEL	PARASCENE
STEERSMAN	UPPERMOST	BLUESTONE	DRIPSTONE	HAILSTONE	LATESCENT	PARASCEVE
SUDORIFIC	USHERETTE	BOATSWAIN	DROPSICAL	HAILSTORM	LEAFSTALK	PARASITIC
SUFFRAGAN	UTTERANCE	BOMBSHELL	DRUGSTORE	HAIRSTYLE	LEGISLATE	PECKSNIFF
SUGARCANE	UTTERLESS	BONDSTONE	DRUMSTICK	HALFSTAFF	LIFESTYLE	PENISTONE
SUPERCOOL	UTTERMOST	BOOKSHELF	DRYASDUST	HALLSTATT	LIMESTONE	PERISCIAN
SUPERETTE	VAPORETTO	BOOKSTALL	EAVESDROP	HAMPSHIRE	LINTSTOCK	PERISCOPE
SUPERFINE	VAPORIFIC	BOOKSTAND	ECOSSAISE	HAMPSTEAD	LIVESTOCK	PERISHING
SUPERNOVA	VAPORIZER	BOOKSTORE	EDDYSTONE	HANDSHAKE	LOADSTONE	PERISTOME
SUPERSEDE	VENERABLE	BRASSERIE	EGRESSION	HANDSPIKE	LOAMSHIRE	PERISTYLE
SUPERSTAR	VENEREOUS	BRASSICAS	ELKOSHITE	HANDSTAND	LOCKSMITH	PHANSIGAR
SUPERVENE	VENTRICLE	BRASSIERE	ELLESMERE	HARDSHELL	LODESTONE	PHARSALIA
SUPERVISE	VICARIOUS	BRASSWARE	EMBASSADE	HARESTANE	LOGISTICS	PIKESTAFF
SURPRISED	VICEREGAL	BRIMSTONE	EMBASSAGE	HARTSHORN	LONGSHORE	PILASTERS
SYBARITIC	VICEREINE	BRITSCHKA	ENDOSPERM	HAWKSBILL	LOUISIANA	PIPESTONE
SYNERGIST	WAFERTHIN	CADASTRAL	EPHESIANS	HEADSCARF	LUTESCENT	PLAUSIBLE
TAMERLANE	WATERBABY	CAKESTAND	EQUISETUM	HEADSTALL	LYMESWOLD	PLAUSIBLY
TAVERNERS	WATERBUTT	CELESTIAL	EXCESSIVE	HEADSTONE	MAELSTROM	PLAUSTRAL
TOBERMORY	WATERFALL	CERUSSITE	EXCISEMAN	HEMISTICH	MAJUSCULE	PLEASANCE
TOLERABLE	WATERFORD	CHINSTRAP	EXCUSABLE	HEXASTICH	MAKESHIFT	PLIMSOLLS
TOLERABLY	WATERFOWL	CHRISTIAN	EXCUSABLY	HIGHSPEED	MAULSTICK	POTASSIUM
TOLERANCE	WATERGATE	CHRISTMAS	EXPISCATE	HINDSIGHT	MEGASCOPE	PRESSGANG
TOLERATED	WATERHOLE	CHRYSALIS	EXPOSITOR	HOARSTONE	MEGASPORE	PRIESTESS
TONBRIDGE	WATERLESS	CLASSICAL	FALDSTOOL	HOLYSTONE	MERESWINE	PRIESTLEY
TOPDRAWER	WATERLILY	CLASSLESS	FARMSTEAD	HOMESTEAD	MILESTONE	PROUSTITE
TOVARISCH	WATERLINE	CLASSMATE	FATISCENT	HORNSTONE	MILKSHAKE	PUISSANCE
TREDRILLE	WATERMARK	CLASSROOM	FEEDSTUFF	HOROSCOPE	MILLSTONE	PUNISHING
TRIERARCH	WATERMILL	CLEPSYDRA	FILMSTRIP	HOURSTONE	MINISKIRT	QUIESCENT
TURNROUND	WATERSHED	CLOISONNÉ	FILOSELLE	IGNESCENT	MINKSTONE	RACKSTRAW
UNCERTAIN	WATERSIDE	COCKSCOMB	FINISHING	IMPASSION	MINUSCULE	RAINSTORM
UNCHRISOM	WATERWEED	COCKSFOOT	FIRESTONE	IMPASSIVE	MODESTINE	RAVISHING
UNCORRECT	WHERRYMAN	COCKSWAIN	FLAGSTAFF	IMPOSTURE	MOLESKINS	RECESSION
UNDERBITE	WHIPROUND	COCUSWOOD	FLAGSTONE	INCESSANT	MONASTERY	RECESSIVE
UNDERBRED	YGGDRASIL	COLOSSEUM	FLAMSTEED	INGESTION	MONASTRAL	RECUSANCE
UNDERCAST	YTTERBIUM	COLOSTOMY	FLOWSTONE	INJUSTICE	MONKSHOOD	REFUSENIK
UNDERCOAT	ACCESSION	COLOSTRUM	FOODSTORE	INNISFAIL	MONOSTICH	REGISSEUR
UNDERDONE	ACCESSORY	COLTSFOOT	FOODSTUFF	INNISFREE	MOONSHINE	REGISTRAR
UNDERFEED	ACOUSTICS	CORKSCREW	FOOTSTALL	INSISTENT	MOONSTONE	REINSTATE
UNDERFELT	ADMISSION	CORNSTALK	FOOTSTOOL	INTESTATE	MORTSTONE	REMISSION
UNDERFLOW	ADVISABLE	CORUSCATE	FORASMUCH	INTESTINE	MUMPSIMUS	RENASCENT
UNDERFOOT	ADVISEDLY	COUNSELOR	FORESHORE	INVISIBLE	MUTOSCOPE	REPOSSESS
UNDERGRAD	AEROSPACE	CROISSANT	FORESIGHT	IRONSIDES	NECESSARY	RESISTANT
UNDERHAND	ALTISSIMO	CROSSBEAM	FORESPEAK	IRONSTONE	NECESSITY	RHAPSODIC
UNDERHUNG	AMBUSCADE	CROSSBILL	FORESPEND	JACKSCREW	NEWSSHEET	RINGSIDER
UNDERLINE	AMIDSHIPS	CROSSBRED	FORESTAGE	JACKSNIPE	NEWSSTALL	ROADSTEAD

ROOTSTOCK	TRANSPOSE	ARMSTRONG	DECATHLON	GAUNTNESS	LOGOTHETE	POLITESSE
ROUSSETTE	TRANSSHIP	ATTITUDES	DEMETRIUS	GAZETTEER	MAINTENON	POLITICAL
RUFESCENT	TRANSVAAL	AUXOTROPH	DEMITASSE	GENETICAL	MALATHION	POLITIQUE
RUNESTAVE	TREASURER	AWESTRUCK	DIASTASIS	GENITALIA	MATUTINAL	POLYTHENE
SALESGIRL	TROOSTITE	BACKTRACK	DIGITALIN	GOBETWEEN	MEDITATOR	POULTERER
SALESLADY	TROSSACHS	BAGATELLE	DIGITALIS	GREATCOAT	MEHITABEL	PRACTICAL
SANDSTONE	TROUSSEAU	BATHTOWEL	DIPHTHONG	GREATNESS	MENSTRUAL	PRACTISED
SANDSTORM	TUMESCENT	BEAUTEOUS	DONATELLO	GREETINGS	MENSTRUUM	PRACTOLOL
SATISFIED	TUNGSTATE	BEAUTIFUL	DOUBTLESS	GUILTLESS	MIDSTREAM	PRINTABLE
SCANSORES	TUNGSTOUS	BEESTINGS	DOWNTREND	HABITABLE	MILITANCY	PROPTOSIS
SCISSORER	TURNSTILE	BELATEDLY	DRAFTSMAN	HABITUATE	MINUTEMAN	PROSTRATE
SEBASTIAN	TURNSTONE	BILATERAL	DRIFTWOOD	HALITOSIS	MISSTROKE	PUNCTILIO
SECESSION	UNMUSICAL	BIRDTABLE	DUNSTABLE	HALOTHANE	MOISTNESS	PUNCTUATE
SENESCENT	VANISHING	BLISTERED	ECTOTHERM	HAMSTRING	MONATOMIC	PURITANIC
SENESCHAL	VARISCITE	BLOATWARE	EIGHTIETH	HAMSTRUNG	MONOTROCH	PYRETHRUM
SERASKIER	VELASQUEZ	BLOWTORCH	EIGHTSOME	HEALTHILY	MONSTROUS	QUANTICAL
SHENSTONE	VELDSKOEN	BLUNTNESS	ELASTOMER	HEARTACHE	MORATORIA	QUANTOCKS
SHIPSHAPE	VENUSBERG	BLUSTERER	ELECTORAL	HEARTBEAT	MORATORIO	QUARTERLY
SHOESHINE	VIGESIMAL	BOUNTEOUS	ELECTRESS	HEARTBURN	MOUSTACHE	QUARTETTE
SIDESWIPE	VIPASSANA	BOUNTIFUL	ELECTRIFY	HEARTFELT	MUNITIONS	QUIETNESS
SILTSTONE	VITASCOPE	BRACTEOLE	ELECTRODE	HEARTHRUG	NABATHEAN	QUINTETTE
SINGSPIEL	VOLKSRAAD	BREATHING	ELECTUARY	HEARTLAND	NEGOTIATE	QUINTROON
SINUSITIS	WASHSTAND	BRISTLING	EMBATTLED	HEARTLESS	NERITIDAE	QUINTUPLE
SLABSTONE	WELDSTADT	BUCKTEETH	ENACTMENT	HEARTWOOD	NIGHTCLUB	QUITTANCE
SLAPSTICK	WHETSTONE	BUCKTHORN	EPISTAXIS	HEMITROPE	NIGHTFALL	RACETRACK
SNOWSHOES	WHIMSICAL	BUMPTIOUS	EPISTOLER	HEMSTITCH	NIGHTFIRE	REACTANCE
SNOWSTORM	WHINSTONE	CAFETERIA	EQUITABLE	HEPATICAL	NIGHTGLOW	REDSTREAK
SOAPSTONE	WHIPSNADE	CAFETIERE	EQUITABLY	HEPATITIS	NIGHTGOWN	REISTAFEL
SOMASCOPE	WHUNSTANE	CAPITULAR	ERGATANER	HERETICAL	NIGHTHAWK	RELATIONS
SONGSMITH	WINDSCALE	CAPITULUM	ERISTICAL	HERITABLE	NIGHTMARE	REPUTABLE
SPONSORED	WINDSWEPT	CARETAKER	EROSTRATE	HESITANCE	NIGHTSPOT	REPUTEDLY
STARSTONE	WITHSTAND	CARTTRACK	ETCETERAS	HESITANCY	NIGHTTIME	REVETMENT
STRESSFUL	WOODSHOCK	CATATONIA	EVENTUATE	HEXATEUCH	NIGHTWORK	RHEOTAXIS
STROSSERS	WORDSMITH	CATATONIC	EXACTMENT	IDENTICAL	NINETIETH	RIGHTEOUS
SWANSDOWN	WORKSPACE	CERATITIS	EXACTNESS	IDENTIKIT	NOMOTHETE	RIGHTHAND
TABASHEER	XEROSTOMA	CERATODUS	EXANTHEMA	IDIOTICON	NOVITIATE	RIGHTNESS
TAOISEACH	YARDSTICK	CHANTEUSE	EXCITABLE	IMMUTABLE	OUGHTNESS	RIGHTWING
TAVISTOCK	YORKSHIRE	CHANTILLY	EXISTENCE	IMMUTABLY	OVERTHROW	ROISTERER
TAYASSUID	ZYGOSPORE	CHARTERED	EXOSTOSIS	IMPATIENT	OVERTONES	SAGITTARY
TEARSHEET	ABLUTIONS	CHARTREUX	EXPATIATE	IMPETUOUS	OVERTRUMP	SAINTFOIN
TELESALES	ABOUTFACE	CHASTENED	EYESTRAIN	IMPOTENCE	PAINTWORK	SAINTHOOD
TELESCOPE	ABOUTTURN	CHATTERER	FACETIOUS	INCITATUS	PALATABLE	SANCTUARY
TELESTICH	ADAPTABLE	CLUSTERED	FAINTNESS	INERTNESS	PANATELLA	SAXITOXIN
THEOSOPHY	ADEPTNESS	COASTLINE	FANATICAL	INFATUATE	PANETTONE	SCANTLING
THERSITES	ADMITTING	COINTREAU	FASTTRACK	INPATIENT	PARATAXIS	SCATTERED
THIRSTILY	ADULTERER	CONSTABLE	FAULTLESS	IRRITABLE	PARATHION	SCENTLESS
THIRSTING	ADULTHOOD	CONSTANCE	FIRSTEVER	IRRITABLY	PARATROOP	SCEPTICAL
THOUSANDS	AEROTAXIS	CONSTANCY	FIRSTHAND	IRRITATED	PAROTITIS	SCINTILLA
THRASHING	AFLATOXIN	CONSTRICT	FIRSTRATE	JEPHTHAHS	PARTTIMER	SCRATCHED
THRASONIC	AIRSTREAM	CONSTRUCT	FLATTENED	JETSTREAM	PATHTRAIN	SCRATCHES
THRESHOLD	ALBATROSS	COUNTDOWN	FLATTENER	JOCKTELEG	PENETRATE	SCRUTATOR
THYESTEAN	ALERTNESS	COUNTLESS	FLATTERED	KERATITIS	PENITENCE	SECATEURS
TIMESHARE	ALLOTMENT	COUNTRIES	FLATTERER	KEYSTROKE	PENSTEMON	SEDITIOUS
TOADSTONE	AMBITIOUS	COURTELLE	FLEETWOOD	LAPSTREAK	PHANTASMA	SHATTERED
TOADSTOOL	ANASTASIA	COURTEOUS	FLINTLOCK	LEASTWAYS	PICKTHANK	SHELTERED
TOMBSTONE	ANNOTATED	COURTESAN	FLUCTUATE	LEASTWISE	PINSTRIPE	SHIFTLESS
TOWNSFOLK	ANNOTATOR	COURTROOM	FLUSTERED	LENGTHILY	PIRATICAL	SHIFTWORK
TRANSCEND	ANTITOXIC	COURTSHIP	FORETASTE	LEVITICUS	PLASTERED	SHINTOISM
TRANSEUNT	ANTITOXIN	COURTYARD	FRACTIOUS	LIENTERIC	PLASTERER	SHORTCAKE
TRANSFORM	APARTHEID	CRAFTSMAN	FROSTBITE	LIGHTFACE	PLASTIQUE	SHORTFALL
TRANSFUSE	APARTMENT	CRUSTACEA	FRUCTIDOR	LIGHTFOOT	PLAYTHING	SHORTHAND
TRANSHUME	APOSTOLIC	CRYPTOGAM	FRUITCAKE	LIGHTLESS	PLENTEOUS	SHORTHAUL
TRANSIENT	APPETIZER	CUNCTATOR	FRUITERER	LIGHTNESS	PLENTIFUL	SHORTHOLD
TRANSLATE	ARBITRAGE	CURETTAGE	FRUITLESS	LIGHTNING	POINTEDLY	SHORTHORN
TRANSMUTE	ARBITRARY	DAUNTLESS	FRUSTRATE	LIGHTSHIP	POINTLESS	SHORTLIST
TRANSPIRE	ARBITRATE	DEBATABLE	GAELTACHT	LIGHTSOME	POINTSMAN	SHORTNESS
TRANSPORT	ARISTOTLE	DEBUTANTE	GALATIANS	LIMITLESS	POLITBURO	SHORTSTAY

SHORTSTOP	UNWATERED	CONFUCIUS	GARRULOUS	PANDURATE	TALMUDIST	RENOVATOR
SHORTTERM	UNWITTING	CONFUSING	GRADUALLY	PARBUCKLE	TELLURIAN	SCRIVENER
SHUTTERED	UPAITHRIC	CONFUSION	GRADUATED	PASTURAGE	TELLURION	SEMIVOWEL
SIDETRACK	UPSETTING	CONJUGATE	GRANULATE	PENDULATE	TELLURIUM	SYNOVITIS
SIGHTLESS	VEGETABLE	CONJURING	GRANULITE	PENDULOUS	TINGUAITE	UNCOVERED
SIGHTSEER	VEGETATOR	CONNUBIAL	GRANULOSE	PENPUSHER	TOLPUDDLE	UNDIVIDED
SKEPTICAL	VERATRINE	CONQUEROR	HACQUETON	PERFUMERY	TREBUCHET	UNINVITED
SKINTIGHT	VERITABLE	CONSULATE	HAMBURGER	PERGUNNAH	TREMULANT	UNSAVOURY
SLANTWISE	VEXATIONS	CONSUMING	HAMMURABI	PERSUADED	TREMULATE	AINSWORTH
SMARTNESS	VEXATIOUS	CONTUMACY	HARQUEBUS	PERTURBED	TREMULOUS	ALLOWABLE
SOLITAIRE	VIENTIANE	CONTUMELY	HAWCUBITE	PERTUSATE	TRIBUNATE	ALLOWANCE
SOMETHING	VOLATIBLE	CONTUSION	HERCULEAN	PERTUSSIS	TRIBUTARY	ARROWHEAD
SOMETIMES	WAISTBAND	CORDUROYS	IMPLUVIUM	PETARIST	TRICUSPID	ARROWROOT
SPARTACUS	WAISTCOAT	CORPULENT	IMPOUNDER	PIROUETTE	TRITURATE	BACKWARDS
SPATTERED	WAISTLINE	CORPUSCLE	IMPRUDENT	POLLUTANT	TRUCULENT	BACKWATER
SPECTACLE	WHEATGERM	CORRUGATE	INCAUTION	POLLUTION	TURBULENT	BACKWOODS
SPECTATOR	WHEATMEAL	CORRUPTER	INCLUDING	PORCUPINE	TURQUOISE	BANDWAGON
SPLITTING	WHISTLING	COSTUMIER	INCLUSION	PORTULACA	UNBOUNDED	BOTSWANAN
SPORTSMAN	WHITTAWER	COTHURNUS	INCLUSIVE	POSTULANT	UNCOUPLED	BRATWURST
SPORTSMEN	WRESTLING	COUTURIER	INERUDITE	POSTULATE	UNCOURTLY	BUCKWHEAT
SPRITEFUL	YACHTSMAN	CRAPULENT	INFLUENCE	POTHUNTER	UNDAUNTED	CARTWHEEL
SPRITSAIL	YACHTSMEN	CRAPULOUS	INFLUENZA	PRECURSOR	UNDOUBTED	CHARWOMAN
SQUATTERS	ACIDULATE	CREDULITY	INOCULATE	PREJUDICE	UNEQUALED	DASHWHEEL
STARTLING	ACIDULOUS	CREDULOUS	INTRUSION	PRELUSORY	UNFOUNDED	DISHWATER
STILTBIRD	AFFLUENCE	CROQUETTE	INTRUSIVE	PRIMULINE	UNTOUCHED	DOWNWARDS
STOUTNESS	AHASUERUS	CUCHULAIN	JACQUERIE	PROFUSELY	UNUNUNIUM	EASTWARDS
STRATAGEM	ANNOUNCER	CURFUFFLE	JIGGUMBOB	PROFUSION	UNUSUALLY	EDELWEISS
STRATEGIC	ARTHURIAN	DAMBUSTER	KERFUFFLE	PROLUSION	UPCOUNTRY	EDGEWORTH
STRETCHED	ASTOUNDED	DEBAUCHED	LABOURITE	PROMUSCIS	URUGUAYAN	ELBOWROOM
STRETCHER	ATAHUALPA	DEBAUCHEE	LAEVULOSE	PULLULATE	VERTUMNUS	ELSEWHERE
STRUTTING	AUTEURISM	DEFAULTER	LANGUAGES	PURSUANCE	VIRGULATE	ENDOWMENT
SUBSTANCE	BANQUETTE	DIFFUSION	LANGUEDOC	QUERULOUS	VIRTUALLY	ERSTWHILE
SUBSTRATA	BECQUEREL	DISBURDEN	LANGUETTE	RAPTUROUS	VITRUVIAN	FIREWATER
SUBSTRATE	BRIQUETTE	DISGUISED	LANGUIDLY	REMOULADE	VOLTURNUS	FIREWORKS
SUMPTUARY	CAGOULARD	DISGUSTED	LEISURELY	RESHUFFLE	VULTURINE	FOLKWEAVE
SUMPTUOUS	CALCULATE	DISPUTANT	LIMBURGER	RESOURCES	WALPURGIS	FOREWOMAN
SUNSTROKE	CALPURNIA	DISTURBED	LIMOUSINE	ROXBURGHE	WELSUMMER	FOURWHEEL
SWEATBAND	CAMBUSCAN	EFFLUENCE	LITHUANIA	SAPSUCKER	WHODUNNIT	FREEWHEEL
SWEETENER	CARBUNCLE	EFFLUVIUM	MACQUARIE	SASQUATCH	ALLEVIATE	GEARWHEEL
SWEETMEAT	CARTULARY	EJACULATE	MANDUCATE	SCHMUTTER	ANTIVENIN	GREYWACKE
SWEETNESS	CELLULITE	ELOCUTION	MARAUDING	SCLAUNDER	ARRIVISTE	HOMEWARDS
SWEETSHOP	CELLULOID	ELOQUENCE	MARQUESAS	SCROUNGER	BEHAVIOUR	IRONWORKS
SWIFTNESS	CELLULOSE	EMOLUMENT	MARQUETRY	SECLUSION	BOLIVIANO	IRRAWADDY
TEMPTRESS	CENTURION	ENCAUSTIC	MARSUPIAL	SELJUKIAN	CANAVERAL	JERKWATER
THIRTIETH	CHALUMEAU	ENCOUNTER	MARSUPIUM	SENSUALLY	DELIVERER	JOBSWORTH
TIGHTENER	CHEQUERED	ENCOURAGE	MASCULINE	SHUBUNKIN	ECHEVERIA	KINSWOMAN
TIGHTHEAD	CHERUBINI	ENTOURAGE	MATHURINE	SINGULTUS	ENLIVENED	LANDWARDS
TIGHTNESS	CHIHUAHUA	EPICUREAN	MAVOURNIN	SIPHUNCLE	EQUIVOCAL	LEFTWARDS
TIGHTROPE	CIRCULATE	ETIQUETTE	MEASURING	SPATULATE	EQUIVOQUE	LILYWHITE
TIMETABLE	COAGULANT	EVOLUTION	MERCURIAL	SPECULATE	EXCAVATOR	MEANWHILE
TOASTRACK	COAGULATE	EXCLUDING	MIDSUMMER	SPELUNKER	GENEVIEVE	OARSWOMAN
TRACTABLE	COLLUSION	EXCLUSION	MISGUIDED	SPODUMENE	GRENVILLE	OVERWEIGH
TRATTORIA	COLLUSIVE	EXCLUSIVE	MUNDUNGUS	SPRAUCHLE	GRIEVANCE	OVERWHELM
TREATMENT	COLOURFUL	EXECUTANT	MURMURING	STATUETTE	GROSVENOR	POSTWOMAN
TREETRUNK	COLOURING	EXECUTION	MUSSULMAN	STATUTORY	IMMOVABLE	RAINWATER
TRIATHLON	COLOURIST	EXECUTIVE	NANTUCKET	STIMULANT	IMMOVABLY	REARWARDS
TRIETERIC	COMMUNION	EXECUTRIX	NEPTUNIUM	STIMULATE	INNOVATOR	RENEWABLE
TURNTABLE	COMMUNISM	EXEQUATUR	NOCTURNAL	STIPULATE	LUBAVITCH	ROADWORKS
TWENTIETH	COMMUNIST	EXHAUSTED	NUMMULITE	SUBJUGATE	NASHVILLE	ROSEWATER
UNALTERED	COMMUNITY	EXTRUSION	NUNCUPATE	SUCCUBINE	NECKVERSE	SALTWATER
UNEATABLE	COMMUTATE	FACTUALLY	OBSCURELY	SUCCULENT	OBLIVIOUS	SALTWORKS
UNFITTING	COMPUTING	FAVOURITE	OBSCURITY	SUCCURSAL	OVERVALUE	SCREWBALL
UNMATCHED	CONCUBINE	FLATULENT	OBTRUSION	SUFFUSION	PALOVERDE	SCREWEDUP
UNNATURAL	CONCUSSED	FORMULATE	OBTRUSIVE	SULFUROUS	RECOVERED	SCREWPINE
UNNOTICED	CONDUCIVE	FORTUNATE	OCCLUSION	SUPPURATE	REDIVIVUS	SCREWTAPE
UNSETTLED	CONDUCTOR	FREQUENCY	OPHIUCHUS	SURMULLET	RELEVANCE	SHIPWRECK
UNTUTORED	CONDUCTUS	GARRULITY	OUTNUMBER	SURQUEDRY	REMOVABLE	SIDEWARDS

SKEWWHIFF	HUNKYDORY	AGREEABLY	BREAKAWAY	EMACIATED	GRIEVANCE	KINGMAKER	
SNOWWHITE	JELLYFISH	ALDEBARAN	BRUMMAGEM	ENCELADUS	GUJARATHI	LACERATED	
SOMEWHERE	LAFAYETTE	ALIPHATIC	CAMERAMAN	ENCHEASON	GYROMANCY	LAGNIAPPE	
STALWORTH	LATHYRISM	ALLEMANDE	CANTHARIS	ENDECAGON	HABITABLE	LAMINATED	
TEESWATER	MALAYSIAN	ALLIGATOR	CANTHARUS	ENDURABLE	HALFBAKED	LANDWARDS	
THROWAWAY	MARTYRDOM	ALLOCARPY	CARACALLA	ENDURANCE	HANSEATIC	LANGUAGES	
THROWBACK	MASSYMORE	ALLOPATHY	CARETAKER	ENIGMATIC	HARIGALDS	LANTHANUM	
THROWDOWN	MOLLYMAWK	ALLOWABLE	CASTRATED	ENJOYABLE	HEARTACHE	LATERALLY	
THROWSTER	MONEYWORT	ALLOWANCE	CATAMARAN	ENSHEATHE	HEDERATED	LAUGHABLE	
ULLSWATER	NEODYMIUM	ALTERABLE	CENTRALLY	EPEOLATRY	HENDIADYS	LEFTWARDS	
WASTWATER	NEWLYWEDS	AMBULANCE	CEROMANCY	EPISTAXIS	HERITABLE	LEHRJAHRE	
WESTWARDS	PACHYDERM	AMYGDALUS	CHALIAPIN	EQUITABLE	HESITANCE	LEVERAGED	
WHITWORTH	PARHYPATE	ANABRANCH	CHAMPAGNE	EQUITABLY	HESITANCY	LIBERALLY	
WIDOWHOOD	PENNYWORT	ANAPLASIA	CHAMPAIGN	ERGATANER	HIGHLANDS	LIBERATED	
ADMIXTURE	PHENYTOIN	ANAPLASTY	CHARLATAN	ESCALATOR	HIMALAYAN	LIBERATOR	
MONOXYLON	PIGGYBACK	ANASTASIA	CHAWBACON	ESMERALDA	HIMALAYAS	LINKLATER	
OBNOXIOUS	PIGGYBANK	ANNOTATED	CHICKADEE	ESOPHAGUS	HINDRANCE	LITERALLY	
TAMOXIFEN	POPPYCOCK	ANNOTATOR	CHIHUAHUA	ESPERANCE	HOLOCAUST	LITHUANIA	
TARAXACUM	PROPYLENE	ANNOYANCE	CHROMATIC	ESPERANTO	HOMEWARDS	LOGICALLY	
ACETYLENE	PUSSYFOOT	ANTENATAL	CHRYSALIS	ESTIMABLE	HONORABLE	LONGRANGE	
ALICYCLIC	READYEARN	ANTIPASTO	CINEMATIC	ETERNALLY	HOTHEADED	LUMINAIRE	
AMARYLLIS	READYMADE	ANTIPATHY	CINERARIA	ETIOLATED	HYLOBATES	LUMINANCE	
AMBLYOPIA	REPAYABLE	APOPHATIC	CLEARANCE	EUPHRATES	HYPOCAUST	LYMPHATIC	
ANNOYANCE	REPAYMENT	APPARATUS	CLEOPATRA	EXCAVATOR	IDEOPATHY	LYRICALLY	
ANONYMITY	RUNNYMEDE	APPLIANCE	COLLEAGUE	EXCITABLE	IDIOMATIC	MACADAMIA	
ANONYMOUS	SALLYPORT	ARAUCARIA	COMICALLY	EXCUSABLE	IGNORAMUS	MACQUARIE	
BELLYACHE	SALLYPOST	AREOPAGUS	COMPLAINT	EXCUSABLY	IGNORANCE	MAGICALLY	
BELLYFLOP	SANNYASIN	ARROGANCE	CONCEALED	EXECRABLE	ILLEGALLY	MAHARAJAH	
BILLYCOCK	SPLAYFOOT	ASPARAGUS	CONFLATED	EXECRABLY	IMBALANCE	MAHARANEE	
BOOBYTRAP	STAGYRITE	ASPIRATOR	CONSTABLE	EXEQUATUR	IMMANACLE	MALLEABLE	
CANDYTUFT	STORYBOOK	ASSONANCE	CONSTANCE	EYESHADOW	IMMORALLY	MATELASSE	
CHARYBDIS	STORYLINE	ASSURANCE	CONSTANCY	FACTUALLY	IMMOVABLE	MATRIARCH	
COLLYRIUM	TACHYLITE	ASTHMATIC	CONTRALTO	FALKLANDS	IMMOVABLY	MAYORALTY	
CONDYLOMA	TACHYLYTE	ATAHUALPA	CORDIALLY	FAVORABLE	IMMUTABLE	MEATBALLS	
CORDYLINE	TRIDYMITE	ATHENAEUM	CRUCIALLY	FAVORABLY	IMMUTABLY	MEDICALLY	
CUBBYHOLE	TUMMYACHE	AUSTRALIA	CRUSTACEA	FIGURANTE	IMPEDANCE	MEDICATED	
CURRYCOMB	WALLYDRAG	AUTOLATRY	CUNCTATOR	FILICALES	IMPERATOR	MEDITATOR	
DAIRYMAID	WITHYWIND	AUTOMAKER	CYNICALLY	FILMMAKER	INCAPABLE	MEHITABEL	
DANDYPRAT	BEELZEBUB	AUTOMATED	DALLIANCE	FIREWATER	INCITATUS	MEMORABLE	
DIONYSIAN	DONIZETTI	AUTOMATIC	DEBATABLE	FLAGRANCE	INCREASED	MENOPAUSE	
DIONYSIUS	EMBEZZLER	AUTOMATON	DEBUTANTE	FLAMMABLE	INCUBATOR	MESSIANIC	
DITHYRAMB	FRIZZANTE	AVAILABLE	DECORATED	FLIPPANCY	INCURABLE	METABASIS	
ECOSYSTEM	NIETZSCHE	AVOIDABLE	DECORATOR	FOOLHARDY	INCURABLY	MIDHEAVEN	
EMBRYONIC	QUIZZICAL	AVOIDANCE	DEDICATED	FORETASTE	INDICATES	MILITANCY	
EMPHYSEMA	SFORZANDO	AXIOMATIC	DEFINABLE	FRAGRANCE	INDICATOR	MINELAYER	
ENJOYABLE	SYNIZESIS	BACKWARDS	DEMITASSE	FRAGRANCY	INEFFABLE	MISCHANCE	
ENJOYMENT	VENEZUELA	BACKWATER	DESIRABLE	FREELANCE	INHUMANLY	MISERABLE	
ENTHYMEME	WHIZZBANG	BAINMARIE	DETONATOR	FREEMASON	INITIALLY	MISERABLY	
EPICYCLIC	**9:6**	BALALAIKA	DIASTASIS	FRIZZANTE	INITIATED	MISPLACED	
EPONYMOUS	ABERRANCE	BALTHAZAR	DIGITALIN	FROGMARCH	INITIATOR	MISSHAPEN	
EURHYTHMY	ABUNDANCE	BANDWAGON	DIGITALIS	GAELTACHT	INNOVATOR	MITHRAISM	
EVERYBODY	ABYSMALLY	BAREFACED	DISCHARGE	GAINSAYER	INORGANIC	MODERATOR	
FAIRYLAND	ACARIASIS	BASICALLY	DISGRACED	GALAPAGOS	INSULATOR	MONOLAYER	
FAIRYTALE	ACONCAGUA	BEEFEATER	DISHWATER	GALDRAGON	INSURANCE	MONOMACHY	
FERRYBOAT	ACROBATIC	BELLYACHE	DISPLACED	GARIBALDI	IRRAWADDY	MONOMANIA	
FORSYTHIA	ADAPTABLE	BIGHEADED	DISPLAYED	GAUDEAMUS	IRRITABLE	MOONRAKER	
GALLYCROW	ADMIRABLE	BILLIARDS	DISTRAINT	GENERALLY	IRRITABLY	MORECAMBE	
GARRYOWEN	ADMIRABLY	BIOGRAPHY	DJELLABAH	GENERATOR	IRRITATED	MORTGAGEE	
GLORYHOLE	ADMIRALTY	BIRDTABLE	DOMINANCE	GENITALIA	ISLAMABAD	MORTGAGOR	
GOSSYPINE	ADRENALIN	BONAPARTE	DOWNWARDS	GEOGRAPHY	ISOCRATES	MOSCHATEL	
GOSSYPIUM	ADVISABLE	BOOBIALLA	DRINKABLE	GLADIATOR	JACARANDA	MOTHBALLS	
HEAVYDUTY	ADVOCATED	BOOKMAKER	DUNSTABLE	GLENGARRY	JERKWATER	MOTHEATEN	
HOLLYHOCK	AEROTAXIS	BOOTLACES	DYSPHAGIA	GLISSANDO	JERUSALEM	MOUSTACHE	
HOLLYWOOD	AFFIDAVIT	BOTSWANAN	DYSPRAXIA	GRADUALLY	JOCULARLY	MUCORALES	
HONEYCOMB	AFRIKAANS	BRADLAUGH	EASTWARDS	GRADUATED	JOUISANCE	MUMCHANCE	
HONEYMOON	AFRIKANER	BREAKABLE	ECOSSAISE	GREENAWAY	JUBILANCE	MUSICALLY	
HONKYTONK	AGREEABLE	BREAKAGES	ELONGATED	GREYWACKE	KHANSAMAH	MUTILATED	

NATURALLY	POLEMARCH	SCHOLARCH	TOLERABLY	BLACKBUCK	JARLSBERG	THROBBING
NAUSEATED	POLONAISE	SCHOLARLY	TOLERANCE	BLOODBATH	LEASEBACK	THROWBACK
NAVIGABLE	POPULARLY	SCIAMACHY	TOLERATED	CALEMBOUR	LUXEMBURG	TITHEBARN
NAVIGATOR	POPULATED	SCIOMANCY	TOOTHACHE	CAMEMBERT	MAGDEBURG	TURNABOUT
NEUCHATEL	PORBEAGLE	SCRUTATOR	TOPDRAWER	CANTABILE	MATCHBOOK	TRILOBITE
NEUTRALLY	PORTRAYAL	SCUDDALER	TOPICALLY	CARAMBOLA	MATCHBOOK	UNDERBITE
NEWSPAPER	POSTCARDS	SEANNACHY	TRACEABLE	CARIBBEAN	MOTORBIKE	UNDERBRED
NICARAGUA	POSTNATAL	SEMBLANCE	TRACTABLE	CHARABANC	MOTORBOAT	UNDOUBTED
NOMINALLY	PRAGMATIC	SEMIRAMIS	TRAINABLE	CHARYBDIS	MYOFIBRIL	VENUSBERG
NOMINATOR	PREGNANCY	SENSUALLY	TRAUMATIC	CHECKBOOK	NEIGHBOUR	VERTEBRAE
NOTEPAPER	PRINTABLE	SEPARABLE	TREGEAGLE	CHEEKBONE	NOTCHBACK	VERTEBRAL
NOVOCAINE	PRISMATIC	SEPARATED	TRIERARCH	CHERUBINI	NUREMBERG	VESTIBULE
NOVODAMUS	PROGRAMME	SEPARATOR	TRIVIALLY	COENOBITE	NUTJOBBER	WAGENBOOM
NUMERAIRE	PSEUDAXIS	SERENADER	TROSSACHS	COENOBIUM	ODDJOBMAN	WAISTBAND
NUMERATOR	PSORIASIS	SEVERALLY	TROUBADOR	COLOMBIAN	OFFENBACH	WALKABOUT
OBEISANCE	PUISSANCE	SEVERANCE	TRUNCATED	COLOMBIER	OTTERBURN	WALLABIES
OCCUPANCY	PURCHASER	SFORZANDO	TUMMYACHE	COLUMBARY	PALPEBRAL	WATERBABY
OFFCHANCE	PURITANIC	SHAMIANAH	TURNTABLE	COLUMBATE	PAPERBACK	WATERBUTT
OFFSEASON	PURSUANCE	SHETLANDS	TYPICALLY	COLUMBIAN	PICKABACK	WHALEBOAT
OLECRANON	PYROMANCY	SHILLABER	ULLSWATER	COLUMBINE	PIGGYBACK	WHALEBONE
OMNIRANGE	PYROMANIA	SHOEMAKER	ULTIMATUM	COLUMBITE	PIGGYBANK	WHEELBASE
OMOPHAGIC	QUADRATIC	SIBILANCE	UNASHAMED	COLUMBIUM	PINCHBECK	WHITEBAIT
OPSIMATHY	QUADRATUS	SIDEWARDS	UNBALANCE	CONCUBINE	POLITBURO	WHIZZBANG
OPTICALLY	QUITTANCE	SIMILARLY	UNDAMAGED	CONNUBIAL	POSSIBLES	WINNEBAGO
ORDINAIRE	RADICALLY	SIMULATED	UNEATABLE	CROOKBACK	POWERBOAT	YOHIMBINE
ORDINANCE	RAINGAUGE	SIMULATOR	UNEQUALED	CROSSBEAM	PROBABLES	YTTERBIUM
ORIFLAMME	RAINWATER	SKIAMACHY	UNRELATED	CROSSBILL	RACCABOUT	AFFLICTED
OROGRAPHY	RATEPAYER	SLAMMAKIN	UNSHEATHE	CROSSBRED	RAZORBILL	AFFRICATE
OUDENARDE	REACHABLE	SLAPHAPPY	UNTENABLE	CROWSBILL	RECUMBENT	AFTERCARE
OVERHASTY	REACTANCE	SOLITAIRE	UNTREATED	CURVEBALL	REFURBISH	AGALACTIC
OVERPAINT	REARRANGE	SOUVLAKIA	UNUSUALLY	DEATHBLOW	REPROBATE	ALICYCLIC
OVERRATED	REARWARDS	SOVENANCE	URTICARIA	DECUMBENT	RIDGEBACK	ALTERCATE
OVERVALUE	RECUSANCE	SPARTACUS	URUGUAYAN	DISEMBARK	ROCAMBOLE	AMBUSCADE
PACEMAKER	REDHEADED	SPATIALLY	UTTERANCE	DOTHEBOYS	ROUNDBACK	AMERICANO
PAGLIACCI	REFINANCE	SPECIALLY	VEGETABLE	ELIZABETH	SAUCEBOAT	AMERICIUM
PAILLASSE	REGULARLY	SPECIALTY	VEGETATOR	ENCUMBENT	SCRAMBLER	ANDROCLES
PALATABLE	REGULATOR	SPECTACLE	VENERABLE	ETHELBERT	SCRAPBOOK	ANGLICISM
PALLIASSE	REISTAFEL	SPECTATOR	VENGEANCE	EVERYBODY	SCREWBALL	ANTARCTIC
PANCHAYAT	RELEVANCE	SPINNAKER	VERITABLE	EXCAMBION	SCRUBBING	APPLICANT
PANORAMIC	REMBRANDT	SQUINANCY	VIGILANCE	FENCIBLES	SHELLBACK	ARABICIZE
PAPARAZZI	REMOVABLE	STANDARDS	VIGILANTE	FERRYBOAT	SHOREBIRD	AUTOSCOPY
PAPARAZZO	RENEWABLE	STANNATOR	VIRTUALLY	FLASHBACK	SHRUBBERY	BANDICOOT
PARABASIS	RENOVATOR	STARGAZER	WALLPAPER	FLASHBULB	SLINGBACK	BARMECIDE
PARATAXIS	REPAYABLE	STIGMATIC	WANCHANCY	FRITHBORH	SOUNDBITE	BARNACLES
PARTIALLY	REPUTABLE	STINGAREE	WASHBASIN	FROSTBITE	SPEEDBOAT	BARRACUDA
PATRIARCH	RESONANCE	STOICALLY	WASTWATER	FUNGIBLES	SPELLBIND	BARRICADE
PEACEABLE	RESONATOR	STORIATED	WESTWARDS	GALLABEAH	SPOONBILL	BARYSCOPE
PEACEABLY	RESTRAINT	STORNAWAY	WHITTAWER	GREENBACK	STEAMBOAT	BEDJACKET
PECULATOR	REYKJAVIK	STRATAGEM	WINDFALLS	GUIDEBOOK	STEENBRAS	BELLICOSE
PEDERASTY	RHEOTAXIS	SUBSTANCE	WOODLANDS	GUTENBERG	STEINBECK	BENBECULA
PENDRAGON	RHEUMATIC	SUFFRAGAN	WORMEATEN	HATCHBACK	STEINBOCK	BICONCAVE
PERCHANCE	ROSEWATER	SUPINATOR	XENOMANIA	HAWCUBITE	STILLBORN	BIFURCATE
PERIPATUS	ROSINANTE	SURCHARGE	YGGDRASIL	HAWKSBILL	STILTBIRD	BILLYCOCK
PERMEABLE	ROZINANTE	TABULATOR	ZYGOMATIC	HEARTBEAT	STINKBIRD	BOCCACCIO
PERSUADED	RUFFIANLY	TACAMAHAC	ABSORBENT	HEARTBURN	STIRABOUT	BRAINCASE
PETULANCE	SACCHARIN	TARAXACUM	ABSORBING	HELLEBORE	STONEBOAT	BRIEFCASE
PHANTASMA	SALERATUS	TEACHABLE	ADVERBIAL	HOBGOBLIN	STOOLBALL	BRITSCHKA
PHARSALIA	SALTWATER	TEESWATER	AITCHBONE	HORSEBACK	STORYBOOK	BROADCAST
PHILLABEG	SANDPAPER	TELEPATHY	AMPHIBIAN	HOUSEBOAT	STROMBOLI	CACHECTIC
PICOFARAD	SANNYASIN	TELESALES	ARCHIBALD	HUCKABACK	STYLOBATE	CAPRICCIO
PIGHEADED	SASQUATCH	THAUMATIN	ARQUEBUSE	HUNCHBACK	SUCCUBINE	CAPRICORN
PIXILATED	SATURATED	THINKABLE	ATTRIBUTE	HYPERBOLA	SWEATBAND	CARPACCIO
PLEASANCE	SCABLANDS	THOUSANDS	AYLESBURY	HYPERBOLE	SYLLABARY	CATCHCROP
PLUMDAMAS	SCALEABLE	THROWAWAY	BARNABITE	IMPROBITY	SYLLABLES	CAVALCADE
PNEUMATIC	SCALLAWAG	TIMETABLE	BILLABONG	INCUMBENT	THIGHBONE	CEVAPCICI
POCKMANKY	SCARLATTI	TINGUAITE	BLACKBALL	INSELBERG	THORNBACK	CHARACTER
POIGNANCY	SCHEMATIC	TOLERABLE	BLACKBIRD	INTERBRED	THORNBILL	CHILDCARE

CLIMACTIC	FORNICATE	MICROCYTE	PROSECUTE	TACTICIAN	CONFIDANT	INCONDITE
CLINICIAN	FRUITCAKE	MINUSCULE	PROTECTOR	TARMACKED	CONFIDENT	INERUDITE
COCKSCOMB	FULLSCALE	MISLOCATE	PUBLICIST	TELESCOPE	CONUNDRUM	INTENDANT
COLLECTED	FUNGICIDE	MISPICKEL	PUBLICITY	TERRACING	COUNTDOWN	INTENDING
COLLECTOR	GALLICISM	MONTACUTE	PUBLICIZE	TERRICOLE	COVERDALE	INTERDICT
COLLOCATE	GALLYCROW	MONTICULE	PUGNACITY	TESTICLES	COWARDICE	INTRODUCE
COMPACTLY	GERMICIDE	MORTICIAN	QUIESCENT	THYLACINE	CRACKDOWN	IPRINDOLE
CONDUCIVE	GRATICULE	MOTORCADE	RADICCHIO	TICTACTOE	CROCODILE	KNOCKDOWN
CONDUCTOR	GREATCOAT	MUTOSCOPE	RECONCILE	TOOTHCOMB	CUSPIDORE	LAMPADARY
CONDUCTUS	GYNOECIUM	MYRMECOID	REFLECTOR	TRANSCEND	CUSTODIAL	LAMPADION
CONFUCIUS	GYROSCOPE	MYSTICISM	REFRACTOR	TREBUCHET	CUSTODIAN	LEGENDARY
CONNECTED	HEADSCARF	NANTUCKET	REJOICING	TRITICALE	CYMBIDIUM	LIMPIDITY
CONNECTOR	HENPECKED	NAUMACHIA	RENASCENT	TUMESCENT	DAMNEDEST	LIQUIDATE
CONSOCIES	HERBICIDE	NEGLECTED	REPERCUSS	UNCHECKED	DEFENDANT	LIQUIDITY
CONVECTOR	HIPPOCRAS	NIGHTCLUB	REPLACING	UNCONCERN	DEFENDERS	LIQUIDIZE
CORKSCREW	HITCHCOCK	OBFUSCATE	REPLICANT	UNDERCAST	DEGRADING	LONGEDFOR
CORRECTED	HONEYCOMB	OCHLOCRAT	REPLICATE	UNDERCOAT	DEMANDING	MAJORDOMO
CORRECTLY	HOOLACHAN	OLIGOCENE	REPROCESS	UNMATCHED	DEOXIDISE	MARAUDING
CORRECTOR	HOROSCOPE	OPHIUCHUS	RESPECTED	UNPRECISE	DEPENDANT	METHADONE
CORUSCATE	HOUSECOAT	OSTRACISE	RESPECTER	UNSHACKLE	DEPENDENT	METHODISM
COXSACKIE	HURRICANE	OSTRACISM	RETRACTOR	UNTOUCHED	DEPENDING	METHODIST
CRITICISM	HURRICANO	OSTRACIZE	RETROCEDE	UNWELCOME	DEPREDATE	MORBIDITY
CRITICIZE	IGNESCENT	PAPERCLIP	RICERCARE	UPPERCASE	DIFFIDENT	MUSCADINE
CURRYCOMB	IMBRICATE	PARASCENE	ROUGHCAST	VARISCITE	DISSIDENT	NEFANDOUS
DAMASCENE	IMBROCATE	PARASCEVE	RUDBECKIA	VELLICATE	DRAVIDIAN	NITHSDALE
DEBAUCHED	IMPEACHER	PARBUCKLE	RUFESCENT	VINDICATE	DROMEDARY	OBCORDATE
DEBAUCHEE	IMPLICATE	PARRICIDE	RUSTICATE	VITASCOPE	DRYASDUST	OFFENDING
DEFALCATE	IMPRECATE	PARTICLES	SAPSUCKER	VORTICISM	EAVESDROP	ORMANDINE
DEFLECTOR	IMPRECISE	PASTICCIO	SARBACANE	WAISTCOAT	EDWARDIAN	ORTHODOXY
DEMARCATE	INCULCATE	PATERCOVE	SCARECROW	WINDSCALE	EIDERDOWN	OSTEODERM
DEMULCENT	INSINCERE	PATRICIAN	SCHNECKEN	WITTICISM	ELUCIDATE	OUTSIDERS
DEPRECATE	INSPECTOR	PATRICIDE	SCOLECITE	ABOUNDING	EMMERDALE	PACHYDERM
DESICCATE	INTERCEDE	PATROCLUS	SCRATCHED	ABSURDITY	ENNERDALE	PALLADIAN
DETRACTOR	INTERCEPT	PENTECOST	SCRATCHES	ACCORDANT	EPICEDIUM	PALLADIUM
DIALECTAL	INTERCITY	PERFECTLY	SENESCENT	ACCORDING	EUCLIDEAN	PERIODATE
DIALECTIC	INTRICACY	PERISCIAN	SENESCHAL	ACCORDION	EXCLUDING	PETHIDINE
DIETICIAN	INTRICATE	PERISCOPE	SEPULCHER	AFTERDAMP	EXTRADITE	PLACIDITY
DIFFICULT	INVOICING	PERSECUTE	SEPULCHRE	ALMANDINE	FACUNDITY	POMPADOUR
DISLOCATE	ISOTACTIC	PESTICIDE	SERVICING	APHRODITE	FARANDOLE	POUJADIST
DUODECIMO	ITALICIZE	PETTICOAT	SHORTCAKE	APPENDAGE	FECUNDITY	PRECEDENT
DUPLICAND	JACKSCREW	PHAGOCYTE	SIMULCAST	ASCENDANT	FORBIDDEN	PRECEDING
DUPLICATE	JAMPACKED	PHENACITE	SKYJACKER	ASCENDING	FRIGIDITY	PREJUDICE
DUPLICITY	KNAPSCULL	PHONECARD	SOLLICKER	ASTRODOME	GABARDINE	PREORDAIN
EMBRACERY	KONISCOPE	PHOTOCOPY	SOMASCOPE	ATTENDANT	GABERDINE	PRESIDENT
EMBRACING	LANDSCAPE	PHYSICIAN	SOPHOCLES	BALLADEER	GERUNDIVE	PRESIDIAL
EMBROCATE	LAODICEAN	PHYSICIST	SPHINCTER	BALLADIST	GIRANDOLE	PRESIDIUM
EMPLECTON	LATESCENT	PICNICKER	SPOROCARP	BEDRIDDEN	GIRONDIST	PROCEDURE
ENCIRCLED	LEUCOCYTE	PILLICOCK	SPRAICKLE	BELVEDERE	GRAVADLAX	PROVEDORE
ENDEICTIC	LITHOCYST	PINCHCOCK	SPRAUCHLE	BLACKDAMP	GRENADIER	PROVIDENT
ENSORCELL	LONGICORN	PINOCCHIO	STAIRCASE	BREAKDOWN	GRENADINE	PROVIDING
ENTRECHAT	LOQUACITY	PISTACHIO	STATOCYST	BRIGADIER	GROUNDHOG	PTERIDIUM
ENTRECÔTE	LUBRICANT	PIZZICATO	STAUNCHLY	BRIGADOON	GROUNDING	QUOTIDIAN
EPICYCLIC	LUBRICATE	PLEIOCENE	STOMACHIC	BURUNDIAN	GROUNDNUT	RANCIDITY
EPINICION	LUTESCENT	PLUTOCRAT	STONECHAT	BYPRODUCT	GROUNDSEL	RECONDITE
ERADICATE	MACROCOSM	POETICIZE	STONECROP	CALENDULA	HABERDINE	RECORDING
EROTICISM	MAJUSCULE	POPPYCOCK	STRETCHED	CAMBODIAN	HAYRADDIN	RECORDIST
EXPISCATE	MANDICATE	PRECOCITY	STRETCHER	CANDIDACY	HAZARDOUS	REDUNDANT
EXPLICATE	MANDUCATE	PREDICANT	SUBJACENT	CANDIDATE	HEAVYDUTY	REGARDANT
EXSICCATE	MASTICATE	PREDICATE	SUFFOCATE	CATHEDRAL	HEBRIDEAN	REGARDFUL
EXTRACTOR	MATRICIDE	PREDICTOR	SUGARCANE	CAVENDISH	HIPPODAME	REGARDING
EXTRICATE	MEGASCOPE	PRELECTOR	SUPERCOOL	CELANDINE	HIRUNDINE	REPRODUCE
FABRICATE	MENDACITY	PREOCCUPY	SUSPECTED	CHURIDARS	HISTIDINE	REWARDING
FATISCENT	MENDICANT	PROCACITY	SUSPICION	CIRCADIAN	HUNKYDORY	ROTUNDATE
FINANCIAL	MENTICIDE	PROJECTED	SYNDICATE	CLAMPDOWN	IMPENDING	ROTUNDITY
FINANCIER	METRICATE	PROJECTOR	SYNOECETE	COLLODION	IMPRUDENT	SANHEDRIM
FLASHCUBE	MICROCHIP	PROLACTIN	SYNTACTIC	COMMODITY	INCARDINE	SANHEDRIN
FORFICATE	MICROCOSM	PROMACHOS	SYRIACISM	COMMODORE	INCLUDING	SANHEDRON

SCORODITE	ASSUREDLY	COTYLEDON	ETCETERAS	INFERENCE	MUNIMENTS	PROPHETIC
SCOUNDREL	ASYMMETRY	COUCHETTE	ETHEREOUS	INFLUENCE	NASEBERRY	PROTHESIS
SCRODDLED	ASYNDETON	COUNSELOR	ETIQUETTE	INFLUENZA	NECKVERSE	PRURIENCE
SECONDARY	AUBRIETIA	COURGETTE	EUHEMERUS	INNKEEPER	NESCIENCE	PUERPERAL
SHAKEDOWN	BACKBENCH	COURTELLE	EUMYCETES	INNOCENCE	NIAISERIE	PURULENCE
SHELDDUCK	BACKPEDAL	COURTEOUS	EVANGELIC	INSOLENCE	NICKNEVEN	QUARTERLY
SHIELDING	BAGATELLE	COURTESAN	EXCISEMAN	INTUMESCE	NICODEMUS	QUARTETTE
SKEDADDLE	BAKSHEESH	COVALENCY	EXISTENCE	IPHIGENIA	NINEPENCE	QUENNELLE
SOLFIDIAN	BANEBERRY	CRANBERRY	EYEOPENER	ISCHAEMIC	NIPCHEESE	QUERCETIN
SOUTHDOWN	BANQUETTE	CRESCELLE	FABACEOUS	ISOSCELES	NORTHEAST	QUERCETUS
SPHENDONE	BAROMETER	CRESCENDO	FEATHERED	JACQUERIE	NORTHERLY	QUINTETTE
SPLENDOUR	BARONETCY	CRICKETER	FEMINEITY	JOBSEEKER	NOTONECTA	RADDLEMAN
SPREADING	BATTLEAXE	CROOKEDLY	FIFTEENTH	JOCKTELEG	NOVELETTE	RASPBERRY
STERADIAN	BEANFEAST	CROQUETTE	FILOSELLE	JUNEBERRY	OBEDIENCE	RATTLEBAG
STEVEDORE	BEAUTEOUS	CROSSEYED	FIRSTEVER	KENTLEDGE	OLEORESIN	READYEARN
STOLIDITY	BECQUEREL	CRYOGENIC	FLATTENED	KILOHERTZ	ONCOMETER	RECOVERED
STUPIDITY	BEEKEEPER	CRYOMETER	FLATTENER	KILOMETER	ONTOGENCY	REDBREAST
SUBSIDIZE	BEELZEBUB	CUTANEOUS	FLATTERED	KILOMETRE	OPENHEART	REDOLENCE
SWANSDOWN	BELATEDLY	CYNEGETIC	FLATTERER	KINTLEDGE	OPPONENTS	REFERENCE
SYMPODIUM	BETHLEHEM	DAREDEVIL	FLECHETTE	KITCHENER	OPTOMETRY	REFUSENIK
TALMUDIST	BILATERAL	DECADENCE	FLUSTERED	KLEMPERER	ORANGEADE	RELIGEUSE
THECODONT	BLINKERED	DECAMERON	FOLKWEAVE	KNACKERED	ORANGEMAN	RENFIERST
THORNDYKE	BLISTERED	DECIDEDLY	FOREBEARS	KNOWLEDGE	ORGANELLE	REPUTEDLY
THREADFIN	BLUEBEARD	DEFERENCE	FOURPENCE	KONIMETER	OUBLIETTE	RESIDENCE
THROWDOWN	BLUEBERRY	DELINEATE	FRAGMENTS	LACKBEARD	OVERHEADS	RESIDENCY
TOLPUDDLE	BLUNDERER	DELIVERER	FRANCESCA	LAFAYETTE	OVERREACH	RETICENCE
TOUCHDOWN	BLUSTERER	DIABLERIE	FREQUENCY	LAMASERAI	OVERREACT	RETRIEVAL
TRAGEDIAN	BOBSLEIGH	DIAERESIS	FRESHENER	LANGUEDOC	OVERWEIGH	RETRIEVER
TRIHEDRON	BOLSHEVIK	DIANOETIC	FRUITERER	LANGUETTE	PADEMELON	REVERENCE
TURBIDITY	BOTTLEFUL	DIATHERMY	GASOMETER	LARGHETTO	PAILLETTE	RIGHTEOUS
UNBENDING	BOUNTEOUS	DIATHESIS	GEARLEVER	LAUNCELOT	PALOVERDE	RIGOLETTO
UNBRIDLED	BOURGEOIS	DILIGENCE	GENTEELLY	LAZARETTO	PANATELLA	RINGFENCE
UNDERDONE	BRACTEOLE	DIOCLETES	GENTLEMAN	LEUKAEMIA	PANTHEISM	ROISTERER
UNFLEDGED	BRASSERIE	DISCREDIT	GENTLEMEN	LIENTERIC	PANTHENOL	ROUNCEVAL
UNHEEDING	BREAKEVEN	DISPLEASE	GEORGETTE	LINDBERGH	PARAMEDIC	ROUNDELAY
UNMINDFUL	BRIDLEWAY	DIVIDENDS	GIGAHERTZ	LIONHEART	PARAMETER	ROUSSETTE
UNTRODDEN	BRIQUETTE	DOCUMENTS	GLAIREOUS	LORGNETTE	PARCHEESI	RUBICELLE
VIDEODISC	BROTHERLY	DONATELLO	GREASEGUN	LUCIFERIN	PARFLECHE	RUDDLEMAN
VIDEODISK	BUBBLEGUM	DONIZETTI	GREYBEARD	LYSIMETER	PARTHENON	RUDIMENTS
WALLYDRAG	BUCKTEETH	DOODLEBUG	GROSVENOR	MADELEINE	PAYCHEQUE	SADDLEBAG
WHITEDAMP	BUMBLEBEE	DOSIMETER	GUILLEMOT	MAINTENON	PEDOMETER	SAGAPENUM
WRONGDOER	CACHAEMIA	DRUNKENLY	HACKBERRY	MAJORETTE	PENDLETON	SALICETUM
ABERNETHY	CAFETERIA	DUNDREARY	HACKNEYED	MANIFESTO	PENITENCE	SALOPETTE
ACCIDENTS	CANALETTO	ECHEVERIA	HACQUETON	MANOMETER	PENSTEMON	SALTPETER
ACQUIESCE	CANAVERAL	EDELWEISS	HAECCEITY	MARQUESAS	PERCHERON	SALTPETRE
ACROPETAL	CANDLELIT	EFFLUENCE	HALFPENNY	MARQUETRY	PERIMETER	SCATTERED
ADHERENCE	CANDLEMAS	ELOQUENCE	HARQUEBUS	MEDIAEVAL	PERPLEXED	SCHLIEREN
ADULTERER	CAPORETTO	EMERGENCE	HECOGENIN	MEGAHERTZ	PHRENETIC	SCHMIEDER
ADVISEDLY	CATALEPSY	EMERGENCY	HEXAMERON	MEKOMETER	PIROUETTE	SCREWEDUP
AESTHETIC	CATTLEMAN	ENERGETIC	HEXAMETER	MELANESIA	PLASTERED	SCRIVENER
AFFLUENCE	CATTLEPEN	ENGINEERS	HEXATEUCH	MENAGERIE	PLASTERER	SCYTHEMAN
AGGRIEVED	CENTREING	ENLIVENED	HEYPRESTO	MENSHEVIK	PLENTEOUS	SEBACEOUS
AHASUERUS	CHALLENGE	ENTELECHY	HODOMETER	METAPELET	PLUMBEOUS	SECATEURS
ALLEGEDLY	CHAMPERTY	ENUCLEATE	HUNDREDTH	MICKLETON	PLUNDERER	SENTIENCE
ALTIMETER	CHANTEUSE	EPAULETTE	HURRIEDLY	MIDDLEMAN	POINTEDLY	SERVIETTE
ANALGESIA	CHARGEFUL	EPHEMERAL	ILLIBERAL	MIDDLESEX	POLICEMAN	SETACEOUS
ANALGESIC	CHARTERED	EPHEMERIS	IMMANENCE	MIDDLETON	POLITESSE	SHARPENER
ANOPHELES	CHASTENED	EPHEMERON	IMMANENCY	MIDINETTE	POLYNESIA	SHATTERED
ANTIHELIX	CHATTERER	EPICLESIS	IMMINENCE	MILOMETER	PONTLEVIS	SHELTERED
ANTISERUM	CHEQUERED	EPIGAEOUS	IMMODESTY	MINUTEMAN	PORIFERAN	SHEPHERDS
ANTIVENIN	CIGARETTE	EPITHESIS	IMPOTENCE	MIRABELLE	PORTREEVE	SHUTTERED
APATHETIC	CINEREOUS	EQUISETUM	IMPUDENCE	MISCREANT	POULTERER	SIMPLETON
APHERESIS	CLUSTERED	ERIOMETER	INCIDENCE	MISONEIST	PRECIEUSE	SINGLESEX
AQUARELLE	COHERENCE	ERRONEOUS	INDECENCY	MISTLETOE	PRIMAEVAL	SINGLETON
AQUILEGIA	COLUMELLA	ESCOPETTE	INDIGENCE	MONOCEROS	PRINCETON	SIXTEENMO
ARBORETUM	CONCIERGE	ESCULENTS	INDOLENCE	MONOMETER	PROCOELUS	SIXTEENTH
ARMAMENTS	CONQUEROR	ESTAFETTE	INDONESIA	MUGGLETON	PROCREATE	SLUMBERER

SOAPBERRY	UNTIMEOUS	INTERFACE	UNCONFINE	EFFULGENT	PROROGATE	BENIGHTED
SOLDIERLY	UNWATERED	INTERFERE	UNDERFEED	ELLINGTON	RADIOGRAM	BIOSPHERE
SONOMETER	USHERETTE	JELLYFISH	UNDERFELT	EMBROGLIO	REDINGOTE	BLACKHEAD
SOUBRETTE	VAPORETTO	JUSTIFIED	UNDERFLOW	ERPINGHAM	REFULGENT	BLASPHEME
SOUTHEAST	VARICELLA	KERFUFFLE	UNDERFOOT	EXPURGATE	RESURGENT	BLASPHEMY
SOUTHERLY	VEHEMENCE	KHALIFATE	UNRUFFLED	FALANGIST	RUDDIGORE	BLEACHERS
SOVEREIGN	VEILLEUSE	KOMINFORM	UNSELFISH	FERINGHEE	SALANGANE	BLOCKHEAD
SPAGHETTI	VENEREOUS	LIGHTFACE	VENTIFACT	FLOODGATE	SALESGIRL	BLUESHIFT
SPATTERED	VESTMENTS	LIGHTFOOT	VERMIFORM	FOREIGNER	SAUVIGNON	BOMBSHELL
SPEAKEASY	VICEREGAL	LIQUEFIED	VERMIFUGE	FUSTIGATE	SCAPEGOAT	BOOKSHELF
SPHACELUS	VICEREINE	MAGNIFIER	VERSIFIER	GALENGALE	SEGREGATE	BRANCHING
SPINNERET	VIRULENCE	MICROFILM	WATERFALL	GALINGALE	SERENGETI	BREATHING
SPLENETIC	VOLAGEOUS	MIDWIFERY	WATERFORD	GEOLOGIST	SOLFEGGIO	BREECHING
SPONGEBAG	VOLTMETER	MISINFORM	WATERFOWL	GREENGAGE	SPRINGALD	BRONCHIAL
SPRITEFUL	WAGONETTE	MORTIFIED	WHEREFORE	HABERGEON	SPRINGBOK	BROUGHTON
SQUIREAGE	WELLBEING	MULTIFORM	WHITEFISH	HARROGATE	SPRINGLET	BUCKTHORN
STABLEBOY	WELTGEIST	NIGHTFALL	WHOLEFOOD	HECTOGRAM	STANDGALE	BUCKWHEAT
STABLELAD	WHICHEVER	NIGHTFIRE	WOMENFOLK	HEMINGWAY	STRAGGLER	CACOPHONY
STABLEMAN	WHOSOEVER	OCULIFORM	WRECKFISH	HISTOGRAM	STRANGELY	CARTWHEEL
STAGGERED	WILDGEESE	PANTOFFLE	WRONGFOOT	HUMONGOUS	STRANGLER	CATECHISM
STAMMERER	WIMBLEDON	PETRIFIED	ABORIGINE	HUMUNGOUS	STRANGLES	CATECHIZE
STANDERBY	WINEBERRY	PITCHFORK	AFTERGLOW	IMBROGLIO	STRANGURY	CHILDHOOD
STATUETTE	WITCHETTY	PROKOFIEV	AGGREGATE	INDULGENT	STRINGENT	CHURCHILL
STIFFENER	ZEITGEIST	PUSSYFOOT	ALPENGLOW	INELEGANT	STRINGOPS	CHURCHMAN
STONKERED	ZUCCHETTO	QUALIFIED	AMBERGRIS	INSTIGATE	STRONGARM	CINEPHILE
STRATEGIC	ZYMOMETER	QUALIFIER	ANALOGOUS	INSURGENT	STRONGYLE	COLOPHONY
STRIDENCY	ABOUTFACE	RECTIFIER	ANGIOGRAM	INTRIGUED	SUBJUGATE	CROTCHETY
SUCCEEDED	AMPLIFIER	RESHUFFLE	ANISOGAMY	INTRIGUER	SUBROGATE	CUBBYHOLE
SUPERETTE	ANGELFISH	RESTIFORM	APOLOGIST	IRVINGISM	SURROGATE	DACHSHUND
SURQUEDRY	BELLYFLOP	RESURFACE	APOLOGIZE	KENTIGERN	SYLLOGISM	DASHWHEEL
SWAGGERER	BLACKFACE	RETROFLEX	ARCTOGAEA	LENINGRAD	SYNANGIUM	DECACHORD
SWEETENER	BLACKFOOT	ROQUEFORT	ARLINGTON	LITURGICS	SYNERGIST	DECATHLON
SWIMMERET	BLINDFOLD	ROUNDFISH	ASTRAGALS	LOHENGRIN	TARRAGONA	DECKCHAIR
SWINGEING	BREAKFAST	SABLEFISH	AUBERGINE	LOWLIGHTS	TERMAGANT	DELIGHTED
SYNIZESIS	CEASEFIRE	SACRIFICE	BEDRAGGLE	MALENGINE	TERMAGENT	DIARRHOEA
SYNTHESIS	CERTIFIED	SAINTFOIN	BELEAGUER	METHEGLIN	TETRAGRAM	DIPHTHONG
SYNTHETIC	CHAUFFEUR	SASSAFRAS	BELONGING	MILLIGRAM	THRONGING	ECOSPHERE
TAILLEFER	CLARIFIER	SATISFIED	BILINGUAL	MISTIGRIS	TRIANGLED	ECTOTHERM
TAOISEACH	CLINGFILM	SCALDFISH	BIOLOGIST	MONERGISM	TRISAGION	ELKOSHITE
TAXIDERMY	COCKSFOOT	SCARIFIER	BORNAGAIN	MONSIGNOR	TURMAGENT	ELSEWHERE
TAXIMETER	COLTSFOOT	SCRUFFILY	CABLEGRAM	MUSKOGEAN	UNDERGRAD	ENLIGHTEN
TEMULENCE	COMINFORM	SERREFILE	CAIRNGORM	NEGLIGENT	VARANGIAN	ENTOPHYTE
TENEMENTS	CROCKFORD	SHAMEFAST	CARTOGRAM	NEOLOGISM	VARIEGATE	EPARCHATE
TERAHERTZ	CROSSFIRE	SHEEPFOLD	CASTIGATE	NEUROGLIA	VERDIGRIS	ERSTWHILE
THACKERAY	CROWSFOOT	SHELLFISH	CENTIGRAM	NEWSAGENT	VESTIGIAL	EXANTHEMA
THRENETIC	CRUCIFORM	SHORTFALL	CHEONGSAM	NIGHTGLOW	VOLGOGRAD	EXOSPHERE
THUNDERER	CUNEIFORM	SMOKEFREE	COLLEGIAN	NIGHTGOWN	VOLTIGEUR	FALSEHOOD
TIERCERON	CURFUFFLE	SNAILFISH	COLLIGATE	NORWEGIAN	VORTIGERN	FAULCHION
TIGHTENER	DANDIFIED	SPECIFICS	CONJUGATE	NYSTAGMUS	WATERGATE	FINISHING
TITTLEBAT	DEVILFISH	SPECIFIED	CONSIGNEE	OBBLIGATO	WHEATGERM	FIRSTHAND
TONOMETER	DIGNIFIED	SPLAYFOOT	CONSIGNOR	OBJURGATE	WOBBEGONG	FLOWCHART
TOURNEDOS	DISAFFIRM	SPOONFEED	CONTAGION	ORPINGTON	WOEBEGONE	FOMALHAUT
TOXIGENIC	DISINFECT	STEADFAST	CORREGGIO	OSTROGOTH	ZOOLOGIST	FORESHORE
TRANSEUNT	EARTHFLAX	STERNFAST	CORRUGATE	OUTRIGGER	ACROPHONY	FOURWHEEL
TRIETERIC	ERUCIFORM	STOCKFISH	COSMOGONY	PACKAGING	ADULTHOOD	FRANCHISE
TRINKETER	FEBRIFUGE	STUPEFIED	COTANGENT	PANTAGAMY	AGUECHEEK	FRATCHETY
TRIPMETER	FIELDFARE	SUPERFINE	DARTAGNAN	PATHOGENY	ALPENHORN	FREEPHONE
TROMPETTE	GLORIFIED	SWORDFISH	DETERGENT	PEKINGESE	AMIDSHIPS	FREEWHEEL
TROPAELIN	GOOSEFOOT	TECTIFORM	DIALOGITE	PELLAGRIN	AMORPHOUS	FREIGHTER
TRUEPENNY	GREENFEED	TERRIFIED	DISENGAGE	PENTAGRAM	ANARCHIST	FRENCHMAN
TRUMPEDUP	HEARTFELT	TESTIFIER	DISFIGURE	PHONOGRAM	ANTIPHONY	FRENCHMEN
TRUMPETER	HEREAFTER	THEREFORE	DISREGARD	PHOTOGENE	APARTHEID	GATESHEAD
TUILLETTE	HORRIFIED	THREEFOLD	DIVERGENT	PHYLOGENY	APPREHEND	GEARSHIFT
UMPTEENTH	HYDROFOIL	TOWNSFOLK	DIVERGING	PICTOGRAM	ARROWHEAD	GEARWHEEL
UNALTERED	IMPERFECT	TRANSFORM	ECOLOGIST	PREFIGURE	ARTICHOKE	GLORYHOLE
UNCOVERED	INNISFAIL	TRANSFUSE	EDDINGTON	PRESSGANG	BACKSHISH	GOOSEHERD
UNHOPEFUL	INNISFREE	TRUNKFISH	EFFINGHAM	PROPAGATE	BEACHHEAD	GREENHEAD

GREENHORN	OVERTHROW	STEELHEAD	ARTERIOLE	CYTOKININ	FIDUCIARY	INCIPIENT
GUILDHALL	OVERWHELM	STINKHORN	ARTHRITIC	DEADLIGHT	FIRELIGHT	INCOMINGS
HALOPHILE	PARACHUTE	STOCKHOLM	ARTHRITIS	DECALITRE	FLYWEIGHT	INCURIOUS
HALOTHANE	PARATHION	STOKEHOLD	ARTIFICER	DEFICIENT	FOOTHILLS	INDELIBLE
HAMPSHIRE	PAROCHIAL	STONEHAND	ASSOCIATE	DEFOLIANT	FORESIGHT	INDELIBLY
HANDSHAKE	PAROCHINE	STRAPHANG	ASTUCIOUS	DEFOLIATE	FORFEITED	INEBRIATE
HARDIHOOD	PERIPHERY	SWINEHERD	ATROCIOUS	DELICIOUS	FORTNIGHT	INFURIATE
HARDSHELL	PERISHING	SYCOPHANT	AUDACIOUS	DELIRIOUS	FRACTIOUS	INGENIOUS
HARTSHORN	PHOSPHATE	TABASHEER	AUTOPILOT	DELPHINUS	FRUCTIDOR	INGRAINED
HAWSEHOLE	PHOSPHENE	TEARSHEET	AUXILIARY	DEPOSITOR	FUGACIOUS	INHERITED
HEALTHILY	PICKTHANK	TELEPHONE	BACKBITER	DESIPIENT	FURACIOUS	INHERITOR
HEARTHRUG	PLAYTHING	TELEPHONY	BASILICAL	DIACRITIC	GALATIANS	INHIBITED
HEDYPHANE	PLOUGHMAN	TELEPHOTO	BASILICON	DIRIGIBLE	GAULEITER	INHIBITOR
HESYCHASM	POLYPHASE	TELOPHASE	BEAUTIFUL	DISGUISED	GENETICAL	INJURIOUS
HESYCHAST	POLYPHONE	THATCHING	BEESTINGS	DISORIENT	GENEVIEVE	INPATIENT
HITCHHIKE	POLYPHONY	THICKHEAD	BEHAVIOUR	DISUNITED	GLEANINGS	INSCRIBED
HOLLYHOCK	POLYTHENE	THRASHING	BEVERIDGE	DIVISIBLE	GLENLIVET	INSIDIOUS
HOLOPHOTE	PRONGHORN	THRESHOLD	BLESSINGS	DOCTRINAL	GOLDFIELD	INSIPIENT
HOMOPHONE	PROUDHORN	TIGHTHEAD	BOLIVIANO	DOLOMITES	GOLDFINCH	INTROITUS
HORSEHAIR	PUNISHING	TIMESHARE	BOTANICAL	DOLOMITIC	GOLDSINNY	INVIDIOUS
HOUSEHOLD	PUSHCHAIR	TISIPHONE	BOUNTIFUL	DOMICILED	GOODNIGHT	INVISIBLE
IDIOPHONE	PYRETHRUM	TOXOPHILY	BOYFRIEND	DOMINICAL	GOONHILLY	IRASCIBLE
IODOPHILE	RACCAHOUT	TRANSHUME	BRANDIRON	DOMINICAN	GRAMPIANS	IRONSIDES
JEPHTHAHS	RAINCHECK	TREACHERY	BRASSICAS	DOWNRIGHT	GRANDIOSE	IRRADIANT
JOSEPHINE	RAVISHING	TRENCHANT	BRASSIERE	DROPPINGS	GRAPHICAL	IRRADIATE
JOSEPHSON	REPECHAGE	TRIATHLON	BRILLIANT	DROPSICAL	GREETINGS	ISOCLINAL
KICKSHAWS	REPREHEND	TRONDHEIM	BRUNHILDE	DYNAMITED	GRENVILLE	JAUNDICED
KISWAHILI	RIDERHOOD	TRUNCHEON	BULLFIGHT	EASTLINGS	GRISAILLE	JUDICIARY
KRUMMHORN	RIGHTHAND	UNDERHAND	BULLFINCH	EBULLIENT	GRUBBINOL	JUDICIOUS
LAMPSHADE	RORSCHACH	UNDERHUNG	BUMPTIOUS	ECARDINES	GUERRILLA	JURIDICAL
LAUNCHING	ROUNDHAND	UNSIGHTLY	CAFETIERE	EFFICIENT	GUMSHIELD	JUVENILIA
LEASEHOLD	ROUNDHEAD	UPAITHRIC	CALORIFIC	EGREGIOUS	HAIRPIECE	KARABINER
LENGTHILY	SAINTHOOD	VANISHING	CAMBRIDGE	EIGHTIETH	HALOBIONT	KERATITIS
LILYWHITE	SAXOPHONE	WATERHOLE	CANONICAL	ELUTRIATE	HANDPIECE	KINGSIZED
LOAMSHIRE	SCONCHEON	WHITEHALL	CAPACIOUS	EMBROIDER	HARDLINER	LABORIOUS
LOGOTHETE	SCORCHING	WHITEHEAD	CAPACITOR	EMBROILED	HEADFIRST	LABYRINTH
LONGCHAMP	SCOTCHMAN	WIDOWHOOD	CAPARISON	EMOLLIATE	HEADLIGHT	LACINIATE
LONGSHORE	SCUNCHEON	WINDCHILL	CAPTAINCY	EMOLLIENT	HEADLINED	LACONICAL
LOOSEHEAD	SEARCHING	WOMANHOOD	CARTRIDGE	EMPIRICAL	HEADPIECE	LAMINITIS
LUSTIHOOD	SELACHION	WOODCHUCK	CATSKILLS	ENGRAINED	HEMSTITCH	LAMPLIGHT
MAKESHIFT	SEMAPHORE	WOODSHOCK	CERATITIS	ENTERITIS	HEPATICAL	LANGRIDGE
MALACHITE	SERAPHINE	XENOPHOBE	CERTAINLY	ENUNCIATE	HEPATITIS	LANGUIDLY
MALATHION	SHEIKHDOM	XEROPHYTE	CERTAINTY	EPHESIANS	HERETICAL	LASTDITCH
MASOCHISM	SHIPSHAPE	XYLOPHONE	CHAFFINCH	EQUALIZER	HIGHLIGHT	LATENIGHT
MASOCHIST	SHOESHINE	YORKSHIRE	CHANTILLY	ERISTICAL	HILARIOUS	LESTRIGON
MEANWHILE	SHORTHAND	ABDOMINAL	CHIPPINGS	ESTAMINET	HILLBILLY	LEVITICUS
MEGAPHONE	SHORTHAUL	ABLUTIONS	CHRONICLE	EUMENIDES	HINDSIGHT	LIMELIGHT
METAPHASE	SHORTHOLD	ABSTAINER	CIVILISED	EURIPIDES	HOBNAILED	LINGFIELD
MILKSHAKE	SHORTHORN	ADENOIDAL	CIVILIZED	EXCALIBUR	HOMICIDAL	LITIGIOUS
MISBEHAVE	SISYPHEAN	ADMONITOR	CLASSICAL	EXCIPIENT	HONORIFIC	LIVRAISON
MONKSHOOD	SKETCHILY	AFFILIATE	COALFIELD	EXCLAIMED	HUMILIATE	LOCALIZED
MONOCHORD	SKETCHMAP	ALEURITIS	COALMINER	EXCORIATE	ICTERIDAE	LOGARITHM
MOONSHINE	SKETCHPAD	ALGORITHM	COCKAIGNE	EXERCISED	IDENTICAL	LONGLIVED
MOUSEHOLE	SKEWWHIFF	ALLEGIANT	COCKFIGHT	EXERCISES	IDENTIKIT	LOUISIANA
MUSICHALL	SLAUGHTER	ALLEVIATE	COLCHICUM	EXHIBITOR	IDIOTICON	LUBAVITCH
NABATHEAN	SLOUGHING	AMBITIOUS	COLERIDGE	EXPATIATE	ILLEGIBLE	LUMBRICUS
NEWSSHEET	SNOWSHOES	ANCIPITAL	COLLOIDAL	EXPEDIENT	ILLEGIBLY	LUXURIANT
NIGHTHAWK	SNOWWHITE	ANTONINUS	COMPLIANT	EXPLOITER	ILLICITLY	LUXURIATE
NOMOTHETE	SOMETHING	APENNINES	CONCEITED	EXPOSITOR	ILLOGICAL	LUXURIOUS
NOOSPHERE	SOMEWHERE	APPARITOR	CONSCIOUS	EYEBRIGHT	IMMEDIACY	MADARIAGA
NOTOCHORD	SPEARHEAD	APPETIZER	CONTAINER	FABULINUS	IMMEDIATE	MAHARISHI
OCTACHORD	SPEECHIFY	APPRAISAL	CONTRIVED	FACETIOUS	IMMUNISER	MALICIOUS
OPPENHEIM	SPRECHERY	ARKWRIGHT	CONTRIVER	FANATICAL	IMPATIENT	MANSFIELD
OPTOPHONE	SPRIGHTLY	ARMADILLO	COPYRIGHT	FATIDICAL	IMPERIOUS	MASEFIELD
OVERSHADE	STAGEHAND	ARRIVISTE	CORNEILLE	FEDUCIARY	IMPOLITIC	MATUTINAL
OVERSHOES	STANCHION	ARSENICAL	CORNFIELD	FERACIOUS	INAUDIBLE	MEDICINAL
OVERSHOOT	STATEHOOD	ARTEMISIA	CUFFLINKS	FEROCIOUS	INAUDIBLY	MELODIOUS

447

MEMORITER	PLAUSIBLE	SIMPLISTE	UNETHICAL	SPRINKLER	CALCULATE	CRIPPLING
MENADIONE	PLAUSIBLY	SINUSITIS	UNINVITED	STEENKIRK	CANNELURE	CROWNLIKE
MENOMINEE	PLENTIFUL	SKEPTICAL	UNLIMITED	UNLUCKILY	CAPILLARY	CRUMBLING
MICROINCH	POLEMICAL	SKINDIVER	UNMUSICAL	VELDSKOEN	CARMELITE	CUCHULAIN
MIDDLINGS	POLITICAL	SKINTIGHT	UNNOTICED	WHITAKERS	CARNELIAN	CURTILAGE
MINACIOUS	POLITIQUE	SOLICITOR	UNREFINED	WOMANKIND	CARTILAGE	CYCLOLITH
MINEFIELD	PORPOISES	SOMETIMES	UNSPOILED	ACETYLENE	CARTULARY	CYMBELINE
MISGUIDED	POTBOILER	SOPORIFIC	UNTRAINED	ACIDULATE	CASTELLAN	DAEDALIAN
MITRAILLE	PRACTICAL	SOUFRIERE	UNTYPICAL	ACIDULOUS	CASTILIAN	DAMSELFLY
MOGADISHU	PRACTISED	SPHERICAL	VAGINITIS	ACTUALITY	CATACLYSM	DANDELION
MONTAIGNE	PRESCIENT	SPILLICAN	VAPORIFIC	AEROPLANE	CATAPLASM	DAUNTLESS
MOONLIGHT	PRINCIPAL	SPILLIKIN	VAPORIZER	ALTIPLANO	CATAPLEXY	DEATHLESS
MOTORISTS	PRINCIPLE	SPLENITIS	VENTRICLE	ALVEOLATE	CEASELESS	DECILLION
MOURNIVAL	PROCLITIC	SPOTLIGHT	VERACIOUS	AMARYLLIS	CELLULITE	DECOLLATE
MUJAHIDIN	PROPRIETY	SQUALIDLY	VERIDICAL	ANABOLISM	CELLULOID	DEFAULTER
MUMPSIMUS	PSYCHICAL	STARLIGHT	VEXATIONS	ANATOLIAN	CELLULOSE	DEUCALION
MUNICIPAL	PTARMIGAN	STOCKINET	VEXATIOUS	ANCILLARY	CERECLOTH	DISABLING
MUNITIONS	PUNCTILIO	STOCKINGS	VICARIOUS	ANIMALISM	CHAIRLIFT	DISBELIEF
NARGHILLY	PYRAMIDAL	STOPLIGHT	VIDELICET	ANIMALITY	CHAMELEON	DISCOLOUR
NASHVILLE	QUADRILLE	STROBILUS	VIENTIANE	ANOMALOUS	CHAMPLAIN	DISHCLOTH
NEFARIOUS	QUANTICAL	STRUMITIS	VIGESIMAL	ANSCHLUSS	CHAMPLEVÉ	DISOBLIGE
NEGOTIATE	QUIZZICAL	SUBEDITOR	VISAGISTE	ANTHOLOGY	CHAROLAIS	DISSOLUTE
NEPHRITIC	QUODLIBET	SUDORIFIC	VIVACIOUS	ANTICLINE	CHECKLIST	DISSOLVED
NEPHRITIS	RADCLIFFE	SUPPLIANT	VOLATIBLE	APPALLING	CHEERLESS	DISTILLER
NERITIDAE	RAPACIOUS	SUPPLICAT	VORACIOUS	APPEALING	CHEVALIER	DIXIELAND
NINETIETH	RECIPIENT	SURFEITED	WAHABIITE	AQUAPLANE	CHILBLAIN	DOUBTLESS
NOTARIKON	RECLAIMED	SURPRISED	WHIMSICAL	ARTILLERY	CHILDLESS	DOWELLING
NOTORIETY	RECLAIMER	SUSTAINED	WHIRLIGIG	ASHMOLEAN	CHILDLIKE	DREAMLAND
NOTORIOUS	REDIVIVUS	SWEEPINGS	WOMANISER	ASSAILANT	CHIPOLATA	DREAMLESS
NOVICIATE	REDUCIBLE	SYBARITIC	WOMANIZER	ASTROLABE	CHISELLER	DWINDLING
NOVITIATE	RELATIONS	SYNOVITIS	XANTHIPPE	ASTROLOGY	CHOCOLATE	EARTHLING
NUMERICAL	RELIGIOSO	SYRPHIDAE	APPLEJACK	ATONALITY	CHOLELITH	EBRILLADE
OBLIVIOUS	RELIGIOUS	TABANIDAE	BLACKJACK	AUTOCLAVE	CILIOLATE	ECTOPLASM
OBNOXIOUS	REMINISCE	TAILLIGHT	CHEAPJACK	AYATOLLAH	CIPOLLINO	EJACULATE
OCCIPITAL	REPUDIATE	TAILPIECE	INTERJECT	BACKCLOTH	CIRCULATE	ELAEOLITE
OCEANIDES	RESILIENT	TAMOXIFEN	KABELJOUW	BACKSLIDE	CLASSLESS	EMBELLISH
OFFICIALS	RETALIATE	TECHNICAL	LJUBLJANA	BALACLAVA	CLEVELAND	ENAMELLED
OFFICIANT	RETINITIS	TECHNIQUE	SURREJOIN	BANDALORE	CLOUDLESS	ENCHILADA
OFFICIATE	RINGSIDER	TENACIOUS	AMELAKITE	BANDOLEER	COACHLOAD	ENGARLAND
OFFICIOUS	ROUNCIVAL	TEREBINTH	ASTRAKHAN	BANDOLERO	COAGULANT	EPHIALTES
ORGANICAL	RUSHLIGHT	THERMIDOR	ATTACKING	BANDOLIER	COAGULATE	EPIPOLISM
ORGANISED	SAGACIOUS	THERSITES	EPINIKION	BANDOLINE	COASTLINE	ESEMPLASY
ORGANISER	SALACIOUS	THINNINGS	FINICKING	BARCELONA	COLORLESS	ESQUILINE
ORGANIZED	SAMARITAN	THIRTIETH	FINICKITY	BATTALION	COMPELLED	ESTABLISH
ORGANIZER	SANDPIPER	TIMEPIECE	GAVELKIND	BEARDLESS	CONDYLOMA	ESTRELDID
ORTANIQUE	SAPODILLA	TIPULIDAE	HAYMAKING	BEDFELLOW	CONGOLESE	ETHNOLOGY
OUTGOINGS	SATIRICAL	TONBRIDGE	HIJACKING	BERKELIUM	CONSULATE	ETYMOLOGY
OUTSKIRTS	SATYRIDAE	TOTALIZER	HUMANKIND	BERYLLIUM	COPROLITE	EVERGLADE
OVERNIGHT	SATYRINAE	TOVARISCH	KNAPSKULL	BICYCLIST	CORALLINE	EXCELLENT
OVERRIDER	SCAGLIOLA	TRACHINUS	LAWMAKING	BLACKLEAD	CORDYLINE	EXEMPLARY
OVERSIGHT	SCALLIONS	TRAMLINES	MINISKIRT	BLACKLIST	CORNELIAN	EXEMPLIFY
OVERSIZED	SCEPTICAL	TRANSIENT	MOLESKINS	BLAMELESS	CORNFLOUR	EYESPLICE
PALAFITTE	SCHEHITAH	TRAPPINGS	NOLLEKENS	BLOODLESS	COROLLARY	FACECLOTH
PARASITIC	SCHOLIAST	TREDRILLE	NUMBSKULL	BOOTBLACK	CORPULENT	FAIRYLAND
PAROTITIS	SCIARIDAE	TRICLINIC	PALANKEEN	BOUNDLESS	CORRELATE	FAITHLESS
PARTRIDGE	SCINTILLA	TRIMMINGS	PANNIKELL	BOXWALLAH	COSMOLOGY	FAULTLESS
PARTTIMER	SCRAPINGS	TROCHILIC	PARTAKING	BRAINLESS	COUNTLESS	FERTILITY
PECUNIARY	SCURRIOUR	TROCHILUS	PERIAKTOS	BRAMBLING	COVELLITE	FERTILIZE
PEMPHIGUS	SEDITIOUS	TWENTIETH	PHENAKISM	BRAZILIAN	CRACKLING	FEUDALISM
PENFRIEND	SEMIFINAL	UMBILICAL	PREDIKANT	BREADLINE	CRAPULENT	FEUILLANT
PENURIOUS	SHECHINAH	UMBILICUS	PROVOKING	BRISTLING	CRAPULOUS	FIBROLINE
PHANSIGAR	SHECHITAH	UNCHRISOM	REWORKING	BROADLOOM	CRASHLAND	FIBROLITE
PHILLIBEG	SHEFFIELD	UNCLAIMED	SELJUKIAN	BRUTALISM	CREDULITY	FILOPLUME
PHLEBITIS	SHOWPIECE	UNDECIDED	SERASKIER	BRUTALITY	CREDULOUS	FIREPLACE
PHRENITIS	SICILIANO	UNDEFILED	SHOLOKHOV	BRUTALIZE	CREPOLINE	FISHPLATE
PIRATICAL	SIDELIGHT	UNDEFINED	SHRINKAGE	CABALLERO	CRIBELLUM	FLABELLUM
PLASTIQUE	SILURIDAE	UNDIVIDED	SHRINKING	CAGOULARD	CRINOLINE	FLAGELLIN

FLAGELLUM	HOPLOLOGY	MENTALITY	PANTALOON	RASKOLNIK	SINGULTUS	TENAILLON
FLATULENT	HORSELESS	MERCILESS	PAPILLOTE	REBELLION	SKINFLINT	TEPHILLIN
FLEDGLING	HOSTILITY	MESOBLAST	PARABLAST	RECALLING	SLEEPLESS	TETRALOGY
FLESHLESS	HOURGLASS	MESSALINA	PARACLETE	RECOLLECT	SMOKELESS	THANKLESS
FLINTLOCK	HOUSELEEK	METALLOID	PARDALOTE	REMOULADE	SMUGGLING	THERALITE
FOLIOLOSE	HYPALLAGE	METROLAND	PARHELION	RENTALLER	SNOWFLAKE	THORNLESS
FOOTPLATE	HYPERLINK	MICROLITE	PATHOLOGY	REPELLENT	SOCIALISM	THRALLDOM
FORECLOSE	HYPOBLAST	MICROLITH	PATROLMAN	REPELLING	SOCIALIST	THRILLANT
FORMALIST	ICHNOLITE	MIRTHLESS	PENDULATE	REPTILIAN	SOCIALITE	THRILLING
FORMALITY	IDIOBLAST	MISFALLEN	PENDULOUS	RESSALDAR	SOCIALIZE	THUMBLING
FORMALIZE	IDIOPLASM	MISOCLERE	PENILLION	RETAILING	SOCIOLECT	TITILLATE
FORMULATE	IMAGELESS	MODELLING	PENNILESS	REVEALING	SOCIOLOGY	TONOPLAST
FORTALICE	IMPELLING	MODILLION	PERCALINE	REVELLING	SOMEPLACE	TOOTHLESS
FORTILAGE	INABILITY	MONGOLIAN	PERCOLATE	RHODOLITE	SOMMELIER	TORTELIER
FOSSILISE	INDWELLER	MONGOLISM	PERICLASE	RICHELIEU	SOMNOLENT	TOUCHLINE
FOUNDLING	INFIELDER	MONOPLANE	PESTILENT	RIDERLESS	SORTILEGE	TOWELLING
FRAGILITY	INOCULATE	MORTALITY	PETILLANT	RIDGELING	SOUNDLESS	TRACKLESS
FRANGLAIS	INQUILINE	MOUSELIKE	PETROLEUM	ROADBLOCK	SPACELESS	TRAFALGAR
FRIESLAND	INSHALLAH	MOUTHLESS	PETROLOGY	ROSTELLUM	SPARKLERS	TRAGELAPH
FRIVOLITY	INTELLECT	MUSSOLINI	PHACOLITE	ROTAPLANE	SPARKLING	TRANSLATE
FRIVOLOUS	INTERLACE	MUSSULMAN	PHIGALIAN	RUGGELACH	SPATULATE	TRAVELERS
FRUGALITY	INTERLARD	MUTUALISM	PHILOLOGY	SACKCLOTH	SPECULATE	TRAVELING
FRUITLESS	INTERLOCK	MYTHOLOGY	PHONOLITE	SACRILEGE	SPICILEGE	TRAVELLER
FULLBLOWN	INTERLOPE	NAMEPLATE	PHONOLOGY	SAILCLOTH	SPINELESS	TREILLAGE
FUSILLADE	INTERLUDE	NATHELESS	PHTHALATE	SALESLADY	STABILITY	TREMBLING
GANGPLANK	INVIOLATE	NATROLITE	PHYCOLOGY	SANDALLED	STABILIZE	TREMOLITE
GARRULITY	ISINGLASS	NEPHALISM	PHYTOLITE	SASSOLITE	STAINLESS	TREMULANT
GARRULOUS	ISRAELITE	NEPHALIST	PIERGLASS	SATELLITE	STARTLING	TREMULATE
GASHOLDER	JAMBALAYA	NEPHELINE	PISTOLEER	SCAMBLING	STATELESS	TREMULOUS
GENEALOGY	JAYWALKER	NEURALGIA	PLUMBLINE	SCANTLING	STATOLITH	TREVELYAN
GENIALITY	JEWELLERY	NEURALGIC	PLURALISM	SCAPOLITE	STERILITY	TRIBALISM
GENTILITY	JOVIALITY	NEUROLOGY	PLURALITY	SCENTLESS	STERILIZE	TRIBOLOGY
GENUFLECT	KEYHOLDER	NEWSFLASH	POINTLESS	SCHEELITE	STIMULANT	TRICKLESS
GERFALCON	LACCOLITE	NICCOLITE	PORCELAIN	SCHELLING	STIMULATE	TRICOLOUR
GIBRALTAR	LAEVULOSE	NIDERLING	PORTULACA	SCHILLING	STIPULATE	TRUCKLOAD
GLABELLAR	LAMPBLACK	NIEBELUNG	POSTILION	SCHMALTZY	STONELESS	TRUCULENT
GONDOLIER	LANDSLIDE	NOISELESS	POSTULANT	SCHOOLBOY	STORYLINE	TURBULENT
GOSPELLER	LATICLAVE	NONILLION	POSTULATE	SCHOOLING	STOWNLINS	TWAYBLADE
GRACELESS	LEGISLATE	NORMALACY	POTHOLING	SCHOOLMAN	STRAPLESS	TWINKLING
GRANULATE	LIABILITY	NORMALITY	POWELLITE	SEMIFLUID	STRIPLING	UNDERLINE
GRANULITE	LIBELLOUS	NORMALIZE	POWERLESS	SEMIGLOSS	STROLLING	UNDERLING
GRANULOSE	LIGHTLESS	NOSEBLEED	PREDILECT	SEMIOLOGY	STUMBLING	UNFAILING
GRAPPLING	LIMITLESS	NOSTALGIA	PREHALLUX	SENSELESS	SUBCELLAR	UNFEELING
GRASSLAND	LINEOLATE	NOSTALGIC	PREPOLLEX	SENSILLUM	SUBDOLOUS	UNHEALTHY
GRIMALKIN	LOBLOLLYS	NOSTOLOGY	PREVALENT	SEPIOLITE	SUCCULENT	UNIVALENT
GRUELLING	LOCELLATE	NUMMULITE	PRICELESS	SERIALIST	SURMULLET	UNSKILLED
GRUMBLING	LOINCLOTH	OCTILLION	PRIMULINE	SERIALIZE	SWADDLING	UNSULLIED
GUIDELINE	LOOKALIKE	OCTOPLOID	PRIVILEGE	SERVILELY	SWOTHLING	UNWILLING
GUILELESS	LOOSELEAF	ODOURLESS	PROPELLED	SERVILITY	SYLPHLIKE	UTTERLESS
GUILTLESS	MACROLOGY	OFFCOLOUR	PROPELLER	SEXUALITY	SYMBOLISM	VACILLATE
GYROPLANE	MADRILENE	OLENELLUS	PROPYLENE	SHAMELESS	SYMBOLIST	VAINGLORY
HAEMALOMA	MAGDALENE	OPOBALSAM	PROSELYTE	SHAPELESS	SYMBOLIZE	VALUELESS
HARIOLATE	MAGNALIUM	OPODELDOC	PROVOLONE	SHASHLICK	SYPHILOMA	VANDALISM
HARMALINE	MAMMALIAN	ORGILLOUS	PUCELLAGE	SHAVELING	TABELLION	VANDALIZE
HEADCLOTH	MANDOLINE	ORICALCHE	PUERILITY	SHEARING	TABLELAND	VARIOLATE
HEARTLAND	MARMALADE	ORTHOLOGY	PULLULATE	SHEERLEGS	TACHILITE	VENIALITY
HEARTLESS	MARSHLAND	OSCILLATE	PUMMELLED	SHIFTLESS	TACHYLITE	VENTILATE
HEATHLAND	MARVELOUS	OTTRELITE	PUNCHLINE	SHOPFLOOR	TACHYLYTE	VERBALIZE
HELVELLYN	MASCULINE	OURSELVES	PUPILLAGE	SHORTLIST	TAHSILDAR	VERMILION
HERBALIST	MATCHLESS	OVERBLOWN	PYGMALION	SHOVELFUL	TAILPLANE	VEXILLARY
HERCULEAN	MATCHLOCK	OVERCLOUD	QUERULOUS	SHOVELLER	TAMERLANE	VIABILITY
HIGHCLASS	MAUSOLEUM	OVERSLEEP	QUICKLIME	SHUFFLING	TANTALITE	VIRGULATE
HIGHFLYER	MAXILLARY	OWLEGLASS	RACIALISM	SIBYLLINE	TANTALIZE	VISUALIZE
HINGELESS	MEDALLION	PALEOLITH	RADIOLOGY	SIGHTLESS	TASSELLED	VITELLIUS
HIPPOLYTA	MEDALLIST	PANELLING	RAMILLIES	SIGNALLER	TASTELESS	VOICELESS
HIPPOLYTE	MELONLIKE	PANELLIST	RANGELAND	SIGNALMAN	TAUTOLOGY	WAGHALTER
HISTOLOGY	MENDELISM	PANTALEON	RANGELAND	SINGALESE	TELEOLOGY	WAGONLOAD

WAISTLINE	DEFORMITY	IMMELMANN	READYMADE	ABOMINATE	CALVINIST	DECENNIAL
WALDFLUTE	DETERMINE	IMPLEMENT	REANIMATE	ABSCONDER	CAMPANILE	DECLINING
WASHCLOTH	DETRIMENT	IMPROMPTU	RECOMMEND	ABSTINENT	CAMPANULA	DEMEANING
WASTELAND	DEVILMENT	INANIMATE	REDEEMING	ACUMINATE	CANNONADE	DEMEANOUR
WATERLESS	DIATOMITE	INCLEMENT	REEXAMINE	ACUTENESS	CANTONESE	DENSENESS
WATERLILY	DIPLOMACY	INCOMMODE	REFORMIST	ADEPTNESS	CARBONADE	DERRINGER
WATERLINE	DISARMING	INCREMENT	REPAYMENT	ADJOINING	CARBONADO	DESIGNATE
WAVELLITE	DISCOMFIT	INFIRMARY	REPRIMAND	AFTERNOON	CARBONARI	DESIGNING
WHISTLING	DISMEMBER	INFIRMITY	REVETMENT	ALERTNESS	CARBONATE	DINGINESS
WINEGLASS	DISSEMBLE	INFORMANT	ROSCOMMON	ALEXANDER	CARBONIZE	DIRTINESS
WORKPLACE	DISTEMPER	INNERMOST	RUNNYMEDE	ALEXANDRA	CARBUNCLE	DISHONEST
WORTHLESS	ECONOMICS	INTERMENT	SACRAMENT	ALOOFNESS	CARCINOMA	DISHONOUR
WRANGLERS	ECONOMIST	JERAHMEEL	SCHLEMIEL	ALTERNATE	CARPENTER	DISMANTLE
WREAKLESS	ECONOMIZE	JESSAMINE	SCHLEMIHL	ALUMINIUM	CARPENTRY	DISPENSER
WRESTLING	EGAREMENT	JIGGUMBOB	SCRIMMAGE	AMARANTIN	CASSANDRA	DISSENTER
ZIBELLINE	ELLESMERE	JUDGEMENT	SCRUMMAGE	AMAZONITE	CASSONADE	DISSONANT
ABASEMENT	ELOPEMENT	KALSOMINE	SEDGEMOOR	AMUSINGLY	CASTANETS	DISTANTLY
ABATEMENT	EMOLUMENT	LADYSMITH	SENTIMENT	ANNOUNCER	CAVERNOUS	DISTENDED
ACADEMIST	ENACTMENT	LANDSMAAL	SEPTEMBER	APPOINTED	CENTENARY	DIZZINESS
ACCLIMATE	ENDOWMENT	LINEAMENT	SEPTIMOLE	APPOINTEE	CERVANTES	DRACONIAN
ACETAMIDE	ENJOYMENT	LOCKSMITH	SHEEPMEAT	ARABINOSE	CEYLONESE	DRAGONFLY
ADORNMENT	ENROLMENT	LODGEMENT	SONGSMITH	ARACHNOID	CHAMINADE	DRAWKNIFE
AFTERMATH	ENTHYMEME	MALLEMUCK	SOPHOMORE	ARAGONITE	CHAVENDER	DULCINIST
AFTERMOST	ENTRAMMEL	MAPPEMOND	SPEARMINT	ARCHANGEL	CHEAPNESS	DUNGENESS
AGAMEMNON	ENTREMETS	MASSYMORE	SPECIMENS	ASHKENAZI	CHICANERY	DUNSINANE
AGREEMENT	ENVERMEIL	MATRIMONY	SPODUMENE	ASPLENIUM	CIRCINATE	EAGERNESS
ALCHEMIST	EPITOMIZE	MATTAMORE	SQUEAMISH	ASTOUNDED	CLARENDON	ECHIDNINE
ALIGNMENT	EPONYMOUS	MELPOMENE	SQUIRMING	ASTRONAUT	CLEANNESS	ELEGANTLY
ALLOTMENT	EQUIPMENT	MERRIMENT	STALEMATE	ASTRONOMY	CLEARNESS	ELEMENTAL
AMAZEMENT	EUDAEMONY	MICROMOLE	STATEMENT	ATTAINDER	CLOSENESS	ELEVENSES
AMENDMENT	EUPHEMISM	MIDSUMMER	STREAMING	AUTHENTIC	COCHINEAL	ELIMINATE
AMUSEMENT	EXACTMENT	MILLAMANT	SUBLIMATE	AVALANCHE	COFFINITE	EMBRANGLE
ANATOMIST	EXANIMATE	MINCEMEAT	SUBLIMELY	AWAKENING	COLONNADE	EMINENTLY
ANATOMIZE	EXCREMENT	MISTEMPER	SUPREMACY	AWARENESS	COLUMNIST	EMPENNAGE
ANDROMEDA	EXTREMELY	MOLLYMAWK	SUPREMELY	BADMINTON	COMMANDER	EMPTINESS
ANNULMENT	EXTREMISM	MRIDAMGAM	SUQUAMISH	BARTENDER	COMMENSAL	ENCHANTED
ANONYMITY	EXTREMIST	NATHEMORE	SWANIMOTE	BASTINADE	COMMUNION	ENCHANTER
ANONYMOUS	EXTREMITY	NEODYMIUM	SWEETMEAT	BASTINADO	COMMUNISM	ENCOUNTER
APARTMENT	FACSIMILE	NEVERMORE	SYNCOMIUM	BEGINNING	COMMUNIST	ENERINITE
ATONEMENT	FIRMAMENT	NIGHTMARE	TESTAMENT	BERGANDER	COMMUNITY	ENGRENAGE
BALTIMORE	FLORIMELL	NURSEMAID	TESTIMONY	BESPANGLE	COMPANIES	ENSCONCED
BENCHMARK	FLOURMILL	NUTRIMENT	THELEMITE	BLACKNESS	COMPANION	ENTRANCED
BERGAMASK	FOGRAMITE	OCKHAMIST	TOBERMORY	BLANDNESS	COMPONENT	EPICENTRE
BERGOMASK	FORASMUCH	OUTERMOST	TRADEMARK	BLATANTLY	CONDENSER	EPIGENOUS
BIRTHMARK	FORCEMEAT	OUTNUMBER	TRANSMUTE	BLINDNESS	CONGENIAL	EROGENOUS
BLACKMAIL	FUNDAMENT	PANDEMIAN	TRASIMENE	BLUFFNESS	CONSENSUS	ESPAGNOLE
BLACKMORE	FURNIMENT	PANTOMIME	TREADMILL	BLUNTNESS	CONSONANT	ESPIONAGE
CARBAMATE	GESSAMINE	PARCHMENT	TREATMENT	BOLOGNESE	CONTENDER	ESPLANADE
CARBAMIDE	GILGAMESH	PARSIMONY	TRIDYMITE	BOSSANOVA	CONTENTED	ESTRANGED
CATCHMENT	GINORMOUS	PASSAMENT	UNANIMITY	BOSSINESS	CONTINENT	EUPHONIUM
CHALUMEAU	GLUTAMINE	PATRIMONY	UNANIMOUS	BOSTONIAN	CONTINUAL	EVIDENTLY
CHAMOMILE	GOLDSMITH	PERFUMERY	UNDERMINE	BRASENOSE	CONTINUUM	EXACTNESS
CHECKMATE	GOSSAMERY	PERGAMENE	UNDERMOST	BREAKNECK	CONVINCED	EXOGENOUS
CLASSMATE	GOTHAMITE	PERSIMMON	UPPERMOST	BRIEFNESS	CORIANDER	EXTRINSIC
COLLIMATE	GREENMAIL	PESSIMISM	UTTERMOST	BRISKNESS	COSMONAUT	FAINTNESS
CONDEMNED	GUACAMOLE	PESSIMIST	VERKAMPTE	BRITANNIA	CRAZINESS	FALERNIAN
CONDIMENT	GUATEMALA	PHARAMOND	VERTUMNUS	BRITANNIC	CRETINOUS	FALSENESS
CONSUMING	HACKAMORE	PHEROMONE	VICTIMIZE	BROMINATE	CRIMINATE	FANDANGLE
CONTEMPER	HALFEMPTY	PIECEMEAL	WATERMARK	BUCCANEER	CRISPNESS	FASCINATE
CONTUMACY	HASHEMITE	PLACEMENT	WATERMILL	BULKINESS	CRUDENESS	FASTENING
CONTUMELY	HATCHMENT	PROLAMINE	WELCOMING	BURKINABE	CULMINATE	FATTENING
COSTUMIER	HINDEMITH	PROSIMIAN	WELSUMMER	BURLINESS	CURRENTLY	FERDINAND
CUSTOMARY	HISTAMINE	PROTAMINE	WHALEMEAT	BYSTANDER	DALTONISM	FERMENTED
CUSTOMIZE	HOCCAMORE	PROXIMATE	WHEATMEAL	CALCANEUM	DARWINIAN	FERVENTLY
CYCLAMATE	HONEYMOON	PROXIMITY	WHOLEMEAL	CALCANEUS	DEACONESS	FESTINATE
DAIRYMAID	HOUSEMAID	QUASIMODO	WILLEMITE	CALCINATE	DEAFENING	FINLANDIA
DEFERMENT	HUMANMADE	QUERIMONY	WORDSMITH	CALVANISM	DEAMINATE	FOGGINESS

FOREANENT	HOBBINOLL	LOWLINESS	OBSTINACY	PROMENADE	SDEIGNFUL	TACKINESS
FORTUNATE	HODMANDOD	LURIDNESS	OBSTINATE	PROMINENT	SEASONING	TANZANIAN
FORWANDER	HOTTENTOT	LUSTINESS	OBTAINING	PROPONENT	SEEMINGLY	TAPDANCER
FRAGONARD	HOUYHNHNM	MACDONALD	OILTANKER	PROVENDER	SEGMENTED	TARDINESS
FRANKNESS	HOYDENISH	MACHINATE	OLIVENITE	PRUDENTLY	SEQUENCER	TASMANIAN
FRESHNESS	HUMDINGER	MACHINERY	OPENENDED	PRYTANEUM	SEQUINNED	TAUCHNITZ
FUGGINESS	HUSBANDLY	MACHINING	OPULENTLY	PUFFINESS	SERBONIAN	TAVERNERS
FULMINANT	HUSBANDRY	MACHINIST	ORIGENIST	PULMONARY	SERMONIZE	TECTONICS
FULMINATE	HUSKINESS	MACKENZIE	ORIGINATE	PULMONATE	SHADINESS	TEKNONYMY
FUSSINESS	HYDRANGEA	MADDENING	OROBANCHE	PUNGENTLY	SHAKINESS	TELLINGLY
FUSTINESS	HYGIENIST	MALIGNANT	ORPHANAGE	PURDONIUM	SHARPNESS	TENSENESS
FUZZINESS	HYPHENATE	MALIGNITY	OUGHTNESS	PYTHONESS	SHEERNESS	TERMINATE
GABIONADE	ICELANDER	MALLANDER	OXYGENATE	QUARENDEN	SHORTNESS	TERPINEOL
GALIONGEE	ICELANDIC	MALLENDER	PAGEANTRY	QUEERNESS	SHOWINESS	TERSENESS
GALLANTLY	IMAGINARY	MANGANATE	PANHANDLE	QUICKNESS	SHUBUNKIN	THELONIUS
GALLANTRY	IMBRANGLE	MANGANESE	PARSONAGE	QUIETNESS	SICKENING	THICKNESS
GALLINULE	IMPOUNDER	MANHANDLE	PASSENGER	RADIANTLY	SILLINESS	THREONINE
GALVANISM	IMPSONITE	MANLINESS	PATERNITY	RAFFINOSE	SIMEONITE	THUMBNAIL
GALVANIZE	INCARNATE	MARTINEAU	PATIENTLY	RANDINESS	SINKANSEN	TIGHTNESS
GARDENING	INCOGNITO	MARTINMAS	PATRONAGE	RATIONALE	SIPHUNCLE	TIMPANIST
GARGANTUA	INDEMNIFY	MASSINGER	PATRONESS	RATIONING	SIRBONIAN	TIPSINESS
GASCONADE	INDEMNITY	MATERNITY	PATRONIZE	READINESS	SLACKNESS	TIREDNESS
GAUDINESS	INDIGNANT	MECHANICS	PAUSANIAS	REASONING	SLEEKNESS	TORBANITE
GAUNTNESS	INDIGNITY	MECHANISM	PAWKINESS	RECKONING	SLIMINESS	TORMENTER
GAWKINESS	INERTNESS	MECHANIZE	PEASANTRY	RECOGNIZE	SLOVENIAN	TORMENTIL
GELIGNITE	INGLENOOK	MEDMENHAM	PECKSNIFF	RECTANGLE	SMALLNESS	TORMENTOR
GENUINELY	INOPINATE	MENNONITE	PELMANISM	REDDENDUM	SMARTNESS	TORMENTUM
GERMANCER	INQUINATE	MERCENARY	PENDENNIS	REDHANDED	SOBERNESS	TOSCANINI
GERMANDER	INSOMNIAC	MERGANSER	PERENNIAL	REEDINESS	SOFTENING	TOTTENHAM
GERMANITE	INSTANTER	MESSENGER	PERGUNNAH	REJOINDER	SOGGINESS	TOUGHNESS
GERMANIUM	INSTANTLY	METRONOME	PERIANDER	REMAINDER	SOLEMNITY	TRETINOIN
GERMINATE	INSWINGER	MEZZANINE	PERMANENT	REMAINING	SOLEMNIZE	TRIBUNATE
GIBEONITE	INTERNODE	MIDIANITE	PERSONAGE	RENCONTRE	SOPPINESS	TRIENNIAL
GIDDINESS	INTRINSIC	MIDWINTER	PERSONATE	REPLENISH	SOSTENUTO	TRITENESS
GLUCINIUM	INVERNESS	MILLENIAL	PERSONIFY	REPUGNANT	SOUNDNESS	TRUTINATE
GLUTINOUS	JACKKNIFE	MILLINERY	PERSONNEL	RETAINING	SOUTENEUR	TUBBINESS
GMELINITE	JACKSNIPE	MISHANDLE	PERTINENT	RETURNING	SPARINGLY	TURBINATE
GODLINESS	JAGGANATH	MISMANAGE	PETTINESS	RIBBONISM	SPELUNKER	TYMPANIST
GOOSANDER	JANSENISM	MISTINESS	PHALANGER	RIGHTNESS	SPICINESS	TYRANNIZE
GOOSENECK	JANSENIST	MODERNISM	PHILANDER	RIPIENIST	SPIKENARD	TYRANNOUS
GOVERNESS	JARGONIZE	MODERNIST	PHITONIUM	RISKINESS	STALENESS	UKRAINIAN
GOVERNING	JERKINESS	MODERNITY	PIQUANTLY	ROSMINIAN	STARKNESS	ULIGINOUS
GRANDNESS	JOBCENTRE	MODERNIZE	PLAINNESS	ROUGHNECK	STAVANGER	ULTRONEUS
GREATNESS	JOBERNOWL	MOISTNESS	PLATONIST	ROUGHNESS	STEEPNESS	UNBEKNOWN
GRIMINESS	JOHANNINE	MONTANISM	PLUMPNESS	ROUMANIAN	STERNNESS	UNBOUNDED
GRUFFNESS	JORDANIAN	MONTANIST	PLUTONIUM	ROUMANSCH	STEVENSON	UNCHANGED
GUARANTEE	JUICINESS	MONZONITE	POISONING	ROUTINELY	STIFFNESS	UNDAUNTED
GUARANTOR	JUSTINIAN	MOODINESS	POISONOUS	ROWDINESS	STILLNESS	UNFOUNDED
HANDINESS	KISSINGER	MORGANITE	POLIANITE	RUNCINATE	STOUTNESS	UNSINNING
HAPPENING	KITTENISH	MORMONISM	POLLINATE	RUSTINESS	STRAINING	UNUNUNIUM
HAPPINESS	KNOWINGLY	MOSKONFYT	POLYANDRY	RUTHENIAN	SUBTENANT	UPCOUNTRY
HARBINGER	LANCINATE	MRIDANGAM	PORRINGER	RUTHENIUM	SUCCENTOR	UREDINIAL
HARDANGER	LANKINESS	MUCKENDER	POTHUNTER	SADDENING	SUCCINATE	URICONIAN
HARDINESS	LAPLANDER	MUDDINESS	POTTINGAR	SALTINESS	SUETONIUS	UROKINASE
HARMONICA	LARGENESS	MUNDUNGUS	PREBENDAL	SANTONICA	SULKINESS	UTICENSIS
HARMONIST	LAWMONGER	MURKINESS	PRECENTOR	SARMENTUM	SULTANATE	VACCINATE
HARMONIUM	LEGIONARY	MUSHINESS	PRECINCTS	SASSENACH	SUNTANNED	VAGUENESS
HARMONIZE	LENIENTLY	MUSTINESS	PRECONISE	SATURNIAN	SUPERNOVA	VALDENSES
HARSHNESS	LIGHTNESS	MUZZINESS	PREMONISH	SATURNINE	SURCINGLE	VALIANTLY
HASTENING	LIGHTNING	NAKEDNESS	PRESENTED	SATURNISM	SURLINESS	VELLENAGE
HASTINESS	LISTENING	NASTINESS	PRESENTER	SAUCINESS	SURRENDER	VERMINOUS
HEADINESS	LOCHINVAR	NATHANIEL	PRESENTLY	SAVERNAKE	SUSPENDED	VIOLENTLY
HEAVINESS	LOFTINESS	NEPTUNIUM	PRETENDER	SCAVENGER	SUSPENDER	VIOLINIST
HERMANDAD	LONDONESE	NOBLENESS	PROCONSUL	SCHLENTER	SUSPENSOR	VIRGINALS
HESSONITE	LONGINGLY	NOISINESS	PROFANELY	SCLAUNDER	SWEETNESS	VIRGINIAN
HIBERNATE	LOOSENESS	OBSCENELY	PROFANITY	SCREENING	SWIFTNESS	VIRGINITY
HIBERNIAN	LOWLANDER	OBSCENITY	PROLONGED	SCROUNGER	SYLVANITE	VIRGINIUM

VISIONARY	BACKWOODS	EASTBOUND	ISOPROPYL	PAREGORIC	SLUGHORNE	ATTEMPTED
VIVIDNESS	BAKEHOUSE	EASYGOING	ISOTROPIC	PARTHOLON	SNOWBOUND	BACKSPACE
VOLCANISM	BALLPOINT	ECTOMORPH	JOBSWORTH	PATCHOULI	SNOWDONIA	BISHOPRIC
VOLTINISM	BAMBOOZLE	EDGEWORTH	KARAKORAM	PATCHOULY	SOFTCOVER	CALLIPERS
VULCANIAN	BARAGOUIN	ELASTOMER	KINKCOUGH	PATRIOTIC	SOLILOQUY	CARYOPSIS
VULCANIST	BAREBONES	ELECTORAL	KINSWOMAN	PEDAGOGUE	SOURDOUGH	CATCHPOLE
VULCANITE	BARTHOLDI	EMBRYONIC	KNEECORDS	PENSIONER	SPASMODIC	CATCHPOLL
VULCANIZE	BARTHOLIN	EMOTIONAL	KNIPHOFIA	PENTHOUSE	SPOFFORTH	CATHEPSIN
VULPINITE	BASEBOARD	EMPANOPLY	LAGOMORPH	PERAEOPOD	SPONSORED	CENTIPEDE
WALDENSES	BASECOURT	ENDOMORPH	LANDLOPER	PERIBOLOS	STALWORTH	CHILOPODA
WAMBENGER	BATHTOWEL	EPISCOPAL	LATECOMER	PERIMORPH	STARBOARD	CHIROPODY
WARMONGER	BEETHOVEN	EPISTOLER	LAWNMOWER	PHELLOGEN	STATIONED	COLLAPSAR
WEAKENING	BILLBOARD	EQUIPOISE	LAZYBONES	PHYLLOPOD	STATIONER	CORRUPTER
WEARINESS	BLOWTORCH	EQUIVOCAL	LEAFMOULD	PINHOOKER	STEGNOSIS	CTESIPHON
WEIRDNESS	BOATHOUSE	EQUIVOQUE	LECANORAM	PLAYHOUSE	STEGNOTIC	DANDYPRAT
WELLKNOWN	BOOKLOVER	ETHANOATE	LEITMOTIF	PLETHORIC	STERCORAL	DAVENPORT
WHIPSNADE	BOONDOCKS	EUCHLORIC	LEITMOTIV	PLIMSOLLS	SULPHONIC	DECOMPOSE
WHITENESS	BOSPHORUS	EXOSTOSIS	LIMEHOUSE	PNEUMONIA	SUNFLOWER	DEVONPORT
WHITENING	BULLDOZER	FACTIONAL	LOBSCOUSE	POLYGONAL	SURFBOARD	DISAPPEAR
WHODUNNIT	CABRIOLET	FARMHOUSE	LOUDMOUTH	POLYMORPH	SYMBIOSIS	DISREPAIR
WHOLENESS	CALABOOSE	FASHIONED	MACARONIC	POMPHOLYX	SYMBIOTIC	DISREPUTE
WILLINGLY	CALEDONIA	FICTIONAL	MACEDOINE	POORHOUSE	SYMPHONIC	DISSIPATE
WINCANTON	CARDBOARD	FIREWORKS	MACEDONIA	PORTFOLIO	SYNAGOGUE	DODDIPOLL
WISCONSIN	CARTHORSE	FLAGEOLET	MADAROSIS	POSTHOUSE	TAILBOARD	DRAINPIPE
WITTINGLY	CASHPOINT	FLOPHOUSE	MALEBOLGE	POSTPONED	THEOSOPHY	DYSPEPSIA
WOODENTOP	CATACOMBS	FOOTLOOSE	MALLEOLUS	POSTWOMAN	THRASONIC	DYSPEPTIC
WOOLINESS	CATALOGUE	FORECOURT	MATAGOURI	PRACTOLOL	TICHBORNE	ECLAMPSIA
WORDINESS	CATAMOUNT	FOREGOING	MAYFLOWER	PRODROMAL	TIMENOGUY	ECTROPION
WULFENITE	CATATONIA	FOREWOMAN	MELANOSIS	PRODROMUS	TOLLHOUSE	ENCOLPION
ZEALANDER	CATATONIC	FRAMBOISE	MELANOTIC	PROGNOSIS	TRATTORIA	ENCOLPIUM
ZEPHANIAH	CERATODUS	FRANCOLIN	MENTIONED	PROPIONIC	TRYPHOEUS	ENCOMPASS
ZINFANDEL	CHARLOTTE	FREEBOARD	MESOMORPH	PROPTOSIS	TURNROUND	ENDOSPERM
ZINKENITE	CHARWOMAN	FROGMOUTH	METABOLIC	PROTHORAX	TURQUOISE	ENDPAPERS
ZIRCONIUM	CHERNOZEM	GARRYOWEN	MILLIONTH	PSEUDONYM	UNALLOYED	ENTROPION
ZOOMANTIC	CHIPBOARD	GLADIOLUS	MISSIONER	PSYCHOSIS	UNEXPOSED	ENTROPIUM
ABANDONED	CHLOROSIS	GLENDOWER	MONATOMIC	PSYCHOTIC	UNOPPOSED	EPEDAPHIC
ABANDONEE	CIRRHOSIS	GOALMOUTH	MONOCOQUE	PYRRHONIC	UNSAVOURY	EPILEPTIC
ACROPOLIS	CLAPBOARD	GOMPHOSIS	MONOLOGUE	QUANTOCKS	UNTUTORED	ESTRAPADE
ACYCLOVIR	CLIPBOARD	GREYHOUND	MORATORIA	RACEHORSE	VERSIONAL	ETHIOPIAN
AFLATOXIN	CLOISONNÉ	GRINGOLET	MORATORIO	REARHORSE	VIEWPOINT	EUTROPHIC
AGINCOURT	CLUBHOUSE	GUILLOCHE	MUCHLOVED	REARMOUSE	VITRIOLIC	EXCULPATE
AINSWORTH	COCKROACH	HALFDOZEN	MUSHROOMS	REINFORCE	VOODOOISM	EXTEMPORE
AIRCOOLED	COOKHOUSE	HALITOSIS	MYOGLOBIN	REREMOUSE	WALLBOARD	EXTIRPATE
ALCOHOLIC	CRANBORNE	HARDBOARD	NEWSHOUND	RHAPSODIC	WAREHOUSE	FALLOPIAN
AMAUROSIS	CROSSOVER	HARDCOVER	NONPROFIT	ROADHOUSE	WASHBOARD	FILLIPEEN
AMBLYOPIA	CRYPTOGAM	HARPOONER	NONSMOKER	ROADWORKS	WAYZGOOSE	FLESHPOTS
AMENHOTEP	DANTHONIA	HAUTMONDE	NUCLEOLUS	RUNAROUND	WEBFOOTED	FORESPEAK
ANAEROBIC	DARTBOARD	HAWTHORNE	OARSWOMAN	SAFFLOWER	WESTBOUND	FORESPEND
ANECDOTAL	DARTMOUTH	HEADBOARD	OASTHOUSE	SALTWORKS	WHIPROUND	FROGSPAWN
ANECDOTES	DASHBOARD	HERODOTUS	OCTAGONAL	SAXITOXIN	WHITWORTH	GALLIPOLI
ANKYLOSIS	DECALOGUE	HETERODOX	OESTROGEN	SCALLOPED	WILLPOWER	GALLOPADE
ANNAPOLIS	DEERHOUND	HETEROSIS	OKEYDOKEY	SCANSORES	WINDHOVER	GODOLPHIN
ANTIGONUS	DEMAGOGUE	HEXAGONAL	OUROBOROS	SCISSORER	WODEHOUSE	GOSSYPINE
ANTINOVEL	DESTROYED	HIDEBOUND	OUROBORUS	SCLEROSIS	WOLFHOUND	GOSSYPIUM
ANTIPODES	DESTROYER	HOARHOUND	OUTGROWTH	SCLEROTAL	WOODBORER	HANDSPIKE
ANTITOXIC	DEVELOPED	HOMEBOUND	OUTROOPER	SCOLIOSIS	WOODHOUSE	HIGHSPEED
ANTITOXIN	DEVELOPER	HOPSCOTCH	OUTSPOKEN	SCOLIOTIC	WOODLOUSE	HOMEOPATH
APERIODIC	DEXTRORSE	HORDEOLUM	OVERBOARD	SECTIONAL	WORKFORCE	HORSEPLAY
APOLLONUS	DIAGNOSIS	HOREHOUND	OVERJOYED	SEMEIOTIC	WORKHORSE	HYDROPULT
APOSTOLIC	DISCLOSED	HYPEROPIA	OVERPOISE	SEMICOLON	WORKHOUSE	INCULPATE
ARISTOTLE	DIZYGOTIC	HYPINOSIS	OVERPOWER	SEMIVOWEL	WYANDOTTE	INTERPLAY
ARTHROPOD	DOSSHOUSE	IBUPROFEN	OVERTONES	SHINTOISM	ZOOSCOPIC	INTERPOSE
ARTHROSIS	DOUKHOBOR	IDEALOGUE	PANEGOISM	SIDEBOARD	ACCOMPANY	INTERPRET
AUTONOMIC	DUCKBOARD	IGUANODON	PARABOLIC	SIDEROSIS	AEROSPACE	JUXTAPOSE
AUTOROUTE	DUMBFOUND	INDECORUM	PARAGOGUE	SIGNBOARD	ANALEPTIC	KIDNAPPED
AYCKBOURN	DUNGEONER	IRONWORKS	PARAMOUNT	SILICOSIS	ASCLEPIUS	KIDNAPPER
BACKBOARD	DYSTROPHY	ISALLOBAR	PARANOIAC	SLOWCOACH	ASTROPHEL	LANGSPIEL

LITHOPONE	UNDERPAID	BERSERKER	CONGERIES	EDITORIAL	GARDEROBE	INAMORATA
LIVERPOOL	UNDERPASS	BETTERTON	CONJURING	EIDOGRAPH	GARGARISM	INAMORATO
MADREPORE	UNHAPPILY	BIRDBRAIN	CONSCRIPT	ELABORATE	GASPEREAU	INCORRECT
MARCHPANE	UNHELPFUL	BIRTHRATE	CONSTRICT	ELATERIUM	GATECRASH	INQUIRING
MARSUPIAL	VERTIPORT	BIZARRELY	CONSTRUCT	ELBOWROOM	GATHERING	INQUORATE
MARSUPIUM	WALLOPING	BLOODROOT	CONVERTED	ELECTRESS	GIBBERISH	INSPIRING
MEGASPORE	WHIRLPOOL	BLUEPRINT	CONVERTER	ELECTRIFY	GINGERADE	INTEGRATE
MELAMPODE	WINCOPIPE	BOANERGES	COOPERATE	ELECTRODE	GLAMORIZE	INTEGRITY
MENIPPEAN	WORKSPACE	BOARDROOM	CORDUROYS	EMBARRASS	GLAMOROUS	INTERRUPT
MERCAPTAN	ZYGOSPORE	BOMBARDON	CORMORANT	ENCHORIAL	GLOMERATE	INUMBRATE
MILLEPEDE	BALDAQUIN	BOOMERANG	CORNBRASH	ENCOURAGE	GLOMERULE	ISODORIAN
MILLEPORE	EXCHEQUER	BORDEREAU	CORNCRAKE	ENDEARING	GLYCERIDE	ISOMERASE
MILLIPEDE	HARLEQUIN	BORDERING	CORNERMAN	ENDOCRINE	GLYCERINE	ITINERANT
MULTIPLEX	MANNEQUIN	BROKERAGE	CORPORATE	ENDOERGIC	GODPARENT	ITINERARY
NUNCUPATE	PALANQUIN	BUCHAREST	CORPOREAL	ENHYDRITE	GOLDCREST	ITINERATE
ORTHOPTER	SOBRIQUET	BULGARIAN	COTHURNUS	ENQUIRIES	GONGORISM	JACKFRUIT
OSTEOPATH	VELASQUEZ	BUTTERBUR	COUNTRIES	ENQUIRING	GOSLARITE	JEQUIRITY
OVERSPEND	ABHORRENT	BUTTERCUP	COURTROOM	ENTOURAGE	GRADGRIND	JESSERANT
OVERSPILL	ACTUARIAL	BUTTERFLY	COUTURIER	ENUMERATE	GREENROOM	JETSTREAM
PALAMPORE	ADUMBRATE	BUTTERNUT	CRITERION	EPHEDRINE	GREGARINE	JITTERBUG
PALEMPORE	AEPYORNIS	CAESAREAN	CURSORILY	EPICUREAN	GREGORIAN	KEPLARIAN
PARHYPATE	AERODROME	CALABRESE	CUTTHROAT	EPIDERMIS	GROCERIES	KEYSTROKE
PASSEPIED	AIRSTREAM	CALDARIUM	CYCLORAMA	EPIPHRAGM	GROSGRAIN	KIESERITE
PHILIPPIC	ALBATROSS	CALIBRATE	DANGEROUS	EROSTRATE	GUARDRAIL	KILDERKIN
PINEAPPLE	ALGEBRAIC	CALPURNIA	DASTARDLY	ERYTHRITE	GUARDROOM	KILLARNEY
PITCHPINE	ALLOGRAFT	CAMCORDER	DAYSPRING	EUCHARIST	GUITARIST	KNOTGRASS
PITCHPOLE	ALLOGRAPH	CANCEROUS	DECLARING	EUPHORBIA	GUTTERING	LABOURITE
PITCHPOLL	AMSTERDAM	CAREERIST	DEHYDRATE	EUSKARIAN	HAIRBRUSH	LAKEFRONT
PORCUPINE	ANCHORAGE	CARTTRACK	DELACROIX	EVAPORATE	HAMADRYAD	LANDDROST
PRECEPTOR	ANCHORITE	CASSEROLE	DEMETRIUS	EVERGREEN	HAMBURGER	LANDGRAVE
PRECIPICE	ANCHORMAN	CASUARINA	DEMOCRACY	EVITERNAL	HAMMERING	LAPSTREAK
PRIMIPARA	ANHYDRIDE	CATARRHAL	DEMURRAGE	EXODERMIS	HAMMURABI	LATHYRISM
PROLEPSIS	ANHYDRITE	CATHARSIS	DENIGRATE	EXONERATE	HAMSTRING	LATTERDAY
QUAILPIPE	ANHYDROUS	CATHARTIC	DEODORANT	EXUBERANT	HAMSTRUNG	LAUNDRESS
RANTIPOLE	ANSWERING	CATHERINE	DEODORIZE	EYESTRAIN	HANDBRAKE	LAZZARONE
RESERPINE	ARBITRAGE	CAUTERIZE	DESCARTES	FACTORIAL	HANKERING	LEAKPROOF
RHODOPSIN	ARBITRARY	CELEBRANT	DESECRATE	FACTORISE	HAYMARKET	LECHEROUS
RIDGEPOLE	ARBITRATE	CELEBRATE	DESPERADO	FASTTRACK	HEADDRESS	LEISURELY
SALLYPORT	ARMSTRONG	CELEBRITY	DESPERATE	FAVOURITE	HECTORING	LETHARGIC
SALLYPOST	ARROWROOT	CELLARIST	DETERRENT	FENUGREEK	HEMITROPE	LETTERBOX
SCHNAPPER	ARTHURIAN	CENTERING	DEUTERIUM	FILIGRAIN	HERBARIUM	LETTERING
SCRAPPING	ASYNERGIA	CENTURION	DEXTERITY	FILTERING	HERBORIST	LIBRARIAN
SCREWPINE	AUCTORIAL	CEREBRATE	DEXTEROUS	FILTERTIP	HESPERIAN	LICKERISH
SCRIMPING	AUSTERITY	CHAMFRAIN	DIANDROUS	FINGERING	HESTERNAL	LIMBURGER
SCRUMPING	AUTEURISM	CHANCROID	DIAPHRAGM	FINGERTIP	HIERARCHY	LINGERING
SHRIMPING	AUTHORESS	CHAPARRAL	DIFFERENT	FIREBRAND	HIMYARITE	LIQUORICE
SINGAPORE	AUTHORITY	CHAPERONE	DINNERSET	FIREBREAK	HINDBRAIN	LIQUORISH
SINGSPIEL	AUTHORIZE	CHARTREUX	DISBURDEN	FIREDRAKE	HISTORIAN	LOGOGRIPH
STANDPIPE	AUTOCRACY	CHECKROOM	DISCARDED	FIREPROOF	HOARFROST	LOITERING
STENOPAIC	AUTOCROSS	CHONDRITE	DISPARAGE	FIRSTRATE	HODIERNAL	LOMBARDIC
STOCKPILE	AUTOGRAPH	CHONDROID	DISPARATE	FISHERMAN	HODOGRAPH	LUCUBRATE
STOVEPIPE	AUXOTROPH	CIMMERIAN	DISPARITY	FLAVORING	HOLDERBAT	LUDICROUS
STRAPPADO	AWESTRUCK	CLAMOROUS	DISPERSAL	FLOWERBED	HOLLERITH	LUMBERING
STRAPPING	AWKWARDLY	CLASSROOM	DISPERSED	FLOWERING	HOLOGRAPH	MAINFRAME
SWORDPLAY	BACHARACH	CLOAKROOM	DISTORTED	FLOWERPOT	HOMEGROWN	MALFORMED
SYLLEPSIS	BACKTRACK	COFFERDAM	DISTURBED	FOOLPROOF	HOMOGRAFT	MANNERING
SYNCOPATE	BACTERIAL	COINTREAU	DITHERING	FOOTBRAKE	HOMOGRAPH	MANNERISM
THERAPIST	BACTERIUM	COLLYRIUM	DITHYRAMB	FOOTPRINT	HOUSEROOM	MANUBRIUM
TOOTHPICK	BALLERINA	COLOURFUL	DOCTORATE	FOREBRAIN	HUNGARIAN	MARGARINE
TRANSPIRE	BANTERING	COLOURING	DOORFRAME	FOREFRONT	HUTTERITE	MARMOREAL
TRANSPORT	BARBARIAN	COLOURIST	DOWNGRADE	FORLORNLY	HYPOCRISY	MARTYRDOM
TRANSPOSE	BARBARISM	COMFORTER	DOWNTREND	FOSSORIAL	HYPOCRITE	MASSORETE
TRIUMPHAL	BARBARITY	CONCERNED	DUIKERBOK	FRATERNAL	HYSTERICS	MASTERFUL
TURBOPROP	BARBARIZE	CONCERTED	DUMBARTON	FREDERICK	IDEOGRAPH	MASTERMAN
TURCOPOLE	BARBAROUS	CONCORDAT	DUNGAREES	FRUSTRATE	IDIOGRAPH	MATHURINE
UNADOPTED	BARMBRACK	CONFIRMED	EALDORMAN	FULLERENE	IMMIGRANT	MAVOURNIN
UNCOUPLED	BEDSPREAD	CONFORMAL	EASTERNER	FULLGROWN	IMMIGRATE	MEANDRIAN

MEASURING	PALSGRAVE	QUIVERING	SPINDRIER	UNGUARDED	ARABESQUE	DEFENSIVE
MELIORATE	PALUDRINE	RACETRACK	SPINDRIFT	UNIFORMED	ASCENSION	DENTISTRY
MELODRAMA	PANDURATE	RANCOROUS	SQUADRONE	UNIFORMLY	ASPERSION	DEPRESSED
MENSTRUAL	PARAGRAPH	RAPTORIAL	STAGIRITE	UNITARIAN	ATAVISTIC	DIFFUSION
MENSTRUUM	PARATROOP	RAPTUROUS	STAGYRITE	UNIVERSAL	ATHEISTIC	DIMENSION
MEPACRINE	PASSERINE	RATHERIPE	STATEROOM	UNLEARNED	ATHELSTAN	DIONYSIAN
MERCERIZE	PASTERNAK	RATHERISH	STILLROOM	UNMARRIED	AXMINSTER	DIONYSIUS
MERCURIAL	PASTORALE	READDRESS	STOCKROOM	UNSPARING	BALLISTIC	DISGUSTED
MEROCRINE	PASTURAGE	RECTORIAL	STOREROOM	UNWORRIED	BAPTISMAL	DISMISSAL
MESMERISM	PATHTRAIN	RECURRENT	SUBCORTEX	VANTBRASS	BARRISTER	DIVERSIFY
MESMERIZE	PATTERNED	RECURRING	SUBMARINE	VELODROME	BEARDSLEY	DIVERSION
METEORITE	PEDIGREES	REDSTREAK	SUBMERGED	VERATRINE	BLINDSPOT	DIVERSITY
METEOROID	PENETRATE	REFERRING	SUBNORMAL	VERBERATE	BLOODSHED	DONCASTER
MIDSTREAM	PEPPERONI	REGUERDON	SUBSCRIBE	VICTORIAN	BLOODSHOT	DRAFTSMAN
MISDIRECT	PEPPERPOT	REHEARSAL	SUBSCRIPT	VICTORINE	BOMBASINE	EARNESTLY
MISFIRING	PEREGRINE	REITERATE	SUBSTRATA	VOLKSRAAD	BOMBASTIC	ECOSYSTEM
MISSTROKE	PERFERVID	RENDERING	SUBSTRATE	VOLTURNUS	BROADSIDE	EGRESSION
MOBOCRACY	PERFORANS	RESOURCES	SUCCURSAL	VOLUCRINE	BUNDESTAG	EIGHTSOME
MOCKERNUT	PERFORATE	RESURRECT	SUFFERING	VULGARIAN	BURLESQUE	EMBASSADE
MONODRAMA	PERFORMED	RETIARIUS	SULFUROUS	VULGARISM	CALLOSITY	EMBASSAGE
MONOGRAPH	PERFORMER	RIGMAROLE	SUMMARILY	VULGARITY	CAMBUSCAN	EMBRASURE
MONOTROCH	PERTURBED	ROSMARINE	SUMMARIZE	VULTURINE	CANVASSER	EMPAESTIC
MONSTROUS	PERVERTED	ROTTERDAM	SUNSCREEN	WAGNERIAN	CARTESIAN	EMPHASIZE
MOTHERING	PETAURIST	ROXBURGHE	SUNSTROKE	WAGNERITE	CASUISTIC	EMPHYSEMA
MOTOCROSS	PHALAROPE	RUBBERIZE	SUPPORTER	WAITERAGE	CASUISTRY	ENCAUSTIC
MUGLARITE	PHANARIOT	SACKERSON	SUPPURATE	WALDGRAVE	CAUCASIAN	ENCLOSURE
MURDERESS	PICTORIAL	SACRARIUM	SYNEDRION	WALPURGIS	CAUCASOID	ENDLESSLY
MURDEROUS	PIGNERATE	SAGEBRUSH	TANGERINE	WANDERING	CERUSSITE	ENGROSSED
MURMURING	PILFERAGE	SALUBRITY	TANTARARA	WANWORTHY	CHEAPSIDE	ENGROSSER
MUSCARINE	PILFERING	SALVARSAN	TARTAREAN	WARTCRESS	CHEMISTRY	EPINASTIC
MUTTERING	PIMPERNEL	SANDARACH	TECTORIAL	WASHERMAN	CHERISHED	EXCELSIOR
MYSTERIES	PINKERTON	SANGFROID	TELEGRAPH	WASSERMAN	CHORISTER	EXCESSIVE
NAPIERIAN	PINSTRIPE	SARTORIAL	TELLURIAN	WESTERNER	CLEANSING	EXCLUSION
NECTARINE	PIPEDREAM	SARTORIUS	TELLURION	WINDBREAK	COALESCED	EXCLUSIVE
NEWMARKET	PISTAREEN	SAUTERNES	TELLURIUM	WISECRACK	COELOSTAT	EXCURSION
NEWSPRINT	PLAYGROUP	SAXIFRAGE	TEMPERATE	WITHDRAWN	COLLISION	EXHAUSTED
NIDDERING	POLVERINE	SCALARIUM	TEMPORARY	WITHERING	COLLUSION	EXPANSION
NIGGARDLY	POLYGRAPH	SCELERATE	TEMPORIZE	WITHERITE	COLLUSIVE	EXPANSIVE
NIPPERKIN	POMOERIUM	SCHNORKEL	TEMPTRESS	WOLVERINE	COLOSSEUM	EXPENSIVE
NOCTURNAL	PONDEROSA	SCHNORRER	TENDERIZE	WONDERFUL	COMMISSAR	EXPLOSION
NOMOCRACY	PONDEROUS	SEAFARING	TENEBROSE	WOODCRAFT	COMPOSING	EXPLOSIVE
NONPAREIL	POPPERING	SEAWORTHY	TENTORIUM	WOOMERANG	COMPOSITE	EXPRESSED
OBSCURELY	PORPORATE	SECTARIAN	TERRARIUM	WUTHERING	COMPOSURE	EXPRESSLY
OBSCURITY	PORTERAGE	SECTORIAL	TERRORISM	YESTERDAY	CONCISELY	EXPULSION
OBSECRATE	POSTERIOR	SEMIBREVE	TERRORIST	YESTEREVE	CONCISION	EXQUISITE
OCTOBRIST	POSTERITY	SENIORITY	TERRORIZE	ZECHARIAH	CONCUSSED	EXTENSILE
OFFSPRING	PRECURSOR	SENSORIUM	TESTDRIVE	ZENOCRATE	CONFESSED	EXTENSION
OLEOGRAPH	PREFERRED	SEPHARDIM	TETRARCHY	ACCESSION	CONFESSOR	EXTENSIVE
OLIGARCHY	PRESCRIBE	SERIGRAPH	TETTEROUS	ACCESSORY	CONFUSING	EXTRUSION
ORATORIAN	PRESERVED	SHELDRAKE	THEOBROMA	ADDRESSED	CONFUSION	FANTASIZE
ORPHARION	PRESERVER	SHEWBREAD	THEOCRACY	ADDRESSEE	CONGESTED	FANTASTIC
OUTSPREAD	PRESERVES	SHIPWRECK	TIGHTROPE	ADMISSION	CONTUSION	FIELDSMAN
OUTTHRUST	PRESHRUNK	SHIVERING	TIMOCRACY	ADVERSARY	CORPOSANT	FILLISTER
OUTWARDLY	PRETERITE	SHOPFRONT	TIPPERARY	ADVERSELY	CORPUSCLE	FLOORSHOW
OUTWORKER	PRETERMIT	SIDETRACK	TOASTRACK	ADVERSITY	CORROSION	FLORESTAN
OVENPROOF	PREVERNAL	SIEGFRIED	TOPIARIST	AFORESAID	CORROSIVE	FLUORSPAR
OVERCROWD	PRIMARILY	SILVEREYE	TREETRUNK	AGGRESSOR	CORTISONE	FOOLISHLY
OVERDRAFT	PROCERITY	SINCERELY	TRICERION	AIMLESSLY	COURTSHIP	FORJASKIT
OVERDRAWN	PROKARYON	SINCERITY	TRIFORIUM	ALABASTER	CRACKSMAN	FORJESKIT
OVERDRESS	PROOFREAD	SISSERARY	TRITURATE	ALONGSIDE	CRAFTSMAN	FRICASSEE
OVERDRIVE	PROPERDIN	SNOWDRIFT	TROPARION	ALTISSIMO	CROISSANT	FROBISHER
OVERGROWN	PROSCRIBE	SOLDERING	TUILERIES	AMBROSIAL	CUPRESSUS	FROISSART
OVERPRINT	PROSTRATE	SOLFERINO	TUTIORISM	AMBROSIAN	CURIOSITY	GARNISHEE
OVERTRUMP	PULVERIZE	SOOTERKIN	UNCHARGED	AMPERSAND	DAMBUSTER	GEODESIST
OVIPAROUS	QUAVERING	SORCERESS	UNCORRECT	ANGUISHED	DECESSION	GLUCOSIDE
OZOCERITE	QUINTROON	SPELDRING	UNCOURTLY	ANIMISTIC	DECURSIVE	GODDESSES
OZOKERITE	QUIVERFUL	SPIDERWEB	UNDERRATE	ANIMOSITY	DECUSSATE	GOOSESTEP

GRANDSIRE	MOYGASHEL	PROTESTER	STATESIDE	WHOLESALE	AUGUSTINE	COMMITTEE
GRAPESHOT	NARCISSUS	PROTOSTAR	STATESMAN	WHOLESOME	AVOCATION	COMMOTION
GRAVESEND	NEBBISHER	PROVISION	STATISTIC	WILLESDEN	BACKSTAGE	COMMUTATE
GRAVESIDE	NECESSARY	PTEROSAUR	STEAMSHIP	WITNESSED	BANDSTAND	COMPETENT
GREENSAND	NECESSITY	PUBLISHED	STEERSMAN	WOLLASTON	BANISTERS	COMPETING
GROTESQUE	NEWCASTLE	PUBLISHER	STEGOSAUR	WORCESTER	BARBITONE	COMPOTIER
GUARDSMAN	NIETZSCHE	PURPOSELY	STRESSFUL	WORRISOME	BARBOTINE	COMPUTING
GYMNASIUM	NIGHTSPOT	QUICKSAND	STROSSERS	YACHTSMAN	BARNSTORM	CONDITION
GYMNASTIC	NIGROSINE	QUICKSTEP	STYLISHLY	YACHTSMEN	BASKETFUL	CONFITEOR
HADROSAUR	OBSESSION	REALISTIC	STYLISTIC	YOUNGSTER	BEATITUDE	CONNOTATE
HAMFISTED	OBSESSIVE	RECESSION	SUBFOSSIL	ZOROASTER	BECHSTEIN	CORNETIST
HARLESTON	OBTRUSION	RECESSIVE	SUCCESSOR	ABDUCTION	BEDSITTER	CORNSTALK
HARVESTER	OBTRUSIVE	RECURSIVE	SUFFUSION	ABOLITION	BEEFSTEAK	COSMETICS
HAVERSACK	OCCLUSION	REFRESHER	SUPERSEDE	ABOUTTURN	BERNSTEIN	COVERTURE
HEARDSMAN	ODALISQUE	REGISSEUR	SUPERSTAR	ACCENTUAL	BETROTHAL	CREMATION
HEAVISIDE	OFFENSIVE	REICHSRAT	SUPPOSING	ACCRETION	BETROTHED	CREMATORY
HERONSHAW	OMBUDSMAN	REICHSTAG	SWEETSHOP	ACOUSTICS	BIMONTHLY	CRENATION
HERPESTES	ONOMASTIC	REMISSION	SWORDSMAN	ACQUITTAL	BIPARTITE	CREPITATE
HEURISTIC	ONTHESPOT	REPOSSESS	SYMPOSIUM	ADDICTION	BISECTION	CROUSTADE
HOLINSHED	OPPRESSED	REPRESENT	TAYASSUID	ADDICTIVE	BLUESTONE	CURETTAGE
HORSESHOE	OPPRESSOR	REPRESSED	TEDIOSITY	ADJECTIVE	BOLECTION	CURVATURE
HYDROSTAT	ORCHESTRA	REPRESSOR	TEIRESIAS	ADMITTING	BONDSTONE	CYCLOTRON
ILCHESTER	ORGIASTIC	REPULSION	TENNESSEE	ADMIXTURE	BOOBYTRAP	DALMATIAN
IMMENSELY	OSTENSIVE	REPULSIVE	THALASSIC	ADORATION	BOOKSTALL	DAMNATION
IMMENSITY	OWNERSHIP	REQUISITE	THIRDSMAN	ADULATION	BOOKSTAND	DEATHTRAP
IMMERSION	PALAESTRA	RETORSION	THREESOME	ADVANTAGE	BOOKSTORE	DEBENTURE
IMPASSION	PALMISTRY	REVERSING	THROWSTER	ADVECTION	BRIMSTONE	DECASTYLE
IMPASSIVE	PARNASITE	REVERSION	THYRISTOR	ADVENTIST	BUCENTAUR	DECEITFUL
IMPRESSED	PARNASSUS	REVULSION	TOOTHSOME	ADVENTIVE	BUCKETFUL	DECEPTION
IMPULSION	PAYMASTER	RHODESIAN	TOWCESTER	ADVENTURE	BUDGETARY	DECEPTIVE
IMPULSIVE	PEEVISHLY	RHYMESTER	TRACKSUIT	ADVERTISE	BUFFETING	DECOCTION
INCESSANT	PEIRASTIC	RIVERSIDE	TRADESMAN	AFFECTING	BYZANTINE	DECONTROL
INCLUSION	PENINSULA	ROUGHSHOD	TRANSSHIP	AFFECTION	CADASTRAL	DECRETALS
INCLUSIVE	PENPUSHER	ROUNDSMAN	TRIBESMAN	AGITATION	CAKESTAND	DECRETORY
INCURSION	PENTOSANE	SACRISTAN	TRIBESMEN	ALBERTINE	CALENTURE	DEDUCTION
INSENSATE	PERTUSATE	SARCASTIC	TRICKSTER	ALLANTOID	CALVITIES	DEDUCTIVE
INTENSELY	PERTUSSIS	SAUCISSON	TRICUSPID	ALLANTOIS	CANDYTUFT	DEFEATISM
INTENSIFY	PERVASION	SCRIMSHAW	TRIMESTER	AMBROTYPE	CARNATION	DEFEATIST
INTENSITY	PERVASIVE	SECESSION	TROOPSHIP	AMIANTHUS	CARPETING	DEFECTION
INTENSIVE	PETERSHAM	SECLUSION	TROUSSEAU	AMPLITUDE	CASSATION	DEFECTIVE
INTERSECT	PHARISAIC	SELFISHLY	UNABASHED	ANCESTRAL	CAUSATION	DEFLATION
INTRUSION	PHILISTER	SEQUESTER	UNBIASSED	ANDANTINO	CAVORTING	DEJECTION
INTRUSIVE	PHOTOSTAT	SHARESMAN	UNCEASING	ANGOSTURA	CEANOTHUS	DENTITION
INVERSION	PLAINSMAN	SHARKSKIN	UNCROSSED	ANIMATION	CELESTIAL	DEPARTURE
JANISSARY	PLAINSONG	SHEEPSKIN	UNDERSEAL	ANOINTING	CERTITUDE	DEPASTURE
KERMESITE	POETASTER	SHELLSUIT	UNDERSELL	APERITIVE	CESSATION	DEPICTION
KLINOSTAT	POINTSMAN	SHORTSTAY	UNDERSIDE	APPERTAIN	CHIEFTAIN	DESERTION
LANCASTER	POLYESTER	SHORTSTOP	UNDERSIGN	APPORTION	CHINATOWN	DESPOTISM
LAVOISIER	POMPOSITY	SIGHTSEER	UNDERSONG	ARCHETYPE	CHINSTRAP	DESTITUTE
LEICESTER	POSSESSED	SINUOSITY	UNDRESSED	ARCHITECT	CHRISTIAN	DESUETUDE
LEPROSERY	POSSESSOR	SLAVISHLY	UPANISHAD	ARGENTINA	CHRISTMAS	DESULTORY
LIGHTSHIP	POTASSIUM	SLINGSHOT	UPHOLSTER	ARGENTINE	CLIENTELE	DETECTION
LIGHTSOME	PRANKSTER	SOLIPSISM	URANISCUS	ARMISTICE	COALITION	DETECTIVE
LIMOUSINE	PRECISELY	SOPHISTER	VALVASSOR	ARRESTING	COARCTATE	DETENTION
LOATHSOME	PRECISIAN	SOPHISTIC	VERBASCUM	ASCERTAIN	COCKATIEL	DETRITION
MADRASSAH	PRECISION	SOPHISTRY	VERBOSITY	ASPARTAME	COEMPTION	DEVASTATE
MADRESSAH	PRECISIVE	SOTTISIER	VESPASIAN	ASSERTING	COGNITION	DEVIATION
MAGNESIUM	PRELUSORY	SOUWESTER	VIPASSANA	ASSERTION	COGNITIVE	DIAMETRIC
MALAYSIAN	PROBOSCIS	SPACESHIP	VISCOSITY	ASSERTIVE	COLLATION	DIANETICS
MARCASITE	PROCESSOR	SPACESUIT	VOUCHSAFE	ASSISTANT	COLLOTYPE	DICHOTOMY
MEDRESSEH	PROFESSED	SPADASSIN	WAPINSHAW	ASSUETUDE	COLOSTOMY	DICTATION
MENUISIER	PROFESSOR	SPEARSIDE	WASPISHLY	ASTROTURF	COLOSTRUM	DIDACTICS
MIDRASHIM	PROFUSELY	SPOILSMAN	WATERSHED	ATHLETICS	COMBATANT	DIETETICS
MINNESOTA	PROFUSION	SPOKESMAN	WATERSIDE	ATTENTION	COMBATIVE	DIGASTRIC
MNEMOSYNE	PROLUSION	SPORTSMAN	WEARISOME	ATTENTIVE	COMINTERN	DIGESTION
MOCCASINS	PROMISING	SPORTSMEN	WEDNESDAY	ATTRITION	COMMITTAL	DIGESTIVE
MONTESPAN	PROMUSCIS	SPRITSAIL	WENCESLAS	ATTUITION	COMMITTED	DIGNITARY

DIRECTION	FARMSTEAD	HARMOTOME	ISOMETRIC	MOLLITIES	PENISTONE	RECAPTURE
DIRECTIVE	FEEDSTUFF	HAUGHTILY	ITERATION	MOMENTARY	PERDITION	RECEPTION
DIRECTORS	FERROTYPE	HEADSTALL	JACKSTRAW	MOMENTOUS	PERISTOME	RECEPTIVE
DIRECTORY	FEUDATORY	HEADSTONE	JAWBATION	MONACTINE	PERISTYLE	RECTITUDE
DISENTOMB	FILMSTRIP	HEMIPTERA	JENNETING	MONASTERY	PERMITTED	REDLETTER
DISPUTANT	FIORITURA	HEMISTICH	JOCKSTRAP	MONASTRAL	PERPETUAL	REDUCTION
DIVERTING	FIRESTONE	HERMITAGE	JUNKETING	MONOSTICH	PETTITOES	REFECTION
DOGMATISM	FLAGITATE	HEXASTICH	KARYOTYPE	MOONSTONE	PHENYTOIN	REFECTORY
DOGMATIZE	FLAGSTAFF	HOARSTONE	KERBSTONE	MORTSTONE	PHILATELY	REFLATION
DORMITION	FLAGSTONE	HOLYSTONE	KNOBSTICK	MOUSETRAP	PHONETICS	REGISTRAR
DORMITORY	FLAMSTEED	HOMESTEAD	KROPOTKIN	MUFFETTEE	PHOTOTUBE	REGRETFUL
DOWNSTAGE	FLEXITIME	HOMOPTERA	LACTATION	MULTITUDE	PHYTOTRON	REINSTATE
DRAMATICS	FLOTATION	HONKYTONK	LAMARTINE	MUSKETEER	PICKETING	REJECTION
DRAMATIST	FLOWSTONE	HORNSTONE	LANDSTURM	MUSKETOON	PIKESTAFF	RELUCTANT
DRAMATIZE	FOLKETING	HORSETAIL	LARGITION	MUSSITATE	PILASTERS	REMONTANT
DRIPSTONE	FOODSTORE	HORTATIVE	LASSITUDE	NARRATION	PIPESTONE	RENDITION
DRUGSTORE	FOODSTUFF	HORTATORY	LATRATION	NARRATIVE	PITUITARY	REPENTANT
DRUMSTICK	FOOTSTALL	HOSPITIUM	LAUDATION	NAUGHTILY	PITUITRIN	REPERTORY
DYSENTERY	FOOTSTOOL	HOURSTONE	LAUDATORY	NEFERTITI	PLACATORY	REPLETION
ECCENTRIC	FORESTAGE	HYPNOTISM	LEAFSTALK	NEGRITUDE	PLAINTIFF	REPLETIVE
EDDYSTONE	FORESTALL	HYPNOTIST	LEUCOTOME	NEOLITHIC	PLAINTIVE	REPORTAGE
EDUCATION	FORESTERS	HYPNOTIZE	LEVANTINE	NEWSSTALL	PLANETARY	REPORTING
EDUCATIVE	FORGATHER	ILLGOTTEN	LEVIATHAN	NEWSSTAND	PLATITUDE	REPTATION
EFFECTIVE	FORGETFUL	IMITATION	LIBERTIES	NICTITATE	PLAUSTRAL	RESENTFUL
EFFECTUAL	FORGETIVE	IMITATIVE	LIBERTINE	NIGHTTIME	PLENITUDE	RESISTANT
EGLANTINE	FORGOTTEN	IMMORTALS	LIFESTYLE	NIGRITUDE	POCKETFUL	RESNATRON
ELEVATION	FORMATION	IMPACTION	LIMESTONE	NONENTITY	POLLUTANT	RESORTING
ELOCUTION	FORMATIVE	IMPARTIAL	LINTSTOCK	NORMATIVE	POLLUTION	RESTITUTE
EMANATION	FORSYTHIA	IMPORTANT	LIPPITUDE	NUTRITION	POPLITEAL	RESULTANT
EMBATTLED	FORTITUDE	IMPORTUNE	LIVESTOCK	NUTRITIVE	POTENTATE	RESULTING
EMULATION	FREESTONE	IMPOSTURE	LOADSTONE	OBJECTIFY	POTENTIAL	RETENTION
ENCANTHIS	FREESTYLE	INANITION	LODESTONE	OBJECTION	PRECATORY	RETENTIVE
ENCRATITE	FRIGATOON	INCAUTION	LOGISTICS	OBJECTIVE	PREDATORY	RETORTION
ENRAPTURE	FRIGHTFUL	INCENTIVE	LONGITUDE	OBREPTION	PREFATORY	REVICTUAL
ENSTATITE	FURNITURE	INCEPTION	LUCRATIVE	OBSTETRIC	PREMATURE	REVOLTING
ENTERTAIN	GALACTOSE	INCEPTIVE	LUCRETIUS	OBVENTION	PREMOTION	RILLETTES
EPILATION	GALANTINE	INDENTURE	LUCTATION	OCCULTIST	PRIESTESS	ROADSTEAD
EPULATION	GALLSTONE	INDICTION	LUNCHTIME	OCTASTICH	PRIESTLEY	ROBERTSON
ERUDITION	GARNITURE	INDUCTION	MACARTHUR	ODELSTING	PRIMITIAE	ROOTSTOCK
ESSENTIAL	GAZETTEER	INDUCTIVE	MACTATION	OFFERTORY	PRIMITIVE	RUINATION
ESTHETICS	GEARSTICK	INFANTILE	MAELSTROM	OLFACTORY	PRIVATEER	RUNESTAVE
EURHYTHMY	GEOMETRIC	INFECTING	MAGNETISM	OPERATING	PRIVATELY	SABBATIAN
EVAGATION	GEOMETRID	INFECTION	MAGNETIZE	OPERATION	PRIVATION	SAGITTARY
EVOCATION	GERIATRIC	INFERTILE	MAGNETRON	OPERATIVE	PRIVATIZE	SALVATION
EVOCATIVE	GESTATION	INFLATION	MAGNITUDE	OPPORTUNE	PROACTIVE	SANDSTONE
EVOCATORY	GIGANTISM	INGESTION	MANDATARY	ORIENTATE	PROBATION	SANDSTORM
EVOLUTION	GLADSTONE	INJECTION	MANDATORY	ORTHOTONE	PROFITEER	SASKATOON
EXARATION	GODFATHER	INJUSTICE	MANGETOUT	OUTFITTER	PROMOTION	SATIATION
EXCEPTION	GODMOTHER	INSERTION	MANHATTAN	OUTOFTOWN	PROMPTING	SCHMUTTER
EXECUTANT	GONIATITE	INSISTENT	MARKETEER	OVERSTATE	PROTOTYPE	SCHNITTKE
EXECUTION	GRADATION	INSTITUTE	MARKETING	OVERSTEER	PROUSTITE	SCHNITZEL
EXECUTIVE	GRAPETREE	INSULTING	MAULSTICK	OVULATION	PULPITEER	SCIENTISM
EXECUTRIX	GRATITUDE	INTENTION	MAURITIAN	OXIDATION	PULSATION	SCIENTIST
EXEMPTION	GRAVITATE	INTESTATE	MAURITIUS	PAKISTANI	PUPPETEER	SCREWTAPE
EXORATION	GUNCOTTON	INTESTINE	MEDIATION	PALESTINE	PURGATIVE	SCRIPTURE
EXPECTANT	GUSTATION	INTUITION	MENTATION	PALMATION	PURGATORY	SCULPTING
EXPECTING	HAEMATITE	INTUITIVE	MESENTERY	PALMITATE	QUOTATION	SCULPTURE
EXPERTISE	HAILSTONE	INUNCTION	MEZZOTINT	PALPATION	QUOTITION	SEABOTTLE
EXPIATION	HAILSTORM	INUSITATE	MICROTOME	PALPITATE	RACKETEER	SEBASTIAN
EXPIATORY	HAIRSTYLE	INVECTIVE	MICROTONE	PANDATION	RACKSTRAW	SECRETARY
EXPLETIVE	HALFSTAFF	INVENTION	MIGRATION	PANETTONE	RACONTEUR	SECRETION
EXPORTING	HALLSTATT	INVENTIVE	MIGRATORY	PARENTAGE	RADIATING	SECRETIVE
EXTORTION	HAMFATTER	INVENTORY	MILESTONE	PARENTING	RADIATION	SEDENTARY
EXUDATION	HAMPSTEAD	INVERTASE	MILLSTONE	PARTITION	RAINSTORM	SEDUCTION
EYELETEER	HANDSTAND	IRONSTONE	MINIATURE	PEACETIME	RASPATORY	SEDUCTIVE
FAIRYTALE	HARESTANE	IRRUPTION	MINKSTONE	PEGMATITE	REALITIES	SELECTING
FALDSTOOL	HARMATTAN	ISOLATION	MODESTINE	PELLITORY	REBOATION	SELECTION

SELECTIVE	THIRSTING	AMBIGUOUS	HOPEFULLY	SIDEBURNS	FESTIVITY	BRIDEWELL
SELLOTAPE	THRIFTILY	AMOROUSLY	HYDRAULIC	SKILFULLY	FORGIVING	BRUSHWOOD
SEMANTEME	THROATILY	ANNAPURNA	ICHNEUMON	SOULFULLY	FURTIVELY	BURROWING
SEMANTICS	THUMBTACK	ANTIQUARY	IMPETUOUS	SPUNCULID	GALLIVANT	CASSOWARY
SEMANTIDE	THYESTEAN	ANTIQUITY	INAUGURAL	STRENUOUS	GALRAVAGE	CATCHWORD
SEMANTRON	THYRATRON	ANXIOUSLY	INDRAUGHT	SULPHURIC	GRAPEVINE	CATERWAUL
SEMIOTICS	TITRATION	ARDUOUSLY	INFATUATE	SUMPTUARY	GUINEVERE	CEDARWOOD
SENSATION	TOADSTONE	ARTICULAR	INGENUITY	SUMPTUOUS	HERBIVORE	CHICKWEED
SENSITIVE	TOADSTOOL	ASSIDUITY	INGENUOUS	SWINBURNE	IMPLUVIUM	CLEARWING
SENSITIZE	TOCCATINA	ASSIDUOUS	INNOCUOUS	TABBOULEH	IMPROVING	CLOCKWISE
SEPULTURE	TOMBSTONE	ATTENUATE	INSINUATE	TACTFULLY	IMPROVISE	CLOCKWORK
SERIATION	TOMENTOSE	ATTITUDES	INSOLUBLE	TARPAULIN	INSOLVENT	COCKSWAIN
SERRATION	TRADITION	AURICULAR	INVOLUCRE	TEARFULLY	INTERVENE	COCUSWOOD
SERVITUDE	TREGETOUR	AVUNCULAR	IRREGULAR	TEDIOUSLY	INTERVIEW	CROSSWALK
SEVENTEEN	TREMATODE	BALEFULLY	JEALOUSLY	TENACULUM	INTROVERT	CROSSWIND
SHENSTONE	TRIBUTARY	BASHFULLY	KLENDUSIC	TENUOUSLY	LEFTOVERS	CROSSWISE
SHORTTERM	TRILITHON	BILIRUBIN	LANDAULET	THEREUPON	LONGEVITY	CROSSWORD
SICCATIVE	TRIPITAKA	BINOCULAR	LANGOUSTE	THESAURUS	MASSIVELY	DRIFTWOOD
SIGNATORY	TROOSTITE	BODYGUARD	LIFEGUARD	THINGUMMY	MICROVOLT	EAGLEWOOD
SIGNATURE	TUNGSTATE	BRATWURST	MANGOUSTE	TOTAQUINE	MILLIVOLT	EARTHWORK
SILTSTONE	TUNGSTOUS	BRUSQUELY	MANOEUVRE	TREASURER	MISGIVING	EARTHWORM
SITUATION	TURNSTILE	BURROUGHS	MARIJUANA	TURNBULLS	MUSCOVADO	FIELDWORK
SLABSTONE	TURNSTONE	CALLOUSLY	MELBOURNE	UNCLOUDED	MUSCOVITE	FLEETWOOD
SLAPSTICK	TURPITUDE	CAPITULAR	MOLECULAR	UNDILUTED	OBSERVANT	FOLLOWING
SLIGHTEST	UMBRATILE	CAPITULUM	MONOCULAR	UNINJURED	PASSIVELY	FORTHWINK
SMALLTIME	UNCERTAIN	CAREFULLY	NERVOUSLY	UNNATURAL	PASSIVITY	FORTHWITH
SNOWSTORM	UNCLOTHED	CARTOUCHE	OBLIQUELY	UNPOPULAR	PENSIVELY	FRAMEWORK
SOAPSTONE	UNDERTAKE	CASSOULET	OBSEQUIES	UNSECURED	PERSEVERE	GLASSWARE
SONNETEER	UNDERTONE	CENTAURUS	OBVIOUSLY	VANCOUVER	PIACEVOLE	GLASSWORT
SPIRITISM	UNEARTHLY	COADJUTOR	OMINOUSLY	VARIOUSLY	PRIMAVERA	GOBETWEEN
SPIRITOUS	UNFITTING	CONCLUDED	ONSLAUGHT	VEHICULAR	RECEIVING	GREENWEED
SPIRITUAL	UNSCATHED	CONCOURSE	OPERCULUM	VENEZUELA	RECONVENE	GREENWICH
SPLINTERS	UNSETTLED	CONGRUENT	ORBICULAR	VESICULAR	REPROVING	GREENWOOD
SPLITTING	UNWITTING	CONGRUOUS	PAINFULLY	VICIOUSLY	RESERVIST	GUESSWORK
SQUATTERS	UNWRITTEN	COPIOUSLY	PALINURUS	WELLBUILT	RESERVOIR	GUNPOWDER
SQUINTING	UPLIFTING	CURIOUSLY	PANTOUFLE	WHEREUPON	RETROVERT	HALLOWEEN
STARSTONE	UPSETTING	DECIDUOUS	PARACUSIS	WILLFULLY	REVOLVING	HALLOWMAS
STATUTORY	URINATION	DEVIOUSLY	PEDICULAR	WISTFULLY	ROOSEVELT	HANDIWORK
STREETAGE	VALENTINE	DIAZEUXIS	PERICUTIN	ACCLIVITY	SCHIAVONE	HARROWING
STREETCAR	VALUATION	DISCOURSE	PIPSQUEAK	AGGRAVATE	SLIVOVICA	HAZELWORT
STRIATION	VARIATION	DOLEFULLY	PITIFULLY	APPROVING	SLIVOVITZ	HEARTWOOD
STRICTURE	VASECTOMY	DUBIOUSLY	PLAYFULLY	ARCHIVIST	SUBDIVIDE	HOLLYWOOD
STRONTIUM	VELVETEEN	DUTIFULLY	POTPOURRI	ARCHIVOLT	SUPERVENE	HOMEOWNER
STRUCTURE	VERNATION	EDINBURGH	PRESCUTUM	BELIEVING	SUPERVISE	HORSEWHIP
STRUTTING	VERSATILE	ELECTUARY	PRONOUNCE	BOULEVARD	SURVIVING	HOUSEWIFE
SUBALTERN	VESTITURE	ENAMOURED	PUNCTUATE	CAPTIVATE	TRANSVAAL	HOUSEWORK
SUBENTIRE	VIBRATILE	ENERGUMEN	QUADRUPED	CAPTIVITY	TSAREVICH	HOWTOWDIE
SUBTITLED	VIBRATION	EVENTUATE	QUADRUPLE	CARNIVORE	UNNERVING	INGROWING
SUCCOTASH	VIBRATORY	EXTENUATE	QUINQUINA	CHARIVARI	UVAROVITE	KITTIWAKE
SUMMATION	VIDEOTAPE	FAMAGUSTA	QUINTUPLE	CHINOVNIK	VITRUVIAN	LAMBSWOOL
SUNBATHER	VIOLATION	FATUOUSLY	RAUCOUSLY	CONCAVITY	ADDERWORT	LANCEWOOD
SUSCITATE	VITIATION	FEARFULLY	REARGUARD	CONVIVIAL	AFTERWORD	LANDOWNER
SYMMETRIC	VOLUNTARY	FIREGUARD	REIMBURSE	CRACOVIAN	BACKSWORD	LASERWORT
TABLATURE	VOLUNTEER	FISHGUARD	RELIQUARY	CULTIVATE	BEACHWEAR	LEASTWAYS
TALKATIVE	WAFERTHIN	FLAVOURED	RELIQUIAE	DECEMVIRI	BILLOWING	LEASTWISE
TARANTASS	WAPENTAKE	FLUCTUATE	RESIDUARY	DECLIVITY	BIRTHWORT	LIVERWORT
TARANTULA	WASHSTAND	FRETFULLY	RETICULAR	DEPRAVITY	BLACKWOOD	LOUSEWORT
TARGETEER	WEIGHTING	FUNICULAR	RETICULUM	DESERVING	BLINDWORM	LYMESWOLD
TARNATION	WELDSTADT	FUNICULUS	RIOTOUSLY	DISCOVERT	BLOATWARE	MARROWFAT
TAVISTOCK	WHETSTONE	FURIOUSLY	RUINOUSLY	DISCOVERY	BLOODWORM	MATCHWOOD
TEAKETTLE	WHINSTONE	GAINFULLY	SAFEGUARD	DISFAVOUR	BOARDWALK	MERESWINE
TELESTICH	WHUNSTANE	GLANDULAR	SANCTUARY	DUBROVNIK	BOATSWAIN	METALWORK
TENTATIVE	WITHSTAND	GLEEFULLY	SANDHURST	EFFLUVIUM	BORROWING	MICROWATT
TERRITORY	WURLITZER	HABITUATE	SCHNAUZER	ENDEAVOUR	BRAINWASH	MICROWAVE
TESTATRIX	XEROSTOMA	HANDCUFFS	SCORBUTIC	ENGRAVING	BRAINWAVE	MILLIWATT
THANATISM	YARDSTICK	HELPFULLY	SCORBUTUS	EVASIVELY	BRASSWARE	MONEYWORT
THIRSTILY	AMBIGUITY	HIDEOUSLY	SERIOUSLY	EXTROVERT	BRICKWORK	MOUTHWASH

NARROWING	METHOXIDE	TRAPEZIUM	AUXILIARY	CARBONADE	CORPORATE	DIXIELAND
NEWLYWEDS	OVEREXERT	TRAPEZIUS	BACHARACH	CARBONADO	CORPOSANT	DOCTORATE
NIGHTWORK	PROLIXITY	TRAPEZOID	BACKBOARD	CARBONARI	CORRELATE	DOORFRAME
NORTHWARD	REFLEXION	TREBIZOND	BACKSPACE	CARBONATE	CORRUGATE	DOWNGRADE
NORTHWEST	REFLEXIVE	**9:7**	BACKSTAGE	CARDBOARD	CORUSCATE	DOWNSTAGE
OTHERWISE	THYROXINE	ABOMINATE	BACKTRACK	CARTILAGE	COSMONAUT	DREAMLAND
PAINTWORK	UNISEXUAL	ABOUTFACE	BALACLAVA	CARTTRACK	COURTYARD	DROMEDARY
PAPERWORK	AESCHYLUS	ACCLIMATE	BANDSTAND	CARTULARY	COVERDALE	DUCKBOARD
PATCHWORK	ANAGLYPTA	ACCOMPANY	BARMBRACK	CASSONADE	CRASHLAND	DUNDREARY
PAULOWNIA	APOCRYPHA	ACCORDANT	BARRICADE	CASSOWARY	CREPITATE	DUNSINANE
PEARLWORT	APOPHYSIS	ACIDULATE	BASEBOARD	CASTIGATE	CRIMINATE	DUPLICAND
PEASEWEEP	AUTOLYCUS	ACUMINATE	BASTINADE	CATAPLASM	CROISSANT	DUPLICATE
PENNYWORK	AUTOLYSIS	ADUMBRATE	BASTINADO	CATERWAUL	CROOKBACK	EBRILLADE
PIECEWORK	BRICKYARD	ADVANTAGE	BATTLEAXE	CAVALCADE	CROSSWALK	ECTOPLASM
PIEPOWDER	CATALYSIS	ADVERSARY	BEANFEAST	CELEBRANT	CROUSTADE	EIDOGRAPH
POKERWORK	CATALYTIC	AEROPLANE	BENCHMARK	CELEBRATE	CUCHULAIN	EJACULATE
QUILLWORT	CHLAMYDES	AEROSPACE	BERGAMASK	CENTENARY	CULMINATE	ELABORATE
RIGHTWING	CLEPSYDRA	AFFILIATE	BERGOMASK	CEREBRATE	CULTIVATE	ELECTUARY
SATINWOOD	CLERGYMAN	AFFRICATE	BICONCAVE	CHAMFRAIN	CURETTAGE	ELIMINATE
SHIFTWORK	COLOCYNTH	AFORESAID	BIFURCATE	CHAMINADE	CURTILAGE	ELUCIDATE
SHIPOWNER	COURTYARD	AFRIKAANS	BILLBOARD	CHAMPLAIN	CURVEBALL	ELUTRIATE
SIDESWIPE	DIAPHYSIS	AFTERCARE	BIRDBRAIN	CHARABANC	CUSTOMARY	EMBARRASS
SLANTWISE	EMPHLYSIS	AFTERDAMP	BIRTHMARK	CHARIVARI	CYCLAMATE	EMBASSADE
SLEEPWALK	EMPLOYEES	AFTERMATH	BIRTHRATE	CHAROLAIS	CYCLORAMA	EMBASSAGE
SNAKEWEED	EPIPHYSIS	AGGRAVATE	BLACKBALL	CHEAPJACK	DAIRYMAID	EMBROCATE
SNEERWELL	EPIPHYTIC	AGGREGATE	BLACKDAMP	CHECKMATE	DARTBOARD	EMMERDALE
SORROWFUL	GINGLYMUS	ALGEBRAIC	BLACKFACE	CHIEFTAIN	DASHBOARD	EMOLLIATE
SOUTHWARD	GRAVEYARD	ALLEGIANT	BLACKJACK	CHILBLAIN	DEAMINATE	EMPENNAGE
SOUTHWARK	GREENYARD	ALLEVIATE	BLACKMAIL	CHILDCARE	DECKCHAIR	ENCHILADA
SOUTHWEST	KILOCYCLE	ALLOGRAFT	BLOATWARE	CHIPBOARD	DECOLLATE	ENCOMPASS
SPEARWORT	LACHRYMAL	ALLOGRAPH	BLOODBATH	CHIPOLATA	DECRETALS	ENCOURAGE
SPEEDWELL	LIVERYMAN	ALTERCATE	BLUEBEARD	CHOCOLATE	DECUSSATE	ENGARLAND
STATEWIDE	MEGACYCLE	ALTERNATE	BOARDWALK	CHURIDARS	DEFALCATE	ENGRENAGE
STINKWOOD	MONOXYLON	ALTIPLANO	BOATSWAIN	CILIOLATE	DEFENDANT	ENNERDALE
STOCKWORK	OCCUPYING	ALVEOLATE	BODYGUARD	CIRCINATE	DEFOLIANT	ENTERTAIN
STONEWALL	OVERLYING	AMBUSCADE	BOLIVIANO	CIRCULATE	DEFOLIATE	ENTOURAGE
STONEWARE	PANEGYRIC	AMERICANO	BOOKSTALL	CLAPBOARD	DEHYDRATE	ENUCLEATE
STONEWARE	PARALYSIS	AMPERSAND	BOOKSTAND	CLASSMATE	DELINEATE	ENUMERATE
STONEWORT	PARALYTIC	ANCHORAGE	BOOMERANG	CLEVELAND	DEMARCATE	ENUNCIATE
STUMPWORK	PARANYMPH	ANCILLARY	BOOTBLACK	CLIPBOARD	DEMOCRACY	EPARCHATE
SUNDOWNER	PRESBYTER	ANISOGAMY	BORNAGAIN	COAGULANT	DEMURRAGE	EPHESIANS
TABLEWARE	PURIFYING	ANTIQUARY	BOULEVARD	COAGULATE	DENIGRATE	EPIPHRAGM
TOUCHWOOD	PYONGYANG	APPENDAGE	BRAINCASE	COARCTATE	DEODORANT	ERADICATE
TRADEWIND	SANTAYANA	APPERTAIN	BRAINWASH	COCKROACH	DEPENDANT	EROSTRATE
TULIPWOOD	SCALLYWAG	APPLEJACK	BRAINWAVE	COCKSWAIN	DEPRECATE	ESEMPLASY
UNCROWNED	STEELYARD	APPLICANT	BRASSWARE	COGNIZANT	DEPREDATE	ESPIONAGE
UNDERWALK	STOCKYARD	AQUAPLANE	BREAKFAST	COLLIGATE	DESECRATE	ESPLANADE
UNDERWEAR	SURVEYING	ARBITRAGE	BRICKYARD	COLLIMATE	DESICCATE	ESTRAPADE
UNDERWENT	SYMPHYSIS	ARBITRARY	BRIEFCASE	COLLOCATE	DESIGNATE	ETHANOATE
UNDERWOOD	SYNCHYSIS	ARBITRATE	BRILLIANT	COLONNADE	DESPERADO	EVAPORATE
UNKNOWING	UNVARYING	ARCHIBALD	BROADCAST	COLUMBARY	DESPERATE	EVENTUATE
WALLOWING	WHERRYMAN	ARCTOGAEA	BROKERAGE	COLUMBATE	DEVASTATE	EVERGLADE
WATCHWORD	AGONIZING	ASCENDANT	BROMINATE	COMBATANT	DIAPHRAGM	EXANIMATE
WATERWEED	APOENZYME	ASCERTAIN	BUCENTAUR	COMMUTATE	DIGNITARY	EXCORIATE
WEDGEWOOD	CHABAZITE	ASHKENAZI	BUDGETARY	COMPLIANT	DIPLOMACY	EXCULPATE
WHIRLWIND	CHALAZION	ASPARTAME	BURKINABE	CONFIDANT	DISEMBARK	EXECUTANT
WHITEWALL	COGNIZANT	ASSAILANT	CAGOULARD	CONJUGATE	DISENGAGE	EXEMPLARY
WHITEWASH	EMBEZZLER	ASSISTANT	CAKESTAND	CONNOTATE	DISLOCATE	EXONERATE
WHITEWING	HAPHAZARD	ASSOCIATE	CALCINATE	CONSONANT	DISPARAGE	EXPATIATE
WHITEWOOD	HYDRAZINE	ASTRAGALS	CALCULATE	CONSULATE	DISPARATE	EXPECTANT
WILLOWING	MONTEZUMA	ASTROLABE	CALIBRATE	CONTUMACY	DISPLEASE	EXPISCATE
WINDSWEPT	ORGANZINE	ASTRONAUT	CANDIDACY	COOPERATE	DISPUTANT	EXPLICATE
WITHYWIND	PROENZYME	ATTENDANT	CANDIDATE	CORMORANT	DISREGARD	EXPURGATE
WORLDWIDE	SCHNOZZLE	ATTENUATE	CANNONADE	CORNBRASH	DISREPAIR	EXSICCATE
YELLOWISH	SHEMOZZLE	AUTOCLAVE	CAPILLARY	CORNCRAKE	DISSIPATE	EXTENUATE
CONNEXION	TRAPEZIAL	AUTOCRACY	CAPTIVATE	CORNSTALK	DISSONANT	EXTIRPATE
INFLEXION	TRAPEZIST	AUTOGRAPH	CARBAMATE	COROLLARY	DITHYRAMB	EXTRICATE

EXUBERANT	GLASSWARE	IDIOBLAST	LACKBEARD	MOTORCADE	PASTORALE	RATIONALE
EYESTRAIN	GLOMERATE	IDIOGRAPH	LAMPADARY	MOUTHWASH	PASTURAGE	READYEARN
FABRICATE	GRAMPIANS	IDIOPLASM	LAMPBLACK	MUSCOVADO	PATHTRAIN	READYMADE
FAIRYLAND	GRANULATE	IMAGINARY	LAMPSHADE	MUSICHALL	PATRONAGE	REANIMATE
FAIRYTALE	GRASSLAND	IMBRICATE	LANCINATE	MUSSITATE	PECUNIARY	REARGUARD
FASCINATE	GRAVEYARD	IMBROCATE	LANDGRAVE	NAMEPLATE	PENDULATE	REDBREAST
FASTTRACK	GRAVITATE	IMMEDIACY	LANDSCAPE	NECESSARY	PENETRATE	REDUNDANT
FEDUCIARY	GREENBACK	IMMEDIATE	LANDSMAAL	NEGOTIATE	PENTOSANE	REGARDANT
FERDINAND	GREENGAGE	IMMELMANN	LATICLAVE	NEWSFLASH	PERCOLATE	REINSTATE
FESTINATE	GREENMAIL	IMMIGRANT	LEAFSTALK	NEWSSTALL	PERFORANS	REITERATE
FEUILLANT	GREENSAND	IMMIGRATE	LEASEBACK	NEWSSTAND	PERFORATE	RELIQUARY
FIDUCIARY	GREENYARD	IMMORTALS	LEASTWAYS	NICTITATE	PERICLASE	RELUCTANT
FIELDFARE	GREYBEARD	IMPLICATE	LEGENDARY	NIGHTFALL	PERIODATE	REMONTANT
FILIGRAIN	GROSGRAIN	IMPORTANT	LEGIONARY	NIGHTHAWK	PERSONAGE	REMOULADE
FIREBRAND	GUARDRAIL	IMPRECATE	LEGISLATE	NIGHTMARE	PERSONATE	REPECHAGE
FIREDRAKE	GUATEMALA	INAMORATA	LIFEGUARD	NITHSDALE	PERTUSATE	REPENTANT
FIREGUARD	GUILDHALL	INAMORATO	LIGHTFACE	NOMOCRACY	PETILLANT	REPLICANT
FIREPLACE	GYROPLANE	INANIMATE	LINEOLATE	NORMALACY	PHARISAIC	REPLICATE
FIRSTHAND	HABITUATE	INCARNATE	LIONHEART	NORTHEAST	PHONECARD	REPORTAGE
FIRSTRATE	HADROSAUR	INCESSANT	LIQUIDATE	NORTHWARD	PHOSPHATE	REPRIMAND
FISHGUARD	HALFSTAFF	INCULCATE	LJUBLJANA	NOTCHBACK	PHTHALATE	REPROBATE
FISHPLATE	HALLSTATT	INCULPATE	LOCELLATE	NOVICIATE	PICKABACK	REPUDIATE
FLAGITATE	HALOTHANE	INDIGNANT	LONGCHAMP	NOVITIATE	PICKTHANK	REPUGNANT
FLAGSTAFF	HAMMURABI	INEBRIATE	LOUISIANA	NUNCUPATE	PIERGLASS	RESIDUARY
FLASHBACK	HANDBRAKE	INELEGANT	LUBRICANT	NURSEMAID	PIGGYBACK	RESISTANT
FLOODGATE	HANDSHAKE	INFATUATE	LUBRICATE	OBBLIGATO	PIGGYBANK	RESULTANT
FLOWCHART	HANDSTAND	INFIRMARY	LUCUBRATE	OBCORDATE	PIGNERATE	RESURFACE
FLUCTUATE	HAPHAZARD	INFORMANT	LUXURIANT	OBFUSCATE	PIKESTAFF	RETALIATE
FOLKWEAVE	HARDBOARD	INFURIATE	LUXURIATE	OBJURGATE	PILFERAGE	RICERCARE
FOMALHAUT	HARESTANE	INNISFAIL	MACDONALD	OBSECRATE	PITUITARY	RIDGEBACK
FOOTBRAKE	HARIOLATE	INOCULATE	MACHINATE	OBSERVANT	PIZZICATO	RIGHTHAND
FOOTPLATE	HARROGATE	INOPINATE	MADARIAGA	OBSTINACY	PLANETARY	RORSCHACH
FOOTSTALL	HATCHBACK	INQUINATE	MAINFRAME	OBSTINATE	POLLINATE	ROTAPLANE
FOREBEARS	HAVERSACK	INQUORATE	MALIGNANT	OFFENBACH	POLLUTANT	ROTUNDATE
FOREBRAIN	HEADBOARD	INSENSATE	MANDATARY	OFFICIALS	POLYGRAPH	ROUGHCAST
FORESTAGE	HEADSCARF	INSINUATE	MANDICATE	OFFICIANT	POLYPHASE	ROUNDBACK
FORESTALL	HEADSTALL	INSTIGATE	MANDUCATE	OFFICIATE	PORCELAIN	ROUNDHAND
FORFICATE	HEARTLAND	INTEGRATE	MANGANATE	OLEOGRAPH	PORPORATE	RUGGELACH
FORMULATE	HEATHLAND	INTENDANT	MARCHPANE	OPENHEART	PORTERAGE	RUNCINATE
FORNICATE	HEDYPHANE	INTERFACE	MARIJUANA	ORANGEADE	PORTULACA	RUNESTAVE
FORTILAGE	HERMITAGE	INTERLACE	MARMALADE	ORIENTATE	POSTULANT	RUSTICATE
FORTUNATE	HESYCHASM	INTERLARD	MARSHLAND	ORIGINATE	POSTULATE	SAFEGUARD
FRAGONARD	HESYCHAST	INTESTATE	MASTICATE	ORPHANAGE	POTENTATE	SAGITTARY
FRANGLAIS	HIBERNATE	INTRICACY	MAXILLARY	OSCILLATE	PREDICANT	SALANGANE
FREEBOARD	HIGHCLASS	INTRICATE	MELIORATE	OSTEOPATH	PREDICATE	SALESLADY
FRIESLAND	HINDBRAIN	INUMBRATE	MELODRAMA	OVERBOARD	PREDIKANT	SANCTUARY
FROGSPAWN	HIPPODAME	INUSITATE	MENDICANT	OVERDRAFT	PREORDAIN	SANDARACH
FROISSART	HODOGRAPH	INVERTASE	MERCENARY	OVERDRAWN	PRESSGANG	SANTAYANA
FRUITCAKE	HOLOGRAPH	INVIOLATE	MESOBLAST	OVERHEADS	PRIMIPARA	SARBACANE
FRUSTRATE	HOMEOPATH	IRRADIANT	METAPHASE	OVERREACH	PROCREATE	SASSENACH
FULLSCALE	HOMOGRAFT	IRRADIATE	METRICATE	OVERREACT	PROMENADE	SAVERNAKE
FULMINANT	HOMOGRAPH	ISINGLASS	METROLAND	OVERSHADE	PROPAGATE	SAXIFRAGE
FULMINATE	HORSEBACK	ISOMERASE	MICROWATT	OVERSTATE	PROROGATE	SCELERATE
FUSILLADE	HORSEHAIR	ITINERANT	MICROWAVE	OWLEGLASS	PROSTRATE	SCHOLIAST
FUSTIGATE	HORSETAIL	ITINERARY	MILKSHAKE	OXYGENATE	PROXIMATE	SCREWBALL
GABIONADE	HOURGLASS	ITINERATE	MILLAMANT	PAKISTANI	PTEROSAUR	SCREWTAPE
GALATIANS	HOUSEMAID	JAGGANATH	MILLIWATT	PALMITATE	PUCELLAGE	SCRIMMAGE
GALENGALE	HUCKABACK	JAMBALAYA	MISBEHAVE	PALPITATE	PULLULATE	SCRUMMAGE
GALINGALE	HUMANMADE	JANISSARY	MISCREANT	PALSGRAVE	PULMONARY	SECONDARY
GALLIVANT	HUMILIATE	JEPHTHAHS	MISLOCATE	PANDURATE	PULMONATE	SECRETARY
GALLOPADE	HUNCHBACK	JESSERANT	MISMANAGE	PANTAGAMY	PUNCTUATE	SEDENTARY
GALRAVAGE	HURRICANE	JUDICIARY	MOBOCRACY	PAPERBACK	PUPILLAGE	SEGREGATE
GANGPLANK	HURRICANO	KHALIFATE	MOLLYMAWK	PARABLAST	PUSHCHAIR	SELLOTAPE
GASCONADE	HYPALLAGE	KICKSHAWS	MOMENTARY	PARAGRAPH	PYONGYANG	SERIGRAPH
GATECRASH	HYPHENATE	KITTIWAKE	MONODRAMA	PARENTAGE	QUICKSAND	SHAMEFAST
GERMINATE	HYPOBLAST	KNOTGRASS	MONOGRAPH	PARHYPATE	RACETRACK	SHELDRAKE
GINGERADE	IDEOGRAPH	LACINIATE	MONOPLANE	PARSONAGE	RANGELAND	SHELLBACK

SHIPSHAPE	SURROGATE	VELLICATE	DEBATABLE	NAVIGABLE	CHAWBACON	QUIZZICAL
SHORTCAKE	SUSCITATE	VENTIFACT	DEFINABLE	NUTJOBBER	CHRONICLE	RESOURCES
SHORTFALL	SWEATBAND	VENTILATE	DESIRABLE	OUTNUMBER	CLASSICAL	SATIRICAL
SHORTHAND	SYCOPHANT	VERBERATE	DIRIGIBLE	PALATABLE	COALESCED	SCEPTICAL
SHORTHAUL	SYLLABARY	VEXILLARY	DISMEMBER	PEACEABLE	COLCHICUM	SCIAMACHY
SHRINKAGE	SYNCOPATE	VIDEOTAPE	DISSEMBLE	PEACEABLY	CONVINCED	SEANNACHY
SICILIANO	SYNDICATE	VIENTIANE	DISTURBED	PERMEABLE	CORPUSCLE	SEQUENCER
SIDEBOARD	TABLELAND	VINDICATE	DIVISIBLE	PERTURBED	CRUSTACEA	SIPHUNCLE
SIDETRACK	TABLEWARE	VIPASSANA	DJELLABAH	PHILLABEG	DISGRACED	SKEPTICAL
SIGNBOARD	TAILBOARD	VIRGINALS	DOODLEBUG	PHILLIBEG	DISPLACED	SKIAMACHY
SIMULCAST	TAILPLANE	VIRGULATE	DOUKHOBOR	PLAUSIBLE	DOMINICAL	SPARTACUS
SISSERARY	TAMERLANE	VISIONARY	DRINKABLE	PLAUSIBLY	DOMINICAN	SPECTACLE
SLEEPWALK	TANTARARA	VOLKSRAAD	DUIKERBOK	PRINTABLE	DROPSICAL	SPHERICAL
SLINGBACK	TAOISEACH	VOLUNTARY	DUNSTABLE	QUODLIBET	EMPIRICAL	SPILLICAN
SLOWCOACH	TARANTASS	VOUCHSAFE	ENDURABLE	RATTLEBAG	ENSCONCED	STREETCAR
SNOWFLAKE	TELEGRAPH	WAISTBAND	ENJOYABLE	REACHABLE	ENTELECHY	SUPPLICAT
SOMEPLACE	TELOPHASE	WAITERAGE	EQUITABLE	REDUCIBLE	ENTRANCED	TAPDANCER
SOUTHEAST	TEMPERATE	WALDGRAVE	EQUITABLY	REMOVABLE	EQUIVOCAL	TARAXACUM
SOUTHWARD	TEMPORARY	WALLBOARD	ESTIMABLE	RENEWABLE	ERISTICAL	TECHNICAL
SOUTHWARK	TERMAGANT	WAPENTAKE	EUPHORBIA	REPAYABLE	FANATICAL	TETRARCHY
SPATULATE	TERMINATE	WASHBOARD	EXCALIBUR	REPUTABLE	FATIDICAL	TOOTHACHE
SPEAKEASY	THEOCRACY	WASHSTAND	EXCITABLE	SADDLEBAG	GAELTACHT	TROSSACHS
SPECULATE	THORNBACK	WASTELAND	EXCUSABLE	SCALEABLE	GENETICAL	TUMMYACHE
SPIKENARD	THRILLANT	WATERBABY	EXCUSABLY	SCHOOLBOY	GERFALCON	UMBILICAL
SPOROCARP	THROWBACK	WATERFALL	EXECRABLE	SEPARABLE	GERMANCER	UMBILICUS
SPRINGALD	THUMBNAIL	WATERGATE	EXECRABLY	SEPTEMBER	GRAPHICAL	UNETHICAL
SPRITSAIL	THUMBTACK	WATERMARK	FAVORABLE	SHILLABER	GREYWACKE	UNMUSICAL
SQUIREAGE	TIMESHARE	WELDSTADT	FAVORABLY	SPONGEBAG	GUILLOCHE	UNNOTICED
STAGEHAND	TIMOCRACY	WHEELBASE	FLAMMABLE	SPRINGBOK	HEARTACHE	UNTYPICAL
STAIRCASE	TIPPERARY	WHIPSNADE	FLOWERBED	STABLEBOY	HEPATICAL	URANISCUS
STALEMATE	TITHEBARN	WHITEBAIT	HABITABLE	TEACHABLE	HERETICAL	VENTRICLE
STANDGALE	TITILLATE	WHITEDAMP	HARQUEBUS	THINKABLE	HIERARCHY	VERBASCUM
STARBOARD	TOASTRACK	WHITEHALL	HERITABLE	TIMETABLE	IDENTICAL	VERIDICAL
STEADFAST	TONOPLAST	WHITEWALL	HOLDERBAT	TITTLEBAT	IDIOTICON	VIDELICET
STEELYARD	TRADEMARK	WHITEWASH	HONORABLE	TOLERABLE	ILLOGICAL	WHIMSICAL
STEGOSAUR	TRAGELAPH	WHIZZBANG	ILLEGIBLE	TOLERABLY	IMMANACLE	ABSCONDER
STENOPAIC	TRANSLATE	WHOLESALE	ILLEGIBLY	TRACEABLE	INVOLUCRE	ADENOIDAL
STERNFAST	TRANSVAAL	WHUNSTANE	IMMOVABLE	TRACTABLE	JAUNDICED	ADVISEDLY
STIMULANT	TREILLAGE	WINDSCALE	IMMOVABLY	TRAINABLE	JURIDICAL	ALEXANDER
STIMULATE	TREMULANT	WINEGLASS	IMMUTABLE	TURNTABLE	KILOCYCLE	ALEXANDRA
STIPULATE	TREMULATE	WINNEBAGO	IMMUTABLY	UNEATABLE	LACONICAL	ALLEGEDLY
STOCKYARD	TRENCHANT	WISECRACK	INAUDIBLE	UNTENABLE	LEVITICUS	AMSTERDAM
STONEHAND	TRIBUNATE	WITHDRAWN	INAUDIBLY	VEGETABLE	LUMBRICUS	ANTIPODES
STONEWALL	TRIBUTARY	WITHSTAND	INCAPABLE	VENERABLE	MEGACYCLE	APERIODIC
STONEWARE	TRIPITAKA	WOODCRAFT	INCURABLE	VERITABLE	MISPLACED	ASSUREDLY
STOOLBALL	TRITICALE	WOOMERANG	INCURABLY	VOLATIBLE	MONOMACHY	ASTOUNDED
STRAPHANG	TRITURATE	WORKPLACE	INDELIBLE	ANNOUNCER	MOUSTACHE	ATTAINDER
STRAPPADO	TRUTINATE	WORKSPACE	INDELIBLY	ARSENICAL	NIETZSCHE	ATTITUDES
STREETAGE	TUNGSTATE	ZENOCRATE	INEFFABLE	ARTIFICER	NOTONECTA	AWKWARDLY
STRONGARM	TURBINATE	ADAPTABLE	INSCRIBED	AUTOLYCUS	NUMERICAL	BACKPEDAL
STYLOBATE	TWAYBLADE	ADMIRABLE	INSOLUBLE	AVALANCHE	OLIGARCHY	BARTENDER
SUBJUGATE	UNCERTAIN	ADMIRABLY	INVISIBLE	BAREFACED	ORGANICAL	BEDRIDDEN
SUBLIMATE	UNDERCAST	ADVISABLE	IRASCIBLE	BASILICAL	ORICALCHE	BELATEDLY
SUBROGATE	UNDERHAND	AGREEABLE	IRRITABLE	BASILICON	OROBANCHE	BERGANDER
SUBSTRATA	UNDERPAID	AGREEABLY	IRRITABLY	BELLYACHE	PAGLIACCI	BEVERIDGE
SUBSTRATE	UNDERPASS	ALLOWABLE	ISALLOBAR	BOCCACCIO	PARFLECHE	BIGHEADED
SUBTENANT	UNDERRATE	ALTERABLE	ISLAMABAD	BOONDOCKS	PASTICCIO	BOMBARDON
SUCCINATE	UNDERTAKE	ANAEROBIC	JIGGUMBOB	BOOTLACES	PIRATICAL	BYSTANDER
SUCCOTASH	UNDERWALK	AVAILABLE	JITTERBUG	BOTANICAL	POLEMICAL	CAMBRIDGE
SUFFOCATE	UPPERCASE	AVOIDABLE	LAUGHABLE	BRASSICAS	POLITICAL	CAMCORDER
SUGARCANE	UROKINASE	BEELZEBUB	LETTERBOX	BUTTERCUP	PRACTICAL	CARTRIDGE
SULTANATE	VACCINATE	BILIRUBIN	MALLEABLE	CAMBUSCAN	PRECINCTS	CASSANDRA
SUMPTUARY	VACILLATE	BIRDTABLE	MEHITABEL	CANONICAL	PROBOSCIS	CERATODUS
SUPPLIANT	VANTBRASS	BREAKABLE	MEMORABLE	CAPRICCIO	PROMUSCIS	CHARYBDIS
SUPPURATE	VARIEGATE	BUMBLEBEE	MISERABLE	CARBUNCLE	PSYCHICAL	CHAVENDER
SUPREMACY	VARIOLATE	BUTTERBUR	MISERABLY	CARPACCIO	QUANTICAL	CHICKADEE
SURFBOARD	VELLENAGE	CONSTABLE	MYOGLOBIN	CARTOUCHE	QUANTOCKS	CHLAMYDES

CLARENDON	MISGUIDED	UNCLOUDED	BLEACHERS	CONCISELY	ELOPEMENT	FURTIVELY
CLEPSYDRA	MISHANDLE	UNDECIDED	BLINDNESS	CONDIMENT	ELSEWHERE	FUSSINESS
COFFERDAM	MUCKENDER	UNDIVIDED	BLOCKHEAD	CONFIDENT	EMBRACERY	FUSTINESS
COLERIDGE	MUJAHIDIN	UNFOUNDED	BLOODLESS	CONFITEOR	EMOLLIENT	FUZZINESS
COLLOIDAL	NERITIDAE	UNGUARDED	BLUFFNESS	CONGOLESE	EMOLUMENT	GALLABEAH
COMMANDER	NIGGARDLY	UNTRODDEN	BLUNTNESS	CONGRUENT	EMPHYSEMA	GASPEREAU
CONCLUDED	OCEANIDES	WEDNESDAY	BOLOGNESE	CONTINENT	EMPLOYEES	GATESHEAD
CONCORDAT	OPENENDED	WILLESDEN	BOMBSHELL	CONTUMELY	EMPTINESS	GAUDINESS
CONTENDER	OPODELDOC	WIMBLEDON	BOOKSHELF	CORNFIELD	ENACTMENT	GAUNTNESS
CORIANDER	OUTWARDLY	YESTERDAY	BORDEREAU	CORPOREAL	ENCUMBENT	GAWKINESS
COTYLEDON	OVERRIDER	ZEALANDER	BOSSINESS	CORPULENT	ENDOSPERM	GAZETTEER
CROOKEDLY	PANHANDLE	ZINFANDEL	BOUNDLESS	COTANGENT	ENDOWMENT	GEARWHEEL
DASTARDLY	PARAMEDIC	ABASEMENT	BOYFRIEND	COUNTLESS	ENDPAPERS	GENEVIEVE
DECIDEDLY	PARTRIDGE	ABATEMENT	BRAINLESS	CRAPULENT	ENGINEERS	GENUFLECT
DISBURDEN	PERIANDER	ABHORRENT	BRASSIERE	CRAZINESS	ENJOYMENT	GENUINELY
DISCARDED	PERSUADED	ABSORBENT	BREAKNECK	CRISPNESS	ENROLMENT	GIDDINESS
DISCREDIT	PHILANDER	ABSTINENT	BRIDEWELL	CROSSBEAM	ENSORCELL	GILGAMESH
DISTENDED	PIEPOWDER	ACETYLENE	BRIEFNESS	CROTCHETY	ENTHYMEME	GOBETWEEN
EMBROIDER	PIGHEADED	ACUTENESS	BRISKNESS	CRUDENESS	ENTREMETS	GODLINESS
ENCELADUS	POINTEDLY	ADEPTNESS	BRUSQUELY	DAMASCENE	ENVERMEIL	GODPARENT
ESTRELDID	POLYANDRY	ADORNMENT	BUCCANEER	DAMNEDEST	EPICUREAN	GOLDCREST
EUMENIDES	PREBENDAL	ADVERSELY	BUCHAREST	DASHWHEEL	EQUIPMENT	GOLDFIELD
EURIPIDES	PRETENDER	AGREEMENT	BUCKTEETH	DAUNTLESS	ETHELBERT	GOOSEHERD
EYESHADOW	PROPERDIN	AGUECHEEK	BUCKWHEAT	DEACONESS	EUCLIDEAN	GOOSENECK
FINLANDIA	PROVENDER	AIRSTREAM	BULKINESS	DEATHLESS	EVASIVELY	GOSSAMERY
FORBIDDEN	PYRAMIDAL	ALERTNESS	BURLINESS	DECUMBENT	EVERGREEN	GOVERNESS
FORWANDER	QUARENDEN	ALIGNMENT	CABALLERO	DEFENDERS	EXACTMENT	GRACELESS
FRUCTIDOR	REDDENDUM	ALLOTMENT	CAESAREAN	DEFERMENT	EXACTNESS	GRANDNESS
GASHOLDER	REDHANDED	ALOOFNESS	CAFETIERE	DEFICIENT	EXANTHEMA	GRAVESEND
GERMANDER	REDHEADED	AMAZEMENT	CALABRESE	DEMULCENT	EXCELLENT	GREATNESS
GOOSANDER	REGUERDON	AMENDMENT	CALCANEUM	DENSENESS	EXCIPIENT	GREENFEED
GUNPOWDER	REJOINDER	AMUSEMENT	CALCANEUS	DEPENDENT	EXCREMENT	GREENHEAD
HAYRADDIN	REMAINDER	ANDROMEDA	CALLIPERS	DESIPIENT	EXOSPHERE	GREENWEED
HENDIADYS	REPUTEDLY	ANNULMENT	CAMEMBERT	DETERGENT	EXPEDIENT	GRIMINESS
HERMANDAD	RESSALDAR	APARTHEID	CANTONESE	DETERRENT	EXTREMELY	GRUFFNESS
HETERODOX	RHAPSODIC	APARTMENT	CARIBBEAN	DETRIMENT	EXTROVERT	GUILELESS
HODMANDOD	RINGSIDER	APPREHEND	CARTWHEEL	DEVILMENT	EYELETEER	GUILTLESS
HOMICIDAL	ROTTERDAM	ARCHITECT	CASTANETS	DIFFERENT	FAINTNESS	GUINEVERE
HOTHEADED	SATYRIDAE	ARROWHEAD	CATAPLEXY	DIFFIDENT	FAITHLESS	GUMSHIELD
HOWTOWDIE	SCHMIEDER	ARTILLERY	CATCHMENT	DINGINESS	FALSENESS	GUTENBERG
HUNDREDTH	SCIARIDAE	ASHMOLEAN	CEASELESS	DIRTINESS	FARMSTEAD	HABERGEON
HURRIEDLY	SCLAUNDER	ATHENAEUM	CENTIPEDE	DISAPPEAR	FATISCENT	HAIRPIECE
HUSBANDLY	SCREWEDUP	ATONEMENT	CEYLONESE	DISCOVERT	FAULTLESS	HALLOWEEN
HUSBANDRY	SEPHARDIM	AUTHORESS	CHALUMEAU	DISCOVERY	FENUGREEK	HAMPSTEAD
ICELANDER	SERENADER	AWARENESS	CHAMELEON	DISHONEST	FILLIPEEN	HANDINESS
ICELANDIC	SHEIKHDOM	BAKSHEESH	CHAMPLEVÉ	DISINFECT	FIREBREAK	HANDPIECE
ICTERIDAE	SILURIDAE	BALLADEER	CHARTREUX	DISORIENT	FIRMAMENT	HAPPINESS
IGUANODON	SKEDADDLE	BANDOLEER	CHAUFFEUR	DISSIDENT	FLAMSTEED	HARDINESS
IMPOUNDER	SPASMODIC	BANDOLERO	CHEAPNESS	DIVERGENT	FLATULENT	HARDSHELL
INFIELDER	SQUALIDLY	BANISTERS	CHEERLESS	DIZZINESS	FLESHLESS	HARSHNESS
IRONSIDES	SUCCEEDED	BEACHHEAD	CHICANERY	DOUBTLESS	FLORIMELL	HASTINESS
IRRAWADDY	SURQUEDRY	BEACHWEAR	CHICKWEED	DOWNTREND	FOGGINESS	HATCHMENT
KENTLEDGE	SURRENDER	BEARDLESS	CHILDLESS	DREAMLESS	FORCEMEAT	HEADDRESS
KEYHOLDER	SUSPENDED	BECHSTEIN	CLASSLESS	DUNGAREES	FOREANENT	HEADINESS
KINTLEDGE	SUSPENDER	BEDSPREAD	CLEANNESS	DUNGENESS	FORESPEAK	HEADPIECE
KNOWLEDGE	SYRPHIDAE	BEEFSTEAK	CLEARNESS	DYSENTERY	FORESPEND	HEARTBEAT
LANGRIDGE	TABANIDAE	BELVEDERE	CLIENTELE	EAGERNESS	FORESTERS	HEARTFELT
LANGUEDOC	TAHSILDAR	BERNSTEIN	CLOSENESS	EBULLIENT	FOURWHEEL	HEARTLESS
LANGUIDLY	THERMIDOR	BIOSPHERE	CLOUDLESS	ECOSPHERE	FRANKNESS	HEAVINESS
LAPLANDER	THRALLDOM	BIZARRELY	COALFIELD	ECTOTHERM	FRATCHETY	HEBRIDEAN
LATTERDAY	TIPULIDAE	BLACKHEAD	COCHINEAL	EFFICIENT	FREEWHEEL	HEMIPTERA
LOMBARDIC	TOLPUDDLE	BLACKLEAD	COINTREAU	EFFULGENT	FRESHNESS	HERCULEAN
LOWLANDER	TONBRIDGE	BLACKNESS	COLORLESS	EGAREMENT	FRUITLESS	HIGHSPEED
MALLANDER	TOURNEDOS	BLAMELESS	COLOSSEUM	EIGHTIETH	FUGGINESS	HINGELESS
MALLENDER	TROUBADOR	BLANDNESS	COMINTERN	ELECTRESS	FULLERENE	HOMESTEAD
MANHANDLE	TRUMPEDUP	BLASPHEME	COMPETENT	ELIZABETH	FUNDAMENT	HOMOPTERA
MARTYRDOM	UNBOUNDED	BLASPHEMY	COMPONENT	ELLESMERE	FURNIMENT	HORSELESS

HOUSELEEK	MACCABEES	OBSCURELY	PRESIDENT	RUNNYMEDE	SPEARHEAD	TIPSINESS
HUSKINESS	MACHINERY	ODOURLESS	PREVALENT	RUSTINESS	SPECIMENS	TIREDNESS
IGNESCENT	MADRILENE	OLIGOCENE	PRICELESS	SACRAMENT	SPEEDWELL	TOOTHLESS
IMAGELESS	MAGDALENE	OPPENHEIM	PRIESTESS	SACRILEGE	SPICILEGE	TOUGHNESS
IMMENSELY	MANGANESE	OSTEODERM	PRIMAVERA	SALTINESS	SPICINESS	TRACKLESS
IMPATIENT	MANLINESS	OUGHTNESS	PRIVATEER	SAUCINESS	SPINELESS	TRANSCEND
IMPERFECT	MANSFIELD	OUTSIDERS	PRIVATELY	SCENTLESS	SPLINTERS	TRANSIENT
IMPLEMENT	MARKETEER	OUTSPREAD	PRIVILEGE	SCONCHEON	SPODUMENE	TRASIMENE
IMPRUDENT	MARMOREAL	OVERDRESS	PROFANELY	SCUNCHEON	SPOONFEED	TRAVELERS
INCIPIENT	MARTINEAU	OVEREXERT	PROFITEER	SEMANTEME	SPRECHERY	TREACHERY
INCLEMENT	MASEFIELD	OVERSLEEP	PROFUSELY	SEMIBREVE	SQUATTERS	TREATMENT
INCORRECT	MASSIVELY	OVERSPEND	PROMINENT	SENESCENT	STAINLESS	TRICKLESS
INCREMENT	MASSORETE	OVERSTEER	PROOFREAD	SENSELESS	STALENESS	TRITENESS
INCUMBENT	MATCHLESS	OVERWHELM	PROPONENT	SENTIMENT	STARKNESS	TRONDHEIM
INDULGENT	MAUSOLEUM	PACHYDERM	PROPRIETY	SERENGETI	STATELESS	TROUSSEAU
INERTNESS	MELPOMENE	PALANKEEN	PROPYLENE	SERVILELY	STATEMENT	TRUCULENT
INPATIENT	MENIPPEAN	PANNIKELL	PROVIDENT	SEVENTEEN	STEELHEAD	TRUNCHEON
INSELBERG	MERCILESS	PANTALEON	PRYTANEUM	SHADINESS	STEEPNESS	TRYPHOEUS
INSINCERE	MERRIMENT	PARACLETE	PUFFINESS	SHAKINESS	STEINBECK	TUBBINESS
INSIPIENT	MESENTERY	PARASCENE	PULPITEER	SHAMELESS	STERNNESS	TUMESCENT
INSISTENT	MIDSTREAM	PARASCEVE	PUPPETEER	SHAPELESS	STIFFNESS	TURBULENT
INSOLVENT	MIDWIFERY	PARCHEESI	PURPOSELY	SHARPNESS	STILLNESS	TURMAGENT
INSURGENT	MILLEPEDE	PARCHMENT	PYTHONESS	SHEEPMEAT	STONELESS	TWENTIETH
INTELLECT	MILLINERY	PASSAMENT	QUEERNESS	SHEERLEGS	STOUTNESS	ULTRONEUS
INTENSELY	MILLIPEDE	PASSIVELY	QUICKNESS	SHEERNESS	STRANGELY	UNCONCERN
INTERCEDE	MINCEMEAT	PATHOGENY	QUIESCENT	SHEFFIELD	STRAPLESS	UNCORRECT
INTERCEPT	MINEFIELD	PATRONESS	QUIETNESS	SHEWBREAD	STRINGENT	UNDERFEED
INTERFERE	MIRTHLESS	PAWKINESS	RACKETEER	SHIFTLESS	STROSSERS	UNDERFELT
INTERJECT	MISDIRECT	PEASEWEEP	RACONTEUR	SHIPWRECK	SUBALTERN	UNDERSEAL
INTERMENT	MISOCLERE	PEDIGREES	RAINCHECK	SHORTNESS	SUBJACENT	UNDERSELL
INTERSECT	MISTINESS	PEKINGESE	RANDINESS	SHORTTERM	SUBLIMELY	UNDERWEAR
INTERVENE	MOISTNESS	PENFRIEND	READDRESS	SHOWINESS	SUCCULENT	UNDERWENT
INTROVERT	MONASTERY	PENNILESS	READINESS	SHOWPIECE	SULKINESS	UNIVALENT
INVERNESS	MOODINESS	PENSIVELY	RECIPIENT	SHRUBBERY	SUNSCREEN	UTTERLESS
JARLSBERG	MOUTHLESS	PERFUMERY	RECOLLECT	SIGHTLESS	SUPERSEDE	VAGUENESS
JERAHMEEL	MUDDINESS	PERGAMENE	RECOMMEND	SIGHTSEER	SUPERVENE	VALUELESS
JERKINESS	MURDERESS	PERIPHERY	RECONVENE	SILLINESS	SUPREMELY	VELVETEEN
JETSTREAM	MURKINESS	PERMANENT	RECUMBENT	SILVEREYE	SURLINESS	VENEZUELA
JEWELLERY	MUSHINESS	PERSEVERE	RECURRENT	SINCERELY	SWEETMEAT	VENUSBERG
JUDGEMENT	MUSKETEER	PERTINENT	REDSTREAK	SINGALESE	SWEETNESS	VIVIDNESS
JUICINESS	MUSKOGEAN	PESTILENT	REEDINESS	SISYPHEAN	SWIFTNESS	VOICELESS
KENTIGERN	MUSTINESS	PETROLEUM	REFULGENT	SLACKNESS	SWINEHERD	VOLTIGEUR
LANKINESS	MUZZINESS	PETTINESS	REGISSEUR	SLEEKNESS	SYNOECETE	VOLUNTEER
LAODICEAN	NABATHEAN	PHILATELY	RENASCENT	SLEEPLESS	TABASHEER	VORTIGERN
LAPSTREAK	NAKEDNESS	PHOSPHENE	REPAYMENT	SLIGHTEST	TACKINESS	WARTCRESS
LARGENESS	NASTINESS	PHOTOGENE	REPELLENT	SLIMINESS	TAILPIECE	WATERLESS
LATESCENT	NATHELESS	PHYLOGENY	REPOSSESS	SMALLNESS	TARDINESS	WATERWEED
LAUNDRESS	NEGLIGENT	PIECEMEAL	REPREHEND	SMARTNESS	TARGETEER	WEARINESS
LEFTOVERS	NEWLYWEDS	PILASTERS	REPRESENT	SMOKELESS	TARTAREAN	WEIRDNESS
LEISURELY	NEWSAGENT	PINCHBECK	REPROCESS	SNAKEWEED	TASTELESS	WHALEMEAT
LEPROSERY	NEWSSHEET	PIPEDREAM	RESILIENT	SNEERWELL	TAVERNERS	WHEATGERM
LIGHTLESS	NINETIETH	PIPSQUEAK	RESURGENT	SOBERNESS	TEARSHEET	WHEATMEAL
LIGHTNESS	NIPCHEESE	PISTAREEN	RESURRECT	SOCIOLECT	TEMPTRESS	WHITAKERS
LIMITLESS	NOBLENESS	PISTOLEER	RETROCEDE	SOGGINESS	TENSENESS	WHITEHEAD
LINEAMENT	NOISELESS	PLACEMENT	RETROVERT	SOMEWHERE	TERMAGENT	WHITENESS
LINGFIELD	NOISINESS	PLAINNESS	REVETMENT	SOMNOLENT	TERPINEOL	WHOLEMEAL
LODGEMENT	NOLLEKENS	PLEIOCENE	RIDERLESS	SONNETEER	TERSENESS	WHOLENESS
LOFTINESS	NOMOTHETE	PLUMPNESS	RIGHTNESS	SOPPINESS	TESTAMENT	WILDGEESE
LOGOTHETE	NONPAREIL	POINTLESS	RISKINESS	SORCERESS	THANKLESS	WINDBREAK
LONDONESE	NOOSPHERE	POLYTHENE	ROADSTEAD	SORTILEGE	THICKHEAD	WINDSWEPT
LOOSEHEAD	NORTHWEST	POPLITEAL	ROOSEVELT	SOUFRIERE	THICKNESS	WOOLINESS
LOOSELEAF	NOSEBLEED	PORTREEVE	ROUGHNECK	SOUNDLESS	THIRTIETH	WORDINESS
LOOSENESS	NOTORIETY	POWERLESS	ROUGHNESS	SOUNDNESS	THORNLESS	WORTHLESS
LOWLINESS	NUREMBERG	PRECEDENT	ROUNDHEAD	SOUTENEUR	THYESTEAN	WRANGLERS
LURIDNESS	NUTRIMENT	PRECISELY	ROUTINELY	SOUTHWEST	TIGHTHEAD	WREAKLESS
LUSTINESS	OBLIQUELY	PREDILECT	ROWDINESS	SPACELESS	TIGHTNESS	YESTEREVE
LUTESCENT	OBSCENELY	PRESCIENT	RUFESCENT	SPARKLERS	TIMEPIECE	BASKETFUL

BEAUTIFUL	BURROUGHS	NICARAGUA	BLOODSHOT	SEPULCHRE	ALBERTINE	AUBERGINE
BOTTLEFUL	CATALOGUE	NOSTALGIA	BRITSCHKA	SHOLOKHOV	ALCHEMIST	AUCTORIAL
BOUNTIFUL	CHAMPAGNE	NOSTALGIC	CATARRHAL	SLAVISHLY	ALMANDINE	AUGUSTINE
BUCKETFUL	COCKAIGNE	OESTROGEN	CEANOTHUS	SLINGSHOT	ALONGSIDE	AUSTERITY
BUTTERFLY	COCKFIGHT	OMOPHAGIC	CHERISHED	SPACESHIP	ALTISSIMO	AUTEURISM
CALORIFIC	COLLEAGUE	ONSLAUGHT	CHIHUAHUA	SPRAUCHLE	ALUMINIUM	AUTHORITY
CHARGEFUL	COPYRIGHT	OUTRIGGER	COURTSHIP	STAUNCHLY	AMAZONITE	AUTHORIZE
COLOURFUL	CORREGGIO	OVERNIGHT	CTESIPHON	STEAMSHIP	AMBIGUITY	AVOCATION
CURFUFFLE	CRYPTOGAM	OVERSIGHT	DEBAUCHED	STOMACHIC	AMBROSIAL	AWAKENING
DAMSELFLY	DEADLIGHT	PARAGOGUE	DEBAUCHEE	STONECHAT	AMBROSIAN	BACKSHISH
DECEITFUL	DECALOGUE	PASSENGER	EFFINGHAM	STRETCHED	AMELAKITE	BACKSLIDE
DISCOMFIT	DEMAGOGUE	PEDAGOGUE	ENCANTHIS	STRETCHER	AMERICIUM	BACTERIAL
DRAGONFLY	DERRINGER	PEMPHIGUS	ENTRECHAT	STYLISHLY	AMIDSHIPS	BACTERIUM
FORGETFUL	DOWNRIGHT	PENDRAGON	EPEDAPHIC	SUNBATHER	AMPHIBIAN	BALALAIKA
FRIGHTFUL	DYSPHAGIA	PHALANGER	ERPINGHAM	SWEETSHOP	AMPLIFIER	BALLADIST
HANDCUFFS	EMBRANGLE	PHANSIGAR	EURHYTHMY	TACAMAHAC	ANABOLISM	BALLERINA
HONORIFIC	ENDECAGON	PHELLOGEN	EUTROPHIC	TOTTENHAM	ANARCHIST	BALLPOINT
IBUPROFEN	ENDOERGIC	PORBEAGLE	FERINGHEE	TRANSSHIP	ANATOLIAN	BANDOLIER
KERFUFFLE	ESOPHAGUS	PORRINGER	FLOORSHOW	TREBUCHET	ANATOMIST	BANDOLINE
KNIPHOFIA	ESTRANGED	POTTINGAR	FOOLISHLY	TRILITHON	ANATOMIZE	BANTERING
LONGEDFOR	EYEBRIGHT	PROLONGED	FORGATHER	TRIUMPHAL	ANCHORITE	BARBARIAN
MARROWFAT	FANDANGLE	PTARMIGAN	FORSYTHIA	TROOPSHIP	ANDANTINO	BARBARISM
MASTERFUL	FIRELIGHT	RECTANGLE	FROBISHER	UNABASHED	ANGELFISH	BARBARITY
MOSKONFYT	FLYWEIGHT	ROXBURGHE	GARNISHEE	UNCLOTHED	ANGLICISM	BARBARIZE
NONPROFIT	FORESIGHT	RUSHLIGHT	GODFATHER	UNEARTHLY	ANHYDRIDE	BARBOTINE
PANTOFFLE	FORTNIGHT	SCAVENGER	GODMOTHER	UNMATCHED	ANHYDRITE	BARMECIDE
PANTOUFLE	GALAPAGOS	SCROUNGER	GODOLPHIN	UNSCATHED	ANIMALISM	BARNABITE
PLENTIFUL	GALDRAGON	SEEMINGLY	GRAPESHOT	UNTOUCHED	ANIMALITY	BATTALION
POCKETFUL	GALIONGEE	SIDELIGHT	GROUNDHOG	UPANISHAD	ANIMATION	BEGINNING
QUIVERFUL	GOODNIGHT	SKINTIGHT	HERONSHAW	WAFERTHIN	ANIMOSITY	BELIEVING
RADCLIFFE	GREASEGUN	SOLFEGGIO	HOLINSHED	WAPINSHAW	ANOINTING	BELONGING
REGARDFUL	HAMBURGER	SPARINGLY	HOOLACHAN	WASPISHLY	ANONYMITY	BERKELIUM
REGRETFUL	HARBINGER	SPOTLIGHT	HORSESHOE	WATERSHED	ANSWERING	BERYLLIUM
REISTAFEL	HARDANGER	STARLIGHT	HORSEWHIP	ABDUCTION	ANTICLINE	BICYCLIST
RESENTFUL	HEADLIGHT	STAVANGER	HOUYHNHNM	ABOLITION	ANTIQUITY	BILLOWING
RESHUFFLE	HIGHLIGHT	STOPLIGHT	IMPEACHER	ABORIGINE	APERITIVE	BIOLOGIST
SDEIGNFUL	HINDSIGHT	STRATAGEM	LEHRJAHRE	ABOUNDING	APHRODITE	BIPARTITE
SHOVELFUL	HUMDINGER	STRATEGIC	LEVIATHAN	ABSORBING	APOLOGIST	BISECTION
SOPORIFIC	HYDRANGEA	SUBMERGED	LIGHTSHIP	ABSURDITY	APOLOGIZE	BLACKBIRD
SORROWFUL	IDEALOGUE	SUFFRAGAN	LOWLIGHTS	ACADEMIST	APPALLING	BLACKLIST
SPRITEFUL	IMBRANGLE	SURCINGLE	MACARTHUR	ACCESSION	APPEALING	BLUEPRINT
STRESSFUL	INDRAUGHT	SYNAGOGUE	MEDMENHAM	ACCLIVITY	APPORTION	BLUESHIFT
SUDORIFIC	INSWINGER	TAILLIGHT	MICROCHIP	ACCORDING	APPROVING	BOBSLEIGH
TAILLEFER	KISSINGER	TELLINGLY	MIDRASHIM	ACCORDION	ARABICIZE	BOLECTION
TAMOXIFEN	KNOWINGLY	TIMENOGUY	MOYGASHEL	ACCRETION	ARAGONITE	BOMBASINE
THREADFIN	LAMPLIGHT	TRAFALGAR	NAUMACHIA	ACETAMIDE	ARCHIVIST	BORDERING
UNHELPFUL	LANGUAGES	TREGEAGLE	NEBBISHER	ACOUSTICS	ARGENTINA	BORROWING
UNHOPEFUL	LATENIGHT	UNCHANGED	NEOLITHIC	ACTUALITY	ARGENTINE	BOSTONIAN
UNMINDFUL	LAWMONGER	UNCHARGED	OPHIUCHUS	ACTUARIAL	ARMISTICE	BRAMBLING
VAPORIFIC	LESTRIGON	UNDAMAGED	OWNERSHIP	ADDICTION	ARRESTING	BRANCHING
WONDERFUL	LETHARGIC	UNFLEDGED	PEEVISHLY	ADDICTIVE	ARTHURIAN	BRAZILIAN
ACONCAGUA	LEVERAGED	VICEREGAL	PENPUSHER	ADJECTIVE	ASCENDING	BREADLINE
AMUSINGLY	LIMBURGER	WALPURGIS	PETERSHAM	ADJOINING	ASCENSION	BREATHING
AQUILEGIA	LIMELIGHT	WAMBENGER	PINOCCHIO	ADMISSION	ASCLEPIUS	BREECHING
ARCHANGEL	LONGINGLY	WARMONGER	PISTACHIO	ADMITTING	ASPERSION	BRIGADIER
AREOPAGUS	MASSINGER	WHIRLIGIG	PROMACHOS	ADORATION	ASPLENIUM	BRISTLING
ARKWRIGHT	MESSENGER	WILLINGLY	PUBLISHED	ADULATION	ASSERTING	BROADSIDE
ASPARAGUS	MONOLOGUE	WITTINGLY	PUBLISHER	ADVECTION	ASSERTION	BRONCHIAL
ASYNERGIA	MONTAIGNE	AMIANTHUS	RADICCHIO	ADVENTIST	ASSERTIVE	BRUTALISM
BANDWAGON	MOONLIGHT	ANGUISHED	REFRESHER	ADVENTIVE	ASSIDUITY	BRUTALITY
BEDRAGGLE	MORTGAGEE	ASTRAKHAN	ROUGHSHOD	ADVERBIAL	ATHLETICS	BRUTALIZE
BESPANGLE	MORTGAGOR	ASTROPHEL	SCRATCHED	ADVERSITY	ATONALITY	BUFFETING
BOANERGES	MRIDAMGAM	BETHLEHEM	SCRATCHES	ADVERTISE	ATTACKING	BULGARIAN
BREAKAGES	MRIDANGAM	BETROTHAL	SCRIMSHAW	AFFECTING	ATTENTION	BURROWING
BRUMMAGEM	MUNDUNGUS	BETROTHED	SELFISHLY	AFFECTION	ATTENTIVE	BURUNDIAN
BUBBLEGUM	NEURALGIA	BIMONTHLY	SENESCHAL	AGITATION	ATTRITION	BYZANTINE
BULLFIGHT	NEURALGIC	BLOODSHED	SEPULCHER	AGONIZING	ATTUITION	CALDARIUM

CALLOSITY	COCKATIEL	COUNTRIES	DEOXIDISE	ECONOMICS	EXCELSIOR	FLOWERING
CALVANISM	COEMPTION	COUTURIER	DEPENDING	ECONOMIST	EXCEPTION	FOGRAMITE
CALVINIST	COENOBITE	COVELLITE	DEPICTION	ECONOMIZE	EXCESSIVE	FOLKETING
CALVITIES	COENOBIUM	COWARDICE	DEPRAVITY	ECOSSAISE	EXCLUDING	FOLLOWING
CAMBODIAN	COFFINITE	CRACKLING	DESERTION	ECTROPION	EXCLUSION	FOOTPRINT
CAMPANILE	COGNITION	CRACOVIAN	DESERVING	EDELWEISS	EXCLUSIVE	FOREGOING
CANTABILE	COGNITIVE	CREDULITY	DESIGNING	EDITORIAL	EXCURSION	FORGETIVE
CAPTIVITY	COLLATION	CREMATION	DESPOTISM	EDUCATION	EXECUTION	FORGIVING
CARBAMIDE	COLLEGIAN	CRENATION	DETECTION	EDUCATIVE	EXECUTIVE	FORMALIST
CARBONIZE	COLLISION	CREPOLINE	DETECTIVE	EDWARDIAN	EXEMPLIFY	FORMALITY
CAREERIST	COLLODION	CRINOLINE	DETENTION	EFFECTIVE	EXEMPTION	FORMALIZE
CARMELITE	COLLUSION	CRIPPLING	DETERMINE	EFFLUVIUM	EXORATION	FORMATION
CARNATION	COLLUSIVE	CRITERION	DETRITION	EGLANTINE	EXPANSION	FORMATIVE
CARNELIAN	COLLYRIUM	CRITICISM	DEUCALION	EGRESSION	EXPANSIVE	FORTALICE
CARPETING	COLOMBIAN	CRITICIZE	DEUTERIUM	ELAEOLITE	EXPECTING	FORTHWINK
CARTESIAN	COLOMBIER	CROCODILE	DEVIATION	ELATERIUM	EXPENSIVE	FORTHWITH
CASHPOINT	COLOURING	CROSSBILL	DEVILFISH	ELECTRIFY	EXPERTISE	FOSSILISE
CASSATION	COLOURIST	CROSSFIRE	DEXTERITY	ELEVATION	EXPIATION	FOSSORIAL
CASTILIAN	COLUMBIAN	CROSSWIND	DIALOGITE	ELKOSHITE	EXPLETIVE	FOUNDLING
CASUARINA	COLUMBINE	CROSSWISE	DIANETICS	ELOCUTION	EXPLOSION	FRAGILITY
CATECHISM	COLUMBITE	CROWNLIKE	DIATOMITE	EMANATION	EXPLOSIVE	FRAMBOISE
CATECHIZE	COLUMBIUM	CROWSBILL	DICTATION	EMBELLISH	EXPORTING	FRANCHISE
CATHERINE	COLUMNIST	CRUMBLING	DIDACTICS	EMBRACING	EXPULSION	FREDERICK
CAUCASIAN	COMBATIVE	CURIOSITY	DIETETICS	EMPHASIZE	EXQUISITE	FRIGIDITY
CAUSATION	COMMODITY	CURSORILY	DIETICIAN	EMULATION	EXTENSILE	FRIVOLITY
CAUTERIZE	COMMOTION	CUSTODIAL	DIFFUSION	ENCHORIAL	EXTENSION	FROSTBITE
CAVENDISH	COMMUNION	CUSTODIAN	DIGESTION	ENCOLPION	EXTENSIVE	FRUGALITY
CAVORTING	COMMUNISM	CUSTOMIZE	DIGESTIVE	ENCOLPIUM	EXTORTION	FUNGICIDE
CEASEFIRE	COMMUNIST	CYCLOLITH	DIGNIFIED	ENCRATITE	EXTRADITE	GABARDINE
CELANDINE	COMMUNITY	CYMBELINE	DIMENSION	ENDEARING	EXTREMISM	GABERDINE
CELEBRITY	COMPANIES	CYMBIDIUM	DIONYSIAN	ENDOCRINE	EXTREMIST	GALANTINE
CELESTIAL	COMPANION	DAEDALIAN	DIONYSIUS	ENERINITE	EXTREMITY	GALLICISM
CELLARIST	COMPETING	DALMATIAN	DIRECTION	ENGRAVING	EXTRUSION	GALVANISM
CELLULITE	COMPLAINT	DALTONISM	DIRECTIVE	ENHYDRITE	EXUDATION	GALVANIZE
CENTERING	COMPOSING	DAMNATION	DISABLING	ENQUIRIES	EYESPLICE	GARDENING
CENTREING	COMPOSITE	DANDELION	DISAFFIRM	ENQUIRING	FACSIMILE	GARGARISM
CENTURION	COMPOTIER	DANDIFIED	DISARMING	ENSTATITE	FACTORIAL	GARRULITY
CERTIFIED	COMPUTING	DARWINIAN	DISBELIEF	ENTROPION	FACTORISE	GATHERING
CERUSSITE	CONCAVITY	DAYSPRING	DISOBLIGE	ENTROPIUM	FACUNDITY	GAVELKIND
CESSATION	CONCISION	DEAFENING	DISPARITY	EPHEDRINE	FALANGIST	GEARSHIFT
CEVAPCICI	CONCUBINE	DECEMVIRI	DISTRAINT	EPICEDIUM	FALERNIAN	GEARSTICK
CHABAZITE	CONDITION	DECENNIAL	DITHERING	EPILATION	FALLOPIAN	GELIGNITE
CHAIRLIFT	CONDUCIVE	DECEPTION	DIVERGING	EPINICION	FANTASIZE	GENIALITY
CHALAZION	CONFUCIUS	DECEPTIVE	DIVERSIFY	EPINIKION	FASTENING	GENTILITY
CHAMOMILE	CONFUSING	DECESSION	DIVERSION	EPIPOLISM	FATTENING	GEODESIST
CHAMPAIGN	CONFUSION	DECILLION	DIVERSITY	EPITOMIZE	FAULCHION	GEOLOGIST
CHEAPSIDE	CONGENIAL	DECLARING	DIVERTING	EPULATION	FAVOURITE	GERMANITE
CHECKLIST	CONGERIES	DECLINING	DOGMATISM	EQUIPOISE	FECUNDITY	GERMANIUM
CHERUBINI	CONJURING	DECLIVITY	DOGMATIZE	EROTICISM	FEMINEITY	GERMICIDE
CHEVALIER	CONNEXION	DECOCTION	DORMITION	ERSTWHILE	FERTILITY	GERUNDIVE
CHILDLIKE	CONNUBIAL	DECURSIVE	DOWELLING	ERUDITION	FERTILIZE	GESSAMINE
CHOLELITH	CONSCRIPT	DEDUCTION	DRACONIAN	ERYTHRITE	FESTIVITY	GESTATION
CHONDRITE	CONSOCIES	DEDUCTIVE	DRAINPIPE	ESQUILINE	FEUDALISM	GIBBERISH
CHRISTIAN	CONSTRICT	DEFEATISM	DRAMATICS	ESSENTIAL	FIBROLINE	GIBEONITE
CHURCHILL	CONSUMING	DEFEATIST	DRAMATIST	ESTABLISH	FIBROLITE	GIGANTISM
CIMMERIAN	CONTAGION	DEFECTION	DRAMATIZE	ESTHETICS	FILTERING	GIRONDIST
CINEPHILE	CONTUSION	DEFECTIVE	DRAVIDIAN	ETHIOPIAN	FINANCIAL	GLAMORIZE
CIPOLLINO	CONVIVIAL	DEFENSIVE	DRAWKNIFE	EUCHARIST	FINANCIER	GLORIFIED
CIRCADIAN	COPROLITE	DEFLATION	DRUMSTICK	EUPHEMISM	FINGERING	GLUCINIUM
CLARIFIER	CORALLINE	DEFORMITY	DULCINIST	EUPHONIUM	FINICKING	GLUCOSIDE
CLEANSING	CORDYLINE	DEGRADING	DUODECIMO	EUSKARIAN	FINICKITY	GLUTAMINE
CLEARWING	CORNELIAN	DEJECTION	DUPLICITY	EVAGATION	FINISHING	GLYCERIDE
CLINGFILM	CORNETIST	DEMANDING	DWINDLING	EVOCATION	FLAVORING	GLYCERINE
CLINICIAN	CORROSION	DEMEANING	EARTHLING	EVOCATIVE	FLEDGLING	GMELINITE
CLOCKWISE	CORROSIVE	DEMETRIUS	EASYGOING	EVOLUTION	FLEXITIME	GOLDSMITH
COALITION	COSMETICS	DENTITION	ECHIDNINE	EXARATION	FLOTATION	GONDOLIER
COASTLINE	COSTUMIER	DEODORIZE	ECOLOGIST	EXCAMBION	FLOURMILL	GONGORISM

GONIATITE	HISTIDINE	INFLEXION	LADYSMITH	MANNERISM	MOLESKINS	OBREPTION
GOSLARITE	HISTORIAN	INGENUITY	LAMARTINE	MANUBRIUM	MOLLITIES	OBSCENITY
GOSSYPINE	HITCHHIKE	INGESTION	LAMPADION	MARAUDING	MONACTINE	OBSCURITY
GOSSYPIUM	HOLLERITH	INGROWING	LANDSLIDE	MARCASITE	MONERGISM	OBSEQUIES
GOTHAMITE	HORRIFIED	INJECTION	LANGSPIEL	MARGARINE	MONGOLIAN	OBSESSION
GOVERNING	HORTATIVE	INJUSTICE	LARGITION	MARKETING	MONGOLISM	OBSESSIVE
GRADATION	HOSPITIUM	INQUILINE	LATHYRISM	MARSUPIAL	MONOSTICH	OBTAINING
GRADGRIND	HOSTILITY	INQUIRING	LATRATION	MARSUPIUM	MONTANISM	OBTRUSION
GRANDSIRE	HOUSEWIFE	INSERTION	LAUDATION	MASCULINE	MONTANIST	OBTRUSIVE
GRANULITE	HOYDENISH	INSOMNIAC	LAUNCHING	MASOCHISM	MONZONITE	OBVENTION
GRAPEVINE	HUMANKIND	INSPIRING	LAVOISIER	MASOCHIST	MOONSHINE	OCCLUSION
GRAPPLING	HUNGARIAN	INSULTING	LAWMAKING	MATERNITY	MORBIDITY	OCCULTIST
GRAVESIDE	HUTTERITE	INTEGRITY	LEASTWISE	MATHURINE	MORGANITE	OCCUPYING
GREENWICH	HYDRAZINE	INTENDING	LENGTHILY	MATRICIDE	MORMONISM	OCKHAMIST
GREGARINE	HYGIENIST	INTENSIFY	LETTERING	MAULSTICK	MORTALITY	OCTASTICH
GREGORIAN	HYPERLINK	INTENSITY	LEVANTINE	MAURITIAN	MORTICIAN	OCTILLION
GRENADIER	HYPNOTISM	INTENSIVE	LIABILITY	MAURITIUS	MORTIFIED	OCTOBRIST
GRENADINE	HYPNOTIST	INTENTION	LIBERTIES	MEANDRIAN	MOTHERING	ODELSTING
GROCERIES	HYPNOTIZE	INTERCITY	LIBERTINE	MEANWHILE	MOTORBIKE	OFFENDING
GROUNDING	HYPOCRISY	INTERDICT	LIBRARIAN	MEASURING	MOUSELIKE	OFFENSIVE
GRUELLING	HYPOCRITE	INTERVIEW	LICKERISH	MECHANICS	MUGLARITE	OFFSPRING
GRUMBLING	HYSTERICS	INTESTINE	LIGHTNING	MECHANISM	MURMURING	OLIVENITE
GUIDELINE	ICHNOLITE	INTRUSION	LILYWHITE	MECHANIZE	MUSCADINE	OPERATING
GUITARIST	IMITATION	INTRUSIVE	LIMOUSINE	MEDALLION	MUSCARINE	OPERATION
GUSTATION	IMITATIVE	INTUITION	LIMPIDITY	MEDALLIST	MUSCOVITE	OPERATIVE
GUTTERING	IMMENSITY	INTUITIVE	LINGERING	MEDIATION	MUSSOLINI	ORATORIAN
GYMNASIUM	IMMERSION	INUNCTION	LIQUEFIED	MELONLIKE	MUTTERING	ORDINAIRE
GYNOECIUM	IMPACTION	INVECTIVE	LIQUIDITY	MENDACITY	MUTUALISM	ORGANZINE
HABERDINE	IMPARTIAL	INVENTION	LIQUIDIZE	MENDELISM	MYSTERIES	ORIGENIST
HAECCEITY	IMPASSION	INVENTIVE	LIQUORICE	MENNONITE	MYSTICISM	ORMANDINE
HAEMATITE	IMPASSIVE	INVERSION	LIQUORISH	MENTALITY	NAPIERIAN	ORPHARION
HALOPHILE	IMPELLING	INVOICING	LISTENING	MENTATION	NARRATION	OSTENSIVE
HAMMERING	IMPENDING	IODOPHILE	LITURGICS	MENTICIDE	NARRATIVE	OSTRACISE
HAMPSHIRE	IMPLUVIUM	IRRUPTION	LOAMSHIRE	MENUISIER	NARROWING	OSTRACISM
HAMSTRING	IMPRECISE	IRVINGISM	LOCKSMITH	MEPACRINE	NATHANIEL	OSTRACIZE
HANDSPIKE	IMPROBITY	ISODORIAN	LOGISTICS	MERCERIZE	NATROLITE	OTHERWISE
HANKERING	IMPROVING	ISOLATION	LOGOGRIPH	MERCURIAL	NAUGHTILY	OTTRELITE
HAPPENING	IMPROVISE	ISRAELITE	LOITERING	MERESWINE	NECESSITY	OVERDRIVE
HARMALINE	IMPSONITE	ITALICIZE	LONGEVITY	MEROCRINE	NECTARINE	OVERLYING
HARMONICA	IMPULSION	ITERATION	LOOKALIKE	MESMERISM	NEFERTITI	OVERPAINT
HARMONIST	IMPULSIVE	JACKKNIFE	LOQUACITY	MESMERIZE	NEODYMIUM	OVERPOISE
HARMONIUM	INABILITY	JACKSNIPE	LUCRATIVE	MESSALINA	NEOLOGISM	OVERPRINT
HARMONIZE	INANITION	JANSENISM	LUCRETIUS	METEORITE	NEPHALISM	OVERSPILL
HARROWING	INCARDINE	JANSENIST	LUCTATION	METHODISM	NEPHALIST	OVERWEIGH
HASHEMITE	INCAUTION	JARGONIZE	LUMBERING	METHODIST	NEPHELINE	OVULATION
HASTENING	INCENTIVE	JAWBATION	LUMINAIRE	METHOXIDE	NEPTUNIUM	OXIDATION
HAUGHTILY	INCEPTION	JELLYFISH	LUNCHTIME	MEZZANINE	NEWSPRINT	OZOCERITE
HAWCUBITE	INCEPTIVE	JENNETING	MACEDOINE	MEZZOTINT	NICCOLITE	OZOKERITE
HAWKSBILL	INCLUDING	JEQUIRITY	MACHINING	MICROFILM	NIDDERING	PACKAGING
HAYMAKING	INCLUSION	JESSAMINE	MACHINIST	MICROLITE	NIDERLING	PALEOLITH
HEALTHILY	INCLUSIVE	JOHANNINE	MACTATION	MICROLITH	NIGHTFIRE	PALESTINE
HEAVISIDE	INCOGNITO	JORDANIAN	MADDENING	MIDIANITE	NIGHTTIME	PALLADIAN
HECTORING	INCONDITE	JOSEPHINE	MADELEINE	MIGRATION	NIGROSINE	PALLADIUM
HEMISTICH	INCURSION	JOVIALITY	MAGNALIUM	MILLENIAL	NONENTITY	PALMATION
HERBALIST	INDEMNIFY	JUNKETING	MAGNESIUM	MINISKIRT	NONILLION	PALPATION
HERBARIUM	INDEMNITY	JUSTIFIED	MAGNETISM	MISFIRING	NORMALITY	PALUDRINE
HERBICIDE	INDICTION	JUSTINIAN	MAGNETIZE	MISGIVING	NORMALIZE	PANDATION
HERBORIST	INDIGNITY	KALSOMINE	MAGNIFIER	MISONEIST	NORMATIVE	PANDEMIAN
HESPERIAN	INDUCTION	KEPLARIAN	MAKESHIFT	MITHRAISM	NORWEGIAN	PANEGOISM
HESSONITE	INDUCTIVE	KERMESITE	MALACHITE	MOCCASINS	NOVOCAINE	PANELLING
HEXASTICH	INERUDITE	KIESERITE	MALATHION	MODELLING	NUMERAIRE	PANELLIST
HIBERNIAN	INFANTILE	KISWAHILI	MALAYSIAN	MODERNISM	NUMMULITE	PANTHEISM
HIJACKING	INFECTING	KITTENISH	MALENGINE	MODERNIST	NUTRITION	PANTOMIME
HIMYARITE	INFECTION	KNOBSTICK	MALIGNITY	MODERNITY	NUTRITIVE	PARANOIAC
HINDEMITH	INFERTILE	LABOURITE	MAMMALIAN	MODERNIZE	OBJECTIFY	PARATHION
HIRUNDINE	INFIRMITY	LACCOLITE	MANDOLINE	MODESTINE	OBJECTION	PARENTING
HISTAMINE	INFLATION	LACTATION	MANNERING	MODILLION	OBJECTIVE	PARHELION

PARNASITE	POPPERING	QUALIFIER	REPULSION	SCHELLING	SHRINKING	STANDPIPE
PAROCHIAL	PORCUPINE	QUAVERING	REPULSIVE	SCHILLING	SHUFFLING	STARTLING
PAROCHINE	POSTERIOR	QUICKLIME	REQUISITE	SCHLEMIEL	SIBYLLINE	STATESIDE
PARRICIDE	POSTERITY	QUINQUINA	RESERPINE	SCHLEMIHL	SICCATIVE	STATEWIDE
PARTAKING	POSTILION	QUIVERING	RESERVIST	SCHOOLING	SICKENING	STATOLITH
PARTITION	POTASSIUM	QUOTATION	RESORTING	SCIENTISM	SIDESWIPE	STEENKIRK
PASSEPIED	POTENTIAL	QUOTIDIAN	RESTRAINT	SCIENTIST	SIEGFRIED	STERADIAN
PASSERINE	POTHOLING	QUOTITION	RESULTING	SCOLECITE	SIMEONITE	STERILITY
PASSIVITY	POUJADIST	RACIALISM	RETAILING	SCORCHING	SINCERITY	STERILIZE
PATERNITY	POWELLITE	RACIALIST	RETAINING	SCORODITE	SINGSPIEL	STILTBIRD
PATRICIAN	PRECEDING	RADIATING	RETENTION	SCRAPPING	SINUOSITY	STINKBIRD
PATRICIDE	PRECIPICE	RADIATION	RETENTIVE	SCREENING	SIRBONIAN	STOCKFISH
PATRONIZE	PRECISIAN	RAMILLIES	RETIARIUS	SCREWPINE	SITUATION	STOCKPILE
PAUSANIAS	PRECISION	RANCIDITY	RETORSION	SCRIMPING	SKETCHILY	STOLIDITY
PEACETIME	PRECISIVE	RAPTORIAL	RETORTION	SCRUBBING	SKEWWHIFF	STORYLINE
PECKSNIFF	PRECOCITY	RATHERIPE	RETURNING	SCRUFFILY	SKINFLINT	STOVEPIPE
PEGMATITE	PRECONISE	RATHERISH	REVEALING	SCRUMPING	SLANTWISE	STOWNLINS
PELMANISM	PREJUDICE	RATIONING	REVELLING	SCULPTING	SLAPSTICK	STRAINING
PENILLION	PREMONISH	RAVISHING	REVERSING	SEAFARING	SLIVOVICA	STRAPPING
PERCALINE	PREMOTION	RAZORBILL	REVERSION	SEARCHING	SLIVOVITZ	STREAMING
PERDITION	PRESCRIBE	REALITIES	REVOLTING	SEASONING	SLOUGHING	STRIATION
PEREGRINE	PRESIDIAL	REASONING	REVOLVING	SEBASTIAN	SLOVENIAN	STRIPLING
PERENNIAL	PRESIDIUM	REBELLION	REVULSION	SECESSION	SMALLTIME	STROLLING
PERISCIAN	PRETERITE	REBOATION	REWARDING	SECLUSION	SMUGGLING	STRONTIUM
PERISHING	PRIMARILY	RECALLING	REWORKING	SECRETION	SNAILFISH	STRUTTING
PERSONIFY	PRIMITIAE	RECEIVING	RHODESIAN	SECRETIVE	SNOWDRIFT	STUMBLING
PERVASION	PRIMITIVE	RECEPTION	RHODOLITE	SECTARIAN	SNOWWHITE	STUPEFIED
PERVASIVE	PRIMULINE	RECEPTIVE	RIBBONISM	SECTORIAL	SOCIALISM	STUPIDITY
PESSIMISM	PRIVATION	RECESSION	RICHELIEU	SEDUCTION	SOCIALIST	SUBDIVIDE
PESSIMIST	PRIVATIZE	RECESSIVE	RIDGELING	SEDUCTIVE	SOCIALITE	SUBENTIRE
PESTICIDE	PROACTIVE	RECKONING	RIGHTWING	SELACHION	SOCIALIZE	SUBMARINE
PETAURIST	PROBATION	RECOGNIZE	RIPIENIST	SELECTING	SOFTENING	SUBSCRIBE
PETHIDINE	PROCACITY	RECONCILE	RIVERSIDE	SELECTION	SOLDERING	SUBSCRIPT
PETRIFIED	PROCERITY	RECONDITE	ROSMARINE	SELECTIVE	SOLEMNITY	SUBSIDIZE
PHACOLITE	PROFANITY	RECORDING	ROSMINIAN	SELJUKIAN	SOLEMNIZE	SUCCUBINE
PHANARIOT	PROFUSION	RECORDIST	ROTUNDITY	SEMANTICS	SOLFERINO	SUETONIUS
PHENACITE	PROKOFIEV	RECTIFIER	ROUMANIAN	SEMANTIDE	SOLFIDIAN	SUFFERING
PHENAKISM	PROLAMINE	RECTORIAL	ROUNDFISH	SEMIOTICS	SOLIPSISM	SUFFUSION
PHIGALIAN	PROLIXITY	RECURRING	RUBBERIZE	SENIORITY	SOLITAIRE	SUMMARILY
PHITONIUM	PROLUSION	RECURSIVE	RUINATION	SENSATION	SOMETHING	SUMMARIZE
PHONETICS	PROMISING	REDEEMING	RUTHENIAN	SENSITIVE	SOMMELIER	SUMMATION
PHONOLITE	PROMOTION	REDUCTION	RUTHENIUM	SENSITIZE	SONGSMITH	SUPERFINE
PHYSICIAN	PROMPTING	REEXAMINE	SABBATIAN	SENSORIUM	SOTTISIER	SUPERVISE
PHYSICIST	PROSCRIBE	REFECTION	SABLEFISH	SEPIOLITE	SOUNDBITE	SUPPOSING
PHYTOLITE	PROSIMIAN	REFERRING	SACRARIUM	SERAPHINE	SOVEREIGN	SUQUAMISH
PICKETING	PROTAMINE	REFLATION	SACRIFICE	SERASKIER	SPARKLING	SURVEYING
PICTORIAL	PROUSTITE	REFLEXION	SADDENING	SERBONIAN	SPEARMINT	SURVIVING
PILFERING	PROVIDING	REFLEXIVE	SALESGIRL	SERIALIST	SPEARSIDE	SUSPICION
PINSTRIPE	PROVISION	REFORMIST	SALUBRITY	SERIALIZE	SPECIFICS	SWADDLING
PITCHPINE	PROVOKING	REFURBISH	SALVATION	SERIATION	SPECIFIED	SWINGEING
PLACIDITY	PROXIMITY	REGARDING	SANTONICA	SERMONIZE	SPEECHIFY	SWORDFISH
PLAINTIFF	PTERIDIUM	REJECTION	SARTORIAL	SERRATION	SPELDRING	SWOTHLING
PLAINTIVE	PUBLICIST	REJOICING	SARTORIUS	SERREFILE	SPELLBIND	SYLLOGISM
PLATONIST	PUBLICITY	RELIQUIAE	SASSOLITE	SERVICING	SPINDRIER	SYLPHLIKE
PLAYTHING	PUBLICIZE	REMAINING	SATELLITE	SERVILITY	SPINDRIFT	SYLVANITE
PLUMBLINE	PUERILITY	REMISSION	SATIATION	SEXUALITY	SPIRITISM	SYMBOLISM
PLURALISM	PUGNACITY	RENDERING	SATISFIED	SHASHLICK	SPLITTING	SYMBOLIST
PLURALITY	PULSATION	RENDITION	SATURNIAN	SHAVELING	SPOONBILL	SYMBOLIZE
PLUTONIUM	PULVERIZE	REPELLING	SATURNINE	SHEARLING	SPREADING	SYMPODIUM
POETICIZE	PUNCHLINE	REPLACING	SATURNISM	SHELLFISH	SQUEAMISH	SYMPOSIUM
POISONING	PUNISHING	REPLENISH	SCALARIUM	SHIELDING	SQUINTING	SYNANGIUM
POLIANITE	PURDONIUM	REPLETION	SCALDFISH	SHINTOISM	SQUIRMING	SYNCOMIUM
POLLUTION	PURGATIVE	REPLETIVE	SCAMBLING	SHIVERING	STABILITY	SYNEDRION
POLONAISE	PURIFYING	REPORTING	SCANTLING	SHOESHINE	STABILIZE	SYNERGIST
POLVERINE	PYGMALION	REPROVING	SCAPOLITE	SHOREBIRD	STAGIRITE	SYRIACISM
POMOERIUM	QUAILPIPE	REPTATION	SCARIFIER	SHORTLIST	STAGYRITE	TABELLION
POMPOSITY	QUALIFIED	REPTILIAN	SCHEELITE	SHRIMPING	STANCHION	TACHILITE

TACHYLITE	TRAPEZIAL	VANDALISM	WELLBUILT	PACEMAKER	CAPITULUM	GLEEFULLY
TACTICIAN	TRAPEZIST	VANDALIZE	WELTGEIST	PARBUCKLE	CARACALLA	GOONHILLY
TALKATIVE	TRAPEZIUM	VANISHING	WHIRLWIND	PICNICKER	CAREFULLY	GOSPELLER
TALMUDIST	TRAPEZIUS	VARANGIAN	WHISTLING	PINHOOKER	CASSOULET	GRADUALLY
TANGERINE	TRAVELING	VARIATION	WHITEFISH	RUDBECKIA	CASTELLAN	GRAVADLAX
TANTALITE	TREADMILL	VARISCITE	WHITENING	SAPSUCKER	CATSKILLS	GRENVILLE
TANTALIZE	TREMBLING	VENIALITY	WHITEWING	SCHNECKEN	CENTRALLY	GRINGOLET
TANZANIAN	TREMOLITE	VERATRINE	WILLEMITE	SCHNORKEL	CHANTILLY	GRISAILLE
TARNATION	TRIBALISM	VERBALIZE	WILLOWING	SHARKSKIN	CHISELLER	GUERRILLA
TASMANIAN	TRICERION	VERBOSITY	WINCOPIPE	SHEEPSKIN	CHRYSALIS	HARIGALDS
TAUCHNITZ	TRIDYMITE	VERMILION	WINDCHILL	SHOEMAKER	COLUMELLA	HELPFULLY
TECTONICS	TRIENNIAL	VERNATION	WITHERING	SHUBUNKIN	COMICALLY	HELVELLYN
TECTORIAL	TRIFORIUM	VERSATILE	WITHERITE	SKYJACKER	COMPELLED	HILLBILLY
TEDIOSITY	TRILOBITE	VERSIFIER	WITHYWIND	SLAMMAKIN	CONCEALED	HOBGOBLIN
TEIRESIAS	TRISAGION	VESPASIAN	WITTICISM	SOLLICKER	CONTRALTO	HOBNAILED
TELESTICH	TROOSTITE	VESTIGIAL	WOLVERINE	SOOTERKIN	CORDIALLY	HOPEFULLY
TELLURIAN	TROPARION	VIABILITY	WOMANKIND	SOUVLAKIA	CORNEILLE	HORDEOLUM
TELLURION	TRUNKFISH	VIBRATILE	WORDSMITH	SPELUNKER	COUNSELOR	HORSEPLAY
TELLURIUM	TSAREVICH	VIBRATION	WORLDWIDE	SPILLIKIN	COURTELLE	HYDRAULIC
TEMPORIZE	TUILERIES	VICEREINE	WRECKFISH	SPINNAKER	CRESCELLE	ILLEGALLY
TENDERIZE	TURBIDITY	VICTIMIZE	WRESTLING	SPRAICKLE	CRIBELLUM	IMBROGLIO
TENTATIVE	TURNSTILE	VICTORIAN	WULFENITE	TARMACKED	CRUCIALLY	IMMORALLY
TENTORIUM	TURQUOISE	VICTORINE	WUTHERING	UNCHECKED	CYNICALLY	INDWELLER
TERRACING	TUTIORISM	VIDEODISC	YARDSTICK	UNSHACKLE	DEATHBLOW	INITIALLY
TERRARIUM	TWINKLING	VIDEODISK	YELLOWISH	ABYSMALLY	DECATHLON	INSHALLAH
TERRIFIED	TYMPANIST	VIEWPOINT	YOHIMBINE	ACROPOLIS	DIGITALIN	INTERPLAY
TERRORISM	TYRANNIZE	VIOLATION	YORKSHIRE	ADMIRALTY	DIGITALIS	IRREGULAR
TERRORIST	UKRAINIAN	VIOLINIST	YTTERBIUM	ADRENALIN	DISTILLER	ISOSCELES
TERRORIZE	UMBRATILE	VIRGINIAN	ZECHARIAH	AESCHYLUS	DOLEFULLY	JERUSALEM
TESTDRIVE	UNANIMITY	VIRGINITY	ZEITGEIST	AFTERGLOW	DOMICILED	JOCKTELEG
TESTIFIER	UNBENDING	VIRGINIUM	ZEPHANIAH	AIRCOOLED	DONATELLO	JUVENILIA
THANATISM	UNCEASING	VISCOSITY	ZIBELLINE	ALCOHOLIC	DUTIFULLY	LANDAULET
THATCHING	UNCONFINE	VISUALIZE	ZINKENITE	ALICYCLIC	EARTHFLAX	LATERALLY
THELEMITE	UNDERBITE	VITELLIUS	ZIRCONIUM	ALPENGLOW	EMBATTLED	LAUNCELOT
THELONIUS	UNDERLINE	VITIATION	ZOOLOGIST	AMARYLLIS	EMBEZZLER	LIBERALLY
THERALITE	UNDERLING	VITRUVIAN	MAHARAJAH	AMYGDALUS	EMBROGLIO	LITERALLY
THERAPIST	UNDERMINE	VOLCANISM	AUTOMAKER	ANDROCLES	EMBROILED	LOBLOLLYS
THIRSTILY	UNDERSIDE	VOLTINISM	BEDJACKET	ANNAPOLIS	ENAMELLED	LOGICALLY
THIRSTING	UNDERSIGN	VOLUCRINE	BERSERKER	ANOPHELES	ENCIRCLED	LYRICALLY
THORNBILL	UNFAILING	VOODOOISM	BOOKMAKER	ANTIHELIX	EPICYCLIC	MAGICALLY
THRASHING	UNFEELING	VORTICISM	CARETAKER	APOSTOLIC	EPISTOLER	MALEBOLGE
THREONINE	UNFITTING	VULCANIAN	COXSACKIE	AQUARELLE	ESMERALDA	MALLEOLUS
THRIFTILY	UNHAPPILY	VULCANIST	FILMMAKER	ARMADILLO	ETERNALLY	MAYORALTY
THRILLING	UNHEEDING	VULCANITE	FORJASKIT	ARTICULAR	EVANGELIC	MEATBALLS
THROATILY	UNITARIAN	VULCANIZE	FORJESKIT	ATAHUALPA	FACTUALLY	MEDICALLY
THROBBING	UNKNOWING	VULGARIAN	GRIMALKIN	AURICULAR	FEARFULLY	METABOLIC
THRONGING	UNLUCKILY	VULGARISM	HALFBAKED	AUSTRALIA	FENCIBLES	METAPELET
THUMBLING	UNMARRIED	VULGARITY	HAYMARKET	AUTOPILOT	FILICALES	METHEGLIN
THYLACINE	UNNERVING	VULPINITE	HENPECKED	AVUNCULAR	FILOSELLE	MIRABELLE
THYROXINE	UNPRECISE	VULTURINE	IDENTIKIT	AYATOLLAH	FLABELLUM	MISFALLEN
TIMPANIST	UNSELFISH	WAGNERIAN	JAMPACKED	BAGATELLE	FLAGELLIN	MITRAILLE
TINGUAITE	UNSINNING	WAGNERITE	JAYWALKER	BALEFULLY	FLAGELLUM	MOLECULAR
TITRATION	UNSPARING	WAHABIITE	JOBSEEKER	BARNACLES	FLAGEOLET	MONOCULAR
TOCCATINA	UNSULLIED	WAISTLINE	KILDERKIN	BARTHOLDI	FOOTHILLS	MONOXYLON
TOOTHPICK	UNUNUNIUM	WALLABIES	KINGMAKER	BARTHOLIN	FRANCOLIN	MOTHBALLS
TOPIARIST	UNVARYING	WALLOPING	KROPOTKIN	BASHFULLY	FRETFULLY	MUCORALES
TORBANITE	UNWILLING	WALLOWING	MISPICKEL	BASICALLY	FUNGIBLES	MULTIPLEX
TORTELIER	UNWITTING	WANDERING	MOONRAKER	BEARDSLEY	FUNICULAR	MUSICALLY
TOSCANINI	UNWORRIED	WATERLILY	NANTUCKET	BEDFELLOW	FUNICULUS	NARGHILLY
TOTAQUINE	UPLIFTING	WATERLINE	NEWMARKET	BELLYFLOP	GAINFULLY	NASHVILLE
TOUCHLINE	UPSETTING	WATERMILL	NIPPERKIN	BINOCULAR	GARIBALDI	NATURALLY
TOWELLING	UREDINIAL	WATERSIDE	NONSMOKER	BOOBIALLA	GENERALLY	NEUROGLIA
TOXOPHILY	URICONIAN	WAVELLITE	NOTARIKON	BOXWALLAH	GENITALIA	NEUTRALLY
TRADEWIND	URINATION	WEAKENING	OILTANKER	BRUNHILDE	GENTEELLY	NIGHTCLUB
TRADITION	UVAROVITE	WEIGHTING	OKEYDOKEY	CABRIOLET	GLABELLAR	NIGHTGLOW
TRAGEDIAN	VALENTINE	WELCOMING	OUTSPOKEN	CANDLELIT	GLADIOLUS	NOMINALLY
TRANSPIRE	VALUATION	WELLBEING	OUTWORKER	CAPITULAR	GLANDULAR	NUCLEOLUS

OLENELLUS	STABLELAD	CRACKSMAN	PRODROMAL	ASSONANCE	EMOTIONAL	INCOMINGS
OPERCULUM	STOICALLY	CRAFTSMAN	PRODROMUS	ASSURANCE	ENDURANCE	INDECENCY
OPTICALLY	STRAGGLER	DRAFTSMAN	PROGRAMME	AVOIDANCE	ENGRAINED	INDIGENCE
ORBICULAR	STRANGLER	EALDORMAN	RADDLEMAN	BACKBENCH	ENLIVENED	INDOLENCE
ORGANELLE	STRANGLES	ELASTOMER	RECLAIMED	BAREBONES	ERGATANER	INFERENCE
OVERVALUE	STROBILUS	ENERGUMEN	RECLAIMER	BEESTINGS	ESCULENTS	INFLUENCE
PADEMELON	SUBCELLAR	ENTRAMMEL	ROSCOMMON	BLESSINGS	ESPERANCE	INFLUENZA
PAINFULLY	SUBTITLED	EPIDERMIS	ROUNDSMAN	BOTSWANAN	ESPERANTO	INGRAINED
PANATELLA	SURMULLET	EXCISEMAN	RUDDLEMAN	BRITANNIA	ESTAMINET	INHUMANLY
PAPERCLIP	SWORDPLAY	EXCLAIMED	SCHOOLMAN	BRITANNIC	EVITERNAL	INNOCENCE
PARABOLIC	SYLLABLES	EXODERMIS	SCOTCHMAN	BULLFINCH	EXISTENCE	INORGANIC
PARTHOLON	TABBOULEH	FIELDSMAN	SCYTHEMAN	BUTTERNUT	EYEOPENER	INSOLENCE
PARTIALLY	TACTFULLY	FISHERMAN	SEMIRAMIS	CALEDONIA	FABULINUS	INSURANCE
PARTICLES	TARPAULIN	FOREWOMAN	SHARESMAN	CALPURNIA	FACTIONAL	IPHIGENIA
PATROCLUS	TASSELLED	FRENCHMAN	SIGNALMAN	CAPTAINCY	FALKLANDS	ISOCLINAL
PEDICULAR	TEARFULLY	FRENCHMEN	SKETCHMAP	CATATONIA	FASHIONED	JACARANDA
PERIBOLOS	TELESALES	GAUDEAMUS	SOMETIMES	CATATONIC	FICTIONAL	JOUISANCE
PHARSALIA	TENACULUM	GENTLEMAN	SPOILSMAN	CEROMANCY	FIFTEENTH	JUBILANCE
PITIFULLY	TENAILLON	GENTLEMEN	SPOKESMAN	CERTAINLY	FIGURANTE	KARABINER
PLAYFULLY	TEPHILLIN	GINGLYMUS	SPORTSMAN	CERTAINTY	FLAGRANCE	KILLARNEY
PLIMSOLLS	TESTICLES	GUARDSMAN	SPORTSMEN	CHAFFINCH	FLATTENED	KITCHENER
POMPHOLYX	TOPICALLY	GUILLEMOT	STABLEMAN	CHALLENGE	FLATTENER	LABYRINTH
PORTFOLIO	TRAVELLER	HALLOWMAS	STATESMAN	CHASTENED	FLIPPANCY	LANDOWNER
POSSIBLES	TREDRILLE	HEARDSMAN	STEERSMAN	CHINOVNIK	FOREIGNER	LANTHANUM
POTBOILER	TRIANGLED	ICHNEUMON	SUBNORMAL	CHIPPINGS	FORLORNLY	LAZYBONES
PRACTOLOL	TRIATHLON	IGNORAMUS	SWORDSMAN	CLEARANCE	FOURPENCE	LITHUANIA
PREHALLUX	TRIVIALLY	ISCHAEMIC	THINGUMMY	CLOISONNÉ	FRAGMENTS	LONGRANGE
PREPOLLEX	TROCHILIC	KHANSAMAH	THIRDSMAN	COALMINER	FRAGRANCE	LUMINANCE
PRIESTLEY	TROCHILUS	KINSWOMAN	TRADESMAN	COHERENCE	FRAGRANCY	MACARONIC
PROBABLES	TROPAELIN	LACHRYMAL	TRIBESMAN	COLOCYNTH	FRATERNAL	MACEDONIA
PROCOELUS	TURNBULLS	LATECOMER	TRIBESMEN	CONCERNED	FREELANCE	MAHARANEE
PROPELLED	TYPICALLY	LEUKAEMIA	UNASHAMED	CONDEMNED	FREQUENCY	MAINTENON
PROPELLER	UNBRIDLED	LIVERYMAN	UNCLAIMED	CONSIGNEE	FRESHENER	MATUTINAL
PUMMELLED	UNCOUPLED	MACADAMIA	UNIFORMED	CONSIGNOR	FRIZZANTE	MAVOURNIN
PUNCTILIO	UNDEFILED	MALFORMED	UNIFORMLY	CONSTANCE	GLEANINGS	MEDICINAL
QUADRILLE	UNDERFLOW	MARTINMAS	VIGESIMAL	CONSTANCY	GLISSANDO	MENOMINEE
QUENNELLE	UNEQUALED	MASTERMAN	WASHERMAN	CONTAINER	GOLDFINCH	MENTIONED
RADICALLY	UNPOPULAR	MIDDLEMAN	WASSERMAN	COTHURNUS	GOLDSINNY	MESSIANIC
RENTALLER	UNRUFFLED	MIDSUMMER	WELSUMMER	COVALENCY	GREETINGS	MICROINCH
RETICULAR	UNSETTLED	MINUTEMAN	WHERRYMAN	CRESCENDO	GRIEVANCE	MIDDLINGS
RETICULUM	UNSKILLED	MONATOMIC	YACHTSMAN	CRYOGENIC	GROSVENOR	MILITANCY
RETROFLEX	UNSPOILED	MORECAMBE	YACHTSMEN	CUFFLINKS	GROUNDNUT	MILLIONTH
ROSTELLUM	UNUSUALLY	MUMPSIMUS	ABANDONED	CYTOKININ	GRUBBINOL	MISCHANCE
ROUNDELAY	VARICELLA	MUSSULMAN	ABANDONEE	DALLIANCE	GYROMANCY	MISSIONER
RUBICELLE	VEHICULAR	NICODEMUS	ABDOMINAL	DANTHONIA	HALFPENNY	MOCKERNUT
SANDALLED	VESICULAR	NOVODAMUS	ABERRANCE	DARTAGNAN	HARDLINER	MONOMANIA
SAPODILLA	VIRTUALLY	NYSTAGMUS	ABSTAINER	DEBUTANTE	HARPOONER	MONSIGNOR
SCINTILLA	VITRIOLIC	OARSWOMAN	ABUNDANCE	DECADENCE	HAUTMONDE	MUMCHANCE
SCRAMBLER	WENCESLAS	ODDJOBMAN	ACCIDENTS	DEFERENCE	HEADLINED	MUNIMENTS
SCRODDLED	WILLFULLY	OMBUDSMAN	ADHERENCE	DELPHINUS	HECOGENIN	NESCIENCE
SCUDDALER	WINDFALLS	ORANGEMAN	AEPYORNIS	DILIGENCE	HESITANCE	NINEPENCE
SEMICOLON	WISTFULLY	ORIFLAMME	AFFLUENCE	DIVIDENDS	HESITANCY	NOCTURNAL
SENSILLUM	ANCHORMAN	PANORAMIC	AFRIKANER	DOCTRINAL	HESTERNAL	OBEDIENCE
SENSUALLY	AUTONOMIC	PARANYMPH	AGAMEMNON	DOCUMENTS	HEXAGONAL	OBEISANCE
SEVERALLY	BAPTISMAL	PARTTIMER	ALLEMANDE	DOMINANCE	HIGHLANDS	OCCUPANCY
SHOVELLER	CACHAEMIA	PATROLMAN	ALLOWANCE	DROPPINGS	HINDRANCE	OCTAGONAL
SIGNALLER	CAMERAMAN	PENSTEMON	AMBULANCE	DRUNKENLY	HODIERNAL	OFFCHANCE
SKILFULLY	CANDLEMAS	PERFORMED	ANABRANCH	DUBROVNIK	HOMEOWNER	OLECRANON
SOPHOCLES	CATACOMBS	PERFORMER	ANNOYANCE	DUNGEONER	IGNORANCE	OMNIRANGE
SOULFULLY	CATTLEMAN	PERSIMMON	ANTIGONUS	EASTERNER	IMBALANCE	ONTOGENCY
SPATIALLY	CHARWOMAN	PLAINSMAN	ANTIVENIN	EASTLINGS	IMMANENCE	OPPONENTS
SPECIALLY	CHRISTMAS	PLOUGHMAN	ANTONINUS	ECARDINES	IMMANENCY	ORDINANCE
SPECIALTY	CHURCHMAN	PLUMDAMAS	APENNINES	EFFLUENCE	IMMINENCE	OUTGOINGS
SPHACELUS	CLERGYMAN	POINTSMAN	APOLLONUS	ELOQUENCE	IMPEDANCE	OVERTONES
SPRINGLET	CONFIRMED	POLICEMAN	APPLIANCE	EMBRYONIC	IMPOTENCE	PANTHENOL
SPRINKLER	CONFORMAL	POSTWOMAN	ARMAMENTS	EMERGENCE	IMPUDENCE	PARTHENON
SPUNCULID	CORNERMAN	PRETERMIT	ARROGANCE	EMERGENCY	INCIDENCE	PASTERNAK

PATTERNED	SHECHINAH	AFTERMOST	BREAKDOWN	CREMATORY	EXPIATORY	HAILSTONE
PAULOWNIA	SHETLANDS	AFTERNOON	BRICKWORK	CRETINOUS	EXTEMPORE	HAILSTORM
PENDENNIS	SHIPOWNER	AFTERWORD	BRIGADOON	CROCKFORD	FABACEOUS	HALOBIONT
PENITENCE	SIBILANCE	AITCHBONE	BRIMSTONE	CROSSWORD	FACECLOTH	HANDIWORK
PENSIONER	SIXTEENMO	ALBATROSS	BROADLOOM	CROWSFOOT	FACETIOUS	HARDIHOOD
PERCHANCE	SIXTEENTH	ALLANTOID	BRUSHWOOD	CRUCIFORM	FALDSTOOL	HARMOTOME
PERGUNNAH	SNOWDONIA	ALLANTOIS	BUCKTHORN	CUBBYHOLE	FALSEHOOD	HARTSHORN
PERSONNEL	SOVENANCE	ALPENHORN	BUMPTIOUS	CUNEIFORM	FARANDOLE	HAWSEHOLE
PETULANCE	SQUINANCY	AMBIGUOUS	CACOPHONY	CURRYCOMB	FERACIOUS	HAZARDOUS
PIMPERNEL	STATIONED	AMBITIOUS	CAIRNGORM	CUSPIDORE	FEROCIOUS	HAZELWORT
PLEASANCE	STATIONER	AMORPHOUS	CALABOOSE	CUTANEOUS	FERRYBOAT	HEADCLOTH
PNEUMONIA	STIFFENER	ANALOGOUS	CALEMBOUR	CUTTHROAT	FEUDATORY	HEADSTONE
POCKMANKY	STOCKINET	ANHYDROUS	CANCEROUS	DANGEROUS	FIELDWORK	HEARTWOOD
POIGNANCY	STOCKINGS	ANOMALOUS	CAPACIOUS	DAVENPORT	FIREPROOF	HELLEBORE
POLYGONAL	STRIDENCY	ANONYMOUS	CAPRICORN	DECACHORD	FIRESTONE	HEMITROPE
POSTPONED	SUBSTANCE	ANTHOLOGY	CARAMBOLA	DECIDUOUS	FLAGSTONE	HERBIVORE
PREGNANCY	SULPHONIC	ANTIPHONY	CARCINOMA	DECOMPOSE	FLEETWOOD	HILARIOUS
PREVERNAL	SUNDOWNER	ARABINOSE	CARNIVORE	DECRETORY	FLESHPOTS	HISTOLOGY
PRONOUNCE	SUNTANNED	ARACHNOID	CASSEROLE	DELACROIX	FLINTLOCK	HITCHCOCK
PROPIONIC	SUSTAINED	ARCHIVOLT	CATCHPOLE	DELICIOUS	FLOWSTONE	HOARFROST
PRURIENCE	SWEEPINGS	ARMSTRONG	CATCHPOLL	DELIRIOUS	FOLIOLOSE	HOARSTONE
PSEUDONYM	SWEETENER	ARROWROOT	CATCHWORD	DEMEANOUR	FOODSTORE	HOBBINOLL
PUISSANCE	SYMPHONIC	ARTERIOLE	CAUCASOID	DESULTORY	FOOLPROOF	HOCCAMORE
PURITANIC	TEMULENCE	ARTICHOKE	CAVERNOUS	DEVONPORT	FOOTLOOSE	HOLLYHOCK
PURSUANCE	TENEMENTS	ASSIDUOUS	CEDARWOOD	DEXTEROUS	FOOTSTOOL	HOLLYWOOD
PURULENCE	TEREBINTH	ASTRODOME	CELLULOID	DIANDROUS	FORECLOSE	HOLOPHOTE
PYROMANCY	THINNINGS	ASTROLOGY	CELLULOSE	DIARRHOEA	FOREFRONT	HOLYSTONE
PYROMANIA	THOUSANDS	ASTRONOMY	CERECLOTH	DICHOTOMY	FORESHORE	HOMEGROWN
PYRRHONIC	THRASONIC	ASTUCIOUS	CHANCROID	DIPHTHONG	FRACTIOUS	HOMOPHONE
QUITTANCE	TIGHTENER	ATROCIOUS	CHAPERONE	DIRECTORS	FRAMEWORK	HONEYCOMB
RASKOLNIK	TOLERANCE	AUDACIOUS	CHECKBOOK	DIRECTORY	FREEPHONE	HONEYMOON
REACTANCE	TOXIGENIC	AUTOCROSS	CHECKROOM	DISCOLOUR	FREESTONE	HONKYTONK
REARRANGE	TRACHINUS	AUTOSCOPY	CHEEKBONE	DISENTOMB	FRIGATOON	HOPLOLOGY
RECUSANCE	TRAMLINES	AUXOTROPH	CHILDHOOD	DISFAVOUR	FRITHBORH	HORNSTONE
REDOLENCE	TRAPPINGS	BACKCLOTH	CHILOPODA	DISHCLOTH	FRIVOLOUS	HOROSCOPE
REFERENCE	TRICLINIC	BACKSWORD	CHINATOWN	DISHONOUR	FUGACIOUS	HORTATORY
REFINANCE	TRIMMINGS	BACKWOODS	CHIROPODY	DODDIPOLL	FULLBLOWN	HOURSTONE
REFUSENIK	TRUEPENNY	BALTIMORE	CHONDROID	DORMITORY	FULLGROWN	HOUSEBOAT
RELEVANCE	UMPTEENTH	BANDALORE	CINEREOUS	DOTHEBOYS	FURACIOUS	HOUSECOAT
REMBRANDT	UNBALANCE	BANDICOOT	CLAMOROUS	DRIFTWOOD	GALACTOSE	HOUSEHOLD
RESIDENCE	UNCROWNED	BARBAROUS	CLAMPDOWN	DRIPSTONE	GALLIPOLI	HOUSEROOM
RESIDENCY	UNDEFINED	BARBITONE	CLASSROOM	DRUGSTORE	GALLSTONE	HOUSEWORK
RESONANCE	UNLEARNED	BARCELONA	CLOAKROOM	EAGLEWOOD	GARDEROBE	HUMONGOUS
RETICENCE	UNREFINED	BARNSTORM	CLOCKWORK	EARTHWORK	GARRULOUS	HUMUNGOUS
REVERENCE	UNTRAINED	BARYSCOPE	COACHLOAD	EARTHWORM	GENEALOGY	HUNKYDORY
RINGFENCE	UTTERANCE	BEAUTEOUS	COCKSCOMB	EDDYSTONE	GINORMOUS	HYDROFOIL
ROSINANTE	VEHEMENCE	BEHAVIOUR	COCKSFOOT	EGREGIOUS	GIRANDOLE	HYPERBOLA
ROZINANTE	VENGEANCE	BELLICOSE	COCUSWOOD	EIDERDOWN	GLADSTONE	HYPERBOLE
RUDIMENTS	VERSIONAL	BILLABONG	COLOPHONY	EIGHTSOME	GLAIREOUS	IDIOPHONE
RUFFIANLY	VERTUMNUS	BILLYCOCK	COLOSTOMY	ELBOWROOM	GLAMOROUS	IMPERIOUS
SAGAPENUM	VESTMENTS	BIRTHWORT	COLTSFOOT	ELECTRODE	GLASSWORT	IMPETUOUS
SATYRINAE	VIGILANCE	BLACKFOOT	COMINFORM	ENDEAVOUR	GLORYHOLE	INCOMMODE
SAUTERNES	VIGILANTE	BLACKMORE	COMMODORE	ENTRECÔTE	GLUTINOUS	INCURIOUS
SAUVIGNON	VIRULENCE	BLACKWOOD	CONDYLOMA	EPIGAEOUS	GOOSEFOOT	INGENIOUS
SCABLANDS	VOLTURNUS	BLINDFOLD	CONGRUOUS	EPIGENOUS	GRANDIOSE	INGENUOUS
SCIOMANCY	WANCHANCY	BLINDWORM	CONSCIOUS	EPONYMOUS	GRANULOSE	INGLENOOK
SCRAPINGS	WESTERNER	BLOODROOT	CORDUROYS	EROGENOUS	GREATCOAT	INJURIOUS
SCRIVENER	WHODUNNIT	BLOODWORM	CORNFLOUR	ERRONEOUS	GREENHORN	INNERMOST
SECTIONAL	WOODLANDS	BLUESTONE	CORTISONE	ERUCIFORM	GREENROOM	INNOCUOUS
SEMBLANCE	XENOMANIA	BOARDROOM	COSMOGONY	ESPAGNOLE	GREENWOOD	INSIDIOUS
SEMIFINAL	ABLUTIONS	BONDSTONE	COSMOLOGY	ETHEREOUS	GUACAMOLE	INTERLOCK
SENTIENCE	ACCESSORY	BOOKSTORE	COUNTDOWN	ETHNOLOGY	GUARDROOM	INTERLOPE
SEQUINNED	ACIDULOUS	BOSSANOVA	COURTEOUS	ETYMOLOGY	GUESSWORK	INTERNODE
SEVERANCE	ACROPHONY	BOUNTEOUS	COURTROOM	EUDAEMONY	GUIDEBOOK	INTERPOSE
SFORZANDO	ADDERWORT	BOURGEOIS	CRACKDOWN	EVERYBODY	GYROSCOPE	INVENTORY
SHAMIANAH	ADULTHOOD	BRACTEOLE	CRAPULOUS	EVOCATORY	HACKAMORE	INVIDIOUS
SHARPENER	AERODROME	BRASENOSE	CREDULOUS	EXOGENOUS	HAEMALOMA	IPRINDOLE

IRONSTONE	METALWORK	OVERBLOWN	PRELUSORY	SETACEOUS	TELEPHONE	VENEREOUS
JOBERNOWL	METEOROID	OVERCLOUD	PRONGHORN	SHAKEDOWN	TELEPHONY	VERACIOUS
JUDICIOUS	METHADONE	OVERCROWD	PROUDHORN	SHEEPFOLD	TELEPHOTO	VERMIFORM
JUXTAPOSE	METRONOME	OVERGROWN	PROVEDORE	SHENSTONE	TELESCOPE	VERMINOUS
KABELJOUW	MICROCOSM	OVERSHOES	PROVOLONE	SHIFTWORK	TENACIOUS	VERTIPORT
KERBSTONE	MICROMOLE	OVERSHOOT	PURGATORY	SHOPFLOOR	TENEBROSE	VEXATIONS
KEYSTROKE	MICROTOME	OVIPAROUS	PUSSYFOOT	SHOPFRONT	TERRICOLE	VEXATIOUS
KNOCKDOWN	MICROTONE	PAINTWORK	QUASIMODO	SHORTHOLD	TERRITORY	VIBRATORY
KOMINFORM	MICROVOLT	PALAMPORE	QUERIMONY	SHORTHORN	TESTIMONY	VICARIOUS
KONISCOPE	MIGRATORY	PALEMPORE	QUERULOUS	SIGNATORY	TETRALOGY	VITASCOPE
KRUMMHORN	MILESTONE	PANETTONE	QUILLWORT	SILTSTONE	TETTEROUS	VIVACIOUS
LABORIOUS	MILLEPORE	PANTALOON	QUINTROON	SINGAPORE	THECODONT	VOLAGEOUS
LAEVULOSE	MILLIVOLT	PAPERWORK	RACCABOUT	SLABSTONE	THEOBROMA	VORACIOUS
LAKEFRONT	MILLSTONE	PAPILLOTE	RACCAHOUT	SNOWSHOES	THEREFORE	WAGENBOOM
LAMBSWOOL	MINACIOUS	PARATROOP	RADIOLOGY	SNOWSTORM	THIGHBONE	WAGONLOAD
LANCEWOOD	MINKSTONE	PARDALOTE	RAFFINOSE	SOAPSTONE	THREEFOLD	WAISTCOAT
LANDDROST	MINNESOTA	PARSIMONY	RAINSTORM	SOCIOLOGY	THREESOME	WALKABOUT
LASERWORT	MISINFORM	PATCHWORK	RANCOROUS	SOMASCOPE	THRESHOLD	WASHCLOTH
LAUDATORY	MISSTROKE	PATERCOVE	RANTIPOLE	SOPHOMORE	THROWDOWN	WATCHWORD
LAZZARONE	MOMENTOUS	PATHOLOGY	RAPACIOUS	SOUTHDOWN	TIGHTROPE	WATERFORD
LEAKPROOF	MONEYWORT	PATRIMONY	RAPTUROUS	SPEARWORT	TISIPHONE	WATERFOWL
LEASEHOLD	MONKSHOOD	PEARLWORT	RASPATORY	SPEEDBOAT	TOADSTONE	WATERHOLE
LECHEROUS	MONOCHORD	PELLITORY	REDINGOTE	SPHENDONE	TOADSTOOL	WAYZGOOSE
LEUCOTOME	MONOTROCH	PENDULOUS	REFECTORY	SPIRITOUS	TOBERMORY	WEARISOME
LIBELLOUS	MONSTROUS	PENISTONE	RELATIONS	SPLAYFOOT	TOMBSTONE	WEDGEWOOD
LIGHTFOOT	MOONSTONE	PENNYWORT	RELIGIOSO	SPLENDOUR	TOMENTOSE	WELLKNOWN
LIGHTSOME	MORTSTONE	PENTECOST	RELIGIOUS	SQUADRONE	TOOTHCOMB	WHALEBOAT
LIMESTONE	MOTOCROSS	PENURIOUS	REPERTORY	STARSTONE	TOOTHSOME	WHALEBONE
LINTSTOCK	MOTORBOAT	PEPPERONI	RESERVOIR	STATEHOOD	TOUCHDOWN	WHEREFORE
LITHOPONE	MOUSEHOLE	PERISCOPE	RESTIFORM	STATEROOM	TOUCHWOOD	WHETSTONE
LITIGIOUS	MULTIFORM	PERISTOME	RIDERHOOD	STATUTORY	TOWNSFOLK	WHINSTONE
LIVERPOOL	MUNITIONS	PETROLOGY	RIDGEPOLE	STEAMBOAT	TRANSFORM	WHIRLPOOL
LIVERWORT	MURDEROUS	PETTICOAT	RIGHTEOUS	STEINBOCK	TRANSPORT	WHITEWOOD
LIVESTOCK	MUSHROOMS	PETTITOES	RIGMAROLE	STEVEDORE	TRANSPOSE	WHOLEFOOD
LOADSTONE	MUSKETOON	PHALAROPE	ROADBLOCK	STILLBORN	TRAPEZOID	WHOLESOME
LOATHSOME	MUTOSCOPE	PHARAMOND	ROCAMBOLE	STILLROOM	TREBIZOND	WIDOWHOOD
LODESTONE	MYRMECOID	PHENYTOIN	ROOTSTOCK	STINKHORN	TREGETOUR	WOBBEGONG
LOINCLOTH	MYTHOLOGY	PHEROMONE	ROQUEFORT	STINKWOOD	TREMATODE	WOEBEGONE
LONGICORN	NATHEMORE	PHILOLOGY	RUDDIGORE	STIRABOUT	TREMULOUS	WOMANHOOD
LONGSHORE	NEFANDOUS	PHONOLOGY	SACKCLOTH	STOCKHOLM	TRETINOIN	WOMENFOLK
LOUSEWORT	NEFARIOUS	PHOTOCOPY	SAGACIOUS	STOCKROOM	TRIBOLOGY	WOODSHOCK
LUDICROUS	NEIGHBOUR	PHYCOLOGY	SAILCLOTH	STOCKWORK	TRICOLOUR	WORRISOME
LUSTIHOOD	NEUROLOGY	PIACEVOLE	SAINTFOIN	STOKEHOLD	TRUCKLOAD	WRONGDOER
LUXURIOUS	NEVERMORE	PIECEWORK	SAINTHOOD	STONEBOAT	TULIPWOOD	WRONGFOOT
LYMESWOLD	NIGHTGOWN	PILLICOCK	SALACIOUS	STONEWORK	TUNGSTOUS	XENOPHOBE
MACROCOSM	NIGHTWORK	PINCHCOCK	SALLYPORT	STONEWORT	TURCOPOLE	XEROSTOMA
MACROLOGY	NOSTOLOGY	PIPESTONE	SALLYPOST	STOREROOM	TURNABOUT	XYLOPHONE
MADREPORE	NOTOCHORD	PITCHFORK	SANDSTONE	STORYBOOK	TURNSTONE	ZYGOSPORE
MAJORDOMO	NOTORIOUS	PITCHPOLE	SANDSTORM	STRENUOUS	TYRANNOUS	AMBLYOPIA
MALICIOUS	OBLIVIOUS	PITCHPOLL	SANGFROID	STRINGOPS	ULIGINOUS	ANAGLYPTA
MANDATORY	OBNOXIOUS	PLACATORY	SASKATOON	STROMBOLI	UNANIMOUS	APOCRYPHA
MANGETOUT	OCTACHORD	PLAINSONG	SATINWOOD	STUMPWORK	UNBEKNOWN	ARTHROPOD
MAPPEMOND	OCTOPLOID	PLAYGROUP	SAUCEBOAT	SUBDOLOUS	UNDERCOAT	BEEKEEPER
MARVELOUS	OCULIFORM	PLENTEOUS	SAXOPHONE	SULFUROUS	UNDERDONE	BIOGRAPHY
MASSYMORE	OFFCOLOUR	PLUMBEOUS	SCAGLIOLA	SUMPTUOUS	UNDERFOOT	BLINDSPOT
MATCHBOOK	OFFERTORY	POISONOUS	SCALLIONS	SUNSTROKE	UNDERMOST	CATALEPSY
MATCHLOCK	OFFICIOUS	POKERWORK	SCAPEGOAT	SUPERCOOL	UNDERSONG	CATTLEPEN
MATCHWOOD	OLFACTORY	POLYPHONE	SCHIAVONE	SUPERNOVA	UNDERTONE	CHALIAPIN
MATRIMONY	OPTOPHONE	POLYPHONY	SCRAPBOOK	SURREJOIN	UNDERWOOD	CONTEMPER
MATTAMORE	ORGILLOUS	POMPADOUR	SCURRIOUR	SWANIMOTE	UNTIMEOUS	DEVELOPED
MEGAPHONE	ORTHODOXY	PONDEROSA	SEBACEOUS	SWANSDOWN	UNWELCOME	DEVELOPER
MEGASCOPE	ORTHOLOGY	PONDEROUS	SEDGEMOOR	SYPHILOMA	UPPERMOST	DISTEMPER
MEGASPORE	ORTHOTONE	POPPYCOCK	SEDITIOUS	TARRAGONA	UTTERMOST	DYSTROPHY
MELAMPODE	OSTROGOTH	POWERBOAT	SEMAPHORE	TAUTOLOGY	VAINGLORY	EMPANOPLY
MELODIOUS	OUTERMOST	PRECATORY	SEMIGLOSS	TAVISTOCK	VASECTOMY	EPISCOPAL
MENADIONE	OUTOFTOWN	PREDATORY	SEMIOLOGY	TECTIFORM	VELDSKOEN	FLOWERPOT
METALLOID	OVENPROOF	PREFATORY	SEPTIMOLE	TELEOLOGY	VELODROME	FLUORSPAR

GEOGRAPHY	ARAUCARIA	ECCENTRIC	LIENTERIC	RASPBERRY	THACKERAY	CIRRHOSIS
HALFEMPTY	BACKWARDS	ECHEVERIA	LINDBERGH	REARHORSE	THESAURUS	CIVILISED
HYPEROPIA	BAINMARIE	ECTOMORPH	LOHENGRIN	REARWARDS	THUNDERER	COLLAPSAR
IMPROMPTU	BANEBERRY	EDGEWORTH	LUCIFERIN	RECOVERED	THYRATRON	COMMENSAL
INNKEEPER	BECQUEREL	EDINBURGH	MACQUARIE	REGISTRAR	TICHBORNE	COMMISSAR
ISOPROPYL	BILATERAL	ELECTORAL	MAELSTROM	REGULARLY	TIERCERON	CONCUSSED
ISOTROPIC	BILLIARDS	ENAMOURED	MAGNETRON	REICHSRAT	TRATTORIA	CONDENSER
KIDNAPPED	BISHOPRIC	ENDOMORPH	MATRIARCH	REIMBURSE	TREASURER	CONFESSED
KIDNAPPER	BLINKERED	EPHEMERAL	MEGAHERTZ	REINFORCE	TRIERARCH	CONFESSOR
LAGNIAPPE	BLISTERED	EPHEMERIS	MELBOURNE	RENFIERST	TRIETERIC	CONSENSUS
LANDLOPER	BLOWTORCH	EPHEMERON	MENAGERIE	RESNATRON	TRIHEDRON	COPIOUSLY
MISSHAPEN	BLUEBERRY	ETCETERAS	MESOMORPH	ROADWORKS	TURBOPROP	COURTESAN
MISTEMPER	BLUNDERER	EUCHLORIC	MILLIGRAM	ROISTERER	UNALTERED	CUPRESSUS
MONTESPAN	BLUSTERER	EUHEMERUS	MISTIGRIS	SACCHARIN	UNCOVERED	CURIOUSLY
MUNICIPAL	BONAPARTE	EXECUTRIX	MONASTRAL	SALTWORKS	UNDERBRED	DEMITASSE
NEWSPAPER	BOOBYTRAP	FEATHERED	MONOCEROS	SANDHURST	UNDERGRAD	DEPRESSED
NIGHTSPOT	BOSPHORUS	FILMSTRIP	MORATORIA	SANHEDRIM	UNINJURED	DEVIOUSLY
NOTEPAPER	BRANDIRON	FIREWORKS	MORATORIO	SANHEDRIN	UNNATURAL	DIAERESIS
ONTHESPOT	BRASSERIE	FLATTENED	MOUSETRAP	SANHEDRON	UNSECURED	DIAGNOSIS
OROGRAPHY	BRATWURST	FLATTERER	MYOFIBRIL	SASSAFRAS	UNTUTORED	DIAPHYSIS
OUTROOPER	BROTHERLY	FLAVOURED	NASEBERRY	SCANSORES	UNWATERED	DIASTASIS
PEPPERPOT	CABLEGRAM	FLUSTERED	NECKVERSE	SCARECROW	UPAITHRIC	DIATHESIS
PERAEOPOD	CADASTRAL	FOOLHARDY	NIAISERIE	SCATTERED	URTICARIA	DINNERSET
PHILIPPIC	CAFETERIA	FROGMARCH	NORTHERLY	SCHLIEREN	VERDIGRIS	DISCLOSED
PHYLLOPOD	CANAVERAL	FRUITERER	OBSTETRIC	SCHNORRER	VERTEBRAE	DISGUISED
PINEAPPLE	CANTHARIS	GALLYCROW	OCHLOCRAT	SCHOLARCH	VERTEBRAL	DISMISSAL
PRINCIPAL	CANTHARUS	GEOMETRIC	OUDENARDE	SCHOLARLY	VOLGOGRAD	DISPENSER
PRINCIPLE	CARTHORSE	GEOMETRID	OUROBOROS	SCISSORER	WALLYDRAG	DISPERSAL
QUADRUPED	CARTOGRAM	GERIATRIC	OUROBORUS	SCOUNDREL	WESTWARDS	DISPERSED
QUADRUPLE	CATAMARAN	GIGAHERTZ	OUTSKIRTS	SEMANTRON	WHITWORTH	DUBIOUSLY
QUINTUPLE	CATCHCROP	GLENGARRY	OVERTHROW	SHATTERED	WINEBERRY	DYSPEPSIA
SANDPAPER	CATHEDRAL	GRAPETREE	PALINURUS	SHELTERED	WOODBORER	ECLAMPSIA
SANDPIPER	CENTAURUS	HACKBERRY	PALOVERDE	SHEPHERDS	WORKFORCE	ELEVENSES
SCALLOPED	CENTIGRAM	HAWTHORNE	PALPEBRAL	SHUTTERED	WORKHORSE	EMPHLYSIS
SCHNAPPER	CHAMPERTY	HEADFIRST	PANEGYRIC	SIDEBURNS	ACARIASIS	ENCHEASON
SKETCHPAD	CHAPARRAL	HEARTHRUG	PAREGORIC	SIDEWARDS	ACQUIESCE	ENDLESSLY
SLAPHAPPY	CHARTERED	HECTOGRAM	PATRIARCH	SIMILARLY	ADDRESSED	ENGROSSED
THEOSOPHY	CHATTERER	HEXAMERON	PELLAGRIN	SLUGHORNE	ADDRESSEE	ENGROSSER
THEREUPON	CHEQUERED	HIPPOCRAS	PENTAGRAM	SLUMBERER	AGGRESSOR	EPICLESIS
TRICUSPID	CHINSTRAP	HISTOGRAM	PERCHERON	SMOKEFREE	AIMLESSLY	EPIPHYSIS
VERKAMPTE	CINERARIA	HOMEWARDS	PERIMORPH	SOAPBERRY	AMAUROSIS	EPITHESIS
WALLPAPER	CLUSTERED	ILLIBERAL	PHONOGRAM	SOLDIERLY	AMOROUSLY	EXERCISED
WHEREUPON	COLOSTRUM	INAUGURAL	PHYTOTRON	SOUTHERLY	ANALGESIA	EXERCISES
XANTHIPPE	CONCIERGE	INDECORUM	PICOFARAD	SPATTERED	ANALGESIC	EXOSTOSIS
ZOOSCOPIC	CONCOURSE	INNISFREE	PICTOGRAM	SPINNERET	ANAPLASIA	EXPRESSED
ARABESQUE	CONQUEROR	INTERBRED	PITUITRIN	SPOFFORTH	ANAPLASTY	EXPRESSLY
BURLESQUE	CONUNDRUM	INTERPRET	PLASTERED	SPONSORED	ANASTASIA	EXTRINSIC
EQUIVOQUE	CORKSCREW	IRONWORKS	PLASTERER	STAGGERED	ANKYLOSIS	FAMAGUSTA
GROTESQUE	CRANBERRY	ISOMETRIC	PLAUSTRAL	STALWORTH	ANTIPASTO	FATUOUSLY
MONOCOQUE	CRANBORNE	JACKSCREW	PLETHORIC	STAMMERER	ANXIOUSLY	FORETASTE
ODALISQUE	CROSSBRED	JACKSTRAW	PLUNDERER	STANDARDS	APHERESIS	FRANCESCA
ORTANIQUE	CYCLOTRON	JACQUERIE	PLUTOCRAT	STANDERBY	APOPHYSIS	FREEMASON
PAYCHEQUE	DANDYPRAT	JOBSWORTH	POLEMARCH	STEENBRAS	APPRAISAL	FRICASSEE
PLASTIQUE	DEATHTRAP	JOCKSTRAP	POLYMORPH	STERCORAL	ARDUOUSLY	FURIOUSLY
POLITIQUE	DECAMERON	JOCULARLY	POPULARLY	STINGAREE	ARRIVISTE	GODDESSES
SOLILOQUY	DECONTROL	JUNEBERRY	PORIFERAN	STONECROP	ARTEMISIA	GOMPHOSIS
TECHNIQUE	DELIVERER	KARAKORAM	POSTCARDS	STONKERED	ARTHROSIS	GROUNDSEL
ADULTERER	DEXTRORSE	KILOHERTZ	POTPOURRI	SULPHURIC	AUTOLYSIS	HALITOSIS
AHASUERUS	DIABLERIE	KLEMPERER	POULTERER	SURCHARGE	CALLOUSLY	HETEROSIS
AINSWORTH	DIAMETRIC	KNACKERED	PREFERRED	SWAGGERER	CANVASSER	HEYPRESTO
ALDEBARAN	DIATHERMY	KNEECORDS	PROTHORAX	SWIMMERET	CAPARISON	HIDEOUSLY
ALLOCARPY	DIGASTRIC	LAGOMORPH	PUERPERAL	SWINBURNE	CARYOPSIS	HYPINOSIS
AMBERGRIS	DISCHARGE	LAMASERAI	PYRETHRUM	SYMMETRIC	CATALYSIS	IMMODESTY
ANCESTRAL	DISCOURSE	LANDWARDS	QUARTERLY	TAXIDERMY	CATHARSIS	IMMUNISER
ANGIOGRAM	DOWNWARDS	LECANORAM	RACEHORSE	TERAHERTZ	CATHEPSIN	IMPRESSED
ANNAPURNA	EASTWARDS	LEFTWARDS	RACKSTRAW	TESTATRIX	CHEONGSAM	INCREASED
ANTISERUM	EAVESDROP	LENINGRAD	RADIOGRAM	TETRAGRAM	CHLOROSIS	INDONESIA

INTRINSIC	RHODOPSIN	ALIPHATIC	CASUISTIC	DISGUSTED	FIREWATER	ISOTACTIC
INTUMESCE	RIOTOUSLY	ALLIGATOR	CASUISTRY	DISHWATER	FLECHETTE	JERKWATER
JEALOUSLY	ROBERTSON	ALLOPATHY	CATALYTIC	DISMANTLE	FLORESTAN	JOBCENTRE
JOSEPHSON	ROUMANSCH	ALTIMETER	CATHARTIC	DISSENTER	FORFEITED	KERATITIS
KLENDUSIC	RUINOUSLY	AMARANTIN	CERATITIS	DISTANTLY	FORGOTTEN	KILOMETER
LANGOUSTE	SACKERSON	AMENHOTEP	CERVANTES	DISTORTED	FREIGHTER	KILOMETRE
LIVRAISON	SALVARSAN	ANALEPTIC	CHARACTER	DISUNITED	GALLANTLY	KLINOSTAT
MADAROSIS	SANNYASIN	ANCIPITAL	CHARLATAN	DIZYGOTIC	GALLANTRY	KONIMETER
MADRASSAH	SAUCISSON	ANECDOTAL	CHARLOTTE	DOLOMITES	GARGANTUA	LACERATED
MADRESSAH	SCLEROSIS	ANECDOTES	CHEMISTRY	DOLOMITIC	GASOMETER	LAFAYETTE
MAHARISHI	SCOLIOSIS	ANIMISTIC	CHORISTER	DONCASTER	GAULEITER	LAMINATED
MANGOUSTE	SERIOUSLY	ANNOTATED	CHROMATIC	DONIZETTI	GENERATOR	LAMINITIS
MANIFESTO	SIDEROSIS	ANNOTATOR	CIGARETTE	DOSIMETER	GEORGETTE	LANCASTER
MARQUESAS	SILICOSIS	ANTARCTIC	CINEMATIC	DUMBARTON	GIBRALTAR	LANGUETTE
MATELASSE	SIMPLISTE	ANTENATAL	CLEOPATRA	DYNAMITED	GLADIATOR	LARGHETTO
MEDRESSEH	SINGLESEX	ANTIPATHY	CLIMACTIC	DYSPEPTIC	GOOSESTEP	LASTDITCH
MELANESIA	SINKANSEN	APATHETIC	COADJUTOR	EARNESTLY	GRADUATED	LAZARETTO
MELANOSIS	SPADASSIN	APOPHATIC	COELOSTAT	ECOSYSTEM	GUARANTEE	LEICESTER
MERGANSER	STEGNOSIS	APPARATUS	COLLECTED	EDDINGTON	GUARANTOR	LEITMOTIF
METABASIS	STEVENSON	APPARITOR	COLLECTOR	ELEGANTLY	GUJARATHI	LEITMOTIV
MIDDLESEX	SUBFOSSIL	APPOINTED	COMFORTER	ELEMENTAL	GUNCOTTON	LENIENTLY
MOGADISHU	SUCCESSOR	APPOINTEE	COMMITTAL	ELLINGTON	GYMNASTIC	LIBERATED
MOTORISTS	SUCCURSAL	ARBORETUM	COMMITTED	ELONGATED	HACQUETON	LIBERATOR
NARCISSUS	SURPRISED	ARISTOTLE	COMMITTEE	EMACIATED	HAMFATTER	LINKLATER
NERVOUSLY	SUSPENSOR	ARLINGTON	COMPACTLY	EMINENTLY	HAMFISTED	LOGARITHM
OBVIOUSLY	SYLLEPSIS	ARTHRITIC	CONCEITED	EMPAESTIC	HANSEATIC	LORGNETTE
OFFSEASON	SYMBIOSIS	ARTHRITIS	CONCERTED	EMPLECTON	HARLESTON	LUBAVITCH
OLEORESIN	SYMPHYSIS	ASPIRATOR	CONDUCTOR	ENCAUSTIC	HARMATTAN	LYMPHATIC
OMINOUSLY	SYNCHYSIS	ASTHMATIC	CONDUCTUS	ENCHANTED	HARVESTER	LYSIMETER
OPOBALSAM	SYNIZESIS	ASYMMETRY	CONFLATED	ENCHANTER	HEDERATED	MAJORETTE
OPPRESSED	SYNTHESIS	ASYNDETON	CONGESTED	ENCOUNTER	HEMSTITCH	MANHATTAN
OPPRESSOR	TEDIOUSLY	ATAVISTIC	CONNECTED	ENDEICTIC	HEPATITIS	MANOMETER
ORGANISED	TENNESSEE	ATHEISTIC	CONNECTOR	ENERGETIC	HEREAFTER	MARQUETRY
ORGANISER	TENUOUSLY	ATHELSTAN	CONTENTED	ENIGMATIC	HERODOTUS	MEDICATED
OVERHASTY	THALASSIC	ATTEMPTED	CONVECTOR	ENLIGHTEN	HERPESTES	MEDITATOR
PAILLASSE	TOVARISCH	AUBRIETIA	CONVERTED	ENSHEATHE	HEURISTIC	MEKOMETER
PALLIASSE	UNBIASSED	AUTHENTIC	CONVERTER	ENTERITIS	HEXAMETER	MELANOTIC
PARABASIS	UNCHRISOM	AUTOLATRY	CORRECTED	EPAULETTE	HODOMETER	MEMORITER
PARACUSIS	UNCROSSED	AUTOMATED	CORRECTLY	EPEOLATRY	HOPSCOTCH	MERCAPTAN
PARALYSIS	UNDRESSED	AUTOMATIC	CORRECTOR	EPHIALTES	HOTTENTOT	MICKLETON
PARNASSUS	UNEXPOSED	AUTOMATON	CORRUPTER	EPICENTRE	HYDROSTAT	MIDDLETON
PEDERASTY	UNIVERSAL	AXIOMATIC	COUCHETTE	EPILEPTIC	HYLOBATES	MIDINETTE
PERTUSSIS	UNOPPOSED	AXMINSTER	COURGETTE	EPINASTIC	IDEOPATHY	MIDWINTER
PHANTASMA	UTICENSIS	BACKBITER	CRICKETER	EPIPHYTIC	IDIOMATIC	MILOMETER
POLITESSE	VALDENSES	BACKWATER	CROQUETTE	EQUISETUM	ILCHESTER	MISTLETOE
POLYNESIA	VALVASSOR	BADMINTON	CRYOMETER	ERIOMETER	ILLGOTTEN	MODERATOR
PORPOISES	VARIOUSLY	BALLISTIC	CUNCTATOR	ESCALATOR	ILLICITLY	MONOMETER
POSSESSED	VICIOUSLY	BANQUETTE	CURRENTLY	ESCOPETTE	IMPERATOR	MOSCHATEL
POSSESSOR	VISAGISTE	BAROMETER	CYNEGETIC	ESTAFETTE	IMPOLITIC	MOTHEATEN
PRACTISED	WALDENSES	BARONETCY	DAMBUSTER	ETIOLATED	INCITATUS	MUFFETTEE
PRECURSOR	WASHBASIN	BARRISTER	DECALITRE	ETIQUETTE	INCUBATOR	MUGGLETON
PROCESSOR	WISCONSIN	BEDSITTER	DECORATED	EUMYCETES	INDICATES	MUTILATED
PROCONSUL	WITNESSED	BEEFEATER	DECORATOR	EUPHRATES	INDICATOR	NAUSEATED
PROFESSED	WOMANISER	BENIGHTED	DEDICATED	EVIDENTLY	INHERITED	NAVIGATOR
PROFESSOR	YGGDRASIL	BETTERTON	DEFAULTER	EXCAVATOR	INHERITOR	NEGLECTED
PROGNOSIS	ABERNETHY	BLATANTLY	DEFLECTOR	EXEQUATUR	INHIBITED	NEPHRITIC
PROLEPSIS	ACQUITTAL	BOMBASTIC	DELIGHTED	EXHAUSTED	INHIBITOR	NEPHRITIS
PROPTOSIS	ACROBATIC	BRIQUETTE	DENTISTRY	EXHIBITOR	INITIATED	NEUCHATEL
PROTHESIS	ACROPETAL	BROUGHTON	DEPOSITOR	EXPLOITER	INITIATOR	NEWCASTLE
PSORIASIS	ADMONITOR	BUNDESTAG	DESCARTES	EXPOSITOR	INNOVATOR	NOMINATOR
PSYCHOSIS	ADVOCATED	CACHECTIC	DETONATOR	EXTRACTOR	INSPECTOR	NOVELETTE
PURCHASER	AESTHETIC	CANALETTO	DETRACTOR	FANTASTIC	INSTANTER	NUMERATOR
RAUCOUSLY	AFFLICTED	CAPACITOR	DIACRITIC	FERMENTED	INSTANTLY	OCCIPITAL
REHEARSAL	AGALACTIC	CAPORETTO	DIALECTAL	FERVENTLY	INSULATOR	ONCOMETER
REMINISCE	ALABASTER	CARPENTER	DIALECTIC	FILLISTER	INTROITUS	ONOMASTIC
REPRESSED	ALEURITIS	CARPENTRY	DIANOETIC	FILTERTIP	IRRITATED	OPSIMATHY
REPRESSOR	ALGORITHM	CASTRATED	DIOCLETES	FINGERTIP	ISOCRATES	OPTOMETRY

OPULENTLY	PROTOSTAR	SIMPLETON	TRUNCATED	BENBECULA	HEARTBURN	PLATITUDE
ORCHESTRA	PRUDENTLY	SIMULATED	TUILLETTE	BILINGUAL	HEAVYDUTY	PLAYHOUSE
ORGIASTIC	PSYCHOTIC	SIMULATOR	ULLSWATER	BLACKBUCK	HEXATEUCH	PLENITUDE
ORPINGTON	PUNGENTLY	SINGLETON	ULTIMATUM	BOATHOUSE	HIDEBOUND	POLITBURO
ORTHOPTER	QUADRATIC	SINGULTUS	UNADOPTED	BRADLAUGH	HOARHOUND	POORHOUSE
OUBLIETTE	QUADRATUS	SINUSITIS	UNCOURTLY	BYPRODUCT	HOLOCAUST	POSTHOUSE
OUTFITTER	QUARTETTE	SLAUGHTER	UNDAUNTED	CALENDULA	HOMEBOUND	PRECIEUSE
OVERRATED	QUERCETIN	SOLICITOR	UNDILUTED	CALENTURE	HOREHOUND	PREFIGURE
PAGEANTRY	QUERCETUS	SONOMETER	UNDOUBTED	CAMPANULA	HYDROPULT	PREMATURE
PAILLETTE	QUICKSTEP	SOPHISTER	UNHEALTHY	CANDYTUFT	HYPOCAUST	PREOCCUPY
PALAESTRA	QUINTETTE	SOPHISTIC	UNINVITED	CANNELURE	IMPORTUNE	PRESHRUNK
PALAFITTE	RADIANTLY	SOPHISTRY	UNLIMITED	CATAMOUNT	IMPOSTURE	PROCEDURE
PALMISTRY	RAINWATER	SOUBRETTE	UNRELATED	CERTITUDE	INDENTURE	PROSECUTE
PARALYTIC	REALISTIC	SOUWESTER	UNSHEATHE	CHANTEUSE	INSTITUTE	RAINGAUGE
PARAMETER	REDLETTER	SPAGHETTI	UNSIGHTLY	CLUBHOUSE	INTERLUDE	REARMOUSE
PARASITIC	REFLECTOR	SPECTATOR	UNTREATED	COMPOSURE	INTERRUPT	RECAPTURE
PAROTITIS	REFRACTOR	SPHINCTER	UNWRITTEN	CONSTRUCT	INTRIGUED	RECTITUDE
PATIENTLY	REGULATOR	SPLENETIC	UPCOUNTRY	CONTINUAL	INTRIGUER	RELIGEUSE
PATRIOTIC	REICHSTAG	SPLENITIS	UPHOLSTER	CONTINUUM	INTRODUCE	REPERCUSS
PAYMASTER	RENCONTRE	SPRIGHTLY	USHERETTE	COOKHOUSE	JACKFRUIT	REPRODUCE
PEASANTRY	RENOVATOR	STANNATOR	VAGINITIS	COVERTURE	KINKCOUGH	REREMOUSE
PECULATOR	RESONATOR	STATISTIC	VALIANTLY	CURVATURE	KNAPSCULL	RESTITUTE
PEDOMETER	RESPECTED	STATUETTE	VAPORETTO	DACHSHUND	KNAPSKULL	REVICTUAL
PEIRASTIC	RESPECTER	STEGNOTIC	VEGETATOR	DARTMOUTH	LANDSTURM	ROADHOUSE
PENDLETON	RETINITIS	STIGMATIC	VIOLENTLY	DEBENTURE	LASSITUDE	RUNAROUND
PERFECTLY	RETRACTOR	STORIATED	VOLTMETER	DEERHOUND	LEAFMOULD	SAGEBRUSH
PERIAKTOS	RHEUMATIC	STRUMITIS	WAGHALTER	DEPARTURE	LIMEHOUSE	SCRIPTURE
PERICUTIN	RHYMESTER	STYLISTIC	WAGONETTE	DEPASTURE	LIPPITUDE	SCULPTURE
PERIMETER	RIGOLETTO	SUBCORTEX	WANWORTHY	DESTITUTE	LOBSCOUSE	SECATEURS
PERIPATUS	RILLETTES	SUBEDITOR	WASTWATER	DESUETUDE	LONGITUDE	SEMIFLUID
PERMITTED	ROSEWATER	SUCCENTOR	WEBFOOTED	DIFFICULT	LOUDMOUTH	SEPULTURE
PERVERTED	ROUSSETTE	SUPERETTE	WINCANTON	DISFIGURE	LUXEMBURG	SERVITUDE
PHILISTER	SACRISTAN	SUPERSTAR	WITCHETTY	DISREPUTE	MAGDEBURG	SHELDDUCK
PHLEBITIS	SALERATUS	SUPINATOR	WOLLASTON	DISSOLUTE	MAGNITUDE	SHELLSUIT
PHOTOSTAT	SALICETUM	SUPPORTER	WOODENTOP	DOSSHOUSE	MAJUSCULE	SIGNATURE
PHRENETIC	SALOPETTE	SURFEITED	WORCESTER	DRYASDUST	MALLEMUCK	SNOWBOUND
PHRENITIS	SALTPETER	SUSPECTED	WORMEATEN	DUMBFOUND	MANNEQUIN	SOBRIQUET
PINKERTON	SALTPETRE	SYBARITIC	WYANDOTTE	EASTBOUND	MATAGOURI	SOSTENUTO
PIQUANTLY	SALTWATER	SYMBIOTIC	YOUNGSTER	EFFECTUAL	MENOPAUSE	SOURDOUGH
PIROUETTE	SAMARITAN	SYNOVITIS	ZOOMANTIC	EMBRASURE	MENSTRUAL	SPACESUIT
PIXILATED	SARCASTIC	SYNTACTIC	ZOROASTER	ENCLOSURE	MENSTRUUM	SPIRITUAL
PNEUMATIC	SARMENTUM	SYNTHETIC	ZUCCHETTO	ENRAPTURE	MINIATURE	STRANGURY
POETASTER	SASQUATCH	TABULATOR	ZYGOMATIC	EXCHEQUER	MINUSCULE	STRICTURE
POLYESTER	SATURATED	TAXIMETER	ZYMOMETER	FARMHOUSE	MONTACUTE	STRUCTURE
POPULATED	SCARLATTI	TEAKETTLE	ABOUTTURN	FEBRIFUGE	MONTEZUMA	TABLATURE
POSTNATAL	SCHEHITAH	TEESWATER	ACCENTUAL	FEEDSTUFF	MONTICULE	TARANTULA
POTHUNTER	SCHEMATIC	TELEPATHY	ADMIXTURE	FILOPLUME	MULTITUDE	TAYASSUID
PRAGMATIC	SCHLENTER	THAUMATIN	ADVENTURE	FIORITURA	NEGRITUDE	TOLLHOUSE
PRANKSTER	SCHMALTZY	THERSITES	AGINCOURT	FLASHBULB	NEWSHOUND	TRACKSUIT
PRECENTOR	SCHMUTTER	THRENETIC	AMPLITUDE	FLASHCUBE	NIEBELUNG	TRANSEUNT
PRECEPTOR	SCHNITTKE	THROWSTER	ANGOSTURA	FLOPHOUSE	NIGRITUDE	TRANSFUSE
PREDICTOR	SCLEROTAL	THYRISTOR	ANSCHLUSS	FOODSTUFF	NUMBSKULL	TRANSHUME
PRELECTOR	SCOLIOTIC	TICTACTOE	ARQUEBUSE	FORASMUCH	OASTHOUSE	TRANSMUTE
PRESBYTER	SCORBUTIC	TOLERATED	ASSUETUDE	FORECOURT	OPPORTUNE	TREETRUNK
PRESCUTUM	SCORBUTUS	TONOMETER	ASTROTURF	FORTITUDE	OTTERBURN	TURNROUND
PRESENTED	SCRUTATOR	TORMENTER	ATTRIBUTE	FROGMOUTH	OUTTHRUST	TURPITUDE
PRESENTER	SEABOTTLE	TORMENTIL	AUTOROUTE	FURNITURE	OVERTRUMP	UNDERHUNG
PRESENTLY	SEAWORTHY	TORMENTOR	AWESTRUCK	GALLINULE	PALANQUIN	UNISEXUAL
PRINCETON	SEGMENTED	TORMENTUM	AYCKBOURN	GARNITURE	PARACHUTE	UNSAVOURY
PRISMATIC	SEMEIOTIC	TOWCESTER	AYLESBURY	GLOMERULE	PARAMOUNT	VEILLEUSE
PROCLITIC	SEPARATED	TRAUMATIC	BAKEHOUSE	GOALMOUTH	PATCHOULI	VELASQUEZ
PROJECTED	SEPARATOR	TRICKSTER	BALDAQUIN	GRATICULE	PATCHOULY	VERMIFUGE
PROJECTOR	SEQUESTER	TRIMESTER	BARAGOUIN	GRATITUDE	PENINSULA	VESTIBULE
PROLACTIN	SERVIETTE	TRINKETER	BARRACUDA	GREYHOUND	PENTHOUSE	VESTITURE
PROPHETIC	SHECHITAH	TRIPMETER	BASECOURT	HAIRBRUSH	PERPETUAL	WALDFLUTE
PROTECTOR	SHORTSTAY	TROMPETTE	BEATITUDE	HAMSTRUNG	PERSECUTE	WAREHOUSE
PROTESTER	SHORTSTOP	TRUMPETER	BELEAGUER	HARLEQUIN	PHOTOTUBE	WATERBUTT

WESTBOUND	SEMIVOWEL	URUGUAYAN	BEACHWEAR	COLLAPSAR	ETHIOPIAN	HOMESTEAD	
WHIPROUND	SPIDERWEB	XEROPHYTE	BEDSPREAD	COLLEGIAN	EUCLIDEAN	HOMICIDAL	
WODEHOUSE	STORNAWAY	APPETIZER	BEEFSTEAK	COLLOIDAL	EUSKARIAN	HOOLACHAN	
WOLFHOUND	SUNFLOWER	BALTHAZAR	BETROTHAL	COLOMBIAN	EVITERNAL	HORSEPLAY	
WOODCHUCK	THROWAWAY	BAMBOOZLE	BILATERAL	COLUMBIAN	EXCISEMAN	HOUSEBOAT	
WOODHOUSE	TOPDRAWER	BULLDOZER	BILINGUAL	COMMENSAL	FACTIONAL	HOUSECOAT	
WOODLOUSE	WHITTAWER	CHERNOZEM	BINOCULAR	COMMISSAR	FACTORIAL	HUNGARIAN	
WORKHOUSE	WILLPOWER	CIVILIZED	BLACKHEAD	COMMITTAL	FALERNIAN	HYDROSTAT	
ACYCLOVIR	AEROTAXIS	EQUALIZER	BLACKLEAD	CONCORDAT	FALLOPIAN	ICTERIDAE	
AFFIDAVIT	AFLATOXIN	HALFDOZEN	BLOCKHEAD	CONFORMAL	FANATICAL	IDENTICAL	
AGGRIEVED	ANTITOXIC	KINGSIZED	BOOBYTRAP	CONGENIAL	FARMSTEAD	ILLIBERAL	
ANTINOVEL	ANTITOXIN	LOCALIZED	BORDEREAU	CONNUBIAL	FATIDICAL	ILLOGICAL	
BEETHOVEN	DIAZEUXIS	MACKENZIE	BOSTONIAN	CONTINUAL	FERRYBOAT	IMPARTIAL	
BOLSHEVIK	DYSPRAXIA	ORGANIZED	BOTANICAL	CONVIVIAL	FICTIONAL	INAUGURAL	
BOOKLOVER	EPISTAXIS	ORGANIZER	BOTSWANAN	CORNELIAN	FIELDSMAN	INSHALLAH	
BREAKEVEN	PARATAXIS	OVERSIZED	BOXWALLAH	CORNERMAN	FINANCIAL	INSOMNIAC	
CONTRIVED	PERPLEXED	PAPARAZZI	BRASSICAS	CORPOREAL	FIREBREAK	INTERPLAY	
CONTRIVER	PSEUDAXIS	PAPARAZZO	BRAZILIAN	COURTESAN	FISHERMAN	IRREGULAR	
CROSSOVER	RHEOTAXIS	SCHNAUZER	BREAKAWAY	CRACKSMAN	FLORESTAN	ISALLOBAR	
DAREDEVIL	SAXITOXIN	SCHNITZEL	BRIDLEWAY	CRACOVIAN	FLUORSPAR	ISLAMABAD	
DISSOLVED	AMBROTYPE	SCHNOZZLE	BRONCHIAL	CRAFTSMAN	FORCEMEAT	ISOCLINAL	
FIRSTEVER	APOENZYME	SHEMOZZLE	BUCKWHEAT	CROSSBEAM	FORESPEAK	ISODORIAN	
GEARLEVER	ARCHETYPE	STARGAZER	BULGARIAN	CRYPTOGAM	FOREWOMAN	JACKSTRAW	
GLENLIVET	CATACLYSM	TOTALIZER	BUNDESTAG	CUSTODIAL	FOSSORIAL	JETSTREAM	
HARDCOVER	COLLOTYPE	VAPORIZER	BURUNDIAN	CUSTODIAN	FRATERNAL	JOCKSTRAP	
LOCHINVAR	CROSSEYED	WOMANIZER	CABLEGRAM	CUTTHROAT	FRENCHMAN	JORDANIAN	
LONGLIVED	DECASTYLE	WURLITZER	CADASTRAL	DAEDALIAN	FUNICULAR	JURIDICAL	
MANOEUVRE	DESTROYED	**9:8**	CAESAREAN	DALMATIAN	GALLABEAH	JUSTINIAN	
MEDIAEVAL	DESTROYER	ABDOMINAL	CAMBODIAN	DANDYPRAT	GASPEREAU	KARAKORAM	
MENSHEVIK	DISPLAYED	ACCENTUAL	CAMBUSCAN	DARTAGNAN	GATESHEAD	KEPLARIAN	
MIDHEAVEN	ENTOPHYTE	ACQUITTAL	CAMERAMAN	DARWINIAN	GENETICAL	KHANSAMAH	
MOURNIVAL	FERROTYPE	ACROPETAL	CANAVERAL	DEATHTRAP	GENTLEMAN	KINSWOMAN	
MUCHLOVED	FREESTYLE	ACTUARIAL	CANDLEMAS	DECENNIAL	GIBRALTAR	KLINOSTAT	
NICKNEVEN	GAINSAYER	ADENOIDAL	CANONICAL	DIALECTAL	GLABELLAR	LACHRYMAL	
OURSELVES	HACKNEYED	ADVERBIAL	CAPITULAR	DIETICIAN	GLANDULAR	LACONICAL	
PERFERVID	HAIRSTYLE	AIRSTREAM	CARIBBEAN	DIONYSIAN	GRAPHICAL	LAMASERAI	
PONTLEVIS	HAMADRYAD	ALDEBARAN	CARNELIAN	DISAPPEAR	GRAVADLAX	LANDSMAAL	
PRESERVED	HIGHFLYER	AMBROSIAL	CARTESIAN	DISMISSAL	GREATCOAT	LAODICEAN	
PRESERVER	HIMALAYAN	AMBROSIAN	CARTOGRAM	DISPERSAL	GREENAWAY	LAPSTREAK	
PRESERVES	HIMALAYAS	AMPHIBIAN	CASTELLAN	DJELLABAH	GREENHEAD	LATTERDAY	
PRIMAEVAL	HIPPOLYTA	AMSTERDAM	CASTILIAN	DOCTRINAL	GREGORIAN	LECANORAM	
REDIVIVUS	HIPPOLYTE	ANATOLIAN	CATAMARAN	DOMINICAL	GUARDSMAN	LENINGRAD	
RETRIEVAL	KARYOTYPE	ANCESTRAL	CATARRHAL	DOMINICAN	HALLOWMAS	LEVIATHAN	
RETRIEVER	LEUCOCYTE	ANCHORMAN	CATHEDRAL	DRACONIAN	HAMADRYAD	LIBRARIAN	
REYKJAVIK	LIFESTYLE	ANCIPITAL	CATTLEMAN	DRAFTSMAN	HAMPSTEAD	LIVERYMAN	
ROUNCEVAL	LITHOCYST	ANECDOTAL	CAUCASIAN	DRAVIDIAN	HARMATTAN	LOCHINVAR	
ROUNCIVAL	MICROCYTE	ANGIOGRAM	CELESTIAL	DROPSICAL	HEARDSMAN	LOOSEHEAD	
SKINDIVER	MINELAYER	ANTENATAL	CENTIGRAM	EALDORMAN	HEARTBEAT	LOOSELEAF	
SOFTCOVER	MNEMOSYNE	APPRAISAL	CHALUMEAU	EARTHFLAX	HEBRIDEAN	MADRASSAH	
VANCOUVER	MONOLAYER	ARROWHEAD	CHAPARRAL	EDITORIAL	HECTOGRAM	MADRESSAH	
WHICHEVER	OVERJOYED	ARSENICAL	CHARLATAN	EDWARDIAN	HEMINGWAY	MAHARAJAH	
WHOSOEVER	PANCHAYAT	ARTHURIAN	CHARWOMAN	EFFECTUAL	HEPATICAL	MALAYSIAN	
WINDHOVER	PERISTYLE	ARTICULAR	CHEONGSAM	EFFINGHAM	HERCULEAN	MAMMALIAN	
BATHTOWEL	PHAGOCYTE	ASHMOLEAN	CHINSTRAP	ELECTORAL	HERETICAL	MANHATTAN	
BREAKAWAY	PORTRAYAL	ASTRAKHAN	CHRISTIAN	ELEMENTAL	HERMANDAD	MARMOREAL	
BRIDLEWAY	PROENZYME	ATHELSTAN	CHRISTMAS	EMOTIONAL	HERONSHAW	MARQUESAS	
GARRYOWEN	PROKARYON	AUCTORIAL	CHURCHMAN	EMPIRICAL	HESPERIAN	MARROWFAT	
GLENDOVER	PROSELYTE	AURICULAR	CIMMERIAN	ENCHORIAL	HESTERNAL	MARSUPIAL	
GREENAWAY	PROTOTYPE	AVUNCULAR	CIRCADIAN	ENTRECHAT	HEXAGONAL	MARTINEAU	
HEMINGWAY	RATEPAYER	AYATOLLAH	CLASSICAL	EPHEMERAL	HIBERNIAN	MARTINMAS	
LAWNMOWER	STATOCYST	BACKPEDAL	CLERGYMAN	EPICUREAN	HIMALAYAN	MASTERMAN	
MAYFLOWER	STRONGYLE	BACTERIAL	CLINICIAN	EPISCOPAL	HIMALAYAS	MATUTINAL	
OUTGROWTH	TACHYLYTE	BALTHAZAR	COACHLOAD	EQUIVOCAL	HIPPOCRAS	MAURITIAN	
OVERPOWER	TEKNONYMY	BAPTISMAL	COCHINEAL	ERISTICAL	HISTOGRAM	MEANDRIAN	
SAFFLOWER	THORNDYKE	BARBARIAN	COELOSTAT	ERPINGHAM	HISTORIAN	MEDIAEVAL	
SCALLAWAG	TREVELYAN	BASILICAL	COFFERDAM	ESSENTIAL	HODIERNAL	MEDICINAL	
SCALLYWAG	UNALLOYED	BEACHHEAD	COINTREAU	ETCETERAS	HOLDERBAT	MEDMENHAM	

MENIPPEAN	PICTORIAL	ROUNDELAY	STEERSMAN	VARANGIAN	ARCHITECT	FIREPLACE
MENSTRUAL	PIECEMEAL	ROUNDHEAD	STERADIAN	VEHICULAR	ARMISTICE	FLAGRANCE
MERCAPTAN	PIPEDREAM	ROUNDSMAN	STERCORAL	VERIDICAL	ARROGANCE	FLASHBACK
MERCURIAL	PIPSQUEAK	RUDDLEMAN	STONEBOAT	VERSIONAL	ASSONANCE	FLINTLOCK
MIDDLEMAN	PIRATICAL	RUTHENIAN	STONECHAT	VERTEBRAE	ASSURANCE	FLIPPANCY
MIDSTREAM	PLAINSMAN	SABBATIAN	STORNAWAY	VERTEBRAL	ATHLETICS	FORASMUCH
MILLENIAL	PLAUSTRAL	SACRISTAN	STREETCAR	VESICULAR	AUTOCRACY	FORTALICE
MILLIGRAM	PLOUGHMAN	SADDLEBAG	SUBCELLAR	VESPASIAN	AVOIDANCE	FOURPENCE
MINCEMEAT	PLUMDAMAS	SALVARSAN	SUBNORMAL	VESTIGIAL	AWESTRUCK	FRAGRANCE
MINUTEMAN	PLUTOCRAT	SAMARITAN	SUCCURSAL	VICEREGAL	BACHARACH	FRAGRANCY
MOLECULAR	POINTSMAN	SARTORIAL	SUFFRAGAN	VICTORIAN	BACKBENCH	FRANCESCA
MONASTRAL	POLEMICAL	SASSAFRAS	SUPERSTAR	VIGESIMAL	BACKSPACE	FREDERICK
MONGOLIAN	POLICEMAN	SATIRICAL	SUPPLICAT	VIRGINIAN	BACKTRACK	FREELANCE
MONOCULAR	POLITICAL	SATURNIAN	SWEETMEAT	VITRUVIAN	BARMBRACK	FREQUENCY
MONTESPAN	POLYGONAL	SATYRIDAE	SWORDPLAY	VOLGOGRAD	BARONETCY	FROGMARCH
MORTICIAN	POPLITEAL	SATYRINAE	SWORDSMAN	VOLKSRAAD	BILLYCOCK	GEARSTICK
MOTORBOAT	PORIFERAN	SAUCEBOAT	SYRPHIDAE	VULCANIAN	BLACKBUCK	GENUFLECT
MOURNIVAL	PORTRAYAL	SCALLAWAG	TABANIDAE	VULGARIAN	BLACKFACE	GOLDFINCH
MOUSETRAP	POSTNATAL	SCALLYWAG	TACAMAHAC	WAGNERIAN	BLACKJACK	GOOSENECK
MRIDAMGAM	POSTWOMAN	SCAPEGOAT	TACTICIAN	WAGONLOAD	BLOWTORCH	GREENBACK
MRIDANGAM	POTENTIAL	SCEPTICAL	TAHSILDAR	WAISTCOAT	BOOTBLACK	GREENWICH
MUNICIPAL	POTTINGAR	SCHEHITAH	TANZANIAN	WALLYDRAG	BREAKNECK	GRIEVANCE
MUSKOGEAN	POWERBOAT	SCHOOLMAN	TARTAREAN	WAPINSHAW	BULLFINCH	GYROMANCY
MUSSULMAN	PRACTICAL	SCIARIDAE	TASMANIAN	WASHERMAN	BYPRODUCT	HAIRPIECE
NABATHEAN	PREBENDAL	SCLEROTAL	TECHNICAL	WASSERMAN	CANDIDACY	HANDPIECE
NAPIERIAN	PRECISIAN	SCOTCHMAN	TECTORIAL	WEDNESDAY	CAPTAINCY	HARMONICA
NERITIDAE	PRESIDIAL	SCRIMSHAW	TEIRESIAS	WENCESLAS	CARTTRACK	HATCHBACK
NOCTURNAL	PREVERNAL	SCYTHEMAN	TELLURIAN	WHALEBOAT	CEROMANCY	HAVERSACK
NORWEGIAN	PRIMAEVAL	SEBASTIAN	TETRAGRAM	WHALEMEAT	CEVAPCICI	HEADPIECE
NUMERICAL	PRIMITIAE	SECTARIAN	THACKERAY	WHEATMEAL	CHAFFINCH	HEMISTICH
OARSWOMAN	PRINCIPAL	SECTIONAL	THICKHEAD	WHERRYMAN	CHEAPJACK	HEMSTITCH
OCCIPITAL	PRODROMAL	SECTORIAL	THIRDSMAN	WHIMSICAL	CLEARANCE	HESITANCE
OCHLOCRAT	PROOFREAD	SELJUKIAN	THROWAWAY	WHITEHEAD	COCKROACH	HESITANCY
OCTAGONAL	PROSIMIAN	SEMIFINAL	THYESTEAN	WHOLEMEAL	COHERENCE	HEXASTICH
ODDJOBMAN	PROTHORAX	SENESCHAL	TIGHTHEAD	WINDBREAK	CONSTANCE	HEXATEUCH
OMBUDSMAN	PROTOSTAR	SERBONIAN	TIPULIDAE	YACHTSMAN	CONSTANCY	HINDRANCE
OPOBALSAM	PSYCHICAL	SHAMIANAH	TITTLEBAT	YESTERDAY	CONSTRICT	HITCHCOCK
ORANGEMAN	PTARMIGAN	SHARESMAN	TOTTENHAM	ZECHARIAH	CONSTRUCT	HOLLYHOCK
ORATORIAN	PUERPERAL	SHECHINAH	TRADESMAN	ZEPHANIAH	CONTUMACY	HOPSCOTCH
ORBICULAR	PYRAMIDAL	SHECHITAH	TRAFALGAR	ASTROLABE	COSMETICS	HORSEBACK
ORGANICAL	QUANTICAL	SHEEPMEAT	TRAGEDIAN	BURKINABE	COVALENCY	HUCKABACK
OUTSPREAD	QUIZZICAL	SHEWBREAD	TRANSVAAL	CATACOMBS	COWARDICE	HUNCHBACK
PALLADIAN	QUOTIDIAN	SHORTSTAY	TRAPEZIAL	FLASHCUBE	CROOKBACK	HYSTERICS
PALPEBRAL	RACKSTRAW	SIGNALMAN	TREVELYAN	GARDEROBE	DALLIANCE	IGNORANCE
PANCHAYAT	RADDLEMAN	SILURIDAE	TRIBESMAN	HAMMURABI	DECADENCE	IMBALANCE
PANDEMIAN	RADIOGRAM	SIRBONIAN	TRIENNIAL	MORECAMBE	DEFERENCE	IMMANENCE
PARANOIAC	RAPTORIAL	SISYPHEAN	TRIUMPHAL	PHOTOTUBE	DEMOCRACY	IMMANENCY
PAROCHIAL	RATTLEBAG	SKEPTICAL	TROUSSEAU	PRESCRIBE	DIANETICS	IMMEDIACY
PASTERNAK	RECTORIAL	SKETCHMAP	TRUCKLOAD	PROSCRIBE	DIDACTICS	IMMINENCE
PATRICIAN	REDSTREAK	SKETCHPAD	UKRAINIAN	STANDERBY	DIETETICS	IMPEDANCE
PATROLMAN	REGISTRAR	SLOVENIAN	UMBILICAL	SUBSCRIBE	DILIGENCE	IMPERFECT
PAUSANIAS	REHEARSAL	SOLFIDIAN	UNDERCOAT	WATERBABY	DIPLOMACY	IMPOTENCE
PEDICULAR	REICHSRAT	SPEARHEAD	UNDERGRAD	XENOPHOBE	DISINFECT	IMPUDENCE
PENTAGRAM	REICHSTAG	SPEEDBOAT	UNDERSEAL	ABERRANCE	DOMINANCE	INCIDENCE
PERENNIAL	RELIQUIAE	SPHERICAL	UNDERWEAR	ABOUTFACE	DRAMATICS	INCORRECT
PERGUNNAH	REPTILIAN	SPILLICAN	UNETHICAL	ABUNDANCE	DRUMSTICK	INDECENCY
PERISCIAN	RESSALDAR	SPIRITUAL	UNISEXUAL	ACOUSTICS	ECONOMICS	INDIGENCE
PERPETUAL	RETICULAR	SPOILSMAN	UNITARIAN	ACQUIESCE	EFFLUENCE	INDOLENCE
PETERSHAM	RETRIEVAL	SPOKESMAN	UNIVERSAL	ADHERENCE	ELOQUENCE	INFERENCE
PETTICOAT	REVICTUAL	SPONGEBAG	UNMUSICAL	AEROSPACE	EMERGENCE	INFLUENCE
PHANSIGAR	RHODESIAN	SPORTSMAN	UNNATURAL	AFFLUENCE	EMERGENCY	INJUSTICE
PHIGALIAN	ROADSTEAD	STABLELAD	UNPOPULAR	ALLOWANCE	ENDURANCE	INNOCENCE
PHONOGRAM	ROSMINIAN	STABLEMAN	UNTYPICAL	AMBULANCE	ESPERANCE	INSOLENCE
PHOTOSTAT	ROTTERDAM	STATESMAN	UPANISHAD	ANABRANCH	ESTHETICS	INSURANCE
PHYSICIAN	ROUMANIAN	STEAMBOAT	UREDINIAL	ANNOYANCE	EXISTENCE	INTELLECT
PICOFARAD	ROUNCEVAL	STEELHEAD	URICONIAN	APPLEJACK	EYESPLICE	INTERDICT
PICTOGRAM	ROUNCIVAL	STEENBRAS	URUGUAYAN	APPLIANCE	FASTTRACK	INTERFACE

INTERJECT	PRECIPICE	STEINBECK	CERTITUDE	MILLIPEDE	ALABASTER	BRUMMAGEM
INTERLACE	PREDILECT	STEINBOCK	CHAMINADE	MOTORCADE	ALEXANDER	BUCCANEER
INTERLOCK	PREGNANCY	STRIDENCY	CHEAPSIDE	MULTITUDE	ALTIMETER	BULLDOZER
INTERSECT	PREJUDICE	SUBSTANCE	CHILOPODA	MUSCOVADO	AMENHOTEP	BUMBLEBEE
INTRICACY	PRONOUNCE	SUPREMACY	CHIROPODY	NEGRITUDE	AMPLIFIER	BYSTANDER
INTRODUCE	PRURIENCE	TAILPIECE	COLONNADE	NEWLYWEDS	ANDROCLES	CABRIOLET
INTUMESCE	PUISSANCE	TAOISEACH	CRESCENDO	NIGRITUDE	ANECDOTES	CALVITIES
JOUISANCE	PURSUANCE	TAVISTOCK	CROUSTADE	ORANGEADE	ANGUISHED	CAMCORDER
JUBILANCE	PURULENCE	TECTONICS	DESPERADO	OUDENARDE	ANNOTATED	CANVASSER
KNOBSTICK	PYROMANCY	TELESTICH	DESUETUDE	OVERHEADS	ANNOUNCER	CARETAKER
LAMPBLACK	QUITTANCE	TEMULENCE	DIVIDENDS	OVERSHADE	ANOPHELES	CARPENTER
LASTDITCH	RACETRACK	THEOCRACY	DOWNGRADE	PALOVERDE	ANTINOVEL	CARTWHEEL
LEASEBACK	RAINCHECK	THORNBACK	DOWNWARDS	PARRICIDE	ANTIPODES	CASSOULET
LIGHTFACE	REACTANCE	THROWBACK	EASTWARDS	PATRICIDE	APENNINES	CASTRATED
LINTSTOCK	RECOLLECT	THUMBTACK	EBRILLADE	PESTICIDE	APPETIZER	CATTLEPEN
LIQUORICE	RECUSANCE	TIMEPIECE	ELECTRODE	PLATITUDE	APPOINTED	CERTIFIED
LITURGICS	REDOLENCE	TIMOCRACY	EMBASSADE	PLENITUDE	APPOINTEE	CERVANTES
LIVESTOCK	REFERENCE	TOASTRACK	ENCHILADA	POSTCARDS	ARCHANGEL	CHARACTER
LOGISTICS	REFINANCE	TOLERANCE	ESMERALDA	PROMENADE	ARCTOGAEA	CHARTERED
LUBAVITCH	REINFORCE	TOOTHPICK	ESPLANADE	QUASIMODO	ARTIFICER	CHASTENED
LUMINANCE	RELEVANCE	TOVARISCH	ESTRAPADE	READYMADE	ASTOUNDED	CHATTERER
MALLEMUCK	REMINISCE	TRIERARCH	EVERGLADE	REARWARDS	ASTROPHEL	CHAVENDER
MATCHLOCK	REPRODUCE	TSAREVICH	EVERYBODY	RECTITUDE	ATTAINDER	CHEQUERED
MATRIARCH	RESIDENCE	UNBALANCE	FALKLANDS	REMBRANDT	ATTEMPTED	CHERISHED
MAULSTICK	RESIDENCY	UNCORRECT	FOOLHARDY	REMOULADE	ATTITUDES	CHERNOZEM
MECHANICS	RESONANCE	UTTERANCE	FORTITUDE	RETROCEDE	AUTOMAKER	CHEVALIER
MICROINCH	RESURFACE	VEHEMENCE	FUNGICIDE	RIVERSIDE	AUTOMATED	CHICKADEE
MILITANCY	RESURRECT	VENGEANCE	FUSILLADE	RUNNYMEDE	AXMINSTER	CHICKWEED
MISCHANCE	RETICENCE	VENTIFACT	GABIONADE	SALESLADY	BACKBITER	CHISELLER
MISDIRECT	REVERENCE	VIGILANCE	GALLOPADE	SCABLANDS	BACKWATER	CHLAMYDES
MOBOCRACY	RIDGEBACK	VIRULENCE	GARIBALDI	SEMANTIDE	BALLADEER	CHORISTER
MONOSTICH	RINGFENCE	WANCHANCY	GASCONADE	SERVITUDE	BANDOLEER	CIVILISED
MONOTROCH	ROADBLOCK	WISECRACK	GERMICIDE	SFORZANDO	BANDOLIER	CIVILIZED
MUMCHANCE	ROOTSTOCK	WOODCHUCK	GINGERADE	SHEPHERDS	BAREBONES	CLARIFIER
NESCIENCE	RORSCHACH	WOODSHOCK	GLISSANDO	SHETLANDS	BAREFACED	CLUSTERED
NINEPENCE	ROUGHNECK	WORKFORCE	GLUCOSIDE	SIDEWARDS	BARNACLES	COALESCED
NOMOCRACY	ROUMANSCH	WORKPLACE	GLYCERIDE	SPEARSIDE	BAROMETER	COALMINER
NORMALACY	ROUNDBACK	WORKSPACE	GRATITUDE	STANDARDS	BARRISTER	COCKATIEL
NOTCHBACK	RUGGELACH	YARDSTICK	GRAVESIDE	STATESIDE	BARTENDER	COLLECTED
OBEDIENCE	SACRIFICE	ACETAMIDE	HARIGALDS	STATEWIDE	BATHTOWEL	COLOMBIER
OBEISANCE	SANDARACH	ALLEMANDE	HAUTMONDE	STRAPPADO	BEARDSLEY	COMFORTER
OBSTINACY	SANTONICA	ALONGSIDE	HEAVISIDE	SUBDIVIDE	BECQUEREL	COMMANDER
OCCUPANCY	SASQUATCH	AMBUSCADE	HERBICIDE	SUPERSEDE	BEDJACKET	COMMITTED
OCTASTICH	SASSENACH	AMPLITUDE	HIGHLANDS	THOUSANDS	BEDRIDDEN	COMMITTEE
OFFCHANCE	SCHOLARCH	ANDROMEDA	HOMEWARDS	TREMATODE	BEDSITTER	COMPANIES
OFFENBACH	SCIOMANCY	ANHYDRIDE	HUMANMADE	TURPITUDE	BEEFEATER	COMPELLED
ONTOGENCY	SEMANTICS	ASSUETUDE	INCOMMODE	TWAYBLADE	BEEKEEPER	COMPOTIER
ORDINANCE	SEMBLANCE	BACKSLIDE	INTERCEDE	UNDERSIDE	BEETHOVEN	CONCEALED
OVERREACH	SEMIOTICS	BACKWARDS	INTERLUDE	WATERSIDE	BELEAGUER	CONCEITED
OVERREACT	SENTIENCE	BACKWOODS	INTERNODE	WELDSTADT	BENIGHTED	CONCERNED
PAGLIACCI	SEVERANCE	BARMECIDE	IRRAWADDY	WESTWARDS	BERGANDER	CONCERTED
PAPERBACK	SHASHLICK	BARRACUDA	JACARANDA	WHIPSNADE	BERSERKER	CONCLUDED
PATRIARCH	SHELDDUCK	BARRICADE	KNEECORDS	WOODLANDS	BETHLEHEM	CONCUSSED
PENITENCE	SHELLBACK	BARTHOLDI	LAMPSHADE	WORLDWIDE	BETROTHED	CONDEMNED
PERCHANCE	SHIPWRECK	BASTINADE	LANDSLIDE	ABANDONED	BIGHEADED	CONDENSER
PETULANCE	SHOWPIECE	BASTINADO	LANDWARDS	ABANDONEE	BLINKERED	CONFESSED
PHONETICS	SIBILANCE	BEATITUDE	LASSITUDE	ABSCONDER	BLISTERED	CONFIRMED
PICKABACK	SIDETRACK	BILLIARDS	LEFTWARDS	ABSTAINER	BLOODSHED	CONFLATED
PIGGYBACK	SLAPSTICK	BROADSIDE	LIPPITUDE	ADDRESSED	BLUNDERER	CONGERIES
PILLICOCK	SLINGBACK	BRUNHILDE	LONGITUDE	ADDRESSEE	BLUSTERER	CONGESTED
PINCHBECK	SLIVOVICA	CANNONADE	MAGNITUDE	ADULTERER	BOANERGES	CONNECTED
PINCHCOCK	SLOWCOACH	CARBAMIDE	MARMALADE	ADVOCATED	BOOKLOVER	CONSIGNEE
PLEASANCE	SOCIOLECT	CARBONADE	MATRICIDE	AFFLICTED	BOOKMAKER	CONSOCIES
POIGNANCY	SOMEPLACE	CARBONADO	MELAMPODE	AFRIKANER	BOOTLACES	CONTAINER
POLEMARCH	SOVENANCE	CASSONADE	MENTICIDE	AGGRIEVED	BREAKAGES	CONTEMPER
POPPYCOCK	SPECIFICS	CAVALCADE	METHOXIDE	AGUECHEEK	BREAKEVEN	CONTENDER
PORTULACA	SQUINANCY	CENTIPEDE	MILLEPEDE	AIRCOOLED	BRIGADIER	CONTENTED

CONTRIVED	EASTERNER	FLATTERED	HAYMARKET	KISSINGER	MOONRAKER	PEDIGREES
CONTRIVER	ECARDINES	FLATTERER	HEADLINED	KITCHENER	MORTGAGEE	PEDOMETER
CONVERTED	ECOSYSTEM	FLAVOURED	HEDERATED	KLEMPERER	MORTIFIED	PENPUSHER
CONVERTER	ELASTOMER	FLOWERBED	HENPECKED	KNACKERED	MOSCHATEL	PENSIONER
CONVINCED	ELEVENSES	FLUSTERED	HEREAFTER	KONIMETER	MOTHEATEN	PERFORMED
CORIANDER	ELONGATED	FORBIDDEN	HERPESTES	LACERATED	MOYGASHEL	PERFORMER
CORKSCREW	EMACIATED	FOREIGNER	HEXAMETER	LAMINATED	MUCHLOVED	PERIANDER
CORRECTED	EMBATTLED	FORFEITED	HIGHFLYER	LANCASTER	MUCKENDER	PERIMETER
CORRUPTER	EMBEZZLER	FORGATHER	HIGHSPEED	LANDAULET	MUCORALES	PERMITTED
COSTUMIER	EMBROIDER	FORGOTTEN	HOBNAILED	LANDLOPER	MUFFETTEE	PERPLEXED
COUNTRIES	EMBROILED	FORWANDER	HODOMETER	LANDOWNER	MULTIPLEX	PERSONNEL
COUTURIER	EMPLOYEES	FOURWHEEL	HOLINSHED	LANGSPIEL	MUSKETEER	PERSUADED
CRICKETER	ENAMELLED	FREEWHEEL	HOMEOWNER	LANGUAGES	MUTILATED	PERTURBED
CROSSBRED	ENAMOURED	FREIGHTER	HORRIFIED	LAPLANDER	MYSTERIES	PERVERTED
CROSSEYED	ENCHANTED	FRENCHMEN	HOTHEADED	LATECOMER	NANTUCKET	PETRIFIED
CROSSOVER	ENCHANTER	FRESHENER	HOUSELEEK	LAVOISIER	NATHANIEL	PETTITOES
CRUSTACEA	ENCIRCLED	FRICASSEE	HUMDINGER	LAWMONGER	NAUSEATED	PHALANGER
CRYOMETER	ENCOUNTER	FROBISHER	HYDRANGEA	LAWNMOWER	NEBBISHER	PHELLOGEN
DAMBUSTER	ENERGUMEN	FRUITERER	HYLOBATES	LAZYBONES	NEGLECTED	PHILANDER
DANDIFIED	ENGRAINED	FUNGIBLES	IBUPROFEN	LEICESTER	NEUCHATEL	PHILISTER
DASHWHEEL	ENGROSSED	GAINSAYER	ICELANDER	LEVERAGED	NEWMARKET	PHILLABEG
DEBAUCHED	ENGROSSER	GALIONGEE	ILCHESTER	LIBERATED	NEWSPAPER	PHILLIBEG
DEBAUCHEE	ENLIGHTEN	GARNISHEE	ILLGOTTEN	LIBERTIES	NEWSSHEET	PICNICKER
DECORATED	ENLIVENED	GARRYOWEN	IMMUNISER	LIMBURGER	NICKNEVEN	PIEPOWDER
DEDICATED	ENQUIRIES	GASHOLDER	IMPEACHER	LINKLATER	NONSMOKER	PIGHEADED
DEFAULTER	ENSCONCED	GASOMETER	IMPOUNDER	LIQUEFIED	NOSEBLEED	PIMPERNEL
DELIGHTED	ENTRAMMEL	GAULEITER	IMPRESSED	LOCALIZED	NOTEPAPER	PINHOOKER
DELIVERER	ENTRANCED	GAZETTEER	INCREASED	LONGLIVED	NUTJOBBER	PISTAREEN
DEPRESSED	EPHIALTES	GEARLEVER	INDICATES	LOWLANDER	OBSEQUIES	PISTOLEER
DERRINGER	EPISTOLER	GEARWHEEL	INDWELLER	LYSIMETER	OCEANIDES	PIXILATED
DESCARTES	EQUALIZER	GENTLEMEN	INFIELDER	MACCABEES	OESTROGEN	PLASTERED
DESTROYED	ERGATANER	GERMANCER	INGRAINED	MAGNIFIER	OILTANKER	PLASTERER
DESTROYER	ERIOMETER	GERMANDER	INHERITED	MAHARANEE	OKEYDOKEY	PLUNDERER
DEVELOPED	ESTAMINET	GLENDOWER	INHIBITED	MALFORMED	ONCOMETER	POETASTER
DEVELOPER	ESTRANGED	GLENLIVET	INITIATED	MALLANDER	OPENENDED	POLYESTER
DIARRHOEA	ETIOLATED	GLORIFIED	INNISFREE	MALLENDER	OPPRESSED	POPULATED
DIGNIFIED	EUMENIDES	GOBETWEEN	INNKEEPER	MANOMETER	ORGANISED	PORPOISES
DINNERSET	EUMYCETES	GODDESSES	INSCRIBED	MARKETEER	ORGANISER	PORRINGER
DIOCLETES	EUPHRATES	GODFATHER	INSTANTER	MASSINGER	ORGANIZED	POSSESSED
DISBELIEF	EURIPIDES	GODMOTHER	INSWINGER	MAYFLOWER	ORGANIZER	POSSIBLES
DISBURDEN	EVERGREEN	GONDOLIER	INTERBRED	MEDICATED	ORTHOPTER	POSTPONED
DISCARDED	EXCHEQUER	GOOSANDER	INTERPRET	MEDRESSEH	OURSELVES	POTBOILER
DISCLOSED	EXCLAIMED	GOOSESTEP	INTERVIEW	MEHITABEL	OUTFITTER	POTHUNTER
DISGRACED	EXERCISED	GOSPELLER	INTRIGUED	MEKOMETER	OUTNUMBER	POULTERER
DISGUISED	EXERCISES	GRADUATED	INTRIGUER	MEMORITER	OUTRIGGER	PRACTISED
DISGUSTED	EXHAUSTED	GRAPETREE	IRONSIDES	MENOMINEE	OUTROOPER	PRANKSTER
DISHWATER	EXPLOITER	GREENFEED	IRRITATED	MENTIONED	OUTSPOKEN	PREFERRED
DISMEMBER	EXPRESSED	GREENWEED	ISOCRATES	MENUISIER	OUTWORKER	PREPOLLEX
DISPENSER	EYELETEER	GRENADIER	ISOSCELES	MERGANSER	OVERJOYED	PRESBYTER
DISPERSED	EYEOPENER	GRINGOLET	JACKSCREW	MESSENGER	OVERPOWER	PRESENTED
DISPLACED	FASHIONED	GROCERIES	JAMPACKED	METAPELET	OVERRATED	PRESENTER
DISPLAYED	FEATHERED	GROUNDSEL	JAUNDICED	MIDDLESEX	OVERRIDER	PRESERVED
DISSENTER	FENCIBLES	GUARANTEE	JAYWALKER	MIDHEAVEN	OVERSHOES	PRESERVER
DISSOLVED	FENUGREEK	GUNPOWDER	JERAHMEEL	MIDSUMMER	OVERSIZED	PRESERVES
DISTEMPER	FERINGHEE	HACKNEYED	JERKWATER	MIDWINTER	OVERSLEEP	PRETENDER
DISTENDED	FERMENTED	HALFBAKED	JERUSALEM	MILOMETER	OVERSTEER	PRIESTLEY
DISTILLER	FILICALES	HALFDOZEN	JOBSEEKER	MINELAYER	OVERTONES	PRIVATEER
DISTORTED	FILLIPEEN	HALLOWEEN	JOCKTELEG	MISFALLEN	PACEMAKER	PROBABLES
DISTURBED	FILLISTER	HAMBURGER	JUSTIFIED	MISGUIDED	PALANKEEN	PROFESSED
DISUNITED	FILMMAKER	HAMFATTER	KARABINER	MISPICKEL	PARAMETER	PROFITEER
DOLOMITES	FINANCIER	HAMFISTED	KEYHOLDER	MISPLACED	PARTICLES	PROJECTED
DOMICILED	FIREWATER	HARBINGER	KIDNAPPED	MISSHAPEN	PARTTIMER	PROKOFIEV
DONCASTER	FIRSTEVER	HARDANGER	KIDNAPPER	MISSIONER	PASSENGER	PROLONGED
DOSIMETER	FLAGEOLET	HARDCOVER	KILLARNEY	MISTEMPER	PASSEPIED	PROPELLED
DUNGAREES	FLAMSTEED	HARDLINER	KILOMETER	MOLLITIES	PATTERNED	PROPELLER
DUNGEONER	FLATTENED	HARPOONER	KINGMAKER	MONOLAYER	PAYMASTER	PROTESTER
DYNAMITED	FLATTENER	HARVESTER	KINGSIZED	MONOMETER	PEASEWEEP	PROVENDER

PUBLISHED	SCISSORER	STAGGERED	TRAMLINES	UNTRAINED	INTENSIFY	HERMITAGE
PUBLISHER	SCLAUNDER	STAMMERER	TRAVELLER	UNTREATED	JACKKNIFE	HISTOLOGY
PULPITEER	SCOUNDREL	STARGAZER	TREASURER	UNTRODDEN	MAKESHIFT	HOPLOLOGY
PUMMELLED	SCRAMBLER	STATIONED	TREBUCHET	UNTUTORED	OBJECTIFY	HYPALLAGE
PUPPETEER	SCRATCHED	STATIONER	TRIANGLED	UNWATERED	OVERDRAFT	INCOMINGS
PURCHASER	SCRATCHES	STAVANGER	TRIBESMEN	UNWORRIED	PECKSNIFF	KENTLEDGE
QUADRUPED	SCRIVENER	STIFFENER	TRICKSTER	UNWRITTEN	PERSONIFY	KINKCOUGH
QUALIFIED	SCRODDLED	STINGAREE	TRIMESTER	UPHOLSTER	PIKESTAFF	KINTLEDGE
QUALIFIER	SCROUNGER	STOCKINET	TRINKETER	VALDENSES	PLAINTIFF	KNOWLEDGE
QUARENDEN	SCUDDALER	STONKERED	TRIPMETER	VANCOUVER	RADCLIFFE	LANGRIDGE
QUICKSTEP	SEGMENTED	STORIATED	TRUMPETER	VAPORIZER	SKEWWHIFF	LINDBERGH
QUODLIBET	SEMIVOWEL	STRAGGLER	TRUNCATED	VELASQUEZ	SNOWDRIFT	LONGRANGE
RACKETEER	SEPARATED	STRANGLER	TUILERIES	VELDSKOEN	SPEECHIFY	MACROLOGY
RAINWATER	SEPTEMBER	STRANGLES	ULLSWATER	VELVETEEN	SPINDRIFT	MADARIAGA
RAMILLIES	SEPULCHER	STRATAGEM	UNABASHED	VERSIFIER	VOUCHSAFE	MALEBOLGE
RATEPAYER	SEQUENCER	STRETCHED	UNADOPTED	VIDELICET	WOODCRAFT	MIDDLINGS
REALITIES	SEQUESTER	STRETCHER	UNALLOYED	VOLTMETER	ADVANTAGE	MISMANAGE
RECLAIMED	SEQUINNED	STUPEFIED	UNALTERED	VOLUNTEER	ANCHORAGE	MYTHOLOGY
RECLAIMER	SERASKIER	SUBCORTEX	UNASHAMED	WAGHALTER	ANTHOLOGY	NEUROLOGY
RECOVERED	SERENADER	SUBMERGED	UNBIASSED	WALDENSES	APPENDAGE	NOSTOLOGY
RECTIFIER	SEVENTEEN	SUBTITLED	UNBOUNDED	WALLABIES	ARBITRAGE	OMNIRANGE
REDHANDED	SHARPENER	SUCCEEDED	UNBRIDLED	WALLPAPER	ASTROLOGY	ORPHANAGE
REDHEADED	SHATTERED	SUNBATHER	UNCHANGED	WAMBENGER	BACKSTAGE	ORTHOLOGY
REDLETTER	SHELTERED	SUNDOWNER	UNCHARGED	WARMONGER	BEESTINGS	OUTGOINGS
REFRESHER	SHILLABER	SUNFLOWER	UNCHECKED	WASTWATER	BEVERIDGE	OVERWEIGH
REISTAFEL	SHIPOWNER	SUNSCREEN	UNCLAIMED	WATERSHED	BLESSINGS	PARENTAGE
REJOINDER	SHOEMAKER	SUNTANNED	UNCLOTHED	WATERWEED	BOBSLEIGH	PARSONAGE
REMAINDER	SHOVELLER	SUPPORTER	UNCLOUDED	WEBFOOTED	BRADLAUGH	PARTRIDGE
RENTALLER	SHUTTERED	SURFEITED	UNCOUPLED	WELSUMMER	BROKERAGE	PASTURAGE
REPRESSED	SIEGFRIED	SURMULLET	UNCOVERED	WESTERNER	CAMBRIDGE	PATHOLOGY
RESOURCES	SIGHTSEER	SURPRISED	UNCROSSED	WHICHEVER	CARTILAGE	PATRONAGE
RESPECTED	SIGNALLER	SURRENDER	UNCROWNED	WHITTAWER	CARTRIDGE	PERSONAGE
RESPECTER	SIMULATED	SUSPECTED	UNDAMAGED	WHOSOEVER	CHALLENGE	PETROLOGY
RETRIEVER	SINGLESEX	SUSPENDED	UNDAUNTED	WILLESDEN	CHAMPAIGN	PHILOLOGY
RETROFLEX	SINGSPIEL	SUSPENDER	UNDECIDED	WILLPOWER	CHIPPINGS	PHONOLOGY
RHYMESTER	SINKANSEN	SUSTAINED	UNDEFILED	WINDHOVER	COLERIDGE	PHYCOLOGY
RICHELIEU	SKINDIVER	SWAGGERER	UNDEFINED	WITNESSED	CONCIERGE	PILFERAGE
RILLETTES	SKYJACKER	SWEETENER	UNDERBRED	WOMANISER	COSMOLOGY	PORTERAGE
RINGSIDER	SLAUGHTER	SWIMMERET	UNDERFEED	WOMANIZER	CURETTAGE	PRIVILEGE
ROISTERER	SLUMBERER	SYLLABLES	UNDILUTED	WOODBORER	CURTILAGE	PUCELLAGE
ROSEWATER	SMOKEFREE	TABASHEER	UNDIVIDED	WORCESTER	DEMURRAGE	PUPILLAGE
SAFFLOWER	SNAKEWEED	TABBOULEH	UNDOUBTED	WORMEATEN	DIAPHRAGM	RADIOLOGY
SALTPETER	SNOWSHOES	TAILLEFER	UNDRESSED	WRONGDOER	DISCHARGE	RAINGAUGE
SALTWATER	SOBRIQUET	TAMOXIFEN	UNEQUALED	YACHTSMEN	DISENGAGE	REARRANGE
SANDALLED	SOFTCOVER	TAPDANCER	UNEXPOSED	YOUNGSTER	DISOBLIGE	REPECHAGE
SANDPAPER	SOLLICKER	TARGETEER	UNFLEDGED	ZEALANDER	DISPARAGE	REPORTAGE
SANDPIPER	SOMETIMES	TARMACKED	UNFOUNDED	ZINFANDEL	DOWNSTAGE	SACRILEGE
SAPSUCKER	SOMMELIER	TASSELLED	UNGUARDED	ZOROASTER	DROPPINGS	SAXIFRAGE
SATISFIED	SONNETEER	TAXIMETER	UNIFORMED	ZYMOMETER	EASTLINGS	SCRAPINGS
SATURATED	SONOMETER	TEARSHEET	UNINJURED	ALLOGRAFT	EDINBURGH	SCRIMMAGE
SAUTERNES	SOPHISTER	TEESWATER	UNINVITED	BLUESHIFT	EMBASSAGE	SCRUMMAGE
SCALLOPED	SOPHOCLES	TELESALES	UNLEARNED	CANDYTUFT	EMPENNAGE	SEMIOLOGY
SCANSORES	SOTTISIER	TENNESSEE	UNLIMITED	CHAIRLIFT	ENCOURAGE	SHEERLEGS
SCARIFIER	SOUWESTER	TERRIFIED	UNMARRIED	DIVERSIFY	ENGRENAGE	SHRINKAGE
SCATTERED	SPATTERED	TESTICLES	UNMATCHED	DRAWKNIFE	ENTOURAGE	SOCIOLOGY
SCAVENGER	SPECIFIED	TESTIFIER	UNNOTICED	ELECTRIFY	EPIPHRAGM	SORTILEGE
SCHLEMIEL	SPELUNKER	THERSITES	UNOPPOSED	EXEMPLIFY	ESPIONAGE	SOURDOUGH
SCHLENTER	SPHINCTER	THROWSTER	UNREFINED	FEEDSTUFF	ETHNOLOGY	SOVEREIGN
SCHLIEREN	SPIDERWEB	THUNDERER	UNRELATED	FLAGSTAFF	ETYMOLOGY	SPICILEGE
SCHMIEDER	SPINDRIER	TIGHTENER	UNRUFFLED	FOODSTUFF	FEBRIFUGE	SQUIREAGE
SCHMUTTER	SPINNAKER	TOLERATED	UNSCATHED	GEARSHIFT	FORESTAGE	STOCKINGS
SCHNAPPER	SPINNERET	TONOMETER	UNSECURED	HALFSTAFF	FORTILAGE	STREETAGE
SCHNAUZER	SPONSORED	TOPDRAWER	UNSETTLED	HANDCUFFS	GALRAVAGE	SURCHARGE
SCHNECKEN	SPOONFEED	TORMENTER	UNSKILLED	HOMOGRAFT	GENEALOGY	SWEEPINGS
SCHNITZEL	SPORTSMEN	TORTELIER	UNSPOILED	HOUSEWIFE	GLEANINGS	TAUTOLOGY
SCHNORKEL	SPRINGLET	TOTALIZER	UNSULLIED	INDEMNIFY	GREENGAGE	TELEOLOGY
SCHNORRER	SPRINKLER	TOWCESTER	UNTOUCHED		GREETINGS	TETRALOGY

THINNINGS	ROXBURGHE	APPERTAIN	CHARYBDIS	EPICLESIS	IMPOLITIC	NIAISERIE
TONBRIDGE	RUSHLIGHT	AQUILEGIA	CHIEFTAIN	EPICYCLIC	INDONESIA	NIPPERKIN
TRAPPINGS	SCHLEMIHL	ARACHNOID	CHILBLAIN	EPIDERMIS	INNISFAIL	NONPAREIL
TREILLAGE	SCIAMACHY	ARAUCARIA	CHINOVNIK	EPILEPTIC	INORGANIC	NONPROFIT
TRIBOLOGY	SEANNACHY	ARTEMISIA	CHLOROSIS	EPINASTIC	INTRINSIC	NOSTALGIA
TRIMMINGS	SEAWORTHY	ARTHRITIC	CHONDROID	EPIPHYSIS	IPHIGENIA	NOSTALGIC
UNDERSIGN	SIDELIGHT	ARTHRITIS	CHROMATIC	EPIPHYTIC	ISCHAEMIC	NURSEMAID
VELLENAGE	SKIAMACHY	ARTHROSIS	CHRYSALIS	EPISTAXIS	ISOMETRIC	OBSTETRIC
VERMIFUGE	SKINTIGHT	ASCERTAIN	CINEMATIC	EPITHESIS	ISOTACTIC	OCTOPLOID
WAITERAGE	SPOTLIGHT	ASTHMATIC	CINERARIA	ESTRELDID	ISOTROPIC	OLEORESIN
WINNEBAGO	STARLIGHT	ASYNERGIA	CIRRHOSIS	EUCHLORIC	JACKFRUIT	OMOPHAGIC
ABERNETHY	STOPLIGHT	ATAVISTIC	CLIMACTIC	EUPHORBIA	JACQUERIE	ONOMASTIC
ALGORITHM	TAILLIGHT	ATHEISTIC	COCKSWAIN	EUTROPHIC	JUVENILIA	OPPENHEIM
ALLOPATHY	TELEPATHY	AUBRIETIA	CORREGGIO	EVANGELIC	KERATITIS	ORGIASTIC
ANTIPATHY	TETRARCHY	AUSTRALIA	COURTSHIP	EXECUTRIX	KILDERKIN	OWNERSHIP
APOCRYPHA	THEOSOPHY	AUTHENTIC	COXSACKIE	EXODERMIS	KLENDUSIC	PALANQUIN
ARKWRIGHT	TOOTHACHE	AUTOLYSIS	CRYOGENIC	EXOSTOSIS	KNIPHOFIA	PANEGYRIC
AVALANCHE	TROSSACHS	AUTOMATIC	CUCHULAIN	EXTRINSIC	KROPOTKIN	PANORAMIC
BELLYACHE	TUMMYACHE	AUTONOMIC	CYNEGETIC	EYESTRAIN	LAMINITIS	PAPERCLIP
BIOGRAPHY	UNHEALTHY	AXIOMATIC	CYTOKININ	FANTASTIC	LEITMOTIF	PARABASIS
BULLFIGHT	UNSHEATHE	BAINMARIE	DAIRYMAID	FILIGRAIN	LEITMOTIV	PARABOLIC
BURROUGHS	WANWORTHY	BALDAQUIN	DANTHONIA	FILMSTRIP	LETHARGIC	PARACUSIS
CARTOUCHE	ACARIASIS	BALLISTIC	DAREDEVIL	FILTERTIP	LEUKAEMIA	PARALYSIS
COCKFIGHT	ACROBATIC	BARAGOUIN	DECKCHAIR	FINGERTIP	LIENTERIC	PARALYTIC
COPYRIGHT	ACROPOLIS	BARTHOLIN	DELACROIX	FINLANDIA	LIGHTSHIP	PARAMEDIC
DEADLIGHT	ACYCLOVIR	BECHSTEIN	DIABLERIE	FLAGELLIN	LITHUANIA	PARASITIC
DOWNRIGHT	ADRENALIN	BERNSTEIN	DIACRITIC	FOREBRAIN	LOHENGRIN	PARATAXIS
DYSTROPHY	AEPYORNIS	BILIRUBIN	DIAERESIS	FORJASKIT	LOMBARDIC	PAREGORIC
ENSHEATHE	AEROTAXIS	BIRDBRAIN	DIAGNOSIS	FORJESKIT	LUCIFERIN	PAROTITIS
ENTELECHY	AESTHETIC	BISHOPRIC	DIALECTIC	FORSYTHIA	LYMPHATIC	PASTICCIO
EYEBRIGHT	AFFIDAVIT	BLACKMAIL	DIAMETRIC	FRANCOLIN	MACADAMIA	PATHTRAIN
FIRELIGHT	AFLATOXIN	BOATSWAIN	DIANOETIC	FRANGLAIS	MACARONIC	PATRIOTIC
FLYWEIGHT	AFORESAID	BOCCACCIO	DIAPHYSIS	GENITALIA	MACEDONIA	PAULOWNIA
FORESIGHT	AGALACTIC	BOLSHEVIK	DIASTASIS	GEOMETRIC	MACKENZIE	PEIRASTIC
FORTNIGHT	ALCOHOLIC	BOMBASTIC	DIATHESIS	GEOMETRID	MACQUARIE	PELLAGRIN
GAELTACHT	ALEURITIS	BORNAGAIN	DIAZEUXIS	GERIATRIC	MADAROSIS	PENDENNIS
GEOGRAPHY	ALGEBRAIC	BOURGEOIS	DIGASTRIC	GODOLPHIN	MANNEQUIN	PERFERVID
GOODNIGHT	ALICYCLIC	BRASSERIE	DIGITALIN	GOMPHOSIS	MAVOURNIN	PERICUTIN
GUILLOCHE	ALIPHATIC	BRITANNIA	DIGITALIS	GREENMAIL	MELANESIA	PERTUSSIS
GUJARATHI	ALLANTOID	BRITANNIC	DISCOMFIT	GRIMALKIN	MELANOSIS	PHARISAIC
HEADLIGHT	ALLANTOIS	CACHAEMIA	DISCREDIT	GROSGRAIN	MELANOTIC	PHARSALIA
HEARTACHE	AMARANTIN	CACHECTIC	DISREPAIR	GUARDRAIL	MENAGERIE	PHENYTOIN
HIERARCHY	AMARYLLIS	CAFETERIA	DIZYGOTIC	GYMNASTIC	MENSHEVIK	PHILIPPIC
HIGHLIGHT	AMAUROSIS	CALEDONIA	DOLOMITIC	HALITOSIS	MESSIANIC	PHLEBITIS
HINDSIGHT	AMBERGRIS	CALORIFIC	DUBROVNIK	HANSEATIC	METABASIS	PHRENETIC
IDEOPATHY	AMBLYOPIA	CALPURNIA	DYSPEPSIA	HARLEQUIN	METABOLIC	PHRENITIS
INDRAUGHT	ANAEROBIC	CANDLELIT	DYSPEPTIC	HAYRADDIN	METALLOID	PINOCCHIO
JEPHTHAHS	ANALEPTIC	CANTHARIS	DYSPHAGIA	HECOGENIN	METEOROID	PISTACHIO
LAMPLIGHT	ANALGESIA	CAPRICCIO	DYSPRAXIA	HEPATITIS	METHEGLIN	PITUITRIN
LATENIGHT	ANALGESIC	CARPACCIO	ECCENTRIC	HETEROSIS	MICROCHIP	PLETHORIC
LIMELIGHT	ANAPLASIA	CARYOPSIS	ECHEVERIA	HEURISTIC	MIDRASHIM	PNEUMATIC
LOGARITHM	ANASTASIA	CASUISTIC	ECLAMPSIA	HINDBRAIN	MISTIGRIS	PNEUMONIA
MAHARISHI	ANIMISTIC	CATALYSIS	EMBROGLIO	HOBGOBLIN	MONATOMIC	POLYNESIA
MOGADISHU	ANKYLOSIS	CATALYTIC	EMBRYONIC	HONORIFIC	MONOMANIA	PONTLEVIS
MONOMACHY	ANNAPOLIS	CATATONIA	EMPAESTIC	HORSEHAIR	MORATARIA	PORCELAIN
MOONLIGHT	ANTARCTIC	CATATONIC	EMPHLYSIS	HORSETAIL	MORATORIO	PORTFOLIO
MOUSTACHE	ANTIHELIX	CATHARSIS	ENCANTHIS	HORSEWHIP	MUJAHIDIN	PRAGMATIC
NIETZSCHE	ANTITOXIC	CATHARTIC	ENCAUSTIC	HOUSEMAID	MYOFIBRIL	PREORDAIN
OLIGARCHY	ANTITOXIN	CATHEPSIN	ENDEICTIC	HOWTOWDIE	MYOGLOBIN	PRETERMIT
ONSLAUGHT	ANTIVENIN	CAUCASOID	ENDOERGIC	HYDRAULIC	MYRMECOID	PRISMATIC
OPSIMATHY	APARTHEID	CELLULOID	ENERGETIC	HYDROFOIL	NAUMACHIA	PROBOSCIS
ORICALCHE	APATHETIC	CERATITIS	ENIGMATIC	HYPEROPIA	NEOLITHIC	PROCLITIC
OROBANCHE	APERIODIC	CHALIAPIN	ENTERITIS	HYPINOSIS	NEPHRITIC	PROGNOSIS
OROGRAPHY	APHERESIS	CHAMFRAIN	ENTERTAIN	ICELANDIC	NEPHRITIS	PROLACTIN
OVERNIGHT	APOPHATIC	CHAMPLAIN	ENVERMEIL	IDENTIKIT	NEURALGIA	PROLEPSIS
OVERSIGHT	APOPHYSIS	CHANCROID	EPEDAPHIC	IDIOMATIC	NEURALGIC	PROMUSCIS
PARFLECHE	APOSTOLIC	CHAROLAIS	EPHEMERIS	IMBROGLIO	NEUROGLIA	PROPERDIN

PROPHETIC	STATISTIC	WHODUNNIT	ARDUOUSLY	CORNFIELD	EXECRABLY	HOBBINOLL
PROPIONIC	STEAMSHIP	WISCONSIN	ARISTOTLE	CORNSTALK	EXPRESSLY	HONORABLE
PROPTOSIS	STEGNOSIS	XENOMANIA	ARMADILLO	CORPUSCLE	EXTENSILE	HOPEFULLY
PROTHESIS	STEGNOTIC	YGGDRASIL	ARTERIOLE	CORRECTLY	EXTREMELY	HOUSEHOLD
PSEUDAXIS	STENOPAIC	ZOOMANTIC	ASSUREDLY	COURTELLE	FACSIMILE	HURRIEDLY
PSORIASIS	STIGMATIC	ZOOSCOPIC	ASTRAGALS	COVERDALE	FACTUALLY	HUSBANDLY
PSYCHOSIS	STOMACHIC	ZYGOMATIC	AVAILABLE	CRESCELLE	FAIRYTALE	HYDROPULT
PSYCHOTIC	STRATEGIC	ARTICHOKE	AVOIDABLE	CROCODILE	FANDANGLE	HYPERBOLA
PUNCTILIO	STRUMITIS	BALALAIKA	AWKWARDLY	CROOKEDLY	FARANDOLE	HYPERBOLE
PURITANIC	STYLISTIC	BOONDOCKS	BAGATELLE	CROSSBILL	FATUOUSLY	ILLEGALLY
PUSHCHAIR	SUBFOSSIL	BRITSCHKA	BALEFULLY	CROSSWALK	FAVORABLE	ILLEGIBLE
PYROMANIA	SUDORIFIC	CHILDLIKE	BAMBOOZLE	CROWSBILL	FAVORABLY	ILLEGIBLY
PYRRHONIC	SULPHONIC	CORNCRAKE	BASHFULLY	CRUCIALLY	FEARFULLY	ILLICITLY
QUADRATIC	SULPHURIC	CROWNLIKE	BASICALLY	CUBBYHOLE	FERVENTLY	IMBRANGLE
QUERCETIN	SURREJOIN	CUFFLINKS	BEDRAGGLE	CURFUFFLE	FILOSELLE	IMMANACLE
RADICCHIO	SYBARITIC	FIREDRAKE	BELATEDLY	CURIOUSLY	FLAMMABLE	IMMENSELY
RASKOLNIK	SYLLEPSIS	FIREWORKS	BENBECULA	CURRENTLY	FLASHBULB	IMMORALLY
REALISTIC	SYMBIOSIS	FOOTBRAKE	BESPANGLE	CURSORILY	FLORIMELL	IMMORTALS
REFUSENIK	SYMBIOTIC	FRUITCAKE	BIMONTHLY	CURVEBALL	FLOURMILL	IMMOVABLE
RESERVOIR	SYMMETRIC	GREYWACKE	BIRDTABLE	CYNICALLY	FOOLISHLY	IMMOVABLY
RETINITIS	SYMPHONIC	HANDBRAKE	BIZARRELY	DAMSELFLY	FOOTHILLS	IMMUTABLE
REYKJAVIK	SYMPHYSIS	HANDSHAKE	BLACKBALL	DASTARDLY	FOOTSTALL	IMMUTABLY
RHAPSODIC	SYNCHYSIS	HANDSPIKE	BLATANTLY	DEBATABLE	FORESTALL	INAUDIBLE
RHEOTAXIS	SYNIZESIS	HITCHHIKE	BLINDFOLD	DECASTYLE	FORLORNLY	INAUDIBLY
RHEUMATIC	SYNOVITIS	IRONWORKS	BOARDWALK	DECIDEDLY	FREESTYLE	INCAPABLE
RHODOPSIN	SYNTACTIC	KEYSTROKE	BOMBSHELL	DECRETALS	FRETFULLY	INCURABLE
RUDBECKIA	SYNTHESIS	KITTIWAKE	BOOBIALLA	DEFINABLE	FULLSCALE	INCURABLY
SACCHARIN	SYNTHETIC	LOOKALIKE	BOOKSHELF	DESIRABLE	FURIOUSLY	INDELIBLE
SAINTFOIN	TARPAULIN	MELONLIKE	BOOKSTALL	DEVIOUSLY	FURTIVELY	INDELIBLY
SANGFROID	TAYASSUID	MILKSHAKE	BRACTEOLE	DIFFICULT	GAINFULLY	INEFFABLE
SANHEDRIM	TEPHILLIN	MISSTROKE	BREAKABLE	DIRIGIBLE	GALENGALE	INFANTILE
SANHEDRIN	TESTATRIX	MOTORBIKE	BRIDEWELL	DISMANTLE	GALINGALE	INFERTILE
SANNYASIN	THALASSIC	MOUSELIKE	BROTHERLY	DISSEMBLE	GALLANTLY	INHUMANLY
SARCASTIC	THAUMATIN	POCKMANKY	BRUSQUELY	DISTANTLY	GALLINULE	INITIALLY
SAXITOXIN	THRASONIC	QUANTOCKS	BUTTERFLY	DIVISIBLE	GALLIPOLI	INSOLUBLE
SCHEMATIC	THREADFIN	ROADWORKS	CALENDULA	DODDIPOLL	GENERALLY	INSTANTLY
SCLEROSIS	THRENETIC	SALTWORKS	CALLOUSLY	DOLEFULLY	GENTEELLY	INTENSELY
SCOLIOSIS	THUMBNAIL	SAVERNAKE	CAMPANILE	DONATELLO	GENUINELY	INVISIBLE
SCOLIOTIC	TORMENTIL	SCHNITTKE	CAMPANULA	DRAGONFLY	GIRANDOLE	IODOPHILE
SCORBUTIC	TOXIGENIC	SHELDRAKE	CANTABILE	DRINKABLE	GLEEFULLY	IPRINDOLE
SEMEIOTIC	TRACKSUIT	SHORTCAKE	CARACALLA	DRUNKENLY	GLOMERULE	IRASCIBLE
SEMIFLUID	TRANSSHIP	SNOWFLAKE	CARAMBOLA	DUBIOUSLY	GLORYHOLE	IRRITABLE
SEMIRAMIS	TRAPEZOID	SUNSTROKE	CARBUNCLE	DUNSTABLE	GOLDFIELD	IRRITABLY
SEPHARDIM	TRATTORIA	SYLPHLIKE	CAREFULLY	DUTIFULLY	GOONHILLY	JEALOUSLY
SHARKSKIN	TRAUMATIC	THORNDYKE	CASSEROLE	EARNESTLY	GRADUALLY	JOCULARLY
SHEEPSKIN	TRETINOIN	TRIPITAKA	CATCHPOLE	ELEGANTLY	GRATICULE	KERFUFFLE
SHELLSUIT	TRICLINIC	UNDERTAKE	CATCHPOLL	EMBRANGLE	GRENVILLE	KILOCYCLE
SHUBUNKIN	TRICUSPID	WAPENTAKE	CATSKILLS	EMINENTLY	GRISAILLE	KISWAHILI
SIDEROSIS	TRIETERIC	ABYSMALLY	CENTRALLY	EMMERDALE	GUACAMOLE	KNAPSCULL
SILICOSIS	TROCHILIC	ADAPTABLE	CERTAINLY	EMPANOPLY	GUATEMALA	KNAPSKULL
SINUSITIS	TRONDHEIM	ADMIRABLE	CHAMOMILE	ENDLESSLY	GUERRILLA	KNOWINGLY
SLAMMAKIN	TROOPSHIP	ADMIRABLY	CHANTILLY	ENDURABLE	GUILDHALL	LANGUIDLY
SNOWDONIA	TROPAELIN	ADVERSELY	CHRONICLE	ENJOYABLE	GUMSHIELD	LATERALLY
SOLFEGGIO	UNCERTAIN	ADVISABLE	CHURCHILL	ENNERDALE	HABITABLE	LAUGHABLE
SOOTERKIN	UNDERPAID	ADVISEDLY	CINEPHILE	ENSORCELL	HAIRSTYLE	LEAFMOULD
SOPHISTIC	UPAITHRIC	AGREEABLE	CLIENTELE	EQUITABLE	HALOPHILE	LEAFSTALK
SOPORIFIC	URTICARIA	AGREEABLY	CLINGFILM	EQUITABLY	HARDSHELL	LEASEHOLD
SOUVLAKIA	UTICENSIS	AIMLESSLY	COALFIELD	ERSTWHILE	HAUGHTILY	LEISURELY
SPACESHIP	VAGINITIS	ALLEGEDLY	COLUMELLA	ESPAGNOLE	HAWKSBILL	LENGTHILY
SPACESUIT	VAPORIFIC	ALLOWABLE	COMICALLY	ESTIMABLE	HAWSEHOLE	LENIENTLY
SPADASSIN	VERDIGRIS	ALTERABLE	COMPACTLY	ETERNALLY	HEADSTALL	LIBERALLY
SPASMODIC	VITRIOLIC	AMOROUSLY	CONCISELY	EVASIVELY	HEALTHILY	LIFESTYLE
SPILLIKIN	WAFERTHIN	AMUSINGLY	CONSTABLE	EVIDENTLY	HEARTFELT	LINGFIELD
SPLENETIC	WALPURGIS	ANXIOUSLY	CONTUMELY	EXCITABLE	HELPFULLY	LITERALLY
SPLENITIS	WASHBASIN	AQUARELLE	COPIOUSLY	EXCUSABLE	HERITABLE	LOGICALLY
SPRITSAIL	WHIRLIGIG	ARCHIBALD	CORDIALLY	EXCUSABLY	HIDEOUSLY	LONGINGLY
SPUNCULID	WHITEBAIT	ARCHIVOLT	CORNEILLE	EXECRABLE	HILLBILLY	LYMESWOLD

LYRICALLY	PASTORALE	RUINOUSLY	TEARFULLY	WELLBUILT	PROENZYME	APPLICANT
MACDONALD	PATCHOULI	SAPODILLA	TEDIOUSLY	WHITEHALL	PROGRAMME	APPREHEND
MAGICALLY	PATCHOULY	SCAGLIOLA	TELLINGLY	WHITEWALL	QUICKLIME	APPROVING
MAJUSCULE	PATIENTLY	SCALEABLE	TENUOUSLY	WHOLESALE	SEMANTEME	AQUAPLANE
MALLEABLE	PEACEABLE	SCHNOZZLE	TERRICOLE	WILLFULLY	SIXTEENMO	ARGENTINA
MANHANDLE	PEACEABLY	SCHOLARLY	THINKABLE	WILLINGLY	SMALLTIME	ARGENTINE
MANSFIELD	PEEVISHLY	SCINTILLA	THIRSTILY	WINDCHILL	SYPHILOMA	ARMSTRONG
MASEFIELD	PENINSULA	SCREWBALL	THORNBILL	WINDFALLS	TAXIDERMY	ARRESTING
MASSIVELY	PENSIVELY	SCRUFFILY	THREEFOLD	WINDSCALE	TEKNONYMY	ASCENDANT
MEANWHILE	PERFECTLY	SEABOTTLE	THRESHOLD	WISTFULLY	THEOBROMA	ASCENDING
MEATBALLS	PERISTYLE	SEEMINGLY	THRIFTILY	WITTINGLY	THINGUMMY	ASSAILANT
MEDICALLY	PERMEABLE	SELFISHLY	THROATILY	WOMENFOLK	THREESOME	ASSERTING
MEGACYCLE	PHILATELY	SENSUALLY	TIMETABLE	AERODROME	TOOTHCOMB	ASSISTANT
MEMORABLE	PIACEVOLE	SEPARABLE	TOLERABLE	AFTERDAMP	TOOTHSOME	ATONEMENT
MICROFILM	PINEAPPLE	SEPTIMOLE	TOLERABLY	ALTISSIMO	TRANSHUME	ATTACKING
MICROMOLE	PIQUANTLY	SERIOUSLY	TOPICALLY	ANISOGAMY	UNWELCOME	ATTENDANT
MICROVOLT	PITCHPOLE	SERREFILE	TOWNSFOLK	APOENZYME	VASECTOMY	AUBERGINE
MILLIVOLT	PITCHPOLL	SERVILELY	TOXOPHILY	ASPARTAME	VELODROME	AUGUSTINE
MINEFIELD	PITIFULLY	SEVERALLY	TRACEABLE	ASTRODOME	WEARISOME	AWAKENING
MINUSCULE	PLAUSIBLE	SHEEPFOLD	TRACTABLE	ASTRONOMY	WHITEDAMP	BALLERINA
MIRABELLE	PLAUSIBLY	SHEFFIELD	TRAINABLE	BLACKDAMP	WHOLESOME	BALLPOINT
MISERABLE	PLAYFULLY	SHEMOZZLE	TREADMILL	BLASPHEME	WORRISOME	BANDOLINE
MISERABLY	PLIMSOLLS	SHORTFALL	TREDRILLE	BLASPHEMY	XEROSTOMA	BANDSTAND
MISHANDLE	POINTEDLY	SHORTHOLD	CARCINOMA	CARCINOMA	ABASEMENT	BANTERING
MITRAILLE	POPULARLY	SIMILARLY	TREGEAGLE	CARCINOMA	ABATEMENT	BARBITONE
MONTICULE	PORBEAGLE	SINCERELY	TRITICALE	COLOSTOMY	ABHORRENT	BARBOTINE
MOTHBALLS	PRECISELY	SIPHUNCLE	TRIVIALLY	CONDYLOMA	ABLUTIONS	BARCELONA
MOUSEHOLE	PRESENTLY	SKEDADDLE	TURCOPOLE	CURRYCOMB	ABORIGINE	BEGINNING
MUSICALLY	PRIMARILY	SKETCHILY	TURNBULLS	CYCLORAMA	ABOUNDING	BELIEVING
MUSICHALL	PRINCIPLE	SKILFULLY	TURNSTILE	DIATHERMY	ABSORBENT	BELONGING
NARGHILLY	PRINTABLE	SLAVISHLY	TURNTABLE	DICHOTOMY	ABSORBING	BILLABONG
NASHVILLE	PRIVATELY	SLEEPWALK	TYPICALLY	DISENTOMB	ABSTINENT	BILLOWING
NATURALLY	PROFANELY	SNEERWELL	UMBRATILE	DITHYRAMB	ACCOMPANY	BLUEPRINT
NAUGHTILY	PROFUSELY	SOLDIERLY	UNCOURTLY	DOORFRAME	ACCORDANT	BLUESTONE
NAVIGABLE	PRUDENTLY	SOULFULLY	UNDERFELT	DUODECIMO	ACCORDING	BOLIVIANO
NERVOUSLY	PUNGENTLY	SOUTHERLY	UNDERSELL	EIGHTSOME	ACETYLENE	BOMBASINE
NEUTRALLY	PURPOSELY	SPARINGLY	UNDERWALK	EMPHYSEMA	ACROPHONY	BONDSTONE
NEWCASTLE	QUADRILLE	SPATIALLY	UNEARTHLY	ENTHYMEME	ADJOINING	BOOKSTAND
NEWSSTALL	QUADRUPLE	SPECIALLY	UNEATABLE	EURHYTHMY	ADMITTING	BOOMERANG
NIGGARDLY	QUARTERLY	SPECTACLE	UNHAPPILY	EXANTHEMA	ADORNMENT	BORDERING
NIGHTFALL	QUENNELLE	SPEEDWELL	UNIFORMLY	FILOPLUME	AEROPLANE	BORROWING
NITHSDALE	QUINTUPLE	SPOONBILL	UNLUCKILY	FLEXITIME	AFFECTING	BOYFRIEND
NOMINALLY	RADIANTLY	SPRAICKLE	UNSHACKLE	HAEMALOMA	AFRIKAANS	BRAMBLING
NORTHERLY	RADICALLY	SPRAUCHLE	UNSIGHTLY	HARMOTOME	AGONIZING	BRANCHING
NUMBSKULL	RANTIPOLE	SPRIGHTLY	UNTENABLE	HIPPODAME	AGREEMENT	BREADLINE
OBLIQUELY	RATIONALE	SPRINGALD	UNUSUALLY	HONEYCOMB	AITCHBONE	BREATHING
OBSCENELY	RAUCOUSLY	SQUALIDLY	VALIANTLY	LEUCOTOME	ALBERTINE	BREECHING
OBSCURELY	RAZORBILL	STANDGALE	VARICELLA	LIGHTSOME	ALIGNMENT	BRILLIANT
OBVIOUSLY	REACHABLE	STAUNCHLY	VARIOUSLY	LOATHSOME	ALLEGIANT	BRIMSTONE
OFFICIALS	RECONCILE	STOCKHOLM	VEGETABLE	LONGCHAMP	ALLOTMENT	BRISTLING
OMINOUSLY	RECTANGLE	STOCKPILE	VENERABLE	LUNCHTIME	ALMANDINE	BUFFETING
OPTICALLY	REDUCIBLE	STOICALLY	VENEZUELA	MAINFRAME	ALTIPLANO	BURROWING
OPULENTLY	REGULARLY	STOKEHOLD	VENTRICLE	MAJORDOMO	AMAZEMENT	BYZANTINE
ORGANELLE	REMOVABLE	STONEWALL	VERITABLE	MELODRAMA	AMENDMENT	CACOPHONY
OUTWARDLY	RENEWABLE	STOOLBALL	VERSATILE	METRONOME	AMERICANO	CAKESTAND
OVERSPILL	REPAYABLE	STRANGELY	VESTIBULE	MICROTOME	AMPERSAND	CARPETING
OVERWHELM	REPUTABLE	STROMBOLI	VIBRATILE	MONODRAMA	AMUSEMENT	CASHPOINT
PAINFULLY	REPUTEDLY	STRONGYLE	VICIOUSLY	MONTEZUMA	ANDANTINO	CASUARINA
PALATABLE	RESHUFFLE	STYLISHLY	VIOLENTLY	MUSHROOMS	ANNAPURNA	CATAMOUNT
PANATELLA	RIDGEPOLE	SUBLIMELY	VIRGINALS	NIGHTTIME	ANNULMENT	CATCHMENT
PANHANDLE	RIGMAROLE	SUMMARILY	VIRTUALLY	ORIFLAMME	ANOINTING	CATHERINE
PANNIKELL	RIOTOUSLY	SUPREMELY	VOLATILE	OVERTRUMP	ANSWERING	CAVORTING
PANTOFFLE	ROCAMBOLE	SURCINGLE	WASPISHLY	PANTAGAMY	ANTICLINE	CELANDINE
PANTOUFLE	ROOSEVELT	TACTFULLY	WATERFALL	PANTOMIME	ANTIPHONY	CELEBRANT
PARBUCKLE	ROUTINELY	TARANTULA	WATERHOLE	PEACETIME	APARTMENT	CENTERING
PARTIALLY	RUBICELLE	TEACHABLE	WATERLILY	PERISTOME	APPALLING	CENTREING
PASSIVELY	RUFFIANLY	TEAKETTLE	WATERMILL	PHANTASMA	APPEALING	CHAMPAGNE

CHAPERONE	DEMEANING	EXCELLENT	GRAMPIANS	IMPORTUNE	LUTESCENT	NEWSAGENT
CHARABANC	DEMULCENT	EXCIPIENT	GRAPEVINE	IMPROVING	LUXURIANT	NEWSHOUND
CHEEKBONE	DEODORANT	EXCLUDING	GRAPPLING	IMPRUDENT	MACEDOINE	NEWSPRINT
CHERUBINI	DEPENDANT	EXCREMENT	GRASSLAND	INCARDINE	MACHINING	NEWSSTAND
CIPOLLINO	DEPENDENT	EXECUTANT	GRAVESEND	INCESSANT	MADDENING	NIDDERING
CLEANSING	DEPENDING	EXPECTANT	GREENSAND	INCIPIENT	MADELEINE	NIDERLING
CLEARWING	DESERVING	EXPECTING	GREGARINE	INCLEMENT	MADRILENE	NIEBELUNG
CLEVELAND	DESIGNING	EXPEDIENT	GRENADINE	INCLUDING	MAGDALENE	NIGROSINE
CLOISONNÉ	DESIPIENT	EXPORTING	GREYHOUND	INCREMENT	MALENGINE	NOLLEKENS
COAGULANT	DETERGENT	EXUBERANT	GROUNDING	INCUMBENT	MALIGNANT	NOVOCAINE
COASTLINE	DETERMINE	FAIRYLAND	GRUELLING	INDIGNANT	MANDOLINE	NUTRIMENT
COCKAIGNE	DETERRENT	FASTENING	GRUMBLING	INDULGENT	MANNERING	OBSERVANT
COGNIZANT	DETRIMENT	FATISCENT	GUIDELINE	INELEGANT	MAPPEMOND	OBTAINING
COLOPHONY	DEVILMENT	FATTENING	GUTTERING	INFECTING	MARAUDING	OCCUPYING
COLOURING	DIFFERENT	FERDINAND	GYROPLANE	INFORMANT	MARCHPANE	ODELSTING
COLUMBINE	DIFFIDENT	FEUILLANT	HABERDINE	INGROWING	MARGARINE	OFFENDING
COMBATANT	DIPHTHONG	FIBROLINE	HAILSTONE	INPATIENT	MARIJUANA	OFFICIANT
COMPETENT	DISABLING	FILTERING	HALFPENNY	INQUILINE	MARKETING	OFFSPRING
COMPETING	DISARMING	FINGERING	HALOBIONT	INQUIRING	MARSHLAND	OLIGOCENE
COMPLAINT	DISORIENT	FINICKING	HALOTHANE	INSIPIENT	MASCULINE	OPERATING
COMPLIANT	DISPUTANT	FINISHING	HAMMERING	INSISTENT	MATHURINE	OPPORTUNE
COMPONENT	DISSIDENT	FIREBRAND	HAMSTRING	INSOLVENT	MATRIMONY	OPTOPHONE
COMPOSING	DISSONANT	FIRESTONE	HAMSTRUNG	INSPIRING	MEASURING	ORGANZINE
COMPUTING	DISTRAINT	FIRMAMENT	HANDSTAND	INSULTING	MEGAPHONE	ORMANDINE
CONCUBINE	DITHERING	FIRSTHAND	HANKERING	INSURGENT	MELBOURNE	ORTHOTONE
CONDIMENT	DIVERGENT	FLAGSTONE	HAPPENING	INTENDANT	MELPOMENE	OVERLYING
CONFIDANT	DIVERGING	FLATULENT	HARESTANE	INTENDING	MENADIONE	OVERPAINT
CONFIDENT	DIVERTING	FLAVORING	HARMALINE	INTERMENT	MENDICANT	OVERPRINT
CONFUSING	DIXIELAND	FLEDGLING	HARROWING	INTERVENE	MEPACRINE	OVERSPEND
CONGRUENT	DOWELLING	FLOWERING	HASTENING	INTESTINE	MERESWINE	PACKAGING
CONJURING	DOWNTREND	FLOWSTONE	HATCHMENT	INVOICING	MEROCRINE	PAKISTANI
CONSONANT	DREAMLAND	FOLKETING	HAWTHORNE	IRONSTONE	MERRIMENT	PALESTINE
CONSUMING	DRIPSTONE	FOLLOWING	HAYMAKING	IRRADIANT	MESSALINA	PALUDRINE
CONTINENT	DUMBFOUND	FOOTPRINT	HEADSTONE	ITINERANT	METHADONE	PANELLING
CORALLINE	DUNSINANE	FOREANENT	HEARTLAND	JENNETING	METROLAND	PANETTONE
CORDYLINE	DUPLICAND	FOREFRONT	HEATHLAND	JESSAMINE	MEZZANINE	PARAMOUNT
CORMORANT	DWINDLING	FOREGOING	HECTORING	JESSERANT	MEZZOTINT	PARASCENE
CORPOSANT	EARTHLING	FORESPEND	HEDYPHANE	JOHANNINE	MICROTONE	PARCHMENT
CORPULENT	EASTBOUND	FORGIVING	HIDEBOUND	JOSEPHINE	MILESTONE	PARENTING
CORTISONE	EASYGOING	FORTHWINK	HIJACKING	JUDGEMENT	MILLAMANT	PAROCHINE
COSMOGONY	EBULLIENT	FOUNDLING	HIRUNDINE	JUNKETING	MILLSTONE	PARSIMONY
COTANGENT	ECHIDNINE	FREEPHONE	HISTAMINE	KALSOMINE	MINKSTONE	PARTAKING
CRACKLING	EDDYSTONE	FREESTONE	HISTIDINE	KERBSTONE	MISCREANT	PASSAMENT
CRANBORNE	EFFICIENT	FRIESLAND	HOARHOUND	LAKEFRONT	MISFIRING	PASSERINE
CRAPULENT	EFFULGENT	FULLERENE	HOARSTONE	LAMARTINE	MISGIVING	PATHOGENY
CRASHLAND	EGAREMENT	FULMINANT	HOLYSTONE	LATESCENT	MNEMOSYNE	PATRIMONY
CREPOLINE	EGLANTINE	FUNDAMENT	HOMEBOUND	LAUNCHING	MOCCASINS	PENFRIEND
CRINOLINE	ELOPEMENT	FURNIMENT	HOMOPHONE	LAWMAKING	MODELLING	PENISTONE
CRIPPLING	EMBRACING	GABARDINE	HONKYTONK	LAZZARONE	MODESTINE	PENTOSANE
CROISSANT	EMOLLIENT	GABERDINE	HOREHOUND	LETTERING	MOLESKINS	PEPPERONI
CROSSWIND	EMOLUMENT	GALANTINE	HORNSTONE	LEVANTINE	MONACTINE	PERCALINE
CRUMBLING	ENACTMENT	GALATIANS	HOURSTONE	LIBERTINE	MONOPLANE	PEREGRINE
CYMBELINE	ENCUMBENT	GALLIVANT	HOUYHNHNM	LIGHTNING	MONTAIGNE	PERFORANS
DACHSHUND	ENDEARING	GALLSTONE	HUMANKIND	LIMESTONE	MOONSHINE	PERGAMENE
DAMASCENE	ENDOCRINE	GANGPLANK	HURRICANE	LIMOUSINE	MOONSTONE	PERISHING
DAYSPRING	ENDOWMENT	GARDENING	HURRICANO	LINEAMENT	MORTSTONE	PERMANENT
DEAFENING	ENGARLAND	GATHERING	HYDRAZINE	LINGERING	MOTHERING	PERTINENT
DECLARING	ENGRAVING	GAVELKIND	HYPERLINK	LISTENING	MUNITIONS	PESTILENT
DECLINING	ENJOYMENT	GESSAMINE	IDIOPHONE	LITHOPONE	MURMURING	PETHIDINE
DECUMBENT	ENQUIRING	GLADSTONE	IGNESCENT	LJUBLJANA	MUSCADINE	PETILLANT
DEERHOUND	ENROLMENT	GLUTAMINE	IMMELMANN	LOADSTONE	MUSCARINE	PHARAMOND
DEFENDANT	EPHEDRINE	GLYCERINE	IMMIGRANT	LODESTONE	MUSSOLINI	PHEROMONE
DEFERMENT	EPHESIANS	GODPARENT	IMPATIENT	LODGEMENT	MUTTERING	PHOSPHENE
DEFICIENT	EQUIPMENT	GOLDSINNY	IMPELLING	LOITERING	NARROWING	PHOTOGENE
DEFOLIANT	ESQUILINE	GOSSYPINE	IMPENDING	LOUISIANA	NECTARINE	PHYLOGENY
DEGRADING	EUDAEMONY	GOVERNING	IMPLEMENT	LUBRICANT	NEGLIGENT	PICKETING
DEMANDING	EXACTMENT	GRADGRIND	IMPORTANT	LUMBERING	NEPHELINE	PICKTHANK

PIGGYBANK	REEXAMINE	SCRAPPING	STRINGENT	TREMBLING	WHITENING	BLACKWOOD
PILFERING	REFERRING	SCREENING	STRIPLING	TREMULANT	WHITEWING	BLINDSPOT
PIPESTONE	REFULGENT	SCREWPINE	STROLLING	TRENCHANT	WHIZZBANG	BLOODROOT
PITCHPINE	REGARDANT	SCRIMPING	STRUTTING	TRUCULENT	WHUNSTANE	BLOODSHOT
PLACEMENT	REGARDING	SCRUBBING	STUMBLING	TRUEPENNY	WILLOWING	BOARDROOM
PLAINSONG	REJOICING	SCRUMPING	SUBJACENT	TUMESCENT	WITHERING	BOLECTION
PLAYTHING	RELATIONS	SCULPTING	SUBMARINE	TURBULENT	WITHSTAND	BOMBARDON
PLEIOCENE	RELUCTANT	SEAFARING	SUBTENANT	TURMAGENT	WITHYWIND	BRANDIRON
PLUMBLINE	REMAINING	SEARCHING	SUCCUBINE	TURNROUND	WOBBEGONG	BRIGADOON
POISONING	REMONTANT	SEASONING	SUCCULENT	TURNSTONE	WOEBEGONE	BROADLOOM
POLLUTANT	RENASCENT	SELECTING	SUFFERING	TWINKLING	WOLFHOUND	BROUGHTON
POLVERINE	RENDERING	SENESCENT	SUGARCANE	UNBENDING	WOLVERINE	BRUSHWOOD
POLYPHONE	REPAYMENT	SENTIMENT	SUPERFINE	UNCEASING	WOMANKIND	CAPACITOR
POLYPHONY	REPELLENT	SERAPHINE	SUPERVENE	UNCONFINE	WOOMERANG	CAPARISON
POLYTHENE	REPELLING	SERVICING	SUPPLIANT	UNDERDONE	WRESTLING	CARNATION
POPPERING	REPENTANT	SHAVELING	SUPPOSING	UNDERHAND	WUTHERING	CASSATION
PORCUPINE	REPLACING	SHEARLING	SURVEYING	UNDERHUNG	XYLOPHONE	CATCHCROP
POSTULANT	REPLICANT	SHENSTONE	SURVIVING	UNDERLINE	YOHIMBINE	CAUSATION
POTHOLING	REPORTING	SHIELDING	SWADDLING	UNDERLING	ZIBELLINE	CEDARWOOD
PRECEDENT	REPREHEND	SHIVERING	SWEATBAND	UNDERMINE	ABDUCTION	CENTURION
PRECEDING	REPRESENT	SHOESHINE	SWINBURNE	UNDERSONG	ABOLITION	CESSATION
PREDICANT	REPRIMAND	SHOPFRONT	SWINGEING	UNDERTONE	ACCESSION	CHALAZION
PREDIKANT	REPROVING	SHORTHAND	SWOTHLING	UNDERWENT	ACCORDION	CHAMELEON
PRESCIENT	REPUGNANT	SHRIMPING	SYCOPHANT	UNFAILING	ACCRETION	CHAWBACON
PRESHRUNK	RESERPINE	SHRINKING	TABLELAND	UNFEELING	ADDICTION	CHECKBOOK
PRESIDENT	RESILIENT	SHUFFLING	TAILPLANE	UNFITTING	ADMISSION	CHECKROOM
PRESSGANG	RESISTANT	SIBYLLINE	TAMERLANE	UNHEEDING	ADMONITOR	CHILDHOOD
PREVALENT	RESORTING	SICILIANO	TANGERINE	UNIVALENT	ADORATION	CLARENDON
PRIMULINE	RESTRAINT	SICKENING	TARRAGONA	UNKNOWING	ADULATION	CLASSROOM
PROLAMINE	RESULTANT	SIDEBURNS	TELEPHONE	UNNERVING	ADULTHOOD	CLOAKROOM
PROMINENT	RESULTING	SILTSTONE	TELEPHONY	UNSINNING	ADVECTION	COADJUTOR
PROMISING	RESURGENT	SKINFLINT	TERMAGANT	UNSPARING	AFFECTION	COALITION
PROMPTING	RETAILING	SLABSTONE	TERMAGENT	UNVARYING	AFTERNOON	COCKSFOOT
PROPONENT	RETAINING	SLOUGHING	TERRACING	UNWILLING	AGAMEMNON	COCUSWOOD
PROPYLENE	RETURNING	SLUGHORNE	TESTAMENT	UNWITTING	AGGRESSOR	COEMPTION
PROTAMINE	REVEALING	SMUGGLING	TESTIMONY	UPLIFTING	AGITATION	COGNITION
PROVIDENT	REVELLING	SNOWBOUND	THATCHING	UPSETTING	ALLIGATOR	COLLATION
PROVIDING	REVERSING	SOAPSTONE	THECODONT	VALENTINE	ALPENGLOW	COLLECTOR
PROVOKING	REVETMENT	SOFTENING	THIGHBONE	VANISHING	ANIMATION	COLLISION
PROVOLONE	REVOLTING	SOLDERING	THIRSTING	VERATRINE	ANNOTATOR	COLLODION
PUNCHLINE	REVOLVING	SOLFERINO	THRASHING	VEXATIONS	APPARITOR	COLLUSION
PUNISHING	REWARDING	SOMETHING	THREONINE	VICEREINE	APPORTION	COLTSFOOT
PURIFYING	REWORKING	SOMNOLENT	THRILLANT	VICTORINE	ARLINGTON	COMMOTION
PYONGYANG	RIDGELING	SPARKLING	THRILLING	VIENTIANE	ARROWROOT	COMMUNION
QUAVERING	RIGHTHAND	SPEARMINT	THROBBING	VIEWPOINT	ARTHROPOD	COMPANION
QUERIMONY	RIGHTWING	SPECIMENS	THRONGING	VIPASSANA	ASCENSION	CONCISION
QUICKSAND	ROSMARINE	SPELDRING	THUMBLING	VOLUCRINE	ASPERSION	CONDITION
QUIESCENT	ROTAPLANE	SPELLBIND	THYLACINE	VULTURINE	ASPIRATOR	CONDUCTOR
QUINQUINA	ROUNDHAND	SPHENDONE	THYROXINE	WAISTBAND	ASSERTION	CONFESSOR
QUIVERING	RUFESCENT	SPLITTING	TICHBORNE	WAISTLINE	ASYNDETON	CONFITEOR
RADIATING	RUNAROUND	SPODUMENE	TISIPHONE	WALLOPING	ATTENTION	CONFUSION
RANGELAND	SACRAMENT	SPREADING	TOADSTONE	WALLOWING	ATTRITION	CONNECTOR
RATIONING	SADDENING	SQUADRONE	TOCCATINA	WANDERING	ATTUITION	CONNEXION
RAVISHING	SALANGANE	SQUINTING	TOMBSTONE	WASHSTAND	AUTOMATON	CONQUEROR
REASONING	SANDSTONE	SQUIRMING	TOSCANINI	WASTELAND	AUTOPILOT	CONSIGNOR
RECALLING	SANTAYANA	STAGEHAND	TOTAQUINE	WATERLINE	AVOCATION	CONTAGION
RECEIVING	SARBACANE	STARSTONE	TOUCHLINE	WEAKENING	BADMINTON	CONTUSION
RECIPIENT	SATURNINE	STARTLING	TOWELLING	WEIGHTING	BANDICOOT	CONVECTOR
RECKONING	SAXOPHONE	STATEMENT	TRADEWIND	WELCOMING	BANDWAGON	CORRECTOR
RECOMMEND	SCALLIONS	STIMULANT	TRANSCEND	WELLBEING	BASILICON	CORROSION
RECONVENE	SCAMBLING	STONEHAND	TRANSEUNT	WESTBOUND	BATTALION	COTYLEDON
RECORDING	SCANTLING	STORYLINE	TRANSIENT	WHALEBONE	BEDFELLOW	COUNSELOR
RECUMBENT	SCHELLING	STOWNLINS	TRASIMENE	WHETSTONE	BELLYFLOP	COURTROOM
RECURRENT	SCHIAVONE	STRAINING	TRAVELING	WHINSTONE	BETTERTON	CREMATION
RECURRING	SCHILLING	STRAPHANG	TREATMENT	WHIPROUND	BISECTION	CRENATION
REDEEMING	SCHOOLING	STRAPPING	TREBIZOND	WHIRLWIND	BLACKFOOT	CRITERION
REDUNDANT	SCORCHING	STREAMING	TREETRUNK	WHISTLING	BLACKWOOD	CROWSFOOT

CTESIPHON	EVOLUTION	HONEYMOON	MAELSTROM	PECULATOR	REPTATION	STORYBOOK
CUNCTATOR	EXARATION	HORSESHOE	MAGNETRON	PENDLETON	REPULSION	STRIATION
CYCLOTRON	EXCAMBION	HOTTENTOT	MAINTENON	PENDRAGON	RESNATRON	SUBEDITOR
DAMNATION	EXCAVATOR	HOUSEROOM	MALATHION	PENILLION	RESONATOR	SUCCENTOR
DANDELION	EXCELSIOR	ICHNEUMON	MARTYRDOM	PENSTEMON	RETENTION	SUCCESSOR
DEATHBLOW	EXCEPTION	IDIOTICON	MATCHBOOK	PEPPERPOT	RETORSION	SUFFUSION
DECAMERON	EXCLUSION	IGUANODON	MATCHWOOD	PERAEOPOD	RETORTION	SUMMATION
DECATHLON	EXCURSION	IMITATION	MEDALLION	PERCHERON	RETRACTOR	SUPERCOOL
DECEPTION	EXECUTION	IMMERSION	MEDIATION	PERDITION	REVERSION	SUPINATOR
DECESSION	EXEMPTION	IMPACTION	MEDITATOR	PERIAKTOS	REVULSION	SUSPENSOR
DECILLION	EXHIBITOR	IMPASSION	MENTATION	PERIBOLOS	RIDERHOOD	SUSPICION
DECOCTION	EXORATION	IMPERATOR	MICKLETON	PERSIMMON	ROBERTSON	SWEETSHOP
DECONTROL	EXPANSION	IMPULSION	MIDDLETON	PERVASION	ROSCOMMON	SYNEDRION
DECORATOR	EXPIATION	INANITION	MIGRATION	PHANARIOT	ROUGHSHOD	TABELLION
DEDUCTION	EXPLOSION	INCAUTION	MISTLETOE	PHYLLOPOD	RUINATION	TABULATOR
DEFECTION	EXPOSITOR	INCEPTION	MODERATOR	PHYTOTRON	SACKERSON	TARNATION
DEFLATION	EXPULSION	INCLUSION	MODILLION	PINKERTON	SAINTHOOD	TELLURION
DEFLECTOR	EXTENSION	INCUBATOR	MONKSHOOD	POLLUTION	SALVATION	TENAILLON
DEJECTION	EXTORTION	INCURSION	MONOCEROS	POSSESSOR	SANHEDRON	TERPINEOL
DENTITION	EXTRACTOR	INDICATOR	MONOXYLON	POSTERIOR	SASKATOON	THEREUPON
DEPICTION	EXTRUSION	INDICTION	MONSIGNOR	POSTILION	SATIATION	THERMIDOR
DEPOSITOR	EXUDATION	INDUCTION	MORTGAGOR	PRACTOLOL	SATINWOOD	THRALLDOM
DESERTION	EYESHADOW	INFECTION	MUGGLETON	PRECENTOR	SAUCISSON	THYRATRON
DETECTION	FALDSTOOL	INFLATION	MUSKETOON	PRECEPTOR	SAUVIGNON	THYRISTOR
DETENTION	FALSEHOOD	INFLEXION	NARRATION	PRECISION	SCARECROW	TICTACTOE
DETONATOR	FAULCHION	INGESTION	NAVIGATOR	PRECURSOR	SCHOOLBOY	TIERCERON
DETRACTOR	FIREPROOF	INGLENOOK	NIGHTGLOW	PREDICTOR	SCONCHEON	TITRATION
DETRITION	FLEETWOOD	INHERITOR	NIGHTSPOT	PRELECTOR	SCRAPBOOK	TOADSTOOL
DEUCALION	FLOORSHOW	INHIBITOR	NOMINATOR	PREMOTION	SCRUTATOR	TORMENTOR
DEVIATION	FLOTATION	INITIATOR	NONILLION	PRINCETON	SCUNCHEON	TOUCHWOOD
DICTATION	FLOWERPOT	INJECTION	NOTARIKON	PRIVATION	SECESSION	TOURNEDOS
DIFFUSION	FOOLPROOF	INNOVATOR	NUMERATOR	PROBATION	SECLUSION	TRADITION
DIGESTION	FOOTSTOOL	INSERTION	NUTRITION	PROCESSOR	SECRETION	TRIATHLON
DIMENSION	FORMATION	INSPECTOR	OBJECTION	PROFESSOR	SEDGEMOOR	TRICERION
DIRECTION	FREEMASON	INSULATOR	OBREPTION	PROFUSION	SEDUCTION	TRIHEDRON
DIVERSION	FRIGATOON	INTENTION	OBSESSION	PROJECTOR	SELACHION	TRILITHON
DORMITION	FRUCTIDOR	INTRUSION	OBTRUSION	PROKARYON	SELECTION	TRISAGION
DOUKHOBOR	GALAPAGOS	INTUITION	OBVENTION	PROLUSION	SEMANTRON	TROPARION
DRIFTWOOD	GALDRAGON	INUNCTION	OCCLUSION	PROMACHOS	SEMICOLON	TROUBADOR
DUIKERBOK	GALLYCROW	INVENTION	OCTILLION	PROMOTION	SENSATION	TRUNCHEON
DUMBARTON	GENERATOR	INVERSION	OFFSEASON	PROTECTOR	SEPARATOR	TULIPWOOD
EAGLEWOOD	GERFALCON	IRRUPTION	OLECRANON	PROVISION	SERIATION	TURBOPROP
EAVESDROP	GESTATION	ISOLATION	ONTHESPOT	PULSATION	SERRATION	UNCHRISOM
ECTROPION	GLADIATOR	ITERATION	OPERATION	PUSSYFOOT	SHEIKHDOM	UNDERFLOW
EDDINGTON	GOOSEFOOT	JAWBATION	OPODELDOC	PYGMALION	SHOLOKHOV	UNDERFOOT
EDUCATION	GRADATION	JIGGUMBOB	OPPRESSOR	QUINTROON	SHOPFLOOR	UNDERWOOD
EGRESSION	GRAPESHOT	JOSEPHSON	ORPHARION	QUOTATION	SHORTSTOP	URINATION
ELBOWROOM	GREENHORN	LACTATION	ORPINGTON	QUOTITION	SIMPLETON	VALUATION
ELEVATION	GREENWOOD	LAMBSWOOL	OUROBOROS	RADIATION	SIMULATOR	VALVASSOR
ELLINGTON	GROSVENOR	LAMPADION	OVENPROOF	REBELLION	SINGLETON	VARIATION
ELOCUTION	GROUNDHOG	LANCEWOOD	OVERSHOOT	REBOATION	SITUATION	VEGETATOR
EMANATION	GRUBBINOL	LANGUEDOC	OVERTHROW	RECEPTION	SLINGSHOT	VERMILION
EMPLECTON	GUARANTOR	LARGITION	OVULATION	RECESSION	SOLICITOR	VERNATION
EMULATION	GUARDROOM	LATRATION	OXIDATION	REDUCTION	SPECTATOR	VIBRATION
ENCHEASON	GUIDEBOOK	LAUDATION	PADEMELON	REFECTION	SPLAYFOOT	VIOLATION
ENCOLPION	GUILLEMOT	LAUNCELOT	PALMATION	REFLATION	SPRINGBOK	VITIATION
ENDECAGON	GUNCOTTON	LEAKPROOF	PALPATION	REFLECTOR	STABLEBOY	WAGENBOOM
ENTROPION	GUSTATION	LESTRIGON	PANDATION	REFLEXION	STANCHION	WEDGEWOOD
EPHEMERON	HABERGEON	LETTERBOX	PANTALEON	REFRACTOR	STANNATOR	WHEREUPON
EPILATION	HACQUETON	LIBERATOR	PANTALOON	REGUERDON	STATEHOOD	WHIRLPOOL
EPINICION	HARDIHOOD	LIGHTFOOT	PANTHENOL	REGULATOR	STATEROOM	WHITEWOOD
EPINIKION	HARLESTON	LIVERPOOL	PARATHION	REJECTION	STEVENSON	WHOLEFOOD
EPULATION	HEARTWOOD	LIVRAISON	PARATROOP	REMISSION	STILLROOM	WIDOWHOOD
ERUDITION	HETERODOX	LONGEDFOR	PARHELION	RENDITION	STINKWOOD	WIMBLEDON
ESCALATOR	HEXAMERON	LUCTATION	PARTHENON	RENOVATOR	STOCKROOM	WINCANTON
EVAGATION	HODMANDOD	LUSTIHOOD	PARTHOLON	REPLETION	STONECROP	WOLLASTON
EVOCATION	HOLLYWOOD	MACTATION	PARTITION	REPRESSOR	STOREROOM	WOMANHOOD

WOODENTOP	TELESCOPE	CALENTURE	DISFIGURE	HACKAMORE	MANOEUVRE	PILASTERS
WRONGFOOT	TIGHTROPE	CALLIPERS	DISREGARD	HACKBERRY	MARQUETRY	PITCHFORK
ALLOCARPY	TRAGELAPH	CAMEMBERT	DORMITORY	HAILSTORM	MASSYMORE	PITUITARY
ALLOGRAPH	VIDEOTAPE	CANNELURE	DROMEDARY	HAMPSHIRE	MATAGOURI	PLACATORY
AMBROTYPE	VITASCOPE	CAPILLARY	DRUGSTORE	HANDIWORK	MATAMORE	PLANETARY
AMIDSHIPS	WINCOPIPE	CAPRICORN	DUCKBOARD	HAPHAZARD	MAXILLARY	POKERWORK
ARCHETYPE	WINDSWEPT	CARBONARI	DUNDREARY	HARDBOARD	MEGASPORE	POLITBURO
ATAHUALPA	XANTHIPPE	CARDBOARD	DYSENTERY	HARTSHORN	MERCENARY	POLYANDRY
AUTOGRAPH	ABOUTTURN	CARNIVORE	EARTHWORK	HAZELWORT	MESENTERY	POTPOURRI
AUTOSCOPE	ACCESSORY	CARPENTRY	EARTHWORM	HEADBOARD	METALWORK	PRECATORY
AUXOTROPH	ADDERWORT	CARTULARY	ECOSPHERE	HEADSCARF	MIDWIFERY	PREDATORY
BARYSCOPE	ADMIXTURE	CASSANDRA	ECTOTHERM	HEARTBURN	MIGRATORY	PREFATORY
COLLOTYPE	ADVENTURE	CASSOWARY	ELECTUARY	HELLEBORE	MILLEPORE	PREFIGURE
CONSCRIPT	ADVERSARY	CASUISTRY	ELLESMERE	HEMIPTERA	MILLINERY	PRELUSORY
DRAINPIPE	AFTERCARE	CATCHWORD	ELSEWHERE	HERBIVORE	MINIATURE	PREMATURE
ECTOMORPH	AFTERWORD	CEASEFIRE	EMBRACERY	HOCCAMORE	MINISKIRT	PRIMAVERA
EIDOGRAPH	AGINCOURT	CENTENARY	EMBRASURE	HOMOPTERA	MISINFORM	PRIMIPARA
ENDOMORPH	ALEXANDRA	CHARIVARI	ENCLOSURE	HORTATORY	MISOCLERE	PROCEDURE
FERROTYPE	ALPENHORN	CHEMISTRY	ENDOSPERM	HOUSEWORK	MOMENTARY	PRONGHORN
GYROSCOPE	ANCILLARY	CHICANERY	ENDPAPERS	HUNKYDORY	MONASTERY	PROUDHORN
HEMITROPE	ANGOSTURA	CHILDCARE	ENGINEERS	HUSBANDRY	MONEYWORT	PROVEDORE
HODOGRAPH	ANTIQUARY	CHIPBOARD	ENRAPTURE	IMAGINARY	MONOCHORD	PULMONARY
HOLOGRAPH	ARBITRARY	CHURIDARS	EPEOLATRY	IMPOSTURE	MULTIFORM	PURGATORY
HOMOGRAPH	ARTILLERY	CLAPBOARD	EPICENTRE	INDENTURE	NASEBERRY	QUILLWORT
HOROSCOPE	ASTROTURF	CLEOPATRA	ERUCIFORM	INFIRMARY	NATHEMORE	RAINSTORM
IDEOGRAPH	ASYMMETRY	CLEPSYDRA	ETHELBERT	INSELBERG	NECESSARY	RASPATORY
IDIOGRAPH	AUTOLATRY	CLIPBOARD	EVOCATORY	INSINCERE	NEVERMORE	RASPBERRY
INTERCEPT	AUXILIARY	CLOCKWORK	EXEMPLARY	INTERFERE	NIGHTFIRE	READYEARN
INTERLOPE	AYCKBOURN	COLUMBARY	EXOSPHERE	INTERLARD	NIGHTMARE	REARGUARD
INTERRUPT	AYLESBURY	COMINFORM	EXPIATORY	INTROVERT	NIGHTWORK	RECAPTURE
JACKSNIPE	BACKBOARD	COMINTERN	EXTEMPORE	INVENTORY	NOOSPHERE	REFECTORY
KARYOTYPE	BACKSWORD	COMMODORE	EXTROVERT	INVOLUCRE	NORTHWARD	RELIQUARY
KONISCOPE	BALTIMORE	COMPOSURE	FEDUCIARY	ITINERARY	NOTOCHORD	RENCONTRE
LAGNIAPPE	BANDALORE	COROLLARY	FEUDATORY	JANISSARY	NUMERAIRE	REPERTORY
LAGOMORPH	BANDOLERO	COURTYARD	FIDUCIARY	JARLSBERG	NUREMBERG	RESIDUARY
LANDSCAPE	BANEBERRY	COVERTURE	FIELDFARE	JEWELLERY	OCTACHORD	RESTIFORM
LOGOGRIPH	BANISTERS	CRANBERRY	FIELDWORK	JOBCENTRE	OCULIFORM	RETROVERT
MEGASCOPE	BARNSTORM	CREMATORY	FIORITURA	JUDICIARY	OFFERTORY	RICERCARE
MESOMORPH	BASEBOARD	CROCKFORD	FIREGUARD	JUNEBERRY	OLFACTORY	ROQUEFORT
MONOGRAPH	BASECOURT	CROSSFIRE	FISHGUARD	KENTIGERN	OPENHEART	RUDDIGORE
MUTOSCOPE	BELVEDERE	CROSSWORD	FLOWCHART	KILOMETRE	OPTOMETRY	SAFEGUARD
OLEOGRAPH	BENCHMARK	CRUCIFORM	FOODSTORE	KOMINFORM	ORCHESTRA	SAGITTARY
PARAGRAPH	BILLBOARD	CUNEIFORM	FOREBEARS	KRUMMHORN	ORDINAIRE	SALESGIRL
PARANYMPH	BIOSPHERE	CURVATURE	FORECOURT	LACKBEARD	OSTEODERM	SALLYPORT
PERIMORPH	BIRTHMARK	CUSPIDORE	FORESHORE	LAMPADARY	OTTERBURN	SALTPETRE
PERISCOPE	BIRTHWORT	CUSTOMARY	FORESTERS	LANDSTURM	OUTSIDERS	SANCTUARY
PHALAROPE	BLACKBIRD	DARTBOARD	FRAGONARD	LASERWORT	OVERBOARD	SANDSTORM
PHOTOCOPY	BLACKMORE	DASHBOARD	FRAMEWORK	LAUDATORY	OVEREXERT	SCRIPTURE
PINSTRIPE	BLEACHERS	DAVENPORT	FREEBOARD	LEFTOVERS	PACHYDERM	SCULPTURE
POLYGRAPH	BLINDWORM	DEBENTURE	FRITHBORH	LEGENDARY	PAGEANTRY	SECATEURS
POLYMORPH	BLOATWARE	DECACHORD	FROISSART	LEGIONARY	PAINTWORK	SECONDARY
PREOCCUPY	BLOODWORM	DECALITRE	FURNITURE	LEHRJAHRE	PALAESTRA	SECRETARY
PROTOTYPE	BLUEBEARD	DECEMVIRI	GALLANTRY	LEPROSERY	PALAMPORE	SEDENTARY
QUAILPIPE	BLUEBERRY	DECRETORY	GARNITURE	LIFEGUARD	PALEMPORE	SEMAPHORE
RATHERIPE	BODYGUARD	DEFENDERS	GLASSWARE	LIONHEART	PALMISTRY	SEPULCHRE
SCREWTAPE	BOOKSTORE	DENTISTRY	GLASSWORT	LIVERWORT	PAPERWORK	SEPULTURE
SELLOTAPE	BOULEVARD	DEPARTURE	GLENGARRY	LOAMSHIRE	PATCHWORK	SHIFTWORK
SERIGRAPH	BRASSIERE	DEPASTURE	GOOSEHERD	LONGICORN	PEARLWORT	SHOREBIRD
SHIPSHAPE	BRASSWARE	DESULTORY	GOSSAMERY	LONGSHORE	PEASANTRY	SHORTHORN
SIDESWIPE	BRICKWORK	DEVONPORT	GRANDSIRE	LOUSEWORT	PECUNIARY	SHORTTERM
SLAPHAPPY	BRICKYARD	DIGNITARY	GRAVEYARD	LUMINAIRE	PELLITORY	SHRUBBERY
SOMASCOPE	BUCKTHORN	DIRECTORS	GREENHORN	LUXEMBURG	PENNYWORT	SIDEBOARD
STANDPIPE	BUDGETARY	DIRECTORY	GREENYARD	MACHINERY	PERFUMERY	SIGNATORY
STOVEPIPE	CABALLERO	DISAFFIRM	GREYBEARD	MADREPORE	PERIPHERY	SIGNATURE
STRINGOPS	CAFETIERE	DISCOVERT	GUESSWORK	MAGDEBURG	PERSEVERE	SIGNBOARD
SUBSCRIPT	CAGOULARD	DISCOVERY	GUINEVERE	MANDATARY	PHONECARD	SINGAPORE
TELEGRAPH	CAIRNGORM	DISEMBARK	GUTENBERG	MANDATORY	PIECEWORK	SISSERARY

SNOWSTORM	VENUSBERG	BOLOGNESE	DEFEATISM	FUSTINESS	INNERMOST	MONTANIST
SOAPBERRY	VERMIFORM	BOSSINESS	DEFEATIST	FUZZINESS	INTERPOSE	MOODINESS
SOLITAIRE	VERTIPORT	BOUNDLESS	DEMITASSE	GALACTOSE	INVERNESS	MORMONISM
SOMEWHERE	VESTITURE	BRAINCASE	DENSENESS	GALLICISM	INVERTASE	MOTOCROSS
SOPHISTRY	VEXILLARY	BRAINLESS	DEOXIDISE	GALVANISM	IRVINGISM	MOUTHLESS
SOPHOMORE	VIBRATORY	BRAINWASH	DESPOTISM	GARGARISM	ISINGLASS	MOUTHWASH
SOUFRIERE	VISIONARY	BRASENOSE	DEVILFISH	GATECRASH	ISOMERASE	MUDDINESS
SOUTHWARD	VOLUNTARY	BRATWURST	DEXTRORSE	GAUDINESS	JANSENISM	MURDERESS
SOUTHWARK	VORTIGERN	BREAKFAST	DINGINESS	GAUNTNESS	JANSENIST	MURKINESS
SPARKLERS	WALLBOARD	BRIEFCASE	DIRTINESS	GAWKINESS	JELLYFISH	MUSHINESS
SPEARWORT	WASHBOARD	BRIEFNESS	DISCOURSE	GEODESIST	JERKINESS	MUSTINESS
SPIKENARD	WATCHWORD	BRISKNESS	DISHONEST	GEOLOGIST	JUICINESS	MUTUALISM
SPLINTERS	WATERFORD	BROADCAST	DISPLEASE	GIBBERISH	JUXTAPOSE	MUZZINESS
SPOROCARP	WATERMARK	BRUTALISM	DIZZINESS	GIDDINESS	KITTENISH	MYSTICISM
SPRECHERY	WHEATGERM	BUCHAREST	DOGMATISM	GIGANTISM	KNOTGRASS	NAKEDNESS
SQUATTERS	WHEREFORE	BULKINESS	DOSSHOUSE	GILGAMESH	LAEVULOSE	NASTINESS
STARBOARD	WHITAKERS	BURLINESS	DOUBTLESS	GIRONDIST	LANDDROST	NATHELESS
STATUTORY	WINEBERRY	CALABOOSE	DRAMATIST	GODLINESS	LANKINESS	NECKVERSE
STEELYARD	WRANGLERS	CALABRESE	DREAMLESS	GOLDCREST	LARGENESS	NEOLOGISM
STEENKIRK	YORKSHIRE	CALVANISM	DRYASDUST	GONGORISM	LATHYRISM	NEPHALISM
STEVEDORE	ZYGOSPORE	CALVINIST	DULCINIST	GOVERNESS	LAUNDRESS	NEPHALIST
STILLBORN	ACADEMIST	CANTONESE	DUNGENESS	GRACELESS	LEASTWISE	NEWSFLASH
STILTBIRD	ACUTENESS	CAREERIST	EAGERNESS	GRANDIOSE	LICKERISH	NIPCHEESE
STINKBIRD	ADEPTNESS	CARTHORSE	ECOLOGIST	GRANDNESS	LIGHTLESS	NOBLENESS
STINKHORN	ADVENTIST	CATACLYSM	ECONOMIST	GRANULOSE	LIGHTNESS	NOISELESS
STOCKWORK	ADVERTISE	CATALEPSY	ECOSSAISE	GREATNESS	LIMEHOUSE	NOISINESS
STOCKYARD	AFTERMOST	CATAPLASM	ECTOPLASM	GRIMINESS	LIMITLESS	NORTHEAST
STONEWARE	ALBATROSS	CATECHISM	EDELWEISS	GRUFFNESS	LIQUORISH	NORTHWEST
STONEWORK	ALCHEMIST	CAVENDISH	ELECTRESS	GUILELESS	LITHOCYST	OASTHOUSE
STONEWORT	ALERTNESS	CEASELESS	EMBARRASS	GUILTLESS	LOBSCOUSE	OCCULTIST
STRANGURY	ALOOFNESS	CELLARIST	EMBELLISH	GUITARIST	LOFTINESS	OCKHAMIST
STRICTURE	ANABOLISM	CELLULOSE	EMPTINESS	HAIRBRUSH	LONDONESE	OCTOBRIST
STRONGARM	ANARCHIST	CEYLONESE	ENCOMPASS	HANDINESS	LOOSENESS	ODOURLESS
STROSSERS	ANATOMIST	CHANTEUSE	EPIPOLISM	HAPPINESS	LOWLINESS	ORIGENIST
STRUCTURE	ANGELFISH	CHEAPNESS	EQUIPOISE	HARDINESS	LURIDNESS	OSTRACISE
STUMPWORK	ANGLICISM	CHECKLIST	EROTICISM	HARMONIST	LUSTINESS	OSTRACISM
SUBALTERN	ANIMALISM	CHEERLESS	ESEMPLASY	HARSHNESS	MACHINIST	OTHERWISE
SUBENTIRE	ANSCHLUSS	CHILDLESS	ESTABLISH	HASTINESS	MACROCOSM	OUGHTNESS
SUMPTUARY	APOLOGIST	CLASSLESS	EUCHARIST	HEADDRESS	MAGNETISM	OUTERMOST
SURFBOARD	ARABINOSE	CLEANNESS	EUPHEMISM	HEADFIRST	MANGANESE	OUTTHRUST
SURQUEDRY	ARCHIVIST	CLEARNESS	EXACTNESS	HEADINESS	MANLINESS	OVERDRESS
SWINEHERD	ARQUEBUSE	CLOCKWISE	EXPERTISE	HEARTLESS	MANNERISM	OVERPOISE
SYLLABARY	AUTEURISM	CLOSENESS	EXTREMISM	HEAVINESS	MASOCHISM	OWLEGLASS
TABLATURE	AUTHORESS	CLOUDLESS	EXTREMIST	HERBALIST	MASOCHIST	PAILLASSE
TABLEWARE	AUTOCROSS	CLUBHOUSE	FACTORISE	HERBORIST	MATCHLESS	PALLIASSE
TAILBOARD	AWARENESS	COLORLESS	FAINTNESS	HESYCHASM	MATELASSE	PANEGOISM
TANTARARA	BACKSHISH	COLOURIST	FAITHLESS	HESYCHAST	MECHANISM	PANELLIST
TAVERNERS	BAKEHOUSE	COLUMNIST	FALANGIST	HIGHCLASS	MEDALLIST	PANTHEISM
TECTIFORM	BAKSHEESH	COMMUNISM	FALSENESS	HINGELESS	MENDELISM	PARABLAST
TEMPORARY	BALLADIST	COMMUNIST	FARMHOUSE	HOARFROST	MENOPAUSE	PARCHEESI
TERRITORY	BARBARISM	CONCOURSE	FAULTLESS	HOLOCAUST	MERCILESS	PATRONESS
THEREFORE	BEANFEAST	CONGOLESE	FEUDALISM	HORSELESS	MESMERISM	PAWKINESS
TIMESHARE	BEARDLESS	COOKHOUSE	FLESHLESS	HOURGLASS	MESOBLAST	PEKINGESE
TIPPERARY	BELLICOSE	CORNBRASH	FLOPHOUSE	HOYDENISH	METAPHASE	PELMANISM
TITHEBARN	BERGAMASK	CORNETIST	FOGGINESS	HUSKINESS	METHODISM	PENNILESS
TOBERMORY	BERGOMASK	COUNTLESS	FOLIOLOSE	HYGIENIST	METHODIST	PENTECOST
TRADEMARK	BICYCLIST	CRAZINESS	FOOTLOOSE	HYPNOTISM	MICROCOSM	PENTHOUSE
TRANSFORM	BIOLOGIST	CRISPNESS	FORECLOSE	HYPNOTIST	MIRTHLESS	PERICLASE
TRANSPIRE	BLACKLIST	CRITICISM	FORMALIST	HYPOBLAST	MISONEIST	PESSIMISM
TRANSPORT	BLACKNESS	CROSSWISE	FOSSILISE	HYPOCAUST	MISTINESS	PESSIMIST
TRAVELERS	BLAMELESS	CRUDENESS	FRAMBOISE	HYPOCRISY	MITHRAISM	PETAURIST
TREACHERY	BLANDNESS	DALTONISM	FRANCHISE	IDIOBLAST	MODERNISM	PETTINESS
TRIBUTARY	BLINDNESS	DAMNEDEST	FRANKNESS	IDIOPLASM	MODERNIST	PHENAKISM
UNCONCERN	BLOODLESS	DAUNTLESS	FRESHNESS	IMAGELESS	MOISTNESS	PHYSICIST
UNSAVOURY	BLUFFNESS	DEACONESS	FRUITLESS	IMPRECISE	MONERGISM	PIERGLASS
UPCOUNTRY	BLUNTNESS	DEATHLESS	FUGGINESS	IMPROVISE	MONGOLISM	PLAINNESS
VAINGLORY	BOATHOUSE	DECOMPOSE	FUSSINESS	INERTNESS	MONTANISM	PLATONIST

PLAYHOUSE	SCENTLESS	SUCCOTASH	VIDEODISC	ANIMALITY	COENOBITE	DISSOLUTE
PLUMPNESS	SCHOLIAST	SULKINESS	VIDEODISK	ANIMOSITY	COFFINITE	DIVERSITY
PLURALISM	SCIENTISM	SUPERVISE	VIOLINIST	ANONYMITY	COLLIGATE	DOCTORATE
POINTLESS	SCIENTIST	SUQUAMISH	VIVIDNESS	ANTIPASTO	COLLIMATE	DOCUMENTS
POLITESSE	SEMIGLOSS	SURLINESS	VOICELESS	ANTIQUITY	COLLOCATE	DONIZETTI
POLONAISE	SENSELESS	SWEETNESS	VOLCANISM	APHRODITE	COLOCYNTH	DUPLICATE
POLYPHASE	SERIALIST	SWIFTNESS	VOLTINISM	ARAGONITE	COLUMBATE	DUPLICITY
PONDEROSA	SHADINESS	SWORDFISH	VOODOOISM	ARBITRATE	COLUMBITE	EDGEWORTH
POORHOUSE	SHAKINESS	SYLLOGISM	VORTICISM	ARMAMENTS	COMMODITY	EIGHTIETH
POSTHOUSE	SHAMEFAST	SYMBOLISM	VULCANIST	ARRIVISTE	COMMUNITY	EJACULATE
POUJADIST	SHAMELESS	SYMBOLIST	VULGARISM	ASSIDUITY	COMMUTATE	ELABORATE
POWERLESS	SHAPELESS	SYNERGIST	WAREHOUSE	ASSOCIATE	COMPOSITE	ELAEOLITE
PRECIEUSE	SHARPNESS	SYRIACISM	WARTCRESS	ATONALITY	CONCAVITY	ELIMINATE
PRECONISE	SHEERNESS	TACKINESS	WATERLESS	ATTENUATE	CONJUGATE	ELIZABETH
PREMONISH	SHELLFISH	TALMUDIST	WAYZGOOSE	ATTRIBUTE	CONNOTATE	ELKOSHITE
PRICELESS	SHIFTLESS	TARANTASS	WEARINESS	AUSTERITY	CONSULATE	ELUCIDATE
PRIESTESS	SHINTOISM	TARDINESS	WEIRDNESS	AUTHORITY	CONTRALTO	ELUTRIATE
PUBLICIST	SHORTLIST	TASTELESS	WELTGEIST	AUTOROUTE	COOPERATE	EMBROCATE
PUFFINESS	SHORTNESS	TELOPHASE	WHEELBASE	BACKCLOTH	COPROLITE	EMOLLIATE
PYTHONESS	SHOWINESS	TEMPTRESS	WHITEFISH	BANQUETTE	CORPORATE	ENCRATITE
QUEERNESS	SIGHTLESS	TENEBROSE	WHITENESS	BARBARITY	CORRELATE	ENERINITE
QUICKNESS	SILLINESS	TENSENESS	WHITEWASH	BARNABITE	CORRUGATE	ENHYDRITE
QUIETNESS	SIMULCAST	TERRORISM	WHOLENESS	BIFURCATE	CORUSCATE	ENSTATITE
RACEHORSE	SINGALESE	TERRORIST	WILDGEESE	BIPARTITE	COUCHETTE	ENTOPHYTE
RACIALISM	SLACKNESS	TERSENESS	WINEGLASS	BIRTHRATE	COURGETTE	ENTRECÔTE
RACIALIST	SLANTWISE	THANATISM	WITTICISM	BLOODBATH	COVELLITE	ENTREMETS
RAFFINOSE	SLEEKNESS	THANKLESS	WODEHOUSE	BONAPARTE	CREDULITY	ENUCLEATE
RANDINESS	SLEEPLESS	THERAPIST	WOODHOUSE	BRIQUETTE	CREPITATE	ENUMERATE
RATHERISH	SLIGHTEST	THICKNESS	WOODLOUSE	BROMINATE	CRIMINATE	ENUNCIATE
READDRESS	SLIMINESS	THORNLESS	WOOLINESS	BRUTALITY	CROQUETTE	EPARCHATE
READINESS	SMALLNESS	TIGHTNESS	WORDINESS	BUCKTEETH	CROTCHETY	EPAULETTE
REARHORSE	SMARTNESS	TIMPANIST	WORKHORSE	CALCINATE	CULMINATE	ERADICATE
REARMOUSE	SMOKELESS	TIPSINESS	WORKHOUSE	CALCULATE	CULTIVATE	EROSTRATE
RECORDIST	SNAILFISH	TIREDNESS	WORTHLESS	CALIBRATE	CURIOSITY	ERYTHRITE
REDBREAST	SOBERNESS	TOLLHOUSE	WREAKLESS	CALLOSITY	CYCLAMATE	ESCOPETTE
REEDINESS	SOCIALISM	TOMENTOSE	WRECKFISH	CANALETTO	CYCLOLITH	ESCULENTS
REFORMIST	SOCIALIST	TONOPLAST	YELLOWISH	CANDIDATE	DARTMOUTH	ESPERANTO
REFURBISH	SOGGINESS	TOOTHLESS	ZEITGEIST	CAPORETTO	DEAMINATE	ESTAFETTE
REIMBURSE	SOLIPSISM	TOPIARIST	ZOOLOGIST	CAPTIVATE	DEBUTANTE	ETHANOATE
RELIGEUSE	SOPPINESS	TOUGHNESS	ABOMINATE	CAPTIVITY	DECLIVITY	ETIQUETTE
RELIGIOSO	SORCERESS	TRACKLESS	ABSURDITY	CARBAMATE	DECOLLATE	EVAPORATE
RENFIERST	SOUNDLESS	TRANSFUSE	ACCIDENTS	CARBONATE	DECUSSATE	EVENTUATE
REPERCUSS	SOUNDNESS	TRANSPOSE	ACCLIMATE	CARMELITE	DEFALCATE	EXANIMATE
REPLENISH	SOUTHEAST	TRAPEZIST	ACCLIVITY	CASTANETS	DEFOLIATE	EXCORIATE
REPOSSESS	SOUTHWEST	TRIBALISM	ACIDULATE	CASTIGATE	DEFORMITY	EXCULPATE
REPROCESS	SPACELESS	TRICKLESS	ACTUALITY	CELEBRATE	DEHYDRATE	EXONERATE
REREMOUSE	SPEAKEASY	TRITENESS	ACUMINATE	CELEBRITY	DELINEATE	EXPATIATE
RESERVIST	SPICINESS	TRUNKFISH	ADMIRALTY	CELLULITE	DEMARCATE	EXPISCATE
RIBBONISM	SPINELESS	TUBBINESS	ADUMBRATE	CEREBRATE	DENIGRATE	EXPLICATE
RIDERLESS	SPIRITISM	TURQUOISE	ADVERSITY	CERECLOTH	DEPRAVITY	EXPURGATE
RIGHTNESS	SQUEAMISH	TUTIORISM	AFFILIATE	CERTAINTY	DEPRECATE	EXQUISITE
RIPIENIST	STAINLESS	TYMPANIST	AFFRICATE	CERUSSITE	DEPREDATE	EXSICCATE
RISKINESS	STAIRCASE	UNDERCAST	AFTERMATH	CHABAZITE	DESECRATE	EXTENUATE
ROADHOUSE	STALENESS	UNDERMOST	AGGRAVATE	CHAMPERTY	DESICCATE	EXTIRPATE
ROUGHCAST	STARKNESS	UNDERPASS	AGGREGATE	CHARLOTTE	DESIGNATE	EXTRADITE
ROUGHNESS	STATELESS	UNPRECISE	AINSWORTH	CHECKMATE	DESPERATE	EXTREMITY
ROUNDFISH	STATOCYST	UNSELFISH	ALLEVIATE	CHIPOLATA	DESTITUTE	EXTRICATE
ROWDINESS	STEADFAST	UPPERCASE	ALTERCATE	CHOCOLATE	DEVASTATE	FABRICATE
RUSTINESS	STEEPNESS	UPPERMOST	ALTERNATE	CHOLELITH	DEXTERITY	FACECLOTH
SABLEFISH	STERNFAST	UROKINASE	ALVEOLATE	CHONDRITE	DIALOGITE	FACUNDITY
SAGEBRUSH	STERNNESS	UTTERLESS	AMAZONITE	CIGARETTE	DIATOMITE	FAMAGUSTA
SALLYPOST	STIFFNESS	UTTERMOST	AMBIGUITY	CILIOLATE	DISHCLOTH	FASCINATE
SALTINESS	STILLNESS	VAGUENESS	AMELAKITE	CIRCINATE	DISLOCATE	FAVOURITE
SANDHURST	STOCKFISH	VALUELESS	ANAGLYPTA	CIRCULATE	DISPARATE	FECUNDITY
SATURNISM	STONELESS	VANDALISM	ANAPLASTY	CLASSMATE	DISPARITY	FEMINEITY
SAUCINESS	STOUTNESS	VANTBRASS	ANCHORITE	COAGULATE	DISREPUTE	FERTILITY
SCALDFISH	STRAPLESS	VEILLEUSE	ANHYDRITE	COARCTATE	DISSIPATE	FESTINATE

FESTIVITY	HINDEMITH	KIESERITE	MORBIDITY	PENDULATE	RIGOLETTO	SUPERETTE
FIBROLITE	HIPPOLYTA	KILOHERTZ	MORGANITE	PENETRATE	ROSINANTE	SUPPURATE
FIFTEENTH	HIPPOLYTE	LABOURITE	MORTALITY	PERCOLATE	ROTUNDATE	SURROGATE
FIGURANTE	HOLLERITH	LABYRINTH	MOTORISTS	PERFORATE	ROTUNDITY	SUSCITATE
FINICKITY	HOLOPHOTE	LACCOLITE	MUGLARITE	PERIODATE	ROUSSETTE	SWANIMOTE
FIRSTRATE	HOMEOPATH	LACINIATE	MUNIMENTS	PERSECUTE	ROZINANTE	SYLVANITE
FISHPLATE	HOSTILITY	LADYSMITH	MUSCOVITE	PERSONATE	RUDIMENTS	SYNCOPATE
FLAGITATE	HUMILIATE	LAFAYETTE	MUSSITATE	PERTUSATE	RUNCINATE	SYNDICATE
FLECHETTE	HUNDREDTH	LANCINATE	NAMEPLATE	PHACOLITE	RUSTICATE	SYNOECETE
FLESHPOTS	HUTTERITE	LANGOUSTE	NATROLITE	PHAGOCYTE	SACKCLOTH	TACHILITE
FLOODGATE	HYPHENATE	LANGUETTE	NECESSITY	PHENACITE	SAILCLOTH	TACHYLITE
FLUCTUATE	HYPOCRITE	LARGHETTO	NEFERTITI	PHONOLITE	SALOPETTE	TACHYLYTE
FOGRAMITE	ICHNOLITE	LAZARETTO	NEGOTIATE	PHOSPHATE	SALUBRITY	TANTALITE
FOOTPLATE	IMBRICATE	LEGISLATE	NICCOLITE	PHTHALATE	SASSOLITE	TAUCHNITZ
FORETASTE	IMBROCATE	LEUCOCYTE	NICTITATE	PHYTOLITE	SATELLITE	TEDIOSITY
FORFICATE	IMMEDIATE	LIABILITY	NINETIETH	PIGNERATE	SCAPOLITE	TELEPHOTO
FORMALITY	IMMENSITY	LILYWHITE	NOMOTHETE	PIROUETTE	SCARLATTI	TEMPERATE
FORMULATE	IMMIGRATE	LIMPIDITY	NONENTITY	PIZZICATO	SCELERATE	TENEMENTS
FORNICATE	IMMODESTY	LINEOLATE	NORMALITY	PLACIDITY	SCHEELITE	TERAHERTZ
FORTHWITH	IMPLICATE	LIQUIDATE	NOTONECTA	PLURALITY	SCOLECITE	TEREBINTH
FORTUNATE	IMPRECATE	LIQUIDITY	NOTORIETY	POLIANITE	SCORODITE	TERMINATE
FRAGILITY	IMPROBITY	LOCELLATE	NOVELETTE	POLLINATE	SEGREGATE	THELEMITE
FRAGMENTS	IMPROMPTU	LOCKSMITH	NOVICIATE	POMPOSITY	SENIORITY	THERALITE
FRATCHETY	IMPSONITE	LOGOTHETE	NOVITIATE	PORPORATE	SEPIOLITE	THIRTIETH
FRIGIDITY	INABILITY	LOINCLOTH	NUMMULITE	POSTERITY	SERENGETI	TINGUAITE
FRIVOLITY	INAMORATA	LONGEVITY	NUNCUPATE	POSTULATE	SERVIETTE	TITILLATE
FRIZZANTE	INAMORATO	LOQUACITY	OBBLIGATO	POTENTATE	SERVILITY	TORBANITE
FROGMOUTH	INANIMATE	LORGNETTE	OBCORDATE	POWELLITE	SEXUALITY	TRANSLATE
FROSTBITE	INCARNATE	LOUDMOUTH	OBFUSCATE	PRECINCTS	SIMEONITE	TRANSMUTE
FRUGALITY	INCOGNITO	LOWLIGHTS	OBJURGATE	PRECOCITY	SIMPLISTE	TREMOLITE
FRUSTRATE	INCONDITE	LUBRICATE	OBSCENITY	PREDICATE	SINCERITY	TREMULATE
FULMINATE	INCULCATE	LUCUBRATE	OBSCURITY	PRETERITE	SINUOSITY	TRIBUNATE
FUSTIGATE	INCULPATE	LUXURIATE	OBSECRATE	PROCACITY	SIXTEENTH	TRIDYMITE
GARRULITY	INDEMNITY	MACHINATE	OBSTINATE	PROCERITY	SLIVOVITZ	TRILOBITE
GELIGNITE	INDIGNITY	MAJORETTE	OFFICIATE	PROCREATE	SNOWWHITE	TRITURATE
GENIALITY	INEBRIATE	MALACHITE	OLIVENITE	PROFANITY	SOCIALITE	TROMPETTE
GENTILITY	INERUDITE	MALIGNITY	OPPONENTS	PROLIXITY	SOLEMNITY	TROOSTITE
GEORGETTE	INFATUATE	MANDICATE	ORIENTATE	PROPAGATE	SONGSMITH	TRUTINATE
GERMANITE	INFIRMITY	MANDUCATE	ORIGINATE	PROPRIETY	SOSTENUTO	TUILLETTE
GERMINATE	INFURIATE	MANGANATE	OSCILLATE	PROROGATE	SOUBRETTE	TUNGSTATE
GIBEONITE	INGENUITY	MANGOUSTE	OSTEOPATH	PROSECUTE	SOUNDBITE	TURBIDITY
GIGAHERTZ	INOCULATE	MANIFESTO	OSTROGOTH	PROSELYTE	SPAGHETTI	TURBINATE
GLOMERATE	INOPINATE	MARCASITE	OTTRELITE	PROSTRATE	SPATULATE	TWENTIETH
GMELINITE	INQUINATE	MASSORETE	OUBLIETTE	PROUSTITE	SPECIALTY	UMPTEENTH
GOALMOUTH	INQUORATE	MASTICATE	OUTGROWTH	PROXIMATE	SPECULATE	UNANIMITY
GOLDSMITH	INSENSATE	MATERNITY	OUTSKIRTS	PROXIMITY	SPOFFORTH	UNDERBITE
GONIATITE	INSINUATE	MAYORALTY	OVERHASTY	PUBLICITY	STABILITY	UNDERRATE
GOSLARITE	INSTIGATE	MEGAHERTZ	OVERSTATE	PUERILITY	STAGIRITE	USHERETTE
GOTHAMITE	INSTITUTE	MELIORATE	OXYGENATE	PUGNACITY	STAGYRITE	UVAROVITE
GRANULATE	INTEGRATE	MENDACITY	OZOCERITE	PULLULATE	STALEMATE	VACCINATE
GRANULITE	INTEGRITY	MENNONITE	OZOKERITE	PULMONATE	STALWORTH	VACILLATE
GRAVITATE	INTENSITY	MENTALITY	PAILLETTE	PUNCTUATE	STATOLITH	VAPORETTO
HABITUATE	INTERCITY	METEORITE	PALAFITTE	QUARTETTE	STATUETTE	VARIEGATE
HAECCEITY	INTESTATE	METRICATE	PALEOLITH	QUINTETTE	STERILITY	VARIOLATE
HAEMATITE	INTRICATE	MICROCYTE	PALMITATE	RANCIDITY	STIMULATE	VARISCITE
HALFEMPTY	INUMBRATE	MICROLITE	PALPITATE	REANIMATE	STIPULATE	VELLICATE
HALLSTATT	INUSITATE	MICROLITH	PANDURATE	RECONDITE	STOLIDITY	VENIALITY
HARIOLATE	INVIOLATE	MICROWATT	PAPILLOTE	REDINGOTE	STUPIDITY	VENTILATE
HARROGATE	IRRADIATE	MIDIANITE	PARACHUTE	REINSTATE	STYLOBATE	VERBERATE
HASHEMITE	ISRAELITE	MIDINETTE	PARACLETE	REITERATE	SUBJUGATE	VERBOSITY
HAWCUBITE	ITINERATE	MILLIONTH	PARDALOTE	REPLICATE	SUBLIMATE	VERKAMPTE
HEADCLOTH	JAGGANATH	MILLIWATT	PARHYPATE	REPROBATE	SUBROGATE	VESTMENTS
HEAVYDUTY	JEQUIRITY	MINNESOTA	PARNASITE	REPUDIATE	SUBSTRATA	VIABILITY
HESSONITE	JOBSWORTH	MISLOCATE	PASSIVITY	REQUISITE	SUBSTRATE	VIGILANTE
HEYPRESTO	JOVIALITY	MODERNITY	PATERNITY	RESTITUTE	SUCCINATE	VINDICATE
HIBERNATE	KERMESITE	MONTACUTE	PEDERASTY	RETALIATE	SUFFOCATE	VIRGINITY
HIMYARITE	KHALIFATE	MONZONITE	PEGMATITE	RHODOLITE	SULTANATE	VIRGULATE

VISAGISTE	BOTTLEFUL	DEUTERIUM	HERBARIUM	NOTORIOUS	REGARDFUL	TRAPEZIUM
VISCOSITY	BOUNTEOUS	DEXTEROUS	HERODOTUS	NOVODAMUS	REGISSEUR	TRAPEZIUS
VULCANITE	BOUNTIFUL	DIANDROUS	HILARIOUS	NUCLEOLUS	REGRETFUL	TREGETOUR
VULGARITY	BUBBLEGUM	DIONYSIUS	HORDEOLUM	NYSTAGMUS	RELIGIOUS	TREMULOUS
VULPINITE	BUCENTAUR	DISCOLOUR	HOSPITIUM	OBLIVIOUS	RESENTFUL	TRICOLOUR
WAGNERITE	BUCKETFUL	DISFAVOUR	HUMONGOUS	OBNOXIOUS	RETIARIUS	TRIFORIUM
WAGONETTE	BUMPTIOUS	DISHONOUR	HUMUNGOUS	ODALISQUE	RETICULUM	TROCHILUS
WAHABIITE	BURLESQUE	DOODLEBUG	IDEALOGUE	OFFCOLOUR	RIGHTEOUS	TRUMPEDUP
WALDFLUTE	BUTTERBUR	EFFLUVIUM	IGNORAMUS	OFFICIOUS	ROSTELLUM	TRYPHOEUS
WASHCLOTH	BUTTERCUP	EGREGIOUS	IMPERIOUS	OLENELLUS	RUTHENIUM	TUNGSTOUS
WATERBUTT	BUTTERNUT	ELATERIUM	IMPETUOUS	OPERCULUM	SACRARIUM	TURNABOUT
WATERGATE	CALCANEUM	ENCELADUS	IMPLUVIUM	OPHIUCHUS	SAGACIOUS	TYRANNOUS
WAVELLITE	CALCANEUS	ENCOLPIUM	INCITATUS	ORGILLOUS	SAGAPENUM	ULIGINOUS
WHITWORTH	CALDARIUM	ENDEAVOUR	INCURIOUS	ORTANIQUE	SALACIOUS	ULTIMATUM
WILLEMITE	CALEMBOUR	ENTROPIUM	INDECORUM	OUROBORUS	SALERATUS	ULTRONEUS
WITCHETTY	CANCEROUS	EPICEDIUM	INGENIOUS	OVERCLOUD	SALICETUM	UMBILICUS
WITHERITE	CANTHARUS	EPIGAEOUS	INGENUOUS	OVERVALUE	SARMENTUM	UNANIMOUS
WORDSMITH	CAPACIOUS	EPIGENOUS	INJURIOUS	OVIPAROUS	SARTORIUS	UNHELPFUL
WULFENITE	CAPITULUM	EPONYMOUS	INNOCUOUS	PALINURUS	SCALARIUM	UNHOPEFUL
WYANDOTTE	CATALOGUE	EQUISETUM	INSIDIOUS	PALLADIUM	SCORBUTUS	UNMINDFUL
XEROPHYTE	CATERWAUL	EQUIVOQUE	INTROITUS	PARAGOGUE	SCREWEDUP	UNTIMEOUS
ZENOCRATE	CAVERNOUS	EROGENOUS	INVIDIOUS	PARNASSUS	SCURRIOUR	UNUNUNIUM
ZINKENITE	CEANOTHUS	ERRONEOUS	JITTERBUG	PATROCLUS	SDEIGNFUL	URANISCUS
ZUCCHETTO	CENTAURUS	ESOPHAGUS	JUDICIOUS	PAYCHEQUE	SEBACEOUS	VENEREOUS
ACIDULOUS	CERATODUS	ETHEREOUS	KABELJOUW	PEDAGOGUE	SEDITIOUS	VERACIOUS
ACONCAGUA	CHARGEFUL	EUHEMERUS	LABORIOUS	PEMPHIGUS	SENSILLUM	VERBASCUM
AESCHYLUS	CHARTREUX	EUPHONIUM	LANTHANUM	PENDULOUS	SENSORIUM	VERMINOUS
AHASUERUS	CHAUFFEUR	EXCALIBUR	LECHEROUS	PENURIOUS	SETACEOUS	VERTUMNUS
ALUMINIUM	CHIHUAHUA	EXEQUATUR	LEVITICUS	PERIPATUS	SHORTHAUL	VEXATIOUS
AMBIGUOUS	CINEREOUS	EXOGENOUS	LIBELLOUS	PETROLEUM	SHOVELFUL	VICARIOUS
AMBITIOUS	CLAMOROUS	FABACEOUS	LITIGIOUS	PHITONIUM	SINGULTUS	VIRGINIUM
AMERICIUM	COENOBIUM	FABULINUS	LUCRETIUS	PLASTIQUE	SOLILOQUY	VITELLIUS
AMIANTHUS	COLCHICUM	FACETIOUS	LUDICROUS	PLAYGROUP	SORROWFUL	VIVACIOUS
AMORPHOUS	COLLEAGUE	FERACIOUS	LUMBRICUS	PLENTEOUS	SOUTENEUR	VOLAGEOUS
AMYGDALUS	COLLYRIUM	FEROCIOUS	LUXURIOUS	PLENTIFUL	SPARTACUS	VOLTIGEUR
ANALOGOUS	COLOSSEUM	FLABELLUM	MACARTHUR	PLUMBEOUS	SPHACELUS	VOLTURNUS
ANHYDROUS	COLOSTRUM	FLAGELLUM	MAGNALIUM	PLUTONIUM	SPIRITOUS	VORACIOUS
ANOMALOUS	COLOURFUL	FOMALHAUT	MAGNESIUM	POCKETFUL	SPLENDOUR	WALKABOUT
ANONYMOUS	COLUMBIUM	FORGETFUL	MALICIOUS	POISONOUS	SPRITEFUL	WONDERFUL
ANTIGONUS	CONDUCTUS	FRACTIOUS	MALLEOLUS	POLITIQUE	STEGOSAUR	YTTERBIUM
ANTISERUM	CONFUCIUS	FRIGHTFUL	MANGETOUT	POMOERIUM	STIRABOUT	ZIRCONIUM
ANTONINUS	CONGRUOUS	FRIVOLOUS	MANUBRIUM	POMPADOUR	STRENUOUS	ADDICTIVE
APOLLONUS	CONSCIOUS	FUGACIOUS	MARSUPIUM	PONDEROUS	STRESSFUL	ADJECTIVE
APPARATUS	CONSENSUS	FUNICULUS	MARVELOUS	POTASSIUM	STROBILUS	ADVENTIVE
ARABESQUE	CONTINUUM	FURACIOUS	MASTERFUL	PREHALLUX	STRONTIUM	APERITIVE
ARBORETUM	CONUNDRUM	GARGANTUA	MAURITIUS	PRESCUTUM	SUBDOLOUS	ASSERTIVE
AREOPAGUS	CORNFLOUR	GARRULOUS	MAUSOLEUM	PRESIDIUM	SUETONIUS	ATTENTIVE
ASCLEPIUS	COSMONAUT	GAUDEAMUS	MELODIOUS	PROCOELUS	SULFUROUS	AUTOCLAVE
ASPARAGUS	COTHURNUS	GERMANIUM	MENSTRUUM	PROCONSUL	SUMPTUOUS	BALACLAVA
ASPLENIUM	COURTEOUS	GINGLYMUS	MINACIOUS	PRODROMUS	SYMPODIUM	BICONCAVE
ASSIDUOUS	CRAPULOUS	GINORMOUS	MOCKERNUT	PRYTANEUM	SYMPOSIUM	BOSSANOVA
ASTRONAUT	CREDULOUS	GLADIOLUS	MOMENTOUS	PTERIDIUM	SYNAGOGUE	BRAINWAVE
ASTUCIOUS	CRETINOUS	GLAIREOUS	MONOCOQUE	PTEROSAUR	SYNANGIUM	CHAMPLEVÉ
ATHENAEUM	CRIBELLUM	GLAMOROUS	MONOLOGUE	PURDONIUM	SYNCOMIUM	COGNITIVE
ATROCIOUS	CUPRESSUS	GLUCINIUM	MONSTROUS	PYRETHRUM	TARAXACUM	COLLUSIVE
AUDACIOUS	CUTANEOUS	GLUTINOUS	MUMPSIMUS	QUADRATUS	TECHNIQUE	COMBATIVE
AUTOLYCUS	CYMBIDIUM	GOSSYPIUM	MUNDUNGUS	QUERCETUS	TELLURIUM	CONDUCIVE
BACTERIUM	DANGEROUS	GREASEGUN	MURDEROUS	QUERULOUS	TENACIOUS	CORROSIVE
BARBAROUS	DECALOGUE	GROTESQUE	NARCISSUS	QUIVERFUL	TENACULUM	DECEPTIVE
BASKETFUL	DECEITFUL	GROUNDNUT	NEFANDOUS	RACCABOUT	TENTORIUM	DECURSIVE
BEAUTEOUS	DECIDUOUS	GYMNASIUM	NEFARIOUS	RACCAHOUT	TERRARIUM	DEDUCTIVE
BEAUTIFUL	DELICIOUS	GYNOECIUM	NEIGHBOUR	RACONTEUR	TETTEROUS	DEFECTIVE
BEELZEBUB	DELIRIOUS	HADROSAUR	NEODYMIUM	RANCOROUS	THELONIUS	DEFENSIVE
BEHAVIOUR	DELPHINUS	HARMONIUM	NEPTUNIUM	RAPACIOUS	THESAURUS	DETECTIVE
BERKELIUM	DEMAGOGUE	HARQUEBUS	NICARAGUA	RAPTUROUS	TIMENOGUY	DIGESTIVE
BERYLLIUM	DEMEANOUR	HAZARDOUS	NICODEMUS	REDDENDUM	TORMENTUM	DIRECTIVE
BOSPHORUS	DEMETRIUS	HEARTHRUG	NIGHTCLUB	REDIVIVUS	TRACHINUS	EDUCATIVE

EFFECTIVE	SUPERNOVA	EMPHASIZE	ASYNERGIA	INFLUENZA	XEROSTOMA	ENERGETIC
EVOCATIVE	TALKATIVE	EPITOMIZE	ATAHUALPA	IPHIGENIA	BEELZEBUB	ENIGMATIC
EXCESSIVE	TENTATIVE	FANTASIZE	AUBRIETIA	JACARANDA	COCKSCOMB	EPEDAPHIC
EXCLUSIVE	TESTDRIVE	FERTILIZE	AUSTRALIA	JAMBALAYA	CURRYCOMB	EPICYCLIC
EXECUTIVE	WALDGRAVE	FORMALIZE	BALACLAVA	JUVENILIA	DISENTOMB	EPILEPTIC
EXPANSIVE	YESTEREVE	GALVANIZE	BALALAIKA	KNIPHOFIA	DITHYRAMB	EPINASTIC
EXPENSIVE	BREAKDOWN	GLAMORIZE	BALLERINA	LEUKAEMIA	FLASHBULB	EPIPHYTIC
EXPLETIVE	CHINATOWN	HARMONIZE	BARCELONA	LITHUANIA	HONEYCOMB	EUCHLORIC
EXPLOSIVE	CLAMPDOWN	HYPNOTIZE	BARRACUDA	LJUBLJANA	JIGGUMBOB	EUTROPHIC
EXTENSIVE	COUNTDOWN	INFLUENZA	BENBECULA	LOUISIANA	NIGHTCLUB	EVANGELIC
FOLKWEAVE	CRACKDOWN	ITALICIZE	BOOBIALLA	MACADAMIA	SPIDERWEB	EXTRINSIC
FORGETIVE	EIDERDOWN	JARGONIZE	BOSSANOVA	MACEDONIA	TOOTHCOMB	FANTASTIC
FORMATIVE	FROGSPAWN	LIQUIDIZE	BRITANNIA	MADARIAGA	ACROBATIC	GEOMETRIC
GENEVIEVE	FULLBLOWN	MAGNETIZE	BRITSCHKA	MARIJUANA	AESTHETIC	GERIATRIC
GERUNDIVE	FULLGROWN	MECHANIZE	CACHAEMIA	MELANESIA	AGALACTIC	GYMNASTIC
HORTATIVE	HOMEGROWN	MERCERIZE	CAFETERIA	MELODRAMA	ALCOHOLIC	HANSEATIC
IMITATIVE	JOBERNOWL	MESMERIZE	CALEDONIA	MESSALINA	ALGEBRAIC	HEURISTIC
IMPASSIVE	KICKSHAWS	MODERNIZE	CALENDULA	MINNESOTA	ALICYCLIC	HONORIFIC
IMPULSIVE	KNOCKDOWN	NORMALIZE	CALPURNIA	MONODRAMA	ALIPHATIC	HYDRAULIC
INCENTIVE	MOLLYMAWK	OSTRACIZE	CAMPANULA	MONOMANIA	ANAEROBIC	ICELANDIC
INCEPTIVE	NIGHTGOWN	PAPARAZZI	CARACALLA	MONTEZUMA	ANALEPTIC	IDIOMATIC
INCLUSIVE	NIGHTHAWK	PAPARAZZO	CARAMBOLA	MORATORIA	ANALGESIC	IMPOLITIC
INDUCTIVE	OUTOFTOWN	PATRONIZE	CARCINOMA	NAUMACHIA	ANIMISTIC	INORGANIC
INTENSIVE	OVERBLOWN	POETICIZE	CASSANDRA	NEURALGIA	ANTARCTIC	INSOMNIAC
INTRUSIVE	OVERCROWD	PRIVATIZE	CASUARINA	NEUROGLIA	ANTITOXIC	INTRINSIC
INTUITIVE	OVERDRAWN	PUBLICIZE	CATATONIA	NICARAGUA	APATHETIC	ISCHAEMIC
INVECTIVE	OVERGROWN	PULVERIZE	CHIHUAHUA	NOSTALGIA	APERIODIC	ISOMETRIC
INVENTIVE	SHAKEDOWN	RECOGNIZE	CHILOPODA	NOTONECTA	APOPHATIC	ISOTACTIC
LANDGRAVE	SOUTHDOWN	RUBBERIZE	CHIPOLATA	ORCHESTRA	APOSTOLIC	ISOTROPIC
LATICLAVE	SWANSDOWN	SCHMALTZY	CINERARIA	PALAESTRA	ARTHRITIC	KLENDUSIC
LUCRATIVE	THROWDOWN	SENSITIZE	CLEOPATRA	PANATELLA	ASTHMATIC	LANGUEDOC
MICROWAVE	TOUCHDOWN	SERIALIZE	CLEPSYDRA	PAULOWNIA	ATAVISTIC	LETHARGIC
MISBEHAVE	UNBEKNOWN	SERMONIZE	COLUMELLA	PENINSULA	ATHEISTIC	LIENTERIC
NARRATIVE	WATERFOWL	SOCIALIZE	CONDYLOMA	PHANTASMA	AUTHENTIC	LOMBARDIC
NORMATIVE	WELLKNOWN	SOLEMNIZE	CRUSTACEA	PHARSALIA	AUTOMATIC	LYMPHATIC
NUTRITIVE	WITHDRAWN	STABILIZE	CYCLORAMA	PNEUMONIA	AUTONOMIC	MACARONIC
OBJECTIVE	BATTLEAXE	STERILIZE	DANTHONIA	POLYNESIA	AXIOMATIC	MELANOTIC
OBSESSIVE	CATAPLEXY	SUBSIDIZE	DIARRHOEA	PONDEROSA	BALLISTIC	MESSIANIC
OBTRUSIVE	ORTHODOXY	SUMMARIZE	DYSPEPSIA	PORTULACA	BISHOPRIC	METABOLIC
OFFENSIVE	CORDUROYS	SYMBOLIZE	DYSPHAGIA	PRIMAVERA	BOMBASTIC	MONATOMIC
OPERATIVE	DOTHEBOYS	TANTALIZE	DYSPRAXIA	PRIMIPARA	BRITANNIC	NEOLITHIC
OSTENSIVE	HELVELLYN	TEMPORIZE	ECHEVERIA	PYROMANIA	CACHECTIC	NEPHRITIC
OVERDRIVE	HENDIADYS	TENDERIZE	ECLAMPSIA	QUINQUINA	CALORIFIC	NEURALGIC
PALSGRAVE	ISOPROPYL	TERRORIZE	EMPHYSEMA	RUDBECKIA	CASUISTIC	NOSTALGIC
PARASCEVE	JAMBALAYA	TYRANNIZE	ENCHILADA	SANTAYANA	CATALYTIC	OBSTETRIC
PATERCOVE	LEASTWAYS	VANDALIZE	ESMERALDA	SANTONICA	CATATONIC	OMOPHAGIC
PERVASIVE	LOBLOLLYS	VERBALIZE	EUPHORBIA	SAPODILLA	CATHARTIC	ONOMASTIC
PLAINTIVE	MOSKONFYT	VICTIMIZE	EXANTHEMA	SCAGLIOLA	CHARABANC	OPODELDOC
PORTREEVE	POMPHOLYX	VISUALIZE	FAMAGUSTA	SCINTILLA	CHROMATIC	ORGIASTIC
PRECISIVE	PSEUDONYM	VULCANIZE	FINLANDIA	SLIVOVICA	CINEMATIC	PANEGYRIC
PRIMITIVE	SILVEREYE	**9:9**	FIORITURA	SNOWDONIA	CLIMACTIC	PANORAMIC
PROACTIVE	ANATOMIZE	ACONCAGUA	FORSYTHIA	SOUVLAKIA	CRYOGENIC	PARABOLIC
PURGATIVE	APOLOGIZE	ALEXANDRA	FRANCESCA	SUBSTRATA	CYNEGETIC	PARALYTIC
RECEPTIVE	ARABICIZE	AMBLYOPIA	GARGANTUA	SUPERNOVA	DIACRITIC	PARAMEDIC
RECESSIVE	ASHKENAZI	ANAGLYPTA	GENITALIA	SYPHILOMA	DIALECTIC	PARANOIAC
RECURSIVE	AUTHORIZE	ANALGESIA	GUATEMALA	TANTARARA	DIAMETRIC	PARASITIC
REFLEXIVE	BARBARIZE	ANAPLASIA	GUERRILLA	TARANTULA	DIANOETIC	PAREGORIC
REPLETIVE	BRUTALIZE	ANASTASIA	HAEMALOMA	TARRAGONA	DIGASTRIC	PATRIOTIC
REPULSIVE	CARBONIZE	ANDROMEDA	HARMONICA	THEOBROMA	DIZYGOTIC	PEIRASTIC
RETENTIVE	CATECHIZE	ANGOSTURA	HEMIPTERA	TOCCATINA	DOLOMITIC	PHARISAIC
RUNESTAVE	CAUTERIZE	ANNAPURNA	HIPPOLYTA	TRATTORIA	DYSPEPTIC	PHILIPPIC
SECRETIVE	CRITICIZE	APOCRYPHA	HOMOPTERA	TRIPITAKA	ECCENTRIC	PHRENETIC
SEDUCTIVE	CUSTOMIZE	AQUILEGIA	HYDRANGEA	URTICARIA	EMBRYONIC	PLETHORIC
SELECTIVE	DEODORIZE	ARAUCARIA	HYPERBOLA	VARICELLA	EMPAESTIC	PNEUMATIC
SEMIBREVE	DOGMATIZE	ARCTOGAEA	HYPEROPIA	VENEZUELA	ENCAUSTIC	PRAGMATIC
SENSITIVE	DRAMATIZE	ARGENTINA	INAMORATA	VIPASSANA	ENDEICTIC	PRISMATIC
SICCATIVE	ECONOMIZE	ARTEMISIA	INDONESIA	XENOMANIA	ENDOERGIC	PROCLITIC

PROPHETIC	ARCHIBALD	CONCERTED	ENAMOURED	HARDIHOOD	MENTIONED	PUMMELLED
PROPIONIC	ARROWHEAD	CONCLUDED	ENCHANTED	HEADBOARD	METALLOID	QUADRUPED
PSYCHOTIC	ARTHROPOD	CONCUSSED	ENCIRCLED	HEADLINED	METEOROID	QUALIFIED
PURITANIC	ASTOUNDED	CONDEMNED	ENGARLAND	HEARTLAND	METROLAND	QUICKSAND
PYRRHONIC	ATTEMPTED	CONFESSED	ENGRAINED	HEARTWOOD	MINEFIELD	RANGELAND
QUADRATIC	AUTOMATED	CONFIRMED	ENGROSSED	HEATHLAND	MISGUIDED	REARGUARD
REALISTIC	BACKBOARD	CONFLATED	ENLIVENED	HEDERATED	MISPLACED	RECLAIMED
RHAPSODIC	BACKSWORD	CONGESTED	ENSCONCED	HENPECKED	MONKSHOOD	RECOMMEND
RHEUMATIC	BANDSTAND	CONNECTED	ENTRANCED	HERMANDAD	MONOCHORD	RECOVERED
SARCASTIC	BAREFACED	CONTENTED	ESTRANGED	HIDEBOUND	MORTIFIED	REDHANDED
SCHEMATIC	BASEBOARD	CONTRIVED	ESTRELDID	HIGHSPEED	MUCHLOVED	REDHEADED
SCOLIOTIC	BEACHHEAD	CONVERTED	ETIOLATED	HOARHOUND	MUTILATED	REPREHEND
SCORBUTIC	BEDSPREAD	CONVINCED	EXCLAIMED	HOBNAILED	MYRMECOID	REPRESSED
SEMEIOTIC	BENIGHTED	CORNFIELD	EXERCISED	HODMANDOD	NAUSEATED	REPRIMAND
SOPHISTIC	BETROTHED	CORRECTED	EXHAUSTED	HOLINSHED	NEGLECTED	RESPECTED
SOPORIFIC	BIGHEADED	COURTYARD	EXPRESSED	HOLLYWOOD	NEWSHOUND	RIDERHOOD
SPASMODIC	BILLBOARD	CRASHLAND	FAIRYLAND	HOMEBOUND	NEWSSTAND	RIGHTHAND
SPLENETIC	BLACKBIRD	CROCKFORD	FALSEHOOD	HOMESTEAD	NORTHWARD	ROADSTEAD
STATISTIC	BLACKHEAD	CROSSBRED	FARMSTEAD	HOREHOUND	NOSEBLEED	ROUGHSHOD
STEGNOTIC	BLACKLEAD	CROSSEYED	FASHIONED	HORRIFIED	NOTOCHORD	ROUNDHAND
STENOPAIC	BLACKWOOD	CROSSWIND	FEATHERED	HOTHEADED	NURSEMAID	ROUNDHEAD
STIGMATIC	BLINDFOLD	CROSSWORD	FERDINAND	HOUSEHOLD	OCTACHORD	RUNAROUND
STOMACHIC	BLINKERED	DACHSHUND	FERMENTED	HOUSEMAID	OCTOPLOID	SAFEGUARD
STRATEGIC	BLISTERED	DAIRYMAID	FIREBRAND	HUMANKIND	OPENENDED	SAINTHOOD
STYLISTIC	BLOCKHEAD	DANDIFIED	FIREGUARD	IMPRESSED	OPPRESSED	SANDALLED
SUDORIFIC	BLOODSHED	DARTBOARD	FIRSTHAND	INCREASED	ORGANISED	SANGFROID
SULPHONIC	BLUEBEARD	DASHBOARD	FISHGUARD	INGRAINED	ORGANIZED	SATINWOOD
SULPHURIC	BODYGUARD	DEBAUCHED	FLAMSTEED	INHERITED	OUTSPREAD	SATISFIED
SYBARITIC	BOOKSTAND	DECACHORD	FLATTENED	INHIBITED	OVERBOARD	SATURATED
SYMBIOTIC	BOULEVARD	DECORATED	FLATTERED	INITIATED	OVERCLOUD	SCALLOPED
SYMMETRIC	BOYFRIEND	DEDICATED	FLAVOURED	INSCRIBED	OVERCROWD	SCATTERED
SYMPHONIC	BRICKYARD	DEERHOUND	FLEETWOOD	INTERBRED	OVERJOYED	SCRATCHED
SYNTACTIC	BRUSHWOOD	DELIGHTED	FLOWERBED	INTERLARD	OVERRATED	SCRODDLED
SYNTHETIC	CAGOULARD	DEPRESSED	FLUSTERED	INTRIGUED	OVERSIZED	SEGMENTED
TACAMAHAC	CAKESTAND	DESTROYED	FORESPEND	IRRITATED	OVERSPEND	SEMIFLUID
THALASSIC	CARDBOARD	DEVELOPED	FORFEITED	ISLAMABAD	PASSEPIED	SEPARATED
THRASONIC	CASTRATED	DIGNIFIED	FRAGONARD	JAMPACKED	PATTERNED	SEQUINNED
THRENETIC	CATCHWORD	DISCARDED	FREEBOARD	JAUNDICED	PENFRIEND	SHATTERED
TOXIGENIC	CAUCASOID	DISCLOSED	FRIESLAND	JUSTIFIED	PERAEOPOD	SHEEPFOLD
TRAUMATIC	CEDARWOOD	DISGRACED	GATESHEAD	KIDNAPPED	PERFERVID	SHEFFIELD
TRICLINIC	CELLULOID	DISGUISED	GAVELKIND	KINGSIZED	PERFORMED	SHELTERED
TRIETERIC	CERTIFIED	DISGUSTED	GEOMETRID	KNACKERED	PERMITTED	SHEWBREAD
TROCHILIC	CHANCROID	DISPERSED	GLORIFIED	LACERATED	PERPLEXED	SHOREBIRD
UPAITHRIC	CHARTERED	DISPLACED	GOLDFIELD	LACKBEARD	PERSUADED	SHORTHAND
VAPORIFIC	CHASTENED	DISPLAYED	GOOSEHERD	LAMINATED	PERTURBED	SHORTHOLD
VIDEODISC	CHEQUERED	DISREGARD	GRADGRIND	LANCEWOOD	PERVERTED	SHUTTERED
VITRIOLIC	CHERISHED	DISSOLVED	GRADUATED	LEAFMOULD	PETRIFIED	SIDEBOARD
ZOOMANTIC	CHICKWEED	DISTENDED	GRASSLAND	LEASEHOLD	PHARAMOND	SIEGFRIED
ZOOSCOPIC	CHILDHOOD	DISTORTED	GRAVESEND	LENINGRAD	PHONECARD	SIGNBOARD
ZYGOMATIC	CHIPBOARD	DISTURBED	GRAVEYARD	LEVERAGED	PHYLLOPOD	SIMULATED
ABANDONED	CHONDROID	DISUNITED	GREENFEED	LIBERATED	PICOFARAD	SKETCHPAD
ADDRESSED	CIVILISED	DIXIELAND	GREENHEAD	LIFEGUARD	PIGHEADED	SNAKEWEED
ADULTHOOD	CIVILIZED	DOMICILED	GREENSAND	LINGFIELD	PIXILATED	SNOWBOUND
ADVOCATED	CLAPBOARD	DOWNTREND	GREENWEED	LIQUEFIED	PLASTERED	SOUTHWARD
AFFLICTED	CLEVELAND	DREAMLAND	GREENWOOD	LOCALIZED	POPULATED	SPATTERED
AFORESAID	CLIPBOARD	DRIFTWOOD	GREENYARD	LONGLIVED	POSSESSED	SPEARHEAD
AFTERWORD	CLUSTERED	DUCKBOARD	GREYBEARD	LOOSEHEAD	POSTPONED	SPECIFIED
AGGRIEVED	COACHLOAD	DUMBFOUND	GREYHOUND	LUSTIHOOD	PRACTISED	SPELLBIND
AIRCOOLED	COALESCED	DUPLICAND	GUMSHIELD	LYMESWOLD	PREFERRED	SPIKENARD
ALLANTOID	COALFIELD	DYNAMITED	HACKNEYED	MACDONALD	PRESENTED	SPONSORED
AMPERSAND	COCUSWOOD	EAGLEWOOD	HALFBAKED	MALFORMED	PRESERVED	SPOONFEED
ANGUISHED	COLLECTED	EASTBOUND	HAMADRYAD	MANSFIELD	PROFESSED	SPRINGALD
ANNOTATED	COMMITTED	ELONGATED	HAMFISTED	MAPPEMOND	PROJECTED	SPUNCULID
APARTHEID	COMPELLED	EMACIATED	HAMPSTEAD	MARSHLAND	PROLONGED	STABLELAD
APPOINTED	CONCEALED	EMBATTLED	HANDSTAND	MASEFIELD	PROOFREAD	STAGEHAND
APPREHEND	CONCEITED	EMBROILED	HAPHAZARD	MATCHWOOD	PROPELLED	STAGGERED
ARACHNOID	CONCERNED	ENAMELLED	HARDBOARD	MEDICATED	PUBLISHED	STARBOARD

STATEHOOD	UNDAUNTED	WITNESSED	APOLOGIZE	BEVERIDGE	CASSONADE	COMMITTEE
STATIONED	UNDECIDED	WOLFHOUND	APPENDAGE	BICONCAVE	CASTIGATE	COMMODORE
STEELHEAD	UNDEFILED	WOMANHOOD	APPLIANCE	BIFURCATE	CATALOGUE	COMMUTATE
STEELYARD	UNDEFINED	WOMANKIND	APPOINTEE	BIOSPHERE	CATCHPOLE	COMPOSITE
STILTBIRD	UNDERBRED	ABANDONEE	AQUAPLANE	BIPARTITE	CATECHIZE	COMPOSURE
STINKBIRD	UNDERFEED	ABERRANCE	AQUARELLE	BIRDTABLE	CATHERINE	CONCIERGE
STINKWOOD	UNDERGRAD	ABOMINATE	ARABESQUE	BIRTHRATE	CAUTERIZE	CONCOURSE
STOCKYARD	UNDERHAND	ABORIGINE	ARABICIZE	BLACKFACE	CAVALCADE	CONCUBINE
STOKEHOLD	UNDERPAID	ABOUTFACE	ARABINOSE	BLACKMORE	CEASEFIRE	CONDUCIVE
STONEHAND	UNDERWOOD	ABUNDANCE	ARAGONITE	BLASPHEME	CELANDINE	CONGOLESE
STONKERED	UNDILUTED	ACCLIMATE	ARBITRAGE	BLOATWARE	CELEBRATE	CONJUGATE
STORIATED	UNDIVIDED	ACETAMIDE	ARBITRATE	BLUESTONE	CELLULITE	CONNOTATE
STRETCHED	UNDOUBTED	ACETYLENE	ARCHETYPE	BOATHOUSE	CELLULOSE	CONSIGNEE
STUPEFIED	UNDRESSED	ACIDULATE	ARGENTINE	BOLOGNESE	CENTIPEDE	CONSTABLE
SUBMERGED	UNEQUALED	ACQUIESCE	ARISTOTLE	BOMBASINE	CEREBRATE	CONSTANCE
SUBTITLED	UNEXPOSED	ACUMINATE	ARMISTICE	BONAPARTE	CERTITUDE	CONSULATE
SUCCEEDED	UNFLEDGED	ADAPTABLE	ARQUEBUSE	BONDSTONE	CERUSSITE	COOKHOUSE
SUNTANNED	UNFOUNDED	ADDICTIVE	ARRIVISTE	BOOKSTORE	CEYLONESE	COOPERATE
SURFBOARD	UNGUARDED	ADDRESSEE	ARROGANCE	BRACTEOLE	CHABAZITE	COPROLITE
SURFEITED	UNIFORMED	ADHERENCE	ARTERIOLE	BRAINCASE	CHALLENGE	CORALLINE
SURPRISED	UNINJURED	ADJECTIVE	ARTICHOKE	BRAINWAVE	CHAMINADE	CORDYLINE
SUSPECTED	UNINVITED	ADMIRABLE	ASPARTAME	BRASENOSE	CHAMOMILE	CORNCRAKE
SUSPENDED	UNLEARNED	ADMIXTURE	ASSERTIVE	BRASSERIE	CHAMPAGNE	CORNEILLE
SUSTAINED	UNLIMITED	ADUMBRATE	ASSOCIATE	BRASSIERE	CHAMPLEVÉ	CORPORATE
SWEATBAND	UNMARRIED	ADVANTAGE	ASSONANCE	BRASSWARE	CHANTEUSE	CORPUSCLE
SWINEHERD	UNMATCHED	ADVENTIVE	ASSUETUDE	BREADLINE	CHAPERONE	CORRELATE
TABLELAND	UNNOTICED	ADVENTURE	ASSURANCE	BREAKABLE	CHARLOTTE	CORROSIVE
TAILBOARD	UNOPPOSED	ADVERTISE	ASTRODOME	BRIEFCASE	CHEAPSIDE	CORRUGATE
TARMACKED	UNREFINED	ADVISABLE	ASTROLABE	BRIMSTONE	CHECKMATE	CORTISONE
TASSELLED	UNRELATED	AERODROME	ATTENTIVE	BRIQUETTE	CHEEKBONE	CORUSCATE
TAYASSUID	UNRUFFLED	AEROPLANE	ATTENUATE	BROADSIDE	CHICKADEE	COUCHETTE
TERRIFIED	UNSCATHED	AEROSPACE	ATTRIBUTE	BROKERAGE	CHILDCARE	COURGETTE
THICKHEAD	UNSECURED	AFFILIATE	AUBERGINE	BROMINATE	CHILDLIKE	COURTELLE
THREEFOLD	UNSETTLED	AFFLUENCE	AUGUSTINE	BRUNHILDE	CHOCOLATE	COVELLITE
THRESHOLD	UNSKILLED	AFFRICATE	AUTHORIZE	BRUTALIZE	CHONDRITE	COVERDALE
TIGHTHEAD	UNSPOILED	AFTERCARE	AUTOCLAVE	BUMBLEBEE	CHRONICLE	COVERTURE
TOLERATED	UNSULLIED	AGGRAVATE	AUTOROUTE	BURKINABE	CIGARETTE	COWARDICE
TOUCHWOOD	UNTOUCHED	AGGREGATE	AVAILABLE	BURLESQUE	CILIOLATE	COXSACKIE
TRADEWIND	UNTRAINED	AGREEABLE	AVALANCHE	BYZANTINE	CINEPHILE	CRANBORNE
TRANSCEND	UNTREATED	AITCHBONE	AVOIDABLE	CAFETIERE	CIRCINATE	CREPITATE
TRAPEZOID	UNTUTORED	ALBERTINE	AVOIDANCE	CALABOOSE	CIRCULATE	CREPOLINE
TREBIZOND	UNWATERED	ALLEMANDE	BACKSLIDE	CALABRESE	CLASSMATE	CRESCELLE
TRIANGLED	UNWORRIED	ALLEVIATE	BACKSPACE	CALCINATE	CLEARANCE	CRIMINATE
TRICUSPID	UPANISHAD	ALLOWABLE	BACKSTAGE	CALCULATE	CLIENTELE	CRINOLINE
TRUCKLOAD	VOLGOGRAD	ALLOWANCE	BAGATELLE	CALENTURE	CLOCKWISE	CRITICIZE
TRUNCATED	VOLKSRAAD	ALMANDINE	BAINMARIE	CALIBRATE	CLOISONNÉ	CROCODILE
TULIPWOOD	WAGONLOAD	ALONGSIDE	BAKEHOUSE	CAMBRIDGE	CLUBHOUSE	CROQUETTE
TURNROUND	WAISTBAND	ALTERABLE	BALTIMORE	CAMPANILE	COAGULATE	CROSSFIRE
UNABASHED	WALLBOARD	ALTERCATE	BAMBOOZLE	CANDIDATE	COARCTATE	CROSSWISE
UNADOPTED	WASHBOARD	ALTERNATE	BANDALORE	CANNELURE	COASTLINE	CROUSTADE
UNALLOYED	WASHSTAND	ALVEOLATE	BANDOLINE	CANNONADE	COCKAIGNE	CROWNLIKE
UNALTERED	WASTELAND	AMAZONITE	BANQUETTE	CANTABILE	COENOBITE	CUBBYHOLE
UNASHAMED	WATCHWORD	AMBROTYPE	BARBARIZE	CANTONESE	COFFINITE	CULMINATE
UNBIASSED	WATERFORD	AMBULANCE	BARBITONE	CAPTIVATE	COGNITIVE	CULTIVATE
UNBOUNDED	WATERSHED	AMBUSCADE	BARBOTINE	CARBAMATE	COHERENCE	CURETTAGE
UNBRIDLED	WATERWEED	AMELAKITE	BARMECIDE	CARBAMIDE	COLERIDGE	CURFUFFLE
UNCHANGED	WEBFOOTED	AMPLITUDE	BARNABITE	CARBONADE	COLLEAGUE	CURTILAGE
UNCHARGED	WEDGEWOOD	ANATOMIZE	BARRICADE	CARBONATE	COLLIGATE	CURVATURE
UNCHECKED	WESTBOUND	ANCHORAGE	BARYSCOPE	CARBONIZE	COLLIMATE	CUSPIDORE
UNCLAIMED	WHIPROUND	ANCHORITE	BASTINADE	CARBUNCLE	COLLOCATE	CUSTOMIZE
UNCLOTHED	WHIRLWIND	ANHYDRIDE	BATTLEAXE	CARMELITE	COLLOTYPE	CYCLAMATE
UNCLOUDED	WHITEHEAD	ANHYDRITE	BEATITUDE	CARNIVORE	COLLUSIVE	CYMBELINE
UNCOUPLED	WHITEWOOD	ANNOYANCE	BEDRAGGLE	CARTHORSE	COLONNADE	DALLIANCE
UNCOVERED	WHOLEFOOD	ANTICLINE	BELLICOSE	CARTILAGE	COLUMBATE	DAMASCENE
UNCROSSED	WIDOWHOOD	APERITIVE	BELLYACHE	CARTOUCHE	COLUMBINE	DEAMINATE
UNCROWNED	WITHSTAND	APHRODITE	BELVEDERE	CARTRIDGE	COLUMBITE	DEBATABLE
UNDAMAGED	WITHYWIND	APOENZYME	BESPANGLE	CASSEROLE	COMBATIVE	DEBAUCHEE

492

DEBENTURE	DOORFRAME	EPAULETTE	FAVOURITE	FURNITURE	GUIDELINE	HUMILIATE
DEBUTANTE	DOSSHOUSE	EPHEDRINE	FEBRIFUGE	FUSILLADE	GUILLOCHE	HURRICANE
DECADENCE	DOWNGRADE	EPICENTRE	FERINGHEE	FUSTIGATE	GUINEVERE	HUTTERITE
DECALITRE	DOWNSTAGE	EPITOMIZE	FERROTYPE	GABARDINE	GYROPLANE	HYDRAZINE
DECALOGUE	DRAINPIPE	EQUIPOISE	FERTILIZE	GABERDINE	GYROSCOPE	HYPALLAGE
DECASTYLE	DRAMATIZE	EQUITABLE	FESTINATE	GABIONADE	HABERDINE	HYPERBOLE
DECEPTIVE	DRAWKNIFE	EQUIVOQUE	FIBROLINE	GALACTOSE	HABITABLE	HYPHENATE
DECOLLATE	DRINKABLE	ERADICATE	FIBROLITE	GALANTINE	HABITUATE	HYPNOTIZE
DECOMPOSE	DRIPSTONE	EROSTRATE	FIELDFARE	GALENGALE	HACKAMORE	HYPOCRITE
DECURSIVE	DRUGSTORE	ERSTWHILE	FIGURANTE	GALINGALE	HAEMATITE	ICHNOLITE
DECUSSATE	DUNSINANE	ERYTHRITE	FILOPLUME	GALIONGEE	HAILSTONE	ICTERIDAE
DEDUCTIVE	DUNSTABLE	ESCOPETTE	FILOSELLE	GALLINULE	HAIRPIECE	IDEALOGUE
DEFALCATE	DUPLICATE	ESPAGNOLE	FIREDRAKE	GALLOPADE	HAIRSTYLE	IDIOPHONE
DEFECTIVE	EBRILLADE	ESPERANCE	FIREPLACE	GALLSTONE	HALOPHILE	IGNORANCE
DEFENSIVE	ECHIDNINE	ESPIONAGE	FIRESTONE	GALRAVAGE	HALOTHANE	ILLEGIBLE
DEFERENCE	ECONOMIZE	ESPLANADE	FIRSTRATE	GALVANIZE	HAMPSHIRE	IMBALANCE
DEFINABLE	ECOSPHERE	ESQUILINE	FISHPLATE	GARDEROBE	HANDBRAKE	IMBRANGLE
DEFOLIATE	ECOSSAISE	ESTAFETTE	FLAGITATE	GARNISHEE	HANDPIECE	IMBRICATE
DEHYDRATE	EDDYSTONE	ESTIMABLE	FLAGRANCE	GARNITURE	HANDSHAKE	IMBROCATE
DELINEATE	EDUCATIVE	ESTRAPADE	FLAGSTONE	GASCONADE	HANDSPIKE	IMITATIVE
DEMAGOGUE	EFFECTIVE	ETHANOATE	FLAMMABLE	GELIGNITE	HARESTANE	IMMANACLE
DEMARCATE	EFFLUENCE	ETIQUETTE	FLASHCUBE	GENEVIEVE	HARIOLATE	IMMANENCE
DEMITASSE	EGLANTINE	EVAPORATE	FLECHETTE	GEORGETTE	HARMALINE	IMMEDIATE
DEMURRAGE	EIGHTSOME	EVENTUATE	FLEXITIME	GERMANITE	HARMONIZE	IMMIGRATE
DENIGRATE	EJACULATE	EVERGLADE	FLOODGATE	GERMICIDE	HARMOTOME	IMMINENCE
DEODORIZE	ELABORATE	EVOCATIVE	FLOPHOUSE	GERMINATE	HARROGATE	IMMOVABLE
DEOXIDISE	ELAEOLITE	EXANIMATE	FLOWSTONE	GERUNDIVE	HASHEMITE	IMMUTABLE
DEPARTURE	ELECTRODE	EXCESSIVE	FLUCTUATE	GESSAMINE	HAUTMONDE	IMPASSIVE
DEPASTURE	ELIMINATE	EXCITABLE	FOGRAMITE	GIBEONITE	HAWCUBITE	IMPEDANCE
DEPRECATE	ELKOSHITE	EXCLUSIVE	FOLIOLOSE	GINGERADE	HAWSEHOLE	IMPLICATE
DEPREDATE	ELLESMERE	EXCORIATE	FOLKWEAVE	GIRANDOLE	HAWTHORNE	IMPORTUNE
DESECRATE	ELOQUENCE	EXCULPATE	FOODSTORE	GLADSTONE	HEADPIECE	IMPOSTURE
DESICCATE	ELSEWHERE	EXCUSABLE	FOOTBRAKE	GLAMORIZE	HEADSTONE	IMPOTENCE
DESIGNATE	ELUCIDATE	EXECRABLE	FOOTLOOSE	GLASSWARE	HEARTACHE	IMPRECATE
DESIRABLE	ELUTRIATE	EXECUTIVE	FOOTPLATE	GLOMERATE	HEAVISIDE	IMPRECISE
DESPERATE	EMBASSADE	EXISTENCE	FORECLOSE	GLOMERULE	HEDYPHANE	IMPROVISE
DESTITUTE	EMBASSAGE	EXONERATE	FORESHORE	GLORYHOLE	HELLEBORE	IMPSONITE
DESUETUDE	EMBRANGLE	EXOSPHERE	FORESTAGE	GLUCOSIDE	HEMITROPE	IMPUDENCE
DETECTIVE	EMBRASURE	EXPANSIVE	FORETASTE	GLUTAMINE	HERBICIDE	IMPULSIVE
DETERMINE	EMBROCATE	EXPATIATE	FORFICATE	GLYCERIDE	HERBIVORE	INANIMATE
DEVASTATE	EMERGENCE	EXPENSIVE	FORGETIVE	GLYCERINE	HERITABLE	INAUDIBLE
DEXTRORSE	EMMERDALE	EXPERTISE	FORMALIZE	GMELINITE	HERMITAGE	INCAPABLE
DIABLERIE	EMOLLIATE	EXPISCATE	FORMATIVE	GONIATITE	HESITANCE	INCARDINE
DIALOGITE	EMPENNAGE	EXPLETIVE	FORMULATE	GOSLARITE	HESSONITE	INCARNATE
DIATOMITE	EMPHASIZE	EXPLICATE	FORNICATE	GOSSYPINE	HIBERNATE	INCENTIVE
DIGESTIVE	ENCLOSURE	EXPLOSIVE	FORTALICE	GOTHAMITE	HIMYARITE	INCEPTIVE
DILIGENCE	ENCOURAGE	EXPURGATE	FORTILAGE	GRANDIOSE	HINDRANCE	INCIDENCE
DIRECTIVE	ENCRATITE	EXQUISITE	FORTITUDE	GRANDSIRE	HIPPODAME	INCLUSIVE
DIRIGIBLE	ENDOCRINE	EXSICCATE	FORTUNATE	GRANULATE	HIPPOLYTE	INCOMMODE
DISCHARGE	ENDURABLE	EXTEMPORE	FOSSILISE	GRANULITE	HIRUNDINE	INCONDITE
DISCOURSE	ENDURANCE	EXTENSILE	FOURPENCE	GRANULOSE	HISTAMINE	INCULCATE
DISENGAGE	ENERINITE	EXTENSIVE	FRAGRANCE	GRAPETREE	HISTIDINE	INCULPATE
DISFIGURE	ENGRENAGE	EXTENUATE	FRAMBOISE	GRAPEVINE	HITCHHIKE	INCURABLE
DISLOCATE	ENHYDRITE	EXTIRPATE	FRANCHISE	GRATICULE	HOARSTONE	INDELIBLE
DISMANTLE	ENJOYABLE	EXTRADITE	FREELANCE	GRATITUDE	HOCCAMORE	INDENTURE
DISOBLIGE	ENNERDALE	EXTRICATE	FREEPHONE	GRAVESIDE	HOLOPHOTE	INDIGENCE
DISPARAGE	ENRAPTURE	EYESPLICE	FREESTONE	GRAVITATE	HOLYSTONE	INDOLENCE
DISPARATE	ENSHEATHE	FABRICATE	FREESTYLE	GREENGAGE	HOMOPHONE	INDUCTIVE
DISPLEASE	ENSTATITE	FACSIMILE	FRICASSEE	GREGARINE	HONORABLE	INEBRIATE
DISREPUTE	ENTHYMEME	FACTORISE	FRIZZANTE	GRENADINE	HORNSTONE	INEFFABLE
DISSEMBLE	ENTOPHYTE	FAIRYTALE	FROSTBITE	GRENVILLE	HOROSCOPE	INERUDITE
DISSIPATE	ENTOURAGE	FANDANGLE	FRUITCAKE	GREYWACKE	HORSESHOE	INFANTILE
DISSOLUTE	ENTRECÔTE	FANTASIZE	FRUSTRATE	GRIEVANCE	HORTATIVE	INFATUATE
DIVISIBLE	ENUCLEATE	FARANDOLE	FULLERENE	GRISAILLE	HOURSTONE	INFERENCE
DOCTORATE	ENUMERATE	FARMHOUSE	FULLSCALE	GROTESQUE	HOUSEWIFE	INFERTILE
DOGMATIZE	ENUNCIATE	FASCINATE	FULMINATE	GUACAMOLE	HOWTOWDIE	INFLUENCE
DOMINANCE	EPARCHATE	FAVORABLE	FUNGICIDE	GUARANTEE	HUMANMADE	INFURIATE

INJUSTICE	KERFUFFLE	LUMINANCE	METHOXIDE	NATROLITE	ORPHANAGE	PENDULATE
INNISFREE	KERMESITE	LUNCHTIME	METRICATE	NAVIGABLE	ORTANIQUE	PENETRATE
INNOCENCE	KEYSTROKE	LUXURIATE	METRONOME	NECKVERSE	ORTHOTONE	PENISTONE
INOCULATE	KHALIFATE	MACEDOINE	MEZZANINE	NECTARINE	OSCILLATE	PENITENCE
INOPINATE	KIESERITE	MACHINATE	MICROCYTE	NEGOTIATE	OSTENSIVE	PENTHOUSE
INQUILINE	KILOCYCLE	MACKENZIE	MICROLITE	NEGRITUDE	OSTRACISE	PENTOSANE
INQUINATE	KILOMETRE	MACQUARIE	MICROMOLE	NEPHELINE	OSTRACIZE	PERCALINE
INQUORATE	KINTLEDGE	MADELEINE	MICROTOME	NERITIDAE	OTHERWISE	PERCHANCE
INSENSATE	KITTIWAKE	MADREPORE	MICROWAVE	NESCIENCE	OTTRELITE	PERCOLATE
INSINCERE	KNOWLEDGE	MADRILENE	MIDIANITE	NEVERMORE	OUBLIETTE	PEREGRINE
INSINUATE	KONISCOPE	MAGDALENE	MIDINETTE	NEWCASTLE	OUDENARDE	PERFORATE
INSOLENCE	LABOURITE	MAGNETIZE	MILESTONE	NIAISERIE	OVERDRIVE	PERGAMENE
INSOLUBLE	LACCOLITE	MAGNITUDE	MILKSHAKE	NICCOLITE	OVERPOISE	PERICLASE
INSTIGATE	LACINIATE	MAHARANEE	MILLEPEDE	NICTITATE	OVERSHADE	PERIODATE
INSTITUTE	LAEVULOSE	MAINFRAME	MILLEPORE	NIETZSCHE	OVERSTATE	PERISCOPE
INSURANCE	LAFAYETTE	MAJORETTE	MILLIPEDE	NIGHTFIRE	OVERVALUE	PERISTOME
INTEGRATE	LAGNIAPPE	MAJUSCULE	MILLSTONE	NIGHTMARE	OXYGENATE	PERISTYLE
INTENSIVE	LAMARTINE	MALACHITE	MINIATURE	NIGHTTIME	OZOCERITE	PERMEABLE
INTERCEDE	LAMPSHADE	MALEBOLGE	MINKSTONE	NIGRITUDE	OZOKERITE	PERSECUTE
INTERFACE	LANCINATE	MALENGINE	MINUSCULE	NIGROSINE	PAILLASSE	PERSEVERE
INTERFERE	LANDGRAVE	MALLEABLE	MIRABELLE	NINEPENCE	PAILLETTE	PERSONAGE
INTERLACE	LANDSCAPE	MANDICATE	MISBEHAVE	NIPCHEESE	PALAFITTE	PERSONATE
INTERLOPE	LANDSLIDE	MANDOLINE	MISCHANCE	NITHSDALE	PALAMPORE	PERTUSATE
INTERLUDE	LANGOUSTE	MANDUCATE	MISERABLE	NOMOTHETE	PALATABLE	PERVASIVE
INTERNODE	LANGRIDGE	MANGANATE	MISHANDLE	NOOSPHERE	PALEMPORE	PESTICIDE
INTERPOSE	LANGUETTE	MANGANESE	MISLOCATE	NORMALIZE	PALESTINE	PETHIDINE
INTERVENE	LASSITUDE	MANGOUSTE	MISMANAGE	NORMATIVE	PALLIASSE	PETULANCE
INTESTATE	LATICLAVE	MANHANDLE	MISOCLERE	NOVELETTE	PALMITATE	PHACOLITE
INTESTINE	LAUGHABLE	MANOEUVRE	MISSTROKE	NOVICIATE	PALOVERDE	PHAGOCYTE
INTRICATE	LAZZARONE	MARCASITE	MISTLETOE	NOVITIATE	PALPITATE	PHALAROPE
INTRODUCE	LEASTWISE	MARCHPANE	MITRAILLE	NOVOCAINE	PALSGRAVE	PHENACITE
INTRUSIVE	LEGISLATE	MARGARINE	MNEMOSYNE	NUMERAIRE	PALUDRINE	PHEROMONE
INTUITIVE	LEHRJAHRE	MARMALADE	MODERNIZE	NUMMULITE	PANDURATE	PHONOLITE
INTUMESCE	LEUCOCYTE	MASCULINE	MODESTINE	NUNCUPATE	PANETTONE	PHOSPHATE
INUMBRATE	LEUCOTOME	MASSORETE	MONACTINE	NUTRITIVE	PANHANDLE	PHOSPHENE
INUSITATE	LEVANTINE	MASSYMORE	MONOCOQUE	OASTHOUSE	PANTOFFLE	PHOTOGENE
INVECTIVE	LIBERTINE	MASTICATE	MONOLOGUE	OBCORDATE	PANTOMIME	PHOTOTUBE
INVENTIVE	LIFESTYLE	MATELASSE	MONOPLANE	OBEDIENCE	PANTOUFLE	PHTHALATE
INVERTASE	LIGHTFACE	MATHURINE	MONTACUTE	OBEISANCE	PAPILLOTE	PHYTOLITE
INVIOLATE	LIGHTSOME	MATRICIDE	MONTAIGNE	OBFUSCATE	PARACHUTE	PIACEVOLE
INVISIBLE	LILYWHITE	MATTAMORE	MONTICULE	OBJECTIVE	PARACLETE	PIGNERATE
INVOLUCRE	LIMEHOUSE	MEANWHILE	MONZONITE	OBJURGATE	PARAGOGUE	PILFERAGE
IODOPHILE	LIMESTONE	MECHANIZE	MOONSHINE	OBSECRATE	PARASCENE	PINEAPPLE
IPRINDOLE	LIMOUSINE	MEGACYCLE	MOONSTONE	OBSESSIVE	PARASCEVE	PINSTRIPE
IRASCIBLE	LINEOLATE	MEGAPHONE	MORECAMBE	OBSTINATE	PARBUCKLE	PIPESTONE
IRONSTONE	LIPPITUDE	MEGASCOPE	MORGANITE	OBTRUSIVE	PARDALOTE	PIROUETTE
IRRADIATE	LIQUIDATE	MEGASPORE	MORTGAGEE	ODALISQUE	PARENTAGE	PITCHPINE
IRRITABLE	LIQUIDIZE	MELAMPODE	MORTSTONE	OFFCHANCE	PARFLECHE	PITCHPOLE
ISOMERASE	LIQUORICE	MELBOURNE	MOTORBIKE	OFFENSIVE	PARHYPATE	PLAINTIVE
ISRAELITE	LITHOPONE	MELIORATE	MOTORCADE	OFFICIATE	PARNASITE	PLASTIQUE
ITALICIZE	LOADSTONE	MELONLIKE	MOUSEHOLE	OLIGOCENE	PAROCHINE	PLATITUDE
ITINERATE	LOAMSHIRE	MELPOMENE	MOUSELIKE	OLIVENITE	PARRICIDE	PLAUSIBLE
JACKKNIFE	LOATHSOME	MEMORABLE	MOUSTACHE	OMNIRANGE	PARSONAGE	PLAYHOUSE
JACKSNIPE	LOBSCOUSE	MENADIONE	MUFFETTEE	OPERATIVE	PARTRIDGE	PLEASANCE
JACQUERIE	LOCELLATE	MENAGERIE	MUGLARITE	OPPORTUNE	PASSERINE	PLEIOCENE
JARGONIZE	LODESTONE	MENNONITE	MULTITUDE	OPTOPHONE	PASTORALE	PLENITUDE
JESSAMINE	LOGOTHETE	MENOMINEE	MUMCHANCE	ORANGEADE	PASTURAGE	PLUMBLINE
JOBCENTRE	LONDONESE	MENOPAUSE	MUSCADINE	ORDINAIRE	PATERCOVE	POETICIZE
JOHANNINE	LONGITUDE	MENTICULE	MUSCARINE	ORDINANCE	PATRICIDE	POLIANITE
JOSEPHINE	LONGRANGE	MEPACRINE	MUSCOVITE	ORGANELLE	PATRONAGE	POLITESSE
JOUISANCE	LONGSHORE	MERCERIZE	MUSSITATE	ORGANZINE	PATRONIZE	POLITIQUE
JUBILANCE	LOOKALIKE	MERESWINE	MUTOSCOPE	ORICALCHE	PAYCHEQUE	POLLINATE
JUXTAPOSE	LORGNETTE	MEROCRINE	NAMEPLATE	ORIENTATE	PEACEABLE	POLONAISE
KALSOMINE	LUBRICATE	MESMERIZE	NARRATIVE	ORIFLAMME	PEACETIME	POLVERINE
KARYOTYPE	LUCRATIVE	METAPHASE	NASHVILLE	ORIGINATE	PEDAGOGUE	POLYPHASE
KENTLEDGE	LUCUBRATE	METEORITE	NATHEMORE	ORMANDINE	PEGMATITE	POLYPHONE
KERBSTONE	LUMINAIRE	METHADONE	NATHEMORE	OROBANCHE	PEKINGESE	POLYTHENE

POORHOUSE	QUINTETTE	RETICENCE	SENSITIVE	SQUADRONE	TACHILITE	TRANSPIRE
PORBEAGLE	QUINTUPLE	RETROCEDE	SENSITIZE	SQUIREAGE	TACHYLITE	TRANSPOSE
PORCUPINE	QUITTANCE	REVERENCE	SENTIENCE	STABILIZE	TACHYLYTE	TRASIMENE
PORPORATE	RACEHORSE	RHODOLITE	SEPARABLE	STAGIRITE	TAILPIECE	TREDRILLE
PORTERAGE	RADCLIFFE	RICERCARE	SEPIOLITE	STAGYRITE	TAILPLANE	TREGEAGLE
PORTREEVE	RAFFINOSE	RIDGEPOLE	SEPTIMOLE	STAIRCASE	TALKATIVE	TREILLAGE
POSTHOUSE	RAINGAUGE	RIGMAROLE	SEPULCHRE	STALEMATE	TAMERLANE	TREMATODE
POSTULATE	RANTIPOLE	RINGFENCE	SEPULTURE	STANDGALE	TANGERINE	TREMOLITE
POTENTATE	RATHERIPE	RIVERSIDE	SERAPHINE	STANDPIPE	TANTALITE	TREMULATE
POWELLITE	RATIONALE	ROADHOUSE	SERIALIZE	STARSTONE	TANTALIZE	TRIBUNATE
PRECIEUSE	REACHABLE	ROCAMBOLE	SERMONIZE	STATESIDE	TEACHABLE	TRIDYMITE
PRECIPICE	REACTANCE	ROSINANTE	SERREFILE	STATEWIDE	TEAKETTLE	TRILOBITE
PRECISIVE	READYMADE	ROSMARINE	SERVIETTE	STATUETTE	TECHNIQUE	TRITICALE
PRECONISE	REANIMATE	ROTAPLANE	SERVITUDE	STERILIZE	TELEPHONE	TRITURATE
PREDICATE	REARHORSE	ROTUNDATE	SEVERANCE	STEVEDORE	TELESCOPE	TROMPETTE
PREFIGURE	REARMOUSE	ROUSSETTE	SHELDRAKE	STIMULATE	TELOPHASE	TROOSTITE
PREJUDICE	REARRANGE	ROXBURGHE	SHEMOZZLE	STINGAREE	TEMPERATE	TRUTINATE
PREMATURE	RECAPTURE	ROZINANTE	SHENSTONE	STIPULATE	TEMPORIZE	TUILLETTE
PRESCRIBE	RECEPTIVE	RUBBERIZE	SHIPSHAPE	STOCKPILE	TEMULENCE	TUMMYACHE
PRETERITE	RECESSIVE	RUBICELLE	SHOESHINE	STONEWARE	TENDERIZE	TUNGSTATE
PRIMITIAE	RECOGNIZE	RUDDIGORE	SHORTCAKE	STORYLINE	TENEBROSE	TURBINATE
PRIMITIVE	RECONCILE	RUNCINATE	SHOWPIECE	STOVEPIPE	TENNESSEE	TURCOPOLE
PRIMULINE	RECONDITE	RUNESTAVE	SHRINKAGE	STREETAGE	TENTATIVE	TURNSTILE
PRINCIPLE	RECONVENE	RUNNYMEDE	SIBILANCE	STRICTURE	TERMINATE	TURNSTONE
PRINTABLE	RECTANGLE	RUSTICATE	SIBYLLINE	STRONGYLE	TERRICOLE	TURNTABLE
PRIVATIZE	RECTITUDE	SACRIFICE	SICCATIVE	STRUCTURE	TERRORIZE	TURPITUDE
PRIVILEGE	RECURSIVE	SACRILEGE	SIDESWIPE	STYLOBATE	TESTDRIVE	TURQUOISE
PROACTIVE	RECUSANCE	SALANGANE	SIGNATURE	SUBDIVIDE	THELEMITE	TWAYBLADE
PROCEDURE	REDINGOTE	SALOPETTE	SILTSTONE	SUBENTIRE	THERALITE	TYRANNIZE
PROCREATE	REDOLENCE	SALTPETRE	SILURIDAE	SUBJUGATE	THEREFORE	UMBRATILE
PROENZYME	REDUCIBLE	SANDSTONE	SILVEREYE	SUBLIMATE	THIGHBONE	UNBALANCE
PROGRAMME	REEXAMINE	SARBACANE	SIMEONITE	SUBMARINE	THINKABLE	UNCONFINE
PROLAMINE	REFERENCE	SASSOLITE	SIMPLISTE	SUBROGATE	THORNDYKE	UNDERBITE
PROMENADE	REFINANCE	SATELLITE	SINGALESE	SUBSCRIBE	THREESOME	UNDERDONE
PRONOUNCE	REFLEXIVE	SATURNINE	SINGAPORE	SUBSIDIZE	THREONINE	UNDERLINE
PROPAGATE	REIMBURSE	SATYRIDAE	SIPHUNCLE	SUBSTANCE	THYLACINE	UNDERMINE
PROPYLENE	REINFORCE	SATYRINAE	SKEDADDLE	SUBSTRATE	THYROXINE	UNDERRATE
PROROGATE	REINSTATE	SAVERNAKE	SLABSTONE	SUCCINATE	TICHBORNE	UNDERSIDE
PROSCRIBE	REITERATE	SAXIFRAGE	SLANTWISE	SUCCUBINE	TICTACTOE	UNDERTAKE
PROSECUTE	RELEVANCE	SAXOPHONE	SLUGHORNE	SUFFOCATE	TIGHTROPE	UNDERTONE
PROSELYTE	RELIGEUSE	SCALEABLE	SMALLTIME	SUGARCANE	TIMEPIECE	UNEATABLE
PROSTRATE	RELIQUIAE	SCAPOLITE	SMOKEFREE	SULTANATE	TIMESHARE	UNPRECISE
PROTAMINE	REMINISCE	SCELERATE	SNOWFLAKE	SUMMARIZE	TIMETABLE	UNSHACKLE
PROTOTYPE	REMOULADE	SCHEELITE	SNOWWHITE	SUNSTROKE	TINGUAITE	UNSHEATHE
PROUSTITE	REMOVABLE	SCHIAVONE	SOAPSTONE	SUPERETTE	TIPULIDAE	UNTENABLE
PROVEDORE	RENCONTRE	SCHNITTKE	SOCIALITE	SUPERFINE	TISIPHONE	UNWELCOME
PROVOLONE	RENEWABLE	SCHNOZZLE	SOCIALIZE	SUPERSEDE	TITILLATE	UPPERCASE
PROXIMATE	REPAYABLE	SCIARIDAE	SOLEMNIZE	SUPERVENE	TOADSTONE	UROKINASE
PRURIENCE	REPECHAGE	SCOLECITE	SOLITAIRE	SUPERVISE	TOLERABLE	USHERETTE
PUBLICIZE	REPLETIVE	SCORODITE	SOMASCOPE	SUPPURATE	TOLERANCE	UTTERANCE
PUCELLAGE	REPLICATE	SCREWPINE	SOMEPLACE	SURCHARGE	TOLLHOUSE	UVAROVITE
PUISSANCE	REPORTAGE	SCREWTAPE	SOMEWHERE	SURCINGLE	TOLPUDDLE	VACCINATE
PULLULATE	REPROBATE	SCRIMMAGE	SOPHOMORE	SURROGATE	TOMBSTONE	VACILLATE
PULMONATE	REPRODUCE	SCRIPTURE	SORTILEGE	SUSCITATE	TOMENTOSE	VALENTINE
PULVERIZE	REPUDIATE	SCRUMMAGE	SOUBRETTE	SWANIMOTE	TONBRIDGE	VANDALIZE
PUNCHLINE	REPULSIVE	SCULPTURE	SOUFRIERE	SWINBURNE	TOOTHACHE	VARIEGATE
PUNCTUATE	REPUTABLE	SEABOTTLE	SOUNDBITE	SYLPHLIKE	TOOTHSOME	VARIOLATE
PUPILLAGE	REQUISITE	SECRETIVE	SOVENANCE	SYLVANITE	TORBANITE	VARISCITE
PURGATIVE	REREMOUSE	SEDUCTIVE	SPATULATE	SYMBOLIZE	TOTAQUINE	VEGETABLE
PURSUANCE	RESERPINE	SEGREGATE	SPEARSIDE	SYNAGOGUE	TOUCHLINE	VEHEMENCE
PURULENCE	RESHUFFLE	SELECTIVE	SPECTACLE	SYNCOPATE	TRACEABLE	VEILLEUSE
QUADRILLE	RESIDENCE	SELLOTAPE	SPECULATE	SYNDICATE	TRACTABLE	VELLENAGE
QUADRUPLE	RESONANCE	SEMANTEME	SPHENDONE	SYNOECETE	TRAINABLE	VELLICATE
QUAILPIPE	RESTITUTE	SEMANTIDE	SPICILEGE	SYRPHIDAE	TRANSFUSE	VELODROME
QUARTETTE	RESURFACE	SEMAPHORE	SPODUMENE	TABANIDAE	TRANSHUME	VENERABLE
QUENNELLE	RETALIATE	SEMBLANCE	SPRAICKLE	TABLATURE	TRANSLATE	VENGEANCE
QUICKLIME	RETENTIVE	SEMIBREVE	SPRAUCHLE	TABLEWARE	TRANSMUTE	VENTILATE

VENTRICLE	WORKFORCE	BREATHING	GRAPPLING	OPERATING	SCANTLING	UNDERLING
VERATRINE	WORKHORSE	BREECHING	GROUNDHOG	OVERLYING	SCHELLING	UNDERSONG
VERBALIZE	WORKHOUSE	BRISTLING	GROUNDING	PACKAGING	SCHILLING	UNFAILING
VERBERATE	WORKPLACE	BUFFETING	GRUELLING	PANELLING	SCHOOLING	UNFEELING
VERITABLE	WORKSPACE	BUNDESTAG	GRUMBLING	PARENTING	SCORCHING	UNFITTING
VERKAMPTE	WORLDWIDE	BURROWING	GUTENBERG	PARTAKING	SCRAPPING	UNHEEDING
VERMIFUGE	WORRISOME	CARPETING	GUTTERING	PERISHING	SCREENING	UNKNOWING
VERSATILE	WULFENITE	CAVORTING	HAMMERING	PHILLABEG	SCRIMPING	UNNERVING
VERTEBRAE	WYANDOTTE	CENTERING	HAMSTRING	PHILLIBEG	SCRUBBING	UNSINNING
VESTIBULE	XANTHIPPE	CENTREING	HAMSTRUNG	PICKETING	SCRUMPING	UNSPARING
VESTITURE	XENOPHOBE	CLEANSING	HANKERING	PILFERING	SCULPTING	UNVARYING
VIBRATILE	XEROPHYTE	CLEARWING	HAPPENING	PLAINSONG	SEAFARING	UNWILLING
VICEREINE	XYLOPHONE	COLOURING	HARROWING	PLAYTHING	SEARCHING	UNWITTING
VICTIMIZE	YESTEREVE	COMPETING	HASTENING	POISONING	SEASONING	UPLIFTING
VICTORINE	YOHIMBINE	COMPOSING	HAYMAKING	POPPERING	SELECTING	UPSETTING
VIDEOTAPE	YORKSHIRE	COMPUTING	HEARTHRUG	POTHOLING	SERVICING	VANISHING
VIENTIANE	ZENOCRATE	CONFUSING	HECTORING	PRECEDING	SHAVELING	VENUSBERG
VIGILANCE	ZIBELLINE	CONJURING	HIJACKING	PRESSGANG	SHEARLING	WALLOPING
VIGILANTE	ZINKENITE	CONSUMING	IMPELLING	PROMISING	SHIELDING	WALLOWING
VINDICATE	ZYGOSPORE	CRACKLING	IMPENDING	PROMPTING	SHIVERING	WALLYDRAG
VIRGULATE	ASTROTURF	CRIPPLING	IMPROVING	PROVIDING	SHRIMPING	WANDERING
VIRULENCE	BOOKSHELF	CRUMBLING	INCLUDING	PROVOKING	SHRINKING	WEAKENING
VISAGISTE	DISBELIEF	DAYSPRING	INFECTING	PUNISHING	SHUFFLING	WEIGHTING
VISUALIZE	FEEDSTUFF	DEAFENING	INGROWING	PURIFYING	SICKENING	WELCOMING
VITASCOPE	FIREPROOF	DECLARING	INQUIRING	PYONGYANG	SLOUGHING	WELLBEING
VOLATIBLE	FLAGSTAFF	DECLINING	INSELBERG	QUAVERING	SMUGGLING	WHIRLIGIG
VOLUCRINE	FOODSTUFF	DEGRADING	INSPIRING	QUIVERING	SOFTENING	WHISTLING
VOUCHSAFE	FOOLPROOF	DEMANDING	INSULTING	RADIATING	SOLDERING	WHITENING
VULCANITE	HALFSTAFF	DEMEANING	INTENDING	RATIONING	SOMETHING	WHITEWING
VULCANIZE	HEADSCARF	DEPENDING	INVOICING	RATTLEBAG	SPARKLING	WHIZZBANG
VULPINITE	LEAKPROOF	DESERVING	JARLSBERG	RAVISHING	SPELDRING	WILLOWING
VULTURINE	LEITMOTIF	DESIGNING	JENNETING	REASONING	SPLITTING	WITHERING
WAGNERITE	LOOSELEAF	DIPHTHONG	JITTERBUG	RECALLING	SPONGEBAG	WOBBEGONG
WAGONETTE	OVENPROOF	DISABLING	JOCKTELEG	RECEIVING	SPREADING	WOOMERANG
WAHABIITE	PECKSNIFF	DISARMING	JUNKETING	RECKONING	SQUINTING	WRESTLING
WAISTLINE	PIKESTAFF	DITHERING	LAUNCHING	RECORDING	SQUIRMING	WUTHERING
WAITERAGE	PLAINTIFF	DIVERGING	LAWMAKING	RECURRING	STARTLING	AFTERMATH
WALDFLUTE	SKEWWHIFF	DIVERTING	LETTERING	REDEEMING	STRAINING	AINSWORTH
WALDGRAVE	ABOUNDING	DOODLEBUG	LIGHTNING	REFERRING	STRAPHANG	ALLOGRAPH
WAPENTAKE	ABSORBING	DOWELLING	LINGERING	REGARDING	STRAPPING	ANABRANCH
WAREHOUSE	ACCORDING	DWINDLING	LISTENING	REICHSTAG	STREAMING	ANGELFISH
WATERGATE	ADJOINING	EARTHLING	LOITERING	REJOICING	STRIPLING	AUTOGRAPH
WATERHOLE	ADMITTING	EASYGOING	LUMBERING	REMAINING	STROLLING	AUXOTROPH
WATERLINE	AFFECTING	EMBRACING	LUXEMBURG	RENDERING	STRUTTING	AYATOLLAH
WATERSIDE	AGONIZING	ENDEARING	MACHINING	REPELLING	STUMBLING	BACHARACH
WAVELLITE	ANOINTING	ENGRAVING	MADDENING	REPLACING	SUFFERING	BACKBENCH
WAYZGOOSE	ANSWERING	ENQUIRING	MAGDEBURG	REPORTING	SUPPOSING	BACKCLOTH
WEARISOME	APPALLING	EXCLUDING	MANNERING	REPROVING	SURVEYING	BACKSHISH
WHALEBONE	APPEALING	EXPECTING	MARAUDING	RESORTING	SURVIVING	BAKSHEESH
WHEELBASE	APPROVING	EXPORTING	MARKETING	RESULTING	SWADDLING	BLOODBATH
WHEREFORE	ARMSTRONG	FASTENING	MEASURING	RETAILING	SWINGEING	BLOWTORCH
WHETSTONE	ARRESTING	FATTENING	MISFIRING	RETAINING	SWOTHLING	BOBSLEIGH
WHINSTONE	ASCENDING	FILTERING	MISGIVING	RETURNING	TERRACING	BOXWALLAH
WHIPSNADE	ASSERTING	FINGERING	MODELLING	REVEALING	THATCHING	BRADLAUGH
WHOLESALE	ATTACKING	FINICKING	MOTHERING	REVELLING	THIRSTING	BRAINWASH
WHOLESOME	AWAKENING	FINISHING	MURMURING	REVERSING	THRASHING	BUCKTEETH
WHUNSTANE	BANTERING	FLAVORING	MUTTERING	REVOLTING	THRILLING	BULLFINCH
WILDGEESE	BEGINNING	FLEDGLING	NARROWING	REVOLVING	THROBBING	CAVENDISH
WILLEMITE	BELIEVING	FLOWERING	NIDDERING	REWARDING	THRONGING	CERECLOTH
WINCOPIPE	BELONGING	FOLKETING	NIDERLING	REWORKING	THUMBLING	CHAFFINCH
WINDSCALE	BILLABONG	FOLLOWING	NIEBELUNG	RIDGELING	TOWELLING	CHOLELITH
WITHERITE	BILLOWING	FOREGOING	NUREMBERG	RIGHTWING	TRAVELING	COCKROACH
WODEHOUSE	BOOMERANG	FORGIVING	OBTAINING	SADDENING	TREMBLING	COLOCYNTH
WOEBEGONE	BORDERING	FOUNDLING	OCCUPYING	SADDLEBAG	TWINKLING	CORNBRASH
WOLVERINE	BORROWING	GARDENING	ODELSTING	SCALLAWAG	UNBENDING	CYCLOLITH
WOODHOUSE	BRAMBLING	GATHERING	OFFENDING	SCALLYWAG	UNCEASING	DARTMOUTH
WOODLOUSE	BRANCHING	GOVERNING	OFFSPRING	SCAMBLING	UNDERHUNG	DEVILFISH

DISHCLOTH	MESOMORPH	TEREBINTH	CARTTRACK	PIECEWORK	ANCESTRAL	DISPERSAL
DJELLABAH	MICROINCH	THIRTIETH	CHEAPJACK	PIGGYBACK	ANCIPITAL	DOCTRINAL
ECTOMORPH	MICROLITH	TOVARISCH	CHECKBOOK	PIGGYBANK	ANECDOTAL	DODDIPOLL
EDGEWORTH	MILLIONTH	TRAGELAPH	CHINOVNIK	PILLICOCK	ANTENATAL	DOMINICAL
EDINBURGH	MONOGRAPH	TRIERARCH	CLOCKWORK	PINCHBECK	ANTINOVEL	DROPSICAL
EIDOGRAPH	MONOSTICH	TRUNKFISH	CORNSTALK	PINCHCOCK	APPRAISAL	EDITORIAL
EIGHTIETH	MONOTROCH	TSAREVICH	CROOKBACK	PIPSQUEAK	ARCHANGEL	EFFECTUAL
ELIZABETH	MOUTHWASH	TWENTIETH	CROSSWALK	PITCHFORK	ARSENICAL	ELECTORAL
EMBELLISH	NEWSFLASH	UMPTEENTH	DISEMBARK	POKERWORK	ASTROPHEL	ELEMENTAL
ENDOMORPH	NINETIETH	UNSELFISH	DRUMSTICK	POPPYCOCK	AUCTORIAL	EMOTIONAL
ESTABLISH	OCTASTICH	WASHCLOTH	DUBROVNIK	PRESHRUNK	BACKPEDAL	EMPIRICAL
FACECLOTH	OFFENBACH	WHITEFISH	DUIKERBOK	RACETRACK	BACTERIAL	ENCHORIAL
FIFTEENTH	OLEOGRAPH	WHITEWASH	EARTHWORK	RAINCHECK	BAPTISMAL	ENSORCELL
FORASMUCH	OSTEOPATH	WHITWORTH	FASTTRACK	RASKOLNIK	BASILICAL	ENTRAMMEL
FORTHWITH	OSTROGOTH	WORDSMITH	FENUGREEK	REDSTREAK	BASKETFUL	ENVERMEIL
FRITHBORH	OUTGROWTH	WRECKFISH	FIELDWORK	REFUSENIK	BATHTOWEL	EPHEMERAL
FROGMARCH	OVERREACH	YELLOWISH	FIREBREAK	REYKJAVIK	BEAUTIFUL	EPISCOPAL
FROGMOUTH	OVERWEIGH	ZECHARIAH	FLASHBACK	RIDGEBACK	BECQUEREL	EQUIVOCAL
GALLABEAH	PALEOLITH	ZEPHANIAH	FLINTLOCK	ROADBLOCK	BETROTHAL	ERISTICAL
GATECRASH	PARAGRAPH	ASHKENAZI	FORESPEAK	ROOTSTOCK	BILATERAL	ESSENTIAL
GIBBERISH	PARANYMPH	BARTHOLDI	FORTHWINK	ROUGHNECK	BILINGUAL	EVITERNAL
GILGAMESH	PATRIARCH	CARBONARI	FRAMEWORK	ROUNDBACK	BLACKBALL	FACTIONAL
GOALMOUTH	PERGUNNAH	CEVAPCICI	FREDERICK	SCRAPBOOK	BLACKMAIL	FACTORIAL
GOLDFINCH	PERIMORPH	CHARIVARI	GANGPLANK	SHASHLICK	BOMBSHELL	FALDSTOOL
GOLDSMITH	POLEMARCH	CHERUBINI	GEARSTICK	SHELDDUCK	BOOKSTALL	FANATICAL
GREENWICH	POLYGRAPH	DECEMVIRI	GOOSENECK	SHELLBACK	BOTANICAL	FATIDICAL
HAIRBRUSH	POLYMORPH	DONIZETTI	GREENBACK	SHIFTWORK	BOTTLEFUL	FICTIONAL
HEADCLOTH	PREMONISH	GALLIPOLI	GUESSWORK	SHIPWRECK	BOUNTIFUL	FINANCIAL
HEMISTICH	RATHERISH	GARIBALDI	GUIDEBOOK	SIDETRACK	BRIDEWELL	FLORIMELL
HEMSTITCH	REFURBISH	GUJARATHI	HANDIWORK	SLAPSTICK	BRONCHIAL	FLOURMILL
HEXASTICH	REPLENISH	HAMMURABI	HATCHBACK	SLEEPWALK	BUCKETFUL	FOOTSTALL
HEXATEUCH	RORSCHACH	KISWAHILI	HAVERSACK	SLINGBACK	CADASTRAL	FOOTSTOOL
HINDEMITH	ROUMANSCH	LAMASERAI	HITCHCOCK	SOUTHWARK	CANAVERAL	FORESTALL
HODOGRAPH	ROUNDFISH	MAHARISHI	HOLLYHOCK	SPRINGBOK	CANONICAL	FORGETFUL
HOLLERITH	RUGGELACH	MATAGOURI	HONKYTONK	STEENKIRK	CARTWHEEL	FOSSORIAL
HOLOGRAPH	SABLEFISH	MUSSOLINI	HORSEBACK	STEINBECK	CATARRHAL	FOURWHEEL
HOMEOPATH	SACKCLOTH	NEFERTITI	HOUSELEEK	STEINBOCK	CATCHPOLL	FRATERNAL
HOMOGRAPH	SAGEBRUSH	PAGLIACCI	HOUSEWORK	STOCKWORK	CATERWAUL	FREEWHEEL
HOPSCOTCH	SAILCLOTH	PAKISTANI	HUCKABACK	STONEWORK	CATHEDRAL	FRIGHTFUL
HOYDENISH	SANDARACH	PAPARAZZI	HUNCHBACK	STORYBOOK	CELESTIAL	GEARWHEEL
HUNDREDTH	SASQUATCH	PARCHEESI	HYPERLINK	STUMPWORK	CHAPARRAL	GENETICAL
IDEOGRAPH	SASSENACH	PATCHOULI	INGLENOOK	TAVISTOCK	CHARGEFUL	GRAPHICAL
IDIOGRAPH	SCALDFISH	PEPPERONI	INTERLOCK	THORNBACK	CHURCHILL	GREENMAIL
INSHALLAH	SCHEHITAH	POTPOURRI	KNOBSTICK	THROWBACK	CLASSICAL	GROUNDSEL
JAGGANATH	SCHOLARCH	SCARLATTI	LAMPBLACK	THUMBTACK	COCHINEAL	GRUBBINOL
JELLYFISH	SERIGRAPH	SERENGETI	LAPSTREAK	TOASTRACK	COCKATIEL	GUARDRAIL
JOBSWORTH	SHAMIANAH	SPAGHETTI	LEAFSTALK	TOOTHPICK	COLLOIDAL	GUILDHALL
KHANSAMAH	SHECHINAH	STROMBOLI	LEASEBACK	TOWNSFOLK	COLOURFUL	HARDSHELL
KINKCOUGH	SHECHITAH	TOSCANINI	LINTSTOCK	TRADEMARK	COMMENSAL	HAWKSBILL
KITTENISH	SHELLFISH	AGUECHEEK	LIVESTOCK	TREETRUNK	COMMITTAL	HEADSTALL
LABYRINTH	SIXTEENTH	APPLEJACK	MALLEMUCK	UNDERWALK	CONFORMAL	HEPATICAL
LADYSMITH	SLOWCOACH	AWESTRUCK	MATCHBOOK	VIDEODISK	CONGENIAL	HERETICAL
LAGOMORPH	SNAILFISH	BACKTRACK	MATCHLOCK	WATERMARK	CONNUBIAL	HESTERNAL
LASTDITCH	SONGSMITH	BARMBRACK	MAULSTICK	WINDBREAK	CONTINUAL	HEXAGONAL
LICKERISH	SOURDOUGH	BEEFSTEAK	MENSHEVIK	WISECRACK	CONVIVIAL	HOBBINOLL
LINDBERGH	SPOFFORTH	BENCHMARK	METALWORK	WOMENFOLK	CORPOREAL	HODIERNAL
LIQUORISH	SQUEAMISH	BERGAMASK	MOLLYMAWK	WOODCHUCK	CROSSBILL	HOMICIDAL
LOCKSMITH	STALWORTH	BERGOMASK	NIGHTHAWK	WOODSHOCK	CROWSBILL	HORSETAIL
LOGOGRIPH	STATOLITH	BILLYCOCK	NIGHTWORK	YARDSTICK	CURVEBALL	HYDROFOIL
LOINCLOTH	STOCKFISH	BIRTHMARK	NOTCHBACK	ABDOMINAL	CUSTODIAL	IDENTICAL
LOUDMOUTH	SUCCOTASH	BLACKBUCK	PAINTWORK	ACCENTUAL	DAREDEVIL	ILLIBERAL
LUBAVITCH	SUQUAMISH	BLACKJACK	PAPERBACK	ACQUITTAL	DASHWHEEL	ILLOGICAL
MADRASSAH	SWORDFISH	BOARDWALK	PAPERWORK	ACROPETAL	DECEITFUL	IMPARTIAL
MADRESSAH	TABBOULEH	BOLSHEVIK	PASTERNAK	ACTUARIAL	DECENNIAL	INAUGURAL
MAHARAJAH	TAOISEACH	BOOTBLACK	PATCHWORK	ADENOIDAL	DECONTROL	INNISFAIL
MATRIARCH	TELEGRAPH	BREAKNECK	PICKABACK	ADVERBIAL	DIALECTAL	ISOCLINAL
MEDRESSEH	TELESTICH	BRICKWORK	PICKTHANK	AMBROSIAL	DISMISSAL	ISOPROPYL

JERAHMEEL	PREVERNAL	TORMENTIL	CALCANEUM	GARGARISM	MUTUALISM	STATEROOM
JOBERNOWL	PRIMAEVAL	TRANSVAAL	CALDARIUM	GERMANIUM	MYSTICISM	STILLROOM
JURIDICAL	PRINCIPAL	TRAPEZIAL	CALVANISM	GIGANTISM	NEODYMIUM	STOCKHOLM
KNAPSCULL	PROCONSUL	TREADMILL	CAPITULUM	GLUCINIUM	NEOLOGISM	STOCKROOM
KNAPSKULL	PRODROMAL	TRIENNIAL	CARTOGRAM	GONGORISM	NEPHALISM	STOREROOM
LACHRYMAL	PSYCHICAL	TRIUMPHAL	CATACLYSM	GOSSYPIUM	NEPTUNIUM	STRATAGEM
LACONICAL	PUERPERAL	UMBILICAL	CATAPLASM	GREENROOM	OCULIFORM	STRONGARM
LAMBSWOOL	PYRAMIDAL	UNDERSEAL	CATECHISM	GUARDROOM	OPERCULUM	STRONTIUM
LANDSMAAL	QUANTICAL	UNDERSELL	CENTIGRAM	GYMNASIUM	OPOBALSAM	SYLLOGISM
LANGSPIEL	QUIVERFUL	UNETHICAL	CHECKROOM	GYNOECIUM	OPPENHEIM	SYMBOLISM
LIVERPOOL	QUIZZICAL	UNHELPFUL	CHEONGSAM	HAILSTORM	OSTEODERM	SYMPODIUM
MARMOREAL	RAPTORIAL	UNHOPEFUL	CHERNOZEM	HARMONIUM	OSTRACISM	SYMPOSIUM
MARSUPIAL	RAZORBILL	UNISEXUAL	CLASSROOM	HECTOGRAM	OVERWHELM	SYNANGIUM
MASTERFUL	RECTORIAL	UNIVERSAL	CLINGFILM	HERBARIUM	PACHYDERM	SYNCOMIUM
MATUTINAL	REGARDFUL	UNMINDFUL	CLOAKROOM	HESYCHASM	PALLADIUM	SYRIACISM
MEDIAEVAL	REGRETFUL	UNMUSICAL	COENOBIUM	HISTOGRAM	PANEGOISM	TARAXACUM
MEDICINAL	REHEARSAL	UNNATURAL	COFFERDAM	HORDEOLUM	PANTHEISM	TECTIFORM
MEHITABEL	REISTAFEL	UNTYPICAL	COLCHICUM	HOSPITIUM	PELMANISM	TELLURIUM
MENSTRUAL	RESENTFUL	UREDINIAL	COLLYRIUM	HOUSEROOM	PENTAGRAM	TENACULUM
MERCURIAL	RETRIEVAL	VERIDICAL	COLOSSEUM	HOUYHNHNM	PESSIMISM	TENTORIUM
MILLENIAL	REVICTUAL	VERSIONAL	COLOSTRUM	HYPNOTISM	PETERSHAM	TERRARIUM
MISPICKEL	ROUNCEVAL	VERTEBRAL	COLUMBIUM	IDIOPLASM	PETROLEUM	TERRORISM
MONASTRAL	ROUNCIVAL	VESTIGIAL	COMINFORM	IMPLUVIUM	PHENAKISM	TETRAGRAM
MOSCHATEL	SALESGIRL	VICEREGAL	COMMUNISM	INDECORUM	PHITONIUM	THANATISM
MOURNIVAL	SARTORIAL	VIGESIMAL	CONTINUUM	IRVINGISM	PHONOGRAM	THRALLDOM
MOYGASHEL	SATIRICAL	WATERFALL	CONUNDRUM	JANSENISM	PICTOGRAM	TORMENTUM
MUNICIPAL	SCEPTICAL	WATERFOWL	COURTROOM	JERUSALEM	PIPEDREAM	TOTTENHAM
MUSICHALL	SCHLEMIEL	WATERMILL	CRIBELLUM	JETSTREAM	PLURALISM	TRANSFORM
MYOFIBRIL	SCHLEMIHL	WHEATMEAL	CRITICISM	KARAKORAM	PLUTONIUM	TRAPEZIUM
NATHANIEL	SCHNITZEL	WHIMSICAL	CROSSBEAM	KOMINFORM	POMOERIUM	TRIBALISM
NEUCHATEL	SCHNORKEL	WHIRLPOOL	CRUCIFORM	LANDSTURM	POTASSIUM	TRIFORIUM
NEWSSTALL	SCLEROTAL	WHITEHALL	CRYPTOGAM	LANTHANUM	PRESCUTUM	TRONDHEIM
NIGHTFALL	SCOUNDREL	WHITEWALL	CUNEIFORM	LATHYRISM	PRESIDIUM	TUTIORISM
NOCTURNAL	SCREWBALL	WHOLEMEAL	CYMBIDIUM	LECANORAM	PRYTANEUM	ULTIMATUM
NONPAREIL	SDEIGNFUL	WINDCHILL	DALTONISM	LOGARITHM	PSEUDONYM	UNCHRISOM
NUMBSKULL	SECTIONAL	WONDERFUL	DEFEATISM	MACROCOSM	PTERIDIUM	UNUNUNIUM
NUMERICAL	SECTORIAL	YGGDRASIL	DESPOTISM	MAELSTROM	PURDONIUM	VANDALISM
OCCIPITAL	SEMIFINAL	ZINFANDEL	DEUTERIUM	MAGNALIUM	PYRETHRUM	VERBASCUM
OCTAGONAL	SEMIVOWEL	AIRSTREAM	DIAPHRAGM	MAGNESIUM	RACIALISM	VERMIFORM
ORGANICAL	SENESCHAL	ALGORITHM	DISAFFIRM	MAGNETISM	RADIOGRAM	VIRGINIUM
OVERSPILL	SHORTFALL	ALUMINIUM	DOGMATISM	MANNERISM	RAINSTORM	VOLCANISM
PALPEBRAL	SHORTHAUL	AMERICIUM	EARTHWORM	MANUBRIUM	REDDENDUM	VOLTINISM
PANNIKELL	SHOVELFUL	AMSTERDAM	ECOSYSTEM	MARSUPIUM	RESTIFORM	VOODOOISM
PANTHENOL	SINGSPIEL	ANABOLISM	ECTOPLASM	MARTYRDOM	RETICULUM	VORTICISM
PAROCHIAL	SKEPTICAL	ANGIOGRAM	ECTOTHERM	MASOCHISM	RIBBONISM	VULGARISM
PERENNIAL	SNEERWELL	ANGLICISM	EFFINGHAM	MAUSOLEUM	ROSTELLUM	WAGENBOOM
PERPETUAL	SORROWFUL	ANIMALISM	EFFLUVIUM	MECHANISM	ROTTERDAM	WHEATGERM
PERSONNEL	SPEEDWELL	ANTISERUM	ELATERIUM	MEDMENHAM	RUTHENIUM	WITTICISM
PICTORIAL	SPHERICAL	ARBORETUM	ELBOWROOM	MENDELISM	SACRARIUM	YTTERBIUM
PIECEMEAL	SPIRITUAL	ASPLENIUM	ENCOLPIUM	MENSTRUUM	SAGAPENUM	ZIRCONIUM
PIMPERNEL	SPOONBILL	ATHENAEUM	ENDOSPERM	MESMERISM	SALICETUM	ABDUCTION
PIRATICAL	SPRITEFUL	AUTEURISM	ENTROPIUM	METHODISM	SANDSTORM	ABOLITION
PITCHPOLL	SPRITSAIL	BACTERIUM	EPICEDIUM	MICROCOSM	SANHEDRIM	ABOUTTURN
PLAUSTRAL	STERCORAL	BARBARISM	EPIPHRAGM	MICROFILM	SARMENTUM	ACCESSION
PLENTIFUL	STONEWALL	BARNSTORM	EPIPOLISM	MIDRASHIM	SATURNISM	ACCORDION
POCKETFUL	STOOLBALL	BERKELIUM	EQUISETUM	MIDSTREAM	SCALARIUM	ACCRETION
POLEMICAL	STRESSFUL	BERYLLIUM	EROTICISM	MILLIGRAM	SCIENTISM	ADDICTION
POLITICAL	SUBFOSSIL	BETHLEHEM	ERPINGHAM	MISINFORM	SENSILLUM	ADMISSION
POLYGONAL	SUBNORMAL	BLINDWORM	ERUCIFORM	MITHRAISM	SENSORIUM	ADORATION
POPLITEAL	SUCCURSAL	BLOODWORM	EUPHEMISM	MODERNISM	SEPHARDIM	ADRENALIN
PORTRAYAL	SUPERCOOL	BOARDROOM	EUPHONIUM	MONERGISM	SHEIKHDOM	ADULATION
POSTNATAL	TECHNICAL	BROADLOOM	EXTREMISM	MONGOLISM	SHINTOISM	ADVECTION
POTENTIAL	TECTORIAL	BRUMMAGEM	FEUDALISM	MONTANISM	SHORTTERM	AFFECTION
PRACTICAL	TERPINEOL	BRUTALISM	FLABELLUM	MORMONISM	SNOWSTORM	AFLATOXIN
PRACTOLOL	THORNBILL	BUBBLEGUM	FLAGELLUM	MRIDAMGAM	SOCIALISM	AFTERNOON
PREBENDAL	THUMBNAIL	CABLEGRAM	GALLICISM	MRIDANGAM	SOLIPSISM	AGAMEMNON
PRESIDIAL	TOADSTOOL	CAIRNGORM	GALVANISM	MULTIFORM	SPIRITISM	AGITATION

ALDEBARAN	CARNELIAN	CTESIPHON	EPILATION	GUARDSMAN	KENTIGERN	NORWEGIAN
ALPENHORN	CARTESIAN	CUCHULAIN	EPINICION	GUNCOTTON	KEPLARIAN	NOTARIKON
AMARANTIN	CASSATION	CUSTODIAN	EPINIKION	GUSTATION	KILDERKIN	NUTRITION
AMBROSIAN	CASTELLAN	CYCLOTRON	EPULATION	HABERGEON	KINSWOMAN	OARSWOMAN
AMPHIBIAN	CASTILIAN	CYTOKININ	ERUDITION	HACQUETON	KNOCKDOWN	OBJECTION
ANATOLIAN	CATAMARAN	DAEDALIAN	ETHIOPIAN	HALFDOZEN	KROPOTKIN	OBREPTION
ANCHORMAN	CATHEPSIN	DALMATIAN	EUCLIDEAN	HALLOWEEN	KRUMMHORN	OBSESSION
ANIMATION	CATTLEMAN	DAMNATION	EUSKARIAN	HARLEQUIN	LACTATION	OBTRUSION
ANTITOXIN	CATTLEPEN	DANDELION	EVAGATION	HARLESTON	LAMPADION	OBVENTION
ANTIVENIN	CAUCASIAN	DARTAGNAN	EVERGREEN	HARMATTAN	LAODICEAN	OCCLUSION
APPERTAIN	CAUSATION	DARWINIAN	EVOCATION	HARTSHORN	LARGITION	OCTILLION
APPORTION	CENTURION	DECAMERON	EVOLUTION	HAYRADDIN	LATRATION	ODDJOBMAN
ARLINGTON	CESSATION	DECATHLON	EXARATION	HEARDSMAN	LAUDATION	OESTROGEN
ARTHURIAN	CHALAZION	DECEPTION	EXCAMBION	HEARTBURN	LESTRIGON	OFFSEASON
ASCENSION	CHALIAPIN	DECESSION	EXCEPTION	HEBRIDEAN	LEVIATHAN	OLECRANON
ASCERTAIN	CHAMELEON	DECILLION	EXCISEMAN	HECOGENIN	LIBRARIAN	OLEORESIN
ASHMOLEAN	CHAMFRAIN	DECOCTION	EXCLUSION	HELVELLYN	LIVERYMAN	OMBUDSMAN
ASPERSION	CHAMPAIGN	DEDUCTION	EXCURSION	HERCULEAN	LIVRAISON	OPERATION
ASSERTION	CHAMPLAIN	DEFECTION	EXECUTION	HESPERIAN	LOHENGRIN	ORANGEMAN
ASTRAKHAN	CHARLATAN	DEFLATION	EXEMPTION	HEXAMERON	LONGICORN	ORATORIAN
ASYNDETON	CHARWOMAN	DEJECTION	EXORATION	HIBERNIAN	LUCIFERIN	ORPHARION
ATHELSTAN	CHAWBACON	DENTITION	EXPANSION	HIMALAYAN	LUCTATION	ORPINGTON
ATTENTION	CHIEFTAIN	DEPICTION	EXPIATION	HINDBRAIN	MACTATION	OTTERBURN
ATTRITION	CHILBLAIN	DESERTION	EXPLOSION	HISTORIAN	MAGNETRON	OUTOFTOWN
ATTUITION	CHINATOWN	DETECTION	EXPULSION	HOBGOBLIN	MAINTENON	OUTSPOKEN
AUTOMATON	CHRISTIAN	DETENTION	EXTENSION	HOMEGROWN	MALATHION	OVERBLOWN
AVOCATION	CHURCHMAN	DETRITION	EXTORTION	HONEYMOON	MALAYSIAN	OVERDRAWN
AYCKBOURN	CIMMERIAN	DEUCALION	EXTRUSION	HOOLACHAN	MAMMALIAN	OVERGROWN
BADMINTON	CIRCADIAN	DEVIATION	EXUDATION	HUNGARIAN	MANHATTAN	OVULATION
BALDAQUIN	CLAMPDOWN	DICTATION	EYESTRAIN	IBUPROFEN	MANNEQUIN	OXIDATION
BANDWAGON	CLARENDON	DIETICIAN	FALERNIAN	ICHNEUMON	MASTERMAN	PADEMELON
BARAGOUIN	CLERGYMAN	DIFFUSION	FALLOPIAN	IDIOTICON	MAURITIAN	PALANKEEN
BARBARIAN	CLINICIAN	DIGESTION	FAULCHION	IGUANODON	MAVOURNIN	PALANQUIN
BARTHOLIN	COALITION	DIGITALIN	FIELDSMAN	ILLGOTTEN	MEANDRIAN	PALLADIAN
BASILICON	COCKSWAIN	DIMENSION	FILIGRAIN	IMITATION	MEDALLION	PALMATION
BATTALION	COEMPTION	DIONYSIAN	FILLIPEEN	IMMELMANN	MEDIATION	PALPATION
BECHSTEIN	COGNITION	DIRECTION	FISHERMAN	IMMERSION	MENIPPEAN	PANDATION
BEDRIDDEN	COLLATION	DISBURDEN	FLAGELLIN	IMPACTION	MENTATION	PANDEMIAN
BEETHOVEN	COLLEGIAN	DIVERSION	FLORESTAN	IMPASSION	MERCAPTAN	PANTALEON
BERNSTEIN	COLLISION	DOMINICAN	FLOTATION	IMPULSION	METHEGLIN	PANTALOON
BETTERTON	COLLODION	DORMITION	FORBIDDEN	INANITION	MICKLETON	PARATHION
BILIRUBIN	COLLUSION	DRACONIAN	FOREBRAIN	INCAUTION	MIDDLEMAN	PARHELION
BIRDBRAIN	COLOMBIAN	DRAFTSMAN	FOREWOMAN	INCEPTION	MIDDLETON	PARTHENON
BISECTION	COLUMBIAN	DRAVIDIAN	FORGOTTEN	INCLUSION	MIDHEAVEN	PARTHOLON
BOATSWAIN	COMINTERN	DUMBARTON	FORMATION	INCURSION	MIGRATION	PARTITION
BOLECTION	COMMOTION	EALDORMAN	FRANCOLIN	INDICTION	MINUTEMAN	PATHTRAIN
BOMBARDON	COMMUNION	ECTROPION	FREEMASON	INDUCTION	MISFALLEN	PATRICIAN
BORNAGAIN	COMPANION	EDDINGTON	FRENCHMAN	INFECTION	MISSHAPEN	PATROLMAN
BOSTONIAN	CONCISION	EDUCATION	FRENCHMEN	INFLATION	MODILLION	PELLAGRIN
BOTSWANAN	CONDITION	EDWARDIAN	FRIGATOON	INFLEXION	MONGOLIAN	PENDLETON
BRANDIRON	CONFUSION	EGRESSION	FROGSPAWN	INGESTION	MONOXYLON	PENDRAGON
BRAZILIAN	CONNEXION	EIDERDOWN	FULLBLOWN	INJECTION	MONTESPAN	PENILLION
BREAKDOWN	CONTAGION	ELEVATION	FULLGROWN	INSERTION	MORTICIAN	PENSTEMON
BREAKEVEN	CONTUSION	ELLINGTON	GALDRAGON	INTENTION	MOTHEATEN	PERCHERON
BRIGADOON	CORNELIAN	ELOCUTION	GARRYOWEN	INTRUSION	MUGGLETON	PERDITION
BROUGHTON	CORNERMAN	EMANATION	GENTLEMAN	INTUITION	MUJAHIDIN	PERICUTIN
BUCKTHORN	CORROSION	EMPLECTON	GENTLEMEN	INUNCTION	MUSKETOON	PERISCIAN
BULGARIAN	COTYLEDON	EMULATION	GERFALCON	INVENTION	MUSKOGEAN	PERSIMMON
BURUNDIAN	COUNTDOWN	ENCHEASON	GESTATION	INVERSION	MUSSULMAN	PERVASION
CAESAREAN	COURTESAN	ENCOLPION	GOBETWEEN	IRRUPTION	MYOGLOBIN	PHELLOGEN
CAMBODIAN	CRACKDOWN	ENDECAGON	GODOLPHIN	ISODORIAN	NABATHEAN	PHENYTOIN
CAMBUSCAN	CRACKSMAN	ENERGUMEN	GRADATION	ISOLATION	NAPIERIAN	PHIGALIAN
CAMERAMAN	CRACOVIAN	ENLIGHTEN	GREASEGUN	ITERATION	NARRATION	PHYSICIAN
CAPARISON	CRAFTSMAN	ENTERTAIN	GREENHORN	JAWBATION	NICKNEVEN	PHYTOTRON
CAPRICORN	CREMATION	ENTROPION	GREGORIAN	JORDANIAN	NIGHTGOWN	PINKERTON
CARIBBEAN	CRENATION	EPHEMERON	GRIMALKIN	JOSEPHSON	NIPPERKIN	PISTAREEN
CARNATION	CRITERION	EPICUREAN	GROSGRAIN	JUSTINIAN	NONILLION	PITUITRIN

PLAINSMAN	RUDDLEMAN	SPORTSMAN	URICONIAN	INCOGNITO	SWEETSHOP	CHATTERER
PLOUGHMAN	RUINATION	SPORTSMEN	URINATION	LARGHETTO	TRANSSHIP	CHAUFFEUR
POINTSMAN	RUTHENIAN	STABLEMAN	URUGUAYAN	LAZARETTO	TROOPSHIP	CHAVENDER
POLICEMAN	SABBATIAN	STANCHION	VALUATION	MAJORDOMO	TRUMPEDUP	CHEVALIER
POLLUTION	SACCHARIN	STATESMAN	VARANGIAN	MANIFESTO	TURBOPROP	CHISELLER
PORCELAIN	SACKERSON	STEERSMAN	VARIATION	MORATORIO	WHITEDAMP	CHORISTER
PORIFERAN	SACRISTAN	STERADIAN	VELDSKOEN	MUSCOVADO	WOODENTOP	CLARIFIER
POSTILION	SAINTFOIN	STEVENSON	VELVETEEN	OBBLIGATO	ABSCONDER	COADJUTOR
POSTWOMAN	SALVARSAN	STILLBORN	VERMILION	PAPARAZZO	ABSTAINER	COALMINER
PRECISIAN	SALVATION	STINKHORN	VERNATION	PASTICCIO	ACYCLOVIR	COLLAPSAR
PRECISION	SAMARITAN	STRIATION	VESPASIAN	PINOCCHIO	ADMONITOR	COLLECTOR
PREMOTION	SANHEDRIN	SUBALTERN	VIBRATION	PISTACHIO	ADULTERER	COLOMBIER
PREORDAIN	SANHEDRON	SUFFRAGAN	VICTORIAN	PIZZICATO	AFRIKANER	COMFORTER
PRINCETON	SANNYASIN	SUFFUSION	VIOLATION	POLITBURO	AGGRESSOR	COMMANDER
PRIVATION	SASKATOON	SUMMATION	VIRGINIAN	PORTFOLIO	ALABASTER	COMMISSAR
PROBATION	SATIATION	SUNSCREEN	VITIATION	PUNCTILIO	ALEXANDER	COMPOTIER
PROFUSION	SATURNIAN	SURREJOIN	VITRUVIAN	QUASIMODO	ALLIGATOR	CONDENSER
PROKARYON	SAUCISSON	SUSPICION	VORTIGERN	RADICCHIO	ALTIMETER	CONDUCTOR
PROLACTIN	SAUVIGNON	SWANSDOWN	VULCANIAN	RELIGIOSO	AMPLIFIER	CONFESSOR
PROLUSION	SAXITOXIN	SWORDSMAN	VULGARIAN	RIGOLETTO	ANNOTATOR	CONFITEOR
PROMOTION	SCHLIEREN	SYNEDRION	WAFERTHIN	SFORZANDO	ANNOUNCER	CONNECTOR
PRONGHORN	SCHNECKEN	TABELLION	WAGNERIAN	SICILIANO	APPARITOR	CONQUEROR
PROPERDIN	SCHOOLMAN	TACTICIAN	WASHBASIN	SIXTEENMO	APPETIZER	CONSIGNOR
PROSIMIAN	SCONCHEON	TAMOXIFEN	WASHERMAN	SOLFEGGIO	ARTICULAR	CONTAINER
PROUDHORN	SCOTCHMAN	TANZANIAN	WASSERMAN	SOLFERINO	ARTIFICER	CONTEMPER
PROVISION	SCUNCHEON	TARNATION	WELLKNOWN	SOSTENUTO	ASPIRATOR	CONTENDER
PTARMIGAN	SCYTHEMAN	TARPAULIN	WHEREUPON	STRAPPADO	ATTAINDER	CONTRIVER
PULSATION	SEBASTIAN	TARTAREAN	WHERRYMAN	TELEPHOTO	AURICULAR	CONVECTOR
PYGMALION	SECESSION	TASMANIAN	WILLESDEN	VAPORETTO	AUTOMAKER	CONVERTER
QUARENDEN	SECLUSION	TELLURIAN	WIMBLEDON	WINNEBAGO	AVUNCULAR	CORIANDER
QUERCETIN	SECRETION	TELLURION	WINCANTON	ZUCCHETTO	AXMINSTER	CORNFLOUR
QUINTROON	SECTARIAN	TENAILLON	WISCONSIN	AFTERDAMP	BACKBITER	CORRECTOR
QUOTATION	SEDUCTION	TEPHILLIN	WITHDRAWN	AMENHOTEP	BACKWATER	CORRUPTER
QUOTIDIAN	SELACHION	THAUMATIN	WOLLASTON	BELLYFLOP	BALLADEER	COSTUMIER
QUOTITION	SELECTION	THEREUPON	WORMEATEN	BLACKDAMP	BALTHAZAR	COUNSELOR
RADDLEMAN	SELJUKIAN	THIRDSMAN	YACHTSMAN	BOOBYTRAP	BANDOLEER	COUTURIER
RADIATION	SEMANTRON	THREADFIN	YACHTSMEN	BUTTERCUP	BANDOLIER	CRICKETER
READYEARN	SEMICOLON	THROWDOWN	ALTIPLANO	CATCHCROP	BAROMETER	CROSSOVER
REBELLION	SENSATION	THYESTEAN	ALTISSIMO	CHINSTRAP	BARRISTER	CRYOMETER
REBOATION	SERBONIAN	THYRATRON	AMERICANO	COURTSHIP	BARTENDER	CUNCTATOR
RECEPTION	SERIATION	TIERCERON	ANDANTINO	DEATHTRAP	BEACHWEAR	DAMBUSTER
RECESSION	SERRATION	TITHEBARN	ANTIPASTO	EAVESDROP	BEDSITTER	DECKCHAIR
REDUCTION	SEVENTEEN	TITRATION	ARMADILLO	FILMSTRIP	BEEFEATER	DECORATOR
REFECTION	SHAKEDOWN	TOUCHDOWN	BANDOLERO	FILTERTIP	BEEKEEPER	DEFAULTER
REFLATION	SHARESMAN	TRADESMAN	BASTINADO	FINGERTIP	BEHAVIOUR	DEFLECTOR
REFLEXION	SHARKSKIN	TRADITION	BOCCACCIO	GOOSESTEP	BELEAGUER	DELIVERER
REGUERDON	SHEEPSKIN	TRAGEDIAN	BOLIVIANO	HORSEWHIP	BERGANDER	DEMEANOUR
REJECTION	SHORTHORN	TRETINOIN	CABALLERO	JOCKSTRAP	BERSERKER	DEPOSITOR
REMISSION	SHUBUNKIN	TREVELYAN	CANALETTO	LIGHTSHIP	BINOCULAR	DERRINGER
RENDITION	SIGNALMAN	TRIATHLON	CAPORETTO	LONGCHAMP	BLUNDERER	DESTROYER
REPLETION	SIMPLETON	TRIBESMAN	CAPRICCIO	MICROCHIP	BLUSTERER	DETONATOR
REPTATION	SINGLETON	TRIBESMEN	CARBONADO	MOUSETRAP	BOOKLOVER	DETRACTOR
REPTILIAN	SINKANSEN	TRICERION	CARPACCIO	OVERSLEEP	BOOKMAKER	DEVELOPER
REPULSION	SIRBONIAN	TRIHEDRON	CIPOLLINO	OVERTRUMP	BRIGADIER	DISAPPEAR
RESNATRON	SISYPHEAN	TRILITHON	CONTRALTO	OWNERSHIP	BUCCANEER	DISCOLOUR
RETENTION	SITUATION	TRISAGION	CORREGGIO	PAPERCLIP	BUCENTAUR	DISFAVOUR
RETORSION	SLAMMAKIN	TROPAELIN	CRESCENDO	PARATROOP	BULLDOZER	DISHONOUR
RETORTION	SLOVENIAN	TROPARION	DESPERADO	PEASEWEEP	BUTTERBUR	DISHWATER
REVERSION	SOLFIDIAN	TRUNCHEON	DONATELLO	PLAYGROUP	BYSTANDER	DISMEMBER
REVULSION	SOOTERKIN	UKRAINIAN	DUODECIMO	QUICKSTEP	CALEMBOUR	DISPENSER
RHODESIAN	SOUTHDOWN	UNBEKNOWN	EMBROGLIO	SCREWEDUP	CAMCORDER	DISREPAIR
RHODOPSIN	SOVEREIGN	UNCERTAIN	ESPERANTO	SHORTSTOP	CANVASSER	DISSENTER
ROBERTSON	SPADASSIN	UNCONCERN	GLISSANDO	SKETCHMAP	CAPACITOR	DISTEMPER
ROSCOMMON	SPILLICAN	UNDERSIGN	HEYPRESTO	SPACESHIP	CAPITULAR	DISTILLER
ROSMINIAN	SPILLIKIN	UNITARIAN	HURRICANO	SPOROCARP	CARETAKER	DONCASTER
ROUMANIAN	SPOILSMAN	UNTRODDEN	IMBROGLIO	STEAMSHIP	CARPENTER	DOSIMETER
ROUNDSMAN	SPOKESMAN	UNWRITTEN	INAMORATO	STONECROP	CHARACTER	DOUKHOBOR

DUNGEONER	HAMFATTER	MALLENDER	PHILANDER	RETICULAR	STAMMERER	VERSIFIER
EASTERNER	HARBINGER	MANOMETER	PHILISTER	RETRACTOR	STANNATOR	VESICULAR
ELASTOMER	HARDANGER	MARKETEER	PICNICKER	RETRIEVER	STARGAZER	VOLTIGEUR
EMBEZZLER	HARDCOVER	MASSINGER	PIEPOWDER	RHYMESTER	STATIONER	VOLTMETER
EMBROIDER	HARDLINER	MAYFLOWER	PINHOOKER	RINGSIDER	STAVANGER	VOLUNTEER
ENCHANTER	HARPOONER	MEDITATOR	PISTOLEER	ROISTERER	STEGOSAUR	WAGHALTER
ENCOUNTER	HARVESTER	MEKOMETER	PLASTERER	ROSEWATER	STIFFENER	WALLPAPER
ENDEAVOUR	HEREAFTER	MEMORITER	PLUNDERER	SAFFLOWER	STRAGGLER	WAMBENGER
ENGROSSER	HEXAMETER	MENUISIER	POETASTER	SALTPETER	STRANGLER	WARMONGER
EPISTOLER	HIGHFLYER	MERGANSER	POLYESTER	SALTWATER	STREETCAR	WASTWATER
EQUALIZER	HODOMETER	MESSENGER	POMPADOUR	SANDPAPER	STRETCHER	WELSUMMER
ERGATANER	HOMEOWNER	MIDSUMMER	PORRINGER	SANDPIPER	SUBCELLAR	WESTERNER
ERIOMETER	HORSEHAIR	MIDWINTER	POSSESSOR	SAPSUCKER	SUBEDITOR	WHICHEVER
ESCALATOR	HUMDINGER	MILOMETER	POSTERIOR	SCARIFIER	SUCCENTOR	WHITTAWER
EXCALIBUR	ICELANDER	MINELAYER	POTBOILER	SCAVENGER	SUCCESSOR	WHOSOEVER
EXCAVATOR	ILCHESTER	MISSIONER	POTHUNTER	SCHLENTER	SUNBATHER	WILLPOWER
EXCELSIOR	IMMUNISER	MISTEMPER	POTTINGAR	SCHMIEDER	SUNDOWNER	WINDHOVER
EXCHEQUER	IMPEACHER	MODERATOR	POULTERER	SCHMUTTER	SUNFLOWER	WOMANISER
EXEQUATUR	IMPERATOR	MOLECULAR	PRANKSTER	SCHNAPPER	SUPERSTAR	WOMANIZER
EXHIBITOR	IMPOUNDER	MONOCULAR	PRECENTOR	SCHNAUZER	SUPINATOR	WOODBORER
EXPLOITER	INCUBATOR	MONOLAYER	PRECEPTOR	SCHNORRER	SUPPORTER	WORCESTER
EXPOSITOR	INDICATOR	MONOMETER	PRECURSOR	SCISSORER	SURRENDER	WRONGDOER
EXTRACTOR	INDWELLER	MONSIGNOR	PREDICTOR	SCLAUNDER	SUSPENDER	WURLITZER
EYELETEER	INFIELDER	MOONRAKER	PRELECTOR	SCRAMBLER	SUSPENSOR	YOUNGSTER
EYEOPENER	INHERITOR	MORTGAGOR	PRESBYTER	SCRIVENER	SWAGGERER	ZEALANDER
FILLISTER	INHIBITOR	MUCKENDER	PRESENTER	SCROUNGER	SWEETENER	ZOROASTER
FILMMAKER	INITIATOR	MUSKETEER	PRESERVER	SCRUTATOR	TABASHEER	ZYMOMETER
FINANCIER	INNKEEPER	NAVIGATOR	PRETENDER	SCUDDALER	TABULATOR	ABLUTIONS
FIREWATER	INNOVATOR	NEBBISHER	PRIVATEER	SCURRIOUR	TAHSILDAR	ACARIASIS
FIRSTEVER	INSPECTOR	NEIGHBOUR	PROCESSOR	SEDGEMOOR	TAILLEFER	ACCIDENTS
FLATTENER	INSTANTER	NEWSPAPER	PROFESSOR	SEPARATOR	TAPDANCER	ACIDULOUS
FLATTERER	INSULATOR	NOMINATOR	PROFITEER	SEPTEMBER	TARGETEER	ACOUSTICS
FLUORSPAR	INSWINGER	NONSMOKER	PROJECTOR	SEPULCHER	TAXIMETER	ACROPOLIS
FOREIGNER	INTRIGUER	NOTEPAPER	PROPELLER	SEQUENCER	TEESWATER	ACUTENESS
FORGATHER	IRREGULAR	NUMERATOR	PROTECTOR	SEQUESTER	TESTIFIER	ADEPTNESS
FORWANDER	ISALLOBAR	NUTJOBBER	PROTESTER	SERASKIER	THERMIDOR	AEPYORNIS
FREIGHTER	JAYWALKER	OFFCOLOUR	PROTOSTAR	SERENADER	THROWSTER	AEROTAXIS
FRESHENER	JERKWATER	OILTANKER	PROVENDER	SHARPENER	THUNDERER	AESCHYLUS
FROBISHER	JOBSEEKER	ONCOMETER	PTEROSAUR	SHILLABER	THYRISTOR	AFRIKAANS
FRUCTIDOR	KARABINER	OPPRESSOR	PUBLISHER	SHIPOWNER	TIGHTENER	AHASUERUS
FRUITERER	KEYHOLDER	ORBICULAR	PULPITEER	SHOEMAKER	TONOMETER	ALBATROSS
FUNICULAR	KIDNAPPER	ORGANISER	PUPPETEER	SHOPFLOOR	TOPDRAWER	ALERTNESS
GAINSAYER	KILOMETER	ORGANIZER	PURCHASER	SHOVELLER	TORMENTER	ALEURITIS
GASHOLDER	KINGMAKER	ORTHOPTER	PUSHCHAIR	SIGHTSEER	TORMENTOR	ALLANTOIS
GASOMETER	KISSINGER	OUTFITTER	QUALIFIER	SIGNALLER	TORTELIER	ALOOFNESS
GAULEITER	KITCHENER	OUTNUMBER	RACKETEER	SIMULATOR	TOTALIZER	AMARYLLIS
GAZETTEER	KLEMPERER	OUTRIGGER	RACONTEUR	SKINDIVER	TOWCESTER	AMAUROSIS
GEARLEVER	KONIMETER	OUTROOPER	RAINWATER	SKYJACKER	TRAFALGAR	AMBERGRIS
GENERATOR	LANCASTER	OUTWORKER	RATEPAYER	SLAUGHTER	TRAVELLER	AMBIGUOUS
GERMANCER	LANDLOPER	OVERPOWER	RECLAIMER	SLUMBERER	TREASURER	AMBITIOUS
GERMANDER	LANDOWNER	OVERRIDER	RECTIFIER	SOFTCOVER	TREGETOUR	AMIANTHUS
GIBRALTAR	LAPLANDER	OVERSTEER	REDLETTER	SOLICITOR	TRICKSTER	AMIDSHIPS
GLABELLAR	LATECOMER	PACEMAKER	REFLECTOR	SOLLICKER	TRICOLOUR	AMORPHOUS
GLADIATOR	LAVOISIER	PARAMETER	REFRACTOR	SOMMELIER	TRIMESTER	AMYGDALUS
GLANDULAR	LAWMONGER	PARTTIMER	REFRESHER	SONNETEER	TRINKETER	ANALOGOUS
GLENDOWER	LAWNMOWER	PASSENGER	REGISSEUR	SONOMETER	TRIPMETER	ANDROCLES
GODFATHER	LEICESTER	PAYMASTER	REGISTRAR	SOPHISTER	TROUBADOR	ANECDOTES
GODMOTHER	LIBERATOR	PECULATOR	REGULATOR	SOTTISIER	TRUMPETER	ANHYDROUS
GONDOLIER	LIMBURGER	PEDICULAR	REJOINDER	SOUTENEUR	ULLSWATER	ANKYLOSIS
GOOSANDER	LINKLATER	PEDOMETER	REMAINDER	SOUWESTER	UNDERWEAR	ANNAPOLIS
GOSPELLER	LOCHINVAR	PENPUSHER	RENOVATOR	SPECTATOR	UNPOPULAR	ANOMALOUS
GRENADIER	LONGEDFOR	PENSIONER	RENTALLER	SPELUNKER	UPHOLSTER	ANONYMOUS
GROSVENOR	LOWLANDER	PERFORMER	REPRESSOR	SPHINCTER	VALVASSOR	ANOPHELES
GUARANTOR	LYSIMETER	PERIANDER	RESERVOIR	SPINDRIER	VANCOUVER	ANSCHLUSS
GUNPOWDER	MACARTHUR	PERIMETER	RESONATOR	SPINNAKER	VAPORIZER	ANTIGONUS
HADROSAUR	MAGNIFIER	PHALANGER	RESPECTER	SPLENDOUR	VEGETATOR	ANTIPODES
HAMBURGER	MALLANDER	PHANSIGAR	RESSALDAR	SPRINKLER	VEHICULAR	ANTONINUS

APENNINES	CARYOPSIS	DENSENESS	ESTHETICS	GRAMPIANS	JEPHTHAHS	MONSTROUS
APHERESIS	CASTANETS	DESCARTES	ETCETERAS	GRANDNESS	JERKINESS	MOODINESS
APOLLONUS	CATACOMBS	DEXTEROUS	ETHEREOUS	GREATNESS	JUDICIOUS	MOTHBALLS
APOPHYSIS	CATALYSIS	DIAERESIS	EUHEMERUS	GREETINGS	JUICINESS	MOTOCROSS
APPARATUS	CATHARSIS	DIAGNOSIS	EUMENIDES	GRIMINESS	KERATITIS	MOTORISTS
AREOPAGUS	CATSKILLS	DIANDROUS	EUMYCETES	GROCERIES	KICKSHAWS	MOUTHLESS
ARMAMENTS	CAVERNOUS	DIANETICS	EUPHRATES	GRUFFNESS	KNEECORDS	MUCORALES
ARTHRITIS	CEANOTHUS	DIAPHYSIS	EURIPIDES	GUILELESS	KNOTGRASS	MUDDINESS
ARTHROSIS	CEASELESS	DIASTASIS	EXACTNESS	GUILTLESS	LABORIOUS	MUMPSIMUS
ASCLEPIUS	CENTAURUS	DIATHESIS	EXERCISES	HALITOSIS	LAMINITIS	MUNDUNGUS
ASPARAGUS	CERATITIS	DIAZEUXIS	EXODERMIS	HALLOWMAS	LANDWARDS	MUNIMENTS
ASSIDUOUS	CERATODUS	DIDACTICS	EXOGENOUS	HANDCUFFS	LANGUAGES	MUNITIONS
ASTRAGALS	CERVANTES	DIETETICS	EXOSTOSIS	HANDINESS	LANKINESS	MURDERESS
ASTUCIOUS	CHAROLAIS	DIGITALIS	FABACEOUS	HAPPINESS	LARGENESS	MURDEROUS
ATHLETICS	CHARYBDIS	DINGINESS	FABULINUS	HARDINESS	LAUNDRESS	MURKINESS
ATROCIOUS	CHEAPNESS	DIOCLETES	FACETIOUS	HARIGALDS	LAZYBONES	MUSHINESS
ATTITUDES	CHEERLESS	DIONYSIUS	FAINTNESS	HARQUEBUS	LEASTWAYS	MUSHROOMS
AUDACIOUS	CHILDLESS	DIRECTORS	FAITHLESS	HARSHNESS	LECHEROUS	MUSTINESS
AUTHORESS	CHIPPINGS	DIRTINESS	FALKLANDS	HASTINESS	LEFTOVERS	MUZZINESS
AUTOCROSS	CHLAMYDES	DIVIDENDS	FALSENESS	HAZARDOUS	LEFTWARDS	MYSTERIES
AUTOLYCUS	CHLOROSIS	DIZZINESS	FAULTLESS	HEADDRESS	LEVITICUS	NAKEDNESS
AUTOLYSIS	CHRISTMAS	DOCUMENTS	FENCIBLES	HEADINESS	LIBELLOUS	NARCISSUS
AWARENESS	CHRYSALIS	DOLOMITES	FERACIOUS	HEARTLESS	LIBERTIES	NASTINESS
BACKWARDS	CHURIDARS	DOTHEBOYS	FEROCIOUS	HEAVINESS	LIGHTLESS	NATHELESS
BACKWOODS	CINEREOUS	DOUBTLESS	FILICALES	HENDIADYS	LIGHTNESS	NEFANDOUS
BANISTERS	CIRRHOSIS	DOWNWARDS	FIREWORKS	HEPATITIS	LIMITLESS	NEFARIOUS
BARBAROUS	CLAMOROUS	DRAMATICS	FLESHLESS	HERODOTUS	LITIGIOUS	NEPHRITIS
BAREBONES	CLASSLESS	DREAMLESS	FLESHPOTS	HERPESTES	LITURGICS	NEWLYWEDS
BARNACLES	CLEANNESS	DROPPINGS	FOGGINESS	HETEROSIS	LOBLOLLYS	NICODEMUS
BEARDLESS	CLEARNESS	DUNGAREES	FOOTHILLS	HIGHCLASS	LOFTINESS	NOBLENESS
BEAUTEOUS	CLOSENESS	DUNGENESS	FOREBEARS	HIGHLANDS	LOGISTICS	NOISELESS
BEESTINGS	CLOUDLESS	EAGERNESS	FORESTERS	HILARIOUS	LOOSENESS	NOISINESS
BILLIARDS	COLORLESS	EASTLINGS	FRACTIOUS	HIMALAYAS	LOWLIGHTS	NOLLEKENS
BLACKNESS	COMPANIES	EASTWARDS	FRAGMENTS	HINGELESS	LOWLINESS	NOTORIOUS
BLAMELESS	CONDUCTUS	ECARDINES	FRANGLAIS	HIPPOCRAS	LUCRETIUS	NOVODAMUS
BLANDNESS	CONFUCIUS	ECONOMICS	FRANKNESS	HOMEWARDS	LUDICROUS	NUCLEOLUS
BLEACHERS	CONGERIES	EDELWEISS	FRESHNESS	HORSELESS	LUMBRICUS	NYSTAGMUS
BLESSINGS	CONGRUOUS	EGREGIOUS	FRIVOLOUS	HOURGLASS	LURIDNESS	OBLIVIOUS
BLINDNESS	CONSCIOUS	ELECTRESS	FRUITLESS	HUMONGOUS	LUSTINESS	OBNOXIOUS
BLOODLESS	CONSENSUS	ELEVENSES	FUGACIOUS	HUMUNGOUS	LUXURIOUS	OBSEQUIES
BLUFFNESS	CONSOCIES	EMBARRASS	FUGGINESS	HUSKINESS	MACCABEES	OCEANIDES
BLUNTNESS	CORDUROYS	EMPHLYSIS	FUNGIBLES	HYLOBATES	MADAROSIS	ODOURLESS
BOANERGES	COSMETICS	EMPLOYEES	FUNICULUS	HYPINOSIS	MALICIOUS	OFFICIALS
BOONDOCKS	COTHURNUS	EMPTINESS	FURACIOUS	HYSTERICS	MALLEOLUS	OFFICIOUS
BOOTLACES	COUNTLESS	ENCANTHIS	FUSSINESS	IGNORAMUS	MANLINESS	OLENELLUS
BOSPHORUS	COUNTRIES	ENCELADUS	FUSTINESS	IMAGELESS	MARQUESAS	OPHIUCHUS
BOSSINESS	COURTEOUS	ENCOMPASS	FUZZINESS	IMMORTALS	MARTINMAS	OPPONENTS
BOUNDLESS	CRAPULOUS	ENDPAPERS	GALAPAGOS	IMPERIOUS	MARVELOUS	ORGILLOUS
BOUNTEOUS	CRAZINESS	ENGINEERS	GALATIANS	IMPETUOUS	MATCHLESS	OUGHTNESS
BOURGEOIS	CREDULOUS	ENQUIRIES	GARRULOUS	INCITATUS	MAURITIUS	OUROBOROS
BRAINLESS	CRETINOUS	ENTERITIS	GAUDEAMUS	INCOMINGS	MEATBALLS	OUROBORUS
BRASSICAS	CRISPNESS	ENTREMETS	GAUDINESS	INCURIOUS	MECHANICS	OURSELVES
BREAKAGES	CRUDENESS	EPHEMERIS	GAUNTNESS	INDICATES	MELANOSIS	OUTGOINGS
BRIEFNESS	CUFFLINKS	EPHESIANS	GAWKINESS	INERTNESS	MELODIOUS	OUTSIDERS
BRISKNESS	CUPRESSUS	EPHIALTES	GIDDINESS	INGENIOUS	MERCILESS	OUTSKIRTS
BULKINESS	CUTANEOUS	EPICLESIS	GINGLYMUS	INGENUOUS	METABASIS	OVERDRESS
BUMPTIOUS	DANGEROUS	EPIDERMIS	GINORMOUS	INJURIOUS	MIDDLINGS	OVERHEADS
BURLINESS	DAUNTLESS	EPIGAEOUS	GLADIOLUS	INNOCUOUS	MINACIOUS	OVERSHOES
BURROUGHS	DEACONESS	EPIGENOUS	GLAIREOUS	INSIDIOUS	MIRTHLESS	OVERTONES
CALCANEUS	DEATHLESS	EPIPHYSIS	GLAMOROUS	INTROITUS	MISTIGRIS	OVIPAROUS
CALLIPERS	DECIDUOUS	EPISTAXIS	GLEANINGS	INVERNESS	MISTINESS	OWLEGLASS
CALVITIES	DECRETALS	EPITHESIS	GLUTINOUS	INVIDIOUS	MOCCASINS	PALINURUS
CANCEROUS	DEFENDERS	EPONYMOUS	GODDESSES	IRONSIDES	MOISTNESS	PARABASIS
CANDLEMAS	DELICIOUS	EROGENOUS	GODLINESS	IRONWORKS	MOLESKINS	PARACUSIS
CANTHARIS	DELIRIOUS	ERRONEOUS	GOMPHOSIS	ISINGLASS	MOLLITIES	PARALYSIS
CANTHARUS	DELPHINUS	ESCULENTS	GOVERNESS	ISOCRATES	MOMENTOUS	PARATAXIS
CAPACIOUS	DEMETRIUS	ESOPHAGUS	GRACELESS	ISOSCELES	MONOCEROS	PARNASSUS

PAROTITIS	RAPACIOUS	SIDEROSIS	SYLLEPSIS	VANTBRASS	ARCHIVIST	CONFIDENT
PARTICLES	RAPTUROUS	SIDEWARDS	SYMBIOSIS	VENEREOUS	ARCHIVOLT	CONGRUENT
PATROCLUS	READDRESS	SIGHTLESS	SYMPHYSIS	VERACIOUS	ARKWRIGHT	CONSCRIPT
PATRONESS	READINESS	SILICOSIS	SYNCHYSIS	VERDIGRIS	ARROWROOT	CONSONANT
PAUSANIAS	REALITIES	SILLINESS	SYNIZESIS	VERMINOUS	ASCENDANT	CONSTRICT
PAWKINESS	REARWARDS	SINGULTUS	SYNOVITIS	VERTUMNUS	ASSAILANT	CONSTRUCT
PEDIGREES	REDIVIVUS	SINUSITIS	SYNTHESIS	VESTMENTS	ASSISTANT	CONTINENT
PEMPHIGUS	REEDINESS	SLACKNESS	TACKINESS	VEXATIONS	ASTRONAUT	COPYRIGHT
PENDENNIS	RELATIONS	SLEEKNESS	TARANTASS	VEXATIOUS	ATONEMENT	CORMORANT
PENDULOUS	RELIGIOUS	SLEEPLESS	TARDINESS	VICARIOUS	ATTENDANT	CORNETIST
PENNILESS	REPERCUSS	SLIMINESS	TASTELESS	VIRGINALS	AUTOPILOT	CORPOSANT
PENURIOUS	REPOSSESS	SMALLNESS	TAVERNERS	VITELLIUS	BALLADIST	CORPULENT
PERFORANS	REPROCESS	SMARTNESS	TECTONICS	VIVACIOUS	BALLPOINT	COSMONAUT
PERIAKTOS	RESOURCES	SMOKELESS	TEIRESIAS	VIVIDNESS	BANDICOOT	COTANGENT
PERIBOLOS	RETIARIUS	SNOWSHOES	TELESALES	VOICELESS	BASECOURT	CRAPULENT
PERIPATUS	RETINITIS	SOBERNESS	TEMPTRESS	VOLAGEOUS	BEANFEAST	CROISSANT
PERTUSSIS	RHEOTAXIS	SOGGINESS	TENACIOUS	VOLTURNUS	BEDJACKET	CROWSFOOT
PETTINESS	RIDERLESS	SOMETIMES	TENEMENTS	VORACIOUS	BICYCLIST	CUTTHROAT
PETTITOES	RIGHTEOUS	SOPHOCLES	TENSENESS	WALDENSES	BIOLOGIST	DAMNEDEST
PHLEBITIS	RIGHTNESS	SOPPINESS	TERSENESS	WALLABIES	BIRTHWORT	DANDYPRAT
PHONETICS	RILLETTES	SORCERESS	TESTICLES	WALPURGIS	BLACKFOOT	DAVENPORT
PHRENITIS	RISKINESS	SOUNDLESS	TETTEROUS	WARTCRESS	BLACKLIST	DEADLIGHT
PIERGLASS	ROADWORKS	SOUNDNESS	THANKLESS	WATERLESS	BLINDSPOT	DECUMBENT
PILASTERS	ROUGHNESS	SPACELESS	THELONIUS	WEARINESS	BLOODROOT	DEFEATIST
PLAINNESS	ROWDINESS	SPARKLERS	THERSITES	WEIRDNESS	BLOODSHOT	DEFENDANT
PLENTEOUS	RUDIMENTS	SPARTACUS	THESAURUS	WENCESLAS	BLUEPRINT	DEFERMENT
PLIMSOLLS	RUSTINESS	SPECIFICS	THICKNESS	WESTWARDS	BLUESHIFT	DEFICIENT
PLUMBEOUS	SAGACIOUS	SPECIMENS	THINNINGS	WHITAKERS	BRATWURST	DEFOLIANT
PLUMDAMAS	SALACIOUS	SPHACELUS	THORNLESS	WHITENESS	BREAKFAST	DEMULCENT
PLUMPNESS	SALERATUS	SPICINESS	THOUSANDS	WHOLENESS	BRILLIANT	DEODORANT
POINTLESS	SALTINESS	SPINELESS	TIGHTNESS	WINDFALLS	BROADCAST	DEPENDANT
POISONOUS	SALTWORKS	SPIRITOUS	TIPSINESS	WINEGLASS	BUCHAREST	DEPENDENT
PONDEROUS	SARTORIUS	SPLENITIS	TIREDNESS	WOODLANDS	BUCKWHEAT	DESIPIENT
PONTLEVIS	SASSAFRAS	SPLINTERS	TOOTHLESS	WOOLINESS	BULLFIGHT	DETERGENT
PORPOISES	SAUCINESS	SQUATTERS	TOUGHNESS	WORDINESS	BUTTERNUT	DETERRENT
POSSIBLES	SAUTERNES	STAINLESS	TOURNEDOS	WORTHLESS	BYPRODUCT	DETRIMENT
POSTCARDS	SCABLANDS	STALENESS	TRACHINUS	WRANGLERS	CABRIOLET	DEVILMENT
POWERLESS	SCALLIONS	STANDARDS	TRACKLESS	WREAKLESS	CALVINIST	DEVONPORT
PRECINCTS	SCANSORES	STARKNESS	TRAMLINES	ABASEMENT	CAMEMBERT	DIFFERENT
PRESERVES	SCENTLESS	STATELESS	TRAPEZIUS	ABATEMENT	CANDLELIT	DIFFICULT
PRICELESS	SCLEROSIS	STEENBRAS	TRAPPINGS	ABHORRENT	CANDYTUFT	DIFFIDENT
PRIESTESS	SCOLIOSIS	STEEPNESS	TRAVELERS	ABSORBENT	CAREERIST	DINNERSET
PROBABLES	SCORBUTUS	STEGNOSIS	TREMULOUS	ABSTINENT	CASHPOINT	DISCOMFIT
PROBOSCIS	SCRAPINGS	STERNNESS	TRICKLESS	ACADEMIST	CASSOULET	DISCOVERT
PROCOELUS	SCRATCHES	STIFFNESS	TRIMMINGS	ACCORDANT	CATAMOUNT	DISCREDIT
PRODROMUS	SEBACEOUS	STILLNESS	TRITENESS	ADDERWORT	CATCHMENT	DISHONEST
PROGNOSIS	SECATEURS	STOCKINGS	TROCHILUS	ADORNMENT	CELEBRANT	DISINFECT
PROLEPSIS	SEDITIOUS	STONELESS	TROSSACHS	ADVENTIST	CELLARIST	DISORIENT
PROMACHOS	SEMANTICS	STOUTNESS	TRYPHOEUS	AFFIDAVIT	CHAIRLIFT	DISPUTANT
PROMUSCIS	SEMIGLOSS	STOWNLINS	TUBBINESS	AFTERMOST	CHECKLIST	DISSIDENT
PROPTOSIS	SEMIOTICS	STRANGLES	TUILERIES	AGINCOURT	COAGULANT	DISSONANT
PROTHESIS	SEMIRAMIS	STRAPLESS	TUNGSTOUS	AGREEMENT	COCKFIGHT	DISTRAINT
PSEUDAXIS	SENSELESS	STRENUOUS	TURNBULLS	ALCHEMIST	COCKSFOOT	DIVERGENT
PSORIASIS	SETACEOUS	STRINGOPS	TYRANNOUS	ALIGNMENT	COELOSTAT	DOWNRIGHT
PSYCHOSIS	SHADINESS	STROBILUS	ULIGINOUS	ALLEGIANT	COGNIZANT	DRAMATIST
PUFFINESS	SHAKINESS	STROSSERS	ULTRONEUS	ALLOGRAFT	COLOURIST	DRYASDUST
PYTHONESS	SHAMELESS	STRUMITIS	UMBILICUS	ALLOTMENT	COLTSFOOT	DULCINIST
QUADRATUS	SHAPELESS	SUBDOLOUS	UNANIMOUS	AMAZEMENT	COLUMNIST	EBULLIENT
QUANTOCKS	SHARPNESS	SUETONIUS	UNDERPASS	AMENDMENT	COMBATANT	ECOLOGIST
QUEERNESS	SHEERLEGS	SULFUROUS	UNTIMEOUS	AMUSEMENT	COMMUNIST	ECONOMIST
QUERCETUS	SHEERNESS	SULKINESS	URANISCUS	ANARCHIST	COMPETENT	EFFICIENT
QUERULOUS	SHEPHERDS	SUMPTUOUS	UTICENSIS	ANATOMIST	COMPLAINT	EFFULGENT
QUICKNESS	SHETLANDS	SURLINESS	UTTERLESS	ANNULMENT	COMPLIANT	EGAREMENT
QUIETNESS	SHIFTLESS	SWEEPINGS	VAGINITIS	APARTMENT	COMPONENT	ELOPEMENT
RAMILLIES	SHORTNESS	SWEETNESS	VAGUENESS	APOLOGIST	CONCORDAT	EMOLLIENT
RANCOROUS	SHOWINESS	SWIFTNESS	VALDENSES	APPLICANT	CONDIMENT	EMOLUMENT
RANDINESS	SIDEBURNS	SYLLABLES	VALUELESS	ARCHITECT	CONFIDANT	ENACTMENT

ENCUMBENT	HARMONIST	JUDGEMENT	OCTOBRIST	REDBREAST	SPLAYFOOT	UTTERMOST
ENDOWMENT	HATCHMENT	KLINOSTAT	OFFICIANT	REDUNDANT	SPOTLIGHT	VENTIFACT
ENJOYMENT	HAYMARKET	LAKEFRONT	ONSLAUGHT	REFORMIST	SPRINGLET	VERTIPORT
ENROLMENT	HAZELWORT	LAMPLIGHT	ONTHESPOT	REFULGENT	STARLIGHT	VIDELICET
ENTRECHAT	HEADFIRST	LANDAULET	OPENHEART	REGARDANT	STATEMENT	VIEWPOINT
EQUIPMENT	HEADLIGHT	LANDDROST	ORIGENIST	REICHSRAT	STATOCYST	VIOLINIST
ESTAMINET	HEARTBEAT	LASERWORT	OUTERMOST	RELUCTANT	STEADFAST	VULCANIST
ETHELBERT	HEARTFELT	LATENIGHT	OUTTHRUST	REMBRANDT	STEAMBOAT	WAISTCOAT
EUCHARIST	HERBALIST	LATESCENT	OVERDRAFT	REMONTANT	STERNFAST	WALKABOUT
EXACTMENT	HERBORIST	LAUNCELOT	OVEREXERT	RENASCENT	STIMULANT	WATERBUTT
EXCELLENT	HESYCHAST	LIGHTFOOT	OVERNIGHT	RENFIERST	STIRABOUT	WELDSTADT
EXCIPIENT	HIGHLIGHT	LIMELIGHT	OVERPAINT	REPAYMENT	STOCKINET	WELLBUILT
EXCREMENT	HINDSIGHT	LINEAMENT	OVERPRINT	REPELLENT	STONEBOAT	WELTGEIST
EXECUTANT	HOARFROST	LIONHEART	OVERREACT	REPENTANT	STONECHAT	WHALEBOAT
EXPECTANT	HOLDERBAT	LITHOCYST	OVERSHOOT	REPLICANT	STONEWORT	WHALEMEAT
EXPEDIENT	HOLOCAUST	LIVERWORT	OVERSIGHT	REPRESENT	STOPLIGHT	WHITEBAIT
EXTREMIST	HOMOGRAFT	LODGEMENT	PANCHAYAT	REPUGNANT	STRINGENT	WHODUNNIT
EXTROVERT	HOTTENTOT	LOUSEWORT	PANELLIST	RESERVIST	SUBJACENT	WINDSWEPT
EXUBERANT	HOUSEBOAT	LUBRICANT	PARABLAST	RESILIENT	SUBSCRIPT	WOODCRAFT
EYEBRIGHT	HOUSECOAT	LUTESCENT	PARAMOUNT	RESISTANT	SUBTENANT	WRONGFOOT
FALANGIST	HYDROPULT	LUXURIANT	PARCHMENT	RESTRAINT	SUCCULENT	ZEITGEIST
FATISCENT	HYDROSTAT	MACHINIST	PASSAMENT	RESULTANT	SUPPLIANT	ZOOLOGIST
FERRYBOAT	HYGIENIST	MAKESHIFT	PEARLWORT	RESURGENT	SUPPLICAT	BORDEREAU
FEUILLANT	HYPNOTIST	MALIGNANT	PENNYWORT	RESURRECT	SURMULLET	CHALUMEAU
FIRELIGHT	HYPOBLAST	MANGETOUT	PENTECOST	RETROVERT	SWEETMEAT	COINTREAU
FIRMAMENT	HYPOCAUST	MARROWFAT	PEPPERPOT	REVETMENT	SWIMMERET	GASPEREAU
FLAGEOLET	IDENTIKIT	MASOCHIST	PERMANENT	RIPIENIST	SYCOPHANT	IMPROMPTU
FLATULENT	IDIOBLAST	MEDALLIST	PERTINENT	ROOSEVELT	SYMBOLIST	MARTINEAU
FLOWCHART	IGNESCENT	MENDICANT	PESSIMIST	ROQUEFORT	SYNERGIST	MOGADISHU
FLOWERPOT	IMMIGRANT	MERRIMENT	PESTILENT	ROUGHCAST	TAILLIGHT	RICHELIEU
FLYWEIGHT	IMPATIENT	MESOBLAST	PETAURIST	RUFESCENT	TALMUDIST	TROUSSEAU
FOMALHAUT	IMPERFECT	METAPELET	PETILLANT	RUSHLIGHT	TEARSHEET	LEITMOTIV
FOOTPRINT	IMPLEMENT	METHODIST	PETTICOAT	SACRAMENT	TERMAGANT	PROKOFIEV
FORCEMEAT	IMPORTANT	MEZZOTINT	PHANARIOT	SALLYPORT	TERMAGENT	SHOLOKHOV
FOREANENT	IMPRUDENT	MICROVOLT	PHOTOSTAT	SALLYPOST	TERRORIST	AFTERGLOW
FORECOURT	INCESSANT	MICROWATT	PHYSICIST	SANDHURST	TESTAMENT	ALPENGLOW
FOREFRONT	INCIPIENT	MILLAMANT	PLACEMENT	SAUCEBOAT	THECODONT	BEDFELLOW
FORESIGHT	INCLEMENT	MILLIVOLT	PLATONIST	SCAPEGOAT	THERAPIST	CORKSCREW
FORJASKIT	INCORRECT	MILLIWATT	PLUTOCRAT	SCHOLIAST	THRILLANT	DEATHBLOW
FORJESKIT	INCREMENT	MINCEMEAT	POLLUTANT	SCIENTIST	TIMPANIST	EYESHADOW
FORMALIST	INCUMBENT	MINISKIRT	POSTULANT	SENESCENT	TITTLEBAT	FLOORSHOW
FORTNIGHT	INDIGNANT	MISCREANT	POUJADIST	SENTIMENT	TONOPLAST	GALLYCROW
FROISSART	INDRAUGHT	MISDIRECT	POWERBOAT	SERIALIST	TOPIARIST	HERONSHAW
FULMINANT	INDULGENT	MISONEIST	PRECEDENT	SHAMEFAST	TRACKSUIT	INTERVIEW
FUNDAMENT	INELEGANT	MOCKERNUT	PREDICANT	SHEEPMEAT	TRANSEUNT	JACKSCREW
FURNIMENT	INFORMANT	MODERNIST	PREDIKANT	SHELLSUIT	TRANSIENT	JACKSTRAW
GAELTACHT	INNERMOST	MONEYWORT	PREDILECT	SHOPFRONT	TRANSPORT	KABELJOUW
GALLIVANT	INPATIENT	MONTANIST	PRESCIENT	SHORTLIST	TRAPEZIST	NIGHTGLOW
GEARSHIFT	INSIPIENT	MOONLIGHT	PRESIDENT	SIDELIGHT	TREATMENT	OVERTHROW
GENUFLECT	INSISTENT	MOSKONFYT	PRETERMIT	SIMULCAST	TREBUCHET	RACKSTRAW
GEODESIST	INSOLVENT	MOTORBOAT	PREVALENT	SKINFLINT	TREMULANT	SCARECROW
GEOLOGIST	INSURGENT	NANTUCKET	PROMINENT	SKINTIGHT	TRENCHANT	SCRIMSHAW
GIRONDIST	INTELLECT	NEGLIGENT	PROPONENT	SLIGHTEST	TRUCULENT	UNDERFLOW
GLASSWORT	INTENDANT	NEPHALIST	PROVIDENT	SLINGSHOT	TUMESCENT	WAPINSHAW
GLENLIVET	INTERCEPT	NEWMARKET	PUBLICIST	SNOWDRIFT	TURBULENT	ANTIHELIX
GODPARENT	INTERDICT	NEWSAGENT	PUSSYFOOT	SOBRIQUET	TURMAGENT	CHARTREUX
GOLDCREST	INTERJECT	NEWSPRINT	QUIESCENT	SOCIALIST	TURNABOUT	DELACROIX
GOODNIGHT	INTERMENT	NEWSSHEET	QUILLWORT	SOCIOLECT	TYMPANIST	EARTHFLAX
GOOSEFOOT	INTERPRET	NIGHTSPOT	QUODLIBET	SOMNOLENT	UNCORRECT	EXECUTRIX
GRAPESHOT	INTERRUPT	NONPROFIT	RACCABOUT	SOUTHEAST	UNDERCAST	GRAVADLAX
GREATCOAT	INTERSECT	NORTHEAST	RACCAHOUT	SOUTHWEST	UNDERCOAT	HETERODOX
GRINGOLET	INTROVERT	NORTHWEST	RACIALIST	SPACESUIT	UNDERFELT	LETTERBOX
GROUNDNUT	IRRADIANT	NUTRIMENT	RECIPIENT	SPEARMINT	UNDERFOOT	MIDDLESEX
GUILLEMOT	ITINERANT	OBSERVANT	RECOLLECT	SPEARWORT	UNDERMOST	MULTIPLEX
GUITARIST	JACKFRUIT	OCCULTIST	RECORDIST	SPEEDBOAT	UNDERWENT	POMPHOLYX
HALLSTATT	JANSENIST	OCHLOCRAT	RECUMBENT	SPINDRIFT	UNIVALENT	PREHALLUX
HALOBIONT	JESSERANT	OCKHAMIST	RECURRENT	SPINNERET	UPPERMOST	PREPOLLEX

PROTHORAX	BLASPHEMY	DASTARDLY	FECUNDITY	IDEOPATHY	LONGINGLY	OPSIMATHY
RETROFLEX	BLATANTLY	DECIDEDLY	FEDUCIARY	ILLEGALLY	LOQUACITY	OPTICALLY
SINGLESEX	BLUEBERRY	DECLIVITY	FEMINEITY	ILLEGIBLY	LYRICALLY	OPTOMETRY
SUBCORTEX	BREAKAWAY	DECRETORY	FERTILITY	ILLICITLY	MACHINERY	OPULENTLY
TESTATRIX	BRIDLEWAY	DEFORMITY	FERVENTLY	IMAGINARY	MACROLOGY	OROGRAPHY
ABERNETHY	BROTHERLY	DEMOCRACY	FESTIVITY	IMMANENCY	MAGICALLY	ORTHODOXY
ABSURDITY	BRUSQUELY	DENTISTRY	FEUDATORY	IMMEDIACY	MALIGNITY	ORTHOLOGY
ABYSMALLY	BRUTALITY	DEPRAVITY	FIDUCIARY	IMMENSELY	MANDATARY	OUTWARDLY
ACCESSORY	BUDGETARY	DESULTORY	FINICKITY	IMMENSITY	MANDATORY	OVERHASTY
ACCLIVITY	BUTTERFLY	DEVIOUSLY	FLIPPANCY	IMMODESTY	MARQUETRY	PAGEANTRY
ACCOMPANY	CACOPHONY	DEXTERITY	FOOLHARDY	IMMORALLY	MASSIVELY	PAINFULLY
ACROPHONY	CALLOSITY	DIATHERMY	FOOLISHLY	IMMOVABLY	MATERNITY	PALMISTRY
ACTUALITY	CALLOUSLY	DICHOTOMY	FORLORNLY	IMMUTABLY	MATRIMONY	PANTAGAMY
ADMIRABLY	CANDIDACY	DIGNITARY	FORMALITY	IMPROBITY	MAXILLARY	PARSIMONY
ADMIRALTY	CAPILLARY	DIPLOMACY	FRAGILITY	INABILITY	MAYORALTY	PARTIALLY
ADVERSARY	CAPTAINCY	DIRECTORY	FRAGRANCY	INAUDIBLY	MEDICALLY	PASSIVELY
ADVERSELY	CAPTIVITY	DISCOVERY	FRATCHETY	INCURABLY	MENDACITY	PASSIVITY
ADVERSITY	CAREFULLY	DISPARITY	FREQUENCY	INDECENCY	MENTALITY	PATCHOULY
ADVISEDLY	CARPENTRY	DISTANTLY	FRETFULLY	INDELIBLY	MERCENARY	PATERNITY
AGREEABLY	CARTULARY	DIVERSIFY	FRIGIDITY	INDEMNIFY	MESENTERY	PATHOGENY
AIMLESSLY	CASSOWARY	DIVERSITY	FRIVOLITY	INDEMNITY	MIDWIFERY	PATHOLOGY
ALLEGEDLY	CASUISTRY	DOLEFULLY	FRUGALITY	INDIGNITY	MIGRATORY	PATIENTLY
ALLOCARPY	CATALEPSY	DORMITORY	FURIOUSLY	INFIRMARY	MILITANCY	PATRIMONY
ALLOPATHY	CATAPLEXY	DRAGONFLY	FURTIVELY	INFIRMITY	MILLINERY	PEACEABLY
AMBIGUITY	CELEBRITY	DROMEDARY	GAINFULLY	INGENUITY	MISERABLY	PEASANTRY
AMOROUSLY	CENTENARY	DRUNKENLY	GALLANTLY	INHUMANLY	MOBOCRACY	PECUNIARY
AMUSINGLY	CENTRALLY	DUBIOUSLY	GALLANTRY	INITIALLY	MODERNITY	PEDERASTY
ANAPLASTY	CEROMANCY	DUNDREARY	GARRULITY	INSTANTLY	MOMENTARY	PEEVISHLY
ANCILLARY	CERTAINLY	DUPLICITY	GENEALOGY	INTEGRITY	MONASTERY	PELLITORY
ANIMALITY	CERTAINTY	DUTIFULLY	GENERALLY	INTENSELY	MONOMACHY	PENSIVELY
ANIMOSITY	CHAMPERTY	DYSENTERY	GENIALITY	INTENSIFY	MORBIDITY	PERFECTLY
ANISOGAMY	CHANTILLY	DYSTROPHY	GENTEELLY	INTENSITY	MORTALITY	PERFUMERY
ANONYMITY	CHEMISTRY	EARNESTLY	GENTILITY	INTERCITY	MUSICALLY	PERIPHERY
ANTHOLOGY	CHICANERY	ELECTRIFY	GENUINELY	INTERPLAY	MYTHOLOGY	PERSONIFY
ANTIPATHY	CHIROPODY	ELECTUARY	GEOGRAPHY	INTRICACY	NARGHILLY	PETROLOGY
ANTIPHONY	COLOPHONY	ELEGANTLY	GLEEFULLY	INVENTORY	NASEBERRY	PHILATELY
ANTIQUARY	COLOSTOMY	EMBRACERY	GLENGARRY	IRRAWADDY	NATURALLY	PHILOLOGY
ANTIQUITY	COLUMBARY	EMERGENCY	GOLDSINNY	IRRITABLY	NAUGHTILY	PHONOLOGY
ANXIOUSLY	COMICALLY	EMINENTLY	GOONHILLY	ITINERARY	NECESSARY	PHOTOCOPY
ARBITRARY	COMMODITY	EMPANOPLY	GOSSAMERY	JANISSARY	NECESSITY	PHYCOLOGY
ARDUOUSLY	COMMUNITY	ENDLESSLY	GRADUALLY	JEALOUSLY	NERVOUSLY	PHYLOGENY
ARTILLERY	COMPACTLY	ENTELECHY	GREENAWAY	JEQUIRITY	NEUROLOGY	PIQUANTLY
ASSIDUITY	CONCAVITY	EPEOLATRY	GYROMANCY	JEWELLERY	NEUTRALLY	PITIFULLY
ASSUREDLY	CONCISELY	EQUITABLY	HACKBERRY	JOCULARLY	NIGGARDLY	PITUITARY
ASTROLOGY	CONSTANCY	ESEMPLASY	HAECCEITY	JOVIALITY	NOMINALLY	PLACATORY
ASTRONOMY	CONTUMACY	ETERNALLY	HALFEMPTY	JUDICIARY	NOMOCRACY	PLACIDITY
ASYMMETRY	CONTUMELY	ETHNOLOGY	HALFPENNY	JUNEBERRY	NONENTITY	PLANETARY
ATONALITY	COPIOUSLY	ETYMOLOGY	HAUGHTILY	KILLARNEY	NORMALACY	PLAUSIBLY
AUSTERITY	CORDIALLY	EUDAEMONY	HEALTHILY	KNOWINGLY	NORMALITY	PLAYFULLY
AUTHORITY	COROLLARY	EURHYTHMY	HEAVYDUTY	LAMPADARY	NORTHERLY	PLURALITY
AUTOCRACY	CORRECTLY	EVASIVELY	HELPFULLY	LANGUIDLY	NOSTOLOGY	POCKMANKY
AUTOLATRY	COSMOGONY	EVERYBODY	HEMINGWAY	LATERALLY	NOTORIETY	POIGNANCY
AUTOSCOPY	COSMOLOGY	EVIDENTLY	HESITANCY	LATTERDAY	OBJECTIFY	POINTEDLY
AUXILIARY	COVALENCY	EVOCATORY	HIDEOUSLY	LAUDATORY	OBLIQUELY	POLYANDRY
AWKWARDLY	CRANBERRY	EXCUSABLY	HIERARCHY	LEGENDARY	OBSCENELY	POLYPHONY
AYLESBURY	CREDULITY	EXECRABLY	HILLBILLY	LEGIONARY	OBSCENITY	POMPOSITY
BALEFULLY	CREMATORY	EXEMPLARY	HISTOLOGY	LEISURELY	OBSCURELY	POPULARLY
BANEBERRY	CROOKEDLY	EXEMPLIFY	HOPEFULLY	LENGTHILY	OBSCURITY	POSTERITY
BARBARITY	CROTCHETY	EXPIATORY	HOPLOLOGY	LENIENTLY	OBSTINACY	PRECATORY
BARONETCY	CRUCIALLY	EXPRESSLY	HORSEPLAY	LEPROSERY	OBVIOUSLY	PRECISELY
BASHFULLY	CURIOSITY	EXTREMELY	HORTATORY	LIABILITY	OCCUPANCY	PRECOCITY
BASICALLY	CURIOUSLY	EXTREMITY	HOSTILITY	LIBERALLY	OFFERTORY	PREDATORY
BEARDSLEY	CURRENTLY	FACTUALLY	HUNKYDORY	LIMPIDITY	OKEYDOKEY	PREFATORY
BELATEDLY	CURSORILY	FACUNDITY	HURRIEDLY	LIQUIDITY	OLFACTORY	PREGNANCY
BIMONTHLY	CUSTOMARY	FATUOUSLY	HUSBANDLY	LITERALLY	OLIGARCHY	PRELUSORY
BIOGRAPHY	CYNICALLY	FAVORABLY	HUSBANDRY	LOGICALLY	OMINOUSLY	PREOCCUPY
BIZARRELY	DAMSELFLY	FEARFULLY	HYPOCRISY	LONGEVITY	ONTOGENCY	PRESENTLY

PRIESTLEY	REGULARLY	SENIORITY	SPEAKEASY	TACTFULLY	TOPICALLY	VIOLENTLY
PRIMARILY	RELIQUARY	SENSUALLY	SPECIALLY	TAUTOLOGY	TOXOPHILY	VIRGINITY
PRIVATELY	REPERTORY	SERIOUSLY	SPECIALTY	TAXIDERMY	TREACHERY	VIRTUALLY
PROCACITY	REPUTEDLY	SERVILELY	SPEECHIFY	TEARFULLY	TRIBOLOGY	VISCOSITY
PROCERITY	RESIDENCY	SERVILITY	SPRECHERY	TEDIOSITY	TRIBUTARY	VISIONARY
PROFANELY	RESIDUARY	SEVERALLY	SPRIGHTLY	TEDIOUSLY	TRIVIALLY	VOLUNTARY
PROFANITY	RIOTOUSLY	SEXUALITY	SQUALIDLY	TEKNONYMY	TRUEPENNY	VULGARITY
PROFUSELY	ROTUNDITY	SHORTSTAY	SQUINANCY	TELEOLOGY	TURBIDITY	WANCHANCY
PROLIXITY	ROUNDELAY	SHRUBBERY	STABILITY	TELEPATHY	TYPICALLY	WANWORTHY
PROPRIETY	ROUTINELY	SIGNATORY	STABLEBOY	TELEPHONY	UNANIMITY	WASPISHLY
PROXIMITY	RUFFIANLY	SIMILARLY	STANDERBY	TELLINGLY	UNCOURTLY	WATERBABY
PRUDENTLY	RUINOUSLY	SINCERELY	STATUTORY	TEMPORARY	UNEARTHLY	WATERLILY
PUBLICITY	SAGITTARY	SINCERITY	STAUNCHLY	TENUOUSLY	UNHAPPILY	WEDNESDAY
PUERILITY	SALESLADY	SINUOSITY	STERILITY	TERRITORY	UNHEALTHY	WILLFULLY
PUGNACITY	SALUBRITY	SISSERARY	STOICALLY	TESTIMONY	UNIFORMLY	WILLINGLY
PULMONARY	SANCTUARY	SKETCHILY	STOLIDITY	TETRALOGY	UNLUCKILY	WINEBERRY
PUNGENTLY	SCHMALTZY	SKIAMACHY	STORNAWAY	TETRARCHY	UNSAVOURY	WISTFULLY
PURGATORY	SCHOLARLY	SKILFULLY	STRANGELY	THACKERAY	UNSIGHTLY	WITCHETTY
PURPOSELY	SCHOOLBOY	SLAPHAPPY	STRANGURY	THEOCRACY	UNUSUALLY	WITTINGLY
PYROMANCY	SCIAMACHY	SLAVISHLY	STRIDENCY	THEOSOPHY	UPCOUNTRY	YESTERDAY
QUARTERLY	SCIOMANCY	SOAPBERRY	STUPIDITY	THINGUMMY	VAINGLORY	GIGAHERTZ
QUERIMONY	SCRUFFILY	SOCIOLOGY	STYLISHLY	THIRSTILY	VALIANTLY	KILOHERTZ
RADIANTLY	SEANNACHY	SOLDIERLY	SUBLIMELY	THRIFTILY	VARIOUSLY	MEGAHERTZ
RADICALLY	SEAWORTHY	SOLEMNITY	SUMMARILY	THROATILY	VASECTOMY	SLIVOVITZ
RADIOLOGY	SECONDARY	SOLILOQUY	SUMPTUARY	THROWAWAY	VENIALITY	TAUCHNITZ
RANCIDITY	SECRETARY	SOPHISTRY	SUPREMACY	TIMENOGUY	VERBOSITY	TERAHERTZ
RASPATORY	SEDENTARY	SOULFULLY	SUPREMELY	TIMOCRACY	VEXILLARY	VELASQUEZ
RASPBERRY	SEEMINGLY	SOUTHERLY	SURQUEDRY	TIPPERARY	VIABILITY	
RAUCOUSLY	SELFISHLY	SPARINGLY	SWORDPLAY	TOBERMORY	VIBRATORY	
REFECTORY	SEMIOLOGY	SPATIALLY	SYLLABARY	TOLERABLY	VICIOUSLY	

10:1

ABBREVIATE	ADDITAMENT	ALDERMANLY	ANACHARSIS	ANTISEPSIS	ARTICULATE
ABDICATION	ADDITIONAL	ALDERWOMAN	ANACLASTIC	ANTISEPTIC	ARTIFICIAL
ABERDEVINE	ADELANTADO	ALECTORIAN	ANACOUSTIC	ANTISOCIAL	ARTOCARPUS
ABERGLAUBE	ADEQUATELY	ALEMBICATE	ANACRUSTIC	ANTISTATIC	ARUNDELIAN
ABERRATION	ADHIBITION	ALEXANDERS	ANADROMOUS	ANTITHESIS	ARYTAENOID
ABHIDHAMMA	ADIAPHORON	ALEXANDRIA	ANADYOMENE	ANTITHETIC	ASAFOETIDA
ABHORRENCE	ADJECTIVAL	ALGOLAGNIA	ANALOGICAL	ANTITRAGUS	ASARABACCA
ABITURIENT	ADJUDICATE	ALGONQUIAN	ANALPHABET	ANTIVENENE	ASBESTOSIS
ABNORMALLY	ADJUSTABLE	ALIENATION	ANALYTICAL	APEMANTHUS	ASCENDANCY
ABOMINABLE	ADJUSTMENT	ALIMENTARY	ANARCHICAL	APHAERESIS	ASCENDENCY
ABOMINABLY	ADMINISTER	ALKALINITY	ANASTIGMAT	APICULTURE	ASCETICISM
ABONNEMENT	ADMIRATION	ALLEGATION	ANASTROPHE	APOCALYPSE	ASCOMYCETE
ABORIGINAL	ADMIRINGLY	ALLEGEANCE	ANATOMICAL	APOCRYPHAL	ASCRIBABLE
ABOVEBOARD	ADMISSIBLE	ALLEGIANCE	ANAXIMENES	APOLAUSTIC	ASPARAGINE
ABRIDGMENT	ADMITTANCE	ALLIGATION	ANCHORETIC	APOLLONIAN	ASPERSIONS
ABROGATION	ADMITTEDLY	ALLOCATION	ANCHYLOSIS	APOLLONIUS	ASPHALTITE
ABRUPTNESS	ADMONITION	ALLOCUTION	ANCIPITOUS	APOLOGETIC	ASPHYXIATE
ABSCISSION	ADOLESCENT	ALLOSAURUS	ANDALUSIAN	APOPEMPTIC	ASPIDISTRA
ABSOLUTELY	ADRAMELECH	ALLOSTERIC	ANDALUSITE	APOPHTHEGM	ASPIRATION
ABSOLUTION	ADRENALINE	ALLOTROPIC	ANDROMACHE	APOPLECTIC	ASSEMBLAGE
ABSOLUTISM	ADRENERGIC	ALLPURPOSE	ANEMOGRAPH	APOSEMATIC	ASSEMBLING
ABSORBANCE	ADULLAMITE	ALLUREMENT	ANEMOMETER	APOSTROPHE	ASSESSMENT
ABSORPTION	ADULTERANT	ALLYCHOLLY	ANESTHESIA	APOTHECARY	ASSEVERATE
ABSTEMIOUS	ADULTERATE	ALMACANTAR	ANESTHETIC	APOTHECIUM	ASSIGNABLE
ABSTENTION	ADULTERESS	ALMSGIVING	ANGIOSPERM	APOTHEOSIS	ASSIGNMENT
ABSTINENCE	ADULTERINE	ALMSHOUSES	ANGLERFISH	APOTROPAIC	ASSIMILATE
ABSTRACTED	ADULTEROUS	ALMUCANTAR	ANGLOPHILE	APPARENTLY	ASSISTANCE
ABUNDANTLY	ADVENTURER	ALPENSTOCK	ANGLOPHOBE	APPARITION	ASSOCIATED
ABYSSINIAN	ADVERSARIA	ALPHONSINE	ANGUILLULA	APPEARANCE	ASSORTMENT
ACANACEOUS	ADVERTISER	ALTAZIMUTH	ANGURVADEL	APPETITIVE	ASSUMPTION
ACCELERATE	AERENCHYMA	ALTERATION	ANGWANTIBO	APPETIZING	ASSUMPTIVE
ACCENTUATE	AEROBATICS	ALTERNATOR	ANHELATION	APPLICABLE	ASTEROIDEA
ACCESSIBLE	AEROPHAGIA	ALTOGETHER	ANIMADVERT	APPLICATOR	ASTIGMATIC
ACCESSIONS	AERUGINOUS	ALTRUISTIC	ANNEXATION	APPOSITION	ASTOMATOUS
ACCIDENTAL	AESTHETICS	ALZHEIMERS	ANNIHILATE	APPRECIATE	ASTONISHED
ACCLIVIOUS	AFFABILITY	AMALGAMATE	ANNOTATION	APPRENTICE	ASTOUNDING
ACCOMPLICE	AFFETTUOSO	AMANUENSIS	ANNUALIZED	APTERYGOTA	ASTRAGALUS
ACCOMPLISH	AFFILIATED	AMARYLLIDS	ANNUNCIATE	AQUAFORTIS	ASTRALAGUS
ACCORDANCE	AFFLICTION	AMATEURISH	ANSCHAUUNG	AQUAMANALE	ASTRINGENT
ACCOUNTANT	AFFORDABLE	AMBARVALIA	ANSWERABLE	AQUAMANILE	ASTROLOGER
ACCOUNTING	AFICIONADO	AMBASSADOR	ANTAGONISE	AQUAMARINE	ASTRONOMER
ACCREDITED	AFRICANDER	AMBIVALENT	ANTAGONISM	ARACOSTYLE	ASTUTENESS
ACCUBATION	AFRICANISM	AMBLYOPSIS	ANTAGONIST	ARAGONITES	ASYMMETRIC
ACCUMULATE	AFRORMOSIA	AMBLYSTOMA	ANTAGONIZE	ARAUCANIAN	ASYNARTETE
ACCURATELY	AFTERBIRTH	AMBOCEPTOR	ANTARCTICA	ARBITRATOR	ATELEIOSIS
ACCUSATION	AFTERHOURS	AMBULACRUM	ANTECEDENT	ARCHBISHOP	ATHANASIAN
ACCUSATIVE	AFTERIMAGE	AMBULATORY	ANTEPENULT	ARCHDEACON	ATMOSPHERE
ACCUSINGLY	AFTERPIECE	AMELIORATE	ANTHELION	ARCHETYPAL	ATRACURIUM
ACCUSTOMED	AFTERSHAVE	AMERINDIAN	ANTHOCLORE	ARCHIMEDES	ATRAMENTAL
ACEPHALOUS	AFTERSHOCK	AMIABILITY	ANTHRACINE	ARCHITRAVE	ATTACHMENT
ACETABULAR	AFTERTASTE	AMMUNITION	ANTHRACITE	AREFACTION	ATTAINABLE
ACETABULUM	AFTERWARDS	AMPELOPSIS	ANTHROPOID	ARENACEOUS	ATTAINMENT
ACHITOPHEL	AGAPANTHUS	AMPHIBIOUS	ANTIADITIS	AREOGRAPHY	ATTENDANCE
ACHROMATIC	AGGRANDISE	AMPHIBRACH	ANTIBARBUS	AREOPAGITE	ATTRACTION
ACOLOUTHOS	AGGRESSION	AMPHICTYON	ANTIBIOTIC	ARGOLEMONO	ATTRACTIVE
ACOTYLEDON	AGGRESSIVE	AMPHIGOURI	ANTICHTHON	ARIMASPIAN	AUCTIONEER
ACQUAINTED	AGONISTICS	AMPHIMACER	ANTICIPATE	ARISTIPPUS	AUDIBILITY
ACROAMATIC	AGRAHAYANA	AMPHIMIXIS	ANTICLIMAX	ARISTOCRAT	AUDITORIUM
ACROBATICS	AGRONOMIST	AMPHINEURA	ANTIFREEZE	ARISTOLOGY	AURIFEROUS
ACROGENOUS	AHITHOPHEL	AMPHITRITE	ANTIMASQUE	ARISTOTLES	AUSPICIOUS
ACROMEGALY	AIRFREIGHT	AMPHITRYON	ANTIMATTER	ARITHMETIC	AUSTRALIAN
ACRONYCHAL	ALABANDINE	AMPHOTERIC	ANTIMONIAN	ARMAGEDDON	AUSTRALORP
ACROTERION	ALABANDITE	AMPLEFORTH	ANTINOMIAN	ARMIPOTENT	AUSTRINGER
ACTIONABLE	ALBIGENSES	AMPUSSYAND	ANTIOCHENE	ARROGANTLY	AUTECOLOGY
ACTIVITIST	ALCAICERIA	AMPUTATION	ANTIOCHIAN	ARSMETRICK	AUTHORISED
ADAMANTINE	ALCHERINGA	AMRITATTVA	ANTIPHONAL	ARTHRALGIA	AUTHORSHIP
ADAPTATION	ALCIBIADES	AMYGDALOID	ANTIPODEAN	ARTHROMERE	AUTOCHTHON
	ALCOHOLISM	ANABAPTIST	ANTIPROTON	ARTHURIANA	AUTOCRATIC
	ALCYONARIA	ANACARDIUM	ANTIQUATED	ARTICULATA	AUTODIDACT

AUTOECIOUS	BARMECIDAL	BILIVERDIN	BOOTLICKER	BURDENSOME	CANTABRIAN
AUTOGENOUS	BARMITZVAH	BINOCULARS	BOOZINGKEN	BUREAUCRAT	CANTALOUPE
AUTOMATION	BAROMETRIC	BINUCLEATE	BORDERLAND	BURGEONING	CANTATRICE
AUTOMATIZE	BARRACKING	BIOCHEMIST	BORDERLINE	BURGLARIZE	CANTERBURY
AUTOMOBILE	BARRACOOTA	BIOGRAPHER	BORDRAGING	BURLINGTON	CANTILEVER
AUTOMOTIVE	BARRACOUTA	BIOLOGICAL	BORROWINGS	BUSHRANGER	CANTILLATE
AUTONOMOUS	BARRAMUNDA	BIOPHYSICS	BOTHERSOME	BUTCHERING	CANTONMENT
AUTOPLASTY	BARRAMUNDI	BIORHYTHMS	BOTTICELLI	BUTTERBAKE	CANVASBACK
AUTOSTRADA	BARRENNESS	BIPARTISAN	BOTTLEHEAD	BUTTERBUMP	CANVASSING
AVANTGARDE	BARYSPHERE	BIPINNARIA	BOTTLENECK	BUTTERFISH	CAOUTCHOUC
AVANTURINE	BASKETBALL	BIRKENHEAD	BOTTOMLESS	BUTTERMERE	CAPABILITY
AVARICIOUS	BASKETWORK	BIRMINGHAM	BOUILLOTTE	BUTTERMILK	CAPACITATE
AVENTURINE	BASSINGTON	BIRTHPLACE	BOURIGNIAN	BUTTONDOWN	CAPERNAITE
AVERRHOISM	BASSOONIST	BIRTHRIGHT	BOUSINGKEN	BUTTONHOLE	CAPERNOITY
AVICULARIA	BATHYSCAPH	BISSEXTILE	BOWDLERISE	BYELECTION	CAPILLAIRE
AVVOGADORE	BATRACHIAN	BITTERLING	BOWDLERIZE	BYSSINOSIS	CAPITALISM
AXINOMANCY	BATTAILOUS	BITTERNESS	BRACHIOPOD	CACHINNATE	CAPITALIST
BABESIASIS	BATTENBERG	BITUMINOUS	BRADYKININ	CACODAEMON	CAPITALIZE
BABIROUSSA	BATTENBURG	BLACKBEARD	BRADYSEISM	CACOGRAPHY	CAPITATION
BABYLONIAN	BATTLEDOOR	BLACKBERRY	BRAGADISME	CACOMISTLE	CAPITELLUM
BABYSITTER	BATTLEDORE	BLACKBOARD	BRAINCHILD	CACUMINOUS	CAPITOLINE
BACCHANTES	BATTLEMENT	BLACKBULLY	BRAININESS	CADAVEROUS	CAPITULARY
BACITRACIN	BATTLESHIP	BLACKENING	BRAINPOWER	CAERPHILLY	CAPITULATE
BACKBITING	BAUDELAIRE	BLACKGUARD	BRAINSTORM	CAESPITOSE	CAPNOMANCY
BACKBLOCKS	BEARGARDEN	BLACKHEART	BRASSBOUND	CALAMANDER	CAPODASTRO
BACKGAMMON	BEAUJOLAIS	BLACKSHIRT	BRATISLAVA	CALAMITOUS	CAPPUCCINO
BACKGROUND	BEAUTICIAN	BLACKSMITH	BRAZILWOOD	CALAMONDIN	CAPREOLATE
BACKHANDED	BEAUTIFIER	BLACKSTONE	BREADFRUIT	CALAVERITE	CAPRICIOUS
BACKHANDER	BEAVERSKIN	BLACKTHORN	BREAKABLES	CALCAREOUS	CAPTIVATED
BACKPACKER	BEDCHAMBER	BLACKWATER	BREAKWATER	CALCEDONIO	CARABINEER
BACKSLIDER	BEDCLOTHES	BLANCMANGE	BREASTBONE	CALCEOLATE	CARABINIER
BACKSTAIRS	BEDEVILLED	BLANQUETTE	BREASTFEED	CALCITONIN	CARACTACUS
BACKSTROKE	BEDRAGGLED	BLASPHEMER	BREASTWORK	CALCULABLE	CARAMELIZE
BADDERLOCK	BEEFBURGER	BLASTOCOEL	BREATHLESS	CALCULATED	CARBURETOR
BAFFLEMENT	BEEFEATERS	BLASTOIDEA	BRESSUMMER	CALCULATOR	CARCINOGEN
BAGASSOSIS	BEEKEEPING	BLEARYEYED	BRICKLAYER	CALEDONIAN	CARDIOGRAM
BAHRAINIAN	BEFOREHAND	BLEPHARISM	BRICKWORKS	CALEFACTOR	CARDIOLOGY
BAILIEWICK	BEHAVIORAL	BLISSFULLY	BRIDEGROOM	CALESCENCE	CARELESSLY
BAILLIWICK	BEHINDHAND	BLISTERING	BRIDESMAID	CALIFORNIA	CARICATURA
BALANCHINE	BELARUSIAN	BLITHERING	BRIDGEHEAD	CALLIATURE	CARICATURE
BALBRIGGAN	BELIEVABLE	BLITZKRIEG	BRIDGETOWN	CALORIFIER	CARMAGNOLE
BALBUTIENT	BELLADONNA	BLOCKHOUSE	BRIDLEPATH	CALUMNIATE	CARNASSIAL
BALDERDASH	BELLAMOURE	BLOODHOUND	BRIGANDINE	CALYDONIAN	CARPATHIAN
BALIBUNTAL	BELLARMINE	BLOODSTAIN	BRIGANTINE	CALYPTRATE	CARPENTIER
BALLISTICS	BELLWETHER	BLOODSTOCK	BRIGHTNESS	CAMBERWELL	CARPHOLOGY
BALLISTITE	BELONGINGS	BLOODSTONE	BRILLIANCE	CAMBRENSIS	CARRAGHEEN
BALLOONING	BELSHAZZAR	BLOOMSBURY	BRITISHISM	CAMELOPARD	CARTHAMINE
BALLOONIST	BENEDICITE	BLOTTESQUE	BROADCLOTH	CAMERLENGO	CARTHUSIAN
BALNEATION	BENEFACTOR	BLUEBONNET	BROADPIECE	CAMERLINGO	CARTOMANCY
BALNEOLOGY	BENEFICENT	BLUEBOTTLE	BROADSHEET	CAMERONIAN	CARTOONIST
BALUSTRADE	BENEFICIAL	BLUEMANTLE	BROADSWORD	CAMOUFLAGE	CARYATIDES
BAMBOOZLED	BENEVOLENT	BLUETHROAT	BROCATELLE	CAMPAIGNER	CASCARILLA
BANDERILLA	BENTHAMITE	BLUNDERING	BROKENDOWN	CAMPANELLA	CASSIABARK
BANDERILLO	BENZEDRINE	BOBBYSOXER	BRONCHITIC	CAMPARADOR	CASSIOPEIA
BANDMASTER	BERMOOTHES	BOISTEROUS	BRONCHITIS	CAMPERDOWN	CASSOLETTE
BANGLADESH	BERNARDINE	BOLLANDIST	BROOMSTICK	CAMPESTRAL	CASSUMUNAR
BANISHMENT	BERSAGLIER	BOLSHEVIST	BROWNLANDS	CAMSTEERIE	CASTRATION
BANKRUPTCY	BESTIALITY	BOMBARDIER	BROWNSTONE	CANCELLOUS	CASUALNESS
BARASINGHA	BESTSELLER	BONDHOLDER	BUCCINATOR	CANCIONERO	CATABOLISM
BARBAROSSA	BETACRUCIS	BONDSWOMAN	BUCEPHALUS	CANCRIZANS	CATACHUMEN
BARBITURIC	BETELGEUSE	BONESHAKER	BUCHMANISM	CANDELABRA	CATAFALQUE
BARCAROLLE	BETELGEUZE	BONNETHEAD	BUCKINGHAM	CANDELILLA	CATALECTIC
BARCHESTER	BEWILDERED	BOOKBINDER	BUCKJUMPER	CANDLEFISH	CATALEPTIC
BAREFOOTED	BEWITCHING	BOOKKEEPER	BUDGERIGAR	CANDLEWICK	CATALOGUER
BAREHEADED	BHADRAPADA	BOOKMARKER	BUFFLEHEAD	CANDYFLOSS	CATAPHRACT
BARELEGGED	BIANNUALLY	BOOKMOBILE	BUFFOONERY	CANECUTTER	CATARRHINE
BARGAINING	BICHROMATE	BOOKSELLER	BULLHEADED	CANEPHORUS	CATASTASIS
BARLEYBREE	BIENNIALLY	BOONDOGGLE	BUMFREEZER	CANNELLONI	CATAWAMPUS
BARLEYCORN	BIJOUTERIE	BOOTLEGGER	BUNDESWEHR	CANNONBALL	CATCHPENNY

CATCRACKER	CHAUDFROID	CINQUEFOIL	COLDSTREAM	COMPOSITOR	CONSISTENT
CATECHUMEN	CHAULMUGRA	CIRCASSIAN	COLEOPTERA	COMPOUNDED	CONSISTORY
CATEGORISE	CHAUTAUQUA	CIRCUITOUS	COLEORHIZA	COMPRADORE	CONSONANCE
CATEGORIZE	CHAUVINISM	CIRCUMCISE	COLLAPSING	COMPREHEND	CONSONANTS
CATENACCIO	CHAUVINIST	CIRCUMFLEX	COLLARBONE	COMPRESSED	CONSORTIUM
CATHOLICON	CHEAPSKATE	CIRCUMFUSE	COLLATERAL	COMPRESSOR	CONSPECTUS
CATHOLICOS	CHECKLATON	CIRCUMVENT	COLLECTING	COMPROMISE	CONSPIRACY
CATTLEGRID	CHECKPOINT	CIRRHOPODA	COLLECTION	COMPULSION	CONSTANTAN
CAUTIONARY	CHEEKINESS	CIRRIPEDEA	COLLECTIVE	COMPULSIVE	CONSTANTIA
CAUTIOUSLY	CHEERFULLY	CIRRIPEDIA	COLLEGIATE	COMPULSORY	CONSTANTLY
CAVALRYMAN	CHEESECAKE	CISLEITHAN	COLLEMBOLA	COMSTOCKER	CONSTITUTE
CAVICORNIA	CHEESEWOOD	CISPONTINE	COLLIMATOR	CONCENTRIC	CONSTRAINT
CECIDOMYIA	CHEIRONOMY	CISTERCIAN	COLLIQUATE	CONCEPTION	CONSTRINGE
CELEBRATED	CHELTENHAM	CITRONELLA	COLLOCUTER	CONCEPTUAL	CONSUETUDE
CELESTIALS	CHEMICALLY	CLADOPHYLL	COLLOQUIAL	CONCERNING	CONSULTANT
CELLOPHANE	CHEMONASTY	CLAIRCOLLE	COLONNADED	CONCERTINA	CONSULTING
CELLULITIS	CHEQUEBOOK	CLAMMINESS	COLORATION	CONCERVATE	CONSUMMATE
CENSORIOUS	CHERIMOYER	CLAMOURING	COLORATURA	CONCESSION	CONTAGIOUS
CENSORSHIP	CHERRYWOOD	CLANSWOMAN	COLOSSALLY	CONCHIGLIE	CONTENTION
CENTENNIAL	CHERSONESE	CLARABELLA	COLOSSIANS	CONCHIOLIN	CONTESTANT
CENTESIMAL	CHERVONETS	CLASPKNIFE	COLOURLESS	CONCHOLOGY	CONTEXTUAL
CENTIGRADE	CHESSBOARD	CLASSICISM	COLPORTAGE	CONCILIATE	CONTIGUITY
CENTILITER	CHESSYLITE	CLASSICIST	COLPORTEUR	CONCINNITY	CONTIGUOUS
CENTILITRE	CHESTERTON	CLASSIFIED	COLPOSCOPE	CONCINNOUS	CONTINENCE
CENTIMETER	CHEVESAILE	CLAVICHORD	COMANCHERO	CONCLUDING	CONTINGENT
CENTIMETRE	CHEVISANCE	CLEARSTORY	COMBUSTION	CONCLUSION	CONTINUANT
CENTRALIZE	CHEVROTAIN	CLEARWATER	COMEDIENNE	CONCLUSIVE	CONTINUING
CENTRIFUGE	CHICHESTER	CLEMENCEAU	COMESTIBLE	CONCOCTION	CONTINUITY
CENTROSOME	CHICKENPOX	CLEMENTINE	COMFORTING	CONCORDANT	CONTINUOUS
CEPHALOPOD	CHIFFCHAFF	CLERESTORY	COMMANDANT	CONCRETION	CONTORTION
CEREBELLUM	CHIFFONIER	CLEROMANCY	COMMANDEER	CONCURRENT	CONTRABAND
CEREMONIAL	CHILDBIRTH	CLEVERNESS	COMMANDING	CONCUSSION	CONTRACTOR
CEREMONIES	CHILDERMAS	CLINGSTONE	COMMENTARY	CONDESCEND	CONTRADICT
CERTIORARI	CHILDISHLY	CLINICALLY	COMMENTATE	CONDIMENTS	CONTRAFLOW
CESTRACION	CHILLINESS	CLOCKMAKER	COMMERCIAL	CONDOLENCE	CONTRAHENT
CHAFFERING	CHIMBORAZO	CLODHOPPER	COMMISSARY	CONDOTTIER	CONTRARILY
CHAIRWOMAN	CHIMNEYPOT	CLOISTERED	COMMISSION	CONDUCTING	CONTRAVENE
CHALCEDONY	CHIMPANZEE	CLOMIPHENE	COMMISSURE	CONDUCTION	CONTRECOUP
CHALLENGED	CHINABERRY	CLOSTRIDIA	COMMITMENT	CONEFLOWER	CONTRIBUTE
CHALLENGER	CHINAGRAPH	CLOUDBERRY	COMMIXTURE	CONFECTION	CONTRITION
CHALYBEATE	CHINASTONE	CLOUDBURST	COMMODIOUS	CONFEDERAL	CONTROLLER
CHAMAELEON	CHINCHILLA	CLOUDINESS	COMMONALTY	CONFERENCE	CONTROVERT
CHAMAEROPS	CHINQUAPIN	CLUMPERTON	COMMONWEAL	CONFERVOID	CONVALESCE
CHAMBERPOT	CHIRICAUNE	CLUMSINESS	COMMUNALLY	CONFESSION	CONVECTION
CHAMBERTIN	CHIROMANCY	CLYDESDALE	COMMUNIQUÉ	CONFIDANTE	CONVENANCE
CHAMBRANLE	CHIRONOMIC	CNIDOBLAST	COMMUTABLE	CONFIDENCE	CONVENIENT
CHAMPIGNON	CHIROPTERA	COADJUTANT	COMPARABLE	CONFISCATE	CONVENTION
CHANCELLOR	CHITARRONE	COARSENESS	COMPARATOR	CONFLICTED	CONVENTUAL
CHANDELIER	CHITTAGONG	COASTGUARD	COMPARISON	CONFLUENCE	CONVERGENT
CHANGEABLE	CHIVALROUS	COATHANGER	COMPASSION	CONFORMIST	CONVERSANT
CHANGELESS	CHLORINATE	COCCINEOUS	COMPATIBLE	CONFORMITY	CONVERSELY
CHANGELING	CHLOROFORM	COCHLEARIA	COMPATRIOT	CONFOUNDED	CONVERSION
CHAPARAJOS	CHOICELESS	COCKABULLY	COMPELLING	CONFUSEDLY	CONVEYABLE
CHAPAREJOS	CHOLALOGUE	COCKALORUM	COMPENDIUM	CONGENITAL	CONVEYANCE
CHAPFALLEN	CHOPSTICKS	COCKATRICE	COMPENSATE	CONGESTION	CONVICTION
CHAPLAINCY	CHREMATIST	COCKCHAFER	COMPETENCE	CONGREGATE	CONVINCING
CHAPTALISE	CHRISTIANA	COCKERNONY	COMPETITOR	CONIFEROUS	CONVOLUTED
CHARDONNAY	CHROMOSOME	CODSWALLOP	COMPLACENT	CONJECTURE	CONVOLVUTE
CHARGEABLE	CHRONICLER	COELACANTH	COMPLANATE	CONNECTING	CONVULSION
CHARGEHAND	CHRONICLES	COETANEOUS	COMPLEMENT	CONNECTION	CONVULSIVE
CHARIOTEER	CHRONOLOGY	COEXISTENT	COMPLETELY	CONNECTIVE	COORDINATE
CHARITABLE	CHRYSIPPUS	COGITATION	COMPLETION	CONNIPTION	COPARCENER
CHARITABLY	CHRYSOLITE	COGNISANCE	COMPLEXION	CONNIVANCE	COPENHAGEN
CHAROLLAIS	CHUCKWALLA	COGNIZANCE	COMPLEXITY	CONQUERING	COPERNICUS
CHARTREUSE	CHURCHGOER	COHERENTLY	COMPLIANCE	CONSCIENCE	COPESETTIC
CHATELAINE	CHURCHYARD	COINCIDENT	COMPLICATE	CONSECRATE	COPPERHEAD
CHATTERBOX	CHURLISHLY	COLBERTINE	COMPLICITY	CONSENSION	COPPERNOSE
CHATTERTON	CINDERELLA	COLCHESTER	COMPLIMENT	CONSEQUENT	COPPERSKIN
CHAUCERIAN	CINECAMERA	COLCHICINE	COMPLUVIUM	CONSIDERED	COPULATION

COPYHOLDER	CROSSBONES	DECOLLATOR	DEPOPULATE	DIASTALTIC	DISENGAGED
COPYWRITER	CROSSBREED	DECOLORATE	DEPORTMENT	DICHROMATE	DISENNOBLE
COQUELICOT	CROSSCHECK	DECOLORIZE	DEPOSITARY	DICHROMISM	DISFIGURED
COQUETTISH	CROSSHATCH	DECOMPOSED	DEPOSITION	DICKCISSEL	DISGRUNTLE
COQUIMBITE	CROSSPIECE	DECORATION	DEPOSITORY	DICTIONARY	DISGUSTING
CORALBERRY	CROSSREFER	DECORATIVE	DEPRECIATE	DICTOGRAPH	DISHABILLE
CORDIALITY	CROSSROADS	DECRESCENT	DEPRESSANT	DICYNODONT	DISHARMONY
CORDIERITE	CROTALARIA	DEDICATION	DEPRESSING	DIDASCALIC	DISHEARTEN
CORDILLERA	CROTALIDAE	DEDUCTIBLE	DEPRESSION	DIDGERIDOO	DISHONESTY
CORDWAINER	CRUIKSHANK	DEEPFREEZE	DEPRESSIVE	DIDUNCULUS	DISHWASHER
CORINTHIAN	CRUSTACEAN	DEEPSEATED	DEPUTATION	DIELECTRIC	DISINCLINE
CORNCOCKLE	CRYOGENICS	DEFACEMENT	DERACINATE	DIFFERENCE	DISINHERIT
CORNFLAKES	CRYOPHORUS	DEFAMATION	DERAILLEUR	DIFFICULTY	DISJOINTED
CORNFLOWER	CRYPTOGRAM	DEFAMATORY	DERAILMENT	DIFFIDENCE	DISLOYALTY
CORNSTALKS	CRYPTOZOIC	DEFEASANCE	DEREGULATE	DIGESTIBLE	DISMANTLED
CORNSTARCH	CTENOPHORA	DEFECATION	DERIVATION	DIGITORIUM	DISMISSIVE
CORNUCOPIA	CTENOPHORE	DEFENSIBLE	DERIVATIVE	DIGRESSION	DISORDERED
COROMANDEL	CUCKOOPINT	DEFICIENCY	DERMATITIS	DILAPIDATE	DISORDERLY
CORONATION	CUCULLATED	DEFILEMENT	DEROGATORY	DILATATION	DISPENSARY
CORPULENCE	CUCURBITAL	DEFINITELY	DESALINATE	DILETTANTE	DISPENSING
CORRECTING	CUDDLESOME	DEFINITION	DESBOROUGH	DILIGENTLY	DISPERSION
CORRECTION	CUIRASSIER	DEFINITIVE	DESCENDANT	DIMINISHED	DISPIRITED
CORRECTIVE	CUISENAIRE	DEFLAGRATE	DESCENDING	DIMINUENDO	DISPOSABLE
CORREGIDOR	CULTIVATED	DEFLECTION	DESCRIBING	DIMINUTION	DISPOSSESS
CORRESPOND	CULTIVATOR	DEFRAYMENT	DESECRATED	DIMINUTIVE	DISPUTABLE
CORRIGENDA	CULVERTAGE	DEGENERACY	DESERVEDLY	DINANDERIE	DISQUALIFY
CORROBOREE	CUMBERLAND	DEGENERATE	DÉSHABILLÉ	DINNERTIME	DISQUIETED
CORRUGATED	CUMBERSOME	DEGRADABLE	DESICCATED	DIOPHANTOS	DISRESPECT
CORRUGATOR	CUMMERBUND	DEHISCENCE	DESIDERATA	DIPHTHERIA	DISRUPTION
CORRUPTING	CUMULATIVE	DEJECTEDLY	DESOLATION	DIPLODOCUS	DISRUPTIVE
CORRUPTION	CURMUDGEON	DELCREDERE	DESPAIRING	DIPLOMATIC	DISSECTION
CORTADERIA	CURMURRING	DELECTABLE	DESPICABLE	DIPSOMANIA	DISSELBOOM
CORYBANTES	CURRENCIES	DELEGATION	DESPITEOUS	DIRECTIONS	DISSEMBLER
CORYBANTIC	CURRICULUM	DELIBERATE	DESPONDENT	DIRECTNESS	DISSENSION
CORYPHAEUS	CURVACEOUS	DELICATELY	DESQUAMATE	DIRECTOIRE	DISSENTING
COSTLINESS	CURVETTING	DELIGATION	DESSIATINE	DIREMPTION	DISSERTATE
COTTIERISM	CUSSEDNESS	DELIGHTFUL	DESSYATINE	DISABILITY	DISSERVICE
COTTONTAIL	CUTTLEBONE	DELINQUENT	DETACHABLE	DISAPPOINT	DISSIDENCE
COTTONWOOD	CUTTLEFISH	DELIRATION	DETACHMENT	DISAPPROVE	DISSILIENT
COUNCILLOR	CYBERNETIC	DELPHINIUM	DETAINMENT	DISARRANGE	DISSIMILAR
COUNSELING	CYCLOPEDIA	DELTIOLOGY	DETECTABLE	DISASTROUS	DISSIPATED
COUNSELLOR	CYCLOSTYLE	DEMIRELIEF	DETERMINED	DISBELIEVE	DISSOCIATE
COUNTERACT	CYNOMOLGUS	DEMOBILISE	DETERMINER	DISBURTHEN	DISSOLVENT
COUNTRYMAN	CYSTOSCOPY	DEMOBILIZE	DETERRENCE	DISCERNING	DISSONANCE
COURAGEOUS	DAMSELFISH	DEMOCRATIC	DETESTABLE	DISCIPLINE	DISSUASION
COURTHOUSE	DARJEELING	DEMOCRITUS	DETONATION	DISCLAIMER	DISTENSION
COUSCOUSOU	DARKHAIRED	DEMODULATE	DETRACTION	DISCLOSURE	DISTILLATE
COVENANTER	DAYDREAMER	DEMOGORGON	DETRUNCATE	DISCOBOLUS	DISTILLERY
COXCOMICAL	DEACTIVATE	DEMOGRAPHY	DEUTOPLASM	DISCOLORED	DISTILLING
CRAFTINESS	DEADLINESS	DEMOISELLE	DEVANAGARI	DISCOMFORT	DISTINCTLY
CRAIGFLUKE	DEADNETTLE	DEMOLITION	DEVASTATED	DISCOMMODE	DISTORTION
CRANKSHAFT	DEALERSHIP	DEMONIACAL	DEVASTAVIT	DISCOMPOSE	DISTRACTED
CRAPULENCE	DEBASEMENT	DEMONOLOGY	DEVELOPING	DISCONCERT	DISTRAUGHT
CRAQUETURE	DEBATEMENT	DEMORALISE	DEVOLUTION	DISCONNECT	DISTRESSED
CREATIVITY	DEBAUCHERY	DEMORALIZE	DEVOTEMENT	DISCONTENT	DISTRIBUTE
CREDENTIAL	DEBILITATE	DENDROPHIS	DEVOTIONAL	DISCOPHORA	DISTRINGAS
CREDITABLE	DEBOUCHURE	DENOUEMENT	DHARMSHALA	DISCORDANT	DISTURBING
CREDITABLY	DEBRIEFING	DENSIMETER	DIABOLICAL	DISCOURAGE	DITHIONATE
CRENELLATE	DECAGRAMME	DENTIFRICE	DIACAUSTIC	DISCOVERER	DIURNALIST
CREOPHAGUS	DECAHEDRON	DEPARTMENT	DIACHRONIC	DISCREETLY	DIVERGENCE
CRETACEOUS	DECAMPMENT	DEPARTURES	DIACONICON	DISCREPANT	DIVINATION
CREWELWORK	DECAPITATE	DEPENDABLE	DIADROMOUS	DISCRETION	DIVISIONAL
CRICKETING	DECATHLETE	DEPENDENCE	DIAGENESIS	DISCURSIVE	DOCIMASTIC
CRIMINALLY	DECELERATE	DEPENDENCY	DIAGNOSTIC	DISCUSSING	DODECANESE
CRISPBREAD	DECENNOVAL	DEPILATION	DIAGONALLY	DISCUSSION	DOGGEDNESS
CRISPINIAN	DECIMALIZE	DEPILATORY	DIALECTICS	DISDAINFUL	DOLCEMENTE
CRISSCROSS	DECIPHERED	DEPLORABLE	DIAPEDESIS	DISEMBOGUE	DOLICHOLIS
CRITICALLY	DECISIVELY	DEPLORABLY	DIAPHANOUS	DISEMBOWEL	DOLICHOTUS
CROCKFORDS	DECLENSION	DEPLOYMENT	DIASKEUAST	DISENCHANT	DOMICILARY

DOMINATING	EFFACEMENT	ENGAGEMENT	ESCULAPIAN	EXPEDITION	FELICITOUS
DOMINATION	EFFECTUATE	ENGENDRURE	ESCUTCHEON	EXPENDABLE	FELLOWSHIP
DONNYBROOK	EFFEMINACY	ENGLISHMAN	ESPADRILLE	EXPERIENCE	FEMININITY
DOORKEEPER	EFFEMINATE	ENGLISHMEN	ESPECIALLY	EXPERIMENT	FENESTELLA
DOORTODOOR	EFFERVESCE	ENGOUEMENT	ESTANCIERO	EXPIRATION	FERNITICLE
DOPPLERITE	EFFICIENCY	ENGROSSING	ESTIMATION	EXPLICABLE	FERRANDINE
DOSTOEVSKY	EFFLEURAGE	ENHYDRITIC	ESTRAMACON	EXPLICITLY	FERTILISED
DOUBLEBASS	EFFORTLESS	ENKEPHALIN	ETEOCRETAN	EXPOSITION	FERTILISER
DOUBLETALK	EFFRONTERY	ENLACEMENT	ETERNALIZE	EXPOSITORY	FERTILIZER
DOUBTFULLY	EFFUSIVELY	ENLÈVEMENT	ETHEOSTOMA	EXPOUNDERS	FESCENNINE
DOVERCOURT	EGOCENTRIC	ENLISTMENT	ETHYLAMINE	EXPRESSION	FETTERLOCK
DOWNMARKET	EGURGITATE	ENORMOUSLY	EUCALYPTOL	EXPRESSIVE	FETTUCCINE
DOWNSIZING	EIGHTEENTH	ENRAPTURED	EUCALYPTUS	EXPRESSMAN	FEUILLETON
DOWNSTAIRS	EISTEDDFOD	ENRICHMENT	EUCHLORINE	EXPRESSWAY	FEVERISHLY
DOWNSTREAM	ELACAMPANE	ENROLLMENT	EUDIOMETER	EXTENDABLE	FIANCHETTO
DRACONITES	ELASTICATE	ENSANGUINE	EUHEMERISM	EXTENSIBLE	FIBERGLASS
DRAGONROOT	ELASTICITY	ENTEROCELE	EULOGISTIC	EXTERNALLY	FIBREGLASS
DRAKESTONE	ELDERBERRY	ENTERPRISE	EUPHONIOUS	EXTINCTION	FIBRILLATE
DRAWBRIDGE	ELECAMPANE	ENTHUSIASM	EUPHROSYNE	EXTINGUISH	FIBROSITIS
DRAWCANSIR	ELECTORATE	ENTHUSIAST	EUROCHEQUE	EXTRACTION	FICKLENESS
DRAWSTRING	ELECTRICAL	ENTICEMENT	EUROCLYDON	EXTRANEOUS	FICTITIOUS
DREADFULLY	ELECTROMER	ENTOMBMENT	EURYPTERUS	EXUBERANCE	FIDDLEWOOD
DREADLOCKS	ELECTRONIC	ENTOMOLOGY	EUSTACHIAN	EXULTATION	FIELDMOUSE
DREAMINESS	ELEGABALUS	ENTRANCING	EUTHANASIA	EYEWITNESS	FIENDISHLY
DREARINESS	ELEMENTARY	ENTREATING	EUTHYNEURA	FABULOUSLY	FIERCENESS
DREARISOME	ELEUSINIAN	ENTREMESSE	EUTRAPELIA	FACESAVING	FIGURATION
DREIKANTER	ELIMINATOR	ENTRENCHED	EVACUATION	FACILITATE	FIGURATIVE
DRESSMAKER	ELLIPTICAL	ENTRYPHONE	EVALUATION	FACILITIES	FIGUREHEAD
DRINKWATER	ELONGATION	EPANOPHORA	EVANESCENT	FACTITIOUS	FILIBUSTER
DROSOPHILA	ELOQUENTLY	EPAULEMENT	EVANGELIST	FAHRENHEIT	FILLIBRUSH
DROWSINESS	ELYTRIFORM	EPENTHETIC	EVANGELIZE	FAIRGROUND	FILTHINESS
DRUMBLEDOR	EMACIATION	EPHRAIMITE	EVAPORATED	FAIRHAIRED	FILTRATION
DRUZHINNIK	EMALANGENI	EPICANTHUS	EVENHANDED	FAITHFULLY	FINGERLING
DUCKBOARDS	EMANCIPATE	EPIDEICTIC	EVENTUALLY	FALDISTORY	FINGERNAIL
DUKKERIPEN	EMARGINATE	EPIDENDRUM	EVERGLADES	FALKLANDER	FINGERPICK
DUMBLEDORE	EMASCULATE	EPIDIDYMUS	EVERYPLACE	FALLACIOUS	FINISTERRE
DUNDERFUNK	EMBANKMENT	EPIDIORITE	EVERYTHING	FALLINGOFF	FIREWALKER
DUNDERHEAD	EMBERGOOSE	EPIGENETIC	EVERYWHERE	FALSETRUTH	FIREWARDEN
DUNDERPATE	EMBITTERED	EPIGLOTTIS	EVISCERATE	FAMILIARLY	FIRTHSOKEN
DUNIWASSAL	EMBLEMATIC	EPILIMNION	EVITERNITY	FAMISHMENT	FISHMONGER
DUODECIMAL	EMBLEMENTS	EPIMENIDES	EXACERBATE	FANATICISM	FISHSELLER
DUPLICATOR	EMBODIMENT	EPIMETHEUS	EXACTITUDE	FANTASTICO	FISTICUFFS
DURABILITY	EMBONPOINT	EPIPHONEMA	EXAGGERATE	FANTOCCINI	FITZGERALD
DUTCHWOMAN	EMBOUCHURE	EPIPLASTRA	EXALTATION	FAREPAYING	FLABBINESS
DUUMVIRATE	EMBROIDERY	EPISCOPATE	EXASPERATE	FARFETCHED	FLAGELLATE
DYNAMITARD	EMBRYOLOGY	EPISPASTIC	EXCAVATION	FARRANDINE	FLAGITIOUS
DYSCRASITE	EMENDATION	EPISTEMICS	EXCELLENCE	FARSIGHTED	FLAGRANTLY
DYSPROSIUM	EMIGRATION	EPISTROPHE	EXCELLENCY	FASCIATION	FLAMBOYANT
DYSTROPHIC	EMISSIVITY	EPITHELIUM	EXCITEMENT	FASCINATED	FLAMEPROOF
EARTHQUAKE	EMMENTALER	EPONYCHIUM	EXCRUCIATE	FASCINATOR	FLAMINGANT
EARTHSHINE	EMMETROPIA	EPROUVETTE	EXECRATION	FASTIDIOUS	FLANCONADE
EARTHWORKS	EMOLUMENTS	EQUANIMITY	EXEMPTNESS	FASTIGIATE	FLAPDOODLE
EASTERLING	EMPEDOCLES	EQUATORIAL	EXENTERATE	FASTMOVING	FLASHINESS
EATANSWILL	EMPFINDUNG	EQUESTRIAN	EXHALATION	FATALISTIC	FLASHPOINT
EBOULEMENT	EMPLASTRUM	EQUITATION	EXHAUSTING	FATALITIES	FLATTERING
EBRACTEATE	EMPLOYMENT	EQUIVALENT	EXHAUSTION	FATHERLAND	FLATULENCE
EBULLIENCE	EMULSIFIER	EQUIVOCATE	EXHAUSTIVE	FATHERLESS	FLAVESCENT
ECARDINATE	ENANTIOSIS	ERGONOMICS	EXHIBITION	FAULTINESS	FLAVOURING
ECCHYMOSIS	ENCAMPMENT	ERIOCAULON	EXHILARATE	FAVORITISM	FLEETINGLY
ECCOPROTIC	ENCASEMENT	ERUBESCENT	EXHUMATION	FAVOURABLE	FLESHINESS
ECHINODERM	ENCEPHALON	ERUCTATION	EXOBIOLOGY	FAVOURABLY	FLICKERING
ECHINOIDEA	ENCHANTING	ERYMANTHUS	EXONERATED	FEARLESSLY	FLIGHTLESS
ECHOPRAXIA	ENCLOISTER	ERYSIPELAS	EXORBITANT	FEARNOUGHT	FLIMSINESS
ECOLOGICAL	ENCOIGNURE	ESCADRILLE	EXOTHERMIC	FEATHERBED	FLINDERSIA
ECONOMICAL	ENCYCLICAL	ESCALATION	EXOTICALLY	FEDERALISM	FLIPPANTLY
ECTHLIPSIS	ENDEARMENT	ESCAPEMENT	EXPATRIATE	FEDERALIST	FLIRTATION
ECUADORIAN	ENDOGAMOUS	ESCARPMENT	EXPECTANCY	FEDERATION	FLOCCULATE
ECUMENICAL	ENDOGENOUS	ESCHAROTIC	EXPEDIENCE	FEEBLENESS	FLOCCULENT
EDULCORATE	ENDOSMOSIS	ESCRITOIRE	EXPEDIENCY	FELICITATE	FLOODLIGHT

FLOORBOARD	FRATRICIDE	GELATINOUS	GONDOLIERS	GUESTHOUSE	HELIOLATER
FLOORCLOTH	FRAUDULENT	GEMINATION	GONFANONER	GUIDELINES	HELIOTROPE
FLORENTINE	FRAUNHOFER	GENERALISE	GONIOMETER	GUILLOTINE	HELLBENDER
FLORIBUNDA	FRAXINELLA	GENERALITY	GONORRHOEA	GUTTIFERAE	HELLESPONT
FLOURISHED	FREEBOOTER	GENERALIZE	GOODFELLOW	GUTTURALLY	HELPLESSLY
FLOWERBEDS	FREEHANDER	GENERATION	GOOSEBERRY	GYMNASTICS	HEMICHORDA
FLUCTUATER	FREEHOLDER	GENERATRIX	GOOSEFLESH	GYMNOSOPHY	HEMIHEDRON
FLUFFINESS	FREELANCER	GENEROSITY	GORGEOUSLY	GYMNOSPERM	HEMIPLEGIA
FLUGELHORN	FREELOADER	GENEROUSLY	GORMANDIZE	GYNECOLOGY	HEMISPHERE
FLUNKEYDOM	FREEMARTIN	GENETHLIAC	GOVERNANCE	GYPSOPHILA	HEMOGLOBIN
FLUTEMOUTH	FREEMASONS	GENEVRETTE	GOVERNESSY	GYROSCOPIC	HEMOPHILIA
FLYCATCHER	FREIGHTAGE	GENICULATE	GOVERNMENT	HABILITATE	HEMORRHAGE
FOLIACEOUS	FREMESCENT	GENTLEFOLK	GRACEFULLY	HABITATION	HENCEFORTH
FONTANELLE	FRENETICAL	GENTLENESS	GRACIOUSLY	HABITUALLY	HENDECAGON
FONTICULUS	FRENZIEDLY	GEOCENTRIC	GRADUALISM	HACKBUTEER	HEPATOCELE
FONTINALIS	FREQUENTED	GEOGRAPHER	GRADUATION	HACKMATACK	HEPHAESTUS
FOODSTUFFS	FREQUENTER	GEOGRAPHIC	GRAMICIDIN	HAEMANTHUS	HEPTAGONAL
FOOTBALLER	FREQUENTLY	GEOLOGICAL	GRAMMARIAN	HAGIOSCOPE	HEPTAMERON
FOOTBRIDGE	FRESHWATER	GEOPHYSICS	GRAMOPHONE	HAIRSPRING	HEPTATEUCH
FOOTLIGHTS	FRICANDEAU	GEORGETOWN	GRANADILLA	HAKENKREUZ	HEPTATHLON
FOOTPRINTS	FRIENDLESS	GEOTHERMAL	GRANDCHILD	HALFDOLLAR	HERBACEOUS
FORBEARING	FRIENDSHIP	GEOTROPISM	GRANDDADDY	HALFHOURLY	HEREABOUTS
FORBIDDING	FRIGHTENED	GERIATRICS	GRANDSTAND	HALFSISTER	HEREDITARY
FORCEFULLY	FRINGILLID	GERMICIDAL	GRANGERISM	HALFYEARLY	HERESIARCH
FOREBITTER	FRISKINESS	GESUNDHEIT	GRANGERIZE	HALIEUTICS	HEROICALLY
FOREBODING	FRITHSOKEN	GETHSEMANE	GRANULATED	HALLELUJAH	HESITANTLY
FORECASTER	FRITILLARY	GETTYSBURG	GRAPEFRUIT	HALLMARKED	HESITATION
FORECASTLE	FROGHOPPER	GETUPANDGO	GRAPHOLOGY	HALLOYSITE	HESPERIDES
FOREDAMNED	FROLICSOME	GHIBELLINE	GRAPTOLITE	HALLUBALOO	HETERODOXY
FOREFATHER	FROMANTEEL	GIARDIASIS	GRASSLANDS	HAMESUCKEN	HETERODYNE
FOREFINGER	FRONTCOURT	GIBBERELLA	GRASSROOTS	HAMMERHEAD	HETEROGAMY
FOREGATHER	FRONTWARDS	GILBERTIAN	GRASSWIDOW	HAMMERLOCK	HEXAVALENT
FOREGROUND	FRUITFULLY	GILBERTINE	GRATEFULLY	HAMSHACKLE	HIERARCHIC
FOREORDAIN	FRUSTRATED	GILLRAVAGE	GRATIFYING	HANDICRAFT	HIEROGLYPH
FORERUNNER	FRUTESCENT	GINGERBEER	GRATILLITY	HANDLEBARS	HIEROMANCY
FORESHADOW	FUDDYDUDDY	GINGERSNAP	GRATUITOUS	HANDMAIDEN	HIEROPHANT
FOREWARNED	FULFILMENT	GINGIVITIS	GRAVEOLENT	HANDPICKED	HIEROSCOPY
FORFAITING	FULIGINOUS	GIRDLERINK	GRAVESTONE	HANDSOMELY	HIGHBINDER
FORFEITURE	FULLLENGTH	GIRLFRIEND	GREEDINESS	HANDSPRING	HIGHFLYING
FORFEUCHEN	FULLYGROWN	GLACIATION	GREENCLOTH	HANGGLIDER	HIGHHANDED
FORFOUGHEN	FUMIGATION	GLAMOURISE	GREENFINCH	HANKYPANKY	HIGHLANDER
FORGIVABLE	FUNCTIONAL	GLASSHOUSE	GREENHEART	HANOVERIAN	HIGHWAYMAN
FORINSECAL	FUNGICIDAL	GLASSINESS	GREENHOUSE	HARASSMENT	HILDEBRAND
FORMIDABLE	FURNISHING	GLASSWORKS	GREENSHANK	HARDBOILED	HINDENBURG
FORTHRIGHT	FUSTANELLA	GLAUCONITE	GREENSTICK	HARDCASTLE	HINDUSTANI
FORTINBRAS	FUSTANELLE	GLEEMAIDEN	GREENSTONE	HARMANBECK	HINTERLAND
FORTISSIMO	FUTURISTIC	GLENDOVEER	GREENSWARD	HARMONIOUS	HIPPARCHUS
FORTUITOUS	GADOLINIUM	GLISTENING	GREGARIOUS	HARRINGTON	HIPPOCRENE
FOSSILIZED	GAINGIVING	GLITTERAND	GRENADIERS	HARTEBEEST	HIPPODROME
FOUDROYANT	GAINSTRIVE	GLITTERATI	GRENADILLA	HARVESTMAN	HIPPOGRIFF
FOUNDATION	GALIMATIAS	GLITTERING	GREYFRIARS	HATEENOUGH	HIPPOGRYPH
FOURCHETTE	GALLABIYAH	GLORIOUSLY	GRIDIRONER	HAUSTELLUM	HIPPOMANES
FOURIERISM	GALLABIYEH	GLOSSINESS	GRIDLOCKED	HAUSTORIUM	HISTOLYSIS
FOURRAGERE	GALLIAMBIC	GLOUCESTER	GRINDSTONE	HEADHUNTED	HISTORICAL
FOURTEENTH	GALRAVITCH	GLUTTONOUS	GRITTINESS	HEADHUNTER	HISTRIONIC
FOXHUNTING	GALSWORTHY	GLYCOLYSIS	GROCETERIA	HEADLIGHTS	HITCHHIKER
FRACTIONAL	GALUMPHING	GLYCOSURIA	GROUNDBAIT	HEADMASTER	HITHERWARD
FRAGMENTAL	GALVANISER	GNOSTICISM	GROUNDLESS	HEADPHONES	HITOPADESA
FRAMBOESIA	GAMEKEEPER	GOALKEEPER	GROUNDLING	HEADSTRONG	HITOPADESA
FRANCHISEE	GANGRENOUS	GOATSBEARD	GROUNDSMAN	HEARTBREAK	HOARSENESS
FRANCHISOR	GARGANTUAN	GOATSUCKER	GROUNDWORK	HEARTINESS	HOBBYHORSE
FRANCISCAN	GARGOUILLE	GOBEMOUCHE	GROVELLING	HEAVENWARD	HODGEPODGE
FRANGIPANE	GARLANDAGE	GODPARENTS	GRUBBINESS	HECTICALLY	HOLOFERNES
FRANGIPANI	GARNIERITE	GOLDDIGGER	GRUMPINESS	HECTOLITRE	HOLOGRAPHY
FRATERETTO	GASCONNADE	GOLDENSEAL	GUACHAMOLE	HEDONISTIC	HOLOHEDRAL
FRATERNISE	GASTEROPOD	GOLDFINGER	GUARANTEED	HEEDLESSLY	HOLOPHOTAL
FRATERNITY	GASTRONOME	GOLDILOCKS	GUARNERIUS	HEIDELBERG	HOLOPHYTIC
FRATERNIZE	GASTRONOMY	GOLDTHREAD	GUATEMALAN	HELICOPTER	HOLOSTERIC
FRATICELLI	GAULTHERIA	GOLIATHISE	GUBERNATOR	HELIOGRAPH	HOMECOMING

HOMELINESS	HYPNOTIZED	IMPRESARIO	INDULGENCE	INSISTENCE	INVIOLABLE
HOMEOPATHY	HYPOCORISM	IMPRESSION	INDUMENTUM	INSOLENTLY	INVITATION
HOMEOUSIAN	HYPODERMIC	IMPRESSIVE	INDUSTRIAL	INSOLVENCY	INVOCATION
HOMEWORKER	HYPOGAEOUS	IMPRIMATUR	INEBRIATED	INSOUCIANT	INVOLUTION
HOMOEOPATH	HYPOGENOUS	IMPROBABLE	INEDUCABLE	INSPECTION	IONOSPHERE
HOMOGENIZE	HYPOTENUSE	IMPROBABLY	INEFFICACY	INSPISSATE	IRIDESCENT
HOMOOUSIAN	HYPOTHESIS	IMPROPERLY	INELIGIBLE	INSTALMENT	IRISHWOMAN
HOMOPHOBIA	HYPSOMETRY	IMPROVISED	INEPTITUDE	INSTIGATOR	IRISHWOMEN
HOMOPHOBIC	HYSTERESIS	IMPRUDENCE	INEQUALITY	INSTRUCTED	IRONICALLY
HOMOPHONIC	HYSTERICAL	IMPUDENTLY	INESCULENT	INSTRUCTOR	IRONMONGER
HOMORELAPS	IATROGENIC	IMPURITIES	INEVITABLE	INSTRUMENT	IRRADICATE
HOMOSEXUAL	ICEBREAKER	IMPUTATION	INEVITABLY	INSUFFLATE	IRRATIONAL
HOMUNCULUS	ICHTHYOSIS	INACCURACY	INEXORABLE	INSULARITY	IRRELEVANT
HONEYBUNCH	ICONOCLAST	INACCURATE	INFALLIBLE	INSULATION	IRREMEDIAL
HONORARIUM	ICONOSCOPE	INACTIVITY	INFALLIBLY	INSURGENCY	IRRESOLUTE
HONOURABLE	ICOSANDRIA	INADEQUACY	INFATUATED	INTAGLIATE	IRREVERENT
HONOURABLY	ICOSOHEDRA	INADEQUATE	INFECTIOUS	INTANGIBLE	IRRIGATION
HONOURLESS	IDEALISTIC	INAPTITUDE	INFEFTMENT	INTEGRATED	IRRITATING
HOODWINKED	IGNIMBRITE	INARTISTIC	INFERNALLY	INTEGUMENT	IRRITATION
HOOTANANNY	IGNORANTLY	INAUGURATE	INFIBULATE	INTELIGENT	ISABELLINE
HOOTENANNY	ILLADVISED	INBREEDING	INFIDELITY	INTEMERATE	ISOLEUCINE
HOOTNANNIE	ILLAQUEATE	INCAPACITY	INFIGHTING	INTEMPERATE	ISOMETRICS
HOPELESSLY	ILLEGALITY	INCAPARINA	INFILTRATE	INTENERATE	ISONIAZIDE
HORIZONTAL	ILLITERACY	INCAUTIOUS	INFINITELY	INTENTNESS	JABBERWOCK
HORNBLENDE	ILLITERATE	INCENDIARY	INFINITIVE	INTERBREED	JACKANAPES
HORNBLOWER	ILLUMINATE	INCESTUOUS	INFLATABLE	INTERCEDER	JACKBOOTED
HORNRIMMED	ILLUMINATI	INCHOATIVE	INFLECTION	INTERCLUDE	JACKHAMMER
HORRENDOUS	ILLUSTRATE	INCIDENTAL	INFLEXIBLE	INTERESTED	JACKSTONES
HORRIFYING	IMAGINABLE	INCINERATE	INFLEXIBLY	INTERFERER	JACKSTRAWS
HORSEDRAWN	IMBECILITY	INCISIVELY	INFLICTION	INTERFERON	JACULATION
HORSELBERG	IMBRICATED	INCITEMENT	INFORMALLY	INTERLEAVE	JAGUARONDI
HORSEPOWER	IMBROCCATA	INCIVILITY	INFRACTION	INTERLOPER	JAGUARUNDI
HORSERIDER	IMMACULACY	INCOHERENT	INFREQUENT	INTERMARRY	JAMESONITE
HORSEWOMAN	IMMACULATE	INCOMPLETE	INFURIATED	INTERMEZZO	JARDINIERE
HOSPITABLE	IMMATERIAL	INCONSTANT	INGEMINATE	INTERNALLY	JARGONELLE
HOSPITABLY	IMMATURITY	INCRASSATE	INGENERATE	INTERNMENT	JAUNTINESS
HOTCHPOTCH	IMMEMORIAL	INCREASING	INGLORIOUS	INTERNODAL	JAYWALKING
HOUSEBOUND	IMMOBILITY	INCREDIBLE	INGRATIATE	INTERPHONE	JEISTIECOR
HOUSECRAFT	IMMOBILIZE	INCREDIBLY	INGREDIENT	INTERSTATE	JEOPARDISE
HOUSEMAIDS	IMMODERATE	INCRESCENT	INHABITANT	INTERSTICE	JEOPARDIZE
HOUSEPROUD	IMMOLATION	INCUBATION	INHALATION	INTERTRIGO	JERRYBUILT
HOVERCRAFT	IMMORALITY	INCUMBENCY	INHERENTLY	INTERTWINE	JIGGAMAREE
HOWLEGLASS	IMMORTELLE	INCUNABULA	INHIBITING	INTERWEAVE	JIGGERMAST
HOWSOMEVER	IMMUNOLOGY	INDAPAMIDE	INHIBITION	INTERWOVEN	JINGOISTIC
HULLABALOO	IMPAIRMENT	INDECENTLY	INHIBITORY	INTESTINAL	JOBSEEKERS
HUMANISTIC	IMPALPABLE	INDECISION	INHUMANITY	INTESTINES	JOCULARITY
HUMANITIES	IMPALUDISM	INDECISIVE	INIMITABLE	INTIMATELY	JOHNSONIAN
HUMBLENESS	IMPARLANCE	INDECOROUS	INIQUITOUS	INTIMATION	JOLTERHEAD
HUMDUDGEON	IMPASSABLE	INDEFINITE	INITIATION	INTIMIDATE	JOURNALESE
HUMIDIFIER	IMPATIENCE	INDELICACY	INITIATIVE	INTINCTION	JOURNALISM
HUMIDISTAT	IMPECCABLE	INDELICATE	INJUNCTION	INTOLERANT	JOURNALIST
HUMORESQUE	IMPECCABLY	INDENTURES	INKSLINGER	INTONATION	JOURNEYMAN
HUMOROUSLY	IMPEDIMENT	INDEXATION	INNERSPACE	INTOXICANT	JOUYSAUNCE
HUMOURLESS	IMPENITENT	INDICATION	INNOCENTLY	INTOXICATE	JUBILANTLY
HUMPBACKED	IMPERATIVE	INDICATIVE	INNOVATION	INTRAURBAN	JUBILATION
HUSBANDAGE	IMPERSONAL	INDICOLITE	INNOVATIVE	INTRIGUING	JUDICATURE
HYALOPHANE	IMPERVIOUS	INDICTABLE	INOPERABLE	INTROSPECT	JUDICIALLY
HYDRAULICS	IMPLACABLE	INDICTMENT	INORDINATE	INUNDATION	JUGENDSTIL
HYDROLYSIS	IMPLACABLY	INDIGENOUS	INOSCULATE	INVALIDATE	JUGGERNAUT
HYDROMETER	IMPLICITLY	INDIGOLITE	INQUIRENDO	INVALIDISM	JUSTICIARY
HYDROPHANE	IMPOLITELY	INDIRECTLY	INQUISITOR	INVALIDITY	KARMATHIAN
HYDROPHYTE	IMPORTANCE	INDISCREET	INSANITARY	INVALUABLE	KARTTIKAYA
HYDROPLANE	IMPOSITION	INDISPOSED	INSATIABLE	INVARIABLE	KATERFELTO
HYDROPONIC	IMPOSSIBLE	INDISTINCT	INSATIABLY	INVARIABLY	KEMPERYMAN
HYGROMETER	IMPOSSIBLY	INDITEMENT	INSECURELY	INVESTMENT	KENILWORTH
HYPAETHRAL	IMPOSTHUME	INDIVIDUAL	INSECURITY	INVETERATE	KENSPECKLE
HYPAETHRON	IMPOTENTLY	INDONESIAN	INSEMINATE	INVIGILATE	KENTUCKIAN
HYPERBOLIC	IMPOVERISH	INDUCEMENT	INSENSIBLE	INVIGORATE	KERSEYMERE
HYPERDULIA	IMPREGNATE	INDUCTANCE	INSIPIDITY	INVINCIBLE	KESSELRING

KETTLEDRUM	LAWBREAKER	LITIGATION	MALEFACTOR	MEAGERNESS	MIDDLEBROW
KEYBOARDER	LAWRENCIUM	LITTLENESS	MALEVOLENT	MEAGRENESS	MIDLOTHIAN
KHIDMUTGAR	LEADERSHIP	LITURGICAL	MALIGNANCY	MEANDERING	MIDSHIPMAN
KIDNAPPING	LEAFHOPPER	LIVELIHOOD	MALINGERER	MEANINGFUL	MIGHTINESS
KIESELGUHR	LEAMINGTON	LIVELINESS	MALLOPHAGA	MEASURABLE	MIGNONETTE
KILMARNOCK	LEBENSRAUM	LIVERWURST	MALMESBURY	MECHANICAL	MILEOMETER
KILOMETRES	LEDERHOSEN	LOCKERROOM	MALODOROUS	MECHANIZED	MILITARISM
KIMBERLITE	LEFTHANDED	LOCKKEEPER	MALTHUSIAN	MEDDLESOME	MILITARIST
KINCHINLAY	LEFTHANDER	LOCOMOTION	MANAGEABLE	MEDICAMENT	MILITIAMAN
KINDLINESS	LEFTWINGER	LOCOMOTIVE	MANAGEMENT	MEDICATION	MILLEFIORI
KINGFISHER	LEGALISTIC	LOCULAMENT	MANAGERESS	MEDIOCRITY	MILLENNIUM
KLANGFARBE	LEGIBILITY	LOGANBERRY	MANAGERIAL	MEDITATION	MILLICURIE
KLEBSIELLA	LEGISLATOR	LOGARITHMS	MANCHESTER	MEDITATIVE	MILLIFARAD
KLOOTCHMAN	LEGITIMACY	LOGGERHEAD	MANCHINEEL	MEDIUMTERM	MILLIHENRY
KNIFEBOARD	LEGITIMATE	LOGISTICAL	MANDEVILLE	MEERSCHAUM	MILLIMETER
KNIGHTHEAD	LEGITIMIZE	LOGORRHOEA	MANDRAGORA	MEGALITHIC	MILLIMETRE
KNIGHTHOOD	LEGUMINOUS	LONELINESS	MANGABEIRA	MEGALOSAUR	MIMEOGRAPH
KNOBKERRIE	LEGWARMERS	LONGCHAMPS	MANGOSTEEN	MEITNERIUM	MINDERERUS
KNOCKABOUT	LEMNISCATE	LONGFELLOW	MANICHAEAN	MELACONITE	MINERALOGY
KOEKSISTER	LENGTHWAYS	LOQUACIOUS	MANICURIST	MELANCHOLY	MINESTRONE
KOOKABURRA	LENGTHWISE	LORDLINESS	MANIFESTLY	MELANESIAN	MINEWORKER
KRIEGSPIEL	LENOCINIUM	LORDOLATRY	MANIPULATE	MELLOWNESS	MINIMALISM
KRUGERRAND	LENTICULAR	LOTOPHAGUS	MANSERVANT	MELOCOTOON	MINIMALIST
KSHATRIYAS	LENTIGINES	LOUISIETTE	MANUSCRIPT	MEMBERSHIP	MINIMARKET
KUOMINTANG	LEONTIASIS	LOVELINESS	MANZANILLA	MEMBRANOUS	MINISTRATE
KURDAITCHA	LEOPARDESS	LUGUBRIOUS	MAQUILLAGE	MEMORANDUM	MINISTROKE
LABORATORY	LEPRECHAUN	LUMBERJACK	MARASCHINO	MENACINGLY	MINUTEBOOK
LACCADIVES	LESBIANISM	LUMINARIST	MARCANTANT	MENDACIOUS	MINUTENESS
LACERATION	LETTERHEAD	LUMINOSITY	MARCESCENT	MENECHMIAN	MIRACULOUS
LACHRYMOSE	LEUCHAEMIA	LUMPECTOMY	MARCIONITE	MENINGITIS	MISCELLANY
LACKADAISY	LEVITATION	LUMPSUCKER	MARGASIRSA	MENORRHOEA	MISCHMETAL
LACKLUSTER	LHERZOLITE	LUPERCALIA	MARGINALIA	MENSTRUATE	MISCONDUCT
LACKLUSTRE	LIBERALISM	LUSITANIAN	MARGINALLY	MEPERIDINE	MISERICORD
LACUSTRINE	LIBERALITY	LUTESTRING	MARGUERITE	MERCANTILE	MISFORTUNE
LADYKILLER	LIBERALIZE	LUXEMBOURG	MARIOLATRY	MERCIFULLY	MISGIVINGS
LAEOTROPIC	LIBERATION	LUXURIANCE	MARIONETTE	MERRYMAKER	MISHGUGGLE
LAMARCKISM	LIBIDINOUS	LYCHNAPSIA	MARKETABLE	MESENTERON	MISHNAYOTH
LAMBREQUIN	LIBRETTIST	LYSENKOISM	MARQUETRIE	MESITYLENE	MISLEADING
LAMENTABLE	LIBREVILLE	MABINOGION	MARSHALSEA	MESOLITHIC	MISMATCHED
LAMENTABLY	LICENTIATE	MACEBEARER	MARTINGALE	METABOLISE	MISOCAPNIC
LAMINATION	LICENTIOUS	MACEDONIAN	MARTINIQUE	METABOLISM	MISOGYNIST
LANCEOLATE	LIEBERMANN	MACKINTOSH	MARVELLOUS	METACARPAL	MISPRISION
LANDAMMANN	LIEUTENANT	MACONOCHIE	MARYLEBONE	METACARPUS	MISSIONARY
LANDLOCKED	LIGHTERMAN	MACROBIOTE	MASCARPONE	METACENTRE	MISTAKENLY
LANDLOUPER	LIGHTHOUSE	MACROCARPA	MASKANONGE	METALEPSIS	MITHRIDATE
LANDLUBBER	LIGHTINGUP	MADAGASCAN	MASKINONGE	METALLURGY	MITIGATING
LANDSTHING	LIGNOCAINE	MADAGASCAR	MASKIROVKA	METAPHRASE	MITIGATION
LANGERHANS	LIKELIHOOD	MAGISTRACY	MASQUERADE	METAPLASIS	MIZZENMAST
LANGUOROUS	LIKEMINDED	MAGISTRAND	MASSASAUGA	METASTABLE	MODERATELY
LANIGEROUS	LILYWHITES	MAGISTRATE	MASTECTOMY	METATARSAL	MODERATION
LANSQUENET	LIMBERNECK	MAGNIFICAT	MASTERMIND	METATARSUS	MODIFIABLE
LANTHANIDE	LIMBURGITE	MAGNIFYING	MASTERWORT	METATHERIA	MOISTURIZE
LARGESCALE	LIMITATION	MAHAYANALI	MASTURBATE	METATHESIS	MOLENDINAR
LARYNGITIS	LIMITROPHE	MAHOMMEDAN	MATCHMAKER	METHEDRINE	MOLYBDENUM
LASCIVIOUS	LINEAMENTS	MAIDENHAIR	MATCHSTALK	METHODICAL	MONANDROUS
LASTMINUTE	LINEOMYCIN	MAIDENHOOD	MATCHSTICK	METHOMANIA	MONARCHIST
LATTERMATH	LINGUISTIC	MAINPERNOR	MATELLASSE	METHUSALEH	MONEGASQUE
LATTICINIO	LINGULELLA	MAINSPRING	MATERIALLY	METHUSELAH	MONETARISM
LAUDERDALE	LIPIZZANER	MAINSTREAM	MATERNALLY	METHYLATED	MONETARIST
LAUNCEGAYE	LIQUESCENT	MAINTAINER	MATRIARCHY	METICULOUS	MONEYMAKER
LAUNCESTON	LIQUIDATOR	MAISONETTE	MATTERHORN	METROPOLIS	MONILIASIS
LAUNDROMAT	LIQUIDIZER	MAKESYSTEM	MATURATION	METTLESOME	MONILIFORM
LAURDALITE	LISTLESSLY	MAKEWEIGHT	MAUPASSANT	MICHAELMAS	MONOACIDIC
LAURENTIAN	LITERATURE	MAKUNOUCHI	MAURITANIA	MICROFICHE	MONOCARPIC
LAURUSTINE	LITHISTADA	MALACOLOGY	MAVOURNEEN	MICROLIGHT	MONOCHROME
LAURVIKITE	LITHOGRAPH	MALAGUETTA	MAXIMALIST	MICROMETER	MONOECIOUS
LAVALLIÈRE	LITHOMARGE	MALAPROPOS	MAXIMILIAN	MICRONESIA	MONOGAMOUS
LAVISHNESS	LITHOPHANE	MALAYALAAM	MAYONNAISE	MICROPHONE	MONOLITHIC
LAWABIDING	LITHUANIAN	MALCONTENT	MEADOWPLAN	MICROSCOPE	

MONOPHONIC	MUTTONHEAD	NIGHTDRESS	OBTUSENESS	OSCULATION	PALMATIFID
MONOPLEGIA	MYCORRHIZA	NIGHTLIGHT	OCCASIONAL	OSCULATORY	PALMATOZOA
MONOPODIUM	MYELINATED	NIGHTSHADE	OCCIDENTAL	OSMETERIUM	PALMERSTON
MONOPOLISE	MYOCARDIAL	NIGHTSHIRT	OCCUPATION	OSMIDROSIS	PALMERWORM
MONOPOLIZE	MYRINGITIS	NIGHTSTICK	OCCURRENCE	OSTENSIBLE	PALUDAMENT
MONOPTERON	MYRIOSCOPE	NIGRESCENT	OCEANARIUM	OSTENSIBLY	PALUSTRINE
MONOPTEROS	MYSTAGOGUE	NIHILISTIC	OCEANGOING	OSTEOBLAST	PALYNOLOGY
MONOTHEISM	MYSTAGOGUS	NIMBLENESS	OCHLOCRACY	OSTEOCOLLA	PANAMANIAN
MONOTONOUS	MYSTERIOUS	NINCOMPOOP	OCTAHEDRON	OSTEOLEPIS	PANARITIUM
MONOVALENT	NAPTHALENE	NINETEENTH	OCTODECIMO	OSTEOPATHY	PANCRATIUM
MONSTRANCE	NARCISSISM	NOBLEWOMAN	ODDFELLOWS	OSTEOPHYTE	PANJANDRUM
MONTAGNARD	NARCOLEPSY	NOMINALIST	ODELSTHING	OSTROGOTHS	PANNICULUS
MONTESSORI	NARROWBOAT	NOMINATION	ODIOUSNESS	OTHERGATES	PANOPTICON
MONTEVERDI	NARROWDALE	NOMINATIVE	ODONTALGIA	OTHERGUESS	PANSOPHIST
MONTEVIDEO	NARROWNESS	NOMOTHETIC	ODONTOLITE	OUANANICHE	PANTAGRUEL
MONTGOMERY	NASTURTIUM	NONALIGNED	ODONTOLOGY	OUGHTLINGS	PANTALOONS
MONTICULUS	NATATORIAL	NONCHALANT	OESOPHAGUS	OUTBALANCE	PANTOGRAPH
MONTRACHET	NATATORIUM	NONFICTION	OFFBALANCE	OUTLANDISH	PANTOSCOPE
MONTSERRAT	NATHELESSE	NONONSENSE	OFFICIALLY	OUTPATIENT	PAPAVERINE
MONUMENTAL	NATIONALLY	NONPAYMENT	OFFLICENCE	OUTPERFORM	PAPERCHASE
MORALITIES	NATIONWIDE	NONPLUSSED	OFFPUTTING	OUTPOURING	PAPERKNIFE
MORATORIUM	NATTERJACK	NONSMOKING	OFFTHECUFF	OUTRAGEOUS	PAPIAMENTO
MORBIDEZZA	NATURALISM	NONSUCCESS	OFFTHEWALL	OUTSPECKLE	PARACELSUS
MORDACIOUS	NATURALIST	NONVINTAGE	OFTENTIMES	OUVIRANDRA	PARADIDDLE
MORGANATIC	NATURALIZE	NONVIOLENT	OIREACHTAS	OVERBOUGHT	PARADOXIDE
MORGANETTA	NATUROPATH	NORBERTINE	OLEAGINOUS	OVERCHARGE	PARADOXINE
MORIGEROUS	NAUSEATING	NORMOBLAST	OLERACEOUS	OVEREATING	PARAENESIS
MORISONIAN	NAUSEATIVE	NORTHANGER	OMBROMETER	OVERLANDER	PARAGLOSSA
MOROSENESS	NAVIGATION	NORTHBOUND	OMBROPHOBE	OVERMATTER	PARAGONITE
MORPHOLOGY	NDRANGHETA	NORTHERNER	OMNIPOTENT	OVERPRAISE	PARAGUAYAN
MORTADELLA	NEAPOLITAN	NORTHSTEAD	OMNISCIENT	OVERRIDING	PARALLELED
MOSASAUROS	NECROMANCY	NORTHWARDS	OMNIVOROUS	OVERSHADOW	PARAMARIBO
MOSSBUNKER	NECROPOLIS	NOSOCOMIAL	OMOPHORION	OVERSLAUGH	PARAMETRIC
MOTHERHOOD	NECTABANUS	NOSOPHOBIA	ONOMASTICS	OVERSPREAD	PARANORMAL
MOTHERLAND	NEEDLECASE	NOTABILITY	OOPHORITIS	OVERSTRAIN	PARAPHASIA
MOTHERLESS	NEEDLEWORK	NOTEWORTHY	OPALESCENT	OVERSTRUNG	PARAPHILIA
MOTHERLIKE	NEFANDROUS	NOTICEABLE	OPENHANDED	OVERSUPPLY	PARAPHONIA
MOTIONLESS	NEGATIVELY	NOTICEABLY	OPENMINDED	OVERTHETOP	PARAPHRASE
MOTIVATION	NEGLECTFUL	NOTIFIABLE	OPHICLEIDE	OVERTHWART	PARAPHYSIS
MOTORCYCLE	NEGLIGENCE	NOTIONALLY	OPHTHALMIC	OVERWEIGHT	PARAPLEGIA
MOUCHARABY	NEGLIGIBLE	NOTORYCTES	OPISOMETER	OVERWORKED	PARAPLEGIC
MOUDIEWART	NEGOTIABLE	NOUAKCHOTT	OPOTHERAPY	OVIPOSITOR	PARAPRAXIS
MOULDINESS	NEGOTIATOR	NOURISHING	OPPOSITION	OWLSPIEGLE	PARARTHRIA
MOULDIWARP	NEIGHBORLY	NOURRITURE	OPPRESSION	OXYGENATOR	PARASCENIA
MOUNTEBANK	NEMATOCYST	NOVACULITE	OPPRESSIVE	OXYMORONIC	PARASELENE
MOURNFULLY	NEOTERICAL	NUCLEONICS	OPPROBRIUM	OZYMANDIAS	PARASTATAL
MOUSEPIECE	NESSELRODE	NUDIBRANCH	OPTIMISTIC	PACESETTER	PARATROOPS
MOUSSELINE	NETHERMOST	NUMBERLESS	ORANGEWOOD	PACIFICISM	PARDONABLE
MOUSTERIAN	NETTLERASH	NUMERATION	ORATORICAL	PADAREWSKI	PARDONABLY
MOUTHORGAN	NETTLETREE	NUMISMATIC	ORCHESTRAL	PADDINGTON	PARENCHYMA
MOUTHPIECE	NETWORKING	NURSERYMAN	ORCHIDEOUS	PADDLEFISH	PARENTHOOD
MOZAMBIQUE	NEURILEMMA	NUTCRACKER	ORDINARILY	PADDYMELON	PARENTLESS
MOZZARELLA	NEUROLEMMA	NUTRITIOUS	ORDINATION	PAEDIATRIC	PARGETTING
MUCKRAKING	NEUTRALISE	NYCTALOPIA	ORDONNANCE	PAGINATION	PARISCHANE
MUDSKIPPER	NEUTRALITY	NYMPHOLEPT	ORDOVICIAN	PAINKILLER	PARISIENNE
MUJAHEDDIN	NEUTRALIZE	OBEDIENTLY	ORIDINANCE	PAINLESSLY	PARKLEAVES
MULIEBRITY	NEUTROPHIL	OBFUSCATED	ORIGINALLY	PAINTBRUSH	PARLIAMENT
MULLIGRUBS	NEWFANGLED	OBJECTLESS	ORIGINATOR	PALAEOTYPE	PARMACITIE
MULTIMEDIA	NEWSAGENTS	OBLIGATION	ORNAMENTAL	PALAESTRAL	PARMIGIANA
MULTIPLIED	NEWSCASTER	OBLIGATORY	OROBRANCHE	PALAGONITE	PARNASSIAN
MULTIPLIER	NEWSLETTER	OBLIGINGLY	OROGENESIS	PALATALISE	PARNELLISM
MUMBLENEWS	NEWSMONGER	OBLITERATE	ORPHEOREON	PALATINATE	PARONYCHIA
MUNIFICENT	NEWSPAPERS	OBLOMOVISM	ORTHOCAINE	PALESTRINA	PARRAMATTA
MUSICOLOGY	NEWSREADER	OBSEQUIOUS	ORTHOCLASE	PALFRENIER	PARTHENOPE
MUSKETEERS	NEWSWORTHY	OBSERVABLE	ORTHOGONAL	PALIMPSEST	PARTIALITY
MUSSORGSKY	NICARAGUAN	OBSERVANCE	ORTHOPNOEA	PALINDROME	PARTICIPLE
MUTABILITY	NICROSILAL	OBSIDIONAL	ORTHOPTICS	PALISANDER	PARTICULAR
MUTILATION	NIDDERLING	OBSTETRICS	OSCILLATOR	PALLBEARER	PARTINGALE
MUTINOUSLY	NIGGERHEAD	OBTAINABLE	OSCITATION	PALLIATIVE	PARVOVIRUS

PASIGRAPHY	PERDITIOUS	PHENOMENON	PLASMODESM	PORRACEOUS	PRESSURIZE
PASQUINADE	PERDURABLE	PHILATELIC	PLASTICINE	PORTAMENTO	PRESUMABLY
PASSAGEWAY	PEREMPTORY	PHILIPPINA	PLASTICITY	PORTCULLIS	PRESUPPOSE
PASSAMEZZO	PERFECTION	PHILIPPINE	PLATELAYER	PORTENTOUS	PRETENSION
PASSIONATE	PERFICIENT	PHILISTINE	PLATINISED	PORTIONIST	PRETINCOLE
PASTEBOARD	PERFIDIOUS	PHILLIPINA	PLATTELAND	PORTMANTLE	PRETTINESS
PASTEURISE	PERFORATED	PHILLIPINE	PLAYFELLOW	PORTMANTUA	PREVAILING
PASTEURIZE	PERFORATOR	PHILLUMENY	PLAYGROUND	PORTSMOUTH	PREVALENCE
PASTORELLA	PERFORMING	PHILOPOENA	PLAYWRIGHT	PORTUGUESE	PREVENANCY
PATAGONIAN	PERIDOTITE	PHILOSOPHY	PLEASANTLY	POSITIVELY	PREVENTION
PATAVINITY	PERIEGESIS	PHILOXENIA	PLEASANTRY	POSITIVIST	PREVENTIVE
PATCHCOCKE	PERIHELION	PHLEBOTOMY	PLEBISCITE	POSSESSION	PREVIOUSLY
PATCHINESS	PERILOUSLY	PHLEGETHON	PLEONASTIC	POSSESSIVE	PRICKLOUSE
PATERNALLY	PERIODICAL	PHLEGMASIA	PLEROPHORY	POSTCHAISE	PRIESTHOOD
PATHFINDER	PERIPHERAL	PHLEGMATIC	PLESIOSAUR	POSTHUMOUS	PRIMORDIAL
PATHOGENIC	PERISHABLE	PHLOGISTIC	PLEXIMETER	POSTILLATE	PRINCIPIUM
PATIBULARY	PERIWINKLE	PHLOGISTON	PLIABILITY	POSTILLION	PRINCIPLED
PATISSERIE	PERMAFROST	PHLOGOPITE	PLIOHIPPUS	POSTLIMINY	PRINCIPLES
PATRIARCHY	PERMANENCE	PHOLIDOSIS	PLOUGHBOTE	POSTMASTER	PRIVATEERS
PATRIOTISM	PERMANENCY	PHONOGRAPH	PLOUGHGATE	POSTMORTEM	PRIVILEGED
PATRONISED	PERMEATION	PHOSPHORUS	PLOUGHWISE	POSTSCRIPT	PRIZEFIGHT
PATRONYMIC	PERMISSION	PHOTODIODE	PLUMASSIER	POTENTIATE	PROAIRESIS
PAWNBROKER	PERMISSIVE	PHOTOGENIC	PLUNDERING	POTENTILLA	PROCEDURAL
PEACEFULLY	PERNICIOUS	PHOTOGRAPH	PLUPERFECT	POURPARLER	PROCEEDING
PEACEMAKER	PERNICKETY	PHOTONASTY	PLUTOCRACY	POWERHOUSE	PROCESSING
PEACHERINO	PERORATION	PHOTOPHORE	POCAHONTAS	POZZUOLANA	PROCESSION
PEASHOOTER	PEROVSKITE	PHRENESIAC	POCKETBOOK	PRAEMUNIRE	PROCLIVITY
PEAUDESOIE	PERPETRATE	PHRENOLOGY	POCKMANTIE	PRAETORIAN	PROCREATOR
PECCADILLO	PERPETUATE	PHYLACTERY	POCKMARKED	PRAETORIUM	PROCRUSTES
PECULATION	PERPETUITY	PHYLLIOPOD	POETASTERY	PRAGMATISM	PROCUMBENT
PECULIARLY	PERPLEXING	PHYSICALLY	POETICALLY	PRAGMATIST	PROCURABLE
PEDESTRIAN	PERPLEXITY	PHYSIOCRAT	POGONOTOMY	PRATINCOLE	PROCURATOR
PEDIATRICS	PERQUISITE	PHYSIOLOGY	POHUTUKAWA	PRAXITELES	PRODIGALLY
PEDICULATE	PERSECUTOR	PHYTOTOXIN	POIGNANTLY	PREARRANGE	PRODIGIOUS
PEDIMENTAL	PERSEPHONE	PIANISSIMO	POIKILITIC	PREBENDARY	PRODUCTION
PEDIPALPUS	PERSEPOLIS	PIANOFORTE	POINSETTIA	PRECARIOUS	PRODUCTIVE
PEELGARLIC	PERSICARIA	PICARESQUE	POINTBLANK	PRECAUTION	PROFESSION
PEJORATIVE	PERSIENNES	PICAYUNISH	POKERFACED	PRECEDENCE	PROFICIENT
PENELOPHON	PERSIFLAGE	PICCADILLY	POLIANTHES	PRECIPITIN	PROFITABLE
PENETRABLE	PERSISTENT	PICCALILLI	POLITENESS	PRECOCIOUS	PROFITABLY
PENETRALIA	PERSONABLE	PICCANINNY	POLITICIAN	PRECURSORY	PROFITLESS
PENICILLIN	PERSONALLY	PICHICIAGO	POLITICIZE	PREDACIOUS	PROFLIGACY
PENINSULAR	PERSTRINGE	PICHICIEGO	POLLINATED	PREDECEASE	PROFLIGATE
PENNILLION	PERSUADING	PICKPOCKET	POLYANTHUS	PREDESTINE	PROFOUNDLY
PENNISETUM	PERSUASION	PICTOGRAPH	POLYCHAETE	PREDICTION	PROFUNDITY
PENSIEROSO	PERSUASIVE	PIGEONHOLE	POLYCHREST	PREDISPOSE	PROGENITOR
PENSIONNAT	PERTINENCE	PILEDRIVER	POLYCHROME	PREDNISONE	PROGESSION
PENTAGONAL	PERVERSELY	PILGARLICK	POLYGAMIST	PREEMINENT	PROGRAMMER
PENTAMERON	PERVERSION	PILGRIMAGE	POLYGAMOUS	PREFERABLE	PROHIBITED
PENTAMETER	PERVERSITY	PILLIWINKS	POLYHEDRON	PREFERABLY	PROJECTILE
PENTATEUCH	PESCADORES	PILLOWCASE	POLYHYMNIA	PREFERENCE	PROJECTING
PENTATHLON	PESTALOZZI	PILLOWSLIP	POLYMERIZE	PREFERMENT	PROJECTION
PENTATONIC	PESTILENCE	PINAKOTHEK	POLYNESIAN	PREHENSILE	PROMENADER
PENTELIKON	PETITIONER	PINCHPENNY	POLYNOMIAL	PREHISTORY	PROMETHEAN
PENTETERIC	PETRARCHAN	PINCUSHION	POLYPHEMUS	PREJUDICED	PROMETHEUS
PENTIMENTO	PETRIFYING	PINNIPEDIA	POLYTHEISM	PRELECTION	PROMETHIUM
PENTSTEMON	PETRISSAGE	PIONEERING	POLYVALENT	PREMARITAL	PROMINENCE
PEPPERCORN	PETROGLYPH	PIPSISSEWA	POMERANIAN	PREMEDICAL	PROMISSORY
PEPPERMILL	PETRONELLA	PIRANDELLO	PONCHIELLI	PREPARATOR	PROMONTORY
PEPPERMINT	PETTICHAPS	PISTILLATE	PONEROLOGY	PREPAYMENT	PROMPTBOOK
PEPPERWORT	PETTYCHAPS	PITCHSTONE	PONTEDERIA	PREPENSELY	PROMPTNESS
PERCENTAGE	PETULANTLY	PITYRIASIS	PONTEFRACT	PREPOSITOR	PROMULGATE
PERCENTILE	PHAELONIAN	PLAGIARISE	PONTICELLO	PREPOSSESS	PRONOUNCED
PERCEPTION	PHAENOTYPE	PLAGIARISM	PONTIFICAL	PREPOTENCE	PROPAGANDA
PERCEPTIVE	PHAGEDAENA	PLAGIARIST	POPULARITY	PRESBYOPIA	PROPAGATOR
PERCIPIENT	PHANTASIME	PLAGIARIZE	POPULARIZE	PRESBYTERY	PROPELLANT
PERCOLATOR	PHANTASIST	PLANCHETTE	POPULATION	PRESCIENCE	PROPELLENT
PERCUSSION	PHARMACIST	PLANOBLAST	PORLOCKING	PRESENTDAY	PROPENSITY
PERDENDOSI	PHENOMENAL	PLANTATION	PORNOCRACY	PRESIDENCY	PROPERTIUS

PROPHETESS	PUNCTULATE	RAWSTHORNE	RELUCTANCE	REVERSIBLE	RUDDERLESS
PROPIONATE	PUNDIGRION	RAZZMATAZZ	REMARKABLE	REVITALIZE	RUDIMENTAL
PROPITIATE	PUNICACEAE	REACTIVATE	REMARKABLY	REVIVALIST	RUDOLPHINE
PROPITIOUS	PUNISHABLE	READERSHIP	REMITTANCE	REVOCATION	RUGGEDNESS
PROPLITEAL	PUNISHMENT	REAMINGBIT	REMONETISE	REVOLUTION	RUMBLOSSOM
PROPORTION	PURITANISM	REAPPRAISE	REMORSEFUL	RHAMPASTOS	RUMBULLION
PROPOSITUS	PURPOSEFUL	REARMAMENT	REMOTENESS	RHAPSODISE	RUMINANTIA
PROPRAETOR	PURSUIVANT	REASONABLE	REMUNERATE	RHAPSODIST	RUMINATION
PROPRIETOR	PUTREFYING	REASONABLY	RENDEZVOUS	RHAPSODIZE	RUMINATIVE
PROPULSION	PUTRESCENT	REASSEMBLE	RENOVATION	RHEOTROPIC	RUPESTRIAN
PROPYLAEUM	PUZZLEMENT	REASSURING	REORGANIZE	RHETORICAL	RUPICOLINE
PROSCENIUM	PYCNOGONID	REBELLIOUS	REPAIRABLE	RHEUMATICS	RUSSIANIZE
PROSCIUTTO	PYRACANTHA	RECEPTACLE	REPARATION	RHEUMATISM	RUTHERFORD
PROSCRIBED	PYRAGYRITE	RECIDIVISM	REPATRIATE	RHEUMATOID	RUTHLESSLY
PROSECUTOR	PYRIDOXINE	RECIDIVIST	REPEATABLE	RHINEGRAVE	SABBATICAL
PROSERPINA	PYROGRAPHY	RECIPROCAL	REPEATEDLY	RHINESTONE	SABRETACHE
PROSERPINE	PYROMANIAC	RECITATION	REPENTANCE	RHINOCEROS	SACCHARASE
PROSILIENT	PYROPHORUS	RECITATIVE	REPERTOIRE	RHINOLALIA	SACCHARIDE
PROSPECTOR	PYTHAGORAS	RECITATIVO	REPETITEUR	RHINOPHYMA	SACCHARINE
PROSPECTUS	PYTHOGENIC	RECKLESSLY	REPETITION	RHIPIPTERA	SACCHAROID
PROSPERINA	QUADRANGLE	RECOGNISED	REPETITIVE	RHOEADALES	SACERDOTAL
PROSPERITY	QUADRATURA	RECOGNIZED	REPORTEDLY	RHYTHMICAL	SACREDNESS
PROSPEROUS	QUADRICEPS	RECOMMENCE	REPOSITORY	RIBOFLAVIN	SACROSANCT
PROSTHESIS	QUADRIREME	RECOMPENSE	REPRESSION	RICHARDSON	SADDLEBACK
PROSTHETIC	QUAESTUARY	RECONCILED	REPRESSIVE	RICHTHOFEN	SADDLEBILL
PROSTITUTE	QUAINTNESS	RECONSIDER	REPRODUCER	RIDICULOUS	SAGITTARIA
PROTAGORAS	QUARANTINE	RECREATION	REPUBLICAN	RIDINGHOOD	SALAMANDER
PROTANOPIA	QUARRENDER	RECRUDESCE	REPUGNANCE	RIGELATION	SALBUTAMOL
PROTANOPIC	QUARTERING	RECUPERATE	REPUTATION	RIGHTFULLY	SALESWOMAN
PROTECTION	QUARTEROON	RECURRENCE	REQUIESCAT	RIGHTWARDS	SALICORNIA
PROTECTIVE	QUATERNARY	REDCURRANT	REREDORTER	RIGOROUSLY	SALIVATION
PROTERVITY	QUEASINESS	REDECORATE	RESCHEDULE	RIJSTTAFEL	SALLENDERS
PROTESTANT	QUEENSBURY	REDEMPTION	RESEARCHER	RINDERPEST	SALMAGUNDI
PROTOPLASM	QUEENSTOWN	REDISCOVER	RESEMBLING	RINGELMANN	SALMANAZAR
PROTRACTED	QUENCHLESS	REDRUTHITE	RESENTMENT	RINGLEADER	SALMONELLA
PROTRACTOR	QUERCITRON	REDUNDANCY	RESERVISTS	RINGMASTER	SALOPETTES
PROTRUSILE	QUERSPRUNG	REELECTION	RESIGNEDLY	RIPSNORTER	SALPINGIAN
PROTRUSION	QUESADILLA	REFERENDUM	RESILIENCE	RITORNELLE	SALTARELLO
PROVEDITOR	QUESTIONER	REFINEMENT	RESISTANCE	RITORNELLO	SALTCELLAR
PROVENANCE	QUICKSANDS	REFLECTING	RESOLUTELY	ROADRUNNER	SALTIGRADE
PROVERBIAL	QUICKTHORN	REFLECTION	RESOLUTION	ROADWORTHY	SALUBRIOUS
PROVIDENCE	QUIESCENCE	REFLECTIVE	RESORCINOL	ROBERTSMAN	SALUTATION
PROVINCIAL	QUIRINALIA	REFRACTION	RESOUNDING	ROBERTSMAN	SALVADORAN
PROVISIONS	QUIZMASTER	REFRACTIVE	RESPECTFUL	ROBUSTIOUS	SAMARSKITE
PRUDENTIAL	RABBINICAL	REFRACTORY	RESPECTING	ROBUSTNESS	SAMOTHRACE
PRZEWALSKI	RACECOURSE	REFRESHING	RESPECTIVE	ROCKABILLY	SANATORIUM
PSALTERIUM	RADICALISM	REFRINGENT	RESPIRATOR	ROCKINGHAM	SANCTIFIED
PSAMMOPHIL	RADIOGRAPH	REFUTATION	RESPONDENT	ROCKSTEADY	SANCTITIES
PSEPHOLOGY	RADIOLARIA	REGARDLESS	RESPONSIVE	ROISTERING	SANCTITUDE
PSEUDOCARP	RAGAMUFFIN	REGENERATE	RESTAURANT	ROLANDSECK	SANDALWOOD
PSILOCYBIN	RAILWAYMAN	REGIMENTAL	RESTLESSLY	ROLLICKING	SANDEMANIA
PSOCOPTERA	RAIYATWARI	REGIMENTED	RESTRAINED	ROMANESQUE	SANDERLING
PSYCHIATRY	RAJPRAMUKH	REGISTERED	RESTRICTED	ROQUELAURE	SANDGROPER
PSYCHOLOGY	RAMPALLIAN	REGRESSION	RESUMPTION	ROSANILINE	SANDINISTA
PSYCHOPATH	RAMSHACKLE	REGRESSIVE	RESUPINATE	ROSECHAFER	SANDWICHES
PSYCHOPOMP	RANDLETREE	REGULARITY	RESURGENCE	ROSEMALING	SANFORISED
PTERANODON	RANDOMNESS	REGULARIZE	RETICULATE	ROTHSCHILD	SANGUINARY
PTERYGOTUS	RANNELTREE	REGULATION	RETINALITE	ROTISSERIE	SANITARIUM
PUBERULENT	RANNLETREE	REITERATED	RETIREMENT	ROTTWEILER	SANITATION
PUBESCENCE	RANTLETREE	REJONEADOR	RETRACTION	ROUGHHOUSE	SANNAYASIN
PUBLISHING	RANUNCULUS	REJUVENATE	RETRAINING	ROUNDABOUT	SAPPERMENT
PUCKERWOOD	RAPPORTEUR	RELATIVELY	RETREATING	ROUNDHOUSE	SAPROPHYTE
PUGNACIOUS	RATIONALLY	RELATIVITY	RETROGRADE	ROUSEABOUT	SARCOCOLLA
PULSATORE	RATTLETRAP	RELAXATION	RETROGRESS	ROUSTABOUT	SARCOLEMMA
PULSOMETER	RAVENOUSLY	RELAXATIVE	RETROSPECT	ROWDYDOWDY	SARMENTOUS
PUMMELLING	RAVENSBILL	RELEGATION	RETURNABLE	ROWLANDSON	SARSQUATCH
PUMPHANDLE	RAVENSDUCK	RELENTLESS	REVELATION	RUBBERNECK	SATISFYING
PUNCHDRUNK	RAVENSTONE	RELINQUISH	REVENGEFUL	RUBIGINOUS	SATURATION
PUNCTUALLY	RAWINSONDE	RELOCATION	REVERENTLY	RUBINSTEIN	SATURNALIA

SATYAGRAHA	SEASONABLY	SHEEPSHANK	SKATEBOARD	SOUTHWARDS	STABILISER
SAUERKRAUT	SECONDBEST	SHELDONIAN	SKEPTICISM	SPACECRAFT	STABILIZER
SAUROPSIDA	SECONDHAND	SHELLSHOCK	SKETCHBOOK	SPALLATION	STADHOLDER
SAVAGENESS	SECONDMENT	SHELLYCOAT	SKEUOMORPH	SPARSENESS	STAGECOACH
SAVONAROLA	SECONDRATE	SHENANIGAN	SKILLFULLY	SPARTACIST	STAGECRAFT
SAXICOLINE	SECRETAIRE	SHERARDISE	SKINDIVING	SPATCHCOCK	STAGGERING
SAXICOLOUS	SECULARIZE	SHIBBOLETH	SKRIMSHANK	SPEAKERINE	STAGNATION
SBUDDIKINS	SECURITIES	SHIELDRAKE	SKUPSHTINA	SPECIALISE	STALACTITE
SCAMMOZZIS	SEDATENESS	SHIFTINESS	SKYSCRAPER	SPECIALISM	STALAGMITE
SCANDALISE	SEDULOUSLY	SHILLELAGH	SLAMMERKIN	SPECIALIST	STALHELMER
SCANDALIZE	SEECATCHIE	SHIMMERING	SLANDEROUS	SPECIALITY	STALLENGER
SCANDALOUS	SEEMLIHEAD	SHIPWRIGHT	SLATTERNLY	SPECIALIZE	STALLINGER
SCANDAROON	SEERSUCKER	SHISHKEBAB	SLEEPINESS	SPECIOUSLY	STAMMERING
SCANDERBEG	SEGREGATED	SHOCKINGLY	SLEEVELESS	SPECTACLED	STANDPOINT
SCANTINESS	SEGUIDILLA	SHOCKPROOF	SLIPSTREAM	SPECTACLES	STANDSTILL
SCAPEGRACE	SEISMOLOGY	SHODDINESS	SLOPPINESS	SPECTATORS	STANISLAUS
SCAPHOPODA	SELEGILINE	SHOESTRING	SLUGGISHLY	SPECULATOR	STAPHYLINE
SCARAMOUCH	SELFESTEEM	SHOPKEEPER	SLUICEGATE	SPEECHLESS	STARVATION
SCARCEMENT	SELFSTYLED	SHOPLIFTER	SLUMBERING	SPEEDINESS	STARVELING
SCARCENESS	SELLINGERS	SHOPSOILED	SMALLSCALE	SPELEOLOGY	STATECRAFT
SCARLATINA	SELTZOGENE	SHOPWALKER	SMARAGDINE	SPELLBOUND	STATIONARY
SCARLETINA	SEMICIRCLE	SHORTBREAD	SMARMINESS	SPENCERIAN	STATIONERY
SCATHELESS	SEMIQUAVER	SHORTENING	SMATTERING	SPENSERIAN	STATISTICS
SCATTERING	SENATORIAL	SHORTLIVED	SMITHEREEN	SPERMACETI	STATOCRACY
SCATURIENT	SENEGALESE	SHORTRANGE	SMOKESTACK	SPERMICIDE	STATUESQUE
SCEPTICISM	SENESCENCE	SHOVELHEAD	SMOOTHNESS	SPERRYLITE	STAUROLITE
SCHALSTEIN	SENSUALITY	SHOVELNOSE	SMORREBROD	SPHACELATE	STAVESACRE
SCHIPPERKE	SENSUOUSLY	SHOWJUMPER	SNAKEMOUTH	SPHALERITE	STEADINESS
SCHISMATIC	SEPARATELY	SHREWDNESS	SNAKESTONE	SPIDERWORT	STEAKHOUSE
SCHLIMAZEL	SEPARATION	SHRIEVALTY	SNAPDRAGON	SPIFLICATE	STEALTHILY
SCHOLAEMIA	SEPARATISM	SHRILLNESS	SNAPHAUNCE	SPILLIKINS	STEELINESS
SCHOLASTIC	SEPARATIST	SHRIVELLED	SNAPHAUNCH	SPINESCENT	STEELWORKS
SCHOOLBOOK	SEPARATRIX	SHROVETIDE	SNEEZEWOOD	SPIRACULUM	STEMWINDER
SCHOOLGIRL	SEPTENNIAL	SHUDDERING	SNIGGERING	SPIRITEDLY	STENOTYPER
SCHOOLMAAM	SEPTUAGINT	SICILIENNE	SNOOTINESS	SPIRITLESS	STENTORIAN
SCHWARZLOT	SEPULCHRAL	SIDEBOARDS	SNORKELING	SPIRITUOUS	STEPFATHER
SCIENTIFIC	SEQUACIOUS	SIDERATION	SNOWBLOWER	SPIRKETING	STEPHANITE
SCINTIGRAM	SEQUENTIAL	SIDEROSTAT	SNOWCAPPED	SPISSITUDE	STEPHENSON
SCLERIASIS	SERMONICAL	SIDESADDLE	SNOWMOBILE	SPITCHCOCK	STEPLADDER
SCOFFINGLY	SERPENTINE	SIDEWINDER	SOBERSIDES	SPITEFULLY	STEPMOTHER
SCOMBRESOX	SERRADELLA	SIGILLARIA	SOFTBOILED	SPLANCHNIC	STEPSISTER
SCOOTERIST	SERRADILLA	SIGNIFICAT	SOGDOLAGER	SPLENDIDLY	STEREOTOMY
SCOPELIDAE	SERRASALMO	SIGNORELLI	SOGDOLIGER	SPLITLEVEL	STEREOTYPE
SCORDATURA	SERVICEMAN	SILHOUETTE	SOGDOLOGER	SPODOMANCY	STEREOTYPY
SCOREBOARD	SERVOMOTOR	SILVERBACK	SOLICITOUS	SPOILSPORT	STERILISER
SCORNFULLY	SETTERWORT	SILVERBELL	SOLICITUDE	SPOKESHAVE	STERILIZER
SCORZONERA	SETTLEMENT	SILVERBILL	SOLIDARITY	SPOLIATION	STERNALGIA
SCOTODINIA	SEVENTIETH	SILVERFISH	SOLIFIDIAN	SPOLIATIVE	STERTEROUS
SCOTSWOMAN	SEXAGESIMA	SILVERSIDE	SOLIVAGANT	SPONGEWARE	STERTOROUS
SCREECHING	SEXDUCTION	SILVERSKIN	SOLUBILITY	SPONGIFORM	STEWARDESS
SCREENPLAY	SEXOLOGIST	SILVERWARE	SOMBRERITE	SPONSIONAL	STIACCIATO
SCRIBBLING	SGANARELLE	SIMILARITY	SOMERSAULT	SPOONERISM	STICHARION
SCRIMSHANK	SHABBINESS	SIMILITUDE	SOMERVILLE	SPORANGIUM	STICKINESS
SCRIPTURAL	SHACKLETON	SIMILLIMUM	SOMNOLENCE	SPORTINGLY	STICKYBEAK
SCRIPTURES	SHADOWLESS	SIMMENTHAL	SONGSTRESS	SPORTSWEAR	STIGMATISE
SCROUNGING	SHAGGYMANE	SIMPLICITY	SONGWRITER	SPOTLESSLY	STIGMATIZE
SCRUPULOUS	SHAGHAIRED	SIMPLISTIC	SOOTHINGLY	SPREAGHERY	STILLBIRTH
SCRUTINEER	SHAKUHACHI	SIMULACRUM	SOOTHSAYER	SPRINGBOKS	STILLICIDE
SCRUTINISE	SHAMEFACED	SIMULATING	SOPHOCLEAN	SPRINGHAAS	STILLIFORM
SCRUTINIZE	SHAMEFULLY	SIMULATION	SOPHOMORIC	SPRINGLESS	STILLSTAND
SCULPTRESS	SHAMPOOING	SINARCHIST	SORDIDNESS	SPRINGLIKE	STINGINESS
SCURRILITY	SHANDRYDAN	SINARQUIST	SOUBRIQUET	SPRINGTAIL	STINGYBARK
SCURRILOUS	SHANDYGAFF	SINFULNESS	SOUNDPROOF	SPRINGTIME	STOCHASTIC
SCUTELLATE	SHARAWADGI	SINGHALESE	SOUNDTRACK	SPRINKLING	STOCKINESS
SDRUCCIOLA	SHARAWAGGI	SINGLENESS	SOURDELINE	SPRUCENESS	STOMATOPOD
SEAMANSHIP	SHATTERING	SINGULARLY	SOUSAPHONE	SPURIOUSLY	STONEBRASH
SEAMSTRESS	SHEARWATER	SINOATRIAL	SOUTERRAIN	SQUEEZEBOX	STONEHENGE
SEANNACHIE	SHECKLATON	SINSEMILLA	SOUTHBOUND	SQUETEAGUE	STONEMASON
SEASONABLE	SHEEPISHLY	SISTERHOOD	SOUTHERNER	SQUIREARCH	STONYHURST

STOREFRONT	SUBORBITAL	SUSCEPTIVE	TARDIGRADE	THERMOSTAT	TOSTICATED
STOREHOUSE	SUBREPTION	SUSPENDERS	TARPAULING	THICKENING	TOUCHANDGO
STOUTHERIE	SUBROUTINE	SUSPENSION	TARTRAZINE	THIMBLEFUL	TOUCHINESS
STOUTHRIEF	SUBSCRIBER	SUSPICIOUS	TASKMASTER	THIMBLEWIT	TOUCHPAPER
STRABISMUS	SUBSECTION	SUSTAINING	TASTEFULLY	THINGUMBOB	TOUCHPIECE
STRABOTOMY	SUBSELLIUM	SUSTENANCE	TATPURUSHA	THIRTEENTH	TOUCHSTONE
STRACCHINO	SUBSEQUENT	SUZERAINTY	TATTERSALL	THIXOTROPY	TOURBILLON
STRAGGLING	SUBSIDENCE	SVADILFARI	TAXONOMIST	THOROUGHLY	TOURMALINE
STRAIGHTEN	SUBSIDIARY	SWAGGERING	TCHOUKBALL	THOUGHTFUL	TOURNAMENT
STRAITENED	SUBSISTENT	SWALLOWING	TECHNETIUM	THOUSANDTH	TOURNIQUET
STRAMONIUM	SUBSPECIES	SWEATSHIRT	TECHNICIAN	THREADBARE	TOWNSWOMAN
STRAPONTIN	SUBSTATION	SWEDENBORG	TECHNOCRAT	THREADLIKE	TOXICOLOGY
STRASBOURG	SUBSTITUTE	SWEEPSTAKE	TECHNOLOGY	THREADWORM	TRACHELATE
STRATEGIST	SUBSTRATUM	SWEETBREAD	TEDDINGTON	THREATENED	TRADITIONS
STRATHSPEY	SUBTENANCY	SWEETBRIAR	TEENYWEENY	THREEPENCE	TRAFFICKER
STRATIOTES	SUBTERFUGE	SWEETENING	TEETHRIDGE	THREEPENNY	TRAGACANTH
STRATOCRAT	SUBTRAHEND	SWEETHEART	TEETOTALER	THREESCORE	TRAGICALLY
STRATOCYST	SUBTROPICS	SWELTERING	TEICHOPSIA	THRENODIAL	TRAITOROUS
STRAVINSKY	SUBVENTION	SWIMMINGLY	TEINOSCOPE	THROMBOSIS	TRAJECTORY
STRAWBERRY	SUBVERSION	SWITCHBACK	TELEBRIDGE	THROUGHOUT	TRAMONTANA
STRAWBOARD	SUBVERSIVE	SWORDSTICK	TELEGRAPHY	THROUGHPUT	TRAMONTANE
STREAMERED	SUCCEEDING	SYMBOLICAL	TELEOSTOME	THROUGHWAY	TRAMPOLINE
STREAMLINE	SUCCESSFUL	SYMPATHISE	TELEPATHIC	THUCYDIDES	TRANQUILLY
STREETLAMP	SUCCESSION	SYMPATHIZE	TELEPHONIC	THUMBIKINS	TRANSCRIBE
STREETWISE	SUCCESSIVE	SYMPHONIUM	TELESCOPIC	THUMBSCREW	TRANSCRIPT
STRELITZIA	SUCCINCTLY	SYMPTOMIZE	TELEVISION	THUNDERBOX	TRANSGRESS
STRENGTHEN	SUDATORIUM	SYNAERESIS	TELIOSPORE	THUNDERING	TRANSIENCE
STREPITANT	SUDDENNESS	SYNCHRONAL	TELPHERAGE	THUNDEROUS	TRANSISTOR
STREPITOSO	SUFFERANCE	SYNCHRONIC	TEMPERANCE	THYSANURAN	TRANSITION
STRICTNESS	SUFFICIENT	SYNCOPATED	TEMPTATION	TICKERTAPE	TRANSITIVE
STRIDENTLY	SUFFRAGIST	SYNCRETISE	TENDERFOOT	TIEBREAKER	TRANSITORY
STRIDEWAYS	SUGARALLIE	SYNECDOCHE	TENDERLOIN	TILLANDSIA	TRANSLATED
STRIDULATE	SUGGESTION	SYNEIDESIS	TENDERNESS	TIMBERYARD	TRANSLATOR
STRIKINGLY	SUGGESTIVE	SYNONYMOUS	TENDRILLED	TIMBROLOGY	TRANSPLANT
STRINDBERG	SULPHUROUS	SYNOSTOSIS	TENEBRIFIC	TIMEKEEPER	TRANSPOSED
STRINGENCY	SULTRINESS	SYNTAGMATA	TENNANTITE	TIMELINESS	TRANSPOSON
STRINGENDO	SUMMERTIME	SYNTERESIS	TENRECIDAE	TIMESAVING	TRANSVERSE
STRINGHALT	SUNBATHING	SYNTHESIZE	TENTERHOOK	TIMESERVER	TRAUMATIZE
STRIPTEASE	SUNGLASSES	SYNTHRONUS	TEPIDARIUM	TIMESWITCH	TRAVANCORE
STROGANOFF	SUPERADDED	SYPHILITIC	TERMINABLE	TINKERBELL	TRAVELATOR
STRONGHOLD	SUPERCARGO	SYSTEMATIC	TERMINALIA	TINTORETTO	TRAVELLERS
STRONGROOM	SUPERGIANT	TABERNACLE	TERMINALLY	TIRAILLEUR	TRAVELLING
STROPHIOLE	SUPERHUMAN	TABLANETTE	TERNEPLATE	TIRELESSLY	TRAVELOGUE
STRUCTURAL	SUPERMODEL	TABLECLOTH	TERRACOTTA	TIROCINIUM	TRAVERTINE
STRULDBERG	SUPERPOWER	TABLESPOON	TERREPLEIN	TITARAKURA	TRAVOLATOR
STRULDBRUG	SUPERSONIC	TABULATION	TERRIFYING	TOCCATELLA	TRECENTIST
STRYCHNINE	SUPERSTORE	TACHOGRAPH	TERTIARIES	TOCOPHEROL	TREKSCHUIT
STUBBORNLY	SUPERTONIC	TACHOMETER	TESCHENITE	TOILETRIES	TREMENDOUS
STUDIOUSLY	SUPERVISED	TACTICALLY	TESTACEOUS	TOILINETTE	TRENCHMORE
STUFFINESS	SUPERVISOR	TACTLESSLY	TESTICULAR	TOLERANTLY	TRENDINESS
STULTIFIED	SUPERWOMAN	TAGLIARINI	THALASSIAN	TOLERATION	TRESPASSER
STUMBLEDOM	SUPPLEJACK	TAILGATING	THALESTRIS	TOLLKEEPER	TRIACONTER
STUPEFYING	SUPPLEMENT	TAILORMADE	THALICTRUM	TOMFOOLERY	TRIANGULAR
STUPENDOUS	SUPPLENESS	TALEBEARER	THALLIFORM	TONGUESTER	TRIANGULUM
STURDINESS	SUPPLICANT	TALLEYRAND	THANKFULLY	TOOTHBRUSH	TRICHOLOGY
STYLISTICS	SUPPLICATE	TAMBERLANE	THAUMASITE	TOOTHPASTE	TRICKINESS
STYLOPISED	SUPPORTING	TAMBOURINE	THEATRICAL	TOPICALITY	TRICLINIUM
SUAVEOLENT	SUPPORTIVE	TAMPERFOOT	THELLUSSON	TOPOGRAPHY	TRIDENTINE
SUBCOMPACT	SUPPOSEDLY	TANAGRIDAE	THEMSELVES	TOPOLOGIST	TRIFOLIATE
SUBHEADING	SUPPRESSED	TANGANYIKA	THEOCRITUS	TOPSYTURVY	TRILATERAL
SUBJECTION	SUPPRESSOR	TANGENTIAL	THEODOLITE	TORBERNITE	TRILINGUAL
SUBJECTIVE	SURFRIDING	TANGLEFOOT	THEOLOGATE	TORCHLIGHT	TRILLIONTH
SUBLIMATER	SURGICALLY	TANNHAUSER	THEOLOGIAN	TORPESCENT	TRIMALCHIO
SUBLIMINAL	SURINAMESE	TANTAMOUNT	THEOLOGISE	TORQUEMADA	TRIMSNITCH
SUBMARINER	SURPASSING	TAPDANCING	THEOLOGIST	TORRENTIAL	TRINACRIAN
SUBMEDIANT	SURPRISING	TAPERECORD	THEREAFTER	TORRICELLI	TRIPARTITE
SUBMERSION	SURREALISM	TAPOTEMENT	THEREANENT	TORTELLINI	TRIPEHOUND
SUBMISSION	SURREALIST	TARADIDDLE	THERMIONIC	TORTUOUSLY	TRIPLICATE
SUBMISSIVE	SURROUNDED	TARANTELLA	THERMISTOR	TOSSICATED	TRIPLICITY

TRIPUDIARY	UNBEARABLY	UNFORESEEN	UPHOLSTERY	VITUPERATE	WESTERNIZE
TRISKELION	UNBEATABLE	UNFRIENDLY	UPPERCLASS	VIVANDIÈRE	WHARFINGER
TRITANOPIA	UNBECOMING	UNFRUITFUL	UPROARIOUS	VIVIPAROUS	WHATSOEVER
TRIUMPHANT	UNBELIEVER	UNGRACIOUS	UPSTANDING	VOCABULARY	WHEATSHEAF
TRIVIALITY	UNBLEACHED	UNGRATEFUL	UROGENITAL	VOCABULIST	WHEATSTONE
TRIVIALIZE	UNBLINKING	UNGROUNDED	UROPOIESIS	VOCATIONAL	WHEELCHAIR
TROCHANTER	UNBLUSHING	UNHAMPERED	UROSTEGITE	VOCIFERATE	WHEELHOUSE
TROCHOTRON	UNCOMMONLY	UNHEARABLE	URTICACEAE	VOCIFEROUS	WHEEZINESS
TROCTOLITE	UNCONFINED	UNHERALDED	USEFULNESS	VOETGANGER	WHEWELLITE
TROGLODYTE	UNCRITICAL	UNHYGIENIC	USQUEBAUGH	VOLATILITY	WHIGGAMORE
TROMBONIST	UNCTUOUSLY	UNICAMERAL	USUCAPTION	VOLLEYBALL	WHILLYWHAW
TROMOMETER	UNCULTURED	UNIFORMITY	USURPATION	VOLUBILITY	WHIRLYBIRD
TROPAEOLUM	UNDECLARED	UNIGENITUS	UTILIZABLE	VOLUMINOUS	WHISPERING
TROPHONIUS	UNDEFEATED	UNILATERAL	VALENTINES	VOLUPTUARY	WHITEHEART
TROPOPAUSE	UNDEFENDED	UNIMPAIRED	VALIDATION	VOLUPTUOUS	WHITETHORN
TROPOPHYTE	UNDENIABLE	UNINFORMED	VALLADOLID	VOLUTATION	WHITEWATER
TROTSKYITE	UNDERBURNT	UNINSPIRED	VANDERBILT	VORAGINOUS	WHITSTABLE
TROUBADOUR	UNDERCLASS	UNINVITING	VARICOSITY	VULCANALIA	WHITTERICK
TROUVAILLE	UNDERCOVER	UNIQUENESS	VARIEGATED	VULNERABLE	WHOLESALER
TRUCULENCE	UNDERCRAFT	UNIVERSITY	VARNISHING	WAGEEARNER	WHOLEWHEAT
TRUSTFULLY	UNDERCROFT	UNLADYLIKE	VASCULITIS	WAINSCOTED	WICKEDNESS
TRUTHFULLY	UNDERFLOOR	UNLEAVENED	VAUDEVILLE	WALDENSIAN	WICKERWORK
TRYPTOPHAN	UNDERLEASE	UNLETTERED	VEGETABLES	WALLACHIAN	WIDDICOMBE
TUBERCULAR	UNDERLINEN	UNLICENSED	VEGETARIAN	WALLFLOWER	WIDESPREAD
TULARAEMIA	UNDERLYING	UNMANNERED	VEGETATION	WAMPUMPEAG	WILDEBEEST
TUMBLEDOWN	UNDERNEATH	UNMANNERLY	VEHEMENTLY	WANCHANCIE	WILDERNESS
TUMESCENCE	UNDERPANTS	UNNUMBERED	VELITATION	WANDERINGS	WILDFOWLER
TUMULTUOUS	UNDERSCORE	UNOBSERVED	VELOCIPEDE	WANDERLUST	WILLIAMSON
TURBULENCE	UNDERSHIRT	UNOCCUPIED	VENERATION	WANDSWORTH	WILLINGDON
TURNAROUND	UNDERSIZED	UNOFFICIAL	VENEZUELAN	WANTHRIVEN	WILLOWHERB
TURPENTINE	UNDERSKIRT	UNORIGINAL	VENTILATOR	WAPENSCHAW	WILLYWILLY
TURRITELLA	UNDERSLUNG	UNORTHODOX	VERIFIABLE	WAPINSCHAW	WINCEYETTE
TURTLEDOVE	UNDERSTAND	UNPLEASANT	VERMICELLI	WAPPENSHAW	WINCHESTER
TURTLEHEAD	UNDERSTATE	UNPREPARED	VERMILLION	WARRANDICE	WINDERMERE
TURTLENECK	UNDERSTEER	UNPROMPTED	VERNACULAR	WASHINGTON	WINDFLOWER
TUTIVILLUS	UNDERSTOOD	UNPROVOKED	VERNISSAGE	WASSAILING	WINDJAMMER
TYMPANITES	UNDERSTUDY	UNPUNCTUAL	VERSAILLES	WASSERMANS	WINDOWPANE
TYMPANITIS	UNDERTAKER	UNREADABLE	VERTEBRATE	WASTEFULLY	WINDOWSILL
TYPESCRIPT	UNDERVALUE	UNREASONED	VERTICALLY	WASTEPAPER	WINDSCREEN
TYPESETTER	UNDERWATER	UNREDEEMED	VESICULATE	WATCHFULLY	WINDSHIELD
TYPEWRITER	UNDERWORLD	UNRELIABLE	VESTIBULUM	WATCHMAKER	WINDSURFER
TYPOGRAPHY	UNDERWRITE	UNRELIEVED	VETERINARY	WATCHTOWER	WINTERTIME
TYRANNICAL	UNDESCRIED	UNREQUITED	VIBRACULUM	WATERBORNE	WISHYWASHY
TYRANNISED	UNDESERVED	UNRESERVED	VIBRAPHONE	WATERBRASH	WITCHCRAFT
UBERMENSCH	UNDETECTED	UNRESOLVED	VIBRATIONS	WATERCOLOR	WITGATBOOM
UBIQUINONE	UNDETERRED	UNREVEALED	VICEGERENT	WATERCRESS	WITHDRAWAL
UBIQUITOUS	UNDIGESTED	UNRIVALLED	VICEREGENT	WATERFRONT	WITSNAPPER
ULCERATION	UNDISPUTED	UNROMANTIC	VICTORIANA	WATERLEVEL	WOFFINGTON
ULSTERETTE	UNDOCTORED	UNRULINESS	VICTORIOUS	WATERMELON	WOLFRAMITE
ULTIMATELY	UNDULATING	UNSALARIED	VICTUALLER	WATERPROOF	WONDERLAND
ULTRABASIC	UNDULATION	UNSCHOOLED	VIDARABINE	WATERSKIER	WONDERMENT
ULTRAFICHE	UNEASINESS	UNSCRAMBLE	VIETNAMESE	WATERSPOUT	WOODENHEAD
ULTRAMAFIC	UNEDIFYING	UNSCRIPTED	VIEWFINDER	WATERTIGHT	WOODPECKER
ULTRASONIC	UNEDUCATED	UNSEASONED	VIGILANTES	WATERWHEEL	WOODPIGEON
ULTRASOUND	UNEMPLOYED	UNSETTLING	VIGOROUSLY	WATERWINGS	WOODWORKER
ULTRONEOUS	UNENVIABLE	UNSHACKLED	VILLAINOUS	WATERWORKS	WOOLLYBACK
UMBELLIFER	UNEQUALLED	UNSLEEPING	VILLANELLE	WATTLEWORK	WOOLLYBUTT
UNABRIDGED	UNEVENNESS	UNSOCIABLE	VILLANOVAN	WAVELENGTH	WORDSWORTH
UNACCENTED	UNEVENTFUL	UNSPECIFIC	VILLEINAGE	WEAPONLESS	WORKAHOLIC
UNAFFECTED	UNEXAMPLED	UNSUITABLE	VINDEMIATE	WEATHERMAN	WORLDCLASS
UNANSWERED	UNEXPECTED	UNSWERVING	VINDICTIVE	WEAVERBIRD	WORSHIPPER
UNARGUABLE	UNEXPLORED	UNTHINKING	VINEGARISH	WEEDKILLER	WORTHINESS
UNASSIGNED	UNFAITHFUL	UNTIDINESS	VIROLOGIST	WEIGHTLESS	WORTHWHILE
UNASSUMING	UNFAMILIAR	UNTRUTHFUL	VIRTUOSITY	WEIMARANER	WRAPAROUND
UNATTACHED	UNFATHOMED	UNUNHEXIUM	VIRTUOUSLY	WELLEARNED	WRETCHEDLY
UNATTENDED	UNFETTERED	UNUNNILIUM	VIRULENTLY	WELLINGTON	WRISTWATCH
UNAVAILING	UNFINISHED	UNWORKABLE	VISIBILITY	WELLSPRING	WRONGDOING
UNBALANCED	UNFLAGGING	UNYIELDING	VISITATION	WELSHWOMAN	WRONGFULLY
UNBEARABLE	UNFLAVORED	UPBRINGING	VITELLICLE	WENTLETRAP	WUNDERKIND

WYCLIFFIAN	BALUSTRADE	CALYDONIAN	CARPATHIAN	FARRANDINE	HARASSMENT
XENOPHOBIA	BAMBOOZLED	CALYPTRATE	CARPENTIER	FARSIGHTED	HARDBOILED
XENOPHOBIC	BANDERILLA	CAMBERWELL	CARPHOLOGY	FASCIATION	HARDCASTLE
XEROPHYTIC	BANDERILLO	CAMBRENSIS	CARRAGHEEN	FASCINATED	HARMANBECK
XEROSTOMIA	BANDMASTER	CAMELOPARD	CARTHAMINE	FASCINATOR	HARMONIOUS
XIPHOPAGUS	BANGLADESH	CAMERLENGO	CARTHUSIAN	FASTIDIOUS	HARRINGTON
YAFFINGALE	BANISHMENT	CAMERLINGO	CARTOMANCY	FASTIGIATE	HARTEBEEST
YARBOROUGH	BANKRUPTCY	CAMERONIAN	CARTOONIST	FASTMOVING	HARVESTMAN
YELLOWBACK	BARASINGHA	CAMOUFLAGE	CARYATIDES	FATALISTIC	HATEENOUGH
YELLOWGIRL	BARBAROSSA	CAMPAIGNER	CASCARILLA	FATALITIES	HAUSTELLUM
YELLOWJACK	BARBITURIC	CAMPANELLA	CASSIABARK	FATHERLAND	HAUSTORIUM
YELLOWLEGS	BARCAROLLE	CAMPARADOR	CASSIOPEIA	FATHERLESS	IATROGENIC
YELLOWROOT	BARCHESTER	CAMPERDOWN	CASSOLETTE	FAULTINESS	JABBERWOCK
YELLOWWOOD	BAREFOOTED	CAMPESTRAL	CASSUMUNAR	FAVORITISM	JACKANAPES
YESTERWEEK	BAREHEADED	CAMSTEERIE	CASTRATION	FAVOURABLE	JACKBOOTED
YESTERYEAR	BARELEGGED	CANCELLOUS	CASUALNESS	FAVOURABLY	JACKHAMMER
YGGDRASILL	BARGAINING	CANCIONERO	CATABOLISM	GADOLINIUM	JACKSTONES
YOUNGBERRY	BARLEYBREE	CANCRIZANS	CATACHUMEN	GAINGIVING	JACKSTRAWS
YOURSELVES	BARLEYCORN	CANDELABRA	CATAFALQUE	GAINSTRIVE	JACULATION
YTHUNDERED	BARMECIDAL	CANDELILLA	CATALECTIC	GALIMATIAS	JAGUARONDI
ZABAGLIONE	BARMITZVAH	CANDLEFISH	CATALEPTIC	GALLABIYAH	JAGUARUNDI
ZAPOROGIAN	BAROMETRIC	CANDLEWICK	CATALOGUER	GALLABIYEH	JAMESONITE
ZEUGLODONT	BARRACKING	CANDYFLOSS	CATAPHRACT	GALLIAMBIC	JARDINIERE
ZIDOVUDINE	BARRACOOTA	CANECUTTER	CATARRHINE	GALRAVITCH	JARGONELLE
ZIMBABWEAN	BARRACOUTA	CANEPHORUS	CATASTASIS	GALSWORTHY	JAUNTINESS
ZINCOGRAPH	BARRAMUNDA	CANNELLONI	CATAWAMPUS	GALUMPHING	JAYWALKING
ZOANTHARIA	BARRAMUNDI	CANNONBALL	CATCHPENNY	GALVANISER	KARMATHIAN
ZOLLVEREIN	BARRENNESS	CANTABRIAN	CATCRACKER	GAMEKEEPER	KARTTIKAYA
ZOOLOGICAL	BARYSPHERE	CANTALOUPE	CATECHUMEN	GANGRENOUS	KATERFELTO
ZOOTHAPSIS	BASKETBALL	CANTATRICE	CATEGORISE	GARGANTUAN	LABORATORY
ZOOTHERAPY	BASKETWORK	CANTERBURY	CATEGORIZE	GARGOUILLE	LACCADIVES
ZUMBOORUCK	BASSINGTON	CANTILEVER	CATENACCIO	GARLANDAGE	LACERATION
ZWITTERION	BASSOONIST	CANTILLATE	CATHOLICON	GARNIERITE	LACHRYMOSE
ZYGODACTYL	BATHYSCAPH	CANTONMENT	CATHOLICOS	GASCONNADE	LACKADAISY
	BATRACHIAN	CANVASBACK	CATTLEGRID	GASTEROPOD	LACKLUSTER
10:2	BATTAILOUS	CANVASSING	CAUTIONARY	GASTRONOME	LACKLUSTRE
BABESIASIS	BATTENBERG	CAOUTCHOUC	CAUTIOUSLY	GASTRONOMY	LACUSTRINE
BABIROUSSA	BATTENBURG	CAPABILITY	CAVALRYMAN	GAULTHERIA	LADYKILLER
BABYLONIAN	BATTLEDOOR	CAPACITATE	CAVICORNIA	HABILITATE	LAEOTROPIC
BABYSITTER	BATTLEDORE	CAPERNAITE	DAMSELFISH	HABITATION	LAMARCKISM
BACCHANTES	BATTLEMENT	CAPERNOITY	DARJEELING	HABITUALLY	LAMBREQUIN
BACITRACIN	BATTLESHIP	CAPILLAIRE	DARKHAIRED	HACKBUTEER	LAMENTABLE
BACKBITING	BAUDELAIRE	CAPITALISM	DAYDREAMER	HACKMATACK	LAMENTABLY
BACKBLOCKS	CACHINNATE	CAPITALIST	EARTHQUAKE	HAEMANTHUS	LAMINATION
BACKGAMMON	CACODAEMON	CAPITALIZE	EARTHSHINE	HAGIOSCOPE	LANCEOLATE
BACKGROUND	CACOGRAPHY	CAPITATION	EARTHWORKS	HAIRSPRING	LANDAMMANN
BACKHANDED	CACOMISTLE	CAPITELLUM	EASTERLING	HAKENKREUZ	LANDLOCKED
BACKHANDER	CACUMINOUS	CAPITOLINE	EATANSWILL	HALFDOLLAR	LANDLOUPER
BACKPACKER	CADAVEROUS	CAPITULARY	FABULOUSLY	HALFHOURLY	LANDLUBBER
BACKSLIDER	CAERPHILLY	CAPITULATE	FACESAVING	HALFSISTER	LANDSTHING
BACKSTAIRS	CAESPITOSE	CAPNOMANCY	FACILITATE	HALFYEARLY	LANGERHANS
BACKSTROKE	CALAMANDER	CAPODASTRO	FACILITIES	HALIEUTICS	LANGUOROUS
BADDERLOCK	CALAMITOUS	CAPPUCCINO	FACTITIOUS	HALLELUJAH	LANIGEROUS
BAFFLEMENT	CALAMONDIN	CAPREOLATE	FAHRENHEIT	HALLMARKED	LANSQUENET
BAGASSOSIS	CALCAREOUS	CAPRICIOUS	FAIRGROUND	HALLOYSITE	LANTHANIDE
BAHRAINIAN	CALCEDONIO	CAPTIVATED	FAIRHAIRED	HALLUBALOO	LARGESCALE
BAILIEWICK	CALCEOLATE	CARABINEER	FAITHFULLY	HAMESUCKEN	LARYNGITIS
BAILLIWICK	CALCITONIN	CARABINIER	FALDISTORY	HAMMERHEAD	LASCIVIOUS
BALANCHINE	CALCULABLE	CARACTACUS	FALKLANDER	HAMMERLOCK	LASTMINUTE
BALBRIGGAN	CALCULATED	CARAMELIZE	FALLACIOUS	HAMSHACKLE	LATTERMATH
BALBUTIENT	CALCULATOR	CARBURETOR	FALLINGOFF	HANDICRAFT	LATTICINIO
BALDERDASH	CALEDONIAN	CARCINOGEN	FALSETRUTH	HANDLEBARS	LAUDERDALE
BALIBUNTAL	CALEFACTOR	CARDIOGRAM	FAMILIARLY	HANDMAIDEN	LAUNCEGAYE
BALLISTICS	CALESCENCE	CARDIOLOGY	FAMISHMENT	HANDPICKED	LAUNCESTON
BALLISTITE	CARELESSLY	CARICATURA	FANATICISM	HANDSOMELY	LAUNDROMAT
BALLOONING	CALIFORNIA	CARICATURE	FANTASTICO	HANDSPRING	LAURDALITE
BALLOONIST	CALLIATURE	CARMAGNOLE	FANTOCCINI	HANGGLIDER	LAURENTIAN
BALNEATION	CALORIFIER	CARNASSIAL	FAREPAYING	HANKYPANKY	LAURUSTINE
BALNEOLOGY	CALUMNIATE	CARNASSIAL	FARFETCHED	HANOVERIAN	LAURVIKITE

LAVALLIÈRE	MARGUERITE	PALATALISE	PARNELLISM	SADDLEBILL	TANAGRIDAE
LAVISHNESS	MARIOLATRY	PALATINATE	PARONYCHIA	SAGITTARIA	TANGANYIKA
LAWABIDING	MARIONETTE	PALESTRINA	PARRAMATTA	SALAMANDER	TANGENTIAL
LAWBREAKER	MARKETABLE	PALFRENIER	PARTHENOPE	SALBUTAMOL	TANGLEFOOT
LAWRENCIUM	MARQUETRIE	PALIMPSEST	PARTIALITY	SALESWOMAN	TANNHAUSER
MABINOGION	MARSHALSEA	PALINDROME	PARTICIPLE	SALICORNIA	TANTAMOUNT
MACEBEARER	MARTINGALE	PALISANDER	PARTICULAR	SALIVATION	TAPDANCING
MACEDONIAN	MARTINIQUE	PALLBEARER	PARTINGALE	SALLENDERS	TAPERECORD
MACKINTOSH	MARVELLOUS	PALLIATIVE	PARVOVIRUS	SALMAGUNDI	TAPOTEMENT
MACONOCHIE	MARYLEBONE	PALMATIFID	PASIGRAPHY	SALMANAZAR	TARADIDDLE
MACROBIOTE	MASCARPONE	PALMATOZOA	PASQUINADE	SALMONELLA	TARANTELLA
MACROCARPA	MASKANONGE	PALMERSTON	PASSAGEWAY	SALOPETTES	TARDIGRADE
MADAGASCAN	MASKINONGE	PALMERWORM	PASSAMEZZO	SALPINGIAN	TARPAULING
MADAGASCAR	MASKIROVKA	PALUDAMENT	PASSIONATE	SALTARELLO	TARTRAZINE
MAGISTRACY	MASQUERADE	PALUSTRINE	PASTEBOARD	SALTCELLAR	TASKMASTER
MAGISTRAND	MASSASAUGA	PALYNOLOGY	PASTEURISE	SALTIGRADE	TASTEFULLY
MAGISTRATE	MASTECTOMY	PANAMANIAN	PASTEURIZE	SALUBRIOUS	TATPURUSHA
MAGNIFICAT	MASTERMIND	PANARITIUM	PASTORELLA	SALUTATION	TATTERSALL
MAGNIFYING	MASTERWORT	PANCRATIUM	PATAGONIAN	SALVADORAN	TAXONOMIST
MAHAYANALI	MASTURBATE	PANJANDRUM	PATAVINITY	SAMARSKITE	VALENTINES
MAHOMMEDAN	MATCHMAKER	PANNICULUS	PATCHCOCKE	SAMOTHRACE	VALIDATION
MAIDENHAIR	MATCHSTALK	PANOPTICON	PATCHINESS	SANATORIUM	VALLADOLID
MAIDENHOOD	MATCHSTICK	PANSOPHIST	PATERNALLY	SANCTIFIED	VANDERBILT
MAINPERNOR	MATELLASSE	PANTAGRUEL	PATHFINDER	SANCTITIES	VARICOSITY
MAINSPRING	MATERIALLY	PANTALOONS	PATHOGENIC	SANCTITUDE	VARIEGATED
MAINSTREAM	MATERNALLY	PANTOGRAPH	PATIBULARY	SANDALWOOD	VARNISHING
MAINTAINER	MATRIARCHY	PANTOSCOPE	PATISSERIE	SANDEMANIA	VASCULITIS
MAISONETTE	MATTERHORN	PAPAVERINE	PATRIARCHY	SANDERLING	VAUDEVILLE
MAKESYSTEM	MATURATION	PAPERCHASE	PATRIOTISM	SANDGROPER	WAGEEARNER
MAKEWEIGHT	MAUPASSANT	PAPERKNIFE	PATRONISED	SANDINISTA	WAINSCOTED
MAKUNOUCHI	MAURITANIA	PAPIAMENTO	PATRONYMIC	SANDWICHES	WALDENSIAN
MALACOLOGY	MAVOURNEEN	PARACELSUS	PAWNBROKER	SANFORISED	WALLACHIAN
MALAGUETTA	MAXIMALIST	PARADIDDLE	RABBINICAL	SANGUINARY	WALLFLOWER
MALAPROPOS	MAXIMILIAN	PARADOXIDE	RACECOURSE	SANITARIUM	WAMPUMPEAG
MALAYALAAM	MAYONNAISE	PARADOXINE	RADICALISM	SANITATION	WANCHANCIE
MALCONTENT	NAPTHALENE	PARAENESIS	RADIOGRAPH	SANNAYASIN	WANDERINGS
MALEFACTOR	NARCISSISM	PARAGLOSSA	RADIOLARIA	SAPPERMENT	WANDERLUST
MALEVOLENT	NARCOLEPSY	PARAGONITE	RAGAMUFFIN	SAPROPHYTE	WANDSWORTH
MALIGNANCY	NARROWBOAT	PARAGUAYAN	RAILWAYMAN	SARCOCOLLA	WANTHRIVEN
MALINGERER	NARROWDALE	PARALLELED	RAIYATWARI	SARCOLEMMA	WAPENSCHAW
MALLOPHAGA	NARROWNESS	PARAMARIBO	RAJPRAMUKH	SARMENTOUS	WAPINSCHAW
MALMESBURY	NASTURTIUM	PARAMETRIC	RAMPALLIAN	SARSQUATCH	WAPPENSHAW
MALODOROUS	NATATORIAL	PARANORMAL	RAMSHACKLE	SATISFYING	WARRANDICE
MALTHUSIAN	NATATORIUM	PARAPHASIA	RANDLETREE	SATURATION	WASHINGTON
MANAGEABLE	NATHELESSE	PARAPHILIA	RANDOMNESS	SATURNALIA	WASSAILING
MANAGEMENT	NATIONALLY	PARAPHONIA	RANNELTREE	SATYAGRAHA	WASSERMANS
MANAGERESS	NATIONWIDE	PARAPHRASE	RANNLETREE	SAUERKRAUT	WASTEFULLY
MANAGERIAL	NATTERJACK	PARAPHYSIS	RANTLETREE	SAUROPSIDA	WASTEPAPER
MANCHESTER	NATURALISM	PARAPLEGIA	RANUNCULUS	SAVAGENESS	WATCHFULLY
MANCHINEEL	NATURALIST	PARAPLEGIC	RAPPORTEUR	SAVONAROLA	WATCHMAKER
MANDEVILLE	NATURALIZE	PARAPRAXIS	RATIONALLY	SAXICOLINE	WATCHTOWER
MANDRAGORA	NATUROPATH	PARARTHRIA	RATTLETRAP	SAXICOLOUS	WATERBORNE
MANGABEIRA	NAUSEATING	PARASCENIA	RAVENOUSLY	TABERNACLE	WATERBRASH
MANGOSTEEN	NAUSEATIVE	PARASELENE	RAVENSBILL	TABLANETTE	WATERCOLOR
MANICHAEAN	NAVIGATION	PARASTATAL	RAVENSDUCK	TABLECLOTH	WATERCRESS
MANICURIST	PACESETTER	PARATROOPS	RAVENSTONE	TABLESPOON	WATERFRONT
MANIFESTLY	PACIFICISM	PARDONABLE	RAWINSONDE	TABULATION	WATERLEVEL
MANIPULATE	PADAREWSKI	PARDONABLY	RAWSTHORNE	TACHOGRAPH	WATERMELON
MANSERVANT	PADDINGTON	PARENCHYMA	RAZZMATAZZ	TACHOMETER	WATERPROOF
MANUSCRIPT	PADDLEFISH	PARENTHOOD	SABBATICAL	TACTICALLY	WATERSKIER
MANZANILLA	PADDYMELON	PARENTLESS	SABRETACHE	TACTLESSLY	WATERSPOUT
MAQUILLAGE	PAEDIATRIC	PARGETTING	SACCHARASE	TAGLIARINI	WATERTIGHT
MARASCHINO	PAGINATION	PARISCHANE	SACCHARIDE	TAILGATING	WATERWHEEL
MARCANTANT	PAINKILLER	PARISIENNE	SACCHARINE	TAILORMADE	WATERWINGS
MARCESCENT	PAINLESSLY	PARKLEAVES	SACCHAROID	TALEBEARER	WATERWORKS
MARCIONITE	PAINTBRUSH	PARLIAMENT	SACERDOTAL	TALLEYRAND	WATTLEWORK
MARGASIRSA	PALAEOTYPE	PARMACITIE	SACREDNESS	TAMBERLANE	WAVELENGTH
MARGINALIA	PALAESTRAL	PARMIGIANA	SACROSANCT	TAMBOURINE	YAFFINGALE
MARGINALLY	PALAGONITE	PARNASSIAN	SADDLEBACK	TAMPERFOOT	YARBOROUGH

□■□□□□□□□□

ZABAGLIONE	ACCUSATION	SCHOLASTIC	ODDFELLOWS	CEPHALOPOD	DEMOBILISE
ZAPOROGIAN	ACCUSATIVE	SCHOOLBOOK	ODELSTHING	CEREBELLUM	DEMOBILIZE
ABBREVIATE	ACCUSINGLY	SCHOOLGIRL	ODIOUSNESS	CEREMONIAL	DEMOCRATIC
ABDICATION	ACCUSTOMED	SCHOOLMAAM	ODONTALGIA	CEREMONIES	DEMOCRITUS
ABERDEVINE	ACEPHALOUS	SCHWARZLOT	ODONTOLITE	CERTIORARI	DEMODULATE
ABERGLAUBE	ACETABULAR	SCIENTIFIC	ODONTOLOGY	CESTRACION	DEMOGORGON
ABERRATION	ACETABULUM	SCINTIGRAM	SDRUCCIOLA	DEACTIVATE	DEMOGRAPHY
ABHIDHAMMA	ACHITOPHEL	SCLERIASIS	AERENCHYMA	DEADLINESS	DEMOISELLE
ABHORRENCE	ACHROMATIC	SCOFFINGLY	AEROBATICS	DEADNETTLE	DEMOLITION
ABITURIENT	ACOLOUTHOS	SCOMBRESOX	AEROPHAGIA	DEALERSHIP	DEMONIACAL
ABNORMALLY	ACOTYLEDON	SCOOTERIST	AERUGINOUS	DEBASEMENT	DEMONOLOGY
ABOMINABLE	ACQUAINTED	SCOPELIDAE	BEARGARDEN	DEBATEMENT	DEMORALISE
ABOMINABLY	ACROAMATIC	SCORDATURA	BEAUJOLAIS	DEBAUCHERY	DEMORALIZE
ABONNEMENT	ACROBATICS	SCOREBOARD	BEAUTICIAN	DEBILITATE	DENDROPHIS
ABORIGINAL	ACROGENOUS	SCORNFULLY	BEAUTIFIER	DEBOUCHURE	DENOUEMENT
ABOVEBOARD	ACROMEGALY	SCORZONERA	BEAVERSKIN	DEBRIEFING	DENSIMETER
ABRIDGMENT	ACRONYCHAL	SCOTODINIA	BEDCHAMBER	DECAGRAMME	DENTIFRICE
ABROGATION	ACROTERION	SCOTSWOMAN	BEDCLOTHES	DECAHEDRON	DEPARTMENT
ABRUPTNESS	ACTIONABLE	SCREECHING	BEDEVILLED	DECAMPMENT	DEPARTURES
ABSCISSION	ACTIVITIST	SCREENPLAY	BEDRAGGLED	DECAPITATE	DEPENDABLE
ABSOLUTELY	ECARDINATE	SCRIBBLING	BEEFBURGER	DECATHLETE	DEPENDENCE
ABSOLUTION	ECCHYMOSIS	SCRIMSHANK	BEEFEATERS	DECELERATE	DEPENDENCY
ABSOLUTISM	ECCOPROTIC	SCRIPTURAL	BEEKEEPING	DECENNOVAL	DEPILATION
ABSORBANCE	ECHINODERM	SCRIPTURES	BEFOREHAND	DECIMALIZE	DEPILATORY
ABSORPTION	ECHINOIDEA	SCROUNGING	BEHAVIORAL	DECIPHERED	DEPLORABLE
ABSTEMIOUS	ECHOPRAXIA	SCRUPULOUS	BEHINDHAND	DECISIVELY	DEPLORABLY
ABSTENTION	ECOLOGICAL	SCRUTINEER	BELARUSIAN	DECLENSION	DEPLOYMENT
ABSTINENCE	ECONOMICAL	SCRUTINISE	BELIEVABLE	DECOLLATOR	DEPOPULATE
ABSTRACTED	ECTHLIPSIS	SCRUTINIZE	BELLADONNA	DECOLORATE	DEPORTMENT
ABUNDANTLY	ECUADORIAN	SCULPTRESS	BELLAMOURE	DECOLORIZE	DEPOSITARY
ABYSSINIAN	ECUMENICAL	SCURRILITY	BELLARMINE	DECOMPOSED	DEPOSITION
EBOULEMENT	ICEBREAKER	SCURRILOUS	BELLWETHER	DECORATION	DEPOSITORY
EBRACTEATE	ICHTHYOSIS	SCUTELLATE	BELONGINGS	DECORATIVE	DEPRECIATE
EBULLIENCE	ICONOCLAST	TCHOUKBALL	BELSHAZZAR	DECRESCENT	DEPRESSANT
OBEDIENTLY	ICONOSCOPE	ADAMANTINE	BENEDICITE	DEDICATION	DEPRESSING
OBFUSCATED	ICOSANDRIA	ADAPTATION	BENEFACTOR	DEDUCTIBLE	DEPRESSION
OBJECTLESS	ICOSOHEDRA	ADDITAMENT	BENEFICENT	DEEPFREEZE	DEPRESSIVE
OBLIGATION	OCCASIONAL	ADDITIONAL	BENEFICIAL	DEEPSEATED	DEPUTATION
OBLIGATORY	OCCIDENTAL	ADELANTADO	BENEVOLENT	DEFACEMENT	DERACINATE
OBLIGINGLY	OCCUPATION	ADEQUATELY	BENTHAMITE	DEFAMATION	DERAILLEUR
OBLITERATE	OCCURRENCE	ADHIBITION	BENZEDRINE	DEFAMATORY	DERAILMENT
OBLOMOVISM	OCEANARIUM	ADIAPHORON	BERMOOTHES	DEFEASANCE	DEREGULATE
OBSEQUIOUS	OCEANGOING	ADJECTIVAL	BERNARDINE	DEFECATION	DERIVATION
OBSERVABLE	OCHLOCRACY	ADJUDICATE	BERSAGLIER	DEFENSIBLE	DERIVATIVE
OBSERVANCE	OCTAHEDRON	ADJUSTABLE	BESTIALITY	DEFICIENCY	DERMATITIS
OBSIDIONAL	OCTODECIMO	ADJUSTMENT	BESTSELLER	DEFILEMENT	DEROGATORY
OBSTETRICS	SCAMMOZZIS	ADMINISTER	BETACRUCIS	DEFINITELY	DESALINATE
OBTAINABLE	SCANDALISE	ADMIRATION	BETELGEUSE	DEFINITION	DESBOROUGH
OBTUSENESS	SCANDALIZE	ADMIRINGLY	BETELGEUZE	DEFINITIVE	DESCENDANT
SBUDDIKINS	SCANDALOUS	ADMISSIBLE	BEWILDERED	DEFLAGRATE	DESCENDING
UBERMENSCH	SCANDAROON	ADMITTANCE	BEWITCHING	DEFLECTION	DESCRIBING
UBIQUINONE	SCANDERBEG	ADMITTEDLY	CECIDOMYIA	DEFRAYMENT	DESECRATED
UBIQUITOUS	SCANTINESS	ADMONITION	CELEBRATED	DEGENERACY	DESERVEDLY
ACANACEOUS	SCAPEGRACE	ADOLESCENT	CELESTIALS	DEGENERATE	DÉSHABILLÉ
ACCELERATE	SCAPHOPODA	ADRAMELECH	CELLOPHANE	DEGRADABLE	DESICCATED
ACCENTUATE	SCARAMOUCH	ADRENALINE	CELLULITIS	DEHISCENCE	DESIDERATA
ACCESSIBLE	SCARCEMENT	ADRENERGIC	CENSORIOUS	DEJECTEDLY	DESOLATION
ACCESSIONS	SCARCENESS	ADULLAMITE	CENSORSHIP	DELCREDERE	DESPAIRING
ACCIDENTAL	SCARLATINA	ADULTERANT	CENTENNIAL	DELECTABLE	DESPICABLE
ACCLIVIOUS	SCARLETINA	ADULTERATE	CENTESIMAL	DELEGATION	DESPITEOUS
ACCOMPLICE	SCATHELESS	ADULTERESS	CENTIGRADE	DELIBERATE	DESPONDENT
ACCOMPLISH	SCATTERING	ADULTERINE	CENTILITER	DELICATELY	DESQUAMATE
ACCORDANCE	SCATURIENT	ADULTEROUS	CENTILITRE	DELIGATION	DESSIATINE
ACCOUNTANT	SCEPTICISM	ADVENTURER	CENTIMETER	DELIGHTFUL	DESSYATINE
ACCOUNTING	SCHALSTEIN	ADVERSARIA	CENTIMETRE	DELINQUENT	DETACHABLE
ACCREDITED	SCHIPPERKE	ADVERTISER	CENTRALIZE	DELIRATION	DETACHMENT
ACCUBATION	SCHISMATIC	EDULCORATE	CENTRIFUGE	DELPHINIUM	DETAINMENT
ACCUMULATE	SCHLIMAZEL	IDEALISTIC	CENTROSOME	DELTIOLOGY	DETECTABLE
ACCURATELY	SCHOLAEMIA	NDRANGHETA	CENTROSOME	DEMIRELIEF	DETERMINED

DETERMINER	HEADSTRONG	LEGUMINOUS	METHEDRINE	PENTAGONAL	PERVERSELY
DETERRENCE	HEARTBREAK	LEGWARMERS	METHODICAL	PENTAMERON	PERVERSION
DETESTABLE	HEARTINESS	LEMNISCATE	METHOMANIA	PENTAMETER	PERVERSITY
DETONATION	HEAVENWARD	LENGTHWAYS	METHUSALEH	PENTATEUCH	PESCADORES
DETRACTION	HECTICALLY	LENGTHWISE	METHUSELAH	PENTATHLON	PESTALOZZI
DETRUNCATE	HECTOLITRE	LENOCINIUM	METHYLATED	PENTATONIC	PESTILENCE
DEUTOPLASM	HEDONISTIC	LENTICULAR	METICULOUS	PENTELIKON	PETITIONER
DEVANAGARI	HEEDLESSLY	LENTIGINES	METROPOLIS	PENTETERIC	PETRARCHAN
DEVASTATED	HEIDELBERG	LEONTIASIS	METTLESOME	PENTIMENTO	PETRIFYING
DEVASTAVIT	HELICOPTER	LEOPARDESS	NEAPOLITAN	PENTSTEMON	PETRISSAGE
DEVELOPING	HELIOGRAPH	LEPRECHAUN	NECROMANCY	PEPPERCORN	PETROGLYPH
DEVOLUTION	HELIOLATER	LESBIANISM	NECROPOLIS	PEPPERMILL	PETRONELLA
DEVOTEMENT	HELIOTROPE	LETTERHEAD	NECTABANUS	PEPPERMINT	PETTICHAPS
DEVOTIONAL	HELLBENDER	LEUCHAEMIA	NEEDLECASE	PEPPERWORT	PETTYCHAPS
FEARLESSLY	HELLESPONT	LEVITATION	NEEDLEWORK	PERCENTAGE	PETULANTLY
FEARNOUGHT	HELPLESSLY	MEADOWPLAN	NEFANDROUS	PERCENTILE	REACTIVATE
FEATHERBED	HEMICHORDA	MEAGERNESS	NEGATIVELY	PERCEPTION	READERSHIP
FEDERALISM	HEMIHEDRON	MEAGRENESS	NEGLECTFUL	PERCEPTIVE	REAMINGBIT
FEDERALIST	HEMIPLEGIA	MEANDERING	NEGLIGENCE	PERCIPIENT	REAPPRAISE
FEDERATION	HEMISPHERE	MEANINGFUL	NEGLIGIBLE	PERCOLATOR	REARMAMENT
FEEBLENESS	HEMOGLOBIN	MEASURABLE	NEGOTIABLE	PERCUSSION	REASONABLE
FELICITATE	HEMOPHILIA	MECHANICAL	NEGOTIATOR	PERDENDOSI	REASONABLY
FELICITOUS	HEMORRHAGE	MECHANIZED	NEIGHBORLY	PERDITIOUS	REASSEMBLE
FELLOWSHIP	HENCEFORTH	MEDDLESOME	NEMATOCYST	PERDURABLE	REASSURING
FEMININITY	HENDECAGON	MEDICAMENT	NEOTERICAL	PEREMPTORY	REBELLIOUS
FENESTELLA	HEPATOCELE	MEDICATION	NESSELRODE	PERFECTION	RECEPTACLE
FERNITICLE	HEPHAESTUS	MEDIOCRITY	NETHERMOST	PERFICIENT	RECIDIVISM
FERRANDINE	HEPTAGONAL	MEDITATION	NETTLERASH	PERFIDIOUS	RECIDIVIST
FERTILISED	HEPTAMERON	MEDITATIVE	NETTLETREE	PERFORATED	RECIPROCAL
FERTILISER	HEPTATEUCH	MEDIUMTERM	NETWORKING	PERFORATOR	RECITATION
FERTILIZER	HEPTATHLON	MEERSCHAUM	NEURILEMMA	PERFORMING	RECITATIVE
FESCENNINE	HERBACEOUS	MEGALITHIC	NEUROLEMMA	PERIDOTITE	RECITATIVO
FETTERLOCK	HEREABOUTS	MEGALOSAUR	NEUTRALISE	PERIEGESIS	RECKLESSLY
FETTUCCINE	HEREDITARY	MEITNERIUM	NEUTRALITY	PERIHELION	RECOGNISED
FEUILLETON	HERESIARCH	MELACONITE	NEUTRALIZE	PERILOUSLY	RECOGNIZED
FEVERISHLY	HEROICALLY	MELANCHOLY	NEUTROPHIL	PERIODICAL	RECOMMENCE
GELATINOUS	HESITANTLY	MELANESIAN	NEWFANGLED	PERIPHERAL	RECOMPENSE
GEMINATION	HESITATION	MELLOWNESS	NEWSAGENTS	PERISHABLE	RECONCILED
GENERALISE	HESPERIDES	MELOCOTOON	NEWSCASTER	PERIWINKLE	RECONSIDER
GENERALITY	HETERODOXY	MEMBERSHIP	NEWSLETTER	PERMAFROST	RECREATION
GENERALIZE	HETERODYNE	MEMBRANOUS	NEWSMONGER	PERMANENCE	RECRUDESCE
GENERATION	HETEROGAMY	MEMORANDUM	NEWSPAPERS	PERMANENCY	RECUPERATE
GENERATRIX	HEXAVALENT	MENACINGLY	NEWSREADER	PERMEATION	RECURRENCE
GENEROSITY	JEISTIECOR	MENDACIOUS	NEWSWORTHY	PERMISSION	REDCURRANT
GENEROUSLY	JEOPARDISE	MENECHMIAN	OESOPHAGUS	PERMISSIVE	REDECORATE
GENETHLIAC	JEOPARDIZE	MENINGITIS	PEACEFULLY	PERNICIOUS	REDEMPTION
GENEVRETTE	JERRYBUILT	MENORRHOEA	PEACEMAKER	PERNICKETY	REDISCOVER
GENICULATE	KEMPERYMAN	MENSTRUATE	PEACHERINO	PERORATION	REDRUTHITE
GENTLEFOLK	KENILWORTH	MEPERIDINE	PEASHOOTER	PEROVSKITE	REDUNDANCY
GENTLENESS	KENSPECKLE	MERCANTILE	PEAUDESOIE	PERPETRATE	REELECTION
GEOCENTRIC	KENTUCKIAN	MERCIFULLY	PECCADILLO	PERPETUATE	REFERENDUM
GEOGRAPHER	KERSEYMERE	MERRYMAKER	PECULATION	PERPETUITY	REFINEMENT
GEOGRAPHIC	KESSELRING	MESENTERON	PECULIARLY	PERPLEXING	REFLECTING
GEOLOGICAL	KETTLEDRUM	MESITYLENE	PEDESTRIAN	PERPLEXITY	REFLECTION
GEOPHYSICS	KEYBOARDER	MESOLITHIC	PEDIATRICS	PERQUISITE	REFLECTIVE
GEORGETOWN	LEADERSHIP	METABOLISE	PEDICULATE	PERSECUTOR	REFRACTION
GEOTHERMAL	LEAFHOPPER	METABOLISM	PEDIMENTAL	PERSEPHONE	REFRACTIVE
GEOTROPISM	LEAMINGTON	METACARPAL	PEDIPALPUS	PERSEPOLIS	REFRACTORY
GERIATRICS	LEBENSRAUM	METACARPUS	PEELGARLIC	PERSICARIA	REFRESHING
GERMICIDAL	LEDERHOSEN	METACENTRE	PEJORATIVE	PERSIENNES	REFRINGENT
GESUNDHEIT	LEFTHANDED	METALEPSIS	PENELOPHON	PERSIFLAGE	REFUTATION
GETHSEMANE	LEFTHANDER	METALLURGY	PENETRABLE	PERSISTENT	REGARDLESS
GETTYSBURG	LEFTWINGER	METAPHRASE	PENETRALIA	PERSONABLE	REGENERATE
GETUPANDGO	LEGALISTIC	METAPLASIS	PENICILLIN	PERSONALLY	REGIMENTAL
HEADHUNTED	LEGIBILITY	METASTABLE	PENINSULAR	PERSTRINGE	REGIMENTED
HEADHUNTER	LEGISLATOR	METATARSAL	PENNILLION	PERSUADING	REGISTERED
HEADLIGHTS	LEGITIMACY	METATARSUS	PENNISETUM	PERSUASION	REGRESSION
HEADMASTER	LEGITIMATE	METATHERIA	PENSIEROSO	PERSUASIVE	REGRESSIVE
HEADPHONES	LEGITIMIZE	METATHESIS	PENSIONNAT	PERTINENCE	REGULARITY

REGULARIZE	RETICULATE	SEVENTIETH	WEIGHTLESS	BHADRAPADA	CHILLINESS
REGULATION	RETINALITE	SEXAGESIMA	WEIMARANER	CHAFFERING	CHIMBORAZO
REITERATED	RETIREMENT	SEXDUCTION	WELLEARNED	CHAIRWOMAN	CHIMNEYPOT
REJONEADOR	RETRACTION	SEXOLOGIST	WELLINGTON	CHALCEDONY	CHIMPANZEE
REJUVENATE	RETRAINING	TECHNETIUM	WELLSPRING	CHALLENGED	CHINABERRY
RELATIVELY	RETREATING	TECHNICIAN	WELSHWOMAN	CHALLENGER	CHINAGRAPH
RELATIVITY	RETROGRADE	TECHNOCRAT	WENTLETRAP	CHALYBEATE	CHINASTONE
RELAXATION	RETROGRESS	TECHNOLOGY	WESTERNIZE	CHAMAELEON	CHINCHILLA
RELAXATIVE	RETROSPECT	TEDDINGTON	XENOPHOBIA	CHAMAEROPS	CHINQUAPIN
RELEGATION	RETURNABLE	TEENYWEENY	XENOPHOBIC	CHAMBERPOT	CHIRICAUNE
RELENTLESS	REVELATION	TEETHRIDGE	XEROPHYTIC	CHAMBERTIN	CHIROMANCY
RELINQUISH	REVENGEFUL	TEETOTALER	XEROSTOMIA	CHAMBRANLE	CHIRONOMIC
RELOCATION	REVERENTLY	TEICHOPSIA	YELLOWBACK	CHAMPIGNON	CHIROPTERA
RELUCTANCE	REVERSIBLE	TEINOSCOPE	YELLOWGIRL	CHANCELLOR	CHITARRONE
REMARKABLE	REVITALIZE	TELEBRIDGE	YELLOWJACK	CHANDELIER	CHITTAGONG
REMARKABLY	REVIVALIST	TELEGRAPHY	YELLOWLEGS	CHANGEABLE	CHIVALROUS
REMITTANCE	REVOCATION	TELEOSTOME	YELLOWROOT	CHANGELESS	CHLORINATE
REMONETISE	REVOLUTION	TELEPATHIC	YELLOWWOOD	CHANGELING	CHLOROFORM
REMORSEFUL	SEAMANSHIP	TELEPHONIC	YESTERWEEK	CHAPARAJOS	CHOICELESS
REMOTENESS	SEAMSTRESS	TELESCOPIC	YESTERYEAR	CHAPAREJOS	CHOLALOGUE
REMUNERATE	SEANNACHIE	TELEVISION	ZEUGLODONT	CHAPFALLEN	CHOPSTICKS
RENDEZVOUS	SEASONABLE	TELIOSPORE	AFFABILITY	CHAPLAINCY	CHREMATIST
RENOVATION	SEASONABLY	TELPHERAGE	AFFETTUOSO	CHAPTALISE	CHRISTIANA
REORGANIZE	SECONDBEST	TEMPERANCE	AFFILIATED	CHARDONNAY	CHROMOSOME
REPAIRABLE	SECONDHAND	TEMPTATION	AFFLICTION	CHARGEABLE	CHRONICLER
REPARATION	SECONDMENT	TENDERFOOT	AFFORDABLE	CHARGEHAND	CHRONICLES
REPATRIATE	SECONDRATE	TENDERLOIN	AFICIONADO	CHARIOTEER	CHRONOLOGY
REPEATABLE	SECRETAIRE	TENDERNESS	AFRICANDER	CHARITABLE	CHRYSIPPUS
REPEATEDLY	SECULARIZE	TENDRILLED	AFRICANISM	CHARITABLY	CHRYSOLITE
REPENTANCE	SECURITIES	TENEBRIFIC	AFRORMOSIA	CHAROLLAIS	CHUCKWALLA
REPERTOIRE	SEDATENESS	TENNANTITE	AFTERBIRTH	CHARTREUSE	CHURCHGOER
REPETITEUR	SEDULOUSLY	TENRECIDAE	AFTERHOURS	CHATELAINE	CHURCHYARD
REPETITION	SEECATCHIE	TENTERHOOK	AFTERIMAGE	CHATTERBOX	CHURLISHLY
REPETITIVE	SEEMLIHEAD	TEPIDARIUM	AFTERPIECE	CHATTERTON	DHARMSHALA
REPORTEDLY	SEERSUCKER	TERMINABLE	AFTERSHAVE	CHAUCERIAN	GHIBELLINE
REPOSITORY	SEGREGATED	TERMINALIA	AFTERSHOCK	CHAUDFROID	KHIDMUTGAR
REPRESSION	SEGUIDILLA	TERMINALLY	AFTERTASTE	CHAULMUGRA	LHERZOLITE
REPRESSIVE	SEISMOLOGY	TERNEPLATE	AFTERWARDS	CHAUTAUQUA	PHAELONIAN
REPRODUCER	SELEGILINE	TERRACOTTA	EFFACEMENT	CHAUVINISM	PHAENOTYPE
REPUBLICAN	SELFESTEEM	TERREPLEIN	EFFECTUATE	CHAUVINIST	PHAGEDAENA
REPUGNANCE	SELFSTYLED	TERRIFYING	EFFEMINACY	CHEAPSKATE	PHANTASIME
REPUTATION	SELLINGERS	TERTIARIES	EFFEMINATE	CHECKLATON	PHANTASIST
REQUIESCAT	SELTZOGENE	TESCHENITE	EFFERVESCE	CHECKPOINT	PHARMACIST
REREDORTER	SEMICIRCLE	TESTACEOUS	EFFICIENCY	CHEEKINESS	PHENOMENAL
RESCHEDULE	SEMIQUAVER	TESTICULAR	EFFLEURAGE	CHEERFULLY	PHENOMENON
RESEARCHER	SENATORIAL	VEGETABLES	EFFORTLESS	CHEESECAKE	PHILATELIC
RESEMBLING	SENEGALESE	VEGETARIAN	EFFRONTERY	CHEESEWOOD	PHILIPPINA
RESENTMENT	SENESCENCE	VEGETATION	EFFUSIVELY	CHEIRONOMY	PHILIPPINE
RESERVISTS	SENSUALITY	VEHEMENTLY	OFFBALANCE	CHELTENHAM	PHILISTINE
RESIGNEDLY	SENSUOUSLY	VELITATION	OFFICIALLY	CHEMICALLY	PHILLIPINA
RESILIENCE	SEPARATELY	VELOCIPEDE	OFFLICENCE	CHEMONASTY	PHILLIPINE
RESISTANCE	SEPARATION	VENERATION	OFFPUTTING	CHEQUEBOOK	PHILLUMENY
RESOLUTELY	SEPARATISM	VENEZUELAN	OFFTHECUFF	CHERIMOYER	PHILOPOENA
RESOLUTION	SEPARATIST	VENTILATOR	OFFTHEWALL	CHERRYWOOD	PHILOSOPHY
RESORCINOL	SEPARATRIX	VERIFIABLE	OFTENTIMES	CHERSONESE	PHILOXENIA
RESOUNDING	SEPTENNIAL	VERMICELLI	AGAPANTHUS	CHERVONETS	PHLEBOTOMY
RESPECTFUL	SEPTUAGINT	VERMILLION	AGGRANDISE	CHESSBOARD	PHLEGETHON
RESPECTING	SEPULCHRAL	VERNACULAR	AGGRESSION	CHESSYLITE	PHLEGMASIA
RESPECTIVE	SEQUACIOUS	VERNISSAGE	AGGRESSIVE	CHESTERTON	PHLEGMATIC
RESPIRATOR	SEQUENTIAL	VERSAILLES	AGONISTICS	CHEVESAILE	PHLOGISTIC
RESPONDENT	SERMONICAL	VERTEBRATE	AGRAHAYANA	CHEVISANCE	PHLOGISTON
RESPONSIVE	SERPENTINE	VERTICALLY	AGRONOMIST	CHEVROTAIN	PHLOGOPITE
RESTAURANT	SERRADELLA	VESICULATE	EGOCENTRIC	CHICHESTER	PHOLIDOSIS
RESTLESSLY	SERRADILLA	VESTIBULUM	EGURGITATE	CHICKENPOX	PHONOGRAPH
RESTRAINED	SERRASALMO	VETERINARY	IGNIMBRITE	CHIFFCHAFF	PHOSPHORUS
RESTRICTED	SERVICEMAN	WEAPONLESS	IGNORANTLY	CHIFFONIER	PHOTODIODE
RESUMPTION	SERVOMOTOR	WEATHERMAN	SGANARELLE	CHILDBIRTH	PHOTOGENIC
RESUPINATE	SETTERWORT	WEAVERBIRD	YGGDRASILL	CHILDERMAS	PHOTOGRAPH
RESURGENCE	SETTLEMENT	WEEDKILLER	AHITHOPHEL	CHILDISHLY	PHOTONASTY

PHOTOPHORE	SHOVELNOSE	WHITETHORN	DIFFICULTY	DISJOINTED	FILTRATION
PHRENESIAC	SHOWJUMPER	WHITEWATER	DIFFIDENCE	DISLOYALTY	FINGERLING
PHRENOLOGY	SHREWDNESS	WHITSTABLE	DIGESTIBLE	DISMANTLED	FINGERNAIL
PHYLACTERY	SHRIEVALTY	WHITTERICK	DIGITORIUM	DISMISSIVE	FINGERPICK
PHYLLIOPOD	SHRILLNESS	WHOLESALER	DIGRESSION	DISORDERED	FINISTERRE
PHYSICALLY	SHRIVELLED	WHOLEWHEAT	DILAPIDATE	DISORDERLY	FIREWALKER
PHYSIOCRAT	SHROVETIDE	AIRFREIGHT	DILATATION	DISPENSARY	FIREWARDEN
PHYSIOLOGY	SHUDDERING	BIANNUALLY	DILETTANTE	DISPENSING	FIRTHSOKEN
PHYTOTOXIN	THALASSIAN	BICHROMATE	DILIGENTLY	DISPERSION	FISHMONGER
RHAMPASTOS	THALESTRIS	BIENNIALLY	DIMINISHED	DISPIRITED	FISHSELLER
RHAPSODISE	THALICTRUM	BIJOUTERIE	DIMINUENDO	DISPOSABLE	FISTICUFFS
RHAPSODIST	THALLIFORM	BILIVERDIN	DIMINUTION	DISPOSSESS	FITZGERALD
RHAPSODIZE	THANKFULLY	BINOCULARS	DIMINUTIVE	DISPUTABLE	GIARDIASIS
RHEOTROPIC	THAUMASITE	BINUCLEATE	DINANDERIE	DISQUALIFY	GIBBERELLA
RHETORICAL	THEATRICAL	BIOCHEMIST	DINNERTIME	DISQUIETED	GILBERTIAN
RHEUMATICS	THELLUSSON	BIOGRAPHER	DIOPHANTOS	DISRESPECT	GILBERTINE
RHEUMATISM	THEMSELVES	BIOLOGICAL	DIPHTHERIA	DISRUPTION	GILLRAVAGE
RHEUMATOID	THEOCRITUS	BIOPHYSICS	DIPLODOCUS	DISRUPTIVE	GINGERBEER
RHINEGRAVE	THEODOLITE	BIORHYTHMS	DIPLOMATIC	DISSECTION	GINGERSNAP
RHINESTONE	THEOLOGATE	BIPARTISAN	DIPSOMANIA	DISSELBOOM	GINGIVITIS
RHINOCEROS	THEOLOGIAN	BIPINNARIA	DIRECTIONS	DISSEMBLER	GIRDLERINK
RHINOLALIA	THEOLOGISE	BIRKENHEAD	DIRECTNESS	DISSENSION	GIRLFRIEND
RHINOPHYMA	THEOLOGIST	BIRMINGHAM	DIRECTOIRE	DISSENTING	HIERARCHIC
RHIPIPTERA	THEREAFTER	BIRTHPLACE	DIREMPTION	DISSERTATE	HIEROGLYPH
RHOEADALES	THEREANENT	BIRTHRIGHT	DISABILITY	DISSERVICE	HIEROMANCY
RHYTHMICAL	THERMIONIC	BISSEXTILE	DISAPPOINT	DISSIDENCE	HIEROPHANT
SHABBINESS	THERMISTOR	BITTERLING	DISAPPROVE	DISSILIENT	HIEROSCOPY
SHACKLETON	THERMOSTAT	BITTERNESS	DISARRANGE	DISSIMILAR	HIGHBINDER
SHADOWLESS	THICKENING	BITUMINOUS	DISASTROUS	DISSIPATED	HIGHFLYING
SHAGGYMANE	THIMBLEFUL	CINDERELLA	DISBELIEVE	DISSOCIATE	HIGHHANDED
SHAGHAIRED	THIMBLEWIT	CINECAMERA	DISBURTHEN	DISSOLVENT	HIGHLANDER
SHAKUHACHI	THINGUMBOB	CINQUEFOIL	DISCERNING	DISSONANCE	HIGHWAYMAN
SHAMEFACED	THIRTEENTH	CIRCASSIAN	DISCIPLINE	DISSUASION	HILDEBRAND
SHAMEFULLY	THIXOTROPY	CIRCUITOUS	DISCLAIMER	DISTENSION	HINDENBURG
SHAMPOOING	THOROUGHLY	CIRCUMCISE	DISCLOSURE	DISTILLATE	HINDUSTANI
SHANDRYDAN	THOUGHTFUL	CIRCUMFLEX	DISCOBOLUS	DISTILLERY	HINTERLAND
SHANDYGAFF	THOUSANDTH	CIRCUMFUSE	DISCOLORED	DISTILLING	HIPPARCHUS
SHARAWADGI	THREADBARE	CIRCUMVENT	DISCOMFORT	DISTINCTLY	HIPPOCRENE
SHARAWAGGI	THREADLIKE	CIRRHOPODA	DISCOMMODE	DISTORTION	HIPPODROME
SHATTERING	THREADWORM	CIRRIPEDEA	DISCOMPOSE	DISTRACTED	HIPPOGRIFF
SHEARWATER	THREATENED	CIRRIPEDIA	DISCONCERT	DISTRAUGHT	HIPPOGRYPH
SHECKLATON	THREEPENCE	CISLEITHAN	DISCONNECT	DISTRESSED	HIPPOMANES
SHEEPISHLY	THREEPENNY	CISPONTINE	DISCONTENT	DISTRIBUTE	HISTOLYSIS
SHEEPSHANK	THREESCORE	CISTERCIAN	DISCOPHORA	DISTRINGAS	HISTORICAL
SHELDONIAN	THRENODIAL	CITRONELLA	DISCORDANT	DISTURBING	HISTRIONIC
SHELLSHOCK	THROMBOSIS	DIABOLICAL	DISCOURAGE	DITHIONATE	HITCHHIKER
SHELLYCOAT	THROUGHOUT	DIACAUSTIC	DISCOVERER	DIURNALIST	HITHERWARD
SHENANIGAN	THROUGHPUT	DIACHRONIC	DISCREETLY	DIVERGENCE	HITOPADESA
SHERARDISE	THROUGHWAY	DIACONICON	DISCREPANT	DIVINATION	HITOPADESA
SHIBBOLETH	THUCYDIDES	DIADROMOUS	DISCRETION	DIVISIONAL	JIGGAMAREE
SHIELDRAKE	THUMBIKINS	DIAGENESIS	DISCURSIVE	EIGHTEENTH	JIGGERMAST
SHIFTINESS	THUMBSCREW	DIAGNOSTIC	DISCUSSING	EISTEDDFOD	JINGOISTIC
SHILLELAGH	THUNDERBOX	DIAGONALLY	DISCUSSION	FIANCHETTO	KIDNAPPING
SHIMMERING	THUNDERING	DIALECTICS	DISDAINFUL	FIBERGLASS	KIESELGUHR
SHIPWRIGHT	THUNDEROUS	DIAPEDESIS	DISEMBOGUE	FIBREGLASS	KILMARNOCK
SHISHKEBAB	THYSANURAN	DIAPHANOUS	DISEMBOWEL	FIBRILLATE	KILOMETRES
SHOCKINGLY	WHARFINGER	DIASKEUAST	DISENCHANT	FIBROSITIS	KIMBERLITE
SHOCKPROOF	WHATSOEVER	DIASTALTIC	DISENGAGED	FICKLENESS	KINCHINLAY
SHODDINESS	WHEATSHEAF	DICHROMATE	DISENNOBLE	FICTITIOUS	KINDLINESS
SHOESTRING	WHEATSTONE	DICHROMISM	DISFIGURED	FIDDLEWOOD	KINGFISHER
SHOPKEEPER	WHEELCHAIR	DICKCISSEL	DISGRUNTLE	FIELDMOUSE	LIBERALISM
SHOPLIFTER	WHEELHOUSE	DICTIONARY	DISGUSTING	FIENDISHLY	LIBERALITY
SHOPSOILED	WHEEZINESS	DICTOGRAPH	DISHABILLE	FIERCENESS	LIBERALIZE
SHOPWALKER	WHEWELLITE	DICYNODONT	DISHARMONY	FIGURATION	LIBERATION
SHORTBREAD	WHIGGAMORE	DIDASCALIC	DISHEARTEN	FIGURATIVE	LIBIDINOUS
SHORTENING	WHILLYWHAW	DIDGERIDOO	DISHONESTY	FIGUREHEAD	LIBRETTIST
SHORTLIVED	WHIRLYBIRD	DIDUNCULUS	DISHWASHER	FILIBUSTER	LIBREVILLE
SHORTRANGE	WHISPERING	DIELECTRIC	DISINCLINE	FILLIBRUSH	LICENTIATE
SHOVELHEAD	WHITEHEART	DIFFERENCE	DISINHERIT	FILTHINESS	LICENTIOUS

LIEBERMANN	MIRACULOUS	RIGHTFULLY	VICTUALLER	ALCOHOLISM	BLUEMANTLE
LIEUTENANT	MISCELLANY	RIGHTWARDS	VIDARABINE	ALCYONARIA	BLUETHROAT
LIGHTERMAN	MISCHMETAL	RIGOROUSLY	VIETNAMESE	ALDERMANLY	BLUNDERING
LIGHTHOUSE	MISCONDUCT	RIJSTTAFEL	VIEWFINDER	ALDERWOMAN	CLADOPHYLL
LIGHTINGUP	MISERICORD	RINDERPEST	VIGILANTES	ALECTORIAN	CLAIRCOLLE
LIGNOCAINE	MISFORTUNE	RINGELMANN	VIGOROUSLY	ALEMBICATE	CLAMMINESS
LIKELIHOOD	MISGIVINGS	RINGLEADER	VILLAINOUS	ALEXANDERS	CLAMOURING
LIKEMINDED	MISHGUGGLE	RINGMASTER	VILLANELLE	ALEXANDRIA	CLANSWOMAN
LILYWHITES	MISHNAYOTH	RIPSNORTER	VILLANOVAN	ALGOLAGNIA	CLARABELLA
LIMBERNECK	MISLEADING	RITORNELLE	VILLEINAGE	ALGONQUIAN	CLASPKNIFE
LIMBURGITE	MISMATCHED	RITORNELLO	VINDEMIATE	ALIENATION	CLASSICISM
LIMITATION	MISOCAPNIC	SICILIENNE	VINDICTIVE	ALIMENTARY	CLASSICIST
LIMITROPHE	MISOGYNIST	SIDEBOARDS	VINEGARISH	ALKALINITY	CLASSIFIED
LINEAMENTS	MISPRISION	SIDERATION	VIROLOGIST	ALLEGATION	CLAVICHORD
LINEOMYCIN	MISSIONARY	SIDEROSTAT	VIRTUOSITY	ALLEGEANCE	CLEARSTORY
LINGUISTIC	MISTAKENLY	SIDESADDLE	VIRTUOUSLY	ALLEGIANCE	CLEARWATER
LINGULELLA	MITHRIDATE	SIDEWINDER	VIRULENTLY	ALLIGATION	CLEMENCEAU
LIPIZZANER	MITIGATING	SIGILLARIA	VISIBILITY	ALLOCATION	CLEMENTINE
LIQUESCENT	MITIGATION	SIGNIFICAT	VISITATION	ALLOCUTION	CLERESTORY
LIQUIDATOR	MIZZENMAST	SIGNORELLI	VITELLICLE	ALLOSAURUS	CLEROMANCY
LIQUIDIZER	NICARAGUAN	SILHOUETTE	VITUPERATE	ALLOSTERIC	CLEVERNESS
LISTLESSLY	NICROSILAL	SILVERBACK	VIVANDIÈRE	ALLOTROPIC	CLINGSTONE
LITERATURE	NIDDERLING	SILVERBELL	VIVIPAROUS	ALLPURPOSE	CLINICALLY
LITHISTADA	NIGGERHEAD	SILVERBILL	WICKEDNESS	ALLUREMENT	CLOCKMAKER
LITHOGRAPH	NIGHTDRESS	SILVERFISH	WICKERWORK	ALLYCHOLLY	CLODHOPPER
LITHOMARGE	NIGHTLIGHT	SILVERSIDE	WIDDICOMBE	ALMACANTAR	CLOISTERED
LITHOPHANE	NIGHTSHADE	SILVERSKIN	WIDESPREAD	ALMSGIVING	CLOMIPHENE
LITHUANIAN	NIGHTSHIRT	SILVERWARE	WILDEBEEST	ALMSHOUSES	CLOSTRIDIA
LITIGATION	NIGHTSTICK	SIMILARITY	WILDERNESS	ALMUCANTAR	CLOUDBERRY
LITTLENESS	NIGRESCENT	SIMILITUDE	WILDFOWLER	ALPENSTOCK	CLOUDBURST
LITURGICAL	NIHILISTIC	SIMILLIMUM	WILLIAMSON	ALPHONSINE	CLOUDINESS
LIVELIHOOD	NIMBLENESS	SIMMENTHAL	WILLINGDON	ALTAZIMUTH	CLUMPERTON
LIVELINESS	NINCOMPOOP	SIMPLICITY	WILLOWHERB	ALTERATION	CLUMSINESS
LIVERWURST	NINETEENTH	SIMPLISTIC	WILLYWILLY	ALTERNATOR	CLYDESDALE
MICHAELMAS	OIREACHTAS	SIMULACRUM	WINCEYETTE	ALTOGETHER	ELACAMPANE
MICROFICHE	PIANISSIMO	SIMULATING	WINCHESTER	ALTRUISTIC	ELASTICATE
MICROLIGHT	PIANOFORTE	SIMULATION	WINDERMERE	ALZHEIMERS	ELASTICITY
MICROMETER	PICARESQUE	SINARCHIST	WINDFLOWER	BLACKBEARD	ELDERBERRY
MICRONESIA	PICAYUNISH	SINARQUIST	WINDJAMMER	BLACKBERRY	ELECAMPANE
MICROPHONE	PICCADILLY	SINFULNESS	WINDOWPANE	BLACKBOARD	ELECTORATE
MICROSCOPE	PICCALILLI	SINGHALESE	WINDOWSILL	BLACKBULLY	ELECTRICAL
MIDDLEBROW	PICCANINNY	SINGLENESS	WINDSCREEN	BLACKENING	ELECTROMER
MIDLOTHIAN	PICHICIAGO	SINGULARLY	WINDSHIELD	BLACKGUARD	ELECTRONIC
MIDSHIPMAN	PICHICIEGO	SINOATRIAL	WINDSURFER	BLACKHEART	ELEGABALUS
MIGHTINESS	PICKPOCKET	SINSEMILLA	WINTERTIME	BLACKSHIRT	ELEMENTARY
MIGNONETTE	PICTOGRAPH	SISTERHOOD	WISHYWASHY	BLACKSMITH	ELEUSINIAN
MILEOMETER	PIGEONHOLE	TICKERTAPE	WITCHCRAFT	BLACKSTONE	ELIMINATOR
MILITARISM	PILEDRIVER	TIEBREAKER	WITGATBOOM	BLACKTHORN	ELLIPTICAL
MILITARIST	PILGARLICK	TILLANDSIA	WITHDRAWAL	BLACKWATER	ELONGATION
MILITIAMAN	PILGRIMAGE	TIMBERYARD	WITSNAPPER	BLANCMANGE	ELOQUENTLY
MILLEFIORI	PILLIWINKS	TIMBROLOGY	XIPHOPAGUS	BLANQUETTE	ELYTRIFORM
MILLENNIUM	PILLOWCASE	TIMEKEEPER	ZIDOVUDINE	BLASPHEMER	FLABBINESS
MILLICURIE	PILLOWSLIP	TIMELINESS	ZIMBABWEAN	BLASTOCOEL	FLAGELLATE
MILLIFARAD	PINAKOTHEK	TIMESAVING	ZINCOGRAPH	BLASTOIDEA	FLAGITIOUS
MILLIHENRY	PINCHPENNY	TIMESERVER	SKATEBOARD	BLEARYEYED	FLAGRANTLY
MILLIMETER	PINCUSHION	TIMESWITCH	SKEPTICISM	BLEPHARISM	FLAMBOYANT
MILLIMETRE	PINNIPEDIA	TINKERBELL	SKETCHBOOK	BLISSFULLY	FLAMEPROOF
MIMEOGRAPH	PIONEERING	TINTORETTO	SKEUOMORPH	BLISTERING	FLAMINGANT
MINDERERUS	PIPSISSEWA	TIRAILLEUR	SKILLFULLY	BLITHERING	FLANCONADE
MINERALOGY	PIRANDELLO	TIRELESSLY	SKINDIVING	BLITZKRIEG	FLAPDOODLE
MINESTRONE	PISTILLATE	TIROCINIUM	SKRIMSHANK	BLOCKHOUSE	FLASHINESS
MINEWORKER	PITCHSTONE	TITARAKURA	SKUPSHTINA	BLOODHOUND	FLASHPOINT
MINIMALISM	PITYRIASIS	VIBRACULUM	SKYSCRAPER	BLOODSTAIN	FLATTERING
MINIMALIST	RIBOFLAVIN	VIBRAPHONE	ALABANDINE	BLOODSTOCK	FLATULENCE
MINIMARKET	RICHARDSON	VIBRATIONS	ALABANDITE	BLOODSTONE	FLAVESCENT
MINISTRATE	RICHTHOFEN	VICEGERENT	ALBIGENSES	BLOOMSBURY	FLAVOURING
MINISTROKE	RIDICULOUS	VICEREGENT	ALCAICERIA	BLOTTESQUE	FLEETINGLY
MINUTEBOOK	RIDINGHOOD	VICTORIANA	ALCHERINGA	BLUEBONNET	FLESHINESS
MINUTENESS	RIGELATION	VICTORIOUS	ALCIBIADES	BLUEBOTTLE	FLICKERING

FLIGHTLESS	PLEBISCITE	EMASCULATE	IMPROPERLY	ANTEPENULT	ENTREMESSE
FLIMSINESS	PLEONASTIC	EMBANKMENT	IMPROVISED	ANTHEOLION	ENTRENCHED
FLINDERSIA	PLEROPHORY	EMBERGOOSE	IMPRUDENCE	ANTHOCLORE	ENTRYPHONE
FLIPPANTLY	PLESIOSAUR	EMBITTERED	IMPUDENTLY	ANTHRACINE	GNOSTICISM
FLIRTATION	PLEXIMETER	EMBLEMATIC	IMPURITIES	ANTHRACITE	INACCURACY
FLOCCULATE	PLIABILITY	EMBLEMENTS	IMPUTATION	ANTHROPOID	INACCURATE
FLOCCULENT	PLIOHIPPUS	EMBODIMENT	OMBROMETER	ANTIADITIS	INACTIVITY
FLOODLIGHT	PLOUGHBOTE	EMBONPOINT	OMBROPHOBE	ANTIBARBUS	INADEQUACY
FLOORBOARD	PLOUGHGATE	EMBOUCHURE	OMNIPOTENT	ANTIBIOTIC	INADEQUATE
FLOORCLOTH	PLOUGHWISE	EMBROIDERY	OMNISCIENT	ANTICHTHON	INAPTITUDE
FLORENTINE	PLUMASSIER	EMBRYOLOGY	OMNIVOROUS	ANTICIPATE	INARTISTIC
FLORIBUNDA	PLUNDERING	EMENDATION	OMOPHORION	ANTICLIMAX	INAUGURATE
FLOURISHED	PLUPERFECT	EMIGRATION	SMALLSCALE	ANTIFREEZE	INBREEDING
FLOWERBEDS	PLUTOCRACY	EMISSIVITY	SMARAGDINE	ANTIMASQUE	INCAPACITY
FLUCTUATER	SLAMMERKIN	EMMENTALER	SMARMINESS	ANTIMATTER	INCAPARINA
FLUFFINESS	SLANDEROUS	EMMETROPIA	SMATTERING	ANTIMONIAN	INCAUTIOUS
FLUGELHORN	SLATTERNLY	EMOLUMENTS	SMITHEREEN	ANTINOMIAN	INCENDIARY
FLUNKEYDOM	SLEEPINESS	EMPEDOCLES	SMOKESTACK	ANTIOCHENE	INCESTUOUS
FLUTEMOUTH	SLEEVELESS	EMPFINDUNG	SMOOTHNESS	ANTIOCHIAN	INCHOATIVE
FLYCATCHER	SLIPSTREAM	EMPLASTRUM	SMORREBROD	ANTIPHONAL	INCIDENTAL
GLACIATION	SLOPPINESS	EMPLOYMENT	UMBELLIFER	ANTIPODEAN	INCINERATE
GLAMOURISE	SLUGGISHLY	EMULSIFIER	ANABAPTIST	ANTIPROTON	INCISIVELY
GLASSHOUSE	SLUICEGATE	IMAGINABLE	ANACARDIUM	ANTIQUATED	INCITEMENT
GLASSINESS	SLUMBERING	IMBECILITY	ANACHARSIS	ANTISEPSIS	INCIVILITY
GLASSWORKS	ULCERATION	IMBRICATED	ANACLASTIC	ANTISEPTIC	INCOHERENT
GLAUCONITE	ULSTERETTE	IMBROCCATA	ANACOUSTIC	ANTISOCIAL	INCOMPLETE
GLEEMAIDEN	ULTIMATELY	IMMACULACY	ANACRUSTIC	ANTISTATIC	INCONSTANT
GLENDOVEER	ULTRABASIC	IMMACULATE	ANADROMOUS	ANTITHESIS	INCRASSATE
GLISTENING	ULTRAFICHE	IMMATERIAL	ANADYOMENE	ANTITHETIC	INCREASING
GLITTERAND	ULTRAMAFIC	IMMATURITY	ANALOGICAL	ANTITRAGUS	INCREDIBLE
GLITTERATI	ULTRASONIC	IMMEMORIAL	ANALPHABET	ANTIVENENE	INCREDIBLY
GLITTERING	ULTRASOUND	IMMOBILITY	ANALYTICAL	CNIDOBLAST	INCRESCENT
GLORIOUSLY	ULTRONEOUS	IMMOBILIZE	ANARCHICAL	ENANTIOSIS	INCUBATION
GLOSSINESS	AMALGAMATE	IMMODERATE	ANASTIGMAT	ENCAMPMENT	INCUMBENCY
GLOUCESTER	AMANUENSIS	IMMOLATION	ANASTROPHE	ENCASEMENT	INCUNABULA
GLUTTONOUS	AMARYLLIDS	IMMORALITY	ANATOMICAL	ENCEPHALON	INDAPAMIDE
GLYCOLYSIS	AMATEURISH	IMMORTELLE	ANAXIMENES	ENCHANTING	INDECENTLY
GLYCOSURIA	AMBARVALIA	IMMUNOLOGY	ANCHORETIC	ENCLOISTER	INDECISION
ILLADVISED	AMBASSADOR	IMPAIRMENT	ANCHYLOSIS	ENCOIGNURE	INDECISIVE
ILLAQUEATE	AMBIVALENT	IMPALPABLE	ANCIPITOUS	ENCYCLICAL	INDECOROUS
ILLEGALITY	AMBLYOPSIS	IMPALUDISM	ANDALUSIAN	ENDEARMENT	INDEFINITE
ILLITERACY	AMBLYSTOMA	IMPARLANCE	ANDALUSITE	ENDOGAMOUS	INDELICACY
ILLITERATE	AMBOCEPTOR	IMPASSABLE	ANDROMACHE	ENDOGENOUS	INDELICATE
ILLUMINATE	AMBULACRUM	IMPATIENCE	ANEMOGRAPH	ENDOSMOSIS	INDENTURES
ILLUMINATI	AMBULATORY	IMPECCABLE	ANEMOMETER	ENGAGEMENT	INDEXATION
ILLUSTRATE	AMELIORATE	IMPECCABLY	ANESTHESIA	ENGENDRURE	INDICATION
KLANGFARBE	AMERINDIAN	IMPEDIMENT	ANESTHETIC	ENGLISHMAN	INDICATIVE
KLEBSIELLA	AMIABILITY	IMPENITENT	ANGIOSPERM	ENGLISHMEN	INDICOLITE
KLOOTCHMAN	AMMUNITION	IMPERATIVE	ANGLERFISH	ENGOUEMENT	INDICTABLE
OLEAGINOUS	AMPELOPSIS	IMPERSONAL	ANGLOPHILE	ENGROSSING	INDICTMENT
OLERACEOUS	AMPHIBIOUS	IMPERVIOUS	ANGLOPHOBE	ENHYDRITIC	INDIGENOUS
PLAGIARISE	AMPHIBRACH	IMPLACABLE	ANGUILLULA	ENKEPHALIN	INDIGOLITE
PLAGIARISM	AMPHICTYON	IMPLACABLY	ANGURVADEL	ENLACEMENT	INDIRECTLY
PLAGIARIST	AMPHIGOURI	IMPLICITLY	ANGWANTIBO	ENLÈVEMENT	INDISCREET
PLAGIARIZE	AMPHIMACER	IMPOLITELY	ANHELATION	ENLISTMENT	INDISPOSED
PLANCHETTE	AMPHIMIXIS	IMPORTANCE	ANIMADVERT	ENORMOUSLY	INDISTINCT
PLANOBLAST	AMPHINEURA	IMPOSITION	ANNEXATION	ENRAPTURED	INDITEMENT
PLANTATION	AMPHITRITE	IMPOSSIBLE	ANNIHILATE	ENRICHMENT	INDIVIDUAL
PLASMODESM	AMPHITRYON	IMPOSSIBLY	ANNOTATION	ENROLLMENT	INDONESIAN
PLASTICINE	AMPHOTERIC	IMPOSTHUME	ANNUALIZED	ENSANGUINE	INDUCEMENT
PLASTICITY	AMPLEFORTH	IMPOTENTLY	ANNUNCIATE	ENTEROCELE	INDUCTANCE
PLATELAYER	AMPUSSYAND	IMPOVERISH	ANSCHAUUNG	ENTERPRISE	INDULGENCE
PLATINISED	AMPUTATION	IMPREGNATE	ANSWERABLE	ENTHUSIASM	INDUMENTUM
PLATTELAND	AMRITATTVA	IMPRESARIO	ANTAGONISE	ENTHUSIAST	INDUSTRIAL
PLAYFELLOW	AMYGDALOID	IMPRESSION	ANTAGONISM	ENTICEMENT	INEBRIATED
PLAYGROUND	EMACIATION	IMPRESSIVE	ANTAGONIST	ENTOMBMENT	INEDUCABLE
PLAYWRIGHT	EMALANGENI	IMPRIMATUR	ANTAGONIZE	ENTOMOLOGY	INEFFICACY
PLEASANTLY	EMANCIPATE	IMPROBABLE	ANTARCTICA	ENTRANCING	INELIGIBLE
PLEASANTRY	EMARGINATE	IMPROBABLY	ANTECEDENT	ENTREATING	INEPTITUDE

INEQUALITY	INSTRUCTED	KNOCKABOUT	UNDESERVED	UNRESERVED	COELACANTH
INESCULENT	INSTRUCTOR	ONOMASTICS	UNDETECTED	UNRESOLVED	COETANEOUS
INEVITABLE	INSTRUMENT	SNAKEMOUTH	UNDETERRED	UNREVEALED	COEXISTENT
INEVITABLY	INSUFFLATE	SNAKESTONE	UNDIGESTED	UNRIVALLED	COGITATION
INEXORABLE	INSULARITY	SNAPDRAGON	UNDISPUTED	UNROMANTIC	COGNISANCE
INFALLIBLE	INSULATION	SNAPHAUNCE	UNDOCTORED	UNRULINESS	COGNIZANCE
INFALLIBLY	INSURGENCY	SNAPHAUNCH	UNDULATING	UNSALARIED	COHERENTLY
INFATUATED	INTAGLIATE	SNEEZEWOOD	UNDULATION	UNSCHOOLED	COINCIDENT
INFECTIOUS	INTANGIBLE	SNIGGERING	UNEASINESS	UNSCRAMBLE	COLBERTINE
INFEFTMENT	INTEGRATED	SNOOTINESS	UNEDIFYING	UNSCRIPTED	COLCHESTER
INFERNALLY	INTEGUMENT	SNORKELING	UNEDUCATED	UNSEASONED	COLCHICINE
INFIBULATE	INTELIGENT	SNOWBLOWER	UNEMPLOYED	UNSETTLING	COLDSTREAM
INFIDELITY	INTEMERATE	SNOWCAPPED	UNENVIABLE	UNSHACKLED	COLEOPTERA
INFIGHTING	INTENDMENT	SNOWMOBILE	UNEQUALLED	UNSHEAPING	COLEORHIZA
INFILTRATE	INTENERATE	UNABRIDGED	UNEVENNESS	UNSLEEPING	COLLAPSING
INFINITELY	INTENTNESS	UNACCENTED	UNEVENTFUL	UNSOCIABLE	COLLARBONE
INFINITIVE	INTERBREED	UNAFFECTED	UNEXAMPLED	UNSPECIFIC	COLLATERAL
INFLATABLE	INTERCEDER	UNANSWERED	UNEXPECTED	UNSUITABLE	COLLECTING
INFLECTION	INTERCLUDE	UNARGUABLE	UNEXPLORED	UNSWERVING	COLLECTION
INFLEXIBLE	INTERESTED	UNASSIGNED	UNFAITHFUL	UNTHINKING	COLLECTIVE
INFLEXIBLY	INTERFERER	UNASSUMING	UNFAMILIAR	UNTIDINESS	COLLEGIATE
INFLICTION	INTERFERON	UNATTACHED	UNFATHOMED	UNTRUTHFUL	COLLEMBOLA
INFORMALLY	INTERLEAVE	UNATTENDED	UNFETTERED	UNUNHEXIUM	COLLIMATOR
INFRACTION	INTERLOPER	UNAVAILING	UNFINISHED	UNUNNILIUM	COLLIQUATE
INFREQUENT	INTERMARRY	UNBALANCED	UNFLAGGING	UNWORKABLE	COLLOCUTER
INFURIATED	INTERMEZZO	UNBEARABLE	UNFLAVORED	UNYIELDING	COLLOQUIAL
INGEMINATE	INTERNALLY	UNBEARABLY	UNFORESEEN	BOBBYSOXER	COLONNADED
INGENERATE	INTERNMENT	UNBEATABLE	UNFRIENDLY	BOISTEROUS	COLORATION
INGLORIOUS	INTERNODAL	UNBECOMING	UNFRUITFUL	BOLLANDIST	COLORATURA
INGRATIATE	INTERPHONE	UNBELIEVER	UNGRACIOUS	BOLSHEVIST	COLOSSALLY
INGREDIENT	INTERSTATE	UNBLEACHED	UNGRATEFUL	BOMBARDIER	COLOSSIANS
INHABITANT	INTERSTICE	UNBLINKING	UNGROUNDED	BONDHOLDER	COLOURLESS
INHALATION	INTERTRIGO	UNBLUSHING	UNHAMPERED	BONDSWOMAN	COLPORTAGE
INHERENTLY	INTERTWINE	UNCOMMONLY	UNHEARABLE	BONESHAKER	COLPORTEUR
INHIBITING	INTERWEAVE	UNCONFINED	UNHERALDED	BONNETHEAD	COLPOSCOPE
INHIBITION	INTERWOVEN	UNCRITICAL	UNHYGIENIC	BOOKBINDER	COMANCHERO
INHIBITORY	INTESTINAL	UNCTUOUSLY	UNICAMERAL	BOOKKEEPER	COMBUSTION
INHUMANITY	INTESTINES	UNCULTURED	UNIFORMITY	BOOKMARKER	COMEDIENNE
INIMITABLE	INTIMATELY	UNDECLARED	UNIGENITUS	BOOKMOBILE	COMESTIBLE
INIQUITOUS	INTIMATION	UNDEFEATED	UNILATERAL	BOOKSELLER	COMFORTING
INITIATION	INTIMIDATE	UNDEFENDED	UNIMPAIRED	BOONDOGGLE	COMMANDANT
INITIATIVE	INTINCTION	UNDENIABLE	UNINFORMED	BOOTLEGGER	COMMANDEER
INJUNCTION	INTOLERANT	UNDERBURNT	UNINSPIRED	BOOTLICKER	COMMANDING
INKSLINGER	INTONATION	UNDERCLASS	UNINVITING	BOOZINGKEN	COMMENTARY
INNERSPACE	INTOXICANT	UNDERCOVER	UNIQUENESS	BORDERLAND	COMMENTATE
INNOCENTLY	INTOXICATE	UNDERCRAFT	UNIVERSITY	BORDERLINE	COMMERCIAL
INNOVATION	INTRAURBAN	UNDERCROFT	UNLADYLIKE	BORDRAGING	COMMISSARY
INNOVATIVE	INTRIGUING	UNDERFLOOR	UNLEAVENED	BORROWINGS	COMMISSION
INOPERABLE	INTROSPECT	UNDERLEASE	UNLETTERED	BOTHERSOME	COMMISSURE
INORDINATE	INUNDATION	UNDERLINEN	UNLICENSED	BOTTICELLI	COMMITMENT
INOSCULATE	INVALIDATE	UNDERLYING	UNMANNERED	BOTTLEHEAD	COMMIXTURE
INQUIRENDO	INVALIDISM	UNDERNEATH	UNMANNERLY	BOTTLENECK	COMMODIOUS
INQUISITOR	INVALIDITY	UNDERPANTS	UNNUMBERED	BOTTOMLESS	COMMONALTY
INSANITARY	INVALUABLE	UNDERSCORE	UNOBSERVED	BOUILLOTTE	COMMONWEAL
INSATIABLE	INVARIABLE	UNDERSHIRT	UNOCCUPIED	BOURIGNIAN	COMMUNALLY
INSATIABLY	INVARIABLY	UNDERSIZED	UNOFFICIAL	BOUSINGKEN	COMMUNIQUÉ
INSECURELY	INVESTMENT	UNDERSKIRT	UNORIGINAL	BOWDLERISE	COMMUTABLE
INSECURITY	INVETERATE	UNDERSLUNG	UNORTHODOX	BOWDLERIZE	COMPARABLE
INSEMINATE	INVIGILATE	UNDERSTAND	UNPLEASANT	COADJUTANT	COMPARATOR
INSENSIBLE	INVIGORATE	UNDERSTATE	UNPREPARED	COARSENESS	COMPARISON
INSIPIDITY	INVINCIBLE	UNDERSTEER	UNPROMPTED	COASTGUARD	COMPASSION
INSISTENCE	INVIOLABLE	UNDERSTOOD	UNPROVOKED	COATHANGER	COMPATIBLE
INSOLENTLY	INVITATION	UNDERSTUDY	UNPUNCTUAL	COCCINEOUS	COMPATRIOT
INSOLVENCY	INVOCATION	UNDERTAKER	UNREADABLE	COCHLEARIA	COMPELLING
INSOUCIANT	INVOLUTION	UNDERVALUE	UNREASONED	COCKABULLY	COMPENDIUM
INSPECTION	KNIFEBOARD	UNDERWATER	UNREDEEMED	COCKALORUM	COMPENSATE
INSPISSATE	KNIGHTHEAD	UNDERWORLD	UNRELIABLE	COCKATRICE	COMPETENCE
INSTALMENT	KNIGHTHOOD	UNDERWRITE	UNRELIEVED	COCKCHAFER	COMPETITOR
INSTIGATOR	KNOBKERRIE	UNDESCRIED	UNREQUITED	CODSWALLOP	COMPLACENT

529

COMPLANATE	CONNECTING	CONVULSION	DONNYBROOK	GONFANONER	JOLTERHEAD
COMPLEMENT	CONNECTION	CONVULSIVE	DOORKEEPER	GONIOMETER	JOURNALESE
COMPLETELY	CONNECTIVE	COORDINATE	DOORTODOOR	GONORRHOEA	JOURNALISM
COMPLETION	CONNIPTION	COPARCENER	DOPPLERITE	GOODFELLOW	JOURNALIST
COMPLEXION	CONNIVANCE	COPENHAGEN	DOSTOEVSKY	GOOSEBERRY	JOURNEYMAN
COMPLEXITY	CONQUERING	COPERNICUS	DOUBLEBASS	GOOSEFLESH	JOUYSAUNCE
COMPLIANCE	CONSCIENCE	COPESETTIC	DOUBLETALK	GORGEOUSLY	KOEKSISTER
COMPLICATE	CONSECRATE	COPPERHEAD	DOUBTFULLY	GORMANDIZE	KOOKABURRA
COMPLICITY	CONSENSION	COPPERNOSE	DOVERCOURT	GOVERNANCE	LOCKERROOM
COMPLIMENT	CONSEQUENT	COPPERSKIN	DOWNMARKET	GOVERNESSY	LOCKKEEPER
COMPLUVIUM	CONSIDERED	COPULATION	DOWNSIZING	GOVERNMENT	LOCOMOTION
COMPOSITOR	CONSISTENT	COPYHOLDER	DOWNSTAIRS	HOARSENESS	LOCOMOTIVE
COMPOUNDED	CONSISTORY	COPYWRITER	DOWNSTREAM	HOBBYHORSE	LOCULAMENT
COMPRADORE	CONSONANCE	COQUELICOT	FOLIACEOUS	HODGEPODGE	LOGANBERRY
COMPREHEND	CONSONANTS	COQUETTISH	FONTANELLE	HOLOFERNES	LOGARITHMS
COMPRESSED	CONSORTIUM	COQUIMBITE	FONTICULUS	HOLOGRAPHY	LOGGERHEAD
COMPRESSOR	CONSPECTUS	CORALBERRY	FONTINALIS	HOLOHEDRAL	LOGISTICAL
COMPROMISE	CONSPIRACY	CORDIALITY	FOODSTUFFS	HOLOPHOTAL	LOGORRHOEA
COMPULSION	CONSTANTAN	CORDIERITE	FOOTBALLER	HOLOPHYTIC	LONELINESS
COMPULSIVE	CONSTANTIA	CORDILLERA	FOOTBRIDGE	HOLOSTERIC	LONGCHAMPS
COMPULSORY	CONSTANTLY	CORDWAINER	FOOTLIGHTS	HOMECOMING	LONGFELLOW
COMSTOCKER	CONSTITUTE	CORINTHIAN	FOOTPRINTS	HOMELINESS	LOQUACIOUS
CONCENTRIC	CONSTRAINT	CORNCOCKLE	FORBEARING	HOMEOPATHY	LORDLINESS
CONCEPTION	CONSTRINGE	CORNFLAKES	FORBIDDING	HOMEOUSIAN	LORDOLATRY
CONCEPTUAL	CONSUETUDE	CORNFLOWER	FORCEFULLY	HOMEWORKER	LOTOPHAGUS
CONCERNING	CONSULTANT	CORNSTALKS	FOREBITTER	HOMOEOPATH	LOUISIETTE
CONCERTINA	CONSULTING	CORNSTARCH	FOREBODING	HOMOGENIZE	LOVELINESS
CONCERVATE	CONSUMMATE	CORNUCOPIA	FORECASTER	HOMOOUSIAN	MODERATELY
CONCESSION	CONTAGIOUS	COROMANDEL	FORECASTLE	HOMOPHOBIA	MODERATION
CONCHIGLIE	CONTENTION	CORONATION	FOREDAMNED	HOMOPHOBIC	MODIFIABLE
CONCHIOLIN	CONTESTANT	CORPULENCE	FOREFATHER	HOMOPHONIC	MODULATION
CONCHOLOGY	CONTEXTUAL	CORRECTING	FOREFINGER	HOMORELAPS	MOISTURIZE
CONCILIATE	CONTIGUITY	CORRECTION	FOREGATHER	HOMOSEXUAL	MOLENDINAR
CONCINNITY	CONTIGUOUS	CORRECTIVE	FOREGROUND	HOMUNCULUS	MOLYBDENUM
CONCINNOUS	CONTINENCE	CORREGIDOR	FOREORDAIN	HONEYBUNCH	MONANDROUS
CONCLUDING	CONTINGENT	CORRESPOND	FORERUNNER	HONORARIUM	MONARCHIST
CONCLUSION	CONTINUANT	CORRIGENDA	FORESHADOW	HONOURABLE	MONEGASQUE
CONCLUSIVE	CONTINUING	CORROBOREE	FOREWARNED	HONOURABLY	MONETARISM
CONCOCTION	CONTINUITY	CORRUGATED	FORFAITING	HONOURLESS	MONETARIST
CONCORDANT	CONTINUOUS	CORRUGATOR	FORFEITURE	HOODWINKED	MONEYMAKER
CONCRETION	CONTORTION	CORRUPTING	FORFEUCHEN	HOOTANANNY	MONILIASIS
CONCURRENT	CONTRABAND	CORRUPTION	FORFOUGHEN	HOOTENANNY	MONILIFORM
CONCUSSION	CONTRACTOR	CORTADERIA	FORGIVABLE	HOOTNANNIE	MONOACIDIC
CONDESCEND	CONTRADICT	CORYBANTES	FORINSECAL	HOPELESSLY	MONOCARPIC
CONDIMENTS	CONTRAFLOW	CORYBANTIC	FORMIDABLE	HORIZONTAL	MONOCHROME
CONDOLENCE	CONTRAHENT	CORYPHAEUS	FORTHRIGHT	HORNBLENDE	MONOECIOUS
CONDOTTIER	CONTRARILY	COSTLINESS	FORTINBRAS	HORNBLOWER	MONOGAMOUS
CONDUCTING	CONTRAVENE	COTTIERISM	FORTISSIMO	HORNRIMMED	MONOLITHIC
CONDUCTION	CONTRECOUP	COTTONTAIL	FORTUITOUS	HORRENDOUS	MONOPHONIC
CONEFLOWER	CONTRIBUTE	COTTONWOOD	FOSSILIZED	HORRIFYING	MONOPLEGIA
CONFECTION	CONTRITION	COUNCILLOR	FOUDROYANT	HORSEDRAWN	MONOPODIUM
CONFEDERAL	CONTROLLER	COUNSELING	FOUNDATION	HORSELBERG	MONOPOLISE
CONFERENCE	CONTROVERT	COUNSELLOR	FOURCHETTE	HORSEPOWER	MONOPOLIZE
CONFERVOID	CONVALESCE	COUNTERACT	FOURIERISM	HORSERIDER	MONOPTERON
CONFESSION	CONVECTION	COUNTRYMAN	FOURRAGERE	HORSEWOMAN	MONOPTEROS
CONFIDANTE	CONVENANCE	COURAGEOUS	FOURTEENTH	HOSPITABLE	MONOTHEISM
CONFIDENCE	CONVENIENT	COURTHOUSE	FOXHUNTING	HOSPITABLY	MONOTONOUS
CONFISCATE	CONVENTION	COUSCOUSOU	GOALKEEPER	HOTCHPOTCH	MONOVALENT
CONFLICTED	CONVENTUAL	COVENANTER	GOATSBEARD	HOUSEBOUND	MONSTRANCE
CONFLUENCE	CONVERGENT	COXCOMICAL	GOATSUCKER	HOUSECRAFT	MONTAGNARD
CONFORMIST	CONVERSANT	DOCIMASTIC	GOBEMOUCHE	HOUSEMAIDS	MONTESSORI
CONFORMITY	CONVERSELY	DODECANESE	GODPARENTS	HOUSEPROUD	MONTEVERDI
CONFOUNDED	CONVERSION	DOGGEDNESS	GOLDDIGGER	HOVERCRAFT	MONTEVIDEO
CONFUSEDLY	CONVEYABLE	DOLCEMENTE	GOLDENSEAL	HOWLEGLASS	MONTGOMERY
CONGENITAL	CONVEYANCE	DOLICHOLIS	GOLDFINGER	HOWSOMEVER	MONTICULUS
CONGESTION	CONVICTION	DOLICHOTUS	GOLDILOCKS	IONOSPHERE	MONTRACHET
CONGREGATE	CONVINCING	DOMICILARY	GOLDTHREAD	JOBSEEKERS	MONTSERRAT
CONIFEROUS	CONVOLUTED	DOMINATING	GOLIATHISE	JOCULARITY	MONUMENTAL
CONJECTURE	CONVOLVUTE	DOMINATION	GONDOLIERS	JOHNSONIAN	MORALITIES

MORATORIUM	POCKETBOOK	ROADRUNNER	TOPICALITY	APOLLONIUS	SPECTACLED
MORBIDEZZA	POCKMANTIE	ROADWORTHY	TOPOGRAPHY	APOLOGETIC	SPECTACLES
MORDACIOUS	POCKMARKED	ROBERDSMAN	TOPOLOGIST	APOPEMPTIC	SPECTATORS
MORGANATIC	POETASTERY	ROBERTSMAN	TOPSYTURVY	APOPHTHEGM	SPECULATOR
MORGANETTA	POETICALLY	ROBUSTIOUS	TORBERNITE	APOPLECTIC	SPEECHLESS
MORIGEROUS	POGONOTOMY	ROBUSTNESS	TORCHLIGHT	APOSEMATIC	SPEEDINESS
MORISONIAN	POHUTUKAWA	ROCKABILLY	TORPESCENT	APOSTROPHE	SPELEOLOGY
MOROSENESS	POIGNANTLY	ROCKINGHAM	TORQUEMADA	APOTHECARY	SPELLBOUND
MORPHOLOGY	POIKILITIC	ROCKSTEADY	TORRENTIAL	APOTHECIUM	SPENCERIAN
MORTADELLA	POINSETTIA	ROISTERING	TORRICELLI	APOTHEOSIS	SPENSERIAN
MOSASAUROS	POINTBLANK	ROLANDSECK	TORTELLINI	APOTROPAIC	SPERMACETI
MOSSBUNKER	POKERFACED	ROLLICKING	TORTUOUSLY	APPARENTLY	SPERMICIDE
MOTHERHOOD	POLIANTHES	ROMANESQUE	TOSSICATED	APPARITION	SPERRYLITE
MOTHERLAND	POLITENESS	ROQUELAURE	TOSTICATED	APPEARANCE	SPHACELATE
MOTHERLESS	POLITICIAN	ROSANILINE	TOUCHANDGO	APPETITIVE	SPHALERITE
MOTHERLIKE	POLITICIZE	ROSECHAFER	TOUCHINESS	APPETIZING	SPIDERWORT
MOTIONLESS	POLLINATED	ROSEMALING	TOUCHPAPER	APPLICABLE	SPIFLICATE
MOTIVATION	POLYANTHUS	ROTHSCHILD	TOUCHPIECE	APPLICATOR	SPILLIKINS
MOTORCYCLE	POLYCHAETE	ROTISSERIE	TOUCHSTONE	APPOSITION	SPINESCENT
MOUCHARABY	POLYCHREST	ROTTWEILER	TOURBILLON	APPRECIATE	SPIRACULUM
MOUDIEWART	POLYCHROME	ROUGHHOUSE	TOURMALINE	APPRENTICE	SPIRITEDLY
MOULDINESS	POLYGAMIST	ROUNDABOUT	TOURNAMENT	APTERYGOTA	SPIRITLESS
MOULDIWARP	POLYGAMOUS	ROUNDHOUSE	TOURNIQUET	EPANOPHORA	SPIRITUOUS
MOUNTEBANK	POLYHEDRON	ROUSEABOUT	TOWNSWOMAN	EPAULEMENT	SPIRKETING
MOURNFULLY	POLYHYMNIA	ROUSTABOUT	TOXICOLOGY	EPENTHETIC	SPISSITUDE
MOUSEPIECE	POLYMERIZE	ROWDYDOWDY	VOCABULARY	EPHRAIMITE	SPITCHCOCK
MOUSSELINE	POLYNESIAN	ROWLANDSON	VOCABULIST	EPICANTHUS	SPITEFULLY
MOUSTERIAN	POLYNOMIAL	SOBERSIDES	VOCATIONAL	EPIDEICTIC	SPLANCHNIC
MOUTHORGAN	POLYPHEMUS	SOFTBOILED	VOCIFERATE	EPIDENDRUM	SPLENDIDLY
MOUTHPIECE	POLYTHEISM	SOGDOLAGER	VOCIFEROUS	EPIDIDYMUS	SPLITLEVEL
MOZAMBIQUE	POLYVALENT	SOGDOLIGER	VOETGANGER	EPIDIORITE	SPODOMANCY
MOZZARELLA	POMERANIAN	SOGDOLOGER	VOLATILITY	EPIGENETIC	SPOILSPORT
NOBLEWOMAN	PONCHIELLI	SOLICITOUS	VOLLEYBALL	EPIGLOTTIS	SPOKESHAVE
NOMINALIST	PONEROLOGY	SOLICITUDE	VOLUBILITY	EPILIMNION	SPOLIATION
NOMINATION	PONTEDERIA	SOLIDARITY	VOLUMINOUS	EPIMENIDES	SPOLIATIVE
NOMINATIVE	PONTEFRACT	SOLIFIDIAN	VOLUPTUARY	EPIMETHEUS	SPONGEWARE
NOMOTHETIC	PONTICELLO	SOLIVAGANT	VOLUPTUOUS	EPIPHONEMA	SPONGIFORM
NONALIGNED	PONTIFICAL	SOLUBILITY	VOLUTATION	EPIPLASTRA	SPONSIONAL
NONCHALANT	POPULARITY	SOMBRERITE	VORAGINOUS	EPISCOPATE	SPOONERISM
NONFICTION	POPULARIZE	SOMERSAULT	WOFFINGTON	EPISPASTIC	SPORANGIUM
NONONSENSE	POPULATION	SOMERVILLE	WOLFRAMITE	EPISTEMICS	SPORTINGLY
NONPAYMENT	PORLOCKING	SOMNOLENCE	WONDERLAND	EPISTROPHE	SPORTSWEAR
NONPLUSSED	PORNOCRACY	SONGSTRESS	WONDERMENT	EPITHELIUM	SPOTLESSLY
NONSMOKING	PORRACEOUS	SONGWRITER	WOODENHEAD	EPONYCHIUM	SPREAGHERY
NONSUCCESS	PORTAMENTO	SOOTHINGLY	WOODPECKER	EPROUVETTE	SPRINGBOKS
NONVINTAGE	PORTCULLIS	SOOTHSAYER	WOODPIGEON	OPALESCENT	SPRINGHAAS
NONVIOLENT	PORTENTOUS	SOPHOCLEAN	WOODWORKER	OPENHANDED	SPRINGLESS
NORBERTINE	PORTIONIST	SOPHOMORIC	WOOLLYBACK	OPENMINDED	SPRINGLIKE
NORMOBLAST	PORTMANTLE	SORDIDNESS	WOOLLYBUTT	OPHICLEIDE	SPRINGTAIL
NORTHANGER	PORTMANTUA	SOUBRIQUET	WORDSWORTH	OPHTHALMIC	SPRINGTIME
NORTHBOUND	PORTSMOUTH	SOUNDPROOF	WORKAHOLIC	OPISOMETER	SPRINKLING
NORTHERNER	PORTUGUESE	SOUNDTRACK	WORLDCLASS	OPOTHERAPY	SPRUCENESS
NORTHSTEAD	POSITIVELY	SOURDELINE	WORSHIPPER	OPPOSITION	SPURIOUSLY
NORTHWARDS	POSITIVIST	SOUSAPHONE	WORTHINESS	OPPRESSION	UPBRINGING
NOSOCOMIAL	POSSESSION	SOUTERRAIN	WORTHWHILE	OPPRESSIVE	UPHOLSTERY
NOSOPHOBIA	POSSESSIVE	SOUTHBOUND	YOUNGBERRY	OPPROBRIUM	UPPERCLASS
NOTABILITY	POSTCHAISE	SOUTHERNER	YOURSELVES	OPTIMISTIC	UPROARIOUS
NOTEWORTHY	POSTHUMOUS	SOUTHWARDS	ZOANTHARIA	SPACECRAFT	UPSTANDING
NOTICEABLE	POSTILLATE	TOCCATELLA	ZOLLVEREIN	SPALLATION	AQUAFORTIS
NOTICEABLY	POSTILLION	TOCOPHEROL	ZOOLOGICAL	SPARSENESS	AQUAMANALE
NOTIFIABLE	POSTLIMINY	TOILETRIES	ZOOTHAPSIS	SPARTACIST	AQUAMANILE
NOTIONALLY	POSTMASTER	TOILINETTE	ZOOTHERAPY	SPATCHCOCK	AQUAMARINE
NOTORYCTES	POSTMORTEM	TOLERANTLY	APEMANTHUS	SPEAKERINE	EQUANIMITY
NOUAKCHOTT	POSTSCRIPT	TOLERATION	APHAERESIS	SPECIALISE	EQUATORIAL
NOURISHING	POTENTIATE	TOLLKEEPER	APICULTURE	SPECIALISM	EQUESTRIAN
NOURRITURE	POTENTILLA	TOMFOOLERY	APOCALYPSE	SPECIALIST	EQUITATION
NOVACULITE	POURPARLER	TONGUESTER	APOCRYPHAL	SPECIALITY	EQUIVALENT
OOPHORITIS	POWERHOUSE	TOOTHBRUSH	APOLAUSTIC	SPECIALIZE	EQUIVOCATE
POCAHONTAS	POZZUOLANA	TOOTHPASTE	APOLLONIAN	SPECIOUSLY	SQUEEZEBOX

SQUETEAGUE	BROADSWORD	FRAMBOESIA	GRATUITOUS	PRAGMATIST	PROCURABLE
SQUIREARCH	BROCATELLE	FRANCHISEE	GRAVEOLENT	PRATINCOLE	PROCURATOR
ARACOSTYLE	BROKENDOWN	FRANCHISOR	GRAVESTONE	PRAXITELES	PRODIGALLY
ARAGONITES	BRONCHITIC	FRANCISCAN	GREEDINESS	PREARRANGE	PRODIGIOUS
ARAUCANIAN	BRONCHITIS	FRANGIPANE	GREENCLOTH	PREBENDARY	PRODUCTION
ARBITRATOR	BROOMSTICK	FRANGIPANI	GREENFINCH	PRECARIOUS	PRODUCTIVE
ARCHBISHOP	BROWNLANDS	FRATERETTO	GREENHEART	PRECAUTION	PROFESSION
ARCHDEACON	BROWNSTONE	FRATERNISE	GREENHOUSE	PRECEDENCE	PROFICIENT
ARCHETYPAL	CRAFTINESS	FRATERNITY	GREENSHANK	PRECIPITIN	PROFITABLE
ARCHIMEDES	CRAIGFLUKE	FRATERNIZE	GREENSTICK	PRECOCIOUS	PROFITABLY
ARCHITRAVE	CRANKSHAFT	FRATICELLI	GREENSTONE	PRECURSORY	PROFITLESS
AREFACTION	CRAPULENCE	FRATRICIDE	GREENSWARD	PREDACIOUS	PROFLIGACY
ARENACEOUS	CRAQUETURE	FRAUDULENT	GREGARIOUS	PREDECEASE	PROFLIGATE
AREOGRAPHY	CREATIVITY	FRAUNHOFER	GRENADIERS	PREDESTINE	PROFOUNDLY
AREOPAGITE	CREDENTIAL	FRAXINELLA	GRENADILLA	PREDICTION	PROFUNDITY
ARGOLEMONO	CREDITABLE	FREEBOOTER	GREYFRIARS	PREDISPOSE	PROGENITOR
ARIMASPIAN	CREDITABLY	FREEHANDER	GRIDIRONER	PREDNISONE	PROGESSION
ARISTIPPUS	CRENELLATE	FREEHOLDER	GRIDLOCKED	PREEMINENT	PROGRAMMER
ARISTOCRAT	CREOPHAGUS	FREELANCER	GRINDSTONE	PREFERABLE	PROHIBITED
ARISTOLOGY	CRETACEOUS	FREELOADER	GRITTINESS	PREFERABLY	PROJECTILE
ARISTOTLES	CREWELWORK	FREEMARTIN	GROCETERIA	PREFERENCE	PROJECTING
ARITHMETIC	CRICKETING	FREEMASONS	GROUNDBAIT	PREFERMENT	PROJECTION
ARMAGEDDON	CRIMINALLY	FREIGHTAGE	GROUNDLESS	PREHENSILE	PROMENADER
ARMIPOTENT	CRISPBREAD	FREMESCENT	GROUNDLING	PREHISTORY	PROMETHEAN
ARROGANTLY	CRISPINIAN	FRENETICAL	GROUNDSMAN	PREJUDICED	PROMETHEUS
ARSMETRICK	CRISSCROSS	FRENZIEDLY	GROUNDWORK	PRELECTION	PROMETHIUM
ARTHRALGIA	CRITICALLY	FREQUENTED	GROVELLING	PREMARITAL	PROMINENCE
ARTHROMERE	CROCKFORDS	FREQUENTER	GRUBBINESS	PREMEDICAL	PROMISSORY
ARTHURIANA	CROSSBONES	FREQUENTLY	GRUMPINESS	PREPARATOR	PROMONTORY
ARTICULATA	CROSSBREED	FRESHWATER	IRIDESCENT	PREPAYMENT	PROMPTBOOK
ARTICULATE	CROSSCHECK	FRICANDEAU	IRISHWOMAN	PREPENSELY	PROMPTNESS
ARTIFICIAL	CROSSHATCH	FRIENDLESS	IRISHWOMEN	PREPOSITOR	PROMULGATE
ARTOCARPUS	CROSSPIECE	FRIENDSHIP	IRONICALLY	PREPOSSESS	PRONOUNCED
ARUNDELIAN	CROSSREFER	FRIGHTENED	IRONMONGER	PREPOTENCE	PROPAGANDA
ARYTAENOID	CROSSROADS	FRINGILLID	IRRADICATE	PRESBYOPIA	PROPAGATOR
BRACHIOPOD	CROTALARIA	FRISKINESS	IRRATIONAL	PRESBYTERY	PROPELLANT
BRADYKININ	CROTALIDAE	FRITHSOKEN	IRRELEVANT	PRESCIENCE	PROPELLENT
BRADYSEISM	CRUIKSHANK	FRITILLARY	IRREMEDIAL	PRESENTDAY	PROPENSITY
BRAGADISME	CRUSTACEAN	FROGHOPPER	IRRESOLUTE	PRESIDENCY	PROPERTIUS
BRAINCHILD	CRYOGENICS	FROLICSOME	IRREVERENT	PRESSURIZE	PROPHETESS
BRAININESS	CRYOPHORUS	FROMANTEEL	IRRIGATION	PRESUMABLY	PROPIONATE
BRAINPOWER	CRYPTOGRAM	FRONTCOURT	IRRITATING	PRESUPPOSE	PROPITIATE
BRAINSTORM	CRYPTOZOIC	FRONTWARDS	IRRITATION	PRETENSION	PROPITIOUS
BRASSBOUND	DRACONITES	FRUITFULLY	KRIEGSPIEL	PRETINCOLE	PROPLITEAL
BRATISLAVA	DRAGONROOT	FRUSTRATED	KRUGERRAND	PRETTINESS	PROPORTION
BRAZILWOOD	DRAKESTONE	FRUTESCENT	ORANGEWOOD	PREVAILING	PROPOSITUS
BREADFRUIT	DRAWBRIDGE	GRACEFULLY	ORATORICAL	PREVALENCE	PROPRAETOR
BREAKABLES	DRAWCANSIR	GRACIOUSLY	ORCHESTRAL	PREVENANCY	PROPRIETOR
BREAKWATER	DRAWSTRING	GRADUALISM	ORCHIDEOUS	PREVENTION	PROPULSION
BREASTBONE	DREADFULLY	GRADUATION	ORDINARILY	PREVENTIVE	PROPYLAEUM
BREASTFEED	DREADLOCKS	GRAMICIDIN	ORDINATION	PREVIOUSLY	PROSCENIUM
BREASTWORK	DREAMINESS	GRAMMARIAN	ORDONNANCE	PRICKLOUSE	PROSCIUTTO
BREATHLESS	DREARINESS	GRAMOPHONE	ORDOVICIAN	PRIESTHOOD	PROSCRIBED
BRESSUMMER	DREARISOME	GRANADILLA	ORIDINANCE	PRIMORDIAL	PROSECUTOR
BRICKLAYER	DREIKANTER	GRANDCHILD	ORIGINALLY	PRINCIPIUM	PROSERPINA
BRICKWORKS	DRESSMAKER	GRANDDADDY	ORIGINATOR	PRINCIPLED	PROSERPINE
BRIDEGROOM	DRINKWATER	GRANDSTAND	ORNAMENTAL	PRINCIPLES	PROSILIENT
BRIDESMAID	DROSOPHILA	GRANGERISM	OROBRANCHE	PRIVATEERS	PROSPECTOR
BRIDGEHEAD	DROWSINESS	GRANGERIZE	OROGENESIS	PRIVILEGED	PROSPECTUS
BRIDLEPATH	DRUMBLEDOR	GRANULATED	ORPHEOREON	PRIZEFIGHT	PROSPERINA
BRIGANDINE	DRUZHINNIK	GRAPEFRUIT	ORTHOCAINE	PROAIRESIS	PROSPERITY
BRIGANTINE	ERGONOMICS	GRAPHOLOGY	ORTHOCLASE	PROCEDURAL	PROSPEROUS
BRIGHTNESS	ERIOCAULON	GRAPTOLITE	ORTHOGONAL	PROCEEDING	PROSTHESIS
BRILLIANCE	ERUBESCENT	GRASSLANDS	ORTHOPNOEA	PROCESSING	PROSTHETIC
BRITISHISM	ERUCTATION	GRASSROOTS	ORTHOPTICS	PROCESSION	PROSTITUTE
BROADCLOTH	ERYMANTHUS	GRASSWIDOW	PRAEMUNIRE	PROCLIVITY	PROTAGORAS
BROADPIECE	ERYSIPELAS	GRATEFULLY	PRAETORIAN	PROCREATOR	PROTANOPIA
BROADSHEET	FRACTIONAL	GRATIFYING	PRAETORIUM	PROCRUSTES	PROTANOPIC
	FRAGMENTAL	GRATILLITY	PRAGMATISM	PROCUMBENT	PROTECTION

PROTECTIVE	TRIPARTITE	ASTRINGENT	OTHERGATES	STONEBRASH	AUSTRALORP
PROTERVITY	TRIPEHOUND	ASTROLOGER	OTHERGUESS	STONEHENGE	AUSTRINGER
PROTESTANT	TRIPLICATE	ASTRONOMER	PTERANODON	STONEMASON	AUTECOLOGY
PROTOPLASM	TRIPLICITY	ASTUTENESS	PTERYGOTUS	STONYHURST	AUTHORISED
PROTRACTED	TRIPUDIARY	ASYMMETRIC	STABILISER	STOREFRONT	AUTHORSHIP
PROTRACTOR	TRISKELION	ASYNARTETE	STABILIZER	STOREHOUSE	AUTOCHTHON
PROTRUSILE	TRITANOPIA	ESCADRILLE	STADHOLDER	STOUTHERIE	AUTOCRATIC
PROTRUSION	TRIUMPHANT	ESCALATION	STAGECOACH	STOUTHRIEF	AUTODIDACT
PROVEDITOR	TRIVIALITY	ESCAPEMENT	STAGECRAFT	STRABISMUS	AUTOECIOUS
PROVENANCE	TRIVIALIZE	ESCARPMENT	STAGGERING	STRABOTOMY	AUTOGENOUS
PROVERBIAL	TROCHANTER	ESCHAROTIC	STAGNATION	STRACCHINO	AUTOMATION
PROVIDENCE	TROCHOTRON	ESCRITOIRE	STALACTITE	STRAGGLING	AUTOMATIZE
PROVINCIAL	TROCTOLITE	ESCULAPIAN	STALAGMITE	STRAIGHTEN	AUTOMOBILE
PROVISIONS	TROGLODYTE	ESCUTCHEON	STALHELMER	STRAITENED	AUTOMOTIVE
PRUDENTIAL	TROMBONIST	ESPADRILLE	STALLENGER	STRAMONIUM	AUTONOMOUS
PRZEWALSKI	TROMOMETER	ESPECIALLY	STALLINGER	STRAPONTIN	AUTOPLASTY
TRACHELATE	TROPAEOLUM	ESTANCIERO	STAMMERING	STRASBOURG	AUTOSTRADA
TRADITIONS	TROPHONIUS	ESTIMATION	STANDPOINT	STRATEGIST	BUCCINATOR
TRAFFICKER	TROPOPAUSE	ESTRAMACON	STANDSTILL	STRATHSPEY	BUCEPHALUS
TRAGACANTH	TROPOPHYTE	ISABELLINE	STANISLAUS	STRATIOTES	BUCHMANISM
TRAGICALLY	TROTSKYITE	ISOLEUCINE	STAPHYLINE	STRATOCRAT	BUCKINGHAM
TRAITOROUS	TROUBADOUR	ISOMETRICS	STARVATION	STRATOCYST	BUCKJUMPER
TRAJECTORY	TROUVAILLE	ISONIAZIDE	STARVELING	STRAVINSKY	BUDGERIGAR
TRAMONTANA	TRUCULENCE	KSHATRIYAS	STATECRAFT	STRAWBERRY	BUFFLEHEAD
TRAMONTANE	TRUSTFULLY	OSCILLATOR	STATIONARY	STRAWBOARD	BUFFOONERY
TRAMPOLINE	TRUTHFULLY	OSCITATION	STATIONERY	STREAMERED	BULLHEADED
TRANQUILLY	TRYPTOPHAN	OSCULATION	STATISTICS	STREAMLINE	BUMFREEZER
TRANSCRIBE	UROGENITAL	OSCULATORY	STATOCRACY	STREETLAMP	BUNDESWEHR
TRANSCRIPT	UROPOIESIS	OSMETERIUM	STATUESQUE	STREETWISE	BURDENSOME
TRANSGRESS	UROSTEGITE	OSMIDROSIS	STAUROLITE	STRELITZIA	BUREAUCRAT
TRANSIENCE	URTICACEAE	OSTENSIBLE	STAVESACRE	STRENGTHEN	BURGEONING
TRANSISTOR	WRAPAROUND	OSTENSIBLY	STEADINESS	STREPITANT	BURGLARIZE
TRANSITION	WRETCHEDLY	OSTEOBLAST	STEAKHOUSE	STREPITOSO	BURLINGTON
TRANSITIVE	WRISTWATCH	OSTEOCOLLA	STEALTHILY	STRICTNESS	BUSHRANGER
TRANSITORY	WRONGDOING	OSTEOLEPIS	STEELINESS	STRIDENTLY	BUTCHERING
TRANSLATED	WRONGFULLY	OSTEOPATHY	STEELWORKS	STRIDEWAYS	BUTTERBAKE
TRANSLATOR	ASAFOETIDA	OSTEOPHYTE	STEMWINDER	STRIDULATE	BUTTERBUMP
TRANSPLANT	ASARABACCA	OSTROGOTHS	STENOTYPER	STRIKINGLY	BUTTERFISH
TRANSPOSED	ASBESTOSIS	PSALTERIUM	STENTORIAN	STRINDBERG	BUTTERMERE
TRANSPOSON	ASCENDANCY	PSAMMOPHIL	STEPFATHER	STRINGENCY	BUTTERMILK
TRANSVERSE	ASCENDENCY	PSEPHOLOGY	STEPHANITE	STRINGENDO	BUTTONDOWN
TRAUMATIZE	ASCETICISM	PSEUDOCARP	STEPHENSON	STRINGHALT	BUTTONHOLE
TRAVANCORE	ASCOMYCETE	PSILOCYBIN	STEPLADDER	STRIPTEASE	CUCKOOPINT
TRAVELATOR	ASCRIBABLE	PSOCOPTERA	STEPMOTHER	STROGANOFF	CUCULLATED
TRAVELLERS	ASPARAGINE	PSYCHIATRY	STEPSISTER	STRONGHOLD	CUCURBITAL
TRAVELLING	ASPERSIONS	PSYCHOLOGY	STEREOTOMY	STRONGROOM	CUDDLESOME
TRAVELOGUE	ASPHALTITE	PSYCHOPATH	STEREOTYPE	STROPHIOLE	CUIRASSIER
TRAVERTINE	ASPHYXIATE	PSYCHOPOMP	STEREOTYPY	STRUCTURAL	CUISENAIRE
TRAVOLATOR	ASPIDISTRA	USEFULNESS	STERILISER	STRULDBERG	CULTIVATED
TRECENTIST	ASPIRATION	USQUEBAUGH	STERILIZER	STRULDBRUG	CULTIVATOR
TREKSCHUIT	ASSEMBLAGE	USUCAPTION	STERNALGIA	STRYCHNINE	CULVERTAGE
TREMENDOUS	ASSEMBLING	USURPATION	STERTOROUS	STUBBORNLY	CUMBERLAND
TRENCHMORE	ASSESSMENT	ATELEIOSIS	STEWARDESS	STUDIOUSLY	CUMBERSOME
TRENDINESS	ASSEVERATE	ATHANASIAN	STIACCIATO	STUFFINESS	CUMMERBUND
TRESPASSER	ASSIGNABLE	ATMOSPHERE	STICHARION	STULTIFIED	CUMULATIVE
TRIACONTER	ASSIGNMENT	ATRACURIUM	STICKINESS	STUMBLEDOM	CURMUDGEON
TRIANGULAR	ASSIMILATE	ATRAMENTAL	STICKYBEAK	STUPEFYING	CURMURRING
TRIANGULUM	ASSISTANCE	ATTACHMENT	STIGMATISE	STUPENDOUS	CURRENCIES
TRICHOLOGY	ASSOCIATED	ATTAINABLE	STIGMATIZE	STURDINESS	CURRICULUM
TRICKINESS	ASSORTMENT	ATTAINMENT	STILLBIRTH	STYLISTICS	CURVACEOUS
TRICLINIUM	ASSUMPTION	ATTENDANCE	STILLICIDE	STYLOPISED	CURVETTING
TRIDENTINE	ASSUMPTIVE	ATTRACTION	STILLIFORM	UTILIZABLE	CUSSEDNESS
TRIFOLIATE	ASTEROIDEA	ATTRACTIVE	STILLSTAND	YTHUNDERED	CUTTLEBONE
TRILATERAL	ASTIGMATIC	CTENOPHORA	STINGINESS	AUCTIONEER	CUTTLEFISH
TRILINGUAL	ASTOMATOUS	CTENOPHORE	STINGYBARK	AUDIBILITY	DUCKBOARDS
TRILLIONTH	ASTONISHED	ETEOCRETAN	STINGYBARK	AUDITORIUM	DUKKERIPEN
TRIMALCHIO	ASTOUNDING	ETERNALIZE	STOCHASTIC	AURIFEROUS	DUMBLEDORE
TRIMSNITCH	ASTRAGALUS	ETHEOSTOMA	STOCKINESS	AUSPICIOUS	DUNDERFUNK
TRINACRIAN	ASTRALAGUS	ETHYLAMINE	STOMATOPOD	AUSTRALIAN	DUNDERHEAD

DUNDERPATE	LUMPECTOMY	QUAINTNESS	SUCCEEDING	VULNERABLE	EXECRATION
DUNIWASSAL	LUMPSUCKER	QUARANTINE	SUCCESSFUL	WUNDERKIND	EXEMPTNESS
DUODECIMAL	LUPERCALIA	QUARRENDER	SUCCESSION	ZUMBOORUCK	EXENTERATE
DUPLICATOR	LUSITANIAN	QUARTERING	SUCCESSIVE	AVANTGARDE	EXHALATION
DURABILITY	LUTESTRING	QUARTEROON	SUCCINCTLY	AVANTURINE	EXHAUSTING
DUTCHWOMAN	LUXEMBOURG	QUATERNARY	SUDATORIUM	AVARICIOUS	EXHAUSTION
DUUMVIRATE	LUXURIANCE	QUEASINESS	SUDDENNESS	AVENTURINE	EXHAUSTIVE
EUCALYPTOL	MUCKRAKING	QUEENSBURY	SUFFERANCE	AVERRHOISM	EXHIBITION
EUCALYPTUS	MUDSKIPPER	QUEENSTOWN	SUFFICIENT	AVICULARIA	EXHILARATE
EUCHLORINE	MUJAHEDDIN	QUENCHLESS	SUFFRAGIST	AVVOGADORE	EXHUMATION
EUDIOMETER	MULIEBRITY	QUERCITRON	SUGARALLIE	EVACUATION	EXOBIOLOGY
EUHEMERISM	MULLIGRUBS	QUERSPRUNG	SUGGESTION	EVALUATION	EXONERATED
EULOGISTIC	MULTIMEDIA	QUESADILLA	SUGGESTIVE	EVANESCENT	EXORBITANT
EUPHONIOUS	MULTIPLIED	QUESTIONER	SULPHUROUS	EVANGELIST	EXOTHERMIC
EUPHROSYNE	MULTIPLIER	QUICKSANDS	SULTRINESS	EVANGELIZE	EXOTICALLY
EUROCHEQUE	MUMBLENEWS	QUICKTHORN	SUMMERTIME	EVAPORATED	EXPATRIATE
EUROCLYDON	MUNIFICENT	QUIESCENCE	SUNBATHING	EVENHANDED	EXPECTANCY
EURYPTERUS	MUSICOLOGY	QUIRINALIA	SUNGLASSES	EVENTUALLY	EXPEDIENCE
EUSTACHIAN	MUSKETEERS	QUIZMASTER	SUPERADDED	EVERGLADES	EXPEDIENCY
EUTHANASIA	MUSSORGSKY	RUBBERNECK	SUPERCARGO	EVERYPLACE	EXPEDITION
EUTHYNEURA	MUTABILITY	RUBIGINOUS	SUPERGIANT	EVERYTHING	EXPENDABLE
EUTRAPELIA	MUTILATION	RUBINSTEIN	SUPERHUMAN	EVERYWHERE	EXPERIENCE
FUDDYDUDDY	MUTINOUSLY	RUDDERLESS	SUPERMODEL	EVISCERATE	EXPERIMENT
FULFILMENT	MUTTONHEAD	RUDIMENTAL	SUPERPOWER	EVITERNITY	EXPIRATION
FULIGINOUS	NUCLEONICS	RUDOLPHINE	SUPERSONIC	OVERBOUGHT	EXPLICABLE
FULLLENGTH	NUDIBRANCH	RUGGEDNESS	SUPERSTORE	OVERCHARGE	EXPLICITLY
FULLYGROWN	NUMBERLESS	RUMBLOSSOM	SUPERTONIC	OVEREATING	EXPOSITION
FUMIGATION	NUMERATION	RUMBULLION	SUPERVISED	OVERLANDER	EXPOSITORY
FUNCTIONAL	NUMISMATIC	RUMINANTIA	SUPERVISOR	OVERMATTER	EXPOUNDERS
FUNGICIDAL	NURSERYMAN	RUMINATION	SUPERWOMAN	OVERPRAISE	EXPRESSION
FURNISHING	NUTCRACKER	RUMINATIVE	SUPPLEJACK	OVERRIDING	EXPRESSIVE
FUSTANELLA	NUTRITIOUS	RUPESTRIAN	SUPPLEMENT	OVERSHADOW	EXPRESSMAN
FUSTANELLE	OUANANICHE	RUPICOLINE	SUPPLENESS	OVERSLAUGH	EXPRESSWAY
FUTURISTIC	OUGHTLINGS	RUSSIANIZE	SUPPLICANT	OVERSPREAD	EXTENDABLE
GUACHAMOLE	OUTBALANCE	RUTHERFORD	SUPPLICATE	OVERSTRAIN	EXTENSIBLE
GUARANTEED	OUTLANDISH	RUTHLESSLY	SUPPORTING	OVERSTRUNG	EXTERNALLY
GUARNERIUS	OUTPATIENT	SUAVEOLENT	SUPPORTIVE	OVERSUPPLY	EXTINCTION
GUATEMALAN	OUTPERFORM	SUBCOMPACT	SUPPOSEDLY	OVERTHETOP	EXTINGUISH
GUBERNATOR	OUTPOURING	SUBHEADING	SUPPRESSED	OVERTHWART	EXTRACTION
GUESTHOUSE	OUTRAGEOUS	SUBJECTION	SUPPRESSOR	OVERWEIGHT	EXTRANEOUS
GUIDELINES	OUTSPECKLE	SUBJECTIVE	SURFRIDING	OVERWORKED	EXUBERANCE
GUILLOTINE	OUVIRANDRA	SUBLIMATER	SURGICALLY	OVIPOSITOR	EXULTATION
GUTTIFERAE	PUBERULENT	SUBLIMINAL	SURINAMESE	SVADILFARI	OXYGENATOR
GUTTURALLY	PUBESCENCE	SUBMARINER	SURPASSING	OWLSPIEGLE	OXYMORONIC
HULLABALOO	PUBLISHING	SUBMEDIANT	SURPRISING	SWAGGERING	BYELECTION
HUMANISTIC	PUCKERWOOD	SUBMERSION	SURREALISM	SWALLOWING	BYSSINOSIS
HUMANITIES	PUGNACIOUS	SUBMISSION	SURREALIST	SWEATSHIRT	CYBERNETIC
HUMBLENESS	PULSATANCE	SUBMISSIVE	SURROUNDED	SWEDENBORG	CYCLOPEDIA
HUMDUDGEON	PULSOMETER	SUBORBITAL	SUSCEPTIVE	SWEEPSTAKE	CYCLOSTYLE
HUMIDIFIER	PUMMELLING	SUBREPTION	SUSPENDERS	SWEETBREAD	CYNOMOLGUS
HUMIDISTAT	PUMPHANDLE	SUBROUTINE	SUSPENSION	SWEETBRIAR	CYSTOSCOPY
HUMORESQUE	PUNCHDRUNK	SUBSCRIBER	SUSPICIOUS	SWEETENING	DYNAMITARD
HUMOROUSLY	PUNCTUALLY	SUBSECTION	SUSTAINING	SWEETHEART	DYSCRASITE
HUMOURLESS	PUNCTULATE	SUBSELLIUM	SUSTENANCE	SWELTERING	DYSPROSIUM
HUMPBACKED	PUNDIGRION	SUBSEQUENT	SUZERAINTY	SWIMMINGLY	DYSTROPHIC
HUSBANDAGE	PUNICACEAE	SUBSIDENCE	TUBERCULAR	SWITCHBACK	EYEWITNESS
JUBILANTLY	PUNISHABLE	SUBSIDIARY	TULARAEMIA	SWORDSTICK	GYMNASTICS
JUBILATION	PUNISHMENT	SUBSISTENT	TUMBLEDOWN	ZWITTERION	GYMNOSOPHY
JUDICATURE	PURITANISM	SUBSPECIES	TUMESCENCE	AXINOMANCY	GYMNOSPERM
JUDICIALLY	PURPOSEFUL	SUBSTATION	TUMULTUOUS	EXACERBATE	GYNECOLOGY
JUGENDSTIL	PURSUIVANT	SUBSTITUTE	TURBULENCE	EXACTITUDE	GYPSOPHILA
JUGGERNAUT	PUTREFYING	SUBSTRATUM	TURNAROUND	EXAGGERATE	GYROSCOPIC
JUSTICIARY	PUTRESCENT	SUBTENANCY	TURPENTINE	EXALTATION	HYALOPHANE
KUOMINTANG	PUZZLEMENT	SUBTERFUGE	TURRITELLA	EXASPERATE	HYDRAULICS
KURDAITCHA	QUADRANGLE	SUBTRAHEND	TURTLEDOVE	EXCAVATION	HYDROLYSIS
LUGUBRIOUS	QUADRATURA	SUBTROPICS	TURTLEHEAD	EXCELLENCE	HYDROMETER
LUMBERJACK	QUADRICEPS	SUBVENTION	TURTLENECK	EXCELLENCY	HYDROPHANE
LUMINARIST	QUADRIREME	SUBVERSION	TUTIVILLUS	EXCITEMENT	HYDROPHYTE
LUMINOSITY	QUAESTUARY	SUBVERSIVE	VULCANALIA	EXCRUCIATE	HYDROPLANE

HYDROPONIC
HYGROMETER
HYPAETHRAL
HYPAETHRON
HYPERBOLIC
HYPERDULIA
HYPNOTIZED
HYPOCORISM
HYPODERMIC
HYPOGAEOUS
HYPOGENOUS
HYPOTENUSE
HYPOTHESIS
HYPSOMETRY
HYSTERESIS
HYSTERICAL
LYCHNAPSIA
LYSENKOISM
MYCORRHIZA
MYELINATED
MYOCARDIAL
MYRINGITIS
MYRIOSCOPE
MYSTAGOGUE
MYSTAGOGUS
MYSTERIOUS
NYCTALOPIA
NYMPHOLEPT
PYCNOGONID
PYRACANTHA
PYRAGYRITE
PYRIDOXINE
PYROGRAPHY
PYROMANIAC
PYROPHORUS
PYTHAGORAS
PYTHOGENIC
SYMBOLICAL
SYMPATHISE
SYMPATHIZE
SYMPHONIUM
SYMPTOMIZE
SYNAERESIS
SYNCHRONAL
SYNCHRONIC
SYNCOPATED
SYNCRETISE
SYNECDOCHE
SYNEIDESIS
SYNONYMOUS
SYNOSTOSIS
SYNTAGMATA
SYNTERESIS
SYNTHESIZE
SYNTHRONUS
SYPHILITIC
SYSTEMATIC
TYMPANITES
TYMPANITIS
TYPESCRIPT
TYPESETTER
TYPEWRITER
TYPOGRAPHY
TYRANNICAL
TYRANNISED
WYCLIFFIAN
ZYGODACTYL
OZYMANDIAS

10:3

ACANACEOUS
ADAMANTINE
ADAPTATION
AGAPANTHUS
ALABANDINE
ALABANDITE
AMALGAMATE
AMANUENSIS
AMARYLLIDS
AMATEURISH
ANABAPTIST
ANACARDIUM
ANACHARSIS
ANACLASTIC
ANACOUSTIC
ANACRUSTIC
ANADROMOUS
ANADYOMENE
ANALOGICAL
ANALPHABET
ANALYTICAL
ANARCHICAL
ANASTIGMAT
ANASTROPHE
ANATOMICAL
ANAXIMENES
ARACOSTYLE
ARAGONITES
ARAUCANIAN
ASAFOETIDA
ASARABACCA
AVANTGARDE
AVANTURINE
AVARICIOUS
BEARGARDEN
BEAUJOLAIS
BEAUTICIAN
BEAUTIFIER
BEAVERSKIN
BHADRAPADA
BIANNUALLY
BLACKBEARD
BLACKBERRY
BLACKBOARD
BLACKBULLY
BLACKENING
BLACKGUARD
BLACKHEART
BLACKSHIRT
BLACKSMITH
BLACKSTONE
BLACKTHORN
BLACKWATER
BLANCMANGE
BLANQUETTE
BLASPHEMER
BLASTOCOEL
BLASTOIDEA
BRACHIOPOD
BRADYKININ
BRADYSEISM
BRAGADISME
BRAINCHILD
BRAININESS
BRAINPOWER
BRAINSTORM
BRASSBOUND

BRATISLAVA
BRAZILWOOD
CHAFFERING
CHAIRWOMAN
CHALCEDONY
CHALLENGED
CHALLENGER
CHALYBEATE
CHAMAELEON
CHAMAEROPS
CHAMBERPOT
CHAMBERTIN
CHAMBRANLE
CHAMPIGNON
CHANCELLOR
CHANDELIER
CHANGEABLE
CHANGELESS
CHANGELING
CHAPARAJOS
CHAPAREJOS
CHAPFALLEN
CHAPLAINCY
CHAPTALISE
CHARDONNAY
CHARGEABLE
CHARGEHAND
CHARIOTEER
CHARITABLE
CHARITABLY
CHAROLLAIS
CHARTREUSE
CHATELAINE
CHATTERBOX
CHATTERTON
CHAUCERIAN
CHAUDFROID
CHAULMUGRA
CHAUTAUQUA
CHAUVINISM
CHAUVINIST
CLADOPHYLL
CLAIRCOLLE
CLAMMINESS
CLAMOURING
CLANSWOMAN
CLARABELLA
CLASPKNIFE
CLASSICISM
CLASSICIST
CLASSIFIED
CLAVICHORD
COADJUTANT
COARSENESS
COASTGUARD
COATHANGER
CRAFTINESS
CRAIGFLUKE
CRANKSHAFT
CRAPULENCE
CRAQUETURE
DEACTIVATE
DEADLINESS
DEADNETTLE
DEALERSHIP
DHARMSHALA
DIABOLICAL
DIACAUSTIC
DIACHRONIC

DIACONICON
DIADROMOUS
DIAGENESIS
DIAGNOSTIC
DIAGONALLY
DIALECTICS
DIAPEDESIS
DIAPHANOUS
DIASKEUAST
DIASTALTIC
DRACONITES
DRAGONROOT
DRAKESTONE
DRAWBRIDGE
DRAWCANSIR
DRAWSTRING
ECARDINATE
ELACAMPANE
ELASTICATE
ELASTICITY
EMACIATION
EMALANGENI
EMANCIPATE
EMARGINATE
EMASCULATE
ENANTIOSIS
EPANOPHORA
EPAULEMENT
EVACUATION
EVALUATION
EVANESCENT
EVANGELIST
EVANGELIZE
EVAPORATED
EXACERBATE
EXACTITUDE
EXAGGERATE
EXALTATION
EXASPERATE
FEARLESSLY
FEARNOUGHT
FEATHERBED
FIANCHETTO
FLABBINESS
FLAGELLATE
FLAGITIOUS
FLAGRANTLY
FLAMBOYANT
FLAMEPROOF
FLAMINGANT
FLANCONADE
FLAPDOODLE
FLASHINESS
FLASHPOINT
FLATTERING
FLATULENCE
FLAVESCENT
FLAVOURING
FRACTIONAL
FRAGMENTAL
FRAMBOESIA
FRANCHISEE
FRANCHISOR
FRANCISCAN
FRANGIPANE
FRANGIPANI
FRATERETTO
FRATERNISE
FRATERNITY

FRATERNIZE
FRATICELLI
FRATRICIDE
FRAUDULENT
FRAUNHOFER
FRAXINELLA
GIARDIASIS
GLACIATION
GLAMOURISE
GLASSHOUSE
GLASSINESS
GLASSWORKS
GLAUCONITE
GOALKEEPER
GOATSBEARD
GOATSUCKER
GRACEFULLY
GRACIOUSLY
GRADUALISM
GRADUATION
GRAMICIDIN
GRAMMARIAN
GRAMOPHONE
GRANADILLA
GRANDCHILD
GRANDDADDY
GRANDSTAND
GRANGERISM
GRANGERIZE
GRANULATED
GRAPEFRUIT
GRAPHOLOGY
GRAPTOLITE
GRASSLANDS
GRASSROOTS
GRASSWIDOW
GRATEFULLY
GRATIFYING
GRATILLITY
GRATUITOUS
GRAVEOLENT
GRAVESTONE
GUACHAMOLE
GUARANTEED
GUARNERIUS
GUATEMALAN
HEADHUNTED
HEADHUNTER
HEADLIGHTS
HEADMASTER
HEADPHONES
HEADSTRONG
HEARTBREAK
HEARTINESS
HEAVENWARD
HOARSENESS
HYALOPHANE
IMAGINABLE
INACCURACY
INACCURATE
INACTIVITY
INADEQUACY
INADEQUATE
INAPTITUDE
INARTISTIC
INAUGURATE
ISABELLINE
KLANGFARBE
LEADERSHIP

LEAFHOPPER
LEAMINGTON
MEADOWPLAN
MEAGERNESS
MEAGRENESS
MEANDERING
MEANINGFUL
MEASURABLE
NEAPOLITAN
OPALESCENT
ORANGEWOOD
ORATORICAL
OUANANICHE
PEACEFULLY
PEACEMAKER
PEACHERINO
PEASHOOTER
PEAUDESOIE
PHAELONIAN
PHAENOTYPE
PHAGEDAENA
PHANTASIME
PHANTASIST
PHARMACIST
PIANISSIMO
PIANOFORTE
PLAGIARISE
PLAGIARISM
PLAGIARIST
PLAGIARIZE
PLANCHETTE
PLANOBLAST
PLANTATION
PLASMODESM
PLASTICINE
PLASTICITY
PLATELAYER
PLATINISED
PLATTELAND
PLAYFELLOW
PLAYGROUND
PLAYWRIGHT
PRAEMUNIRE
PRAETORIAN
PRAETORIUM
PRAGMATISM
PRAGMATIST
PRATINCOLE
PRAXITELES
PSALTERIUM
PSAMMOPHIL
QUADRANGLE
QUADRATURA
QUADRICEPS
QUADRIREME
QUAESTUARY
QUAINTNESS
QUARANTINE
QUARRENDER
QUARTERING
QUARTEROON
QUATERNARY
REACTIVATE
READERSHIP
REAMINGBIT
REAPPRAISE
REARMAMENT
REASONABLE
REASONABLY

REASSEMBLE	STAGNATION	UNASSIGNED	LIBERALITY	UNBECOMING	CACOMISTLE
REASSURING	STALACTITE	UNASSUMING	LIBERALIZE	UNBELIEVER	CACUMINOUS
RHAMPASTOS	STALAGMITE	UNATTACHED	LIBERATION	UNBLEACHED	CECIDOMYIA
RHAPSODISE	STALHELMER	UNATTENDED	LIBIDINOUS	UNBLINKING	COCCINEOUS
RHAPSODIST	STALLENGER	UNAVAILING	LIBRETTIST	UNBLUSHING	COCHLEARIA
RHAPSODIZE	STALLINGER	WEAPONLESS	LIBREVILLE	UPBRINGING	COCKABULLY
ROADRUNNER	STAMMERING	WEATHERMAN	MABINOGION	VIBRACULUM	COCKALORUM
ROADWORTHY	STANDPOINT	WEAVERBIRD	NOBLEWOMAN	VIBRAPHONE	COCKATRICE
SCAMMOZZIS	STANDSTILL	WHARFINGER	OMBROMETER	VIBRATIONS	COCKCHAFER
SCANDALISE	STANISLAUS	WHATSOEVER	OMBROPHOBE	ZABAGLIONE	COCKERNONY
SCANDALIZE	STAPHYLINE	WRAPAROUND	PUBERULENT	ACCELERATE	CUCKOOPINT
SCANDALOUS	STARVATION	ZOANTHARIA	PUBESCENCE	ACCENTUATE	CUCULLATED
SCANDAROON	STARVELING	ABBREVIATE	PUBLISHING	ACCESSIBLE	CUCURBITAL
SCANDERBEG	STATECRAFT	ALBIGENSES	RABBINICAL	ACCESSIONS	CYCLOPEDIA
SCANTINESS	STATIONARY	AMBARVALIA	REBELLIOUS	ACCIDENTAL	CYCLOSTYLE
SCAPEGRACE	STATIONERY	AMBASSADOR	RIBOFLAVIN	ACCLIVIOUS	DECAGRAMME
SCAPHOPODA	STATISTICS	AMBIVALENT	ROBERDSMAN	ACCOMPLICE	DECAHEDRON
SCARAMOUCH	STATOCRACY	AMBLYOPSIS	ROBERTSMAN	ACCOMPLISH	DECAMPMENT
SCARCEMENT	STATUESQUE	AMBLYSTOMA	ROBUSTIOUS	ACCORDANCE	DECAPITATE
SCARCENESS	STAUROLITE	AMBOCEPTOR	ROBUSTNESS	ACCOUNTANT	DECATHLETE
SCARLATINA	STAVESACRE	AMBULACRUM	RUBBERNECK	ACCOUNTING	DECELERATE
SCARLETINA	SUAVEOLENT	AMBULATORY	RUBIGINOUS	ACCREDITED	DECENNOVAL
SCATHELESS	SVADILFARI	ARBITRATOR	RUBINSTEIN	ACCUBATION	DECIMALIZE
SCATTERING	SWAGGERING	ASBESTOSIS	SABBATICAL	ACCUMULATE	DECIPHERED
SCATURIENT	SWALLOWING	BABESIASIS	SABRETACHE	ACCURATELY	DECISIVELY
SEAMANSHIP	THALASSIAN	BABIROUSSA	SOBERSIDES	ACCUSATION	DECLENSION
SEAMSTRESS	THALESTRIS	BABYLONIAN	SUBCOMPACT	ACCUSATIVE	DECOLLATOR
SEANNACHIE	THALICTRUM	BABYSITTER	SUBHEADING	ACCUSINGLY	DECOLORATE
SEASONABLE	THALLIFORM	BOBBYSOXER	SUBJECTION	ACCUSTOMED	DECOLORIZE
SEASONABLY	THANKFULLY	CYBERNETIC	SUBJECTIVE	ALCAICERIA	DECOMPOSED
SGANARELLE	THAUMASITE	DEBASEMENT	SUBLIMATER	ALCHERINGA	DECORATION
SHABBINESS	TRACHELATE	DEBATEMENT	SUBLIMINAL	ALCIBIADES	DECORATIVE
SHACKLETON	TRADITIONS	DEBAUCHERY	SUBMARINER	ALCOHOLISM	DECRESCENT
SHADOWLESS	TRAFFICKER	DEBILITATE	SUBMEDIANT	ALCYONARIA	DICHROMATE
SHAGGYMANE	TRAGACANTH	DEBOUCHURE	SUBMERSION	ANCHORETIC	DICHROMISM
SHAGHAIRED	TRAGICALLY	DEBRIEFING	SUBMISSION	ANCHYLOSIS	DICKCISSEL
SHAKUHACHI	TRAITOROUS	EMBANKMENT	SUBMISSIVE	ANCIPITOUS	DICTIONARY
SHAMEFACED	TRAJECTORY	EMBERGOOSE	SUBORBITAL	ARCHBISHOP	DICTOGRAPH
SHAMEFULLY	TRAMONTANA	EMBITTERED	SUBREPTION	ARCHDEACON	DICYNODONT
SHAMPOOING	TRAMONTANE	EMBLEMATIC	SUBROUTINE	ARCHETYPAL	DOCIMASTIC
SHANDRYDAN	TRAMPOLINE	EMBLEMENTS	SUBSCRIBER	ARCHIMEDES	DUCKBOARDS
SHANDYGAFF	TRANQUILLY	EMBODIMENT	SUBSECTION	ARCHITRAVE	ECCHYMOSIS
SHARAWADGI	TRANSCRIBE	EMBONPOINT	SUBSELLIUM	ASCENDANCY	ECCOPROTIC
SHARAWAGGI	TRANSCRIPT	EMBOUCHURE	SUBSEQUENT	ASCENDENCY	ENCAMPMENT
SHATTERING	TRANSGRESS	EMBROIDERY	SUBSIDENCE	ASCETICISM	ENCASEMENT
SKATEBOARD	TRANSIENCE	EMBRYOLOGY	SUBSIDIARY	ASCOMYCETE	ENCEPHALON
SLAMMERKIN	TRANSISTOR	FABULOUSLY	SUBSISTENT	ASCRIBABLE	ENCHANTING
SLANDEROUS	TRANSITION	FIBERGLASS	SUBSPECIES	AUCTIONEER	ENCLOISTER
SLATTERNLY	TRANSITIVE	FIBREGLASS	SUBSTATION	BACCHANTES	ENCOIGNURE
SMALLSCALE	TRANSITORY	FIBRILLATE	SUBSTITUTE	BACITRACIN	ENCYCLICAL
SMARAGDINE	TRANSLATED	FIBROSITIS	SUBSTRATUM	BACKBITING	ESCADRILLE
SMARMINESS	TRANSLATOR	GIBBERELLA	SUBTENANCY	BACKBLOCKS	ESCALATION
SMATTERING	TRANSPLANT	GOBEMOUCHE	SUBTERFUGE	BACKGAMMON	ESCAPEMENT
SNAKEMOUTH	TRANSPOSED	GUBERNATOR	SUBTRAHEND	BACKGROUND	ESCARPMENT
SNAKESTONE	TRANSPOSON	HABILITATE	SUBTROPICS	BACKHANDED	ESCHAROTIC
SNAPDRAGON	TRANSVERSE	HABITATION	SUBVENTION	BACKHANDER	ESCRITOIRE
SNAPHAUNCE	TRAUMATIZE	HABITUALLY	SUBVERSION	BACKPACKER	ESCULAPIAN
SNAPHAUNCH	TRAVANCORE	HOBBYHORSE	SUBVERSIVE	BACKSLIDER	ESCUTCHEON
SPACECRAFT	TRAVELATOR	IMBECILITY	TABERNACLE	BACKSTAIRS	EUCALYPTOL
SPALLATION	TRAVELLERS	IMBRICATED	TABLANETTE	BACKSTROKE	EUCALYPTUS
SPARSENESS	TRAVELLING	IMBROCCATA	TABLECLOTH	BICHROMATE	EUCHLORINE
SPARTACIST	TRAVELOGUE	INBREEDING	TABLESPOON	BUCCINATOR	EXCAVATION
SPATCHCOCK	TRAVERTINE	JABBERWOCK	TABULATION	BUCEPHALUS	EXCELLENCE
STABILISER	TRAVOLATOR	JOBSEEKERS	TUBERCULAR	BUCHMANISM	EXCELLENCY
STABILIZER	UNABRIDGED	JUBILANTLY	UMBELLIFER	BUCKINGHAM	EXCITEMENT
STADHOLDER	UNACCENTED	JUBILATION	UNBALANCED	BUCKJUMPER	EXCRUCIATE
STAGECOACH	UNAFFECTED	LABORATORY	UNBEARABLE	CACHINNATE	FACESAVING
STAGECRAFT	UNANSWERED	LEBENSRAUM	UNBEARABLY	CACODAEMON	FACILITATE
STAGGERING	UNARGUABLE	LIBERALISM	UNBEATABLE	CACOGRAPHY	FACILITIES

FACTITIOUS	NECROPOLIS	SECONDMENT	ENDOGENOUS	MUDSKIPPER	UNDERVALUE
FICKLENESS	NECTABANUS	SECONDRATE	ENDOSMOSIS	NIDDERLING	UNDERWATER
FICTITIOUS	NICARAGUAN	SECRETAIRE	EUDIOMETER	NUDIBRANCH	UNDERWORLD
HACKBUTEER	NICROSILAL	SECULARIZE	FEDERALISM	ODDFELLOWS	UNDERWRITE
HACKMATACK	NUCLEONICS	SECURITIES	FEDERALIST	ORDINARILY	UNDESCRIED
HECTICALLY	NYCTALOPIA	SICILIENNE	FEDERATION	ORDINATION	UNDESERVED
HECTOLITRE	OCCASIONAL	SUCCEEDING	FIDDLEWOOD	ORDONNANCE	UNDETECTED
INCAPACITY	OCCIDENTAL	SUCCESSFUL	FUDDYDUDDY	ORDOVICIAN	UNDETERRED
INCAPARINA	OCCIDENTAL	SUCCESSION	GADOLINIUM	PADAREWSKI	UNDIGESTED
INCAUTIOUS	OCCURRENCE	SUCCESSIVE	GODPARENTS	PADDINGTON	UNDISPUTED
INCENDIARY	ORCHESTRAL	SUCCINCTLY	HEDONISTIC	PADDLEFISH	UNDOCTORED
INCESTUOUS	ORCHIDEOUS	TACHOGRAPH	HODGEPODGE	PADDYMELON	UNDULATING
INCHOATIVE	OSCILLATOR	TACHOMETER	HYDRAULICS	PEDESTRIAN	UNDULATION
INCIDENTAL	OSCITATION	TACTICALLY	HYDROLYSIS	PEDIATRICS	VIDARABINE
INCINERATE	OSCULATION	TACTLESSLY	HYDROMETER	PEDICULATE	WIDDICOMBE
INCISIVELY	OSCULATORY	TECHNETIUM	HYDROPHANE	PEDIMENTAL	WIDESPREAD
INCITEMENT	PACESETTER	TECHNICIAN	HYDROPHYTE	PEDIPALPUS	ZIDOVUDINE
INCIVILITY	PACIFICISM	TECHNOCRAT	HYDROPLANE	RADICALISM	ABERDEVINE
INCOHERENT	PECCADILLO	TECHNOLOGY	HYDROPONIC	RADIOGRAPH	ABERGLAUBE
INCOMPLETE	PECULATION	TICKERTAPE	INDAPAMIDE	RADIOLARIA	ABERRATION
INCONSTANT	PECULIARLY	TOCCATELLA	INDECENTLY	REDCURRANT	ACEPHALOUS
INCRASSATE	PICARESQUE	TOCOPHEROL	INDECISION	REDECORATE	ACETABULAR
INCREASING	PICAYUNISH	ULCERATION	INDECISIVE	REDEMPTION	ACETABULUM
INCREDIBLE	PICCADILLY	UNCOMMONLY	INDECOROUS	REDISCOVER	ADELANTADO
INCREDIBLY	PICCALILLI	UNCONFINED	INDEFINITE	REDRUTHITE	ADEQUATELY
INCRESCENT	PICCANINNY	UNCRITICAL	INDELICACY	REDUNDANCY	ALECTORIAN
INCUBATION	PICHICIAGO	UNCTUOUSLY	INDELICATE	RIDICULOUS	ALEMBICATE
INCUMBENCY	PICHICIEGO	UNCULTURED	INDENTURES	RIDINGHOOD	ALEXANDERS
INCUNABULA	PICKPOCKET	VICEGERENT	INDEXATION	RUDDERLESS	ALEXANDRIA
JACKANAPES	PICTOGRAPH	VICEREGENT	INDICATION	RUDIMENTAL	AMELIORATE
JACKBOOTED	POCAHONTAS	VICTORIANA	INDICATIVE	RUDOLPHINE	AMERINDIAN
JACKHAMMER	POCKETBOOK	VICTORIOUS	INDICOLITE	SADDLEBACK	ANEMOGRAPH
JACKSTONES	POCKMANTIE	VICTUALLER	INDICTABLE	SADDLEBILL	ANEMOMETER
JACKSTRAWS	POCKMARKED	VOCABULARY	INDICTMENT	SEDATENESS	ANESTHESIA
JACULATION	PUCKERWOOD	VOCABULIST	INDIGENOUS	SEDULOUSLY	ANESTHETIC
JOCULARITY	PYCNOGONID	VOCATIONAL	INDIGOLITE	SIDEBOARDS	APEMANTHUS
LACCADIVES	RACECOURSE	VOCIFERATE	INDIRECTLY	SIDERATION	AREFACTION
LACERATION	RECEPTACLE	VOCIFEROUS	INDISCREET	SIDEROSTAT	ARENACEOUS
LACHRYMOSE	RECIDIVISM	WICKEDNESS	INDISPOSED	SIDESADDLE	AREOGRAPHY
LACKADAISY	RECIDIVIST	WICKERWORK	INDISTINCT	SIDEWINDER	AREOPAGITE
LACKLUSTER	RECIPROCAL	WYCLIFFIAN	INDITEMENT	SUDATORIUM	ATELEIOSIS
LACKLUSTRE	RECITATION	ABDICATION	INDIVIDUAL	SUDDENNESS	AVENTURINE
LACUSTRINE	RECITATIVE	ADDITAMENT	INDONESIAN	TEDDINGTON	AVERRHOISM
LICENTIATE	RECITATIVO	ADDITIONAL	INDUCEMENT	UNDECLARED	BEEFBURGER
LICENTIOUS	RECKLESSLY	ALDERMANLY	INDUCTANCE	UNDEFEATED	BEEFEATERS
LOCKERROOM	RECOGNISED	ALDERWOMAN	INDULGENCE	UNDEFENDED	BEEKEEPING
LOCKKEEPER	RECOGNIZED	ANDALUSIAN	INDUMENTUM	UNDENIABLE	BIENNIALLY
LOCOMOTION	RECOMMENCE	ANDALUSITE	INDUSTRIAL	UNDERBURNT	BLEARYEYED
LOCOMOTIVE	RECOMPENSE	ANDROMACHE	JUDICATURE	UNDERCLASS	BLEPHARISM
LOCULAMENT	RECONCILED	AUDIBILITY	JUDICIALLY	UNDERCOVER	BREADFRUIT
LYCHNAPSIA	RECONSIDER	AUDITORIUM	KIDNAPPING	UNDERCRAFT	BREAKABLES
MACEBEARER	RECREATION	BADDERLOCK	LADYKILLER	UNDERCROFT	BREAKWATER
MACEDONIAN	RECRUDESCE	BEDCHAMBER	LEDERHOSEN	UNDERFLOOR	BREASTBONE
MACKINTOSH	RECUPERATE	BEDCLOTHES	MADAGASCAN	UNDERLEASE	BREASTFEED
MACONOCHIE	RECURRENCE	BEDEVILLED	MADAGASCAR	UNDERLINEN	BREASTWORK
MACROBIOTE	RICHARDSON	BEDRAGGLED	MEDDLESOME	UNDERLYING	BREATHLESS
MACROCARPA	RICHTHOFEN	BUDGERIGAR	MEDICAMENT	UNDERNEATH	BRESSUMMER
MECHANICAL	ROCKABILLY	CADAVEROUS	MEDICATION	UNDERPANTS	BYELECTION
MECHANIZED	ROCKINGHAM	CODSWALLOP	MEDIOCRITY	UNDERSCORE	CAERPHILLY
MICHAELMAS	ROCKSTEADY	CUDDLESOME	MEDITATION	UNDERSHIRT	CAESPITOSE
MICROFICHE	SACCHARASE	DEDICATION	MEDITATIVE	UNDERSIZED	CHEAPSKATE
MICROLIGHT	SACCHARIDE	DEDUCTIBLE	MEDIUMTERM	UNDERSKIRT	CHECKLATON
MICROMETER	SACCHARINE	DIDASCALIC	MIDDLEBROW	UNDERSLUNG	CHECKPOINT
MICRONESIA	SACCHAROID	DIDGERIDOO	MIDLOTHIAN	UNDERSTAND	CHEEKINESS
MICROPHONE	SACERDOTAL	DIDUNCULUS	MIDSHIPMAN	UNDERSTATE	CHEERFULLY
MICROSCOPE	SACREDNESS	DODECANESE	MODERATELY	UNDERSTEER	CHEESECAKE
MUCKRAKING	SACROSANCT	ELDERBERRY	MODERATION	UNDERSTOOD	CHEESEWOOD
MYCORRHIZA	SECONDBEST	ENDEARMENT	MODIFIABLE	UNDERSTUDY	CHEIRONOMY
NECROMANCY	SECONDHAND	ENDOGAMOUS	MODULATION	UNDERTAKER	CHELTENHAM

CHEMICALLY	FLEETINGLY	OPENHANDED	PRESUMABLY	STEAKHOUSE	VOETGANGER
CHEMONASTY	FLESHINESS	OPENMINDED	PRESUPPOSE	STEALTHILY	WEEDKILLER
CHEQUEBOOK	FREEBOOTER	OVERBOUGHT	PRETENSION	STEELINESS	WHEATSHEAF
CHERIMOYER	FREEHANDER	OVERCHARGE	PRETINCOLE	STEELWORKS	WHEATSTONE
CHERRYWOOD	FREEHOLDER	OVEREATING	PRETTINESS	STEMWINDER	WHEELCHAIR
CHERSONESE	FREELANCER	OVERLANDER	PREVAILING	STENOTYPER	WHEELHOUSE
CHERVONETS	FREELOADER	OVERMATTER	PREVALENCE	STENTORIAN	WHEEZINESS
CHESSBOARD	FREEMARTIN	OVERPRAISE	PREVENANCY	STEPFATHER	WHEWELLITE
CHESSYLITE	FREEMASONS	OVERRIDING	PREVENTION	STEPHANITE	WRETCHEDLY
CHESTERTON	FREIGHTAGE	OVERSHADOW	PREVENTIVE	STEPHENSON	AFFABILITY
CHEVESAILE	FREMESCENT	OVERSLAUGH	PREVIOUSLY	STEPLADDER	AFFETTUOSO
CHEVISANCE	FRENETICAL	OVERSPREAD	PSEPHOLOGY	STEPMOTHER	AFFILIATED
CHEVROTAIN	FRENZIEDLY	OVERSTRAIN	PSEUDOCARP	STEPSISTER	AFFLICTION
CLEARSTORY	FREQUENTED	OVERSTRUNG	PTERANODON	STEREOTOMY	AFFORDABLE
CLEARWATER	FREQUENTER	OVERSUPPLY	PTERYGOTUS	STEREOTYPE	BAFFLEMENT
CLEMENCEAU	FREQUENTLY	OVERTHETOP	QUEASINESS	STEREOTYPY	BEFOREHAND
CLEMENTINE	FRESHWATER	OVERTHWART	QUEENSBURY	STERILISER	BUFFLEHEAD
CLERESTORY	GLEEMAIDEN	OVERWEIGHT	QUEENSTOWN	STERILIZER	BUFFOONERY
CLEROMANCY	GLENDOVEER	OVERWORKED	QUENCHLESS	STERNALGIA	DEFACEMENT
CLEVERNESS	GREEDINESS	PAEDIATRIC	QUERCITRON	STERTEROUS	DEFAMATION
COELACANTH	GREENCLOTH	PEELGARLIC	QUERSPRUNG	STERTOROUS	DEFAMATORY
COETANEOUS	GREENFINCH	PHENOMENAL	QUESADILLA	STEWARDESS	DEFEASANCE
COEXISTENT	GREENHEART	PHENOMENON	QUESTIONER	SWEATSHIRT	DEFECATION
CREATIVITY	GREENHOUSE	PLEASANTLY	REELECTION	SWEDENBORG	DEFENSIBLE
CREDENTIAL	GREENSHANK	PLEASANTRY	RHEOTROPIC	SWEEPSTAKE	DEFICIENCY
CREDITABLE	GREENSTICK	PLEBISCITE	RHETORICAL	SWEETBREAD	DEFILEMENT
CREDITABLY	GREENSTONE	PLEONASTIC	RHEUMATICS	SWEETBRIAR	DEFINITELY
CRENELLATE	GREENSWARD	PLEROPHORY	RHEUMATISM	SWEETENING	DEFINITION
CREOPHAGUS	GREGARIOUS	PLESIOSAUR	RHEUMATOID	SWEETHEART	DEFINITIVE
CRETACEOUS	GRENADIERS	PLEXIMETER	SCEPTICISM	SWELTERING	DEFLAGRATE
CREWELWORK	GRENADILLA	POETASTERY	SEECATCHIE	TEENYWEENY	DEFLECTION
CTENOPHORA	GREYFRIARS	POETICALLY	SEEMLIHEAD	TEETHRIDGE	DEFRAYMENT
CTENOPHORE	GUESTHOUSE	PREARRANGE	SEERSUCKER	TEETOTALER	DIFFERENCE
DEEPFREEZE	HAEMANTHUS	PREBENDARY	SHEARWATER	THEATRICAL	DIFFICULTY
DEEPSEATED	HEEDLESSLY	PRECARIOUS	SHECKLATON	THELLUSSON	DIFFIDENCE
DIELECTRIC	HIERARCHIC	PRECAUTION	SHEEPISHLY	THEMSELVES	EFFACEMENT
DREADFULLY	HIEROGLYPH	PRECEDENCE	SHEEPSHANK	THEOCRITUS	EFFECTUATE
DREADLOCKS	HIEROMANCY	PRECIPITIN	SHELDONIAN	THEODOLITE	EFFEMINACY
DREAMINESS	HIEROPHANT	PRECOCIOUS	SHELLSHOCK	THEOLOGATE	EFFEMINATE
DREARINESS	HIEROSCOPY	PRECURSORY	SHELLYCOAT	THEOLOGIAN	EFFERVESCE
DREARISOME	ICEBREAKER	PREDACIOUS	SHENANIGAN	THEOLOGISE	EFFICIENCY
DREIKANTER	IDEALISTIC	PREDECEASE	SHERARDISE	THEOLOGIST	EFFLEURAGE
DRESSMAKER	INEBRIATED	PREDESTINE	SKEPTICISM	THEREAFTER	EFFORTLESS
ELECAMPANE	INEDUCABLE	PREDICTION	SKETCHBOOK	THEREANENT	EFFRONTERY
ELECTORATE	INEFFICACY	PREDISPOSE	SKEUOMORPH	THERMIONIC	EFFUSIVELY
ELECTRICAL	INELIGIBLE	PREDNISONE	SLEEPINESS	THERMISTOR	INFALLIBLE
ELECTROMER	INEPTITUDE	PREEMINENT	SLEEVELESS	THERMOSTAT	INFALLIBLY
ELECTRONIC	INEQUALITY	PREFERABLE	SNEEZEWOOD	TIEBREAKER	INFATUATED
ELEGABALUS	INESCULENT	PREFERABLY	SPEAKERINE	TRECENTIST	INFECTIOUS
ELEMENTARY	INEVITABLE	PREFERENCE	SPECIALISE	TREKSCHUIT	INFEFTMENT
ELEUSINIAN	INEVITABLY	PREFERMENT	SPECIALISM	TREMENDOUS	INFERNALLY
EMENDATION	INEXORABLE	PREHENSILE	SPECIALIST	TRENCHMORE	INFIBULATE
EPENTHETIC	KIESELGUHR	PREHISTORY	SPECIALITY	TRENDINESS	INFIDELITY
ETEOCRETAN	KLEBSIELLA	PREJUDICED	SPECIALIZE	TRESPASSER	INFIGHTING
ETERNALIZE	KOEKSISTER	PRELECTION	SPECIOUSLY	UBERMENSCH	INFILTRATE
EVENHANDED	LAEOTROPIC	PREMARITAL	SPECTACLED	UNEASINESS	INFINITELY
EVENTUALLY	LHERZOLITE	PREMEDICAL	SPECTACLES	UNEDIFYING	INFINITIVE
EVERGLADES	LIEBERMANN	PREPARATOR	SPECTATORS	UNEDUCATED	INFLATABLE
EVERYPLACE	LIEUTENANT	PREPAYMENT	SPECULATOR	UNEMPLOYED	INFLECTION
EVERYTHING	MEERSCHAUM	PREPENSELY	SPEECHLESS	UNENVIABLE	INFLEXIBLE
EVERYWHERE	MYELINATED	PREPOSITOR	SPEEDINESS	UNEQUALLED	INFLEXIBLY
EXECRATION	NEEDLECASE	PREPOSSESS	SPELEOLOGY	UNEVENNESS	INFLICTION
EXEMPTNESS	NEEDLEWORK	PREPOTENCE	SPELLBOUND	UNEVENTFUL	INFORMALLY
EXENTERATE	OBEDIENTLY	PRESBYOPIA	SPENCERIAN	UNEXAMPLED	INFRACTION
EYEWITNESS	OCEANARIUM	PRESBYTERY	SPENSERIAN	UNEXPECTED	INFREQUENT
FEEBLENESS	OCEANGOING	PRESCIENCE	SPERMACETI	UNEXPLORED	INFURIATED
FIELDMOUSE	ODELSTHING	PRESENTDAY	SPERMICIDE	USEFULNESS	LEFTHANDED
FIENDISHLY	OLEAGINOUS	PRESIDENCY	SPERRYLITE	VIETNAMESE	LEFTHANDER
FIERCENESS	OLERACEOUS	PRESSURIZE	STEADINESS	VIEWFINDER	LEFTWINGER

NEFANDROUS	FIGUREHEAD	REGISTERED	INHIBITION	BRITISHISM	FRICANDEAU
OBFUSCATED	HAGIOSCOPE	REGRESSION	INHIBITORY	CHICHESTER	FRIENDLESS
OFFBALANCE	HIGHBINDER	REGRESSIVE	INHUMANITY	CHICKENPOX	FRIENDSHIP
OFFICIALLY	HIGHFLYING	REGULARITY	JOHNSONIAN	CHIFFCHAFF	FRIGHTENED
OFFLICENCE	HIGHHANDED	REGULARIZE	KSHATRIYAS	CHIFFONIER	FRINGILLID
OFFPUTTING	HIGHLANDER	REGULATION	MAHAYANALI	CHILDBIRTH	FRISKINESS
OFFTHECUFF	HIGHWAYMAN	RIGELATION	MAHOMMEDAN	CHILDERMAS	FRITHSOKEN
OFFTHEWALL	HYGROMETER	RIGHTFULLY	NIHILISTIC	CHILDISHLY	FRITILLARY
REFERENDUM	INGEMINATE	RIGHTWARDS	OCHLOCRACY	CHILLINESS	GAINGIVING
REFINEMENT	INGENERATE	RIGOROUSLY	OPHICLEIDE	CHIMBORAZO	GAINSTRIVE
REFLECTING	INGLORIOUS	RUGGEDNESS	OPHTHALMIC	CHIMNEYPOT	GHIBELLINE
REFLECTION	INGRATIATE	SAGITTARIA	OTHERGATES	CHIMPANZEE	GLISTENING
REFLECTIVE	INGREDIENT	SEGREGATED	OTHERGUESS	CHINABERRY	GLITTERAND
REFRACTION	JAGUARONDI	SEGUIDILLA	POHUTUKAWA	CHINAGRAPH	GLITTERATI
REFRACTIVE	JAGUARUNDI	SIGILLARIA	SCHALSTEIN	CHINASTONE	GLITTERING
REFRACTORY	JIGGAMAREE	SIGNIFICAT	SCHIPPERKE	CHINCHILLA	GRIDIRONER
REFRESHING	JIGGERMAST	SIGNORELLI	SCHISMATIC	CHINQUAPIN	GRIDLOCKED
REFRINGENT	JUGENDSTIL	SOGDOLAGER	SCHLIMAZEL	CHIRICAUNE	GRINDSTONE
REFUTATION	JUGGERNAUT	SOGDOLIGER	SCHOLAEMIA	CHIROMANCY	GRITTINESS
SOFTBOILED	LEGALISTIC	SOGDOLOGER	SCHOLASTIC	CHIRONOMIC	GUIDELINES
SUFFERANCE	LEGIBILITY	SUGARALLIE	SCHOOLBOOK	CHIROPTERA	GUILLOTINE
SUFFICIENT	LEGISLATOR	SUGGESTION	SCHOOLGIRL	CHITARRONE	HAIRSPRING
SUFFRAGIST	LEGITIMACY	SUGGESTIVE	SCHOOLMAAM	CHITTAGONG	HEIDELBERG
UNFAITHFUL	LEGITIMATE	TAGLIARINI	SCHWARZLOT	CHIVALROUS	INIMITABLE
UNFAMILIAR	LEGITIMIZE	UNGRACIOUS	SPHACELATE	CLINGSTONE	INIQUITOUS
UNFATHOMED	LEGUMINOUS	UNGRATEFUL	SPHALERITE	CLINICALLY	INITIATION
UNFETTERED	LEGWARMERS	UNGROUNDED	TCHOUKBALL	CNIDOBLAST	INITIATIVE
UNFINISHED	LIGHTERMAN	VEGETABLES	UNHAMPERED	COINCIDENT	IRIDESCENT
UNFLAGGING	LIGHTHOUSE	VEGETARIAN	UNHEARABLE	CRICKETING	IRISHWOMAN
UNFLAVORED	LIGHTINGUP	VEGETATION	UNHERALDED	CRIMINALLY	IRISHWOMEN
UNFORESEEN	LIGNOCAINE	VIGILANTES	UNHYGIENIC	CRISPBREAD	JEISTIECOR
UNFRIENDLY	LOGANBERRY	VIGOROUSLY	UPHOLSTERY	CRISPINIAN	KHIDMUTGAR
UNFRUITFUL	LOGARITHMS	WAGEEARNER	VEHEMENTLY	CRISSCROSS	KNIFEBOARD
WOFFINGTON	LOGGERHEAD	YGGDRASILL	YTHUNDERED	CRITICALLY	KNIGHTHEAD
YAFFINGALE	LOGISTICAL	ZYGODACTYL	ABITURIENT	CUIRASSIER	KNIGHTHOOD
AGGRANDISE	LOGORRHOEA	ABHIDHAMMA	ADIAPHORON	CUISENAIRE	KRIEGSPIEL
AGGRESSION	LUGUBRIOUS	ABHORRENCE	AFICIONADO	DRINKWATER	MAIDENHAIR
AGGRESSIVE	MAGISTRACY	ACHITOPHEL	AHITHOPHEL	ELIMINATOR	MAIDENHOOD
ALGOLAGNIA	MAGISTRAND	ACHROMATIC	ALIENATION	EMIGRATION	MAINPERNOR
ALGONQUIAN	MAGISTRATE	ADHIBITION	ALIMENTARY	EMISSIVITY	MAINSPRING
ANGIOSPERM	MAGNIFICAT	ANHELATION	AMIABILITY	EPICANTHUS	MAINSTREAM
ANGLERFISH	MAGNIFYING	APHAERESIS	ANIMADVERT	EPIDEICTIC	MAINTAINER
ANGLOPHILE	MEGALITHIC	ATHANASIAN	APICULTURE	EPIDENDRUM	MAISONETTE
ANGLOPHOBE	MEGALOSAUR	BAHRAINIAN	ARIMASPIAN	EPIDIDYMUS	MEITNERIUM
ANGUILLULA	MIGHTINESS	BEHAVIORAL	ARISTIPPUS	EPIDIORITE	MOISTURIZE
ANGURVADEL	MIGNONETTE	BEHINDHAND	ARISTOCRAT	EPIGENETIC	NEIGHBORLY
ANGWANTIBO	NEGATIVELY	COHERENTLY	ARISTOLOGY	EPIGLOTTIS	ODIOUSNESS
ARGOLEMONO	NEGLECTFUL	DEHISCENCE	ARISTOTLES	EPILIMNION	OPISOMETER
BAGASSOSIS	NEGLIGENCE	ECHINODERM	ARITHMETIC	EPIMENIDES	ORIDINANCE
COGITATION	NEGLIGIBLE	ECHINOIDEA	AVICULARIA	EPIMETHEUS	ORIGINALLY
COGNISANCE	NEGOTIABLE	ECHOPRAXIA	AXINOMANCY	EPIPHONEMA	ORIGINATOR
COGNIZANCE	NEGOTIATOR	ENHYDRITIC	BAILIEWICK	EPIPLASTRA	OVIPOSITOR
DEGENERACY	NIGGERHEAD	EPHRAIMITE	BAILLIWICK	EPISCOPATE	PAINKILLER
DEGENERATE	NIGHTDRESS	ETHEOSTOMA	BLISSFULLY	EPISPASTIC	PAINLESSLY
DEGRADABLE	NIGHTLIGHT	ETHYLAMINE	BLISTERING	EPISTEMICS	PAINTBRUSH
DIGESTIBLE	NIGHTSHADE	EUHEMERISM	BLITHERING	EPISTROPHE	PHILATELIC
DIGITORIUM	NIGHTSHIRT	EXHALATION	BLITZKRIEG	EPITHELIUM	PHILIPPINA
DIGRESSION	NIGHTSTICK	EXHAUSTING	BOISTEROUS	ERIOCAULON	PHILIPPINE
DOGGEDNESS	NIGRESCENT	EXHAUSTION	BRICKLAYER	EVISCERATE	PHILISTINE
EIGHTEENTH	OUGHTLINGS	EXHAUSTIVE	BRICKWORKS	EVITERNITY	PHILLIPINA
ENGAGEMENT	PAGINATION	EXHIBITION	BRIDEGROOM	FAIRGROUND	PHILLIPINE
ENGENDRURE	PIGEONHOLE	EXHILARATE	BRIDESMAID	FAIRHAIRED	PHILLUMENY
ENGLISHMAN	POGONOTOMY	EXHUMATION	BRIDGEHEAD	FAITHFULLY	PHILOPOENA
ENGLISHMEN	PUGNACIOUS	FAHRENHEIT	BRIDGETOWN	FLICKERING	PHILOSOPHY
ENGOUEMENT	RAGAMUFFIN	ICHTHYOSIS	BRIDLEPATH	FLIGHTLESS	PHILOXENIA
ENGROSSING	REGARDLESS	INHABITANT	BRIGANDINE	FLIMSINESS	PLIABILITY
ERGONOMICS	REGENERATE	INHALATION	BRIGANTINE	FLINDERSIA	PLIOHIPPUS
FIGURATION	REGIMENTAL	INHERENTLY	BRIGHTNESS	FLIPPANTLY	POIGNANTLY
FIGURATIVE	REGIMENTED	INHIBITING	BRILLIANCE	FLIRTATION	POIKILITIC

POINSETTIA	TAILORMADE	MUJAHEDDIN	CALLIATURE	FELICITATE	MALAYALAAM
POINTBLANK	TEICHOPSIA	OBJECTLESS	CALORIFIER	FELICITOUS	MALCONTENT
PRICKLOUSE	TEINOSCOPE	PEJORATIVE	CALUMNIATE	FELLOWSHIP	MALEFACTOR
PRIESTHOOD	THICKENING	RAJPRAMUKH	CALYDONIAN	FILIBUSTER	MALEVOLENT
PRIMORDIAL	THIMBLEFUL	REJONEADOR	CALYPTRATE	FILLIBRUSH	MALIGNANCY
PRINCIPIUM	THIMBLEWIT	REJUVENATE	CELEBRATED	FILTHINESS	MALINGERER
PRINCIPLED	THINGUMBOB	RIJSTTAFEL	CELESTIALS	FILTRATION	MALLOPHAGA
PRINCIPLES	THIRTEENTH	ALKALINITY	CELLOPHANE	FOLIACEOUS	MALMESBURY
PRIVATEERS	THIXOTROPY	DUKKERIPEN	CELLULITIS	FULFILMENT	MALODOROUS
PRIVILEGED	TOILETRIES	ENKEPHALIN	CHLORINATE	FULIGINOUS	MALTHUSIAN
PRIZEFIGHT	TOILINETTE	HAKENKREUZ	CHLOROFORM	FULLLENGTH	MELACONITE
PSILOCYBIN	TRIACONTER	INKSLINGER	COLBERTINE	FULLYGROWN	MELANCHOLY
QUICKSANDS	TRIANGULAR	LIKELIHOOD	COLCHESTER	GALIMATIAS	MELANESIAN
QUICKTHORN	TRIANGULUM	LIKEMINDED	COLCHICINE	GALLABIYAH	MELLOWNESS
QUIESCENCE	TRICHOLOGY	MAKESYSTEM	COLDSTREAM	GALLABIYEH	MELOCOTOON
QUIRINALIA	TRICKINESS	MAKEWEIGHT	COLEOPTERA	GALLIAMBIC	MILEOMETER
QUIZMASTER	TRICLINIUM	MAKUNOUCHI	COLEORHIZA	GALRAVITCH	MILITARISM
RAILWAYMAN	TRIDENTINE	POKERFACED	COLLAPSING	GALSWORTHY	MILITARIST
RAIYATWARI	TRIFOLIATE	ALLEGATION	COLLARBONE	GALUMPHING	MILITIAMAN
REITERATED	TRILATERAL	ALLEGEANCE	COLLATERAL	GALVANISER	MILLEFIORI
RHINEGRAVE	TRILINGUAL	ALLEGIANCE	COLLECTING	GELATINOUS	MILLENNIUM
RHINESTONE	TRILLIONTH	ALLIGATION	COLLECTION	GILBERTIAN	MILLICURIE
RHINOCEROS	TRIMALCHIO	ALLOCATION	COLLECTIVE	GILBERTINE	MILLIFARAD
RHINOLALIA	TRIMSNITCH	ALLOCUTION	COLLEGIATE	GILLRAVAGE	MILLIHENRY
RHINOPHYMA	TRINACRIAN	ALLOSAURUS	COLLEMBOLA	GOLDDIGGER	MILLIMETER
RHIPIPTERA	TRIPARTITE	ALLOSTERIC	COLLIMATOR	GOLDENSEAL	MILLIMETRE
ROISTERING	TRIPEHOUND	ALLOTROPIC	COLLIQUATE	GOLDFINGER	MOLENDINAR
SCIENTIFIC	TRIPLICATE	ALLPURPOSE	COLLOCUTER	GOLDILOCKS	MOLYBDENUM
SCINTIGRAM	TRIPLICITY	ALLUREMENT	COLLOQUIAL	GOLDTHREAD	MULIEBRITY
SEISMOLOGY	TRIPUDIARY	ALLYCHOLLY	COLONNADED	GOLIATHISE	MULLIGRUBS
SHIBBOLETH	TRISKELION	BALANCHINE	COLORATION	HALFDOLLAR	MULTIMEDIA
SHIELDRAKE	TRITANOPIA	BALBRIGGAN	COLORATURA	HALFHOURLY	MULTIPLIED
SHIFTINESS	TRIUMPHANT	BALBUTIENT	COLOSSALLY	HALFSISTER	MULTIPLIER
SHILLELAGH	TRIVIALITY	BALDERDASH	COLOSSIANS	HALFYEARLY	OBLIGATION
SHIMMERING	TRIVIALIZE	BALIBUNTAL	COLOURLESS	HALIEUTICS	OBLIGATORY
SHIPWRIGHT	UBIQUINONE	BALLISTICS	COLPORTAGE	HALLELUJAH	OBLIGINGLY
SHISHKEBAB	UBIQUITOUS	BALLISTITE	COLPORTEUR	HALLMARKED	OBLITERATE
SKILLFULLY	UNICAMERAL	BALLOONING	COLPOSCOPE	HALLOYSITE	OBLOMOVISM
SKINDIVING	UNIFORMITY	BALLOONIST	CULTIVATED	HALLUBALOO	OWLSPIEGLE
SLIPSTREAM	UNIGENITUS	BALNEATION	CULTIVATOR	HELICOPTER	PALAEOTYPE
SMITHEREEN	UNILATERAL	BALNEOLOGY	CULVERTAGE	HELIOGRAPH	PALAESTRAL
SNIGGERING	UNIMPAIRED	BALUSTRADE	DELCREDERE	HELIOLATER	PALAGONITE
SPIDERWORT	UNINFORMED	BELARUSIAN	DELECTABLE	HELIOTROPE	PALATALISE
SPIFLICATE	UNINSPIRED	BELIEVABLE	DELEGATION	HELLBENDER	PALATINATE
SPILLIKINS	UNINVITING	BELLADONNA	DELIBERATE	HELLESPONT	PALESTRINA
SPINESCENT	UNIQUENESS	BELLAMOURE	DELICATELY	HELPLESSLY	PALFRENIER
SPIRACULUM	UNIVERSITY	BELLARMINE	DELIGATION	HILDEBRAND	PALIMPSEST
SPIRITEDLY	UTILIZABLE	BELLWETHER	DELIGHTFUL	HOLOFERNES	PALINDROME
SPIRITLESS	WAINSCOTED	BELONGINGS	DELINQUENT	HOLOGRAPHY	PALISANDER
SPIRITUOUS	WEIGHTLESS	BELSHAZZAR	DELIRATION	HOLOHEDRAL	PALLBEARER
SPIRKETING	WEIMARANER	BILIVERDIN	DELPHINIUM	HOLOPHOTAL	PALLIATIVE
SPISSITUDE	WHIGGAMORE	BOLLANDIST	DELTIOLOGY	HOLOPHYTIC	PALMATIFID
SPITCHCOCK	WHILLYWHAW	BOLSHEVIST	DILAPIDATE	HOLOSTERIC	PALMATOZOA
SPITEFULLY	WHIRLYBIRD	BULLHEADED	DILATATION	HULLABALOO	PALMERSTON
STIACCIATO	WHISPERING	CALAMANDER	DILETTANTE	ILLADVISED	PALMERWORM
STICHARION	WHITEHEART	CALAMITOUS	DILIGENTLY	ILLAQUEATE	PALUDAMENT
STICKINESS	WHITETHORN	CALAMONDIN	DOLCEMENTE	ILLEGALITY	PALUSTRINE
STICKYBEAK	WHITEWATER	CALAVERITE	DOLICHOLIS	ILLITERACY	PALYNOLOGY
STIGMATISE	WHITSTABLE	CALCAREOUS	DOLICHOTUS	ILLITERATE	PHLEBOTOMY
STIGMATIZE	WHITTERICK	CALCEDONIO	ELLIPTICAL	ILLUMINATE	PHLEGETHON
STILLBIRTH	WRISTWATCH	CALCEOLATE	ENLACEMENT	ILLUMINATI	PHLEGMASIA
STILLICIDE	ZWITTERION	CALCITONIN	ENLÈVEMENT	ILLUSTRATE	PHLEGMATIC
STILLIFORM	ADJECTIVAL	CALCULABLE	ENLISTMENT	JOLTERHEAD	PHLOGISTIC
STILLSTAND	ADJUDICATE	CALCULATED	EULOGISTIC	KILMARNOCK	PHLOGISTON
STINGINESS	ADJUSTABLE	CALCULATOR	FALDISTORY	KILOMETRES	PHLOGOPITE
STINGYBARK	ADJUSTMENT	CALEDONIAN	FALKLANDER	LILYWHITES	PILEDRIVER
SWIMMINGLY	BIJOUTERIE	CALEFACTOR	FALLACIOUS	MALACOLOGY	PILGARLICK
SWITCHBACK	DEJECTEDLY	CALESCENCE	FALLINGOFF	MALAGUETTA	PILGRIMAGE
TAILGATING	INJUNCTION	CALIFORNIA	FALSETRUTH	MALAPROPOS	PILLIWINKS

PILLOWCASE	SOLIVAGANT	ADMIRINGLY	COMPLIANCE	HOMEWORKER	PUMPHANDLE
PILLOWSLIP	SOLUBILITY	ADMISSIBLE	COMPLICATE	HOMOEOPATH	RAMPALLIAN
POLIANTHES	SPLANCHNIC	ADMITTANCE	COMPLICITY	HOMOGENIZE	RAMSHACKLE
POLITENESS	SPLENDIDLY	ADMITTEDLY	COMPLIMENT	HOMOOUSIAN	REMARKABLE
POLITICIAN	SPLITLEVEL	ADMONITION	COMPLUVIUM	HOMOPHOBIA	REMARKABLY
POLITICIZE	SULPHUROUS	ALMACANTAR	COMPOSITOR	HOMOPHOBIC	REMITTANCE
POLLINATED	SULTRINESS	ALMSGIVING	COMPOUNDED	HOMOPHONIC	REMONETISE
POLYANTHUS	TALEBEARER	ALMSHOUSES	COMPRADORE	HOMORELAPS	REMORSEFUL
POLYCHAETE	TALLEYRAND	ALMUCANTAR	COMPREHEND	HOMOSEXUAL	REMOTENESS
POLYCHREST	TELEBRIDGE	AMMUNITION	COMPRESSED	HOMUNCULUS	REMUNERATE
POLYCHROME	TELEGRAPHY	ARMAGEDDON	COMPRESSOR	HUMANISTIC	ROMANESQUE
POLYGAMIST	TELEOSTOME	ARMIPOTENT	COMPROMISE	HUMANITIES	RUMBLOSSOM
POLYGAMOUS	TELEPATHIC	ATMOSPHERE	COMPULSION	HUMBLENESS	RUMBULLION
POLYHEDRON	TELEPHONIC	BAMBOOZLED	COMPULSIVE	HUMDUDGEON	RUMINANTIA
POLYHYMNIA	TELESCOPIC	BOMBARDIER	COMPULSORY	HUMIDIFIER	RUMINATION
POLYMERIZE	TELEVISION	BUMFREEZER	COMSTOCKER	HUMIDISTAT	RUMINATIVE
POLYNESIAN	TELIOSPORE	CAMBERWELL	CUMBERLAND	HUMORESQUE	SAMARSKITE
POLYNOMIAL	TELPHERAGE	CAMBRENSIS	CUMBERSOME	HUMOROUSLY	SAMOTHRACE
POLYPHEMUS	TILLANDSIA	CAMELOPARD	CUMMERBUND	HUMOURLESS	SEMICIRCLE
POLYTHEISM	TOLERANTLY	CAMERLENGO	CUMULATIVE	HUMPBACKED	SEMIQUAVER
POLYVALENT	TOLERATION	CAMERLINGO	DAMSELFISH	IMMACULACY	SIMILARITY
PULSATANCE	TOLLKEEPER	CAMERONIAN	DEMIRELIEF	IMMACULATE	SIMILITUDE
PULSOMETER	TULARAEMIA	CAMOUFLAGE	DEMOBILISE	IMMATERIAL	SIMILLIMUM
RELATIVELY	UNLADYLIKE	CAMPAIGNER	DEMOBILIZE	IMMATURITY	SIMMENTHAL
RELATIVITY	UNLEAVENED	CAMPANELLA	DEMOCRATIC	IMMEMORIAL	SIMPLICITY
RELAXATION	UNLETTERED	CAMPARADOR	DEMOCRITUS	IMMOBILITY	SIMPLISTIC
RELAXATIVE	UNLICENSED	CAMPERDOWN	DEMODULATE	IMMOBILIZE	SIMULACRUM
RELEGATION	VALENTINES	CAMPESTRAL	DEMOGORGON	IMMODERATE	SIMULATING
RELENTLESS	VALIDATION	CAMSTEERIE	DEMOGRAPHY	IMMOLATION	SIMULATION
RELINQUISH	VALLADOLID	COMANCHERO	DEMOISELLE	IMMORALITY	SOMBRERITE
RELOCATION	VELITATION	COMBUSTION	DEMOLITION	IMMORTELLE	SOMERSAULT
RELUCTANCE	VELOCIPEDE	COMEDIENNE	DEMONIACAL	IMMUNOLOGY	SOMERVILLE
ROLANDSECK	VILLAINOUS	COMESTIBLE	DEMONOLOGY	JAMESONITE	SOMNOLENCE
ROLLICKING	VILLANELLE	COMFORTING	DEMORALISE	KEMPERYMAN	SUMMERTIME
SALAMANDER	VILLANOVAN	COMMANDANT	DEMORALIZE	KIMBERLITE	SYMBOLICAL
SALBUTAMOL	VILLEINAGE	COMMANDEER	DIMINISHED	LAMARCKISM	SYMPATHISE
SALESWOMAN	VOLATILITY	COMMANDING	DIMINUENDO	LAMBREQUIN	SYMPATHIZE
SALICORNIA	VOLLEYBALL	COMMENTARY	DIMINUTION	LAMENTABLE	SYMPHONIUM
SALIVATION	VOLUBILITY	COMMENTATE	DIMINUTIVE	LAMENTABLY	SYMPTOMIZE
SALLENDERS	VOLUMINOUS	COMMERCIAL	DOMICILARY	LAMINATION	TAMBERLANE
SALMAGUNDI	VOLUPTUARY	COMMISSARY	DOMINATING	LEMNISCATE	TAMBOURINE
SALMANAZAR	VOLUPTUOUS	COMMISSION	DOMINATION	LIMBERNECK	TAMPERFOOT
SALMONELLA	VOLUTATION	COMMISSURE	DUMBLEDORE	LIMBURGITE	TEMPERANCE
SALOPETTES	VULCANALIA	COMMITMENT	EMMENTALER	LIMITATION	TEMPTATION
SALPINGIAN	VULNERABLE	COMMIXTURE	EMMETROPIA	LIMITROPHE	TIMBERYARD
SALTARELLO	WALDENSIAN	COMMODIOUS	FAMILIARLY	LUMBERJACK	TIMBROLOGY
SALTCELLAR	WALLACHIAN	COMMONALTY	FAMISHMENT	LUMINARIST	TIMEKEEPER
SALTIGRADE	WALLFLOWER	COMMONWEAL	FEMININITY	LUMINOSITY	TIMELINESS
SALUBRIOUS	WELLEARNED	COMMUNALLY	FUMIGATION	LUMPECTOMY	TIMESAVING
SALUTATION	WELLINGTON	COMMUNIQUÉ	GAMEKEEPER	LUMPSUCKER	TIMESERVER
SALVADORAN	WELLSPRING	COMMUTABLE	GEMINATION	MEMBERSHIP	TIMESWITCH
SCLERIASIS	WELSHWOMAN	COMPARABLE	GYMNASTICS	MEMBRANOUS	TOMFOOLERY
SELEGILINE	WILDEBEEST	COMPARATOR	GYMNOSOPHY	MEMORANDUM	TUMBLEDOWN
SELFESTEEM	WILDERNESS	COMPARISON	GYMNOSPERM	MIMEOGRAPH	TUMESCENCE
SELFSTYLED	WILDFOWLER	COMPASSION	HAMESUCKEN	MUMBLENEWS	TUMULTUOUS
SELLINGERS	WILLIAMSON	COMPATIBLE	HAMMERHEAD	NEMATOCYST	TYMPANITES
SELTZOGENE	WILLINGDON	COMPATRIOT	HAMMERLOCK	NIMBLENESS	TYMPANITIS
SILHOUETTE	WILLOWHERB	COMPELLING	HAMSHACKLE	NOMINALIST	UNMANNERED
SILVERBACK	WILLYWILLY	COMPENDIUM	HEMICHORDA	NOMINATION	UNMANNERLY
SILVERBELL	WOLFRAMITE	COMPENSATE	HEMIHEDRON	NOMINATIVE	WAMPUMPEAG
SILVERBILL	YELLOWBACK	COMPETENCE	HEMIPLEGIA	NOMOTHETIC	ZIMBABWEAN
SILVERFISH	YELLOWGIRL	COMPETITOR	HEMISPHERE	NUMBERLESS	ZUMBOORUCK
SILVERSIDE	YELLOWJACK	COMPLACENT	HEMOGLOBIN	NUMERATION	ABNORMALLY
SILVERSKIN	YELLOWLEGS	COMPLANATE	HEMOPHILIA	NUMISMATIC	ANNEXATION
SILVERWARE	YELLOWROOT	COMPLEMENT	HEMORRHAGE	NYMPHOLEPT	ANNIHILATE
SOLICITOUS	YELLOWWOOD	COMPLETELY	HOMECOMING	OSMETERIUM	ANNOTATION
SOLICITUDE	ZOLLVEREIN	COMPLETION	HOMELINESS	OSMIDROSIS	ANNUALIZED
SOLIDARITY	ADMINISTER	COMPLEXION	HOMEOPATHY	POMERANIAN	ANNUNCIATE
SOLIFIDIAN	ADMIRATION	COMPLEXITY	HOMEOUSIAN	PUMMELLING	BANDERILLA

BANDERILLO	CONCLUSION	CONTINUANT	GENETHLIAC	MANAGEABLE	NINCOMPOOP
BANDMASTER	CONCLUSIVE	CONTINUING	GENEVRETTE	MANAGEMENT	NINETEENTH
BANGLADESH	CONCOCTION	CONTINUITY	GENICULATE	MANAGERESS	NONALIGNED
BANISHMENT	CONCORDANT	CONTINUOUS	GENTLEFOLK	MANAGERIAL	NONCHALANT
BANKRUPTCY	CONCRETION	CONTORTION	GENTLENESS	MANCHESTER	NONFICTION
BENEDICITE	CONCURRENT	CONTRABAND	GINGERBEER	MANCHINEEL	NONONSENSE
BENEFACTOR	CONCUSSION	CONTRACTOR	GINGERSNAP	MANDEVILLE	NONPAYMENT
BENEFICENT	CONDESCEND	CONTRADICT	GINGIVITIS	MANDRAGORA	NONPLUSSED
BENEFICIAL	CONDIMENTS	CONTRAFLOW	GONDOLIERS	MANGABEIRA	NONSMOKING
BENEVOLENT	CONDOLENCE	CONTRAHENT	GONFANONER	MANGOSTEEN	NONSUCCESS
BENTHAMITE	CONDOTTIER	CONTRARILY	GONIOMETER	MANICHAEAN	NONVINTAGE
BENZEDRINE	CONDUCTING	CONTRAVENE	GONORRHOEA	MANICURIST	NONVIOLENT
BINOCULARS	CONDUCTION	CONTRECOUP	GYNECOLOGY	MANIFESTLY	OMNIPOTENT
BINUCLEATE	CONEFLOWER	CONTRIBUTE	HANDICRAFT	MANIPULATE	OMNISCIENT
BONDHOLDER	CONFECTION	CONTRITION	HANDLEBARS	MANSERVANT	OMNIVOROUS
BONDSWOMAN	CONFEDERAL	CONTROLLER	HANDMAIDEN	MANUSCRIPT	ORNAMENTAL
BONESHAKER	CONFERENCE	CONTROVERT	HANDPICKED	MANZANILLA	PANAMANIAN
BONNETHEAD	CONFERVOID	CONVALESCE	HANDSOMELY	MENACINGLY	PANARITIUM
BUNDESWEHR	CONFESSION	CONVECTION	HANDSPRING	MENDACIOUS	PANCRATIUM
CANCELLOUS	CONFIDANTE	CONVENANCE	HANGGLIDER	MENECHMIAN	PANJANDRUM
CANCIONERO	CONFIDENCE	CONVENIENT	HANKYPANKY	MENINGITIS	PANNICULUS
CANCRIZANS	CONFISCATE	CONVENTION	HANOVERIAN	MENORRHOEA	PANOPTICON
CANDELABRA	CONFLICTED	CONVENTUAL	HENCEFORTH	MENSTRUATE	PANSOPHIST
CANDELILLA	CONFLUENCE	CONVERGENT	HENDECAGON	MINDERERUS	PANTAGRUEL
CANDLEFISH	CONFORMIST	CONVERSANT	HINDENBURG	MINERALOGY	PANTALOONS
CANDLEWICK	CONFORMITY	CONVERSELY	HINDUSTANI	MINESTRONE	PANTOGRAPH
CANDYFLOSS	CONFOUNDED	CONVERSION	HINTERLAND	MINEWORKER	PANTOSCOPE
CANECUTTER	CONFUSEDLY	CONVEYABLE	HONEYBUNCH	MINIMALISM	PENELOPHON
CANEPHORUS	CONGENITAL	CONVEYANCE	HONORARIUM	MINIMALIST	PENETRABLE
CANNELLONI	CONGESTION	CONVICTION	HONOURABLE	MINIMARKET	PENETRALIA
CANNONBALL	CONGREGATE	CONVINCING	HONOURABLY	MINISTRATE	PENICILLIN
CANTABRIAN	CONIFEROUS	CONVOLUTED	HONOURLESS	MINISTROKE	PENINSULAR
CANTALOUPE	CONJECTURE	CONVOLVUTE	IGNIMBRITE	MINUTEBOOK	PENNILLION
CANTATRICE	CONNECTING	CONVULSION	IGNORANTLY	MINUTENESS	PENNISETUM
CANTERBURY	CONNECTION	CONVULSIVE	INNERSPACE	MONANDROUS	PENSIEROSO
CANTILEVER	CONNECTIVE	CYNOMOLGUS	INNOCENTLY	MONARCHIST	PENSIONNAT
CANTILLATE	CONNIPTION	DENDROPHIS	INNOVATION	MONEGASQUE	PENTAGONAL
CANTONMENT	CONNIVANCE	DENOUEMENT	INNOVATIVE	MONETARISM	PENTAMERON
CANVASBACK	CONQUERING	DENSIMETER	IONOSPHERE	MONETARIST	PENTAMETER
CANVASSING	CONSCIENCE	DENTIFRICE	JINGOISTIC	MONEYMAKER	PENTATEUCH
CENSORIOUS	CONSECRATE	DINANDERIE	KENILWORTH	MONILIASIS	PENTATHLON
CENSORSHIP	CONSENSION	DINNERTIME	KENSPECKLE	MONILIFORM	PENTATONIC
CENTENNIAL	CONSEQUENT	DONNYBROOK	KENTUCKIAN	MONOACIDIC	PENTELIKON
CENTESIMAL	CONSIDERED	DUNDERFUNK	KINCHINLAY	MONOCARPIC	PENTETERIC
CENTIGRADE	CONSISTENT	DUNDERHEAD	KINDLINESS	MONOCHROME	PENTIMENTO
CENTILITER	CONSISTORY	DUNDERPATE	KINGFISHER	MONOECIOUS	PENTSTEMON
CENTILITRE	CONSONANCE	DUNIWASSAL	LANCEOLATE	MONOGAMOUS	PINAKOTHEK
CENTIMETER	CONSONANTS	DYNAMITARD	LANDAMMANN	MONOLITHIC	PINCHPENNY
CENTIMETRE	CONSORTIUM	FANATICISM	LANDLOCKED	MONOPHONIC	PINCUSHION
CENTRALIZE	CONSPECTUS	FANTASTICO	LANDLOUPER	MONOPLEGIA	PINNIPEDIA
CENTRIFUGE	CONSPIRACY	FANTOCCINI	LANDLUBBER	MONOPODIUM	PONCHIELLI
CENTROSOME	CONSTANTAN	FENESTELLA	LANDSTHING	MONOPOLISE	PONEROLOGY
CINDERELLA	CONSTANTIA	FINGERLING	LANGERHANS	MONOPOLIZE	PONTEDERIA
CINECAMERA	CONSTANTLY	FINGERNAIL	LANGUOROUS	MONOPTERON	PONTEFRACT
CINQUEFOIL	CONSTITUTE	FINGERPICK	LANIGEROUS	MONOPTEROS	PONTICELLO
CONCENTRIC	CONSTRAINT	FINISTERRE	LANSQUENET	MONOTHEISM	PONTIFICAL
CONCEPTION	CONSTRINGE	FONTANELLE	LANTHANIDE	MONOTONOUS	PUNCHDRUNK
CONCEPTUAL	CONSUETUDE	FONTICULUS	LENGTHWAYS	MONOVALENT	PUNCTUALLY
CONCERNING	CONSULTANT	FONTINALIS	LENGTHWISE	MONSTRANCE	PUNCTULATE
CONCERTINA	CONSULTING	FUNCTIONAL	LENOCINIUM	MONTAGNARD	PUNDIGRION
CONCERVATE	CONSUMMATE	FUNGICIDAL	LENTICULAR	MONTESSORI	PUNICACEAE
CONCESSION	CONTAGIOUS	GANGRENOUS	LENTIGINES	MONTEVERDI	PUNISHABLE
CONCHIGLIE	CONTENTION	GENERALISE	LINEAMENTS	MONTEVIDEO	PUNISHMENT
CONCHIOLIN	CONTESTANT	GENERALITY	LINEOMYCIN	MONTGOMERY	RANDLETREE
CONCHOLOGY	CONTEXTUAL	GENERALIZE	LINGUISTIC	MONTICULUS	RANDOMNESS
CONCILIATE	CONTIGUITY	GENERATION	LINGULELLA	MONTRACHET	RANNELTREE
CONCINNITY	CONTIGUOUS	GENERATRIX	LONELINESS	MONTSERRAT	RANNLETREE
CONCINNOUS	CONTINENCE	GENEROSITY	LONGCHAMPS	MONUMENTAL	RANTLETREE
CONCLUDING	CONTINGENT	GENEROUSLY	LONGFELLOW	MUNIFICENT	RANUNCULUS

RENDEZVOUS	VANDERBILT	BOOKMOBILE	FOODSTUFFS	PHOSPHORUS	PROSCENIUM
RENOVATION	VENERATION	BOOKSELLER	FOOTBALLER	PHOTODIODE	PROSCIUTTO
RINDERPEST	VENEZUELAN	BOONDOGGLE	FOOTBRIDGE	PHOTOGENIC	PROSCRIBED
RINGELMANN	VENTILATOR	BOOTLEGGER	FOOTLIGHTS	PHOTOGRAPH	PROSECUTOR
RINGLEADER	VINDEMIATE	BOOTLICKER	FOOTPRINTS	PHOTONASTY	PROSERPINA
RINGMASTER	VINDICTIVE	BOOZINGKEN	FROGHOPPER	PHOTOPHORE	PROSERPINE
SANATORIUM	VINEGARISH	BROADCLOTH	FROLICSOME	PIONEERING	PROSILIENT
SANCTIFIED	WANCHANCIE	BROADPIECE	FROMANTEEL	PLOUGHBOTE	PROSPECTOR
SANCTITIES	WANDERINGS	BROADSHEET	FRONTCOURT	PLOUGHGATE	PROSPECTUS
SANCTITUDE	WANDERLUST	BROADSWORD	FRONTWARDS	PLOUGHWISE	PROSPERINA
SANDALWOOD	WANDSWORTH	BROCATELLE	GEOCENTRIC	PROAIRESIS	PROSPERITY
SANDEMANIA	WANTHRIVEN	BROKENDOWN	GEOGRAPHER	PROCEDURAL	PROSPEROUS
SANDERLING	WENTLETRAP	BRONCHITIC	GEOGRAPHIC	PROCEEDING	PROSTHESIS
SANDGROPER	WINCEYETTE	BRONCHITIS	GEOLOGICAL	PROCESSING	PROSTHETIC
SANDINISTA	WINCHESTER	BROOMSTICK	GEOPHYSICS	PROCESSION	PROSTITUTE
SANDWICHES	WINDERMERE	BROWNLANDS	GEORGETOWN	PROCLIVITY	PROTAGORAS
SANFORISED	WINDFLOWER	BROWNSTONE	GEOTHERMAL	PROCREATOR	PROTANOPIA
SANGUINARY	WINDJAMMER	CAOUTCHOUC	GEOTROPISM	PROCRUSTES	PROTANOPIC
SANITARIUM	WINDOWPANE	CHOICELESS	GLORIOUSLY	PROCUMBENT	PROTECTION
SANITATION	WINDOWSILL	CHOLALOGUE	GLOSSINESS	PROCURABLE	PROTECTIVE
SANNAYASIN	WINDSCREEN	CHOPSTICKS	GLOUCESTER	PROCURATOR	PROTERVITY
SENATORIAL	WINDSHIELD	CLOCKMAKER	GNOSTICISM	PRODIGALLY	PROTESTANT
SENEGALESE	WINDSURFER	CLODHOPPER	GOODFELLOW	PRODIGIOUS	PROTOPLASM
SENESCENCE	WINTERTIME	CLOISTERED	GOOSEBERRY	PRODUCTION	PROTRACTED
SENSUALITY	WONDERLAND	CLOMIPHENE	GOOSEFLESH	PRODUCTIVE	PROTRACTOR
SENSUOUSLY	WONDERMENT	CLOSTRIDIA	GROCETERIA	PROFESSION	PROTRUSILE
SINARCHIST	WUNDERKIND	CLOUDBERRY	GROUNDBAIT	PROFICIENT	PROTRUSION
SINARQUIST	XENOPHOBIA	CLOUDBURST	GROUNDLESS	PROFITABLE	PROVEDITOR
SINFULNESS	XENOPHOBIC	CLOUDINESS	GROUNDLING	PROFITABLY	PROVENANCE
SINGHALESE	ZINCOGRAPH	COORDINATE	GROUNDSMAN	PROFITLESS	PROVERBIAL
SINGLENESS	ABOMINABLE	CROCKFORDS	GROUNDWORK	PROFLIGACY	PROVIDENCE
SINGULARLY	ABOMINABLY	CROSSBONES	GROVELLING	PROFLIGATE	PROVINCIAL
SINOATRIAL	ABONNEMENT	CROSSBREED	HOODWINKED	PROFOUNDLY	PROVISIONS
SINSEMILLA	ABORIGINAL	CROSSCHECK	HOOTANANNY	PROFUNDITY	PSOCOPTERA
SONGSTRESS	ABOVEBOARD	CROSSHATCH	HOOTENANNY	PROGENITOR	REORGANIZE
SONGWRITER	ACOLOUTHOS	CROSSPIECE	HOOTNANNIE	PROGESSION	RHOEADALES
SUNBATHING	ACOTYLEDON	CROSSREFER	ICONOCLAST	PROGRAMMER	SCOFFINGLY
SUNGLASSES	ADOLESCENT	CROSSROADS	ICONOSCOPE	PROHIBITED	SCOMBRESOX
SYNAERESIS	AGONISTICS	CROTALARIA	ICOSANDRIA	PROJECTILE	SCOOTERIST
SYNCHRONAL	APOCALYPSE	CROTALIDAE	ICOSOHEDRA	PROJECTING	SCOPELIDAE
SYNCHRONIC	APOCRYPHAL	DIOPHANTOS	INOPERABLE	PROJECTION	SCORDATURA
SYNCOPATED	APOLAUSTIC	DOORKEEPER	INORDINATE	PROMENADER	SCOREBOARD
SYNCRETISE	APOLLONIAN	DOORTODOOR	INOSCULATE	PROMETHEAN	SCORNFULLY
SYNECDOCHE	APOLLONIUS	DROSOPHILA	IRONICALLY	PROMETHEUS	SCORZONERA
SYNEIDESIS	APOLOGETIC	DROWSINESS	IRONMONGER	PROMETHIUM	SCOTODINIA
SYNONYMOUS	APOPEMPTIC	DUODECIMAL	ISOLEUCINE	PROMINENCE	SCOTSWOMAN
SYNOSTOSIS	APOPHTHEGM	EBOULEMENT	ISOMETRICS	PROMISSORY	SHOCKINGLY
SYNTAGMATA	APOPLECTIC	ECOLOGICAL	ISONIAZIDE	PROMONTORY	SHOCKPROOF
SYNTERESIS	APOSEMATIC	ECONOMICAL	JEOPARDISE	PROMPTBOOK	SHODDINESS
SYNTHESIZE	APOSTROPHE	EGOCENTRIC	JEOPARDIZE	PROMPTNESS	SHOESTRING
SYNTHRONUS	APOTHECARY	ELONGATION	KLOOTCHMAN	PROMULGATE	SHOPKEEPER
TANAGRIDAE	APOTHECIUM	ELOQUENTLY	KNOBKERRIE	PRONOUNCED	SHOPLIFTER
TANGANYIKA	APOTHEOSIS	EMOLUMENTS	KNOCKABOUT	PROPAGANDA	SHOPSOILED
TANGENTIAL	APOTROPAIC	ENORMOUSLY	KOOKABURRA	PROPAGATOR	SHOPWALKER
TANGLEFOOT	BIOCHEMIST	EPONYCHIUM	KUOMINTANG	PROPELLANT	SHORTBREAD
TANNHAUSER	BIOGRAPHER	EXOBIOLOGY	LEONTIASIS	PROPELLENT	SHORTENING
TANTAMOUNT	BIOLOGICAL	EXONERATED	LEOPARDESS	PROPENSITY	SHORTLIVED
TENDERFOOT	BIOPHYSICS	EXORBITANT	MYOCARDIAL	PROPERTIUS	SHORTRANGE
TENDERLOIN	BIORHYTHMS	EXOTHERMIC	NEOTERICAL	PROPHETESS	SHOVELHEAD
TENDERNESS	BLOCKHOUSE	EXOTICALLY	ODONTALGIA	PROPIONATE	SHOVELNOSE
TENDRILLED	BLOODHOUND	FLOCCULATE	ODONTOLITE	PROPITIATE	SHOWJUMPER
TENEBRIFIC	BLOODSTAIN	FLOCCULENT	ODONTOLOGY	PROPITIOUS	SLOPPINESS
TENNANTITE	BLOODSTOCK	FLOODLIGHT	OMOPHORION	PROPLITEAL	SMOKESTACK
TENRECIDAE	BLOODSTONE	FLOORBOARD	ONOMASTICS	PROPORTION	SMOOTHNESS
TENTERHOOK	BLOOMSBURY	FLOORCLOTH	OPOTHERAPY	PROPOSITUS	SMORREBROD
TINKERBELL	BLOTTESQUE	FLORENTINE	OROBRANCHE	PROPRAETOR	SNOOTINESS
TINTORETTO	BOOKBINDER	FLORIBUNDA	OROGENESIS	PROPRIETOR	SNORKELING
TONGUESTER	BOOKKEEPER	FLOURISHED	PHOLIDOSIS	PROPULSION	SNOWBLOWER
UNNUMBERED	BOOKMARKER	FLOWERBEDS	PHONOGRAPH	PROPYLAEUM	SNOWCAPPED

SNOWMOBILE	AMPELOPSIS	DEPLORABLE	HYPOTENUSE	REPENTANCE	WAPENSCHAW
SOOTHINGLY	AMPHIBIOUS	DEPLORABLY	HYPOTHESIS	REPERTOIRE	WAPINSCHAW
SOOTHSAYER	AMPHIBRACH	DEPLOYMENT	HYPSOMETRY	REPETITEUR	WAPPENSHAW
SPODOMANCY	AMPHICTYON	DEPOPULATE	IMPAIRMENT	REPETITION	XIPHOPAGUS
SPOILSPORT	AMPHIGOURI	DEPORTMENT	IMPALPABLE	REPETITIVE	ZAPOROGIAN
SPOKESHAVE	AMPHIMACER	DEPOSITARY	IMPALUDISM	REPORTEDLY	ACQUAINTED
SPOLIATION	AMPHIMIXIS	DEPOSITION	IMPARLANCE	REPOSITORY	COQUELICOT
SPOLIATIVE	AMPHINEURA	DEPOSITORY	IMPASSABLE	REPRESSION	COQUETTISH
SPONGEWARE	AMPHITRITE	DEPRECIATE	IMPATIENCE	REPRESSIVE	COQUIMBITE
SPONGIFORM	AMPHITRYON	DEPRESSANT	IMPECCABLE	REPRODUCER	INQUIRENDO
SPONSIONAL	AMPHOTERIC	DEPRESSING	IMPECCABLY	REPUBLICAN	INQUISITOR
SPOONERISM	AMPLEFORTH	DEPRESSION	IMPEDIMENT	REPUGNANCE	LIQUESCENT
SPORANGIUM	AMPUSSYAND	DEPRESSIVE	IMPENITENT	REPUTATION	LIQUIDATOR
SPORTINGLY	AMPUTATION	DEPUTATION	IMPERATIVE	RIPSNORTER	LIQUIDIZER
SPORTSWEAR	APPARENTLY	DIPHTHERIA	IMPERSONAL	RUPESTRIAN	LOQUACIOUS
SPOTLESSLY	APPARITION	DIPLODOCUS	IMPERVIOUS	RUPICOLINE	MAQUILLAGE
STOCHASTIC	APPEARANCE	DIPLOMATIC	IMPLACABLE	SAPPERMENT	REQUIESCAT
STOCKINESS	APPETITIVE	DIPSOMANIA	IMPLACABLY	SAPROPHYTE	ROQUELAURE
STOMATOPOD	APPETIZING	DOPPLERITE	IMPLICITLY	SEPARATELY	SEQUACIOUS
STONEBRASH	APPLICABLE	DUPLICATOR	IMPOLITELY	SEPARATION	SEQUENTIAL
STONEHENGE	APPLICATOR	EMPEDOCLES	IMPORTANCE	SEPARATISM	USQUEBAUGH
STONEMASON	APPOSITION	EMPFINDUNG	IMPOSITION	SEPARATIST	ABRIDGMENT
STONYHURST	APPRECIATE	EMPLASTRUM	IMPOSSIBLE	SEPARATRIX	ABROGATION
STOREFRONT	APPRENTICE	EMPLOYMENT	IMPOSSIBLY	SEPTENNIAL	ABRUPTNESS
STOREHOUSE	ASPARAGINE	ESPADRILLE	IMPOSTHUME	SEPTUAGINT	ACROAMATIC
STOUTHERIE	ASPERSIONS	ESPECIALLY	IMPOTENTLY	SEPULCHRAL	ACROBATICS
STOUTHRIEF	ASPHALTITE	EUPHONIOUS	IMPOVERISH	SOPHOCLEAN	ACROGENOUS
SWORDSTICK	ASPHYXIATE	EUPHROSYNE	IMPREGNATE	SOPHOMORIC	ACROMEGALY
THOROUGHLY	ASPIDISTRA	EXPATRIATE	IMPRESARIO	SUPERADDED	ACRONYCHAL
THOUGHTFUL	ASPIRATION	EXPECTANCY	IMPRESSION	SUPERCARGO	ACROTERION
THOUSANDTH	BIPARTISAN	EXPEDIENCE	IMPRESSIVE	SUPERGIANT	ADRAMELECH
TOOTHBRUSH	BIPINNARIA	EXPEDIENCY	IMPRIMATUR	SUPERHUMAN	ADRENALINE
TOOTHPASTE	CAPABILITY	EXPEDITION	IMPROBABLE	SUPERMODEL	ADRENERGIC
TROCHANTER	CAPACITATE	EXPENDABLE	IMPROBABLY	SUPERPOWER	AERENCHYMA
TROCHOTRON	CAPERNAITE	EXPERIENCE	IMPROPERLY	SUPERSONIC	AEROBATICS
TROCTOLITE	CAPERNOITY	EXPERIMENT	IMPROVISED	SUPERSTORE	AEROPHAGIA
TROGLODYTE	CAPILLAIRE	EXPIRATION	IMPRUDENCE	SUPERTONIC	AERUGINOUS
TROMBONIST	CAPITALISM	EXPLICABLE	IMPUDENTLY	SUPERVISED	AFRICANDER
TROMOMETER	CAPITALIST	EXPLICITLY	IMPURITIES	SUPERVISOR	AFRICANISM
TROPAEOLUM	CAPITALIZE	EXPOSITION	IMPUTATION	SUPERWOMAN	AFRORMOSIA
TROPHONIUS	CAPITATION	EXPOSITORY	LEPRECHAUN	SUPPLEJACK	AGRAHAYANA
TROPOPAUSE	CAPITELLUM	EXPOUNDERS	LIPIZZANER	SUPPLEMENT	AGRONOMIST
TROPOPHYTE	CAPITOLINE	EXPRESSION	LUPERCALIA	SUPPLENESS	AIRFREIGHT
TROTSKYITE	CAPITULARY	EXPRESSIVE	MEPERIDINE	SUPPLICANT	AMRITATTVA
TROUBADOUR	CAPITULATE	EXPRESSMAN	NAPTHALENE	SUPPLICATE	ARROGANTLY
TROUVAILLE	CAPNOMANCY	EXPRESSWAY	OOPHORITIS	SUPPORTING	ATRACURIUM
UNOBSERVED	CAPODASTRO	GYPSOPHILA	OPPOSITION	SUPPORTIVE	ATRAMENTAL
UNOCCUPIED	CAPPUCCINO	HEPATOCELE	OPPRESSION	SUPPOSEDLY	AURIFEROUS
UNOFFICIAL	CAPREOLATE	HEPHAESTUS	OPPRESSIVE	SUPPRESSED	BARASINGHA
UNORIGINAL	CAPRICIOUS	HEPTAGONAL	OPPROBRIUM	SUPPRESSOR	BARBAROSSA
UNORTHODOX	CAPTIVATED	HEPTAMERON	ORPHEOREON	SYPHILITIC	BARBITURIC
UROGENITAL	CEPHALOPOD	HEPTATEUCH	PAPAVERINE	TAPDANCING	BARCAROLLE
UROPOIESIS	COPARCENER	HEPTATHLON	PAPERCHASE	TAPERECORD	BARCHESTER
UROSTEGITE	COPENHAGEN	HIPPARCHUS	PAPERKNIFE	TAPOTEMENT	BAREFOOTED
WHOLESALER	COPERNICUS	HIPPOCRENE	PAPIAMENTO	TEPIDARIUM	BAREHEADED
WHOLEWHEAT	COPESETTIC	HIPPODROME	PEPPERCORN	TOPICALITY	BARELEGGED
WOODENHEAD	COPPERHEAD	HIPPOGRIFF	PEPPERMILL	TOPOGRAPHY	BARGAINING
WOODPECKER	COPPERNOSE	HIPPOGRYPH	PEPPERMINT	TOPOLOGIST	BARLEYBREE
WOODPIGEON	COPPERSKIN	HIPPOMANES	PEPPERWORT	TOPSYTURVY	BARLEYCORN
WOODWORKER	COPULATION	HOPELESSLY	PIPSISSEWA	TYPESCRIPT	BARMECIDAL
WOOLLYBACK	COPYHOLDER	HYPAETHRAL	POPULARITY	TYPESETTER	BARMITZVAH
WOOLLYBUTT	COPYWRITER	HYPAETHRON	POPULARIZE	TYPEWRITER	BAROMETRIC
WRONGDOING	DEPARTMENT	HYPERBOLIC	POPULATION	TYPOGRAPHY	BARRACKING
WRONGFULLY	DEPARTURES	HYPERDULIA	RAPPORTEUR	UNPLEASANT	BARRACOOTA
ZOOLOGICAL	DEPENDABLE	HYPNOTIZED	REPAIRABLE	UNPREPARED	BARRACOUTA
ZOOTHAPSIS	DEPENDENCE	HYPOCORISM	REPARATION	UNPROMPTED	BARRAMUNDA
ZOOTHERAPY	DEPENDENCY	HYPODERMIC	REPATRIATE	UNPROVOKED	BARRAMUNDI
ALPENSTOCK	DEPILATION	HYPOGAEOUS	REPEATABLE	UNPUNCTUAL	BARRENNESS
ALPHONSINE	DEPILATORY	HYPOGENOUS	REPEATEDLY	UPPERCLASS	BARYSPHERE

BERMOOTHES	CORNSTARCH	FORECASTER	JERRYBUILT	PARANORMAL	PERORATION
BERNARDINE	CORNUCOPIA	FORECASTLE	KARMATHIAN	PARAPHASIA	PEROVSKITE
BERSAGLIER	COROMANDEL	FOREDAMNED	KARTTIKAYA	PARAPHILIA	PERPETRATE
BIRKENHEAD	CORONATION	FOREFATHER	KERSEYMERE	PARAPHONIA	PERPETUATE
BIRMINGHAM	CORPULENCE	FOREFINGER	KURDAITCHA	PARAPHRASE	PERPETUITY
BIRTHPLACE	CORRECTING	FOREGATHER	LARGESCALE	PARAPHYSIS	PERPLEXING
BIRTHRIGHT	CORRECTION	FOREGROUND	LARYNGITIS	PARAPLEGIA	PERPLEXITY
BORDERLAND	CORRECTIVE	FOREORDAIN	LORDLINESS	PARAPLEGIC	PERQUISITE
BORDERLINE	CORREGIDOR	FORERUNNER	LORDOLATRY	PARAPRAXIS	PERSECUTOR
BORDRAGING	CORRESPOND	FORESHADOW	MARASCHINO	PARARTHRIA	PERSEPHONE
BORROWINGS	CORRIGENDA	FOREWARNED	MARCANTANT	PARASCENIA	PERSEPOLIS
BURDENSOME	CORROBOREE	FORFAITING	MARCESCENT	PARASELENE	PERSICARIA
BUREAUCRAT	CORRUGATED	FORFEITURE	MARCIONITE	PARASTATAL	PERSIENNES
BURGEONING	CORRUGATOR	FORFEUCHEN	MARGASIRSA	PARATROOPS	PERSIFLAGE
BURGLARIZE	CORRUPTING	FORFOUGHEN	MARGINALIA	PARDONABLE	PERSISTENT
BURLINGTON	CORRUPTION	FORGIVABLE	MARGINALLY	PARDONABLY	PERSONABLE
CARABINEER	CORTADERIA	FORINSECAL	MARGUERITE	PARENCHYMA	PERSONALLY
CARABINIER	CORYBANTES	FORMIDABLE	MARIOLATRY	PARENTHOOD	PERSTRINGE
CARACTACUS	CORYBANTIC	FORTHRIGHT	MARIONETTE	PARENTLESS	PERSUADING
CARAMELIZE	CORYPHAEUS	FORTINBRAS	MARKETABLE	PARGETTING	PERSUASION
CARBURETOR	CURMUDGEON	FORTISSIMO	MARQUETRIE	PARISCHANE	PERSUASIVE
CARCINOGEN	CURMURRING	FORTUITOUS	MARSHALSEA	PARISIENNE	PERTINENCE
CARDIOGRAM	CURRENCIES	FURNISHING	MARTINGALE	PARKLEAVES	PERVERSELY
CARDIOLOGY	CURRICULUM	GARGANTUAN	MARTINIQUE	PARLIAMENT	PERVERSION
CARELESSLY	CURVACEOUS	GARGOUILLE	MARVELLOUS	PARMACITIE	PERVERSITY
CARICATURA	CURVETTING	GARLANDAGE	MARYLEBONE	PARMIGIANA	PHRENESIAC
CARICATURE	DARJEELING	GARNIERITE	MERCANTILE	PARNASSIAN	PHRENOLOGY
CARMAGNOLE	DARKHAIRED	GERIATRICS	MERCIFULLY	PARNELLISM	PIRANDELLO
CARNASSIAL	DERACINATE	GERMICIDAL	MERRYMAKER	PARONYCHIA	PORLOCKING
CARPATHIAN	DERAILLEUR	GIRDLERINK	MIRACULOUS	PARRAMATTA	PORNOCRACY
CARPENTIER	DERAILMENT	GIRLFRIEND	MORALITIES	PARTHENOPE	PORRACEOUS
CARPHOLOGY	DEREGULATE	GORGEOUSLY	MORATORIUM	PARTIALITY	PORTAMENTO
CARRAGHEEN	DERIVATION	GORMANDIZE	MORBIDEZZA	PARTICIPLE	PORTCULLIS
CARTHAMINE	DERIVATIVE	GYROSCOPIC	MORDACIOUS	PARTICULAR	PORTENTOUS
CARTHUSIAN	DERMATITIS	HARASSMENT	MORGANATIC	PARTINGALE	PORTIONIST
CARTOMANCY	DEROGATORY	HARDBOILED	MORGANETTA	PARVOVIRUS	PORTMANTLE
CARTOONIST	DIRECTIONS	HARDCASTLE	MORIGEROUS	PERCENTAGE	PORTMANTUA
CARYATIDES	DIRECTNESS	HARMANBECK	MORISONIAN	PERCENTILE	PORTSMOUTH
CEREBELLUM	DIRECTOIRE	HARMONIOUS	MOROSENESS	PERCEPTION	PORTUGUESE
CEREMONIAL	DIREMPTION	HARRINGTON	MORPHOLOGY	PERCEPTIVE	PURITANISM
CEREMONIES	DURABILITY	HARTEBEEST	MORTADELLA	PERCIPIENT	PURPOSEFUL
CERTIORARI	EARTHQUAKE	HARVESTMAN	MYRINGITIS	PERCOLATOR	PURSUIVANT
CHREMATIST	EARTHSHINE	HERBACEOUS	MYRIOSCOPE	PERCUSSION	PYRACANTHA
CHRISTIANA	EARTHWORKS	HEREABOUTS	NARCISSISM	PERDENDOSI	PYRAGYRITE
CHROMOSOME	EBRACTEATE	HEREDITARY	NARCOLEPSY	PERDITIOUS	PYRIDOXINE
CHRONICLER	ENRAPTURED	HERESIARCH	NARROWBOAT	PERDURABLE	PYROGRAPHY
CHRONICLES	ENRICHMENT	HEROICALLY	NARROWDALE	PEREMPTORY	PYROMANIAC
CHRONOLOGY	ENROLLMENT	HORIZONTAL	NARROWNESS	PERFECTION	PYROPHORUS
CHRYSIPPUS	EPROUVETTE	HORNBLENDE	NDRANGHETA	PERFICIENT	REREDORTER
CHRYSOLITE	EUROCHEQUE	HORNBLOWER	NORBERTINE	PERFIDIOUS	SARCOCOLLA
CIRCASSIAN	EUROCLYDON	HORNRIMMED	NORMOBLAST	PERFORATED	SARCOLEMMA
CIRCUITOUS	EURYPTERUS	HORRENDOUS	NORTHANGER	PERFORATOR	SARMENTOUS
CIRCUMCISE	FAREPAYING	HORRIFYING	NORTHBOUND	PERFORMING	SARSQUATCH
CIRCUMFLEX	FARFETCHED	HORSEDRAWN	NORTHERNER	PERIDOTITE	SCREECHING
CIRCUMFUSE	FARRANDINE	HORSELBERG	NORTHSTEAD	PERIEGESIS	SCREENPLAY
CIRCUMVENT	FARSIGHTED	HORSEPOWER	NORTHWARDS	PERIHELION	SCRIBBLING
CIRRHOPODA	FERNITICLE	HORSERIDER	NURSERYMAN	PERILOUSLY	SCRIMSHANK
CIRRIPEDEA	FERRANDINE	HORSEWOMAN	OIREACHTAS	PERIODICAL	SCRIPTURAL
CIRRIPEDIA	FERTILISED	IRRADICATE	PARACELSUS	PERIPHERAL	SCRIPTURES
CORALBERRY	FERTILISER	IRRATIONAL	PARADIDDLE	PERISHABLE	SCROUNGING
CORDIALITY	FERTILIZER	IRRELEVANT	PARADOXIDE	PERIWINKLE	SCRUPULOUS
CORDIERITE	FIREWALKER	IRREMEDIAL	PARADOXINE	PERMAFROST	SCRUTINEER
CORDILLERA	FIREWARDEN	IRRESOLUTE	PARAENESIS	PERMANENCE	SCRUTINISE
CORDWAINER	FIRTHSOKEN	IRREVERENT	PARAGLOSSA	PERMANENCY	SCRUTINIZE
CORINTHIAN	FORBEARING	IRRIGATION	PARAGONITE	PERMEATION	SDRUCCIOLA
CORNCOCKLE	FORBIDDING	IRRITATING	PARAGUAYAN	PERMISSION	SERMONICAL
CORNFLAKES	FORCEFULLY	IRRITATION	PARALLELED	PERMISSIVE	SERPENTINE
CORNFLOWER	FOREBITTER	JARDINIERE	PARAMARIBO	PERNICIOUS	SERRADELLA
CORNSTALKS	FOREBODING	JARGONELLE	PARAMETRIC	PERNICKETY	SERRADILLA

SERRASALMO	SURROUNDED	VERTICALLY	DESALINATE	DISPENSARY	HISTORICAL
SERVICEMAN	TARADIDDLE	VIROLOGIST	DESBOROUGH	DISPENSING	HISTRIONIC
SERVOMOTOR	TARANTELLA	VIRTUOSITY	DESCENDANT	DISPERSION	HOSPITABLE
SHREWDNESS	TARDIGRADE	VIRTUOUSLY	DESCENDING	DISPIRITED	HOSPITABLY
SHRIEVALTY	TARPAULING	VIRULENTLY	DESCRIBING	DISPOSABLE	HUSBANDAGE
SHRILLNESS	TARTRAZINE	VORAGINOUS	DESECRATED	DISPOSSESS	HYSTERESIS
SHRIVELLED	TERMINABLE	WARRANDICE	DESERVEDLY	DISPUTABLE	HYSTERICAL
SHROVETIDE	TERMINALIA	WORDSWORTH	DÉSHABILLÉ	DISQUALIFY	INSANITARY
SKRIMSHANK	TERMINALLY	WORKAHOLIC	DESICCATED	DISQUIETED	INSATIABLE
SORDIDNESS	TERNEPLATE	WORLDCLASS	DESIDERATA	DISRESPECT	INSATIABLY
SPREAGHERY	TERRACOTTA	WORSHIPPER	DESOLATION	DISRUPTION	INSECURELY
SPRINGBOKS	TERREPLEIN	WORTHINESS	DESPAIRING	DISRUPTIVE	INSECURITY
SPRINGHAAS	TERRIFYING	WORTHWHILE	DESPICABLE	DISSECTION	INSEMINATE
SPRINGLESS	TERTIARIES	XEROPHYTIC	DESPITEOUS	DISSELBOOM	INSENSIBLE
SPRINGLIKE	THREADBARE	XEROSTOMIA	DESPONDENT	DISSEMBLER	INSIPIDITY
SPRINGTAIL	THREADLIKE	YARBOROUGH	DESQUAMATE	DISSENSION	INSISTENCE
SPRINGTIME	THREADWORM	ABSCISSION	DESSIATINE	DISSENTING	INSOLENTLY
SPRINKLING	THREATENED	ABSOLUTELY	DESSYATINE	DISSERTATE	INSOLVENCY
SPRUCENESS	THREEPENCE	ABSOLUTION	DISABILITY	DISSERVICE	INSOUCIANT
STRABISMUS	THREEPENNY	ABSOLUTISM	DISAPPOINT	DISSIDENCE	INSPECTION
STRABOTOMY	THREESCORE	ABSORBANCE	DISAPPROVE	DISSILIENT	INSPISSATE
STRACCHINO	THRENODIAL	ABSORPTION	DISARRANGE	DISSIMILAR	INSTALMENT
STRAGGLING	THROMBOSIS	ABSTEMIOUS	DISASTROUS	DISSIPATED	INSTIGATOR
STRAIGHTEN	THROUGHOUT	ABSTENTION	DISBELIEVE	DISSOCIATE	INSTRUCTED
STRAITENED	THROUGHPUT	ABSTINENCE	DISBURTHEN	DISSOLVENT	INSTRUCTOR
STRAMONIUM	THROUGHWAY	ABSTRACTED	DISCERNING	DISSONANCE	INSTRUMENT
STRAPONTIN	TIRAILLEUR	AESTHETICS	DISCIPLINE	DISSUASION	INSUFFLATE
STRASBOURG	TIRELESSLY	ANSCHAUUNG	DISCLAIMER	DISTENSION	INSULARITY
STRATEGIST	TIROCINIUM	ANSWERABLE	DISCLOSURE	DISTILLATE	INSULATION
STRATHSPEY	TORBERNITE	ARSMETRICK	DISCOBOLUS	DISTILLERY	INSURGENCY
STRATIOTES	TORCHLIGHT	ASSEMBLAGE	DISCOLORED	DISTILLING	JUSTICIARY
STRATOCRAT	TORPESCENT	ASSEMBLING	DISCOMFORT	DISTINCTLY	KESSELRING
STRATOCYST	TORQUEMADA	ASSESSMENT	DISCOMMODE	DISTORTION	LASCIVIOUS
STRAVINSKY	TORRENTIAL	ASSEVERATE	DISCOMPOSE	DISTRACTED	LASTMINUTE
STRAWBERRY	TORRICELLI	ASSIGNABLE	DISCONCERT	DISTRAUGHT	LESBIANISM
STRAWBOARD	TORTELLINI	ASSIGNMENT	DISCONNECT	DISTRESSED	LISTLESSLY
STREAMERED	TORTUOUSLY	ASSIMILATE	DISCONTENT	DISTRIBUTE	LUSITANIAN
STREAMLINE	TURBULENCE	ASSISTANCE	DISCOPHORA	DISTRINGAS	LYSENKOISM
STREETLAMP	TURNAROUND	ASSOCIATED	DISCORDANT	DISTURBING	MASCARPONE
STREETWISE	TURPENTINE	ASSORTMENT	DISCOURAGE	DOSTOEVSKY	MASKANONGE
STRELITZIA	TURRITELLA	ASSUMPTION	DISCOVERER	DYSCRASITE	MASKINONGE
STRENGTHEN	TURTLEDOVE	ASSUMPTIVE	DISCREETLY	DYSPROSIUM	MASKIROVKA
STREPITANT	TURTLEHEAD	AUSPICIOUS	DISCREPANT	DYSTROPHIC	MASQUERADE
STREPITOSO	TURTLENECK	AUSTRALIAN	DISCRETION	EASTERLING	MASSASAUGA
STRICTNESS	TYRANNICAL	AUSTRALORP	DISCURSIVE	EISTEDDFOD	MASTECTOMY
STRIDENTLY	TYRANNISED	AUSTRINGER	DISCUSSING	ENSANGUINE	MASTERMIND
STRIDEWAYS	UNREADABLE	BASKETBALL	DISCUSSION	EUSTACHIAN	MASTERWORT
STRIDULATE	UNREASONED	BASKETWORK	DISDAINFUL	FASCIATION	MASTURBATE
STRIKINGLY	UNREDEEMED	BASSINGTON	DISEMBOGUE	FASCINATED	MESENTERON
STRINDBERG	UNRELIABLE	BASSOONIST	DISEMBOWEL	FASCINATOR	MESITYLENE
STRINGENCY	UNRELIEVED	BESTIALITY	DISENCHANT	FASTIDIOUS	MESOLITHIC
STRINGENDO	UNREQUITED	BESTSELLER	DISENGAGED	FASTIGIATE	MISCELLANY
STRINGHALT	UNRESERVED	BISSEXTILE	DISENNOBLE	FASTMOVING	MISCHMETAL
STRIPTEASE	UNRESOLVED	BUSHRANGER	DISFIGURED	FESCENNINE	MISCONDUCT
STROGANOFF	UNREVEALED	BYSSINOSIS	DISGRUNTLE	FISHMONGER	MISERICORD
STRONGHOLD	UNRIVALLED	CASCARILLA	DISGUSTING	FISHSELLER	MISFORTUNE
STRONGROOM	UNROMANTIC	CASSIABARK	DISHABILLE	FISTICUFFS	MISGIVINGS
STROPHIOLE	UNRULINESS	CASSIOPEIA	DISHARMONY	FOSSILIZED	MISHGUGGLE
STRUCTURAL	UPROARIOUS	CASSOLETTE	DISHEARTEN	FUSTANELLA	MISHNAYOTH
STRULDBERG	VARICOSITY	CASSUMUNAR	DISHONESTY	FUSTANELLE	MISLEADING
STRULDBRUG	VARIEGATED	CASTRATION	DISHWASHER	GASCONNADE	MISMATCHED
STRYCHNINE	VARNISHING	CASUALNESS	DISINCLINE	GASTEROPOD	MISOCAPNIC
SURFRIDING	VERIFIABLE	CESTRACION	DISINHERIT	GASTRONOME	MISOGYNIST
SURGICALLY	VERMICELLI	CISLEITHAN	DISJOINTED	GASTRONOMY	MISPRISION
SURINAMESE	VERMILLION	CISPONTINE	DISLOYALTY	GESUNDHEIT	MISSIONARY
SURPASSING	VERNACULAR	CISTERCIAN	DISMANTLED	HESITANTLY	MISTAKENLY
SURPRISING	VERNISSAGE	COSTLINESS	DISMISSIVE	HESITATION	MOSASAUROS
SURREALISM	VERSAILLES	CUSSEDNESS	DISORDERED	HESPERIDES	MOSSBUNKER
SURREALIST	VERTEBRATE	CYSTOSCOPY	DISORDERLY	HISTOLYSIS	MUSICOLOGY

MUSKETEERS	SISTERHOOD	ANTHROPOID	BATTENBERG	ENTICEMENT	INTERTRIGO
MUSSORGSKY	SUSCEPTIVE	ANTIADITIS	BATTENBURG	ENTOMBMENT	INTERTWINE
MYSTAGOGUE	SUSPENDERS	ANTIBARBUS	BATTLEDOOR	ENTOMOLOGY	INTERWEAVE
MYSTAGOGUS	SUSPENSION	ANTIBIOTIC	BATTLEDORE	ENTRANCING	INTERWOVEN
MYSTERIOUS	SUSPICIOUS	ANTICHTHON	BATTLEMENT	ENTREATING	INTESTINAL
NASTURTIUM	SUSTAINING	ANTICIPATE	BATTLESHIP	ENTREMESSE	INTESTINES
NESSELRODE	SUSTENANCE	ANTICLIMAX	BETACRUCIS	ENTRENCHED	INTIMATELY
NOSOCOMIAL	SYSTEMATIC	ANTIFREEZE	BETELGEUSE	ENTRYPHONE	INTIMATION
NOSOPHOBIA	TASKMASTER	ANTIMASQUE	BETELGEUZE	ESTANCIERO	INTIMIDATE
OBSEQUIOUS	TASTEFULLY	ANTIMATTER	BITTERLING	ESTIMATION	INTINCTION
OBSERVABLE	TESCHENITE	ANTIMONIAN	BITTERNESS	ESTRAMACON	INTOLERANT
OBSERVANCE	TESTACEOUS	ANTINOMIAN	BITUMINOUS	EUTHANASIA	INTONATION
OBSIDIONAL	TESTICULAR	ANTIOCHENE	BOTHERSOME	EUTHYNEURA	INTOXICANT
OBSTETRICS	TOSSICATED	ANTIOCHIAN	BOTTICELLI	EUTRAPELIA	INTOXICATE
OESOPHAGUS	TOSTICATED	ANTIPHONAL	BOTTLEHEAD	EXTENDABLE	INTRAURBAN
PASIGRAPHY	ULSTERETTE	ANTIPODEAN	BOTTLENECK	EXTENSIBLE	INTRIGUING
PASQUINADE	UNSALARIED	ANTIPROTON	BOTTOMLESS	EXTERNALLY	INTROSPECT
PASSAGEWAY	UNSCHOOLED	ANTIQUATED	BUTCHERING	EXTINCTION	KATERFELTO
PASSAMEZZO	UNSCRAMBLE	ANTISEPSIS	BUTTERBAKE	EXTINGUISH	KETTLEDRUM
PASSIONATE	UNSCRIPTED	ANTISEPTIC	BUTTERBUMP	EXTRACTION	LATTERMATH
PASTEBOARD	UNSEASONED	ANTISOCIAL	BUTTERFISH	EXTRANEOUS	LATTICINIO
PASTEURISE	UNSETTLING	ANTISTATIC	BUTTERMERE	FATALISTIC	LETTERHEAD
PASTEURIZE	UNSHACKLED	ANTITHESIS	BUTTERMILK	FATALITIES	LITERATURE
PASTORELLA	UNSLEEPING	ANTITHETIC	BUTTONDOWN	FATHERLAND	LITHISTADA
PESCADORES	UNSOCIABLE	ANTITRAGUS	BUTTONHOLE	FATHERLESS	LITHOGRAPH
PESTALOZZI	UNSPECIFIC	ANTIVENENE	CATABOLISM	FETTERLOCK	LITHOMARGE
PESTILENCE	UNSUITABLE	APTERYGOTA	CATACHUMEN	FETTUCCINE	LITHOPHANE
PISTILLATE	UNSWERVING	ARTHRALGIA	CATAFALQUE	FITZGERALD	LITHUANIAN
POSITIVELY	UPSTANDING	ARTHROMERE	CATALECTIC	FUTURISTIC	LITIGATION
POSITIVIST	VASCULITIS	ARTHURIANA	CATALEPTIC	GETHSEMANE	LITTLENESS
POSSESSION	VESICULATE	ARTICULATA	CATALOGUER	GETTYSBURG	LITURGICAL
POSSESSIVE	VESTIBULUM	ARTICULATE	CATAPHRACT	GETUPANDGO	LOTOPHAGUS
POSTCHAISE	VISIBILITY	ARTIFICIAL	CATARRHINE	GUTTIFERAE	LUTESTRING
POSTHUMOUS	VISITATION	ARTOCARPUS	CATASTASIS	GUTTURALLY	MATCHMAKER
POSTILLATE	WASHINGTON	ASTEROIDEA	CATAWAMPUS	HATEENOUGH	MATCHSTALK
POSTILLION	WASSAILING	ASTIGMATIC	CATCHPENNY	HETERODOXY	MATCHSTICK
POSTLIMINY	WASSERMANS	ASTOMATOUS	CATCRACKER	HETERODYNE	MATELLASSE
POSTMASTER	WASTEFULLY	ASTONISHED	CATECHUMEN	HETEROGAMY	MATERIALLY
POSTMORTEM	WASTEPAPER	ASTOUNDING	CATEGORISE	HITCHHIKER	MATERNALLY
POSTSCRIPT	WESTERNIZE	ASTRAGALUS	CATEGORIZE	HITHERWARD	MATRIARCHY
RESCHEDULE	WISHYWASHY	ASTRALAGUS	CATENACCIO	HITOPADESA	MATTERHORN
RESEARCHER	YESTERWEEK	ASTRINGENT	CATHOLICON	HITOPODESA	MATURATION
RESEMBLING	YESTERYEAR	ASTROLOGER	CATHOLICOS	HOTCHPOTCH	METABOLISE
RESENTMENT	ACTIONABLE	ASTRONOMER	CATTLEGRID	IATROGENIC	METABOLISM
RESERVISTS	ACTIVITIST	ASTUTENESS	CITRONELLA	INTAGLIATE	METACARPAL
RESIGNEDLY	AFTERBIRTH	ATTACHMENT	COTTIERISM	INTANGIBLE	METACARPUS
RESILIENCE	AFTERHOURS	ATTAINABLE	COTTONTAIL	INTEGRATED	METACENTRE
RESISTANCE	AFTERIMAGE	ATTAINMENT	COTTONWOOD	INTEGUMENT	METALEPSIS
RESOLUTELY	AFTERPIECE	ATTENDANCE	CUTTLEBONE	INTELIGENT	METALLURGY
RESOLUTION	AFTERSHAVE	ATTRACTION	CUTTLEFISH	INTEMERATE	METAPHRASE
RESORCINOL	AFTERSHOCK	ATTRACTIVE	DETACHABLE	INTENDMENT	METAPLASIS
RESOUNDING	AFTERTASTE	AUTECOLOGY	DETACHMENT	INTENERATE	METASTABLE
RESPECTFUL	AFTERWARDS	AUTHORISED	DETAINMENT	INTENTNESS	METATARSAL
RESPECTING	ALTAZIMUTH	AUTHORSHIP	DETECTABLE	INTERBREED	METATARSUS
RESPECTIVE	ALTERATION	AUTOCHTHON	DETERMINED	INTERCEDER	METATHERIA
RESPIRATOR	ALTERNATOR	AUTOCRATIC	DETERMINER	INTERCLUDE	METATHESIS
RESPONDENT	ALTOGETHER	AUTODIDACT	DETERRENCE	INTERESTED	METHEDRINE
RESPONSIVE	ALTRUISTIC	AUTOECIOUS	DETESTABLE	INTERFERER	METHODICAL
RESTAURANT	ANTAGONISE	AUTOGENOUS	DETONATION	INTERFERON	METHOMANIA
RESTLESSLY	ANTAGONISM	AUTOMATION	DETRACTION	INTERLEAVE	METHUSALEH
RESTRAINED	ANTAGONIST	AUTOMATIZE	DETRUNCATE	INTERLOPER	METHUSELAH
RESTRICTED	ANTAGONIZE	AUTOMOBILE	DITHIONATE	INTERMARRY	METHYLATED
RESUMPTION	ANTARCTICA	AUTOMOTIVE	DUTCHWOMAN	INTERMEZZO	METICULOUS
RESUPINATE	ANTECEDENT	AUTONOMOUS	EATANSWILL	INTERNALLY	METROPOLIS
RESURGENCE	ANTEPENULT	AUTOPLASTY	ECTHLIPSIS	INTERNMENT	METTLESOME
ROSANILINE	ANTHEOLION	AUTOSTRADA	ENTEROCELE	INTERNODAL	MITHRIDATE
ROSECHAFER	ANTHOCLORE	BATHYSCAPH	ENTERPRISE	INTERPHONE	MITIGATING
ROSEMALING	ANTHRACINE	BATRACHIAN	ENTHUSIASM	INTERSTATE	MITIGATION
RUSSIANIZE	ANTHRACITE	BATTAILOUS	ENTHUSIAST	INTERSTICE	MOTHERHOOD

MOTHERLAND	PATRIOTISM	WATERCRESS	EQUANIMITY	NEURILEMMA	TRUSTFULLY
MOTHERLESS	PATRONISED	WATERFRONT	EQUATORIAL	NEUROLEMMA	TRUTHFULLY
MOTHERLIKE	PATRONYMIC	WATERLEVEL	EQUESTRIAN	NEUTRALISE	UNUNHEXIUM
MOTIONLESS	PETITIONER	WATERMELON	EQUITATION	NEUTRALITY	UNUNNILIUM
MOTIVATION	PETRARCHAN	WATERPROOF	EQUIVALENT	NEUTRALIZE	USUCAPTION
MOTORCYCLE	PETRIFYING	WATERSKIER	EQUIVOCATE	NEUTROPHIL	USURPATION
MUTABILITY	PETRISSAGE	WATERSPOUT	ERUBESCENT	NOUAKCHOTT	VAUDEVILLE
MUTILATION	PETROGLYPH	WATERTIGHT	ERUCTATION	NOURISHING	YOUNGBERRY
MUTINOUSLY	PETRONELLA	WATERWHEEL	EXUBERANCE	NOURRITURE	YOURSELVES
MUTTONHEAD	PETTICHAPS	WATERWINGS	EXULTATION	PLUMASSIER	ZEUGLODONT
NATATORIAL	PETTYCHAPS	WATERWORKS	FAULTINESS	PLUNDERING	ADVENTURER
NATATORIUM	PETULANTLY	WATTLEWORK	FEUILLETON	PLUPERFECT	ADVERSARIA
NATHELESSE	PITCHSTONE	WITCHCRAFT	FLUCTUATER	PLUTOCRACY	ADVERTISER
NATIONALLY	PITYRIASIS	WITGATBOOM	FLUFFINESS	POURPARLER	AVVOGADORE
NATIONWIDE	POTENTIATE	WITHDRAWAL	FLUGELHORN	PRUDENTIAL	CAVALRYMAN
NATTERJACK	POTENTILLA	WITSNAPPER	FLUNKEYDOM	ROUGHHOUSE	CAVICORNIA
NATURALISM	PUTREFYING	ABUNDANTLY	FLUTEMOUTH	ROUNDABOUT	COVENANTER
NATURALIST	PUTRESCENT	ADULLAMITE	FOUDROYANT	ROUNDHOUSE	DEVANAGARI
NATURALIZE	PYTHAGORAS	ADULTERANT	FOUNDATION	ROUSEABOUT	DEVASTATED
NATUROPATH	PYTHOGENIC	ADULTERATE	FOURCHETTE	ROUSTABOUT	DEVASTAVIT
NETHERMOST	RATIONALLY	ADULTERESS	FOURIERISM	SAUERKRAUT	DEVELOPING
NETTLERASH	RATTLETRAP	ADULTERINE	FOURRAGERE	SAUROPSIDA	DEVOLUTION
NETTLETREE	RETICULATE	ADULTEROUS	FOURTEENTH	SBUDDIKINS	DEVOTEMENT
NETWORKING	RETINALITE	AQUAFORTIS	FRUITFULLY	SCULPTRESS	DEVOTIONAL
NOTABILITY	RETIREMENT	AQUAMANALE	FRUSTRATED	SCURRILITY	DIVERGENCE
NOTEWORTHY	RETRACTION	AQUAMANILE	FRUTESCENT	SCURRILOUS	DIVINATION
NOTICEABLE	RETRAINING	AQUAMARINE	GAULTHERIA	SCUTELLATE	DIVISIONAL
NOTICEABLY	RETREATING	ARUNDELIAN	GLUTTONOUS	SHUDDERING	DOVERCOURT
NOTIFIABLE	RETROGRADE	BAUDELAIRE	GRUBBINESS	SKUPSHTINA	FAVORITISM
NOTIONALLY	RETROGRESS	BLUEBONNET	GRUMPINESS	SLUGGISHLY	FAVOURABLE
NOTORYCTES	RETROSPECT	BLUEBOTTLE	HAUSTELLUM	SLUICEGATE	FAVOURABLY
NUTCRACKER	RETURNABLE	BLUEMANTLE	HAUSTORIUM	SLUMBERING	FEVERISHLY
NUTRITIOUS	RITORNELLE	BLUETHROAT	HOUSEBOUND	SOUBRIQUET	GOVERNANCE
OBTAINABLE	RITORNELLO	BLUNDERING	HOUSECRAFT	SOUNDPROOF	GOVERNESSY
OBTUSENESS	ROTHSCHILD	BOUILLOTTE	HOUSEMAIDS	SOUNDTRACK	GOVERNMENT
OCTAHEDRON	ROTISSERIE	BOURIGNIAN	HOUSEPROUD	SOURDELINE	HOVERCRAFT
OCTODECIMO	ROTTWEILER	BOUSINGKEN	INUNDATION	SOUSAPHONE	INVALIDATE
OFTENTIMES	RUTHERFORD	CAUTIONARY	JAUNTINESS	SOUTERRAIN	INVALIDISM
OPTIMISTIC	RUTHLESSLY	CAUTIOUSLY	JOURNALESE	SOUTHBOUND	INVALIDITY
ORTHOCAINE	SATISFYING	CHUCKWALLA	JOURNALISM	SOUTHERNER	INVALUABLE
ORTHOCLASE	SATURATION	CHURCHGOER	JOURNALIST	SOUTHWARDS	INVARIABLE
ORTHOGONAL	SATURNALIA	CHURCHYARD	JOURNEYMAN	SPURIOUSLY	INVARIABLY
ORTHOPNOEA	SATYAGRAHA	CHURLISHLY	JOUYSAUNCE	SQUEEZEBOX	INVESTMENT
ORTHOPTICS	SETTERWORT	CLUMPERTON	KRUGERRAND	SQUETEAGUE	INVETERATE
OSTENSIBLE	SETTLEMENT	CLUMSINESS	LAUDERDALE	SQUIREARCH	INVIGILATE
OSTENSIBLY	TATPURUSHA	COUNCILLOR	LAUNCEGAYE	STUBBORNLY	INVIGORATE
OSTEOBLAST	TATTERSALL	COUNSELING	LAUNCESTON	STUDIOUSLY	INVINCIBLE
OSTEOCOLLA	TITARAKURA	COUNSELLOR	LAUNDROMAT	STUFFINESS	INVIOLABLE
OSTEOLEPIS	TUTIVILLUS	COUNTERACT	LAURDALITE	STULTIFIED	INVITATION
OSTEOPATHY	ULTIMATELY	COUNTRYMAN	LAURENTIAN	STUMBLEDOM	INVOCATION
OSTEOPHYTE	ULTRABASIC	COURAGEOUS	LAURUSTINE	STUPEFYING	INVOLUTION
OSTROGOTHS	ULTRAFICHE	COURTHOUSE	LAURVIKITE	STUPENDOUS	LAVALLIÈRE
OUTBALANCE	ULTRAMAFIC	COUSCOUSOU	LEUCHAEMIA	STURDINESS	LAVISHNESS
OUTLANDISH	ULTRASONIC	CRUIKSHANK	LOUISIETTE	THUCYDIDES	LEVITATION
OUTPATIENT	ULTRASOUND	CRUSTACEAN	MAUPASSANT	THUMBIKINS	LIVELIHOOD
OUTPERFORM	ULTRONEOUS	DEUTOPLASM	MAURITANIA	THUMBSCREW	LIVELINESS
OUTPOURING	UNTHINKING	DIURNALIST	MOUCHARABY	THUNDERBOX	LIVERWURST
OUTRAGEOUS	UNTIDINESS	DOUBLEBASS	MOUDIEWART	THUNDERING	LOVELINESS
OUTSPECKLE	UNTRUTHFUL	DOUBLETALK	MOULDINESS	THUNDEROUS	MAVOURNEEN
PATAGONIAN	URTICACEAE	DOUBTFULLY	MOULDIWARP	TOUCHANDGO	NAVIGATION
PATAVINITY	VETERINARY	DRUMBLEDOR	MOUNTEBANK	TOUCHINESS	NOVACULITE
PATCHCOCKE	VITELLICLE	DRUZHINNIK	MOURNFULLY	TOUCHPAPER	OUVIRANDRA
PATCHINESS	VITUPERATE	DUUMVIRATE	MOUSEPIECE	TOUCHPIECE	RAVENOUSLY
PATERNALLY	WATCHFULLY	EBULLIENCE	MOUSSELINE	TOUCHSTONE	RAVENSBILL
PATHFINDER	WATCHMAKER	ECUADORIAN	MOUSTERIAN	TOURBILLON	RAVENSDUCK
PATHOGENIC	WATCHTOWER	ECUMENICAL	MOUTHORGAN	TOURMALINE	RAVENSTONE
PATIBULARY	WATERBORNE	EDULCORATE	MOUTHPIECE	TOURNAMENT	REVELATION
PATISSERIE	WATERBRASH	EGURGITATE	NAUSEATING	TOURNIQUET	REVENGEFUL
PATRIARCHY	WATERCOLOR	EMULSIFIER	NAUSEATIVE	TRUCULENCE	REVERENTLY

REVERSIBLE	GLYCOLYSIS	BAGASSOSIS	DEVASTATED	INCAPACITY	MUTABILITY
REVITALIZE	GLYCOSURIA	BALANCHINE	DEVASTAVIT	INCAPARINA	NATATORIAL
REVIVALIST	JAYWALKING	BARASINGHA	DIDASCALIC	INCAUTIOUS	NATATORIUM
REVOCATION	KEYBOARDER	BEHAVIORAL	DILAPIDATE	INDAPAMIDE	NDRANGHETA
REVOLUTION	MAYONNAISE	BELARUSIAN	DILATATION	INFALLIBLE	NEFANDROUS
SAVAGENESS	OXYGENATOR	BETACRUCIS	DINANDERIE	INFALLIBLY	NEGATIVELY
SAVONAROLA	OXYMORONIC	BIPARTISAN	DISABILITY	INFATUATED	NEMATOCYST
SEVENTIETH	OZYMANDIAS	BLEARYEYED	DISAPPOINT	INHABITANT	NICARAGUAN
VIVANDIÈRE	PHYLACTERY	BREADFRUIT	DISAPPROVE	INHALATION	NONALIGNED
VIVIPAROUS	PHYLLIOPOD	BREAKABLES	DISARRANGE	INSANITARY	NOTABILITY
WAVELENGTH	PHYSICALLY	BREAKWATER	DISASTROUS	INSATIABLE	NOUAKCHOTT
BEWILDERED	PHYSIOCRAT	BREASTBONE	DREADFULLY	INSATIABLY	NOVACULITE
BEWITCHING	PHYSIOLOGY	BREASTFEED	DREADLOCKS	INTAGLIATE	OBTAINABLE
BOWDLERISE	PHYTOTOXIN	BREASTWORK	DREAMINESS	INTANGIBLE	OCCASIONAL
BOWDLERIZE	PSYCHIATRY	BREATHLESS	DREARINESS	INVALIDATE	OCEANARIUM
DOWNMARKET	PSYCHOLOGY	BROADCLOTH	DREARISOME	INVALIDISM	OCEANGOING
DOWNSIZING	PSYCHOPATH	BROADPIECE	DURABILITY	INVALIDITY	OCTAHEDRON
DOWNSTAIRS	PSYCHOPOMP	BROADSHEET	DYNAMITARD	INVALUABLE	OLEAGINOUS
DOWNSTREAM	RHYTHMICAL	BROADSWORD	EATANSWILL	INVARIABLE	ORNAMENTAL
HOWLEGLASS	SKYSCRAPER	CADAVEROUS	EBRACTEATE	INVARIABLY	PADAREWSKI
HOWSOMEVER	STYLISTICS	CALAMANDER	ECUADORIAN	IRRADICATE	PALAEOTYPE
LAWABIDING	STYLOPISED	CALAMITOUS	EFFACEMENT	IRRATIONAL	PALAESTRAL
LAWBREAKER	THYSANURAN	CALAMONDIN	EMBANKMENT	KSHATRIYAS	PALAGONITE
LAWRENCIUM	TRYPTOPHAN	CALAVERITE	ENCAMPMENT	LAMARCKISM	PALATALISE
NEWFANGLED	UNYIELDING	CAPABILITY	ENCASEMENT	LAVALLIÈRE	PALATINATE
NEWSAGENTS	ALZHEIMERS	CAPACITATE	ENGAGEMENT	LAWABIDING	PANAMANIAN
NEWSCASTER	MIZZENMAST	CARABINEER	ENLACEMENT	LEGALISTIC	PANARITIUM
NEWSLETTER	MOZAMBIQUE	CARABINIER	ENRAPTURED	LOGANBERRY	PAPAVERINE
NEWSMONGER	MOZZARELLA	CARACTACUS	ENSANGUINE	LOGARITHMS	PARACELSUS
NEWSPAPERS	POZZUOLANA	CARAMELIZE	EQUANIMITY	MADAGASCAN	PARADIDDLE
NEWSREADER	PRZEWALSKI	CATABOLISM	EQUATORIAL	MADAGASCAR	PARADOXIDE
NEWSWORTHY	PUZZLEMENT	CATACHUMEN	ESCADRILLE	MAHAYANALI	PARADOXINE
PAWNBROKER	RAZZMATAZZ	CATAFALQUE	ESCALATION	MALACOLOGY	PARAENESIS
POWERHOUSE	SUZERAINTY	CATALECTIC	ESCAPEMENT	MALAGUETTA	PARAGLOSSA
RAWINSONDE	**10:4**	CATALEPTIC	ESCARPMENT	MALAPROPOS	PARAGONITE
RAWSTHORNE		CATALOGUER	ESPADRILLE	MALAYALAAM	PARAGUAYAN
ROWDYDOWDY	ADIAPHORON	CATAPHRACT	ESTANCIERO	MANAGEABLE	PARALLELED
ROWLANDSON	ADRAMELECH	CATARRHINE	EUCALYPTOL	MANAGEMENT	PARAMARIBO
TOWNSWOMAN	AFFABILITY	CATASTASIS	EUCALYPTUS	MANAGERESS	PARAMETRIC
UNWORKABLE	AGRAHAYANA	CATAWAMPUS	EXCAVATION	MANAGERIAL	PARANORMAL
COXCOMICAL	ALCAICERIA	CAVALRYMAN	EXHALATION	MARASCHINO	PARAPHASIA
FOXHUNTING	ALKALINITY	CHEAPSKATE	EXHAUSTING	MEGALITHIC	PARAPHILIA
HEXAVALENT	ALMACANTAR	CLEARSTORY	EXHAUSTION	MEGALOSAUR	PARAPHONIA
LUXEMBOURG	ALTAZIMUTH	CLEARWATER	EXHAUSTIVE	MELACONITE	PARAPHRASE
LUXURIANCE	AMBARVALIA	COMANCHERO	EXPATRIATE	MELANCHOLY	PARAPHYSIS
MAXIMALIST	AMBASSADOR	COPARCENER	FANATICISM	MELANESIAN	PARAPLEGIA
MAXIMILIAN	AMIABILITY	CORALBERRY	FATALISTIC	MENACINGLY	PARAPLEGIC
SAXICOLINE	ANDALUSIAN	CREATIVITY	FATALITIES	METABOLISE	PARAPRAXIS
SAXICOLOUS	ANDALUSITE	DEBASEMENT	GELATINOUS	METABOLISM	PARARTHRIA
SEXAGESIMA	ANTAGONISE	DEBATEMENT	HARASSMENT	METACARPAL	PARASCENIA
SEXDUCTION	ANTAGONISM	DEBAUCHERY	HEPATOCELE	METACARPUS	PARASELENE
SEXOLOGIST	ANTAGONIST	DECAGRAMME	HEXAVALENT	METACENTRE	PARASTATAL
TAXONOMIST	ANTAGONIZE	DECAHEDRON	HUMANISTIC	METALEPSIS	PARATROOPS
TOXICOLOGY	ANTARCTICA	DECAMPMENT	HUMANITIES	METALLURGY	PATAGONIAN
ABYSSINIAN	APHAERESIS	DECAPITATE	HYPAETHRAL	METAPHRASE	PATAVINITY
AMYGDALOID	APPARENTLY	DECATHLETE	HYPAETHRON	METAPLASIS	PICARESQUE
ARYTAENOID	APPARITION	DEFACEMENT	IDEALISTIC	METASTABLE	PICAYUNISH
ASYMMETRIC	AQUAFORTIS	DEFAMATION	ILLADVISED	METATARSAL	PINAKOTHEK
ASYNARTETE	AQUAMANALE	DEFAMATORY	ILLAQUEATE	METATARSUS	PIRANDELLO
CLYDESDALE	AQUAMANILE	DEPARTMENT	IMMACULACY	METATHERIA	PLEASANTLY
CRYOGENICS	AQUAMARINE	DEPARTURES	IMMACULATE	METATHESIS	PLEASANTRY
CRYOPHORUS	ARMAGEDDON	DERACINATE	IMMATERIAL	MIRACULOUS	PLIABILITY
CRYPTOGRAM	ASPARAGINE	DERAILLEUR	IMMATURITY	MONANDROUS	POCAHONTAS
CRYPTOZOIC	ATHANASIAN	DERAILMENT	IMPAIRMENT	MONARCHIST	PREARRANGE
DAYDREAMER	ATRACURIUM	DESALINATE	IMPALPABLE	MORALITIES	PROAIRESIS
ELYTRIFORM	ATRAMENTAL	DETACHABLE	IMPALUDISM	MORATORIUM	PYRACANTHA
ERYMANTHUS	ATTACHMENT	DETACHMENT	IMPARLANCE	MOSASAUROS	PYRAGYRITE
ERYSIPELAS	ATTAINABLE	DETAINMENT	IMPASSABLE	MOZAMBIQUE	QUEASINESS
FLYCATCHER	ATTAINMENT	DEVANAGARI	IMPATIENCE	MUJAHEDDIN	RAGAMUFFIN

REGARDLESS	TYRANNISED	KNOBKERRIE	BLACKBERRY	CRICKETING	GRACIOUSLY
RELATIVELY	UNBALANCED	LAMBREQUIN	BLACKBOARD	CROCKFORDS	GROCETERIA
RELATIVITY	UNEASINESS	LAWBREAKER	BLACKBULLY	DEACTIVATE	GUACHAMOLE
RELAXATION	UNFAITHFUL	LESBIANISM	BLACKENING	DELCREDERE	HENCEFORTH
RELAXATIVE	UNFAMILIAR	LIEBERMANN	BLACKGUARD	DESCENDANT	HITCHHIKER
REMARKABLE	UNFATHOMED	LIMBERNECK	BLACKHEART	DESCENDING	HOTCHPOTCH
REMARKABLY	UNHAMPERED	LIMBURGITE	BLACKSHIRT	DESCRIBING	INACCURACY
REPAIRABLE	UNLADYLIKE	LUMBERJACK	BLACKSMITH	DIACAUSTIC	INACCURATE
REPARATION	UNMANNERED	MEMBERSHIP	BLACKSTONE	DIACHRONIC	INACTIVITY
REPATRIATE	UNMANNERLY	MEMBRANOUS	BLACKTHORN	DIACONICON	KINCHINLAY
ROLANDSECK	UNSALARIED	MORBIDEZZA	BLACKWATER	DISCERNING	KNOCKABOUT
ROMANESQUE	VIDARABINE	MUMBLENEWS	BLOCKHOUSE	DISCIPLINE	LACCADIVES
ROSANILINE	VIVANDIÈRE	NIMBLENESS	BRACHIOPOD	DISCLAIMER	LANCEOLATE
SALAMANDER	VOCABULARY	NORBERTINE	BRICKLAYER	DISCLOSURE	LASCIVIOUS
SAMARSKITE	VOCABULIST	NUMBERLESS	BRICKWORKS	DISCOBOLUS	LEUCHAEMIA
SANATORIUM	VOCATIONAL	OFFBALANCE	BROCATELLE	DISCOLORED	MALCONTENT
SAVAGENESS	VOLATILITY	OROBRANCHE	BUCCINATOR	DISCOMFORT	MANCHESTER
SCHALSTEIN	VORAGINOUS	OUTBALANCE	BUTCHERING	DISCOMMODE	MANCHINEEL
SEDATENESS	WHEATSHEAF	PLEBISCITE	CALCAREOUS	DISCOMPOSE	MARCANTANT
SENATORIAL	WHEATSTONE	PREBENDARY	CALCEDONIO	DISCONCERT	MARCESCENT
SEPARATELY	ZABAGLIONE	RABBINICAL	CALCEOLATE	DISCONNECT	MARCIONITE
SEPARATION	ALABANDINE	RUBBERNECK	CALCITONIN	DISCONTENT	MASCARPONE
SEPARATISM	ALABANDITE	RUMBLOSSOM	CALCULABLE	DISCOPHORA	MATCHMAKER
SEPARATIST	ANABAPTIST	RUMBULLION	CALCULATED	DISCORDANT	MATCHSTALK
SEPARATRIX	BALBRIGGAN	SABBATICAL	CALCULATOR	DISCOURAGE	MATCHSTICK
SEXAGESIMA	BALBUTIENT	SALBUTAMOL	CANCELLOUS	DISCOVERER	MERCANTILE
SHEARWATER	BAMBOOZLED	SHABBINESS	CANCIONERO	DISCREETLY	MERCIFULLY
SINARCHIST	BARBAROSSA	SHIBBOLETH	CANCRIZANS	DISCREPANT	MISCELLANY
SINARQUIST	BARBITURIC	SOMBRERITE	CARCINOGEN	DISCRETION	MISCHMETAL
SPEAKERINE	BOBBYSOXER	SOUBRIQUET	CASCARILLA	DISCURSIVE	MISCONDUCT
SPHACELATE	BOMBARDIER	STABILISER	CATCHPENNY	DISCUSSING	MOUCHARABY
SPHALERITE	CAMBERWELL	STABILIZER	CATCRACKER	DISCUSSION	MYOCARDIAL
SPLANCHNIC	CAMBRENSIS	STUBBORNLY	CHECKLATON	DOLCEMENTE	NARCISSISM
STEADINESS	CARBURETOR	SUNBATHING	CHECKPOINT	DRACONITES	NARCOLEPSY
STEAKHOUSE	COLBERTINE	SYMBOLICAL	CHICHESTER	DUTCHWOMAN	NINCOMPOOP
STEALTHILY	COMBUSTION	TAMBERLANE	CHICKENPOX	DYSCRASITE	NONCHALANT
STIACCIATO	CUMBERLAND	TAMBOURINE	CHUCKWALLA	EGOCENTRIC	NUTCRACKER
STRABISMUS	CUMBERSOME	TIEBREAKER	CIRCASSIAN	ELACAMPANE	PANCRATIUM
STRABOTOMY	DESBOROUGH	TIMBERYARD	CIRCUITOUS	ELECAMPANE	PATCHCOCKE
STRACCHINO	DIABOLICAL	TIMBROLOGY	CIRCUMCISE	ELECTORATE	PATCHINESS
STRAGGLING	DISBELIEVE	TORBERNITE	CIRCUMFLEX	ELECTRICAL	PEACEFULLY
STRAIGHTEN	DISBURTHEN	TUMBLEDOWN	CIRCUMFUSE	ELECTROMER	PEACEMAKER
STRAITENED	DOUBLEBASS	TURBULENCE	CIRCUMVENT	ELECTRONIC	PEACHERINO
STRAMONIUM	DOUBLETALK	UNABRIDGED	CLOCKMAKER	EMACIATION	PECCADILLO
STRAPONTIN	DOUBTFULLY	UNOBSERVED	COCCINEOUS	EPICANTHUS	PERCENTAGE
STRASBOURG	DUMBLEDORE	YARBOROUGH	COLCHESTER	ERUCTATION	PERCENTILE
STRATEGIST	ERUBESCENT	ZIMBABWEAN	COLCHICINE	EVACUATION	PERCEPTION
STRATHSPEY	EXOBIOLOGY	ZUMBOORUCK	CONCENTRIC	EXACERBATE	PERCEPTIVE
STRATIOTES	EXUBERANCE	ABSCISSION	CONCEPTION	EXACTITUDE	PERCIPIENT
STRATOCRAT	FEEBLENESS	AFICIONADO	CONCEPTUAL	EXECRATION	PERCOLATOR
STRATOCYST	FLABBINESS	ALECTORIAN	CONCERNING	FASCIATION	PERCUSSION
STRAVINSKY	FORBEARING	ANACARDIUM	CONCERTINA	FASCINATED	PESCADORES
STRAWBERRY	FORBIDDING	ANACHARSIS	CONCERVATE	FASCINATOR	PICCADILLY
STRAWBOARD	GHIBELLINE	ANACLASTIC	CONCESSION	FESCENNINE	PICCALILLI
SUDATORIUM	GIBBERELLA	ANACOUSTIC	CONCHIGLIE	FLICKERING	PICCANINNY
SUGARALLIE	GILBERTIAN	ANACRUSTIC	CONCHIOLIN	FLOCCULATE	PINCHPENNY
SWEATSHIRT	GILBERTINE	ANSCHAUUNG	CONCHOLOGY	FLOCCULENT	PINCUSHION
SYNAERESIS	GRUBBINESS	APICULTURE	CONCILIATE	FLUCTUATER	PITCHSTONE
TANAGRIDAE	HERBACEOUS	APOCALYPSE	CONCINNITY	FLYCATCHER	PONCHIELLI
TARADIDDLE	HOBBYHORSE	APOCRYPHAL	CONCINNOUS	FORCEFULLY	PRECARIOUS
TARANTELLA	HUMBLENESS	ARACOSTYLE	CONCLUDING	FRACTIONAL	PRECAUTION
THEATRICAL	HUSBANDAGE	AVICULARIA	CONCLUSION	FRICANDEAU	PRECEDENCE
TIRAILLEUR	ICEBREAKER	BACCHANTES	CONCLUSIVE	FUNCTIONAL	PRECIPITIN
TITARAKURA	INEBRIATED	BARCAROLLE	CONCOCTION	GASCONNADE	PRECOCIOUS
TRIACONTER	ISABELLINE	BARCHESTER	CONCORDANT	GEOCENTRIC	PRECURSORY
TRIANGULAR	JABBERWOCK	BEDCHAMBER	CONCRETION	GLACIATION	PRICKLOUSE
TRIANGULUM	KEYBOARDER	BEDCLOTHES	CONCURRENT	GLYCOLYSIS	PROCEDURAL
TULARAEMIA	KIMBERLITE	BIOCHEMIST	CONCUSSION	GLYCOSURIA	PROCEEDING
TYRANNICAL	KLEBSIELLA	BLACKBEARD	COXCOMICAL	GRACEFULLY	PROCESSING

PROCESSION	TOUCHPAPER	CONDIMENTS	INEDUCABLE	SANDERLING	ADVERSARIA
PROCLIVITY	TOUCHPIECE	CONDOLENCE	IRIDESCENT	SANDGROPER	ADVERTISER
PROCREATOR	TOUCHSTONE	CONDOTTIER	JARDINIERE	SANDINISTA	AERENCHYMA
PROCRUSTES	TRACHELATE	CONDUCTING	KHIDMUTGAR	SANDWICHES	AFFETTUOSO
PROCUMBENT	TRECENTIST	CONDUCTION	KINDLINESS	SBUDDIKINS	AFTERBIRTH
PROCURABLE	TRICHOLOGY	CORDIALITY	KURDAITCHA	SEXDUCTION	AFTERHOURS
PROCURATOR	TRICKINESS	CORDIERITE	LANDAMMANN	SHADOWLESS	AFTERIMAGE
PSOCOPTERA	TRICLINIUM	CORDILLERA	LANDLOCKED	SHODDINESS	AFTERPIECE
PSYCHIATRY	TROCHANTER	CORDWAINER	LANDLOUPER	SHUDDERING	AFTERSHAVE
PSYCHOLOGY	TROCHOTRON	CREDENTIAL	LANDLUBBER	SOGDOLAGER	AFTERSHOCK
PSYCHOPATH	TROCTOLITE	CREDITABLE	LANDSTHING	SOGDOLIGER	AFTERTASTE
PSYCHOPOMP	TRUCULENCE	CREDITABLY	LAUDERDALE	SOGDOLOGER	AFTERWARDS
PUNCHDRUNK	UNACCENTED	CUDDLESOME	LEADERSHIP	SORDIDNESS	ALDERMANLY
PUNCTUALLY	UNICAMERAL	DAYDREAMER	LORDLINESS	SPIDERWORT	ALDERWOMAN
PUNCTULATE	UNOCCUPIED	DEADLINESS	LORDOLATRY	SPODOMANCY	ALIENATION
QUICKSANDS	UNSCHOOLED	DEADNETTLE	MAIDENHAIR	STADHOLDER	ALLEGATION
QUICKTHORN	UNSCRAMBLE	DENDROPHIS	MAIDENHOOD	STUDIOUSLY	ALLEGEANCE
REACTIVATE	UNSCRIPTED	DIADROMOUS	MANDEVILLE	SUDDENNESS	ALLEGIANCE
REDCURRANT	USUCAPTION	DISDAINFUL	MANDRAGORA	SVADILFARI	ALPENSTOCK
RESCHEDULE	VASCULITIS	DUNDERFUNK	MEADOWPLAN	SWEDENBORG	ALTERATION
SACCHARASE	VULCANALIA	DUNDERHEAD	MEDDLESOME	TAPDANCING	ALTERNATOR
SACCHARIDE	WANCHANCIE	DUNDERPATE	MENDACIOUS	TARDIGRADE	AMPELOPSIS
SACCHARINE	WATCHFULLY	DUODECIMAL	MIDDLEBROW	TEDDINGTON	ANHELATION
SACCHAROID	WATCHMAKER	EPIDEICTIC	MINDERERUS	TENDERFOOT	ANNEXATION
SANCTIFIED	WATCHTOWER	EPIDENDRUM	MORDACIOUS	TENDERLOIN	ANTECEDENT
SANCTITIES	WINCEYETTE	EPIDIDYMUS	MOUDIEWART	TENDERNESS	ANTEPENULT
SANCTITUDE	WINCHESTER	EPIDIORITE	NEEDLECASE	TENDRILLED	APPEARANCE
SARCOCOLLA	WITCHCRAFT	FALDISTORY	NEEDLEWORK	TRADITIONS	APPETITIVE
SARCOLEMMA	ZINCOGRAPH	FIDDLEWOOD	NIDDERLING	TRIDENTINE	APPETIZING
SEECATCHIE	ANADROMOUS	FOODSTUFFS	OBEDIENTLY	UNEDIFYING	APTERYGOTA
SHACKLETON	ANADYOMENE	FOUDROYANT	ORIDINANCE	UNEDUCATED	ASBESTOSIS
SHECKLATON	BADDERLOCK	FUDDYDUDDY	PADDINGTON	VANDERBILT	ASCENDANCY
SHOCKINGLY	BALDERDASH	GIRDLERINK	PADDLEFISH	VAUDEVILLE	ASCENDENCY
SHOCKPROOF	BANDERILLA	GOLDDIGGER	PADDYMELON	VINDEMIATE	ASCETICISM
SPACECRAFT	BANDERILLO	GOLDENSEAL	PAEDIATRIC	VINDICTIVE	ASPERSIONS
SPECIALISE	BANDMASTER	GOLDFINGER	PARDONABLE	WALDENSIAN	ASSEMBLAGE
SPECIALISM	BAUDELAIRE	GOLDILOCKS	PARDONABLY	WANDERINGS	ASSEMBLING
SPECIALIST	BHADRAPADA	GOLDTHREAD	PERDENDOSI	WANDERLUST	ASSESSMENT
SPECIALITY	BONDHOLDER	GONDOLIERS	PERDITIOUS	WANDSWORTH	ASSEVERATE
SPECIALIZE	BONDSWOMAN	GOODFELLOW	PERDURABLE	WEEDKILLER	ASTEROIDEA
SPECIOUSLY	BORDERLAND	GRADUALISM	PREDACIOUS	WIDDICOMBE	ATTENDANCE
SPECTACLED	BORDERLINE	GRADUATION	PREDECEASE	WILDEBEEST	AUTECOLOGY
SPECTACLES	BORDRAGING	GRIDIRONER	PREDESTINE	WILDERNESS	BABESIASIS
SPECTATORS	BOWDLERISE	GRIDLOCKED	PREDICTION	WILDFOWLER	BAREFOOTED
SPECULATOR	BOWDLERIZE	GUIDELINES	PREDISPOSE	WINDERMERE	BAREHEADED
STICHARION	BRADYKININ	HANDICRAFT	PREDNISONE	WINDFLOWER	BARELEGGED
STICKINESS	BRADYSEISM	HANDLEBARS	PRODIGALLY	WINDJAMMER	BEDEVILLED
STICKYBEAK	BRIDEGROOM	HANDMAIDEN	PRODIGIOUS	WINDOWPANE	BENEDICITE
STOCHASTIC	BRIDESMAID	HANDPICKED	PRODUCTION	WINDOWSILL	BENEFACTOR
STOCKINESS	BRIDGEHEAD	HANDSOMELY	PRODUCTIVE	WINDSCREEN	BENEFICENT
SUBCOMPACT	BRIDGETOWN	HANDSPRING	PRUDENTIAL	WINDSHIELD	BENEFICIAL
SUCCEEDING	BRIDLEPATH	HARDBOILED	PUNDIGRION	WINDSURFER	BENEVOLENT
SUCCESSFUL	BUNDESWEHR	HARDCASTLE	QUADRANGLE	WONDERLAND	BETELGEUSE
SUCCESSION	BURDENSOME	HEADHUNTED	QUADRATURA	WONDERMENT	BETELGEUZE
SUCCESSIVE	CANDELABRA	HEADHUNTER	QUADRICEPS	WOODENHEAD	BLUEBONNET
SUCCINCTLY	CANDELILLA	HEADLIGHTS	QUADRIREME	WOODPECKER	BLUEBOTTLE
SUSCEPTIVE	CANDLEFISH	HEADMASTER	RANDLETREE	WOODPIGEON	BLUEMANTLE
SYNCHRONAL	CANDLEWICK	HEADPHONES	RANDOMNESS	WOODWORKER	BLUETHROAT
SYNCHRONIC	CANDYFLOSS	HEADSTRONG	READERSHIP	WORDSWORTH	BONESHAKER
SYNCOPATED	CARDIOGRAM	HEEDLESSLY	RENDEZVOUS	WUNDERKIND	BUCEPHALUS
SYNCRETISE	CARDIOLOGY	HEIDELBERG	RINDERPEST	YGGDRASILL	BUREAUCRAT
TEICHOPSIA	CINDERELLA	HENDECAGON	ROADRUNNER	ACCELERATE	CALEDONIAN
TESCHENITE	CLADOPHYLL	HILDEBRAND	ROADWORTHY	ACCENTUATE	CALEFACTOR
THICKENING	CLODHOPPER	HINDENBURG	ROWDYDOWDY	ACCESSIBLE	CALESCENCE
THUCYDIDES	CLYDESDALE	HINDUSTANI	RUDDERLESS	ACCESSIONS	CAMELOPARD
TOCCATELLA	CNIDOBLAST	HOODWINKED	SADDLEBACK	ADJECTIVAL	CAMERLENGO
TORCHLIGHT	COADJUTANT	HUMDUDGEON	SADDLEBILL	ADRENALINE	CAMERLINGO
TOUCHANDGO	COLDSTREAM	INADEQUACY	SANDALWOOD	ADRENERGIC	CAMERONIAN
TOUCHINESS	CONDESCEND	INADEQUATE	SANDEMANIA	ADVENTURER	CANECUTTER

CANEPHORUS	EFFERVESCE	GENEROUSLY	INSENSIBLE	MALEFACTOR	PRAEMUNIRE
CAPERNAITE	ELDERBERRY	GENETHLIAC	INTEGRATED	MALEVOLENT	PRAETORIAN
CAPERNOITY	EMBERGOOSE	GENEVRETTE	INTEGUMENT	MATELLASSE	PRAETORIUM
CARELESSLY	EMMENTALER	GLEEMAIDEN	INTELLIGENT	MATERIALLY	PREEMINENT
CATECHUMEN	EMMETROPIA	GOBEMOUCHE	INTEMERATE	MATERNALLY	PRIESTHOOD
CATEGORISE	EMPEDOCLES	GOVERNANCE	INTENDMENT	MENECHMIAN	PRZEWALSKI
CATEGORIZE	ENCEPHALON	GOVERNESSY	INTENERATE	MEPERIDINE	PUBERULENT
CATENACCIO	ENDEARMENT	GOVERNMENT	INTENTNESS	MESENTERON	PUBESCENCE
CELEBRATED	ENGENDRURE	GREEDINESS	INTERBREED	MILEOMETER	QUAESTUARY
CELESTIALS	ENKEPHALIN	GREENCLOTH	INTERCEDER	MIMEOGRAPH	QUEENSBURY
CEREBELLUM	ENLÈVEMENT	GREENFINCH	INTERCLUDE	MINERALOGY	QUEENSTOWN
CEREMONIAL	ENTEROCELE	GREENHEART	INTERESTED	MINESTRONE	QUIESCENCE
CEREMONIES	ENTERPRISE	GREENHOUSE	INTERFERER	MINEWORKER	RACECOURSE
CHEEKINESS	EQUESTRIAN	GREENSHANK	INTERFERON	MISERICORD	RAVENOUSLY
CHEERFULLY	ESPECIALLY	GREENSTICK	INTERLEAVE	MODERATELY	RAVENSBILL
CHEESECAKE	ETHEOSTOMA	GREENSTONE	INTERLOPER	MODERATION	RAVENSDUCK
CHEESEWOOD	EUHEMERISM	GREENSWARD	INTERMARRY	MOLENDINAR	RAVENSTONE
CHREMATIST	EXCELLENCE	GUBERNATOR	INTERMEZZO	MONEGASQUE	REBELLIOUS
CINECAMERA	EXCELLENCY	GYNECOLOGY	INTERNALLY	MONETARISM	RECEPTACLE
COHERENTLY	EXPECTANCY	HAKENKREUZ	INTERNMENT	MONETARIST	REDECORATE
COLEOPTERA	EXPEDIENCE	HAMESUCKEN	INTERNODAL	MONEYMAKER	REDEMPTION
COLEORHIZA	EXPEDIENCY	HATEENOUGH	INTERPHONE	NINETEENTH	REFERENDUM
COMEDIENNE	EXPEDITION	HEREABOUTS	INTERSTATE	NOTEWORTHY	REGENERATE
COMESTIBLE	EXPENDABLE	HEREDITARY	INTERSTICE	NUMERATION	RELEGATION
CONEFLOWER	EXPERIENCE	HERESIARCH	INTERTRIGO	OBJECTLESS	RELENTLESS
COPENHAGEN	EXPERIMENT	HETERODOXY	INTERTWINE	OBSEQUIOUS	REPEATABLE
COPERNICUS	EXTENDABLE	HETERODYNE	INTERWEAVE	OBSERVABLE	REPEATEDLY
COPESETTIC	EXTENSIBLE	HETEROGAMY	INTERWOVEN	OBSERVANCE	REPENTANCE
COVENANTER	EXTERNALLY	HOMECOMING	INTESTINAL	OFTENTIMES	REPERTOIRE
CYBERNETIC	FACESAVING	HOMELINESS	INTESTINES	OIREACHTAS	REPETITEUR
DECELERATE	FAREPAYING	HOMEOPATHY	INVESTMENT	OSMETERIUM	REPETITION
DECENNOVAL	FEDERALISM	HOMEOUSIAN	INVETERATE	OSTENSIBLE	REPETITIVE
DEFEASANCE	FEDERALIST	HOMEWORKER	IRRELEVANT	OSTENSIBLY	REREDORTER
DEFECATION	FEDERATION	HONEYBUNCH	IRREMEDIAL	OSTEOBLAST	RESEARCHER
DEFENSIBLE	FENESTELLA	HOPELESSLY	IRRESOLUTE	OSTEOCOLLA	RESEMBLING
DEGENERACY	FEVERISHLY	HOVERCRAFT	IRREVERENT	OSTEOLEPIS	RESENTMENT
DEGENERATE	FIBERGLASS	HYPERBOLIC	JAMESONITE	OSTEOPATHY	RESERVISTS
DEJECTEDLY	FIREWALKER	HYPERDULIA	JUGENDSTIL	OSTEOPHYTE	REVELATION
DELECTABLE	FIREWARDEN	ILLEGALITY	KATERFELTO	OTHERGATES	REVENGEFUL
DELEGATION	FLEETINGLY	IMBECILITY	KRIEGSPIEL	OTHERGUESS	REVERENTLY
DEPENDABLE	FOREBITTER	IMMEMORIAL	LACERATION	PACESETTER	REVERSIBLE
DEPENDENCE	FOREBODING	IMPECCABLE	LAMENTABLE	PALESTRINA	RHOEADALES
DEPENDENCY	FORECASTER	IMPECCABLY	LAMENTABLY	PAPERCHASE	RIGELATION
DEREGULATE	FORECASTLE	IMPEDIMENT	LEBENSRAUM	PAPERKNIFE	ROBERDSMAN
DESECRATED	FOREDAMNED	IMPENITENT	LEDERHOSEN	PARENCHYMA	ROBERTSMAN
DESERVEDLY	FOREFATHER	IMPERATIVE	LIBERALISM	PARENTHOOD	ROSECHAFER
DETECTABLE	FOREFINGER	IMPERSONAL	LIBERALITY	PARENTLESS	ROSEMALING
DETERMINED	FOREGATHER	IMPERVIOUS	LIBERALIZE	PATERNALLY	RUPESTRIAN
DETERMINER	FOREGROUND	INCENDIARY	LIBERATION	PEDESTRIAN	SACERDOTAL
DETERRENCE	FOREORDAIN	INCESTUOUS	LICENTIATE	PENELOPHON	SALESWOMAN
DETESTABLE	FORERUNNER	INDECENTLY	LICENTIOUS	PENETRABLE	SAUERKRAUT
DEVELOPING	FORESHADOW	INDECISION	LIKELIHOOD	PENETRALIA	SCIENTIFIC
DIGESTIBLE	FOREWARNED	INDECISIVE	LIKEMINDED	PEREMPTORY	SCLERIASIS
DILETTANTE	FREEBOOTER	INDECOROUS	LINEAMENTS	PHAELONIAN	SCREECHING
DIRECTIONS	FREEHANDER	INDEFINITE	LINEOMYCIN	PHAENOTYPE	SCREENPLAY
DIRECTNESS	FREEHOLDER	INDELICACY	LITERATURE	PHLEBOTOMY	SELEGILINE
DIRECTOIRE	FREELANCER	INDELICATE	LIVELIHOOD	PHLEGETHON	SENEGALESE
DIREMPTION	FREELOADER	INDENTURES	LIVELINESS	PHLEGMASIA	SENESCENCE
DISEMBOGUE	FREEMARTIN	INDEXATION	LIVERWURST	PHLEGMATIC	SEVENTIETH
DISEMBOWEL	FREEMASONS	INFECTIOUS	LONELINESS	PHRENESIAC	SHEEPISHLY
DISENCHANT	FRIENDLESS	INFEFTMENT	LOVELINESS	PHRENOLOGY	SHEEPSHANK
DISENGAGED	FRIENDSHIP	INFERNALLY	LUPERCALIA	PIGEONHOLE	SHIELDRAKE
DISENNOBLE	GAMEKEEPER	INGEMINATE	LUTESTRING	PILEDRIVER	SHOESTRING
DIVERGENCE	GENERALISE	INGENERATE	LUXEMBOURG	POKERFACED	SHREWDNESS
DODECANESE	GENERALITY	INHERENTLY	LYSENKOISM	POMERANIAN	SIDEBOARDS
DOVERCOURT	GENERALIZE	INNERSPACE	MACEBEARER	PONEROLOGY	SIDERATION
EFFECTUATE	GENERATION	INSECURELY	MACEDONIAN	POTENTIATE	SIDEROSTAT
EFFEMINACY	GENERATRIX	INSECURITY	MAKESYSTEM	POTENTILLA	SIDESADDLE
EFFEMINATE	GENEROSITY	INSEMINATE	MAKEWEIGHT	POWERHOUSE	SIDEWINDER

SLEEPINESS	TUBERCULAR	VENEZUELAN	HALFHOURLY	DIAGONALLY	ORIGINALLY
SLEEVELESS	TUMESCENCE	VETERINARY	HALFSISTER	DIDGERIDOO	ORIGINATOR
SNEEZEWOOD	TYPESCRIPT	VICEGERENT	HALFYEARLY	DISGRUNTLE	OROGENESIS
SOBERSIDES	TYPESETTER	VICEREGENT	INEFFICACY	DISGUSTING	OXYGENATOR
SOMERSAULT	TYPEWRITER	VINEGARISH	KNIFEBOARD	DOGGEDNESS	PARGETTING
SOMERVILLE	ULCERATION	VITELLICLE	LEAFHOPPER	DRAGONROOT	PHAGEDAENA
SPEECHLESS	UMBELLIFER	WAGEEARNER	MISFORTUNE	ELEGABALUS	PILGARLICK
SPEEDINESS	UNBEARABLE	WAPENSCHAW	NEWFANGLED	EMIGRATION	PILGRIMAGE
SPLENDIDLY	UNBEARABLY	WATERBORNE	NONFICTION	EPIGENETIC	PLAGIARISE
SPREAGHERY	UNBEATABLE	WATERBRASH	ODDFELLOWS	EPIGLOTTIS	PLAGIARISM
SQUEEZEBOX	UNBECOMING	WATERCOLOR	PALFRENIER	EXAGGERATE	PLAGIARIST
SQUETEAGUE	UNBELIEVER	WATERCRESS	PERFECTION	FINGERLING	PLAGIARIZE
STEELINESS	UNDECLARED	WATERFRONT	PERFICIENT	FINGERNAIL	POIGNANTLY
STEELWORKS	UNDEFEATED	WATERLEVEL	PERFIDIOUS	FINGERPICK	PRAGMATISM
STREAMERED	UNDEFENDED	WATERMELON	PERFORATED	FLAGELLATE	PRAGMATIST
STREAMLINE	UNDENIABLE	WATERPROOF	PERFORATOR	FLAGITIOUS	PROGENITOR
STREETLAMP	UNDERBURNT	WATERSKIER	PERFORMING	FLAGRANTLY	PROGESSION
STREETWISE	UNDERCLASS	WATERSPOUT	PREFERABLE	FLIGHTLESS	PROGRAMMER
STRELITZIA	UNDERCOVER	WATERTIGHT	PREFERABLY	FLUGELHORN	RINGELMANN
STRENGTHEN	UNDERCRAFT	WATERWHEEL	PREFERENCE	FORGIVABLE	RINGLEADER
STREPITANT	UNDERCROFT	WATERWINGS	PREFERMENT	FRAGMENTAL	RINGMASTER
STREPITOSO	UNDERFLOOR	WATERWORKS	PROFESSION	FRIGHTENED	ROUGHHOUSE
SUPERADDED	UNDERLEASE	WAVELENGTH	PROFICIENT	FROGHOPPER	RUGGEDNESS
SUPERCARGO	UNDERLINEN	WHEELCHAIR	PROFITABLE	FUNGICIDAL	SANGUINARY
SUPERGIANT	UNDERLYING	WHEELHOUSE	PROFITABLY	GANGRENOUS	SHAGGYMANE
SUPERHUMAN	UNDERNEATH	WHEEZINESS	PROFITLESS	GARGANTUAN	SHAGHAIRED
SUPERMODEL	UNDERPANTS	WIDESPREAD	PROFLIGACY	GARGOUILLE	SINGHALESE
SUPERPOWER	UNDERSCORE	AIRFREIGHT	PROFLIGATE	GEOGRAPHER	SINGLENESS
SUPERSONIC	UNDERSHIRT	AREFACTION	PROFOUNDLY	GEOGRAPHIC	SINGULARLY
SUPERSTORE	UNDERSIZED	ASAFOETIDA	PROFUNDITY	GINGERBEER	SLUGGISHLY
SUPERTONIC	UNDERSKIRT	BAFFLEMENT	SANFORISED	GINGERSNAP	SNIGGERING
SUPERVISED	UNDERSLUNG	BEEFBURGER	SCOFFINGLY	GINGIVITIS	SONGSTRESS
SUPERVISOR	UNDERSTAND	BEEFEATERS	SELFESTEEM	GORGEOUSLY	SONGWRITER
SUPERWOMAN	UNDERSTATE	BUFFLEHEAD	SELFSTYLED	GREGARIOUS	STAGECOACH
SUZERAINTY	UNDERSTEER	BUFFOONERY	SHIFTINESS	HANGGLIDER	STAGECRAFT
SWEEPSTAKE	UNDERSTOOD	BUMFREEZER	SINFULNESS	HODGEPODGE	STAGGERING
SWEETBREAD	UNDERSTUDY	CHAFFERING	SPIFLICATE	IMAGINABLE	STAGNATION
SWEETBRIAR	UNDERTAKER	CHIFFCHAFF	STUFFINESS	JARGONELLE	STIGMATISE
SWEETENING	UNDERVALUE	CHIFFONIER	SUFFERANCE	JIGGAMAREE	STIGMATIZE
SWEETHEART	UNDERWATER	COMFORTING	SUFFICIENT	JIGGERMAST	SUGGESTION
SYNECDOCHE	UNDERWORLD	CONFECTION	SUFFRAGIST	JINGOISTIC	SUGGESTIVE
SYNEIDESIS	UNDERWRITE	CONFEDERAL	SURFRIDING	JUGGERNAUT	SUNGLASSES
TABERNACLE	UNDESCRIED	CONFERENCE	TOMFOOLERY	KINGFISHER	SURGICALLY
TALEBEARER	UNDESERVED	CONFERVOID	TRAFFICKER	KNIGHTHEAD	SWAGGERING
TAPERECORD	UNDETECTED	CONFESSION	TRIFOLIATE	KNIGHTHOOD	TANGANYIKA
TELEBRIDGE	UNDETERRED	CONFIDANTE	UNAFFECTED	KRUGERRAND	TANGENTIAL
TELEGRAPHY	UNFETTERED	CONFIDENCE	UNIFORMITY	LANGERHANS	TANGLEFOOT
TELEOSTOME	UNHEARABLE	CONFISCATE	UNOFFICIAL	LANGUOROUS	TONGUESTER
TELEPATHIC	UNHERALDED	CONFLICTED	USEFULNESS	LARGESCALE	TRAGACANTH
TELEPHONIC	UNLEAVENED	CONFLUENCE	WOFFINGTON	LENGTHWAYS	TRAGICALLY
TELESCOPIC	UNLETTERED	CONFORMIST	WOLFRAMITE	LENGTHWISE	TROGLODYTE
TELEVISION	UNREADABLE	CONFORMITY	YAFFINGALE	LINGUISTIC	UNIGENITUS
TENEBRIFIC	UNREASONED	CONFOUNDED	AMYGDALOID	LINGULELLA	UROGENITAL
THREADBARE	UNREDEEMED	CONFUSEDLY	ARAGONITES	LOGGERHEAD	WEIGHTLESS
THREADLIKE	UNRELIABLE	CRAFTINESS	BANGLADESH	LONGCHAMPS	WHIGGAMORE
THREADWORM	UNRELIEVED	DIFFERENCE	BARGAINING	LONGFELLOW	WITGATBOOM
THREATENED	UNREQUITED	DIFFICULTY	BIOGRAPHER	MANGABEIRA	ZEUGLODONT
THREEPENCE	UNRESERVED	DIFFIDENCE	BRAGADISME	MANGOSTEEN	ALCHERINGA
THREEPENNY	UNRESOLVED	DISFIGURED	BRIGANDINE	MARGASIRSA	ALPHONSINE
THREESCORE	UNREVEALED	EMPFINDUNG	BRIGANTINE	MARGINALIA	ALZHEIMERS
THRENODIAL	UNSEASONED	FARFETCHED	BRIGHTNESS	MARGINALLY	AMPHIBIOUS
TIMEKEEPER	UNSETTLING	FLUFFINESS	BUDGERIGAR	MARGUERITE	AMPHIBRACH
TIMELINESS	UPPERCLASS	FORFAITING	BURGEONING	MEAGERNESS	AMPHICTYON
TIMESAVING	VALENTINES	FORFEITURE	BURGLARIZE	MEAGRENESS	AMPHIGOURI
TIMESERVER	VEGETABLES	FORFEUCHEN	CONGENITAL	MISGIVINGS	AMPHIMACER
TIMESWITCH	VEGETARIAN	FORFOUGHEN	CONGESTION	MORGANATIC	AMPHIMIXIS
TIRELESSLY	VEGETATION	FULFILMENT	CONGREGATE	MORGANETTA	AMPHINEURA
TOLERANTLY	VEHEMENTLY	GONFANONER	DIAGENESIS	NEIGHBORLY	AMPHITRITE
TOLERATION	VENERATION	HALFDOLLAR	DIAGNOSTIC	NIGGERHEAD	AMPHITRYON

AMPHOTERIC	LIGHTINGUP	UNTHINKING	AUDIBILITY	DIMINISHED	HEMISPHERE
ANCHORETIC	LITHISTADA	WASHINGTON	AUDITORIUM	DIMINUENDO	HESITANTLY
ANCHYLOSIS	LITHOGRAPH	WISHYWASHY	AURIFEROUS	DIMINUTION	HESITATION
ANTHEOLION	LITHOMARGE	WITHDRAWAL	BABIROUSSA	DIMINUTIVE	HORIZONTAL
ANTHOCLORE	LITHOPHANE	XIPHOPAGUS	BACITRACIN	DISINCLINE	HUMIDIFIER
ANTHRACINE	LITHUANIAN	ABDICATION	BALIBUNTAL	DISINHERIT	HUMIDISTAT
ANTHRACITE	LYCHNAPSIA	ABHIDHAMMA	BANISHMENT	DIVINATION	IGNIMBRITE
ANTHROPOID	MECHANICAL	ABRIDGMENT	BEHINDHAND	DIVISIONAL	ILLITERACY
ARCHBISHOP	MECHANIZED	ACCIDENTAL	BELIEVABLE	DOCIMASTIC	ILLITERATE
ARCHDEACON	METHEDRINE	ACHITOPHEL	BEWILDERED	DOLICHOLIS	INCIDENTAL
ARCHETYPAL	METHODICAL	ACTIONABLE	BEWITCHING	DOLICHOTUS	INCINERATE
ARCHIMEDES	METHOMANIA	ACTIVITIST	BILIVERDIN	DOMICILARY	INCISIVELY
ARCHITRAVE	METHUSALEH	ADDITAMENT	BIPINNARIA	DOMINATING	INCITEMENT
ARTHRALGIA	METHUSELAH	ADDITIONAL	BOUILLOTTE	DOMINATION	INCIVILITY
ARTHROMERE	METHYLATED	ADHIBITION	BRAINCHILD	DREIKANTER	INDICATION
ARTHURIANA	MICHAELMAS	ADMINISTER	BRAININESS	DUNIWASSAL	INDICATIVE
ASPHALTITE	MIGHTINESS	ADMIRATION	BRAINPOWER	ECHINODERM	INDICOLITE
ASPHYXIATE	MISHGUGGLE	ADMIRINGLY	BRAINSTORM	ECHINOIDEA	INDICTABLE
AUTHORISED	MISHNAYOTH	ADMISSIBLE	CALIFORNIA	EFFICIENCY	INDICTMENT
AUTHORSHIP	MITHRIDATE	ADMITTANCE	CAPILLAIRE	ELLIPTICAL	INDIGENOUS
BATHYSCAPH	MOTHERHOOD	ADMITTEDLY	CAPITALISM	EMBITTERED	INDIGOLITE
BICHROMATE	MOTHERLAND	AFFILIATED	CAPITALIST	ENLISTMENT	INDIRECTLY
BOTHERSOME	MOTHERLESS	AFRICANDER	CAPITALIZE	ENRICHMENT	INDISCREET
BUCHMANISM	MOTHERLIKE	AFRICANISM	CAPITATION	ENTICEMENT	INDISPOSED
BUSHRANGER	NATHELESSE	ALBIGENSES	CAPITELLUM	EQUITATION	INDISTINCT
CACHINNATE	NETHERMOST	ALCIBIADES	CAPITOLINE	EQUIVALENT	INDITEMENT
CATHOLICON	NIGHTDRESS	ALLIGATION	CAPITULARY	EQUIVOCATE	INDIVIDUAL
CATHOLICOS	NIGHTLIGHT	AMBIVALENT	CAPITULATE	ESTIMATION	INFIBULATE
CEPHALOPOD	NIGHTSHADE	AMRITATTVA	CARICATURA	EUDIOMETER	INFIDELITY
COCHLEARIA	NIGHTSHIRT	ANCIPITOUS	CARICATURE	EXCITEMENT	INFIGHTING
DÉSHABILLÉ	NIGHTSTICK	ANGIOSPERM	CAVICORNIA	EXHIBITION	INFILTRATE
DICHROMATE	OOPHORITIS	ANNIHILATE	CECIDOMYIA	EXHILARATE	INFINITELY
DICHROMISM	ORCHESTRAL	ANTIADITIS	CHAIRWOMAN	EXPIRATION	INFINITIVE
DIPHTHERIA	ORCHIDEOUS	ANTIBARBUS	CHEIRONOMY	EXTINCTION	INHIBITING
DISHABILLE	ORPHEOREON	ANTIBIOTIC	CHOICELESS	EXTINGUISH	INHIBITION
DISHARMONY	ORTHOCAINE	ANTICHTHON	CHRISTIANA	FACILITATE	INHIBITORY
DISHEARTEN	ORTHOCLASE	ANTICIPATE	CLAIRCOLLE	FACILITIES	INSIPIDITY
DISHONESTY	ORTHOGONAL	ANTICLIMAX	CLOISTERED	FAMILIARLY	INSISTENCE
DISHWASHER	ORTHOPNOEA	ANTIFREEZE	COGITATION	FAMISHMENT	INTIMATELY
DITHIONATE	ORTHOPTICS	ANTIMASQUE	CONIFEROUS	FELICITATE	INTIMATION
ECCHYMOSIS	OUGHTLINGS	ANTIMATTER	CORINTHIAN	FELICITOUS	INTIMIDATE
ECTHLIPSIS	PATHFINDER	ANTIMONIAN	CRAIGFLUKE	FEMININITY	INTINCTION
EIGHTEENTH	PATHOGENIC	ANTINOMIAN	CRUIKSHANK	FEUILLETON	INVIGILATE
ENCHANTING	PICHICIAGO	ANTIOCHENE	DEBILITATE	FILIBUSTER	INVIGORATE
ENTHUSIASM	PICHICIEGO	ANTIOCHIAN	DECIMALIZE	FINISTERRE	INVINCIBLE
ENTHUSIAST	PREHENSILE	ANTIPHONAL	DECIPHERED	FOLIACEOUS	INVIOLABLE
ESCHAROTIC	PREHISTORY	ANTIPODEAN	DECISIVELY	FORINSECAL	INVITATION
EUCHLORINE	PROHIBITED	ANTIPROTON	DEDICATION	FREIGHTAGE	IRRIGATION
EUPHONIOUS	PYTHAGORAS	ANTIQUATED	DEFICIENCY	FRUITFULLY	IRRITATING
EUPHROSYNE	PYTHOGENIC	ANTISEPSIS	DEFILEMENT	FULIGINOUS	IRRITATION
EUTHANASIA	RICHARDSON	ANTISEPTIC	DEFINITELY	FUMIGATION	JUBILANTLY
EUTHYNEURA	RICHTHOFEN	ANTISOCIAL	DEFINITION	GALIMATIAS	JUBILATION
FATHERLAND	RIGHTFULLY	ANTISTATIC	DEFINITIVE	GEMINATION	JUDICATURE
FATHERLESS	RIGHTWARDS	ANTITHESIS	DEHISCENCE	GENICULATE	JUDICIALLY
FISHMONGER	ROTHSCHILD	ANTITHETIC	DELIBERATE	GERIATRICS	KENILWORTH
FISHSELLER	RUTHERFORD	ANTITRAGUS	DELICATELY	GOLIATHISE	LAMINATION
FOXHUNTING	RUTHLESSLY	ANTIVENENE	DELIGATION	GONIOMETER	LANIGEROUS
GETHSEMANE	SILHOUETTE	ARBITRATOR	DELIGHTFUL	HABILITATE	LAVISHNESS
HEPHAESTUS	SOPHOCLEAN	ARMIPOTENT	DELINQUENT	HABITATION	LEGIBILITY
HIGHBINDER	SOPHOMORIC	ARTICULATA	DELIRATION	HABITUALLY	LEGISLATOR
HIGHFLYING	SUBHEADING	ARTICULATE	DEMIRELIEF	HAGIOSCOPE	LEGITIMACY
HIGHHANDED	SYPHILITIC	ARTIFICIAL	DEPILATION	HALIEUTICS	LEGITIMATE
HIGHLANDER	TACHOGRAPH	ASPIDISTRA	DEPILATORY	HELICOPTER	LEGITIMIZE
HIGHWAYMAN	TACHOMETER	ASPIRATION	DERIVATION	HELIOGRAPH	LEVITATION
HITHERWARD	TECHNETIUM	ASSIGNABLE	DERIVATIVE	HELIOLATER	LIBIDINOUS
INCHOATIVE	TECHNICIAN	ASSIGNMENT	DESICCATED	HELIOTROPE	LIMITATION
LACHRYMOSE	TECHNOCRAT	ASSIMILATE	DESIDERATA	HEMICHORDA	LIMITROPHE
LIGHTERMAN	TECHNOLOGY	ASSISTANCE	DIGITORIUM	HEMIHEDRON	LIPIZZANER
LIGHTHOUSE	UNSHACKLED	ASTIGMATIC	DILIGENTLY	HEMIPLEGIA	LITIGATION

LOGISTICAL	OBSIDIONAL	REMITTANCE	STRIPTEASE	CUCKOOPINT	ANALOGICAL
LOUISIETTE	OCCIDENTAL	RESIGNEDLY	SURINAMESE	DARKHAIRED	ANALPHABET
LUMINARIST	OFFICIALLY	RESILIENCE	TELIOSPORE	DICKCISSEL	ANALYTICAL
LUMINOSITY	OMNIPOTENT	RESISTANCE	TEPIDARIUM	DRAKESTONE	ANGLERFISH
LUSITANIAN	OMNISCIENT	RETICULATE	TOPICALITY	DUCKBOARDS	ANGLOPHILE
MABINOGION	OMNIVOROUS	RETINALITE	TOXICOLOGY	DUKKERIPEN	ANGLOPHOBE
MAGISTRACY	OPHICLEIDE	RETIREMENT	TRAITOROUS	FALKLANDER	APOLAUSTIC
MAGISTRAND	OPTIMISTIC	REVITALIZE	TUTIVILLUS	FICKLENESS	APOLLONIAN
MAGISTRATE	ORDINARILY	REVIVALIST	ULTIMATELY	HACKBUTEER	APOLLONIUS
MALIGNANCY	ORDINATION	RIDICULOUS	UNDIGESTED	HACKMATACK	APOLOGETIC
MALINGERER	OSCILLATOR	RIDINGHOOD	UNDISPUTED	HANKYPANKY	APPLICABLE
MANICHAEAN	OSCITATION	ROTISSERIE	UNFINISHED	JACKANAPES	APPLICATOR
MANICURIST	OSMIDROSIS	RUBIGINOUS	UNLICENSED	JACKBOOTED	ATELEIOSIS
MANIFESTLY	OUVIRANDRA	RUBINSTEIN	UNRIVALLED	JACKHAMMER	BAILIEWICK
MANIPULATE	PACIFICISM	RUDIMENTAL	UNTIDINESS	JACKSTONES	BAILLIWICK
MARIOLATRY	PAGINATION	RUMINANTIA	UNYIELDING	JACKSTRAWS	BALLISTICS
MARIONETTE	PALIMPSEST	RUMINATION	URTICACEAE	KOEKSISTER	BALLISTITE
MAXIMALIST	PALINDROME	RUMINATIVE	VALIDATION	KOOKABURRA	BALLOONING
MAXIMILIAN	PALISANDER	RUPICOLINE	VARICOSITY	LACKADAISY	BALLOONIST
MEDICAMENT	PAPIAMENTO	SAGITTARIA	VARIEGATED	LACKLUSTER	BARLEYBREE
MEDICATION	PARISCHANE	SALICORNIA	VELITATION	LACKLUSTRE	BARLEYCORN
MEDIOCRITY	PARISIENNE	SALIVATION	VERIFIABLE	LOCKERROOM	BELLADONNA
MEDITATION	PASIGRAPHY	SANITARIUM	VESICULATE	LOCKKEEPER	BELLAMOURE
MEDITATIVE	PATIBULARY	SANITATION	VIGILANTES	MACKINTOSH	BELLARMINE
MEDIUMTERM	PATISSERIE	SATISFYING	VISIBILITY	MARKETABLE	BELLWETHER
MENINGITIS	PEDIATRICS	SAXICOLINE	VISITATION	MASKANONGE	BIOLOGICAL
MESITYLENE	PEDICULATE	SAXICOLOUS	VIVIPAROUS	MASKINONGE	BOLLANDIST
METICULOUS	PEDIMENTAL	SCHIPPERKE	VOCIFERATE	MASKIROVKA	BRILLIANCE
MILITARISM	PEDIPALPUS	SCHISMATIC	VOCIFEROUS	MUCKRAKING	BULLHEADED
MILITARIST	PENICILLIN	SCRIBBLING	WAPINSCHAW	MUSKETEERS	BURLINGTON
MILITIAMAN	PENINSULAR	SCRIMSHANK	CONJECTURE	PARKLEAVES	BYELECTION
MINIMALISM	PERIDOTITE	SCRIPTURAL	DARJEELING	PICKPOCKET	CALLIATURE
MINIMALIST	PERIEGESIS	SCRIPTURES	DISJOINTED	POCKETBOOK	CELLOPHANE
MINIMARKET	PERIHELION	SEMICIRCLE	PANJANDRUM	POCKMANTIE	CELLULITIS
MINISTRATE	PERILOUSLY	SEMIQUAVER	PREJUDICED	POCKMARKED	CHALCEDONY
MINISTROKE	PERIODICAL	SHRIEVALTY	PROJECTILE	POIKILITIC	CHALLENGED
MITIGATING	PERIPHERAL	SHRILLNESS	PROJECTING	PUCKERWOOD	CHALLENGER
MITIGATION	PERISHABLE	SHRIVELLED	PROJECTION	RECKLESSLY	CHALYBEATE
MODIFIABLE	PERIWINKLE	SICILIENNE	SUBJECTION	ROCKABILLY	CHELTENHAM
MONILIASIS	PETITIONER	SIGILLARIA	SUBJECTIVE	ROCKINGHAM	CHILDBIRTH
MONILIFORM	POLIANTHES	SIMILARITY	TRAJECTORY	ROCKSTEADY	CHILDERMAS
MORIGEROUS	POLITENESS	SIMILITUDE	BACKBITING	SHAKUHACHI	CHILDISHLY
MORISONIAN	POLITICIAN	SIMILLIMUM	BACKBLOCKS	SMOKESTACK	CHILLINESS
MOTIONLESS	POLITICIZE	SKRIMSHANK	BACKGAMMON	SNAKEMOUTH	CHOLALOGUE
MOTIVATION	POSITIVELY	SLUICEGATE	BACKGROUND	SNAKESTONE	CISLEITHAN
MULIEBRITY	POSITIVIST	SOLICITOUS	BACKHANDED	SPOKESHAVE	COELACANTH
MUNIFICENT	PUNICACEAE	SOLICITUDE	BACKHANDER	TASKMASTER	COLLAPSING
MUSICOLOGY	PUNISHABLE	SOLIDARITY	BACKPACKER	TICKERTAPE	COLLARBONE
MUTILATION	PUNISHMENT	SOLIFIDIAN	BACKSLIDER	TINKERBELL	COLLATERAL
MUTINOUSLY	PURITANISM	SOLIVAGANT	BACKSTAIRS	TREKSCHUIT	COLLECTING
MYRINGITIS	PYRIDOXINE	SPLITLEVEL	BACKSTROKE	WICKEDNESS	COLLECTION
MYRIOSCOPE	QUAINTNESS	SPOILSPORT	BANKRUPTCY	WICKERWORK	COLLECTIVE
NATIONALLY	RADICALISM	SPRINGBOKS	BASKETBALL	WORKAHOLIC	COLLEGIATE
NATIONWIDE	RADIOGRAPH	SPRINGHAAS	BASKETWORK	ACCLIVIOUS	COLLEMBOLA
NAVIGATION	RADIOLARIA	SPRINGLESS	BEEKEEPING	ACOLOUTHOS	COLLIMATOR
NIHILISTIC	RATIONALLY	SPRINGLIKE	BIRKENHEAD	ADELANTADO	COLLIQUATE
NOMINALIST	RAWINSONDE	SPRINGTAIL	BOOKBINDER	ADOLESCENT	COLLOCUTER
NOMINATION	RECIDIVISM	SPRINGTIME	BOOKKEEPER	ADULLAMITE	COLLOQUIAL
NOMINATIVE	RECIDIVIST	SPRINKLING	BOOKMARKER	ADULTERANT	CYCLOPEDIA
NOTICEABLE	RECIPROCAL	SQUIREARCH	BOOKMOBILE	ADULTERATE	CYCLOSTYLE
NOTICEABLY	RECITATION	STRICTNESS	BOOKSELLER	ADULTERESS	DEALERSHIP
NOTIFIABLE	RECITATIVE	STRIDENTLY	BROKENDOWN	ADULTERINE	DECLENSION
NOTIONALLY	RECITATIVO	STRIDEWAYS	BUCKINGHAM	ADULTEROUS	DEFLAGRATE
NUDIBRANCH	REDISCOVER	STRIDULATE	BUCKJUMPER	AFFLICTION	DEFLECTION
NUMISMATIC	REFINEMENT	STRIKINGLY	COCKABILLY	AMALGAMATE	DEPLORABLE
OBLIGATION	REGIMENTAL	STRINDBERG	COCKALORUM	AMBLYOPSIS	DEPLORABLY
OBLIGATORY	REGIMENTED	STRINGENCY	COCKATRICE	AMBLYSTOMA	DEPLOYMENT
OBLIGINGLY	REGISTERED	STRINGENDO	COCKCHAFER	AMELIORATE	DIALECTICS
OBLITERATE	RELINQUISH	STRINGHALT	COCKERNONY	AMPLEFORTH	DIELECTRIC

DIPLODOCUS	MILLIFARAD	STALAGMITE	YELLOWROOT	EPIMETHEUS	SCAMMOZZIS
DIPLOMATIC	MILLIHENRY	STALHELMER	YELLOWWOOD	ERYMANTHUS	SCOMBRESOX
DISLOYALTY	MILLIMETER	STALLENGER	ZOLLVEREIN	EXEMPTNESS	SEAMANSHIP
DUPLICATOR	MILLIMETRE	STALLINGER	ZOOLOGICAL	FLAMBOYANT	SEAMSTRESS
EBULLIENCE	MISLEADING	STILLBIRTH	ABOMINABLE	FLAMEPROOF	SEEMLIHEAD
ECOLOGICAL	MOULDINESS	STILLICIDE	ABOMINABLY	FLAMINGANT	SERMONICAL
EDULCORATE	MOULDIWARP	STILLIFORM	ADAMANTINE	FLIMSINESS	SHAMEFACED
EFFLEURAGE	MULLIGRUBS	STILLSTAND	ALEMBICATE	FORMIDABLE	SHAMEFULLY
EMALANGENI	MYELINATED	STULTIFIED	ALIMENTARY	FRAMBOESIA	SHAMPOOING
EMBLEMATIC	NEGLECTFUL	STYLISTICS	ANEMOGRAPH	FREMESCENT	SHIMMERING
EMBLEMENTS	NEGLIGENCE	STYLOPISED	ANEMOMETER	FROMANTEEL	SIMMENTHAL
EMOLUMENTS	NEGLIGIBLE	SUBLIMATER	ANIMADVERT	GERMICIDAL	SLAMMERKIN
EMPLASTRUM	NOBLEWOMAN	SUBLIMINAL	APEMANTHUS	GLAMOURISE	SLUMBERING
EMPLOYMENT	NUCLEONICS	SWALLOWING	ARIMASPIAN	GORMANDIZE	STAMMERING
EMULSIFIER	OCHLOCRACY	SWELTERING	ARSMETRICK	GRAMICIDIN	STEMWINDER
ENCLOISTER	ODELSTHING	TABLANETTE	ASYMMETRIC	GRAMMARIAN	STOMATOPOD
ENGLISHMAN	OFFLICENCE	TABLECLOTH	BARMECIDAL	GRAMOPHONE	STUMBLEDOM
ENGLISHMEN	OPALESCENT	TABLESPOON	BARMITZVAH	GRUMPINESS	SUBMARINER
EPILIMNION	OUTLANDISH	TAGLIARINI	BERMOOTHES	HAEMANTHUS	SUBMEDIANT
EVALUATION	PALLBEARER	TAILGATING	BIRMINGHAM	HAMMERHEAD	SUBMERSION
EXALTATION	PALLIATIVE	TAILORMADE	CARMAGNOLE	HAMMERLOCK	SUBMISSION
EXPLICABLE	PARLIAMENT	TALLEYRAND	CHAMAELEON	HARMANBECK	SUBMISSIVE
EXPLICITLY	PEELGARLIC	THALASSIAN	CHAMAEROPS	HARMONIOUS	SUMMERTIME
EXULTATION	PHILATELIC	THALESTRIS	CHAMBERPOT	INIMITABLE	SWIMMINGLY
FALLACIOUS	PHILIPPINA	THALICTRUM	CHAMBERTIN	ISOMETRICS	TERMINABLE
FALLINGOFF	PHILIPPINE	THALLIFORM	CHAMBRANLE	KARMATHIAN	TERMINALIA
FAULTINESS	PHILISTINE	THELLUSSON	CHAMPIGNON	KILMARNOCK	TERMINALLY
FELLOWSHIP	PHILLIPINA	TILLANDSIA	CHEMICALLY	KUOMINTANG	THEMSELVES
FIELDMOUSE	PHILLIPINE	TOILETRIES	CHEMONASTY	LEAMINGTON	THIMBLEFUL
FILLIBRUSH	PHILLUMENY	TOILINETTE	CHIMBORAZO	MALMESBURY	THIMBLEWIT
FROLICSOME	PHILOPOENA	TOLLKEEPER	CHIMNEYPOT	MISMATCHED	THUMBIKINS
FULLLENGTH	PHILOSOPHY	TRILATERAL	CHIMPANZEE	NORMOBLAST	THUMBSCREW
FULLYGROWN	PHILOXENIA	TRILINGUAL	CLAMMINESS	ONOMASTICS	TRAMONTANA
GALLABIYAH	PHOLIDOSIS	TRILLIONTH	CLAMOURING	OXYMORONIC	TRAMONTANE
GALLABIYEH	PHYLACTERY	UNBLEACHED	CLEMENCEAU	OZYMANDIAS	TRAMPOLINE
GALLIAMBIC	PHYLLIOPOD	UNBLINKING	CLEMENTINE	PALMATIFID	TREMENDOUS
GARLANDAGE	PILLIWINKS	UNBLUSHING	CLOMIPHENE	PALMATOZOA	TRIMALCHIO
GAULTHERIA	PILLOWCASE	UNFLAGGING	CLUMPERTON	PALMERSTON	TRIMSNITCH
GEOLOGICAL	PILLOWSLIP	UNFLAVORED	CLUMSINESS	PALMERWORM	TROMBONIST
GILLRAVAGE	POLLINATED	UNILATERAL	COMMANDANT	PARMACITIE	TROMOMETER
GIRLFRIEND	PORLOCKING	UNPLEASANT	COMMANDEER	PARMIGIANA	UNEMPLOYED
GOALKEEPER	PRELECTION	UNSLEEPING	COMMANDING	PERMAFROST	UNIMPAIRED
GUILLOTINE	PSALTERIUM	UTILIZABLE	COMMENTARY	PERMANENCE	VERMICELLI
HALLELUJAH	PSILOCYBIN	VALLADOLID	COMMENTATE	PERMANENCY	VERMILLION
HALLMARKED	PUBLISHING	VILLAINOUS	COMMERCIAL	PERMEATION	WEIMARANER
HALLOYSITE	RAILWAYMAN	VILLANELLE	COMMISSARY	PERMISSION	ABONNEMENT
HALLUBALOO	REELECTION	VILLANOVAN	COMMISSION	PERMISSIVE	ABUNDANTLY
HELLBENDER	REFLECTING	VILLEINAGE	COMMISSURE	PLUMASSIER	ACANACEOUS
HELLESPONT	REFLECTION	VOLLEYBALL	COMMITMENT	PREMARITAL	AGONISTICS
HOWLEGLASS	REFLECTIVE	WALLACHIAN	COMMIXTURE	PREMEDICAL	AMANUENSIS
HULLABALOO	ROLLICKING	WALLFLOWER	COMMODIOUS	PRIMORDIAL	ARENACEOUS
HYALOPHANE	ROWLANDSON	WELLEARNED	COMMONALTY	PROMENADER	ARUNDELIAN
IMPLACABLE	SALLENDERS	WELLINGTON	COMMONWEAL	PROMETHEAN	ASYNARTETE
IMPLACABLY	SCHLIMAZEL	WELLSPRING	COMMUNALLY	PROMETHEUS	AVANTGARDE
IMPLICITLY	SCULPTRESS	WHILLYWHAW	COMMUNIQUÉ	PROMETHIUM	AVANTURINE
INELIGIBLE	SELLINGERS	WHOLESALER	COMMUTABLE	PROMINENCE	AVENTURINE
INFLATABLE	SHELDONIAN	WHOLEWHEAT	CRIMINALLY	PROMISSORY	AXINOMANCY
INFLECTION	SHELLSHOCK	WILLIAMSON	CUMMERBUND	PROMONTORY	BALNEATION
INFLEXIBLE	SHELLYCOAT	WILLINGDON	CURMUDGEON	PROMPTBOOK	BALNEOLOGY
INFLEXIBLY	SHILLELAGH	WILLOWHERB	CURMURRING	PROMPTNESS	BERNARDINE
INFLICTION	SKILLFULLY	WILLYWILLY	DERMATITIS	PROMULGATE	BIANNUALLY
INGLORIOUS	SMALLSCALE	WOOLLYBACK	DISMANTLED	PSAMMOPHIL	BIENNIALLY
ISOLEUCINE	SPALLATION	WOOLLYBUTT	DISMISSIVE	PUMMELLING	BLANCMANGE
MALLOPHAGA	SPELEOLOGY	WORLDCLASS	DRUMBLEDOR	REAMINGBIT	BLANQUETTE
MELLOWNESS	SPELLBOUND	WYCLIFFIAN	DUUMVIRATE	RHAMPASTOS	BLUNDERING
MIDLOTHIAN	SPILLIKINS	YELLOWBACK	ECUMENICAL	SALMAGUNDI	BONNETHEAD
MILLEFIORI	SPOLIATION	YELLOWGIRL	ELEMENTARY	SALMANAZAR	BOONDOGGLE
MILLENNIUM	SPOLIATIVE	YELLOWJACK	ELIMINATOR	SALMONELLA	BRONCHITIC
MILLICURIE	STALACTITE	YELLOWLEGS	EPIMENIDES	SARMENTOUS	BRONCHITIS

CANNELLONI	FRANCHISEE	PARNASSIAN	STENTORIAN	ACROMEGALY	COLONNADED
CANNONBALL	FRANCHISOR	PARNELLISM	STINGINESS	ACRONYCHAL	COLORATION
CAPNOMANCY	FRANCISCAN	PAWNBROKER	STINGYBARK	ACROTERION	COLORATURA
CARNASSIAL	FRANGIPANE	PENNILLION	STONEBRASH	ADMONITION	COLOSSALLY
CHANCELLOR	FRANGIPANI	PENNISETUM	STONEHENGE	AEROBATICS	COLOSSIANS
CHANDELIER	FRENETICAL	PERNICIOUS	STONEMASON	AEROPHAGIA	COLOURLESS
CHANGEABLE	FRENZIEDLY	PERNICKETY	STONYHURST	AFFORDABLE	COROMANDEL
CHANGELESS	FRINGILLID	PHANTASIME	TANNHAUSER	AFRORMOSIA	CORONATION
CHANGELING	FRONTCOURT	PHANTASIST	TEENYWEENY	AGRONOMIST	CREOPHAGUS
CHINABERRY	FRONTWARDS	PHENOMENAL	TEINOSCOPE	ALCOHOLISM	CRYOGENICS
CHINAGRAPH	FURNISHING	PHENOMENON	TENNANTITE	ALGOLAGNIA	CRYOPHORUS
CHINASTONE	GAINGIVING	PHONOGRAPH	TERNEPLATE	ALGONQUIAN	CYNOMOLGUS
CHINCHILLA	GAINSTRIVE	PIANISSIMO	THANKFULLY	ALLOCATION	DEBOUCHURE
CHINQUAPIN	GARNIERITE	PIANOFORTE	THINGUMBOB	ALLOCUTION	DECOLLATOR
CLANSWOMAN	GLENDOVEER	PINNIPEDIA	THUNDERBOX	ALLOSAURUS	DECOLORATE
CLINGSTONE	GRANADILLA	PIONEERING	THUNDERING	ALLOSTERIC	DECOLORIZE
CLINICALLY	GRANDCHILD	PLANCHETTE	THUNDEROUS	ALLOTROPIC	DECOMPOSED
COGNISANCE	GRANDDADDY	PLANOBLAST	TOWNSWOMAN	ALTOGETHER	DECORATION
COGNIZANCE	GRANDSTAND	PLANTATION	TRANQUILLY	AMBOCEPTOR	DECORATIVE
COINCIDENT	GRANGERISM	PLUNDERING	TRANSCRIBE	ANNOTATION	DEMOBILISE
CONNECTING	GRANGERIZE	POINSETTIA	TRANSCRIPT	APPOSITION	DEMOBILIZE
CONNECTION	GRANULATED	POINTBLANK	TRANSGRESS	AREOGRAPHY	DEMOCRATIC
CONNECTIVE	GRENADIERS	PORNOCRACY	TRANSIENCE	AREOPAGITE	DEMOCRITUS
CONNIPTION	GRENADILLA	PRINCIPIUM	TRANSISTOR	ARGOLEMONO	DEMODULATE
CONNIVANCE	GRINDSTONE	PRINCIPLED	TRANSITION	ARROGANTLY	DEMOGORGON
CORNCOCKLE	GYMNASTICS	PRINCIPLES	TRANSITIVE	ARTOCARPUS	DEMOGRAPHY
CORNFLAKES	GYMNOSOPHY	PRONOUNCED	TRANSITORY	ASCOMYCETE	DEMOISELLE
CORNFLOWER	GYMNOSPERM	PUGNACIOUS	TRANSLATED	ASSOCIATED	DEMOLITION
CORNSTALKS	HORNBLENDE	PYCNOGONID	TRANSLATOR	ASSORTMENT	DEMONIACAL
CORNSTARCH	HORNBLOWER	QUENCHLESS	TRANSPLANT	ASTOMATOUS	DEMONOLOGY
CORNUCOPIA	HORNRIMMED	RANNELTREE	TRANSPOSED	ASTONISHED	DEMORALISE
COUNCILLOR	HYPNOTIZED	RANNLETREE	TRANSPOSON	ASTOUNDING	DEMORALIZE
COUNSELING	ICONOCLAST	RHINEGRAVE	TRANSVERSE	ATMOSPHERE	DENOUEMENT
COUNSELLOR	ICONOSCOPE	RHINESTONE	TRENCHMORE	AUTOCHTHON	DEPOPULATE
COUNTERACT	INUNDATION	RHINOCEROS	TRENDINESS	AUTOCRATIC	DEPORTMENT
COUNTRYMAN	IRONICALLY	RHINOLALIA	TRINACRIAN	AUTODIDACT	DEPOSITARY
CRANKSHAFT	IRONMONGER	RHINOPHYMA	TURNAROUND	AUTOECIOUS	DEPOSITION
CRENELLATE	ISONIAZIDE	ROUNDABOUT	UNANSWERED	AUTOGENOUS	DEPOSITORY
CTENOPHORA	JAUNTINESS	ROUNDHOUSE	UNENVIABLE	AUTOMATION	DEROGATORY
CTENOPHORE	JOHNSONIAN	SANNAYASIN	UNINFORMED	AUTOMATIZE	DESOLATION
DINNERTIME	KIDNAPPING	SCANDALISE	UNINSPIRED	AUTOMOBILE	DETONATION
DONNYBROOK	KLANGFARBE	SCANDALIZE	UNINVITING	AUTOMOTIVE	DEVOLUTION
DOWNMARKET	LAUNCEGAYE	SCANDALOUS	UNUNHEXIUM	AUTONOMOUS	DEVOTEMENT
DOWNSIZING	LAUNCESTON	SCANDAROON	UNUNNILIUM	AUTOPLASTY	DEVOTIONAL
DOWNSTAIRS	LAUNDROMAT	SCANDERBEG	VARNISHING	AUTOSTRADA	DISORDERED
DOWNSTREAM	LEMNISCATE	SCANTINESS	VERNACULAR	AVVOGADORE	DISORDERLY
DRINKWATER	LEONTIASIS	SCINTIGRAM	VERNISSAGE	BAROMETRIC	ECCOPROTIC
ECONOMICAL	LIGNOCAINE	SEANNACHIE	VULNERABLE	BEFOREHAND	ECHOPRAXIA
ELONGATION	MAGNIFICAT	SGANARELLE	WAINSCOTED	BELONGINGS	EFFORTLESS
EMANCIPATE	MAGNIFYING	SHANDRYDAN	WRONGDOING	BIJOUTERIE	EMBODIMENT
EMENDATION	MAINPERNOR	SHANDYGAFF	WRONGFULLY	BINOCULARS	EMBONPOINT
ENANTIOSIS	MAINSPRING	SHENANIGAN	YOUNGBERRY	BLOODHOUND	EMBOUCHURE
EPANOPHORA	MAINSTREAM	SIGNIFICAT	ZOANTHARIA	BLOODSTAIN	ENCOIGNURE
EPENTHETIC	MAINTAINER	SIGNORELLI	ABHORRENCE	BLOODSTOCK	ENDOGAMOUS
EPONYCHIUM	MEANDERING	SKINDIVING	ABNORMALLY	BLOODSTONE	ENDOGENOUS
EVANESCENT	MEANINGFUL	SLANDEROUS	ABROGATION	BLOOMSBURY	ENDOSMOSIS
EVANGELIST	MIGNONETTE	SOMNOLENCE	ABSOLUTELY	BROOMSTICK	ENGOUEMENT
EVANGELIZE	MOUNTEBANK	SOUNDPROOF	ABSOLUTION	CACODAEMON	ENROLLMENT
EVENHANDED	ODONTALGIA	SOUNDTRACK	ABSOLUTISM	CACOGRAPHY	ENTOMBMENT
EVENTUALLY	ODONTOLITE	SPENCERIAN	ABSORBANCE	CACOMISTLE	ENTOMOLOGY
EXENTERATE	ODONTOLOGY	SPENSERIAN	ABSORPTION	CALORIFIER	EPROUVETTE
EXONERATED	OPENHANDED	SPINESCENT	ACCOMPLICE	CAMOUFLAGE	ERGONOMICS
FERNITICLE	OPENMINDED	SPONGEWARE	ACCOMPLISH	CAPODASTRO	ERIOCAULON
FIANCHETTO	ORANGEWOOD	SPONGIFORM	ACCORDANCE	CHLORINATE	ETEOCRETAN
FIENDISHLY	OUANANICHE	SPONSIONAL	ACCOUNTANT	CHLOROFORM	EULOGISTIC
FLANCONADE	PAINKILLER	STANDPOINT	ACCOUNTING	CHROMOSOME	EUROCHEQUE
FLINDERSIA	PAINLESSLY	STANDSTILL	ACROAMATIC	CHRONICLER	EUROCLYDON
FLUNKEYDOM	PAINTBRUSH	STANISLAUS	ACROBATICS	CHRONICLES	EXPOSITION
FOUNDATION	PANNICULUS	STENOTYPER	ACROGENOUS	CHRONOLOGY	EXPOSITORY

557

EXPOUNDERS	INSOLVENCY	PHLOGOPITE	THROMBOSIS	COMPLANATE	INEPTITUDE
FAVORITISM	INSOUCIANT	PLEONASTIC	THROUGHOUT	COMPLEMENT	INOPERABLE
FAVOURABLE	INTOLERANT	PLIOHIPPUS	THROUGHPUT	COMPLETELY	INSPECTION
FAVOURABLY	INTONATION	POGONOTOMY	THROUGHWAY	COMPLETION	INSPISSATE
FLOODLIGHT	INTOXICANT	PYROGRAPHY	TIROCINIUM	COMPLEXION	JEOPARDISE
FLOORBOARD	INTOXICATE	PYROMANIAC	TOCOPHEROL	COMPLEXITY	JEOPARDIZE
FLOORCLOTH	INVOCATION	PYROPHORUS	TOPOGRAPHY	COMPLIANCE	KEMPERYMAN
GADOLINIUM	INVOLUTION	RECOGNISED	TOPOLOGIST	COMPLICATE	LEOPARDESS
GONORRHOEA	IONOSPHERE	RECOGNIZED	TYPOGRAPHY	COMPLICITY	LUMPECTOMY
GYROSCOPIC	KILOMETRES	RECOMMENCE	UNCOMMONLY	COMPLIMENT	LUMPSUCKER
HANOVERIAN	KLOOTCHMAN	RECOMPENSE	UNCONFINED	COMPLUVIUM	MAUPASSANT
HEDONISTIC	LABORATORY	RECONCILED	UNDOCTORED	COMPOSITOR	MISPRISION
HEMOGLOBIN	LAEOTROPIC	RECONSIDER	UNFORESEEN	COMPOUNDED	MORPHOLOGY
HEMOPHILIA	LENOCINIUM	REJONEADOR	UNROMANTIC	COMPRADORE	NEAPOLITAN
HEMORRHAGE	LOCOMOTION	RELOCATION	UNSOCIABLE	COMPREHEND	NONPAYMENT
HEROICALLY	LOCOMOTIVE	REMONETISE	UNWORKABLE	COMPRESSED	NONPLUSSED
HITOPADESA	LOGORRHOEA	REMORSEFUL	UPHOLSTERY	COMPRESSOR	NYMPHOLEPT
HITOPODESA	LOTOPHAGUS	REMOTENESS	UPROARIOUS	COMPROMISE	OFFPUTTING
HOLOFERNES	MACONOCHIE	RENOVATION	VELOCIPEDE	COMPULSION	OMOPHORION
HOLOGRAPHY	MAHOMMEDAN	REPORTEDLY	VIGOROUSLY	COMPULSIVE	OUTPATIENT
HOLOHEDRAL	MALODOROUS	REPOSITORY	VIROLOGIST	COMPULSORY	OUTPERFORM
HOLOPHOTAL	MAVOURNEEN	RESOLUTELY	XENOPHOBIA	COPPERHEAD	OUTPOURING
HOLOPHYTIC	MAYONNAISE	RESOLUTION	XENOPHOBIC	COPPERNOSE	OVIPOSITOR
HOLOSTERIC	MELOCOTOON	RESORCINOL	XEROPHYTIC	COPPERSKIN	PEPPERCORN
HOMOEOPATH	MEMORANDUM	RESOUNDING	XEROSTOMIA	CORPULENCE	PEPPERMILL
HOMOGENIZE	MENORRHOEA	REVOCATION	ZAPOROGIAN	CRAPULENCE	PEPPERMINT
HOMOOUSIAN	MESOLITHIC	REVOLUTION	ZIDOVUDINE	CRYPTOGRAM	PEPPERWORT
HOMOPHOBIA	MISOCAPNIC	RHEOTROPIC	ZYGODACTYL	CRYPTOZOIC	PERPETRATE
HOMOPHOBIC	MISOGYNIST	RIBOFLAVIN	ACEPHALOUS	DEEPFREEZE	PERPETUATE
HOMOPHONIC	MONOACIDIC	RIGOROUSLY	ADAPTATION	DEEPSEATED	PERPETUITY
HOMORELAPS	MONOCARPIC	RITORNELLE	AGAPANTHUS	DELPHINIUM	PERPLEXING
HOMOSEXUAL	MONOCHROME	RITORNELLO	ALLPURPOSE	DESPAIRING	PERPLEXITY
HONORARIUM	MONOECIOUS	RUDOLPHINE	APOPEMPTIC	DESPICABLE	PLUPERFECT
HONOURABLE	MONOGAMOUS	SALOPETTES	APOPHTHEGM	DESPITEOUS	PREPARATOR
HONOURABLY	MONOLITHIC	SAMOTHRACE	APOPLECTIC	DESPONDENT	PREPAYMENT
HONOURLESS	MONOPHONIC	SAVONAROLA	AUSPICIOUS	DIAPEDESIS	PREPENSELY
HUMORESQUE	MONOPLEGIA	SCHOLAEMIA	BIOPHYSICS	DIAPHANOUS	PREPOSITOR
HUMOROUSLY	MONOPODIUM	SCHOLASTIC	BLEPHARISM	DIOPHANTOS	PREPOSSESS
HUMOURLESS	MONOPOLISE	SCHOOLBOOK	CAMPAIGNER	DISPENSARY	PREPOTENCE
HYPOCORISM	MONOPOLIZE	SCHOOLGIRL	CAMPANELLA	DISPENSING	PROPAGANDA
HYPODERMIC	MONOPTERON	SCHOOLMAAM	CAMPARADOR	DISPERSION	PROPAGATOR
HYPOGAEOUS	MONOPTEROS	SCOOTERIST	CAMPERDOWN	DISPIRITED	PROPELLANT
HYPOGENOUS	MONOTHEISM	SCROUNGING	CAMPESTRAL	DISPOSABLE	PROPELLENT
HYPOTENUSE	MONOTONOUS	SECONDBEST	CAPPUCCINO	DISPOSSESS	PROPENSITY
HYPOTHESIS	MONOVALENT	SECONDHAND	CARPATHIAN	DISPUTABLE	PROPERTIUS
IGNORANTLY	MOROSENESS	SECONDMENT	CARPENTIER	DOPPLERITE	PROPHETESS
IMMOBILITY	MOTORCYCLE	SECONDRATE	CARPHOLOGY	DYSPROSIUM	PROPIONATE
IMMOBILIZE	MYCORRHIZA	SEXOLOGIST	CHAPARAJOS	EPIPHONEMA	PROPITIATE
IMMODERATE	NEGOTIABLE	SHROVETIDE	CHAPAREJOS	EPIPLASTRA	PROPITIOUS
IMMOLATION	NEGOTIATOR	SINOATRIAL	CHAPFALLEN	EVAPORATED	PROPLITEAL
IMMORALITY	NOMOTHETIC	SMOOTHNESS	CHAPLAINCY	FLAPDOODLE	PROPORTION
IMMORTELLE	NONONSENSE	SNOOTINESS	CHAPTALISE	FLIPPANTLY	PROPOSITUS
IMPOLITELY	NOSOCOMIAL	SPOONERISM	CHOPSTICKS	GEOPHYSICS	PROPRAETOR
IMPORTANCE	NOSOPHOBIA	STROGANOFF	CISPONTINE	GODPARENTS	PROPRIETOR
IMPOSITION	NOTORYCTES	STRONGHOLD	COLPORTAGE	GRAPEFRUIT	PROPULSION
IMPOSSIBLE	OBLOMOVISM	STRONGROOM	COLPORTEUR	GRAPHOLOGY	PROPYLAEUM
IMPOSSIBLY	OCTODECIMO	STROPHIOLE	COLPOSCOPE	GRAPTOLITE	PSEPHOLOGY
IMPOSTHUME	ODIOUSNESS	SUBORBITAL	COMPARABLE	HELPLESSLY	PUMPHANDLE
IMPOTENTLY	OESOPHAGUS	SYNONYMOUS	COMPARATOR	HESPERIDES	PURPOSEFUL
IMPOVERISH	OPPOSITION	SYNOSTOSIS	COMPARISON	HIPPARCHUS	RAJPRAMUKH
INCOHERENT	ORDONNANCE	TAPOTEMENT	COMPASSION	HIPPOCRENE	RAMPALLIAN
INCOMPLETE	ORDOVICIAN	TAXONOMIST	COMPATIBLE	HIPPODROME	RAPPORTEUR
INCONSTANT	PANOPTICON	TCHOUKBALL	COMPATRIOT	HIPPOGRIFF	REAPPRAISE
INDONESIAN	PARONYCHIA	THEOCRITUS	COMPELLING	HIPPOGRYPH	RESPECTFUL
INFORMALLY	PEJORATIVE	THEODOLITE	COMPENDIUM	HIPPOMANES	RESPECTING
INNOCENTLY	PERORATION	THEOLOGATE	COMPENSATE	HOSPITABLE	RESPECTIVE
INNOVATION	PEROVSKITE	THEOLOGIAN	COMPETENCE	HOSPITABLY	RESPIRATOR
INNOVATIVE	PHLOGISTIC	THEOLOGISE	COMPETITOR	HUMPBACKED	RESPONDENT
INSOLENTLY	PHLOGISTON	THEOLOGIST	COMPLACENT	INAPTITUDE	RESPONSIVE

RHAPSODISE	TROPOPHYTE	BATRACHIAN	DISRUPTIVE	HORRIFYING	NECROPOLIS
RHAPSODIST	TRYPTOPHAN	BEARGARDEN	DIURNALIST	HYDRAULICS	NEURILEMMA
RHAPSODIZE	TURPENTINE	BEDRAGGLED	DOORKEEPER	HYDROLYSIS	NEUROLEMMA
RHIPIPTERA	TYMPANITES	BIORHYTHMS	DOORTODOOR	HYDROMETER	NICROSILAL
SALPINGIAN	TYMPANITIS	BORROWINGS	ECARDINATE	HYDROPHANE	NIGRESCENT
SAPPERMENT	UNSPECIFIC	BOURIGNIAN	EFFRONTERY	HYDROPHYTE	NOURISHING
SCAPEGRACE	UROPOIESIS	CAERPHILLY	EGURGITATE	HYDROPLANE	NOURRITURE
SCAPHOPODA	WAMPUMPEAG	CAPREOLATE	EMARGINATE	HYDROPONIC	NUTRITIOUS
SCEPTICISM	WAPPENSHAW	CAPRICIOUS	EMBROIDERY	HYGROMETER	OLERACEOUS
SCOPELIDAE	WEAPONLESS	CARRAGHEEN	EMBRYOLOGY	IATROGENIC	OMBROMETER
SERPENTINE	WRAPAROUND	CHARDONNAY	ENGROSSING	IMBRICATED	OMBROPHOBE
SHIPWRIGHT	ADEQUATELY	CHARGEABLE	ENORMOUSLY	IMBROCCATA	OPPRESSION
SHOPKEEPER	CHEQUEBOOK	CHARGEHAND	ENTRANCING	IMPREGNATE	OPPRESSIVE
SHOPLIFTER	CINQUEFOIL	CHARIOTEER	ENTREATING	IMPRESARIO	OPPROBRIUM
SHOPSOILED	CONQUERING	CHARITABLE	ENTREMESSE	IMPRESSION	OSTROGOTHS
SHOPWALKER	CRAQUETURE	CHARITABLY	ENTRENCHED	IMPRESSIVE	OUTRAGEOUS
SIMPLICITY	DESQUAMATE	CHAROLLAIS	ENTRYPHONE	IMPRIMATUR	OVERBOUGHT
SIMPLISTIC	DISQUALIFY	CHARTREUSE	EPHRAIMITE	IMPROBABLE	OVERCHARGE
SKEPTICISM	DISQUIETED	CHERIMOYER	ESCRITOIRE	IMPROBABLY	OVEREATING
SKUPSHTINA	ELOQUENTLY	CHERRYWOOD	ESTRAMACON	IMPROPERLY	OVERLANDER
SLIPSTREAM	FREQUENTED	CHERSONESE	ETERNALIZE	IMPROVISED	OVERMATTER
SLOPPINESS	FREQUENTER	CHERVONETS	EUTRAPELIA	IMPRUDENCE	OVERPRAISE
SNAPDRAGON	FREQUENTLY	CHIRICAUNE	EVERGLADES	INARTISTIC	OVERRIDING
SNAPHAUNCE	INEQUALITY	CHIROMANCY	EVERYPLACE	INBREEDING	OVERSHADOW
SNAPHAUNCH	INIQUITOUS	CHIRONOMIC	EVERYTHING	INCRASSATE	OVERSLAUGH
STAPHYLINE	MARQUETRIE	CHIROPTERA	EVERYWHERE	INCREASING	OVERSPREAD
STEPFATHER	MASQUERADE	CHURCHGOER	EXCRUCIATE	INCREDIBLE	OVERSTRAIN
STEPHANITE	PASQUINADE	CHURCHYARD	EXORBITANT	INCREDIBLY	OVERSTRUNG
STEPHENSON	PERQUISITE	CHURLISHLY	EXPRESSION	INCRESCENT	OVERSUPPLY
STEPLADDER	TORQUEMADA	CIRRHOPODA	EXPRESSIVE	INFRACTION	OVERTHETOP
STEPMOTHER	UBIQUINONE	CIRRIPEDEA	EXPRESSMAN	INFREQUENT	OVERTHWART
STEPSISTER	UBIQUITOUS	CIRRIPEDIA	EXPRESSWAY	INGRATIATE	OVERWEIGHT
STUPEFYING	UNEQUALLED	CITRONELLA	EXTRACTION	INGREDIENT	OVERWORKED
STUPENDOUS	UNIQUENESS	CLARABELLA	EXTRANEOUS	INORDINATE	PARRAMATTA
SULPHUROUS	ABBREVIATE	CLERESTORY	FAHRENHEIT	INTRAURBAN	PATRIARCHY
SUPPLEJACK	ABERDEVINE	CLEROMANCY	FAIRGROUND	INTRIGUING	PATRIOTISM
SUPPLEMENT	ABERGLAUBE	COARSENESS	FAIRHAIRED	INTROSPECT	PATRONISED
SUPPLENESS	ABERRATION	COORDINATE	FARRANDINE	JERRYBUILT	PATRONYMIC
SUPPLICANT	ABORIGINAL	CORRECTING	FEARLESSLY	JOURNALESE	PETRARCHAN
SUPPLICATE	ACCREDITED	CORRECTION	FEARNOUGHT	JOURNALISM	PETRIFYING
SUPPORTING	ACHROMATIC	CORRECTIVE	FERRANDINE	JOURNALIST	PETRISSAGE
SUPPORTIVE	AGGRANDISE	CORREGIDOR	FIBREGLASS	JOURNEYMAN	PETROGLYPH
SUPPOSEDLY	AGGRESSION	CORRESPOND	FIBRILLATE	LAURDALITE	PETRONELLA
SUPPRESSED	AGGRESSIVE	CORRIGENDA	FIBROSITIS	LAURENTIAN	PHARMACIST
SUPPRESSOR	ALTRUISTIC	CORROBOREE	FIERCENESS	LAURUSTINE	PLEROPHORY
SURPASSING	AMARYLLIDS	CORRUGATED	FLIRTATION	LAURVIKITE	PORRACEOUS
SURPRISING	AMERINDIAN	CORRUGATOR	FLORENTINE	LAWRENCIUM	POURPARLER
SUSPENDERS	ANARCHICAL	CORRUPTING	FLORIBUNDA	LEPRECHAUN	PTERANODON
SUSPENSION	ANDROMACHE	CORRUPTION	FOURCHETTE	LHERZOLITE	PTERYGOTUS
SUSPICIOUS	APPRECIATE	COURAGEOUS	FOURIERISM	LIBRETTIST	PUTREFYING
SYMPATHISE	APPRENTICE	COURTHOUSE	FOURRAGERE	LIBREVILLE	PUTRESCENT
SYMPATHIZE	ASARABACCA	CUIRASSIER	FOURTEENTH	MACROBIOTE	QUARANTINE
SYMPHONIUM	ASCRIBABLE	CURRENCIES	GALRAVITCH	MACROCARPA	QUARRENDER
SYMPTOMIZE	ASTRAGALUS	CURRICULUM	GEORGETOWN	MATRIARCHY	QUARTERING
TAMPERFOOT	ASTRALAGUS	DEBRIEFING	GIARDIASIS	MAURITANIA	QUARTEROON
TARPAULING	ASTRINGENT	DECRESCENT	GLORIOUSLY	MEERSCHAUM	QUERCITRON
TATPURUSHA	ASTROLOGER	DEFRAYMENT	GUARANTEED	MERRYMAKER	QUERSPRUNG
TELPHERAGE	ASTRONOMER	DEGRADABLE	GUARNERIUS	METROPOLIS	QUIRINALIA
TEMPERANCE	ATTRACTION	DEPRECIATE	HAIRSPRING	MICROFICHE	REARMAMENT
TEMPTATION	ATTRACTIVE	DEPRESSANT	HARRINGTON	MICROLIGHT	RECREATION
TORPESCENT	AVARICIOUS	DEPRESSING	HEARTBREAK	MICROMETER	RECRUDESCE
TRIPARTITE	AVERRHOISM	DEPRESSION	HEARTINESS	MICRONESIA	REDRUTHITE
TRIPEHOUND	BAHRAINIAN	DEPRESSIVE	HIERARCHIC	MICROPHONE	REFRACTION
TRIPLICATE	BARRACKING	DETRACTION	HIEROGLYPH	MICROSCOPE	REFRACTIVE
TRIPLICITY	BARRACOOTA	DETRUNCATE	HIEROMANCY	MOURNFULLY	REFRACTORY
TRIPUDIARY	BARRACOUTA	DHARMSHALA	HIEROPHANT	NARROWBOAT	REFRESHING
TROPAEOLUM	BARRAMUNDA	DIGRESSION	HIEROSCOPY	NARROWDALE	REFRINGENT
TROPHONIUS	BARRAMUNDI	DISRESPECT	HOARSENESS	NARROWNESS	REGRESSION
TROPOPAUSE	BARRENNESS	DISRUPTION	HORRENDOUS	NECROMANCY	REGRESSIVE

REORGANIZE	STOREHOUSE	BASSOONIST	CUSSEDNESS	HOUSEMAIDS	PERSUASIVE
REPRESSION	STURDINESS	BELSHAZZAR	DAMSELFISH	HOUSEPROUD	PHOSPHORUS
REPRESSIVE	SUBREPTION	BERSAGLIER	DENSIMETER	HOWSOMEVER	PHYSICALLY
REPRODUCER	SUBROUTINE	BISSEXTILE	DESSIATINE	HYPSOMETRY	PHYSIOCRAT
RETRACTION	SURREALISM	BLASPHEMER	DESSYATINE	ICOSANDRIA	PHYSIOLOGY
RETRAINING	SURREALIST	BLASTOCOEL	DIASKEUAST	ICOSOHEDRA	PIPSISSEWA
RETREATING	SURROUNDED	BLASTOIDEA	DIASTALTIC	INESCULENT	PLASMODESM
RETROGRADE	SWORDSTICK	BLISSFULLY	DIPSOMANIA	INKSLINGER	PLASTICINE
RETROGRESS	TENRECIDAE	BLISTERING	DISSECTION	INOSCULATE	PLASTICITY
RETROSPECT	TERRACOTTA	BOISTEROUS	DISSELBOOM	IRISHWOMAN	PLESIOSAUR
SABRETACHE	TERREPLEIN	BOLSHEVIST	DISSEMBLER	IRISHWOMEN	POSSESSION
SACREDNESS	TERRIFYING	BOUSINGKEN	DISSENSION	JEISTIECOR	POSSESSIVE
SACROSANCT	THEREAFTER	BRASSBOUND	DISSENTING	JOBSEEKERS	PRESBYOPIA
SAPROPHYTE	THEREANENT	BRESSUMMER	DISSERTATE	KENSPECKLE	PRESBYTERY
SAUROPSIDA	THERMIONIC	BYSSINOSIS	DISSERVICE	KERSEYMERE	PRESCIENCE
SCARAMOUCH	THERMISTOR	CAESPITOSE	DISSIDENCE	KESSELRING	PRESENTDAY
SCARCEMENT	THERMOSTAT	CAMSTEERIE	DISSILIENT	KIESELGUHR	PRESIDENCY
SCARCENESS	THIRTEENTH	CASSIABARK	DISSIMILAR	LANSQUENET	PRESSURIZE
SCARLATINA	THOROUGHLY	CASSIOPEIA	DISSIPATED	MAISONETTE	PRESUMABLY
SCARLETINA	TORRENTIAL	CASSOLETTE	DISSOCIATE	MANSERVANT	PRESUPPOSE
SCORDATURA	TORRICELLI	CASSUMUNAR	DISSOLVENT	MARSHALSEA	PROSCENIUM
SCOREBOARD	TOURBILLON	CENSORIOUS	DISSONANCE	MASSASAUGA	PROSCIUTTO
SCORNFULLY	TOURMALINE	CENSORSHIP	DISSUASION	MEASURABLE	PROSCRIBED
SCORZONERA	TOURNAMENT	CHESSBOARD	DRESSMAKER	MENSTRUATE	PROSECUTOR
SCURRILITY	TOURNIQUET	CHESSYLITE	DROSOPHILA	MIDSHIPMAN	PROSERPINA
SCURRILOUS	TURRITELLA	CHESTERTON	ELASTICATE	MISSIONARY	PROSERPINE
SECRETAIRE	UBERMENSCH	CLASPKNIFE	ELASTICITY	MOISTURIZE	PROSILIENT
SEERSUCKER	ULTRABASIC	CLASSICISM	EMASCULATE	MONSTRANCE	PROSPECTOR
SEGREGATED	ULTRAFICHE	CLASSICIST	EMISSIVITY	MOSSBUNKER	PROSPECTUS
SERRADELLA	ULTRAMAFIC	CLASSIFIED	EPISCOPATE	MOUSEPIECE	PROSPERINA
SERRADILLA	ULTRASONIC	CLOSTRIDIA	EPISPASTIC	MOUSSELINE	PROSPERITY
SERRASALMO	ULTRASOUND	COASTGUARD	EPISTEMICS	MOUSTERIAN	PROSPEROUS
SHARAWADGI	ULTRONEOUS	CODSWALLOP	EPISTROPHE	MUDSKIPPER	PROSTHESIS
SHARAWAGGI	UNARGUABLE	COMSTOCKER	ERYSIPELAS	MUSSORGSKY	PROSTHETIC
SHERARDISE	UNCRITICAL	CONSCIENCE	EVISCERATE	NAUSEATING	PROSTITUTE
SHORTBREAD	UNFRIENDLY	CONSECRATE	EXASPERATE	NAUSEATIVE	PULSATANCE
SHORTENING	UNFRUITFUL	CONSENSION	FALSETRUTH	NESSELRODE	PULSOMETER
SHORTLIVED	UNGRACIOUS	CONSEQUENT	FARSIGHTED	NEWSAGENTS	PURSUIVANT
SHORTRANGE	UNGRATEFUL	CONSIDERED	FLASHINESS	NEWSCASTER	QUESADILLA
SMARAGDINE	UNGROUNDED	CONSISTENT	FLASHPOINT	NEWSLETTER	QUESTIONER
SMARMINESS	UNORIGINAL	CONSISTORY	FLESHINESS	NEWSMONGER	RAMSHACKLE
SMORREBROD	UNORTHODOX	CONSONANCE	FOSSILIZED	NEWSPAPERS	RAWSTHORNE
SNORKELING	UNPREPARED	CONSONANTS	FRESHWATER	NEWSREADER	REASONABLE
SOURDELINE	UNPROMPTED	CONSORTIUM	FRISKINESS	NEWSWORTHY	REASONABLY
SPARSENESS	UNPROVOKED	CONSPECTUS	FRUSTRATED	NONSMOKING	REASSEMBLE
SPARTACIST	UNTRUTHFUL	CONSPIRACY	GALSWORTHY	NONSUCCESS	REASSURING
SPERMACETI	UPBRINGING	CONSTANTAN	GLASSHOUSE	NURSERYMAN	RIJSTTAFEL
SPERMICIDE	USURPATION	CONSTANTIA	GLASSINESS	OPISOMETER	RIPSNORTER
SPERRYLITE	VIBRACULUM	CONSTANTLY	GLASSWORKS	OUTSPECKLE	ROISTERING
SPIRACULUM	VIBRAPHONE	CONSTITUTE	GLISTENING	OWLSPIEGLE	ROUSEABOUT
SPIRITEDLY	VIBRATIONS	CONSTRAINT	GLOSSINESS	PANSOPHIST	ROUSTABOUT
SPIRITLESS	WARRANDICE	CONSTRINGE	GNOSTICISM	PASSAGEWAY	RUSSIANIZE
SPIRITUOUS	WHARFINGER	CONSUETUDE	GOOSEBERRY	PASSAMEZZO	SARSQUATCH
SPIRKETING	WHIRLYBIRD	CONSULTANT	GOOSEFLESH	PASSIONATE	SEASONABLE
SPORANGIUM	YOURSELVES	CONSULTING	GRASSLANDS	PEASHOOTER	SEASONABLY
SPORTINGLY	ABYSSINIAN	CONSUMMATE	GRASSROOTS	PENSIEROSO	SEISMOLOGY
SPORTSWEAR	ALMSGIVING	COUSCOUSOU	GRASSWIDOW	PENSIONNAT	SENSUALITY
SPURIOUSLY	ALMSHOUSES	CRISPBREAD	GUESTHOUSE	PERSECUTOR	SENSUOUSLY
STARVATION	ANASTIGMAT	CRISPINIAN	GYPSOPHILA	PERSEPHONE	SHISHKEBAB
STARVELING	ANASTROPHE	CRISSCROSS	HAMSHACKLE	PERSEPOLIS	SINSEMILLA
STEREOTOMY	ANESTHESIA	CROSSBONES	HAUSTELLUM	PERSICARIA	SKYSCRAPER
STEREOTYPE	ANESTHETIC	CROSSBREED	HAUSTORIUM	PERSIENNES	SOUSAPHONE
STEREOTYPY	APOSEMATIC	CROSSCHECK	HORSEDRAWN	PERSIFLAGE	SPISSITUDE
STERILISER	APOSTROPHE	CROSSHATCH	HORSELBERG	PERSISTENT	SUBSCRIBER
STERILIZER	ARISTIPPUS	CROSSPIECE	HORSEPOWER	PERSONABLE	SUBSECTION
STERNALGIA	ARISTOCRAT	CROSSREFER	HORSERIDER	PERSONALLY	SUBSELLIUM
STERTEROUS	ARISTOLOGY	CROSSROADS	HORSEWOMAN	PERSTRINGE	SUBSEQUENT
STERTOROUS	ARISTOTLES	CRUSTACEAN	HOUSEBOUND	PERSUADING	SUBSIDENCE
STOREFRONT	BASSINGTON	CUISENAIRE	HOUSECRAFT	PERSUASION	SUBSIDIARY

SUBSISTENT	BUTTERBAKE	COSTLINESS	FOOTLIGHTS	LASTMINUTE	PARTICIPLE
SUBSPECIES	BUTTERBUMP	COTTIERISM	FOOTPRINTS	LATTERMATH	PARTICULAR
SUBSTATION	BUTTERFISH	COTTONTAIL	FORTHRIGHT	LATTICINIO	PARTINGALE
SUBSTITUTE	BUTTERMERE	COTTONWOOD	FORTINBRAS	LEFTHANDED	PASTEBOARD
SUBSTRATUM	BUTTERMILK	CRETACEOUS	FORTISSIMO	LEFTHANDER	PASTEURISE
THYSANURAN	BUTTONDOWN	CRITICALLY	FORTUITOUS	LEFTWINGER	PASTEURIZE
TOPSYTURVY	BUTTONHOLE	CROTALARIA	FRATERETTO	LENTICULAR	PASTORELLA
TOSSICATED	CANTABRIAN	CROTALIDAE	FRATERNISE	LENTIGINES	PENTAGONAL
TRESPASSER	CANTALOUPE	CULTIVATED	FRATERNITY	LETTERHEAD	PENTAMERON
TRISKELION	CANTATRICE	CULTIVATOR	FRATERNIZE	LISTLESSLY	PENTAMETER
TRUSTFULLY	CANTERBURY	CUTTLEBONE	FRATICELLI	LITTLENESS	PENTATEUCH
UNASSIGNED	CANTILEVER	CUTTLEFISH	FRATRICIDE	MALTHUSIAN	PENTATHLON
UNASSUMING	CANTILLATE	CYSTOSCOPY	FRITHSOKEN	MARTINGALE	PENTATONIC
UROSTEGITE	CANTONMENT	DELTIOLOGY	FRITILLARY	MARTINIQUE	PENTELIKON
VERSAILLES	CAPTIVATED	DENTIFRICE	FRUTESCENT	MASTECTOMY	PENTETERIC
WASSAILING	CARTHAMINE	DEUTOPLASM	FUSTANELLA	MASTERMIND	PENTIMENTO
WASSERMANS	CARTHUSIAN	DICTIONARY	FUSTANELLE	MASTERWORT	PENTSTEMON
WELSHWOMAN	CARTOMANCY	DICTOGRAPH	GASTEROPOD	MASTURBATE	PERTINENCE
WHISPERING	CARTOONIST	DISTENSION	GASTRONOME	MATTERHORN	PESTALOZZI
WITSNAPPER	CASTRATION	DISTILLATE	GASTRONOMY	MEITNERIUM	PESTILENCE
WORSHIPPER	CATTLEGRID	DISTILLERY	GENTLEFOLK	METTLESOME	PETTICHAPS
WRISTWATCH	CAUTIONARY	DISTILLING	GENTLENESS	MISTAKENLY	PETTYCHAPS
ABITURIENT	CAUTIOUSLY	DISTINCTLY	GEOTHERMAL	MONTAGNARD	PHOTODIODE
ABSTEMIOUS	CENTENNIAL	DISTORTION	GEOTROPISM	MONTESSORI	PHOTOGENIC
ABSTENTION	CENTESIMAL	DISTRACTED	GETTYSBURG	MONTEVERDI	PHOTOGRAPH
ABSTINENCE	CENTIGRADE	DISTRAUGHT	GLITTERAND	MONTEVIDEO	PHOTONASTY
ABSTRACTED	CENTILITER	DISTRESSED	GLITTERATI	MONTGOMERY	PHOTOPHORE
ACETABULAR	CENTILITRE	DISTRIBUTE	GLITTERING	MONTICULUS	PHYTOTOXIN
ACETABULUM	CENTIMETER	DISTRINGAS	GLUTTONOUS	MONTRACHET	PICTOGRAPH
ACOTYLEDON	CENTIMETRE	DISTURBING	GOATSBEARD	MONTSERRAT	PISTILLATE
AESTHETICS	CENTRALIZE	DOSTOEVSKY	GOATSUCKER	MORTADELLA	PLATELAYER
AHITHOPHEL	CENTRIFUGE	DYSTROPHIC	GRATEFULLY	MOUTHORGAN	PLATINISED
AMATEURISH	CENTROSOME	EARTHQUAKE	GRATIFYING	MOUTHPIECE	PLATTELAND
ANATOMICAL	CERTIORARI	EARTHSHINE	GRATILLITY	MULTIMEDIA	PLUTOCRACY
APOTHECARY	CESTRACION	EARTHWORKS	GRATUITOUS	MULTIPLIED	POETASTERY
APOTHECIUM	CHATELAINE	EASTERLING	GRITTINESS	MULTIPLIER	POETICALLY
APOTHEOSIS	CHATTERBOX	EISTEDDFOD	GUATEMALAN	MUTTONHEAD	PONTEDERIA
APOTROPAIC	CHATTERTON	ELYTRIFORM	GUTTIFERAE	MYSTAGOGUE	PONTEFRACT
ARITHMETIC	CHITARRONE	EPITHELIUM	GUTTURALLY	MYSTAGOGUS	PONTICELLO
ARYTAENOID	CHITTAGONG	EUSTACHIAN	HARTEBEEST	MYSTERIOUS	PONTIFICAL
AUCTIONEER	CISTERCIAN	EVITERNITY	HECTICALLY	NAPTHALENE	PORTAMENTO
AUSTRALIAN	COATHANGER	EXOTHERMIC	HECTOLITRE	NASTURTIUM	PORTCULLIS
AUSTRALORP	COETANEOUS	EXOTICALLY	HEPTAGONAL	NATTERJACK	PORTENTOUS
AUSTRINGER	CONTAGIOUS	FACTITIOUS	HEPTAMERON	NECTABANUS	PORTIONIST
BATTAILOUS	CONTENTION	FAITHFULLY	HEPTATEUCH	NEOTERICAL	PORTMANTLE
BATTENBERG	CONTESTANT	FANTASTICO	HEPTATHLON	NETTLERASH	PORTMANTUA
BATTENBURG	CONTEXTUAL	FANTOCCINI	HINTERLAND	NETTLETREE	PORTSMOUTH
BATTLEDOOR	CONTIGUITY	FASTIDIOUS	HISTOLYSIS	NEUTRALISE	PORTUGUESE
BATTLEDORE	CONTIGUOUS	FASTIGIATE	HISTORICAL	NEUTRALITY	POSTCHAISE
BATTLEMENT	CONTINENCE	FASTMOVING	HISTRIONIC	NEUTRALIZE	POSTHUMOUS
BATTLESHIP	CONTINGENT	FEATHERBED	HOOTANANNY	NEUTROPHIL	POSTILLATE
BENTHAMITE	CONTINUANT	FERTILISED	HOOTENANNY	NORTHANGER	POSTILLION
BESTIALITY	CONTINUING	FERTILISER	HOOTNANNIE	NORTHBOUND	POSTLIMINY
BESTSELLER	CONTINUITY	FERTILIZER	HYSTERESIS	NORTHERNER	POSTMASTER
BIRTHPLACE	CONTINUOUS	FETTERLOCK	HYSTERICAL	NORTHSTEAD	POSTMORTEM
BIRTHRIGHT	CONTORTION	FETTUCCINE	ICHTHYOSIS	NORTHWARDS	POSTSCRIPT
BITTERLING	CONTRABAND	FICTITIOUS	INITIATION	NYCTALOPIA	PRATINCOLE
BITTERNESS	CONTRACTOR	FILTHINESS	INITIATIVE	OBSTETRICS	PRETENSION
BLITHERING	CONTRADICT	FILTRATION	INSTALMENT	OFFTHECUFF	PRETINCOLE
BLITZKRIEG	CONTRAFLOW	FIRTHSOKEN	INSTIGATOR	OFFTHEWALL	PRETTINESS
BLOTTESQUE	CONTRAHENT	FISTICUFFS	INSTRUCTED	OPHTHALMIC	PROTAGORAS
BOOTLEGGER	CONTRARILY	FLATTERING	INSTRUCTOR	OPOTHERAPY	PROTANOPIA
BOOTLICKER	CONTRAVENE	FLATULENCE	INSTRUMENT	ORATORICAL	PROTANOPIC
BOTTICELLI	CONTRECOUP	FLUTEMOUTH	JOLTERHEAD	PANTAGRUEL	PROTECTION
BOTTLEHEAD	CONTRIBUTE	FONTANELLE	JUSTICIARY	PANTALOONS	PROTECTIVE
BOTTLENECK	CONTRITION	FONTICULUS	KARTTIKAYA	PANTOGRAPH	PROTERVITY
BOTTOMLESS	CONTROLLER	FONTINALIS	KENTUCKIAN	PANTOSCOPE	PROTESTANT
BRATISLAVA	CONTROVERT	FOOTBALLER	KETTLEDRUM	PARTHENOPE	PROTOPLASM
BRITISHISM	CORTADERIA	FOOTBRIDGE	LANTHANIDE	PARTIALITY	PROTRACTED

PROTRACTOR	TASTEFULLY	ADJUSTMENT	GROUNDSMAN	PLOUGHWISE	UNDULATING
PROTRUSILE	TATTERSALL	AERUGINOUS	GROUNDWORK	POHUTUKAWA	UNDULATION
PROTRUSION	TEETHRIDGE	ALLUREMENT	HOMUNCULUS	POPULARITY	UNNUMBERED
QUATERNARY	TEETOTALER	ALMUCANTAR	ILLUMINATE	POPULARIZE	UNPUNCTUAL
RANTLETREE	TENTERHOOK	AMBULACRUM	ILLUMINATI	POPULATION	UNRULINESS
RATTLETRAP	TERTIARIES	AMBULATORY	ILLUSTRATE	PSEUDOCARP	UNSUITABLE
REITERATED	TESTACEOUS	AMMUNITION	IMMUNOLOGY	RANUNCULUS	USQUEBAUGH
RESTAURANT	TESTICULAR	AMPUSSYAND	IMPUDENTLY	RECUPERATE	VIRULENTLY
RESTLESSLY	TINTORETTO	AMPUTATION	IMPURITIES	RECURRENCE	VITUPERATE
RESTRAINED	TOOTHBRUSH	ANGUILLULA	IMPUTATION	REDUNDANCY	VOLUBILITY
RESTRICTED	TOOTHPASTE	ANGURVADEL	INAUGURATE	REFUTATION	VOLUMINOUS
RHETORICAL	TORTELLINI	ANNUALIZED	INCUBATION	REGULARITY	VOLUPTUARY
RHYTHMICAL	TORTUOUSLY	ANNUNCIATE	INCUMBENCY	REGULARIZE	VOLUPTUOUS
ROTTWEILER	TOSTICATED	ARAUCANIAN	INCUNABULA	REGULATION	VOLUTATION
SALTARELLO	TRITANOPIA	ASSUMPTION	INDUCEMENT	REJUVENATE	YTHUNDERED
SALTCELLAR	TROTSKYITE	ASSUMPTIVE	INDUCTANCE	RELUCTANCE	ABOVEBOARD
SALTIGRADE	TRUTHFULLY	ASTUTENESS	INDULGENCE	REMUNERATE	BEAVERSKIN
SCATHELESS	TURTLEDOVE	BALUSTRADE	INDUMENTUM	REPUBLICAN	CANVASBACK
SCATTERING	TURTLEHEAD	BEAUJOLAIS	INDUSTRIAL	REPUGNANCE	CANVASSING
SCATURIENT	TURTLENECK	BEAUTICIAN	INFURIATED	REPUTATION	CHEVESAILE
SCOTODINIA	ULSTERETTE	BEAUTIFIER	INHUMANITY	REQUIESCAT	CHEVISANCE
SCOTSWOMAN	UNATTACHED	BINUCLEATE	INJUNCTION	RESUMPTION	CHEVROTAIN
SCUTELLATE	UNATTENDED	BITUMINOUS	INQUIRENDO	RESUPINATE	CHIVALROUS
SELTZOGENE	UNCTUOUSLY	CACUMINOUS	INQUISITOR	RESURGENCE	CLAVICHORD
SEPTENNIAL	UPSTANDING	CALUMNIATE	INSUFFLATE	RETURNABLE	CLEVERNESS
SEPTUAGINT	VENTILATOR	CAOUTCHOUC	INSULARITY	RHEUMATICS	CONVALESCE
SETTERWORT	VERTEBRATE	CASUALNESS	INSULATION	RHEUMATISM	CONVECTION
SETTLEMENT	VERTICALLY	CHAUCERIAN	INSURGENCY	RHEUMATOID	CONVENANCE
SHATTERING	VESTIBULUM	CHAUDFROID	JACULATION	ROBUSTIOUS	CONVENIENT
SISTERHOOD	VICTORIANA	CHAULMUGRA	JAGUARONDI	ROBUSTNESS	CONVENTION
SKATEBOARD	VICTORIOUS	CHAUTAUQUA	JAGUARUNDI	ROQUELAURE	CONVENTUAL
SKETCHBOOK	VICTUALLER	CHAUVINISM	JOCULARITY	SALUBRIOUS	CONVERGENT
SLATTERNLY	VIETNAMESE	CHAUVINIST	LACUSTRINE	SALUTATION	CONVERSANT
SMATTERING	VIRTUOSITY	CLOUDBERRY	LEGUMINOUS	SATURATION	CONVERSELY
SMITHEREEN	VIRTUOUSLY	CLOUDBURST	LIEUTENANT	SATURNALIA	CONVERSION
SOFTBOILED	VOETGANGER	CLOUDINESS	LIQUESCENT	SCRUPULOUS	CONVEYABLE
SOOTHINGLY	WANTHRIVEN	COPULATION	LIQUIDATOR	SCRUTINEER	CONVEYANCE
SOOTHSAYER	WASTEFULLY	COQUELICOT	LIQUIDIZER	SCRUTINISE	CONVICTION
SOUTERRAIN	WASTEPAPER	COQUETTISH	LITURGICAL	SCRUTINIZE	CONVINCING
SOUTHBOUND	WATTLEWORK	COQUIMBITE	LOCULAMENT	SDRUCCIOLA	CONVOLUTED
SOUTHERNER	WEATHERMAN	CUCULLATED	LOQUACIOUS	SECULARIZE	CONVOLVUTE
SOUTHWARDS	WENTLETRAP	CUCURBITAL	LUGUBRIOUS	SECURITIES	CONVULSION
SPATCHCOCK	WESTERNIZE	CUMULATIVE	LUXURIANCE	SEDULOUSLY	CONVULSIVE
SPITCHCOCK	WHATSOEVER	DEDUCTIBLE	MAKUNOUCHI	SEGUIDILLA	CULVERTAGE
SPITEFULLY	WHITEHEART	DEPUTATION	MANUSCRIPT	SEPULCHRAL	CURVACEOUS
SPOTLESSLY	WHITETHORN	DIDUNCULUS	MAQUILLAGE	SEQUACIOUS	CURVETTING
STATECRAFT	WHITEWATER	EBOULEMENT	MATURATION	SEQUENTIAL	FLAVESCENT
STATIONARY	WHITSTABLE	EFFUSIVELY	MINUTEBOOK	SIMULACRUM	FLAVOURING
STATIONERY	WHITTERICK	ELEUSINIAN	MINUTENESS	SIMULATING	GALVANISER
STATISTICS	WINTERTIME	EPAULEMENT	MODULATION	SIMULATION	GRAVEOLENT
STATOCRACY	WORTHINESS	ESCULAPIAN	MONUMENTAL	SKEUOMORPH	GRAVESTONE
STATUESQUE	WORTHWHILE	ESCUTCHEON	NATURALISM	SOLUBILITY	GROVELLING
SUBTENANCY	WRETCHEDLY	EXHUMATION	NATURALIST	SPRUCENESS	HARVESTMAN
SUBTERFUGE	YESTERWEEK	FABULOUSLY	NATURALIZE	STAUROLITE	HEAVENWARD
SUBTRAHEND	YESTERYEAR	FIGURATION	NATUROPATH	STOUTHERIE	INEVITABLE
SUBTROPICS	ZOOTHAPSIS	FIGURATIVE	OBFUSCATED	STOUTHRIEF	INEVITABLY
SULTRINESS	ZOOTHERAPY	FIGUREHEAD	OBTUSENESS	STRUCTURAL	MARVELLOUS
SUSTAINING	ZWITTERION	FLOURISHED	OCCUPATION	STRULDBERG	NONVINTAGE
SUSTENANCE	ABRUPTNESS	FRAUDULENT	OCCURRENCE	STRULDBRUG	NONVIOLENT
SWITCHBACK	ACCUBATION	FRAUNHOFER	OSCULATION	TABULATION	PARVOVIRUS
SYNTAGMATA	ACCUMULATE	FUTURISTIC	OSCULATORY	THAUMASITE	PERVERSELY
SYNTERESIS	ACCURATELY	GALUMPHING	PALUDAMENT	THOUGHTFUL	PERVERSION
SYNTHESIZE	ACCUSATION	GESUNDHEIT	PALUSTRINE	THOUSANDTH	PERVERSITY
SYNTHRONUS	ACCUSATIVE	GETUPANDGO	PEAUDESOIE	TRAUMATIZE	PREVAILING
SYSTEMATIC	ACCUSINGLY	GLAUCONITE	PECULATION	TRIUMPHANT	PREVALENCE
TACTICALLY	ACCUSTOMED	GLOUCESTER	PECULIARLY	TROUBADOUR	PREVENANCY
TACTLESSLY	ACQUAINTED	GROUNDBAIT	PETULANTLY	TROUVAILLE	PREVENTION
TANTAMOUNT	ADJUDICATE	GROUNDLESS	PLOUGHBOTE	TUMULTUOUS	PREVENTIVE
TARTRAZINE	ADJUSTABLE	GROUNDLING	PLOUGHGATE	UNCULTURED	PREVIOUSLY

PRIVATEERS	PRAXITELES	**10:5**	CARMAGNOLE	ERYMANTHUS	KIDNAPPING
PRIVILEGED	THIXOTROPY	ACANACEOUS	CARNASSIAL	ESCHAROTIC	KILMARNOCK
PROVEDITOR	UNEXAMPLED	ACETABULAR	CARPATHIAN	ESTRAMACON	KOOKABURRA
PROVENANCE	UNEXPECTED	ACETABULUM	CARRAGHEEN	EUSTACHIAN	KURDAITCHA
PROVERBIAL	UNEXPLORED	ACQUAINTED	CARYATIDES	EUTHANASIA	LACCADIVES
PROVIDENCE	ALCYONARIA	ACROAMATIC	CASCARILLA	EUTRAPELIA	LACKADAISY
PROVINCIAL	ALLYCHOLLY	ADAMANTINE	CASUALNESS	EXTRACTION	LANDAMMANN
PROVISIONS	BABYLONIAN	ADELANTADO	CEPHALOPOD	EXTRANEOUS	LEGWARMERS
SALVADORAN	BABYSITTER	AGAPANTHUS	CHAMAELEON	FALLACIOUS	LEOPARDESS
SERVICEMAN	BARYSPHERE	AGGRANDISE	CHAMAEROPS	FANTASTICO	LINEAMENTS
SERVOMOTOR	CALYDONIAN	ALABANDINE	CHAPARAJOS	FARRANDINE	LOQUACIOUS
SHOVELHEAD	CALYPTRATE	ALABANDITE	CHAPAREJOS	FERRANDINE	MANGABEIRA
SHOVELNOSE	CARYATIDES	ALEXANDERS	CHINABERRY	FLYCATCHER	MANZANILLA
SILVERBACK	CHRYSIPPUS	ALEXANDRIA	CHINAGRAPH	FOLIACEOUS	MARCANTANT
SILVERBELL	CHRYSOLITE	ANABAPTIST	CHINASTONE	FONTANELLE	MARGASIRSA
SILVERBILL	COPYHOLDER	ANACARDIUM	CHITARRONE	FORFAITING	MASCARPONE
SILVERFISH	COPYWRITER	ANGWANTIBO	CHIVALROUS	FRICANDEAU	MASKANONGE
SILVERSIDE	CORYBANTES	ANIMADVERT	CHOLALOGUE	FROMANTEEL	MASSASAUGA
SILVERSKIN	CORYBANTIC	ANNUALIZED	CIRCASSIAN	FUSTANELLA	MAUPASSANT
SILVERWARE	CORYPHAEUS	ANTIADITIS	CLARABELLA	FUSTANELLE	MECHANICAL
STAVESACRE	DICYNODONT	APEMANTHUS	COCKABULLY	GALLABIYAH	MECHANIZED
SUAVEOLENT	ENCYCLICAL	APOCALYPSE	COCKALORUM	GALLABIYEH	MENDACIOUS
SUBVENTION	ENHYDRITIC	APOLAUSTIC	COCKATRICE	GALRAVITCH	MERCANTILE
SUBVERSION	ETHYLAMINE	APPEARANCE	COELACANTH	GALVANISER	MICHAELMAS
SUBVERSIVE	EURYPTERUS	AREFACTION	COETANEOUS	GARGANTUAN	MISMATCHED
TRAVANCORE	GREYFRIARS	ARENACEOUS	COLLAPSING	GARLANDAGE	MISTAKENLY
TRAVELATOR	JOUYSAUNCE	ARIMASPIAN	COLLARBONE	GERIATRICS	MONOACIDIC
TRAVELLERS	LADYKILLER	ARYTAENOID	COLLATERAL	GODPARENTS	MONTAGNARD
TRAVELLING	LARYNGITIS	ASARABACCA	COMMANDANT	GOLIATHISE	MORDACIOUS
TRAVELOGUE	LILYWHITES	ASPHALTITE	COMMANDEER	GONFANONER	MORGANATIC
TRAVERTINE	MARYLEBONE	ASTRAGALUS	COMMANDING	GORMANDIZE	MORGANETTA
TRAVOLATOR	MOLYBDENUM	ASTRALAGUS	COMPARABLE	GRANADILLA	MORTADELLA
TRIVIALITY	PALYNOLOGY	ASYNARTETE	COMPARATOR	GREGARIOUS	MOZZARELLA
TRIVIALIZE	PITYRIASIS	ATTRACTION	COMPARISON	GRENADIERS	MYOCARDIAL
UNAVAILING	PLAYFELLOW	ATTRACTIVE	COMPASSION	GRENADILLA	MYSTAGOGUE
UNEVENNESS	PLAYGROUND	BAHRAINIAN	COMPATIBLE	GUARANTEED	MYSTAGOGUS
UNEVENTFUL	PLAYWRIGHT	BARBAROSSA	COMPATRIOT	GYMNASTICS	NECTABANUS
UNIVERSITY	POLYANTHUS	BARCAROLLE	CONTAGIOUS	HAEMANTHUS	NEWFANGLED
WEAVERBIRD	POLYCHAETE	BARGAINING	CONVALESCE	HARMANBECK	NEWSAGENTS
ANGWANTIBO	POLYCHREST	BARRACKING	CORTADERIA	HEPHAESTUS	NONPAYMENT
ANSWERABLE	POLYCHROME	BARRACOOTA	COURAGEOUS	HEPTAGONAL	NYCTALOPIA
BROWNLANDS	POLYGAMIST	BARRACOUTA	CRETACEOUS	HEPTAMERON	OFFBALANCE
BROWNSTONE	POLYGAMOUS	BARRAMUNDA	CROTALARIA	HEPTATEUCH	OIREACHTAS
CREWELWORK	POLYHEDRON	BARRAMUNDI	CROTALIDAE	HEPTATHLON	OLERACEOUS
DRAWBRIDGE	POLYHYMNIA	BATRACHIAN	CUIRASSIER	HERBACEOUS	ONOMASTICS
DRAWCANSIR	POLYMERIZE	BATTAILOUS	CURVACEOUS	HEREABOUTS	OUANANICHE
DRAWSTRING	POLYNESIAN	BEDRAGGLED	DEFEASANCE	HIERARCHY	OUTBALANCE
DROWSINESS	POLYNOMIAL	BELLADONNA	DEFLAGRATE	HIPPARCHUS	OUTLANDISH
EYEWITNESS	POLYPHEMUS	BELLAMOURE	DEFRAYMENT	HOOTANANNY	OUTPATIENT
FLOWERBEDS	POLYTHEISM	BELLARMINE	DEGRADABLE	HULLABALOO	OUTRAGEOUS
JAYWALKING	POLYVALENT	BERNARDINE	DERMATITIS	HUSBANDAGE	OZYMANDIAS
LEGWARMERS	RAIYATWARI	BERSAGLIER	DÉSHABILLÉ	HYDRAULICS	PALMATIFID
NETWORKING	SATYAGRAHA	BOLLANDIST	DESPAIRING	ICOSANDRIA	PALMATOZOA
SCHWARZLOT	STRYCHNINE	BOMBARDIER	DETRACTION	IMPLACABLE	PANJANDRUM
SHOWJUMPER	UNHYGIENIC	BRAGADISME	DIACAUSTIC	IMPLACABLY	PANTAGRUEL
SNOWBLOWER	BENZEDRINE	BRIGANDINE	DISDAINFUL	INCRASSATE	PANTALOONS
SNOWCAPPED	BOOZINGKEN	BRIGANTINE	DISHABILLE	INFLATABLE	PAPIAMENTO
SNOWMOBILE	BRAZILWOOD	BROCATELLE	DISHARMONY	INFRACTION	PARMACITIE
STEWARDESS	DRUZHINNIK	BUREAUCRAT	DISMANTLED	INGRATIATE	PARNASSIAN
UNSWERVING	FITZGERALD	CALCAREOUS	ELACAMPANE	INSTALMENT	PARRAMATTA
VIEWFINDER	MANZANILLA	CAMPAIGNER	ELECAMPANE	INTRAURBAN	PASSAGEWAY
WHEWELLITE	MIZZENMAST	CAMPANELLA	ELEGABALUS	JACKANAPES	PASSAMEZZO
ALEXANDERS	MOZZARELLA	CAMPARADOR	EMALANGENI	JAGUARONDI	PECCADILLO
ALEXANDRIA	POZZUOLANA	CANTABRIAN	EMPLASTRUM	JAGUARUNDI	PEDIATRICS
ANAXIMENES	PRIZEFIGHT	CANTALOUPE	ENCHANTING	JAYWALKING	PENTAGONAL
COEXISTENT	PUZZLEMENT	CANTATRICE	ENDEARMENT	JEOPARDISE	PENTAMERON
FRAXINELLA	QUIZMASTER	CANVASBACK	ENTRANCING	JEOPARDIZE	PENTAMETER
INEXORABLE	RAZZMATAZZ	CANVASSING	EPHRAIMITE	JIGGAMAREE	PENTATEUCH
PLEXIMETER			EPICANTHUS	KARMATHIAN	PENTATHLON

563

PENTATONIC	SERRASALMO	UNLEAVENED	FLAMBOYANT	VOCABULARY	DETACHABLE
PERMAFROST	SGANARELLE	UNREADABLE	FOOTBALLER	VOCABULIST	DETACHMENT
PERMANENCE	SHARAWADGI	UNREASONED	FOOTBRIDGE	VOLUBILITY	DETECTABLE
PERMANENCY	SHARAWAGGI	UNSEASONED	FOREBITTER	ABDICATION	DICKCISSEL
PESCADORES	SHENANIGAN	UNSHACKLED	FOREBODING	ADJECTIVAL	DIRECTIONS
PESTALOZZI	SHERARDISE	UPROARIOUS	FRAMBOESIA	AFRICANDER	DIRECTNESS
PETRARCHAN	SINOATRIAL	UPSTANDING	FREEBOOTER	AFRICANISM	DIRECTOIRE
PHILATELIC	SMARAGDINE	USUCAPTION	GRUBBINESS	ALLOCATION	DODECANESE
PHYLACTERY	SOUSAPHONE	VALLADOLID	HACKBUTEER	ALLOCUTION	DOLICHOLIS
PICCADILLY	SPIRACULUM	VERNACULAR	HARDBOILED	ALLYCHOLLY	DOLICHOTUS
PICCALILLI	SPORANGIUM	VERSAILLES	HELLBENDER	ALMACANTAR	DOMICILARY
PICCANINNY	SPREAGHERY	VIBRACULUM	HIGHBINDER	ALMUCANTAR	DRAWCANSIR
PILGARLICK	STALACTITE	VIBRAPHONE	HORNBLENDE	AMBOCEPTOR	EBRACTEATE
PLUMASSIER	STALAGMITE	VIBRATIONS	HORNBLOWER	ANARCHICAL	EDULCORATE
POETASTERY	STEWARDESS	VILLAINOUS	HUMPBACKED	ANTECEDENT	EFFACEMENT
POLIANTHES	STOMATOPOD	VILLANELLE	IMMOBILITY	ANTICHTHON	EFFECTUATE
POLYANTHUS	STREAMERED	VILLANOVAN	IMMOBILIZE	ANTICIPATE	EFFICIENCY
PORRACEOUS	STREAMLINE	VULCANALIA	INCUBATION	ANTICLIMAX	EMANCIPATE
PORTAMENTO	SUBMARINER	WALLACHIAN	INFIBULATE	ARAUCANIAN	EMASCULATE
PRECARIOUS	SUNBATHING	WARRANDICE	INHABITANT	ARTICULATA	ENCYCLICAL
PRECAUTION	SURPASSING	WASSAILING	INHIBITING	ARTICULATE	ENLACEMENT
PREDACIOUS	SUSTAINING	WEIMARANER	INHIBITION	ARTOCARPUS	ENRICHMENT
PREMARITAL	SYMPATHISE	WITGATBOOM	INHIBITORY	ASSOCIATED	ENTICEMENT
PREPARATOR	SYMPATHIZE	WORKAHOLIC	JACKBOOTED	ATRACURIUM	EPISCOPATE
PREPAYMENT	SYNTAGMATA	WRAPAROUND	LAWABIDING	ATTACHMENT	ERIOCAULON
PREVAILING	TABLANETTE	ZIMBABWEAN	LEGIBILITY	AUTECOLOGY	ESPECIALLY
PREVALENCE	TANGANYIKA	ACCUBATION	LUGUBRIOUS	AUTOCHTHON	ETEOCRETAN
PRIVATEERS	TANTAMOUNT	ACROBATICS	MACEBEARER	AUTOCRATIC	EUROCHEQUE
PROPAGANDA	TAPDANCING	ADHIBITION	METABOLISE	BETACRUCIS	EUROCLYDON
PROPAGATOR	TARPAULING	AEROBATICS	METABOLISM	BINOCULARS	EVISCERATE
PROTAGORAS	TENNANTITE	AFFABILITY	MOLYBDENUM	BINUCLEATE	EXPECTANCY
PROTANOPIA	TERRACOTTA	ALCIBIADES	MOSSBUNKER	BLANCMANGE	FELICITATE
PROTANOPIC	TESTACEOUS	ALEMBICATE	MUTABILITY	BRONCHITIC	FELICITOUS
PTERANODON	THALASSIAN	AMIABILITY	NOTABILITY	BRONCHITIS	FIANCHETTO
PUGNACIOUS	THREADBARE	ANTIBARBUS	NUDIBRANCH	CANECUTTER	FIERCENESS
PULSATANCE	THREADLIKE	ANTIBIOTIC	OVERBOUGHT	CAPACITATE	FLANCONADE
PYTHAGORAS	THREADWORM	ARCHBISHOP	PALLBEARER	CARACTACUS	FLOCCULATE
QUARANTINE	THREATENED	AUDIBILITY	PATIBULARY	CARICATURA	FLOCCULENT
QUESADILLA	THYSANURAN	BACKBITING	PAWNBROKER	CARICATURE	FORECASTER
RAIYATWARI	TILLANDSIA	BACKBLOCKS	PHLEBOTOMY	CATACHUMEN	FORECASTLE
RAMPALLIAN	TOCCATELLA	BALIBUNTAL	PLIABILITY	CATECHUMEN	FOURCHETTE
REFRACTION	TRAGACANTH	BEEFBURGER	PRESBYOPIA	CAVICORNIA	FRANCHISEE
REFRACTIVE	TRAVANCORE	BLUEBONNET	PRESBYTERY	CHALCEDONY	FRANCHISOR
REFRACTORY	TRILATERAL	BLUEBOTTLE	REPUBLICAN	CHANCELLOR	FRANCISCAN
REPEATABLE	TRIMALCHIO	BOOKBINDER	SALUBRIOUS	CHAUCERIAN	GENICULATE
REPEATEDLY	TRINACRIAN	CAPABILITY	SCOMBRESOX	CHINCHILLA	GLAUCONITE
RESEARCHER	TRIPARTITE	CARABINEER	SCRIBBLING	CHOICELESS	GLOUCESTER
RESTAURANT	TRITANOPIA	CARABINIER	SHABBINESS	CHURCHGOER	GYNECOLOGY
RETRACTION	TROPAEOLUM	CATABOLISM	SHIBBOLETH	CHURCHYARD	HARDCASTLE
RETRAINING	TURNAROUND	CELEBRATED	SIDEBOARDS	CINECAMERA	HELICOPTER
RHOEADALES	TYMPANITES	CEREBELLUM	SLUMBERING	COCKCHAFER	HEMICHORDA
RICHARDSON	TYMPANITIS	CHAMBERPOT	SNOWBLOWER	COINCIDENT	HOMECOMING
ROCKABILLY	ULTRABASIC	CHAMBERTIN	SOFTBOILED	CONSCIENCE	HYPOCORISM
ROWLANDSON	ULTRAFICHE	CHAMBRANLE	SOLUBILITY	CORNCOCKLE	IMBECILITY
SABBATICAL	ULTRAMAFIC	CHIMBORAZO	STRABISMUS	COUNCILLOR	IMMACULACY
SALMAGUNDI	ULTRASONIC	CORYBANTES	STRABOTOMY	COUSCOUSOU	IMMACULATE
SALMANAZAR	ULTRASOUND	CORYBANTIC	STUBBORNLY	DEDICATION	IMPECCABLE
SALTARELLO	UNAVAILING	DELIBERATE	STUMBLEDOM	DEDUCTIBLE	IMPECCABLY
SALVADORAN	UNBEARABLE	DEMOBILISE	TALEBEARER	DEFACEMENT	INACCURACY
SANDALWOOD	UNBEARABLY	DEMOBILIZE	TELEBRIDGE	DEFECATION	INACCURATE
SANNAYASIN	UNBEATABLE	DISABILITY	TENEBRIFIC	DEFICIENCY	INDECENTLY
SATYAGRAHA	UNEXAMPLED	DRAWBRIDGE	THIMBLEFUL	DEJECTEDLY	INDECISION
SCARAMOUCH	UNFLAGGING	DRUMBLEDOR	THIMBLEWIT	DELECTABLE	INDECISIVE
SCHWARZLOT	UNFLAVORED	DUCKBOARDS	THUMBIKINS	DELICATELY	INDECOROUS
SEAMANSHIP	UNGRACIOUS	DURABILITY	THUMBSCREW	DEMOCRATIC	INDICATION
SEECATCHIE	UNGRATEFUL	EXHIBITION	TOURBILLON	DEMOCRITUS	INDICATIVE
SEQUACIOUS	UNHEARABLE	EXORBITANT	TROMBONIST	DERACINATE	INDICOLITE
SERRADELLA	UNICAMERAL	FILIBUSTER	TROUBADOUR	DESECRATED	INDICTABLE
SERRADILLA	UNILATERAL	FLABBINESS	VISIBILITY	DESICCATED	INDICTMENT

INDUCEMENT	RIDICULOUS	BROADPIECE	MEANDERING	ADOLESCENT	CANNELLONI
INDUCTANCE	ROSECHAFER	BROADSHEET	MOULDINESS	AGGRESSION	CANTERBURY
INESCULENT	RUPICOLINE	BROADSWORD	MOULDIWARP	AGGRESSIVE	CAPREOLATE
INFECTIOUS	SALICORNIA	CACODAEMON	OBSIDIONAL	ALCHERINGA	CARPENTIER
INNOCENTLY	SALTCELLAR	CALEDONIAN	OCCIDENTAL	ALIMENTARY	CENTENNIAL
INOSCULATE	SAXICOLINE	CALYDONIAN	OCTODECIMO	ALZHEIMERS	CENTESIMAL
INSECURELY	SAXICOLOUS	CAPODASTRO	OSMIDROSIS	AMATEURISH	CHATELAINE
INSECURITY	SCARCEMENT	CECIDOMYIA	PALUDAMENT	AMPLEFORTH	CHEVESAILE
INVOCATION	SCARCENESS	CHANDELIER	PARADIDDLE	ANGLERFISH	CINDERELLA
JUDICATURE	SDRUCCIOLA	CHARDONNAY	PARADOXIDE	ANSWERABLE	CISLEITHAN
JUDICIALLY	SEMICIRCLE	CHAUDFROID	PARADOXINE	ANTHEOLION	CISTERCIAN
LAUNCEGAYE	SKETCHBOOK	CHILDBIRTH	PEAUDESOIE	APHAERESIS	CLEMENCEAU
LAUNCESTON	SKYSCRAPER	CHILDERMAS	PERIDOTITE	APOPEMPTIC	CLEMENTINE
LENOCINIUM	SLUICEGATE	CHILDISHLY	PILEDRIVER	APOSEMATIC	CLERESTORY
LONGCHAMPS	SNOWCAPPED	CLOUDBERRY	PLUNDERING	APPRECIATE	CLEVERNESS
MALACOLOGY	SOLICITOUS	CLOUDBURST	PSEUDOCARP	APPRENTICE	CLYDESDALE
MANICHAEAN	SOLICITUDE	CLOUDINESS	PYRIDOXINE	ARCHETYPAL	COCKERNONY
MANICURIST	SPATCHCOCK	COMEDIENNE	RECIDIVISM	ARSMETRICK	COLBERTINE
MEDICAMENT	SPEECHLESS	COORDINATE	RECIDIVIST	ATELEIOSIS	COLLECTING
MEDICATION	SPENCERIAN	DEMODULATE	REREDORTER	AUTOECIOUS	COLLECTION
MELACONITE	SPHACELATE	DESIDERATA	ROUNDABOUT	BADDERLOCK	COLLECTIVE
MELOCOTOON	SPITCHCOCK	DREADFULLY	ROUNDHOUSE	BALDERDASH	COLLEGIATE
MENACINGLY	SPRUCENESS	DREADLOCKS	SBUDDIKINS	BALNEATION	COLLEMBOLA
MENECHMIAN	STIACCIATO	ECARDINATE	SCANDALISE	BALNEOLOGY	COMMENTARY
METACARPAL	STRACCHINO	ECUADORIAN	SCANDALIZE	BANDERILLA	COMMENTATE
METACARPUS	STRICTNESS	EMBODIMENT	SCANDALOUS	BANDERILLO	COMMERCIAL
METACENTRE	STRUCTURAL	EMENDATION	SCANDAROON	BARLEYBREE	COMPELLING
METICULOUS	STRYCHNINE	EMPEDOCLES	SCANDERBEG	BARLEYCORN	COMPENDIUM
MIRACULOUS	SUBSCRIBER	ENHYDRITIC	SCORDATURA	BARMECIDAL	COMPENSATE
MISOCAPNIC	SWITCHBACK	ESCADRILLE	SHANDRYDAN	BARRENNESS	COMPETENCE
MONOCARPIC	SYNECDOCHE	ESPADRILLE	SHANDYGAFF	BASKETBALL	COMPETITOR
MONOCHROME	THEOCRITUS	EXPEDIENCE	SHELDONIAN	BASKETWORK	CONCENTRIC
MUSICOLOGY	TIROCINIUM	EXPEDIENCY	SHODDINESS	BATTENBERG	CONCEPTION
NEWSCASTER	TOPICALITY	EXPEDITION	SHUDDERING	BATTENBURG	CONCEPTUAL
NOSOCOMIAL	TOXICOLOGY	FIELDMOUSE	SKINDIVING	BAUDELAIRE	CONCERNING
NOTICEABLE	TRENCHMORE	FIENDISHLY	SLANDEROUS	BEAVERSKIN	CONCERTINA
NOTICEABLY	TRIACONTER	FLAPDOODLE	SNAPDRAGON	BEEFEATERS	CONCERVATE
NOVACULITE	UNACCENTED	FLINDERSIA	SOLIDARITY	BEEKEEPING	CONCESSION
OBJECTLESS	UNBECOMING	FLOODLIGHT	SOUNDPROOF	BELIEVABLE	CONDESCEND
OFFICIALLY	UNDECLARED	FOREDAMNED	SOUNDTRACK	BENZEDRINE	CONFECTION
OPHICLEIDE	UNDOCTORED	FOUNDATION	SOURDELINE	BIRKENHEAD	CONFEDERAL
OVERCHARGE	UNLICENSED	FRAUDULENT	SPEEDINESS	BISSEXTILE	CONFERENCE
PARACELSUS	UNOCCUPIED	GIARDIASIS	STANDPOINT	BITTERLING	CONFERVOID
PEDICULATE	UNSOCIABLE	GLENDOVEER	STANDSTILL	BITTERNESS	CONFESSION
PENICILLIN	URTICACEAE	GOLDDIGGER	STEADINESS	BONNETHEAD	CONGENITAL
PLANCHETTE	VARICOSITY	GRANDCHILD	STRIDENTLY	BORDERLAND	CONGESTION
POLYCHAETE	VELOCIPEDE	GRANDDADDY	STRIDEWAYS	BORDERLINE	CONJECTURE
POLYCHREST	VESICULATE	GRANDSTAND	STRIDULATE	BOTHERSOME	CONNECTING
POLYCHROME	WRETCHEDLY	GREEDINESS	STURDINESS	BRIDEGROOM	CONNECTION
PORTCULLIS	ABERDEVINE	GRINDSTONE	SWORDSTICK	BRIDESMAID	CONNECTIVE
POSTCHAISE	ABHIDHAMMA	HALFDOLLAR	TARADIDDLE	BROKENDOWN	CONSECRATE
PRESCIENCE	ABRIDGMENT	HEREDITARY	TEPIDARIUM	BUDGERIGAR	CONSENSION
PRINCIPIUM	ABUNDANTLY	HUMIDIFIER	THEODOLITE	BUNDESWEHR	CONSEQUENT
PRINCIPLED	ACCIDENTAL	HUMIDISTAT	THUNDERBOX	BURDENSOME	CONTENTION
PRINCIPLES	ADJUDICATE	HYPODERMIC	THUNDERING	BURGEONING	CONTESTANT
PROSCENIUM	AMYGDALOID	ILLADVISED	THUNDEROUS	BUTTERBAKE	CONTEXTUAL
PROSCIUTTO	ARCHDEACON	IMMODERATE	TRENDINESS	BUTTERBUMP	CONVECTION
PROSCRIBED	ARUNDELIAN	IMPEDIMENT	UNLADYLIKE	BUTTERFISH	CONVENANCE
PUNICACEAE	ASPIDISTRA	IMPUDENTLY	UNREDEEMED	BUTTERMERE	CONVENIENT
PYRACANTHA	AUTODIDACT	INCIDENTAL	UNTIDINESS	BUTTERMILK	CONVENTION
QUENCHLESS	BENEDICITE	INFIDELITY	VALIDATION	BYELECTION	CONVENTUAL
QUERCITRON	BLOODHOUND	INORDINATE	WITHDRAWAL	CALCEDONIO	CONVERGENT
RACECOURSE	BLOODSTAIN	INUNDATION	WORLDCLASS	CALCEOLATE	CONVERSANT
RADICALISM	BLOODSTOCK	IRRADICATE	ZYGODACTYL	CAMBERWELL	CONVERSELY
REDECORATE	BLOODSTONE	LAUNDROMAT	ABBREVIATE	CAMPERDOWN	CONVERSION
RELOCATION	BLUNDERING	LAURDALITE	ABOVEBOARD	CAMPESTRAL	CONVEYABLE
RELUCTANCE	BOONDOGGLE	LIBIDINOUS	ABSTEMIOUS	CANCELLOUS	CONVEYANCE
RETICULATE	BREADFRUIT	MACEDONIAN	ABSTENTION	CANDELABRA	COPPERHEAD
REVOCATION	BROADCLOTH	MALODOROUS	ACCREDITED	CANDELILLA	COPPERNOSE

COPPERSKIN	EMBLEMATIC	GUIDELINES	KRUGERRAND	OBSTETRICS	PRETENSION
COQUELICOT	EMBLEMENTS	HALIEUTICS	LANCEOLATE	ODDFELLOWS	PREVENANCY
COQUETTISH	ENTREATING	HALLELUJAH	LANGERHANS	OPALESCENT	PREVENTION
CORRECTING	ENTREMESSE	HAMMERHEAD	LARGESCALE	OPPRESSION	PREVENTIVE
CORRECTION	ENTRENCHED	HAMMERLOCK	LATTERMATH	OPPRESSIVE	PRIZEFIGHT
CORRECTIVE	EPIDEICTIC	HARTEBEEST	LAUDERDALE	ORCHESTRAL	PROCEDURAL
CORREGIDOR	EPIDENDRUM	HARVESTMAN	LAURENTIAN	OROGENESIS	PROCEEDING
CORRESPOND	EPIGENETIC	HATEENOUGH	LAWRENCIUM	ORPHEOREON	PROCESSING
CREDENTIAL	EPIMENIDES	HEAVENWARD	LEADERSHIP	OUTPERFORM	PROCESSION
CRENELLATE	EPIMETHEUS	HEIDELBERG	LEPRECHAUN	OVEREATING	PROFESSION
CREWELWORK	ERUBESCENT	HELLESPONT	LETTERHEAD	OXYGENATOR	PROGENITOR
CUISENAIRE	EVANESCENT	HENCEFORTH	LIBRETTIST	PALAEOTYPE	PROGESSION
CULVERTAGE	EVITERNITY	HENDECAGON	LIBREVILLE	PALAESTRAL	PROJECTILE
CUMBERLAND	EXACERBATE	HESPERIDES	LIEBERMANN	PALMERSTON	PROJECTING
CUMBERSOME	EXONERATED	HILDEBRAND	LIMBERNECK	PALMERWORM	PROJECTION
CUMMERBUND	EXPRESSION	HINDENBURG	LIQUESCENT	PARAENESIS	PROMENADER
CURRENCIES	EXPRESSIVE	HINTERLAND	LOCKERROOM	PARGETTING	PROMETHEAN
CURVETTING	EXPRESSMAN	HITHERWARD	LOGGERHEAD	PARNELLISM	PROMETHEUS
CUSSEDNESS	EXPRESSWAY	HODGEPODGE	LUMBERJACK	PASTEBOARD	PROMETHIUM
DAMSELFISH	EXUBERANCE	HOMOEOPATH	LUMPECTOMY	PASTEURISE	PROPELLANT
DARJEELING	FAHRENHEIT	HOOTENANNY	MAIDENHAIR	PASTEURIZE	PROPELLENT
DEALERSHIP	FALSETRUTH	HORRENDOUS	MAIDENHOOD	PEACEFULLY	PROPENSITY
DECLENSION	FARFETCHED	HORSEDRAWN	MALMESBURY	PEACEMAKER	PROPERTIUS
DECRESCENT	FATHERLAND	HORSELBERG	MANDEVILLE	PENTELIKON	PROSECUTOR
DEFLECTION	FATHERLESS	HORSEPOWER	MANSERVANT	PENTETERIC	PROSERPINA
DEPRECIATE	FESCENNINE	HORSERIDER	MARCESCENT	PEPPERCORN	PROSERPINE
DEPRESSANT	FETTERLOCK	HORSEWOMAN	MARKETABLE	PEPPERMILL	PROTECTION
DEPRESSING	FIBREGLASS	HOUSEBOUND	MARVELLOUS	PEPPERMINT	PROTECTIVE
DEPRESSION	FINGERLING	HOUSECRAFT	MASTECTOMY	PEPPERWORT	PROTERVITY
DEPRESSIVE	FINGERNAIL	HOUSEMAIDS	MASTERMIND	PERCENTAGE	PROTESTANT
DESCENDANT	FINGERPICK	HOUSEPROUD	MASTERWORT	PERCENTILE	PROVEDITOR
DESCENDING	FLAGELLATE	HOWLEGLASS	MATTERHORN	PERCEPTION	PROVENANCE
DIAGENESIS	FLAMEPROOF	HYPAETHRAL	MEAGERNESS	PERCEPTIVE	PROVERBIAL
DIALECTICS	FLAVESCENT	HYPAETHRON	MEMBERSHIP	PERDENDOSI	PRUDENTIAL
DIAPEDESIS	FLORENTINE	HYSTERESIS	METHEDRINE	PERFECTION	PUCKERWOOD
DIDGERIDOO	FLOWERBEDS	HYSTERICAL	MILLEFIORI	PERIEGESIS	PUMMELLING
DIELECTRIC	FLUGELHORN	IMPREGNATE	MILLENNIUM	PERMEATION	PUTREFYING
DIFFERENCE	FLUTEMOUTH	IMPRESARIO	MINDERERUS	PERPETRATE	PUTRESCENT
DIGRESSION	FORBEARING	IMPRESSION	MISCELLANY	PERPETUATE	QUATERNARY
DINNERTIME	FORCEFULLY	IMPRESSIVE	MISLEADING	PERPETUITY	RANNELTREE
DISBELIEVE	FORFEITURE	INADEQUACY	MIZZENMAST	PERSECUTOR	READERSHIP
DISCERNING	FORFEUCHEN	INADEQUATE	MONOECIOUS	PERSEPHONE	RECREATION
DISHEARTEN	FRATERETTO	INBREEDING	MONTESSORI	PERSEPOLIS	REELECTION
DISPENSARY	FRATERNISE	INCREASING	MONTEVERDI	PERVERSELY	REFLECTING
DISPENSING	FRATERNITY	INCREDIBLE	MONTEVIDEO	PERVERSION	REFLECTION
DISPERSION	FRATERNIZE	INCREDIBLY	MOTHERHOOD	PERVERSITY	REFLECTIVE
DISRESPECT	FREMESCENT	INCRESCENT	MOTHERLAND	PHAGEDAENA	REFRESHING
DISSECTION	FRENETICAL	INFLECTION	MOTHERLESS	PIONEERING	REGRESSION
DISSELBOOM	FRUTESCENT	INFLEXIBLE	MOTHERLIKE	PLATELAYER	REGRESSIVE
DISSEMBLER	GASTEROPOD	INFLEXIBLY	MOUSEPIECE	PLUPERFECT	REITERATED
DISSENSION	GEOCENTRIC	INFREQUENT	MULIEBRITY	POCKETBOOK	RENDEZVOUS
DISSENTING	GHIBELLINE	INGREDIENT	MUSKETEERS	PONTEDERIA	REPRESSION
DISSERTATE	GIBBERELLA	INOPERABLE	MYSTERIOUS	PONTEFRACT	REPRESSIVE
DISSERVICE	GILBERTIAN	INSPECTION	NATHELESSE	PORTENTOUS	RESPECTFUL
DISTENSION	GILBERTINE	IRIDESCENT	NATTERJACK	POSSESSION	RESPECTING
DOGGEDNESS	GINGERBEER	ISABELLINE	NAUSEATING	POSSESSIVE	RESPECTIVE
DOLCEMENTE	GINGERSNAP	ISOLEUCINE	NAUSEATIVE	PREBENDARY	RETREATING
DRAKESTONE	GOLDENSEAL	ISOMETRICS	NEGLECTFUL	PRECEDENCE	RHINEGRAVE
DUKKERIPEN	GOOSEBERRY	JABBERWOCK	NEOTERICAL	PREDECEASE	RHINESTONE
DUNDERFUNK	GOOSEFLESH	JIGGERMAST	NESSELRODE	PREDESTINE	RINDERPEST
DUNDERHEAD	GORGEOUSLY	JOBSEEKERS	NETHERMOST	PREFERABLE	RINGELMANN
DUNDERPATE	GRACEFULLY	JOLTERHEAD	NIDDERLING	PREFERABLY	ROQUELAURE
DUODECIMAL	GRAPEFRUIT	JUGGERNAUT	NIGGERHEAD	PREFERENCE	ROUSEABOUT
EASTERLING	GRATEFULLY	KEMPERYMAN	NIGRESCENT	PREFERMENT	RUBBERNECK
ECUMENICAL	GRAVEOLENT	KERSEYMERE	NOBLEWOMAN	PREHENSILE	RUDDERLESS
EFFLEURAGE	GRAVESTONE	KESSELRING	NORBERTINE	PRELECTION	RUGGEDNESS
EGOCENTRIC	GROCETERIA	KIESELGUHR	NUCLEONICS	PREMEDICAL	RUTHERFORD
EISTEDDFOD	GROVELLING	KIMBERLITE	NUMBERLESS	PREPENSELY	SABRETACHE
ELEMENTARY	GUATEMALAN	KNIFEBOARD	NURSERYMAN	PRESENTDAY	SACREDNESS

SALLENDERS	SUBSELLIUM	UNEVENNESS	DEEPFREEZE	BEARGARDEN	MADAGASCAN
SANDEMANIA	SUBSEQUENT	UNEVENTFUL	FLUFFINESS	BRIDGEHEAD	MADAGASCAR
SANDERLING	SUBTENANCY	UNIGENITUS	FOREFATHER	BRIDGETOWN	MALAGUETTA
SAPPERMENT	SUBTERFUGE	UNIVERSITY	FOREFINGER	CACOGRAPHY	MALIGNANCY
SARMENTOUS	SUBVENTION	UNPLEASANT	GIRLFRIEND	CATEGORISE	MANAGEABLE
SCAPEGRACE	SUBVERSION	UNPREPARED	GOLDFINGER	CATEGORIZE	MANAGEMENT
SCOPELIDAE	SUBVERSIVE	UNSLEEPING	GOODFELLOW	CHANGEABLE	MANAGERESS
SCOREBOARD	SUCCEEDING	UNSPECIFIC	GREYFRIARS	CHANGELESS	MANAGERIAL
SCREECHING	SUCCESSFUL	UNSWERVING	HIGHFLYING	CHANGELING	MISHGUGGLE
SCREENPLAY	SUCCESSION	UNYIELDING	HOLOFERNES	CHARGEABLE	MISOGYNIST
SCUTELLATE	SUCCESSIVE	UROGENITAL	INDEFINITE	CHARGEHAND	MITIGATING
SECRETAIRE	SUDDENNESS	USQUEBAUGH	INEFFICACY	CLINGSTONE	MITIGATION
SEGREGATED	SUFFERANCE	VANDERBILT	INFEFTMENT	CRAIGFLUKE	MONEGASQUE
SELFESTEEM	SUGGESTION	VARIEGATED	INSUFFLATE	CRYOGENICS	MONOGAMOUS
SEPTENNIAL	SUGGESTIVE	VAUDEVILLE	KINGFISHER	DECAGRAMME	MONTGOMERY
SEQUENTIAL	SUMMERTIME	VERTEBRATE	LONGFELLOW	DELEGATION	MORIGEROUS
SERPENTINE	SURREALISM	VILLEINAGE	MALEFACTOR	DELIGATION	NAVIGATION
SETTERWORT	SURREALIST	VINDEMIATE	MANIFESTLY	DELIGHTFUL	OBLIGATION
SHAMEFACED	SUSCEPTIVE	VOLLEYBALL	MODIFIABLE	DEMOGORGON	OBLIGATORY
SHAMEFULLY	SUSPENDERS	VULNERABLE	MUNIFICENT	DEMOGRAPHY	OBLIGINGLY
SHOVELHEAD	SUSPENSION	WAGEEARNER	NOTIFIABLE	DEREGULATE	OLEAGINOUS
SHOVELNOSE	SUSTENANCE	WALDENSIAN	PACIFICISM	DEROGATORY	ORANGEWOOD
SHRIEVALTY	SWEDENBORG	WANDERINGS	PATHFINDER	DILIGENTLY	PALAGONITE
SILVERBACK	SYNAERESIS	WANDERLUST	PLAYFELLOW	EGURGITATE	PARAGLOSSA
SILVERBELL	SYNTERESIS	WAPPENSHAW	RIBOFLAVIN	ELONGATION	PARAGONITE
SILVERBILL	SYSTEMATIC	WASSERMANS	SCOFFINGLY	EMARGINATE	PARAGUAYAN
SILVERFISH	TABLECLOTH	WASTEFULLY	SOLIFIDIAN	ENDOGAMOUS	PASIGRAPHY
SILVERSIDE	TABLESPOON	WASTEPAPER	STEPFATHER	ENDOGENOUS	PATAGONIAN
SILVERSKIN	TALLEYRAND	WEAVERBIRD	STUFFINESS	ENGAGEMENT	PEELGARLIC
SILVERWARE	TAMBERLANE	WELLEARNED	TRAFFICKER	EULOGISTIC	PHLEGETHON
SIMMENTHAL	TAMPERFOOT	WESTERNIZE	UNAFFECTED	EVANGELIST	PHLEGMASIA
SINSEMILLA	TANGENTIAL	WHEWELLITE	UNDEFEATED	EVANGELIZE	PHLEGMATIC
SISTERHOOD	TASTEFULLY	WHITEHEART	UNDEFENDED	EVERGLADES	PHLOGISTIC
SKATEBOARD	TATTERSALL	WHITETHORN	UNINFORMED	EXAGGERATE	PHLOGISTON
SMOKESTACK	TEMPERANCE	WHITEWATER	UNOFFICIAL	FAIRGROUND	PHLOGOPITE
SNAKEMOUTH	TENDERFOOT	WHOLESALER	VERIFIABLE	FITZGERALD	PLAYGROUND
SNAKESTONE	TENDERLOIN	WHOLEWHEAT	VIEWFINDER	FOREGATHER	PLOUGHBOTE
SOUTERRAIN	TENDERNESS	WICKEDNESS	VOCIFERATE	FOREGROUND	PLOUGHGATE
SPACECRAFT	TENRECIDAE	WICKERWORK	VOCIFEROUS	FRANGIPANE	PLOUGHWISE
SPELEOLOGY	TENTERHOOK	WILDEBEEST	WALLFLOWER	FRANGIPANI	POLYGAMIST
SPIDERWORT	TERNEPLATE	WILDERNESS	WHARFINGER	FREIGHTAGE	POLYGAMOUS
SPINESCENT	TERREPLEIN	WINCEYETTE	WILDFOWLER	FRINGILLID	PYRAGYRITE
SPITEFULLY	THALESTRIS	WINDERMERE	WINDFLOWER	FULIGINOUS	PYROGRAPHY
SPOKESHAVE	THEREAFTER	WINTERTIME	ABERGLAUBE	FUMIGATION	RECOGNISED
SQUEEZEBOX	THEREANENT	WONDERLAND	ABROGATION	GAINGIVING	RECOGNIZED
STAGECOACH	THREEPENCE	WONDERMENT	ACROGENOUS	GEORGETOWN	RELEGATION
STAGECRAFT	THREEPENNY	WOODENHEAD	AERUGINOUS	GRANGERISM	REORGANIZE
STATECRAFT	THREESCORE	WUNDERKIND	ALBIGENSES	GRANGERIZE	REPUGNANCE
STAVESACRE	TICKERTAPE	YESTERWEEK	ALLEGATION	HANGGLIDER	RESIGNEDLY
STEREOTOMY	TIMBERYARD	YESTERYEAR	ALLEGEANCE	HEMOGLOBIN	RUBIGINOUS
STEREOTYPE	TINKERBELL	ANTIFREEZE	ALLEGIANCE	HOLOGRAPHY	SANDGROPER
STEREOTYPY	TOILETRIES	AQUAFORTIS	ALLIGATION	HOMOGENIZE	SAVAGENESS
STONEBRASH	TORBERNITE	ARTIFICIAL	ALMSGIVING	HYPOGAEOUS	SELEGILINE
STONEHENGE	TORPESCENT	AURIFEROUS	ALTOGETHER	HYPOGENOUS	SENEGALESE
STONEMASON	TORRENTIAL	BAREFOOTED	AMALGAMATE	ILLEGALITY	SEXAGESIMA
STOREFRONT	TORTELLINI	BENEFACTOR	ANTAGONISE	INAUGURATE	SHAGGYMANE
STOREHOUSE	TRAJECTORY	BENEFICENT	ANTAGONISM	INDIGENOUS	SLUGGISHLY
STREETLAMP	TRAVELATOR	BENEFICIAL	ANTAGONIST	INDIGOLITE	SNIGGERING
STREETWISE	TRAVELLERS	CALEFACTOR	ANTAGONIZE	INFIGHTING	SPONGEWARE
STUPEFYING	TRAVELLING	CALIFORNIA	AREOGRAPHY	INTAGLIATE	SPONGIFORM
STUPENDOUS	TRAVELOGUE	CATAFALQUE	ARMAGEDDON	INTEGRATED	STAGGERING
SUAVEOLENT	TRAVERTINE	CHAFFERING	ARROGANTLY	INTEGUMENT	STINGINESS
SUBHEADING	TRECENTIST	CHAPFALLEN	ASSIGNABLE	INVIGILATE	STINGYBARK
SUBJECTION	TREMENDOUS	CHIFFCHAFF	ASSIGNMENT	INVIGORATE	STRAGGLING
SUBJECTIVE	TRIDENTINE	CHIFFONIER	ASTIGMATIC	IRRIGATION	STROGANOFF
SUBMEDIANT	TRIPEHOUND	CONEFLOWER	AUTOGENOUS	KLANGFARBE	SWAGGERING
SUBMERSION	TURPENTINE	CONIFEROUS	AVVOGADORE	KRIEGSPIEL	TAILGATING
SUBREPTION	ULSTERETTE	CORNFLAKES	BACKGAMMON	LANIGEROUS	TANAGRIDAE
SUBSECTION	UNBLEACHED	CORNFLOWER	BACKGROUND	LITIGATION	TELEGRAPHY

THINGUMBOB	DIAPHANOUS	NONCHALANT	SYNTHRONUS	AUSPICIOUS	CONFIDANTE
THOUGHTFUL	DIOPHANTOS	NORTHANGER	TANNHAUSER	AVARICIOUS	CONFIDENCE
TOPOGRAPHY	DRUZHINNIK	NORTHBOUND	TEETHRIDGE	BAILIEWICK	CONFISCATE
TYPOGRAPHY	DUTCHWOMAN	NORTHERNER	TEICHOPSIA	BALLISTICS	CONNIPTION
UNARGUABLE	EARTHQUAKE	NORTHSTEAD	TELPHERAGE	BALLISTITE	CONNIVANCE
UNDIGESTED	EARTHSHINE	NORTHWARDS	TESCHENITE	BARBITURIC	CONSIDERED
UNHYGIENIC	EARTHWORKS	NYMPHOLEPT	TOOTHBRUSH	BARMITZVAH	CONSISTENT
VICEGERENT	EPIPHONEMA	OCTAHEDRON	TOOTHPASTE	BASSINGTON	CONSISTORY
VINEGARISH	EPITHELIUM	OFFTHECUFF	TORCHLIGHT	BESTIALITY	CONTIGUITY
VOETGANGER	EVENHANDED	OFFTHEWALL	TOUCHANDGO	BIRMINGHAM	CONTIGUOUS
VORAGINOUS	EXOTHERMIC	OMOPHORION	TOUCHINESS	BOOZINGKEN	CONTINENCE
WHIGGAMORE	FAIRHAIRED	OPENHANDED	TOUCHPAPER	BOTTICELLI	CONTINGENT
WRONGDOING	FAITHFULLY	OPHTHALMIC	TOUCHPIECE	BOURIGNIAN	CONTINUANT
WRONGFULLY	FEATHERBED	OPOTHERAPY	TOUCHSTONE	BOUSINGKEN	CONTINUING
YOUNGBERRY	FILTHINESS	PARTHENOPE	TRACHELATE	BRATISLAVA	CONTINUITY
ZABAGLIONE	FIRTHSOKEN	PATCHCOCKE	TRICHOLOGY	BRAZILWOOD	CONTINUOUS
ACEPHALOUS	FLASHINESS	PATCHINESS	TROCHANTER	BRITISHISM	CONVICTION
AESTHETICS	FLASHPOINT	PEACHERINO	TROCHOTRON	BUCCINATOR	CONVINCING
AGRAHAYANA	FLESHINESS	PEASHOOTER	TROPHONIUS	BUCKINGHAM	COQUIMBITE
AHITHOPHEL	FLIGHTLESS	PERIHELION	TRUTHFULLY	BURLINGTON	CORDIALITY
ALCOHOLISM	FORTHRIGHT	PINCHPENNY	UNSCHOOLED	BYSSINOSIS	CORDIERITE
ALMSHOUSES	FREEHANDER	PITCHSTONE	UNUNHEXIUM	CACHINNATE	CORDILLERA
ANACHARSIS	FREEHOLDER	PLIOHIPPUS	WANCHANCIE	CALCITONIN	CORRIGENDA
ANNIHILATE	FRESHWATER	POCAHONTAS	WANTHRIVEN	CALLIATURE	COTTIERISM
ANSCHAUUNG	FRIGHTENED	POLYHEDRON	WATCHFULLY	CANCIONERO	CREDITABLE
APOPHTHEGM	FRITHSOKEN	POLYHYMNIA	WATCHMAKER	CANTILEVER	CREDITABLY
APOTHECARY	FROGHOPPER	PONCHIELLI	WATCHTOWER	CANTILLATE	CRIMINALLY
APOTHECIUM	GEOPHYSICS	POSTHUMOUS	WEATHERMAN	CAPRICIOUS	CRITICALLY
APOTHEOSIS	GEOTHERMAL	PROPHETESS	WEIGHTLESS	CAPTIVATED	CULTIVATED
ARITHMETIC	GRAPHOLOGY	PSEPHOLOGY	WELSHWOMAN	CARCINOGEN	CULTIVATOR
BACCHANTES	GUACHAMOLE	PSYCHIATRY	WINCHESTER	CARDIOGRAM	CURRICULUM
BACKHANDED	HALFHOURLY	PSYCHOLOGY	WITCHCRAFT	CARDIOLOGY	DEBRIEFING
BACKHANDER	HAMSHACKLE	PSYCHOPATH	WORSHIPPER	CASSIABARK	DELTIOLOGY
BARCHESTER	HEADHUNTED	PSYCHOPOMP	WORTHINESS	CASSIOPEIA	DEMOISELLE
BAREHEADED	HEADHUNTER	PUMPHANDLE	WORTHWHILE	CAUTIONARY	DENSIMETER
BEDCHAMBER	HEMIHEDRON	PUNCHDRUNK	ZOOTHAPSIS	CAUTIOUSLY	DENTIFRICE
BELSHAZZAR	HIGHHANDED	RAMSHACKLE	ZOOTHERAPY	CENTIGRADE	DERAILLEUR
BENTHAMITE	HITCHHIKER	RESCHEDULE	ABOMINABLE	CENTILITER	DERAILMENT
BIOCHEMIST	HOLOHEDRAL	RHYTHMICAL	ABOMINABLY	CENTILITRE	DESPICABLE
BIOPHYSICS	HOTCHPOTCH	ROUGHHOUSE	ABORIGINAL	CENTIMETER	DESPITEOUS
BIORHYTHMS	ICHTHYOSIS	SACCHARASE	ABSCISSION	CENTIMETRE	DESSIATINE
BIRTHPLACE	INCOHERENT	SACCHARIDE	ABSTINENCE	CERTIORARI	DETAINMENT
BIRTHRIGHT	IRISHWOMAN	SACCHARINE	ACCLIVIOUS	CHARIOTEER	DICTIONARY
BLEPHARISM	IRISHWOMEN	SACCHAROID	AFFLICTION	CHARITABLE	DIFFICULTY
BLITHERING	JACKHAMMER	SCAPHOPODA	AFICIONADO	CHARITABLY	DIFFIDENCE
BOLSHEVIST	KINCHINLAY	SCATHELESS	AGONISTICS	CHEMICALLY	DISCIPLINE
BONDHOLDER	KNIGHTHEAD	SHAGHAIRED	ALCAICERIA	CHERIMOYER	DISFIGURED
BRACHIOPOD	KNIGHTHOOD	SHISHKEBAB	AMELIORATE	CHEVISANCE	DISMISSIVE
BRIGHTNESS	LANTHANIDE	SINGHALESE	AMERINDIAN	CHIRICAUNE	DISPIRITED
BULLHEADED	LEAFHOPPER	SMITHEREEN	AMPHIBIOUS	CIRRIPEDEA	DISSIDENCE
BUTCHERING	LEFTHANDED	SNAPHAUNCE	AMPHIBRACH	CIRRIPEDIA	DISSILIENT
CARPHOLOGY	LEFTHANDER	SNAPHAUNCH	AMPHICTYON	CLAVICHORD	DISSIMILAR
CARTHAMINE	LEUCHAEMIA	SOOTHINGLY	AMPHIGOURI	CLINICALLY	DISSIPATED
CARTHUSIAN	MALTHUSIAN	SOOTHSAYER	AMPHIMACER	CLOMIPHENE	DISTILLATE
CATCHPENNY	MANCHESTER	SOUTHBOUND	AMPHIMIXIS	COCCINEOUS	DISTILLERY
CHICHESTER	MANCHINEEL	SOUTHERNER	AMPHINEURA	COEXISTENT	DISTILLING
CIRRHOPODA	MARSHALSEA	SOUTHWARDS	AMPHITRITE	COGNISANCE	DISTINCTLY
CLODHOPPER	MATCHMAKER	STADHOLDER	AMPHITRYON	COGNIZANCE	DITHIONATE
COATHANGER	MATCHSTALK	STALHELMER	ANAXIMENES	COLLIMATOR	DUPLICATOR
COLCHESTER	MATCHSTICK	STAPHYLINE	ANGUILLULA	COLLIQUATE	ELIMINATOR
COLCHICINE	MIDSHIPMAN	STEPHANITE	APPLICABLE	COMMISSARY	EMACIATION
CONCHIGLIE	MISCHMETAL	STEPHENSON	APPLICATOR	COMMISSION	EMPFINDUNG
CONCHIOLIN	MORPHOLOGY	STICHARION	ARCHIMEDES	COMMISSURE	ENCOIGNURE
CONCHOLOGY	MOUCHARABY	STOCHASTIC	ARCHITRAVE	COMMITMENT	ENGLISHMAN
COPYHOLDER	MOUTHORGAN	SULPHUROUS	ASCRIBABLE	COMMIXTURE	ENGLISHMEN
DARKHAIRED	MOUTHPIECE	SYMPHONIUM	ASTRINGENT	CONCILIATE	EPIDIDYMUS
DECAHEDRON	MUJAHEDDIN	SYNCHRONAL	ATTAINABLE	CONCINNITY	EPIDIORITE
DELPHINIUM	NAPTHALENE	SYNCHRONIC	ATTAINMENT	CONCINNOUS	EPILIMNION
DIACHRONIC	NEIGHBORLY	SYNTHESIZE	AUCTIONEER	CONDIMENTS	ERYSIPELAS

ESCRITOIRE	INEVITABLY	ORIGINALLY	PRECIPITIN	STUDIOUSLY	BLACKBEARD
EXOBIOLOGY	INFLICTION	ORIGINATOR	PREDICTION	STYLISTICS	BLACKBERRY
EXOTICALLY	INIMITABLE	PADDINGTON	PREDISPOSE	SUBLIMATER	BLACKBOARD
EXPLICABLE	INITIATION	PAEDIATRIC	PREHISTORY	SUBLIMINAL	BLACKBULLY
EXPLICITLY	INITIATIVE	PALLIATIVE	PRESIDENCY	SUBMISSION	BLACKENING
EYEWITNESS	INQUIRENDO	PANNICULUS	PRETINCOLE	SUBMISSIVE	BLACKGUARD
FACTITIOUS	INQUISITOR	PARLIAMENT	PREVIOUSLY	SUBSIDENCE	BLACKHEART
FALDISTORY	INSPISSATE	PARMIGIANA	PRIVILEGED	SUBSIDIARY	BLACKSHIRT
FALLINGOFF	INSTIGATOR	PARTIALITY	PROAIRESIS	SUBSISTENT	BLACKSMITH
FARSIGHTED	INTRIGUING	PARTICIPLE	PRODIGALLY	SUCCINCTLY	BLACKSTONE
FASCIATION	IRONICALLY	PARTICULAR	PRODIGIOUS	SUFFICIENT	BLACKTHORN
FASCINATED	ISONIAZIDE	PARTINGALE	PROFICIENT	SURGICALLY	BLACKWATER
FASCINATOR	JARDINIERE	PASSIONATE	PROFITABLE	SUSPICIOUS	BLOCKHOUSE
FASTIDIOUS	JUSTICIARY	PATRIARCHY	PROFITABLY	SVADILFARI	BOOKKEEPER
FASTIGIATE	KUOMINTANG	PATRIOTISM	PROFITLESS	SYNEIDESIS	BREAKABLES
FERNITICLE	LASCIVIOUS	PENNILLION	PROHIBITED	SYPHILITIC	BREAKWATER
FERTILISED	LATTICINIO	PENNISETUM	PROMINENCE	TACTICALLY	BRICKLAYER
FERTILISER	LEAMINGTON	PENSIEROSO	PROMISSORY	TAGLIARINI	BRICKWORKS
FERTILIZER	LEMNISCATE	PENSIONNAT	PROPIONATE	TARDIGRADE	CHECKLATON
FIBRILLATE	LENTICULAR	PENTIMENTO	PROPITIATE	TEDDINGTON	CHECKPOINT
FICTITIOUS	LENTIGINES	PERCIPIENT	PROPITIOUS	TERMINABLE	CHEEKINESS
FILLIBRUSH	LESBIANISM	PERDITIOUS	PROSILIENT	TERMINALIA	CHICKENPOX
FISTICUFFS	LIQUIDATOR	PERFICIENT	PROVIDENCE	TERMINALLY	CHUCKWALLA
FLAGITIOUS	LIQUIDIZER	PERFIDIOUS	PROVINCIAL	TERRIFYING	CLOCKMAKER
FLAMINGANT	LITHISTADA	PERMISSION	PROVISIONS	TERTIARIES	CRANKSHAFT
FLORIBUNDA	MACKINTOSH	PERMISSIVE	PUBLISHING	TESTICULAR	CRICKETING
FONTICULUS	MAGNIFICAT	PERNICIOUS	PUNDIGRION	THALICTRUM	CROCKFORDS
FONTINALIS	MAGNIFYING	PERNICKETY	QUIRINALIA	TIRAILLEUR	CRUIKSHANK
FORBIDDING	MAQUILLAGE	PERSICARIA	RABBINICAL	TOILINETTE	DIASKEUAST
FORGIVABLE	MARCIONITE	PERSIENNES	REAMINGBIT	TORRICELLI	DOORKEEPER
FORMIDABLE	MARGINALIA	PERSIFLAGE	REFRINGENT	TOSSICATED	DREIKANTER
FORTINBRAS	MARGINALLY	PERSISTENT	REPAIRABLE	TOSTICATED	DRINKWATER
FORTISSIMO	MARTINGALE	PERTINENCE	REQUIESCAT	TRADITIONS	FLICKERING
FOSSILIZED	MARTINIQUE	PESTILENCE	RESPIRATOR	TRAGICALLY	FLUNKEYDOM
FOURIERISM	MASKINONGE	PETRIFYING	RHIPIPTERA	TRILINGUAL	FRISKINESS
FRATICELLI	MASKIROVKA	PETRISSAGE	ROCKINGHAM	TRIVIALITY	GAMEKEEPER
FRAXINELLA	MATRIARCHY	PETTICHAPS	ROLLICKING	TRIVIALIZE	GOALKEEPER
FRITILLARY	MAURITANIA	PHILIPPINA	RUSSIANIZE	TURRITELLA	KNOBKERRIE
FROLICSOME	MEANINGFUL	PHILIPPINE	SALPINGIAN	UNBLINKING	KNOCKABOUT
FULFILMENT	MERCIFULLY	PHILISTINE	SALTIGRADE	UNCRITICAL	LADYKILLER
FUNGICIDAL	MILLICURIE	PHOLIDOSIS	SANDINISTA	UNEDIFYING	LOCKKEEPER
FURNISHING	MILLIFARAD	PHYSICALLY	SCHLIMAZEL	UNFAITHFUL	MUDSKIPPER
GALLIAMBIC	MILLIHENRY	PHYSIOCRAT	SEGUIDILLA	UNFRIENDLY	NOUAKCHOTT
GARNIERITE	MILLIMETER	PHYSIOLOGY	SELLINGERS	UNORIGINAL	PAINKILLER
GERMICIDAL	MILLIMETRE	PIANISSIMO	SERVICEMAN	UNSUITABLE	PINAKOTHEK
GINGIVITIS	MISGIVINGS	PICHICIAGO	SIGNIFICAT	UNTHINKING	PRICKLOUSE
GLACIATION	MISSIONARY	PICHICIEGO	SORDIDNESS	UPBRINGING	QUICKSANDS
GLORIOUSLY	MONTICULUS	PILLIWINKS	SPECIALISE	UTILIZABLE	QUICKTHORN
GOLDILOCKS	MORBIDEZZA	PINNIPEDIA	SPECIALISM	VARNISHING	SHACKLETON
GRACIOUSLY	MOUDIEWART	PIPSISSEWA	SPECIALIST	VENTILATOR	SHECKLATON
GRAMICIDIN	MULLIGRUBS	PISTILLATE	SPECIALITY	VERMICELLI	SHOCKINGLY
GRATIFYING	MULTIMEDIA	PLAGIARISE	SPECIALIZE	VERMILLION	SHOCKPROOF
GRATILLITY	MULTIPLIED	PLAGIARISM	SPECIOUSLY	VERNISSAGE	SHOPKEEPER
GRIDIRONER	MULTIPLIER	PLAGIARIST	SPIRITEDLY	VERTICALLY	SNORKELING
GUTTIFERAE	MYELINATED	PLATINISED	SPIRITLESS	VESTIBULUM	SPEAKERINE
HANDICRAFT	NARCISSISM	PLEBISCITE	SPIRITUOUS	VINDICTIVE	SPIRKETING
HARRINGTON	NEGLIGENCE	PLESIOSAUR	SPOLIATION	WASHINGTON	STEAKHOUSE
HECTICALLY	NEGLIGIBLE	PLEXIMETER	SPOLIATIVE	WELLINGTON	STICKINESS
HEROICALLY	NEURILEMMA	POETICALLY	SPURIOUSLY	WIDDICOMBE	STICKYBEAK
HORRIFYING	NONFICTION	POIKILITIC	STABILISER	WILLIAMSON	STOCKINESS
HOSPITABLE	NONVINTAGE	POLLINATED	STABILIZER	WILLINGDON	STRIKINGLY
HOSPITABLY	NONVIOLENT	PONTICELLO	STANISLAUS	WOFFINGTON	THANKFULLY
IMAGINABLE	NOURISHING	PONTIFICAL	STATIONARY	WYCLIFFIAN	THICKENING
IMBRICATED	NUTRITIOUS	PORTIONIST	STATIONERY	YAFFINGALE	TIMEKEEPER
IMPAIRMENT	OBEDIENTLY	POSTILLATE	STATISTICS	BEAUJOLAIS	TOLLKEEPER
IMPLICITLY	OBTAINABLE	POSTILLION	STERILISER	BUCKJUMPER	TRICKINESS
IMPRIMATUR	OFFLICENCE	PRATINCOLE	STERILIZER	COADJUTANT	TRISKELION
INELIGIBLE	ORCHIDEOUS	PRAXITELES	STRAIGHTEN	SHOWJUMPER	WEEDKILLER
INEVITABLE	ORIDINANCE	PRECIPITIN	STRAITENED	WINDJAMMER	ABSOLUTELY

ABSOLUTION	COMPLIMENT	GENTLEFOLK	METALLURGY	SADDLEBILL	TOPOLOGIST
ABSOLUTISM	COMPLUVIUM	GENTLENESS	METTLESOME	SCARLATINA	TRICLINIUM
ACCELERATE	CONCLUDING	GIRDLERINK	MIDDLEBROW	SCARLETINA	TRILLIONTH
ADULLAMITE	CONCLUSION	GRIDLOCKED	MODULATION	SCHALSTEIN	TRIPLICATE
AFFILIATED	CONCLUSIVE	GUILLOTINE	MONILIASIS	SCHOLAEMIA	TRIPLICITY
ALGOLAGNIA	CONFLICTED	HABILITATE	MONILIFORM	SCHOLASTIC	TROGLODYTE
ALKALINITY	CONFLUENCE	HANDLEBARS	MONOLITHIC	SECULARIZE	TUMBLEDOWN
AMBULACRUM	COPULATION	HEADLIGHTS	MORALITIES	SEDULOUSLY	TUMULTUOUS
AMBULATORY	CORALBERRY	HEEDLESSLY	MUMBLENEWS	SEEMLIHEAD	TURTLEDOVE
AMPELOPSIS	COSTLINESS	HELPLESSLY	MUTILATION	SEPULCHRAL	TURTLEHEAD
ANACLASTIC	CUCULLATED	HIGHLANDER	NEEDLECASE	SETTLEMENT	TURTLENECK
ANDALUSIAN	CUDDLESOME	HOMELINESS	NEEDLEWORK	SEXOLOGIST	UMBELLIFER
ANDALUSITE	CUMULATIVE	HOPELESSLY	NETTLERASH	SHELLSHOCK	UNBALANCED
ANHELATION	CUTTLEBONE	HUMBLENESS	NETTLETREE	SHELLYCOAT	UNBELIEVER
APOLLONIAN	CUTTLEFISH	IDEALISTIC	NEWSLETTER	SHIELDRAKE	UNCULTURED
APOLLONIUS	DEADLINESS	IMMOLATION	NIHILISTIC	SHILLELAGH	UNDULATING
APOPLECTIC	DEBILITATE	IMPALPABLE	NIMBLENESS	SHOPLIFTER	UNDULATION
ARGOLEMONO	DECELERATE	IMPALUDISM	NONALIGNED	SHRILLNESS	UNRELIABLE
BABYLONIAN	DECOLLATOR	IMPOLITELY	NONPLUSSED	SICILIENNE	UNRELIEVED
BAFFLEMENT	DECOLORATE	INDELICACY	OSCILLATOR	SIGILLARIA	UNRULINESS
BAILLIWICK	DECOLORIZE	INDELICATE	OSCULATION	SIMILARITY	UNSALARIED
BANGLADESH	DEFILEMENT	INDULGENCE	OSCULATORY	SIMILITUDE	UPHOLSTERY
BARELEGGED	DEMOLITION	INFALLIBLE	OVERLANDER	SIMILLIMUM	VIGILANTES
BATTLEDOOR	DEPILATION	INFALLIBLY	PADDLEFISH	SIMPLICITY	VIROLOGIST
BATTLEDORE	DEPILATORY	INFILTRATE	PAINLESSLY	SIMPLISTIC	VIRULENTLY
BATTLEMENT	DESALINATE	INHALATION	PARALLELED	SIMULACRUM	VITELLICLE
BATTLESHIP	DESOLATION	INKSLINGER	PARKLEAVES	SIMULATING	WATTLEWORK
BEDCLOTHES	DEVELOPING	INSOLENTLY	PECULATION	SIMULATION	WAVELENGTH
BETELGEUSE	DEVOLUTION	INSOLVENCY	PECULIARLY	SINGLENESS	WENTLETRAP
BETELGEUZE	DISCLAIMER	INSULARITY	PENELOPHON	SKILLFULLY	WHEELCHAIR
BEWILDERED	DISCLOSURE	INSULATION	PERILOUSLY	SMALLSCALE	WHEELHOUSE
BOOTLEGGER	DOPPLERITE	INTELIGENT	PERPLEXING	SPALLATION	WHILLYWHAW
BOOTLICKER	DOUBLEBASS	INTOLERANT	PERPLEXITY	SPELLBOUND	WHIRLYBIRD
BOTTLEHEAD	DOUBLETALK	INVALIDATE	PETULANTLY	SPHALERITE	WOOLLYBACK
BOTTLENECK	DUMBLEDORE	INVALIDISM	PHAELONIAN	SPIFLICATE	WOOLLYBUTT
BOUILLOTTE	EBOULEMENT	INVALIDITY	PHILLIPINA	SPILLIKINS	ZEUGLODONT
BOWDLERISE	EBULLIENCE	INVALUABLE	PHILLIPINE	SPOILSPORT	ACCOMPLICE
BOWDLERIZE	ECTHLIPSIS	INVOLUTION	PHILLUMENY	SPOTLESSLY	ACCOMPLISH
BRIDLEPATH	ENROLLMENT	IRRELEVANT	PHYLLIOPOD	STALLENGER	ACCUMULATE
BRILLIANCE	EPAULEMENT	JACULATION	POPULARITY	STALLINGER	ACROMEGALY
BUFFLEHEAD	EPIGLOTTIS	JOCULARITY	POPULARIZE	STEALTHILY	ADRAMELECH
BURGLARIZE	EPIPLASTRA	JUBILANTLY	POPULATION	STEELINESS	ANTIMASQUE
CAMELOPARD	ESCALATION	JUBILATION	POSTLIMINY	STEELWORKS	ANTIMATTER
CANDLEFISH	ESCULAPIAN	KENILWORTH	PROCLIVITY	STEPLADDER	ANTIMONIAN
CANDLEWICK	ETHYLAMINE	KETTLEDRUM	PROFLIGACY	STILLBIRTH	AQUAMANALE
CAPILLAIRE	EUCALYPTOL	KINDLINESS	PROFLIGATE	STILLICIDE	AQUAMANILE
CARELESSLY	EUCALYPTUS	LACKLUSTER	PROPLITEAL	STILLIFORM	AQUAMARINE
CATALECTIC	EUCHLORINE	LACKLUSTRE	PUZZLEMENT	STILLSTAND	ASCOMYCETE
CATALEPTIC	EXCELLENCE	LANDLOCKED	RANDLETREE	STRELITZIA	ASSEMBLAGE
CATALOGUER	EXCELLENCY	LANDLOUPER	RANNLETREE	STRULDBERG	ASSEMBLING
CATTLEGRID	EXHALATION	LANDLUBBER	RANTLETREE	STRULDBRUG	ASSIMILATE
CAVALRYMAN	EXHILARATE	LAVALLIÈRE	RATTLETRAP	SUNGLASSES	ASSUMPTION
CHALLENGED	FABULOUSLY	LEGALISTIC	REBELLIOUS	SUPPLEJACK	ASSUMPTIVE
CHALLENGER	FACILITATE	LIKELIHOOD	RECKLESSLY	SUPPLEMENT	ASTOMATOUS
CHAPLAINCY	FACILITIES	LISTLESSLY	REGULARITY	SUPPLENESS	ASYMMETRIC
CHAULMUGRA	FALKLANDER	LITTLENESS	REGULARIZE	SUPPLICANT	ATRAMENTAL
CHILLINESS	FAMILIARLY	LIVELIHOOD	REGULATION	SUPPLICATE	AUTOMATION
CHURLISHLY	FATALISTIC	LIVELINESS	RESILIENCE	SWALLOWING	AUTOMATIZE
COCHLEARIA	FATALITIES	LOCULAMENT	RESOLUTELY	TABULATION	AUTOMOBILE
COMPLACENT	FEARLESSLY	LONELINESS	RESOLUTION	TACTLESSLY	AUTOMOTIVE
COMPLANATE	FEEBLENESS	LORDLINESS	RESTLESSLY	TANGLEFOOT	BANDMASTER
COMPLEMENT	FEUILLETON	LOVELINESS	REVELATION	THALLIFORM	BAROMETRIC
COMPLETELY	FICKLENESS	MARYLEBONE	REVOLUTION	THELLUSSON	BITUMINOUS
COMPLETION	FIDDLEWOOD	MATELLASSE	RIGELATION	THEOLOGATE	BLOOMSBURY
COMPLEXION	FOOTLIGHTS	MEDDLESOME	RINGLEADER	THEOLOGIAN	BLUEMANTLE
COMPLEXITY	FREELANCER	MEGALITHIC	RUDOLPHINE	THEOLOGISE	BOOKMARKER
COMPLIANCE	FREELOADER	MEGALOSAUR	RUMBLOSSOM	THEOLOGIST	BOOKMOBILE
COMPLICATE	FULLLENGTH	MESOLITHIC	RUTHLESSLY	TIMELINESS	BROOMSTICK
COMPLICITY	GADOLINIUM	METALEPSIS	SADDLEBACK	TIRELESSLY	BUCHMANISM

CACOMISTLE	LEGUMINOUS	STAMMERING	DEADNETTLE	GROUNDSMAN	OCEANARIUM
CACUMINOUS	LIKEMINDED	STEPMOTHER	DECENNOVAL	GROUNDWORK	OCEANGOING
CALAMANDER	LOCOMOTION	STIGMATISE	DEFENSIBLE	GUARNERIUS	OFTENTIMES
CALAMITOUS	LOCOMOTIVE	STIGMATIZE	DEFINITELY	HAKENKREUZ	ORDINARILY
CALAMONDIN	LUXEMBOURG	STRAMONIUM	DEFINITION	HEDONISTIC	ORDINATION
CALUMNIATE	MAHOMMEDAN	SWIMMINGLY	DEFINITIVE	HOMUNCULUS	ORDONNANCE
CARAMELIZE	MAXIMALIST	TASKMASTER	DEGENERACY	HOOTNANNIE	OSTENSIBLE
CEREMONIAL	MAXIMILIAN	THAUMATOSE	DEGENERATE	HUMANISTIC	OSTENSIBLY
CEREMONIES	MINIMALISM	THERMIONIC	DELINQUENT	HUMANITIES	PAGINATION
CHREMATIST	MINIMALIST	THERMISTOR	DEMONIACAL	IMMUNOLOGY	PALINDROME
CHROMOSOME	MINIMARKET	THERMOSTAT	DEMONOLOGY	IMPENITENT	PALYNOLOGY
CLAMMINESS	MONUMENTAL	THROMBOSIS	DEPENDABLE	INCENDIARY	PARANORMAL
COROMANDEL	MOZAMBIQUE	TOURMALINE	DEPENDENCE	INCINERATE	PARENCHYMA
CYNOMOLGUS	NEWSMONGER	TRAUMATIZE	DEPENDENCY	INCONSTANT	PARENTHOOD
DECAMPMENT	NONSMOKING	TRIUMPHANT	DETONATION	INCUNABULA	PARENTLESS
DECIMALIZE	OBLOMOVISM	UBERMENSCH	DEVANAGARI	INDENTURES	PARONYCHIA
DECOMPOSED	OPENMINDED	ULTIMATELY	DIAGNOSTIC	INDONESIAN	PENINSULAR
DEFAMATION	OPTIMISTIC	UNCOMMONLY	DICYNODONT	INFINITELY	PHAENOTYPE
DEFAMATORY	ORNAMENTAL	UNFAMILIAR	DIDUNCULUS	INFINITIVE	PHRENESIAC
DHARMSHALA	OVERMATTER	UNHAMPERED	DIMINISHED	INGENERATE	PHRENOLOGY
DIREMPTION	PALIMPSEST	UNNUMBERED	DIMINUENDO	INJUNCTION	PIRANDELLO
DISEMBOGUE	PANAMANIAN	UNROMANTIC	DIMINUTION	INSANITARY	PLEONASTIC
DISEMBOWEL	PARAMARIBO	VEHEMENTLY	DIMINUTIVE	INSENSIBLE	POGONOTOMY
DOCIMASTIC	PARAMETRIC	VOLUMINOUS	DINANDERIE	INTANGIBLE	POIGNANTLY
DOWNMARKET	PEDIMENTAL	ABONNEMENT	DISENCHANT	INTENDMENT	POLYNESIAN
DREAMINESS	PEREMPTORY	ACCENTUATE	DISENGAGED	INTENERATE	POLYNOMIAL
DYNAMITARD	PHARMACIST	ACRONYCHAL	DISENNOBLE	INTENTNESS	POTENTIATE
EFFEMINACY	PLASMODESM	ADMINISTER	DISINCLINE	INTINCTION	POTENTILLA
EFFEMINATE	POCKMANTIE	ADMONITION	DISINHERIT	INTONATION	PREDNISONE
ENCAMPMENT	POCKMARKED	ADRENALINE	DIURNALIST	INVINCIBLE	QUAINTNESS
ENORMOUSLY	POLYMERIZE	ADRENERGIC	DIVINATION	JOURNALESE	QUEENSBURY
ENTOMBMENT	PORTMANTLE	ADVENTURER	DOMINATING	JOURNALISM	QUEENSTOWN
ENTOMOLOGY	PORTMANTUA	AERENCHYMA	DOMINATION	JOURNALIST	RANUNCULUS
ESTIMATION	POSTMASTER	AGRONOMIST	EATANSWILL	JOURNEYMAN	RAVENOUSLY
EUHEMERISM	POSTMORTEM	ALGONQUIAN	ECHINODERM	JUGENDSTIL	RAVENSBILL
EXHUMATION	PRAEMUNIRE	ALIENATION	ECHINOIDEA	LAMENTABLE	RAVENSDUCK
FASTMOVING	PRAGMATISM	ALPENSTOCK	EMBANKMENT	LAMENTABLY	RAVENSTONE
FISHMONGER	PRAGMATIST	AMMUNITION	EMBONPOINT	LAMINATION	RAWINSONDE
FRAGMENTAL	PREEMINENT	ANNUNCIATE	EMMENTALER	LARYNGITIS	RECONCILED
FREEMARTIN	PSAMMOPHIL	ANTINOMIAN	ENGENDRURE	LEBENSRAUM	RECONSIDER
FREEMASONS	PYROMANIAC	ASCENDANCY	ENSANGUINE	LICENTIATE	REDUNDANCY
GALIMATIAS	QUIZMASTER	ASCENDENCY	EQUANIMITY	LICENTIOUS	REFINEMENT
GALUMPHING	RAGAMUFFIN	ASTONISHED	ERGONOMICS	LOGANBERRY	REGENERATE
GLEEMAIDEN	RAZZMATAZZ	ATHANASIAN	ESTANCIERO	LUMINARIST	REJONEADOR
GOBEMOUCHE	REARMAMENT	ATTENDANCE	ETERNALIZE	LUMINOSITY	RELENTLESS
GRAMMARIAN	RECOMMENCE	AUTONOMOUS	EXPENDABLE	LYCHNAPSIA	RELINQUISH
HACKMATACK	RECOMPENSE	BALANCHINE	EXTENDABLE	LYSENKOISM	REMONETISE
HALLMARKED	REDEMPTION	BEHINDHAND	EXTENSIBLE	MABINOGION	REMUNERATE
HANDMAIDEN	REGIMENTAL	BELONGINGS	EXTINCTION	MACONOCHIE	REPENTANCE
HEADMASTER	REGIMENTED	BIANNUALLY	EXTINGUISH	MAKUNOUCHI	RESENTMENT
IGNIMBRITE	RESEMBLING	BIENNIALLY	FEARNOUGHT	MALINGERER	RETINALITE
ILLUMINATE	RESUMPTION	BIPINNARIA	FEMININITY	MAYONNAISE	REVENGEFUL
ILLUMINATI	RHEUMATICS	BRAINCHILD	FORINSECAL	MEITNERIUM	RIDINGHOOD
IMMEMORIAL	RHEUMATISM	BRAININESS	FRAUNHOFER	MELANCHOLY	RIPSNORTER
INCOMPLETE	RHEUMATOID	BRAINPOWER	FRIENDLESS	MELANESIAN	ROLANDSECK
INCUMBENCY	RINGMASTER	BRAINSTORM	FRIENDSHIP	MENINGITIS	ROMANESQUE
INDUMENTUM	ROSEMALING	BROWNLANDS	GEMINATION	MESENTERON	ROSANILINE
INGEMINATE	RUDIMENTAL	BROWNSTONE	GESUNDHEIT	MISHNAYOTH	RUBINSTEIN
INHUMANITY	SALAMANDER	CATENACCIO	GREENCLOTH	MOLENDINAR	RUMINANTIA
INSEMINATE	SCAMMOZZIS	CHIMNEYPOT	GREENFINCH	MONANDROUS	RUMINATION
INTEMERATE	SCRIMSHANK	CHRONICLER	GREENHEART	MOURNFULLY	RUMINATIVE
INTIMATELY	SEISMOLOGY	CHRONICLES	GREENHOUSE	MUTINOUSLY	SAVONAROLA
INTIMATION	SHIMMERING	CHRONOLOGY	GREENSHANK	MYRINGITIS	SCIENTIFIC
INTIMIDATE	SKRIMSHANK	COLONNADED	GREENSTICK	NDRANGHETA	SCORNFULLY
IRONMONGER	SLAMMERKIN	COMANCHERO	GREENSTONE	NEFANDROUS	SEANNACHIE
IRREMEDIAL	SMARMINESS	COPENHAGEN	GREENSWARD	NOMINALIST	SECONDBEST
KHIDMUTGAR	SNOWMOBILE	CORINTHIAN	GROUNDBAIT	NOMINATION	SECONDHAND
KILOMETRES	SPERMACETI	CORONATION	GROUNDLESS	NOMINATIVE	SECONDMENT
LASTMINUTE	SPERMICIDE	COVENANTER	GROUNDLING	NONONSENSE	SECONDRATE

SEVENTIETH	ARACOSTYLE	COTTONWOOD	GLYCOSURIA	MARIONETTE	PERCOLATOR
SPLANCHNIC	ARAGONITES	COXCOMICAL	GONDOLIERS	MEADOWPLAN	PERFORATED
SPLENDIDLY	ASAFOETIDA	CTENOPHORA	GONIOMETER	MEDIOCRITY	PERFORATOR
SPOONERISM	ASTROLOGER	CTENOPHORE	GRAMOPHONE	MELLOWNESS	PERFORMING
SPRINGBOKS	ASTRONOMER	CUCKOOPINT	GYMNOSOPHY	METHODICAL	PERIODICAL
SPRINGHAAS	AUTHORISED	CYCLOPEDIA	GYMNOSPERM	METHOMANIA	PERSONABLE
SPRINGLESS	AUTHORSHIP	CYCLOSTYLE	GYPSOPHILA	METROPOLIS	PERSONALLY
SPRINGLIKE	AXINOMANCY	CYSTOSCOPY	HAGIOSCOPE	MICROFICHE	PETROGLYPH
SPRINGTAIL	BALLOONING	DEPLORABLE	HALLOYSITE	MICROLIGHT	PETRONELLA
SPRINGTIME	BALLOONIST	DEPLORABLY	HARMONIOUS	MICROMETER	PHENOMENAL
SPRINKLING	BAMBOOZLED	DEPLOYMENT	HECTOLITRE	MICRONESIA	PHENOMENON
STAGNATION	BASSOONIST	DESBOROUGH	HELIOGRAPH	MICROPHONE	PHILOPOENA
STERNALGIA	BERMOOTHES	DESPONDENT	HELIOLATER	MICROSCOPE	PHILOSOPHY
STRENGTHEN	BIOLOGICAL	DEUTOPLASM	HELIOTROPE	MIDLOTHIAN	PHILOXENIA
STRINDBERG	BORROWINGS	DIABOLICAL	HIEROGLYPH	MIGNONETTE	PHONOGRAPH
STRINGENCY	BOTTOMLESS	DIACONICON	HIEROMANCY	MILEOMETER	PHOTODIODE
STRINGENDO	BUFFOONERY	DIAGONALLY	HIEROPHANT	MIMEOGRAPH	PHOTOGENIC
STRINGHALT	BUTTONDOWN	DICTOGRAPH	HIEROSCOPY	MISCONDUCT	PHOTOGRAPH
STRONGHOLD	BUTTONHOLE	DIPLODOCUS	HIPPOCRENE	MISFORTUNE	PHOTONASTY
STRONGROOM	CANNONBALL	DIPLOMATIC	HIPPODROME	MOTIONLESS	PHOTOPHORE
SURINAMESE	CANTONMENT	DIPSOMANIA	HIPPOGRIFF	MUSSORGSKY	PHYTOTOXIN
SYNONYMOUS	CAPNOMANCY	DISCOBOLUS	HIPPOGRYPH	MUTTONHEAD	PIANOFORTE
TARANTELLA	CARTOMANCY	DISCOLORED	HIPPOMANES	MYRIOSCOPE	PICTOGRAPH
TAXONOMIST	CARTOONIST	DISCOMFORT	HISTOLYSIS	NARCOLEPSY	PIGEONHOLE
TECHNETIUM	CASSOLETTE	DISCOMMODE	HISTORICAL	NARROWBOAT	PILLOWCASE
TECHNICIAN	CATHOLICON	DISCOMPOSE	HOMEOPATHY	NARROWDALE	PILLOWSLIP
TECHNOCRAT	CATHOLICOS	DISCONCERT	HOMEOUSIAN	NARROWNESS	PLANOBLAST
TECHNOLOGY	CELLOPHANE	DISCONNECT	HOMOOUSIAN	NATIONALLY	PLEROPHORY
THRENODIAL	CENSORIOUS	DISCONTENT	HOWSOMEVER	NATIONWIDE	PLUTOCRACY
TOURNAMENT	CENSORSHIP	DISCOPHORA	HYALOPHANE	NEAPOLITAN	PORLOCKING
TOURNIQUET	CHAROLLAIS	DISCORDANT	HYDROLYSIS	NECROMANCY	PORNOCRACY
TRIANGULAR	CHEMONASTY	DISCOURAGE	HYDROMETER	NECROPOLIS	PRECOCIOUS
TRIANGULUM	CHIROMANCY	DISCOVERER	HYDROPHANE	NETWORKING	PREPOSITOR
TYRANNICAL	CHIRONOMIC	DISHONESTY	HYDROPHYTE	NEUROLEMMA	PREPOSSESS
TYRANNISED	CHIROPTERA	DISJOINTED	HYDROPLANE	NICROSILAL	PREPOTENCE
UNCONFINED	CISPONTINE	DISLOYALTY	HYDROPONIC	NINCOMPOOP	PRIMORDIAL
UNDENIABLE	CITRONELLA	DISPOSABLE	HYGROMETER	NORMOBLAST	PROFOUNDLY
UNFINISHED	CLADOPHYLL	DISPOSSESS	HYPNOTIZED	NOTIONALLY	PROMONTORY
UNMANNERED	CLAMOURING	DISSOCIATE	HYPSOMETRY	OCHLOCRACY	PRONOUNCED
UNMANNERLY	CLEROMANCY	DISSOLVENT	IATROGENIC	OMBROMETER	PROPORTION
UNPUNCTUAL	CNIDOBLAST	DISSONANCE	ICONOCLAST	OMBROPHOBE	PROPOSITUS
UNUNNILIUM	COLEOPTERA	DISTORTION	ICONOSCOPE	OOPHORITIS	PROTOPLASM
VALENTINES	COLEORHIZA	DOSTOEVSKY	ICOSOHEDRA	OPISOMETER	PSILOCYBIN
VIETNAMESE	COLLOCUTER	DRACONITES	IMBROCCATA	OPPROBRIUM	PSOCOPTERA
VIVANDIÈRE	COLLOQUIAL	DRAGONROOT	IMPROBABLE	ORATORICAL	PULSOMETER
WAPENSCHAW	COLPORTAGE	DROSOPHILA	IMPROBABLY	ORTHOCAINE	PURPOSEFUL
WAPINSCHAW	COLPORTEUR	ECOLOGICAL	IMPROPERLY	ORTHOCLASE	PYCNOGONID
WITSNAPPER	COLPOSCOPE	ECONOMICAL	IMPROVISED	ORTHOGONAL	PYTHOGENIC
YTHUNDERED	COMFORTING	EFFRONTERY	INCHOATIVE	ORTHOPNOEA	RADIOGRAPH
ACHROMATIC	COMMODIOUS	EMBROIDERY	INEXORABLE	ORTHOPTICS	RADIOLARIA
ACOLOUTHOS	COMMONALLY	EMPLOYMENT	INGLORIOUS	OSTEOBLAST	RANDOMNESS
ACTIONABLE	COMMONWEAL	ENCLOISTER	INTROSPECT	OSTEOCOLLA	RAPPORTEUR
ALCYONARIA	COMPOSITOR	ENGROSSING	INVIOLABLE	OSTEOLEPIS	RATIONALLY
ALPHONSINE	COMPOUNDED	EPANOPHORA	JARGONELLE	OSTEOPATHY	REASONABLE
AMPHOTERIC	CONCOCTION	ETHEOSTOMA	JINGOISTIC	OSTEOPHYTE	REASONABLY
ANACOUSTIC	CONCORDANT	EUDIOMETER	KEYBOARDER	OSTROGOTHS	REPRODUCER
ANALOGICAL	CONDOLENCE	EUPHONIOUS	LIGNOCAINE	OUTPOURING	RESPONDENT
ANATOMICAL	CONDOTTIER	EVAPORATED	LINEOMYCIN	OVIPOSITOR	RESPONSIVE
ANCHORETIC	CONFORMIST	FANTOCCINI	LITHOGRAPH	OXYMORONIC	RETROGRADE
ANDROMACHE	CONFORMITY	FELLOWSHIP	LITHOMARGE	PANSOPHIST	RETROGRESS
ANEMOGRAPH	CONFOUNDED	FIBROSITIS	LITHOPHANE	PANTOGRAPH	RETROSPECT
ANEMOMETER	CONSONANCE	FLAVOURING	LORDOLATRY	PANTOSCOPE	RHETORICAL
ANGIOSPERM	CONSONANTS	FOREORDAIN	MACROBIOTE	PARDONABLE	RHINOCEROS
ANGLOPHILE	CONSORTIUM	FORFOUGHEN	MACROCARPA	PARDONABLY	RHINOLALIA
ANGLOPHOBE	CONTORTION	GARGOUILLE	MAISONETTE	PARVOVIRUS	RHINOPHYMA
ANTHOCLORE	CONVOLUTED	GASCONNADE	MALCONTENT	PASTORELLA	SACROSANCT
ANTIOCHENE	CONVOLVUTE	GEOLOGICAL	MALLOPHAGA	PATHOGENIC	SALMONELLA
ANTIOCHIAN	CORROBOREE	GLAMOURISE	MANGOSTEEN	PATRONISED	SANFORISED
APOLOGETIC	COTTONTAIL	GLYCOLYSIS	MARIOLATRY	PATRONYMIC	SAPROPHYTE

SARCOCOLLA
SARCOLEMMA
SAUROPSIDA
SCHOOLBOOK
SCHOOLGIRL
SCHOOLMAAM
SCOTODINIA
SEASONABLE
SEASONABLY
SERMONICAL
SERVOMOTOR
SHADOWLESS
SIGNORELLI
SILHOUETTE
SKEUOMORPH
SOGDOLAGER
SOGDOLIGER
SOGDOLOGER
SOMNOLENCE
SOPHOCLEAN
SOPHOMORIC
SPODOMANCY
STATOCRACY
STENOTYPER
STYLOPISED
SUBCOMPACT
SUBROUTINE
SUPPORTING
SUPPORTIVE
SUPPOSEDLY
SURROUNDED
SYMBOLICAL
SYNCOPATED
TACHOGRAPH
TACHOMETER
TAILORMADE
TAMBOURINE
TEETOTALER
TEINOSCOPE
TELEOSTOME
TELIOSPORE
THIXOTROPY
THOROUGHLY
TINTORETTO
TOMFOOLERY
TRAMONTANA
TRAMONTANE
TRAVOLATOR
TRIFOLIATE
TROMOMETER
TROPOPAUSE
TROPOPHYTE
ULTRONEOUS
UNGROUNDED
UNIFORMITY
UNPROMPTED
UNPROVOKED
UROPOIESIS
VICTORIANA
VICTORIOUS
WEAPONLESS
WILLOWHERB
WINDOWPANE
WINDOWSILL
XIPHOPAGUS
YARBOROUGH
YELLOWBACK
YELLOWGIRL
YELLOWJACK

YELLOWLEGS
YELLOWROOT
YELLOWWOOD
ZINCOGRAPH
ZOOLOGICAL
ZUMBOORUCK
ABRUPTNESS
ADIAPHORON
AEROPHAGIA
ANALPHABET
ANCIPITOUS
ANTEPENULT
ANTIPHONAL
ANTIPODEAN
ANTIPROTON
AREOPAGITE
ARMIPOTENT
AUTOPLASTY
BACKPACKER
BLASPHEMER
BUCEPHALUS
CAERPHILLY
CAESPITOSE
CALYPTRATE
CANEPHORUS
CATAPHRACT
CHAMPIGNON
CHEAPSKATE
CHIMPANZEE
CLASPKNIFE
CLUMPERTON
CONSPECTUS
CONSPIRACY
CORYPHAEUS
CREOPHAGUS
CRISPBREAD
CRISPINIAN
CRYOPHORUS
DECAPITATE
DECIPHERED
DEPOPULATE
DILAPIDATE
DISAPPOINT
DISAPPROVE
ECCOPROTIC
ECHOPRAXIA
ELLIPTICAL
ENCEPHALON
ENKEPHALIN
ENRAPTURED
EPISPASTIC
ESCAPEMENT
EURYPTERUS
EXASPERATE
EXEMPTNESS
FAREPAYING
FLIPPANTLY
FOOTPRINTS
GETUPANDGO
GRUMPINESS
HANDPICKED
HEADPHONES
HEMIPLEGIA
HEMOPHILIA
HITOPADESA
HITOPODESA
HOLOPHOTAL
HOLOPHYTIC
HOMOPHOBIA

HOMOPHOBIC
HOMOPHONIC
INCAPACITY
INCAPARINA
INDAPAMIDE
INSIPIDITY
KENSPECKLE
LOTOPHAGUS
MAINPERNOR
MALAPROPOS
MANIPULATE
METAPHRASE
METAPLASIS
MONOPHONIC
MONOPLEGIA
MONOPODIUM
MONOPOLISE
MONOPOLIZE
MONOPTERON
MONOPTEROS
NEWSPAPERS
NOSOPHOBIA
OCCUPATION
OESOPHAGUS
OWLSPIEGLE
PANOPTICON
PARAPHASIA
PARAPHILIA
PARAPHONIA
PARAPHRASE
PARAPHYSIS
PARAPLEGIA
PARAPLEGIC
PARAPRAXIS
PEDIPALPUS
PERIPHERAL
PHOSPHORUS
PICKPOCKET
POLYPHEMUS
POURPARLER
PROMPTBOOK
PROMPTNESS
PROSPECTOR
PROSPECTUS
PROSPERINA
PROSPERITY
PROSPEROUS
PYROPHORUS
REAPPRAISE
RECEPTACLE
RECIPROCAL
RECUPERATE
RESUPINATE
RHAMPASTOS
SALOPETTES
SCHIPPERKE
SCRIPTURAL
SCRIPTURES
SCRUPULOUS
SCULPTRESS
SHAMPOOING
SHEEPISHLY
SHEEPSHANK
SLEEPINESS
SLOPPINESS
STRAPONTIN

STREPITANT
STREPITOSO
STRIPTEASE
STROPHIOLE
SUBSPECIES
SWEEPSTAKE
TELEPATHIC
TELEPHONIC
TOCOPHEROL
TRAMPOLINE
TRESPASSER
UNEMPLOYED
UNEXPECTED
UNEXPLORED
UNIMPAIRED
USURPATION
VITUPERATE
VIVIPAROUS
VOLUPTUARY
VOLUPTUOUS
WHISPERING
WOODPECKER
WOODPIGEON
XENOPHOBIA
XENOPHOBIC
XEROPHYTIC
ANTIQUATED
BLANQUETTE
CHINQUAPIN
ILLAQUEATE
LANSQUENET
OBSEQUIOUS
SARSQUATCH
SEMIQUAVER
TRANQUILLY
UNREQUITED
ABERRATION
ABHORRENCE
ABNORMALLY
ABSORBANCE
ABSORPTION
ABSTRACTED
ACCORDANCE
ACCURATELY
ADMIRATION
ADMIRINGLY
ADVERSARIA
ADVERTISER
AFFORDABLE
AFRORMOSIA
AFTERBIRTH
AFTERHOURS
AFTERIMAGE
AFTERPIECE
AFTERSHAVE
AFTERSHOCK
AFTERTASTE
AFTERWARDS
AIRFREIGHT
ALDERMANLY
ALDERWOMAN
ALLUREMENT
ALTERATION
ALTERNATOR
AMBARVALIA
ANACRUSTIC
ANADROMOUS
ANGURVADEL
ANTARCTICA

ANTHRACINE
ANTHRACITE
ANTHROPOID
APOCRYPHAL
APOTROPAIC
APPARENTLY
APPARITION
APTERYGOTA
ARTHRALGIA
ARTHROMERE
ASPARAGINE
ASPERSIONS
ASPIRATION
ASSORTMENT
ASTEROIDEA
AUSTRALIAN
AUSTRALORP
AUSTRINGER
AVERRHOISM
BABIROUSSA
BALBRIGGAN
BANKRUPTCY
BEFOREHAND
BELARUSIAN
BHADRAPADA
BICHROMATE
BIOGRAPHER
BIPARTISAN
BLEARYEYED
BORDRAGING
BUMFREEZER
BUSHRANGER
CALORIFIER
CAMBRENSIS
CAMERLENGO
CAMERLINGO
CAMERONIAN
CANCRIZANS
CAPERNAITE
CAPERNOITY
CASTRATION
CATARRHINE
CATCRACKER
CENTRALIZE
CENTRIFUGE
CENTROSOME
CESTRACION
CHAIRWOMAN
CHEERFULLY
CHEIRONOMY
CHERRYWOOD
CHEVROTAIN
CHLORINATE
CHLOROFORM
CLAIRCOLLE
CLEARSTORY
CLEARWATER
COHERENTLY
COLORATION
COLORATURA
COMPRADORE
COMPREHEND
COMPRESSED
COMPRESSOR
COMPROMISE
CONCRETION
CONGREGATE
CONTRABAND
CONTRACTOR

CONTRADICT
CONTRAFLOW
CONTRAHENT
CONTRARILY
CONTRAVENE
CONTRECOUP
CONTRIBUTE
CONTRITION
CONTROLLER
CONTROVERT
COPARCENER
COPERNICUS
CUCURBITAL
CYBERNETIC
DAYDREAMER
DECORATION
DECORATIVE
DELCREDERE
DELIRATION
DEMIRELIEF
DEMORALISE
DEMORALIZE
DENDROPHIS
DEPARTMENT
DEPARTURES
DEPORTMENT
DESCRIBING
DESERVEDLY
DETERMINED
DETERMINER
DETERRENCE
DIADROMOUS
DICHROMATE
DICHROMISM
DISARRANGE
DISCREETLY
DISCREPANT
DISCRETION
DISGRUNTLE
DISORDERED
DISORDERLY
DISTRACTED
DISTRAUGHT
DISTRESSED
DISTRIBUTE
DISTRINGAS
DIVERGENCE
DOVERCOURT
DREARINESS
DREARISOME
DYSCRASITE
DYSPROSIUM
DYSTROPHIC
EFFERVESCE
EFFORTLESS
ELDERBERRY
ELYTRIFORM
EMBERGOOSE
EMIGRATION
ENTEROCELE
ENTERPRISE
ESCARPMENT
EUPHROSYNE
EXECRATION
EXPERIENCE
EXPERIMENT
EXPIRATION
EXTERNALLY
FAVORITISM

FEDERALISM	INSTRUMENT	NEUTRALIZE	RITORNELLE	UNABRIDGED	ANTISEPSIS
FEDERALIST	INSURGENCY	NEUTROPHIL	RITORNELLO	UNDERBURNT	ANTISEPTIC
FEDERATION	INTERBREED	NEWSREADER	ROADRUNNER	UNDERCLASS	ANTISOCIAL
FEVERISHLY	INTERCEDER	NICARAGUAN	ROBERDSMAN	UNDERCOVER	ANTISTATIC
FIBERGLASS	INTERCLUDE	NOTORYCTES	ROBERTSMAN	UNDERCRAFT	APPOSITION
FIGURATION	INTERESTED	NOURRITURE	SACERDOTAL	UNDERCROFT	ASBESTOSIS
FIGURATIVE	INTERFERER	NUMERATION	SAMARSKITE	UNDERFLOOR	ASSESSMENT
FIGUREHEAD	INTERFERON	NUTCRACKER	SATURATION	UNDERLEASE	ASSISTANCE
FILTRATION	INTERLEAVE	OBSERVABLE	SATURNALIA	UNDERLINEN	ATMOSPHERE
FLAGRANTLY	INTERLOPER	OBSERVANCE	SAUERKRAUT	UNDERLYING	AUTOSTRADA
FLOORBOARD	INTERMARRY	OCCURRENCE	SCLERIASIS	UNDERNEATH	BABESIASIS
FLOORCLOTH	INTERMEZZO	OROBRANCHE	SCURRILITY	UNDERPANTS	BABYSITTER
FLOURISHED	INTERNALLY	OTHERGATES	SCURRILOUS	UNDERSCORE	BACKSLIDER
FORERUNNER	INTERNMENT	OTHERGUESS	SECURITIES	UNDERSHIRT	BACKSTAIRS
FOUDROYANT	INTERNODAL	OUVIRANDRA	SEPARATELY	UNDERSIZED	BACKSTROKE
FOURRAGERE	INTERPHONE	OVERRIDING	SEPARATION	UNDERSKIRT	BAGASSOSIS
FRATRICIDE	INTERSTATE	PADAREWSKI	SEPARATISM	UNDERSLUNG	BALUSTRADE
FUTURISTIC	INTERSTICE	PALFRENIER	SEPARATIST	UNDERSTAND	BANISHMENT
GANGRENOUS	INTERTRIGO	PANARITIUM	SEPARATRIX	UNDERSTATE	BARASINGHA
GASTRONOME	INTERTWINE	PANCRATIUM	SHEARWATER	UNDERSTEER	BARYSPHERE
GASTRONOMY	INTERWEAVE	PAPERCHASE	SIDERATION	UNDERSTOOD	BESTSELLER
GENERALISE	INTERWOVEN	PAPERKNIFE	SIDEROSTAT	UNDERSTUDY	BLISSFULLY
GENERALITY	INVARIABLE	PARARTHRIA	SINARCHIST	UNDERTAKER	BONDSWOMAN
GENERALIZE	INVARIABLY	PATERNALLY	SINARQUIST	UNDERVALUE	BONESHAKER
GENERATION	KATERFELTO	PEJORATIVE	SMORREBROD	UNDERWATER	BOOKSELLER
GENERATRIX	LABORATORY	PERORATION	SOBERSIDES	UNDERWORLD	BRASSBOUND
GENEROSITY	LACERATION	PICARESQUE	SOMBRERITE	UNDERWRITE	BREASTBONE
GENEROUSLY	LACHRYMOSE	PILGRIMAGE	SOMERSAULT	UNFORESEEN	BREASTFEED
GEOGRAPHER	LAMARCKISM	PITYRIASIS	SOMERVILLE	UNHERALDED	BREASTWORK
GEOGRAPHIC	LAMBREQUIN	POKERFACED	SOUBRIQUET	UNSCRAMBLE	BRESSUMMER
GEOTROPISM	LAWBREAKER	POMERANIAN	SPERRYLITE	UNSCRIPTED	CALESCENCE
GILLRAVAGE	LEDERHOSEN	PONEROLOGY	SQUIREARCH	UNWORKABLE	CATASTASIS
GONORRHOEA	LIBERALISM	POWERHOUSE	STAUROLITE	UPPERCLASS	CELESTIALS
GOVERNANCE	LIBERALITY	PREARRANGE	SUBORBITAL	VENERATION	CHEESECAKE
GOVERNESSY	LIBERALIZE	PROCREATOR	SUBTRAHEND	VETERINARY	CHEESEWOOD
GOVERNMENT	LIBERATION	PROCRUSTES	SUBTROPICS	VICEREGENT	CHERSONESE
GUBERNATOR	LITERATURE	PROGRAMMER	SUFFRAGIST	VIDARABINE	CHESSBOARD
HEMORRHAGE	LITURGICAL	PROPRAETOR	SUGARALLIE	VIGOROUSLY	CHESSYLITE
HETERODOXY	LIVERWURST	PROPRIETOR	SULTRINESS	WATERBORNE	CHOPSTICKS
HETERODYNE	LOGARITHMS	PROTRACTED	SUPERADDED	WATERBRASH	CHRISTIANA
HETEROGAMY	LOGORRHOEA	PROTRACTOR	SUPERCARGO	WATERCOLOR	CHRYSIPPUS
HISTRIONIC	LUPERCALIA	PROTRUSILE	SUPERGIANT	WATERCRESS	CHRYSOLITE
HOMORELAPS	LUXURIANCE	PROTRUSION	SUPERHUMAN	WATERFRONT	CLANSWOMAN
HONORARIUM	MANDRAGORA	PUBERULENT	SUPERMODEL	WATERLEVEL	CLASSICISM
HORNRIMMED	MATERIALLY	QUADRANGLE	SUPERPOWER	WATERMELON	CLASSICIST
HOVERCRAFT	MATERNALLY	QUADRATURA	SUPERSONIC	WATERPROOF	CLASSIFIED
HUMORESQUE	MATURATION	QUADRICEPS	SUPERSTORE	WATERSKIER	CLOISTERED
HUMOROUSLY	MEAGRENESS	QUADRIREME	SUPERTONIC	WATERSPOUT	CLUMSINESS
HYPERBOLIC	MEMBRANOUS	QUARRENDER	SUPERVISED	WATERTIGHT	COARSENESS
HYPERDULIA	MEMORANDUM	RAJPRAMUKH	SUPERVISOR	WATERWHEEL	COLDSTREAM
ICEBREAKER	MENORRHOEA	RECURRENCE	SUPERWOMAN	WATERWINGS	COLOSSALLY
IGNORANTLY	MEPERIDINE	REFERENDUM	SUPPRESSED	WATERWORKS	COLOSSIANS
IMMORALITY	MINERALOGY	REGARDLESS	SUPPRESSOR	WOLFRAMITE	COMESTIBLE
IMMORTELLE	MISERICORD	REMARKABLE	SURFRIDING	YGGDRASILL	COPESETTIC
IMPARLANCE	MISPRISION	REMARKABLY	SURPRISING	ZAPOROGIAN	CORNSTALKS
IMPERATIVE	MITHRIDATE	REMORSEFUL	SUZERAINTY	ABYSSINIAN	CORNSTARCH
IMPERSONAL	MODERATELY	REPARATION	SYNCRETISE	ACCESSIBLE	COUNSELING
IMPERVIOUS	MODERATION	REPERTOIRE	TABERNACLE	ACCESSIONS	COUNSELLOR
IMPORTANCE	MONARCHIST	REPORTEDLY	TAPERECORD	ACCUSATION	CRISSCROSS
IMPURITIES	MONTRACHET	RESERVISTS	TARTRAZINE	ACCUSATIVE	CROSSBONES
INDIRECTLY	MOTORCYCLE	RESORCINOL	TENDRILLED	ACCUSINGLY	CROSSBREED
INEBRIATED	MUCKRAKING	RESTRAINED	TIEBREAKER	ACCUSTOMED	CROSSCHECK
INFERNALLY	MYCORRHIZA	RESTRICTED	TIMBROLOGY	ADJUSTABLE	CROSSHATCH
INFORMALLY	NATURALISM	RESURGENCE	TITARAKURA	ADJUSTMENT	CROSSPIECE
INFURIATED	NATURALIST	RETIREMENT	TOLERANTLY	ADMISSIBLE	CROSSREFER
INHERENTLY	NATURALIZE	RETURNABLE	TOLERATION	ALLOSAURUS	CROSSROADS
INNERSPACE	NATUROPATH	REVERENTLY	TUBERCULAR	ALLOSTERIC	DEBASEMENT
INSTRUCTED	NEUTRALISE	REVERSIBLE	TULARAEMIA	AMBASSADOR	DECISIVELY
INSTRUCTOR	NEUTRALITY	RIGOROUSLY	ULCERATION	AMPUSSYAND	DEEPSEATED

DEHISCENCE	INDISTINCT	POINSETTIA	TREKSCHUIT	BEAUTICIAN	EPENTHETIC
DEPOSITARY	INDUSTRIAL	PORTSMOUTH	TRIMSNITCH	BEAUTIFIER	EPISTEMICS
DEPOSITION	INSISTENCE	POSTSCRIPT	TROTSKYITE	BEWITCHING	EPISTROPHE
DEPOSITORY	INTESTINAL	PRESSURIZE	TUMESCENCE	BLASTOCOEL	EQUATORIAL
DETESTABLE	INTESTINES	PRIESTHOOD	TYPESCRIPT	BLASTOIDEA	EQUITATION
DEVASTATED	INVESTMENT	PUBESCENCE	TYPESETTER	BLISTERING	ERUCTATION
DEVASTAVIT	IONOSPHERE	PUNISHABLE	UNANSWERED	BLOTTESQUE	ESCUTCHEON
DIDASCALIC	IRRESOLUTE	PUNISHMENT	UNASSIGNED	BLUETHROAT	EVENTUALLY
DIGESTIBLE	JACKSTONES	QUAESTUARY	UNASSUMING	BOISTEROUS	EXACTITUDE
DISASTROUS	JACKSTRAWS	QUEASINESS	UNDESCRIED	BREATHLESS	EXALTATION
DIVISIONAL	JAMESONITE	QUERSPRUNG	UNDESERVED	CAMSTEERIE	EXCITEMENT
DOWNSIZING	JOHNSONIAN	QUIESCENCE	UNDISPUTED	CAOUTCHOUC	EXENTERATE
DOWNSTAIRS	JOUYSAUNCE	QUIESCENCE	UNEASINESS	CAPITALISM	EXPATRIATE
DOWNSTREAM	KLEBSIELLA	REASSEMBLE	UNINSPIRED	CAPITALIST	EXULTATION
DRAWSTRING	KOEKSISTER	REASSURING	UNOBSERVED	CAPITALIZE	FANATICISM
DRESSMAKER	LACUSTRINE	REDISCOVER	UNRESERVED	CAPITATION	FAULTINESS
DROWSINESS	LANDSTHING	REGISTERED	UNRESOLVED	CAPITELLUM	FLATTERING
EFFUSIVELY	LAVISHNESS	REPOSITORY	WAINSCOTED	CAPITOLINE	FLEETINGLY
ELEUSINIAN	LEGISLATOR	RESISTANCE	WANDSWORTH	CAPITULARY	FLIRTATION
EMISSIVITY	LOGISTICAL	RHAPSODISE	WELLSPRING	CAPITULATE	FLUCTUATER
EMULSIFIER	LOUISIETTE	RHAPSODIST	WHATSOEVER	CHAPTALISE	FOURTEENTH
ENCASEMENT	LUMPSUCKER	RHAPSODIZE	WHITSTABLE	CHARTREUSE	FRACTIONAL
ENDOSMOSIS	LUTESTRING	ROBUSTIOUS	WIDESPREAD	CHATTERBOX	FRONTCOURT
ENLISTMENT	MAGISTRACY	ROBUSTNESS	WINDSCREEN	CHATTERTON	FRONTWARDS
EQUESTRIAN	MAGISTRAND	ROCKSTEADY	WINDSHIELD	CHAUTAUQUA	FRUITFULLY
EXPOSITION	MAGISTRATE	ROTHSCHILD	WINDSURFER	CHELTENHAM	FRUSTRATED
EXPOSITORY	MAINSPRING	ROTISSERIE	WORDSWORTH	CHESTERTON	FUNCTIONAL
FACESAVING	MAINSTREAM	RUPESTRIAN	XEROSTOMIA	CHITTAGONG	GAULTHERIA
FAMISHMENT	MAKESYSTEM	SALESWOMAN	YOURSELVES	CLOSTRIDIA	GELATINOUS
FENESTELLA	MANUSCRIPT	SATISFYING	ACHITOPHEL	COASTGUARD	GENETHLIAC
FINISTERRE	MARASCHINO	SCHISMATIC	ACROTERION	COGITATION	GLISTENING
FISHSELLER	MEERSCHAUM	SCOTSWOMAN	ADAPTATION	COMSTOCKER	GLITTERAND
FLIMSINESS	METASTABLE	SEAMSTRESS	ADDITAMENT	CONSTANTAN	GLITTERATI
FOODSTUFFS	MINESTRONE	SEERSUCKER	ADDITIONAL	CONSTANTIA	GLITTERING
FORESHADOW	MINISTRATE	SELFSTYLED	ADMITTANCE	CONSTANTLY	GLUTTONOUS
GAINSTRIVE	MINISTROKE	SENESCENCE	ADMITTEDLY	CONSTITUTE	GNOSTICISM
GETHSEMANE	MONTSERRAT	SHOESTRING	ADULTERANT	CONSTRAINT	GOLDTHREAD
GLASSHOUSE	MORISONIAN	SHOPSOILED	ADULTERATE	CONSTRINGE	GRAPTOLITE
GLASSINESS	MOROSENESS	SIDESADDLE	ADULTERESS	COUNTERACT	GRITTINESS
GLASSWORKS	MOSASAUROS	SKUPSHTINA	ADULTERINE	COUNTRYMAN	GUESTHOUSE
GLOSSINESS	MOUSSELINE	SLIPSTREAM	ADULTEROUS	COURTHOUSE	HABITATION
GOATSBEARD	NUMISMATIC	SONGSTRESS	AFFETTUOSO	CRAFTINESS	HABITUALLY
GOATSUCKER	OBFUSCATED	SPARSENESS	ALECTORIAN	CREATIVITY	HAUSTELLUM
GRASSLANDS	OBTUSENESS	SPENSERIAN	ALLOTROPIC	CRUSTACEAN	HAUSTORIUM
GRASSROOTS	OCCASIONAL	SPISSITUDE	AMPUTATION	CRYPTOGRAM	HEARTBREAK
GRASSWIDOW	ODELSTHING	SPONSIONAL	AMRITATTVA	CRYPTOZOIC	HEARTINESS
GYROSCOPIC	OMNISCIENT	STEPSISTER	ANASTIGMAT	DEACTIVATE	HEPATOCELE
HAIRSPRING	OPPOSITION	STRASBOURG	ANASTROPHE	DEBATEMENT	HESITANTLY
HALFSISTER	OVERSHADOW	SYNOSTOSIS	ANESTHESIA	DECATHLETE	HESITATION
HAMESUCKEN	OVERSLAUGH	TELESCOPIC	ANESTHETIC	DEPUTATION	HYPOTENUSE
HANDSOMELY	OVERSPREAD	THEMSELVES	ANNOTATION	DEVOTEMENT	HYPOTHESIS
HANDSPRING	OVERSTRAIN	THOUSANDTH	ANTITHESIS	DEVOTIONAL	ILLITERACY
HARASSMENT	OVERSTRUNG	TIMESAVING	ANTITHETIC	DIASTALTIC	ILLITERATE
HEADSTRONG	OVERSUPPLY	TIMESERVER	ANTITRAGUS	DIGITORIUM	IMMATERIAL
HEMISPHERE	PACESETTER	TIMESWITCH	APOSTROPHE	DILATATION	IMMATURITY
HERESIARCH	PALESTRINA	TOWNSWOMAN	APPETITIVE	DILETTANTE	IMPATIENCE
HOARSENESS	PALISANDER	TRANSCRIBE	APPETIZING	DIPHTHERIA	IMPOTENTLY
HOLOSTERIC	PALUSTRINE	TRANSCRIPT	ARBITRATOR	DOORTODOOR	IMPUTATION
HOMOSEXUAL	PARASCENIA	TRANSGRESS	ARISTIPPUS	DOUBTFULLY	INACTIVITY
ILLUSTRATE	PARASELENE	TRANSIENCE	ARISTOCRAT	EIGHTEENTH	INAPTITUDE
IMPASSABLE	PARASTATAL	TRANSISTOR	ARISTOLOGY	ELASTICATE	INARTISTIC
IMPOSITION	PARISCHANE	TRANSITION	ARISTOTLES	ELASTICITY	INCITEMENT
IMPOSSIBLE	PARISIENNE	TRANSITIVE	ASCETICISM	ELECTORATE	INDITEMENT
IMPOSSIBLY	PATISSERIE	TRANSITORY	ASTUTENESS	ELECTRICAL	INEPTITUDE
IMPOSTHUME	PEDESTRIAN	TRANSLATED	AUDITORIUM	ELECTROMER	INFATUATED
INCESTUOUS	PENTSTEMON	TRANSLATOR	AVANTGARDE	ELECTRONIC	INSATIABLE
INCISIVELY	PERISHABLE	TRANSPLANT	AVANTURINE	EMBITTERED	INSATIABLY
INDISCREET	PLEASANTLY	TRANSPOSED	AVENTURINE	EMMETROPIA	INVETERATE
INDISPOSED	PLEASANTRY	TRANSPOSON	BACITRACIN	ENANTIOSIS	INVITATION

IRRATIONAL	PAINTBRUSH	SCEPTICISM	VEGETATION	CURMURRING	MASTURBATE
IRRITATING	PALATALISE	SCINTIGRAM	VELITATION	DEBAUCHERY	MAVOURNEEN
IRRITATION	PALATINATE	SCOOTERIST	VISITATION	DEBOUCHURE	MEASURABLE
JAUNTINESS	PARATROOPS	SCRUTINEER	VOCATIONAL	DENOUEMENT	MEDIUMTERM
JEISTIECOR	PENETRABLE	SCRUTINISE	VOLATILITY	DESQUAMATE	METHUSALEH
KARTTIKAYA	PENETRALIA	SCRUTINIZE	VOLUTATION	DETRUNCATE	METHUSELAH
KLOOTCHMAN	PERSTRINGE	SEDATENESS	WHEATSHEAF	DISBURTHEN	NASTURTIUM
KSHATRIYAS	PETITIONER	SENATORIAL	WHEATSTONE	DISCURSIVE	NONSUCCESS
LAEOTROPIC	PHANTASIME	SHATTERING	WHITTERICK	DISCUSSING	ODIOUSNESS
LEGITIMACY	PHANTASIST	SHIFTINESS	WRISTWATCH	DISCUSSION	OFFPUTTING
LEGITIMATE	PLANTATION	SHORTBREAD	ZOANTHARIA	DISGUSTING	PASQUINADE
LEGITIMIZE	PLASTICINE	SHORTENING	ZWITTERION	DISPUTABLE	PERCUSSION
LENGTHWAYS	PLASTICITY	SHORTLIVED	ABITURIENT	DISQUALIFY	PERDURABLE
LENGTHWISE	PLATTELAND	SHORTRANGE	ACCOUNTANT	DISQUIETED	PERQUISITE
LEONTIASIS	POHUTUKAWA	SKEPTICISM	ACCOUNTING	DISRUPTION	PERSUADING
LEVITATION	POINTBLANK	SLATTERNLY	ADEQUATELY	DISRUPTIVE	PERSUASION
LIEUTENANT	POLITENESS	SMATTERING	ALLPURPOSE	DISSUASION	PERSUASIVE
LIGHTERMAN	POLITICIAN	SMOOTHNESS	ALTRUISTIC	DISTURBING	PINCUSHION
LIGHTHOUSE	POLITICIZE	SNOOTINESS	AMANUENSIS	ELOQUENTLY	PORTUGUESE
LIGHTINGUP	POLYTHEISM	SPARTACIST	APICULTURE	EMBOUCHURE	POZZUOLANA
LIMITATION	POSITIVELY	SPECTACLED	ARTHURIANA	EMOLUMENTS	PRECURSORY
LIMITROPHE	POSITIVIST	SPECTACLES	ASTOUNDING	ENGOUEMENT	PREJUDICED
LUSITANIAN	PRAETORIAN	SPECTATORS	AVICULARIA	ENTHUSIASM	PRESUMABLY
MAINTAINER	PRAETORIUM	SPLITLEVEL	BALBUTIENT	ENTHUSIAST	PRESUPPOSE
MEDITATION	PRETTINESS	SPORTINGLY	BIJOUTERIE	EPROUVETTE	PROCUMBENT
MEDITATIVE	PROSTHESIS	SPORTSWEAR	CALCULABLE	EVACUATION	PROCURABLE
MENSTRUATE	PROSTHETIC	SQUETEAGUE	CALCULATED	EVALUATION	PROCURATOR
MESITYLENE	PROSTITUTE	STENTORIAN	CALCULATOR	EXCRUCIATE	PRODUCTION
METATARSAL	PSALTERIUM	STERTEROUS	CAMOUFLAGE	EXHAUSTING	PRODUCTIVE
METATARSUS	PUNCTUALLY	STERTOROUS	CAPPUCCINO	EXHAUSTION	PROFUNDITY
METATHERIA	PUNCTULATE	STOUTHERIE	CARBURETOR	EXHAUSTIVE	PROMULGATE
METATHESIS	PURITANISM	STOUTHRIEF	CASSUMUNAR	EXPOUNDERS	PROPULSION
MIGHTINESS	QUARTERING	STRATEGIST	CELLULITIS	FAVOURABLE	PURSUIVANT
MILITARISM	QUARTEROON	STRATHSPEY	CHEQUEBOOK	FAVOURABLY	RECRUDESCE
MILITARIST	QUESTIONER	STRATIOTES	CINQUEFOIL	FETTUCCINE	REDCURRANT
MILITIAMAN	RAWSTHORNE	STRATOCRAT	CIRCUITOUS	FLATULENCE	REDRUTHITE
MINUTEBOOK	REACTIVATE	STRATOCYST	CIRCUMCISE	FORTUITOUS	RESOUNDING
MINUTENESS	RECITATION	STULTIFIED	CIRCUMFLEX	FOXHUNTING	RUMBULLION
MOISTURIZE	RECITATIVE	SUBSTATION	CIRCUMFUSE	FREQUENTED	SALBUTAMOL
MONETARISM	RECITATIVO	SUBSTITUTE	CIRCUMVENT	FREQUENTER	SANGUINARY
MONETARIST	REFUTATION	SUBSTRATUM	COLOURLESS	FREQUENTLY	SCATURIENT
MONOTHEISM	RELATIVELY	SUDATORIUM	COMBUSTION	GRADUALISM	SCROUNGING
MONOTONOUS	RELATIVITY	SWEATSHIRT	COMMUNALLY	GRADUATION	SENSUALITY
MONSTRANCE	REMITTANCE	SWEETBREAD	COMMUNIQUÉ	GRANULATED	SENSUOUSLY
MORATORIUM	REMOTENESS	SWEETBRIAR	COMMUTABLE	GRATUITOUS	SEPTUAGINT
MOUNTEBANK	REPATRIATE	SWEETENING	COMPULSION	GUTTURALLY	SEXDUCTION
MOUSTERIAN	REPETITEUR	SWEETHEART	COMPULSIVE	HALLUBALOO	SHAKUHACHI
NATATORIAL	REPETITION	SWELTERING	COMPULSORY	HINDUSTANI	SINFULNESS
NATATORIUM	REPETITIVE	SYMPTOMIZE	CONCURRENT	HONOURABLE	SINGULARLY
NEGATIVELY	REPUTATION	TAPOTEMENT	CONCUSSION	HONOURABLY	SPECULATOR
NEGOTIABLE	REVITALIZE	TEMPTATION	CONDUCTING	HONOURLESS	STATUESQUE
NEGOTIATOR	RHEOTROPIC	THEATRICAL	CONDUCTION	HUMDUDGEON	TATPURUSHA
NEMATOCYST	RICHTHOFEN	THIRTEENTH	CONFUSEDLY	HUMOURLESS	TCHOUKBALL
NIGHTDRESS	RIGHTFULLY	TRAITOROUS	CONQUERING	IMPRUDENCE	THROUGHOUT
NIGHTLIGHT	RIGHTWARDS	TROCTOLITE	CONSUETUDE	INCAUTIOUS	THROUGHPUT
NIGHTSHADE	RIJSTTAFEL	TRUSTFULLY	CONSULTANT	INEDUCABLE	THROUGHWAY
NIGHTSHIRT	ROISTERING	TRYPTOPHAN	CONSULTING	INEQUALITY	TONGUESTER
NIGHTSTICK	ROUSTABOUT	UNATTACHED	CONSUMMATE	INIQUITOUS	TORQUEMADA
NINETEENTH	SAGITTARIA	UNATTENDED	CONVULSION	INSOUCIANT	TORTUOUSLY
NOMOTHETIC	SALUTATION	UNDETECTED	CONVULSIVE	KENTUCKIAN	TRIPUDIARY
OBLITERATE	SAMOTHRACE	UNDETERRED	CORNUCOPIA	LANGUOROUS	TRUCULENCE
ODONTALGIA	SANATORIUM	UNFATHOMED	CORPULENCE	LAURUSTINE	TURBULENCE
ODONTOLITE	SANCTIFIED	UNFETTERED	CORRUGATED	LIMBURGITE	UBIQUINONE
ODONTOLOGY	SANCTITIES	UNLETTERED	CORRUGATOR	LINGUISTIC	UBIQUITOUS
OSCITATION	SANCTITUDE	UNORTHODOX	CORRUPTING	LINGULELLA	UNBLUSHING
OSMETERIUM	SANITARIUM	UNSETTLING	CORRUPTION	LITHUANIAN	UNCTUOUSLY
OUGHTLINGS	SANITATION	UROSTEGITE	CRAPULENCE	MARGUERITE	UNEDUCATED
OVERTHETOP	SCANTINESS	VEGETABLES	CRAQUETURE	MARQUETRIE	UNEQUALLED
OVERTHWART	SCATTERING	VEGETARIAN	CURMUDGEON	MASQUERADE	UNFRUITFUL

UNIQUENESS	CODSWALLOP	GETTYSBURG	AMBULATORY	CASSIABARK	DEVANAGARI
UNTRUTHFUL	COPYWRITER	HALFYEARLY	AMPUTATION	CASTRATION	DIAPHANOUS
USEFULNESS	CORDWAINER	HANKYPANKY	AMRITATTVA	CATAFALQUE	DIASTALTIC
VASCULITIS	DISHWASHER	HOBBYHORSE	AMYGDALOID	CATAWAMPUS	DILATATION
VICTUALLER	DUNIWASSAL	HONEYBUNCH	ANACHARSIS	CATCRACKER	DIOPHANTOS
VIRTUOSITY	FIREWALKER	JERRYBUILT	ANACLASTIC	CATENACCIO	DISCLAIMER
VIRTUOUSLY	FIREWARDEN	MAHAYANALI	ANHELATION	CENTRALIZE	DISHEARTEN
WAMPUMPEAG	FOREWARNED	MALAYALAAM	ANNEXATION	CESTRACION	DISHWASHER
ACTIVIST	GALSWORTHY	MERRYMAKER	ANNOTATION	CHAPFALLEN	DISQUALIFY
AMBIVALENT	HIGHWAYMAN	METHYLATED	ANSCHAUUNG	CHAPLAINCY	DISSUASION
ANTIVENENE	HOMEWORKER	MONEYMAKER	ANTHRACINE	CHAPTALISE	DISTRACTED
ASSEVERATE	HOODWINKED	PADDYMELON	ANTHRACITE	CHAUTAUQUA	DISTRAUGHT
BEDEVILLED	LEFTWINGER	PETTYCHAPS	ANTIBARBUS	CHIMPANZEE	DIURNALIST
BEHAVIORAL	LILYWHITES	PICAYUNISH	ANTIMASQUE	CHITTAGONG	DIVINATION
BENEVOLENT	MAKEWEIGHT	PROPYLAEUM	ANTIMATTER	CHREMATIST	DOCIMASTIC
BILIVERDIN	MINEWORKER	PTERYGOTUS	AQUAMANALE	CINECAMERA	DODECANESE
CADAVEROUS	NEWSWORTHY	ROWDYDOWDY	AQUAMANILE	COATHANGER	DOMINATING
CALAVERITE	NOTEWORTHY	STONYHURST	AQUAMARINE	CODSWALLOP	DOMINATION
CHAUVINISM	OVERWEIGHT	TEENYWEENY	ARAUCANIAN	COGITATION	DOWNMARKET
CHAUVINIST	OVERWORKED	THUCYDIDES	AREOPAGITE	COLORATION	DRAWCANSIR
CHERVONETS	PERIWINKLE	TOPSYTURVY	ARROGANTLY	COLORATURA	DREIKANTER
DERIVATION	PLAYWRIGHT	WILLYWILLY	ARTHRALGIA	COMPLACENT	DUNIWASSAL
DERIVATIVE	PRZEWALSKI	WISHYWASHY	ARTOCARPUS	COMPLANATE	DYSCRASITE
DUUMVIRATE	RAILWAYMAN	ALTAZIMUTH	ASPARAGINE	COMPRADORE	ELONGATION
ENLÈVEMENT	ROADWORTHY	BLITZKRIEG	ASPIRATION	CONSTANTAN	EMACIATION
EQUIVALENT	ROTTWEILER	FRENZIEDLY	ASTOMATOUS	CONSTANTIA	EMENDATION
EQUIVOCATE	SANDWICHES	HORIZONTAL	ATHANASIAN	CONSTANTLY	EMIGRATION
EXCAVATION	SHIPWRIGHT	LHERZOLITE	AUSTRALIAN	CONTRABAND	ENDOGAMOUS
GENEVRETTE	SHOPWALKER	LIPIZZANER	AUSTRALORP	CONTRACTOR	ENTREATING
HANOVERIAN	SHREWDNESS	SCORZONERA	AUTOMATION	CONTRADICT	EPIPLASTRA
HEXAVALENT	SIDEWINDER	SELTZOGENE	AUTOMATIZE	CONTRAFLOW	EPISPASTIC
IMPOVERISH	SONGWRITER	SNEEZEWOOD	AVVOGADORE	CONTRAHENT	EQUITATION
INCIVILITY	STEMWINDER	VENEZUELAN	BACCHANTES	CONTRARILY	EQUIVALENT
INDIVIDUAL	STRAWBERRY	WHEEZINESS	BACKGAMMON	CONTRAVENE	ERIOCAULON
INNOVATION	STRAWBOARD	**10:6**	BACKHANDED	COPULATION	ERUCTATION
INNOVATIVE	TYPEWRITER	ABDICATION	BACKHANDER	CORDIALITY	ESCALATION
IRREVERENT	WOODWORKER	ABERRATION	BACKPACKER	CORDWAINER	ESCULAPIAN
LAURVIKITE	ANNEXATION	ABROGATION	BALNEATION	COROMANDEL	ESTIMATION
MALEVOLENT	INDEXATION	ABSTRACTED	BANDMASTER	CORONATION	ETERNALIZE
MONOVALENT	INTOXICANT	ABUNDANTLY	BANGLADESH	CORYBANTES	ETHYLAMINE
MOTIVATION	INTOXICATE	ACCUBATION	BEARGARDEN	CORYBANTIC	EVACUATION
OMNIVOROUS	RELAXATION	ACCURATELY	BEDCHAMBER	COVENANTER	EVALUATION
ORDOVICIAN	RELAXATIVE	ACCUSATION	BEEFEATERS	CRUSTACEAN	EVENHANDED
PAPAVERINE	ACOTYLEDON	ACCUSATIVE	BELSHAZZAR	CUMULATIVE	EXALTATION
PATAVINITY	AMARYLLIDS	ACEPHALOUS	BENEFACTOR	DARKHAIRED	EXCAVATION
PEROVSKITE	AMBLYOPSIS	ACROBATICS	BENTHAMITE	DECIMALIZE	EXECRATION
POLYVALENT	AMBLYSTOMA	ADAPTATION	BESTIALITY	DECORATION	EXHALATION
REJUVENATE	ANADYOMENE	ADDITAMENT	BHADRAPADA	DECORATIVE	EXHILARATE
RENOVATION	ANALYTICAL	ADEQUATELY	BIOGRAPHER	DEDICATION	EXHUMATION
REVIVALIST	ANCHYLOSIS	ADMIRATION	BLEPHARISM	DEFAMATION	EXPIRATION
SALIVATION	ASPHYXIATE	ADRENALINE	BLUEMANTLE	DEFAMATORY	EXULTATION
SHRIVELLED	BATHYSCAPH	ADULLAMITE	BOOKMARKER	DEFECATION	FACESAVING
SHROVETIDE	BOBBYSOXER	AEROBATICS	BORDRAGING	DELEGATION	FAIRHAIRED
SLEEVELESS	BRADYKININ	AFRICANDER	BREAKABLES	DELICATELY	FALKLANDER
SOLIVAGANT	BRADYSEISM	AFRICANISM	BUCHMANISM	DELIGATION	FAREPAYING
STARVATION	CANDYFLOSS	AGRAHAYANA	BURGLARIZE	DELIRATION	FASCIATION
STARVELING	CHALYBEATE	ALGOLAGNIA	BUSHRANGER	DEMORALISE	FEDERALISM
STRAVINSKY	DESSYATINE	ALIENATION	CACODAEMON	DEMORALIZE	FEDERALIST
TELEVISION	DONNYBROOK	ALLEGATION	CALAMANDER	DEPILATION	FEDERATION
TROUVAILLE	ECCHYMOSIS	ALLIGATION	CALEFACTOR	DEPILATORY	FIGURATION
TUTIVILLUS	EMBRYOLOGY	ALLOCATION	CALLIATURE	DEPUTATION	FIGURATIVE
UNENVIABLE	ENTRYPHONE	ALLOSAURUS	CAPITALISM	DERIVATION	FILTRATION
UNINVITING	EPONYCHIUM	ALMACANTAR	CAPITALIST	DERIVATIVE	FIREWALKER
UNREVEALED	EUTHYNEURA	ALMUCANTAR	CAPITALIZE	DEROGATORY	FIREWARDEN
UNRIVALLED	EVERYPLACE	ALTERATION	CAPITATION	DESOLATION	FLAGRANTLY
ZIDOVUDINE	EVERYTHING	AMALGAMATE	CAPODASTRO	DESQUAMATE	FLIPPANTLY
ZOLLVEREIN	EVERYWHERE	AMBIVALENT	CARICATURA	DESSIATINE	FLIRTATION
BELLWETHER	FUDDYDUDDY	AMBULACRUM	CARICATURE	DESSYATINE	FOOTBALLER
CATAWAMPUS	FULLYGROWN		CARTHAMINE	DETONATION	FORBEARING

FORECASTER	INITIATIVE	METATARSUS	PALUDAMENT	REGULARIZE	SNAPHAUNCE
FORECASTLE	INNOVATION	MILITARISM	PANAMANIAN	REGULATION	SNAPHAUNCH
FOREDAMNED	INNOVATIVE	MILITARIST	PANCRATIUM	RELAXATION	SNOWCAPPED
FOREFATHER	INSULARITY	MINERALOGY	PARAMARIBO	RELAXATIVE	SOLIDARITY
FOREGATHER	INSULATION	MINIMALISM	PARLIAMENT	RELEGATION	SOLIVAGANT
FOREWARNED	INTIMATELY	MINIMALIST	PARTIALITY	RELOCATION	SPALLATION
FOUNDATION	INTIMATION	MINIMARKET	PATRIARCHY	RENOVATION	SPARTACIST
FOURRAGERE	INTONATION	MISHNAYOTH	PECULATION	REORGANIZE	SPECIALISE
FREEHANDER	INUNDATION	MISLEADING	PEDIPALPUS	REPARATION	SPECIALISM
FREELANCER	INVITATION	MISOCAPNIC	PEELGARLIC	REPUTATION	SPECIALIST
FREEMARTIN	INVOCATION	MITIGATING	PEJORATIVE	RESTRAINED	SPECIALITY
FREEMASONS	IRRIGATION	MITIGATION	PERMEATION	RETINALITE	SPECIALIZE
FUMIGATION	IRRITATING	MODERATELY	PERORATION	RETREATING	SPECTACLED
GALIMATIAS	IRRITATION	MODERATION	PERSUADING	REVELATION	SPECTACLES
GALLIAMBIC	ISONIAZIDE	MODULATION	PERSUASION	REVITALIZE	SPECTATORS
GEMINATION	JACKHAMMER	MONEGASQUE	PERSUASIVE	REVIVALIST	SPERMACETI
GENERALISE	JACULATION	MONETARISM	PETULANTLY	REVOCATION	SPOLIATION
GENERALITY	JOCULARITY	MONETARIST	PHANTASIME	RHAMPASTOS	SPOLIATIVE
GENERALIZE	JOURNALESE	MONOCARPIC	PHANTASIST	RHEUMATICS	STAGNATION
GENERATION	JOURNALISM	MONOGAMOUS	PHARMACIST	RHEUMATISM	STARVATION
GENERATRIX	JOURNALIST	MONOVALENT	PLAGIARISE	RHEUMATOID	STEPFATHER
GEOGRAPHER	JOUYSAUNCE	MONTRACHET	PLAGIARISM	RIGELATION	STEPHANITE
GEOGRAPHIC	JUBILANTLY	MOSASAUROS	PLAGIARIST	RINGMASTER	STEPLADDER
GETUPANDGO	JUBILATION	MOTIVATION	PLAGIARIZE	ROSEMALING	STERNALGIA
GILLRAVAGE	JUDICATURE	MOUCHARABY	PLANTATION	ROUNDABOUT	STICHARION
GLACIATION	KEYBOARDER	MUCKRAKING	PLEASANTLY	ROUSEABOUT	STIGMATISE
GLEEMAIDEN	KNOCKABOUT	MUTILATION	PLEASANTRY	ROUSTABOUT	STIGMATIZE
GRADUALISM	LABORATORY	NAPTHALENE	PLEONASTIC	RUMINANTIA	STOCHASTIC
GRADUATION	LACERATION	NATURALISM	POCKMANTIE	RUMINATION	STROGANOFF
GRAMMARIAN	LAMINATION	NATURALIST	POCKMARKED	RUMINATIVE	SUBHEADING
GUACHAMOLE	LANTHANIDE	NATURALIZE	POIGNANTLY	RUSSIANIZE	SUBSTATION
HABITATION	LAURDALITE	NAUSEATING	POLYGAMIST	SACCHARASE	SUBTRAHEND
HACKMATACK	LEFTHANDED	NAUSEATIVE	POLYGAMOUS	SACCHARIDE	SUFFRAGIST
HALLMARKED	LEFTHANDER	NAVIGATION	POLYVALENT	SACCHARINE	SUGARALLIE
HAMSHACKLE	LESBIANISM	NEUTRALISE	POMERANIAN	SACCHAROID	SUNGLASSES
HANDMAIDEN	LEUCHAEMIA	NEUTRALITY	POPULARITY	SALAMANDER	SUPERADDED
HARDCASTLE	LEVITATION	NEUTRALIZE	POPULARIZE	SALIVATION	SURINAMESE
HEADMASTER	LIBERALISM	NEWSCASTER	POPULATION	SALUTATION	SURREALISM
HESITANTLY	LIBERALITY	NEWSPAPERS	PORTMANTLE	SANITARIUM	SURREALIST
HESITATION	LIBERALIZE	NICARAGUAN	PORTMANTUA	SANITATION	SUZERAINTY
HEXAVALENT	LIBERATION	NOMINALIST	POSTMASTER	SATURATION	TABULATION
HIGHHANDED	LIMITATION	NOMINATION	POURPARLER	SAVONAROLA	TAGLIARINI
HIGHLANDER	LITERATURE	NOMINATIVE	PRAGMATISM	SCANDALISE	TAILGATING
HIGHWAYMAN	LITHUANIAN	NONCHALANT	PRAGMATIST	SCANDALIZE	TANNHAUSER
HITOPADESA	LITIGATION	NORTHANGER	PROGRAMMER	SCANDALOUS	TARTRAZINE
HONORARIUM	LOCULAMENT	NUMERATION	PROPRAETOR	SCANDAROON	TASKMASTER
HOOTNANNIE	LUMINARIST	NUTCRACKER	PROTRACTED	SCARLATINA	TELEPATHIC
HUMPBACKED	LUSITANIAN	OBLIGATION	PROTRACTOR	SCHOLAEMIA	TEMPTATION
HYPOGAEOUS	LYCHNAPSIA	OBLIGATORY	PRZEWALSKI	SCHOLASTIC	TEPIDARIUM
IGNORANTLY	MADAGASCAN	OCCUPATION	PUMPHANDLE	SCORDATURA	TERTIARIES
ILLEGALITY	MADAGASCAR	OCEANARIUM	PUNICACEAE	SEANNACHIE	THAUMASITE
IMMOLATION	MAHAYANALI	ODONTALGIA	PURITANISM	SECULARIZE	THEREAFTER
IMMORALITY	MAINTAINER	OPENHANDED	PYRACANTHA	SENEGALESE	THEREANENT
IMPERATIVE	MALAYALAAM	OPHTHALMIC	PYROMANIAC	SENSUALITY	THOUSANDTH
IMPUTATION	MALEFACTOR	ORDINARILY	QUADRANGLE	SEPARATELY	TIMESAVING
INCAPACITY	MANDRAGORA	ORDINATION	QUADRATURA	SEPARATION	TITARAKURA
INCAPARINA	MARSHALSEA	OROBRANCHE	QUIZMASTER	SEPARATISM	TOLERANTLY
INCHOATIVE	MATRIARCHY	OSCITATION	RADICALISM	SEPARATIST	TOLERATION
INCREASING	MATURATION	OSCULATION	RAILWAYMAN	SEPARATRIX	TOPICALITY
INCUBATION	MAXIMALIST	OSCULATORY	RAJPRAMUKH	SEPTUAGINT	TOUCHANDGO
INCUNABULA	MEDICAMENT	OUVIRANDRA	RAMSHACKLE	SHAGHAIRED	TOURMALINE
INDAPAMIDE	MEDICATION	OVEREATING	RAZZMATAZZ	SHOPWALKER	TOURNAMENT
INDEXATION	MEDITATION	OVERLANDER	REARMAMENT	SIDERATION	TRAUMATIZE
INDICATION	MEDITATIVE	OVERMATTER	RECITATION	SIDESADDLE	TRESPASSER
INDICATIVE	MEMBRANOUS	PAEDIATRIC	RECITATIVE	SIMILARITY	TRIVIALITY
INEQUALITY	MEMORANDUM	PAGINATION	RECITATIVO	SIMULACRUM	TRIVIALIZE
INHALATION	METACARPAL	PALATALISE	RECREATION	SIMULATING	TROCHANTER
INHUMANITY	METACARPUS	PALISANDER	REFUTATION	SIMULATION	TROUBADOUR
INITIATION	METATARSAL	PALLIATIVE	REGULARITY	SINGHALESE	TROUVAILLE

TULARAEMIA	COCKABULLY	STRAWBOARD	CONNECTING	HIPPOCRENE	PARMACITIE
ULCERATION	CORALBERRY	SUBORBITAL	CONNECTION	HOMUNCULUS	PARTICIPLE
ULTIMATELY	CORROBOREE	SWEETBREAD	CONNECTIVE	HOUSECRAFT	PARTICULAR
UNATTACHED	CRISPBREAD	SWEETBRIAR	CONSECRATE	HOVERCRAFT	PATCHCOCKE
UNBALANCED	CROSSBONES	THROMBOSIS	CONVECTION	ICONOCLAST	PERFECTION
UNBLEACHED	CROSSBREED	TOOTHBRUSH	CONVICTION	IMBRICATED	PERFICIENT
UNDULATING	CUCURBITAL	ULTRABASIC	COPARCENER	IMBROCCATA	PERNICIOUS
UNDULATION	DÉSHABILLÉ	UNDERBURNT	CORNUCOPIA	IMPECCABLE	PERNICKETY
UNEQUALLED	DISCOBOLUS	UNNUMBERED	CORRECTING	IMPECCABLY	PERSECUTOR
UNHERALDED	DISEMBOGUE	USQUEBAUGH	CORRECTION	IMPLACABLE	PERSICARIA
UNIMPAIRED	DISEMBOWEL	VERTEBRATE	CORRECTIVE	IMPLACABLY	PETTICHAPS
UNPLEASANT	DISHABILLE	VESTIBULUM	CRETACEOUS	IMPLICITLY	PETTYCHAPS
UNRIVALLED	DONNYBROOK	WATERBORNE	CRISSCROSS	INDISCREET	PHYLACTERY
UNROMANTIC	ELDERBERRY	WATERBRASH	CRITICALLY	INEDUCABLE	PHYSICALLY
UNSALARIED	ELEGABALUS	WILDEBEEST	CROSSCHECK	INFLECTION	PICHICIAGO
UNSCRAMBLE	ENTOMBMENT	YOUNGBERRY	CURRICULUM	INFLICTION	PICHICIEGO
URTICACEAE	FILLIBRUSH	ZIMBABWEAN	CURVACEOUS	INFRACTION	PLUTOCRACY
USURPATION	FLOORBOARD	ACANACEOUS	DEBAUCHERY	INJUNCTION	POETICALLY
VALIDATION	FLORIBUNDA	AERENCHYMA	DEBOUCHURE	INSOUCIANT	PONTICELLO
VEGETABLES	GALLABIYAH	AFFLICTION	DEFLECTION	INSPECTION	PORLOCKING
VEGETARIAN	GALLABIYEH	ALCAICERIA	DEHISCENCE	INTERCEDER	PORNOCRACY
VEGETATION	GOATSBEARD	AMPHICTYON	DEPRECIATE	INTERCLUDE	PORRACEOUS
VELITATION	GOOSEBERRY	ANNUNCIATE	DESICCATED	INTINCTION	POSTSCRIPT
VENERATION	HALLUBALOO	ANTARCTICA	DESPICABLE	INVINCIBLE	PRECOCIOUS
VICTUALLER	HARTEBEEST	ANTHOCLORE	DETRACTION	IRONICALLY	PREDACIOUS
VIDARABINE	HEARTBREAK	ANTIOCHENE	DIALECTICS	JUSTICIARY	PREDECEASE
VIETNAMESE	HEREABOUTS	ANTIOCHIAN	DIDASCALIC	KENTUCKIAN	PREDICTION
VIGILANTES	HILDEBRAND	APPLICABLE	DIDUNCULUS	KLOOTCHMAN	PRELECTION
VINEGARISH	HONEYBUNCH	APPLICATOR	DIELECTRIC	LAMARCKISM	PRODUCTION
VISITATION	HOUSEBOUND	APPRECIATE	DIFFICULTY	LATTICINIO	PRODUCTIVE
VIVIPAROUS	HULLABALOO	AREFACTION	DISENCHANT	LENTICULAR	PROFICIENT
VOETGANGER	HYPERBOLIC	ARENACEOUS	DISINCLINE	LEPRECHAUN	PROJECTILE
VOLUTATION	IGNIMBRITE	ATTRACTION	DISSECTION	LIGNOCAINE	PROJECTING
WAGEEARNER	IMPROBABLE	ATTRACTIVE	DISSOCIATE	LOQUACIOUS	PROJECTION
WANCHANCIE	IMPROBABLY	AUSPICIOUS	DOVERCOURT	LUMPECTOMY	PROSECUTOR
WELLEARNED	INCUMBENCY	AUTOECIOUS	DUODECIMAL	LUPERCALIA	PROTECTION
WHIGGAMORE	INTERBREED	AVARICIOUS	DUPLICATOR	MACROCARPA	PROTECTIVE
WILLIAMSON	JERRYBUILT	BALANCHINE	EMBOUCHURE	MANUSCRIPT	PSILOCYBIN
WINDJAMMER	KNIFEBOARD	BARMECIDAL	EPONYCHIUM	MARASCHINO	PUBESCENCE
WITSNAPPER	KOOKABURRA	BARRACKING	ESCUTCHEON	MASTECTOMY	PUGNACIOUS
WOLFRAMITE	LOGANBERRY	BARRACOOTA	ESTANCIERO	MEDIOCRITY	QUIESCENCE
YGGDRASILL	LUXEMBOURG	BARRACOUTA	EUSTACHIAN	MEERSCHAUM	RANUNCULUS
ZOOTHAPSIS	MACROBIOTE	BATRACHIAN	EXCRUCIATE	MELANCHOLY	RECONCILED
ZYGODACTYL	MANGABEIRA	BEWITCHING	EXOTICALLY	MENDACIOUS	REDISCOVER
ABOVEBOARD	MOZAMBIQUE	BOTTICELLI	EXPLICABLE	MILLICURIE	REELECTION
ABSORBANCE	MULIEBRITY	BRAINCHILD	EXPLICITLY	MONARCHIST	REFLECTING
ACETABULAR	NECTABANUS	BROADCLOTH	EXTINCTION	MONOACIDIC	REFLECTION
ACETABULUM	NEIGHBORLY	BYELECTION	EXTRACTION	MONOECIOUS	REFLECTIVE
AFTERBIRTH	NORMOBLAST	CALESCENCE	FALLACIOUS	MONTICULUS	REFRACTION
AMPHIBIOUS	NORTHBOUND	CAOUTCHOUC	FANTOCCINI	MORDACIOUS	REFRACTIVE
AMPHIBRACH	OPPROBRIUM	CAPPUCCINO	FETTUCCINE	MOTORCYCLE	REFRACTORY
ASARABACCA	OSTEOBLAST	CAPRICIOUS	FISTICUFFS	NEGLECTFUL	RESORCINOL
ASCRIBABLE	PAINTBRUSH	CHEMICALLY	FLOORCLOTH	NONFICTION	RESPECTFUL
ASSEMBLAGE	PASTEBOARD	CHIFFCHAFF	FOLIACEOUS	NONSUCCESS	RESPECTING
ASSEMBLING	PLANOBLAST	CHIRICAUNE	FONTICULUS	NOUAKCHOTT	RESPECTIVE
BLACKBEARD	POINTBLANK	CLAIRCOLLE	FRATICELLI	OBFUSCATED	RETRACTION
BLACKBERRY	PROHIBITED	CLAVICHORD	FROLICSOME	OCHLOCRACY	RHINOCEROS
BLACKBOARD	RESEMBLING	CLINICALLY	FRONTCOURT	OFFLICENCE	ROLLICKING
BLACKBULLY	ROCKABILLY	COELACANTH	FUNGICIDAL	OIREACHTAS	ROTHSCHILD
BRASSBOUND	SCOREBOARD	COLLECTING	GERMICIDAL	OLERACEOUS	SARCOCOLLA
CANTABRIAN	SCRIBBLING	COLLECTION	GRAMICIDIN	OMNISCIENT	SCREECHING
CHALYBEATE	SHORTBREAD	COLLECTIVE	GRANDCHILD	ORTHOCAINE	SDRUCCIOLA
CHESSBOARD	SKATEBOARD	COLLOCUTER	GREENCLOTH	ORTHOCLASE	SENESCENCE
CHILDBIRTH	SOUTHBOUND	COMANCHERO	GYROSCOPIC	OSTEOCOLLA	SEPULCHRAL
CHINABERRY	SPELLBOUND	CONCOCTION	HANDICRAFT	PANNICULUS	SEQUACIOUS
CLARABELLA	STILLBIRTH	CONDUCTING	HECTICALLY	PAPERCHASE	SERVICEMAN
CLOUDBERRY	STONEBRASH	CONDUCTION	HENDECAGON	PARASCENIA	SEXDUCTION
CLOUDBURST	STRASBOURG	CONFECTION	HERBACEOUS	PARENCHYMA	SINARCHIST
CNIDOBLAST	STRAWBERRY	CONJECTURE	HEROICALLY	PARISCHANE	SOPHOCLEAN

SPACECRAFT	ASCENDENCY	MORBIDEZZA	ABONNEMENT	BOTTLEHEAD	CONQUERING
SPIRACULUM	ATTENDANCE	MORTADELLA	ACCELERATE	BOTTLENECK	CONSPECTUS
SPLANCHNIC	BEHINDHAND	NEFANDROUS	ACCIDENTAL	BOWDLERISE	CONSUETUDE
STAGECOACH	BELLADONNA	NIGHTDRESS	ACROGENOUS	BOWDLERIZE	CONTRECOUP
STAGECRAFT	BENZEDRINE	ORCHIDEOUS	ACROMEGALY	BRIDGEHEAD	COPESETTIC
STALACTITE	BEWILDERED	PALINDROME	ACROTERION	BRIDGETOWN	CORDIERITE
STATECRAFT	BRAGADISME	PECCADILLO	ADRAMELECH	BRIDLEPATH	COTTIERISM
STATOCRACY	CALCEDONIO	PERFIDIOUS	ADRENERGIC	BUFFLEHEAD	COUNSELING
STIACCIATO	COMMODIOUS	PERIODICAL	ADULTERANT	BULLHEADED	COUNSELLOR
STRACCHINO	CONFEDERAL	PESCADORES	ADULTERATE	BUMFREEZER	COUNTERACT
SUBJECTION	CONFIDANTE	PHAGEDAENA	ADULTERESS	BUTCHERING	CRAQUETURE
SUBJECTIVE	CONFIDENCE	PHOLIDOSIS	ADULTERINE	CADAVEROUS	CRICKETING
SUBSECTION	CONSIDERED	PHOTODIODE	ADULTEROUS	CALAVERITE	CRYOGENICS
SUFFICIENT	CORTADERIA	PICCADILLY	AESTHETICS	CAMBRENSIS	CUDDLESOME
SUPERCARGO	CURMUDGEON	PIRANDELLO	AIRFREIGHT	CAMSTEERIE	CUTTLEBONE
SURGICALLY	CUSSEDNESS	PONTEDERIA	ALBIGENSES	CANDLEFISH	CUTTLEFISH
SUSPICIOUS	DEGRADABLE	PRECEDENCE	ALLEGEANCE	CANDLEWICK	DARJEELING
TABLECLOTH	DEPENDABLE	PREJUDICED	ALLUREMENT	CAPITELLUM	DAYDREAMER
TACTICALLY	DEPENDENCE	PREMEDICAL	ALTOGETHER	CARAMELIZE	DEADNETTLE
TELESCOPIC	DEPENDENCY	PRESIDENCY	AMANUENSIS	CARELESSLY	DEBASEMENT
TENRECIDAE	DIAPEDESIS	PROCEDURAL	AMBOCEPTOR	CATALECTIC	DEBATEMENT
TERRACOTTA	DIFFIDENCE	PROVEDITOR	ANTECEDENT	CATALEPTIC	DEBRIEFING
TESTACEOUS	DINANDERIE	PROVIDENCE	ANTEPENULT	CATTLEGRID	DECAHEDRON
TESTICULAR	DIPLODOCUS	PUNCHDRUNK	ANTISEPSIS	CEREBELLUM	DECELERATE
THALICTRUM	DISORDERED	QUESADILLA	ANTISEPTIC	CHAFFERING	DEEPSEATED
TORRICELLI	DISORDERLY	RECRUDESCE	ANTIVENENE	CHALCEDONY	DEFACEMENT
TOSSICATED	DISSIDENCE	REDUNDANCY	APOPLECTIC	CHALLENGED	DEFILEMENT
TOSTICATED	DOGGEDNESS	REGARDLESS	APOTHECARY	CHALLENGER	DEGENERACY
TRAGACANTH	EISTEDDFOD	REPRODUCER	APOTHECIUM	CHAMAELEON	DEGENERATE
TRAGICALLY	ENGENDRURE	RHOEADALES	APOTHEOSIS	CHAMAEROPS	DELCREDERE
TRAJECTORY	EPIDIDYMUS	ROBERDSMAN	APPARENTLY	CHAMBERPOT	DELIBERATE
TRANSCRIBE	EXPENDABLE	ROLANDSECK	ARCHDEACON	CHAMBERTIN	DEMIRELIEF
TRANSCRIPT	EXTENDABLE	ROWDYDOWDY	ARGOLEMONO	CHANCELLOR	DENOUEMENT
TREKSCHUIT	FASTIDIOUS	RUGGEDNESS	ARMAGEDDON	CHANDELIER	DESIDERATA
TRINACRIAN	FORBIDDING	SACERDOTAL	ARUNDELIAN	CHANGEABLE	DEVOTEMENT
TUBERCULAR	FORMIDABLE	SACREDNESS	ARYTAENOID	CHANGELESS	DIASKEUAST
TUMESCENCE	FRIENDLESS	SALVADORAN	ASAFOETIDA	CHANGELING	DILIGENTLY
TYPESCRIPT	FRIENDSHIP	SCOTODINIA	ASSEVERATE	CHARGEABLE	DISCREETLY
UNDERCLASS	FUDDYDUDDY	SECONDBEST	ASTUTENESS	CHARGEHAND	DISCREPANT
UNDERCOVER	GESUNDHEIT	SECONDHAND	ASYMMETRIC	CHATTERBOX	DISCRETION
UNDERCRAFT	GRANADILLA	SECONDMENT	ATRAMENTAL	CHATTERTON	DISTRESSED
UNDERCROFT	GRANDDADDY	SECONDRATE	AURIFEROUS	CHAUCERIAN	DOORKEEPER
UNDESCRIED	GRENADIERS	SEGUIDILLA	AUTOGENOUS	CHEESECAKE	DOPPLERITE
UNEDUCATED	GRENADILLA	SERRADELLA	BAFFLEMENT	CHEESEWOOD	DOSTOEVSKY
UNGRACIOUS	GROUNDBAIT	SERRADILLA	BAILIEWICK	CHELTENHAM	DOUBLEBASS
UNPUNCTUAL	GROUNDLESS	SHIELDRAKE	BARCHESTER	CHEQUEBOOK	DOUBLETALK
UNSHACKLED	GROUNDLING	SHREWDNESS	BAREHEADED	CHESTERTON	DUMBLEDORE
UNSPECIFIC	GROUNDSMAN	SORDIDNESS	BARELEGGED	CHICHESTER	EBOULEMENT
UPPERCLASS	GROUNDWORK	SPLENDIDLY	BAROMETRIC	CHICKENPOX	EFFACEMENT
VERMICELLI	HIPPODROME	STRINDBERG	BATTLEDOOR	CHILDERMAS	EIGHTEENTH
VERNACULAR	HORSEDRAWN	STRULDBERG	BATTLEDORE	CHIMNEYPOT	ELOQUENTLY
VERTICALLY	HUMDUDGEON	STRULDBRUG	BATTLEMENT	CHOICELESS	ENCASEMENT
VIBRACULUM	HYPERDULIA	SUBMEDIANT	BATTLESHIP	CINQUEFOIL	ENDOGENOUS
VINDICTIVE	IMPRUDENCE	SUBSIDENCE	BEEKEEPING	CLUMPERTON	ENGAGEMENT
WAINSCOTED	INCENDIARY	SUBSIDIARY	BEFOREHAND	COARSENESS	ENGOUEMENT
WALLACHIAN	INCREDIBLE	SYNECDOCHE	BELLWETHER	COCHLEARIA	ENLACEMENT
WATERCOLOR	INCREDIBLY	SYNEIDESIS	BESTSELLER	COHERENTLY	ENLÈVEMENT
WATERCRESS	INGREDIENT	THREADBARE	BILIVERDIN	COLCHESTER	ENTICEMENT
WHEELCHAIR	INTENDMENT	THREADLIKE	BIOCHEMIST	COMPLEMENT	EPAULEMENT
WIDDICOMBE	JUGENDSTIL	THREADWORM	BLACKENING	COMPLETELY	EPISTEMICS
WINDSCREEN	LACCADIVES	THUCYDIDES	BLISTERING	COMPLETION	EPITHELIUM
WITCHCRAFT	LACKADAISY	TRIPUDIARY	BLITHERING	COMPLEXION	ESCAPEMENT
WORLDCLASS	LIQUIDATOR	UNREADABLE	BLOTTESQUE	COMPLEXITY	EUHEMERISM
ACCORDANCE	LIQUIDIZER	VALLADOLID	BLUNDERING	COMPREHEND	EVANGELIST
ACCREDITED	METHEDRINE	VIVANDIÈRE	BOISTEROUS	COMPRESSED	EVANGELIZE
AFFORDABLE	METHODICAL	WICKEDNESS	BOLSHEVIST	COMPRESSOR	EVISCERATE
ANIMADVERT	MOLENDINAR	WRONGDOING	BOOKKEEPER	CONCRETION	EXAGGERATE
ANTIADITIS	MOLYBDENUM	YTHUNDERED	BOOKSELLER	CONGREGATE	EXASPERATE
ASCENDANCY	MONANDROUS	ABERDEVINE	BOOTLEGGER	CONIFEROUS	EXCITEMENT

EXENTERATE	IMPUDENTLY	MONUMENTAL	PROSCENIUM	SMATTERING	TUMBLEDOWN
EXOTHERMIC	INBREEDING	MORIGEROUS	PROSPECTOR	SMITHEREEN	TURTLEDOVE
FEARLESSLY	INCIDENTAL	MOROSENESS	PROSPECTUS	SMORREBROD	TURTLEHEAD
FEATHERBED	INCINERATE	MOUDIEWART	PROSPERINA	SNEEZEWOOD	TURTLENECK
FEEBLENESS	INCITEMENT	MOUNTEBANK	PROSPERITY	SNIGGERING	TYPESETTER
FICKLENESS	INCOHERENT	MOUSSELINE	PROSPEROUS	SNORKELING	UBERMENSCH
FIDDLEWOOD	INDECENTLY	MOUSTERIAN	PSALTERIUM	SOMBRERITE	UNACCENTED
FIERCENESS	INDIGENOUS	MUJAHEDDIN	PUZZLEMENT	SOURDELINE	UNAFFECTED
FIGUREHEAD	INDIRECTLY	MUMBLENEWS	QUARRENDER	SOUTHERNER	UNATTENDED
FISHSELLER	INDITEMENT	NEEDLECASE	QUARTERING	SPARSENESS	UNDEFEATED
FITZGERALD	INDONESIAN	NEEDLEWORK	QUARTEROON	SPEAKERINE	UNDEFENDED
FLATTERING	INDUCEMENT	NETTLERASH	RANDLETREE	SPENCERIAN	UNDESERVED
FLICKERING	INDUMENTUM	NETTLETREE	RANNLETREE	SPENSERIAN	UNDETECTED
FLINDERSIA	INFIDELITY	NEWSLETTER	RANTLETREE	SPHACELATE	UNDETERRED
FLUNKEYDOM	INGENERATE	NEWSREADER	RATTLETRAP	SPHALERITE	UNDIGESTED
FOURIERISM	INHERENTLY	NIMBLENESS	REASSEMBLE	SPIRKETING	UNEXPECTED
FOURTEENTH	INNOCENTLY	NINETEENTH	RECKLESSLY	SPONGEWARE	UNFORESEEN
FRAGMENTAL	INSOLENTLY	NORTHERNER	RECUPERATE	SPOONERISM	UNFRIENDLY
FREQUENTED	INTEMERATE	NOTICEABLE	REFERENDUM	SPOTLESSLY	UNIQUENESS
FREQUENTER	INTENERATE	NOTICEABLY	REFINEMENT	SPRUCENESS	UNLICENSED
FREQUENTLY	INTERESTED	OBEDIENTLY	REGENERATE	SQUETEAGUE	UNOBSERVED
FULLLENGTH	INTOLERANT	OBLITERATE	REGIMENTAL	SQUIREARCH	UNREDEEMED
GAMEKEEPER	INVETERATE	OBTUSENESS	REGIMENTED	STAGGERING	UNRESERVED
GANGRENOUS	IRRELEVANT	OCCIDENTAL	REJONEADOR	STALHELMER	UNREVEALED
GARNIERITE	IRREMEDIAL	OCTAHEDRON	REJUVENATE	STALLENGER	UNSLEEPING
GENTLEFOLK	IRREVERENT	OCTODECIMO	REMONETISE	STAMMERING	UNUNHEXIUM
GENTLENESS	JOBSEEKERS	OFFTHECUFF	REMOTENESS	STARVELING	UROSTEGITE
GEORGETOWN	JOURNEYMAN	OFFTHEWALL	REMUNERATE	STATUESQUE	VEHEMENTLY
GEOTHERMAL	KENSPECKLE	OPOTHERAPY	REQUIESCAT	STEPHENSON	VICEGERENT
GETHSEMANE	KETTLEDRUM	ORANGEWOOD	RESCHEDULE	STERTEROUS	VICEREGENT
GIRDLERINK	KILOMETRES	ORNAMENTAL	RESTLESSLY	STRATEGIST	VIRULENTLY
GLISTENING	KNOBKERRIE	OSMETERIUM	RETIREMENT	STRIDENTLY	VITUPERATE
GLITTERAND	LAMBREQUIN	OUTSPECKLE	REVERENTLY	STRIDEWAYS	VOCIFERATE
GLITTERATI	LANIGEROUS	OVERWEIGHT	RINGLEADER	SUBSPECIES	VOCIFEROUS
GLITTERING	LAUNCEGAYE	PACESETTER	ROISTERING	SUCCEEDING	WATTLEWORK
GLOUCESTER	LAUNCESTON	PADAREWSKI	ROMANESQUE	SUPPLEJACK	WAVELENGTH
GOALKEEPER	LAWBREAKER	PADDLEFISH	ROTTWEILER	SUPPLEMENT	WEATHERMAN
GOODFELLOW	LIEUTENANT	PAINLESSLY	RUDIMENTAL	SUPPLENESS	WENTLETRAP
GRANGERISM	LIGHTERMAN	PALFRENIER	RUTHLESSLY	SUPPRESSED	WHISPERING
GRANGERIZE	LISTLESSLY	PALLBEARER	SADDLEBACK	SUPPRESSOR	WHITTERICK
GUARNERIUS	LITTLENESS	PAPAVERINE	SADDLEBILL	SWAGGERING	WINCHESTER
HALFYEARLY	LOCKKEEPER	PARACELSUS	SALOPETTES	SWEETENING	WOODPECKER
HANDLEBARS	LONGFELLOW	PARAMETRIC	SALTCELLAR	SWELTERING	YOURSELVES
HANOVERIAN	MACEBEARER	PARASELENE	SAVAGENESS	SYNCRETISE	ZOLLVEREIN
HAUSTELLUM	MAINPERNOR	PARKLEAVES	SCANDERBEG	SYNTHESIZE	ZOOTHERAPY
HEEDLESSLY	MAKEWEIGHT	PARTHENOPE	SCARCEMENT	TACTLESSLY	ZWITTERION
HELLBENDER	MANAGEABLE	PEACHERINO	SCARCENESS	TALEBEARER	AMPLEFORTH
HELPLESSLY	MANAGEMENT	PEAUDESOIE	SCARLETINA	TANGLEFOOT	BLISSFULLY
HEMIHEDRON	MANAGERESS	PEDIMENTAL	SCATHELESS	TAPERECORD	BREADFRUIT
HEPHAESTUS	MANAGERIAL	PENSIEROSO	SCATTERING	TAPOTEMENT	CAMOUFLAGE
HOARSENESS	MANCHESTER	PERIHELION	SCOOTERIST	TECHNETIUM	CANDYFLOSS
HOLOFERNES	MANIFESTLY	PERPLEXING	SEDATENESS	TELPHERAGE	CHAUDFROID
HOLOHEDRAL	MARGUERITE	PERPLEXITY	SETTLEMENT	TESCHENITE	CHEERFULLY
HOMOGENIZE	MARQUETRIE	PERSIENNES	SEXAGESIMA	THEMSELVES	CRAIGFLUKE
HOMORELAPS	MARYLEBONE	PHLEGETHON	SHATTERING	THICKENING	CROCKFORDS
HOMOSEXUAL	MASQUERADE	PHRENESIAC	SHILLELAGH	THIRTEENTH	DENTIFRICE
HOPELESSLY	MEAGRENESS	PICARESQUE	SHIMMERING	THUNDERBOX	DOUBTFULLY
HUMBLENESS	MEANDERING	PIONEERING	SHOPKEEPER	THUNDERING	DREADFULLY
HUMORESQUE	MEDDLESOME	PLATTELAND	SHORTENING	THUNDEROUS	FAITHFULLY
HYPODERMIC	MEITNERIUM	PLAYFELLOW	SHRIVELLED	TIEBREAKER	FORCEFULLY
HYPOGENOUS	MELANESIAN	PLUNDERING	SHROVETIDE	TIMEKEEPER	FRUITFULLY
HYPOTENUSE	METACENTRE	POINSETTIA	SHUDDERING	TIMESERVER	GOOSEFLESH
ICEBREAKER	METALEPSIS	POLITENESS	SINGLENESS	TIRELESSLY	GRACEFULLY
ILLITERACY	METTLESOME	POLYHEDRON	SLAMMERKIN	TOLLKEEPER	GRAPEFRUIT
ILLITERATE	MICHAELMAS	POLYMERIZE	SLANDEROUS	TONGUESTER	GRATEFULLY
IMMATERIAL	MIDDLEBROW	POLYNESIAN	SLATTERNLY	TORQUEMADA	GRATIFYING
IMMODERATE	MINUTEBOOK	PROCEEDING	SLEEVELESS	TRACHELATE	GREENFINCH
IMPOTENTLY	MINUTENESS	PROCREATOR	SLUICEGATE	TRISKELION	GUTTIFERAE
IMPOVERISH	MONTSERRAT	PROPHETESS	SLUMBERING	TROPAEOLUM	HENCEFORTH

HORRIFYING	COLLEGIATE	PHONOGRAPH	ANTIPHONAL	HOMOPHOBIC	STONYHURST
INSUFFLATE	CONTAGIOUS	PHOTOGENIC	ANTITHESIS	HOMOPHONIC	STOREHOUSE
INTERFERER	CONTIGUITY	PHOTOGRAPH	ANTITHETIC	HYPOTHESIS	STOUTHERIE
INTERFERON	CONTIGUOUS	PICTOGRAPH	ATTACHMENT	ICOSOHEDRA	STOUTHRIEF
KATERFELTO	CORREGIDOR	PORTUGUESE	AUTOCHTHON	INFIGHTING	STRATHSPEY
KLANGFARBE	CORRIGENDA	PRODIGALLY	AVERRHOISM	LAVISHNESS	STROPHIOLE
MAGNIFICAT	CORRUGATED	PRODIGIOUS	BANISHMENT	LEDERHOSEN	STRYCHNINE
MAGNIFYING	CORRUGATOR	PROPAGANDA	BLACKHEART	LENGTHWAYS	SUPERHUMAN
MERCIFULLY	COURAGEOUS	PROPAGATOR	BLASPHEMER	LENGTHWISE	SWEETHEART
MICROFICHE	DEFLAGRATE	PROTAGORAS	BLOCKHOUSE	LIGHTHOUSE	SWITCHBACK
MILLEFIORI	DICTOGRAPH	PTERYGOTUS	BLOODHOUND	LILYWHITES	TELEPHONIC
MILLIFARAD	DISENGAGED	PUNDIGRION	BLUETHROAT	LONGCHAMPS	THOUGHTFUL
MOURNFULLY	DISFIGURED	PYCNOGONID	BONESHAKER	LOTOPHAGUS	TOCOPHEROL
PEACEFULLY	DIVERGENCE	PYTHAGORAS	BREATHLESS	MANICHAEAN	TRENCHMORE
PERMAFROST	ECOLOGICAL	PYTHOGENIC	BRONCHITIC	MENECHMIAN	TRIPEHOUND
PERSIFLAGE	EMBERGOOSE	RADIOGRAPH	BRONCHITIS	METAPHRASE	UNFATHOMED
PETRIFYING	ENCOIGNURE	RESURGENCE	BUCEPHALUS	METATHERIA	UNORTHODOX
PIANOFORTE	ENSANGUINE	RETROGRADE	CAERPHILLY	METATHESIS	WHEELHOUSE
POKERFACED	EXTINGUISH	RETROGRESS	CANEPHORUS	MILLIHENRY	WHITEHEART
PONTEFRACT	FARSIGHTED	REVENGEFUL	CATACHUMEN	MONOCHROME	WINDSHIELD
PONTIFICAL	FASTIGIATE	RHINEGRAVE	CATAPHRACT	MONOPHONIC	WORKAHOLIC
PRIZEFIGHT	FIBERGLASS	RIDINGHOOD	CATECHUMEN	MONOTHEISM	WRETCHEDLY
PUTREFYING	FIBREGLASS	SALMAGUNDI	CHINCHILLA	NOMOTHETIC	XENOPHOBIA
RIGHTFULLY	FULLYGROWN	SALTIGRADE	CHURCHGOER	NOSOPHOBIA	XENOPHOBIC
SATISFYING	GEOLOGICAL	SATYAGRAHA	CHURCHYARD	OESOPHAGUS	XEROPHYTIC
SCORNFULLY	HELIOGRAPH	SCAPEGRACE	COCKCHAFER	OVERCHARGE	ZOANTHARIA
SHAMEFACED	HEPTAGONAL	SEGREGATED	COPENHAGEN	OVERSHADOW	ABYSSINIAN
SHAMEFULLY	HIEROGLYPH	SMARAGDINE	CORYPHAEUS	OVERTHETOP	ACCUSINGLY
SIGNIFICAT	HIPPOGRIFF	SPREAGHERY	COURTHOUSE	OVERTHWART	ACQUAINTED
SKILLFULLY	HIPPOGRYPH	SPRINGBOKS	CREOPHAGUS	PARAPHASIA	ACTIVITIST
SPITEFULLY	HOWLEGLASS	SPRINGHAAS	CROSSHATCH	PARAPHILIA	ADDITIONAL
STOREFRONT	IATROGENIC	SPRINGLESS	CRYOPHORUS	PARAPHONIA	ADHIBITION
STUPEFYING	IMPREGNATE	SPRINGLIKE	DECATHLETE	PARAPHRASE	ADJUDICATE
TASTEFULLY	INDULGENCE	SPRINGTAIL	DECIPHERED	PARAPHYSIS	ADMINISTER
TERRIFYING	INELIGIBLE	SPRINGTIME	DELIGHTFUL	PERIPHERAL	ADMIRINGLY
THANKFULLY	INSTIGATOR	STALAGMITE	DETACHABLE	PERISHABLE	ADMONITION
TRUSTFULLY	INSURGENCY	STRAGGLING	DETACHMENT	PHOSPHORUS	AERUGINOUS
TRUTHFULLY	INTANGIBLE	STRAIGHTEN	DIPHTHERIA	PLANCHETTE	AFFABILITY
ULTRAFICHE	INTRIGUING	STRENGTHEN	DISINHERIT	PLOUGHBOTE	AFFILIATED
UNCONFINED	LARYNGITIS	STRINGENCY	DOLICHOLIS	PLOUGHGATE	AFTERIMAGE
UNDERFLOOR	LENTIGINES	STRINGENDO	DOLICHOTUS	PLOUGHWISE	ALCIBIADES
UNEDIFYING	LITHOGRAPH	STRINGHALT	ENCEPHALON	POLYCHAETE	ALEMBICATE
WASTEFULLY	LITURGICAL	STRONGHOLD	ENKEPHALIN	POLYCHREST	ALKALINITY
WATCHFULLY	MALINGERER	STRONGROOM	ENRICHMENT	POLYCHROME	ALLEGIANCE
WATERFRONT	MENINGITIS	SUPERGIANT	EPENTHETIC	POLYPHEMUS	ALMSGIVING
WRONGFULLY	MIMEOGRAPH	SYNTAGMATA	EUROCHEQUE	POLYTHEISM	ALTAZIMUTH
WYCLIFFIAN	MONTAGNARD	TACHOGRAPH	FAMISHMENT	POSTCHAISE	ALTRUISTIC
ABORIGINAL	MULLIGRUBS	TARDIGRADE	FIANCHETTO	POWERHOUSE	ALZHEIMERS
ABRIDGMENT	MYRINGITIS	THROUGHOUT	FORESHADOW	PROSTHESIS	AMIABILITY
AMPHIGOURI	MYSTAGOGUE	THROUGHPUT	FOURCHETTE	PROSTHETIC	AMMUNITION
ANALOGICAL	MYSTAGOGUS	THROUGHWAY	FRANCHISEE	PUNISHABLE	ANASTIGMAT
ANEMOGRAPH	NDRANGHETA	TRANSGRESS	FRANCHISOR	PUNISHMENT	ANCIPITOUS
APOLOGETIC	NEGLIGENCE	TRIANGULAR	FRAUNHOFER	PYROPHORUS	ANNIHILATE
ASTRAGALUS	NEGLIGIBLE	TRIANGULUM	FREIGHTAGE	QUENCHLESS	ANTIBIOTIC
AVANTGARDE	NEWSAGENTS	UNFLAGGING	GAULTHERIA	RAWSTHORNE	ANTICIPATE
BEDRAGGLED	OCEANGOING	UNORIGINAL	GENETHLIAC	RICHTHOFEN	APPARITION
BELONGINGS	ORTHOGONAL	VARIEGATED	GLASSHOUSE	ROSECHAFER	APPETITIVE
BERSAGLIER	OSTROGOTHS	ZINCOGRAPH	GOLDTHREAD	ROUGHHOUSE	APPETIZING
BETELGEUSE	OTHERGATES	ZOOLOGICAL	GREENHEART	ROUNDHOUSE	APPOSITION
BETELGEUZE	OTHERGUESS	ABHIDHAMMA	GREENHOUSE	SAMOTHRACE	ARCHBISHOP
BIOLOGICAL	OUTRAGEOUS	ADIAPHORON	GUESTHOUSE	SHAKUHACHI	ARISTIPPUS
BLACKGUARD	PANTAGRUEL	AEROPHAGIA	HEADPHONES	SKETCHBOOK	ARTIFICIAL
BOURIGNIAN	PANTOGRAPH	AFTERHOURS	HEMICHORDA	SKUPSHTINA	ASCETICISM
BRIDEGROOM	PARMIGIANA	ALLYCHOLLY	HEMOPHILIA	SMOOTHNESS	ASPIDISTRA
CARMAGNOLE	PASSAGEWAY	ANALPHABET	HITCHHIKER	SPATCHCOCK	ASSIMILATE
CARRAGHEEN	PATHOGENIC	ANARCHICAL	HOBBYHORSE	SPEECHLESS	ASSOCIATED
CENTIGRADE	PENTAGONAL	ANESTHESIA	HOLOPHOTAL	SPITCHCOCK	ASTONISHED
CHINAGRAPH	PERIEGESIS	ANESTHETIC	HOLOPHYTIC	STEAKHOUSE	ATELEIOSIS
COASTGUARD	PETROGLYPH	ANTICHTHON	HOMOPHOBIA	STONEHENGE	AUDIBILITY

AUSTRINGER	CONTRIBUTE	ENCLOISTER	HALFSISTER	IRRATIONAL	OBLIGINGLY
AUTODIDACT	CONTRITION	EPHRAIMITE	HANDPICKED	JAUNTINESS	OBSIDIONAL
BABESIASIS	COORDINATE	EPIDEICTIC	HEADLIGHTS	JEISTIECOR	OCCASIONAL
BABYSITTER	COSTLINESS	EQUANIMITY	HEARTINESS	JINGOISTIC	OFFICIALLY
BACKBITING	COUNCILLOR	ESPECIALLY	HEDONISTIC	JUDICIALLY	OLEAGINOUS
BAHRAINIAN	CRAFTINESS	EULOGISTIC	HEREDITARY	KARTTIKAYA	OPENMINDED
BAILLIWICK	CREATIVITY	EXACTITUDE	HERESIARCH	KINCHINLAY	OPPOSITION
BALBRIGGAN	CRISPINIAN	EXHIBITION	HIGHBINDER	KINDLINESS	OPTIMISTIC
BARASINGHA	DEACTIVATE	EXORBITANT	HISTRIONIC	KINGFISHER	ORDOVICIAN
BARGAINING	DEADLINESS	EXPEDIENCE	HOMELINESS	KLEBSIELLA	OVERRIDING
BATTAILOUS	DEBILITATE	EXPEDIENCY	HOODWINKED	KOEKSISTER	OWLSPIEGLE
BEAUTICIAN	DECAPITATE	EXPEDITION	HORNRIMMED	KURDAITCHA	PACIFICISM
BEAUTIFIER	DECISIVELY	EXPERIENCE	HUMANISTIC	LADYKILLER	PAINKILLER
BEDEVILLED	DEFICIENCY	EXPERIMENT	HUMANITIES	LASTMINUTE	PALATINATE
BEHAVIORAL	DEFINITELY	EXPOSITION	HUMIDIFIER	LAURVIKITE	PANARITIUM
BENEDICITE	DEFINITION	EXPOSITORY	HUMIDISTAT	LAWABIDING	PARADIDDLE
BENEFICENT	DEFINITIVE	FACILITATE	IDEALISTIC	LEFTWINGER	PARISIENNE
BENEFICIAL	DELPHINIUM	FACILITIES	ILLUMINATE	LEGALISTIC	PASQUINADE
BIENNIALLY	DEMOBILISE	FAMILIARLY	ILLUMINATI	LEGIBILITY	PATAVINITY
BITUMINOUS	DEMOBILIZE	FANATICISM	IMBECILITY	LEGITIMACY	PATCHINESS
BOOKBINDER	DEMOLITION	FATALISTIC	IMMOBILITY	LEGITIMATE	PATHFINDER
BOOTLICKER	DEMONIACAL	FATALITIES	IMMOBILIZE	LEGITIMIZE	PECULIARLY
BRACHIOPOD	DEPOSITARY	FAULTINESS	IMPATIENCE	LEGUMINOUS	PENICILLIN
BRAININESS	DEPOSITION	FAVORITISM	IMPEDIMENT	LENOCINIUM	PERIWINKLE
BRILLIANCE	DEPOSITORY	FELICITATE	IMPENITENT	LEONTIASIS	PERQUISITE
CACOMISTLE	DERACINATE	FELICITOUS	IMPOLITELY	LIBIDINOUS	PETITIONER
CACUMINOUS	DESALINATE	FEMININITY	IMPOSITION	LIGHTINGUP	PHILLIPINA
CAESPITOSE	DESCRIBING	FEVERISHLY	IMPURITIES	LIKELIHOOD	PHILLIPINE
CALAMITOUS	DESPAIRING	FIENDISHLY	INACTIVITY	LIKEMINDED	PHLOGISTIC
CALORIFIER	DEVOTIONAL	FILTHINESS	INAPTITUDE	LINGUISTIC	PHLOGISTON
CAMPAIGNER	DICKCISSEL	FLABBINESS	INARTISTIC	LIVELIHOOD	PHYLLIOPOD
CANCRIZANS	DILAPIDATE	FLASHINESS	INCISIVELY	LIVELINESS	PILGRIMAGE
CAPABILITY	DIMINISHED	FLEETINGLY	INCIVILITY	LOGARITHMS	PITYRIASIS
CAPACITATE	DISABILITY	FLESHINESS	INDECISION	LONELINESS	PLASTICINE
CARABINEER	DISDAINFUL	FLIMSINESS	INDECISIVE	LORDLINESS	PLASTICITY
CARABINIER	DISJOINTED	FLOURISHED	INDEFINITE	LOUISIETTE	PLIABILITY
CENTRIFUGE	DISQUIETED	FLUFFINESS	INDELICACY	LOVELINESS	PLIOHIPPUS
CHAMPIGNON	DISTRIBUTE	FOOTLIGHTS	INDELICATE	LUXURIANCE	POLITICIAN
CHAUVINISM	DISTRINGAS	FOREBITTER	INDIVIDUAL	MANCHINEEL	POLITICIZE
CHAUVINIST	DIVISIONAL	FOREFINGER	INEBRIATED	MATERIALLY	PONCHIELLI
CHEEKINESS	DOMICILARY	FORFAITING	INEFFICACY	MAXIMILIAN	POSITIVELY
CHILDISHLY	DOWNSIZING	FORFEITURE	INEPTITUDE	MEGALITHIC	POSITIVIST
CHILLINESS	DREAMINESS	FORTUITOUS	INFINITELY	MENACINGLY	POSTLIMINY
CHLORINATE	DREARINESS	FRACTIONAL	INFINITIVE	MEPERIDINE	PREDNISONE
CHRONICLER	DREARISOME	FRANCISCAN	INFURIATED	MESOLITHIC	PREEMINENT
CHRONICLES	DROWSINESS	FRANGIPANE	INGEMINATE	MIDSHIPMAN	PRESCIENCE
CHRYSIPPUS	DRUZHINNIK	FRANGIPANI	INHABITANT	MIGHTINESS	PRETTINESS
CHURLISHLY	DURABILITY	FRATRICIDE	INHIBITING	MILITIAMAN	PREVAILING
CIRCUITOUS	DUUMVIRATE	FRENZIEDLY	INHIBITION	MISERICORD	PRINCIPIUM
CISLEITHAN	DYNAMITARD	FRINGILLID	INHIBITORY	MISPRISION	PRINCIPLED
CLAMMINESS	EBULLIENCE	FRISKINESS	INIQUITOUS	MITHRIDATE	PRINCIPLES
CLASSICISM	ECARDINATE	FULIGINOUS	INKSLINGER	MODIFIABLE	PROCLIVITY
CLASSICIST	ECTHLIPSIS	FUNCTIONAL	INORDINATE	MONILIASIS	PROFLIGACY
CLASSIFIED	EFFEMINACY	FUTURISTIC	INSANITARY	MONILIFORM	PROFLIGATE
CLOUDINESS	EFFEMINATE	GADOLINIUM	INSATIABLE	MONOLITHIC	PROPLITEAL
CLUMSINESS	EFFICIENCY	GAINGIVING	INSATIABLY	MORALITIES	PROPRIETOR
COINCIDENT	EFFUSIVELY	GELATINOUS	INSEMINATE	MOULDINESS	PROSCIUTTO
COLCHICINE	EGURGITATE	GIARDIASIS	INSIPIDITY	MOULDIWARP	PROSTITUTE
COMEDIENNE	ELASTICATE	GLASSINESS	INTELIGENT	MUDSKIPPER	PSYCHIATRY
COMPLIANCE	ELASTICITY	GLOSSINESS	INTIMIDATE	MUNIFICENT	PURSUIVANT
COMPLICATE	ELEUSINIAN	GNOSTICISM	INTOXICANT	MUTABILITY	QUADRICEPS
COMPLICITY	ELYTRIFORM	GOLDDIGGER	INTOXICATE	NEGATIVELY	QUADRIREME
COMPLIMENT	EMANCIPATE	GOLDFINGER	INVALIDATE	NEGOTIABLE	QUEASINESS
CONCHIGLIE	EMARGINATE	GRATUITOUS	INVALIDISM	NEGOTIATOR	QUERCITRON
CONCHIOLIN	EMBODIMENT	GREEDINESS	INVALIDITY	NIHILISTIC	QUESTIONER
CONFLICTED	EMBROIDERY	GRITTINESS	INVARIABLE	NONALIGNED	REACTIVATE
CONSCIENCE	EMISSIVITY	GRUBBINESS	INVARIABLY	NOTABILITY	RECIDIVISM
CONSPIRACY	EMULSIFIER	GRUMPINESS	INVIGILATE	NOTIFIABLE	RECIDIVIST
CONSTITUTE	ENANTIOSIS	HABILITATE	IRRADICATE	NOURRITURE	RELATIVELY

583

RELATIVITY	STILLICIDE	UNUNNILIUM	CANTALOUPE	FLAGELLATE	OUTBALANCE
REPETITEUR	STILLIFORM	UROPOIESIS	CANTILEVER	FLATULENCE	OVERSLAUGH
REPETITION	STINGINESS	VELOCIPEDE	CANTILLATE	FLOODLIGHT	PANTALOONS
REPETITIVE	STOCKINESS	VERIFIABLE	CAPILLAIRE	FLUGELHORN	PARAGLOSSA
REPOSITORY	STRABISMUS	VERSAILLES	CASSOLETTE	FOSSILIZED	PARALLELED
RESILIENCE	STRATIOTES	VETERINARY	CASUALNESS	FRITILLARY	PARAPLEGIA
RESTRICTED	STRAVINSKY	VIEWFINDER	CATHOLICON	FULFILMENT	PARAPLEGIC
RESUPINATE	STRELITZIA	VILLAINOUS	CATHOLICOS	GHIBELLINE	PARNELLISM
RETRAINING	STREPITANT	VILLEINAGE	CELLULITIS	GLYCOLYSIS	PENNILLION
ROSANILINE	STREPITOSO	VISIBILITY	CENTILITER	GOLDILOCKS	PENTELIKON
RUBIGINOUS	STRIKINGLY	VOCATIONAL	CENTILITRE	GONDOLIERS	PERCOLATOR
SANCTIFIED	STUFFINESS	VOLATILITY	CEPHALOPOD	GRANULATED	PESTALOZZI
SANCTITIES	STULTIFIED	VOLUBILITY	CHAROLLAIS	GRASSLANDS	PESTILENCE
SANCTITUDE	STURDINESS	VOLUMINOUS	CHATELAINE	GRATILLITY	PICCALILLI
SANDWICHES	SUBSTITUTE	VORAGINOUS	CHECKLATON	GROVELLING	PISTILLATE
SANGUINARY	SULTRINESS	WASSAILING	CHIVALROUS	GUIDELINES	PLATELAYER
SBUDDIKINS	SUPPLICANT	WEEDKILLER	CHOLALOGUE	HALLELUJAH	POIKILITIC
SCANTINESS	SUPPLICATE	WHARFINGER	COCKALORUM	HANGGLIDER	POSTILLATE
SCEPTICISM	SURFRIDING	WHEEZINESS	COMPELLING	HECTOLITRE	POSTILLION
SCINTIGRAM	SURPRISING	WOODPIGEON	COMPULSION	HEIDELBERG	PREVALENCE
SCLERIASIS	SUSTAINING	WORSHIPPER	COMPULSIVE	HELIOLATER	PRICKLOUSE
SCOFFINGLY	SWIMMINGLY	WORTHINESS	COMPULSORY	HEMIPLEGIA	PRIVILEGED
SCRUTINEER	TARADIDDLE	BLITZKRIEG	CONCILIATE	HEMOGLOBIN	PROMULGATE
SCRUTINISE	TECHNICIAN	BRADYKININ	CONDOLENCE	HIGHFLYING	PROPELLANT
SCRUTINIZE	TELEVISION	CLASPKNIFE	CONEFLOWER	HISTOLYSIS	PROPELLENT
SCURRILITY	TENDRILLED	EMBANKMENT	CONSULTANT	HORNBLENDE	PROPULSION
SCURRILOUS	THALLIFORM	HAKENKREUZ	CONSULTING	HORNBLOWER	PROPYLAEUM
SECURITIES	THERMIONIC	LYSENKOISM	CONVALESCE	HORSELBERG	PROSILIENT
SEEMLIHEAD	THERMISTOR	MISTAKENLY	CONVOLUTED	HYDROLYSIS	PUMMELLING
SELEGILINE	THUMBIKINS	PAPERKNIFE	CONVOLVUTE	IMPARLANCE	RADIOLARIA
SEMICIRCLE	TIMELINESS	REMARKABLE	CONVULSION	INFALLIBLE	RAMPALLIAN
SHABBINESS	TIROCINIUM	REMARKABLY	CONVULSIVE	INFALLIBLY	RANNELTREE
SHEEPISHLY	TOUCHINESS	SAUERKRAUT	COQUELICOT	INSTALMENT	REBELLIOUS
SHIFTINESS	TOURBILLON	SHISHKEBAB	CORDILLERA	INTAGLIATE	REPUBLICAN
SHOCKINGLY	TOURNIQUET	SPRINKLING	CORNFLAKES	INTERLEAVE	RHINOLALIA
SHODDINESS	TRAFFICKER	TCHOUKBALL	CORNFLOWER	INTERLOPER	RIBOFLAVIN
SHOPLIFTER	TRANSIENCE	TROTSKYITE	CORPULENCE	INVIOLABLE	RINGELMANN
SICILIENNE	TRANSISTOR	UNWORKABLE	CRAPULENCE	ISABELLINE	ROQUELAURE
SIDEWINDER	TRANSITION	ABERGLAUBE	CRENELLATE	JAYWALKING	RUMBULLION
SIMILITUDE	TRANSITIVE	ACOTYLEDON	CREWELWORK	KESSELRING	SANDALWOOD
SIMPLICITY	TRANSITORY	AMARYLLIDS	CROTALARIA	KIESELGUHR	SARCOLEMMA
SIMPLISTIC	TRENDINESS	ANCHYLOSIS	CROTALIDAE	LAVALLIÈRE	SCHOOLBOOK
SKEPTICISM	TRICKINESS	ANGUILLULA	CUCULLATED	LEGISLATOR	SCHOOLGIRL
SKINDIVING	TRICLINIUM	ANNUALIZED	DAMSELFISH	LINGULELLA	SCHOOLMAAM
SLEEPINESS	TRILLIONTH	ANTICLIMAX	DECOLLATOR	LORDOLATRY	SCOPELIDAE
SLOPPINESS	TRIPLICATE	APICULTURE	DERAILLEUR	MAQUILLAGE	SCUTELLATE
SLUGGISHLY	TRIPLICITY	APOCALYPSE	DERAILMENT	MARIOLATRY	SHACKLETON
SMARMINESS	TUTIVILLUS	ASPHALTITE	DIABOLICAL	MARVELLOUS	SHECKLATON
SNOOTINESS	UBIQUINONE	ASTRAGALUS	DISBELIEVE	MATELLASSE	SHORTLIVED
SOLICITOUS	UBIQUITOUS	ASTROLOGER	DISCOLORED	METALLURGY	SHOVELHEAD
SOLICITUDE	UNABRIDGED	AUTOPLASTY	DISSELBOOM	METAPLASIS	SHOVELNOSE
SOLIFIDIAN	UNASSIGNED	AVICULARIA	DISSILIENT	METHYLATED	SHRILLNESS
SOLUBILITY	UNAVAILING	BACKBLOCKS	DISSOLVENT	MICROLIGHT	SIGILLARIA
SOOTHINGLY	UNBELIEVER	BACKSLIDER	DISTILLATE	MISCELLANY	SIMILLIMUM
SOUBRIQUET	UNDENIABLE	BAUDELAIRE	DISTILLERY	MONOPLEGIA	SINFULNESS
SPEEDINESS	UNEASINESS	BINUCLEATE	DISTILLING	NARCOLEPSY	SINGULARLY
SPERMICIDE	UNENVIABLE	BOUILLOTTE	DREADLOCKS	NATHELESSE	SNOWBLOWER
SPIFLICATE	UNFAMILIAR	BRAZILWOOD	DRUMBLEDOR	NEAPOLITAN	SOGDOLAGER
SPILLIKINS	UNFINISHED	BRICKLAYER	ENCYCLICAL	NESSELRODE	SOGDOLIGER
SPISSITUDE	UNFRUITFUL	BROWNLANDS	ENROLLMENT	NEURILEMMA	SOGDOLIGER
SPONGIFORM	UNHYGIENIC	CALCULABLE	EUROCLYDON	NEUROLEMMA	SOMNOLENCE
SPONSIONAL	UNINVITING	CALCULATED	EVERGLADES	NIGHTLIGHT	SPECULATOR
SPORTINGLY	UNOFFICIAL	CALCULATOR	EXCELLENCE	NYCTALOPIA	SPLITLEVEL
STALLINGER	UNRELIABLE	CAMERLENGO	EXCELLENCY	ODDFELLOWS	STABILISER
STEADINESS	UNRELIEVED	CAMERLINGO	FERTILISED	OFFBALANCE	STABILIZER
STEELINESS	UNRULINESS	CANCELLOUS	FERTILISER	OPHICLEIDE	STERILISER
STEMWINDER	UNSCRIPTED	CANDELABRA	FERTILIZER	OSCILLATOR	STERILIZER
STEPSISTER	UNSOCIABLE	CANDELILLA	FEUILLETON	OSTEOLEPIS	STUMBLEDOM
STICKINESS	UNTIDINESS	CANNELLONI	FIBRILLATE	OUGHTLINGS	SUBSELLIUM

SVADILFARI	CIRCUMFLEX	NINCOMPOOP	ALEXANDERS	CONCINNITY	EXPOUNDERS
SYMBOLICAL	CIRCUMFUSE	NUMISMATIC	ALEXANDRIA	CONCINNOUS	EXTERNALLY
SYPHILITIC	CIRCUMVENT	OMBROMETER	ALIMENTARY	CONGENITAL	EXTRANEOUS
THIMBLEFUL	CLEROMANCY	OPISOMETER	ALPHONSINE	CONSENSION	FAHRENHEIT
THIMBLEWIT	CLOCKMAKER	PADDYMELON	ALTERNATOR	CONSONANCE	FALLINGOFF
TIRAILLEUR	COLLEMBOLA	PAPIAMENTO	AMERINDIAN	CONSONANTS	FARRANDINE
TORCHLIGHT	COLLIMATOR	PARRAMATTA	AMPHINEURA	CONTENTION	FASCINATED
TORTELLINI	CONDIMENTS	PASSAMEZZO	ANGWANTIBO	CONTINENCE	FASCINATOR
TRANSLATED	CONSUMMATE	PEACEMAKER	APEMANTHUS	CONTINGENT	FERRANDINE
TRANSLATOR	COQUIMBITE	PENTAMERON	APPRENTICE	CONTINUANT	FESCENNINE
TRAVELATOR	COXCOMICAL	PENTAMETER	ARAGONITES	CONTINUING	FLAMINGANT
TRAVELLERS	DENSIMETER	PENTIMENTO	ASSIGNABLE	CONTINUITY	FLORENTINE
TRAVELLING	DETERMINED	PHENOMENAL	ASSIGNMENT	CONTINUOUS	FONTANELLE
TRAVELOGUE	DETERMINER	PHENOMENON	ASTOUNDING	CONVENANCE	FONTINALIS
TRAVOLATOR	DIPLOMATIC	PHLEGMASIA	ASTRINGENT	CONVENIENT	FORTINBRAS
TRIFOLIATE	DIPSOMANIA	PHLEGMATIC	ASTRONOMER	CONVENTION	FOXHUNTING
TRIMALCHIO	DISCOMFORT	PLEXIMETER	ATTAINABLE	CONVENTUAL	FRAXINELLA
TRUCULENCE	DISCOMMODE	PORTAMENTO	ATTAINMENT	CONVINCING	FRICANDEAU
TURBULENCE	DISCOMPOSE	PORTSMOUTH	BARRENNESS	COPERNICUS	FROMANTEEL
UMBELLIFER	DISSEMBLER	PRESUMABLY	BASSINGTON	COTTONTAIL	FUSTANELLA
UNDECLARED	DISSIMILAR	PROCUMBENT	BATTENBERG	COTTONWOOD	FUSTANELLE
UNDERLEASE	DOLCEMENTE	PULSOMETER	BATTENBURG	CREDENTIAL	GALVANISER
UNDERLINEN	DRESSMAKER	RANDOMNESS	BIPINNARIA	CRIMINALLY	GARGANTUAN
UNDERLYING	ECCHYMOSIS	RECOMMENCE	BIRKENHEAD	CUISENAIRE	GARLANDAGE
UNEMPLOYED	ECONOMICAL	RHYTHMICAL	BIRMINGHAM	CURRENCIES	GASCONNADE
UNEXPLORED	ELACAMPANE	SANDEMANIA	BOLLANDIST	CYBERNETIC	GEOCENTRIC
UNYIELDING	ELECAMPANE	SCARAMOUCH	BOOZINGKEN	DECENNOVAL	GOLDENSEAL
USEFULNESS	EMBLEMATIC	SCHISMATIC	BOUSINGKEN	DECLENSION	GONFANONER
VASCULITIS	EMBLEMENTS	SCHLIMAZEL	BRIGANDINE	DESCENDANT	GORMANDIZE
VENTILATOR	EMOLUMENTS	SERVOMOTOR	BRIGANTINE	DESCENDING	GOVERNANCE
VERMILLION	ENDOSMOSIS	SINSEMILLA	BROKENDOWN	DESPONDENT	GOVERNESSY
VITELLICLE	ENTREMESSE	SKEUOMORPH	BUCCINATOR	DETAINMENT	GOVERNMENT
WALLFLOWER	EPILIMNION	SNAKEMOUTH	BUCKINGHAM	DETRUNCATE	GUARANTEED
WATERLEVEL	ESTRAMACON	SOPHOMORIC	BURDENSOME	DIACONICON	GUBERNATOR
WHEWELLITE	EUDIOMETER	SPODOMANCY	BURLINGTON	DIAGENESIS	HAEMANTHUS
WINDFLOWER	FIELDMOUSE	STONEMASON	BUTTONDOWN	DIAGONALLY	HARMANBECK
ZABAGLIONE	FLUTEMOUTH	STREAMERED	BUTTONHOLE	DISCONCERT	HARMONIOUS
ABNORMALLY	GONIOMETER	STREAMLINE	BYSSINOSIS	DISCONNECT	HARRINGTON
ABSTEMIOUS	GUATEMALAN	SUBCOMPACT	CACHINNATE	DISCONTENT	HATEENOUGH
ACHROMATIC	HEPTAMERON	SUBLIMATER	CALUMNIATE	DISENNOBLE	HEAVENWARD
ACROAMATIC	HIEROMANCY	SUBLIMINAL	CAMPANELLA	DISHONESTY	HINDENBURG
AFRORMOSIA	HIPPOMANES	SUPERMODEL	CANNONBALL	DISMANTLED	HOOTANANNY
ALDERMANLY	HOUSEMAIDS	SYSTEMATIC	CANTONMENT	DISPENSARY	HOOTENANNY
AMPHIMACER	HOWSOMEVER	TACHOMETER	CAPERNAITE	DISPENSING	HORRENDOUS
AMPHIMIXIS	HYDROMETER	TANTAMOUNT	CAPERNOITY	DISSENSION	HUSBANDAGE
ANATOMICAL	HYGROMETER	TROMOMETER	CARCINOGEN	DISSENTING	ICOSANDRIA
ANAXIMENES	HYPSOMETRY	ULTRAMAFIC	CARPENTIER	DISSONANCE	IMAGINABLE
ANDROMACHE	IMPRIMATUR	UNCOMMONLY	CENTENNIAL	DISTENSION	INFERNALLY
ANEMOMETER	INFORMALLY	UNEXAMPLED	CHEMONASTY	DISTINCTLY	INTERNALLY
APOPEMPTIC	INTERMARRY	UNICAMERAL	CHIRONOMIC	DRACONITES	INTERNMENT
APOSEMATIC	INTERMEZZO	UNPROMPTED	CISPONTINE	DRAGONROOT	INTERNODAL
ARCHIMEDES	JIGGAMAREE	VINDEMIATE	CITRONELLA	ECUMENICAL	JACKANAPES
ARITHMETIC	LANDAMMANN	WAMPUMPEAG	CLEMENCEAU	EFFRONTERY	JARDINIERE
ASTIGMATIC	LINEAMENTS	WATCHMAKER	CLEMENTINE	EGOCENTRIC	JARGONELLE
AXINOMANCY	LINEOMYCIN	WATERMELON	COCCINEOUS	ELEMENTARY	KUOMINTANG
BARRAMUNDA	LITHOMARGE	ABOMINABLE	COETANEOUS	ELIMINATOR	LAURENTIAN
BARRAMUNDI	MAHOMMEDAN	ABOMINABLY	COLONNADED	EMALANGENI	LAWRENCIUM
BELLAMOURE	MATCHMAKER	ABSTENTION	COMMANDANT	EMPFINDUNG	LEAMINGTON
BLANCMANGE	MEDIUMTERM	ABSTINENCE	COMMANDEER	ENCHANTING	MACKINTOSH
BOTTOMLESS	MERRYMAKER	ACCOUNTANT	COMMANDING	ENTRANCING	MAIDENHAIR
CAPNOMANCY	METHOMANIA	ACCOUNTING	COMMENTARY	ENTRENCHED	MAIDENHOOD
CARTOMANCY	MICROMETER	ACTIONABLE	COMMENTATE	EPICANTHUS	MAISONETTE
CASSUMUNAR	MILEOMETER	ADAMANTINE	COMMONALTY	EPIDENDRUM	MALCONTENT
CENTIMETER	MILLIMETER	ADELANTADO	COMMONWEAL	EPIGENETIC	MALIGNANCY
CENTIMETRE	MILLIMETRE	AGAPANTHUS	COMMUNALLY	EPIMENIDES	MANZANILLA
CHAULMUGRA	MISCHMETAL	AGGRANDISE	COMMUNIQUÉ	ERYMANTHUS	MARCANTANT
CHERIMOYER	MONEYMAKER	ALABANDINE	COMPENDIUM	EUPHONIOUS	MARGINALIA
CHIROMANCY	MULTIMEDIA	ALABANDITE	COMPENSATE	EUTHANASIA	MARGINALLY
CIRCUMCISE	NECROMANCY	ALCYONARIA	CONCENTRIC	EUTHYNEURA	MARIONETTE

MARTINGALE	PREVENTION	TENNANTITE	APOLLONIAN	CHERVONETS	FOREBODING
MARTINIQUE	PREVENTIVE	TERMINABLE	APOLLONIUS	CHEVROTAIN	FOUDROYANT
MASKANONGE	PROFUNDITY	TERMINALIA	APOTROPAIC	CHIFFONIER	FRAMBOESIA
MASKINONGE	PROGENITOR	TERMINALLY	AQUAFORTIS	CHIMBORAZO	FREEBOOTER
MATERNALLY	PROMENADER	THYSANURAN	ARISTOCRAT	CHLOROFORM	FREEHOLDER
MAYONNAISE	PROMINENCE	TILLANDSIA	ARISTOLOGY	CHROMOSOME	FREELOADER
MEANINGFUL	PROMONTORY	TOILINETTE	ARISTOTLES	CHRONOLOGY	FROGHOPPER
MECHANICAL	PROPENSITY	TORRENTIAL	ARMIPOTENT	CHRYSOLITE	GALSWORTHY
MECHANIZED	PROTANOPIA	TRAMONTANA	ARTHROMERE	CIRRHOPODA	GASTRONOME
MERCANTILE	PROTANOPIC	TRAMONTANE	ASTEROIDEA	CLODHOPPER	GASTRONOMY
MICRONESIA	PROVENANCE	TRAVANCORE	AUCTIONEER	COMPROMISE	GENEROSITY
MIGNONETTE	PROVINCIAL	TRECENTIST	AUDITORIUM	COMSTOCKER	GENEROUSLY
MILLENNIUM	PRUDENTIAL	TREMENDOUS	AUTECOLOGY	CONCHOLOGY	GEOTROPISM
MISCONDUCT	PTERANODON	TRIDENTINE	AUTOMOBILE	CONTROLLER	GLAUCONITE
MIZZENMAST	QUARANTINE	TRILINGUAL	AUTOMOTIVE	CONTROVERT	GLENDOVEER
MORGANATIC	QUIRINALIA	TRIMSNITCH	AUTONOMOUS	COPYHOLDER	GLORIOUSLY
MORGANETTA	RABBINICAL	TRITANOPIA	BABIROUSSA	CORNCOCKLE	GLUTTONOUS
MOTIONLESS	RATIONALLY	TURPENTINE	BABYLONIAN	COUSCOUSOU	GOBEMOUCHE
MUTTONHEAD	REAMINGBIT	TYMPANITES	BALLOONING	CRYPTOGRAM	GORGEOUSLY
MYELINATED	REASONABLE	TYMPANITIS	BALLOONIST	CRYPTOZOIC	GRACIOUSLY
NATIONALLY	REASONABLY	TYRANNICAL	BALNEOLOGY	CUCKOOPINT	GRAPHOLOGY
NATIONWIDE	RECOGNISED	TYRANNISED	BAMBOOZLED	CYNOMOLGUS	GRAPTOLITE
NEWFANGLED	RECOGNIZED	ULTRONEOUS	BAREFOOTED	DECOLORATE	GRAVEOLENT
NONVINTAGE	REFRINGENT	UNBLINKING	BASSOONIST	DECOLORIZE	GRIDLOCKED
NOTIONALLY	REPUGNANCE	UNDERNEATH	BEAUJOLAIS	DELTIOLOGY	GUILLOTINE
OBTAINABLE	RESIGNEDLY	UNEVENNESS	BEDCLOTHES	DEMOGORGON	GYNECOLOGY
ORDONNANCE	RESOUNDING	UNEVENTFUL	BENEVOLENT	DEMONOLOGY	HALFDOLLAR
ORIDINANCE	RESPONDENT	UNIGENITUS	BERMOOTHES	DENDROPHIS	HALFHOURLY
ORIGINALLY	RESPONSIVE	UNMANNERED	BICHROMATE	DEVELOPING	HANDSOMELY
ORIGINATOR	RETURNABLE	UNMANNERLY	BLASTOCOEL	DIADROMOUS	HARDBOILED
OROGENESIS	RITORNELLE	UNTHINKING	BLASTOIDEA	DIAGNOSTIC	HAUSTORIUM
OUANANICHE	RITORNELLO	UPBRINGING	BLUEBONNET	DICHROMATE	HELICOPTER
OUTLANDISH	ROCKINGHAM	UPSTANDING	BLUEBOTTLE	DICHROMISM	HEPATOCELE
OXYGENATOR	ROWLANDSON	UROGENITAL	BONDHOLDER	DICTIONARY	HETERODOXY
OZYMANDIAS	SALLENDERS	VILLANELLE	BOOKMOBILE	DICYNODONT	HETERODYNE
PADDINGTON	SALMANAZAR	VILLANOVAN	BOONDOGGLE	DIGITORIUM	HETEROGAMY
PANJANDRUM	SALMONELLA	VULCANALIA	BUFFOONERY	DISCLOSURE	HITOPODESA
PARAENESIS	SALPINGIAN	WALDENSIAN	BURGEONING	DITHIONATE	HOMECOMING
PARDONABLE	SANDINISTA	WAPPENSHAW	CALAMONDIN	DOORTODOOR	HOMEWORKER
PARDONABLY	SARMENTOUS	WARRANDICE	CALCEOLATE	DUCKBOARDS	HOMOEOPATH
PARTINGALE	SATURNALIA	WASHINGTON	CALEDONIAN	DYSPROSIUM	HORIZONTAL
PATERNALLY	SCREENPLAY	WEAPONLESS	CALIFORNIA	DYSTROPHIC	HUMOROUSLY
PATRONISED	SCROUNGING	WELLINGTON	CALYDONIAN	ECHINODERM	HYPOCORISM
PATRONYMIC	SEAMANSHIP	WILLINGDON	CAMELOPARD	ECHINOIDEA	IMMEMORIAL
PERCENTAGE	SEASONABLE	WOFFINGTON	CAMERONIAN	ECUADORIAN	IMMUNOLOGY
PERCENTILE	SEASONABLY	WOODENHEAD	CANCIONERO	EDULCORATE	INDECOROUS
PERDENDOSI	SELLINGERS	YAFFINGALE	CAPITOLINE	ELECTORATE	INDICOLITE
PERMANENCE	SEPTENNIAL	ACHITOPHEL	CAPREOLATE	EMBRYOLOGY	INDIGOLITE
PERMANENCY	SEQUENTIAL	AFICIONADO	CARDIOGRAM	EMPEDOCLES	INVIGORATE
PERSONABLE	SERMONICAL	AGRONOMIST	CARDIOLOGY	ENORMOUSLY	IRONMONGER
PERSONALLY	SERPENTINE	AHITHOPHEL	CARPHOLOGY	ENTEROCELE	IRRESOLUTE
PERTINENCE	SHENANIGAN	ALCOHOLISM	CARTOONIST	ENTOMOLOGY	JACKBOOTED
PETRONELLA	SIMMENTHAL	ALECTORIAN	CASSIOPEIA	EPIDIORITE	JAMESONITE
PHOTONASTY	SPORANGIUM	ALMSHOUSES	CATABOLISM	EPIGLOTTIS	JOHNSONIAN
PICCANINNY	STUPENDOUS	AMBLYOPSIS	CATALOGUER	EPIPHONEMA	LANCEOLATE
PIGEONHOLE	SUBTENANCY	AMELIORATE	CATEGORISE	EPISCOPATE	LANDLOCKED
PLATINISED	SUBVENTION	AMPELOPSIS	CATEGORIZE	EQUATORIAL	LANDLOUPER
POLIANTHES	SUCCINCTLY	ANADROMOUS	CAUTIONARY	EQUIVOCATE	LANGUOROUS
POLLINATED	SUDDENNESS	ANADYOMENE	CAUTIOUSLY	ERGONOMICS	LEAFHOPPER
POLYANTHUS	SUSPENDERS	ANTAGONISE	CAVICORNIA	EUCHLORINE	LHERZOLITE
PORTENTOUS	SUSPENSION	ANTAGONISM	CECIDOMYIA	EUPHROSYNE	LOCOMOTION
PRATINCOLE	SUSTENANCE	ANTAGONIST	CENTROSOME	EXOBIOLOGY	LOCOMOTIVE
PREBENDARY	SWEDENBORG	ANTAGONIZE	CEREMONIAL	FABULOUSLY	LUMINOSITY
PREHENSILE	TABERNACLE	ANTHEOLION	CEREMONIES	FASTMOVING	MABINOGION
PREPENSELY	TABLANETTE	ANTHROPOID	CERTIORARI	FEARNOUGHT	MACEDONIAN
PRESENTDAY	TANGANYIKA	ANTIMONIAN	CHARDONNAY	FISHMONGER	MACONOCHIE
PRETENSION	TANGENTIAL	ANTINOMIAN	CHARIOTEER	FLAMBOYANT	MAKUNOUCHI
PRETINCOLE	TAPDANCING	ANTIPODEAN	CHEIRONOMY	FLANCONADE	MALACOLOGY
PREVENANCY	TEDDINGTON	ANTISOCIAL	CHERSONESE	FLAPDOODLE	MALEVOLENT

MALODOROUS	POGONOTOMY	STUDIOUSLY	CLADOPHYLL	MULTIPLIER	WIDESPREAD
MARCIONITE	POLYNOMIAL	SUAVEOLENT	CLOMIPHENE	NECROPOLIS	XIPHOPAGUS
MEGALOSAUR	PONEROLOGY	SUBTROPICS	COLEOPTERA	OMBROPHOBE	ALGONQUIAN
MELACONITE	PORTIONIST	SUDATORIUM	COLLAPSING	ORTHOPNOEA	COLLIQUATE
MELOCOTOON	POSTMORTEM	SWALLOWING	CONCEPTION	ORTHOPTICS	COLLOQUIAL
METABOLISE	POZZUOLANA	SYMPHONIUM	CONCEPTUAL	OSTEOPATHY	CONSEQUENT
METABOLISM	PRAETORIAN	SYMPTOMIZE	CONNIPTION	OSTEOPHYTE	DELINQUENT
MINEWORKER	PRAETORIUM	TAXONOMIST	CORRUPTING	OVERSPREAD	EARTHQUAKE
MISSIONARY	PREVIOUSLY	TECHNOCRAT	CORRUPTION	PALIMPSEST	INADEQUACY
MONOPODIUM	PROPIONATE	TECHNOLOGY	CROSSPIECE	PANSOPHIST	INADEQUATE
MONOPOLISE	PSAMMOPHIL	TEICHOPSIA	CTENOPHORA	PERCEPTION	INFREQUENT
MONOPOLIZE	PSEPHOLOGY	THEODOLITE	CTENOPHORE	PERCEPTIVE	RELINQUISH
MONOTONOUS	PSEUDOCARP	THEOLOGATE	CYCLOPEDIA	PERCIPIENT	SINARQUIST
MONTGOMERY	PSYCHOLOGY	THEOLOGIAN	DECAMPMENT	PEREMPTORY	SUBSEQUENT
MORATORIUM	PSYCHOPATH	THEOLOGISE	DECOMPOSED	PERSEPHONE	ABHORRENCE
MORISONIAN	PSYCHOPOMP	THEOLOGIST	DEUTOPLASM	PERSEPOLIS	ABITURIENT
MORPHOLOGY	PYRIDOXINE	THERMOSTAT	DIREMPTION	PHILIPPINA	ALCHERINGA
MOUTHORGAN	RACECOURSE	THRENODIAL	DISAPPOINT	PHILIPPINE	ALLOTROPIC
MUSICOLOGY	RAVENOUSLY	TIMBROLOGY	DISAPPROVE	PHILOPOENA	ALLPURPOSE
MUTINOUSLY	REDECORATE	TOMFOOLERY	DISCIPLINE	PHOTOPHORE	ANACARDIUM
NATATORIAL	REREDORTER	TOPOLOGIST	DISCOPHORA	PINCHPENNY	ANASTROPHE
NATATORIUM	RHAPSODISE	TORTUOUSLY	DISRUPTION	PINNIPEDIA	ANCHORETIC
NATUROPATH	RHAPSODIST	TOXICOLOGY	DISRUPTIVE	PLEROPHORY	ANGLERFISH
NEMATOCYST	RHAPSODIZE	TRAITOROUS	DISSIPATED	PRECIPITIN	ANSWERABLE
NEUTROPHIL	RIGOROUSLY	TRAMPOLINE	DROSOPHILA	PRESUPPOSE	ANTIFREEZE
NEWSMONGER	RIPSNORTER	TRIACONTER	EMBONPOINT	PROTOPLASM	ANTIPROTON
NEWSWORTHY	ROADWORTHY	TRICHOLOGY	ENCAMPMENT	PSOCOPTERA	ANTITRAGUS
NONSMOKING	RUMBLOSSOM	TROCHOTRON	ENTERPRISE	QUERSPRUNG	APHAERESIS
NONVIOLENT	RUPICOLINE	TROCTOLITE	ENTRYPHONE	RECOMPENSE	APOSTROPHE
NOSOCOMIAL	SALICORNIA	TROGLODYTE	EPANOPHORA	REDEMPTION	APPEARANCE
NOTEWORTHY	SANATORIUM	TROMBONIST	ERYSIPELAS	RESUMPTION	ARBITRATOR
NUCLEONICS	SAXICOLINE	TROPHONIUS	ESCARPMENT	RHINOPHYMA	AREOGRAPHY
NYMPHOLEPT	SAXICOLOUS	TRYPTOPHAN	EUTRAPELIA	RHIPIPTERA	ARTHURIANA
OBLOMOVISM	SCAMMOZZIS	UNBECOMING	EVERYPLACE	RUDOLPHINE	ASYNARTETE
ODONTOLITE	SCAPHOPODA	UNCTUOUSLY	FLAMEPROOF	SAPROPHYTE	AUTHORISED
ODONTOLOGY	SCORZONERA	UNINFORMED	FLASHPOINT	SAUROPSIDA	AUTHORSHIP
OMNIPOTENT	SEDULOUSLY	UNRESOLVED	GALUMPHING	SCHIPPERKE	AUTOCRATIC
OMNIVOROUS	SEISMOLOGY	UNSCHOOLED	GRAMOPHONE	SHOCKPROOF	BACITRACIN
OMOPHORION	SELTZOGENE	VARICOSITY	GYPSOPHILA	SOUNDPROOF	BACKGROUND
ORPHEOREON	SENATORIAL	VIGOROUSLY	HAIRSPRING	SOUSAPHONE	BADDERLOCK
OVERBOUGHT	SENSUOUSLY	VIROLOGIST	HANDSPRING	STANDPOINT	BALDERDASH
OVERWORKED	SEXOLOGIST	VIRTUOSITY	HANKYPANKY	STYLOPISED	BANDERILLA
PALAEOTYPE	SHAMPOOING	VIRTUOUSLY	HEMISPHERE	SUBREPTION	BANDERILLO
PALAGONITE	SHELDONIAN	WHATSOEVER	HIEROPHANT	SUPERPOWER	BARBAROSSA
PALYNOLOGY	SHIBBOLETH	WILDFOWLER	HODGEPODGE	SUSCEPTIVE	BARCAROLLE
PARADOXIDE	SHOPSOILED	WOODWORKER	HOMEOPATHY	SYNCOPATED	BEAVERSKIN
PARADOXINE	SIDEBOARDS	ZAPOROGIAN	HORSEPOWER	TERNEPLATE	BELLARMINE
PARAGONITE	SIDEROSTAT	ZEUGLODONT	HOTCHPOTCH	TERREPLEIN	BERNARDINE
PARANORMAL	SNOWMOBILE	ZUMBOORUCK	HOUSEPROUD	THREEPENCE	BETACRUCIS
PASSIONATE	SOFTBOILED	ABSORPTION	HYALOPHANE	THREEPENNY	BIRTHRIGHT
PATAGONIAN	SPECIOUSLY	ACCOMPLICE	HYDROPHANE	TOOTHPASTE	BITTERLING
PATRIOTISM	SPELEOLOGY	ACCOMPLISH	HYDROPHYTE	TOUCHPAPER	BITTERNESS
PEASHOOTER	SPURIOUSLY	AFTERPIECE	HYDROPLANE	TOUCHPIECE	BOMBARDIER
PENELOPHON	STADHOLDER	ANABAPTIST	HYDROPONIC	TRANSPLANT	BORDERLAND
PENSIONNAT	STATIONARY	ANGLOPHILE	IMPALPABLE	TRANSPOSED	BORDERLINE
PERIDOTITE	STATIONERY	ANGLOPHOBE	IMPROPERLY	TRANSPOSON	BOTHERSOME
PERILOUSLY	STAUROLITE	ASSUMPTION	INCOMPLETE	TRIUMPHANT	BUDGERIGAR
PHAELONIAN	STENTORIAN	ASSUMPTIVE	INDISPOSED	TROPOPAUSE	BUTTERBAKE
PHAENOTYPE	STEPMOTHER	ATMOSPHERE	INTERPHONE	TROPOPHYTE	BUTTERBUMP
PHLEBOTOMY	STEREOTOMY	BARYSPHERE	IONOSPHERE	UNDERPANTS	BUTTERFISH
PHLOGOPITE	STEREOTYPE	BIRTHPLACE	KIDNAPPING	UNDISPUTED	BUTTERMERE
PHRENOLOGY	STEREOTYPY	BRAINPOWER	LITHOPHANE	UNHAMPERED	BUTTERMILK
PHYSIOCRAT	STERTOROUS	BROADPIECE	MAINSPRING	UNINSPIRED	CACOGRAPHY
PHYSIOLOGY	STRABOTOMY	CATCHPENNY	MALLOPHAGA	UNPREPARED	CALCAREOUS
PICKPOCKET	STRAMONIUM	CELLOPHANE	METROPOLIS	USUCAPTION	CAMBERWELL
PINAKOTHEK	STRAPONTIN	CHECKPOINT	MICROPHONE	VIBRAPHONE	CAMPARADOR
PLASMODESM	STRATOCRAT	CHIROPTERA	MOUSEPIECE	WASTEPAPER	CAMPERDOWN
PLESIOSAUR	STRATOCYST	CIRRIPEDEA	MOUTHPIECE	WATERPROOF	CANTERBURY
POCAHONTAS	STUBBORNLY	CIRRIPEDIA	MULTIPLIED	WELLSPRING	CARBURETOR

CASCARILLA	DIFFERENCE	GRASSROOTS	MEASURABLE	PREPARATOR	SUBVERSIVE
CATARRHINE	DINNERTIME	GREGARIOUS	MEMBERSHIP	PRIMORDIAL	SUFFERANCE
CAVALRYMAN	DISARRANGE	GREYFRIARS	MENORRHOEA	PROAIRESIS	SUMMERTIME
CELEBRATED	DISBURTHEN	GRIDIRONER	MENSTRUATE	PROCURABLE	SUPPORTING
CENSORIOUS	DISCERNING	GUTTURALLY	MINDERERUS	PROCURATOR	SUPPORTIVE
CENSORSHIP	DISCORDANT	HAMMERHEAD	MISFORTUNE	PROPERTIUS	SYNAERESIS
CHAMBRANLE	DISCURSIVE	HAMMERLOCK	MONSTRANCE	PROPORTION	SYNCHRONAL
CHAPARAJOS	DISHARMONY	HEMORRHAGE	MOTHERHOOD	PROSCRIBED	SYNCHRONIC
CHAPAREJOS	DISPERSION	HESPERIDES	MOTHERLAND	PROSERPINA	SYNTERESIS
CHARTREUSE	DISPIRITED	HIERARCHIC	MOTHERLESS	PROSERPINE	SYNTHRONUS
CHITARRONE	DISSERTATE	HINTERLAND	MOTHERLIKE	PROTERVITY	TAILORMADE
CINDERELLA	DISSERVICE	HIPPARCHUS	MOZZARELLA	PROVERBIAL	TAMBERLANE
CISTERCIAN	DISTORTION	HISTORICAL	MUSSORGSKY	PUCKERWOOD	TAMPERFOOT
CLEVERNESS	DISTURBING	HITHERWARD	MYCORRHIZA	PYROGRAPHY	TANAGRIDAE
CLOSTRIDIA	DRAWBRIDGE	HOLOGRAPHY	MYOCARDIAL	QUATERNARY	TATPURUSHA
COCKERNONY	DUKKERIPEN	HONOURABLE	MYSTERIOUS	RAPPORTEUR	TATTERSALL
COLBERTINE	DUNDERFUNK	HONOURABLY	NASTURTIUM	READERSHIP	TEETHRIDGE
COLEORHIZA	DUNDERHEAD	HONOURLESS	NATTERJACK	REAPPRAISE	TELEBRIDGE
COLLARBONE	DUNDERPATE	HORSERIDER	NEOTERICAL	RECIPROCAL	TELEGRAPHY
COLOURLESS	EASTERLING	HUMOURLESS	NETHERMOST	RECURRENCE	TEMPERANCE
COLPORTAGE	ECCOPROTIC	HYSTERESIS	NETWORKING	REDCURRANT	TENDERFOOT
COLPORTEUR	ECHOPRAXIA	HYSTERICAL	NIDDERLING	REITERATED	TENDERLOIN
COMFORTING	ELECTRICAL	IMPAIRMENT	NIGGERHEAD	REPAIRABLE	TENDERNESS
COMMERCIAL	ELECTROMER	INEXORABLE	NORBERTINE	REPATRIATE	TENEBRIFIC
COMPARABLE	ELECTRONIC	INGLORIOUS	NUDIBRANCH	RESEARCHER	TENTERHOOK
COMPARATOR	EMMETROPIA	INOPERABLE	NUMBERLESS	RESPIRATOR	THEATRICAL
COMPARISON	ENDEARMENT	INQUIRENDO	NURSERYMAN	RHEOTROPIC	THEOCRITUS
CONCERNING	ENHYDRITIC	INTEGRATED	OCCURRENCE	RHETORICAL	TICKERTAPE
CONCERTINA	EPISTROPHE	JABBERWOCK	OOPHORITIS	RICHARDSON	TIMBERYARD
CONCERVATE	ESCADRILLE	JAGUARONDI	ORATORICAL	RINDERPEST	TINKERBELL
CONCORDANT	ESCHAROTIC	JAGUARUNDI	OSMIDROSIS	RUBBERNECK	TINTORETTO
CONCURRENT	ESPADRILLE	JEOPARDISE	OUTPERFORM	RUDDERLESS	TOPOGRAPHY
CONFERENCE	ETEOCRETAN	JEOPARDIZE	OVERPRAISE	RUTHERFORD	TORBERNITE
CONFERVOID	EVAPORATED	JIGGERMAST	OXYMORONIC	SALTARELLO	TRAVERTINE
CONFORMIST	EVITERNITY	JOLTERHEAD	PALMERSTON	SALUBRIOUS	TRIPARTITE
CONFORMITY	EXACERBATE	JUGGERNAUT	PALMERWORM	SANDERLING	TURNAROUND
CONSORTIUM	EXONERATED	KEMPERYMAN	PARAPRAXIS	SANDGROPER	TYPEWRITER
CONSTRAINT	EXPATRIATE	KILMARNOCK	PARATROOPS	SANFORISED	TYPOGRAPHY
CONSTRINGE	EXUBERANCE	KIMBERLITE	PASIGRAPHY	SAPPERMENT	ULSTERETTE
CONTORTION	FAIRGROUND	KRUGERRAND	PASTORELLA	SCATURIENT	UNBEARABLE
CONVERGENT	FATHERLAND	KSHATRIYAS	PAWNBROKER	SCHWARZLOT	UNBEARABLY
CONVERSANT	FATHERLESS	LAEOTROPIC	PENETRABLE	SCOMBRESOX	UNHEARABLE
CONVERSELY	FAVOURABLE	LANGERHANS	PENETRALIA	SETTERWORT	UNIFORMITY
CONVERSION	FAVOURABLY	LATTERMATH	PEPPERCORN	SGANARELLE	UNIVERSITY
COPPERHEAD	FETTERLOCK	LAUDERDALE	PEPPERMILL	SHANDRYDAN	UNSWERVING
COPPERNOSE	FINGERLING	LAUNDROMAT	PEPPERMINT	SHERARDISE	UPROARIOUS
COPPERSKIN	FINGERNAIL	LEADERSHIP	PEPPERWORT	SHIPWRIGHT	VANDERBILT
COPYWRITER	FINGERPICK	LEGWARMERS	PERDURABLE	SHORTRANGE	VICTORIANA
COUNTRYMAN	FLOWERBEDS	LEOPARDESS	PERFORATED	SIGNORELLI	VICTORIOUS
CROSSREFER	FOOTBRIDGE	LETTERHEAD	PERFORATOR	SILVERBACK	VULNERABLE
CROSSROADS	FOOTPRINTS	LIEBERMANN	PERFORMING	SILVERBELL	WANDERINGS
CULVERTAGE	FOREGROUND	LIMBERNECK	PERSTRINGE	SILVERBILL	WANDERLUST
CUMBERLAND	FOREORDAIN	LIMBURGITE	PERVERSELY	SILVERFISH	WANTHRIVEN
CUMBERSOME	FORTHRIGHT	LIMITROPHE	PERVERSION	SILVERSIDE	WASSERMANS
CUMMERBUND	FRATERETTO	LOCKERROOM	PERVERSITY	SILVERSKIN	WEAVERBIRD
CURMURRING	FRATERNISE	LOGGERHEAD	PETRARCHAN	SILVERWARE	WEIMARANER
DEALERSHIP	FRATERNITY	LOGORRHOEA	PILEDRIVER	SISTERHOOD	WESTERNIZE
DECAGRAMME	FRATERNIZE	LUGUBRIOUS	PILGARLICK	SKYSCRAPER	WICKERWORK
DEEPFREEZE	FRUSTRATED	LUMBERJACK	PLAYGROUND	SNAPDRAGON	WILDERNESS
DEMOCRATIC	GASTEROPOD	MALAPROPOS	PLAYWRIGHT	SONGWRITER	WINDERMERE
DEMOCRITUS	GENEVRETTE	MANSERVANT	PLUPERFECT	SOUTERRAIN	WINTERTIME
DEMOGRAPHY	GIBBERELLA	MASCARPONE	PREARRANGE	SPIDERWORT	WITHDRAWAL
DEPLORABLE	GILBERTIAN	MASKIROVKA	PRECARIOUS	STEWARDESS	WONDERLAND
DEPLORABLY	GILBERTINE	MASTERMIND	PRECURSORY	SUBMARINER	WONDERMENT
DESBOROUGH	GINGERBEER	MASTERWORT	PREFERABLE	SUBMERSION	WRAPAROUND
DESECRATED	GINGERSNAP	MASTURBATE	PREFERABLY	SUBSCRIBER	WUNDERKIND
DETERRENCE	GIRLFRIEND	MATTERHORN	PREFERENCE	SUBSTRATUM	YARBOROUGH
DIACHRONIC	GODPARENTS	MAVOURNEEN	PREFERMENT	SUBTERFUGE	YESTERWEEK
DIDGERIDOO	GONORRHOEA	MEAGERNESS	PREMARITAL	SUBVERSION	YESTERYEAR

ABSCISSION	CONDESCEND	GREENSWARD	PANTOSCOPE	SOBERSIDES	ADMITTANCE
ACCESSIBLE	CONFESSION	GRINDSTONE	PARNASSIAN	SOMERSAULT	ADMITTEDLY
ACCESSIONS	CONFISCATE	GYMNASTICS	PATISSERIE	SOOTHSAYER	ADVENTURER
ADMISSIBLE	CONFUSEDLY	GYMNOSOPHY	PENINSULAR	SPINESCENT	ADVERTISER
ADOLESCENT	CONGESTION	GYMNOSPERM	PENNISETUM	SPOILSPORT	AFFETTUOSO
ADVERSARIA	CONSISTENT	HAGIOSCOPE	PERCUSSION	SPOKESHAVE	AFTERTASTE
AFTERSHAVE	CONSISTORY	HARASSMENT	PERMISSION	SPORTSWEAR	ALLOSTERIC
AFTERSHOCK	CONTESTANT	HARVESTMAN	PERMISSIVE	STANDSTILL	AMPHITRITE
AGGRESSION	CORRESPOND	HELLESPONT	PEROVSKITE	STANISLAUS	AMPHITRYON
AGGRESSIVE	CRANKSHAFT	HIEROSCOPY	PERSISTENT	STATISTICS	AMPHOTERIC
AGONISTICS	CRUIKSHANK	HINDUSTANI	PETRISSAGE	STAVESACRE	ANALYTICAL
ALPENSTOCK	CUIRASSIER	ICONOSCOPE	PHILISTINE	STILLSTAND	ANTISTATIC
AMBASSADOR	CYCLOSTYLE	IMPASSABLE	PHILOSOPHY	STYLISTICS	APOPHTHEGM
AMBLYSTOMA	CYSTOSCOPY	IMPERSONAL	PIANISSIMO	SUBMISSION	ARCHETYPAL
AMPUSSYAND	DECRESCENT	IMPOSSIBLE	PINCUSHION	SUBMISSIVE	ARCHITRAVE
ANGIOSPERM	DEFEASANCE	IMPOSSIBLY	PIPSISSEWA	SUBSISTENT	ARSMETRICK
ARACOSTYLE	DEFENSIBLE	IMPRESARIO	PITCHSTONE	SUCCESSFUL	ASBESTOSIS
ARIMASPIAN	DEMOISELLE	IMPRESSION	PLEBISCITE	SUCCESSION	ASSISTANCE
ASPERSIONS	DEPRESSANT	IMPRESSIVE	PLUMASSIER	SUCCESSIVE	ASSORTMENT
ASSESSMENT	DEPRESSING	INCONSTANT	POETASTERY	SUGGESTION	AUTOSTRADA
BAGASSOSIS	DEPRESSION	INCRASSATE	POSSESSION	SUGGESTIVE	BACKSTAIRS
BALLISTICS	DEPRESSIVE	INCRESCENT	POSSESSIVE	SUPERSONIC	BACKSTROKE
BALLISTITE	DHARMSHALA	INNERSPACE	PREDESTINE	SUPERSTORE	BALBUTIENT
BATHYSCAPH	DIGRESSION	INQUISITOR	PREDISPOSE	SUPPOSEDLY	BALUSTRADE
BLACKSHIRT	DISCUSSING	INSENSIBLE	PREHISTORY	SURPASSING	BARBITURIC
BLACKSMITH	DISCUSSION	INSPISSATE	PREPOSITOR	SWEATSHIRT	BARMITZVAH
BLACKSTONE	DISGUSTING	INTERSTATE	PREPOSSESS	SWEEPSTAKE	BASKETBALL
BLOODSTAIN	DISMISSIVE	INTERSTICE	PROCESSING	SWORDSTICK	BASKETWORK
BLOODSTOCK	DISPOSABLE	INTROSPECT	PROCESSION	TABLESPOON	BIJOUTERIE
BLOODSTONE	DISPOSSESS	IRIDESCENT	PROFESSION	TEINOSCOPE	BIPARTISAN
BLOOMSBURY	DISRESPECT	KRIEGSPIEL	PROGESSION	TELEOSTOME	BLACKTHORN
BOBBYSOXER	DRAKESTONE	LARGESCALE	PROMISSORY	TELIOSPORE	BONNETHEAD
BRADYSEISM	EARTHSHINE	LAURUSTINE	PROPOSITUS	THALASSIAN	BREASTBONE
BRAINSTORM	EATANSWILL	LEBENSRAUM	PROTESTANT	THALESTRIS	BREASTFEED
BRATISLAVA	EMPLASTRUM	LEMNISCATE	PROVISIONS	THREESCORE	BREASTWORK
BRIDESMAID	ENGLISHMAN	LIQUESCENT	PUBLISHING	THUMBSCREW	BRIGHTNESS
BRITISHISM	ENGLISHMEN	LITHISTADA	PURPOSEFUL	TORPESCENT	BROCATELLE
BROADSHEET	ENGROSSING	MALMESBURY	PUTRESCENT	TOUCHSTONE	CALCITONIN
BROADSWORD	ENTHUSIASM	MANGOSTEEN	QUEENSBURY	ULTRASONIC	CALYPTRATE
BROOMSTICK	ENTHUSIAST	MARCESCENT	QUEENSTOWN	ULTRASOUND	CANTATRICE
BROWNSTONE	ERUBESCENT	MARGASIRSA	QUICKSANDS	UNBLUSHING	CARACTACUS
BUNDESWEHR	ETHEOSTOMA	MASSASAUGA	RAVENSBILL	UNDERSCORE	CARPATHIAN
CAMPESTRAL	EVANESCENT	MATCHSTALK	RAVENSDUCK	UNDERSHIRT	CARYATIDES
CANVASBACK	EXHAUSTING	MATCHSTICK	RAVENSTONE	UNDERSIZED	CATASTASIS
CANVASSING	EXHAUSTION	MAUPASSANT	RAWINSONDE	UNDERSKIRT	CELESTIALS
CARNASSIAL	EXHAUSTIVE	METHUSALEH	RECONSIDER	UNDERSLUNG	CHARITABLE
CENTESIMAL	EXPRESSION	METHUSELAH	REFRESHING	UNDERSTAND	CHARITABLY
CHEAPSKATE	EXPRESSIVE	MICROSCOPE	REGRESSION	UNDERSTATE	CHOPSTICKS
CHEVESAILE	EXPRESSMAN	MONTESSORI	REGRESSIVE	UNDERSTEER	CHRISTIANA
CHEVISANCE	EXPRESSWAY	MYRIOSCOPE	REMORSEFUL	UNDERSTOOD	CLOISTERED
CHINASTONE	EXTENSIBLE	NARCISSISM	REPRESSION	UNDERSTUDY	COCKATRICE
CIRCASSIAN	FALDISTORY	NICROSILAL	REPRESSIVE	UNREASONED	COLDSTREAM
CLEARSTORY	FANTASTICO	NIGHTSHADE	RETROSPECT	UNSEASONED	COLLATERAL
CLERESTORY	FIBROSITIS	NIGHTSHIRT	REVERSIBLE	UPHOLSTERY	COMESTIBLE
CLINGSTONE	FIRTHSOKEN	NIGHTSTICK	RHINESTONE	VARNISHING	COMMITMENT
CLYDESDALE	FLAVESCENT	NIGRESCENT	ROTISSERIE	VERNISSAGE	COMMUTABLE
COEXISTENT	FORINSECAL	NONONSENSE	RUBINSTEIN	WAPENSCHAW	COMPATIBLE
COGNISANCE	FORTISSIMO	NORTHSTEAD	SACROSANCT	WAPINSCHAW	COMPATRIOT
COLOSSALLY	FREMESCENT	NOURISHING	SAMARSKITE	WATERSKIER	COMPETENCE
COLOSSIANS	FRITHSOKEN	ODIOUSNESS	SCHALSTEIN	WATERSPOUT	COMPETITOR
COLPOSCOPE	FRUTESCENT	ONOMASTICS	SCRIMSHANK	WHEATSHEAF	CONDOTTIER
COMBUSTION	FURNISHING	OPALESCENT	SELFESTEEM	WHEATSTONE	COQUETTISH
COMMISSARY	GETTYSBURG	OPPRESSION	SERRASALMO	WHOLESALER	CORINTHIAN
COMMISSION	GLYCOSURIA	OPPRESSIVE	SHEEPSHANK	ABRUPTNESS	CORNSTALKS
COMMISSURE	GRANDSTAND	ORCHESTRAL	SHELLSHOCK	ACCENTUATE	CORNSTARCH
COMPASSION	GRAVESTONE	OSTENSIBLE	SKRIMSHANK	ACCUSTOMED	CREDITABLE
COMPOSITOR	GREENSHANK	OSTENSIBLY	SMALLSCALE	ADJECTIVAL	CREDITABLY
CONCESSION	GREENSTICK	OVIPOSITOR	SMOKESTACK	ADJUSTABLE	CURVETTING
CONCUSSION	GREENSTONE	PALAESTRAL	SNAKESTONE	ADJUSTMENT	DEDUCTIBLE

DEJECTEDLY	INCESTUOUS	PARENTHOOD	SEVENTIETH	ANTIQUATED	IMMATURITY
DELECTABLE	INDENTURES	PARENTLESS	SHOESTRING	APOLAUSTIC	IMPALUDISM
DEPARTMENT	INDICTABLE	PARGETTING	SINOATRIAL	ARTICULATA	INACCURACY
DEPARTURES	INDICTMENT	PEDESTRIAN	SLIPSTREAM	ARTICULATE	INACCURATE
DEPORTMENT	INDISTINCT	PEDIATRICS	SONGSTRESS	ATRACURIUM	INAUGURATE
DERMATITIS	INDUCTANCE	PENTATEUCH	SOUNDTRACK	AVANTURINE	INESCULENT
DESPITEOUS	INDUSTRIAL	PENTATHLON	SPIRITEDLY	AVENTURINE	INFATUATED
DETECTABLE	INEVITABLE	PENTATONIC	SPIRITLESS	BALIBUNTAL	INFIBULATE
DETESTABLE	INEVITABLY	PENTETERIC	SPIRITUOUS	BANKRUPTCY	INOSCULATE
DEVASTATED	INFECTIOUS	PENTSTEMON	STEALTHILY	BEEFBURGER	INSECURELY
DEVASTAVIT	INFEFTMENT	PERDITIOUS	STENOTYPER	BELARUSIAN	INSECURITY
DIGESTIBLE	INFILTRATE	PERPETRATE	STOMATOPOD	BIANNUALLY	INSTRUCTED
DILETTANTE	INFLATABLE	PERPETUATE	STRAITENED	BINOCULARS	INSTRUCTOR
DIRECTIONS	INGRATIATE	PERPETUITY	STREETLAMP	BLANQUETTE	INSTRUMENT
DIRECTNESS	INIMITABLE	PHILATELIC	STREETWISE	BRESSUMMER	INTEGUMENT
DIRECTOIRE	INSISTENCE	PHYTOTOXIN	STRICTNESS	BUCKJUMPER	INTRAURBAN
DISASTROUS	INTENTNESS	POCKETBOOK	STRIPTEASE	BUREAUCRAT	INVALUABLE
DISPUTABLE	INTERTRIGO	POTENTIATE	STRUCTURAL	CANECUTTER	INVOLUTION
DOWNSTAIRS	INTERTWINE	POTENTILLA	SUNBATHING	CAPITULARY	ISOLEUCINE
DOWNSTREAM	INTESTINAL	PRAXITELES	SUPERTONIC	CAPITULATE	KHIDMUTGAR
DRAWSTRING	INTESTINES	PREPOTENCE	SYMPATHISE	CARTHUSIAN	LACKLUSTER
EBRACTEATE	INVESTMENT	PRIESTHOOD	SYMPATHIZE	CHINQUAPIN	LACKLUSTRE
EFFECTUATE	ISOMETRICS	PRIVATEERS	SYNOSTOSIS	CLAMOURING	LANDLUBBER
EFFORTLESS	JACKSTONES	PROFITABLE	TARANTELLA	COADJUTANT	LANSQUENET
ELLIPTICAL	JACKSTRAWS	PROFITABLY	TEETOTALER	COMPLUVIUM	LUMPSUCKER
EMBITTERED	KARMATHIAN	PROFITLESS	THIXOTROPY	COMPOUNDED	MALAGUETTA
EMMENTALER	KNIGHTHEAD	PROMETHEAN	THREATENED	CONCLUDING	MALTHUSIAN
ENLISTMENT	KNIGHTHOOD	PROMETHEUS	TOCCATELLA	CONCLUSION	MANICURIST
ENRAPTURED	LACUSTRINE	PROMETHIUM	TOILETRIES	CONCLUSIVE	MANIPULATE
EPIMETHEUS	LAMENTABLE	PROMPTBOOK	TOPSYTURVY	CONFLUENCE	METICULOUS
EQUESTRIAN	LAMENTABLY	PROMPTNESS	TRADITIONS	CONFOUNDED	MIRACULOUS
ESCRITOIRE	LANDSTHING	PROPITIATE	TRILATERAL	DEMODULATE	MISHGUGGLE
EURYPTERUS	LIBRETTIST	PROPITIOUS	TUMULTUOUS	DEPOPULATE	MOISTURIZE
EVERYTHING	LICENTIATE	PULSATANCE	TURRITELLA	DEREGULATE	MOSSBUNKER
EXEMPTNESS	LICENTIOUS	QUAESTUARY	UNBEATABLE	DEVOLUTION	NONPLUSSED
EXPECTANCY	LOGISTICAL	QUAINTNESS	UNCRITICAL	DIACAUSTIC	NOVACULITE
EYEWITNESS	LUTESTRING	QUICKTHORN	UNCULTURED	DIMINUENDO	OBSEQUIOUS
FACTITIOUS	MAGISTRACY	RAIYATWARI	UNDERTAKER	DIMINUTION	OUTPOURING
FALSETRUTH	MAGISTRAND	RECEPTACLE	UNDOCTORED	DIMINUTIVE	OVERSUPPLY
FARFETCHED	MAGISTRATE	REDRUTHITE	UNFAITHFUL	DISCOURAGE	PARAGUAYAN
FENESTELLA	MAINSTREAM	REGISTERED	UNFETTERED	DISGRUNTLE	PASTEURISE
FERNITICLE	MARKETABLE	RELENTLESS	UNGRATEFUL	EFFLEURAGE	PASTEURIZE
FICTITIOUS	MAURITANIA	RELUCTANCE	UNILATERAL	EMASCULATE	PATIBULARY
FINISTERRE	MESENTERON	REMITTANCE	UNLETTERED	EVENTUALLY	PEDICULATE
FLAGITIOUS	METASTABLE	REPEATABLE	UNSETTLING	FILIBUSTER	PHILLUMENY
FLIGHTLESS	MIDLOTHIAN	REPEATEDLY	UNSUITABLE	FLAVOURING	PICAYUNISH
FLYCATCHER	MINESTRONE	REPENTANCE	UNTRUTHFUL	FLOCCULATE	POHUTUKAWA
FOODSTUFFS	MINISTRATE	REPERTOIRE	VALENTINES	FLOCCULENT	PORTCULLIS
FRENETICAL	MINISTROKE	REPORTEDLY	VIBRATIONS	FLUCTUATER	POSTHUMOUS
FRIGHTENED	MISMATCHED	RESENTMENT	VOLUPTUARY	FORERUNNER	PRAEMUNIRE
GAINSTRIVE	MONOPTERON	RESISTANCE	VOLUPTUOUS	FORFEUCHEN	PRECAUTION
GERIATRICS	MONOPTEROS	RIJSTTAFEL	WATCHTOWER	FORFOUGHEN	PRESSURIZE
GOLIATHISE	MUSKETEERS	ROBERTSMAN	WATERTIGHT	FRAUDULENT	PROCRUSTES
GROCETERIA	NUTRITIOUS	ROBUSTIOUS	WEIGHTLESS	GARGOUILLE	PROFOUNDLY
HEADSTRONG	OBJECTLESS	ROBUSTNESS	WHITETHORN	GENICULATE	PRONOUNCED
HELIOTROPE	OBSTETRICS	ROCKSTEADY	WHITSTABLE	GLAMOURISE	PROTRUSILE
HEPTATEUCH	ODELSTHING	RUPESTRIAN	WITGATBOOM	GOATSUCKER	PROTRUSION
HEPTATHLON	OFFPUTTING	SABBATICAL	XEROSTOMIA	HABITUALLY	PUBERULENT
HOLOSTERIC	OFTENTIMES	SABRETACHE	ABSOLUTELY	HACKBUTEER	PUNCTUALLY
HOSPITABLE	OUTPATIENT	SAGITTARIA	ABSOLUTION	HALIEUTICS	PUNCTULATE
HOSPITABLY	OVERSTRAIN	SALBUTAMOL	ABSOLUTISM	HAMESUCKEN	RAGAMUFFIN
HYPAETHRAL	OVERSTRUNG	SCIENTIFIC	ACCUMULATE	HEADHUNTED	REASSURING
HYPAETHRON	PALESTRINA	SCRIPTURAL	ACOLOUTHOS	HEADHUNTER	RESOLUTELY
HYPNOTIZED	PALMATIFID	SCRIPTURES	ALLOCUTION	HOMEOUSIAN	RESOLUTION
ILLUSTRATE	PALMATOZOA	SCULPTRESS	AMATEURISH	HOMOOUSIAN	RESTAURANT
IMMORTELLE	PALUSTRINE	SEAMSTRESS	ANACOUSTIC	HYDRAULICS	RETICULATE
IMPORTANCE	PANOPTICON	SECRETAIRE	ANACRUSTIC	ILLAQUEATE	REVOLUTION
IMPOSTHUME	PARARTHRIA	SEECATCHIE	ANDALUSIAN	IMMACULACY	RIDICULOUS
INCAUTIOUS	PARASTATAL	SELFSTYLED	ANDALUSITE	IMMACULATE	ROADRUNNER

SARSQUATCH	BLACKWATER	YELLOWJACK	**10:7**	BLANCMANGE	CORRUGATED
SCRUPULOUS	BONDSWOMAN	YELLOWLEGS	ABERGLAUBE	BONESHAKER	CORRUGATOR
SEERSUCKER	BORROWINGS	YELLOWROOT	ABHIDHAMMA	BREAKWATER	CORYPHAEUS
SEMIQUAVER	BREAKWATER	YELLOWWOOD	ABNORMALLY	BRICKLAYER	CREDITABLE
SHOWJUMPER	BRICKWORKS	ASPHYXIATE	ABOMINABLE	BRILLIANCE	CREDITABLY
SILHOUETTE	CHAIRWOMAN	BISSEXTILE	ABOMINABLY	BROWNLANDS	CREOPHAGUS
STRIDULATE	CHUCKWALLA	COMMIXTURE	ABSORBANCE	BUCCINATOR	CRIMINALLY
SUBROUTINE	CLANSWOMAN	CONTEXTUAL	ACCORDANCE	BUCEPHALUS	CRITICALLY
SULPHUROUS	CLEARWATER	INFLEXIBLE	ACHROMATIC	BULLHEADED	CROSSHATCH
SURROUNDED	DRINKWATER	INFLEXIBLY	ACROAMATIC	CACOGRAPHY	CROTALARIA
TAMBOURINE	DUTCHWOMAN	PHILOXENIA	ACTIONABLE	CALCULABLE	CUCULLATED
TARPAULING	EARTHWORKS	ACRONYCHAL	ADJUSTABLE	CALCULATED	CUISENAIRE
THELLUSSON	EVERYWHERE	APOCRYPHAL	ADMITTANCE	CALCULATOR	CULTIVATED
THINGUMBOB	FELLOWSHIP	APTERYGOTA	ADVERSARIA	CAMPARADOR	CULTIVATOR
THOROUGHLY	FRESHWATER	ASCOMYCETE	AEROPHAGIA	CANDELABRA	DAYDREAMER
TRANQUILLY	FRONTWARDS	BARLEYBREE	AFFILIATED	CAPERNAITE	DECAGRAMME
UNARGUABLE	GLASSWORKS	BARLEYCORN	AFFORDABLE	CAPILLAIRE	DECOLLATOR
UNASSUMING	GRASSWIDOW	BIOPHYSICS	AFTERTASTE	CAPNOMANCY	DEEPSEATED
UNGROUNDED	HORSEWOMAN	BIORHYTHMS	AFTERWARDS	CAPTIVATED	DEFEASANCE
UNOCCUPIED	INTERWEAVE	BLEARYEYED	ALCIBIADES	CARACTACUS	DEGRADABLE
UNREQUITED	INTERWOVEN	CHERRYWOOD	ALCYONARIA	CARTOMANCY	DELECTABLE
VENEZUELAN	IRISHWOMAN	CHESSYLITE	ALDERMANLY	CATASTASIS	DEMOCRATIC
VESICULATE	IRISHWOMEN	CONVEYABLE	ALLEGEANCE	CELEBRATED	DEMOGRAPHY
VOCABULARY	KENILWORTH	CONVEYANCE	ALLEGIANCE	CHAMBRANLE	DEMONIACAL
VOCABULIST	LIVERWURST	DEFRAYMENT	ALTERNATOR	CHANGEABLE	DEPENDABLE
WINDSURFER	MEADOWPLAN	DEPLOYMENT	AMBARVALIA	CHAPARAJOS	DEPLORABLE
ZIDOVUDINE	MELLOWNESS	DISLOYALTY	AMBASSADOR	CHARGEABLE	DEPLORABLY
ABBREVIATE	NARROWBOAT	EMPLOYMENT	AMPHIMACER	CHARITABLE	DESECRATED
ACCLIVIOUS	NARROWDALE	EUCALYPTOL	ANALPHABET	CHARITABLY	DESICCATED
AMBARVALIA	NARROWNESS	EUCALYPTUS	ANDROMACHE	CHATELAINE	DESPICABLE
ANGURVADEL	NOBLEWOMAN	GEOPHYSICS	ANGURVADEL	CHECKLATON	DETACHABLE
BELIEVABLE	NORTHWARDS	HALLOYSITE	ANSWERABLE	CHEMICALLY	DETECTABLE
CAPTIVATED	PILLIWINKS	ICHTHYOSIS	ANTIQUATED	CHEMONASTY	DETESTABLE
CONNIVANCE	PILLOWCASE	KERSEYMERE	ANTISTATIC	CHEVESAILE	DEVASTATED
CULTIVATED	PILLOWSLIP	LACHRYMOSE	ANTITRAGUS	CHEVISANCE	DEVASTAVIT
CULTIVATOR	RIGHTWARDS	MAKESYSTEM	APOSEMATIC	CHINQUAPIN	DIAGONALLY
DESERVEDLY	SALESWOMAN	MESITYLENE	APPEARANCE	CHIRICAUNE	DIDASCALIC
DISCOVERER	SCOTSWOMAN	MISOGYNIST	APPLICABLE	CHIROMANCY	DILETTANTE
EFFERVESCE	SHADOWLESS	NONPAYMENT	APPLICATOR	CHUCKWALLA	DIPLOMATIC
EPROUVETTE	SHARAWADGI	NOTORYCTES	ARBITRATOR	CLEARWATER	DIPSOMANIA
FORGIVABLE	SHARAWAGGI	PARONYCHIA	ARCHDEACON	CLEROMANCY	DISARRANGE
GALRAVITCH	SHEARWATER	POLYHYMNIA	AREOGRAPHY	CLINICALLY	DISENGAGED
GINGIVITIS	SOUTHWARDS	PREPAYMENT	ASARABACCA	CLOCKMAKER	DISLOYALTY
ILLADVISED	STEELWORKS	PRESBYOPIA	ASCENDANCY	COCHLEARIA	DISPOSABLE
IMPERVIOUS	SUPERWOMAN	PRESBYTERY	ASCRIBABLE	COCKCHAFER	DISPUTABLE
IMPROVISED	TEENYWEENY	PYRAGYRITE	ASSIGNABLE	COELACANTH	DISSIPATED
INSOLVENCY	TIMESWITCH	SANNAYASIN	ASSISTANCE	COGNISANCE	DISSONANCE
LASCIVIOUS	TOWNSWOMAN	SHAGGYMANE	ASSOCIATED	COGNIZANCE	DOWNSTAIRS
LIBREVILLE	UNANSWERED	SHANDYGAFF	ASTIGMATIC	COLLIMATOR	DRESSMAKER
MANDEVILLE	UNDERWATER	SHELLYCOAT	ASTRAGALUS	COLONNADED	DRINKWATER
MISGIVINGS	UNDERWORLD	SPERRYLITE	ASTRALAGUS	COLOSSALLY	DUCKBOARDS
MONTEVERDI	UNDERWRITE	STAPHYLINE	ATTAINABLE	COMMONALTY	DUPLICATOR
MONTEVIDEO	WANDSWORTH	STICKYBEAK	ATTENDANCE	COMMUNALLY	ECHOPRAXIA
OBSERVABLE	WATERWHEEL	STINGYBARK	AUTOCRATIC	COMMUTABLE	ELEGABALUS
OBSERVANCE	WATERWINGS	SYNONYMOUS	AUTOPLASTY	COMPARABLE	ELIMINATOR
PARVOVIRUS	WATERWORKS	TALLEYRAND	AVANTGARDE	COMPARATOR	EMBLEMATIC
RESERVISTS	WELSHWOMAN	UNLADYLIKE	AVICULARIA	COMPLIANCE	EMMENTALER
SHRIEVALTY	WHITEWATER	VOLLEYBALL	AXINOMANCY	CONFIDANTE	ENCEPHALON
SOMERVILLE	WHOLEWHEAT	WHILLYWHAW	BABESIASIS	CONNIVANCE	ENKEPHALIN
SUPERVISED	WILLOWHERB	WHIRLYBIRD	BACITRACIN	CONSONANCE	ESPECIALLY
SUPERVISOR	WILLYWILLY	WINCEYETTE	BACKSTAIRS	CONSONANTS	ESTRAMACON
TRANSVERSE	WINDOWPANE	WOOLLYBACK	BAREHEADED	CONSTRAINT	EUTHANASIA
UNDERVALUE	WINDOWSILL	WOOLLYBUTT	BAUDELAIRE	CONVENANCE	EVAPORATED
UNFLAVORED	WISHYWASHY	COGNIZANCE	BELIEVABLE	CONVEYABLE	EVENTUALLY
UNLEAVENED	WORDSWORTH	LIPIZZANER	BIANNUALLY	CONVEYANCE	EVERGLADES
UNPROVOKED	WORTHWHILE	RENDEZVOUS	BIENNIALLY	COPENHAGEN	EXONERATED
VAUDEVILLE	WRISTWATCH	SQUEEZEBOX	BIPINNARIA	CORNFLAKES	EXOTICALLY
AFTERWARDS	YELLOWBACK	UTILIZABLE	BLACKWATER	CORNSTALKS	EXPECTANCY
ALDERWOMAN	YELLOWGIRL			CORNSTARCH	EXPENDABLE

EXPLICABLE	INFATUATED	NECROMANCY	PREFERABLE	SHAKUHACHI	UNENVIABLE
EXTENDABLE	INFERNALLY	NECTABANUS	PREFERABLY	SHAMEFACED	UNHEARABLE
EXTERNALLY	INFLATABLE	NEGOTIABLE	PREPARATOR	SHARAWADGI	UNPREPARED
EXUBERANCE	INFORMALLY	NEGOTIATOR	PRESUMABLY	SHARAWAGGI	UNREADABLE
FAMILIARLY	INFURIATED	NEWSREADER	PREVENANCY	SHEARWATER	UNRELIABLE
FASCINATED	INIMITABLE	NORTHWARDS	PROCREATOR	SHECKLATON	UNREVEALED
FASCINATOR	INOPERABLE	NOTICEABLE	PROCURABLE	SHORTRANGE	UNSOCIABLE
FAVOURABLE	INSATIABLE	NOTICEABLY	PROCURATOR	SHRIEVALTY	UNSUITABLE
FAVOURABLY	INSATIABLY	NOTIFIABLE	PRODIGALLY	SIDEBOARDS	UNWORKABLE
FLUCTUATER	INSTIGATOR	NOTIONALLY	PROFITABLE	SIGILLARIA	USQUEBAUGH
FONTINALIS	INTEGRATED	NUDIBRANCH	PROFITABLY	SINGULARLY	UTILIZABLE
FORESHADOW	INTERMARRY	NUMISMATIC	PROMENADER	SKYSCRAPER	VARIEGATED
FORGIVABLE	INTERNALLY	OBFUSCATED	PROPAGANDA	SNAPDRAGON	VENTILATOR
FORMIDABLE	INVALUABLE	OBSERVABLE	PROPAGATOR	SOGDOLAGER	VERIFIABLE
FREELOADER	INVARIABLE	OBSERVANCE	PROPYLAEUM	SOMERSAULT	VERTICALLY
FRESHWATER	INVARIABLY	OBTAINABLE	PROVENANCE	SOOTHSAYER	VULCANALIA
FRONTWARDS	INVIOLABLE	OESOPHAGUS	PSYCHIATRY	SOUTHWARDS	VULNERABLE
FRUSTRATED	IRONICALLY	OFFBALANCE	PULSATANCE	SPECULATOR	WASTEPAPER
GIARDIASIS	JACKANAPES	OFFICIALLY	PUNCTUALLY	SPODOMANCY	WATCHMAKER
GOVERNANCE	JIGGAMAREE	ORDONNANCE	PUNISHABLE	SQUETEAGUE	WEIMARANER
GRANDDADDY	JUDICIALLY	ORIDINANCE	PYROGRAPHY	SQUIREARCH	WHITEWATER
GRANULATED	KLANGFARBE	ORIGINALLY	QUICKSANDS	STAVESACRE	WHITSTABLE
GRASSLANDS	LACKADAISY	ORIGINATOR	QUIRINALIA	STONEMASON	WHOLESALER
GUATEMALAN	LAMENTABLE	ORTHOCAINE	RADIOLARIA	SUBLIMATER	WISHYWASHY
GUBERNATOR	LAMENTABLY	OSCILLATOR	RATIONALLY	SUBSTRATUM	WITHDRAWAL
GUTTURALLY	LAWBREAKER	OSTEOPATHY	REAPPRAISE	SUBTENANCY	WRISTWATCH
HABITUALLY	LEGISLATOR	OTHERGATES	REASONABLE	SUFFERANCE	XIPHOPAGUS
HALFYEARLY	LEONTIASIS	OUTBALANCE	REASONABLY	SUPERCARGO	ZOANTHARIA
HALLUBALOO	LIGNOCAINE	OVERCHARGE	RECEPTACLE	SURGICALLY	AUTOMOBILE
HANKYPANKY	LIPIZZANER	OVERPRAISE	REDUNDANCY	SUSTENANCE	BARLEYBREE
HECTICALLY	LIQUIDATOR	OVERSHADOW	REITERATED	SYNCOPATED	BASKETBALL
HELIOLATER	LITHOMARGE	OVERSLAUGH	REJONEADOR	SYSTEMATIC	BATTENBERG
HENDECAGON	LONGCHAMPS	OXYGENATOR	RELUCTANCE	TABERNACLE	BATTENBURG
HERESIARCH	LORDOLATRY	PALLBEARER	REMARKABLE	TACTICALLY	BLOOMSBURY
HEROICALLY	LOTOPHAGUS	PARAGUAYAN	REMARKABLY	TALEBEARER	BOOKMOBILE
HIEROMANCY	LUPERCALIA	PARAPHASIA	REMITTANCE	TEETOTALER	BREAKABLES
HIPPOMANES	LUXURIANCE	PARAPRAXIS	REPAIRABLE	TELEGRAPHY	BREASTBONE
HOLOGRAPHY	MACEBEARER	PARASTATAL	REPEATABLE	TEMPERANCE	BUTTERBAKE
HOMEOPATHY	MACROCARPA	PARDONABLE	REPENTANCE	TERMINABLE	BUTTERBUMP
HONOURABLE	MALIGNANCY	PARDONABLY	REPUGNANCE	TERMINALIA	CANNONBALL
HONOURABLY	MANAGEABLE	PARKLEAVES	RESISTANCE	TERMINALLY	CANTERBURY
HOOTANANNY	MANICHAEAN	PARRAMATTA	RESPIRATOR	TIEBREAKER	CANVASBACK
HOOTENANNY	MARGINALIA	PASIGRAPHY	RETURNABLE	TOOTHPASTE	CASSIABARK
HOSPITABLE	MARGINALLY	PATERNALLY	RHINOLALIA	TOPOGRAPHY	CHEQUEBOOK
HOSPITABLY	MARIOLATRY	PEACEMAKER	RHOEADALES	TOSSICATED	COLLARBONE
HOUSEMAIDS	MARKETABLE	PECULIARLY	RIBOFLAVIN	TOSTICATED	COLLEMBOLA
HULLABALOO	MASSASAUGA	PENETRABLE	RIGHTWARDS	TOUCHPAPER	CONTRABAND
ICEBREAKER	MATCHMAKER	PENETRALIA	RIJSTTAFEL	TRAGACANTH	CONTRIBUTE
IMAGINABLE	MATELLASSE	PERCOLATOR	RINGLEADER	TRAGICALLY	COQUIMBITE
IMBRICATED	MATERIALLY	PERDURABLE	ROQUELAURE	TRANSLATED	CUMMERBUND
IMPALPABLE	MATERNALLY	PERFORATED	ROSECHAFER	TRANSLATOR	CUTTLEBONE
IMPARLANCE	MAURITANIA	PERFORATOR	SABRETACHE	TRAVELATOR	DESCRIBING
IMPASSABLE	MAYONNAISE	PERISHABLE	SACROSANCT	TRAVOLATOR	DISSELBOOM
IMPECCABLE	MEASURABLE	PERSICARIA	SAGITTARIA	TROPOPAUSE	DISSEMBLER
IMPECCABLY	MERRYMAKER	PERSONABLE	SALBUTAMOL	TYPOGRAPHY	DISTRIBUTE
IMPLACABLE	METAPLASIS	PERSONALLY	SALMANAZAR	ULTRABASIC	DISTURBING
IMPLACABLY	METASTABLE	PHAGEDAENA	SANDEMANIA	ULTRAMAFIC	DOUBLEBASS
IMPORTANCE	METHOMANIA	PHLEGMASIA	SANNAYASIN	UNARGUABLE	EXACERBATE
IMPRESARIO	METHUSALEH	PHLEGMATIC	SARSQUATCH	UNBEARABLE	FLOWERBEDS
IMPRIMATUR	METHYLATED	PHOTONASTY	SATURNALIA	UNBEARABLY	FORTINBRAS
IMPROBABLE	MILITIAMAN	PHYSICALLY	SCHISMATIC	UNBEATABLE	GETTYSBURG
IMPROBABLY	MILLIFARAD	PITYRIASIS	SCHLIMAZEL	UNDECLARED	GINGERBEER
INDICTABLE	MODIFIABLE	PLATELAYER	SCLERIASIS	UNDEFEATED	GROUNDBAIT
INDUCTANCE	MONEYMAKER	POETICALLY	SEASONABLE	UNDENIABLE	HANDLEBARS
INEBRIATED	MONILIASIS	POKERFACED	SEASONABLY	UNDERPANTS	HARMANBECK
INEDUCABLE	MONSTRANCE	POLLINATED	SECRETAIRE	UNDERTAKER	HEIDELBERG
INEVITABLE	MORGANATIC	POLYCHAETE	SEGREGATED	UNDERVALUE	HINDENBURG
INEVITABLY	MYELINATED	POSTCHAISE	SEMIQUAVER	UNDERWATER	HORSELBERG
INEXORABLE	NATIONALLY	PREARRANGE	SERRASALMO	UNEDUCATED	INCUNABULA

KNOCKABOUT	BEAUTICIAN	HAMESUCKEN	PROTRACTOR	ARMAGEDDON	JEOPARDIZE
LANDLUBBER	BENEDICITE	HAMSHACKLE	PROVINCIAL	ASTOUNDING	KETTLEDRUM
MALMESBURY	BENEFACTOR	HANDPICKED	PSEUDOCARP	AUTODIDACT	LAUDERDALE
MARYLEBONE	BENEFICENT	HEPATOCELE	PUNICACEAE	AVVOGADORE	LAWABIDING
MASTURBATE	BENEFICIAL	HIERARCHIC	PUTRESCENT	BALDERDASH	LEOPARDESS
MIDDLEBROW	BLASTOCOEL	HIEROSCOPY	QUADRICEPS	BANGLADESH	MEPERIDINE
MINUTEBOOK	BOOTLICKER	HIPPARCHUS	RAMSHACKLE	BATTLEDOOR	MISCONDUCT
MOUNTEBANK	BUREAUCRAT	HUMPBACKED	RESEARCHER	BATTLEDORE	MISLEADING
NARROWBOAT	CALEFACTOR	ICONOSCOPE	RESTRICTED	BERNARDINE	MITHRIDATE
PLOUGHBOTE	CAPPUCCINO	IMBROCCATA	SANDWICHES	BOLLANDIST	MONOPODIUM
POCKETBOOK	CATALECTIC	INCAPACITY	SCEPTICISM	BOMBARDIER	MUJAHEDDIN
PROCUMBENT	CATCRACKER	INCRESCENT	SEANNACHIE	BRIGANDINE	MYOCARDIAL
PROMPTBOOK	CATENACCIO	INDELICACY	SEECATCHIE	BROKENDOWN	NARROWDALE
PROVERBIAL	CESTRACION	INDELICATE	SEERSUCKER	BUTTONDOWN	OCTAHEDRON
QUEENSBURY	CHEESECAKE	INDIRECTLY	SHELLYCOAT	CAMPERDOWN	OUTLANDISH
RAVENSBILL	CHRONICLER	INEFFICACY	SIMPLICITY	CHALCEDONY	OVERRIDING
ROUNDABOUT	CHRONICLES	INSTRUCTED	SIMULACRUM	CLYDESDALE	OZYMANDIAS
ROUSEABOUT	CIRCUMCISE	INSTRUCTOR	SKEPTICISM	COINCIDENT	PANJANDRUM
ROUSTABOUT	CISTERCIAN	INTOXICANT	SMALLSCALE	COMMANDANT	PARADIDDLE
SADDLEBACK	CLASSICISM	INTOXICATE	SPARTACIST	COMMANDEER	PERDENDOSI
SADDLEBILL	CLASSICIST	IRIDESCENT	SPATCHCOCK	COMMANDING	PERSUADING
SCHOOLBOOK	CLEMENCEAU	IRRADICATE	SPECTACLED	COMPENDIUM	PLASMODESM
SECONDBEST	COLCHICINE	ISOLEUCINE	SPECTACLES	COMPRADORE	POLYHEDRON
SILVERBACK	COLPOSCOPE	KENSPECKLE	SPERMACETI	CONCLUDING	PREBENDARY
SILVERBELL	COMMERCIAL	LANDLOCKED	SPERMICIDE	CONCORDANT	PRIMORDIAL
SILVERBILL	COMPLACENT	LARGESCALE	SPIFLICATE	CONTRADICT	PROCEEDING
SKETCHBOOK	COMPLICATE	LAWRENCIUM	SPINESCENT	DECAHEDRON	PROFUNDITY
SMORREBROD	COMPLICITY	LEMNISCATE	SPITCHCOCK	DELCREDERE	RAVENSDUCK
SNOWMOBILE	COMSTOCKER	LIQUESCENT	STILLICIDE	DESCENDANT	RESCHEDULE
SPRINGBOKS	CONDESCEND	LUMPSUCKER	STRATOCRAT	DESCENDING	RESOUNDING
STICKYBEAK	CONFISCATE	MACONOCHIE	STRATOCYST	DESPONDENT	RESPONDENT
STINGYBARK	CONFLICTED	MALEFACTOR	SUBSPECIES	DICYNODONT	RHAPSODISE
STRINDBERG	CONSPECTUS	MARCESCENT	SUCCINCTLY	DILAPIDATE	RHAPSODIST
STRULDBERG	CONTRACTOR	MICROSCOPE	SUPPLICANT	DISCORDANT	RHAPSODIZE
STRULDBRUG	CONTRECOUP	MISERICORD	SUPPLICATE	DOORTODOOR	RICHARDSON
SWEDENBORG	CONVINCING	MISMATCHED	TAPDANCING	DUMBLEDORE	ROWLANDSON
SWITCHBACK	CORNCOCKLE	MONTRACHET	TAPERECORD	ECHINODERM	SALLENDERS
TCHOUKBALL	CRUSTACEAN	MUNIFICENT	TECHNICIAN	EISTEDDFOD	SHERARDISE
THREADBARE	CURRENCIES	MYRIOSCOPE	TECHNOCRAT	EMBROIDERY	SIDESADDLE
TINKERBELL	CYSTOSCOPY	NEEDLECASE	TEINOSCOPE	EMPFINDUNG	SMARAGDINE
VANDERBILT	DECRESCENT	NEMATOCYST	THREESCORE	EPIDENDRUM	SOLIFIDIAN
VEGETABLES	DETRUNCATE	NIGRESCENT	THUMBSCREW	EXPOUNDERS	STEPLADDER
VIDARABINE	DISCONCERT	NONSUCCESS	TORPESCENT	FARRANDINE	STEWARDESS
VOLLEYBALL	DISTINCTLY	NOTORYCTES	TRAFFICKER	FERRANDINE	STUPENDOUS
WEAVERBIRD	DISTRACTED	NUTCRACKER	TRAVANCORE	FORBIDDING	SUBHEADING
WHIRLYBIRD	ELASTICATE	OCTODECIMO	TRIMALCHIO	FOREBODING	SUCCEEDING
WITGATBOOM	ELASTICITY	OFFTHECUFF	TRIPLICATE	FOREORDAIN	SUPERADDED
WOOLLYBACK	EMPEDOCLES	OPALESCENT	TRIPLICITY	FRICANDEAU	SURFRIDING
WOOLLYBUTT	ENTEROCELE	ORDOVICIAN	UNAFFECTED	GARLANDAGE	SUSPENDERS
YELLOWBACK	ENTRANCING	OUTSPECKLE	UNATTACHED	GORMANDIZE	TARADIDDLE
ABSTRACTED	ENTRENCHED	PACIFICISM	UNBLEACHED	HEMIHEDRON	THRENODIAL
ACRONYCHAL	EPIDEICTIC	PANTOSCOPE	UNDERSCORE	HETERODOXY	TILLANDSIA
ADJUDICATE	EQUIVOCATE	PARONYCHIA	UNDETECTED	HETERODYNE	TREMENDOUS
ADOLESCENT	ERUBESCENT	PEPPERCORN	UNEXPECTED	HITOPADESA	TROGLODYTE
ALEMBICATE	EVANESCENT	PETRARCHAN	UNOFFICIAL	HITOPODESA	TROUBADOUR
AMBULACRUM	FANATICISM	PHARMACIST	URTICACEAE	HOLOHEDRAL	TUMBLEDOWN
ANTHRACINE	FANTOCCINI	PHYSIOCRAT	WAPENSCHAW	HORRENDOUS	TURTLEDOVE
ANTHRACITE	FARFETCHED	PICKPOCKET	WAPINSCHAW	HUSBANDAGE	UNABRIDGED
ANTISOCIAL	FETTUCCINE	PILLOWCASE	WOODPECKER	ICOSANDRIA	UNYIELDING
APOPLECTIC	FLAVESCENT	PLASTICINE	ZYGODACTYL	IMPALUDISM	UPSTANDING
APOTHECARY	FLYCATCHER	PLASTICITY	AGGRANDISE	INBREEDING	WARRANDICE
APOTHECIUM	FORFEUCHEN	PLEBISCITE	ALABANDINE	INDIVIDUAL	ZEUGLODONT
ARISTOCRAT	FRATRICIDE	POLITICIAN	ALABANDITE	INSIPIDITY	ZIDOVUDINE
ARTIFICIAL	FREMESCENT	POLITICIZE	ALEXANDERS	INTIMIDATE	ABHORRENCE
ASCETICISM	FRUTESCENT	PRATINCOLE	ALEXANDRIA	INVALIDATE	ABSTINENCE
ASCOMYCETE	GNOSTICISM	PRETINCOLE	AMERINDIAN	INVALIDISM	ACANACEOUS
BACKPACKER	GOATSUCKER	PROSPECTOR	ANACARDIUM	INVALIDITY	ACOTYLEDON
BARLEYCORN	GRIDLOCKED	PROSPECTUS	ANTECEDENT	IRREMEDIAL	ADMITTEDLY
BATHYSCAPH	HAGIOSCOPE	PROTRACTED	ANTIPODEAN	JEOPARDISE	ALCAICERIA

ALLOSTERIC	CONSIDERED	EXPEDIENCY	KATERFELTO	PARISIENNE	RESURGENCE
AMPHINEURA	CONTINENCE	EXPERIENCE	KLEBSIELLA	PASSAGEWAY	REVENGEFUL
AMPHOTERIC	CONVALESCE	EXTRANEOUS	LANSQUENET	PASSAMEZZO	RHINOCEROS
ANAXIMENES	COPARCENER	FENESTELLA	LEUCHAEMIA	PASTORELLA	RITORNELLE
ANCHORETIC	CORALBERRY	FEUILLETON	LINEAMENTS	PATHOGENIC	RITORNELLO
ANEMOMETER	CORPULENCE	FIANCHETTO	LINGULELLA	PATISSERIE	ROCKSTEADY
ANESTHESIA	CORRIGENDA	FINISTERRE	LOCKKEEPER	PENNISETUM	ROTISSERIE
ANESTHETIC	CORTADERIA	FLATULENCE	LOGANBERRY	PENTAMERON	SALMONELLA
ANTIFREEZE	COURAGEOUS	FOLIACEOUS	LOUISIETTE	PENTAMETER	SALTARELLO
ANTITHESIS	CRAPULENCE	FONTANELLE	MAHOMMEDAN	PENTATEUCH	SARCOLEMMA
ANTITHETIC	CRETACEOUS	FORINSECAL	MAISONETTE	PENTETERIC	SCHIPPERKE
APHAERESIS	CROSSREFER	FOURCHETTE	MALAGUETTA	PENTIMENTO	SCHOLAEMIA
APOLOGETIC	CURVACEOUS	FOURTEENTH	MALINGERER	PENTSTEMON	SCOMBRESOX
ARCHIMEDES	CYBERNETIC	FRAMBOESIA	MANGABEIRA	PERIEGESIS	SENESCENCE
ARENACEOUS	CYCLOPEDIA	FRATERETTO	MARIONETTE	PERIPHERAL	SERRADELLA
ARITHMETIC	DECIPHERED	FRATICELLI	MESENTERON	PERMANENCE	SERVICEMAN
ASCENDENCY	DEEPFREEZE	FRAXINELLA	METATHERIA	PERMANENCY	SGANARELLE
BETELGEUSE	DEFICIENCY	FRENZIEDLY	METATHESIS	PERTINENCE	SHACKLETON
BETELGEUZE	DEHISCENCE	FRIGHTENED	METHUSELAH	PESTILENCE	SHISHKEBAB
BEWILDERED	DEJECTEDLY	FUSTANELLA	MICROMETER	PETRONELLA	SHOPKEEPER
BIJOUTERIE	DEMOISELLE	FUSTANELLE	MICRONESIA	PHENOMENAL	SICILIENNE
BINUCLEATE	DENSIMETER	GAMEKEEPER	MIGNONETTE	PHENOMENON	SIGNORELLI
BLACKBEARD	DEPENDENCE	GAULTHERIA	MILEOMETER	PHILATELIC	SILHOUETTE
BLACKBERRY	DEPENDENCY	GENEVRETTE	MILLIHENRY	PHILOXENIA	SOMNOLENCE
BLACKHEART	DESERVEDLY	GIBBERELLA	MILLIMETER	PHOTOGENIC	SPIRITEDLY
BLANQUETTE	DESPITEOUS	GOALKEEPER	MILLIMETRE	PINCHPENNY	SPLITLEVEL
BLASPHEMER	DETERRENCE	GOATSBEARD	MINDERERUS	PINNIPEDIA	SQUEEZEBOX
BLEARYEYED	DIAGENESIS	GODPARENTS	MISCHMETAL	PIRANDELLO	STONEHENGE
BOOKKEEPER	DIAPEDESIS	GONIOMETER	MISTAKENLY	PLANCHETTE	STOUTHERIE
BOTTICELLI	DIFFERENCE	GOOSEBERRY	MOLYBDENUM	PLEXIMETER	STRAITENED
BRADYSEISM	DIFFIDENCE	GOVERNESSY	MONOPLEGIA	POLYPHEMUS	STRAWBERRY
BROCATELLE	DIMINUENDO	GREENHEART	MONOPTERON	POLYTHEISM	STREAMERED
BUMFREEZER	DINANDERIE	GROCETERIA	MONOPTEROS	PONCHIELLI	STRINGENCY
CACODAEMON	DIPHTHERIA	GUTTIFERAE	MONOTHEISM	PONTEDERIA	STRINGENDO
CALCAREOUS	DISCOVERER	HARTEBEEST	MONTEVERDI	PONTICELLO	STRIPTEASE
CALESCENCE	DISCREETLY	HEMIPLEGIA	MORBIDEZZA	PORRACEOUS	STUMBLEDOM
CAMERLENGO	DISHONESTY	HEPTAMERON	MORGANETTA	PORTAMENTO	SUBSIDENCE
CAMPANELLA	DISINHERIT	HEPTATEUCH	MORTADELLA	PRAXITELES	SUPPOSEDLY
CAMSTEERIE	DISORDERED	HERBACEOUS	MOZZARELLA	PRECEDENCE	SWEETHEART
CANTILEVER	DISORDERLY	HOLOSTERIC	MULTIMEDIA	PREDECEASE	SYNAERESIS
CARBURETOR	DISQUIETED	HORNBLENDE	MUSKETEERS	PREFERENCE	SYNEIDESIS
CASSOLETTE	DISSIDENCE	HOWSOMEVER	NARCOLEPSY	PREPOTENCE	SYNTERESIS
CATCHPENNY	DIVERGENCE	HYDROMETER	NATHELESSE	PRESCIENCE	TABLANETTE
CENTIMETER	DOLCEMENTE	HYGROMETER	NEGLIGENCE	PRESIDENCY	TACHOMETER
CENTIMETRE	DOORKEEPER	HYPOGAEOUS	NEURILEMMA	PREVALENCE	TARANTELLA
CHALYBEATE	DRUMBLEDOR	HYPOTHESIS	NEUROLEMMA	PRIVATEERS	TEENYWEENY
CHAPAREJOS	EBRACTEATE	HYPSOMETRY	NEWSAGENTS	PRIVILEGED	TESTACEOUS
CHARTREUSE	EBULLIENCE	HYSTERESIS	NINETEENTH	PROAIRESIS	THIMBLEFUL
CHINABERRY	EFFERVESCE	IATROGENIC	NOMOTHETIC	PROMINENCE	THIMBLEWIT
CINDERELLA	EFFICIENCY	ICOSOHEDRA	NONONSENSE	PROPRAETOR	THIRTEENTH
CIRRIPEDEA	EIGHTEENTH	ILLAQUEATE	OCCURRENCE	PROPRIETOR	THREATENED
CIRRIPEDIA	ELDERBERRY	IMMORTELLE	OFFLICENCE	PROSTHESIS	THREEPENCE
CITRONELLA	EMBITTERED	IMPATIENCE	OLERACEOUS	PROSTHETIC	THREEPENNY
CLARABELLA	EMBLEMENTS	IMPROPERLY	OMBROMETER	PROVIDENCE	TIMEKEEPER
CLOISTERED	EMOLUMENTS	IMPRUDENCE	OPHICLEIDE	PUBESCENCE	TINTORETTO
CLOUDBERRY	ENTREMESSE	INCUMBENCY	OPISOMETER	PULSOMETER	TOCCATELLA
COCCINEOUS	EPENTHETIC	INDULGENCE	ORCHIDEOUS	PURPOSEFUL	TOCOPHEROL
COETANEOUS	EPIGENETIC	INQUIRENDO	OROGENESIS	PYTHOGENIC	TOILINETTE
COLLATERAL	EPROUVETTE	INSISTENCE	OSTEOLEPIS	QUIESCENCE	TOLLKEEPER
COMEDIENNE	ERYSIPELAS	INSOLVENCY	OUTRAGEOUS	RECOMMENCE	TORRICELLI
COMPETENCE	ETEOCRETAN	INSURGENCY	OVERTHETOP	RECOMPENSE	TRANSIENCE
CONDIMENTS	EUDIOMETER	INTERCEDER	OWLSPIEGLE	RECRUDESCE	TRANSVERSE
CONDOLENCE	EUROCHEQUE	INTERFERER	PADDYMELON	RECURRENCE	TRILATERAL
CONFEDERAL	EURYPTERUS	INTERFERON	PAPIAMENTO	REGISTERED	TROMOMETER
CONFERENCE	EUTHYNEURA	INTERLEAVE	PARAENESIS	REMORSEFUL	TRUCULENCE
CONFIDENCE	EUTRAPELIA	INTERMEZZO	PARALLELED	REPEATEDLY	TULARAEMIA
CONFLUENCE	EXCELLENCE	INTERWEAVE	PARAPLEGIA	REPORTEDLY	TUMESCENCE
CONFUSEDLY	EXCELLENCY	JARGONELLE	PARAPLEGIC	RESIGNEDLY	TURBULENCE
CONSCIENCE	EXPEDIENCE	JEISTIECOR	PARASCENIA	RESILIENCE	TURRITELLA

ULSTERETTE	TANGLEFOOT	REAMINGBIT	CELLOPHANE	LEPRECHAUN	SOUSAPHONE
ULTRONEOUS	TENDERFOOT	REFRINGENT	CHARGEHAND	LETTERHEAD	SPLANCHNIC
UNANSWERED	THALLIFORM	ROCKINGHAM	CHIFFCHAFF	LIKELIHOOD	SPOKESHAVE
UNBELIEVER	THEREAFTER	SALPINGIAN	CLADOPHYLL	LITHOPHANE	SPREAGHERY
UNDERLEASE	WYCLIFFIAN	SCHOOLGIRL	CLAVICHORD	LIVELIHOOD	SPRINGHAAS
UNDERNEATH	ACROMEGALY	SCINTIGRAM	CLOMIPHENE	LOGGERHEAD	STEALTHILY
UNFETTERED	ALGOLAGNIA	SCROUNGING	COLEORHIZA	LOGORRHOEA	STRACCHINO
UNGRATEFUL	ANASTIGMAT	SELLINGERS	COMANCHERO	MAIDENHAIR	STRAIGHTEN
UNHAMPERED	APTERYGOTA	SELTZOGENE	COMPREHEND	MAIDENHOOD	STRINGHALT
UNHYGIENIC	AREOPAGITE	SEPTUAGINT	CONTRAHENT	MALLOPHAGA	STRONGHOLD
UNICAMERAL	ASPARAGINE	SEXOLOGIST	COPPERHEAD	MARASCHINO	SUBTRAHEND
UNILATERAL	ASTRINGENT	SHANDYGAFF	CORINTHIAN	MATTERHORN	SUNBATHING
UNLEAVENED	BALBRIGGAN	SLUICEGATE	CRANKSHAFT	MEERSCHAUM	SWEATSHIRT
UNLETTERED	BARELEGGED	SOLIVAGANT	CROSSCHECK	MELANCHOLY	SYMPATHISE
UNMANNERED	BASSINGTON	SPORANGIUM	CRUIKSHANK	MENORRHOEA	SYMPATHIZE
UNMANNERLY	BEDRAGGLED	STRATEGIST	CTENOPHORA	MICROPHONE	TENTERHOOK
UNNUMBERED	BIRMINGHAM	SUFFRAGIST	CTENOPHORE	MIDLOTHIAN	THROUGHOUT
UNREDEEMED	BOONDOGGLE	TEDDINGTON	DEBAUCHERY	MONARCHIST	THROUGHPUT
UNRELIEVED	BOOTLEGGER	THEOLOGATE	DEBOUCHURE	MOTHERHOOD	THROUGHWAY
UROPOIESIS	BOOZINGKEN	THEOLOGIAN	DHARMSHALA	MUTTONHEAD	TREKSCHUIT
VENEZUELAN	BORDRAGING	THEOLOGISE	DISCOPHORA	MYCORRHIZA	TRIUMPHANT
VERMICELLI	BOUSINGKEN	THEOLOGIST	DISENCHANT	NDRANGHETA	TROPOPHYTE
VILLANELLE	BUCKINGHAM	THOROUGHLY	DROSOPHILA	NIGGERHEAD	TURTLEHEAD
WATERLEVEL	BURLINGTON	TOPOLOGIST	DUNDERHEAD	NIGHTSHADE	UNBLUSHING
WATERMELON	CAMPAIGNER	TRILINGUAL	EARTHSHINE	NIGHTSHIRT	UNDERSHIRT
WHATSOEVER	CARDIOGRAM	UNASSIGNED	EMBOUCHURE	NOUAKCHOTT	UNFAITHFUL
WHITEHEART	CATALOGUER	UNFLAGGING	ENGLISHMAN	NOURISHING	UNTRUTHFUL
WILDEBEEST	CATTLEGRID	UPBRINGING	ENGLISHMEN	ODELSTHING	VARNISHING
WINCEYETTE	CHAMPIGNON	UROSTEGITE	ENTRYPHONE	OIREACHTAS	VIBRAPHONE
WRETCHEDLY	CHITTAGONG	VICEREGENT	EPANOPHORA	OMBROPHOBE	WALLACHIAN
YOUNGBERRY	CHURCHGOER	VIROLOGIST	EPIMETHEUS	OSTEOPHYTE	WATERWHEEL
YTHUNDERED	CONCHIGLIE	WASHINGTON	EPONYCHIUM	PANSOPHIST	WHEATSHEAF
ANGLERFISH	CONGREGATE	WELLINGTON	ESCUTCHEON	PAPERCHASE	WHEELCHAIR
BEAUTIFIER	CONTINGENT	WILLINGDON	EUSTACHIAN	PARARTHRIA	WHITETHORN
BREASTFEED	CONVERGENT	WOFFINGTON	EVERYTHING	PARENCHYMA	WHOLEWHEAT
BUTTERFISH	CRYPTOGRAM	WOODPIGEON	EVERYWHERE	PARENTHOOD	WILLOWHERB
CALORIFIER	CURMUDGEON	YAFFINGALE	FAHRENHEIT	PARISCHANE	WOODENHEAD
CANDLEFISH	DEVANAGARI	YELLOWGIRL	FARSIGHTED	PENTATHLON	WORTHWHILE
CENTRIFUGE	EMALANGENI	ZAPOROGIAN	FIGUREHEAD	PERSEPHONE	ABBREVIATE
CHLOROFORM	FALLINGOFF	AERENCHYMA	FLUGELHORN	PETTICHAPS	ABITURIENT
CINQUEFOIL	FLAMINGANT	AFTERSHAVE	FURNISHING	PETTYCHAPS	ABORIGINAL
CIRCUMFLEX	FOOTLIGHTS	AFTERSHOCK	GALUMPHING	PHOTOPHORE	ABSTEMIOUS
CIRCUMFUSE	FORFOUGHEN	ANGLOPHILE	GESUNDHEIT	PIGEONHOLE	ACCESSIBLE
CLASSIFIED	FOURRAGERE	ANGLOPHOBE	GOLIATHISE	PINCUSHION	ACCESSIONS
CONTRAFLOW	GOLDDIGGER	ANTIOCHENE	GONORRHOEA	PLEROPHORY	ACCLIVIOUS
CUTTLEFISH	HARRINGTON	ANTIOCHIAN	GRAMOPHONE	PRIESTHOOD	ACCREDITED
DAMSELFISH	HEADLIGHTS	APOPHTHEGM	GRANDCHILD	PROMETHEAN	ADJECTIVAL
DEBRIEFING	HETEROGAMY	ATMOSPHERE	GREENSHANK	PROMETHEUS	ADMISSIBLE
DISCOMFORT	HUMDUDGEON	BALANCHINE	GYPSOPHILA	PROMETHIUM	ADVERTISER
DUNDERFUNK	INTELIGENT	BARYSPHERE	HAMMERHEAD	PUBLISHING	AFTERBIRTH
ELYTRIFORM	KIESELGUHR	BATRACHIAN	HEMISPHERE	QUICKTHORN	AFTERPIECE
EMULSIFIER	LAUNCEGAYE	BEFOREHAND	HEMORRHAGE	REDRUTHITE	AIRFREIGHT
GENTLEFOLK	LEAMINGTON	BEHINDHAND	HEPTATHLON	REFRESHING	ALCHERINGA
HUMIDIFIER	LIMBURGITE	BEWITCHING	HIEROPHANT	RHINOPHYMA	AMPHIBIOUS
MONILIFORM	MABINOGION	BIRKENHEAD	HYALOPHANE	RIDINGHOOD	AMPHIMIXIS
OUTPERFORM	MANDRAGORA	BLACKSHIRT	HYDROPHANE	ROTHSCHILD	ANALOGICAL
PADDLEFISH	MARTINGALE	BLACKTHORN	HYDROPHYTE	RUDOLPHINE	ANALYTICAL
PLUPERFECT	MEANINGFUL	BONNETHEAD	HYPAETHRAL	SAPROPHYTE	ANARCHICAL
RAGAMUFFIN	MISHGUGGLE	BOTTLEHEAD	HYPAETHRON	SCREECHING	ANATOMICAL
RUTHERFORD	MUSSORGSKY	BRAINCHILD	IMPOSTHUME	SCRIMSHANK	ANNUALIZED
SANCTIFIED	NEWFANGLED	BRIDGEHEAD	INTERPHONE	SECONDHAND	ANNUNCIATE
SHOPLIFTER	NICARAGUAN	BRITISHISM	IONOSPHERE	SEEMLIHEAD	ANTIADITIS
SILVERFISH	NONALIGNED	BROADSHEET	JOLTERHEAD	SEPULCHRAL	ANTICLIMAX
SPONGIFORM	PADDINGTON	BUFFLEHEAD	KARMATHIAN	SHEEPSHANK	APPRECIATE
STILLIFORM	PARTINGALE	BUTTONHOLE	KLOOTCHMAN	SHELLSHOCK	ARAGONITES
STULTIFIED	PLOUGHGATE	CAOUTCHOUC	KNIGHTHEAD	SHOVELHEAD	ARTHURIANA
SUBTERFUGE	PROFLIGACY	CARPATHIAN	KNIGHTHOOD	SINARCHIST	ASPERSIONS
SVADILFARI	PROFLIGATE	CARRAGHEEN	LANDSTHING	SISTERHOOD	ASPHYXIATE
TAMPERFOOT	PROMULGATE	CATARRHINE	LANGERHANS	SKRIMSHANK	ASTEROIDEA

AUSPICIOUS	DEPRECIATE	GIRLFRIEND	LUGUBRIOUS	PILEDRIVER	SOBERSIDES
AUTHORISED	DERMATITIS	GLEEMAIDEN	MACROBIOTE	PILLIWINKS	SOFTBOILED
AUTOECIOUS	DÉSHABILLÉ	GONDOLIERS	MAGNIFICAT	PLATINISED	SOGDOLIGER
AVARICIOUS	DETERMINED	GRAMICIDIN	MAINTAINER	PLAYWRIGHT	SOMERVILLE
BACKSLIDER	DETERMINER	GRANADILLA	MAKEWEIGHT	POIKILITIC	SONGWRITER
BALBUTIENT	DIABOLICAL	GRASSWIDOW	MANDEVILLE	PONTIFICAL	SPLENDIDLY
BANDERILLA	DIACONICON	GREENFINCH	MANZANILLA	POTENTIATE	STABILISER
BANDERILLO	DIDGERIDOO	GREGARIOUS	MARGASIRSA	POTENTILLA	STABILIZER
BARMECIDAL	DIGESTIBLE	GRENADIERS	MARTINIQUE	PRECARIOUS	STERILISER
BELONGINGS	DIRECTIONS	GRENADILLA	MECHANICAL	PRECIPITIN	STERILIZER
BIOLOGICAL	DISBELIEVE	GREYFRIARS	MECHANIZED	PRECOCIOUS	STIACCIATO
BIPARTISAN	DISCLAIMER	GUIDELINES	MENDACIOUS	PREDACIOUS	STILLBIRTH
BIRTHRIGHT	DISHABILLE	HANDMAIDEN	MENINGITIS	PREJUDICED	STROPHIOLE
BLASTOIDEA	DISPIRITED	HANGGLIDER	METHODICAL	PREMARITAL	STYLOPISED
BORROWINGS	DISSILIENT	HARDBOILED	MICROFICHE	PREMEDICAL	SUBLIMINAL
BRADYKININ	DISSIMILAR	HARMONIOUS	MICROLIGHT	PREPOSITOR	SUBMARINER
BRAGADISME	DISSOCIATE	HECTOLITRE	MILLEFIORI	PRIZEFIGHT	SUBMEDIANT
BROADPIECE	DRACONITES	HEMOPHILIA	MISGIVINGS	PRODIGIOUS	SUBORBITAL
BRONCHITIC	DRAWBRIDGE	HESPERIDES	MOLENDINAR	PROFICIENT	SUBSCRIBER
BRONCHITIS	DUKKERIPEN	HISTORICAL	MONOACIDIC	PROGENITOR	SUBSIDIARY
BUDGERIGAR	DUODECIMAL	HITCHHIKER	MONOECIOUS	PROHIBITED	SUFFICIENT
CAERPHILLY	ECHINOIDEA	HORSERIDER	MONTEVIDEO	PROPITIATE	SUPERGIANT
CALUMNIATE	ECOLOGICAL	HYPNOTIZED	MORDACIOUS	PROPITIOUS	SUPERVISED
CAMERLINGO	ECONOMICAL	HYSTERICAL	MOUSEPIECE	PROPOSITUS	SUPERVISOR
CANDELILLA	ECUMENICAL	ILLADVISED	MOUTHPIECE	PROSCRIBED	SUSPICIOUS
CAPRICIOUS	ELECTRICAL	IMPERVIOUS	MOZAMBIQUE	PROSILIENT	SUZERAINTY
CARYATIDES	ELLIPTICAL	IMPLICITLY	MYRINGITIS	PROVEDITOR	SYMBOLICAL
CASCARILLA	ENCYCLICAL	IMPOSSIBLE	MYSTERIOUS	PROVISIONS	SYPHILITIC
CATHOLICON	ENHYDRITIC	IMPOSSIBLY	NEAPOLITAN	PUGNACIOUS	TANAGRIDAE
CATHOLICOS	ENTHUSIASM	IMPROVISED	NEGLIGIBLE	QUESADILLA	TEETHRIDGE
CELESTIALS	ENTHUSIAST	INCAUTIOUS	NEOTERICAL	RABBINICAL	TELEBRIDGE
CELLULITIS	EPIMENIDES	INCENDIARY	NICROSILAL	REBELLIOUS	TENEBRIFIC
CENSORIOUS	ESCADRILLE	INCREDIBLE	NIGHTLIGHT	RECOGNISED	TENRECIDAE
CENTESIMAL	ESPADRILLE	INCREDIBLY	NUTRITIOUS	RECOGNIZED	THEATRICAL
CENTILITER	ESTANCIERO	INDISTINCT	OBSEQUIOUS	RECONCILED	THEOCRITUS
CENTILITRE	EUPHONIOUS	INELIGIBLE	OFTENTIMES	RECONSIDER	THUCYDIDES
CHAPLAINCY	EXCRUCIATE	INFALLIBLE	OMNISCIENT	REPATRIATE	TIMESWITCH
CHILDBIRTH	EXPATRIATE	INFALLIBLY	OOPHORITIS	REPUBLICAN	TORCHLIGHT
CHINCHILLA	EXPLICITLY	INFECTIOUS	ORATORICAL	RESERVISTS	TOUCHPIECE
CHOPSTICKS	EXTENSIBLE	INFLEXIBLE	OSTENSIBLE	RESORCINOL	TRADITIONS
CHRISTIANA	FACTITIOUS	INFLEXIBLY	OSTENSIBLY	RESTRAINED	TRANQUILLY
CLOSTRIDIA	FAIRHAIRED	INGLORIOUS	OUANANICHE	REVERSIBLE	TRIFOLIATE
COLLEGIATE	FALLACIOUS	INGRATIATE	OUGHTLINGS	RHETORICAL	TRIMSNITCH
COLOSSIANS	FASTIDIOUS	INGREDIENT	OUTPATIENT	RHYTHMICAL	TRIPUDIARY
COMESTIBLE	FASTIGIATE	INQUISITOR	OVERWEIGHT	ROBUSTIOUS	TROUVAILLE
COMMODIOUS	FERNITICLE	INSENSIBLE	OVIPOSITOR	ROCKABILLY	TYMPANITES
COMMUNIQUÉ	FERTILISED	INSOUCIANT	PALMATIFID	ROTTWEILER	TYMPANITIS
COMPARISON	FERTILISER	INTAGLIATE	PANOPTICON	SABBATICAL	TYPEWRITER
COMPATIBLE	FERTILIZER	INTANGIBLE	PARAPHILIA	SALUBRIOUS	TYRANNICAL
COMPETITOR	FIBROSITIS	INTESTINAL	PARMACITIE	SANDINISTA	TYRANNISED
COMPOSITOR	FICTITIOUS	INTESTINES	PARMIGIANA	SANFORISED	ULTRAFICHE
CONCILIATE	FLAGITIOUS	INVINCIBLE	PARTICIPLE	SCATURIENT	UMBELLIFER
CONGENITAL	FLOODLIGHT	JARDINIERE	PARVOVIRUS	SCIENTIFIC	UNCONFINED
CONSTRINGE	FOOTBRIDGE	JUSTICIARY	PATRONISED	SCOPELIDAE	UNCRITICAL
CONTAGIOUS	FOOTPRINTS	KSHATRIYAS	PECCADILLO	SCOTODINIA	UNDERLINEN
CONVENIENT	FORTHRIGHT	LACCADIVES	PENTELIKON	SDRUCCIOLA	UNDERSIZED
COPERNICUS	FOSSILIZED	LARYNGITIS	PERCIPIENT	SEGUIDILLA	UNGRACIOUS
COPYWRITER	FRANCHISEE	LASCIVIOUS	PERDITIOUS	SEQUACIOUS	UNIGENITUS
COQUELICOT	FRANCHISOR	LATTICINIO	PERFICIENT	SERMONICAL	UNIMPAIRED
CORDWAINER	FRENETICAL	LAVALLIÈRE	PERFIDIOUS	SERRADILLA	UNINSPIRED
CORREGIDOR	FUNGICIDAL	LENTIGINES	PERIODICAL	SEVENTIETH	UNORIGINAL
COXCOMICAL	GALLABIYAH	LIBREVILLE	PERNICIOUS	SHAGHAIRED	UNREQUITED
CROSSPIECE	GALLABIYEH	LICENTIATE	PERSTRINGE	SHENANIGAN	UNSPECIFIC
CROTALIDAE	GALRAVITCH	LICENTIOUS	PHOTODIODE	SHIPWRIGHT	UPROARIOUS
CUCURBITAL	GALVANISER	LILYWHITES	PICCADILLY	SHOPSOILED	UROGENITAL
DARKHAIRED	GARGOUILLE	LIQUIDIZER	PICCALILLI	SHORTLIVED	VALENTINES
DEDUCTIBLE	GEOLOGICAL	LITURGICAL	PICCANINNY	SIGNIFICAT	VASCULITIS
DEFENSIBLE	GERMICIDAL	LOGISTICAL	PICHICIAGO	SIMILLIMUM	VAUDEVILLE
DEMOCRITUS	GINGIVITIS	LOQUACIOUS	PICHICIEGO	SINSEMILLA	VIBRATIONS

VICTORIANA	AUSTRALIAN	CRAIGFLUKE	GHIBELLINE	MAXIMILIAN	PLATTELAND
VICTORIOUS	AUSTRALORP	CRENELLATE	GOODFELLOW	MESITYLENE	PLAYFELLOW
VINDEMIATE	AUTECOLOGY	CUMBERLAND	GOOSEFLESH	METABOLISE	PLIABILITY
VITELLICLE	BADDERLOCK	CYNOMOLGUS	GRADUALISM	METABOLISM	POINTBLANK
VIVANDIÈRE	BALNEOLOGY	DARJEELING	GRAPHOLOGY	METICULOUS	POLYVALENT
WANDERINGS	BATTAILOUS	DECATHLETE	GRAPTOLITE	MICHAELMAS	PONEROLOGY
WANTHRIVEN	BEAUJOLAIS	DECIMALIZE	GRATILLITY	MINERALOGY	PORTCULLIS
WATERTIGHT	BEDEVILLED	DELTIOLOGY	GRAVEOLENT	MINIMALISM	POSTILLATE
WATERWINGS	BENEVOLENT	DEMIRELIEF	GREENCLOTH	MINIMALIST	POSTILLION
WILLYWILLY	BERSAGLIER	DEMOBILISE	GROUNDLESS	MIRACULOUS	POZZUOLANA
WINDSHIELD	BESTIALITY	DEMOBILIZE	GROUNDLING	MISCELLANY	PREVAILING
ZABAGLIONE	BESTSELLER	DEMODULATE	GROVELLING	MONOPOLISE	PROFITLESS
ZOOLOGICAL	BINOCULARS	DEMONOLOGY	GYNECOLOGY	MONOPOLIZE	PROPELLANT
LUMBERJACK	BIRTHPLACE	DEMORALISE	HALFDOLLAR	MONOVALENT	PROPELLENT
NATTERJACK	BITTERLING	DEMORALIZE	HAMMERLOCK	MORPHOLOGY	PROTOPLASM
SUPPLEJACK	BONDHOLDER	DEPOPULATE	HAUSTELLUM	MOTHERLAND	PRZEWALSKI
YELLOWJACK	BOOKSELLER	DERAILLEUR	HEXAVALENT	MOTHERLESS	PSEPHOLOGY
BARRACKING	BORDERLAND	DEREGULATE	HIEROGLYPH	MOTHERLIKE	PSYCHOLOGY
CHEAPSKATE	BORDERLINE	DEUTOPLASM	HINTERLAND	MOTIONLESS	PUBERULENT
JAYWALKING	BOTTOMLESS	DIASTALTIC	HOMORELAPS	MOUSSELINE	PUMMELLING
JOBSEEKERS	BRATISLAVA	DISABILITY	HONOURLESS	MULTIPLIED	PUNCTULATE
KARTTIKAYA	BREATHLESS	DISCIPLINE	HOWLEGLASS	MULTIPLIER	QUENCHLESS
KENTUCKIAN	BROADCLOTH	DISINCLINE	HUMOURLESS	MUSICOLOGY	RADICALISM
LAMARCKISM	CALCEOLATE	DISQUALIFY	HYDRAULICS	MUTABILITY	RAMPALLIAN
LAURVIKITE	CAMOUFLAGE	DISTILLATE	HYDROPLANE	NAPTHALENE	REGARDLESS
MUCKRAKING	CANCELLOUS	DISTILLERY	ICONOCLAST	NATURALISM	RELENTLESS
NETWORKING	CANDYFLOSS	DISTILLING	ILLEGALITY	NATURALIST	RESEMBLING
NONSMOKING	CANNELLONI	DIURNALIST	IMBECILITY	NATURALIZE	RETICULATE
PERNICKETY	CANTILLATE	DOMICILARY	IMMACULACY	NEUTRALISE	RETINALITE
PEROVSKITE	CAPABILITY	DURABILITY	IMMACULATE	NEUTRALITY	REVITALIZE
POHUTUKAWA	CAPITALISM	EASTERLING	IMMOBILITY	NEUTRALIZE	REVIVALIST
PORLOCKING	CAPITALIST	EFFORTLESS	IMMOBILIZE	NIDDERLING	RIDICULOUS
ROLLICKING	CAPITALIZE	EMASCULATE	IMMORALITY	NOMINALIST	ROSANILINE
SAMARSKITE	CAPITELLUM	EMBRYOLOGY	IMMUNOLOGY	NONCHALANT	ROSEMALING
SBUDDIKINS	CAPITOLINE	ENTOMOLOGY	INCIVILITY	NONVIOLENT	RUDDERLESS
SPILLIKINS	CAPITULARY	EPITHELIUM	INCOMPLETE	NORMOBLAST	RUMBULLION
THUMBIKINS	CAPITULATE	EQUIVALENT	INDICOLITE	NOTABILITY	RUPICOLINE
TITARAKURA	CAPREOLATE	ETERNALIZE	INDIGOLITE	NOVACULITE	SALTCELLAR
UNBLINKING	CARAMELIZE	EVANGELIST	INEQUALITY	NUMBERLESS	SANDERLING
UNDERSKIRT	CARDIOLOGY	EVANGELIZE	INESCULENT	NYMPHOLEPT	SAXICOLINE
UNSHACKLED	CARPHOLOGY	EVERYPLACE	INFIBULATE	OBJECTLESS	SAXICOLOUS
UNTHINKING	CATABOLISM	EXOBIOLOGY	INFIDELITY	ODDFELLOWS	SCANDALISE
WATERSKIER	CATAFALQUE	FATHERLAND	INOSCULATE	ODONTALGIA	SCANDALIZE
WUNDERKIND	CENTRALIZE	FATHERLESS	INSUFFLATE	ODONTOLITE	SCANDALOUS
ACCOMPLICE	CEREBELLUM	FEDERALISM	INTERCLUDE	ODONTOLOGY	SCATHELESS
ACCOMPLISH	CHAMAELEON	FEDERALIST	INVIGILATE	OPHTHALMIC	SCRIBBLING
ACCUMULATE	CHANCELLOR	FETTERLOCK	IRRESOLUTE	ORTHOCLASE	SCRUPULOUS
ACEPHALOUS	CHANDELIER	FIBERGLASS	ISABELLINE	OSTEOBLAST	SCURRILITY
ADRAMELECH	CHANGELESS	FIBREGLASS	JOURNALESE	PAINKILLER	SCURRILOUS
ADRENALINE	CHANGELING	FIBRILLATE	JOURNALISM	PALATALISE	SCUTELLATE
AFFABILITY	CHAPFALLEN	FINGERLING	JOURNALIST	PALYNOLOGY	SEISMOLOGY
ALCOHOLISM	CHAPTALISE	FIREWALKER	KIMBERLITE	PARACELSUS	SELEGILINE
AMARYLLIDS	CHAROLLAIS	FISHSELLER	LADYKILLER	PARASELENE	SENEGALESE
AMBIVALENT	CHESSYLITE	FLAGELLATE	LANCEOLATE	PARENTLESS	SENSUALITY
AMIABILITY	CHOICELESS	FLIGHTLESS	LAURDALITE	PARNELLISM	SHADOWLESS
AMYGDALOID	CHRONOLOGY	FLOCCULATE	LEGIBILITY	PARTIALITY	SHIBBOLETH
ANGUILLULA	CHRYSOLITE	FLOCCULENT	LHERZOLITE	PATIBULARY	SHILLELAGH
ANNIHILATE	CNIDOBLAST	FLOORCLOTH	LIBERALISM	PEDICULATE	SHOPWALKER
ANTHEOLION	CODSWALLOP	FOOTBALLER	LIBERALITY	PEDIPALPUS	SHRIVELLED
ANTHOCLORE	COLOURLESS	FRAUDULENT	LIBERALIZE	PENICILLIN	SINGHALESE
ARISTOLOGY	COMPELLING	FREEHOLDER	LONGFELLOW	PENNILLION	SLEEVELESS
ARTHRALGIA	CONCHOLOGY	FRIENDLESS	MALACOLOGY	PERIHELION	SNORKELING
ARTICULATA	CONTROLLER	FRINGILLID	MALAYALAAM	PERSIFLAGE	SOLUBILITY
ARTICULATE	COPYHOLDER	FRITILLARY	MALEVOLENT	PETROGLYPH	SOPHOCLEAN
ARUNDELIAN	CORDIALITY	GENERALISE	MANIPULATE	PHRENOLOGY	SOURDELINE
ASSEMBLAGE	CORDILLERA	GENERALITY	MAQUILLAGE	PHYSIOLOGY	SPECIALISE
ASSEMBLING	COUNCILLOR	GENERALIZE	MARSHALSEA	PILGARLICK	SPECIALISM
ASSIMILATE	COUNSELING	GENETHLIAC	MARVELLOUS	PISTILLATE	SPECIALIST
AUDIBILITY	COUNSELLOR	GENICULATE	MAXIMALIST	PLANOBLAST	SPECIALITY

SPECIALIZE	VERSAILLES	DECAMPMENT	INTERNMENT	UNASSUMING	BRAININESS
SPEECHLESS	VESICULATE	DEFACEMENT	INVESTMENT	UNBECOMING	BRIGHTNESS
SPELEOLOGY	VICTUALLER	DEFILEMENT	JACKHAMMER	UNIFORMITY	BUCHMANISM
SPERRYLITE	VISIBILITY	DEFRAYMENT	JIGGERMAST	UNSCRAMBLE	BUFFOONERY
SPHACELATE	VOCABULARY	DENOUEMENT	KERSEYMERE	VIETNAMESE	BURGEONING
SPIRITLESS	VOCABULIST	DEPARTMENT	LACHRYMOSE	WASSERMANS	BUSHRANGER
SPRINGLESS	VOLATILITY	DEPLOYMENT	LANDAMMANN	WHIGGAMORE	CACHINNATE
SPRINGLIKE	VOLUBILITY	DEPORTMENT	LATTERMATH	WILLIAMSON	CACUMINOUS
SPRINKLING	WANDERLUST	DERAILMENT	LEGITIMACY	WINDERMERE	CALAMANDER
STADHOLDER	WASSAILING	DESQUAMATE	LEGITIMATE	WINDJAMMER	CALAMONDIN
STALHELMER	WEAPONLESS	DETACHMENT	LEGITIMIZE	WOLFRAMITE	CALEDONIAN
STANISLAUS	WEEDKILLER	DETAINMENT	LEGWARMERS	WONDERMENT	CALYDONIAN
STAPHYLINE	WEIGHTLESS	DEVOTEMENT	LIEBERMANN	ABRUPTNESS	CAMBRENSIS
STARVELING	WHEWELLITE	DIADROMOUS	LOCULAMENT	ABUNDANTLY	CAMERONIAN
STAUROLITE	WONDERLAND	DICHROMATE	MANAGEMENT	ABYSSINIAN	CANCIONERO
STERNALGIA	WORLDCLASS	DICHROMISM	MASTERMIND	ACCIDENTAL	CARABINEER
STRAGGLING	YELLOWLEGS	DISCOMMODE	MEDICAMENT	ACCUSINGLY	CARABINIER
STREAMLINE	YOURSELVES	DISHARMONY	MENECHMIAN	ACQUAINTED	CARMAGNOLE
STREETLAMP	ABONNEMENT	EBOULEMENT	MIZZENMAST	ACROGENOUS	CARTOONIST
STRIDULATE	ABRIDGMENT	EFFACEMENT	MONOGAMOUS	ADMIRINGLY	CASUALNESS
SUAVEOLENT	ADDITAMENT	EMBANKMENT	MONTGOMERY	AERUGINOUS	CAUTIONARY
SUBSELLIUM	ADJUSTMENT	EMBODIMENT	NETHERMOST	AFICIONADO	CENTENNIAL
SUGARALLIE	ADULLAMITE	EMPLOYMENT	NONPAYMENT	AFRICANDER	CEREMONIAL
SURREALISM	AFTERIMAGE	ENCAMPMENT	NOSOCOMIAL	AFRICANISM	CEREMONIES
SURREALIST	AGRONOMIST	ENCASEMENT	PALUDAMENT	ALBIGENSES	CHALLENGED
TABLECLOTH	ALLUREMENT	ENDEARMENT	PARLIAMENT	ALKALINITY	CHALLENGER
TAMBERLANE	ALTAZIMUTH	ENDOGAMOUS	PEPPERMILL	ALMACANTAR	CHARDONNAY
TARPAULING	ALZHEIMERS	ENGAGEMENT	PEPPERMINT	ALMUCANTAR	CHAUVINISM
TECHNOLOGY	AMALGAMATE	ENGOUEMENT	PERFORMING	AMANUENSIS	CHAUVINIST
TENDERLOIN	ANADROMOUS	ENLACEMENT	PHILLUMENY	ANTAGONISE	CHEEKINESS
TENDRILLED	ANADYOMENE	ENLÈVEMENT	PILGRIMAGE	ANTAGONISM	CHEIRONOMY
TERNEPLATE	ANTINOMIAN	ENLISTMENT	POLYGAMIST	ANTAGONIST	CHELTENHAM
TERREPLEIN	ARGOLEMONO	ENRICHMENT	POLYGAMOUS	ANTAGONIZE	CHERSONESE
THEMSELVES	ARTHROMERE	ENROLLMENT	POLYHYMNIA	ANTEPENULT	CHERVONETS
THEODOLITE	ASSESSMENT	ENTICEMENT	POLYNOMIAL	ANTIMONIAN	CHICKENPOX
THREADLIKE	ASSIGNMENT	ENTOMBMENT	POSTHUMOUS	ANTIVENENE	CHIFFONIER
TIMBROLOGY	ASSORTMENT	EPAULEMENT	POSTLIMINY	APOLLONIAN	CHILLINESS
TIRAILLEUR	ATTACHMENT	EPHRAIMITE	PREFERMENT	APOLLONIUS	CHIMPANZEE
TOMFOOLERY	ATTAINMENT	EPISTEMICS	PREPAYMENT	APPARENTLY	CHLORINATE
TOPICALITY	AUTONOMOUS	EQUANIMITY	PROGRAMMER	AQUAMANALE	CLAMMINESS
TORTELLINI	BACKGAMMON	ERGONOMICS	PUNISHMENT	AQUAMANILE	CLASPKNIFE
TOURBILLON	BAFFLEMENT	ESCAPEMENT	PUZZLEMENT	ARAUCANIAN	CLEVERNESS
TOURMALINE	BANISHMENT	ESCARPMENT	RAJPRAMUKH	ARROGANTLY	CLOUDINESS
TOXICOLOGY	BATTLEMENT	ETHYLAMINE	REARMAMENT	ARYTAENOID	CLUMSINESS
TRACHELATE	BEDCHAMBER	EXCITEMENT	REASSEMBLE	ASTUTENESS	COARSENESS
TRAMPOLINE	BELLARMINE	EXPERIMENT	REFINEMENT	ATRAMENTAL	COATHANGER
TRANSPLANT	BENTHAMITE	FAMISHMENT	RESENTMENT	AUCTIONEER	COCKERNONY
TRAVELLERS	BICHROMATE	FOREDAMNED	RETIREMENT	AUSTRINGER	COHERENTLY
TRAVELLING	BIOCHEMIST	FULFILMENT	RINGELMANN	AUTOGENOUS	COMPLANATE
TRICHOLOGY	BLACKSMITH	GALLIAMBIC	SAPPERMENT	BABYLONIAN	COMPOUNDED
TRISKELION	BRESSUMMER	GETHSEMANE	SCARCEMENT	BACCHANTES	CONCERNING
TRIVIALITY	BRIDESMAID	GOVERNMENT	SCHOOLMAAM	BACKHANDED	CONCINNITY
TRIVIALIZE	BUCKJUMPER	GUACHAMOLE	SECONDMENT	BACKHANDER	CONCINNOUS
TROCTOLITE	BUTTERMERE	HANDSOMELY	SETTLEMENT	BAHRAINIAN	CONFOUNDED
TUTIVILLUS	BUTTERMILK	HARASSMENT	SHAGGYMANE	BALIBUNTAL	CONSTANTAN
UNAVAILING	CANTONMENT	HOMECOMING	SHOWJUMPER	BALLOONING	CONSTANTIA
UNDERCLASS	CARTHAMINE	HORNRIMMED	STALAGMITE	BALLOONIST	CONSTANTLY
UNDERFLOOR	CATAWAMPUS	IMPAIRMENT	SUPPLEMENT	BARASINGHA	COORDINATE
UNDERSLUNG	CECIDOMYIA	IMPEDIMENT	SURINAMESE	BARGAINING	COPPERNOSE
UNEQUALLED	CINECAMERA	INCITEMENT	SYMPTOMIZE	BARRENNESS	COROMANDEL
UNFAMILIAR	COMMITMENT	INDAPAMIDE	SYNONYMOUS	BASSOONIST	CORYBANTES
UNHERALDED	COMPLEMENT	INDICTMENT	SYNTAGMATA	BITTERNESS	CORYBANTIC
UNLADYLIKE	COMPLIMENT	INDITEMENT	TAILORMADE	BITUMINOUS	COSTLINESS
UNRESOLVED	COMPROMISE	INDUCEMENT	TAPOTEMENT	BLACKENING	COVENANTER
UNRIVALLED	CONFORMIST	INFEFTMENT	TAXONOMIST	BLUEBONNET	CRAFTINESS
UNSETTLING	CONFORMITY	INSTALMENT	THINGUMBOB	BLUEMANTLE	CRISPINIAN
UNUNNILIUM	CONSUMMATE	INSTRUMENT	TORQUEMADA	BOOKBINDER	CRYOGENICS
UPPERCLASS	DEBASEMENT	INTEGUMENT	TOURNAMENT	BOTTLENECK	CUSSEDNESS
VERMILLION	DEBATEMENT	INTENDMENT	TRENCHMORE	BOURIGNIAN	DEADLINESS

DELPHINIUM	FULLLENGTH	LEFTHANDER	PASQUINADE	SEDATENESS	TRICLINIUM
DERACINATE	GADOLINIUM	LEFTWINGER	PASSIONATE	SEPTENNIAL	TROCHANTER
DESALINATE	GANGRENOUS	LEGUMINOUS	PATAGONIAN	SHABBINESS	TROMBONIST
DIAPHANOUS	GASCONNADE	LENOCINIUM	PATAVINITY	SHELDONIAN	TROPHONIUS
DICTIONARY	GASTRONOME	LESBIANISM	PATCHINESS	SHIFTINESS	TURTLENECK
DILIGENTLY	GASTRONOMY	LIBIDINOUS	PATHFINDER	SHOCKINGLY	UBERMENSCH
DIOPHANTOS	GELATINOUS	LIEUTENANT	PEDIMENTAL	SHODDINESS	UBIQUINONE
DIRECTNESS	GENTLENESS	LIGHTINGUP	PENSIONNAT	SHORTENING	UNACCENTED
DISCERNING	GETUPANDGO	LIKEMINDED	PERIWINKLE	SHOVELNOSE	UNATTENDED
DISCONNECT	GLASSINESS	LIMBERNECK	PERSIENNES	SHREWDNESS	UNBALANCED
DISDAINFUL	GLAUCONITE	LITHUANIAN	PETULANTLY	SHRILLNESS	UNDEFENDED
DISGRUNTLE	GLISTENING	LITTLENESS	PHAELONIAN	SIDEWINDER	UNEASINESS
DISJOINTED	GLOSSINESS	LIVELINESS	PICAYUNISH	SINFULNESS	UNEVENNESS
DISTRINGAS	GLUTTONOUS	LONELINESS	PLEASANTLY	SINGLENESS	UNFRIENDLY
DITHIONATE	GOLDFINGER	LORDLINESS	PLEASANTRY	SLEEPINESS	UNGROUNDED
DODECANESE	GREEDINESS	LOVELINESS	POCAHONTAS	SLOPPINESS	UNIQUENESS
DOGGEDNESS	GRITTINESS	LUSITANIAN	POCKMANTIE	SMARMINESS	UNLICENSED
DRAWCANSIR	GRUBBINESS	MACEDONIAN	POIGNANTLY	SMOOTHNESS	UNROMANTIC
DREAMINESS	GRUMPINESS	MAHAYANALI	POLITENESS	SNOOTINESS	UNRULINESS
DREARINESS	HEADHUNTED	MANCHINEEL	POMERANIAN	SOOTHINGLY	UNTIDINESS
DREIKANTER	HEADHUNTER	MARCIONITE	PORTIONIST	SORDIDNESS	USEFULNESS
DROWSINESS	HEARTINESS	MAVOURNEEN	PORTMANTLE	SPARSENESS	VEHEMENTLY
DRUZHINNIK	HELLBENDER	MEAGERNESS	PORTMANTUA	SPEEDINESS	VETERINARY
ECARDINATE	HESITANTLY	MEAGRENESS	PRAEMUNIRE	SPORTINGLY	VIEWFINDER
EFFEMINACY	HIGHBINDER	MELACONITE	PREEMINENT	SPRUCENESS	VIGILANTES
EFFEMINATE	HIGHHANDED	MELLOWNESS	PRETTINESS	STALLENGER	VILLAINOUS
ELEUSINIAN	HIGHLANDER	MEMBRANOUS	PROFOUNDLY	STALLINGER	VILLEINAGE
ELOQUENTLY	HOARSENESS	MEMORANDUM	PROMPTNESS	STATIONARY	VIRULENTLY
EMARGINATE	HOMELINESS	MENACINGLY	PRONOUNCED	STATIONERY	VOETGANGER
ENCOIGNURE	HOMOGENIZE	METACENTRE	PROPIONATE	STEADINESS	VOLUMINOUS
ENDOGENOUS	HOODWINKED	MIGHTINESS	PROSCENIUM	STEELINESS	VORAGINOUS
EPILIMNION	HOOTNANNIE	MILLENNIUM	PUMPHANDLE	STEMWINDER	WANCHANCIE
EPIPHONEMA	HORIZONTAL	MINUTENESS	PURITANISM	STEPHANITE	WAVELENGTH
EVENHANDED	HUMBLENESS	MISOGYNIST	PYRACANTHA	STEPHENSON	WESTERNIZE
EVITERNITY	HYPOGENOUS	MISSIONARY	PYROMANIAC	STICKINESS	WHARFINGER
EXEMPTNESS	HYPOTENUSE	MONOTONOUS	QUADRANGLE	STINGINESS	WHEEZINESS
EYEWITNESS	IGNORANTLY	MONTAGNARD	QUAINTNESS	STOCKINESS	WICKEDNESS
FALKLANDER	ILLUMINATE	MONUMENTAL	QUARRENDER	STRAMONIUM	WILDERNESS
FAULTINESS	ILLUMINATI	MORISONIAN	QUATERNARY	STRAPONTIN	WORTHINESS
FEEBLENESS	IMPOTENTLY	MOROSENESS	QUEASINESS	STRAVINSKY	ABOVEBOARD
FEMININITY	IMPREGNATE	MOSSBUNKER	RANDOMNESS	STRICTNESS	ACCUSTOMED
FESCENNINE	IMPUDENTLY	MOULDINESS	REFERENDUM	STRIDENTLY	ADDITIONAL
FICKLENESS	INCIDENTAL	MUMBLENEWS	REGIMENTAL	STRIKINGLY	ADIAPHORON
FIERCENESS	INDECENTLY	NARROWNESS	REGIMENTED	STROGANOFF	AFRORMOSIA
FILTHINESS	INDEFINITE	NEWSMONGER	REJUVENATE	STRYCHNINE	AFTERHOURS
FINGERNAIL	INDIGENOUS	NIMBLENESS	REMOTENESS	STUFFINESS	ALDERWOMAN
FISHMONGER	INDUMENTUM	NORTHANGER	REORGANIZE	STURDINESS	ALLOTROPIC
FLABBINESS	INGEMINATE	NUCLEONICS	RESUPINATE	SUDDENNESS	ALLYCHOLLY
FLAGRANTLY	INHERENTLY	OBEDIENTLY	RETRAINING	SULTRINESS	AMPHIGOURI
FLANCONADE	INHUMANITY	OBLIGINGLY	REVERENTLY	SUPPLENESS	AMPLEFORTH
FLASHINESS	INKSLINGER	OBTUSENESS	ROADRUNNER	SURROUNDED	ANASTROPHE
FLEETINGLY	INNOCENTLY	OCCIDENTAL	ROBUSTNESS	SUSTAINING	ANCHYLOSIS
FLESHINESS	INORDINATE	ODIOUSNESS	RUBBERNECK	SWEETENING	ANTIBIOTIC
FLIMSINESS	INSEMINATE	OLEAGINOUS	RUBIGINOUS	SWIMMINGLY	ANTIPHONAL
FLIPPANTLY	INSOLENTLY	OPENHANDED	RUDIMENTAL	SYMPHONIUM	ANTIPROTON
FLUFFINESS	INTENTNESS	OPENMINDED	RUGGEDNESS	TENDERNESS	APOSTROPHE
FOREFINGER	IRONMONGER	ORNAMENTAL	RUMINANTIA	TESCHENITE	APOTHEOSIS
FORERUNNER	JAMESONITE	OROBRANCHE	RUSSIANIZE	THEREANENT	ASBESTOSIS
FRAGMENTAL	JAUNTINESS	ORTHOPNOEA	SACREDNESS	THICKENING	ASTROLOGER
FRATERNISE	JOHNSONIAN	OUVIRANDRA	SALAMANDER	THOUSANDTH	ASTRONOMER
FRATERNITY	JUBILANTLY	OVERLANDER	SANGUINARY	TIMELINESS	ATELEIOSIS
FRATERNIZE	JUGGERNAUT	PALAGONITE	SAVAGENESS	TIROCINIUM	AVERRHOISM
FREEHANDER	KILMARNOCK	PALATINATE	SCANTINESS	TOLERANTLY	BACKBLOCKS
FREELANCER	KINCHINLAY	PALFRENIER	SCARCENESS	TORBERNITE	BACKGROUND
FREQUENTED	KINDLINESS	PALISANDER	SCOFFINGLY	TOUCHANDGO	BAGASSOSIS
FREQUENTER	LANTHANIDE	PANAMANIAN	SCORZONERA	TOUCHINESS	BARBAROSSA
FREQUENTLY	LASTMINUTE	PAPERKNIFE	SCRUTINEER	TRENDINESS	BARCAROLLE
FRISKINESS	LAVISHNESS	PARAGONITE	SCRUTINISE	TRIACONTER	BAREFOOTED
FULIGINOUS	LEFTHANDED	PARTHENOPE	SCRUTINIZE	TRICKINESS	BARRACOOTA

BARRACOUTA	ENDOSMOSIS	LUXEMBOURG	ROWDYDOWDY	VALLADOLID	FROGHOPPER
BEHAVIORAL	EPISTROPHE	LYSENKOISM	SACERDOTAL	VILLANOVAN	GEOGRAPHER
BELLADONNA	ESCHAROTIC	MALAPROPOS	SALESWOMAN	VOCATIONAL	GEOGRAPHIC
BELLAMOURE	ESCRITOIRE	MASKANONGE	SALVADORAN	WAINSCOTED	GEOTROPISM
BLACKBOARD	FAIRGROUND	MASKINONGE	SANDGROPER	WALLFLOWER	GYMNOSPERM
BLOCKHOUSE	FIELDMOUSE	MASKIROVKA	SARCOCOLLA	WANDSWORTH	HELICOPTER
BLOODHOUND	FIRTHSOKEN	METROPOLIS	SCARAMOUCH	WATCHTOWER	HELLESPONT
BOBBYSOXER	FLAPDOODLE	MONOPHONIC	SCOREBOARD	WATERBORNE	HOMOEOPATH
BONDSWOMAN	FLASHPOINT	MYSTAGOGUE	SCOTSWOMAN	WATERCOLOR	INNERSPACE
BOUILLOTTE	FLOORBOARD	MYSTAGOGUS	SERVOMOTOR	WATERWORKS	INTROSPECT
BRACHIOPOD	FLUTEMOUTH	NECROPOLIS	SHAMPOOING	WELSHWOMAN	KIDNAPPING
BRAINPOWER	FOREGROUND	NEIGHBORLY	SKATEBOARD	WHEELHOUSE	KRIEGSPIEL
BRASSBOUND	FRACTIONAL	NOBLEWOMAN	SKEUOMORPH	WIDDICOMBE	LEAFHOPPER
BRICKWORKS	FRAUNHOFER	NORTHBOUND	SNAKEMOUTH	WINDFLOWER	LYCHNAPSIA
BYSSINOSIS	FREEBOOTER	NOSOPHOBIA	SNOWBLOWER	WORDSWORTH	MASCARPONE
CALCEDONIO	FRITHSOKEN	NYCTALOPIA	SOGDOLOGER	WORKAHOLIC	MEADOWPLAN
CALCITONIN	FRONTCOURT	OBSIDIONAL	SOPHOMORIC	WRAPAROUND	METALEPSIS
CANEPHORUS	FUNCTIONAL	OCCASIONAL	SOUTHBOUND	WRONGDOING	MIDSHIPMAN
CANTALOUPE	GASTEROPOD	OCEANGOING	SPELLBOUND	XENOPHOBIA	MISOCAPNIC
CAPERNOITY	GLASSHOUSE	ORTHOGONAL	SPONSIONAL	XENOPHOBIC	MUDSKIPPER
CARCINOGEN	GLASSWORKS	OSMIDROSIS	STAGECOACH	XEROSTOMIA	NATUROPATH
CEPHALOPOD	GOLDILOCKS	OSTEOCOLLA	STANDPOINT	YARBOROUGH	NEUTROPHIL
CHAIRWOMAN	GONFANONER	OSTROGOTHS	STEAKHOUSE	ACHITOPHEL	NEWSPAPERS
CHECKPOINT	GRASSROOTS	OXYMORONIC	STEELWORKS	AHITHOPHEL	NINCOMPOOP
CHERIMOYER	GREENHOUSE	PALMATOZOA	STOMATOPOD	ALLPURPOSE	OVERSUPPLY
CHESSBOARD	GRIDIRONER	PANTALOONS	STOREHOUSE	AMBLYOPSIS	PENELOPHON
CHIRONOMIC	GUESTHOUSE	PARAGLOSSA	STRASBOURG	AMBOCEPTOR	PHILIPPINA
CHOLALOGUE	GYMNOSOPHY	PARAPHONIA	STRATIOTES	AMPELOPSIS	PHILIPPINE
CLAIRCOLLE	GYROSCOPIC	PARATROOPS	STRAWBOARD	ANGIOSPERM	PHILLIPINA
CLANSWOMAN	HATEENOUGH	PASTEBOARD	SUPERMODEL	ANTHROPOID	PHILLIPINE
COCKALORUM	HEADPHONES	PATCHCOCKE	SUPERPOWER	ANTICIPATE	PHLOGOPITE
CONCHIOLIN	HEMICHORDA	PAWNBROKER	SUPERSONIC	ANTISEPSIS	PLIOHIPPUS
CONEFLOWER	HEMOGLOBIN	PEASHOOTER	SUPERTONIC	ANTISEPTIC	PREDISPOSE
CORNFLOWER	HENCEFORTH	PENTAGONAL	SUPERWOMAN	APOCRYPHAL	PRESUPPOSE
CORNUCOPIA	HEPTAGONAL	PENTATONIC	SYNCHRONAL	APOPEMPTIC	PRINCIPIUM
CORROBOREE	HEREABOUTS	PERSEPOLIS	SYNCHRONIC	APOTROPAIC	PRINCIPLED
COURTHOUSE	HISTRIONIC	PESCADORES	SYNECDOCHE	ARIMASPIAN	PRINCIPLES
CROCKFORDS	HOBBYHORSE	PESTALOZZI	SYNOSTOSIS	ARISTIPPUS	PROSERPINA
CROSSBONES	HODGEPODGE	PETITIONER	SYNTHRONUS	BANKRUPTCY	PROSERPINE
CROSSROADS	HOLOPHOTAL	PHILOPOENA	TANTAMOUNT	BEEKEEPING	PSAMMOPHIL
CRYOPHORUS	HOMOPHOBIA	PHILOSOPHY	TELEPHONIC	BHADRAPADA	PSYCHOPATH
DECENNOVAL	HOMOPHOBIC	PHOLIDOSIS	TELESCOPIC	BIOGRAPHER	PSYCHOPOMP
DECOMPOSED	HOMOPHONIC	PHOSPHORUS	TERRACOTTA	BRIDLEPATH	RETROSPECT
DESBOROUGH	HORNBLOWER	PHYLLIOPOD	THERMIONIC	CAMELOPARD	RINDERPEST
DEVOTIONAL	HORSEPOWER	PHYTOTOXIN	THROMBOSIS	CASSIOPEIA	SCAPHOPODA
DIACHRONIC	HORSEWOMAN	PIANOFORTE	TOWNSWOMAN	CATALEPTIC	SCREENPLAY
DIPLODOCUS	HOTCHPOTCH	PLAYGROUND	TRANSPOSED	CHRYSIPPUS	SNOWCAPPED
DIRECTOIRE	HOUSEBOUND	PORTSMOUTH	TRANSPOSON	CIRRHOPODA	SPOILSPORT
DISAPPOINT	HYDROPONIC	POWERHOUSE	TRAVELOGUE	CLODHOPPER	SUBCOMPACT
DISCOBOLUS	HYPERBOLIC	PRESBYOPIA	TRILLIONTH	CORRESPOND	SUBTROPICS
DISCOLORED	ICHTHYOSIS	PRICKLOUSE	TRIPEHOUND	CUCKOOPINT	TABLESPOON
DISEMBOGUE	IMPERSONAL	PROTAGORAS	TRITANOPIA	DENDROPHIS	TEICHOPSIA
DISEMBOWEL	INDISPOSED	PROTANOPIA	TROPAEOLUM	DEVELOPING	TELIOSPORE
DISENNOBLE	INTERLOPER	PROTANOPIC	TURNAROUND	DISCOMPOSE	TRYPTOPHAN
DIVISIONAL	INTERNODAL	PTERANODON	ULTRASONIC	DISCREPANT	UNEXAMPLED
DOLICHOLIS	INTERWOVEN	PTERYGOTUS	ULTRASOUND	DISRESPECT	UNOCCUPIED
DOLICHOTUS	IRISHWOMAN	PYCNOGONID	UNCOMMONLY	DYSTROPHIC	UNPROMPTED
DOVERCOURT	IRISHWOMEN	PYROPHORUS	UNDERCOVER	ECTHLIPSIS	UNSCRIPTED
DREADLOCKS	IRRATIONAL	PYTHAGORAS	UNDERWORLD	ELACAMPANE	UNSLEEPING
DUTCHWOMAN	JACKBOOTED	QUESTIONER	UNDOCTORED	ELACAMPANE	VELOCIPEDE
EARTHWORKS	JACKSTONES	RAWINSONDE	UNEMPLOYED	EMANCIPATE	WAMPUMPEAG
ECCHYMOSIS	JAGUARONDI	RAWSTHORNE	UNEXPLORED	EPISCOPATE	WATERSPOUT
ECCOPROTIC	KENILWORTH	RECIPROCAL	UNFATHOMED	ESCULAPIAN	WINDOWPANE
ELECTROMER	KNIFEBOARD	REDISCOVER	UNFLAVORED	EUCALYPTOL	WITSNAPPER
ELECTRONIC	LAEOTROPIC	REPERTOIRE	UNORTHODOX	EUCALYPTUS	WORSHIPPER
EMBERGOOSE	LAUNDROMAT	RHEOTROPIC	UNPROVOKED	FINGERPICK	ZOOTHAPSIS
EMBONPOINT	LEDERHOSEN	RICHTHOFEN	UNREASONED	FRANGIPANE	LAMBREQUIN
EMMETROPIA	LIGHTHOUSE	ROUGHHOUSE	UNSCHOOLED	FRANGIPANI	SOUBRIQUET
ENANTIOSIS	LIMITROPHE	ROUNDHOUSE	UNSEASONED		TOURNIQUET

ACCELERATE	CHESTERTON	FITZGERALD	INDUSTRIAL	MORATORIUM	PORNOCRACY
ACROTERION	CHILDERMAS	FLAMEPROOF	INFILTRATE	MORIGEROUS	POSTMORTEM
ADRENERGIC	CHIMBORAZO	FLATTERING	INGENERATE	MOUCHARABY	POSTSCRIPT
ADULTERANT	CHINAGRAPH	FLAVOURING	INSECURELY	MOUSTERIAN	POURPARLER
ADULTERATE	CHITARRONE	FLICKERING	INSECURITY	MOUTHORGAN	PRAETORIAN
ADULTERESS	CHIVALROUS	FLINDERSIA	INSULARITY	MULIEBRITY	PRAETORIUM
ADULTERINE	CLAMOURING	FORBEARING	INTEMERATE	MULLIGRUBS	PRESSURIZE
ADULTEROUS	CLUMPERTON	FOREWARNED	INTENERATE	NATATORIAL	PROSPERINA
ALECTORIAN	COCKATRICE	FOURIERISM	INTERBREED	NATATORIUM	PROSPERITY
AMATEURISH	COLDSTREAM	FREEMARTIN	INTERTRIGO	NEFANDROUS	PROSPEROUS
AMELIORATE	COMPATRIOT	FULLYGROWN	INTOLERANT	NESSELRODE	PSALTERIUM
AMPHIBRACH	CONCURRENT	GAINSTRIVE	INTRAURBAN	NETTLERASH	PUNCHDRUNK
AMPHITRITE	CONIFEROUS	GALSWORTHY	INVETERATE	NEWSWORTHY	PUNDIGRION
AMPHITRYON	CONQUERING	GARNIERITE	INVIGORATE	NIGHTDRESS	PYRAGYRITE
ANACHARSIS	CONSECRATE	GEOTHERMAL	IRREVERENT	NORTHERNER	QUADRIREME
ANEMOGRAPH	CONSPIRACY	GERIATRICS	ISOMETRICS	NOTEWORTHY	QUARTERING
ANTIBARBUS	CONTRARILY	GIRDLERINK	JACKSTRAWS	OBLITERATE	QUARTEROON
AQUAFORTIS	CORDIERITE	GLAMOURISE	JOCULARITY	OBSTETRICS	QUERSPRUNG
AQUAMARINE	COTTIERISM	GLITTERAND	KESSELRING	OCEANARIUM	RADIOGRAPH
ARCHITRAVE	COUNTERACT	GLITTERATI	KEYBOARDER	OCHLOCRACY	REASSURING
ARSMETRICK	CRISPBREAD	GLITTERING	KNOBKERRIE	OMNIVOROUS	RECUPERATE
ARTOCARPUS	CRISSCROSS	GOLDTHREAD	KRUGERRAND	OMOPHORION	REDCURRANT
ASSEVERATE	CROSSBREED	GRAMMARIAN	LACUSTRINE	OPOTHERAPY	REDECORATE
ATRACURIUM	CURMURRING	GRANGERISM	LANGUOROUS	OPPROBRIUM	REGENERATE
AUDITORIUM	DECELERATE	GRANGERIZE	LANIGEROUS	ORDINARILY	REGULARITY
AURIFEROUS	DECOLORATE	GRAPEFRUIT	LEBENSRAUM	ORPHEOREON	REGULARIZE
AUTOSTRADA	DECOLORIZE	GUARNERIUS	LIGHTERMAN	OSMETERIUM	REMUNERATE
AVANTURINE	DEFLAGRATE	HAIRSPRING	LITHOGRAPH	OUTPOURING	REREDORTER
AVENTURINE	DEGENERACY	HAKENKREUZ	LOCKERROOM	OVERSPREAD	RESTAURANT
BACKSTROKE	DEGENERATE	HALLMARKED	LUMINARIST	OVERSTRAIN	RETROGRADE
BALUSTRADE	DELIBERATE	HANDICRAFT	LUTESTRING	OVERSTRUNG	RETROGRESS
BEARGARDEN	DEMOGORGON	HANDSPRING	MAGISTRACY	OVERWORKED	RHINEGRAVE
BEEFBURGER	DENTIFRICE	HANOVERIAN	MAGISTRAND	PAINTBRUSH	RIPSNORTER
BENZEDRINE	DESIDERATA	HAUSTORIUM	MAGISTRATE	PALESTRINA	ROADWORTHY
BILIVERDIN	DESPAIRING	HEADSTRONG	MAINPERNOR	PALINDROME	ROISTERING
BLEPHARISM	DICTOGRAPH	HEARTBREAK	MAINSPRING	PALUSTRINE	RUPESTRIAN
BLISTERING	DIGITORIUM	HELIOGRAPH	MAINSTREAM	PANTAGRUEL	SACCHARASE
BLITHERING	DISAPPROVE	HELIOTROPE	MALODOROUS	PANTOGRAPH	SACCHARIDE
BLITZKRIEG	DISASTROUS	HILDEBRAND	MANAGERESS	PAPAVERINE	SACCHARINE
BLUETHROAT	DISCOURAGE	HIPPOCRENE	MANAGERIAL	PARAMARIBO	SACCHAROID
BLUNDERING	DISHEARTEN	HIPPODROME	MANICURIST	PARANORMAL	SALICORNIA
BOISTEROUS	DONNYBROOK	HIPPOGRIFF	MANUSCRIPT	PARAPHRASE	SALTIGRADE
BOOKMARKER	DOPPLERITE	HIPPOGRYPH	MARGUERITE	PASTEURISE	SAMOTHRACE
BOWDLERISE	DOWNMARKET	HOLOFERNES	MASQUERADE	PASTEURIZE	SANATORIUM
BOWDLERIZE	DOWNSTREAM	HOMEWORKER	MATRIARCHY	PATRIARCHY	SANITARIUM
BREADFRUIT	DRAGONROOT	HONORARIUM	MEANDERING	PEACHERINO	SATYAGRAHA
BRIDEGROOM	DRAWSTRING	HORSEDRAWN	MEDIOCRITY	PEDESTRIAN	SAUERKRAUT
BURGLARIZE	DUUMVIRATE	HOUSECRAFT	MEITNERIUM	PEDIATRICS	SAVONAROLA
BUTCHERING	ECUADORIAN	HOUSEPROUD	METACARPAL	PEELGARLIC	SCANDAROON
CADAVEROUS	EDULCORATE	HOVERCRAFT	METACARPUS	PENSIEROSO	SCANDERBEG
CALAVERITE	EFFLEURAGE	HYPOCORISM	METAPHRASE	PERMAFROST	SCAPEGRACE
CALIFORNIA	ELECTORATE	HYPODERMIC	METATARSAL	PERPETRATE	SCATTERING
CALYPTRATE	ENGENDRURE	IGNIMBRITE	METATARSUS	PHONOGRAPH	SCOOTERIST
CANTABRIAN	ENTERPRISE	ILLITERACY	METHEDRINE	PHOTOGRAPH	SCULPTRESS
CANTATRICE	EPIDIORITE	ILLITERATE	MILITARISM	PICTOGRAPH	SEAMSTRESS
CATAPHRACT	EQUATORIAL	ILLUSTRATE	MILITARIST	PIONEERING	SECONDRATE
CATEGORISE	EQUESTRIAN	IMMATERIAL	MIMEOGRAPH	PLAGIARISE	SECULARIZE
CATEGORIZE	EUCHLORINE	IMMATURITY	MINESTRONE	PLAGIARISM	SEMICIRCLE
CAVICORNIA	EUHEMERISM	IMMEMORIAL	MINEWORKER	PLAGIARIST	SENATORIAL
CENTIGRADE	EVISCERATE	IMMODERATE	MINIMARKET	PLAGIARIZE	SHATTERING
CERTIORARI	EXAGGERATE	IMPOVERISH	MINISTRATE	PLUNDERING	SHIELDRAKE
CHAFFERING	EXASPERATE	INACCURACY	MINISTROKE	PLUTOCRACY	SHIMMERING
CHAMAEROPS	EXENTERATE	INACCURATE	MOISTURIZE	POCKMARKED	SHOCKPROOF
CHAMBERPOT	EXHILARATE	INAUGURATE	MONANDROUS	POLYCHREST	SHOESTRING
CHAMBERTIN	EXOTHERMIC	INCAPARINA	MONETARISM	POLYCHROME	SHORTBREAD
CHATTERBOX	FALSETRUTH	INCINERATE	MONETARIST	POLYMERIZE	SHUDDERING
CHATTERTON	FEATHERBED	INCOHERENT	MONOCARPIC	PONTEFRACT	SIMILARITY
CHAUCERIAN	FILLIBRUSH	INDECOROUS	MONOCHROME	POPULARITY	SINOATRIAL
CHAUDFROID	FIREWARDEN	INDISCREET	MONTSERRAT	POPULARIZE	SLAMMERKIN

SLANDEROUS	UNRESERVED	CHURLISHLY	FATALISTIC	METTLESOME	RINGMASTER
SLATTERNLY	UNSALARIED	CIRCASSIAN	FEARLESSLY	MISPRISION	ROBERDSMAN
SLIPSTREAM	VEGETARIAN	COLCHESTER	FELLOWSHIP	MONEGASQUE	ROBERTSMAN
SLUMBERING	VERTEBRATE	COLLAPSING	FEVERISHLY	MONTESSORI	ROLANDSECK
SMATTERING	VICEGERENT	COMMISSARY	FIENDISHLY	NARCISSISM	ROMANESQUE
SMITHEREEN	VINEGARISH	COMMISSION	FILIBUSTER	NEWSCASTER	RUMBLOSSOM
SNIGGERING	VITUPERATE	COMMISSURE	FLOURISHED	NIHILISTIC	RUTHLESSLY
SOLIDARITY	VIVIPAROUS	COMPASSION	FORECASTER	NONPLUSSED	SAUROPSIDA
SOMBRERITE	VOCIFERATE	COMPENSATE	FORECASTLE	OPPRESSION	SCHOLASTIC
SONGSTRESS	VOCIFEROUS	COMPRESSED	FORTISSIMO	OPPRESSIVE	SEAMANSHIP
SOUNDPROOF	WAGEEARNER	COMPRESSOR	FRANCISCAN	OPTIMISTIC	SEXAGESIMA
SOUNDTRACK	WATERBRASH	COMPULSION	FREEMASONS	PAINLESSLY	SHEEPISHLY
SOUTERRAIN	WATERCRESS	COMPULSIVE	FRIENDSHIP	PALIMPSEST	SIDEROSTAT
SOUTHERNER	WATERFRONT	COMPULSORY	FROLICSOME	PALMERSTON	SILVERSIDE
SPACECRAFT	WATERPROOF	CONCESSION	FUTURISTIC	PARNASSIAN	SILVERSKIN
SPEAKERINE	WEATHERMAN	CONCLUSION	GENEROSITY	PEAUDESOIE	SIMPLISTIC
SPENCERIAN	WELLEARNED	CONCLUSIVE	GEOPHYSICS	PERCUSSION	SLUGGISHLY
SPENSERIAN	WELLSPRING	CONCUSSION	GINGERSNAP	PERMISSION	SPOTLESSLY
SPHALERITE	WHISPERING	CONFESSION	GLOUCESTER	PERMISSIVE	STATUESQUE
SPOONERISM	WHITTERICK	CONSENSION	GOLDENSEAL	PERQUISITE	STEPSISTER
STAGECRAFT	WIDESPREAD	CONVERSANT	GROUNDSMAN	PERSUASION	STOCHASTIC
STAGGERING	WINDSCREEN	CONVERSELY	HALFSISTER	PERSUASIVE	STRABISMUS
STAMMERING	WINDSURFER	CONVERSION	HALLOYSITE	PERVERSELY	STRATHSPEY
STATECRAFT	WITCHCRAFT	CONVULSION	HARDCASTLE	PERVERSION	SUBMERSION
STATOCRACY	WOODWORKER	CONVULSIVE	HEADMASTER	PERVERSITY	SUBMISSION
STENTORIAN	YELLOWROOT	COPPERSKIN	HEDONISTIC	PETRISSAGE	SUBMISSIVE
STERTEROUS	ZINCOGRAPH	CUDDLESOME	HEEDLESSLY	PHANTASIME	SUBVERSION
STERTOROUS	ZOLLVEREIN	CUIRASSIER	HELPLESSLY	PHANTASIST	SUBVERSIVE
STICHARION	ZOOTHERAPY	CUMBERSOME	HEPHAESTUS	PHLOGISTIC	SUCCESSFUL
STONEBRASH	ZUMBOORUCK	DEALERSHIP	HOMEOUSIAN	PHLOGISTON	SUCCESSION
STOREFRONT	ZWITTERION	DECLENSION	HOMOOUSIAN	PHRENESIAC	SUCCESSIVE
STOUTHRIEF	ABSCISSION	DEPRESSANT	HOPELESSLY	PIANISSIMO	SUNGLASSES
STRONGROOM	ADMINISTER	DEPRESSING	HUMANISTIC	PICARESQUE	SUPPRESSED
STUBBORNLY	AGGRESSION	DEPRESSION	HUMIDISTAT	PILLOWSLIP	SUPPRESSOR
SUDATORIUM	AGGRESSIVE	DEPRESSIVE	HUMORESQUE	PIPSISSEWA	SURPASSING
SULPHUROUS	ALPHONSINE	DIACAUSTIC	IDEALISTIC	PLEONASTIC	SURPRISING
SWAGGERING	ALTRUISTIC	DIAGNOSTIC	IMPRESSION	PLESIOSAUR	SUSPENSION
SWEETBREAD	ANACLASTIC	DICKCISSEL	IMPRESSIVE	PLUMASSIER	SYNTHESIZE
SWEETBRIAR	ANACOUSTIC	DIGRESSION	INARTISTIC	POLYNESIAN	TACTLESSLY
SWELTERING	ANACRUSTIC	DIMINISHED	INCRASSATE	POSSESSION	TASKMASTER
TACHOGRAPH	ANDALUSIAN	DISCLOSURE	INCREASING	POSSESSIVE	TATTERSALL
TAGLIARINI	ANDALUSITE	DISCURSIVE	INDECISION	POSTMASTER	TELEVISION
TALLEYRAND	ANTIMASQUE	DISCUSSING	INDECISIVE	PRECURSORY	THALASSIAN
TAMBOURINE	APOLAUSTIC	DISCUSSION	INDONESIAN	PREDNISONE	THAUMASITE
TARDIGRADE	ARCHBISHOP	DISHWASHER	INSPISSATE	PREHENSILE	THELLUSSON
TELPHERAGE	ASPIDISTRA	DISMISSIVE	INTERESTED	PREPENSELY	THERMISTOR
TEPIDARIUM	ASTONISHED	DISPENSARY	JINGOISTIC	PREPOSSESS	THERMOSTAT
TERTIARIES	ATHANASIAN	DISPENSING	JUGENDSTIL	PRETENSION	TIRELESSLY
THIXOTROPY	AUTHORSHIP	DISPERSION	KINGFISHER	PROCESSING	TONGUESTER
THUNDERBOX	BANDMASTER	DISPOSSESS	KOEKSISTER	PROCESSION	TRANSISTOR
THUNDERING	BARCHESTER	DISSENSION	LACKLUSTER	PROCRUSTES	TRESPASSER
THUNDEROUS	BATTLESHIP	DISSUASION	LACKLUSTRE	PROFESSION	UNDIGESTED
TIMESERVER	BEAVERSKIN	DISTENSION	LAUNCESTON	PROGESSION	UNFINISHED
TOILETRIES	BELARUSIAN	DISTRESSED	LEADERSHIP	PROMISSORY	UNFORESEEN
TOOTHBRUSH	BIOPHYSICS	DOCIMASTIC	LEGALISTIC	PROPENSITY	UNIVERSITY
TRAITOROUS	BLOTTESQUE	DREARISOME	LINGUISTIC	PROPULSION	UNPLEASANT
TRANSCRIBE	BOTHERSOME	DUNIWASSAL	LISTLESSLY	PROTRUSILE	VARICOSITY
TRANSCRIPT	BURDENSOME	DYSCRASITE	LUMINOSITY	PROTRUSION	VERNISSAGE
TRANSGRESS	CACOMISTLE	DYSPROSIUM	MADAGASCAN	QUIZMASTER	VIRTUOSITY
TRINACRIAN	CANVASSING	ENCLOISTER	MADAGASCAR	READERSHIP	WALDENSIAN
TYPESCRIPT	CAPODASTRO	ENGROSSING	MAKESYSTEM	RECKLESSLY	WAPPENSHAW
UNDERCRAFT	CARELESSLY	EPIPLASTRA	MALTHUSIAN	REGRESSION	WINCHESTER
UNDERCROFT	CARNASSIAL	EPISPASTIC	MANCHESTER	REGRESSIVE	WINDOWSILL
UNDERWRITE	CARTHUSIAN	EULOGISTIC	MANIFESTLY	REPRESSION	YGGDRASILL
UNDESCRIED	CENSORSHIP	EUPHROSYNE	MAUPASSANT	REPRESSIVE	ABDICATION
UNDESERVED	CENTROSOME	EXPRESSION	MEDDLESOME	REQUIESCAT	ABERRATION
UNDETERRED	CHICHESTER	EXPRESSIVE	MEGALOSAUR	RESPONSIVE	ABROGATION
UNINFORMED	CHILDISHLY	EXPRESSMAN	MELANESIAN	RESTLESSLY	ABSOLUTELY
UNOBSERVED	CHROMOSOME	EXPRESSWAY	MEMBERSHIP	RHAMPASTOS	ABSOLUTION

ABSOLUTISM	AUTOMATION	CONCEPTION	DEPOSITARY	EXPEDITION	IMPURITIES
ABSORPTION	AUTOMATIZE	CONCEPTUAL	DEPOSITION	EXPIRATION	IMPUTATION
ABSTENTION	AUTOMOTIVE	CONCERTINA	DEPOSITORY	EXPOSITION	INAPTITUDE
ACCOUNTANT	BABYSITTER	CONCOCTION	DEPUTATION	EXPOSITORY	INCHOATIVE
ACCOUNTING	BACKBITING	CONCRETION	DERIVATION	EXTINCTION	INCONSTANT
ACCUBATION	BALLISTICS	CONDOTTIER	DERIVATIVE	EXTRACTION	INCUBATION
ACCURATELY	BALLISTITE	CONDUCTING	DEROGATORY	EXULTATION	INDEXATION
ACCUSATION	BALNEATION	CONDUCTION	DESOLATION	FACILITATE	INDICATION
ACCUSATIVE	BAROMETRIC	CONFECTION	DESSIATINE	FACILITIES	INDICATIVE
ACOLOUTHOS	BEDCLOTHES	CONGESTION	DESSYATINE	FALDISTORY	INEPTITUDE
ACROBATICS	BEEFEATERS	CONJECTURE	DETONATION	FANTASTICO	INFIGHTING
ACTIVITIST	BELLWETHER	CONNECTING	DETRACTION	FASCIATION	INFINITELY
ADAMANTINE	BERMOOTHES	CONNECTION	DEVOLUTION	FATALITIES	INFINITIVE
ADAPTATION	BIORHYTHMS	CONNECTIVE	DIALECTICS	FAVORITISM	INFLECTION
ADELANTADO	BISSEXTILE	CONNIPTION	DIELECTRIC	FEDERATION	INFLICTION
ADEQUATELY	BLACKSTONE	CONSISTENT	DILATATION	FELICITATE	INFRACTION
ADHIBITION	BLOODSTAIN	CONSISTORY	DIMINUTION	FELICITOUS	INHABITANT
ADMIRATION	BLOODSTOCK	CONSORTIUM	DIMINUTIVE	FIGURATION	INHALATION
ADMONITION	BLOODSTONE	CONSTITUTE	DINNERTIME	FIGURATIVE	INHIBITING
AEROBATICS	BLUEBOTTLE	CONSUETUDE	DIREMPTION	FILTRATION	INHIBITION
AESTHETICS	BRAINSTORM	CONSULTANT	DISBURTHEN	FLIRTATION	INHIBITORY
AFFLICTION	BRIDGETOWN	CONSULTING	DISCONTENT	FLORENTINE	INIQUITOUS
AGAPANTHUS	BRIGANTINE	CONTENTION	DISCRETION	FOREBITTER	INITIATION
AGONISTICS	BROOMSTICK	CONTESTANT	DISGUSTING	FOREFATHER	INITIATIVE
ALIENATION	BROWNSTONE	CONTEXTUAL	DISMANTLED	FOREGATHER	INJUNCTION
ALIMENTARY	BYELECTION	CONTORTION	DISRUPTION	FORFAITING	INNOVATION
ALLEGATION	CAESPITOSE	CONTRITION	DISRUPTIVE	FORFEITURE	INNOVATIVE
ALLIGATION	CALAMITOUS	CONVECTION	DISSECTION	FORTUITOUS	INSANITARY
ALLOCATION	CALLIATURE	CONVENTION	DISSENTING	FOUNDATION	INSPECTION
ALLOCUTION	CAMPESTRAL	CONVENTUAL	DISSERTATE	FOXHUNTING	INSULATION
ALPENSTOCK	CANECUTTER	CONVICTION	DISTORTION	FREIGHTAGE	INTERSTATE
ALTERATION	CAPACITATE	COPESETTIC	DIVINATION	FROMANTEEL	INTERSTICE
ALTOGETHER	CAPITATION	COPULATION	DOMINATING	FUMIGATION	INTIMATELY
AMBLYSTOMA	CARICATURA	COQUETTISH	DOMINATION	GALIMATIAS	INTIMATION
AMBULATORY	CARICATURE	CORONATION	DOUBLETALK	GARGANTUAN	INTINCTION
AMMUNITION	CARPENTIER	CORRECTING	DRAKESTONE	GEMINATION	INTONATION
AMPHICTYON	CASTRATION	CORRECTION	DYNAMITARD	GENERATION	INUNDATION
AMPUTATION	CHARIOTEER	CORRECTIVE	EFFRONTERY	GENERATRIX	INVITATION
AMRITATTVA	CHEVROTAIN	CORRUPTING	EGOCENTRIC	GEOCENTRIC	INVOCATION
ANABAPTIST	CHINASTONE	CORRUPTION	EGURGITATE	GEORGETOWN	INVOLUTION
ANCIPITOUS	CHIROPTERA	COTTONTAIL	ELEMENTARY	GILBERTIAN	IRRIGATION
ANGWANTIBO	CHREMATIST	CRAQUETURE	ELONGATION	GILBERTINE	IRRITATING
ANHELATION	CIRCUITOUS	CREDENTIAL	EMACIATION	GLACIATION	IRRITATION
ANNEXATION	CISLEITHAN	CRICKETING	EMENDATION	GRADUATION	JACULATION
ANNOTATION	CISPONTINE	CULVERTAGE	EMIGRATION	GRANDSTAND	JUBILATION
ANTARCTICA	CLEARSTORY	CUMULATIVE	EMPLASTRUM	GRATUITOUS	JUDICATURE
ANTICHTHON	CLEMENTINE	CURVETTING	ENCHANTING	GRAVESTONE	KHIDMUTGAR
ANTIMATTER	CLERESTORY	CYCLOSTYLE	ENTREATING	GREENSTICK	KILOMETRES
APEMANTHUS	CLINGSTONE	DEADNETTLE	EPICANTHUS	GREENSTONE	KUOMINTANG
APICULTURE	COADJUTANT	DEBILITATE	EPIGLOTTIS	GRINDSTONE	KURDAITCHA
APPARITION	COEXISTENT	DECAPITATE	EQUITATION	GUARANTEED	LABORATORY
APPETITIVE	COGITATION	DECORATION	ERUCTATION	GUILLOTINE	LACERATION
APPOSITION	COLBERTINE	DECORATIVE	ERYMANTHUS	GYMNASTICS	LAMINATION
APPRENTICE	COLEOPTERA	DEDICATION	ESCALATION	HABILITATE	LAURENTIAN
ARACOSTYLE	COLLECTING	DEFAMATION	ESTIMATION	HABITATION	LAURUSTINE
AREFACTION	COLLECTION	DEFAMATORY	ETHEOSTOMA	HACKBUTEER	LEVITATION
ARISTOTLES	COLLECTIVE	DEFECATION	EVACUATION	HACKMATACK	LIBERATION
ARMIPOTENT	COLORATION	DEFINITELY	EVALUATION	HAEMANTHUS	LIBRETTIST
ASAFOETIDA	COLORATURA	DEFINITION	EXACTITUDE	HALIEUTICS	LIMITATION
ASPHALTITE	COLPORTAGE	DEFINITIVE	EXALTATION	HARVESTMAN	LITERATURE
ASPIRATION	COLPORTEUR	DEFLECTION	EXCAVATION	HEREDITARY	LITHISTADA
ASSUMPTION	COMBUSTION	DELEGATION	EXECRATION	HESITATION	LITIGATION
ASSUMPTIVE	COMFORTING	DELICATELY	EXHALATION	HINDUSTANI	LOCOMOTION
ASTOMATOUS	COMMENTARY	DELIGATION	EXHAUSTING	HUMANITIES	LOCOMOTIVE
ASYMMETRIC	COMMENTATE	DELIGHTFUL	EXHAUSTION	IMMOLATION	LOGARITHMS
ASYNARTETE	COMMIXTURE	DELIRATION	EXHAUSTIVE	IMPENITENT	LUMPECTOMY
ATTRACTION	COMPLETELY	DEMOLITION	EXHIBITION	IMPERATIVE	MACKINTOSH
ATTRACTIVE	COMPLETION	DEPILATION	EXHUMATION	IMPOLITELY	MALCONTENT
AUTOCHTHON	CONCENTRIC	DEPILATORY	EXORBITANT	IMPOSITION	MANGOSTEEN

MARCANTANT	PERCENTILE	REFLECTING	SMOKESTACK	TRANSITIVE	CONTIGUOUS
MARQUETRIE	PERCEPTION	REFLECTION	SNAKESTONE	TRANSITORY	CONTINUANT
MASTECTOMY	PERCEPTIVE	REFLECTIVE	SOLICITOUS	TRAUMATIZE	CONTINUING
MATCHSTALK	PEREMPTORY	REFRACTION	SOLICITUDE	TRAVERTINE	CONTINUITY
MATCHSTICK	PERFECTION	REFRACTIVE	SPALLATION	TRECENTIST	CONTINUOUS
MATURATION	PERIDOTITE	REFRACTORY	SPECTATORS	TRIDENTINE	CONVOLUTED
MEDICATION	PERMEATION	REFUTATION	SPIRKETING	TRIPARTITE	COUSCOUSOU
MEDITATION	PERORATION	REGULATION	SPISSITUDE	TROCHOTRON	CURRICULUM
MEDITATIVE	PERSISTENT	RELAXATION	SPOLIATION	TURPENTINE	DELINQUENT
MEDIUMTERM	PHAENOTYPE	RELAXATIVE	SPOLIATIVE	TYPESETTER	DEPARTURES
MEGALITHIC	PHILISTINE	RELEGATION	SPRINGTAIL	UBIQUITOUS	DIASKEUAST
MELOCOTOON	PHLEBOTOMY	RELOCATION	SPRINGTIME	ULCERATION	DIDUNCULUS
MERCANTILE	PHLEGETHON	REMONETISE	STAGNATION	ULTIMATELY	DIFFICULTY
MESOLITHIC	PHYLACTERY	RENOVATION	STALACTITE	UNDERSTAND	DISFIGURED
MISFORTUNE	PINAKOTHEK	REPARATION	STANDSTILL	UNDERSTATE	DISTRAUGHT
MITIGATING	PITCHSTONE	REPETITEUR	STARVATION	UNDERSTEER	DOUBTFULLY
MITIGATION	PLANTATION	REPETITION	STATISTICS	UNDERSTOOD	DREADFULLY
MODERATELY	POETASTERY	REPETITIVE	STEPFATHER	UNDERSTUDY	EARTHQUAKE
MODERATION	POGONOTOMY	REPOSITORY	STEPMOTHER	UNDULATING	EFFECTUATE
MODULATION	POINSETTIA	REPUTATION	STEREOTOMY	UNDULATION	ENORMOUSLY
MONOLITHIC	POLIANTHES	RESOLUTELY	STEREOTYPE	UNEVENTFUL	ENRAPTURED
MORALITIES	POLYANTHUS	RESOLUTION	STEREOTYPY	UNFRUITFUL	ENSANGUINE
MOTIVATION	POPULATION	RESPECTFUL	STIGMATISE	UNINVITING	ERIOCAULON
MUTILATION	PORTENTOUS	RESPECTING	STIGMATIZE	UNPUNCTUAL	EXTINGUISH
NASTURTIUM	PRAGMATISM	RESPECTIVE	STILLSTAND	UPHOLSTERY	FABULOUSLY
NAUSEATING	PRAGMATIST	RESUMPTION	STRABOTOMY	USUCAPTION	FAITHFULLY
NAUSEATIVE	PRECAUTION	RETRACTION	STRELITZIA	USURPATION	FEARNOUGHT
NAVIGATION	PREDESTINE	RETREATING	STRENGTHEN	VALIDATION	FISTICUFFS
NEGLECTFUL	PREDICTION	REVELATION	STREPITANT	VEGETATION	FLORIBUNDA
NETTLETREE	PREHISTORY	REVOCATION	STREPITOSO	VELITATION	FONTICULUS
NEWSLETTER	PRELECTION	REVOLUTION	STYLISTICS	VENERATION	FOODSTUFFS
NIGHTSTICK	PRESBYTERY	RHEUMATICS	SUBJECTION	VINDICTIVE	FORCEFULLY
NOMINATION	PRESENTDAY	RHEUMATISM	SUBJECTIVE	VISITATION	FRUITFULLY
NOMINATIVE	PREVENTION	RHEUMATOID	SUBREPTION	VOLUTATION	FUDDYDUDDY
NONFICTION	PREVENTIVE	RHINESTONE	SUBROUTINE	WENTLETRAP	GENEROUSLY
NONVINTAGE	PRODUCTION	RHIPIPTERA	SUBSECTION	WHEATSTONE	GLORIOUSLY
NORBERTINE	PRODUCTIVE	RIGELATION	SUBSISTENT	WINTERTIME	GLYCOSURIA
NORTHSTEAD	PROJECTILE	RUBINSTEIN	SUBSTATION	ACCENTUATE	GOBEMOUCHE
NOURRITURE	PROJECTING	RUMINATION	SUBSTITUTE	ACETABULAR	GORGEOUSLY
NUMERATION	PROJECTION	RUMINATIVE	SUBVENTION	ACETABULUM	GRACEFULLY
OBLIGATION	PROMONTORY	SALIVATION	SUGGESTION	ADVENTURER	GRACIOUSLY
OBLIGATORY	PROPERTIUS	SALOPETTES	SUGGESTIVE	AFFETTUOSO	GRATEFULLY
OCCUPATION	PROPHETESS	SALUTATION	SUMMERTIME	ALGONQUIAN	HALFHOURLY
OFFPUTTING	PROPLITEAL	SANCTITIES	SUPERSTORE	ALLOSAURUS	HALLELUJAH
OMNIPOTENT	PROPORTION	SANCTITUDE	SUPPORTING	ALMSHOUSES	HOMUNCULUS
ONOMASTICS	PROSTITUTE	SANITATION	SUPPORTIVE	ANSCHAUUNG	HONEYBUNCH
OPPOSITION	PROTECTION	SARMENTOUS	SUSCEPTIVE	BABIROUSSA	HUMOROUSLY
ORCHESTRAL	PROTECTIVE	SATURATION	SWEEPSTAKE	BARBITURIC	HYPERDULIA
ORDINATION	PROTESTANT	SCARLATINA	SWORDSTICK	BARRAMUNDA	INADEQUACY
ORTHOPTICS	PRUDENTIAL	SCARLETINA	SYNCRETISE	BARRAMUNDI	INADEQUATE
OSCITATION	PSOCOPTERA	SCHALSTEIN	TABULATION	BETACRUCIS	INCESTUOUS
OSCULATION	QUADRATURA	SCORDATURA	TAILGATING	BLACKBULLY	INDENTURES
OSCULATORY	QUARANTINE	SECURITIES	TANGENTIAL	BLACKGUARD	INFREQUENT
OVEREATING	QUEENSTOWN	SELFESTEEM	TECHNETIUM	BLISSFULLY	INTRIGUING
OVERMATTER	QUERCITRON	SEPARATELY	TELEOSTOME	CASSUMUNAR	JAGUARUNDI
PACESETTER	RANDLETREE	SEPARATION	TELEPATHIC	CATACHUMEN	JERRYBUILT
PAEDIATRIC	RANNELTREE	SEPARATISM	TEMPTATION	CATECHUMEN	JOUYSAUCE
PAGINATION	RANNLETREE	SEPARATIST	TENNANTITE	CAUTIOUSLY	KOOKABURRA
PALAEOTYPE	RANTLETREE	SEPARATRIX	THALESTRIS	CHAULMUGRA	LANDLOUPER
PALAESTRAL	RAPPORTEUR	SEQUENTIAL	THALICTRUM	CHAUTAUQUA	LENTICULAR
PALLIATIVE	RATTLETRAP	SERPENTINE	THOUGHTFUL	CHEERFULLY	LIVERWURST
PANARITIUM	RAVENSTONE	SEXDUCTION	TICKERTAPE	CLOUDBURST	MAKUNOUCHI
PANCRATIUM	RAZZMATAZZ	SHROVETIDE	TOLERATION	COASTGUARD	MENSTRUATE
PARAMETRIC	RECITATION	SIDERATION	TORRENTIAL	COCKABULLY	MERCIFULLY
PARGETTING	RECITATIVE	SIMILITUDE	TOUCHSTONE	COLLIQUATE	METALLURGY
PATRIOTISM	RECITATIVO	SIMMENTHAL	TRAJECTORY	COLLOCUTER	MILLICURIE
PECULATION	RECREATION	SIMULATING	TRAMONTANA	COLLOQUIAL	MONTICULUS
PEJORATIVE	REDEMPTION	SIMULATION	TRAMONTANE	CONSEQUENT	MOSASAUROS
PERCENTAGE	REELECTION	SKUPSHTINA	TRANSITION	CONTIGUITY	MOURNFULLY

MUTINOUSLY	VOLUPTUOUS	JABBERWOCK	MAGNIFYING	ASPHYXIATE	COLPORTAGE
OTHERGUESS	WASTEFULLY	LENGTHWAYS	MISHNAYOTH	ASSEMBLAGE	COMMANDANT
OVERBOUGHT	WATCHFULLY	LENGTHWISE	MOTORCYCLE	ASSEVERATE	COMMENTARY
PANNICULUS	WRONGFULLY	MASTERWORT	NURSERYMAN	ASSIMILATE	COMMENTATE
PARTICULAR	ABERDEVINE	MOUDIEWART	PARAPHYSIS	AUTODIDACT	COMMISSARY
PEACEFULLY	ALMSGIVING	MOULDIWARP	PATRONYMIC	AUTOSTRADA	COMPENSATE
PENINSULAR	ANIMADVERT	NATIONWIDE	PETRIFYING	BALDERDASH	COMPLANATE
PERILOUSLY	BOLSHEVIST	NEEDLEWORK	PSILOCYBIN	BALUSTRADE	COMPLICATE
PERPETUATE	CIRCUMVENT	OFFTHEWALL	PUTREFYING	BASKETBALL	CONCERVATE
PERPETUITY	COMPLUVIUM	ORANGEWOOD	RAILWAYMAN	BATHYSCAPH	CONCILIATE
PERSECUTOR	CONCERVATE	OVERTHWART	SATISFYING	BEAUJOLAIS	CONCORDANT
PORTUGUESE	CONFERVOID	PADAREWSKI	SELFSTYLED	BEFOREHAND	CONFISCATE
PREVIOUSLY	CONTRAVENE	PALMERWORM	SHANDRYDAN	BEHINDHAND	CONGREGATE
PROCEDURAL	CONTROVERT	PEPPERWORT	STENOTYPER	BHADRAPADA	CONSECRATE
PROSCIUTTO	CONVOLVUTE	PLOUGHWISE	STUPEFYING	BICHROMATE	CONSPIRACY
PROSECUTOR	CREATIVITY	PUCKERWOOD	TANGANYIKA	BINOCULARS	CONSULTANT
QUAESTUARY	DEACTIVATE	RAIYATWARI	TERRIFYING	BINUCLEATE	CONSUMMATE
RACECOURSE	DECISIVELY	SANDALWOOD	TIMBERYARD	BIRTHPLACE	CONTESTANT
RANUNCULUS	DISSERVICE	SETTERWORT	TROTSKYITE	BLACKBEARD	CONTINUANT
RAVENOUSLY	DISSOLVENT	SILVERWARE	UNDERLYING	BLACKBOARD	CONTRABAND
RELINQUISH	DOSTOEVSKY	SNEEZEWOOD	UNEDIFYING	BLACKGUARD	CONVERSANT
REPRODUCER	EFFUSIVELY	SPIDERWORT	XEROPHYTIC	BLACKHEART	COORDINATE
RIGHTFULLY	EMISSIVITY	SPONGEWARE	YESTERYEAR	BLOODSTAIN	COTTONTAIL
RIGOROUSLY	FACESAVING	SPORTSWEAR	APPETIZING	BORDERLAND	COUNTERACT
SALMAGUNDI	FASTMOVING	STREETWISE	BAMBOOZLED	BRATISLAVA	CRANKSHAFT
SCORNFULLY	GAINGIVING	STRIDEWAYS	BARMITZVAH	BRIDESMAID	CRENELLATE
SCRIPTURAL	GILLRAVAGE	SWALLOWING	BELSHAZZAR	BRIDLEPATH	CROSSROADS
SCRIPTURES	GLENDOVEER	THREADWORM	CANCRIZANS	BUTTERBAKE	CRUIKSHANK
SEDULOUSLY	INACTIVITY	WATTLEWORK	CRYPTOZOIC	CACHINNATE	CULVERTAGE
SENSUOUSLY	INCISIVELY	WHILLYWHAW	DOWNSIZING	CALCEOLATE	CUMBERLAND
SHAMEFULLY	IRRELEVANT	WICKERWORK	ISONIAZIDE	CALUMNIATE	DEACTIVATE
SINARQUIST	MANSERVANT	WILDFOWLER	SCAMMOZZIS	CALYPTRATE	DEBILITATE
SKILLFULLY	NEGATIVELY	YELLOWWOOD	SCHWARZLOT	CAMELOPARD	DECAPITATE
SNAPHAUNCE	OBLOMOVISM	YESTERWEEK	TARTRAZINE	CAMOUFLAGE	DECELERATE
SNAPHAUNCH	POSITIVELY	ZIMBABWEAN		CANCRIZANS	DECOLORATE
SPECIOUSLY	POSITIVIST	COMPLEXION	**10:8**	CANNONBALL	DEFLAGRATE
SPIRACULUM	PROCLIVITY	COMPLEXITY	ABBREVIATE	CANTILLATE	DEGENERACY
SPIRITUOUS	PROTERVITY	HOMOSEXUAL	ABOVEBOARD	CANVASBACK	DEGENERATE
SPITEFULLY	PURSUIVANT	PARADOXIDE	ACCELERATE	CAPACITATE	DELIBERATE
SPURIOUSLY	REACTIVATE	PARADOXINE	ACCENTUATE	CAPITULARY	DEMODULATE
STONYHURST	RECIDIVISM	PERPLEXING	ACCOUNTANT	CAPITULATE	DEPOPULATE
STRUCTURAL	RECIDIVIST	PERPLEXITY	ACCUMULATE	CAPREOLATE	DEPOSITARY
STUDIOUSLY	RELATIVELY	PYRIDOXINE	ACROMEGALY	CASSIABARK	DEPRECIATE
SUBSEQUENT	RELATIVITY	UNUNHEXIUM	ADELANTADO	CATAPHRACT	DEPRESSANT
SUPERHUMAN	RENDEZVOUS	AGRAHAYANA	ADJUDICATE	CAUTIONARY	DERACINATE
TANNHAUSER	SKINDIVING	AMPUSSYAND	ADULTERANT	CELESTIALS	DEREGULATE
TASTEFULLY	TIMESAVING	APOCALYPSE	ADULTERATE	CELLOPHANE	DESALINATE
TATPURUSHA	UNSWERVING	ARCHETYPAL	AFICIONADO	CENTIGRADE	DESCENDANT
TESTICULAR	BAILIEWICK	CAVALRYMAN	AFTERIMAGE	CERTIORARI	DESIDERATA
THANKFULLY	BAILLIWICK	CHIMNEYPOT	AFTERSHAVE	CHALYBEATE	DESQUAMATE
THYSANURAN	BASKETWORK	CHURCHYARD	AGRAHAYANA	CHARGEHAND	DETRUNCATE
TOPSYTURVY	BRAZILWOOD	COUNTRYMAN	ALEMBICATE	CHAROLLAIS	DEUTOPLASM
TORTUOUSLY	BREASTWORK	EPIDIDYMUS	ALIMENTARY	CHEAPSKATE	DEVANAGARI
TRIANGULAR	BROADSWORD	EUROCLYDON	AMALGAMATE	CHEESECAKE	DHARMSHALA
TRIANGULUM	BUNDESWEHR	FAREPAYING	AMELIORATE	CHESSBOARD	DIASKEUAST
TRUSTFULLY	CAMBERWELL	FLAMBOYANT	AMPHIBRACH	CHEVROTAIN	DICHROMATE
TRUTHFULLY	CANDLEWICK	FLUNKEYDOM	AMPUSSYAND	CHIFFCHAFF	DICTIONARY
TUBERCULAR	CHEESEWOOD	FOUDROYANT	ANEMOGRAPH	CHIMBORAZO	DICTOGRAPH
TUMULTUOUS	CHERRYWOOD	GLYCOLYSIS	ANNIHILATE	CHINAGRAPH	DILAPIDATE
UNCTUOUSLY	COMMONWEAL	GRATIFYING	ANNUNCIATE	CHLORINATE	DISCORDANT
UNCULTURED	COTTONWOOD	HIGHFLYING	ANTICIPATE	CHRISTIANA	DISCOURAGE
UNDERBURNT	CREWELWORK	HIGHWAYMAN	APOTHECARY	CHURCHYARD	DISCREPANT
UNDISPUTED	EATANSWILL	HISTOLYSIS	APOTROPAIC	CLYDESDALE	DISENCHANT
VERNACULAR	FIDDLEWOOD	HOLOPHYTIC	APPRECIATE	CNIDOBLAST	DISPENSARY
VESTIBULUM	GREENSWARD	HORRIFYING	AQUAMANALE	COADJUTANT	DISSERTATE
VIBRACULUM	GROUNDWORK	HYDROLYSIS	ARCHITRAVE	COASTGUARD	DISSOCIATE
VIGOROUSLY	HEAVENWARD	JOURNEYMAN	ARTHURIANA	COLLEGIATE	DISTILLATE
VIRTUOUSLY	HITHERWARD	KEMPERYMAN	ARTICULATA	COLLIQUATE	DITHIONATE
VOLUPTUARY	INTERTWINE	LINEOMYCIN	ARTICULATE	COLOSSIANS	DOMICILARY

DOUBLEBASS	GREYFRIARS	INTERWEAVE	MOULDIWARP	PUNCTULATE	STREETLAMP
DOUBLETALK	GROUNDBAIT	INTIMIDATE	MOUNTEBANK	PURSUIVANT	STREPITANT
DUNDERPATE	HABILITATE	INTOLERANT	NARROWDALE	QUAESTUARY	STRIDEWAYS
DUUMVIRATE	HACKMATACK	INTOXICANT	NATTERJACK	QUATERNARY	STRIDULATE
DYNAMITARD	HANDICRAFT	INTOXICATE	NATUROPATH	RADIOGRAPH	STRINGHALT
EARTHQUAKE	HANDLEBARS	INVALIDATE	NEEDLECASE	RAIYATWARI	STRIPTEASE
EBRACTEATE	HEAVENWARD	INVETERATE	NETTLERASH	RAZZMATAZZ	SUBCOMPACT
ECARDINATE	HELIOGRAPH	INVIGILATE	NIGHTSHADE	REACTIVATE	SUBMEDIANT
EDULCORATE	HEMORRHAGE	INVIGORATE	NONCHALANT	RECUPERATE	SUBSIDIARY
EFFECTUATE	HEREDITARY	IRRADICATE	NONVINTAGE	REDCURRANT	SUPERGIANT
EFFEMINACY	HETEROGAMY	IRRELEVANT	NORMOBLAST	REDECORATE	SUPPLEJACK
EFFEMINATE	HIEROPHANT	JACKSTRAWS	OBLITERATE	REGENERATE	SUPPLICANT
EFFLEURAGE	HILDEBRAND	JIGGERMAST	OCHLOCRACY	REJUVENATE	SUPPLICATE
EGURGITATE	HINDUSTANI	JUGGERNAUT	OFFTHEWALL	REMUNERATE	SVADILFARI
ELACAMPANE	HINTERLAND	JUSTICIARY	OPOTHERAPY	REPATRIATE	SWEEPSTAKE
ELASTICATE	HITHERWARD	KARTTIKAYA	ORTHOCLASE	RESTAURANT	SWEETHEART
ELECAMPANE	HOMOEOPATH	KNIFEBOARD	OSTEOBLAST	RESUPINATE	SWITCHBACK
ELECTORATE	HOMORELAPS	KRUGERRAND	OVERSTRAIN	RETICULATE	SYNTAGMATA
ELEMENTARY	HORSEDRAWN	KUOMINTANG	OVERTHWART	RETROGRADE	TACHOGRAPH
EMANCIPATE	HOUSECRAFT	LANCEOLATE	PALATINATE	RHINEGRAVE	TAILORMADE
EMARGINATE	HOVERCRAFT	LANDAMMANN	PANTOGRAPH	RINGELMANN	TALLEYRAND
EMASCULATE	HOWLEGLASS	LANGERHANS	PAPERCHASE	ROCKSTEADY	TAMBERLANE
ENTHUSIASM	HUSBANDAGE	LARGESCALE	PARAPHRASE	SACCHARASE	TARDIGRADE
ENTHUSIAST	HYALOPHANE	LATTERMATH	PARISCHANE	SADDLEBACK	TATTERSALL
EPISCOPATE	HYDROPHANE	LAUDERDALE	PARMIGIANA	SALTIGRADE	TCHOUKBALL
EQUIVOCATE	HYDROPLANE	LAUNCEGAYE	PARTINGALE	SANGUINARY	TELPHERAGE
EVERYPLACE	ICONOCLAST	LEBENSRAUM	PASQUINADE	SATYAGRAHA	TERNEPLATE
EVISCERATE	ILLAQUEATE	LEGITIMACY	PASSIONATE	SAUERKRAUT	THEOLOGATE
EXACERBATE	ILLITERACY	LEGITIMATE	PASTEBOARD	SCAPEGRACE	THREADBARE
EXAGGERATE	ILLITERATE	LEMNISCATE	PATIBULARY	SCHOOLMAAM	TICKERTAPE
EXASPERATE	ILLUMINATE	LENGTHWAYS	PEDICULATE	SCOREBOARD	TIMBERYARD
EXCRUCIATE	ILLUMINATI	LEPRECHAUN	PERCENTAGE	SCRIMSHANK	TORQUEMADA
EXENTERATE	ILLUSTRATE	LICENTIATE	PERPETRATE	SCUTELLATE	TRACHELATE
EXHILARATE	IMBROCCATA	LIEBERMANN	PERPETUATE	SECONDHAND	TRAMONTANA
EXORBITANT	IMMACULACY	LIEUTENANT	PERSIFLAGE	SECONDRATE	TRAMONTANE
EXPATRIATE	IMMACULATE	LITHISTADA	PETRISSAGE	SHAGGYMANE	TRANSPLANT
FACILITATE	IMMODERATE	LITHOGRAPH	PETTICHAPS	SHANDYGAFF	TRIFOLIATE
FASTIGIATE	IMPREGNATE	LITHOPHANE	PETTYCHAPS	SHEEPSHANK	TRIPLICATE
FATHERLAND	INACCURACY	LUMBERJACK	PHONOGRAPH	SHIELDRAKE	TRIPUDIARY
FELICITATE	INACCURATE	MAGISTRACY	PHOTOGRAPH	SHILLELAGH	TRIUMPHANT
FIBERGLASS	INADEQUACY	MAGISTRAND	PICHICIAGO	SILVERBACK	UNDERCLASS
FIBREGLASS	INADEQUATE	MAGISTRATE	PICTOGRAPH	SILVERWARE	UNDERCRAFT
FIBRILLATE	INAUGURATE	MAHAYANALI	PILGRIMAGE	SKATEBOARD	UNDERLEASE
FINGERNAIL	INCENDIARY	MAIDENHAIR	PILLOWCASE	SKRIMSHANK	UNDERNEATH
FITZGERALD	INCINERATE	MALAYALAAM	PISTILLATE	SLUICEGATE	UNDERSTAND
FLAGELLATE	INCONSTANT	MALLOPHAGA	PLANOBLAST	SMALLSCALE	UNDERSTATE
FLAMBOYANT	INCRASSATE	MANIPULATE	PLATTELAND	SMOKESTACK	UNPLEASANT
FLAMINGANT	INDELICACY	MANSERVANT	PLESIOSAUR	SOLIVAGANT	UPPERCLASS
FLANCONADE	INDELICATE	MAQUILLAGE	PLOUGHGATE	SOUNDTRACK	VERNISSAGE
FLOCCULATE	INEFFICACY	MARCANTANT	PLUTOCRACY	SOUTERRAIN	VERTEBRATE
FLOORBOARD	INFIBULATE	MARTINGALE	POHUTUKAWA	SPACECRAFT	VESICULATE
FOREORDAIN	INFILTRATE	MASQUERADE	POINTBLANK	SPHACELATE	VETERINARY
FOUDROYANT	INGEMINATE	MASTURBATE	PONTEFRACT	SPIFLICATE	VICTORIANA
FRANGIPANE	INGENERATE	MATCHSTALK	PORNOCRACY	SPOKESHAVE	VILLEINAGE
FRANGIPANI	INGRATIATE	MAUPASSANT	POSTILLATE	SPONGEWARE	VINDEMIATE
FREIGHTAGE	INHABITANT	MEERSCHAUM	POTENTIATE	SPRINGHAAS	VITUPERATE
FRITILLARY	INNERSPACE	MEGALOSAUR	POZZUOLANA	SPRINGTAIL	VOCABULARY
GARLANDAGE	INORDINATE	MENSTRUATE	PREBENDARY	STAGECOACH	VOCIFERATE
GASCONNADE	INOSCULATE	METAPHRASE	PREDECEASE	STAGECRAFT	VOLLEYBALL
GENICULATE	INSANITARY	MIMEOGRAPH	PROFLIGACY	STANISLAUS	VOLUPTUARY
GETHSEMANE	INSEMINATE	MINISTRATE	PROFLIGATE	STATECRAFT	WASSERMANS
GILLRAVAGE	INSOUCIANT	MISCELLANY	PROMULGATE	STATIONARY	WATERBRASH
GLITTERAND	INSPISSATE	MISSIONARY	PROPELLANT	STATOCRACY	WHEELCHAIR
GLITTERATI	INSUFFLATE	MITHRIDATE	PROPIONATE	STIACCIATO	WHITEHEART
GOATSBEARD	INTAGLIATE	MIZZENMAST	PROPITIATE	STILLSTAND	WINDOWPANE
GRANDSTAND	INTEMERATE	MONTAGNARD	PROTESTANT	STINGYBARK	WITCHCRAFT
GREENHEART	INTENERATE	MOTHERLAND	PROTOPLASM	STONEBRASH	WONDERLAND
GREENSHANK	INTERLEAVE	MOUCHARABY	PSEUDOCARP	STRAWBOARD	WOOLLYBACK
GREENSWARD	INTERSTATE	MOUDIEWART	PSYCHOPATH	STRAWBOARD	WORLDCLASS

YAFFINGALE	IMPASSABLE	REASONABLY	FORINSECAL	ARCHIMEDES	INTERNODAL
YELLOWBACK	IMPECCABLE	REASSEMBLE	FRANCISCAN	ARMAGEDDON	KEYBOARDER
YELLOWJACK	IMPECCABLY	REMARKABLE	FREELANCER	ASTEROIDEA	LEFTHANDED
ZINCOGRAPH	IMPLACABLE	REMARKABLY	FRENETICAL	BACKHANDED	LEFTHANDER
ZOOTHERAPY	IMPLACABLY	REPAIRABLE	GEOLOGICAL	BACKHANDER	LIKEMINDED
ABOMINABLE	IMPOSSIBLE	REPEATABLE	GOBEMOUCHE	BACKSLIDER	MAHOMMEDAN
ABOMINABLY	IMPOSSIBLY	RETURNABLE	GOLDILOCKS	BAREHEADED	MEMORANDUM
ACCESSIBLE	IMPROBABLE	REVERSIBLE	HISTORICAL	BARMECIDAL	MONOACIDIC
ACTIONABLE	IMPROBABLY	SCANDERBEG	HYSTERICAL	BEARGARDEN	MONTEVIDEO
ADJUSTABLE	INCREDIBLE	SEASONABLE	JEISTIECOR	BILIVERDIN	MUJAHEDDIN
ADMISSIBLE	INCREDIBLY	SEASONABLY	KURDAITCHA	BLASTOIDEA	MULTIMEDIA
AFFORDABLE	INDICTABLE	SHISHKEBAB	LINEOMYCIN	BONDHOLDER	NEWSREADER
ANALPHABET	INEDUCABLE	SQUEEZEBOX	LITURGICAL	BOOKBINDER	OPENHANDED
ANSWERABLE	INELIGIBLE	SUBSCRIBER	LOGISTICAL	BULLHEADED	OPENMINDED
ANTIBARBUS	INEVITABLE	TERMINABLE	MADAGASCAN	CALAMANDER	OUVIRANDRA
APPLICABLE	INEVITABLY	THINGUMBOB	MADAGASCAR	CALAMONDIN	OVERLANDER
ASCRIBABLE	INEXORABLE	THUNDERBOX	MAGNIFICAT	CAMPARADOR	OVERSHADOW
ASSIGNABLE	INFALLIBLE	UNARGUABLE	MAKUNOUCHI	CARYATIDES	PALISANDER
ATTAINABLE	INFALLIBLY	UNBEARABLE	MATRIARCHY	CIRRIPEDEA	PARADIDDLE
BEDCHAMBER	INFLATABLE	UNBEARABLY	MECHANICAL	CIRRIPEDIA	PATHFINDER
BELIEVABLE	INFLEXIBLE	UNBEATABLE	METHODICAL	CLOSTRIDIA	PINNIPEDIA
CALCULABLE	INFLEXIBLY	UNDENIABLE	MICROFICHE	COLONNADED	PRESENTDAY
CANDELABRA	INIMITABLE	UNENVIABLE	MOTORCYCLE	COMPOUNDED	PROFOUNDLY
CHANGEABLE	INOPERABLE	UNHEARABLE	NEOTERICAL	CONFOUNDED	PROMENADER
CHARGEABLE	INSATIABLE	UNREADABLE	ORATORICAL	CONFUSEDLY	PTERANODON
CHARITABLE	INSATIABLY	UNRELIABLE	OROBRANCHE	COPYHOLDER	PUMPHANDLE
CHARITABLY	INSENSIBLE	UNSCRAMBLE	OUANANICHE	COROMANDEL	QUARRENDER
CHATTERBOX	INTANGIBLE	UNSOCIABLE	PANOPTICON	CORREGIDOR	RECONSIDER
COMESTIBLE	INTRAURBAN	UNSUITABLE	PATCHCOCKE	CROTALIDAE	REFERENDUM
COMMUTABLE	INVALUABLE	UNWORKABLE	PATRIARCHY	CYCLOPEDIA	REJONEADOR
COMPARABLE	INVARIABLE	UTILIZABLE	PERIODICAL	DEJECTEDLY	REPEATEDLY
COMPATIBLE	INVARIABLY	VERIFIABLE	POKERFACED	DESERVEDLY	REPORTEDLY
CONVEYABLE	INVINCIBLE	VULNERABLE	PONTIFICAL	DIDGERIDOO	RESIGNEDLY
CREDITABLE	INVIOLABLE	WHITSTABLE	PREJUDICED	DRAWBRIDGE	RINGLEADER
CREDITABLY	LAMENTABLE	XENOPHOBIA	PREMEDICAL	DRUMBLEDOR	SALAMANDER
DEDUCTIBLE	LAMENTABLY	XENOPHOBIC	PRONOUNCED	ECHINOIDEA	SCOPELIDAE
DEFENSIBLE	LANDLUBBER	AMPHIMACER	RABBINICAL	EPIMENIDES	SHANDRYDAN
DEGRADABLE	MANAGEABLE	ANALOGICAL	RECEPTACLE	EUROCLYDON	SHARAWADGI
DELECTABLE	MARKETABLE	ANALYTICAL	RECIPROCAL	EVENHANDED	SIDESADDLE
DEPENDABLE	MEASURABLE	ANARCHICAL	REPRODUCER	EVERGLADES	SIDEWINDER
DEPLORABLE	METASTABLE	ANATOMICAL	REPUBLICAN	FALKLANDER	SOBERSIDES
DEPLORABLY	MODIFIABLE	ANDROMACHE	REQUIESCAT	FIREWARDEN	SPIRITEDLY
DESPICABLE	NEGLIGIBLE	ARCHDEACON	RHETORICAL	FLAPDOODLE	SPLENDIDLY
DETACHABLE	NEGOTIABLE	ASARABACCA	RHYTHMICAL	FLUNKEYDOM	STADHOLDER
DETECTABLE	NOSOPHOBIA	BACITRACIN	SABBATICAL	FOOTBRIDGE	STEMWINDER
DETESTABLE	NOTICEABLE	BACKBLOCKS	SABRETACHE	FORESHADOW	STEPLADDER
DIGESTIBLE	NOTICEABLY	BETACRUCIS	SEMICIRCLE	FREEHANDER	STUMBLEDOM
DISENNOBLE	NOTIFIABLE	BIOLOGICAL	SERMONICAL	FREEHOLDER	SUPERADDED
DISPOSABLE	OBSERVABLE	CARACTACUS	SHAKUHACHI	FREELOADER	SUPERMODEL
DISPUTABLE	OBTAINABLE	CATENACCIO	SHAMEFACED	FRENZIEDLY	SUPPOSEDLY
EXPENDABLE	OSTENSIBLE	CATHOLICON	SIGNIFICAT	FUDDYDUDDY	SURROUNDED
EXPLICABLE	OSTENSIBLY	CATHOLICOS	STAVESACRE	FUNGICIDAL	TANAGRIDAE
EXTENDABLE	PARDONABLE	CHOPSTICKS	SYMBOLICAL	GERMICIDAL	TARADIDDLE
EXTENSIBLE	PARDONABLY	COPERNICUS	SYNECDOCHE	GETUPANDGO	TEETHRIDGE
FAVOURABLE	PENETRABLE	COQUELICOT	TABERNACLE	GLEEMAIDEN	TELEBRIDGE
FAVOURABLY	PERDURABLE	COXCOMICAL	THEATRICAL	GRAMICIDIN	TENRECIDAE
FEATHERBED	PERISHABLE	DEMONIACAL	TYRANNICAL	GRANDDADDY	THOUSANDTH
FORGIVABLE	PERSONABLE	DIABOLICAL	ULTRAFICHE	GRASSWIDOW	THUCYDIDES
FORMIDABLE	PREFERABLE	DIACONICON	UNBALANCED	HANDMAIDEN	TOUCHANDGO
GALLIAMBIC	PREFERABLY	DIPLODOCUS	UNCRITICAL	HANGGLIDER	UNATTENDED
HEMOGLOBIN	PRESUMABLY	DREADLOCKS	VITELLICLE	HELLBENDER	UNDEFENDED
HOMOPHOBIA	PROCURABLE	ECOLOGICAL	WANCHANCIE	HESPERIDES	UNFRIENDLY
HOMOPHOBIC	PROFITABLE	ECONOMICAL	ZOOLOGICAL	HIGHBINDER	UNGROUNDED
HONOURABLE	PROFITABLY	ECUMENICAL	ACOTYLEDON	HIGHHANDED	UNHERALDED
HONOURABLY	PROSCRIBED	ELECTRICAL	ADMITTEDLY	HIGHLANDER	UNORTHODOX
HOSPITABLE	PSILOCYBIN	ELLIPTICAL	AFRICANDER	HODGEPODGE	VIEWFINDER
HOSPITABLY	PUNISHABLE	ENCYCLICAL	ALCIBIADES	HORSERIDER	WILLINGDON
IMAGINABLE	REAMINGBIT	ESTRAMACON	AMBASSADOR	ICOSOHEDRA	WRETCHEDLY
IMPALPABLE	REASONABLE	FERNITICLE	ANGURVADEL	INTERCEDER	ABITURIENT

ABONNEMENT	CARABINEER	DEFACEMENT	EXCITEMENT	HOARSENESS	MANICHAEAN
ABRIDGMENT	CARRAGHEEN	DEFILEMENT	EXEMPTNESS	HOMELINESS	MARCESCENT
ABRUPTNESS	CASSIOPEIA	DEFINITELY	EXPERIMENT	HONOURLESS	MAVOURNEEN
ABSOLUTELY	CASUALNESS	DEFRAYMENT	EXPOUNDERS	HORSELBERG	MEAGERNESS
ACCURATELY	CHAMAELEON	DELCREDERE	EYEWITNESS	HUMBLENESS	MEAGRENESS
ADDITAMENT	CHANGELESS	DELICATELY	FAHRENHEIT	HUMDUDGEON	MEDICAMENT
ADEQUATELY	CHARIOTEER	DELINQUENT	FAMISHMENT	HUMOURLESS	MEDIUMTERM
ADJUSTMENT	CHEEKINESS	DENOUEMENT	FATHERLESS	IMPAIRMENT	MELLOWNESS
ADOLESCENT	CHERSONESE	DEPARTMENT	FAULTINESS	IMPEDIMENT	MESITYLENE
ADRAMELECH	CHERVONETS	DEPLOYMENT	FEEBLENESS	IMPENITENT	MIGHTINESS
ADULTERESS	CHILLINESS	DEPORTMENT	FICKLENESS	IMPOLITELY	MINUTENESS
AFTERPIECE	CHIROPTERA	DERAILLEUR	FIERCENESS	INCISIVELY	MODERATELY
ALEXANDERS	CHOICELESS	DERAILMENT	FIGUREHEAD	INCITEMENT	MONOVALENT
ALLUREMENT	CINECAMERA	DESPONDENT	FILTHINESS	INCOHERENT	MONTGOMERY
ALZHEIMERS	CIRCUMVENT	DETACHMENT	FLABBINESS	INCOMPLETE	MOROSENESS
AMBIVALENT	CLAMMINESS	DETAINMENT	FLASHINESS	INCRESCENT	MOTHERLESS
ANADYOMENE	CLEMENCEAU	DEVOTEMENT	FLAVESCENT	INDICTMENT	MOTIONLESS
ANGIOSPERM	CLEVERNESS	DIRECTNESS	FLESHINESS	INDISCREET	MOULDINESS
ANIMADVERT	CLOMIPHENE	DISBELIEVE	FLIGHTLESS	INDITEMENT	MOUSEPIECE
ANTECEDENT	CLOUDINESS	DISCONCERT	FLIMSINESS	INDUCEMENT	MOUTHPIECE
ANTIFREEZE	CLUMSINESS	DISCONNECT	FLOCCULENT	INESCULENT	MUMBLENEWS
ANTIOCHENE	COARSENESS	DISCONTENT	FLOWERBEDS	INFEFTMENT	MUNIFICENT
ANTIPODEAN	COEXISTENT	DISPOSSESS	FLUFFINESS	INFINITELY	MUSKETEERS
ANTIVENENE	COINCIDENT	DISRESPECT	FOURRAGERE	INFREQUENT	MUTTONHEAD
APOPHTHEGM	COLDSTREAM	DISSILIENT	FRAUDULENT	INGREDIENT	NAPTHALENE
ARMIPOTENT	COLEOPTERA	DISSOLVENT	FREMESCENT	INSECURELY	NARROWNESS
ARTHROMERE	COLOURLESS	DISTILLERY	FRICANDEAU	INSTALMENT	NDRANGHETA
ASCOMYCETE	COLPORTEUR	DODECANESE	FRIENDLESS	INSTRUMENT	NEGATIVELY
ASSESSMENT	COMANCHERO	DOGGEDNESS	FRISKINESS	INTEGUMENT	NEWSPAPERS
ASSIGNMENT	COMMANDEER	DOWNSTREAM	FROMANTEEL	INTELIGENT	NIGGERHEAD
ASSORTMENT	COMMITMENT	DREAMINESS	FRUTESCENT	INTENDMENT	NIGHTDRESS
ASTRINGENT	COMMONWEAL	DREARINESS	FULFILMENT	INTENTNESS	NIGRESCENT
ASTUTENESS	COMPLACENT	DROWSINESS	GENTLENESS	INTERBREED	NIMBLENESS
ASYNARTETE	COMPLEMENT	DUNDERHEAD	GESUNDHEIT	INTERNMENT	NONPAYMENT
ATMOSPHERE	COMPLETELY	EBOULEMENT	GINGERBEER	INTIMATELY	NONSUCCESS
ATTACHMENT	COMPLIMENT	ECHINODERM	GIRLFRIEND	INTROSPECT	NONVIOLENT
ATTAINMENT	COMPREHEND	EFFACEMENT	GLASSINESS	INVESTMENT	NORTHSTEAD
AUCTIONEER	CONCURRENT	EFFORTLESS	GLENDOVEER	IONOSPHERE	NUMBERLESS
BAFFLEMENT	CONDESCEND	EFFRONTERY	GLOSSINESS	IRIDESCENT	NYMPHOLEPT
BALBUTIENT	CONSEQUENT	EFFUSIVELY	GOLDENSEAL	IRREVERENT	OBJECTLESS
BANGLADESH	CONSISTENT	EMALANGENI	GOLDTHREAD	JARDINIERE	OBTUSENESS
BANISHMENT	CONTINGENT	EMBANKMENT	GONDOLIERS	JAUNTINESS	ODIOUSNESS
BARRENNESS	CONTRAHENT	EMBODIMENT	GOOSEFLESH	JOBSEEKERS	OMNIPOTENT
BARYSPHERE	CONTRAVENE	EMBROIDERY	GOVERNMENT	JOLTERHEAD	OMNISCIENT
BATTENBERG	CONTROVERT	EMPLOYMENT	GRAVEOLENT	JOURNALESE	OPALESCENT
BATTLEMENT	CONVENIENT	ENCAMPMENT	GREEDINESS	KERSEYMERE	ORPHEOREON
BEEFEATERS	CONVERGENT	ENCASEMENT	GRENADIERS	KINDLINESS	OTHERGUESS
BENEFICENT	CONVERSELY	ENDEARMENT	GRITTINESS	KNIGHTHEAD	OUTPATIENT
BENEVOLENT	COPPERHEAD	ENGAGEMENT	GROUNDLESS	LAVALLIÈRE	OVERSPREAD
BIRKENHEAD	CORDILLERA	ENGOUEMENT	GRUBBINESS	LAVISHNESS	PALIMPSEST
BITTERNESS	CORYPHAEUS	ENLACEMENT	GRUMPINESS	LEGWARMERS	PALUDAMENT
BONNETHEAD	COSTLINESS	ENLÈVEMENT	GUARANTEED	LEOPARDESS	PARASELENE
BOTTLEHEAD	CRAFTINESS	ENLISTMENT	GYMNOSPERM	LETTERHEAD	PARENTLESS
BOTTLENECK	CRISPBREAD	ENRICHMENT	HACKBUTEER	LIMBERNECK	PARLIAMENT
BOTTOMLESS	CROSSBREED	ENROLLMENT	HAKENKREUZ	LIQUESCENT	PATCHINESS
BRAININESS	CROSSCHECK	ENTEROCELE	HAMMERHEAD	LITTLENESS	PERCIPIENT
BREASTFEED	CROSSPIECE	ENTICEMENT	HANDSOMELY	LIVELINESS	PERFICIENT
BREATHLESS	CRUSTACEAN	ENTOMBMENT	HARASSMENT	LOCULAMENT	PERNICKETY
BRIDGEHEAD	CURMUDGEON	EPAULEMENT	HARMANBECK	LOGGERHEAD	PERSISTENT
BRIGHTNESS	CUSSEDNESS	EPIMETHEUS	HARTEBEEST	LONELINESS	PERVERSELY
BROADPIECE	DEADLINESS	EPIPHONEMA	HEARTBREAK	LORDLINESS	PHAGEDAENA
BROADSHEET	DEBASEMENT	EQUIVALENT	HEARTINESS	LOVELINESS	PHILLUMENY
BUFFLEHEAD	DEBATEMENT	ERUBESCENT	HEIDELBERG	MAINSTREAM	PHILOPOENA
BUFFOONERY	DEBAUCHERY	ESCAPEMENT	HEMISPHERE	MALCONTENT	PHYLACTERY
BUNDESWEHR	DECAMPMENT	ESCARPMENT	HEPATOCELE	MALEVOLENT	PICHICIEGO
BUTTERMERE	DECATHLETE	ESCUTCHEON	HEXAVALENT	MANAGEMENT	PIPSISSEWA
CAMBERWELL	DECISIVELY	ESTANCIERO	HIPPOCRENE	MANAGERESS	PLASMODESM
CANCIONERO	DECRESCENT	EVANESCENT	HITOPADESA	MANCHINEEL	PLUPERFECT
CANTONMENT	DEEPFREEZE	EVERYWHERE	HITOPODESA	MANGOSTEEN	POETASTERY

POLITENESS	SCHALSTEIN	SULTRINESS	DISDAINFUL	FULLLENGTH	ASTONISHED
POLYCHAETE	SCORZONERA	SUPPLEMENT	EISTEDDFOD	GOLDDIGGER	AUTHORSHIP
POLYCHREST	SCRUTINEER	SUPPLENESS	FISTICUFFS	GOLDFINGER	AUTOCHTHON
POLYVALENT	SCULPTRESS	SURINAMESE	FOODSTUFFS	HEMIPLEGIA	BATTLESHIP
PORTUGUESE	SEAMSTRESS	SUSPENDERS	FRAUNHOFER	HENDECAGON	BEDCLOTHES
POSITIVELY	SECONDBEST	SWEETBREAD	MEANINGFUL	INKSLINGER	BELLWETHER
PREEMINENT	SECONDMENT	TAPOTEMENT	NEGLECTFUL	IRONMONGER	BERMOOTHES
PREFERMENT	SEDATENESS	TEENYWEENY	PALMATIFID	KHIDMUTGAR	BIOGRAPHER
PREPAYMENT	SEEMLIHEAD	TENDERNESS	PURPOSEFUL	LEFTWINGER	BIORHYTHMS
PREPENSELY	SELFESTEEM	TERREPLEIN	RAGAMUFFIN	LIGHTINGUP	BIRMINGHAM
PREPOSSESS	SELLINGERS	THEREANENT	REMORSEFUL	LOTOPHAGUS	BUCKINGHAM
PRESBYTERY	SELTZOGENE	TIMELINESS	RESPECTFUL	MAKEWEIGHT	CENSORSHIP
PRETTINESS	SENEGALESE	TINKERBELL	REVENGEFUL	MENACINGLY	CHELTENHAM
PRIVATEERS	SEPARATELY	TIRAILLEUR	RICHTHOFEN	MICROLIGHT	CHILDISHLY
PROCUMBENT	SETTLEMENT	TOMFOOLERY	RIJSTTAFEL	MISHGUGGLE	CHURLISHLY
PROFICIENT	SEVENTIETH	TORPESCENT	ROSECHAFER	MONOPLEGIA	CISLEITHAN
PROFITLESS	SHABBINESS	TOUCHINESS	SCIENTIFIC	MOUTHORGAN	DEALERSHIP
PROMETHEAN	SHADOWLESS	TOUCHPIECE	SUCCESSFUL	MYSTAGOGUE	DENDROPHIS
PROMETHEUS	SHIBBOLETH	TOURNAMENT	TENEBRIFIC	MYSTAGOGUS	DIMINISHED
PROMPTNESS	SHIFTINESS	TRANSGRESS	THIMBLEFUL	NEWSMONGER	DISBURTHEN
PROPELLENT	SHODDINESS	TRAVELLERS	THOUGHTFUL	NIGHTLIGHT	DISHWASHER
PROPHETESS	SHORTBREAD	TRENDINESS	ULTRAMAFIC	NORTHANGER	DYSTROPHIC
PROPLITEAL	SHOVELHEAD	TRICKINESS	UMBELLIFER	OBLIGINGLY	ENTRENCHED
PROPYLAEUM	SHREWDNESS	TURTLEHEAD	UNEVENTFUL	ODONTALGIA	EPICANTHUS
PROSILIENT	SHRILLNESS	TURTLENECK	UNFAITHFUL	OESOPHAGUS	ERYMANTHUS
PSOCOPTERA	SILVERBELL	ULTIMATELY	UNFRUITFUL	OVERBOUGHT	FARFETCHED
PUBERULENT	SINFULNESS	UNDERSTEER	UNGRATEFUL	OVERWEIGHT	FELLOWSHIP
PUNICACEAE	SINGHALESE	UNEASINESS	UNSPECIFIC	OWLSPIEGLE	FEVERISHLY
PUNISHMENT	SINGLENESS	UNEVENNESS	UNTRUTHFUL	PARAPLEGIA	FIENDISHLY
PUTRESCENT	SLEEPINESS	UNFORESEEN	WINDSURFER	PARAPLEGIC	FLOURISHED
PUZZLEMENT	SLEEVELESS	UNIQUENESS	ACCUSINGLY	PLAYWRIGHT	FLYCATCHER
QUADRICEPS	SLIPSTREAM	UNRULINESS	ADMIRINGLY	PRIVILEGED	FOOTLIGHTS
QUADRIREME	SLOPPINESS	UNTIDINESS	ADRENERGIC	PRIZEFIGHT	FOREFATHER
QUAINTNESS	SMARMINESS	UPHOLSTERY	AEROPHAGIA	QUADRANGLE	FOREGATHER
QUEASINESS	SMITHEREEN	URTICACEAE	AIRFREIGHT	SCOFFINGLY	FORFEUCHEN
QUENCHLESS	SMOOTHNESS	USEFULNESS	ANTITRAGUS	SHARAWAGGI	FORFOUGHEN
RANDOMNESS	SNOOTINESS	VELOCIPEDE	ARTHRALGIA	SHENANIGAN	FRIENDSHIP
RAPPORTEUR	SONGSTRESS	VICEGERENT	ASTRALAGUS	SHIPWRIGHT	GEOGRAPHER
REARMAMENT	SOPHOCLEAN	VICEREGENT	ASTROLOGER	SHOCKINGLY	GEOGRAPHIC
REFINEMENT	SORDIDNESS	VIETNAMESE	AUSTRINGER	SNAPDRAGON	HAEMANTHUS
REFRINGENT	SPARSENESS	VIVANDIÈRE	BALBRIGGAN	SOGDOLAGER	HEADLIGHTS
REGARDLESS	SPEECHLESS	WAMPUMPEAG	BARASINGHA	SOGDOLIGER	HIERARCHIC
RELATIVELY	SPEEDINESS	WATERCRESS	BARELEGGED	SOGDOLOGER	HIPPARCHUS
RELENTLESS	SPERMACETI	WATERWHEEL	BEEFBURGER	SOOTHINGLY	KINGFISHER
REMOTENESS	SPINESCENT	WEAPONLESS	BIRTHRIGHT	SPORTINGLY	LEADERSHIP
REPETITEUR	SPIRITLESS	WEIGHTLESS	BOONDOGGLE	SQUETEAGUE	LOGARITHMS
RESENTMENT	SPORTSWEAR	WHEATSHEAF	BOOTLEGGER	STALLENGER	MACONOCHIE
RESOLUTELY	SPREAGHERY	WHEEZINESS	BUDGERIGAR	STALLINGER	MEGALITHIC
RESPONDENT	SPRINGLESS	WHOLEWHEAT	BUSHRANGER	STERNALGIA	MEMBERSHIP
RETIREMENT	SPRUCENESS	WICKEDNESS	CARCINOGEN	STRIKINGLY	MESOLITHIC
RETROGRESS	STATIONERY	WIDESPREAD	CHALLENGED	SWIMMINGLY	MISMATCHED
RETROSPECT	STEADINESS	WILDEBEEST	CHALLENGER	TORCHLIGHT	MONOLITHIC
RHIPIPTERA	STEELINESS	WILDERNESS	CHAULMUGRA	TRAVELOGUE	MONTRACHET
RINDERPEST	STEWARDESS	WILLOWHERB	CHOLALOGUE	UNABRIDGED	NEUTROPHIL
ROBUSTNESS	STICKINESS	WINDERMERE	COATHANGER	VOETGANGER	PARONYCHIA
ROLANDSECK	STICKYBEAK	WINDSCREEN	COPENHAGEN	WATERTIGHT	PENELOPHON
RUBBERNECK	STINGINESS	WINDSHIELD	CREOPHAGUS	WAVELENGTH	PETRARCHAN
RUBINSTEIN	STOCKINESS	WONDERMENT	CYNOMOLGUS	WHARFINGER	PHLEGETHON
RUDDERLESS	STRICTNESS	WOODENHEAD	DEMOGORGON	XIPHOPAGUS	PINAKOTHEK
RUGGEDNESS	STRINDBERG	WOODPIGEON	DISEMBOGUE	ACHITOPHEL	POLIANTHES
SACREDNESS	STRULDBERG	WORTHINESS	DISENGAGED	ACOLOUTHOS	POLYANTHUS
SALLENDERS	STUFFINESS	YELLOWLEGS	DISTRAUGHT	ACRONYCHAL	PSAMMOPHIL
SAPPERMENT	STURDINESS	YESTERWEEK	DISTRINGAS	AGAPANTHUS	READERSHIP
SAVAGENESS	SUAVEOLENT	YESTERYEAR	FEARNOUGHT	AHITHOPHEL	RESEARCHER
SCANTINESS	SUBSEQUENT	ZIMBABWEAN	FISHMONGER	ALTOGETHER	ROCKINGHAM
SCARCEMENT	SUBSISTENT	ZOLLVEREIN	FLEETINGLY	ANTICHTHON	SANDWICHES
SCARCENESS	SUBTRAHEND	COCKCHAFER	FLOODLIGHT	APEMANTHUS	SEAMANSHIP
SCATHELESS	SUDDENNESS	CROSSREFER	FOREFINGER	APOCRYPHAL	SEANNACHIE
SCATURIENT	SUFFICIENT	DELIGHTFUL	FORTHRIGHT	ARCHBISHOP	SEECATCHIE

SHEEPISHLY	AMATEURISH	BACKBITING	CANDLEWICK	COMMANDING	CORRUPTION
SIMMENTHAL	AMERINDIAN	BACKSTAIRS	CANTABRIAN	COMMERCIAL	COTTIERISM
SLUGGISHLY	AMIABILITY	BAHRAINIAN	CANTATRICE	COMMISSION	COUNSELING
STEPFATHER	AMMUNITION	BAILIEWICK	CANVASSING	COMPASSION	CREATIVITY
STEPMOTHER	AMPHITRITE	BAILLIWICK	CAPABILITY	COMPATRIOT	CREDENTIAL
STRENGTHEN	AMPUTATION	BALANCHINE	CAPERNAITE	COMPELLING	CRICKETING
TELEPATHIC	ANABAPTIST	BALLISTICS	CAPERNOITY	COMPENDIUM	CRISPINIAN
THOROUGHLY	ANACARDIUM	BALLISTITE	CAPILLAIRE	COMPLETION	CRYOGENICS
TRIMALCHIO	ANDALUSIAN	BALLOONING	CAPITALISM	COMPLEXION	CUCKOOPINT
TRYPTOPHAN	ANDALUSITE	BALLOONIST	CAPITALIST	COMPLEXITY	CUIRASSIER
UNATTACHED	ANGLERFISH	BALNEATION	CAPITALIZE	COMPLICITY	CUISENAIRE
UNBLEACHED	ANGLOPHILE	BARGAINING	CAPITATION	COMPLUVIUM	CUMULATIVE
UNFINISHED	ANGWANTIBO	BARRACKING	CAPITOLINE	COMPROMISE	CURMURRING
WAPENSCHAW	ANHELATION	BASSOONIST	CAPPUCCINO	COMPULSION	CURRENCIES
WAPINSCHAW	ANNEXATION	BATRACHIAN	CARABINIER	COMPULSIVE	CURVETTING
WAPPENSHAW	ANNOTATION	BAUDELAIRE	CARAMELIZE	CONCEPTION	CUTTLEFISH
WHILLYWHAW	ANTAGONISE	BEAUTICIAN	CARNASSIAL	CONCERNING	DAMSELFISH
ABDICATION	ANTAGONISM	BEAUTIFIER	CARPATHIAN	CONCERTINA	DARJEELING
ABERDEVINE	ANTAGONIST	BEEKEEPING	CARPENTIER	CONCESSION	DEBRIEFING
ABERRATION	ANTAGONIZE	BELARUSIAN	CARTHAMINE	CONCINNITY	DECIMALIZE
ABROGATION	ANTARCTICA	BELLARMINE	CARTHUSIAN	CONCLUDING	DECLENSION
ABSCISSION	ANTHEOLION	BENEDICITE	CARTOONIST	CONCLUSION	DECOLORIZE
ABSOLUTION	ANTHRACINE	BENEFICIAL	CASTRATION	CONCLUSIVE	DECORATION
ABSOLUTISM	ANTHRACITE	BENTHAMITE	CATABOLISM	CONCOCTION	DECORATIVE
ABSORPTION	ANTIMONIAN	BENZEDRINE	CATARRHINE	CONCRETION	DEDICATION
ABSTENTION	ANTINOMIAN	BERNARDINE	CATEGORISE	CONCUSSION	DEFAMATION
ABYSSINIAN	ANTIOCHIAN	BERSAGLIER	CATEGORIZE	CONDOTTIER	DEFECATION
ACCOMPLICE	ANTISOCIAL	BESTIALITY	CENTENNIAL	CONDUCTING	DEFINITION
ACCOMPLISH	APOLLONIAN	BEWITCHING	CENTRALIZE	CONDUCTION	DEFINITIVE
ACCOUNTING	APOLLONIUS	BIOCHEMIST	CEREMONIAL	CONFECTION	DEFLECTION
ACCUBATION	APOTHECIUM	BIOPHYSICS	CEREMONIES	CONFESSION	DELEGATION
ACCUSATION	APPARITION	BISSEXTILE	CESTRACION	CONFORMIST	DELIGATION
ACCUSATIVE	APPETITIVE	BITTERLING	CHAFFERING	CONFORMITY	DELIRATION
ACROBATICS	APPETIZING	BLACKENING	CHANDELIER	CONGESTION	DELPHINIUM
ACROTERION	APPOSITION	BLACKSHIRT	CHANGELING	CONNECTING	DEMIRELIEF
ACTIVITIST	APPRENTICE	BLACKSMITH	CHAPTALISE	CONNECTION	DEMOBILISE
ADAMANTINE	AQUAMANILE	BLEPHARISM	CHATELAINE	CONNECTIVE	DEMOBILIZE
ADAPTATION	AQUAMARINE	BLISTERING	CHAUCERIAN	CONNIPTION	DEMOLITION
ADHIBITION	ARAUCANIAN	BLITHERING	CHAUVINISM	CONQUERING	DEMORALISE
ADMIRATION	AREFACTION	BLITZKRIEG	CHAUVINIST	CONSENSION	DEMORALIZE
ADMONITION	AREOPAGITE	BLUNDERING	CHECKPOINT	CONSORTIUM	DENTIFRICE
ADRENALINE	ARIMASPIAN	BOLLANDIST	CHESSYLITE	CONSTRAINT	DEPILATION
ADULLAMITE	ARSMETRICK	BOLSHEVIST	CHEVESAILE	CONSULTING	DEPOSITION
ADULTERINE	ARTIFICIAL	BOMBARDIER	CHIFFONIER	CONTENTION	DEPRESSING
AEROBATICS	ARUNDELIAN	BOOKMOBILE	CHREMATIST	CONTIGUITY	DEPRESSION
AESTHETICS	ASAFOETIDA	BORDERLINE	CHRYSOLITE	CONTINUING	DEPRESSIVE
AFFABILITY	ASCETICISM	BORDRAGING	CIRCASSIAN	CONTINUITY	DEPUTATION
AFFLICTION	ASPARAGINE	BOURIGNIAN	CIRCUMCISE	CONTORTION	DERIVATION
AFRICANISM	ASPHALTITE	BOWDLERISE	CISPONTINE	CONTRADICT	DERIVATIVE
AGGRANDISE	ASPIRATION	BOWDLERIZE	CISTERCIAN	CONTRARILY	DESCENDING
AGGRESSION	ASSEMBLING	BRADYSEISM	CLAMOURING	CONTRITION	DESCRIBING
AGGRESSIVE	ASSUMPTION	BRAINCHILD	CLASPKNIFE	CONVECTION	DESOLATION
AGONISTICS	ASSUMPTIVE	BRIGANDINE	CLASSICISM	CONVENTION	DESPAIRING
AGRONOMIST	ASTOUNDING	BRIGANTINE	CLASSICIST	CONVERSION	DESSIATINE
ALABANDINE	ATHANASIAN	BRITISHISM	CLASSIFIED	CONVICTION	DESSYATINE
ALABANDITE	ATRACURIUM	BROOMSTICK	CLEMENTINE	CONVINCING	DETONATION
ALCOHOLISM	ATTRACTION	BUCHMANISM	COCKATRICE	CONVULSION	DETRACTION
ALECTORINE	ATTRACTIVE	BURGEONING	COGITATION	CONVULSIVE	DEVELOPING
ALGONQUIAN	AUDIBILITY	BURGLARIZE	COLBERTINE	COPULATION	DEVOLUTION
ALIENATION	AUDITORIUM	BUTCHERING	COLCHICINE	COQUETTISH	DIALECTICS
ALKALINITY	AUSTRALIAN	BUTTERFISH	COLEORHIZA	COQUIMBITE	DICHROMISM
ALLEGATION	AUTOMATION	BUTTERMILK	COLLAPSING	CORDIALITY	DIGITORIUM
ALLIGATION	AUTOMATIZE	BYELECTION	COLLECTING	CORDIERITE	DIGRESSION
ALLOCATION	AUTOMOBILE	CALAVERITE	COLLECTION	CORINTHIAN	DILATATION
ALLOCUTION	AUTOMOTIVE	CALEDONIAN	COLLECTIVE	CORONATION	DIMINUTION
ALMSGIVING	AVANTURINE	CALORIFIER	COLLOQUIAL	CORRECTING	DIMINUTIVE
ALPHONSINE	AVENTURINE	CALYDONIAN	COLORATION	CORRECTION	DINNERTIME
ALTERATION	AVERRHOISM	CAMERONIAN	COMBUSTION	CORRECTIVE	DIRECTOIRE
AMARYLLIDS	BABYLONIAN	CANDLEFISH	COMFORTING	CORRUPTING	DIREMPTION

DISABILITY	ESCRITOIRE	FRATERNISE	HYDRAULICS	INVALIDITY	MAINSPRING
DISAPPOINT	ESCULAPIAN	FRATERNITY	HYPOCORISM	INVITATION	MALTHUSIAN
DISCERNING	ESTIMATION	FRATERNIZE	IGNIMBRITE	INVOCATION	MANAGERIAL
DISCIPLINE	ETERNALIZE	FRATRICIDE	ILLEGALITY	INVOLUTION	MANGABEIRA
DISCRETION	ETHYLAMINE	FUMIGATION	IMBECILITY	IRREMEDIAL	MANICURIST
DISCURSIVE	EUCHLORINE	FURNISHING	IMMATERIAL	IRRIGATION	MANUSCRIPT
DISCUSSING	EUHEMERISM	GADOLINIUM	IMMATURITY	IRRITATING	MARASCHINO
DISCUSSION	EUSTACHIAN	GAINGIVING	IMMEMORIAL	IRRITATION	MARCIONITE
DISGUSTING	EVACUATION	GAINSTRIVE	IMMOBILITY	ISABELLINE	MARGUERITE
DISINCLINE	EVALUATION	GALIMATIAS	IMMOBILIZE	ISOLEUCINE	MASTERMIND
DISMISSIVE	EVANGELIST	GALUMPHING	IMMOLATION	ISOMETRICS	MATCHSTICK
DISPENSING	EVANGELIZE	GARNIERITE	IMMORALITY	ISONIAZIDE	MATURATION
DISPERSION	EVERYTHING	GEMINATION	IMPALUDISM	JACULATION	MAXIMALIST
DISQUALIFY	EVITERNITY	GENERALISE	IMPERATIVE	JAMESONITE	MAXIMILIAN
DISRUPTION	EXALTATION	GENERALITY	IMPOSITION	JAYWALKING	MAYONNAISE
DISRUPTIVE	EXCAVATION	GENERALIZE	IMPOVERISH	JEOPARDISE	MEANDERING
DISSECTION	EXECRATION	GENERATION	IMPRESSION	JEOPARDIZE	MEDICATION
DISSENSION	EXHALATION	GENEROSITY	IMPRESSIVE	JERRYBUILT	MEDIOCRITY
DISSENTING	EXHAUSTING	GENETHLIAC	IMPURITIES	JOCULARITY	MEDITATION
DISSERVICE	EXHAUSTION	GEOPHYSICS	IMPUTATION	JOHNSONIAN	MEDITATIVE
DISSUASION	EXHAUSTIVE	GEOTROPISM	INACTIVITY	JOURNALISM	MEITNERIUM
DISTENSION	EXHIBITION	GERIATRICS	INBREEDING	JOURNALIST	MELACONITE
DISTILLING	EXHUMATION	GHIBELLINE	INCAPACITY	JUBILATION	MELANESIAN
DISTORTION	EXPEDITION	GILBERTIAN	INCAPARINA	KARMATHIAN	MENECHMIAN
DISTURBING	EXPIRATION	GILBERTINE	INCHOATIVE	KENTUCKIAN	MEPERIDINE
DIURNALIST	EXPOSITION	GIRDLERINK	INCIVILITY	KESSELRING	MERCANTILE
DIVINATION	EXPRESSION	GLACIATION	INCREASING	KIDNAPPING	METABOLISE
DOMINATING	EXPRESSIVE	GLAMOURISE	INCUBATION	KIMBERLITE	METABOLISM
DOMINATION	EXTINCTION	GLAUCONITE	INDAPAMIDE	KRIEGSPIEL	METHEDRINE
DOPPLERITE	EXTINGUISH	GLISTENING	INDECISION	LACERATION	MIDLOTHIAN
DOWNSIZING	EXTRACTION	GLITTERING	INDECISIVE	LACKADAISY	MILITARISM
DOWNSTAIRS	EXULTATION	GNOSTICISM	INDEFINITE	LACUSTRINE	MILITARIST
DRAWSTRING	FACESAVING	GOLIATHISE	INDEXATION	LAMARCKISM	MILLENNIUM
DROSOPHILA	FACILITIES	GORMANDIZE	INDICATION	LAMINATION	MINIMALISM
DURABILITY	FANATICISM	GRADUALISM	INDICATIVE	LANDSTHING	MINIMALIST
DYSCRASITE	FANTASTICO	GRADUATION	INDICOLITE	LANTHANIDE	MISLEADING
DYSPROSIUM	FANTOCCINI	GRAMMARIAN	INDIGOLITE	LAURDALITE	MISOGYNIST
EARTHSHINE	FAREPAYING	GRANDCHILD	INDONESIAN	LAURENTIAN	MISPRISION
EASTERLING	FARRANDINE	GRANGERISM	INDUSTRIAL	LAURUSTINE	MITIGATING
EATANSWILL	FASCIATION	GRANGERIZE	INEQUALITY	LAURVIKITE	MITIGATION
ECUADORIAN	FASTMOVING	GRAPTOLITE	INFIDELITY	LAWABIDING	MODERATION
ELASTICITY	FATALITIES	GRATIFYING	INFIGHTING	LAWRENCIUM	MODULATION
ELEUSINIAN	FAVORITISM	GRATILLITY	INFINITIVE	LEGIBILITY	MOISTURIZE
ELONGATION	FEDERALISM	GREENSTICK	INFLECTION	LEGITIMIZE	MONARCHIST
EMACIATION	FEDERALIST	GROUNDLING	INFLICTION	LENGTHWISE	MONETARISM
EMBONPOINT	FEDERATION	GROVELLING	INFRACTION	LENOCINIUM	MONETARIST
EMENDATION	FEMININITY	GUARNERIUS	INHALATION	LESBIANISM	MONOPODIUM
EMIGRATION	FERRANDINE	GUILLOTINE	INHIBITING	LEVITATION	MONOPOLISE
EMISSIVITY	FESCENNINE	GYMNASTICS	INHIBITION	LHERZOLITE	MONOPOLIZE
EMULSIFIER	FETTUCCINE	GYPSOPHILA	INHUMANITY	LIBERALISM	MONOTHEISM
ENCHANTING	FIGURATION	HABITATION	INITIATION	LIBERALITY	MORALITIES
ENGROSSING	FIGURATIVE	HAIRSPRING	INITIATIVE	LIBERALIZE	MORATORIUM
ENSANGUINE	FILTRATION	HALIEUTICS	INJUNCTION	LIBERATION	MORISONIAN
ENTERPRISE	FINGERLING	HALLOYSITE	INNOVATION	LIBRETTIST	MOTHERLIKE
ENTRANCING	FINGERPICK	HANDSPRING	INNOVATIVE	LIGNOCAINE	MOTIVATION
ENTREATING	FLASHPOINT	HANOVERIAN	INSECURITY	LIMBURGITE	MOUSSELINE
EPHRAIMITE	FLATTERING	HAUSTORIUM	INSIPIDITY	LIMITATION	MOUSTERIAN
EPIDIORITE	FLAVOURING	HESITATION	INSPECTION	LITHUANIAN	MUCKRAKING
EPILIMNION	FLICKERING	HIGHFLYING	INSULARITY	LITIGATION	MULIEBRITY
EPISTEMICS	FLIRTATION	HIPPOGRIFF	INSULATION	LOCOMOTION	MULTIPLIED
EPITHELIUM	FLORENTINE	HOMECOMING	INTERSTICE	LOCOMOTIVE	MULTIPLIER
EPONYCHIUM	FORBEARING	HOMEOUSIAN	INTERTRIGO	LUMINARIST	MUTABILITY
EQUANIMITY	FORBIDDING	HOMOGENIZE	INTERTWINE	LUMINOSITY	MUTILATION
EQUATORIAL	FOREBODING	HOMOOUSIAN	INTIMATION	LUSITANIAN	MYCORRHIZA
EQUESTRIAN	FORFAITING	HONORARIUM	INTINCTION	LUTESTRING	MYOCARDIAL
EQUITATION	FORTISSIMO	HORRIFYING	INTONATION	LYSENKOISM	NARCISSISM
ERGONOMICS	FOUNDATION	HOUSEMAIDS	INTRIGUING	MABINOGION	NASTURTIUM
ERUCTATION	FOURIERISM	HUMANITIES	INUNDATION	MACEDONIAN	NATATORIAL
ESCALATION	FOXHUNTING	HUMIDIFIER	INVALIDISM	MAGNIFYING	NATATORIUM

NATIONWIDE	PANSOPHIST	PLASTICITY	PROTRUSION	REVITALIZE	SEXOLOGIST
NATURALISM	PAPAVERINE	PLEBISCITE	PROVERBIAL	REVIVALIST	SHAMPOOING
NATURALIST	PAPERKNIFE	PLIABILITY	PROVINCIAL	REVOCATION	SHATTERING
NATURALIZE	PARADOXIDE	PLOUGHWISE	PRUDENTIAL	REVOLUTION	SHELDONIAN
NAUSEALISM	PARADOXINE	PLUMASSIER	PSALTERIUM	RHAPSODISE	SHERARDISE
NAUSEATIVE	PARAGONITE	PLUNDERING	PUBLISHING	RHAPSODIST	SHERARDISE
NAVIGATION	PARAMARIBO	POLITICIAN	PUMMELLING	RHAPSODIZE	SHIMMERING
NETWORKING	PARGETTING	POLITICIZE	PUNDIGRION	RHEUMATICS	SHOESTRING
NEUTRALISE	PARNASSIAN	POLYGAMIST	PURITANISM	RHEUMATISM	SHORTENING
NEUTRALITY	PARNELLISM	POLYMERIZE	PUTREFYING	RIGELATION	SHROVETIDE
NEUTRALIZE	PARTIALITY	POLYNESIAN	PYRAGYRITE	ROISTERING	SHUDDERING
NIDDERLING	PASTEURISE	POLYNOMIAL	PYRIDOXINE	ROLLICKING	SIDERATION
NIGHTSHIRT	PASTEURIZE	POLYTHEISM	PYROMANIAC	ROSANILINE	SILVERBILL
NIGHTSTICK	PATAGONIAN	POMERANIAN	QUARANTINE	ROSEMALING	SILVERFISH
NOMINALIST	PATAVINITY	POPULARITY	QUARTERING	ROTHSCHILD	SILVERSIDE
NOMINATION	PATRIOTISM	POPULARIZE	RADICALISM	RUDOLPHINE	SIMILARITY
NOMINATIVE	PEACHERINO	POPULATION	RAMPALLIAN	RUMBULLION	SIMPLICITY
NONFICTION	PECULATION	PORLOCKING	RAVENSBILL	RUMINATION	SIMULATING
NONSMOKING	PEDESTRIAN	PORTIONIST	REAPPRAISE	RUMINATIVE	SIMULATION
NORBERTINE	PEDIATRICS	POSITIVIST	REASSURING	RUPESTRIAN	SINARCHIST
NOSOCOMIAL	PEJORATIVE	POSSESSION	RECIDIVISM	RUPICOLINE	SINARQUIST
NOTABILITY	PENNILLION	POSSESSIVE	RECIDIVIST	RUSSIANIZE	SINOATRIAL
NOURISHING	PEPPERMILL	POSTCHAISE	RECITATION	SACCHARIDE	SKEPTICISM
NOVACULITE	PEPPERMINT	POSTILLION	RECITATIVE	SACCHARINE	SKINDIVING
NUCLEONICS	PERCENTILE	POSTLIMINY	RECITATIVO	SADDLEBILL	SKUPSHTINA
NUMERATION	PERCEPTION	POSTSCRIPT	RECREATION	SALINGIAN	SLUMBERING
OBLIGATION	PERCEPTIVE	PRAEMUNIRE	REDEMPTION	SALPINGIAN	SMARAGDINE
OBLOMOVISM	PERCUSSION	PRAETORIAN	REDRUTHITE	SALIVATION	SMATTERING
OBSTETRICS	PERFECTION	PRAETORIUM	REELECTION	SALUTATION	SNIGGERING
OCCUPATION	PERFORMING	PRAGMATISM	REFLECTING	SAMARSKITE	SNORKELING
OCEANARIUM	PERIDOTITE	PRAGMATIST	REFLECTION	SANATORIUM	SNOWMOBILE
OCEANGOING	PERIHELION	PRECAUTION	REFLECTIVE	SANCTIFIED	SOLIDARITY
OCTODECIMO	PERMEATION	PREDESTINE	REFRACTION	SANCTITIES	SOLIFIDIAN
ODELSTHING	PERMISSION	PREDICTION	REFRACTIVE	SANDERLING	SOLUBILITY
ODONTOLITE	PERMISSIVE	PREHENSILE	REFRESHING	SANITARIUM	SOMBRERITE
OFFPUTTING	PERORATION	PRELECTION	REFUTATION	SANITATION	SOURDELINE
OMOPHORION	PEROVSKITE	PRESSURIZE	REGRESSION	SATISFYING	SPALLATION
ONOMASTICS	PERPETUITY	PRETENSION	REGRESSIVE	SATURATION	SPARTACIST
OPHICLEIDE	PERPLEXING	PREVAILING	REGULARITY	SAUROPSIDA	SPEAKERINE
OPPOSITION	PERPLEXITY	PREVENTION	REGULARIZE	SAXICOLINE	SPECIALISE
OPPRESSION	PERQUISITE	PREVENTIVE	REGULATION	SBUDDIKINS	SPECIALISM
OPPRESSIVE	PERSUADING	PRIMORDIAL	RELATIVITY	SCANDALISE	SPECIALIST
OPPROBRIUM	PERSUASION	PRINCIPIUM	RELAXATION	SCANDALIZE	SPECIALITY
ORDINARILY	PERSUASIVE	PROCEEDING	RELAXATIVE	SCARLATINA	SPECIALIZE
ORDINATION	PERVERSION	PROCESSING	RELEGATION	SCARLETINA	SPENCERIAN
ORDOVICIAN	PERVERSITY	PROCESSION	RELINQUISH	SCATTERING	SPENSERIAN
ORTHOCAINE	PETRIFYING	PROCLIVITY	RELOCATION	SCEPTICISM	SPERMICIDE
ORTHOPTICS	PHAELONIAN	PRODUCTION	REMONETISE	SCHOOLGIRL	SPERRYLITE
OSCITATION	PHANTASIME	PRODUCTIVE	RENOVATION	SCOOTERIST	SPHALERITE
OSCULATION	PHANTASIST	PROFESSION	REORGANIZE	SCREECHING	SPILLIKINS
OSMETERIUM	PHARMACIST	PROFUNDITY	REPARATION	SCRIBBLING	SPIRKETING
OUTLANDISH	PHILIPPINA	PROGESSION	REPERTOIRE	SCROUNGING	SPOLIATION
OUTPOURING	PHILIPPINE	PROJECTILE	REPETITION	SCRUTINISE	SPOLIATIVE
OVEREATING	PHILISTINE	PROJECTING	REPETITIVE	SCRUTINIZE	SPOONERISM
OVERPRAISE	PHILLIPINA	PROJECTION	REPRESSION	SCURRILITY	SPORANGIUM
OVERRIDING	PHILLIPINE	PROMETHIUM	REPRESSIVE	SECRETAIRE	SPRINGLIKE
OZYMANDIAS	PHLOGOPITE	PROPENSITY	REPUTATION	SECULARIZE	SPRINGTIME
PACIFICISM	PHRENESIAC	PROPERTIUS	RESEMBLING	SECURITIES	SPRINKLING
PADDLEFISH	PIANISSIMO	PROPORTION	RESOLUTION	SELEGILINE	STAGGERING
PAGINATION	PICAYUNISH	PROPULSION	RESOUNDING	SENATORIAL	STAGNATION
PALAGONITE	PILGARLICK	PROSCENIUM	RESPECTING	SENSUALITY	STALACTITE
PALATALISE	PINCUSHION	PROSERPINA	RESPECTIVE	SEPARATION	STALAGMITE
PALESTRINA	PIONEERING	PROSERPINE	RESPONSIVE	SEPARATISM	STAMMERING
PALFRENIER	PLAGIARISE	PROSPERINA	RESUMPTION	SEPARATIST	STANDPOINT
PALLIATIVE	PLAGIARISM	PROSPERITY	RETINALITE	SEPTENNIAL	STANDSTILL
PALUSTRINE	PLAGIARIST	PROTECTION	RETRACTION	SEPTUAGINT	STAPHYLINE
PANAMANIAN	PLAGIARIZE	PROTECTIVE	RETRAINING	SEQUENTIAL	STARVATION
PANARITIUM	PLANTATION	PROTERVITY	RETREATING	SERPENTINE	STARVELING
PANCRATIUM	PLASTICINE	PROTRUSILE	REVELATION	SEXAGESIMA	STATISTICS
				SEXDUCTION	STAUROLITE

STEALTHILY	TAMBOURINE	UNDERWRITE	ZWITTERION	ARISTOTLES	EMMENTALER
STENTORIAN	TANGANYIKA	UNDESCRIED	CHAPARAJOS	ASTRAGALUS	EMPEDOCLES
STEPHANITE	TANGENTIAL	UNDULATING	CHAPAREJOS	BAMBOOZLED	ENCEPHALON
STICHARION	TAPDANCING	UNDULATION	HALLELUJAH	BANDERILLA	ENKEPHALIN
STIGMATISE	TARPAULING	UNEDIFYING	BACKPACKER	BANDERILLO	ERIOCAULON
STIGMATIZE	TARTRAZINE	UNFAMILIAR	BEAVERSKIN	BARCAROLLE	ERYSIPELAS
STILLICIDE	TAXONOMIST	UNFLAGGING	BONESHAKER	BEDEVILLED	ESCADRILLE
STOUTHRIEF	TECHNETIUM	UNIFORMITY	BOOKMARKER	BEDRAGGLED	ESPADRILLE
STRACCHINO	TECHNICIAN	UNINVITING	BOOTLICKER	BESTSELLER	ESPECIALLY
STRAGGLING	TELEVISION	UNIVERSITY	BOOZINGKEN	BIANNUALLY	EUTRAPELIA
STRAMONIUM	TEMPTATION	UNLADYLIKE	BOUSINGKEN	BIENNIALLY	EVENTUALLY
STRATEGIST	TENNANTITE	UNOCCUPIED	CATCRACKER	BLACKBULLY	EXOTICALLY
STREAMLINE	TEPIDARIUM	UNOFFICIAL	CLOCKMAKER	BLISSFULLY	EXTERNALLY
STREETWISE	TERRIFYING	UNSALARIED	COMSTOCKER	BOOKSELLER	FAITHFULLY
STRYCHNINE	TERTIARIES	UNSETTLING	COPPERSKIN	BOTTICELLI	FENESTELLA
STULTIFIED	TESCHENITE	UNSLEEPING	CORNCOCKLE	BREAKABLES	FISHSELLER
STUPEFYING	THALASSIAN	UNSWERVING	CORNFLAKES	BROCATELLE	FONTANELLE
STYLISTICS	THAUMASITE	UNTHINKING	DOWNMARKET	BUCEPHALUS	FONTICULUS
SUBHEADING	THEODOLITE	UNUNHEXIUM	DRESSMAKER	CAERPHILLY	FONTINALIS
SUBJECTION	THEOLOGIAN	UNUNNILIUM	FIREWALKER	CAMPANELLA	FOOTBALLER
SUBJECTIVE	THEOLOGISE	UNYIELDING	FIRTHSOKEN	CANDELILLA	FORCEFULLY
SUBMERSION	THEOLOGIST	UPBRINGING	FRITHSOKEN	CAPITELLUM	FRATICELLI
SUBMISSION	THICKENING	UPSTANDING	GOATSUCKER	CASCARILLA	FRAXINELLA
SUBMISSIVE	THREADLIKE	UROSTEGITE	GRIDLOCKED	CEREBELLUM	FRINGILLID
SUBREPTION	THRENODIAL	USUCAPTION	HALLMARKED	CHANCELLOR	FRUITFULLY
SUBROUTINE	THUMBIKINS	USURPATION	HAMESUCKEN	CHAPFALLEN	FUSTANELLA
SUBSECTION	THUNDERING	VALIDATION	HAMSHACKLE	CHEERFULLY	FUSTANELLE
SUBSELLIUM	TIMESAVING	VANDERBILT	HANDPICKED	CHEMICALLY	GARGOUILLE
SUBSPECIES	TIROCINIUM	VARICOSITY	HITCHHIKER	CHINCHILLA	GIBBERELLA
SUBSTATION	TOILETRIES	VARNISHING	HOMEWORKER	CHRONICLER	GOODFELLOW
SUBTROPICS	TOLERATION	VEGETARIAN	HOODWINKED	CHRONICLES	GRACEFULLY
SUBVENTION	TOPICALITY	VEGETATION	HUMPBACKED	CHUCKWALLA	GRANADILLA
SUBVERSION	TOPOLOGIST	VELITATION	ICEBREAKER	CINDERELLA	GRATEFULLY
SUBVERSIVE	TORBERNITE	VENERATION	KENSPECKLE	CIRCUMFLEX	GRENADILLA
SUCCEEDING	TORRENTIAL	VERMILLION	LANDLOCKED	CITRONELLA	GUATEMALAN
SUCCESSION	TORTELLINI	VIDARABINE	LAWBREAKER	CLAIRCOLLE	GUTTURALLY
SUCCESSIVE	TOURMALINE	VINDICTIVE	LUMPSUCKER	CLARABELLA	HABITUALLY
SUDATORIUM	TRAMPOLINE	VINEGARISH	MATCHMAKER	CLINICALLY	HALFDOLLAR
SUFFRAGIST	TRANSCRIBE	VIROLOGIST	MERRYMAKER	COCKABULLY	HALLUBALOO
SUGGESTION	TRANSCRIPT	VIRTUOSITY	MINEWORKER	CODSWALLOP	HARDBOILED
SUGGESTIVE	TRANSITION	VISIBILITY	MINIMARKET	COLOSSALLY	HAUSTELLUM
SUMMERTIME	TRANSITIVE	VISITATION	MONEYMAKER	COMMONALTY	HECTICALLY
SUNBATHING	TRAUMATIZE	VOCABULIST	MOSSBUNKER	COMMUNALLY	HEMOPHILIA
SUPPORTING	TRAVELLING	VOLATILITY	NUTCRACKER	CONCHIGLIE	HEPTATHLON
SUPPORTIVE	TRAVERTINE	VOLUBILITY	OUTSPECKLE	CONCHIOLIN	HEROICALLY
SURFRIDING	TRECENTIST	VOLUTATION	OVERWORKED	CONTRAFLOW	HOMUNCULUS
SURPASSING	TRICLINIUM	WALDENSIAN	PAWNBROKER	CONTROLLER	HULLABALOO
SURPRISING	TRIDENTINE	WALLACHIAN	PEACEMAKER	CORNSTALKS	HYPERBOLIC
SURREALISM	TRINACRIAN	WARRANDICE	PENTELIKON	COUNCILLOR	HYPERDULIA
SURREALIST	TRIPARTITE	WASSAILING	PERIWINKLE	COUNSELLOR	IMMORTELLE
SUSCEPTIVE	TRIPLICITY	WATERSKIER	PICKPOCKET	CRIMINALLY	INFERNALLY
SUSPENSION	TRISKELION	WEAVERBIRD	POCKMARKED	CRITICALLY	INFORMALLY
SUSTAINING	TRIVIALITY	WELLSPRING	RAMSHACKLE	CURRICULUM	INTERNALLY
SWAGGERING	TRIVIALIZE	WESTERNIZE	SEERSUCKER	DEMOISELLE	IRONICALLY
SWALLOWING	TROCTOLITE	WHEWELLITE	SHOPWALKER	DÉSHABILLÉ	JARGONELLE
SWEATSHIRT	TROMBONIST	WHIRLYBIRD	SILVERSKIN	DIAGONALLY	JUDICIALLY
SWEETBRIAR	TROPHONIUS	WHISPERING	SLAMMERKIN	DIDASCALIC	KATERFELTO
SWEETENING	TROTSKYITE	WHITTERICK	TIEBREAKER	DIDUNCULUS	KINCHINLAY
SWELTERING	TURPENTINE	WINDOWSILL	TRAFFICKER	DIFFICULTY	KLEBSIELLA
SWORDSTICK	TYPESCRIPT	WINTERTIME	UNDERTAKER	DISCOBOLUS	LADYKILLER
SYMPATHISE	ULCERATION	WOLFRAMITE	UNPROVOKED	DISHABILLE	LENTICULAR
SYMPATHIZE	UNASSUMING	WORTHWHILE	WATCHMAKER	DISLOYALTY	LIBREVILLE
SYMPHONIUM	UNAVAILING	WRONGDOING	WOODPECKER	DISMANTLED	LINGULELLA
SYMPTOMIZE	UNBECOMING	WUNDERKIND	WOODWORKER	DISSEMBLER	LONGFELLOW
SYNCRETISE	UNBLINKING	WYCLIFFIAN	ABNORMALLY	DISSIMILAR	LUPERCALIA
SYNTHESIZE	UNBLUSHING	YELLOWGIRL	ACETABULAR	DOLICHOLIS	MANDEVILLE
TABULATION	UNDERLYING	YGGDRASILL	ACETABULUM	DOUBTFULLY	MANZANILLA
TAGLIARINI	UNDERSHIRT	ZAPOROGIAN	ALLYCHOLLY	DREADFULLY	MARGINALIA
TAILGATING	UNDERSKIRT	ZIDOVUDINE	AMBARVALIA	ELEGABALUS	MARGINALLY

MATERIALLY	SALTCELLAR	VULCANALIA	PATRONYMIC	CAVICORNIA	FLATULENCE
MATERNALLY	SARCOCOLLA	WASTEFULLY	PENTSTEMON	CHAMBRANLE	FLORIBUNDA
MEADOWPLAN	SATURNALIA	WATCHFULLY	POLYPHEMUS	CHAMPIGNON	FOOTPRINTS
MERCIFULLY	SCHWARZLOT	WATERCOLOR	PROGRAMMER	CHAPLAINCY	FOREDAMNED
METHUSALEH	SCORNFULLY	WATERMELON	RAILWAYMAN	CHARDONNAY	FORERUNNER
METHUSELAH	SCREENPLAY	WEEDKILLER	ROBERDSMAN	CHEVISANCE	FOREWARNED
METROPOLIS	SEGUIDILLA	WHOLESALER	ROBERTSMAN	CHIROMANCY	FOURTEENTH
MONTICULUS	SELFSTYLED	WILDFOWLER	SALBUTAMOL	CLEROMANCY	FRACTIONAL
MORTADELLA	SERRADELLA	WILLYWILLY	SALESWOMAN	COELACANTH	FRIGHTENED
MOURNFULLY	SERRADILLA	WORKAHOLIC	SARCOLEMMA	COGNISANCE	FUNCTIONAL
MOZZARELLA	SERRASALMO	WRONGFULLY	SCHOLAEMIA	COGNIZANCE	GINGERSNAP
NATIONALLY	SGANARELLE	ABHIDHAMMA	SCOTSWOMAN	COMEDIENNE	GODPARENTS
NECROPOLIS	SHAMEFULLY	ACCUSTOMED	SERVICEMAN	COMPETENCE	GONFANONER
NEWFANGLED	SHOPSOILED	ALDERWOMAN	SIMILLIMUM	COMPLIANCE	GOVERNANCE
NICROSILAL	SHRIEVALTY	ANASTIGMAT	STALHELMER	CONDIMENTS	GRASSLANDS
NOTIONALLY	SHRIVELLED	ANTICLIMAX	STRABISMUS	CONDOLENCE	GREENFINCH
OFFICIALLY	SIGNORELLI	ASTRONOMER	SUPERHUMAN	CONFERENCE	GRIDIRONER
ORIGINALLY	SINSEMILLA	BACKGAMMON	SUPERWOMAN	CONFIDANTE	GUIDELINES
OSTEOCOLLA	SKILLFULLY	BLASPHEMER	TOWNSWOMAN	CONFIDENCE	HANKYPANKY
PADDYMELON	SOFTBOILED	BONDSWOMAN	TULARAEMIA	CONFLUENCE	HEADPHONES
PAINKILLER	SOMERVILLE	BRESSUMMER	UNFATHOMED	CONNIVANCE	HEPTAGONAL
PANNICULUS	SPECTACLED	CACODAEMON	UNINFORMED	CONSCIENCE	HIEROMANCY
PARALLELED	SPECTACLES	CATACHUMEN	UNREDEEMED	CONSONANCE	HIPPOMANES
PARAPHILIA	SPIRACULUM	CATECHUMEN	WEATHERMAN	CONSONANTS	HISTRIONIC
PARTICULAR	SPITEFULLY	CAVALRYMAN	WELSHWOMAN	CONSTRINGE	HOLOFERNES
PASTORELLA	SUGARALLIE	CENTESIMAL	WIDDICOMBE	CONTINENCE	HOMOPHONIC
PATERNALLY	SURGICALLY	CHAIRWOMAN	WINDJAMMER	CONVENANCE	HONEYBUNCH
PEACEFULLY	TACTICALLY	CHILDERMAS	XEROSTOMIA	CONVEYANCE	HOOTANANNY
PECCADILLO	TARANTELLA	CHIRONOMIC	ABHORRENCE	COPARCENER	HOOTENANNY
PEELGARLIC	TASTEFULLY	CLANSWOMAN	ABORIGINAL	CORDWAINER	HOOTNANNIE
PENETRALIA	TEETOTALER	COUNTRYMAN	ABSORBANCE	CORPULENCE	HORNBLENDE
PENICILLIN	TENDRILLED	DAYDREAMER	ABSTINENCE	CORRIGENDA	HYDROPONIC
PENINSULAR	TERMINALIA	DECAGRAMME	ACCORDANCE	CRAPULENCE	IATROGENIC
PENTATHLON	TERMINALLY	DISCLAIMER	ADDITIONAL	CROSSBONES	IMPARLANCE
PERSEPOLIS	TESTICULAR	DUODECIMAL	ADMITTANCE	DEFEASANCE	IMPATIENCE
PERSONALLY	THANKFULLY	DUTCHWOMAN	ALCHERINGA	DEFICIENCY	IMPERSONAL
PETRONELLA	TOCCATELLA	ELECTROMER	ALDERMANLY	DEHISCENCE	IMPORTANCE
PHILATELIC	TORRICELLI	ENGLISHMAN	ALGOLAGNIA	DEPENDENCE	IMPRUDENCE
PHYSICALLY	TOURBILLON	ENGLISHMEN	ALLEGEANCE	DEPENDENCY	INCUMBENCY
PICCADILLY	TRAGICALLY	EPIDIDYMUS	ALLEGIANCE	DETERMINED	INDISTINCT
PICCALILLI	TRANQUILLY	EXOTHERMIC	ANAXIMENES	DETERMINER	INDUCTANCE
PILLOWSLIP	TRIANGULAR	EXPRESSMAN	ANTIPHONAL	DETERRENCE	INDULGENCE
PIRANDELLO	TRIANGULUM	GEOTHERMAL	APPEARANCE	DEVOTIONAL	INQUIRENDO
PLAYFELLOW	TROPAEOLUM	GROUNDSMAN	ASCENDANCY	DIACHRONIC	INSISTENCE
POETICALLY	TROUVAILLE	HARVESTMAN	ASCENDENCY	DIFFERENCE	INSOLVENCY
PONCHIELLI	TRUSTFULLY	HIGHWAYMAN	ASSISTANCE	DIFFIDENCE	INSURGENCY
PONTICELLO	TRUTHFULLY	HORNRIMMED	ATTENDANCE	DILETTANTE	INTESTINAL
PORTCULLIS	TUBERCULAR	HORSEWOMAN	AXINOMANCY	DIMINUENDO	INTESTINES
POTENTILLA	TURRITELLA	HYPODERMIC	BARRAMUNDA	DIPSOMANIA	IRRATIONAL
POURPARLER	TUTIVILLUS	IRISHWOMAN	BARRAMUNDI	DISARRANGE	JACKSTONES
PRAXITELES	UNDERVALUE	IRISHWOMEN	BELLADONNA	DISSIDENCE	JAGUARONDI
PRINCIPLED	UNEQUALLED	JACKHAMMER	BELONGINGS	DISSONANCE	JAGUARUNDI
PRINCIPLES	UNEXAMPLED	JOURNEYMAN	BLANCMANGE	DIVERGENCE	JOUYSAUNCE
PRODIGALLY	UNREVEALED	KEMPERYMAN	BLUEBONNET	DIVISIONAL	LANSQUENET
PUNCTUALLY	UNRIVALLED	KLOOTCHMAN	BORROWINGS	DOLCEMENTE	LATTICINIO
QUESADILLA	UNSCHOOLED	LAUNDROMAT	BRADYKININ	DRUZHINNIK	LENTIGINES
QUIRINALIA	UNSHACKLED	LEUCHAEMIA	BRILLIANCE	EBULLIENCE	LINEAMENTS
RANUNCULUS	VALLADOLID	LIGHTERMAN	BROWNLANDS	EFFICIENCY	LIPIZZANER
RATIONALLY	VAUDEVILLE	LONGCHAMPS	CALCEDONIO	EIGHTEENTH	LUXURIANCE
RECONCILED	VEGETABLES	MICHAELMAS	CALCITONIN	ELECTRONIC	MAINPERNOR
RHINOLALIA	VENEZUELAN	MIDSHIPMAN	CALESCENCE	EMBLEMENTS	MAINTAINER
RHOEADALES	VERMICELLI	MILITIAMAN	CALIFORNIA	EMOLUMENTS	MALIGNANCY
RIGHTFULLY	VERNACULAR	NEURILEMMA	CAMERLENGO	EXCELLENCE	MASKANONGE
RITORNELLE	VERSAILLES	NEUROLEMMA	CAMERLINGO	EXCELLENCY	MASKINONGE
RITORNELLO	VERTICALLY	NOBLEWOMAN	CAMPAIGNER	EXPECTANCY	MAURITANIA
ROCKABILLY	VESTIBULUM	NURSERYMAN	CAPNOMANCY	EXPEDIENCE	METHOMANIA
ROTTWEILER	VIBRACULUM	OFTENTIMES	CARTOMANCY	EXPEDIENCY	MILLIHENRY
SALMONELLA	VICTUALLER	OPHTHALMIC	CASSUMUNAR	EXPERIENCE	MISGIVINGS
SALTARELLO	VILLANELLE	PARANORMAL	CATCHPENNY	EXUBERANCE	MISOCAPNIC

MISTAKENLY	QUIESCENCE	UNLEAVENED	BREASTWORK	COURAGEOUS	GANGRENOUS
MOLENDINAR	RAWINSONDE	UNORIGINAL	BRIDEGROOM	CRETACEOUS	GASTRONOME
MOLYBDENUM	RECOMMENCE	UNREASONED	BRIDGETOWN	CREWELWORK	GASTRONOMY
MONOPHONIC	RECOMPENSE	UNSEASONED	BROADCLOTH	CRISSCROSS	GELATINOUS
MONSTRANCE	RECURRENCE	VALENTINES	BROADSWORD	CRYPTOZOIC	GENTLEFOLK
NECROMANCY	REDUNDANCY	VOCATIONAL	BROKENDOWN	CTENOPHORA	GEORGETOWN
NECTABANUS	RELUCTANCE	WAGEEARNER	BROWNSTONE	CTENOPHORE	GLUTTONOUS
NEGLIGENCE	REMITTANCE	WANDERINGS	BURDENSOME	CUDDLESOME	GONORRHOEA
NEWSAGENTS	REPENTANCE	WATERWINGS	BUTTONDOWN	CUMBERSOME	GRAMOPHONE
NINETEENTH	REPUGNANCE	WEIMARANER	BUTTONHOLE	CURVACEOUS	GRAPHOLOGY
NONALIGNED	RESILIENCE	WELLEARNED	CACUMINOUS	CUTTLEBONE	GRASSROOTS
NONONSENSE	RESISTANCE	ABSTEMIOUS	CADAVEROUS	CYSTOSCOPY	GRATUITOUS
NORTHERNER	RESORCINOL	ACANACEOUS	CAESPITOSE	DEFAMATORY	GRAVESTONE
NUDIBRANCH	RESTRAINED	ACCESSIONS	CALAMITOUS	DELTIOLOGY	GREENCLOTH
OBSERVANCE	RESURGENCE	ACCLIVIOUS	CALCAREOUS	DEMONOLOGY	GREENSTONE
OBSIDIONAL	ROADRUNNER	ACEPHALOUS	CAMPERDOWN	DEPILATORY	GREGARIOUS
OCCASIONAL	SACROSANCT	ACROGENOUS	CANCELLOUS	DEPOSITORY	GRINDSTONE
OCCURRENCE	SALICORNIA	ADULTEROUS	CANDYFLOSS	DEROGATORY	GROUNDWORK
OFFBALANCE	SALMAGUNDI	AERUGINOUS	CANNELLONI	DESPITEOUS	GUACHAMOLE
OFFLICENCE	SANDEMANIA	AFFETTUOSO	CAOUTCHOUC	DIADROMOUS	GYNECOLOGY
ORDONNANCE	SCOTODINIA	AFTERSHOCK	CAPRICIOUS	DIAPHANOUS	HAGIOSCOPE
ORIDINANCE	SENESCENCE	ALLPURPOSE	CARDIOLOGY	DICYNODONT	HAMMERLOCK
ORTHOGONAL	SHORTRANGE	ALPENSTOCK	CARMAGNOLE	DIRECTIONS	HARMONIOUS
OUGHTLINGS	SICILIENNE	AMBLYSTOMA	CARPHOLOGY	DISAPPROVE	HEADSTRONG
OUTBALANCE	SLATTERNLY	AMBULATORY	CENSORIOUS	DISASTROUS	HELIOTROPE
OXYMORONIC	SNAPHAUNCE	AMPHIBIOUS	CENTROSOME	DISCOMFORT	HELLESPONT
PAPIAMENTO	SNAPHAUNCH	AMYGDALOID	CHALCEDONY	DISCOMMODE	HERBACEOUS
PARAPHONIA	SOMNOLENCE	ANADROMOUS	CHAMAEROPS	DISCOMPOSE	HETERODOXY
PARASCENIA	SOUTHERNER	ANCIPITOUS	CHAUDFROID	DISCOPHORA	HIEROSCOPY
PARISIENNE	SPLANCHNIC	ANGLOPHOBE	CHEESEWOOD	DISHARMONY	HIPPODROME
PATHOGENIC	SPODOMANCY	ANTHOCLORE	CHEIRONOMY	DISSELBOOM	HORRENDOUS
PENSIONNAT	SPONSIONAL	ANTHROPOID	CHEQUEBOOK	DONNYBROOK	HOUSEPROUD
PENTAGONAL	STONEHENGE	APTERYGOTA	CHERRYWOOD	DOORTODOOR	HYPOGAEOUS
PENTATONIC	STRAITENED	ARENACEOUS	CHINASTONE	DRAGONROOT	HYPOGENOUS
PENTIMENTO	STRINGENCY	ARGOLEMONO	CHITARRONE	DRAKESTONE	ICONOSCOPE
PERMANENCE	STRINGENDO	ARISTOLOGY	CHITTAGONG	DREARISOME	IMMUNOLOGY
PERMANENCY	STUBBORNLY	ARYTAENOID	CHIVALROUS	DUMBLEDORE	IMPERVIOUS
PERSIENNES	SUBLIMINAL	ASPERSIONS	CHLOROFORM	ELYTRIFORM	INCAUTIOUS
PERSTRINGE	SUBMARINER	ASTOMATOUS	CHROMOSOME	EMBERGOOSE	INCESTUOUS
PERTINENCE	SUBSIDENCE	AURIFEROUS	CHRONOLOGY	EMBRYOLOGY	INDECOROUS
PESTILENCE	SUBTENANCY	AUSPICIOUS	CHURCHGOER	ENDOGAMOUS	INDIGENOUS
PETITIONER	SUFFERANCE	AUSTRALORP	CINQUEFOIL	ENDOGENOUS	INFECTIOUS
PHENOMENAL	SUPERSONIC	AUTECOLOGY	CIRCUITOUS	ENTOMOLOGY	INGLORIOUS
PHENOMENON	SUPERTONIC	AUTOECIOUS	CIRRHOPODA	ENTRYPHONE	INHIBITORY
PHILOXENIA	SUSTENANCE	AUTOGENOUS	CLAVICHORD	EPANOPHORA	INIQUITOUS
PHOTOGENIC	SUZERAINTY	AUTONOMOUS	CLEARSTORY	ETHEOSTOMA	INTERPHONE
PICCANINNY	SYNCHRONAL	AVARICIOUS	CLERESTORY	EUPHONIOUS	JABBERWOCK
PILLIWINKS	SYNCHRONIC	AVVOGADORE	CLINGSTONE	EXOBIOLOGY	KILMARNOCK
PINCHPENNY	SYNTHRONUS	BACKSTROKE	COCCINEOUS	EXPOSITORY	KNIGHTHOOD
POLYHYMNIA	TELEPHONIC	BADDERLOCK	COCKERNONY	EXTRANEOUS	KNOCKABOUT
PORTAMENTO	TEMPERANCE	BALNEOLOGY	COETANEOUS	FACTITIOUS	LABORATORY
PREARRANGE	THERMIONIC	BARLEYCORN	COLLARBONE	FALDISTORY	LACHRYMOSE
PRECEDENCE	THIRTEENTH	BARRACOOTA	COLLEMBOLA	FALLACIOUS	LANGUOROUS
PREFERENCE	THREATENED	BASKETWORK	COLPOSCOPE	FALLINGOFF	LANIGEROUS
PREPOTENCE	THREEPENCE	BATTAILOUS	COMMODIOUS	FASTIDIOUS	LASCIVIOUS
PRESCIENCE	THREEPENNY	BATTLEDOOR	COMPRADORE	FELICITOUS	LEGUMINOUS
PRESIDENCY	TRAGACANTH	BATTLEDORE	COMPULSORY	FETTERLOCK	LIBIDINOUS
PREVALENCE	TRANSIENCE	BITUMINOUS	CONCHOLOGY	FICTITIOUS	LICENTIOUS
PREVENANCY	TRILLIONTH	BLACKSTONE	CONCINNOUS	FIDDLEWOOD	LIKELIHOOD
PROMINENCE	TRUCULENCE	BLACKTHORN	CONFERVOID	FLAGITIOUS	LIVELIHOOD
PROPAGANDA	TUMESCENCE	BLASTOCOEL	CONIFEROUS	FLAMEPROOF	LOCKERROOM
PROVENANCE	TURBULENCE	BLOODSTOCK	CONSISTORY	FLOORCLOTH	LOGORRHOEA
PROVIDENCE	ULTRASONIC	BLOODSTONE	CONTAGIOUS	FLUGELHORN	LOQUACIOUS
PUBESCENCE	UNASSIGNED	BLUETHROAT	CONTIGUOUS	FOLIACEOUS	LUGUBRIOUS
PULSATANCE	UNCOMMONLY	BOISTEROUS	CONTINUOUS	FORTUITOUS	LUMPECTOMY
PYCNOGONID	UNCONFINED	BOTHERSOME	CONTRECOUP	FREEMASONS	MACKINTOSH
PYTHOGENIC	UNDERLINEN	BRAINSTORM	COPPERNOSE	FROLICSOME	MACROBIOTE
QUESTIONER	UNDERPANTS	BRAZILWOOD	CORRESPOND	FULIGINOUS	MAIDENHOOD
QUICKSANDS	UNHYGIENIC	BREASTBONE	COTTONWOOD	FULLYGROWN	MALACOLOGY

MALODOROUS	PARTHENOPE	RUTHERFORD	THIXOTROPY	CHRYSIPPUS	MARTINIQUE
MANDRAGORA	PEAUDESOIE	SACCHAROID	THREADWORM	CLODHOPPER	MONEGASQUE
MARVELLOUS	PENSIEROSO	SALUBRIOUS	THREESCORE	CORNUCOPIA	MOZAMBIQUE
MARYLEBONE	PEPPERCORN	SANDALWOOD	THROUGHOUT	DEMOGRAPHY	PICARESQUE
MASCARPONE	PEPPERWORT	SARMENTOUS	THUNDEROUS	DOORKEEPER	ROMANESQUE
MASTECTOMY	PERDENDOSI	SAVONAROLA	TIMBROLOGY	DUKKERIPEN	STATUESQUE
MASTERWORT	PERDITIOUS	SAXICOLOUS	TOUCHSTONE	EMMETROPIA	ADIAPHORON
MATTERHORN	PEREMPTORY	SCANDALOUS	TOXICOLOGY	EPISTROPHE	ADVENTURER
MEDDLESOME	PERFIDIOUS	SCANDAROON	TRADITIONS	FROGHOPPER	ADVERSARIA
MELANCHOLY	PERMAFROST	SCAPHOPODA	TRAITOROUS	GAMEKEEPER	AFTERBIRTH
MELOCOTOON	PERNICIOUS	SCHOOLBOOK	TRAJECTORY	GASTEROPOD	AFTERWARDS
MEMBRANOUS	PERSEPHONE	SCRUPULOUS	TRANSITORY	GOALKEEPER	ALCAICERIA
MENDACIOUS	PHLEBOTOMY	SCURRILOUS	TRAVANCORE	GYMNOSOPHY	ALCYONARIA
MENORRHOEA	PHOTODIODE	SDRUCCIOLA	TREMENDOUS	GYROSCOPIC	ALEXANDRIA
METICULOUS	PHOTOPHORE	SEISMOLOGY	TRENCHMORE	HOLOGRAPHY	ALLOSAURUS
METTLESOME	PHRENOLOGY	SEQUACIOUS	TRICHOLOGY	INTERLOPER	ALLOSTERIC
MICROPHONE	PHYSIOLOGY	SETTERWORT	TROUBADOUR	JACKANAPES	AMBULACRUM
MICROSCOPE	PIGEONHOLE	SHELLSHOCK	TUMBLEDOWN	LAEOTROPIC	AMPHOTERIC
MILLEFIORI	PITCHSTONE	SHELLYCOAT	TUMULTUOUS	LANDLOUPER	AMPLEFORTH
MINERALOGY	PLEROPHORY	SHOCKPROOF	TURTLEDOVE	LEAFHOPPER	ARISTOCRAT
MINESTRONE	PLOUGHBOTE	SHOVELNOSE	UBIQUINONE	LIMITROPHE	ASYMMETRIC
MINISTROKE	POCKETBOOK	SISTERHOOD	UBIQUITOUS	LOCKKEEPER	AVANTGARDE
MINUTEBOOK	POGONOTOMY	SKETCHBOOK	ULTRONEOUS	MALAPROPOS	AVICULARIA
MIRACULOUS	POLYCHROME	SLANDEROUS	UNDERCROFT	METACARPAL	BARBITURIC
MISERICORD	POLYGAMOUS	SNAKESTONE	UNDERFLOOR	METACARPUS	BARLEYBREE
MISHNAYOTH	PONEROLOGY	SNEEZEWOOD	UNDERSCORE	MONOCARPIC	BAROMETRIC
MONANDROUS	PORRACEOUS	SOLICITOUS	UNDERSTOOD	MUDSKIPPER	BEHAVIORAL
MONILIFORM	PORTENTOUS	SOUNDPROOF	UNGRACIOUS	NARCOLEPSY	BEWILDERED
MONOCHROME	POSTHUMOUS	SOUSAPHONE	UPROARIOUS	NYCTALOPIA	BIJOUTERIE
MONOECIOUS	PRATINCOLE	SPATCHCOCK	VIBRAPHONE	OSTEOLEPIS	BIPINNARIA
MONOGAMOUS	PRECARIOUS	SPECTATORS	VIBRATIONS	OVERSUPPLY	BLACKBERRY
MONOTONOUS	PRECOCIOUS	SPELEOLOGY	VICTORIOUS	PARTICIPLE	BRICKWORKS
MONTESSORI	PRECURSORY	SPIDERWORT	VILLAINOUS	PASIGRAPHY	BUREAUCRAT
MORDACIOUS	PREDACIOUS	SPIRITUOUS	VIVIPAROUS	PEDIPALPUS	CAMPESTRAL
MORIGEROUS	PREDISPOSE	SPITCHCOCK	VOCIFEROUS	PHILOSOPHY	CAMSTEERIE
MORPHOLOGY	PREDNISONE	SPOILSPORT	VOLUMINOUS	PHYLLIOPOD	CANEPHORUS
MOTHERHOOD	PREHISTORY	SPONGIFORM	VOLUPTUOUS	PLIOHIPPUS	CARDIOGRAM
MUSICOLOGY	PRESUPPOSE	SPRINGBOKS	VORAGINOUS	PRESBYOPIA	CATTLEGRID
MYRIOSCOPE	PRETINCOLE	STEREOTOMY	WATERFRONT	PROTANOPIA	CHILDBIRTH
MYSTERIOUS	PRIESTHOOD	STERTEROUS	WATERPROOF	PROTANOPIC	CHINABERRY
NARROWBOAT	PRODIGIOUS	STERTOROUS	WATERSPOUT	PYROGRAPHY	CLOISTERED
NEEDLEWORK	PROMISSORY	STILLIFORM	WATTLEWORK	RHEOTROPIC	CLOUDBERRY
NEFANDROUS	PROMONTORY	STOREFRONT	WHEATSTONE	SANDGROPER	CLOUDBURST
NESSELRODE	PROMPTBOOK	STRABOTOMY	WHIGGAMORE	SHOPKEEPER	COCHLEARIA
NETHERMOST	PROPITIOUS	STREPITOSO	WHITETHORN	SHOWJUMPER	COCKALORUM
NINCOMPOOP	PROSPEROUS	STROGANOFF	WICKERWORK	SKYSCRAPER	COLLATERAL
NOUAKCHOTT	PROVISIONS	STRONGHOLD	WITGATBOOM	SNOWCAPPED	CONCENTRIC
NUTRITIOUS	PSEPHOLOGY	STRONGROOM	YELLOWROOT	STENOTYPER	CONFEDERAL
OBLIGATORY	PSYCHOLOGY	STROPHIOLE	YELLOWWOOD	STOMATOPOD	CONSIDERED
OBSEQUIOUS	PSYCHOPOMP	STUPENDOUS	ZABAGLIONE	STRATHSPEY	CORALBERRY
ODDFELLOWS	PUCKERWOOD	SULPHUROUS	ZEUGLODONT	TELEGRAPHY	CORNSTARCH
ODONTOLOGY	PUGNACIOUS	SUPERSTORE	ALLOTROPIC	TELESCOPIC	CORROBOREE
OLEAGINOUS	QUARTEROON	SUSPICIOUS	ANASTROPHE	THROUGHPUT	CORTADERIA
OLERACEOUS	QUEENSTOWN	SWEDENBORG	APOCALYPSE	TIMEKEEPER	CROCKFORDS
OMBROPHOBE	QUICKTHORN	SYNONYMOUS	APOSTROPHE	TOLLKEEPER	CROTALARIA
OMNIVOROUS	RAVENSTONE	TABLECLOTH	ARCHETYPAL	TOPOGRAPHY	CRYOPHORUS
ORANGEWOOD	REBELLIOUS	TABLESPOON	AREOGRAPHY	TOUCHPAPER	CRYPTOGRAM
ORCHIDEOUS	REFRACTORY	TAMPERFOOT	ARISTIPPUS	TRITANOPIA	DARKHAIRED
ORTHOPNOEA	RENDEZVOUS	TANGLEFOOT	ARTOCARPUS	TYPOGRAPHY	DECAHEDRON
OSCULATORY	REPOSITORY	TAPERECORD	BOOKKEEPER	WASTEPAPER	DECIPHERED
OUTPERFORM	RHEUMATOID	TECHNOLOGY	BRACHIOPOD	WITSNAPPER	DEPARTURES
OUTRAGEOUS	RHINESTONE	TEINOSCOPE	BUCKJUMPER	WORSHIPPER	DIELECTRIC
PALINDROME	RIDICULOUS	TELEOSTOME	CACOGRAPHY	ANTIMASQUE	DINANDERIE
PALMERWORM	RIDINGHOOD	TELIOSPORE	CATAWAMPUS	BLOTTESQUE	DIPHTHERIA
PALYNOLOGY	ROBUSTIOUS	TENDERFOOT	CEPHALOPOD	CATAFALQUE	DISCOLORED
PANTALOONS	ROUNDABOUT	TENDERLOIN	CHAMBERPOT	CHAUTAUQUA	DISCOVERER
PANTOSCOPE	ROUSEABOUT	TENTERHOOK	CHICKENPOX	COMMUNIQUÉ	DISFIGURED
PARATROOPS	ROUSTABOUT	TESTACEOUS	CHIMNEYPOT	EUROCHEQUE	DISINHERIT
PARENTHOOD	RUBIGINOUS	THALLIFORM	CHINQUAPIN	HUMORESQUE	DISORDERED

DISORDERLY	NEIGHBORLY	SUPERCARGO	CAUTIOUSLY	OROGENESIS	TRANSPOSON
DUCKBOARDS	NETTLETREE	TALEBEARER	CHEMONASTY	OSMIDROSIS	TRESPASSER
EARTHWORKS	NORTHWARDS	TECHNOCRAT	COMPARISON	PADAREWSKI	TYRANNISED
EGOCENTRIC	OCTAHEDRON	THALESTRIS	COMPRESSED	PAINLESSLY	UBERMENSCH
ELDERBERRY	ORCHESTRAL	THALICTRUM	COMPRESSOR	PARACELSUS	ULTRABASIC
EMBITTERED	OVERCHARGE	THUMBSCREW	CONVALESCE	PARAENESIS	UNCTUOUSLY
EMPLASTRUM	PAEDIATRIC	THYSANURAN	COUSCOUSOU	PARAGLOSSA	UNLICENSED
ENRAPTURED	PALAESTRAL	TOCOPHEROL	DECOMPOSED	PARAPHASIA	UROPOIESIS
EPIDENDRUM	PALLBEARER	TOPSYTURVY	DIAGENESIS	PARAPHYSIS	VIGOROUSLY
EURYPTERUS	PANJANDRUM	TRANSVERSE	DIAPEDESIS	PATRONISED	VIRTUOUSLY
FAIRHAIRED	PARAMETRIC	TRILATERAL	DICKCISSEL	PERIEGESIS	WILLIAMSON
FAMILIARLY	PARARTHRIA	TROCHOTRON	DISHONESTY	PERILOUSLY	WISHYWASHY
FINISTERRE	PARVOVIRUS	UNANSWERED	DISTRESSED	PHLEGMASIA	ZOOTHAPSIS
FORTINBRAS	PATISSERIE	UNCULTURED	DOSTOEVSKY	PHOLIDOSIS	ABSTRACTED
FRONTWARDS	PECULIARLY	UNDECLARED	DRAWCANSIR	PHOTONASTY	ABUNDANTLY
GAULTHERIA	PENTAMERON	UNDERBURNT	DUNIWASSAL	PITYRIASIS	ACCIDENTAL
GENERATRIX	PENTETERIC	UNDERWORLD	ECCHYMOSIS	PLATINISED	ACCREDITED
GEOCENTRIC	PERIPHERAL	UNDETERRED	ECTHLIPSIS	PREVIOUSLY	ACHROMATIC
GLASSWORKS	PERSICARIA	UNDOCTORED	EFFERVESCE	PROAIRESIS	ACQUAINTED
GLYCOSURIA	PESCADORES	UNEXPLORED	ENANTIOSIS	PROSTHESIS	ACROAMATIC
GOOSEBERRY	PHOSPHORUS	UNFETTERED	ENDOSMOSIS	PRZEWALSKI	ADMINISTER
GROCETERIA	PHYSIOCRAT	UNFLAVORED	ENORMOUSLY	RAVENOUSLY	AFFILIATED
GUTTIFERAE	PIANOFORTE	UNHAMPERED	ENTREMESSE	RECKLESSLY	ALMACANTAR
HALFHOURLY	POLYHEDRON	UNICAMERAL	EUTHANASIA	RECOGNISED	ALMUCANTAR
HALFYEARLY	PONTEDERIA	UNILATERAL	FABULOUSLY	RECRUDESCE	ALTERNATOR
HEMICHORDA	PROCEDURAL	UNIMPAIRED	FEARLESSLY	RESERVISTS	ALTRUISTIC
HEMIHEDRON	PROTAGORAS	UNINSPIRED	FERTILISED	RESTLESSLY	AMBOCEPTOR
HENCEFORTH	PYROPHORUS	UNLETTERED	FERTILISER	RICHARDSON	AMRITATTVA
HEPTAMERON	PYTHAGORAS	UNMANNERED	FLINDERSIA	RIGOROUSLY	ANACLASTIC
HERESIARCH	QUERCITRON	UNMANNERLY	FRAMBOESIA	ROWLANDSON	ANACOUSTIC
HOBBYHORSE	RACECOURSE	UNNUMBERED	FRANCHISEE	RUMBLOSSOM	ANACRUSTIC
HOLOHEDRAL	RADIOLARIA	UNPREPARED	FRANCHISOR	RUTHLESSLY	ANCHORETIC
HOLOSTERIC	RANDLETREE	WANDSWORTH	GALVANISER	SANDINISTA	ANEMOMETER
HYPAETHRAL	RANNELTREE	WATERBORNE	GENEROUSLY	SANFORISED	ANESTHETIC
HYPAETHRON	RANNLETREE	WATERWORKS	GIARDIASIS	SANNAYASIN	ANTIADITIS
ICOSANDRIA	RANTLETREE	WENTLETRAP	GLORIOUSLY	SCLERIASIS	ANTIBIOTIC
IMPRESARIO	RATTLETRAP	WORDSWORTH	GLYCOLYSIS	SCOMBRESOX	ANTIMATTER
IMPROPERLY	RAWSTHORNE	YOUNGBERRY	GORGEOUSLY	SEDULOUSLY	ANTIPROTON
INDENTURES	REGISTERED	YTHUNDERED	GOVERNESSY	SENSUOUSLY	ANTIQUATED
INTERFERER	RHINOCEROS	ZOANTHARIA	GRACIOUSLY	SPECIOUSLY	ANTISEPTIC
INTERFERON	RIGHTWARDS	ADVERTISER	HEEDLESSLY	SPOTLESSLY	ANTISTATIC
INTERMARRY	ROTISSERIE	AFRORMOSIA	HELPLESSLY	SPURIOUSLY	ANTITHETIC
JIGGAMAREE	SAGITTARIA	AFTERTASTE	HISTOLYSIS	STABILISER	APOLAUSTIC
KENILWORTH	SALVADORAN	ALBIGENSES	HOPELESSLY	STEPHENSON	APOLOGETIC
KETTLEDRUM	SCHIPPERKE	ALMSHOUSES	HUMOROUSLY	STERILISER	APOPEMPTIC
KILOMETRES	SCINTIGRAM	AMANUENSIS	HYDROLYSIS	STONEMASON	APOPLECTIC
KLANGFARBE	SCRIPTURAL	AMBLYOPSIS	HYPOTHESIS	STRAVINSKY	APOSEMATIC
KNOBKERRIE	SCRIPTURES	AMPELOPSIS	HYSTERESIS	STUDIOUSLY	APPARENTLY
KOOKABURRA	SEPARATRIX	ANACHARSIS	ICHTHYOSIS	STYLOPISED	APPLICATOR
LITHOMARGE	SEPULCHRAL	ANCHYLOSIS	ILLADVISED	SUNGLASSES	AQUAFORTIS
LIVERWURST	SHAGHAIRED	ANESTHESIA	IMPROVISED	SUPERVISED	ARAGONITES
LOGANBERRY	SIDEBOARDS	ANTISEPSIS	INDISPOSED	SUPERVISOR	ARBITRATOR
MACEBEARER	SIGILLARIA	ANTITHESIS	LEDERHOSEN	SUPPRESSED	ARITHMETIC
MACROCARPA	SIMULACRUM	APHAERESIS	LEONTIASIS	SUPPRESSOR	ARROGANTLY
MALINGERER	SINGULARLY	APOTHEOSIS	LISTLESSLY	SYNAERESIS	ASPIDISTRA
MARGARSIRA	SKEUOMORPH	ASBESTOSIS	LYCHNAPSIA	SYNEIDESIS	ASSOCIATED
MARQUETRIE	SMORREBROD	ATELEIOSIS	MARSHALSEA	SYNOSTOSIS	ASTIGMATIC
MESENTERON	SOPHOMORIC	AUTHORISED	MATELLASSE	SYNTERESIS	ATRAMENTAL
METALLURGY	SOUTHWARDS	AUTOPLASTY	METALEPSIS	TACTLESSLY	AUTOCRATIC
METATHERIA	SQUIREARCH	BABESIASIS	METAPLASIS	TANNHAUSER	BABYSITTER
MIDDLEBROW	STEELWORKS	BABIROUSSA	METATARSAL	TATPURUSHA	BACCHANTES
MILLICURIE	STILLBIRTH	BAGASSOSIS	METATARSUS	TEICHOPSIA	BALIBUNTAL
MILLIFARAD	STONYHURST	BARBAROSSA	METATHESIS	THELLUSSON	BANDMASTER
MINDERERUS	STOUTHERIE	BIPARTISAN	MICRONESIA	THROMBOSIS	BANKRUPTCY
MONOPTERON	STRATOCRAT	BRAGADISME	MONILIASIS	TILLANDSIA	BARCHESTER
MONOPTEROS	STRAWBERRY	BYSSINOSIS	MUSSORGSKY	TIRELESSLY	BAREFOOTED
MONTEVERDI	STREAMERED	CAMBRENSIS	MUTINOUSLY	TOOTHPASTE	BASSINGTON
MONTSERRAT	STRUCTURAL	CARELESSLY	NATHELESSE	TORTUOUSLY	BENEFACTOR
MOSASAUROS	STRULDBRUG	CATASTASIS	NONPLUSSED	TRANSPOSED	BLACKWATER

BLANQUETTE	DESICCATED	FUTURISTIC	LIQUIDATOR	PHLOGISTIC	SIMPLISTIC
BLUEBOTTLE	DEVASTATED	GALRAVITCH	LORDOLATRY	PHLOGISTON	SONGWRITER
BLUEMANTLE	DIACAUSTIC	GALSWORTHY	LOUISIETTE	PLANCHETTE	SPECULATOR
BOUILLOTTE	DIAGNOSTIC	GENEVRETTE	MAISONETTE	PLEASANTLY	STEPSISTER
BREAKWATER	DIASTALTIC	GINGIVITIS	MAKESYSTEM	PLEASANTRY	STOCHASTIC
BRONCHITIC	DILIGENTLY	GLOUCESTER	MALAGUETTA	PLEONASTIC	STRAIGHTEN
BRONCHITIS	DIOPHANTOS	GONIOMETER	MALEFACTOR	PLEXIMETER	STRAPONTIN
BUCCINATOR	DIPLOMATIC	GRANULATED	MANCHESTER	POCAHONTAS	STRATIOTES
BURLINGTON	DISCREETLY	GUBERNATOR	MANIFESTLY	POCKMANTIE	STRIDENTLY
CACOMISTLE	DISGRUNTLE	HALFSISTER	MARIOLATRY	POIGNANTLY	SUBLIMATER
CALCULATED	DISHEARTEN	HARDCASTLE	MARIONETTE	POIKILITIC	SUBORBITAL
CALCULATOR	DISJOINTED	HARRINGTON	MENINGITIS	POINSETTIA	SUBSTRATUM
CALEFACTOR	DISPIRITED	HEADHUNTED	METACENTRE	POLLINATED	SUCCINCTLY
CANECUTTER	DISQUIETED	HEADHUNTER	METHYLATED	PORTMANTLE	SYNCOPATED
CAPODASTRO	DISSIPATED	HEADMASTER	MICROMETER	PORTMANTUA	SYPHILITIC
CAPTIVATED	DISTINCTLY	HECTOLITRE	MIGNONETTE	POSTMASTER	SYSTEMATIC
CARBURETOR	DISTRACTED	HEDONISTIC	MILEOMETER	POSTMORTEM	TABLANETTE
CASSOLETTE	DOCIMASTIC	HELICOPTER	MILLIMETER	PRECIPITIN	TACHOMETER
CATALECTIC	DOLICHOTUS	HELIOLATER	MILLIMETRE	PREMARITAL	TASKMASTER
CATALEPTIC	DRACONITES	HEPHAESTUS	MISCHMETAL	PREPARATOR	TEDDINGTON
CELEBRATED	DREIKANTER	HESITANTLY	MONUMENTAL	PREPOSITOR	TERRACOTTA
CELLULITIS	DRINKWATER	HOLOPHOTAL	MORGANATIC	PROCREATOR	THEOCRITUS
CENTILITER	DUPLICATOR	HOLOPHYTIC	MORGANETTA	PROCRUSTES	THEREAFTER
CENTILITRE	ECCOPROTIC	HOMEOPATHY	MYELINATED	PROCURATOR	THERMISTOR
CENTIMETER	ELIMINATOR	HORIZONTAL	MYRINGITIS	PROGENITOR	THERMOSTAT
CENTIMETRE	ELOQUENTLY	HOTCHPOTCH	NEAPOLITAN	PROHIBITED	TIMESWITCH
CHAMBERTIN	EMBLEMATIC	HUMANISTIC	NEGOTIATOR	PROPAGATOR	TINTORETTO
CHATTERTON	ENCLOISTER	HUMIDISTAT	NEWSCASTER	PROPOSITUS	TOILINETTE
CHECKLATON	ENHYDRITIC	HYDROMETER	NEWSLETTER	PROPRAETOR	TOLERANTLY
CHESTERTON	EPENTHETIC	HYGROMETER	NEWSWORTHY	PROPRIETOR	TONGUESTER
CHICHESTER	EPIDEICTIC	HYPSOMETRY	NIHILISTIC	PROSCIUTTO	TOSSICATED
CLEARWATER	EPIGENETIC	IDEALISTIC	NOMOTHETIC	PROSECUTOR	TOSTICATED
CLUMPERTON	EPIGLOTTIS	IGNORANTLY	NOTEWORTHY	PROSPECTOR	TRANSISTOR
COHERENTLY	EPIPLASTRA	IMBRICATED	NOTORYCTES	PROSPECTUS	TRANSLATED
COLCHESTER	EPISPASTIC	IMPLICITLY	NUMISMATIC	PROSTHETIC	TRANSLATOR
COLLIMATOR	EPROUVETTE	IMPOTENTLY	OBEDIENTLY	PROTRACTED	TRAVELATOR
COLLOCUTER	ESCHAROTIC	IMPRIMATUR	OBFUSCATED	PROTRACTOR	TRAVOLATOR
COMPARATOR	ETEOCRETAN	IMPUDENTLY	OCCIDENTAL	PROVEDITOR	TRIACONTER
COMPETITOR	EUCALYPTOL	INARTISTIC	OIREACHTAS	PSYCHIATRY	TRIMSNITCH
COMPOSITOR	EUCALYPTUS	INCIDENTAL	OMBROMETER	PTERYGOTUS	TROCHANTER
CONFLICTED	EUDIOMETER	INDECENTLY	OOPHORITIS	PULSOMETER	TROMOMETER
CONGENITAL	EULOGISTIC	INDIRECTLY	OPISOMETER	PYRACANTHA	TYMPANITES
CONSPECTUS	EVAPORATED	INDUMENTUM	OPTIMISTIC	QUIZMASTER	TYMPANITIS
CONSTANTAN	EXONERATED	INEBRIATED	ORIGINATOR	REGIMENTAL	TYPESETTER
CONSTANTIA	EXPLICITLY	INFATUATED	ORNAMENTAL	REGIMENTED	TYPEWRITER
CONSTANTLY	FARSIGHTED	INFURIATED	OSCILLATOR	REITERATED	ULSTERETTE
CONTRACTOR	FASCINATED	INHERENTLY	OSTEOPATHY	REREDORTER	UNACCENTED
CONVOLUTED	FASCINATOR	INNOCENTLY	OSTROGOTHS	RESPIRATOR	UNAFFECTED
COPESETTIC	FATALISTIC	INQUISITOR	OTHERGATES	RESTRICTED	UNDEFEATED
COPYWRITER	FEUILLETON	INSOLENTLY	OVERMATTER	REVERENTLY	UNDERWATER
CORRUGATED	FIANCHETTO	INSTIGATOR	OVERTHETOP	RHAMPASTOS	UNDETECTED
CORRUGATOR	FIBROSITIS	INSTRUCTED	OVIPOSITOR	RINGMASTER	UNDIGESTED
CORYBANTES	FILIBUSTER	INSTRUCTOR	OXYGENATOR	RIPSNORTER	UNDISPUTED
CORYBANTIC	FLAGRANTLY	INTEGRATED	PACESETTER	ROADWORTHY	UNEDUCATED
COVENANTER	FLIPPANTLY	INTERESTED	PADDINGTON	RUDIMENTAL	UNEXPECTED
CROSSHATCH	FLUCTUATER	JACKBOOTED	PALMERSTON	RUMINANTIA	UNIGENITUS
CUCULLATED	FOREBITTER	JINGOISTIC	PARASTATAL	SACERDOTAL	UNPROMPTED
CUCURBITAL	FORECASTER	JUBILANTLY	PARMACITIE	SALOPETTES	UNREQUITED
CULTIVATED	FORECASTLE	JUGENDSTIL	PARRAMATTA	SARSQUATCH	UNROMANTIC
CULTIVATOR	FOURCHETTE	KOEKSISTER	PEASHOOTER	SCHISMATIC	UNSCRIPTED
CYBERNETIC	FRAGMENTAL	LACKLUSTER	PEDIMENTAL	SCHOLASTIC	UROGENITAL
DEADNETTLE	FRATERETTO	LACKLUSTRE	PENNISETUM	SEGREGATED	VARIEGATED
DECOLLATOR	FREEBOOTER	LARYNGITIS	PENTAMETER	SERVOMOTOR	VASCULITIS
DEEPSEATED	FREEMARTIN	LAUNCESTON	PERCOLATOR	SHACKLETON	VEHEMENTLY
DEMOCRATIC	FREQUENTED	LEAMINGTON	PERFORATED	SHEARWATER	VENTILATOR
DEMOCRITUS	FREQUENTER	LEGALISTIC	PERFORATOR	SHECKLATON	VIGILANTES
DENSIMETER	FREQUENTLY	LEGISLATOR	PERSECUTOR	SHOPLIFTER	VIRULENTLY
DERMATITIS	FRESHWATER	LILYWHITES	PETULANTLY	SIDEROSTAT	WAINSCOTED
DESECRATED	FRUSTRATED	LINGUISTIC	PHLEGMATIC	SILHOUETTE	WASHINGTON

WELLINGTON	FILLIBRUSH	SOUTHBOUND	THIMBLEWIT	**10:9**	CANTABRIAN
WHITEWATER	FLUTEMOUTH	SPELLBOUND	THROUGHWAY	ABORIGINAL	CARDIOGRAM
WINCEYETTE	FOREGROUND	SPISSITUDE	WALLFLOWER	ABYSSINIAN	CARNASSIAL
WINCHESTER	FORFEITURE	STEAKHOUSE	WATCHTOWER	ACCIDENTAL	CARPATHIAN
WOFFINGTON	FRONTCOURT	STOREHOUSE	WINDFLOWER	ACETABULAR	CARTHUSIAN
WRISTWATCH	GARGANTUAN	STRASBOURG	WITHDRAWAL	ACRONYCHAL	CASSUMUNAR
XEROPHYTIC	GETTYSBURG	SUBSTITUTE	AMPHIMIXIS	ADDITIONAL	CAVALRYMAN
ZYGODACTYL	GLASSHOUSE	SUBTERFUGE	BOBBYSOXER	ADJECTIVAL	CENTENNIAL
ABERGLAUBE	GRAPEFRUIT	TANTAMOUNT	ECHOPRAXIA	ALDERWOMAN	CENTESIMAL
AFTERHOURS	GREENHOUSE	TITARAKURA	PARAPRAXIS	ALECTORIAN	CEREMONIAL
ALTAZIMUTH	GUESTHOUSE	TOOTHBRUSH	PHYTOTOXIN	ALGONQUIAN	CHAIRWOMAN
AMPHIGOURI	HATEENOUGH	TOURNIQUET	AERENCHYMA	ALMACANTAR	CHARDONNAY
AMPHINEURA	HEPTATEUCH	TREKSCHUIT	AMPHICTYON	ALMUCANTAR	CHAUCERIAN
ANGUILLULA	HEREABOUTS	TRILINGUAL	AMPHITRYON	AMERINDIAN	CHELTENHAM
ANSCHAUUNG	HINDENBURG	TRIPEHOUND	ARACOSTYLE	ANALOGICAL	CHILDERMAS
ANTEPENULT	HOMOSEXUAL	TROPOPAUSE	BLEARYEYED	ANALYTICAL	CIRCASSIAN
APICULTURE	HOUSEBOUND	TURNAROUND	BRICKLAYER	ANARCHICAL	CISLEITHAN
BACKGROUND	HYPOTENUSE	ULTRASOUND	CECIDOMYIA	ANASTIGMAT	CISTERCIAN
BARRACOUTA	IMPOSTHUME	UNDERSLUNG	CHERIMOYER	ANATOMICAL	CLANSWOMAN
BATTENBURG	INAPTITUDE	UNDERSTUDY	CLADOPHYLL	ANDALUSIAN	CLEMENCEAU
BELLAMOURE	INCUNABULA	UNPUNCTUAL	CYCLOSTYLE	ANTICLIMAX	COLDSTREAM
BETELGEUSE	INDIVIDUAL	USQUEBAUGH	EUPHROSYNE	ANTIMONIAN	COLLATERAL
BETELGEUZE	INEPTITUDE	WANDERLUST	GALLABIYAH	ANTINOMIAN	COLLOQUIAL
BLOCKHOUSE	INTERCLUDE	WHEELHOUSE	GALLABIYEH	ANTIOCHIAN	COMMERCIAL
BLOODHOUND	IRRESOLUTE	WOOLLYBUTT	HETERODYNE	ANTIPHONAL	COMMONWEAL
BLOOMSBURY	JUDICATURE	WRAPAROUND	HIEROGLYPH	ANTIPODEAN	CONCEPTUAL
BRASSBOUND	KIESELGUHR	YARBOROUGH	HIPPOGRYPH	ANTISOCIAL	CONFEDERAL
BREADFRUIT	LAMBREQUIN	ZUMBOORUCK	HYDROPHYTE	APOCRYPHAL	CONGENITAL
BUTTERBUMP	LASTMINUTE	ADJECTIVAL	KSHATRIYAS	APOLLONIAN	CONSTANTAN
CALLIATURE	LIGHTHOUSE	BARMITZVAH	NEMATOCYST	ARAUCANIAN	CONTEXTUAL
CANTALOUPE	LITERATURE	CANTILEVER	OSTEOPHYTE	ARCHETYPAL	CONVENTUAL
CANTERBURY	LUXEMBOURG	DECENNOVAL	PALAEOTYPE	ARIMASPIAN	COPPERHEAD
CARICATURA	MALMESBURY	DEVASTAVIT	PARAGUAYAN	ARISTOCRAT	CORINTHIAN
CARICATURE	MASSASAUGA	HOWSOMEVER	PARENCHYMA	ARTIFICIAL	COUNTRYMAN
CATALOGUER	MISCONDUCT	INTERWOVEN	PETROGLYPH	ARUNDELIAN	COXCOMICAL
CENTRIFUGE	MISFORTUNE	LACCADIVES	PHAENOTYPE	ATHANASIAN	CREDENTIAL
CHARTREUSE	MULLIGRUBS	MASKIROVKA	PLATELAYER	ATRAMENTAL	CRISPBREAD
CHIRICAUNE	NICARAGUAN	PARKLEAVES	RHINOPHYMA	AUSTRALIAN	CRISPINIAN
CIRCUMFUSE	NORTHBOUND	PILEDRIVER	SAPROPHYTE	BABYLONIAN	CROTALIDAE
COLORATURA	NOURRITURE	REDISCOVER	SOOTHSAYER	BAHRAINIAN	CRUSTACEAN
COMMISSURE	OFFTHECUFF	RIBOFLAVIN	STEREOTYPE	BALBRIGGAN	CRYPTOGRAM
COMMIXTURE	OVERSLAUGH	SEMIQUAVER	STEREOTYPY	BALIBUNTAL	CUCURBITAL
CONCEPTUAL	OVERSTRUNG	SHORTLIVED	STRATOCYST	BARMECIDAL	DECENNIACAL
CONJECTURE	PAINTBRUSH	SPLITLEVEL	TROGLODYTE	BARMITZVAH	DEMONIACAL
CONSTITUTE	PANTAGRUEL	THEMSELVES	TROPOPHYTE	BATRACHIAN	DEVOTIONAL
CONSUETUDE	PENTATEUCH	TIMESERVER	UNEMPLOYED	BEAUTICIAN	DIABOLICAL
CONTEXTUAL	PLAYGROUND	UNBELIEVER	ANNUALIZED	BEHAVIORAL	DISSIMILAR
CONTRIBUTE	PORTSMOUTH	UNDERCOVER	BELSHAZZAR	BELARUSIAN	DISTRINGAS
CONVENTUAL	POWERHOUSE	UNDESERVED	BUMFREEZER	BELSHAZZAR	DIVISIONAL
CONVOLVUTE	PRICKLOUSE	UNOBSERVED	CHIMPANZEE	BENEFICIAL	DOWNSTREAM
COURTHOUSE	PROSTITUTE	UNRELIEVED	FERTILIZER	BIOLOGICAL	DUNDERHEAD
CRAIGFLUKE	PUNCHDRUNK	UNRESERVED	FOSSILIZED	BIPARTISAN	DUNIWASSAL
CRAQUETURE	QUADRATURA	UNRESOLVED	HYPNOTIZED	BIRKENHEAD	DUODECIMAL
CUMMERBUND	QUEENSBURY	VILLANOVAN	INTERMEZZO	BIRMINGHAM	DUTCHWOMAN
DEBOUCHURE	QUERSPRUNG	WANTHRIVEN	LIQUIDIZER	BLUETHROAT	ECOLOGICAL
DESBOROUGH	RAJPRAMUKH	WATERLEVEL	MECHANIZED	BONDSWOMAN	ECONOMICAL
DISCLOSURE	RAVENSDUCK	WHATSOEVER	MORBIDEZZA	BONNETHEAD	ECUADORIAN
DISTRIBUTE	RESCHEDULE	YOURSELVES	PALMATOZOA	BOTTLEHEAD	ECUMENICAL
DOVERCOURT	ROQUELAURE	BRAINPOWER	PASSAMEZZO	BOURIGNIAN	ELECTRICAL
DUNDERFUNK	ROUGHHOUSE	CONEFLOWER	PESTALOZZI	BRIDGEHEAD	ELEUSINIAN
EMBOUCHURE	ROUNDHOUSE	CORNFLOWER	RECOGNIZED	BUCKINGHAM	ELLIPTICAL
EMPFINDUNG	SANCTITUDE	DISEMBOWEL	SALMANAZAR	BUDGERIGAR	ENCYCLICAL
ENCOIGNURE	SCARAMOUCH	EXPRESSWAY	SCAMMOZZIS	BUFFLEHEAD	ENGLISHMAN
ENGENDRURE	SCORDATURA	HORNBLOWER	SCHLIMAZEL	BUREAUCRAT	EQUATORIAL
EUTHYNEURA	SIMILITUDE	HORSEPOWER	STABILIZER	CALEDONIAN	EQUESTRIAN
EXACTITUDE	SNAKEMOUTH	PASSAGEWAY	STERILIZER	CALYDONIAN	ERYSIPELAS
FAIRGROUND	SOLICITUDE	ROWDYDOWDY	STRELITZIA	CAMERONIAN	ESCULAPIAN
FALSETRUTH	SOMERSAULT	SNOWBLOWER	UNDERSIZED	CAMPESTRAL	ETEOCRETAN
FIELDMOUSE	SOUBRIQUET	SUPERPOWER		CANTABRIAN	EUSTACHIAN

EXPRESSMAN	KSHATRIYAS	PARANORMAL	SEPTENNIAL	VENEZUELAN	BLOODSTOCK
EXPRESSWAY	LAUNDROMAT	PARASTATAL	SEPULCHRAL	VERNACULAR	BOTTLENECK
FIGUREHEAD	LAURENTIAN	PARNASSIAN	SEQUENTIAL	VILLANOVAN	BRILLIANCE
FORINSECAL	LETTERHEAD	PARTICULAR	SERMONICAL	VOCATIONAL	BROADPIECE
FORTINBRAS	LIGHTERMAN	PASSAGEWAY	SERVICEMAN	WALDENSIAN	BROOMSTICK
FRACTIONAL	LITHUANIAN	PATAGONIAN	SHANDRYDAN	WALLACHIAN	CALESCENCE
FRAGMENTAL	LITURGICAL	PEDESTRIAN	SHELDONIAN	WAMPUMPEAG	CANDLEWICK
FRANCISCAN	LOGGERHEAD	PEDIMENTAL	SHELLYCOAT	WAPENSCHAW	CANTATRICE
FRENETICAL	LOGISTICAL	PENINSULAR	SHENANIGAN	WAPINSCHAW	CANVASBACK
FRICANDEAU	LUSITANIAN	PENSIONNAT	SHISHKEBAB	WAPPENSHAW	CAPNOMANCY
FUNCTIONAL	MACEDONIAN	PENTAGONAL	SHORTBREAD	WEATHERMAN	CARTOMANCY
FUNGICIDAL	MADAGASCAN	PERIODICAL	SHOVELHEAD	WELSHWOMAN	CATAPHRACT
GALIMATIAS	MADAGASCAR	PERIPHERAL	SIDEROSTAT	WENTLETRAP	CHAPLAINCY
GALLABIYAH	MAGNIFICAT	PETRARCHAN	SIGNIFICAT	WHEATSHEAF	CHEVISANCE
GARGANTUAN	MAHOMMEDAN	PHAELONIAN	SIMMENTHAL	WHILLYWHAW	CHIROMANCY
GENETHLIAC	MAINSTREAM	PHENOMENAL	SINOATRIAL	WHOLEWHEAT	CLEROMANCY
GEOLOGICAL	MALAYALAAM	PHRENESIAC	SLIPSTREAM	WIDESPREAD	COCKATRICE
GEOTHERMAL	MALTHUSIAN	PHYSIOCRAT	SOLIFIDIAN	WITHDRAWAL	COGNISANCE
GERMICIDAL	MALTHUSIAN				
GERMICIDAL	MANAGERIAL	POCAHONTAS	SOPHOCLEAN	WOODENHEAD	COGNIZANCE
GILBERTIAN	MANAGERIAL	POLITICIAN	SPENCERIAN	WYCLIFFIAN	COMPETENCE
GINGERSNAP	MANICHAEAN	POLYNESIAN	SPENSERIAN	YESTERYEAR	COMPLIANCE
GOLDENSEAL	MAXIMILIAN	POLYNOMIAL	SPONSIONAL	ZAPOROGIAN	CONDOLENCE
GOLDTHREAD	MEADOWPLAN	POMERANIAN	SPORTSWEAR	ZIMBABWEAN	CONFERENCE
GRAMMARIAN	MECHANICAL	PONTIFICAL	SPRINGHAAS	ZOOLOGICAL	CONFIDENCE
GROUNDSMAN	MELANESIAN	PRAETORIAN	STENTORIAN	ABERGLAUBE	CONFLUENCE
GUATEMALAN	MENECHMIAN	PREMARITAL	STICKYBEAK	ANGLOPHOBE	CONNIVANCE
GUTTIFERAE	METACARPAL	PREMEDICAL	STRATOCRAT	ANGWANTIBO	CONSCIENCE
HALFDOLLAR	METATARSAL	PRESENTDAY	STRUCTURAL	KLANGFARBE	CONSONANCE
HALLELUJAH	METHODICAL	PRIMORDIAL	SUBLIMINAL	MOUCHARABY	CONSPIRACY
HAMMERHEAD	METHUSELAH	PROCEDURAL	SUBORBITAL	MULLIGRUBS	CONTINENCE
HANOVERIAN	MICHAELMAS	PROMETHEAN	SUPERHUMAN	OMBROPHOBE	CONTRADICT
HARVESTMAN	MIDLOTHIAN	PROPLITEAL	SUPERWOMAN	PARAMARIBO	CONVALESCE
HEARTBREAK	MIDSHIPMAN	PROTAGORAS	SWEETBREAD	TRANSCRIBE	CONVENANCE
HEPTAGONAL	MILITIAMAN	PROVERBIAL	SWEETBRIAR	WIDDICOMBE	CONVEYANCE
HIGHWAYMAN	MILLIFARAD	PROVINCIAL	SYMBOLICAL	ABHORRENCE	CORNSTARCH
HISTORICAL	MISCHMETAL	PRUDENTIAL	SYNCHRONAL	ABSORBANCE	CORPULENCE
HOLOHEDRAL	MOLENDINAR	PUNICACEAE	TANAGRIDAE	ABSTINENCE	COUNTERACT
HOLOPHOTAL	MONTSERRAT	PYROMANIAC	TANGENTIAL	ACCOMPLICE	CRAPULENCE
HOMEOUSIAN	MONUMENTAL	PYTHAGORAS	TECHNICIAN	ACCORDANCE	CROSSCHECK
HOMOOUSIAN	MORISONIAN	RABBINICAL	TECHNOCRAT	ACROBATICS	CROSSHATCH
HOMOSEXUAL	MOUSTERIAN	RAILWAYMAN	TENRECIDAE	ADMITTANCE	CROSSPIECE
HORIZONTAL	MOUTHORGAN	RAMPALLIAN	TESTICULAR	ADRAMELECH	CRYOGENICS
HORSEWOMAN	MUTTONHEAD	RATTLETRAP	THALASSIAN	AEROBATICS	DEFEASANCE
HUMIDISTAT	MYOCARDIAL	RECIPROCAL	THEATRICAL	AESTHETICS	DEFICIENCY
HYPAETHRAL	NARROWBOAT	REGIMENTAL	THEOLOGIAN	AFTERPIECE	DEGENERACY
HYSTERICAL	NATATORIAL	REPUBLICAN	THERMOSTAT	AFTERSHOCK	DEHISCENCE
IMMATERIAL	NEAPOLITAN	REQUIESCAT	THRENODIAL	AGONISTICS	DENTIFRICE
IMMEMORIAL	NEOTERICAL	RHETORICAL	THROUGHWAY	ALLEGEANCE	DEPENDENCE
IMPERSONAL	NICARAGUAN	RHYTHMICAL	THYSANURAN	ALLEGIANCE	DEPENDENCY
INCIDENTAL	NICROSILAL	ROBERDSMAN	TORRENTIAL	ALPENSTOCK	DETERRENCE
INDIVIDUAL	NIGGERHEAD	ROBERTSMAN	TOWNSWOMAN	AMPHIBRACH	DIALECTICS
INDONESIAN	NOBLEWOMAN	ROCKINGHAM	TRIANGULAR	ANTARCTICA	DIFFERENCE
INDUSTRIAL	NORTHSTEAD	RUDIMENTAL	TRILATERAL	APPEARANCE	DIFFIDENCE
INTERNODAL	NOSOCOMIAL	RUPESTRIAN	TRILINGUAL	APPRENTICE	DISCONNECT
INTESTINAL	NURSERYMAN	SABBATICAL	TRINACRIAN	ARSMETRICK	DISRESPECT
INTRAURBAN	OBSIDIONAL	SACERDOTAL	TRYPTOPHAN	ASARABACCA	DISSERVICE
IRISHWOMAN	OCCASIONAL	SALESWOMAN	TUBERCULAR	ASCENDANCY	DISSIDENCE
IRRATIONAL	OCCIDENTAL	SALMANAZAR	TURTLEHEAD	ASCENDENCY	DISSONANCE
IRREMEDIAL	OIREACHTAS	SALPINGIAN	TYRANNICAL	ASSISTANCE	DIVERGENCE
JOHNSONIAN	ORATORICAL	SALTCELLAR	UNCRITICAL	ATTENDANCE	EBULLIENCE
JOLTERHEAD	ORCHESTRAL	SALVADORAN	UNFAMILIAR	AUTODIDACT	EFFEMINACY
JOURNEYMAN	ORDOVICIAN	SCHOOLMAAM	UNICAMERAL	AXINOMANCY	EFFERVESCE
KARMATHIAN	ORNAMENTAL	SCINTIGRAM	UNILATERAL	BADDERLOCK	EFFICIENCY
KEMPERYMAN	ORTHOGONAL	SCOPELIDAE	UNOFFICIAL	BAILIEWICK	EPISTEMICS
KENTUCKIAN	OVERSPREAD	SCOTSWOMAN	UNORIGINAL	BAILIWICK	ERGONOMICS
KHIDMUTGAR	OZYMANDIAS	SCREENPLAY	UNPUNCTUAL	BALLISTICS	EVERYPLACE
KINCHINLAY	PALAESTRAL	SCRIPTURAL	UROGENITAL	BANKRUPTCY	EXCELLENCE
KLOOTCHMAN	PANAMANIAN	SEEMLIHEAD	URTICACEAE	BIOPHYSICS	EXCELLENCY
KNIGHTHEAD	PARAGUAYAN	SENATORIAL	VEGETARIAN	BIRTHPLACE	EXPECTANCY

EXPEDIENCE	OCHLOCRACY	STATOCRACY	ISONIAZIDE	ASSOCIATED	CANTILEVER
EXPEDIENCY	OFFBALANCE	STRINGENCY	JAGUARONDI	ASTEROIDEA	CAPTIVATED
EXPERIENCE	OFFLICENCE	STYLISTICS	JAGUARUNDI	ASTONISHED	CARABINEER
EXUBERANCE	ONOMASTICS	SUBCOMPACT	LANTHANIDE	ASTROLOGER	CARABINIER
FANTASTICO	ORDONNANCE	SUBSIDENCE	LITHISTADA	ASTRONOMER	CARCINOGEN
FETTERLOCK	ORIDINANCE	SUBTENANCY	MASQUERADE	AUCTIONEER	CARPENTIER
FINGERPICK	ORTHOPTICS	SUBTROPICS	MONTEVERDI	AUSTRINGER	CARRAGHEEN
FLATULENCE	OUTBALANCE	SUFFERANCE	NATIONWIDE	AUTHORISED	CARYATIDES
GALRAVITCH	PEDIATRICS	SUPPLEJACK	NESSELRODE	BABYSITTER	CATACHUMEN
GEOPHYSICS	PENTATEUCH	SUSTENANCE	NIGHTSHADE	BACCHANTES	CATALOGUER
GERIATRICS	PERMANENCE	SWITCHBACK	NORTHWARDS	BACKHANDED	CATCRACKER
GOVERNANCE	PERMANENCY	SWORDSTICK	OPHICLEIDE	BACKHANDER	CATECHUMEN
GREENFINCH	PERTINENCE	TEMPERANCE	PARADOXIDE	BACKPACKER	CELEBRATED
GREENSTICK	PESTILENCE	THREEPENCE	PASQUINADE	BACKSLIDER	CENTILITER
GYMNASTICS	PILGARLICK	TIMESWITCH	PHOTODIODE	BAMBOOZLED	CENTIMETER
HACKMATACK	PLUPERFECT	TOUCHPIECE	PROPAGANDA	BANDMASTER	CEREMONIES
HALIEUTICS	PLUTOCRACY	TRANSIENCE	QUICKSANDS	BARCHESTER	CHALLENGED
HAMMERLOCK	PONTEFRACT	TRIMSNITCH	RAWINSONDE	BAREFOOTED	CHALLENGER
HARMANBECK	PORNOCRACY	TRUCULENCE	RETROGRADE	BAREHEADED	CHANDELIER
HEPTATEUCH	PRECEDENCE	TUMESCENCE	RIGHTWARDS	BARELEGGED	CHAPFALLEN
HERESIARCH	PREFERENCE	TURBULENCE	ROCKSTEADY	BARLEYBREE	CHARIOTEER
HIEROMANCY	PREPOTENCE	TURTLENECK	ROWDYDOWDY	BEARGARDEN	CHERIMOYER
HONEYBUNCH	PRESCIENCE	UBERMENSCH	SACCHARIDE	BEAUTIFIER	CHICHESTER
HOTCHPOTCH	PRESIDENCY	WARRANDICE	SALMAGUNDI	BEDCHAMBER	CHIFFONIER
HYDRAULICS	PREVALENCE	WHITTERICK	SALTIGRADE	BEDCLOTHES	CHIMPANZEE
ILLITERACY	PREVENANCY	WOOLLYBACK	SANCTITUDE	BEDEVILLED	CHRONICLER
IMMACULACY	PROFLIGACY	WRISTWATCH	SAUROPSIDA	BEDRAGGLED	CHRONICLES
IMPARLANCE	PROMINENCE	YELLOWBACK	SCAPHOPODA	BEEFBURGER	CHURCHGOER
IMPATIENCE	PROVENANCE	YELLOWJACK	SHROVETIDE	BELLWETHER	CIRCUMFLEX
IMPORTANCE	PROVIDENCE	ZUMBOORUCK	SIDEBOARDS	BERMOOTHES	CIRRIPEDEA
IMPRUDENCE	PUBESCENCE	ADELANTADO	SILVERSIDE	BERSAGLIER	CLASSIFIED
INACCURACY	PULSATANCE	AFICIONADO	SIMILITUDE	BESTSELLER	CLEARWATER
INADEQUACY	QUIESCENCE	AFTERWARDS	SOLICITUDE	BEWILDERED	CLOCKMAKER
INCUMBENCY	RAVENSDUCK	AMARYLLIDS	SOUTHWARDS	BIOGRAPHER	CLODHOPPER
INDELICACY	RECOMMENCE	ASAFOETIDA	SPERMICIDE	BLACKWATER	CLOISTERED
INDISTINCT	RECRUDESCE	AUTOSTRADA	SPISSITUDE	BLASPHEMER	COATHANGER
INDUCTANCE	RECURRENCE	AVANTGARDE	STILLICIDE	BLASTOCOEL	COCKCHAFER
INDULGENCE	REDUNDANCY	BALUSTRADE	STRINGENDO	BLASTOIDEA	COLCHESTER
INEFFICACY	RELUCTANCE	BARRAMUNDA	TAILORMADE	BLEARYEYED	COLLOCUTER
INNERSPACE	REMITTANCE	BARRAMUNDI	TARDIGRADE	BLITZKRIEG	COLONNADED
INSISTENCE	REPENTANCE	BHADRAPADA	TORQUEMADA	BLUEBONNET	COMMANDEER
INSOLVENCY	REPUGNANCE	BROWNLANDS	UNDERSTUDY	BOBBYSOXER	COMPOUNDED
INSURGENCY	RESILIENCE	CENTIGRADE	VELOCIPEDE	BOMBARDIER	COMPRESSED
INTERSTICE	RESISTANCE	CIRRHOPODA	ABSTRACTED	BONDHOLDER	COMSTOCKER
INTROSPECT	RESURGENCE	CONSUETUDE	ACCREDITED	BONESHAKER	CONDOTTIER
ISOMETRICS	RETROSPECT	CORRIGENDA	ACCUSTOMED	BOOKBINDER	CONEFLOWER
JABBERWOCK	RHEUMATICS	CROCKFORDS	ACHITOPHEL	BOOKKEEPER	CONFLICTED
JOUYSAUNCE	ROLANDSECK	CROSSROADS	ACQUAINTED	BOOKMARKER	CONFOUNDED
KILMARNOCK	RUBBERNECK	DIMINUENDO	ADMINISTER	BOOKSELLER	CONSIDERED
LEGITIMACY	SACROSANCT	DISCOMMODE	ADVENTURER	BOOTLEGGER	CONTROLLER
LIMBERNECK	SADDLEBACK	DUCKBOARDS	ADVERTISER	BOOTLICKER	CONVOLUTED
LUMBERJACK	SAMOTHRACE	EXACTITUDE	AFFILIATED	BOOZINGKEN	COPARCENER
LUXURIANCE	SARSQUATCH	FLANCONADE	AFRICANDER	BOUSINGKEN	COPENHAGEN
MAGISTRACY	SCAPEGRACE	FLORIBUNDA	AHITHOPHEL	BRAINPOWER	COPYHOLDER
MALIGNANCY	SCARAMOUCH	FLOWERBEDS	ALBIGENSES	BREAKABLES	COPYWRITER
MATCHSTICK	SENESCENCE	FRATRICIDE	ALCIBIADES	BREAKWATER	CORDWAINER
MISCONDUCT	SHELLSHOCK	FRONTWARDS	ALMSHOUSES	BREASTFEED	CORNFLAKES
MONSTRANCE	SILVERBACK	FUDDYDUDDY	ALTOGETHER	BRESSUMMER	CORNFLOWER
MOUSEPIECE	SMOKESTACK	GASCONNADE	AMPHIMACER	BRICKLAYER	COROMANDEL
MOUTHPIECE	SNAPHAUNCE	GRANDDADDY	ANALPHABET	BROADSHEET	CORROBOREE
NATTERJACK	SNAPHAUNCH	GRASSLANDS	ANAXIMENES	BUCKJUMPER	CORRUGATED
NECROMANCY	SOMNOLENCE	HEMICHORDA	ANEMOMETER	BULLHEADED	CORYBANTES
NEGLIGENCE	SOUNDTRACK	HORNBLENDE	ANGURVADEL	BUMFREEZER	COVENANTER
NIGHTSTICK	SPATCHCOCK	HOUSEMAIDS	ANNUALIZED	BUSHRANGER	CROSSBONES
NUCLEONICS	SPITCHCOCK	INAPTITUDE	ANTIMATTER	CALAMANDER	CROSSBREED
NUDIBRANCH	SPODOMANCY	INDAPAMIDE	ANTIQUATED	CALCULATED	CROSSREFER
OBSERVANCE	SQUIREARCH	INEPTITUDE	ARAGONITES	CALORIFIER	CUCULLATED
OBSTETRICS	STAGECOACH	INQUIRENDO	ARCHIMEDES	CAMPAIGNER	CUIRASSIER
OCCURRENCE	STATISTICS	INTERCLUDE	ARISTOTLES	CANECUTTER	CULTIVATED

CURRENCIES	FIREWALKER	HELLBENDER	LILYWHITES	PAWNBROKER	SANDWICHES
DARKHAIRED	FIREWARDEN	HESPERIDES	LIPIZZANER	PEACEMAKER	SANFORISED
DAYDREAMER	FIRTHSOKEN	HIGHBINDER	LIQUIDIZER	PEASHOOTER	SCANDERBEG
DECIPHERED	FISHMONGER	HIGHHANDED	LOCKKEEPER	PENTAMETER	SCHLIMAZEL
DECOMPOSED	FISHSELLER	HIGHLANDER	LOGORRHOEA	PERFORATED	SCRIPTURES
DEEPSEATED	FLOURISHED	HIPPOMANES	LUMPSUCKER	PERSIENNES	SCRUTINEER
DEMIRELIEF	FLUCTUATER	HITCHHIKER	MACEBEARER	PESCADORES	SECURITIES
DENSIMETER	FLYCATCHER	HOLOFERNES	MAINTAINER	PETITIONER	SEERSUCKER
DEPARTURES	FOOTBALLER	HOMEWORKER	MAKESYSTEM	PICKPOCKET	SEGREGATED
DESECRATED	FOREBITTER	HOODWINKED	MALINGERER	PILEDRIVER	SELFESTEEM
DESICCATED	FORECASTER	HORNBLOWER	MANCHESTER	PINAKOTHEK	SELFSTYLED
DETERMINED	FOREDAMNED	HORNRIMMED	MANCHINEEL	PLATELAYER	SEMIQUAVER
DETERMINER	FOREFATHER	HORSEPOWER	MANGOSTEEN	PLATINISED	SHAGHAIRED
DEVASTATED	FOREFINGER	HORSERIDER	MARSHALSEA	PLEXIMETER	SHAMEFACED
DICKCISSEL	FOREGATHER	HOWSOMEVER	MATCHMAKER	PLUMASSIER	SHEARWATER
DIMINISHED	FORERUNNER	HUMANITIES	MAVOURNEEN	POCKMARKED	SHOPKEEPER
DISBURTHEN	FOREWARNED	HUMIDIFIER	MECHANIZED	POKERFACED	SHOPLIFTER
DISCLAIMER	FORFEUCHEN	HUMPBACKED	MENORRHOEA	POLIANTHES	SHOPSOILED
DISCOLORED	FORFOUGHEN	HYDROMETER	MERRYMAKER	POLLINATED	SHOPWALKER
DISCOVERER	FOSSILIZED	HYGROMETER	METHUSALEH	POSTMASTER	SHORTLIVED
DISEMBOWEL	FRANCHISEE	HYPNOTIZED	METHYLATED	POSTMORTEM	SHOWJUMPER
DISENGAGED	FRAUNHOFER	ICEBREAKER	MICROMETER	POURPARLER	SHRIVELLED
DISFIGURED	FREEBOOTER	ILLADVISED	MILEOMETER	PRAXITELES	SIDEWINDER
DISHEARTEN	FREEHANDER	IMBRICATED	MILLIMETER	PREJUDICED	SKYSCRAPER
DISHWASHER	FREEHOLDER	IMPROVISED	MINEWORKER	PRINCIPLED	SMITHEREEN
DISJOINTED	FREELANCER	IMPURITIES	MINIMARKET	PRINCIPLES	SNOWBLOWER
DISMANTLED	FREELOADER	INDENTURES	MISMATCHED	PRIVILEGED	SNOWCAPPED
DISORDERED	FREQUENTED	INDISCREET	MONEYMAKER	PROCRUSTES	SOBERSIDES
DISPIRITED	FREQUENTER	INDISPOSED	MONTEVIDEO	PROGRAMMER	SOFTBOILED
DISQUIETED	FRESHWATER	INEBRIATED	MONTRACHET	PROHIBITED	SOGDOLAGER
DISSEMBLER	FRIGHTENED	INFATUATED	MORALITIES	PROMENADER	SOGDOLIGER
DISSIPATED	FRITHSOKEN	INFURIATED	MOSSBUNKER	PRONOUNCED	SOGDOLOGER
DISTRACTED	FROGHOPPER	INKSLINGER	MUDSKIPPER	PROSCRIBED	SONGWRITER
DISTRESSED	FROMANTEEL	INSTRUCTED	MULTIPLIED	PROTRACTED	SOOTHSAYER
DOORKEEPER	FRUSTRATED	INTEGRATED	MULTIPLIER	PULSOMETER	SOUBRIQUET
DOWNMARKET	GALLABIYEH	INTERBREED	MYELINATED	QUARRENDER	SOUTHERNER
DRACONITES	GALVANISER	INTERCEDER	NETTLETREE	QUESTIONER	SPECTACLED
DREIKANTER	GAMEKEEPER	INTERESTED	NEWFANGLED	QUIZMASTER	SPECTACLES
DRESSMAKER	GEOGRAPHER	INTERFERER	NEWSCASTER	RANDLETREE	SPLITLEVEL
DRINKWATER	GINGERBEER	INTERLOPER	NEWSLETTER	RANNELTREE	STABILISER
DUKKERIPEN	GLEEMAIDEN	INTERWOVEN	NEWSMONGER	RANNLETREE	STABILIZER
ECHINOIDEA	GLENDOVEER	INTESTINES	NEWSREADER	RANTLETREE	STADHOLDER
ELECTROMER	GLOUCESTER	IRISHWOMEN	NONALIGNED	RECOGNISED	STALHELMER
EMBITTERED	GOALKEEPER	JACKANAPES	NONPLUSSED	RECOGNIZED	STALLENGER
EMMENTALER	GOATSUCKER	JACKBOOTED	NORTHANGER	RECONCILED	STALLINGER
EMPEDOCLES	GOLDDIGGER	JACKHAMMER	NORTHERNER	RECONSIDER	STEMWINDER
EMULSIFIER	GOLDFINGER	JACKSTONES	NOTORYCTES	REDISCOVER	STENOTYPER
ENCLOISTER	GONFANONER	JIGGAMAREE	NUTCRACKER	REGIMENTED	STEPFATHER
ENGLISHMEN	GONIOMETER	KEYBOARDER	OBFUSCATED	REGISTERED	STEPLADDER
ENRAPTURED	GONORRHOEA	KILOMETRES	OFTENTIMES	REITERATED	STEPMOTHER
ENTRENCHED	GRANULATED	KINGFISHER	OMBROMETER	REPRODUCER	STEPSISTER
EPIMENIDES	GRIDIRONER	KOEKSISTER	OPENHANDED	REREDORTER	STERILISER
EUDIOMETER	GRIDLOCKED	KRIEGSPIEL	OPENMINDED	RESEARCHER	STERILIZER
EVAPORATED	GUARANTEED	LACCADIVES	OPISOMETER	RESTRAINED	STOUTHRIEF
EVENHANDED	GUIDELINES	LACKBUTEER	ORTHOPNOEA	RESTRICTED	STRAIGHTEN
EVERGLADES	HACKBUTEER	LACKLUSTER	OTHERGATES	RHOEADALES	STRAITENED
EXONERATED	HALFSISTER	LADYKILLER	OVERLANDER	RICHTHOFEN	STRATHSPEY
FACILITIES	HALLMARKED	LANDLOCKED	OVERMATTER	RIJSTTAFEL	STRATIOTES
FAIRHAIRED	HAMESUCKEN	LANDLOUPER	OVERWORKED	RINGLEADER	STREAMERED
FALKLANDER	HANDMAIDEN	LANDLUBBER	PACESETTER	RINGMASTER	STRENGTHEN
FARFETCHED	HANDPICKED	LANSQUENET	PAINKILLER	RIPSNORTER	STULTIFIED
FARSIGHTED	HANGGLIDER	LAWBREAKER	PALFRENIER	ROADRUNNER	STYLOPISED
FASCINATED	HARDBOILED	LEAFHOPPER	PALISANDER	ROSECHAFER	SUBLIMATER
FATALITIES	HEADHUNTED	LEDERHOSEN	PALLBEARER	ROTTWEILER	SUBMARINER
FEATHERBED	HEADMASTER	LEFTHANDED	PANTAGRUEL	SALAMANDER	SUBSCRIBER
FERTILISED	HEADMISTER	LEFTHANDER	PARALLELED	SALOPETTES	SUBSPECIES
FERTILISER	HEADPHONES	LEFTWINGER	PARKLEAVES	SANCTIFIED	SUNGLASSES
FERTILIZER	HELICOPTER	LENTIGINES	PATHFINDER	SANCTITIES	SUPERADDED
FILIBUSTER	HELIOLATER	LIKEMINDED	PATRONISED	SANDGROPER	SUPERMODEL

SUPERPOWER	UNEQUALLED	WITSNAPPER	HUSBANDAGE	EPISTROPHE	ANACOUSTIC
SUPERVISED	UNEXAMPLED	WOODPECKER	IMMUNOLOGY	FEARNOUGHT	ANACRUSTIC
SUPPRESSED	UNEXPECTED	WOODWORKER	INTERTRIGO	FLOODLIGHT	ANCHORETIC
SURROUNDED	UNEXPLORED	WORSHIPPER	LITHOMARGE	FORTHRIGHT	ANCHYLOSIS
SYNCOPATED	UNFATHOMED	YESTERWEEK	MALACOLOGY	GALSWORTHY	ANESTHESIA
TACHOMETER	UNFETTERED	YOURSELVES	MALLOPHAGA	GOBEMOUCHE	ANESTHETIC
TALEBEARER	UNFINISHED	YTHUNDERED	MAQUILLAGE	GYMNOSOPHY	ANTHROPOID
TANNHAUSER	UNFLAVORED	CHIFFCHAFF	MASKANONGE	HOLOGRAPHY	ANTIADITIS
TASKMASTER	UNFORESEEN	CLASPKNIFE	MASKINONGE	HOMEOPATHY	ANTIBIOTIC
TEETOTALER	UNGROUNDED	CRANKSHAFT	MASSASAUGA	KIESELGUHR	ANTISEPSIS
TENDRILLED	UNHAMPERED	DISQUALIFY	METALLURGY	KURDAITCHA	ANTISEPTIC
TERTIARIES	UNHERALDED	FALLINGOFF	MINERALOGY	LIMITROPHE	ANTISTATIC
THEMSELVES	UNIMPAIRED	FISTICUFFS	MISGIVINGS	MAKEWEIGHT	ANTITHESIS
THEREAFTER	UNINFORMED	FOODSTUFFS	MORPHOLOGY	MAKUNOUCHI	ANTITHETIC
THREATENED	UNINSPIRED	HANDICRAFT	MUSICOLOGY	MATRIARCHY	APHAERESIS
THUCYDIDES	UNLEAVENED	HIPPOGRIFF	NONVINTAGE	MICROFICHE	APOLAUSTIC
THUMBSCREW	UNLETTERED	HOUSECRAFT	ODONTOLOGY	MICROLIGHT	APOLOGETIC
TIEBREAKER	UNLICENSED	HOVERCRAFT	OUGHTLINGS	NEWSWORTHY	APOPEMPTIC
TIMEKEEPER	UNMANNERED	OFFTHECUFF	OVERCHARGE	NIGHTLIGHT	APOPLECTIC
TIMESERVER	UNNUMBERED	PAPERKNIFE	OVERSLAUGH	NOTEWORTHY	APOSEMATIC
TOILETRIES	UNOBSERVED	SHANDYGAFF	PALYNOLOGY	OROBRANCHE	APOTHEOSIS
TOLLKEEPER	UNOCCUPIED	SPACECRAFT	PERCENTAGE	OSTEOPATHY	APOTROPAIC
TONGUESTER	UNPREPARED	STAGECRAFT	PERSIFLAGE	OSTROGOTHS	AQUAFORTIS
TOSSICATED	UNPROMPTED	STATECRAFT	PERSTRINGE	OUANANICHE	ARITHMETIC
TOSTICATED	UNPROVOKED	STROGANOFF	PETRISSAGE	OVERBOUGHT	ARTHRALGIA
TOUCHPAPER	UNREASONED	UNDERCRAFT	PHRENOLOGY	OVERWEIGHT	ARYTAENOID
TOURNIQUET	UNREDEEMED	UNDERCROFT	PHYSIOLOGY	PASIGRAPHY	ASBESTOSIS
TRAFFICKER	UNRELIEVED	WITCHCRAFT	PICHICIAGO	PATRIARCHY	ASTIGMATIC
TRANSLATED	UNREQUITED	AFTERIMAGE	PICHICIEGO	PHILOSOPHY	ASYMMETRIC
TRANSPOSED	UNRESERVED	ALCHERINGA	PILGRIMAGE	PLAYWRIGHT	ATELEIOSIS
TRESPASSER	UNRESOLVED	APOPHTHEGM	PONEROLOGY	PRIZEFIGHT	AUTHORSHIP
TRIACONTER	UNREVEALED	ARISTOLOGY	PREARRANGE	PYRACANTHA	AUTOCRATIC
TROCHANTER	UNRIVALLED	ASSEMBLAGE	PSEPHOLOGY	PYROGRAPHY	AVICULARIA
TROMOMETER	UNSALARIED	AUTECOLOGY	PSYCHOLOGY	ROADWORTHY	BABESIASIS
TYMPANITES	UNSCHOOLED	BALNEOLOGY	SEISMOLOGY	SABRETACHE	BACITRACIN
TYPESETTER	UNSCRIPTED	BELONGINGS	SHARAWADGI	SATYAGRAHA	BAGASSOSIS
TYPEWRITER	UNSEASONED	BLANCMANGE	SHARAWAGGI	SHAKUHACHI	BARBITURIC
TYRANNISED	UNSHACKLED	BORROWINGS	SHILLELAGH	SHIPWRIGHT	BAROMETRIC
UMBELLIFER	VALENTINES	CAMERLENGO	SHORTRANGE	SYNECDOCHE	BATTLESHIP
UNABRIDGED	VARIEGATED	CAMERLINGO	SPELEOLOGY	TATPURUSHA	BEAUJOLAIS
UNACCENTED	VEGETABLES	CAMOUFLAGE	STONEHENGE	TELEGRAPHY	BEAVERSKIN
UNAFFECTED	VERSAILLES	CARDIOLOGY	SUBTERFUGE	TOPOGRAPHY	BETACRUCIS
UNANSWERED	VICTUALLER	CARPHOLOGY	SUPERCARGO	TORCHLIGHT	BIJOUTERIE
UNASSIGNED	VIEWFINDER	CENTRIFUGE	TECHNOLOGY	TYPOGRAPHY	BILIVERDIN
UNATTACHED	VIGILANTES	CHRONOLOGY	TEETHRIDGE	ULTRAFICHE	BIPINNARIA
UNATTENDED	VOETGANGER	COLPORTAGE	TELEBRIDGE	WATERTIGHT	BLOODSTAIN
UNBALANCED	WAGEEARNER	CONCHOLOGY	TELPHERAGE	WISHYWASHY	BRADYKININ
UNBELIEVER	WAINSCOTED	CONSTRINGE	TIMBROLOGY	ACHROMATIC	BREADFRUIT
UNBLEACHED	WALLFLOWER	CULVERTAGE	TOUCHANDGO	ACROAMATIC	BRIDESMAID
UNCONFINED	WANTHRIVEN	DELTIOLOGY	TOXICOLOGY	ADRENERGIC	BRONCHITIC
UNCULTURED	WASTEPAPER	DEMONOLOGY	TRICHOLOGY	ADVERSARIA	BRONCHITIS
UNDECLARED	WATCHMAKER	DESBOROUGH	USQUEBAUGH	AEROPHAGIA	BYSSINOSIS
UNDEFEATED	WATCHTOWER	DISARRANGE	VERNISSAGE	AFRORMOSIA	CALAMONDIN
UNDEFENDED	WATERLEVEL	DISCOURAGE	VILLEINAGE	ALCAICERIA	CALCEDONIO
UNDERCOVER	WATERSKIER	DRAWBRIDGE	WANDERINGS	ALCYONARIA	CALCITONIN
UNDERLINEN	WATERWHEEL	EFFLEURAGE	WATERWINGS	ALEXANDRIA	CALIFORNIA
UNDERSIZED	WEEDKILLER	EMBRYOLOGY	YARBOROUGH	ALGOLAGNIA	CAMBRENSIS
UNDERSTEER	WEIMARANER	ENTOMOLOGY	YELLOWLEGS	ALLOSTERIC	CAMSTEERIE
UNDERTAKER	WELLEARNED	EXOBIOLOGY	AIRFREIGHT	ALLOTROPIC	CASSIOPEIA
UNDERWATER	WHARFINGER	FOOTBRIDGE	ANASTROPHE	ALTRUISTIC	CATALECTIC
UNDESCRIED	WHATSOEVER	FREIGHTAGE	ANDROMACHE	AMANUENSIS	CATALEPTIC
UNDESERVED	WHITEWATER	GARLANDAGE	APOSTROPHE	AMBARVALIA	CATASTASIS
UNDETECTED	WHOLESALER	GETUPANDGO	AREOGRAPHY	AMBLYOPSIS	CATENACCIO
UNDETERRED	WILDFOWLER	GILLRAVAGE	BARASINGHA	AMPELOPSIS	CATTLEGRID
UNDIGESTED	WINCHESTER	GRAPHOLOGY	BIRTHRIGHT	AMPHIMIXIS	CAVICORNIA
UNDISPUTED	WINDFLOWER	GYNECOLOGY	BUNDESWEHR	AMPHOTERIC	CECIDOMYIA
UNDOCTORED	WINDJAMMER	HATEENOUGH	CACOGRAPHY	AMYGDALOID	CELLULITIS
UNEDUCATED	WINDSCREEN	HEMORRHAGE	DEMOGRAPHY	ANACHARSIS	CENSORSHIP
UNEMPLOYED	WINDSURFER	HODGEPODGE	DISTRAUGHT	ANACLASTIC	CHAMBERTIN

CHAROLLAIS	FAHRENHEIT	LYCHNAPSIA	PERIEGESIS	SPRINGTAIL	MASKIROVKA
CHAUDFROID	FATALISTIC	MACONOCHIE	PERSEPOLIS	STERNALGIA	MINISTROKE
CHEVROTAIN	FELLOWSHIP	MAIDENHAIR	PERSICARIA	STOCHASTIC	MOTHERLIKE
CHINQUAPIN	FIBROSITIS	MARGINALIA	PHILATELIC	STOUTHERIE	MUSSORGSKY
CHIRONOMIC	FINGERNAIL	MARQUETRIE	PHILOXENIA	STRAPONTIN	PADAREWSKI
CINQUEFOIL	FLINDERSIA	MAURITANIA	PHLEGMASIA	STRELITZIA	PATCHCOCKE
CIRRIPEDIA	FONTINALIS	MEGALITHIC	PHLEGMATIC	SUGARALLIE	PILLIWINKS
CLOSTRIDIA	FOREORDAIN	MEMBERSHIP	PHLOGISTIC	SUPERSONIC	PRZEWALSKI
COCHLEARIA	FRAMBOESIA	MENINGITIS	PHOLIDOSIS	SUPERTONIC	RAJPRAMUKH
CONCENTRIC	FREEMARTIN	MESOLITHIC	PHOTOGENIC	SYNAERESIS	SCHIPPERKE
CONCHIGLIE	FRIENDSHIP	METALEPSIS	PHYTOTOXIN	SYNCHRONIC	SHIELDRAKE
CONCHIOLIN	FRINGILLID	METAPLASIS	PILLOWSLIP	SYNEIDESIS	SPRINGBOKS
CONFERVOID	FUTURISTIC	METATHERIA	PINNIPEDIA	SYNOSTOSIS	SPRINGLIKE
CONSTANTIA	GALLIAMBIC	METATHESIS	PITYRIASIS	SYNTERESIS	STEELWORKS
COPESETTIC	GAULTHERIA	METHOMANIA	PLEONASTIC	SYPHILITIC	STRAVINSKY
COPPERSKIN	GENERATRIX	METROPOLIS	POCKMANTIE	SYSTEMATIC	SWEEPSTAKE
CORNUCOPIA	GEOCENTRIC	MICRONESIA	POIKILITIC	TEICHOPSIA	TANGANYIKA
CORTADERIA	GEOGRAPHIC	MILLICURIE	POINSETTIA	TELEPATHIC	THREADLIKE
CORYBANTIC	GESUNDHEIT	MISOCAPNIC	POLYHYMNIA	TELEPHONIC	UNLADYLIKE
COTTONTAIL	GIARDIASIS	MONILIASIS	PONTEDERIA	TELESCOPIC	WATERWORKS
CROTALARIA	GINGIVITIS	MONOACIDIC	PORTCULLIS	TENDERLOIN	ABNORMALLY
CRYPTOZOIC	GLYCOLYSIS	MONOCARPIC	PRECIPITIN	TENEBRIFIC	ABOMINABLE
CYBERNETIC	GLYCOSURIA	MONOLITHIC	PRESBYOPIA	TERMINALIA	ABOMINABLY
CYCLOPEDIA	GRAMICIDIN	MONOPHONIC	PROAIRESIS	TERREPLEIN	ABSOLUTELY
DEALERSHIP	GRAPEFRUIT	MONOPLEGIA	PROSTHESIS	THALESTRIS	ABUNDANTLY
DEMOCRATIC	GROCETERIA	MORGANATIC	PROSTHETIC	THERMIONIC	ACCESSIBLE
DENDROPHIS	GROUNDBAIT	MUJAHEDDIN	PROTANOPIA	THIMBLEWIT	ACCURATELY
DERMATITIS	GYROSCOPIC	MULTIMEDIA	PROTANOPIC	THROMBOSIS	ACCUSINGLY
DEVASTAVIT	HEDONISTIC	MYRINGITIS	PSAMMOPHIL	TILLANDSIA	ACROMEGALY
DIACAUSTIC	HEMIPLEGIA	NECROPOLIS	PSILOCYBIN	TREKSCHUIT	ACTIONABLE
DIACHRONIC	HEMOGLOBIN	NEUTROPHIL	PYCNOGONID	TRIMALCHIO	ADEQUATELY
DIAGENESIS	HEMOPHILIA	NIHILISTIC	PYTHOGENIC	TRITANOPIA	ADJUSTABLE
DIAGNOSTIC	HIERARCHIC	NOMOTHETIC	QUIRINALIA	TULARAEMIA	ADMIRINGLY
DIAPEDESIS	HISTOLYSIS	NOSOPHOBIA	RADIOLARIA	TYMPANITIS	ADMISSIBLE
DIASTALTIC	HISTRIONIC	NUMISMATIC	RAGAMUFFIN	ULTRABASIC	ADMITTEDLY
DIDASCALIC	HOLOPHYTIC	NYCTALOPIA	READERSHIP	ULTRAMAFIC	AFFORDABLE
DIELECTRIC	HOLOSTERIC	ODONTALGIA	REAMINGBIT	ULTRASONIC	ALDERMANLY
DINANDERIE	HOMOPHOBIA	OOPHORITIS	RHEOTROPIC	UNHYGIENIC	ALLYCHOLLY
DIPHTHERIA	HOMOPHOBIC	OPHTHALMIC	RHEUMATOID	UNROMANTIC	ANGLOPHILE
DIPLOMATIC	HOMOPHONIC	OPTIMISTIC	RHINOLALIA	UNSPECIFIC	ANGUILLULA
DIPSOMANIA	HOOTNANNIE	OROGENESIS	RIBOFLAVIN	UROPOIESIS	ANSWERABLE
DISINHERIT	HUMANISTIC	OSMIDROSIS	ROTISSERIE	VALLADOLID	ANTEPENULT
DOCIMASTIC	HYDROLYSIS	OSTEOLEPIS	RUBINSTEIN	VASCULITIS	APPARENTLY
DOLICHOLIS	HYDROPONIC	OVERSTRAIN	RUMINANTIA	VULCANALIA	APPLICABLE
DRAWCANSIR	HYPERBOLIC	OXYMORONIC	SACCHAROID	WANCHANCIE	AQUAMANALE
DRUZHINNIK	HYPERDULIA	PAEDIATRIC	SAGITTARIA	WHEELCHAIR	AQUAMANILE
DYSTROPHIC	HYPODERMIC	PALMATIFID	SALICORNIA	WORKAHOLIC	ARACOSTYLE
ECCHYMOSIS	HYPOTHESIS	PARAENESIS	SANDEMANIA	XENOPHOBIA	ARROGANTLY
ECCOPROTIC	HYSTERESIS	PARAMETRIC	SANNAYASIN	XENOPHOBIC	ASCRIBABLE
ECHOPRAXIA	IATROGENIC	PARAPHASIA	SATURNALIA	XEROPHYTIC	ASSIGNABLE
ECTHLIPSIS	ICHTHYOSIS	PARAPHILIA	SCAMMOZZIS	XEROSTOMIA	ATTAINABLE
EGOCENTRIC	ICOSANDRIA	PARAPHONIA	SCHALSTEIN	ZOANTHARIA	AUTOMOBILE
ELECTRONIC	IDEALISTIC	PARAPHYSIS	SCHISMATIC	ZOLLVEREIN	BANDERILLA
EMBLEMATIC	IMPRESARIO	PARAPLEGIA	SCHOLAEMIA	ZOOTHAPSIS	BANDERILLO
EMMETROPIA	INARTISTIC	PARAPLEGIC	SCHOLASTIC	BACKBLOCKS	BARCAROLLE
ENANTIOSIS	JINGOISTIC	PARAPRAXIS	SCIENTIFIC	BACKSTROKE	BASKETBALL
ENDOSMOSIS	JUGENDSTIL	PARARTHRIA	SCLERIASIS	BRICKWORKS	BELIEVABLE
ENHYDRITIC	KNOBKERRIE	PARASCENIA	SCOTODINIA	BUTTERBAKE	BIANNUALLY
ENKEPHALIN	LAEOTROPIC	PARMACITIE	SEAMANSHIP	CHEESECAKE	BIENNIALLY
EPENTHETIC	LAMBREQUIN	PARONYCHIA	SEANNACHIE	CHOPSTICKS	BISSEXTILE
EPIDEICTIC	LARYNGITIS	PATHOGENIC	SEECATCHIE	CORNSTALKS	BLACKBULLY
EPIGENETIC	LATTICINIO	PATISSERIE	SEPARATRIX	CRAIGFLUKE	BLISSFULLY
EPIGLOTTIS	LEADERSHIP	PATRONYMIC	SIGILLARIA	DOSTOEVSKY	BLUEBOTTLE
EPISPASTIC	LEGALISTIC	PEAUDESOIE	SILVERSKIN	DREADLOCKS	BLUEMANTLE
ESCHAROTIC	LEONTIASIS	PEELGARLIC	SIMPLISTIC	EARTHQUAKE	BOOKMOBILE
EULOGISTIC	LEUCHAEMIA	PENETRALIA	SLAMMERKIN	EARTHWORKS	BOONDOGGLE
EUTHANASIA	LINEOMYCIN	PENICILLIN	SOPHOMORIC	GLASSWORKS	BOTTICELLI
EUTRAPELIA	LINGUISTIC	PENTATONIC	SOUTERRAIN	GOLDILOCKS	BRAINCHILD
EXOTHERMIC	LUPERCALIA	PENTETERIC	SPLANCHNIC	HANKYPANKY	BROCATELLE

BUTTERMILK	DESPICABLE	GRACEFULLY	INSATIABLE	ORDINARILY	REASONABLY
BUTTONHOLE	DETACHABLE	GRACIOUSLY	INSATIABLY	ORIGINALLY	REASSEMBLE
CACOMISTLE	DETECTABLE	GRANADILLA	INSECURELY	OSTENSIBLE	RECEPTACLE
CAERPHILLY	DETESTABLE	GRANDCHILD	INSENSIBLE	OSTENSIBLY	RECKLESSLY
CALCULABLE	DHARMSHALA	GRATEFULLY	INSOLENTLY	OSTEOCOLLA	RELATIVELY
CAMBERWELL	DIAGONALLY	GRENADILLA	INTANGIBLE	OUTSPECKLE	REMARKABLE
CAMPANELLA	DIGESTIBLE	GUACHAMOLE	INTERNALLY	OVERSUPPLY	REMARKABLY
CANDELILLA	DILIGENTLY	GUTTURALLY	INTIMATELY	OWLSPIEGLE	REPAIRABLE
CANNONBALL	DISCREETLY	GYPSOPHILA	INVALUABLE	PAINLESSLY	REPEATABLE
CARELESSLY	DISENNOBLE	HABITUALLY	INVARIABLE	PARADIDDLE	REPEATEDLY
CARMAGNOLE	DISGRUNTLE	HALFHOURLY	INVARIABLY	PARDONABLE	REPORTEDLY
CASCARILLA	DISHABILLE	HALFYEARLY	INVINCIBLE	PARDONABLY	RESCHEDULE
CAUTIOUSLY	DISORDERLY	HAMSHACKLE	INVIOLABLE	PARTICIPLE	RESIGNEDLY
CELESTIALS	DISPOSABLE	HANDSOMELY	IRONICALLY	PARTINGALE	RESOLUTELY
CHAMBRANLE	DISPUTABLE	HARDCASTLE	JARGONELLE	PASTORELLA	RESTLESSLY
CHANGEABLE	DISTINCTLY	HECTICALLY	JERRYBUILT	PATERNALLY	RETURNABLE
CHARGEABLE	DOUBLETALK	HEEDLESSLY	JUBILANTLY	PEACEFULLY	REVERENTLY
CHARITABLE	DOUBTFULLY	HELPLESSLY	JUDICIALLY	PECCADILLO	REVERSIBLE
CHARITABLY	DREADFULLY	HEPATOCELE	KENSPECKLE	PECULIARLY	RIGHTFULLY
CHEERFULLY	DROSOPHILA	HEROICALLY	KLEBSIELLA	PENETRABLE	RIGOROUSLY
CHEMICALLY	EATANSWILL	HESITANTLY	LAMENTABLE	PEPPERMILL	RITORNELLE
CHEVESAILE	EFFUSIVELY	HONOURABLE	LAMENTABLY	PERCENTILE	RITORNELLO
CHILDISHLY	ELOQUENTLY	HONOURABLY	LARGESCALE	PERDURABLE	ROCKABILLY
CHINCHILLA	ENORMOUSLY	HOPELESSLY	LAUDERDALE	PERILOUSLY	ROTHSCHILD
CHUCKWALLA	ENTEROCELE	HOSPITABLE	LIBREVILLE	PERISHABLE	RUTHLESSLY
CHURLISHLY	ESCADRILLE	HOSPITABLY	LINGULELLA	PERIWINKLE	SADDLEBILL
CINDERELLA	ESPADRILLE	HUMOROUSLY	LISTLESSLY	PERSONABLE	SALMONELLA
CITRONELLA	ESPECIALLY	IGNORANTLY	MAHAYANALI	PERSONALLY	SALTARELLO
CLADOPHYLL	EVENTUALLY	IMAGINABLE	MANAGEABLE	PERVERSELY	SARCOCOLLA
CLAIRCOLLE	EXOTICALLY	IMMORTELLE	MANDEVILLE	PETRONELLA	SAVONAROLA
CLARABELLA	EXPENDABLE	IMPALPABLE	MANIFESTLY	PETULANTLY	SCOFFINGLY
CLINICALLY	EXPLICABLE	IMPASSABLE	MANZANILLA	PHYSICALLY	SCORNFULLY
CLYDESDALE	EXPLICITLY	IMPECCABLE	MARGINALLY	PICCADILLY	SDRUCCIOLA
COCKABULLY	EXTENDABLE	IMPECCABLY	MARKETABLE	PICCALILLI	SEASONABLE
COHERENTLY	EXTENSIBLE	IMPLACABLE	MARTINGALE	PIGEONHOLE	SEASONABLY
COLLEMBOLA	EXTERNALLY	IMPLACABLY	MATCHSTALK	PIRANDELLO	SEDULOUSLY
COLOSSALLY	FABULOUSLY	IMPLICITLY	MATERIALLY	PLEASANTLY	SEGUIDILLA
COMESTIBLE	FAITHFULLY	IMPOLITELY	MATERNALLY	POETICALLY	SEMICIRCLE
COMMUNALLY	FAMILIARLY	IMPOSSIBLE	MEASURABLE	POIGNANTLY	SENSUOUSLY
COMMUTABLE	FAVOURABLE	IMPOSSIBLY	MELANCHOLY	PONCHIELLI	SEPARATELY
COMPARABLE	FAVOURABLY	IMPOTENTLY	MENACINGLY	PONTICELLO	SERRADELLA
COMPATIBLE	FEARLESSLY	IMPROBABLE	MERCANTILE	PORTMANTLE	SERRADILLA
COMPLETELY	FENESTELLA	IMPROBABLY	MERCIFULLY	POSITIVELY	SGANARELLE
CONFUSEDLY	FERNITICLE	IMPROPERLY	METASTABLE	POTENTILLA	SHAMEFULLY
CONSTANTLY	FEVERISHLY	IMPUDENTLY	MISHGUGGLE	PRATINCOLE	SHEEPISHLY
CONTRARILY	FIENDISHLY	INCISIVELY	MISTAKENLY	PREFERABLE	SHOCKINGLY
CONVERSELY	FITZGERALD	INCREDIBLE	MODERATELY	PREFERABLY	SIDESADDLE
CONVEYABLE	FLAGRANTLY	INCREDIBLY	MODIFIABLE	PREHENSILE	SIGNORELLI
CORNCOCKLE	FLAPDOODLE	INCUNABULA	MORTADELLA	PREPENSELY	SILVERBELL
CREDITABLE	FLEETINGLY	INDECENTLY	MOTORCYCLE	PRESUMABLY	SILVERBILL
CREDITABLY	FLIPPANTLY	INDICTABLE	MOURNFULLY	PRETINCOLE	SINGULARLY
CRIMINALLY	FONTANELLE	INDIRECTLY	MOZZARELLA	PREVIOUSLY	SINSEMILLA
CRITICALLY	FORCEFULLY	INEDUCABLE	MUTINOUSLY	PROCURABLE	SKILLFULLY
CYCLOSTYLE	FORECASTLE	INELIGIBLE	NARROWDALE	PRODIGALLY	SLATTERNLY
DEADNETTLE	FORGIVABLE	INEVITABLE	NATIONALLY	PROFITABLE	SLUGGISHLY
DECISIVELY	FORMIDABLE	INEVITABLY	NEGATIVELY	PROFITABLY	SMALLSCALE
DEDUCTIBLE	FRATICELLI	INEXORABLE	NEGLIGIBLE	PROFOUNDLY	SNOWMOBILE
DEFENSIBLE	FRAXINELLA	INFALLIBLE	NEGOTIABLE	PROJECTILE	SOMERSAULT
DEFINITELY	FRENZIEDLY	INFALLIBLY	NEIGHBORLY	PROTRUSILE	SOMERVILLE
DEGRADABLE	FREQUENTLY	INFERNALLY	NOTICEABLE	PUMPHANDLE	SOOTHINGLY
DEJECTEDLY	FRUITFULLY	INFINITELY	NOTICEABLY	PUNCTUALLY	SPECIOUSLY
DELECTABLE	FUSTANELLA	INFLATABLE	NOTIFIABLE	PUNISHABLE	SPIRITEDLY
DELICATELY	FUSTANELLE	INFLEXIBLE	NOTIONALLY	QUADRANGLE	SPITEFULLY
DEMOISELLE	GARGOUILLE	INFLEXIBLY	OBEDIENTLY	QUESADILLA	SPLENDIDLY
DEPENDABLE	GENEROUSLY	INFORMALLY	OBLIGINGLY	RAMSHACKLE	SPORTINGLY
DEPLORABLE	GENTLEFOLK	INHERENTLY	OBSERVABLE	RATIONALLY	SPOTLESSLY
DEPLORABLY	GIBBERELLA	INIMITABLE	OBTAINABLE	RAVENOUSLY	SPURIOUSLY
DESERVEDLY	GLORIOUSLY	INNOCENTLY	OFFICIALLY	RAVENSBILL	STANDSTILL
DÉSHABILLÉ	GORGEOUSLY	INOPERABLE	OFFTHEWALL	REASONABLE	STEALTHILY

STRIDENTLY	WATCHFULLY	ACCOUNTANT	BORDRAGING	CONTESTANT	DISTURBING
STRIKINGLY	WHITSTABLE	ACCOUNTING	BRASSBOUND	CONTINGENT	DOMINATING
STRINGHALT	WILLYWILLY	ADAMANTINE	BREASTBONE	CONTINUANT	DOWNSIZING
STRONGHOLD	WINDOWSILL	ADDITAMENT	BRIGANDINE	CONTINUING	DRAKESTONE
STROPHIOLE	WINDSHIELD	ADJUSTMENT	BRIGANTINE	CONTRABAND	DRAWSTRING
STUBBORNLY	WORTHWHILE	ADOLESCENT	BROWNSTONE	CONTRAHENT	DUNDERFUNK
STUDIOUSLY	WRETCHEDLY	ADRENALINE	BURGEONING	CONTRAVENE	EARTHSHINE
SUCCINCTLY	WRONGFULLY	ADULTERANT	BUTCHERING	CONVENIENT	EASTERLING
SUPPOSEDLY	YAFFINGALE	ADULTERINE	CANCRIZANS	CONVERGENT	EBOULEMENT
SURGICALLY	YGGDRASILL	AGRAHAYANA	CANNELLONI	CONVERSANT	EFFACEMENT
SWIMMINGLY	ABHIDHAMMA	ALABANDINE	CANTONMENT	CONVINCING	ELACAMPANE
TABERNACLE	AERENCHYMA	ALLUREMENT	CANVASSING	CORRECTING	ELECAMPANE
TACTICALLY	AMBLYSTOMA	ALMSGIVING	CAPITOLINE	CORRESPOND	EMALANGENI
TACTLESSLY	BIORHYTHMS	ALPHONSINE	CAPPUCCINO	CORRUPTING	EMBANKMENT
TARADIDDLE	BOTHERSOME	AMBIVALENT	CARTHAMINE	COUNSELING	EMBODIMENT
TARANTELLA	BRAGADISME	AMPUSSYAND	CATARRHINE	CRICKETING	EMBONPOINT
TASTEFULLY	BURDENSOME	ANADYOMENE	CATCHPENNY	CRUIKSHANK	EMPFINDUNG
TATTERSALL	BUTTERBUMP	ANSCHAUUNG	CELLOPHANE	CUCKOOPINT	EMPLOYMENT
TCHOUKBALL	CENTROSOME	ANTECEDENT	CHAFFERING	CUMBERLAND	ENCAMPMENT
TERMINABLE	CHEIRONOMY	ANTHRACINE	CHALCEDONY	CUMMERBUND	ENCASEMENT
TERMINALLY	CHROMOSOME	ANTIOCHENE	CHANGELING	CURMURRING	ENCHANTING
THANKFULLY	CUDDLESOME	ANTIVENENE	CHARGEHAND	CURVETTING	ENDEARMENT
THOROUGHLY	CUMBERSOME	APPETIZING	CHATELAINE	CUTTLEBONE	ENGAGEMENT
TINKERBELL	DECAGRAMME	AQUAMARINE	CHECKPOINT	DARJEELING	ENGOUEMENT
TIRELESSLY	DINNERTIME	ARGOLEMONO	CHINASTONE	DEBASEMENT	ENGROSSING
TOCCATELLA	DREARISOME	ARMIPOTENT	CHIRICAUNE	DEBATEMENT	ENLACEMENT
TOLERANTLY	EPIPHONEMA	ARTHURIANA	CHITARRONE	DEBRIEFING	ENLÈVEMENT
TORRICELLI	ETHEOSTOMA	ASPARAGINE	CHITTAGONG	DECAMPMENT	ENLISTMENT
TORTUOUSLY	FORTISSIMO	ASPERSIONS	CHRISTIANA	DECRESCENT	ENRICHMENT
TRAGICALLY	FROLICSOME	ASSEMBLING	CIRCUMVENT	DEFACEMENT	ENROLLMENT
TRANQUILLY	GASTRONOME	ASSESSMENT	CISPONTINE	DEFILEMENT	ENSANGUINE
TROUVAILLE	GASTRONOMY	ASSIGNMENT	CLAMOURING	DEFRAYMENT	ENTICEMENT
TRUSTFULLY	HETEROGAMY	ASSORTMENT	CLEMENTINE	DELINQUENT	ENTOMBMENT
TRUTHFULLY	HIPPODROME	ASTOUNDING	CLINGSTONE	DENOUEMENT	ENTRANCING
TURRITELLA	IMPOSTHUME	ASTRINGENT	CLOMIPHENE	DEPARTMENT	ENTREATING
ULTIMATELY	LOGARITHMS	ATTACHMENT	COADJUTANT	DEPLOYMENT	ENTRYPHONE
UNARGUABLE	LUMPECTOMY	ATTAINMENT	COCKERNONY	DEPORTMENT	EPAULEMENT
UNBEARABLE	MASTECTOMY	AVANTURINE	COEXISTENT	DEPRESSANT	EQUIVALENT
UNBEARABLY	MEDDLESOME	AVENTURINE	COINCIDENT	DEPRESSING	ERUBESCENT
UNBEATABLE	METTLESOME	BACKBITING	COLBERTINE	DERAILMENT	ESCAPEMENT
UNCOMMONLY	MONOCHROME	BACKGROUND	COLCHICINE	DESCENDANT	ESCARPMENT
UNCTUOUSLY	NEURILEMMA	BAFFLEMENT	COLLAPSING	DESCENDING	ETHYLAMINE
UNDENIABLE	NEUROLEMMA	BALANCHINE	COLLARBONE	DESCRIBING	EUCHLORINE
UNDERWORLD	OCTODECIMO	BALBUTIENT	COLLECTING	DESPAIRING	EUPHROSYNE
UNENVIABLE	PALINDROME	BALLOONING	COLOSSIANS	DESPONDENT	EVANESCENT
UNFRIENDLY	PARENCHYMA	BANISHMENT	COMEDIENNE	DESSIATINE	EVERYTHING
UNHEARABLE	PHANTASIME	BARGAINING	COMFORTING	DESSYATINE	EXCITEMENT
UNMANNERLY	PHLEBOTOMY	BARRACKING	COMMANDANT	DETACHMENT	EXHAUSTING
UNREADABLE	PIANISSIMO	BATTLEMENT	COMMANDING	DETAINMENT	EXORBITANT
UNRELIABLE	POGONOTOMY	BEEKEEPING	COMMITMENT	DEVELOPING	EXPERIMENT
UNSCRAMBLE	POLYCHROME	BEFOREHAND	COMPELLING	DEVOTEMENT	FACESAVING
UNSOCIABLE	PSYCHOPOMP	BEHINDHAND	COMPLACENT	DICYNODONT	FAIRGROUND
UNSUITABLE	QUADRIREME	BELLADONNA	COMPLEMENT	DIRECTIONS	FAMISHMENT
UNWORKABLE	RHINOPHYMA	BELLARMINE	COMPLIMENT	DISAPPOINT	FANTOCCINI
UTILIZABLE	SARCOLEMMA	BENEFICENT	COMPREHEND	DISCERNING	FAREPAYING
VANDERBILT	SERRASALMO	BENEVOLENT	CONCERNING	DISCIPLINE	FARRANDINE
VAUDEVILLE	SEXAGESIMA	BENZEDRINE	CONCERTINA	DISCONTENT	FASTMOVING
VEHEMENTLY	SPRINGTIME	BERNARDINE	CONCLUDING	DISCORDANT	FATHERLAND
VERIFIABLE	STEREOTOMY	BEWITCHING	CONCORDANT	DISCREPANT	FERRANDINE
VERMICELLI	STRABOTOMY	BITTERLING	CONCURRENT	DISCUSSING	FESCENNINE
VERTICALLY	STREETLAMP	BLACKENING	CONDESCEND	DISENCHANT	FETTUCCINE
VIGOROUSLY	SUMMERTIME	BLACKSTONE	CONDUCTING	DISGUSTING	FINGERLING
VILLANELLE	TELEOSTOME	BLISTERING	CONNECTING	DISHARMONY	FLAMBOYANT
VIRTUOUSLY	WINTERTIME	BLITHERING	CONQUERING	DISINCLINE	FLAMINGANT
VIRULENTLY	ABERDEVINE	BLOODHOUND	CONSEQUENT	DISPENSING	FLASHPOINT
VITELLICLE	ABITURIENT	BLOODSTONE	CONSISTENT	DISSENTING	FLATTERING
VOLLEYBALL	ABONNEMENT	BLUNDERING	CONSTRAINT	DISSILIENT	FLAVESCENT
VULNERABLE	ABRIDGMENT	BORDERLAND	CONSULTANT	DISSOLVENT	FLAVOURING
WASTEFULLY	ACCESSIONS	BORDERLINE	CONSULTING	DISTILLING	FLICKERING

FLOCCULENT	INCRESCENT	MISCELLANY	PLATTELAND	SATISFYING	SUFFICIENT
FLORENTINE	INDICTMENT	MISFORTUNE	PLAYGROUND	SAXICOLINE	SUNBATHING
FORBEARING	INDITEMENT	MISLEADING	PLUNDERING	SBUDDIKINS	SUPERGIANT
FORBIDDING	INDUCEMENT	MITIGATING	POINTBLANK	SCARCEMENT	SUPPLEMENT
FOREBODING	INESCULENT	MONOVALENT	POLYVALENT	SCARLATINA	SUPPLICANT
FOREGROUND	INFEFTMENT	MOTHERLAND	PORLOCKING	SCARLETINA	SUPPORTING
FORFAITING	INFIGHTING	MOUNTEBANK	POSTLIMINY	SCATTERING	SURFRIDING
FOUDROYANT	INFREQUENT	MOUSSELINE	POZZUOLANA	SCATURIENT	SURPASSING
FOXHUNTING	INGREDIENT	MUCKRAKING	PREDESTINE	SCREECHING	SURPRISING
FRANGIPANE	INHABITANT	MUNIFICENT	PREDNISONE	SCRIBBLING	SUSTAINING
FRANGIPANI	INHIBITING	NAPTHALENE	PREEMINENT	SCRIMSHANK	SWAGGERING
FRAUDULENT	INSOUCIANT	NAUSEATING	PREFERMENT	SCROUNGING	SWALLOWING
FREEMASONS	INSTALMENT	NETWORKING	PREPAYMENT	SECONDHAND	SWEETENING
FREMESCENT	INSTRUMENT	NIDDERLING	PREVAILING	SECONDMENT	SWELTERING
FRUTESCENT	INTEGUMENT	NIGRESCENT	PROCEEDING	SELEGILINE	TAGLIARINI
FULFILMENT	INTELIGENT	NONCHALANT	PROCESSING	SELTZOGENE	TAILGATING
FURNISHING	INTENDMENT	NONPAYMENT	PROCUMBENT	SEPTUAGINT	TALLEYRAND
GAINGIVING	INTERNMENT	NONSMOKING	PROFICIENT	SERPENTINE	TAMBERLANE
GALUMPHING	INTERPHONE	NONVIOLENT	PROJECTING	SETTLEMENT	TAMBOURINE
GETHSEMANE	INTERTWINE	NORBERTINE	PROPELLANT	SHAGGYMANE	TANTAMOUNT
GHIBELLINE	INTOLERANT	NORTHBOUND	PROPELLENT	SHAMPOOING	TAPDANCING
GILBERTINE	INTOXICANT	NOURISHING	PROSERPINA	SHATTERING	TAPOTEMENT
GIRDLERINK	INTRIGUING	OCEANGOING	PROSERPINE	SHEEPSHANK	TARPAULING
GIRLFRIEND	INVESTMENT	ODELSTHING	PROSILIENT	SHIMMERING	TARTRAZINE
GLISTENING	IRIDESCENT	OFFPUTTING	PROSPERINA	SHOESTRING	TEENYWEENY
GLITTERAND	IRRELEVANT	OMNIPOTENT	PROTESTANT	SHORTENING	TERRIFYING
GLITTERING	IRREVERENT	OMNISCIENT	PROVISIONS	SHUDDERING	THEREANENT
GOVERNMENT	IRRITATING	OPALESCENT	PUBERULENT	SICILIENNE	THICKENING
GRAMOPHONE	ISABELLINE	ORTHOCAINE	PUBLISHING	SIMULATING	THREEPENNY
GRANDSTAND	ISOLEUCINE	OUTPATIENT	PUMMELLING	SKINDIVING	THUMBIKINS
GRATIFYING	JAYWALKING	OUTPOURING	PUNCHDRUNK	SKRIMSHANK	THUNDERING
GRAVEOLENT	KESSELRING	OVEREATING	PUNISHMENT	SKUPSHTINA	TIMESAVING
GRAVESTONE	KIDNAPPING	OVERRIDING	PURSUIVANT	SLUMBERING	TORPESCENT
GREENSHANK	KRUGERRAND	OVERSTRUNG	PUTREFYING	SMARAGDINE	TORTELLINI
GREENSTONE	KUOMINTANG	PALESTRINA	PUTRESCENT	SMATTERING	TOUCHSTONE
GRINDSTONE	LACUSTRINE	PALUDAMENT	PUZZLEMENT	SNAKESTONE	TOURMALINE
GROUNDLING	LANDAMMANN	PALUSTRINE	PYRIDOXINE	SNIGGERING	TOURNAMENT
GROVELLING	LANDSTHING	PANTALOONS	QUARANTINE	SNORKELING	TRADITIONS
GUILLOTINE	LANGERHANS	PAPAVERINE	QUARTERING	SOLIVAGANT	TRAMONTANA
HAIRSPRING	LAURUSTINE	PARADOXINE	QUERSPRUNG	SOURDELINE	TRAMONTANE
HANDSPRING	LAWABIDING	PARASELENE	RAVENSTONE	SOUSAPHONE	TRAMPOLINE
HARASSMENT	LIEBERMANN	PARGETTING	RAWSTHORNE	SOUTHBOUND	TRANSPLANT
HEADSTRONG	LIEUTENANT	PARISCHANE	REARMAMENT	SPEAKERINE	TRAVELLING
HELLESPONT	LIGNOCAINE	PARISIENNE	REASSURING	SPELLBOUND	TRAVERTINE
HETERODYNE	LIQUESCENT	PARLIAMENT	REDCURRANT	SPILLIKINS	TRIDENTINE
HEXAVALENT	LITHOPHANE	PARMIGIANA	REFINEMENT	SPINESCENT	TRIPEHOUND
HIEROPHANT	LOCULAMENT	PEACHERINO	REFLECTING	SPIRKETING	TRIUMPHANT
HIGHFLYING	LUTESTRING	PEPPERMINT	REFRESHING	SPRINKLING	TURNAROUND
HILDEBRAND	MAGISTRAND	PERCIPIENT	REFRINGENT	STAGGERING	TURPENTINE
HINDUSTANI	MAGNIFYING	PERFICIENT	RESEMBLING	STAMMERING	UBIQUINONE
HINTERLAND	MAINSPRING	PERFORMING	RESENTMENT	STANDPOINT	ULTRASOUND
HIPPOCRENE	MALCONTENT	PERPLEXING	RESOUNDING	STAPHYLINE	UNASSUMING
HOMECOMING	MALEVOLENT	PERSEPHONE	RESPECTING	STARVELING	UNAVAILING
HOOTANANNY	MANAGEMENT	PERSISTENT	RESPONDENT	STILLSTAND	UNBECOMING
HOOTENANNY	MANSERVANT	PERSUADING	RESTAURANT	STOREFRONT	UNBLINKING
HORRIFYING	MARASCHINO	PETRIFYING	RETIREMENT	STRACCHINO	UNBLUSHING
HOUSEBOUND	MARCANTANT	PHAGEDAENA	RETRAINING	STRAGGLING	UNDERBURNT
HYALOPHANE	MARCESCENT	PHILIPPINA	RETREATING	STREAMLINE	UNDERLYING
HYDROPHANE	MARYLEBONE	PHILIPPINE	RHINESTONE	STREPITANT	UNDERSLUNG
HYDROPLANE	MASCARPONE	PHILISTINE	RINGELMANN	STRYCHNINE	UNDERSTAND
IMPAIRMENT	MASTERMIND	PHILLIPINA	ROISTERING	STUPEFYING	UNDULATING
IMPEDIMENT	MAUPASSANT	PHILLIPINE	ROLLICKING	SUAVEOLENT	UNEDIFYING
IMPENITENT	MEANDERING	PHILLUMENY	ROSANILINE	SUBHEADING	UNFLAGGING
INBREEDING	MEDICAMENT	PHILOPOENA	ROSEMALING	SUBMEDIANT	UNINVITING
INCAPARINA	MEPERIDINE	PICCANINNY	RUDOLPHINE	SUBROUTINE	UNPLEASANT
INCITEMENT	MESITYLENE	PINCHPENNY	RUPICOLINE	SUBSEQUENT	UNSETTLING
INCOHERENT	METHEDRINE	PIONEERING	SACCHARINE	SUBSISTENT	UNSLEEPING
INCONSTANT	MICROPHONE	PITCHSTONE	SANDERLING	SUBTRAHEND	UNSWERVING
INCREASING	MINESTRONE	PLASTICINE	SAPPERMENT	SUCCEEDING	UNTHINKING

UNYIELDING	ARCHDEACON	CONDUCTION	DISTORTION	HEPTATHLON	MODERATION
UPBRINGING	AREFACTION	CONFECTION	DIVINATION	HESITATION	MODULATION
UPSTANDING	ARMAGEDDON	CONFESSION	DOMINATION	HULLABALOO	MONOPTERON
VARNISHING	ASPIRATION	CONGESTION	DONNYBROOK	HUMDUDGEON	MONOPTEROS
VIBRAPHONE	ASSUMPTION	CONNECTION	DOORTODOOR	HYPAETHRON	MOSASAUROS
VIBRATIONS	ATTRACTION	CONNIPTION	DRAGONROOT	IMMOLATION	MOTHERHOOD
VICEGERENT	AUTOCHTHON	CONSENSION	DRUMBLEDOR	IMPOSITION	MOTIVATION
VICEREGENT	AUTOMATION	CONTENTION	DUPLICATOR	IMPRESSION	MUTILATION
VICTORIANA	BACKGAMMON	CONTORTION	EISTEDDFOD	IMPUTATION	NAVIGATION
VIDARABINE	BALNEATION	CONTRACTOR	ELIMINATOR	INCUBATION	NEGOTIATOR
WASSAILING	BASSINGTON	CONTRAFLOW	ELONGATION	INDECISION	NINCOMPOOP
WASSERMANS	BATTLEDOOR	CONTRITION	EMACIATION	INDEXATION	NOMINATION
WATERBORNE	BENEFACTOR	CONVECTION	EMENDATION	INDICATION	NONFICTION
WATERFRONT	BRACHIOPOD	CONVENTION	EMIGRATION	INFLECTION	NUMERATION
WELLSPRING	BRAZILWOOD	CONVERSION	ENCEPHALON	INFLICTION	OBLIGATION
WHEATSTONE	BRIDEGROOM	CONVICTION	EPILIMNION	INFRACTION	OCCUPATION
WHISPERING	BUCCINATOR	CONVULSION	EQUITATION	INHALATION	OCTAHEDRON
WINDOWPANE	BURLINGTON	COPULATION	ERIOCAULON	INHIBITION	OMOPHORION
WONDERLAND	BYELECTION	COQUELICOT	ERUCTATION	INITIATION	OPPOSITION
WONDERMENT	CACODAEMON	CORONATION	ESCALATION	INJUNCTION	OPPRESSION
WRAPAROUND	CALCULATOR	CORRECTION	ESCUTCHEON	INNOVATION	ORANGEWOOD
WRONGDOING	CALEFACTOR	CORREGIDOR	ESTIMATION	INQUISITOR	ORDINATION
WUNDERKIND	CAMPARADOR	CORRUGATOR	ESTRAMACON	INSPECTION	ORIGINATOR
ZABAGLIONE	CAPITATION	CORRUPTION	EUCALYPTOL	INSTIGATOR	ORPHEOREON
ZEUGLODONT	CARBURETOR	COTTONWOOD	EUROCLYDON	INSTRUCTOR	OSCILLATOR
ZIDOVUDINE	CASTRATION	COUNCILLOR	EVACUATION	INSULATION	OSCITATION
ABDICATION	CATHOLICON	COUNSELLOR	EVALUATION	INTERFERON	OSCULATION
ABERRATION	CATHOLICOS	COUSCOUSOU	EXALTATION	INTIMATION	OVERSHADOW
ABROGATION	CEPHALOPOD	CULTIVATOR	EXCAVATION	INTINCTION	OVERTHETOP
ABSCISSION	CESTRACION	CURMUDGEON	EXECRATION	INTONATION	OVIPOSITOR
ABSOLUTION	CHAMAELEON	DECAHEDRON	EXHALATION	INUNDATION	OXYGENATOR
ABSORPTION	CHAMBERPOT	DECLENSION	EXHAUSTION	INVITATION	PADDINGTON
ABSTENTION	CHAMPIGNON	DECOLLATOR	EXHIBITION	INVOCATION	PADDYMELON
ACCUBATION	CHANCELLOR	DECORATION	EXHUMATION	INVOLUTION	PAGINATION
ACCUSATION	CHAPARAJOS	DEDICATION	EXPEDITION	IRRIGATION	PALMATOZOA
ACOLOUTHOS	CHAPAREJOS	DEFAMATION	EXPIRATION	IRRITATION	PALMERSTON
ACOTYLEDON	CHATTERBOX	DEFECATION	EXPOSITION	JACULATION	PANOPTICON
ACROTERION	CHATTERTON	DEFINITION	EXPRESSION	JEISTIECOR	PARENTHOOD
ADAPTATION	CHECKLATON	DEFLECTION	EXTINCTION	JUBILATION	PECULATION
ADHIBITION	CHEESEWOOD	DELEGATION	EXTRACTION	KNIGHTHOOD	PENELOPHON
ADIAPHORON	CHEQUEBOOK	DELIGATION	EXULTATION	LACERATION	PENNILLION
ADMIRATION	CHERRYWOOD	DELIRATION	FASCIATION	LAMINATION	PENTAMERON
ADMONITION	CHESTERTON	DEMOGORGON	FASCINATOR	LAUNCESTON	PENTATHLON
AFFLICTION	CHICKENPOX	DEMOLITION	FEDERATION	LEAMINGTON	PENTELIKON
AGGRESSION	CHIMNEYPOT	DEPILATION	FEUILLETON	LEGISLATOR	PENTSTEMON
ALIENATION	CLUMPERTON	DEPOSITION	FIDDLEWOOD	LEVITATION	PERCEPTION
ALLEGATION	CODSWALLOP	DEPRESSION	FIGURATION	LIBERATION	PERCOLATOR
ALLIGATION	COGITATION	DEPUTATION	FILTRATION	LIKELIHOOD	PERCUSSION
ALLOCATION	COLLECTION	DERIVATION	FLAMEPROOF	LIMITATION	PERFECTION
ALLOCUTION	COLLIMATOR	DESOLATION	FLIRTATION	LIQUIDATOR	PERFORATOR
ALTERATION	COLORATION	DETONATION	FLUNKEYDOM	LITIGATION	PERIHELION
ALTERNATOR	COMBUSTION	DETRACTION	FORESHADOW	LIVELIHOOD	PERMEATION
AMBASSADOR	COMMISSION	DEVOLUTION	FOUNDATION	LOCKERROOM	PERMISSION
AMBOCEPTOR	COMPARATOR	DIACONICON	FRANCHISOR	LOCOMOTION	PERORATION
AMMUNITION	COMPARISON	DIDGERIDOO	FUMIGATION	LONGFELLOW	PERSECUTOR
AMPHICTYON	COMPASSION	DIGRESSION	GASTEROPOD	MABINOGION	PERSUASION
AMPHITRYON	COMPATRIOT	DILATATION	GEMINATION	MAIDENHOOD	PERVERSION
AMPUTATION	COMPETITOR	DIMINUTION	GENERATION	MAINPERNOR	PHENOMENON
ANHELATION	COMPLETION	DIOPHANTOS	GLACIATION	MALAPROPOS	PHLEGETHON
ANNEXATION	COMPLEXION	DIREMPTION	GOODFELLOW	MALEFACTOR	PHLOGISTON
ANNOTATION	COMPOSITOR	DISCRETION	GRADUATION	MATURATION	PHYLLIOPOD
ANTHEOLION	COMPRESSOR	DISCUSSION	GRASSWIDOW	MEDICATION	PINCUSHION
ANTICHTHON	COMPULSION	DISPERSION	GUBERNATOR	MEDITATION	PLANTATION
ANTIPROTON	CONCEPTION	DISRUPTION	HABITATION	MELOCOTOON	PLAYFELLOW
APPARITION	CONCESSION	DISSECTION	HALLUBALOO	MESENTERON	POCKETBOOK
APPLICATOR	CONCLUSION	DISSELBOOM	HARRINGTON	MIDDLEBROW	POLYHEDRON
APPOSITION	CONCOCTION	DISSENSION	HEMIHEDRON	MINUTEBOOK	POPULATION
ARBITRATOR	CONCRETION	DISSUASION	HENDECAGON	MISPRISION	POSSESSION
ARCHBISHOP	CONCUSSION	DISTENSION	HEPTAMERON	MITIGATION	POSTILLION

PRECAUTION	SALIVATION	TRAVOLATOR	QUADRICEPS	CERTIORARI	EXPOSITORY
PREDICTION	SALUTATION	TRISKELION	RADIOGRAPH	CHAULMUGRA	EXPOUNDERS
PRELECTION	SANDALWOOD	TROCHOTRON	SKEUOMORPH	CHESSBOARD	FALDISTORY
PREPARATOR	SANITATION	ULCERATION	STEREOTYPE	CHINABERRY	FINISTERRE
PREPOSITOR	SATURATION	UNDERFLOOR	STEREOTYPY	CHIROPTERA	FLOORBOARD
PRETENSION	SCANDAROON	UNDERSTOOD	TACHOGRAPH	CHLOROFORM	FLUGELHORN
PREVENTION	SCHOOLBOOK	UNDULATION	TEINOSCOPE	CHURCHYARD	FORFEITURE
PRIESTHOOD	SCHWARZLOT	UNORTHODOX	THIXOTROPY	CINECAMERA	FOURRAGERE
PROCESSION	SCOMBRESOX	USUCAPTION	TICKERTAPE	CLAVICHORD	FRITILLARY
PROCREATOR	SEPARATION	USURPATION	TRANSCRIPT	CLEARSTORY	FRONTCOURT
PROCURATOR	SERVOMOTOR	VALIDATION	TYPESCRIPT	CLERESTORY	GETTYSBURG
PRODUCTION	SEXDUCTION	VEGETATION	ZINCOGRAPH	CLOUDBERRY	GOATSBEARD
PROFESSION	SHACKLETON	VELITATION	ZOOTHERAPY	COASTGUARD	GONDOLIERS
PROGENITOR	SHECKLATON	VENERATION	ABOVEBOARD	COLEOPTERA	GOOSEBERRY
PROGESSION	SHOCKPROOF	VENTILATOR	AFTERHOURS	COLORATURA	GREENHEART
PROJECTION	SIDERATION	VERMILLION	ALEXANDERS	COMANCHERO	GREENSWARD
PROMPTBOOK	SIMULATION	VISITATION	ALIMENTARY	COMMENTARY	GRENADIERS
PROPAGATOR	SISTERHOOD	VOLUTATION	ALZHEIMERS	COMMISSARY	GREYFRIARS
PROPORTION	SKETCHBOOK	WASHINGTON	AMBULATORY	COMMISSURE	GROUNDWORK
PROPRAETOR	SMORREBROD	WATERCOLOR	AMPHIGOURI	COMMIXTURE	GYMNOSPERM
PROPRIETOR	SNAPDRAGON	WATERMELON	AMPHINEURA	COMPRADORE	HANDLEBARS
PROPULSION	SNEEZEWOOD	WATERPROOF	ANGIOSPERM	COMPULSORY	HEAVENWARD
PROSECUTOR	SOUNDPROOF	WELLINGTON	ANIMADVERT	CONJECTURE	HECTOLITRE
PROSPECTOR	SPALLATION	WILLIAMSON	ANTHOCLORE	CONSISTORY	HEIDELBERG
PROTECTION	SPECULATOR	WILLINGDON	APICULTURE	CONTROVERT	HEMISPHERE
PROTRACTOR	SPOLIATION	WITGATBOOM	APOTHECARY	CORALBERRY	HEREDITARY
PROTRUSION	SQUEEZEBOX	WOFFINGTON	ARTHROMERE	CORDILLERA	HINDENBURG
PROVEDITOR	STAGNATION	WOODPIGEON	ASPIDISTRA	CRAQUETURE	HITHERWARD
PTERANODON	STARVATION	YELLOWROOT	ATMOSPHERE	CREWELWORK	HORSELBERG
PUCKERWOOD	STEPHENSON	YELLOWWOOD	AUSTRALORP	CTENOPHORA	HYPSOMETRY
PUNDIGRION	STICHARION	ZWITTERION	AVVOGADORE	CTENOPHORE	ICOSOHEDRA
QUARTEROON	STOMATOPOD	ANEMOGRAPH	BACKSTAIRS	CUISENAIRE	INCENDIARY
QUERCITRON	STONEMASON	BATHYSCAPH	BARLEYCORN	DEBAUCHERY	INHIBITORY
RECITATION	STRONGROOM	CANTALOUPE	BARYSPHERE	DEBOUCHURE	INSANITARY
RECREATION	STUMBLEDOM	CHAMAEROPS	BASKETWORK	DEFAMATORY	INTERMARRY
REDEMPTION	SUBJECTION	CHINAGRAPH	BATTENBERG	DELCREDERE	IONOSPHERE
REELECTION	SUBMERSION	COLPOSCOPE	BATTENBURG	DEPILATORY	JARDINIERE
REFLECTION	SUBMISSION	CYSTOSCOPY	BATTLEDORE	DEPOSITARY	JOBSEEKERS
REFRACTION	SUBREPTION	DICTOGRAPH	BAUDELAIRE	DEPOSITORY	JUDICATURE
REFUTATION	SUBSECTION	HAGIOSCOPE	BEEFEATERS	DEROGATORY	JUSTICIARY
REGRESSION	SUBSTATION	HELIOGRAPH	BELLAMOURE	DEVANAGARI	KERSEYMERE
REGULATION	SUBVENTION	HELIOTROPE	BINOCULARS	DICTIONARY	KNIFEBOARD
REJONEADOR	SUBVERSION	HIEROGLYPH	BLACKBEARD	DIRECTOIRE	KOOKABURRA
RELAXATION	SUCCESSION	HIEROSCOPY	BLACKBERRY	DISCLOSURE	LABORATORY
RELEGATION	SUGGESTION	HIPPOGRYPH	BLACKBOARD	DISCOMFORT	LACKLUSTRE
RELOCATION	SUPERVISOR	HOMORELAPS	BLACKGUARD	DISCONCERT	LAVALLIÈRE
RENOVATION	SUPPRESSOR	ICONOSCOPE	BLACKHEART	DISCOPHORA	LEGWARMERS
REPARATION	SUSPENSION	LITHOGRAPH	BLACKSHIRT	DISPENSARY	LITERATURE
REPETITION	TABLESPOON	LONGCHAMPS	BLACKTHORN	DISTILLERY	LOGANBERRY
REPRESSION	TABULATION	MACROCARPA	BLOOMSBURY	DOMICILARY	LORDOLATRY
REPUTATION	TAMPERFOOT	MANUSCRIPT	BRAINSTORM	DOVERCOURT	LUXEMBOURG
RESOLUTION	TANGLEFOOT	MICROSCOPE	BREASTWORK	DOWNSTAIRS	MALMESBURY
RESORCINOL	TEDDINGTON	MIMEOGRAPH	BROADSWORD	DUMBLEDORE	MANDRAGORA
RESPIRATOR	TELEVISION	MYRIOSCOPE	BUFFOONERY	DYNAMITARD	MANGABEIRA
RESUMPTION	TEMPTATION	NYMPHOLEPT	BUTTERMERE	ECHINODERM	MARIOLATRY
RETRACTION	TENDERFOOT	OPOTHERAPY	CALLIATURE	EFFRONTERY	MASTERWORT
REVELATION	TENTERHOOK	PALAEOTYPE	CAMELOPARD	ELDERBERRY	MATTERHORN
REVOCATION	THELLUSSON	PANTOGRAPH	CANCIONERO	ELEMENTARY	MEDIUMTERM
REVOLUTION	THERMISTOR	PANTOSCOPE	CANDELABRA	ELYTRIFORM	METACENTRE
RHAMPASTOS	THINGUMBOB	PARATROOPS	CANTERBURY	EMBOUCHURE	MILLEFIORI
RHINOCEROS	THUNDERBOX	PARTHENOPE	CAPILLAIRE	EMBROIDERY	MILLIHENRY
RICHARDSON	TOCOPHEROL	PETROGLYPH	CAPITULARY	ENCOIGNURE	MILLIMETRE
RIDINGHOOD	TOLERATION	PETTICHAPS	CAPODASTRO	ENGENDRURE	MISERICORD
RIGELATION	TOURBILLON	PETTYCHAPS	CARICATURA	EPANOPHORA	MISSIONARY
ROWLANDSON	TRANSISTOR	PHAENOTYPE	CARICATURE	EPIPLASTRA	MONILIFORM
RUMBLOSSOM	TRANSITION	PHONOGRAPH	CASSIABARK	ESCRITOIRE	MONTAGNARD
RUMBULLION	TRANSLATOR	PHOTOGRAPH	CAUTIONARY	ESTANCIERO	MONTESSORI
RUMINATION	TRANSPOSON	PICTOGRAPH	CENTILITRE	EUTHYNEURA	MONTGOMERY
SALBUTAMOL	TRAVELATOR	POSTSCRIPT	CENTIMETRE	EVERYWHERE	MOUDIEWART

MOULDIWARP	STRAWBOARD	BARBAROSSA	DISCOMPOSE	HOBBYHORSE	NARCOLEPSY
MUSKETEERS	STRINDBERG	BARRENNESS	DISPOSSESS	HOMELINESS	NARROWNESS
NEEDLEWORK	STRULDBERG	BASSOONIST	DIURNALIST	HONOURLESS	NATHELESSE
NEWSPAPERS	SUBSIDIARY	BETELGEUSE	DODECANESE	HOWLEGLASS	NATURALISM
NIGHTSHIRT	SUPERSTORE	BIOCHEMIST	DOGGEDNESS	HUMBLENESS	NATURALIST
NOURRITURE	SUSPENDERS	BITTERNESS	DOUBLEBASS	HUMOURLESS	NEEDLECASE
OBLIGATORY	SVADILFARI	BLEPHARISM	DREAMINESS	HYPOCORISM	NEMATOCYST
OSCULATORY	SWEATSHIRT	BLOCKHOUSE	DREARINESS	HYPOTENUSE	NETHERMOST
OUTPERFORM	SWEDENBORG	BOLLANDIST	DROWSINESS	ICONOCLAST	NETTLERASH
OUVIRANDRA	SWEETHEART	BOLSHEVIST	EFFORTLESS	IMPALUDISM	NEUTRALISE
OVERTHWART	TAPERECORD	BOTTOMLESS	EMBERGOOSE	IMPOVERISH	NIGHTDRESS
PALMERWORM	TELIOSPORE	BOWDLERISE	ENTERPRISE	INTENTNESS	NIMBLENESS
PASTEBOARD	THALLIFORM	BRADYSEISM	ENTHUSIASM	INVALIDISM	NOMINALIST
PATIBULARY	THREADBARE	BRAININESS	ENTHUSIAST	JAUNTINESS	NONONSENSE
PEPPERCORN	THREADWORM	BREATHLESS	ENTREMESSE	JEOPARDISE	NONSUCCESS
PEPPERWORT	THREESCORE	BRIGHTNESS	EUHEMERISM	JIGGERMAST	NORMOBLAST
PEREMPTORY	TIMBERYARD	BRITISHISM	EVANGELIST	JOURNALESE	NUMBERLESS
PHOTOPHORE	TITARAKURA	BUCHMANISM	EXEMPTNESS	JOURNALISM	OBJECTLESS
PHYLACTERY	TOMFOOLERY	BUTTERFISH	EXTINGUISH	JOURNALIST	OBLOMOVISM
PLEASANTRY	TRAJECTORY	CAESPITOSE	EYEWITNESS	KINDLINESS	OBTUSENESS
PLEROPHORY	TRANSITORY	CANDLEFISH	FANATICISM	LACHRYMOSE	ODIOUSNESS
POETASTERY	TRAVANCORE	CANDYFLOSS	FATHERLESS	LACKADAISY	ORTHOCLASE
PRAEMUNIRE	TRAVELLERS	CAPITALISM	FAULTINESS	LAMARCKISM	OSTEOBLAST
PREBENDARY	TRENCHMORE	CAPITALIST	FAVORITISM	LAVISHNESS	OTHERGUESS
PRECURSORY	TRIPUDIARY	CARTOONIST	FEDERALISM	LENGTHWISE	OUTLANDISH
PREHISTORY	UNDERSCORE	CASUALNESS	FEDERALIST	LEOPARDESS	OVERPRAISE
PRESBYTERY	UNDERSHIRT	CATABOLISM	FEEBLENESS	LESBIANISM	PACIFICISM
PRIVATEERS	UNDERSKIRT	CATEGORISE	FIBERGLASS	LIBERALISM	PADDLEFISH
PROMISSORY	UPHOLSTERY	CHANGELESS	FIBREGLASS	LIBRETTIST	PAINTBRUSH
PROMONTORY	VETERINARY	CHAPTALISE	FICKLENESS	LIGHTHOUSE	PALATALISE
PSEUDOCARP	VIVANDIÈRE	CHARTREUSE	FIELDMOUSE	LITTLENESS	PALIMPSEST
PSOCOPTERA	VOCABULARY	CHAUVINISM	FIERCENESS	LIVELINESS	PANSOPHIST
PSYCHIATRY	VOLUPTUARY	CHAUVINIST	FILLIBRUSH	LIVERWURST	PAPERCHASE
QUADRATURA	WATTLEWORK	CHEEKINESS	FILTHINESS	LONELINESS	PARAGLOSSA
QUAESTUARY	WEAVERBIRD	CHERSONESE	FLABBINESS	LORDLINESS	PARAPHRASE
QUATERNARY	WHIGGAMORE	CHILLINESS	FLASHINESS	LOVELINESS	PARENTLESS
QUEENSBURY	WHIRLYBIRD	CHOICELESS	FLESHINESS	LUMINARIST	PARNELLISM
QUICKTHORN	WHITEHEART	CHREMATIST	FLIGHTLESS	LYSENKOISM	PASTEURISE
RAIYATWARI	WHITETHORN	CIRCUMCISE	FLIMSINESS	MACKINTOSH	PATCHINESS
REFRACTORY	WICKERWORK	CIRCUMFUSE	FLUFFINESS	MANAGERESS	PATRIOTISM
REPERTOIRE	WILLOWHERB	CLAMMINESS	FOURIERISM	MANICURIST	PENSIEROSO
REPOSITORY	WINDERMERE	CLASSICISM	FRATERNISE	MARGASIRSA	PERDENDOSI
RHIPIPTERA	YELLOWBIRD	CLASSICIST	FRIENDLESS	MATELLASSE	PERMAFROST
ROQUELAURE	YOUNGBERRY	CLEVERNESS	FRISKINESS	MAXIMALIST	PHANTASISE
RUTHERFORD	ABRUPTNESS	CLOUDBURST	GENERALISE	MAYONNAISE	PHARMACIST
SALLENDERS	ABSOLUTISM	CLOUDINESS	GENTLENESS	MEAGERNESS	PICAYUNISH
SANGUINARY	ACCOMPLISH	CLUMSINESS	GEOTROPISM	MEAGRENESS	PILLOWCASE
SCHOOLGIRL	ACTIVITIST	CNIDOBLAST	GLAMOURISE	MELLOWNESS	PLAGIARISE
SCORDATURA	ADULTERESS	COARSENESS	GLASSHOUSE	METABOLISE	PLAGIARISM
SCOREBOARD	AFFETTUOSO	COLOURLESS	GLASSINESS	METABOLISM	PLAGIARIST
SCORZONERA	AFRICANISM	COMPROMISE	GLOSSINESS	METAPHRASE	PLANOBLAST
SECRETAIRE	AGGRANDISE	CONFORMIST	GNOSTICISM	MIGHTINESS	PLASMODESM
SELLINGERS	AGRONOMIST	COPPERNOSE	GOLIATHISE	MILITARISM	PLOUGHWISE
SETTERWORT	ALCOHOLISM	COQUETTISH	GOOSEFLESH	MILITARIST	POLITENESS
SILVERWARE	ALLPURPOSE	COSTLINESS	GOVERNESSY	MINIMALISM	POLYCHREST
SKATEBOARD	AMATEURISH	COTTIERISM	GRADUALISM	MINIMALIST	POLYGAMIST
SPECTATORS	ANABAPTIST	COURTHOUSE	GRANGERISM	MINUTENESS	POLYTHEISM
SPIDERWORT	ANGLERFISH	CRAFTINESS	GREEDINESS	MISOGYNIST	PORTIONIST
SPOILSPORT	ANTAGONISE	CRISSCROSS	GREENHOUSE	MIZZENMAST	PORTUGUESE
SPONGEWARE	ANTAGONISM	CUSSEDNESS	GRITTINESS	MONARCHIST	POSITIVIST
SPONGIFORM	ANTAGONIST	CUTTLEFISH	GROUNDLESS	MONETARISM	POSTCHAISE
SPREAGHERY	APOCALYPSE	DAMSELFISH	GRUBBINESS	MONETARIST	POWERHOUSE
STATIONARY	ASCETICISM	DEADLINESS	GRUMPINESS	MONOPOLISE	PRAGMATISM
STATIONERY	ASTUTENESS	DEMOBILISE	GUESTHOUSE	MONOTHEISM	PRAGMATIST
STAVESACRE	AVERRHOISM	DEMORALISE	HARTEBEEST	MOROSENESS	PREDECEASE
STILLIFORM	BABIROUSSA	DEUTOPLASM	HEARTINESS	MOTHERLESS	PREDISPOSE
STINGYBARK	BALDERDASH	DIASKEUAST	HITOPADESA	MOTIONLESS	PREPOSSESS
STRASBOURG	BALLOONIST	DICHROMISM	HITOPODESA	MOULDINESS	PRESUPPOSE
STRAWBERRY	BANGLADESH	DIRECTNESS	HOARSENESS	NARCISSISM	PRETTINESS

PRICKLOUSE	SMOOTHNESS	VIROLOGIST	CANTILLATE	DILETTANTE	GLAUCONITE
PROFITLESS	SNOOTINESS	VOCABULIST	CAPABILITY	DISABILITY	GLITTERATI
PROMPTNESS	SONGSTRESS	WANDERLUST	CAPACITATE	DISHONESTY	GODPARENTS
PROPHETESS	SORDIDNESS	WATERBRASH	CAPERNAITE	DISLOYALTY	GRAPTOLITE
PROTOPLASM	SPARSENESS	WATERCRESS	CAPERNOITY	DISSERTATE	GRASSROOTS
PURITANISM	SPARTACIST	WEAPONLESS	CAPITULATE	DISSOCIATE	GRATILLITY
QUAINTNESS	SPECIALISE	WEIGHTLESS	CAPREOLATE	DISTILLATE	GREENCLOTH
QUEASINESS	SPECIALISM	WHEELHOUSE	CASSOLETTE	DISTRIBUTE	HABILITATE
QUENCHLESS	SPECIALIST	WHEEZINESS	CHALYBEATE	DITHIONATE	HALLOYSITE
RACECOURSE	SPEECHLESS	WICKEDNESS	CHEAPSKATE	DOLCEMENTE	HEADLIGHTS
RADICALISM	SPEEDINESS	WILDEBEEST	CHEMONASTY	DOPPLERITE	HENCEFORTH
RANDOMNESS	SPIRITLESS	WILDERNESS	CHERVONETS	DUNDERPATE	HEREABOUTS
REAPPRAISE	SPOONERISM	WORLDCLASS	CHESSYLITE	DURABILITY	HOMOEOPATH
RECIDIVISM	SPRINGLESS	WORTHINESS	CHILDBIRTH	DUUMVIRATE	HYDROPHYTE
RECIDIVIST	SPRUCENESS	ABBREVIATE	CHLORINATE	DYSCRASITE	IGNIMBRITE
RECOMPENSE	STEADINESS	ACCELERATE	CHRYSOLITE	EBRACTEATE	ILLAQUEATE
REGARDLESS	STEAKHOUSE	ACCENTUATE	COELACANTH	ECARDINATE	ILLEGALITY
RELENTLESS	STEELINESS	ACCUMULATE	COLLEGIATE	EDULCORATE	ILLITERATE
RELINQUISH	STEWARDESS	ADJUDICATE	COLLIQUATE	EFFECTUATE	ILLUMINATE
REMONETISE	STICKINESS	ADULLAMITE	COMMENTATE	EFFEMINATE	ILLUMINATI
REMOTENESS	STIGMATISE	ADULTERATE	COMMONALTY	EGURGITATE	ILLUSTRATE
RETROGRESS	STINGINESS	AFFABILITY	COMPENSATE	EIGHTEENTH	IMBECILITY
REVIVALIST	STOCKINESS	AFTERBIRTH	COMPLANATE	ELASTICATE	IMBROCCATA
RHAPSODISE	STONEBRASH	AFTERTASTE	COMPLEXITY	ELASTICITY	IMMACULATE
RHAPSODIST	STONYHURST	ALABANDITE	COMPLICATE	ELECTORATE	IMMATURITY
RHEUMATISM	STOREHOUSE	ALEMBICATE	COMPLICITY	EMANCIPATE	IMMOBILITY
RINDERPEST	STRATEGIST	ALKALINITY	CONCERVATE	EMARGINATE	IMMODERATE
ROBUSTNESS	STRATOCYST	ALTAZIMUTH	CONCILIATE	EMASCULATE	IMMORALITY
ROUGHHOUSE	STREETWISE	AMALGAMATE	CONCINNITY	EMBLEMENTS	IMPREGNATE
ROUNDHOUSE	STREPITOSO	AMELIORATE	CONDIMENTS	EMISSIVITY	INACCURATE
RUDDERLESS	STRICTNESS	AMIABILITY	CONFIDANTE	EMOLUMENTS	INACTIVITY
RUGGEDNESS	STRIPTEASE	AMPHITRITE	CONFISCATE	EPHRAIMITE	INADEQUATE
SACCHARASE	STUFFINESS	AMPLEFORTH	CONFORMITY	EPIDIORITE	INAUGURATE
SACREDNESS	STURDINESS	ANDALUSITE	CONGREGATE	EPISCOPATE	INCAPACITY
SAVAGENESS	SUDDENNESS	ANNIHILATE	CONSECRATE	EPROUVETTE	INCINERATE
SCANDALISE	SUFFRAGIST	ANNUNCIATE	CONSONANTS	EQUANIMITY	INCIVILITY
SCANTINESS	SULTRINESS	ANTHRACITE	CONSTITUTE	EQUIVOCATE	INCOMPLETE
SCARCENESS	SUPPLENESS	ANTICIPATE	CONSUMMATE	EVISCERATE	INCRASSATE
SCATHELESS	SURINAMESE	APPRECIATE	CONTIGUITY	EVITERNITY	INDEFINITE
SCEPTICISM	SURREALISM	APTERYGOTA	CONTINUITY	EXACERBATE	INDELICATE
SCOOTERIST	SURREALIST	AREOPAGITE	CONTRIBUTE	EXAGGERATE	INDICOLITE
SCRUTINISE	SYMPATHISE	ARTICULATA	CONVOLVUTE	EXASPERATE	INDIGOLITE
SCULPTRESS	SYNCRETISE	ARTICULATE	COORDINATE	EXCRUCIATE	INEQUALITY
SEAMSTRESS	TAXONOMIST	ASCOMYCETE	COQUIMBITE	EXENTERATE	INFIBULATE
SECONDBEST	TENDERNESS	ASPHALTITE	CORDIALITY	EXHILARATE	INFIDELITY
SEDATENESS	THEOLOGISE	ASPHYXIATE	CORDIERITE	EXPATRIATE	INFILTRATE
SENEGALESE	THEOLOGIST	ASSEVERATE	CREATIVITY	FACILITATE	INGEMINATE
SEPARATISM	TIMELINESS	ASSIMILATE	CRENELLATE	FALSETRUTH	INGENERATE
SEPARATIST	TOOTHBRUSH	ASYNARTETE	DEACTIVATE	FASTIGIATE	INGRATIATE
SEXOLOGIST	TOPOLOGIST	AUDIBILITY	DEBILITATE	FELICITATE	INHUMANITY
SHABBINESS	TOUCHINESS	AUTOPLASTY	DECAPITATE	FEMININITY	INORDINATE
SHADOWLESS	TRANSGRESS	BALLISTITE	DECATHLETE	FIANCHETTO	INOSCULATE
SHERARDISE	TRANSVERSE	BARRACOOTA	DECELERATE	FIBRILLATE	INSECURITY
SHIFTINESS	TRECENTIST	BARRACOUTA	DECOLORATE	FLAGELLATE	INSEMINATE
SHODDINESS	TRENDINESS	BENEDICITE	DEFLAGRATE	FLOCCULATE	INSIPIDITY
SHOVELNOSE	TRICKINESS	BENTHAMITE	DEGENERATE	FLOORCLOTH	INSPISSATE
SHREWDNESS	TROMBONIST	BESTIALITY	DELIBERATE	FLUTEMOUTH	INSUFFLATE
SHRILLNESS	TROPOPAUSE	BICHROMATE	DEMODULATE	FOOTLIGHTS	INSULARITY
SILVERFISH	UNDERCLASS	BINUCLEATE	DEPOPULATE	FOOTPRINTS	INTAGLIATE
SINARCHIST	UNDERLEASE	BLACKSMITH	DEPRECIATE	FOURCHETTE	INTEMERATE
SINARQUIST	UNEASINESS	BLANQUETTE	DERACINATE	FOURTEENTH	INTENERATE
SINFULNESS	UNEVENNESS	BOUILLOTTE	DEREGULATE	FRATERETTO	INTERSTATE
SINGHALESE	UNIQUENESS	BRIDLEPATH	DESALINATE	FRATERNITY	INTIMIDATE
SINGLENESS	UNRULINESS	BROADCLOTH	DESIDERATA	FULLLENGTH	INTOXICATE
SKEPTICISM	UNTIDINESS	CACHINNATE	DESQUAMATE	GARNIERITE	INVALIDATE
SLEEPINESS	UPPERCLASS	CALAVERITE	DETRUNCATE	GENERALITY	INVALIDITY
SLEEVELESS	USEFULNESS	CALCEOLATE	DICHROMATE	GENEROSITY	INVETERATE
SLOPPINESS	VIETNAMESE	CALUMNIATE	DIFFICULTY	GENEVRETTE	INVIGILATE
SMARMINESS	VINEGARISH	CALYPTRATE	DILAPIDATE	GENICULATE	INVIGORATE

IRRADICATE	PERQUISITE	SPIFLICATE	ACETABULUM	CONTINUOUS	HONORARIUM
IRRESOLUTE	PERVERSITY	STALACTITE	ACROGENOUS	CONTRECOUP	HORRENDOUS
JAMESONITE	PHLOGOPITE	STALAGMITE	ADULTEROUS	COPERNICUS	HOUSEPROUD
JOCULARITY	PHOTONASTY	STAUROLITE	AERUGINOUS	CORYPHAEUS	HUMORESQUE
KATERFELTO	PIANOFORTE	STEPHANITE	AGAPANTHUS	COURAGEOUS	HYPOGAEOUS
KENILWORTH	PISTILLATE	STIACCIATO	ALLOSAURUS	CREOPHAGUS	HYPOGENOUS
KIMBERLITE	PLANCHETTE	STILLBIRTH	AMBULACRUM	CRETACEOUS	IMPERVIOUS
LANCEOLATE	PLASTICITY	STRIDULATE	AMPHIBIOUS	CRYOPHORUS	IMPRIMATUR
LASTMINUTE	PLEBISCITE	SUBSTITUTE	ANACARDIUM	CURRICULUM	INCAUTIOUS
LATTERMATH	PLIABILITY	SUPPLICATE	ANADROMOUS	CURVACEOUS	INCESTUOUS
LAURDALITE	PLOUGHBOTE	SUZERAINTY	ANCIPITOUS	CYNOMOLGUS	INDECOROUS
LAURVIKITE	PLOUGHGATE	SYNTAGMATA	ANTIBARBUS	DELIGHTFUL	INDIGENOUS
LEGIBILITY	POLYCHAETE	TABLANETTE	ANTIMASQUE	DELPHINIUM	INDUMENTUM
LEGITIMATE	POPULARITY	TABLECLOTH	ANTITRAGUS	DEMOCRITUS	INFECTIOUS
LEMNISCATE	PORTAMENTO	TENNANTITE	APEMANTHUS	DERAILLEUR	INGLORIOUS
LHERZOLITE	PORTSMOUTH	TERNEPLATE	APOLLONIUS	DESPITEOUS	INIQUITOUS
LIBERALITY	POSTILLATE	TERRACOTTA	APOTHECIUM	DIADROMOUS	JUGGERNAUT
LICENTIATE	POTENTIATE	TESCHENITE	ARENACEOUS	DIAPHANOUS	KETTLEDRUM
LIMBURGITE	PROCLIVITY	THAUMASITE	ARISTIPPUS	DIDUNCULUS	KNOCKABOUT
LINEAMENTS	PROFLIGATE	THEODOLITE	ARTOCARPUS	DIGITORIUM	LANGUOROUS
LOUISIETTE	PROFUNDITY	THEOLOGATE	ASTOMATOUS	DIPLODOCUS	LANIGEROUS
LUMINOSITY	PROMULGATE	THIRTEENTH	ASTRAGALUS	DISASTROUS	LASCIVIOUS
MACROBIOTE	PROPENSITY	THOUSANDTH	ASTRALAGUS	DISCOBOLUS	LAWRENCIUM
MAGISTRATE	PROPIONATE	TINTORETTO	ATRACURIUM	DISDAINFUL	LEBENSRAUM
MAISONETTE	PROPITIATE	TOILINETTE	AUDITORIUM	DISEMBOGUE	LEGUMINOUS
MALAGUETTA	PROSCIUTTO	TOOTHPASTE	AURIFEROUS	DOLICHOTUS	LENOCINIUM
MANIPULATE	PROSPERITY	TOPICALITY	AUSPICIOUS	DYSPROSIUM	LEPRECHAUN
MARCIONITE	PROSTITUTE	TORBERNITE	AUTOECIOUS	ELEGABALUS	LIBIDINOUS
MARGUERITE	PROTERVITY	TRACHELATE	AUTOGENOUS	EMPLASTRUM	LICENTIOUS
MARIONETTE	PSYCHOPATH	TRAGACANTH	AUTONOMOUS	ENDOGAMOUS	LIGHTINGUP
MASTURBATE	PUNCTULATE	TRIFOLIATE	AVARICIOUS	ENDOGENOUS	LOQUACIOUS
MEDIOCRITY	PYRAGYRITE	TRILLIONTH	BATTAILOUS	EPICANTHUS	LOTOPHAGUS
MELACONITE	REACTIVATE	TRIPARTITE	BITUMINOUS	EPIDENDRUM	LUGUBRIOUS
MENSTRUATE	RECUPERATE	TRIPLICATE	BLOTTESQUE	EPIDIDYMUS	MALODOROUS
MIGNONETTE	REDECORATE	TRIPLICITY	BOISTEROUS	EPIMETHEUS	MARTINIQUE
MINISTRATE	REDRUTHITE	TRIVIALITY	BUCEPHALUS	EPITHELIUM	MARVELLOUS
MISHNAYOTH	REGENERATE	TROCTOLITE	CACUMINOUS	EPONYCHIUM	MEANINGFUL
MITHRIDATE	REGULARITY	TROGLODYTE	CADAVEROUS	ERYMANTHUS	MEERSCHAUM
MORGANETTA	REJUVENATE	TROPOPHYTE	CALAMITOUS	EUCALYPTUS	MEGALOSAUR
MULIEBRITY	RELATIVITY	TROTSKYITE	CALCAREOUS	EUPHONIOUS	MEITNERIUM
MUTABILITY	REMUNERATE	ULSTERETTE	CANCELLOUS	EUROCHEQUE	MEMBRANOUS
NATUROPATH	REPATRIATE	UNDERNEATH	CANEPHORUS	EURYPTERUS	MEMORANDUM
NDRANGHETA	RESERVISTS	UNDERPANTS	CAOUTCHOUC	EXTRANEOUS	MENDACIOUS
NEUTRALITY	RESUPINATE	UNDERSTATE	CAPITELLUM	FACTITIOUS	METACARPUS
NEWSAGENTS	RETICULATE	UNDERWRITE	CAPRICIOUS	FALLACIOUS	METATARSUS
NINETEENTH	RETINALITE	UNIFORMITY	CARACTACUS	FASTIDIOUS	METICULOUS
NOTABILITY	SAMARSKITE	UNIVERSITY	CATAFALQUE	FELICITOUS	MILLENNIUM
NOUAKCHOTT	SANDINISTA	UROSTEGITE	CATAWAMPUS	FICTITIOUS	MINDERERUS
NOVACULITE	SAPROPHYTE	VARICOSITY	CENSORIOUS	FLAGITIOUS	MIRACULOUS
OBLITERATE	SCURRILITY	VERTEBRATE	CEREBELLUM	FOLIACEOUS	MOLYBDENUM
ODONTOLITE	SCUTELLATE	VESICULATE	CHAUTAUQUA	FONTICULUS	MONANDROUS
OSTEOPHYTE	SECONDRATE	VINDEMIATE	CHIVALROUS	FORTUITOUS	MONEGASQUE
PALAGONITE	SENSUALITY	VIRTUOSITY	CHOLALOGUE	FULIGINOUS	MONOECIOUS
PALATINATE	SEVENTIETH	VISIBILITY	CHRYSIPPUS	GADOLINIUM	MONOGAMOUS
PAPIAMENTO	SHIBBOLETH	VITUPERATE	CIRCUITOUS	GANGRENOUS	MONOPODIUM
PARAGONITE	SHRIEVALTY	VOCIFERATE	COCCINEOUS	GELATINOUS	MONOTONOUS
PARRAMATTA	SILHOUETTE	VOLATILITY	COCKALORUM	GLUTTONOUS	MONTICULUS
PARTIALITY	SIMILARITY	VOLUBILITY	COETANEOUS	GRATUITOUS	MORATORIUM
PASSIONATE	SIMPLICITY	WANDSWORTH	COLPORTEUR	GREGARIOUS	MORDACIOUS
PATAVINITY	SLUICEGATE	WAVELENGTH	COMMODIOUS	GUARNERIUS	MORIGEROUS
PEDICULATE	SNAKEMOUTH	WHEWELLITE	COMMUNIQUÉ	HAEMANTHUS	MOZAMBIQUE
PENTIMENTO	SOLIDARITY	WINCEYETTE	COMPENDIUM	HAKENKREUZ	MYSTAGOGUE
PERIDOTITE	SOLUBILITY	WOLFRAMITE	COMPLUVIUM	HARMONIOUS	MYSTAGOGUS
PERNICKETY	SOMBRERITE	WOOLLYBUTT	CONCINNOUS	HAUSTELLUM	MYSTERIOUS
PEROVSKITE	SPECIALITY	WORDSWORTH	CONIFEROUS	HAUSTORIUM	NASTURTIUM
PERPETRATE	SPERMACETI	ABSTEMIOUS	CONSORTIUM	HEPHAESTUS	NATATORIUM
PERPETUATE	SPERRYLITE	ACANACEOUS	CONSPECTUS	HERBACEOUS	NECTABANUS
PERPETUITY	SPHACELATE	ACCLIVIOUS	CONTAGIOUS	HIPPARCHUS	NEFANDROUS
PERPLEXITY	SPHALERITE	ACEPHALOUS	CONTIGUOUS	HOMUNCULUS	NEGLECTFUL

NUTRITIOUS	SALUBRIOUS	UPROARIOUS	REFLECTIVE	JEOPARDIZE	BARRACOUTA
OBSEQUIOUS	SANATORIUM	VESTIBULUM	REFRACTIVE	LEGITIMIZE	BARRAMUNDA
OCEANARIUM	SANITARIUM	VIBRACULUM	REGRESSIVE	LIBERALIZE	BELLADONNA
OESOPHAGUS	SARMENTOUS	VICTORIOUS	RELAXATIVE	MOISTURIZE	BHADRAPADA
OLEAGINOUS	SAUERKRAUT	VILLAINOUS	REPETITIVE	MONOPOLIZE	BIPINNARIA
OLERACEOUS	SAXICOLOUS	VIVIPAROUS	REPRESSIVE	MORBIDEZZA	BLASTOIDEA
OMNIVOROUS	SCANDALOUS	VOCIFEROUS	RESPECTIVE	MYCORRHIZA	BRATISLAVA
OPPROBRIUM	SCRUPULOUS	VOLUMINOUS	RESPONSIVE	NATURALIZE	CALIFORNIA
ORCHIDEOUS	SCURRILOUS	VOLUPTUOUS	RHINEGRAVE	NEUTRALIZE	CAMPANELLA
OSMETERIUM	SEQUACIOUS	VORAGINOUS	RUMINATIVE	PASSAMEZZO	CANDELABRA
OUTRAGEOUS	SIMILLIMUM	WATERSPOUT	SPOKESHAVE	PASTEURIZE	CANDELILLA
PANARITIUM	SIMULACRUM	XIPHOPAGUS	SPOLIATIVE	PESTALOZZI	CARICATURA
PANCRATIUM	SLANDEROUS	ACCUSATIVE	SUBJECTIVE	PLAGIARIZE	CASCARILLA
PANJANDRUM	SOLICITOUS	AFTERSHAVE	SUBMISSIVE	POLITICIZE	CASSIOPEIA
PANNICULUS	SPIRACULUM	AGGRESSIVE	SUBVERSIVE	POLYMERIZE	CAVICORNIA
PARACELSUS	SPIRITUOUS	AMRITATTVA	SUCCESSIVE	POPULARIZE	CECIDOMYIA
PARVOVIRUS	SPORANGIUM	APPETITIVE	SUGGESTIVE	PRESSURIZE	CHAULMUGRA
PEDIPALPUS	SQUETEAGUE	ARCHITRAVE	SUPPORTIVE	RAZZMATAZZ	CHAUTAUQUA
PENNISETUM	STANISLAUS	ASSUMPTIVE	SUSCEPTIVE	REGULARIZE	CHINCHILLA
PERDITIOUS	STATUESQUE	ATTRACTIVE	TOPSYTURVY	REORGANIZE	CHIROPTERA
PERFIDIOUS	STERTEROUS	AUTOMOTIVE	TRANSITIVE	REVITALIZE	CHRISTIANA
PERNICIOUS	STERTOROUS	BRATISLAVA	TURTLEDOVE	RHAPSODIZE	CHUCKWALLA
PHOSPHORUS	STRABISMUS	COLLECTIVE	VINDICTIVE	RUSSIANIZE	CINDERELLA
PICARESQUE	STRAMONIUM	COMPULSIVE	BRIDGETOWN	SCANDALIZE	CINECAMERA
PLESIOSAUR	STRULDBRUG	CONCLUSIVE	BROKENDOWN	SCRUTINIZE	CIRRHOPODA
PLIOHIPPUS	STUPENDOUS	CONNECTIVE	BUTTONDOWN	SECULARIZE	CIRRIPEDEA
POLYANTHUS	SUBSELLIUM	CONVULSIVE	CAMPERDOWN	SPECIALIZE	CIRRIPEDIA
POLYGAMOUS	SUBSTRATUM	CORRECTIVE	FULLYGROWN	STIGMATIZE	CITRONELLA
POLYPHEMUS	SUCCESSFUL	CUMULATIVE	GEORGETOWN	SYMPATHIZE	CLARABELLA
PORRACEOUS	SUDATORIUM	DECORATIVE	HORSEDRAWN	SYMPTOMIZE	CLOSTRIDIA
PORTENTOUS	SULPHUROUS	DEFINITIVE	JACKSTRAWS	SYNTHESIZE	COCHLEARIA
PORTMANTUA	SUSPICIOUS	DEPRESSIVE	MUMBLENEWS	TRAUMATIZE	COLEOPTERA
POSTHUMOUS	SYMPHONIUM	DERIVATIVE	ODDFELLOWS	TRIVIALIZE	COLEORHIZA
PRAETORIUM	SYNONYMOUS	DIMINUTIVE	PIPSISSEWA	WESTERNIZE	COLLEMBOLA
PRECARIOUS	SYNTHRONUS	DISAPPROVE	POHUTUKAWA		COLORATURA
PRECOCIOUS	TECHNETIUM	DISBELIEVE	QUEENSTOWN	**10:10**	CONCERTINA
PREDACIOUS	TEPIDARIUM	DISCURSIVE	TUMBLEDOWN	ABHIDHAMMA	CONSTANTIA
PRINCIPIUM	TESTACEOUS	DISMISSIVE	HETERODOXY	ADVERSARIA	CORDILLERA
PRODIGIOUS	THALICTRUM	DISRUPTIVE	KARTTIKAYA	AERENCHYMA	CORNUCOPIA
PROMETHEUS	THEOCRITUS	EXHAUSTIVE	LAUNCEGAYE	AEROPHAGIA	CORRIGENDA
PROMETHIUM	THIMBLEFUL	EXPRESSIVE	LENGTHWAYS	AFRORMOSIA	CORTADERIA
PROPERTIUS	THOUGHTFUL	FIGURATIVE	STRIDEWAYS	AGRAHAYANA	CROTALARIA
PROPITIOUS	THROUGHOUT	GAINSTRIVE	ZYGODACTYL	ALCAICERIA	CTENOPHORA
PROPOSITUS	THROUGHPUT	IMPERATIVE	ANTAGONIZE	ALCHERINGA	CYCLOPEDIA
PROPYLAEUM	THUNDEROUS	IMPRESSIVE	ANTIFREEZE	ALCYONARIA	DESIDERATA
PROSCENIUM	TIRAILLEUR	INCHOATIVE	AUTOMATIZE	ALEXANDRIA	DHARMSHALA
PROSPECTUS	TIROCINIUM	INDECISIVE	BETELGEUZE	ALGOLAGNIA	DIPHTHERIA
PROSPEROUS	TRAITOROUS	INDICATIVE	BOWDLERIZE	AMBARVALIA	DIPSOMANIA
PSALTERIUM	TRAVELOGUE	INFINITIVE	BURGLARIZE	AMBLYSTOMA	DISCOPHORA
PTERYGOTUS	TREMENDOUS	INITIATIVE	CAPITALIZE	AMPHINEURA	DROSOPHILA
PUGNACIOUS	TRIANGULUM	INNOVATIVE	CARAMELIZE	AMRITATTVA	ECHINOIDEA
PURPOSEFUL	TRICLINIUM	INTERLEAVE	CATEGORIZE	ANESTHESIA	ECHOPRAXIA
PYROPHORUS	TROPAEOLUM	INTERWEAVE	CENTRALIZE	ANGUILLULA	EMMETROPIA
RANUNCULUS	TROPHONIUS	LOCOMOTIVE	CHIMBORAZO	ANTARCTICA	EPANOPHORA
RAPPORTEUR	TROUBADOUR	MEDITATIVE	COLEORHIZA	APTERYGOTA	EPIPHONEMA
REBELLIOUS	TUMULTUOUS	NAUSEATIVE	DECIMALIZE	ARTHRALGIA	EPIPLASTRA
REFERENDUM	TUTIVILLUS	NOMINATIVE	DECOLORIZE	ARTHURIANA	ETHEOSTOMA
REMORSEFUL	UBIQUITOUS	OPPRESSIVE	DEEPFREEZE	ARTICULATA	EUTHANASIA
RENDEZVOUS	ULTRONEOUS	PALLIATIVE	DEMOBILIZE	ASAFOETIDA	EUTHYNEURA
REPETITEUR	UNDERVALUE	PEJORATIVE	DEMORALIZE	ASARABACCA	EUTRAPELIA
RESPECTFUL	UNEVENTFUL	PERCEPTIVE	ETERNALIZE	ASPIDISTRA	FENESTELLA
REVENGEFUL	UNFAITHFUL	PERMISSIVE	EVANGELIZE	ASTEROIDEA	FLINDERSIA
RIDICULOUS	UNFRUITFUL	PERSUASIVE	FRATERNIZE	AUTOSTRADA	FLORIBUNDA
ROBUSTIOUS	UNGRACIOUS	POSSESSIVE	GENERALIZE	AVICULARIA	FRAMBOESIA
ROMANESQUE	UNGRATEFUL	PREVENTIVE	GORMANDIZE	BABIROUSSA	FRAXINELLA
ROUNDABOUT	UNIGENITUS	PRODUCTIVE	GRANGERIZE	BANDERILLA	FUSTANELLA
ROUSEABOUT	UNTRUTHFUL	PROTECTIVE	HOMOGENIZE	BARASINGHA	GAULTHERIA
ROUSTABOUT	UNUNHEXIUM	RECITATIVE	IMMOBILIZE	BARBAROSSA	GIBBERELLA
RUBIGINOUS	UNUNNILIUM	RECITATIVO	INTERMEZZO	BARRACOOTA	GLYCOSURIA

GONORRHOEA	PARMIGIANA	TEICHOPSIA	ELECTRONIC	SCHISMATIC	BUFFLEHEAD
GRANADILLA	PARONYCHIA	TERMINALIA	EMBLEMATIC	SCHOLASTIC	BULLHEADED
GRENADILLA	PARRAMATTA	TERRACOTTA	ENHYDRITIC	SCIENTIFIC	CALCULATED
GROCETERIA	PASTORELLA	TILLANDSIA	EPENTHETIC	SIMPLISTIC	CAMELOPARD
GYPSOPHILA	PENETRALIA	TITARAKURA	EPIDEICTIC	SOPHOMORIC	CAPTIVATED
HEMICHORDA	PERSICARIA	TOCCATELLA	EPIGENETIC	SPLANCHNIC	CATTLEGRID
HEMIPLEGIA	PETRONELLA	TORQUEMADA	EPISPASTIC	STOCHASTIC	CELEBRATED
HEMOPHILIA	PHAGEDAENA	TRAMONTANA	ESCHAROTIC	SUPERSONIC	CEPHALOPOD
HITOPADESA	PHILIPPINA	TRITANOPIA	EULOGISTIC	SUPERTONIC	CHALLENGED
HITOPODESA	PHILLIPINA	TULARAEMIA	EXOTHERMIC	SYNCHRONIC	CHARGEHAND
HOMOPHOBIA	PHILOPOENA	TURRITELLA	FATALISTIC	SYPHILITIC	CHAUDFROID
HYPERDULIA	PHILOXENIA	VICTORIANA	FUTURISTIC	SYSTEMATIC	CHEESEWOOD
ICOSANDRIA	PHLEGMASIA	VULCANALIA	GALLIAMBIC	TELEPATHIC	CHERRYWOOD
ICOSOHEDRA	PINNIPEDIA	XENOPHOBIA	GENETHLIAC	TELEPHONIC	CHESSBOARD
IMBROCCATA	PIPSISSEWA	XEROSTOMIA	GEOCENTRIC	TELESCOPIC	CHURCHYARD
INCAPARINA	POHUTUKAWA	ZOANTHARIA	GEOGRAPHIC	TENEBRIFIC	CLASSIFIED
INCUNABULA	POINSETTIA	SHISHKEBAB	GYROSCOPIC	THERMIONIC	CLAVICHORD
KARTTIKAYA	POLYHYMNIA	THINGUMBOB	HEDONISTIC	ULTRABASIC	CLOISTERED
KLEBSIELLA	PONTEDERIA	WILLOWHERB	HIERARCHIC	ULTRAMAFIC	COASTGUARD
KOOKABURRA	PORTMANTUA	ACHROMATIC	HISTRIONIC	ULTRASONIC	COLONNADED
KURDAITCHA	POTENTILLA	ACROAMATIC	HOLOPHYTIC	UNHYGIENIC	COMPOUNDED
LEUCHAEMIA	POZZUOLANA	ADRENERGIC	HOLOSTERIC	UNROMANTIC	COMPREHEND
LINGULELLA	PRESBYOPIA	ALLOSTERIC	HOMOPHOBIC	UNSPECIFIC	COMPRESSED
LITHISTADA	PROPAGANDA	ALLOTROPIC	HOMOPHONIC	WORKAHOLIC	CONDESCEND
LOGORRHOEA	PROSERPINA	ALTRUISTIC	HUMANISTIC	XENOPHOBIC	CONFERVOID
LUPERCALIA	PROSPERINA	AMPHOTERIC	HYDROPONIC	XEROPHYTIC	CONFLICTED
LYCHNAPSIA	PROTANOPIA	ANACLASTIC	HYPERBOLIC	ABOVEBOARD	CONFOUNDED
MACROCARPA	PSOCOPTERA	ANACOUSTIC	HYPODERMIC	ABSTRACTED	CONSIDERED
MALAGUETTA	PYRACANTHA	ANACRUSTIC	IATROGENIC	ACCREDITED	CONTRABAND
MALLOPHAGA	QUADRATURA	ANCHORETIC	IDEALISTIC	ACCUSTOMED	CONVOLUTED
MANDRAGORA	QUESADILLA	ANESTHETIC	INARTISTIC	ACQUAINTED	COPPERHEAD
MANGABEIRA	QUIRINALIA	ANTIBIOTIC	JINGOISTIC	AFFILIATED	CORRESPOND
MANZANILLA	RADIOLARIA	ANTISEPTIC	LAEOTROPIC	AMPUSSYAND	CORRUGATED
MARGASIRSA	RHINOLALIA	ANTISTATIC	LEGALISTIC	AMYGDALOID	COTTONWOOD
MARGINALIA	RHINOPHYMA	ANTITHETIC	LINGUISTIC	ANNUALIZED	CRISPBREAD
MARSHALSEA	RHIPIPTERA	APOLAUSTIC	MEGALITHIC	ANTHROPOID	CROSSBREED
MASKIROVKA	RUMINANTIA	APOLOGETIC	MESOLITHIC	ANTIQUATED	CUCULLATED
MASSASAUGA	SAGITTARIA	APOPEMPTIC	MISOCAPNIC	ARYTAENOID	CULTIVATED
MAURITANIA	SALICORNIA	APOPLECTIC	MONOACIDIC	ASSOCIATED	CUMBERLAND
MENORRHOEA	SALMONELLA	APOSEMATIC	MONOCARPIC	ASTONISHED	CUMMERBUND
METATHERIA	SANDEMANIA	APOTROPAIC	MONOLITHIC	AUTHORISED	DARKHAIRED
METHOMANIA	SANDINISTA	ARITHMETIC	MONOPHONIC	BACKGROUND	DECIPHERED
MICRONESIA	SARCOCOLLA	ASTIGMATIC	MORGANATIC	BACKHANDED	DECOMPOSED
MONOPLEGIA	SARCOLEMMA	ASYMMETRIC	NIHILISTIC	BAMBOOZLED	DEEPSEATED
MORBIDEZZA	SATURNALIA	AUTOCRATIC	NOMOTHETIC	BAREFOOTED	DESECRATED
MORGANETTA	SATYAGRAHA	BARBITURIC	NUMISMATIC	BAREHEADED	DESICCATED
MORTADELLA	SAUROPSIDA	BAROMETRIC	OPHTHALMIC	BARELEGGED	DETERMINED
MOZZARELLA	SAVONAROLA	BRONCHITIC	OPTIMISTIC	BEDEVILLED	DEVASTATED
MULTIMEDIA	SCAPHOPODA	CAOUTCHOUC	OXYMORONIC	BEDRAGGLED	DIMINISHED
MYCORRHIZA	SCARLATINA	CATALECTIC	PAEDIATRIC	BEFOREHAND	DISCOLORED
NDRANGHETA	SCARLETINA	CATALEPTIC	PARAMETRIC	BEHINDHAND	DISENGAGED
NEURILEMMA	SCHOLAEMIA	CHIRONOMIC	PARAPLEGIC	BEWILDERED	DISFIGURED
NEUROLEMMA	SCORDATURA	CONCENTRIC	PATHOGENIC	BIRKENHEAD	DISJOINTED
NOSOPHOBIA	SCORZONERA	COPESETTIC	PATRONYMIC	BLACKBEARD	DISMANTLED
NYCTALOPIA	SCOTODINIA	CORYBANTIC	PEELGARLIC	BLACKBOARD	DISORDERED
ODONTALGIA	SDRUCCIOLA	CRYPTOZOIC	PENTATONIC	BLACKGUARD	DISPIRITED
ORTHOPNOEA	SEGUIDILLA	CYBERNETIC	PENTETERIC	BLEARYEYED	DISQUIETED
OSTEOCOLLA	SERRADELLA	DEMOCRATIC	PHILATELIC	BLOODHOUND	DISSIPATED
OUVIRANDRA	SERRADILLA	DIACAUSTIC	PHLEGMATIC	BONNETHEAD	DISTRACTED
PALESTRINA	SEXAGESIMA	DIACHRONIC	PHLOGISTIC	BORDERLAND	DISTRESSED
PALMATOZOA	SIGILLARIA	DIAGNOSTIC	PHOTOGENIC	BOTTLEHEAD	DUNDERHEAD
PARAGLOSSA	SINSEMILLA	DIASTALTIC	PHRENESIAC	BRACHIOPOD	DYNAMITARD
PARAPHASIA	SKUPSHTINA	DIDASCALIC	PLEONASTIC	BRAINCHILD	EISTEDDFOD
PARAPHILIA	STERNALGIA	DIELECTRIC	POIKILITIC	BRASSBOUND	EMBITTERED
PARAPHONIA	STRELITZIA	DIPLOMATIC	PROSTHETIC	BRAZILWOOD	ENRAPTURED
PARAPLEGIA	SYNTAGMATA	DOCIMASTIC	PROTANOPIC	BREASTFEED	ENTRENCHED
PARARTHRIA	TANGANYIKA	DYSTROPHIC	PYROMANIAC	BRIDESMAID	EVAPORATED
PARASCENIA	TARANTELLA	ECCOPROTIC	PYTHOGENIC	BRIDGEHEAD	EVENHANDED
PARENCHYMA	TATPURUSHA	EGOCENTRIC	RHEOTROPIC	BROADSWORD	EXONERATED

FAIRGROUND	LIKEMINDED	SECONDHAND	UNDETECTED	ACCORDANCE	ASPHYXIATE
FAIRHAIRED	LIVELIHOOD	SEEMLIHEAD	UNDETERRED	ACCUMULATE	ASSEMBLAGE
FARFETCHED	LOGGERHEAD	SEGREGATED	UNDIGESTED	ACCUSATIVE	ASSEVERATE
FARSIGHTED	MAGISTRAND	SELFSTYLED	UNDISPUTED	ACTIONABLE	ASSIGNABLE
FASCINATED	MAIDENHOOD	SHAGHAIRED	UNDOCTORED	ADAMANTINE	ASSIMILATE
FATHERLAND	MASTERMIND	SHAMEFACED	UNEDUCATED	ADJUDICATE	ASSISTANCE
FEATHERBED	MECHANIZED	SHOPSOILED	UNEMPLOYED	ADJUSTABLE	ASSUMPTIVE
FERTILISED	METHYLATED	SHORTBREAD	UNEQUALLED	ADMISSIBLE	ASYNARTETE
FIDDLEHEAD	MILLIFARAD	SHORTLIVED	UNEXAMPLED	ADMITTANCE	ATMOSPHERE
FIGUREHEAD	MISERICORD	SHOVELHEAD	UNEXPECTED	ADRENALINE	ATTAINABLE
FITZGERALD	MISMATCHED	SHRIVELLED	UNEXPLORED	ADULLAMITE	ATTENDANCE
FLOORBOARD	MONTAGNARD	SISTERHOOD	UNFATHOMED	ADULTERATE	ATTRACTIVE
FLOURISHED	MOTHERHOOD	SKATEBOARD	UNFETTERED	ADULTERINE	AUTOMATIZE
FOREDAMNED	MOTHERLAND	SMORREBROD	UNFINISHED	AFFORDABLE	AUTOMOBILE
FOREGROUND	MULTIPLIED	SNEEZEWOOD	UNFLAVORED	AFTERIMAGE	AUTOMOTIVE
FOREWARNED	MUTTONHEAD	SNOWCAPPED	UNGROUNDED	AFTERPIECE	AVANTGARDE
FOSSILIZED	MYELINATED	SOFTBOILED	UNHAMPERED	AFTERSHAVE	AVANTURINE
FREQUENTED	NEWFANGLED	SOUTHBOUND	UNHERALDED	AFTERTASTE	AVENTURINE
FRIGHTENED	NIGGERHEAD	SPECTACLED	UNIMPAIRED	AGGRANDISE	AVVOGADORE
FRINGILLID	NONALIGNED	SPELLBOUND	UNINFORMED	AGGRESSIVE	BACKSTROKE
FRUSTRATED	NONPLUSSED	STILLSTAND	UNINSPIRED	ALABANDINE	BALANCHINE
GASTEROPOD	NORTHBOUND	STOMATOPOD	UNLEAVENED	ALABANDITE	BALLISTITE
GIRLFRIEND	NORTHSTEAD	STRAITENED	UNLETTERED	ALEMBICATE	BALUSTRADE
GLITTERAND	OBFUSCATED	STRAWBOARD	UNLICENSED	ALLEGEANCE	BARCAROLLE
GOATSBEARD	OPENHANDED	STREAMERED	UNMANNERED	ALLEGIANCE	BARLEYBREE
GOLDTHREAD	OPENMINDED	STRONGHOLD	UNNUMBERED	ALLPURPOSE	BARYSPHERE
GRANDCHILD	ORANGEWOOD	STULTIFIED	UNOBSERVED	ALPHONSINE	BATTLEDORE
GRANDSTAND	OVERSPREAD	STYLOPISED	UNOCCUPIED	AMALGAMATE	BAUDELAIRE
GRANULATED	OVERWORKED	SUBTRAHEND	UNPREPARED	AMELIORATE	BELIEVABLE
GREENSWARD	PALMATIFID	SUPERADDED	UNPROMPTED	AMPHITRITE	BELLAMOURE
GRIDLOCKED	PARALLELED	SUPERVISED	UNPROVOKED	ANADYOMENE	BELLARMINE
GUARANTEED	PARENTHOOD	SUPPRESSED	UNREASONED	ANASTROPHE	BENEDICITE
HALLMARKED	PASTEBOARD	SURROUNDED	UNREDEEMED	ANDALUSITE	BENTHAMITE
HAMMERHEAD	PATRONISED	SWEETBREAD	UNRELIEVED	ANDROMACHE	BENZEDRINE
HANDPICKED	PERFORATED	SYNCOPATED	UNREQUITED	ANGLOPHILE	BERNARDINE
HARDBOILED	PHYLLIOPOD	TALLEYRAND	UNRESERVED	ANGLOPHOBE	BETELGEUSE
HEADHUNTED	PLATINISED	TAPERECORD	UNRESOLVED	ANNIHILATE	BETELGEUZE
HEAVENWARD	PLATTELAND	TENDRILLED	UNREVEALED	ANNUNCIATE	BICHROMATE
HIGHHANDED	PLAYGROUND	THREATENED	UNRIVALLED	ANSWERABLE	BIJOUTERIE
HILDEBRAND	POCKMARKED	TIMBERYARD	UNSALARIED	ANTAGONISE	BINUCLEATE
HINTERLAND	POKERFACED	TOSSICATED	UNSCHOOLED	ANTAGONIZE	BIRTHPLACE
HITHERWARD	POLLINATED	TOSTICATED	UNSCRIPTED	ANTHOCLORE	BISSEXTILE
HOODWINKED	PREJUDICED	TRANSLATED	UNSEASONED	ANTHRACINE	BLACKSTONE
HORNRIMMED	PRIESTHOOD	TRANSPOSED	UNSHACKLED	ANTHRACITE	BLANCMANGE
HOUSEBOUND	PRINCIPLED	TRIPEHOUND	VALLADOLID	ANTICIPATE	BLANQUETTE
HOUSEPROUD	PRIVILEGED	TURNAROUND	VARIEGATED	ANTIFREEZE	BLOCKHOUSE
HUMPBACKED	PROHIBITED	TURTLEHEAD	WAINSCOTED	ANTIMASQUE	BLOODSTONE
HYPNOTIZED	PRONOUNCED	TYRANNISED	WEAVERBIRD	ANTIOCHENE	BLOTTESQUE
ILLADVISED	PROSCRIBED	ULTRASOUND	WELLEARNED	ANTIVENENE	BLUEBOTTLE
IMBRICATED	PROTRACTED	UNABRIDGED	WHIRLYBIRD	APICULTURE	BLUEMANTLE
IMPROVISED	PUCKERWOOD	UNACCENTED	WIDESPREAD	APOCALYPSE	BOOKMOBILE
INDISPOSED	PYCNOGONID	UNAFFECTED	WINDSHIELD	APOSTROPHE	BOONDOGGLE
INEBRIATED	RECOGNISED	UNANSWERED	WONDERLAND	APPEARANCE	BORDERLINE
INFATUATED	RECOGNIZED	UNASSIGNED	WOODENHEAD	APPETITIVE	BOTHERSOME
INFURIATED	RECONCILED	UNATTACHED	WRAPAROUND	APPLICABLE	BOUILLOTTE
INSTRUCTED	REGIMENTED	UNATTENDED	WUNDERKIND	APPRECIATE	BOWDLERISE
INTEGRATED	REGISTERED	UNBALANCED	YELLOWWOOD	APPRENTICE	BOWDLERIZE
INTERBREED	REITERATED	UNBLEACHED	YTHUNDERED	AQUAMANALE	BRAGADISME
INTERESTED	RESTRAINED	UNCONFINED	ABBREVIATE	AQUAMANILE	BREASTBONE
JACKBOOTED	RESTRICTED	UNCULTURED	ABERDEVINE	AQUAMARINE	BRIGANDINE
JOLTERHEAD	RHEUMATOID	UNDECLARED	ABERGLAUBE	ARACOSTYLE	BRIGANTINE
KNIFEBOARD	RIDINGHOOD	UNDEFEATED	ABHORRENCE	ARCHITRAVE	BRILLIANCE
KNIGHTHEAD	ROTHSCHILD	UNDEFENDED	ABOMINABLE	AREOPAGITE	BROADPIECE
KNIGHTHOOD	RUTHERFORD	UNDERSIZED	ABSORBANCE	ARTHROMERE	BROCATELLE
KRUGERRAND	SACCHAROID	UNDERSTAND	ABSTINENCE	ARTICULATE	BROWNSTONE
LANDLOCKED	SANCTIFIED	UNDERSTOOD	ACCELERATE	ASCOMYCETE	BURDENSOME
LEFTHANDED	SANDALWOOD	UNDERWORLD	ACCENTUATE	ASCRIBABLE	BURGLARIZE
LETTERHEAD	SANFORISED	UNDESCRIED	ACCESSIBLE	ASPARAGINE	BUTTERBAKE
LIKELIHOOD	SCOREBOARD	UNDESERVED	ACCOMPLICE	ASPHALTITE	BUTTERMERE

BUTTONHOLE	CLYDESDALE	CRAPULENCE	DILAPIDATE	ENTRYPHONE	FREIGHTAGE
CACHINNATE	COCKATRICE	CRAQUETURE	DILETTANTE	EPHRAIMITE	FROLICSOME
CACOMISTLE	COGNISANCE	CREDITABLE	DIMINUTIVE	EPIDIORITE	FUSTANELLE
CAESPITOSE	COGNIZANCE	CRENELLATE	DINANDERIE	EPISCOPATE	GAINSTRIVE
CALAVERITE	COLBERTINE	CROSSPIECE	DINNERTIME	EPISTROPHE	GARGOUILLE
CALCEOLATE	COLCHICINE	CROTALIDAE	DIRECTOIRE	EPROUVETTE	GARLANDAGE
CALCULABLE	COLLARBONE	CTENOPHORE	DISAPPROVE	EQUIVOCATE	GARNIERITE
CALESCENCE	COLLECTIVE	CUDDLESOME	DISARRANGE	ESCADRILLE	GASCONNADE
CALLIATURE	COLLEGIATE	CUISENAIRE	DISBELIEVE	ESCRITOIRE	GASTRONOME
CALUMNIATE	COLLIQUATE	CULVERTAGE	DISCIPLINE	ESPADRILLE	GENERALISE
CALYPTRATE	COLPORTAGE	CUMBERSOME	DISCLOSURE	ETERNALIZE	GENERALIZE
CAMOUFLAGE	COLPOSCOPE	CUMULATIVE	DISCOMMODE	ETHYLAMINE	GENEVRETTE
CAMSTEERIE	COMEDIENNE	CUTTLEBONE	DISCOMPOSE	EUCHLORINE	GENICULATE
CANTALOUPE	COMESTIBLE	CYCLOSTYLE	DISCOURAGE	EUPHROSYNE	GETHSEMANE
CANTATRICE	COMMENTATE	DEACTIVATE	DISCURSIVE	EUROCHEQUE	GHIBELLINE
CANTILLATE	COMMISSURE	DEADNETTLE	DISEMBOGUE	EVANGELIZE	GILBERTINE
CAPACITATE	COMMIXTURE	DEBILITATE	DISENNOBLE	EVERYPLACE	GILLRAVAGE
CAPERNAITE	COMMUNIQUÉ	DEBOUCHURE	DISGRUNTLE	EVERYWHERE	GLAMOURISE
CAPILLAIRE	COMMUTABLE	DECAGRAMME	DISHABILLE	EVISCERATE	GLASSHOUSE
CAPITALIZE	COMPARABLE	DECAPITATE	DISINCLINE	EXACERBATE	GLAUCONITE
CAPITOLINE	COMPATIBLE	DECATHLETE	DISMISSIVE	EXACTITUDE	GOBEMOUCHE
CAPITULATE	COMPENSATE	DECELERATE	DISPOSABLE	EXAGGERATE	GOLIATHISE
CAPREOLATE	COMPETENCE	DECIMALIZE	DISPUTABLE	EXASPERATE	GORMANDIZE
CARAMELIZE	COMPLANATE	DECOLORATE	DISRUPTIVE	EXCELLENCE	GOVERNANCE
CARICATURE	COMPLIANCE	DECOLORIZE	DISSERTATE	EXCRUCIATE	GRAMOPHONE
CARMAGNOLE	COMPLICATE	DECORATIVE	DISSERVICE	EXENTERATE	GRANGERIZE
CARTHAMINE	COMPRADORE	DEDUCTIBLE	DISSIDENCE	EXHAUSTIVE	GRAPTOLITE
CASSOLETTE	COMPROMISE	DEEPFREEZE	DISSOCIATE	EXHILARATE	GRAVESTONE
CATAFALQUE	COMPULSIVE	DEFEASANCE	DISSONANCE	EXPATRIATE	GREENHOUSE
CATARRHINE	CONCERVATE	DEFENSIBLE	DISTILLATE	EXPEDIENCE	GREENSTONE
CATEGORISE	CONCHIGLIE	DEFINITIVE	DISTRIBUTE	EXPENDABLE	GRINDSTONE
CATEGORIZE	CONCILIATE	DEFLAGRATE	DITHIONATE	EXPERIENCE	GUACHAMOLE
CELLOPHANE	CONCLUSIVE	DEGENERATE	DIVERGENCE	EXPLICABLE	GUESTHOUSE
CENTIGRADE	CONDOLENCE	DEGRADABLE	DODECANESE	EXPRESSIVE	GUILLOTINE
CENTILITRE	CONFERENCE	DEHISCENCE	DOLCEMENTE	EXTENDABLE	GUTTIFERAE
CENTIMETRE	CONFIDANTE	DELCREDERE	DOPPLERITE	EXTENSIBLE	HABILITATE
CENTRALIZE	CONFIDENCE	DELECTABLE	DRAKESTONE	EXUBERANCE	HAGIOSCOPE
CENTRIFUGE	CONFISCATE	DELIBERATE	DRAWBRIDGE	FACILITATE	HALLOYSITE
CENTROSOME	CONFLUENCE	DEMOBILISE	DREARISOME	FARRANDINE	HAMSHACKLE
CHALYBEATE	CONGREGATE	DEMOBILIZE	DUMBLEDORE	FASTIGIATE	HARDCASTLE
CHAMBRANLE	CONJECTURE	DEMODULATE	DUNDERPATE	FAVOURABLE	HECTOLITRE
CHANGEABLE	CONNECTIVE	DEMOISELLE	DUUMVIRATE	FELICITATE	HELIOTROPE
CHARGEABLE	CONNIVANCE	DEMORALISE	DYSCRASITE	FERNITICLE	HEMISPHERE
CHARITABLE	CONSCIENCE	DEMORALIZE	EARTHQUAKE	FERRANDINE	HEMORRHAGE
CHARTREUSE	CONSECRATE	DENTIFRICE	EARTHSHINE	FESCENNINE	HEPATOCELE
CHATELAINE	CONSONANCE	DEPENDABLE	EBRACTEATE	FETTUCCINE	HETERODYNE
CHEAPSKATE	CONSTITUTE	DEPENDENCE	EBULLIENCE	FIBRILLATE	HIPPOCRENE
CHEESECAKE	CONSTRINGE	DEPLORABLE	ECARDINATE	FIELDMOUSE	HIPPODROME
CHERSONESE	CONSUETUDE	DEPOPULATE	EDULCORATE	FIGURATIVE	HOBBYHORSE
CHESSYLITE	CONSUMMATE	DEPRECIATE	EFFECTUATE	FINISTERRE	HODGEPODGE
CHEVESAILE	CONTINENCE	DEPRESSIVE	EFFEMINATE	FLAGELLATE	HOMOGENIZE
CHEVISANCE	CONTRAVENE	DERACINATE	EFFERVESCE	FLANCONADE	HONOURABLE
CHIMPANZEE	CONTRIBUTE	DEREGULATE	EFFLEURAGE	FLAPDOODLE	HOOTNANNIE
CHINASTONE	CONVALESCE	DERIVATIVE	EGURGITATE	FLATULENCE	HORNBLENDE
CHIRICAUNE	CONVENANCE	DESALINATE	ELACAMPANE	FLOCCULATE	HOSPITABLE
CHITARRONE	CONVEYABLE	DÉSHABILLÉ	ELASTICATE	FLORENTINE	HUMORESQUE
CHLORINATE	CONVEYANCE	DESPICABLE	ELECAMPANE	FONTANELLE	HUSBANDAGE
CHOLALOGUE	CONVOLVUTE	DESQUAMATE	ELECTORATE	FOOTBRIDGE	HYALOPHANE
CHROMOSOME	CONVULSIVE	DESSIATINE	EMANCIPATE	FORECASTLE	HYDROPHANE
CHRYSOLITE	COORDINATE	DESSYATINE	EMARGINATE	FORFEITURE	HYDROPHYTE
CIRCUMCISE	COPPERNOSE	DETACHABLE	EMASCULATE	FORGIVABLE	HYDROPLANE
CIRCUMFUSE	COQUIMBITE	DETECTABLE	EMBERGOOSE	FORMIDABLE	HYPOTENUSE
CISPONTINE	CORDIERITE	DETERRENCE	EMBOUCHURE	FOURCHETTE	ICONOSCOPE
CLAIRCOLLE	CORNCOCKLE	DETESTABLE	ENCOIGNURE	FOURRAGERE	IGNIMBRITE
CLASPKNIFE	CORPULENCE	DETRUNCATE	ENGENDRURE	FRANCHISEE	ILLAQUEATE
CLEMENTINE	CORRECTIVE	DICHROMATE	ENSANGUINE	FRANGIPANE	ILLITERATE
CLINGSTONE	CORROBOREE	DIFFERENCE	ENTEROCELE	FRATERNISE	ILLUMINATE
CLOMIPHENE	COURTHOUSE	DIFFIDENCE	ENTERPRISE	FRATERNIZE	ILLUSTRATE
	CRAIGFLUKE	DIGESTIBLE	ENTREMESSE	FRATRICIDE	IMAGINABLE

IMMACULATE	INTERLEAVE	MACROBIOTE	NEEDLECASE	PATCHCOCKE	PREDISPOSE
IMMOBILIZE	INTERPHONE	MAGISTRATE	NEGLIGENCE	PATISSERIE	PREDNISONE
IMMODERATE	INTERSTATE	MAISONETTE	NEGLIGIBLE	PEAUDESOIE	PREFERABLE
IMMORTELLE	INTERSTICE	MANAGEABLE	NEGOTIABLE	PEDICULATE	PREFERENCE
IMPALPABLE	INTERTWINE	MANDEVILLE	NESSELRODE	PEJORATIVE	PREHENSILE
IMPARLANCE	INTERWEAVE	MANIPULATE	NETTLETREE	PENETRABLE	PREPOTENCE
IMPASSABLE	INTIMIDATE	MAQUILLAGE	NEUTRALISE	PERCENTAGE	PRESCIENCE
IMPATIENCE	INTOXICATE	MARCIONITE	NEUTRALIZE	PERCENTILE	PRESSURIZE
IMPECCABLE	INVALIDATE	MARGUERITE	NIGHTSHADE	PERCEPTIVE	PRESUPPOSE
IMPERATIVE	INVALUABLE	MARIONETTE	NOMINATIVE	PERDURABLE	PRETINCOLE
IMPLACABLE	INVARIABLE	MARKETABLE	NONONSENSE	PERIDOTITE	PREVALENCE
IMPORTANCE	INVETERATE	MARQUETRIE	NONVINTAGE	PERISHABLE	PREVENTIVE
IMPOSSIBLE	INVIGILATE	MARTINGALE	NORBERTINE	PERIWINKLE	PRICKLOUSE
IMPOSTHUME	INVIGORATE	MARTINIQUE	NOTICEABLE	PERMANENCE	PROCURABLE
IMPREGNATE	INVINCIBLE	MARYLEBONE	NOTIFIABLE	PERMISSIVE	PRODUCTIVE
IMPRESSIVE	INVIOLABLE	MASCARPONE	NOURRITURE	PEROVSKITE	PROFITABLE
IMPROBABLE	IONOSPHERE	MASKANONGE	NOVACULITE	PERPETRATE	PROFLIGATE
IMPRUDENCE	IRRADIATE	MASKINONGE	OBLITERATE	PERPETUATE	PROJECTILE
INACCURATE	IRRESOLUTE	MASQUERADE	OBSERVABLE	PERQUISITE	PROMINENCE
INADEQUATE	ISABELLINE	MASTURBATE	OBSERVANCE	PERSEPHONE	PROMULGATE
INAPTITUDE	ISOLEUCINE	MATELLASSE	OBTAINABLE	PERSIFLAGE	PROPIONATE
INAUGURATE	ISONIAZIDE	MAYONNAISE	OCCURRENCE	PERSONABLE	PROPITIATE
INCHOATIVE	JAMESONITE	MEASURABLE	ODONTOLITE	PERSTRINGE	PROSERPINE
INCINERATE	JARDINIERE	MEDDLESOME	OFFBALANCE	PERSUASIVE	PROSTITUTE
INCOMPLETE	JARGONELLE	MEDITATIVE	OFFLICENCE	PERTINENCE	PROTECTIVE
INCRASSATE	JEOPARDISE	MELACONITE	OMBROPHOBE	PESTILENCE	PROTRUSILE
INCREDIBLE	JEOPARDIZE	MENSTRUATE	OPHICLEIDE	PETRISSAGE	PROVENANCE
INDAPAMIDE	JIGGAMAREE	MEPERIDINE	OPPRESSIVE	PHAENOTYPE	PROVIDENCE
INDECISIVE	JOURNALESE	MERCANTILE	ORDONNANCE	PHANTASIME	PUBESCENCE
INDEFINITE	JOUYSAUNCE	MESITYLENE	ORIDINANCE	PHILIPPINE	PULSATANCE
INDELICATE	JUDICATURE	METABOLISE	OROBRANCHE	PHILISTINE	PUMPHANDLE
INDICATIVE	KENSPECKLE	METACENTRE	ORTHOCAINE	PHILLIPINE	PUNCTULATE
INDICOLITE	KERSEYMERE	METAPHRASE	ORTHOCLASE	PHLOGOPITE	PUNICACEAE
INDICTABLE	KIMBERLITE	METASTABLE	OSTENSIBLE	PHOTODIODE	PUNISHABLE
INDIGOLITE	KLANGFARBE	METHEDRINE	OSTEOPHYTE	PHOTOPHORE	PYRAGYRITE
INDUCTANCE	KNOBKERRIE	METTLESOME	OUANANICHE	PIANOFORTE	PYRIDOXINE
INDULGENCE	LACHRYMOSE	MICROFICHE	OUTBALANCE	PICARESQUE	QUADRANGLE
INEDUCABLE	LACKLUSTRE	MICROPHONE	OUTSPECKLE	PIGEONHOLE	QUADRIREME
INELIGIBLE	LACUSTRINE	MICROSCOPE	OVERCHARGE	PILGRIMAGE	QUARANTINE
INEPTITUDE	LAMENTABLE	MIGNONETTE	OVERPRAISE	PILLOWCASE	QUIESCENCE
INEVITABLE	LANCEOLATE	MILLICURIE	OWLSPIEGLE	PISTILLATE	RACECOURSE
INEXORABLE	LANTHANIDE	MILLIMETRE	PALAEOTYPE	PITCHSTONE	RAMSHACKLE
INFALLIBLE	LARGESCALE	MINESTRONE	PALAGONITE	PLAGIARISE	RANDLETREE
INFIBULATE	LASTMINUTE	MINISTRATE	PALATALISE	PLAGIARIZE	RANNELTREE
INFILTRATE	LAUDERDALE	MINISTROKE	PALATINATE	PLANCHETTE	RANNLETREE
INFINITIVE	LAUNCEGAYE	MISFORTUNE	PALINDROME	PLASTICINE	RANTLETREE
INFLATABLE	LAURDALITE	MISHGUGGLE	PALLIATIVE	PLEBISCITE	RAVENSTONE
INFLEXIBLE	LAURUSTINE	MITHRIDATE	PALUSTRINE	PLOUGHBOTE	RAWINSONDE
INGEMINATE	LAURVIKITE	MODIFIABLE	PANTOSCOPE	PLOUGHGATE	RAWSTHORNE
INGENERATE	LAVALLIÈRE	MOISTURIZE	PAPAVERINE	PLOUGHWISE	REACTIVATE
INGRATIATE	LEGITIMATE	MONEGASQUE	PAPERCHASE	POCKMANTIE	REAPPRAISE
INIMITABLE	LEGITIMIZE	MONOCHROME	PAPERKNIFE	POLITICIZE	REASONABLE
INITIATIVE	LEMNISCATE	MONOPOLISE	PARADIDDLE	POLYCHAETE	REASSEMBLE
INNERSPACE	LENGTHWISE	MONOPOLIZE	PARADOXIDE	POLYCHROME	RECEPTACLE
INNOVATIVE	LHERZOLITE	MONSTRANCE	PARADOXINE	POLYMERIZE	RECITATIVE
INOPERABLE	LIBERALIZE	MOTHERLIKE	PARAGONITE	POPULARIZE	RECOMMENCE
INORDINATE	LIBREVILLE	MOTORCYCLE	PARAPHRASE	PORTMANTLE	RECOMPENSE
INOSCULATE	LICENTIATE	MOUSEPIECE	PARASELENE	PORTUGUESE	RECRUDESCE
INSATIABLE	LIGHTHOUSE	MOUSSELINE	PARDONABLE	POSSESSIVE	RECUPERATE
INSEMINATE	LIGNOCAINE	MOUTHPIECE	PARISCHANE	POSTCHAISE	RECURRENCE
INSENSIBLE	LIMBURGITE	MOZAMBIQUE	PARISIENNE	POSTILLATE	REDECORATE
INSISTENCE	LIMITROPHE	MYRIOSCOPE	PARMACITIE	POTENTIATE	REDRUTHITE
INSPISSATE	LITERATURE	MYSTAGOGUE	PARTHENOPE	POWERHOUSE	REFLECTIVE
INSUFFLATE	LITHOMARGE	NAPTHALENE	PARTICIPLE	PRAEMUNIRE	REFRACTIVE
INTAGLIATE	LITHOPHANE	NARROWDALE	PARTINGALE	PRATINCOLE	REGENERATE
INTANGIBLE	LOCOMOTIVE	NATHELESSE	PASQUINADE	PREARRANGE	REGRESSIVE
INTEMERATE	LOUISIETTE	NATIONWIDE	PASSIONATE	PRECEDENCE	REGULARIZE
INTENERATE	LUXURIANCE	NATURALIZE	PASTEURISE	PREDECEASE	REJUVENATE
INTERCLUDE	MACONOCHIE	NAUSEATIVE	PASTEURIZE	PREDESTINE	RELAXATIVE

RELUCTANCE	SENEGALESE	SUBSTITUTE	TRIDENTINE	WINDERMERE	DEBRIEFING
REMARKABLE	SENESCENCE	SUBTERFUGE	TRIFOLIATE	WINDOWPANE	DEPRESSING
REMITTANCE	SERPENTINE	SUBVERSIVE	TRIPARTITE	WINTERTIME	DESCENDING
REMONETISE	SGANARELLE	SUCCESSIVE	TRIPLICATE	WOLFRAMITE	DESCRIBING
REMUNERATE	SHAGGYMANE	SUFFERANCE	TRIVIALIZE	WORTHWHILE	DESPAIRING
REORGANIZE	SHERARDISE	SUGARALLIE	TROCTOLITE	YAFFINGALE	DEVELOPING
REPAIRABLE	SHIELDRAKE	SUGGESTIVE	TROGLODYTE	ZABAGLIONE	DISCERNING
REPATRIATE	SHORTRANGE	SUMMERTIME	TROPOPAUSE	ZIDOVUDINE	DISCUSSING
REPEATABLE	SHOVELNOSE	SUPERSTORE	TROPOPHYTE	CHIFFCHAFF	DISGUSTING
REPENTANCE	SHROVETIDE	SUPPLICATE	TROTSKYITE	DEMIRELIEF	DISPENSING
REPERTOIRE	SICILIENNE	SUPPORTIVE	TROUVAILLE	FALLINGOFF	DISSENTING
REPETITIVE	SIDESADDLE	SURINAMESE	TRUCULENCE	FLAMEPROOF	DISTILLING
REPRESSIVE	SILHOUETTE	SUSCEPTIVE	TUMESCENCE	HIPPOGRIFF	DISTURBING
REPUGNANCE	SILVERSIDE	SUSTENANCE	TURBULENCE	OFFTHECUFF	DOMINATING
RESCHEDULE	SILVERWARE	SWEEPSTAKE	TURPENTINE	SHANDYGAFF	DOWNSIZING
RESILIENCE	SIMILITUDE	SYMPATHISE	TURTLEDOVE	SHOCKPROOF	DRAWSTRING
RESISTANCE	SINGHALESE	SYMPATHIZE	UBIQUINONE	SOUNDPROOF	EASTERLING
RESPECTIVE	SLUICEGATE	SYMPTOMIZE	ULSTERETTE	STROGANOFF	EMPFINDUNG
RESPONSIVE	SMALLSCALE	SYNCRETISE	ULTRAFICHE	WATERPROOF	ENCHANTING
RESUPINATE	SMARAGDINE	SYNECDOCHE	UNARGUABLE	WHEATSHEAF	ENGROSSING
RESURGENCE	SNAKESTONE	SYNTHESIZE	UNBEARABLE	ACCOUNTING	ENTRANCING
RETICULATE	SNAPHAUNCE	TABERNACLE	UNBEATABLE	ALMSGIVING	ENTREATING
RETINALITE	SNOWMOBILE	TABLANETTE	UNDENIABLE	ANSCHAUUNG	EVERYTHING
RETROGRADE	SOLICITUDE	TAILORMADE	UNDERLEASE	APPETIZING	EXHAUSTING
RETURNABLE	SOMBRERITE	TAMBERLANE	UNDERSCORE	ASSEMBLING	FACESAVING
REVERSIBLE	SOMERVILLE	TAMBOURINE	UNDERSTATE	ASTOUNDING	FAREPAYING
REVITALIZE	SOMNOLENCE	TANAGRIDAE	UNDERVALUE	BACKBITING	FASTMOVING
RHAPSODISE	SOURDELINE	TARADIDDLE	UNDERWRITE	BALLOONING	FINGERLING
RHAPSODIZE	SOUSAPHONE	TARDIGRADE	UNENVIABLE	BARGAINING	FLATTERING
RHINEGRAVE	SPEAKERINE	TARTRAZINE	UNHEARABLE	BARRACKING	FLAVOURING
RHINESTONE	SPECIALISE	TEINOSCOPE	UNLADYLIKE	BATTENBERG	FLICKERING
RITORNELLE	SPECIALIZE	TELEBRIDGE	UNREADABLE	BATTENBURG	FORBEARING
ROMANESQUE	SPERMICIDE	TELEOSTOME	UNRELIABLE	BEEKEEPING	FORBIDDING
ROQUELAURE	SPERRYLITE	TELIOSPORE	UNSCRAMBLE	BEWITCHING	FOREBODING
ROSANILINE	SPHACELATE	TELPHERAGE	UNSOCIABLE	BITTERLING	FORFAITING
ROTISSERIE	SPHALERITE	TEMPERANCE	UNSUITABLE	BLACKENING	FOXHUNTING
ROUGHHOUSE	SPIFLICATE	TENNANTITE	UNWORKABLE	BLISTERING	FURNISHING
ROUNDHOUSE	SPISSITUDE	TENRECIDAE	UROSTEGITE	BLITHERING	GAINGIVING
RUDOLPHINE	SPOKESHAVE	TERMINABLE	URTICACEAE	BLITZKRIEG	GALUMPHING
RUMINATIVE	SPOLIATIVE	TERNEPLATE	UTILIZABLE	BLUNDERING	GETTYSBURG
RUPICOLINE	SPONGEWARE	TESCHENITE	VAUDEVILLE	BORDRAGING	GLISTENING
RUSSIANIZE	SPRINGLIKE	THAUMASITE	VELOCIPEDE	BURGEONING	GLITTERING
SABRETACHE	SPRINGTIME	THEODOLITE	VERIFIABLE	BUTCHERING	GRATIFYING
SACCHARASE	SQUETEAGUE	THEOLOGATE	VERNISSAGE	CANVASSING	GROUNDLING
SACCHARIDE	STALACTITE	THEOLOGISE	VERTEBRATE	CHAFFERING	GROVELLING
SACCHARINE	STALAGMITE	THREADBARE	VESICULATE	CHANGELING	HAIRSPRING
SALTIGRADE	STAPHYLINE	THREADLIKE	VIBRAPHONE	CHITTAGONG	HANDSPRING
SAMARSKITE	STATUESQUE	THREEPENCE	VIDARABINE	CLAMOURING	HEADSTRONG
SAMOTHRACE	STAUROLITE	THREESCORE	VIETNAMESE	COLLAPSING	HEIDELBERG
SANCTITUDE	STAVESACRE	TICKERTAPE	VILLANELLE	COLLECTING	HIGHFLYING
SAPROPHYTE	STEAKHOUSE	TOILINETTE	VILLEINAGE	COMFORTING	HINDENBURG
SAXICOLINE	STEPHANITE	TOOTHPASTE	VINDEMIATE	COMMANDING	HOMECOMING
SCANDALISE	STEREOTYPE	TORBERNITE	VINDICTIVE	COMPELLING	HORRIFYING
SCANDALIZE	STIGMATISE	TOUCHPIECE	VITELLICLE	CONCERNING	HORSELBERG
SCAPEGRACE	STIGMATIZE	TOUCHSTONE	VITUPERATE	CONCLUDING	INBREEDING
SCHIPPERKE	STILLICIDE	TOURMALINE	VIVANDIÈRE	CONDUCTING	INCREASING
SCOPELIDAE	STONEHENGE	TRACHELATE	VOCIFERATE	CONNECTING	INFIGHTING
SCRUTINISE	STOREHOUSE	TRAMONTANE	VULNERABLE	CONQUERING	INHIBITING
SCRUTINIZE	STOUTHERIE	TRAMPOLINE	WANCHANCIE	CONSULTING	INTRIGUING
SCUTELLATE	STREAMLINE	TRANSCRIBE	WARRANDICE	CONTINUING	IRRITATING
SEANNACHIE	STREETWISE	TRANSIENCE	WATERBORNE	CONVINCING	JAYWALKING
SEASONABLE	STRIDULATE	TRANSITIVE	WESTERNIZE	CORRECTING	KESSELRING
SECONDRATE	STRIPTEASE	TRANSVERSE	WHEATSTONE	CORRUPTING	KIDNAPPING
SECRETAIRE	STROPHIOLE	TRAUMATIZE	WHEELHOUSE	COUNSELING	KUOMINTANG
SECULARIZE	STRYCHNINE	TRAVANCORE	WHEWELLITE	CRICKETING	LANDSTHING
SEECATCHIE	SUBJECTIVE	TRAVELOGUE	WHIGGAMORE	CURMURRING	LAWABIDING
SELEGILINE	SUBMISSIVE	TRAVERTINE	WHITSTABLE	CURVETTING	LUTESTRING
SELTZOGENE	SUBROUTINE	TRENCHMORE	WINCEYETTE	DARJEELING	LUXEMBOURG
SEMICIRCLE	SUBSIDENCE				MAGNIFYING

MAINSPRING	STRAGGLING	CHILDBIRTH	SILVERFISH	BADDERLOCK	TURTLENECK
MEANDERING	STRASBOURG	CHINAGRAPH	SKEUOMORPH	BAILIEWICK	WATTLEWORK
MISLEADING	STRINDBERG	COELACANTH	SNAKEMOUTH	BAILLIWICK	WHITTERICK
MITIGATING	STRULDBRUG	COQUETTISH	SNAPHAUNCH	BASKETWORK	WICKERWORK
MUCKRAKING	STRULDBRUG	CORNSTARCH	SQUIREARCH	BLOODSTOCK	WOOLLYBACK
NAUSEATING	STUPEFYING	CROSSHATCH	STAGECOACH	BOTTLENECK	YELLOWBACK
NETWORKING	SUBHEADING	CUTTLEFISH	STILLBIRTH	BREASTWORK	YELLOWJACK
NIDDERLING	SUCCEEDING	DAMSELFISH	STONEBRASH	BROOMSTICK	YESTERWEEK
NONSMOKING	SUNBATHING	DESBOROUGH	TABLECLOTH	BUTTERMILK	ZUMBOORUCK
NOURISHING	SUPPORTING	DICTOGRAPH	TACHOGRAPH	CANDLEWICK	ABORIGINAL
OCEANGOING	SURFRIDING	EIGHTEENTH	THIRTEENTH	CANVASBACK	ACCIDENTAL
ODELSTHING	SURPASSING	EXTINGUISH	THOUSANDTH	CASSIABARK	ACHITOPHEL
OFFPUTTING	SURPRISING	FALSETRUTH	TIMESWITCH	CHEQUEBOOK	ACRONYCHAL
OUTPOURING	SUSTAINING	FILLIBRUSH	TOOTHBRUSH	CREWELWORK	ADDITIONAL
OVEREATING	SWAGGERING	FLOORCLOTH	TRAGACANTH	CROSSCHECK	ADJECTIVAL
OVERRIDING	SWALLOWING	FLUTEMOUTH	TRILLIONTH	CRUIKSHANK	AHITHOPHEL
OVERSTRUNG	SWEDENBORG	FOURTEENTH	TRIMSNITCH	DONNYBROOK	ANALOGICAL
PARGETTING	SWEETENING	FULLLENGTH	UBERMENSCH	DOUBLETALK	ANALYTICAL
PERFORMING	SWELTERING	GALLABIYAH	UNDERNEATH	DRUZHINNIK	ANARCHICAL
PERPLEXING	TAILGATING	GALLABIYEH	USQUEBAUGH	DUNDERFUNK	ANATOMICAL
PERSUADING	TAPDANCING	GALRAVITCH	VINEGARISH	FETTERLOCK	ANGURVADEL
PETRIFYING	TARPAULING	GOOSEFLESH	WANDSWORTH	FINGERPICK	ANTIPHONAL
PIONEERING	TERRIFYING	GREENCLOTH	WATERBRASH	GENTLEFOLK	ANTISOCIAL
PLUNDERING	THICKENING	GREENFINCH	WAVELENGTH	GIRDLERINK	APOCRYPHAL
PORLOCKING	THUNDERING	HALLELUJAH	WORDSWORTH	GREENSHANK	ARCHETYPAL
PREVAILING	TIMESAVING	HATEENOUGH	WRISTWATCH	GREENSTICK	ARTIFICIAL
PROCEEDING	TRAVELLING	HELIOGRAPH	YARBOROUGH	GROUNDWORK	ATRAMENTAL
PROCESSING	UNASSUMING	HENCEFORTH	ZINCOGRAPH	HACKMATACK	BALIBUNTAL
PROJECTING	UNAVAILING	HEPTATEUCH	AMPHIGOURI	HAMMERLOCK	BARMECIDAL
PUBLISHING	UNBECOMING	HERESIARCH	BARRAMUNDI	HARMANBECK	BASKETBALL
PUMMELLING	UNBLINKING	HIEROGLYPH	BOTTICELLI	HEARTBREAK	BEHAVIORAL
PUTREFYING	UNBLUSHING	HIPPOGRYPH	CANNELLONI	JABBERWOCK	BENEFICIAL
QUARTERING	UNDERLYING	HOMOEOPATH	CERTIORARI	KILMARNOCK	BIOLOGICAL
QUERSPRUNG	UNDERSLUNG	HONEYBUNCH	DEVANAGARI	LIMBERNECK	BLASTOCOEL
REASSURING	UNDULATING	HOTCHPOTCH	EMALANGENI	LUMBERJACK	CAMBERWELL
REFLECTING	UNEDIFYING	IMPOVERISH	FANTOCCINI	MATCHSTALK	CAMPESTRAL
REFRESHING	UNFLAGGING	KENILWORTH	FRANGIPANI	MATCHSTICK	CANNONBALL
RESEMBLING	UNINVITING	LATTERMATH	FRATICELLI	MINUTEBOOK	CARNASSIAL
RESOUNDING	UNSETTLING	LITHOGRAPH	GLITTERATI	MOUNTEBANK	CENTENNIAL
RESPECTING	UNSLEEPING	MACKINTOSH	HINDUSTANI	NATTERJACK	CENTESIMAL
RETRAINING	UNSWERVING	METHUSALEH	ILLUMINATI	NEEDLEWORK	CEREMONIAL
RETREATING	UNTHINKING	METHUSELAH	JAGUARONDI	NIGHTSTICK	CINQUEFOIL
ROISTERING	UNYIELDING	MIMEOGRAPH	JAGUARUNDI	PILGARLICK	CLADOPHYLL
ROLLICKING	UPBRINGING	MISHNAYOTH	MAHAYANALI	PINAKOTHEK	COLLATERAL
ROSEMALING	UPSTANDING	NATUROPATH	MAKUNOUCHI	POCKETBOOK	COLLOQUIAL
SANDERLING	VARNISHING	NETTLERASH	MILLEFIORI	POINTBLANK	COMMERCIAL
SATISFYING	WAMPUMPEAG	NINETEENTH	MONTESSORI	PROMPTBOOK	COMMONWEAL
SCANDERBEG	WASSAILING	NUDIBRANCH	MONTEVERDI	PUNCHDRUNK	CONCEPTUAL
SCATTERING	WELLSPRING	OUTLANDISH	PADAREWSKI	RAVENSDUCK	CONFEDERAL
SCREECHING	WHISPERING	OVERSLAUGH	PERDENDOSI	ROLANDSECK	CONGENITAL
SCRIBBLING	WRONGDOING	PADDLEFISH	PESTALOZZI	RUBBERNECK	CONTEXTUAL
SCROUNGING	ACCOMPLISH	PAINTBRUSH	PICCALILLI	SADDLEBACK	CONVENTUAL
SHAMPOOING	ADRAMELECH	PANTOGRAPH	PONCHIELLI	SCHOOLBOOK	COROMANDEL
SHATTERING	AFTERBIRTH	PENTATEUCH	PRZEWALSKI	SCRIMSHANK	COTTONTAIL
SHIMMERING	ALTAZIMUTH	PETROGLYPH	RAIYATWARI	SHEEPSHANK	COXCOMICAL
SHOESTRING	AMATEURISH	PHONOGRAPH	SALMAGUNDI	SHELLSHOCK	CREDENTIAL
SHORTENING	AMPHIBRACH	PHOTOGRAPH	SHAKUHACHI	SILVERBACK	CUCURBITAL
SHUDDERING	AMPLEFORTH	PICAYUNISH	SHARAWADGI	SKETCHBOOK	DECENNOVAL
SIMULATING	ANEMOGRAPH	PICTOGRAPH	SHARAWAGGI	SKRIMSHANK	DELIGHTFUL
SKINDIVING	ANGLERFISH	PORTSMOUTH	SIGNORELLI	SMOKESTACK	DEMONIACAL
SLUMBERING	BALDERDASH	PSYCHOPATH	SPERMACETI	SOUNDTRACK	DEVOTIONAL
SMATTERING	BANGLADESH	RADIOGRAPH	SVADILFARI	SPATCHCOCK	DIABOLICAL
SNIGGERING	BARMITZVAH	RAJPRAMUKH	TAGLIARINI	SPITCHCOCK	DICKCISSEL
SNORKELING	BATHYSCAPH	RELINQUISH	TORRICELLI	STICKYBEAK	DISDAINFUL
SPIRKETING	BLACKSMITH	SARSQUATCH	TORTELLINI	STINGYBARK	DISEMBOWEL
SPRINKLING	BRIDLEPATH	SCARAMOUCH	VERMICELLI	SUPPLEJACK	DIVISIONAL
STAGGERING	BROADCLOTH	SEVENTIETH	AFTERSHOCK	SWITCHBACK	DUNIWASSAL
STAMMERING	BUTTERFISH	SHIBBOLETH	ALPENSTOCK	SWORDSTICK	DUODECIMAL
STARVELING	CANDLEFISH	SHILLELAGH	ARSMETRICK	TENTERHOOK	EATANSWILL

ECOLOGICAL	PARASTATAL	TRILINGUAL	DYSPROSIUM	PATRIOTISM	ACCUSATION
ECONOMICAL	PEDIMENTAL	TYRANNICAL	ECHINODERM	PENNISETUM	ACOTYLEDON
ECUMENICAL	PENTAGONAL	UNCRITICAL	ELYTRIFORM	PLAGIARISM	ACROTERION
ELECTRICAL	PEPPERMILL	UNEVENTFUL	EMPLASTRUM	PLASMODESM	ADAPTATION
ELLIPTICAL	PERIODICAL	UNFAITHFUL	ENTHUSIASM	POLYTHEISM	ADHIBITION
ENCYCLICAL	PERIPHERAL	UNFRUITFUL	EPIDENDRUM	POSTMORTEM	ADIAPHORON
EQUATORIAL	PHENOMENAL	UNGRATEFUL	EPITHELIUM	PRAETORIUM	ADMIRATION
EUCALYPTOL	POLYNOMIAL	UNICAMERAL	EPONYCHIUM	PRAGMATISM	ADMONITION
FINGERNAIL	PONTIFICAL	UNILATERAL	EUHEMERISM	PRINCIPIUM	AFFLICTION
FORINSECAL	PREMARITAL	UNOFFICIAL	FANATICISM	PROMETHIUM	AGGRESSION
FRACTIONAL	PREMEDICAL	UNORIGINAL	FAVORITISM	PROPYLAEUM	ALDERWOMAN
FRAGMENTAL	PRIMORDIAL	UNPUNCTUAL	FEDERALISM	PROSCENIUM	ALECTORIAN
FRENETICAL	PROCEDURAL	UNTRUTHFUL	FLUNKEYDOM	PROTOPLASM	ALGONQUIAN
FROMANTEEL	PROPLITEAL	UROGENITAL	FOURIERISM	PSALTERIUM	ALIENATION
FUNCTIONAL	PROVERBIAL	VOCATIONAL	GADOLINIUM	PURITANISM	ALLEGATION
FUNGICIDAL	PROVINCIAL	VOLLEYBALL	GEOTROPISM	RADICALISM	ALLIGATION
GEOLOGICAL	PRUDENTIAL	WATERLEVEL	GNOSTICISM	RECIDIVISM	ALLOCATION
GEOTHERMAL	PSAMMOPHIL	WATERWHEEL	GRADUALISM	REFERENDUM	ALLOCUTION
GERMICIDAL	PURPOSEFUL	WINDOWSILL	GRANGERISM	RHEUMATISM	ALTERATION
GOLDENSEAL	RABBINICAL	WITHDRAWAL	GYMNOSPERM	ROCKINGHAM	AMERINDIAN
HEPTAGONAL	RAVENSBILL	YELLOWGIRL	HAUSTELLUM	RUMBLOSSOM	AMMUNITION
HISTORICAL	RECIPROCAL	YGGDRASILL	HAUSTORIUM	SANATORIUM	AMPHICTYON
HOLOHEDRAL	REGIMENTAL	ZOOLOGICAL	HONORARIUM	SANITARIUM	AMPHITRYON
HOLOPHOTAL	REMORSEFUL	ZYGODACTYL	HYPOCORISM	SCEPTICISM	AMPUTATION
HOMOSEXUAL	RESORCINOL	ABSOLUTISM	IMPALUDISM	SCHOOLMAAM	ANDALUSIAN
HORIZONTAL	RESPECTFUL	ACETABULUM	INDUMENTUM	SCINTIGRAM	ANHELATION
HYPAETHRAL	REVENGEFUL	AFRICANISM	INVALIDISM	SELFESTEEM	ANNEXATION
HYSTERICAL	RHETORICAL	ALCOHOLISM	JOURNALISM	SEPARATISM	ANNOTATION
IMMATERIAL	RHYTHMICAL	AMBULACRUM	KETTLEDRUM	SIMILLIMUM	ANTHEOLION
IMMEMORIAL	RIJSTTAFEL	ANACARDIUM	LAMARCKISM	SIMULACRUM	ANTICHTHON
IMPERSONAL	RUDIMENTAL	ANGIOSPERM	LAWRENCIUM	SKEPTICISM	ANTIMONIAN
INCIDENTAL	SABBATICAL	ANTAGONISM	LEBENSRAUM	SLIPSTREAM	ANTINOMIAN
INDIVIDUAL	SACERDOTAL	APOPHTHEGM	LENOCINIUM	SPECIALISM	ANTIOCHIAN
INDUSTRIAL	SADDLEBILL	APOTHECIUM	LESBIANISM	SPIRACULUM	ANTIPODEAN
INTERNODAL	SALBUTAMOL	ASCETICISM	LIBERALISM	SPONGIFORM	ANTIPROTON
INTESTINAL	SCHLIMAZEL	ATRACURIUM	LOCKERROOM	SPOONERISM	APOLLONIAN
IRRATIONAL	SCHOOLGIRL	AUDITORIUM	LYSENKOISM	SPORANGIUM	APPARITION
IRREMEDIAL	SCRIPTURAL	AVERRHOISM	MAINSTREAM	STILLIFORM	APPOSITION
JUGENDSTIL	SENATORIAL	BIRMINGHAM	MAKESYSTEM	STRAMONIUM	ARAUCANIAN
KRIEGSPIEL	SEPTENNIAL	BLEPHARISM	MALAYALAAM	STRONGROOM	ARCHDEACON
LITURGICAL	SEPULCHRAL	BRADYSEISM	MEDIUMTERM	STUMBLEDOM	AREFACTION
LOGISTICAL	SEQUENTIAL	BRAINSTORM	MEERSCHAUM	SUBSELLIUM	ARIMASPIAN
MANAGERIAL	SERMONICAL	BRIDEGROOM	MEITNERIUM	SUBSTRATUM	ARMAGEDDON
MANCHINEEL	SILVERBELL	BRITISHISM	MEMORANDUM	SUDATORIUM	ARUNDELIAN
MEANINGFUL	SILVERBILL	BUCHMANISM	METABOLISM	SURREALISM	ASPIRATION
MECHANICAL	SIMMENTHAL	BUCKINGHAM	MILITARISM	SYMPHONIUM	ASSUMPTION
METACARPAL	SINOATRIAL	CAPITALISM	MILLENNIUM	TECHNETIUM	ATHANASIAN
METATARSAL	SPLITLEVEL	CAPITELLUM	MINIMALISM	TEPIDARIUM	ATTRACTION
METHODICAL	SPONSIONAL	CARDIOGRAM	MOLYBDENUM	THALICTRUM	AUSTRALIAN
MISCHMETAL	SPRINGTAIL	CATABOLISM	MONETARISM	THALLIFORM	AUTOCHTHON
MONUMENTAL	STANDSTILL	CEREBELLUM	MONILIFORM	THREADWORM	AUTOMATION
MYOCARDIAL	STRUCTURAL	CHAUVINISM	MONOPODIUM	TIROCINIUM	BABYLONIAN
NATATORIAL	SUBLIMINAL	CHELTENHAM	MONOTHEISM	TRIANGULUM	BACITRACIN
NEGLECTFUL	SUBORBITAL	CHLOROFORM	MORATORIUM	TRICLINIUM	BACKGAMMON
NEOTERICAL	SUCCESSFUL	CLASSICISM	NARCISSISM	TROPAEOLUM	BAHRAINIAN
NEUTROPHIL	SUPERMODEL	COCKALORUM	NASTURTIUM	UNUNHEXIUM	BALBRIGGAN
NICROSILAL	SYMBOLICAL	COLDSTREAM	NATATORIUM	UNUNNILIUM	BALNEATION
NOSOCOMIAL	SYNCHRONAL	COMPENDIUM	NATURALISM	VESTIBULUM	BARLEYCORN
OBSIDIONAL	TANGENTIAL	COMPLUVIUM	OBLOMOVISM	VIBRACULUM	BASSINGTON
OCCASIONAL	TATTERSALL	CONSORTIUM	OCEANARIUM	WITGATBOOM	BATRACHIAN
OCCIDENTAL	TCHOUKBALL	COTTIERISM	OPPROBRIUM	ABDICATION	BEARGARDEN
OFFTHEWALL	THEATRICAL	CRYPTOGRAM	OSMETERIUM	ABERRATION	BEAUTICIAN
ORATORICAL	THIMBLEFUL	CURRICULUM	OUTPERFORM	ABROGATION	BEAVERSKIN
ORCHESTRAL	THOUGHTFUL	DELPHINIUM	PACIFICISM	ABSCISSION	BELARUSIAN
ORNAMENTAL	THRENODIAL	DEUTOPLASM	PALMERWORM	ABSOLUTION	BILIVERDIN
ORTHOGONAL	TINKERBELL	DICHROMISM	PANARITIUM	ABSORPTION	BIPARTISAN
PALAESTRAL	TOCOPHEROL	DIGITORIUM	PANCRATIUM	ABSTENTION	BLACKTHORN
PANTAGRUEL	TORRENTIAL	DISSELBOOM	PANJANDRUM	ABYSSINIAN	BLOODSTAIN
PARANORMAL	TRILATERAL	DOWNSTREAM	PARNELLISM	ACCUBATION	BONDSWOMAN

BOOZINGKEN	CONTENTION	ENGLISHMEN	HEMOGLOBIN	LITIGATION	PENTAMERON
BOURIGNIAN	CONTORTION	ENKEPHALIN	HENDECAGON	LOCOMOTION	PENTATHLON
BOUSINGKEN	CONTRITION	EPILIMNION	HEPTAMERON	LUSITANIAN	PENTELIKON
BRADYKININ	CONVECTION	EQUESTRIAN	HEPTATHLON	MABINOGION	PENTSTEMON
BRIDGETOWN	CONVENTION	EQUITATION	HESITATION	MACEDONIAN	PEPPERCORN
BROKENDOWN	CONVERSION	ERIOCAULON	HIGHWAYMAN	MADAGASCAN	PERCEPTION
BURLINGTON	CONVICTION	ERUCTATION	HOMEOUSIAN	MAHOMMEDAN	PERCUSSION
BUTTONDOWN	CONVULSION	ESCALATION	HOMOOUSIAN	MALTHUSIAN	PERFECTION
BYELECTION	COPENHAGEN	ESCULAPIAN	HORSEDRAWN	MANGOSTEEN	PERIHELION
CACODAEMON	COPPERSKIN	ESCUTCHEON	HORSEWOMAN	MANICHAEAN	PERMEATION
CALAMONDIN	COPULATION	ESTIMATION	HUMDUDGEON	MATTERHORN	PERMISSION
CALCITONIN	CORINTHIAN	ESTRAMACON	HYPAETHRON	MATURATION	PERORATION
CALEDONIAN	CORONATION	ETEOCRETAN	IMMOLATION	MAVOURNEEN	PERSUASION
CALYDONIAN	CORRECTION	EUROCLYDON	IMPOSITION	MAXIMILIAN	PERVERSION
CAMERONIAN	CORRUPTION	EUSTACHIAN	IMPRESSION	MEADOWPLAN	PETRARCHAN
CAMPERDOWN	COUNTRYMAN	EVACUATION	IMPUTATION	MEDICATION	PHAELONIAN
CANTABRIAN	CRISPINIAN	EVALUATION	INCUBATION	MEDITATION	PHENOMENON
CAPITATION	CRUSTACEAN	EXALTATION	INDECISION	MELANESIAN	PHLEGETHON
CARCINOGEN	CURMUDGEON	EXCAVATION	INDEXATION	MELOCOTOON	PHLOGISTON
CARPATHIAN	DECAHEDRON	EXECRATION	INDICATION	MENECHMIAN	PHYTOTOXIN
CARRAGHEEN	DECLENSION	EXHALATION	INDONESIAN	MESENTERON	PINCUSHION
CARTHUSIAN	DECORATION	EXHAUSTION	INFLECTION	MIDLOTHIAN	PLANTATION
CASTRATION	DEDICATION	EXHIBITION	INFLICTION	MIDSHIPMAN	POLITICIAN
CATACHUMEN	DEFAMATION	EXHUMATION	INFRACTION	MILITIAMAN	POLYHEDRON
CATECHUMEN	DEFECATION	EXPEDITION	INHALATION	MISPRISION	POLYNESIAN
CATHOLICON	DEFINITION	EXPIRATION	INHIBITION	MITIGATION	POMERANIAN
CAVALRYMAN	DEFLECTION	EXPOSITION	INITIATION	MODERATION	POPULATION
CESTRACION	DELEGATION	EXPRESSION	INJUNCTION	MODULATION	POSSESSION
CHAIRWOMAN	DELIGATION	EXPRESSMAN	INNOVATION	MONOPTERON	POSTILLION
CHAMAELEON	DELIRATION	EXTINCTION	INSPECTION	MORISONIAN	PRAETORIAN
CHAMBERTIN	DEMOGORGON	EXTRACTION	INSULATION	MOTIVATION	PRECAUTION
CHAMPIGNON	DEMOLITION	EXULTATION	INTERFERON	MOUSTERIAN	PRECIPITIN
CHAPFALLEN	DEPILATION	FASCIATION	INTERWOVEN	MOUTHORGAN	PREDICTION
CHATTERTON	DEPOSITION	FEDERATION	INTIMATION	MUJAHEDDIN	PRELECTION
CHAUCERIAN	DEPRESSION	FEUILLETON	INTINCTION	MUTILATION	PRETENSION
CHECKLATON	DEPUTATION	FIGURATION	INTONATION	NAVIGATION	PREVENTION
CHESTERTON	DERIVATION	FILTRATION	INTRAURBAN	NEAPOLITAN	PROCESSION
CHEVROTAIN	DESOLATION	FIREWARDEN	INUNDATION	NICARAGUAN	PRODUCTION
CHINQUAPIN	DETONATION	FIRTHSOKEN	INVITATION	NOBLEWOMAN	PROFESSION
CIRCASSIAN	DETRACTION	FLIRTATION	INVOCATION	NOMINATION	PROGESSION
CISLEITHAN	DEVOLUTION	FLUGELHORN	INVOLUTION	NONFICTION	PROJECTION
CISTERCIAN	DIACONICON	FOREORDAIN	IRISHWOMAN	NUMERATION	PROMETHEAN
CLANSWOMAN	DIGRESSION	FORFEUCHEN	IRISHWOMEN	NURSERYMAN	PROPORTION
CLUMPERTON	DILATATION	FORFOUGHEN	IRRIGATION	OBLIGATION	PROPULSION
COGITATION	DIMINUTION	FOUNDATION	IRRITATION	OCCUPATION	PROTECTION
COLLECTION	DIREMPTION	FRANCISCAN	JACULATION	OCTAHEDRON	PROTRUSION
COLORATION	DISBURTHEN	FREEMARTIN	JOHNSONIAN	OMOPHORION	PSILOCYBIN
COMBUSTION	DISCRETION	FRITHSOKEN	JOURNEYMAN	OPPOSITION	PTERANODON
COMMISSION	DISCUSSION	FULLYGROWN	JUBILATION	OPPRESSION	PUNDIGRION
COMPARISON	DISHEARTEN	FUMIGATION	KARMATHIAN	ORDINATION	QUARTEROON
COMPASSION	DISPERSION	GARGANTUAN	KEMPERYMAN	ORDOVICIAN	QUEENSTOWN
COMPLETION	DISRUPTION	GEMINATION	KENTUCKIAN	ORPHEOREON	QUERCITRON
COMPLEXION	DISSECTION	GENERATION	KLOOTCHMAN	OSCITATION	QUICKTHORN
COMPULSION	DISSENSION	GEORGETOWN	LACERATION	OSCULATION	RAGAMUFFIN
CONCEPTION	DISSUASION	GILBERTIAN	LAMBREQUIN	OVERSTRAIN	RAILWAYMAN
CONCESSION	DISTENSION	GLACIATION	LAMINATION	PADDINGTON	RAMPALLIAN
CONCHIOLIN	DISTORTION	GLEEMAIDEN	LANDAMMANN	PADDYMELON	RECITATION
CONCLUSION	DIVINATION	GRADUATION	LAUNCESTON	PAGINATION	RECREATION
CONCOCTION	DOMINATION	GRAMICIDIN	LAURENTIAN	PALMERSTON	REDEMPTION
CONCRETION	DUKKERIPEN	GRAMMARIAN	LEAMINGTON	PANAMANIAN	REELECTION
CONCUSSION	DUTCHWOMAN	GROUNDSMAN	LEDERHOSEN	PANOPTICON	REFLECTION
CONDUCTION	ECUADORIAN	GUATEMALAN	LEPRECHAUN	PARAGUAYAN	REFRACTION
CONFECTION	ELEUSINIAN	HABITATION	LEVITATION	PARNASSIAN	REFUTATION
CONFESSION	ELONGATION	HAMESUCKEN	LIBERATION	PATAGONIAN	REGRESSION
CONGESTION	EMACIATION	HANDMAIDEN	LIEBERMANN	PECULATION	REGULATION
CONNECTION	EMENDATION	HANOVERIAN	LIGHTERMAN	PEDESTRIAN	RELAXATION
CONNIPTION	EMIGRATION	HARRINGTON	LIMITATION	PENELOPHON	RELEGATION
CONSENSION	ENCEPHALON	HARVESTMAN	LINEOMYCIN	PENICILLIN	RELOCATION
CONSTANTAN	ENGLISHMAN	HEMIHEDRON	LITHUANIAN	PENNILLION	RENOVATION

REPARATION	SUBSTATION	ARGOLEMONO	LIGHTINGUP	BUNDESWEHR	DISSIMILAR
REPETITION	SUBVENTION	BANDERILLO	MEMBERSHIP	BUSHRANGER	DOORKEEPER
REPRESSION	SUBVERSION	CALCEDONIO	MOULDIWARP	CALAMANDER	DOORTODOOR
REPUBLICAN	SUCCESSION	CAMERLENGO	NINCOMPOOP	CALCULATOR	DRAWCANSIR
REPUTATION	SUGGESTION	CAMERLINGO	OVERTHETOP	CALEFACTOR	DREIKANTER
RESOLUTION	SUPERHUMAN	CANCIONERO	PILLOWSLIP	CALORIFIER	DRESSMAKER
RESUMPTION	SUPERWOMAN	CAPODASTRO	PSEUDOCARP	CAMPAIGNER	DRINKWATER
RETRACTION	SUSPENSION	CAPPUCCINO	PSYCHOPOMP	CAMPARADOR	DRUMBLEDOR
REVELATION	TABLESPOON	CATENACCIO	RATTLETRAP	CANECUTTER	DUPLICATOR
REVOCATION	TABULATION	CHIMBORAZO	READERSHIP	CANTILEVER	ELECTROMER
REVOLUTION	TECHNICIAN	COMANCHERO	SEAMANSHIP	CARABINEER	ELIMINATOR
RIBOFLAVIN	TEDDINGTON	DIDGERIDOO	STREETLAMP	CARABINIER	EMMENTALER
RICHARDSON	TELEVISION	DIMINUENDO	WENTLETRAP	CARBURETOR	EMULSIFIER
RICHTHOFEN	TEMPTATION	ESTANCIERO	ACETABULAR	CARPENTIER	ENCLOISTER
RIGELATION	TENDERLOIN	FANTASTICO	ADMINISTER	CASSUMUNAR	EUDIOMETER
RINGELMANN	TERREPLEIN	FIANCHETTO	ADVENTURER	CATALOGUER	FALKLANDER
ROBERDSMAN	THALASSIAN	FORTISSIMO	ADVERTISER	CATCRACKER	FASCINATOR
ROBERTSMAN	THELLUSSON	FRATERETTO	AFRICANDER	CENTILITER	FERTILISER
ROWLANDSON	THEOLOGIAN	GETUPANDGO	ALMACANTAR	CENTIMETER	FERTILIZER
RUBINSTEIN	THYSANURAN	HALLUBALOO	ALMUCANTAR	CHALLENGER	FILIBUSTER
RUMBULLION	TOLERATION	HULLABALOO	ALTERNATOR	CHANCELLOR	FIREWALKER
RUMINATION	TOURBILLON	IMPRESARIO	ALTOGETHER	CHANDELIER	FISHMONGER
RUPESTRIAN	TOWNSWOMAN	INQUIRENDO	AMBASSADOR	CHARIOTEER	FISHSELLER
SALESWOMAN	TRANSITION	INTERMEZZO	AMBOCEPTOR	CHERIMOYER	FLUCTUATER
SALIVATION	TRANSPOSON	INTERTRIGO	AMPHIMACER	CHICHESTER	FLYCATCHER
SALPINGIAN	TRINACRIAN	KATERFELTO	ANEMOMETER	CHIFFONIER	FOOTBALLER
SALUTATION	TRISKELION	LATTICINIO	ANTIMATTER	CHRONICLER	FOREBITTER
SALVADORAN	TROCHOTRON	MARASCHINO	APPLICATOR	CHURCHGOER	FORECASTER
SANITATION	TRYPTOPHAN	MONTEVIDEO	ARBITRATOR	CLEARWATER	FOREFATHER
SANNAYASIN	TUMBLEDOWN	OCTODECIMO	ASTROLOGER	CLOCKMAKER	FOREFINGER
SATURATION	ULCERATION	PAPIAMENTO	ASTRONOMER	CLODHOPPER	FOREGATHER
SCANDAROON	UNDERLINEN	PARAMARIBO	AUCTIONEER	COATHANGER	FORERUNNER
SCHALSTEIN	UNDULATION	PASSAMEZZO	AUSTRINGER	COCKCHAFER	FRANCHISOR
SCOTSWOMAN	UNFORESEEN	PEACHERINO	BABYSITTER	COLCHESTER	FRAUNHOFER
SEPARATION	USUCAPTION	PECCADILLO	BACKHANDER	COLLIMATOR	FREEBOOTER
SERVICEMAN	USURPATION	PENSIEROSO	BACKPACKER	COLLOCUTER	FREEHANDER
SEXDUCTION	VALIDATION	PENTIMENTO	BACKSLIDER	COLPORTEUR	FREEHOLDER
SHACKLETON	VEGETARIAN	PIANISSIMO	BANDMASTER	COMMANDEER	FREELANCER
SHANDRYDAN	VEGETATION	PICHICIAGO	BARCHESTER	COMPARATOR	FREELOADER
SHECKLATON	VELITATION	PICHICIEGO	BATTLEDOOR	COMPETITOR	FREQUENTER
SHELDONIAN	VENERATION	PIRANDELLO	BEAUTIFIER	COMPOSITOR	FRESHWATER
SHENANIGAN	VENEZUELAN	PONTICELLO	BEDCHAMBER	COMPRESSOR	FROGHOPPER
SIDERATION	VERMILLION	PORTAMENTO	BEEFBURGER	COMSTOCKER	GALVANISER
SILVERSKIN	VILLANOVAN	PROSCIUTTO	BELLWETHER	CONDOTTIER	GAMEKEEPER
SIMULATION	VISITATION	RECITATIVO	BELSHAZZAR	CONEFLOWER	GEOGRAPHER
SLAMMERKIN	VOLUTATION	RITORNELLO	BENEFACTOR	CONTRACTOR	GINGERBEER
SMITHEREEN	WALDENSIAN	SALTARELLO	BERSAGLIER	CONTROLLER	GLENDOVEER
SNAPDRAGON	WALLACHIAN	SERRASALMO	BESTSELLER	COPARCENER	GLOUCESTER
SOLIFIDIAN	WANTHRIVEN	STIACCIATO	BIOGRAPHER	COPYHOLDER	GOALKEEPER
SOPHOCLEAN	WASHINGTON	STRACCHINO	BLACKWATER	COPYWRITER	GOATSUCKER
SOUTERRAIN	WATERMELON	STREPITOSO	BLASPHEMER	CORDWAINER	GOLDDIGGER
SPALLATION	WEATHERMAN	STRINGENDO	BOBBYSOXER	CORNFLOWER	GOLDFINGER
SPENCERIAN	WELLINGTON	SUPERCARGO	BOMBARDIER	CORREGIDOR	GONFANONER
SPENSERIAN	WELSHWOMAN	TINTORETTO	BONDHOLDER	CORRUGATOR	GONIOMETER
SPOLIATION	WHITETHORN	TOUCHANDGO	BONESHAKER	COUNCILLOR	GRIDIRONER
STAGNATION	WILLIAMSON	TRIMALCHIO	BOOKBINDER	COUNSELLOR	GUBERNATOR
STARVATION	WILLINGDON	ARCHBISHOP	BOOKKEEPER	COVENANTER	HACKBUTEER
STENTORIAN	WINDSCREEN	AUSTRALORP	BOOKMARKER	CROSSREFER	HALFDOLLAR
STEPHENSON	WOFFINGTON	AUTHORSHIP	BOOKSELLER	CUIRASSIER	HALFSISTER
STICHARION	WOODPIGEON	BATTLESHIP	BOOTLEGGER	CULTIVATOR	HANGGLIDER
STONEMASON	WYCLIFFIAN	BUTTERBUMP	BOOTLICKER	DAYDREAMER	HEADHUNTER
STRAIGHTEN	ZAPOROGIAN	CENSORSHIP	BRAINPOWER	DECOLLATOR	HEADMASTER
STRAPONTIN	ZIMBABWEAN	CODSWALLOP	BREAKWATER	DENSIMETER	HELICOPTER
STRENGTHEN	ZOLLVEREIN	CONTRECOUP	BRESSUMMER	DERAILLEUR	HELIOLATER
SUBJECTION	ZWITTERION	DEALERSHIP	BRICKLAYER	DETERMINER	HELLBENDER
SUBMERSION	ADELANTADO	FELLOWSHIP	BUCCINATOR	DISCLAIMER	HIGHBINDER
SUBMISSION	AFFETTUOSO	FRIENDSHIP	BUCKJUMPER	DISCOVERER	HIGHLANDER
SUBREPTION	AFICIONADO	GINGERSNAP	BUDGERIGAR	DISHWASHER	HITCHHIKER
SUBSECTION	ANGWANTIBO	LEADERSHIP	BUMFREEZER	DISSEMBLER	HOMEWORKER

HORNBLOWER	ORIGINATOR	SERVOMOTOR	UNDERCOVER	ANCIPITOUS	CANEPHORUS
HORSEPOWER	OSCILLATOR	SHEARWATER	UNDERFLOOR	ANTIADITIS	CAPRICIOUS
HORSERIDER	OVERLANDER	SHOPKEEPER	UNDERSTEER	ANTIBARBUS	CARACTACUS
HOWSOMEVER	OVERMATTER	SHOPLIFTER	UNDERTAKER	ANTISEPSIS	CARYATIDES
HUMIDIFIER	OVIPOSITOR	SHOPWALKER	UNDERWATER	ANTITHESIS	CASUALNESS
HYDROMETER	OXYGENATOR	SHOWJUMPER	UNFAMILIAR	ANTITRAGUS	CATASTASIS
HYGROMETER	PACESETTER	SIDEWINDER	VENTILATOR	APEMANTHUS	CATAWAMPUS
ICEBREAKER	PAINKILLER	SKYSCRAPER	VERNACULAR	APHAERESIS	CATHOLICOS
IMPRIMATUR	PALFRENIER	SNOWBLOWER	VICTUALLER	APOLLONIUS	CELESTIALS
INKSLINGER	PALISANDER	SOGDOLAGER	VIEWFINDER	APOTHEOSIS	CELLULITIS
INQUISITOR	PALLBEARER	SOGDOLIGER	VOETGANGER	AQUAFORTIS	CENSORIOUS
INSTIGATOR	PARTICULAR	SOGDOLOGER	WAGEEARNER	ARAGONITES	CEREMONIES
INSTRUCTOR	PATHFINDER	SONGWRITER	WALLFLOWER	ARCHIMEDES	CHAMAEROPS
INTERCEDER	PAWNBROKER	SOOTHSAYER	WASTEPAPER	ARENACEOUS	CHANGELESS
INTERFERER	PEACEMAKER	SOUTHERNER	WATCHMAKER	ARISTIPPUS	CHAPARAJOS
INTERLOPER	PEASHOOTER	SPECULATOR	WATCHTOWER	ARISTOTLES	CHAPAREJOS
IRONMONGER	PENINSULAR	SPORTSWEAR	WATERCOLOR	ARTOCARPUS	CHAROLLAIS
JACKHAMMER	PENTAMETER	STABILISER	WATERSKIER	ASBESTOSIS	CHEEKINESS
JEISTIECOR	PERCOLATOR	STABILIZER	WEEDKILLER	ASPERSIONS	CHERVONETS
KEYBOARDER	PERFORATOR	STADHOLDER	WEIMARANER	ASTOMATOUS	CHILDERMAS
KHIDMUTGAR	PERSECUTOR	STALHELMER	WHARFINGER	ASTRAGALUS	CHILLINESS
KIESELGUHR	PETITIONER	STALLENGER	WHATSOEVER	ASTRALAGUS	CHIVALROUS
KINGFISHER	PILEDRIVER	STALLINGER	WHEELCHAIR	ASTUTENESS	CHOICELESS
KOEKSISTER	PLATELAYER	STEMWINDER	WHITEWATER	ATELEIOSIS	CHOPSTICKS
LACKLUSTER	PLESIOSAUR	STENOTYPER	WHOLESALER	AURIFEROUS	CHRONICLES
LADYKILLER	PLEXIMETER	STEPFATHER	WILDFOWLER	AUSPICIOUS	CHRYSIPPUS
LANDLOUPER	PLUMASSIER	STEPLADDER	WINCHESTER	AUTOECIOUS	CIRCUITOUS
LANDLUBBER	POSTMASTER	STEPMOTHER	WINDFLOWER	AUTOGENOUS	CLAMMINESS
LAWBREAKER	POURPARLER	STEPSISTER	WINDJAMMER	AUTONOMOUS	CLEVERNESS
LEAFHOPPER	PREPARATOR	STERILISER	WINDSURFER	AVARICIOUS	CLOUDINESS
LEFTHANDER	PREPOSITOR	STERILIZER	WITSNAPPER	BABESIASIS	CLUMSINESS
LEFTWINGER	PROCREATOR	SUBLIMATER	WOODPECKER	BACCHANTES	COARSENESS
LEGISLATOR	PROCURATOR	SUBMARINER	WOODWORKER	BACKBLOCKS	COCCINEOUS
LENTICULAR	PROGENITOR	SUBSCRIBER	WORSHIPPER	BACKSTAIRS	COETANEOUS
LIPIZZANER	PROGRAMMER	SUPERPOWER	YESTERYEAR	BAGASSOSIS	COLOSSIANS
LIQUIDATOR	PROMENADER	SUPERVISOR	ABRUPTNESS	BALLISTICS	COLOURLESS
LIQUIDIZER	PROPAGATOR	SUPPRESSOR	ABSTEMIOUS	BARRENNESS	COMMODIOUS
LOCKKEEPER	PROPRAETOR	SWEETBRIAR	ACANACEOUS	BATTAILOUS	CONCINNOUS
LUMPSUCKER	PROPRIETOR	TACHOMETER	ACCESSIONS	BEAUJOLAIS	CONDIMENTS
MACEBEARER	PROSECUTOR	TALEBEARER	ACCLIVIOUS	BEDCLOTHES	CONIFEROUS
MADAGASCAR	PROSPECTOR	TANNHAUSER	ACEPHALOUS	BEEFEATERS	CONSONANTS
MAIDENHAIR	PROTRACTOR	TASKMASTER	ACOLOUTHOS	BELONGINGS	CONSPECTUS
MAINPERNOR	PROVEDITOR	TEETOTALER	ACROBATICS	BERMOOTHES	CONTAGIOUS
MAINTAINER	PULSOMETER	TESTICULAR	ACROGENOUS	BETACRUCIS	CONTIGUOUS
MALEFACTOR	QUARRENDER	THEREAFTER	ADULTERESS	BINOCULARS	CONTINUOUS
MALINGERER	QUESTIONER	THERMISTOR	ADULTEROUS	BIOPHYSICS	COPERNICUS
MANCHESTER	QUIZMASTER	TIEBREAKER	AEROBATICS	BIORHYTHMS	CORNFLAKES
MATCHMAKER	RAPPORTEUR	TIMEKEEPER	AERUGINOUS	BITTERNESS	CORNSTALKS
MEGALOSAUR	RECONSIDER	TIMESERVER	AESTHETICS	BITUMINOUS	CORYBANTES
MERRYMAKER	REDISCOVER	TIRAILLEUR	AFTERHOURS	BOISTEROUS	CORYPHAEUS
MICROMETER	REJONEADOR	TOLLKEEPER	AFTERWARDS	BORROWINGS	COSTLINESS
MILEOMETER	REPETITEUR	TONGUESTER	AGAPANTHUS	BOTTOMLESS	COURAGEOUS
MILLIMETER	REPRODUCER	TOUCHPAPER	AGONISTICS	BRAININESS	CRAFTINESS
MINEWORKER	REREDORTER	TRAFFICKER	ALBIGENSES	BREAKABLES	CREOPHAGUS
MOLENDINAR	RESEARCHER	TRANSISTOR	ALCIBIADES	BREATHLESS	CRETACEOUS
MONEYMAKER	RESPIRATOR	TRANSLATOR	ALEXANDERS	BRICKWORKS	CRISSCROSS
MOSSBUNKER	RINGLEADER	TRAVELATOR	ALLOSAURUS	BRIGHTNESS	CROCKFORDS
MUDSKIPPER	RINGMASTER	TRAVOLATOR	ALMSHOUSES	BRONCHITIS	CROSSBONES
MULTIPLIER	RIPSNORTER	TRESPASSER	ALZHEIMERS	BROWNLANDS	CROSSROADS
NEGOTIATOR	ROADRUNNER	TRIACONTER	AMANUENSIS	BUCEPHALUS	CRYOGENICS
NEWSCASTER	ROSECHAFER	TRIANGULAR	AMARYLLIDS	BYSSINOSIS	CRYOPHORUS
NEWSLETTER	ROTTWEILER	TROCHANTER	AMBLYOPSIS	CACUMINOUS	CURRENCIES
NEWSMONGER	SALAMANDER	TROMOMETER	AMPELOPSIS	CADAVEROUS	CURVACEOUS
NEWSREADER	SALMANAZAR	TROUBADOUR	AMPHIBIOUS	CALAMITOUS	CUSSEDNESS
NORTHANGER	SALTCELLAR	TUBERCULAR	AMPHIMIXIS	CALCAREOUS	CYNOMOLGUS
NORTHERNER	SANDGROPER	TYPESETTER	ANACHARSIS	CAMBRENSIS	DEADLINESS
NUTCRACKER	SCRUTINEER	TYPEWRITER	ANADROMOUS	CANCELLOUS	DEMOCRITUS
OMBROMETER	SEERSUCKER	UMBELLIFER	ANAXIMENES	CANCRIZANS	DENDROPHIS
OPISOMETER	SEMIQUAVER	UNBELIEVER	ANCHYLOSIS	CANDYFLOSS	DEPARTURES

DERMATITIS	FICTITIOUS	HOARSENESS	MANAGERESS	OOPHORITIS	PROSTHESIS
DESPITEOUS	FIERCENESS	HOLOFERNES	MARVELLOUS	ORCHIDEOUS	PROTAGORAS
DIADROMOUS	FILTHINESS	HOMELINESS	MEAGERNESS	OROGENESIS	PROVISIONS
DIAGENESIS	FISTICUFFS	HOMORELAPS	MEAGRENESS	ORTHOPTICS	PTERYGOTUS
DIALECTICS	FLABBINESS	HOMUNCULUS	MELLOWNESS	OSMIDROSIS	PUGNACIOUS
DIAPEDESIS	FLAGITIOUS	HONOURLESS	MEMBRANOUS	OSTEOLEPIS	PYROPHORUS
DIAPHANOUS	FLASHINESS	HORRENDOUS	MENDACIOUS	OSTROGOTHS	PYTHAGORAS
DIDUNCULUS	FLESHINESS	HOUSEMAIDS	MENINGITIS	OTHERGATES	QUADRICEPS
DIOPHANTOS	FLIGHTLESS	HOWLEGLASS	METACARPUS	OTHERGUESS	QUAINTNESS
DIPLODOCUS	FLIMSINESS	HUMANITIES	METALEPSIS	OUGHTLINGS	QUEASINESS
DIRECTIONS	FLOWERBEDS	HUMBLENESS	METAPLASIS	OUTRAGEOUS	QUENCHLESS
DIRECTNESS	FLUFFINESS	HUMOURLESS	METATARSUS	OZYMANDIAS	QUICKSANDS
DISASTROUS	FOLIACEOUS	HYDRAULICS	METATHESIS	PANNICULUS	RANDOMNESS
DISCOBOLUS	FONTICULUS	HYDROLYSIS	METICULOUS	PANTALOONS	RANUNCULUS
DISPOSSESS	FONTINALIS	HYPOGAEOUS	METROPOLIS	PARACELSUS	REBELLIOUS
DISTRINGAS	FOODSTUFFS	HYPOGENOUS	MICHAELMAS	PARAENESIS	REGARDLESS
DOGGEDNESS	FOOTLIGHTS	HYPOTHESIS	MIGHTINESS	PARAPHYSIS	RELENTLESS
DOLICHOLIS	FOOTPRINTS	HYSTERESIS	MINDERERUS	PARAPRAXIS	REMOTENESS
DOLICHOTUS	FORTINBRAS	ICHTHYOSIS	MINUTENESS	PARATROOPS	RENDEZVOUS
DOUBLEBASS	FORTUITOUS	IMPERVIOUS	MIRACULOUS	PARENTLESS	RESERVISTS
DOWNSTAIRS	FREEMASONS	IMPURITIES	MISGIVINGS	PARKLEAVES	RETROGRESS
DRACONITES	FRIENDLESS	INCAUTIOUS	MONANDROUS	PARVOVIRUS	RHAMPASTOS
DREADLOCKS	FRISKINESS	INCESTUOUS	MONILIASIS	PATCHINESS	RHEUMATICS
DREAMINESS	FRONTWARDS	INDECOROUS	MONOECIOUS	PEDIATRICS	RHINOCEROS
DREARINESS	FULIGINOUS	INDENTURES	MONOGAMOUS	PEDIPALPUS	RHOEADALES
DROWSINESS	GALIMATIAS	INDIGENOUS	MONOPTEROS	PERDITIOUS	RIDICULOUS
DUCKBOARDS	GANGRENOUS	INFECTIOUS	MONOTONOUS	PERFIDIOUS	RIGHTWARDS
EARTHWORKS	GELATINOUS	INGLORIOUS	MONTICULUS	PERIEGESIS	ROBUSTIOUS
ECCHYMOSIS	GENTLENESS	INIQUITOUS	MORALITIES	PERNICIOUS	ROBUSTNESS
ECTHLIPSIS	GEOPHYSICS	INTENTNESS	MORDACIOUS	PERSEPOLIS	RUBIGINOUS
EFFORTLESS	GERIATRICS	INTESTINES	MORIGEROUS	PERSIENNES	RUDDERLESS
ELEGABALUS	GIARDIASIS	ISOMETRICS	MOROSENESS	PESCADORES	RUGGEDNESS
EMBLEMENTS	GINGIVITIS	JACKANAPES	MOSASAUROS	PETTICHAPS	SACREDNESS
EMOLUMENTS	GLASSINESS	JACKSTONES	MOTHERLESS	PETTYCHAPS	SALLENDERS
EMPEDOCLES	GLASSWORKS	JACKSTRAWS	MOTIONLESS	PHOLIDOSIS	SALOPETTES
ENANTIOSIS	GLOSSINESS	JAUNTINESS	MOULDINESS	PHOSPHORUS	SALUBRIOUS
ENDOGAMOUS	GLUTTONOUS	JOBSEEKERS	MULLIGRUBS	PILLIWINKS	SANCTITIES
ENDOGENOUS	GLYCOLYSIS	KILOMETRES	MUMBLENEWS	PITYRIASIS	SANDWICHES
ENDOSMOSIS	GODPARENTS	KINDLINESS	MUSKETEERS	PLIOHIPPUS	SARMENTOUS
EPICANTHUS	GOLDILOCKS	KSHATRIYAS	MYRINGITIS	POCAHONTAS	SAVAGENESS
EPIDIDYMUS	GONDOLIERS	LACCADIVES	MYSTAGOGUS	POLIANTHES	SAXICOLOUS
EPIGLOTTIS	GRASSLANDS	LANGERHANS	MYSTERIOUS	POLITENESS	SBUDDIKINS
EPIMENIDES	GRASSROOTS	LANGUOROUS	NARROWNESS	POLYANTHUS	SCAMMOZZIS
EPIMETHEUS	GRATUITOUS	LANIGEROUS	NECROPOLIS	POLYGAMOUS	SCANDALOUS
EPISTEMICS	GREEDINESS	LARYNGITIS	NECTABANUS	POLYPHEMUS	SCANTINESS
ERGONOMICS	GREGARIOUS	LASCIVIOUS	NEFANDROUS	PORRACEOUS	SCARCENESS
ERYMANTHUS	GRENADIERS	LAVISHNESS	NEWSAGENTS	PORTCULLIS	SCATHELESS
ERYSIPELAS	GREYFRIARS	LEGUMINOUS	NEWSPAPERS	PORTENTOUS	SCLERIASIS
EUCALYPTUS	GRITTINESS	LEGWARMERS	NIGHTDRESS	POSTHUMOUS	SCRIPTURES
EUPHONIOUS	GROUNDLESS	LENGTHWAYS	NIMBLENESS	PRAXITELES	SCRUPULOUS
EURYPTERUS	GRUBBINESS	LENTIGINES	NONSUCCESS	PRECARIOUS	SCULPTRESS
EVERGLADES	GRUMPINESS	LEONTIASIS	NORTHWARDS	PRECOCIOUS	SCURRILOUS
EXEMPTNESS	GUARNERIUS	LEOPARDESS	NOTORYCTES	PREDACIOUS	SEAMSTRESS
EXPOUNDERS	GUIDELINES	LIBIDINOUS	NUCLEONICS	PREPOSSESS	SECURITIES
EXTRANEOUS	GYMNASTICS	LICENTIOUS	NUMBERLESS	PRETTINESS	SEDATENESS
EYEWITNESS	HAEMANTHUS	LILYWHITES	NUTRITIOUS	PRINCIPLES	SELLINGERS
FACILITIES	HALIEUTICS	LINEAMENTS	OBJECTLESS	PRIVATEERS	SEQUACIOUS
FACTITIOUS	HANDLEBARS	LITTLENESS	OBSEQUIOUS	PROAIRESIS	SHABBINESS
FALLACIOUS	HARMONIOUS	LIVELINESS	OBSTETRICS	PROCRUSTES	SHADOWLESS
FASTIDIOUS	HEADLIGHTS	LOGARITHMS	OBTUSENESS	PRODIGIOUS	SHIFTINESS
FATALITIES	HEADPHONES	LONELINESS	ODDFELLOWS	PROFITLESS	SHODDINESS
FATHERLESS	HEARTINESS	LONGCHAMPS	ODIOUSNESS	PROMETHEUS	SHREWDNESS
FAULTINESS	HEPHAESTUS	LOQUACIOUS	OESOPHAGUS	PROMPTNESS	SHRILLNESS
FEEBLENESS	HERBACEOUS	LORDLINESS	OFTENTIMES	PROPERTIUS	SIDEBOARDS
FELICITOUS	HEREABOUTS	LOTOPHAGUS	OIREACHTAS	PROPHETESS	SINFULNESS
FIBERGLASS	HESPERIDES	LOVELINESS	OLEAGINOUS	PROPITIOUS	SINGLENESS
FIBREGLASS	HIPPARCHUS	LUGUBRIOUS	OLERACEOUS	PROPOSITUS	SLANDEROUS
FIBROSITIS	HIPPOMANES	MALAPROPOS	OMNIVOROUS	PROSPECTUS	SLEEPINESS
FICKLENESS	HISTOLYSIS	MALODOROUS	ONOMASTICS	PROSPEROUS	SLEEVELESS

SLOPPINESS	TRAITOROUS	ANALPHABET	CONVENIENT	ESCARPMENT	IRREVERENT
SMARMINESS	TRANSGRESS	ANASTIGMAT	CONVERGENT	EVANESCENT	JERRYBUILT
SMOOTHNESS	TRAVELLERS	ANIMADVERT	CONVERSANT	EVANGELIST	JIGGERMAST
SNOOTINESS	TREMENDOUS	ANTAGONIST	COQUELICOT	EXCITEMENT	JOURNALIST
SOBERSIDES	TRENDINESS	ANTECEDENT	COUNTERACT	EXORBITANT	JUGGERNAUT
SOLICITOUS	TRICKINESS	ANTEPENULT	CRANKSHAFT	EXPERIMENT	KNOCKABOUT
SONGSTRESS	TROPHONIUS	ARISTOCRAT	CUCKOOPINT	FAHRENHEIT	LANSQUENET
SORDIDNESS	TUMULTUOUS	ARMIPOTENT	DEBASEMENT	FAMISHMENT	LAUNDROMAT
SOUTHWARDS	TUTIVILLUS	ASSESSMENT	DEBATEMENT	FEARNOUGHT	LIBRETTIST
SPARSENESS	TYMPANITES	ASSIGNMENT	DECAMPMENT	FEDERALIST	LIEUTENANT
SPECTACLES	TYMPANITIS	ASSORTMENT	DECRESCENT	FLAMBOYANT	LIQUESCENT
SPECTATORS	UBIQUITOUS	ASTRINGENT	DEFACEMENT	FLAMINGANT	LIVERWURST
SPEECHLESS	ULTRONEOUS	ATTACHMENT	DEFILEMENT	FLASHPOINT	LOCULAMENT
SPEEDINESS	UNDERCLASS	ATTAINMENT	DEFRAYMENT	FLAVESCENT	LUMINARIST
SPILLIKINS	UNDERPANTS	AUTODIDACT	DELINQUENT	FLOCCULENT	MAGNIFICAT
SPIRITLESS	UNEASINESS	BAFFLEMENT	DENOUEMENT	FLOODLIGHT	MAKEWEIGHT
SPIRITUOUS	UNEVENNESS	BALBUTIENT	DEPARTMENT	FORTHRIGHT	MALCONTENT
SPRINGBOKS	UNGRACIOUS	BALLOONIST	DEPLOYMENT	FOUDROYANT	MALEVOLENT
SPRINGHAAS	UNIGENITUS	BANISHMENT	DEPORTMENT	FRAUDULENT	MANAGEMENT
SPRINGLESS	UNIQUENESS	BASSOONIST	DEPRESSANT	FREMESCENT	MANICURIST
SPRUCENESS	UNRULINESS	BATTLEMENT	DERAILMENT	FRONTCOURT	MANSERVANT
STANISLAUS	UNTIDINESS	BENEFICENT	DESCENDANT	FRUTESCENT	MANUSCRIPT
STATISTICS	UPPERCLASS	BENEVOLENT	DESPONDENT	FULFILMENT	MARCANTANT
STEADINESS	UPROARIOUS	BIOCHEMIST	DETACHMENT	GESUNDHEIT	MARCESCENT
STEELINESS	UROPOIESIS	BIRTHRIGHT	DETAINMENT	GOVERNMENT	MASTERWORT
STEELWORKS	USEFULNESS	BLACKHEART	DEVASTAVIT	GRAPEFRUIT	MAUPASSANT
STERTEROUS	VALENTINES	BLACKSHIRT	DEVOTEMENT	GRAVEOLENT	MAXIMALIST
STERTOROUS	VASCULITIS	BLUEBONNET	DIASKEUAST	GREENHEART	MEDICAMENT
STEWARDESS	VEGETABLES	BLUETHROAT	DICYNODONT	GROUNDBAIT	MICROLIGHT
STICKINESS	VERSAILLES	BOLLANDIST	DISAPPOINT	HANDICRAFT	MILITARIST
STINGINESS	VIBRATIONS	BOLSHEVIST	DISCOMFORT	HARASSMENT	MINIMALIST
STOCKINESS	VICTORIOUS	BREADFRUIT	DISCONCERT	HARTEBEEST	MINIMARKET
STRABISMUS	VIGILANTES	BROADSHEET	DISCONNECT	HELLESPONT	MISCONDUCT
STRATIOTES	VILLAINOUS	BUREAUCRAT	DISCONTENT	HEXAVALENT	MISOGYNIST
STRICTNESS	VIVIPAROUS	CANTONMENT	DISCORDANT	HIEROPHANT	MIZZENMAST
STRIDEWAYS	VOCIFEROUS	CAPITALIST	DISCREPANT	HOUSECRAFT	MONARCHIST
STUFFINESS	VOLUMINOUS	CARTOONIST	DISENCHANT	HOVERCRAFT	MONETARIST
STUPENDOUS	VOLUPTUOUS	CATAPHRACT	DISINHERIT	HUMIDISTAT	MONOVALENT
STURDINESS	VORAGINOUS	CHAMBERPOT	DISRESPECT	ICONOCLAST	MONTRACHET
STYLISTICS	WANDERINGS	CHAUVINIST	DISSILIENT	IMPAIRMENT	MONTSERRAT
SUBSPECIES	WASSERMANS	CHECKPOINT	DISSOLVENT	IMPEDIMENT	MOUDIEWART
SUBTROPICS	WATERCRESS	CHIMNEYPOT	DISTRAUGHT	IMPENITENT	MUNIFICENT
SUDDENNESS	WATERWINGS	CHREMATIST	DIURNALIST	INCITEMENT	NARROWBOAT
SULPHUROUS	WATERWORKS	CIRCUMVENT	DOVERCOURT	INCOHERENT	NATURALIST
SULTRINESS	WEAPONLESS	CLASSICIST	DOWNMARKET	INCONSTANT	NEMATOCYST
SUNGLASSES	WEIGHTLESS	CLOUDBURST	DRAGONROOT	INCRESCENT	NETHERMOST
SUPPLENESS	WHEEZINESS	CNIDOBLAST	EBOULEMENT	INDICTMENT	NIGHTLIGHT
SUSPENDERS	WICKEDNESS	COADJUTANT	EFFACEMENT	INDISCREET	NIGHTSHIRT
SUSPICIOUS	WILDERNESS	COEXISTENT	EMBANKMENT	INDISTINCT	NIGRESCENT
SYNAERESIS	WORLDCLASS	COINCIDENT	EMBODIMENT	INDITEMENT	NOMINALIST
SYNEIDESIS	WORTHINESS	COMMANDANT	EMBONPOINT	INDUCEMENT	NONCHALANT
SYNONYMOUS	XIPHOPAGUS	COMMITMENT	EMPLOYMENT	INESCULENT	NONPAYMENT
SYNOSTOSIS	YELLOWLEGS	COMPATRIOT	ENCAMPMENT	INFEFTMENT	NONVIOLENT
SYNTERESIS	YOURSELVES	COMPLACENT	ENCASEMENT	INFREQUENT	NORMOBLAST
SYNTHRONUS	ZOOTHAPSIS	COMPLEMENT	ENDEARMENT	INGREDIENT	NOUAKCHOTT
TENDERNESS	ABITURIENT	COMPLIMENT	ENGAGEMENT	INHABITANT	NYMPHOLEPT
TERTIARIES	ABONNEMENT	CONCORDANT	ENGOUEMENT	INSOUCIANT	OMNIPOTENT
TESTACEOUS	ABRIDGMENT	CONCURRENT	ENLACEMENT	INSTALMENT	OMNISCIENT
THALESTRIS	ACCOUNTANT	CONFORMIST	ENLÈVEMENT	INSTRUMENT	OPALESCENT
THEMSELVES	ACTIVITIST	CONSEQUENT	ENLISTMENT	INTEGUMENT	OSTEOBLAST
THEOCRITUS	ADDITAMENT	CONSISTENT	ENRICHMENT	INTELIGENT	OUTPATIENT
THROMBOSIS	ADJUSTMENT	CONSTRAINT	ENROLLMENT	INTENDMENT	OVERBOUGHT
THUCYDIDES	ADOLESCENT	CONSULTANT	ENTHUSIAST	INTERNMENT	OVERTHWART
THUMBIKINS	ADULTERANT	CONTESTANT	ENTICEMENT	INTOLERANT	OVERWEIGHT
THUNDEROUS	AGRONOMIST	CONTINGENT	ENTOMBMENT	INTOXICANT	PALIMPSEST
TIMELINESS	AIRFREIGHT	CONTINUANT	EPAULEMENT	INTROSPECT	PALUDAMENT
TOILETRIES	ALLUREMENT	CONTRADICT	EQUIVALENT	INVESTMENT	PANSOPHIST
TOUCHINESS	AMBIVALENT	CONTRAHENT	ERUBESCENT	IRIDESCENT	PARLIAMENT
TRADITIONS	ANABAPTIST	CONTROVERT	ESCAPEMENT	IRRELEVANT	PENSIONNAT

PEPPERMINT	SHELLYCOAT	VANDERBILT	AUTOPLASTY	CREATIVITY	FAITHFULLY
PEPPERWORT	SHIPWRIGHT	VICEGERENT	AXINOMANCY	CREDITABLY	FALDISTORY
PERCIPIENT	SIDEROSTAT	VICEREGENT	BALNEOLOGY	CRIMINALLY	FAMILIARLY
PERFICIENT	SIGNIFICAT	VIROLOGIST	BANKRUPTCY	CRITICALLY	FAVOURABLY
PERMAFROST	SINARCHIST	VOCABULIST	BESTIALITY	CYSTOSCOPY	FEARLESSLY
PERSISTENT	SINARQUIST	WANDERLUST	BIANNUALLY	DEBAUCHERY	FEMININITY
PHANTASIST	SOLIVAGANT	WATERFRONT	BIENNIALLY	DECISIVELY	FEVERISHLY
PHARMACIST	SOMERSAULT	WATERSPOUT	BLACKBERRY	DEFAMATORY	FIENDISHLY
PHYSIOCRAT	SOUBRIQUET	WATERTIGHT	BLACKBULLY	DEFICIENCY	FLAGRANTLY
PICKPOCKET	SPACECRAFT	WHITEHEART	BLISSFULLY	DEFINITELY	FLEETINGLY
PLAGIARIST	SPARTACIST	WHOLEWHEAT	BLOOMSBURY	DEGENERACY	FLIPPANTLY
PLANOBLAST	SPECIALIST	WILDEBEEST	BUFFOONERY	DEJECTEDLY	FORCEFULLY
PLAYWRIGHT	SPIDERWORT	WITCHCRAFT	CACOGRAPHY	DELICATELY	FRATERNITY
PLUPERFECT	SPINESCENT	WONDERMENT	CAERPHILLY	DELTIOLOGY	FRENZIEDLY
POLYCHREST	SPOILSPORT	WOOLLYBUTT	CANTERBURY	DEMOGRAPHY	FREQUENTLY
POLYGAMIST	STAGECRAFT	YELLOWROOT	CAPABILITY	DEMONOLOGY	FRITILLARY
POLYVALENT	STANDPOINT	ZEUGLODONT	CAPERNOITY	DEPENDENCY	FRUITFULLY
PONTEFRACT	STATECRAFT	CLEMENCEAU	CAPITULARY	DEPILATORY	FUDDYDUDDY
PORTIONIST	STONYHURST	COUSCOUSOU	CAPNOMANCY	DEPLORABLY	GALSWORTHY
POSITIVIST	STOREFRONT	FRICANDEAU	CARDIOLOGY	DEPOSITARY	GASTRONOMY
POSTSCRIPT	STRATEGIST	CONTRAFLOW	CARELESSLY	DEPOSITORY	GENERALITY
PRAGMATIST	STRATOCRAT	FORESHADOW	CARPHOLOGY	DEROGATORY	GENEROSITY
PREEMINENT	STRATOCYST	GOODFELLOW	CARTOMANCY	DESERVEDLY	GENEROUSLY
PREFERMENT	STREPITANT	GRASSWIDOW	CATCHPENNY	DIAGONALLY	GLORIOUSLY
PREPAYMENT	STRINGHALT	LONGFELLOW	CAUTIONARY	DICTIONARY	GOOSEBERRY
PRIZEFIGHT	SUAVEOLENT	MIDDLEBROW	CAUTIOUSLY	DIFFICULTY	GORGEOUSLY
PROCUMBENT	SUBCOMPACT	OVERSHADOW	CHALCEDONY	DILIGENTLY	GOVERNESSY
PROFICIENT	SUBMEDIANT	PLAYFELLOW	CHAPLAINCY	DISABILITY	GRACEFULLY
PROPELLANT	SUBSEQUENT	THUMBSCREW	CHARDONNAY	DISCREETLY	GRACIOUSLY
PROPELLENT	SUBSISTENT	WAPENSCHAW	CHARITABLY	DISHARMONY	GRANDDADDY
PROSILIENT	SUFFICIENT	WAPINSCHAW	CHEERFULLY	DISHONESTY	GRAPHOLOGY
PROTESTANT	SUFFRAGIST	WAPPENSHAW	CHEIRONOMY	DISLOYALTY	GRATEFULLY
PUBERULENT	SUPERGIANT	WHILLYWHAW	CHEMICALLY	DISORDERLY	GRATILLITY
PUNISHMENT	SUPPLEMENT	ANTICLIMAX	CHEMONASTY	DISPENSARY	GUTTURALLY
PURSUIVANT	SUPPLICANT	CHATTERBOX	CHILDISHLY	DISQUALIFY	GYMNOSOPHY
PUTRESCENT	SURREALIST	CHICKENPOX	CHINABERRY	DISTILLERY	GYNECOLOGY
PUZZLEMENT	SWEATSHIRT	CIRCUMFLEX	CHIROMANCY	DISTINCTLY	HABITUALLY
REAMINGBIT	SWEETHEART	GENERATRIX	CHRONOLOGY	DOMICILARY	HALFHOURLY
REARMAMENT	TAMPERFOOT	SCOMBRESOX	CHURLISHLY	DOSTOEVSKY	HALFYEARLY
RECIDIVIST	TANGLEFOOT	SEPARATRIX	CLEARSTORY	DOUBTFULLY	HANDSOMELY
REFINEMENT	TANTAMOUNT	SQUEEZEBOX	CLERESTORY	DREADFULLY	HANKYPANKY
REFRINGENT	TAPOTEMENT	THUNDERBOX	CLEROMANCY	DURABILITY	HECTICALLY
REQUIESCAT	TAXONOMIST	UNORTHODOX	CLINICALLY	EFFEMINACY	HEEDLESSLY
RESENTMENT	TECHNOCRAT	ABNORMALLY	CLOUDBERRY	EFFICIENCY	HELPLESSLY
RESPONDENT	TENDERFOOT	ABOMINABLY	COCKABULLY	EFFRONTERY	HEREDITARY
RESTAURANT	THEOLOGIST	ABSOLUTELY	COCKERNONY	EFFUSIVELY	HEROICALLY
RETIREMENT	THEREANENT	ABUNDANTLY	COHERENTLY	ELASTICITY	HESITANTLY
RETROSPECT	THERMOSTAT	ACCURATELY	COLOSSALLY	ELDERBERRY	HETERODOXY
REVIVALIST	THIMBLEWIT	ACCUSINGLY	COMMENTARY	ELEMENTARY	HETEROGAMY
RHAPSODIST	THROUGHOUT	ACROMEGALY	COMMISSARY	ELOQUENTLY	HIEROMANCY
RINDERPEST	THROUGHPUT	ADEQUATELY	COMMONALTY	EMBROIDERY	HIEROSCOPY
ROUNDABOUT	TOPOLOGIST	ADMIRINGLY	COMMUNALLY	EMBRYOLOGY	HOLOGRAPHY
ROUSEABOUT	TORCHLIGHT	ADMITTEDLY	COMPLETELY	EMISSIVITY	HOMEOPATHY
ROUSTABOUT	TORPESCENT	AFFABILITY	COMPLEXITY	ENORMOUSLY	HONOURABLY
SACROSANCT	TOURNAMENT	ALDERMANLY	COMPLICITY	ENTOMOLOGY	HOOTANANNY
SAPPERMENT	TOURNIQUET	ALIMENTARY	COMPULSORY	EQUANIMITY	HOOTENANNY
SAUERKRAUT	TRANSCRIPT	ALKALINITY	CONCHOLOGY	ESPECIALLY	HOPELESSLY
SCARCEMENT	TRANSPLANT	ALLYCHOLLY	CONCINNITY	EVENTUALLY	HOSPITABLY
SCATURIENT	TRECENTIST	AMBULATORY	CONFORMITY	EVITERNITY	HUMOROUSLY
SCHWARZLOT	TREKSCHUIT	AMIABILITY	CONFUSEDLY	EXCELLENCY	HYPSOMETRY
SCOOTERIST	TRIUMPHANT	APOTHECARY	CONSISTORY	EXOBIOLOGY	IGNORANTLY
SECONDBEST	TROMBONIST	APPARENTLY	CONSPIRACY	EXOTICALLY	ILLEGALITY
SECONDMENT	TYPESCRIPT	AREOGRAPHY	CONSTANTLY	EXPECTANCY	ILLITERACY
SEPARATIST	UNDERBURNT	ARISTOLOGY	CONTIGUITY	EXPEDIENCY	IMBECILITY
SEPTUAGINT	UNDERCRAFT	ARROGANTLY	CONTINUITY	EXPLICITLY	IMMACULACY
SETTERWORT	UNDERCROFT	ASCENDANCY	CONTRARILY	EXPOSITORY	IMMATURITY
SETTLEMENT	UNDERSHIRT	ASCENDENCY	CONVERSELY	EXPRESSWAY	IMMOBILITY
SEXOLOGIST	UNDERSKIRT	AUDIBILITY	CORALBERRY	EXTERNALLY	IMMORALITY
	UNPLEASANT	AUTECOLOGY	CORDIALITY	FABULOUSLY	IMMUNOLOGY

IMPECCABLY	LEGITIMACY	OSCULATORY	PRESENTDAY	SEPARATELY	THROUGHWAY
IMPLACABLY	LIBERALITY	OSTENSIBLY	PRESIDENCY	SHAMEFULLY	TIMBROLOGY
IMPLICITLY	LISTLESSLY	OSTEOPATHY	PRESUMABLY	SHEEPISHLY	TIRELESSLY
IMPOLITELY	LOGANBERRY	OVERSUPPLY	PREVENANCY	SHOCKINGLY	TOLERANTLY
IMPOSSIBLY	LORDOLATRY	PAINLESSLY	PREVIOUSLY	SHRIEVALTY	TOMFOOLERY
IMPOTENTLY	LUMINOSITY	PALYNOLOGY	PROCLIVITY	SIMILARITY	TOPICALITY
IMPROBABLY	LUMPECTOMY	PARDONABLY	PRODIGALLY	SIMPLICITY	TOPOGRAPHY
IMPROPERLY	MAGISTRACY	PARTIALITY	PROFITABLY	SINGULARLY	TOPSYTURVY
IMPUDENTLY	MALACOLOGY	PASIGRAPHY	PROFLIGACY	SKILLFULLY	TORTUOUSLY
INACCURACY	MALIGNANCY	PASSAGEWAY	PROFOUNDLY	SLATTERNLY	TOXICOLOGY
INACTIVITY	MALMESBURY	PATAVINITY	PROFUNDITY	SLUGGISHLY	TRAGICALLY
INADEQUACY	MANIFESTLY	PATERNALLY	PROMISSORY	SOLIDARITY	TRAJECTORY
INCAPACITY	MARGINALLY	PATIBULARY	PROMONTORY	SOLUBILITY	TRANQUILLY
INCENDIARY	MARIOLATRY	PATRIARCHY	PROPENSITY	SOOTHINGLY	TRANSITORY
INCISIVELY	MASTECTOMY	PEACEFULLY	PROSPERITY	SPECIALITY	TRICHOLOGY
INCIVILITY	MATERIALLY	PECULIARLY	PROTERVITY	SPECIOUSLY	TRIPLICITY
INCREDIBLY	MATERNALLY	PEREMPTORY	PSEPHOLOGY	SPELEOLOGY	TRIPUDIARY
INCUMBENCY	MATRIARCHY	PERILOUSLY	PSYCHIATRY	SPIRITEDLY	TRIVIALITY
INDECENTLY	MEDIOCRITY	PERMANENCY	PSYCHOLOGY	SPITEFULLY	TRUSTFULLY
INDELICACY	MELANCHOLY	PERNICKETY	PUNCTUALLY	SPLENDIDLY	TRUTHFULLY
INDIRECTLY	MENACINGLY	PERPETUITY	PYROGRAPHY	SPODOMANCY	TYPOGRAPHY
INEFFICACY	MERCIFULLY	PERPLEXITY	QUAESTUARY	SPORTINGLY	ULTIMATELY
INEQUALITY	METALLURGY	PERSONALLY	QUATERNARY	SPOTLESSLY	UNBEARABLY
INEVITABLY	MILLIHENRY	PERVERSELY	QUEENSBURY	SPREAGHERY	UNCOMMONLY
INFALLIBLY	MINERALOGY	PERVERSITY	RATIONALLY	SPURIOUSLY	UNCTUOUSLY
INFERNALLY	MISCELLANY	PETULANTLY	RAVENOUSLY	STATIONARY	UNDERSTUDY
INFIDELITY	MISSIONARY	PHILLUMENY	REASONABLY	STATIONERY	UNFRIENDLY
INFINITELY	MISTAKENLY	PHILOSOPHY	RECKLESSLY	STATOCRACY	UNIFORMITY
INFLEXIBLY	MODERATELY	PHLEBOTOMY	REDUNDANCY	STEALTHILY	UNIVERSITY
INFORMALLY	MONTGOMERY	PHOTONASTY	REFRACTORY	STEREOTOMY	UNMANNERLY
INHERENTLY	MORPHOLOGY	PHRENOLOGY	REGULARITY	STEREOTYPY	UPHOLSTERY
INHIBITORY	MOUCHARABY	PHYLACTERY	RELATIVELY	STRABOTOMY	VARICOSITY
INHUMANITY	MOURNFULLY	PHYSICALLY	RELATIVITY	STRATHSPEY	VEHEMENTLY
INNOCENTLY	MULIEBRITY	PHYSIOLOGY	REMARKABLY	STRAVINSKY	VERTICALLY
INSANITARY	MUSICOLOGY	PICCADILLY	REPEATEDLY	STRAWBERRY	VETERINARY
INSATIABLY	MUSSORGSKY	PICCANINNY	REPORTEDLY	STRIDENTLY	VIGOROUSLY
INSECURELY	MUTABILITY	PINCHPENNY	REPOSITORY	STRIKINGLY	VIRTUOSITY
INSECURITY	MUTINOUSLY	PLASTICITY	RESIGNEDLY	STRINGENCY	VIRTUOUSLY
INSIPIDITY	NARCOLEPSY	PLEASANTLY	RESOLUTELY	STUBBORNLY	VIRULENTLY
INSOLENTLY	NATIONALLY	PLEASANTRY	RESTLESSLY	STUDIOUSLY	VISIBILITY
INSOLVENCY	NECROMANCY	PLEROPHORY	REVERENTLY	SUBSIDIARY	VOCABULARY
INSULARITY	NEGATIVELY	PLIABILITY	RIGHTFULLY	SUBTENANCY	VOLATILITY
INSURGENCY	NEIGHBORLY	PLUTOCRACY	RIGOROUSLY	SUCCINCTLY	VOLUBILITY
INTERMARRY	NEUTRALITY	POETASTERY	ROADWORTHY	SUPPOSEDLY	VOLUPTUARY
INTERNALLY	NEWSWORTHY	POETICALLY	ROCKABILLY	SURGICALLY	WASTEFULLY
INTIMATELY	NOTABILITY	POGONOTOMY	ROCKSTEADY	SUZERAINTY	WATCHFULLY
INVALIDITY	NOTEWORTHY	POIGNANTLY	ROWDYDOWDY	SWIMMINGLY	WILLYWILLY
INVARIABLY	NOTICEABLY	PONEROLOGY	RUTHLESSLY	TACTICALLY	WISHYWASHY
IRONICALLY	NOTIONALLY	POPULARITY	SANGUINARY	TACTLESSLY	WRETCHEDLY
JOCULARITY	OBEDIENTLY	PORNOCRACY	SCOFFINGLY	TASTEFULLY	WRONGFULLY
JUBILANTLY	OBLIGATORY	POSITIVELY	SCORNFULLY	TECHNOLOGY	YOUNGBERRY
JUDICIALLY	OBLIGINGLY	POSTLIMINY	SCREENPLAY	TEENYWEENY	ZOOTHERAPY
JUSTICIARY	OCHLOCRACY	PREBENDARY	SCURRILITY	TELEGRAPHY	HAKENKREUZ
KINCHINLAY	ODONTOLOGY	PRECURSORY	SEASONABLY	TERMINALLY	RAZZMATAZZ
LABORATORY	OFFICIALLY	PREFERABLY	SEDULOUSLY	THANKFULLY	
LACKADAISY	OPOTHERAPY	PREHISTORY	SEISMOLOGY	THIXOTROPY	
LAMENTABLY	ORDINARILY	PREPENSELY	SENSUALITY	THOROUGHLY	
LEGIBILITY	ORIGINALLY	PRESBYTERY	SENSUOUSLY	THREEPENNY	

11:1

ABANDONMENT	AFFLIICTION	ANGELOLATRY	ARGENTINIAN	BATHYSPHERE	BRILLIANTLY
ABBREVIATED	AFGHANISTAN	ANISOCERCAL	ARISTOCRACY	BATTLEDRESS	BRISTLECONE
ABECEDARIAN	AFTERSCHOOL	ANNABERGITE	ARQUEBUSIER	BATTLEFIELD	BRITTLENESS
ABIOGENESIS	AGGLOMERATE	ANNIVERSARY	ARRANGEMENT	BATTLEFRONT	BROADCASTER
ABIOGENETIC	AGGLUTINANT	ANONYMOUSLY	ARRHENOTOKY	BATTLEMENTS	BROADMINDED
ABLACTATION	AGGLUTINATE	ANSWERPHONE	ARRIVEDERCI	BEACHCOMBER	BROBDINGNAG
ABNORMALITY	AGGRAVATING	ANTECEDENCE	ARTHRAPODAL	BEASTLINESS	BROTHERHOOD
ABOMINATION	AGGRAVATION	ANTECHAMBER	ARTHRODESIS	BEAUMONTAGE	BRUCELLOSIS
ABORTIONIST	AGGREGATION	ANTEPENDIUM	ARTHROSPORE	BEAUTIFULLY	BULLFIGHTER
ABRACADABRA	AGNOSTICISM	ANTHESTERIA	ARTICULATED	BEHAVIOURAL	BUMBERSHOOT
ABRIDGEMENT	AGONOTHETES	ANTHOCYANIN	ARTILLERIST	BELEAGUERED	BUPRESTIDAE
ABSENTEEISM	AGORAPHOBIA	ANTHOLOGIZE	ARTIODACTYL	BELLEROPHON	BUREAUCRACY
ABSORPTANCE	AGRICULTURE	ANTHONOMOUS	ASCLEPIADES	BELLETTRIST	BURGOMASTER
ABSTRACTION	AGROSTOLOGY	ANTHRACOSIS	ASPERGILLUM	BELLIGERENT	BUSHWHACKER
ACADEMICIAN	AGUARDIENTE	ANTIBURGHER	ASPERGILLUS	BELLYTIMBER	BUSINESSMAN
ACADEMICISM	AIGUILLETTE	ANTICYCLONE	ASPERSORIUM	BELORUSSIAN	BUTTONQUAIL
ACATALECTIC	AILUROPHILE	ANTINEUTRON	ASPHETERISM	BENEDICTINE	CABBALISTIC
ACCELERATOR	AIRCRAFTMAN	ANTIPHONARY	ASSASSINATE	BENEDICTION	CACOGASTRIC
ACCESSORIES	AIRSICKNESS	ANTIPHRASIS	ASSEMBLYMAN	BENEFICIARY	CACOPHONOUS
ACCIPITRINE	ALBIGENSIAN	ANTIPYRETIC	ASSIDUOUSLY	BENEFICIATE	CALCEOLARIA
ACCLAMATION	ALBUGINEOUS	ANTIQUARIAN	ASSIGNATION	BENEVOLENCE	CALCULATING
ACCLIMATION	ALBUMINURIA	ANTIRRHINUM	ASSIMILATED	BEREAVEMENT	CALCULATION
ACCLIMATISE	ALCYONARIAN	ANTISTHENES	ASSOCIATION	BERGSCHRUND	CALEFACIENT
ACCLIMATIZE	ALEXANDRINE	ANTISTROPHE	ASSYTHEMENT	BESIEGEMENT	CALENDERING
ACCOMMODATE	ALEXANDRITE	ANTONOMASIA	ASTIGMATISM	BESSARABIAN	CALIBRATION
ACCOMPANIST	ALIFANFARON	APATOSAURUS	ASTONISHING	BESTSELLING	CALIFORNIUM
ACCORDINGLY	ALLEGORICAL	APHANIPTERA	ASTRINGENCY	BEWILDERING	CALLANETICS
ACCOUNTABLE	ALLELOMORPH	APHRODISIAC	ATHARVAVEDA	BIBLIOPHILE	CALLIGRAPHY
ACCOUNTANCY	ALLEVIATION	APLANOSPORE	ATHERINIDAE	BICARBONATE	CALLIPYGEAN
ACCRESCENCE	ALPHABETIZE	APOCALYPTIC	ATHERMANOUS	BICENTENARY	CALLISTEMON
ACCULTURATE	ALTERCATION	APODYTERIUM	ATMOSPHERIC	BIELORUSSIA	CALLITRICHE
ACCUMULATOR	ALTERNATELY	APOLLINARIS	ATRABILIOUS	BIFURCATION	CALLOUSNESS
ACHIEVEMENT	ALTERNATING	APOLLONICON	ATROCIOUSLY	BILIOUSNESS	CAMALDOLITE
ACINACIFORM	ALTERNATION	APOMORPHINE	ATTENTIVELY	BILLIONAIRE	CAMARADERIE
ACKNOWLEDGE	ALTERNATIVE	APONEUROSIS	ATTENUATION	BIMILLENARY	CAMERAWOMAN
ACOLOUTHITE	AMBIVALENCE	APOPHYLLITE	ATTESTATION	BIOCHEMICAL	CAMEROONIAN
ACQUIESCENT	AMELANCHIER	APOSIOPESIS	ATTRIBUTION	BIRDWATCHER	CAMOUFLAGED
ACQUISITION	AMERCIAMENT	APOSTROPHUS	ATTRIBUTIVE	BITTERSWEET	CAMPANOLOGY
ACQUISITIVE	AMERICANISM	APPALLINGLY	AUDACIOUSLY	BLACKFELLOW	CAMPESTRIAN
ACRIFLAVINE	AMINOBUTENE	APPARATCHIK	AUDIOVISUAL	BLACKMAILER	CAMPHORATED
ACRIMONIOUS	AMOBARBITAL	APPEARANCES	AUGUSTINIAN	BLADDERWORT	CANDESCENCE
ACROCENTRIC	AMONTILLADO	APPEASEMENT	AURIGNACIAN	BLAMEWORTHY	CANDIDATURE
ACTUALITIES	AMPHETAMINE	APPELLATION	AUXANOMETER	BLANKURSINE	CANDLELIGHT
ACUPUNCTURE	AMPHIBOLOGY	APPELLATIVE	AVERRUNCATE	BLASPHEMOUS	CANDLESTICK
ADIAPHORIST	AMPHISBAENA	APPLERINGIE	AVOIRDUPOIS	BLESSEDNESS	CANNIBALISM
ADJOURNMENT	AMPHISBOENA	APPLICATION	AWKWARDNESS	BLOCKBUSTER	CANNIBALIZE
ADJUDICATOR	AMPLEXICAUL	APPOINTMENT	AXEROPHTHOL	BLOODSPORTS	CAPACITANCE
ADOLESCENCE	AMYLOPECTIN	APPRECIABLE	AZOTOBACTER	BLOODSTREAM	CAPACITATOR
ADOPTIANISM	ANACHRONISM	APPRECIABLY	BACCHANALIA	BLOODSUCKER	CAPERNOITED
ADOPTIONISM	ANACOLUTHIA	APPRENTICED	BACKBENCHER	BLUNDERBORE	CAPERNOITIE
ADULLAMITES	ANACREONTIC	APPROACHING	BACKFIELDER	BODHISATTVA	CAPRICCIOSO
ADULTERATED	ANADIPLOSIS	APPROBATION	BACKPACKING	BOMBARDMENT	CAPTIVATING
ADUMBRATION	ANAESTHESIA	APPROPRIATE	BACKSLIDING	BOOKBINDING	CAPTIVATION
ADVANCEMENT	ANAESTHETIC	APPROVINGLY	BADDELEYITE	BOOKKEEPING	CARABINIERE
ADVENTURESS	ANAGNORISIS	APPROXIMATE	BADTEMPERED	BOOKSELLERS	CARAVANNING
ADVENTUROUS	ANAPHYLAXIS	APPURTENANT	BALISTRARIA	BORBORYGMUS	CARBORUNDUM
ADVERBIALLY	ANAPLEROSIS	ARBITRAGEUR	BALLBEARING	BOTANOMANCY	CARBURETTOR
ADVERTISING	ANAPLEROTIC	ARBITRAMENT	BANDEIRANTE	BOURGEOISIE	CARDIOGRAPH
AERODYNAMIC	ANASTOMOSIS	ARBITRARILY	BANGLADESHI	BOUTONNIERE	CARDOPHAGUS
AERONAUTICS	ANAXIMANDER	ARBITRATION	BANNOCKBURN	BOYSENBERRY	CAREFULNESS
AESCULAPIAN	ANDROGENOUS	ARCHAEOLOGY	BARBASTELLE	BRAGGADOCIO	CARMINATIVE
AESCULAPIUS	ANDROGYNOUS	ARCHEGONIAL	BARBITURATE	BRANDENBURG	CARNAPTIOUS
AFFECTATION	ANENCEPHALY	ARCHEGONIUM	BARNSTORMER	BRAZZAVILLE	CARNIVOROUS
AFFILIATION	ANESTHETIST	ARCHENTERON	BARTHOLOMEW	BREADCRUMBS	CAROLINGIAN
AFFIRMATION	ANESTHETIZE	ARCHILOCHUS	BARYCENTRIC	BREADWINNER	CARRIAGEWAY
AFFIRMATIVE	ANFRACTUOUS	ARGATHELIAN	BASKERVILLE	BREASTPLATE	CARSICKNESS
			BASHFULNESS	BREATHALYSE	CARTOGRAPHY

CASSITERITE	CHRISTENING	COMMANDMENT	CONSCIOUSLY	COPPERPLATE	CYLINDRICAL
CASTELLATED	CHRISTMASSY	COMMEMORATE	CONSECUTIVE	COPROPHAGAN	CYMOPHANOUS
CATACAUSTIC	CHRISTOPHER	COMMENDABLE	CONSEQUENCE	COPROSTEROL	CYTOGENESIS
CATACHRESIS	CHROMOPLAST	COMMENDABLY	CONSERVANCY	CORDWAINERS	DACTYLOGRAM
CATACLYSMIC	CHRONICALLY	COMMENTATOR	CONSIDERATE	CORINTHIANS	DANGEROUSLY
CATADROMOUS	CHRONOMETER	COMMINATION	CONSIDERING	CORNERSTONE	DARDANELLES
CATALLACTIC	CHRYSAROBIN	COMMISERATE	CONSIGNMENT	CORPORATION	DEBILITATED
CATASTROPHE	CHRYSOPRASE	COMMONPLACE	CONSILIENCE	CORRECTNESS	DECAPITATED
CATCHPHRASE	CILOFIBRATE	COMMONSENSE	CONSISTENCE	CORRELATION	DECARBONATE
CATEGORICAL	CINQUECENTO	COMMUNALISM	CONSISTENCY	CORROBORATE	DECARBONIZE
CATERPILLAR	CIRCULARIZE	COMMUNICANT	CONSOLATION	CORRUGATION	DECEITFULLY
CATHOLICISM	CIRCULATING	COMMUNICATE	CONSOLIDATE	CORRUPTIBLE	DECEPTIVELY
CAULIFLOWER	CIRCULATION	COMMUTATION	CONSPICUOUS	COTTONMOUTH	DECLAMATION
CAUSTICALLY	CIRCULATORY	COMPARATIVE	CONSPIRATOR	COULOMMIERS	DECLAMATORY
CEASELESSLY	CIRCUMCISER	COMPARTMENT	CONSTANTINE	COUNSELLING	DECLARATION
CELEBRATION	CIRCUMFLECT	COMPENDIOUS	CONSTELLATE	COUNTENANCE	DECLARATIVE
CENTENARIAN	CIRCUMSPECT	COMPETENTLY	CONSTERNATE	COUNTERFEIT	DECONSTRUCT
CENTERPIECE	CIRRHIPEDEA	COMPETITION	CONSTIPATED	COUNTERFOIL	DECORATIONS
CENTREBOARD	CIRRHIPEDIA	COMPETITIVE	CONSTITUENT	COUNTERFORT	DECORTICATE
CENTREPIECE	CITIZENSHIP	COMPILATION	CONSTRAINED	COUNTERGLOW	DECREPITATE
CENTRIFUGAL	CITLALEPETL	COMPILEMENT	CONSTRICTED	COUNTERHAND	DECREPITUDE
CENTRIPETAL	CITRONELLAL	COMPLACENCY	CONSTRICTOR	COUNTERMAND	DEERSTALKER
CENTUMVIRUS	CLADOSPORUM	COMPLAISANT	CONSTRUCTOR	COUNTERPANE	DEFENCELESS
CENTURIATOR	CLAIRSCHACH	COMPLICATED	CONSTUPRATE	COUNTERPART	DEFENSELESS
CERARGYRITE	CLAIRVOYANT	COMPLIMENTS	CONSULTANCY	COUNTERSIGN	DEFENSIVELY
CEREBRATION	CLANDESTINE	COMPOSITION	CONSUMABLES	COUNTERSINK	DEFERENTIAL
CEREMONIOUS	CLANJAMFRAY	COMPOTATION	CONSUMERISM	COUNTRIFIED	DEFOLIATION
CERTIFIABLE	CLAPPERCLAW	COMPRIMARIO	CONSUMPTION	COUNTRYSIDE	DEFORMATION
CERTIFICATE	CLARENCIEUX	COMPTROLLER	CONSUMPTIVE	COURTEOUSLY	DEGLUTINATE
CESAREWITCH	CLEANLINESS	COMPUNCTION	CONTAINMENT	COURTLINESS	DEGLUTITION
CHAIRPERSON	CLEANSHAVEN	COMPUTATION	CONTAMINANT	COXWAINLESS	DEGRADATION
CHALLENGING	CLIFFHANGER	COMPUTERIZE	CONTAMINATE	CRACKERJACK	DEGRINGOLER
CHAMBERLAIN	CLIMACTERIC	COMRADESHIP	CONTEMPLANT	CRACKHALTER	DEHORTATIVE
CHAMBERMAID	CLIMATOLOGY	COMSTOCKERY	CONTEMPLATE	CRACOVIENNE	DEHYDRATION
CHANCELLERY	CLINOCHLORE	CONCEALMENT	CONTENEMENT	CRATERELLUS	DEIFICATION
CHANTARELLE	CLIOMETRICS	CONCEIVABLE	CONTENTEDLY	CREDENTIALS	DELECTATION
CHANTERELLE	COACHFELLOW	CONCEIVABLY	CONTENTIOUS	CREDIBILITY	DELETERIOUS
CHANTICLEER	COAGULATION	CONCENTRATE	CONTENTMENT	CREDULOUSLY	DELICIOUSLY
CHARACINOID	COALESCENCE	CONCEPTICLE	CONTINENTAL	CRÉMAILLÈRE	DELICTATION
CHARGEPAYER	COBBLESTONE	CONCILIATOR	CONTINGENCE	CREMATORIUM	DELINEATION
CHARISMATIC	COCKLESHELL	CONCISENESS	CONTINGENCY	CRENELLATED	DELINQUENCY
CHARLEMAGNE	COEFFICIENT	CONCOMITANT	CONTINUALLY	CREPITATION	DELITESCENT
CHAULMOOGRA	COENOBITISM	CONCORDANCE	CONTINUANCE	CREPUSCULAR	DELIVERANCE
CHAULMOUGRA	COEXISTENCE	CONCURRENCE	CONTRACTION	CRESCENTADE	DEMAGOGUERY
CHEERLEADER	COGNOSCENTE	CONDITIONAL	CONTRACTUAL	CRESTFALLEN	DEMARCATION
CHEESECLOTH	COGNOSCENTI	CONDITIONER	CONTRAPTION	CRIMINOLOGY	DEMIBASTION
CHEIROGNOMY	COHORTATIVE	CONDOLENCES	CONTRASTING	CRITHOMANCY	DEMOGRAPHIC
CHIAROSCURO	COINCIDENCE	CONDOMINIUM	CONTRAYERVA	CRITICASTER	DEMONOMANIA
CHIASTOLITE	COLDBLOODED	CONDOTTIERE	CONTRETEMPS	CROCIDOLITE	DEMONSTRATE
CHICHEVACHE	COLEORRHIZA	CONDOTTIORE	CONTRIBUTOR	CROCODILIAN	DEMORALIZED
CHICKENFEED	COLLABORATE	CONDUCTANCE	CONTRIVANCE	CROMWELLIAN	DEMOSTHENES
CHILDMINDER	COLLAPSIBLE	CONDUCTRESS	CONTROVERSY	CROOKEDNESS	DEMOSTHENIC
CHILLINGHAM	COLLECTANEA	CONFABULATE	CONTUBERNAL	CROSSLEGGED	DENDRACHATE
CHINOISERIE	COLLENCHYMA	CONFARREATE	CONURBATION	CRUCIFIXION	DENOMINATOR
CHIPPENDALE	COLLOCATION	CONFEDERACY	CONVALLARIA	CRYSTALLINE	DENUMERABLE
CHIROGRAPHY	COLONIALISM	CONFEDERATE	CONVENIENCE	CRYSTALLISE	DEOXYGENATE
CHIROPODIST	COLONIALIST	CONFIDENTLY	CONVENTICLE	CRYSTALLIZE	DEPARTEMENT
CHITTERLING	COLORIMETER	CONFINEMENT	CONVERGENCE	CULMINATION	DEPHLEGMATE
CHLOROPHYLL	COLOURBLIND	CONFUTATION	CONVERTIBLE	CULPABILITY	DEPORTATION
CHOCKABLOCK	COLUMBARIUM	CONGRESSMAN	CONVOCATION	CULTIVATION	DEPREDATION
CHOIRMASTER	COMBINATION	CONJECTURAL	CONVOLUTION	CULVERINEER	DEPRIVATION
CHOLESTEROL	COMBUSTIBLE	CONJUGATION	CONVOLVULUS	CURNAPTIOUS	DERANGEMENT
CHOLINERGIC	COMESTIBLES	CONJUNCTION	CONVULSIONS	CURTAILMENT	DERELICTION
CHONDROSTEI	COMEUPPANCE	CONJUNCTURE	COOPERATION	CUSTOMARILY	DERMATOLOGY
CHORDOPHONE	COMFORTABLE	CONNECTICUT	COOPERATIVE	CYBERNETICS	DESCENDANTS
CHOROGRAPHY	COMFORTABLY	CONNOISSEUR	COORDINATED	CYCLOALKANE	DESCRIPTION
CHRISMATION	COMFORTLESS	CONNOTATION	COORDINATES	CYCLOSTYLED	DESCRIPTIVE

DESECRATION	DISCOLOURED	DREADLOCKED	ENCHANTRESS	ETYMOLOGIST	FAMILIARIZE
DESEGREGATE	DISCONTINUE	DREADNOUGHT	ENCHIRIDION	EUCALYPTOLE	FANATICALLY
DESELECTION	DISCOTHEQUE	DRESSMAKING	ENCHONDROMA	EUCHARISTIC	FANFARONADE
DESERPIDINE	DISCOURTESY	DRINKDRIVER	ENCOURAGING	EUCHROMATIN	FARINACEOUS
DESEXUALIZE	DISCREPANCY	DRUNKENNESS	ENCROACHING	EUPHEMISTIC	FARKLEBERRY
DESICCATION	DISEMBODIED	DRYCLEANERS	ENCUMBRANCE	EURHYTHMICS	FARRAGINOUS
DESIGNATION	DISENCUMBER	DRYCLEANING	ENDOCARDIUM	EVANGELICAL	FARREACHING
DESPERATELY	DISENTANGLE	DUBIOUSNESS	ENDORSEMENT	EVAPORATION	FARTHERMOST
DESPERATION	DISFIGURING	DUMBFOUNDED	ENDOTHERMIC	EVASIVENESS	FARTHINGALE
DESPONDENCY	DISGRACEFUL	DUNIEWASSAL	ENDOTROPHIC	EVENTRATION	FASCINATING
DESTABILIZE	DISGRUNTLED	DUPLICATING	ENFEOFFMENT	EVENTUALITY	FASCINATION
DESTINATION	DISHEVELLED	DUPLICATION	ENFORCEABLE	EVERLASTING	FASHIONABLE
DESTITUTION	DISHONESTLY	DUSTWRAPPER	ENFORCEMENT	EVISCERATED	FASHIONABLY
DESTRUCTION	DISILLUSION	DYAESTHESIA	ENFOULDERED	EXAGGERATED	FATUOUSNESS
DESTRUCTIVE	DISIMPRISON	DYSFUNCTION	ENFRANCHISE	EXAMINATION	FAULTFINDER
DETERIORATE	DISINCLINED	DYSLOGISTIC	ENGHALSKRUG	EXANTHEMATA	FAULTLESSLY
DETERMINANT	DISINTEREST	EARNESTNESS	ENGINEERING	EXASPERATED	FAUXBOURDON
DETERMINATE	DISJUNCTION	EARTHENWARE	ENHANCEMENT	EXCEEDINGLY	FAVOURITISM
DETERMINING	DISJUNCTIVE	EARTHSHAKER	ENJAMBEMENT	EXCEPTIONAL	FEASIBILITY
DETESTATION	DISLOCATION	EASTERNMOST	ENKEPHALINE	EXCESSIVELY	FEATURELESS
DETRIMENTAL	DISOBEDIENT	ECCALEOBION	ENLARGEMENT	EXCLAMATION	FEHMGERICHT
DEUTERONOMY	DISORGANIZE	ECTOTROPHIC	ENLIGHTENED	EXCLUSIVELY	FERNITICKLE
DEUTSCHMARK	DISORIENTED	EDIFICATION	ENNEAHEDRON	EXCRESCENCE	FEROCIOUSLY
DEVALUATION	DISPARAGING	EDUCATIONAL	ENSLAVEMENT	EXECUTIONER	FERRONNIÈRE
DEVASTATING	DISPENSABLE	EFFECTIVELY	ENTABLATURE	EXHILARATED	FESTINATELY
DEVASTATION	DISPERSABLE	EFFECTUALLY	ENTABLEMENT	EXHORTATION	FESTSCHRIFT
DEVELOPMENT	DISPLEASURE	EFFICACIOUS	ENTERTAINER	EXONERATION	FIDDLEDEDEE
DEVIOUSNESS	DISPOSITION	EFFICIENTLY	ENTHRALLING	EXORBITANCE	FIELDWORKER
DEVITRIFIED	DISPUTATION	EGALITARIAN	ENTITLEMENT	EXOSKELETON	FILAMENTOUS
DIAGNOSTICS	DISQUIETING	EGOTISTICAL	ENUMERATION	EXPECTANTLY	FILLIBUSTER
DIAMONDBACK	DISREGARDED	EINSTEINIUM	ENUNCIATION	EXPECTATION	FINANCIALLY
DIAPHORESIS	DISSEMINATE	EJACULATION	ENVIRONMENT	EXPECTORANT	FINGERPRINT
DIAPHORETIC	DISSEPIMENT	ELABORATELY	EOANTHROPUS	EXPECTORATE	FINGERSTALL
DIARTHROSIS	DISSERTATOR	ELABORATION	EPAMINONDAS	EXPEDITIOUS	FIRECRACKER
DIASCORDIUM	DISSIMULATE	ELASTOPLAST	EPANALEPSIS	EXPENDITURE	FIRELIGHTER
DIATESSARON	DISSIPATION	ELECTRICIAN	EPICHEIREMA	EXPERIENCED	FISHANDCHIP
DIATESSERON	DISSOLUTION	ELECTRICITY	EPIDIASCOPE	EXPLANATION	FISHMONGERS
DICEPHALOUS	DISTASTEFUL	ELECTROCUTE	EPIGENESIST	EXPLANATORY	FISSIONABLE
DICHROMATIC	DISTINCTION	ELECTROLIER	EPINEPHRINE	EXPLORATION	FITZWILLIAM
DICOTYLEDON	DISTINCTIVE	ELECTROLYTE	EPITHYMETIC	EXPLORATORY	FLABBERGAST
DICTATORIAL	DISTINGUISH	ELECTRONICS	EPOCHMAKING	EXPONENTIAL	FLAMBOYANCE
DIFFERENTLY	DISTRACTION	ELECTROTINT	EQUIDISTANT	EXPOSTULATE	FLAMBOYANTE
DIFFIDENTLY	DISTRESSING	ELEPHANTINE	EQUILATERAL	EXPROPRIATE	FLANKERBACK
DIFFRACTION	DISTRIBUTED	ELEUTHERIAN	EQUILIBRIST	EXPURGATION	FLANNELETTE
DILAPIDATED	DISTRIBUTOR	ELIGIBILITY	EQUILIBRIUM	EXQUISITELY	FLAVOURSOME
DIMENSIONAL	DISTRUSTFUL	ELIMINATION	EQUINOCTIAL	EXTEMPORISE	FLEXIBILITY
DIMERCAPROL	DISTURBANCE	ELIZABETHAN	EQUIPOLLENT	EXTEMPORIZE	FLICKERTAIL
DINNYHAUSER	DITHELETISM	ELUCIDATION	EQUIVALENCE	EXTENSIVELY	FLIRTATIOUS
DINNYHAYSER	DITTOGRAPHY	EMBARKATION	EQUIVOCALLY	EXTENUATING	FLORILEGIUM
DIORTHOTIC	DIVORCEMENT	EMBARRASSED	ERADICATION	EXTENUATION	FLOURISHING
DIPHYCERCAL	DOCTRINAIRE	EMBELLISHED	EREMACAUSIS	EXTERMINATE	FLUCTUATING
DIPLOMATICS	DOCUMENTARY	EMBOÎTEMENT	ERIODENDRON	EXTERNALIZE	FLUCTUATION
DIPLOMATIST	DODECASTYLE	EMBROCATION	ERRATICALLY	EXTORTIONER	FLUORESCENT
DIPROTODONT	DOLABRIFORM	EMMENAGOGUE	ERRONEOUSLY	EXTRADITION	FLUOROMETER
DIPSOMANIAC	DOMESTICATE	EMMENTHALER	ERYMANTHIAN	EXTRAPOLATE	FLUOROSCOPE
DIPTEROCARP	DOMESTICITY	EMOTIONALLY	ERYTHROCYTE	EXTRAVAGANT	FOMENTATION
DIRECTIONAL	DOMINEERING	EMPHYTEUSIS	ESCARMOUCHE	EXTROGENOUS	FOOLISHNESS
DIRECTORATE	DOUBLECHECK	EMPIECEMENT	ESCHATOLOGY	EXTROVERTED	FOOTBALLING
DISABLEMENT	DOUBLECROSS	EMPIRICUTIC	ESCHERICHIA	EYECATCHING	FOOTWASHING
DISAFFECTED	DOUROUCOULI	EMPLACEMENT	ESPIEGLERIE	FABRICATION	FORAMINIFER
DISAGREEING	DOWNHEARTED	EMPOWERMENT	ESSENTIALLY	FACETIOUSLY	FORBEARANCE
DISAPPROVAL	DOWNTRODDEN	EMPTYHANDED	ESTABLISHED	FACTFINDING	FORBIDDANCE
DISARMAMENT	DRACUNCULUS	EMPYROMANCY	ESTABLISHER	FACULTATIVE	FORECASTING
DISBELIEVER	DRAGGLETAIL	ENARTHROSIS	ESTRAMAZONE	FAIRWEATHER	FORECLOSURE
DISCERNIBLE	DRAGONNADES	ENCAPSULATE	ESTRANGHELO	FALLIBILITY	FOREFATHERS
DISCERNMENT	DRASTICALLY	ENCEPHALOMA	ETHNOGRAPHY	FAMILIARISE	FORESEEABLE
DISCIPLINED	DRAUGHTSMAN	ENCHANTMENT	ETHNOLOGIST	FAMILIARITY	FORESHORTEN

FORESTATION	GATECRASHER	HABILIMENTS	HISTORIATED	IDENTICALLY	INCANTATION
FORETHOUGHT	GEGENSCHEIN	HAEMOGLOBIN	HISTRIONICS	IDENTIFYING	INCAPSULATE
FOREWARNING	GELSEMININE	HAEMOPHILIA	HOBBLEDEHOY	IDEOLOGICAL	INCARCERATE
FORFOUGHTEN	GENEALOGIST	HAEMORRHAGE	HOGGISHNESS	IDEOPRAXIST	INCARNADINE
FORGIVENESS	GENERALIZED	HAEMORRHOID	HOHENLINDEN	IDIOGRAPHIC	INCARNATION
FORLORNNESS	GENERICALLY	HAGIOGRAPHA	HOLLANDAISE	IDIOTICALLY	INCESSANTLY
FORMULATION	GENETICALLY	HAGIOGRAPHY	HOLOTHURIAN	IDOLIZATION	INCINERATOR
FORNICATION	GENOUILLÈRE	HAIRDRESSER	HOMEOPATHIC	IDYLLICALLY	INCLINATION
FORTHCOMING	GENTLEMANLY	HAIRRAISING	HOMOEOPATHY	IGNOMINIOUS	INCOHERENCE
FORTNIGHTLY	GENTLEWOMAN	HALBSTARKER	HOMOGENEITY	IGNORANTINE	INCOMPETENT
FORTUNATELY	GENUFLEXION	HALFBROTHER	HOMOGENEOUS	ILLMANNERED	INCOMPOSITE
FORTUNELOUD	GENUINENESS	HALFHEARTED	HOMOGENIZED	ILLOGICALLY	INCONGRUITY
FOTHERGILLA	GEOMETRICAL	HALFHOLIDAY	HOMOIOUSIAN	ILLUMINANCE	INCONGRUOUS
FOULMOUTHED	GEOSYNCLINE	HALLEFLINTA	HOMOPHONOUS	ILLUMINATED	INCONSTANCY
FOUNDATIONS	GERMINATION	HALLUCINATE	HOMOTHERMAL	ILLUSIONARY	INCONTINENT
FRAGMENTARY	GERONTOLOGY	HAMMERCLOTH	HOMOTHERMIC	ILLUSIONISM	INCORPORATE
FRANKFURTER	GERRYMANDER	HANDCRAFTED	HONEYCOMBED	ILLUSIONIST	INCORPOREAL
FRANKLINITE	GESTATORIAL	HANDICAPPED	HONEYMOONER	ILLUSTRATOR	INCORRECTLY
FRANTICALLY	GESTICULATE	HANDICAPPER	HONEYSUCKLE	ILLUSTRIOUS	INCREDULITY
FRATERNALLY	GHASTLINESS	HANDWRITING	HOOLIGANISM	ILLYWHACKER	INCREDULOUS
FRAUDULENCE	GIBBERELLIN	HANDWRITTEN	HOOTANANNIE	IMAGINATION	INCREMENTAL
FREEMASONRY	GIGGLESTICK	HANGGLIDING	HOOTENANNIE	IMAGINATIVE	INCRIMINATE
FREETHINKER	GIGGLESWICK	HAPHAZARDLY	HORNSWOGGLE	IMMEDIATELY	INCUNABULUM
FRENCHWOMAN	GIGGLEWATER	HARDHITTING	HORSERACING	IMMIGRATION	INDEFINABLE
FRENCHWOMEN	GILLYFLOWER	HARDICANUTE	HORSERADISH	IMMORTALISE	INDENTATION
FRIGATEBIRD	GINGERBREAD	HARDPRESSED	HORSERIDING	IMMORTALITY	INDEPENDENT
FRIGHTENING	GIRDLESTEAD	HARDWORKING	HOSPITALITY	IMMORTALIZE	INDEXLINKED
FRIGHTFULLY	GLADWELLISE	HAREBRAINED	HOSPITALIZE	IMPARTIALLY	INDIARUBBER
FRIVOLOUSLY	GLASTONBURY	HARIOLATION	HOSPITALLER	IMPASSIONED	INDIFFERENT
FRONTRUNNER	GLIMMERGOWK	HARPSICHORD	HOSTILITIES	IMPASSIVELY	INDIGESTION
FROSTBITTEN	GLOSSOLALIA	HATCHETTITE	HOUSEFATHER	IMPATIENTLY	INDIGNANTLY
FRUGIVOROUS	GLUCOSAMINE	HAUGHTINESS	HOUSEHOLDER	IMPEACHMENT	INDIGNATION
FRUITLESSLY	GNATHONICAL	HEALTHINESS	HOUSEKEEPER	IMPECUNIOUS	INDIVISIBLE
FRUSTRATING	GODDAUGHTER	HEARTBROKEN	HOUSEMASTER	IMPEDIMENTA	INDIVISIBLY
FRUSTRATION	GODFORSAKEN	HEARTLESSLY	HOUSEMOTHER	IMPERFORATE	INDOMITABLE
FULFILLMENT	GONFALONIER	HEAVYHANDED	HOUSEPARENT	IMPERIALISM	INDUBITABLE
FULLBLOODED	GOODLOOKING	HEAVYWEIGHT	HUCKLEBERRY	IMPERIALIST	INDUBITABLY
FULMINATION	GOODNATURED	HEBDOMADARY	HUCKSTERAGE	IMPERIOUSLY	INDULGENTLY
FUNAMBULIST	GORDONSTOUN	HECKELPHONE	HUMGRUFFIAN	IMPERMANENT	INDUPLICATE
FUNCTIONARY	GRALLATORES	HELPFULNESS	HUMILIATING	IMPERMEABLE	INDUSTRIOUS
FUNCTIONING	GRAMMALOGUE	HEMERALOPIA	HUMILIATION	IMPERSONATE	INEBRIATION
FUNDAMENTAL	GRAMMATICAL	HEMIANOPSIA	HUMMINGBIRD	IMPERTINENT	INEFFECTIVE
FUNDRAISING	GRANDFATHER	HEMOPHILIAC	HUNDREDFOLD	IMPETUOSITY	INEFFECTUAL
FURNISHINGS	GRANDMASTER	HEMORRHOIDS	HURTLEBERRY	IMPETUOUSLY	INEFFICIENT
FURTHERANCE	GRANDMOTHER	HEPATOSCOPY	HUSBANDLAND	IMPIGNORATE	INELUCTABLE
FURTHERMORE	GRAPHICALLY	HEPPLEWHITE	HYDROCARBON	IMPLAUSIBLE	INEQUITABLE
FURTHERMOST	GRASSHOPPER	HERBIVOROUS	HYDROGENATE	IMPLEMENTAL	INESCAPABLE
FURTHERSOME	GRAVEDIGGER	HERPETOLOGY	HYDROMEDUSA	IMPLICATION	INESSENTIAL
FURTIVENESS	GRAVIMETRIC	HERRINGBONE	HYDROPHOBIA	IMPORTANTLY	INESTIMABLE
FUSTILARIAN	GRAVITATION	HETEROGRAFT	HYDROPHOBIC	IMPORTATION	INEXCITABLE
GABERLUNZIE	GREASEPAINT	HETEROSCIAN	HYDROPONICS	IMPORTUNATE	INEXCUSABLE
GALLIBAGGER	GREENBOTTLE	HEXADECIMAL	HYDROSTATIC	IMPRACTICAL	INEXCUSABLY
GALLIBEGGAR	GREENGROCER	HIBERNATING	HYDROSTATIC	IMPRECATION	INEXPEDIENT
GALLIGANTUS	GREENOCKITE	HIBERNATION	HYMNOLOGIST	IMPRECISION	INEXPENSIVE
GALLIMAUFRY	GREGARINIDA	HIDEOUSNESS	HYOPLASTRON	IMPREGNABLE	INFANGTHIEF
GALLOVIDIAN	GRENZGANGER	HIGHLIGHTER	HYPERBOREAN	IMPROPRIETY	INFANTICIDE
GALLOWGLASS	GROUNDSHEET	HIGHPITCHED	HYPERMARKET	IMPROVEMENT	INFANTRYMAN
GALLYBAGGER	GROUNDSPEED	HIGHPOWERED	HYPERTROPHY	IMPROVIDENT	INFATUATION
GALLYBEGGAR	GROUNDSWELL	HIGHPROFILE	HYPHENATION	IMPRUDENTLY	INFERIORITY
GAMETANGIUM	GUADALCANAL	HIGHQUALITY	HYPOCORISMA	IMPULSIVELY	INFERTILITY
GAMETOPHYTE	GUBERNATION	HIGHRANKING	HYPOTENSION	INADVERTENT	INFESTATION
GAMMERSTANG	GUESSTIMATE	HILARIOUSLY	HYPOTHECATE	INADVISABLE	INFILTRATOR
GAMOGENESIS	GULLIBILITY	HINDERLANDS	HYPOTHERMIA	INALIENABLE	INFLAMMABLE
GARNISHMENT	GUTTERSNIPE	HIPPOCAMPUS	ICHTHYOLITE	INATTENTION	INFLUENTIAL
GARRULOUSLY	GUTTURALISE	HIPPOCRATES	ICHTHYORNIS	INATTENTIVE	INFORMALITY
GASTRECTOMY	GYNAECOLOGY	HIPPOCRATIC	ICONOGRAPHY	INAUTHENTIC	INFORMATICS
GASTRONOMIC	HABERDASHER	HISTOLOGIST	ICONOSTASIS	INCALESCENT	INFORMATION

INFORMATIVE	INTERRELATE	KINDERSPIEL	LOCORESTIVE	MARLBOROUGH	MICTURITION
INFREQUENCY	INTERROGATE	KINDHEARTED	LOGARITHMIC	MARSHMALLOW	MIDDENSTEAD
INFURIATING	INTERRUPTER	KINNIKINICK	LOGGERHEADS	MASCULINITY	MIDDLEMARCH
INGENIOUSLY	INTERSPERSE	KIRKPATRICK	LOGODAEDALY	MASKALLONGE	MIDDLESIZED
INGRATITUDE	INTERVENING	KITCHENETTE	LOGOGRAPHER	MASOCHISTIC	MILLIAMPERE
INGREDIENTS	INTERVIEWEE	KLEPTOMANIA	LONGANIMITY	MASQUERADER	MILLIONAIRE
INHABITABLE	INTERVIEWER	KNUCKLEBALL	LONGAWAITED	MASSIVENESS	MILQUETOAST
INHABITANTS	INTOLERABLE	KOMMERSBUCH	LONGINQUITY	MASTERFULLY	MINESWEEPER
INHERITANCE	INTOLERABLY	KOTABOTHRON	LONGLASTING	MASTERPIECE	MINIATURIST
INJUDICIOUS	INTOLERANCE	KRIEGSSPIEL	LONGRUNNING	MASTICATION	MINIATURIZE
INNUMERABLE	INTOXICATED	KULTURKREIS	LONGSIGHTED	MATERIALISE	MINISTERIAL
INOCULATION	INTOXIMETER	KWASHIORKOR	LONGSLEEVED	MATERIALISM	MINISTERING
INOFFENSIVE	INTRACTABLE	LABORIOUSLY	LOOSESTRIFE	MATERIALIST	MINNESINGER
INOPERATIVE	INTRADERMAL	LABORSAVING	LOUDSPEAKER	MATERIALIZE	MISALLIANCE
INOPPORTUNE	INTRAVENOUS	LACONICALLY	LOUISIANIAN	MATHEMATICS	MISANTHROPE
INQUIRINGLY	INTREPIDITY	LAMENTATION	LUBRICATION	MATRIARCHAL	MISANTHROPY
INQUISITION	INTRICATELY	LAMMERGEIER	LUMINESCENT	MATRICULATE	MISBEGOTTEN
INQUISITIVE	INTROVERTED	LAMMERGEYER	LUXEMBURGER	MATRIMONIAL	MISBEHAVIOR
INSCRIPTION	INTUITIVELY	LAMPLIGHTER	LUXULYANITE	MAURETANIAN	MISCARRIAGE
INSCRUTABLE	INVESTIGATE	LAMPROPHYRE	LUXURIANTLY	MAURITANIAN	MISCHIEVOUS
INSECTICIDE	INVESTITURE	LANDSKNECHT	LUXURIOUSLY	MEADOWSWEET	MISCONSTRUE
INSECTIVORE	INVIGILATOR	LAPIDESCENT	LYCANTHROPE	MEANDERINGS	MISDEMEANOR
INSENSITIVE	INVINCIBLES	LARYNGISMUS	LYCANTHROPY	MEANINGLESS	MISERICORDE
INSEPARABLE	INVOLUNTARY	LASERPICIUM	LYCHNOSCOPE	MEASURELESS	MISERLINESS
INSIDIOUSLY	INVOLVEMENT	LATERIGRADE	MACADAMIZED	MEASUREMENT	MISFEASANCE
INSINCERITY	IPECACUANHA	LATERITIOUS	MACERANDUBA	MECKLENBURG	MISIDENTIFY
INSINUATING	IRIDESCENCE	LATIFUNDIUM	MACHAIRODUS	MEDIASTINUM	MISSISSIPPI
INSINUATION	IRONMONGERS	LATROCINIUM	MACHINATION	MEDICINALLY	MISSPELLING
INSISTENTLY	IRONMONGERY	LATTICEWORK	MACROBIOTIC	MEDIUMSIZED	MISTRUSTFUL
INSOUCIANCE	IRRADIATION	LAUNDERETTE	MACROGAMETE	MEGALOMANIA	MOCKINGBIRD
INSPIRATION	IRREDENTIST	LAWBREAKING	MACROSCOPIC	MEGALOMANIC	MODELMOLEST
INSTABILITY	IRREDUCIBLE	LAWLESSNESS	MAGISTERIAL	MEGALOPOLIS	MODERNISTIC
INSTALLMENT	IRREFUTABLE	LEADSWINGER	MAGISTRATES	MEGATHERIUM	MOISTURIZER
INSTANTIATE	IRREGULARLY	LEASEHOLDER	MAGLEMOSIAN	MEKHITARIST	MOLESTATION
INSTIGATION	IRRELEVANCE	LEATHERBACK	MAGNANIMITY	MELANCHOLIA	MOLLYCODDLE
INSTINCTIVE	IRRELIGIOUS	LEATHERETTE	MAGNANIMOUS	MELANCHOLY	MOMENTARILY
INSTITUTION	IRREPARABLE	LEATHERHEAD	MAGNIFICENT	MELANOCHROI	MONARCHICAL
INSTRUCTION	IRREPARABLY	LEATHERNECK	MAINTENANCE	MELLIFLUOUS	MONCHIQUITE
INSTRUCTIVE	IRREVERENCE	LEATHERWOOD	MAISTERDOME	MELODIOUSLY	MONEYLENDER
INSTRUMENTS	IRREVOCABLE	LECITHINASE	MAKEBELIEVE	MEMORABILIA	MONEYMAKING
INSULTINGLY	ISOELECTRIC	LECTURESHIP	MALADJUSTED	MENDELEVIUM	MONOCHINOUS
INSUPERABLE	ISOLECITHAL	LEFTLUGGAGE	MALAKATOONE	MENDELSSOHN	MONOCHROMAT
INTEGRATION	ISOMORPHOUS	LEGERDEMAIN	MALAPROPISM	MENSURATION	MONOGRAMMED
INTELLIGENT	ISOXSUPRINE	LEGIONNAIRE	MALEDICTION	MENTHOLATED	MONOLINGUAL
INTEMPERATE	ISTIOPHORUS	LEGISLATION	MALEFACTION	MENTONNIÈRE	MONONGAHELA
INTENSIVELY	ITHYPHALLIC	LEGISLATIVE	MALEVOLENCE	MEPROBAMATE	MONONUCLEAR
INTENTIONAL	ITHYPHALLUS	LEGISLATURE	MALFEASANCE	MERCHANDISE	MONOPSONIST
INTERACTION	JABBERWOCKY	LENGTHENING	MALFUNCTION	MERCHANDIZE	MONOTHELITE
INTERACTIVE	JACQUEMINOT	LENGTHINESS	MALICIOUSLY	MERCHANTMAN	MONOTREMATA
INTERCALARY	JACTITATION	LENTIGINOSE	MALPRACTICE	MERCILESSLY	MONSTROSITY
INTERCEPTOR	JAMAHIRIYAH	LEPIDOPTERA	MANCIPATION	MERITORIOUS	MONTESQUIEU
INTERCHANGE	JERRYMANDER	LEPIDOSIREN	MANEUVERING	MERRYMAKING	MONTGOLFIER
INTERCOSTAL	JINRICKSHAW	LETTERPRESS	MANGALSUTRA	METACARPALS	MONTMORENCY
INTERCOURSE	JOSEPHINITE	LEVELHEADED	MANIPULATOR	METACENTRIC	MOONLIGHTER
INTERESTING	JUDICIOUSLY	LIBERTARIAN	MANTELLETTA	METAGENESIS	MORGENSTERN
INTERGLOSSA	JUSTIFIABLE	LICKSPITTLE	MANTELPIECE	METALWORKER	MOSSTROOPER
INTERGROWTH	JUSTIFIABLY	LIGHTHEADED	MANTELSHELF	METAPHYSICS	MOUNTAINEER
INTERLACING	KALASHNIKOV	LIGHTWEIGHT	MANUFACTURE	METATARSALS	MOUNTAINOUS
INTERLEUKIN	KAMELAUKION	LILLIPUTIAN	MANUMISSION	METEOROLOGY	MOXIBUSTION
INTERLINGUA	KATABOTHRON	LINDISFARNE	MAQUILADORA	METHODOLOGY	MOZAMBIQUAN
INTERMINGLE	KATAVOTHRON	LINGUISTICS	MARCONIGRAM	METRICATION	MUDSLINGING
INTERNALIZE	KETAVOTHRON	LIQUIDAMBAR	MARGINALIST	MICHURINISM	MULTIRACIAL
INTERNECINE	KIDDLEYWINK	LIQUIDATION	MARGINALIZE	MICROGAMETE	MULTISTOREY
INTERNUNCIO	KILIMANJARO	LITERALNESS	MARIONBERRY	MICROSCOPIC	MUNCHHAUSEN
INTERPOLATE	KILOCALORIE	LITHOGRAPHY	MARIONETTES	MICROSECOND	MUNIFICENCE
INTERPRETER	KIMERIDGIAN	LITTÉRATEUR	MARIVAUDAGE	MICROTUBULE	MUNITIONIZE
INTERREGNUM	KINCHINMORT	LIVINGSTONE	MARKETPLACE	MICROVILLUS	MURMURATION

MUSCHELKALK	NUMISMATIST	OSTEOPATHIC	PARVANIMITY	PERSONALIST	POLTERGEIST
MUSKELLUNGE	NUTCRACKERS	OSTEOPLASTY	PASSACAGLIA	PERSONALITY	POLYHYDROXY
MYCOLOGICAL	NUTRITIONAL	OSTRACODERM	PASSIVENESS	PERSONALIZE	POLYMORPHIC
MYCOPHAGIST	NYMPHOMANIA	OSTREOPHAGE	PASTEURELLA	PERSONIFIED	POLYSTYRENE
MYTHOLOGIZE	OARSMANSHIP	OUAGADOUGOU	PASTOURELLE	PERSPECTIVE	POLYTECHNIC
MYXOMATOSIS	OBJECTIVELY	OUTDISTANCE	PATERNALISM	PERSPICUITY	POLYTRICHUM
NAPHTHALENE	OBJECTIVITY	OUTMANEUVER	PATERNOSTER	PERSPICUOUS	POMEGRANATE
NARRAGANSET	OBLITERATED	OUTPOURINGS	PATHOLOGIST	PERTINACITY	POMPELMOOSE
NATIONALISM	OBMUTESCENT	OUTSTANDING	PATRIARCHAL	PERTINENTLY	POMPELMOUSE
NATIONALIST	OBSERVATION	OVARIECTOMY	PATRONISING	PESSIMISTIC	PONDEROUSLY
NATIONALITY	OBSERVATORY	OVERBALANCE	PATRONIZING	PETITMAITRE	PONTIFICATE
NATIONALIZE	OBSESSIVELY	OVERBEARING	PAWNBROKERS	PETRODOLLAR	PORNOGRAPHY
NATIONSTATE	OBSOLESCENT	OVERCROWDED	PEACEKEEPER	PETTICOATED	PORTERHOUSE
NATURALNESS	OBSTETRICAL	OVERDRAUGHT	PECULIARITY	PETTIFOGGER	PORTLANDIAN
NATUROPATHY	OBSTINATELY	OVEREXPOSED	PEDAGOGICAL	PHALANSTERY	PORTMANTEAU
NAUGHTINESS	OBSTRICTION	OVERFISHING	PEDESTRIANS	PHARISAICAL	PORTRAITIST
NEANDERTHAL	OBSTRUCTION	OVERFLOWING	PEDETENTOUS	PHARYNGITIS	PORTRAITURE
NEARSIGHTED	OBSTRUCTIVE	OVERHANGING	PEEVISHNESS	PHILANDERER	POSSESSIONS
NECESSARILY	OBTEMPERATE	OVERLAPPING	PELARGONIUM	PHILATELIST	POSSIBILITY
NECESSITATE	OBVIOUSNESS	OVERLEARNED	PELOPONNESE	PHILIPPIANS	POTAMOGETON
NECESSITOUS	OCHLOCRATIC	OVERMANNING	PENETRATING	PHILIPPINES	POTENTIALLY
NECROBIOSIS	OCTASTICHON	OVERPAYMENT	PENETRATION	PHILLIPSITE	PRACTICABLE
NECROMANCER	ODONTOBLAST	OVERSTUFFED	PENICILLATE	PHILOCTETES	PRACTICALLY
NEEDLEPOINT	ODONTOPHORE	OVERTURNING	PENITENTIAL	PHILOLOGIST	PRECAUTIONS
NEEDLESTICK	OFFENSIVELY	OVERWEENING	PENNYFATHER	PHILOSOPHER	PRECIPITATE
NEEDLEWOMAN	OFFHANDEDLY	OVERWHELMED	PENSIONABLE	PHONETICIAN	PRECIPITOUS
NEGOTIATING	OFFICIALDOM	OVERWROUGHT	PENSIVENESS	PHONOFIDDLE	PRECONCEIVE
NEGOTIATION	OFFICIALESE	OVERZEALOUS	PENTATHLETE	PHOTOCOPIER	PREDECESSOR
NEIGHBORING	OFFICIOUSLY	OXODIZATION	PENTAVALENT	PHOTOFINISH	PREDESTINED
NEIGHBOURLY	OLIGOCHAETE	OXYRHYNCHUS	PENTECONTER	PHOTOGRAPHY	PREDICAMENT
NERVOUSNESS	OMMATOPHORE	PACIFICALLY	PENTECOSTAL	PHOTOSPHERE	PREDICATIVE
NETHERLANDS	OMNIPOTENCE	PAEDIATRICS	PENTHESILEA	PHRASEOLOGY	PREDICTABLE
NETHERLINGS	OMNIPRESENT	PAEDOTROPHY	PENTONVILLE	PHTHIRIASIS	PREDICTABLY
NEUROLOGIST	OMNISCIENCE	PAINKILLING	PENULTIMATE	PHYLLOCLADE	PREDOMINANT
NEUTRALISED	ONEIRODYNIA	PAINSTAKING	PERAMBULATE	PHYSIOGNOMY	PREDOMINATE
NEVERENDING	ONEIROMANCY	PALEOGRAPHY	PERCEFOREST	PICKELHAUBE	PREEMINENCE
NEWSCASTING	ONOMASTICON	PALEOLITHIC	PERCEPTIBLE	PICKYOUROWN	PREHISTORIC
NIACINAMIDE	ONTOLOGICAL	PALESTINIAN	PERCEPTIBLY	PICTURESQUE	PREJUDICIAL
NICKELODEON	OPALESCENCE	PAMPELMOOSE	PERCHLORATE	PIEDMONTITE	PRELIBATION
NICKNACKERY	OPERATIONAL	PAMPELMOUSE	PERCIPIENCE	PIERREPOINT	PRELIMINARY
NIERSTEINER	OPINIONATED	PAMPHLETEER	PERCOLATION	PINACOTHECA	PREMATURELY
NIGHTINGALE	OPPIGNORATE	PANDEMONIUM	PERDUELLION	PINNYWINKLE	PREMEDITATE
NIGHTMARISH	OPPORTUNELY	PANOMPHAEAN	PEREGRINATE	PISCATORIAL	PREMIERSHIP
NIKETHAMIDE	OPPORTUNISM	PANTALETTES	PERENNIALLY	PISSASPHALT	PREMONITION
NIPFARTHING	OPPORTUNIST	PAPERWEIGHT	PERESTROIKA	PITCHBLENDE	PREMONITORY
NOISELESSLY	OPPORTUNITY	PARABLEPSIS	PERFORATION	PLAGIARISED	PREOCCUPIED
NOMENCLATOR	OPPROBRIOUS	PARABOLANUS	PERFORMANCE	PLAGIOSTOMI	PREPARATION
NONCHALANCE	OPTOMETRIST	PARACETAMOL	PERFUNCTORY	PLANETARIUM	PREPARATIVE
NONDESCRIPT	ORCHESTRATE	PARACHUTIST	PERICARDIUM	PLANTAGENET	PREPARATORY
NONETHELESS	ORCHESTRINA	PARACROSTIC	PERIGORDIAN	PLANTIGRADE	PREPOLLENCE
NONEXISTENT	ORCHESTRION	PARADOXICAL	PERIODONTIC	PLATERESQUE	PREPOSITION
NONFEASANCE	ORDERLINESS	PARALEIPSIS	PERIPATETIC	PLATYRRHINE	PREROGATIVE
NONSENSICAL	ORGANICALLY	PARAMASTOID	PERIPHRASIS	PLAYFULNESS	PRESENTABLE
NORTHCLIFFE	ORGANIZAION	PARAMEDICAL	PERISSOLOGY	PLEASURABLE	PRESENTMENT
NORTHEASTER	ORIENTALISM	PARANEPHROS	PERISTALITH	PLEBEIANISE	PRESSURIZED
NORTHWESTER	ORIENTALIST	PARASITOSIS	PERISTALSIS	PLEISTOCENE	PRESTIGIOUS
NOSTRADAMUS	ORIENTATION	PARATROOPER	PERITONAEUM	PLEURODYNIA	PRESTISSIMO
NOTHINGNESS	ORIGINALITY	PARATYPHOID	PERITONITIS	PLOUGHSHARE	PRESTONPANS
NOTICEBOARD	ORIGINATING	PARENTHESIS	PERLUSTRATE	POCOCURANTE	PRESTRESSED
NOTORIOUSLY	ORIGINATION	PARISHIONER	PERMANENTLY	PODSNAPPERY	PRESUMPTION
NOTOTHERIUM	ORNITHOLOGY	PARLIPOMENA	PERMISSIBLE	POINTLESSLY	PRESUMPTIVE
NOURISHMENT	ORNITHOPTER	PARONOMASIA	PERMUTATION	POLICEWOMAN	PRETENSIONS
NOVELETTISH	ORTHOCENTRE	PARTICIPANT	PERPETRATOR	POLIORCETIC	PRETENTIOUS
NUCLEOPLASM	ORTHOGRAPHY	PARTICIPATE	PERPETUALLY	POLITICALLY	PRETERITION
NUMBERPLATE	ORTHOPAEDIC	PARTICIPIAL	PERSECUTION	POLITICIANS	PREVARICATE
NUMERICALLY	OSCILLATION	PARTNERSHIP	PERSEVERING	POLLENBRUSH	PREVENTABLE
NUMISMATICS	OSTENTATION	PARTURITION	PERSISTENCE	POLLINATION	PRICKLINESS

PRIMIGENIAL	PUBLISHABLE	RECRUITMENT	RETALIATORY	SAPROLEGNIA	SELFISHNESS
PRINCIPALLY	PULCHRITUDE	RECTANGULAR	RETARDATION	SAPROPHYTIC	SELFRESPECT
PRISCIANIST	PUNCHINELLO	RECTIFIABLE	RETINACULUM	SARCENCHYME	SELFSERVICE
PRIZEWINNER	PUNCTILIOUS	RECTILINEAR	RETINOSCOPY	SARCOPHAGUS	SEMITRAILER
PROBABILITY	PUNCTUALITY	RECURRENTLY	RETINOSPORA	SATIRICALLY	SEMPITERNAL
PROBATIONER	PUNCTUATION	REDOUBTABLE	RETRACTABLE	SAUSAGEMEAT	SEMPITERNUM
PROCEEDINGS	PURITANICAL	REDUPLICATE	RETRIBUTION	SAVOURINESS	SENNACHERIB
PROCREATION	PURPOSELESS	REFLEXOLOGY	RETRIBUTIVE	SAXOPHONIST	SENSATIONAL
PROCRUSTEAN	PURPRESTURE	REFOCILLATE	RETRIEVABLE	SCAFFOLDING	SENSIBILITY
PROCUREMENT	PYELOGRAPHY	REFORMATION	RETROACTIVE	SCALPRIFORM	SENSITIVELY
PRODIGALISE	PYRARGYRITE	REFORMATORY	RETROROCKET	SCANDALIZED	SENSITIVITY
PRODIGALITY	PYTHONESQUE	REFRESHMENT	REVALUATION	SCANDANAVIA	SENTENTIOUS
PROFESSEDLY	QUADRENNIAL	REFRIGERANT	REVELATIONS	SCANDINAVIA	SENTIMENTAL
PROFICIENCY	QUADRENNIUM	REFRIGERATE	REVENDICATE	SCARABAEOID	SEPIOSTAIRE
PROFITEROLE	QUADRUPLETS	REFURBISHED	REVERBERATE	SCARBOROUGH	SEPTENARIUS
PROFUSENESS	QUALITATIVE	REGIMENTALS	REVERENTIAL	SCAREMONGER	SEPTENTRION
PROGENITRIX	QUARRELLING	REGISTERING	REVISIONISM	SCATTERGOOD	SEPTICAEMIA
PROGNATHOUS	QUARRELSOME	REGRETFULLY	REVOLUTIONS	SCATTERLING	SEQUESTRATE
PROGRESSION	QUARRINGTON	REGRETTABLE	RHABDOMANCY	SCEPTICALLY	SERENDIPITY
PROGRESSIVE	QUARTERBACK	REGRETTABLY	RHAPSODICAL	SCEUOPHYLAX	SERICULTURE
PROHIBITION	QUARTERDECK	REGURGITATE	RHEUMATICKY	SCHECKLATON	SERIOUSNESS
PROHIBITIVE	QUERULOUSLY	REICHENBACH	RHOPALOCERA	SCHISTOSOMA	SERVICEABLE
PROLEGOMENA	QUESTIONING	REINCARNATE	RIBONUCLEIC	SCHISTOSOME	SESQUIOXIDE
PROLETARIAN	QUICKSILVER	REITERATION	RIDDLEMEREE	SCHOLARSHIP	SEVENTEENTH
PROLETARIAT	QUINTUPLETS	RELEASEMENT	RIFACIMENTO	SCHOTTISCHE	SEVERALFOLD
PROLIFERATE	RABELAISIAN	RELIABILITY	RIGHTANGLED	SCHRECKLICH	SEXOLOGICAL
PROLOCUTION	RADIOACTIVE	RELIGIOUSLY	RIGHTEOUSLY	SCHWARMEREI	SEXTODECIMO
PROMINENTLY	RADIOCARBON	RELUCTANTLY	RIGHTHANDED	SCIENTOLOGY	SHAFTESBURY
PROMISCUITY	RADIOGRAPHY	REMEMBRANCE	RIGHTHANDER	SCINTILLATE	SHAKESPEARE
PROMISCUOUS	RADIOLOGIST	REMINISCENT	RIGHTWINGER	SCIREFACIAS	SHALLOWNESS
PROMOTIONAL	RAFFISHNESS	REMONSTRATE	RINFORZANDO	SCITAMINEAE	SHAMELESSLY
PROMPTITUDE	RALLENTANDO	REMORSELESS	RINTHEREOUT	SCLERODERMA	SHAPELINESS
PROOFREADER	RAMGUNSHOCH	RENAISSANCE	ROBESPIERRE	SCOLECIFORM	SHAREHOLDER
PROPAGATION	RANGEFINDER	REORIENTATE	ROCKEFELLER	SCOLOPENDRA	SHEATHKNIFE
PROPHETICAL	RAPSCALLION	REPETITIOUS	RODOMONTADE	SCOPOLAMINE	SHENANIGANS
PROPHYLAXIS	RAPTUROUSLY	REPLACEABLE	ROGUISHNESS	SCOREKEEPER	SHEPHERDESS
PROPINQUITY	RASTAFARIAN	REPLACEMENT	ROMANTICISM	SCOUTMASTER	SHINPLASTER
PROPOSITION	RATATOUILLE	REPRESENTED	ROMANTICIZE	SCREAMINGLY	SHIPBUILDER
PROPRIETARY	RATIOCINATE	REPROACHFUL	ROSICRUCIAN	SCREWDRIVER	SHIPWRECKED
PROROGATION	RATIONALITY	REPUDIATION	ROTOGRAVURE	SCRIMSHANDY	SHITTIMWOOD
PROSAICALLY	RATIONALIZE	REQUIREMENT	ROTTENSTONE	SCRIPTORIUM	SHOPLIFTING
PROSECUTION	RATTLESNAKE	REQUISITION	RUDESHEIMER	SCRUFFINESS	SHORTCHANGE
PROSELYTISM	RAUCOUSNESS	RESEMBLANCE	RUDIMENTARY	SCRUMPTIOUS	SHORTCOMING
PROSELYTIZE	RAVISHINGLY	RESENTFULLY	RUMBUSTIOUS	SCULDUDDERY	SHORTHANDED
PROSPECTIVE	RAZZAMATAZZ	RESERVATION	RUMFRUCTION	SCULDUGGERY	SHOVELBOARD
PROSTHETICS	REACTIONARY	RESIDENTIAL	RUMGUMPTION	SCULLABOGUE	SHOWERPROOF
PROSTRATION	READABILITY	RESIGNATION	SABBATARIAN	SCUPPERNONG	SHOWJUMPING
PROTAGONIST	REALIGNMENT	RESISTIVITY	SACHERTORTE	SCUTTLEBUTT	SHOWMANSHIP
PROTEROZOIC	REALIZATION	RESOURCEFUL	SACRAMENTAL	SCYPHISTOMA	SHUNAMITISM
PROTOCOCCUS	REALPOLITIK	RESPECTABLE	SACRIFICIAL	SEARCHLIGHT	SHUTTLECOCK
PROTONOTARY	REANIMATION	RESPECTABLY	SADDLEHORSE	SEASICKNESS	SIGHTSCREEN
PROTRACTING	REAPPRAISAL	RESPIRATION	SAGACIOUSLY	SECONDARILY	SIGHTSEEING
PROTRACTION	REASSURANCE	RESPIRATORY	SAGITTARIUS	SECONDCLASS	SIGNIFICANT
PROTUBERANT	REBARBATIVE	RESPLENDENT	SAINTLINESS	SECRETARIAL	SILLIMANITE
PROVISIONAL	RECANTATION	RESPONSIBLE	SAINTPAULIA	SECRETARIAT	SILVERBERRY
PROVISIONER	RECEPTIVITY	RESPONSIBLY	SALACIOUSLY	SECRETIVELY	SILVERPOINT
PROVOCATION	RECESSIONAL	RESPONSIONS	SALESPERSON	SEDIMENTARY	SILVERSMITH
PROVOCATIVE	RECIPROCATE	RESTATEMENT	SALINOMETER	SEGREGATION	SINGAPOREAN
PRZEWALSKIS	RECIPROCITY	RESTITUTION	SALPINGITIS	SEIGNIORAGE	SINGLESTICK
PSEUDOLOGIA	RECLAMATION	RESTIVENESS	SALTIMBANCO	SEISMOGRAPH	SINGULARITY
PSEUDOMORPH	RECOGNITION	RESTORATION	SALTIMBOCCA	SELAGINELLA	SINISTRORSE
PSITTACOSIS	RECONDITION	RESTORATIVE	SALVADORIAN	SELECTIVELY	SKEPTICALLY
PSYCHEDELIC	RECONNOITER	RESTRICTION	SALVOGUNNER	SELECTIVITY	SKETCHINESS
PSYCHIATRIC	RECONNOITRE	RESTRICTIVE	SANDERSWOOD	SELFCONTROL	SKIDBLADNIR
PTERODACTYL	RECONSTRUCT	RESTRUCTURE	SANGUINEOUS	SELFDEFENCE	SKILLIGALEE
PTOCHOCRACY	RECOVERABLE	RESUSCITATE	SANSEVIERIA	SELFEVIDENT	SKILLIGOLEE
PUBLICATION	RECRIMINATE	RETALIATION	SAPONACEOUS	SELFIMPOSED	SKIMMINGTON

SKULDUDDERY	SRANANTONGO	SUBDIVISION	SYMMETRICAL	TETRADRACHM	TRADITIONAL
SKULDUGGERY	STADTHOLDER	SUBDOMINANT	SYMPATHETIC	TETRAHEDRON	TRAFFICATOR
SLEEPWALKER	STAGFLATION	SUBITANEOUS	SYMPATHISER	THALIDOMIDE	TRAGELAPHUS
SLENDERNESS	STAIRCARPET	SUBJUGATION	SYMPATHIZER	THALLOPHYTE	TRANQUILITY
SLEUTHHOUND	STAKEHOLDER	SUBJUNCTIVE	SYMPLEGADES	THANATOPSIS	TRANSACTION
SLIGHTINGLY	STALLHOLDER	SUBLIMATION	SYMPOSIARCH	THANKLESSLY	TRANSCEIVER
SLUMBERWEAR	STANDARDIZE	SUBMERGENCE	SYMPTOMATIC	THAUMATROPE	TRANSDERMAL
SLUMGULLION	STANDOFFISH	SUBMULTIPLE	SYNCHROMESH	THEATERGOER	TRANSFERRED
SMALLHOLDER	STANDPATTER	SUBORDINATE	SYNCHRONISE	THEATREGOER	TRANSFERRIN
SMITHEREENS	STATELINESS	SUBPANATION	SYNCHRONISM	THEATRICALS	TRANSFIGURE
SMITHSONIAN	STATISTICAL	SUBSERVIENT	SYNCHRONIZE	THENCEFORTH	TRANSFORMED
SMITHSONITE	STEADFASTLY	SUBSISTENCE	SYNCHRONOUS	THEOBROMINE	TRANSFORMER
SMOKESCREEN	STEAMROLLER	SUBSTANDARD	SYNCOPATION	THEOLOGICAL	TRANSFUSION
SMORGASBORD	STEATOPYGIA	SUBSTANTIAL	SYNDICALISM	THEOPNEUSTY	TRANSILIENT
SMOULDERING	STEEPLEJACK	SUBSTANTIVE	SYNDICATION	THEORETICAL	TRANSLATION
SNICKERSNEE	STEGANOGRAM	SUBTRACTION	SYNTHESIZED	THERAPEUTAE	TRANSLUCENT
SNORKELLING	STEGANOPODE	SUBTROPICAL	SYNTHESIZER	THERAPEUTIC	TRANSMITTED
SOCIABILITY	STEINBERGER	SUBUNGULATA	SYSTEMATIZE	THEREABOUTS	TRANSMITTER
SOCIOLOGIST	STELLIONATE	SUCCEDANEUM	TABERNACLES	THERMOMETER	TRANSPARENT
SOCKDALAGER	STENOCHROME	SUDETENLAND	TACHYCARDIA	THERMOPYLAE	TRANSPONDER
SOCKDOLAGER	STENOGRAPHY	SUFFICIENCY	TACHYGRAPHY	THESMOTHETE	TRANSPORTED
SOCKDOLIGER	STEPBROTHER	SUFFOCATING	TACITURNITY	THIGMOTAXIS	TRANSPORTER
SOCKDOLOGER	STEREOGRAPH	SUFFOCATION	TAGLIATELLE	THINGAMABOB	TRANSURANIC
SOLILOQUIZE	STEREOMETER	SUFFRAGETTE	TANGIBILITY	THINGAMAJIG	TRANSVERSAL
SOLIPSISTIC	STEREOSCOPE	SUGARCOATED	TANTALIZING	THINGLINESS	TREACHEROUS
SOROPTIMIST	STEREOTYPED	SUGGESTIBLE	TARATANTARA	THINGUMAJIG	TREACHETOUR
SORROWFULLY	STETHOSCOPE	SUITABILITY	TARRADIDDLE	THISTLEDOWN	TREASONABLE
SOUNDLESSLY	STICKLEBACK	SUMMERHOUSE	TASTELESSLY	THOROUGHPIN	TREECREEPER
SOUTHAMPTON	STILBESTROL	SUMPTUOUSLY	TATTERSALLS	THOUGHTLESS	TRENCHERMAN
SOUTHWESTER	STIMULATION	SUNDRENCHED	TAUROBOLIUM	THREATENING	TREPIDATION
SOVEREIGNTY	STIPENDIARY	SUPERALTERN	TAUTOCHRONE	THRIFTINESS	TREPONEMATA
SPACESAVING	STIPULATION	SUPERCHARGE	TAXIDERMIST	THROGMORTON	TRESPASSING
SPANGCOCKLE	STOCKBROKER	SUPERCHERIE	TCHAIKOVSKY	THUNDERBIRD	TRIBULATION
SPARROWHAWK	STOCKHAUSEN	SUPERFICIAL	TEASPOONFUL	THUNDERBOLT	TRICERATOPS
SPATTERDASH	STOCKHOLDER	SUPERFICIES	TECHNICALLY	THUNDERCLAP	TRICHINELLA
SPATTERDOCK	STOCKJOBBER	SUPERFLUITY	TECTIBRANCH	THUNDERHEAD	TRICHINOSED
SPECIALIZED	STOCKTAKING	SUPERFLUOUS	TEDIOUSNESS	THYROTROPIN	TRICHOPTERA
SPECTACULAR	STOOLPIGEON	SUPERIMPOSE	TEENYBOPPER	TICKTACKTOE	TRIMESTRIAL
SPECULATION	STOREKEEPER	SUPERINTEND	TEETOTALLER	TIDDLEYWINK	TRINCOMALEE
SPECULATIVE	STORYTELLER	SUPERIORITY	TEGUCIGALPA	TIGGYWINKLE	TRINIDADIAN
SPEECHCRAFT	STRADUARIUS	SUPERLATIVE	TÉLÉFÉRIQUE	TIGHTFISTED	TRINITARIAN
SPEEDOMETER	STRAITLACED	SUPERMARKET	TELEGRAPHER	TIGHTLIPPED	TRINOBANTES
SPELLBINDER	STRAMINEOUS	SUPERSCRIBE	TELEGRAPHIC	TIMBROMANIA	TRIPHIBIOUS
SPENDTHRIFT	STRANDLOPER	SUPERSCRIPT	TELEKINESIS	TIMBROPHILY	TRIPTOLEMUS
SPERMATOZOA	STRANGENESS	SUPERSEDEAS	TELEPHONIST	TIMEKEEPING	TRITAGONIST
SPERMICIDAL	STRANGEWAYS	SUPERSEDERE	TELEPRINTER	TIMESHARING	TRIUMVIRATE
SPERMOPHILE	STRANGULATE	SUPERTANKER	TELEWORKING	TIRONENSIAN	TROMPELOEIL
SPESSARTITE	STRAPHANGER	SUPERVISION	TELOCENTRIC	TITILLATION	TROPHOBLAST
SPHRAGISTIC	STRATEGICAL	SUPERVISORY	TEMPERAMENT	TITLEHOLDER	TROPOSPHERE
SPIFFLICATE	STREAMLINED	SUPPEDANEUM	TEMPERATURE	TOASTMASTER	TROUBLESOME
SPIRITUALLY	STREETLIGHT	SUPPOSITION	TEMPESTUOUS	TOBACCONIST	TROUBLESPOT
SPIROCHAETE	STRENUOUSLY	SUPPOSITORY	TEMPORARILY	TOBOGGANING	TRUCULENTLY
SPITSTICKER	STRETCHABLE	SUPPRESSION	TENACIOUSLY	TONSILLITIS	TRUSTEESHIP
SPLUTTERING	STRETCHLESS	SUPPURATION	TENDENTIOUS	TOPLOFTICAL	TRUSTWORTHY
SPOKESWOMAN	STRIKEBOUND	SURROUNDING	TENSIOMETER	TOPOGRAPHER	TRYPANOSOMA
SPONDULICKS	STRINGBOARD	SURTARBRAND	TENTATIVELY	TORRIDONIAN	TRYPANOSOME
SPONDYLITIS	STRINGENTLY	SURTURBRAND	TENTERHOOKS	TORTICOLLIS	TSCHERNOSEM
SPONSORSHIP	STRINGYBARK	SURVEILLANT	TENUOUSNESS	TORTICULLUS	TURBELLARIA
SPONTANEITY	STROBOSCOPE	SUSCEPTIBLE	TERMINATION	TOSTICATION	TURRICULATE
SPONTANEOUS	STRONGYLOID	SUSTAINABLE	TERMINOLOGY	TOTALIZATOR	TWELVEMONTH
SPORTSFIELD	STROPHILLUS	SUSURRATION	TERPSICHORE	TOURBILLION	TYPESETTING
SPORTSWOMAN	STRUTHIONES	SVARABHAKTI	TERREMOTIVE	TOWNSPEOPLE	TYPEWRITTEN
SPREADSHEET	STYLISHNESS	SWALLOWABLE	TERRESTRIAL	TOXICOGENIC	TYPOGRAPHER
SPRINGBOARD	STYLIZATION	SWITCHBOARD	TERRITORIAL	TOXOPHILITE	TYPOGRAPHIC
SPRINGCLEAN	STYLOPODIUM	SWITZERLAND	TESSARAGLOT	TRACASSERIE	TYRANNOSAUR
SPRINGHOUSE	STYMPHALIAN	SWORDSWOMAN	TESSELLATED	TRACHEOTOMY	TYROGLYPHID
SPRINGINESS	SUBCONTRACT	SYCOPHANTIC	TESTIMONIAL	TRACKLEMENT	TYRONENSIAN

ULOTRICHALE	UNFAVORABLE	UTRICULARIA	WELLBEHAVED	BACKPACKING	CARNIVOROUS
ULTRAMARINE	UNFLAPPABLE	VACCINATION	WELLDEFINED	BACKSLIDING	CAROLINGIAN
ULTRAMODERN	UNFLINCHING	VACILLATING	WELLDRESSED	BADDELEYITE	CARRIAGEWAY
ULTRAVIOLET	UNFORTUNATE	VACILLATION	WELLFOUNDED	BADTEMPERED	CARSICKNESS
UNALIENABLE	UNFULFILLED	VACUOUSNESS	WELLINGTONS	BALISTRARIA	CARTOGRAPHY
UNALTERABLE	UNFURNISHED	VALEDICTION	WELLMEANING	BALLBEARING	CASSITERITE
UNAMBIGUOUS	UNGETATABLE	VALEDICTORY	WENSLEYDALE	BANDEIRANTE	CASTELLATED
UNANIMOUSLY	UNGODLINESS	VALLAMBROSA	WESTERNMOST	BANGLADESHI	CATACAUSTIC
UNANNOUNCED	UNHAPPINESS	VALLISNERIA	WESTMINSTER	BANNOCKBURN	CATACHRESIS
UNASSERTIVE	UNIFICATION	VARANGARIAN	WESTPHALIAN	BARBASTELLE	CATACLYSMIC
UNAUTHENTIC	UNIMPORTANT	VARIABILITY	WHEELBARROW	BARBITURATE	CATADROMOUS
UNAVAILABLE	UNIMPRESSED	VARIEGATION	WHEELWRIGHT	BARNSTORMER	CATALLACTIC
UNAVOIDABLE	UNINHABITED	VARIOLATION	WHEREABOUTS	BARTHOLOMEW	CATASTROPHE
UNAVOIDABLY	UNINHIBITED	VARSOVIENNE	WHEREWITHAL	BARYCENTRIC	CATCHPHRASE
UNBEFITTING	UNINITIATED	VASOPRESSIN	WHIGMALEERY	BASHFULNESS	CATEGORICAL
UNBLEMISHED	UNIVERSALLY	VENDEMIAIRE	WHISKERANDO	BASKERVILLE	CATERPILLAR
UNBREAKABLE	UNJUSTIFIED	VENTILATION	WHISTLESTOP	BATHYSPHERE	CATHOLICISM
UNCASTRATED	UNMITIGATED	VENTURESOME	WHITEBOYISM	BATTLEDRESS	CAULIFLOWER
UNCERTAINTY	UNMOTIVATED	VERBIGERATE	WHITECHAPEL	BATTLEFIELD	CAUSTICALLY
UNCHRISTIAN	UNNATURALLY	VERMICULITE	WHITECOLLAR	BATTLEFRONT	DACTYLOGRAM
UNCIVILISED	UNNECESSARY	VERSATILITY	WHITEFRIARS	BATTLEMENTS	DANGEROUSLY
UNCIVILIZED	UNOBSERVANT	VERTIGINOUS	WHITETHROAT	CABBALISTIC	DARDANELLES
UNCLEANNESS	UNOBTRUSIVE	VESPERTINAL	WHITLEATHER	CACOGASTRIC	EARNESTNESS
UNCLUTTERED	UNPALATABLE	VESUVIANITE	WHITSUNTIDE	CACOPHONOUS	EARTHENWARE
UNCOMMITTED	UNPATRIOTIC	VICARIOUSLY	WHITTINGTON	CALCEOLARIA	EARTHSHAKER
UNCONCEALED	UNPERTURBED	VICHYSOISSE	WIDERANGING	CALCULATING	EASTERNMOST
UNCONCERNED	UNPRACTICAL	VICIOUSNESS	WIENERWURST	CALCULATION	FABRICATION
UNCONFIRMED	UNPRINTABLE	VICISSITUDE	WILBERFORCE	CALEFACIENT	FACETIOUSLY
UNCONNECTED	UNPROTECTED	VIDEOCAMERA	WILLINGNESS	CALENDERING	FACTFINDING
UNCONQUERED	UNPUBLISHED	VINAIGRETTE	WINDBREAKER	CALIBRATION	FACULTATIVE
UNCONSCIOUS	UNQUALIFIED	VINBLASTINE	WINDCHEATER	CALIFORNIUM	FAIRWEATHER
UNCONTESTED	UNREALISTIC	VINCRISTINE	WINDLESTRAW	CALLANETICS	FALLIBILITY
UNCONVERTED	UNREASONING	VINDICATION	WINDOWFRAME	CALLIGRAPHY	FAMILIARISE
UNCONVINCED	UNREHEARSED	VIOLINCELLO	WINDOWLEDGE	CALLIPYGEAN	FAMILIARITY
UNCOUNTABLE	UNRELENTING	VIOLONCELLO	WINDSURFING	CALLISTEMON	FAMILIARIZE
UNCOUTHNESS	UNREMITTING	VISCOUNTESS	WINTERBERRY	CALLITRICHE	FANATICALLY
UNCRUSHABLE	UNREPENTANT	VITAMINIZED	WINTERGREEN	CALLOUSNESS	FANFARONADE
UNDEMANDING	UNRIGHTEOUS	VIVACIOUSLY	WISHTONWISH	CAMALDOLITE	FARINACEOUS
UNDERCHARGE	UNSATISFIED	VIVISECTION	WISTFULNESS	CAMARADERIE	FARKLEBERRY
UNDERCOOKED	UNSATURATED	VOLCANOLOGY	WITCHDOCTOR	CAMERAWOMAN	FARRAGINOUS
UNDERGROUND	UNSCHEDULED	VOLKSKAMMER	WITENAGEMOT	CAMEROONIAN	FARREACHING
UNDERGROWTH	UNSHAKEABLE	VOLUNTARILY	WITHERSHINS	CAMOUFLAGED	FARTHERMOST
UNDERHANDED	UNSHELTERED	VOLUNTARISM	WITHHOLDING	CAMPANOLOGY	FARTHINGALE
UNDERMANNED	UNSHRINKING	VOORTREKKER	WOMANLINESS	CAMPESTRIAN	FASCINATING
UNDERSIGNED	UNSOLICITED	VORACIOUSLY	WONDERFULLY	CAMPHORATED	FASCINATION
UNDERSTATED	UNSPEAKABLE	VOTERIGGING	WOODCARVING	CANDESCENCE	FASHIONABLE
UNDERTAKING	UNSPECIFIED	VULCANOLOGY	WORKMANLIKE	CANDIDATURE	FASHIONABLY
UNDERVALUED	UNSTOPPABLE	WAINSCOTING	WORKMANSHIP	CANDLELIGHT	FATUOUSNESS
UNDERWEIGHT	UNSUPPORTED	WAKEFULNESS	WORKSTATION	CANDLESTICK	FAULTFINDER
UNDERWRITER	UNSURPASSED	WALDSTERBEN	WORLDFAMOUS	CANNIBALISM	FAULTLESSLY
UNDESERVING	UNSUSPECTED	WAPPENSCHAW	WORLDLINESS	CANNIBALIZE	FAUXBOURDON
UNDESIRABLE	UNSWEETENED	WAREHOUSING	WORRYTROUGH	CAPACITANCE	FAVOURITISM
UNDEVELOPED	UNTHINKABLE	WARMHEARTED	WRONGHEADED	CAPACITATOR	GABERLUNZIE
UNDIGNIFIED	UNTOUCHABLE	WASHERWOMAN	XENODOCHIUM	CAPERNOITED	GALLIBAGGER
UNDISCLOSED	UNTRAMELLED	WASHLEATHER	XEROPHILOUS	CAPERNOITIE	GALLIBEGGAR
UNDISGUISED	UNUNQUADIUM	WASTEBASKET	XEROTHERMIC	CAPRICCIOSO	GALLIGANTUS
UNDISTURBED	UNUTTERABLE	WATERCOLOUR	XEROTRIPSIS	CAPTIVATING	GALLIMAUFRY
UNDOUBTEDLY	UNVARNISHED	WATERCOURSE	XYLOGRAPHER	CAPTIVATION	GALLOVIDIAN
UNDRINKABLE	UNWARRANTED	WATEREDDOWN	YELLOWPLUSH	CARABINIERE	GALLOWGLASS
UNEMOTIONAL	UNWELCOMING	WATERLOGGED	YELLOWSTONE	CARAVANNING	GALLYBAGGER
UNENDURABLE	UNWHOLESOME	WATERMEADOW	ZOOPLANKTON	CARBORUNDUM	GALLYBEGGAR
UNENVELOPED	UNWITTINGLY	WATERSKIING	ZOROASTRIAN	CARBURETTOR	GAMETANGIUM
UNEQUIVOCAL	UPHOLSTERER	WATERSPLASH	ZWISCHENZUG	CARDIOGRAPH	GAMETOPHYTE
UNESSENTIAL	UPRIGHTNESS	WAYWARDNESS	**11:2**	CARDOPHAGUS	GAMMERSTANG
UNEXPLAINED	USELESSNESS	WEATHERCOCK	BACCHANALIA	CAREFULNESS	GAMOGENESIS
UNEXPRESSED	UTILITARIAN	WEIGHBRIDGE	BACKBENCHER	CARMINATIVE	GARNISHMENT
UNFAILINGLY	UTILIZATION	WELLADVISED	BACKFIELDER	CARNAPTIOUS	GARRULOUSLY

GASTRECTOMY	MACHINATION	NATURALNESS	RATIONALITY	WAREHOUSING	ACRIFLAVINE
GASTRONOMIC	MACROBIOTIC	NATUROPATHY	RATIONALIZE	WARMHEARTED	ACRIMONIOUS
GATECRASHER	MACROGAMETE	NAUGHTINESS	RATTLESNAKE	WASHERWOMAN	ACROCENTRIC
HABERDASHER	MACROSCOPIC	OARSMANSHIP	RAUCOUSNESS	WASHLEATHER	ACTUALITIES
HABILIMENTS	MAGISTERIAL	PACIFICALLY	RAVISHINGLY	WASTEBASKET	ACUPUNCTURE
HAEMOGLOBIN	MAGISTRATES	PAEDIATRICS	RAZZAMATAZZ	WATERCOLOUR	ECCALEOBION
HAEMOPHILIA	MAGLEMOSIAN	PAEDOTROPHY	SABBATARIAN	WATERCOURSE	ECTOTROPHIC
HAEMORRHAGE	MAGNANIMITY	PAINKILLING	SACHERTORTE	WATEREDDOWN	ICHTHYOLITE
HAEMORRHOID	MAGNANIMOUS	PAINSTAKING	SACRAMENTAL	WATERLOGGED	ICHTHYORNIS
HAGIOGRAPHA	MAGNIFICENT	PALEOGRAPHY	SACRIFICIAL	WATERMEADOW	ICONOGRAPHY
HAGIOGRAPHY	MAINTENANCE	PALEOLITHIC	SADDLEHORSE	WATERSKIING	ICONOSTASIS
HAIRDRESSER	MAISTERDOME	PALESTINIAN	SAGACIOUSLY	WATERSPLASH	OCHLOCRATIC
HAIRRAISING	MAKEBELIEVE	PAMPELMOOSE	SAGITTARIUS	WAYWARDNESS	OCTASTICHON
HALBSTARKER	MALADJUSTED	PAMPELMOUSE	SAINTLINESS	ABANDONMENT	SCAFFOLDING
HALFBROTHER	MALAKATOONE	PAMPHLETEER	SAINTPAULIA	ABBREVIATED	SCALPRIFORM
HALFHEARTED	MALAPROPISM	PANDEMONIUM	SALACIOUSLY	ABECEDARIAN	SCANDALIZED
HALFHOLIDAY	MALEDICTION	PANOMPHAEAN	SALESPERSON	ABIOGENESIS	SCANDANAVIA
HALLEFLINTA	MALEFACTION	PANTALETTES	SALINOMETER	ABIOGENETIC	SCANDINAVIA
HALLUCINATE	MALEVOLENCE	PAPERWEIGHT	SALPINGITIS	ABLACTATION	SCARABAEOID
HAMMERCLOTH	MALFEASANCE	PARABLEPSIS	SALTIMBANCO	ABNORMALITY	SCARBOROUGH
HANDCRAFTED	MALFUNCTION	PARABOLANUS	SALTIMBOCCA	ABOMINATION	SCAREMONGER
HANDICAPPED	MALICIOUSLY	PARACETAMOL	SALVADORIAN	ABORTIONIST	SCATTERGOOD
HANDICAPPER	MALPRACTICE	PARACHUTIST	SALVOGUNNER	ABRACADABRA	SCATTERLING
HANDWRITING	MANCIPATION	PARACROSTIC	SANDERSWOOD	ABRIDGEMENT	SCEPTICALLY
HANDWRITTEN	MANEUVERING	PARADOXICAL	SANGUINEOUS	ABSENTEEISM	SCEUOPHYLAX
HANGGLIDING	MANGALSUTRA	PARALEIPSIS	SANSEVIERIA	ABSORPTANCE	SCHECKLATON
HAPHAZARDLY	MANIPULATOR	PARAMASTOID	SAPONACEOUS	ABSTRACTION	SCHISTOSOMA
HARDHITTING	MANTELLETTA	PARAMEDICAL	SAPROLEGNIA	OBJECTIVELY	SCHISTOSOME
HARDICANUTE	MANTELPIECE	PARANEPHROS	SAPROPHYTIC	OBJECTIVITY	SCHOLARSHIP
HARDPRESSED	MANTELSHELF	PARASITOSIS	SARCENCHYME	OBLITERATED	SCHOTTISCHE
HARDWORKING	MANUFACTURE	PARATROOPER	SARCOPHAGUS	OBMUTESCENT	SCHRECKLICH
HAREBRAINED	MANUMISSION	PARATYPHOID	SATIRICALLY	OBSERVATION	SCHWARMEREI
HARIOLATION	MAQUILADORA	PARENTHESIS	SAUSAGEMEAT	OBSERVATORY	SCIENTOLOGY
HARPSICHORD	MARCONIGRAM	PARISHIONER	SAVOURINESS	OBSESSIVELY	SCINTILLATE
HATCHETTITE	MARGINALIST	PARLIPOMENA	SAXOPHONIST	OBSOLESCENT	SCIREFACIAS
HAUGHTINESS	MARGINALIZE	PARONOMASIA	TABERNACLES	OBSTETRICAL	SCITAMINEAE
JABBERWOCKY	MARIONBERRY	PARTICIPANT	TACHYCARDIA	OBSTINATELY	SCLERODERMA
JACQUEMINOT	MARIONETTES	PARTICIPATE	TACHYGRAPHY	OBSTRICTION	SCOLECIFORM
JACTITATION	MARIVAUDAGE	PARTICIPIAL	TACITURNITY	OBSTRUCTION	SCOLOPENDRA
JAMAHIRIYAH	MARKETPLACE	PARTNERSHIP	TAGLIATELLE	OBSTRUCTIVE	SCOPOLAMINE
KALASHNIKOV	MARLBOROUGH	PARTURITION	TANGIBILITY	OBTEMPERATE	SCOREKEEPER
KAMELAUKION	MARSHMALLOW	PARVANIMITY	TANTALIZING	OBVIOUSNESS	SCOUTMASTER
KATABOTHRON	MASCULINITY	PASSACAGLIA	TARATANTARA	ACADEMICIAN	SCREAMINGLY
KATAVOTHRON	MASKALLONGE	PASSIVENESS	TARRADIDDLE	ACADEMICISM	SCREWDRIVER
LABORIOUSLY	MASOCHISTIC	PASTEURELLA	TASTELESSLY	ACATALECTIC	SCRIMSHANDY
LABORSAVING	MASQUERADER	PASTOURELLE	TATTERSALLS	ACCELERATOR	SCRIPTORIUM
LACONICALLY	MASSIVENESS	PATERNALISM	TAUROBOLIUM	ACCESSORIES	SCRUFFINESS
LAMENTATION	MASTERFULLY	PATERNOSTER	TAUTOCHRONE	ACCIPITRINE	SCRUMPTIOUS
LAMMERGEIER	MASTERPIECE	PATHOLOGIST	TAXIDERMIST	ACCLAMATION	SCULDUDDERY
LAMMERGEYER	MASTICATION	PATRIARCHAL	VACCINATION	ACCLIMATION	SCULDUGGERY
LAMPLIGHTER	MATERIALISE	PATRONISING	VACILLATING	ACCLIMATISE	SCULLABOGUE
LAMPROPHYRE	MATERIALISM	PATRONIZING	VACILLATION	ACCLIMATIZE	SCUPPERNONG
LANDSKNECHT	MATERIALIST	PAWNBROKERS	VACUOUSNESS	ACCOMMODATE	SCUTTLEBUTT
LAPIDESCENT	MATERIALIZE	RABELAISIAN	VALEDICTION	ACCOMPANIST	SCYPHISTOMA
LARYNGISMUS	MATHEMATICS	RADIOACTIVE	VALEDICTORY	ACCORDINGLY	TCHAIKOVSKY
LASERPICIUM	MATRIARCHAL	RADIOCARBON	VALLAMBROSA	ACCOUNTABLE	ADIAPHORIST
LATERIGRADE	MATRICULATE	RADIOGRAPHY	VALLISNERIA	ACCOUNTANCY	ADJOURNMENT
LATERITIOUS	MATRIMONIAL	RADIOLOGIST	VARANGARIAN	ACCRESCENCE	ADJUDICATOR
LATIFUNDIUM	MAURETANIAN	RAFFISHNESS	VARIABILITY	ACCULTURATE	ADOLESCENCE
LATROCINIUM	MAURITANIAN	RALLENTANDO	VARIEGATION	ACCUMULATOR	ADOPTIANISM
LATTICEWORK	NAPHTHALENE	RAMGUNSHOCH	VARIOLATION	ACHIEVEMENT	ADOPTIONISM
LAUNDERETTE	NARRAGANSET	RANGEFINDER	VARSOVIENNE	ACINACIFORM	ADULLAMITES
LAWBREAKING	NATIONALISM	RAPSCALLION	VASOPRESSIN	ACKNOWLEDGE	ADULTERATED
LAWLESSNESS	NATIONALIST	RAPTUROUSLY	WAINSCOTING	ACOLOUTHITE	ADUMBRATION
MACADAMIZED	NATIONALITY	RASTAFARIAN	WAKEFULNESS	ACQUIESCENT	ADVANCEMENT
MACERANDUBA	NATIONALIZE	RATATOUILLE	WALDSTERBEN	ACQUISITION	ADVENTURESS
MACHAIRODUS	NATIONSTATE	RATIOCINATE	WAPPENSCHAW	ACQUISITIVE	ADVENTUROUS

ADVERBIALLY	DECORATIONS	DETERMINATE	LECITHINASE	NEGOTIATION	PERSONALIZE
ADVERTISING	DECORTICATE	DETERMINING	LECTURESHIP	NEIGHBORING	PERSONIFIED
EDIFICATION	DECREPITATE	DETESTATION	LEFTLUGGAGE	NEIGHBOURLY	PERSPECTIVE
EDUCATIONAL	DECREPITUDE	DETRIMENTAL	LEGERDEMAIN	NERVOUSNESS	PERSPICUITY
IDENTICALLY	DEERSTALKER	DEUTERONOMY	LEGIONNAIRE	NETHERLANDS	PERSPICUOUS
IDENTIFYING	DEFENCELESS	DEUTSCHMARK	LEGISLATION	NETHERLINGS	PERTINACITY
IDEOLOGICAL	DEFENSELESS	DEVALUATION	LEGISLATIVE	NEUROLOGIST	PERTINENTLY
IDEOPRAXIST	DEFENSIVELY	DEVASTATING	LEGISLATURE	NEUTRALISED	PESSIMISTIC
IDIOGRAPHIC	DEFERENTIAL	DEVASTATION	LENGTHENING	NEVERENDING	PETITMAITRE
IDIOTICALLY	DEFOLIATION	DEVELOPMENT	LENGTHINESS	NEWSCASTING	PETRODOLLAR
IDOLIZATION	DEFORMATION	DEVIOUSNESS	LENTIGINOSE	PEACEKEEPER	PETTICOATED
IDYLLICALLY	DEGLUTINATE	DEVITRIFIED	LEPIDOPTERA	PECULIARITY	PETTIFOGGER
ODONTOBLAST	DEGLUTITION	FEASIBILITY	LEPIDOSIREN	PEDAGOGICAL	REACTIONARY
ODONTOPHORE	DEGRADATION	FEATURELESS	LETTERPRESS	PEDESTRIANS	READABILITY
AERODYNAMIC	DEGRINGOLER	FEHMGERICHT	LEVELHEADED	PEDETENTOUS	REALIGNMENT
AERONAUTICS	DEHORTATIVE	FERNITICKLE	MEADOWSWEET	PEEVISHNESS	REALIZATION
AESCULAPIAN	DEHYDRATION	FEROCIOUSLY	MEANDERINGS	PELARGONIUM	REALPOLITIK
AESCULAPIUS	DEIFICATION	FERRONNIÈRE	MEANINGLESS	PELOPONNESE	REANIMATION
BEACHCOMBER	DELECTATION	FESTINATELY	MEASURELESS	PENETRATING	REAPPRAISAL
BEASTLINESS	DELETERIOUS	FESTSCHRIFT	MEASUREMENT	PENETRATION	REASSURANCE
BEAUMONTAGE	DELICIOUSLY	GEGENSCHEIN	MECKLENBURG	PENICILLATE	REBARBATIVE
BEAUTIFULLY	DELICTATION	GELSEMININE	MEDIASTINUM	PENITENTIAL	RECANTATION
BEHAVIOURAL	DELINEATION	GENEALOGIST	MEDICINALLY	PENNYFATHER	RECEPTIVITY
BELEAGUERED	DELINQUENCY	GENERALIZED	MEDIUMSIZED	PENSIONABLE	RECESSIONAL
BELLEROPHON	DELITESCENT	GENERICALLY	MEGALOMANIA	PENSIVENESS	RECIPROCATE
BELLETTRIST	DELIVERANCE	GENETICALLY	MEGALOMANIC	PENTATHLETE	RECIPROCITY
BELLIGERENT	DEMAGOGUERY	GENOUILLÈRE	MEGALOPOLIS	PENTAVALENT	RECLAMATION
BELLYTIMBER	DEMARCATION	GENTLEMANLY	MEGATHERIUM	PENTECONTER	RECOGNITION
BELORUSSIAN	DEMIBASTION	GENTLEWOMAN	MEKHITARIST	PENTECOSTAL	RECONDITION
BENEDICTINE	DEMOGRAPHIC	GENUFLEXION	MELANCHOLIA	PENTHESILEA	RECONNOITER
BENEDICTION	DEMONOMANIA	GENUINENESS	MELANCHOLIC	PENTONVILLE	RECONNOITRE
BENEFICIARY	DEMONSTRATE	GEOMETRICAL	MELANOCHROI	PENULTIMATE	RECONSTRUCT
BENEFICIATE	DEMORALIZED	GEOSYNCLINE	MELLIFLUOUS	PERAMBULATE	RECOVERABLE
BENEVOLENCE	DEMOSTHENES	GERMINATION	MELODIOUSLY	PERCEFOREST	RECRIMINATE
BEREAVEMENT	DEMOSTHENIC	GERONTOLOGY	MEMORABILIA	PERCEPTIBLE	RECRUITMENT
BERGSCHRUND	DENDRACHATE	GERRYMANDER	MENDELEVIUM	PERCEPTIBLY	RECTANGULAR
BESIEGEMENT	DENOMINATOR	GESTATORIAL	MENDELSSOHN	PERCHLORATE	RECTIFIABLE
BESSARABIAN	DENUMERABLE	GESTICULATE	MENSURATION	PERCIPIENCE	RECTILINEAR
BESTSELLING	DEOXYGENATE	HEALTHINESS	MENTHOLATED	PERCOLATION	RECURRENTLY
BEWILDERING	DEPARTEMENT	HEARTBROKEN	MENTONNIÈRE	PERDUELLION	REDOUBTABLE
CEASELESSLY	DEPHLEGMATE	HEARTLESSLY	MEPROBAMATE	PEREGRINATE	REDUPLICATE
CELEBRATION	DEPORTATION	HEAVYHANDED	MERCHANDISE	PERENNIALLY	REFLEXOLOGY
CENTENARIAN	DEPREDATION	HEAVYWEIGHT	MERCHANDIZE	PERESTROIKA	REFOCILLATE
CENTERPIECE	DEPRIVATION	HEBDOMADARY	MERCHANTMAN	PERFORATION	REFORMATION
CENTREBOARD	DERANGEMENT	HECKELPHONE	MERCILESSLY	PERFORMANCE	REFORMATORY
CENTREPIECE	DERELICTION	HELPFULNESS	MERITORIOUS	PERFUNCTORY	REFRESHMENT
CENTRIFUGAL	DERMATOLOGY	HEMERALOPIA	MERRYMAKING	PERICARDIUM	REFRIGERANT
CENTRIPETAL	DESCENDANTS	HEMIANOPSIA	METACARPALS	PERIGORDIAN	REFRIGERATE
CENTUMVIRUS	DESCRIPTION	HEMOPHILIAC	METACENTRIC	PERIODONTIC	REFURBISHED
CENTURIATOR	DESCRIPTIVE	HEMORRHOIDS	METAGENESIS	PERIPATETIC	REGIMENTALS
CERARGYRITE	DESECRATION	HEPATOSCOPY	METALWORKER	PERIPHRASIS	REGISTERING
CEREBRATION	DESEGREGATE	HEPPLEWHITE	METAPHYSICS	PERISSOLOGY	REGRETFULLY
CEREMONIOUS	DESELECTION	HERBIVOROUS	METATARSALS	PERISTALITH	REGRETTABLE
CERTIFIABLE	DESERPIDINE	HERPETOLOGY	METEOROLOGY	PERISTALSIS	REGRETTABLY
CERTIFICATE	DESEXUALIZE	HERRINGBONE	METHODOLOGY	PERITONAEUM	REGURGITATE
CESAREWITCH	DESICCATION	HETEROGRAFT	METRICATION	PERITONITIS	REICHENBACH
DEBILITATED	DESIGNATION	HETEROSCIAN	NEANDERTHAL	PERLUSTRATE	REINCARNATE
DECAPITATED	DESPERATELY	HEXADECIMAL	NEARSIGHTED	PERMANENTLY	REITERATION
DECARBONATE	DESPERATION	JERRYMANDER	NECESSARILY	PERMISSIBLE	RELEASEMENT
DECARBONIZE	DESPONDENCY	KETAVOTHRON	NECESSITATE	PERMUTATION	RELIABILITY
DECEITFULLY	DESTABILIZE	LEADSWINGER	NECESSITOUS	PERPETRATOR	RELIGIOUSLY
DECEPTIVELY	DESTINATION	LEASEHOLDER	NECROBIOSIS	PERPETUALLY	RELUCTANTLY
DECLAMATION	DESTITUTION	LEATHERBACK	NECROMANCER	PERSECUTION	REMEMBRANCE
DECLAMATORY	DESTRUCTION	LEATHERETTE	NEEDLEPOINT	PERSEVERING	REMINISCENT
DECLARATION	DESTRUCTIVE	LEATHERHEAD	NEEDLESTICK	PERSISTENCE	REMONSTRATE
DECLARATIVE	DETERIORATE	LEATHERNECK	NEEDLEWOMAN	PERSONALIST	REMORSELESS
DECONSTRUCT	DETERMINANT	LEATHERWOOD	NEGOTIATING	PERSONALITY	RENAISSANCE

REORIENTATE	SELFDEFENCE	VENTILATION	CHARACINOID	SHAPELINESS	WHITSUNTIDE
REPETITIOUS	SELFEVIDENT	VENTURESOME	CHARGEPAYER	SHAREHOLDER	WHITTINGTON
REPLACEABLE	SELFIMPOSED	VERBIGERATE	CHARISMATIC	SHEATHKNIFE	AIGUILLETTE
REPLACEMENT	SELFISHNESS	VERMICULITE	CHARLEMAGNE	SHENANIGANS	AILUROPHILE
REPRESENTED	SELFRESPECT	VERSATILITY	CHAULMOOGRA	SHEPHERDESS	AIRCRAFTMAN
REPROACHFUL	SELFSERVICE	VERTIGINOUS	CHAULMOUGRA	SHINPLASTER	AIRSICKNESS
REPUDIATION	SEMITRAILER	VESPERTINAL	CHEERLEADER	SHIPBUILDER	BIBLIOPHILE
REQUIREMENT	SEMPITERNAL	VESUVIANITE	CHEESECLOTH	SHIPWRECKED	BICARBONATE
REQUISITION	SEMPITERNUM	WEATHERCOCK	CHEIROGNOMY	SHITTIMWOOD	BICENTENARY
RESEMBLANCE	SENNACHERIB	WEIGHBRIDGE	CHIAROSCURO	SHOPLIFTING	BIELORUSSIA
RESENTFULLY	SENSATIONAL	WELLADVISED	CHIASTOLITE	SHORTCHANGE	BIFURCATION
RESERVATION	SENSIBILITY	WELLBEHAVED	CHICHEVACHE	SHORTCOMING	BILIOUSNESS
RESIDENTIAL	SENSITIVELY	WELLDEFINED	CHICKENFEED	SHORTHANDED	BILLIONAIRE
RESIGNATION	SENSITIVITY	WELLDRESSED	CHILDMINDER	SHOVELBOARD	BIMILLENARY
RESISTIVITY	SENTENTIOUS	WELLFOUNDED	CHILLINGHAM	SHOWERPROOF	BIOCHEMICAL
RESOURCEFUL	SENTIMENTAL	WELLINGTONS	CHINOISERIE	SHOWJUMPING	BIRDWATCHER
RESPECTABLE	SEPIOSTAIRE	WELLMEANING	CHIPPENDALE	SHOWMANSHIP	BITTERSWEET
RESPECTABLY	SEPTENARIUS	WENSLEYDALE	CHIROGRAPHY	SHUNAMITISM	CILOFIBRATE
RESPIRATION	SEPTENTRION	WESTERNMOST	CHIROPODIST	SHUTTLECOCK	CINQUECENTO
RESPIRATORY	SEPTICAEMIA	WESTMINSTER	CHITTERLING	THALIDOMIDE	CIRCULARIZE
RESPLENDENT	SEQUESTRATE	WESTPHALIAN	CHLOROPHYLL	THALLOPHYTE	CIRCULATING
RESPONSIBLE	SERENDIPITY	XENODOCHIUM	CHOCKABLOCK	THANATOPSIS	CIRCULATION
RESPONSIBLY	SERICULTURE	XEROPHILOUS	CHOIRMASTER	THANKLESSLY	CIRCULATORY
RESPONSIONS	SERIOUSNESS	XEROTHERMIC	CHOLESTEROL	THAUMATROPE	CIRCUMCISER
RESTATEMENT	SERVICEABLE	XEROTRIPSIS	CHOLINERGIC	THEATERGOER	CIRCUMFLECT
RESTITUTION	SESQUIOXIDE	YELLOWPLUSH	CHONDROSTEI	THEATREGOER	CIRCUMSPECT
RESTIVENESS	SEVENTEENTH	YELLOWSTONE	CHORDOPHONE	THEATRICALS	CIRRHIPEDEA
RESTORATION	SEVERALFOLD	AFFECTATION	CHOROGRAPHY	THENCEFORTH	CIRRHIPEDIA
RESTORATIVE	SEXOLOGICAL	AFFILIATION	CHRISMATION	THEOBROMINE	CITIZENSHIP
RESTRICTION	SEXTODECIMO	AFFIRMATION	CHRISTENING	THEOLOGICAL	CITLALEPETL
RESTRICTIVE	TEASPOONFUL	AFFIRMATIVE	CHRISTMASSY	THEOPNEUSTY	CITRONELLAL
RESTRUCTURE	TECHNICALLY	AFFLIICTION	CHRISTOPHER	THEORETICAL	DIAGNOSTICS
RESUSCITATE	TECTIBRANCH	AFGHANISTAN	CHROMOPLAST	THERAPEUTAE	DIAMONDBACK
RETALIATION	TEDIOUSNESS	AFTERSCHOOL	CHRONICALLY	THERAPEUTIC	DIAPHORESIS
RETALIATORY	TEENYBOPPER	EFFECTIVELY	CHRONOMETER	THEREABOUTS	DIAPHORETIC
RETARDATION	TEETOTALLER	EFFECTUALLY	CHRYSAROBIN	THERMOMETER	DIARTHROSIS
RETINACULUM	TEGUCICALPA	EFFICACIOUS	CHRYSOPRASE	THERMOPYLAE	DIASCORDIUM
RETINOSCOPY	TÉLÉFÉRIQUE	EFFICIENTLY	GHASTLINESS	THESMOTHETE	DIATESSARON
RETINOSPORA	TELEGRAPHER	OFFENSIVELY	PHALANSTERY	THIGMOTAXIS	DIATESSERON
RETRACTABLE	TELEGRAPHIC	OFFHANDEDLY	PHARISAICAL	THINGAMABOB	DICEPHALOUS
RETRIBUTION	TELEKINESIS	OFFICIALDOM	PHARYNGITIS	THINGAMAJIG	DICHROMATIC
RETRIBUTIVE	TELEPHONIST	OFFICIALESE	PHILANDERER	THINGLINESS	DICOTYLEDON
RETRIEVABLE	TELEPRINTER	OFFICIOUSLY	PHILATELIST	THINGUMAJIG	DICTATORIAL
RETROACTIVE	TELEWORKING	AGGLOMERATE	PHILIPPIANS	THISTLEDOWN	DIFFERENTLY
RETROROCKET	TELOCENTRIC	AGGLUTINANT	PHILIPPINES	THOROUGHPIN	DIFFIDENTLY
REVALUATION	TEMPERAMENT	AGGLUTINATE	PHILLIPSITE	THOUGHTLESS	DIFFRACTION
REVELATIONS	TEMPERATURE	AGGRAVATING	PHILOCTETES	THREATENING	DILAPIDATED
REVENDICATE	TEMPESTUOUS	AGGRAVATION	PHILOLOGIST	THRIFTINESS	DIMENSIONAL
REVERBERATE	TEMPORARILY	AGGREGATION	PHILOSOPHER	THROGMORTON	DIMERCAPROL
REVERENTIAL	TENACIOUSLY	AGNOSTICISM	PHONETICIAN	THUNDERBIRD	DINNYHAUSER
REVISIONISM	TENDENTIOUS	AGONOTHETES	PHONOFIDDLE	THUNDERBOLT	DINNYHAYSER
REVOLUTIONS	TENSIOMETER	AGORAPHOBIA	PHOTOCOPIER	THUNDERCLAP	DIORTHORTIC
SEARCHLIGHT	TENTATIVELY	AGRICULTURE	PHOTOFINISH	THUNDERHEAD	DIPHYCERCAL
SEASICKNESS	TENTERHOOKS	AGROSTOLOGY	PHOTOGRAPHY	THYROTROPIN	DIPLOMATICS
SECONDARILY	TENUOUSNESS	AGUARDIENTE	PHOTOSPHERE	WHEELBARROW	DIPLOMATIST
SECONDCLASS	TERMINATION	EGALITARIAN	PHRASEOLOGY	WHEELWRIGHT	DIPROTODONT
SECRETARIAL	TERMINOLOGY	EGOTISTICAL	PHTHIRIASIS	WHEREABOUTS	DIPSOMANIAC
SECRETARIAT	TERPSICHORE	IGNOMINIOUS	PHYLLOCLADE	WHEREWITHAL	DIPTEROCARP
SECRETIVELY	TERREMOTIVE	IGNORANTINE	PHYSIOGNOMY	WHIGMALEERY	DIRECTIONAL
SEDIMENTARY	TERRESTRIAL	CHAIRPERSON	RHABDOMANCY	WHISKERANDO	DIRECTORATE
SEGREGATION	TERRITORIAL	CHALLENGING	RHAPSODICAL	WHISTLESTOP	DISABLEMENT
SEIGNIORAGE	TESSARAGLOT	CHAMBERLAIN	RHEUMATICKY	WHITEBOYISM	DISAFFECTED
SEISMOGRAPH	TESSELLATED	CHAMBERMAID	RHOPALOCERA	WHITECHAPEL	DISAGREEING
SELAGINELLA	TESTIMONIAL	CHANCELLERY	SHAFTESBURY	WHITECOLLAR	DISAPPROVAL
SELECTIVELY	TETRADRACHM	CHANTARELLE	SHAKESPEARE	WHITEFRIARS	DISARMAMENT
SELECTIVITY	TETRAHEDRON	CHANTERELLE	SHALLOWNESS	WHITETHROAT	DISBELIEVER
SELFCONTROL	VENDEMIAIRE	CHANTICLEER	SHAMELESSLY	WHITLEATHER	DISCERNIBLE

DISCERNMENT	GIGGLESTICK	MISANTHROPE	VICHYSOISSE	BLOODSUCKER	PLANETARIUM
DISCIPLINED	GIGGLESWICK	MISANTHROPY	VICIOUSNESS	BLUNDERBORE	PLANTAGENET
DISCOLOURED	GIGGLEWATER	MISBEGOTTEN	VICISSITUDE	CLADOSPORUM	PLANTIGRADE
DISCONTINUE	GILLYFLOWER	MISBEHAVIOR	VIDEOCAMERA	CLAIRSCHACH	PLATERESQUE
DISCOTHEQUE	GINGERBREAD	MISCARRIAGE	VINAIGRETTE	CLAIRVOYANT	PLATYRRHINE
DISCOURTESY	GIRDLESTEAD	MISCHIEVOUS	VINBLASTINE	CLANDESTINE	PLAYFULNESS
DISCREPANCY	HIBERNATING	MISCONSTRUE	VINCRISTINE	CLANJAMFRAY	PLEASURABLE
DISEMBODIED	HIBERNATION	MISDEMEANOR	VINDICATION	CLAPPERCLAW	PLEBEIANISE
DISENCUMBER	HIDEOUSNESS	MISERICORDE	VIOLINCELLO	CLARENCIEUX	PLEISTOCENE
DISENTANGLE	HIGHLIGHTER	MISERLINESS	VIOLONCELLO	CLEANLINESS	PLEURODYNIA
DISFIGURING	HIGHPITCHED	MISFEASANCE	VISCOUNTESS	CLEANSHAVEN	PLOUGHSHARE
DISGRACEFUL	HIGHPOWERED	MISIDENTIFY	VITAMINIZED	CLIFFHANGER	SLEEPWALKER
DISGRUNTLED	HIGHPROFILE	MISSISSIPPI	VIVACIOUSLY	CLIMACTERIC	SLENDERNESS
DISHEVELLED	HIGHQUALITY	MISSPELLING	VIVISECTION	CLIMATOLOGY	SLEUTHHOUND
DISHONESTLY	HIGHRANKING	MISTRUSTFUL	WIDERANGING	CLINOCHLORE	SLIGHTINGLY
DISILLUSION	HILARIOUSLY	NIACINAMIDE	WIENERWURST	CLIOMETRICS	SLUMBERWEAR
DISIMPRISON	HINDERLANDS	NICKELODEON	WILBERFORCE	ELABORATELY	SLUMGULLION
DISINCLINED	HIPPOCAMPUS	NICKNACKERY	WILLINGNESS	ELABORATION	ULOTRICHALE
DISINTEREST	HIPPOCRATES	NIERSTEINER	WINDBREAKER	ELASTOPLAST	ULTRAMARINE
DISJUNCTION	HIPPOCRATIC	NIGHTINGALE	WINDCHEATER	ELECTRICIAN	ULTRAMODERN
DISJUNCTIVE	HISTOLOGIST	NIGHTMARISH	WINDLESTRAW	ELECTRICITY	ULTRAVIOLET
DISLOCATION	HISTORIATED	NIKETHAMIDE	WINDOWFRAME	ELECTROCUTE	AMBIVALENCE
DISOBEDIENT	HISTRIONICS	NIPFARTHING	WINDOWLEDGE	ELECTROLIER	AMELANCHIER
DISORGANIZE	JINRICKSHAW	PICKELHAUBE	WINDSURFING	ELECTROLYTE	AMERCIAMENT
DISORIENTED	KIDDLEYWINK	PICKYOUROWN	WINTERBERRY	ELECTRONICS	AMERICANISM
DISPARAGING	KILIMANJARO	PICTURESQUE	WINTERGREEN	ELECTROTINT	AMINOBUTENE
DISPENSABLE	KILOCALORIE	PIEDMONTITE	WISHTONWISH	ELEPHANTINE	AMMOPHILOUS
DISPERSABLE	KIMERIDGIAN	PIERREPOINT	WISTFULNESS	ELEUTHERIAN	AMOBARBITAL
DISPLEASURE	KINCHINMORT	PINACOTHECA	WITCHDOCTOR	ELIGIBILITY	AMONTILLADO
DISPOSITION	KINDERSPIEL	PINNYWINKLE	WITENAGEMOT	ELIMINATION	AMPHETAMINE
DISPUTATION	KINDHEARTED	PISCATORIAL	WITHERSHINS	ELIZABETHAN	AMPHIBOLOGY
DISQUIETING	KINNIKINICK	PISSASPHALT	WITHHOLDING	ELUCIDATION	AMPHISBAENA
DISREGARDED	KIRKPATRICK	PITCHBLENDE	EJACULATION	FLABBERGAST	AMPHISBOENA
DISSEMINATE	KITCHENETTE	RIBONUCLEIC	SKEPTICALLY	FLAMBOYANCE	AMPLEXICAUL
DISSEPIMENT	LIBERTARIAN	RIDDLEMEREE	SKETCHINESS	FLAMBOYANTE	AMYLOPECTIN
DISSERTATOR	LICKSPITTLE	RIFACIMENTO	SKIDBLADNIR	FLANKERBACK	EMBARKATION
DISSIMULATE	LIGHTHEADED	RIGHTANGLED	SKILLIGALEE	FLANNELETTE	EMBARRASSED
DISSIPATION	LIGHTWEIGHT	RIGHTEOUSLY	SKILLIGOLEE	FLAVOURSOME	EMBELLISHED
DISSOLUTION	LILLIPUTIAN	RIGHTHANDED	SKIMMINGTON	FLEXIBILITY	EMBOÎTEMENT
DISTASTEFUL	LINDISFARNE	RIGHTHANDER	SKULDUDDERY	FLICKERTAIL	EMBROCATION
DISTINCTION	LINGUISTICS	RIGHTWINGER	SKULDUGGERY	FLIRTATIOUS	EMMENAGOGUE
DISTINCTIVE	LIQUIDAMBAR	RINFORZANDO	ALBIGENSIAN	FLORILEGIUM	EMMENTHALER
DISTINGUISH	LIQUIDATION	RINTHEREOUT	ALBUGINEOUS	FLOURISHING	EMOTIONALLY
DISTRACTION	LITERALNESS	SIGHTSCREEN	ALBUMINURIA	FLUCTUATING	EMPHYTEUSIS
DISTRESSING	LITHOGRAPHY	SIGHTSEEING	ALCYONARIAN	FLUCTUATION	EMPIECEMENT
DISTRIBUTED	LITTÉRATEUR	SIGNIFICANT	ALEXANDRINE	FLUORESCENT	EMPIRICUTIC
DISTRIBUTOR	LIVINGSTONE	SILLIMANITE	ALEXANDRITE	FLUOROMETER	EMPLACEMENT
DISTRUSTFUL	MICHURINISM	SILVERBERRY	ALIFANFARON	FLUOROSCOPE	EMPOWERMENT
DISTURBANCE	MICROGAMETE	SILVERPOINT	ALLEGORICAL	GLADWELLISE	EMPTYHANDED
DITHELETISM	MICROSCOPIC	SILVERSMITH	ALLELOMORPH	GLASTONBURY	EMPYROMANCY
DITTOGRAPHY	MICROSECOND	SINGAPOREAN	ALLEVIATION	GLIMMERGOWK	IMAGINATION
DIVORCEMENT	MICROTUBULE	SINGLESTICK	ALPHABETIZE	GLOSSOLALIA	IMAGINATIVE
EINSTEINIUM	MICROVILLUS	SINGULARITY	ALTERCATION	GLUCOSAMINE	IMMEDIATELY
FIDDLEDEDEE	MICTURITION	SINISTRORSE	ALTERNATELY	ILLMANNERED	IMMIGRATION
FIELDWORKER	MIDDENSTEAD	TICKTACKTOE	ALTERNATING	ILLOGICALLY	IMMORTALISE
FILAMENTOUS	MIDDLEMARCH	TIDDLEYWINK	ALTERNATION	ILLUMINANCE	IMMORTALITY
FILLIBUSTER	MIDDLESIZED	TIGGYWINKLE	ALTERNATIVE	ILLUMINATED	IMMORTALIZE
FINANCIALLY	MILLIAMPERE	TIGHTFISTED	BLACKFELLOW	ILLUSIONARY	IMPARTIALLY
FINGERPRINT	MILLIONAIRE	TIGHTLIPPED	BLACKMAILER	ILLUSIONISM	IMPASSIONED
FINGERSTALL	MILQUETOAST	TIMBROMANIA	BLADDERWORT	ILLUSIONIST	IMPASSIVELY
FIRECRACKER	MINESWEEPER	TIMBROPHILY	BLAMEWORTHY	ILLUSTRATOR	IMPATIENTLY
FIRELIGHTER	MINIATURIST	TIMEKEEPING	BLANKURSINE	ILLUSTRIOUS	IMPEACHMENT
FISHANDCHIP	MINIATURIZE	TIMESHARING	BLASPHEMOUS	ILLYWHACKER	IMPECUNIOUS
FISHMONGERS	MINISTERIAL	TIRONENSIAN	BLESSEDNESS	KLEPTOMANIA	IMPEDIMENTA
FISSIONABLE	MINISTERING	TITILLATION	BLOCKBUSTER	OLIGOCHAETE	IMPERFORATE
FITZWILLIAM	MINNESINGER	TITLEHOLDER	BLOODSPORTS	PLAGIARISED	IMPERIALISM
GIBBERELLIN	MISALLIANCE	VICARIOUSLY	BLOODSTREAM	PLAGIOSTOMI	IMPERIALIST

IMPERIOUSLY	ANTICYCLONE	INCONSTANCY	INOPERATIVE	INTRADERMAL	UNDEVELOPED
IMPERMANENT	ANTINEUTRON	INCONTINENT	INOPPORTUNE	INTRAVENOUS	UNDIGNIFIED
IMPERMEABLE	ANTIPHONARY	INCORPORATE	INQUIRINGLY	INTREPIDITY	UNDISCLOSED
IMPERSONATE	ANTIPHRASIS	INCORPOREAL	INQUISITION	INTRICATELY	UNDISGUISED
IMPERTINENT	ANTIPYRETIC	INCORRECTLY	INQUISITIVE	INTROVERTED	UNDISTURBED
IMPETUOSITY	ANTIQUARIAN	INCREDULITY	INSCRIPTION	INTUITIVELY	UNDOUBTEDLY
IMPETUOUSLY	ANTIRRHINUM	INCREDULOUS	INSCRUTABLE	INVESTIGATE	UNDRINKABLE
IMPIGNORATE	ANTISTHENES	INCREMENTAL	INSECTICIDE	INVESTITURE	UNEMOTIONAL
IMPLAUSIBLE	ANTISTROPHE	INCRIMINATE	INSECTIVORE	INVIGILATOR	UNENDURABLE
IMPLEMENTAL	ANTONOMASIA	INCUNABULUM	INSENSITIVE	INVINCIBLES	UNENVELOPED
IMPLICATION	ENARTHROSIS	INDEFINABLE	INSEPARABLE	INVOLUNTARY	UNEQUIVOCAL
IMPORTANTLY	ENCAPSULATE	INDENTATION	INSIDIOUSLY	INVOLVEMENT	UNESSENTIAL
IMPORTATION	ENCEPHALOMA	INDEPENDENT	INSINCERITY	KNUCKLEBALL	UNEXPLAINED
IMPORTUNATE	ENCHANTMENT	INDEXLINKED	INSINUATING	ONEIRODYNIA	UNEXPRESSED
IMPRACTICAL	ENCHANTRESS	INDIARUBBER	INSINUATION	ONEIROMANCY	UNFAILINGLY
IMPRECATION	ENCHIRIDION	INDIFFERENT	INSISTENTLY	ONOMASTICON	UNFAVORABLE
IMPRECISION	ENCHONDROMA	INDIGESTION	INSOUCIANCE	ONTOLOGICAL	UNFLAPPABLE
IMPREGNABLE	ENCOURAGING	INDIGNANTLY	INSPIRATION	SNICKERSNEE	UNFLINCHING
IMPROPRIETY	ENCROACHING	INDIGNATION	INSTABILITY	SNORKELLING	UNFORTUNATE
IMPROVEMENT	ENCUMBRANCE	INDIVISIBLE	INSTALLMENT	UNALIENABLE	UNFULFILLED
IMPROVIDENT	ENDOCARDIUM	INDIVISIBLY	INSTANTIATE	UNALTERABLE	UNFURNISHED
IMPRUDENTLY	ENDORSEMENT	INDOMITABLE	INSTIGATION	UNAMBIGUOUS	UNGETATABLE
IMPULSIVELY	ENDOTHERMIC	INDUBITABLE	INSTINCTIVE	UNANIMOUSLY	UNGODLINESS
OMMATOPHORE	ENDOTROPHIC	INDUBITABLY	INSTITUTION	UNANNOUNCED	UNHAPPINESS
OMNIPOTENCE	ENFEOFFMENT	INDULGENTLY	INSTRUCTION	UNASSERTIVE	UNIFICATION
OMNIPRESENT	ENFORCEABLE	INDUPLICATE	INSTRUCTIVE	UNAUTHENTIC	UNIMPORTANT
OMNISCIENCE	ENFORCEMENT	INDUSTRIOUS	INSTRUMENTS	UNAVAILABLE	UNIMPRESSED
SMALLHOLDER	ENFOULDERED	INEBRIATION	INSULTINGLY	UNAVOIDABLE	UNINHABITED
SMITHEREENS	ENFRANCHISE	INEFFECTIVE	INSUPERABLE	UNAVOIDABLY	UNINHIBITED
SMITHSONIAN	ENGHALSKRUG	INEFFECTUAL	INTEGRATION	UNBEFITTING	UNINITIATED
SMITHSONITE	ENGINEERING	INEFFICIENT	INTELLIGENT	UNBLEMISHED	UNIVERSALLY
SMOKESCREEN	ENHANCEMENT	INELUCTABLE	INTEMPERATE	UNBREAKABLE	UNJUSTIFIED
SMORGASBORD	ENJAMBEMENT	INEQUITABLE	INTENSIVELY	UNCASTRATED	UNMITIGATED
SMOULDERING	ENKEPHALINE	INESCAPABLE	INTENTIONAL	UNCERTAINTY	UNMOTIVATED
ANACHRONISM	ENLARGEMENT	INESSENTIAL	INTERACTION	UNCHRISTIAN	UNNATURALLY
ANACOLUTHIA	ENLIGHTENED	INESTIMABLE	INTERACTIVE	UNCIVILISED	UNNECESSARY
ANACREONTIC	ENNEAHEDRON	INEXCITABLE	INTERCALARY	UNCIVILIZED	UNOBSERVANT
ANADIPLOSIS	ENSLAVEMENT	INEXCUSABLE	INTERCEPTOR	UNCLEANNESS	UNOBTRUSIVE
ANAESTHESIA	ENTABLATURE	INEXCUSABLY	INTERCHANGE	UNCLUTTERED	UNPALATABLE
ANAESTHETIC	ENTABLEMENT	INEXPEDIENT	INTERCOSTAL	UNCOMMITTED	UNPATRIOTIC
ANAGNORISIS	ENTERTAINER	INEXPENSIVE	INTERCOURSE	UNCONCEALED	UNPERTURBED
ANAPHYLAXIS	ENTHRALLING	INFANGTHIEF	INTERESTING	UNCONCERNED	UNPRACTICAL
ANAPLEROSIS	ENTITLEMENT	INFANTICIDE	INTERGLOSSA	UNCONFIRMED	UNPRINTABLE
ANAPLEROTIC	ENUMERATION	INFANTRYMAN	INTERGROWTH	UNCONNECTED	UNPROTECTED
ANASTOMOSIS	ENUNCIATION	INFATUATION	INTERLACING	UNCONQUERED	UNPUBLISHED
ANAXIMANDER	ENVIRONMENT	INFERIORITY	INTERLEUKIN	UNCONSCIOUS	UNQUALIFIED
ANDROGENOUS	GNATHONICAL	INFERTILITY	INTERLINGUA	UNCONTESTED	UNREALISTIC
ANDROGYNOUS	INADVERTENT	INFESTATION	INTERMINGLE	UNCONVERTED	UNREASONING
ANENCEPHALY	INADVISABLE	INFILTRATOR	INTERNALIZE	UNCONVINCED	UNREHEARSED
ANESTHETIST	INALIENABLE	INFLAMMABLE	INTERNECINE	UNCOUNTABLE	UNRELENTING
ANESTHETIZE	INATTENTION	INFLUENTIAL	INTERNUNCIO	UNCOUTHNESS	UNREMITTING
ANFRACTUOUS	INATTENTIVE	INFORMALITY	INTERPOLATE	UNCRUSHABLE	UNREPENTANT
ANGELOLATRY	INAUTHENTIC	INFORMATICS	INTERPRETER	UNDEMANDING	UNRIGHTEOUS
ANISOCERCAL	INCALESCENT	INFORMATION	INTERREGNUM	UNDERCHARGE	UNSATISFIED
ANNABERGITE	INCANTATION	INFORMATIVE	INTERRELATE	UNDERCOOKED	UNSATURATED
ANNIVERSARY	INCAPSULATE	INFREQUENCY	INTERROGATE	UNDERGROUND	UNSCHEDULED
ANONYMOUSLY	INCARCERATE	INFURIATING	INTERRUPTER	UNDERGROWTH	UNSHAKEABLE
ANSWERPHONE	INCARNADINE	INGENIOUSLY	INTERSPERSE	UNDERHANDED	UNSHELTERED
ANTECEDENCE	INCARNATION	INGRATITUDE	INTERVENING	UNDERMANNED	UNSHRINKING
ANTECHAMBER	INCESSANTLY	INGREDIENTS	INTERVIEWEE	UNDERSIGNED	UNSOLICITED
ANTEPENDIUM	INCINERATOR	INHABITABLE	INTERVIEWER	UNDERSTATED	UNSPEAKABLE
ANTHESTERIA	INCLINATION	INHABITANTS	INTOLERABLE	UNDERTAKING	UNSPECIFIED
ANTHOCYANIN	INCOHERENCE	INHERITANCE	INTOLERABLY	UNDERVALUED	UNSTOPPABLE
ANTHOLOGIZE	INCOMPETENT	INJUDICIOUS	INTOLERANCE	UNDERWEIGHT	UNSUPPORTED
ANTHONOMOUS	INCOMPOSITE	INNUMERABLE	INTOXICATED	UNDERWRITER	UNSURPASSED
ANTHRACOSIS	INCONGRUITY	INOCULATION	INTOXIMETER	UNDESERVING	UNSUSPECTED
ANTIBURGHER	INCONGRUOUS	INOFFENSIVE	INTRACTABLE	UNDESIRABLE	UNSWEETENED

UNTHINKABLE	COMPETENTLY	CONSTERNATE	COUNTERFEIT	HOMOEOPATHY	MONTESQUIEU
UNTOUCHABLE	COMPETITION	CONSTIPATED	COUNTERFOIL	HOMOGENEITY	MONTGOLFIER
UNTRAMELLED	COMPETITIVE	CONSTITUENT	COUNTERFORT	HOMOGENEOUS	MONTMORENCY
UNUNQUADIUM	COMPILATION	CONSTRAINED	COUNTERGLOW	HOMOGENIZED	MOONLIGHTER
UNUTTERABLE	COMPILEMENT	CONSTRICTED	COUNTERHAND	HOMOIOUSIAN	MORGENSTERN
UNVARNISHED	COMPLACENCY	CONSTRICTOR	COUNTERMAND	HOMOPHONOUS	MOSSTROOPER
UNWARRANTED	COMPLAISANT	CONSTRUCTOR	COUNTERPANE	HOMOTHERMAL	MOUNTAINEER
UNWELCOMING	COMPLICATED	CONSTUPRATE	COUNTERPART	HOMOTHERMIC	MOUNTAINOUS
UNWHOLESOME	COMPLIMENTS	CONSULTANCY	COUNTERSIGN	HONEYCOMBED	MOXIBUSTION
UNWITTINGLY	COMPOSITION	CONSUMABLES	COUNTERSINK	HONEYMOONER	MOZAMBIQUAN
BODHISATTVA	COMPOTATION	CONSUMERISM	COUNTRIFIED	HONEYSUCKLE	NOISELESSLY
BOMBARDMENT	COMPRIMARIO	CONSUMPTION	COUNTRYSIDE	HOOLIGANISM	NOMENCLATOR
BOOKBINDING	COMPTROLLER	CONSUMPTIVE	COURTEOUSLY	HOOTANANNIE	NONCHALANCE
BOOKKEEPING	COMPUNCTION	CONTAINMENT	COURTLINESS	HOOTENANNIE	NONDESCRIPT
BOOKSELLERS	COMPUTATION	CONTAMINANT	COXWAINLESS	HORNSWOGGLE	NONETHELESS
BORBORYGMUS	COMPUTERIZE	CONTAMINATE	DOCTRINAIRE	HORSERACING	NONEXISTENT
BOTANOMANCY	COMRADESHIP	CONTEMPLANT	DOCUMENTARY	HORSERADISH	NONFEASANCE
BOURGEOISIE	COMSTOCKERY	CONTEMPLATE	DODECASTYLE	HORSERIDING	NONSENSICAL
BOUTONNIERE	CONCEALMENT	CONTENEMENT	DOLABRIFORM	HOSPITALITY	NORTHCLIFFE
BOYSENBERRY	CONCEIVABLE	CONTENTEDLY	DOMESTICATE	HOSPITALIZE	NORTHEASTER
COACHFELLOW	CONCEIVABLY	CONTENTIOUS	DOMESTICITY	HOSPITALLER	NORTHWESTER
COAGULATION	CONCENTRATE	CONTENTMENT	DOMINEERING	HOSTILITIES	NOSTRADAMUS
COALESCENCE	CONCEPTICLE	CONTINENTAL	DOUBLECHECK	HOUSEFATHER	NOTHINGNESS
COBBLESTONE	CONCILIATOR	CONTINGENCE	DOUBLECROSS	HOUSEHOLDER	NOTICEBOARD
COCKLESHELL	CONCISENESS	CONTINGENCY	DOUROUCOULI	HOUSEKEEPER	NOTORIOUSLY
COEFFICIENT	CONCOMITANT	CONTINUALLY	DOWNHEARTED	HOUSEMASTER	NOTOTHERIUM
COENOBITISM	CONCORDANCE	CONTINUANCE	DOWNTRODDEN	HOUSEMOTHER	NOURISHMENT
COEXISTENCE	CONCURRENCE	CONTRACTION	EOANTHROPUS	HOUSEPARENT	NOVELETTISH
COGNOSCENTE	CONDITIONAL	CONTRACTUAL	FOMENTATION	JOSEPHINITE	POCOCURANTE
COGNOSCENTI	CONDITIONER	CONTRAPTION	FOOLISHNESS	KOMMERSBUCH	PODSNAPPERY
COHORTATIVE	CONDOLENCES	CONTRASTING	FOOTBALLING	KOTABOTHRON	POINTLESSLY
COINCIDENCE	CONDOMINIUM	CONTRAYERVA	FOOTWASHING	LOCORESTIVE	POLICEWOMAN
COLDBLOODED	CONDOTTIERE	CONTRETEMPS	FORAMINIFER	LOGARITHMIC	POLIORCETIC
COLEORRHIZA	CONDOTTIORE	CONTRIBUTOR	FORBEARANCE	LOGGERHEADS	POLITICALLY
COLLABORATE	CONDUCTANCE	CONTRIVANCE	FORBIDDANCE	LOGODAEDALY	POLITICIANS
COLLAPSIBLE	CONDUCTRESS	CONTROVERSY	FORECASTING	LOGOGRAPHER	POLLENBRUSH
COLLECTANEA	CONFABULATE	CONTUBERNAL	FORECLOSURE	LONGANIMITY	POLLINATION
COLLENCHYMA	CONFARREATE	CONURBATION	FOREFATHERS	LONGAWAITED	POLTERGEIST
COLLOCATION	CONFEDERACY	CONVALLARIA	FORESEEABLE	LONGINQUITY	POLYHYDROXY
COLONIALISM	CONFEDERATE	CONVENIENCE	FORESHORTEN	LONGLASTING	POLYMORPHIC
COLONIALIST	CONFIDENTLY	CONVENTICLE	FORESTATION	LONGRUNNING	POLYSTYRENE
COLORIMETER	CONFINEMENT	CONVERGENCE	FORETHOUGHT	LONGSIGHTED	POLYTECHNIC
COLOURBLIND	CONFUTATION	CONVERTIBLE	FOREWARNING	LONGSLEEVED	POLYTRICHUM
COLUMBARIUM	CONGRESSMAN	CONVOCATION	FORFOUGHTEN	LOOSESTRIFE	POMEGRANATE
COMBINATION	CONJECTURAL	CONVOLUTION	FORGIVENESS	LOUDSPEAKER	POMPELMOOSE
COMBUSTIBLE	CONJUGATION	CONVOLVULUS	FORLORNNESS	LOUISIANIAN	POMPELMOUSE
COMESTIBLES	CONJUNCTION	CONVULSIONS	FORMULATION	MOCKINGBIRD	PONDEROUSLY
COMEUPPANCE	CONJUNCTURE	COOPERATION	FORNICATION	MODELMOLEST	PONTIFICATE
COMFORTABLE	CONNECTICUT	COOPERATIVE	FORTHCOMING	MODERNISTIC	PORNOGRAPHY
COMFORTABLY	CONNOISSEUR	COORDINATED	FORTNIGHTLY	MOISTURIZER	PORTERHOUSE
COMFORTLESS	CONNOTATION	COORDINATES	FORTUNATELY	MOLESTATION	PORTLANDIAN
COMMANDMENT	CONSCIOUSLY	COPPERPLATE	FORTUNELOUD	MOLLYCODDLE	PORTMANTEAU
COMMEMORATE	CONSECUTIVE	COPROPHAGAN	FOTHERGILLA	MOMENTARILY	PORTRAITIST
COMMENDABLE	CONSEQUENCE	COPROSTEROL	FOULMOUTHED	MONARCHICAL	PORTRAITURE
COMMENDABLY	CONSERVANCY	CORDWAINERS	FOUNDATIONS	MONCHIQUITE	POSSESSIONS
COMMENTATOR	CONSIDERATE	CORINTHIANS	GODDAUGHTER	MONEYLENDER	POSSIBILITY
COMMINATION	CONSIDERING	CORNERSTONE	GODFORSAKEN	MONEYMAKING	POTAMOGETON
COMMISERATE	CONSIGNMENT	CORPORATION	GONFALONIER	MONOCHINOUS	POTENTIALLY
COMMONPLACE	CONSILIENCE	CORRECTNESS	GOODLOOKING	MONOCHROMAT	ROBESPIERRE
COMMONSENSE	CONSISTENCE	CORRELATION	GOODNATURED	MONOGRAMMED	ROCKEFELLER
COMMUNALISM	CONSISTENCY	CORROBORATE	GORDONSTOUN	MONOLINGUAL	RODOMONTADE
COMMUNICANT	CONSOLATION	CORRUGATION	HOBBLEDEHOY	MONONGAHELA	ROGUISHNESS
COMMUNICATE	CONSOLIDATE	CORRUPTIBLE	HOGGISHNESS	MONONUCLEAR	ROMANTICISM
COMMUTATION	CONSPICUOUS	COTTONMOUTH	HOHENLINDEN	MONOPSONIST	ROMANTICIZE
COMPARATIVE	CONSPIRATOR	COULOMMIERS	HOLLANDAISE	MONOTHELITE	ROSICRUCIAN
COMPARTMENT	CONSTANTINE	COUNSELLING	HOLOTHURIAN	MONOTREMATA	ROTOGRAVURE
COMPENDIOUS	CONSTELLATE	COUNTENANCE	HOMEOPATHIC	MONSTROSITY	ROTTENSTONE

SOCIABILITY	APPLICATION	UPRIGHTNESS	CROOKEDNESS	IRONMONGERY	PRESTRESSED
SOCIOLOGIST	APPOINTMENT	EQUIDISTANT	CROSSLEGGED	IRRADIATION	PRESUMPTION
SOCKDALAGER	APPRECIABLE	EQUILATERAL	CRUCIFIXION	IRREDENTIST	PRESUMPTIVE
SOCKDOLAGER	APPRECIABLY	EQUILIBRIST	CRYSTALLINE	IRREDUCIBLE	PRETENSIONS
SOCKDOLIGER	APPRENTICED	EQUILIBRIUM	CRYSTALLISE	IRREFUTABLE	PRETENTIOUS
SOCKDOLOGER	APPROACHING	EQUINOCTIAL	CRYSTALLIZE	IRREGULARLY	PRETERITION
SOLILOQUIZE	APPROBATION	EQUIPOLLENT	DRACUNCULUS	IRRELEVANCE	PREVARICATE
SOLIPSISTIC	APPROPRIATE	EQUIVALENCE	DRAGGLETAIL	IRRELIGIOUS	PREVENTABLE
SOROPTIMIST	APPROVINGLY	EQUIVOCALLY	DRAGONNADES	IRREPARABLE	PRICKLINESS
SORROWFULLY	APPROXIMATE	ARBITRAGEUR	DRASTICALLY	IRREPARABLY	PRIMIGENIAL
SOUNDLESSLY	APPURTENANT	ARBITRAMENT	DRAUGHTSMAN	IRREVERENCE	PRINCIPALLY
SOUTHAMPTON	EPAMINONDAS	ARBITRARILY	DREADLOCKED	IRREVOCABLE	PRISCIANIST
SOUTHWESTER	EPANALEPSIS	ARBITRATION	DREADNOUGHT	KRIEGSSPIEL	PRIZEWINNER
SOVEREIGNTY	EPICHEIREMA	ARCHAEOLOGY	DRESSMAKING	ORCHESTRATE	PROBABILITY
TOASTMASTER	EPIDIASCOPE	ARCHEGONIAL	DRINKDRIVER	ORCHESTRINA	PROBATIONER
TOBACCONIST	EPIGENESIST	ARCHEGONIUM	DRUNKENNESS	ORCHESTRION	PROCEEDINGS
TOBOGGANING	EPINEPHRINE	ARCHENTERON	DRYCLEANERS	ORDERLINESS	PROCREATION
TONSILLITIS	EPITHYMETIC	ARCHILOCHUS	DRYCLEANING	ORGANICALLY	PROCRUSTEAN
TOPLOFTICAL	EPOCHMAKING	ARCHIPELAGO	ERADICATION	ORGANIZAION	PROCUREMENT
TOPOGRAPHER	IPECACUANHA	ARGATHELIAN	EREMACAUSIS	ORIENTALISM	PRODIGALISE
TORRIDONIAN	OPALESCENCE	ARGENTINIAN	ERIODENDRON	ORIENTALIST	PRODIGALITY
TORTICOLLIS	OPERATIONAL	ARISTOCRACY	ERRATICALLY	ORIENTATION	PROFESSEDLY
TORTICULLUS	OPINIONATED	ARQUEBUSIER	ERRONEOUSLY	ORIGINALITY	PROFICIENCY
TOSTICATION	OPPIGNORATE	ARRANGEMENT	ERYMANTHIAN	ORIGINATING	PROFITEROLE
TOTALIZATOR	OPPORTUNELY	ARRHENOTOKY	ERYTHROCYTE	ORIGINATION	PROFUSENESS
TOURBILLION	OPPORTUNISM	ARRIVEDERCI	FRAGMENTARY	ORNITHOLOGY	PROGENITRIX
TOWNSPEOPLE	OPPORTUNIST	ARTHRAPODAL	FRANKFURTER	ORNITHOPTER	PROGNATHOUS
TOXICOGENIC	OPPORTUNITY	ARTHRODESIS	FRANKLINITE	ORTHOCENTRE	PROGRESSION
TOXOPHILITE	OPPROBRIOUS	ARTHROSPORE	FRANTICALLY	ORTHOGRAPHY	PROGRESSIVE
VOLCANOLOGY	OPTOMETRIST	ARTICULATED	FRATERNALLY	ORTHOPAEDIC	PROHIBITION
VOLKSKAMMER	SPACESAVING	ARTILLERIST	FRAUDULENCE	PRACTICABLE	PROHIBITIVE
VOLUNTARILY	SPANGCOCKLE	ARTIODACTYL	FREEMASONRY	PRACTICALLY	PROLEGOMENA
VOLUNTARISM	SPARROWHAWK	BRAGGADOCIO	FREETHINKER	PRECAUTIONS	PROLETARIAN
VOORTREKKER	SPATTERDASH	BRANDENBURG	FRENCHWOMAN	PRECIPITATE	PROLETARIAT
VORACIOUSLY	SPATTERDOCK	BRAZZAVILLE	FRENCHWOMEN	PRECIPITOUS	PROLIFERATE
VOTERIGGING	SPECIALIZED	BREADCRUMBS	FRIGATEBIRD	PRECONCEIVE	PROLOCUTION
WOMANLINESS	SPECTACULAR	BREADWINNER	FRIGHTENING	PREDECESSOR	PROMINENTLY
WONDERFULLY	SPECULATION	BREASTPLATE	FRIGHTFULLY	PREDESTINED	PROMISCUITY
WOODCARVING	SPECULATIVE	BREATHALYSE	FRIVOLOUSLY	PREDICAMENT	PROMISCUOUS
WORKMANLIKE	SPEECHCRAFT	BRILLIANTLY	FRONTRUNNER	PREDICATIVE	PROMOTIONAL
WORKMANSHIP	SPEEDOMETER	BRISTLECONE	FROSTBITTEN	PREDICTABLE	PROMPTITUDE
WORKSTATION	SPELLBINDER	BRITTLENESS	FRUGIVOROUS	PREDICTABLY	PROOFREADER
WORLDFAMOUS	SPENDTHRIFT	BROADCASTER	FRUITLESSLY	PREDOMINANT	PROPAGATION
WORLDLINESS	SPERMATOZOA	BROADMINDED	FRUSTRATING	PREDOMINATE	PROPHETICAL
WORRYTROUGH	SPERMICIDAL	BRODBINGNAG	FRUSTRATION	PREEMINENCE	PROPHYLAXIS
ZOOPLANKTON	SPERMOPHILE	BROTHERHOOD	GRALLATORES	PREHISTORIC	PROPINQUITY
ZOROASTRIAN	SPESSARTITE	BRUCELLOSIS	GRAMMALOGUE	PREJUDICIAL	PROPOSITION
APATOSAURUS	SPHRAGISTIC	CRACKERJACK	GRAMMATICAL	PRELIBATION	PROPRIETARY
APHANIPTERA	SPIFFLICATE	CRACKHALTER	GRANDFATHER	PRELIMINARY	PROROGATION
APHRODISIAC	SPIRITUALLY	CRACOVIENNE	GRANDMASTER	PREMATURELY	PROSAICALLY
APLANOSPORE	SPIROCHAETE	CRATERELLUS	GRANDMOTHER	PREMEDITATE	PROSECUTION
APOCALYPTIC	SPITSTICKER	CREDENTIALS	GRAPHICALLY	PREMIERSHIP	PROSELYTISM
APODYTERIUM	SPLUTTERING	CREDIBILITY	GRASSHOPPER	PREMONITION	PROSELYTIZE
APOLLINARIS	SPOKESWOMAN	CREDULOUSLY	GRAVEDIGGER	PREMONITORY	PROSPECTIVE
APOLLONICON	SPONDULICKS	CRÉMAILLÈRE	GRAVIMETRIC	PREOCCUPIED	PROSTHETICS
APOMORPHINE	SPONDYLITIS	CREMATORIUM	GRAVITATION	PREPARATION	PROSTRATION
APONEUROSIS	SPONSORSHIP	CRENELLATED	GREASEPAINT	PREPARATIVE	PROTAGONIST
APOPHYLLITE	SPONTANEITY	CREPITATION	GREENBOTTLE	PREPARATORY	PROTEROZOIC
APOSIOPESIS	SPONTANEOUS	CREPUSCULAR	GREENGROCER	PREPOLLENCE	PROTOCOCCUS
APOSTROPHUS	SPORTSFIELD	CRESCENTADE	GREENOCKITE	PREPOSITION	PROTONOTARY
APPALLINGLY	SPORTSWOMAN	CRESTFALLEN	GREGARINIDA	PREROGATIVE	PROTRACTING
APPARATCHIK	SPREADSHEET	CRIMINOLOGY	GRENZGANGER	PRESENTABLE	PROTRACTION
APPEARANCES	SPRINGBOARD	CRITHOMANCY	GROUNDSHEET	PRESENTMENT	PROTUBERANT
APPEASEMENT	SPRINGCLEAN	CRITICASTER	GROUNDSPEED	PRESSURIZED	PROVISIONAL
APPELLATION	SPRINGHOUSE	CROCIDOLITE	GROUNDSWELL	PRESTIGIOUS	PROVISIONER
APPELLATIVE	SPRINGINESS	CROCODILIAN	IRIDESCENCE	PRESTISSIMO	PROVOCATION
APPLERINGIE	UPHOLSTERER	CROMWELLIAN	IRONMONGERS	PRESTONPANS	PROVOCATIVE

PRZEWALSKIS	ASSASSINATE	STEATOPYGIA	BUSINESSMAN	MUSCHELKALK	SUGARCOATED
SRANANTONGO	ASSEMBLYMAN	STEEPLEJACK	BUTTONQUAIL	MUSKELLUNGE	SUGGESTIBLE
TRACASSERIE	ASSIDUOUSLY	STEGANOGRAM	CULMINATION	NUCLEOPLASM	SUITABILITY
TRACHEOTOMY	ASSIGNATION	STEGANOPODE	CULPABILITY	NUMBERPLATE	SUMMERHOUSE
TRACKLEMENT	ASSIMILATED	STEINBERGER	CULTIVATION	NUMERICALLY	SUMPTUOUSLY
TRADITIONAL	ASSOCIATION	STELLIONATE	CULVERINEER	NUMISMATICS	SUNDRENCHED
TRAFFICATOR	ASSYTHEMENT	STENOCHROME	CURNAPTIOUS	NUMISMATIST	SUPERALTERN
TRAGELAPHUS	ASTIGMATISM	STENOGRAPHY	CURTAILMENT	NUTCRACKERS	SUPERCHARGE
TRANQUILITY	ASTONISHING	STEPBROTHER	CUSTOMARILY	NUTRITIONAL	SUPERCHERIE
TRANSACTION	ASTRINGENCY	STEREOGRAPH	DUBIOUSNESS	OUAGADOUGOU	SUPERFICIAL
TRANSCEIVER	ESCARMOUCHE	STEREOMETER	DUMBFOUNDED	OUTDISTANCE	SUPERFICIES
TRANSDERMAL	ESCHATOLOGY	STEREOSCOPE	DUNIEWASSAL	OUTMANEUVER	SUPERFLUITY
TRANSFERRED	ESCHERICHIA	STEREOTYPED	DUPLICATING	OUTPOURINGS	SUPERFLUOUS
TRANSFERRIN	ESPIEGLERIE	STETHOSCOPE	DUPLICATION	OUTSTANDING	SUPERIMPOSE
TRANSFIGURE	ESSENTIALLY	STICKLEBACK	DUSTWRAPPER	PUBLICATION	SUPERINTEND
TRANSFORMED	ESTABLISHED	STILBESTROL	EUCALYPTOLE	PUBLISHABLE	SUPERIORITY
TRANSFORMER	ESTABLISHER	STIMULATION	EUCHARISTIC	PULCHRITUDE	SUPERLATIVE
TRANSFUSION	ESTRAMAZONE	STIPENDIARY	EUCHROMATIN	PUNCHINELLO	SUPERMARKET
TRANSILIENT	ESTRANGHELO	STIPULATION	EUPHEMISTIC	PUNCTILIOUS	SUPERSCRIBE
TRANSLATION	ISOELECTRIC	STOCKBROKER	EURHYTHMICS	PUNCTUALITY	SUPERSCRIPT
TRANSLUCENT	ISOLECITHAL	STOCKHAUSEN	FULFILLMENT	PUNCTUATION	SUPERSEDEAS
TRANSMITTED	ISOMORPHOUS	STOCKHOLDER	FULLBLOODED	PURITANICAL	SUPERSEDERE
TRANSMITTER	ISOXSUPRINE	STOCKJOBBER	FULMINATION	PURPOSELESS	SUPERTANKER
TRANSPARENT	ISTIOPHORUS	STOCKTAKING	FUNAMBULIST	PURPRESTURE	SUPERVISION
TRANSPONDER	OSCILLATION	STOOLPIGEON	FUNCTIONARY	QUADRENNIAL	SUPERVISORY
TRANSPORTED	OSTENTATION	STOREKEEPER	FUNCTIONING	QUADRENNIUM	SUPPEDANEUM
TRANSPORTER	OSTEOPATHIC	STORYTELLER	FUNDAMENTAL	QUADRUPLETS	SUPPOSITION
TRANSURANIC	OSTEOPLASTY	STRADUARIUS	FUNDRAISING	QUALITATIVE	SUPPOSITORY
TRANSVERSAL	OSTRACODERM	STRAITLACED	FURNISHINGS	QUARRELLING	SUPPRESSION
TREACHEROUS	OSTREOPHAGE	STRAMINEOUS	FURTHERANCE	QUARRELSOME	SUPPURATION
TREACHETOUR	PSEUDOLOGIA	STRANDLOPER	FURTHERMORE	QUARRINGTON	SURROUNDING
TREASONABLE	PSEUDOMORPH	STRANGENESS	FURTHERMOST	QUARTERBACK	SURTARBRAND
TREECREEPER	PSITTACOSIS	STRANGEWAYS	FURTHERSOME	QUARTERDECK	SURTURBRAND
TRENCHERMAN	PSYCHEDELIC	STRANGULATE	FURTIVENESS	QUERULOUSLY	SURVEILLANT
TREPIDATION	PSYCHIATRIC	STRAPHANGER	FUSTILARIAN	QUESTIONING	SUSCEPTIBLE
TREPONEMATA	TSCHERNOSEM	STRATEGICAL	GUADALCANAL	QUICKSILVER	SUSTAINABLE
TRESPASSING	USELESSNESS	STREAMLINED	GUBERNATION	QUINTUPLETS	SUSURRATION
TRIBULATION	ATHARVAVEDA	STREETLIGHT	GUESSTIMATE	RUDESHEIMER	TURBELLARIA
TRICERATOPS	ATHERINIDAE	STRENUOUSLY	GULLIBILITY	RUDIMENTARY	TURRICULATE
TRICHINELLA	ATHERMANOUS	STRETCHABLE	GUTTERSNIPE	RUMBUSTIOUS	VULCANOLOGY
TRICHINOSED	ATMOSPHERIC	STRETCHLESS	GUTTURALISE	RUMFRUCTION	AVERRUNCATE
TRICHOPTERA	ATRABILIOUS	STRIKEBOUND	HUCKLEBERRY	RUMGUMPTION	AVOIRDUPOIS
TRIMESTRIAL	ATROCIOUSLY	STRINGBOARD	HUCKSTERAGE	SUBCONTRACT	EVANGELICAL
TRINCOMALEE	ATTENTIVELY	STRINGENTLY	HUMGRUFFIAN	SUBDIVISION	EVAPORATION
TRINIDADIAN	ATTENUATION	STRINGYBARK	HUMILIATING	SUBDOMINANT	EVASIVENESS
TRINITARIAN	ATTESTATION	STROBOSCOPE	HUMILIATION	SUBITANEOUS	EVENTRATION
TRINOBANTES	ATTRIBUTION	STRONGYLOID	HUMMINGBIRD	SUBJUGATION	EVENTUALITY
TRIPHIBIOUS	ATTRIBUTIVE	STROPHILLUS	HUNDREDFOLD	SUBJUNCTIVE	EVERLASTING
TRIPTOLEMUS	ETHNOGRAPHY	STRUTHIONES	HURTLEBERRY	SUBLIMATION	EVISCERATED
TRITAGONIST	ETHNOLOGIST	STYLISHNESS	HUSBANDLAND	SUBMERGENCE	OVARIECTOMY
TRIUMVIRATE	ETYMOLOGIST	STYLIZATION	JUDICIOUSLY	SUBMULTIPLE	OVERBALANCE
TROMPELOEIL	ITHYPHALLIC	STYLOPODIUM	JUSTIFIABLE	SUBORDINATE	OVERBEARING
TROPHOBLAST	ITHYPHALLUS	STYMPHALIAN	JUSTIFIABLY	SUBPANATION	OVERCROWDED
TROPOSPHERE	PTERODACTYL	UTILITARIAN	KULTURKREIS	SUBSERVIENT	OVERDRAUGHT
TROUBLESOME	PTOCHOCRACY	UTILIZATION	LUBRICATION	SUBSISTENCE	OVEREXPOSED
TROUBLESPOT	STADTHOLDER	UTRICULARIA	LUMINESCENT	SUBSTANDARD	OVERFISHING
TRUCULENTLY	STAGFLATION	AUDACIOUSLY	LUXEMBURGER	SUBSTANTIAL	OVERFLOWING
TRUSTEESHIP	STAIRCARPET	AUDIOVISUAL	LUXULYANITE	SUBSTANTIVE	OVERHANGING
TRUSTWORTHY	STAKEHOLDER	AUGUSTINIAN	LUXURIANTLY	SUBTRACTION	OVERLAPPING
TRYPANOSOMA	STALLHOLDER	AURIGNACIAN	LUXURIOUSLY	SUBTROPICAL	OVERLEARNED
TRYPANOSOME	STANDARDIZE	AUXANOMETER	MUDSLINGING	SUBUNGULATA	OVERMANNING
WRONGHEADED	STANDOFFISH	BULLFIGHTER	MULTIRACIAL	SUCCEDANEUM	OVERPAYMENT
ASCLEPIADES	STANDPATTER	BUMBERSHOOT	MULTISTOREY	SUDETENLAND	OVERSTUFFED
ASPERGILLUM	STATELINESS	BUPRESTIDAE	MUNCHHAUSEN	SUFFICIENCY	OVERTURNING
ASPERGILLUS	STATISTICAL	BUREAUCRACY	MUNIFICENCE	SUFFOCATING	OVERWEENING
ASPERSORIUM	STEADFASTLY	BURGOMASTER	MUNITIONIZE	SUFFOCATION	OVERWHELMED
ASPHETERISM	STEAMROLLER	BUSHWHACKER	MURMURATION	SUFFRAGETTE	OVERWROUGHT

OVERZEALOUS	EYECATCHING	ANADIPLOSIS	EJACULATION	MEADOWSWEET	SPATTERDOCK
SVARABHAKTI	GYNAECOLOGY	ANAESTHESIA	ELABORATELY	MEANDERINGS	SRANANTONGO
AWKWARDNESS	HYDROCARBON	ANAESTHETIC	ELABORATION	MEANINGLESS	STADTHOLDER
KWASHIORKOR	HYDROGENATE	ANAGNORISIS	ELASTOPLAST	MEASURELESS	STAGFLATION
SWALLOWABLE	HYDROMEDUSA	ANAPHYLAXIS	ENARTHROSIS	MEASUREMENT	STAIRCARPET
SWITCHBOARD	HYDROPHIDAE	ANAPLEROSIS	EOANTHROPUS	NEANDERTHAL	STAKEHOLDER
SWITZERLAND	HYDROPHOBIA	ANAPLEROTIC	EPAMINONDAS	NEARSIGHTED	STALLHOLDER
SWORDSWOMAN	HYDROPHOBIC	ANASTOMOSIS	EPANALEPSIS	NIACINAMIDE	STANDARDIZE
TWELVEMONTH	HYDROPONICS	ANAXIMANDER	ERADICATION	OPALESCENCE	STANDOFFISH
ZWISCHENZUG	HYDROSTATIC	APATOSAURUS	EVANGELICAL	OUAGADOUGOU	STANDPATTER
AXEROPHTHOL	HYMNOLOGIST	BEACHCOMBER	EVAPORATION	OVARIECTOMY	STATELINESS
EXAGGERATED	HYOPLASTRON	BEASTLINESS	EVASIVENESS	PEACEKEEPER	STATISTICAL
EXAMINATION	HYPERBOREAN	BEAUMONTAGE	EXAGGERATED	PHALANSTERY	SVARABHAKTI
EXANTHEMATA	HYPERMARKET	BEAUTIFULLY	EXAMINATION	PHARISAICAL	SWALLOWABLE
EXASPERATED	HYPERTROPHY	BLACKFELLOW	EXANTHEMATA	PHARYNGITIS	TEASPOONFUL
EXCEEDINGLY	HYPHENATION	BLACKMAILER	EXASPERATED	PLAGIARISED	THALIDOMIDE
EXCEPTIONAL	HYPOCORISMA	BLADDERWORT	FEASIBILITY	PLAGIOSTOMI	THALLOPHYTE
EXCESSIVELY	HYPOTENSION	BLAMEWORTHY	FEATURELESS	PLANETARIUM	THANATOPSIS
EXCLAMATION	HYPOTHECATE	BLANKURSINE	FLABBERGAST	PLANTAGENET	THANKLESSLY
EXCLUSIVELY	HYPOTHERMIA	BLASPHEMOUS	FLAMBOYANCE	PLANTIGRADE	THAUMATROPE
EXCRESCENCE	LYCANTHROPE	BRAGGADOCIO	FLAMBOYANTE	PLATERESQUE	TOASTMASTER
EXECUTIONER	LYCANTHROPY	BRANDENBURG	FLANKERBACK	PLATYRRHINE	TRACASSERIE
EXHILARATED	LYCHNOSCOPE	BRAZZAVILLE	FLANNELETTE	PLAYFULNESS	TRACHEOTOMY
EXHORTATION	MYCOLOGICAL	CEASELESSLY	FLAVOURSOME	PRACTICABLE	TRACKLEMENT
EXONERATION	MYCOPHAGIST	CHAIRPERSON	FRAGMENTARY	PRACTICALLY	TRADITIONAL
EXORBITANCE	MYTHOLOGIZE	CHALLENGING	FRANKFURTER	QUADRENNIAL	TRAFFICATOR
EXOSKELETON	MYXOMATOSIS	CHAMBERLAIN	FRANKLINITE	QUADRENNIUM	TRAGELAPHUS
EXPECTANTLY	NYMPHOMANIA	CHAMBERMAID	FRANTICALLY	QUADRUPLETS	TRANQUILITY
EXPECTATION	PYELOGRAPHY	CHANCELLERY	FRATERNALLY	QUALITATIVE	TRANSACTION
EXPECTORANT	PYRARGYRITE	CHANTARELLE	FRAUDULENCE	QUARRELLING	TRANSCEIVER
EXPECTORATE	PYTHONESQUE	CHANTERELLE	GHASTLINESS	QUARRELSOME	TRANSDERMAL
EXPEDITIOUS	SYCOPHANTIC	CHANTICLEER	GLADWELLISE	QUARRINGTON	TRANSFERRED
EXPENDITURE	SYMMETRICAL	CHARACINOID	GLASTONBURY	QUARTERBACK	TRANSFERRIN
EXPERIENCED	SYMPATHETIC	CHARGEPAYER	GNATHONICAL	QUARTERDECK	TRANSFIGURE
EXPLANATION	SYMPATHISER	CHARISMATIC	GRALLATORES	REACTIONARY	TRANSFORMED
EXPLANATORY	SYMPATHIZER	CHARLEMAGNE	GRAMMALOGUE	READABILITY	TRANSFORMER
EXPLORATION	SYMPLEGADES	CHAULMOOGRA	GRAMMATICAL	REALIGNMENT	TRANSFUSION
EXPLORATORY	SYMPOSIARCH	CHAULMOUGRA	GRANDFATHER	REALIZATION	TRANSILIENT
EXPONENTIAL	SYMPTOMATIC	CLADOSPORUM	GRANDMASTER	REALPOLITIK	TRANSLATION
EXPOSTULATE	SYNCHROMESH	CLAIRSCHACH	GRANDMOTHER	REANIMATION	TRANSLUCENT
EXPROPRIATE	SYNCHRONISE	CLAIRVOYANT	GRAPHICALLY	REAPPRAISAL	TRANSMITTED
EXPURGATION	SYNCHRONISM	CLANDESTINE	GRASSHOPPER	REASSURANCE	TRANSMITTER
EXQUISITELY	SYNCHRONIZE	CLANJAMFRAY	GRAVEDIGGER	RHABDOMANCY	TRANSPARENT
EXTEMPORISE	SYNCHRONOUS	CLAPPERCLAW	GRAVIMETRIC	RHAPSODICAL	TRANSPONDER
EXTEMPORIZE	SYNCOPATION	CLARENCIEUX	GRAVITATION	SCAFFOLDING	TRANSPORTED
EXTENSIVELY	SYNDICALISM	COACHFELLOW	GUADALCANAL	SCALPRIFORM	TRANSPORTER
EXTENUATING	SYNDICATION	COAGULATION	HEALTHINESS	SCANDALIZED	TRANSURANIC
EXTENUATION	SYNTHESIZED	COALESCENCE	HEARTBROKEN	SCANDANAVIA	TRANSVERSAL
EXTERMINATE	SYNTHESIZER	CRACKERJACK	HEARTLESSLY	SCANDINAVIA	UNALIENABLE
EXTERNALIZE	SYSTEMATIZE	CRACKHALTER	HEAVYHANDED	SCARABAEOID	UNALTERABLE
EXTORTIONER	TYPESETTING	CRACOVIENNE	HEAVYWEIGHT	SCARBOROUGH	UNAMBIGUOUS
EXTRADITION	TYPEWRITTEN	CRATERELLUS	IMAGINATION	SCAREMONGER	UNANIMOUSLY
EXTRAPOLATE	TYPOGRAPHER	DIAGNOSTICS	IMAGINATIVE	SCATTERGOOD	UNANNOUNCED
EXTRAVAGANT	TYPOGRAPHIC	DIAMONDBACK	INADVERTENT	SCATTERLING	UNASSERTIVE
EXTROGENOUS	TYRANNOSAUR	DIAPHORESIS	INADVISABLE	SEARCHLIGHT	UNAUTHENTIC
EXTROVERTED	TYROGLYPHID	DIAPHORETIC	INALIENABLE	SEASICKNESS	UNAVAILABLE
OXODIZATION	TYRONENSIAN	DIARTHROSIS	INATTENTION	SHAFTESBURY	UNAVOIDABLE
OXYRHYNCHUS	XYLOGRAPHER	DIASCORDIUM	INATTENTIVE	SHAKESPEARE	UNAVOIDABLY
CYBERNETICS	AZOTOBACTER	DIATESSARON	INAUTHENTIC	SHALLOWNESS	WEATHERCOCK
CYCLOALKANE	**11:3**	DIATESSERON	KWASHIORKOR	SHAMELESSLY	ABBREVIATED
CYCLOSTYLED	ABANDONMENT	DRACUNCULUS	LEADSWINGER	SHAPELINESS	ALBIGENSIAN
CYLINDRICAL	ACADEMICIAN	DRAGGLETAIL	LEASEHOLDER	SHAREHOLDER	ALBUGINEOUS
CYMOPHANOUS	ACADEMICISM	DRAGONNADES	LEATHERBACK	SMALLHOLDER	ALBUMINURIA
CYTOGENESIS	ACATALECTIC	DRASTICALLY	LEATHERETTE	SPACESAVING	AMBIVALENCE
DYAESTHESIA	ANACHRONISM	DRAUGHTSMAN	LEATHERHEAD	SPANGCOCKLE	ARBITRAGEUR
DYSFUNCTION	ANACOLUTHIA	DYAESTHESIA	LEATHERNECK	SPARROWHAWK	ARBITRAMENT
DYSLOGISTIC	ANACREONTIC	EGALITARIAN	LEATHERWOOD	SPATTERDASH	ARBITRARILY

ARBITRATION	ACCOMPANIST	EXCLAMATION	NICKNACKERY	UNCONSCIOUS	ORDERLINESS
BIBLIOPHILE	ACCORDINGLY	EXCLUSIVELY	NUCLEOPLASM	UNCONTESTED	PEDAGOGICAL
CABBALISTIC	ACCOUNTABLE	EXCRESCENCE	ORCHESTRATE	UNCONVERTED	PEDESTRIANS
COBBLESTONE	ACCOUNTANCY	FACETIOUSLY	ORCHESTRINA	UNCONVINCED	PEDETENTOUS
CYBERNETICS	ACCRESCENCE	FACTFINDING	ORCHESTRION	UNCOUNTABLE	PODSNAPPERY
DEBILITATED	ACCULTURATE	FACULTATIVE	OSCILLATION	UNCOUTHNESS	RADIOACTIVE
DUBIOUSNESS	ACCUMULATOR	HECKELPHONE	PACIFICALLY	UNCRUSHABLE	RADIOCARBON
EMBARKATION	ALCYONARIAN	HUCKLEBERRY	PECULIARITY	VACCINATION	RADIOGRAPHY
EMBARRASSED	ARCHAEOLOGY	HUCKSTERAGE	PICKELHAUBE	VACILLATING	RADIOLOGIST
EMBELLISHED	ARCHEGONIAL	INCALESCENT	PICKYOUROWN	VACILLATION	REDOUBTABLE
EMBOÎTEMENT	ARCHEGONIUM	INCANTATION	PICTURESQUE	VACUOUSNESS	REDUPLICATE
EMBROCATION	ARCHENTERON	INCAPSULATE	POCOCURANTE	VICARIOUSLY	RIDDLEMEREE
FABRICATION	ARCHILOCHUS	INCARCERATE	RECANTATION	VICHYSOISSE	RODOMONTADE
GABERLUNZIE	ARCHIPELAGO	INCARNADINE	RECEPTIVITY	VICIOUSNESS	RUDESHEIMER
GIBBERELLIN	ASCLEPIADES	INCARNATION	RECESSIONAL	VICISSITUDE	RUDIMENTARY
GUBERNATION	BACCHANALIA	INCESSANTLY	RECIPROCATE	ANDROGENOUS	SADDLEHORSE
HABERDASHER	BACKBENCHER	INCINERATOR	RECIPROCITY	ANDROGYNOUS	SEDIMENTARY
HABILIMENTS	BACKFIELDER	INCLINATION	RECLAMATION	AUDACIOUSLY	SUDETENLAND
HEBDOMADARY	BACKPACKING	INCOHERENCE	RECOGNITION	AUDIOVISUAL	TEDIOUSNESS
HIBERNATING	BACKSLIDING	INCOMPETENT	RECONDITION	BADDELEYITE	TIDDLEYWINK
HIBERNATION	BICARBONATE	INCOMPOSITE	RECONNOITER	BADTEMPERED	UNDEMANDING
HOBBLEDEHOY	BICENTENARY	INCONGRUITY	RECONNOITRE	BODHISATTVA	UNDERCHARGE
JABBERWOCKY	CACOGASTRIC	INCONGRUOUS	RECONSTRUCT	DODECASTYLE	UNDERCOOKED
LABORIOUSLY	CACOPHONOUS	INCONSTANCY	RECOVERABLE	ENDOCARDIUM	UNDERGROUND
LABORSAVING	COCKLESHELL	INCONTINENT	RECRIMINATE	ENDORSEMENT	UNDERGROWTH
LIBERTARIAN	CYCLOALKANE	INCORPORATE	RECRUITMENT	ENDOTHERMIC	UNDERHANDED
LUBRICATION	CYCLOSTYLED	INCORPOREAL	RECTANGULAR	ENDOTROPHIC	UNDERMANNED
PUBLICATION	DACTYLOGRAM	INCORRECTLY	RECTIFIABLE	FIDDLEDEDEE	UNDERSIGNED
PUBLISHABLE	DECAPITATED	INCREDULITY	RECTILINEAR	GODDAUGHTER	UNDERSTATED
RABELAISIAN	DECARBONATE	INCREDULOUS	RECURRENTLY	GODFORSAKEN	UNDERTAKING
REBARBATIVE	DECARBONIZE	INCREMENTAL	ROCKEFELLER	HIDEOUSNESS	UNDERVALUED
RIBONUCLEIC	DECEITFULLY	INCRIMINATE	SACHERTORTE	HYDROCARBON	UNDERWEIGHT
ROBESPIERRE	DECEPTIVELY	INCUNABULUM	SACRAMENTAL	HYDROGENATE	UNDERWRITER
SABBATARIAN	DECLAMATION	JACQUEMINOT	SACRIFICIAL	HYDROMEDUSA	UNDESERVING
SUBCONTRACT	DECLAMATORY	JACTITATION	SECONDARILY	HYDROPHIDAE	UNDESIRABLE
SUBDIVISION	DECLARATION	LACONICALLY	SECONDCLASS	HYDROPHOBIA	UNDEVELOPED
SUBDOMINANT	DECLARATIVE	LECITHINASE	SECRETARIAL	HYDROPHOBIC	UNDIGNIFIED
SUBITANEOUS	DECONSTRUCT	LECTURESHIP	SECRETARIAT	HYDROPONICS	UNDISCLOSED
SUBJUGATION	DECORATIONS	LICKSPITTLE	SECRETIVELY	HYDROSTATIC	UNDISGUISED
SUBJUNCTIVE	DECORTICATE	LOCORESTIVE	SOCIABILITY	INDEFINABLE	UNDISTURBED
SUBLIMATION	DECREPITATE	LYCANTHROPE	SOCIOLOGIST	INDENTATION	UNDOUBTEDLY
SUBMERGENCE	DECREPITUDE	LYCANTHROPY	SOCKDALAGER	INDEPENDENT	UNDRINKABLE
SUBMULTIPLE	DICEPHALOUS	LYCHNOSCOPE	SOCKDOLAGER	INDEXLINKED	VIDEOCAMERA
SUBORDINATE	DICHROMATIC	MACADAMIZED	SOCKDOLIGER	INDIARUBBER	WIDERANGING
SUBPANATION	DICOTYLEDON	MACERANDUBA	SOCKDOLOGER	INDIFFERENT	ABECEDARIAN
SUBSERVIENT	DICTATORIAL	MACHAIRODUS	SUCCEDANEUM	INDIGESTION	ALEXANDRINE
SUBSISTENCE	DOCTRINAIRE	MACHINATION	SYCOPHANTIC	INDIGNANTLY	ALEXANDRITE
SUBSTANDARD	DOCUMENTARY	MACROBIOTIC	TACHYCARDIA	INDIGNATION	AMELANCHIER
SUBSTANTIAL	ECCALEOBION	MACROGAMETE	TACHYGRAPHY	INDIVISIBLE	AMERCIAMENT
SUBSTANTIVE	ENCAPSULATE	MACROSCOPIC	TACITURNITY	INDIVISIBLY	AMERICANISM
SUBTRACTION	ENCEPHALOMA	MECKLENBURG	TECHNICALLY	INDOMITABLE	ANENCEPHALY
SUBTROPICAL	ENCHANTMENT	MICHURINISM	TECTIBRANCH	INDUBITABLE	ANESTHETIST
SUBUNGULATA	ENCHANTRESS	MICROGAMETE	TICKTACKTOE	INDUBITABLY	ANESTHETIZE
TABERNACLES	ENCHIRIDION	MICROSCOPIC	TSCHERNOSEM	INDULGENTLY	AVERRUNCATE
TOBACCONIST	ENCHONDROMA	MICROSECOND	UNCASTRATED	INDUPLICATE	AXEROPHTHOL
TOBOGGANING	ENCOURAGING	MICROTUBULE	UNCERTAINTY	INDUSTRIOUS	BIELORUSSIA
UNBEFITTING	ENCROACHING	MICROVILLUS	UNCHRISTIAN	JUDICIOUSLY	BLESSEDNESS
UNBLEMISHED	ENCUMBRANCE	MICTURITION	UNCIVILISED	KIDDLEYWINK	BREADCRUMBS
UNBREAKABLE	ESCARMOUCHE	MOCKINGBIRD	UNCIVILIZED	MEDIASTINUM	BREADWINNER
ACCELERATOR	ESCHATOLOGY	MYCOLOGICAL	UNCLEANNESS	MEDICINALLY	BREASTPLATE
ACCESSORIES	ESCHERICHIA	MYCOPHAGIST	UNCLUTTERED	MEDIUMSIZED	BREATHALYSE
ACCIPITRINE	EUCALYPTOLE	NECESSARILY	UNCOMMITTED	MIDDENSTEAD	CHEERLEADER
ACCLAMATION	EUCHARISTIC	NECESSITATE	UNCONCEALED	MIDDLEMARCH	CHEESECLOTH
ACCLIMATION	EUCHROMATIN	NECESSITOUS	UNCONCERNED	MIDDLESIZED	CHEIROGNOMY
ACCLIMATISE	EXCEEDINGLY	NECROBIOSIS	UNCONFIRMED	MODELMOLEST	CLEANLINESS
ACCLIMATIZE	EXCEPTIONAL	NECROMANCER	UNCONNECTED	MODERNISTIC	CLEANSHAVEN
ACCOMMODATE	EXCESSIVELY	NICKELODEON	UNCONQUERED	MUDSLINGING	COEFFICIENT

COENOBITISM	KLEPTOMANIA	PRESTIGIOUS	THERAPEUTIC	INFURIATING	LEGISLATIVE
COEXISTENCE	NEEDLEPOINT	PRESTISSIMO	THEREABOUTS	LEFTLUGGAGE	LEGISLATURE
CREDENTIALS	NEEDLESTICK	PRESTONPANS	THERMOMETER	OFFENSIVELY	LIGHTHEADED
CREDIBILITY	NEEDLEWOMAN	PRESTRESSED	THERMOPYLAE	OFFHANDEDLY	LIGHTWEIGHT
CREDULOUSLY	NIERSTEINER	PRESUMPTION	THESMOTHETE	OFFICIALDOM	LOGARITHMIC
CRÉMAILLÈRE	ONEIRODYNIA	PRESUMPTIVE	TREACHEROUS	OFFICIALESE	LOGGERHEADS
CREMATORIUM	ONEIROMANCY	PRETENSIONS	TREACHETOUR	OFFICIOUSLY	LOGODAEDALY
CRENELLATED	OPERATIONAL	PRETENTIOUS	TREASONABLE	RAFFISHNESS	LOGOGRAPHER
CREPITATION	OVERBALANCE	PRETERITION	TREECREEPER	REFLEXOLOGY	MAGISTERIAL
CREPUSCULAR	OVERBEARING	PREVARICATE	TRENCHERMAN	REFOCILLATE	MAGISTRATES
CRESCENTADE	OVERCROWDED	PREVENTABLE	TREPIDATION	REFORMATION	MAGLEMOSIAN
CRESTFALLEN	OVERDRAUGHT	PSEUDOLOGIA	TREPONEMATA	REFORMATORY	MAGNANIMITY
DEERSTALKER	OVEREXPOSED	PSEUDOMORPH	TRESPASSING	REFRESHMENT	MAGNANIMOUS
DREADLOCKED	OVERFISHING	PTERODACTYL	TWELVEMONTH	REFRIGERANT	MAGNIFICENT
DREADNOUGHT	OVERFLOWING	PYELOGRAPHY	UNEMOTIONAL	REFRIGERATE	MEGALOMANIA
DRESSMAKING	OVERHANGING	QUERULOUSLY	UNENDURABLE	REFURBISHED	MEGALOMANIC
ELECTRICIAN	OVERLAPPING	QUESTIONING	UNENVELOPED	RIFACIMENTO	MEGALOPOLIS
ELECTRICITY	OVERLEARNED	RHEUMATICKY	UNEQUIVOCAL	SUFFICIENCY	MEGATHERIUM
ELECTROCUTE	OVERMANNING	SCEPTICALLY	UNESSENTIAL	SUFFOCATING	NEGOTIATING
ELECTROLIER	OVERPAYMENT	SCEUOPHYLAX	UNEXPLAINED	SUFFOCATION	NEGOTIATION
ELECTROLYTE	OVERSTUFFED	SHEATHKNIFE	UNEXPRESSED	SUFFRAGETTE	NIGHTINGALE
ELECTRONICS	OVERTURNING	SHENANIGANS	USELESSNESS	UNFAILINGLY	NIGHTMARISH
ELECTROTINT	OVERWEENING	SHEPHERDESS	WHEELBARROW	UNFAVORABLE	ORGANICALLY
ELEPHANTINE	OVERWHELMED	SKEPTICALLY	WHEELWRIGHT	UNFLAPPABLE	ORGANIZAION
ELEUTHERIAN	OVERWROUGHT	SKETCHINESS	WHEREABOUTS	UNFLINCHING	REGIMENTALS
EREMACAUSIS	OVERZEALOUS	SLEEPWALKER	WHEREWITHAL	UNFORTUNATE	REGISTERING
EVENTRATION	PAEDIATRICS	SLENDERNESS	WIENERWURST	UNFULFILLED	REGRETFULLY
EVENTUALITY	PAEDOTROPHY	SLEUTHHOUND	AFFECTATION	UNFURNISHED	REGRETTABLE
EVERLASTING	PEEVISHNESS	SPECIALIZED	AFFILIATION	AFGHANISTAN	REGRETTABLY
EXECUTIONER	PIEDMONTITE	SPECTACULAR	AFFIRMATION	AGGLOMERATE	REGURGITATE
EYECATCHING	PIERREPOINT	SPECULATION	AFFIRMATIVE	AGGLUTINANT	RIGHTANGLED
FIELDWORKER	PLEASURABLE	SPECULATIVE	AFFLIICTION	AGGLUTINATE	RIGHTEOUSLY
FLEXIBILITY	PLEBEIANISE	SPEECHCRAFT	ANFRACTUOUS	AGGRAVATING	RIGHTHANDED
FREEMASONRY	PLEISTOCENE	SPEEDOMETER	BIFURCATION	AGGRAVATION	RIGHTHANDER
FREETHINKER	PLEURODYNIA	SPELLBINDER	DEFENCELESS	AGGREGATION	RIGHTWINGER
FRENCHWOMAN	PRECAUTIONS	SPENDTHRIFT	DEFENSELESS	AIGUILLETTE	ROGUISHNESS
FRENCHWOMEN	PRECIPITATE	SPERMATOZOA	DEFENSIVELY	ANGELOLATRY	SAGACIOUSLY
GREASEPAINT	PRECIPITOUS	SPERMICIDAL	DEFERENTIAL	ARGATHELIAN	SAGITTARIUS
GREENBOTTLE	PRECONCEIVE	SPERMOPHILE	DEFOLIATION	ARGENTINIAN	SEGREGATION
GREENGROCER	PREDECESSOR	SPESSARTITE	DEFORMATION	AUGUSTINIAN	SIGHTSCREEN
GREENOCKITE	PREDESTINED	STEADFASTLY	DIFFERENTLY	COGNOSCENTE	SIGHTSEEING
GREGARINIDA	PREDICAMENT	STEAMROLLER	DIFFIDENTLY	COGNOSCENTI	SIGNIFICANT
GRENZGANGER	PREDICATIVE	STEATOPYGIA	DIFFRACTION	DEGLUTINATE	SUGARCOATED
GUESSTIMATE	PREDICTABLE	STEEPLEJACK	EFFECTIVELY	DEGLUTITION	SUGGESTIBLE
HAEMOGLOBIN	PREDICTABLY	STEGANOGRAM	EFFECTUALLY	DEGRADATION	TAGLIATELLE
HAEMOPHILIA	PREDOMINANT	STEGANOPODE	EFFICACIOUS	DEGRINGOLER	TEGUCICALPA
HAEMORRHAGE	PREDOMINATE	STEINBERGER	EFFICIENTLY	ENGHALSKRUG	TIGGYWINKLE
HAEMORRHOID	PREEMINENCE	STELLIONATE	ENFEOFFMENT	ENGINEERING	TIGHTFISTED
IDENTICALLY	PREHISTORIC	STENOCHROME	ENFORCEABLE	GEGENSCHEIN	TIGHTLIPPED
IDENTIFYING	PREJUDICIAL	STENOGRAPHY	ENFORCEMENT	GIGGLESTICK	UNGETATABLE
IDEOLOGICAL	PRELIBATION	STEPBROTHER	ENFOULDERED	GIGGLESWICK	UNGODLINESS
IDEOPRAXIST	PRELIMINARY	STEREOGRAPH	ENFRANCHISE	GIGGLEWATER	ACHIEVEMENT
INEBRIATION	PREMATURELY	STEREOMETER	INFANGTHIEF	HAGIOGRAPHA	APHANIPTERA
INEFFECTIVE	PREMEDITATE	STEREOSCOPE	INFANTICIDE	HAGIOGRAPHY	APHRODISIAC
INEFFECTUAL	PREMIERSHIP	STEREOTYPED	INFANTRYMAN	HIGHLIGHTER	ATHARVAVEDA
INEFFICIENT	PREMONITION	STETHOSCOPE	INFATUATION	HIGHPITCHED	ATHERINIDAE
INELUCTABLE	PREMONITORY	TEENYBOPPER	INFERIORITY	HIGHPOWERED	ATHERMANOUS
INEQUITABLE	PREOCCUPIED	TEETOTALLER	INFERTILITY	HIGHPROFILE	BEHAVIOURAL
INESCAPABLE	PREPARATION	THEATERGOER	INFESTATION	HIGHQUALITY	COHORTATIVE
INESSENTIAL	PREPARATIVE	THEATREGOER	INFILTRATOR	HIGHRANKING	DEHORTATIVE
INESTIMABLE	PREPARATORY	THEATRICALS	INFLAMMABLE	HOGGISHNESS	DEHYDRATION
INEXCITABLE	PREPOLLENCE	THENCEFORTH	INFLUENTIAL	INGENIOUSLY	ENHANCEMENT
INEXCUSABLE	PREPOSITION	THEOBROMINE	INFORMALITY	INGRATITUDE	ETHNOGRAPHY
INEXCUSABLY	PREROGATIVE	THEOLOGICAL	INFORMATICS	INGREDIENTS	ETHNOLOGIST
INEXPEDIENT	PRESENTABLE	THEOPNEUSTY	INFORMATION	LEGERDEMAIN	EXHILARATED
INEXPENSIVE	PRESENTMENT	THEORETICAL	INFORMATIVE	LEGIONNAIRE	EXHORTATION
IPECACUANHA	PRESSURIZED	THERAPEUTAE	INFREQUENCY	LEGISLATION	FEHMGERICHT

HOHENLINDEN	FRIGATEBIRD	SNICKERSNEE	MEKHITARIST	FILLIBUSTER	PELOPONNESE
ICHTHYOLITE	FRIGHTENING	SPIFFLICATE	NIKETHAMIDE	FULFILLMENT	POLICEWOMAN
ICHTHYORNIS	FRIGHTFULLY	SPIRITUALLY	WAKEFULNESS	FULLBLOODED	POLIORCETIC
INHABITABLE	FRIVOLOUSLY	SPIROCHAETE	ABLACTATION	FULMINATION	POLITICALLY
INHABITANTS	GLIMMERGOWK	SPITSTICKER	AILUROPHILE	GALLIBAGGER	POLITICIANS
INHERITANCE	HAIRDRESSER	STICKLEBACK	ALLEGORICAL	GALLIBEGGAR	POLLENBRUSH
ITHYPHALLIC	HAIRRAISING	STILBESTROL	ALLELOMORPH	GALLIGANTUS	POLLINATION
ITHYPHALLUS	IDIOGRAPHIC	STIMULATION	ALLEVIATION	GALLIMAUFRY	POLTERGEIST
OCHLOCRATIC	IDIOTICALLY	STIPENDIARY	APLANOSPORE	GALLOVIDIAN	POLYHYDROXY
SCHECKLATON	IRIDESCENCE	STIPULATION	BALISTRARIA	GALLOWGLASS	POLYMORPHIC
SCHISTOSOMA	KRIEGSSPIEL	SUITABILITY	BALLBEARING	GALLYBAGGER	POLYSTYRENE
SCHISTOSOME	MAINTENANCE	SWITCHBOARD	BELEAGUERED	GALLYBEGGAR	POLYTECHNIC
SCHOLARSHIP	MAISTERDOME	SWITZERLAND	BELLEROPHON	GELSEMININE	POLYTRICHUM
SCHOTTISCHE	MOISTURIZER	THIGMOTAXIS	BELLETTRIST	GILLYFLOWER	PULCHRITUDE
SCHRECKLICH	NEIGHBORING	THINGAMABOB	BELLIGERENT	GULLIBILITY	RALLENTANDO
SCHWARMEREI	NEIGHBOURLY	THINGAMAJIG	BELLYTIMBER	HALBSTARKER	RELEASEMENT
SPHRAGISTIC	NOISELESSLY	THINGLINESS	BELORUSSIAN	HALFBROTHER	RELIABILITY
TCHAIKOVSKY	OLIGOCHAETE	THINGUMAJIG	BILIOUSNESS	HALFHEARTED	RELIGIOUSLY
UNHAPPINESS	OPINIONATED	THISTLEDOWN	BILLIONAIRE	HALFHOLIDAY	RELUCTANTLY
UPHOLSTERER	ORIENTALISM	TRIBULATION	BULLFIGHTER	HALLEFLINTA	SALACIOUSLY
ABIOGENESIS	ORIENTALIST	TRICERATOPS	CALCEOLARIA	HALLUCINATE	SALESPERSON
ABIOGENETIC	ORIENTATION	TRICHINELLA	CALCULATING	HELPFULNESS	SALINOMETER
ACINACIFORM	ORIGINALITY	TRICHINOSED	CALCULATION	HILARIOUSLY	SALPINGITIS
ADIAPHORIST	ORIGINATING	TRICHOPTERA	CALEFACIENT	HOLLANDAISE	SALTIMBANCO
ALIFANFARON	ORIGINATION	TRIMESTRIAL	CALENDERING	HOLOTHURIAN	SALTIMBOCCA
AMINOBUTENE	PAINKILLING	TRINCOMALEE	CALIBRATION	ILLMANNERED	SALVADORIAN
ANISOCERCAL	PAINSTAKING	TRINIDADIAN	CALIFORNIUM	ILLOGICALLY	SALVOGUNNER
ARISTOCRACY	PHILANDERER	TRINITARIAN	CALLANETICS	ILLUMINANCE	SCLERODERMA
BRILLIANTLY	PHILATELIST	TRINOBANTES	CALLIGRAPHY	ILLUMINATED	SELAGINELLA
BRISTLECONE	PHILIPPIANS	TRIPHIBIOUS	CALLIPYGEAN	ILLUSIONARY	SELECTIVELY
BRITTLENESS	PHILIPPINES	TRIPTOLEMUS	CALLISTEMON	ILLUSIONISM	SELECTIVITY
CHIAROSCURO	PHILLIPSITE	TRITAGONIST	CALLITRICHE	ILLUSIONIST	SELFCONTROL
CHIASTOLITE	PHILOCTETES	TRIUMVIRATE	CALLOUSNESS	ILLUSTRATOR	SELFDEFENCE
CHICHEVACHE	PHILOLOGIST	UNIFICATION	CELEBRATION	ILLUSTRIOUS	SELFEVIDENT
CHICKENFEED	PHILOSOPHER	UNIMPORTANT	CHLOROPHYLL	ILLYWHACKER	SELFIMPOSED
CHILDMINDER	POINTLESSLY	UNIMPRESSED	CILOFIBRATE	KALASHNIKOV	SELFISHNESS
CHILLINGHAM	PRICKLINESS	UNINHABITED	COLDBLOODED	KILIMANJARO	SELFRESPECT
CHINOISERIE	PRIMIGENIAL	UNINHIBITED	COLEORRHIZA	KILOCALORIE	SELFSERVICE
CHIPPENDALE	PRINCIPALLY	UNINITIATED	COLLABORATE	KULTURKREIS	SILLIMANITE
CHIROGRAPHY	PRISCIANIST	UNIVERSALLY	COLLAPSIBLE	LILLIPUTIAN	SILVERBERRY
CHIROPODIST	PRIZEWINNER	UTILITARIAN	COLLECTANEA	MALADJUSTED	SILVERPOINT
CHITTERLING	PSITTACOSIS	UTILIZATION	COLLENCHYMA	MALAKATOONE	SILVERSMITH
CLIFFHANGER	QUICKSILVER	WAINSCOTING	COLLOCATION	MALAPROPISM	SOLILOQUIZE
CLIMACTERIC	QUINTUPLETS	WEIGHBRIDGE	COLONIALISM	MALEDICTION	SOLIPSISTIC
CLIMATOLOGY	REICHENBACH	WHIGMALEERY	COLONIALIST	MALEFACTION	SPLUTTERING
CLINOCHLORE	REINCARNATE	WHISKERANDO	COLORIMETER	MALEVOLENCE	TÉLÉFÉRIQUE
CLIOMETRICS	REITERATION	WHISTLESTOP	COLOURBLIND	MALFEASANCE	TELEGRAPHER
COINCIDENCE	SAINTLINESS	WHITEBOYISM	COLUMBARIUM	MALFUNCTION	TELEGRAPHIC
CRIMINOLOGY	SAINTPAULIA	WHITECHAPEL	CULMINATION	MALICIOUSLY	TELEKINESIS
CRITHOMANCY	SCIENTOLOGY	WHITECOLLAR	CULPABILITY	MALPRACTICE	TELEPHONIST
CRITICASTER	SCINTILLATE	WHITEFRIARS	CULTIVATION	MELANCHOLIA	TELEPRINTER
DEIFICATION	SCIREFACIAS	WHITETHROAT	CULVERINEER	MELANCHOLIC	TELEWORKING
DRINKDRIVER	SCITAMINEAE	WHITLEATHER	CYLINDRICAL	MELANOCHROI	TELOCENTRIC
EDIFICATION	SEIGNIORAGE	WHITSUNTIDE	DELECTATION	MELLIFLUOUS	VALEDICTION
ELIGIBILITY	SEISMOGRAPH	WHITTINGTON	DELETERIOUS	MELODIOUSLY	VALEDICTORY
ELIMINATION	SHINPLASTER	ZWISCHENZUG	DELICIOUSLY	MILLIAMPERE	VALLAMBROSA
ELIZABETHAN	SHIPBUILDER	ADJOURNMENT	DELICTATION	MILLIONAIRE	VALLISNERIA
EPICHEIREMA	SHIPWRECKED	ADJUDICATOR	DELINEATION	MILQUETOAST	VOLCANOLOGY
EPIDIASCOPE	SHITTIMWOOD	ENJAMBEMENT	DELINQUENCY	MOLESTATION	VOLKSKAMMER
EPIGENESIST	SKIDBLADNIR	INJUDICIOUS	DELITESCENT	MOLLYCODDLE	VOLUNTARILY
EPINEPHRINE	SKILLIGALEE	OBJECTIVELY	DELIVERANCE	MULTIRACIAL	VOLUNTARISM
EPITHYMETIC	SKILLIGOLEE	OBJECTIVITY	DILAPIDATED	MULTISTOREY	VULCANOLOGY
ERIODENDRON	SKIMMINGTON	UNJUSTIFIED	DOLABRIFORM	OBLITERATED	WALDSTERBEN
EVISCERATED	SLIGHTINGLY	ACKNOWLEDGE	ENLARGEMENT	PALEOGRAPHY	WELLADVISED
FAIRWEATHER	SMITHEREENS	AWKWARDNESS	ENLIGHTENED	PALEOLITHIC	WELLBEHAVED
FLICKERTAIL	SMITHSONIAN	ENKEPHALINE	FALLIBILITY	PALESTINIAN	WELLDEFINED
FLIRTATIOUS	SMITHSONITE	MAKEBELIEVE	FILAMENTOUS	PELARGONIUM	WELLDRESSED

WELLFOUNDED	DEMONOMANIA	PAMPHLETEER	CONCENTRATE	CONTENTMENT	HUNDREDFOLD
WELLINGTONS	DEMONSTRATE	POMEGRANATE	CONCEPTICLE	CONTINENTAL	IGNOMINIOUS
WELLMEANING	DEMORALIZED	POMPELMOOSE	CONCILIATOR	CONTINGENCE	IGNORANTINE
WILBERFORCE	DEMOSTHENES	POMPELMOUSE	CONCISENESS	CONTINGENCY	INNUMERABLE
WILLINGNESS	DEMOSTHENIC	RAMGUNSHOCH	CONCOMITANT	CONTINUALLY	JINRICKSHAW
XYLOGRAPHER	DIMENSIONAL	REMEMBRANCE	CONCORDANCE	CONTINUANCE	KINCHINMORT
YELLOWPLUSH	DIMERCAPROL	REMINISCENT	CONCURRENCE	CONTRACTION	KINDERSPIEL
YELLOWSTONE	DOMESTICATE	REMONSTRATE	CONDITIONAL	CONTRACTUAL	KINDHEARTED
AMMOPHILOUS	DOMESTICITY	REMORSELESS	CONDITIONER	CONTRAPTION	KINNIKINICK
ATMOSPHERIC	DOMINEERING	ROMANTICISM	CONDOLENCES	CONTRASTING	LANDSKNECHT
BIMILLENARY	DUMBFOUNDED	ROMANTICIZE	CONDOMINIUM	CONTRAYERVA	LENGTHENING
BOMBARDMENT	EMMENAGOGUE	RUMBUSTIOUS	CONDOTTIERE	CONTRETEMPS	LENGTHINESS
BUMBERSHOOT	EMMENTHALER	RUMFRUCTION	CONDOTTIORE	CONTRIBUTOR	LENTIGINOSE
CAMALDOLITE	FAMILIARISE	RUMGUMPTION	CONDUCTANCE	CONTRIVANCE	LINDISFARNE
CAMARADERIE	FAMILIARITY	SEMITRAILER	CONDUCTRESS	CONTROVERSY	LINGUISTICS
CAMERAWOMAN	FAMILIARIZE	SEMPITERNAL	CONFABULATE	CONTUBERNAL	LONGANIMITY
CAMEROONIAN	FOMENTATION	SEMPITERNUM	CONFARREATE	CONURBATION	LONGAWAITED
CAMOUFLAGED	GAMETANGIUM	SUMMERHOUSE	CONFEDERACY	CONVALLARIA	LONGINQUITY
CAMPANOLOGY	GAMETOPHYTE	SUMPTUOUSLY	CONFEDERATE	CONVENIENCE	LONGLASTING
CAMPESTRIAN	GAMMERSTANG	SYMMETRICAL	CONFIDENTLY	CONVENTICLE	LONGRUNNING
CAMPHORATED	GAMOGENESIS	SYMPATHETIC	CONFINEMENT	CONVERGENCE	LONGSIGHTED
COMBINATION	HAMMERCLOTH	SYMPATHISER	CONFUTATION	CONVERTIBLE	LONGSLEEVED
COMBUSTIBLE	HEMERALOPIA	SYMPATHIZER	CONGRESSMAN	CONVOCATION	MANCIPATION
COMESTIBLES	HEMIANOPSIA	SYMPLEGADES	CONJECTURAL	CONVOLUTION	MANEUVERING
COMEUPPANCE	HEMOPHILIAC	SYMPOSIARCH	CONJUGATION	CONVOLVULUS	MANGALSUTRA
COMFORTABLE	HEMORRHOIDS	SYMPTOMATIC	CONJUNCTION	CONVULSIONS	MANIPULATOR
COMFORTABLY	HOMEOPATHIC	TEMPERAMENT	CONJUNCTURE	DANGEROUSLY	MANTELLETTA
COMFORTLESS	HOMOEOPATHY	TEMPERATURE	CONNECTICUT	DENDRACHATE	MANTELPIECE
COMMANDMENT	HOMOGENEITY	TEMPESTUOUS	CONNOISSEUR	DENOMINATOR	MANTELSHELF
COMMEMORATE	HOMOGENEOUS	TEMPORARILY	CONNOTATION	DENUMERABLE	MANUFACTURE
COMMENDABLE	HOMOGENIZED	TIMBROMANIA	CONSCIOUSLY	DINNYHAUSER	MANUMISSION
COMMENDABLY	HOMOIOUSIAN	TIMBROPHILY	CONSECUTIVE	DINNYHAYSER	MENDELEVIUM
COMMENTATOR	HOMOPHONOUS	TIMEKEEPING	CONSEQUENCE	DUNIEWASSAL	MENDELSSOHN
COMMINATION	HOMOTHERMAL	TIMESHARING	CONSERVANCY	EINSTEINIUM	MENSURATION
COMMISERATE	HOMOTHERMIC	UNMITIGATED	CONSIDERATE	ENNEAHEDRON	MENTHOLATED
COMMONPLACE	HUMGRUFFIAN	UNMOTIVATED	CONSIDERING	FANATICALLY	MENTONNIÈRE
COMMONSENSE	HUMILIATING	WOMANLINESS	CONSIGNMENT	FANFARONADE	MINESWEEPER
COMMUNALISM	HUMILIATION	ABNORMALITY	CONSILIENCE	FINANCIALLY	MINIATURIST
COMMUNICANT	HUMMINGBIRD	AGNOSTICISM	CONSISTENCE	FINGERPRINT	MINIATURIZE
COMMUNICATE	HYMNOLOGIST	ANNABERGITE	CONSISTENCY	FINGERSTALL	MINISTERIAL
COMMUTATION	IMMEDIATELY	ANNIVERSARY	CONSOLATION	FUNAMBULIST	MINISTERING
COMPARATIVE	IMMIGRATION	BANDEIRANTE	CONSOLIDATE	FUNCTIONARY	MINNESINGER
COMPARTMENT	IMMORTALISE	BANGLADESHI	CONSPICUOUS	FUNCTIONING	MONARCHICAL
COMPENDIOUS	IMMORTALITY	BANNOCKBURN	CONSPIRATOR	FUNDAMENTAL	MONCHIQUITE
COMPETENTLY	IMMORTALIZE	BENEDICTINE	CONSTANTINE	FUNDRAISING	MONEYLENDER
COMPETITION	JAMAHIRIYAH	BENEDICTION	CONSTELLATE	GENEALOGIST	MONEYMAKING
COMPETITIVE	KAMELAUKION	BENEFICIARY	CONSTERNATE	GENERALIZED	MONOCHINOUS
COMPILATION	KIMERIDGIAN	BENEFICIATE	CONSTIPATED	GENERICALLY	MONOCHROMAT
COMPILEMENT	KOMMERSBUCH	BENEVOLENCE	CONSTITUENT	GENETICALLY	MONOGRAMMED
COMPLACENCY	LAMENTATION	CANDESCENCE	CONSTRAINED	GENOUILLÈRE	MONOLINGUAL
COMPLAISANT	LAMMERGEIER	CANDIDATURE	CONSTRICTED	GENTLEMANLY	MONONGAHELA
COMPLICATED	LAMMERGEYER	CANDLELIGHT	CONSTRICTOR	GENTLEWOMAN	MONONUCLEAR
COMPLIMENTS	LAMPLIGHTER	CANDLESTICK	CONSTRUCTOR	GENUFLEXION	MONOPSONIST
COMPOSITION	LAMPROPHYRE	CANNIBALISM	CONSTUPRATE	GENUINENESS	MONOTHELITE
COMPOTATION	LUMINESCENT	CANNIBALIZE	CONSULTANCY	GINGERBREAD	MONOTREMATA
COMPRIMARIO	MEMORABILIA	CENTENARIAN	CONSUMABLES	GONFALONIER	MONSTROSITY
COMPTROLLER	MOMENTARILY	CENTERPIECE	CONSUMERISM	GYNAECOLOGY	MONTESQUIEU
COMPUNCTION	NOMENCLATOR	CENTREBOARD	CONSUMPTION	HANDCRAFTED	MONTGOLFIER
COMPUTATION	NUMBERPLATE	CENTREPIECE	CONSUMPTIVE	HANDICAPPED	MONTMORENCY
COMPUTERIZE	NUMERICALLY	CENTRIFUGAL	CONTAINMENT	HANDICAPPER	MUNCHHAUSEN
COMRADESHIP	NUMISMATICS	CENTRIPETAL	CONTAMINANT	HANDWRITING	MUNIFICENCE
COMSTOCKERY	NUMISMATIST	CENTUMVIRUS	CONTAMINATE	HANDWRITTEN	MUNITIONIZE
CYMOPHANOUS	NYMPHOMANIA	CENTURIATOR	CONTEMPLANT	HANGGLIDING	NONCHALANCE
DEMAGOGUERY	OBMUTESCENT	CINQUECENTO	CONTEMPLATE	HINDERLANDS	NONDESCRIPT
DEMARCATION	OMMATOPHORE	CONCEALMENT	CONTENEMENT	HONEYCOMBED	NONETHELESS
DEMIBASTION	PAMPELMOOSE	CONCEIVABLE	CONTENTEDLY	HONEYMOONER	NONEXISTENT
DEMOGRAPHIC	PAMPELMOUSE	CONCEIVABLY	CONTENTIOUS	HONEYSUCKLE	NONFEASANCE

NONSENSICAL	TENUOUSNESS	CROCIDOLITE	PROFICIENCY	SPONDYLITIS	COPPERPLATE
OMNIPOTENCE	TONSILLITIS	CROCODILIAN	PROFITEROLE	SPONSORSHIP	COPROPHAGAN
OMNIPRESENT	UNNATURALLY	CROMWELLIAN	PROFUSENESS	SPONTANEITY	COPROSTEROL
OMNISCIENCE	UNNECESSARY	CROOKEDNESS	PROGENITRIX	SPONTANEOUS	DEPARTEMENT
ORNITHOLOGY	VENDEMIAIRE	CROSSLEGGED	PROGNATHOUS	SPORTSFIELD	DEPHLEGMATE
ORNITHOPTER	VENTILATION	DEOXYGENATE	PROGRESSION	SPORTSWOMAN	DEPORTATION
PANDEMONIUM	VENTURESOME	DIORTHORTIC	PROGRESSIVE	STOCKBROKER	DEPREDATION
PANOMPHAEAN	VINAIGRETTE	EGOTISTICAL	PROHIBITION	STOCKHAUSEN	DEPRIVATION
PANTALETTES	VINBLASTINE	EMOTIONALLY	PROHIBITIVE	STOCKHOLDER	DIPHYCERCAL
PENETRATING	VINCRISTINE	EPOCHMAKING	PROLEGOMENA	STOCKJOBBER	DIPLOMATICS
PENETRATION	VINDICATION	EXONERATION	PROLETARIAN	STOCKTAKING	DIPLOMATIST
PENICILLATE	WENSLEYDALE	EXORBITANCE	PROLETARIAT	STOOLPIGEON	DIPROTODONT
PENITENTIAL	WINDBREAKER	EXOSKELETON	PROLIFERATE	STOREKEEPER	DIPSOMANIAC
PENNYFATHER	WINDCHEATER	FLORILEGIUM	PROLOCUTION	STORYTELLER	DIPTEROCARP
PENSIONABLE	WINDLESTRAW	FLOURISHING	PROMINENTLY	SWORDSWOMAN	DUPLICATING
PENSIVENESS	WINDOWFRAME	FOOLISHNESS	PROMISCUITY	THOROUGHPIN	DUPLICATION
PENTATHLETE	WINDOWLEDGE	FOOTBALLING	PROMISCUOUS	THOUGHTLESS	EMPHYTEUSIS
PENTAVALENT	WINDSURFING	FOOTWASHING	PROMOTIONAL	TROMPELOEIL	EMPIECEMENT
PENTECONTER	WINTERBERRY	FRONTRUNNER	PROMPTITUDE	TROPHOBLAST	EMPIRICUTIC
PENTECOSTAL	WINTERGREEN	FROSTBITTEN	PROOFREADER	TROPOSPHERE	EMPLACEMENT
PENTHESILEA	WONDERFULLY	GEOMETRICAL	PROPAGATION	TROUBLESOME	EMPOWERMENT
PENTONVILLE	XENODOCHIUM	GEOSYNCLINE	PROPHETICAL	TROUBLESPOT	EMPTYHANDED
PENULTIMATE	ABOMINATION	GLOSSOLALIA	PROPHYLAXIS	ULOTRICHALE	EMPYROMANCY
PINACOTHECA	ABORTIONIST	GOODLOOKING	PROPINQUITY	UNOBSERVANT	ESPIEGLERIE
PINNYWINKLE	ACOLOUTHITE	GOODNATURED	PROPOSITION	UNOBTRUSIVE	EUPHEMISTIC
PONDEROUSLY	ADOLESCENCE	GROUNDSHEET	PROPRIETARY	VIOLINCELLO	EXPECTANTLY
PONTIFICATE	ADOPTIANISM	GROUNDSPEED	PROROGATION	VIOLONCELLO	EXPECTATION
PUNCHINELLO	ADOPTIONISM	GROUNDSWELL	PROSAICALLY	VOORTREKKER	EXPECTORANT
PUNCTILIOUS	AGONOTHETES	HOOLIGANISM	PROSECUTION	WOODCARVING	EXPECTORATE
PUNCTUALITY	AGORAPHOBIA	HOOTANANNIE	PROSELYTISM	WRONGHEADED	EXPEDITIOUS
PUNCTUATION	AMOBARBITAL	HOOTENANNIE	PROSELYTIZE	ZOOPLANKTON	EXPENDITURE
RANGEFINDER	AMONTILLADO	HYOPLASTRON	PROSPECTIVE	ALPHABETIZE	EXPERIENCED
RENAISSANCE	ANONYMOUSLY	ICONOGRAPHY	PROSTHETICS	AMPHETAMINE	EXPLANATION
RINFORZANDO	APOCALYPTIC	ICONOSTASIS	PROSTRATION	AMPHIBOLOGY	EXPLANATORY
RINTHEREOUT	APODYTERIUM	IDOLIZATION	PROTAGONIST	AMPHISBAENA	EXPLORATION
SANDERSWOOD	APOLLINARIS	INOCULATION	PROTEROZOIC	AMPHISBOENA	EXPLORATORY
SANGUINEOUS	APOLLONICON	INOFFENSIVE	PROTOCOCCUS	AMPLEXICAUL	EXPONENTIAL
SANSEVIERIA	APOMORPHINE	INOPERATIVE	PROTONOTARY	APPALLINGLY	EXPOSTULATE
SENNACHERIB	APONEUROSIS	INOPPORTUNE	PROTRACTING	APPARATCHIK	EXPROPRIATE
SENSATIONAL	APOPHYLLITE	IRONMONGERS	PROTRACTION	APPEARANCES	EXPURGATION
SENSIBILITY	APOSIOPESIS	IRONMONGERY	PROTUBERANT	APPEASEMENT	HAPHAZARDLY
SENSITIVELY	APOSTROPHUS	ISOELECTRIC	PROVISIONAL	APPELLATION	HEPATOSCOPY
SENSITIVITY	AVOIRDUPOIS	ISOLECITHAL	PROVISIONER	APPELLATIVE	HEPPLEWHITE
SENTENTIOUS	AZOTOBACTER	ISOMORPHOUS	PROVOCATION	APPLERINGIE	HIPPOCAMPUS
SENTIMENTAL	BIOCHEMICAL	ISOXSUPRINE	PROVOCATIVE	APPLICATION	HIPPOCRATES
SINGAPOREAN	BLOCKBUSTER	LOOSESTRIFE	PTOCHOCRACY	APPOINTMENT	HIPPOCRATIC
SINGLESTICK	BLOODSPORTS	MOONLIGHTER	REORIENTATE	APPRECIABLE	HYPERBOREAN
SINGULARITY	BLOODSTREAM	ODONTOBLAST	RHOPALOCERA	APPRECIABLY	HYPERMARKET
SINISTRORSE	BLOODSUCKER	ODONTOPHORE	SCOLECIFORM	APPRENTICED	HYPERTROPHY
SUNDRENCHED	BOOKBINDING	ONOMASTICON	SCOLOPENDRA	APPROACHING	HYPHENATION
SYNCHROMESH	BOOKKEEPING	OXODIZATION	SCOPOLAMINE	APPROBATION	HYPOCORISMA
SYNCHRONISE	BOOKSELLERS	PHONETICIAN	SCOREKEEPER	APPROPRIATE	HYPOTENSION
SYNCHRONISM	BROADCASTER	PHONOFIDDLE	SCOUTMASTER	APPROVINGLY	HYPOTHECATE
SYNCHRONIZE	BROADMINDED	PHOTOCOPIER	SHOPLIFTING	APPROXIMATE	HYPOTHERMIA
SYNCHRONOUS	BRODBINGNAG	PHOTOFINISH	SHORTCHANGE	APPURTENANT	IMPARTIALLY
SYNCOPATION	BROTHERHOOD	PHOTOGRAPHY	SHORTCOMING	ASPERGILLUM	IMPASSIONED
SYNDICALISM	CHOCKABLOCK	PHOTOSPHERE	SHORTHANDED	ASPERGILLUS	IMPASSIVELY
SYNDICATION	CHOIRMASTER	PLOUGHSHARE	SHOVELBOARD	ASPERSORIUM	IMPATIENTLY
SYNTHESIZED	CHOLESTEROL	PROBABILITY	SHOWERPROOF	ASPHETERISM	IMPEACHMENT
SYNTHESIZER	CHOLINERGIC	PROBATIONER	SHOWJUMPING	BUPRESTIDAE	IMPECUNIOUS
TANGIBILITY	CHONDROSTEI	PROCEEDINGS	SHOWMANSHIP	CAPACITANCE	IMPEDIMENTA
TANTALIZING	CHORDOPHONE	PROCREATION	SMOKESCREEN	CAPACITATOR	IMPERFORATE
TENACIOUSLY	CHOROGRAPHY	PROCRUSTEAN	SMORGASBORD	CAPERNOITED	IMPERIALISM
TENDENTIOUS	COOPERATION	PROCUREMENT	SMOULDERING	CAPERNOITIE	IMPERIALIST
TENSIOMETER	COOPERATIVE	PRODIGALISE	SNORKELLING	CAPRICCIOSO	IMPERIOUSLY
TENTATIVELY	COORDINATED	PRODIGALITY	SPOKESWOMAN	CAPTIVATING	IMPERMANENT
TENTERHOOKS	COORDINATES	PROFESSEDLY	SPONDULICKS	CAPTIVATION	IMPERMEABLE

IMPERSONATE	SUPPEDANEUM	CARDOPHAGUS	FORBEARANCE	MARKETPLACE	PERMUTATION
IMPERTINENT	SUPPOSITION	CAREFULNESS	FORBIDDANCE	MARLBOROUGH	PERPETRATOR
IMPETUOSITY	SUPPOSITORY	CARMINATIVE	FORECASTING	MARSHMALLOW	PERPETUALLY
IMPETUOUSLY	SUPPRESSION	CARNAPTIOUS	FORECLOSURE	MERCHANDISE	PERSECUTION
IMPIGNORATE	SUPPURATION	CARNIVOROUS	FOREFATHERS	MERCHANDIZE	PERSEVERING
IMPLAUSIBLE	TOPLOFTICAL	CAROLINGIAN	FORESEEABLE	MERCHANTMAN	PERSISTENCE
IMPLEMENTAL	TOPOGRAPHER	CARRIAGEWAY	FORESHORTEN	MERCILESSLY	PERSONALIST
IMPLICATION	TYPESETTING	CARSICKNESS	FORESTATION	MERITORIOUS	PERSONALITY
IMPORTANTLY	TYPEWRITTEN	CARTOGRAPHY	FORETHOUGHT	MERRYMAKING	PERSONALIZE
IMPORTATION	TYPOGRAPHER	CERARGYRITE	FOREWARNING	MORGENSTERN	PERSONIFIED
IMPORTUNATE	TYPOGRAPHIC	CEREBRATION	FORFOUGHTEN	MURMURATION	PERSPECTIVE
IMPRACTICAL	UNPALATABLE	CEREMONIOUS	FORGIVENESS	NARRAGANSET	PERSPICUITY
IMPRECATION	UNPATRIOTIC	CERTIFIABLE	FORLORNNESS	NERVOUSNESS	PERSPICUOUS
IMPRECISION	UNPERTURBED	CERTIFICATE	FORMULATION	NORTHCLIFFE	PERTINACITY
IMPREGNABLE	UNPRACTICAL	CHRISMATION	FORNICATION	NORTHEASTER	PERTINENTLY
IMPROPRIETY	UNPRINTABLE	CHRISTENING	FORTHCOMING	NORTHWESTER	PHRASEOLOGY
IMPROVEMENT	UNPROTECTED	CHRISTMASSY	FORTNIGHTLY	OARSMANSHIP	PORNOGRAPHY
IMPROVIDENT	UNPUBLISHED	CHRISTOPHER	FORTUNATELY	PARABLEPSIS	PORTERHOUSE
IMPRUDENTLY	WAPPENSCHAW	CHROMOPLAST	FORTUNELOUD	PARABOLANUS	PORTLANDIAN
IMPULSIVELY	ACQUIESCENT	CHRONICALLY	FURNISHINGS	PARACETAMOL	PORTMANTEAU
LAPIDESCENT	ACQUISITION	CHRONOMETER	FURTHERANCE	PARACHUTIST	PORTRAITIST
LEPIDOPTERA	ACQUISITIVE	CHRYSAROBIN	FURTHERMORE	PARACROSTIC	PORTRAITURE
LEPIDOSIREN	ARQUEBUSIER	CHRYSOPRASE	FURTHERMOST	PARADOXICAL	PURITANICAL
MEPROBAMATE	EXQUISITELY	CIRCULARIZE	FURTHERSOME	PARALEIPSIS	PURPOSELESS
NAPHTHALENE	INQUIRINGLY	CIRCULATING	FURTIVENESS	PARAMASTOID	PURPRESTURE
NIPFARTHING	INQUISITION	CIRCULATION	GARNISHMENT	PARAMEDICAL	PYRARGYRITE
OPPIGNORATE	INQUISITIVE	CIRCULATORY	GARRULOUSLY	PARANEPHROS	SARCENCHYME
OPPORTUNELY	LIQUIDAMBAR	CIRCUMCISER	GERMINATION	PARASITOSIS	SARCOPHAGUS
OPPORTUNISM	LIQUIDATION	CIRCUMFLECT	GERONTOLOGY	PARATROOPER	SCREAMINGLY
OPPORTUNIST	MAQUILADORA	CIRCUMSPECT	GERRYMANDER	PARATYPHOID	SCREWDRIVER
OPPORTUNITY	REQUIREMENT	CIRRHIPEDEA	GIRDLESTEAD	PARENTHESIS	SCRIMSHANDY
OPPROBRIOUS	REQUISITION	CIRRHIPEDIA	GORDONSTOUN	PARISHIONER	SCRIPTORIUM
PAPERWEIGHT	SEQUESTRATE	CORDWAINERS	HARDHITTING	PARLIPOMENA	SCRUFFINESS
RAPSCALLION	UNQUALIFIED	CORINTHIANS	HARDICANUTE	PARONOMASIA	SCRUMPTIOUS
RAPTUROUSLY	ABRACADABRA	CORNERSTONE	HARDPRESSED	PARTICIPANT	SERENDIPITY
REPETITIOUS	ABRIDGEMENT	CORPORATION	HARDWORKING	PARTICIPATE	SERICULTURE
REPLACEABLE	ACRIFLAVINE	CORRECTNESS	HAREBRAINED	PARTICIPIAL	SERIOUSNESS
REPLACEMENT	ACRIMONIOUS	CORRELATION	HARIOLATION	PARTNERSHIP	SERVICEABLE
REPRESENTED	ACROCENTRIC	CORROBORATE	HARPSICHORD	PARTURITION	SOROPTIMIST
REPROACHFUL	AERODYNAMIC	CORRUGATION	HERBIVOROUS	PARVANIMITY	SORROWFULLY
REPUDIATION	AERONAUTICS	CORRUPTIBLE	HERPETOLOGY	PERAMBULATE	SPREADSHEET
SAPONACEOUS	AGRICULTURE	CURNAPTIOUS	HERRINGBONE	PERCEFOREST	SPRINGBOARD
SAPROLEGNIA	AGROSTOLOGY	CURTAILMENT	HORNSWOGGLE	PERCEPTIBLE	SPRINGCLEAN
SAPROPHYTIC	AIRCRAFTMAN	DARDANELLES	HORSERACING	PERCEPTIBLY	SPRINGHOUSE
SEPIOSTAIRE	AIRSICKNESS	DERANGEMENT	HORSERADISH	PERCHLORATE	SPRINGINESS
SEPTENARIUS	ARRANGEMENT	DERELICTION	HORSERIDING	PERCIPIENCE	STRADUARIUS
SEPTENTRION	ARRHENOTOKY	DERMATOLOGY	HURTLEBERRY	PERCOLATION	STRAITLACED
SEPTICAEMIA	ARRIVEDERCI	DIRECTIONAL	IRRADIATION	PERDUELLION	STRAMINEOUS
SUPERALTERN	ATRABILIOUS	DIRECTORATE	IRREDENTIST	PEREGRINATE	STRANDLOPER
SUPERCHARGE	ATROCIOUSLY	EARNESTNESS	IRREDUCIBLE	PERENNIALLY	STRANGENESS
SUPERCHERIE	AURIGNACIAN	EARTHENWARE	IRREFUTABLE	PERESTROIKA	STRANGEWAYS
SUPERFICIAL	BARBASTELLE	EARTHSHAKER	IRREGULARLY	PERFORATION	STRANGULATE
SUPERFICIES	BARBITURATE	ERRATICALLY	IRRELEVANCE	PERFORMANCE	STRAPHANGER
SUPERFLUITY	BARNSTORMER	ERRONEOUSLY	IRRELIGIOUS	PERFUNCTORY	STRATEGICAL
SUPERFLUOUS	BARTHOLOMEW	EURHYTHMICS	IRREPARABLE	PERICARDIUM	STREAMLINED
SUPERIMPOSE	BARYCENTRIC	FARINACEOUS	IRREPARABLE	PERIGORDIAN	STREETLIGHT
SUPERINTEND	BEREAVEMENT	FARKLEBERRY	IRREVERENCE	PERIODONTIC	STRENUOUSLY
SUPERIORITY	BERGSCHRUND	FARRAGINOUS	IRREVOCABLE	PERIPATETIC	STRETCHABLE
SUPERLATIVE	BIRDWATCHER	FARREACHING	JERRYMANDER	PERIPHRASIS	STRETCHLESS
SUPERMARKET	BORBORYGMUS	FARTHERMOST	KIRKPATRICK	PERISSOLOGY	STRIKEBOUND
SUPERSCRIBE	BUREAUCRACY	FARTHINGALE	LARYNGISMUS	PERISTALITH	STRINGBOARD
SUPERSCRIPT	BURGOMASTER	FERNITICKLE	MARCONIGRAM	PERISTALSIS	STRINGENTLY
SUPERSEDEAS	CARABINIERE	FEROCIOUSLY	MARGINALIST	PERITONAEUM	STRINGYBARK
SUPERSEDERE	CARAVANNING	FERRONNIÈRE	MARGINALIZE	PERITONITIS	STROBOSCOPE
SUPERTANKER	CARBORUNDUM	FIRECRACKER	MARIONBERRY	PERLUSTRATE	STRONGYLOID
SUPERVISION	CARBURETTOR	FIRELIGHTER	MARIONETTES	PERMANENTLY	STROPHILLUS
SUPERVISORY	CARDIOGRAPH	FORAMINIFER	MARIVAUDAGE	PERMISSIBLE	STRUTHIONES

SURROUNDING	ASSYTHEMENT	DISPUTATION	INSTRUCTIVE	RESPONSIBLE	ANTIPHONARY
SURTARBRAND	BASHFULNESS	DISQUIETING	INSTRUMENTS	RESPONSIBLY	ANTIPHRASIS
SURTURBRAND	BASKERVILLE	DISREGARDED	INSULTINGLY	RESPONSIONS	ANTIPYRETIC
SURVEILLANT	BESIEGEMENT	DISSEMINATE	INSUPERABLE	RESTATEMENT	ANTIQUARIAN
TARATANTARA	BESSARABIAN	DISSEPIMENT	JOSEPHINITE	RESTITUTION	ANTIRRHINUM
TARRADIDDLE	BESTSELLING	DISSERTATOR	JUSTIFIABLE	RESTIVENESS	ANTISTHENES
TERMINATION	BUSHWHACKER	DISSIMULATE	JUSTIFIABLY	RESTORATION	ANTISTROPHE
TERMINOLOGY	BUSINESSMAN	DISSIPATION	LASERPICIUM	RESTORATIVE	ANTONOMASIA
TERPSICHORE	CASSITERITE	DISSOLUTION	MASCULINITY	RESTRICTION	ARTHRAPODAL
TERREMOTIVE	CASTELLATED	DISTASTEFUL	MASKALLONGE	RESTRICTIVE	ARTHRODESIS
TERRESTRIAL	CESAREWITCH	DISTINCTION	MASOCHISTIC	RESTRUCTURE	ARTHROSPORE
TERRITORIAL	CUSTOMARILY	DISTINCTIVE	MASQUERADER	RESUSCITATE	ARTICULATED
THREATENING	DESCENDANTS	DISTINGUISH	MASSIVENESS	ROSICRUCIAN	ARTILLERIST
THRIFTINESS	DESCRIPTION	DISTRACTION	MASTERFULLY	SESQUIOXIDE	ARTIODACTYL
THROGMORTON	DESCRIPTIVE	DISTRESSING	MASTERPIECE	SUSCEPTIBLE	ASTIGMATISM
TIRONENSIAN	DESECRATION	DISTRIBUTED	MASTICATION	SUSTAINABLE	ASTONISHING
TORRIDONIAN	DESEGREGATE	DISTRIBUTOR	MISALLIANCE	SUSURRATION	ASTRINGENCY
TORTICOLLIS	DESELECTION	DISTRUSTFUL	MISANTHROPE	SYSTEMATIZE	ATTENTIVELY
TORTICULLUS	DESERPIDINE	DISTURBANCE	MISANTHROPY	TASTELESSLY	ATTENUATION
TURBELLARIA	DESICCATION	DUSTWRAPPER	MISBEGOTTEN	TESSARAGLOT	ATTESTATION
TURRICULATE	DESEXUALIZE	DYSFUNCTION	MISBEHAVIOR	TESSELLATED	ATTRIBUTION
TYRANNOSAUR	DESIGNATION	DYSLOGISTIC	MISCARRIAGE	TESTIMONIAL	ATTRIBUTIVE
TYROGLYPHID	DESPERATELY	EASTERNMOST	MISCHIEVOUS	TOSTICATION	BATHYSPHERE
TYRONENSIAN	DESPERATION	ENSLAVEMENT	MISCONSTRUE	UNSATISFIED	BATTLEDRESS
UNREALISTIC	DESPONDENCY	ESSENTIALLY	MISDEMEANOR	UNSATURATED	BATTLEFIELD
UNREASONING	DESTABILIZE	FASCINATING	MISERICORDE	UNSCHEDULED	BATTLEFRONT
UNREHEARSED	DESTINATION	FASCINATION	MISERLINESS	UNSHAKEABLE	BATTLEMENTS
UNRELENTING	DESTITUTION	FASHIONABLE	MISFEASANCE	UNSHELTERED	BITTERSWEET
UNREMITTING	DESTRUCTION	FASHIONABLY	MISIDENTIFY	UNSHRINKING	BOTANOMANCY
UNREPENTANT	DESTRUCTIVE	FESTINATELY	MISSISSIPPI	UNSOLICITED	BUTTONQUAIL
UNRIGHTEOUS	DISABLEMENT	FESTSCHRIFT	MISSPELLING	UNSPEAKABLE	CATACAUSTIC
UPRIGHTNESS	DISAFFECTED	FISHANDCHIP	MISTRUSTFUL	UNSPECIFIED	CATACHRESIS
UTRICULARIA	DISAGREEING	FISHMONGERS	MOSSTROOPER	UNSTOPPABLE	CATACLYSMIC
VARANGARIAN	DISAPPROVAL	FISSIONABLE	MUSCHELKALK	UNSUPPORTED	CATADROMOUS
VARIABILITY	DISARMAMENT	FUSTILARIAN	MUSKELLUNGE	UNSURPASSED	CATALLACTIC
VARIEGATION	DISBELIEVER	GASTRECTOMY	NOSTRADAMUS	UNSUSPECTED	CATASTROPHE
VARIOLATION	DISCERNIBLE	GASTRONOMIC	OBSERVATION	UNSWEETENED	CATCHPHRASE
VARSOVIENNE	DISCERNMENT	GESTATORIAL	OBSERVATORY	VASOPRESSIN	CATEGORICAL
VERBIGERATE	DISCIPLINED	GESTICULATE	OBSESSIVELY	VESPERTINAL	CATERPILLAR
VERMICULITE	DISCOLOURED	HISTOLOGIST	OBSOLESCENT	VESUVIANITE	CATHOLICISM
VERSATILITY	DISCONTINUE	HISTORIATED	OBSTETRICAL	VISCOUNTESS	CITIZENSHIP
VERTIGINOUS	DISCOTHEQUE	HISTRIONICS	OBSTINATELY	WASHERWOMAN	CITLALEPETL
VORACIOUSLY	DISCOURTESY	HOSPITALITY	OBSTRICTION	WASHLEATHER	CITRONELLAL
WAREHOUSING	DISCREPANCY	HOSPITALIZE	OBSTRUCTION	WASTEBASKET	COTTONMOUTH
WARMHEARTED	DISEMBODIED	HOSPITALLER	OBSTRUCTIVE	WESTERNMOST	CYTOGENESIS
WORKMANLIKE	DISENCUMBER	HOSTILITIES	PASSACAGLIA	WESTMINSTER	DETERIORATE
WORKMANSHIP	DISENTANGLE	HUSBANDLAND	PASSIVENESS	WESTPHALIAN	DETERMINANT
WORKSTATION	DISFIGURING	INSCRIPTION	PASTEURELLA	WISHTONWISH	DETERMINATE
WORLDFAMOUS	DISGRACEFUL	INSCRUTABLE	PASTOURELLE	WISTFULNESS	DETERMINING
WORLDLINESS	DISGRUNTLED	INSECTICIDE	PESSIMISTIC	ACTUALITIES	DETESTATION
WORRYTROUGH	DISHEVELLED	INSECTIVORE	PISCATORIAL	AFTERSCHOOL	DETRIMENTAL
XEROPHILOUS	DISHONESTLY	INSENSITIVE	PISSASPHALT	ALTERCATION	DITHELETISM
XEROTHERMIC	DISILLUSION	INSEPARABLE	POSSESSIONS	ALTERNATELY	DITTOGRAPHY
XEROTRIPSIS	DISIMPRISON	INSIDIOUSLY	POSSIBILITY	ALTERNATING	ECTOTROPHIC
ZOROASTRIAN	DISINCLINED	INSINCERITY	RASTAFARIAN	ALTERNATION	ENTABLATURE
ABSENTEEISM	DISINTEREST	INSINUATING	RESEMBLANCE	ALTERNATIVE	ENTABLEMENT
ABSORPTANCE	DISJUNCTION	INSINUATION	RESENTFULLY	ANTECEDENCE	ENTERTAINER
ABSTRACTION	DISJUNCTIVE	INSISTENTLY	RESERVATION	ANTECHAMBER	ENTHRALLING
AESCULAPIAN	DISLOCATION	INSOUCIANCE	RESIDENTIAL	ANTEPENDIUM	ENTITLEMENT
AESCULAPIUS	DISOBEDIENT	INSPIRATION	RESIGNATION	ANTHESTERIA	ESTABLISHED
ANSWERPHONE	DISORGANIZE	INSTABILITY	RESISTIVITY	ANTHOCYANIN	ESTABLISHER
ASSASSINATE	DISORIENTED	INSTALLMENT	RESOURCEFUL	ANTHOLOGIZE	ESTRAMAZONE
ASSEMBLYMAN	DISPARAGING	INSTANTIATE	RESPECTABLE	ANTHONOMOUS	ESTRANGHELO
ASSIDUOUSLY	DISPENSABLE	INSTIGATION	RESPECTABLY	ANTHRACOSIS	EXTEMPORISE
ASSIGNATION	DISPERSABLE	INSTINCTIVE	RESPIRATION	ANTIBURGHER	EXTEMPORIZE
ASSIMILATED	DISPLEASURE	INSTITUTION	RESPIRATORY	ANTICYCLONE	EXTENSIVELY
ASSOCIATION	DISPOSITION	INSTRUCTION	RESPLENDENT	ANTINEUTRON	EXTENUATING

EXTENUATION	KOTABOTHRON	PETTICOATED	COUNTERFOIL	SAUSAGEMEAT	BEWILDERING
EXTERMINATE	LATERIGRADE	PETTIFOGGER	COUNTERFORT	SCULDUDDERY	DOWNHEARTED
EXTERNALIZE	LATERITIOUS	PHTHIRIASIS	COUNTERGLOW	SCULDUGGERY	DOWNTRODDEN
EXTORTIONER	LATIFUNDIUM	PITCHBLENDE	COUNTERHAND	SCULLABOGUE	LAWBREAKING
EXTRADITION	LATROCINIUM	POTAMOGETON	COUNTERMAND	SCUPPERNONG	LAWLESSNESS
EXTRAPOLATE	LATTICEWORK	POTENTIALLY	COUNTERPANE	SCUTTLEBUTT	NEWSCASTING
EXTRAVAGANT	LETTERPRESS	PYTHONESQUE	COUNTERPART	SHUNAMITISM	PAWNBROKERS
EXTROGENOUS	LITERALNESS	RATATOUILLE	COUNTERSIGN	SHUTTLECOCK	TOWNSPEOPLE
EXTROVERTED	LITHOGRAPHY	RATIOCINATE	COUNTERSINK	SKULDUDDERY	UNWARRANTED
FATUOUSNESS	LITTÉRATEUR	RATIONALITY	COUNTRIFIED	SKULDUGGERY	UNWELCOMING
FITZWILLIAM	MATERIALISE	RATIONALIZE	COUNTRYSIDE	SLUMBERWEAR	UNWHOLESOME
FOTHERGILLA	MATERIALISM	RATTLESNAKE	COURTEOUSLY	SLUMGULLION	UNWITTINGLY
GATECRASHER	MATERIALIST	RETALIATION	COURTLINESS	SOUNDLESSLY	AUXANOMETER
GUTTERSNIPE	MATERIALIZE	RETALIATORY	CRUCIFIXION	SOUTHAMPTON	COXWAINLESS
GUTTURALISE	MATHEMATICS	RETARDATION	DEUTERONOMY	SOUTHWESTER	HEXADECIMAL
HATCHETTITE	MATRIARCHAL	RETINACULUM	DEUTSCHMARK	TAUROBOLIUM	LUXEMBURGER
HETEROGRAFT	MATRICULATE	RETINOSCOPY	DOUBLECHECK	TAUTOCHRONE	LUXULYANITE
HETEROSCIAN	MATRIMONIAL	RETINOSPORA	DOUBLECROSS	THUNDERBIRD	LUXURIANTLY
INTEGRATION	METACARPALS	RETRACTABLE	DOUROUCOULI	THUNDERBOLT	LUXURIOUSLY
INTELLIGENT	METACENTRIC	RETRIBUTION	DRUNKENNESS	THUNDERCLAP	MOXIBUSTION
INTEMPERATE	METAGENESIS	RETRIBUTIVE	EDUCATIONAL	THUNDERHEAD	MYXOMATOSIS
INTENSIVELY	METALWORKER	RETRIEVABLE	ELUCIDATION	TOURBILLION	SAXOPHONIST
INTENTIONAL	METAPHYSICS	RETROACTIVE	ENUMERATION	TRUCULENTLY	SEXOLOGICAL
INTERACTION	METATARSALS	RETROROCKET	ENUNCIATION	TRUSTEESHIP	SEXTODECIMO
INTERACTIVE	METEOROLOGY	ROTOGRAVURE	EQUIDISTANT	TRUSTWORTHY	TAXIDERMIST
INTERCALARY	METHODOLOGY	ROTTENSTONE	EQUILIBRIST	UNUNQUADIUM	TOXICOGENIC
INTERCEPTOR	METRICATION	SATIRICALLY	EQUILIBRIUM	UNUTTERABLE	TOXOPHILITE
INTERCHANGE	MYTHOLOGIZE	TATTERSALLS	EQUINOCTIAL	ADVANCEMENT	AMYLOPECTIN
INTERCOSTAL	NATIONALISM	TETRADRACHM	EQUIPOLLENT	ADVENTURESS	BOYSENBERRY
INTERCOURSE	NATIONALIST	TETRAHEDRON	EQUIVALENCE	ADVENTUROUS	CRYSTALLINE
INTERESTING	NATIONALITY	TITILLATION	EQUIVOCALLY	ADVERBIALLY	CRYSTALLISE
INTERGLOSSA	NATIONALIZE	TITLEHOLDER	FAULTFINDER	ADVERTISING	CRYSTALLIZE
INTERGROWTH	NATIONSTATE	TOTALIZATOR	FAULTLESSLY	DEVALUATION	DRYCLEANERS
INTERLACING	NATURALNESS	ULTRAMARINE	FAUXBOURDON	DEVASTATING	DRYCLEANING
INTERLEUKIN	NATUROPATHY	ULTRAMODERN	FLUCTUATING	DEVASTATION	ERYMANTHIAN
INTERLINGUA	NETHERLANDS	ULTRAVIOLET	FLUCTUATION	DEVELOPMENT	ERYTHROCYTE
INTERMINGLE	NETHERLINGS	UNTHINKABLE	FLUORESCENT	DEVIOUSNESS	ETYMOLOGIST
INTERNALIZE	NOTHINGNESS	UNTOUCHABLE	FLUOROMETER	DEVITRIFIED	IDYLLICALLY
INTERNECINE	NOTICEBOARD	UNTRAMELLED	FLUOROSCOPE	DIVORCEMENT	OXYRHYNCHUS
INTERNUNCIO	NOTORIOUSLY	VITAMINIZED	FOULMOUTHED	ENVIRONMENT	PHYLLOCLADE
INTERPOLATE	NOTOTHERIUM	VOTERIGGING	FOUNDATIONS	FAVOURITISM	PHYSIOGNOMY
INTERPRETER	NUTCRACKERS	WATERCOLOUR	FRUGIVOROUS	INVESTIGATE	PSYCHEDELIC
INTERREGNUM	NUTRITIONAL	WATERCOURSE	FRUITLESSLY	INVESTITURE	PSYCHIATRIC
INTERRELATE	OBTEMPERATE	WATEREDDOWN	FRUSTRATING	INVIGILATOR	SCYPHISTOMA
INTERROGATE	OCTASTICHON	WATERLOGGED	FRUSTRATION	INVINCIBLES	STYLISHNESS
INTERRUPTER	ONTOLOGICAL	WATERMEADOW	GLUCOSAMINE	INVOLUNTARY	STYLIZATION
INTERSPERSE	OPTOMETRIST	WATERSKIING	HAUGHTINESS	INVOLVEMENT	STYLOPODIUM
INTERVENING	ORTHOCENTRE	WATERSPLASH	HOUSEFATHER	LEVELHEADED	STYMPHALIAN
INTERVIEWEE	ORTHOGRAPHY	WITCHDOCTOR	HOUSEHOLDER	LIVINGSTONE	THYROTROPIN
INTERVIEWER	ORTHOPAEDIC	WITENAGEMOT	HOUSEKEEPER	NEVERENDING	TRYPANOSOMA
INTOLERABLE	OSTENTATION	WITHERSHINS	HOUSEMASTER	NOVELETTISH	TRYPANOSOME
INTOLERABLY	OSTEOPATHIC	WITHHOLDING	HOUSEMOTHER	OBVIOUSNESS	WAYWARDNESS
INTOLERANCE	OSTEOPLASTY	ACUPUNCTURE	HOUSEPARENT	RAVISHINGLY	MOZAMBIQUAN
INTOXICATED	OSTRACODERM	ADULLAMITES	KNUCKLEBALL	REVALUATION	PRZEWALSKIS
INTOXIMETER	OSTREOPHAGE	ADULTERATED	LAUNDERETTE	REVELATIONS	RAZZAMATAZZ
INTRACTABLE	OUTDISTANCE	ADUMBRATION	LOUDSPEAKER	REVENDICATE	**11:4**
INTRADERMAL	OUTMANEUVER	AGUARDIENTE	LOUISIANIAN	REVERBERATE	ABLACTATION
INTRAVENOUS	OUTPOURINGS	BLUNDERBORE	MAURETANIAN	REVERENTIAL	ABRACADABRA
INTREPIDITY	OUTSTANDING	BOURGEOISIE	MAURITANIAN	REVISIONISM	ADIAPHORIST
INTRICATELY	PATERNALISM	BOUTONNIERE	MOUNTAINEER	REVOLUTIONS	ADVANCEMENT
INTROVERTED	PATERNOSTER	BRUCELLOSIS	MOUNTAINOUS	SAVOURINESS	AGUARDIENTE
INTUITIVELY	PATHOLOGIST	CAULIFLOWER	NAUGHTINESS	SEVENTEENTH	ANNABERGITE
ISTIOPHORUS	PATRIARCHAL	CAUSTICALLY	NEUROLOGIST	SEVERALFOLD	APHANIPTERA
KATABOTHRON	PATRONISING	COULOMMIERS	NEUTRALISED	SOVEREIGNTY	APLANOSPORE
KATAVOTHRON	PATRONIZING	COUNSELLING	NOURISHMENT	UNVARNISHED	APPALLINGLY
KETAVOTHRON	PETITMAITRE	COUNTENANCE	RAUCOUSNESS	VIVACIOUSLY	APPARATCHIK
KITCHENETTE	PETRODOLLAR	COUNTERFEIT		VIVISECTION	ARGATHELIAN

ARRANGEMENT	FILAMENTOUS	PARALEIPSIS	VICARIOUSLY	BLOCKBUSTER	FUNCTIONING
ASSASSINATE	FINANCIALLY	PARAMASTOID	VINAIGRETTE	BRUCELLOSIS	GLUCOSAMINE
ATHARVAVEDA	FORAMINIFER	PARAMEDICAL	VITAMINIZED	CALCEOLARIA	HATCHETTITE
ATRABILIOUS	FUNAMBULIST	PARANEPHROS	VIVACIOUSLY	CALCULATING	INOCULATION
AUDACIOUSLY	GREASEPAINT	PARASITOSIS	VORACIOUSLY	CALCULATION	INSCRIPTION
AUXANOMETER	GYNAECOLOGY	PARATROOPER	WOMANLINESS	CATCHPHRASE	INSCRUTABLE
BEHAVIOURAL	HEPATOSCOPY	PARATYPHOID	AMOBARBITAL	CHICHEVACHE	IPECACUANHA
BICARBONATE	HEXADECIMAL	PEDAGOGICAL	BARBASTELLE	CHICKENFEED	KINCHINMORT
BOTANOMANCY	HILARIOUSLY	PELARGONIUM	BARBITURATE	CHOCKABLOCK	KITCHENETTE
BREADCRUMBS	IMPARTIALLY	PERAMBULATE	BOMBARDMENT	CIRCULARIZE	KNUCKLEBALL
BREADWINNER	IMPASSIONED	PHRASEOLOGY	BORBORYGMUS	CIRCULATING	MANCIPATION
BREASTPLATE	IMPASSIVELY	PINACOTHECA	BROBDINGNAG	CIRCULATION	MARCONIGRAM
BREATHALYSE	IMPATIENTLY	PLEASURABLE	BUMBERSHOOT	CIRCULATORY	MASCULINITY
BROADCASTER	INCALESCENT	POTAMOGETON	CABBALISTIC	CIRCUMCISER	MERCHANDISE
BROADMINDED	INCANTATION	PYRARGYRITE	CARBORUNDUM	CIRCUMFLECT	MERCHANDIZE
CAMALDOLITE	INCAPSULATE	RATATOUILLE	CARBURETTOR	CIRCUMSPECT	MERCHANTMAN
CAMARADERIE	INCARCERATE	REBARBATIVE	COBBLESTONE	COACHFELLOW	MERCILESSLY
CAPACITANCE	INCARNADINE	RECANTATION	COMBINATION	CONCEALMENT	MISCARRIAGE
CAPACITATOR	INCARNATION	RENAISSANCE	COMBUSTIBLE	CONCEIVABLE	MISCHIEVOUS
CARABINIERE	INFANGTHIEF	RETALIATION	DISBELIEVER	CONCEIVABLY	MISCONSTRUE
CARAVANNING	INFANTICIDE	RETALIATORY	DOUBLECHECK	CONCENTRATE	MONCHIQUITE
CATACAUSTIC	INFANTRYMAN	RETARDATION	DOUBLECROSS	CONCEPTICLE	MUNCHHAUSEN
CATACHRESIS	INFATUATION	REVALUATION	DUMBFOUNDED	CONCILIATOR	MUSCHELKALK
CATACLYSMIC	INHABITABLE	RIFACIMENTO	ELABORATELY	CONCISENESS	NIACINAMIDE
CATADROMOUS	INHABITANTS	ROMANTICISM	ELABORATION	CONCOMITANT	NONCHALANCE
CATALLACTIC	IRRADIATION	ROMANTICIZE	FLABBERGAST	CONCORDANCE	NUTCRACKERS
CATASTROPHE	JAMAHIRIYAH	SAGACIOUSLY	FORBEARANCE	CONCURRENCE	PEACEKEEPER
CERARGYRITE	KALASHNIKOV	SALACIOUSLY	FORBIDDANCE	CRACKERJACK	PERCEFOREST
CESAREWITCH	KATABOTHRON	SELAGINELLA	GIBBERELLIN	CRACKHALTER	PERCEPTIBLE
CHIAROSCURO	KATAVOTHRON	SHEATHKNIFE	HALBSTARKER	CRACOVIENNE	PERCEPTIBLY
CHIASTOLITE	KETAVOTHRON	STEADFASTLY	HERBIVOROUS	CROCIDOLITE	PERCHLORATE
CLEANLINESS	KOTABOTHRON	STEAMROLLER	HOBBLEDEHOY	CROCODILIAN	PERCIPIENCE
CLEANSHAVEN	LOGARITHMIC	STEATOPYGIA	HUSBANDLAND	CRUCIFIXION	PERCOLATION
DECAPITATED	LYCANTHROPE	STRADUARIUS	INEBRIATION	DESCENDANTS	PISCATORIAL
DECARBONATE	LYCANTHROPY	STRAITLACED	JABBERWOCKY	DESCRIPTION	PITCHBLENDE
DECARBONIZE	MACADAMIZED	STRAMINEOUS	LAWBREAKING	DESCRIPTIVE	PRACTICABLE
DEMAGOGUERY	MALADJUSTED	STRANDLOPER	MISBEGOTTEN	DISCERNIBLE	PRACTICALLY
DEMARCATION	MALAKATOONE	STRANGENESS	MISBEHAVIOR	DISCERNMENT	PRECAUTIONS
DEPARTEMENT	MALAPROPISM	STRANGEWAYS	NUMBERPLATE	DISCIPLINED	PRECIPITATE
DERANGEMENT	MEGALOMANIA	STRANGULATE	PLEBEIANISE	DISCOLOURED	PRECIPITOUS
DEVALUATION	MEGALOMANIC	STRAPHANGER	PROBABILITY	DISCONTINUE	PRECONCEIVE
DEVASTATING	MEGALOPOLIS	STRATEGICAL	PROBATIONER	DISCOTHEQUE	PRICKLINESS
DEVASTATION	MEGATHERIUM	SUGARCOATED	RHABDOMANCY	DISCOURTESY	PROCEEDINGS
DILAPIDATED	MELANCHOLIA	TARATANTARA	RUMBUSTIOUS	DISCREPANCY	PROCREATION
DISABLEMENT	MELANCHOLIC	TCHAIKOVSKY	SABBATARIAN	DRACUNCULUS	PROCRUSTEAN
DISAFFECTED	MELANOCHROI	TENACIOUSLY	TIMBROMANIA	DRYCLEANERS	PROCUREMENT
DISAGREEING	METACARPALS	THEATERGOER	TIMBROPHILY	DRYCLEANING	PSYCHEDELIC
DISAPPROVAL	METACENTRIC	THEATREGOER	TRIBULATION	EDUCATIONAL	PSYCHIATRIC
DISARMAMENT	METAGENESIS	THEATRICALS	TURBELLARIA	EJACULATION	PTOCHOCRACY
DOLABRIFORM	METALWORKER	TOBACCONIST	UNOBSERVANT	ELECTRICIAN	PULCHRITUDE
DREADLOCKED	METAPHYSICS	TOTALIZATOR	UNOBTRUSIVE	ELECTRICITY	PUNCHINELLO
DREADNOUGHT	METATARSALS	TREACHEROUS	VERBIGERATE	ELECTROCUTE	PUNCTILIOUS
ECCALEOBION	MISALLIANCE	TREACHETOUR	VINBLASTINE	ELECTROLIER	PUNCTUALITY
EMBARKATION	MISANTHROPE	TREASONABLE	WILBERFORCE	ELECTROLYTE	PUNCTUATION
EMBARRASSED	MISANTHROPY	TYRANNOSAUR	ABECEDARIAN	ELECTRONICS	QUICKSILVER
ENCAPSULATE	MONARCHICAL	UNCASTRATED	AESCULAPIAN	ELECTROTINT	RAUCOUSNESS
ENHANCEMENT	MOZAMBIQUAN	UNFAILINGLY	AESCULAPIUS	ELUCIDATION	REACTIONARY
ENJAMBEMENT	OCTASTICHON	UNFAVORABLE	AIRCRAFTMAN	EPICHEIREMA	REICHENBACH
ENLARGEMENT	OMMATOPHORE	UNHAPPINESS	ANACHRONISM	EPOCHMAKING	SARCENCHYME
ENTABLATURE	ORGANICALLY	UNNATURALLY	ANACOLUTHIA	EXECUTIONER	SARCOPHAGUS
ENTABLEMENT	ORGANIZAION	UNPALATABLE	ANACREONTIC	EYECATCHING	SNICKERSNEE
ERRATICALLY	PARABLEPSIS	UNPATRIOTIC	APOCALYPTIC	FASCINATING	SPACESAVING
ESCARMOUCHE	PARABOLANUS	UNSATISFIED	BACCHANALIA	FASCINATION	SPECIALIZED
ESTABLISHED	PARACETAMOL	UNSATURATED	BEACHCOMBER	FLICKERTAIL	SPECTACULAR
ESTABLISHER	PARACHUTIST	UNVARNISHED	BIOCHEMICAL	FLUCTUATING	SPECULATION
EUCALYPTOLE	PARACROSTIC	UNWARRANTED	BLACKFELLOW	FLUCTUATION	SPECULATIVE
FANATICALLY	PARADOXICAL	VARANGARIAN	BLACKMAILER	FUNCTIONARY	STICKLEBACK

STOCKBROKER	GOODLOOKING	SYNDICALISM	CAPERNOITIE	EXTEMPORIZE	INDEXLINKED
STOCKHAUSEN	GOODNATURED	SYNDICATION	CAREFULNESS	EXTENSIVELY	INFERIORITY
STOCKHOLDER	GORDONSTOUN	TENDENTIOUS	CATEGORICAL	EXTENUATING	INFERTILITY
STOCKJOBBER	GUADALCANAL	TIDDLEYWINK	CATERPILLAR	EXTENUATION	INFESTATION
STOCKTAKING	HANDCRAFTED	TRADITIONAL	CELEBRATION	EXTERMINATE	INGENIOUSLY
SUBCONTRACT	HANDICAPPED	VENDEMIAIRE	CEREBRATION	EXTERNALIZE	INHERITANCE
SUCCEDANEUM	HANDICAPPER	VINDICATION	CEREMONIOUS	FACETIOUSLY	INSECTICIDE
SUSCEPTIBLE	HANDWRITING	WALDSTERBEN	CHEERLEADER	FIRECRACKER	INSECTIVORE
SYNCHROMESH	HANDWRITTEN	WINDBREAKER	CHEESECLOTH	FIRELIGHTER	INSENSITIVE
SYNCHRONISE	HARDHITTING	WINDCHEATER	COLEORRHIZA	FOMENTATION	INSEPARABLE
SYNCHRONISM	HARDICANUTE	WINDLESTRAW	COMESTIBLES	FORECASTING	INTEGRATION
SYNCHRONIZE	HARDPRESSED	WINDOWFRAME	COMEUPPANCE	FORECLOSURE	INTELLIGENT
SYNCHRONOUS	HARDWORKING	WINDOWLEDGE	CYBERNETICS	FOREFATHERS	INTEMPERATE
SYNCOPATION	HEBDOMADARY	WINDSURFING	DECEITFULLY	FORESEEABLE	INTENSIVELY
TRACASSERIE	HINDERLANDS	WONDERFULLY	DECEPTIVELY	FORESHORTEN	INTENTIONAL
TRACHEOTOMY	HUNDREDFOLD	WOODCARVING	DEFENCELESS	FORESTATION	INTERACTION
TRACKLEMENT	INADVERTENT	ABSENTEEISM	DEFENSELESS	FORETHOUGHT	INTERACTIVE
TRICERATOPS	INADVISABLE	ACCELERATOR	DEFENSIVELY	FOREWARNING	INTERCALARY
TRICHINELLA	IRIDESCENCE	ACCESSORIES	DEFERENTIAL	FREEMASONRY	INTERCEPTOR
TRICHINOSED	KIDDLEYWINK	ADVENTURESS	DELECTATION	FREETHINKER	INTERCHANGE
TRICHOPTERA	KINDERSPIEL	ADVENTUROUS	DELETERIOUS	GABERLUNZIE	INTERCOSTAL
TRUCULENTLY	KINDHEARTED	ADVERBIALLY	DERELICTION	GAMETANGIUM	INTERCOURSE
UNSCHEDULED	LANDSKNECHT	ADVERTISING	DESECRATION	GAMETOPHYTE	INTERESTING
VACCINATION	LEADSWINGER	AFFECTATION	DESEGREGATE	GATECRASHER	INTERGLOSSA
VINCRISTINE	LINDISFARNE	AFTERSCHOOL	DESELECTION	GEGENSCHEIN	INTERGROWTH
VISCOUNTESS	LOUDSPEAKER	ALLEGORICAL	DESERPIDINE	GENEALOGIST	INTERLACING
VOLCANOLOGY	MEADOWSWEET	ALLELOMORPH	DESEXUALIZE	GENERALIZED	INTERLEUKIN
VULCANOLOGY	MENDELEVIUM	ALLEVIATION	DETERIORATE	GENERICALLY	INTERLINGUA
WITCHDOCTOR	MENDELSSOHN	ALTERCATION	DETERMINANT	GENETICALLY	INTERMINGLE
ACADEMICIAN	MIDDENSTEAD	ALTERNATELY	DETERMINATE	GREENBOTTLE	INTERNALIZE
ACADEMICISM	MIDDLEMARCH	ALTERNATING	DETERMINING	GREENGROCER	INTERNECINE
ANADIPLOSIS	MIDDLESIZED	ALTERNATION	DETESTATION	GREENOCKITE	INTERNUNCIO
APODYTERIUM	MISDEMEANOR	ALTERNATIVE	DEVELOPMENT	GUBERNATION	INTERPOLATE
BADDELEYITE	NEEDLEPOINT	ANAESTHESIA	DICEPHALOUS	HABERDASHER	INTERPRETER
BANDEIRANTE	NEEDLESTICK	ANAESTHETIC	DIMENSIONAL	HAREBRAINED	INTERREGNUM
BIRDWATCHER	NEEDLEWOMAN	ANGELOLATRY	DIMERCAPROL	HEMERALOPIA	INTERRELATE
BLADDERWORT	NONDESCRIPT	ANTECEDENCE	DIRECTIONAL	HETEROGRAFT	INTERROGATE
CANDESCENCE	OUTDISTANCE	ANTECHAMBER	DIRECTORATE	HETEROSCIAN	INTERRUPTER
CANDIDATURE	OXODIZATION	ANTEPENDIUM	DISEMBODIED	HIBERNATING	INTERSPERSE
CANDLELIGHT	PAEDIATRICS	APPEARANCES	DISENCUMBER	HIBERNATION	INTERVENING
CANDLESTICK	PAEDOTROPHY	APPEASEMENT	DISENTANGLE	HIDEOUSNESS	INTERVIEWEE
CARDIOGRAPH	PANDEMONIUM	APPELLATION	DODECASTYLE	HOHENLINDEN	INTERVIEWER
CARDOPHAGUS	PERDUELLION	APPELLATIVE	DOMESTICATE	HOMEOPATHIC	INVESTIGATE
CLADOSPORUM	PIEDMONTITE	ARGENTINIAN	DOMESTICITY	HONEYCOMBED	INVESTITURE
COLDBLOODED	PONDEROUSLY	ASPERGILLUM	DYAESTHESIA	HONEYMOONER	IRREDENTIST
CONDITIONAL	PREDECESSOR	ASPERGILLUS	EFFECTIVELY	HONEYSUCKLE	IRREDUCIBLE
CONDITIONER	PREDESTINED	ASPERSORIUM	EFFECTUALLY	HYPERBOREAN	IRREFUTABLE
CONDOLENCES	PREDICAMENT	ASSEMBLYMAN	EMBELLISHED	HYPERMARKET	IRREGULARLY
CONDOMINIUM	PREDICATIVE	ATHERINIDAE	EMMENAGOGUE	HYPERTROPHY	IRRELEVANCE
CONDOTTIERE	PREDICTABLE	ATHERMANOUS	EMMENTHALER	IMMEDIATELY	IRRELIGIOUS
CONDOTTIORE	PREDICTABLY	ATTENTIVELY	ENCEPHALOMA	IMPEACHMENT	IRREPARABLE
CONDUCTANCE	PREDOMINANT	ATTENUATION	ENFEOFFMENT	IMPECUNIOUS	IRREPARABLY
CONDUCTRESS	PREDOMINATE	ATTESTATION	ENKEPHALINE	IMPEDIMENTA	IRREVERENCE
CORDWAINERS	PRODIGALISE	BELEAGUERED	ENNEAHEDRON	IMPERFORATE	IRREVOCABLE
CREDENTIALS	PRODIGALITY	BENEDICTINE	ENTERTAINER	IMPERIALISM	ISOELECTRIC
CREDIBILITY	QUADRENNIAL	BENEDICTION	ESSENTIALLY	IMPERIALIST	JOSEPHINITE
CREDULOUSLY	QUADRENNIUM	BENEFICIARY	EXCEEDINGLY	IMPERIOUSLY	KAMELAUKION
DARDANELLES	QUADRUPLETS	BENEFICIATE	EXCEPTIONAL	IMPERMANENT	KIMERIDGIAN
DENDRACHATE	READABILITY	BENEVOLENCE	EXCESSIVELY	IMPERMEABLE	KRIEGSSPIEL
EPIDIASCOPE	RIDDLEMEREE	BEREAVEMENT	EXPECTANTLY	IMPERSONATE	LAMENTATION
ERADICATION	SADDLEHORSE	BICENTENARY	EXPECTATION	IMPERTINENT	LASERPICIUM
FIDDLEDEDEE	SANDERSWOOD	BUREAUCRACY	EXPECTORANT	IMPETUOSITY	LATERIGRADE
FUNDAMENTAL	SKIDBLADNIR	CALEFACIENT	EXPECTORATE	IMPETUOUSLY	LATERITIOUS
FUNDRAISING	STADTHOLDER	CALENDERING	EXPEDITIOUS	INCESSANTLY	LEGERDEMAIN
GIRDLESTEAD	SUBDIVISION	CAMERAWOMAN	EXPENDITURE	INDEFINABLE	LEVELHEADED
GLADWELLISE	SUBDOMINANT	CAMEROONIAN	EXPERIENCED	INDENTATION	LIBERTARIAN
GODDAUGHTER	SUNDRENCHED	CAPERNOITED	EXTEMPORISE	INDEPENDENT	LITERALNESS

LUXEMBURGER	REMEMBRANCE	UNBEFITTING	FULFILLMENT	GIGGLEWATER	ANTHRACOSIS
MACERANDUBA	REPETITIOUS	UNCERTAINTY	GODFORSAKEN	GINGERBREAD	ARCHAEOLOGY
MAKEBELIEVE	RESEMBLANCE	UNDEMANDING	GONFALONIER	GREGARINIDA	ARCHEGONIAL
MALEDICTION	RESENTFULLY	UNDERCHARGE	HALFBROTHER	HANGGLIDING	ARCHEGONIUM
MALEFACTION	RESERVATION	UNDERCOOKED	HALFHEARTED	HAUGHTINESS	ARCHENTERON
MALEVOLENCE	REVELATIONS	UNDERGROUND	HALFHOLIDAY	HOGGISHNESS	ARCHILOCHUS
MANEUVERING	REVENDICATE	UNDERGROWTH	INEFFECTIVE	HUMGRUFFIAN	ARCHIPELAGO
MATERIALISE	REVERBERATE	UNDERHANDED	INEFFECTUAL	IMAGINATION	ARRHENOTOKY
MATERIALISM	REVERENTIAL	UNDERMANNED	INEFFICIENT	IMAGINATIVE	ARTHRAPODAL
MATERIALIST	ROBESPIERRE	UNDERSIGNED	INOFFENSIVE	LENGTHENING	ARTHRODESIS
MATERIALIZE	RUDESHEIMER	UNDERSTATED	MALFEASANCE	LENGTHINESS	ARTHROSPORE
METEOROLOGY	SALESPERSON	UNDERTAKING	MALFUNCTION	LINGUISTICS	ASPHETERISM
MINESWEEPER	SCHECKLATON	UNDERVALUED	MISFEASANCE	LOGGERHEADS	BASHFULNESS
MISERICORDE	SCIENTOLOGY	UNDERWEIGHT	NIPFARTHING	LONGANIMITY	BATHYSPHERE
MISERLINESS	SCLERODERMA	UNDERWRITER	NONFEASANCE	LONGAWAITED	BODHISATTVA
MODELMOLEST	SCREAMINGLY	UNDESERVING	PERFORATION	LONGINQUITY	BUSHWHACKER
MODERNISTIC	SCREWDRIVER	UNDESIRABLE	PERFORMANCE	LONGLASTING	CATHOLICISM
MOLESTATION	SELECTIVELY	UNDEVELOPED	PERFUNCTORY	LONGRUNNING	DEPHLEGMATE
MOMENTARILY	SELECTIVITY	UNGETATABLE	PROFESSEDLY	LONGSIGHTED	DICHROMATIC
MONEYLENDER	SERENDIPITY	UNNECESSARY	PROFICIENCY	LONGSLEEVED	DIPHYCERCAL
MONEYMAKING	SEVENTEENTH	UNPERTURBED	PROFITEROLE	MANGALSUTRA	DISHEVELLED
NECESSARILY	SEVERALFOLD	UNREALISTIC	PROFUSENESS	MARGINALIST	DISHONESTLY
NECESSITATE	SLEEPWALKER	UNREASONING	RAFFISHNESS	MARGINALIZE	DITHELETISM
NECESSITOUS	SOVEREIGNTY	UNREHEARSED	RINFORZANDO	MORGENSTERN	EMPHYTEUSIS
NEVERENDING	SPEECHCRAFT	UNRELENTING	RUMFRUCTION	NAUGHTINESS	ENCHANTMENT
NIKETHAMIDE	SPEEDOMETER	UNREMITTING	SCAFFOLDING	NEIGHBORING	ENCHANTRESS
NOMENCLATOR	SPREADSHEET	UNREPENTANT	SELFCONTROL	NEIGHBOURLY	ENCHIRIDION
NONETHELESS	STEEPLEJACK	UNWELCOMING	SELFDEFENCE	OLIGOCHAETE	ENCHONDROMA
NONEXISTENT	STREAMLINED	VALEDICTION	SELFEVIDENT	ORIGINALITY	ENGHALSKRUG
NOVELETTISH	STREETLIGHT	VALEDICTORY	SELFIMPOSED	ORIGINATING	ENTHRALLING
NUMERICALLY	STRENUOUSLY	VIDEOCAMERA	SELFISHNESS	ORIGINATION	ESCHATOLOGY
OBJECTIVELY	STRETCHABLE	VOTERIGGING	SELFRESPECT	OUAGADOUGOU	ESCHERICHIA
OBJECTIVITY	STRETCHLESS	WAKEFULNESS	SELFSERVICE	PLAGIARISED	EUCHARISTIC
OBSERVATION	SUDETENLAND	WAREHOUSING	SHAFTESBURY	PLAGIOSTOMI	EUCHROMATIN
OBSERVATORY	SUPERALTERN	WATERCOLOUR	SPIFFLICATE	PROGENITRIX	EUPHEMISTIC
OBSESSIVELY	SUPERCHARGE	WATERCOURSE	SUFFICIENCY	PROGNATHOUS	EURHYTHMICS
OBTEMPERATE	SUPERCHERIE	WATEREDDOWN	SUFFOCATING	PROGRESSION	FASHIONABLE
OFFENSIVELY	SUPERFICIAL	WATERLOGGED	SUFFOCATION	PROGRESSIVE	FASHIONABLY
ORDERLINESS	SUPERFICIES	WATERMEADOW	SUFFRAGETTE	RAMGUNSHOCH	FISHANDCHIP
ORIENTALISM	SUPERFLUITY	WATERSKIING	TRAFFICATOR	RANGEFINDER	FISHMONGERS
ORIENTALIST	SUPERFLUOUS	WATERSPLASH	UNIFICATION	RUMGUMPTION	FOTHERGILLA
ORIENTATION	SUPERIMPOSE	WHEELBARROW	ANAGNORISIS	SANGUINEOUS	HAPHAZARDLY
OSTENTATION	SUPERINTEND	WHEELWRIGHT	BANGLADESHI	SEIGNIORAGE	HIGHLIGHTER
OSTEOPATHIC	SUPERIORITY	WIDERANGING	BERGSCHRUND	SINGAPOREAN	HIGHPITCHED
OSTEOPLASTY	SUPERLATIVE	WITENAGEMOT	BRAGGADOCIO	SINGLESTICK	HIGHPOWERED
PALEOGRAPHY	SUPERMARKET	ALIFANFARON	BURGOMASTER	SINGULARITY	HIGHPROFILE
PALEOLITHIC	SUPERSCRIBE	CLIFFHANGER	COAGULATION	SLIGHTINGLY	HIGHQUALITY
PALESTINIAN	SUPERSCRIPT	COEFFICIENT	CONGRESSMAN	STAGFLATION	HIGHRANKING
PAPERWEIGHT	SUPERSEDEAS	COMFORTABLE	DANGEROUSLY	STEGANOGRAM	HYPHENATION
PARENTHESIS	SUPERSEDERE	COMFORTABLY	DIAGNOSTICS	STEGANOPODE	LIGHTHEADED
PATERNALISM	SUPERTANKER	COMFORTLESS	DISGRACEFUL	SUGGESTIBLE	LIGHTWEIGHT
PATERNOSTER	SUPERVISION	CONFABULATE	DISGRUNTLED	TANGIBILITY	LITHOGRAPHY
PEDESTRIANS	SUPERVISORY	CONFARREATE	DRAGGLETAIL	THIGMOTAXIS	LYCHNOSCOPE
PEDETENTOUS	TABERNACLES	CONFEDERACY	DRAGONNADES	TIGGYWINKLE	MACHAIRODUS
PENETRATING	TÉLÉFÉRIQUE	CONFEDERATE	ELIGIBILITY	TRAGELAPHUS	MACHINATION
PENETRATION	TELEGRAPHER	CONFIDENTLY	EPIGENESIST	WEIGHBRIDGE	MATHEMATICS
PEREGRINATE	TELEGRAPHIC	CONFINEMENT	EXAGGERATED	WHIGMALEERY	MEKHITARIST
PERENNIALLY	TELEKINESIS	CONFUTATION	FINGERPRINT	AFGHANISTAN	METHODOLOGY
PERESTROIKA	TELEPHONIST	DEIFICATION	FINGERSTALL	ALPHABETIZE	MICHURINISM
POMEGRANATE	TELEPRINTER	DIFFERENTLY	FORGIVENESS	AMPHETAMINE	MYTHOLOGIZE
POTENTIALLY	TELEWORKING	DIFFIDENTLY	FRAGMENTARY	AMPHIBOLOGY	NAPHTHALENE
PREEMINENCE	THREATENING	DIFFRACTION	FRIGATEBIRD	AMPHISBAENA	NETHERLANDS
PRZEWALSKIS	TIMEKEEPING	DISFIGURING	FRIGHTENING	AMPHISBOENA	NETHERLINGS
RABELAISIAN	TIMESHARING	DYSFUNCTION	FRIGHTFULLY	ANTHESTERIA	NIGHTINGALE
RECEPTIVITY	TREECREEPER	EDIFICATION	FRUGIVOROUS	ANTHOCYANIN	NIGHTMARISH
RECESSIONAL	TYPESETTING	FANFARONADE	GIGGLESTICK	ANTHOLOGIZE	NOTHINGNESS
RELEASEMENT	TYPEWRITTEN	FORFOUGHTEN	GIGGLESWICK	ANTHONOMOUS	OFFHANDEDLY

ORCHESTRATE	ARTIODACTYL	FAMILIARIZE	NOTICEBOARD	SCRIMSHANDY	HECKELPHONE
ORCHESTRINA	ASSIDUOUSLY	FARINACEOUS	NUMISMATICS	SCRIPTORIUM	HUCKLEBERRY
ORCHESTRION	ASSIGNATION	FRUITLESSLY	NUMISMATIST	SEDIMENTARY	HUCKSTERAGE
ORTHOCENTRE	ASSIMILATED	HABILIMENTS	OBLITERATED	SEMITRAILER	KIRKPATRICK
ORTHOGRAPHY	ASTIGMATISM	HAGIOGRAPHA	OBVIOUSNESS	SEPIOSTAIRE	LICKSPITTLE
ORTHOPAEDIC	AUDIOVISUAL	HAGIOGRAPHY	OFFICIALDOM	SERICULTURE	MARKETPLACE
PATHOLOGIST	AURIGNACIAN	HARIOLATION	OFFICIALESE	SERIOUSNESS	MASKALLONGE
PHTHIRIASIS	AVOIRDUPOIS	HEMIANOPSIA	OFFICIOUSLY	SINISTRORSE	MECKLENBURG
PREHISTORIC	BALISTRARIA	HUMILIATING	OMNIPOTENCE	SOCIABILITY	MOCKINGBIRD
PROHIBITION	BESIEGEMENT	HUMILIATION	OMNIPRESENT	SOCIOLOGIST	MUSKELLUNGE
PROHIBITIVE	BEWILDERING	IMMIGRATION	OMNISCIENCE	SOLILOQUIZE	NICKELODEON
PYTHONESQUE	BILIOUSNESS	IMPIGNORATE	ONEIRODYNIA	SOLIPSISTIC	NICKNACKERY
RIGHTANGLED	BIMILLENARY	INCINERATOR	ONEIROMANCY	SPRINGBOARD	PICKELHAUBE
RIGHTEOUSLY	BUSINESSMAN	INDIARUBBER	OPPIGNORATE	SPRINGCLEAN	PICKYOUROWN
RIGHTHANDED	CALIBRATION	INDIFFERENT	ORNITHOLOGY	SPRINGHOUSE	ROCKEFELLER
RIGHTHANDER	CALIFORNIUM	INDIGESTION	ORNITHOPTER	SPRINGINESS	SHAKESPEARE
RIGHTWINGER	CHAIRPERSON	INDIGNANTLY	OSCILLATION	STAIRCARPET	SMOKESCREEN
SACHERTORTE	CHEIROGNOMY	INDIGNATION	PACIFICALLY	STEINBERGER	SOCKDALAGER
SIGHTSCREEN	CHOIRMASTER	INDIVISIBLE	PARISHIONER	STRIKEBOUND	SOCKDOLAGER
SIGHTSEEING	CHRISMATION	INDIVISIBLY	PENICILLATE	STRINGBOARD	SOCKDOLIGER
TACHYCARDIA	CHRISTENING	INFILTRATOR	PENITENTIAL	STRINGENTLY	SOCKDOLOGER
TACHYGRAPHY	CHRISTMASSY	INSIDIOUSLY	PERICARDIUM	STRINGYBARK	SPOKESWOMAN
TECHNICALLY	CHRISTOPHER	INSINCERITY	PERIGORDIAN	SUBITANEOUS	STAKEHOLDER
TIGHTFISTED	CITIZENSHIP	INSINUATING	PERIODONTIC	TACITURNITY	TICKTACKTOE
TIGHTLIPPED	CLAIRSCHACH	INSINUATION	PERIPATETIC	TAXIDERMIST	VOLKSKAMMER
TSCHERNOSEM	CLAIRVOYANT	INSISTENTLY	PERIPHRASIS	TEDIOUSNESS	WORKMANLIKE
UNCHRISTIAN	CORINTHIANS	INVIGILATOR	PERISSOLOGY	THRIFTINESS	WORKMANSHIP
UNSHAKEABLE	CYLINDRICAL	INVINCIBLES	PERISTALITH	TITILLATION	WORKSTATION
UNSHELTERED	DEBILITATED	ISTIOPHORUS	PERISTALSIS	TOXICOGENIC	ACCLAMATION
UNSHRINKING	DELICIOUSLY	JUDICIOUSLY	PERITONAEUM	UNCIVILISED	ACCLIMATION
UNTHINKABLE	DELICTATION	KILIMANJARO	PERITONITIS	UNCIVILIZED	ACCLIMATISE
UNWHOLESOME	DELINEATION	LAPIDESCENT	PETITMAITRE	UNDIGNIFIED	ACCLIMATIZE
VICHYSOISSE	DELINQUENCY	LATIFUNDIUM	PLEISTOCENE	UNDISCLOSED	ACOLOUTHITE
WASHERWOMAN	DELITESCENT	LECITHINASE	POLICEWOMAN	UNDISGUISED	ADOLESCENCE
WASHLEATHER	DELIVERANCE	LEGIONNAIRE	POLIORCETIC	UNDISTURBED	ADULLAMITES
WISHTONWISH	DEMIBASTION	LEGISLATION	POLITICALLY	UNMITIGATED	ADULTERATED
WITHERSHINS	DESICCATION	LEGISLATIVE	POLITICIANS	UNRIGHTEOUS	AFFLIICTION
WITHHOLDING	DESIGNATION	LEGISLATURE	PURITANICAL	UNWITTINGLY	AGGLOMERATE
ABRIDGEMENT	DEVIOUSNESS	LEPIDOPTERA	RADIOACTIVE	UPRIGHTNESS	AGGLUTINANT
ACCIPITRINE	DEVITRIFIED	LEPIDOSIREN	RADIOCARBON	UTRICULARIA	AGGLUTINATE
ACHIEVEMENT	DISILLUSION	LIVINGSTONE	RADIOGRAPHY	VACILLATING	AMELANCHIER
ACRIFLAVINE	DISIMPRISON	LOUISIANIAN	RADIOLOGIST	VACILLATION	AMPLEXICAUL
ACRIMONIOUS	DISINCLINED	LUMINESCENT	RATIOCINATE	VARIABILITY	AMYLOPECTIN
AFFILIATION	DISINTEREST	MAGISTERIAL	RATIONALITY	VARIEGATION	APOLLINARIS
AFFIRMATION	DOMINEERING	MAGISTRATES	RATIONALIZE	VARIOLATION	APOLLONICON
AFFIRMATIVE	DUBIOUSNESS	MALICIOUSLY	RAVISHINGLY	VICIOUSNESS	APPLERINGIE
AGRICULTURE	DUNIEWASSAL	MANIPULATOR	RECIPROCATE	VICISSITUDE	APPLICATION
ALBIGENSIAN	EFFICACIOUS	MARIONBERRY	RECIPROCITY	VIVISECTION	ASCLEPIADES
AMBIVALENCE	EFFICIENTLY	MARIONETTES	REGIMENTALS	CONJECTURAL	BALLBEARING
ANNIVERSARY	EMPIECEMENT	MARIVAUDAGE	REGISTERING	CONJUGATION	BELLEROPHON
ANTIBURGHER	EMPIRICUTIC	MEDIASTINUM	RELIABILITY	CONJUNCTION	BELLETTRIST
ANTICYCLONE	ENGINEERING	MEDICINALLY	RELIGIOUSLY	CONJUNCTURE	BELLIGERENT
ANTINEUTRON	ENLIGHTENED	MEDIUMSIZED	REMINISCENT	DISJUNCTION	BELLYTIMBER
ANTIPHONARY	ENTITLEMENT	MERITORIOUS	RESIDENTIAL	DISJUNCTIVE	BIBLIOPHILE
ANTIPHRASIS	ENVIRONMENT	MINIATURIST	RESIGNATION	PREJUDICIAL	BIELORUSSIA
ANTIPYRETIC	EQUIDISTANT	MINIATURIZE	RESISTIVITY	SUBJUGATION	BILLIONAIRE
ANTIQUARIAN	EQUILATERAL	MINISTERIAL	RETINACULUM	SUBJUNCTIVE	BRILLIANTLY
ANTIRRHINUM	EQUILIBRIST	MINISTERING	RETINOSCOPY	BACKBENCHER	BULLFIGHTER
ANTISTHENES	EQUILIBRIUM	MISIDENTIFY	RETINOSPORA	BACKFIELDER	CALLANETICS
ANTISTROPHE	EQUINOCTIAL	MOXIBUSTION	REVISIONISM	BACKPACKING	CALLIGRAPHY
ARBITRAGEUR	EQUIPOLLENT	MUNIFICENCE	ROSICRUCIAN	BACKSLIDING	CALLIPYGEAN
ARBITRAMENT	EQUIVALENCE	MUNITIONIZE	RUDIMENTARY	BASKERVILLE	CALLISTEMON
ARBITRARILY	EQUIVOCALLY	NATIONALISM	SAGITTARIUS	BOOKBINDING	CALLITRICHE
ARBITRATION	ESPIEGLERIE	NATIONALIST	SALINOMETER	BOOKKEEPING	CALLOUSNESS
ARRIVEDERCI	EXHILARATED	NATIONALITY	SATIRICALLY	BOOKSELLERS	CAULIFLOWER
ARTICULATED	FAMILIARISE	NATIONALIZE	SCHISTOSOMA	COCKLESHELL	CHALLENGING
ARTILLERIST	FAMILIARITY	NATIONSTATE	SCHISTOSOME	FARKLEBERRY	CHILDMINDER

CHILLINGHAM	INFLAMMABLE	SUBLIMATION	ERYMANTHIAN	AMONTILLADO	FORNICATION
CHOLESTEROL	INFLUENTIAL	SWALLOWABLE	ETYMOLOGIST	ANENCEPHALY	FOUNDATIONS
CHOLINERGIC	ISOLECITHAL	TAGLIATELLE	EXAMINATION	ANONYMOUSLY	FRANKFURTER
CITLALEPETL	LAWLESSNESS	THALIDOMIDE	FEHMGERICHT	APONEUROSIS	FRANKLINITE
COALESCENCE	LILLIPUTIAN	THALLOPHYTE	FLAMBOYANCE	BANNOCKBURN	FRANTICALLY
COLLABORATE	MAGLEMOSIAN	TITLEHOLDER	FLAMBOYANTE	BARNSTORMER	FRENCHWOMAN
COLLAPSIBLE	MARLBOROUGH	TOPLOFTICAL	FORMULATION	BLANKURSINE	FRENCHWOMEN
COLLECTANEA	MELLIFLUOUS	TWELVEMONTH	FULMINATION	BLUNDERBORE	FRONTRUNNER
COLLENCHYMA	MILLIAMPERE	UNALIENABLE	GAMMERSTANG	BRANDENBURG	FURNISHINGS
COLLOCATION	MILLIONAIRE	UNALTERABLE	GEOMETRICAL	CANNIBALISM	GARNISHMENT
COULOMMIERS	MOLLYCODDLE	UNBLEMISHED	GERMINATION	CANNIBALIZE	GRANDFATHER
CYCLOALKANE	NUCLEOPLASM	UNCLEANNESS	GLIMMERGOWK	CARNAPTIOUS	GRANDMASTER
CYCLOSTYLED	OCHLOCRATIC	UNCLUTTERED	GRAMMALOGUE	CARNIVOROUS	GRANDMOTHER
DECLAMATION	OPALESCENCE	UNFLAPPABLE	GRAMMATICAL	CHANCELLERY	GRENZGANGER
DECLAMATORY	PARLIPOMENA	UNFLINCHING	HAEMOGLOBIN	CHANTARELLE	HORNSWOGGLE
DECLARATION	PERLUSTRATE	USELESSNESS	HAEMOPHILIA	CHANTERELLE	HYMNOLOGIST
DECLARATIVE	PHALANSTERY	UTILITARIAN	HAEMORRHAGE	CHANTICLEER	ICONOGRAPHY
DEGLUTINATE	PHILANDERER	UTILIZATION	HAEMORRHOID	CHINOISERIE	ICONOSTASIS
DEGLUTITION	PHILATELIST	VALLAMBROSA	HAMMERCLOTH	CHONDROSTEI	IDENTICALLY
DIPLOMATICS	PHILIPPIANS	VALLISNERIA	HUMMINGBIRD	CLANDESTINE	IDENTIFYING
DIPLOMATIST	PHILIPPINES	VIOLINCELLO	ILLMANNERED	CLANJAMFRAY	IRONMONGERS
DISLOCATION	PHILLIPSITE	VIOLONCELLO	ISOMORPHOUS	CLINOCHLORE	IRONMONGERY
DUPLICATING	PHILOCTETES	WELLADVISED	KOMMERSBUCH	COENOBITISM	KINNIKINICK
DUPLICATION	PHILOLOGIST	WELLBEHAVED	LAMMERGEIER	COGNOSCENTE	LAUNDERETTE
DYSLOGISTIC	PHILOSOPHER	WELLDEFINED	LAMMERGEYER	COGNOSCENTI	MAGNANIMITY
EGALITARIAN	PHYLLOCLADE	WELLDRESSED	MURMURATION	COINCIDENCE	MAGNANIMOUS
EMPLACEMENT	POLLENBRUSH	WELLFOUNDED	ONOMASTICON	CONNECTICUT	MAGNIFICENT
ENSLAVEMENT	POLLINATION	WELLINGTONS	OUTMANEUVER	CONNOISSEUR	MAINTENANCE
EXCLAMATION	PRELIBATION	WELLMEANING	PERMANENTLY	CONNOTATION	MEANDERINGS
EXCLUSIVELY	PRELIMINARY	WILLINGNESS	PERMISSIBLE	CORNERSTONE	MEANINGLESS
EXPLANATION	PROLEGOMENA	WORLDFAMOUS	PERMUTATION	COUNSELLING	MINNESINGER
EXPLANATORY	PROLETARIAN	WORLDLINESS	PREMATURELY	COUNTENANCE	MOONLIGHTER
EXPLORATION	PROLETARIAT	YELLOWPLUSH	PREMEDITATE	COUNTERFEIT	MOUNTAINEER
EXPLORATORY	PROLIFERATE	YELLOWSTONE	PREMIERSHIP	COUNTERFOIL	MOUNTAINOUS
FALLIBILITY	PROLOCUTION	ABOMINATION	PREMONITION	COUNTERFORT	NEANDERTHAL
FAULTFINDER	PUBLICATION	ADUMBRATION	PREMONITORY	COUNTERGLOW	ODONTOBLAST
FAULTLESSLY	PUBLISHABLE	APOMORPHINE	PRIMIGENIAL	COUNTERHAND	ODONTOPHORE
FIELDWORKER	PYELOGRAPHY	BLAMEWORTHY	PROMINENTLY	COUNTERMAND	OPINIONATED
FILLIBUSTER	QUALITATIVE	CARMINATIVE	PROMISCUITY	COUNTERPANE	PAINKILLING
FOOLISHNESS	RALLENTANDO	CHAMBERLAIN	PROMISCUOUS	COUNTERPART	PAINSTAKING
FORLORNNESS	REALIGNMENT	CHAMBERMAID	PROMOTIONAL	COUNTERSIGN	PAWNBROKERS
FOULMOUTHED	REALIZATION	CLIMACTERIC	PROMPTITUDE	COUNTERSINK	PENNYFATHER
FULLBLOODED	REALPOLITIK	CLIMATOLOGY	SHAMELESSLY	COUNTRIFIED	PHONETICIAN
GALLIBAGGER	RECLAMATION	COMMANDMENT	SKIMMINGTON	COUNTRYSIDE	PHONOFIDDLE
GALLIBEGGAR	REFLEXOLOGY	COMMEMORATE	SLUMBERWEAR	CRENELLATED	PINNYWINKLE
GALLIGANTUS	REPLACEABLE	COMMENDABLE	SLUMGULLION	CURNAPTIOUS	PLANETARIUM
GALLIMAUFRY	REPLACEMENT	COMMENDABLY	STIMULATION	DINNYHAUSER	PLANTAGENET
GALLOVIDIAN	SCALPRIFORM	COMMENTATOR	STYMPHALIAN	DINNYHAYSER	PLANTIGRADE
GALLOWGLASS	SCOLECIFORM	COMMINATION	SUBMERGENCE	DOWNHEARTED	POINTLESSLY
GALLYBAGGER	SCOLOPENDRA	COMMISERATE	SUBMULTIPLE	DOWNTRODDEN	PORNOGRAPHY
GALLYBEGGAR	SCULDUDDERY	COMMONPLACE	SUMMERHOUSE	DRINKDRIVER	PRINCIPALLY
GILLYFLOWER	SCULDUGGERY	COMMONSENSE	SYMMETRICAL	DRUNKENNESS	QUINTUPLETS
GRALLATORES	SCULLABOGUE	COMMUNALISM	TERMINATION	EARNESTNESS	REANIMATION
GULLIBILITY	SHALLOWNESS	COMMUNICANT	TERMINOLOGY	ENUNCIATION	REINCARNATE
HALLEFLINTA	SILLIMANITE	COMMUNICATE	TRIMESTRIAL	EOANTHROPUS	SAINTLINESS
HALLUCINATE	SKILLIGALEE	COMMUTATION	TROMPELOEIL	EPANALEPSIS	SAINTPAULIA
HEALTHINESS	SKILLIGOLEE	CRÉMAILLÈRE	UNAMBIGUOUS	EPINEPHRINE	SCANDALIZED
HOLLANDAISE	SKULDUDDERY	CREMATORIUM	UNEMOTIONAL	ETHNOGRAPHY	SCANDANAVIA
HOOLIGANISM	SKULDUGGERY	CRIMINOLOGY	UNIMPORTANT	ETHNOLOGIST	SCANDINAVIA
IDOLIZATION	SMALLHOLDER	CROMWELLIAN	UNIMPRESSED	EVANGELICAL	SCINTILLATE
IDYLLICALLY	SPELLBINDER	CULMINATION	VERMICULITE	EVENTRATION	SENNACHERIB
IMPLAUSIBLE	STALLHOLDER	DERMATOLOGY	WARMHEARTED	EVENTUALITY	SHENANIGANS
IMPLEMENTAL	STELLIONATE	DIAMONDBACK	ABANDONMENT	EXANTHEMATA	SHINPLASTER
IMPLICATION	STILBESTROL	ELIMINATION	ACINACIFORM	EXONERATION	SHUNAMITISM
INALIENABLE	STYLISHNESS	ENUMERATION	ACKNOWLEDGE	FERNITICKLE	SIGNIFICANT
INCLINATION	STYLIZATION	EPAMINONDAS	AGONOTHETES	FLANKERBACK	SLENDERNESS
INELUCTABLE	STYLOPODIUM	EREMACAUSIS	AMINOBUTENE	FLANNELETTE	SOUNDLESSLY

SPANGCOCKLE
SPENDTHRIFT
SPONDULICKS
SPONDYLITIS
SPONSORSHIP
SPONTANEITY
SPONTANEOUS
SRANANTONGO
STANDARDIZE
STANDOFFISH
STANDPATTER
STENOCHROME
STENOGRAPHY
TEENYBOPPER
THANATOPSIS
THANKLESSLY
THENCEFORTH
THINGAMABOB
THINGAMAJIG
THINGLINESS
THINGUMAJIG
THUNDERBIRD
THUNDERBOLT
THUNDERCLAP
THUNDERHEAD
TOWNSPEOPLE
TRANQUILITY
TRANSACTION
TRANSCEIVER
TRANSDERMAL
TRANSFERRED
TRANSFERRIN
TRANSFIGURE
TRANSFORMED
TRANSFORMER
TRANSFUSION
TRANSILIENT
TRANSLATION
TRANSLUCENT
TRANSMITTED
TRANSMITTER
TRANSPARENT
TRANSPONDER
TRANSPORTED
TRANSPORTER
TRANSURANIC
TRANSVERSAL
TRENCHERMAN
TRINCOMALEE
TRINIDADIAN
TRINITARIAN
TRINOBANTES
UNANIMOUSLY
UNANNOUNCED
UNENDURABLE
UNENVELOPED
UNINHABITED
UNINHIBITED
UNINITIATED
UNUNQUADIUM
WAINSCOTING
WIENERWURST
WRONGHEADED
ABIOGENESIS
ABIOGENETIC
ABNORMALITY
ABSORPTANCE

ACCOMMODATE
ACCOMPANIST
ACCORDINGLY
ACCOUNTABLE
ACCOUNTANCY
ACROCENTRIC
ADJOURNMENT
AERODYNAMIC
AERONAUTICS
AGNOSTICISM
AGROSTOLOGY
AMMOPHILOUS
ANTONOMASIA
APPOINTMENT
ASSOCIATION
ASTONISHING
ATMOSPHERIC
ATROCIOUSLY
BELORUSSIAN
BLOODSPORTS
BLOODSTREAM
BLOODSUCKER
CACOGASTRIC
CACOPHONOUS
CAMOUFLAGED
CAROLINGIAN
CHLOROPHYLL
CHROMOPLAST
CHRONICALLY
CHRONOMETER
CILOFIBRATE
CLIOMETRICS
COHORTATIVE
COLONIALISM
COLONIALIST
COLORIMETER
COLOURBLIND
CROOKEDNESS
CYMOPHANOUS
CYTOGENESIS
DECONSTRUCT
DECORATIONS
DECORTICATE
DEFOLIATION
DEFORMATION
DEHORTATIVE
DEMOGRAPHIC
DEMONOMANIA
DEMONSTRATE
DEMORALIZED
DEMOSTHENES
DEMOSTHENIC
DENOMINATOR
DEPORTATION
DICOTYLEDON
DISOBEDIENT
DISORGANIZE
DISORIENTED
DIVORCEMENT
ECTOTROPHIC
EMBOÎTEMENT
EMPOWERMENT
ENCOURAGING
ENDOCARDIUM
ENDORSEMENT
ENDOTHERMIC
ENDOTROPHIC

ENFORCEABLE
ENFORCEMENT
ENFOULDERED
ERIODENDRON
ERRONEOUSLY
EXHORTATION
EXPONENTIAL
EXPOSTULATE
EXTORTIONER
FAVOURITISM
FEROCIOUSLY
FLUORESCENT
FLUOROMETER
FLUOROSCOPE
GAMOGENESIS
GENOUILLÈRE
GERONTOLOGY
HEMOPHILIAC
HEMORRHOIDS
HOLOTHURIAN
HOMOEOPATHY
HOMOGENEITY
HOMOGENEOUS
HOMOGENIZED
HOMOIOUSIAN
HOMOPHONOUS
HOMOTHERMAL
HOMOTHERMIC
HYPOCORISMA
HYPOTENSION
HYPOTHECATE
HYPOTHERMIA
IDEOLOGICAL
IDEOPRAXIST
IDIOGRAPHIC
IDIOTICALLY
IGNOMINIOUS
IGNORANTINE
ILLOGICALLY
IMMORTALISE
IMMORTALITY
IMMORTALIZE
IMPORTANTLY
IMPORTATION
IMPORTUNATE
INCOHERENCE
INCOMPETENT
INCOMPOSITE
INCONGRUITY
INCONGRUOUS
INCONSTANCY
INCONTINENT
INCORPORATE
INCORPOREAL
INCORRECTLY
INDOMITABLE
INFORMALITY
INFORMATICS
INFORMATION
INFORMATIVE
INSOUCIANCE
INTOLERABLE
INTOLERABLY
INTOLERANCE
INTOXICATED
INTOXIMETER
INVOLUNTARY

INVOLVEMENT
KILOCALORIE
LABORIOUSLY
LABORSAVING
LACONICALLY
LOCORESTIVE
LOGODAEDALY
LOGOGRAPHER
MASOCHISTIC
MELODIOUSLY
MEMORABILIA
MONOCHINOUS
MONOCHROMAT
MONOGRAMMED
MONOLINGUAL
MONONGAHELA
MONONUCLEAR
MONOPSONIST
MONOTHELITE
MONOTREMATA
MYCOLOGICAL
MYCOPHAGIST
MYXOMATOSIS
NEGOTIATING
NEGOTIATION
NOTORIOUSLY
NOTOTHERIUM
OBSOLESCENT
ONTOLOGICAL
OPPORTUNELY
OPPORTUNISM
OPPORTUNIST
OPPORTUNITY
OPTOMETRIST
PANOMPHAEAN
PARONOMASIA
PELOPONNESE
POCOCURANTE
PREOCCUPIED
PROOFREADER
RECOGNITION
RECONDITION
RECONNOITER
RECONNOITRE
RECONSTRUCT
RECOVERABLE
REDOUBTABLE
REFOCILLATE
REFORMATION
REFORMATORY
REMONSTRATE
REMORSELESS
RESOURCEFUL
REVOLUTIONS
RIBONUCLEIC
RODOMONTADE
ROTOGRAVURE
SAPONACEOUS
SAVOURINESS
SAXOPHONIST
SCHOLARSHIP
SCHOTTISCHE
SECONDARILY
SECONDCLASS
SEXOLOGICAL
SOROPTIMIST
STOOLPIGEON

STROBOSCOPE
STRONGYLOID
STROPHILLUS
SUBORDINATE
SYCOPHANTIC
TELOCENTRIC
THEOBROMINE
THEOLOGICAL
THEOPNEUSTY
THEORETICAL
THROGMORTON
TIRONENSIAN
TOBOGGANING
TOPOGRAPHER
TOXOPHILITE
TYPOGRAPHER
TYPOGRAPHIC
TYROGLYPHID
TYRONENSIAN
UNCOMMITTED
UNCONCEALED
UNCONCERNED
UNCONFIRMED
UNCONNECTED
UNCONQUERED
UNCONSCIOUS
UNCONTESTED
UNCONVERTED
UNCONVINCED
UNCOUNTABLE
UNCOUTHNESS
UNDOUBTEDLY
UNFORTUNATE
UNGODLINESS
UNMOTIVATED
UNSOLICITED
UNTOUCHABLE
UPHOLSTERER
VASOPRESSIN
XENODOCHIUM
XEROPHILOUS
XEROTHERMIC
XEROTRIPSIS
XYLOGRAPHER
ZOROASTRIAN
ACUPUNCTURE
ADOPTIANISM
ADOPTIONISM
ANAPHYLAXIS
ANAPLEROSIS
ANAPLEROTIC
APOPHYLLITE
CAMPANOLOGY
CAMPESTRIAN
CAMPHORATED
CHIPPENDALE
CLAPPERCLAW
COMPARATIVE
COMPARTMENT
COMPENDIOUS
COMPETENTLY
COMPETITION
COMPETITIVE
COMPILATION
COMPILEMENT
COMPLACENCY
COMPLAISANT

COMPLICATED
COMPLIMENTS
COMPOSITION
COMPOTATION
COMPRIMARIO
COMPTROLLER
COMPUNCTION
COMPUTATION
COMPUTERIZE
COOPERATION
COOPERATIVE
COPPERPLATE
CORPORATION
CREPITATION
CREPUSCULAR
CULPABILITY
DESPERATELY
DESPERATION
DESPONDENCY
DIAPHORESIS
DIAPHORETIC
DISPARAGING
DISPENSABLE
DISPERSABLE
DISPLEASURE
DISPOSITION
DISPUTATION
ELEPHANTINE
EVAPORATION
GRAPHICALLY
HARPSICHORD
HELPFULNESS
HEPPLEWHITE
HERPETOLOGY
HIPPOCAMPUS
HIPPOCRATES
HIPPOCRATIC
HOSPITALITY
HOSPITALIZE
HOSPITALLER
HYOPLASTRON
INOPERATIVE
INOPPORTUNE
INSPIRATION
KLEPTOMANIA
LAMPLIGHTER
LAMPROPHYRE
MALPRACTICE
NYMPHOMANIA
OUTPOURINGS
PAMPELMOOSE
PAMPELMOUSE
PAMPHLETEER
PERPETRATOR
PERPETUALLY
POMPELMOOSE
POMPELMOUSE
PREPARATION
PREPARATIVE
PREPARATORY
PREPOLLENCE
PREPOSITION
PROPAGATION
PROPHETICAL
PROPHYLAXIS
PROPINQUITY
PROPOSITION

PROPRIETARY	SESQUIOXIDE	DISREGARDED	MATRIARCHAL	REGRETTABLE	TURRICULATE
PURPOSELESS	UNEQUIVOCAL	DOUROUCOULI	MATRICULATE	REGRETTABLY	ULTRAMARINE
PURPRESTURE	ABBREVIATED	EMBROCATION	MATRIMONIAL	REORIENTATE	ULTRAMODERN
REAPPRAISAL	ABORTIONIST	ENARTHROSIS	MAURETANIAN	REPRESENTED	ULTRAVIOLET
RESPECTABLE	ACCRESCENCE	ENCROACHING	MAURITANIAN	REPROACHFUL	UNBREAKABLE
RESPECTABLY	AGGRAVATING	ENFRANCHISE	MEPROBAMATE	RETRACTABLE	UNCRUSHABLE
RESPIRATION	AGGRAVATION	ESTRAMAZONE	MERRYMAKING	RETRIBUTION	UNDRINKABLE
RESPIRATORY	AGGREGATION	ESTRANGHELO	METRICATION	RETRIBUTIVE	UNPRACTICAL
RESPLENDENT	AGORAPHOBIA	EVERLASTING	MICROGAMETE	RETRIEVABLE	UNPRINTABLE
RESPONSIBLE	AMERCIAMENT	EXCRESCENCE	MICROSCOPIC	RETROACTIVE	UNPROTECTED
RESPONSIBLY	AMERICANISM	EXORBITANCE	MICROSECOND	RETROROCKET	UNTRAMELLED
RESPONSIONS	ANDROGENOUS	EXPROPRIATE	MICROTUBULE	SACRAMENTAL	VOORTREKKER
RHAPSODICAL	ANDROGYNOUS	EXTRADITION	MICROVILLUS	SACRIFICIAL	WHEREABOUTS
RHOPALOCERA	ANFRACTUOUS	EXTRAPOLATE	NARRAGANSET	SAPROLEGNIA	WHEREWITHAL
SALPINGITIS	APHRODISIAC	EXTRAVAGANT	NEARSIGHTED	SAPROPHYTIC	WORRYTROUGH
SCEPTICALLY	APPRECIABLE	EXTROGENOUS	NECROBIOSIS	SCARABAEOID	AIRSICKNESS
SCOPOLAMINE	APPRECIABLY	EXTROVERTED	NECROMANCER	SCARBOROUGH	ANASTOMOSIS
SCUPPERNONG	APPRENTICED	FABRICATION	NEUROLOGIST	SCAREMONGER	ANESTHETIST
SCYPHISTOMA	APPROACHING	FAIRWEATHER	NIERSTEINER	SCHRECKLICH	ANESTHETIZE
SEMPITERNAL	APPROBATION	FARRAGINOUS	NOURISHMENT	SCIREFACIAS	ANISOCERCAL
SEMPITERNUM	APPROPRIATE	FARREACHING	NUTRITIONAL	SCOREKEEPER	APOSIOPESIS
SHAPELINESS	APPROVINGLY	FERRONNIÈRE	OPERATIONAL	SEARCHLIGHT	APOSTROPHUS
SHEPHERDESS	APPROXIMATE	FLIRTATIOUS	OPPROBRIOUS	SECRETARIAL	ARISTOCRACY
SHIPBUILDER	ASTRINGENCY	FLORILEGIUM	OSTRACODERM	SECRETARIAT	BEASTLINESS
SHIPWRECKED	ATTRIBUTION	GARRULOUSLY	OSTREOPHAGE	SECRETIVELY	BESSARABIAN
SHOPLIFTING	ATTRIBUTIVE	GERRYMANDER	OVARIECTOMY	SEGREGATION	BLASPHEMOUS
SKEPTICALLY	AVERRUNCATE	HAIRDRESSER	OVERBALANCE	SHAREHOLDER	BLESSEDNESS
STEPBROTHER	AXEROPHTHOL	HAIRRAISING	OVERBEARING	SHORTCHANGE	BOYSENBERRY
STIPENDIARY	BOURGEOISIE	HEARTBROKEN	OVERCROWDED	SHORTCOMING	BRISTLECONE
STIPULATION	BUPRESTIDAE	HEARTLESSLY	OVERDRAUGHT	SHORTHANDED	CARSICKNESS
SUBPANATION	CAPRICCIOSO	HERRINGBONE	OVEREXPOSED	SMORGASBORD	CASSITERITE
SUMPTUOUSLY	CARRIAGEWAY	HYDROCARBON	OVERFISHING	SNORKELLING	CAUSTICALLY
SUPPEDANEUM	CHARACINOID	HYDROGENATE	OVERFLOWING	SORROWFULLY	CEASELESSLY
SUPPOSITION	CHARGEPAYER	HYDROMEDUSA	OVERHANGING	SPARROWHAWK	COMSTOCKERY
SUPPOSITORY	CHARISMATIC	HYDROPHIDAE	OVERLAPPING	SPERMATOZOA	CONSCIOUSLY
SUPPRESSION	CHARLEMAGNE	HYDROPHOBIA	OVERLEARNED	SPERMICIDAL	CONSECUTIVE
SUPPURATION	CHIROGRAPHY	HYDROPHOBIC	OVERMANNING	SPERMOPHILE	CONSEQUENCE
SYMPATHETIC	CHIROPODIST	HYDROPONICS	OVERPAYMENT	SPHRAGISTIC	CONSERVANCY
SYMPATHISER	CHORDOPHONE	HYDROSTATIC	OVERSTUFFED	SPIRITUALLY	CONSIDERATE
SYMPATHIZER	CHOROGRAPHY	IMPRACTICAL	OVERTURNING	SPIROCHAETE	CONSIDERING
SYMPLEGADES	CIRRHIPEDEA	IMPRECATION	OVERWEENING	SPORTSFIELD	CONSIGNMENT
SYMPOSIARCH	CIRRHIPEDIA	IMPRECISION	OVERWHELMED	SPORTSWOMAN	CONSILIENCE
SYMPTOMATIC	CITRONELLAL	IMPREGNABLE	OVERWROUGHT	STEREOGRAPH	CONSISTENCE
TEMPERAMENT	CLARENCIEUX	IMPROPRIETY	OVERZEALOUS	STEREOMETER	CONSISTENCY
TEMPERATURE	COMRADESHIP	IMPROVEMENT	OXYRHYNCHUS	STEREOSCOPE	CONSOLATION
TEMPESTUOUS	COORDINATED	IMPROVIDENT	PATRIARCHAL	STEREOTYPED	CONSOLIDATE
TEMPORARILY	COORDINATES	IMPRUDENTLY	PATRONISING	STOREKEEPER	CONSPICUOUS
TERPSICHORE	COPROPHAGAN	INCREDULITY	PATRONIZING	STORYTELLER	CONSPIRATOR
TREPIDATION	COPROSTEROL	INCREDULOUS	PETRODOLLAR	SURROUNDING	CONSTANTINE
TREPONEMATA	CORRECTNESS	INCREMENTAL	PHARISAICAL	SVARABHAKTI	CONSTELLATE
TRIPHIBIOUS	CORRELATION	INCRIMINATE	PHARYNGITIS	SWORDSWOMAN	CONSTERNATE
TRIPTOLEMUS	CORROBORATE	INFREQUENCY	PIERREPOINT	TARRADIDDLE	CONSTIPATED
TROPHOBLAST	CORRUGATION	INGRATITUDE	PREROGATIVE	TAUROBOLIUM	CONSTITUENT
TROPOSPHERE	CORRUPTIBLE	INGREDIENTS	PROROGATION	TERREMOTIVE	CONSTRAINED
TRYPANOSOMA	COURTEOUSLY	INTRACTABLE	PTERODACTYL	TERRESTRIAL	CONSTRICTED
TRYPANOSOME	COURTLINESS	INTRADERMAL	QUARRELLING	TERRITORIAL	CONSTRICTOR
UNSPEAKABLE	DECREPITATE	INTRAVENOUS	QUARRELSOME	TETRADRACHM	CONSTRUCTOR
UNSPECIFIED	DECREPITUDE	INTREPIDITY	QUARRINGTON	TETRAHEDRON	CONSTUPRATE
VESPERTINAL	DEERSTALKER	INTRICATELY	QUARTERBACK	THERAPEUTAE	CONSULTANCY
WAPPENSCHAW	DEGRADATION	INTROVERTED	QUARTERDECK	THERAPEUTIC	CONSUMABLES
ZOOPLANKTON	DEGRINGOLER	JERRYMANDER	QUERULOUSLY	THEREABOUTS	CONSUMERISM
CINQUECENTO	DEPREDATION	JINRICKSHAW	RECRIMINATE	THERMOMETER	CONSUMPTION
DISQUIETING	DEPRIVATION	LATROCINIUM	RECRUITMENT	THERMOPYLAE	CONSUMPTIVE
INEQUITABLE	DETRIMENTAL	LUBRICATION	REFRESHMENT	THOROUGHPIN	CRESCENTADE
JACQUEMINOT	DIARTHROSIS	MACROBIOTIC	REFRIGERANT	THYROTROPIN	CRESTFALLEN
MASQUERADER	DIORTHORTIC	MACROGAMETE	REFRIGERATE	TORRIDONIAN	CROSSLEGGED
MILQUETOAST	DIPROTODONT	MACROSCOPIC	REGRETFULLY	TOURBILLION	CRYSTALLINE

CRYSTALLISE	PERSEVERING	ZWISCHENZUG	DESTRUCTION	INATTENTIVE	PETTIFOGGER
CRYSTALLIZE	PERSISTENCE	ABSTRACTION	DESTRUCTIVE	INSTABILITY	PHOTOCOPIER
DIASCORDIUM	PERSONALIST	ACATALECTIC	DEUTERONOMY	INSTALLMENT	PHOTOFINISH
DIPSOMANIAC	PERSONALITY	APATOSAURUS	DEUTSCHMARK	INSTANTIATE	PHOTOGRAPHY
DISSEMINATE	PERSONALIZE	AZOTOBACTER	DIATESSARON	INSTIGATION	PHOTOSPHERE
DISSEPIMENT	PERSONIFIED	BADTEMPERED	DIATESSERON	INSTINCTIVE	PICTURESQUE
DISSERTATOR	PERSPECTIVE	BARTHOLOMEW	DICTATORIAL	INSTITUTION	PLATERESQUE
DISSIMULATE	PERSPICUITY	BATTLEDRESS	DIPTEROCARP	INSTRUCTION	PLATYRRHINE
DISSIPATION	PERSPICUOUS	BATTLEFIELD	DISTASTEFUL	INSTRUCTIVE	POLTERGEIST
DISSOLUTION	PESSIMISTIC	BATTLEFRONT	DISTINCTION	INSTRUMENTS	PONTIFICATE
DRASTICALLY	PHYSIOGNOMY	BATTLEMENTS	DISTINCTIVE	JACTITATION	PORTERHOUSE
DRESSMAKING	PISSASPHALT	BESTSELLING	DISTINGUISH	JUSTIFIABLE	PORTLANDIAN
EINSTEINIUM	PODSNAPPERY	BITTERSWEET	DISTRACTION	JUSTIFIABLY	PORTMANTEAU
ELASTOPLAST	POSSESSIONS	BOUTONNIERE	DISTRESSING	KULTURKREIS	PORTRAITIST
EVASIVENESS	POSSIBILITY	BRITTLENESS	DISTRIBUTED	LATTICEWORK	PORTRAITURE
EVISCERATED	PRESENTABLE	BROTHERHOOD	DISTRIBUTOR	LEATHERBACK	PRETENSIONS
EXASPERATED	PRESENTMENT	BUTTONQUAIL	DISTRUSTFUL	LEATHERETTE	PRETENTIOUS
EXOSKELETON	PRESSURIZED	CAPTIVATING	DISTURBANCE	LEATHERHEAD	PRETERITION
FEASIBILITY	PRESTIGIOUS	CAPTIVATION	DITTOGRAPHY	LEATHERNECK	PROTAGONIST
FISSIONABLE	PRESTISSIMO	CARTOGRAPHY	DOCTRINAIRE	LEATHERWOOD	PROTEROZOIC
FROSTBITTEN	PRESTONPANS	CASTELLATED	DUSTWRAPPER	LECTURESHIP	PROTOCOCCUS
FRUSTRATING	PRESTRESSED	CENTENARIAN	EARTHENWARE	LEFTLUGGAGE	PROTONOTARY
FRUSTRATION	PRESUMPTION	CENTERPIECE	EARTHSHAKER	LENTIGINOSE	PROTRACTING
GELSEMININE	PRESUMPTIVE	CENTREBOARD	EASTERNMOST	LETTERPRESS	PROTRACTION
GEOSYNCLINE	PRISCIANIST	CENTREPIECE	EGOTISTICAL	LITTÉRATEUR	PROTUBERANT
GHASTLINESS	PROSAICALLY	CENTRIFUGAL	EMOTIONALLY	MANTELLETTA	PSITTACOSIS
GLASTONBURY	PROSECUTION	CENTRIPETAL	EMPTYHANDED	MANTELPIECE	RAPTUROUSLY
GLOSSOLALIA	PROSELYTISM	CENTUMVIRUS	EPITHYMETIC	MANTELSHELF	RASTAFARIAN
GRASSHOPPER	PROSELYTIZE	CENTURIATOR	ERYTHROCYTE	MASTERFULLY	RATTLESNAKE
GUESSTIMATE	PROSPECTIVE	CERTIFIABLE	FACTFINDING	MASTERPIECE	RECTANGULAR
HORSERACING	PROSTHETICS	CERTIFICATE	FARTHERMOST	MASTICATION	RECTIFIABLE
HORSERADISH	PROSTRATION	CHITTERLING	FARTHINGALE	MENTHOLATED	RECTILINEAR
HORSERIDING	QUESTIONING	CONTAINMENT	FEATURELESS	MENTONNIÈRE	REITERATION
HOUSEFATHER	RAPSCALLION	CONTAMINANT	FESTINATELY	MICTURITION	RESTATEMENT
HOUSEHOLDER	REASSURANCE	CONTAMINATE	FESTSCHRIFT	MISTRUSTFUL	RESTITUTION
HOUSEKEEPER	SANSEVIERIA	CONTEMPLANT	FOOTBALLING	MONTESQUIEU	RESTIVENESS
HOUSEMASTER	SAUSAGEMEAT	CONTEMPLATE	FOOTWASHING	MONTGOLFIER	RESTORATION
HOUSEMOTHER	SEASICKNESS	CONTENEMENT	FORTHCOMING	MONTMORENCY	RESTORATIVE
HOUSEPARENT	SEISMOGRAPH	CONTENTEDLY	FORTNIGHTLY	MULTIRACIAL	RESTRICTION
INESCAPABLE	SENSATIONAL	CONTENTIOUS	FORTUNATELY	MULTISTOREY	RESTRICTIVE
INESSENTIAL	SENSIBILITY	CONTENTMENT	FORTUNELOUD	NEUTRALISED	RESTRUCTURE
INESTIMABLE	SENSITIVELY	CONTINENTAL	FRATERNALLY	NORTHCLIFFE	RINTHEREOUT
KWASHIORKOR	SENSITIVITY	CONTINGENCE	FURTHERANCE	NORTHEASTER	ROTTENSTONE
LEASEHOLDER	SPESSARTITE	CONTINGENCY	FURTHERMORE	NORTHWESTER	SALTIMBANCO
LOOSESTRIFE	SUBSERVIENT	CONTINUALLY	FURTHERMOST	NOSTRADAMUS	SALTIMBOCCA
MAISTERDOME	SUBSISTENCE	CONTINUANCE	FURTHERSOME	OBSTETRICAL	SCATTERGOOD
MARSHMALLOW	SUBSTANDARD	CONTRACTION	FURTIVENESS	OBSTINATELY	SCATTERLING
MASSIVENESS	SUBSTANTIAL	CONTRACTUAL	FUSTILARIAN	OBSTRICTION	SCITAMINEAE
MEASURELESS	SUBSTANTIVE	CONTRAPTION	GASTRECTOMY	OBSTRUCTION	SCUTTLEBUTT
MEASUREMENT	TEASPOONFUL	CONTRASTING	GASTRONOMIC	OBSTRUCTIVE	SENTENTIOUS
MENSURATION	TENSIOMETER	CONTRAYERVA	GENTLEMANLY	PANTALETTES	SENTIMENTAL
MISSISSIPPI	TESSARAGLOT	CONTRETEMPS	GENTLEWOMAN	PARTICIPANT	SEPTENARIUS
MISSPELLING	TESSELLATED	CONTRIBUTOR	GESTATORIAL	PARTICIPATE	SEPTENTRION
MOISTURIZER	THESMOTHETE	CONTRIVANCE	GESTICULATE	PARTICIPIAL	SEPTICAEMIA
MONSTROSITY	THISTLEDOWN	CONTROVERSY	GNATHONICAL	PARTNERSHIP	SEXTODECIMO
MOSSTROOPER	TOASTMASTER	CONTUBERNAL	GUTTERSNIPE	PARTURITION	SHITTIMWOOD
MUDSLINGING	TONSILLITIS	COTTONMOUTH	GUTTURALISE	PASTEURELLA	SHUTTLECOCK
NEWSCASTING	TRESPASSING	CRATERELLUS	HISTOLOGIST	PASTOURELLE	SKETCHINESS
NOISELESSLY	TRUSTEESHIP	CRITHOMANCY	HISTORIATED	PENTATHLETE	SMITHEREENS
NONSENSICAL	TRUSTWORTHY	CRITICASTER	HISTRIONICS	PENTAVALENT	SMITHSONIAN
OARSMANSHIP	UNASSERTIVE	CULTIVATION	HOOTANANNIE	PENTECONTER	SMITHSONITE
OUTSTANDING	UNESSENTIAL	CURTAILMENT	HOOTENANNIE	PENTECOSTAL	SOUTHAMPTON
PASSACAGLIA	VARSOVIENNE	CUSTOMARILY	HOSTILITIES	PENTHESILEA	SOUTHWESTER
PASSIVENESS	VERSATILITY	DACTYLOGRAM	HURTLEBERRY	PENTONVILLE	SPATTERDASH
PENSIONABLE	WENSLEYDALE	DESTABILIZE	ICHTHYOLITE	PERTINACITY	SPATTERDOCK
PENSIVENESS	WHISKERANDO	DESTINATION	ICHTHYORNIS	PERTINENTLY	SPITSTICKER
PERSECUTION	WHISTLESTOP	DESTITUTION	INATTENTION	PETTICOATED	STATELINESS

STATISTICAL	COLUMBARIUM	RESUSCITATE	SURVEILLANT	APOCALYPTIC	EXTRADITION
STETHOSCOPE	CONURBATION	RHEUMATICKY	UNAVAILABLE	APPEARANCES	EXTRAPOLATE
SUBTRACTION	DENUMERABLE	ROGUISHNESS	UNAVOIDABLE	APPEASEMENT	EXTRAVAGANT
SUBTROPICAL	DOCUMENTARY	SCEUOPHYLAX	UNAVOIDABLY	ARCHAEOLOGY	EYECATCHING
SUITABILITY	DRAUGHTSMAN	SCOUTMASTER	UNIVERSALLY	AWKWARDNESS	FANFARONADE
SURTARBRAND	ELEUTHERIAN	SCRUFFINESS	ANSWERPHONE	BARBASTELLE	FARRAGINOUS
SURTURBRAND	ENCUMBRANCE	SCRUMPTIOUS	AWKWARDNESS	BELEAGUERED	FISHANDCHIP
SUSTAINABLE	EXPURGATION	SEQUESTRATE	COXWAINLESS	BEREAVEMENT	FRIGATEBIRD
SWITCHBOARD	EXQUISITELY	SLEUTHHOUND	SCHWARMEREI	BESSARABIAN	FUNDAMENTAL
SWITZERLAND	FACULTATIVE	SMOULDERING	SHOWERPROOF	BOMBARDMENT	GENEALOGIST
SYNTHESIZED	FATUOUSNESS	SPLUTTERING	SHOWJUMPING	BUREAUCRACY	GESTATORIAL
SYNTHESIZER	FLOURISHING	STRUTHIONES	SHOWMANSHIP	CABBALISTIC	GODDAUGHTER
SYSTEMATIZE	FRAUDULENCE	SUBUNGULATA	UNSWEETENED	CALLANETICS	GONFALONIER
TANTALIZING	GENUFLEXION	SUSURRATION	WAYWARDNESS	CAMPANOLOGY	GREGARINIDA
TASTELESSLY	GENUINENESS	TEGUCICALPA	ALEXANDRINE	CARNAPTIOUS	GUADALCANAL
TATTERSALLS	GROUNDSHEET	TENUOUSNESS	ALEXANDRITE	CHARACINOID	HAPHAZARDLY
TAUTOCHRONE	GROUNDSPEED	THAUMATROPE	ANAXIMANDER	CITLALEPETL	HEMIANOPSIA
TECTIBRANCH	GROUNDSWELL	THOUGHTLESS	COEXISTENCE	CLIMACTERIC	HOLLANDAISE
TEETOTALLER	ILLUMINANCE	TRIUMVIRATE	DEOXYGENATE	CLIMATOLOGY	HOOTANANNIE
TENTATIVELY	ILLUMINATED	TROUBLESOME	FAUXBOURDON	COLLABORATE	HUSBANDLAND
TENTERHOOKS	ILLUSIONARY	TROUBLESPOT	FLEXIBILITY	COLLAPSIBLE	ILLMANNERED
TESTIMONIAL	ILLUSIONISM	UNAUTHENTIC	INEXCITABLE	COMMANDMENT	IMPEACHMENT
TORTICOLLIS	ILLUSIONIST	UNFULFILLED	INEXCUSABLE	COMPARATIVE	IMPLAUSIBLE
TORTICULLUS	ILLUSTRATOR	UNFURNISHED	INEXCUSABLY	COMPARTMENT	IMPRACTICAL
TOSTICATION	ILLUSTRIOUS	UNJUSTIFIED	INEXPEDIENT	COMRADESHIP	INDIARUBBER
TRITAGONIST	IMPULSIVELY	UNPUBLISHED	INEXPENSIVE	CONFABULATE	INFLAMMABLE
ULOTRICHALE	INAUTHENTIC	UNQUALIFIED	ISOXSUPRINE	CONFARREATE	INGRATITUDE
UNSTOPPABLE	INCUNABULUM	UNSUPPORTED	UNEXPLAINED	CONTAINMENT	INSTABILITY
UNUTTERABLE	INDUBITABLE	UNSURPASSED	UNEXPRESSED	CONTAMINANT	INSTALLMENT
VENTILATION	INDUBITABLY	UNSUSPECTED	ALCYONARIAN	CONTAMINATE	INSTANTIATE
VENTURESOME	INDULGENTLY	VACUOUSNESS	ASSYTHEMENT	CONVALLARIA	INTRACTABLE
VERTIGINOUS	INDUPLICATE	VESUVIANITE	BARYCENTRIC	COXWAINLESS	INTRADERMAL
WASTEBASKET	INDUSTRIOUS	VOLUNTARILY	CHRYSAROBIN	CRÉMAILLÈRE	INTRAVENOUS
WEATHERCOCK	INFURIATING	VOLUNTARISM	CHRYSOPRASE	CREMATORIUM	IPECACUANHA
WESTERNMOST	INJUDICIOUS	CONVALLARIA	DEHYDRATION	CULPABILITY	LONGANIMITY
WESTMINSTER	INNUMERABLE	CONVENIENCE	EMPYROMANCY	CURNAPTIOUS	LONGAWAITED
WESTPHALIAN	INQUIRINGLY	CONVENTICLE	ILLYWHACKER	CURTAILMENT	MACHAIRODUS
WHITEBOYISM	INQUISITION	CONVERGENCE	ITHYPHALLIC	DARDANELLES	MAGNANIMITY
WHITECHAPEL	INQUISITIVE	CONVERTIBLE	ITHYPHALLUS	DECLAMATION	MAGNANIMOUS
WHITECOLLAR	INSULTINGLY	CONVOCATION	LARYNGISMUS	DECLAMATORY	MANGALSUTRA
WHITEFRIARS	INSUPERABLE	CONVOLUTION	PLAYFULNESS	DECLARATION	MASKALLONGE
WHITETHROAT	INTUITIVELY	CONVOLVULUS	POLYHYDROXY	DECLARATIVE	MEDIASTINUM
WHITLEATHER	LIQUIDAMBAR	CONVULSIONS	POLYMORPHIC	DEGRADATION	MINIATURIST
WHITSUNTIDE	LIQUIDATION	CULVERINEER	POLYSTYRENE	DERMATOLOGY	MINIATURIZE
WHITTINGTON	LUXULYANITE	FLAVOURSOME	POLYTECHNIC	DESTABILIZE	MISCARRIAGE
WINTERBERRY	LUXURIANTLY	FRIVOLOUSLY	POLYTRICHUM	DICTATORIAL	NARRAGANSET
WINTERGREEN	LUXURIOUSLY	GRAVEDIGGER	BRAZZAVILLE	DISPARAGING	NIPFARTHING
WISTFULNESS	MANUFACTURE	GRAVIMETRIC	ELIZABETHAN	DISTASTEFUL	OFFHANDEDLY
ACCULTURATE	MANUMISSION	GRAVITATION	FITZWILLIAM	EDUCATIONAL	ONOMASTICON
ACCUMULATOR	MAQUILADORA	HEAVYHANDED	PRIZEWINNER	ELIZABETHAN	OPERATIONAL
ACQUIESCENT	NATURALNESS	HEAVYWEIGHT	RAZZAMATAZZ	EMPLACEMENT	OSTRACODERM
ACQUISITION	NATUROPATHY	NERVOUSNESS		ENCHANTMENT	OUAGADOUGOU
ACQUISITIVE	OBMUTESCENT	PARVANIMITY	**11:5**	ENCHANTRESS	OUTMANEUVER
ACTUALITIES	PECULIARITY	PEEVISHNESS	ACATALECTIC	ENFRANCHISE	PANTALETTES
ADJUDICATOR	PENULTIMATE	PREVARICATE	ACCLAMATION	ENGHALSKRUG	PARVANIMITY
AIGUILLETTE	PLEURODYNIA	PREVENTABLE	ACINACIFORM	ENNEAHEDRON	PASSACAGLIA
AILUROPHILE	PLOUGHSHARE	PROVISIONAL	ACTUALITIES	ENSLAVEMENT	PENTATHLETE
ALBUGINEOUS	PSEUDOLOGIA	PROVISIONER	AFGHANISTAN	EPANALEPSIS	PENTAVALENT
ALBUMINURIA	PSEUDOMORPH	PROVOCATION	AGGRAVATING	EREMACAUSIS	PERMANENTLY
APPURTENANT	RECURRENTLY	PROVOCATIVE	AGGRAVATION	ERYMANTHIAN	PHALANSTERY
ARQUEBUSIER	REDUPLICATE	SALVADORIAN	AGORAPHOBIA	ESCHATOLOGY	PHILANDERER
AUGUSTINIAN	REFURBISHED	SALVOGUNNER	ALEXANDRINE	ESTRAMAZONE	PHILATELIST
BEAUMONTAGE	REGURGITATE	SERVICEABLE	ALEXANDRITE	ESTRANGHELO	PISCATORIAL
BEAUTIFULLY	RELUCTANTLY	SHOVELBOARD	ALIFANFARON	EUCHARISTIC	PISSASPHALT
BIFURCATION	REPUDIATION	SILVERBERRY	ALPHABETIZE	EXCLAMATION	PRECAUTIONS
CHAULMOOGRA	REQUIREMENT	SILVERPOINT	AMELANCHIER	EXPLANATION	PREMATURELY
CHAULMOUGRA	REQUISITION	SILVERSMITH	AMOBARBITAL	EXPLANATORY	PREPARATION
			ANFRACTUOUS		

PREPARATIVE	UNPRACTICAL	TOURBILLION	JUDICIOUSLY	ASSIDUOUSLY	SKULDUDDERY
PREPARATORY	UNQUALIFIED	TROUBLESOME	KILOCALORIE	BENEDICTINE	SKULDUGGERY
PREVARICATE	UNREALISTIC	TROUBLESPOT	MALICIOUSLY	BENEDICTION	SLENDERNESS
PROBABILITY	UNREASONING	UNAMBIGUOUS	MASOCHISTIC	BLADDERWORT	SOCKDALAGER
PROBATIONER	UNSHAKEABLE	UNPUBLISHED	MEDICINALLY	BLOODSPORTS	SOCKDOLAGER
PROPAGATION	UNTRAMELLED	WELLBEHAVED	METACARPALS	BLOODSTREAM	SOCKDOLIGER
PROSAICALLY	VALLAMBROSA	WINDBREAKER	METACENTRIC	BLOODSUCKER	SOCKDOLOGER
PROTAGONIST	VARIABILITY	ABLACTATION	MONOCHINOUS	BLUNDERBORE	SOUNDLESSLY
RASTAFARIAN	VERSATILITY	ABRACADABRA	MONOCHROMAT	BRANDENBURG	SPEEDOMETER
RAZZAMATAZZ	VOLCANOLOGY	ACROCENTRIC	NEWSCASTING	BREADCRUMBS	SPENDTHRIFT
READABILITY	VULCANOLOGY	AFFECTATION	NOTICEBOARD	BREADWINNER	SPONDULICKS
RECLAMATION	WAYWARDNESS	AGRICULTURE	OBJECTIVELY	BROADCASTER	SPONDYLITIS
RECTANGULAR	WELLADVISED	AMERCIAMENT	OBJECTIVITY	BROADMINDED	STANDARDIZE
RELEASEMENT	ZOROASTRIAN	ANENCEPHALY	OFFICIALDOM	BROBDINGNAG	STANDOFFISH
RELIABILITY	ADUMBRATION	ANTECEDENCE	OFFICIALESE	CATADROMOUS	STANDPATTER
REPLACEABLE	ANNABERGITE	ANTECHAMBER	OFFICIOUSLY	CHILDMINDER	STEADFASTLY
REPLACEMENT	ANTIBURGHER	ANTICYCLONE	OVERCROWDED	CHONDROSTEI	STRADUARIUS
RESTATEMENT	ATRABILIOUS	ARTICULATED	PARACETAMOL	CHORDOPHONE	SWORDSWOMAN
RETRACTABLE	BACKBENCHER	ASSOCIATION	PARACHUTIST	CLANDESTINE	TAXIDERMIST
RHOPALOCERA	BALLBEARING	ATROCIOUSLY	PARACROSTIC	COORDINATED	THUNDERBIRD
SABBATARIAN	BOOKBINDING	AUDACIOUSLY	PENICILLATE	COORDINATES	THUNDERBOLT
SACRAMENTAL	CALIBRATION	BARYCENTRIC	PERICARDIUM	DEHYDRATION	THUNDERCLAP
SALVADORIAN	CARABINIERE	CAPACITANCE	PINACOTHECA	DREADLOCKED	THUNDERHEAD
SAUSAGEMEAT	CELEBRATION	CAPACITATOR	POCOCURANTE	DREADNOUGHT	UNENDURABLE
SCARABAEOID	CEREBRATION	CATACAUSTIC	POLICEWOMAN	EQUIDISTANT	UNGODLINESS
SCHWARMEREI	CHAMBERLAIN	CATACHRESIS	PREOCCUPIED	ERIODENDRON	VALEDICTION
SCITAMINEAE	CHAMBERMAID	CATACLYSMIC	PRINCIPALLY	EXPEDITIOUS	VALEDICTORY
SCREAMINGLY	COLDBLOODED	CHANCELLERY	PRISCIANIST	FIELDWORKER	WELLDEFINED
SENNACHERIB	DEMIBASTION	COINCIDENCE	RAPSCALLION	FOUNDATIONS	WELLDRESSED
SENSATIONAL	DISABLEMENT	CONSCIOUSLY	REFOCILLATE	FRAUDULENCE	WORLDFAMOUS
SHENANIGANS	DISOBEDIENT	CRESCENTADE	REINCARNATE	GRANDFATHER	WORLDLINESS
SHUNAMITISM	DOLABRIFORM	DELECTATION	RELUCTANTLY	GRANDMASTER	XENODOCHIUM
SINGAPOREAN	ENTABLATURE	DELICIOUSLY	RIFACIMENTO	GRANDMOTHER	ABBREVIATED
SOCIABILITY	ENTABLEMENT	DELICTATION	ROSICRUCIAN	HAIRDRESSER	ABECEDARIAN
SPHRAGISTIC	ESTABLISHED	DESECRATION	SAGACIOUSLY	HEXADECIMAL	ACADEMICIAN
SPREADSHEET	ESTABLISHER	DESICCATION	SALACIOUSLY	IMMEDIATELY	ACADEMICISM
SRANANTONGO	EXORBITANCE	DIASCORDIUM	SCHECKLATON	IMPEDIMENTA	ACCRESCENCE
STEGANOGRAM	FAUXBOURDON	DIRECTIONAL	SEARCHLIGHT	INJUDICIOUS	ACHIEVEMENT
STEGANOPODE	FLABBERGAST	DIRECTORATE	SELECTIVELY	INSIDIOUSLY	ADOLESCENCE
STREAMLINED	FLAMBOYANCE	DODECASTYLE	SELECTIVITY	IRRADIATION	AGGREGATION
SUBPANATION	FLAMBOYANTE	EFFECTIVELY	SELFCONTROL	IRREDENTIST	AMPHETAMINE
SUITABILITY	FOOTBALLING	EFFECTUALLY	SERICULTURE	IRREDUCIBLE	AMPLEXICAUL
SURTARBRAND	FULLBLOODED	EFFICACIOUS	SKETCHINESS	LAPIDESCENT	ANSWERPHONE
SUSTAINABLE	HALFBROTHER	EFFICIENTLY	SPEECHCRAFT	LAUNDERETTE	ANTHESTERIA
SVARABHAKTI	HAREBRAINED	ENDOCARDIUM	SWITCHBOARD	LEPIDOPTERA	APONEUROSIS
SYMPATHETIC	INDUBITABLE	ENUNCIATION	TEGUCICALPA	LEPIDOSIREN	APPLERINGIE
SYMPATHISER	INDUBITABLY	EVISCERATED	TELOCENTRIC	LOGODAEDALY	APPRECIABLE
SYMPATHIZER	INHABITABLE	EXPECTANTLY	TENACIOUSLY	MACADAMIZED	APPRECIABLY
TANTALIZING	INHABITANTS	EXPECTATION	THENCEFORTH	MALADJUSTED	APPRENTICED
TARRADIDDLE	KATABOTHRON	EXPECTORANT	TOBACCONIST	MALEDICTION	ARCHEGONIAL
TENTATIVELY	KOTABOTHRON	EXPECTORATE	TOXICOGENIC	MEANDERINGS	ARCHEGONIUM
TESSARAGLOT	MAKEBELIEVE	FEROCIOUSLY	TREACHEROUS	MELODIOUSLY	ARCHENTERON
TETRADRACHM	MARLBOROUGH	FIRECRACKER	TREACHETOUR	MISIDENTIFY	ARQUEBUSIER
TETRAHEDRON	MOXIBUSTION	FORECASTING	TREECREEPER	NEANDERTHAL	ARRHENOTOKY
THANATOPSIS	OVERBALANCE	FORECLOSURE	TRENCHERMAN	OVERDRAUGHT	ASCLEPIADES
THERAPEUTAE	OVERBEARING	FRENCHWOMAN	TRINCOMALEE	PARADOXICAL	ASPHETERISM
THERAPEUTIC	PARABLEPSIS	FRENCHWOMEN	UNNECESSARY	PSEUDOLOGIA	BADDELEYITE
THREATENING	PARABOLANUS	GATECRASHER	UTRICULARIA	PSEUDOMORPH	BADTEMPERED
TRACASSERIE	PAWNBROKERS	HANDCRAFTED	VIVACIOUSLY	REPUDIATION	BANDEIRANTE
TRITAGONIST	SCARBOROUGH	HYPOCORISMA	VORACIOUSLY	RESIDENTIAL	BASKERVILLE
TRYPANOSOMA	SHIPBUILDER	IMPECUNIOUS	WINDCHEATER	RHABDOMANCY	BELLEROPHON
TRYPANOSOME	SKIDBLADNIR	INESCAPABLE	WOODCARVING	SCANDALIZED	BELLETTRIST
ULTRAMARINE	SLUMBERWEAR	INEXCITABLE	ZWISCHENZUG	SCANDANAVIA	BESIEGEMENT
ULTRAMODERN	STEPBROTHER	INEXCUSABLE	ABANDONMENT	SCANDINAVIA	BITTERSWEET
ULTRAVIOLET	STILBESTROL	INEXCUSABLY	ABRIDGEMENT	SCULDUDDERY	BLAMEWORTHY
UNAVAILABLE	STROBOSCOPE	INSECTICIDE	ADJUDICATOR	SCULDUGGERY	BOYSENBERRY
UNFLAPPABLE	THEOBROMINE	INSECTIVORE	AERODYNAMIC	SELFDEFENCE	BRUCELLOSIS

BUMBERSHOOT	DISCERNIBLE	JABBERWOCKY	POLLENBRUSH	SMOKESCREEN	WONDERFULLY
BUPRESTIDAE	DISCERNMENT	KINDERSPIEL	POLTERGEIST	SPACESAVING	ACRIFLAVINE
CALCEOLARIA	DISHEVELLED	KOMMERSBUCH	POMPELMOOSE	SPOKESWOMAN	BACKFIELDER
CAMPESTRIAN	DISPENSABLE	LAMMERGEIER	POMPELMOUSE	STAKEHOLDER	BASHFULNESS
CANDESCENCE	DISPERSABLE	LAMMERGEYER	PONDEROUSLY	STATELINESS	BENEFICIARY
CASTELLATED	DISREGARDED	LAWLESSNESS	PORTERHOUSE	STEREOGRAPH	BENEFICIATE
CEASELESSLY	DISSEMINATE	LEASEHOLDER	POSSESSIONS	STEREOMETER	BULLFIGHTER
CENTENARIAN	DISSEPIMENT	LETTERPRESS	PREDECESSOR	STEREOSCOPE	CALEFACIENT
CENTERPIECE	DISSERTATOR	LITTÉRATEUR	PREDESTINED	STEREOTYPED	CALIFORNIUM
CHOLESTEROL	DITHELETISM	LOGGERHEADS	PREMEDITATE	STIPENDIARY	CAREFULNESS
CLARENCIEUX	DUNIEWASSAL	LOOSESTRIFE	PRESENTABLE	STOREKEEPER	CILOFIBRATE
COALESCENCE	EARNESTNESS	MAGLEMOSIAN	PRESENTMENT	STREETLIGHT	CLIFFHANGER
COLLECTANEA	EASTERNMOST	MALFEASANCE	PRETENSIONS	SUBMERGENCE	COEFFICIENT
COLLENCHYMA	EMPIECEMENT	MANTELLETTA	PRETENTIOUS	SUBSERVIENT	DISAFFECTED
COMMEMORATE	ENUMERATION	MANTELPIECE	PRETERITION	SUCCEDANEUM	DUMBFOUNDED
COMMENDABLE	EPIGENESIST	MANTELSHELF	PREVENTABLE	SUGGESTIBLE	FACTFINDING
COMMENDABLY	EPINEPHRINE	MARKETPLACE	PRIZEWINNER	SUMMERHOUSE	FOREFATHERS
COMMENTATOR	ESCHERICHIA	MASTERFULLY	PROCEEDINGS	SUPPEDANEUM	GENUFLEXION
COMPENDIOUS	ESPIEGLERIE	MASTERPIECE	PROFESSEDLY	SURVEILLANT	HELPFULNESS
COMPETENTLY	EUPHEMISTIC	MATHEMATICS	PROGENITRIX	SUSCEPTIBLE	INDEFINABLE
COMPETITION	EXCEEDINGLY	MAURETANIAN	PROLEGOMENA	SYMMETRICAL	INDIFFERENT
COMPETITIVE	EXCRESCENCE	MENDELEVIUM	PROLETARIAN	SYSTEMATIZE	INEFFECTIVE
CONCEALMENT	EXONERATION	MENDELSSOHN	PROLETARIAT	TASTELESSLY	INEFFECTUAL
CONCEIVABLE	FARREACHING	MIDDENSTEAD	PROSECUTION	TATTERSALLS	INEFFICIENT
CONCEIVABLY	FINGERPRINT	MINNESINGER	PROSELYTISM	TEMPERAMENT	INOFFENSIVE
CONCENTRATE	FINGERSTALL	MISBEGOTTEN	PROSELYTIZE	TEMPERATURE	IRREFUTABLE
CONCEPTICLE	FORBEARANCE	MISBEHAVIOR	PROTEROZOIC	TEMPESTUOUS	LATIFUNDIUM
CONFEDERACY	FOTHERGILLA	MISDEMEANOR	RALLENTANDO	TENDENTIOUS	MALEFACTION
CONFEDERATE	FRATERNALLY	MISFEASANCE	RANGEFINDER	TENTERHOOKS	MANUFACTURE
CONJECTURAL	GAMMERSTANG	MONTESQUIEU	REFLEXOLOGY	TERREMOTIVE	MUNIFICENCE
CONNECTICUT	GELSEMININE	MORGENSTERN	REFRESHMENT	TERRESTRIAL	OVERFISHING
CONSECUTIVE	GEOMETRICAL	MUSKELLUNGE	REGRETFULLY	TESSELLATED	OVERFLOWING
CONSEQUENCE	GIBBERELLIN	NETHERLANDS	REGRETTABLE	THEREABOUTS	PACIFICALLY
CONSERVANCY	GINGERBREAD	NETHERLINGS	REGRETTABLY	TITLEHOLDER	PLAYFULNESS
CONTEMPLANT	GRAVEDIGGER	NICKELODEON	REITERATION	TRAGELAPHUS	PROOFREADER
CONTEMPLATE	GUTTERSNIPE	NOISELESSLY	REPRESENTED	TRICERATOPS	SCAFFOLDING
CONTENEMENT	GYNAECOLOGY	NONDESCRIPT	RESPECTABLE	TRIMESTRIAL	SCRUFFINESS
CONTENTEDLY	HALLEFLINTA	NONFEASANCE	RESPECTABLY	TSCHERNOSEM	SPIFFLICATE
CONTENTIOUS	HAMMERCLOTH	NONSENSICAL	ROCKEFELLER	TURBELLARIA	STAGFLATION
CONTENTMENT	HECKELPHONE	NUCLEOPLASM	ROTTENSTONE	UNBLEMISHED	TÉLÉFÉRIQUE
CONVENIENCE	HERPETOLOGY	NUMBERPLATE	SACHERTORTE	UNBREAKABLE	THRIFTINESS
CONVENTICLE	HINDERLANDS	OBSTETRICAL	SANDERSWOOD	UNCLEANNESS	TRAFFICATOR
CONVERGENCE	HOMOEOPATHY	OPALESCENCE	SANSEVIERIA	UNIVERSALLY	UNBEFITTING
CONVERTIBLE	HOOTENANNIE	ORCHESTRATE	SARCENCHYME	UNSHELTERED	WAKEFULNESS
COOPERATION	HORSERACING	ORCHESTRINA	SCAREMONGER	UNSPEAKABLE	WELLFOUNDED
COOPERATIVE	HORSERADISH	ORCHESTRION	SCHRECKLICH	UNSPECIFIED	WISTFULNESS
COPPERPLATE	HORSERIDING	OSTREOPHAGE	SCIREFACIAS	UNSWEETENED	ABIOGENESIS
CORNERSTONE	HOUSEFATHER	OVEREXPOSED	SCOLECIFORM	USELESSNESS	ABIOGENETIC
CORRECTNESS	HOUSEHOLDER	PAMPELMOOSE	SCOREKEEPER	VARIEGATION	ALBIGENSIAN
CORRELATION	HOUSEKEEPER	PAMPELMOUSE	SECRETARIAL	VENDEMIAIRE	ALBUGINEOUS
CRATERELLUS	HOUSEMASTER	PANDEMONIUM	SECRETARIAT	VESPERTINAL	ALLEGORICAL
CREDENTIALS	HOUSEMOTHER	PASTEURELLA	SECRETIVELY	WAPPENSCHAW	ASSIGNATION
CRENELLATED	HOUSEPARENT	PEACEKEEPER	SEGREGATION	WASHERWOMAN	ASTIGMATISM
CULVERINEER	HYPHENATION	PENTECONTER	SELFEVIDENT	WASTEBASKET	AURIGNACIAN
DANGEROUSLY	IMPLEMENTAL	PENTECOSTAL	SENTENTIOUS	WESTERNMOST	BOURGEOISIE
DECREPITATE	IMPRECATION	PERCEFOREST	SEPTENARIUS	WHEREABOUTS	BRAGGADOCIO
DECREPITUDE	IMPRECISION	PERCEPTIBLE	SEPTENTRION	WHEREWITHAL	CACOGASTRIC
DEPREDATION	IMPREGNABLE	PERCEPTIBLY	SEQUESTRATE	WHITEBOYISM	CATEGORICAL
DESCENDANTS	INCREDULITY	PERPETRATOR	SHAKESPEARE	WHITECHAPEL	CHARGEPAYER
DESPERATELY	INCREDULOUS	PERPETUALLY	SHAMELESSLY	WHITECOLLAR	CYTOGENESIS
DESPERATION	INCREMENTAL	PERSECUTION	SHAPELINESS	WHITEFRIARS	DEMAGOGUERY
DEUTERONOMY	INFREQUENCY	PERSEVERING	SHAREHOLDER	WHITETHROAT	DEMOGRAPHIC
DIATESSARON	INGREDIENTS	PHONETICIAN	SHOVELBOARD	WIENERWURST	DESEGREGATE
DIATESSERON	INOPERATIVE	PICKELHAUBE	SHOWERPROOF	WILBERFORCE	DESIGNATION
DIFFERENTLY	INTREPIDITY	PLANETARIUM	SILVERBERRY	WINTERBERRY	DISAGREEING
DIPTEROCARP	IRIDESCENCE	PLATERESQUE	SILVERPOINT	WINTERGREEN	DRAGGLETAIL
DISBELIEVER	ISOLECITHAL	PLEBEIANISE	SILVERSMITH	WITHERSHINS	DRAUGHTSMAN

ENLIGHTENED	CIRRHIPEDEA	PROPHETICAL	BIBLIOPHILE	DISTINCTION	IDOLIZATION
EVANGELICAL	CIRRHIPEDIA	PROPHYLAXIS	BILLIONAIRE	DISTINCTIVE	IMAGINATION
EXAGGERATED	COACHFELLOW	PSYCHEDELIC	BODHISATTVA	DISTINGUISH	IMAGINATIVE
FEHMGERICHT	CRITHOMANCY	PSYCHIATRIC	CALLIGRAPHY	DUPLICATING	IMPLICATION
GAMOGENESIS	DIAPHORESIS	PTOCHOCRACY	CALLIPYGEAN	DUPLICATION	INALIENABLE
HANGGLIDING	DIAPHORETIC	PULCHRITUDE	CALLISTEMON	EDIFICATION	INCLINATION
HOMOGENEITY	DOWNHEARTED	PUNCHINELLO	CALLITRICHE	EGALITARIAN	INCRIMINATE
HOMOGENEOUS	EARTHENWARE	REICHENBACH	CANDIDATURE	EGOTISTICAL	INQUIRINGLY
HOMOGENIZED	EARTHSHAKER	RINTHEREOUT	CANNIBALISM	ELIGIBILITY	INQUISITION
IDIOGRAPHIC	ELEPHANTINE	SCYPHISTOMA	CANNIBALIZE	ELIMINATION	INQUISITIVE
ILLOGICALLY	EPICHEIREMA	SHEPHERDESS	CAPRICCIOSO	ELUCIDATION	INSPIRATION
IMMIGRATION	EPITHYMETIC	SLIGHTINGLY	CAPTIVATING	EMBOÎTEMENT	INSTIGATION
IMPIGNORATE	EPOCHMAKING	SMITHEREENS	CAPTIVATION	EMOTIONALLY	INSTINCTIVE
INDIGESTION	ERYTHROCYTE	SMITHSONIAN	CARDIOGRAPH	ENCHIRIDION	INSTITUTION
INDIGNANTLY	FARTHERMOST	SMITHSONITE	CARMINATIVE	EPAMINONDAS	INTRICATELY
INDIGNATION	FARTHINGALE	SOUTHAMPTON	CARNIVOROUS	EPIDIASCOPE	INTUITIVELY
INTEGRATION	FORTHCOMING	SOUTHWESTER	CARRIAGEWAY	ERADICATION	JACTITATION
INVIGILATOR	FRIGHTENING	STETHOSCOPE	CARSICKNESS	EVASIVENESS	JINRICKSHAW
IRREGULARLY	FRIGHTFULLY	SYNCHROMESH	CASSITERITE	EXAMINATION	JUSTIFIABLE
KRIEGSSPIEL	FURTHERANCE	SYNCHRONISE	CAULIFLOWER	EXQUISITELY	JUSTIFIABLY
LOGOGRAPHER	FURTHERMORE	SYNCHRONISM	CERTIFIABLE	FABRICATION	KINNIKINICK
METAGENESIS	FURTHERMOST	SYNCHRONIZE	CERTIFICATE	FALLIBILITY	LATTICEWORK
MONOGRAMMED	FURTHERSOME	SYNCHRONOUS	CHARISMATIC	FASCINATING	LENTIGINOSE
MONTGOLFIER	GNATHONICAL	SYNTHESIZED	CHOLINERGIC	FASCINATION	LILLIPUTIAN
OPPIGNORATE	GRAPHICALLY	SYNTHESIZER	COEXISTENCE	FASHIONABLE	LINDISFARNE
PEDAGOGICAL	HALFHEARTED	TRACHEOTOMY	COMBINATION	FASHIONABLY	LIQUIDAMBAR
PEREGRINATE	HALFHOLIDAY	TRICHINELLA	COMMINATION	FEASIBILITY	LIQUIDATION
PERIGORDIAN	HARDHITTING	TRICHINOSED	COMMISERATE	FERNITICKLE	LONGINQUITY
PLOUGHSHARE	HATCHETTITE	TRICHOPTERA	COMPILATION	FESTINATELY	LUBRICATION
POMEGRANATE	HAUGHTINESS	TRIPHIBIOUS	COMPLEMENT	FILLIBUSTER	MACHINATION
RECOGNITION	ICHTHYOLITE	TROPHOBLAST	CONCILIATOR	FISSIONABLE	MAGNIFICENT
RELIGIOUSLY	ICHTHYORNIS	UNINHABITED	CONCISENESS	FLEXIBILITY	MANCIPATION
RESIGNATION	INCOHERENCE	UNINHIBITED	CONDITIONAL	FLORILEGIUM	MAQUILADORA
ROTOGRAVURE	JAMAHIRIYAH	UNREHEARSED	CONDITIONER	FOOLISHNESS	MARGINALIST
SELAGINELLA	KINCHINMORT	UNSCHEDULED	CONFIDENTLY	FORBIDDANCE	MARGINALIZE
SLUMGULLION	KINDHEARTED	WAREHOUSING	CONFINEMENT	FORGIVENESS	MASSIVENESS
SMORGASBORD	KITCHENETTE	WARMHEARTED	CONSIDERATE	FORNICATION	MASTICATION
SPANGCOCKLE	KWASHIORKOR	WEATHERCOCK	CONSIDERING	FRUGIVOROUS	MATRIARCHAL
TELEGRAPHER	LEATHERBACK	WEIGHBRIDGE	CONSIGNMENT	FULFILLMENT	MATRICULATE
TELEGRAPHIC	LEATHERETTE	WITCHDOCTOR	CONSILIENCE	FULMINATION	MATRIMONIAL
THINGAMABOB	LEATHERHEAD	WITHHOLDING	CONSISTENCE	FURNISHINGS	MAURITANIAN
THINGAMAJIG	LEATHERNECK	ABOMINATION	CONSISTENCY	FURTIVENESS	MEANINGLESS
THINGLINESS	LEATHERWOOD	ACCLIMATION	CONTINENTAL	FUSTILARIAN	MEKHITARIST
THINGUMAJIG	MARSHMALLOW	ACCLIMATISE	CONTINGENCE	GALLIBAGGER	MELLIFLUOUS
THOUGHTLESS	MENTHOLATED	ACCLIMATIZE	CONTINGENCY	GALLIBEGGAR	MERCILESSLY
THROGMORTON	MERCHANDISE	ACQUIESCENT	CONTINUALLY	GALLIGANTUS	METRICATION
TOBOGGANING	MERCHANDIZE	ACQUISITION	CONTINUANCE	GALLIMAUFRY	MILLIAMPERE
TOPOGRAPHER	MERCHANTMAN	ACQUISITIVE	CREDIBILITY	GARNISHMENT	MILLIONAIRE
TYPOGRAPHER	MISCHIEVOUS	AFFLIICTION	CREPITATION	GENUINENESS	MISSISSIPPI
TYPOGRAPHIC	MONCHIQUITE	AIGUILLETTE	CRIMINOLOGY	GERMINATION	MOCKINGBIRD
TYROGLYPHID	MUNCHHAUSEN	AIRSICKNESS	CRITICASTER	GESTICULATE	MULTIRACIAL
UNDIGNIFIED	MUSCHELKALK	AMERICANISM	CROCIDOLITE	GRAVIMETRIC	MULTISTOREY
UNRIGHTEOUS	NAUGHTINESS	AMPHIBOLOGY	CRUCIFIXION	GRAVITATION	NIACINAMIDE
UPRIGHTNESS	NEIGHBORING	AMPHISBAENA	CULMINATION	GULLIBILITY	NOTHINGNESS
WRONGHEADED	NEIGHBOURLY	AMPHISBOENA	CULTIVATION	HANDICAPPED	NOURISHMENT
XYLOGRAPHER	NONCHALANCE	ANADIPLOSIS	DECEITFULLY	HANDICAPPER	NUTRITIONAL
ANACHRONISM	NORTHCLIFFE	ANAXIMANDER	DEGRINGOLER	HARDICANUTE	OBSTINATELY
ANAPHYLAXIS	NORTHEASTER	APOSIOPESIS	DEIFICATION	HERBIVOROUS	OPINIONATED
APOPHYLLITE	NORTHWESTER	APPLICATION	DEPRIVATION	HERRINGBONE	ORIGINALITY
BACCHANALIA	NYMPHOMANIA	APPOINTMENT	DESTINATION	HOGGISHNESS	ORIGINATING
BARTHOLOMEW	OVERHANGING	ARCHILOCHUS	DESTITUTION	HOMOIOUSIAN	ORIGINATION
BEACHCOMBER	OXYRHYNCHUS	ARCHIPELAGO	DETRIMENTAL	HOOLIGANISM	OUTDISTANCE
BIOCHEMICAL	PAMPHLETEER	ASTRINGENCY	DIFFIDENTLY	HOSPITALITY	OVARIECTOMY
BROTHERHOOD	PENTHESILEA	ATTRIBUTION	DISCIPLINED	HOSPITALIZE	OXODIZATION
CAMPHORATED	PERCHLORATE	ATTRIBUTIVE	DISFIGURING	HOSPITALLER	PAEDIATRICS
CATCHPHRASE	PITCHBLENDE	BARBITURATE	DISSIMULATE	HOSTILITIES	PARLIPOMENA
CHICHEVACHE	POLYHYDROXY	BELLIGERENT	DISSIPATION	HUMMINGBIRD	PARTICIPANT

PARTICIPATE	RESTITUTION	VALLISNERIA	BEWILDERING	INCALESCENT	SMOULDERING
PARTICIPIAL	RESTIVENESS	VENTILATION	BIMILLENARY	INDULGENTLY	SOLILOQUIZE
PASSIVENESS	RETRIBUTION	VERBIGERATE	BRILLIANTLY	INFILTRATOR	SPELLBINDER
PATRIARCHAL	RETRIBUTIVE	VERMICULITE	CAMALDOLITE	INSULTINGLY	STALLHOLDER
PEEVISHNESS	RETRIEVABLE	VERTIGINOUS	CANDLELIGHT	INTELLIGENT	STELLIONATE
PENSIONABLE	ROGUISHNESS	VINAIGRETTE	CANDLESTICK	INTOLERABLE	STOOLPIGEON
PENSIVENESS	SACRIFICIAL	VINDICATION	CAROLINGIAN	INTOLERABLY	SWALLOWABLE
PERCIPIENCE	SALPINGITIS	VIOLINCELLO	CATALLACTIC	INTOLERANCE	SYMPLEGADES
PERMISSIBLE	SALTIMBANCO	WELLINGTONS	CHALLENGING	INVOLUNTARY	THALLOPHYTE
PERSISTENCE	SALTIMBOCCA	WILLINGNESS	CHARLEMAGNE	INVOLVEMENT	THEOLOGICAL
PERTINACITY	SEASICKNESS	CLANJAMFRAY	CHAULMOOGRA	IRRELEVANCE	TIDDLEYWINK
PERTINENTLY	SELFIMPOSED	SHOWJUMPING	CHAULMOUGRA	IRRELIGIOUS	TITILLATION
PESSIMISTIC	SELFISHNESS	BLACKFELLOW	CHILLINGHAM	ISOELECTRIC	TOTALIZATOR
PETTICOATED	SEMPITERNAL	BLACKMAILER	COBBLESTONE	KAMELAUKION	UNFULFILLED
PETTIFOGGER	SEMPITERNUM	BLANKURSINE	COCKLESHELL	KIDDLEYWINK	UNPALATABLE
PHARISAICAL	SENSIBILITY	BLOCKBUSTER	COMPLACENCY	LAMPLIGHTER	UNRELENTING
PHILIPPIANS	SENSITIVELY	BOOKKEEPING	COMPLAISANT	LEFTLUGGAGE	UNSOLICITED
PHILIPPINES	SENSITIVITY	CHICKENFEED	COMPLICATED	LEVELHEADED	UNWELCOMING
PHTHIRIASIS	SENTIMENTAL	CHOCKABLOCK	COMPLIMENTS	LONGLASTING	UPHOLSTERER
PHYSIOGNOMY	SEPTICAEMIA	CRACKERJACK	DEBILITATED	LUXULYANITE	VACILLATING
PLAGIARISED	SERVICEABLE	CRACKHALTER	DEFOLIATION	MECKLENBURG	VACILLATION
PLAGIOSTOMI	SIGNIFICANT	CROOKEDNESS	DEPHLEGMATE	MEGALOMANIA	VINBLASTINE
POLLINATION	SILLIMANITE	DRINKDRIVER	DERELICTION	MEGALOMANIC	WASHLEATHER
PONTIFICATE	SPECIALIZED	DRUNKENNESS	DESELECTION	MEGALOPOLIS	WENSLEYDALE
POSSIBILITY	SPIRITUALLY	EXOSKELETON	DEVALUATION	METALWORKER	WHEELBARROW
PRECIPITATE	STATISTICAL	FLANKERBACK	DEVELOPMENT	MIDDLEMARCH	WHEELWRIGHT
PRECIPITOUS	STRAITLACED	FLICKERTAIL	DISILLUSION	MIDDLESIZED	WHITLEATHER
PREDICAMENT	STYLISHNESS	FRANKFURTER	DISPLEASURE	MISALLIANCE	WINDLESTRAW
PREDICATIVE	STYLIZATION	FRANKLINITE	DOUBLECHECK	MODELMOLEST	ZOOPLANKTON
PREDICTABLE	SUBDIVISION	KNUCKLEBALL	DOUBLECROSS	MONOLINGUAL	ACCOMMODATE
PREDICTABLY	SUBLIMATION	MALAKATOONE	DRYCLEANERS	MOONLIGHTER	ACCOMPANIST
PREHISTORIC	SUBSISTENCE	PAINKILLING	DRYCLEANING	MUDSLINGING	ACCUMULATOR
PRELIBATION	SUFFICIENCY	PRICKLINESS	ECCALEOBION	MYCOLOGICAL	ACRIMONIOUS
PRELIMINARY	SYNDICALISM	QUICKSILVER	EMBELLISHED	NEEDLEPOINT	ALBUMINURIA
PREMIERSHIP	SYNDICATION	SNICKERSNEE	EQUILATERAL	NEEDLESTICK	ASSEMBLYMAN
PRIMIGENIAL	TAGLIATELLE	SNORKELLING	EQUILIBRIST	NEEDLEWOMAN	ASSIMILATED
PRODIGALISE	TANGIBILITY	STICKLEBACK	EQUILIBRIUM	NOVELETTISH	BEAUMONTAGE
PRODIGALITY	TCHAIKOVSKY	STOCKBROKER	EUCALYPTOLE	OBSOLESCENT	CEREMONIOUS
PROFICIENCY	TECTIBRANCH	STOCKHAUSEN	EVERLASTING	ONTOLOGICAL	CHROMOPLAST
PROFITEROLE	TENSIOMETER	STOCKHOLDER	EXHILARATED	OSCILLATION	CLIOMETRICS
PROHIBITION	TERMINATION	STOCKJOBBER	FACULTATIVE	OVERLAPPING	COLUMBARIUM
PROHIBITIVE	TERMINOLOGY	STOCKTAKING	FAMILIARISE	OVERLEARNED	DENOMINATOR
PROLIFERATE	TERRITORIAL	STRIKEBOUND	FAMILIARITY	PARALEIPSIS	DENUMERABLE
PROMINENTLY	TESTIMONIAL	TELEKINESIS	FAMILIARIZE	PECULIARITY	DISEMBODIED
PROMISCUITY	THALIDOMIDE	THANKLESSLY	FARKLEBERRY	PENULTIMATE	DISIMPRISON
PROMISCUOUS	TONSILLITIS	TIMEKEEPING	FIDDLEDEDEE	PHILLIPSITE	DOCUMENTARY
PROPINQUITY	TORRIDONIAN	TRACKLEMENT	FIRELIGHTER	PHYLLOCLADE	ENCUMBRANCE
PROVISIONAL	TORTICOLLIS	WHISKERANDO	GENTLEMANLY	PORTLANDIAN	ENJAMBEMENT
PROVISIONER	TORTICULLUS	ACCELERATOR	GENTLEWOMAN	RABELAISIAN	EXTEMPORISE
PUBLICATION	TOSTICATION	ACCULTURATE	GIGGLESTICK	RATTLESNAKE	EXTEMPORIZE
PUBLISHABLE	TRADITIONAL	ADULLAMITES	GIGGLESWICK	RESPLENDENT	FILAMENTOUS
QUALITATIVE	TREPIDATION	AFFILIATION	GIGGLEWATER	RETALIATION	FISHMONGERS
RAFFISHNESS	TRINIDADIAN	ALLELOMORPH	GIRDLESTEAD	RETALIATORY	FORAMINIFER
REALIGNMENT	TRINITARIAN	ANAPLEROSIS	GOODLOOKING	REVALUATION	FOULMOUTHED
REALIZATION	TURRICULATE	ANAPLEROTIC	GRALLATORES	REVELATIONS	FRAGMENTARY
REANIMATION	UNALIENABLE	ANGELOLATRY	HABILIMENTS	REVOLUTIONS	FREEMASONRY
RECRIMINATE	UNANIMOUSLY	APOLLINARIS	HEPPLEWHITE	RIDDLEMEREE	FUNAMBULIST
RECTIFIABLE	UNDRINKABLE	APOLLONICON	HIGHLIGHTER	SADDLEHORSE	GLIMMERGOWK
RECTILINEAR	UNFAILINGLY	APPALLINGLY	HOBBLEDEHOY	SCHOLARSHIP	GRAMMALOGUE
REFRIGERANT	UNFLINCHING	APPELLATION	HUCKLEBERRY	SCULLABOGUE	GRAMMATICAL
REFRIGERATE	UNIFICATION	APPELLATIVE	HUMILIATING	SEXOLOGICAL	IGNOMINIOUS
RENAISSANCE	UNINITIATED	ARTILLERIST	HUMILIATION	SHALLOWNESS	ILLUMINANCE
REORIENTATE	UNPRINTABLE	BANGLADESHI	HURTLEBERRY	SHOPLIFTING	ILLUMINATED
REQUIREMENT	UNTHINKABLE	BATTLEDRESS	HYOPLASTRON	SINGLESTICK	INCOMPETENT
REQUISITION	UTILITARIAN	BATTLEFIELD	IDEOLOGICAL	SKILLIGALEE	INCOMPOSITE
RESPIRATION	UTILIZATION	BATTLEFRONT	IDYLLICALLY	SKILLIGOLEE	INDOMITABLE
RESPIRATORY	VACCINATION	BATTLEMENTS	IMPULSIVELY	SMALLHOLDER	INNUMERABLE

INTEMPERATE	ATTENTIVELY	INFANTICIDE	SPRINGCLEAN	CARBORUNDUM	ELABORATELY
IRONMONGERS	ATTENUATION	INFANTRYMAN	SPRINGHOUSE	CARDOPHAGUS	ELABORATION
IRONMONGERY	AUXANOMETER	INGENIOUSLY	SPRINGINESS	CARTOGRAPHY	EMBROCATION
KILIMANJARO	BICENTENARY	INSENSITIVE	STEINBERGER	CATHOLICISM	ENCHONDROMA
LUXEMBURGER	BOTANOMANCY	INSINCERITY	STRANDLOPER	CHINOISERIE	ENCROACHING
MANUMISSION	BUSINESSMAN	INSINUATING	STRANGENESS	CHIROGRAPHY	ENFEOFFMENT
MONTMORENCY	CALENDERING	INSINUATION	STRANGEWAYS	CHIROPODIST	ETHNOGRAPHY
MOZAMBIQUAN	CHRONICALLY	INTENSIVELY	STRANGULATE	CHOROGRAPHY	ETHNOLOGIST
MYXOMATOSIS	CHRONOMETER	INTENTIONAL	STRENUOUSLY	CITRONELLAL	ETYMOLOGIST
OARSMANSHIP	CLEANLINESS	INVINCIBLES	STRINGBOARD	CLADOSPORUM	EVAPORATION
OBTEMPERATE	CLEANSHAVEN	LACONICALLY	STRINGENTLY	CLINOCHLORE	EXPLORATION
OPTOMETRIST	COLONIALISM	LAMENTATION	STRINGYBARK	COENOBITISM	EXPLORATORY
OVERMANNING	COLONIALIST	LARYNGISMUS	STRONGYLOID	COGNOSCENTE	EXPROPRIATE
PANOMPHAEAN	CORINTHIANS	LIVINGSTONE	SUBUNGULATA	COGNOSCENTI	EXTROGENOUS
PARAMASTOID	CYLINDRICAL	LUMINESCENT	TECHNICALLY	COLEORRHIZA	EXTROVERTED
PARAMEDICAL	DECONSTRUCT	LYCANTHROPE	TIRONENSIAN	COLLOCATION	FATUOUSNESS
PERAMBULATE	DEFENCELESS	LYCANTHROPY	TYRANNOSAUR	COMFORTABLE	FERRONNIÈRE
PIEDMONTITE	DEFENSELESS	LYCHNOSCOPE	TYRONENSIAN	COMFORTABLY	FLAVOURSOME
POLYMORPHIC	DEFENSIVELY	MELANCHOLIA	UNANNOUNCED	COMFORTLESS	FORFOUGHTEN
PORTMANTEAU	DELINEATION	MELANCHOLIC	UNCONCEALED	COMMONPLACE	FORLORNNESS
POTAMOGETON	DELINQUENCY	MELANOCHROI	UNCONCERNED	COMMONSENSE	FRIVOLOUSLY
PREEMINENCE	DEMONOMANIA	MISANTHROPE	UNCONFIRMED	COMPOSITION	GALLOVIDIAN
REGIMENTALS	DEMONSTRATE	MISANTHROPY	UNCONNECTED	COMPOTATION	GALLOWGLASS
REMEMBRANCE	DERANGEMENT	MONONGAHELA	UNCONQUERED	CONCOMITANT	GLUCOSAMINE
RESEMBLANCE	DIAGNOSTICS	MONONUCLEAR	UNCONSCIOUS	CONCORDANCE	GODFORSAKEN
RHEUMATICKY	DIMENSIONAL	NICKNACKERY	UNCONTESTED	CONDOLENCES	GORDONSTOUN
RODOMONTADE	DISENCUMBER	NOMENCLATOR	UNCONVERTED	CONDOMINIUM	HAEMOGLOBIN
RUDIMENTARY	DISENTANGLE	OFFENSIVELY	UNCONVINCED	CONDOTTIERE	HAEMOPHILIA
SCRIMSHANDY	DISINCLINED	ORGANICALLY	VARANGARIAN	CONDOTTIORE	HAEMORRHAGE
SCRUMPTIOUS	DISINTEREST	ORGANIZAION	VOLUNTARILY	CONNOISSEUR	HAEMORRHOID
SEDIMENTARY	DOMINEERING	ORIENTALISM	VOLUNTARISM	CONNOTATION	HAGIOGRAPHA
SEISMOGRAPH	EMMENAGOGUE	ORIENTALIST	WITENAGEMOT	CONSOLATION	HAGIOGRAPHY
SHOWMANSHIP	EMMENTHALER	ORIENTATION	WOMANLINESS	CONSOLIDATE	HARIOLATION
SKIMMINGTON	ENGINEERING	OSTENTATION	ACKNOWLEDGE	CONVOCATION	HEBDOMADARY
SPERMATOZOA	ENHANCEMENT	PARANEPHROS	ACOLOUTHITE	CONVOLUTION	HIDEOUSNESS
SPERMICIDAL	EQUINOCTIAL	PARENTHESIS	AGGLOMERATE	CONVOLVULUS	HIPPOCAMPUS
SPERMOPHILE	ERRONEOUSLY	PARONOMASIA	AGONOTHETES	COPROPHAGAN	HIPPOCRATES
STEAMROLLER	ESSENTIALLY	PARTNERSHIP	ALCYONARIAN	COPROSTEROL	HIPPOCRATIC
STRAMINEOUS	EXPENDITURE	PERENNIALLY	AMINOBUTENE	CORPORATION	HISTOLOGIST
THAUMATROPE	EXPONENTIAL	PODSNAPPERY	ANACOLUTHIA	CORROBORATE	HISTORIATED
THERMOMETER	EXTENSIVELY	POTENTIALLY	ANDROGENOUS	COTTONMOUTH	HOMEOPATHIC
THERMOPYLAE	EXTENUATING	PROGNATHOUS	ANDROGYNOUS	COULOMMIERS	HYDROCARBON
THESMOTHETE	EXTENUATION	RECANTATION	ANISOCERCAL	CRACOVIENNE	HYDROGENATE
THIGMOTAXIS	FARINACEOUS	RECONDITION	ANTHOCYANIN	CROCODILIAN	HYDROMEDUSA
TRIUMVIRATE	FINANCIALLY	RECONNOITER	ANTHOLOGIZE	CUSTOMARILY	HYDROPHIDAE
UNCOMMITTED	FLANNELETTE	RECONNOITRE	ANTHONOMOUS	CYCLOALKANE	HYDROPHOBIA
UNDEMANDING	FOMENTATION	RECONSTRUCT	APATOSAURUS	CYCLOSTYLED	HYDROPHOBIC
UNREMITTING	FORTNIGHTLY	REMINISCENT	APHRODISIAC	DESPONDENCY	HYDROPONICS
VITAMINIZED	GEGENSCHEIN	REMONSTRATE	APOMORPHINE	DEVIOUSNESS	HYDROSTATIC
WELLMEANING	GERONTOLOGY	RESENTFULLY	APPROACHING	DIAMONDBACK	HYMNOLOGIST
WESTMINSTER	GOODNATURED	RETINACULUM	APPROBATION	DIPLOMATICS	ICONOGRAPHY
WHIGMALEERY	GREENBOTTLE	RETINOSCOPY	APPROPRIATE	DIPLOMATIST	ICONOSTASIS
WORKMANLIKE	GREENGROCER	RETINOSPORA	APPROVINGLY	DIPROTODONT	IMPROPRIETY
WORKMANSHIP	GREENOCKITE	REVENDICATE	APPROXIMATE	DIPSOMANIAC	IMPROVEMENT
ABSENTEEISM	GROUNDSHEET	RIBONUCLEIC	ARTIODACTYL	DISCOLOURED	IMPROVIDENT
ADVANCEMENT	GROUNDSPEED	ROMANTICISM	AUDIOVISUAL	DISCONTINUE	INTROVERTED
ADVENTURESS	GROUNDSWELL	ROMANTICIZE	AXEROPHTHOL	DISCOTHEQUE	ISOMORPHOUS
ADVENTUROUS	HOHENLINDEN	SALINOMETER	AZOTOBACTER	DISCOURTESY	ISTIOPHORUS
AERONAUTICS	INCANTATION	SAPONACEOUS	BANNOCKBURN	DISHONESTLY	LATROCINIUM
ANAGNORISIS	INCINERATOR	SCIENTOLOGY	BIELORUSSIA	DISLOCATION	LEGIONNAIRE
ANTINEUTRON	INCONGRUITY	SECONDARILY	BILIOUSNESS	DISPOSITION	LITHOGRAPHY
ANTONOMASIA	INCONGRUOUS	SECONDCLASS	BORBORYGMUS	DISSOLUTION	MACROBIOTIC
APHANIPTERA	INCONSTANCY	SEIGNIORAGE	BOUTONNIERE	DITTOGRAPHY	MACROGAMETE
APLANOSPORE	INCONTINENT	SERENDIPITY	BURGOMASTER	DOUROUCOULI	MACROSCOPIC
ARGENTINIAN	INCUNABULUM	SEVENTEENTH	BUTTONQUAIL	DRAGONNADES	MARCONIGRAM
ARRANGEMENT	INDENTATION	SPRINGBOARD	CALLOUSNESS	DUBIOUSNESS	MARIONBERRY
ASTONISHING	INFANGTHIEF	SPRINGBOARD	CALLOUSNESS	DYSLOGISTIC	MARIONETTES

MEADOWSWEET	PROMOTIONAL	UNEMOTIONAL	MYCOPHAGIST	ALTERNATION	DEPORTATION
MENTONNIÈRE	PROPOSITION	UNPROTECTED	OMNIPOTENCE	ALTERNATIVE	DESCRIPTION
MEPROBAMATE	PROROGATION	UNSTOPPABLE	OMNIPRESENT	ANACREONTIC	DESCRIPTIVE
METEOROLOGY	PROTOCOCCUS	UNWHOLESOME	OVERPAYMENT	ANTHRACOSIS	DESERPIDINE
METHODOLOGY	PROTONOTARY	VACUOUSNESS	PELOPONNESE	ANTIRRHINUM	DESTRUCTION
MICROGAMETE	PROVOCATION	VARIOLATION	PERIPATETIC	APPARATCHIK	DESTRUCTIVE
MICROSCOPIC	PROVOCATIVE	VARSOVIENNE	PERIPHRASIS	APPURTENANT	DETERIORATE
MICROSECOND	PTERODACTYL	VICIOUSNESS	PERSPECTIVE	ARTHRAPODAL	DETERMINANT
MICROTUBULE	PURPOSELESS	VIDEOCAMERA	PERSPICUITY	ARTHRODESIS	DETERMINATE
MICROVILLUS	PYELOGRAPHY	VIOLONCELLO	PERSPICUOUS	ARTHROSPORE	DETERMINING
MISCONSTRUE	PYTHONESQUE	VISCOUNTESS	PROMPTITUDE	ASPERGILLUM	DICHROMATIC
MYTHOLOGIZE	RADIOACTIVE	WINDOWFRAME	PROSPECTIVE	ASPERGILLUS	DIFFRACTION
NATIONALISM	RADIOCARBON	WINDOWLEDGE	REALPOLITIK	ASPERSORIUM	DIMERCAPROL
NATIONALIST	RADIOGRAPHY	YELLOWPLUSH	REAPPRAISAL	ATHARVAVEDA	DISARMAMENT
NATIONALITY	RADIOLOGIST	YELLOWSTONE	RECEPTIVITY	ATHERINIDAE	DISCREPANCY
NATIONALIZE	RATIOCINATE	ACCIPITRINE	RECIPROCATE	ATHERMANOUS	DISGRACEFUL
NATIONSTATE	RATIONALITY	ADIAPHORIST	RECIPROCITY	AVERRUNCATE	DISGRUNTLED
NECROBIOSIS	RATIONALIZE	AMMOPHILOUS	REDUPLICATE	AVOIRDUPOIS	DISORGANIZE
NECROMANCER	RAUCOUSNESS	ANTEPENDIUM	SAXOPHONIST	BELORUSSIAN	DISORIENTED
NERVOUSNESS	REPROACHFUL	ANTIPHONARY	SCALPRIFORM	BICARBONATE	DISTRACTION
NEUROLOGIST	RESPONSIBLE	ANTIPHRASIS	SCRIPTORIUM	BIFURCATION	DISTRESSING
OBVIOUSNESS	RESPONSIBLY	ANTIPYRETIC	SCUPPERNONG	CAMARADERIE	DISTRIBUTED
OCHLOCRATIC	RESPONSIONS	BACKPACKING	SHINPLASTER	CAMERAWOMAN	DISTRIBUTOR
OLIGOCHAETE	RESTORATION	BLASPHEMOUS	SLEEPWALKER	CAMEROONIAN	DISTRUSTFUL
OPPROBRIOUS	RESTORATIVE	CACOPHONOUS	SOLIPSISTIC	CAPERNOITED	DIVORCEMENT
ORTHOCENTRE	RETROACTIVE	CHIPPENDALE	SOROPTIMIST	CAPERNOITIE	DOCTRINAIRE
ORTHOGRAPHY	RETROROCKET	CLAPPERCLAW	STEEPLEJACK	CATERPILLAR	EMBARKATION
ORTHOPAEDIC	RINFORZANDO	CONSPICUOUS	STRAPHANGER	CENTREBOARD	EMBARRASSED
OSTEOPATHIC	SALVOGUNNER	CONSPIRATOR	STROPHILLUS	CENTREPIECE	EMPIRICUTIC
OSTEOPLASTY	SAPROLEGNIA	CYMOPHANOUS	STYMPHALIAN	CENTRIFUGAL	EMPYROMANCY
OUTPOURINGS	SAPROPHYTIC	DECAPITATED	SYCOPHANTIC	CENTRIPETAL	ENDORSEMENT
PAEDOTROPHY	SARCOPHAGUS	DECEPTIVELY	TEASPOONFUL	CERARGYRITE	ENFORCEABLE
PALEOGRAPHY	SCEUOPHYLAX	DICEPHALOUS	TELEPHONIST	CESAREWITCH	ENFORCEMENT
PALEOLITHIC	SCOLOPENDRA	DILAPIDATED	TELEPRINTER	CHAIRPERSON	ENLARGEMENT
PASTOURELLE	SCOPOLAMINE	DISAPPROVAL	THEOPNEUSTY	CHEERLEADER	ENTERTAINER
PATHOLOGIST	SEPIOSTAIRE	ENCAPSULATE	TOXOPHILITE	CHEIROGNOMY	ENTHRALLING
PATRONISING	SERIOUSNESS	ENCEPHALOMA	TRESPASSING	CHIAROSCURO	ENVIRONMENT
PATRONIZING	SEXTODECIMO	ENKEPHALINE	TROMPELOEIL	CHLOROPHYLL	ESCARMOUCHE
PENTONVILLE	SOCIOLOGIST	EQUIPOLLENT	UNEXPLAINED	CHOIRMASTER	EUCHROMATIN
PERCOLATION	SORROWFULLY	EXASPERATED	UNEXPRESSED	CLAIRSCHACH	EXHORTATION
PERFORATION	SPIROCHAETE	EXCEPTIONAL	UNHAPPINESS	CLAIRVOYANT	EXPERIENCED
PERFORMANCE	STENOCHROME	HARDPRESSED	UNIMPORTANT	COHORTATIVE	EXPURGATION
PERIODONTIC	STENOGRAPHY	HEMOPHILIAC	UNIMPRESSED	COLORIMETER	EXTERMINATE
PERSONALIST	STYLOPODIUM	HIGHPITCHED	UNREPENTANT	COMPRIMARIO	EXTERNALIZE
PERSONALITY	SUBCONTRACT	HIGHPOWERED	UNSUPPORTED	CONGRESSMAN	EXTORTIONER
PERSONALIZE	SUBDOMINANT	HIGHPROFILE	VASOPRESSIN	CONTRACTION	FLOURISHING
PERSONIFIED	SUFFOCATING	HOMOPHONOUS	WESTPHALIAN	CONTRACTUAL	FLUORESCENT
PETRODOLLAR	SUFFOCATION	IDEOPRAXIST	XEROPHILOUS	CONTRAPTION	FLUOROMETER
PHILOCTETES	SUPPOSITION	INCAPSULATE	ANTIQUARIAN	CONTRASTING	FLUOROSCOPE
PHILOLOGIST	SUPPOSITORY	INDEPENDENT	HIGHQUALITY	CONTRAYERVA	FUNDRAISING
PHILOSOPHER	SURROUNDING	INDUPLICATE	TRANQUILITY	CONTRETEMPS	GABERLUNZIE
PHONOFIDDLE	SYMPOSIARCH	INEXPEDIENT	UNUNQUADIUM	CONTRIBUTOR	GASTRECTOMY
PHOTOCOPIER	SYNCOPATION	INEXPENSIVE	ABNORMALITY	CONTRIVANCE	GASTRONOMIC
PHOTOFINISH	TAUROBOLIUM	INOPPORTUNE	ABSORPTANCE	CONTROVERSY	GENERALIZED
PHOTOGRAPHY	TAUTOCHRONE	INSEPARABLE	ABSTRACTION	CONURBATION	GENERICALLY
PHOTOSPHERE	TEDIOUSNESS	INSUPERABLE	ACCORDINGLY	CYBERNETICS	GUBERNATION
POLIORCETIC	TEETOTALLER	IRREPARABLE	ADVERBIALLY	DECARBONATE	HABERDASHER
PORNOGRAPHY	TEMPORARILY	IRREPARABLY	ADVERTISING	DECARBONIZE	HAIRRAISING
PRECONCEIVE	TENUOUSNESS	ITHYPHALLIC	AFFIRMATION	DECORTICATE	HEMERALOPIA
PREDOMINANT	THOROUGHPIN	ITHYPHALLUS	AFFIRMATIVE	DEFERENTIAL	HEMORRHOIDS
PREDOMINATE	THYROTROPIN	JOSEPHINITE	AFTERSCHOOL	DEFORMATION	HETEROGRAFT
PREMONITION	TOPLOFTICAL	KIRKPATRICK	AGUARDIENTE	DEHORTATIVE	HETEROSCIAN
PREMONITORY	TREPONEMATA	MALAPROPISM	AILUROPHILE	DEMARCATION	HIBERNATING
PREPOLLENCE	TRINOBANTES	MANIPULATOR	AIRCRAFTMAN	DEMORALIZED	HIBERNATION
PREPOSITION	TROPOSPHERE	METAPHYSICS	ALTERCATION	DENDRACHATE	HIGHRANKING
PREROGATIVE	UNAVOIDABLE	MISSPELLING	ALTERNATELY	DEPARTEMENT	HILARIOUSLY
PROLOCUTION	UNAVOIDABLY	MONOPSONIST	ALTERNATING	DEPARTEMENT	HISTRIONICS

HUMGRUFFIAN	INTERVIEWER	QUADRENNIUM	UNDERSIGNED	EXPOSTULATE	PLEISTOCENE
HUNDREDFOLD	KIMERIDGIAN	QUADRUPLETS	UNDERSTATED	FESTSCHRIFT	POLYSTYRENE
HYPERBOREAN	LABORIOUSLY	QUARRELLING	UNDERTAKING	FORESEEABLE	PRESSURIZED
HYPERMARKET	LABORSAVING	QUARRELSOME	UNDERVALUED	FORESHORTEN	RAVISHINGLY
HYPERTROPHY	LAMPROPHYRE	QUARRINGTON	UNDERWEIGHT	FORESTATION	REASSURANCE
IGNORANTINE	LASERPICIUM	REBARBATIVE	UNDERWRITER	GLOSSOLALIA	RECESSIONAL
IMMORTALISE	LATERIGRADE	RECURRENTLY	UNFORTUNATE	GRASSHOPPER	REGISTERING
IMMORTALITY	LATERITIOUS	REFORMATION	UNFURNISHED	GREASEPAINT	RESISTIVITY
IMMORTALIZE	LAWBREAKING	REFORMATORY	UNPERTURBED	GUESSTIMATE	RESUSCITATE
IMPARTIALLY	LEGERDEMAIN	REFURBISHED	UNSHRINKING	HALBSTARKER	REVISIONISM
IMPERFORATE	LIBERTARIAN	REGURGITATE	UNSURPASSED	HARPSICHORD	RHAPSODICAL
IMPERIALISM	LITERALNESS	REMORSELESS	UNVARNISHED	HORNSWOGGLE	ROBESPIERRE
IMPERIALIST	LOCORESTIVE	RESERVATION	UNWARRANTED	HUCKSTERAGE	RUDESHEIMER
IMPERIOUSLY	LOGARITHMIC	RESTRICTION	VICARIOUSLY	ILLUSIONARY	SALESPERSON
IMPERMANENT	LONGRUNNING	RESTRICTIVE	VINCRISTINE	ILLUSIONISM	SCHISTOSOMA
IMPERMEABLE	LUXURIANTLY	RESTRUCTURE	VOTERIGGING	ILLUSIONIST	SCHISTOSOME
IMPERSONATE	LUXURIOUSLY	RETARDATION	WATERCOLOUR	ILLUSTRATOR	SELFSERVICE
IMPERTINENT	MACERANDUBA	REVERBERATE	WATERCOURSE	ILLUSTRIOUS	SINISTRORSE
IMPORTANTLY	MALPRACTICE	REVERENTIAL	WATEREDDOWN	IMPASSIONED	SPESSARTITE
IMPORTATION	MATERIALISE	RUMFRUCTION	WATERLOGGED	IMPASSIVELY	SPITSTICKER
IMPORTUNATE	MATERIALISM	SATIRICALLY	WATERMEADOW	INCESSANTLY	SPONSORSHIP
INCARCERATE	MATERIALIST	SCLERODERMA	WATERSKIING	INDUSTRIOUS	TERPSICHORE
INCARNADINE	MATERIALIZE	SELFRESPECT	WATERSPLASH	INESSENTIAL	TIMESHARING
INCARNATION	MEMORABILIA	SEVERALFOLD	WIDERANGING	INFESTATION	TOWNSPEOPLE
INCORPORATE	MISERICORDE	SOVEREIGNTY	ACCESSORIES	INSISTENTLY	TRANSACTION
INCORPOREAL	MISERLINESS	SPARROWHAWK	AGNOSTICISM	INVESTIGATE	TRANSCEIVER
INCORRECTLY	MISTRUSTFUL	STAIRCARPET	AGROSTOLOGY	INVESTITURE	TRANSDERMAL
INEBRIATION	MODERNISTIC	SUBORDINATE	ANAESTHESIA	ISOXSUPRINE	TRANSFERRED
INFERIORITY	MONARCHICAL	SUBTRACTION	ANAESTHETIC	KALASHNIKOV	TRANSFERRIN
INFERTILITY	NATURALNESS	SUBTROPICAL	ANTISTHENES	LANDSKNECHT	TRANSFIGURE
INFORMALITY	NATUROPATHY	SUFFRAGETTE	ANTISTROPHE	LEADSWINGER	TRANSFORMED
INFORMATICS	NEUTRALISED	SUGARCOATED	ASSASSINATE	LEGISLATION	TRANSFORMER
INFORMATION	NEVERENDING	SUNDRENCHED	ATMOSPHERIC	LEGISLATIVE	TRANSFUSION
INFORMATIVE	NOSTRADAMUS	SUPERALTERN	ATTESTATION	LEGISLATURE	TRANSILIENT
INFURIATING	NOTORIOUSLY	SUPERCHARGE	AUGUSTINIAN	LICKSPITTLE	TRANSLATION
INHERITANCE	NUMERICALLY	SUPERCHERIE	BACKSLIDING	LONGSIGHTED	TRANSLUCENT
INSCRIPTION	NUTCRACKERS	SUPERFICIAL	BALISTRARIA	LONGSLEEVED	TRANSMITTED
INSCRUTABLE	OBSERVATION	SUPERFICIES	BARNSTORMER	LOUDSPEAKER	TRANSMITTER
INSTRUCTION	OBSERVATORY	SUPERFLUITY	BERGSCHRUND	LOUISIANIAN	TRANSPARENT
INSTRUCTIVE	OBSTRICTION	SUPERFLUOUS	BESTSELLING	MAGISTERIAL	TRANSPONDER
INSTRUMENTS	OBSTRUCTION	SUPERIMPOSE	BLESSEDNESS	MAGISTRATES	TRANSPORTED
INTERACTION	OBSTRUCTIVE	SUPERINTEND	BOOKSELLERS	MINESWEEPER	TRANSPORTER
INTERACTIVE	ONEIRODYNIA	SUPERIORITY	BREASTPLATE	MINISTERIAL	TRANSURANIC
INTERCALARY	ONEIROMANCY	SUPERLATIVE	CATASTROPHE	MINISTERING	TRANSVERSAL
INTERCEPTOR	OPPORTUNELY	SUPERMARKET	CHEESECLOTH	MOLESTATION	TREASONABLE
INTERCHANGE	OPPORTUNISM	SUPERSCRIBE	CHIASTOLITE	NEARSIGHTED	TYPESETTING
INTERCOSTAL	OPPORTUNIST	SUPERSCRIPT	CHRISMATION	NECESSARILY	UNASSERTIVE
INTERCOURSE	OPPORTUNITY	SUPERSEDEAS	CHRISTENING	NECESSITATE	UNCASTRATED
INTERESTING	ORDERLINESS	SUPERSEDERE	CHRISTMASSY	NECESSITOUS	UNDESERVING
INTERGLOSSA	PAPERWEIGHT	SUPERTANKER	CHRISTOPHER	NIERSTEINER	UNDESIRABLE
INTERGROWTH	PATERNALISM	SUPERVISION	CHRYSAROBIN	NUMISMATICS	UNDISCLOSED
INTERLACING	PATERNOSTER	SUPERVISORY	CHRYSOPRASE	NUMISMATIST	UNDISGUISED
INTERLEUKIN	PELARGONIUM	SUPPRESSION	COMESTIBLES	OBSESSIVELY	UNDISTURBED
INTERLINGUA	PIERREPOINT	SUSURRATION	COUNSELLING	OCTASTICHON	UNESSENTIAL
INTERMINGLE	PLEURODYNIA	TABERNACLES	CROSSLEGGED	OMNISCIENCE	UNJUSTIFIED
INTERNALIZE	PORTRAITIST	THEORETICAL	DEERSTALKER	OVERSTUFFED	UNOBSERVANT
INTERNECINE	PORTRAITURE	TIMBROMANIA	DEMOSTHENES	PAINSTAKING	UNSUSPECTED
INTERNUNCIO	PROCREATION	TIMBROPHILY	DEMOSTHENIC	PALESTINIAN	VICISSITUDE
INTERPOLATE	PROCRUSTEAN	ULOTRICHALE	DETESTATION	PARASITOSIS	VIVISECTION
INTERPRETER	PROGRESSION	UNCERTAINTY	DEUTSCHMARK	PARISHIONER	VOLKSKAMMER
INTERREGNUM	PROGRESSIVE	UNCHRISTIAN	DEVASTATING	PEDESTRIANS	WAINSCOTING
INTERRELATE	PROPRIETARY	UNDERCHARGE	DEVASTATION	PERESTROIKA	WALDSTERBEN
INTERROGATE	PROTRACTING	UNDERCOOKED	DOMESTICATE	PERISSOLOGY	WHITSUNTIDE
INTERRUPTER	PROTRACTION	UNDERGROUND	DOMESTICITY	PERISTALITH	WINDSURFING
INTERSPERSE	PURPRESTURE	UNDERGROWTH	DRESSMAKING	PERISTALSIS	WORKSTATION
INTERVENING	PYRARGYRITE	UNDERHANDED	DYAESTHESIA	PHRASEOLOGY	ABORTIONIST
INTERVIEWEE	QUADRENNIAL	UNDERMANNED	EXCESSIVELY	PLEASURABLE	ADOPTIANISM

ADOPTIONISM	ELECTRICITY	MEGATHERIUM	RIGHTHANDER	UNSATURATED	DRACUNCULUS
ADULTERATED	ELECTROCUTE	MERITORIOUS	RIGHTWINGER	UNUTTERABLE	DYSFUNCTION
AMONTILLADO	ELECTROLIER	METATARSALS	SAGITTARIUS	UNWITTINGLY	EJACULATION
ANASTOMOSIS	ELECTROLYTE	MOISTURIZER	SAINTLINESS	VOORTREKKER	ENCOURAGING
ANESTHETIST	ELECTRONICS	MONOTHELITE	SAINTPAULIA	WHISTLESTOP	ENFOULDERED
ANESTHETIZE	ELECTROTINT	MONOTREMATA	SCATTERGOOD	WHITTINGTON	EXCLUSIVELY
APOSTROPHUS	ELEUTHERIAN	MONSTROSITY	SCATTERLING	WISHTONWISH	EXECUTIONER
ARBITRAGEUR	ENARTHROSIS	MOSSTROOPER	SCEPTICALLY	XEROTHERMIC	FAVOURITISM
ARBITRAMENT	ENDOTHERMIC	MOUNTAINEER	SCHOTTISCHE	XEROTRIPSIS	FEATURELESS
ARBITRARILY	ENDOTROPHIC	MOUNTAINOUS	SCINTILLATE	ACCOUNTABLE	FORMULATION
ARBITRATION	ENTITLEMENT	MUNITIONIZE	SCOUTMASTER	ACCOUNTANCY	FORTUNATELY
ARGATHELIAN	EOANTHROPUS	NAPHTHALENE	SCUTTLEBUTT	ACUPUNCTURE	FORTUNELOUD
ARISTOCRACY	ERRATICALLY	NEGOTIATING	SEMITRAILER	ADJOURNMENT	GARRULOUSLY
ASSYTHEMENT	EVENTRATION	NEGOTIATION	SHAFTESBURY	AESCULAPIAN	GENOUILLÈRE
BEASTLINESS	EVENTUALITY	NIGHTINGALE	SHEATHKNIFE	AESCULAPIUS	GUTTURALISE
BEAUTIFULLY	EXANTHEMATA	NIGHTMARISH	SHITTIMWOOD	AGGLUTINANT	HALLUCINATE
BREATHALYSE	FACETIOUSLY	NIKETHAMIDE	SHORTCHANGE	AGGLUTINATE	IMPRUDENTLY
BRISTLECONE	FANATICALLY	NONETHELESS	SHORTCOMING	CALCULATING	INELUCTABLE
BRITTLENESS	FAULTFINDER	NOTOTHERIUM	SHORTHANDED	CALCULATION	INEQUITABLE
CAUSTICALLY	FAULTLESSLY	OBLITERATED	SHUTTLECOCK	CAMOUFLAGED	INFLUENTIAL
CHANTARELLE	FLIRTATIOUS	OBMUTESCENT	SIGHTSCREEN	CARBURETTOR	INOCULATION
CHANTERELLE	FLUCTUATING	ODONTOBLAST	SIGHTSEEING	CENTUMVIRUS	INSOUCIANCE
CHANTICLEER	FLUCTUATION	ODONTOPHORE	SKEPTICALLY	CENTURIATOR	JACQUEMINOT
CHITTERLING	FORETHOUGHT	OMMATOPHORE	SLEUTHHOUND	CINQUECENTO	KULTURKREIS
COMPTROLLER	FRANTICALLY	ORNITHOLOGY	SPATTERDASH	CIRCULARIZE	LECTURESHIP
COMSTOCKERY	FREETHINKER	ORNITHOPTER	SPATTERDOCK	CIRCULATING	LINGUISTICS
CONSTANTINE	FRONTRUNNER	OUTSTANDING	SPECTACULAR	CIRCULATION	MALFUNCTION
CONSTELLATE	FROSTBITTEN	OVERTURNING	SPLUTTERING	CIRCULATORY	MANEUVERING
CONSTERNATE	FRUITLESSLY	PARATROOPER	SPONTANEITY	CIRCUMCISER	MASCULINITY
CONSTIPATED	FRUSTRATING	PARATYPHOID	SPONTANEOUS	CIRCUMFLECT	MASQUERADER
CONSTITUENT	FRUSTRATION	PEDETENTOUS	SPORTSFIELD	CIRCUMSPECT	MEASURELESS
CONSTRAINED	FUNCTIONARY	PENETRATING	SPORTSWOMAN	COAGULATION	MEASUREMENT
CONSTRICTED	FUNCTIONING	PENETRATION	STADTHOLDER	COLOURBLIND	MEDIUMSIZED
CONSTRICTOR	GAMETANGIUM	PENITENTIAL	STEATOPYGIA	COMBUSTIBLE	MENSURATION
CONSTRUCTOR	GAMETOPHYTE	PERITONAEUM	STRATEGICAL	COMEUPPANCE	MICHURINISM
CONSTUPRATE	GENETICALLY	PERITONITIS	STRETCHABLE	COMMUNALISM	MICTURITION
COUNTENANCE	GHASTLINESS	PETITMAITRE	STRETCHLESS	COMMUNICANT	MILQUETOAST
COUNTERFEIT	GLASTONBURY	PLANTAGENET	STRUTHIONES	COMMUNICATE	MURMURATION
COUNTERFOIL	HEALTHINESS	PLANTIGRADE	SUBITANEOUS	COMMUTATION	PARTURITION
COUNTERFORT	HEARTBROKEN	POINTLESSLY	SUBSTANDARD	COMPUNCTION	PERDUELLION
COUNTERGLOW	HEARTLESSLY	POLITICALLY	SUBSTANTIAL	COMPUTATION	PERFUNCTORY
COUNTERHAND	HEPATOSCOPY	POLITICIANS	SUBSTANTIVE	COMPUTERIZE	PERLUSTRATE
COUNTERMAND	HOLOTHURIAN	POLYTECHNIC	SUDETENLAND	CONCURRENCE	PERMUTATION
COUNTERPANE	HOMOTHERMAL	POLYTRICHUM	SUMPTUOUSLY	CONDUCTANCE	PICTURESQUE
COUNTERPART	HOMOTHERMIC	PRACTICABLE	SYMPTOMATIC	CONDUCTRESS	PREJUDICIAL
COUNTERSIGN	HYPOTENSION	PRACTICALLY	TACITURNITY	CONFUTATION	PRESUMPTION
COUNTERSINK	HYPOTHECATE	PRESTIGIOUS	TARATANTARA	CONJUGATION	PRESUMPTIVE
COUNTRIFIED	HYPOTHERMIA	PRESTISSIMO	THEATERGOER	CONJUNCTION	PROCUREMENT
COUNTRYSIDE	IDENTICALLY	PRESTONPANS	THEATREGOER	CONJUNCTURE	PROFUSENESS
COURTEOUSLY	IDENTIFYING	PRESTRESSED	THEATRICALS	CONSULTANCY	PROTUBERANT
COURTLINESS	IDIOTICALLY	PROSTHETICS	THISTLEDOWN	CONSUMABLES	QUERULOUSLY
CRESTFALLEN	IMPATIENTLY	PROSTRATION	TICKTACKTOE	CONSUMERISM	RAMGUNSHOCH
CRYSTALLINE	IMPETUOSITY	PSITTACOSIS	TIGHTFISTED	CONSUMPTION	RAPTUROUSLY
CRYSTALLISE	IMPETUOUSLY	PUNCTILIOUS	TIGHTLIPPED	CONSUMPTIVE	RECRUITMENT
CRYSTALLIZE	INATTENTION	PUNCTUALITY	TOASTMASTER	CONTUBERNAL	REDOUBTABLE
DELETERIOUS	INATTENTIVE	PUNCTUATION	TRIPTOLEMUS	CONVULSIONS	RESOURCEFUL
DELITESCENT	INAUTHENTIC	PURITANICAL	TRUSTEESHIP	CORRUGATION	RUMBUSTIOUS
DEVITRIFIED	INESTIMABLE	QUARTERBACK	TRUSTWORTHY	CORRUPTIBLE	RUMGUMPTION
DIARTHROSIS	INFATUATION	QUARTERDECK	UNALTERABLE	CREDULOUSLY	SANGUINEOUS
DICOTYLEDON	KLEPTOMANIA	QUESTIONING	UNAUTHENTIC	CREPUSCULAR	SAVOURINESS
DIORTHORTIC	LECITHINASE	QUINTUPLETS	UNGETATABLE	DEGLUTINATE	SESQUIOXIDE
DOWNTRODDEN	LENGTHENING	RATATOUILLE	UNMITIGATED	DEGLUTITION	SINGULARITY
DRASTICALLY	LENGTHINESS	REACTIONARY	UNMOTIVATED	DISJUNCTION	SPECULATION
ECTOTROPHIC	LIGHTHEADED	REPETITIOUS	UNNATURALLY	DISJUNCTIVE	SPECULATIVE
EINSTEINIUM	LIGHTWEIGHT	RIGHTANGLED	UNOBTRUSIVE	DISPUTATION	STIMULATION
ELASTOPLAST	MAINTENANCE	RIGHTEOUSLY	UNPATRIOTIC	DISQUIETING	STIPULATION
ELECTRICIAN	MAISTERDOME	RIGHTHANDED	UNSATISFIED	DISTURBANCE	SUBJUGATION

SUBJUNCTIVE	INTOXICATED	CAMERAWOMAN	INTERACTION	REINCARNATE	BLOCKBUSTER
SUBMULTIPLE	INTOXIMETER	CARAVANNING	INTERACTIVE	REPROACHFUL	CANNIBALISM
SUPPURATION	NONEXISTENT	CARRIAGEWAY	IRREPARABLE	RETINACULUM	CANNIBALIZE
SURTURBRAND	ANONYMOUSLY	CATACAUSTIC	IRREPARABLY	RETROACTIVE	COENOBITISM
TRIBULATION	APODYTERIUM	CHANTARELLE	KAMELAUKION	REVELATIONS	COLLABORATE
TRUCULENTLY	BATHYSPHERE	CHOCKABLOCK	KILIMANJARO	RHEUMATICKY	COLUMBARIUM
UNCLUTTERED	BELLYTIMBER	CHRYSAROBIN	KILOCALORIE	RIGHTANGLED	CONFABULATE
UNCOUNTABLE	DACTYLOGRAM	CLANJAMFRAY	KIRKPATRICK	SAPONACEOUS	CONTUBERNAL
UNCOUTHNESS	DEOXYGENATE	COMPLACENCY	LITERALNESS	SCANDALIZED	CONURBATION
UNCRUSHABLE	DINNYHAUSER	COMPLAISANT	LOGODAEDALY	SCANDANAVIA	CORROBORATE
UNDOUBTEDLY	DINNYHAYSER	CONCEALMENT	LONGLASTING	SCHOLARSHIP	CREDIBILITY
UNEQUIVOCAL	DIPHYCERCAL	CONSTANTINE	MACADAMIZED	SCULLABOGUE	CULPABILITY
UNTOUCHABLE	EMPHYTEUSIS	CONTRACTION	MACERANDUBA	SEVERALFOLD	DECARBONATE
VENTURESOME	EMPTYHANDED	CONTRACTUAL	MALAKATOONE	SHOWMANSHIP	DECARBONIZE
ALLEVIATION	EURHYTHMICS	CONTRAPTION	MALEFACTION	SMORGASBORD	DESTABILIZE
AMBIVALENCE	GALLYBAGGER	CONTRASTING	MALFEASANCE	SOCKDALAGER	DISEMBODIED
ANNIVERSARY	GALLYBEGGAR	CONTRAYERVA	MALPRACTICE	SOUTHAMPTON	ELIGIBILITY
ARRIVEDERCI	GEOSYNCLINE	CORDWAINERS	MANUFACTURE	SPECIALIZED	ELIZABETHAN
BEHAVIOURAL	GERRYMANDER	CRYSTALLINE	MARIVAUDAGE	SPECTACULAR	ENCUMBRANCE
BENEVOLENCE	GILLYFLOWER	CRYSTALLISE	MATRIARCHAL	SPERMATOZOA	ENJAMBEMENT
CARAVANNING	HEAVYHANDED	CRYSTALLIZE	MEMORABILIA	SPESSARTITE	FALLIBILITY
DELIVERANCE	HEAVYWEIGHT	CYCLOALKANE	MERCHANDISE	SPONTANEITY	FEASIBILITY
EQUIVALENCE	HONEYCOMBED	DECORATIONS	MERCHANDIZE	SPONTANEOUS	FILLIBUSTER
EQUIVOCALLY	HONEYMOONER	DEMIBASTION	MERCHANTMAN	STANDARDIZE	FLEXIBILITY
INADVERTENT	HONEYSUCKLE	DEMORALIZED	METACARPALS	SUBITANEOUS	FROSTBITTEN
INADVISABLE	JERRYMANDER	DENDRACHATE	METATARSALS	SUBSTANDARD	FUNAMBULIST
INDIVISIBLE	MERRYMAKING	DIFFRACTION	MILLIAMPERE	SUBSTANTIAL	GALLIBAGGER
INDIVISIBLY	MOLLYCODDLE	DISGRACEFUL	MISFEASANCE	SUBSTANTIVE	GALLIBEGGAR
IRREVERENCE	MONEYLENDER	DISTRACTION	MOUNTAINEER	SUBTRACTION	GALLYBAGGER
IRREVOCABLE	MONEYMAKING	DODECASTYLE	MOUNTAINOUS	SUFFRAGETTE	GALLYBEGGAR
KATAVOTHRON	PENNYFATHER	EFFICACIOUS	MYXOMATOSIS	SUPERALTERN	GREENBOTTLE
KETAVOTHRON	PHARYNGITIS	ELEPHANTINE	NATURALNESS	TAGLIATELLE	GULLIBILITY
MALEVOLENCE	PICKYOUROWN	EMMENAGOGUE	NEUTRALISED	TARATANTARA	HEARTBROKEN
MARIVAUDAGE	PINNYWINKLE	ENCROACHING	NEWSCASTING	THAUMATROPE	HYPERBOREAN
RECOVERABLE	PLATYRRHINE	ENDOCARDIUM	NICKNACKERY	THEREABOUTS	INSTABILITY
TWELVEMONTH	STORYTELLER	ENTHRALLING	NONCHALANCE	THINGAMABOB	LUXEMBURGER
UNCIVILISED	TACHYCARDIA	EPIDIASCOPE	NONFEASANCE	THINGAMAJIG	MACROBIOTIC
UNCIVILIZED	TACHYGRAPHY	EQUILATERAL	NOSTRADAMUS	TICKTACKTOE	MEPROBAMATE
UNDEVELOPED	TEENYBOPPER	EQUIVALENCE	NUTCRACKERS	TRANSACTION	MOZAMBIQUAN
UNENVELOPED	TIGGYWINKLE	EVERLASTING	OARSMANSHIP	TRESPASSING	NECROBIOSIS
UNFAVORABLE	VICHYSOISSE	EXHILARATED	OUTSTANDING	UNBREAKABLE	NEIGHBORING
VESUVIANITE	WORRYTROUGH	FARINACEOUS	OVERBALANCE	UNCLEANNESS	NEIGHBOURLY
BIRDWATCHER	BRAZZAVILLE	FARREACHING	OVERHANGING	UNDEMANDING	OPPROBRIOUS
BUSHWHACKER	CITIZENSHIP	FLIRTATIOUS	OVERLAPPING	UNGETATABLE	PERAMBULATE
CORDWAINERS	GRENZGANGER	FOOTBALLING	OVERMANNING	UNINHABITED	PITCHBLENDE
CROMWELLIAN	OVERZEALOUS	FOOTWASHING	OVERPAYMENT	UNPALATABLE	POSSIBILITY
DUSTWRAPPER	SWITZERLAND	FORBEARANCE	PAEDIATRICS	UNSPEAKABLE	PRELIBATION
EMPOWERMENT	**11:6**	FORECASTING	PARAMASTOID	VINBLASTINE	PROBABILITY
FAIRWEATHER	ABRACADABRA	FOREFATHERS	PATRIARCHAL	WHEREABOUTS	PROHIBITION
FITZWILLIAM	ABSTRACTION	FOREWARNING	PERICARDIUM	WHIGMALEERY	PROHIBITIVE
FOOTWASHING	ADULLAMITES	FOUNDATIONS	PERIPATETIC	WIDERANGING	PROTUBERANT
FOREWARNING	AERONAUTICS	FREEMASONRY	PLAGIARISED	WITENAGEMOT	READABILITY
GLADWELLISE	AIRCRAFTMAN	FUNDRAISING	PLANTAGENET	WOODCARVING	REBARBATIVE
HANDWRITING	AMBIVALENCE	GAMETANGIUM	PODSNAPPERY	WORKMANLIKE	REDOUBTABLE
HANDWRITTEN	ANTHRACOSIS	GENERALIZED	PORTLANDIAN	WORKMANSHIP	REFURBISHED
HARDWORKING	APPARATCHIK	GOODNATURED	PORTMANTEAU	ZOOPLANKTON	RELIABILITY
ILLYWHACKER	APPROACHING	GRALLATORES	PORTRAITIST	ADVERBIALLY	REMEMBRANCE
OVERWEENING	ARTHROPODAL	GRAMMALOGUE	PORTRAITURE	ALPHABETIZE	RESEMBLANCE
OVERWHELMED	BACCHANALIA	GRAMMATICAL	PROGNATHOUS	AMINOBUTENE	RETRIBUTION
OVERWROUGHT	BACKPACKING	HAIRRAISING	PROTRACTING	AMPHIBOLOGY	RETRIBUTIVE
PRZEWALSKIS	BANGLADESHI	HEMERALOPIA	PROTRACTION	APPROBATION	REVERBERATE
SCREWDRIVER	BIRDWATCHER	HIGHRANKING	PRZEWALSKIS	ARQUEBUSIER	SCARABAEOID
SHIPWRECKED	BRAGGADOCIO	HYOPLASTRON	PSITTACOSIS	ASSEMBLYMAN	SENSIBILITY
TELEWORKING	BRAZZAVILLE	IGNORANTINE	PURITANICAL	ATTRIBUTION	SOCIABILITY
TYPEWRITTEN	CACOGASTRIC	INCUNABULUM	RABELAISIAN	ATTRIBUTIVE	SPELLBINDER
DESEXUALIZE	CALEFACIENT	INESCAPABLE	RADIOACTIVE	AZOTOBACTER	STEINBERGER
INDEXLINKED	CAMARADERIE	INSEPARABLE	RAPSCALLION	BICARBONATE	STOCKBROKER

SUITABILITY	FABRICATION	PREDICTABLY	AGUARDIENTE	TRINIDADIAN	COUNSELLING
SVARABHAKTI	FESTSCHRIFT	PREOCCUPIED	APHRODISIAC	WELLADVISED	COUNTENANCE
TANGIBILITY	FINANCIALLY	PROFICIENCY	ARTIODACTYL	WITCHDOCTOR	COUNTERFEIT
TAUROBOLIUM	FORNICATION	PROLOCUTION	AVOIRDUPOIS	ABIOGENESIS	COUNTERFOIL
TECTIBRANCH	FORTHCOMING	PROSECUTION	BEWILDERING	ABIOGENETIC	COUNTERFORT
TEENYBOPPER	GESTICULATE	PROTOCOCCUS	CALENDERING	ACCELERATOR	COUNTERGLOW
TRINOBANTES	GYNAECOLOGY	PROVOCATION	CAMALDOLITE	ACQUIESCENT	COUNTERHAND
UNDOUBTEDLY	HALLUCINATE	PROVOCATIVE	CANDIDATURE	ACROCENTRIC	COUNTERMAND
VARIABILITY	HANDICAPPED	PUBLICATION	COMRADESHIP	ADULTERATED	COUNTERPANE
WASTEBASKET	HANDICAPPER	RADIOCARBON	CONFEDERACY	ALBIGENSIAN	COUNTERPART
WEIGHBRIDGE	HARDICANUTE	RATIOCINATE	CONFEDERATE	ANACREONTIC	COUNTERSIGN
WHEELBARROW	HIPPOCAMPUS	REPLACEABLE	CONFIDENTLY	ANAPLEROSIS	COUNTERSINK
WHITEBOYISM	HIPPOCRATES	REPLACEMENT	CONSIDERATE	ANAPLEROTIC	COURTEOUSLY
ACINACIFORM	HIPPOCRATIC	RESPECTABLE	CONSIDERING	ANENCEPHALY	CRACKERJACK
ADVANCEMENT	HONEYCOMBED	RESPECTABLY	CROCIDOLITE	ANNABERGITE	CRESCENTADE
AIRSICKNESS	HYDROCARBON	RESUSCITATE	CROCODILIAN	ANNIVERSARY	CROMWELLIAN
ALTERCATION	IMPEACHMENT	RETRACTABLE	CYLINDRICAL	ANTECEDENCE	CROOKEDNESS
AMERICANISM	IMPLICATION	SCHRECKLICH	DEGRADATION	ANTEPENDIUM	CYTOGENESIS
ANFRACTUOUS	IMPRACTICAL	SCOLECIFORM	DEPREDATION	ANTINEUTRON	DEFERENTIAL
ANISOCERCAL	IMPRECATION	SEASICKNESS	DIFFIDENTLY	ARCHAEOLOGY	DELETERIOUS
ANTHOCYANIN	IMPRECISION	SENNACHERIB	DRINKDRIVER	ARRIVEDERCI	DELINEATION
APPLICATION	INCARCERATE	SEPTICAEMIA	ELUCIDATION	BACKBENCHER	DELITESCENT
APPRECIABLE	INELUCTABLE	SERVICEABLE	EXCEEDINGLY	BALLBEARING	DELIVERANCE
APPRECIABLY	INSINCERITY	SHORTCHANGE	EXPENDITURE	BARYCENTRIC	DENUMERABLE
BANNOCKBURN	INSOUCIANCE	SHORTCOMING	EXTRADITION	BATTLEDRESS	DEPHLEGMATE
BEACHCOMBER	INTERCALARY	SPANGCOCKLE	FORBIDDANCE	BATTLEFIELD	DESELECTION
BERGSCHRUND	INTERCEPTOR	SPIROCHAETE	GRAVEDIGGER	BATTLEFRONT	DISCREPANCY
BIFURCATION	INTERCHANGE	STAIRCARPET	GROUNDSHEET	BATTLEMENTS	DISOBEDIENT
BREADCRUMBS	INTERCOSTAL	STENOCHROME	GROUNDSPEED	BESTSELLING	DISPLEASURE
BROADCASTER	INTERCOURSE	STRETCHABLE	GROUNDSWELL	BIOCHEMICAL	DISTRESSING
CAPRICCIOSO	INTRACTABLE	STRETCHLESS	HABERDASHER	BLADDERWORT	DOCUMENTARY
CARSICKNESS	INTRICATELY	SUFFICIENCY	IMPRUDENTLY	BLESSEDNESS	DOMINEERING
CHARACINOID	INVINCIBLES	SUFFOCATING	INCREDULITY	BLUNDERBORE	DOUBLECHECK
CLIMACTERIC	IPECACUANHA	SUFFOCATION	INCREDULOUS	BOOKKEEPING	DOUBLECROSS
CLINOCHLORE	ISOLECITHAL	SUGARCOATED	INGREDIENTS	BOOKSELLERS	DOWNHEARTED
COLLECTANEA	JINRICKSHAW	SUPERCHARGE	INTRADERMAL	BOURGEOISIE	DRUNKENNESS
COLLOCATION	LATROCINIUM	SUPERCHERIE	LEGERDEMAIN	BRANDENBURG	DRYCLEANERS
CONDUCTANCE	LATTICEWORK	SYNDICALISM	LIQUIDAMBAR	BROTHERHOOD	DRYCLEANING
CONDUCTRESS	LUBRICATION	SYNDICATION	LIQUIDATION	BUSINESSMAN	EARTHENWARE
CONJECTURAL	MASTICATION	TACHYCARDIA	METHODOLOGY	CANDLELIGHT	ECCALEOBION
CONNECTICUT	MATRICULATE	TAUTOCHRONE	OUAGADOUGOU	CANDLESTICK	EINSTEINIUM
CONSECUTIVE	MELANCHOLIA	TOBACCONIST	PERIODONTIC	CENTREBOARD	EMPOWERMENT
CONVOCATION	MELANCHOLIC	TORTICOLLIS	PETRODOLLAR	CENTREPIECE	ENGINEERING
CORRECTNESS	METRICATION	TORTICULLUS	PREJUDICIAL	CESAREWITCH	EPICHEIREMA
CRITICASTER	MOLLYCODDLE	TOSTICATION	PREMEDITATE	CHALLENGING	ERIODENDRON
DEFENCELESS	MONARCHICAL	TRANSCEIVER	PTERODACTYL	CHAMBERLAIN	ERRONEOUSLY
DEIFICATION	NOMENCLATOR	TURRICULATE	RECONDITION	CHAMBERMAID	EVANGELICAL
DEMARCATION	NORTHCLIFFE	UNCONCEALED	RETARDATION	CHANCELLERY	EVISCERATED
DESICCATION	OCHLOCRATIC	UNCONCERNED	REVENDICATE	CHANTERELLE	EXAGGERATED
DEUTSCHMARK	OLIGOCHAETE	UNDERCHARGE	SALVADORIAN	CHARGEPAYER	EXASPERATED
DIMERCAPROL	OMNISCIENCE	UNDERCOOKED	SCREWDRIVER	CHARLEMAGNE	EXOSKELETON
DIPHYCERCAL	ORTHOCENTRE	UNDISCLOSED	SECONDARILY	CHEESECLOTH	EXPONENTIAL
DISENCUMBER	OSTRACODERM	UNIFICATION	SECONDCLASS	CHICHEVACHE	FAIRWEATHER
DISINCLINED	PARTICIPANT	UNPRACTICAL	SERENDIPITY	CHICKENFEED	FARKLEBERRY
DISLOCATION	PARTICIPATE	UNSPECIFIED	SEXTODECIMO	CHIPPENDALE	FARTHERMOST
DIVORCEMENT	PARTICIPIAL	UNTOUCHABLE	SMOULDERING	CHITTERLING	FEHMGERICHT
DUPLICATING	PASSACAGLIA	UNWELCOMING	SPREADSHEET	CINQUECENTO	FIDDLEDEDEE
DUPLICATION	PENTECONTER	VERMICULITE	STRANDLOPER	CITIZENSHIP	FILAMENTOUS
EDIFICATION	PENTECOSTAL	VIDEOCAMERA	SUBORDINATE	CLANDESTINE	FLABBERGAST
EMBROCATION	PERSECUTION	VINDICATION	SUCCEDANEUM	CLAPPERCLAW	FLANKERBACK
EMPIECEMENT	PETTICOATED	WAINSCOTING	SUPPEDANEUM	CLIOMETRICS	FLANNELETTE
EMPLACEMENT	PHILOCTETES	WATERCOLOUR	TARRADIDDLE	COBBLESTONE	FLICKERTAIL
ENFORCEABLE	PHOTOCOPIER	WATERCOURSE	TETRADRACHM	COCKLESHELL	FLUORESCENT
ENFORCEMENT	PREDECESSOR	WHITECHAPEL	THALIDOMIDE	CONGRESSMAN	FORESEEABLE
ENHANCEMENT	PREDICAMENT	WHITECOLLAR	TORRIDONIAN	CONSTELLATE	FRAGMENTARY
ERADICATION	PREDICATIVE	ABECEDARIAN	TRANSDERMAL	CONSTERNATE	FURTHERANCE
EREMACAUSIS	PREDICTABLE	ACCORDINGLY	TREPIDATION	CONTRETEMPS	FURTHERMORE

FURTHERMOST	MAKEBELIEVE	RIDDLEMEREE	VIVISECTION	AGGREGATION	PROLEGOMENA
FURTHERSOME	MASQUERADER	RIGHTEOUSLY	WARMHEARTED	ANDROGENOUS	PROPAGATION
GAMOGENESIS	MEANDERINGS	RINTHEREOUT	WASHLEATHER	ANDROGYNOUS	PROROGATION
GASTRECTOMY	MECKLENBURG	RUDIMENTARY	WATEREDDOWN	ARCHEGONIAL	PROTAGONIST
GENTLEMANLY	METACENTRIC	SADDLEHORSE	WEATHERCOCK	ARCHEGONIUM	PYELOGRAPHY
GENTLEWOMAN	METAGENESIS	SCATTERGOOD	WELLBEHAVED	ARRANGEMENT	PYRARGYRITE
GIGGLESTICK	MIDDLEMARCH	SCATTERLING	WELLDEFINED	ASPERGILLUM	RADIOGRAPHY
GIGGLESWICK	MIDDLESIZED	SCUPPERNONG	WELLMEANING	ASPERGILLUS	REALIGNMENT
GIGGLEWATER	MILQUETOAST	SEDIMENTARY	WENSLEYDALE	BELEAGUERED	REFRIGERANT
GIRDLESTEAD	MISIDENTIFY	SELFDEFENCE	WHISKERANDO	BELLIGERENT	REFRIGERATE
GLADWELLISE	MISSPELLING	SELFRESPECT	WHITLEATHER	BESIEGEMENT	REGURGITATE
GLIMMERGOWK	MUSCHELKALK	SELFSERVICE	WINDLESTRAW	CALLIGRAPHY	SALVOGUNNER
GREASEPAINT	NEANDERTHAL	SHAFTESBURY	BLACKFELLOW	CARTOGRAPHY	SAUSAGEMEAT
HALFHEARTED	NEEDLEPOINT	SHEPHERDESS	CAMOUFLAGED	CERARGYRITE	SEGREGATION
HATCHETTITE	NEEDLESTICK	SINGLESTICK	CAULIFLOWER	CHIROGRAPHY	SPHRAGISTIC
HEPPLEWHITE	NEEDLEWOMAN	SLENDERNESS	CERTIFIABLE	CHOROGRAPHY	SPRINGBOARD
HEXADECIMAL	NEVERENDING	SLUMBERWEAR	CERTIFICATE	CONJUGATION	SPRINGCLEAN
HOBBLEDEHOY	NORTHEASTER	SMITHEREENS	COACHFELLOW	CONSIGNMENT	SPRINGHOUSE
HOMOGENEITY	NOTICEBOARD	SNICKERSNEE	CRESTFALLEN	CORRUGATION	SPRINGINESS
HOMOGENEOUS	NOVELETTISH	SNORKELLING	CRUCIFIXION	DEOXYGENATE	STENOGRAPHY
HOMOGENIZED	OBLITERATED	SOVEREIGNTY	DISAFFECTED	DERANGEMENT	STRANGENESS
HUCKLEBERRY	OBMUTESCENT	SPATTERDASH	ENFEOFFMENT	DISFIGURING	STRANGEWAYS
HUNDREDFOLD	OBSOLESCENT	SPATTERDOCK	FAULTFINDER	DISORGANIZE	STRANGULATE
HURTLEBERRY	OPTOMETRIST	STILBESTROL	FRANKFURTER	DISREGARDED	STRINGBOARD
HYPOTENSION	OVARIECTOMY	STRATEGICAL	GILLYFLOWER	DITTOGRAPHY	STRINGENTLY
INADVERTENT	OVERBEARING	STRIKEBOUND	GRANDFATHER	DYSLOGISTIC	STRINGYBARK
INALIENABLE	OVERLEARNED	SUDETENLAND	HALLEFLINTA	ENLARGEMENT	STRONGYLOID
INATTENTION	OVERWEENING	SUNDRENCHED	HOUSEFATHER	ESPIEGLERIE	SUBJUGATION
INATTENTIVE	OVERZEALOUS	SUPPRESSION	IMPERFORATE	ETHNOGRAPHY	SUBUNGULATA
INCALESCENT	PARACETAMOL	SWITZERLAND	INDIFFERENT	EXPURGATION	TACHYGRAPHY
INCINERATOR	PARALEIPSIS	SYMPLEGADES	JUSTIFIABLE	EXTROGENOUS	TOBOGGANING
INCOHERENCE	PARAMEDICAL	SYNTHESIZED	JUSTIFIABLY	FARRAGINOUS	TRITAGONIST
INDEPENDENT	PARANEPHROS	SYNTHESIZER	MAGNIFICENT	GALLIGANTUS	UNDERGROUND
INDIGESTION	PARTNERSHIP	TAXIDERMIST	MELLIFLUOUS	GREENGROCER	UNDERGROWTH
INEFFECTIVE	PEDETENTOUS	TÉLÉFÉRIQUE	PENNYFATHER	GRENZGANGER	UNDISGUISED
INEFFECTUAL	PENITENTIAL	TELOCENTRIC	PERCEFOREST	HAEMOGLOBIN	VARANGARIAN
INESSENTIAL	PENTHESILEA	THEATERGOER	PETTIFOGGER	HAGIOGRAPHA	VARIEGATION
INEXPEDIENT	PERDUELLION	THENCEFORTH	PHONOFIDDLE	HAGIOGRAPHY	VERBIGERATE
INEXPENSIVE	PERSPECTIVE	THEORETICAL	PHOTOFINISH	HOOLIGANISM	VERTIGINOUS
INFLUENTIAL	PHRASEOLOGY	THUNDERBIRD	PONTIFICATE	HYDROGENATE	VINAIGRETTE
INNUMERABLE	PIERREPOINT	THUNDERBOLT	PROLIFERATE	ICONOGRAPHY	ADIAPHORIST
INOFFENSIVE	POLICEWOMAN	THUNDERCLAP	RANGEFINDER	IMPREGNABLE	AMMOPHILOUS
INSUPERABLE	POLYTECHNIC	THUNDERHEAD	RASTAFARIAN	INCONGRUITY	ANESTHETIST
INTERESTING	PREMIERSHIP	TIDDLEYWINK	RECTIFIABLE	INCONGRUOUS	ANESTHETIZE
INTOLERABLE	PROCEEDINGS	TIMEKEEPING	ROCKEFELLER	INDULGENTLY	ANTECHAMBER
INTOLERABLY	PROCREATION	TIRONENSIAN	SACRIFICIAL	INFANGTHIEF	ANTIPHONARY
INTOLERANCE	PROGRESSION	TRACHEOTOMY	SCIREFACIAS	INSTIGATION	ANTIPHRASIS
IRREDENTIST	PROGRESSIVE	TROMPELOEIL	SCRUFFINESS	INTERGLOSSA	ARGATHELIAN
IRRELEVANCE	PROPHETICAL	TRUSTEESHIP	SIGNIFICANT	INTERGROWTH	ASSYTHEMENT
IRREVERENCE	PROSPECTIVE	TWELVEMONTH	STEADFASTLY	LARYNGISMUS	BLASPHEMOUS
ISOELECTRIC	PSYCHEDELIC	TYPESETTING	SUPERFICIAL	LENTIGINOSE	BREATHALYSE
JACQUEMINOT	PURPRESTURE	TYRONENSIAN	SUPERFICIES	LITHOGRAPHY	BUSHWHACKER
KIDDLEYWINK	QUADRENNIAL	UNALIENABLE	SUPERFLUITY	LIVINGSTONE	CACOPHONOUS
KINDHEARTED	QUADRENNIUM	UNALTERABLE	SUPERFLUOUS	MACROGAMETE	CATACHRESIS
KITCHENETTE	QUARRELLING	UNASSERTIVE	TIGHTFISTED	MICROGAMETE	CLIFFHANGER
LAPIDESCENT	QUARRELSOME	UNDESERVING	TOPLOFTICAL	MISBEGOTTEN	CRACKHALTER
LAUNDERETTE	QUARTERBACK	UNDEVELOPED	TRANSFERRED	MONONGAHELA	CYMOPHANOUS
LAWBREAKING	QUARTERDECK	UNENVELOPED	TRANSFERRIN	NARRAGANSET	DIARTHROSIS
LEATHERBACK	RATTLESNAKE	UNESSENTIAL	TRANSFIGURE	ORTHOGRAPHY	DICEPHALOUS
LEATHERETTE	RECOVERABLE	UNNECESSARY	TRANSFORMED	PALEOGRAPHY	DINNYHAUSER
LEATHERHEAD	REGIMENTALS	UNOBSERVANT	TRANSFORMER	PELARGONIUM	DINNYHAYSER
LEATHERNECK	REICHENBACH	UNREHEARSED	TRANSFUSION	PHOTOGRAPHY	DIORTHORTIC
LEATHERWOOD	REORIENTATE	UNRELENTING	UNCONFIRMED	PORNOGRAPHY	DRAUGHTSMAN
LOCORESTIVE	RESIDENTIAL	UNREPENTANT	UNFULFILLED	PREROGATIVE	ELEUTHERIAN
LUMINESCENT	RESPLENDENT	UNSCHEDULED	WHITEFRIARS	PRIMIGENIAL	EMPTYHANDED
MAINTENANCE	RETRIEVABLE	UNSWEETENED	WORLDFAMOUS	PRODIGALISE	ENARTHROSIS
MAISTERDOME	REVERENTIAL	UNUTTERABLE	ABRIDGEMENT	PRODIGALITY	ENCEPHALOMA

ENDOTHERMIC	SPEECHCRAFT	CAROLINGIAN	FARTHINGALE	JUDICIOUSLY	PROSAICALLY
ENKEPHALINE	STADTHOLDER	CAUSTICALLY	FEROCIOUSLY	KIMERIDGIAN	PSYCHIATRIC
ENLIGHTENED	STAKEHOLDER	CENTRIFUGAL	FIRELIGHTER	KINCHINMORT	PUNCHINELLO
ENNEAHEDRON	STALLHOLDER	CENTRIPETAL	FITZWILLIAM	KWASHIORKOR	PUNCTILIOUS
EOANTHROPUS	STOCKHAUSEN	CHANTICLEER	FLOURISHING	LABORIOUSLY	QUARRINGTON
EXANTHEMATA	STOCKHOLDER	CHILLINGHAM	FORAMINIFER	LACONICALLY	QUESTIONING
FORESHORTEN	STRAPHANGER	CHINOISERIE	FORTNIGHTLY	LAMPLIGHTER	REACTIONARY
FORETHOUGHT	STROPHILLUS	CHRONICALLY	FRANTICALLY	LATERIGRADE	RECRUITMENT
FREETHINKER	STRUTHIONES	CILOFIBRATE	FUNCTIONARY	LATERITIOUS	REFOCILLATE
FRENCHWOMAN	STYMPHALIAN	CIRRHIPEDEA	FUNCTIONING	LINGUISTICS	RELIGIOUSLY
FRENCHWOMEN	SWITCHBOARD	CIRRHIPEDIA	GENERICALLY	LOGARITHMIC	REMINISCENT
GRASSHOPPER	SYCOPHANTIC	COEFFICIENT	GENETICALLY	LONGSIGHTED	REPETITIOUS
HEALTHINESS	TELEPHONIST	COINCIDENCE	GENOUILLÈRE	LOUISIANIAN	REPUDIATION
HEAVYHANDED	TETRAHEDRON	COLONIALISM	GRAPHICALLY	LUXURIANTLY	RESTRICTION
HEMOPHILIAC	THOUGHTLESS	COLONIALIST	HABILIMENTS	LUXURIOUSLY	RESTRICTIVE
HOLOTHURIAN	TIMESHARING	COLORIMETER	HARDHITTING	MACHAIRODUS	RETALIATION
HOMOPHONOUS	TITLEHOLDER	COMPLICATED	HARPSICHORD	MALEDICTION	RETALIATORY
HOMOTHERMAL	TOXOPHILITE	COMPLIMENTS	HIGHLIGHTER	MALICIOUSLY	REVISIONISM
HOMOTHERMIC	TREACHEROUS	COMPRIMARIO	HIGHPITCHED	MANUMISSION	RIFACIMENTO
HOUSEHOLDER	TREACHETOUR	CONCEIVABLE	HILARIOUSLY	MATERIALISE	SAGACIOUSLY
HYPOTHECATE	TRENCHERMAN	CONCEIVABLY	HISTRIONICS	MATERIALISM	SALACIOUSLY
HYPOTHERMIA	UNAUTHENTIC	CONNOISSEUR	HUMILIATING	MATERIALIST	SANGUINEOUS
ILLYWHACKER	UNDERHANDED	CONSCIOUSLY	HUMILIATION	MATERIALIZE	SATIRICALLY
INAUTHENTIC	UNRIGHTEOUS	CONSPICUOUS	IDENTICALLY	MEDICINALLY	SCANDINAVIA
ITHYPHALLIC	UPRIGHTNESS	CONSPIRATOR	IDENTIFYING	MELODIOUSLY	SCEPTICALLY
ITHYPHALLUS	WESTPHALIAN	CONSTIPATED	IDIOTICALLY	MISCHIEVOUS	SCINTILLATE
JOSEPHINITE	WINDCHEATER	CONSTITUENT	IDYLLICALLY	MISERICORDE	SCYPHISTOMA
KALASHNIKOV	WRONGHEADED	CONTAINMENT	IGNOMINIOUS	MONCHIQUITE	SEIGNIORAGE
LEASEHOLDER	XEROPHILOUS	CONTRIBUTOR	ILLOGICALLY	MONOLINGUAL	SELAGINELLA
LECITHINASE	XEROTHERMIC	CONTRIVANCE	ILLUMINANCE	MOONLIGHTER	SESQUIOXIDE
LENGTHENING	ZWISCHENZUG	COORDINATED	ILLUMINATED	MUDSLINGING	SHITTIMWOOD
LENGTHINESS	ABORTIONIST	COORDINATES	ILLUSIONARY	MUNIFICENCE	SHOPLIFTING
LEVELHEADED	ACCIPITRINE	COXWAINLESS	ILLUSIONISM	MUNITIONIZE	SKEPTICALLY
LIGHTHEADED	ADJUDICATOR	CRÉMAILLÈRE	ILLUSIONIST	NEARSIGHTED	SKILLIGALEE
MASOCHISTIC	ADOPTIANISM	CURTAILMENT	IMMEDIATELY	NEGOTIATING	SKILLIGOLEE
MEGATHERIUM	ADOPTIONISM	DEBILITATED	IMPATIENTLY	NEGOTIATION	SKIMMINGTON
METAPHYSICS	AFFILIATION	DECAPITATED	IMPEDIMENTA	NIGHTINGALE	SPERMICIDAL
MISBEHAVIOR	AFFLIICTION	DEFOLIATION	IMPERIALISM	NONEXISTENT	STELLIONATE
MONOCHINOUS	ALBUGINEOUS	DELICIOUSLY	IMPERIALIST	NOTORIOUSLY	STRAMINEOUS
MONOCHROMAT	ALBUMINURIA	DENOMINATOR	IMPERIOUSLY	NUMERICALLY	SUPERIMPOSE
MONOTHELITE	ALLEVIATION	DERELICTION	INADVISABLE	OBSTRICTION	SUPERINTEND
MUNCHHAUSEN	AMERCIAMENT	DESCRIPTION	INDEFINABLE	OFFICIALDOM	SUPERIORITY
MYCOPHAGIST	AMONTILLADO	DESCRIPTIVE	INDIVISIBLE	OFFICIALESE	SURVEILLANT
NAPHTHALENE	APHANIPTERA	DETERIORATE	INDIVISIBLY	OFFICIOUSLY	SUSTAINABLE
NIKETHAMIDE	APOLLINARIS	DILAPIDATED	INDOMITABLE	ORGANICALLY	TECHNICALLY
NONETHELESS	ASSIMILATED	DISORIENTED	INDUBITABLE	ORGANIZAION	TEGUCICALPA
NOTOTHERIUM	ASSOCIATION	DISQUIETING	INDUBITABLY	OVERFISHING	TELEKINESIS
ORNITHOLOGY	ASTONISHING	DISTRIBUTED	INEBRIATION	PACIFICALLY	TENACIOUSLY
ORNITHOPTER	ATHERINIDAE	DISTRIBUTOR	INEFFICIENT	PAINKILLING	TERPSICHORE
OVERWHELMED	ATRABILIOUS	DOCTRINAIRE	INEQUITABLE	PARASITOSIS	TOTALIZATOR
PARACHUTIST	ATROCIOUSLY	DRASTICALLY	INESTIMABLE	PECULIARITY	TOURBILLION
PARISHIONER	AUDACIOUSLY	EFFICIENTLY	INEXCITABLE	PENICILLATE	TRAFFICATOR
PERIPHRASIS	BACKFIELDER	EMPIRICUTIC	INFERIORITY	PERSPICUITY	TRANSILIENT
PLOUGHSHARE	BANDEIRANTE	ENUNCIATION	INFURIATING	PERSPICUOUS	TRICHINELLA
PROSTHETICS	BEAUTIFULLY	EQUIDISTANT	INGENIOUSLY	PHILLIPSITE	TRICHINOSED
RAVISHINGLY	BEHAVIOURAL	EQUILIBRIST	INHABITABLE	PLANTIGRADE	TRIPHIBIOUS
RIGHTHANDED	BENEDICTINE	EQUILIBRIUM	INHABITANTS	PLEBEIANISE	ULOTRICHALE
RIGHTHANDER	BENEDICTION	ERRATICALLY	INHERITANCE	POLITICALLY	UNAMBIGUOUS
RUDESHEIMER	BENEFICIARY	EXORBITANCE	INJUDICIOUS	POLITICIANS	UNAVAILABLE
SAXOPHONIST	BENEFICIATE	EXPEDITIOUS	INSCRIPTION	PRACTICABLE	UNAVOIDABLE
SEARCHLIGHT	BOOKBINDING	EXPERIENCED	INSIDIOUSLY	PRACTICALLY	UNAVOIDABLY
SHAREHOLDER	BRILLIANTLY	FACETIOUSLY	INTOXICATED	PREEMINENCE	UNBEFITTING
SHEATHKNIFE	BROBDINGNAG	FACTFINDING	INTOXIMETER	PRESTIGIOUS	UNCHRISTIAN
SHORTHANDED	BULLFIGHTER	FAMILIARISE	INVIGILATOR	PRESTISSIMO	UNCIVILISED
SKETCHINESS	CAPACITANCE	FAMILIARITY	IRRADIATION	PRINCIPALLY	UNCIVILIZED
SLEUTHHOUND	CAPACITATOR	FAMILIARIZE	IRRELIGIOUS	PRISCIANIST	UNDESIRABLE
SMALLHOLDER	CARABINIERE	FANATICALLY	JAMAHIRIYAH	PROPRIETARY	UNEQUIVOCAL

UNINHIBITED	COAGULATION	INOCULATION	SOUNDLESSLY	CHAULMOOGRA	MARSHMALLOW
UNMITIGATED	COLDBLOODED	INSTALLMENT	SPECULATION	CHAULMOUGRA	MATHEMATICS
UNMOTIVATED	COMPILATION	INTELLIGENT	SPECULATIVE	CHILDMINDER	MATRIMONIAL
UNREMITTING	COMPILEMENT	INTERLACING	SPIFFLICATE	CHOIRMASTER	MEDIUMSIZED
UNSATISFIED	CONCILIATOR	INTERLEUKIN	STAGFLATION	CHRISMATION	MERRYMAKING
UNSHRINKING	CONDOLENCES	INTERLINGUA	STATELINESS	CIRCUMCISER	MISDEMEANOR
UNSOLICITED	CONSILIENCE	KNUCKLEBALL	STEEPLEJACK	CIRCUMFLECT	MODELMOLEST
VALEDICTION	CONSOLATION	LEGISLATION	STICKLEBACK	CIRCUMSPECT	MONEYMAKING
VALEDICTORY	CONSOLIDATE	LEGISLATIVE	STIMULATION	COMMEMORATE	NECROMANCER
VESUVIANITE	CONSULTANCY	LEGISLATURE	STIPULATION	CONCOMITANT	NIGHTMARISH
VICARIOUSLY	CONVALLARIA	LONGSLEEVED	SUBMULTIPLE	CONDOMINIUM	NUMISMATICS
VINCRISTINE	CONVOLUTION	MANGALSUTRA	SUPERLATIVE	CONSUMABLES	NUMISMATIST
VITAMINIZED	CONVOLVULUS	MANTELLETTA	TANTALIZING	CONSUMERISM	PANDEMONIUM
VIVACIOUSLY	CONVULSIONS	MANTELPIECE	TASTELESSLY	CONSUMPTION	PESSIMISTIC
VORACIOUSLY	CORRELATION	MANTELSHELF	TESSELLATED	CONSUMPTIVE	PETITMAITRE
VOTERIGGING	COURTLINESS	MAQUILADORA	THANKLESSLY	CONTAMINANT	PREDOMINANT
WESTMINSTER	CREDULOUSLY	MASCULINITY	THINGLINESS	CONTAMINATE	PREDOMINATE
WHITTINGTON	CRENELLATED	MASKALLONGE	THISTLEDOWN	CONTEMPLANT	PRELIMINARY
MALADJUSTED	CROSSLEGGED	MENDELEVIUM	TIGHTLIPPED	CONTEMPLATE	PRESUMPTION
STOCKJOBBER	DACTYLOGRAM	MENDELSSOHN	TITILLATION	COULOMMIERS	PRESUMPTIVE
EMBARKATION	DISABLEMENT	MERCILESSLY	TONSILLITIS	CUSTOMARILY	RAZZAMATAZZ
HOUSEKEEPER	DISBELIEVER	MISALLIANCE	TRACKLEMENT	DECLAMATION	REANIMATION
KINNIKINICK	DISCOLOURED	MISERLINESS	TRAGELAPHUS	DECLAMATORY	RECLAMATION
LANDSKNECHT	DISILLUSION	MONEYLENDER	TRANSLATION	DEFORMATION	RECRIMINATE
PEACEKEEPER	DISSOLUTION	MUSKELLUNGE	TRANSLUCENT	DETERMINANT	REFORMATION
SCHECKLATON	DITHELETISM	MYTHOLOGIZE	TRIBULATION	DETERMINATE	REFORMATORY
SCOREKEEPER	DRAGGLETAIL	NEUROLOGIST	TROUBLESOME	DETERMINING	RUMGUMPTION
STOREKEEPER	DREADLOCKED	NICKELODEON	TROUBLESPOT	DETRIMENTAL	SACRAMENTAL
TCHAIKOVSKY	EJACULATION	NOISELESSLY	TRUCULENTLY	DIPLOMATICS	SALTIMBANCO
UNSHAKEABLE	EMBELLISHED	ORDERLINESS	TURBELLARIA	DIPLOMATIST	SALTIMBOCCA
VOLKSKAMMER	ENFOULDERED	OSCILLATION	TYROGLYPHID	DIPSOMANIAC	SCAREMONGER
ACATALECTIC	ENGHALSKRUG	OVERFLOWING	UNEXPLAINED	DISARMAMENT	SCITAMINEAE
ACRIFLAVINE	ENTABLATURE	PALEOLITHIC	UNFAILINGLY	DISSEMINATE	SCOUTMASTER
ACTUALITIES	ENTABLEMENT	PAMPELMOOSE	UNGODLINESS	DISSIMULATE	SCREAMINGLY
AESCULAPIAN	ENTITLEMENT	PAMPELMOUSE	UNPUBLISHED	DRESSMAKING	SELFIMPOSED
AESCULAPIUS	EPANALEPSIS	PAMPHLETEER	UNQUALIFIED	EPOCHMAKING	SENTIMENTAL
AIGUILLETTE	ESTABLISHED	PANTALETTES	UNREALISTIC	ESCARMOUCHE	SHUNAMITISM
ANACOLUTHIA	ESTABLISHER	PARABLEPSIS	UNSHELTERED	ESTRAMAZONE	SILLIMANITE
ANTHOLOGIST	ETHNOLOGIST	PATHOLOGIST	UNWHOLESOME	EUPHEMISTIC	STREAMLINED
APOCALYPTIC	ETYMOLOGIST	PERCHLORATE	VACILLATING	EXCLAMATION	SUBDOMINANT
APPALLINGLY	FAULTLESSLY	PERCOLATION	VACILLATION	EXTERMINATE	SUBLIMATION
APPELLATION	FLORILEGIUM	PHILOLOGIST	VARIOLATION	FUNDAMENTAL	SUPERMARKET
APPELLATIVE	FORECLOSURE	PICKELHAUBE	VENTILATION	GALLIMAUFRY	SYSTEMATIZE
ARCHILOCHUS	FORMULATION	POINTLESSLY	WATERLOGGED	GELSEMININE	TERREMOTIVE
ARTILLERIST	FRANKLINITE	POMPELMOOSE	WHISTLESTOP	GERRYMANDER	TESTIMONIAL
BACKSLIDING	FRIVOLOUSLY	POMPELMOUSE	WOMANLINESS	GRANDMASTER	THROGMORTON
BADDELEYITE	FRUITLESSLY	PREPOLLENCE	WORLDLINESS	GRANDMOTHER	TOASTMASTER
BEASTLINESS	FULFILLMENT	PRICKLINESS	ABNORMALITY	GRAVIMETRIC	TRANSMITTED
BIMILLENARY	FULLBLOODED	PROSELYTISM	ACADEMICIAN	HEBDOMADARY	TRANSMITTER
BRISTLECONE	FUSTILARIAN	PROSELYTIZE	ACADEMICISM	HONEYMOONER	ULTRAMARINE
BRITTLENESS	GABERLUNZIE	QUERULOUSLY	ACCLAMATION	HOUSEMASTER	ULTRAMODERN
BRUCELLOSIS	GARRULOUSLY	RADIOLOGIST	ACCLIMATION	HOUSEMOTHER	UNANIMOUSLY
CABBALISTIC	GENEALOGIST	RECTILINEAR	ACCLIMATISE	HYDROMEDUSA	UNBLEMISHED
CALCULATING	GENUFLEXION	REDUPLICATE	ACCLIMATIZE	HYPERMARKET	UNCOMMITTED
CALCULATION	GHASTLINESS	RHOPALOCERA	ACCOMMODATE	IMPERMANENT	UNDERMANNED
CASTELLATED	GONFALONIER	SAINTLINESS	AFFIRMATION	IMPERMEABLE	UNTRAMELLED
CATACLYSMIC	GUADALCANAL	SAPROLEGNIA	AFFIRMATIVE	IMPLEMENTAL	VALLAMBROSA
CATALLACTIC	HANGGLIDING	SCOPOLAMINE	AGGLOMERATE	INCREMENTAL	VENDEMIAIRE
CATHOLICISM	HARIOLATION	SCUTTLEBUTT	ANAXIMANDER	INCRIMINATE	WATERMEADOW
CEASELESSLY	HEARTLESSLY	SHAMELESSLY	ANONYMOUSLY	INFLAMMABLE	ABOMINATION
CHEERLEADER	HECKELPHONE	SHAPELINESS	ASTIGMATISM	INFORMALITY	ACCOUNTABLE
CIRCULARIZE	HISTOLOGIST	SHINPLASTER	ATHERMANOUS	INFORMATICS	ACCOUNTANCY
CIRCULATING	HOHENLINDEN	SHOVELBOARD	BADTEMPERED	INFORMATION	ACUPUNCTURE
CIRCULATION	HOSTILITIES	SHUTTLECOCK	BLACKMAILER	INFORMATIVE	AFGHANISTAN
CIRCULATORY	HYMNOLOGIST	SINGULARITY	BROADMINDED	INTERMINGLE	ALCYONARIAN
CITLALEPETL	INDEXLINKED	SKIDBLADNIR	BURGOMASTER	JERRYMANDER	ALEXANDRINE
CLEANLINESS	INDUPLICATE	SOCIOLOGIST	CENTUMVIRUS	MAGLEMOSIAN	ALEXANDRITE

695

ALIFANFARON	DISCONTINUE	MAGNANIMOUS	RECONNOITER	BILLIONAIRE	KATABOTHRON
ALTERNATELY	DISHONESTLY	MALFUNCTION	RECONNOITRE	BOTANOMANCY	KATAVOTHRON
ALTERNATING	DISJUNCTION	MARCONIGRAM	RECTANGULAR	CALCEOLARIA	KETAVOTHRON
ALTERNATION	DISJUNCTIVE	MARGINALIST	RESIGNATION	CALIFORNIUM	KLEPTOMANIA
ALTERNATIVE	DISPENSABLE	MARGINALIZE	RESPONSIBLE	CAMEROONIAN	KOTABOTHRON
AMELANCHIER	DISTINCTION	MARIONBERRY	RESPONSIBLY	CAMPHORATED	LAMPROPHYRE
ANTHONOMOUS	DISTINCTIVE	MARIONETTES	RESPONSIONS	CARDIOGRAPH	LEPIDOPTERA
APPOINTMENT	DISTINGUISH	MEANINGLESS	ROTTENSTONE	CATEGORICAL	LEPIDOSIREN
APPRENTICED	DRACUNCULUS	MENTONNIÈRE	SALPINGITIS	CEREMONIOUS	LYCHNOSCOPE
ARCHENTERON	DRAGONNADES	MIDDENSTEAD	SARCENCHYME	CHEIROGNOMY	MALEVOLENCE
ARRHENOTOKY	DREADNOUGHT	MISCONSTRUE	SENTENTIOUS	CHIAROSCURO	MARLBOROUGH
ASSIGNATION	DYSFUNCTION	MOCKINGBIRD	SEPTENARIUS	CHLOROPHYLL	MEGALOMANIA
ASTRINGENCY	ELIMINATION	MODERNISTIC	SEPTENTRION	CHORDOPHONE	MEGALOMANIC
AURIGNACIAN	ENCHANTMENT	MORGENSTERN	SHENANIGANS	CHROMOPLAST	MEGALOPOLIS
BOUTONNIERE	ENCHANTRESS	NATIONALISM	SRANANTONGO	CHRONOMETER	MELANOCHROI
BOYSENBERRY	ENCHONDROMA	NATIONALIST	STEGANOGRAM	CHRYSOPRASE	MENTHOLATED
BUTTONQUAIL	ENFRANCHISE	NATIONALITY	STEGANOPODE	COMSTOCKERY	MERITORIOUS
CALLANETICS	EPAMINONDAS	NATIONALIZE	STIPENDIARY	CONTROVERSY	MILLIONAIRE
CAMPANOLOGY	EPIGENESIST	NATIONSTATE	SUBCONTRACT	CRITHOMANCY	MONTGOLFIER
CAPERNOITED	ERYMANTHIAN	NIACINAMIDE	SUBJUNCTIVE	DEMAGOGUERY	MONTMORENCY
CAPERNOITIE	ESTRANGHELO	NONSENSICAL	SUBPANATION	DEMONOMANIA	MYCOLOGICAL
CARMINATIVE	EXAMINATION	NOTHINGNESS	TABERNACLES	DEVELOPMENT	NATUROPATHY
CENTENARIAN	EXPLANATION	OBSTINATELY	TENDENTIOUS	DIAGNOSTICS	NUCLEOPLASM
CHOLINERGIC	EXPLANATORY	OFFHANDEDLY	TERMINATION	DIAPHORESIS	NYMPHOMANIA
CITRONELLAL	EXTERNALIZE	OPPIGNORATE	TERMINOLOGY	DIAPHORETIC	ODONTOBLAST
CLARENCIEUX	FASCINATING	ORIGINALITY	THEOPNEUSTY	DIASCORDIUM	ODONTOPHORE
COLLENCHYMA	FASCINATION	ORIGINATING	TREPONEMATA	DICHROMATIC	OMMATOPHORE
COMBINATION	FERRONNIÈRE	ORIGINATION	TRYPANOSOMA	DUMBFOUNDED	OMNIPOTENCE
COMMANDMENT	FESTINATELY	OUTMANEUVER	TRYPANOSOME	ELASTOPLAST	ONEIRODYNIA
COMMENDABLE	FISHANDCHIP	PARVANIMITY	TYRANNOSAUR	EMOTIONALLY	ONEIROMANCY
COMMENDABLY	FORTUNATELY	PATERNALISM	UNCONNECTED	EMPYROMANCY	ONTOLOGICAL
COMMENTATOR	FORTUNELOUD	PATERNOSTER	UNCOUNTABLE	ENVIRONMENT	OPINIONATED
COMMINATION	FULMINATION	PATRONISING	UNDIGNIFIED	EQUINOCTIAL	OSTREOPHAGE
COMMONPLACE	GENUINENESS	PATRONIZING	UNDRINKABLE	EQUIPOLLENT	PARABOLANUS
COMMONSENSE	GEOSYNCLINE	PENTONVILLE	UNFLINCHING	EQUIVOCALLY	PARADOXICAL
COMMUNALISM	GERMINATION	PERENNIALLY	UNFURNISHED	EUCHROMATIN	PARONOMASIA
COMMUNICANT	GORDONSTOUN	PERFUNCTORY	UNPRINTABLE	FASHIONABLE	PEDAGOGICAL
COMMUNICATE	GUBERNATION	PERMANENTLY	UNTHINKABLE	FASHIONABLY	PELOPONNESE
COMPENDIOUS	HEMIANOPSIA	PERSONALIST	UNVARNISHED	FAUXBOURDON	PENSIONABLE
COMPUNCTION	HERRINGBONE	PERSONALITY	VACCINATION	FISHMONGERS	PERIGORDIAN
CONCENTRATE	HIBERNATING	PERSONALIZE	VIOLINCELLO	FISSIONABLE	PERITONAEUM
CONFINEMENT	HIBERNATION	PERSONIFIED	VIOLONCELLO	FLAMBOYANCE	PERITONITIS
CONJUNCTION	HOLLANDAISE	PERTINACITY	VOLCANOLOGY	FLAMBOYANTE	PHYLLOCLADE
CONJUNCTURE	HOOTANANNIE	PERTINENTLY	VULCANOLOGY	FLUOROMETER	PHYSIOGNOMY
CONTENEMENT	HOOTENANNIE	PHALANSTERY	WAPPENSCHAW	FLUOROSCOPE	PICKYOUROWN
CONTENTEDLY	HUMMINGBIRD	PHARYNGITIS	WELLINGTONS	FOULMOUTHED	PIEDMONTITE
CONTENTIOUS	HUSBANDLAND	PHILANDERER	WILLINGNESS	GAMETOPHYTE	PINACOTHECA
CONTENTMENT	HYPHENATION	POLLENBRUSH	ABANDONMENT	GASTRONOMIC	PLAGIOSTOMI
CONTINENTAL	ILLMANNERED	POLLINATION	ACRIMONIOUS	GLASTONBURY	PLEUROTOMIA
CONTINGENCE	IMAGINATION	PRECONCEIVE	AILUROPHILE	GLOSSOLALIA	POLYMORPHIC
CONTINGENCY	IMAGINATIVE	PREMONITION	ALLEGORICAL	GNATHONICAL	POTAMOGETON
CONTINUALLY	IMPIGNORATE	PREMONITORY	ALLELOMORPH	GOODLOOKING	PRESTONPANS
CONTINUANCE	INCARNADINE	PRESENTABLE	ANAGNORISIS	GREENOCKITE	PSEUDOLOGIA
CONVENIENCE	INCARNATION	PRESENTMENT	ANASTOMOSIS	HALFHOLIDAY	PSEUDOMORPH
CONVENTICLE	INCLINATION	PRETENSIONS	ANGELOLATRY	HARDWORKING	PTOCHOCRACY
COTTONMOUTH	INDIGNANTLY	PRETENTIOUS	ANTONOMASIA	HEPATOSCOPY	RATATOUILLE
CREDENTIALS	INDIGNATION	PREVENTABLE	APLANOSPORE	HETEROGRAFT	REALPOLITIK
CRIMINOLOGY	INSTANTIATE	PROGENITRIX	APOLLONICON	HETEROSCIAN	RETINOSCOPY
CULMINATION	INSTINCTIVE	PROMINENTLY	APOSIOPESIS	HIGHPOWERED	RETINOSPORA
CYBERNETICS	INTERNALIZE	PROPINQUITY	ARISTOCRACY	HOMOEOPATHY	RHABDOMANCY
DARDANELLES	INTERNECINE	PROTONOTARY	ARTHRODESIS	HOMOIOUSIAN	RHAPSODICAL
DEGRINGOLER	INTERNUNCIO	PYTHONESQUE	ARTHROSPORE	HYPOCORISMA	RODOMONTADE
DESCENDANTS	LEGIONNAIRE	RALLENTANDO	AUXANOMETER	IDEOLOGICAL	SALINOMETER
DESIGNATION	LONGANIMITY	RAMGUNSHOCH	BARTHOLOMEW	INOPPORTUNE	SCAFFOLDING
DESPONDENCY	LONGINQUITY	RATIONALITY	BEAUMONTAGE	IRONMONGERS	SCARBOROUGH
DESTINATION	MACHINATION	RATIONALIZE	BENEVOLENCE	IRONMONGERY	SCLERODERMA
DIAMONDBACK	MAGNANIMITY	RECOGNITION	BIBLIOPHILE	IRREVOCABLE	SEISMOGRAPH

SELFCONTROL	COPROPHAGAN	TOWNSPEOPLE	COPPERPLATE	GATECRASHER	NIPFARTHING
SEXOLOGICAL	CORRUPTIBLE	TRANSPARENT	CORNERSTONE	GIBBERELLIN	NUMBERPLATE
SHALLOWNESS	CURNAPTIOUS	TRANSPONDER	CORPORATION	GINGERBREAD	OMNIPRESENT
SOCKDOLAGER	DECREPITATE	TRANSPORTED	COUNTRIFIED	GODFORSAKEN	OVERCROWDED
SOCKDOLIGER	DECREPITUDE	TRANSPORTER	COUNTRYSIDE	GREGARINIDA	OVERDRAUGHT
SOCKDOLOGER	DESERPIDINE	UNFLAPPABLE	CRATERELLUS	GUTTERSNIPE	OVERWROUGHT
SOLILOQUIZE	DISAPPROVAL	UNHAPPINESS	CULVERINEER	GUTTURALISE	PARACROSTIC
SPARROWHAWK	DISCIPLINED	UNSTOPPABLE	DANGEROUSLY	HAEMORRHAGE	PARATROOPER
SPEEDOMETER	DISIMPRISON	UNSUPPORTED	DECLARATION	HAEMORRHOID	PARTURITION
SPERMOPHILE	DISSEPIMENT	UNSURPASSED	DECLARATIVE	HAIRDRESSER	PAWNBROKERS
SPONSORSHIP	DISSIPATION	UNSUSPECTED	DEHYDRATION	HALFBROTHER	PENETRATING
STANDOFFISH	EPINEPHRINE	CONSEQUENCE	DEMOGRAPHIC	HAMMERCLOTH	PENETRATION
STEATOPYGIA	EXPROPRIATE	DELINQUENCY	DESECRATION	HANDCRAFTED	PEREGRINATE
STEREOGRAPH	EXTEMPORISE	INFREQUENCY	DESEGREGATE	HANDWRITING	PERFORATION
STEREOMETER	EXTEMPORIZE	UNCONQUERED	DESPERATELY	HANDWRITTEN	PERFORMANCE
STEREOSCOPE	EXTRAPOLATE	ADJOURNMENT	DESPERATION	HARDPRESSED	PHTHIRIASIS
STEREOTYPED	HAEMOPHILIA	ADUMBRATION	DEUTERONOMY	HAREBRAINED	PICTURESQUE
STETHOSCOPE	HOMEOPATHIC	AMOBARBITAL	DEVITRIFIED	HEMORRHOIDS	PLATERESQUE
STROBOSCOPE	HOUSEPARENT	ANACHRONISM	DIFFERENTLY	HIGHPROFILE	PLATYRRHINE
SUBTROPICAL	HYDROPHIDAE	ANSWERPHONE	DIPTEROCARP	HINDERLANDS	POLIORCETIC
SWALLOWABLE	HYDROPHOBIA	ANTIRRHINUM	DISAGREEING	HISTORIATED	POLTERGEIST
SYMPTOMATIC	HYDROPHOBIC	APOMORPHINE	DISCERNIBLE	HORSERACING	POLYTRICHUM
TEASPOONFUL	HYDROPONICS	APOSTROPHUS	DISCERNMENT	HORSERADISH	POMEGRANATE
TELEWORKING	IMPROPRIETY	APPEARANCES	DISPARAGING	HORSERIDING	PONDEROUSLY
TENSIOMETER	INCOMPETENT	APPLERINGIE	DISPERSABLE	IDEOPRAXIST	PORTERHOUSE
THALLOPHYTE	INCOMPOSITE	ARBITRAGEUR	DISSERTATOR	IDIOGRAPHIC	PREPARATION
THEOLOGICAL	INCORPORATE	ARBITRAMENT	DISTURBANCE	IMMIGRATION	PREPARATIVE
THERMOMETER	INCORPOREAL	ARBITRARILY	DOLABRIFORM	INCORRECTLY	PREPARATORY
THERMOPYLAE	INTEMPERATE	ARBITRATION	DOWNTRODDEN	INDIARUBBER	PRESTRESSED
THESMOTHETE	INTERPOLATE	AWKWARDNESS	DUSTWRAPPER	INOPERATIVE	PRETERITION
THIGMOTAXIS	INTERPRETER	BASKERVILLE	EASTERNMOST	INQUIRINGLY	PREVARICATE
TIMBROMANIA	INTREPIDITY	BELLEROPHON	ECTOTROPHIC	INSPIRATION	PROCUREMENT
TIMBROPHILY	ISTIOPHORUS	BESSARABIAN	ELABORATELY	INTEGRATION	PROOFREADER
TOXICOGENIC	LASERPICIUM	BIELORUSSIA	ELABORATION	INTERREGNUM	PROSTRATION
TREASONABLE	LICKSPITTLE	BITTERSWEET	ELECTRICIAN	INTERRELATE	PROTEROZOIC
TRICHOPTERA	LILLIPUTIAN	BOMBARDMENT	ELECTRICITY	INTERROGATE	PULCHRITUDE
TRINCOMALEE	LOUDSPEAKER	BORBORYGMUS	ELECTROCUTE	INTERRUPTER	RAPTUROUSLY
TRIPTOLEMUS	MANCIPATION	BUMBERSHOOT	ELECTROLIER	ISOMORPHOUS	REAPPRAISAL
TROPHOBLAST	OBTEMPERATE	CALIBRATION	ELECTROLYTE	JABBERWOCKY	RECIPROCATE
UNANNOUNCED	ORTHOPAEDIC	CARBORUNDUM	ELECTRONICS	KINDERSPIEL	RECIPROCITY
UNFAVORABLE	OSTEOPATHIC	CARBURETTOR	ELECTROTINT	KOMMERSBUCH	RECURRENTLY
UNIMPORTANT	OSTEOPLASTY	CATADROMOUS	EMBARRASSED	KULTURKREIS	REITERATION
WAREHOUSING	PANOMPHAEAN	CELEBRATION	ENCHIRIDION	LAMMERGEIER	REQUIREMENT
WELLFOUNDED	PARLIPOMENA	CENTERPIECE	ENCOURAGING	LAMMERGEYER	RESOURCEFUL
WISHTONWISH	PERCEPTIBLE	CENTURIATOR	ENDOTROPHIC	LECTURESHIP	RESPIRATION
WITHHOLDING	PERCEPTIBLY	CEREBRATION	ENUMERATION	LETTERPRESS	RESPIRATORY
XENODOCHIUM	PERCIPIENCE	CHONDROSTEI	ERYTHROCYTE	LITTÉRATEUR	RESTORATION
ABSORPTANCE	PHILIPPIANS	COLEORRHIZA	ESCHERICHIA	LOGGERHEADS	RESTORATIVE
ACCOMPANIST	PHILIPPINES	COLOURBLIND	EUCHARISTIC	LOGOGRAPHER	RETROROCKET
AGORAPHOBIA	PRECIPITATE	COMFORTABLE	EVAPORATION	MALAPROPISM	RINFORZANDO
AMYLOPECTIN	PRECIPITOUS	COMFORTABLY	EVENTRATION	MASTERFULLY	ROSICRUCIAN
ANADIPLOSIS	ROBESPIERRE	COMFORTLESS	EXONERATION	MASTERPIECE	ROTOGRAVURE
APPROPRIATE	SAINTPAULIA	COMPARATIVE	EXPLORATION	MEASURELESS	SACHERTORTE
ARCHIPELAGO	SALESPERSON	COMPARTMENT	EXPLORATORY	MEASUREMENT	SANDERSWOOD
ASCLEPIADES	SAPROPHYTIC	COMPTROLLER	FANFARONADE	MENSURATION	SAVOURINESS
ATMOSPHERIC	SARCOPHAGUS	CONCORDANCE	FAVOURITISM	METEOROLOGY	SCALPRIFORM
AXEROPHTHOL	SCEUOPHYLAX	CONCURRENCE	FEATURELESS	MICHURINISM	SCHWARMEREI
CALLIPYGEAN	SCOLOPENDRA	CONFARREATE	FINGERPRINT	MICTURITION	SEMITRAILER
CARDOPHAGUS	SCRUMPTIOUS	CONSERVANCY	FINGERSTALL	MISCARRIAGE	SHIPWRECKED
CARNAPTIOUS	SINGAPOREAN	CONSTRAINED	FIRECRACKER	MONOGRAMMED	SHOWERPROOF
CATCHPHRASE	STANDPATTER	CONSTRICTED	FORLORNNESS	MONOTREMATA	SILVERBERRY
CATERPILLAR	STOOLPIGEON	CONSTRICTOR	FOTHERGILLA	MONSTROSITY	SILVERPOINT
CHAIRPERSON	STYLOPODIUM	CONSTRUCTOR	FRATERNALLY	MOSSTROOPER	SILVERSMITH
CHIROPODIST	SUSCEPTIBLE	CONVERGENCE	FRONTRUNNER	MULTIRACIAL	STEAMROLLER
COLLAPSIBLE	SYNCOPATION	CONVERTIBLE	FRUSTRATING	MURMURATION	STEPBROTHER
COMEUPPANCE	THERAPEUTAE	COOPERATION	FRUSTRATION	NETHERLANDS	SUBMERGENCE
CONCEPTICLE	THERAPEUTIC	COOPERATIVE	GAMMERSTANG	NETHERLINGS	SUBSERVIENT

SUMMERHOUSE	BLOODSPORTS	KRIEGSSPIEL	SIGHTSCREEN	BELLETTRIST	ESCHATOLOGY
SUPPURATION	BLOODSTREAM	LABORSAVING	SIGHTSEEING	BELLYTIMBER	ESSENTIALLY
SURTARBRAND	BLOODSUCKER	LAWLESSNESS	SMITHSONIAN	BICENTENARY	EURHYTHMICS
SURTURBRAND	BODHISATTVA	LINDISFARNE	SMITHSONITE	BREASTPLATE	EXCEPTIONAL
SUSURRATION	BUPRESTIDAE	LOOSESTRIFE	SMOKESCREEN	CALLITRICHE	EXECUTIONER
SYNCHROMESH	CALLISTEMON	MACROSCOPIC	SOLIPSISTIC	CASSITERITE	EXHORTATION
SYNCHRONISE	CAMPESTRIAN	MEDIASTINUM	SPACESAVING	CATASTROPHE	EXPECTANTLY
SYNCHRONISM	CANDESCENCE	MICROSCOPIC	SPOKESWOMAN	CHIASTOLITE	EXPECTATION
SYNCHRONIZE	CHARISMATIC	MICROSECOND	SPORTSFIELD	CHRISTENING	EXPECTORANT
SYNCHRONOUS	CHOLESTEROL	MINNESINGER	SPORTSWOMAN	CHRISTMASSY	EXPECTORATE
TATTERSALLS	CLADOSPORUM	MISSISSIPPI	STATISTICAL	CHRISTOPHER	EXPOSTULATE
TELEGRAPHER	CLAIRSCHACH	MONOPSONIST	STYLISHNESS	CLIMATOLOGY	EXTORTIONER
TELEGRAPHIC	CLEANSHAVEN	MONTESQUIEU	SUBSISTENCE	COHORTATIVE	EYECATCHING
TELEPRINTER	COALESCENCE	MULTISTOREY	SUGGESTIBLE	COMESTIBLES	FACULTATIVE
TEMPERAMENT	COEXISTENCE	NECESSARILY	SUPERSCRIBE	COMMUTATION	FERNITICKLE
TEMPERATURE	COGNOSCENTE	NECESSITATE	SUPERSCRIPT	COMPETENTLY	FOMENTATION
TEMPORARILY	COGNOSCENTI	NECESSITOUS	SUPERSEDEAS	COMPETITION	FORESTATION
TENTERHOOKS	COMBUSTIBLE	NONDESCRIPT	SUPERSEDERE	COMPETITIVE	FRIGATEBIRD
TESSARAGLOT	COMMISERATE	NOURISHMENT	SUPPOSITION	COMPOTATION	FRIGHTENING
THEATREGOER	COMPOSITION	OBSESSIVELY	SUPPOSITORY	COMPUTATION	FRIGHTFULLY
THEATRICALS	CONCISENESS	OFFENSIVELY	SWORDSWOMAN	COMPUTERIZE	GEOMETRICAL
THEOBROMINE	CONSISTENCE	ONOMASTICON	SYMPOSIARCH	CONDITIONAL	GERONTOLOGY
TOPOGRAPHER	CONSISTENCY	OPALESCENCE	TEMPESTUOUS	CONDITIONER	GESTATORIAL
TREECREEPER	COPROSTEROL	ORCHESTRATE	TERRESTRIAL	CONDOTTIERE	GRAVITATION
TRICERATOPS	CREPUSCULAR	ORCHESTRINA	TRACASSERIE	CONDOTTIORE	GUESSTIMATE
TSCHERNOSEM	CYCLOSTYLED	ORCHESTRION	TRIMESTRIAL	CONFUTATION	HALBSTARKER
TYPEWRITTEN	DECONSTRUCT	OUTDISTANCE	TROPOSPHERE	CONNOTATION	HAUGHTINESS
TYPOGRAPHER	DEFENSELESS	PEEVISHNESS	UNCONSCIOUS	CORINTHIANS	HERPETOLOGY
TYPOGRAPHIC	DEFENSIVELY	PERISSOLOGY	UNCRUSHABLE	CREMATORIUM	HOSPITALITY
UNEXPRESSED	DEMONSTRATE	PERLUSTRATE	UNDERSIGNED	CREPITATION	HOSPITALIZE
UNIMPRESSED	DIATESSARON	PERMISSIBLE	UNDERSTATED	DECEITFULLY	HOSPITALLER
UNIVERSALLY	DIATESSERON	PERSISTENCE	UNREASONING	DECEPTIVELY	HUCKSTERAGE
UNOBTRUSIVE	DIMENSIONAL	PHARISAICAL	UPHOLSTERER	DECORTICATE	HYPERTROPHY
UNPATRIOTIC	DISPOSITION	PHILOSOPHER	USELESSNESS	DEERSTALKER	ILLUSTRATOR
UNWARRANTED	DISTASTEFUL	PHOTOSPHERE	VALLISNERIA	DEGLUTINATE	ILLUSTRIOUS
VASOPRESSIN	EARNESTNESS	PISSASPHALT	VICHYSOISSE	DEGLUTITION	IMMORTALISE
VENTURESOME	EARTHSHAKER	POSSESSIONS	VICISSITUDE	DEHORTATIVE	IMMORTALITY
VESPERTINAL	EGOTISTICAL	PREDESTINED	WATERSKIING	DELECTATION	IMMORTALIZE
VOORTREKKER	ENCAPSULATE	PREHISTORIC	WATERSPLASH	DELICTATION	IMPARTIALLY
WASHERWOMAN	ENDORSEMENT	PREPOSITION	ZOROASTRIAN	DEMOSTHENES	IMPERTINENT
WAYWARDNESS	EXCESSIVELY	PROFESSEDLY	ABLACTATION	DEMOSTHENIC	IMPORTANTLY
WELLDRESSED	EXCLUSIVELY	PROFUSENESS	ABSENTEEISM	DEPARTEMENT	IMPORTATION
WESTERNMOST	EXCRESCENCE	PROMISCUITY	ACCULTURATE	DEPORTATION	IMPORTUNATE
WIENERWURST	EXQUISITELY	PROMISCUOUS	ADVENTURESS	DERMATOLOGY	INCANTATION
WILBERFORCE	EXTENSIVELY	PROPOSITION	ADVENTUROUS	DESTITUTION	INCONTINENT
WINDBREAKER	FOOLISHNESS	PROVISIONAL	ADVERTISING	DETESTATION	INDENTATION
WINTERBERRY	FURNISHINGS	PROVISIONER	AFFECTATION	DEVASTATING	INDUSTRIOUS
WINTERGREEN	GARNISHMENT	PUBLISHABLE	AGGLUTINANT	DEVASTATION	INFANTICIDE
WITHERSHINS	GEGENSCHEIN	PURPOSELESS	AGGLUTINATE	DICTATORIAL	INFANTRYMAN
WONDERFULLY	GLUCOSAMINE	QUICKSILVER	AGNOSTICISM	DIPROTODONT	INFERTILITY
XEROTRIPSIS	HOGGISHNESS	RAFFISHNESS	AGONOTHETES	DIRECTIONAL	INFESTATION
XYLOGRAPHER	HONEYSUCKLE	RECESSIONAL	AGROSTOLOGY	DIRECTORATE	INFILTRATOR
ACCESSORIES	HYDROSTATIC	RECONSTRUCT	AMPHETAMINE	DISCOTHEQUE	INGRATITUDE
ACCRESCENCE	ICONOSTASIS	REFRESHMENT	ANAESTHESIA	DISENTANGLE	INSECTICIDE
ACQUISITION	IMPASSIONED	RELEASEMENT	ANAESTHETIC	DISINTEREST	INSECTIVORE
ACQUISITIVE	IMPASSIVELY	REMONSTRATE	ANTISTHENES	DISPUTATION	INSISTENTLY
ADOLESCENCE	IMPERSONATE	REMORSELESS	ANTISTROPHE	DOMESTICATE	INSTITUTION
AFTERSCHOOL	IMPULSIVELY	RENAISSANCE	APODYTERIUM	DOMESTICITY	INSULTINGLY
AMPHISBAENA	INCAPSULATE	REPRESENTED	APPURTENANT	DYAESTHESIA	INTENTIONAL
AMPHISBOENA	INCESSANTLY	REQUISITION	ARGENTINIAN	EDUCATIONAL	INTUITIVELY
ANTHESTERIA	INCONSTANCY	ROGUISHNESS	ASPHETERISM	EFFECTIVELY	INVESTIGATE
APATOSAURUS	INQUISITION	RUMBUSTIOUS	ATTENTIVELY	EFFECTUALLY	INVESTITURE
APPEASEMENT	INQUISITIVE	SCRIMSHANDY	ATTESTATION	EGALITARIAN	JACTITATION
ASPERSORIUM	INSENSITIVE	SELFISHNESS	AUGUSTINIAN	EMBOÎTEMENT	LAMENTATION
ASSASSINATE	INTENSIVELY	SEPIOSTAIRE	BALISTRARIA	EMMENTHALER	LIBERTARIAN
BARBASTELLE	INTERSPERSE	SEQUESTRATE	BARBITURATE	EMPHYTEUSIS	LYCANTHROPE
BATHYSPHERE	IRIDESCENCE	SHAKESPEARE	BARNSTORMER	ENTERTAINER	LYCANTHROPY

MAGISTERIAL	RESENTFULLY	WALDSTERBEN	MANIPULATOR	APPROVINGLY	PAPERWEIGHT
MAGISTRATES	RESISTIVITY	WHITETHROAT	MISTRUSTFUL	ATHARVAVEDA	PINNYWINKLE
MARKETPLACE	RESTATEMENT	WORKSTATION	MOISTURIZER	AUDIOVISUAL	PRIZEWINNER
MAURETANIAN	RESTITUTION	WORRYTROUGH	MONONUCLEAR	BEREAVEMENT	RIGHTWINGER
MAURITANIAN	ROMANTICISM	ACCUMULATOR	MOXIBUSTION	CAPTIVATING	SLEEPWALKER
MEKHITARIST	ROMANTICIZE	ACOLOUTHITE	NERVOUSNESS	CAPTIVATION	SORROWFULLY
MICROTUBULE	SABBATARIAN	AGRICULTURE	OBSTRUCTION	CARNIVOROUS	SOUTHWESTER
MINIATURIST	SAGITTARIUS	ANTIBURGHER	OBSTRUCTIVE	CLAIRVOYANT	TIGGYWINKLE
MINIATURIZE	SCHISTOSOMA	ANTIQUARIAN	OBVIOUSNESS	CRACOVIENNE	TRUSTWORTHY
MINISTERIAL	SCHISTOSOME	APONEUROSIS	OUTPOURINGS	CULTIVATION	UNDERWEIGHT
MINISTERING	SCHOTTISCHE	ARTICULATED	OVERTURNING	DEPRIVATION	UNDERWRITER
MISANTHROPE	SCIENTOLOGY	ASSIDUOUSLY	PASTEURELLA	DISHEVELLED	WHEELWRIGHT
MISANTHROPY	SCRIPTORIUM	ATTENUATION	PASTOURELLE	ENSLAVEMENT	WHEREWITHAL
MOLESTATION	SECRETARIAL	AVERRUNCATE	PLAYFULNESS	EVASIVENESS	WINDOWFRAME
MOMENTARILY	SECRETARIAT	BASHFULNESS	PLEASURABLE	EXTRAVAGANT	WINDOWLEDGE
NAUGHTINESS	SECRETIVELY	BELORUSSIAN	POCOCURANTE	EXTROVERTED	YELLOWPLUSH
NIERSTEINER	SELECTIVELY	BILIOUSNESS	PRECAUTIONS	FORGIVENESS	YELLOWSTONE
NUTRITIONAL	SELECTIVITY	BLANKURSINE	PRESSURIZED	FRUGIVOROUS	AMPLEXICAUL
OBJECTIVELY	SEMPITERNAL	BUREAUCRACY	PROCRUSTEAN	FURTIVENESS	APPROXIMATE
OBJECTIVITY	SEMPITERNUM	CALLOUSNESS	PUNCTUALITY	GALLOVIDIAN	OVEREXPOSED
OBSTETRICAL	SENSATIONAL	CAREFULNESS	PUNCTUATION	HERBIVOROUS	REFLEXOLOGY
OCTASTICHON	SENSITIVELY	CONSTUPRATE	QUADRUPLETS	IMPROVEMENT	AERODYNAMIC
OPERATIONAL	SENSITIVITY	DESEXUALIZE	QUINTUPLETS	IMPROVIDENT	ANAPHYLAXIS
OPPORTUNELY	SEVENTEENTH	DESTRUCTION	RAUCOUSNESS	INTERVENING	ANTICYCLONE
OPPORTUNISM	SINISTRORSE	DESTRUCTIVE	REASSURANCE	INTERVIEWEE	ANTIPYRETIC
OPPORTUNIST	SLIGHTINGLY	DEVALUATION	RESTRUCTURE	INTERVIEWER	APOPHYLLITE
OPPORTUNITY	SOROPTIMIST	DEVIOUSNESS	REVALUATION	INTRAVENOUS	DICOTYLEDON
ORIENTALISM	SPENDTHRIFT	DISCOURTESY	REVOLUTIONS	INTROVERTED	EPITHYMETIC
ORIENTALIST	SPIRITUALLY	DISGRUNTLED	RIBONUCLEIC	INVOLVEMENT	EUCALYPTOLE
ORIENTATION	SPITSTICKER	DISTRUSTFUL	RUMFRUCTION	MANEUVERING	ICHTHYOLITE
OSTENTATION	SPLUTTERING	DOUROUCOULI	SCULDUDDERY	MASSIVENESS	ICHTHYORNIS
OVERSTUFFED	STOCKTAKING	DUBIOUSNESS	SCULDUGGERY	MICROVILLUS	LUXULYANITE
PAEDOTROPHY	STORYTELLER	EVENTUALITY	SERICULTURE	OBSERVATION	OXYRHYNCHUS
PAINSTAKING	STRAITLACED	EXTENUATING	SERIOUSNESS	OBSERVATORY	PARATYPHOID
PALESTINIAN	STREETLIGHT	EXTENUATION	SHIPBUILDER	PASSIVENESS	POLYHYDROXY
PARENTHESIS	SUPERTANKER	FATUOUSNESS	SHOWJUMPING	PENSIVENESS	PROPHYLAXIS
PEDESTRIANS	SYMMETRICAL	FLAVOURSOME	SKULDUDDERY	PENTAVALENT	SPONDYLITIS
PENTATHLETE	SYMPATHETIC	FLUCTUATING	SKULDUGGERY	PERSEVERING	HAPHAZARDLY
PENULTIMATE	SYMPATHISER	FLUCTUATION	SLUMGULLION	RESERVATION	IDOLIZATION
PERESTROIKA	SYMPATHIZER	FORFOUGHTEN	SPONDULICKS	RESTIVENESS	OXODIZATION
PERISTALITH	TEETOTALLER	FRAUDULENCE	STRADUARIUS	SANSEVIERIA	REALIZATION
PERISTALSIS	TENTATIVELY	GODDAUGHTER	STRENUOUSLY	SELFEVIDENT	STYLIZATION
PERMUTATION	TERRITORIAL	HELPFULNESS	SUMPTUOUSLY	SUBDIVISION	UTILIZATION
PERPETRATOR	THANATOPSIS	HIDEOUSNESS	SURROUNDING	SUPERVISION	**11:7**
PERPETUALLY	THREATENING	HIGHQUALITY	TACITURNITY	SUPERVISORY	ABECEDARIAN
PHILATELIST	THRIFTINESS	HUMGRUFFIAN	TEDIOUSNESS	TRANSVERSAL	ABLACTATION
PHONETICIAN	THYROTROPIN	IMPECUNIOUS	TENUOUSNESS	TRIUMVIRATE	ABNORMALITY
PISCATORIAL	TRADITIONAL	IMPETUOSITY	THINGUMAJIG	ULTRAVIOLET	ABOMINATION
PLANETARIUM	TRINITARIAN	IMPETUOUSLY	THOROUGHPIN	UNCONVERTED	ACCLAMATION
PLEISTOCENE	UNCASTRATED	IMPLAUSIBLE	TRANQUILITY	UNCONVINCED	ACCLIMATION
POLYSTYRENE	UNCERTAINTY	INEXCUSABLE	TRANSURANIC	UNDERVALUED	ACCLIMATISE
POTENTIALLY	UNCLUTTERED	INEXCUSABLY	UNENDURABLE	VARSOVIENNE	ACCLIMATIZE
PREMATURELY	UNCONTESTED	INFATUATION	UNNATURALLY	ACKNOWLEDGE	ACCOMPANIST
PROBATIONER	UNCOUTHNESS	INSCRUTABLE	UNSATURATED	BLAMEWORTHY	ACRIFLAVINE
PROFITEROLE	UNDERTAKING	INSINUATING	UNUNQUADIUM	BREADWINNER	ADOPTIANISM
PROLETARIAN	UNDISTURBED	INSINUATION	UTRICULARIA	DUNIEWASSAL	ADUMBRATION
PROLETARIAT	UNEMOTIONAL	INSTRUCTION	VACUOUSNESS	FIELDWORKER	AESCULAPIAN
PROMOTIONAL	UNFORTUNATE	INSTRUCTIVE	VICIOUSNESS	GALLOWGLASS	AESCULAPIUS
PROMPTITUDE	UNINITIATED	INSTRUMENTS	VISCOUNTESS	HEAVYWEIGHT	AFFECTATION
QUALITATIVE	UNJUSTIFIED	INVOLUNTARY	WAKEFULNESS	HORNSWOGGLE	AFFILIATION
RECANTATION	UNPERTURBED	IRREDUCIBLE	WHITSUNTIDE	LEADSWINGER	AFFIRMATION
RECEPTIVITY	UNPROTECTED	IRREFUTABLE	WINDSURFING	LIGHTWEIGHT	AFFIRMATIVE
REGISTERING	UNWITTINGLY	IRREGULARLY	WISTFULNESS	LONGAWAITED	AGGRAVATING
REGRETFULLY	UTILITARIAN	ISOXSUPRINE	ABBREVIATED	MEADOWSWEET	AGGRAVATION
REGRETTABLE	VERSATILITY	LATIFUNDIUM	ACHIEVEMENT	METALWORKER	AGGREGATION
REGRETTABLY	VOLUNTARILY	LEFTLUGGAGE	AGGRAVATING	MINESWEEPER	ALCYONARIAN
RELUCTANTLY	VOLUNTARISM	LONGRUNNING	AGGRAVATION	NORTHWESTER	ALLEVIATION

ALTERCATION	COMBINATION	DISENTANGLE	FLUCTUATION	IMMORTALIZE	MATERIALIST
ALTERNATELY	COMMINATION	DISLOCATION	FOMENTATION	IMPERIALISM	MATERIALIZE
ALTERNATING	COMMUNALISM	DISORGANIZE	FORESTATION	IMPERIALIST	MATHEMATICS
ALTERNATION	COMMUTATION	DISPARAGING	FORMULATION	IMPERMANENT	MAURETANIAN
ALTERNATIVE	COMPARATIVE	DISPLEASURE	FORNICATION	IMPLICATION	MAURITANIAN
AMERCIAMENT	COMPILATION	DISPUTATION	FORTUNATELY	IMPORTANTLY	MEKHITARIST
AMERICANISM	COMPOTATION	DISREGARDED	FRUSTRATING	IMPORTATION	MENSURATION
AMPHETAMINE	COMPUTATION	DISSIPATION	FRUSTRATION	IMPRECATION	MEPROBAMATE
ANAXIMANDER	CONFUTATION	DOWNHEARTED	FULMINATION	INCANTATION	MERRYMAKING
ANTECHAMBER	CONJUGATION	DRESSMAKING	FUSTILARIAN	INCARNADINE	METRICATION
ANTIQUARIAN	CONNOTATION	DRYCLEANERS	GALLIBAGGER	INCARNATION	MICROGAMETE
APATOSAURUS	CONSOLATION	DRYCLEANING	GALLIGANTUS	INCESSANTLY	MISBEHAVIOR
APPEARANCES	CONSTRAINED	DUNIEWASSAL	GALLIMAUFRY	INCLINATION	MOLESTATION
APPELLATION	CONSUMABLES	DUPLICATING	GALLYBAGGER	INDENTATION	MOMENTARILY
APPELLATIVE	CONURBATION	DUPLICATION	GATECRASHER	INDIGNANTLY	MONEYMAKING
APPLICATION	CONVOCATION	DUSTWRAPPER	GERMINATION	INDIGNATION	MONOGRAMMED
APPROBATION	COOPERATION	EDIFICATION	GERRYMANDER	INEBRIATION	MONONGAHELA
ARBITRAGEUR	COOPERATIVE	EJACULATION	GLUCOSAMINE	INFATUATION	MULTIRACIAL
ARBITRAMENT	CORPORATION	ELABORATELY	GRANDFATHER	INFESTATION	MUNCHHAUSEN
ARBITRARILY	CORRELATION	ELABORATION	GRANDMASTER	INFORMALITY	MURMURATION
ARBITRATION	CORRUGATION	ELIMINATION	GRAVITATION	INFORMATICS	MYCOPHAGIST
ARTIODACTYL	CRACKHALTER	ELUCIDATION	GRENZGANGER	INFORMATION	NAPHTHALENE
ASSIGNATION	CREPITATION	EMBARKATION	GUBERNATION	INFORMATIVE	NARRAGANSET
ASSOCIATION	CRESTFALLEN	EMBARRASSED	GUTTURALISE	INFURIATING	NATIONALISM
ASTIGMATISM	CRITICASTER	EMBROCATION	HABERDASHER	INOCULATION	NATIONALIST
ATHARVAVEDA	CULMINATION	EMPTYHANDED	HALBSTARKER	INOPERATIVE	NATIONALITY
ATHERMANOUS	CULTIVATION	ENCEPHALOMA	HALFHEARTED	INSINUATING	NATIONALIZE
ATTENUATION	CUSTOMARILY	ENCOURAGING	HANDCRAFTED	INSINUATION	NECESSARILY
ATTESTATION	CYMOPHANOUS	ENKEPHALINE	HANDICAPPED	INSPIRATION	NECROMANCER
AURIGNACIAN	DECLAMATION	ENTABLATURE	HANDICAPPER	INSTIGATION	NEGOTIATING
AZOTOBACTER	DECLAMATORY	ENTERTAINER	HAPHAZARDLY	INTEGRATION	NEGOTIATION
BALLBEARING	DECLARATION	ENUMERATION	HARDICANUTE	INTERCALARY	NIACINAMIDE
BESSARABIAN	DECLARATIVE	ENUNCIATION	HAREBRAINED	INTERLACING	NIGHTMARISH
BIFURCATION	DEERSTALKER	EPOCHMAKING	HARIOLATION	INTERNALIZE	NIKETHAMIDE
BLACKMAILER	DEFOLIATION	ERADICATION	HEAVYHANDED	INTRICATELY	NORTHEASTER
BODHISATTVA	DEFORMATION	EREMACAUSIS	HEBDOMADARY	IRRADIATION	NUMISMATICS
BREATHALYSE	DEGRADATION	ESTRAMAZONE	HIBERNATING	ITHYPHALLIC	NUMISMATIST
BRILLIANTLY	DEHORTATIVE	EVAPORATION	HIBERNATION	ITHYPHALLUS	OBSERVATION
BROADCASTER	DEHYDRATION	EVENTRATION	HIGHQUALITY	JACTITATION	OBSERVATORY
BURGOMASTER	DEIFICATION	EVENTUALITY	HIPPOCAMPUS	JERRYMANDER	OBSTINATELY
BUSHWHACKER	DELECTATION	EXAMINATION	HOMEOPATHIC	KINDHEARTED	OFFICIALDOM
CALCULATING	DELICTATION	EXCLAMATION	HOOLIGANISM	LABORSAVING	OFFICIALESE
CALCULATION	DELINEATION	EXHORTATION	HOOTANANNIE	LAMENTATION	ORIENTALISM
CALIBRATION	DEMARCATION	EXONERATION	HOOTENANNIE	LAWBREAKING	ORIENTALIST
CANDIDATURE	DEMOGRAPHIC	EXPECTANTLY	HORSERACING	LEGISLATION	ORIENTATION
CANNIBALISM	DEPORTATION	EXPECTATION	HORSERADISH	LEGISLATIVE	ORIGINALITY
CANNIBALIZE	DEPREDATION	EXPLANATION	HOSPITALITY	LEGISLATURE	ORIGINATING
CAPTIVATING	DEPRIVATION	EXPLANATORY	HOSPITALIZE	LIBERTARIAN	ORIGINATION
CAPTIVATION	DESECRATION	EXPLORATION	HOSPITALLER	LIQUIDAMBAR	ORTHOPAEDIC
CARMINATIVE	DESEXUALIZE	EXPLORATORY	HOUSEFATHER	LIQUIDATION	OSCILLATION
CATALLACTIC	DESICCATION	EXPURGATION	HOUSEMASTER	LITTÉRATEUR	OSTENTATION
CELEBRATION	DESIGNATION	EXTENUATING	HOUSEPARENT	LOGOGRAPHER	OSTEOPATHIC
CENTENARIAN	DESPERATELY	EXTENUATION	HUMILIATING	LONGAWAITED	OVERBEARING
CEREBRATION	DESPERATION	EXTERNALIZE	HUMILIATION	LOUISIANIAN	OVERDRAUGHT
CHOIRMASTER	DESTINATION	EXTRAVAGANT	HYDROCARBON	LUBRICATION	OVERLEARNED
CHRISMATION	DETESTATION	FABRICATION	HYPERMARKET	LUXULYANITE	OVERZEALOUS
CIRCULARIZE	DEVALUATION	FACULTATIVE	HYPHENATION	LUXURIANTLY	OXODIZATION
CIRCULATING	DEVASTATING	FAIRWEATHER	IDEOPRAXIST	MACHINATION	PAINSTAKING
CIRCULATION	DEVASTATION	FAMILIARISE	IDIOGRAPHIC	MACROGAMETE	PASSACAGLIA
CIRCULATORY	DICEPHALOUS	FAMILIARITY	IDOLIZATION	MANCIPATION	PATERNALISM
CLIFFHANGER	DIMERCAPROL	FAMILIARIZE	ILLYWHACKER	MARGINALIST	PECULIARITY
COAGULATION	DINNYHAUSER	FASCINATING	IMAGINATION	MARGINALIZE	PENETRATING
COHORTATIVE	DINNYHAYSER	FASCINATION	IMAGINATIVE	MARSHMALLOW	PENETRATION
COLLOCATION	DIPLOMATICS	FESTINATELY	IMMEDIATELY	MASTICATION	PENNYFATHER
COLONIALISM	DIPLOMATIST	FIRECRACKER	IMMIGRATION	MATERIALISE	PENTAVALENT
COLONIALIST	DIPSOMANIAC	FLUCTUATING	IMMORTALISE	MATERIALISM	PERCOLATION
COLUMBARIUM	DISARMAMENT	FLUCTUATING	IMMORTALITY	MATERIALISM	PERFORATION

PERISTALITH	SAGITTARIUS	TRAGELAPHUS	MARIONBERRY	CREPUSCULAR	MANUFACTURE
PERISTALSIS	SAINTPAULIA	TRANSLATION	MEMORABILIA	DENDRACHATE	MELANOCHROI
PERMUTATION	SCARABAEOID	TRANSPARENT	NOTICEBOARD	DERELICTION	MICROSCOPIC
PERSONALIST	SCIREFACIAS	TREPIDATION	ODONTOBLAST	DESELECTION	MISERICORDE
PERSONALITY	SCOPOLAMINE	TRIBULATION	POLLENBRUSH	DESTRUCTION	MONONUCLEAR
PERSONALIZE	SCOUTMASTER	TRICERATOPS	SALTIMBANCO	DESTRUCTIVE	MUNIFICENCE
PERTINACITY	SECONDARILY	TRINIDADIAN	SALTIMBOCCA	DIFFRACTION	NICKNACKERY
PETITMAITRE	SECRETARIAL	TRINITARIAN	SCULLABOGUE	DISGRACEFUL	NONDESCRIPT
PHARISAICAL	SECRETARIAT	TRINOBANTES	SHOVELBOARD	DISJUNCTION	NUMERICALLY
PLANETARIUM	SEGREGATION	TYPOGRAPHER	SILVERBERRY	DISJUNCTIVE	NUTCRACKERS
PLEBEIANISE	SEMITRAILER	TYPOGRAPHIC	SPRINGBOARD	DISTINCTION	OBSTRICTION
POLLINATION	SEPTENARIUS	ULTRAMARINE	STRIKEBOUND	DISTINCTIVE	OBSTRUCTION
POMEGRANATE	SEPTICAEMIA	UNCERTAINTY	STRINGBOARD	DISTRACTION	OBSTRUCTIVE
PREDICAMENT	SHINPLASTER	UNDERHANDED	SURTARBRAND	DOUBLECHECK	OPALESCENCE
PREDICATIVE	SHORTHANDED	UNDERMANNED	SURTURBRAND	DOUBLECROSS	ORGANICALLY
PRELIBATION	SILLIMANITE	UNDERTAKING	SWITCHBOARD	DOUROUCOULI	OVARIECTOMY
PREPARATION	SINGULARITY	UNDERVALUED	THEREABOUTS	DRACUNCULUS	PACIFICALLY
PREPARATIVE	SKIDBLADNIR	UNEXPLAINED	TRIPHIBIOUS	DRASTICALLY	PERFUNCTORY
PREPARATORY	SLEEPWALKER	UNIFICATION	TROPHOBLAST	DYSFUNCTION	PERSPECTIVE
PREROGATIVE	SPACESAVING	UNREHEARSED	UNINHABITED	EFFICACIOUS	PERSPICUITY
PRISCIANIST	SPECULATION	UNSURPASSED	UNINHIBITED	EMPIRICUTIC	PERSPICUOUS
PROCREATION	SPECULATIVE	UNUNQUADIUM	VALLAMBROSA	ENCROACHING	PHYLLOCLADE
PRODIGALISE	STAGFLATION	UNWARRANTED	WHEREABOUTS	ENFRANCHISE	POLIORCETIC
PRODIGALITY	STAIRCARPET	UTILITARIAN	WINTERBERRY	EQUINOCTIAL	POLITICALLY
PROLETARIAN	STANDPATTER	UTILIZATION	ABSTRACTION	EQUIVOCALLY	POLITICIANS
PROLETARIAT	STEADFASTLY	VACCINATION	ACCRESCENCE	ERRATICALLY	POLYTECHNIC
PROPAGATION	STIMULATION	VACILLATING	ACUPUNCTURE	EXCRESCENCE	PRACTICABLE
PROROGATION	STIPULATION	VACILLATION	ADJUDICATOR	EYECATCHING	PRACTICALLY
PROSTRATION	STOCKHAUSEN	VARANGARIAN	ADOLESCENCE	FANATICALLY	PRECONCEIVE
PROVOCATION	STOCKTAKING	VARIEGATION	AFFLIICTION	FARINACEOUS	PROMISCUITY
PROVOCATIVE	STRADUARIUS	VARIOLATION	AFTERSCHOOL	FARREACHING	PROMISCUOUS
PSYCHIATRIC	STRAPHANGER	VENTILATION	AMELANCHIER	FRANTICALLY	PROSAICALLY
PTERODACTYL	STYLIZATION	VESUVIANITE	ANTHRACOSIS	GASTRECTOMY	PROSPECTIVE
PUBLICATION	STYMPHALIAN	VIDEOCAMERA	ANTICYCLONE	GEGENSCHEIN	PROTRACTING
PUNCTUALITY	SUBJUGATION	VINDICATION	APPROACHING	GENERICALLY	PROTRACTION
PUNCTUATION	SUBLIMATION	VOLKSKAMMER	ARISTOCRACY	GENETICALLY	PSITTACOSIS
QUALITATIVE	SUBPANATION	VOLUNTARILY	BACKPACKING	GEOSYNCLINE	PTOCHOCRACY
RADIOCARBON	SUCCEDANEUM	VOLUNTARISM	BENEDICTINE	GRAPHICALLY	RADIOACTIVE
RASTAFARIAN	SUFFOCATING	WARMHEARTED	BENEDICTION	GREENOCKITE	REPROACHFUL
RATIONALITY	SUFFOCATION	WASHLEATHER	BENEFICIARY	GUADALCANAL	RESOURCEFUL
RATIONALIZE	SUPERLATIVE	WASTEBASKET	BENEFICIATE	HAMMERCLOTH	RESTRICTION
RAZZAMATAZZ	SUPERMARKET	WELLMEANING	BUREAUCRACY	HARPSICHORD	RESTRICTIVE
REALIZATION	SUPERTANKER	WESTPHALIAN	CALEFACIENT	HEXADECIMAL	RESTRUCTURE
REANIMATION	SUPPEDANEUM	WHEELBARROW	CANDESCENCE	IDENTICALLY	RETINACULUM
REAPPRAISAL	SUPPURATION	WHITLEATHER	CAPRICCIOSO	IDIOTICALLY	RETROACTIVE
REBARBATIVE	SUSURRATION	WORKSTATION	CAUSTICALLY	IDYLLICALLY	RIBONUCLEIC
RECANTATION	SYCOPHANTIC	WORLDFAMOUS	CHANTICLEER	ILLOGICALLY	RUMFRUCTION
RECLAMATION	SYNCOPATION	XYLOGRAPHER	CHEESECLOTH	INEFFECTIVE	SAPONACEOUS
REFORMATION	SYNDICALISM	AMOBARBITAL	CHRONICALLY	INEFFECTUAL	SARCENCHYME
REFORMATORY	SYNDICATION	AMPHISBAENA	CINQUECENTO	INEFFICIENT	SATIRICALLY
REITERATION	SYSTEMATIZE	AMPHISBOENA	CIRCUMCISER	INJUDICIOUS	SCEPTICALLY
RELUCTANTLY	TABERNACLES	BOYSENBERRY	CLAIRSCHACH	INSTINCTIVE	SECONDCLASS
REPUDIATION	TACHYCARDIA	CENTREBOARD	CLARENCIEUX	INSTRUCTION	SIGHTSCREEN
RESERVATION	TEETOTALLER	CHOCKABLOCK	COALESCENCE	INSTRUCTIVE	SKEPTICALLY
RESIGNATION	TELEGRAPHER	CILOFIBRATE	COEFFICIENT	INTERACTION	SMOKESCREEN
RESPIRATION	TELEGRAPHIC	COLOURBLIND	COGNOSCENTE	INTERACTIVE	SPECTACULAR
RESPIRATORY	TEMPERAMENT	CONTRIBUTOR	COGNOSCENTI	INTOXICATED	SPEECHCRAFT
RESTORATION	TEMPERATURE	DISTRIBUTED	COLLENCHYMA	IRIDESCENCE	SPERMICIDAL
RESTORATIVE	TEMPORARILY	DISTRIBUTOR	COMPLACENCY	IRREDUCIBLE	SPRINGCLEAN
RETALIATION	TERMINATION	DISTURBANCE	COMPLICATED	IRREVOCABLE	SUBJUNCTIVE
RETALIATORY	TESSARAGLOT	EQUILIBRIST	COMPUNCTION	ISOELECTRIC	SUBTRACTION
RETARDATION	TIMESHARING	EQUILIBRIUM	COMSTOCKERY	LACONICALLY	SUPERSCRIBE
REVALUATION	TITILLATION	FARKLEBERRY	CONJUNCTION	MACROSCOPIC	SUPERSCRIPT
RIGHTHANDED	TOASTMASTER	GINGERBREAD	CONJUNCTURE	MALEDICTION	TECHNICALLY
RIGHTHANDER	TOBOGGANING	HUCKLEBERRY	CONSPICUOUS	MALEFACTION	TEGUCICALPA
ROTOGRAVURE	TOPOGRAPHER	HURTLEBERRY	CONTRACTION	MALFUNCTION	TERPSICHORE
SABBATARIAN	TOSTICATION	INCUNABULUM	CONTRACTUAL	MALPRACTICE	TICKTACKTOE

TRAFFICATOR	ABRIDGEMENT	DEFENCELESS	HEARTLESSLY	NORTHWESTER	SIGHTSEEING
TRANSACTION	ABSENTEEISM	DEFENSELESS	HEAVYWEIGHT	NOTOTHERIUM	SMOULDERING
ULOTRICHALE	ACATALECTIC	DEOXYGENATE	HOMOTHERMAL	OBTEMPERATE	SOUNDLESSLY
UNCONSCIOUS	ACHIEVEMENT	DEPARTEMENT	HOMOTHERMIC	OMNIPRESENT	SOUTHWESTER
UNFLINCHING	ADVANCEMENT	DERANGEMENT	HOUSEKEEPER	ORTHOCENTRE	SPLUTTERING
UNSOLICITED	AGGLOMERATE	DESEGREGATE	HUCKSTERAGE	OUTMANEUVER	STEEPLEJACK
VALEDICTION	ALPHABETIZE	DETRIMENTAL	HYDROGENATE	OVERWEENING	STEINBERGER
VALEDICTORY	AMYLOPECTIN	DIFFERENTLY	HYDROMEDUSA	OVERWHELMED	STICKLEBACK
VIOLINCELLO	ANDROGENOUS	DIFFIDENTLY	HYPOTHECATE	PAMPHLETEER	STOREKEEPER
VIOLONCELLO	ANESTHETIST	DIPHYCERCAL	HYPOTHERMIA	PANTALETTES	STORYTELLER
VIVISECTION	ANESTHETIZE	DISABLEMENT	IMPATIENTLY	PAPERWEIGHT	STRANGENESS
XENODOCHIUM	ANISOCERCAL	DISAFFECTED	IMPERMEABLE	PARABLEPSIS	STRANGEWAYS
ABRACADABRA	APODYTERIUM	DISAGREEING	IMPLEMENTAL	PASSIVENESS	STRINGENTLY
ALEXANDRINE	APPEASEMENT	DISHEVELLED	IMPROVEMENT	PEACEKEEPER	SUPERSEDEAS
ALEXANDRITE	APPURTENANT	DISHONESTLY	IMPRUDENTLY	PENSIVENESS	SUPERSEDERE
ANTECEDENCE	ARCHIPELAGO	DISINTEREST	INAUTHENTIC	PERMANENTLY	TASTELESSLY
ARRIVEDERCI	ARGATHELIAN	DISORIENTED	INCARCERATE	PERSEVERING	TETRAHEDRON
ARTHRODESIS	ARRANGEMENT	DISQUIETING	INCOMPETENT	PERTINENTLY	THANKLESSLY
AWKWARDNESS	ARTILLERIST	DITHELETISM	INCORRECTLY	PHILATELIST	THEATREGOER
BANGLADESHI	ASPHETERISM	DIVORCEMENT	INCREMENTAL	PICTURESQUE	THEOPNEUSTY
BATTLEDRESS	ASSYTHEMENT	DOMINEERING	INDIFFERENT	PLATERESQUE	THERAPEUTAE
BLESSEDNESS	BACKFIELDER	DRAGGLETAIL	INDULGENTLY	POINTLESSLY	THERAPEUTIC
BOMBARDMENT	BADDELEYITE	EFFICIENTLY	INSINCERITY	PREDECESSOR	THISTLEDOWN
BRAGGADOCIO	BELLIGERENT	ELEUTHERIAN	INSISTENTLY	PRESTRESSED	THREATENING
CAMARADERIE	BEREAVEMENT	ELIZABETHAN	INTEMPERATE	PRIMIGENIAL	TIMEKEEPING
COINCIDENCE	BESIEGEMENT	EMBOÎTEMENT	INTERCEPTOR	PROCUREMENT	TOWNSPEOPLE
COMMANDMENT	BEWILDERING	EMPHYTEUSIS	INTERLEUKIN	PROFITEROLE	TRACKLEMENT
COMMENDABLE	BICENTENARY	EMPIECEMENT	INTERNECINE	PROFUSENESS	TRANSCEIVER
COMMENDABLY	BIMILLENARY	EMPLACEMENT	INTERREGNUM	PROLIFERATE	TRANSDERMAL
COMPENDIOUS	BLACKFELLOW	ENDORSEMENT	INTERRELATE	PROMINENTLY	TRANSFERRED
CONCORDANCE	BLASPHEMOUS	ENDOTHERMIC	INTERVENING	PROOFREADER	TRANSFERRIN
CROOKEDNESS	BOOKKEEPING	ENFORCEABLE	INTRADERMAL	PROPRIETARY	TRANSVERSAL
DESCENDANTS	BRISTLECONE	ENFORCEMENT	INTRAVENOUS	PROSTHETICS	TREACHEROUS
DESPONDENCY	BRITTLENESS	ENGINEERING	INTROVERTED	PROTUBERANT	TREACHETOUR
DIAMONDBACK	CALENDERING	ENHANCEMENT	INVOLVEMENT	PURPOSELESS	TREECREEPER
DILAPIDATED	CALLANETICS	ENJAMBEMENT	KNUCKLEBALL	PYTHONESQUE	TRENCHERMAN
DISOBEDIENT	CARBURETTOR	ENLARGEMENT	LATTICEWORK	RECURRENTLY	TREPONEMATA
ENCHONDROMA	CASSITERITE	ENNEAHEDRON	LECTURESHIP	REFRIGERANT	TROUBLESOME
ENFOULDERED	CEASELESSLY	ENSLAVEMENT	LEGERDEMAIN	REFRIGERATE	TROUBLESPOT
FIDDLEDEDEE	CHAIRPERSON	ENTABLEMENT	LENGTHENING	REGISTERING	TRUCULENTLY
FISHANDCHIP	CHEERLEADER	ENTITLEMENT	LEVELHEADED	RELEASEMENT	TRUSTEESHIP
FORBIDDANCE	CHOLINERGIC	EPANALEPSIS	LIGHTHEADED	REMORSELESS	UNAUTHENTIC
HOBBLEDEHOY	CHRISTENING	EPIGENESIST	LIGHTWEIGHT	REPLACEABLE	UNCONCEALED
HOLLANDAISE	CITLALEPETL	EVASIVENESS	LOGODAEDALY	REPLACEMENT	UNCONCERNED
HUNDREDFOLD	CITRONELLAL	EXANTHEMATA	LONGSLEEVED	REPRESENTED	UNCONNECTED
HUSBANDLAND	COACHFELLOW	EXPERIENCED	LOUDSPEAKER	REQUIREMENT	UNCONTESTED
INEXPEDIENT	COMMISERATE	EXTROGENOUS	MAGISTERIAL	RESTATEMENT	UNCONVERTED
KIMERIDGIAN	COMPETENTLY	EXTROVERTED	MANEUVERING	RESTIVENESS	UNDERWEIGHT
NOSTRADAMUS	COMPILEMENT	FAULTLESSLY	MARIONETTES	REVERBERATE	UNEXPRESSED
OFFHANDEDLY	COMPUTERIZE	FEATURELESS	MASSIVENESS	ROCKEFELLER	UNIMPRESSED
ONEIRODYNIA	COMRADESHIP	FLORILEGIUM	MEASURELESS	RUDESHEIMER	UNPROTECTED
PARAMEDICAL	CONCISENESS	FORESEEABLE	MEASUREMENT	SACRAMENTAL	UNSHAKEABLE
PHILANDERER	CONDOLENCES	FORGIVENESS	MEGATHERIUM	SALESPERSON	UNSUSPECTED
PLEURODYNIA	CONFEDERACY	FORTUNELOUD	MENDELEVIUM	SAPROLEGNIA	UNTRAMELLED
POLYHYDROXY	CONFEDERATE	FRIGATEBIRD	MERCILESSLY	SAUSAGEMEAT	UNWHOLESOME
PROCEEDINGS	CONFIDENTLY	FRIGHTENING	MICROSECOND	SCOLOPENDRA	VASOPRESSIN
PSYCHEDELIC	CONFINEMENT	FRUITLESSLY	MINESWEEPER	SCOREKEEPER	VENTURESOME
RHAPSODICAL	CONSIDERATE	FUNDAMENTAL	MINISTERIAL	SCUTTLEBUTT	VERBIGERATE
SCLERODERMA	CONSIDERING	FURTIVENESS	MINISTERING	SEMPITERNAL	VOORTREKKER
SCULDUDDERY	CONSUMERISM	GALLIBEGGAR	MISCHIEVOUS	SEMPITERNUM	WALDSTERBEN
SKULDUDDERY	CONTENEMENT	GALLYBEGGAR	MISDEMEANOR	SENTIMENTAL	WATERMEADOW
STIPENDIARY	CONTINENTAL	GENUFLEXION	MONEYLENDER	SERVICEABLE	WELLDRESSED
UNAVOIDABLE	CONTUBERNAL	GENUINENESS	MONOTHELITE	SEVENTEENTH	WHISTLESTOP
UNAVOIDABLY	CRATERELLUS	GIBBERELLIN	MONOTREMATA	SEXTODECIMO	WINDBREAKER
UNSCHEDULED	CROSSLEGGED	GRAVIMETRIC	NIERSTEINER	SHAMELESSLY	WINDCHEATER
WATEREDDOWN	CYBERNETICS	HAIRDRESSER	NOISELESSLY	SHIPWRECKED	WRONGHEADED
WAYWARDNESS	DARDANELLES	HARDPRESSED	NONETHELESS	SHUTTLECOCK	XEROTHERMIC

ZWISCHENZUG	PHARYNGITIS	LOGGERHEADS	AMMOPHILOUS	DESERPIDINE	HEALTHINESS
AIRCRAFTMAN	PHYSIOGNOMY	LYCANTHROPE	AMPLEXICAUL	DESTABILIZE	HEMOPHILIAC
ALIFANFARON	PLANTAGENET	LYCANTHROPY	APHRODISIAC	DETERMINANT	HISTORIATED
BATTLEFIELD	PLANTIGRADE	MELANCHOLIA	APPALLINGLY	DETERMINATE	HOHENLINDEN
BATTLEFRONT	POLTERGEIST	MELANCHOLIC	APPLERINGIE	DETERMINING	HORSERIDING
BEAUTIFULLY	POTAMOGETON	MISANTHROPE	APPRECIABLE	DEVITRIFIED	HOSTILITIES
CENTRIFUGAL	PRESTIGIOUS	MISANTHROPY	APPRECIABLY	DIMENSIONAL	IMPARTIALLY
CIRCUMFLECT	RECTANGULAR	MONARCHICAL	APPROVINGLY	DIRECTIONAL	IMPASSIONED
DECEITFULLY	SALPINGITIS	NOURISHMENT	APPROXIMATE	DISBELIEVER	IMPASSIVELY
ENFEOFFMENT	SCULDUGGERY	OLIGOCHAETE	ARGENTINIAN	DISPOSITION	IMPERTINENT
FRIGHTFULLY	SEISMOGRAPH	PANOMPHAEAN	ASCLEPIADES	DISSEMINATE	IMPRECISION
HUMGRUFFIAN	SEXOLOGICAL	PARENTHESIS	ASPERGILLUM	DISSEPIMENT	IMPROVIDENT
IDENTIFYING	SKILLIGALEE	PEEVISHNESS	ASPERGILLUS	DOLABRIFORM	IMPULSIVELY
LINDISFARNE	SKILLIGOLEE	PENTATHLETE	ASSASSINATE	DOMESTICATE	INCONTINENT
MASTERFULLY	SKULDUGGERY	PICKELHAUBE	ATTENTIVELY	DOMESTICITY	INCRIMINATE
REGRETFULLY	STEREOGRAPH	PORTERHOUSE	AUDIOVISUAL	DYSLOGISTIC	INDEXLINKED
RESENTFULLY	STRATEGICAL	PUBLISHABLE	AUGUSTINIAN	EDUCATIONAL	INDUPLICATE
SELFDEFENCE	SUBMERGENCE	RAFFISHNESS	BACKSLIDING	EFFECTIVELY	INFANTICIDE
SHOPLIFTING	SUFFRAGETTE	REFRESHMENT	BEASTLINESS	EINSTEINIUM	INFERTILITY
SORROWFULLY	SYMPLEGADES	ROGUISHNESS	BELLYTIMBER	ELECTRICIAN	INGRATITUDE
SPORTSFIELD	THEOLOGICAL	SADDLEHORSE	BREADWINNER	ELECTRICITY	INGREDIENTS
STANDOFFISH	THOROUGHPIN	SAPROPHYTIC	BROADMINDED	ELIGIBILITY	INQUIRINGLY
THENCEFORTH	TOXICOGENIC	SARCOPHAGUS	CABBALISTIC	EMBELLISHED	INQUISITION
WELLDEFINED	UNAMBIGUOUS	SCEUOPHYLAX	CATERPILLAR	ENCHIRIDION	INQUISITIVE
WILBERFORCE	UNMITIGATED	SCRIMSHANDY	CATHOLICISM	EPICHEIREMA	INSECTICIDE
WINDOWFRAME	VOTERIGGING	SELFISHNESS	CENTURIATOR	ESCHERICHIA	INSECTIVORE
WONDERFULLY	WELLINGTONS	SENNACHERIB	CERTIFIABLE	ESSENTIALLY	INSENSITIVE
ASTRINGENCY	WILLINGNESS	SHORTCHANGE	CERTIFICATE	ESTABLISHED	INSOUCIANCE
BULLFIGHTER	WINTERGREEN	SLEUTHHOUND	CHARACINOID	ESTABLISHER	INSTABILITY
CARDIOGRAPH	WITENAGEMOT	SPENDTHRIFT	CHILDMINDER	EUCHARISTIC	INSULTINGLY
CARRIAGEWAY	AGONOTHETES	SPIROCHAETE	CLEANLINESS	EUPHEMISTIC	INTELLIGENT
CHEIROGNOMY	AGORAPHOBIA	SPRINGHOUSE	COENOBITISM	EXCEEDINGLY	INTENSIVELY
CONTINGENCE	ANAESTHESIA	STENOCHROME	COMESTIBLES	EXCEPTIONAL	INTENTIONAL
CONTINGENCY	ANAESTHETIC	STRETCHABLE	COMMUNICANT	EXCESSIVELY	INTERLINGUA
CONVERGENCE	ANTIRRHINUM	STRETCHLESS	COMMUNICATE	EXCLUSIVELY	INTERMINGLE
DEGRINGOLER	ANTISTHENES	STYLISHNESS	COMPETITION	EXECUTIONER	INTERVIEWEE
DEMAGOGUERY	ATMOSPHERIC	SUMMERHOUSE	COMPETITIVE	EXPENDITURE	INTERVIEWER
DEPHLEGMATE	AXEROPHTHOL	SUPERCHARGE	COMPLAISANT	EXQUISITELY	INTREPIDITY
DISTINGUISH	BERGSCHRUND	SUPERCHERIE	COMPOSITION	EXTENSIVELY	INTUITIVELY
EMMENAGOGUE	CARDOPHAGUS	SVARABHAKTI	CONCILIATOR	EXTERMINATE	INVESTIGATE
ESTRANGHELO	CATCHPHRASE	SYMPATHETIC	CONCOMITANT	EXTORTIONER	INVESTITURE
FIRELIGHTER	CLEANSHAVEN	SYMPATHISER	CONDITIONAL	EXTRADITION	INVINCIBLES
FORFOUGHTEN	CLINOCHLORE	SYMPATHIZER	CONDITIONER	FALLIBILITY	ISOLECITHAL
FORTNIGHTLY	COPROPHAGAN	TAUTOCHRONE	CONDOMINIUM	FARRAGINOUS	JOSEPHINITE
FOTHERGILLA	CORINTHIANS	TENTERHOOKS	CONSILIENCE	FAULTFINDER	JUSTIFIABLE
GALLOWGLASS	DEMOSTHENES	UNCOUTHNESS	CONSOLIDATE	FAVOURITISM	JUSTIFIABLY
GODDAUGHTER	DEMOSTHENIC	UNCRUSHABLE	CONSTRICTED	FEASIBILITY	KINNIKINICK
HERRINGBONE	DEUTSCHMARK	UNDERCHARGE	CONSTRICTOR	FERNITICKLE	LARYNGISMUS
HETEROGRAFT	DISCOTHEQUE	UNTOUCHABLE	CONTAMINANT	FINANCIALLY	LASERPICIUM
HIGHLIGHTER	DYAESTHESIA	WELLBEHAVED	CONTAMINATE	FLEXIBILITY	LATROCINIUM
HUMMINGBIRD	EARTHSHAKER	WHITECHAPEL	CONVENIENCE	FRANKLINITE	LEADSWINGER
IDEOLOGICAL	EMMENTHALER	WHITETHROAT	CORDWAINERS	FREETHINKER	LECITHINASE
IRRELIGIOUS	EPINEPHRINE	ABBREVIATED	COUNTRIFIED	FROSTBITTEN	LENGTHINESS
LAMMERGEIER	EURHYTHMICS	ACADEMICIAN	COURTLINESS	FUNDRAISING	LENTIGINOSE
LAMMERGEYER	FESTSCHRIFT	ACADEMICISM	CRACOVIENNE	GALLOVIDIAN	LICKSPITTLE
LAMPLIGHTER	FOOLISHNESS	ACCORDINGLY	CREDIBILITY	GELSEMININE	LONGANIMITY
LATERIGRADE	FURNISHINGS	ACINACIFORM	CROCODILIAN	GHASTLINESS	MACROBIOTIC
LEFTLUGGAGE	GARNISHMENT	ACQUISITION	CRUCIFIXION	GRAVEDIGGER	MAGNANIMITY
LONGSIGHTED	HAEMOPHILIA	ACQUISITIVE	CULPABILITY	GREGARINIDA	MAGNANIMOUS
MEANINGLESS	HEMORRHOIDS	ACTUALITIES	CULVERINEER	GUESSTIMATE	MAGNIFICENT
MOCKINGBIRD	HOGGISHNESS	ADVERBIALLY	DECEPTIVELY	GULLIBILITY	MARCONIGRAM
MOONLIGHTER	HYDROPHIDAE	ADVERTISING	DECORTICATE	HAIRRAISING	MASCULINITY
MYCOLOGICAL	HYDROPHOBIA	AFGHANISTAN	DECREPITATE	HALLUCINATE	MASOCHISTIC
NEARSIGHTED	HYDROPHOBIC	AGGLUTINANT	DECREPITUDE	HANDWRITING	MICHURINISM
NOTHINGNESS	IMPEACHMENT	AGGLUTINATE	DEFENSIVELY	HANDWRITTEN	MICROVILLUS
ONTOLOGICAL	INTERCHANGE	AGNOSTICISM	DEGLUTINATE	HANGGLIDING	MICTURITION
PEDAGOGICAL	ISTIOPHORUS	AGUARDIENTE	DEGLUTITION	HAUGHTINESS	MINNESINGER

MISALLIANCE	PROHIBITIVE	STATELINESS	XEROTRIPSIS	FULFILLMENT	SOCKDOLIGER
MISERLINESS	PROMOTIONAL	STOOLPIGEON	AIRSICKNESS	GENERALIZED	SOCKDOLOGER
MODERNISTIC	PROMPTITUDE	STROPHILLUS	BANNOCKBURN	GENOUILLÈRE	SPECIALIZED
MONOCHINOUS	PROPOSITION	STRUTHIONES	CARSICKNESS	GILLYFLOWER	SPONDULICKS
MOUNTAINEER	PROVISIONAL	SUBDIVISION	JINRICKSHAW	GLADWELLISE	SPONDYLITIS
MOUNTAINOUS	PROVISIONER	SUBDOMINANT	KULTURKREIS	GLOSSOLALIA	STRAITLACED
MOZAMBIQUAN	PULCHRITUDE	SUBORDINATE	SCHRECKLICH	GRAMMALOGUE	STRANDLOPER
NAUGHTINESS	QUICKSILVER	SUFFICIENCY	SEASICKNESS	HAEMOGLOBIN	STREAMLINED
NECESSITATE	RABELAISIAN	SUITABILITY	SHEATHKNIFE	HALFHOLIDAY	STREETLIGHT
NECESSITOUS	RANGEFINDER	SUPERFICIAL	UNBREAKABLE	HALLEFLINTA	SUPERALTERN
NECROBIOSIS	RATIOCINATE	SUPERFICIES	UNDRINKABLE	HELPFULNESS	SUPERFLUITY
NUTRITIONAL	RAVISHINGLY	SUPERVISION	UNSPEAKABLE	HEMERALOPIA	SUPERFLUOUS
OBJECTIVELY	READABILITY	SUPERVISORY	UNTHINKABLE	HINDERLANDS	SURVEILLANT
OBJECTIVITY	RECEPTIVITY	SUPPOSITION	WATERSKIING	INSTALLMENT	TESSELLATED
OBSESSIVELY	RECESSIONAL	SUPPOSITORY	ACCUMULATOR	INTERGLOSSA	TONSILLITIS
OCTASTICHON	RECOGNITION	SYMPOSIARCH	ACKNOWLEDGE	INVIGILATOR	TOURBILLION
OFFENSIVELY	RECONDITION	TANGIBILITY	AGRICULTURE	IRREGULARLY	TRANSILIENT
OMNISCIENCE	RECRIMINATE	TANTALIZING	AIGUILLETTE	KILOCALORIE	TRIPTOLEMUS
OPERATIONAL	RECTIFIABLE	TARRADIDDLE	AMBIVALENCE	LITERALNESS	TROMPELOEIL
ORDERLINESS	RECTILINEAR	TELEPRINTER	AMONTILLADO	MAKEBELIEVE	TURBELLARIA
PALEOLITHIC	REDUPLICATE	TENTATIVELY	ANADIPLOSIS	MALEVOLENCE	UNAVAILABLE
PALESTINIAN	REFURBISHED	THEATRICALS	ANAPHYLAXIS	MANIPULATOR	UNCIVILISED
PARALEIPSIS	REGURGITATE	THINGLINESS	ANGELOLATRY	MANTELLETTA	UNCIVILIZED
PARISHIONER	RELIABILITY	THRIFTINESS	APOPHYLLITE	MASKALLONGE	UNDEVELOPED
PARTICIPANT	REQUISITION	TIGGYWINKLE	ARTICULATED	MELLIFLUOUS	UNDISCLOSED
PARTICIPATE	RESISTIVITY	TIGHTFISTED	ASSEMBLYMAN	MENTHOLATED	UNENVELOPED
PARTICIPIAL	RESUSCITATE	TIGHTLIPPED	ASSIMILATED	MISSPELLING	UTRICULARIA
PARTURITION	REVENDICATE	TOXOPHILITE	ATRABILIOUS	MONTGOLFIER	WAKEFULNESS
PARVANIMITY	RIGHTWINGER	TRADITIONAL	BARTHOLOMEW	MUSCHELKALK	WHIGMALEERY
PATRONISING	ROBESPIERRE	TRANQUILITY	BASHFULNESS	MUSKELLUNGE	WINDOWLEDGE
PATRONIZING	ROMANTICISM	TRANSFIGURE	BENEVOLENCE	NATURALNESS	WISTFULNESS
PENULTIMATE	ROMANTICIZE	TRANSMITTED	BESTSELLING	NETHERLANDS	WITHHOLDING
PERCIPIENCE	SACRIFICIAL	TRANSMITTER	BOOKSELLERS	NETHERLINGS	ADULLAMITES
PEREGRINATE	SAINTLINESS	TRIUMVIRATE	BRUCELLOSIS	NEUTRALISED	ALLELOMORPH
PERENNIALLY	SANSEVIERIA	TYPEWRITTEN	CALCEOLARIA	NOMENCLATOR	ANASTOMOSIS
PERSONIFIED	SAVOURINESS	ULTRAVIOLET	CAMOUFLAGED	NONCHALANCE	ANTONOMASIA
PESSIMISTIC	SCALPRIFORM	UNBLEMISHED	CANDLELIGHT	NORTHCLIFFE	AUXANOMETER
PHONETICIAN	SCHOTTISCHE	UNCOMMITTED	CAREFULNESS	OSTEOPLASTY	BATTLEMENTS
PHONOFIDDLE	SCITAMINEAE	UNCONFIRMED	CASTELLATED	OVERBALANCE	BIOCHEMICAL
PHOTOFINISH	SCOLECIFORM	UNCONVINCED	CAULIFLOWER	PAINKILLING	BOTANOMANCY
PHTHIRIASIS	SCREAMINGLY	UNDERSIGNED	CHANCELLERY	PARABOLANUS	CHARISMATIC
PINNYWINKLE	SCRUFFINESS	UNDIGNIFIED	CONCEALMENT	PENICILLATE	CHARLEMAGNE
POLYTRICHUM	SECRETIVELY	UNEMOTIONAL	CONSTELLATE	PERDUELLION	CHRISTMASSY
PONTIFICATE	SELECTIVELY	UNFAILINGLY	CONVALLARIA	PITCHBLENDE	CHRONOMETER
PORTRAITIST	SELECTIVITY	UNFULFILLED	COUNSELLING	PLAYFULNESS	CLANJAMFRAY
PORTRAITURE	SELFEVIDENT	UNFURNISHED	CRÉMAILLÈRE	PREPOLLENCE	COLORIMETER
POSSIBILITY	SENSATIONAL	UNGODLINESS	CRENELLATED	PROPHYLAXIS	COMPLIMENTS
POTENTIALLY	SENSIBILITY	UNHAPPINESS	CROMWELLIAN	PRZEWALSKIS	COMPRIMARIO
PRECIPITATE	SENSITIVELY	UNINITIATED	CRYSTALLINE	PSEUDOLOGIA	COTTONMOUTH
PRECIPITOUS	SENSITIVITY	UNJUSTIFIED	CRYSTALLISE	PUNCTILIOUS	COULOMMIERS
PREDOMINANT	SERENDIPITY	UNPATRIOTIC	CRYSTALLIZE	QUARRELLING	CRITHOMANCY
PREDOMINATE	SHAPELINESS	UNPUBLISHED	CURTAILMENT	QUARRELSOME	DEMONOMANIA
PREJUDICIAL	SHENANIGANS	UNQUALIFIED	CYCLOALKANE	RAPSCALLION	DICHROMATIC
PRELIMINARY	SHIPBUILDER	UNREALISTIC	DEMORALIZED	REALPOLITIK	EMPYROMANCY
PREMEDITATE	SHUNAMITISM	UNSPECIFIED	DICOTYLEDON	REFOCILLATE	EPITHYMETIC
PREMONITION	SIGNIFICANT	UNVARNISHED	DISCIPLINED	RESEMBLANCE	EUCHROMATIN
PREMONITORY	SKETCHINESS	UNWITTINGLY	DISINCLINED	SCAFFOLDING	FLUOROMETER
PREPOSITION	SLIGHTINGLY	VARIABILITY	ENTHRALLING	SCANDALIZED	GENTLEMANLY
PRETERITION	SOCIABILITY	VARSOVIENNE	EQUIPOLLENT	SCHECKLATON	HABILIMENTS
PREVARICATE	SOLIPSISTIC	VENDEMIAIRE	EQUIVALENCE	SCINTILLATE	IMPEDIMENTA
PRICKLINESS	SOROPTIMIST	VERSATILITY	ESPIEGLERIE	SEARCHLIGHT	INESTIMABLE
PRIZEWINNER	SOVEREIGNTY	VERTIGINOUS	EVANGELICAL	SERICULTURE	INFLAMMABLE
PROBABILITY	SPELLBINDER	VICISSITUDE	EXOSKELETON	SEVERALFOLD	INSTRUMENTS
PROBATIONER	SPHRAGISTIC	WHEREWITHAL	FITZWILLIAM	SLUMGULLION	INTOXIMETER
PROFICIENCY	SPIFFLICATE	WOMANLINESS	FLANNELETTE	SNORKELLING	JACQUEMINOT
PROGENITRIX	SPITSTICKER	WORLDLINESS	FOOTBALLING	SOCKDALAGER	KLEPTOMANIA
PROHIBITION	SPRINGINESS	XEROPHILOUS	FRAUDULENCE	SOCKDOLAGER	MACADAMIZED

MEGALOMANIA	CONSTANTINE	KILIMANJARO	SUBSTANDARD	CAMALDOLITE	FIELDWORKER
MEGALOMANIC	CONTAINMENT	KINCHINMORT	SUBSTANTIAL	CAMEROONIAN	FORECLOSURE
MIDDLEMARCH	COORDINATED	KITCHENETTE	SUBSTANTIVE	CAMPANOLOGY	FORESHORTEN
MILLIAMPERE	COORDINATES	LANDSKNECHT	SUDETENLAND	CAPERNOITED	FORETHOUGHT
NYMPHOMANIA	COUNTENANCE	LATIFUNDIUM	SUNDRENCHED	CAPERNOITIE	FORTHCOMING
ONEIROMANCY	COXWAINLESS	LEGIONNAIRE	SUPERINTEND	CARNIVOROUS	FRIVOLOUSLY
PAMPELMOOSE	CRESCENTADE	LONGRUNNING	SURROUNDING	CATADROMOUS	FRUGIVOROUS
PAMPELMOUSE	CYTOGENESIS	MACERANDUBA	SUSTAINABLE	CHAULMOOGRA	FULLBLOODED
PARONOMASIA	DEFERENTIAL	MAINTENANCE	TARATANTARA	CHAULMOUGRA	FUNCTIONARY
PERFORMANCE	DENOMINATOR	MECKLENBURG	TELEKINESIS	CHIASTOLITE	FUNCTIONING
POMPELMOOSE	DISCERNIBLE	MEDICINALLY	TELOCENTRIC	CHIROPODIST	GARRULOUSLY
POMPELMOUSE	DISCERNMENT	MENTONNIÈRE	TIRONENSIAN	CHONDROSTEI	GENEALOGIST
PSEUDOMORPH	DISGRUNTLED	MERCHANDISE	TREASONABLE	CHRISTOPHER	GERONTOLOGY
RHABDOMANCY	DOCTRINAIRE	MERCHANDIZE	TRICHINELLA	CLAIRVOYANT	GESTATORIAL
RIDDLEMEREE	DOCUMENTARY	MERCHANTMAN	TRICHINOSED	CLIMATOLOGY	GONFALONIER
RIFACIMENTO	DRAGONNADES	METACENTRIC	TSCHERNOSEM	COLDBLOODED	GOODLOOKING
SALINOMETER	DRUNKENNESS	METAGENESIS	TYRONENSIAN	COLLABORATE	GRANDMOTHER
SCHWARMEREI	EARTHENWARE	MILLIONAIRE	UNALIENABLE	COMMEMORATE	GRASSHOPPER
SHITTIMWOOD	EASTERNMOST	MISIDENTIFY	UNCLEANNESS	COMPTROLLER	GREENBOTTLE
SHOWJUMPING	ELEPHANTINE	MONOLINGUAL	UNDEMANDING	CONSCIOUSLY	GYNAECOLOGY
SOUTHAMPTON	EMOTIONALLY	MUDSLINGING	UNESSENTIAL	CORROBORATE	HALFBROTHER
SPEEDOMETER	ENVIRONMENT	NEVERENDING	UNRELENTING	COURTEOUSLY	HEMIANOPSIA
STEREOMETER	ERIODENDRON	NIGHTINGALE	UNREPENTANT	CREDULOUSLY	HERBIVOROUS
SUPERIMPOSE	EXPONENTIAL	OARSMANSHIP	UNSHRINKING	CREMATORIUM	HERPETOLOGY
SYMPTOMATIC	FACTFINDING	OPINIONATED	VALLISNERIA	CRIMINOLOGY	HIGHPROFILE
TENSIOMETER	FARTHINGALE	OUTSTANDING	VISCOUNTESS	CROCIDOLITE	HILARIOUSLY
THERMOMETER	FASHIONABLE	OVERHANGING	VITAMINIZED	DACTYLOGRAM	HISTOLOGIST
THINGAMABOB	FASHIONABLY	OVERMANNING	WESTERNMOST	DANGEROUSLY	HISTRIONICS
THINGAMAJIG	FERRONNIÈRE	OXYRHYNCHUS	WESTMINSTER	DECARBONATE	HOMOPHONOUS
THINGUMAJIG	FILAMENTOUS	PEDETENTOUS	WHITSUNTIDE	DECARBONIZE	HONEYCOMBED
TIMBROMANIA	FISHMONGERS	PELOPONNESE	WHITTINGTON	DELICIOUSLY	HONEYMOONER
TRINCOMALEE	FISSIONABLE	PENITENTIAL	WIDERANGING	DERMATOLOGY	HORNSWOGGLE
TWELVEMONTH	FORAMINIFER	PENSIONABLE	WISHTONWISH	DETERIORATE	HOUSEHOLDER
ABANDONMENT	FORLORNNESS	PERITONAEUM	WORKMANLIKE	DEUTERONOMY	HOUSEMOTHER
ABIOGENESIS	FRAGMENTARY	PERITONITIS	WORKMANSHIP	DICTATORIAL	HYDROPONICS
ABIOGENETIC	FRATERNALLY	PIEDMONTITE	ZOOPLANKTON	DIORTHORTIC	HYMNOLOGIST
ACRIMONIOUS	GAMETANGIUM	PORTLANDIAN	ABORTIONIST	DIPROTODONT	HYPERBOREAN
ACROCENTRIC	GAMOGENESIS	PORTMANTEAU	ACCESSORIES	DIPTEROCARP	ICHTHYOLITE
ADJOURNMENT	GASTRONOMIC	PREEMINENCE	ACCOMMODATE	DIRECTORATE	ICHTHYORNIS
AERODYNAMIC	GLASTONBURY	PRESTONPANS	ADIAPHORIST	DISCOLOURED	ILLUSIONARY
ALBIGENSIAN	GNATHONICAL	PUNCHINELLO	ADOPTIONISM	DISEMBODIED	ILLUSIONISM
ALBUGINEOUS	HIGHRANKING	PURITANICAL	AGROSTOLOGY	DOWNTRODDEN	ILLUSIONIST
ALBUMINURIA	HOMOGENEITY	QUADRENNIAL	AMPHIBOLOGY	DREADLOCKED	IMPERFORATE
ANTEPENDIUM	HOMOGENEOUS	QUADRENNIUM	ANACHRONISM	DREADNOUGHT	IMPERIOUSLY
APOLLINARIS	HOMOGENIZED	QUARRINGTON	ANACREONTIC	ECCALEOBION	IMPERSONATE
APOLLONICON	HYPOTENSION	REALIGNMENT	ANONYMOUSLY	ECTOTROPHIC	IMPETUOSITY
ATHERINIDAE	IGNOMINIOUS	REGIMENTALS	ANTHOLOGIZE	ELECTROCUTE	IMPETUOUSLY
AVERRUNCATE	IGNORANTINE	REICHENBACH	ANTHONOMOUS	ELECTROLIER	IMPIGNORATE
BACCHANALIA	ILLMANNERED	REORIENTATE	ANTIPHONARY	ELECTROLYTE	INCOMPOSITE
BACKBENCHER	ILLUMINANCE	RESIDENTIAL	APOSTROPHUS	ELECTRONICS	INCORPORATE
BARYCENTRIC	ILLUMINATED	RESPLENDENT	ARCHAEOLOGY	ELECTROTINT	INCORPOREAL
BEAUMONTAGE	IMPECUNIOUS	REVERENTIAL	ARCHEGONIAL	ENDOTROPHIC	INFERIORITY
BILLIONAIRE	IMPREGNABLE	RIGHTANGLED	ARCHEGONIUM	EPAMINONDAS	INGENIOUSLY
BOOKBINDING	INALIENABLE	RODOMONTADE	ARCHILOCHUS	ERRONEOUSLY	INSIDIOUSLY
BOUTONNIERE	INATTENTION	RUDIMENTARY	ARRHENOTOKY	ERYTHROCYTE	INTERCOSTAL
BRANDENBURG	INATTENTIVE	SANGUINEOUS	ASPERSORIUM	ESCARMOUCHE	INTERCOURSE
BRODBINGNAG	INDEFINABLE	SCANDANAVIA	ASSIDUOUSLY	ESCHATOLOGY	INTERPOLATE
CARABINIERE	INDEPENDENT	SCANDINAVIA	ATROCIOUSLY	ETHNOLOGIST	INTERROGATE
CARAVANNING	INESSENTIAL	SEDIMENTARY	AUDACIOUSLY	ETYMOLOGIST	JUDICIOUSLY
CAROLINGIAN	INEXPENSIVE	SELAGINELLA	BARNSTORMER	EXPECTORANT	KWASHIORKOR
CEREMONIOUS	INFLUENTIAL	SELFCONTROL	BEACHCOMBER	EXPECTORATE	LABORIOUSLY
CHALLENGING	INOFFENSIVE	SHOWMANSHIP	BEHAVIOURAL	EXTEMPORISE	LEASEHOLDER
CHICKENFEED	INVOLUNTARY	SKIMMINGTON	BELLEROPHON	EXTEMPORIZE	LUXURIOUSLY
CHILLINGHAM	IRONMONGERS	SPONTANEITY	BICARBONATE	EXTRAPOLATE	MAGLEMOSIAN
CHIPPENDALE	IRONMONGERY	SPONTANEOUS	BLAMEWORTHY	FACETIOUSLY	MALAPROPISM
CITIZENSHIP	IRREDENTIST	STRAMINEOUS	BOURGEOISIE	FANFARONADE	MALICIOUSLY
CONSIGNMENT	KALASHNIKOV	SUBITANEOUS	CACOPHONOUS	FEROCIOUSLY	MATRIMONIAL

MELODIOUSLY	REVISIONISM	TRUSTWORTHY	INESCAPABLE	ANTIPHRASIS	EXHILARATED
METALWORKER	RHOPALOCERA	TRYPANOSOMA	INSCRIPTION	ANTIPYRETIC	EXPROPRIATE
METEOROLOGY	RIGHTEOUSLY	TRYPANOSOME	INTERSPERSE	ANTISTROPHE	FARTHERMOST
METHODOLOGY	SAGACIOUSLY	TYRANNOSAUR	ISOMORPHOUS	APONEUROSIS	FEHMGERICHT
MISBEGOTTEN	SALACIOUSLY	ULTRAMODERN	ISOXSUPRINE	APPROPRIATE	FLABBERGAST
MODELMOLEST	SALVADORIAN	UNANIMOUSLY	LAMPROPHYRE	BALISTRARIA	FLANKERBACK
MOLLYCODDLE	SAXOPHONIST	UNDERCOOKED	LEPIDOPTERA	BANDEIRANTE	FLAVOURSOME
MONOPSONIST	SCAREMONGER	UNREASONING	LETTERPRESS	BLADDERWORT	FLICKERTAIL
MONSTROSITY	SCHISTOSOMA	UNSUPPORTED	MANTELPIECE	BLANKURSINE	FORBEARANCE
MOSSTROOPER	SCHISTOSOME	UNWELCOMING	MARKETPLACE	BLUNDERBORE	FOREWARNING
MUNITIONIZE	SCIENTOLOGY	VICARIOUSLY	MASTERPIECE	BREADCRUMBS	FURTHERANCE
MYTHOLOGIZE	SCRIPTORIUM	VICHYSOISSE	MEGALOPOLIS	BROTHERHOOD	FURTHERMORE
NEIGHBORING	SEIGNIORAGE	VIVACIOUSLY	NATUROPATHY	CALIFORNIUM	FURTHERMOST
NEIGHBOURLY	SESQUIOXIDE	VOLCANOLOGY	NEEDLEPOINT	CALLIGRAPHY	FURTHERSOME
NEUROLOGIST	SHAREHOLDER	VORACIOUSLY	NUCLEOPLASM	CALLITRICHE	GEOMETRICAL
NICKELODEON	SHORTCOMING	VULCANOLOGY	NUMBERPLATE	CAMPHORATED	GLIMMERGOWK
NOTORIOUSLY	SINGAPOREAN	WAINSCOTING	ODONTOPHORE	CARTOGRAPHY	GREENGROCER
OFFICIOUSLY	SMALLHOLDER	WATERCOLOUR	OMMATOPHORE	CATACHRESIS	HAEMORRHAGE
OPPIGNORATE	SMITHSONIAN	WATERCOURSE	OSTREOPHAGE	CATASTROPHE	HAEMORRHOID
ORNITHOLOGY	SMITHSONITE	WATERLOGGED	OVEREXPOSED	CATEGORICAL	HAGIOGRAPHA
ORNITHOPTER	SOCIOLOGIST	WHITEBOYISM	OVERLAPPING	CHAMBERLAIN	HAGIOGRAPHY
OSTRACODERM	SPANGCOCKLE	WHITECOLLAR	PARANEPHROS	CHAMBERMAID	HARDWORKING
OUAGADOUGOU	STADTHOLDER	WITCHDOCTOR	PARATYPHOID	CHANTARELLE	HEARTBROKEN
OVERCROWDED	STAKEHOLDER	AILUROPHILE	PHILIPPIANS	CHANTERELLE	HIPPOCRATES
OVERFLOWING	STALLHOLDER	ANENCEPHALY	PHILIPPINES	CHIROGRAPHY	HIPPOCRATIC
OVERWROUGHT	STEAMROLLER	ANSWERPHONE	PHILLIPSITE	CHITTERLING	HYPERTROPHY
PANDEMONIUM	STEGANOGRAM	APHANIPTERA	PHOTOSPHERE	CHOROGRAPHY	HYPOCORISMA
PARACROSTIC	STEGANOPODE	APOMORPHINE	PIERREPOINT	CHRYSAROBIN	ICONOGRAPHY
PARATROOPER	STELLIONATE	APOSIOPESIS	PISSASPHALT	CLAPPERCLAW	ILLUSTRATOR
PARLIPOMENA	STEPBROTHER	ARTHRAPODAL	PODSNAPPERY	COLEORRHIZA	ILLUSTRIOUS
PATERNOSTER	STOCKHOLDER	BADTEMPERED	PRESUMPTION	CONCURRENCE	IMPROPRIETY
PATHOLOGIST	STOCKJOBBER	BATHYSPHERE	PRESUMPTIVE	CONFARREATE	INADVERTENT
PAWNBROKERS	STRENUOUSLY	BIBLIOPHILE	PRINCIPALLY	CONSPIRATOR	INCINERATOR
PELARGONIUM	STYLOPODIUM	BLOODSPORTS	QUADRUPLETS	CONSTERNATE	INCOHERENCE
PENTECONTER	SUGARCOATED	BREASTPLATE	QUINTUPLETS	COUNTERFEIT	INCONGRUITY
PENTECOSTAL	SUMPTUOUSLY	CENTERPIECE	RUMGUMPTION	COUNTERFOIL	INCONGRUOUS
PERCEFOREST	SUPERIORITY	CENTREPIECE	SELFIMPOSED	COUNTERFORT	INDUSTRIOUS
PERCHLORATE	SYNCHROMESH	CENTRIPETAL	SHAKESPEARE	COUNTERGLOW	INFANTRYMAN
PERIODONTIC	SYNCHRONISE	CHARGEPAYER	SHOWERPROOF	COUNTERHAND	INFILTRATOR
PERISSOLOGY	SYNCHRONISM	CHLOROPHYLL	SILVERPOINT	COUNTERMAND	INNUMERABLE
PETRODOLLAR	SYNCHRONIZE	CHORDOPHONE	SPERMOPHILE	COUNTERPANE	INOPPORTUNE
PETTICOATED	SYNCHRONOUS	CHROMOPLAST	STEATOPYGIA	COUNTERPART	INSEPARABLE
PETTIFOGGER	TAUROBOLIUM	CHRYSOPRASE	SUBTROPICAL	COUNTERSIGN	INSUPERABLE
PHILOLOGIST	TCHAIKOVSKY	CIRRHIPEDEA	THALLOPHYTE	COUNTERSINK	INTERGROWTH
PHILOSOPHER	TEASPOONFUL	CIRRHIPEDIA	THERMOPYLAE	CRACKERJACK	INTERPRETER
PHOTOCOPIER	TEENYBOPPER	CLADOSPORUM	TIMBROPHILY	CYLINDRICAL	INTOLERABLE
PHRASEOLOGY	TELEPHONIST	COMEUPPANCE	TRICHOPTERA	DELETERIOUS	INTOLERABLY
PISCATORIAL	TENACIOUSLY	COMMONPLACE	TROPOSPHERE	DELIVERANCE	INTOLERANCE
PLEISTOCENE	TERMINOLOGY	CONSTIPATED	UNFLAPPABLE	DENUMERABLE	IRREPARABLE
PONDEROUSLY	TERREMOTIVE	CONSTUPRATE	UNSTOPPABLE	DIAPHORESIS	IRREPARABLY
PROLEGOMENA	TERRITORIAL	CONSUMPTION	WATERSPLASH	DIAPHORETIC	IRREVERENCE
PROTAGONIST	TESTIMONIAL	CONSUMPTIVE	YELLOWPLUSH	DIARTHROSIS	JAMAHIRIYAH
PROTEROZOIC	THALIDOMIDE	CONTEMPLANT	BUTTONQUAIL	DIASCORDIUM	LAUNDERETTE
PROTOCOCCUS	THANATOPSIS	CONTEMPLATE	LONGINQUITY	DISAPPROVAL	LEATHERBACK
PROTONOTARY	THEOBROMINE	CONTRAPTION	MONCHIQUITE	DISCOURTESY	LEATHERETTE
QUERULOUSLY	THROGMORTON	COPPERPLATE	MONTESQUIEU	DISIMPRISON	LEATHERHEAD
QUESTIONING	TITLEHOLDER	DESCRIPTION	PROPINQUITY	DITTOGRAPHY	LEATHERNECK
RADIOLOGIST	TOBACCONIST	DESCRIPTIVE	SOLILOQUIZE	DRINKDRIVER	LEATHERWOOD
RAPTUROUSLY	TORRIDONIAN	DEVELOPMENT	ACCELERATOR	EMPOWERMENT	LITHOGRAPHY
REACTIONARY	TORTICOLLIS	DISCREPANCY	ADULTERATED	ENARTHROSIS	MACHAIRODUS
RECIPROCATE	TRACHEOTOMY	ELASTOPLAST	ALLEGORICAL	ENCUMBRANCE	MAGISTRATES
RECIPROCITY	TRANSFORMED	EUCALYPTOLE	ANAGNORISIS	ENDOCARDIUM	MAISTERDOME
RECONNOITER	TRANSFORMER	FINGERPRINT	ANAPLEROSIS	EOANTHROPUS	MARLBOROUGH
RECONNOITRE	TRANSPONDER	GAMETOPHYTE	ANAPLEROTIC	ETHNOGRAPHY	MASQUERADER
REFLEXOLOGY	TRANSPORTED	GREASEPAINT	ANNABERGITE	EVISCERATED	MATRIARCHAL
RELIGIOUSLY	TRANSPORTER	HECKELPHONE	ANNIVERSARY	EXAGGERATED	MEANDERINGS
RETROROCKET	TRITAGONIST	HOMOEOPATHY	ANTIBURGHER	EXASPERATED	MERITORIOUS

METACARPALS	TACITURNITY	DIATESSERON	MORGENSTERN	VINCRISTINE	DISSERTATOR
METATARSALS	TAXIDERMIST	DISPENSABLE	MOXIBUSTION	WAPPENSCHAW	DISTASTEFUL
MISCARRIAGE	TECTIBRANCH	DISPERSABLE	NATIONSTATE	WINDLESTRAW	DRAUGHTSMAN
MOISTURIZER	TÉLÉFÉRIQUE	DISTRESSING	NEEDLESTICK	WITHERSHINS	EARNESTNESS
MONOCHROMAT	TELEWORKING	DISTRUSTFUL	NERVOUSNESS	YELLOWSTONE	EGOTISTICAL
MONTMORENCY	TETRADRACHM	DODECASTYLE	NEWSCASTING	ABSORPTANCE	ENCHANTMENT
NEANDERTHAL	THEATERGOER	DUBIOUSNESS	NONEXISTENT	ACCIPITRINE	ENCHANTRESS
OBLITERATED	THUNDERBIRD	ENGHALSKRUG	NONFEASANCE	ACCOUNTABLE	ENLIGHTENED
OBSTETRICAL	THUNDERBOLT	EPIDIASCOPE	NONSENSICAL	ACCOUNTANCY	EQUILATERAL
OCHLOCRATIC	THUNDERCLAP	EQUIDISTANT	OBMUTESCENT	ACOLOUTHITE	ERYMANTHIAN
OPPROBRIOUS	THUNDERHEAD	EVERLASTING	OBSOLESCENT	ANFRACTUOUS	EXORBITANCE
ORTHOGRAPHY	THYROTROPIN	FATUOUSNESS	OBVIOUSNESS	ANTHESTERIA	EXPEDITIOUS
OUTPOURINGS	TRANSURANIC	FINGERSTALL	OVERFISHING	APPARATCHIK	FLIRTATIOUS
OVERTURNING	UNALTERABLE	FLOURISHING	PARAMASTOID	APPOINTMENT	FOREFATHERS
PAEDOTROPHY	UNASSERTIVE	FLUORESCENT	PENTHESILEA	APPRENTICED	FOUNDATIONS
PALEOGRAPHY	UNCASTRATED	FLUOROSCOPE	PERMISSIBLE	ARCHENTERON	GOODNATURED
PARTNERSHIP	UNDERGROUND	FOOTWASHING	PHALANSTERY	BARBASTELLE	GRALLATORES
PASTEURELLA	UNDERGROWTH	FORECASTING	PLAGIOSTOMI	BELLETTRIST	GRAMMATICAL
PASTOURELLE	UNDERWRITER	FREEMASONRY	PLOUGHSHARE	BIRDWATCHER	HARDHITTING
PATRIARCHAL	UNDESERVING	GAMMERSTANG	POSSESSIONS	BLOODSTREAM	HATCHETTITE
PEDESTRIANS	UNDESIRABLE	GIGGLESTICK	PRESTISSIMO	BUPRESTIDAE	HIGHPITCHED
PERESTROIKA	UNENDURABLE	GIGGLESWICK	PRETENSIONS	CALLISTEMON	HYDROSTATIC
PERICARDIUM	UNFAVORABLE	GIRDLESTEAD	PROCRUSTEAN	CAMPESTRIAN	ICONOSTASIS
PERIGORDIAN	UNIMPORTANT	GODFORSAKEN	PROFESSEDLY	CAPACITANCE	IMPRACTICAL
PERIPHRASIS	UNNATURALLY	GORDONSTOUN	PROGRESSION	CAPACITATOR	INCONSTANCY
PERPETRATOR	UNOBSERVANT	GROUNDSHEET	PROGRESSIVE	CARNAPTIOUS	INDOMITABLE
PHOTOGRAPHY	UNSATURATED	GROUNDSPEED	PURPRESTURE	CHOLESTEROL	INDUBITABLE
PLAGIARISED	UNUTTERABLE	GROUNDSWELL	RAMGUNSHOCH	CLIMACTERIC	INDUBITABLY
PLATYRRHINE	VINAIGRETTE	GUTTERSNIPE	RATTLESNAKE	CLIOMETRICS	INELUCTABLE
PLEASURABLE	WEATHERCOCK	HEPATOSCOPY	RAUCOUSNESS	COEXISTENCE	INEQUITABLE
POCOCURANTE	WEIGHBRIDGE	HETEROSCIAN	REMINISCENT	COLLECTANEA	INEXCITABLE
POLYMORPHIC	WHEELWRIGHT	HIDEOUSNESS	RENAISSANCE	COMBUSTIBLE	INFANGTHIEF
PORNOGRAPHY	WHISKERANDO	HYOPLASTRON	RESPONSIBLE	COMFORTABLE	INHABITABLE
PREMIERSHIP	WHITEFRIARS	IMPLAUSIBLE	RESPONSIBLY	COMFORTABLY	INHABITANTS
PRESSURIZED	WINDSURFING	INADVISABLE	RESPONSIONS	COMFORTLESS	INHERITANCE
PYELOGRAPHY	WOODCARVING	INCALESCENT	RETINOSCOPY	COMMENTATOR	INSCRUTABLE
QUARTERBACK	WORRYTROUGH	INDIGESTION	RETINOSPORA	COMPARTMENT	INSTANTIATE
QUARTERDECK	ACQUIESCENT	INDIVISIBLE	ROTTENSTONE	CONCENTRATE	INTRACTABLE
RADIOGRAPHY	APLANOSPORE	INDIVISIBLY	SANDERSWOOD	CONCEPTICLE	IRREFUTABLE
REASSURANCE	ARTHROSPORE	INEXCUSABLE	SCYPHISTOMA	CONDOTTIERE	KATABOTHRON
RECOVERABLE	ASTONISHING	INEXCUSABLY	SELFRESPECT	CONDOTTIORE	KATAVOTHRON
REINCARNATE	BELORUSSIAN	INTERESTING	SERIOUSNESS	CONDUCTANCE	KETAVOTHRON
REMEMBRANCE	BILIOUSNESS	KINDERSPIEL	SHAFTESBURY	CONDUCTRESS	KIRKPATRICK
RINTHEREOUT	BITTERSWEET	KOMMERSBUCH	SILVERSMITH	CONJECTURAL	KOTABOTHRON
SCARBOROUGH	BUMBERSHOOT	KRIEGSSPIEL	SINGLESTICK	CONNECTICUT	LATERITIOUS
SCATTERGOOD	BUSINESSMAN	LAPIDESCENT	SMORGASBORD	CONSISTENCE	LOGARITHMIC
SCATTERLING	CACOGASTRIC	LAWLESSNESS	SPREADSHEET	CONSISTENCY	LOOSESTRIFE
SCHOLARSHIP	CALLOUSNESS	LEPIDOSIREN	STEREOSCOPE	CONSTITUENT	MALAKATOONE
SCREWDRIVER	CANDLESTICK	LINGUISTICS	STETHOSCOPE	CONSULTANCY	MEDIASTINUM
SCUPPERNONG	CHIAROSCURO	LIVINGSTONE	STILBESTROL	CONTENTEDLY	MILQUETOAST
SELFSERVICE	CHINOISERIE	LOCORESTIVE	STROBOSCOPE	CONTENTIOUS	MULTISTOREY
SHEPHERDESS	CIRCUMSPECT	LONGLASTING	SUPPRESSION	CONTENTMENT	MYXOMATOSIS
SINISTRORSE	CLANDESTINE	LUMINESCENT	SYNTHESIZED	CONTRETEMPS	NIPFARTHING
SLENDERNESS	COBBLESTONE	LYCHNOSCOPE	SYNTHESIZER	CONVENTICLE	NOVELETTISH
SLUMBERWEAR	COCKLESHELL	MALFEASANCE	TATTERSALLS	CONVERTIBLE	OMNIPOTENCE
SMITHEREENS	COLLAPSIBLE	MANGALSUTRA	TEDIOUSNESS	COPROSTEROL	ONOMASTICON
SNICKERSNEE	COMMONSENSE	MANTELSHELF	TENUOUSNESS	CORRECTNESS	OPTOMETRIST
SPATTERDASH	CONGRESSMAN	MANUMISSION	TRACASSERIE	CORRUPTIBLE	ORCHESTRATE
SPATTERDOCK	CONNOISSEUR	MEADOWSWEET	TRESPASSING	CREDENTIALS	ORCHESTRINA
SPESSARTITE	CONTRASTING	MEDIUMSIZED	UNCHRISTIAN	CURNAPTIOUS	ORCHESTRION
SPONSORSHIP	CONVULSIONS	MENDELSSOHN	UNIVERSALLY	CYCLOSTYLED	OUTDISTANCE
STANDARDIZE	CORNERSTONE	MIDDENSTEAD	UNNECESSARY	DEBILITATED	PAEDIATRICS
STENOGRAPHY	DELITESCENT	MIDDLESIZED	UNSATISFIED	DECAPITATED	PARACETAMOL
STOCKBROKER	DEMIBASTION	MISCONSTRUE	USELESSNESS	DECONSTRUCT	PARASITOSIS
SWITZERLAND	DEVIOUSNESS	MISFEASANCE	VACUOUSNESS	DECORATIONS	PERCEPTIBLE
SYMMETRICAL	DIAGNOSTICS	MISSISSIPPI	VICIOUSNESS	DEMONSTRATE	PERCEPTIBLY
TACHYGRAPHY	DIATESSARON	MISTRUSTFUL	VINBLASTINE	DISCONTINUE	PERIPATETIC

PERLUSTRATE	UNRIGHTEOUS	MALADJUSTED	HIGHPOWERED	BILLIONAIRE	DITTOGRAPHY
PERSISTENCE	UNSHELTERED	MARIVAUDAGE	JABBERWOCKY	BOTANOMANCY	DOCTRINAIRE
PHILOCTETES	UNSWEETENED	MATRICULATE	NEEDLEWOMAN	CALCEOLARIA	DRAGONNADES
PINACOTHECA	UPHOLSTERER	MICROTUBULE	POLICEWOMAN	CALLIGRAPHY	DRASTICALLY
PRECAUTIONS	UPRIGHTNESS	MINIATURIST	SHALLOWNESS	CAMOUFLAGED	EARTHSHAKER
PREDESTINED	VESPERTINAL	MINIATURIZE	SPARROWHAWK	CAMPHORATED	EFFECTUALLY
PREDICTABLE	ZOROASTRIAN	OPPORTUNELY	SPOKESWOMAN	CAPACITANCE	EMMENTHALER
PREDICTABLY	ACCULTURATE	OPPORTUNISM	SPORTSWOMAN	CAPACITATOR	EMOTIONALLY
PREHISTORIC	ADVENTURESS	OPPORTUNIST	SWALLOWABLE	CARDOPHAGUS	EMPYROMANCY
PRESENTABLE	ADVENTUROUS	OPPORTUNITY	SWORDSWOMAN	CARTOGRAPHY	ENCUMBRANCE
PRESENTMENT	AERONAUTICS	OVERSTUFFED	WASHERWOMAN	CASTELLATED	ENFORCEABLE
PRETENTIOUS	AMINOBUTENE	PARACHUTIST	WIENERWURST	CAUSTICALLY	EQUIVOCALLY
PREVENTABLE	ANACOLUTHIA	PERAMBULATE	PARADOXICAL	CENTURIATOR	ERRATICALLY
PROGNATHOUS	ANTINEUTRON	PERPETUALLY	ANDROGYNOUS	CERTIFIABLE	ESSENTIALLY
PROPHETICAL	ARQUEBUSIER	PERSECUTION	ANTHOCYANIN	CHARGEPAYER	ETHNOGRAPHY
RALLENTANDO	ATTRIBUTION	PICKYOUROWN	APOCALYPTIC	CHARISMATIC	EUCHROMATIN
RECONSTRUCT	ATTRIBUTIVE	PREMATURELY	BORBORYGMUS	CHARLEMAGNE	EVISCERATED
RECRUITMENT	AVOIRDUPOIS	PREOCCUPIED	CALLIPYGEAN	CHEERLEADER	EXAGGERATED
REDOUBTABLE	BARBITURATE	PROLOCUTION	CATACLYSMIC	CHICHEVACHE	EXASPERATED
REGRETTABLE	BELEAGUERED	PROSECUTION	CERARGYRITE	CHIROGRAPHY	EXHILARATED
REGRETTABLY	BIELORUSSIA	RATATOUILLE	CONTRAYERVA	CHOROGRAPHY	EXORBITANCE
REMONSTRATE	BLOCKBUSTER	RESTITUTION	COUNTRYSIDE	CHRISTMASSY	FANATICALLY
REPETITIOUS	BLOODSUCKER	RETRIBUTION	FLAMBOYANCE	CHRONICALLY	FASHIONABLE
RESPECTABLE	CARBORUNDUM	RETRIBUTIVE	FLAMBOYANTE	CLEANSHAVEN	FASHIONABLY
RESPECTABLY	CATACAUSTIC	ROSICRUCIAN	KIDDLEYWINK	COLLECTANEA	FINANCIALLY
RETRACTABLE	CONFABULATE	SALVOGUNNER	METAPHYSICS	COMEUPPANCE	FISSIONABLE
REVELATIONS	CONSECUTIVE	SPIRITUALLY	OVERPAYMENT	COMFORTABLE	FLAMBOYANCE
REVOLUTIONS	CONSEQUENCE	STRANGULATE	POLYSTYRENE	COMFORTABLY	FLAMBOYANTE
RHEUMATICKY	CONSTRUCTOR	SUBUNGULATA	PROSELYTISM	COMMENDABLE	FORBEARANCE
RUMBUSTIOUS	CONTINUALLY	TORTICULLUS	PROSELYTIZE	COMMENDABLY	FORBIDDANCE
SACHERTORTE	CONTINUANCE	TRANSFUSION	PYRARGYRITE	COMMENTATOR	FORESEEABLE
SCRUMPTIOUS	CONVOLUTION	TRANSLUCENT	STRINGYBARK	COMPLICATED	FRANTICALLY
SENTENTIOUS	DELINQUENCY	TURRICULATE	STRONGYLOID	COMPRIMARIO	FRATERNALLY
SEPIOSTAIRE	DESTITUTION	UNANNOUNCED	TIDDLEYWINK	CONCEIVABLE	FURTHERANCE
SEPTENTRION	DISENCUMBER	UNCONQUERED	TYROGLYPHID	CONCEIVABLY	GENERICALLY
SEQUESTRATE	DISFIGURING	UNDISGUISED	WENSLEYDALE	CONCILIATOR	GENETICALLY
SPERMATOZOA	DISILLUSION	UNDISTURBED	ORGANIZAION	CONCORDANCE	GENTLEMANLY
SRANANTONGO	DISSIMULATE	UNFORTUNATE	RINFORZANDO	CONDUCTANCE	GIGGLEWATER
STATISTICAL	DISSOLUTION	UNOBTRUSIVE	TOTALIZATOR	CONSERVANCY	GLOSSOLALIA
STEREOTYPED	DUMBFOUNDED	UNPERTURBED	**11:8**	CONSPIRATOR	GODFORSAKEN
SUBCONTRACT	EFFECTUALLY	VERMICULITE	ABBREVIATED	CONSTIPATED	GRAPHICALLY
SUBMULTIPLE	ENCAPSULATE	WAREHOUSING	ABRACADABRA	CONSULTANCY	GREASEPAINT
SUBSISTENCE	EXPOSTULATE	WELLFOUNDED	ABSORPTANCE	CONTINUALLY	GUADALCANAL
SUGGESTIBLE	FAUXBOURDON	BASKERVILLE	ACCELERATOR	CONTINUANCE	HAGIOGRAPHA
SUSCEPTIBLE	FILLIBUSTER	BRAZZAVILLE	ACCOUNTABLE	CONTRIVANCE	HAGIOGRAPHY
TAGLIATELLE	FOULMOUTHED	CENTUMVIRUS	ACCOUNTANCY	CONVALLARIA	HINDERLANDS
TEMPESTUOUS	FRANKFURTER	CHICHEVACHE	ACCUMULATOR	COORDINATED	HIPPOCRATES
TENDENTIOUS	FRONTRUNNER	CONCEIVABLE	ADJUDICATOR	COORDINATES	HIPPOCRATIC
TERRESTRIAL	FUNAMBULIST	CONCEIVABLY	ADULTERATED	COPROPHAGAN	HISTORIATED
THAUMATROPE	GABERLUNZIE	CONSERVANCY	ADVERBIALLY	COUNTENANCE	HOLLANDAISE
THEORETICAL	GESTICULATE	CONTRIVANCE	AERODYNAMIC	CRENELLATED	HOMOEOPATHY
THESMOTHETE	HOLOTHURIAN	CONTROVERSY	ALIFANFARON	CRITHOMANCY	HYDROSTATIC
THIGMOTAXIS	HOMOIOUSIAN	CONVOLVULUS	AMPHISBAENA	DEBILITATED	ICONOGRAPHY
THOUGHTLESS	HONEYSUCKLE	IRRELEVANCE	ANAPHYLAXIS	DECAPITATED	ICONOSTASIS
TOPLOFTICAL	IMPORTUNATE	PENTONVILLE	ANGELOLATRY	DELIVERANCE	IDENTICALLY
TRIMESTRIAL	INCAPSULATE	RETRIEVABLE	ANTHOCYANIN	DEMONOMANIA	IDIOTICALLY
TYPESETTING	INCREDULITY	SUBSERVIENT	ANTIPHRASIS	DENOMINATOR	IDYLLICALLY
UNBEFITTING	INCREDULOUS	UNEQUIVOCAL	ANTONOMASIA	DENUMERABLE	ILLOGICALLY
UNCLUTTERED	INDIARUBBER	UNMOTIVATED	APOLLINARIS	DESCENDANTS	ILLUMINANCE
UNCOUNTABLE	INFREQUENCY	WELLADVISED	APPRECIABLE	DIATESSARON	ILLUMINATED
UNDERSTATED	INSTITUTION	CAMERAWOMAN	APPRECIABLY	DICHROMATIC	ILLUSTRATOR
UNDOUBTEDLY	INTERNUNCIO	CESAREWITCH	ARTICULATED	DILAPIDATED	IMPARTIALLY
UNGETATABLE	INTERRUPTER	FRENCHWOMAN	ASCLEPIADES	DISCREPANCY	IMPERMEABLE
UNPALATABLE	IPECACUANHA	FRENCHWOMEN	ASSIMILATED	DISPENSABLE	IMPREGNABLE
UNPRACTICAL	KAMELAUKION	GENTLEWOMAN	BACCHANALIA	DISPERSABLE	INADVISABLE
UNPRINTABLE	LILLIPUTIAN	GIGGLEWATER	BALISTRARIA	DISSERTATOR	INALIENABLE
UNREMITTING	LUXEMBURGER	HEPPLEWHITE	BANDEIRANTE	DISTURBANCE	INCINERATOR

INCONSTANCY	NYMPHOMANIA	SCANDANAVIA	UNPRINTABLE	CATHOLICISM	RETINOSCOPY
INDEFINABLE	OBLITERATED	SCANDINAVIA	UNSATURATED	CERTIFICATE	RETROROCKET
INDOMITABLE	OCHLOCRATIC	SCEPTICALLY	UNSHAKEABLE	CHIAROSCURO	REVENDICATE
INDUBITABLE	OLIGOCHAETE	SCHECKLATON	UNSPEAKABLE	CLAPPERCLAW	RHOPALOCERA
INDUBITABLY	ONEIROMANCY	SCRIMSHANDY	UNSTOPPABLE	COMMUNICANT	ROMANTICISM
INELUCTABLE	OPINIONATED	SEPIOSTAIRE	UNTHINKABLE	COMMUNICATE	ROMANTICIZE
INEQUITABLE	ORGANICALLY	SERVICEABLE	UNTOUCHABLE	CONSTRICTED	ROSICRUCIAN
INESCAPABLE	ORGANIZAION	SHORTCHANGE	UNUTTERABLE	CONSTRICTOR	SACRIFICIAL
INESTIMABLE	ORTHOGRAPHY	SKEPTICALLY	UTRICULARIA	CONSTRUCTOR	SCIREFACIAS
INEXCITABLE	OSTEOPLASTY	SKILLIGALEE	VENDEMIAIRE	DECORTICATE	SEXTODECIMO
INEXCUSABLE	OUTDISTANCE	SOCKDALAGER	WATERMEADOW	DELITESCENT	SHIPWRECKED
INEXCUSABLY	OVERBALANCE	SOCKDOLAGER	WELLBEHAVED	DIPTEROCARP	SHUTTLECOCK
INFILTRATOR	PACIFICALLY	SPIRITUALLY	WHISKERANDO	DISAFFECTED	SIGNIFICANT
INFLAMMABLE	PALEOGRAPHY	SPIROCHAETE	WHITECHAPEL	DOMESTICATE	SPANGCOCKLE
INHABITABLE	PANOMPHAEAN	STENOGRAPHY	WINDBREAKER	DOMESTICITY	SPIFFLICATE
INHABITANTS	PARABOLANUS	STRAITLACED	WINDCHEATER	DREADLOCKED	SPITSTICKER
INHERITANCE	PARACETAMOL	STRETCHABLE	WRONGHEADED	ELECTRICIAN	STEREOSCOPE
INNUMERABLE	PARONOMASIA	SUGARCOATED	BANNOCKBURN	ELECTRICITY	STETHOSCOPE
INSCRUTABLE	PENSIONABLE	SUPERCHARGE	BESSARABIAN	ELECTROCUTE	STROBOSCOPE
INSEPARABLE	PERENNIALLY	SUSTAINABLE	BLUNDERBORE	EPIDIASCOPE	SUNDRENCHED
INSOUCIANCE	PERFORMANCE	SVARABHAKTI	BRANDENBURG	ERYTHROCYTE	SUPERFICIAL
INSUPERABLE	PERIPHRASIS	SWALLOWABLE	COMESTIBLES	ESCHERICHIA	SUPERFICIES
INTERCHANGE	PERITONAEUM	SYMPLEGADES	CONSUMABLES	FERNITICKLE	TABERNACLES
INTOLERABLE	PERPETRATOR	SYMPOSIARCH	DIAMONDBACK	FIRECRACKER	THEATRICALS
INTOLERABLY	PERPETUALLY	SYMPTOMATIC	ECCALEOBION	FISHANDCHIP	THUNDERCLAP
INTOLERANCE	PETTICOATED	TACHYGRAPHY	FLANKERBACK	FLUORESCENT	TRANSLUCENT
INTOXICATED	PHOTOGRAPHY	TATTERSALLS	FRIGATEBIRD	FLUOROSCOPE	UNCONNECTED
INTRACTABLE	PHTHIRIASIS	TECHNICALLY	GLASTONBURY	HEPATOSCOPY	UNPROTECTED
INVIGILATOR	PICKELHAUBE	TECTIBRANCH	HERRINGBONE	HETEROSCIAN	UNSUSPECTED
IPECACUANHA	PLEASURABLE	TEGUCICALPA	HUMMINGBIRD	HIGHPITCHED	WAPPENSCHAW
IRREFUTABLE	POCOCURANTE	TESSELLATED	INDIARUBBER	HONEYSUCKLE	WEATHERCOCK
IRREGULARLY	POLITICALLY	TETRADRACHM	INVINCIBLES	HORSERACING	WITCHDOCTOR
IRRELEVANCE	PORNOGRAPHY	THIGMOTAXIS	KNUCKLEBALL	HYPOTHECATE	ACCOMMODATE
IRREPARABLE	POTENTIALLY	THINGAMABOB	KOMMERSBUCH	ILLYWHACKER	ANTEPENDIUM
IRREPARABLY	PRACTICABLE	THINGAMAJIG	LEATHERBACK	INCALESCENT	BACKSLIDING
IRREVOCABLE	PRACTICALLY	THINGUMAJIG	MECKLENBURG	INCORRECTLY	BOOKBINDING
JUSTIFIABLE	PREDICTABLE	TIMBROMANIA	MICROTUBULE	INDUPLICATE	CHIPPENDALE
JUSTIFIABLY	PREDICTABLY	TOTALIZATOR	MOCKINGBIRD	INFANTICIDE	CHIROPODIST
KLEPTOMANIA	PRESENTABLE	TRAFFICATOR	QUARTERBACK	INSECTICIDE	CONSOLIDATE
LACONICALLY	PREVENTABLE	TRANSURANIC	REICHENBACH	INTERLACING	DESERPIDINE
LEGIONNAIRE	PRINCIPALLY	TREASONABLE	SCUTTLEBUTT	INTERNECINE	DIASCORDIUM
LEVELHEADED	PROOFREADER	TRINCOMALEE	SHAFTESBURY	LAPIDESCENT	DIPROTODONT
LIGHTHEADED	PROPHYLAXIS	TURBELLARIA	SMORGASBORD	LASERPICIUM	DISEMBODIED
LINDISFARNE	PROSAICALLY	UNALIENABLE	STICKLEBACK	LUMINESCENT	DOWNTRODDEN
LITHOGRAPHY	PUBLISHABLE	UNALTERABLE	STOCKJOBBER	LYCHNOSCOPE	ENCHIRIDION
LOUDSPEAKER	PYELOGRAPHY	UNAVAILABLE	STRINGYBARK	MAGNIFICENT	ENDOCARDIUM
MAGISTRATES	RADIOGRAPHY	UNAVOIDABLE	THUNDERBIRD	MATRIARCHAL	ENNEAHEDRON
MAINTENANCE	RALLENTANDO	UNAVOIDABLY	THUNDERBOLT	MICROSECOND	ERIODENDRON
MALFEASANCE	REASSURANCE	UNBREAKABLE	ACADEMICIAN	MULTIRACIAL	FACTFINDING
MANIPULATOR	RECOVERABLE	UNCASTRATED	ACADEMICISM	OBMUTESCENT	GALLOVIDIAN
MASQUERADER	RECTIFIABLE	UNCONCEALED	ACATALECTIC	OBSOLESCENT	HANGGLIDING
MEDICINALLY	REDOUBTABLE	UNCOUNTABLE	ACQUIESCENT	OCTASTICHON	HEBDOMADARY
MEGALOMANIA	REGRETTABLE	UNCRUSHABLE	AGNOSTICISM	OXYRHYNCHUS	HORSERADISH
MEGALOMANIC	REGRETTABLY	UNDERCHARGE	AMPLEXICAUL	PATRIARCHAL	HORSERIDING
MENTHOLATED	REMEMBRANCE	UNDERSTATED	AMYLOPECTIN	PERTINACITY	HYDROMEDUSA
MIDDLEMARCH	RENAISSANCE	UNDESIRABLE	APPARATCHIK	PHONETICIAN	IMPROVIDENT
MILLIONAIRE	REPLACEABLE	UNDRINKABLE	ARCHILOCHUS	PLEISTOCENE	INCARNADINE
MISALLIANCE	RESEMBLANCE	UNENDURABLE	ARTIODACTYL	POLYTRICHUM	INDEPENDENT
MISDEMEANOR	RESPECTABLE	UNFAVORABLE	AURIGNACIAN	PONTIFICATE	INTREPIDITY
MISFEASANCE	RESPECTABLY	UNFLAPPABLE	AVERRUNCATE	PREJUDICIAL	LATIFUNDIUM
NATUROPATHY	RETRACTABLE	UNGETATABLE	AZOTOBACTER	PREVARICATE	LOGODAEDALY
NETHERLANDS	RETRIEVABLE	UNINITIATED	BACKBENCHER	PROTOCOCCUS	MACERANDUBA
NOMENCLATOR	RHABDOMANCY	UNIVERSALLY	BIRDWATCHER	PTERODACTYL	MAISTERDOME
NONCHALANCE	RINFORZANDO	UNMITIGATED	BLOODSUCKER	RECIPROCATE	MAQUILADORA
NONFEASANCE	SALTIMBANCO	UNMOTIVATED	BRISTLECONE	RECIPROCITY	MARIVAUDAGE
NOSTRADAMUS	SARCOPHAGUS	UNNATURALLY	BUSHWHACKER	REDUPLICATE	MERCHANDISE
NUMERICALLY	SATIRICALLY	UNPALATABLE	CATALLACTIC	REMINISCENT	MERCHANDIZE

MOLLYCODDLE	CAMARADERIE	FRAUDULENCE	RINTHEREOUT	HIGHPROFILE	PATHOLOGIST
NEVERENDING	CANDESCENCE	GAMOGENESIS	ROBESPIERRE	HUMGRUFFIAN	PETTIFOGGER
NICKELODEON	CARRIAGEWAY	HABILIMENTS	SALINOMETER	HUNDREDFOLD	PHILOLOGIST
OSTRACODERM	CATACHRESIS	HIGHPOWERED	SANGUINEOUS	MONTGOLFIER	QUARRINGTON
OUTSTANDING	CENTRIPETAL	HOBBLEDEHOY	SANSEVIERIA	OVERSTUFFED	RADIOLOGIST
PERICARDIUM	CHANTARELLE	HOMOGENEITY	SAPONACEOUS	PERSONIFIED	RIGHTANGLED
PERIGORDIAN	CHANTERELLE	HOMOGENEOUS	SCARABAEOID	SCALPRIFORM	SAPROLEGNIA
PHONOFIDDLE	CHINOISERIE	HOUSEKEEPER	SCHWARMEREI	SCOLECIFORM	SCATTERGOOD
PORTLANDIAN	CHOLESTEROL	HUCKLEBERRY	SCLERODERMA	SEVERALFOLD	SCULDUGGERY
QUARTERDECK	CHRONOMETER	HURTLEBERRY	SCOREKEEPER	STANDOFFISH	SHENANIGANS
RESPLENDENT	CINQUECENTO	ILLMANNERED	SELAGINELLA	UNDIGNIFIED	SKIMMINGTON
SCAFFOLDING	CIRRHIPEDEA	IMPEDIMENTA	SELFDEFENCE	UNJUSTIFIED	SKULDUGGERY
SCULDUDDERY	CIRRHIPEDIA	INCOHERENCE	SENNACHERIB	UNQUALIFIED	SOCIOLOGIST
SELFEVIDENT	CLIMACTERIC	INFREQUENCY	SEPTICAEMIA	UNSATISFIED	SOVEREIGNTY
SHEPHERDESS	COALESCENCE	INGREDIENTS	SEVENTEENTH	UNSPECIFIED	STEGANOGRAM
SKIDBLADNIR	COEXISTENCE	INSTRUMENTS	SHAKESPEARE	WINDSURFING	STOOLPIGEON
SKULDUDDERY	COGNOSCENTE	INTERPRETER	SIGHTSEEING	ANNABERGITE	TESSARAGLOT
SPATTERDASH	COGNOSCENTI	INTERSPERSE	SILVERBERRY	ANTHOLOGIZE	THEATERGOER
SPATTERDOCK	COINCIDENCE	INTERVIEWEE	SMITHEREENS	ANTIBURGHER	THEATREGOER
STANDARDIZE	COLORIMETER	INTERVIEWER	SPEEDOMETER	ARBITRAGEUR	TRANSFIGURE
STYLOPODIUM	COMMONSENSE	INTOXIMETER	SPONTANEITY	BORBORYGMUS	UNDERSIGNED
SUBSTANDARD	COMPLACENCY	IRIDESCENCE	SPONTANEOUS	BROBDINGNAG	VOTERIGGING
SUPERSEDEAS	COMPLIMENTS	IRREVERENCE	STEREOMETER	CALLIPYGEAN	WATERLOGGED
SUPERSEDERE	CONCURRENCE	KITCHENETTE	STOREKEEPER	CAROLINGIAN	WHITTINGTON
SURROUNDING	CONFARREATE	LAMMERGEIER	STRAMINEOUS	CHALLENGING	WIDERANGING
TARRADIDDLE	CONSEQUENCE	LAMMERGEYER	SUBITANEOUS	CHILLINGHAM	ACOLOUTHITE
TETRAHEDRON	CONSILIENCE	LANDSKNECHT	SUBMERGENCE	COUNTERGLOW	AFTERSCHOOL
THISTLEDOWN	CONSISTENCE	LAUNDERETTE	SUBSISTENCE	CROSSLEGGED	AILUROPHILE
TRINIDADIAN	CONSISTENCY	LEATHERETTE	SUFFICIENCY	DACTYLOGRAM	AMELANCHIER
ULTRAMODERN	CONTENTEDLY	LOGGERHEADS	SUFFRAGETTE	DESEGREGATE	ANENCEPHALY
UNDEMANDING	CONTINGENCE	LONGSLEEVED	SUPERCHERIE	DISPARAGING	ANSWERPHONE
UNUNQUADIUM	CONTINGENCY	MALEVOLENCE	SYMPATHETIC	ENCOURAGING	APOMORPHINE
WATEREDDOWN	CONTRAYERVA	MANTELLETTA	TAGLIATELLE	ETHNOLOGIST	APPROACHING
WENSLEYDALE	CONTRETEMPS	MARIONBERRY	TELEKINESIS	ETYMOLOGIST	ASTONISHING
WITHHOLDING	CONTROVERSY	METAGENESIS	TENSIOMETER	EXTRAVAGANT	BATHYSPHERE
ABIOGENESIS	CONVENIENCE	MINESWEEPER	THERMOMETER	FARTHINGALE	BIBLIOPHILE
ABIOGENETIC	CONVERGENCE	MONTMORENCY	TOXICOGENIC	FISHMONGERS	BROTHERHOOD
ABSENTEEISM	COPROSTEROL	MUNIFICENCE	TRACASSERIE	FLABBERGAST	BULLFIGHTER
ACCRESCENCE	CRACOVIENNE	OFFHANDEDLY	TREECREEPER	FLORILEGIUM	BUMBERSHOOT
ACKNOWLEDGE	CYTOGENESIS	OMNIPOTENCE	TRICHINELLA	GALLIBAGGER	CHLOROPHYLL
ADOLESCENCE	DELINQUENCY	OMNISCIENCE	TRIPTOLEMUS	GALLIBEGGAR	CHORDOPHONE
AGONOTHETES	DEMOSTHENES	OPALESCENCE	UNCLUTTERED	GALLYBAGGER	CLAIRSCHACH
AGUARDIENTE	DEMOSTHENIC	ORTHOPAEDIC	UNCONQUERED	GALLYBEGGAR	COCKLESHELL
AIGUILLETTE	DESPONDENCY	PARENTHESIS	UNDOUBTEDLY	GAMETANGIUM	COLEORRHIZA
ALBUGINEOUS	DIAPHORESIS	PASTEURELLA	UNRIGHTEOUS	GENEALOGIST	COLLENCHYMA
AMBIVALENCE	DIAPHORETIC	PASTOURELLE	UNSHELTERED	GLIMMERGOWK	COUNTERHAND
ANAESTHESIA	DIATESSERON	PEACEKEEPER	UNSWEETENED	GRAVEDIGGER	DENDRACHATE
ANAESTHETIC	DICOTYLEDON	PERCIPIENCE	UPHOLSTERER	HISTOLOGIST	DOUBLECHECK
ANTECEDENCE	DISAGREEING	PERIPATETIC	VALLISNERIA	HORNSWOGGLE	ENCROACHING
ANTHESTERIA	DISBELIEVER	PERSISTENCE	VARSOVIENNE	HYMNOLOGIST	ENFRANCHISE
ANTIPYRETIC	DISCOTHEQUE	PHILANDERER	VINAIGRETTE	INTELLIGENT	ERYMANTHIAN
ANTISTHENES	DISGRACEFUL	PHILOCTETES	VIOLINCELLO	INTERREGNUM	ESTRANGHELO
APOSIOPESIS	DISTASTEFUL	PITCHBLENDE	VIOLONCELLO	INTERROGATE	EYECATCHING
ARCHENTERON	DYAESTHESIA	PLANTAGENET	WHIGMALEERY	INVESTIGATE	FARREACHING
ARRIVEDERCI	ENFOULDERED	POLIORCETIC	WINDOWLEDGE	IRONMONGERS	FIRELIGHTER
ARTHRODESIS	ENLIGHTENED	POLTERGEIST	WINTERBERRY	IRONMONGERY	FLOURISHING
ASTRINGENCY	EPITHYMETIC	POTAMOGETON	WITENAGEMOT	KIMERIDGIAN	FOOTWASHING
ATMOSPHERIC	EQUILATERAL	PRECONCEIVE	ACINACIFORM	LEFTLUGGAGE	FOREFATHERS
AUXANOMETER	EQUIVALENCE	PREEMINENCE	CHICKENFEED	MARCONIGRAM	FORFOUGHTEN
BADTEMPERED	ESPIEGLERIE	PREPOLLENCE	CLANJAMFRAY	MONOLINGUAL	FORTNIGHTLY
BANGLADESHI	EXCRESCENCE	PROFESSEDLY	COUNTERFEIT	MUDSLINGING	GAMETOPHYTE
BARBASTELLE	EXOSKELETON	PROFICIENCY	COUNTERFOIL	MYCOPHAGIST	GEGENSCHEIN
BATTLEMENTS	FARINACEOUS	PSYCHEDELIC	COUNTERFORT	MYTHOLOGIZE	GODDAUGHTER
BELEAGUERED	FARKLEBERRY	PUNCHINELLO	COUNTRIFIED	NEUROLOGIST	GROUNDSHEET
BENEVOLENCE	FIDDLEDEDEE	RESOURCEFUL	DEVITRIFIED	NIGHTINGALE	HAEMORRHAGE
BOYSENBERRY	FLANNELETTE	RIDDLEMEREE	DOLABRIFORM	OVERHANGING	HAEMORRHOID
CALLISTEMON	FLUOROMETER	RIFACIMENTO	HANDCRAFTED	PASSACAGLIA	HARPSICHORD

HECKELPHONE	BOURGEOISIE	HALFHOLIDAY	PERMISSIBLE	TONSILLITIS	BACKFIELDER
HEPPLEWHITE	BOUTONNIERE	HALLEFLINTA	PETITMAITRE	TOPLOFTICAL	BESTSELLING
HIGHLIGHTER	BRAZZAVILLE	HAREBRAINED	PHARISAICAL	TRANSCEIVER	BLACKFELLOW
INFANGTHIEF	BUPRESTIDAE	HEAVYWEIGHT	PHARYNGITIS	TRANSILIENT	BOOKSELLERS
ISOMORPHOUS	CALEFACIENT	HEXADECIMAL	PHILIPPIANS	TRIPHIBIOUS	BREASTPLATE
KATABOTHRON	CALLITRICHE	HOMOGENIZED	PHILIPPINES	UNCERTAINTY	BREATHALYSE
KATAVOTHRON	CANDLELIGHT	HYDROPHIDAE	PLAGIARISED	UNCIVILISED	CAMALDOLITE
KETAVOTHRON	CAPERNOITED	HYPOCORISMA	POLITICIANS	UNCIVILIZED	CAMPANOLOGY
KOTABOTHRON	CAPERNOITIE	IDEOLOGICAL	POSSESSIONS	UNCONSCIOUS	CANNIBALISM
LAMPLIGHTER	CAPRICCIOSO	IGNOMINIOUS	PRECAUTIONS	UNDERWEIGHT	CANNIBALIZE
LAMPROPHYRE	CARABINIERE	ILLUSTRIOUS	PREDESTINED	UNDERWRITER	CATERPILLAR
LEATHERHEAD	CARNAPTIOUS	IMPECUNIOUS	PRESSURIZED	UNDISGUISED	CHAMBERLAIN
LOGARITHMIC	CATEGORICAL	IMPLAUSIBLE	PRESTIGIOUS	UNEXPLAINED	CHANCELLERY
LONGSIGHTED	CENTERPIECE	IMPRACTICAL	PRETENSIONS	UNINHABITED	CHANTICLEER
MANTELSHELF	CENTREPIECE	IMPROPRIETY	PRETENTIOUS	UNINHIBITED	CHEESECLOTH
MELANOCHROI	CENTUMVIRUS	INDIVISIBLE	PROCEEDINGS	UNPRACTICAL	CHIASTOLITE
MONONGAHELA	CEREMONIOUS	INDIVISIBLY	PROPHETICAL	UNSOLICITED	CHITTERLING
MOONLIGHTER	CESAREWITCH	INDUSTRIOUS	PUNCTILIOUS	VESPERTINAL	CHOCKABLOCK
NEARSIGHTED	CIRCUMCISER	INEFFICIENT	PURITANICAL	VICHYSOISSE	CHROMOPLAST
NIPFARTHING	CLARENCIEUX	INEXPEDIENT	RATATOUILLE	VITAMINIZED	CIRCUMFLECT
ODONTOPHORE	COEFFICIENT	INJUDICIOUS	REALPOLITIK	WATERSKIING	CITRONELLAL
OMMATOPHORE	COLLAPSIBLE	INSTANTIATE	REAPPRAISAL	WEIGHBRIDGE	CLIMATOLOGY
OSTREOPHAGE	COMBUSTIBLE	IRREDUCIBLE	RECONNOITER	WELLADVISED	CLINOCHLORE
OVERFISHING	COMPENDIOUS	IRRELIGIOUS	RECONNOITRE	WELLDEFINED	COACHFELLOW
PARANEPHROS	CONCEPTICLE	JACQUEMINOT	REPETITIOUS	WHEELWRIGHT	COLONIALISM
PARATYPHOID	CONDOTTIERE	JAMAHIRIYAH	RESPONSIBLE	WHITEFRIARS	COLONIALIST
PHOTOSPHERE	CONDOTTIORE	KALASHNIKOV	RESPONSIBLY	CRACKERJACK	COLOURBLIND
PINACOTHECA	CONNECTICUT	LATERITIOUS	RESPONSIONS	KILIMANJARO	COMFORTLESS
PISSASPHALT	CONSTRAINED	LEPIDOSIREN	REVELATIONS	STEEPLEJACK	COMMONPLACE
PLATYRRHINE	CONTENTIOUS	LIGHTWEIGHT	REVOLUTIONS	BACKPACKING	COMMUNALISM
PLOUGHSHARE	CONVENTICLE	LONGAWAITED	RHAPSODICAL	COMSTOCKERY	COMPTROLLER
POLYTECHNIC	CONVERTIBLE	MACADAMIZED	RHEUMATICKY	CYCLOALKANE	CONFABULATE
PROGNATHOUS	CONVULSIONS	MAKEBELIEVE	RUDESHEIMER	DRESSMAKING	CONSTELLATE
RAMGUNSHOCH	CORINTHIANS	MANTELPIECE	RUMBUSTIOUS	ENGHALSKRUG	CONTEMPLANT
REPROACHFUL	CORRUPTIBLE	MASTERPIECE	SALPINGITIS	EPOCHMAKING	CONTEMPLATE
SARCENCHYME	COULOMMIERS	MEANDERINGS	SCANDALIZED	GOODLOOKING	COPPERPLATE
SPARROWHAWK	CREDENTIALS	MEDIASTINUM	SCREWDRIVER	GREENOCKITE	COUNSELLING
SPERMOPHILE	CURNAPTIOUS	MEDIUMSIZED	SCRUMPTIOUS	HARDWORKING	COXWAINLESS
SPREADSHEET	CYLINDRICAL	MEMORABILIA	SEARCHLIGHT	HIGHRANKING	CRACKHALTER
TERPSICHORE	DECORATIONS	MENTONNIÈRE	SEMITRAILER	KAMELAUKION	CRATERELLUS
THALLOPHYTE	DELETERIOUS	MERITORIOUS	SENTENTIOUS	LAWBREAKING	CREDIBILITY
THESMOTHETE	DEMORALIZED	MIDDLESIZED	SEXOLOGICAL	MERRYMAKING	CRÉMAILLÈRE
THOROUGHPIN	DISCERNIBLE	MISCARRIAGE	SOCKDOLIGER	MONEYMAKING	CRESTFALLEN
THUNDERHEAD	DISCIPLINED	MISSISSIPPI	SPECIALIZED	MUSCHELKALK	CRIMINOLOGY
TIMBROPHILY	DISCONTINUE	MOISTURIZER	SPERMICIDAL	NICKNACKERY	CROCIDOLITE
TROPOSPHERE	DISIMPRISON	MONARCHICAL	SPONDULICKS	NUTCRACKERS	CROCODILIAN
ULOTRICHALE	DISINCLINED	MYCOLOGICAL	SPONDYLITIS	PAINSTAKING	CROMWELLIAN
UNFLINCHING	DISOBEDIENT	NETHERLINGS	SPORTSFIELD	PAWNBROKERS	CRYSTALLINE
WITHERSHINS	DRINKDRIVER	NEUTRALISED	STATISTICAL	STOCKTAKING	CRYSTALLISE
XENODOCHIUM	EFFICACIOUS	NIERSTEINER	STIPENDIARY	TELEWORKING	CRYSTALLIZE
ACRIMONIOUS	EGOTISTICAL	NONSENSICAL	STRATEGICAL	TICKTACKTOE	CULPABILITY
ADULLAMITES	ENTERTAINER	NORTHCLIFFE	STREAMLINED	UNDERTAKING	DARDANELLES
ALLEGORICAL	EVANGELICAL	OBSTETRICAL	STREETLIGHT	UNSHRINKING	DEERSTALKER
AMOBARBITAL	EXPEDITIOUS	ONOMASTICON	SUBMULTIPLE	VOORTREKKER	DEFENCELESS
ANAGNORISIS	EXPROPRIATE	ONTOLOGICAL	SUBSERVIENT	ZOOPLANKTON	DEFENSELESS
ANTIRRHINUM	FEHMGERICHT	OPPROBRIOUS	SUBTROPICAL	ABNORMALITY	DERMATOLOGY
APOLLONICON	FERRONNIÈRE	OUTPOURINGS	SUGGESTIBLE	AGROSTOLOGY	DESEXUALIZE
APPRENTICED	FLIRTATIOUS	PAPERWEIGHT	SUSCEPTIBLE	AMMOPHILOUS	DESTABILIZE
APPROPRIATE	FORAMINIFER	PARADOXICAL	SYMMETRICAL	AMONTILLADO	DICEPHALOUS
ATHERINIDAE	FOTHERGILLA	PARAMEDICAL	SYMPATHISER	AMPHIBOLOGY	DISHEVELLED
ATRABILIOUS	FOUNDATIONS	PEDAGOGICAL	SYMPATHIZER	ANTICYCLONE	DISSIMULATE
BASKERVILLE	FURNISHINGS	PEDESTRIANS	SYNTHESIZED	APOPHYLLITE	ELASTOPLAST
BATTLEFIELD	GENERALIZED	PENTHESILEA	SYNTHESIZER	ARCHAEOLOGY	ELECTROLIER
BENEFICIARY	GEOMETRICAL	PENTONVILLE	TÉLÉFÉRIQUE	ARCHIPELAGO	ELECTROLYTE
BENEFICIATE	GNATHONICAL	PERCEPTIBLE	TENDENTIOUS	ARGATHELIAN	ELIGIBILITY
BIOCHEMICAL	GRAMMATICAL	PERCEPTIBLY	THEOLOGICAL	ASPERGILLUM	ENCAPSULATE
BLACKMAILER	HAEMOPHILIA	PERITONITIS	THEORETICAL	ASPERGILLUS	ENCEPHALOMA

ENKEPHALINE	MICROVILLUS	SLEEPWALKER	BELLYTIMBER	MAGNANIMOUS	AWKWARDNESS
ENTHRALLING	MISSPELLING	SLUMGULLION	BEREAVEMENT	MEASUREMENT	BASHFULNESS
EQUIPOLLENT	MODELMOLEST	SMALLHOLDER	BESIEGEMENT	MEPROBAMATE	BEASTLINESS
ESCHATOLOGY	MONONUCLEAR	SNORKELLING	BLASPHEMOUS	MICROGAMETE	BICARBONATE
EVENTUALITY	MONOTHELITE	SOCIABILITY	BOMBARDMENT	MONOGRAMMED	BICENTENARY
EXPOSTULATE	NAPHTHALENE	SPRINGCLEAN	CATADROMOUS	MONOTREMATA	BILIOUSNESS
EXTERNALIZE	NATIONALISM	STADTHOLDER	CHAMBERMAID	NIACINAMIDE	BIMILLENARY
EXTRAPOLATE	NATIONALIST	STAKEHOLDER	COMMANDMENT	NIKETHAMIDE	BLESSEDNESS
FALLIBILITY	NATIONALITY	STALLHOLDER	COMPARTMENT	NOURISHMENT	BREADWINNER
FEASIBILITY	NATIONALIZE	STEAMROLLER	COMPILEMENT	OVERPAYMENT	BRILLIANTLY
FEATURELESS	NONETHELESS	STOCKHOLDER	CONCEALMENT	PARLIPOMENA	BRITTLENESS
FITZWILLIAM	NUCLEOPLASM	STORYTELLER	CONFINEMENT	PARVANIMITY	BROADMINDED
FLEXIBILITY	NUMBERPLATE	STRANGULATE	CONSIGNMENT	PENULTIMATE	CACOPHONOUS
FOOTBALLING	ODONTOBLAST	STRETCHLESS	CONTAINMENT	PREDICAMENT	CALIFORNIUM
FORTUNELOUD	OFFICIALDOM	STRONGYLOID	CONTENEMENT	PRESENTMENT	CALLOUSNESS
FUNAMBULIST	OFFICIALESE	STROPHILLUS	CONTENTMENT	PROCUREMENT	CAMEROONIAN
GALLOWGLASS	ORIENTALISM	STYMPHALIAN	COUNTERMAND	PROLEGOMENA	CARAVANNING
GENOUILLÈRE	ORIENTALIST	SUBUNGULATA	CURTAILMENT	REALIGNMENT	CARBORUNDUM
GEOSYNCLINE	ORIGINALITY	SUDETENLAND	DEPARTEMENT	RECRUITMENT	CAREFULNESS
GERONTOLOGY	ORNITHOLOGY	SUITABILITY	DEPHLEGMATE	REFRESHMENT	CARSICKNESS
GESTICULATE	OVERWHELMED	SURVEILLANT	DERANGEMENT	RELEASEMENT	CHARACINOID
GIBBERELLIN	OVERZEALOUS	SWITZERLAND	DEUTSCHMARK	REPLACEMENT	CHEIROGNOMY
GLADWELLISE	PAINKILLING	SYNDICALISM	DEVELOPMENT	REQUIREMENT	CHILDMINDER
GULLIBILITY	PATERNALISM	TANGIBILITY	DISABLEMENT	RESTATEMENT	CHRISTENING
GUTTURALISE	PENICILLATE	TAUROBOLIUM	DISARMAMENT	SAUSAGEMEAT	CLEANLINESS
GYNAECOLOGY	PENTATHLETE	TEETOTALLER	DISCERNMENT	SCOPOLAMINE	CLIFFHANGER
HAMMERCLOTH	PENTAVALENT	TERMINOLOGY	DISENCUMBER	SHORTCOMING	COMPETENTLY
HEMOPHILIAC	PERAMBULATE	THOUGHTLESS	DISSEPIMENT	SILVERSMITH	CONCISENESS
HERPETOLOGY	PERDUELLION	TITLEHOLDER	DIVORCEMENT	SOROPTIMIST	CONDOLENCES
HIGHQUALITY	PERISSOLOGY	TORTICOLLIS	EASTERNMOST	SYNCHROMESH	CONDOMINIUM
HOSPITALITY	PERISTALITH	TORTICULLUS	EMBOÎTEMENT	TAXIDERMIST	CONFIDENTLY
HOSPITALIZE	PERISTALSIS	TOURBILLION	EMPIECEMENT	TEMPERAMENT	CONSTERNATE
HOSPITALLER	PERSONALIST	TOXOPHILITE	EMPLACEMENT	THALIDOMIDE	CONTAMINANT
HOUSEHOLDER	PERSONALITY	TRANQUILITY	EMPOWERMENT	THEOBROMINE	CONTAMINATE
HUSBANDLAND	PERSONALIZE	TROPHOBLAST	ENCHANTMENT	TRACKLEMENT	CONTINENTAL
ICHTHYOLITE	PETRODOLLAR	TURRICULATE	ENDORSEMENT	TREPONEMATA	CORDWAINERS
IMMORTALISE	PHILATELIST	UNDERVALUED	ENFEOFFMENT	UNWELCOMING	CORRECTNESS
IMMORTALITY	PHRASEOLOGY	UNFULFILLED	ENFORCEMENT	VIDEOCAMERA	COURTLINESS
IMMORTALIZE	PHYLLOCLADE	UNTRAMELLED	ENHANCEMENT	VOLKSKAMMER	CROOKEDNESS
IMPERIALISM	POSSIBILITY	VARIABILITY	ENJAMBEMENT	WESTERNMOST	CULVERINEER
IMPERIALIST	PROBABILITY	VERMICULITE	ENLARGEMENT	WORLDFAMOUS	CYMOPHANOUS
INCAPSULATE	PRODIGALISE	VERSATILITY	ENSLAVEMENT	ABORTIONIST	DECARBONATE
INCREDULITY	PRODIGALITY	VOLCANOLOGY	ENTABLEMENT	ACCOMPANIST	DECARBONIZE
INCREDULOUS	PUNCTUALITY	VULCANOLOGY	ENTITLEMENT	ACCORDINGLY	DEGLUTINATE
INFERTILITY	PURPOSELESS	WATERCOLOUR	ENVIRONMENT	ADOPTIANISM	DEOXYGENATE
INFORMALITY	QUADRUPLETS	WATERSPLASH	EURHYTHMICS	ADOPTIONISM	DETERMINANT
INSTABILITY	QUARRELLING	WESTPHALIAN	EXANTHEMATA	AGGLUTINANT	DETERMINATE
INTERCALARY	QUICKSILVER	WHITECOLLAR	FARTHERMOST	AGGLUTINATE	DETERMINING
INTERNALIZE	QUINTUPLETS	WORKMANLIKE	FORTHCOMING	AIRSICKNESS	DETRIMENTAL
INTERPOLATE	RAPSCALLION	XEROPHILOUS	FULFILLMENT	AMERICANISM	DEUTERONOMY
INTERRELATE	RATIONALITY	YELLOWPLUSH	FURTHERMORE	ANACHRONISM	DEVIOUSNESS
ITHYPHALLIC	RATIONALIZE	ABANDONMENT	FURTHERMOST	ANACREONTIC	DIFFERENTLY
ITHYPHALLUS	READABILITY	ABRIDGEMENT	GARNISHMENT	ANAXIMANDER	DIFFIDENTLY
LEASEHOLDER	REFLEXOLOGY	ACHIEVEMENT	GLUCOSAMINE	ANDROGENOUS	DIPSOMANIAC
MARGINALIST	REFOCILLATE	ADJOURNMENT	GUESSTIMATE	ANDROGYNOUS	DISENTANGLE
MARGINALIZE	RELIABILITY	ADVANCEMENT	HIPPOCAMPUS	ANTIPHONARY	DISORGANIZE
MARKETPLACE	REMORSELESS	AMERCIAMENT	HONEYCOMBED	APPALLINGLY	DISORIENTED
MARSHMALLOW	RIBONUCLEIC	AMPHETAMINE	IMPEACHMENT	APPEARANCES	DISSEMINATE
MATERIALISE	ROCKEFELLER	ANTECHAMBER	IMPROVEMENT	APPLERINGIE	DRUNKENNESS
MATERIALISM	SCATTERLING	ANTHONOMOUS	INSTALLMENT	APPROVINGLY	DRYCLEANERS
MATERIALIST	SCHRECKLICH	APPEASEMENT	INVOLVEMENT	APPURTENANT	DRYCLEANING
MATERIALIZE	SCIENTOLOGY	APPOINTMENT	KINCHINMORT	ARCHEGONIAL	DUBIOUSNESS
MATRICULATE	SCINTILLATE	APPROXIMATE	LEGERDEMAIN	ARCHEGONIUM	DUMBFOUNDED
MEANINGLESS	SECONDCLASS	ARBITRAMENT	LIQUIDAMBAR	ARGENTINIAN	EARNESTNESS
MEASURELESS	SENSIBILITY	ARRANGEMENT	LONGANIMITY	ASSASSINATE	EFFICIENTLY
METEOROLOGY	SHAREHOLDER	ASSYTHEMENT	MACROGAMETE	ATHERMANOUS	EINSTEINIUM
METHODOLOGY	SHIPBUILDER	BEACHCOMBER	MAGNANIMITY	AUGUSTINIAN	ELECTRONICS

EMPTYHANDED	INDIGNANTLY	PERTINENTLY	STELLIONATE	ANAPLEROTIC	MELANCHOLIC
EPAMINONDAS	INDULGENTLY	PHOTOFINISH	STRANGENESS	ANASTOMOSIS	MICROSCOPIC
EVASIVENESS	INQUIRINGLY	PHYSIOGNOMY	STRAPHANGER	ANTHRACOSIS	MILQUETOAST
EXCEEDINGLY	INSISTENTLY	PINNYWINKLE	STRINGENTLY	ANTISTROPHE	MISERICORDE
EXPECTANTLY	INSULTINGLY	PLAYFULNESS	STYLISHNESS	APONEUROSIS	MONOCHROMAT
EXPERIENCED	INTERLINGUA	PLEBEIANISE	SUBDOMINANT	ARTHRAPODAL	MOSSTROOPER
EXTERMINATE	INTERMINGLE	POMEGRANATE	SUBORDINATE	BARTHOLOMEW	MULTISTOREY
EXTROGENOUS	INTERNUNCIO	PREDOMINANT	SUCCEDANEUM	BLOODSPORTS	MYXOMATOSIS
FANFARONADE	INTERVENING	PREDOMINATE	SUPERTANKER	BRAGGADOCIO	NECROBIOSIS
FARRAGINOUS	INTRAVENOUS	PRELIMINARY	SUPPEDANEUM	BRUCELLOSIS	NEEDLEPOINT
FATUOUSNESS	JERRYMANDER	PRICKLINESS	SYCOPHANTIC	CAMERAWOMAN	NEEDLEWOMAN
FAULTFINDER	JOSEPHINITE	PRIMIGENIAL	SYNCHRONISE	CATASTROPHE	NOTICEBOARD
FOOLISHNESS	KINNIKINICK	PRISCIANIST	SYNCHRONISM	CAULIFLOWER	NUTRITIONAL
FOREWARNING	LATROCINIUM	PRIZEWINNER	SYNCHRONIZE	CENTREBOARD	OPERATIONAL
FORGIVENESS	LAWLESSNESS	PROFUSENESS	SYNCHRONOUS	CHAULMOOGRA	OVEREXPOSED
FORLORNNESS	LEADSWINGER	PROMINENTLY	TACITURNITY	CHRYSAROBIN	PAEDOTROPHY
FRANKLINITE	LEATHERNECK	PROTAGONIST	TEASPOONFUL	CLADOSPORUM	PAMPELMOOSE
FREETHINKER	LECITHINASE	QUADRENNIAL	TEDIOUSNESS	COLDBLOODED	PAMPELMOUSE
FRIGHTENING	LENGTHENING	QUADRENNIUM	TELEPHONIST	CONDITIONAL	PARASITOSIS
FRONTRUNNER	LENGTHINESS	QUESTIONING	TELEPRINTER	CONDITIONER	PARATROOPER
FUNCTIONARY	LENTIGINOSE	RAFFISHNESS	TENUOUSNESS	COTTONMOUTH	PARISHIONER
FUNCTIONING	LITERALNESS	RANGEFINDER	TESTIMONIAL	DEGRINGOLER	PERESTROIKA
FUNDAMENTAL	LONGRUNNING	RATIOCINATE	THINGLINESS	DIARTHROSIS	PIERREPOINT
FURTIVENESS	LOUISIANIAN	RATTLESNAKE	THREATENING	DIMENSIONAL	POLICEWOMAN
GABERLUNZIE	LUXULYANITE	RAUCOUSNESS	THRIFTINESS	DIRECTIONAL	POMPELMOOSE
GALLIGANTUS	LUXURIANTLY	RAVISHINGLY	TIGGYWINKLE	DISAPPROVAL	POMPELMOUSE
GELSEMININE	MASCULINITY	REACTIONARY	TOBACCONIST	DOUROUCOULI	PORTERHOUSE
GENUINENESS	MASSIVENESS	RECRIMINATE	TOBOGGANING	EDUCATIONAL	PREHISTORIC
GERRYMANDER	MATRIMONIAL	RECTILINEAR	TORRIDONIAN	EMMENAGOGUE	PROBATIONER
GHASTLINESS	MAURETANIAN	RECURRENTLY	TRANSPONDER	ENARTHROSIS	PROMOTIONAL
GONFALONIER	MAURITANIAN	REINCARNATE	TRINOBANTES	EOANTHROPUS	PROVISIONAL
GREGARINIDA	MICHURINISM	RELUCTANTLY	TRITAGONIST	EXCEPTIONAL	PROVISIONER
GRENZGANGER	MINNESINGER	REPRESENTED	TRUCULENTLY	EXECUTIONER	PSEUDOLOGIA
GUTTERSNIPE	MISERLINESS	RESTIVENESS	UNANNOUNCED	EXTORTIONER	PSEUDOMORPH
HALLUCINATE	MONEYLENDER	REVISIONISM	UNAUTHENTIC	FREEMASONRY	PSITTACOSIS
HARDICANUTE	MONOCHINOUS	RIGHTHANDED	UNCLEANNESS	FRENCHWOMAN	RECESSIONAL
HAUGHTINESS	MONOPSONIST	RIGHTHANDER	UNCONVINCED	FRENCHWOMEN	SACHERTORTE
HEALTHINESS	MOUNTAINEER	RIGHTWINGER	UNCOUTHNESS	FULLBLOODED	SADDLEHORSE
HEAVYHANDED	MOUNTAINOUS	ROGUISHNESS	UNDERHANDED	GASTRONOMIC	SALTIMBOCCA
HELPFULNESS	MUNITIONIZE	SACRAMENTAL	UNDERMANNED	GENTLEWOMAN	SCARBOROUGH
HIDEOUSNESS	NARRAGANSET	SAINTLINESS	UNFAILINGLY	GILLYFLOWER	SCULLABOGUE
HISTRIONICS	NATURALNESS	SALVOGUNNER	UNFORTUNATE	GRALLATORES	SELFIMPOSED
HOGGISHNESS	NAUGHTINESS	SAVOURINESS	UNGODLINESS	GRAMMALOGUE	SENSATIONAL
HOHENLINDEN	NECROMANCER	SAXOPHONIST	UNHAPPINESS	GREENGROCER	SHOVELBOARD
HOMOPHONOUS	NERVOUSNESS	SCAREMONGER	UNREASONING	HAEMOGLOBIN	SILVERPOINT
HOOLIGANISM	NOTHINGNESS	SCITAMINEAE	UNWARRANTED	HEARTBROKEN	SINISTRORSE
HOOTANANNIE	OBVIOUSNESS	SCOLOPENDRA	UNWITTINGLY	HEMERALOPIA	SKILLIGOLEE
HOOTENANNIE	OPPORTUNELY	SCREAMINGLY	UPRIGHTNESS	HEMORRHOIDS	SLEUTHHOUND
HYDROGENATE	OPPORTUNISM	SCRUFFINESS	USELESSNESS	HONEYMOONER	SOCKDOLOGER
HYDROPONICS	OPPORTUNIST	SCUPPERNONG	VACUOUSNESS	HYDROPHOBIA	SPERMATOZOA
ILLUSIONARY	OPPORTUNITY	SEASICKNESS	VERTIGINOUS	HYDROPHOBIC	SPOKESWOMAN
ILLUSIONISM	ORDERLINESS	SELFISHNESS	VESUVIANITE	HYPERTROPHY	SPORTSWOMAN
ILLUSIONIST	ORTHOCENTRE	SENTIMENTAL	VICIOUSNESS	IMPASSIONED	SPRINGBOARD
IMPATIENTLY	OVERMANNING	SERIOUSNESS	WAKEFULNESS	INTENTIONAL	SPRINGHOUSE
IMPERMANENT	OVERTURNING	SHALLOWNESS	WAYWARDNESS	INTERGLOSSA	SRANANTONGO
IMPERSONATE	OVERWEENING	SHAPELINESS	WELLFOUNDED	INTERGROWTH	STOCKBROKER
IMPERTINENT	PALESTINIAN	SHEATHKNIFE	WELLMEANING	ISTIOPHORUS	STRANDLOPER
IMPLEMENTAL	PANDEMONIUM	SHORTHANDED	WILLINGNESS	JABBERWOCKY	STRIKEBOUND
IMPORTANTLY	PASSIVENESS	SILLIMANITE	WISTFULNESS	KILOCALORIE	STRINGBOARD
IMPORTUNATE	PEEVISHNESS	SKETCHINESS	WOMANLINESS	MACHAIRODUS	STRUTHIONES
IMPRUDENTLY	PELARGONIUM	SLENDERNESS	WORLDLINESS	MACROBIOTIC	SUMMERHOUSE
INAUTHENTIC	PELOPONNESE	SLIGHTINGLY	ZWISCHENZUG	MACROSCOPIC	SWITCHBOARD
INCESSANTLY	PENSIVENESS	SMITHSONIAN	AGORAPHOBIA	MALAKATOONE	SWORDSWOMAN
INCONTINENT	PENTECONTER	SMITHSONITE	ALLELOMORPH	MARLBOROUGH	TENTERHOOKS
INCREMENTAL	PEREGRINATE	SPELLBINDER	AMPHISBOENA	MASKALLONGE	THENCEFORTH
INCRIMINATE	PERIODONTIC	SPRINGINESS	ANADIPLOSIS	MEGALOPOLIS	THEREABOUTS
INDEXLINKED	PERMANENTLY	STATELINESS	ANAPLEROSIS	MELANCHOLIA	THYROTROPIN

TOWNSPEOPLE	RETINOSPORA	COLUMBARIUM	HYDROCARBON	PROFITEROLE	TRANSVERSAL
TRADITIONAL	SELFRESPECT	COMMEMORATE	HYPERBOREAN	PROLETARIAN	TREACHEROUS
TRICHINOSED	SERENDIPITY	COMMISERATE	HYPERMARKET	PROLETARIAT	TRENCHERMAN
TROMPELOEIL	SHOWJUMPING	COMPUTERIZE	HYPOTHERMIA	PROLIFERATE	TRIMESTRIAL
TSCHERNOSEM	SOUTHAMPTON	CONCENTRATE	ICHTHYORNIS	PROTUBERANT	TRINITARIAN
TWELVEMONTH	STEGANOPODE	CONDUCTRESS	IMPERFORATE	PTOCHOCRACY	TRIUMVIRATE
ULTRAVIOLET	SUPERIMPOSE	CONFEDERACY	IMPIGNORATE	PYRARGYRITE	TRUSTWORTHY
UNDERCOOKED	TEENYBOPPER	CONFEDERATE	INCARCERATE	RADIOCARBON	ULTRAMARINE
UNDERGROUND	TELEGRAPHER	CONSIDERATE	INCORPORATE	RASTAFARIAN	UNCONCERNED
UNDERGROWTH	TELEGRAPHIC	CONSIDERING	INCORPOREAL	RECONSTRUCT	UNCONFIRMED
UNDEVELOPED	THANATOPSIS	CONSTUPRATE	INDIFFERENT	REFRIGERANT	UNCONVERTED
UNDISCLOSED	TIGHTLIPPED	CONSUMERISM	INFERIORITY	REFRIGERATE	UNDISTURBED
UNEMOTIONAL	TIMEKEEPING	CONTUBERNAL	INSINCERITY	REGISTERING	UNPERTURBED
UNENVELOPED	TOPOGRAPHER	CORROBORATE	INTEMPERATE	REMONSTRATE	UNREHEARSED
UNEQUIVOCAL	TRAGELAPHUS	CREMATORIUM	INTRADERMAL	REVERBERATE	UNSUPPORTED
UNPATRIOTIC	TYPOGRAPHER	CUSTOMARILY	INTROVERTED	SABBATARIAN	UTILITARIAN
WASHERWOMAN	TYPOGRAPHIC	DECONSTRUCT	ISOXSUPRINE	SAGITTARIUS	VALLAMBROSA
WHEREABOUTS	TYROGLYPHID	DEMONSTRATE	KINDHEARTED	SALESPERSON	VARANGARIAN
WILBERFORCE	XEROTRIPSIS	DETERIORATE	KIRKPATRICK	SALVADORIAN	VERBIGERATE
WORRYTROUGH	XYLOGRAPHER	DICTATORIAL	KULTURKREIS	SCRIPTORIUM	VOLUNTARILY
AESCULAPIAN	MOZAMBIQUAN	DIORTHORTIC	KWASHIORKOR	SECONDARILY	VOLUNTARISM
AESCULAPIUS	ABECEDARIAN	DIPHYCERCAL	LATERIGRADE	SECRETARIAL	WALDSTERBEN
APLANOSPORE	ACCESSORIES	DIRECTORATE	LETTERPRESS	SECRETARIAT	WARMHEARTED
APOCALYPTIC	ACCIPITRINE	DISFIGURING	LIBERTARIAN	SEIGNIORAGE	WHEELBARROW
APOSTROPHUS	ACCULTURATE	DISINTEREST	LOOSESTRIFE	SEISMOGRAPH	WHITETHROAT
ARTHROSPORE	ADIAPHORIST	DISREGARDED	LUXEMBURGER	SEMPITERNAL	WINDOWFRAME
AVOIRDUPOIS	ADVENTURESS	DOMINEERING	LYCANTHROPE	SEMPITERNUM	WINTERGREEN
BELLEROPHON	ADVENTUROUS	DOUBLECROSS	LYCANTHROPY	SEPTENARIUS	XEROTHERMIC
BOOKKEEPING	AGGLOMERATE	DOWNHEARTED	MAGISTERIAL	SEPTENTRION	ZOROASTRIAN
CHRISTOPHER	ALCYONARIAN	EGALITARIAN	MANEUVERING	SEQUESTRATE	ADVERTISING
CIRCUMSPECT	ALEXANDRINE	ELEUTHERIAN	MEGATHERIUM	SHOWERPROOF	AFGHANISTAN
CITLALEPETL	ALEXANDRITE	ENCHANTRESS	MEKHITARIST	SIGHTSCREEN	ALBIGENSIAN
COUNTERPANE	ANISOCERCAL	ENCHONDROMA	METALWORKER	SINGAPOREAN	ANNIVERSARY
COUNTERPART	ANTIQUARIAN	ENDOTHERMIC	MINIATURIST	SINGULARITY	APHRODISIAC
DEMOGRAPHIC	APODYTERIUM	ENGINEERING	MINIATURIZE	SMOKESCREEN	ARQUEBUSIER
DIMERCAPROL	ARBITRARILY	EPICHEIREMA	MINISTERIAL	SMOULDERING	AUDIOVISUAL
DUSTWRAPPER	ARISTOCRACY	EPINEPHRINE	MINISTERING	SPEECHCRAFT	BELORUSSIAN
ECTOTROPHIC	ARTILLERIST	EQUILIBRIST	MISANTHROPE	SPENDTHRIFT	BIELORUSSIA
ENDOTROPHIC	ASPERSORIUM	EQUILIBRIUM	MISANTHROPY	SPLUTTERING	BLANKURSINE
EPANALEPSIS	ASPHETERISM	EXPECTORANT	MOMENTARILY	STAIRCARPET	BLOCKBUSTER
GRASSHOPPER	BALLBEARING	EXPECTORATE	NECESSARILY	STEINBERGER	BROADCASTER
GROUNDSPEED	BARBITURATE	EXTEMPORISE	NEIGHBORING	STENOCHROME	BURGOMASTER
HANDICAPPED	BARNSTORMER	EXTEMPORIZE	NIGHTMARISH	STEREOGRAPH	BUSINESSMAN
HANDICAPPER	BATTLEDRESS	EXTROVERTED	NONDESCRIPT	STRADUARIUS	CABBALISTIC
HEMIANOPSIA	BATTLEFRONT	FAMILIARISE	NOTOTHERIUM	SUBCONTRACT	CATACAUSTIC
IDIOGRAPHIC	BELLETTRIST	FAMILIARITY	OBTEMPERATE	SUPERIORITY	CATACLYSMIC
INTERCEPTOR	BELLIGERENT	FAMILIARIZE	OPPIGNORATE	SUPERMARKET	CEASELESSLY
INTERRUPTER	BERGSCHRUND	FAUXBOURDON	OPTOMETRIST	SUPERSCRIBE	CHOIRMASTER
KINDERSPIEL	BEWILDERING	FESTSCHRIFT	ORCHESTRATE	SUPERSCRIPT	CHONDROSTEI
KRIEGSSPIEL	BLAMEWORTHY	FIELDWORKER	ORCHESTRINA	SURTARBRAND	CITIZENSHIP
LOGOGRAPHER	BLOODSTREAM	FINGERPRINT	ORCHESTRION	SURTURBRAND	COMPLAISANT
MALAPROPISM	BUREAUCRACY	FORESHORTEN	OVERBEARING	TACHYCARDIA	COMRADESHIP
METACARPALS	CALENDERING	FRANKFURTER	OVERLEARNED	TAUTOCHRONE	CONGRESSMAN
MILLIAMPERE	CAMPESTRIAN	FRUGIVOROUS	PAEDIATRICS	TEMPORARILY	CONNOISSEUR
ORNITHOPTER	CARDIOGRAPH	FUSTILARIAN	PECULIARITY	TERRESTRIAL	COUNTERSIGN
OVERLAPPING	CARNIVOROUS	GESTATORIAL	PERCEFOREST	TERRITORIAL	COUNTERSINK
PARABLEPSIS	CASSITERITE	GINGERBREAD	PERCHLORATE	THAUMATROPE	COUNTRYSIDE
PARALEIPSIS	CATCHPHRASE	HALBSTARKER	PERLUSTRATE	THROGMORTON	CRITICASTER
PARTICIPANT	CENTENARIAN	HALFHEARTED	PERSEVERING	TIMESHARING	DISHONESTLY
PARTICIPATE	CERARGYRITE	HAPHAZARDLY	PICKYOUROWN	TRANSDERMAL	DISILLUSION
PARTICIPIAL	CHAIRPERSON	HERBIVOROUS	PISCATORIAL	TRANSFERRED	DISPLEASURE
PHILOSOPHER	CHOLINERGIC	HETEROGRAFT	PLANETARIUM	TRANSFERRIN	DISTRESSING
PHOTOCOPIER	CHRYSOPRASE	HOLOTHURIAN	PLANTIGRADE	TRANSFORMED	DRAUGHTSMAN
PODSNAPPERY	CILOFIBRATE	HOMOTHERMAL	POLLENBRUSH	TRANSFORMER	DUNIEWASSAL
POLYMORPHIC	CIRCULARIZE	HOMOTHERMIC	POLYHYDROXY	TRANSPARENT	DYSLOGISTIC
PREOCCUPIED	CLIOMETRICS	HOUSEPARENT	POLYSTYRENE	TRANSPORTED	EMBARRASSED
PRESTONPANS	COLLABORATE	HUCKSTERAGE	PREMATURELY	TRANSPORTER	EMBELLISHED

EPIGENESIST
ESTABLISHED
ESTABLISHER
EUCHARISTIC
EUPHEMISTIC
FAULTLESSLY
FILLIBUSTER
FLAVOURSOME
FORECLOSURE
FRUITLESSLY
FUNDRAISING
FURTHERSOME
GATECRASHER
GRANDMASTER
HABERDASHER
HAIRDRESSER
HAIRRAISING
HARDPRESSED
HEARTLESSLY
HOMOIOUSIAN
HOUSEMASTER
HYPOTENSION
IMPETUOSITY
IMPRECISION
INCOMPOSITE
INEXPENSIVE
INOFFENSIVE
INTERCOSTAL
JINRICKSHAW
LARYNGISMUS
LECTURESHIP
MAGLEMOSIAN
MALADJUSTED
MANUMISSION
MASOCHISTIC
MENDELSSOHN
MERCILESSLY
METAPHYSICS
METATARSALS
MODERNISTIC
MONSTROSITY
NOISELESSLY
NORTHEASTER
NORTHWESTER
OARSMANSHIP
OMNIPRESENT
PARACROSTIC
PARTNERSHIP
PATERNOSTER
PATRONISING
PENTECOSTAL
PESSIMISTIC
PHILLIPSITE
PICTURESQUE
PLATERESQUE
POINTLESSLY
PREDECESSOR
PREMIERSHIP
PRESTISSIMO
PRESTRESSED
PROGRESSION
PROGRESSIVE
PRZEWALSKIS
PYTHONESQUE
QUARRELSOME
RABELAISIAN
REFURBISHED

SCHISTOSOMA
SCHISTOSOME
SCHOLARSHIP
SCHOTTISCHE
SCOUTMASTER
SHAMELESSLY
SHINPLASTER
SHOWMANSHIP
SNICKERSNEE
SOLIPSISTIC
SOUNDLESSLY
SOUTHWESTER
SPHRAGISTIC
SPONSORSHIP
STEADFASTLY
SUBDIVISION
SUPERVISION
SUPERVISORY
SUPPRESSION
TASTELESSLY
THANKLESSLY
TIGHTFISTED
TIRONENSIAN
TOASTMASTER
TRANSFUSION
TRESPASSING
TROUBLESOME
TROUBLESPOT
TRUSTEESHIP
TRYPANOSOMA
TRYPANOSOME
TYRANNOSAUR
TYRONENSIAN
UNBLEMISHED
UNCONTESTED
UNEXPRESSED
UNFURNISHED
UNIMPRESSED
UNNECESSARY
UNOBTRUSIVE
UNPUBLISHED
UNREALISTIC
UNSURPASSED
UNVARNISHED
UNWHOLESOME
VASOPRESSIN
VENTURESOME
WAREHOUSING
WASTEBASKET
WELLDRESSED
WESTMINSTER
WHISTLESTOP
WORKMANSHIP
ABLACTATION
ABOMINATION
ABSTRACTION
ACCLAMATION
ACCLIMATION
ACCLIMATISE
ACCLIMATIZE
ACQUISITION
ACQUISITIVE
ACROCENTRIC
ACTUALITIES
ACUPUNCTURE
ADUMBRATION
AERONAUTICS

AFFECTATION
AFFILIATION
AFFIRMATION
AFFIRMATIVE
AFFLIICTION
AGGRAVATING
AGGRAVATION
AGGREGATION
AGRICULTURE
AIRCRAFTMAN
ALLEVIATION
ALPHABETIZE
ALTERCATION
ALTERNATELY
ALTERNATING
ALTERNATION
ALTERNATIVE
AMINOBUTENE
ANACOLUTHIA
ANESTHETIST
ANESTHETIZE
ANTINEUTRON
APHANIPTERA
APPELLATION
APPELLATIVE
APPLICATION
APPROBATION
ARBITRATION
ARRHENOTOKY
ASSIGNATION
ASSOCIATION
ASTIGMATISM
ATTENUATION
ATTESTATION
ATTRIBUTION
ATTRIBUTIVE
AXEROPHTHOL
BARYCENTRIC
BEAUMONTAGE
BENEDICTINE
BENEDICTION
BIFURCATION
BODHISATTVA
CACOGASTRIC
CALCULATING
CALCULATION
CALIBRATION
CALLANETICS
CANDIDATURE
CANDLESTICK
CAPTIVATING
CAPTIVATION
CARBURETTOR
CARMINATIVE
CELEBRATION
CEREBRATION
CHRISMATION
CIRCULATING
CIRCULATION
CIRCULATORY
CLANDESTINE
COAGULATION
COBBLESTONE
COENOBITISM
COHORTATIVE
COLLOCATION
COMBINATION

COMMINATION
COMMUTATION
COMPARATIVE
COMPETITION
COMPETITIVE
COMPILATION
COMPOSITION
COMPOTATION
COMPUNCTION
COMPUTATION
CONCOMITANT
CONFUTATION
CONJUGATION
CONJUNCTION
CONJUNCTURE
CONNOTATION
CONSECUTIVE
CONSOLATION
CONSTANTINE
CONSUMPTION
CONSUMPTIVE
CONTRACTION
CONTRACTUAL
CONTRAPTION
CONTRASTING
CONURBATION
CONVOCATION
CONVOLUTION
COOPERATION
COOPERATIVE
CORNERSTONE
CORPORATION
CORRELATION
CORRUGATION
CREPITATION
CRESCENTADE
CULMINATION
CULTIVATION
CYBERNETICS
DECLAMATION
DECLAMATORY
DECLARATION
DECLARATIVE
DECREPITATE
DECREPITUDE
DEFERENTIAL
DEFOLIATION
DEFORMATION
DEGLUTITION
DEGRADATION
DEHORTATIVE
DEHYDRATION
DEIFICATION
DELECTATION
DELICTATION
DELINEATION
DEMARCATION
DEMIBASTION
DEPORTATION
DEPREDATION
DEPRIVATION
DERELICTION
DESCRIPTION
DESCRIPTIVE
DESECRATION
DESELECTION
DESICCATION

DESIGNATION
DESPERATELY
DESPERATION
DESTINATION
DESTITUTION
DESTRUCTION
DESTRUCTIVE
DETESTATION
DEVALUATION
DEVASTATING
DEVASTATION
DIAGNOSTICS
DIFFRACTION
DIPLOMATICS
DIPLOMATIST
DISCOURTESY
DISGRUNTLED
DISJUNCTION
DISJUNCTIVE
DISLOCATION
DISPOSITION
DISPUTATION
DISQUIETING
DISSIPATION
DISSOLUTION
DISTINCTION
DISTINCTIVE
DISTRACTION
DISTRUSTFUL
DITHELETISM
DOCUMENTARY
DODECASTYLE
DRAGGLETAIL
DUPLICATING
DUPLICATION
DYSFUNCTION
EDIFICATION
EJACULATION
ELABORATELY
ELABORATION
ELECTROTINT
ELEPHANTINE
ELIMINATION
ELIZABETHAN
ELUCIDATION
EMBARKATION
EMBROCATION
ENTABLATURE
ENUMERATION
ENUNCIATION
EQUIDISTANT
EQUINOCTIAL
ERADICATION
EUCALYPTOLE
EVAPORATION
EVENTRATION
EVERLASTING
EXAMINATION
EXCLAMATION
EXHORTATION
EXONERATION
EXPECTATION
EXPENDITURE
EXPLANATION
EXPLANATORY
EXPLORATION
EXPLORATORY

EXPONENTIAL
EXPURGATION
EXQUISITELY
EXTENUATING
EXTENUATION
EXTRADITION
FABRICATION
FACULTATIVE
FAIRWEATHER
FASCINATING
FASCINATION
FAVOURITISM
FESTINATELY
FILAMENTOUS
FINGERSTALL
FLICKERTAIL
FLUCTUATING
FLUCTUATION
FOMENTATION
FORECASTING
FORESTATION
FORMULATION
FORNICATION
FORTUNATELY
FOULMOUTHED
FRAGMENTARY
FROSTBITTEN
FRUSTRATING
FRUSTRATION
FULMINATION
GAMMERSTANG
GASTRECTOMY
GERMINATION
GIGGLESTICK
GIRDLESTEAD
GORDONSTOUN
GRANDFATHER
GRANDMOTHER
GRAVIMETRIC
GRAVITATION
GREENBOTTLE
GUBERNATION
HALFBROTHER
HANDWRITING
HANDWRITTEN
HARDHITTING
HARIOLATION
HATCHETTITE
HIBERNATING
HIBERNATION
HOMEOPATHIC
HOSTILITIES
HOUSEFATHER
HOUSEMOTHER
HUMILIATING
HUMILIATION
HYOPLASTRON
HYPHENATION
IDOLIZATION
IGNORANTINE
IMAGINATION
IMAGINATIVE
IMMEDIATELY
IMMIGRATION
IMPLICATION
IMPORTATION
IMPRECATION

INADVERTENT	MALPRACTICE	PORTMANTEAU	RESPIRATORY	TRANSLATION	DECEITFULLY
INATTENTION	MANCIPATION	PORTRAITIST	RESTITUTION	TRANSMITTED	DELICIOUSLY
INATTENTIVE	MANUFACTURE	PORTRAITURE	RESTORATION	TRANSMITTER	DEMAGOGUERY
INCANTATION	MARIONETTES	PRECIPITATE	RESTORATIVE	TREACHETOUR	DINNYHAUSER
INCARNATION	MASTICATION	PRECIPITOUS	RESTRICTION	TREPIDATION	DISCOLOURED
INCLINATION	MATHEMATICS	PREDICATIVE	RESTRICTIVE	TRIBULATION	DISTINGUISH
INCOMPETENT	MENSURATION	PRELIBATION	RESTRUCTURE	TRICERATOPS	DISTRIBUTED
INDENTATION	MERCHANTMAN	PREMEDITATE	RESUSCITATE	TRICHOPTERA	DISTRIBUTOR
INDIGESTION	METACENTRIC	PREMONITION	RETALIATION	TYPESETTING	DRACUNCULUS
INDIGNATION	METRICATION	PREMONITORY	RETALIATORY	TYPEWRITTEN	DREADNOUGHT
INEBRIATION	MICTURITION	PREPARATION	RETARDATION	UNASSERTIVE	EMPHYTEUSIS
INEFFECTIVE	MIDDENSTEAD	PREPARATIVE	RETRIBUTION	UNBEFITTING	EMPIRICUTIC
INEFFECTUAL	MISBEGOTTEN	PREPARATORY	RETRIBUTIVE	UNCHRISTIAN	EREMACAUSIS
INESSENTIAL	MISCONSTRUE	PREPOSITION	RETROACTIVE	UNCOMMITTED	ERRONEOUSLY
INFATUATION	MISIDENTIFY	PREROGATIVE	REVALUATION	UNESSENTIAL	ESCARMOUCHE
INFESTATION	MISTRUSTFUL	PRESUMPTION	REVERENTIAL	UNIFICATION	FACETIOUSLY
INFLUENTIAL	MOLESTATION	PRESUMPTIVE	RODOMONTADE	UNIMPORTANT	FEROCIOUSLY
INFORMATICS	MORGENSTERN	PRETERITION	ROTTENSTONE	UNRELENTING	FORETHOUGHT
INFORMATION	MOXIBUSTION	PROCREATION	RUDIMENTARY	UNREMITTING	FRIGHTFULLY
INFORMATIVE	MURMURATION	PROCRUSTEAN	RUMFRUCTION	UNREPENTANT	FRIVOLOUSLY
INFURIATING	NATIONSTATE	PROGENITRIX	RUMGUMPTION	UTILIZATION	GALLIMAUFRY
INGRATITUDE	NEANDERTHAL	PROHIBITION	SCYPHISTOMA	VACCINATION	GARRULOUSLY
INOCULATION	NECESSITATE	PROHIBITIVE	SEDIMENTARY	VACILLATING	GOODNATURED
INOPERATIVE	NECESSITOUS	PROLOCUTION	SEGREGATION	VACILLATION	HILARIOUSLY
INOPPORTUNE	NEEDLESTICK	PROMPTITUDE	SELFCONTROL	VALEDICTION	IMPERIOUSLY
INQUISITION	NEGOTIATING	PROPAGATION	SERICULTURE	VALEDICTORY	IMPETUOUSLY
INQUISITIVE	NEGOTIATION	PROPOSITION	SHOPLIFTING	VARIEGATION	INCONGRUITY
INSCRIPTION	NEWSCASTING	PROPRIETARY	SHUNAMITISM	VARIOLATION	INCONGRUOUS
INSENSITIVE	NONEXISTENT	PROROGATION	SINGLESTICK	VENTILATION	INCUNABULUM
INSINUATING	NOVELETTISH	PROSECUTION	SPECULATION	VICISSITUDE	INGENIOUSLY
INSINUATION	NUMISMATICS	PROSELYTISM	SPECULATIVE	VINBLASTINE	INSIDIOUSLY
INSPIRATION	NUMISMATIST	PROSELYTIZE	SPESSARTITE	VINCRISTINE	INTERCOURSE
INSTIGATION	OBSERVATION	PROSPECTIVE	STAGFLATION	VINDICATION	INTERLEUKIN
INSTINCTIVE	OBSERVATORY	PROSTHETICS	STANDPATTER	VISCOUNTESS	JUDICIOUSLY
INSTITUTION	OBSTINATELY	PROSTRATION	STEPBROTHER	VIVISECTION	LABORIOUSLY
INSTRUCTION	OBSTRICTION	PROTONOTARY	STILBESTROL	WAINSCOTING	LONGINQUITY
INSTRUCTIVE	OBSTRUCTION	PROTRACTING	STIMULATION	WASHLEATHER	LUXURIOUSLY
INTEGRATION	OBSTRUCTIVE	PROTRACTION	STIPULATION	WELLINGTONS	MALICIOUSLY
INTERACTION	ORIENTATION	PROVOCATION	STYLIZATION	WHEREWITHAL	MANGALSUTRA
INTERACTIVE	ORIGINATING	PROVOCATIVE	SUBJUGATION	WHITLEATHER	MASTERFULLY
INTERESTING	ORIGINATION	PSYCHIATRIC	SUBJUNCTIVE	WHITSUNTIDE	MELLIFLUOUS
INTRICATELY	OSCILLATION	PUBLICATION	SUBLIMATION	WINDLESTRAW	MELODIOUSLY
INVESTITURE	OSTENTATION	PULCHRITUDE	SUBPANATION	WORKSTATION	MONCHIQUITE
INVOLUNTARY	OSTEOPATHIC	PUNCTUATION	SUBSTANTIAL	YELLOWSTONE	MONTESQUIEU
IRRADIATION	OVARIECTOMY	PURPRESTURE	SUBSTANTIVE	ALBUMINURIA	MUNCHHAUSEN
IRREDENTIST	OXODIZATION	QUALITATIVE	SUBTRACTION	ANFRACTUOUS	MUSKELLUNGE
ISOELECTRIC	PALEOLITHIC	RADIOACTIVE	SUFFOCATING	ANONYMOUSLY	NEIGHBOURLY
ISOLECITHAL	PAMPHLETEER	RAZZAMATAZZ	SUFFOCATION	APATOSAURUS	NOTORIOUSLY
JACTITATION	PANTALETTES	REALIZATION	SUPERALTERN	ASSIDUOUSLY	OFFICIOUSLY
LAMENTATION	PARACHUTIST	REANIMATION	SUPERINTEND	ATROCIOUSLY	OUAGADOUGOU
LEGISLATION	PARAMASTOID	REBARBATIVE	SUPERLATIVE	AUDACIOUSLY	OUTMANEUVER
LEGISLATIVE	PARTURITION	RECANTATION	SUPPOSITION	BEAUTIFULLY	OVERDRAUGHT
LEGISLATURE	PEDETENTOUS	RECLAMATION	SUPPOSITORY	BEHAVIOURAL	OVERWROUGHT
LEPIDOPTERA	PENETRATING	RECOGNITION	SUPPURATION	BREADCRUMBS	PERSPICUITY
LICKSPITTLE	PENETRATION	RECONDITION	SUSURRATION	BUTTONQUAIL	PERSPICUOUS
LILLIPUTIAN	PENITENTIAL	REFORMATION	SYNCOPATION	CENTRIFUGAL	PONDEROUSLY
LINGUISTICS	PENNYFATHER	REFORMATORY	SYNDICATION	CHAULMOUGRA	PROMISCUITY
LIQUIDATION	PERCOLATION	REGIMENTALS	SYSTEMATIZE	CONJECTURAL	PROMISCUOUS
LITTÉRATEUR	PERFORATION	REGURGITATE	TARATANTARA	CONSCIOUSLY	PROPINQUITY
LIVINGSTONE	PERFUNCTORY	REITERATION	TELOCENTRIC	CONSPICUOUS	QUERULOUSLY
LOCORESTIVE	PERMUTATION	REORIENTATE	TEMPERATURE	CONSTITUENT	RAPTUROUSLY
LONGLASTING	PERSECUTION	REPUDIATION	TERMINATION	CONTRIBUTOR	RECTANGULAR
LUBRICATION	PERSPECTIVE	REQUISITION	TERREMOTIVE	CONVOLVULUS	REGRETFULLY
MACHINATION	PHALANSTERY	RESERVATION	TITILLATION	COURTEOUSLY	RELIGIOUSLY
MALEDICTION	PIEDMONTITE	RESIDENTIAL	TOSTICATION	CREDULOUSLY	RESENTFULLY
MALEFACTION	PLAGIOSTOMI	RESIGNATION	TRACHEOTOMY	CREPUSCULAR	RETINACULUM
MALFUNCTION	POLLINATION	RESPIRATION	TRANSACTION	DANGEROUSLY	RIGHTEOUSLY

SAGACIOUSLY	KIDDLEYWINK	CHAMBERLAIN	EXPECTORANT	NOTICEBOARD	SHOVELBOARD
SAINTPAULIA	LATTICEWORK	CHAMBERMAID	EXPECTORATE	NUCLEOPLASM	SIGNIFICANT
SALACIOUSLY	LEATHERWOOD	CHIPPENDALE	EXPOSTULATE	NUMBERPLATE	SPARROWHAWK
SOLILOQUIZE	MEADOWSWEET	CHROMOPLAST	EXPROPRIATE	OBTEMPERATE	SPATTERDASH
SORROWFULLY	OVERCROWDED	CHRYSOPRASE	EXTERMINATE	ODONTOBLAST	SPEECHCRAFT
SPECTACULAR	OVERFLOWING	CILOFIBRATE	EXTRAPOLATE	OPPIGNORATE	SPIFFLICATE
STOCKHAUSEN	SANDERSWOOD	CLAIRSCHACH	EXTRAVAGANT	ORCHESTRATE	SPRINGBOARD
STRENUOUSLY	SHITTIMWOOD	CLAIRVOYANT	FANFARONADE	OSTREOPHAGE	STEEPLEJACK
SUMPTUOUSLY	SLUMBERWEAR	COLLABORATE	FARTHINGALE	PARTICIPANT	STELLIONATE
SUPERFLUITY	STRANGEWAYS	COMMEMORATE	FINGERSTALL	PARTICIPATE	STEREOGRAPH
SUPERFLUOUS	TIDDLEYWINK	COMMISERATE	FLABBERGAST	PEDESTRIANS	STICKLEBACK
TEMPESTUOUS	WISHTONWISH	COMMONPLACE	FLANKERBACK	PENICILLATE	STIPENDIARY
TENACIOUSLY	CRUCIFIXION	COMMUNICANT	FLICKERTAIL	PENULTIMATE	STRANGEWAYS
THEOPNEUSTY	GENUFLEXION	COMMUNICATE	FRAGMENTARY	PERAMBULATE	STRANGULATE
THERAPEUTAE	IDEOPRAXIST	COMPLAISANT	FUNCTIONARY	PERCHLORATE	STRINGBOARD
THERAPEUTIC	SESQUIOXIDE	CONCENTRATE	GALLOWGLASS	PEREGRINATE	STRINGYBARK
UNAMBIGUOUS	ASSEMBLYMAN	CONCOMITANT	GAMMERSTANG	PERLUSTRATE	SUBCONTRACT
UNANIMOUSLY	BADDELEYITE	CONFABULATE	GESTICULATE	PHILIPPIANS	SUBDOMINANT
UNSCHEDULED	CLAIRVOYANT	CONFARREATE	GUESSTIMATE	PHYLLOCLADE	SUBORDINATE
VICARIOUSLY	CYCLOSTYLED	CONFEDERACY	HAEMORRHAGE	PISSASPHALT	SUBSTANDARD
VIVACIOUSLY	DINNYHAYSER	CONFEDERATE	HALLUCINATE	PLANTIGRADE	SUBUNGULATA
VORACIOUSLY	IDENTIFYING	CONSIDERATE	HEBDOMADARY	PLOUGHSHARE	SUDETENLAND
WATERCOURSE	INFANTRYMAN	CONSOLIDATE	HETEROGRAFT	POLITICIANS	SURTARBRAND
WIENERWURST	ONEIRODYNIA	CONSTELLATE	HUCKSTERAGE	POMEGRANATE	SURTURBRAND
WONDERFULLY	PLEURODYNIA	CONSTERNATE	HUSBANDLAND	PONTIFICATE	SURVEILLANT
ACRIFLAVINE	SAPROPHYTIC	CONSTUPRATE	HYDROGENATE	PRECIPITATE	SWITCHBOARD
ATHARVAVEDA	SCEUOPHYLAX	CONTAMINANT	HYPOTHECATE	PREDOMINANT	SWITZERLAND
ATTENTIVELY	STEATOPYGIA	CONTAMINATE	ILLUSIONARY	PREDOMINATE	TARATANTARA
DECEPTIVELY	STEREOTYPED	CONTEMPLANT	IMPERFORATE	PRELIMINARY	THEATRICALS
DEFENSIVELY	THERMOPYLAE	CONTEMPLATE	IMPERSONATE	PREMEDITATE	TREPONEMATA
EFFECTIVELY	WHITEBOYISM	COPPERPLATE	IMPIGNORATE	PRESTONPANS	TRIUMVIRATE
EXCESSIVELY	ESTRAMAZONE	CORINTHIANS	IMPORTUNATE	PREVARICATE	TROPHOBLAST
EXCLUSIVELY	PATRONIZING	CORROBORATE	INCAPSULATE	PROLIFERATE	TURRICULATE
EXTENSIVELY	PROTEROZOIC	COUNTERHAND	INCARCERATE	PROPRIETARY	TYRANNOSAUR
IMPASSIVELY	TANTALIZING	COUNTERMAND	INCORPORATE	PROTONOTARY	ULOTRICHALE
IMPULSIVELY	**11:9**	COUNTERPANE	INCRIMINATE	PROTUBERANT	UNFORTUNATE
INSECTIVORE	ACCOMMODATE	COUNTERPART	INDUPLICATE	PTOCHOCRACY	UNIMPORTANT
INTENSIVELY	ACCULTURATE	CRACKERJACK	INSTANTIATE	QUARTERBACK	UNNECESSARY
INTUITIVELY	AGGLOMERATE	CREDENTIALS	INTEMPERATE	RATIOCINATE	UNOBSERVANT
LABORSAVING	AGGLUTINANT	CRESCENTADE	INTERCALARY	RATTLESNAKE	UNREPENTANT
MENDELEVIUM	AGGLUTINATE	CYCLOALKANE	INTERPOLATE	RAZZAMATAZZ	VERBIGERATE
MISBEHAVIOR	AMONTILLADO	DECARBONATE	INTERRELATE	REACTIONARY	WATERSPLASH
MISCHIEVOUS	AMPLEXICAUL	DECORTICATE	INTERROGATE	RECIPROCATE	WENSLEYDALE
OBJECTIVELY	ANENCEPHALY	DECREPITATE	INVESTIGATE	RECRIMINATE	WHITEFRIARS
OBJECTIVITY	ANNIVERSARY	DEGLUTINATE	INVOLUNTARY	REDUPLICATE	WINDOWFRAME
OBSESSIVELY	ANTIPHONARY	DEMONSTRATE	KILIMANJARO	REFOCILLATE	ABRACADABRA
OFFENSIVELY	APPROPRIATE	DENDRACHATE	KNUCKLEBALL	REFRIGERANT	ACCOUNTABLE
RECEPTIVITY	APPROXIMATE	DEOXYGENATE	LATERIGRADE	REFRIGERATE	AGORAPHOBIA
RESISTIVITY	APPURTENANT	DEPHLEGMATE	LEATHERBACK	REGIMENTALS	ANTECHAMBER
ROTOGRAVURE	ARCHIPELAGO	DESEGREGATE	LECITHINASE	REGURGITATE	APPRECIABLE
SECRETIVELY	ARISTOCRACY	DETERIORATE	LEFTLUGGAGE	REICHENBACH	APPRECIABLY
SELECTIVELY	ASSASSINATE	DETERMINANT	LEGERDEMAIN	REINCARNATE	BEACHCOMBER
SELECTIVITY	AVERRUNCATE	DETERMINATE	LOGGERHEADS	REMONSTRATE	BELLYTIMBER
SELFSERVICE	BARBITURATE	DEUTSCHMARK	LOGODAEDALY	REORIENTATE	CERTIFIABLE
SENSITIVELY	BEAUMONTAGE	DIAMONDBACK	MARIVAUDAGE	RESUSCITATE	CHRYSAROBIN
SENSITIVITY	BENEFICIARY	DIPTEROCARP	MARKETPLACE	REVENDICATE	COLLAPSIBLE
SPACESAVING	BENEFICIATE	DIRECTORATE	MATRICULATE	REVERBERATE	COMBUSTIBLE
TCHAIKOVSKY	BICARBONATE	DISSEMINATE	MEPROBAMATE	RODOMONTADE	COMFORTABLE
TENTATIVELY	BICENTENARY	DISSIMULATE	METACARPALS	RUDIMENTARY	COMFORTABLY
UNDESERVING	BIMILLENARY	DOCUMENTARY	METATARSALS	SCINTILLATE	COMMENDABLE
UNOBSERVANT	BREASTPLATE	DOMESTICATE	MILQUETOAST	SECONDCLASS	COMMENDABLY
WOODCARVING	BUREAUCRACY	DRAGGLETAIL	MISCARRIAGE	SEDIMENTARY	CONCEIVABLE
BITTERSWEET	BUTTONQUAIL	EARTHENWARE	MONOTREMATA	SEIGNIORAGE	CONCEIVABLY
BLADDERWORT	CARDIOGRAPH	ELASTOPLAST	MUSCHELKALK	SEISMOGRAPH	CONVERTIBLE
EARTHENWARE	CATCHPHRASE	ENCAPSULATE	NATIONSTATE	SEQUESTRATE	CORRUPTIBLE
GIGGLESWICK	CENTREBOARD	EQUIDISTANT	NECESSITATE	SHAKESPEARE	DENUMERABLE
GROUNDSWELL	CERTIFICATE	EXANTHEMATA	NIGHTINGALE	SHENANIGANS	DISCERNIBLE

DISENCUMBER	RESPECTABLE	INTERNUNCIO	HOUSEHOLDER	BATHYSPHERE	DESPERATELY
DISPENSABLE	RESPECTABLY	JABBERWOCKY	HYDROPHIDAE	BATTLEDRESS	DEVELOPMENT
DISPERSABLE	RESPONSIBLE	LANDSKNECHT	JERRYMANDER	BATTLEFIELD	DEVIOUSNESS
ENFORCEABLE	RESPONSIBLY	MONARCHICAL	LEASEHOLDER	BEASTLINESS	DISABLEMENT
FASHIONABLE	RETRACTABLE	MYCOLOGICAL	LEVELHEADED	BELLIGERENT	DISARMAMENT
FASHIONABLY	RETRIEVABLE	NECROMANCER	LIGHTHEADED	BEREAVEMENT	DISCERNMENT
FISSIONABLE	SERVICEABLE	NONSENSICAL	MACHAIRODUS	BESIEGEMENT	DISCOURTESY
FORESEEABLE	STOCKJOBBER	OBSTETRICAL	MASQUERADER	BILIOUSNESS	DISINTEREST
HAEMOGLOBIN	STRETCHABLE	ONOMASTICON	MOLLYCODDLE	BITTERSWEET	DISOBEDIENT
HONEYCOMBED	SUGGESTIBLE	ONTOLOGICAL	MONEYLENDER	BLESSEDNESS	DISSEPIMENT
HYDROCARBON	SUSCEPTIBLE	PARADOXICAL	OFFHANDEDLY	BLOODSTREAM	DIVORCEMENT
HYDROPHOBIA	SUSTAINABLE	PARAMEDICAL	OFFICIALDOM	BOMBARDMENT	DOUBLECHECK
HYDROPHOBIC	SWALLOWABLE	PEDAGOGICAL	ORTHOPAEDIC	BOOKSELLERS	DRUNKENNESS
IMPERMEABLE	THINGAMABOB	PHARISAICAL	OVERCROWDED	BOUTONNIERE	DRYCLEANERS
IMPLAUSIBLE	TREASONABLE	PROPHETICAL	PHONOFIDDLE	BRITTLENESS	DUBIOUSNESS
IMPREGNABLE	UNALIENABLE	PROTOCOCCUS	PROFESSEDLY	CALEFACIENT	EARNESTNESS
INADVISABLE	UNALTERABLE	PURITANICAL	PROOFREADER	CALLIPYGEAN	EFFECTIVELY
INALIENABLE	UNAVAILABLE	RHAPSODICAL	RANGEFINDER	CALLOUSNESS	ELABORATELY
INDEFINABLE	UNAVOIDABLE	RHEUMATICKY	RIGHTHANDED	CARABINIERE	EMBOÎTEMENT
INDIARUBBER	UNAVOIDABLY	SALTIMBOCCA	RIGHTHANDER	CAREFULNESS	EMPIECEMENT
INDIVISIBLE	UNBREAKABLE	SCHOTTISCHE	SCOLOPENDRA	CARSICKNESS	EMPLACEMENT
INDIVISIBLY	UNCOUNTABLE	SEXOLOGICAL	SHAREHOLDER	CENTERPIECE	EMPOWERMENT
INDOMITABLE	UNCRUSHABLE	SPONDULICKS	SHIPBUILDER	CENTREPIECE	ENCHANTMENT
INDUBITABLE	UNDESIRABLE	STATISTICAL	SHORTHANDED	CHANCELLERY	ENCHANTRESS
INDUBITABLY	UNDISTURBED	STRAITLACED	SMALLHOLDER	CHANTICLEER	ENDORSEMENT
INELUCTABLE	UNDRINKABLE	STRATEGICAL	SPELLBINDER	CHICKENFEED	ENFEOFFMENT
INEQUITABLE	UNENDURABLE	SUBTROPICAL	SPERMICIDAL	CIRCUMFLECT	ENFORCEMENT
INESCAPABLE	UNFAVORABLE	SYMMETRICAL	STADTHOLDER	CIRCUMSPECT	ENHANCEMENT
INESTIMABLE	UNFLAPPABLE	TETRADRACHM	STAKEHOLDER	CITLALEPETL	ENJAMBEMENT
INEXCITABLE	UNGETATABLE	THEOLOGICAL	STALLHOLDER	CLARENCIEUX	ENLARGEMENT
INEXCUSABLE	UNPALATABLE	THEORETICAL	STOCKHOLDER	CLEANLINESS	ENSLAVEMENT
INEXCUSABLY	UNPERTURBED	TOPLOFTICAL	SYMPLEGADES	COCKLESHELL	ENTABLEMENT
INFLAMMABLE	UNPRINTABLE	UNANNOUNCED	TACHYCARDIA	COEFFICIENT	ENTITLEMENT
INHABITABLE	UNSHAKEABLE	UNCONVINCED	TARRADIDDLE	COMFORTLESS	ENVIRONMENT
INNUMERABLE	UNSPEAKABLE	UNEQUIVOCAL	TITLEHOLDER	COMMANDMENT	EPICHEIREMA
INSCRUTABLE	UNSTOPPABLE	UNPRACTICAL	TRANSPONDER	COMPARTMENT	EQUIPOLLENT
INSEPARABLE	UNTHINKABLE	ACKNOWLEDGE	UNDERHANDED	COMPILEMENT	ESTRANGHELO
INSUPERABLE	UNTOUCHABLE	ANAXIMANDER	UNDOUBTEDLY	COMSTOCKERY	EVASIVENESS
INTOLERABLE	UNUTTERABLE	ARTHRAPODAL	WATERMEADOW	CONCEALMENT	EXCESSIVELY
INTOLERABLY	WALDSTERBEN	ASCLEPIADES	WEIGHBRIDGE	CONCISENESS	EXCLUSIVELY
INTRACTABLE	ALLEGORICAL	ATHERINIDAE	WELLFOUNDED	CONDOTTIERE	EXQUISITELY
IRREDUCIBLE	ANISOCERCAL	BACKFIELDER	WINDOWLEDGE	CONDUCTRESS	EXTENSIVELY
IRREFUTABLE	APOLLONICON	BROADMINDED	WRONGHEADED	CONFINEMENT	FATUOUSNESS
IRREPARABLE	APPEARANCES	BUPRESTIDAE	ABANDONMENT	CONNOISSEUR	FEATURELESS
IRREPARABLY	APPRENTICED	CARBORUNDUM	ABRIDGEMENT	CONSIGNMENT	FERRONNIÈRE
IRREVOCABLE	BIOCHEMICAL	CHEERLEADER	ACHIEVEMENT	CONSTITUENT	FESTINATELY
JUSTIFIABLE	BRAGGADOCIO	CHILDMINDER	ACQUIESCENT	CONTAINMENT	FISHMONGERS
JUSTIFIABLY	CALLITRICHE	CIRRHIPEDEA	ADJOURNMENT	CONTENEMENT	FLUORESCENT
LIQUIDAMBAR	CATEGORICAL	CIRRHIPEDIA	ADVANCEMENT	CONTENTMENT	FOOLISHNESS
PENSIONABLE	CHICHEVACHE	COLDBLOODED	ADVENTURESS	CORDWAINERS	FOREFATHERS
PERCEPTIBLE	CONCEPTICLE	CONTENTEDLY	AIRSICKNESS	CORRECTNESS	FORGIVENESS
PERCEPTIBLY	CONDOLENCES	DICOTYLEDON	ALTERNATELY	COULOMMIERS	FORLORNNESS
PERMISSIBLE	CONNECTICUT	DISREGARDED	AMERCIAMENT	COUNTERFEIT	FORTUNATELY
PLEASURABLE	CONVENTICLE	DOWNTRODDEN	AMINOBUTENE	COURTLINESS	FULFILLMENT
PRACTICABLE	CYLINDRICAL	DRAGONNADES	AMPHISBAENA	COXWAINLESS	FURTIVENESS
PREDICTABLE	DIPHYCERCAL	DUMBFOUNDED	AMPHISBOENA	CRÉMAILLÈRE	GARNISHMENT
PREDICTABLY	EGOTISTICAL	EMPTYHANDED	APHANIPTERA	CROOKEDNESS	GEGENSCHEIN
PRESENTABLE	ESCARMOUCHE	EPAMINONDAS	APPEASEMENT	CULVERINEER	GENOUILLÈRE
PREVENTABLE	EVANGELICAL	FAULTFINDER	APPOINTMENT	CURTAILMENT	GENUINENESS
PUBLISHABLE	EXPERIENCED	FAUXBOURDON	ARBITRAGEUR	DECEPTIVELY	GHASTLINESS
RADIOCARBON	FEHMGERICHT	FIDDLEDEDEE	ARBITRAMENT	DEFENCELESS	GINGERBREAD
RECOVERABLE	GEOMETRICAL	FULLBLOODED	ARRANGEMENT	DEFENSELESS	GIRDLESTEAD
RECTIFIABLE	GNATHONICAL	GERRYMANDER	ASSYTHEMENT	DEFENSIVELY	GROUNDSHEET
REDOUBTABLE	GRAMMATICAL	HALFHOLIDAY	ATHARVAVEDA	DELITESCENT	GROUNDSPEED
REGRETTABLE	GREENGROCER	HAPHAZARDLY	ATTENTIVELY	DEMAGOGUERY	GROUNDSWELL
REGRETTABLY	IDEOLOGICAL	HEAVYHANDED	AWKWARDNESS	DEPARTEMENT	HAUGHTINESS
REPLACEABLE	IMPRACTICAL	HOHENLINDEN	BASHFULNESS	DERANGEMENT	HEALTHINESS

HELPFULNESS	NICKELODEON	RHOPALOCERA	UNGODLINESS	PAPERWEIGHT	OSTEOPATHIC
HIDEOUSNESS	NICKNACKERY	RIBONUCLEIC	UNHAPPINESS	PETTIFOGGER	OXYRHYNCHUS
HOGGISHNESS	NONETHELESS	ROGUISHNESS	UPRIGHTNESS	PSEUDOLOGIA	PALEOLITHIC
HOUSEPARENT	NONEXISTENT	SAINTLINESS	USELESSNESS	RAVISHINGLY	PARTNERSHIP
HYPERBOREAN	NOTHINGNESS	SAUSAGEMEAT	VACUOUSNESS	RIGHTWINGER	PATRIARCHAL
IMMEDIATELY	NOURISHMENT	SAVOURINESS	VICIOUSNESS	SARCOPHAGUS	PENNYFATHER
IMPASSIVELY	NUTCRACKERS	SCITAMINEAE	VIDEOCAMERA	SCAREMONGER	PHILOSOPHER
IMPEACHMENT	OBJECTIVELY	SCRUFFINESS	VISCOUNTESS	SCREAMINGLY	POLYMORPHIC
IMPERMANENT	OBMUTESCENT	SCULDUDDERY	WAKEFULNESS	SCULLABOGUE	POLYTRICHUM
IMPERTINENT	OBSESSIVELY	SCULDUGGERY	WAYWARDNESS	SEARCHLIGHT	PREMIERSHIP
IMPROPRIETY	OBSOLESCENT	SEASICKNESS	WHIGMALEERY	SLIGHTINGLY	REFURBISHED
IMPROVEMENT	OBSTINATELY	SECRETIVELY	WILLINGNESS	SOCKDALAGER	SCHOLARSHIP
IMPROVIDENT	OBVIOUSNESS	SELECTIVELY	WINTERGREEN	SOCKDOLAGER	SHOWMANSHIP
IMPULSIVELY	OFFENSIVELY	SELFEVIDENT	WISTFULNESS	SOCKDOLIGER	SPONSORSHIP
INADVERTENT	OFFICIALESE	SELFISHNESS	WOMANLINESS	SOCKDOLOGER	STEPBROTHER
INCALESCENT	OLIGOCHAETE	SELFRESPECT	WORLDLINESS	STEATOPYGIA	SUNDRENCHED
INCOMPETENT	OMNIPRESENT	SENSITIVELY	DISGRACEFUL	STEINBERGER	TELEGRAPHER
INCONTINENT	OPPORTUNELY	SERIOUSNESS	DISTASTEFUL	STRAPHANGER	TELEGRAPHIC
INCORPOREAL	ORDERLINESS	SHALLOWNESS	DISTRUSTFUL	STREETLIGHT	TOPOGRAPHER
INDEPENDENT	OSTRACODERM	SHAPELINESS	FORAMINIFER	UNDERWEIGHT	TRAGELAPHUS
INDIFFERENT	OVERPAYMENT	SHEPHERDESS	GALLIMAUFRY	UNFAILINGLY	TRUSTEESHIP
INEFFICIENT	PAMPHLETEER	SIGHTSCREEN	MISTRUSTFUL	UNWITTINGLY	TYPOGRAPHER
INEXPEDIENT	PANOMPHAEAN	SINGAPOREAN	NORTHCLIFFE	WATERLOGGED	TYPOGRAPHIC
INSTALLMENT	PARLIPOMENA	SKETCHINESS	OVERSTUFFED	WHEELWRIGHT	TYROGLYPHID
INTELLIGENT	PASSIVENESS	SKULDUDDERY	REPROACHFUL	ANACOLUTHIA	UNBLEMISHED
INTENSIVELY	PAWNBROKERS	SKULDUGGERY	RESOURCEFUL	ANTIBURGHER	UNFURNISHED
INTRICATELY	PEEVISHNESS	SLENDERNESS	TEASPOONFUL	APOSTROPHUS	UNPUBLISHED
INTUITIVELY	PELOPONNESE	SLUMBERWEAR	ACCORDINGLY	APPARATCHIK	UNVARNISHED
INVOLVEMENT	PENSIVENESS	SMITHEREENS	APPALLINGLY	ARCHILOCHUS	WAPPENSCHAW
IRONMONGERS	PENTATHLETE	SMOKESCREEN	APPLERINGIE	AXEROPHTHOL	WASHLEATHER
IRONMONGERY	PENTAVALENT	SPIROCHAETE	APPROVINGLY	BACKBENCHER	WHEREWITHAL
KULTURKREIS	PERCEFOREST	SPORTSFIELD	CAMOUFLAGED	BELLEROPHON	WHITLEATHER
LAPIDESCENT	PERITONAEUM	SPREADSHEET	CANDLELIGHT	BIRDWATCHER	WORKMANSHIP
LAWLESSNESS	PHALANSTERY	SPRINGCLEAN	CARDOPHAGUS	CHILLINGHAM	XYLOGRAPHER
LEATHERHEAD	PHOTOSPHERE	SPRINGINESS	CENTRIFUGAL	CHRISTOPHER	ABECEDARIAN
LEATHERNECK	PINACOTHECA	STATELINESS	CHARLEMAGNE	CITIZENSHIP	ABLACTATION
LENGTHINESS	PLAYFULNESS	STOOLPIGEON	CHAULMOOGRA	COMRADESHIP	ABNORMALITY
LEPIDOPTERA	PLEISTOCENE	STRANGENESS	CHAULMOUGRA	DEMOGRAPHIC	ABOMINATION
LETTERPRESS	PODSNAPPERY	STRETCHLESS	CHOLINERGIC	ECTOTROPHIC	ABORTIONIST
LITERALNESS	POLYSTYRENE	STYLISHNESS	CLIFFHANGER	ELIZABETHAN	ABSENTEEISM
LITTÉRATEUR	PORTMANTEAU	SUBSERVIENT	COPROPHAGAN	EMBELLISHED	ABSTRACTION
LUMINESCENT	PREDICAMENT	SUCCEDANEUM	CROSSLEGGED	ENDOTROPHIC	ACADEMICIAN
MACROGAMETE	PREMATURELY	SUPERALTERN	DISENTANGLE	ESCHERICHIA	ACADEMICISM
MAGNIFICENT	PRESENTMENT	SUPERINTEND	DREADNOUGHT	ESTABLISHED	ACCESSORIES
MAKEBELIEVE	PRICKLINESS	SUPERSEDEAS	EMMENAGOGUE	ESTABLISHER	ACCIPITRINE
MANTELPIECE	PROCRUSTEAN	SUPERSEDERE	EXCEEDINGLY	FAIRWEATHER	ACCLAMATION
MANTELSHELF	PROCUREMENT	SUPPEDANEUM	FORETHOUGHT	FISHANDCHIP	ACCLIMATION
MASSIVENESS	PROFUSENESS	SYNCHROMESH	GALLIBAGGER	FOULMOUTHED	ACCLIMATISE
MASTERPIECE	PROLEGOMENA	TEDIOUSNESS	GALLIBEGGAR	GATECRASHER	ACCLIMATIZE
MEADOWSWEET	PURPOSELESS	TEMPERAMENT	GALLYBAGGER	GRANDFATHER	ACCOMPANIST
MEANINGLESS	QUADRUPLETS	TENTATIVELY	GALLYBEGGAR	GRANDMOTHER	ACOLOUTHITE
MEASURELESS	QUARTERDECK	TENUOUSNESS	GRAMMALOGUE	HABERDASHER	ACQUISITION
MEASUREMENT	QUINTUPLETS	THESMOTHETE	GRAVEDIGGER	HALFBROTHER	ACQUISITIVE
MENTONNIÈRE	RAFFISHNESS	THINGLINESS	GRENZGANGER	HIGHPITCHED	ACRIFLAVINE
MICROGAMETE	RAUCOUSNESS	THOUGHTLESS	HEAVYWEIGHT	HOBBLEDEHOY	ACTUALITIES
MIDDENSTEAD	REALIGNMENT	THRIFTINESS	HORNSWOGGLE	HOMEOPATHIC	ADIAPHORIST
MILLIAMPERE	RECRUITMENT	THUNDERHEAD	INQUIRINGLY	HOUSEFATHER	ADOPTIANISM
MISERLINESS	RECTILINEAR	TRACKLEMENT	INSULTINGLY	HOUSEMOTHER	ADOPTIONISM
MODELMOLEST	REFRESHMENT	TRANSILIENT	INTERLINGUA	IDIOGRAPHIC	ADUMBRATION
MONONGAHELA	RELEASEMENT	TRANSLUCENT	INTERMINGLE	ISOLECITHAL	ADVERTISING
MONONUCLEAR	REMINISCENT	TRANSPARENT	LEADSWINGER	JINRICKSHAW	AERONAUTICS
MORGENSTERN	REMORSELESS	TRICHOPTERA	LIGHTWEIGHT	LECTURESHIP	AESCULAPIAN
MOUNTAINEER	REPLACEMENT	TROMPELOEIL	LUXEMBURGER	LOGOGRAPHER	AESCULAPIUS
NAPHTHALENE	REQUIREMENT	TROPOSPHERE	MINNESINGER	MATRIARCHAL	AFFECTATION
NATURALNESS	RESPLENDENT	ULTRAMODERN	OUAGADOUGOU	NEANDERTHAL	AFFILIATION
NAUGHTINESS	RESTATEMENT	UNCLEANNESS	OVERDRAUGHT	OARSMANSHIP	AFFIRMATION
NERVOUSNESS	RESTIVENESS	UNCOUTHNESS	OVERWROUGHT	OCTASTICHON	AFFIRMATIVE

AFFLIICTION	BIFURCATION	CONSIDERING	DESTABILIZE	ENDOCARDIUM	FRANKLINITE
AGGRAVATING	BILLIONAIRE	CONSOLATION	DESTINATION	ENFRANCHISE	FRIGATEBIRD
AGGRAVATION	BLANKURSINE	CONSTANTINE	DESTITUTION	ENGINEERING	FRIGHTENING
AGGREGATION	BOOKBINDING	CONSUMERISM	DESTRUCTION	ENKEPHALINE	FRUSTRATING
AGNOSTICISM	BOOKKEEPING	CONSUMPTION	DESTRUCTIVE	ENTHRALLING	FRUSTRATION
AILUROPHILE	CALCULATING	CONSUMPTIVE	DETERMINING	ENUMERATION	FULMINATION
ALBIGENSIAN	CALCULATION	CONTRACTION	DETESTATION	ENUNCIATION	FUNAMBULIST
ALCYONARIAN	CALENDERING	CONTRAPTION	DEVALUATION	EPIGENESIST	FUNCTIONING
ALEXANDRINE	CALIBRATION	CONTRASTING	DEVASTATING	EPINEPHRINE	FUNDRAISING
ALEXANDRITE	CALIFORNIUM	CONURBATION	DEVASTATION	EPOCHMAKING	FUSTILARIAN
ALLEVIATION	CALLANETICS	CONVOCATION	DEVITRIFIED	EQUILIBRIST	GALLOVIDIAN
ALPHABETIZE	CAMALDOLITE	CONVOLUTION	DIAGNOSTICS	EQUILIBRIUM	GAMETANGIUM
ALTERCATION	CAMEROONIAN	COOPERATION	DIASCORDIUM	EQUINOCTIAL	GELSEMININE
ALTERNATING	CAMPESTRIAN	COOPERATIVE	DICTATORIAL	ERADICATION	GENEALOGIST
ALTERNATION	CANDLESTICK	CORPORATION	DIFFRACTION	ERYMANTHIAN	GENUFLEXION
ALTERNATIVE	CANNIBALISM	CORRELATION	DIPLOMATICS	ETHNOLOGIST	GEOSYNCLINE
AMELANCHIER	CANNIBALIZE	CORRUGATION	DIPLOMATIST	ETYMOLOGIST	GERMINATION
AMERICANISM	CAPTIVATING	COUNSELLING	DIPSOMANIAC	EURHYTHMICS	GESTATORIAL
AMPHETAMINE	CAPTIVATION	COUNTERSIGN	DISAGREEING	EVAPORATION	GIGGLESTICK
ANACHRONISM	CARAVANNING	COUNTERSINK	DISEMBODIED	EVENTRATION	GIGGLESWICK
ANESTHETIST	CARMINATIVE	COUNTRIFIED	DISFIGURING	EVENTUALITY	GLADWELLISE
ANESTHETIZE	CAROLINGIAN	COUNTRYSIDE	DISILLUSION	EVERLASTING	GLUCOSAMINE
ANNABERGITE	CASSITERITE	CREDIBILITY	DISJUNCTION	EXAMINATION	GONFALONIER
ANTEPENDIUM	CATHOLICISM	CREMATORIUM	DISJUNCTIVE	EXCLAMATION	GOODLOOKING
ANTHOLOGIZE	CELEBRATION	CREPITATION	DISLOCATION	EXHORTATION	GRAVITATION
ANTIQUARIAN	CENTENARIAN	CROCIDOLITE	DISORGANIZE	EXONERATION	GREASEPAINT
APHRODISIAC	CERARGYRITE	CROCODILIAN	DISPARAGING	EXPECTATION	GREENOCKITE
APODYTERIUM	CEREBRATION	CROMWELLIAN	DISPOSITION	EXPLANATION	GREGARINIDA
APOMORPHINE	CHALLENGING	CRUCIFIXION	DISPUTATION	EXPLORATION	GUBERNATION
APOPHYLLITE	CHIASTOLITE	CRYSTALLINE	DISQUIETING	EXPONENTIAL	GULLIBILITY
APPELLATION	CHIROPODIST	CRYSTALLISE	DISSIPATION	EXPURGATION	GUTTERSNIPE
APPELLATIVE	CHITTERLING	CRYSTALLIZE	DISSOLUTION	EXTEMPORISE	GUTTURALISE
APPLICATION	CHRISMATION	CULMINATION	DISTINCTION	EXTEMPORIZE	HAIRRAISING
APPROACHING	CHRISTENING	CULPABILITY	DISTINCTIVE	EXTENUATING	HANDWRITING
APPROBATION	CIRCULARIZE	CULTIVATION	DISTINGUISH	EXTENUATION	HANGGLIDING
ARBITRARILY	CIRCULATING	CUSTOMARILY	DISTRACTION	EXTERNALIZE	HARDHITTING
ARBITRATION	CIRCULATION	CYBERNETICS	DISTRESSING	EXTRADITION	HARDWORKING
ARCHEGONIAL	CLANDESTINE	DECARBONIZE	DITHELETISM	EYECATCHING	HARIOLATION
ARCHEGONIUM	CLIOMETRICS	DECLAMATION	DOCTRINAIRE	FABRICATION	HATCHETTITE
ARGATHELIAN	COAGULATION	DECLARATION	DOMESTICITY	FACTFINDING	HEMOPHILIAC
ARGENTINIAN	COENOBITISM	DECLARATIVE	DOMINEERING	FACULTATIVE	HEMORRHOIDS
ARQUEBUSIER	COHORTATIVE	DEFERENTIAL	DRESSMAKING	FALLIBILITY	HEPPLEWHITE
ARTILLERIST	COLEORRHIZA	DEFOLIATION	DRYCLEANING	FAMILIARISE	HETEROSCIAN
ASPERSORIUM	COLLOCATION	DEFORMATION	DUPLICATING	FAMILIARITY	HIBERNATING
ASPHETERISM	COLONIALISM	DEGLUTITION	DUPLICATION	FAMILIARIZE	HIBERNATION
ASSIGNATION	COLONIALIST	DEGRADATION	DYSFUNCTION	FARREACHING	HIGHPROFILE
ASSOCIATION	COLOURBLIND	DEHORTATIVE	ECCALEOBION	FASCINATING	HIGHQUALITY
ASTIGMATISM	COLUMBARIUM	DEHYDRATION	EDIFICATION	FASCINATION	HIGHRANKING
ASTONISHING	COMBINATION	DEIFICATION	EGALITARIAN	FAVOURITISM	HISTOLOGIST
ATTENUATION	COMMINATION	DELECTATION	EINSTEINIUM	FEASIBILITY	HISTRIONICS
ATTESTATION	COMMUNALISM	DELICTATION	EJACULATION	FESTSCHRIFT	HOLLANDAISE
ATTRIBUTION	COMMUTATION	DELINEATION	ELABORATION	FINGERPRINT	HOLOTHURIAN
ATTRIBUTIVE	COMPARATIVE	DEMARCATION	ELECTRICIAN	FITZWILLIAM	HOMOGENEITY
AUGUSTINIAN	COMPETITION	DEMIBASTION	ELECTRICITY	FLEXIBILITY	HOMOIOUSIAN
AURIGNACIAN	COMPETITIVE	DEPORTATION	ELECTROLIER	FLORILEGIUM	HOOLIGANISM
BACKPACKING	COMPILATION	DEPREDATION	ELECTRONICS	FLOURISHING	HORSERACING
BACKSLIDING	COMPOSITION	DEPRIVATION	ELECTROTINT	FLUCTUATING	HORSERADISH
BADDELEYITE	COMPOTATION	DERELICTION	ELEPHANTINE	FLUCTUATION	HORSERIDING
BALLBEARING	COMPUNCTION	DESCRIPTION	ELEUTHERIAN	FOMENTATION	HOSPITALITY
BELLETTRIST	COMPUTATION	DESCRIPTIVE	ELIGIBILITY	FOOTBALLING	HOSPITALIZE
BELORUSSIAN	COMPUTERIZE	DESECRATION	ELIMINATION	FOOTWASHING	HOSTILITIES
BENEDICTINE	CONDOMINIUM	DESELECTION	ELUCIDATION	FORECASTING	HUMGRUFFIAN
BENEDICTION	CONFUTATION	DESERPIDINE	EMBARKATION	FORESTATION	HUMILIATING
BESSARABIAN	CONJUGATION	DESEXUALIZE	EMBROCATION	FOREWARNING	HUMILIATION
BESTSELLING	CONJUNCTION	DESICCATION	ENCHIRIDION	FORMULATION	HUMMINGBIRD
BEWILDERING	CONNOTATION	DESIGNATION	ENCOURAGING	FORNICATION	HYDROPONICS
BIBLIOPHILE	CONSECUTIVE	DESPERATION	ENCROACHING	FORTHCOMING	HYMNOLOGIST

HYPHENATION	INSTRUCTIVE	MATRIMONIAL	OPPORTUNIST	PISCATORIAL	RATIONALIZE
HYPOTENSION	INTEGRATION	MAURETANIAN	OPPORTUNITY	PLANETARIUM	READABILITY
ICHTHYOLITE	INTERACTION	MAURITANIAN	OPTOMETRIST	PLATYRRHINE	REALIZATION
IDENTIFYING	INTERACTIVE	MEGATHERIUM	ORCHESTRINA	PLEBEIANISE	REANIMATION
IDEOPRAXIST	INTERESTING	MEKHITARIST	ORCHESTRION	POLLINATION	REBARBATIVE
IDOLIZATION	INTERLACING	MENDELEVIUM	ORGANIZAION	POLTERGEIST	RECANTATION
IGNORANTINE	INTERNALIZE	MENSURATION	ORIENTALISM	PORTLANDIAN	RECEPTIVITY
ILLUSIONISM	INTERNECINE	MERCHANDISE	ORIENTALIST	PORTRAITIST	RECIPROCITY
ILLUSIONIST	INTERVENING	MERCHANDIZE	ORIENTATION	POSSIBILITY	RECLAMATION
IMAGINATION	INTREPIDITY	MERRYMAKING	ORIGINALITY	PRECONCEIVE	RECOGNITION
IMAGINATIVE	IRRADIATION	METAPHYSICS	ORIGINATING	PREDICATIVE	RECONDITION
IMMIGRATION	IRREDENTIST	METRICATION	ORIGINATION	PREJUDICIAL	REFORMATION
IMMORTALISE	ISOXSUPRINE	MICHURINISM	OSCILLATION	PRELIBATION	REGISTERING
IMMORTALITY	JACTITATION	MICTURITION	OSTENTATION	PREMONITION	REITERATION
IMMORTALIZE	JOSEPHINITE	MILLIONAIRE	OUTSTANDING	PREOCCUPIED	RELIABILITY
IMPERIALISM	KAMELAUKION	MINIATURIST	OVERBEARING	PREPARATION	REPUDIATION
IMPERIALIST	KIDDLEYWINK	MINIATURIZE	OVERFISHING	PREPARATIVE	REQUISITION
IMPETUOSITY	KIMERIDGIAN	MINISTERIAL	OVERFLOWING	PREPOSITION	RESERVATION
IMPLICATION	KINDERSPIEL	MINISTERING	OVERHANGING	PREROGATIVE	RESIDENTIAL
IMPORTATION	KINNIKINICK	MISBEHAVIOR	OVERLAPPING	PRESTISSIMO	RESIGNATION
IMPRECATION	KIRKPATRICK	MISIDENTIFY	OVERMANNING	PRESUMPTION	RESISTIVITY
IMPRECISION	KRIEGSSPIEL	MISSPELLING	OVERTURNING	PRESUMPTIVE	RESPIRATION
INATTENTION	LABORSAVING	MOCKINGBIRD	OVERWEENING	PRETERITION	RESTITUTION
INATTENTIVE	LAMENTATION	MOLESTATION	OXODIZATION	PRIMIGENIAL	RESTORATION
INCANTATION	LAMMERGEIER	MOMENTARILY	PAEDIATRICS	PRISCIANIST	RESTORATIVE
INCARNADINE	LASERPICIUM	MONCHIQUITE	PAINKILLING	PROBABILITY	RESTRICTION
INCARNATION	LATIFUNDIUM	MONEYMAKING	PAINSTAKING	PROCREATION	RESTRICTIVE
INCLINATION	LATROCINIUM	MONOPSONIST	PALESTINIAN	PRODIGALISE	RETALIATION
INCOMPOSITE	LAWBREAKING	MONOTHELITE	PANDEMONIUM	PRODIGALITY	RETARDATION
INCONGRUITY	LEGIONNAIRE	MONSTROSITY	PARACHUTIST	PROGRESSION	RETRIBUTION
INCREDULITY	LEGISLATION	MONTESQUIEU	PARTICIPIAL	PROGRESSIVE	RETRIBUTIVE
INDENTATION	LEGISLATIVE	MONTGOLFIER	PARTURITION	PROHIBITION	RETROACTIVE
INDIGESTION	LENGTHENING	MOXIBUSTION	PARVANIMITY	PROHIBITIVE	REVALUATION
INDIGNATION	LIBERTARIAN	MUDSLINGING	PATERNALISM	PROLETARIAN	REVERENTIAL
INEBRIATION	LILLIPUTIAN	MULTIRACIAL	PATHOLOGIST	PROLETARIAT	REVISIONISM
INEFFECTIVE	LINGUISTICS	MUNITIONIZE	PATRONISING	PROLOCUTION	ROMANTICISM
INESSENTIAL	LIQUIDATION	MURMURATION	PATRONIZING	PROMISCUITY	ROMANTICIZE
INEXPENSIVE	LOCORESTIVE	MYCOPHAGIST	PECULIARITY	PROPAGATION	ROSICRUCIAN
INFANGTHIEF	LONGANIMITY	MYTHOLOGIZE	PELARGONIUM	PROPINQUITY	RUMFRUCTION
INFANTICIDE	LONGINQUITY	NATIONALISM	PENETRATING	PROPOSITION	RUMGUMPTION
INFATUATION	LONGLASTING	NATIONALIST	PENETRATION	PROROGATION	SABBATARIAN
INFERIORITY	LONGRUNNING	NATIONALITY	PENITENTIAL	PROSECUTION	SACRIFICIAL
INFERTILITY	LOOSESTRIFE	NATIONALIZE	PERCOLATION	PROSELYTISM	SAGITTARIUS
INFESTATION	LOUISIANIAN	NECESSARILY	PERDUELLION	PROSELYTIZE	SALVADORIAN
INFLUENTIAL	LUBRICATION	NEEDLEPOINT	PERESTROIKA	PROSPECTIVE	SAXOPHONIST
INFORMALITY	LUXULYANITE	NEEDLESTICK	PERFORATION	PROSTHETICS	SCAFFOLDING
INFORMATICS	MACHINATION	NEGOTIATING	PERICARDIUM	PROSTRATION	SCATTERLING
INFORMATION	MAGISTERIAL	NEGOTIATION	PERIGORDIAN	PROTAGONIST	SCHRECKLICH
INFORMATIVE	MAGLEMOSIAN	NEIGHBORING	PERISTALITH	PROTRACTING	SCIREFACIAS
INFURIATING	MAGNANIMITY	NEUROLOGIST	PERMUTATION	PROTRACTION	SCOPOLAMINE
INOCULATION	MALAPROPISM	NEVERENDING	PERSECUTION	PROVOCATION	SCRIPTORIUM
INOFFENSIVE	MALEDICTION	NEWSCASTING	PERSEVERING	PROVOCATIVE	SECONDARILY
INOPERATIVE	MALEFACTION	NIACINAMIDE	PERSONALIST	PUBLICATION	SECRETARIAL
INQUISITION	MALFUNCTION	NIGHTMARISH	PERSONALITY	PUNCTUALITY	SECRETARIAT
INQUISITIVE	MALPRACTICE	NIKETHAMIDE	PERSONALIZE	PUNCTUATION	SEGREGATION
INSCRIPTION	MANCIPATION	NIPFARTHING	PERSONIFIED	PYRARGYRITE	SELECTIVITY
INSECTICIDE	MANEUVERING	NONDESCRIPT	PERSPECTIVE	QUADRENNIAL	SELFSERVICE
INSENSITIVE	MANUMISSION	NOTOTHERIUM	PERSPICUITY	QUADRENNIUM	SENSIBILITY
INSINCERITY	MARGINALIST	NOVELETTISH	PERTINACITY	QUALITATIVE	SENSITIVITY
INSINUATING	MARGINALIZE	NUMISMATICS	PHILATELIST	QUARRELLING	SEPIOSTAIRE
INSINUATION	MASCULINITY	NUMISMATIST	PHILLIPSITE	QUESTIONING	SEPTENARIUS
INSPIRATION	MASTICATION	OBJECTIVITY	PHILOLOGIST	RABELAISIAN	SEPTENTRION
INSTABILITY	MATERIALISE	OBSERVATION	PHONETICIAN	RADIOACTIVE	SERENDIPITY
INSTIGATION	MATERIALISM	OBSTRICTION	PHOTOCOPIER	RADIOLOGIST	SESQUIOXIDE
INSTINCTIVE	MATERIALIST	OBSTRUCTION	PHOTOFINISH	RAPSCALLION	SEXTODECIMO
INSTITUTION	MATERIALIZE	OBSTRUCTIVE	PIEDMONTITE	RASTAFARIAN	SHEATHKNIFE
INSTRUCTION	MATHEMATICS	OPPORTUNISM	PIERREPOINT	RATIONALITY	SHOPLIFTING

SHORTCOMING	TACITURNITY	VACILLATING	SUPERMARKET	INCUNABULUM	UNCONCEALED
SHOWJUMPING	TANGIBILITY	VACILLATION	SUPERTANKER	INVINCIBLES	UNFULFILLED
SHUNAMITISM	TANTALIZING	VALEDICTION	SVARABHAKTI	ITHYPHALLIC	UNIVERSALLY
SIGHTSEEING	TAUROBOLIUM	VARANGARIAN	TIGGYWINKLE	ITHYPHALLUS	UNNATURALLY
SILLIMANITE	TAXIDERMIST	VARIABILITY	UNDERCOOKED	LACONICALLY	UNSCHEDULED
SILVERPOINT	TELEPHONIST	VARIEGATION	VOORTREKKER	MARSHMALLOW	UNTRAMELLED
SILVERSMITH	TELEWORKING	VARIOLATION	WASTEBASKET	MASTERFULLY	VIOLINCELLO
SINGLESTICK	TEMPORARILY	VENDEMIAIRE	WINDBREAKER	MEDICINALLY	VIOLONCELLO
SINGULARITY	TERMINATION	VENTILATION	ADVERBIALLY	MEGALOPOLIS	WHITECOLLAR
SLUMGULLION	TERREMOTIVE	VERMICULITE	ASPERGILLUM	MELANCHOLIA	WONDERFULLY
SMITHSONIAN	TERRESTRIAL	VERSATILITY	ASPERGILLUS	MELANCHOLIC	AERODYNAMIC
SMITHSONITE	TERRITORIAL	VESUVIANITE	BACCHANALIA	MEMORABILIA	AIRCRAFTMAN
SMOULDERING	TESTIMONIAL	VINBLASTINE	BARBASTELLE	MICROVILLUS	ASSEMBLYMAN
SNORKELLING	THALIDOMIDE	VINCRISTINE	BASKERVILLE	NUMERICALLY	BARNSTORMER
SOCIABILITY	THEOBROMINE	VINDICATION	BEAUTIFULLY	ORGANICALLY	BARTHOLOMEW
SOCIOLOGIST	THREATENING	VIVISECTION	BLACKFELLOW	PACIFICALLY	BORBORYGMUS
SOLILOQUIZE	THUNDERBIRD	VOLUNTARILY	BLACKMAILER	PASSACAGLIA	BREADCRUMBS
SOROPTIMIST	TIDDLEYWINK	VOLUNTARISM	BRAZZAVILLE	PASTEURELLA	BUSINESSMAN
SPACESAVING	TIMBROPHILY	VOTERIGGING	CATERPILLAR	PASTOURELLE	CALLISTEMON
SPECULATION	TIMEKEEPING	WAINSCOTING	CAUSTICALLY	PENTHESILEA	CAMERAWOMAN
SPECULATIVE	TIMESHARING	WAREHOUSING	CHANTARELLE	PENTONVILLE	CATACLYSMIC
SPENDTHRIFT	TIRONENSIAN	WATERSKIING	CHANTERELLE	PERENNIALLY	CONGRESSMAN
SPERMOPHILE	TITILLATION	WELLMEANING	CHRONICALLY	PERPETUALLY	CONTRETEMPS
SPESSARTITE	TOBACCONIST	WESTPHALIAN	CITRONELLAL	PETRODOLLAR	DRAUGHTSMAN
SPLUTTERING	TOBOGGANING	WHITEBOYISM	CLAPPERCLAW	POLITICALLY	ENDOTHERMIC
SPONTANEITY	TORRIDONIAN	WHITSUNTIDE	COACHFELLOW	POTENTIALLY	FRENCHWOMAN
STAGFLATION	TOSTICATION	WIDERANGING	COMESTIBLES	PRACTICALLY	FRENCHWOMEN
STANDARDIZE	TOURBILLION	WINDSURFING	COMPTROLLER	PRINCIPALLY	GASTRONOMIC
STANDOFFISH	TOXOPHILITE	WISHTONWISH	CONSUMABLES	PROSAICALLY	GENTLEWOMAN
STIMULATION	TRANQUILITY	WITHERSHINS	CONTINUALLY	PSYCHEDELIC	HEXADECIMAL
STIPULATION	TRANSACTION	WITHHOLDING	CONVOLVULUS	PUNCHINELLO	HOMOTHERMAL
STOCKTAKING	TRANSFUSION	WOODCARVING	COUNTERGLOW	RATATOUILLE	HOMOTHERMIC
STRADUARIUS	TRANSLATION	WORKMANLIKE	CRATERELLUS	RECTANGULAR	HYPOTHERMIA
STYLIZATION	TREPIDATION	WORKSTATION	CREPUSCULAR	REGRETFULLY	INFANTRYMAN
STYLOPODIUM	TRESPASSING	XENODOCHIUM	CRESTFALLEN	RESENTFULLY	INTRADERMAL
STYMPHALIAN	TRIBULATION	ZOROASTRIAN	CYCLOSTYLED	RETINACULUM	LARYNGISMUS
SUBDIVISION	TRIMESTRIAL	THINGAMAJIG	DARDANELLES	RIGHTANGLED	LOGARITHMIC
SUBJUGATION	TRINIDADIAN	THINGUMAJIG	DECEITFULLY	ROCKEFELLER	MERCHANTMAN
SUBJUNCTIVE	TRINITARIAN	BLOODSUCKER	DEGRINGOLER	SAINTPAULIA	MONOCHROMAT
SUBLIMATION	TRITAGONIST	BUSHWHACKER	DISGRUNTLED	SATIRICALLY	MONOGRAMMED
SUBPANATION	TYPESETTING	DEERSTALKER	DISHEVELLED	SCEPTICALLY	NEEDLEWOMAN
SUBSTANTIAL	TYRONENSIAN	DREADLOCKED	DRACUNCULUS	SCEUOPHYLAX	NOSTRADAMUS
SUBSTANTIVE	ULTRAMARINE	EARTHSHAKER	DRASTICALLY	SELAGINELLA	OVERWHELMED
SUBTRACTION	UNASSERTIVE	FERNITICKLE	EFFECTUALLY	SEMITRAILER	PARACETAMOL
SUFFOCATING	UNBEFITTING	FIELDWORKER	EMMENTHALER	SKEPTICALLY	POLICEWOMAN
SUFFOCATION	UNCHRISTIAN	FIRECRACKER	EMOTIONALLY	SKILLIGALEE	RUDESHEIMER
SUITABILITY	UNDEMANDING	FREETHINKER	EQUIVOCALLY	SKILLIGOLEE	SEPTICAEMIA
SUPERFICIAL	UNDERTAKING	GODFORSAKEN	ERRATICALLY	SORROWFULLY	SPOKESWOMAN
SUPERFICIES	UNDESERVING	HALBSTARKER	ESSENTIALLY	SPECTACULAR	SPORTSWOMAN
SUPERFLUITY	UNDIGNIFIED	HEARTBROKEN	FANATICALLY	SPIRITUALLY	SWORDSWOMAN
SUPERIORITY	UNESSENTIAL	HONEYSUCKLE	FINANCIALLY	STEAMROLLER	TRANSDERMAL
SUPERLATIVE	UNFLINCHING	HYPERMARKET	FOTHERGILLA	STORYTELLER	TRANSFORMED
SUPERSCRIBE	UNIFICATION	ILLYWHACKER	FRANTICALLY	STROPHILLUS	TRANSFORMER
SUPERSCRIPT	UNJUSTIFIED	INDEXLINKED	FRATERNALLY	TABERNACLES	TRENCHERMAN
SUPERVISION	UNOBTRUSIVE	INTERLEUKIN	FRIGHTFULLY	TAGLIATELLE	TRIPTOLEMUS
SUPPOSITION	UNQUALIFIED	KALASHNIKOV	GENERICALLY	TATTERSALLS	UNCONFIRMED
SUPPRESSION	UNREASONING	KWASHIORKOR	GENETICALLY	TECHNICALLY	VOLKSKAMMER
SUPPURATION	UNRELENTING	LOUDSPEAKER	GIBBERELLIN	TEETOTALLER	WASHERWOMAN
SURROUNDING	UNREMITTING	METALWORKER	GLOSSOLALIA	TEGUCICALPA	WITENAGEMOT
SUSURRATION	UNSATISFIED	PINNYWINKLE	GRAPHICALLY	TESSARAGLOT	XEROTHERMIC
SYNCHRONISE	UNSHRINKING	PRZEWALSKIS	HAEMOPHILIA	THERMOPYLAE	ABSORPTANCE
SYNCHRONISM	UNSPECIFIED	RETROROCKET	HOSPITALLER	THUNDERCLAP	ACCOUNTANCY
SYNCHRONIZE	UNUNQUADIUM	SHIPWRECKED	IDENTICALLY	TORTICOLLIS	ACCRESCENCE
SYNCOPATION	UNWELCOMING	SLEEPWALKER	IDIOTICALLY	TORTICULLUS	ADOLESCENCE
SYNDICALISM	UTILITARIAN	SPANGCOCKLE	IDYLLICALLY	TRICHINELLA	AGUARDIENTE
SYNDICATION	UTILIZATION	SPITSTICKER	ILLOGICALLY	TRINCOMALEE	AMBIVALENCE
SYSTEMATIZE	VACCINATION	STOCKBROKER	IMPARTIALLY	ULTRAVIOLET	ANTECEDENCE

ANTHOCYANIN	EXECUTIONER	ONEIROMANCY	UNEXPLAINED	DIPROTODONT	MAQUILADORA
ANTIRRHINUM	EXORBITANCE	OPALESCENCE	UNSWEETENED	DOLABRIFORM	MELLIFLUOUS
ANTISTHENES	EXTORTIONER	OPERATIONAL	VARSOVIENNE	DOUBLECROSS	MENDELSSOHN
ASTRINGENCY	FLAMBOYANCE	OUTDISTANCE	VESPERTINAL	EASTERNMOST	MERITORIOUS
BANDEIRANTE	FLAMBOYANTE	OUTPOURINGS	WELLDEFINED	EFFICACIOUS	METEOROLOGY
BATTLEMENTS	FORBEARANCE	OVERBALANCE	WHISKERANDO	ENCEPHALOMA	METHODOLOGY
BENEVOLENCE	FORBIDDANCE	OVERLEARNED	ACINACIFORM	ENCHONDROMA	MICROSECOND
BOTANOMANCY	FRAUDULENCE	PARABOLANUS	ACRIMONIOUS	EPIDIASCOPE	MISANTHROPE
BREADWINNER	FREEMASONRY	PARISHIONER	ADVENTUROUS	ESCHATOLOGY	MISANTHROPY
BROBDINGNAG	FRONTRUNNER	PERCIPIENCE	AFTERSCHOOL	ESTRAMAZONE	MISCHIEVOUS
CANDESCENCE	FURNISHINGS	PERFORMANCE	AGROSTOLOGY	EUCALYPTOLE	MONOCHINOUS
CAPACITANCE	FURTHERANCE	PERSISTENCE	ALBUGINEOUS	EXPEDITIOUS	MOUNTAINOUS
CINQUECENTO	GENTLEMANLY	PHILIPPINES	AMMOPHILOUS	EXPLANATORY	NECESSITOUS
COALESCENCE	GUADALCANAL	PITCHBLENDE	AMPHIBOLOGY	EXPLORATORY	OBSERVATORY
COEXISTENCE	HABILIMENTS	PLANTAGENET	ANDROGENOUS	EXTROGENOUS	ODONTOPHORE
COGNOSCENTE	HALLEFLINTA	PLEURODYNIA	ANDROGYNOUS	FARINACEOUS	OMMATOPHORE
COGNOSCENTI	HAREBRAINED	POCOCURANTE	ANFRACTUOUS	FARRAGINOUS	OPPROBRIOUS
COINCIDENCE	HINDERLANDS	POLYTECHNIC	ANSWERPHONE	FARTHERMOST	ORNITHOLOGY
COLLECTANEA	HONEYMOONER	PREDESTINED	ANTHONOMOUS	FILAMENTOUS	OVARIECTOMY
COMEUPPANCE	HOOTANANNIE	PREEMINENCE	ANTICYCLONE	FLAVOURSOME	OVERZEALOUS
COMMONSENSE	HOOTENANNIE	PREPOLLENCE	APLANOSPORE	FLIRTATIOUS	PAMPELMOOSE
COMPLACENCY	ICHTHYORNIS	PRIZEWINNER	ARCHAEOLOGY	FLUOROSCOPE	PARAMASTOID
COMPLIMENTS	ILLUMINANCE	PROBATIONER	ARRHENOTOKY	FORTUNELOUD	PARATYPHOID
CONCORDANCE	IMPASSIONED	PROCEEDINGS	ARTHROSPORE	FOUNDATIONS	PEDETENTOUS
CONCURRENCE	IMPEDIMENTA	PROFICIENCY	ATHERMANOUS	FRUGIVOROUS	PERFUNCTORY
CONDITIONAL	INCOHERENCE	PROMOTIONAL	ATRABILIOUS	FURTHERMORE	PERISSOLOGY
CONDITIONER	INCONSTANCY	PROVISIONAL	AVOIRDUPOIS	FURTHERMOST	PERSPICUOUS
CONDUCTANCE	INFREQUENCY	PROVISIONER	BATTLEFRONT	FURTHERSOME	PHRASEOLOGY
CONSEQUENCE	INGREDIENTS	RALLENTANDO	BLADDERWORT	GASTRECTOMY	PHYSIOGNOMY
CONSERVANCY	INHABITANTS	REASSURANCE	BLASPHEMOUS	GERONTOLOGY	PICKYOUROWN
CONSILIENCE	INHERITANCE	RECESSIONAL	BLUNDERBORE	GLIMMERGOWK	PLAGIOSTOMI
CONSISTENCE	INSOUCIANCE	REMEMBRANCE	BRISTLECONE	GORDONSTOUN	POLYHYDROXY
CONSISTENCY	INSTRUMENTS	RENAISSANCE	BROTHERHOOD	GYNAECOLOGY	POMPELMOOSE
CONSTRAINED	INTENTIONAL	RESEMBLANCE	BUMBERSHOOT	HAEMORRHOID	POSSESSIONS
CONSULTANCY	INTERCHANGE	RHABDOMANCY	CACOPHONOUS	HAMMERCLOTH	PRECAUTIONS
CONTINGENCE	INTERREGNUM	RIFACIMENTO	CAMPANOLOGY	HARPSICHORD	PRECIPITOUS
CONTINGENCY	INTOLERANCE	RINFORZANDO	CAPRICCIOSO	HECKELPHONE	PREMONITORY
CONTINUANCE	IPECACUANHA	SALTIMBANCO	CARNAPTIOUS	HEPATOSCOPY	PREPARATORY
CONTRIVANCE	IRIDESCENCE	SALVOGUNNER	CARNIVOROUS	HERBIVOROUS	PRESTIGIOUS
CONTUBERNAL	IRRELEVANCE	SAPROLEGNIA	CATADROMOUS	HERPETOLOGY	PRETENSIONS
CONVENIENCE	IRREVERENCE	SCRIMSHANDY	CEREMONIOUS	HERRINGBONE	PRETENTIOUS
CONVERGENCE	JACQUEMINOT	SELFDEFENCE	CHARACINOID	HOMOGENEOUS	PROFITEROLE
COUNTENANCE	KLEPTOMANIA	SEMPITERNAL	CHEESECLOTH	HOMOPHONOUS	PROGNATHOUS
CRACOVIENNE	MAINTENANCE	SEMPITERNUM	CHEIROGNOMY	HUNDREDFOLD	PROMISCUOUS
CRITHOMANCY	MALEVOLENCE	SENSATIONAL	CHOCKABLOCK	IGNOMINIOUS	PROTEROZOIC
DELINQUENCY	MALFEASANCE	SEVENTEENTH	CHORDOPHONE	ILLUSTRIOUS	PUNCTILIOUS
DELIVERANCE	MASKALLONGE	SHORTCHANGE	CIRCULATORY	IMPECUNIOUS	QUARRELSOME
DEMONOMANIA	MEANDERINGS	SKIDBLADNIR	CLIMATOLOGY	INCONGRUOUS	RAMGUNSHOCH
DEMOSTHENES	MEDIASTINUM	SNICKERSNEE	CLINOCHLORE	INCREDULOUS	REFLEXOLOGY
DEMOSTHENIC	MEGALOMANIA	SOVEREIGNTY	COBBLESTONE	INDUSTRIOUS	REFORMATORY
DESCENDANTS	MEGALOMANIC	SRANANTONGO	COMPENDIOUS	INJUDICIOUS	REPETITIOUS
DESPONDENCY	MISALLIANCE	STREAMLINED	CONDOTTIORE	INSECTIVORE	RESPIRATORY
DIMENSIONAL	MISDEMEANOR	STRUTHIONES	CONSPICUOUS	INTRAVENOUS	RESPONSIONS
DIRECTIONAL	MISFEASANCE	SUBMERGENCE	CONTENTIOUS	IRRELIGIOUS	RETALIATORY
DISCIPLINED	MONTMORENCY	SUBSISTENCE	CONVULSIONS	ISOMORPHOUS	RETINOSCOPY
DISCONTINUE	MUNIFICENCE	SUFFICIENCY	CORNERSTONE	KINCHINMORT	RETINOSPORA
DISCREPANCY	MUSKELLUNGE	TECTIBRANCH	COUNTERFOIL	LATERITIOUS	REVELATIONS
DISINCLINED	NETHERLANDS	TIMBROMANIA	COUNTERFORT	LATTICEWORK	REVOLUTIONS
DISTURBANCE	NETHERLINGS	TOXICOGENIC	CRIMINOLOGY	LEATHERWOOD	RINTHEREOUT
EDUCATIONAL	NIERSTEINER	TRADITIONAL	CURNAPTIOUS	LENTIGINOSE	ROTTENSTONE
EMPYROMANCY	NONCHALANCE	TRANSURANIC	CYMOPHANOUS	LIVINGSTONE	RUMBUSTIOUS
ENCUMBRANCE	NONFEASANCE	TWELVEMONTH	DECLAMATORY	LYCANTHROPE	SANDERSWOOD
ENLIGHTENED	NUTRITIONAL	UNCERTAINTY	DECORATIONS	LYCANTHROPY	SANGUINEOUS
ENTERTAINER	NYMPHOMANIA	UNCONCERNED	DELETERIOUS	LYCHNOSCOPE	SAPONACEOUS
EQUIVALENCE	OMNIPOTENCE	UNDERMANNED	DERMATOLOGY	MAGNANIMOUS	SCALPRIFORM
EXCEPTIONAL	OMNISCIENCE	UNDERSIGNED	DEUTERONOMY	MAISTERDOME	SCARABAEOID
EXCRESCENCE	ONEIRODYNIA	UNEMOTIONAL	DICEPHALOUS	MALAKATOONE	SCATTERGOOD

SCHISTOSOMA	CALLIGRAPHY	ATMOSPHERIC	PROGENITRIX	CYTOGENESIS	RAPTUROUSLY
SCHISTOSOME	CARTOGRAPHY	BADTEMPERED	PSEUDOMORPH	DANGEROUSLY	REAPPRAISAL
SCIENTOLOGY	CATASTROPHE	BALISTRARIA	PSYCHIATRIC	DELICIOUSLY	RELIGIOUSLY
SCOLECIFORM	CHIROGRAPHY	BARYCENTRIC	RIDDLEMEREE	DIAPHORESIS	RIGHTEOUSLY
SCRUMPTIOUS	CHOROGRAPHY	BEHAVIOURAL	ROBESPIERRE	DIARTHROSIS	SAGACIOUSLY
SCUPPERNONG	DITTOGRAPHY	BELEAGUERED	SACHERTORTE	DINNYHAUSER	SALACIOUSLY
SCYPHISTOMA	DUSTWRAPPER	BLOODSPORTS	SADDLEHORSE	DINNYHAYSER	SALESPERSON
SENTENTIOUS	EOANTHROPUS	BOYSENBERRY	SANSEVIERIA	DISIMPRISON	SELFIMPOSED
SEVERALFOLD	ETHNOGRAPHY	CACOGASTRIC	SCHWARMEREI	DUNIEWASSAL	SHAMELESSLY
SHITTIMWOOD	GRASSHOPPER	CALCEOLARIA	SCLERODERMA	DYAESTHESIA	SOUNDLESSLY
SHOWERPROOF	HAGIOGRAPHA	CAMARADERIE	SELFCONTROL	EMBARRASSED	STOCKHAUSEN
SHUTTLECOCK	HAGIOGRAPHY	CENTUMVIRUS	SENNACHERIB	EMPHYTEUSIS	STRENUOUSLY
SMORGASBORD	HANDICAPPED	CHINOISERIE	SILVERBERRY	ENARTHROSIS	SUMPTUOUSLY
SPATTERDOCK	HANDICAPPER	CHOLESTEROL	SINISTRORSE	EPANALEPSIS	SYMPATHISER
SPONTANEOUS	HEMERALOPIA	CLADOSPORUM	STEGANOGRAM	EREMACAUSIS	TASTELESSLY
STEGANOPODE	HIPPOCAMPUS	CLANJAMFRAY	STILBESTROL	ERRONEOUSLY	TCHAIKOVSKY
STENOCHROME	HOUSEKEEPER	CLIMACTERIC	SUPERCHARGE	FACETIOUSLY	TELEKINESIS
STEREOSCOPE	HYPERTROPHY	COMPRIMARIO	SUPERCHERIE	FAULTLESSLY	TENACIOUSLY
STETHOSCOPE	ICONOGRAPHY	CONJECTURAL	SYMPOSIARCH	FEROCIOUSLY	THANATOPSIS
STRAMINEOUS	LITHOGRAPHY	CONTRAYERVA	TELOCENTRIC	FRIVOLOUSLY	THANKLESSLY
STROBOSCOPE	MACROSCOPIC	CONTROVERSY	TETRAHEDRON	FRUITLESSLY	THEOPNEUSTY
STRONGYLOID	MICROSCOPIC	CONVALLARIA	THENCEFORTH	GAMOGENESIS	TRANSVERSAL
SUBITANEOUS	MINESWEEPER	COPROSTEROL	TRACASSERIE	GARRULOUSLY	TRICHINOSED
SUPERFLUOUS	MISSISSIPPI	DACTYLOGRAM	TRANSFERRED	HAIRDRESSER	TSCHERNOSEM
SUPERIMPOSE	MOSSTROOPER	DIATESSARON	TRANSFERRIN	HARDPRESSED	UNANIMOUSLY
SUPERVISORY	ORTHOGRAPHY	DIATESSERON	TURBELLARIA	HEARTLESSLY	UNCIVILISED
SUPPOSITORY	PAEDOTROPHY	DIMERCAPROL	UNCLUTTERED	HEMIANOPSIA	UNDISCLOSED
SYNCHRONOUS	PALEOGRAPHY	DISCOLOURED	UNCONQUERED	HILARIOUSLY	UNDISGUISED
TAUTOCHRONE	PARATROOPER	ENFOULDERED	UNDERCHARGE	HYPOCORISMA	UNEXPRESSED
TEMPESTUOUS	PEACEKEEPER	ENGHALSKRUG	UNSHELTERED	ICONOSTASIS	UNIMPRESSED
TENDENTIOUS	PHOTOGRAPHY	ENNEAHEDRON	UPHOLSTERER	IMPERIOUSLY	UNREHEARSED
TENTERHOOKS	PORNOGRAPHY	EQUILATERAL	UTRICULARIA	IMPETUOUSLY	UNSURPASSED
TERMINOLOGY	PYELOGRAPHY	ERIODENDRON	VALLISNERIA	INGENIOUSLY	VASOPRESSIN
TERPSICHORE	RADIOGRAPHY	ESPIEGLERIE	WATERCOURSE	INSIDIOUSLY	VICARIOUSLY
THAUMATROPE	SCOREKEEPER	FARKLEBERRY	WHEELBARROW	INTERGLOSSA	VICHYSOISSE
THEATERGOER	STAIRCARPET	GOODNATURED	WIENERWURST	JUDICIOUSLY	VIVACIOUSLY
THEATREGOER	STENOGRAPHY	GRALLATORES	WILBERFORCE	LABORIOUSLY	VORACIOUSLY
THISTLEDOWN	STEREOTYPED	GRAVIMETRIC	WINDLESTRAW	LUXURIOUSLY	WELLADVISED
THUNDERBOLT	STOREKEEPER	HIGHPOWERED	WINTERBERRY	MALICIOUSLY	WELLDRESSED
TRACHEOTOMY	STRANDLOPER	HUCKLEBERRY	ABIOGENESIS	MELODIOUSLY	XEROTRIPSIS
TREACHEROUS	SUBMULTIPLE	HURTLEBERRY	ANADIPLOSIS	MERCILESSLY	ABBREVIATED
TREACHETOUR	TACHYGRAPHY	HYOPLASTRON	ANAESTHESIA	METAGENESIS	ABIOGENETIC
TRICERATOPS	TEENYBOPPER	ILLMANNERED	ANAGNORISIS	MUNCHHAUSEN	ACATALECTIC
TRIPHIBIOUS	THOROUGHPIN	INTERCOURSE	ANAPLEROSIS	MYXOMATOSIS	ACCELERATOR
TROUBLESOME	THYROTROPIN	INTERSPERSE	ANASTOMOSIS	NARRAGANSET	ACCUMULATOR
TRYPANOSOMA	TIGHTLIPPED	IRREGULARLY	ANONYMOUSLY	NECROBIOSIS	ADJUDICATOR
TRYPANOSOME	TOWNSPEOPLE	ISOELECTRIC	ANTHRACOSIS	NEUTRALISED	ADULLAMITES
UNAMBIGUOUS	TREECREEPER	ISTIOPHORUS	ANTIPHRASIS	NOISELESSLY	ADULTERATED
UNCONSCIOUS	TROUBLESPOT	KATABOTHRON	ANTONOMASIA	NOTORIOUSLY	AFGHANISTAN
UNRIGHTEOUS	UNDEVELOPED	KATAVOTHRON	APONEUROSIS	OFFICIOUSLY	AGONOTHETES
UNWHOLESOME	UNENVELOPED	KETAVOTHRON	APOSIOPESIS	OSTEOPLASTY	AIGUILLETTE
VALEDICTORY	WHITECHAPEL	KILOCALORIE	ARTHRODESIS	OVEREXPOSED	AMOBARBITAL
VALLAMBROSA	DISCOTHEQUE	KOTABOTHRON	ASSIDUOUSLY	PARABLEPSIS	AMYLOPECTIN
VENTURESOME	PICTURESQUE	LEPIDOSIREN	ATROCIOUSLY	PARALEIPSIS	ANACREONTIC
VERTIGINOUS	PLATERESQUE	LINDISFARNE	AUDACIOUSLY	PARASITOSIS	ANAESTHETIC
VOLCANOLOGY	PYTHONESQUE	MARCONIGRAM	BANGLADESHI	PARENTHESIS	ANAPLEROTIC
VULCANOLOGY	TÉLÉFÉRIQUE	MARIONBERRY	BIELORUSSIA	PARONOMASIA	ANGELOLATRY
WATERCOLOUR	ACROCENTRIC	MELANOCHROI	BOURGEOISIE	PERIPHRASIS	ANTIPYRETIC
WATEREDDOWN	ALBUMINURIA	METACENTRIC	BRUCELLOSIS	PERISTALSIS	APOCALYPTIC
WEATHERCOCK	ALIFANFARON	MIDDLEMARCH	CATACHRESIS	PHTHIRIASIS	ARTICULATED
WELLINGTONS	ALLELOMORPH	MISCONSTRUE	CEASELESSLY	PLAGIARISED	ARTIODACTYL
WESTERNMOST	ANTHESTERIA	MISERICORDE	CHAIRPERSON	POINTLESSLY	ASSIMILATED
WHITETHROAT	ANTINEUTRON	MULTISTOREY	CHRISTMASSY	PONDEROUSLY	AUXANOMETER
WORLDFAMOUS	APATOSAURUS	NEIGHBOURLY	CIRCUMCISER	PREDECESSOR	AZOTOBACTER
XEROPHILOUS	APOLLINARIS	PARANEPHROS	CONSCIOUSLY	PRESTRESSED	BLAMEWORTHY
YELLOWSTONE	ARCHENTERON	PHILANDERER	COURTEOUSLY	PSITTACOSIS	BLOCKBUSTER
ANTISTROPHE	ARRIVEDERCI	PREHISTORIC	CREDULOUSLY	QUERULOUSLY	BODHISATTVA

BRILLIANTLY	EXPECTANTLY	MENTHOLATED	TESSELLATED	GLASTONBURY	BREATHALYSE
BROADCASTER	EXTROVERTED	MISBEGOTTEN	THERAPEUTAE	HARDICANUTE	CHARGEPAYER
BULLFIGHTER	FILLIBUSTER	MODERNISTIC	THERAPEUTIC	HYDROMEDUSA	CHLOROPHYLL
BURGOMASTER	FIRELIGHTER	MOONLIGHTER	THERMOMETER	INEFFECTUAL	COLLENCHYMA
CABBALISTIC	FLANNELETTE	NATUROPATHY	THROGMORTON	INGRATITUDE	DODECASTYLE
CAMPHORATED	FLUOROMETER	NEARSIGHTED	TICKTACKTOE	INOPPORTUNE	ELECTROLYTE
CAPACITATOR	FORESHORTEN	NOMENCLATOR	TIGHTFISTED	INVESTITURE	ERYTHROCYTE
CAPERNOITED	FORFOUGHTEN	NORTHEASTER	TOASTMASTER	KOMMERSBUCH	GAMETOPHYTE
CAPERNOITIE	FORTNIGHTLY	NORTHWESTER	TONSILLITIS	LEGISLATURE	JAMAHIRIYAH
CARBURETTOR	FRANKFURTER	OBLITERATED	TOTALIZATOR	MACERANDUBA	LAMMERGEYER
CASTELLATED	FROSTBITTEN	OCHLOCRATIC	TRAFFICATOR	MANUFACTURE	LAMPROPHYRE
CATACAUSTIC	FUNDAMENTAL	OPINIONATED	TRANSMITTED	MARLBOROUGH	SARCENCHYME
CATALLACTIC	GALLIGANTUS	ORNITHOPTER	TRANSMITTER	MECKLENBURG	THALLOPHYTE
CENTRIPETAL	GIGGLEWATER	ORTHOCENTRE	TRANSPORTED	MICROTUBULE	DEMORALIZED
CENTURIATOR	GODDAUGHTER	PANTALETTES	TRANSPORTER	MONOLINGUAL	GABERLUNZIE
CESAREWITCH	GRANDMASTER	PARACROSTIC	TRINOBANTES	MOZAMBIQUAN	GENERALIZED
CHARISMATIC	GREENBOTTLE	PATERNOSTER	TRUCULENTLY	PAMPELMOUSE	HOMOGENIZED
CHOIRMASTER	HALFHEARTED	PENTECONTER	TRUSTWORTHY	PICKELHAUBE	MACADAMIZED
CHONDROSTEI	HANDCRAFTED	PENTECOSTAL	TYPEWRITTEN	POLLENBRUSH	MEDIUMSIZED
CHRONOMETER	HANDWRITTEN	PERIODONTIC	UNAUTHENTIC	POMPELMOUSE	MIDDLESIZED
COLORIMETER	HIGHLIGHTER	PERIPATETIC	UNCASTRATED	PORTERHOUSE	MOISTURIZER
COMMENTATOR	HIPPOCRATES	PERITONITIS	UNCOMMITTED	PORTRAITURE	PRESSURIZED
COMPETENTLY	HIPPOCRATIC	PERMANENTLY	UNCONNECTED	PROMPTITUDE	SCANDALIZED
COMPLICATED	HISTORIATED	PERPETRATOR	UNCONTESTED	PULCHRITUDE	SPECIALIZED
CONCILIATOR	HOMOEOPATHY	PERTINENTLY	UNCONVERTED	PURPRESTURE	SPERMATOZOA
CONFIDENTLY	HOUSEMASTER	PESSIMISTIC	UNDERSTATED	RECONSTRUCT	SYMPATHIZER
CONSPIRATOR	HYDROSTATIC	PETITMAITRE	UNDERWRITER	RESTRUCTURE	SYNTHESIZED
CONSTIPATED	ILLUMINATED	PETTICOATED	UNINHABITED	ROTOGRAVURE	SYNTHESIZER
CONSTRICTED	ILLUSTRATOR	PHARYNGITIS	UNINHIBITED	SCARBOROUGH	UNCIVILIZED
CONSTRICTOR	IMPATIENTLY	PHILOCTETES	UNINITIATED	SCUTTLEBUTT	VITAMINIZED
CONSTRUCTOR	IMPLEMENTAL	POLIORCETIC	UNMITIGATED	SERICULTURE	ZWISCHENZUG
CONTINENTAL	IMPORTANTLY	POTAMOGETON	UNMOTIVATED	SHAFTESBURY	**11:10**
CONTRIBUTOR	IMPRUDENTLY	PROMINENTLY	UNPATRIOTIC	SLEUTHHOUND	ABECEDARIAN
COORDINATED	INAUTHENTIC	PTERODACTYL	UNPROTECTED	SPRINGHOUSE	ACADEMICIAN
COORDINATES	INCESSANTLY	QUARRINGTON	UNREALISTIC	STRIKEBOUND	AESCULAPIAN
CRACKHALTER	INCINERATOR	REALPOLITIK	UNSATURATED	SUMMERHOUSE	AFGHANISTAN
CRENELLATED	INCORRECTLY	RECONNOITER	UNSOLICITED	TEMPERATURE	AIRCRAFTMAN
CRITICASTER	INCREMENTAL	RECONNOITRE	UNSUPPORTED	THEREABOUTS	ALBIGENSIAN
DEBILITATED	INDIGNANTLY	RECURRENTLY	UNSUSPECTED	TRANSFIGURE	ALCYONARIAN
DECAPITATED	INDULGENTLY	RELUCTANTLY	UNWARRANTED	UNDERGROUND	ALLEGORICAL
DENOMINATOR	INFILTRATOR	REPRESENTED	VINAIGRETTE	UNDERVALUED	AMOBARBITAL
DETRIMENTAL	INSISTENTLY	SACRAMENTAL	WARMHEARTED	VICISSITUDE	ANISOCERCAL
DIAPHORETIC	INTERCEPTOR	SALINOMETER	WESTMINSTER	WHEREABOUTS	ANTIQUARIAN
DICHROMATIC	INTERCOSTAL	SALPINGITIS	WHISTLESTOP	WORRYTROUGH	APHRODISIAC
DIFFERENTLY	INTERPRETER	SAPROPHYTIC	WHITTINGTON	YELLOWPLUSH	ARCHEGONIAL
DIFFIDENTLY	INTERRUPTER	SCHECKLATON	WINDCHEATER	CLEANSHAVEN	ARGATHELIAN
DILAPIDATED	INTOXICATED	SCOUTMASTER	WITCHDOCTOR	DISAPPROVAL	ARGENTINIAN
DIORTHORTIC	INTOXIMETER	SENTIMENTAL	ZOOPLANKTON	DISBELIEVER	ARTHRAPODAL
DISAFFECTED	INTROVERTED	SHINPLASTER	ACUPUNCTURE	DRINKDRIVER	ASSEMBLYMAN
DISHONESTLY	INVIGILATOR	SKIMMINGTON	AGRICULTURE	LONGSLEEVED	ATHERINIDAE
DISORIENTED	KINDHEARTED	SOLIPSISTIC	AUDIOVISUAL	OUTMANEUVER	AUDIOVISUAL
DISSERTATOR	KITCHENETTE	SOUTHAMPTON	BANNOCKBURN	QUICKSILVER	AUGUSTINIAN
DISTRIBUTED	LAMPLIGHTER	SOUTHWESTER	BERGSCHRUND	SCANDANAVIA	AURIGNACIAN
DISTRIBUTOR	LAUNDERETTE	SPEEDOMETER	BRANDENBURG	SCANDINAVIA	BEHAVIOURAL
DOWNHEARTED	LEATHERETTE	SPHRAGISTIC	CANDIDATURE	SCREWDRIVER	BELORUSSIAN
DYSLOGISTIC	LICKSPITTLE	SPONDYLITIS	CHIAROSCURO	TRANSCEIVER	BESSARABIAN
EFFICIENTLY	LONGAWAITED	STANDPATTER	CONJUNCTURE	WELLBEHAVED	BIOCHEMICAL
EMPIRICUTIC	LONGSIGHTED	STEADFASTLY	CONTRACTUAL	CARRIAGEWAY	BLOODSTREAM
EPITHYMETIC	LUXURIANTLY	STEREOMETER	COTTONMOUTH	CAULIFLOWER	BROBDINGNAG
EUCHARISTIC	MACROBIOTIC	STRINGENTLY	DECONSTRUCT	GILLYFLOWER	BUPRESTIDAE
EUCHROMATIN	MAGISTRATES	SUFFRAGETTE	DECREPITUDE	INTERGROWTH	BUSINESSMAN
EUPHEMISTIC	MALADJUSTED	SUGARCOATED	DISPLEASURE	INTERVIEWEE	CALLIPYGEAN
EVISCERATED	MANGALSUTRA	SYCOPHANTIC	DOUROUCOULI	INTERVIEWER	CAMERAWOMAN
EXAGGERATED	MANIPULATOR	SYMPATHETIC	ELECTROCUTE	UNDERGROWTH	CAMEROONIAN
EXASPERATED	MANTELLETTA	SYMPTOMATIC	ENTABLATURE	ANAPHYLAXIS	CAMPESTRIAN
EXHILARATED	MARIONETTES	TELEPRINTER	EXPENDITURE	PROPHYLAXIS	CAROLINGIAN
EXOSKELETON	MASOCHISTIC	TENSIOMETER	FORECLOSURE	THIGMOTAXIS	CARRIAGEWAY

CATEGORICAL	HYDROPHIDAE	PROLETARIAN	TRINITARIAN	CONVENIENCE	NUMISMATICS
CATERPILLAR	HYPERBOREAN	PROLETARIAT	TYRONENSIAN	CONVERGENCE	OMNIPOTENCE
CENTENARIAN	IDEOLOGICAL	PROMOTIONAL	UNCHRISTIAN	COUNTENANCE	OMNISCIENCE
CENTRIFUGAL	IMPLEMENTAL	PROPHETICAL	UNEMOTIONAL	CRACKERJACK	ONEIROMANCY
CENTRIPETAL	IMPRACTICAL	PROVISIONAL	UNEQUIVOCAL	CRITHOMANCY	OPALESCENCE
CHILLINGHAM	INCORPOREAL	PURITANICAL	UNESSENTIAL	CYBERNETICS	OUTDISTANCE
CITRONELLAL	INCREMENTAL	QUADRENNIAL	UNPRACTICAL	DECONSTRUCT	OVERBALANCE
CLANJAMFRAY	INEFFECTUAL	RABELAISIAN	UTILITARIAN	DELINQUENCY	PAEDIATRICS
CLAPPERCLAW	INESSENTIAL	RASTAFARIAN	VARANGARIAN	DELIVERANCE	PERCIPIENCE
CONDITIONAL	INFANTRYMAN	REAPPRAISAL	VESPERTINAL	DESPONDENCY	PERFORMANCE
CONGRESSMAN	INFLUENTIAL	RECESSIONAL	WAPPENSCHAW	DIAGNOSTICS	PERSISTENCE
CONJECTURAL	INTENTIONAL	RECTANGULAR	WASHERWOMAN	DIAMONDBACK	PINACOTHECA
CONTINENTAL	INTERCOSTAL	RECTILINEAR	WESTPHALIAN	DIPLOMATICS	PREEMINENCE
CONTRACTUAL	INTRADERMAL	RESIDENTIAL	WHEREWITHAL	DISCREPANCY	PREPOLLENCE
CONTUBERNAL	ISOLECITHAL	REVERENTIAL	WHITECOLLAR	DISTURBANCE	PROFICIENCY
COPROPHAGAN	JAMAHIRIYAH	RHAPSODICAL	WHITETHROAT	DOUBLECHECK	PROSTHETICS
CREPUSCULAR	JINRICKSHAW	ROSICRUCIAN	WINDLESTRAW	ELECTRONICS	PTOCHOCRACY
CROCODILIAN	KIMERIDGIAN	SABBATARIAN	ZOROASTRIAN	EMPYROMANCY	QUARTERBACK
CROMWELLIAN	LEATHERHEAD	SACRAMENTAL	BREADCRUMBS	ENCUMBRANCE	QUARTERDECK
CYLINDRICAL	LIBERTARIAN	SACRIFICIAL	MACERANDUBA	EQUIVALENCE	RAMGUNSHOCH
DACTYLOGRAM	LILLIPUTIAN	SALVADORIAN	PICKELHAUBE	EURHYTHMICS	REASSURANCE
DEFERENTIAL	LIQUIDAMBAR	SAUSAGEMEAT	SUPERSCRIBE	EXCRESCENCE	RECONSTRUCT
DETRIMENTAL	LOUISIANIAN	SCEUOPHYLAX	ABSORPTANCE	EXORBITANCE	REICHENBACH
DICTATORIAL	MAGISTERIAL	SCIREFACIAS	ACCOUNTANCY	FLAMBOYANCE	REMEMBRANCE
DIMENSIONAL	MAGLEMOSIAN	SCITAMINEAE	ACCRESCENCE	FLANKERBACK	RENAISSANCE
DIPHYCERCAL	MARCONIGRAM	SECRETARIAL	ADOLESCENCE	FORBEARANCE	RESEMBLANCE
DIPSOMANIAC	MATRIARCHAL	SECRETARIAT	AERONAUTICS	FORBIDDANCE	RHABDOMANCY
DIRECTIONAL	MATRIMONIAL	SEMPITERNAL	AMBIVALENCE	FRAUDULENCE	SALTIMBANCO
DISAPPROVAL	MAURETANIAN	SENSATIONAL	ANTECEDENCE	FURTHERANCE	SALTIMBOCCA
DRAUGHTSMAN	MAURITANIAN	SENTIMENTAL	ARISTOCRACY	GIGGLESTICK	SCHRECKLICH
DUNIEWASSAL	MERCHANTMAN	SEXOLOGICAL	ARRIVEDERCI	GIGGLESWICK	SELFDEFENCE
EDUCATIONAL	MIDDENSTEAD	SINGAPOREAN	ASTRINGENCY	HISTRIONICS	SELFRESPECT
EGALITARIAN	MINISTERIAL	SLUMBERWEAR	BENEVOLENCE	HYDROPONICS	SELFSERVICE
EGOTISTICAL	MONARCHICAL	SMITHSONIAN	BOTANOMANCY	ILLUMINANCE	SHUTTLECOCK
ELECTRICIAN	MONOCHROMAT	SPECTACULAR	BUREAUCRACY	INCOHERENCE	SINGLESTICK
ELEUTHERIAN	MONOLINGUAL	SPERMICIDAL	CALLANETICS	INCONSTANCY	SPATTERDOCK
ELIZABETHAN	MONONUCLEAR	SPOKESWOMAN	CANDESCENCE	INFORMATICS	STEEPLEJACK
EPAMINONDAS	MOZAMBIQUAN	SPORTSWOMAN	CANDLESTICK	INFREQUENCY	STICKLEBACK
EQUILATERAL	MULTIRACIAL	SPRINGCLEAN	CAPACITANCE	INHERITANCE	SUBCONTRACT
EQUINOCTIAL	MYCOLOGICAL	STATISTICAL	CENTERPIECE	INSOUCIANCE	SUBMERGENCE
ERYMANTHIAN	NEANDERTHAL	STEGANOGRAM	CENTREPIECE	INTOLERANCE	SUBSISTENCE
EVANGELICAL	NEEDLEWOMAN	STRATEGICAL	CESAREWITCH	IRIDESCENCE	SUFFICIENCY
EXCEPTIONAL	NONSENSICAL	STYMPHALIAN	CHOCKABLOCK	IRRELEVANCE	SYMPOSIARCH
EXPONENTIAL	NUTRITIONAL	SUBSTANTIAL	CIRCUMFLECT	IRREVERENCE	TECTIBRANCH
FITZWILLIAM	OBSTETRICAL	SUBTROPICAL	CIRCUMSPECT	KINNIKINICK	WEATHERCOCK
FRENCHWOMAN	ONTOLOGICAL	SUPERFICIAL	CLAIRSCHACH	KIRKPATRICK	WILBERFORCE
FUNDAMENTAL	OPERATIONAL	SUPERSEDEAS	CLIOMETRICS	KOMMERSBUCH	AMONTILLADO
FUSTILARIAN	PALESTINIAN	SWORDSWOMAN	COALESCENCE	LEATHERBACK	ATHARVAVEDA
GALLIBEGGAR	PANOMPHAEAN	SYMMETRICAL	COEXISTENCE	LEATHERNECK	COUNTRYSIDE
GALLOVIDIAN	PARADOXICAL	TERRESTRIAL	COINCIDENCE	LINGUISTICS	CRESCENTADE
GALLYBEGGAR	PARAMEDICAL	TERRITORIAL	COMEUPPANCE	MAINTENANCE	DECREPITUDE
GENTLEWOMAN	PARTICIPIAL	TESTIMONIAL	COMMONPLACE	MALEVOLENCE	FANFARONADE
GEOMETRICAL	PATRIARCHAL	THEOLOGICAL	COMPLACENCY	MALFEASANCE	GREGARINIDA
GESTATORIAL	PEDAGOGICAL	THEORETICAL	CONCORDANCE	MALPRACTICE	HEMORRHOIDS
GINGERBREAD	PENITENTIAL	THERAPEUTAE	CONCURRENCE	MANTELPIECE	HINDERLANDS
GIRDLESTEAD	PENTECOSTAL	THERMOPYLAE	CONDUCTANCE	MARKETPLACE	INFANTICIDE
GNATHONICAL	PERIGORDIAN	THUNDERCLAP	CONFEDERACY	MASTERPIECE	INGRATITUDE
GRAMMATICAL	PETRODOLLAR	THUNDERHEAD	CONSEQUENCE	MATHEMATICS	INSECTICIDE
GUADALCANAL	PHARISAICAL	TIRONENSIAN	CONSERVANCY	METAPHYSICS	LATERIGRADE
HALFHOLIDAY	PHONETICIAN	TOPLOFTICAL	CONSILIENCE	MIDDLEMARCH	LOGGERHEADS
HEMOPHILIAC	PISCATORIAL	TORRIDONIAN	CONSISTENCE	MISALLIANCE	MISERICORDE
HETEROSCIAN	POLICEWOMAN	TRADITIONAL	CONSISTENCY	MISFEASANCE	NETHERLANDS
HEXADECIMAL	PORTLANDIAN	TRANSDERMAL	CONSULTANCY	MONTMORENCY	NIACINAMIDE
HOLOTHURIAN	PORTMANTEAU	TRANSVERSAL	CONTINGENCE	MUNIFICENCE	NIKETHAMIDE
HOMOIOUSIAN	PREJUDICIAL	TRENCHERMAN	CONTINGENCY	NEEDLESTICK	PHYLLOCLADE
HOMOTHERMAL	PRIMIGENIAL	TRIMESTRIAL	CONTINUANCE	NONCHALANCE	PITCHBLENDE
HUMGRUFFIAN	PROCRUSTEAN	TRINIDADIAN	CONTRIVANCE	NONFEASANCE	PLANTIGRADE

PROMPTITUDE	CLIFFHANGER	EXECUTIONER	HOSTILITIES	NIERSTEINER	SIGHTSCREEN
PULCHRITUDE	COLDBLOODED	EXHILARATED	HOUSEFATHER	NORTHEASTER	SKILLIGALEE
RALLENTANDO	COLLECTANEA	EXPERIENCED	HOUSEHOLDER	NORTHWESTER	SKILLIGOLEE
RINFORZANDO	COLORIMETER	EXTORTIONER	HOUSEKEEPER	OBLITERATED	SLEEPWALKER
RODOMONTADE	COMESTIBLES	EXTROVERTED	HOUSEMASTER	OPINIONATED	SMALLHOLDER
SCRIMSHANDY	COMPLICATED	FAIRWEATHER	HOUSEMOTHER	ORNITHOPTER	SMOKESCREEN
SESQUIOXIDE	COMPTROLLER	FAULTFINDER	HYPERMARKET	OUTMANEUVER	SNICKERSNEE
STEGANOPODE	CONDITIONER	FIDDLEDEDEE	ILLMANNERED	OVERCROWDED	SOCKDALAGER
THALIDOMIDE	CONDOLENCES	FIELDWORKER	ILLUMINATED	OVEREXPOSED	SOCKDOLAGER
VICISSITUDE	CONSTIPATED	FILLIBUSTER	ILLYWHACKER	OVERLEARNED	SOCKDOLIGER
WHISKERANDO	CONSTRAINED	FIRECRACKER	IMPASSIONED	OVERSTUFFED	SOCKDOLOGER
WHITSUNTIDE	CONSTRICTED	FIRELIGHTER	INDEXLINKED	OVERWHELMED	SOUTHWESTER
ABBREVIATED	CONSUMABLES	FLUOROMETER	INDIARUBBER	PAMPHLETEER	SPECIALIZED
ACCESSORIES	COORDINATED	FORAMINIFER	INFANGTHIEF	PANTALETTES	SPEEDOMETER
ACTUALITIES	COORDINATES	FORESHORTEN	INTERPRETER	PARATROOPER	SPELLBINDER
ADULLAMITES	COUNTRIFIED	FORFOUGHTEN	INTERRUPTER	PARISHIONER	SPITSTICKER
ADULTERATED	CRACKHALTER	FOULMOUTHED	INTERVIEWEE	PATERNOSTER	SPREADSHEET
AGONOTHETES	CRENELLATED	FRANKFURTER	INTERVIEWER	PEACEKEEPER	STADTHOLDER
AMELANCHIER	CRESTFALLEN	FREETHINKER	INTOXICATED	PENNYFATHER	STAIRCARPET
ANAXIMANDER	CRITICASTER	FRENCHWOMEN	INTOXIMETER	PENTECONTER	STAKEHOLDER
ANTECHAMBER	CROSSLEGGED	FRONTRUNNER	INTROVERTED	PENTHESILEA	STALLHOLDER
ANTIBURGHER	CULVERINEER	FROSTBITTEN	INVINCIBLES	PERSONIFIED	STANDPATTER
ANTISTHENES	CYCLOSTYLED	FULLBLOODED	JERRYMANDER	PETTICOATED	STEAMROLLER
APPEARANCES	DARDANELLES	GALLIBAGGER	KINDERSPIEL	PETTIFOGGER	STEINBERGER
APPRENTICED	DEBILITATED	GALLYBAGGER	KINDHEARTED	PHILANDERER	STEPBROTHER
ARQUEBUSIER	DECAPITATED	GATECRASHER	KRIEGSSPIEL	PHILOCTETES	STEREOMETER
ARTICULATED	DEERSTALKER	GENERALIZED	LAMMERGEIER	PHILOSOPHER	STEREOTYPED
ASCLEPIADES	DEGRINGOLER	GERRYMANDER	LAMMERGEYER	PHOTOCOPIER	STOCKBROKER
ASSIMILATED	DEMORALIZED	GIGGLEWATER	LAMPLIGHTER	PLAGIARISED	STOCKHAUSEN
AUXANOMETER	DEMOSTHENES	GILLYFLOWER	LEADSWINGER	PLANTAGENET	STOCKHOLDER
AZOTOBACTER	DEVITRIFIED	GODDAUGHTER	LEASEHOLDER	PREDESTINED	STOCKJOBBER
BACKBENCHER	DILAPIDATED	GODFORSAKEN	LEPIDOSIREN	PREOCCUPIED	STOREKEEPER
BACKFIELDER	DINNYHAUSER	GONFALONIER	LEVELHEADED	PRESSURIZED	STORYTELLER
BADTEMPERED	DINNYHAYSER	GOODNATURED	LIGHTHEADED	PRESTRESSED	STRAITLACED
BARNSTORMER	DISAFFECTED	GRALLATORES	LOGOGRAPHER	PRIZEWINNER	STRANDLOPER
BARTHOLOMEW	DISBELIEVER	GRANDFATHER	LONGAWAITED	PROBATIONER	STRAPHANGER
BEACHCOMBER	DISCIPLINED	GRANDMASTER	LONGSIGHTED	PROOFREADER	STREAMLINED
BELEAGUERED	DISCOLOURED	GRANDMOTHER	LONGSLEEVED	PROVISIONER	STRUTHIONES
BELLYTIMBER	DISEMBODIED	GRASSHOPPER	LOUDSPEAKER	QUICKSILVER	SUGARCOATED
BIRDWATCHER	DISENCUMBER	GRAVEDIGGER	LUXEMBURGER	RANGEFINDER	SUNDRENCHED
BITTERSWEET	DISGRUNTLED	GREENGROCER	MACADAMIZED	RECONNOITER	SUPERFICIES
BLACKMAILER	DISHEVELLED	GRENZGANGER	MAGISTRATES	REFURBISHED	SUPERMARKET
BLOCKBUSTER	DISINCLINED	GROUNDSHEET	MALADJUSTED	REPRESENTED	SUPERTANKER
BLOODSUCKER	DISORIENTED	GROUNDSPEED	MARIONETTES	RETROROCKET	SYMPATHISER
BREADWINNER	DISREGARDED	HABERDASHER	MASQUERADER	RIDDLEMEREE	SYMPATHIZER
BROADCASTER	DISTRIBUTED	HAIRDRESSER	MEADOWSWEET	RIGHTANGLED	SYMPLEGADES
BROADMINDED	DOWNHEARTED	HALBSTARKER	MEDIUMSIZED	RIGHTHANDED	SYNTHESIZED
BULLFIGHTER	DOWNTRODDEN	HALFBROTHER	MENTHOLATED	RIGHTHANDER	SYNTHESIZER
BURGOMASTER	DRAGONNADES	HALFHEARTED	METALWORKER	RIGHTWINGER	TABERNACLES
BUSHWHACKER	DREADLOCKED	HANDCRAFTED	MIDDLESIZED	ROCKEFELLER	TEENYBOPPER
CAMOUFLAGED	DRINKDRIVER	HANDICAPPED	MINESWEEPER	RUDESHEIMER	TEETOTALLER
CAMPHORATED	DUMBFOUNDED	HANDICAPPER	MINNESINGER	SALINOMETER	TELEGRAPHER
CAPERNOITED	DUSTWRAPPER	HANDWRITTEN	MISBEGOTTEN	SALVOGUNNER	TELEPRINTER
CASTELLATED	EARTHSHAKER	HARDPRESSED	MOISTURIZER	SCANDALIZED	TENSIOMETER
CAULIFLOWER	ELECTROLIER	HAREBRAINED	MONEYLENDER	SCAREMONGER	TESSELLATED
CHANTICLEER	EMBARRASSED	HEARTBROKEN	MONOGRAMMED	SCHWARMEREI	THEATERGOER
CHARGEPAYER	EMBELLISHED	HEAVYHANDED	MONTESQUIEU	SCOREKEEPER	THEATREGOER
CHEERLEADER	EMMENTHALER	HIGHLIGHTER	MONTGOLFIER	SCOUTMASTER	THERMOMETER
CHICKENFEED	EMPTYHANDED	HIGHPITCHED	MOONLIGHTER	SCREWDRIVER	TIGHTFISTED
CHILDMINDER	ENFOULDERED	HIGHPOWERED	MOSSTROOPER	SELFIMPOSED	TIGHTLIPPED
CHOIRMASTER	ENLIGHTENED	HIPPOCRATES	MOUNTAINEER	SEMITRAILER	TITLEHOLDER
CHONDROSTEI	ENTERTAINER	HISTORIATED	MULTISTOREY	SHAREHOLDER	TOASTMASTER
CHRISTOPHER	ESTABLISHED	HOHENLINDEN	MUNCHHAUSEN	SHINPLASTER	TOPOGRAPHER
CHRONOMETER	ESTABLISHER	HOMOGENIZED	NARRAGANSET	SHIPBUILDER	TRANSCEIVER
CIRCUMCISER	EVISCERATED	HONEYCOMBED	NEARSIGHTED	SHIPWRECKED	TRANSFERRED
CIRRHIPEDEA	EXAGGERATED	HONEYMOONER	NECROMANCER	SHORTHANDED	TRANSFORMED
CLEANSHAVEN	EXASPERATED	HOSPITALLER	NEUTRALISED	SHORTHANDED	TRANSFORMER

TRANSMITTED	UNTRAMELLED	PROCEEDINGS	AERODYNAMIC	DIARTHROSIS	METAGENESIS
TRANSMITTER	UNVARNISHED	REFLEXOLOGY	AGORAPHOBIA	DICHROMATIC	MICROSCOPIC
TRANSPONDER	UNWARRANTED	SCARBOROUGH	ALBUMINURIA	DIORTHORTIC	MODERNISTIC
TRANSPORTED	UPHOLSTERER	SCIENTOLOGY	AMYLOPECTIN	DRAGGLETAIL	MYXOMATOSIS
TRANSPORTER	VITAMINIZED	SEIGNIORAGE	ANACOLUTHIA	DYAESTHESIA	NECROBIOSIS
TREECREEPER	VOLKSKAMMER	SHORTCHANGE	ANACREONTIC	DYSLOGISTIC	NYMPHOMANIA
TRICHINOSED	VOORTREKKER	SRANANTONGO	ANADIPLOSIS	ECTOTROPHIC	OARSMANSHIP
TRINCOMALEE	WALDSTERBEN	SUPERCHARGE	ANAESTHESIA	EMPHYTEUSIS	OCHLOCRATIC
TRINOBANTES	WARMHEARTED	TERMINOLOGY	ANAESTHETIC	EMPIRICUTIC	ONEIRODYNIA
TSCHERNOSEM	WASHLEATHER	UNDERCHARGE	ANAGNORISIS	ENARTHROSIS	ORTHOPAEDIC
TYPEWRITTEN	WASTEBASKET	VOLCANOLOGY	ANAPHYLAXIS	ENDOTHERMIC	OSTEOPATHIC
TYPOGRAPHER	WATERLOGGED	VULCANOLOGY	ANAPLEROSIS	ENDOTROPHIC	PALEOLITHIC
ULTRAVIOLET	WELLADVISED	WEIGHBRIDGE	ANAPLEROTIC	EPANALEPSIS	PARABLEPSIS
UNANNOUNCED	WELLBEHAVED	WINDOWLEDGE	ANASTOMOSIS	EPITHYMETIC	PARACROSTIC
UNBLEMISHED	WELLDEFINED	WORRYTROUGH	ANTHESTERIA	EREMACAUSIS	PARALEIPSIS
UNCASTRATED	WELLDRESSED	ANTISTROPHE	ANTHOCYANIN	ESCHERICHIA	PARAMASTOID
UNCIVILISED	WELLFOUNDED	BANGLADESHI	ANTHRACOSIS	ESPIEGLERIE	PARASITOSIS
UNCIVILIZED	WESTMINSTER	BLAMEWORTHY	ANTIPHRASIS	EUCHARISTIC	PARATYPHOID
UNCLUTTERED	WHITECHAPEL	CALLIGRAPHY	ANTIPYRETIC	EUCHROMATIN	PARENTHESIS
UNCOMMITTED	WHITLEATHER	CALLITRICHE	ANTONOMASIA	EUPHEMISTIC	PARONOMASIA
UNCONCEALED	WINDBREAKER	CANDLELIGHT	APOCALYPTIC	FISHANDCHIP	PARTNERSHIP
UNCONCERNED	WINDCHEATER	CARTOGRAPHY	APOLLINARIS	FLICKERTAIL	PASSACAGLIA
UNCONFIRMED	WINTERGREEN	CATASTROPHE	APONEUROSIS	GABERLUNZIE	PERIODONTIC
UNCONNECTED	WRONGHEADED	CHICHEVACHE	APOSIOPESIS	GAMOGENESIS	PERIPATETIC
UNCONQUERED	XYLOGRAPHER	CHIROGRAPHY	APPARATCHIK	GASTRONOMIC	PERIPHRASIS
UNCONTESTED	FESTSCHRIFT	CHOROGRAPHY	APPLERINGIE	GEGENSCHEIN	PERISTALSIS
UNCONVERTED	HETEROGRAFT	DITTOGRAPHY	ARTHRODESIS	GIBBERELLIN	PERITONITIS
UNCONVINCED	LOOSESTRIFE	DREADNOUGHT	ATMOSPHERIC	GLOSSOLALIA	PESSIMISTIC
UNDERCOOKED	MISIDENTIFY	ESCARMOUCHE	AVOIRDUPOIS	GRAVIMETRIC	PHARYNGITIS
UNDERHANDED	NORTHCLIFFE	ETHNOGRAPHY	BACCHANALIA	HAEMOGLOBIN	PHTHIRIASIS
UNDERMANNED	SHEATHKNIFE	FEHMGERICHT	BALISTRARIA	HAEMOPHILIA	PLEURODYNIA
UNDERSIGNED	SPEECHCRAFT	FORETHOUGHT	BARYCENTRIC	HAEMORRHOID	POLIORCETIC
UNDERSTATED	SPENDTHRIFT	HAGIOGRAPHA	BIELORUSSIA	HEMERALOPIA	POLYMORPHIC
UNDERVALUED	ACKNOWLEDGE	HAGIOGRAPHY	BOURGEOISIE	HEMIANOPSIA	POLYTECHNIC
UNDERWRITER	AGROSTOLOGY	HEAVYWEIGHT	BRAGGADOCIO	HIPPOCRATIC	PREHISTORIC
UNDEVELOPED	AMPHIBOLOGY	HOMOEOPATHY	BRUCELLOSIS	HOMEOPATHIC	PREMIERSHIP
UNDIGNIFIED	ARCHAEOLOGY	HYPERTROPHY	BUTTONQUAIL	HOMOTHERMIC	PROGENITRIX
UNDISCLOSED	ARCHIPELAGO	ICONOGRAPHY	CABBALISTIC	HOOTANANNIE	PROPHYLAXIS
UNDISGUISED	BEAUMONTAGE	IPECACUANHA	CACOGASTRIC	HOOTENANNIE	PROTEROZOIC
UNDISTURBED	CAMPANOLOGY	LANDSKNECHT	CALCEOLARIA	HYDROPHOBIA	PRZEWALSKIS
UNENVELOPED	CLIMATOLOGY	LIGHTWEIGHT	CAMARADERIE	HYDROPHOBIC	PSEUDOLOGIA
UNEXPLAINED	COUNTERSIGN	LITHOGRAPHY	CAPERNOITIE	HYDROSTATIC	PSITTACOSIS
UNEXPRESSED	CRIMINOLOGY	MENDELSSOHN	CATACAUSTIC	HYPOTHERMIA	PSYCHEDELIC
UNFULFILLED	DERMATOLOGY	NATUROPATHY	CATACHRESIS	ICHTHYORNIS	PSYCHIATRIC
UNFURNISHED	ESCHATOLOGY	ORTHOGRAPHY	CATACLYSMIC	ICONOSTASIS	REALPOLITIK
UNIMPRESSED	FURNISHINGS	OVERDRAUGHT	CATALLACTIC	IDIOGRAPHIC	RIBONUCLEIC
UNINHABITED	GERONTOLOGY	OVERWROUGHT	CHAMBERLAIN	INAUTHENTIC	SAINTPAULIA
UNINHIBITED	GYNAECOLOGY	PAEDOTROPHY	CHAMBERMAID	INTERLEUKIN	SALPINGITIS
UNINITIATED	HAEMORRHAGE	PALEOGRAPHY	CHARACINOID	INTERNUNCIO	SANSEVIERIA
UNJUSTIFIED	HERPETOLOGY	PAPERWEIGHT	CHARISMATIC	ISOELECTRIC	SAPROLEGNIA
UNMITIGATED	HUCKSTERAGE	PHOTOGRAPHY	CHINOISERIE	ITHYPHALLIC	SAPROPHYTIC
UNMOTIVATED	INTERCHANGE	PORNOGRAPHY	CHOLINERGIC	KILOCALORIE	SCANDANAVIA
UNPERTURBED	LEFTLUGGAGE	PYELOGRAPHY	CHRYSAROBIN	KLEPTOMANIA	SCANDINAVIA
UNPROTECTED	MARIVAUDAGE	RADIOGRAPHY	CIRRHIPEDIA	KULTURKREIS	SCARABAEOID
UNPUBLISHED	MARLBOROUGH	SCHOTTISCHE	CITIZENSHIP	LECTURESHIP	SCHOLARSHIP
UNQUALIFIED	MASKALLONGE	SEARCHLIGHT	CLIMACTERIC	LEGERDEMAIN	SENNACHERIB
UNREHEARSED	MEANDERINGS	STENOGRAPHY	COMPRIMARIO	LOGARITHMIC	SEPTICAEMIA
UNSATISFIED	METEOROLOGY	STREETLIGHT	COMRADESHIP	MACROBIOTIC	SHOWMANSHIP
UNSATURATED	METHODOLOGY	TACHYGRAPHY	CONVALLARIA	MACROSCOPIC	SKIDBLADNIR
UNSCHEDULED	MISCARRIAGE	TETRADRACHM	COUNTERFEIT	MASOCHISTIC	SOLIPSISTIC
UNSHELTERED	MUSKELLUNGE	TRUSTWORTHY	COUNTERFOIL	MEGALOMANIA	SPHRAGISTIC
UNSOLICITED	NETHERLINGS	UNDERWEIGHT	CYTOGENESIS	MEGALOMANIC	SPONDYLITIS
UNSPECIFIED	ORNITHOLOGY	WHEELWRIGHT	DEMOGRAPHIC	MEGALOPOLIS	SPONSORSHIP
UNSUPPORTED	OSTREOPHAGE	ABIOGENESIS	DEMONOMANIA	MELANCHOLIA	STEATOPYGIA
UNSURPASSED	OUTPOURINGS	ABIOGENETIC	DEMOSTHENIC	MELANCHOLIC	STRONGYLOID
UNSUSPECTED	PERISSOLOGY	ACATALECTIC	DIAPHORESIS	MEMORABILIA	SUPERCHERIE
UNSWEETENED	PHRASEOLOGY	ACROCENTRIC	DIAPHORETIC	METACENTRIC	SYCOPHANTIC

SYMPATHETIC	CEASELESSLY	FASHIONABLE	INFLAMMABLE	PERCEPTIBLY	SOUNDLESSLY
SYMPTOMATIC	CERTIFIABLE	FASHIONABLY	INGENIOUSLY	PERENNIALLY	SPANGCOCKLE
TACHYCARDIA	CHANTARELLE	FAULTLESSLY	INHABITABLE	PERMANENTLY	SPERMOPHILE
TELEGRAPHIC	CHANTERELLE	FERNITICKLE	INNUMERABLE	PERMISSIBLE	SPIRITUALLY
TELEKINESIS	CHIPPENDALE	FEROCIOUSLY	INQUIRINGLY	PERPETUALLY	SPORTSFIELD
TELOCENTRIC	CHLOROPHYLL	FESTINATELY	INSCRUTABLE	PERTINENTLY	STEADFASTLY
THANATOPSIS	CHRONICALLY	FINANCIALLY	INSEPARABLE	PHONOFIDDLE	STRENUOUSLY
THERAPEUTIC	COCKLESHELL	FINGERSTALL	INSIDIOUSLY	PINNYWINKLE	STRETCHABLE
THIGMOTAXIS	COLLAPSIBLE	FISSIONABLE	INSISTENTLY	PISSASPHALT	STRINGENTLY
THINGAMAJIG	COMBUSTIBLE	FORESEEABLE	INSULTINGLY	PLEASURABLE	SUBMULTIPLE
THINGUMAJIG	COMFORTABLE	FORTNIGHTLY	INSUPERABLE	POINTLESSLY	SUGGESTIBLE
THOROUGHPIN	COMFORTABLY	FORTUNATELY	INTENSIVELY	POLITICALLY	SUMPTUOUSLY
THYROTROPIN	COMMENDABLE	FOTHERGILLA	INTERMINGLE	PONDEROUSLY	SUSCEPTIBLE
TIMBROMANIA	COMMENDABLY	FRANTICALLY	INTOLERABLE	POTENTIALLY	SUSTAINABLE
TONSILLITIS	COMPETENTLY	FRATERNALLY	INTOLERABLY	PRACTICABLE	SWALLOWABLE
TORTICOLLIS	CONCEIVABLE	FRIGHTFULLY	INTRACTABLE	PRACTICALLY	TAGLIATELLE
TOXICOGENIC	CONCEIVABLY	FRIVOLOUSLY	INTRICATELY	PREDICTABLE	TARRADIDDLE
TRACASSERIE	CONCEPTICLE	FRUITLESSLY	INTUITIVELY	PREDICTABLY	TASTELESSLY
TRANSFERRIN	CONFIDENTLY	GARRULOUSLY	IRREDUCIBLE	PREMATURELY	TATTERSALLS
TRANSURANIC	CONSCIOUSLY	GENERICALLY	IRREFUTABLE	PRESENTABLE	TECHNICALLY
TROMPELOEIL	CONTENTEDLY	GENETICALLY	IRREGULARLY	PREVENTABLE	TEMPORARILY
TRUSTEESHIP	CONTINUALLY	GENTLEMANLY	IRREPARABLE	PRINCIPALLY	TENACIOUSLY
TURBELLARIA	CONVENTICLE	GRAPHICALLY	IRREPARABLY	PROFESSEDLY	TENTATIVELY
TYPOGRAPHIC	CONVERTIBLE	GREENBOTTLE	IRREVOCABLE	PROFITEROLE	THANKLESSLY
TYROGLYPHID	CORRUPTIBLE	GROUNDSWELL	JUDICIOUSLY	PROMINENTLY	THEATRICALS
UNAUTHENTIC	COURTEOUSLY	HAPHAZARDLY	JUSTIFIABLE	PROSAICALLY	THUNDERBOLT
UNPATRIOTIC	CREDENTIALS	HEARTLESSLY	JUSTIFIABLY	PUBLISHABLE	TIGGYWINKLE
UNREALISTIC	CREDULOUSLY	HIGHPROFILE	KNUCKLEBALL	PUNCHINELLO	TIMBROPHILY
UTRICULARIA	CUSTOMARILY	HILARIOUSLY	LABORIOUSLY	QUERULOUSLY	TOWNSPEOPLE
VALLISNERIA	DANGEROUSLY	HONEYSUCKLE	LACONICALLY	RAPTUROUSLY	TREASONABLE
VASOPRESSIN	DECEITFULLY	HORNSWOGGLE	LICKSPITTLE	RATATOUILLE	TRICHINELLA
WORKMANSHIP	DECEPTIVELY	HUNDREDFOLD	LOGODAEDALY	RAVISHINGLY	TRUCULENTLY
XEROTHERMIC	DEFENSIVELY	IDENTICALLY	LUXURIANTLY	RECOVERABLE	ULOTRICHALE
XEROTRIPSIS	DELICIOUSLY	IDIOTICALLY	LUXURIOUSLY	RECTIFIABLE	UNALIENABLE
ARRHENOTOKY	DENUMERABLE	IDYLLICALLY	MALICIOUSLY	RECURRENTLY	UNALTERABLE
JABBERWOCKY	DESPERATELY	ILLOGICALLY	MANTELSHELF	REDOUBTABLE	UNANIMOUSLY
PERESTROIKA	DIFFERENTLY	IMMEDIATELY	MASTERFULLY	REGIMENTALS	UNAVAILABLE
RATTLESNAKE	DIFFIDENTLY	IMPARTIALLY	MEDICINALLY	REGRETFULLY	UNAVOIDABLE
RHEUMATICKY	DISCERNIBLE	IMPASSIVELY	MELODIOUSLY	REGRETTABLE	UNAVOIDABLY
SPONDULICKS	DISENTANGLE	IMPATIENTLY	MERCILESSLY	REGRETTABLY	UNBREAKABLE
TCHAIKOVSKY	DISHONESTLY	IMPERIOUSLY	METACARPALS	RELIGIOUSLY	UNCOUNTABLE
TENTERHOOKS	DISPENSABLE	IMPERMEABLE	METATARSALS	RELUCTANTLY	UNCRUSHABLE
WORKMANLIKE	DISPERSABLE	IMPETUOUSLY	MICROTUBULE	REPLACEABLE	UNDESIRABLE
ACCORDINGLY	DODECASTYLE	IMPLAUSIBLE	MOLLYCODDLE	RESENTFULLY	UNDOUBTEDLY
ACCOUNTABLE	DOUROUCOULI	IMPORTANTLY	MOMENTARILY	RESPECTABLE	UNDRINKABLE
ADVERBIALLY	DRASTICALLY	IMPREGNABLE	MONONGAHELA	RESPECTABLY	UNENDURABLE
AILUROPHILE	EFFECTIVELY	IMPRUDENTLY	MUSCHELKALK	RESPONSIBLE	UNFAILINGLY
ALTERNATELY	EFFECTUALLY	IMPULSIVELY	NECESSARILY	RESPONSIBLY	UNFAVORABLE
ANENCEPHALY	EFFICIENTLY	INADVISABLE	NEIGHBOURLY	RETRACTABLE	UNFLAPPABLE
ANONYMOUSLY	ELABORATELY	INALIENABLE	NIGHTINGALE	RETRIEVABLE	UNGETATABLE
APPALLINGLY	EMOTIONALLY	INCESSANTLY	NOISELESSLY	RIGHTEOUSLY	UNIVERSALLY
APPRECIABLE	ENFORCEABLE	INCORRECTLY	NOTORIOUSLY	SAGACIOUSLY	UNNATURALLY
APPRECIABLY	EQUIVOCALLY	INDEFINABLE	NUMERICALLY	SALACIOUSLY	UNPALATABLE
APPROVINGLY	ERRATICALLY	INDIGNANTLY	OBJECTIVELY	SATIRICALLY	UNPRINTABLE
ARBITRARILY	ERRONEOUSLY	INDIVISIBLE	OBSESSIVELY	SCEPTICALLY	UNSHAKEABLE
ASSIDUOUSLY	ESSENTIALLY	INDIVISIBLY	OBSTINATELY	SCREAMINGLY	UNSPEAKABLE
ATROCIOUSLY	ESTRANGHELO	INDOMITABLE	OFFENSIVELY	SECONDARILY	UNSTOPPABLE
ATTENTIVELY	EUCALYPTOLE	INDUBITABLE	OFFHANDEDLY	SECRETIVELY	UNTHINKABLE
AUDACIOUSLY	EXCEEDINGLY	INDUBITABLY	OFFICIOUSLY	SELAGINELLA	UNTOUCHABLE
BARBASTELLE	EXCESSIVELY	INDULGENTLY	OPPORTUNELY	SELECTIVELY	UNUTTERABLE
BASKERVILLE	EXCLUSIVELY	INELUCTABLE	ORGANICALLY	SENSITIVELY	UNWITTINGLY
BATTLEFIELD	EXPECTANTLY	INEQUITABLE	PACIFICALLY	SERVICEABLE	VICARIOUSLY
BEAUTIFULLY	EXQUISITELY	INESCAPABLE	PASTEURELLA	SEVERALFOLD	VIOLINCELLO
BIBLIOPHILE	EXTENSIVELY	INESTIMABLE	PASTOURELLE	SHAMELESSLY	VIOLONCELLO
BRAZZAVILLE	FACETIOUSLY	INEXCITABLE	PENSIONABLE	SKEPTICALLY	VIVACIOUSLY
BRILLIANTLY	FANATICALLY	INEXCUSABLE	PENTONVILLE	SLIGHTINGLY	VOLUNTARILY
CAUSTICALLY	FARTHINGALE	INEXCUSABLY	PERCEPTIBLE	SORROWFULLY	VORACIOUSLY

WENSLEYDALE	BEREAVEMENT	DISAGREEING	GEOSYNCLINE	NEGOTIATING	SCATTERLING
WONDERFULLY	BERGSCHRUND	DISARMAMENT	GLUCOSAMINE	NEIGHBORING	SCOPOLAMINE
CHEIROGNOMY	BESIEGEMENT	DISCERNMENT	GOODLOOKING	NEVERENDING	SCUPPERNONG
COLLENCHYMA	BESTSELLING	DISFIGURING	GREASEPAINT	NEWSCASTING	SELFEVIDENT
DEUTERONOMY	BEWILDERING	DISOBEDIENT	HAIRRAISING	NIPFARTHING	SHENANIGANS
ENCEPHALOMA	BLANKURSINE	DISPARAGING	HANDWRITING	NONEXISTENT	SHOPLIFTING
ENCHONDROMA	BOMBARDMENT	DISQUIETING	HANGGLIDING	NOURISHMENT	SHORTCOMING
EPICHEIREMA	BOOKBINDING	DISSEPIMENT	HARDHITTING	OBMUTESCENT	SHOWJUMPING
FLAVOURSOME	BOOKKEEPING	DISTRESSING	HARDWORKING	OBSOLESCENT	SIGHTSEEING
FURTHERSOME	BRISTLECONE	DIVORCEMENT	HECKELPHONE	OMNIPRESENT	SIGNIFICANT
GASTRECTOMY	CALCULATING	DOMINEERING	HERRINGBONE	ORCHESTRINA	SILVERPOINT
HYPOCORISMA	CALEFACIENT	DRESSMAKING	HIBERNATING	ORIGINATING	SLEUTHHOUND
MAISTERDOME	CALENDERING	DRYCLEANING	HIGHRANKING	OUTSTANDING	SMITHEREENS
OVARIECTOMY	CAPTIVATING	DUPLICATING	HORSERACING	OVERBEARING	SMOULDERING
PHYSIOGNOMY	CARAVANNING	ELECTROTINT	HORSERIDING	OVERFISHING	SNORKELLING
PLAGIOSTOMI	CHALLENGING	ELEPHANTINE	HOUSEPARENT	OVERFLOWING	SPACESAVING
PRESTISSIMO	CHARLEMAGNE	EMBOÎTEMENT	HUMILIATING	OVERHANGING	SPLUTTERING
QUARRELSOME	CHITTERLING	EMPIECEMENT	HUSBANDLAND	OVERLAPPING	STOCKTAKING
SARCENCHYME	CHORDOPHONE	EMPLACEMENT	IDENTIFYING	OVERMANNING	STRIKEBOUND
SCHISTOSOMA	CHRISTENING	EMPOWERMENT	IGNORANTINE	OVERPAYMENT	SUBDOMINANT
SCHISTOSOME	CIRCULATING	ENCHANTMENT	IMPEACHMENT	OVERTURNING	SUBSERVIENT
SCLERODERMA	CLAIRVOYANT	ENCOURAGING	IMPERMANENT	OVERWEENING	SUDETENLAND
SCYPHISTOMA	CLANDESTINE	ENCROACHING	IMPERTINENT	PAINKILLING	SUFFOCATING
SEXTODECIMO	COBBLESTONE	ENDORSEMENT	IMPROVEMENT	PAINSTAKING	SUPERINTEND
STENOCHROME	COEFFICIENT	ENFEOFFMENT	IMPROVIDENT	PARLIPOMENA	SURROUNDING
TRACHEOTOMY	COLOURBLIND	ENFORCEMENT	INADVERTENT	PARTICIPANT	SURTARBRAND
TROUBLESOME	COMMANDMENT	ENGINEERING	INCALESCENT	PATRONISING	SURTURBRAND
TRYPANOSOMA	COMMUNICANT	ENHANCEMENT	INCARNADINE	PATRONIZING	SURVEILLANT
TRYPANOSOME	COMPARTMENT	ENJAMBEMENT	INCOMPETENT	PEDESTRIANS	SWITZERLAND
UNWHOLESOME	COMPILEMENT	ENKEPHALINE	INCONTINENT	PENETRATING	TANTALIZING
VENTURESOME	COMPLAISANT	ENLARGEMENT	INDEPENDENT	PENTAVALENT	TAUTOCHRONE
WINDOWFRAME	CONCEALMENT	ENSLAVEMENT	INDIFFERENT	PERSEVERING	TELEWORKING
ABANDONMENT	CONCOMITANT	ENTABLEMENT	INEFFICIENT	PHILIPPIANS	TEMPERAMENT
ABRIDGEMENT	CONFINEMENT	ENTHRALLING	INEXPEDIENT	PIERREPOINT	THEOBROMINE
ACCIPITRINE	CONSIDERING	ENTITLEMENT	INFURIATING	PLATYRRHINE	THREATENING
ACHIEVEMENT	CONSIGNMENT	ENVIRONMENT	INOPPORTUNE	PLEISTOCENE	TIDDLEYWINK
ACQUIESCENT	CONSTANTINE	EPINEPHRINE	INSINUATING	POLITICIANS	TIMEKEEPING
ACRIFLAVINE	CONSTITUENT	EPOCHMAKING	INSTALLMENT	POLYSTYRENE	TIMESHARING
ADJOURNMENT	CONTAINMENT	EQUIDISTANT	INTELLIGENT	POSSESSIONS	TOBOGGANING
ADVANCEMENT	CONTAMINANT	EQUIPOLLENT	INTERESTING	PRECAUTIONS	TRACKLEMENT
ADVERTISING	CONTEMPLANT	ESTRAMAZONE	INTERLACING	PREDICAMENT	TRANSILIENT
AGGLUTINANT	CONTENEMENT	EVERLASTING	INTERNECINE	PREDOMINANT	TRANSLUCENT
AGGRAVATING	CONTENTMENT	EXPECTORANT	INTERVENING	PRESENTMENT	TRANSPARENT
ALEXANDRINE	CONTRASTING	EXTENUATING	INVOLVEMENT	PRESTONPANS	TRESPASSING
ALTERNATING	CONVULSIONS	EXTRAVAGANT	ISOXSUPRINE	PRETENSIONS	TYPESETTING
AMERCIAMENT	CORINTHIANS	EYECATCHING	KIDDLEYWINK	PROCUREMENT	ULTRAMARINE
AMINOBUTENE	CORNERSTONE	FACTFINDING	LABORSAVING	PROLEGOMENA	UNBEFITTING
AMPHETAMINE	COUNSELLING	FARREACHING	LAPIDESCENT	PROTRACTING	UNDEMANDING
AMPHISBAENA	COUNTERHAND	FASCINATING	LAWBREAKING	PROTUBERANT	UNDERGROUND
AMPHISBOENA	COUNTERMAND	FINGERPRINT	LENGTHENING	QUARRELLING	UNDERTAKING
ANSWERPHONE	COUNTERPANE	FLOURISHING	LINDISFARNE	QUESTIONING	UNDESERVING
ANTICYCLONE	COUNTERSINK	FLUCTUATING	LIVINGSTONE	REALIGNMENT	UNFLINCHING
APOMORPHINE	CRACOVIENNE	FLUORESCENT	LONGLASTING	RECRUITMENT	UNIMPORTANT
APPEASEMENT	CRYSTALLINE	FOOTBALLING	LONGRUNNING	REFRESHMENT	UNOBSERVANT
APPOINTMENT	CURTAILMENT	FOOTWASHING	LUMINESCENT	REFRIGERANT	UNREASONING
APPROACHING	CYCLOALKANE	FORECASTING	MAGNIFICENT	REGISTERING	UNRELENTING
APPURTENANT	DECORATIONS	FOREWARNING	MALAKATOONE	RELEASEMENT	UNREMITTING
ARBITRAMENT	DELITESCENT	FORTHCOMING	MANEUVERING	REMINISCENT	UNREPENTANT
ARRANGEMENT	DEPARTEMENT	FOUNDATIONS	MEASUREMENT	REPLACEMENT	UNSHRINKING
ASSYTHEMENT	DERANGEMENT	FRIGHTENING	MERRYMAKING	REQUIREMENT	UNWELCOMING
ASTONISHING	DESERPIDINE	FRUSTRATING	MICROSECOND	RESPLENDENT	VACILLATING
BACKPACKING	DETERMINANT	FULFILLMENT	MINISTERING	RESPONSIONS	VARSOVIENNE
BACKSLIDING	DETERMINING	FUNCTIONING	MISSPELLING	RESTATEMENT	VINBLASTINE
BALLBEARING	DEVASTATING	FUNDRAISING	MONEYMAKING	REVELATIONS	VINCRISTINE
BATTLEFRONT	DEVELOPMENT	GAMMERSTANG	MUDSLINGING	REVOLUTIONS	VOTERIGGING
BELLIGERENT	DIPROTODONT	GARNISHMENT	NAPHTHALENE	ROTTENSTONE	WAINSCOTING
BENEDICTINE	DISABLEMENT	GELSEMININE	NEEDLEPOINT	SCAFFOLDING	WAREHOUSING

WATERSKIING	COMMINATION	DIFFRACTION	IMAGINATION	OBSERVATION	RETRIBUTION
WELLINGTONS	COMMUTATION	DIMERCAPROL	IMMIGRATION	OBSTRICTION	REVALUATION
WELLMEANING	COMPETITION	DISILLUSION	IMPLICATION	OBSTRUCTION	RUMFRUCTION
WIDERANGING	COMPILATION	DISIMPRISON	IMPORTATION	OCTASTICHON	RUMGUMPTION
WINDSURFING	COMPOSITION	DISJUNCTION	IMPRECATION	OFFICIALDOM	SALESPERSON
WITHERSHINS	COMPOTATION	DISLOCATION	IMPRECISION	ONOMASTICON	SANDERSWOOD
WITHHOLDING	COMPUNCTION	DISPOSITION	INATTENTION	ORCHESTRION	SCATTERGOOD
WOODCARVING	COMPUTATION	DISPUTATION	INCANTATION	ORGANIZAION	SCHECKLATON
YELLOWSTONE	CONCILIATOR	DISSERTATOR	INCARNATION	ORIENTATION	SEGREGATION
ABLACTATION	CONFUTATION	DISSIPATION	INCINERATOR	ORIGINATION	SELFCONTROL
ABOMINATION	CONJUGATION	DISSOLUTION	INCLINATION	OSCILLATION	SEPTENTRION
ABSTRACTION	CONJUNCTION	DISTINCTION	INDENTATION	OSTENTATION	SHITTIMWOOD
ACCELERATOR	CONNOTATION	DISTRACTION	INDIGESTION	OUAGADOUGOU	SHOWERPROOF
ACCLAMATION	CONSOLATION	DISTRIBUTOR	INDIGNATION	OXODIZATION	SKIMMINGTON
ACCLIMATION	CONSPIRATOR	DUPLICATION	INEBRIATION	PARACETAMOL	SLUMGULLION
ACCUMULATOR	CONSTRICTOR	DYSFUNCTION	INFATUATION	PARANEPHROS	SOUTHAMPTON
ACQUISITION	CONSTRUCTOR	ECCALEOBION	INFESTATION	PARTURITION	SPECULATION
ADJUDICATOR	CONSUMPTION	EDIFICATION	INFILTRATOR	PENETRATION	SPERMATOZOA
ADUMBRATION	CONTRACTION	EJACULATION	INFORMATION	PERCOLATION	STAGFLATION
AFFECTATION	CONTRAPTION	ELABORATION	INOCULATION	PERDUELLION	STILBESTROL
AFFILIATION	CONTRIBUTOR	ELIMINATION	INQUISITION	PERFORATION	STIMULATION
AFFIRMATION	CONURBATION	ELUCIDATION	INSCRIPTION	PERMUTATION	STIPULATION
AFFLIICTION	CONVOCATION	EMBARKATION	INSINUATION	PERPETRATOR	STOOLPIGEON
AFTERSCHOOL	CONVOLUTION	EMBROCATION	INSPIRATION	PERSECUTION	STYLIZATION
AGGRAVATION	COOPERATION	ENCHIRIDION	INSTIGATION	POLLINATION	SUBDIVISION
AGGREGATION	COPROSTEROL	ENNEAHEDRON	INSTITUTION	POTAMOGETON	SUBJUGATION
ALIFANFARON	CORPORATION	ENUMERATION	INSTRUCTION	PREDECESSOR	SUBLIMATION
ALLEVIATION	CORRELATION	ENUNCIATION	INTEGRATION	PRELIBATION	SUBPANATION
ALTERCATION	CORRUGATION	ERADICATION	INTERACTION	PREMONITION	SUBTRACTION
ALTERNATION	COUNTERGLOW	ERIODENDRON	INTERCEPTOR	PREPARATION	SUFFOCATION
ANTINEUTRON	CREPITATION	EVAPORATION	INVIGILATOR	PREPOSITION	SUPERVISION
APOLLONICON	CRUCIFIXION	EVENTRATION	IRRADIATION	PRESUMPTION	SUPPOSITION
APPELLATION	CULMINATION	EXAMINATION	JACQUEMINOT	PRETERITION	SUPPRESSION
APPLICATION	CULTIVATION	EXCLAMATION	JACTITATION	PROCREATION	SUPPURATION
APPROBATION	DECLAMATION	EXHORTATION	KALASHNIKOV	PROGRESSION	SUSURRATION
ARBITRATION	DECLARATION	EXONERATION	KAMELAUKION	PROHIBITION	SYNCOPATION
ARCHENTERON	DEFOLIATION	EXOSKELETON	KATABOTHRON	PROLOCUTION	SYNDICATION
ASSIGNATION	DEFORMATION	EXPECTATION	KATAVOTHRON	PROPAGATION	TERMINATION
ASSOCIATION	DEGLUTITION	EXPLANATION	KETAVOTHRON	PROPOSITION	TESSARAGLOT
ATTENUATION	DEGRADATION	EXPLORATION	KOTABOTHRON	PROROGATION	TETRAHEDRON
ATTESTATION	DEHYDRATION	EXPURGATION	KWASHIORKOR	PROSECUTION	THINGAMABOB
ATTRIBUTION	DEIFICATION	EXTENUATION	LAMENTATION	PROSTRATION	THROGMORTON
AXEROPHTHOL	DELECTATION	EXTRADITION	LEATHERWOOD	PROTRACTION	TICKTACKTOE
BELLEROPHON	DELICTATION	FABRICATION	LEGISLATION	PROVOCATION	TITILLATION
BENEDICTION	DELINEATION	FASCINATION	LIQUIDATION	PUBLICATION	TOSTICATION
BIFURCATION	DEMARCATION	FAUXBOURDON	LUBRICATION	PUNCTUATION	TOTALIZATOR
BLACKFELLOW	DEMIBASTION	FLUCTUATION	MACHINATION	QUARRINGTON	TOURBILLION
BROTHERHOOD	DENOMINATOR	FOMENTATION	MALEDICTION	RADIOCARBON	TRAFFICATOR
BUMBERSHOOT	DEPORTATION	FORESTATION	MALEFACTION	RAPSCALLION	TRANSACTION
CALCULATION	DEPREDATION	FORMULATION	MALFUNCTION	REALIZATION	TRANSFUSION
CALIBRATION	DEPRIVATION	FORNICATION	MANCIPATION	REANIMATION	TRANSLATION
CALLISTEMON	DERELICTION	FRUSTRATION	MANIPULATOR	RECANTATION	TREPIDATION
CAPACITATOR	DESCRIPTION	FULMINATION	MANUMISSION	RECLAMATION	TRIBULATION
CAPTIVATION	DESECRATION	GENUFLEXION	MARSHMALLOW	RECOGNITION	TROUBLESPOT
CARBURETTOR	DESELECTION	GERMINATION	MASTICATION	RECONDITION	UNIFICATION
CELEBRATION	DESICCATION	GRAVITATION	MELANOCHROI	REFORMATION	UTILIZATION
CENTURIATOR	DESIGNATION	GUBERNATION	MENSURATION	REITERATION	VACCINATION
CEREBRATION	DESPERATION	HARIOLATION	METRICATION	REPUDIATION	VACILLATION
CHAIRPERSON	DESTINATION	HIBERNATION	MICTURITION	REQUISITION	VALEDICTION
CHOLESTEROL	DESTITUTION	HOBBLEDEHOY	MISBEHAVIOR	RESERVATION	VARIEGATION
CHRISMATION	DESTRUCTION	HUMILIATION	MISDEMEANOR	RESIGNATION	VARIOLATION
CIRCULATION	DETESTATION	HYDROCARBON	MOLESTATION	RESPIRATION	VENTILATION
COACHFELLOW	DEVALUATION	HYOPLASTRON	MOXIBUSTION	RESTITUTION	VINDICATION
COAGULATION	DEVASTATION	HYPHENATION	MURMURATION	RESTORATION	VIVISECTION
COLLOCATION	DIATESSARON	HYPOTENSION	NEGOTIATION	RESTRICTION	WATERMEADOW
COMBINATION	DIATESSERON	IDOLIZATION	NICKELODEON	RETALIATION	WHEELBARROW
COMMENTATOR	DICOTYLEDON	ILLUSTRATOR	NOMENCLATOR	RETARDATION	WHISTLESTOP

WHITTINGTON	COUNTERFORT	PAWNBROKERS	ACADEMICISM	EPIGENESIST	MYCOPHAGIST
WITCHDOCTOR	COUNTERPART	PERFUNCTORY	ACCLIMATISE	EQUILIBRIST	NATIONALISM
WITENAGEMOT	CRÉMAILLÈRE	PETITMAITRE	ACCOMPANIST	ETHNOLOGIST	NATIONALIST
WORKSTATION	DECLAMATORY	PHALANSTERY	ADIAPHORIST	ETYMOLOGIST	NATURALNESS
ZOOPLANKTON	DEMAGOGUERY	PHOTOSPHERE	ADOPTIANISM	EVASIVENESS	NAUGHTINESS
ALLELOMORPH	DEUTSCHMARK	PLOUGHSHARE	ADOPTIONISM	EXTEMPORISE	NERVOUSNESS
CARDIOGRAPH	DIPTEROCARP	PODSNAPPERY	ADVENTURESS	FAMILIARISE	NEUROLOGIST
CONTRETEMPS	DISPLEASURE	PORTRAITURE	AGNOSTICISM	FARTHERMOST	NIGHTMARISH
EPIDIASCOPE	DOCTRINAIRE	PRELIMINARY	AIRSICKNESS	FATUOUSNESS	NONETHELESS
FLUOROSCOPE	DOCUMENTARY	PREMONITORY	AMERICANISM	FAVOURITISM	NOTHINGNESS
GUTTERSNIPE	DOLABRIFORM	PREPARATORY	ANACHRONISM	FEATURELESS	NOVELETTISH
HEPATOSCOPY	DRYCLEANERS	PROPRIETARY	ANESTHETIST	FLABBERGAST	NUCLEOPLASM
LYCANTHROPE	EARTHENWARE	PROTONOTARY	ARTILLERIST	FOOLISHNESS	NUMISMATIST
LYCANTHROPY	ENTABLATURE	PURPRESTURE	ASPHETERISM	FORGIVENESS	OBVIOUSNESS
LYCHNOSCOPE	EXPENDITURE	REACTIONARY	ASTIGMATISM	FORLORNNESS	ODONTOBLAST
MISANTHROPE	EXPLANATORY	RECONNOITRE	AWKWARDNESS	FUNAMBULIST	OFFICIALESE
MISANTHROPY	EXPLORATORY	REFORMATORY	BASHFULNESS	FURTHERMOST	OPPORTUNISM
MISSISSIPPI	FARKLEBERRY	RESPIRATORY	BATTLEDRESS	FURTIVENESS	OPPORTUNIST
NONDESCRIPT	FERRONNIÈRE	RESTRUCTURE	BEASTLINESS	GALLOWGLASS	OPTOMETRIST
PSEUDOMORPH	FISHMONGERS	RETALIATORY	BELLETTRIST	GENEALOGIST	ORDERLINESS
RETINOSCOPY	FORECLOSURE	RETINOSPORA	BILIOUSNESS	GENUINENESS	ORIENTALISM
SEISMOGRAPH	FOREFATHERS	RHOPALOCERA	BLESSEDNESS	GHASTLINESS	ORIENTALIST
STEREOGRAPH	FRAGMENTARY	ROBESPIERRE	BREATHALYSE	GLADWELLISE	PAMPELMOOSE
STEREOSCOPE	FREEMASONRY	ROTOGRAVURE	BRITTLENESS	GUTTURALISE	PAMPELMOUSE
STETHOSCOPE	FRIGATEBIRD	RUDIMENTARY	CALLOUSNESS	HAUGHTINESS	PARACHUTIST
STROBOSCOPE	FUNCTIONARY	SCALPRIFORM	CANNIBALISM	HEALTHINESS	PASSIVENESS
SUPERSCRIPT	FURTHERMORE	SCOLECIFORM	CAPRICCIOSO	HELPFULNESS	PATERNALISM
TEGUCICALPA	GALLIMAUFRY	SCOLOPENDRA	CAREFULNESS	HIDEOUSNESS	PATHOLOGIST
THAUMATROPE	GENOUILLÈRE	SCULDUDDERY	CARSICKNESS	HISTOLOGIST	PEEVISHNESS
TRICERATOPS	GLASTONBURY	SCULDUGGERY	CATCHPHRASE	HOGGISHNESS	PELOPONNESE
ABRACADABRA	HARPSICHORD	SEDIMENTARY	CATHOLICISM	HOLLANDAISE	PENSIVENESS
ACINACIFORM	HEBDOMADARY	SEPIOSTAIRE	CHIROPODIST	HOOLIGANISM	PERCEFOREST
ACUPUNCTURE	HUCKLEBERRY	SERICULTURE	CHRISTMASSY	HORSERADISH	PERSONALIST
AGRICULTURE	HUMMINGBIRD	SHAFTESBURY	CHROMOPLAST	HYDROMEDUSA	PHILATELIST
ANGELOLATRY	HURTLEBERRY	SHAKESPEARE	CHRYSOPRASE	HYMNOLOGIST	PHILOLOGIST
ANNIVERSARY	ILLUSIONARY	SHOVELBOARD	CLEANLINESS	IDEOPRAXIST	PHOTOFINISH
ANTIPHONARY	INSECTIVORE	SILVERBERRY	COENOBITISM	ILLUSIONISM	PLAYFULNESS
APHANIPTERA	INTERCALARY	SKULDUDDERY	COLONIALISM	ILLUSIONIST	PLEBEIANISE
APLANOSPORE	INVESTITURE	SKULDUGGERY	COLONIALIST	IMMORTALISE	POLLENBRUSH
ARTHROSPORE	INVOLUNTARY	SMORGASBORD	COMFORTLESS	IMPERIALISM	POLTERGEIST
BANNOCKBURN	IRONMONGERS	SPRINGBOARD	COMMONSENSE	IMPERIALIST	POMPELMOOSE
BATHYSPHERE	IRONMONGERY	STIPENDIARY	COMMUNALISM	INTERCOURSE	POMPELMOUSE
BENEFICIARY	KILIMANJARO	STRINGBOARD	CONCISENESS	INTERGLOSSA	PORTERHOUSE
BICENTENARY	KINCHINMORT	STRINGYBARK	CONDUCTRESS	INTERSPERSE	PORTRAITIST
BILLIONAIRE	LAMPROPHYRE	SUBSTANDARD	CONSUMERISM	IRREDENTIST	PRICKLINESS
BIMILLENARY	LATTICEWORK	SUPERALTERN	CONTROVERSY	LAWLESSNESS	PRISCIANIST
BLADDERWORT	LEGIONNAIRE	SUPERSEDERE	CORRECTNESS	LECITHINASE	PRODIGALISE
BLUNDERBORE	LEGISLATURE	SUPERVISORY	COURTLINESS	LENGTHINESS	PROFUSENESS
BOOKSELLERS	LEPIDOPTERA	SUPPOSITORY	COXWAINLESS	LENTIGINOSE	PROSELYTISM
BOUTONNIERE	MANGALSUTRA	SWITCHBOARD	CROOKEDNESS	LETTERPRESS	PROTAGONIST
BOYSENBERRY	MANUFACTURE	TARATANTARA	CRYSTALLISE	LITERALNESS	PURPOSELESS
BRANDENBURG	MAQUILADORA	TEMPERATURE	DEFENCELESS	MALAPROPISM	RADIOLOGIST
CANDIDATURE	MARIONBERRY	TERPSICHORE	DEFENSELESS	MARGINALIST	RAFFISHNESS
CARABINIERE	MECKLENBURG	THUNDERBIRD	DEVIOUSNESS	MASSIVENESS	RAUCOUSNESS
CENTREBOARD	MENTONNIÈRE	TRANSFIGURE	DIPLOMATIST	MATERIALISE	REMORSELESS
CHANCELLERY	MILLIAMPERE	TRICHOPTERA	DISCOURTESY	MATERIALISM	RESTIVENESS
CHAULMOOGRA	MILLIONAIRE	TROPOSPHERE	DISINTEREST	MATERIALIST	REVISIONISM
CHAULMOUGRA	MOCKINGBIRD	ULTRAMODERN	DISTINGUISH	MEANINGLESS	ROGUISHNESS
CHIAROSCURO	MORGENSTERN	UNNECESSARY	DITHELETISM	MEASURELESS	ROMANTICISM
CIRCULATORY	NICKNACKERY	VALEDICTORY	DOUBLECROSS	MEKHITARIST	SADDLEHORSE
CLINOCHLORE	NOTICEBOARD	VENDEMIAIRE	DRUNKENNESS	MERCHANDISE	SAINTLINESS
COMSTOCKERY	NUTCRACKERS	VIDEOCAMERA	DUBIOUSNESS	MICHURINISM	SAVOURINESS
CONDOTTIERE	OBSERVATORY	WHIGMALEERY	EARNESTNESS	MILQUETOAST	SAXOPHONIST
CONDOTTIORE	ODONTOPHORE	WHITEFRIARS	EASTERNMOST	MINIATURIST	SCRUFFINESS
CONJUNCTURE	OMMATOPHORE	WINTERBERRY	ELASTOPLAST	MISERLINESS	SEASICKNESS
CORDWAINERS	ORTHOCENTRE	ABORTIONIST	ENCHANTRESS	MODELMOLEST	SECONDCLASS
COULOMMIERS	OSTRACODERM	ABSENTEEISM	ENFRANCHISE	MONOPSONIST	SELFISHNESS

SERIOUSNESS	ALEXANDRITE	ELECTROLYTE	INVESTIGATE	RECEPTIVITY	WHEREABOUTS
SHALLOWNESS	ANNABERGITE	ELIGIBILITY	JOSEPHINITE	RECIPROCATE	ACRIMONIOUS
SHAPELINESS	APOPHYLLITE	ENCAPSULATE	KITCHENETTE	RECIPROCITY	ADVENTUROUS
SHEPHERDESS	APPROPRIATE	ERYTHROCYTE	LAUNDERETTE	RECRIMINATE	AESCULAPIUS
SHUNAMITISM	APPROXIMATE	EVENTUALITY	LEATHERETTE	REDUPLICATE	ALBUGINEOUS
SINISTRORSE	ASSASSINATE	EXANTHEMATA	LONGANIMITY	REFOCILLATE	AMMOPHILOUS
SKETCHINESS	AVERRUNCATE	EXPECTORATE	LONGINQUITY	REFRIGERATE	AMPLEXICAUL
SLENDERNESS	BADDELEYITE	EXPOSTULATE	LUXULYANITE	REGURGITATE	ANDROGENOUS
SOCIOLOGIST	BANDEIRANTE	EXPROPRIATE	MACROGAMETE	REINCARNATE	ANDROGYNOUS
SOROPTIMIST	BARBITURATE	EXTERMINATE	MAGNANIMITY	RELIABILITY	ANFRACTUOUS
SPATTERDASH	BATTLEMENTS	EXTRAPOLATE	MANTELLETTA	REMONSTRATE	ANTEPENDIUM
SPRINGHOUSE	BENEFICIATE	FALLIBILITY	MASCULINITY	REORIENTATE	ANTHONOMOUS
SPRINGINESS	BICARBONATE	FAMILIARITY	MATRICULATE	RESISTIVITY	ANTIRRHINUM
STANDOFFISH	BLOODSPORTS	FEASIBILITY	MEPROBAMATE	RESUSCITATE	APATOSAURUS
STATELINESS	BREASTPLATE	FLAMBOYANTE	MICROGAMETE	REVENDICATE	APODYTERIUM
STRANGENESS	CAMALDOLITE	FLANNELETTE	MONCHIQUITE	REVERBERATE	APOSTROPHUS
STRETCHLESS	CASSITERITE	FLEXIBILITY	MONOTHELITE	RIFACIMENTO	ARBITRAGEUR
STYLISHNESS	CERARGYRITE	FRANKLINITE	MONOTREMATA	SACHERTORTE	ARCHEGONIUM
SUMMERHOUSE	CERTIFICATE	GAMETOPHYTE	MONSTROSITY	SCINTILLATE	ARCHILOCHUS
SUPERIMPOSE	CHEESECLOTH	GESTICULATE	NATIONALITY	SCUTTLEBUTT	ASPERGILLUM
SYNCHROMESH	CHIASTOLITE	GREENOCKITE	NATIONSTATE	SELECTIVITY	ASPERGILLUS
SYNCHRONISE	CILOFIBRATE	GUESSTIMATE	NECESSITATE	SENSIBILITY	ASPERSORIUM
SYNCHRONISM	CINQUECENTO	GULLIBILITY	NUMBERPLATE	SENSITIVITY	ATHERMANOUS
SYNDICALISM	CITLALEPETL	HABILIMENTS	OBJECTIVITY	SEQUESTRATE	ATRABILIOUS
TAXIDERMIST	COGNOSCENTE	HALLEFLINTA	OBTEMPERATE	SERENDIPITY	BLASPHEMOUS
TEDIOUSNESS	COGNOSCENTI	HALLUCINATE	OLIGOCHAETE	SEVENTEENTH	BORBORYGMUS
TELEPHONIST	COLLABORATE	HAMMERCLOTH	OPPIGNORATE	SILLIMANITE	CACOPHONOUS
TENUOUSNESS	COMMEMORATE	HARDICANUTE	OPPORTUNITY	SILVERSMITH	CALIFORNIUM
THINGLINESS	COMMISERATE	HATCHETTITE	ORCHESTRATE	SINGULARITY	CARBORUNDUM
THOUGHTLESS	COMMUNICATE	HEPPLEWHITE	ORIGINALITY	SMITHSONITE	CARDOPHAGUS
THRIFTINESS	COMPLIMENTS	HIGHQUALITY	OSTEOPLASTY	SOCIABILITY	CARNAPTIOUS
TOBACCONIST	CONCENTRATE	HOMOGENEITY	PARTICIPATE	SOVEREIGNTY	CARNIVOROUS
TRITAGONIST	CONFABULATE	HOSPITALITY	PARVANIMITY	SPESSARTITE	CATADROMOUS
TROPHOBLAST	CONFARREATE	HYDROGENATE	PECULIARITY	SPIFFLICATE	CENTUMVIRUS
UNCLEANNESS	CONFEDERATE	HYPOTHECATE	PENICILLATE	SPIROCHAETE	CEREMONIOUS
UNCOUTHNESS	CONSIDERATE	ICHTHYOLITE	PENTATHLETE	SPONTANEITY	CLADOSPORUM
UNGODLINESS	CONSOLIDATE	IMMORTALITY	PENULTIMATE	STELLIONATE	CLARENCIEUX
UNHAPPINESS	CONSTELLATE	IMPEDIMENTA	PERAMBULATE	STRANGULATE	COLUMBARIUM
UPRIGHTNESS	CONSTERNATE	IMPERFORATE	PERCHLORATE	SUBORDINATE	COMPENDIOUS
USELESSNESS	CONSTUPRATE	IMPERSONATE	PEREGRINATE	SUBUNGULATA	CONDOMINIUM
VACUOUSNESS	CONTAMINATE	IMPETUOSITY	PERISTALITH	SUFFRAGETTE	CONNECTICUT
VALLAMBROSA	CONTEMPLATE	IMPIGNORATE	PERLUSTRATE	SUITABILITY	CONNOISSEUR
VICHYSOISSE	COPPERPLATE	IMPORTUNATE	PERSONALITY	SUPERFLUITY	CONSPICUOUS
VICIOUSNESS	CORROBORATE	IMPROPRIETY	PERSPICUITY	SUPERIORITY	CONTENTIOUS
VISCOUNTESS	COTTONMOUTH	INCAPSULATE	PERTINACITY	SVARABHAKTI	CONVOLVULUS
VOLUNTARISM	CREDIBILITY	INCARCERATE	PHILLIPSITE	TACITURNITY	CRATERELLUS
WAKEFULNESS	CROCIDOLITE	INCOMPOSITE	PIEDMONTITE	TANGIBILITY	CREMATORIUM
WATERCOURSE	CULPABILITY	INCONGRUITY	POCOCURANTE	THALLOPHYTE	CURNAPTIOUS
WATERSPLASH	DECARBONATE	INCORPORATE	POMEGRANATE	THENCEFORTH	CYMOPHANOUS
WAYWARDNESS	DECORTICATE	INCREDULITY	PONTIFICATE	THEOPNEUSTY	DELETERIOUS
WESTERNMOST	DECREPITATE	INCRIMINATE	POSSIBILITY	THEREABOUTS	DIASCORDIUM
WHITEBOYISM	DEGLUTINATE	INDUPLICATE	PRECIPITATE	THESMOTHETE	DICEPHALOUS
WIENERWURST	DEMONSTRATE	INFERIORITY	PREDOMINATE	TOXOPHILITE	DISCONTINUE
WILLINGNESS	DENDRACHATE	INFERTILITY	PREMEDITATE	TRANQUILITY	DISCOTHEQUE
WISHTONWISH	DEOXYGENATE	INFORMALITY	PREVARICATE	TREPONEMATA	DISGRACEFUL
WISTFULNESS	DEPHLEGMATE	INGREDIENTS	PROBABILITY	TRIUMVIRATE	DISTASTEFUL
WOMANLINESS	DESCENDANTS	INHABITANTS	PRODIGALITY	TURRICULATE	DISTRUSTFUL
WORLDLINESS	DESEGREGATE	INSINCERITY	PROLIFERATE	TWELVEMONTH	DRACUNCULUS
YELLOWPLUSH	DETERIORATE	INSTABILITY	PROMISCUITY	UNCERTAINTY	EFFICACIOUS
ABNORMALITY	DETERMINATE	INSTANTIATE	PROPINQUITY	UNDERGROWTH	EINSTEINIUM
ACCOMMODATE	DIRECTORATE	INSTRUMENTS	PUNCTUALITY	UNFORTUNATE	EMMENAGOGUE
ACCULTURATE	DISSEMINATE	INTEMPERATE	PYRARGYRITE	VARIABILITY	ENDOCARDIUM
ACOLOUTHITE	DISSIMULATE	INTERGROWTH	QUADRUPLETS	VERBIGERATE	ENGHALSKRUG
AGGLOMERATE	DOMESTICATE	INTERPOLATE	QUINTUPLETS	VERMICULITE	EOANTHROPUS
AGGLUTINATE	DOMESTICITY	INTERRELATE	RATIOCINATE	VERSATILITY	EQUILIBRIUM
AGUARDIENTE	ELECTRICITY	INTERROGATE	RATIONALITY	VESUVIANITE	EXPEDITIOUS
AIGUILLETTE	ELECTROCUTE	INTREPIDITY	READABILITY	VINAIGRETTE	EXTROGENOUS

733

FARINACEOUS	PRESTIGIOUS	CONSUMPTIVE	CRYSTALLIZE	HEMIANOPSIA	ACROCENTRIC
FARRAGINOUS	PRETENTIOUS	CONTRAYERVA	DECARBONIZE	HYDROMEDUSA	AERODYNAMIC
FILAMENTOUS	PROGNATHOUS	COOPERATIVE	DESEXUALIZE	HYDROPHOBIA	ANACREONTIC
FLIRTATIOUS	PROMISCUOUS	DECLARATIVE	DESTABILIZE	HYPOCORISMA	ANAESTHETIC
FLORILEGIUM	PROTOCOCCUS	DEHORTATIVE	DISORGANIZE	HYPOTHERMIA	ANAPLEROTIC
FORTUNELOUD	PUNCTILIOUS	DESCRIPTIVE	EXTEMPORIZE	IMPEDIMENTA	ANTIPYRETIC
FRUGIVOROUS	PYTHONESQUE	DESTRUCTIVE	EXTERNALIZE	INTERGLOSSA	APHRODISIAC
GALLIGANTUS	QUADRENNIUM	DISJUNCTIVE	FAMILIARIZE	INTERLINGUA	APOCALYPTIC
GAMETANGIUM	REPETITIOUS	DISTINCTIVE	HOSPITALIZE	IPECACUANHA	ATMOSPHERIC
GORDONSTOUN	REPROACHFUL	FACULTATIVE	IMMORTALIZE	KLEPTOMANIA	BARYCENTRIC
GRAMMALOGUE	RESOURCEFUL	IMAGINATIVE	INTERNALIZE	LEPIDOPTERA	CABBALISTIC
HERBIVOROUS	RETINACULUM	INATTENTIVE	MARGINALIZE	MACERANDUBA	CACOGASTRIC
HIPPOCAMPUS	RINTHEREOUT	INEFFECTIVE	MATERIALIZE	MANGALSUTRA	CATACAUSTIC
HOMOGENEOUS	RUMBUSTIOUS	INEXPENSIVE	MERCHANDIZE	MANTELLETTA	CATACLYSMIC
HOMOPHONOUS	SAGITTARIUS	INFORMATIVE	MINIATURIZE	MAQUILADORA	CATALLACTIC
IGNOMINIOUS	SANGUINEOUS	INOFFENSIVE	MUNITIONIZE	MEGALOMANIA	CHARISMATIC
ILLUSTRIOUS	SAPONACEOUS	INOPERATIVE	MYTHOLOGIZE	MELANCHOLIA	CHOLINERGIC
IMPECUNIOUS	SARCOPHAGUS	INQUISITIVE	NATIONALIZE	MEMORABILIA	CLIMACTERIC
INCONGRUOUS	SCRIPTORIUM	INSENSITIVE	PERSONALIZE	MONONGAHELA	DEMOGRAPHIC
INCREDULOUS	SCRUMPTIOUS	INSTINCTIVE	PROSELYTIZE	MONOTREMATA	DEMOSTHENIC
INCUNABULUM	SCULLABOGUE	INSTRUCTIVE	RATIONALIZE	NYMPHOMANIA	DIAPHORETIC
INDUSTRIOUS	SEMPITERNUM	INTERACTIVE	RAZZAMATAZZ	ONEIRODYNIA	DICHROMATIC
INJUDICIOUS	SENTENTIOUS	LEGISLATIVE	ROMANTICIZE	ORCHESTRINA	DIORTHORTIC
INTERLINGUA	SEPTENARIUS	LOCORESTIVE	SOLILOQUIZE	PARLIPOMENA	DIPSOMANIAC
INTERREGNUM	SPONTANEOUS	MAKEBELIEVE	STANDARDIZE	PARONOMASIA	DYSLOGISTIC
INTRAVENOUS	STRADUARIUS	OBSTRUCTIVE	SYNCHRONIZE	PASSACAGLIA	ECTOTROPHIC
IRRELIGIOUS	STRAMINEOUS	PERSPECTIVE	SYSTEMATIZE	PASTEURELLA	EMPIRICUTIC
ISOMORPHOUS	STROPHILLUS	PRECONCEIVE		PENTHESILEA	ENDOTHERMIC
ISTIOPHORUS	STYLOPODIUM	PREDICATIVE	**11:11**	PERESTROIKA	ENDOTROPHIC
ITHYPHALLUS	SUBITANEOUS	PREPARATIVE	ABRACADABRA	PINACOTHECA	EPITHYMETIC
LARYNGISMUS	SUCCEDANEUM	PREROGATIVE	AGORAPHOBIA	PLEURODYNIA	EUCHARISTIC
LASERPICIUM	SUPERFLUOUS	PRESUMPTIVE	ALBUMINURIA	PROLEGOMENA	EUPHEMISTIC
LATERITIOUS	SUPPEDANEUM	PROGRESSIVE	AMPHISBAENA	PSEUDOLOGIA	GASTRONOMIC
LATIFUNDIUM	SYNCHRONOUS	PROHIBITIVE	AMPHISBOENA	RETINOSPORA	GRAVIMETRIC
LATROCINIUM	TAUROBOLIUM	PROSPECTIVE	ANACOLUTHIA	RHOPALOCERA	HEMOPHILIAC
LITTÉRATEUR	TEASPOONFUL	PROVOCATIVE	ANAESTHESIA	SAINTPAULIA	HIPPOCRATIC
MACHAIRODUS	TÉLÉFÉRIQUE	QUALITATIVE	ANTHESTERIA	SALTIMBOCCA	HOMEOPATHIC
MAGNANIMOUS	TEMPESTUOUS	RADIOACTIVE	ANTONOMASIA	SANSEVIERIA	HOMOTHERMIC
MEDIASTINUM	TENDENTIOUS	REBARBATIVE	APHANIPTERA	SAPROLEGNIA	HYDROPHOBIC
MEGATHERIUM	TORTICULLUS	RESTORATIVE	ATHARVAVEDA	SCANDANAVIA	HYDROSTATIC
MELLIFLUOUS	TRAGELAPHUS	RESTRICTIVE	BACCHANALIA	SCANDINAVIA	IDIOGRAPHIC
MENDELEVIUM	TREACHEROUS	RETRIBUTIVE	BALISTRARIA	SCHISTOSOMA	INAUTHENTIC
MERITORIOUS	TREACHETOUR	RETROACTIVE	BIELORUSSIA	SCLERODERMA	ISOELECTRIC
MICROVILLUS	TRIPHIBIOUS	SPECULATIVE	BODHISATTVA	SCOLOPENDRA	ITHYPHALLIC
MISCHIEVOUS	TRIPTOLEMUS	SUBJUNCTIVE	CALCEOLARIA	SCYPHISTOMA	LOGARITHMIC
MISCONSTRUE	TYRANNOSAUR	SUBSTANTIVE	CHAULMOOGRA	SELAGINELLA	MACROBIOTIC
MISTRUSTFUL	UNAMBIGUOUS	SUPERLATIVE	CHAULMOUGRA	SEPTICAEMIA	MACROSCOPIC
MONOCHINOUS	UNCONSCIOUS	TERREMOTIVE	CIRRHIPEDEA	SPERMATOZOA	MASOCHISTIC
MOUNTAINOUS	UNRIGHTEOUS	UNASSERTIVE	CIRRHIPEDIA	STEATOPYGIA	MEGALOMANIC
NECESSITOUS	UNUNQUADIUM	UNOBTRUSIVE	COLEORRHIZA	SUBUNGULATA	MELANCHOLIC
NOSTRADAMUS	VERTIGINOUS	GLIMMERGOWK	COLLECTANEA	TACHYCARDIA	METACENTRIC
NOTOTHERIUM	WATERCOLOUR	PICKYOUROWN	COLLENCHYMA	TARATANTARA	MICROSCOPIC
OPPROBRIOUS	WORLDFAMOUS	SPARROWHAWK	CONTRAYERVA	TEGUCICALPA	MODERNISTIC
OVERZEALOUS	XENODOCHIUM	THISTLEDOWN	CONVALLARIA	TIMBROMANIA	OCHLOCRATIC
OXYRHYNCHUS	XEROPHILOUS	WATEREDDOWN	DEMONOMANIA	TREPONEMATA	ORTHOPAEDIC
PANDEMONIUM	ZWISCHENZUG	POLYHYDROXY	DYAESTHESIA	TRICHINELLA	OSTEOPATHIC
PARABOLANUS	ACQUISITIVE	ARTIODACTYL	ENCEPHALOMA	TRICHOPTERA	PALEOLITHIC
PEDETENTOUS	AFFIRMATIVE	PTERODACTYL	ENCHONDROMA	TRYPANOSOMA	PARACROSTIC
PELARGONIUM	ALTERNATIVE	STRANGEWAYS	EPICHEIREMA	TURBELLARIA	PERIODONTIC
PERICARDIUM	APPELLATIVE	ACCLIMATIZE	ESCHERICHIA	UTRICULARIA	PERIPATETIC
PERITONAEUM	ATTRIBUTIVE	ALPHABETIZE	EXANTHEMATA	VALLAMBROSA	PESSIMISTIC
PERSPICUOUS	BODHISATTVA	ANESTHETIZE	FOTHERGILLA	VALLISNERIA	POLIORCETIC
PICTURESQUE	CARMINATIVE	ANTHOLOGIZE	GLOSSOLALIA	VIDEOCAMERA	POLYMORPHIC
PLANETARIUM	COHORTATIVE	CANNIBALIZE	GREGARINIDA	SENNACHERIB	POLYTECHNIC
PLATERESQUE	COMPARATIVE	CIRCULARIZE	HAEMOPHILIA	THINGAMABOB	PREHISTORIC
POLYTRICHUM	COMPETITIVE	COLEORRHIZA	HAGIOGRAPHA	ABIOGENETIC	PROTEROZOIC
PRECIPITOUS	CONSECUTIVE	COMPUTERIZE	HALLEFLINTA	ACATALECTIC	PSYCHEDELIC
			HEMERALOPIA		

PSYCHIATRIC	DUMBFOUNDED	OVEREXPOSED	UNCONCERNED	ACOLOUTHITE	CAPACITANCE
RIBONUCLEIC	EMBARRASSED	OVERLEARNED	UNCONFIRMED	ACQUISITIVE	CAPERNOITIE
SAPROPHYTIC	EMBELLISHED	OVERSTUFFED	UNCONNECTED	ACRIFLAVINE	CARABINIERE
SOLIPSISTIC	EMPTYHANDED	OVERWHELMED	UNCONQUERED	ACUPUNCTURE	CARMINATIVE
SPHRAGISTIC	ENFOULDERED	PARAMASTOID	UNCONTESTED	ADOLESCENCE	CASSITERITE
SYCOPHANTIC	ENLIGHTENED	PARATYPHOID	UNCONVERTED	AFFIRMATIVE	CATASTROPHE
SYMPATHETIC	ESTABLISHED	PERSONIFIED	UNCONVINCED	AGGLOMERATE	CATCHPHRASE
SYMPTOMATIC	EVISCERATED	PETTICOATED	UNDERCOOKED	AGGLUTINATE	CENTERPIECE
TELEGRAPHIC	EXAGGERATED	PLAGIARISED	UNDERGROUND	AGRICULTURE	CENTREPIECE
TELOCENTRIC	EXASPERATED	PREDESTINED	UNDERHANDED	AGUARDIENTE	CERARGYRITE
THERAPEUTIC	EXHILARATED	PREOCCUPIED	UNDERMANNED	AIGUILLETTE	CERTIFIABLE
TOXICOGENIC	EXPERIENCED	PRESSURIZED	UNDERSIGNED	AILUROPHILE	CERTIFICATE
TRANSURANIC	EXTROVERTED	PRESTRESSED	UNDERSTATED	ALEXANDRINE	CHANTARELLE
TYPOGRAPHIC	FORTUNELOUD	REFURBISHED	UNDERVALUED	ALEXANDRITE	CHANTERELLE
UNAUTHENTIC	FOULMOUTHED	REPRESENTED	UNDEVELOPED	ALPHABETIZE	CHARLEMAGNE
UNPATRIOTIC	FRIGATEBIRD	RIGHTANGLED	UNDIGNIFIED	ALTERNATIVE	CHIASTOLITE
UNREALISTIC	FULLBLOODED	RIGHTHANDED	UNDISCLOSED	AMBIVALENCE	CHICHEVACHE
XEROTHERMIC	GENERALIZED	SANDERSWOOD	UNDISGUISED	AMINOBUTENE	CHINOISERIE
ABBREVIATED	GINGERBREAD	SCANDALIZED	UNDISTURBED	AMPHETAMINE	CHIPPENDALE
ADULTERATED	GIRDLESTEAD	SCARABAEOID	UNENVELOPED	ANESTHETIZE	CHORDOPHONE
APPRENTICED	GOODNATURED	SCATTERGOOD	UNEXPLAINED	ANNABERGITE	CHRYSOPRASE
ARTICULATED	GROUNDSPEED	SELFIMPOSED	UNEXPRESSED	ANSWERPHONE	CILOFIBRATE
ASSIMILATED	HAEMORRHOID	SEVERALFOLD	UNFULFILLED	ANTECEDENCE	CIRCULARIZE
BADTEMPERED	HALFHEARTED	SHIPWRECKED	UNFURNISHED	ANTHOLOGIZE	CLANDESTINE
BATTLEFIELD	HANDCRAFTED	SHITTIMWOOD	UNIMPRESSED	ANTICYCLONE	CLINOCHLORE
BELEAGUERED	HANDICAPPED	SHORTHANDED	UNINHABITED	ANTISTROPHE	COALESCENCE
BERGSCHRUND	HARDPRESSED	SHOVELBOARD	UNINHIBITED	APLANOSPORE	COBBLESTONE
BROADMINDED	HAREBRAINED	SLEUTHHOUND	UNINITIATED	APOMORPHINE	COEXISTENCE
BROTHERHOOD	HARPSICHORD	SMORGASBORD	UNJUSTIFIED	APOPHYLLITE	COGNOSCENTE
CAMOUFLAGED	HEAVYHANDED	SPECIALIZED	UNMITIGATED	APPELLATIVE	COHORTATIVE
CAMPHORATED	HIGHPITCHED	SPORTSFIELD	UNMOTIVATED	APPLERINGIE	COINCIDENCE
CAPERNOITED	HIGHPOWERED	SPRINGBOARD	UNPERTURBED	APPRECIABLE	COLLABORATE
CASTELLATED	HISTORIATED	STEREOTYPED	UNPROTECTED	APPROPRIATE	COLLAPSIBLE
CENTREBOARD	HOMOGENIZED	STRAITLACED	UNPUBLISHED	APPROXIMATE	COMBUSTIBLE
CHAMBERMAID	HONEYCOMBED	STREAMLINED	UNQUALIFIED	ARTHROSPORE	COMEUPPANCE
CHARACINOID	HUMMINGBIRD	STRIKEBOUND	UNREHEARSED	ASSASSINATE	COMFORTABLE
CHICKENFEED	HUNDREDFOLD	STRINGBOARD	UNSATISFIED	ATHERINIDAE	COMMEMORATE
COLDBLOODED	HUSBANDLAND	STRONGYLOID	UNSATURATED	ATTRIBUTIVE	COMMENDABLE
COLOURBLIND	ILLMANNERED	SUBSTANDARD	UNSCHEDULED	AVERRUNCATE	COMMISERATE
COMPLICATED	ILLUMINATED	SUDETENLAND	UNSHELTERED	BADDELEYITE	COMMONPLACE
CONSTIPATED	IMPASSIONED	SUGARCOATED	UNSOLICITED	BANDEIRANTE	COMMONSENSE
CONSTRAINED	INDEXLINKED	SUNDRENCHED	UNSPECIFIED	BARBASTELLE	COMMUNICATE
CONSTRICTED	INTOXICATED	SUPERINTEND	UNSUPPORTED	BARBITURATE	COMPARATIVE
COORDINATED	INTROVERTED	SURTARBRAND	UNSURPASSED	BASKERVILLE	COMPETITIVE
COUNTERHAND	KINDHEARTED	SURTURBRAND	UNSUSPECTED	BATHYSPHERE	COMPUTERIZE
COUNTERMAND	LEATHERHEAD	SWITCHBOARD	UNSWEETENED	BEAUMONTAGE	CONCEIVABLE
COUNTRIFIED	LEATHERWOOD	SWITZERLAND	UNTRAMELLED	BENEDICTINE	CONCENTRATE
CRENELLATED	LEVELHEADED	SYNTHESIZED	UNVARNISHED	BENEFICIATE	CONCEPTICLE
CROSSLEGGED	LIGHTHEADED	TESSELLATED	UNWARRANTED	BENEVOLENCE	CONCORDANCE
CYCLOSTYLED	LONGAWAITED	THUNDERBIRD	VITAMINIZED	BIBLIOPHILE	CONCURRENCE
DEBILITATED	LONGSIGHTED	THUNDERHEAD	WARMHEARTED	BICARBONATE	CONDOTTIERE
DECAPITATED	LONGSLEEVED	TIGHTFISTED	WATERLOGGED	BILLIONAIRE	CONDOTTIORE
DEMORALIZED	MACADAMIZED	TIGHTLIPPED	WELLADVISED	BLANKURSINE	CONDUCTANCE
DEVITRIFIED	MALADJUSTED	TRANSFERRED	WELLBEHAVED	BLUNDERBORE	CONFABULATE
DILAPIDATED	MEDIUMSIZED	TRANSFORMED	WELLDEFINED	BOURGEOISIE	CONFARREATE
DISAFFECTED	MENTHOLATED	TRANSMITTED	WELLDRESSED	BOUTONNIERE	CONFEDERATE
DISCIPLINED	MICROSECOND	TRANSPORTED	WELLFOUNDED	BRAZZAVILLE	CONJUNCTURE
DISCOLOURED	MIDDLEHAND	TRICHINOSED	WRONGHEADED	BREASTPLATE	CONSECUTIVE
DISEMBODIED	MIDDLESIZED	TYROGLYPHID	ABSORPTANCE	BREATHALYSE	CONSEQUENCE
DISGRUNTLED	MOCKINGBIRD	UNANNOUNCED	ACCIPITRINE	BRISTLECONE	CONSIDERATE
DISHEVELLED	MONOGRAMMED	UNBLEMISHED	ACCLIMATISE	BUPRESTIDAE	CONSILIENCE
DISINCLINED	NEARSIGHTED	UNCASTRATED	ACCLIMATIZE	CALLITRICHE	CONSISTENCE
DISORIENTED	NEUTRALISED	UNCIVILISED	ACCOMMODATE	CAMALDOLITE	CONSOLIDATE
DISREGARDED	NOTICEBOARD	UNCIVILIZED	ACCOUNTABLE	CAMARADERIE	CONSTANTINE
DISTRIBUTED	OBLITERATED	UNCLUTTERED	ACCRESCENCE	CANDESCENCE	CONSTELLATE
DOWNHEARTED	OPINIONATED	UNCOMMITTED	ACCULTURATE	CANDIDATURE	CONSTERNATE
DREADLOCKED	OVERCROWDED	UNCONCEALED	ACKNOWLEDGE	CANNIBALIZE	CONSTUPRATE

CONSUMPTIVE	ELECTROLYTE	HALLUCINATE	INSENSITIVE	MASKALLONGE	PEREGRINATE
CONTAMINATE	ELEPHANTINE	HARDICANUTE	INSEPARABLE	MASTERPIECE	PERFORMANCE
CONTEMPLATE	EMMENAGOGUE	HATCHETTITE	INSOUCIANCE	MATERIALISE	PERLUSTRATE
CONTINGENCE	ENCAPSULATE	HECKELPHONE	INSTANTIATE	MATERIALIZE	PERMISSIBLE
CONTINUANCE	ENCUMBRANCE	HEPPLEWHITE	INSTINCTIVE	MATRICULATE	PERSISTENCE
CONTRIVANCE	ENFORCEABLE	HERRINGBONE	INSTRUCTIVE	MENTONNIÈRE	PERSONALIZE
CONVENIENCE	ENFRANCHISE	HIGHPROFILE	INSUPERABLE	MEPROBAMATE	PERSPECTIVE
CONVENTICLE	ENKEPHALINE	HOLLANDAISE	INTEMPERATE	MERCHANDISE	PETITMAITRE
CONVERGENCE	ENTABLATURE	HONEYSUCKLE	INTERACTIVE	MERCHANDIZE	PHILLIPSITE
CONVERTIBLE	EPIDIASCOPE	HOOTANANNIE	INTERCHANGE	MICROGAMETE	PHONOFIDDLE
COOPERATIVE	EPINEPHRINE	HOOTENANNIE	INTERCOURSE	MICROTUBULE	PHOTOSPHERE
COPPERPLATE	EQUIVALENCE	HORNSWOGGLE	INTERMINGLE	MILLIAMPERE	PHYLLOCLADE
CORNERSTONE	ERYTHROCYTE	HOSPITALIZE	INTERNALIZE	MILLIONAIRE	PICKELHAUBE
CORROBORATE	ESCARMOUCHE	HUCKSTERAGE	INTERNECINE	MINIATURIZE	PICTURESQUE
CORRUPTIBLE	ESPIEGLERIE	HYDROGENATE	INTERPOLATE	MISALLIANCE	PIEDMONTITE
COUNTENANCE	ESTRAMAZONE	HYDROPHIDAE	INTERRELATE	MISANTHROPE	PINNYWINKLE
COUNTERPANE	EUCALYPTOLE	HYPOTHECATE	INTERROGATE	MISCARRIAGE	PITCHBLENDE
COUNTRYSIDE	EXCRESCENCE	ICHTHYOLITE	INTERSPERSE	MISCONSTRUE	PLANTIGRADE
CRACOVIENNE	EXORBITANCE	IGNORANTINE	INTERVIEWEE	MISERICORDE	PLATERESQUE
CRÉMAILLÈRE	EXPECTORATE	ILLUMINANCE	INTOLERABLE	MISFEASANCE	PLATYRRHINE
CRESCENTADE	EXPENDITURE	IMAGINATIVE	INTOLERANCE	MOLLYCODDLE	PLEASURABLE
CROCIDOLITE	EXPOSTULATE	IMMORTALISE	INTRACTABLE	MONCHIQUITE	PLEBEIANISE
CRYSTALLINE	EXPROPRIATE	IMMORTALIZE	INVESTIGATE	MONOTHELITE	PLEISTOCENE
CRYSTALLISE	EXTEMPORISE	IMPERFORATE	INVESTITURE	MUNIFICENCE	PLOUGHSHARE
CRYSTALLIZE	EXTEMPORIZE	IMPERMEABLE	IRIDESCENCE	MUNITIONIZE	POCOCURANTE
CYCLOALKANE	EXTERMINATE	IMPERSONATE	IRREDUCIBLE	MUSKELLUNGE	POLYSTYRENE
DECARBONATE	EXTERNALIZE	IMPIGNORATE	IRREFUTABLE	MYTHOLOGIZE	POMEGRANATE
DECARBONIZE	EXTRAPOLATE	IMPLAUSIBLE	IRRELEVANCE	NAPHTHALENE	POMPELMOOSE
DECLARATIVE	FACULTATIVE	IMPORTUNATE	IRREPARABLE	NATIONALIZE	POMPELMOUSE
DECORTICATE	FAMILIARISE	IMPREGNABLE	IRREVERENCE	NATIONSTATE	PONTIFICATE
DECREPITATE	FAMILIARIZE	INADVISABLE	IRREVOCABLE	NECESSITATE	PORTERHOUSE
DECREPITUDE	FANFARONADE	INALIENABLE	ISOXSUPRINE	NIACINAMIDE	PORTRAITURE
DEGLUTINATE	FARTHINGALE	INATTENTIVE	JOSEPHINITE	NIGHTINGALE	PRACTICABLE
DEHORTATIVE	FASHIONABLE	INCAPSULATE	JUSTIFIABLE	NIKETHAMIDE	PRECIPITATE
DELIVERANCE	FERNITICKLE	INCARCERATE	KILOCALORIE	NONCHALANCE	PRECONCEIVE
DEMONSTRATE	FERRONNIÈRE	INCARNADINE	KITCHENETTE	NONFEASANCE	PREDICATIVE
DENDRACHATE	FIDDLEDEDEE	INCOHERENCE	LAMPROPHYRE	NORTHCLIFFE	PREDICTABLE
DENUMERABLE	FISSIONABLE	INCOMPOSITE	LATERIGRADE	NUMBERPLATE	PREDOMINATE
DEOXYGENATE	FLAMBOYANCE	INCORPORATE	LAUNDERETTE	OBSTRUCTIVE	PREEMINENCE
DEPHLEGMATE	FLAMBOYANTE	INCRIMINATE	LEATHERETTE	OBTEMPERATE	PREMEDITATE
DESCRIPTIVE	FLANNELETTE	INDEFINABLE	LECITHINASE	ODONTOPHORE	PREPARATIVE
DESEGREGATE	FLAVOURSOME	INDIVISIBLE	LEFTLUGGAGE	OFFICIALESE	PREPOLLENCE
DESERPIDINE	FLUOROSCOPE	INDOMITABLE	LEGIONNAIRE	OLIGOCHAETE	PREROGATIVE
DESEXUALIZE	FORBEARANCE	INDUBITABLE	LEGISLATIVE	OMMATOPHORE	PRESENTABLE
DESTABILIZE	FORBIDDANCE	INDUPLICATE	LEGISLATURE	OMNIPOTENCE	PRESUMPTIVE
DESTRUCTIVE	FORECLOSURE	INEFFECTIVE	LENTIGINOSE	OMNISCIENCE	PREVARICATE
DETERIORATE	FORESEEABLE	INELUCTABLE	LICKSPITTLE	OPALESCENCE	PREVENTABLE
DETERMINATE	FRANKLINITE	INEQUITABLE	LINDISFARNE	OPPIGNORATE	PRODIGALISE
DIRECTORATE	FRAUDULENCE	INESCAPABLE	LIVINGSTONE	ORCHESTRATE	PROFITEROLE
DISCERNIBLE	FURTHERANCE	INESTIMABLE	LOCORESTIVE	ORTHOCENTRE	PROGRESSIVE
DISCONTINUE	FURTHERMORE	INEXCITABLE	LOOSESTRIFE	OSTREOPHAGE	PROHIBITIVE
DISCOTHEQUE	FURTHERSOME	INEXCUSABLE	LUXULYANITE	OUTDISTANCE	PROLIFERATE
DISENTANGLE	GABERLUNZIE	INEXPENSIVE	LYCANTHROPE	OVERBALANCE	PROMPTITUDE
DISJUNCTIVE	GAMETOPHYTE	INFANTICIDE	LYCHNOSCOPE	PAMPELMOOSE	PROSELYTIZE
DISORGANIZE	GELSEMININE	INFLAMMABLE	MACROGAMETE	PAMPELMOUSE	PROSPECTIVE
DISPENSABLE	GENOUILLÈRE	INFORMATIVE	MAINTENANCE	PARTICIPATE	PROVOCATIVE
DISPERSABLE	GEOSYNCLINE	INGRATITUDE	MAISTERDOME	PASTOURELLE	PUBLISHABLE
DISPLEASURE	GESTICULATE	INHABITABLE	MAKEBELIEVE	PELOPONNESE	PULCHRITUDE
DISSEMINATE	GLADWELLISE	INHERITANCE	MALAKATOONE	PENICILLATE	PURPRESTURE
DISSIMULATE	GLUCOSAMINE	INNUMERABLE	MALEVOLENCE	PENSIONABLE	PYRARGYRITE
DISTINCTIVE	GRAMMALOGUE	INOFFENSIVE	MALFEASANCE	PENTATHLETE	PYTHONESQUE
DISTURBANCE	GREENBOTTLE	INOPERATIVE	MALPRACTICE	PENTONVILLE	QUALITATIVE
DOCTRINAIRE	GREENOCKITE	INOPPORTUNE	MANTELPIECE	PENULTIMATE	QUARRELSOME
DODECASTYLE	GUESSTIMATE	INQUISITIVE	MANUFACTURE	PERAMBULATE	RADIOACTIVE
DOMESTICATE	GUTTERSNIPE	INSCRUTABLE	MARGINALIZE	PERCEPTIBLE	RATATOUILLE
EARTHENWARE	GUTTURALISE	INSECTICIDE	MARIVAUDAGE	PERCHLORATE	RATIOCINATE
ELECTROCUTE	HAEMORRHAGE	INSECTIVORE	MARKETPLACE	PERCIPIENCE	RATIONALIZE

RATTLESNAKE	SPECULATIVE	UNASSERTIVE	CHRISTENING	MONEYMAKING	WIDERANGING
REASSURANCE	SPERMOPHILE	UNAVAILABLE	CIRCULATING	MUDSLINGING	WINDSURFING
REBARBATIVE	SPESSARTITE	UNAVOIDABLE	CONSIDERING	NEGOTIATING	WITHHOLDING
RECIPROCATE	SPIFFLICATE	UNBREAKABLE	CONTRASTING	NEIGHBORING	WOODCARVING
RECONNOITRE	SPIROCHAETE	UNCOUNTABLE	COUNSELLING	NEVERENDING	ZWISCHENZUG
RECOVERABLE	SPRINGHOUSE	UNCRUSHABLE	DETERMINING	NEWSCASTING	ALLELOMORPH
RECRIMINATE	STANDARDIZE	UNDERCHARGE	DEVASTATING	NIPFARTHING	CARDIOGRAPH
RECTIFIABLE	STEGANOPODE	UNDESIRABLE	DISAGREEING	ORIGINATING	CESAREWITCH
REDOUBTABLE	STELLIONATE	UNDRINKABLE	DISFIGURING	OUTSTANDING	CHEESECLOTH
REDUPLICATE	STENOCHROME	UNENDURABLE	DISPARAGING	OVERBEARING	CLAIRSCHACH
REFOCILLATE	STEREOSCOPE	UNFAVORABLE	DISQUIETING	OVERFISHING	COTTONMOUTH
REFRIGERATE	STETHOSCOPE	UNFLAPPABLE	DISTRESSING	OVERFLOWING	DISTINGUISH
REGRETTABLE	STRANGULATE	UNFORTUNATE	DOMINEERING	OVERHANGING	HAMMERCLOTH
REGURGITATE	STRETCHABLE	UNGETATABLE	DRESSMAKING	OVERLAPPING	HORSERADISH
REINCARNATE	STROBOSCOPE	UNOBTRUSIVE	DRYCLEANING	OVERMANNING	INTERGROWTH
REMEMBRANCE	SUBJUNCTIVE	UNPALATABLE	DUPLICATING	OVERTURNING	JAMAHIRIYAH
REMONSTRATE	SUBMERGENCE	UNPRINTABLE	ENCOURAGING	OVERWEENING	KOMMERSBUCH
RENAISSANCE	SUBMULTIPLE	UNSHAKEABLE	ENCROACHING	PAINKILLING	MARLBOROUGH
REORIENTATE	SUBORDINATE	UNSPEAKABLE	ENGHALSKRUG	PAINSTAKING	MIDDLEMARCH
REPLACEABLE	SUBSISTENCE	UNSTOPPABLE	ENGINEERING	PATRONISING	NIGHTMARISH
RESEMBLANCE	SUBSTANTIVE	UNTHINKABLE	ENTHRALLING	PATRONIZING	NOVELETTISH
RESPECTABLE	SUFFRAGETTE	UNTOUCHABLE	EPOCHMAKING	PENETRATING	PERISTALITH
RESPONSIBLE	SUGGESTIBLE	UNUTTERABLE	EVERLASTING	PERSEVERING	PHOTOFINISH
RESTORATIVE	SUMMERHOUSE	UNWHOLESOME	EXTENUATING	PROTRACTING	POLLENBRUSH
RESTRICTIVE	SUPERCHARGE	VARSOVIENNE	EYECATCHING	QUARRELLING	PSEUDOMORPH
RESTRUCTURE	SUPERCHERIE	VENDEMIAIRE	FACTFINDING	QUESTIONING	RAMGUNSHOCH
RESUSCITATE	SUPERIMPOSE	VENTURESOME	FARREACHING	REGISTERING	REICHENBACH
RETRACTABLE	SUPERLATIVE	VERBIGERATE	FASCINATING	SCAFFOLDING	SCARBOROUGH
RETRIBUTIVE	SUPERSCRIBE	VERMICULITE	FLOURISHING	SCATTERING	SCHRECKLICH
RETRIEVABLE	SUPERSEDERE	VESUVIANITE	FLUCTUATING	SCUPPERNONG	SEISMOGRAPH
RETROACTIVE	SUSCEPTIBLE	VICHYSOISSE	FOOTBALLING	SHOPLIFTING	SEVENTEENTH
REVENDICATE	SUSTAINABLE	VICISSITUDE	FOOTWASHING	SHORTCOMING	SILVERSMITH
REVERBERATE	SWALLOWABLE	VINAIGRETTE	FORECASTING	SHOWJUMPING	SPATTERDASH
RIDDLEMEREE	SYNCHRONISE	VINBLASTINE	FOREWARNING	SIGHTSEEING	STANDOFFISH
ROBESPIERRE	SYNCHRONIZE	VINCRISTINE	FORTHCOMING	SMOULDERING	STEREOGRAPH
RODOMONTADE	SYSTEMATIZE	WATERCOURSE	FRIGHTENING	SNORKELLING	SYMPOSIARCH
ROMANTICIZE	TAGLIATELLE	WEIGHBRIDGE	FRUSTRATING	SPACESAVING	SYNCHROMESH
ROTOGRAVURE	TARRADIDDLE	WENSLEYDALE	FUNDRAISING	SPLUTTERING	TECTIBRANCH
ROTTENSTONE	TAUTOCHRONE	WHITSUNTIDE	GAMMERSTANG	STOCKTAKING	THENCEFORTH
SACHERTORTE	TÉLÉFÉRIQUE	WILBERFORCE	GOODLOOKING	SUFFOCATING	TWELVEMONTH
SADDLEHORSE	TEMPERATURE	WINDOWFRAME	HAIRRAISING	SURROUNDING	UNDERGROWTH
SARCENCHYME	TERPSICHORE	WINDOWLEDGE	HANDWRITING	TANTALIZING	WATERSPLASH
SCHISTOSOME	TERREMOTIVE	WORKMANLIKE	HANGGLIDING	TELEWORKING	WISHTONWISH
SCHOTTISCHE	THALIDOMIDE	YELLOWSTONE	HARDHITTING	THINGAMAJIG	WORRYTROUGH
SCINTILLATE	THALLOPHYTE	INFANGTHIEF	HARDWORKING	THINGUMAJIG	YELLOWPLUSH
SCITAMINEAE	THAUMATROPE	MANTELSHELF	HIBERNATING	THREATENING	ARRIVEDERCI
SCOPOLAMINE	THEOBROMINE	SHOWERPROOF	HIGHRANKING	TIMEKEEPING	BANGLADESHI
SCULLABOGUE	THERAPEUTAE	ADVERTISING	HORSERACING	TIMESHARING	CHONDROSTEI
SEIGNIORAGE	THERMOPYLAE	AGGRAVATING	HORSERIDING	TOBOGGANING	COGNOSCENTI
SELFDEFENCE	THESMOTHETE	ALTERNATING	HUMILIATING	TRESPASSING	DOUROUCOULI
SELFSERVICE	TICKTACKTOE	APPROACHING	IDENTIFYING	TYPESETTING	MELANOCHROI
SEPIOSTAIRE	TIGGYWINKLE	ASTONISHING	INFURIATING	UNBEFITTING	MISSISSIPPI
SEQUESTRATE	TOWNSPEOPLE	BACKPACKING	INSINUATING	UNDEMANDING	PLAGIOSTOMI
SERICULTURE	TOXOPHILITE	BACKSLIDING	INTERESTING	UNDERTAKING	SCHWARMEREI
SERVICEABLE	TRACASSERIE	BALLBEARING	INTERLACING	UNDESERVING	SVARABHAKTI
SESQUIOXIDE	TRANSFIGURE	BESTSELLING	INTERVENING	UNFLINCHING	APPARATCHIK
SHAKESPEARE	TREASONABLE	BEWILDERING	LABORSAVING	UNREASONING	CANDLESTICK
SHEATHKNIFE	TRINCOMALEE	BOOKBINDING	LAWBREAKING	UNRELENTING	CHOCKABLOCK
SHORTCHANGE	TRIUMVIRATE	BOOKKEEPING	LENGTHENING	UNREMITTING	COUNTERSINK
SILLIMANITE	TROPOSPHERE	BRANDENBURG	LONGLASTING	UNSHRINKING	CRACKERJACK
SINISTRORSE	TROUBLESOME	BROBDINGNAG	LONGRUNNING	UNWELCOMING	DEUTSCHMARK
SKILLIGALEE	TRYPANOSOME	CALCULATING	MANEUVERING	VACILLATING	DIAMONDBACK
SKILLIGOLEE	TURRICULATE	CALENDERING	MECKLENBURG	VOTERIGGING	DOUBLECHECK
SMITHSONITE	ULOTRICHALE	CAPTIVATING	MERRYMAKING	WAINSCOTING	FLANKERBACK
SNICKERSNEE	ULTRAMARINE	CARAVANNING	MINISTERING	WAREHOUSING	GIGGLESTICK
SOLILOQUIZE	UNALIENABLE	CHALLENGING	MISSPELLING	WATERSKIING	GIGGLESWICK
SPANGCOCKLE	UNALTERABLE	CHITTERLING	MISSPELLING	WELLMEANING	GLIMMERGOWK

KIDDLEYWINK	EXCEPTIONAL	RHAPSODICAL	DIASCORDIUM	ACCLAMATION	COMMINATION
KINNIKINICK	EXPONENTIAL	SACRAMENTAL	DITHELETISM	ACCLIMATION	COMMUTATION
KIRKPATRICK	FINGERSTALL	SACRIFICIAL	DOLABRIFORM	ACQUISITION	COMPETITION
LATTICEWORK	FLICKERTAIL	SECRETARIAL	EINSTEINIUM	ADUMBRATION	COMPILATION
LEATHERBACK	FUNDAMENTAL	SELFCONTROL	ENDOCARDIUM	AESCULAPIAN	COMPOSITION
LEATHERNECK	GEOMETRICAL	SEMPITERNAL	EQUILIBRIUM	AFFECTATION	COMPOTATION
MUSCHELKALK	GESTATORIAL	SENSATIONAL	FAVOURITISM	AFFILIATION	COMPUNCTION
NEEDLESTICK	GNATHONICAL	SENTIMENTAL	FITZWILLIAM	AFFIRMATION	COMPUTATION
QUARTERBACK	GRAMMATICAL	SEXOLOGICAL	FLORILEGIUM	AFFLIICTION	CONFUTATION
QUARTERDECK	GROUNDSWELL	SPERMICIDAL	GAMETANGIUM	AFGHANISTAN	CONGRESSMAN
REALPOLITIK	GUADALCANAL	STATISTICAL	HOOLIGANISM	AGGRAVATION	CONJUGATION
SHUTTLECOCK	HEXADECIMAL	STILBESTROL	ILLUSIONISM	AGGREGATION	CONJUNCTION
SINGLESTICK	HOMOTHERMAL	STRATEGICAL	IMPERIALISM	AIRCRAFTMAN	CONNOTATION
SPARROWHAWK	IDEOLOGICAL	SUBSTANTIAL	INCUNABULUM	ALBIGENSIAN	CONSOLATION
SPATTERDOCK	IMPLEMENTAL	SUBTROPICAL	INTERREGNUM	ALCYONARIAN	CONSUMPTION
STEEPLEJACK	IMPRACTICAL	SUPERFICIAL	LASERPICIUM	ALIFANFARON	CONTRACTION
STICKLEBACK	INCORPOREAL	SYMMETRICAL	LATIFUNDIUM	ALLEVIATION	CONTRAPTION
STRINGYBARK	INCREMENTAL	TEASPOONFUL	LATROCINIUM	ALTERCATION	CONURBATION
TIDDLEYWINK	INEFFECTUAL	TERRESTRIAL	MALAPROPISM	ALTERNATION	CONVOCATION
WEATHERCOCK	INESSENTIAL	TERRITORIAL	MARCONIGRAM	AMYLOPECTIN	CONVOLUTION
AFTERSCHOOL	INFLUENTIAL	TESTIMONIAL	MATERIALISM	ANTHOCYANIN	COOPERATION
ALLEGORICAL	INTENTIONAL	THEOLOGICAL	MEDIASTINUM	ANTINEUTRON	COPROPHAGAN
AMOBARBITAL	INTERCOSTAL	THEORETICAL	MEGATHERIUM	ANTIQUARIAN	CORPORATION
AMPLEXICAUL	INTRADERMAL	TOPLOFTICAL	MENDELEVIUM	APOLLONICON	CORRELATION
ANISOCERCAL	ISOLECITHAL	TRADITIONAL	MICHURINISM	APPELLATION	CORRUGATION
ARCHEGONIAL	KINDERSPIEL	TRANSDERMAL	NATIONALISM	APPLICATION	COUNTERSIGN
ARTHRAPODAL	KNUCKLEBALL	TRANSVERSAL	NOTOTHERIUM	APPROBATION	CREPITATION
ARTIODACTYL	KRIEGSSPIEL	TRIMESTRIAL	NUCLEOPLASM	ARBITRATION	CRESTFALLEN
AUDIOVISUAL	MAGISTERIAL	TROMPELOEIL	OFFICIALDOM	ARCHENTERON	CROCODILIAN
AXEROPHTHOL	MATRIARCHAL	UNEMOTIONAL	OPPORTUNISM	ARGATHELIAN	CROMWELLIAN
BEHAVIOURAL	MATRIMONIAL	UNEQUIVOCAL	ORIENTALISM	ARGENTINIAN	CRUCIFIXION
BIOCHEMICAL	MINISTERIAL	UNESSENTIAL	OSTRACODERM	ASSEMBLYMAN	CULMINATION
BUTTONQUAIL	MISTRUSTFUL	UNPRACTICAL	PANDEMONIUM	ASSIGNATION	CULTIVATION
CATEGORICAL	MONARCHICAL	VESPERTINAL	PATERNALISM	ASSOCIATION	DECLAMATION
CENTRIFUGAL	MONOLINGUAL	WHEREWITHAL	PELARGONIUM	ATTENUATION	DECLARATION
CENTRIPETAL	MULTIRACIAL	WHITECHAPEL	PERICARDIUM	ATTESTATION	DEFOLIATION
CHLOROPHYLL	MYCOLOGICAL	ABSENTEEISM	PERITONAEUM	ATTRIBUTION	DEFORMATION
CHOLESTEROL	NEANDERTHAL	ACADEMICISM	PLANETARIUM	AUGUSTINIAN	DEGLUTITION
CITLALEPETL	NONSENSICAL	ACINACIFORM	POLYTRICHUM	AURIGNACIAN	DEGRADATION
CITRONELLAL	NUTRITIONAL	ADOPTIANISM	PROSELYTISM	BANNOCKBURN	DEHYDRATION
COCKLESHELL	OBSTETRICAL	ADOPTIONISM	QUADRENNIUM	BELLEROPHON	DEIFICATION
CONDITIONAL	ONTOLOGICAL	AGNOSTICISM	RETINACULUM	BELORUSSIAN	DELECTATION
CONJECTURAL	OPERATIONAL	AMERICANISM	REVISIONISM	BENEDICTION	DELICTATION
CONTINENTAL	PARACETAMOL	ANACHRONISM	ROMANTICISM	BESSARABIAN	DELINEATION
CONTRACTUAL	PARADOXICAL	ANTEPENDIUM	SCALPRIFORM	BIFURCATION	DEMARCATION
CONTUBERNAL	PARAMEDICAL	ANTIRRHINUM	SCOLECIFORM	BUSINESSMAN	DEMIBASTION
COPROSTEROL	PARTICIPIAL	APODYTERIUM	SCRIPTORIUM	CALCULATION	DEPORTATION
COUNTERFOIL	PATRIARCHAL	ARCHEGONIUM	SEMPITERNUM	CALIBRATION	DEPREDATION
CYLINDRICAL	PEDAGOGICAL	ASPERGILLUM	SHUNAMITISM	CALLIPYGEAN	DEPRIVATION
DEFERENTIAL	PENITENTIAL	ASPERSORIUM	STEGANOGRAM	CALLISTEMON	DERELICTION
DETRIMENTAL	PENTECOSTAL	ASPHETERISM	STYLOPODIUM	CAMERAWOMAN	DESCRIPTION
DICTATORIAL	PHARISAICAL	ASTIGMATISM	SUCCEDANEUM	CAMEROONIAN	DESECRATION
DIMENSIONAL	PISCATORIAL	BLOODSTREAM	SUPPEDANEUM	CAMPESTRIAN	DESELECTION
DIMERCAPROL	PREJUDICIAL	CALIFORNIUM	SYNCHRONISM	CAPTIVATION	DESICCATION
DIPHYCERCAL	PRIMIGENIAL	CANNIBALISM	SYNDICALISM	CAROLINGIAN	DESIGNATION
DIRECTIONAL	PROMOTIONAL	CARBORUNDUM	TAUROBOLIUM	CELEBRATION	DESPERATION
DISAPPROVAL	PROPHETICAL	CATHOLICISM	TETRADRACHM	CENTENARIAN	DESTINATION
DISGRACEFUL	PROVISIONAL	CHILLINGHAM	TSCHERNOSEM	CEREBRATION	DESTITUTION
DISTASTEFUL	PTERODACTYL	CLADOSPORUM	UNUNQUADIUM	CHAIRPERSON	DESTRUCTION
DISTRUSTFUL	PURITANICAL	COENOBITISM	VOLUNTARISM	CHAMBERLAIN	DETESTATION
DRAGGLETAIL	QUADRENNIAL	COLONIALISM	WHITEBOYISM	CHRISMATION	DEVALUATION
DUNIEWASSAL	REAPPRAISAL	COLUMBARIUM	XENODOCHIUM	CHRYSAROBIN	DEVASTATION
EDUCATIONAL	RECESSIONAL	COMMUNALISM	ABECEDARIAN	CIRCULATION	DIATESSARON
EGOTISTICAL	REPROACHFUL	CONDOMINIUM	ABLACTATION	CLEANSHAVEN	DIATESSERON
EQUILATERAL	RESIDENTIAL	CONSUMERISM	ABOMINATION	COAGULATION	DICOTYLEDON
EQUINOCTIAL	RESOURCEFUL	CREMATORIUM	ABSTRACTION	COLLOCATION	DIFFRACTION
EVANGELICAL	REVERENTIAL	DACTYLOGRAM	ACADEMICIAN	COMBINATION	DISILLUSION

DISIMPRISON	GIBBERELLIN	LUBRICATION	PROPOSITION	SUPERVISION	RIFACIMENTO
DISJUNCTION	GODFORSAKEN	MACHINATION	PROROGATION	SUPPOSITION	RINFORZANDO
DISLOCATION	GORDONSTOUN	MAGLEMOSIAN	PROSECUTION	SUPPRESSION	SALTIMBANCO
DISPOSITION	GRAVITATION	MALEDICTION	PROSTRATION	SUPPURATION	SEXTODECIMO
DISPUTATION	GUBERNATION	MALEFACTION	PROTRACTION	SUSURRATION	SRANANTONGO
DISSIPATION	HAEMOGLOBIN	MALFUNCTION	PROVOCATION	SWORDSWOMAN	VIOLINCELLO
DISSOLUTION	HANDWRITTEN	MANCIPATION	PUBLICATION	SYNCOPATION	VIOLONCELLO
DISTINCTION	HARIOLATION	MANUMISSION	PUNCTUATION	SYNDICATION	WHISKERANDO
DISTRACTION	HEARTBROKEN	MASTICATION	QUARRINGTON	TERMINATION	CITIZENSHIP
DOWNTRODDEN	HETEROSCIAN	MAURETANIAN	RABELAISIAN	TETRAHEDRON	COMRADESHIP
DRAUGHTSMAN	HIBERNATION	MAURITANIAN	RADIOCARBON	THISTLEDOWN	DIPTEROCARP
DUPLICATION	HOHENLINDEN	MENDELSSOHN	RAPSCALLION	THOROUGHPIN	FISHANDCHIP
DYSFUNCTION	HOLOTHURIAN	MENSURATION	RASTAFARIAN	THROGMORTON	LECTURESHIP
ECCALEOBION	HOMOIOUSIAN	MERCHANTMAN	REALIZATION	THYROTROPIN	OARSMANSHIP
EDIFICATION	HUMGRUFFIAN	METRICATION	REANIMATION	TIRONENSIAN	PARTNERSHIP
EGALITARIAN	HUMILIATION	MICTURITION	RECANTATION	TITILLATION	PREMIERSHIP
EJACULATION	HYDROCARBON	MISBEGOTTEN	RECLAMATION	TORRIDONIAN	SCHOLARSHIP
ELABORATION	HYOPLASTRON	MOLESTATION	RECOGNITION	TOSTICATION	SHOWMANSHIP
ELECTRICIAN	HYPERBOREAN	MORGENSTERN	RECONDITION	TOURBILLION	SPONSORSHIP
ELEUTHERIAN	HYPHENATION	MOXIBUSTION	REFORMATION	TRANSACTION	THUNDERCLAP
ELIMINATION	HYPOTENSION	MOZAMBIQUAN	REITERATION	TRANSFERRIN	TRUSTEESHIP
ELIZABETHAN	IDOLIZATION	MUNCHHAUSEN	REPUDIATION	TRANSFUSION	WHISTLESTOP
ELUCIDATION	IMAGINATION	MURMURATION	REQUISITION	TRANSLATION	WORKMANSHIP
EMBARKATION	IMMIGRATION	NEEDLEWOMAN	RESERVATION	TRENCHERMAN	ACCELERATOR
EMBROCATION	IMPLICATION	NEGOTIATION	RESIGNATION	TREPIDATION	ACCUMULATOR
ENCHIRIDION	IMPORTATION	NICKELODEON	RESPIRATION	TRIBULATION	ADJUDICATOR
ENNEAHEDRON	IMPRECATION	OBSERVATION	RESTITUTION	TRINIDADIAN	AMELANCHIER
ENUMERATION	IMPRECISION	OBSTRICTION	RESTORATION	TRINITARIAN	ANAXIMANDER
ENUNCIATION	INATTENTION	OBSTRUCTION	RESTRICTION	TYPEWRITTEN	ANTECHAMBER
ERADICATION	INCANTATION	OCTASTICHON	RETALIATION	TYRONENSIAN	ANTIBURGHER
ERIODENDRON	INCARNATION	ONOMASTICON	RETARDATION	ULTRAMODERN	ARBITRAGEUR
ERYMANTHIAN	INCLINATION	ORCHESTRION	RETRIBUTION	UNCHRISTIAN	ARQUEBUSIER
EUCHROMATIN	INDENTATION	ORGANIZAION	REVALUATION	UNIFICATION	AUXANOMETER
EVAPORATION	INDIGESTION	ORIENTATION	ROSICRUCIAN	UTILITARIAN	AZOTOBACTER
EVENTRATION	INDIGNATION	ORIGINATION	RUMFRUCTION	UTILIZATION	BACKBENCHER
EXAMINATION	INEBRIATION	OSCILLATION	RUMGUMPTION	VACCINATION	BACKFIELDER
EXCLAMATION	INFANTRYMAN	OSTENTATION	SABBATARIAN	VACILLATION	BARNSTORMER
EXHORTATION	INFATUATION	OXODIZATION	SALESPERSON	VALEDICTION	BEACHCOMBER
EXONERATION	INFESTATION	PALESTINIAN	SALVADORIAN	VARANGARIAN	BELLYTIMBER
EXOSKELETON	INFORMATION	PANOMPHAEAN	SCHECKLATON	VARIEGATION	BIRDWATCHER
EXPECTATION	INOCULATION	PARTURITION	SEGREGATION	VARIOLATION	BLACKMAILER
EXPLANATION	INQUISITION	PENETRATION	SEPTENTRION	VASOPRESSIN	BLOCKBUSTER
EXPLORATION	INSCRIPTION	PERCOLATION	SIGHTSCREEN	VENTILATION	BLOODSUCKER
EXPURGATION	INSINUATION	PERDUELLION	SINGAPOREAN	VINDICATION	BREADWINNER
EXTENUATION	INSPIRATION	PERFORATION	SKIMMINGTON	VIVISECTION	BROADCASTER
EXTRADITION	INSTIGATION	PERIGORDIAN	SLUMGULLION	WALDSTERBEN	BULLFIGHTER
FABRICATION	INSTITUTION	PERMUTATION	SMITHSONIAN	WASHERWOMAN	BURGOMASTER
FASCINATION	INSTRUCTION	PERSECUTION	SMOKESCREEN	WATEREDDOWN	BUSHWHACKER
FAUXBOURDON	INTEGRATION	PHONETICIAN	SOUTHAMPTON	WESTPHALIAN	CAPACITATOR
FLUCTUATION	INTERACTION	PICKYOUROWN	SPECULATION	WHITTINGTON	CARBURETTOR
FOMENTATION	INTERLEUKIN	POLICEWOMAN	SPOKESWOMAN	WINTERGREEN	CATERPILLAR
FORESHORTEN	IRRADIATION	POLLINATION	SPORTSWOMAN	WORKSTATION	CAULIFLOWER
FORESTATION	JACTITATION	POTAMOGETON	SPRINGCLEAN	ZOOPLANKTON	CENTURIATOR
FORFOUGHTEN	KAMELAUKION	PRELIBATION	STAGFLATION	ZOROASTRIAN	CHANTICLEER
FORMULATION	KATABOTHRON	PREMONITION	STIMULATION	AMONTILLADO	CHARGEPAYER
FORNICATION	KATAVOTHRON	PREPARATION	STIPULATION	ARCHIPELAGO	CHEERLEADER
FRENCHWOMAN	KETAVOTHRON	PREPOSITION	STOCKHAUSEN	BRAGGADOCIO	CHILDMINDER
FRENCHWOMEN	KIMERIDGIAN	PRESUMPTION	STOOLPIGEON	CAPRICCIOSO	CHOIRMASTER
FROSTBITTEN	KOTABOTHRON	PRETERITION	STYLIZATION	CHIAROSCURO	CHRISTOPHER
FRUSTRATION	LAMENTATION	PROCREATION	STYMPHALIAN	CINQUECENTO	CHRONOMETER
FULMINATION	LEGERDEMAIN	PROCRUSTEAN	SUBDIVISION	COMPRIMARIO	CIRCUMCISER
FUSTILARIAN	LEGISLATION	PROGRESSION	SUBJUGATION	ESTRANGHELO	CLIFFHANGER
GALLOVIDIAN	LEPIDOSIREN	PROHIBITION	SUBLIMATION	INTERNUNCIO	COLORIMETER
GEGENSCHEIN	LIBERTARIAN	PROLETARIAN	SUBPANATION	KILIMANJARO	COMMENTATOR
GENTLEWOMAN	LILLIPUTIAN	PROLOCUTION	SUBTRACTION	PRESTISSIMO	COMPTROLLER
GENUFLEXION	LIQUIDATION	PROPAGATION	SUFFOCATION	PUNCHINELLO	CONCILIATOR
GERMINATION	LOUISIANIAN	PROPAGATION	SUPERALTERN	RALLENTANDO	CONDITIONER

CONNOISSEUR	HOUSEMOTHER	RECTILINEAR	TYPOGRAPHER	CACOPHONOUS	EPAMINONDAS
CONSPIRATOR	ILLUSTRATOR	RIGHTHANDER	TYRANNOSAUR	CALLANETICS	EPANALEPSIS
CONSTRICTOR	ILLYWHACKER	RIGHTWINGER	UNDERWRITER	CALLOUSNESS	EREMACAUSIS
CONSTRUCTOR	INCINERATOR	ROCKEFELLER	UPHOLSTERER	CARDOPHAGUS	EURHYTHMICS
CONTRIBUTOR	INDIARUBBER	RUDESHEIMER	VOLKSKAMMER	CAREFULNESS	EVASIVENESS
CRACKHALTER	INFILTRATOR	SALINOMETER	VOORTREKKER	CARNAPTIOUS	EXPEDITIOUS
CREPUSCULAR	INTERCEPTOR	SALVOGUNNER	WASHLEATHER	CARNIVOROUS	EXTROGENOUS
CRITICASTER	INTERPRETER	SCAREMONGER	WATERCOLOUR	CARSICKNESS	FARINACEOUS
CULVERINEER	INTERRUPTER	SCOREKEEPER	WESTMINSTER	CATACHRESIS	FARRAGINOUS
DEERSTALKER	INTERVIEWER	SCOUTMASTER	WHITECOLLAR	CATADROMOUS	FATUOUSNESS
DEGRINGOLER	INTOXIMETER	SCREWDRIVER	WHITLEATHER	CENTUMVIRUS	FEATURELESS
DENOMINATOR	INVIGILATOR	SEMITRAILER	WINDBREAKER	CEREMONIOUS	FILAMENTOUS
DINNYHAUSER	JERRYMANDER	SHAREHOLDER	WINDCHEATER	CLEANLINESS	FISHMONGERS
DINNYHAYSER	KWASHIORKOR	SHINPLASTER	WITCHDOCTOR	CLIOMETRICS	FLIRTATIOUS
DISBELIEVER	LAMMERGEIER	SHIPBUILDER	XYLOGRAPHER	COMESTIBLES	FOOLISHNESS
DISENCUMBER	LAMMERGEYER	SKIDBLADNIR	ABIOGENESIS	COMFORTLESS	FOREFATHERS
DISSERTATOR	LAMPLIGHTER	SLEEPWALKER	ACCESSORIES	COMPENDIOUS	FORGIVENESS
DISTRIBUTOR	LEADSWINGER	SLUMBERWEAR	ACRIMONIOUS	COMPLIMENTS	FORLORNNESS
DRINKDRIVER	LEASEHOLDER	SMALLHOLDER	ACTUALITIES	CONCISENESS	FOUNDATIONS
DUSTWRAPPER	LIQUIDAMBAR	SOCKDALAGER	ADULLAMITES	CONDOLENCES	FRUGIVOROUS
EARTHSHAKER	LITTÉRATEUR	SOCKDOLAGER	ADVENTURESS	CONDUCTRESS	FURNISHINGS
ELECTROLIER	LOGOGRAPHER	SOCKDOLIGER	ADVENTUROUS	CONSPICUOUS	FURTIVENESS
EMMENTHALER	LOUDSPEAKER	SOCKDOLOGER	AERONAUTICS	CONSUMABLES	GALLIGANTUS
ENTERTAINER	LUXEMBURGER	SOUTHWESTER	AESCULAPIUS	CONTENTIOUS	GALLOWGLASS
ESTABLISHER	MANIPULATOR	SPECTACULAR	AGONOTHETES	CONTRETEMPS	GAMOGENESIS
EXECUTIONER	MASQUERADER	SPEEDOMETER	AIRSICKNESS	CONVOLVULUS	GENUINENESS
EXTORTIONER	METALWORKER	SPELLBINDER	ALBUGINEOUS	CONVULSIONS	GHASTLINESS
FAIRWEATHER	MINESWEEPER	SPITSTICKER	AMMOPHILOUS	COORDINATES	GRALLATORES
FAULTFINDER	MINNESINGER	STADTHOLDER	ANADIPLOSIS	CORDWAINERS	HABILIMENTS
FIELDWORKER	MISBEHAVIOR	STAKEHOLDER	ANAGNORISIS	CORINTHIANS	HAUGHTINESS
FILLIBUSTER	MISDEMEANOR	STALLHOLDER	ANAPHYLAXIS	CORRECTNESS	HEALTHINESS
FIRECRACKER	MOISTURIZER	STANDPATTER	ANAPLEROSIS	COULOMMIERS	HELPFULNESS
FIRELIGHTER	MONEYLENDER	STEAMROLLER	ANASTOMOSIS	COURTLINESS	HEMORRHOIDS
FLUOROMETER	MONONUCLEAR	STEINBERGER	ANDROGENOUS	COXWAINLESS	HERBIVOROUS
FORAMINIFER	MONTGOLFIER	STEPBROTHER	ANDROGYNOUS	CRATERELLUS	HIDEOUSNESS
FRANKFURTER	MOONLIGHTER	STEREOMETER	ANFRACTUOUS	CREDENTIALS	HINDERLANDS
FREETHINKER	MOSSTROOPER	STOCKBROKER	ANTHONOMOUS	CROOKEDNESS	HIPPOCAMPUS
FRONTRUNNER	MOUNTAINEER	STOCKHOLDER	ANTHRACOSIS	CURNAPTIOUS	HIPPOCRATES
GALLIBAGGER	NECROMANCER	STOCKJOBBER	ANTIPHRASIS	CYBERNETICS	HISTRIONICS
GALLIBEGGAR	NIERSTEINER	STOREKEEPER	ANTISTHENES	CYMOPHANOUS	HOGGISHNESS
GALLYBAGGER	NOMENCLATOR	STORYTELLER	APATOSAURUS	CYTOGENESIS	HOMOGENEOUS
GALLYBEGGAR	NORTHEASTER	STRANDLOPER	APOLLINARIS	DARDANELLES	HOMOPHONOUS
GATECRASHER	NORTHWESTER	STRAPHANGER	APONEUROSIS	DECORATIONS	HOSTILITIES
GERRYMANDER	ORNITHOPTER	SUPERTANKER	APOSIOPESIS	DEFENCELESS	HYDROPONICS
GIGGLEWATER	OUTMANEUVER	SYMPATHISER	APOSTROPHUS	DEFENSELESS	ICHTHYORNIS
GILLYFLOWER	PAMPHLETEER	SYMPATHIZER	APPEARANCES	DELETERIOUS	ICONOSTASIS
GODDAUGHTER	PARATROOPER	SYNTHESIZER	ARCHILOCHUS	DEMOSTHENES	IGNOMINIOUS
GONFALONIER	PARISHIONER	TEENYBOPPER	ARTHRODESIS	DESCENDANTS	ILLUSTRIOUS
GRANDFATHER	PATERNOSTER	TEETOTALLER	ASCLEPIADES	DEVIOUSNESS	IMPECUNIOUS
GRANDMASTER	PEACEKEEPER	TELEGRAPHER	ASPERGILLUS	DIAGNOSTICS	INCONGRUOUS
GRANDMOTHER	PENNYFATHER	TELEPRINTER	ATHERMANOUS	DIAPHORESIS	INCREDULOUS
GRASSHOPPER	PENTECONTER	TENSIOMETER	ATRABILIOUS	DIARTHROSIS	INDUSTRIOUS
GRAVEDIGGER	PERPETRATOR	THEATERGOER	AVOIRDUPOIS	DICEPHALOUS	INFORMATICS
GREENGROCER	PETRODOLLAR	THEATREGOER	AWKWARDNESS	DIPLOMATICS	INGREDIENTS
GRENZGANGER	PETTIFOGGER	THERMOMETER	BASHFULNESS	DOUBLECROSS	INHABITANTS
HABERDASHER	PHILANDERER	TITLEHOLDER	BATTLEDRESS	DRACUNCULUS	INJUDICIOUS
HAIRDRESSER	PHILOSOPHER	TOASTMASTER	BATTLEMENTS	DRAGONNADES	INSTRUMENTS
HALBSTARKER	PHOTOCOPIER	TOPOGRAPHER	BEASTLINESS	DRUNKENNESS	INTRAVENOUS
HALFBROTHER	PREDECESSOR	TOTALIZATOR	BILIOUSNESS	DRYCLEANERS	INVINCIBLES
HANDICAPPER	PRIZEWINNER	TRAFFICATOR	BLASPHEMOUS	DUBIOUSNESS	IRONMONGERS
HIGHLIGHTER	PROBATIONER	TRANSCEIVER	BLESSEDNESS	EARNESTNESS	IRRELIGIOUS
HONEYMOONER	PROOFREADER	TRANSFORMER	BLOODSPORTS	EFFICACIOUS	ISOMORPHOUS
HOSPITALLER	PROVISIONER	TRANSMITTER	BOOKSELLERS	ELECTRONICS	ISTIOPHORUS
HOUSEFATHER	QUICKSILVER	TRANSPONDER	BORBORYGMUS	EMPHYTEUSIS	ITHYPHALLUS
HOUSEHOLDER	RANGEFINDER	TRANSPORTER	BREADCRUMBS	ENARTHROSIS	KULTURKREIS
HOUSEKEEPER	RECONNOITER	TREACHETOUR	BRITTLENESS	ENCHANTRESS	LARYNGISMUS
HOUSEMASTER	RECTANGULAR	TREECREEPER	BRUCELLOSIS	EOANTHROPUS	LATERITIOUS

LAWLESSNESS	PHILOCTETES	STRANGEWAYS	ADIAPHORIST	EASTERNMOST	KINCHINMORT
LENGTHINESS	PHTHIRIASIS	STRETCHLESS	ADJOURNMENT	ELASTOPLAST	LANDSKNECHT
LETTERPRESS	PLAYFULNESS	STROPHILLUS	ADVANCEMENT	ELECTROTINT	LAPIDESCENT
LINGUISTICS	POLITICIANS	STRUTHIONES	AGGLUTINANT	EMBOÎTEMENT	LIGHTWEIGHT
LITERALNESS	POSSESSIONS	STYLISHNESS	AMERCIAMENT	EMPIECEMENT	LUMINESCENT
LOGGERHEADS	PRECAUTIONS	SUBITANEOUS	ANESTHETIST	EMPLACEMENT	MAGNIFICENT
MACHAIRODUS	PRECIPITOUS	SUPERFICIES	APPEASEMENT	EMPOWERMENT	MARGINALIST
MAGISTRATES	PRESTIGIOUS	SUPERFLUOUS	APPOINTMENT	ENCHANTMENT	MATERIALIST
MAGNANIMOUS	PRESTONPANS	SUPERSEDEAS	APPURTENANT	ENDORSEMENT	MEADOWSWEET
MARIONETTES	PRETENSIONS	SYMPLEGADES	ARBITRAMENT	ENFEOFFMENT	MEASUREMENT
MASSIVENESS	PRETENTIOUS	SYNCHRONOUS	ARRANGEMENT	ENFORCEMENT	MEKHITARIST
MATHEMATICS	PRICKLINESS	TABERNACLES	ARTILLERIST	ENHANCEMENT	MILQUETOAST
MEANDERINGS	PROCEEDINGS	TATTERSALLS	ASSYTHEMENT	ENJAMBEMENT	MINIATURIST
MEANINGLESS	PROFUSENESS	TEDIOUSNESS	BATTLEFRONT	ENLARGEMENT	MODELMOLEST
MEASURELESS	PROGNATHOUS	TELEKINESIS	BELLETTRIST	ENSLAVEMENT	MONOCHROMAT
MEGALOPOLIS	PROMISCUOUS	TEMPESTUOUS	BELLIGERENT	ENTABLEMENT	MONOPSONIST
MELLIFLUOUS	PROPHYLAXIS	TENDENTIOUS	BEREAVEMENT	ENTITLEMENT	MYCOPHAGIST
MERITORIOUS	PROSTHETICS	TENTERHOOKS	BESIEGEMENT	ENVIRONMENT	NARRAGANSET
METACARPALS	PROTOCOCCUS	TENUOUSNESS	BITTERSWEET	EPIGENESIST	NATIONALIST
METAGENESIS	PRZEWALSKIS	THANATOPSIS	BLADDERWORT	EQUIDISTANT	NEEDLEPOINT
METAPHYSICS	PSITTACOSIS	THEATRICALS	BOMBARDMENT	EQUILIBRIST	NEUROLOGIST
METATARSALS	PUNCTILIOUS	THEREABOUTS	BUMBERSHOOT	EQUIPOLLENT	NONDESCRIPT
MICROVILLUS	PURPOSELESS	THIGMOTAXIS	CALEFACIENT	ETHNOLOGIST	NONEXISTENT
MISCHIEVOUS	QUADRUPLETS	THINGLINESS	CANDLELIGHT	ETYMOLOGIST	NOURISHMENT
MISERLINESS	QUINTUPLETS	THOUGHTLESS	CHIROPODIST	EXPECTORANT	NUMISMATIST
MONOCHINOUS	RAFFISHNESS	THRIFTINESS	CHROMOPLAST	EXTRAVAGANT	OBMUTESCENT
MOUNTAINOUS	RAUCOUSNESS	TONSILLITIS	CIRCUMFLECT	FARTHERMOST	OBSOLESCENT
MYXOMATOSIS	REGIMENTALS	TORTICOLLIS	CIRCUMSPECT	FEHMGERICHT	ODONTOBLAST
NATURALNESS	REMORSELESS	TORTICULLUS	CLAIRVOYANT	FESTSCHRIFT	OMNIPRESENT
NAUGHTINESS	REPETITIOUS	TRAGELAPHUS	COEFFICIENT	FINGERPRINT	OPPORTUNIST
NECESSITOUS	RESPONSIONS	TREACHEROUS	COLONIALIST	FLABBERGAST	OPTOMETRIST
NECROBIOSIS	RESTIVENESS	TRICERATOPS	COMMANDMENT	FLUORESCENT	ORIENTALIST
NERVOUSNESS	REVELATIONS	TRINOBANTES	COMMUNICANT	FORETHOUGHT	OVERDRAUGHT
NETHERLANDS	REVOLUTIONS	TRIPHIBIOUS	COMPARTMENT	FULFILLMENT	OVERPAYMENT
NETHERLINGS	ROGUISHNESS	TRIPTOLEMUS	COMPILEMENT	FUNAMBULIST	OVERWROUGHT
NONETHELESS	RUMBUSTIOUS	UNAMBIGUOUS	COMPLAISANT	FURTHERMOST	PAPERWEIGHT
NOSTRADAMUS	SAGITTARIUS	UNCLEANNESS	CONCEALMENT	GARNISHMENT	PARACHUTIST
NOTHINGNESS	SAINTLINESS	UNCONSCIOUS	CONCOMITANT	GENEALOGIST	PARTICIPANT
NUMISMATICS	SALPINGITIS	UNCOUTHNESS	CONFINEMENT	GREASEPAINT	PATHOLOGIST
NUTCRACKERS	SANGUINEOUS	UNGODLINESS	CONNECTICUT	GROUNDSHEET	PENTAVALENT
OBVIOUSNESS	SAPONACEOUS	UNHAPPINESS	CONSIGNMENT	HEAVYWEIGHT	PERCEFOREST
OPPROBRIOUS	SARCOPHAGUS	UNRIGHTEOUS	CONSTITUENT	HETEROGRAFT	PERSONALIST
ORDERLINESS	SAVOURINESS	UPRIGHTNESS	CONTAINMENT	HISTOLOGIST	PHILATELIST
OUTPOURINGS	SCIREFACIAS	USELESSNESS	CONTAMINANT	HOUSEPARENT	PHILOLOGIST
OVERZEALOUS	SCRUFFINESS	VACUOUSNESS	CONTEMPLANT	HYMNOLOGIST	PIERREPOINT
OXYRHYNCHUS	SCRUMPTIOUS	VERTIGINOUS	CONTENEMENT	HYPERMARKET	PISSASPHALT
PAEDIATRICS	SEASICKNESS	VICIOUSNESS	CONTENTMENT	IDEOPRAXIST	PLANTAGENET
PANTALETTES	SECONDCLASS	VISCOUNTESS	COUNTERFEIT	ILLUSIONIST	POLTERGEIST
PARABLEPSIS	SELFISHNESS	WAKEFULNESS	COUNTERFORT	IMPEACHMENT	PORTRAITIST
PARABOLANUS	SENTENTIOUS	WAYWARDNESS	COUNTERPART	IMPERIALIST	PREDICAMENT
PARALEIPSIS	SEPTENARIUS	WELLINGTONS	CURTAILMENT	IMPERMANENT	PREDOMINANT
PARANEPHROS	SERIOUSNESS	WHEREABOUTS	DECONSTRUCT	IMPERTINENT	PRESENTMENT
PARASITOSIS	SHALLOWNESS	WHITEFRIARS	DELITESCENT	IMPROVEMENT	PRISCIANIST
PARENTHESIS	SHAPELINESS	WILLINGNESS	DEPARTEMENT	IMPROVIDENT	PROCUREMENT
PASSIVENESS	SHENANIGANS	WISTFULNESS	DERANGEMENT	INADVERTENT	PROLETARIAT
PAWNBROKERS	SHEPHERDESS	WITHERSHINS	DETERMINANT	INCALESCENT	PROTAGONIST
PEDESTRIANS	SKETCHINESS	WOMANLINESS	DEVELOPMENT	INCOMPETENT	PROTUBERANT
PEDETENTOUS	SLENDERNESS	WORLDFAMOUS	DIPLOMATIST	INCONTINENT	RADIOLOGIST
PEEVISHNESS	SMITHEREENS	WORLDLINESS	DIPROTODONT	INDEPENDENT	REALIGNMENT
PENSIVENESS	SPONDULICKS	XEROPHILOUS	DISABLEMENT	INDIFFERENT	RECONSTRUCT
PERIPHRASIS	SPONDYLITIS	XEROTRIPSIS	DISARMAMENT	INEFFICIENT	RECRUITMENT
PERISTALSIS	SPONTANEOUS	ABANDONMENT	DISCERNMENT	INEXPEDIENT	REFRESHMENT
PERITONITIS	SPRINGINESS	ABORTIONIST	DISINTEREST	INSTALLMENT	REFRIGERANT
PERSPICUOUS	STATELINESS	ABRIDGEMENT	DISOBEDIENT	INTELLIGENT	RELEASEMENT
PHARYNGITIS	STRADUARIUS	ACCOMPANIST	DISSEPIMENT	INVOLVEMENT	REMINISCENT
PHILIPPIANS	STRAMINEOUS	ACHIEVEMENT	DIVORCEMENT	IRREDENTIST	REPLACEMENT
PHILIPPINES	STRANGENESS	ACQUIESCENT	DREADNOUGHT	JACQUEMINOT	REQUIREMENT

RESPLENDENT	SCEUOPHYLAX	CREDULOUSLY	FRIGHTFULLY	INSISTENTLY	PAEDOTROPHY
RESTATEMENT	ABNORMALITY	CRIMINOLOGY	FRIVOLOUSLY	INSTABILITY	PALEOGRAPHY
RETROROCKET	ACCORDINGLY	CRITHOMANCY	FRUITLESSLY	INSULTINGLY	PARVANIMITY
RINTHEREOUT	ACCOUNTANCY	CULPABILITY	FUNCTIONARY	INTENSIVELY	PECULIARITY
SAUSAGEMEAT	ADVERBIALLY	CUSTOMARILY	GALLIMAUFRY	INTERCALARY	PERCEPTIBLY
SAXOPHONIST	AGROSTOLOGY	DANGEROUSLY	GARRULOUSLY	INTOLERABLY	PERENNIALLY
SCUTTLEBUTT	ALTERNATELY	DECEITFULLY	GASTRECTOMY	INTREPIDITY	PERFUNCTORY
SEARCHLIGHT	AMPHIBOLOGY	DECEPTIVELY	GENERICALLY	INTRICATELY	PERISSOLOGY
SECRETARIAT	ANENCEPHALY	DECLAMATORY	GENETICALLY	INTUITIVELY	PERMANENTLY
SELFEVIDENT	ANGELOLATRY	DEFENSIVELY	GENTLEMANLY	INVOLUNTARY	PERPETUALLY
SELFRESPECT	ANNIVERSARY	DELICIOUSLY	GERONTOLOGY	IRONMONGERY	PERSONALITY
SIGNIFICANT	ANONYMOUSLY	DELINQUENCY	GLASTONBURY	IRREGULARLY	PERSPICUITY
SILVERPOINT	ANTIPHONARY	DEMAGOGUERY	GRAPHICALLY	IRREPARABLY	PERTINACITY
SOCIOLOGIST	APPALLINGLY	DERMATOLOGY	GULLIBILITY	JABBERWOCKY	PERTINENTLY
SOROPTIMIST	APPRECIABLY	DESPERATELY	GYNAECOLOGY	JUDICIOUSLY	PHALANSTERY
SPEECHCRAFT	APPROVINGLY	DESPONDENCY	HAGIOGRAPHY	JUSTIFIABLY	PHOTOGRAPHY
SPENDTHRIFT	ARBITRARILY	DEUTERONOMY	HALFHOLIDAY	LABORIOUSLY	PHRASEOLOGY
SPREADSHEET	ARCHAEOLOGY	DIFFERENTLY	HAPHAZARDLY	LACONICALLY	PHYSIOGNOMY
STAIRCARPET	ARISTOCRACY	DIFFIDENTLY	HEARTLESSLY	LITHOGRAPHY	PODSNAPPERY
STREETLIGHT	ARRHENOTOKY	DISCOURTESY	HEBDOMADARY	LOGODAEDALY	POINTLESSLY
SUBCONTRACT	ASSIDUOUSLY	DISCREPANCY	HEPATOSCOPY	LONGANIMITY	POLITICALLY
SUBDOMINANT	ASTRINGENCY	DISHONESTLY	HERPETOLOGY	LONGINQUITY	POLYHYDROXY
SUBSERVIENT	ATROCIOUSLY	DITTOGRAPHY	HIGHQUALITY	LUXURIANTLY	PONDEROUSLY
SUPERMARKET	ATTENTIVELY	DOCUMENTARY	HILARIOUSLY	LUXURIOUSLY	PORNOGRAPHY
SUPERSCRIPT	AUDACIOUSLY	DOMESTICITY	HOBBLEDEHOY	LYCANTHROPY	POSSIBILITY
SURVEILLANT	BEAUTIFULLY	DRASTICALLY	HOMOEOPATHY	MAGNANIMITY	POTENTIALLY
TAXIDERMIST	BENEFICIARY	EFFECTIVELY	HOMOGENEITY	MALICIOUSLY	PRACTICALLY
TELEPHONIST	BICENTENARY	EFFECTUALLY	HOSPITALITY	MARIONBERRY	PREDICTABLY
TEMPERAMENT	BIMILLENARY	EFFICIENTLY	HUCKLEBERRY	MASCULINITY	PRELIMINARY
TESSARAGLOT	BLAMEWORTHY	ELABORATELY	HURTLEBERRY	MASTERFULLY	PREMATURELY
THUNDERBOLT	BOTANOMANCY	ELECTRICITY	HYPERTROPHY	MEDICINALLY	PREMONITORY
TOBACCONIST	BOYSENBERRY	ELIGIBILITY	ICONOGRAPHY	MELODIOUSLY	PREPARATORY
TRACKLEMENT	BRILLIANTLY	EMOTIONALLY	IDENTICALLY	MERCILESSLY	PRINCIPALLY
TRANSILIENT	BUREAUCRACY	EMPYROMANCY	IDIOTICALLY	METEOROLOGY	PROBABILITY
TRANSLUCENT	CALLIGRAPHY	EQUIVOCALLY	IDYLLICALLY	METHODOLOGY	PRODIGALITY
TRANSPARENT	CAMPANOLOGY	ERRATICALLY	ILLOGICALLY	MISANTHROPY	PROFESSEDLY
TRITAGONIST	CARRIAGEWAY	ERRONEOUSLY	ILLUSIONARY	MISIDENTIFY	PROFICIENCY
TROPHOBLAST	CARTOGRAPHY	ESCHATOLOGY	IMMEDIATELY	MOMENTARILY	PROMINENTLY
TROUBLESPOT	CAUSTICALLY	ESSENTIALLY	IMMORTALITY	MONSTROSITY	PROMISCUITY
ULTRAVIOLET	CEASELESSLY	ETHNOGRAPHY	IMPARTIALLY	MONTMORENCY	PROPINQUITY
UNDERWEIGHT	CHANCELLERY	EVENTUALITY	IMPASSIVELY	MULTISTOREY	PROPRIETARY
UNIMPORTANT	CHEIROGNOMY	EXCEEDINGLY	IMPATIENTLY	NATIONALITY	PROSAICALLY
UNOBSERVANT	CHIROGRAPHY	EXCESSIVELY	IMPERIOUSLY	NATUROPATHY	PROTONOTARY
UNREPENTANT	CHOROGRAPHY	EXCLUSIVELY	IMPETUOSITY	NECESSARILY	PTOCHOCRACY
WASTEBASKET	CHRISTMASSY	EXPECTANTLY	IMPETUOUSLY	NEIGHBOURLY	PUNCTUALITY
WESTERNMOST	CHRONICALLY	EXPLANATORY	IMPORTANTLY	NICKNACKERY	PYELOGRAPHY
WHEELWRIGHT	CIRCULATORY	EXPLORATORY	IMPROPRIETY	NOISELESSLY	QUERULOUSLY
WHITETHROAT	CLANJAMFRAY	EXQUISITELY	IMPRUDENTLY	NOTORIOUSLY	RADIOGRAPHY
WIENERWURST	CLIMATOLOGY	EXTENSIVELY	IMPULSIVELY	NUMERICALLY	RAPTUROUSLY
WITENAGEMOT	COMFORTABLY	FACETIOUSLY	INCESSANTLY	OBJECTIVELY	RATIONALITY
MONTESQUIEU	COMMENDABLY	FALLIBILITY	INCONGRUITY	OBJECTIVITY	RAVISHINGLY
OUAGADOUGOU	COMPETENTLY	FAMILIARITY	INCONSTANCY	OBSERVATORY	REACTIONARY
PORTMANTEAU	COMPLACENCY	FANATICALLY	INCORRECTLY	OBSESSIVELY	READABILITY
KALASHNIKOV	COMSTOCKERY	FARKLEBERRY	INCREDULITY	OBSTINATELY	RECEPTIVITY
BARTHOLOMEW	CONCEIVABLY	FASHIONABLY	INDIGNANTLY	OFFENSIVELY	RECIPROCITY
BLACKFELLOW	CONFEDERACY	FAULTLESSLY	INDIVISIBLY	OFFHANDEDLY	RECURRENTLY
CLAPPERCLAW	CONFIDENTLY	FEASIBILITY	INDUBITABLY	OFFICIOUSLY	REFLEXOLOGY
COACHFELLOW	CONSCIOUSLY	FEROCIOUSLY	INDULGENTLY	ONEIROMANCY	REFORMATORY
COUNTERGLOW	CONSERVANCY	FESTINATELY	INEXCUSABLY	OPPORTUNELY	REGRETFULLY
JINRICKSHAW	CONSISTENCY	FINANCIALLY	INFERIORITY	OPPORTUNITY	REGRETTABLY
MARSHMALLOW	CONSULTANCY	FLEXIBILITY	INFERTILITY	ORGANICALLY	RELIABILITY
WAPPENSCHAW	CONTENTEDLY	FORTNIGHTLY	INFORMALITY	ORIGINALITY	RELIGIOUSLY
WATERMEADOW	CONTINGENCY	FORTUNATELY	INFREQUENCY	ORNITHOLOGY	RELUCTANTLY
WHEELBARROW	CONTINUALLY	FRAGMENTARY	INGENIOUSLY	ORTHOGRAPHY	RESENTFULLY
WINDLESTRAW	CONTROVERSY	FRANTICALLY	INQUIRINGLY	OSTEOPLASTY	RESISTIVITY
CLARENCIEUX	COURTEOUSLY	FRATERNALLY	INSIDIOUSLY	OVARIECTOMY	RESPECTABLY
PROGENITRIX	CREDIBILITY	FREEMASONRY	INSINCERITY	PACIFICALLY	RESPIRATORY

RESPONSIBLY	SECONDARILY	SLIGHTINGLY	SUPERIORITY	TRACHEOTOMY	VICARIOUSLY
RETALIATORY	SECRETIVELY	SOCIABILITY	SUPERVISORY	TRANQUILITY	VIVACIOUSLY
RETINOSCOPY	SEDIMENTARY	SORROWFULLY	SUPPOSITORY	TRUCULENTLY	VOLCANOLOGY
RHABDOMANCY	SELECTIVELY	SOUNDLESSLY	TACHYGRAPHY	TRUSTWORTHY	VOLUNTARILY
RHEUMATICKY	SELECTIVITY	SOVEREIGNTY	TACITURNITY	UNANIMOUSLY	VORACIOUSLY
RIGHTEOUSLY	SENSIBILITY	SPIRITUALLY	TANGIBILITY	UNAVOIDABLY	VULCANOLOGY
RUDIMENTARY	SENSITIVELY	SPONTANEITY	TASTELESSLY	UNCERTAINTY	WHIGMALEERY
SAGACIOUSLY	SENSITIVITY	STEADFASTLY	TCHAIKOVSKY	UNDOUBTEDLY	WINTERBERRY
SALACIOUSLY	SERENDIPITY	STENOGRAPHY	TECHNICALLY	UNFAILINGLY	WONDERFULLY
SATIRICALLY	SHAFTESBURY	STIPENDIARY	TEMPORARILY	UNIVERSALLY	RAZZAMATAZZ
SCEPTICALLY	SHAMELESSLY	STRENUOUSLY	TENACIOUSLY	UNNATURALLY	
SCIENTOLOGY	SILVERBERRY	STRINGENTLY	TENTATIVELY	UNNECESSARY	
SCREAMINGLY	SINGULARITY	SUFFICIENCY	TERMINOLOGY	UNWITTINGLY	
SCRIMSHANDY	SKEPTICALLY	SUITABILITY	THANKLESSLY	VALEDICTORY	
SCULDUDDERY	SKULDUDDERY	SUMPTUOUSLY	THEOPNEUSTY	VARIABILITY	
SCULDUGGERY	SKULDUGGERY	SUPERFLUITY	TIMBROPHILY	VERSATILITY	

12:1

ABBREVIATION	ANDOUILLETTE	ATMOSPHERICS	BLOODTHIRSTY	CHAMPIONSHIP
ABOLITIONIST	ANDROSTERONE	ATTRACTIVELY	BLUESTOCKING	CHARACTERIZE
ABSQUATULATE	ANECATHARSIS	ATTRIBUTABLE	BOISTEROUSLY	CHARTERHOUSE
ACADEMICALLY	ANEMOPHILOUS	AUGMENTATION	BOOBYTRAPPED	CHASTISEMENT
ACCELERATION	ANNIHILATION	AUGMENTATIVE	BOONDOGGLING	CHAUVINISTIC
ACCENTUATION	ANNOUNCEMENT	AUSCULTATION	BOUGAINVILLE	CHEERFULNESS
ACCIDENTALLY	ANNUNCIATION	AUSPICIOUSLY	BOULEVARDIER	CHEESEBURGER
ACCOMPANYING	ANTAGONISTIC	AUSTRALASIAN	BRACHYCEPHAL	CHEESEMONGER
ACCOMPLISHED	ANTANANARIVO	AUSTRONESIAN	BRAINWASHING	CHEESEPARING
ACCORDIONIST	ANTEDILUVIAN	AUTHENTICATE	BRANCHIOPODA	CHEMOTHERAPY
ACCOUCHEMENT	ANTEMERIDIAN	AUTHENTICITY	BREAKTHROUGH	CHESTERFIELD
ACCOUTREMENT	ANTHELMINTIC	AUTOHYPNOSIS	BREASTPLOUGH	CHILDBEARING
ACCUMULATION	ANTHROPOLOGY	AVAILABILITY	BREASTSUMMER	CHILDISHNESS
ACCUSATORIAL	ANTIAIRCRAFT	AWARDWINNING	BREATHALYSER	CHIROPRACTIC
ACETALDEHYDE	ANTIBACCHIUS	AWAYABSOLUTE	BREATHLESSLY	CHIROPRACTOR
ACHLAMYDEOUS	ANTIBARBARUS	AWEINSPIRING	BREATHTAKING	CHITTERLINGS
ACKNOWLEDGED	ANTICIPATION	AYUNTAMIENTO	BRICKFIELDER	CHLORINATION
ACQUAINTANCE	ANTICIPATORY	BABINGTONITE	BRILLIANTINE	CHLOROPICRIN
ACQUIESCENCE	ANTILEGOMENA	BACCHANALIAN	BROADCASTING	CHONDRIOSOME
ADAPTABILITY	ANTIMACASSAR	BACKBREAKING	BRONTOSAURUS	CHOREOGRAPHY
ADDITIONALLY	ANTIMETABOLE	BACKWARDNESS	BUCKLEBEGGAR	CHORIZONTIST
ADJECTIVALLY	ANTIMNEMONIC	BACKWOODSMAN	BUNKOSTEERER	CHREMATISTIC
ADJUDICATION	ANTINEUTRINO	BACTERIOLOGY	BUREAUCRATIC	CHRESTOMATHY
ADMINISTRATE	ANTIPARTICLE	BACTERIOSTAT	BUSINESSLIKE	CHRISTIANITY
ADMONISHMENT	ANTIRACHITIC	BAIRNSFATHER	BUTTERSCOTCH	CHURCHWARDEN
ADSCITITIOUS	ANTISTROPHON	BAMBOCCIADES	BYELORUSSIAN	CHURLISHNESS
ADULTERATION	ANTITHROMBIN	BANANALANDER	CABINETMAKER	CIRCASSIENNE
ADVANTAGEOUS	ANTONINIANUS	BANDERSNATCH	CALCEAMENTUM	CIRCUMCISION
ADVANTAGIOUS	APFELSTRUDEL	BANTAMWEIGHT	CALLIGRAPHIC	CIRCUMGYRATE
ADVENTITIOUS	APLANOGAMETE	BARBERMONGER	CALLISTHENES	CIRCUMSCRIBE
ADVISABILITY	APOLLINARIAN	BARNSTORMING	CALUMNIATION	CIRCUMSTANCE
AECIDIOSPORE	APOSTROPHISE	BARORECEPTOR	CAMERAPERSON	CIVILISATION
AERODYNAMICS	APPENDECTOMY	BARRANQUILLA	CAMIKNICKERS	CIVILIZATION
AERONAUTICAL	APPENDICITIS	BATTLEGROUND	CAMPANULARIA	CLAIRVOYANCE
AETHRIOSCOPE	APPOGGIATURA	BEACONSFIELD	CAMPODEIFORM	CLAIRVOYANCY
AFFECTIONATE	APPRECIATION	BEAUMARCHAIS	CANCELLATION	CLAMJAMPHRIE
AFORETHOUGHT	APPRECIATIVE	BEAUMONTAGUE	CANONIZATION	CLANNISHNESS
AFTEREFFECTS	APPREHENSION	BEAUMONTIQUE	CANTANKEROUS	CLAPPERBOARD
AFTERTHOUGHT	APPREHENSIVE	BEHAVIOURISM	CANTILEVERED	CLARINETTIST
AGALMATOLITE	APPROACHABLE	BELLIGERENCY	CAPERCAILLIE	CLASSIFIABLE
AGAMOGENETIC	APPURTENANCE	BENEFACTRESS	CAPERCAILZIE	CLAUDICATION
AGATHODAIMON	ARBORESCENCE	BENEVOLENTLY	CAPITULATION	CLAVICEMBALO
AGGRESSIVELY	ARCHILOCHIAN	BENZOPHENONE	CARAVANSERAI	CLEARSIGHTED
AGRIBUSINESS	ARCHIPELAGOS	BENZOQUINONE	CARBOHYDRATE	CLEISTOGAMIC
AGRICULTURAL	ARCHITECTURE	BERTHOLLETIA	CARCINOGENIC	CLOTHESHORSE
AIRCRAFTSMAN	ARFVEDSONITE	BERTILLONAGE	CARDINDEXING	COCCIDIOSTAT
ALEXIPHARMIC	ARISTOCRATIC	BESSERWISSER	CARDIOLOGIST	CODIFICATION
ALIMENTATIVE	ARISTOLOCHIA	BETHLEHEMITE	CARDIOMEGALY	COHABITATION
ALLITERATION	ARISTOPHANES	BEWILDERMENT	CARELESSNESS	COINCIDENTAL
ALPHABETICAL	ARISTOTELEAN	BIBLIOGRAPHY	CARICATURIST	COLDSHOULDER
ALPHANUMERIC	ARITHMETICAL	BIBLIOPEGIST	CARLOVINGIAN	COLLABORATOR
AMALGAMATION	AROMATHERAPY	BICAMERALISM	CARPETBAGGER	COLLECTIVELY
AMARANTACEAE	ARSENOPYRITE	BICENTENNIAL	CARPOPHAGOUS	COLLECTORATE
AMBASSADRESS	ARTHROPLASTY	BIELORUSSIAN	CARRIWITCHET	COLLOQUIALLY
AMBIDEXTROUS	ARTICULATION	BILLINGSGATE	CARTHAGINIAN	COLLUCTATION
AMBULANCEMAN	ARTIFICIALLY	BIOCHEMISTRY	CARTOGRAPHER	COLLYWOBBLES
AMELIORATION	ARTILLERYMAN	BIODIVERSITY	CARTOGRAPHIC	COLONIZATION
AMPHISBAENIC	ARTIODACTYLA	BIOFLAVONOID	CASSITERIDES	COLOQUINTIDA
AMPHISTOMOUS	ARTISTICALLY	BIOGRAPHICAL	CASTERBRIDGE	COMBINATIONS
AMPHITHEATER	ASPARAGINASE	BIPROPELLANT	CATADIOPTRIC	COMMANDMENTS
AMPHITHEATRE	ASPHYXIATION	BIRDWATCHING	CATAPHYSICAL	COMMENCEMENT
ANAESTHETISE	ASSIMILATION	BLABBERMOUTH	CATASTROPHIC	COMMENDATION
ANAESTHETIST	ASSUEFACTION	BLACKCURRANT	CATHETOMETER	COMMENDATORY
ANAESTHETIZE	ASTONISHMENT	BLANDISHMENT	CAUTIOUSNESS	COMMENSURATE
ANAMORPHOSIS	ASTROLOGICAL	BLEFUSCUDIAN	CEREBROTONIC	COMMERCIALLY
ANASTIGMATIC	ASTRONOMICAL	BLENNORRHOEA	CEREMONIALLY	COMMISSARIAT
ANCHORPERSON	ASTROPHYSICS	BLETHERSKATE	CHAIRMANSHIP	COMMISSIONED
	ASYMMETRICAL	BLOODLETTING	CHALCOPYRITE	COMMISSIONER
	ATHEROMATOUS	BLOODSTAINED	CHALICOTHERE	COMMONWEALTH

COMMUNICABLE	CONTRIBUTORY	DEPRECIATORY	DONNERWETTER	ERATOSTHENES
COMPANIONWAY	CONTRITURATE	DEREGULATION	DORSIVENTRAL	ERYTHROMYCIN
COMPELLATION	CONTROLLABLE	DERESTRICTED	DOUBLEDECKER	ESCAPOLOGIST
COMPENSATION	CONTUMACIOUS	DESIDERATIVE	DOUBLEGLAZED	ESCHSCHOLZIA
COMPENSATORY	CONVALESCENT	DESIRABILITY	DRAMATICALLY	ESPAGNOLETTE
COMPLACENTLY	CONVALESCING	DESSERTSPOON	DRAMATURGIST	ESSENTIALITY
COMPLETENESS	CONVENIENCES	DEUTERANOPIA	DRESSINGDOWN	ESTHETICALLY
COMPLICATION	CONVENIENTLY	DEUTEROSCOPY	DRINKDRIVING	ESTRANGEMENT
COMPROMISING	CONVENTIONAL	DIAGRAMMATIC	DUNNIEWASSAL	ETEPIMELETIC
COMPURGATION	CONVERSATION	DIALECTICIAN	DYSTELEOLOGY	ETHEROMANIAC
CONCENTRATED	CONVEYANCING	DICHROMATISM	EAVESDROPPER	ETHNOLOGICAL
CONCILIATION	CONVINCINGLY	DICTATORSHIP	ECCENTRICITY	ETYMOLOGICAL
CONCILIATORY	CONVIVIALITY	DIENCEPHALON	ECCLESIASTES	ETYMOLOGICON
CONCLUSIVELY	COORDINATION	DIFFERENTIAL	ECCLESIASTIC	EULENSPIEGEL
CONCURRENTLY	COSCINOMANCY	DILAPIDATION	ECONOMICALLY	EVENHANDEDLY
CONDEMNATION	COSMOPOLITAN	DILATORINESS	ECSTATICALLY	EVENTEMPERED
CONDENSATION	COSTERMONGER	DIPLOGENESIS	EDUCATIONIST	EVOLUTIONARY
CONDUCTIVITY	COUNTERBLAST	DIPRIONIDIAN	EFFERVESCENT	EXACERBATION
CONFECTIONER	COUNTERCLAIM	DIRECTORSHIP	EFFORTLESSLY	EXAGGERATION
CONFESSIONAL	COUNTERMARCH	DISACCHARIDE	EGYPTOLOGIST	EXASPERATING
CONFIDENTIAL	COUNTERPOINT	DISADVANTAGE	ELASMOBRANCH	EXASPERATION
CONFIRMATION	COUNTERPOISE	DISAGREEABLE	ELECTRICALLY	EXCHANGEABLE
CONFIRMATORY	COURAGEOUSLY	DISAGREEMENT	ELECTROLYSIS	EXCITABILITY
CONFISCATION	COURTMARTIAL	DISAPPEARING	ELECTROPLATE	EXCRUCIATING
CONGENITALLY	COVETOUSNESS	DISAPPOINTED	ELECTROTONUS	EXCRUCIATION
CONGLOMERATE	CRASHLANDING	DISASSOCIATE	ELEEMOSYNARY	EXHAUSTIVELY
CONGRATULATE	CRASSAMENTUM	DISASTROUSLY	EMANCIPATION	EXHIBITIONER
CONGREGATION	CREATIVENESS	DISCIPLINARY	EMASCULATION	EXHILARATING
CONQUISTADOR	CREMAILLIÈRE	DISCOMEDUSAE	EMBARRASSING	EXHILARATION
CONSCRIPTION	CRISTOBALITE	DISCOMFITURE	EMBEZZLEMENT	EXPERIMENTAL
CONSECRATION	CROSSBENCHER	DISCOMYCETES	EMBROIDERESS	EXPLOITATION
CONSEQUENCES	CROSSCOUNTRY	DISCONCERTED	EMPHATICALLY	EXSERVICEMAN
CONSEQUENTLY	CROSSEXAMINE	DISCONNECTED	ENANTIOMORPH	EXSUFFLICATE
CONSERVATION	CROSSSECTION	DISCONSOLATE	ENANTIOPATHY	EXTENSIONIST
CONSERVATISM	CRYPTOGRAPHY	DISCONTENTED	ENCHEIRIDION	EXTENSOMETER
CONSERVATIVE	CUCKOOFLOWER	DISCOURAGING	ENCIRCLEMENT	EXTINGUISHER
CONSERVATORY	CYMOTRICHOUS	DISCOURTEOUS	ENCROACHMENT	EXTORTIONATE
CONSIDERABLE	CZECHOSLOVAK	DISCRIMINATE	ENCYCLOPEDIA	EXTRADITABLE
CONSIDERABLY	DAGUERROTYPE	DISDAINFULLY	ENCYCLOPEDIC	EXTRAVAGANCE
CONSISTENTLY	DARLINGTONIA	DISEMBARRASS	ENERGYSAVING	EXTRAVAGANZA
CONSOCIATION	DEAMBULATORY	DISENCHANTED	ENGLISHWOMAN	FAINTHEARTED
CONSOLIDATED	DEASPIRATION	DISFRANCHISE	ENGLISHWOMEN	FAITHFULNESS
CONSOLIDATOR	DEBILITATING	DISHONORABLE	ENHYPOSTASIA	FARTHINGLAND
CONSPECTUITY	DECAPITATION	DISHONORABLY	ENTANGLEMENT	FASTIDIOUSLY
CONSPIRACIST	DECELERATION	DISINCENTIVE	ENTEROMORPHA	FEARLESSNESS
CONSTABULARY	DECENTRALISE	DISINFECTANT	ENTEROPNEUST	FEATHERBRAIN
CONSTIPATION	DECENTRALIZE	DISINGENUOUS	ENTERPRISING	FEHMGERICHTE
CONSTITUENCY	DECIPHERABLE	DISINTEGRATE	ENTERTAINING	FELDSPATHOID
CONSTITUENTS	DECIPHERMENT	DISOBEDIENCE	ENTHUSIASTIC	FERMENTATION
CONSTITUTION	DECONGESTANT	DISORGANIZED	ENTOMOLOGIST	FIDDLESTICKS
CONSTRICTION	DECORATIVELY	DISORIENTATE	ENTOMOSTRACA	FIGURATIVELY
CONSTRUCTION	DEFLATIONARY	DISPENSATION	ENTOPLASTRON	FINALIZATION
CONSTRUCTIVE	DEGENERATION	DISPLACEMENT	ENTREATINGLY	FIRSTFOOTING
CONSULTATION	DEHUMIDIFIER	DISPOSSESSED	ENTRENCHMENT	FLAGELLATION
CONSULTATIVE	DELIBERATELY	DISQUISITION	ENTREPRENEUR	FLAMBOYANTLY
CONSUMMATION	DELIBERATION	DISRESPECTFUL	EPACRIDACEAE	FLITTERMOUSE
CONTABESCENT	DELICATESSEN	DISREPUTABLE	EPANORTHOSIS	FLORICULTURE
CONTAMINATED	DEMILITARIZE	DISSATISFIED	EPENCEPHALON	FLUORESCENCE
CONTEMPORARY	DEMIMONDAINE	DISSERTATION	EPIDEICTICAL	FLUORIDATION
CONTEMPTIBLE	DEMONSTRABLE	DISSOCIATION	EPIGRAMMATIC	FLUVIOMARINE
CONTEMPTUOUS	DEMONSTRABLY	DISTILLATION	EPILEPTIFORM	FOOTSLOGGING
CONTERMINOUS	DEMONSTRATOR	DISTINCTNESS	EPIPHENOMENA	FORCEFULNESS
CONTIGNATION	DENDROLOGIST	DISTRIBUTION	EPISCOPALIAN	FORMALDEHYDE
CONTINUATION	DENOMINATION	DISTRIBUTIVE	EPISTEMOLOGY	FORTUITOUSLY
CONTINUOUSLY	DENUNCIATION	DIVERTICULUM	EPISTOLATERS	FOTHERINGHAY
CONTRAPPOSTO	DEPARTMENTAL	DIVERTIMENTO	EPITHALAMION	FRACTIONALLY
CONTRAPUNTAL	DEPOPULATION	DOGMATICALLY	EPITHALAMIUM	FRANKALMOIGN
CONTRARINESS	DEPRECIATION	DOLPHINARIUM	EQUIVOCATION	FRANKENSTEIN
CONTRIBUTION	DEPRECIATION	DOMESTICATED	EQUIVOCATORY	FRANKINCENSE

FRAUENDIENST	HAIRSPLITTER	HYDROQUINONE	INCAPACITATE	INSTRUMENTAL
FREIGHTLINER	HALLANSHAKER	HYDROTHERAPY	INCAUTIOUSLY	INSUFFERABLE
FRIENDLINESS	HALLUCINOGEN	HYGIENICALLY	INCIDENTALLY	INSUFFERABLY
FRONTIERSMAN	HAMARTHRITIS	HYMENOPTERAN	INCINERATION	INSUFFICIENT
FRONTISPIECE	HAMBLETONIAN	HYMNOGRAPHER	INCOHERENTLY	INSURRECTION
FRUITFULNESS	HAMMERHEADED	HYPERACIDITY	INCOMPARABLE	INTELLECTUAL
FRUMENTATION	HANDKERCHIEF	HYPERBOLICAL	INCOMPARABLY	INTELLIGENCE
FULMINATIONS	HAPPENSTANCE	HYPERPYRETIC	INCOMPATIBLE	INTELLIGIBLE
FUNCTIONALLY	HAPPYGOLUCKY	HYPERSARCOMA	INCOMPETENCE	INTEMPERANCE
FUNCTIONLESS	HAPTOTROPISM	HYPERTENSION	INCOMPLETELY	INTENERATION
FUNDAMENTALS	HARMONIOUSLY	HYPNOTHERAPY	INCONCLUSIVE	INTERCEPTION
FUSTILLIRIAN	HARNESSMAKER	HYPNOTICALLY	INCONSEQUENT	INTERCESSION
GAINSBOROUGH	HARUMFRODITE	HYPOCHONDRIA	INCONSISTENT	INTERCHANGED
GALLIGASKINS	HEADMISTRESS	HYPOCRITICAL	INCONSOLABLE	INTERFERENCE
GALLINACEOUS	HEADQUARTERS	HYPOTHECATOR	INCONTINENCE	INTERGLACIAL
GALLIVANTING	HEARTSTRINGS	HYPOTHETICAL	INCONVENIENT	INTERJECTION
GALVANOMETER	HEARTWARMING	HYSTERECTOMY	INCORPORATED	INTERLOCUTOR
GAMESMANSHIP	HELIOGABALUS	HYSTERICALLY	INCORRIGIBLE	INTERMEDIARY
GAMOSEPALOUS	HELIOTROPISM	IAMBOGRAPHER	INCORRIGIBLY	INTERMEDIATE
GASTARBEITER	HELLGRAMMITE	ICHTHYOCOLLA	INCREASINGLY	INTERMINABLE
GASTROSOPHER	HELPLESSNESS	ICHTHYOPSIDA	INCRUSTATION	INTERMINABLY
GENEALOGICAL	HEMICHORDATA	ICONOCLASTIC	INCUNABULIST	INTERMISSION
GENETHLIACON	HENCEFORWARD	IDEALIZATION	INDEBTEDNESS	INTERMITTENT
GENTLETAMPER	HEPHTHEMIMER	IDENTIFIABLE	INDECLINABLE	INTERPRETING
GEOGRAPHICAL	HEREDITAMENT	IDIOSYNCRASY	INDEFENSIBLE	INTERRELATED
GEOLOGICALLY	HEREDITARIAN	IDIOTHERMOUS	INDEFINITELY	INTERROGATOR
GEOMETRICIAN	HERMENEUTICS	ILLEGIBILITY	INDEPENDENCE	INTERRUPTION
GEOPHYSICIST	HERMENEUTIST	ILLEGITIMACY	INDIFFERENCE	INTERSECTION
GERIATRICIAN	HERMETICALLY	ILLEGITIMATE	INDIGESTIBLE	INTERSPERSED
GERONTOCRACY	HEROICOMICAL	ILLOGICALITY	INDISCRETION	INTERSTELLAR
GESELLSCHAFT	HETEROCLITIC	ILLUMINATING	INDISPUTABLE	INTERVENTION
GIBRALTARIAN	HETEROCONTAE	ILLUMINATION	INDISPUTABLY	INTIMIDATING
GIGANTOMACHY	HETEROGAMETE	ILLUSTRATION	INDISSOLUBLE	INTIMIDATION
GLADIATORIAL	HETEROPHORIA	ILLUSTRATIVE	INDISTINCTLY	INTOXICATING
GLOBETROTTER	HETEROPLASIA	IMMACULATELY	INDIVIDUALLY	INTOXICATION
GLOCKENSPIEL	HETEROSEXUAL	IMMEASURABLE	INDOCTRINATE	INTRANSIGENT
GLUBBDUBDRIB	HETEROSOMATA	IMMEASURABLY	INDUSTRIALLY	INTRANSITIVE
GLYCOPROTEIN	HIERARCHICAL	IMMODERATELY	INEFFICIENCY	INTRAUTERINE
GLYNDEBOURNE	HIEROGLYPHIC	IMMODERATION	INERADICABLE	INTRODUCTION
GLYPTOGRAPHY	HIEROGRAMMAT	IMMUNIZATION	INESCUTCHEON	INTRODUCTORY
GOBBLEDEGOOK	HIEROPHANTIC	IMMUNOLOGIST	INEXACTITUDE	INTROVERSION
GOBBLEDYGOOK	HIGHFALUTING	IMMUTABILITY	INEXPERIENCE	INTUITIONISM
GONADOTROPIN	HILDEBRANDIC	IMPARTIALITY	INEXPLICABLE	INVALIDATION
GONDWANALAND	HINDQUARTERS	IMPENETRABLE	INEXPLICABLY	INVERTEBRATE
GOOSEPIMPLES	HIPPOCRATISE	IMPERFECTION	INEXTRICABLE	INVESTIGATOR
GOVERNMENTAL	HIPPOCREPIAN	IMPERFECTIVE	INEXTRICABLY	INVIGORATING
GRACEFULNESS	HIPPOPOTAMUS	IMPERISHABLE	INFELICITOUS	INVIGORATION
GRACIOUSNESS	HISTIOPHORUS	IMPERSONALLY	INFILTRATION	INVISIBILITY
GRANDISONIAN	HISTORICALLY	IMPERSONATOR	INFLAMMATION	INVULNERABLE
GRANDMONTINE	HOBBIDIDANCE	IMPERTINENCE	INFLAMMATORY	IRASCIBILITY
GRANDPARENTS	HOLIDAYMAKER	IMPLANTATION	INFLATIONARY	IRRATIONALLY
GRAPHOLOGIST	HOMESICKNESS	IMPOLITENESS	INFORMIDABLE	IRREDEEMABLE
GRASSWIDOWER	HOMOEOPATHIC	IMPOVERISHED	INFOTAINMENT	IRREGULARITY
GRATEFULNESS	HOMOTHERMOUS	IMPREGNATION	INFREQUENTLY	IRRESISTIBLE
GREENGROCERS	HOPELESSNESS	IMPRESSIVELY	INFRINGEMENT	IRRESOLUTELY
GREENGROCERY	HORIZONTALLY	IMPRISONMENT	INGRATIATING	IRRESOLUTION
GRISEOFULVIN	HORRIFICALLY	IMPROVIDENCE	INHARMONIOUS	IRRESOLVABLE
GROSSULARITE	HORSEMANSHIP	INACCESSIBLE	INHOSPITABLE	IRRESPECTIVE
GUARDIANSHIP	HORTICULTURE	INACCURATELY	INNATTENTIVE	IRREVERENTLY
GUILDENSTERN	HOUSEBREAKER	INADEQUATELY	INNOMINABLES	IRREVERSIBLE
GYMNOSOPHIST	HOUSEKEEPING	INADMISSIBLE	INORDINATELY	IRRITABILITY
GYNECOLOGIST	HOUSETOHOUSE	INADVERTENCE	INSALUBRIOUS	ISHMAELITISH
HABERDASHERS	HOUSEWARMING	INAPPLICABLE	INSEMINATION	ISOBILATERAL
HABERDASHERY	HUDIBRASTICS	INARTICULATE	INSOLUBILITY	ISOLATIONISM
HAEMATEMESIS	HUMANITARIAN	INAUGURATION	INSPECTORATE	ISOLATIONIST
HAEMOPHILIAC	HUMANIZATION	INAUSPICIOUS	INSTALLATION	JENNYSPINNER
HAEMORRHOIDS	HYDROCHLORIC	INCALCULABLE	INSTAURATION	JOURNALISTIC
HAIRDRESSERS	HYDROGEOLOGY	INCANDESCENT	INSTRUCTIONS	JURISDICTION
HAIRDRESSING	HYDROGRAPHER	INCAPABILITY	INSTRUCTRESS	KALEIDOSCOPE

KALISTOCRACY	MANIPULATION	MODIFICATION	OBSOLETENESS	PAPILIONIDAE
KATHAREVOUSA	MANIPULATIVE	MOISTURIZING	OBSTETRICIAN	PARACENTESIS
KATZENJAMMER	MANOEUVRABLE	MONOSYLLABIC	OBSTREPEROUS	PARALIPOMENA
KERAUNOGRAPH	MANSLAUGHTER	MONOSYLLABLE	OCCASIONALLY	PARAMAGNETIC
KILLIKINNICK	MANUFACTURER	MONOTONOUSLY	OCCUPATIONAL	PARAMILITARY
KINAESTHETIC	MARCOBRUNNER	MONTESSORIAN	OCEANOGRAPHY	PARANTHELIUM
KINDERGARTEN	MARCONIGRAPH	MOONLIGHTING	OCTASTROPHIC	PARENTHESIZE
KIRSCHWASSER	MARKSMANSHIP	MOSBOLLETJIE	OCTOGENARIAN	PARKINSONISM
KLEPTOMANIAC	MARLINESPIKE	MOTORCYCLIST	OLDFASHIONED	PARSIMONIOUS
KLETTERSCHUE	MARRIAGEABLE	MOUSQUETAIRE	OMBUDSPERSON	PARTICOLORED
KLIPSPRINGER	MARSEILLAISE	MOUTHBROODER	ONCORHYNCHUS	PARTICULARLY
LABANOTATION	MASSERANDUBA	MUCILAGINOUS	ONEIROCRITIC	PARTISANSHIP
LABOURSAVING	MASSPRODUCED	MUDDLEHEADED	ONOMATOPOEIA	PASQUEFLOWER
LABYRINTHINE	MASTERSTROKE	MUGGLETONIAN	ONOMATOPOEIC	PASSEMEASURE
LALLAPALOOZA	MASTIGOPHORA	MULLIGATAWNY	ONYCHOPHORAN	PASSEPARTOUT
LAMELLICORNE	MASTURBATION	MULTICOLORED	OPHIOGLOSSUM	PASSIONATELY
LAMENTATIONS	MATHEMATICAL	MULTIFARIOUS	OPINIONATIVE	PASSIONFRUIT
LAMPADEDROMY	MEANINGFULLY	MULTIGRAVIDA	OPISTHOGRAPH	PATHETICALLY
LANCASTERIAN	MECHANICALLY	MULTILATERAL	OPPRESSIVELY	PATHOLOGICAL
LANGUEDOCIAN	MECHITHARIST	MULTIPLICITY	OREOPITHECUS	PEACEFULNESS
LASCIVIOUSLY	MELODRAMATIC	MUNICIPALITY	OREOPITHEOUS	PEACEKEEPING
LATIROSTRATE	MENSTRUATION	MUSICOLOGIST	ORGANISATION	PECTORILOQUY
LAUREATESHIP	MERCANTILISM	MUTESSARIFAT	ORGANIZATION	PEDANTICALLY
LEGALIZATION	MERETRICIOUS	MYRINGOSCOPE	ORIENTEERING	PEDIATRICIAN
LEGIONNAIRES	MERISTEMATIC	MYSTERIOUSLY	ORNITHOGALUM	PEDICELLARIA
LEGITIMATELY	MERITRICIOUS	MYTHOLOGICAL	ORTHODONTICS	PENALIZATION
LEIOTRICHOUS	MERRYTHOUGHT	NARCISSISTIC	ORTHOGENESIS	PENITENTIARY
LEPIDOMELANE	MERVEILLEUSE	NATURALISTIC	ORTHOPAEDICS	PENNSYLVANIA
LEXICOGRAPHY	MESOTHELIOMA	NAVIGABILITY	ORTHOPAEDIST	PERADVENTURE
LICKTRENCHER	METAGNATHOUS	NEIGHBORHOOD	ORTHOPTEROUS	PERAMBULATOR
LIFELESSNESS	METALLOPHONE	NEIGHBOURING	ORTHORHOMBIC	PERCEPTIVELY
LIGHTHEARTED	METALLURGIST	NEOCLASSICAL	ORTHOTONESIS	PERCEPTIVITY
LILLIBULLERO	METAMORPHISM	NEOPLATONISM	OSCILLOSCOPE	PEREMPTORILY
LILLIBURLERO	METAMORPHOSE	NEPENTHACEAE	OSSIFICATION	PERGAMENEOUS
LINCOLNSHIRE	METAPHORICAL	NEPHELOMETER	OSTENTATIOUS	PERICARDITIS
LIQUEFACTION	METAPHYSICAL	NEUROFIBROMA	OSTEOMALACIA	PERIODICALLY
LISTLESSNESS	METHODICALLY	NEUROLOGICAL	OSTEOPOROSIS	PERIODONTICS
LITHOGRAPHIC	METHOTREXATE	NEUROSCIENCE	OSTEOSARCOMA	PERIOSTRACUM
LITHOLATROUS	METICULOUSLY	NEUROTICALLY	OTHERWORLDLY	PERIPHRASTIC
LIVERPUDLIAN	METROPOLITAN	NEVERTHELESS	OUTBUILDINGS	PERISTERONIC
LONGDISTANCE	MICHELANGELO	NEWFOUNDLAND	OUTMANOEUVRE	PERMANGANATE
LONGITUDINAL	MICROBREWERY	NEWSPAPERMAN	OUTRAGEOUSLY	PERMEABILITY
LONGSHOREMAN	MICROCLIMATE	NIGHTCLOTHES	OUTSTRETCHED	PERMITTIVITY
LONGSTANDING	MIDDLEWEIGHT	NIMBOSTRATUS	OVERCROWDING	PERNOCTATION
LOXODROMICAL	MILITARISTIC	NOCONFIDENCE	OVERDRESSING	PERPETRATION
LUGUBRIOUSLY	MILLILAMBERT	NOMENCLATURE	OVERESTIMATE	PERSEVERANCE
LUMINESCENCE	MINDBOGGLING	NONAGENARIAN	OVEREXERTION	PERSISTENTLY
LUMINISCENCE	MINDFULLNESS	NONALCOHOLIC	OVERPOWERING	PERSONALIZED
LUXEMBOURGER	MINERALOGIST	NONCHALANTLY	OVERSCUTCHED	PERSPICACITY
LUXULLIANITE	MINICOMPUTER	NONCOMMITTAL	OVERSTRAINED	PERSPIRATION
LYMANTRIIDAE	MINISTRATION	NONDIRECTIVE	OVERWHELMING	PERSUASIVELY
MACABERESQUE	MIRACULOUSLY	NONEXISTENCE	OXYACETYLENE	PERSULPHURIC
MACHAIRODONT	MISADVENTURE	NONFLAMMABLE	PACIFICATION	PERTINACIOUS
MACMILLANITE	MISANTHROPIC	NONOBJECTIVE	PAINLESSNESS	PERTURBATION
MACROCEPHALY	MISAPPREHEND	NONRESIDENCE	PALEONTOLOGY	PERVERSENESS
MACROPODIDAE	MISBEHAVIOUR	NONRESISTANT	PALINGENESIA	PERVICACIOUS
MADEMOISELLE	MISCALCULATE	NORTHEASTERN	PALINGENESIS	PESTILENTIAL
MAGNETICALLY	MISDELIVERED	NORTHERNMOST	PALPITATIONS	PETRIFACTION
MAGNIFICENCE	MISDEMEANOUR	NORTHWESTERN	PALUDAMENTUM	PETTIFOGGERS
MAGNILOQUENT	MISINTERPRET	NOTIFICATION	PANAESTHESIA	PETTIFOGGERY
MAJESTICALLY	MISPLACEMENT	NUTRITIONIST	PANATHENAEAN	PETTIFOGGING
MALACOSTRACA	MISPRONOUNCE	NYCHTHEMERON	PANCHATANTRA	PHARMACOLOGY
MALFORMATION	MISQUOTATION	NYCTITROPISM	PANCHROMATIC	PHENOMENALLY
MALLEABILITY	MISREPRESENT	NYMPHOMANIAC	PANDAEMONIUM	PHILANTHROPY
MALLOPHAGOUS	MISSTATEMENT	OBEDIENTIARY	PANDANACEOUS	PHILHARMONIC
MALNUTRITION	MISTREATMENT	OBLITERATION	PANPHARMACON	PHILISTINISM
MALPRACTICES	MITRAILLEUSE	OBSEQUIOUSLY	PANTECHNICON	PHILODENDRON
MALTREATMENT	MNEMOTECHNIC	OBSERVANTINE	PANTISOCRACY	PHILOLOGICAL
MANGELWURZEL	MOBILIZATION	OBSOLESCENCE	PANTOPHAGOUS	PHILOSOPHIZE

PHLEBOTOMIST	PREMAXILLARY	PSYCHIATRIST	REMEMBRANCER	SCOPOPHILIAC
PHONETICALLY	PREMONSTRANT	PSYCHOLOGIST	REMINISCENCE	SCREENWRITER
PHOSPHOLIPID	PREPAREDNESS	PSYCHOPATHIC	REMONSTRANCE	SCRIMSHANDER
PHOSPHORENCE	PREPONDERANT	PTERIDOPHYTE	REMUNERATION	SCRIMSHANKER
PHOSPHORESCE	PREPONDERATE	PTERIDOSPERM	REMUNERATIVE	SCRIPTWRITER
PHOTOGLYPHIC	PREPONDERENT	PTERODACTYLE	RENOUNCEMENT	SCRUPULOUSLY
PHOTOGRAPHER	PREPOSSESSED	PUGNACIOUSLY	RENUNCIATION	SCURRILOUSLY
PHOTOGRAPHIC	PREPOSTEROUS	PUMPERNICKEL	REPATRIATION	SECESSIONIST
PHOTOGRAVURE	PREREQUISITE	PURIFICATION	REPERCUSSION	SECRETARIATE
PHRONTISTERY	PRESBYTERIAN	PURPOSEBUILT	REPOSSESSION	SECTARIANISM
PHYCOXANTHIN	PRESCRIPTION	PURPOSEFULLY	REPROCESSING	SEGMENTATION
PHYSIOLOGIST	PRESCRIPTIVE	PUTREFACTION	REPRODUCTION	SELFADHESIVE
PHYTOBENTHOS	PRESENTATION	PYROCATECHOL	REPRODUCTIVE	SELFCATERING
PHYTONADIONE	PRESENTIMENT	PYROTECHNICS	RESETTLEMENT	SELFEMPLOYED
PHYTOPHAGOUS	PRESERVATION	PYTHONOMORPH	RESIPISCENCE	SELFINTEREST
PIGMENTATION	PRESERVATIVE	QUADRAGESIMA	RESPECTFULLY	SELFPORTRAIT
PINNIEWINKLE	PRESIDENTIAL	QUADRAPHONIC	RESPECTIVELY	SEMANTICALLY
PISCICULTURE	PRESTRICTION	QUADRIPLEGIA	RESPONDENTIA	SEMICIRCULAR
PITTERPATTER	PRESUMPTUOUS	QUANTIFIABLE	RESTAURATEUR	SEMIDETACHED
PLACENTIFORM	PREVARICATOR	QUANTITATIVE	RESTLESSNESS	SEMIPRECIOUS
PLAINCLOTHES	PREVENTATIVE	QUARTERFINAL	RESURRECTION	SEPTEMBRISER
PLASTERSTONE	PRIGGISHNESS	QUARTERLIGHT	RESUSCITATED	SEPTUAGESIMA
PLAUSIBILITY	PRIMIGRAVIDA	QUARTERSTAFF	RETARDEDNESS	SEQUENTIALLY
PLECTOGNATHI	PRINCIPALITY	QUESTIONABLE	RETICULATION	SEQUESTRATOR
PLEIOCHASIUM	PRIZEFIGHTER	QUINQUENNIAL	RETRENCHMENT	SERASKIERATE
POGONOPHORAN	PRIZEWINNING	QUINTESSENCE	REVERSIONARY	SERVICEBERRY
POIKILOTHERM	PROBATIONARY	QUIXOTICALLY	RHADAMANTHUS	SERVICEWOMAN
POINTILLISME	PROCESSIONAL	RACKETEERING	RHAMPHOTHECA	SESQUIALTERA
POLARIZATION	PROCLAMATION	RADIOBIOLOGY	RHINORRHOEAL	SESQUITERTIA
POLICYMAKING	PRODIGIOUSLY	RADIOGRAPHER	RHIPIDOPTERA	SEXAGENARIAN
POLYETHYLENE	PRODUCTIVITY	RADIOISOTOPE	RHODODENDRON	SHAMEFACEDLY
POLYNEURITIS	PROFESSIONAL	RADIOTHERAPY	RHYTHMICALLY	SHAREHOLDING
POLYPETALOUS	PROFESSORIAL	RAMBUNCTIOUS	RHYTIDECTOMY	SHARPSHOOTER
POLYRIBOSOME	PROFICIENTLY	RAMIFICATION	RIDICULOUSLY	SHEEPISHNESS
POLYSYLLABIC	PROFITEERING	RATIFICATION	RISORGIMENTO	SHILLYSHALLY
POLYSYLLABLE	PROGESTERONE	READJUSTMENT	RODOMONTADER	SHIPBUILDING
POLYSYNDETON	PROGRAMMABLE	REAPPEARANCE	ROLLERBLADER	SHIRTSLEEVES
POLYURETHANE	PROGYMNASIUM	RECALCITRANT	ROLLERBLADES	SHIRTWAISTER
POPOCATEPETL	PROLEGOMENON	RECAPITULATE	ROMANTICALLY	SHORTCIRCUIT
PORNOGRAPHIC	PROLETARIATE	RECEIVERSHIP	RONCESVALLES	SHORTCOMINGS
POSSESSIVELY	PROLIFICALLY	RECEPTIONIST	ROOMINGHOUSE	SHORTSIGHTED
POSTGRADUATE	PROLONGATION	RECHARGEABLE	RUTHLESSNESS	SHORTSLEEVED
POSTHUMOUSLY	PROPAGANDISM	RECIPROCALLY	SACRILEGIOUS	SHORTSTAFFED
POSTLIMINARY	PROPAGANDIST	RECKLESSNESS	SADISTICALLY	SHOSTAKOVICH
POSTMISTRESS	PROPHYLACTIC	RECOGNIZABLE	SALESMANSHIP	SHUFFLEBOARD
POSTPONEMENT	PROPITIATION	RECOGNIZANCE	SALTATORIOUS	SIDEWHISKERS
POSTPOSITIVE	PROPITIATORY	RECOLLECTION	SALVATIONIST	SIGNIFICANCE
POSTPRANDIAL	PROPITIOUSLY	RECONSTITUTE	SARDANAPALUS	SILVERHAIRED
POTAMOLOGIST	PROPORTIONAL	RECORDPLAYER	SARDONICALLY	SIMULTANEOUS
POTENTIALITY	PROPRIETRESS	RECREATIONAL	SARRUSOPHONE	SINANTHROPUS
POTICHOMANIA	PROSCRIPTION	RECRUDESCENT	SARSAPARILLA	SINGLEDECKER
POWERSHARING	PROSOPOPOEIA	RECUPERATION	SATISFACTION	SINGLEHANDED
PRACTICALITY	PROSTITUTION	RECUPERATIVE	SATISFACTORY	SINGLEMINDED
PRACTICIONER	PROTACTINIUM	REDEMPTIONER	SAUROGNATHAE	SIPHONOPHORA
PRACTITIONER	PROTECTIVELY	REDEPLOYMENT	SCANDALOUSLY	SIPHONOSTELE
PRAISEWORTHY	PROTECTORATE	REDINTEGRATE	SCANDINAVIAN	SIPUNCULACEA
PRALLTRILLER	PROTESTATION	REDISCOVERED	SCAPULIMANCY	SITTLICHKEIT
PRASEODYMIUM	PROTHALAMION	REDISTRIBUTE	SCATTERBRAIN	SIVAPITHECUS
PRAXINOSCOPE	PROTHALAMIUM	REFLATIONARY	SCATTERMOUCH	SKUTTERUDITE
PRECARIOUSLY	PROTHONOTARY	REFLECTIVITY	SCHEHERAZADE	SLEDGEHAMMER
PRECOCIOUSLY	PROTOPLASMAL	REFRIGERATED	SCHILLERSPAR	SLEEPWALKING
PRECONDITION	PROTOPLASMIC	REFRIGERATOR	SCHINDYLESIS	SLOCKDOLAGER
PREDESTINATE	PROTUBERANCE	REGENERATION	SCHIZOMYCETE	SLOCKDOLIGER
PREDETERMINE	PROVERBIALLY	REGISTRATION	SCHNEIDERIAN	SLOCKDOLOGER
PREDILECTION	PROVIDENTIAL	REHABILITATE	SCHOOLMASTER	SLOVENLINESS
PREDOMINANCE	PSEPHOLOGIST	REINVIGORATE	SCHOPENHAUER	SLUBBERINGLY
PREFERENTIAL	PSEUDONYMOUS	REJUVENATION	SCINTILLATOR	SMALLHOLDING
PREGUSTATION	PSIPHENOMENA	RELATIONSHIP	SCLERENCHYMA	SNOBBISHNESS
PREHISTORIAN		RELENTLESSLY	SCLERODERMIA	SNOWBOARDING

SOCIOLOGICAL	STRANGLEHOLD	TAMARICACEAE	TRANSFERENCE	UNDISCHARGED
SOLICITATION	STRANGLEWEED	TAPERECORDER	TRANSGRESSOR	UNECONOMICAL
SOLICITOUSLY	STRATOSPHERE	TAPSALTEERIE	TRANSITIONAL	UNEMPLOYMENT
SOMATOPLEURE	STREPITATION	TAPSLETEERIE	TRANSLATABLE	UNEXPECTEDLY
SOMNAMBULISM	STREPSIPTERA	TARAMASALATA	TRANSLUCENCE	UNEXPURGATED
SOMNAMBULIST	STREPTOMYCIN	TAUTOLOGICAL	TRANSMIGRATE	UNFATHOMABLE
SOPHISTICATE	STREPTONEURA	TECHNICALITY	TRANSMISSION	UNFAVOURABLE
SOUTHCOTTIAN	STRIDULATION	TECHNOLOGIST	TRANSMOGRIFY	UNFREQUENTED
SOUTHEASTERN	STRIGIFORMES	TEETERTOTTER	TRANSOCEANIC	UNIDENTIFIED
SOUTHERNMOST	STRINGCOURSE	TELEASTHETIC	TRANSPARENCY	UNILATERALLY
SOUTHERNWOOD	STROMATOLITE	TELEGRAPHESE	TRANSPONTINE	UNIMAGINABLE
SOUTHWESTERN	STRONGMINDED	TELEGRAPHIST	TRANSVESTISM	UNIMPORTANCE
SPACIOUSNESS	STRONTIANITE	TELEOSAURIAN	TRANSVESTITE	UNINTERESTED
SPATANGOIDEA	STROPHANTHUS	TELEUTOSPORE	TREMENDOUSLY	UNIVERSALIST
SPECIFICALLY	STRUCTURALLY	TERCENTENARY	TRICENTENARY	UNMANAGEABLE
SPECIOUSNESS	STUBBORNNESS	TERGIVERSATE	TRICHOLOGIST	UNMISTAKABLE
SPECKTIONEER	STUDDINGSAIL	TERRIFICALLY	TRICHOPHYTON	UNNEIGHBORLY
SPECTROMETER	STUDIOUSNESS	TERRITORIALS	TRIGONOMETRY	UNOBSTRUCTED
SPECTROSCOPE	STUPEFACTION	TESTAMENTARY	TRIUMPHANTLY	UNOBTAINABLE
SPELEOLOGIST	SUBARRHATION	TESTOSTERONE	TROCHELMINTH	UNOFFICIALLY
SPELLCHECKER	SUBCOMMITTEE	TETRACYCLINE	TROCHOSPHERE	UNOPPRESSIVE
SPERMATOCYTE	SUBCONSCIOUS	TETRAHEDRITE	TROPHALLAXIS	UNPARALLELED
SPERMATOZOID	SUBCONTINENT	TETRODOTOXIN	TROUBLEMAKER	UNPARDONABLE
SPERMATOZOON	SUBCUTANEOUS	THANKFULNESS	TRUTHFULNESS	UNPOPULARITY
SPHACELATION	SUBHASTATION	THANKSGIVING	TUBERCULOSIS	UNPREJUDICED
SPHAIRISTIKE	SUBJECTIVELY	THAUMATURGIC	TURACOVERDIN	UNPRETENDING
SPIEGELEISEN	SUBJECTIVITY	THAUMATURGUS	TURBIDIMETER	UNPRINCIPLED
SPINECHILLER	SUBLAPSARIAN	THEATRICALLY	TURBOCHARGER	UNPRODUCTIVE
SPINSTERHOOD	SUBMINIATURE	THEOPHYLLINE	UINTATHERIUM	UNPROFITABLE
SPIRITUALISM	SUBMISSIVELY	THEORETICIAN	ULOTRICHALES	UNREASONABLE
SPIRITUALIST	SUBSCRIPTION	THERAPEUTICS	ULTRAMONTANE	UNRECOGNISED
SPIRITUALITY	SUBSEQUENTLY	THEREAGAINST	UMBRADARLING	UNRECOGNIZED
SPITEFULNESS	SUBSERVIENCE	THERMOSTATIC	UNACCEPTABLE	UNRESERVEDLY
SPLENOMEGALY	SUBSIDIARITY	THESMOPHORIA	UNACCUSTOMED	UNRESPONSIVE
SPOKESPERSON	SUBSTANTIATE	THESSALONIAN	UNACQUAINTED	UNRESTRAINED
SPORADICALLY	SUBSTITUTION	THICKSKINNED	UNANSWERABLE	UNRESTRICTED
SPORTSGROUND	SUBSTITUTIVE	THIGMOTROPIC	UNAPPARELLED	UNRETURNABLE
SPREADEAGLED	SUBSTRUCTURE	THIRDBOROUGH	UNAPPETIZING	UNSATISFYING
SPRECHGESANG	SUBTERRANEAN	THOROUGHBRED	UNATTAINABLE	UNSCIENTIFIC
SPURIOUSNESS	SUCCESSFULLY	THOROUGHFARE	UNATTRACTIVE	UNSCRUPULOUS
SPURTLEBLADE	SUCCESSIVELY	THOROUGHNESS	UNAUTHORISED	UNSEASONABLE
SQUIRRELFISH	SUCCUSSATION	THOUGHTFULLY	UNAUTHORIZED	UNSUCCESSFUL
STAGGERINGLY	SUFFICIENTLY	THREADNEEDLE	UNBELIEVABLE	UNSURPRISING
STAKHANOVITE	SUGGESTIVELY	THREEQUARTER	UNBELIEVABLY	UNSUSPECTING
STANISLAVSKI	SULPHONAMIDE	THUNDERCLOUD	UNCHALLENGED	UNUTTERABLES
STATISTICIAN	SUPERANNUATE	THUNDERFLASH	UNCHANGEABLE	UPROARIOUSLY
STEALTHINESS	SUPERCHARGED	THUNDERSTORM	UNCHARITABLE	URBANIZATION
STEEPLECHASE	SUPERCHARGER	THYSANOPTERA	UNCHARITABLY	URTRICULARIA
STEGOPHOLIST	SUPERCILIARY	TIGHTFITTING	UNCLASSIFIED	USERFRIENDLY
STELLENBOSCH	SUPERCILIOUS	TIMELESSNESS	UNCONSIDERED	VAINGLORIOUS
STENOGRAPHER	SUPERHIGHWAY	TITANOSAURUS	UNCONTROLLED	VALENCIENNES
STENTORPHONE	SUPERNACULUM	TOBACCONISTS	UNCONVERSANT	VAPORIZATION
STEPDAUGHTER	SUPERNATURAL	TOGETHERNESS	UNCONVINCING	VARICOLOURED
STEREOPHONIC	SUPERSTITION	TORRICELLIAN	UNCTUOUSNESS	VEHMGERICHTE
STEREOPTICON	SUPERSTRATUM	TOTALITARIAN	UNCULTIVATED	VENEPUNCTURE
STEREOSCOPIC	SUPPLICATION	TOXICOLOGIST	UNDEMOCRATIC	VENGEFULNESS
STEREOTYPING	SURMOUNTABLE	TRABECULATED	UNDERACHIEVE	VENTRIPOTENT
STERNUTATION	SURPRISINGLY	TRACTABILITY	UNDERCLOTHES	VERIFICATION
STERNWHEELER	SURREALISTIC	TRADESCANTIA	UNDERCURRENT	VERMICULTURE
STILBOESTROL	SURROUNDINGS	TRADESPEOPLE	UNDEREXPOSED	VERUMONTANUM
STOCKBREEDER	SURVEILLANCE	TRALATICIOUS	UNDERGARMENT	VETERINARIAN
STOCKINGETTE	SUSPICIOUSLY	TRALATITIOUS	UNDERPINNING	VIBRATIUNCLE
STONECHATTER	SWASHBUCKLER	TRANQUILIZER	UNDERSKINKER	VILIFICATION
STORMTROOPER	SWIZZLESTICK	TRANQUILLISE	UNDERSTAFFED	VILLEGIATURA
STRADIVARIUS	SYMBOLICALLY	TRANQUILLITY	UNDERWRITTEN	VINDICTIVELY
STRAIGHTAWAY	SYNADELPHITE	TRANQUILLIZE	UNDESERVEDLY	VITUPERATION
STRAIGHTEDGE	SYNTAGMATITE	TRANSACTIONS	UNDETECTABLE	VITUPERATIVE
STRAIGHTNESS	TACTLESSNESS	TRANSCENDENT	UNDETERMINED	VOCIFERATION
STRAITJACKET	TAGLIACOTIAN	TRANSFERABLE	UNDIMINISHED	VOCIFEROUSLY

VOLUPTUOUSLY	CARDINDEXING	LASCIVIOUSLY	PARTISANSHIP	ACCUSATORIAL
WALLYDRAIGLE	CARDIOLOGIST	LATIROSTRATE	PASQUEFLOWER	ACETALDEHYDE
WAREHOUSEMAN	CARDIOMEGALY	LAUREATESHIP	PASSEMEASURE	ACHLAMYDEOUS
WASHINGTONIA	CARELESSNESS	MACABERESQUE	PASSEPARTOUT	ACKNOWLEDGED
WATCHFULNESS	CARICATURIST	MACHAIRODONT	PASSIONATELY	ACQUAINTANCE
WATERCARRIER	CARLOVINGIAN	MACMILLANITE	PASSIONFRUIT	ACQUIESCENCE
WEATHERPROOF	CARPETBAGGER	MACROCEPHALY	PATHETICALLY	ECCENTRICITY
WEIGHTLIFTER	CARPOPHAGOUS	MACROPODIDAE	PATHOLOGICAL	ECCLESIASTES
WELLBALANCED	CARRIWITCHET	MADEMOISELLE	RACKETEERING	ECCLESIASTIC
WELLINFORMED	CARTHAGINIAN	MAGNETICALLY	RADIOBIOLOGY	ECONOMICALLY
WELLINGTONIA	CARTOGRAPHER	MAGNIFICENCE	RADIOGRAPHER	ECSTATICALLY
WELTERWEIGHT	CARTOGRAPHIC	MAGNILOQUENT	RADIOISOTOPE	ICHTHYOCOLLA
WHIGMALEERIE	CASSITERIDES	MAJESTICALLY	RADIOTHERAPY	ICHTHYOPSIDA
WHIMSICALITY	CASTERBRIDGE	MALACOSTRACA	RAMBUNCTIOUS	ICONOCLASTIC
WHIPPOORWILL	CATADIOPTRIC	MALFORMATION	RAMIFICATION	OCCASIONALLY
WHOLEHEARTED	CATAPHYSICAL	MALLEABILITY	RATIFICATION	OCCUPATIONAL
WICKETKEEPER	CATASTROPHIC	MALLOPHAGOUS	SACRILEGIOUS	OCEANOGRAPHY
WILLIEWAUGHT	CATHETOMETER	MALNUTRITION	SADISTICALLY	OCTASTROPHIC
WILTSHIREMAN	CAUTIOUSNESS	MALPRACTICES	SALESMANSHIP	OCTOGENARIAN
WINTERHALTER	DAGUERROTYPE	MALTREATMENT	SALTATORIOUS	SCANDALOUSLY
WOLLASTONITE	DARLINGTONIA	MANGELWURZEL	SALVATIONIST	SCANDINAVIAN
WOLSTENHOLME	EAVESDROPPER	MANIPULATION	SARDANAPALUS	SCAPULIMANCY
WOODBURYTYPE	FAINTHEARTED	MANIPULATIVE	SARDONICALLY	SCATTERBRAIN
WRETCHEDNESS	FAITHFULNESS	MANOEUVRABLE	SARRUSOPHONE	SCATTERMOUCH
XANTHOPTERIN	FARTHINGLAND	MANSLAUGHTER	SARSAPARILLA	SCHEHERAZADE
XIPHISTERNUM	FASTIDIOUSLY	MANUFACTURER	SATISFACTION	SCHILLERSPAR
YELLOWHAMMER	GAINSBOROUGH	MARCOBRUNNER	SATISFACTORY	SCHINDYLESIS
YORKSHIREMAN	GALLIGASKINS	MARCONIGRAPH	SAUROGNATHAE	SCHIZOMYCETE
YOUTHFULNESS	GALLINACEOUS	MARKSMANSHIP	TACTLESSNESS	SCHNEIDERIAN
ZALAMBDODONT	GALLIVANTING	MARLINESPIKE	TAGLIACOTIAN	SCHOOLMASTER
ZARATHUSTRIC	GALVANOMETER	MARRIAGEABLE	TAMARICACEAE	SCHOPENHAUER
	GAMESMANSHIP	MARSEILLAISE	TAPERECORDER	SCINTILLATOR
12:2	GAMOSEPALOUS	MASSERANDUBA	TAPSALTEERIE	SCLERENCHYMA
BABINGTONITE	GASTARBEITER	MASSPRODUCED	TAPSLETEERIE	SCLERODERMIA
BACCHANALIAN	GASTROSOPHER	MASTERSTROKE	TARAMASALATA	SCOPOPHILIAC
BACKBREAKING	HABERDASHERS	MASTIGOPHORA	TAUTOLOGICAL	SCREENWRITER
BACKWARDNESS	HABERDASHERY	MASTURBATION	VAINGLORIOUS	SCRIMSHANDER
BACKWOODSMAN	HAEMATEMESIS	MATHEMATICAL	VALENCIENNES	SCRIMSHANKER
BACTERIOLOGY	HAEMOPHILIAC	NARCISSISTIC	VAPORIZATION	SCRIPTWRITER
BACTERIOSTAT	HAEMORRHOIDS	NATURALISTIC	VARICOLOURED	SCRUPULOUSLY
BAIRNSFATHER	HAIRDRESSERS	NAVIGABILITY	WALLYDRAIGLE	SCURRILOUSLY
BAMBOCCIADES	HAIRDRESSING	PACIFICATION	WAREHOUSEMAN	ADAPTABILITY
BANANALANDER	HAIRSPLITTER	PAINLESSNESS	WASHINGTONIA	ADDITIONALLY
BANDERSNATCH	HALLANSHAKER	PALEONTOLOGY	WATCHFULNESS	ADJECTIVALLY
BANTAMWEIGHT	HALLUCINOGEN	PALINGENESIA	WATERCARRIER	ADJUDICATION
BARBERMONGER	HAMARTHRITIS	PALINGENESIS	XANTHOPTERIN	ADMINISTRATE
BARNSTORMING	HAMBLETONIAN	PALPITATIONS	ZALAMBDODONT	ADMONISHMENT
BARORECEPTOR	HAMMERHEADED	PALUDAMENTUM	ZARATHUSTRIC	ADSCITITIOUS
BARRANQUILLA	HANDKERCHIEF	PANAESTHESIA	ABBREVIATION	ADULTERATION
BATTLEGROUND	HAPPENSTANCE	PANATHENAEAN	ABOLITIONIST	ADVANTAGEOUS
CABINETMAKER	HAPPYGOLUCKY	PANCHATANTRA	ABSQUATULATE	ADVANTAGIOUS
CALCEAMENTUM	HAPTOTROPISM	PANCHROMATIC	OBEDIENTIARY	ADVENTITIOUS
CALLIGRAPHIC	HARMONIOUSLY	PANDAEMONIUM	OBLITERATION	ADVISABILITY
CALLISTHENES	HARNESSMAKER	PANDANACEOUS	OBSEQUIOUSLY	EDUCATIONIST
CALUMNIATION	HARUMFRODITE	PANPHARMACON	OBSERVANTINE	IDEALIZATION
CAMERAPERSON	IAMBOGRAPHER	PANTECHNICON	OBSOLESCENCE	IDENTIFIABLE
CAMIKNICKERS	KALEIDOSCOPE	PANTISOCRACY	OBSOLETENESS	IDIOSYNCRASY
CAMPANULARIA	KALISTOCRACY	PANTOPHAGOUS	OBSTETRICIAN	IDIOTHERMOUS
CAMPODEIFORM	KATHAREVOUSA	PAPILIONIDAE	OBSTREPEROUS	AECIDIOSPORE
CANCELLATION	KATZENJAMMER	PARACENTESIS	ACADEMICALLY	AERODYNAMICS
CANONIZATION	LABANOTATION	PARALIPOMENA	ACCELERATION	AERONAUTICAL
CANTANKEROUS	LABOURSAVING	PARAMAGNETIC	ACCENTUATION	AETHRIOSCOPE
CANTILEVERED	LABYRINTHINE	PARAMILITARY	ACCIDENTALLY	BEACONSFIELD
CAPERCAILLIE	LALLAPALOOZA	PARANTHELIUM	ACCOMPANYING	BEAUMARCHAIS
CAPERCAILZIE	LAMELLICORNE	PARENTHESIZE	ACCOMPLISHED	BEAUMONTAGUE
CAPITULATION	LAMENTATIONS	PARKINSONISM	ACCORDIONIST	BEAUMONTIQUE
CARAVANSERAI	LAMPADEDROMY	PARSIMONIOUS	ACCOUCHEMENT	BEHAVIOURISM
CARBOHYDRATE	LANCASTERIAN	PARTICOLORED	ACCOUTREMENT	BELLIGERENCY
CARCINOGENIC	LANGUEDOCIAN	PARTICULARLY	ACCUMULATION	BENEFACTRESS

BENEVOLENTLY	HEMICHORDATA	PERADVENTURE	REMONSTRANCE	VERMICULTURE
BENZOPHENONE	HENCEFORWARD	PERAMBULATOR	REMUNERATION	VERUMONTANUM
BENZOQUINONE	HEPHTHEMIMER	PERCEPTIVELY	REMUNERATIVE	VETERINARIAN
BERTHOLLETIA	HEREDITAMENT	PERCEPTIVITY	RENOUNCEMENT	WEATHERPROOF
BERTILLONAGE	HEREDITARIAN	PEREMPTORILY	RENUNCIATION	WEIGHTLIFTER
BESSERWISSER	HERMENEUTICS	PERGAMENEOUS	REPATRIATION	WELLBALANCED
BETHLEHEMITE	HERMENEUTIST	PERICARDITIS	REPERCUSSION	WELLINFORMED
BEWILDERMENT	HERMETICALLY	PERIODICALLY	REPOSSESSION	WELLINGTONIA
CEREBROTONIC	HEROICOMICAL	PERIODONTICS	REPROCESSING	WELTERWEIGHT
CEREMONIALLY	HETEROCLITIC	PERIOSTRACUM	REPRODUCTION	YELLOWHAMMER
DEAMBULATORY	HETEROCONTAE	PERIPHRASTIC	REPRODUCTIVE	AFFECTIONATE
DEASPIRATION	HETEROGAMETE	PERISTERONIC	RESETTLEMENT	AFORETHOUGHT
DEBILITATING	HETEROPHORIA	PERMANGANATE	RESIPISCENCE	AFTEREFFECTS
DECAPITATION	HETEROPLASIA	PERMEABILITY	RESPECTFULLY	AFTERTHOUGHT
DECELERATION	HETEROSEXUAL	PERMITTIVITY	RESPECTIVELY	EFFERVESCENT
DECENTRALISE	HETEROSOMATA	PERNOCTATION	RESPONDENTIA	EFFORTLESSLY
DECENTRALIZE	JENNYSPINNER	PERPETRATION	RESTAURATEUR	AGALMATOLITE
DECIPHERABLE	KERAUNOGRAPH	PERSEVERANCE	RESTLESSNESS	AGAMOGENETIC
DECIPHERMENT	LEGALIZATION	PERSISTENTLY	RESURRECTION	AGATHODAIMON
DECONGESTANT	LEGIONNAIRES	PERSONALIZED	RESUSCITATED	AGGRESSIVELY
DECORATIVELY	LEGITIMATELY	PERSPICACITY	RETARDEDNESS	AGRIBUSINESS
DEFLATIONARY	LEIOTRICHOUS	PERSPIRATION	RETICULATION	AGRICULTURAL
DEGENERATION	LEPIDOMELANE	PERSUASIVELY	RETRENCHMENT	EGYPTOLOGIST
DEHUMIDIFIER	LEXICOGRAPHY	PERSULPHURIC	REVERSIONARY	CHAIRMANSHIP
DELIBERATELY	MEANINGFULLY	PERTINACIOUS	SECESSIONIST	CHALCOPYRITE
DELIBERATION	MECHANICALLY	PERTURBATION	SECRETARIATE	CHALICOTHERE
DELICATESSEN	MECHITHARIST	PERVERSENESS	SECTARIANISM	CHAMPIONSHIP
DEMILITARIZE	MELODRAMATIC	PERVICACIOUS	SEGMENTATION	CHARACTERIZE
DEMIMONDAINE	MENSTRUATION	PESTILENTIAL	SELFADHESIVE	CHARTERHOUSE
DEMONSTRABLE	MERCANTILISM	PETRIFACTION	SELFCATERING	CHASTISEMENT
DEMONSTRABLY	MERETRICIOUS	PETTIFOGGERS	SELFEMPLOYED	CHAUVINISTIC
DEMONSTRATOR	MERISTEMATIC	PETTIFOGGERY	SELFINTEREST	CHEERFULNESS
DENDROLOGIST	MERITRICIOUS	PETTIFOGGING	SELFPORTRAIT	CHEESEBURGER
DENOMINATION	MERRYTHOUGHT	READJUSTMENT	SEMANTICALLY	CHEESEMONGER
DENUNCIATION	MERVEILLEUSE	REAPPEARANCE	SEMICIRCULAR	CHEESEPARING
DEPARTMENTAL	MESOTHELIOMA	RECALCITRANT	SEMIDETACHED	CHEMOTHERAPY
DEPOPULATION	METAGNATHOUS	RECAPITULATE	SEMIPRECIOUS	CHESTERFIELD
DEPRECIATION	METALLOPHONE	RECEIVERSHIP	SEPTEMBRISER	CHILDBEARING
DEPRECIATORY	METALLURGIST	RECEPTIONIST	SEPTUAGESIMA	CHILDISHNESS
DEREGULATION	METAMORPHISM	RECHARGEABLE	SEQUENTIALLY	CHIROPRACTIC
DERESTRICTED	METAMORPHOSE	RECIPROCALLY	SEQUESTRATOR	CHIROPRACTOR
DESIDERATIVE	METAPHORICAL	RECKLESSNESS	SERASKIERATE	CHITTERLINGS
DESIRABILITY	METAPHYSICAL	RECOGNIZABLE	SERVICEBERRY	CHLORINATION
DESSERTSPOON	METHODICALLY	RECOGNIZANCE	SERVICEWOMAN	CHLOROPICRIN
DEUTERANOPIA	METHOTREXATE	RECOLLECTION	SESQUIALTERA	CHONDRIOSOME
DEUTEROSCOPY	METICULOUSLY	RECONSTITUTE	SESQUITERTIA	CHOREOGRAPHY
FEARLESSNESS	METROPOLITAN	RECORDPLAYER	SEXAGENARIAN	CHORIZONTIST
FEATHERBRAIN	NEIGHBORHOOD	RECREATIONAL	TECHNICALITY	CHREMATISTIC
FEHMGERICHTE	NEIGHBOURING	RECRUDESCENT	TECHNOLOGIST	CHRESTOMATHY
FELDSPATHOID	NEOCLASSICAL	RECUPERATION	TEETERTOTTER	CHRISTIANITY
FERMENTATION	NEOPLATONISM	RECUPERATIVE	TELEASTHETIC	CHURCHWARDEN
GENEALOGICAL	NEPENTHACEAE	REDEMPTIONER	TELEGRAPHESE	CHURLISHNESS
GENETHLIACON	NEPHELOMETER	REDEPLOYMENT	TELEGRAPHIST	PHARMACOLOGY
GENTLETAMPER	NEUROFIBROMA	REDINTEGRATE	TELEOSAURIAN	PHENOMENALLY
GEOGRAPHICAL	NEUROLOGICAL	REDISCOVERED	TELEUTOSPORE	PHILANTHROPY
GEOLOGICALLY	NEUROSCIENCE	REDISTRIBUTE	TERCENTENARY	PHILHARMONIC
GEOMETRICIAN	NEUROTICALLY	REFLATIONARY	TERGIVERSATE	PHILISTINISM
GEOPHYSICIST	NEVERTHELESS	REFLECTIVITY	TERRIFICALLY	PHILODENDRON
GERIATRICIAN	NEWFOUNDLAND	REFRIGERATED	TERRITORIALS	PHILOLOGICAL
GERONTOCRACY	NEWSPAPERMAN	REFRIGERATOR	TESTAMENTARY	PHILOSOPHIZE
GESELLSCHAFT	PEACEFULNESS	REGENERATION	TESTOSTERONE	PHLEBOTOMIST
HEADMISTRESS	PEACEKEEPING	REGISTRATION	TETRACYCLINE	PHONETICALLY
HEADQUARTERS	PECTORILOQUY	REHABILITATE	TETRAHEDRITE	PHOSPHOLIPID
HEARTSTRINGS	PEDANTICALLY	REINVIGORATE	TETRODOTOXIN	PHOSPHORENCE
HEARTWARMING	PEDIATRICIAN	RELATIONSHIP	VEHMGERICHTE	PHOSPHORESCE
HELIOGABALUS	PEDICELLARIA	RELENTLESSLY	VENEPUNCTURE	PHOTOGLYPHIC
HELIOTROPISM	PENALIZATION	REMEMBRANCER	VENGEFULNESS	PHOTOGRAPHER
HELLGRAMMITE	PENITENTIARY	REMINISCENCE	VENTRIPOTENT	PHOTOGRAPHIC
HELPLESSNESS	PENNSYLVANIA		VERIFICATION	PHOTOGRAVURE

PHRONTISTERY	BIRDWATCHING	FIRSTFOOTING	SINANTHROPUS	GLYCOPROTEIN
PHYCOXANTHIN	CIRCASSIENNE	GIBRALTARIAN	SINGLEDECKER	GLYNDEBOURNE
PHYSIOLOGIST	CIRCUMCISION	GIGANTOMACHY	SINGLEHANDED	GLYPTOGRAPHY
PHYTOBENTHOS	CIRCUMGYRATE	HIERARCHICAL	SINGLEMINDED	ILLEGIBILITY
PHYTONADIONE	CIRCUMSCRIBE	HIEROGLYPHIC	SIPHONOPHORA	ILLEGITIMACY
PHYTOPHAGOUS	CIRCUMSTANCE	HIEROGRAMMAT	SIPHONOSTELE	ILLEGITIMATE
RHADAMANTHUS	CIVILISATION	HIEROPHANTIC	SIPUNCULACEA	ILLOGICALITY
RHAMPHOTHECA	CIVILIZATION	HIGHFALUTING	SITTLICHKEIT	ILLUMINATING
RHINORRHOEAL	DIAGRAMMATIC	HILDEBRANDIC	SIVAPITHECUS	ILLUMINATION
RHIPIDOPTERA	DIALECTICIAN	HINDQUARTERS	TIGHTFITTING	ILLUSTRATION
RHODODENDRON	DICHROMATISM	HIPPOCRATISE	TIMELESSNESS	ILLUSTRATIVE
RHYTHMICALLY	DICTATORSHIP	HIPPOCREPIAN	TITANOSAURUS	KLEPTOMANIAC
RHYTIDECTOMY	DIENCEPHALON	HIPPOPOTAMUS	UINTATHERIUM	KLETTERSCHUE
SHAMEFACEDLY	DIFFERENTIAL	HISTIOPHORUS	VIBRATIUNCLE	KLIPSPRINGER
SHAREHOLDING	DILAPIDATION	HISTORICALLY	VILIFICATION	OLDFASHIONED
SHARPSHOOTER	DILATORINESS	KILLIKINNICK	VILLEGIATURA	PLACENTIFORM
SHEEPISHNESS	DIPLOGENESIS	KINAESTHETIC	VINDICTIVELY	PLAINCLOTHES
SHILLYSHALLY	DIPRIONIDIAN	KINDERGARTEN	VITUPERATION	PLASTERSTONE
SHIPBUILDING	DIRECTORSHIP	KIRSCHWASSER	VITUPERATIVE	PLAUSIBILITY
SHIRTSLEEVES	DISACCHARIDE	LICKTRENCHER	WICKETKEEPER	PLECTOGNATHI
SHIRTWAISTER	DISADVANTAGE	LIFELESSNESS	WILLIEWAUGHT	PLEIOCHASIUM
SHORTCIRCUIT	DISAGREEABLE	LIGHTHEARTED	WILTSHIREMAN	SLEDGEHAMMER
SHORTCOMINGS	DISAGREEMENT	LILLIBULLERO	WINTERHALTER	SLEEPWALKING
SHORTSIGHTED	DISAPPEARING	LILLIBURLERO	XIPHISTERNUM	SLOCKDOLAGER
SHORTSLEEVED	DISAPPOINTED	LINCOLNSHIRE	SKUTTERUDITE	SLOCKDOLIGER
SHORTSTAFFED	DISASSOCIATE	LIQUEFACTION	ALEXIPHARMIC	SLOCKDOLOGER
SHOSTAKOVICH	DISASTROUSLY	LISTLESSNESS	ALIMENTATION	SLOVENLINESS
SHUFFLEBOARD	DISCIPLINARY	LITHOGRAPHIC	ALLITERATION	SLUBBERINGLY
THANKFULNESS	DISCOMEDUSAE	LITHOLATROUS	ALPHABETICAL	ULOTRICHALES
THANKSGIVING	DISCOMFITURE	LIVERPUDLIAN	ALPHANUMERIC	ULTRAMONTANE
THAUMATURGIC	DISCOMYCETES	MICHELANGELO	BLABBERMOUTH	AMALGAMATION
THAUMATURGUS	DISCONCERTED	MICROBREWERY	BLACKCURRANT	AMARANTACEAE
THEATRICALLY	DISCONNECTED	MICROCLIMATE	BLANDISHMENT	AMBASSADRESS
THEOPHYLLINE	DISCONSOLATE	MIDDLEWEIGHT	BLEFUSCUDIAN	AMBIDEXTROUS
THEORETICIAN	DISCONTENTED	MILITARISTIC	BLENNORRHOEA	AMBULANCEMAN
THERAPEUTICS	DISCOURAGING	MILLILAMBERT	BLETHERSKATE	AMELIORATION
THEREAGAINST	DISCOURTEOUS	MINDBOGGLING	BLOODLETTING	AMPHISBAENIC
THERMOSTATIC	DISCRIMINATE	MINDFULLNESS	BLOODSTAINED	AMPHISTOMOUS
THESMOPHORIA	DISDAINFULLY	MINERALOGIST	BLOODTHIRSTY	AMPHITHEATER
THESSALONIAN	DISEMBARRASS	MINICOMPUTER	BLUESTOCKING	AMPHITHEATRE
THICKSKINNED	DISENCHANTED	MINISTRATION	CLAIRVOYANCE	EMANCIPATION
THIGMOTROPIC	DISFRANCHISE	MIRACULOUSLY	CLAIRVOYANCY	EMASCULATION
THIRDBOROUGH	DISHONORABLE	MISADVENTURE	CLAMJAMPHRIE	EMBARRASSING
THOROUGHBRED	DISHONORABLY	MISANTHROPIC	CLANNISHNESS	EMBEZZLEMENT
THOROUGHFARE	DISINCENTIVE	MISAPPREHEND	CLAPPERBOARD	EMBROIDERESS
THOROUGHNESS	DISINFECTANT	MISBEHAVIOUR	CLARINETTIST	EMPHATICALLY
THOUGHTFULLY	DISINGENUOUS	MISCALCULATE	CLASSIFIABLE	IMMACULATELY
THREADNEEDLE	DISINTEGRATE	MISDELIVERED	CLAUDICATION	IMMEASURABLE
THREEQUARTER	DISOBEDIENCE	MISDEMEANOUR	CLAVICEMBALO	IMMEASURABLY
THUNDERCLOUD	DISORGANIZED	MISINTERPRET	CLEARSIGHTED	IMMODERATELY
THUNDERFLASH	DISORIENTATE	MISPLACEMENT	CLEISTOGAMIC	IMMODERATION
THUNDERSTORM	DISPENSATION	MISPRONOUNCE	CLOTHESHORSE	IMMUNIZATION
THYSANOPTERA	DISPLACEMENT	MISQUOTATION	ELASMOBRANCH	IMMUNOLOGIST
WHIGMALEERIE	DISPOSSESSED	MISREPRESENT	ELECTRICALLY	IMMUTABILITY
WHIMSICALITY	DISQUISITION	MISSTATEMENT	ELECTROLYSIS	IMPARTIALITY
WHIPPOORWILL	DISREPECTFUL	MISTREATMENT	ELECTROPLATE	IMPENETRABLE
WHOLEHEARTED	DISREPUTABLE	MITRAILLEUSE	ELECTROTONUS	IMPERFECTION
AIRCRAFTSMAN	DISSATISFIED	NIGHTCLOTHES	ELEEMOSYNARY	IMPERFECTIVE
BIBLIOGRAPHY	DISSERTATION	NIMBOSTRATUS	FLAGELLATION	IMPERISHABLE
BIBLIOPEGIST	DISSOCIATION	PIGMENTATION	FLAMBOYANTLY	IMPERSONALLY
BICAMERALISM	DISTILLATION	PINNIEWINKLE	FLITTERMOUSE	IMPERSONATOR
BICENTENNIAL	DISTINCTNESS	PISCICULTURE	FLORICULTURE	IMPERTINENCE
BIELORUSSIAN	DISTRIBUTION	PITTERPATTER	FLUORESCENCE	IMPLANTATION
BILLINGSGATE	DISTRIBUTIVE	RIDICULOUSLY	FLUORIDATION	IMPOLITENESS
BIOCHEMISTRY	DIVERTICULUM	RISORGIMENTO	FLUVIOMARINE	IMPOVERISHED
BIODIVERSITY	DIVERTIMENTO	SIDEWHISKERS	GLADIATORIAL	IMPREGNATION
BIOFLAVONOID	FIDDLESTICKS	SIGNIFICANCE	GLOBETROTTER	IMPRESSIVELY
BIOGRAPHICAL	FIGURATIVELY	SILVERHAIRED	GLOCKENSPIEL	IMPRISONMENT
BIPROPELLANT	FINALIZATION	SIMULTANEOUS	GLUBBDUBDRIB	IMPROVIDENCE

OMBUDSPERSON	INCALCULABLE	INSTAURATION	UNAUTHORIZED	UNSUCCESSFUL
SMALLHOLDING	INCANDESCENT	INSTRUCTIONS	UNBELIEVABLE	UNSURPRISING
UMBRADARLING	INCAPABILITY	INSTRUCTRESS	UNBELIEVABLY	UNSUSPECTING
ANAESTHETISE	INCAPACITATE	INSTRUMENTAL	UNCHALLENGED	UNUTTERABLES
ANAESTHETIST	INCAUTIOUSLY	INSUFFERABLE	UNCHANGEABLE	BOISTEROUSLY
ANAESTHETIZE	INCIDENTALLY	INSUFFERABLY	UNCHARITABLE	BOOBYTRAPPED
ANAMORPHOSIS	INCINERATION	INSUFFICIENT	UNCHARITABLY	BOONDOGGLING
ANASTIGMATIC	INCOHERENTLY	INSURRECTION	UNCLASSIFIED	BOUGAINVILLE
ANCHORPERSON	INCOMPARABLE	INTELLECTUAL	UNCONSIDERED	BOULEVARDIER
ANDOUILLETTE	INCOMPARABLY	INTELLIGENCE	UNCONTROLLED	COCCIDIOSTAT
ANDROSTERONE	INCOMPATIBLE	INTELLIGIBLE	UNCONVERSANT	CODIFICATION
ANECATHARSIS	INCOMPETENCE	INTEMPERANCE	UNCONVINCING	COHABITATION
ANEMOPHILOUS	INCOMPLETELY	INTENERATION	UNCTUOUSNESS	COINCIDENTAL
ANNIHILATION	INCONCLUSIVE	INTERCEPTION	UNCULTIVATED	COLDSHOULDER
ANNOUNCEMENT	INCONSEQUENT	INTERCESSION	UNDEMOCRATIC	COLLABORATOR
ANNUNCIATION	INCONSISTENT	INTERCHANGED	UNDERACHIEVE	COLLECTIVELY
ANTAGONISTIC	INCONSOLABLE	INTERFERENCE	UNDERCLOTHES	COLLECTORATE
ANTANANARIVO	INCONTINENCE	INTERGLACIAL	UNDERCURRENT	COLLOQUIALLY
ANTEDILUVIAN	INCONVENIENT	INTERJECTION	UNDEREXPOSED	COLLUCTATION
ANTEMERIDIAN	INCORPORATED	INTERLOCUTOR	UNDERGARMENT	COLLYWOBBLES
ANTHELMINTIC	INCORRIGIBLE	INTERMEDIARY	UNDERPINNING	COLONIZATION
ANTHROPOLOGY	INCORRIGIBLY	INTERMEDIATE	UNDERSKINKER	COLOQUINTIDA
ANTIAIRCRAFT	INCREASINGLY	INTERMINABLE	UNDERSTAFFED	COMBINATIONS
ANTIBACCHIUS	INCRUSTATION	INTERMINABLY	UNDERWRITTEN	COMMANDMENTS
ANTIBARBARUS	INCUNABULIST	INTERMISSION	UNDESERVEDLY	COMMENCEMENT
ANTICIPATION	INDEBTEDNESS	INTERMITTENT	UNDETECTABLE	COMMENDATION
ANTICIPATORY	INDECLINABLE	INTERPRETING	UNDETERMINED	COMMENDATORY
ANTILEGOMENA	INDEFENSIBLE	INTERRELATED	UNDIMINISHED	COMMENSURATE
ANTIMACASSAR	INDEFINITELY	INTERROGATOR	UNDISCHARGED	COMMERCIALLY
ANTIMETABOLE	INDEPENDENCE	INTERRUPTION	UNECONOMICAL	COMMISSARIAT
ANTIMNEMONIC	INDIFFERENCE	INTERSECTION	UNEMPLOYMENT	COMMISSIONED
ANTINEUTRINO	INDIGESTIBLE	INTERSPERSED	UNEXPECTEDLY	COMMISSIONER
ANTIPARTICLE	INDISCRETION	INTERSTELLAR	UNEXPURGATED	COMMONWEALTH
ANTIRACHITIC	INDISPUTABLE	INTERVENTION	UNFATHOMABLE	COMMUNICABLE
ANTISTROPHON	INDISPUTABLY	INTIMIDATING	UNFAVOURABLE	COMPANIONWAY
ANTITHROMBIN	INDISSOLUBLE	INTIMIDATION	UNFREQUENTED	COMPELLATION
ANTONINIANUS	INDISTINCTLY	INTOXICATING	UNIDENTIFIED	COMPENSATION
ENANTIOMORPH	INDIVIDUALLY	INTOXICATION	UNILATERALLY	COMPENSATORY
ENANTIOPATHY	INDOCTRINATE	INTRANSIGENT	UNIMAGINABLE	COMPLACENTLY
ENCHEIRIDION	INDUSTRIALLY	INTRANSITIVE	UNIMPORTANCE	COMPLETENESS
ENCIRCLEMENT	INEFFICIENCY	INTRAUTERINE	UNINTERESTED	COMPLICATION
ENCROACHMENT	INERADICABLE	INTRODUCTION	UNIVERSALIST	COMPROMISING
ENCYCLOPEDIA	INESCUTCHEON	INTRODUCTORY	UNMANAGEABLE	COMPURGATION
ENCYCLOPEDIC	INEXACTITUDE	INTROVERSION	UNMISTAKABLE	CONCENTRATED
ENERGYSAVING	INEXPERIENCE	INTUITIONISM	UNNEIGHBORLY	CONCILIATION
ENGLISHWOMAN	INEXPLICABLE	INVALIDATION	UNOBSTRUCTED	CONCILIATORY
ENGLISHWOMEN	INEXPLICABLY	INVERTEBRATE	UNOBTAINABLE	CONCLUSIVELY
ENHYPOSTASIA	INEXTRICABLE	INVESTIGATOR	UNOFFICIALLY	CONCURRENTLY
ENTANGLEMENT	INEXTRICABLY	INVIGORATING	UNOPPRESSIVE	CONDEMNATION
ENTEROMORPHA	INFELICITOUS	INVIGORATION	UNPARALLELED	CONDENSATION
ENTEROPNEUST	INFILTRATION	INVISIBILITY	UNPARDONABLE	CONDUCTIVITY
ENTERPRISING	INFLAMMATION	INVULNERABLE	UNPOPULARITY	CONFECTIONER
ENTERTAINING	INFLAMMATORY	MNEMOTECHNIC	UNPREJUDICED	CONFESSIONAL
ENTHUSIASTIC	INFLATIONARY	ONCORHYNCHUS	UNPRETENDING	CONFIDENTIAL
ENTOMOLOGIST	INFORMIDABLE	ONEIROCRITIC	UNPRINCIPLED	CONFIRMATION
ENTOMOSTRACA	INFOTAINMENT	ONOMATOPOEIA	UNPRODUCTIVE	CONFIRMATORY
ENTOPLASTRON	INFREQUENTLY	ONOMATOPOEIC	UNPROFITABLE	CONFISCATION
ENTREATINGLY	INFRINGEMENT	ONYCHOPHORAN	UNREASONABLE	CONGENITALLY
ENTRENCHMENT	INGRATIATING	SNOBBISHNESS	UNRECOGNISED	CONGLOMERATE
ENTREPRENEUR	INHARMONIOUS	SNOWBOARDING	UNRECOGNIZED	CONGRATULATE
INACCESSIBLE	INHOSPITABLE	UNACCEPTABLE	UNRESERVEDLY	CONGREGATION
INACCURATELY	INNATTENTIVE	UNACCUSTOMED	UNRESPONSIVE	CONQUISTADOR
INADEQUATELY	INNOMINABLES	UNACQUAINTED	UNRESTRAINED	CONSCRIPTION
INADMISSIBLE	INORDINATELY	UNANSWERABLE	UNRESTRICTED	CONSECRATION
INADVERTENCE	INSALUBRIOUS	UNAPPARELLED	UNRETURNABLE	CONSEQUENCES
INAPPLICABLE	INSEMINATION	UNAPPETIZING	UNSATISFYING	CONSEQUENTLY
INARTICULATE	INSOLUBILITY	UNATTAINABLE	UNSCIENTIFIC	CONSERVATION
INAUGURATION	INSPECTORATE	UNATTRACTIVE	UNSCRUPULOUS	CONSERVATISM
INAUSPICIOUS	INSTALLATION	UNAUTHORISED	UNSEASONABLE	CONSERVATIVE

CONSERVATORY	FOTHERINGHAY	PORNOGRAPHIC	OPHIOGLOSSUM	CRASSAMENTUM
CONSIDERABLE	GOBBLEDEGOOK	POSSESSIVELY	OPINIONATIVE	CREATIVENESS
CONSIDERABLY	GOBBLEDYGOOK	POSTGRADUATE	OPISTHOGRAPH	CREMAILLIÈRE
CONSISTENTLY	GONADOTROPIN	POSTHUMOUSLY	OPPRESSIVELY	CRISTOBALITE
CONSOCIATION	GONDWANALAND	POSTLIMINARY	SPACIOUSNESS	CROSSBENCHER
CONSOLIDATED	GOOSEPIMPLES	POSTMISTRESS	SPATANGOIDEA	CROSSCOUNTRY
CONSOLIDATOR	GOVERNMENTAL	POSTPONEMENT	SPECIFICALLY	CROSSEXAMINE
CONSPECTUITY	HOBBIDIDANCE	POSTPOSITIVE	SPECIOUSNESS	CROSSSECTION
CONSPIRACIST	HOLIDAYMAKER	POSTPRANDIAL	SPECKTIONEER	CRYPTOGRAPHY
CONSTABULARY	HOMESICKNESS	POTAMOLOGIST	SPECTROMETER	DRAMATICALLY
CONSTIPATION	HOMOEOPATHIC	POTENTIALITY	SPECTROSCOPE	DRAMATURGIST
CONSTITUENCY	HOMOTHERMOUS	POTICHOMANIA	SPELEOLOGIST	DRESSINGDOWN
CONSTITUENTS	HOPELESSNESS	POWERSHARING	SPELLCHECKER	DRINKDRIVING
CONSTITUTION	HORIZONTALLY	RODOMONTADER	SPERMATOCYTE	ERATOSTHENES
CONSTRICTION	HORRIFICALLY	ROLLERBLADER	SPERMATOZOID	ERYTHROMYCIN
CONSTRUCTION	HORSEMANSHIP	ROLLERBLADES	SPERMATOZOON	FRACTIONALLY
CONSTRUCTIVE	HORTICULTURE	ROMANTICALLY	SPHACELATION	FRANKALMOIGN
CONSULTATION	HOUSEBREAKER	RONCESVALLES	SPHAIRISTIKE	FRANKENSTEIN
CONSULTATIVE	HOUSEKEEPING	ROOMINGHOUSE	SPIEGELEISEN	FRANKINCENSE
CONSUMMATION	HOUSETOHOUSE	SOCIOLOGICAL	SPINECHILLER	FRAUENDIENST
CONTABESCENT	HOUSEWARMING	SOLICITATION	SPINSTERHOOD	FREIGHTLINER
CONTAMINATED	JOURNALISTIC	SOLICITOUSLY	SPIRITUALISM	FRIENDLINESS
CONTEMPORARY	LONGDISTANCE	SOMATOPLEURE	SPIRITUALIST	FRONTIERSMAN
CONTEMPTIBLE	LONGITUDINAL	SOMNAMBULISM	SPIRITUALITY	FRONTISPIECE
CONTEMPTUOUS	LONGSHOREMAN	SOMNAMBULIST	SPITEFULNESS	FRUITFULNESS
CONTERMINOUS	LONGSTANDING	SOPHISTICATE	SPLENOMEGALY	FRUMENTATION
CONTIGNATION	LOXODROMICAL	SOUTHCOTTIAN	SPOKESPERSON	GRACEFULNESS
CONTINUATION	MOBILIZATION	SOUTHEASTERN	SPORADICALLY	GRACIOUSNESS
CONTINUOUSLY	MODIFICATION	SOUTHERNMOST	SPORTSGROUND	GRANDISONIAN
CONTRAPPOSTO	MOISTURIZING	SOUTHERNWOOD	SPREADEAGLED	GRANDMONTINE
CONTRAPUNTAL	MONOSYLLABIC	SOUTHWESTERN	SPRECHGESANG	GRANDPARENTS
CONTRARINESS	MONOSYLLABLE	TOBACCONISTS	SPURIOUSNESS	GRAPHOLOGIST
CONTRIBUTION	MONOTONOUSLY	TOGETHERNESS	SPURTLEBLADE	GRASSWIDOWER
CONTRIBUTORY	MONTESSORIAN	TORRICELLIAN	UPROARIOUSLY	GRATEFULNESS
CONTRITURATE	MOONLIGHTING	TOTALITARIAN	EQUIVOCATION	GREENGROCERS
CONTROLLABLE	MOSBOLLETJIE	TOXICOLOGIST	EQUIVOCATORY	GREENGROCERY
CONTUMACIOUS	MOTORCYCLIST	VOCIFERATION	SQUIRRELFISH	GRISEOFULVIN
CONVALESCENT	MOUSQUETAIRE	VOCIFEROUSLY	ARBORESCENCE	GROSSULARITE
CONVALESCING	MOUTHBROODER	VOLUPTUOUSLY	ARCHILOCHIAN	IRASCIBILITY
CONVENIENCES	NOCONFIDENCE	WOLLASTONITE	ARCHIPELAGOS	IRRATIONALLY
CONVENIENTLY	NOMENCLATURE	WOLSTENHOLME	ARCHITECTURE	IRREDEEMABLE
CONVENTIONAL	NONAGENARIAN	WOODBURYTYPE	ARFVEDSONITE	IRREGULARITY
CONVERSATION	NONALCOHOLIC	YORKSHIREMAN	ARISTOCRATIC	IRRESISTIBLE
CONVEYANCING	NONCHALANTLY	YOUTHFULNESS	ARISTOLOCHIA	IRRESOLUTELY
CONVINCINGLY	NONCOMMITTAL	APFELSTRUDEL	ARISTOPHANES	IRRESOLUTION
CONVIVIALITY	NONDIRECTIVE	APLANOGAMETE	ARISTOTELEAN	IRRESOLVABLE
COORDINATION	NONEXISTENCE	APOLLINARIAN	ARITHMETICAL	IRRESPECTIVE
COSCINOMANCY	NONFLAMMABLE	APOSTROPHISE	AROMATHERAPY	IRREVERENTLY
COSMOPOLITAN	NONOBJECTIVE	APPENDECTOMY	ARSENOPYRITE	IRREVERSIBLE
COSTERMONGER	NONRESIDENCE	APPENDICITIS	ARTHROPLASTY	IRRITABILITY
COUNTERBLAST	NONRESISTANT	APPOGGIATURA	ARTICULATION	OREOPITHECUS
COUNTERCLAIM	NORTHEASTERN	APPRECIATION	ARTIFICIALLY	OREOPITHEOUS
COUNTERMARCH	NORTHERNMOST	APPRECIATIVE	ARTILLERYMAN	ORGANISATION
COUNTERPOINT	NORTHWESTERN	APPREHENSION	ARTIODACTYLA	ORGANIZATION
COUNTERPOISE	NOTIFICATION	APPREHENSIVE	ARTISTICALLY	ORIENTEERING
COURAGEOUSLY	POGONOPHORAN	APPROACHABLE	BRACHYCEPHAL	ORNITHOGALUM
COURTMARTIAL	POIKILOTHERM	APPURTENANCE	BRAINWASHING	ORTHODONTICS
COVETOUSNESS	POINTILLISME	EPACRIDACEAE	BRANCHIOPODA	ORTHOGENESIS
DOGMATICALLY	POLARIZATION	EPANORTHOSIS	BREAKTHROUGH	ORTHOPAEDICS
DOLPHINARIUM	POLICYMAKING	EPENCEPHALON	BREASTPLOUGH	ORTHOPAEDIST
DOMESTICATED	POLYETHYLENE	EPIDEICTICAL	BREASTSUMMER	ORTHOPTEROUS
DONNERWETTER	POLYNEURITIS	EPIGRAMMATIC	BREATHALYSER	ORTHORHOMBIC
DORSIVENTRAL	POLYPETALOUS	EPILEPTIFORM	BREATHLESSLY	ORTHOTONESIS
DOUBLEDECKER	POLYRIBOSOME	EPIPHENOMENA	BREATHTAKING	PRACTICALITY
DOUBLEGLAZED	POLYSYLLABIC	EPISCOPALIAN	BRICKFIELDER	PRACTICIONER
FOOTSLOGGING	POLYSYLLABLE	EPISTEMOLOGY	BRILLIANTINE	PRACTITIONER
FORCEFULNESS	POLYSYNDETON	EPISTOLATERS	BROADCASTING	PRAISEWORTHY
FORMALDEHYDE	POLYURETHANE	EPITHALAMION	BRONTOSAURUS	PRALLTRILLER
FORTUITOUSLY	POPOCATEPETL	EPITHALAMIUM	CRASHLANDING	PRASEODYMIUM

PRAXINOSCOPE	PROTHALAMION	OSTENTATIOUS	STUPEFACTION	QUIXOTICALLY
PRECARIOUSLY	PROTHALAMIUM	OSTEOMALACIA	AUGMENTATION	RUTHLESSNESS
PRECOCIOUSLY	PROTHONOTARY	OSTEOPOROSIS	AUGMENTATIVE	SUBARRHATION
PRECONDITION	PROTOPLASMAL	OSTEOSARCOMA	AUSCULTATION	SUBCOMMITTEE
PREDESTINATE	PROTOPLASMIC	PSEPHOLOGIST	AUSPICIOUSLY	SUBCONSCIOUS
PREDETERMINE	PROTUBERANCE	PSEUDONYMOUS	AUSTRALASIAN	SUBCONTINENT
PREDILECTION	PROVERBIALLY	PSIPHENOMENA	AUSTRONESIAN	SUBCUTANEOUS
PREDOMINANCE	PROVIDENTIAL	PSYCHIATRIST	AUTHENTICATE	SUBHASTATION
PREFERENTIAL	TRABECULATED	PSYCHOLOGIST	AUTHENTICITY	SUBJECTIVELY
PREGUSTATION	TRACTABILITY	PSYCHOPATHIC	AUTOHYPNOSIS	SUBJECTIVITY
PREHISTORIAN	TRADESCANTIA	USERFRIENDLY	BUCKLEBEGGAR	SUBLAPSARIAN
PREMAXILLARY	TRADESPEOPLE	ATHEROMATOUS	BUNKOSTEERER	SUBMINIATURE
PREMONSTRANT	TRALATICIOUS	ATMOSPHERICS	BUREAUCRATIC	SUBMISSIVELY
PREPAREDNESS	TRALATITIOUS	ATTRACTIVELY	BUSINESSLIKE	SUBSCRIPTION
PREPONDERANT	TRANQUILIZER	ATTRIBUTABLE	BUTTERSCOTCH	SUBSEQUENTLY
PREPONDERATE	TRANQUILLISE	ETEPIMELETIC	CUCKOOFLOWER	SUBSERVIENCE
PREPONDERENT	TRANQUILLITY	ETHEROMANIAC	CURMUDGEONLY	SUBSIDIARITY
PREPOSSESSED	TRANQUILLIZE	ETHNOLOGICAL	DUNNIEWASSAL	SUBSTANTIATE
PREPOSTEROUS	TRANSACTIONS	ETYMOLOGICAL	EULENSPIEGEL	SUBSTITUTION
PREREQUISITE	TRANSCENDENT	ETYMOLOGICON	FULMINATIONS	SUBSTITUTIVE
PRESBYTERIAN	TRANSFERABLE	OTHERWORLDLY	FUNCTIONALLY	SUBSTRUCTURE
PRESCRIPTION	TRANSFERENCE	PTERIDOPHYTE	FUNCTIONLESS	SUBTERRANEAN
PRESCRIPTIVE	TRANSGRESSOR	PTERIDOSPERM	FUNDAMENTALS	SUCCESSFULLY
PRESENTATION	TRANSITIONAL	PTERODACTYLE	FUSTILLIRIAN	SUCCESSIVELY
PRESENTIMENT	TRANSLATABLE	STAGGERINGLY	GUARDIANSHIP	SUCCUSSATION
PRESERVATION	TRANSLUCENCE	STAKHANOVITE	GUILDENSTERN	SUFFICIENTLY
PRESERVATIVE	TRANSMIGRATE	STANISLAVSKI	HUDIBRASTICS	SUGGESTIVELY
PRESIDENTIAL	TRANSMISSION	STATISTICIAN	HUMANITARIAN	SULPHONAMIDE
PRESTRICTION	TRANSMOGRIFY	STEALTHINESS	HUMANIZATION	SUPERANNUATE
PRESUMPTUOUS	TRANSOCEANIC	STEEPLECHASE	JURISDICTION	SUPERCHARGED
PREVARICATOR	TRANSPARENCY	STEGOPHOLIST	LUGUBRIOUSLY	SUPERCHARGER
PREVENTATIVE	TRANSPONTINE	STELLENBOSCH	LUMINESCENCE	SUPERCILIARY
PRIGGISHNESS	TRANSVESTISM	STENOGRAPHER	LUMINISCENCE	SUPERCILIOUS
PRIMIGRAVIDA	TRANSVESTITE	STENTORPHONE	LUXEMBOURGER	SUPERHIGHWAY
PRINCIPALITY	TREMENDOUSLY	STEPDAUGHTER	LUXULLIANITE	SUPERNACULUM
PRIZEFIGHTER	TRICENTENARY	STEREOPHONIC	MUCILAGINOUS	SUPERNATURAL
PRIZEWINNING	TRICHOLOGIST	STEREOPTICON	MUDDLEHEADED	SUPERSTITION
PROBATIONARY	TRICHOPHYTON	STEREOSCOPIC	MUGGLETONIAN	SUPERSTRATUM
PROCESSIONAL	TRIGONOMETRY	STEREOTYPING	MULLIGATAWNY	SUPPLICATION
PROCLAMATION	TRIUMPHANTLY	STERNUTATION	MULTICOLORED	SURMOUNTABLE
PRODIGIOUSLY	TROCHELMINTH	STERNWHEELER	MULTIFARIOUS	SURPRISINGLY
PRODUCTIVITY	TROCHOSPHERE	STILBOESTROL	MULTIGRAVIDA	SURREALISTIC
PROFESSIONAL	TROPHALLAXIS	STOCKBREEDER	MULTILATERAL	SURROUNDINGS
PROFESSORIAL	TROUBLEMAKER	STOCKINGETTE	MULTIPLICITY	SURVEILLANCE
PROFICIENTLY	TRUTHFULNESS	STONECHATTER	MUNICIPALITY	SUSPICIOUSLY
PROFITEERING	URBANIZATION	STORMTROOPER	MUSICOLOGIST	TUBERCULOSIS
PROGESTERONE	URTRICULARIA	STRADIVARIUS	MUTESSARIFAT	TURACOVERDIN
PROGRAMMABLE	WRETCHEDNESS	STRAIGHTAWAY	NUTRITIONIST	TURBIDIMETER
PROGYMNASIUM	ASPARAGINASE	STRAIGHTEDGE	OUTBUILDINGS	TURBOCHARGER
PROLEGOMENON	ASPHYXIATION	STRAIGHTNESS	OUTMANOEUVRE	AVAILABILITY
PROLETARIATE	ASSIMILATION	STRAITJACKET	OUTRAGEOUSLY	EVENHANDEDLY
PROLIFICALLY	ASSUEFACTION	STRANGLEHOLD	OUTSTRETCHED	EVENTEMPERED
PROLONGATION	ASTONISHMENT	STRANGLEWEED	PUGNACIOUSLY	EVOLUTIONARY
PROMULGATION	ASTROLOGICAL	STRATOSPHERE	PUMPERNICKEL	OVERCROWDING
PROPAGANDISM	ASTRONOMICAL	STREPITATION	PURIFICATION	OVERDRESSING
PROPAGANDIST	ASTROPHYSICS	STREPSIPTERA	PURPOSEBUILT	OVERESTIMATE
PROPHYLACTIC	ASYMMETRICAL	STREPTOMYCIN	PURPOSEFULLY	OVEREXERTION
PROPITIATION	ESCAPOLOGIST	STREPTONEURA	PUTREFACTION	OVERPOWERING
PROPITIATORY	ESCHSCHOLZIA	STRIDULATION	QUADRAGESIMA	OVERSCUTCHED
PROPITIOUSLY	ESPAGNOLETTE	STRIGIFORMES	QUADRAPHONIC	OVERSTRAINED
PROPORTIONAL	ESSENTIALITY	STRINGCOURSE	QUADRIPLEGIA	OVERWHELMING
PROPRIETRESS	ESTHETICALLY	STROMATOLITE	QUANTIFIABLE	AWARDWINNING
PROSCRIPTION	ESTRANGEMENT	STRONGMINDED	QUANTITATIVE	AWAYABSOLUTE
PROSOPOPOEIA	ISHMAELITISH	STRONTIANITE	QUARTERFINAL	AWEINSPIRING
PROSTITUTION	ISOBILATERAL	STROPHANTHUS	QUARTERLIGHT	SWASHBUCKLER
PROTACTINIUM	ISOLATIONISM	STRUCTURALLY	QUARTERSTAFF	SWIZZLESTICK
PROTECTIVELY	ISOLATIONIST	STUBBORNNESS	QUESTIONABLE	EXACERBATION
PROTECTORATE	OSCILLOSCOPE	STUDDINGSAIL	QUINQUENNIAL	EXAGGERATION
PROTESTATION	OSSIFICATION	STUDIOUSNESS	QUINTESSENCE	EXASPERATING

EXASPERATION	AMALGAMATION	GRANDISONIAN	TRACTABILITY	SUBMINIATURE
EXCHANGEABLE	AMARANTACEAE	GRANDMONTINE	TRADESCANTIA	SUBMISSIVELY
EXCITABILITY	ANAESTHETISE	GRANDPARENTS	TRADESPEOPLE	SUBSCRIPTION
EXCRUCIATING	ANAESTHETIST	GRAPHOLOGIST	TRALATICIOUS	SUBSEQUENTLY
EXCRUCIATION	ANAESTHETIZE	GRASSWIDOWER	TRALATITIOUS	SUBSERVIENCE
EXHAUSTIVELY	ANAMORPHOSIS	GRATEFULNESS	TRANQUILIZER	SUBSIDIARITY
EXHIBITIONER	ANASTIGMATIC	GUARDIANSHIP	TRANQUILLISE	SUBSTANTIATE
EXHILARATING	AVAILABILITY	HEADMISTRESS	TRANQUILLITY	SUBSTITUTION
EXHILARATION	AWARDWINNING	HEADQUARTERS	TRANQUILLIZE	SUBSTITUTIVE
EXPERIMENTAL	AWAYABSOLUTE	HEARTSTRINGS	TRANSACTIONS	SUBSTRUCTURE
EXPLOITATION	BEACONSFIELD	HEARTWARMING	TRANSCENDENT	SUBTERRANEAN
EXSERVICEMAN	BEAUMARCHAIS	INACCESSIBLE	TRANSFERABLE	TOBACCONISTS
EXSUFFLICATE	BEAUMONTAGUE	INACCURATELY	TRANSFERENCE	TUBERCULOSIS
EXTENSIONIST	BEAUMONTIQUE	INADEQUATELY	TRANSGRESSOR	UMBRADARLING
EXTENSOMETER	BLABBERMOUTH	INADMISSIBLE	TRANSITIONAL	UNBELIEVABLE
EXTINGUISHER	BLACKCURRANT	INADVERTENCE	TRANSLATABLE	UNBELIEVABLY
EXTORTIONATE	BLANDISHMENT	INAPPLICABLE	TRANSLUCENCE	URBANIZATION
EXTRADITABLE	BRACHYCEPHAL	INARTICULATE	TRANSMIGRATE	VIBRATIUNCLE
EXTRAVAGANCE	BRAINWASHING	INAUGURATION	TRANSMISSION	ACCELERATION
EXTRAVAGANZA	BRANCHIOPODA	INAUSPICIOUS	TRANSMOGRIFY	ACCENTUATION
OXYACETYLENE	CHAIRMANSHIP	IRASCIBILITY	TRANSOCEANIC	ACCIDENTALLY
AYUNTAMIENTO	CHALCOPYRITE	MEANINGFULLY	TRANSPARENCY	ACCOMPANYING
BYELORUSSIAN	CHALICOTHERE	PEACEFULNESS	TRANSPONTINE	ACCOMPLISHED
CYMOTRICHOUS	CHAMPIONSHIP	PEACEKEEPING	TRANSVESTISM	ACCORDIONIST
DYSTELEOLOGY	CHARACTERIZE	PHARMACOLOGY	TRANSVESTITE	ACCOUCHEMENT
GYMNOSOPHIST	CHARTERHOUSE	PLACENTIFORM	UNACCEPTABLE	ACCOUTREMENT
GYNECOLOGIST	CHASTISEMENT	PLAINCLOTHES	UNACCUSTOMED	ACCUMULATION
HYDROCHLORIC	CHAUVINISTIC	PLASTERSTONE	UNACQUAINTED	ACCUSATORIAL
HYDROGEOLOGY	CLAIRVOYANCE	PLAUSIBILITY	UNANSWERABLE	AECIDIOSPORE
HYDROGRAPHER	CLAIRVOYANCY	PRACTICALITY	UNAPPARELLED	ANCHORPERSON
HYDROQUINONE	CLAMJAMPHRIE	PRACTICIONER	UNAPPETIZING	ARCHILOCHIAN
HYDROTHERAPY	CLANNISHNESS	PRACTITIONER	UNATTAINABLE	ARCHIPELAGOS
HYGIENICALLY	CLAPPERBOARD	PRAISEWORTHY	UNATTRACTIVE	ARCHITECTURE
HYMENOPTERAN	CLARINETTIST	PRALLTRILLER	UNAUTHORISED	BACCHANALIAN
HYMNOGRAPHER	CLASSIFIABLE	PRASEODYMIUM	UNAUTHORIZED	BACKBREAKING
HYPERACIDITY	CLAUDICATION	PRAXINOSCOPE	WEATHERPROOF	BACKWARDNESS
HYPERBOLICAL	CLAVICEMBALO	QUADRAGESIMA	ABBREVIATION	BACKWOODSMAN
HYPERPYRETIC	CRASHLANDING	QUADRAPHONIC	AMBASSADRESS	BACTERIOLOGY
HYPERSARCOMA	CRASSAMENTUM	QUADRIPLEGIA	AMBIDEXTROUS	BACTERIOSTAT
HYPERTENSION	DEAMBULATORY	QUANTIFIABLE	AMBULANCEMAN	BICAMERALISM
HYPNOTHERAPY	DEASPIRATION	QUANTITATIVE	ARBORESCENCE	BICENTENNIAL
HYPNOTICALLY	DIAGRAMMATIC	QUARTERFINAL	BABINGTONITE	BUCKLEBEGGAR
HYPOCHONDRIA	DIALECTICIAN	QUARTERLIGHT	BIBLIOGRAPHY	COCCIDIOSTAT
HYPOCRITICAL	DRAMATICALLY	QUARTERSTAFF	BIBLIOPEGIST	CUCKOOFLOWER
HYPOTHECATOR	DRAMATURGIST	READJUSTMENT	CABINETMAKER	DECAPITATION
HYPOTHETICAL	ELASMOBRANCH	REAPPEARANCE	DEBILITATING	DECELERATION
HYSTERECTOMY	EMANCIPATION	RHADAMANTHUS	EMBARRASSING	DECENTRALISE
HYSTERICALLY	EMASCULATION	RHAMPHOTHECA	EMBEZZLEMENT	DECENTRALIZE
LYMANTRIIDAE	ENANTIOMORPH	SCANDALOUSLY	EMBROIDERESS	DECIPHERABLE
MYRINGOSCOPE	ENANTIOPATHY	SCANDINAVIAN	GIBRALTARIAN	DECIPHERMENT
MYSTERIOUSLY	EPACRIDACEAE	SCAPULIMANCY	GOBBLEDEGOOK	DECONGESTANT
MYTHOLOGICAL	EPANORTHOSIS	SCATTERBRAIN	GOBBLEDYGOOK	DECORATIVELY
NYCHTHEMERON	ERATOSTHENES	SCATTERMOUCH	HABERDASHERS	DICHROMATISM
NYCTITROPISM	EXACERBATION	SHAMEFACEDLY	HABERDASHERY	DICTATORSHIP
NYMPHOMANIAC	EXAGGERATION	SHAREHOLDING	HOBBIDIDANCE	ECCENTRICITY
PYROCATECHOL	EXASPERATING	SHARPSHOOTER	LABANOTATION	ECCLESIASTES
PYROTECHNICS	EXASPERATION	SMALLHOLDING	LABOURSAVING	ECCLESIASTIC
PYTHONOMORPH	FEARLESSNESS	SPACIOUSNESS	LABYRINTHINE	ENCHEIRIDION
SYMBOLICALLY	FEATHERBRAIN	SPATANGOIDEA	MOBILIZATION	ENCIRCLEMENT
SYNADELPHITE	FLAGELLATION	STAGGERINGLY	OMBUDSPERSON	ENCROACHMENT
SYNTAGMATITE	FLAMBOYANTLY	STAKHANOVITE	SUBARRHATION	ENCYCLOPEDIA
CZECHOSLOVAK	FRACTIONALLY	STANISLAVSKI	SUBCOMMITTEE	ENCYCLOPEDIC
	FRANKALMOIGN	STATISTICIAN	SUBCONSCIOUS	ESCAPOLOGIST
12:3	FRANKENSTEIN	SWASHBUCKLER	SUBCONTINENT	ESCHSCHOLZIA
ACADEMICALLY	FRANKINCENSE	THANKFULNESS	SUBCUTANEOUS	EXCHANGEABLE
ADAPTABILITY	FRAUENDIENST	THANKSGIVING	SUBHASTATION	EXCITABILITY
AGALMATOLITE	GLADIATORIAL	THAUMATURGIC	SUBJECTIVELY	EXCRUCIATING
AGAMOGENETIC	GRACEFULNESS	THAUMATURGUS	SUBJECTIVITY	EXCRUCIATION
AGATHODAIMON	GRACIOUSNESS	TRABECULATED	SUBLAPSARIAN	INCALCULABLE

INCANDESCENT	SUCCUSSATION	UNDEREXPOSED	INEXPLICABLY	SPERMATOCYTE
INCAPABILITY	TACTLESSNESS	UNDERGARMENT	INEXTRICABLE	SPERMATOZOID
INCAPACITATE	TECHNICALITY	UNDERPINNING	INEXTRICABLY	SPERMATOZOON
INCAUTIOUSLY	TECHNOLOGIST	UNDERSKINKER	KLEPTOMANIAC	STEALTHINESS
INCIDENTALLY	UNCHALLENGED	UNDERSTAFFED	KLETTERSCHUE	STEEPLECHASE
INCINERATION	UNCHANGEABLE	UNDERSTRATED	MNEMOTECHNIC	STEGOPHOLIST
INCOHERENTLY	UNCHARITABLE	UNDERWRITTEN	OBEDIENTIARY	STELLENBOSCH
INCOMPARABLE	UNCHARITABLY	UNDESERVEDLY	OCEANOGRAPHY	STENOGRAPHER
INCOMPARABLY	UNCLASSIFIED	UNDETECTABLE	ONEIROCRITIC	STENTORPHONE
INCOMPATIBLE	UNCONSIDERED	UNDETERMINED	OREOPITHECUS	STEPDAUGHTER
INCOMPETENCE	UNCONTROLLED	UNDIMINISHED	OREOPITHEOUS	STEREOPHONIC
INCOMPLETELY	UNCONVERSANT	UNDISCHARGED	OVERCROWDING	STEREOPTICON
INCONCLUSIVE	UNCONVINCING	ACETALDEHYDE	OVERDRESSING	STEREOSCOPIC
INCONSEQUENT	UNCTUOUSNESS	ALEXIPHARMIC	OVERESTIMATE	STEREOTYPING
INCONSISTENT	UNCULTIVATED	AMELIORATION	OVEREXERTION	STERNUTATION
INCONSOLABLE	VOCIFERATION	ANECATHARSIS	OVERPOWERING	STERNWHEELER
INCONTINENCE	VOCIFEROUSLY	ANEMOPHILOUS	OVERSCUTCHED	TEETERTOTTER
INCONVENIENT	WICKETKEEPER	AWEINSPIRING	OVERSTRAINED	THEATRICALLY
INCORPORATED	ADDITIONALLY	BIELORUSSIAN	OVERWHELMING	THEOPHYLLINE
INCORRIGIBLE	ANDOUILLETTE	BLEFUSCUDIAN	PHENOMENALLY	THEORETICIAN
INCORRIGIBLY	ANDROSTERONE	BLENNORRHOEA	PLECTOGNATHI	THERAPEUTICS
INCREASINGLY	CODIFICATION	BLETHERSKATE	PLEIOCHASIUM	THEREAGAINST
INCRUSTATION	FIDDLESTICKS	BREAKTHROUGH	PRECARIOUSLY	THERMOSTATIC
INCUNABULIST	HUDIBRASTICS	BREASTPLOUGH	PRECOCIOUSLY	THESMOPHORIA
LICKTRENCHER	HYDROCHLORIC	BREASTSUMMER	PRECONDITION	THESSALONIAN
MACABERESQUE	HYDROGEOLOGY	BREATHALYSER	PREDESTINATE	TREMENDOUSLY
MACHAIRODONT	HYDROGRAPHER	BREATHLESSLY	PREDETERMINE	UNECONOMICAL
MACMILLANITE	HYDROQUINONE	BREATHTAKING	PREDILECTION	UNEMPLOYMENT
MACROCEPHALY	HYDROTHERAPY	BYELORUSSIAN	PREDOMINANCE	UNEXPECTEDLY
MACROPODIDAE	INDEBTEDNESS	CHEERFULNESS	PREFERENTIAL	UNEXPURGATED
MECHANICALLY	INDECLINABLE	CHEESEBURGER	PREGUSTATION	USERFRIENDLY
MECHITHARIST	INDEFENSIBLE	CHEESEMONGER	PREHISTORIAN	WRETCHEDNESS
MICHELANGELO	INDEFINITELY	CHEESEPARING	PREMAXILLARY	AFFECTIONATE
MICROBREWERY	INDEPENDENCE	CHEMOTHERAPY	PREMONSTRANT	APFELSTRUDEL
MICROCLIMATE	INDIFFERENCE	CHESTERFIELD	PREPAREDNESS	ARFVEDSONITE
MUCILAGINOUS	INDIGESTIBLE	CLEARSIGHTED	PREPONDERANT	DEFLATIONARY
NOCONFIDENCE	INDISCRETION	CLEISTOGAMIC	PREPONDERATE	DIFFERENTIAL
NYCHTHEMERON	INDISPUTABLE	CREATIVENESS	PREPONDERENT	EFFERVESCENT
NYCTITROPISM	INDISPUTABLY	CREMAILLIÈRE	PREPOSSESSED	EFFORTLESSLY
OCCASIONALLY	INDISSOLUBLE	CZECHOSLOVAK	PREPOSTEROUS	INFELICITOUS
OCCUPATIONAL	INDISTINCTLY	DIENCEPHALON	PREREQUISITE	INFILTRATION
ONCORHYNCHUS	INDIVIDUALLY	DRESSINGDOWN	PRESBYTERIAN	INFLAMMATION
OSCILLOSCOPE	INDOCTRINATE	ELECTRICALLY	PRESCRIPTION	INFLAMMATORY
PACIFICATION	INDUSTRIALLY	ELECTROLYSIS	PRESCRIPTIVE	INFLATIONARY
PECTORILOQUY	MADEMOISELLE	ELECTROPLATE	PRESENTATION	INFORMIDABLE
RACKETEERING	MIDDLEWEIGHT	ELECTROTONUS	PRESENTIMENT	INFOTAINMENT
RECALCITRANT	MODIFICATION	ELEEMOSYNARY	PRESERVATION	INFREQUENTLY
RECAPITULATE	MUDDLEHEADED	ENERGYSAVING	PRESERVATIVE	INFRINGEMENT
RECEIVERSHIP	OLDFASHIONED	EPENCEPHALON	PRESIDENTIAL	LIFELESSNESS
RECEPTIONIST	PEDANTICALLY	ETEPIMELETIC	PRESTRICTION	REFLATIONARY
RECHARGEABLE	PEDIATRICIAN	EVENHANDEDLY	PRESUMPTUOUS	REFLECTIVITY
RECIPROCALLY	PEDICELLARIA	EVENTEMPERED	PREVARICATOR	REFRIGERATED
RECKLESSNESS	RADIOBIOLOGY	FREIGHTLINER	PREVENTATIVE	REFRIGERATOR
RECOGNIZABLE	RADIOGRAPHER	GREENGROCERS	PSEPHOLOGIST	SUFFICIENTLY
RECOGNIZANCE	RADIOISOTOPE	GREENGROCERY	PSEUDONYMOUS	UNFATHOMABLE
RECOLLECTION	RADIOTHERAPY	HAEMATEMESIS	PTERIDOPHYTE	UNFAVOURABLE
RECONSTITUTE	REDEMPTIONER	HAEMOPHILIAC	PTERIDOSPERM	UNFREQUENTED
RECORDPLAYER	REDEPLOYMENT	HAEMORRHOIDS	PTERODACTYLE	AGGRESSIVELY
RECREATIONAL	REDINTEGRATE	HIERARCHICAL	QUESTIONABLE	AUGMENTATION
RECRUDESCENT	REDISCOVERED	HIEROGLYPHIC	SHEEPISHNESS	AUGMENTATIVE
RECUPERATION	REDISTRIBUTE	HIEROGRAMMAT	SLEDGEHAMMER	DAGUERROTYPE
RECUPERATIVE	RIDICULOUSLY	HIEROPHANTIC	SLEEPWALKING	DEGENERATION
SACRILEGIOUS	RODOMONTADER	IDEALIZATION	SPECIFICALLY	DOGMATICALLY
SECESSIONIST	SADISTICALLY	IDENTIFIABLE	SPECIOUSNESS	ENGLISHWOMAN
SECRETARIATE	SIDEWHISKERS	INEFFICIENCY	SPECKTIONEER	ENGLISHWOMEN
SECTARIANISM	UNDEMOCRATIC	INERADICABLE	SPECTROMETER	FIGURATIVELY
SOCIOLOGICAL	UNDERACHIEVE	INESCUTCHEON	SPECTROSCOPE	GIGANTOMACHY
SUCCESSFULLY	UNDERCLOTHES	INEXACTITUDE	SPELEOLOGIST	HIGHFALUTING
SUCCESSIVELY	UNDERCURRENT	INEXPERIENCE	SPELLCHECKER	HYGIENICALLY
		INEXPLICABLE		

757

INGRATIATING	CHITTERLINGS	THIGMOTROPIC	ILLUSTRATION	WALLYDRAIGLE
LEGALIZATION	COINCIDENTAL	THIRDBOROUGH	ILLUSTRATIVE	WELLBALANCED
LEGIONNAIRES	CRISTOBALITE	TRICENTENARY	KALEIDOSCOPE	WELLINFORMED
LEGITIMATELY	DRINKDRIVING	TRICHOLOGIST	KALISTOCRACY	WELLINGTONIA
LIGHTHEARTED	EPIDEICTICAL	TRICHOPHYTON	KILLIKINNICK	WELTERWEIGHT
LUGUBRIOUSLY	EPIGRAMMATIC	TRIGONOMETRY	LALLAPALOOZA	WILLIEWAUGHT
MAGNETICALLY	EPILEPTIFORM	TRIUMPHANTLY	LILLIBULLERO	WILTSHIREMAN
MAGNIFICENCE	EPIPHENOMENA	UNIDENTIFIED	LILLIBURLERO	WOLLASTONITE
MAGNILOQUENT	EPISCOPALIAN	UNILATERALLY	MALACOSTRACA	WOLSTENHOLME
MUGGLETONIAN	EPISTEMOLOGY	UNIMAGINABLE	MALFORMATION	YELLOWHAMMER
NIGHTCLOTHES	EPISTOLATERS	UNIMPORTANCE	MALLEABILITY	ZALAMBDODONT
ORGANISATION	EPITHALAMION	UNINTERESTED	MALLOPHAGOUS	ADMINISTRATE
ORGANIZATION	EPITHALAMIUM	UNIVERSALIST	MALNUTRITION	ADMONISHMENT
PIGMENTATION	FAINTHEARTED	VAINGLORIOUS	MALPRACTICES	ATMOSPHERICS
POGONOPHORAN	FAITHFULNESS	WEIGHTLIFTER	MALTREATMENT	BAMBOCCIADES
PUGNACIOUSLY	FLITTERMOUSE	WHIGMALEERIE	MELODRAMATIC	CAMERAPERSON
REGENERATION	FRIENDLINESS	WHIMSICALITY	MILITARISTIC	CAMIKNICKERS
REGISTRATION	GAINSBOROUGH	WHIPPOORWILL	MILLILAMBERT	CAMPANULARIA
SEGMENTATION	GRISEOFULVIN	ADJECTIVALLY	MULLIGATAWNY	CAMPODEIFORM
SIGNIFICANCE	GUILDENSTERN	ADJUDICATION	MULTICOLORED	COMBINATIONS
SUGGESTIVELY	HAIRDRESSERS	MAJESTICALLY	MULTIFARIOUS	COMMANDMENTS
TAGLIACOTIAN	HAIRDRESSING	REJUVENATION	MULTIGRAVIDA	COMMENCEMENT
TIGHTFITTING	HAIRSPLITTER	ACKNOWLEDGED	MULTILATERAL	COMMENDATION
TOGETHERNESS	IDIOSYNCRASY	ALLITERATION	MULTIPLICITY	COMMENDATORY
ACHLAMYDEOUS	IDIOTHERMOUS	APLANOGAMETE	OBLITERATION	COMMENSURATE
ATHEROMATOUS	KLIPSPRINGER	BELLIGERENCY	PALEONTOLOGY	COMMERCIALLY
BEHAVIOURISM	LEIOTRICHOUS	BILLINGSGATE	PALINGENESIA	COMMISSARIAT
COHABITATION	MOISTURIZING	CALCEAMENTUM	PALINGENESIS	COMMISSIONED
DEHUMIDIFIER	NEIGHBORHOOD	CALLIGRAPHIC	PALPITATIONS	COMMISSIONER
ENHYPOSTASIA	NEIGHBOURING	CALLISTHENES	PALUDAMENTUM	COMMONWEALTH
ETHEROMANIAC	OPINIONATIVE	CALUMNIATION	PHLEBOTOMIST	COMMUNICABLE
ETHNOLOGICAL	OPISTHOGRAPH	CHLORINATION	POLARIZATION	COMPANIONWAY
EXHAUSTIVELY	ORIENTEERING	CHLOROPICRIN	POLICYMAKING	COMPELLATION
EXHIBITIONER	PAINLESSNESS	COLDSHOULDER	POLYETHYLENE	COMPENSATION
EXHILARATING	PHILANTHROPY	COLLABORATOR	POLYNEURITIS	COMPENSATORY
EXHILARATION	PHILHARMONIC	COLLECTIVELY	POLYPETALOUS	COMPLACENTLY
FEHMGERICHTE	PHILISTINISM	COLLECTORATE	POLYRIBOSOME	COMPLETENESS
ICHTHYOCOLLA	PHILODENDRON	COLLOQUIALLY	POLYSYLLABIC	COMPLICATION
ICHTHYOPSIDA	PHILOLOGICAL	COLLUCTATION	POLYSYLLABLE	COMPROMISING
INHARMONIOUS	PHILOSOPHIZE	COLLYWOBBLES	POLYSYNDETON	COMPURGATION
INHOSPITABLE	POIKILOTHERM	COLONIZATION	POLYURETHANE	CYMOTRICHOUS
ISHMAELITISH	POINTILLISME	COLOQUINTIDA	RELATIONSHIP	DEMILITARIZE
OPHIOGLOSSUM	PRIGGISHNESS	DELIBERATELY	RELENTLESSLY	DEMIMONDAINE
OTHERWORLDLY	PRIMIGRAVIDA	DELIBERATION	ROLLERBLADER	DEMONSTRABLE
REHABILITATE	PRINCIPALITY	DELICATESSEN	ROLLERBLADES	DEMONSTRABLY
SCHEHERAZADE	PRIZEFIGHTER	DILAPIDATION	SALESMANSHIP	DEMONSTRATOR
SCHILLERSPAR	PRIZEWINNING	DILATORINESS	SALTATORIOUS	DOMESTICATED
SCHINDYLESIS	PSIPHENOMENA	DOLPHINARIUM	SALVATIONIST	GAMESMANSHIP
SCHIZOMYCETE	QUINQUENNIAL	EULENSPIEGEL	SCLERENCHYMA	GAMOSEPALOUS
SCHNEIDERIAN	QUINTESSENCE	FELDSPATHOID	SCLERODERMIA	GYMNOSOPHIST
SCHOOLMASTER	QUIXOTICALLY	FULMINATIONS	SELFADHESIVE	HAMARTHRITIS
SCHOPENHAUER	REINVIGORATE	GALLIGASKINS	SELFCATERING	HAMBLETONIAN
SPHACELATION	RHINORRHOEAL	GALLINACEOUS	SELFEMPLOYED	HAMMERHEADED
SPHAIRISTIKE	RHIPIDOPTERA	GALLIVANTING	SELFINTEREST	HEMICHORDATA
VEHMGERICHTE	SCINTILLATOR	GALVANOMETER	SELFPORTRAIT	HOMESICKNESS
ALIMENTATIVE	SHILLYSHALLY	HALLANSHAKER	SILVERHAIRED	HOMOEOPATHIC
ARISTOCRATIC	SHIPBUILDING	HALLUCINOGEN	SOLICITATION	HOMOTHERMOUS
ARISTOLOCHIA	SHIRTSLEEVES	HELIOGABALUS	SOLICITOUSLY	HUMANITARIAN
ARISTOPHANES	SHIRTWAISTER	HELIOTROPISM	SPLENOMEGALY	HUMANIZATION
ARISTOTELEAN	SPIEGELEISEN	HELLGRAMMITE	SULPHONAMIDE	HYMENOPTERAN
ARITHMETICAL	SPINECHILLER	HELPLESSNESS	TELEASTHETIC	HYMNOGRAPHER
BAIRNSFATHER	SPINSTERHOOD	HILDEBRANDIC	TELEGRAPHESE	IAMBOGRAPHER
BOISTEROUSLY	SPIRITUALISM	HOLIDAYMAKER	TELEGRAPHIST	IMMACULATELY
BRICKFIELDER	SPIRITUALIST	ILLEGIBILITY	TELEOSAURIAN	IMMEASURABLE
BRILLIANTINE	SPIRITUALITY	ILLEGITIMACY	TELEUTOSPORE	IMMEASURABLY
CHILDBEARING	SPITEFULNESS	ILLEGITIMATE	VALENCIENNES	IMMODERATELY
CHILDISHNESS	STILBOESTROL	ILLOGICALITY	VILIFICATION	IMMODERATION
CHIROPRACTIC	SWIZZLESTICK	ILLUMINATING	VILLEGIATURA	IMMUNIZATION
CHIROPRACTOR	THICKSKINNED	ILLUMINATION	VOLUPTUOUSLY	IMMUNOLOGIST

IMMUTABILITY	CONSEQUENTLY	INNOMINABLES	XANTHOPTERIN	PROGYMNASIUM
LAMELLICORNE	CONSERVATION	JENNYSPINNER	ABOLITIONIST	PROLEGOMENON
LAMENTATIONS	CONSERVATISM	KINAESTHETIC	AFORETHOUGHT	PROLETARIATE
LAMPADEDROMY	CONSERVATORY	KINDERGARTEN	APOLLINARIAN	PROLIFICALLY
LUMINESCENCE	CONSIDERABLE	LANCASTERIAN	APOSTROPHISE	PROLONGATION
LUMINISCENCE	CONSIDERABLY	LANGUEDOCIAN	AROMATHERAPY	PROMULGATION
LYMANTRIIDAE	CONSISTENTLY	LINCOLNSHIRE	BIOCHEMISTRY	PROPAGANDISM
NIMBOSTRATUS	CONSOCIATION	LONGDISTANCE	BIODIVERSITY	PROPAGANDIST
NOMENCLATURE	CONSOLIDATED	LONGITUDINAL	BIOFLAVONOID	PROPHYLACTIC
NYMPHOMANIAC	CONSOLIDATOR	LONGSHOREMAN	BIOGRAPHICAL	PROPITIATION
PUMPERNICKEL	CONSPECTUITY	LONGSTANDING	BLOODLETTING	PROPITIATORY
RAMBUNCTIOUS	CONSPIRACIST	MANGELWURZEL	BLOODSTAINED	PROPITIOUSLY
RAMIFICATION	CONSTABULARY	MANIPULATION	BLOODTHIRSTY	PROPORTIONAL
REMEMBRANCER	CONSTIPATION	MANIPULATIVE	BOOBYTRAPPED	PROPRIETRESS
REMINISCENCE	CONSTITUENCY	MANOEUVRABLE	BOONDOGGLING	PROSCRIPTION
REMONSTRANCE	CONSTITUENTS	MANSLAUGHTER	BROADCASTING	PROSOPOPOEIA
REMUNERATION	CONSTITUTION	MANUFACTURER	BRONTOSAURUS	PROSTITUTION
REMUNERATIVE	CONSTRICTION	MENSTRUATION	CHONDRIOSOME	PROTACTINIUM
ROMANTICALLY	CONSTRUCTION	MINDBOGGLING	CHOREOGRAPHY	PROTECTIVELY
SEMANTICALLY	CONSTRUCTIVE	MINDFULLNESS	CHORIZONTIST	PROTECTORATE
SEMICIRCULAR	CONSULTATION	MINERALOGIST	CLOTHESHORSE	PROTESTATION
SEMIDETACHED	CONSULTATIVE	MINICOMPUTER	COORDINATION	PROTHALAMION
SEMIPRECIOUS	CONSUMMATION	MINISTRATION	CROSSBENCHER	PROTHALAMIUM
SIMULTANEOUS	CONTABESCENT	MONOSYLLABIC	CROSSCOUNTRY	PROTHONOTARY
SOMATOPLEURE	CONTAMINATED	MONOSYLLABLE	CROSSEXAMINE	PROTOPLASMAL
SOMNAMBULISM	CONTEMPORARY	MONOTONOUSLY	CROSSSECTION	PROTOPLASMIC
SOMNAMBULIST	CONTEMPTIBLE	MONTESSORIAN	ECONOMICALLY	PROTUBERANCE
SYMBOLICALLY	CONTEMPTUOUS	MUNICIPALITY	EVOLUTIONARY	PROVERBIALLY
TAMARICACEAE	CONTERMINOUS	NONAGENARIAN	FLORICULTURE	PROVIDENTIAL
TIMELESSNESS	CONTIGNATION	NONALCOHOLIC	FOOTSLOGGING	RHODODENDRON
UNMANAGEABLE	CONTINUATION	NONCHALANTLY	FRONTIERSMAN	ROOMINGHOUSE
UNMISTAKABLE	CONTINUOUSLY	NONCOMMITTAL	FRONTISPIECE	SCOPOPHILIAC
ANNIHILATION	CONTRAPPOSTO	NONDIRECTIVE	GEOGRAPHICAL	SHORTCIRCUIT
ANNOUNCEMENT	CONTRAPUNTAL	NONEXISTENCE	GEOLOGICALLY	SHORTCOMINGS
ANNUNCIATION	CONTRARINESS	NONFLAMMABLE	GEOMETRICIAN	SHORTSIGHTED
BANANALANDER	CONTRIBUTION	NONOBJECTIVE	GEOPHYSICIST	SHORTSLEEVED
BANDERSNATCH	CONTRIBUTORY	NONRESIDENCE	GLOBETROTTER	SHORTSTAFFED
BANTAMWEIGHT	CONTRITURATE	NONRESISTANT	GLOCKENSPIEL	SHOSTAKOVICH
BENEFACTRESS	CONTROLLABLE	ORNITHOGALUM	GOOSEPIMPLES	SLOCKDOLAGER
BENEVOLENTLY	CONTUMACIOUS	PANAESTHESIA	GROSSULARITE	SLOCKDOLIGER
BENZOPHENONE	CONVALESCENT	PANATHENAEAN	ICONOCLASTIC	SLOCKDOLOGER
BENZOQUINONE	CONVALESCING	PANCHATANTRA	INORDINATELY	SLOVENLINESS
BUNKOSTEERER	CONVENIENCES	PANCHROMATIC	ISOBILATERAL	SNOBBISHNESS
CANCELLATION	CONVENIENTLY	PANDAEMONIUM	ISOLATIONISM	SNOWBOARDING
CANONIZATION	CONVENTIONAL	PANDANACEOUS	ISOLATIONIST	SPOKESPERSON
CANTANKEROUS	CONVERSATION	PANPHARMACON	MOONLIGHTING	SPORADICALLY
CANTILEVERED	CONVEYANCING	PANTECHNICON	NEOCLASSICAL	SPORTSGROUND
CONCENTRATED	CONVINCINGLY	PANTISOCRACY	NEOPLATONISM	STOCKBREEDER
CONCILIATION	CONVIVIALITY	PANTOPHAGOUS	ONOMATOPOEIA	STOCKINGETTE
CONCILIATORY	DENDROLOGIST	PENALIZATION	ONOMATOPOEIC	STONECHATTER
CONCLUSIVELY	DENOMINATION	PENITENTIARY	PHONETICALLY	STORMTROOPER
CONCURRENTLY	DENUNCIATION	PENNSYLVANIA	PHOSPHOLIPID	THOROUGHBRED
CONDEMNATION	DONNERWETTER	PINNIEWINKLE	PHOSPHORENCE	THOROUGHFARE
CONDENSATION	DUNNIEWASSAL	RENOUNCEMENT	PHOSPHORESCE	THOROUGHNESS
CONDUCTIVITY	FINALIZATION	RENUNCIATION	PHOTOGLYPHIC	THOUGHTFULLY
CONFECTIONER	FUNCTIONALLY	RONCESVALLES	PHOTOGRAPHER	TROCHELMINTH
CONFESSIONAL	FUNCTIONLESS	SINANTHROPUS	PHOTOGRAPHIC	TROCHOSPHERE
CONFIDENTIAL	FUNDAMENTALS	SINGLEDECKER	PHOTOGRAVURE	TROPHALLAXIS
CONFIRMATION	GENEALOGICAL	SINGLEHANDED	PROBATIONARY	TROUBLEMAKER
CONFIRMATORY	GENETHLIACON	SINGLEMINDED	PROCESSIONAL	ULOTRICHALES
CONFISCATION	GENTLETAMPER	SYNADELPHITE	PROCLAMATION	UNOBSTRUCTED
CONGENITALLY	GONADOTROPIN	SYNTAGMATITE	PRODIGIOUSLY	UNOBTAINABLE
CONGLOMERATE	GONDWANALAND	UINTATHERIUM	PRODUCTIVITY	UNOFFICIALLY
CONGRATULATE	GYNECOLOGIST	UNNEIGHBORLY	PROFESSIONAL	UNOPPRESSIVE
CONGREGATION	HANDKERCHIEF	VENEPUNCTURE	PROFESSORIAL	WHOLEHEARTED
CONQUISTADOR	HENCEFORWARD	VENGEFULNESS	PROFICIENTLY	WOODBURYTYPE
CONSCRIPTION	HINDQUARTERS	VENTRIPOTENT	PROFITEERING	ALPHABETICAL
CONSECRATION	INNATTENTIVE	VINDICTIVELY	PROGESTERONE	ALPHANUMERIC
CONSEQUENCES		WINTERHALTER	PROGRAMMABLE	AMPHISBAENIC

AMPHISTOMOUS	REPERCUSSION	CEREMONIALLY	PARALIPOMENA	STREPTOMYCIN
AMPHITHEATER	REPOSSESSION	CHREMATISTIC	PARAMAGNETIC	STREPTONEURA
AMPHITHEATRE	REPROCESSING	CHRESTOMATHY	PARAMILITARY	STRIDULATION
APPENDECTOMY	REPRODUCTION	CHRISTIANITY	PARANTHELIUM	STRIGIFORMES
APPENDICITIS	REPRODUCTIVE	CIRCASSIENNE	PARENTHESIZE	STRINGCOURSE
APPOGGIATURA	SEPTEMBRISER	CIRCUMCISION	PARKINSONISM	STROMATOLITE
APPRECIATION	SEPTUAGESIMA	CIRCUMGYRATE	PARSIMONIOUS	STRONGMINDED
APPRECIATIVE	SIPHONOPHORA	CIRCUMSCRIBE	PARTICOLORED	STRONTIANITE
APPREHENSION	SIPHONOSTELE	CIRCUMSTANCE	PARTICULARLY	STROPHANTHUS
APPREHENSIVE	SIPUNCULACEA	CURMUDGEONLY	PARTISANSHIP	STRUCTURALLY
APPROACHABLE	SOPHISTICATE	DARLINGTONIA	PERADVENTURE	SURMOUNTABLE
APPURTENANCE	SUPERANNUATE	DEREGULATION	PERAMBULATOR	SURPRISINGLY
ASPARAGINASE	SUPERCHARGED	DERESTRICTED	PERCEPTIVELY	SURREALISTIC
ASPHYXIATION	SUPERCHARGER	DIRECTORSHIP	PERCEPTIVITY	SURROUNDINGS
BIPROPELLANT	SUPERCILIARY	DORSIVENTRAL	PEREMPTORILY	SURVEILLANCE
CAPERCAILLIE	SUPERCILIOUS	FARTHINGLAND	PERGAMENEOUS	TARAMASALATA
CAPERCAILZIE	SUPERHIGHWAY	FERMENTATION	PERICARDITIS	TERCENTENARY
CAPITULATION	SUPERNACULUM	FIRSTFOOTING	PERIODICALLY	TERGIVERSATE
DEPARTMENTAL	SUPERNATURAL	FORCEFULNESS	PERIODONTICS	TERRIFICALLY
DEPOPULATION	SUPERSTITION	FORMALDEHYDE	PERIOSTRACUM	TERRITORIALS
DEPRECIATION	SUPERSTRATUM	FORTUITOUSLY	PERIPHRASTIC	THREADNEEDLE
DEPRECIATORY	SUPPLICATION	GERIATRICIAN	PERISTERONIC	THREEQUARTER
DIPLOGENESIS	TAPERECORDER	GERONTOCRACY	PERMANGANATE	TORRICELLIAN
DIPRIONIDIAN	TAPSALTEERIE	HARMONIOUSLY	PERMEABILITY	TURACOVERDIN
EMPHATICALLY	TAPSLETEERIE	HARNESSMAKER	PERMITTIVITY	TURBIDIMETER
ESPAGNOLETTE	UNPARALLELED	HARUMFRODITE	PERNOCTATION	TURBOCHARGER
EXPERIMENTAL	UNPARDONABLE	HEREDITAMENT	PERPETRATION	UNREASONABLE
EXPLOITATION	UNPOPULARITY	HEREDITARIAN	PERSEVERANCE	UNRECOGNISED
HAPPENSTANCE	UNPREJUDICED	HERMENEUTICS	PERSISTENTLY	UNRECOGNIZED
HAPPYGOLUCKY	UNPRETENDING	HERMENEUTIST	PERSONALIZED	UNRESERVEDLY
HAPTOTROPISM	UNPRINCIPLED	HERMETICALLY	PERSPICACITY	UNRESPONSIVE
HEPHTHEMIMER	UNPRODUCTIVE	HEROICOMICAL	PERSPIRATION	UNRESTRAINED
HIPPOCRATISE	UNPROFITABLE	HORIZONTALLY	PERSUASIVELY	UNRESTRICTED
HIPPOCREPIAN	VAPORIZATION	HORRIFICALLY	PERSULPHURIC	UNRETURNABLE
HIPPOPOTAMUS	XIPHISTERNUM	HORSEMANSHIP	PERTINACIOUS	UPROARIOUSLY
HOPELESSNESS	ACQUAINTANCE	HORTICULTURE	PERTURBATION	VARICOLOURED
HYPERACIDITY	ACQUIESCENCE	IRRATIONALLY	PERVERSENESS	VERIFICATION
HYPERBOLICAL	LIQUEFACTION	IRREDEEMABLE	PERVICACIOUS	VERMICULTURE
HYPERPYRETIC	SEQUENTIALLY	IRREGULARITY	PHRONTISTERY	VERUMONTANUM
HYPERSARCOMA	SEQUESTRATOR	IRRESISTIBLE	PORNOGRAPHIC	WAREHOUSEMAN
HYPERTENSION	AERODYNAMICS	IRRESOLUTELY	PURIFICATION	YORKSHIREMAN
HYPNOTHERAPY	AERONAUTICAL	IRRESOLUTION	PURPOSEBUILT	ZARATHUSTRIC
HYPNOTICALLY	AGRIBUSINESS	IRRESOLVABLE	PURPOSEFULLY	ABSQUATULATE
HYPOCHONDRIA	AGRICULTURAL	IRRESPECTIVE	PYROCATECHOL	ADSCITITIOUS
HYPOCRITICAL	AIRCRAFTSMAN	IRREVERENTLY	PYROTECHNICS	ARSENOPYRITE
HYPOTHECATOR	BARBERMONGER	IRREVERSIBLE	SARDANAPALUS	ASSIMILATION
HYPOTHETICAL	BARNSTORMING	IRRITABILITY	SARDONICALLY	ASSUEFACTION
IMPARTIALITY	BARORECEPTOR	JURISDICTION	SARRUSOPHONE	AUSCULTATION
IMPENETRABLE	BARRANQUILLA	KERAUNOGRAPH	SARSAPARILLA	AUSPICIOUSLY
IMPERFECTION	BERTHOLLETIA	KIRSCHWASSER	SCREENWRITER	AUSTRALASIAN
IMPERFECTIVE	BERTILLONAGE	MARCOBRUNNER	SCRIMSHANDER	AUSTRONESIAN
IMPERISHABLE	BIRDWATCHING	MARCONIGRAPH	SCRIMSHANKER	BESSERWISSER
IMPERSONALLY	BUREAUCRATIC	MARKSMANSHIP	SCRIPTWRITER	BUSINESSLIKE
IMPERSONATOR	CARAVANSERAI	MARLINESPIKE	SCRUPULOUSLY	CASSITERIDES
IMPERTINENCE	CARBOHYDRATE	MARRIAGEABLE	SERASKIERATE	CASTERBRIDGE
IMPLANTATION	CARCINOGENIC	MARSEILLAISE	SERVICEBERRY	COSCINOMANCY
IMPOLITENESS	CARDINDEXING	MERCANTILISM	SERVICEWOMAN	COSMOPOLITAN
IMPOVERISHED	CARDIOLOGIST	MERETRICIOUS	SPREADEAGLED	COSTERMONGER
IMPREGNATION	CARDIOMEGALY	MERISTEMATIC	SPRECHGESANG	DESIDERATIVE
IMPRESSIVELY	CARELESSNESS	MERITRICIOUS	STRADIVARIUS	DESIRABILITY
IMPRISONMENT	CARICATURIST	MERRYTHOUGHT	STRAIGHTAWAY	DESSERTSPOON
IMPROVIDENCE	CARLOVINGIAN	MERVEILLEUSE	STRAIGHTEDGE	DISACCHARIDE
LEPIDOMELANE	CARPETBAGGER	MIRACULOUSLY	STRAIGHTNESS	DISADVANTAGE
NEPENTHACEAE	CARPOPHAGOUS	MYRINGOSCOPE	STRAITJACKET	DISAGREEABLE
NEPHELOMETER	CARRIWITCHET	NARCISSISTIC	STRANGLEHOLD	DISAGREEMENT
OPPRESSIVELY	CARTHAGINIAN	NORTHEASTERN	STRANGLEWEED	DISAPPEARING
PAPILIONIDAE	CARTOGRAPHER	NORTHERNMOST	STRATOSPHERE	DISAPPOINTED
POPOCATEPETL	CARTOGRAPHIC	NORTHWESTERN	STREPITATION	DISASSOCIATE
REPATRIATION	CEREBROTONIC	PARACENTESIS	STREPSIPTERA	DISASTROUSLY

DISCIPLINARY	MASTIGOPHORA	ANTANANARIVO	HETEROSEXUAL	ORTHOPTEROUS
DISCOMEDUSAE	MASTURBATION	ANTEDILUVIAN	HETEROSOMATA	ORTHORHOMBIC
DISCOMFITURE	MESOTHELIOMA	ANTEMERIDIAN	INTELLECTUAL	ORTHOTONESIS
DISCOMYCETES	MISADVENTURE	ANTHELMINTIC	INTELLIGENCE	OSTENTATIOUS
DISCONCERTED	MISANTHROPIC	ANTHROPOLOGY	INTELLIGIBLE	OSTEOMALACIA
DISCONNECTED	MISAPPREHEND	ANTIAIRCRAFT	INTEMPERANCE	OSTEOPOROSIS
DISCONSOLATE	MISBEHAVIOUR	ANTIBACCHIUS	INTENERATION	OSTEOSARCOMA
DISCONTENTED	MISCALCULATE	ANTIBARBARUS	INTERCEPTION	OUTBUILDINGS
DISCOURAGING	MISDELIVERED	ANTICIPATION	INTERCESSION	OUTMANOEUVRE
DISCOURTEOUS	MISDEMEANOUR	ANTICIPATORY	INTERCHANGED	OUTRAGEOUSLY
DISCRIMINATE	MISINTERPRET	ANTILEGOMENA	INTERFERENCE	OUTSTRETCHED
DISDAINFULLY	MISPLACEMENT	ANTIMACASSAR	INTERGLACIAL	PATHETICALLY
DISEMBARRASS	MISPRONOUNCE	ANTIMETABOLE	INTERJECTION	PATHOLOGICAL
DISENCHANTED	MISQUOTATION	ANTIMNEMONIC	INTERLOCUTOR	PETRIFACTION
DISFRANCHISE	MISREPRESENT	ANTINEUTRINO	INTERMEDIARY	PETTIFOGGERS
DISHONORABLE	MISSTATEMENT	ANTIPARTICLE	INTERMEDIATE	PETTIFOGGERY
DISHONORABLY	MISTREATMENT	ANTIRACHITIC	INTERMINABLE	PETTIFOGGING
DISINCENTIVE	MOSBOLLETJIE	ANTISTROPHON	INTERMINABLY	PITTERPATTER
DISINFECTANT	MUSICOLOGIST	ANTITHROMBIN	INTERMISSION	POTAMOLOGIST
DISINGENUOUS	MYSTERIOUSLY	ANTONINIANUS	INTERMITTENT	POTENTIALITY
DISINTEGRATE	OBSEQUIOUSLY	ARTHROPLASTY	INTERPRETING	POTICHOMANIA
DISOBEDIENCE	OBSERVANTINE	ARTICULATION	INTERRELATED	PUTREFACTION
DISORGANIZED	OBSOLESCENCE	ARTIFICIALLY	INTERROGATOR	PYTHONOMORPH
DISORIENTATE	OBSOLETENESS	ARTILLERYMAN	INTERRUPTION	RATIFICATION
DISPENSATION	OBSTETRICIAN	ARTIODACTYLA	INTERSECTION	RETARDEDNESS
DISPLACEMENT	OBSTREPEROUS	ARTISTICALLY	INTERSPERSED	RETICULATION
DISPOSSESSED	OSSIFICATION	ASTONISHMENT	INTERSTELLAR	RETRENCHMENT
DISQUISITION	PASQUEFLOWER	ASTROLOGICAL	INTERVENTION	RUTHLESSNESS
DISREPECTFUL	PASSEMEASURE	ASTRONOMICAL	INTIMIDATING	SATISFACTION
DISREPUTABLE	PASSEPARTOUT	ASTROPHYSICS	INTIMIDATION	SATISFACTORY
DISSATISFIED	PASSIONATELY	ATTRACTIVELY	INTOXICATING	SITTLICHKEIT
DISSERTATION	PASSIONFRUIT	ATTRIBUTABLE	INTOXICATION	TETRACYCLINE
DISSOCIATION	PESTILENTIAL	AUTHENTICATE	INTRANSIGENT	TETRAHEDRITE
DISTILLATION	PISCICULTURE	AUTHENTICITY	INTRANSITIVE	TETRODOTOXIN
DISTINCTNESS	POSSESSIVELY	AUTOHYPNOSIS	INTRAUTERINE	TITANOSAURUS
DISTRIBUTION	POSTGRADUATE	BATTLEGROUND	INTRODUCTION	TOTALITARIAN
DISTRIBUTIVE	POSTHUMOUSLY	BETHLEHEMITE	INTRODUCTORY	ULTRAMONTANE
DYSTELEOLOGY	POSTLIMINARY	BUTTERSCOTCH	INTROVERSION	URTRICULARIA
ECSTATICALLY	POSTMISTRESS	CATADIOPTRIC	INTUITIONISM	VETERINARIAN
ESSENTIALITY	POSTPONEMENT	CATAPHYSICAL	KATHAREVOUSA	VITUPERATION
EXSERVICEMAN	POSTPOSITIVE	CATASTROPHIC	KATZENJAMMER	VITUPERATIVE
EXSUFFLICATE	POSTPRANDIAL	CATHETOMETER	LATIROSTRATE	WATCHFULNESS
FASTIDIOUSLY	RESETTLEMENT	ENTANGLEMENT	LITHOGRAPHIC	WATERCARRIER
FUSTILLIRIAN	RESIPISCENCE	ENTEROMORPHA	LITHOLATROUS	ADULTERATION
GASTARBEITER	RESPECTFULLY	ENTEROPNEUST	MATHEMATICAL	AYUNTAMIENTO
GASTROSOPHER	RESPECTIVELY	ENTERPRISING	METAGNATHOUS	BLUESTOCKING
GESELLSCHAFT	RESPONDENTIA	ENTERTAINING	METALLOPHONE	BOUGAINVILLE
HISTIOPHORUS	RESTAURATEUR	ENTHUSIASTIC	METALLURGIST	BOULEVARDIER
HISTORICALLY	RESTLESSNESS	ENTOMOLOGIST	METAMORPHISM	CAUTIOUSNESS
HYSTERECTOMY	RESURRECTION	ENTOMOSTRACA	METAMORPHOSE	CHURCHWARDEN
HYSTERICALLY	RESUSCITATED	ENTOPLASTRON	METAPHORICAL	CHURLISHNESS
INSALUBRIOUS	RISORGIMENTO	ENTREATINGLY	METAPHYSICAL	COUNTERBLAST
INSEMINATION	SESQUIALTERA	ENTRENCHMENT	METHODICALLY	COUNTERCLAIM
INSOLUBILITY	SESQUITERTIA	ENTREPRENEUR	METHOTREXATE	COUNTERMARCH
INSPECTORATE	SUSPICIOUSLY	ESTHETICALLY	METICULOUSLY	COUNTERPOINT
INSTALLATION	TESTAMENTARY	ESTRANGEMENT	METROPOLITAN	COUNTERPOISE
INSTAURATION	TESTOSTERONE	EXTENSIONIST	MITRAILLEUSE	COURAGEOUSLY
INSTRUCTIONS	UNSATISFYING	EXTENSOMETER	MOTORCYCLIST	COURTMARTIAL
INSTRUCTRESS	UNSCIENTIFIC	EXTINGUISHER	MUTESSARIFAT	DEUTERANOPIA
INSTRUMENTAL	UNSCRUPULOUS	EXTORTIONATE	MYTHOLOGICAL	DEUTEROSCOPY
INSUFFERABLE	UNSEASONABLE	EXTRADITABLE	NATURALISTIC	DOUBLEDECKER
INSUFFERABLY	UNSUCCESSFUL	EXTRAVAGANCE	NOTIFICATION	DOUBLEGLAZED
INSUFFICIENT	UNSURPRISING	EXTRAVAGANZA	NUTRITIONIST	EDUCATIONIST
INSURRECTION	UNSUSPECTING	FOTHERINGHAY	OCTASTROPHIC	EQUIVOCATION
LASCIVIOUSLY	WASHINGTONIA	HETEROCLITIC	OCTOGENARIAN	EQUIVOCATORY
LISTLESSNESS	AETHRIOSCOPE	HETEROCONTAE	ORTHODONTICS	FLUORESCENCE
MASSERANDUBA	AFTEREFFECTS	HETEROGAMETE	ORTHOGENESIS	FLUORIDATION
MASSPRODUCED	AFTERTHOUGHT	HETEROPHORIA	ORTHOPAEDICS	FLUVIOMARINE
MASTERSTROKE	ANTAGONISTIC	HETEROPLASIA	ORTHOPAEDIST	FRUITFULNESS

FRUMENTATION	SEXAGENARIAN	GONADOTROPIN	SPHACELATION	BRICKFIELDER
GLUBBDUBDRIB	TOXICOLOGIST	HAMARTHRITIS	SPHAIRISTIKE	CALCEAMENTUM
HOUSEBREAKER	ASYMMETRICAL	HUMANITARIAN	STEALTHINESS	CANCELLATION
HOUSEKEEPING	CRYPTOGRAPHY	HUMANIZATION	STRADIVARIUS	CARCINOGENIC
HOUSETOHOUSE	EGYPTOLOGIST	IDEALIZATION	STRAIGHTAWAY	CIRCASSIENNE
HOUSEWARMING	ERYTHROMYCIN	IMMACULATELY	STRAIGHTEDGE	CIRCUMCISION
JOURNALISTIC	ETYMOLOGICAL	IMPARTIALITY	STRAIGHTNESS	CIRCUMGYRATE
LAUREATESHIP	ETYMOLOGICON	INCALCULABLE	STRAITJACKET	CIRCUMSCRIBE
MOUSQUETAIRE	GLYCOPROTEIN	INCANDESCENT	STRANGLEHOLD	CIRCUMSTANCE
MOUTHBROODER	GLYNDEBOURNE	INCAPABILITY	STRANGLEWEED	COCCIDIOSTAT
NEUROFIBROMA	GLYPTOGRAPHY	INCAPACITATE	STRATOSPHERE	CONCENTRATED
NEUROLOGICAL	ONYCHOPHORAN	INCAUTIOUSLY	SUBARRHATION	CONCILIATION
NEUROSCIENCE	OXYACETYLENE	INHARMONIOUS	SYNADELPHITE	CONCILIATORY
NEUROTICALLY	PHYCOXANTHIN	INNATTENTIVE	TAMARICACEAE	CONCLUSIVELY
SAUROGNATHAE	PHYSIOLOGIST	INSALUBRIOUS	TARAMASALATA	CONCURRENTLY
SCURRILOUSLY	PHYTOBENTHOS	INVALIDATION	THEATRICALLY	COSCINOMANCY
SHUFFLEBOARD	PHYTONADIONE	IRRATIONALLY	TITANOSAURUS	CZECHOSLOVAK
SKUTTERUDITE	PHYTOPHAGOUS	KERAUNOGRAPH	TOBACCONISTS	DISCIPLINARY
SLUBBERINGLY	PSYCHIATRIST	KINAESTHETIC	TOTALITARIAN	DISCOMEDUSAE
SOUTHCOTTIAN	PSYCHOLOGIST	LABANOTATION	TURACOVERDIN	DISCOMFITURE
SOUTHEASTERN	PSYCHOPATHIC	LEGALIZATION	UNFATHOMABLE	DISCOMYCETES
SOUTHERNMOST	RHYTHMICALLY	LYMANTRIIDAE	UNFAVOURABLE	DISCONCERTED
SOUTHERNWOOD	RHYTIDECTOMY	MACABERESQUE	UNMANAGEABLE	DISCONNECTED
SOUTHWESTERN	THYSANOPTERA	MALACOSTRACA	UNPARALLELED	DISCONSOLATE
SPURIOUSNESS		METAGNATHOUS	UNPARDONABLE	DISCONTENTED
SPURTLEBLADE	**12:4**	METALLOPHONE	UNSATISFYING	DISCOURAGING
SQUIRRELFISH	ADVANTAGEOUS	METALLURGIST	URBANIZATION	DISCOURTEOUS
STUBBORNNESS	ADVANTAGIOUS	METAMORPHISM	ZALAMBDODONT	DISCRIMINATE
STUDDINGSAIL	AMBASSADRESS	METAMORPHOSE	ZARATHUSTRIC	EDUCATIONIST
STUDIOUSNESS	ANTAGONISTIC	METAPHORICAL	BAMBOCCIADES	ELECTRICALLY
STUPEFACTION	ANTANANARIVO	METAPHYSICAL	BARBERMONGER	ELECTROLYSIS
TAUTOLOGICAL	APLANOGAMETE	MIRACULOUSLY	BLABBERMOUTH	ELECTROPLATE
THUNDERCLOUD	ASPARAGINASE	MISADVENTURE	BOOBYTRAPPED	ELECTROTONUS
THUNDERFLASH	BANANALANDER	MISANTHROPIC	CARBOHYDRATE	EPACRIDACEAE
THUNDERSTORM	BEHAVIOURISM	MISAPPREHEND	COMBINATIONS	EXACERBATION
TRUTHFULNESS	BICAMERALISM	NONAGENARIAN	DOUBLEDECKER	FORCEFULNESS
UNUTTERABLES	BREAKTHROUGH	NONALCOHOLIC	DOUBLEGLAZED	FRACTIONALLY
YOUTHFULNESS	BREASTPLOUGH	OCCASIONALLY	GLOBETROTTER	FUNCTIONALLY
ADVANTAGEOUS	BREASTSUMMER	OCEANOGRAPHY	GLUBBDUBDRIB	FUNCTIONLESS
ADVANTAGIOUS	BREATHALYSER	OCTASTROPHIC	GOBBLEDEGOOK	GLOCKENSPIEL
ADVENTITIOUS	BREATHLESSLY	ORGANISATION	GOBBLEDYGOOK	GLYCOPROTEIN
ADVISABILITY	BREATHTAKING	ORGANIZATION	HAMBLETONIAN	GRACEFULNESS
CIVILISATION	BROADCASTING	OXYACETYLENE	HOBBIDIDANCE	GRACIOUSNESS
CIVILIZATION	CARAVANSERAI	PANAESTHESIA	IAMBOGRAPHER	HENCEFORWARD
COVETOUSNESS	CATADIOPTRIC	PANATHENAEAN	ISOBILATERAL	INACCESSIBLE
DIVERTICULUM	CATAPHYSICAL	PARACENTESIS	MISBEHAVIOUR	INACCURATELY
DIVERTIMENTO	CATASTROPHIC	PARALIPOMENA	MOSBOLLETJIE	LANCASTERIAN
EAVESDROPPER	CLEARSIGHTED	PARAMAGNETIC	NIMBOSTRATUS	LASCIVIOUSLY
GOVERNMENTAL	COHABITATION	PARAMILITARY	OUTBUILDINGS	LINCOLNSHIRE
INVALIDATION	CREATIVENESS	PARANTHELIUM	PROBATIONARY	MARCOBRUNNER
INVERTEBRATE	DECAPITATION	PEDANTICALLY	RAMBUNCTIOUS	MARCONIGRAPH
INVESTIGATOR	DEPARTMENTAL	PENALIZATION	SLUBBERINGLY	MERCANTILISM
INVIGORATING	DILAPIDATION	PERADVENTURE	SNOBBISHNESS	MISCALCULATE
INVIGORATION	DILATORINESS	PERAMBULATOR	STUBBORNNESS	NARCISSISTIC
INVISIBILITY	DISACCHARIDE	POLARIZATION	SYMBOLICALLY	NEOCLASSICAL
INVULNERABLE	DISADVANTAGE	POTAMOLOGIST	TRABECULATED	NONCHALANTLY
LIVERPUDLIAN	DISAGREEABLE	RECALCITRANT	TURBIDIMETER	NONCOMMITTAL
NAVIGABILITY	DISAGREEMENT	RECAPITULATE	TURBOCHARGER	ONYCHOPHORAN
NEVERTHELESS	DISAPPEARING	REHABILITATE	UNOBSTRUCTED	PANCHATANTRA
REVERSIONARY	DISAPPOINTED	RELATIONSHIP	UNOBTAINABLE	PANCHROMATIC
SIVAPITHECUS	DISASSOCIATE	REPATRIATION	ADSCITITIOUS	PEACEFULNESS
BEWILDERMENT	DISASTROUSLY	RETARDEDNESS	AIRCRAFTSMAN	PEACEKEEPING
NEWFOUNDLAND	EMBARRASSING	ROMANTICALLY	ANECATHARSIS	PERCEPTIVELY
NEWSPAPERMAN	ENTANGLEMENT	SEMANTICALLY	AUSCULTATION	PERCEPTIVITY
POWERSHARING	ESCAPOLOGIST	SERASKIERATE	BACCHANALIAN	PHYCOXANTHIN
LEXICOGRAPHY	ESPAGNOLETTE	SEXAGENARIAN	BEACONSFIELD	PISCICULTURE
LOXODROMICAL	EXHAUSTIVELY	SINANTHROPUS	BIOCHEMISTRY	PLACENTIFORM
LUXEMBOURGER	FINALIZATION	SIVAPITHECUS	BLACKCURRANT	PLECTOGNATHI
LUXULLIANITE	GIGANTOMACHY	SOMATOPLEURE	BRACHYCEPHAL	PRACTICALITY

PRACTICIONER	INADMISSIBLE	COVETOUSNESS	INDEBTEDNESS	PEREMPTORILY
PRACTITIONER	INADVERTENCE	DECELERATION	INDECLINABLE	PHLEBOTOMIST
PRECARIOUSLY	KINDERGARTEN	DECENTRALISE	INDEFENSIBLE	POTENTIALITY
PRECOCIOUSLY	MIDDLEWEIGHT	DECENTRALIZE	INDEFINITELY	POWERSHARING
PRECONDITION	MINDBOGGLING	DEGENERATION	INDEPENDENCE	RECEIVERSHIP
PROCESSIONAL	MINDFULLNESS	DEREGULATION	INFELICITOUS	RECEPTIONIST
PROCLAMATION	MISDELIVERED	DERESTRICTED	INSEMINATION	REDEMPTIONER
PSYCHIATRIST	MISDEMEANOUR	DIRECTORSHIP	INTELLECTUAL	REDEPLOYMENT
PSYCHOLOGIST	MUDDLEHEADED	DISEMBARRASS	INTELLIGENCE	REGENERATION
PSYCHOPATHIC	NONDIRECTIVE	DISENCHANTED	INTELLIGIBLE	RELENTLESSLY
RONCESVALLES	OBEDIENTIARY	DIVERTICULUM	INTEMPERANCE	REMEMBRANCER
SLOCKDOLAGER	PANDAEMONIUM	DIVERTIMENTO	INTENERATION	REPERCUSSION
SLOCKDOLIGER	PANDANACEOUS	DOMESTICATED	INTERCEPTION	RESETTLEMENT
SLOCKDOLOGER	PREDESTINATE	EAVESDROPPER	INTERCESSION	REVERSIONARY
SPACIOUSNESS	PREDETERMINE	ECCENTRICITY	INTERCHANGED	SALESMANSHIP
SPECIFICALLY	PREDILECTION	EFFERVESCENT	INTERFERENCE	SCHEHERAZADE
SPECIOUSNESS	PREDOMINANCE	ELEEMOSYNARY	INTERGLACIAL	SCLERENCHYMA
SPECKTIONEER	PRODIGIOUSLY	EMBEZZLEMENT	INTERJECTION	SCLERODERMIA
SPECTROMETER	PRODUCTIVITY	ENTEROMORPHA	INTERLOCUTOR	SCREENWRITER
SPECTROSCOPE	QUADRAGESIMA	ENTEROPNEUST	INTERMEDIARY	SECESSIONIST
STOCKBREEDER	QUADRAPHONIC	ENTERPRISING	INTERMEDIATE	SHEEPISHNESS
STOCKINGETTE	QUADRIPLEGIA	ENTERTAINING	INTERMINABLE	SIDEWHISKERS
SUBCOMMITTEE	READJUSTMENT	ESSENTIALITY	INTERMINABLY	SLEEPWALKING
SUBCONSCIOUS	RHADAMANTHUS	ETHEROMANIAC	INTERMISSION	SPIEGELEISEN
SUBCONTINENT	RHODODENDRON	EULENSPIEGEL	INTERMITTENT	SPLENOMEGALY
SUBCUTANEOUS	SARDANAPALUS	EXPERIMENTAL	INTERPRETING	SPREADEAGLED
SUCCESSFULLY	SARDONICALLY	EXSERVICEMAN	INTERRELATED	SPRECHGESANG
SUCCESSIVELY	SLEDGEHAMMER	EXTENSIONIST	INTERROGATOR	STEEPLECHASE
SUCCUSSATION	STUDDINGSAIL	EXTENSOMETER	INTERRUPTION	STREPITATION
TERCENTENARY	STUDIOUSNESS	FRIENDLINESS	INTERSECTION	STREPSIPTERA
THICKSKINNED	TRADESCANTIA	GAMESMANSHIP	INTERSPERSED	STREPTOMYCIN
TRACTABILITY	TRADESPEOPLE	GENEALOGICAL	INTERSTELLAR	STREPTONEURA
TRICENTENARY	UNIDENTIFIED	GENETHLIACON	INTERVENTION	SUPERANNUATE
TRICHOLOGIST	VINDICTIVELY	GESELLSCHAFT	INVERTEBRATE	SUPERCHARGED
TRICHOPHYTON	WOODBURYTYPE	GOVERNMENTAL	INVESTIGATOR	SUPERCHARGER
TROCHELMINTH	ACCELERATION	GREENGROCERS	IRREDEEMABLE	SUPERCILIARY
TROCHOSPHERE	ACCENTUATION	GREENGROCERY	IRREGULARITY	SUPERCILIOUS
UNACCEPTABLE	ADJECTIVALLY	GYNECOLOGIST	IRRESISTIBLE	SUPERHIGHWAY
UNACCUSTOMED	ADVENTITIOUS	HABERDASHERS	IRRESOLUTELY	SUPERNACULUM
UNACQUAINTED	AFFECTIONATE	HABERDASHERY	IRRESOLUTION	SUPERNATURAL
UNECONOMICAL	AFTEREFFECTS	HEREDITAMENT	IRRESOLVABLE	SUPERSTITION
UNSCIENTIFIC	AFTERTHOUGHT	HEREDITARIAN	IRRESPECTIVE	SUPERSTRATUM
UNSCRUPULOUS	ANAESTHETISE	HETEROCLITIC	IRREVERENTLY	TAPERECORDER
WATCHFULNESS	ANAESTHETIST	HETEROCONTAE	IRREVERSIBLE	TELEASTHETIC
ACADEMICALLY	ANAESTHETIZE	HETEROGAMETE	KALEIDOSCOPE	TELEGRAPHESE
BANDERSNATCH	ANTEDILUVIAN	HETEROPHORIA	LAMELLICORNE	TELEGRAPHIST
BIODIVERSITY	ANTEMERIDIAN	HETEROPLASIA	LAMENTATIONS	TELEOSAURIAN
BIRDWATCHING	APFELSTRUDEL	HETEROSEXUAL	LIFELESSNESS	TELEUTOSPORE
CARDINDEXING	APPENDECTOMY	HETEROSOMATA	LIVERPUDLIAN	THREADNEEDLE
CARDIOLOGIST	APPENDICITIS	HOMESICKNESS	LUXEMBOURGER	THREEQUARTER
CARDIOMEGALY	ARSENOPYRITE	HOPELESSNESS	MADEMOISELLE	TIMELESSNESS
COLDSHOULDER	ATHEROMATOUS	HYMENOPTERAN	MAJESTICALLY	TOGETHERNESS
CONDEMNATION	BENEFACTRESS	HYPERACIDITY	MERETRICIOUS	TUBERCULOSIS
CONDENSATION	BENEVOLENTLY	HYPERBOLICAL	MINERALOGIST	UNBELIEVABLE
CONDUCTIVITY	BICENTENNIAL	HYPERPYRETIC	MUTESSARIFAT	UNBELIEVABLY
DENDROLOGIST	BLUESTOCKING	HYPERSARCOMA	NEPENTHACEAE	UNDEMOCRATIC
DISDAINFULLY	BUREAUCRATIC	HYPERTENSION	NEVERTHELESS	UNDERACHIEVE
EPIDEICTICAL	CAMERAPERSON	ILLEGIBILITY	NOMENCLATURE	UNDERCLOTHES
FELDSPATHOID	CAPERCAILLIE	ILLEGITIMACY	NONEXISTENCE	UNDERCURRENT
FIDDLESTICKS	CAPERCAILZIE	ILLEGITIMATE	OBSEQUIOUSLY	UNDEREXPOSED
FUNDAMENTALS	CARELESSNESS	IMMEASURABLE	OBSERVANTINE	UNDERGARMENT
GLADIATORIAL	CEREBROTONIC	IMMEASURABLY	ORIENTEERING	UNDERPINNING
GONDWANALAND	CEREMONIALLY	IMPENETRABLE	OSTENTATIOUS	UNDERSKINKER
HANDKERCHIEF	CHEERFULNESS	IMPERFECTION	OSTEOMALACIA	UNDERSTAFFED
HEADMISTRESS	CHEESEBURGER	IMPERFECTIVE	OSTEOPOROSIS	UNDERWRITTEN
HEADQUARTERS	CHEESEMONGER	IMPERISHABLE	OSTEOSARCOMA	UNDESERVEDLY
HILDEBRANDIC	CHEESEPARING	IMPERSONALLY	OTHERWORLDLY	UNDETECTABLE
HINDQUARTERS	CHREMATISTIC	IMPERSONATOR	PALEONTOLOGY	UNDETERMINED
INADEQUATELY	CHRESTOMATHY	IMPERTINENCE	PARENTHESIZE	UNNEIGHBORLY

UNREASONABLE	SINGLEHANDED	RUTHLESSNESS	DEMIMONDAINE	ONEIROCRITIC
UNRECOGNISED	SINGLEMINDED	SIPHONOPHORA	DESIDERATIVE	OPHIOGLOSSUM
UNRECOGNIZED	STAGGERINGLY	SIPHONOSTELE	DESIRABILITY	ORNITHOGALUM
UNRESERVEDLY	STEGOPHOLIST	SOPHISTICATE	DISINCENTIVE	OSCILLOSCOPE
UNRESPONSIVE	SUGGESTIVELY	SUBHASTATION	DISINFECTANT	OSSIFICATION
UNRESTRAINED	TERGIVERSATE	TECHNICALITY	DISINGENUOUS	PACIFICATION
UNRESTRICTED	THIGMOTROPIC	TECHNOLOGIST	DISINTEGRATE	PALINGENESIA
UNRETURNABLE	TRIGONOMETRY	TIGHTFITTING	ENCIRCLEMENT	PALINGENESIS
UNSEASONABLE	VENGEFULNESS	UNCHALLENGED	EQUIVOCATION	PAPILIONIDAE
VALENCIENNES	WEIGHTLIFTER	UNCHANGEABLE	EQUIVOCATORY	PEDIATRICIAN
VENEPUNCTURE	WHIGMALEERIE	UNCHARITABLE	EXCITABILITY	PEDICELLARIA
VETERINARIAN	AETHRIOSCOPE	UNCHARITABLY	EXHIBITIONER	PENITENTIARY
WAREHOUSEMAN	ALPHABETICAL	WASHINGTONIA	EXHILARATING	PERICARDITIS
WATERCARRIER	ALPHANUMERIC	XIPHISTERNUM	EXHILARATION	PERIODICALLY
BIOFLAVONOID	AMPHISBAENIC	ACCIDENTALLY	EXTINGUISHER	PERIODONTICS
BLEFUSCUDIAN	AMPHISTOMOUS	ADDITIONALLY	FREIGHTLINER	PERIOSTRACUM
CONFECTIONER	AMPHITHEATER	ADMINISTRATE	FRUITFULNESS	PERIPHRASTIC
CONFESSIONAL	AMPHITHEATRE	ADVISABILITY	GERIATRICIAN	PERISTERONIC
CONFIDENTIAL	ANCHORPERSON	AECIDIOSPORE	HELIOGABALUS	PLAINCLOTHES
CONFIRMATION	ANTHELMINTIC	AGRIBUSINESS	HELIOTROPISM	PLEIOCHASIUM
CONFIRMATORY	ANTHROPOLOGY	AGRICULTURAL	HEMICHORDATA	POLICYMAKING
CONFISCATION	ARCHILOCHIAN	ALLITERATION	HOLIDAYMAKER	POTICHOMANIA
DIFFERENTIAL	ARCHIPELAGOS	AMBIDEXTROUS	HORIZONTALLY	PRAISEWORTHY
DISFRANCHISE	ARCHITECTURE	ANNIHILATION	HUDIBRASTICS	PURIFICATION
INEFFICIENCY	ARTHROPLASTY	ANTIAIRCRAFT	HYGIENICALLY	RADIOBIOLOGY
MALFORMATION	ASPHYXIATION	ANTIBACCHIUS	INCIDENTALLY	RADIOGRAPHER
NEWFOUNDLAND	AUTHENTICATE	ANTIBARBARUS	INCINERATION	RADIOISOTOPE
NONFLAMMABLE	AUTHENTICITY	ANTICIPATION	INDIFFERENCE	RADIOTHERAPY
OLDFASHIONED	BETHLEHEMITE	ANTICIPATORY	INDIGESTIBLE	RAMIFICATION
PREFERENTIAL	CATHETOMETER	ANTILEGOMENA	INDISCRETION	RATIFICATION
PROFESSIONAL	DICHROMATISM	ANTIMACASSAR	INDISPUTABLE	RECIPROCALLY
PROFESSORIAL	DISHONORABLE	ANTIMETABOLE	INDISPUTABLY	REDINTEGRATE
PROFICIENTLY	DISHONORABLY	ANTIMNEMONIC	INDISSOLUBLE	REDISCOVERED
PROFITEERING	EMPHATICALLY	ANTINEUTRINO	INDISTINCTLY	REDISTRIBUTE
SELFADHESIVE	ENCHEIRIDION	ANTIPARTICLE	INDIVIDUALLY	REGISTRATION
SELFCATERING	ENTHUSIASTIC	ANTIRACHITIC	INFILTRATION	REMINISCENCE
SELFEMPLOYED	ESCHSCHOLZIA	ANTISTROPHON	INTIMIDATING	RESIPISCENCE
SELFINTEREST	ESTHETICALLY	ANTITHROMBIN	INTIMIDATION	RETICULATION
SELFPORTRAIT	EXCHANGEABLE	ARTICULATION	INVIGORATING	RIDICULOUSLY
SHUFFLEBOARD	FOTHERINGHAY	ARTIFICIALLY	INVIGORATION	SADISTICALLY
SUFFICIENTLY	HEPHTHEMIMER	ARTILLERYMAN	INVISIBILITY	SATISFACTION
UNOFFICIALLY	HIGHFALUTING	ARTIODACTYLA	IRRITABILITY	SATISFACTORY
BIOGRAPHICAL	KATHAREVOUSA	ARTISTICALLY	JURISDICTION	SCHILLERSPAR
BOUGAINVILLE	LIGHTHEARTED	ASSIMILATION	KALISTOCRACY	SCHINDYLESIS
CONGENITALLY	LITHOGRAPHIC	AVAILABILITY	LATIROSTRATE	SCHIZOMYCETE
CONGLOMERATE	LITHOLATROUS	AWEINSPIRING	LEGIONNAIRES	SCRIMSHANDER
CONGRATULATE	MACHAIRODONT	BABINGTONITE	LEGITIMATELY	SCRIMSHANKER
CONGREGATION	MATHEMATICAL	BEWILDERMENT	LEPIDOMELANE	SCRIPTWRITER
DIAGRAMMATIC	MECHANICALLY	BRAINWASHING	LEXICOGRAPHY	SEMICIRCULAR
EPIGRAMMATIC	MECHITHARIST	BUSINESSLIKE	LUMINESCENCE	SEMIDETACHED
EXAGGERATION	METHODICALLY	CABINETMAKER	LUMINISCENCE	SEMIPRECIOUS
FLAGELLATION	METHOTREXATE	CAMIKNICKERS	MANIPULATION	SOCIOLOGICAL
GEOGRAPHICAL	MICHELANGELO	CAPITULATION	MANIPULATIVE	SOLICITATION
LANGUEDOCIAN	MYTHOLOGICAL	CARICATURIST	MERISTEMATIC	SOLICITOUSLY
LONGDISTANCE	NEPHELOMETER	CHAIRMANSHIP	MERITRICIOUS	SQUIRRELFISH
LONGITUDINAL	NIGHTCLOTHES	CHRISTIANITY	METICULOUSLY	STRIDULATION
LONGSHOREMAN	NYCHTHEMERON	CIVILISATION	MILITARISTIC	STRIGIFORMES
LONGSTANDING	ORTHODONTICS	CIVILIZATION	MINICOMPUTER	STRINGCOURSE
MANGELWURZEL	ORTHOGENESIS	CLAIRVOYANCE	MINISTRATION	TOXICOLOGIST
MUGGLETONIAN	ORTHOPAEDICS	CLAIRVOYANCY	MISINTERPRET	UNDIMINISHED
NEIGHBORHOOD	ORTHOPAEDIST	CLEISTOGAMIC	MOBILIZATION	UNDISCHARGED
NEIGHBOURING	ORTHOPTEROUS	CODIFICATION	MODIFICATION	UNMISTAKABLE
PERGAMENEOUS	ORTHORHOMBIC	DEBILITATING	MUCILAGINOUS	VARICOLOURED
PREGUSTATION	ORTHOTONESIS	DECIPHERABLE	MUNICIPALITY	VERIFICATION
PRIGGISHNESS	PATHETICALLY	DECIPHERMENT	MUSICOLOGIST	VILIFICATION
PROGESTERONE	PATHOLOGICAL	DELIBERATELY	MYRINGOSCOPE	VOCIFERATION
PROGRAMMABLE	PREHISTORIAN	DELIBERATION	NAVIGABILITY	VOCIFEROUSLY
PROGYMNASIUM	PYTHONOMORPH	DELICATESSEN	NOTIFICATION	SUBJECTIVELY
SINGLEDECKER	RECHARGEABLE	DEMILITARIZE	OBLITERATION	SUBJECTIVITY

BACKBREAKING	KILLIKINNICK	CURMUDGEONLY	DUNNIEWASSAL	THUNDERSTORM
BACKWARDNESS	LALLAPALOOZA	DEAMBULATORY	ECONOMICALLY	TRANQUILIZER
BACKWOODSMAN	LILLIBULLERO	DOGMATICALLY	EMANCIPATION	TRANQUILLISE
BUCKLEBEGGAR	LILLIBURLERO	DRAMATICALLY	ENANTIOMORPH	TRANQUILLITY
BUNKOSTEERER	MALLEABILITY	DRAMATURGIST	ENANTIOPATHY	TRANQUILLIZE
CUCKOOFLOWER	MALLOPHAGOUS	ETYMOLOGICAL	EPANORTHOSIS	TRANSACTIONS
LICKTRENCHER	MARLINESPIKE	ETYMOLOGICON	EPENCEPHALON	TRANSCENDENT
MARKSMANSHIP	MILLILAMBERT	FEHMGERICHTE	ETHNOLOGICAL	TRANSFERABLE
PARKINSONISM	MULLIGATAWNY	FERMENTATION	EVENHANDEDLY	TRANSFERENCE
POIKILOTHERM	PHILANTHROPY	FLAMBOYANTLY	EVENTEMPERED	TRANSGRESSOR
RACKETEERING	PHILHARMONIC	FORMALDEHYDE	FAINTHEARTED	TRANSITIONAL
RECKLESSNESS	PHILISTINISM	FRUMENTATION	FRANKALMOIGN	TRANSLATABLE
SPOKESPERSON	PHILODENDRON	FULMINATIONS	FRANKENSTEIN	TRANSLUCENCE
STAKHANOVITE	PHILOLOGICAL	GEOMETRICIAN	FRANKINCENSE	TRANSMIGRATE
WICKETKEEPER	PHILOSOPHIZE	HAEMATEMESIS	FRONTIERSMAN	TRANSMISSION
YORKSHIREMAN	PRALLTRILLER	HAEMOPHILIAC	FRONTISPIECE	TRANSMOGRIFY
ABOLITIONIST	PROLEGOMENON	HAEMORRHOIDS	GAINSBOROUGH	TRANSOCEANIC
ACHLAMYDEOUS	PROLETARIATE	HAMMERHEADED	GLYNDEBOURNE	TRANSPARENCY
ADULTERATION	PROLIFICALLY	HARMONIOUSLY	GRANDISONIAN	TRANSPONTINE
AGALMATOLITE	PROLONGATION	HERMENEUTICS	GRANDMONTINE	TRANSVESTISM
AMALGAMATION	REFLATIONARY	HERMENEUTIST	GRANDPARENTS	TRANSVESTITE
AMELIORATION	REFLECTIVITY	HERMETICALLY	GYMNOSOPHIST	UNANSWERABLE
APOLLINARIAN	ROLLERBLADER	ISHMAELITISH	HARNESSMAKER	UNINTERESTED
BELLIGERENCY	ROLLERBLADES	MACMILLANITE	HYMNOGRAPHER	VAINGLORIOUS
BIBLIOGRAPHY	SHILLYSHALLY	MNEMOTECHNIC	HYPNOTHERAPY	ACCOMPANYING
BIBLIOPEGIST	SMALLHOLDING	ONOMATOPOEIA	HYPNOTICALLY	ACCOMPLISHED
BIELORUSSIAN	SPELEOLOGIST	ONOMATOPOEIC	ICONOCLASTIC	ACCORDIONIST
BILLINGSGATE	SPELLCHECKER	OUTMANOEUVRE	IDENTIFIABLE	ACCOUCHEMENT
BOULEVARDIER	STELLENBOSCH	PERMANGANATE	JENNYSPINNER	ACCOUTREMENT
BRILLIANTINE	STILBOESTROL	PERMEABILITY	MAGNETICALLY	ADMONISHMENT
BYELORUSSIAN	SUBLAPSARIAN	PERMITTIVITY	MAGNIFICENCE	AERODYNAMICS
CALLIGRAPHIC	TAGLIACOTIAN	PIGMENTATION	MAGNILOQUENT	AERONAUTICAL
CALLISTHENES	TRALATICIOUS	PREMAXILLARY	MALNUTRITION	ANDOUILLETTE
CARLOVINGIAN	TRALATITIOUS	PREMONSTRANT	MEANINGFULLY	ANNOUNCEMENT
CHALCOPYRITE	UNCLASSIFIED	PRIMIGRAVIDA	MOONLIGHTING	ANTONINIANUS
CHALICOTHERE	UNILATERALLY	PROMULGATION	OPINIONATIVE	APPOGGIATURA
CHILDBEARING	VILLEGIATURA	RHAMPHOTHECA	PAINLESSNESS	ARBORESCENCE
CHILDISHNESS	WALLYDRAIGLE	ROOMINGHOUSE	PENNSYLVANIA	ASTONISHMENT
COLLABORATOR	WELLBALANCED	SEGMENTATION	PERNOCTATION	ATMOSPHERICS
COLLECTIVELY	WELLINFORMED	SHAMEFACEDLY	PHENOMENALLY	AUTOHYPNOSIS
COLLECTORATE	WELLINGTONIA	SUBMINIATURE	PHONETICALLY	BARORECEPTOR
COLLOQUIALLY	WHOLEHEARTED	SUBMISSIVELY	PINNIEWINKLE	BLOODLETTING
COLLUCTATION	WILLIEWAUGHT	SURMOUNTABLE	POINTILLISME	BLOODSTAINED
COLLYWOBBLES	WOLLASTONITE	TREMENDOUSLY	PORNOGRAPHIC	BLOODTHIRSTY
DARLINGTONIA	YELLOWHAMMER	UNEMPLOYMENT	PRINCIPALITY	CANONIZATION
DEFLATIONARY	AGAMOGENETIC	UNIMAGINABLE	PUGNACIOUSLY	CHLORINATION
DIALECTICIAN	ALIMENTATIVE	UNIMPORTANCE	QUANTIFIABLE	CHLOROPICRIN
DIPLOGENESIS	ANAMORPHOSIS	VEHMGERICHTE	QUANTITATIVE	COLONIZATION
ECCLESIASTES	ANEMOPHILOUS	VERMICULTURE	QUINQUENNIAL	COLOQUINTIDA
ECCLESIASTIC	AROMATHERAPY	WHIMSICALITY	QUINTESSENCE	CYMOTRICHOUS
ENGLISHWOMAN	ASYMMETRICAL	ACKNOWLEDGED	REINVIGORATE	DECONGESTANT
ENGLISHWOMEN	AUGMENTATION	AYUNTAMIENTO	RHINORRHOEAL	DECORATIVELY
EPILEPTIFORM	AUGMENTATIVE	BARNSTORMING	SCANDALOUSLY	DEMONSTRABLE
EVOLUTIONARY	CHAMPIONSHIP	BLANDISHMENT	SCANDINAVIAN	DEMONSTRABLY
EXPLOITATION	CHEMOTHERAPY	BLENNORRHOEA	SCHNEIDERIAN	DEMONSTRATOR
GALLIGASKINS	CLAMJAMPHRIE	BOONDOGGLING	SCINTILLATOR	DENOMINATION
GALLINACEOUS	COMMANDMENTS	BRANCHIOPODA	SIGNIFICANCE	DEPOPULATION
GALLIVANTING	COMMENCEMENT	BRONTOSAURUS	SOMNAMBULISM	DISOBEDIENCE
GEOLOGICALLY	COMMENDATION	CHONDRIOSOME	SOMNAMBULIST	DISORGANIZED
GUILDENSTERN	COMMENDATORY	CLANNISHNESS	SPINECHILLER	DISORIENTATE
HALLANSHAKER	COMMENSURATE	COINCIDENTAL	SPINSTERHOOD	EFFORTLESSLY
HALLUCINOGEN	COMMERCIALLY	COUNTERBLAST	STANISLAVSKI	ENTOMOLOGIST
HELLGRAMMITE	COMMISSARIAT	COUNTERCLAIM	STENOGRAPHER	ENTOMOSTRACA
IMPLANTATION	COMMISSIONED	COUNTERMARCH	STENTORPHONE	ENTOPLASTRON
INFLAMMATION	COMMISSIONER	COUNTERPOINT	STONECHATTER	EXTORTIONATE
INFLAMMATORY	COMMONWEALTH	COUNTERPOISE	THANKFULNESS	FLUORESCENCE
INFLATIONARY	COMMUNICABLE	DIENCEPHALON	THANKSGIVING	FLUORIDATION
ISOLATIONISM	COSMOPOLITAN	DONNERWETTER	THUNDERCLOUD	GAMOSEPALOUS
ISOLATIONIST	CREMAILLIÈRE	DRINKDRIVING	THUNDERFLASH	GERONTOCRACY

HEROICOMICAL	RODOMONTADER	PROPAGANDIST	COURTMARTIAL	NEUROTICALLY
HOMOEOPATHIC	SCHOOLMASTER	PROPHYLACTIC	DEPRECIATION	NONRESIDENCE
HOMOTHERMOUS	SCHOPENHAUER	PROPITIATION	DEPRECIATORY	NONRESISTANT
HYPOCHONDRIA	STROMATOLITE	PROPITIATORY	DIPRIONIDIAN	NUTRITIONIST
HYPOCRITICAL	STRONGMINDED	PROPITIOUSLY	DISREPECTFUL	OPPRESSIVELY
HYPOTHECATOR	STRONTIANITE	PROPORTIONAL	DISREPUTABLE	OUTRAGEOUSLY
HYPOTHETICAL	STROPHANTHUS	PROPRIETRESS	EMBROIDERESS	OVERCROWDING
IDIOSYNCRASY	THEOPHYLLINE	PSEPHOLOGIST	ENCROACHMENT	OVERDRESSING
IDIOTHERMOUS	THEORETICIAN	PSIPHENOMENA	ENERGYSAVING	OVERESTIMATE
ILLOGICALITY	UNCONSIDERED	PUMPERNICKEL	ENTREATINGLY	OVEREXERTION
IMMODERATELY	UNCONTROLLED	PURPOSEBUILT	ENTRENCHMENT	OVERPOWERING
IMMODERATION	UNCONVERSANT	PURPOSEFULLY	ENTREPRENEUR	OVERSCUTCHED
IMPOLITENESS	UNCONVINCING	REAPPEARANCE	ESTRANGEMENT	OVERSTRAINED
IMPOVERISHED	UNPOPULARITY	RESPECTFULLY	EXCRUCIATING	OVERWHELMING
INCOHERENTLY	UPROARIOUSLY	RESPECTIVELY	EXCRUCIATION	PETRIFACTION
INCOMPARABLE	VAPORIZATION	RESPONDENTIA	EXTRADITABLE	PHARMACOLOGY
INCOMPARABLY	ADAPTABILITY	RHIPIDOPTERA	EXTRAVAGANCE	PREREQUISITE
INCOMPATIBLE	AUSPICIOUSLY	SCAPULIMANCY	EXTRAVAGANZA	PTERIDOPHYTE
INCOMPETENCE	CAMPANULARIA	SCOPOPHILIAC	FEARLESSNESS	PTERIDOSPERM
INCOMPLETELY	CAMPODEIFORM	SHIPBUILDING	FLORICULTURE	PTERODACTYLE
INCONCLUSIVE	CARPETBAGGER	STEPDAUGHTER	GIBRALTARIAN	PUTREFACTION
INCONSEQUENT	CARPOPHAGOUS	STUPEFACTION	GUARDIANSHIP	QUARTERFINAL
INCONSISTENT	CLAPPERBOARD	SULPHONAMIDE	HAIRDRESSERS	QUARTERLIGHT
INCONSOLABLE	COMPANIONWAY	SUPPLICATION	HAIRDRESSING	QUARTERSTAFF
INCONTINENCE	COMPELLATION	SURPRISINGLY	HAIRSPLITTER	RECREATIONAL
INCONVENIENT	COMPENSATION	SUSPICIOUSLY	HEARTSTRINGS	RECRUDESCENT
INCORPORATED	COMPENSATORY	TROPHALLAXIS	HEARTWARMING	REFRIGERATED
INCORRIGIBLE	COMPLACENTLY	UNAPPARELLED	HIERARCHICAL	REFRIGERATOR
INCORRIGIBLY	COMPLETENESS	UNAPPETIZING	HIEROGLYPHIC	REPROCESSING
INDOCTRINATE	COMPLICATION	UNOPPRESSIVE	HIEROGRAMMAT	REPRODUCTION
INFORMIDABLE	COMPROMISING	WHIPPOORWILL	HIEROPHANTIC	REPRODUCTIVE
INFOTAINMENT	COMPURGATION	ABSQUATULATE	HORRIFICALLY	RETRENCHMENT
INHOSPITABLE	CRYPTOGRAPHY	CONQUISTADOR	HYDROCHLORIC	SACRILEGIOUS
INNOMINABLES	DISPENSATION	DISQUISITION	HYDROGEOLOGY	SARRUSOPHONE
INSOLUBILITY	DISPLACEMENT	MISQUOTATION	HYDROGRAPHER	SAUROGNATHAE
INTOXICATING	DISPOSSESSED	PASQUEFLOWER	HYDROQUINONE	SCURRILOUSLY
INTOXICATION	DOLPHINARIUM	SESQUIALTERA	HYDROTHERAPY	SECRETARIATE
LABOURSAVING	EGYPTOLOGIST	SESQUITERTIA	IMPREGNATION	SHAREHOLDING
LEIOTRICHOUS	EPIPHENOMENA	ABBREVIATION	IMPRESSIVELY	SHARPSHOOTER
LOXODROMICAL	ETEPIMELETIC	AFORETHOUGHT	IMPRISONMENT	SHIRTSLEEVES
MANOEUVRABLE	GEOPHYSICIST	AGGRESSIVELY	IMPROVIDENCE	SHIRTWAISTER
MELODRAMATIC	GLYPTOGRAPHY	AMARANTACEAE	INARTICULATE	SHORTCIRCUIT
MESOTHELIOMA	GRAPHOLOGIST	ANDROSTERONE	INCREASINGLY	SHORTCOMINGS
MONOSYLLABIC	HAPPENSTANCE	APPRECIATION	INCRUSTATION	SHORTSIGHTED
MONOSYLLABLE	HAPPYGOLUCKY	APPRECIATIVE	INERADICABLE	SHORTSLEEVED
MONOTONOUSLY	HELPLESSNESS	APPREHENSION	INFREQUENTLY	SHORTSTAFFED
MOTORCYCLIST	HIPPOCRATISE	APPREHENSIVE	INFRINGEMENT	SPERMATOCYTE
NOCONFIDENCE	HIPPOCREPIAN	APPROACHABLE	INGRATIATING	SPERMATOZOID
NONOBJECTIVE	HIPPOPOTAMUS	ASTROLOGICAL	INORDINATELY	SPERMATOZOON
OBSOLESCENCE	INAPPLICABLE	ASTRONOMICAL	INTRANSIGENT	SPIRITUALISM
OBSOLETENESS	INSPECTORATE	ASTROPHYSICS	INTRANSITIVE	SPIRITUALIST
OCTOGENARIAN	KLEPTOMANIAC	ATTRACTIVELY	INTRAUTERINE	SPIRITUALITY
ONCORHYNCHUS	KLIPSPRINGER	ATTRIBUTABLE	INTRODUCTION	SPORADICALLY
OREOPITHECUS	LAMPADEDROMY	AWARDWINNING	INTRODUCTORY	SPORTSGROUND
OREOPITHEOUS	MALPRACTICES	BAIRNSFATHER	INTROVERSION	SPURIOUSNESS
PHRONTISTERY	MISPLACEMENT	BARRANQUILLA	JOURNALISTIC	SPURTLEBLADE
POGONOPHORAN	MISPRONOUNCE	BIPROPELLANT	LAUREATESHIP	STEREOPHONIC
POPOCATEPETL	NEOPLATONISM	CARRIWITCHET	MACROCEPHALY	STEREOPTICON
PYROCATECHOL	NYMPHOMANIAC	CHARACTERIZE	MACROPODIDAE	STEREOSCOPIC
PYROTECHNICS	PALPITATIONS	CHARTERHOUSE	MARRIAGEABLE	STEREOTYPING
RECOGNIZABLE	PANPHARMACON	CHIROPRACTIC	MERRYTHOUGHT	STERNUTATION
RECOGNIZANCE	PERPETRATION	CHIROPRACTOR	METROPOLITAN	STERNWHEELER
RECOLLECTION	PREPAREDNESS	CHOREOGRAPHY	MICROBREWERY	STORMTROOPER
RECONSTITUTE	PREPONDERANT	CHORIZONTIST	MICROCLIMATE	SURREALISTIC
RECORDPLAYER	PREPONDERATE	CHURCHWARDEN	MISREPRESENT	SURROUNDINGS
REMONSTRANCE	PREPONDERENT	CHURLISHNESS	MITRAILLEUSE	TERRIFICALLY
RENOUNCEMENT	PREPOSSESSED	CLARINETTIST	NEUROFIBROMA	TERRITORIALS
REPOSSESSION	PREPOSTEROUS	COORDINATION	NEUROLOGICAL	TETRACYCLINE
RISORGIMENTO	PROPAGANDISM	COURAGEOUSLY	NEUROSCIENCE	TETRAHEDRITE

TETRODOTOXIN	DISSERTATION	SHOSTAKOVICH	FAITHFULNESS	POSTLIMINARY
THERAPEUTICS	DISSOCIATION	SUBSCRIPTION	FARTHINGLAND	POSTMISTRESS
THEREAGAINST	DORSIVENTRAL	SUBSEQUENTLY	FASTIDIOUSLY	POSTPONEMENT
THERMOSTATIC	DRESSINGDOWN	SUBSERVIENCE	FEATHERBRAIN	POSTPOSITIVE
THIRDBOROUGH	ELASMOBRANCH	SUBSIDIARITY	FLITTERMOUSE	POSTPRANDIAL
THOROUGHBRED	EMASCULATION	SUBSTANTIATE	FOOTSLOGGING	PROTACTINIUM
THOROUGHFARE	EPISCOPALIAN	SUBSTITUTION	FORTUITOUSLY	PROTECTIVELY
THOROUGHNESS	EPISTEMOLOGY	SUBSTITUTIVE	FUSTILLIRIAN	PROTECTORATE
TORRICELLIAN	EPISTOLATERS	SUBSTRUCTURE	GASTARBEITER	PROTESTATION
ULTRAMONTANE	EXASPERATING	SWASHBUCKLER	GASTROSOPHER	PROTHALAMION
UMBRADARLING	EXASPERATION	TAPSALTEERIE	GENTLETAMPER	PROTHALAMIUM
UNFREQUENTED	FIRSTFOOTING	TAPSLETEERIE	GRATEFULNESS	PROTHONOTARY
UNPREJUDICED	GOOSEPIMPLES	THESMOPHORIA	HAPTOTROPISM	PROTOPLASMAL
UNPRETENDING	GRASSWIDOWER	THESSALONIAN	HISTIOPHORUS	PROTOPLASMIC
UNPRINCIPLED	GRISEOFULVIN	THYSANOPTERA	HISTORICALLY	PROTUBERANCE
UNPRODUCTIVE	GROSSULARITE	WOLSTENHOLME	HORTICULTURE	RESTAURATEUR
UNPROFITABLE	HORSEMANSHIP	ACETALDEHYDE	HYSTERECTOMY	RESTLESSNESS
URTRICULARIA	HOUSEBREAKER	AGATHODAIMON	HYSTERICALLY	RHYTHMICALLY
USERFRIENDLY	HOUSEKEEPING	ARITHMETICAL	ICHTHYOCOLLA	RHYTIDECTOMY
VIBRATIUNCLE	HOUSETOHOUSE	AUSTRALASIAN	ICHTHYOPSIDA	SALTATORIOUS
ANASTIGMATIC	HOUSEWARMING	AUSTRONESIAN	INSTALLATION	SCATTERBRAIN
APOSTROPHISE	INESCUTCHEON	BACTERIOLOGY	INSTAURATION	SCATTERMOUCH
ARISTOCRATIC	IRASCIBILITY	BACTERIOSTAT	INSTRUCTIONS	SECTARIANISM
ARISTOLOCHIA	KIRSCHWASSER	BANTAMWEIGHT	INSTRUCTRESS	SEPTEMBRISER
ARISTOPHANES	MANSLAUGHTER	BATTLEGROUND	INSTRUMENTAL	SEPTUAGESIMA
ARISTOTELEAN	MARSEILLAISE	BERTHOLLETIA	KLETTERSCHUE	SITTLICHKEIT
BESSERWISSER	MASSERANDUBA	BERTILLONAGE	LISTLESSNESS	SKUTTERUDITE
BOISTEROUSLY	MASSPRODUCED	BLETHERSKATE	MALTREATMENT	SOUTHCOTTIAN
CASSITERIDES	MENSTRUATION	BUTTERSCOTCH	MASTERSTROKE	SOUTHEASTERN
CHASTISEMENT	MISSTATEMENT	CANTANKEROUS	MASTIGOPHORA	SOUTHERNMOST
CHESTERFIELD	MOISTURIZING	CANTILEVERED	MASTURBATION	SOUTHERNWOOD
CLASSIFIABLE	MOUSQUETAIRE	CARTHAGINIAN	MISTREATMENT	SOUTHWESTERN
CONSCRIPTION	NEWSPAPERMAN	CARTOGRAPHER	MONTESSORIAN	SPATANGOIDEA
CONSECRATION	OPISTHOGRAPH	CARTOGRAPHIC	MOUTHBROODER	SPITEFULNESS
CONSEQUENCES	OUTSTRETCHED	CASTERBRIDGE	MULTICOLORED	STATISTICIAN
CONSEQUENTLY	PARSIMONIOUS	CAUTIOUSNESS	MULTIFARIOUS	SUBTERRANEAN
CONSERVATION	PASSEMEASURE	CHITTERLINGS	MULTIGRAVIDA	SYNTAGMATITE
CONSERVATISM	PASSEPARTOUT	CLOTHESHORSE	MULTILATERAL	TACTLESSNESS
CONSERVATIVE	PASSIONATELY	CONTABESCENT	MULTIPLICITY	TAUTOLOGICAL
CONSERVATORY	PASSIONFRUIT	CONTAMINATED	MYSTERIOUSLY	TEETERTOTTER
CONSIDERABLE	PERSEVERANCE	CONTEMPORARY	NORTHEASTERN	TESTAMENTARY
CONSIDERABLY	PERSISTENTLY	CONTEMPTIBLE	NORTHERNMOST	TESTOSTERONE
CONSISTENTLY	PERSONALIZED	CONTEMPTUOUS	NORTHWESTERN	TRUTHFULNESS
CONSOCIATION	PERSPICACITY	CONTERMINOUS	NYCTITROPISM	UINTATHERIUM
CONSOLIDATED	PERSPIRATION	CONTIGNATION	OBSTETRICIAN	ULOTRICHALES
CONSOLIDATOR	PERSUASIVELY	CONTINUATION	OBSTREPEROUS	UNATTAINABLE
CONSPECTUITY	PERSULPHURIC	CONTINUOUSLY	PANTECHNICON	UNATTRACTIVE
CONSPIRACIST	PHOSPHOLIPID	CONTRAPPOSTO	PANTISOCRACY	UNCTUOUSNESS
CONSTABULARY	PHOSPHORENCE	CONTRAPUNTAL	PANTOPHAGOUS	UNUTTERABLES
CONSTIPATION	PHOSPHORESCE	CONTRARINESS	PARTICOLORED	VENTRIPOTENT
CONSTITUENCY	PHYSIOLOGIST	CONTRIBUTION	PARTICULARLY	WEATHERPROOF
CONSTITUENTS	PLASTERSTONE	CONTRIBUTORY	PARTISANSHIP	WELTERWEIGHT
CONSTITUTION	POSSESSIVELY	CONTRITURATE	PECTORILOQUY	WILTSHIREMAN
CONSTRICTION	PRASEODYMIUM	CONTROLLABLE	PERTINACIOUS	WINTERHALTER
CONSTRUCTION	PRESBYTERIAN	CONTUMACIOUS	PERTURBATION	WRETCHEDNESS
CONSTRUCTIVE	PRESCRIPTION	COSTERMONGER	PESTILENTIAL	XANTHOPTERIN
CONSULTATION	PRESCRIPTIVE	DEUTERANOPIA	PETTIFOGGERS	YOUTHFULNESS
CONSULTATIVE	PRESENTATION	DEUTEROSCOPY	PETTIFOGGERY	ACCUMULATION
CONSUMMATION	PRESENTIMENT	DICTATORSHIP	PETTIFOGGING	ACCUSATORIAL
CRASHLANDING	PRESERVATION	DISTILLATION	PHOTOGLYPHIC	ACQUAINTANCE
CRASSAMENTUM	PRESERVATIVE	DISTINCTNESS	PHOTOGRAPHER	ACQUIESCENCE
CRISTOBALITE	PRESIDENTIAL	DISTRIBUTION	PHOTOGRAPHIC	ADJUDICATION
CROSSBENCHER	PRESTRICTION	DISTRIBUTIVE	PHOTOGRAVURE	AMBULANCEMAN
CROSSCOUNTRY	PRESUMPTUOUS	DYSTELEOLOGY	PHYTOBENTHOS	ANNUNCIATION
CROSSEXAMINE	PROSCRIPTION	ECSTATICALLY	PHYTONADIONE	APPURTENANCE
CROSSSECTION	PROSOPOPOEIA	EPITHALAMION	PHYTOPHAGOUS	ASSUEFACTION
DEASPIRATION	PROSTITUTION	EPITHALAMIUM	PITTERPATTER	BEAUMARCHAIS
DESSERTSPOON	QUESTIONABLE	ERATOSTHENES	POSTGRADUATE	BEAUMONTAGUE
DISSATISFIED	SARSAPARILLA	ERYTHROMYCIN	POSTHUMOUSLY	BEAUMONTIQUE

CALUMNIATION	CONVALESCING	BARRANQUILLA	ONOMATOPOEIC	DELIBERATELY
CHAUVINISTIC	CONVENIENCES	BOUGAINVILLE	OUTMANOEUVRE	DELIBERATION
CLAUDICATION	CONVENIENTLY	BUREAUCRATIC	OUTRAGEOUSLY	DISOBEDIENCE
DAGUERROTYPE	CONVENTIONAL	CAMPANULARIA	PANDAEMONIUM	EXHIBITIONER
DEHUMIDIFIER	CONVERSATION	CANTANKEROUS	PANDANACEOUS	FLAMBOYANTLY
DENUNCIATION	CONVEYANCING	CHARACTERIZE	PEDIATRICIAN	GLUBBDUBDRIB
EXSUFFLICATE	CONVINCINGLY	CIRCASSIENNE	PERGAMENEOUS	HUDIBRASTICS
FIGURATIVELY	CONVIVIALITY	COLLABORATOR	PERMANGANATE	INDEBTEDNESS
FRAUENDIENST	FLUVIOMARINE	COMMANDMENTS	PHILANTHROPY	LUGUBRIOUSLY
HARUMFRODITE	GALVANOMETER	COMPANIONWAY	PRECARIOUSLY	MACABERESQUE
ILLUMINATING	MERVEILLEUSE	CONTABESCENT	PREMAXILLARY	MINDBOGGLING
ILLUMINATION	PERVERSENESS	CONTAMINATED	PREPAREDNESS	NONOBJECTIVE
ILLUSTRATION	PERVICACIOUS	CONVALESCENT	PREVARICATOR	PHLEBOTOMIST
ILLUSTRATIVE	PREVARICATOR	CONVALESCING	PROBATIONARY	PRESBYTERIAN
IMMUNIZATION	PREVENTATIVE	COURAGEOUSLY	PROPAGANDISM	REHABILITATE
IMMUNOLOGIST	PROVERBIALLY	CREMAILLIÈRE	PROPAGANDIST	SHIPBUILDING
IMMUTABILITY	PROVIDENTIAL	DEFLATIONARY	PROTACTINIUM	SLUBBERINGLY
INAUGURATION	SALVATIONIST	DICTATORSHIP	PUGNACIOUSLY	SNOBBISHNESS
INAUSPICIOUS	SERVICEBERRY	DISDAINFULLY	RECHARGEABLE	SNOWBOARDING
INCUNABULIST	SERVICEWOMAN	DISSATISFIED	REFLATIONARY	STILBOESTROL
INDUSTRIALLY	SILVERHAIRED	DOGMATICALLY	RESTAURATEUR	STUBBORNNESS
INSUFFERABLE	SLOVENLINESS	DRAMATICALLY	RHADAMANTHUS	TROUBLEMAKER
INSUFFERABLY	SURVEILLANCE	DRAMATURGIST	SALTATORIOUS	WELLBALANCED
INSUFFICIENT	UNIVERSALIST	ECSTATICALLY	SALVATIONIST	WOODBURYTYPE
INSURRECTION	SNOWBOARDING	EDUCATIONIST	SARDANAPALUS	ADJECTIVALLY
INTUITIONISM	ALEXIPHARMIC	EMPHATICALLY	SARSAPARILLA	AFFECTIONATE
INVULNERABLE	INEXACTITUDE	ESTRANGEMENT	SECTARIANISM	AGRICULTURAL
LIQUEFACTION	INEXPERIENCE	EXCHANGEABLE	SELFADHESIVE	ANTICIPATION
LUGUBRIOUSLY	INEXPLICABLE	EXTRADITABLE	SOMNAMBULISM	ANTICIPATORY
LUXULLIANITE	INEXPLICABLY	EXTRAVAGANCE	SOMNAMBULIST	ARTICULATION
MANUFACTURER	INEXTRICABLE	EXTRAVAGANZA	SPATANGOIDEA	BRANCHIOPODA
NATURALISTIC	INEXTRICABLY	FORMALDEHYDE	SPORADICALLY	CARICATURIST
OCCUPATIONAL	PRAXINOSCOPE	FUNDAMENTALS	SPREADEAGLED	CHALCOPYRITE
OMBUDSPERSON	QUIXOTICALLY	GALVANOMETER	SUBHASTATION	CHURCHWARDEN
PALUDAMENTUM	UNEXPECTEDLY	GASTARBEITER	SUBLAPSARIAN	COINCIDENTAL
PLAUSIBILITY	UNEXPURGATED	GENEALOGICAL	SYNTAGMATITE	CONSCRIPTION
PSEUDONYMOUS	AWAYABSOLUTE	GERIATRICIAN	TAPSALTEERIE	DELICATESSEN
RECUPERATION	ENCYCLOPEDIA	GIBRALTARIAN	TELEASTHETIC	DIENCEPHALON
RECUPERATIVE	ENCYCLOPEDIC	HAEMATEMESIS	TESTAMENTARY	DIRECTORSHIP
REJUVENATION	ENHYPOSTASIA	HALLANSHAKER	TETRACYCLINE	DISACCHARIDE
REMUNERATION	LABYRINTHINE	HIERARCHICAL	TETRAHEDRITE	EMANCIPATION
REMUNERATIVE	POLYETHYLENE	IMMEASURABLE	THERAPEUTICS	EMASCULATION
RENUNCIATION	POLYNEURITIS	IMMEASURABLY	THREADNEEDLE	ENCYCLOPEDIA
RESURRECTION	POLYPETALOUS	IMPLANTATION	THYSANOPTERA	ENCYCLOPEDIC
RESUSCITATED	POLYRIBOSOME	INERADICABLE	TRALATICIOUS	EPENCEPHALON
SCRUPULOUSLY	POLYSYLLABIC	INEXACTITUDE	TRALATITIOUS	EPISCOPALIAN
SEQUENTIALLY	POLYSYLLABLE	INFLAMMATION	UINTATHERIUM	GYNECOLOGIST
SEQUESTRATOR	POLYSYNDETON	INFLAMMATORY	ULTRAMONTANE	HEMICHORDATA
SIMULTANEOUS	POLYURETHANE	INFLATIONARY	UMBRADARLING	HYPOCHONDRIA
SIPUNCULACEA	BENZOPHENONE	INGRATIATING	UNCHALLENGED	HYPOCRITICAL
STRUCTURALLY	BENZOQUINONE	INSTALLATION	UNCHANGEABLE	IMMACULATELY
THAUMATURGIC	KATZENJAMMER	INSTAURATION	UNCHARITABLE	INACCESSIBLE
THAUMATURGUS	PRIZEFIGHTER	INTRANSIGENT	UNCHARITABLY	INACCURATELY
THOUGHTFULLY	PRIZEWINNING	INTRANSITIVE	UNCLASSIFIED	INDECLINABLE
TRIUMPHANTLY	SWIZZLESTICK	INTRAUTERINE	UNILATERALLY	INDOCTRINATE
TROUBLEMAKER		ISHMAELITISH	UNIMAGINABLE	INESCUTCHEON
UNAUTHORISED	**12:5**	ISOLATIONISM	UNREASONABLE	IRASCIBILITY
UNAUTHORIZED	ACETALDEHYDE	ISOLATIONIST	UNSEASONABLE	KIRSCHWASSER
UNCULTIVATED	ACHLAMYDEOUS	KATHAREVOUSA	UPROARIOUSLY	LEXICOGRAPHY
UNSUCCESSFUL	ACQUAINTANCE	LALLAPALOOZA	VIBRATIUNCLE	MALACOSTRACA
UNSURPRISING	ALPHABETICAL	LAMPADEDROMY	WOLLASTONITE	METICULOUSLY
UNSUSPECTING	ALPHANUMERIC	LANCASTERIAN	AGRIBUSINESS	MINICOMPUTER
VERUMONTANUM	AMARANTACEAE	MACHAIRODONT	ANTIBACCHIUS	MIRACULOUSLY
VITUPERATION	ANECATHARSIS	MECHANICALLY	ANTIBARBARUS	MUNICIPALITY
VITUPERATIVE	ANTIAIRCRAFT	MERCANTILISM	BACKBREAKING	MUSICOLOGIST
VOLUPTUOUSLY	AROMATHERAPY	MISCALCULATE	BLABBERMOUTH	OVERCROWDING
ARFVEDSONITE	ATTRACTIVELY	MITRAILLEUSE	CEREBROTONIC	OXYACETYLENE
CLAVICEMBALO	AWAYABSOLUTE	OLDFASHIONED	COHABITATION	PARACENTESIS
CONVALESCENT	BANTAMWEIGHT	ONOMATOPOEIA	DEAMBULATORY	PEDICELLARIA

PERICARDITIS
POLICYMAKING
POPOCATEPETL
POTICHOMANIA
PRESCRIPTION
PRESCRIPTIVE
PRINCIPALITY
PROSCRIPTION
PYROCATECHOL
RETICULATION
RIDICULOUSLY
SELFCATERING
SEMICIRCULAR
SOLICITATION
SOLICITOUSLY
SPHACELATION
SPRECHGESANG
STRUCTURALLY
SUBSCRIPTION
TOBACCONISTS
TOXICOLOGIST
TURACOVERDIN
UNACCEPTABLE
UNACCUSTOMED
UNRECOGNISED
UNRECOGNIZED
UNSUCCESSFUL
VARICOLOURED
WRETCHEDNESS
ACCIDENTALLY
ADJUDICATION
AECIDIOSPORE
AERODYNAMICS
AMBIDEXTROUS
ANTEDILUVIAN
AWARDWINNING
BLANDISHMENT
BLOODLETTING
BLOODSTAINED
BLOODTHIRSTY
BOONDOGGLING
BROADCASTING
CATADIOPTRIC
CHILDBEARING
CHILDISHNESS
CHONDRIOSOME
CLAUDICATION
COORDINATION
DESIDERATIVE
DISADVANTAGE
GLYNDEBOURNE
GONADOTROPIN
GRANDISONIAN
GRANDMONTINE
GRANDPARENTS
GUARDIANSHIP
GUILDENSTERN
HAIRDRESSERS
HAIRDRESSING
HEREDITAMENT
HEREDITARIAN
HOLIDAYMAKER
IMMODERATELY
IMMODERATION
INCIDENTALLY
INORDINATELY
IRREDEEMABLE
LEPIDOMELANE
LONGDISTANCE

LOXODROMICAL
MELODRAMATIC
MISADVENTURE
OMBUDSPERSON
OVERDRESSING
PALUDAMENTUM
PERADVENTURE
PSEUDONYMOUS
SCANDALOUSLY
SCANDINAVIAN
SEMIDETACHED
STEPDAUGHTER
STRADIVARIUS
STRIDULATION
STUDDINGSAIL
SYNADELPHITE
THIRDBOROUGH
THUNDERCLOUD
THUNDERFLASH
THUNDERSTORM
ABBREVIATION
ACADEMICALLY
AFORETHOUGHT
AGGRESSIVELY
ALIMENTATIVE
ANTHELMINTIC
APPRECIATION
APPRECIATIVE
APPREHENSION
APPREHENSIVE
ARFVEDSONITE
ASSUEFACTION
AUGMENTATION
AUGMENTATIVE
AUTHENTICATE
AUTHENTICITY
BACTERIOLOGY
BACTERIOSTAT
BANDERSNATCH
BARBERMONGER
BESSERWISSER
BOULEVARDIER
BUTTERSCOTCH
CALCEAMENTUM
CANCELLATION
CARPETBAGGER
CASTERBRIDGE
CATHETOMETER
CHOREOGRAPHY
COLLECTIVELY
COLLECTORATE
COMMENCEMENT
COMMENDATION
COMMENDATORY
COMMENSURATE
COMMERCIALLY
COMPELLATION
COMPENSATION
COMPENSATORY
CONCENTRATED
CONDEMNATION
CONDENSATION
CONFECTIONER
CONFESSIONAL
CONGENITALLY
CONSECRATION
CONSEQUENCES
CONSEQUENTLY
CONSERVATION

CONSERVATISM
CONSERVATIVE
CONSERVATORY
CONTEMPORARY
CONTEMPTIBLE
CONTEMPTUOUS
CONTERMINOUS
CONVENIENCES
CONVENIENTLY
CONVENTIONAL
CONVERSATION
CONVEYANCING
COSTERMONGER
DAGUERROTYPE
DEPRECIATION
DEPRECIATORY
DESSERTSPOON
DEUTERANOPIA
DEUTEROSCOPY
DIALECTICIAN
DIFFERENTIAL
DISPENSATION
DISREPECTFUL
DISREPUTABLE
DISSERTATION
DYSTELEOLOGY
ECCLESIASTES
ECCLESIASTIC
ENCHEIRIDION
ENTREATINGLY
ENTRENCHMENT
ENTREPRENEUR
EPIDEICTICAL
EPILEPTIFORM
ESTHETICALLY
EXACERBATION
FERMENTATION
FLAGELLATION
FORCEFULNESS
FOTHERINGHAY
FRAUENDIENST
FRUMENTATION
GEOMETRICIAN
GLOBETROTTER
GOOSEPIMPLES
GRACEFULNESS
GRATEFULNESS
GRISEOFULVIN
HAMMERHEADED
HAPPENSTANCE
HARNESSMAKER
HENCEFORWARD
HERMENEUTICS
HERMENEUTIST
HERMETICALLY
HILDEBRANDIC
HOMOEOPATHIC
HORSEMANSHIP
HOUSEBREAKER
HOUSEKEEPING
HOUSETOHOUSE
HOUSEWARMING
HYGIENICALLY
HYSTERECTOMY
HYSTERICALLY
IMPREGNATION
IMPRESSIVELY
INADEQUATELY

INCREASINGLY
INFREQUENTLY
INSPECTORATE
KATZENJAMMER
KINAESTHETIC
KINDERGARTEN
LAUREATESHIP
LIQUEFACTION
MAGNETICALLY
MALLEABILITY
MANGELWURZEL
MANOEUVRABLE
MARSEILLAISE
MASSERANDUBA
MASTERSTROKE
MATHEMATICAL
MERVEILLEUSE
MICHELANGELO
MISBEHAVIOUR
MISDELIVERED
MISDEMEANOUR
MISREPRESENT
MONTESSORIAN
MYSTERIOUSLY
NEPHELOMETER
NONRESIDENCE
NONRESISTANT
OBSTETRICIAN
OPPRESSIVELY
OVERESTIMATE
OVEREXERTION
PANAESTHESIA
PANTECHNICON
PASSEMEASURE
PASSEPARTOUT
PATHETICALLY
PEACEFULNESS
PEACEKEEPING
PERCEPTIVELY
PERCEPTIVITY
PERMEABILITY
PERPETRATION
PERSEVERANCE
PERVERSENESS
PHONETICALLY
PIGMENTATION
PITTERPATTER
PLACENTIFORM
POLYETHYLENE
POSSESSIVELY
PRASEODYMIUM
PREDESTINATE
PREDETERMINE
PREFERENTIAL
PREREQUISITE
PRESENTATION
PRESENTIMENT
PRESERVATION
PRESERVATIVE
PREVENTATIVE
PRIZEFIGHTER
PRIZEWINNING
PROCESSIONAL
PROFESSIONAL
PROFESSORIAL
PROGESTERONE
PROLEGOMENON
PROLETARIATE
PROTECTIVELY

PROTECTORATE
PROTESTATION
PROVERBIALLY
PUMPERNICKEL
PUTREFACTION
RACKETEERING
RECREATIONAL
REFLECTIVITY
RESPECTFULLY
RESPECTIVELY
RETRENCHMENT
ROLLERBLADER
ROLLERBLADES
RONCESVALLES
SCHNEIDERIAN
SCREENWRITER
SECRETARIATE
SEGMENTATION
SELFEMPLOYED
SEPTEMBRISER
SEQUENTIALLY
SEQUESTRATOR
SHAMEFACEDLY
SHAREHOLDING
SILVERHAIRED
SLOVENLINESS
SPELEOLOGIST
SPINECHILLER
SPITEFULNESS
SPOKESPERSON
STEREOPHONIC
STEREOPTICON
STEREOSCOPIC
STEREOTYPING
STONECHATTER
STUPEFACTION
SUBJECTIVELY
SUBJECTIVITY
SUBSEQUENTLY
SUBSERVIENCE
SUBTERRANEAN
SUCCESSFULLY
SUCCESSIVELY
SUGGESTIVELY
SURREALISTIC
SURVEILLANCE
TEETERTOTTER
TERCENTENARY
THEREAGAINST
THREEQUARTER
TRABECULATED
TRADESCANTIA
TRADESPEOPLE
TREMENDOUSLY
TRICENTENARY
UNFREQUENTED
UNIDENTIFIED
UNIVERSALIST
UNPREJUDICED
UNPRETENDING
VENGEFULNESS
VILLEGIATURA
WELTERWEIGHT
WHOLEHEARTED
WICKETKEEPER
WINTERHALTER
ARTIFICIALLY
BENEFACTRESS
CODIFICATION

EXSUFFLICATE	BERTHOLLETIA	ADSCITITIOUS	GALLIVANTING	PROFITEERING
HIGHFALUTING	BIOCHEMISTRY	ALEXIPHARMIC	GLADIATORIAL	PROLIFICALLY
INDEFENSIBLE	BLETHERSKATE	AMELIORATION	GRACIOUSNESS	PROPITIATION
INDEFINITELY	BRACHYCEPHAL	AMPHISBAENIC	HEROICOMICAL	PROPITIATORY
INDIFFERENCE	CARTHAGINIAN	AMPHISTOMOUS	HISTIOPHORUS	PROPITIOUSLY
INEFFICIENCY	CLOTHESHORSE	AMPHITHEATER	HOBBIDIDANCE	PROVIDENTIAL
INSUFFERABLE	CRASHLANDING	AMPHITHEATRE	HORRIFICALLY	PTERIDOPHYTE
INSUFFERABLY	CZECHOSLOVAK	ARCHILOCHIAN	HORTICULTURE	PTERIDOSPERM
INSUFFICIENT	DOLPHINARIUM	ARCHIPELAGOS	IMPRISONMENT	RECEIVERSHIP
MANUFACTURER	EPIPHENOMENA	ARCHITECTURE	INFRINGEMENT	REFRIGERATED
MINDFULLNESS	EPITHALAMION	ATTRIBUTABLE	INTUITIONISM	REFRIGERATOR
MODIFICATION	EPITHALAMIUM	AUSPICIOUSLY	ISOBILATERAL	RHIPIDOPTERA
NOTIFICATION	ERYTHROMYCIN	BELLIGERENCY	KALEIDOSCOPE	RHYTIDECTOMY
OSSIFICATION	EVENHANDEDLY	BERTILLONAGE	KILLIKINNICK	ROOMINGHOUSE
PACIFICATION	FAITHFULNESS	BIBLIOGRAPHY	LASCIVIOUSLY	SACRILEGIOUS
PURIFICATION	FARTHINGLAND	BIBLIOPEGIST	LILLIBULLERO	SELFINTEREST
RAMIFICATION	FEATHERBRAIN	BILLINGSGATE	LILLIBURLERO	SERVICEBERRY
RATIFICATION	GEOPHYSICIST	BIODIVERSITY	LONGITUDINAL	SERVICEWOMAN
SHUFFLEBOARD	GRAPHOLOGIST	CALLIGRAPHIC	MACMILLANITE	SIGNIFICANCE
UNOFFICIALLY	ICHTHYOCOLLA	CALLISTHENES	MAGNIFICENCE	SOPHISTICATE
USERFRIENDLY	ICHTHYOPSIDA	CANTILEVERED	MAGNILOQUENT	SPACIOUSNESS
VERIFICATION	INCOHERENTLY	CARCINOGENIC	MARLINESPIKE	SPECIFICALLY
VILIFICATION	MOUTHBROODER	CARDINDEXING	MARRIAGEABLE	SPECIOUSNESS
VOCIFERATION	NEIGHBORHOOD	CARDIOLOGIST	MASTIGOPHORA	SPHAIRISTIKE
VOCIFEROUSLY	NEIGHBOURING	CARDIOMEGALY	MEANINGFULLY	SPIRITUALISM
AMALGAMATION	NONCHALANTLY	CARRIWITCHET	MECHITHARIST	SPIRITUALIST
ANTAGONISTIC	NORTHEASTERN	CASSITERIDES	MILLILAMBERT	SPIRITUALITY
APPOGGIATURA	NORTHERNMOST	CAUTIOUSNESS	MULLIGATAWNY	SPURIOUSNESS
DEREGULATION	NORTHWESTERN	CHALICOTHERE	MULTICOLORED	STANISLAVSKI
DISAGREEABLE	NYMPHOMANIAC	CHORIZONTIST	MULTIFARIOUS	STATISTICIAN
DISAGREEMENT	ONYCHOPHORAN	CLARINETTIST	MULTIGRAVIDA	STRAIGHTAWAY
ENERGYSAVING	PANCHATANTRA	CLAVICEMBALO	MULTILATERAL	STRAIGHTEDGE
ESPAGNOLETTE	PANCHROMATIC	COCCIDIOSTAT	MULTIPLICITY	STRAIGHTNESS
EXAGGERATION	PANPHARMACON	COMBINATIONS	NARCISSISTIC	STRAITJACKET
FEHMGERICHTE	PHILHARMONIC	COMMISSARIAT	NONDIRECTIVE	STUDIOUSNESS
FREIGHTLINER	POSTHUMOUSLY	COMMISSIONED	NUTRITIONIST	SUBMINIATURE
HELLGRAMMITE	PROPHYLACTIC	COMMISSIONER	NYCTITROPISM	SUBMISSIVELY
ILLEGIBILITY	PROTHALAMION	CONCILIATION	OBEDIENTIARY	SUBSIDIARITY
ILLEGITIMACY	PROTHALAMIUM	CONCILIATORY	OPINIONATIVE	SUFFICIENTLY
ILLEGITIMATE	PROTHONOTARY	CONFIDENTIAL	PALPITATIONS	SUSPICIOUSLY
ILLOGICALITY	PSEPHOLOGIST	CONFIRMATION	PANTISOCRACY	TAGLIACOTIAN
INAUGURATION	PSIPHENOMENA	CONFIRMATORY	PARKINSONISM	TERGIVERSATE
INDIGESTIBLE	PSYCHIATRIST	CONFISCATION	PARSIMONIOUS	TERRIFICALLY
INVIGORATING	PSYCHOLOGIST	CONSIDERABLE	PARTICOLORED	TERRITORIALS
INVIGORATION	PSYCHOPATHIC	CONSIDERABLY	PARTICULARLY	TORRICELLIAN
IRREGULARITY	RHYTHMICALLY	CONSISTENTLY	PARTISANSHIP	TURBIDIMETER
METAGNATHOUS	SCHEHERAZADE	CONTIGNATION	PASSIONATELY	UNNEIGHBORLY
NAVIGABILITY	SOUTHCOTTIAN	CONTINUATION	PASSIONFRUIT	UNPRINCIPLED
NONAGENARIAN	SOUTHEASTERN	CONTINUOUSLY	PERMITTIVITY	UNSCIENTIFIC
OCTOGENARIAN	SOUTHERNMOST	CONVINCINGLY	PERSISTENTLY	URTRICULARIA
POSTGRADUATE	SOUTHERNWOOD	CONVIVIALITY	PERTINACIOUS	VERMICULTURE
PRIGGISHNESS	SOUTHWESTERN	COSCINOMANCY	PERVICACIOUS	VINDICTIVELY
RECOGNIZABLE	STAKHANOVITE	DARLINGTONIA	PESTILENTIAL	WASHINGTONIA
RECOGNIZANCE	SULPHONAMIDE	DIPRIONIDIAN	PETRIFACTION	WELLINFORMED
SEXAGENARIAN	SWASHBUCKLER	DISCIPLINARY	PETTIFOGGERS	WELLINGTONIA
SLEDGEHAMMER	TRICHOLOGIST	DISTILLATION	PETTIFOGGERY	WILLIEWAUGHT
SPIEGELEISEN	TRICHOPHYTON	DISTINCTNESS	PETTIFOGGING	XIPHISTERNUM
STAGGERINGLY	TROCHELMINTH	DORSIVENTRAL	PHILISTINISM	CLAMJAMPHRIE
STRIGIFORMES	TROCHOSPHERE	DUNNIEWASSAL	PHYSIOLOGIST	READJUSTMENT
TELEGRAPHESE	TROPHALLAXIS	ENGLISHWOMAN	PINNIEWINKLE	BLACKCURRANT
TELEGRAPHIST	TRUTHFULNESS	ENGLISHWOMEN	PISCICULTURE	BREAKTHROUGH
THOUGHTFULLY	WAREHOUSEMAN	ETEPIMELETIC	POIKILOTHERM	BRICKFIELDER
VAINGLORIOUS	WATCHFULNESS	FASTIDIOUSLY	PRAXINOSCOPE	CAMIKNICKERS
VEHMGERICHTE	WEATHERPROOF	FLORICULTURE	PREDILECTION	DRINKDRIVING
AGATHODAIMON	WEIGHTLIFTER	FLUVIOMARINE	PREHISTORIAN	FRANKALMOIGN
ANNIHILATION	XANTHOPTERIN	FULMINATIONS	PRESIDENTIAL	FRANKENSTEIN
ARITHMETICAL	YOUTHFULNESS	FUSTILLIRIAN	PRIMIGRAVIDA	FRANKINCENSE
AUTOHYPNOSIS	ABOLITIONIST	GALLIGASKINS	PRODIGIOUSLY	GLOCKENSPIEL
BACCHANALIAN	ACQUIESCENCE	GALLINACEOUS	PROFICIENTLY	HANDKERCHIEF

SLOCKDOLAGER	MIDDLEWEIGHT	ENTOMOSTRACA	BICENTENNIAL	PARENTHESIZE
SLOCKDOLIGER	MISPLACEMENT	HARUMFRODITE	BLENNORRHOEA	PEDANTICALLY
SLOCKDOLOGER	MOBILIZATION	HEADMISTRESS	BRAINWASHING	PHRONTISTERY
SPECKTIONEER	MOONLIGHTING	ILLUMINATING	BUSINESSLIKE	PLAINCLOTHES
STOCKBREEDER	MUCILAGINOUS	ILLUMINATION	CABINETMAKER	POGONOPHORAN
STOCKINGETTE	MUDDLEHEADED	INADMISSIBLE	CANONIZATION	POLYNEURITIS
THANKFULNESS	MUGGLETONIAN	INCOMPARABLE	CLANNISHNESS	POTENTIALITY
THANKSGIVING	NEOCLASSICAL	INCOMPARABLY	COLONIZATION	RECONSTITUTE
THICKSKINNED	NEOPLATONISM	INCOMPATIBLE	DECENTRALISE	REDINTEGRATE
ACCELERATION	NONALCOHOLIC	INCOMPETENCE	DECENTRALIZE	REGENERATION
AMBULANCEMAN	NONFLAMMABLE	INCOMPLETELY	DECONGESTANT	RELENTLESSLY
ANTILEGOMENA	OBSOLESCENCE	INNOMINABLES	DEGENERATION	REMINISCENCE
APFELSTRUDEL	OBSOLETENESS	INSEMINATION	DEMONSTRABLE	REMONSTRANCE
APOLLINARIAN	OSCILLOSCOPE	INTEMPERANCE	DEMONSTRABLY	REMUNERATION
ARTILLERYMAN	PAINLESSNESS	INTIMIDATING	DEMONSTRATOR	REMUNERATIVE
AVAILABILITY	PAPILIONIDAE	INTIMIDATION	DENUNCIATION	RENUNCIATION
BATTLEGROUND	PARALIPOMENA	LUXEMBOURGER	DISENCHANTED	ROMANTICALLY
BETHLEHEMITE	PENALIZATION	MADEMOISELLE	DISINCENTIVE	SCHINDYLESIS
BEWILDERMENT	POSTLIMINARY	METAMORPHISM	DISINFECTANT	SEMANTICALLY
BIOFLAVONOID	PRALLTRILLER	METAMORPHOSE	DISINGENUOUS	SINANTHROPUS
BRILLIANTINE	PROCLAMATION	PARAMAGNETIC	DISINTEGRATE	SIPUNCULACEA
BUCKLEBEGGAR	RECALCITRANT	PARAMILITARY	ECCENTRICITY	SPLENOMEGALY
CARELESSNESS	RECKLESSNESS	PERAMBULATOR	ENTANGLEMENT	STERNUTATION
CHURLISHNESS	RECOLLECTION	PEREMPTORILY	ESSENTIALITY	STERNWHEELER
CIVILISATION	RESTLESSNESS	PHARMACOLOGY	EULENSPIEGEL	STRANGLEHOLD
CIVILIZATION	RUTHLESSNESS	POSTMISTRESS	EXTENSIONIST	STRANGLEWEED
COMPLACENTLY	SCHILLERSPAR	POTAMOLOGIST	EXTENSOMETER	STRINGCOURSE
COMPLETENESS	SHILLYSHALLY	REDEMPTIONER	EXTINGUISHER	STRONGMINDED
COMPLICATION	SIMULTANEOUS	REMEMBRANCER	FRIENDLINESS	STRONTIANITE
CONCLUSIVELY	SINGLEDECKER	RODOMONTADER	GERONTOCRACY	TECHNICALITY
CONGLOMERATE	SINGLEHANDED	SCRIMSHANDER	GIGANTOMACHY	TECHNOLOGIST
DEBILITATING	SINGLEMINDED	SCRIMSHANKER	GREENGROCERS	TITANOSAURUS
DECELERATION	SITTLICHKEIT	SPERMATOCYTE	GREENGROCERY	UNCONSIDERED
DEMILITARIZE	SMALLHOLDING	SPERMATOZOID	HUMANITARIAN	UNCONTROLLED
DISPLACEMENT	SPELLCHECKER	SPERMATOZOON	HUMANIZATION	UNCONVERSANT
DOUBLEDECKER	STEALTHINESS	STORMTROOPER	HYMENOPTERAN	UNCONVINCING
DOUBLEGLAZED	STELLENBOSCH	STROMATOLITE	IMMUNIZATION	UNMANAGEABLE
EXHILARATING	SUPPLICATION	TARAMASALATA	IMMUNOLOGIST	URBANIZATION
EXHILARATION	TACTLESSNESS	THAUMATURGIC	IMPENETRABLE	VALENCIENNES
FEARLESSNESS	TAPSLETEERIE	THAUMATURGUS	INCANDESCENT	ACKNOWLEDGED
FIDDLESTICKS	TIMELESSNESS	THERMOSTATIC	INCINERATION	AGAMOGENETIC
FINALIZATION	TOTALITARIAN	THESMOPHORIA	INCONCLUSIVE	ANAMORPHOSIS
GENTLETAMPER	UNBELIEVABLE	THIGMOTROPIC	INCONSEQUENT	ANCHORPERSON
GESELLSCHAFT	UNBELIEVABLY	TRIUMPHANTLY	INCONSISTENT	ANDROSTERONE
GOBBLEDEGOOK	UNCULTIVATED	UNDEMOCRATIC	INCONSOLABLE	ANEMOPHILOUS
GOBBLEDYGOOK	ACCOMPANYING	UNDIMINISHED	INCONTINENCE	APPROACHABLE
HAMBLETONIAN	ACCOMPLISHED	VERUMONTANUM	INCONVENIENT	ARTIODACTYLA
HELPLESSNESS	ACCUMULATION	WHIGMALEERIE	INCUNABULIST	ASTROLOGICAL
HOPELESSNESS	AGALMATOLITE	ZALAMBDODONT	INTENERATION	ASTRONOMICAL
IDEALIZATION	ANTEMERIDIAN	ACCENTUATION	JOURNALISTIC	ASTROPHYSICS
IMPOLITENESS	ANTIMACASSAR	ADMINISTRATE	LABANOTATION	BAMBOCCIADES
INCALCULABLE	ANTIMETABOLE	ADMONISHMENT	LAMENTATIONS	BEACONSFIELD
INFELICITOUS	ANTIMNEMONIC	ADVANTAGEOUS	LUMINESCENCE	BENZOPHENONE
INFILTRATION	ASSIMILATION	ADVANTAGIOUS	LUMINISCENCE	BENZOQUINONE
INSALUBRIOUS	ASYMMETRICAL	ADVENTITIOUS	LYMANTRIIDAE	BIELORUSSIAN
INSOLUBILITY	BEAUMARCHAIS	AERONAUTICAL	MISANTHROPIC	BIPROPELLANT
INTELLECTUAL	BEAUMONTAGUE	ANNUNCIATION	MISINTERPRET	BUNKOSTEERER
INTELLIGENCE	BEAUMONTIQUE	ANTANANARIVO	MYRINGOSCOPE	BYELORUSSIAN
INTELLIGIBLE	BICAMERALISM	ANTINEUTRINO	NEPENTHACEAE	CAMPODEIFORM
INVALIDATION	CALUMNIATION	ANTONINIANUS	NOCONFIDENCE	CARBOHYDRATE
INVULNERABLE	CEREMONIALLY	APLANOGAMETE	NOMENCLATURE	CARLOVINGIAN
LAMELLICORNE	CHREMATISTIC	APPENDECTOMY	OCEANOGRAPHY	CARPOPHAGOUS
LEGALIZATION	DEHUMIDIFIER	APPENDICITIS	ORGANISATION	CARTOGRAPHER
LIFELESSNESS	DEMIMONDAINE	ARSENOPYRITE	ORGANIZATION	CARTOGRAPHIC
LISTLESSNESS	DENOMINATION	ASTONISHMENT	ORIENTEERING	CHEMOTHERAPY
LUXULLIANITE	DISEMBARRASS	AWEINSPIRING	OSTENTATIOUS	CHIROPRACTIC
MANSLAUGHTER	ELASMOBRANCH	BABINGTONITE	PALINGENESIA	CHIROPRACTOR
METALLOPHONE	ELEEMOSYNARY	BAIRNSFATHER	PALINGENESIS	COLLOQUIALLY
METALLURGIST	ENTOMOLOGIST	BANANALANDER	PARANTHELIUM	COMMONWEALTH

CONSOCIATION	METHOTREXATE	RADIOISOTOPE	OCCUPATIONAL	ANTIRACHITIC
CONSOLIDATED	METROPOLITAN	RADIOTHERAPY	OREOPITHECUS	APPURTENANCE
CONSOLIDATOR	MICROBREWERY	REPROCESSING	OREOPITHEOUS	ARBORESCENCE
COSMOPOLITAN	MICROCLIMATE	REPRODUCTION	OVERPOWERING	ARTHROPLASTY
CUCKOOFLOWER	MNEMOTECHNIC	REPRODUCTIVE	PERIPHRASTIC	ASPARAGINASE
DIPLOGENESIS	MOSBOLLETJIE	RESPONDENTIA	PERSPICACITY	ATHEROMATOUS
DISCOMEDUSAE	MYTHOLOGICAL	RHINORRHOEAL	PERSPIRATION	AUSTRALASIAN
DISCOMFITURE	NEUROFIBROMA	RHODODENDRON	PHOSPHOLIPID	AUSTRONESIAN
DISCOMYCETES	NEUROLOGICAL	SARDONICALLY	PHOSPHORESCE	BARORECEPTOR
DISCONCERTED	NEUROSCIENCE	SAUROGNATHAE	PHOSPHORESCE	BIOGRAPHICAL
DISCONNECTED	NEUROTICALLY	SCHOOLMASTER	POLYPETALOUS	CAMERAPERSON
DISCONSOLATE	NEWFOUNDLAND	SCOPOPHILIAC	POSTPONEMENT	CAPERCAILLIE
DISCONTENTED	NIMBOSTRATUS	SIPHONOPHORA	POSTPOSITIVE	CAPERCAILZIE
DISCOURAGING	NONCOMMITTAL	SIPHONOSTELE	POSTPRANDIAL	CHAIRMANSHIP
DISCOURTEOUS	OPHIOGLOSSUM	SOCIOLOGICAL	REAPPEARANCE	CHEERFULNESS
DISHONORABLE	ORTHODONTICS	STEGOPHOLIST	RECAPITULATE	CHLORINATION
DISHONORABLY	ORTHOGENESIS	STENOGRAPHER	RECEPTIONIST	CHLOROPICRIN
DISPOSSESSED	ORTHOPAEDICS	SUBCOMMITTEE	RECIPROCALLY	CLAIRVOYANCE
DISSOCIATION	ORTHOPAEDIST	SUBCONSCIOUS	RECUPERATION	CLAIRVOYANCY
ECONOMICALLY	ORTHOPTEROUS	SUBCONTINENT	RECUPERATIVE	CLEARSIGHTED
EMBROIDERESS	ORTHORHOMBIC	SURMOUNTABLE	REDEPLOYMENT	COMPROMISING
ENCROACHMENT	ORTHOTONESIS	SURROUNDINGS	RESIPISCENCE	CONGRATULATE
EPANORTHOSIS	OSTEOMALACIA	SYMBOLICALLY	RHAMPHOTHECA	CONGREGATION
ERATOSTHENES	OSTEOPOROSIS	TAUTOLOGICAL	SCHOPENHAUER	CONTRAPPOSTO
ETHNOLOGICAL	OSTEOSARCOMA	TELEOSAURIAN	SCRIPTWRITER	CONTRAPUNTAL
ETYMOLOGICAL	PALEONTOLOGY	TESTOSTERONE	SCRUPULOUSLY	CONTRARINESS
ETYMOLOGICON	PANTOPHAGOUS	TETRODOTOXIN	SELFPORTRAIT	CONTRIBUTION
EXPLOITATION	PATHOLOGICAL	THOROUGHBRED	SEMIPRECIOUS	CONTRIBUTORY
GEOLOGICALLY	PECTORILOQUY	THOROUGHFARE	SHARPSHOOTER	CONTRITURATE
GLYCOPROTEIN	PERIODICALLY	THOROUGHNESS	SHEEPISHNESS	CONTROLLABLE
GYMNOSOPHIST	PERIODONTICS	TRIGONOMETRY	SIVAPITHECUS	DECORATIVELY
HAEMOPHILIAC	PERIOSTRACUM	TURBOCHARGER	SLEEPWALKING	DENDROLOGIST
HAEMORRHOIDS	PERNOCTATION	UNECONOMICAL	STEEPLECHASE	DEPARTMENTAL
HAPTOTROPISM	PERSONALIZED	UNPRODUCTIVE	STREPITATION	DESIRABILITY
HARMONIOUSLY	PHENOMENALLY	UNPROFITABLE	STREPSIPTERA	DIAGRAMMATIC
HELIOGABALUS	PHILODENDRON	YELLOWHAMMER	STREPTOMYCIN	DICHROMATISM
HELIOTROPISM	PHILOLOGICAL	ANTIPARTICLE	STREPTONEURA	DISCRIMINATE
HIEROGLYPHIC	PHILOSOPHIZE	CATAPHYSICAL	STROPHANTHUS	DISFRANCHISE
HIEROGRAMMAT	PHOTOGLYPHIC	CHAMPIONSHIP	THEOPHYLLINE	DISORGANIZED
HIEROPHANTIC	PHOTOGRAPHER	CLAPPERBOARD	UNAPPARELLED	DISORIENTATE
HIPPOCRATISE	PHOTOGRAPHIC	CONSPECTUITY	UNAPPETIZING	DISTRIBUTION
HIPPOCREPIAN	PHOTOGRAVURE	CONSPIRACIST	UNEMPLOYMENT	DISTRIBUTIVE
HIPPOPOTAMUS	PHYCOXANTHIN	DEASPIRATION	UNEXPECTEDLY	DIVERTICULUM
HISTORICALLY	PHYTOBENTHOS	DECAPITATION	UNEXPURGATED	DIVERTIMENTO
HYDROCHLORIC	PHYTONADIONE	DECIPHERABLE	UNIMPORTANCE	EFFERVESCENT
HYDROGEOLOGY	PHYTOPHAGOUS	DECIPHERMENT	UNOPPRESSIVE	EFFORTLESSLY
HYDROGRAPHER	PLEIOCHASIUM	DEPOPULATION	UNPOPULARITY	EMBARRASSING
HYDROQUINONE	PORNOGRAPHIC	DILAPIDATION	VENEPUNCTURE	ENCIRCLEMENT
HYDROTHERAPY	PRECOCIOUSLY	DISAPPEARING	VITUPERATION	ENTEROMORPHA
HYMNOGRAPHER	PRECONDITION	DISAPPOINTED	VITUPERATIVE	ENTEROPNEUST
HYPNOTHERAPY	PREDOMINANCE	ENHYPOSTASIA	VOLUPTUOUSLY	ENTERPRISING
HYPNOTICALLY	PREMONSTRANT	ENTOPLASTRON	WHIPPOORWILL	ENTERTAINING
IAMBOGRAPHER	PREPONDERANT	ESCAPOLOGIST	COLOQUINTIDA	EPACRIDACEAE
ICONOCLASTIC	PREPONDERATE	EXASPERATING	HEADQUARTERS	EPIGRAMMATIC
IMPROVIDENCE	PREPONDERENT	EXASPERATION	HINDQUARTERS	ETHEROMANIAC
INTRODUCTION	PREPOSSESSED	INAPPLICABLE	MOUSQUETAIRE	EXPERIMENTAL
INTRODUCTORY	PREPOSTEROUS	INCAPABILITY	OBSEQUIOUSLY	EXSERVICEMAN
INTROVERSION	PROLONGATION	INCAPACITATE	QUINQUENNIAL	EXTORTIONATE
LEGIONNAIRES	PROPORTIONAL	INDEPENDENCE	TRANQUILIZER	FIGURATIVELY
LINCOLNSHIRE	PROSOPOPOEIA	INEXPERIENCE	TRANQUILLISE	FLUORESCENCE
LITHOGRAPHIC	PROTOPLASMAL	INEXPLICABLE	TRANQUILLITY	FLUORIDATION
LITHOLATROUS	PROTOPLASMIC	INEXPLICABLY	TRANQUILLIZE	GASTROSOPHER
MACROCEPHALY	PTERODACTYLE	MANIPULATION	UNACQUAINTED	GEOGRAPHICAL
MACROPODIDAE	PURPOSEBUILT	MANIPULATIVE	ACCORDIONIST	GOVERNMENTAL
MALFORMATION	PURPOSEFULLY	MASSPRODUCED	AETHRIOSCOPE	HABERDASHERS
MALLOPHAGOUS	PYTHONOMORPH	METAPHORICAL	AFTEREFFECTS	HABERDASHERY
MARCOBRUNNER	QUIXOTICALLY	METAPHYSICAL	AFTERTHOUGHT	HAMARTHRITIS
MARCONIGRAPH	RADIOBIOLOGY	MISAPPREHEND	AIRCRAFTSMAN	HETEROCLITIC
METHODICALLY	RADIOGRAPHER	NEWSPAPERMAN	ANTHROPOLOGY	HETEROCONTAE

HETEROGAMETE	QUADRAGESIMA	CRASSAMENTUM	SATISFACTION	COUNTERPOISE
HETEROPHORIA	QUADRAPHONIC	CROSSBENCHER	SATISFACTORY	COURTMARTIAL
HETEROPLASIA	QUADRIPLEGIA	CROSSCOUNTRY	SECESSIONIST	COVETOUSNESS
HETEROSEXUAL	RECORDPLAYER	CROSSEXAMINE	SERASKIERATE	CREATIVENESS
HETEROSOMATA	REPERCUSSION	CROSSSECTION	SPINSTERHOOD	CRISTOBALITE
HYPERACIDITY	RESURRECTION	DERESTRICTED	THESSALONIAN	CRYPTOGRAPHY
HYPERBOLICAL	RETARDEDNESS	DISASSOCIATE	TRANSACTIONS	CYMOTRICHOUS
HYPERPYRETIC	REVERSIONARY	DISASTROUSLY	TRANSCENDENT	DILATORINESS
HYPERSARCOMA	RISORGIMENTO	DOMESTICATED	TRANSFERABLE	EGYPTOLOGIST
HYPERTENSION	SCLERENCHYMA	DRESSINGDOWN	TRANSFERENCE	ELECTRICALLY
IMPARTIALITY	SCLERODERMIA	EAVESDROPPER	TRANSGRESSOR	ELECTROLYSIS
IMPERFECTION	SCURRILOUSLY	ESCHSCHOLZIA	TRANSITIONAL	ELECTROPLATE
IMPERFECTIVE	SQUIRRELFISH	FELDSPATHOID	TRANSLATABLE	ELECTROTONUS
IMPERISHABLE	SUBARRHATION	FOOTSLOGGING	TRANSLUCENCE	ENANTIOMORPH
IMPERSONALLY	SUPERANNUATE	GAINSBOROUGH	TRANSMIGRATE	ENANTIOPATHY
IMPERSONATOR	SUPERCHARGED	GAMESMANSHIP	TRANSMISSION	EPISTEMOLOGY
IMPERTINENCE	SUPERCHARGER	GAMOSEPALOUS	TRANSMOGRIFY	EPISTOLATERS
INCORPORATED	SUPERCILIARY	GRASSWIDOWER	TRANSOCEANIC	EVENTEMPERED
INCORRIGIBLE	SUPERCILIOUS	GROSSULARITE	TRANSPARENCY	EXCITABILITY
INCORRIGIBLY	SUPERHIGHWAY	HAIRSPLITTER	TRANSPONTINE	FAINTHEARTED
INFORMIDABLE	SUPERNACULUM	HOMESICKNESS	TRANSVESTISM	FIRSTFOOTING
INHARMONIOUS	SUPERNATURAL	IDIOSYNCRASY	TRANSVESTITE	FLITTERMOUSE
INSTRUCTIONS	SUPERSTITION	ILLUSTRATION	UNANSWERABLE	FRACTIONALLY
INSTRUCTRESS	SUPERSTRATUM	ILLUSTRATIVE	UNDESERVEDLY	FRONTIERSMAN
INSTRUMENTAL	SURPRISINGLY	INAUSPICIOUS	UNDISCHARGED	FRONTISPIECE
INSURRECTION	TAMARICACEAE	INDISCRETION	UNMISTAKABLE	FRUITFULNESS
INTERCEPTION	TAPERECORDER	INDISPUTABLE	UNOBSTRUCTED	FUNCTIONALLY
INTERCESSION	THEORETICIAN	INDISPUTABLY	UNRESERVEDLY	FUNCTIONLESS
INTERCHANGED	TUBERCULOSIS	INDISSOLUBLE	UNRESPONSIVE	GENETHLIACON
INTERFERENCE	ULOTRICHALES	INDISTINCTLY	UNRESTRAINED	GLYPTOGRAPHY
INTERGLACIAL	UNDERACHIEVE	INDUSTRIALLY	UNRESTRICTED	HEARTSTRINGS
INTERJECTION	UNDERCLOTHES	INHOSPITABLE	UNSUSPECTING	HEARTWARMING
INTERLOCUTOR	UNDERCURRENT	INVESTIGATOR	WHIMSICALITY	HEPHTHEMIMER
INTERMEDIARY	UNDEREXPOSED	INVISIBILITY	WILTSHIREMAN	HOMOTHERMOUS
INTERMEDIATE	UNDERGARMENT	IRRESISTIBLE	YORKSHIREMAN	HYPOTHECATOR
INTERMINABLE	UNDERPINNING	IRRESOLUTELY	ADAPTABILITY	HYPOTHETICAL
INTERMINABLY	UNDERSKINKER	IRRESOLUTION	ADDITIONALLY	IDENTIFIABLE
INTERMISSION	UNDERSTAFFED	IRRESOLVABLE	ADULTERATION	IDIOTHERMOUS
INTERMITTENT	UNDERWRITTEN	IRRESPECTIVE	ALLITERATION	IMMUTABILITY
INTERPRETING	UNPARALLELED	JURISDICTION	ANASTIGMATIC	INARTICULATE
INTERRELATED	UNPARDONABLE	KALISTOCRACY	ANTITHROMBIN	INEXTRICABLE
INTERROGATOR	UNSCRUPULOUS	KLIPSPRINGER	APOSTROPHISE	INEXTRICABLY
INTERRUPTION	UNSURPRISING	LONGSHOREMAN	ARISTOCRATIC	INFOTAINMENT
INTERSECTION	VAPORIZATION	LONGSTANDING	ARISTOLOCHIA	INNATTENTIVE
INTERSPERSED	VENTRIPOTENT	MAJESTICALLY	ARISTOPHANES	IRRATIONALLY
INTERSTELLAR	VETERINARIAN	MARKSMANSHIP	ARISTOTELEAN	IRRITABILITY
INTERVENTION	WATERCARRIER	MERISTEMATIC	AYUNTAMIENTO	KLEPTOMANIAC
INVERTEBRATE	ACCUSATORIAL	MINISTRATION	BOISTEROUSLY	KLETTERSCHUE
LABYRINTHINE	ADVISABILITY	MONOSYLLABIC	BREATHALYSER	LEGITIMATELY
LATIROSTRATE	AMBASSADRESS	MONOSYLLABLE	BREATHLESSLY	LEIOTRICHOUS
LIVERPUDLIAN	ANAESTHETISE	MUTESSARIFAT	BREATHTAKING	LICKTRENCHER
MALPRACTICES	ANAESTHETIST	OCCASIONALLY	BRONTOSAURUS	LIGHTHEARTED
MALTREATMENT	ANAESTHETIZE	OCTASTROPHIC	CAPITULATION	MENSTRUATION
MINERALOGIST	ANTISTROPHON	OVERSCUTCHED	CHARTERHOUSE	MERETRICIOUS
MISPRONOUNCE	ARTISTICALLY	OVERSTRAINED	CHASTISEMENT	MERITRICIOUS
MISTREATMENT	ATMOSPHERICS	PENNSYLVANIA	CHESTERFIELD	MESOTHELIOMA
MOTORCYCLIST	BARNSTORMING	PERISTERONIC	CHITTERLINGS	MILITARISTIC
NATURALISTIC	BLUESTOCKING	PLAUSIBILITY	CONSTABULARY	MISSTATEMENT
NEVERTHELESS	BREASTPLOUGH	POLYSYLLABIC	CONSTIPATION	MOISTURIZING
OBSERVANTINE	BREASTSUMMER	POLYSYLLABLE	CONSTITUENCY	MONOTONOUSLY
OBSTREPEROUS	CATASTROPHIC	POLYSYNDETON	CONSTITUENTS	NIGHTCLOTHES
ONCORHYNCHUS	CHEESEBURGER	PRAISEWORTHY	CONSTITUTION	NYCHTHEMERON
ONEIROCRITIC	CHEESEMONGER	REDISCOVERED	CONSTRICTION	OBLITERATION
OTHERWORLDLY	CHEESEPARING	REDISTRIBUTE	CONSTRUCTION	OPISTHOGRAPH
POLARIZATION	CHRESTOMATHY	REGISTRATION	CONSTRUCTIVE	ORNITHOGALUM
POLYRIBOSOME	CHRISTIANITY	REPOSSESSION	COUNTERBLAST	OUTSTRETCHED
POWERSHARING	CLASSIFIABLE	RESUSCITATED	COUNTERCLAIM	PANATHENAEAN
PROGRAMMABLE	CLEISTOGAMIC	SADISTICALLY	COUNTERMARCH	PENITENTIARY
PROPRIETRESS	COLDSHOULDER	SALESMANSHIP	COUNTERPOINT	PLASTERSTONE

PLECTOGNATHI	CIRCUMSTANCE	OVERWHELMING	EPIGRAMMATIC	STROMATOLITE
POINTILLISME	COLLUCTATION	SIDEWHISKERS	EPITHALAMION	SUBSTANTIATE
PRACTICALITY	COMMUNICABLE	INTOXICATING	EPITHALAMIUM	SUPERANNUATE
PRACTICIONER	COMPURGATION	INTOXICATION	EVENHANDEDLY	SURREALISTIC
PRACTITIONER	CONCURRENTLY	NONEXISTENCE	EXCITABILITY	TAGLIACOTIAN
PRESTRICTION	CONDUCTIVITY	ASPHYXIATION	EXHILARATING	TARAMASALATA
PROSTITUTION	CONQUISTADOR	BOOBYTRAPPED	EXHILARATION	THAUMATURGIC
PYROTECHNICS	CONSULTATION	COLLYWOBBLES	FIGURATIVELY	THAUMATURGUS
QUANTIFIABLE	CONSULTATIVE	HAPPYGOLUCKY	FRANKALMOIGN	THEREAGAINST
QUANTITATIVE	CONSUMMATION	JENNYSPINNER	GEOGRAPHICAL	THESSALONIAN
QUARTERFINAL	CONTUMACIOUS	MERRYTHOUGHT	GLADIATORIAL	TRACTABILITY
QUARTERLIGHT	CURMUDGEONLY	PROGYMNASIUM	GONDWANALAND	TRANSACTIONS
QUARTERSTAFF	DISQUISITION	WALLYDRAIGLE	HIGHFALUTING	TROPHALLAXIS
QUESTIONABLE	ENTHUSIASTIC	EMBEZZLEMENT	HOLIDAYMAKER	UNAPPARELLED
QUINTESSENCE	EVOLUTIONARY	HORIZONTALLY	HYPERACIDITY	UNATTAINABLE
RELATIONSHIP	EXCRUCIATING	SCHIZOMYCETE	IMMUTABILITY	UNDERACHIEVE
REPATRIATION	EXCRUCIATION	SWIZZLESTICK	INCAPABILITY	UNMANAGEABLE
RESETTLEMENT	EXHAUSTIVELY		INCAPACITATE	UNOBTAINABLE
SCATTERBRAIN	FORTUITOUSLY	**12:6**	INCREASINGLY	UNPARALLELED
SCATTERMOUCH	HALLUCINOGEN	ABSQUATULATE	INCUNABULIST	WELLBALANCED
SCINTILLATOR	INCAUTIOUSLY	ACCUSATORIAL	INFOTAINMENT	WHIGMALEERIE
SHIRTSLEEVES	INCRUSTATION	ADAPTABILITY	IRRITABILITY	ALPHABETICAL
SHIRTWAISTER	KERAUNOGRAPH	ADVISABILITY	JOURNALISTIC	ATTRIBUTABLE
SHORTCIRCUIT	LABOURSAVING	AERONAUTICAL	LAUREATESHIP	AWAYABSOLUTE
SHORTCOMINGS	LANGUEDOCIAN	AGALMATOLITE	MALLEABILITY	CHILDBEARING
SHORTSIGHTED	MALNUTRITION	AIRCRAFTSMAN	MALPRACTICES	COLLABORATOR
SHORTSLEEVED	MASTURBATION	AMALGAMATION	MANSLAUGHTER	CONTABESCENT
SHORTSTAFFED	MISQUOTATION	AMBULANCEMAN	MANUFACTURER	CROSSBENCHER
SHOSTAKOVICH	OUTBUILDINGS	ANTANANARIVO	MARRIAGEABLE	DISEMBARRASS
SKUTTERUDITE	PASQUEFLOWER	ANTIBACCHIUS	MILITARISTIC	GAINSBOROUGH
SOMATOPLEURE	PERSUASIVELY	ANTIBARBARUS	MINERALOGIST	HILDEBRANDIC
SPECTROMETER	PERSULPHURIC	ANTIMACASSAR	MISPLACEMENT	HOUSEBREAKER
SPECTROSCOPE	PERTURBATION	ANTIPARTICLE	MISSTATEMENT	HYPERBOLICAL
SPORTSGROUND	POLYURETHANE	ANTIRACHITIC	MUCILAGINOUS	LILLIBULLERO
SPURTLEBLADE	PREGUSTATION	APPROACHABLE	NATURALISTIC	LILLIBURLERO
STENTORPHONE	PRESUMPTUOUS	ASPARAGINASE	NAVIGABILITY	LUXEMBOURGER
STRATOSPHERE	PRODUCTIVITY	AUSTRALASIAN	NEOCLASSICAL	MARCOBRUNNER
SUBSTANTIATE	PROMULGATION	AVAILABILITY	NEOPLATONISM	MICROBREWERY
SUBSTITUTION	PROTUBERANCE	AYUNTAMIENTO	NEWSPAPERMAN	MOUTHBROODER
SUBSTITUTIVE	RAMBUNCTIOUS	BACCHANALIAN	NONCHALANTLY	NEIGHBORHOOD
SUBSTRUCTURE	RECRUDESCENT	BACKWARDNESS	NONFLAMMABLE	NEIGHBOURING
THEATRICALLY	RENOUNCEMENT	BANANALANDER	OCCUPATIONAL	PERAMBULATOR
TIGHTFITTING	SARRUSOPHONE	BEAUMARCHAIS	PALUDAMENTUM	PHYTOBENTHOS
TOGETHERNESS	SCAPULIMANCY	BENEFACTRESS	PANCHATANTRA	PROTUBERANCE
TRACTABILITY	SEPTUAGESIMA	BIOFLAVONOID	PANPHARMACON	RADIOBIOLOGY
UNATTAINABLE	SESQUIALTERA	BIOGRAPHICAL	PARAMAGNETIC	REMEMBRANCER
UNATTRACTIVE	SESQUITERTIA	BIRDWATCHING	PERICARDITIS	STOCKBREEDER
UNAUTHORISED	SUBCUTANEOUS	CALCEAMENTUM	PERMEABILITY	SWASHBUCKLER
UNAUTHORIZED	SUCCUSSATION	CAMERAPERSON	PERSUASIVELY	THIRDBOROUGH
UNDETECTABLE	TELEUTOSPORE	CARAVANSERAI	PHARMACOLOGY	ZALAMBDODONT
UNDETERMINED	UNCTUOUSNESS	CARICATURIST	PHILHARMONIC	ACCOUCHEMENT
UNFATHOMABLE	BEHAVIOURISM	CARTHAGINIAN	POPOCATEPETL	ANNUNCIATION
UNINTERESTED	BENEVOLENTLY	CHREMATISTIC	PROCLAMATION	APPRECIATION
UNOBTAINABLE	CARAVANSERAI	CLAMJAMPHRIE	PROGRAMMABLE	APPRECIATIVE
UNRETURNABLE	CHAUVINISTIC	COMPLACENTLY	PROTHALAMION	ATTRACTIVELY
UNSATISFYING	EQUIVOCATION	CONGRATULATE	PROTHALAMIUM	AUSPICIOUSLY
UNUTTERABLES	EQUIVOCATORY	CONSTABULARY	PYROCATECHOL	BAMBOCCIADES
WOLSTENHOLME	IMPOVERISHED	CONTRAPPOSTO	QUADRAGESIMA	BLACKCURRANT
ZARATHUSTRIC	INADVERTENCE	CONTRAPUNTAL	QUADRAPHONIC	BROADCASTING
ABSQUATULATE	INDIVIDUALLY	CONTRARINESS	RECREATIONAL	CAPERCAILLIE
ACCOUCHEMENT	IRREVERENTLY	CRASSAMENTUM	SCANDALOUSLY	CAPERCAILZIE
ACCOUTREMENT	IRREVERSIBLE	DECORATIVELY	SELFCATERING	CHALICOTHERE
ANDOUILLETTE	REINVIGORATE	DELICATESSEN	SEPTUAGESIMA	CHARACTERIZE
ANNOUNCEMENT	REJUVENATION	DESIRABILITY	SHOSTAKOVICH	CLAVICEMBALO
AUSCULTATION	UNFAVOURABLE	DIAGRAMMATIC	SPERMATOCYTE	COLLECTIVELY
BLEFUSCUDIAN	BACKWARDNESS	DISFRANCHISE	SPERMATOZOID	COLLECTORATE
CIRCUMCISION	BACKWOODSMAN	DISPLACEMENT	SPERMATOZOON	COLLUCTATION
CIRCUMGYRATE	BIRDWATCHING	ENCROACHMENT	STAKHANOVITE	CONDUCTIVITY
CIRCUMSCRIBE	GONDWANALAND	ENTREATINGLY	STEPDAUGHTER	CONFECTIONER

CONSECRATION	SPELLCHECKER	RETARDEDNESS	DOUBLEGLAZED	PASQUEFLOWER
CONSOCIATION	SPINECHILLER	RHIPIDOPTERA	DUNNIEWASSAL	PEDICELLARIA
CROSSCOUNTRY	STONECHATTER	RHODODENDRON	EPENCEPHALON	PENITENTIARY
DENUNCIATION	SUBJECTIVELY	RHYTIDECTOMY	EPIPHENOMENA	PINNIEWINKLE
DEPRECIATION	SUBJECTIVITY	SCHINDYLESIS	EPISTEMOLOGY	PLASTERSTONE
DEPRECIATORY	SUFFICIENTLY	SELFADHESIVE	EVENTEMPERED	POLYNEURITIS
DIALECTICIAN	SUPERCHARGED	SLOCKDOLAGER	EXAGGERATION	POLYPETALOUS
DISACCHARIDE	SUPERCHARGER	SLOCKDOLIGER	EXASPERATING	PRAISEWORTHY
DISENCHANTED	SUPERCILIARY	SLOCKDOLOGER	EXASPERATION	PSIPHENOMENA
DISINCENTIVE	SUPERCILIOUS	SPORADICALLY	FEARLESSNESS	PYROTECHNICS
DISSOCIATION	SUSPICIOUSLY	SPREADEAGLED	FEATHERBRAIN	QUARTERFINAL
ENCIRCLEMENT	TETRACYCLINE	SUBSIDIARITY	FEHMGERICHTE	QUARTERLIGHT
ESCHSCHOLZIA	TOBACCONISTS	TETRODOTOXIN	FIDDLESTICKS	QUARTERSTAFF
EXCRUCIATING	TORRICELLIAN	THREADNEEDLE	FLITTERMOUSE	QUINTESSENCE
EXCRUCIATION	TRABECULATED	TURBIDIMETER	FLUORESCENCE	REAPPEARANCE
FLORICULTURE	TRANSCENDENT	UMBRADARLING	FRANKENSTEIN	RECKLESSNESS
HALLUCINOGEN	TUBERCULOSIS	UNPARDONABLE	GAMOSEPALOUS	RECUPERATION
HEROICOMICAL	TURBOCHARGER	UNPRODUCTIVE	GENTLETAMPER	RECUPERATIVE
HIPPOCRATISE	UNDERCLOTHES	WALLYDRAIGLE	GLOCKENSPIEL	REGENERATION
HIPPOCREPIAN	UNDERCURRENT	ACCELERATION	GLYNDEBOURNE	REJUVENATION
HORTICULTURE	UNDISCHARGED	ACCIDENTALLY	GOBBLEDEGOOK	REMUNERATION
HYDROCHLORIC	UNSUCCESSFUL	ACQUIESCENCE	GOBBLEDYGOOK	REMUNERATIVE
ICONOCLASTIC	URTRICULARIA	ADULTERATION	GUILDENSTERN	RESTLESSNESS
INCALCULABLE	VALENCIENNES	AFTEREFFECTS	HAMBLETONIAN	RUTHLESSNESS
INCONCLUSIVE	VERMICULTURE	ALLITERATION	HANDKERCHIEF	SCATTERBRAIN
INDISCRETION	VINDICTIVELY	AMBIDEXTROUS	HELPLESSNESS	SCATTERMOUCH
INEXACTITUDE	WATERCARRIER	ANTEMERIDIAN	HOPELESSNESS	SCHEHERAZADE
INSPECTORATE	ACCORDIONIST	ANTILEGOMENA	IMMODERATELY	SCHOPENHAUER
INTERCEPTION	APPENDECTOMY	ANTIMETABOLE	IMMODERATION	SCLERENCHYMA
INTERCESSION	APPENDICITIS	ANTINEUTRINO	IMPENETRABLE	SEMIDETACHED
INTERCHANGED	ARFVEDSONITE	ARBORESCENCE	IMPOVERISHED	SEXAGENARIAN
MACROCEPHALY	ARTIODACTYLA	ASYMMETRICAL	INACCESSIBLE	SINGLEDECKER
MICROCLIMATE	BEWILDERMENT	BARORECEPTOR	INADVERTENCE	SINGLEHANDED
MOTORCYCLIST	CAMPODEIFORM	BATTLEGROUND	INCIDENTALLY	SINGLEMINDED
MULTICOLORED	COCCIDIOSTAT	BETHLEHEMITE	INCINERATION	SKUTTERUDITE
NIGHTCLOTHES	CONFIDENTIAL	BICAMERALISM	INCOHERENTLY	SLEDGEHAMMER
NOMENCLATURE	CONSIDERABLE	BIOCHEMISTRY	INDEFENSIBLE	SLUBBERINGLY
NONALCOHOLIC	CONSIDERABLY	BLABBERMOUTH	INDEPENDENCE	SOUTHEASTERN
OVERSCUTCHED	CURMUDGEONLY	BLETHERSKATE	INDIGESTIBLE	SOUTHERNMOST
PANTECHNICON	DRINKDRIVING	BOISTEROUSLY	INEXPERIENCE	SOUTHERNWOOD
PARTICOLORED	EAVESDROPPER	BUCKLEBEGGAR	INTENERATION	SPHACELATION
PARTICULARLY	EXTRADITABLE	BUSINESSLIKE	IRREDEEMABLE	SPIEGELEISEN
PERNOCTATION	FASTIDIOUSLY	CABINETMAKER	IRREVERENTLY	STAGGERINGLY
PERVICACIOUS	FRIENDLINESS	CARELESSNESS	IRREVERSIBLE	STELLENBOSCH
PISCICULTURE	GLUBBDUBDRIB	CHARTERHOUSE	ISHMAELITISH	SYNADELPHITE
PLAINCLOTHES	HABERDASHERS	CHEESEBURGER	KLETTERSCHUE	TACTLESSNESS
PLEIOCHASIUM	HABERDASHERY	CHEESEMONGER	LANGUEDOCIAN	TAPERECORDER
PRECOCIOUSLY	HOBBIDIDANCE	CHEESEPARING	LIFELESSNESS	TAPSLETEERIE
PRODUCTIVITY	INCANDESCENT	CHESTERFIELD	LISTLESSNESS	THEORETICIAN
PROFICIENTLY	INERADICABLE	CHITTERLINGS	LUMINESCENCE	THUNDERCLOUD
PROTACTINIUM	INTRODUCTION	CLAPPERBOARD	MACABERESQUE	THUNDERFLASH
PROTECTIVELY	INTRODUCTORY	CLOTHESHORSE	MALTREATMENT	THUNDERSTORM
PROTECTORATE	JURISDICTION	COMPLETENESS	MIDDLEWEIGHT	TIMELESSNESS
PUGNACIOUSLY	KALEIDOSCOPE	CONGREGATION	MISTREATMENT	TROCHELMINTH
RECALCITRANT	LAMPADEDROMY	CONSPECTUITY	MUDDLEHEADED	UNACCEPTABLE
REDISCOVERED	METHODICALLY	COUNTERBLAST	MUGGLETONIAN	UNAPPETIZING
REFLECTIVITY	ORTHODONTICS	COUNTERCLAIM	NONAGENARIAN	UNDEREXPOSED
RENUNCIATION	PERIODICALLY	COUNTERMARCH	NORTHEASTERN	UNDESERVEDLY
REPERCUSSION	PERIODONTICS	COUNTERPOINT	NORTHERNMOST	UNDETECTABLE
REPROCESSING	PHILODENDRON	COUNTERPOISE	OBEDIENTIARY	UNDETERMINED
RESPECTFULLY	PRESIDENTIAL	CROSSEXAMINE	OBLITERATION	UNEXPECTEDLY
RESPECTIVELY	PROVIDENTIAL	DECELERATION	OBSOLESCENCE	UNINTERESTED
RESUSCITATED	PTERIDOPHYTE	DEGENERATION	OBSOLETENESS	UNRESERVEDLY
SERVICEBERRY	PTERIDOSPERM	DELIBERATELY	OBSTREPEROUS	UNSCIENTIFIC
SERVICEWOMAN	PTERODACTYLE	DELIBERATION	OCTOGENARIAN	UNUTTERABLES
SHORTCIRCUIT	RECORDPLAYER	DESIDERATIVE	OXYACETYLENE	VEHMGERICHTE
SHORTCOMINGS	RECRUDESCENT	DIENCEPHALON	PAINLESSNESS	VITUPERATION
SIPUNCULACEA	REPRODUCTION	DISOBEDIENCE	PANDAEMONIUM	VITUPERATIVE
SOUTHCOTTIAN	REPRODUCTIVE	DOUBLEDECKER	PARACENTESIS	VOCIFERATION

VOCIFEROUSLY	EXTINGUISHER	GENETHLIACON	CATADIOPTRIC	HOMESICKNESS
WEATHERPROOF	GALLIGASKINS	HEMICHORDATA	CHAMPIONSHIP	HUMANITARIAN
WILLIEWAUGHT	GEOLOGICALLY	HEPHTHEMIMER	CHASTISEMENT	HUMANIZATION
WOLSTENHOLME	GREENGROCERS	HOMOTHERMOUS	CHAUVINISTIC	IDEALIZATION
ASSUEFACTION	GREENGROCERY	HYPOCHONDRIA	CHILDISHNESS	IDENTIFIABLE
BRICKFIELDER	HAPPYGOLUCKY	HYPOTHECATOR	CHLORINATION	ILLEGIBILITY
CHEERFULNESS	HELIOGABALUS	HYPOTHETICAL	CHURLISHNESS	ILLEGITIMACY
DISINFECTANT	HIEROGLYPHIC	IDIOTHERMOUS	CIVILISATION	ILLEGITIMATE
EXSUFFLICATE	HIEROGRAMMAT	KIRSCHWASSER	CIVILIZATION	ILLOGICALITY
FAITHFULNESS	HYDROGEOLOGY	LIGHTHEARTED	CLANNISHNESS	ILLUMINATING
FIRSTFOOTING	HYDROGRAPHER	LONGSHOREMAN	CLASSIFIABLE	ILLUMINATION
FORCEFULNESS	HYMNOGRAPHER	MESOTHELIOMA	CLAUDICATION	IMMUNIZATION
FRUITFULNESS	IAMBOGRAPHER	METAPHORICAL	CODIFICATION	IMPERISHABLE
GRACEFULNESS	IMPREGNATION	METAPHYSICAL	COHABITATION	IMPOLITENESS
GRATEFULNESS	INTERGLACIAL	MISBEHAVIOUR	COINCIDENTAL	INADMISSIBLE
HARUMFRODITE	LITHOGRAPHIC	NYCHTHEMERON	COLONIZATION	INARTICULATE
HENCEFORWARD	MASTIGOPHORA	ONCORHYNCHUS	COMPLICATION	INDEFINITELY
HORRIFICALLY	MULLIGATAWNY	OPISTHOGRAPH	CONQUISTADOR	INDIVIDUALLY
IMPERFECTION	MULTIGRAVIDA	ORNITHOGALUM	CONSPIRACIST	INEFFICIENCY
IMPERFECTIVE	MYRINGOSCOPE	OVERWHELMING	CONSTIPATION	INFELICITOUS
INDIFFERENCE	OPHIOGLOSSUM	PANATHENAEAN	CONSTITUENCY	INNOMINABLES
INSUFFERABLE	ORTHOGENESIS	PERIPHRASTIC	CONSTITUENTS	INORDINATELY
INSUFFERABLY	OUTRAGEOUSLY	PHOSPHOLIPID	CONSTITUTION	INSEMINATION
INSUFFICIENT	PALINGENESIA	PHOSPHORENCE	CONTRIBUTION	INTIMIDATING
INTERFERENCE	PALINGENESIS	PHOSPHORESCE	CONTRIBUTORY	INTIMIDATION
LIQUEFACTION	PHOTOGLYPHIC	POTICHOMANIA	CONTRITURATE	INTOXICATING
MAGNIFICENCE	PHOTOGRAPHER	RHAMPHOTHECA	COORDINATION	INTOXICATION
MULTIFARIOUS	PHOTOGRAPHIC	SHAREHOLDING	CREATIVENESS	INVALIDATION
NEUROFIBROMA	PHOTOGRAVURE	SIDEWHISKERS	CREMAILLIÈRE	INVISIBILITY
NOCONFIDENCE	PORNOGRAPHIC	SMALLHOLDING	DEASPIRATION	IRASCIBILITY
PEACEFULNESS	PRIMIGRAVIDA	SPRECHGESANG	DEBILITATING	IRRATIONALLY
PETRIFACTION	PRODIGIOUSLY	STROPHANTHUS	DECAPITATION	IRRESISTIBLE
PETTIFOGGERS	PROLEGOMENON	SUPERHIGHWAY	DEHUMIDIFIER	LABYRINTHINE
PETTIFOGGERY	PROPAGANDISM	TETRAHEDRITE	DEMILITARIZE	LEGALIZATION
PETTIFOGGING	PROPAGANDIST	THEOPHYLLINE	DENOMINATION	LEGITIMATELY
PRIZEFIGHTER	RADIOGRAPHER	THOUGHTFULLY	DILAPIDATION	LONGDISTANCE
PROLIFICALLY	REFRIGERATED	TOGETHERNESS	DISCRIMINATE	LUMINISCENCE
PUTREFACTION	REFRIGERATOR	UNAUTHORISED	DISDAINFULLY	MACHAIRODONT
SATISFACTION	RISORGIMENTO	UNAUTHORIZED	DISORIENTATE	MARSEILLAISE
SATISFACTORY	SAUROGNATHAE	UNFATHOMABLE	DISQUISITION	MERVEILLEUSE
SHAMEFACEDLY	STENOGRAPHER	WHOLEHEARTED	DISTRIBUTION	MITRAILLEUSE
SIGNIFICANCE	STRAIGHTAWAY	WILTSHIREMAN	DISTRIBUTIVE	MOBILIZATION
SPECIFICALLY	STRAIGHTEDGE	WRETCHEDNESS	DOLPHINARIUM	MODIFICATION
SPITEFULNESS	STRAIGHTNESS	YORKSHIREMAN	DRESSINGDOWN	MOONLIGHTING
STUPEFACTION	STRANGLEHOLD	ZARATHUSTRIC	EMANCIPATION	MUNICIPALITY
TERRIFICALLY	STRANGLEWEED	ACQUAINTANCE	EMBROIDERESS	NONEXISTENCE
THANKFULNESS	STRINGCOURSE	ADDITIONALLY	ENANTIOMORPH	NOTIFICATION
TIGHTFITTING	STRONGMINDED	ADJUDICATION	ENANTIOPATHY	OCCASIONALLY
TRANSFERABLE	SYNTAGMATITE	ADMINISTRATE	ENCHEIRIDION	OREOPITHECUS
TRANSFERENCE	TRANSGRESSOR	ADMONISHMENT	EPACRIDACEAE	OREOPITHEOUS
TRUTHFULNESS	UNDERGARMENT	AECIDIOSPORE	EPIDEICTICAL	ORGANISATION
UNPROFITABLE	UNIMAGINABLE	AETHRIOSCOPE	EXHIBITIONER	ORGANIZATION
VENGEFULNESS	UNNEIGHBORLY	ANASTIGMATIC	EXPERIMENTAL	OSSIFICATION
WATCHFULNESS	VILLEGIATURA	ANDOUILLETTE	EXPLOITATION	OUTBUILDINGS
YOUTHFULNESS	ANTITHROMBIN	ANNIHILATION	FARTHINGLAND	PACIFICATION
AGAMOGENETIC	APPREHENSION	ANTEDILUVIAN	FINALIZATION	PAPILIONIDAE
APPOGGIATURA	APPREHENSIVE	ANTIAIRCRAFT	FLUORIDATION	PARALIPOMENA
BABINGTONITE	BRANCHIOPODA	ANTICIPATION	FORTUITOUSLY	PARAMILITARY
BELLIGERENCY	BREATHALYSER	ANTICIPATORY	FRACTIONALLY	PENALIZATION
CALLIGRAPHIC	BREATHLESSLY	ANTONINIANUS	FRANKINCENSE	PERSPICACITY
CARTOGRAPHER	BREATHTAKING	APOLLINARIAN	FRONTIERSMAN	PERSPIRATION
CARTOGRAPHIC	CARBOHYDRATE	ARTIFICIALLY	FRONTISPIECE	PLAUSIBILITY
CONTIGNATION	CATAPHYSICAL	ASSIMILATION	FUNCTIONALLY	POINTILLISME
COURAGEOUSLY	CHURCHWARDEN	ASTONISHMENT	FUNCTIONLESS	POLARIZATION
DECONGESTANT	COLDSHOULDER	BEHAVIOURISM	GRANDISONIAN	POLYRIBOSOME
DIPLOGENESIS	DECIPHERABLE	BLANDISHMENT	GUARDIANSHIP	POSTLIMINARY
DISINGENUOUS	DECIPHERMENT	BOUGAINVILLE	HEADMISTRESS	POSTMISTRESS
DISORGANIZED	FAINTHEARTED	BRILLIANTINE	HEREDITAMENT	PRACTICALITY
ENTANGLEMENT	FREIGHTLINER	CANONIZATION	HEREDITARIAN	PRACTICIONER

PRACTITIONER	ARCHILOCHIAN	RECOLLECTION	RHYTHMICALLY	FULMINATIONS
PRIGGISHNESS	ARTILLERYMAN	REDEPLOYMENT	SALESMANSHIP	GALLINACEOUS
PRINCIPALITY	ASTROLOGICAL	SACRILEGIOUS	SELFEMPLOYED	GALVANOMETER
PROPRIETRESS	AUSCULTATION	SCAPULIMANCY	SEPTEMBRISER	GOVERNMENTAL
PROSTITUTION	BERTILLONAGE	SCHILLERSPAR	SOMNAMBULISM	HALLANSHAKER
PSYCHIATRIST	BLOODLETTING	SCHOOLMASTER	SOMNAMBULIST	HAPPENSTANCE
PURIFICATION	CANCELLATION	SHUFFLEBOARD	SUBCOMMITTEE	HARMONIOUSLY
QUADRIPLEGIA	CANTILEVERED	SOCIOLOGICAL	TESTAMENTARY	HERMENEUTICS
QUANTIFIABLE	COMPELLATION	SPURTLEBLADE	TRANSMIGRATE	HERMENEUTIST
QUANTITATIVE	CONCILIATION	STEEPLECHASE	TRANSMISSION	HYGIENICALLY
QUESTIONABLE	CONCILIATORY	SWIZZLESTICK	TRANSMOGRIFY	IMPLANTATION
RADIOISOTOPE	CONSOLIDATED	SYMBOLICALLY	ULTRAMONTANE	INFRINGEMENT
RAMIFICATION	CONSOLIDATOR	TAPSALTEERIE	ALIMENTATIVE	INTRANSIGENT
RATIFICATION	CONSULTATION	TAUTOLOGICAL	ALPHANUMERIC	INTRANSITIVE
RECAPITULATE	CONSULTATIVE	TRANSLATABLE	AMARANTACEAE	INVULNERABLE
REHABILITATE	CONVALESCENT	TRANSLUCENCE	ANNOUNCEMENT	KATZENJAMMER
REINVIGORATE	CONVALESCING	TROUBLEMAKER	ANTIMNEMONIC	KERAUNOGRAPH
RELATIONSHIP	CRASHLANDING	UNCHALLENGED	ASTRONOMICAL	LEGIONNAIRES
REMINISCENCE	DISTILLATION	UNEMPLOYMENT	AUGMENTATION	MARCONIGRAPH
RESIPISCENCE	DYSTELEOLOGY	VAINGLORIOUS	AUGMENTATIVE	MARLINESPIKE
SCANDINAVIAN	ENCYCLOPEDIA	ACADEMICALLY	AUTHENTICATE	MEANINGFULLY
SCHNEIDERIAN	ENCYCLOPEDIC	ACHLAMYDEOUS	AUTHENTICITY	MECHANICALLY
SCINTILLATOR	ENTOPLASTRON	ARITHMETICAL	BARRANQUILLA	MERCANTILISM
SCURRILOUSLY	ETHNOLOGICAL	BANTAMWEIGHT	BEACONSFIELD	METAGNATHOUS
SEMICIRCULAR	ETYMOLOGICAL	CHAIRMANSHIP	BILLINGSGATE	OUTMANOEUVRE
SESQUIALTERA	ETYMOLOGICON	CIRCUMCISION	CALUMNIATION	PALEONTOLOGY
SESQUITERTIA	FLAGELLATION	CIRCUMGYRATE	CAMIKNICKERS	PANDANACEOUS
SHEEPISHNESS	FOOTSLOGGING	CIRCUMSCRIBE	CAMPANULARIA	PARKINSONISM
SITTLICHKEIT	FORMALDEHYDE	CIRCUMSTANCE	CANTANKEROUS	PERMANGANATE
SIVAPITHECUS	FUSTILLIRIAN	CONDEMNATION	CARCINOGENIC	PERSONALIZED
SNOBBISHNESS	GENEALOGICAL	CONSUMMATION	CARDINDEXING	PERTINACIOUS
SOLICITATION	GESELLSCHAFT	CONTAMINATED	CLARINETTIST	PHILANTHROPY
SOLICITOUSLY	GIBRALTARIAN	CONTEMPORARY	COMBINATIONS	PHYTONADIONE
STOCKINGETTE	INAPPLICABLE	CONTEMPTIBLE	COMMANDMENTS	PIGMENTATION
STRADIVARIUS	INDECLINABLE	CONTEMPTUOUS	COMMENCEMENT	PLACENTIFORM
STREPITATION	INEXPLICABLE	CONTUMACIOUS	COMMENDATION	PRAXINOSCOPE
STRIGIFORMES	INEXPLICABLY	COURTMARTIAL	COMMENDATORY	PRECONDITION
STUDDINGSAIL	INSTALLATION	DISCOMEDUSAE	COMMENSURATE	PREMONSTRANT
SUBSTITUTION	INTELLECTUAL	DISCOMFITURE	COMMONWEALTH	PREPONDERANT
SUBSTITUTIVE	INTELLIGENCE	DISCOMYCETES	COMMUNICABLE	PREPONDERATE
SUPPLICATION	INTELLIGIBLE	ECONOMICALLY	COMPANIONWAY	PREPONDERENT
SURPRISINGLY	INTERLOCUTOR	ETEPIMELETIC	COMPENSATION	PRESENTATION
SURVEILLANCE	ISOBILATERAL	FUNDAMENTALS	COMPENSATORY	PRESENTIMENT
TAMARICACEAE	LAMELLICORNE	GAMESMANSHIP	CONCENTRATED	PREVENTATIVE
TECHNICALITY	LINCOLNSHIRE	GRANDMONTINE	CONDENSATION	PROLONGATION
TOTALITARIAN	LITHOLATROUS	HORSEMANSHIP	CONGENITALLY	PYTHONOMORPH
TRANSITIONAL	LUXULLIANITE	INFLAMMATION	CONTINUATION	RAMBUNCTIOUS
ULOTRICHALES	MACMILLANITE	INFLAMMATORY	CONTINUOUSLY	RECOGNIZABLE
UNBELIEVABLE	MAGNILOQUENT	INFORMIDABLE	CONVENIENCES	RECOGNIZANCE
UNBELIEVABLY	MANGELWURZEL	INHARMONIOUS	CONVENIENTLY	RENOUNCEMENT
UNDIMINISHED	METALLOPHONE	INTERMEDIARY	CONVENTIONAL	RESPONDENTIA
UNOFFICIALLY	METALLURGIST	INTERMEDIATE	CONVINCINGLY	RETRENCHMENT
UNSATISFYING	MICHELANGELO	INTERMINABLE	COSCINOMANCY	ROOMINGHOUSE
URBANIZATION	MILLILAMBERT	INTERMINABLY	DARLINGTONIA	SARDANAPALUS
VAPORIZATION	MISCALCULATE	INTERMISSION	DISCONCERTED	SARDONICALLY
VENTRIPOTENT	MISDELIVERED	INTERMITTENT	DISCONNECTED	SCREENWRITER
VERIFICATION	MOSBOLLETJIE	MARKSMANSHIP	DISCONSOLATE	SEGMENTATION
VETERINARIAN	MULTILATERAL	MATHEMATICAL	DISCONTENTED	SELFINTEREST
VILIFICATION	MYTHOLOGICAL	MISDEMEANOUR	DISHONORABLE	SEQUENTIALLY
WHIMSICALITY	NEPHELOMETER	NONCOMMITTAL	DISHONORABLY	SIPHONOPHORA
INTERJECTION	NEUROLOGICAL	OSTEOMALACIA	DISPENSATION	SIPHONOSTELE
NONOBJECTIVE	OSCILLOSCOPE	PARSIMONIOUS	DISTINCTNESS	SLOVENLINESS
UNPREJUDICED	PATHOLOGICAL	PASSEMEASURE	ENTRENCHMENT	SPATANGOIDEA
HOUSEKEEPING	PERSULPHURIC	PERGAMENEOUS	ESPAGNOLETTE	SUBCONSCIOUS
KILLIKINNICK	PESTILENTIAL	PHENOMENALLY	ESTRANGEMENT	SUBCONTINENT
PEACEKEEPING	PHILOLOGICAL	PREDOMINANCE	EXCHANGEABLE	SUBMINIATURE
SERASKIERATE	POIKILOTHERM	PRESUMPTUOUS	FERMENTATION	SUPERNACULUM
ACETALDEHYDE	PREDILECTION	PROGYMNASIUM	FRAUENDIENST	SUPERNATURAL
ANTHELMINTIC	PROMULGATION	RHADAMANTHUS	FRUMENTATION	TERCENTENARY

THYSANOPTERA	FLUVIOMARINE	SPELEOLOGIST	INCOMPETENCE	CHONDRIOSOME
TREMENDOUSLY	GASTROSOPHER	SPLENOMEGALY	INCOMPLETELY	COMMERCIALLY
TRICENTENARY	GLYPTOGRAPHY	SPURIOUSNESS	INCORPORATED	COMPURGATION
TRIGONOMETRY	GONADOTROPIN	STENTORPHONE	INDISPUTABLE	CONCURRENTLY
UNCHANGEABLE	GRACIOUSNESS	STEREOPHONIC	INDISPUTABLY	CONFIRMATION
UNECONOMICAL	GRAPHOLOGIST	STEREOPTICON	INHOSPITABLE	CONFIRMATORY
UNIDENTIFIED	GRISEOFULVIN	STEREOSCOPIC	INTEMPERANCE	CONSCRIPTION
UNPRINCIPLED	GYNECOLOGIST	STEREOTYPING	INTERPRETING	CONSERVATION
WASHINGTONIA	HETEROCLITIC	STILBOESTROL	IRRESPECTIVE	CONSERVATISM
WELLINFORMED	HETEROCONTAE	STRATOSPHERE	KLIPSPRINGER	CONSERVATIVE
WELLINGTONIA	HETEROGAMETE	STUBBORNNESS	LALLAPALOOZA	CONSERVATORY
AGATHODAIMON	HETEROPHORIA	STUDIOUSNESS	LIVERPUDLIAN	CONSTRICTION
AMELIORATION	HETEROPLASIA	SULPHONAMIDE	MACROPODIDAE	CONSTRUCTION
ANTAGONISTIC	HETEROSEXUAL	TECHNOLOGIST	MALLOPHAGOUS	CONSTRUCTIVE
ANTHROPOLOGY	HETEROSOMATA	THERMOSTATIC	METROPOLITAN	CONTERMINOUS
APLANOGAMETE	HISTIOPHORUS	THESMOPHORIA	MISAPPREHEND	CONVERSATION
ARISTOCRATIC	HOMOEOPATHIC	THIGMOTROPIC	MISREPRESENT	COSTERMONGER
ARISTOLOCHIA	HORIZONTALLY	TITANOSAURUS	MULTIPLICITY	CYMOTRICHOUS
ARISTOPHANES	HYMENOPTERAN	TOXICOLOGIST	ORTHOPAEDICS	DAGUERROTYPE
ARISTOTELEAN	IMMUNOLOGIST	TRANSOCEANIC	ORTHOPAEDIST	DESSERTSPOON
ARSENOPYRITE	INVIGORATING	TRICHOLOGIST	ORTHOPTEROUS	DEUTERANOPIA
ARTHROPLASTY	INVIGORATION	TRICHOPHYTON	OSTEOPOROSIS	DEUTEROSCOPY
ATHEROMATOUS	IRRESOLUTELY	TROCHOSPHERE	PANTOPHAGOUS	DIFFERENTIAL
AUSTRONESIAN	IRRESOLUTION	TURACOVERDIN	PASSEPARTOUT	DISAGREEABLE
BACKWOODSMAN	IRRESOLVABLE	UNCTUOUSNESS	PERCEPTIVELY	DISAGREEMENT
BEAUMONTAGUE	KLEPTOMANIAC	UNDEMOCRATIC	PERCEPTIVITY	DISSERTATION
BEAUMONTIQUE	LABANOTATION	UNFAVOURABLE	PEREMPTORILY	DONNERWETTER
BENEVOLENTLY	LATIROSTRATE	UNIMPORTANCE	PHYTOPHAGOUS	ELECTRICALLY
BERTHOLLETIA	LEPIDOMELANE	UNRECOGNISED	PROSOPOPOEIA	ELECTROLYSIS
BIBLIOGRAPHY	LEXICOGRAPHY	UNRECOGNIZED	PROTOPLASMAL	ELECTROPLATE
BIBLIOPEGIST	MADEMOISELLE	VARICOLOURED	PROTOPLASMIC	ELECTROTONUS
BLENNORRHOEA	MALACOSTRACA	VERUMONTANUM	REDEMPTIONER	EMBARRASSING
BOONDOGGLING	METAMORPHISM	WAREHOUSEMAN	SARSAPARILLA	EPANORTHOSIS
BRONTOSAURUS	METAMORPHOSE	WHIPPOORWILL	SCOPOPHILIAC	ERYTHROMYCIN
CARDIOLOGIST	MINDBOGGLING	XANTHOPTERIN	STEGOPHOLIST	EXACERBATION
CARDIOMEGALY	MINICOMPUTER	ACCOMPANYING	SUBLAPSARIAN	FOTHERINGHAY
CAUTIOUSNESS	MISPRONOUNCE	ACCOMPLISHED	THERAPEUTICS	GASTARBEITER
CEREMONIALLY	MISQUOTATION	ALEXIPHARMIC	TRANSPARENCY	HAEMORRHOIDS
CHALCOPYRITE	MONOTONOUSLY	ANEMOPHILOUS	TRANSPONTINE	HAIRDRESSERS
CHLOROPICRIN	MUSICOLOGIST	ARCHIPELAGOS	TRIUMPHANTLY	HAIRDRESSING
CHOREOGRAPHY	NYMPHOMANIAC	ASTROPHYSICS	UNDERPINNING	HAMMERHEADED
COMPROMISING	OCEANOGRAPHY	ATMOSPHERICS	UNRESPONSIVE	HELLGRAMMITE
CONGLOMERATE	ONEIROCRITIC	BENZOPHENONE	UNSURPRISING	HIERARCHICAL
CONTROLLABLE	ONYCHOPHORAN	BIPROPELLANT	UNSUSPECTING	HISTORICALLY
COVETOUSNESS	OPINIONATIVE	CARPOPHAGOUS	BENZOQUINONE	HUDIBRASTICS
CRISTOBALITE	OVERPOWERING	CHIROPRACTIC	COLLOQUIALLY	HYPOCRITICAL
CRYPTOGRAPHY	PASSIONATELY	CHIROPRACTOR	CONSEQUENCES	HYSTERECTOMY
CUCKOOFLOWER	PASSIONFRUIT	COSMOPOLITAN	CONSEQUENTLY	HYSTERICALLY
CZECHOSLOVAK	PHLEBOTOMIST	DISAPPEARING	HYDROQUINONE	INCORRIGIBLE
DEMIMONDAINE	PHYSIOLOGIST	DISAPPOINTED	INADEQUATELY	INCORRIGIBLY
DENDROLOGIST	PLECTOGNATHI	DISCIPLINARY	INFREQUENTLY	INEXTRICABLE
DICHROMATISM	POGONOPHORAN	DISREPECTFUL	PREREQUISITE	INEXTRICABLY
DILATORINESS	POSTPONEMENT	DISREPUTABLE	SUBSEQUENTLY	INSURRECTION
DIPRIONIDIAN	POSTPOSITIVE	ENTERPRISING	THREEQUARTER	INTERRELATED
EGYPTOLOGIST	POTAMOLOGIST	ENTREPRENEUR	UNFREQUENTED	INTERROGATOR
ELASMOBRANCH	PRASEODYMIUM	EPILEPTIFORM	ANAMORPHOSIS	INTERRUPTION
ELEEMOSYNARY	PROTHONOTARY	FELDSPATHOID	ANCHORPERSON	KATHAREVOUSA
ENHYPOSTASIA	PSEPHOLOGIST	GLYCOPROTEIN	APOSTROPHISE	KINDERGARTEN
ENTEROMORPHA	PSEUDONYMOUS	GOOSEPIMPLES	BACKBREAKING	LABOURSAVING
ENTEROPNEUST	PSYCHOLOGIST	GRANDPARENTS	BACTERIOLOGY	LEIOTRICHOUS
ENTOMOLOGIST	PSYCHOPATHIC	HAEMOPHILIAC	BACTERIOSTAT	LICKTRENCHER
ENTOMOSTRACA	RODOMONTADER	HAIRSPLITTER	BANDERSNATCH	LOXODROMICAL
EPISCOPALIAN	SCHIZOMYCETE	HIEROPHANTIC	BARBERMONGER	LUGUBRIOUSLY
EPISTOLATERS	SCLERODERMIA	HIPPOPOTAMUS	BESSERWISSER	MALFORMATION
EQUIVOCATION	SELFPORTRAIT	HYPERPYRETIC	BIELORUSSIAN	MASSERANDUBA
EQUIVOCATORY	SNOWBOARDING	INAUSPICIOUS	BUTTERSCOTCH	MASSPRODUCED
ESCAPOLOGIST	SOMATOPLEURE	INCOMPARABLE	BYELORUSSIAN	MASTERSTROKE
ETHEROMANIAC	SPACIOUSNESS	INCOMPARABLY	CASTERBRIDGE	MASTURBATION
FLAMBOYANTLY	SPECIOUSNESS	INCOMPATIBLE	CEREBROTONIC	MELODRAMATIC

MENSTRUATION	BAIRNSFATHER	POSSESSIVELY	AMPHITHEATER	ILLUSTRATIVE
MERETRICIOUS	BLEFUSCUDIAN	POWERSHARING	AMPHITHEATRE	IMPARTIALITY
MERITRICIOUS	BLOODSTAINED	PREDESTINATE	ANAESTHETISE	IMPERTINENCE
MYSTERIOUSLY	BUNKOSTEERER	PREGUSTATION	ANAESTHETIST	INCAUTIOUSLY
NONDIRECTIVE	CALLISTHENES	PREHISTORIAN	ANAESTHETIZE	INCONTINENCE
ORTHORHOMBIC	CIRCASSIENNE	PREPOSSESSED	ANECATHARSIS	INDEBTEDNESS
OUTSTRETCHED	CLEARSIGHTED	PREPOSTEROUS	ANTISTROPHON	INDISTINCTLY
OVERCROWDING	COMMISSARIAT	PROCESSIONAL	APPURTENANCE	INDOCTRINATE
OVERDRESSING	COMMISSIONED	PROFESSIONAL	ARCHITECTURE	INDUSTRIALLY
PANCHROMATIC	COMMISSIONER	PROFESSORIAL	AROMATHERAPY	INFILTRATION
PECTORILOQUY	CONFESSIONAL	PROGESTERONE	ARTISTICALLY	INFLATIONARY
PERTURBATION	CONFISCATION	PROTESTATION	BARNSTORMING	INGRATIATING
PERVERSENESS	CONSISTENTLY	PURPOSEBUILT	BICENTENNIAL	INNATTENTIVE
PITTERPATTER	CROSSSECTION	PURPOSEFULLY	BLOODTHIRSTY	INTUITIONISM
POLYURETHANE	DEMONSTRABLE	RECONSTITUTE	BLUESTOCKING	INVERTEBRATE
POSTGRADUATE	DEMONSTRABLY	REMONSTRANCE	BOOBYTRAPPED	INVESTIGATOR
POSTPRANDIAL	DEMONSTRATOR	REPOSSESSION	BREAKTHROUGH	ISOLATIONISM
PRECARIOUSLY	DISASSOCIATE	REVERSIONARY	BREASTPLOUGH	ISOLATIONIST
PREFERENTIAL	DISPOSSESSED	RONCESVALLES	BREASTSUMMER	KALISTOCRACY
PREPAREDNESS	ECCLESIASTES	SARRUSOPHONE	CARPETBAGGER	LAMENTATIONS
PRESCRIPTION	ECCLESIASTIC	SCRIMSHANDER	CASSITERIDES	LONGITUDINAL
PRESCRIPTIVE	ENGLISHWOMAN	SCRIMSHANKER	CATASTROPHIC	LONGSTANDING
PRESERVATION	ENGLISHWOMEN	SECESSIONIST	CATHETOMETER	LYMANTRIIDAE
PRESERVATIVE	ENTHUSIASTIC	SEQUESTRATOR	CHEMOTHERAPY	MAGNETICALLY
PRESTRICTION	ERATOSTHENES	SHARPSHOOTER	CHRESTOMATHY	MAJESTICALLY
PREVARICATOR	EULENSPIEGEL	SHIRTSLEEVES	CHRISTIANITY	MALNUTRITION
PROPORTIONAL	EXHAUSTIVELY	SHORTSIGHTED	CLEISTOGAMIC	MECHITHARIST
PROSCRIPTION	EXTENSIONIST	SHORTSLEEVED	DECENTRALISE	MERISTEMATIC
PROVERBIALLY	EXTENSOMETER	SHORTSTAFFED	DECENTRALIZE	MERRYTHOUGHT
PUMPERNICKEL	GYMNOSOPHIST	SOPHISTICATE	DEFLATIONARY	METHOTREXATE
RECHARGEABLE	HARNESSMAKER	SPOKESPERSON	DEPARTMENTAL	MINISTRATION
RECIPROCALLY	HEARTSTRINGS	SPORTSGROUND	DERESTRICTED	MISANTHROPIC
REPATRIATION	HYPERSARCOMA	STANISLAVSKI	DICTATORSHIP	MISINTERPRET
RESURRECTION	IMMEASURABLE	STATISTICIAN	DIRECTORSHIP	MNEMOTECHNIC
RHINORRHOEAL	IMMEASURABLY	STREPSIPTERA	DISASTROUSLY	NEPENTHACEAE
ROLLERBLADER	IMPERSONALLY	SUBHASTATION	DISINTEGRATE	NEUROTICALLY
ROLLERBLADES	IMPERSONATOR	SUBMISSIVELY	DISSATISFIED	NEVERTHELESS
SECTARIANISM	IMPRESSIVELY	SUCCESSFULLY	DIVERTICULUM	NUTRITIONIST
SEMIPRECIOUS	IMPRISONMENT	SUCCESSIVELY	DIVERTIMENTO	NYCTITROPISM
SILVERHAIRED	INCONSEQUENT	SUCCUSSATION	DOGMATICALLY	OBSTETRICIAN
SPECTROMETER	INCONSISTENT	SUGGESTIVELY	DOMESTICATED	OCTASTROPHIC
SPECTROSCOPE	INCONSOLABLE	SUPERSTITION	DRAMATICALLY	ONOMATOPOEIA
SPHAIRISTIKE	INCRUSTATION	SUPERSTRATUM	DRAMATURGIST	ONOMATOPOEIC
SQUIRRELFISH	INDISSOLUBLE	TELEASTHETIC	ECCENTRICITY	ORIENTEERING
SUBARRHATION	INTERSECTION	TELEOSAURIAN	ECSTATICALLY	ORTHOTONESIS
SUBSCRIPTION	INTERSPERSED	TESTOSTERONE	EDUCATIONIST	OSTENTATIOUS
SUBSERVIENCE	INTERSTELLAR	THANKSGIVING	EFFORTLESSLY	OVERSTRAINED
SUBSTRUCTURE	JENNYSPINNER	THICKSKINNED	EMPHATICALLY	PALPITATIONS
SUBTERRANEAN	KINAESTHETIC	TRADESCANTIA	ENTERTAINING	PARANTHELIUM
TEETERTOTTER	LANCASTERIAN	TRADESPEOPLE	ESSENTIALITY	PARENTHESIZE
TELEGRAPHESE	MONTESSORIAN	UNCLASSIFIED	ESTHETICALLY	PATHETICALLY
TELEGRAPHIST	MUTESSARIFAT	UNCONSIDERED	EVOLUTIONARY	PEDANTICALLY
THEATRICALLY	NARCISSISTIC	UNDERSKINKER	EXTORTIONATE	PEDIATRICIAN
UNATTRACTIVE	NEUROSCIENCE	UNDERSTAFFED	GEOMETRICIAN	PERISTERONIC
UNCHARITABLE	NIMBOSTRATUS	UNREASONABLE	GERIATRICIAN	PERMITTIVITY
UNCHARITABLY	NONRESIDENCE	UNSEASONABLE	GERONTOCRACY	PERPETRATION
UNIVERSALIST	NONRESISTANT	WOLLASTONITE	GIGANTOMACHY	PHONETICALLY
UNOPPRESSIVE	OLDFASHIONED	XIPHISTERNUM	GLOBETROTTER	PHRONTISTERY
UPROARIOUSLY	OMBUDSPERSON	ABOLITIONIST	HAEMATEMESIS	POLYETHYLENE
USERFRIENDLY	OPPRESSIVELY	ACCENTUATION	HAMARTHRITIS	POTENTIALITY
WELTERWEIGHT	OSTEOSARCOMA	ACCOUTREMENT	HAPTOTROPISM	PRALLTRILLER
WINTERHALTER	OVERESTIMATE	ADJECTIVALLY	HELIOTROPISM	PREDETERMINE
AGGRESSIVELY	PANAESTHESIA	ADSCITITIOUS	HERMETICALLY	PROBATIONARY
AMBASSADRESS	PANTISOCRACY	ADVANTAGEOUS	HOUSETOHOUSE	PROFITEERING
AMPHISBAENIC	PARTISANSHIP	ADVANTAGIOUS	HYDROTHERAPY	PROLETARIATE
AMPHISTOMOUS	PERIOSTRACUM	ADVENTITIOUS	HYPERTENSION	PROPITIATION
ANDROSTERONE	PERSISTENTLY	AFFECTIONATE	HYPNOTHERAPY	PROPITIATORY
APFELSTRUDEL	PHILISTINISM	AFORETHOUGHT	HYPNOTICALLY	PROPITIOUSLY
AWEINSPIRING	PHILOSOPHIZE	AFTERTHOUGHT	ILLUSTRATION	QUIXOTICALLY

RACKETEERING
RADIOTHERAPY
RECEPTIONIST
REDINTEGRATE
REDISTRIBUTE
REFLATIONARY
REGISTRATION
RELENTLESSLY
RESETTLEMENT
ROMANTICALLY
SADISTICALLY
SALTATORIOUS
SALVATIONIST
SCRIPTWRITER
SECRETARIATE
SEMANTICALLY
SIMULTANEOUS
SINANTHROPUS
SPECKTIONEER
SPINSTERHOOD
SPIRITUALISM
SPIRITUALIST
SPIRITUALITY
STEALTHINESS
STORMTROOPER
STRAITJACKET
STREPTOMYCIN
STREPTONEURA
STRONTIANITE
STRUCTURALLY
SUBCUTANEOUS
TELEUTOSPORE
TERRITORIALS
TRALATICIOUS
TRALATITIOUS
UINTATHERIUM
UNCONTROLLED
UNCULTIVATED
UNILATERALLY
UNMISTAKABLE
UNOBSTRUCTED
UNPRETENDING
UNRESTRAINED
UNRESTRICTED
VIBRATIUNCLE
VOLUPTUOUSLY
WEIGHTLIFTER
WICKETKEEPER
ACCUMULATION
AGRIBUSINESS
AGRICULTURAL
ARTICULATION
BUREAUCRATIC
CAPITULATION
COLOQUINTIDA
CONCLUSIVELY
DEAMBULATORY
DEPOPULATION
DEREGULATION
DISCOURAGING
DISCOURTEOUS
EMASCULATION
GROSSULARITE
HEADQUARTERS
HINDQUARTERS
IMMACULATELY
INACCURATELY
INAUGURATION
INESCUTCHEON

INSALUBRIOUS
INSOLUBILITY
INSTAURATION
INSTRUCTIONS
INSTRUCTRESS
INSTRUMENTAL
INTRAUTERINE
IRREGULARITY
MANIPULATION
MANIPULATIVE
MANOEUVRABLE
METICULOUSLY
MINDFULLNESS
MIRACULOUSLY
MOISTURIZING
MOUSQUETAIRE
NEWFOUNDLAND
OBSEQUIOUSLY
POSTHUMOUSLY
QUINQUENNIAL
READJUSTMENT
RESTAURATEUR
RETICULATION
RIDICULOUSLY
SCRUPULOUSLY
SHIPBUILDING
STERNUTATION
STRIDULATION
SURMOUNTABLE
SURROUNDINGS
THOROUGHBRED
THOROUGHFARE
THOROUGHNESS
TRANQUILIZER
TRANQUILLISE
TRANQUILLITY
TRANQUILLIZE
UNACCUSTOMED
UNACQUAINTED
UNEXPURGATED
UNPOPULARITY
UNRETURNABLE
UNSCRUPULOUS
VENEPUNCTURE
WOODBURYTYPE
ABBREVIATION
BIODIVERSITY
BOULEVARDIER
CARLOVINGIAN
CLAIRVOYANCE
CLAIRVOYANCY
CONVIVIALITY
DISADVANTAGE
DORSIVENTRAL
EFFERVESCENT
EXSERVICEMAN
EXTRAVAGANCE
EXTRAVAGANZA
GALLIVANTING
IMPROVIDENCE
INCONVENIENT
INTERVENTION
INTROVERSION
LASCIVIOUSLY
MISADVENTURE
OBSERVANTINE
PERADVENTURE
PERSEVERANCE
RECEIVERSHIP

TERGIVERSATE
TRANSVESTISM
TRANSVESTITE
UNCONVERSANT
UNCONVINCING
ACKNOWLEDGED
AWARDWINNING
BRAINWASHING
CARRIWITCHET
COLLYWOBBLES
GRASSWIDOWER
HEARTWARMING
HOUSEWARMING
NORTHWESTERN
OTHERWORLDLY
PRIZEWINNING
SHIRTWAISTER
SLEEPWALKING
SOUTHWESTERN
STERNWHEELER
UNANSWERABLE
UNDERWRITTEN
YELLOWHAMMER
ASPHYXIATION
OVEREXERTION
PHYCOXANTHIN
PREMAXILLARY
AERODYNAMICS
AUTOHYPNOSIS
BRACHYCEPHAL
CONVEYANCING
ENERGYSAVING
GEOPHYSICIST
ICHTHYOCOLLA
ICHTHYOPSIDA
IDIOSYNCRASY
MONOSYLLABIC
MONOSYLLABLE
PENNSYLVANIA
POLICYMAKING
POLYSYLLABIC
POLYSYLLABLE
POLYSYNDETON
PRESBYTERIAN
PROPHYLACTIC
SHILLYSHALLY
CHORIZONTIST
EMBEZZLEMENT

12:7

ACCOMPANYING
ADVANTAGEOUS
ADVANTAGIOUS
AMBASSADRESS
ARTIODACTYLA
ASSUEFACTION
BOULEVARDIER
BRAINWASHING
BREATHALYSER
BRILLIANTINE
BROADCASTING
CAPERCAILLIE
CAPERCAILZIE
CHAIRMANSHIP
COMBINATIONS
CONTUMACIOUS
CONVEYANCING
COURTMARTIAL
CRASHLANDING

DEUTERANOPIA
DISADVANTAGE
DISEMBARRASS
DISORGANIZED
EMBARRASSING
ENTERTAINING
ENTOPLASTRON
EXTRAVAGANCE
EXTRAVAGANZA
FELDSPATHOID
FULMINATIONS
GALLIGASKINS
GALLINACEOUS
GALLIVANTING
GAMESMANSHIP
GRANDPARENTS
GUARDIANSHIP
HABERDASHERS
HABERDASHERY
HEADQUARTERS
HEARTWARMING
HELIOGABALUS
HELLGRAMMITE
HINDQUARTERS
HORSEMANSHIP
HOUSEWARMING
HUDIBRASTICS
HYPERSARCOMA
INCOMPARABLE
INCOMPARABLY
INCOMPATIBLE
ISOBILATERAL
LALLAPALOOZA
LAMENTATIONS
LIQUEFACTION
LITHOLATROUS
LONGSTANDING
MALTREATMENT
MARKSMANSHIP
MASSERANDUBA
MATHEMATICAL
MELODRAMATIC
METAGNATHOUS
MICHELANGELO
MILLILAMBERT
MISBEHAVIOUR
MISTREATMENT
MULLIGATAWNY
MULTIFARIOUS
MULTILATERAL
MUTESSARIFAT
NORTHEASTERN
OBSERVANTINE
ORTHOPAEDICS
ORTHOPAEDIST
OSTENTATIOUS
OSTEOMALACIA
OSTEOSARCOMA
PALPITATIONS
PANDANACEOUS
PARTISANSHIP
PASSEPARTOUT
PERSONALIZED
PERTINACIOUS
PERVICACIOUS
PETRIFACTION
PHYCOXANTHIN
PHYTONADIONE
POSTGRADUATE

POSTPRANDIAL
PROLETARIATE
PROPAGANDISM
PROPAGANDIST
PSYCHIATRIST
PTERODACTYLE
PUTREFACTION
REAPPEARANCE
RHADAMANTHUS
SALESMANSHIP
SARDANAPALUS
SARSAPARILLA
SATISFACTION
SATISFACTORY
SECRETARIATE
SESQUIALTERA
SHAMEFACEDLY
SHIRTWAISTER
SIMULTANEOUS
SLEEPWALKING
SNOWBOARDING
SOUTHEASTERN
STROPHANTHUS
STUPEFACTION
SUBCUTANEOUS
SUPERNACULUM
SUPERNATURAL
TELEGRAPHESE
TELEGRAPHIST
TELEOSAURIAN
TRANSLATABLE
TRANSPARENCY
UMBRADARLING
UNACQUAINTED
UNATTRACTIVE
UNDERGARMENT
UNMISTAKABLE
WATERCARRIER
ADAPTABILITY
ADVISABILITY
AMPHISBAENIC
AVAILABILITY
BUCKLEBEGGAR
CARPETBAGGER
CASTERBRIDGE
CHEESEBURGER
CONSTABULARY
CONTRIBUTION
CONTRIBUTORY
CRISTOBALITE
DESIRABILITY
DISTRIBUTION
DISTRIBUTIVE
ELASMOBRANCH
EXACERBATION
EXCITABILITY
GASTARBEITER
GLYNDEBOURNE
ILLEGIBILITY
IMMUTABILITY
INCAPABILITY
INCUNABULIST
INSALUBRIOUS
INSOLUBILITY
INVISIBILITY
IRASCIBILITY
IRRITABILITY
MALLEABILITY
MASTURBATION

NAVIGABILITY	PHARMACOLOGY	APPREHENSIVE	INCONVENIENT	PROVIDENTIAL
PERMEABILITY	PRACTICALITY	APPURTENANCE	INDEBTEDNESS	PURPOSEBUILT
PERTURBATION	PRACTICIONER	ARCHIPELAGOS	INDIFFERENCE	PURPOSEFULLY
PLAUSIBILITY	PURIFICATION	ARCHITECTURE	INNATTENTIVE	QUINQUENNIAL
POLYRIBOSOME	PYROTECHNICS	ARITHMETICAL	INSUFFERABLE	RACKETEERING
PROVERBIALLY	RAMBUNCTIOUS	ARTILLERYMAN	INSUFFERABLY	RECEIVERSHIP
ROLLERBLADER	RAMIFICATION	BACKBREAKING	INSURRECTION	RECOLLECTION
ROLLERBLADES	RATIFICATION	BELLIGERENCY	INTELLECTUAL	RECRUDESCENT
SEPTEMBRISER	RENOUNCEMENT	BEWILDERMENT	INTEMPERANCE	REDINTEGRATE
SOMNAMBULISM	RETRENCHMENT	BICENTENNIAL	INTERCEPTION	REFRIGERATED
SOMNAMBULIST	SITTLICHKEIT	BIODIVERSITY	INTERCESSION	REFRIGERATOR
TRACTABILITY	STRINGCOURSE	BIPROPELLANT	INTERFERENCE	REPOSSESSION
ADJUDICATION	SUPPLICATION	BLOODLETTING	INTERJECTION	REPROCESSING
ANNOUNCEMENT	TAGLIACOTIAN	CAMPODEIFORM	INTERMEDIARY	RESURRECTION
ANTIBACCHIUS	TAMARICACEAE	CANTILEVERED	INTERMEDIATE	RETARDEDNESS
ANTIMACASSAR	TAPERECORDER	CASSITERIDES	INTERRELATED	RHODODENDRON
ANTIRACHITIC	TECHNICALITY	CHILDBEARING	INTERSECTION	RHYTIDECTOMY
APPROACHABLE	TRADESCANTIA	CLARINETTIST	INTERVENTION	SACRILEGIOUS
ARISTOCRATIC	TRANSACTIONS	CLAVICEMBALO	INTROVERSION	SCHILLERSPAR
ARTIFICIALLY	TRANSOCEANIC	CONFIDENTIAL	INVERTEBRATE	SEMIPRECIOUS
BAMBOCCIADES	ULOTRICHALES	CONSIDERABLE	INVULNERABLE	SERVICEBERRY
BARORECEPTOR	UNDEMOCRATIC	CONSIDERABLY	IRREDEEMABLE	SERVICEWOMAN
BENEFACTRESS	UNDERACHIEVE	CONTABESCENT	IRRESPECTIVE	SHUFFLEBOARD
BLEFUSCUDIAN	UNDETECTABLE	CONVALESCENT	KATHAREVOUSA	SOUTHWESTERN
BRACHYCEPHAL	UNEXPECTEDLY	CONVALESCING	LAMPADEDROMY	SPINSTERHOOD
BUREAUCRATIC	UNOFFICIALLY	COURAGEOUSLY	LICKTRENCHER	SPREADEAGLED
CIRCUMCISION	UNPRINCIPLED	CROSSBENCHER	LIGHTHEARTED	SPURTLEBLADE
CLAUDICATION	VERIFICATION	CROSSSECTION	MACROCEPHALY	SQUIRRELFISH
CODIFICATION	VILIFICATION	DECIPHERABLE	MARLINESPIKE	STEEPLECHASE
COMMENCEMENT	WHIMSICALITY	DECIPHERMENT	MERISTEMATIC	STILBOESTROL
COMMERCIALLY	ACETALDEHYDE	DECONGESTANT	MESOTHELIOMA	SWIZZLESTICK
COMPLACENTLY	AGATHODAIMON	DIFFERENTIAL	MISADVENTURE	TERGIVERSATE
COMPLICATION	CARDINDEXING	DIPLOGENESIS	MISDEMEANOUR	TESTAMENTARY
CONFISCATION	COINCIDENTAL	DISAGREEABLE	MISINTERPRET	TETRAHEDRITE
CONSPECTUITY	COMMANDMENTS	DISAGREEMENT	MNEMOTECHNIC	THERAPEUTICS
CONVINCINGLY	COMMENDATION	DISAPPEARING	MOUSQUETAIRE	TOGETHERNESS
DISCONCERTED	COMMENDATORY	DISCOMEDUSAE	NONDIRECTIVE	TORRICELLIAN
DISPLACEMENT	DEHUMIDIFIER	DISINCENTIVE	NONOBJECTIVE	TRANSCENDENT
DISTINCTNESS	DILAPIDATION	DISINFECTANT	NORTHWESTERN	TRANSFERABLE
ENCROACHMENT	DISOBEDIENCE	DISINGENUOUS	NYCHTHEMERON	TRANSFERENCE
ENTRENCHMENT	DOUBLEDECKER	DISINTEGRATE	ORIENTEERING	TRANSVESTISM
EPIDEICTICAL	EMBROIDERESS	DISORIENTATE	ORTHOGENESIS	TRANSVESTITE
EQUIVOCATION	EPACRIDACEAE	DISREPECTFUL	OUTRAGEOUSLY	TROUBLEMAKER
EQUIVOCATORY	FLUORIDATION	DORSIVENTRAL	OUTSTRETCHED	UNANSWERABLE
HETEROCLITIC	FORMALDEHYDE	DYSTELEOLOGY	OVERDRESSING	UNBELIEVABLE
HETEROCONTAE	FRAUENDIENST	EFFERVESCENT	OVEREXERTION	UNBELIEVABLY
HIERARCHICAL	GOBBLEDEGOOK	ETEPIMELETIC	OVERWHELMING	UNCONVERSANT
HOMESICKNESS	GOBBLEDYGOOK	FAINTHEARTED	PALINGENESIA	UNILATERALLY
HYPERACIDITY	INDIVIDUALLY	FRONTIERSMAN	PALINGENESIS	UNOPPRESSIVE
ILLOGICALITY	INTIMIDATING	FUNDAMENTALS	PANATHENAEAN	UNPRETENDING
INARTICULATE	INTIMIDATION	HAEMATEMESIS	PASSEMEASURE	UNSUCCESSFUL
INCAPACITATE	INVALIDATION	HAIRDRESSERS	PEACEKEEPING	UNSUSPECTING
INEFFICIENCY	LANGUEDOCIAN	HAIRDRESSING	PERADVENTURE	WHOLEHEARTED
INFELICITOUS	PRASEODYMIUM	HEPHTHEMIMER	PERGAMENEOUS	WRETCHEDNESS
INSTRUCTIONS	PRECONDITION	HERMENEUTICS	PERISTERONIC	AFTEREFFECTS
INSTRUCTRESS	PREPONDERANT	HERMENEUTIST	PERSEVERANCE	AIRCRAFTSMAN
INTOXICATING	PREPONDERATE	HOMOTHERMOUS	PESTILENTIAL	BAIRNSFATHER
INTOXICATION	PREPONDERENT	HOUSEKEEPING	PHENOMENALLY	CLASSIFIABLE
MALPRACTICES	RESPONDENTIA	HYDROGEOLOGY	PHILODENDRON	CUCKOOFLOWER
MANUFACTURER	SCHNEIDERIAN	HYPERTENSION	PHYTOBENTHOS	DISCOMFITURE
MISCALCULATE	SCLERODERMIA	HYPOTHECATOR	POLYURETHANE	GRISEOFULVIN
MISPLACEMENT	SINGLEDECKER	HYPOTHETICAL	PREDETERMINE	IDENTIFIABLE
MODIFICATION	TREMENDOUSLY	HYSTERECTOMY	PREDILECTION	PASQUEFLOWER
NEUROSCIENCE	ZALAMBDODONT	IDIOTHERMOUS	PREFERENTIAL	QUANTIFIABLE
NOTIFICATION	AGAMOGENETIC	IMPERFECTION	PREPAREDNESS	STRIGIFORMES
ONEIROCRITIC	ALPHABETICAL	IMPERFECTIVE	PRESIDENTIAL	WELLINFORMED
OSSIFICATION	ANTIMNEMONIC	INCANDESCENT	PROFITEERING	ANASTIGMATIC
PACIFICATION	APPENDECTOMY	INCOMPETENCE	PROPRIETRESS	ANTILEGOMENA
PERSPICACITY	APPREHENSION	INCONSEQUENT	PROTUBERANCE	APLANOGAMETE

ASPARAGINASE	CARPOPHAGOUS	ANNUNCIATION	GRASSWIDOWER	PATHETICALLY
BATTLEGROUND	CHEMOTHERAPY	APPENDICITIS	HALLUCINOGEN	PECTORILOQUY
BIBLIOGRAPHY	DISACCHARIDE	APPOGGIATURA	HARMONIOUSLY	PEDANTICALLY
BILLINGSGATE	DISENCHANTED	APPRECIATION	HERMETICALLY	PERIODICALLY
BOONDOGGLING	ENGLISHWOMAN	APPRECIATIVE	HISTORICALLY	PHONETICALLY
CARTHAGINIAN	ENGLISHWOMEN	ARTISTICALLY	HOBBIDIDANCE	PHRONTISTERY
CHOREOGRAPHY	ESCHSCHOLZIA	ASPHYXIATION	HORRIFICALLY	POTENTIALITY
CIRCUMGYRATE	HAEMOPHILIAC	AUSPICIOUSLY	HYGIENICALLY	PRECARIOUSLY
COMPURGATION	HAMARTHRITIS	AWARDWINNING	HYPNOTICALLY	PRECOCIOUSLY
CONGREGATION	HAMMERHEADED	BACTERIOLOGY	HYPOCRITICAL	PREDOMINANCE
CRYPTOGRAPHY	HIEROPHANTIC	BACTERIOSTAT	HYSTERICALLY	PREMAXILLARY
CURMUDGEONLY	HYDROCHLORIC	BRANCHIOPODA	IMPARTIALITY	PRESCRIPTION
DARLINGTONIA	HYDROTHERAPY	BRICKFIELDER	IMPERTINENCE	PRESCRIPTIVE
DOUBLEGLAZED	HYPNOTHERAPY	CALUMNIATION	IMPROVIDENCE	PRESTRICTION
ESTRANGEMENT	INTERCHANGED	CAMIKNICKERS	INAPPLICABLE	PREVARICATOR
EXCHANGEABLE	MALLOPHAGOUS	CARLOVINGIAN	INAUSPICIOUS	PRIZEFIGHTER
GLYPTOGRAPHY	MECHITHARIST	CARRIWITCHET	INCAUTIOUSLY	PRIZEWINNING
HETEROGAMETE	MERRYTHOUGHT	CHONDRIOSOME	INCONSISTENT	PROBATIONARY
INFRINGEMENT	MISANTHROPIC	CHRISTIANITY	INCONTINENCE	PRODIGIOUSLY
KINDERGARTEN	MUDDLEHEADED	CLEARSIGHTED	INCORRIGIBLE	PROFICIENTLY
LEXICOGRAPHY	NEPENTHACEAE	COCCIDIOSTAT	INCORRIGIBLY	PROLIFICALLY
MARRIAGEABLE	NEVERTHELESS	COLOQUINTIDA	INDECLINABLE	PROPITIATION
MEANINGFULLY	OLDFASHIONED	COMMUNICABLE	INDISTINCTLY	PROPITIATORY
MINDBOGGLING	ORTHORHOMBIC	COMPANIONWAY	INERADICABLE	PROPITIOUSLY
MOONLIGHTING	PANTECHNICON	CONCILIATION	INEXPLICABLE	PROSCRIPTION
MUCILAGINOUS	PANTOPHAGOUS	CONCILIATORY	INEXPLICABLY	PUGNACIOUSLY
OCEANOGRAPHY	PARANTHELIUM	CONGENITALLY	INEXTRICABLE	QUIXOTICALLY
PARAMAGNETIC	PARENTHESIZE	CONSCRIPTION	INEXTRICABLY	RADIOBIOLOGY
PERMANGANATE	PHYTOPHAGOUS	CONSOCIATION	INFLATIONARY	RECALCITRANT
PLECTOGNATHI	PLEIOCHASIUM	CONSOLIDATED	INFORMIDABLE	RECEPTIONIST
PROLONGATION	POLYETHYLENE	CONSOLIDATOR	INFOTAINMENT	RECOGNIZABLE
PROMULGATION	POWERSHARING	CONSTRICTION	INGRATIATING	RECOGNIZANCE
QUADRAGESIMA	RADIOTHERAPY	CONTAMINATED	INHOSPITABLE	REFLATIONARY
RECHARGEABLE	SCOPOPHILIAC	CONVENIENCES	INSUFFICIENT	RENUNCIATION
REINVIGORATE	SCRIMSHANDER	CONVENIENTLY	INTELLIGENCE	REPATRIATION
ROOMINGHOUSE	SCRIMSHANKER	CONVIVIALITY	INTELLIGIBLE	RESUSCITATED
SEPTUAGESIMA	SELFADHESIVE	CYMOTRICHOUS	INTERMINABLE	REVERSIONARY
SPATANGOIDEA	SHARPSHOOTER	DEFLATIONARY	INTERMINABLY	RHYTHMICALLY
SPORTSGROUND	SILVERHAIRED	DENUNCIATION	INTERMISSION	RISORGIMENTO
SPRECHGESANG	SINANTHROPUS	DEPRECIATION	INTERMITTENT	ROMANTICALLY
THANKSGIVING	SINGLEHANDED	DEPRECIATORY	INTUITIONISM	SADISTICALLY
THEREAGAINST	SLEDGEHAMMER	DISSATISFIED	INVESTIGATOR	SALVATIONIST
THOROUGHBRED	SPELLCHECKER	DISSOCIATION	ISOLATIONISM	SARDONICALLY
THOROUGHFARE	SPINECHILLER	DIVERTICULUM	ISOLATIONIST	SCAPULIMANCY
THOROUGHNESS	STEALTHINESS	DIVERTIMENTO	JURISDICTION	SECESSIONIST
UNCHANGEABLE	STEGOPHOLIST	DOGMATICALLY	KILLIKINNICK	SECTARIANISM
UNMANAGEABLE	STERNWHEELER	DOMESTICATED	LAMELLICORNE	SEMANTICALLY
UNRECOGNISED	STONECHATTER	DRAMATICALLY	LASCIVIOUSLY	SERASKIERATE
UNRECOGNIZED	STRAIGHTAWAY	ECCLESIASTES	LEIOTRICHOUS	SHIPBUILDING
WASHINGTONIA	STRAIGHTEDGE	ECCLESIASTIC	LUGUBRIOUSLY	SHORTCIRCUIT
WELLINGTONIA	STRAIGHTNESS	ECONOMICALLY	LUXULLIANITE	SHORTSIGHTED
ACCOUCHEMENT	SUBARRHATION	ECSTATICALLY	MADEMOISELLE	SIDEWHISKERS
AFORETHOUGHT	SUPERCHARGED	EDUCATIONIST	MAGNETICALLY	SIGNIFICANCE
AFTERTHOUGHT	SUPERCHARGER	ELECTRICALLY	MAGNIFICENCE	SPECIFICALLY
ALEXIPHARMIC	TRIUMPHANTLY	EMPHATICALLY	MAJESTICALLY	SPECKTIONEER
AMPHITHEATER	TURBOCHARGER	ENTHUSIASTIC	MARCONIGRAPH	SPHAIRISTIKE
AMPHITHEATRE	UINTATHERIUM	ESSENTIALITY	MECHANICALLY	SPORADICALLY
ANAESTHETISE	UNDISCHARGED	ESTHETICALLY	MERETRICIOUS	STREPSIPTERA
ANAESTHETIST	UNNEIGHBORLY	EVOLUTIONARY	MERITRICIOUS	STRONTIANITE
ANAESTHETIZE	WINTERHALTER	EXCRUCIATING	METHODICALLY	SUBMINIATURE
ANECATHARSIS	YELLOWHAMMER	EXCRUCIATION	MISDELIVERED	SUBSCRIPTION
ANEMOPHILOUS	ABBREVIATION	EXSERVICEMAN	MYSTERIOUSLY	SUBSIDIARITY
AROMATHERAPY	ABOLITIONIST	EXTENSIONIST	NEUROFIBROMA	SUFFICIENTLY
ASTROPHYSICS	ACADEMICALLY	EXTORTIONATE	NEUROTICALLY	SUPERCILIARY
ATMOSPHERICS	ACCORDIONIST	EXTRADITABLE	NOCONFIDENCE	SUPERCILIOUS
BENZOPHENONE	ADJECTIVALLY	FASTIDIOUSLY	NONRESIDENCE	SUPERHIGHWAY
BETHLEHEMITE	ADSCITITIOUS	FOTHERINGHAY	NONRESISTANT	SUSPICIOUSLY
BLOODTHIRSTY	ADVENTITIOUS	GEOLOGICALLY	NUTRITIONIST	SYMBOLICALLY
BREAKTHROUGH	AFFECTIONATE	GOOSEPIMPLES	OBSEQUIOUSLY	TERRIFICALLY

THEATRICALLY	ENTOMOLOGIST	REHABILITATE	KLEPTOMANIAC	INSEMINATION
TIGHTFITTING	EPISTOLATERS	RELENTLESSLY	LEGITIMATELY	LABYRINTHINE
TRALATICIOUS	EPITHALAMION	RESETTLEMENT	LEPIDOMELANE	LEGIONNAIRES
TRALATITIOUS	EPITHALAMIUM	RETICULATION	MALFORMATION	LINCOLNSHIRE
TRANQUILIZER	ESCAPOLOGIST	RIDICULOUSLY	MINICOMPUTER	MISPRONOUNCE
TRANQUILLISE	EXSUFFLICATE	SCANDALOUSLY	NONCOMMITTAL	MONOTONOUSLY
TRANQUILLITY	FLAGELLATION	SCINTILLATOR	NONFLAMMABLE	NEWFOUNDLAND
TRANQUILLIZE	FRANKALMOIGN	SCRUPULOUSLY	NYMPHOMANIAC	NONAGENARIAN
TRANSMIGRATE	FRIENDLINESS	SCURRILOUSLY	PALUDAMENTUM	OBEDIENTIARY
TRANSMISSION	FUSTILLIRIAN	SHIRTSLEEVES	PANDAEMONIUM	OCTOGENARIAN
TURBIDIMETER	GENETHLIACON	SHORTSLEEVED	POLICYMAKING	OPINIONATIVE
UNATTAINABLE	GRAPHOLOGIST	SLOVENLINESS	POSTHUMOUSLY	PARACENTESIS
UNCHARITABLE	GROSSULARITE	SPELEOLOGIST	POSTLIMINARY	PASSIONATELY
UNCHARITABLY	GYNECOLOGIST	SPHACELATION	PROCLAMATION	PASSIONFRUIT
UNCONSIDERED	HAIRSPLITTER	SPIEGELEISEN	PROGRAMMABLE	PENITENTIARY
UNCONVINCING	HIEROGLYPHIC	STANISLAVSKI	PROGYMNASIUM	POLYSYNDETON
UNCULTIVATED	HIGHFALUTING	STRANGLEHOLD	PROTHONOTARY	POSTPONEMENT
UNDERPINNING	ICONOCLASTIC	STRANGLEWEED	PSEUDONYMOUS	PROGYMNASIUM
UNIMAGINABLE	IMMACULATELY	STRIDULATION	SPLENOMEGALY	PSIPHENOMENA
UNOBTAINABLE	IMMUNOLOGIST	SURREALISTIC	STRONGMINDED	PUMPERNICKEL
UNPROFITABLE	INCOMPLETELY	SURVEILLANCE	SUBCOMMITTEE	REJUVENATION
UPROARIOUSLY	INCONCLUSIVE	SYNADELPHITE	SYNTAGMATITE	RODOMONTADER
USERFRIENDLY	INSTALLATION	TECHNOLOGIST	ACCIDENTALLY	SAUROGNATHAE
VALENCIENNES	INTERGLACIAL	THESSALONIAN	ACQUAINTANCE	SCANDINAVIAN
VIBRATIUNCLE	IRREGULARITY	TOXICOLOGIST	AERODYNAMICS	SCHOPENHAUER
VILLEGIATURA	IRRESOLUTELY	TRICHOLOGIST	AMBULANCEMAN	SCLERENCHYMA
WILTSHIREMAN	IRRESOLUTION	TROCHELMINTH	ANTAGONISTIC	SEXAGENARIAN
YORKSHIREMAN	IRRESOLVABLE	TROPHALLAXIS	ANTANANARIVO	STAKHANOVITE
KATZENJAMMER	ISHMAELITISH	UNCHALLENGED	ANTONINIANUS	STELLENBOSCH
STRAITJACKET	JOURNALISTIC	UNDERCLOTHES	APOLLINARIAN	STOCKINGETTE
CANTANKEROUS	MACMILLANITE	UNPARALLELED	AUSTRONESIAN	STUDDINGSAIL
SHOSTAKOVICH	MANIPULATION	UNPOPULARITY	BACCHANALIAN	SUBSTANTIATE
THICKSKINNED	MANIPULATIVE	VARICOLOURED	BEAUMONTAGUE	SULPHONAMIDE
UNDERSKINNER	MARSEILLAISE	WEIGHTLIFTER	BEAUMONTIQUE	SUPERANNUATE
WICKETKEEPER	MERVEILLEUSE	WELLBALANCED	BOUGAINVILLE	SURMOUNTABLE
ACCOMPLISHED	METICULOUSLY	WHIGMALEERIE	CARAVANSERAI	SURROUNDINGS
ACCUMULATION	MICROCLIMATE	AMALGAMATION	CEREMONIALLY	THREADNEEDLE
ACKNOWLEDGED	MINDFULLNESS	ANTHELMINTIC	CHAUVINISTIC	UNDIMINISHED
AGRICULTURAL	MINERALOGIST	ATHEROMATOUS	CHLORINATION	UNSCIENTIFIC
ANDOUILLETTE	MIRACULOUSLY	AYUNTAMIENTO	CONDEMNATION	VENEPUNCTURE
ANNIHILATION	MITRAILLEUSE	BARBERMONGER	CONTIGNATION	VERUMONTANUM
ANTEDILUVIAN	MONOSYLLABIC	BIOCHEMISTRY	COORDINATION	VETERINARIAN
ARISTOLOCHIA	MONOSYLLABLE	CALCEAMENTUM	DEMIMONDAINE	WOLSTENHOLME
ARTICULATION	MOSBOLLETJIE	CARDIOMEGALY	DENOMINATION	ADDITIONALLY
ASSIMILATION	MULTIPLICITY	CHEESEMONGER	DIPRIONIDIAN	AECIDIOSPORE
AUSTRALASIAN	MUSICOLOGIST	CLAMJAMPHRIE	DISCONNECTED	AETHRIOSCOPE
BANANALANDER	NATURALISTIC	COMPROMISING	DISDAINFULLY	APOSTROPHISE
BENEVOLENTLY	NIGHTCLOTHES	CONFIRMATION	DISFRANCHISE	ARCHILOCHIAN
BERTHOLLETIA	NOMENCLATURE	CONFIRMATORY	DOLPHINARIUM	ASTROLOGICAL
BERTILLONAGE	NONCHALANTLY	CONGLOMERATE	DRESSINGDOWN	ASTRONOMICAL
BREATHLESSLY	OPHIOGLOSSUM	CONSUMMATION	EPIPHENOMENA	BACKWOODSMAN
CANCELLATION	OUTBUILDINGS	CONTERMINOUS	EVENHANDEDLY	BARNSTORMING
CAPITULATION	PARAMILITARY	COSTERMONGER	FARTHINGLAND	BEHAVIOURISM
CARDIOLOGIST	PEDICELLARIA	CRASSAMENTUM	FRANKENSTEIN	BLUESTOCKING
COMPELLATION	PENNSYLVANIA	DEPARTMENTAL	FRANKINCENSE	CARCINOGENIC
CONTROLLABLE	PHOTOGLYPHIC	DIAGRAMMATIC	GLOCKENSPIEL	CATADIOPTRIC
CREMAILLIÈRE	PHYSIOLOGIST	DICHROMATISM	GONDWANALAND	CATHETOMETER
DEAMBULATORY	PLAINCLOTHES	DISCRIMINATE	GUILDENSTERN	CEREBROTONIC
DENDROLOGIST	POINTILLISME	ENTEROMORPHA	HORIZONTALLY	CHALICOTHERE
DEPOPULATION	POLYSYLLABIC	EPIGRAMMATIC	IDIOSYNCRASY	CHAMPIONSHIP
DEREGULATION	POLYSYLLABLE	EPISTEMOLOGY	ILLUMINATING	CHORIZONTIST
DISCIPLINARY	POTAMOLOGIST	ETHEROMANIAC	ILLUMINATION	CHRESTOMATHY
DISTILLATION	PROPHYLACTIC	EVENTEMPERED	IMPREGNATION	CLAIRVOYANCE
EFFORTLESSLY	PROTHALAMION	EXPERIMENTAL	INCIDENTALLY	CLAIRVOYANCY
EGYPTOLOGIST	PROTHALAMIUM	FLUVIOMARINE	INDEFENSIBLE	CLEISTOGAMIC
EMASCULATION	PROTOPLASMAL	GOVERNMENTAL	INDEFINITELY	COLDSHOULDER
EMBEZZLEMENT	PROTOPLASMIC	INFLAMMATION	INDEPENDENCE	COLLABORATOR
ENCIRCLEMENT	PSEPHOLOGIST	INFLAMMATORY	INNOMINABLES	
ENTANGLEMENT	PSYCHOLOGIST	INSTRUMENTAL	INORDINATELY	

783

COLLYWOBBLES	MULTICOLORED	TETRODOTOXIN	QUADRAPHONIC	EAVESDROPPER
COSCINOMANCY	MYRINGOSCOPE	THIRDBOROUGH	QUADRIPLEGIA	ECCENTRICITY
COSMOPOLITAN	MYTHOLOGICAL	THYSANOPTERA	RECORDPLAYER	ENCHEIRIDION
CROSSCOUNTRY	NEIGHBORHOOD	TOBACCONISTS	SELFEMPLOYED	ENTERPRISING
DEUTEROSCOPY	NEIGHBOURING	TRANSMOGRIFY	SOMATOPLEURE	ENTREPRENEUR
DICTATORSHIP	NEPHELOMETER	TRANSPONTINE	SPOKESPERSON	EXAGGERATION
DIRECTORSHIP	NEUROLOGICAL	TRIGONOMETRY	STEREOPHONIC	EXASPERATING
DISAPPOINTED	NONALCOHOLIC	ULTRAMONTANE	STEREOPTICON	EXASPERATION
DISASSOCIATE	OCCASIONALLY	UNAUTHORISED	THESMOPHORIA	EXHILARATING
DISHONORABLE	ONOMATOPOEIA	UNAUTHORIZED	TRADESPEOPLE	EXHILARATION
DISHONORABLY	ONOMATOPOEIC	UNECONOMICAL	TRICHOPHYTON	FEATHERBRAIN
ELECTROLYSIS	OPISTHOGRAPH	UNEMPLOYMENT	UNACCEPTABLE	FEHMGERICHTE
ELECTROPLATE	ORNITHOGALUM	UNFATHOMABLE	UNSCRUPULOUS	FLITTERMOUSE
ELECTROTONUS	ORTHODONTICS	UNPARDONABLE	VENTRIPOTENT	GEOMETRICIAN
ENANTIOMORPH	ORTHOTONESIS	UNREASONABLE	XANTHOPTERIN	GERIATRICIAN
ENANTIOPATHY	OSCILLOSCOPE	UNRESPONSIVE	BARRANQUILLA	GLOBETROTTER
ENCYCLOPEDIA	OSTEOPOROSIS	UNSEASONABLE	ACCELERATION	GLYCOPROTEIN
ENCYCLOPEDIC	OTHERWORLDLY	VAINGLORIOUS	ACCOUTREMENT	GREENGROCERS
ERYTHROMYCIN	OUTMANOEUVRE	WHIPPOORWILL	ADULTERATION	GREENGROCERY
ESPAGNOLETTE	OVERCROWDING	ANAMORPHOSIS	ALLITERATION	HAEMORRHOIDS
ETHNOLOGICAL	PANCHROMATIC	ANCHORPERSON	AMELIORATION	HANDKERCHIEF
ETYMOLOGICAL	PANTISOCRACY	ANTHROPOLOGY	ANTEMERIDIAN	HAPTOTROPISM
ETYMOLOGICON	PAPILIONIDAE	ANTICIPATION	ANTIAIRCRAFT	HARUMFRODITE
EXTENSOMETER	PARSIMONIOUS	ANTICIPATORY	ANTIBARBARUS	HELIOTROPISM
FIRSTFOOTING	PARTICOLORED	ARISTOPHANES	ANTIPARTICLE	HIEROGRAMMAT
FOOTSLOGGING	PATHOLOGICAL	ARSENOPYRITE	ANTISTROPHON	HILDEBRANDIC
FRACTIONALLY	PERIODONTICS	ARTHROPLASTY	ANTITHROMBIN	HIPPOCRATISE
FUNCTIONALLY	PETTIFOGGERS	AUTOHYPNOSIS	BACKWARDNESS	HIPPOCREPIAN
FUNCTIONLESS	PETTIFOGGERY	AWEINSPIRING	BEAUMARCHAIS	HOUSEBREAKER
GAINSBOROUGH	PETTIFOGGING	BIBLIOPEGIST	BICAMERALISM	HYDROGRAPHER
GALVANOMETER	PHILOLOGICAL	BIOGRAPHICAL	BLABBERMOUTH	HYMNOGRAPHER
GENEALOGICAL	PHILOSOPHIZE	BREASTPLOUGH	BLENNORRHOEA	IAMBOGRAPHER
GERONTOCRACY	PHOSPHOLIPID	CAMERAPERSON	BLETHERSKATE	ILLUSTRATION
GIGANTOMACHY	PHOSPHORENCE	CHALCOPYRITE	BOISTEROUSLY	ILLUSTRATIVE
GRANDMONTINE	PHOSPHORESCE	CHEESEPARING	BOOBYTRAPPED	IMMODERATELY
GYMNOSOPHIST	POIKILOTHERM	CHLOROPICRIN	CALLIGRAPHIC	IMMODERATION
HAPPYGOLUCKY	POTICHOMANIA	CONSTIPATION	CARTOGRAPHER	IMPOVERISHED
HEMICHORDATA	PRAXINOSCOPE	CONTEMPORARY	CARTOGRAPHIC	INACCURATELY
HENCEFORWARD	PROLEGOMENON	CONTEMPTIBLE	CATASTROPHIC	INADVERTENCE
HEROICOMICAL	PROSOPOPOEIA	CONTEMPTUOUS	CHARTERHOUSE	INAUGURATION
HIPPOPOTAMUS	PTERIDOPHYTE	CONTRAPPOSTO	CHESTERFIELD	INCINERATION
HOUSETOHOUSE	PTERIDOSPERM	CONTRAPUNTAL	CHIROPRACTIC	INCOHERENTLY
HYPERBOLICAL	PYTHONOMORPH	DIENCEPHALON	CHIROPRACTOR	INDISCRETION
HYPOCHONDRIA	QUESTIONABLE	EMANCIPATION	CHITTERLINGS	INDOCTRINATE
ICHTHYOCOLLA	RECIPROCALLY	ENTEROPNEUST	CLAPPERBOARD	INDUSTRIALLY
ICHTHYOPSIDA	REDEPLOYMENT	EPENCEPHALON	CONCURRENTLY	INEXPERIENCE
IMPERSONALLY	REDISCOVERED	EPISCOPALIAN	CONSECRATION	INFILTRATION
IMPERSONATOR	RELATIONSHIP	EULENSPIEGEL	CONSPIRACIST	INSTAURATION
IMPRISONMENT	RHAMPHOTHECA	GAMOSEPALOUS	CONTRARINESS	INTENERATION
INCONSOLABLE	RHIPIDOPTERA	GEOGRAPHICAL	COUNTERBLAST	INTERPRETING
INCORPORATED	SALTATORIOUS	HETEROPHORIA	COUNTERCLAIM	INVIGORATING
INDISSOLUBLE	SARRUSOPHONE	HETEROPLASIA	COUNTERMARCH	INVIGORATION
INHARMONIOUS	SHAREHOLDING	HISTIOPHORUS	COUNTERPOINT	IRREVERENTLY
INTERLOCUTOR	SHORTCOMINGS	HOMOEOPATHIC	COUNTERPOISE	IRREVERSIBLE
INTERROGATOR	SIPHONOPHORA	HYMENOPTERAN	DAGUERROTYPE	KLETTERSCHUE
IRRATIONALLY	SIPHONOSTELE	INTERSPERSED	DEASPIRATION	KLIPSPRINGER
KALEIDOSCOPE	SLOCKDOLAGER	JENNYSPINNER	DECELERATION	LITHOGRAPHIC
KALISTOCRACY	SLOCKDOLIGER	MUNICIPALITY	DECENTRALISE	LYMANTRIIDAE
KERAUNOGRAPH	SLOCKDOLOGER	NEWSPAPERMAN	DECENTRALIZE	MACABERESQUE
LONGSHOREMAN	SMALLHOLDING	OBSTREPEROUS	DEGENERATION	MACHAIRODONT
LOXODROMICAL	SOCIOLOGICAL	OMBUDSPERSON	DELIBERATELY	MALNUTRITION
LUXEMBOURGER	SOUTHCOTTIAN	ONYCHOPHORAN	DELIBERATION	MARCOBRUNNER
MACROPODIDAE	SPECTROMETER	PARALIPOMENA	DERESTRICTED	METAMORPHISM
MAGNILOQUENT	SPECTROSCOPE	PERSULPHURIC	DESIDERATIVE	METAMORPHOSE
MASSPRODUCED	STREPTOMYCIN	PITTERPATTER	DILATORINESS	METHOTREXATE
MASTIGOPHORA	STREPTONEURA	POGONOPHORAN	DISASTROUSLY	MICROBREWERY
METALLOPHONE	TAUTOLOGICAL	PRESUMPTUOUS	DISCOURAGING	MILITARISTIC
METAPHORICAL	TELEUTOSPORE	PRINCIPALITY	DISCOURTEOUS	MINISTRATION
METROPOLITAN	TERRITORIALS	PSYCHOPATHIC	DRINKDRIVING	MISAPPREHEND

MISREPRESENT	UNRESTRICTED	HEADMISTRESS	UNACCUSTOMED	FORTUITOUSLY
MOISTURIZING	UNRETURNABLE	HELPLESSNESS	UNCLASSIFIED	FREIGHTLINER
MOUTHBROODER	UNSURPRISING	HETEROSEXUAL	UNIVERSALIST	FRUMENTATION
MULTIGRAVIDA	UNUTTERABLES	HETEROSOMATA	UNSATISFYING	GENTLETAMPER
NORTHERNMOST	VEHMGERICHTE	HOPELESSNESS	ABSQUATULATE	GIBRALTARIAN
NYCTITROPISM	VITUPERATION	IMPERISHABLE	ACCUSATORIAL	GLADIATORIAL
OBLITERATION	VITUPERATIVE	IMPRESSIVELY	AGALMATOLITE	GONADOTROPIN
OBSTETRICIAN	VOCIFERATION	INACCESSIBLE	ALIMENTATIVE	HAMBLETONIAN
OCTASTROPHIC	VOCIFEROUSLY	INADMISSIBLE	AMARANTACEAE	HEARTSTRINGS
OVERSTRAINED	WALLYDRAIGLE	INCREASINGLY	AMPHISTOMOUS	HEREDITAMENT
PANPHARMACON	WEATHERPROOF	INDIGESTIBLE	ANDROSTERONE	HEREDITARIAN
PEDIATRICIAN	WOODBURYTYPE	INTRANSIGENT	ANTIMETABOLE	HUMANITARIAN
PERICARDITIS	ACQUIESCENCE	INTRANSITIVE	APFELSTRUDEL	ILLEGITIMACY
PERIPHRASTIC	ADMINISTRATE	IRRESISTIBLE	ARISTOTELEAN	ILLEGITIMATE
PERPETRATION	ADMONISHMENT	LABOURSAVING	ASYMMETRICAL	IMPENETRABLE
PERSPIRATION	AGGRESSIVELY	LATIROSTRATE	ATTRACTIVELY	IMPLANTATION
PHILHARMONIC	AGRIBUSINESS	LIFELESSNESS	AUGMENTATION	IMPOLITENESS
PHOTOGRAPHER	ARBORESCENCE	LISTLESSNESS	AUGMENTATIVE	INCRUSTATION
PHOTOGRAPHIC	ARFVEDSONITE	LONGDISTANCE	AUSCULTATION	INESCUTCHEON
PHOTOGRAVURE	ASTONISHMENT	LUMINESCENCE	AUTHENTICATE	INEXACTITUDE
PLASTERSTONE	AWAYABSOLUTE	LUMINISCENCE	AUTHENTICITY	INSPECTORATE
PORNOGRAPHIC	BANDERSNATCH	MALACOSTRACA	BABINGTONITE	INTERSTELLAR
PRALLTRILLER	BEACONSFIELD	MASTERSTROKE	BIRDWATCHING	INTRAUTERINE
PRIMIGRAVIDA	BLANDISHMENT	MONTESSORIAN	BLOODSTAINED	KINAESTHETIC
QUARTERFINAL	BREASTSUMMER	NARCISSISTIC	BREATHTAKING	LABANOTATION
QUARTERLIGHT	BRONTOSAURUS	NEOCLASSICAL	BUNKOSTEERER	LANCASTERIAN
QUARTERSTAFF	BUSINESSLIKE	NONEXISTENCE	CABINETMAKER	LAUREATESHIP
RADIOGRAPHER	BUTTERSCOTCH	OBSOLESCENCE	CALLISTHENES	MERCANTILISM
RECUPERATION	CARELESSNESS	OPPRESSIVELY	CARICATURIST	MISQUOTATION
RECUPERATIVE	CHASTISEMENT	ORGANISATION	CHARACTERIZE	MISSTATEMENT
REDISTRIBUTE	CHILDISHNESS	PAINLESSNESS	CHREMATISTIC	MUGGLETONIAN
REGENERATION	CHURLISHNESS	PARKINSONISM	COHABITATION	NEOPLATONISM
REGISTRATION	CIRCASSIENNE	PERSUASIVELY	COLLECTIVELY	NIMBOSTRATUS
REMEMBRANCER	CIRCUMSCRIBE	PERVERSENESS	COLLECTORATE	OBSOLETENESS
REMUNERATION	CIRCUMSTANCE	POSSESSIVELY	COLLUCTATION	OCCUPATIONAL
REMUNERATIVE	CIVILISATION	POSTMISTRESS	COMPLETENESS	OREOPITHECUS
RESTAURATEUR	CLANNISHNESS	POSTPOSITIVE	CONCENTRATED	OREOPITHEOUS
RHINORRHOEAL	CLOTHESHORSE	PREMONSTRANT	CONDUCTIVITY	ORTHOPTEROUS
SCATTERBRAIN	COMMENSURATE	PREPOSSESSED	CONFECTIONER	OVERESTIMATE
SCATTERMOUCH	COMMISSARIAT	PRIGGISHNESS	CONGRATULATE	OXYACETYLENE
SCHEHERAZADE	COMMISSIONED	PROCESSIONAL	CONSISTENTLY	PALEONTOLOGY
SELFPORTRAIT	COMMISSIONER	PROFESSIONAL	CONSTITUENCY	PANAESTHESIA
SEMICIRCULAR	COMPENSATION	PROFESSORIAL	CONSTITUENTS	PANCHATANTRA
SKUTTERUDITE	COMPENSATORY	QUINTESSENCE	CONSTITUTION	PERCEPTIVELY
SLUBBERINGLY	CONCLUSIVELY	RADIOISOTOPE	CONSULTATION	PERCEPTIVITY
SOUTHERNMOST	CONDENSATION	READJUSTMENT	CONSULTATIVE	PEREMPTORILY
SOUTHERNWOOD	CONFESSIONAL	RECKLESSNESS	CONTRITURATE	PERIOSTRACUM
STAGGERINGLY	CONQUISTADOR	REMINISCENCE	CONVENTIONAL	PERMITTIVITY
STENOGRAPHER	CONVERSATION	RESIPISCENCE	DEBILITATING	PERNOCTATION
STENTORPHONE	CZECHOSLOVAK	RESTLESSNESS	DECAPITATION	PERSISTENTLY
STOCKBREEDER	DISCONSOLATE	RUTHLESSNESS	DECORATIVELY	PHILANTHROPY
STORMTROOPER	DISPENSATION	SHEEPISHNESS	DELICATESSEN	PHILISTINISM
STUBBORNNESS	DISPOSSESSED	SHILLYSHALLY	DEMILITARIZE	PHLEBOTOMIST
SUBTERRANEAN	DISQUISITION	SNOBBISHNESS	DEMONSTRABLE	PIGMENTATION
THUNDERCLOUD	ELEEMOSYNARY	STEREOSCOPIC	DEMONSTRABLY	PLACENTIFORM
THUNDERFLASH	ENERGYSAVING	STRATOSPHERE	DEMONSTRATOR	POLYPETALOUS
THUNDERSTORM	ENHYPOSTASIA	SUBCONSCIOUS	DESSERTSPOON	POPOCATEPETL
TRANSGRESSOR	ENTOMOSTRACA	SUBLAPSARIAN	DIALECTICIAN	PRACTITIONER
UNAPPARELLED	FEARLESSNESS	SUBMISSIVELY	DISCONTENTED	PREDESTINATE
UNCONTROLLED	FIDDLESTICKS	SUCCESSFULLY	DISSERTATION	PREGUSTATION
UNDERWRITTEN	FLUORESCENCE	SUCCESSIVELY	ENTREATINGLY	PREHISTORIAN
UNDESERVEDLY	FRONTISPIECE	SUCCUSSATION	EPANORTHOSIS	PREPOSTEROUS
UNDETERMINED	GASTROSOPHER	SURPRISINGLY	EPILEPTIFORM	PRESBYTERIAN
UNEXPURGATED	GEOPHYSICIST	TACTLESSNESS	ERATOSTHENES	PRESENTATION
UNIMPORTANCE	GESELLSCHAFT	TARAMASALATA	EXHAUSTIVELY	PRESENTIMENT
UNINTERESTED	GRANDISONIAN	THERMOSTATIC	EXHIBITIONER	PREVENTATIVE
UNOBSTRUCTED	HALLANSHAKER	TIMELESSNESS	EXPLOITATION	PRODUCTIVITY
UNRESERVEDLY	HAPPENSTANCE	TITANOSAURUS	FERMENTATION	PROGESTERONE
UNRESTRAINED	HARNESSMAKER	TROCHOSPHERE	FIGURATIVELY	PROPORTIONAL

PROSTITUTION
PROTACTINIUM
PROTECTIVELY
PROTECTORATE
PROTESTATION
PYROCATECHOL
QUANTITATIVE
RECAPITULATE
RECONSTITUTE
RECREATIONAL
REDEMPTIONER
REFLECTIVITY
REMONSTRANCE
RESPECTFULLY
RESPECTIVELY
SEGMENTATION
SELFCATERING
SELFINTEREST
SEMIDETACHED
SEQUENTIALLY
SEQUESTRATOR
SESQUITERTIA
SHORTSTAFFED
SIVAPITHECUS
SOLICITATION
SOLICITOUSLY
SOPHISTICATE
SPERMATOCYTE
SPERMATOZOID
SPERMATOZOON
STATISTICIAN
STEREOTYPING
STERNUTATION
STREPITATION
STROMATOLITE
SUBCONTINENT
SUBHASTATION
SUBJECTIVELY
SUBJECTIVITY
SUBSTITUTION
SUBSTITUTIVE
SUGGESTIVELY
SUPERSTITION
SUPERSTRATUM
TAPSALTEERIE
TAPSLETEERIE
TEETERTOTTER
TELEASTHETIC
TERCENTENARY
TESTOSTERONE
THAUMATURGIC
THAUMATURGUS
THEORETICIAN
THIGMOTROPIC
THOUGHTFULLY
TOTALITARIAN
TRANSITIONAL
TRICENTENARY
UNAPPETIZING
UNDERSTAFFED
UNIDENTIFIED
VINDICTIVELY
WOLLASTONITE
XIPHISTERNUM
ACCENTUATION
AERONAUTICAL
ALPHANUMERIC
ANTINEUTRINO
ATTRIBUTABLE

BENZOQUINONE
BIELORUSSIAN
BLACKCURRANT
BYELORUSSIAN
CAMPANULARIA
CAUTIOUSNESS
CHEERFULNESS
COLLOQUIALLY
CONSEQUENCES
CONSEQUENTLY
CONSTRUCTION
CONSTRUCTIVE
CONTINUATION
CONTINUOUSLY
COVETOUSNESS
DISREPUTABLE
DRAMATURGIST
EXTINGUISHER
FAITHFULNESS
FLORICULTURE
FORCEFULNESS
FRUITFULNESS
GLUBBDUBDRIB
GRACEFULNESS
GRACIOUSNESS
GRATEFULNESS
HORTICULTURE
HYDROQUINONE
IMMEASURABLE
IMMEASURABLY
INADEQUATELY
INCALCULABLE
INDISPUTABLE
INDISPUTABLY
INFREQUENTLY
INTERRUPTION
INTRODUCTION
INTRODUCTORY
LILLIBULLERO
LILLIBURLERO
LIVERPUDLIAN
LONGITUDINAL
MANSLAUGHTER
MENSTRUATION
METALLURGIST
OVERSCUTCHED
PARTICULARLY
PEACEFULNESS
PERAMBULATOR
PISCICULTURE
POLYNEURITIS
PREREQUISITE
REPERCUSSION
REPRODUCTION
REPRODUCTIVE
SIPUNCULACEA
SPACIOUSNESS
SPECIOUSNESS
SPIRITUALISM
SPIRITUALIST
SPIRITUALITY
SPITEFULNESS
SPURIOUSNESS
STEPDAUGHTER
STRUCTURALLY
STUDIOUSNESS
SUBSEQUENTLY
SUBSTRUCTURE
SWASHBUCKLER

THANKFULNESS
THREEQUARTER
TRABECULATED
TRANSLUCENCE
TRUTHFULNESS
TUBERCULOSIS
UNCTUOUSNESS
UNDERCURRENT
UNFAVOURABLE
UNFREQUENTED
UNPREJUDICED
UNPRODUCTIVE
URTRICULARIA
VENGEFULNESS
VERMICULTURE
VOLUPTUOUSLY
WAREHOUSEMAN
WATCHFULNESS
YOUTHFULNESS
ZARATHUSTRIC
BIOFLAVONOID
CONSERVATION
CONSERVATISM
CONSERVATIVE
CONSERVATORY
CREATIVENESS
MANOEUVRABLE
PRESERVATION
PRESERVATIVE
RONCESVALLES
STRADIVARIUS
SUBSERVIENCE
TURACOVERDIN
BANTAMWEIGHT
BESSERWISSER
CHURCHWARDEN
COMMONWEALTH
DONNERWETTER
DUNNIEWASSAL
KIRSCHWASSER
MANGELWURZEL
MIDDLEWEIGHT
OVERPOWERING
PINNIEWINKLE
PRAISEWORTHY
SCREENWRITER
SCRIPTWRITER
WELTERWEIGHT
WILLIEWAUGHT
AMBIDEXTROUS
CROSSEXAMINE
UNDEREXPOSED
ACHLAMYDEOUS
CARBOHYDRATE
CATAPHYSICAL
DISCOMYCETES
FLAMBOYANTLY
HOLIDAYMAKER
HYPERPYRETIC
METAPHYSICAL
MOTORCYCLIST
ONCORHYNCHUS
SCHINDYLESIS
TETRACYCLINE
THEOPHYLLINE
CANONIZATION
CIVILIZATION
COLONIZATION
FINALIZATION

HUMANIZATION
IDEALIZATION
IMMUNIZATION
LEGALIZATION
MOBILIZATION
ORGANIZATION
PENALIZATION
POLARIZATION
URBANIZATION
VAPORIZATION

12:8

ABBREVIATION
ACCELERATION
ACCENTUATION
ACCUMULATION
ADJUDICATION
ADULTERATION
AERODYNAMICS
AGATHODAIMON
ALEXIPHARMIC
ALIMENTATIVE
ALLITERATION
AMALGAMATION
AMARANTACEAE
AMELIORATION
AMPHISBAENIC
ANECATHARSIS
ANNIHILATION
ANNUNCIATION
ANTANANARIVO
ANTICIPATION
ANTICIPATORY
ANTIMACASSAR
ANTIMETABOLE
APLANOGAMETE
APOLLINARIAN
APPOGGIATURA
APPRECIATION
APPRECIATIVE
ARTICULATION
ASPHYXIATION
ASSIMILATION
ATHEROMATOUS
AUGMENTATION
AUGMENTATIVE
AUSCULTATION
AUSTRALASIAN
BACCHANALIAN
BACKBREAKING
BAIRNSFATHER
BANANALANDER
BICAMERALISM
BLOODSTAINED
BOOBYTRAPPED
BREATHTAKING
BRONTOSAURUS
CALLIGRAPHIC
CALUMNIATION
CANCELLATION
CANONIZATION
CAPITULATION
CARPETBAGGER
CARPOPHAGOUS
CARTOGRAPHER
CARTOGRAPHIC
CHEESEPARING
CHILDBEARING
CHIROPRACTIC

CHIROPRACTOR
CHLORINATION
CHRISTIANITY
CHURCHWARDEN
CIVILISATION
CIVILIZATION
CLAUDICATION
CODIFICATION
COHABITATION
COLLUCTATION
COLONIZATION
COMMENDATION
COMMENDATORY
COMMISSARIAT
COMPELLATION
COMPENSATION
COMPENSATORY
COMPLICATION
COMPURGATION
CONCILIATION
CONCILIATORY
CONDEMNATION
CONDENSATION
CONFIRMATION
CONFIRMATORY
CONFISCATION
CONGREGATION
CONSECRATION
CONSERVATION
CONSERVATISM
CONSERVATIVE
CONSERVATORY
CONSOCIATION
CONSPIRACIST
CONSTIPATION
CONSULTATION
CONSULTATIVE
CONSUMMATION
CONTIGNATION
CONTINUATION
CONVERSATION
CONVIVIALITY
COORDINATION
CRISTOBALITE
CROSSEXAMINE
DEAMBULATORY
DEASPIRATION
DEBILITATING
DECAPITATION
DECELERATION
DECENTRALISE
DECENTRALIZE
DEGENERATION
DELIBERATELY
DELIBERATION
DEMILITARIZE
DENOMINATION
DENUNCIATION
DEPOPULATION
DEPRECIATION
DEPRECIATORY
DEREGULATION
DESIDERATIVE
DICHROMATISM
DILAPIDATION
DISACCHARIDE
DISAPPEARING
DISCOURAGING
DISENCHANTED

DISPENSATION	IMPREGNATION	PASSEMEASURE	SEGMENTATION	COUNTERBLAST
DISSERTATION	INACCURATELY	PASSIONATELY	SEMIDETACHED	FEATHERBRAIN
DISSOCIATION	INADEQUATELY	PENALIZATION	SEXAGENARIAN	GLUBBDUBDRIB
DISTILLATION	INAUGURATION	PERIPHRASTIC	SHORTSTAFFED	HELIOGABALUS
DOLPHINARIUM	INCINERATION	PERMANGANATE	SILVERHAIRED	INVERTEBRATE
DUNNIEWASSAL	INCRUSTATION	PERNOCTATION	SINGLEHANDED	NEUROFIBROMA
ECCLESIASTES	INFILTRATION	PERPETRATION	SLEDGEHAMMER	PURPOSEBUILT
ECCLESIASTIC	INFLAMMATION	PERSPICACITY	SOLICITATION	SCATTERBRAIN
EMANCIPATION	INFLAMMATORY	PERSPIRATION	SPHACELATION	SERVICEBERRY
EMASCULATION	INGRATIATING	PERTURBATION	SPIRITUALISM	SHUFFLEBOARD
ENERGYSAVING	INNOMINABLES	PHOTOGRAPHER	SPIRITUALIST	SPURTLEBLADE
ENTHUSIASTIC	INORDINATELY	PHOTOGRAPHIC	SPIRITUALITY	STELLENBOSCH
EPACRIDACEAE	INSEMINATION	PHOTOGRAVURE	SPREADEAGLED	UNNEIGHBORLY
EPISCOPALIAN	INSTALLATION	PHYTOPHAGOUS	STANISLAVSKI	ACADEMICALLY
EPISTOLATERS	INSTAURATION	PIGMENTATION	STENOGRAPHER	ACQUIESCENCE
EPITHALAMION	INTENERATION	PITTERPATTER	STERNUTATION	AMBULANCEMAN
EPITHALAMIUM	INTERCHANGED	PLEIOCHASIUM	STONECHATTER	ANTIAIRCRAFT
EQUIVOCATION	INTERGLACIAL	POLARIZATION	STRADIVARIUS	ANTIBACCHIUS
EQUIVOCATORY	INTIMIDATING	POLICYMAKING	STRAITJACKET	APPENDECTOMY
ESSENTIALITY	INTIMIDATION	POLYPETALOUS	STREPITATION	APPENDICITIS
ETHEROMANIAC	INTOXICATING	PORNOGRAPHIC	STRIDULATION	ARBORESCENCE
EXACERBATION	INTOXICATION	POTENTIALITY	STRONTIANITE	ARCHILOCHIAN
EXAGGERATION	INVALIDATION	POWERSHARING	SUBARRHATION	ARCHITECTURE
EXASPERATING	INVIGORATING	PRACTICALITY	SUBHASTATION	ARTIODACTYLA
EXASPERATION	INVIGORATION	PREGUSTATION	SUBLAPSARIAN	ARTISTICALLY
EXCRUCIATING	IRREGULARITY	PRESENTATION	SUBMINIATURE	ASSUEFACTION
EXCRUCIATION	KATZENJAMMER	PRESERVATION	SUBSIDIARITY	BEAUMARCHAIS
EXHILARATING	KINDERGARTEN	PRESERVATIVE	SUBTERRANEAN	BIRDWATCHING
EXHILARATION	KIRSCHWASSER	PREVENTATIVE	SUCCUSSATION	BLUESTOCKING
EXPLOITATION	KLEPTOMANIAC	PRIMIGRAVIDA	SULPHONAMIDE	BUTTERSCOTCH
FAINTHEARTED	LABANOTATION	PRINCIPALITY	SUPERCHARGED	CAMIKNICKERS
FERMENTATION	LABOURSAVING	PROCLAMATION	SUPERCHARGER	CIRCUMSCRIBE
FINALIZATION	LEGALIZATION	PROGYMNASIUM	SUPPLICATION	COMMUNICABLE
FLAGELLATION	LEGIONNAIRES	PROLONGATION	SYNTAGMATITE	CONSTRICTION
FLAMBOYANTLY	LEGITIMATELY	PROMULGATION	TAMARICACEAE	CONSTRUCTION
FLUORIDATION	LIGHTHEARTED	PROPHYLACTIC	TARAMASALATA	CONSTRUCTIVE
FLUVIOMARINE	LITHOGRAPHIC	PROPITIATION	TECHNICALITY	CONTUMACIOUS
FRUMENTATION	LUXULLIANITE	PROPITIATORY	THEREAGAINST	COUNTERCLAIM
GAMOSEPALOUS	MACMILLANITE	PROTESTATION	THREEQUARTER	CROSSSECTION
GENTLETAMPER	MALFORMATION	PROTHALAMION	TITANOSAURUS	CYMOTRICHOUS
GIBRALTARIAN	MALLOPHAGOUS	PROTHALAMIUM	TOTALITARIAN	DISASSOCIATE
GONDWANALAND	MANIPULATION	PROTOPLASMAL	TRADESCANTIA	DISCOMYCETES
GROSSULARITE	MANIPULATIVE	PROTOPLASMIC	TRIUMPHANTLY	DISFRANCHISE
HEREDITAMENT	MASTURBATION	PSYCHOPATHIC	TURBOCHARGER	DISINFECTANT
HEREDITARIAN	MECHITHARIST	PURIFICATION	UNDERSTAFFED	DISREPECTFUL
HETEROGAMETE	MENSTRUATION	QUANTITATIVE	UNDISCHARGED	DIVERTICULUM
HIEROGRAMMAT	MINISTRATION	RADIOGRAPHER	UNIVERSALIST	DOGMATICALLY
HIEROPHANTIC	MISDEMEANOUR	RAMIFICATION	UNPOPULARITY	DOMESTICATED
HILDEBRANDIC	MISQUOTATION	RATIFICATION	UNRESTRAINED	DRAMATICALLY
HIPPOCRATISE	MOBILIZATION	RECUPERATION	UNUTTERABLES	ECONOMICALLY
HOMOEOPATHIC	MODIFICATION	RECUPERATIVE	URBANIZATION	ECSTATICALLY
HUMANITARIAN	MULTIGRAVIDA	REGENERATION	VAPORIZATION	ELECTRICALLY
HUMANIZATION	MUNICIPALITY	REGISTRATION	VERIFICATION	EMPHATICALLY
HYDROGRAPHER	NEPENTHACEAE	REJUVENATION	VETERINARIAN	ESTHETICALLY
HYMNOGRAPHER	NOMENCLATURE	REMEMBRANCER	VILIFICATION	EXSERVICEMAN
IAMBOGRAPHER	NONAGENARIAN	REMUNERATION	VILLEGIATURA	FLUORESCENCE
ICONOCLASTIC	NONCHALANTLY	REMUNERATIVE	VITUPERATION	FRANKINCENSE
IDEALIZATION	NOTIFICATION	RENUNCIATION	VITUPERATIVE	GALLINACEOUS
ILLOGICALITY	NYMPHOMANIAC	REPATRIATION	VOCIFERATION	GEOLOGICALLY
ILLUMINATING	OBLITERATION	RESTAURATEUR	WALLYDRAIGLE	GERONTOCRACY
ILLUMINATION	OCTOGENARIAN	RETICULATION	WELLBALANCED	GESELLSCHAFT
ILLUSTRATION	OPINIONATIVE	RONCESVALLES	WHIMSICALITY	HANDKERCHIEF
ILLUSTRATIVE	ORGANISATION	SAUROGNATHAE	WHOLEHEARTED	HERMETICALLY
IMMACULATELY	ORGANIZATION	SCANDINAVIAN	WILLIEWAUGHT	HISTORICALLY
IMMODERATELY	OSSIFICATION	SCHEHERAZADE	WINTERHALTER	HORRIFICALLY
IMMODERATION	OVERSTRAINED	SCHOOLMASTER	YELLOWHAMMER	HYGIENICALLY
IMMUNIZATION	PACIFICATION	SCRIMSHANDER	ANTIBARBARUS	HYPNOTICALLY
IMPARTIALITY	PANCHATANTRA	SCRIMSHANKER	CLAPPERBOARD	HYPOTHECATOR
IMPLANTATION	PANTOPHAGOUS	SECTARIANISM	COLLYWOBBLES	HYSTERECTOMY

HYSTERICALLY	SARDONICALLY	ACETALDEHYDE	GASTARBEITER	RELENTLESSLY
ICHTHYOCOLLA	SATISFACTION	ACKNOWLEDGED	GOBBLEDEGOOK	RENOUNCEMENT
IDIOSYNCRASY	SATISFACTORY	AMPHITHEATER	GOVERNMENTAL	RESETTLEMENT
IMPERFECTION	SCLERENCHYMA	AMPHITHEATRE	HAMMERHEADED	RESPONDENTIA
IMPERFECTIVE	SEMANTICALLY	ANAESTHETISE	HETEROSEXUAL	SCHNEIDERIAN
INAPPLICABLE	SEMICIRCULAR	ANAESTHETIST	HIPPOCREPIAN	SCLERODERMIA
INAUSPICIOUS	SEMIPRECIOUS	ANAESTHETIZE	HOUSEBREAKER	SELFADHESIVE
INERADICABLE	SHAMEFACEDLY	ANCHORPERSON	HOUSEKEEPING	SELFCATERING
INESCUTCHEON	SIGNIFICANCE	ANDROSTERONE	HYDROTHERAPY	SELFINTEREST
INEXPLICABLE	SPECIFICALLY	ANNOUNCEMENT	HYPNOTHERAPY	SEPTUAGESIMA
INEXPLICABLY	SPORADICALLY	ARISTOTELEAN	IMPOLITENESS	SERASKIERATE
INEXTRICABLE	STEEPLECHASE	AROMATHERAPY	INCOHERENTLY	SESQUITERTIA
INEXTRICABLY	STEREOSCOPIC	ATMOSPHERICS	INCOMPLETELY	SHIRTSLEEVES
INSUFFICIENT	STUPEFACTION	AUSTRONESIAN	INDISCRETION	SHORTSLEEVED
INSURRECTION	SUBCONSCIOUS	BANTAMWEIGHT	INFREQUENTLY	SINGLEDECKER
INTELLECTUAL	SUBSTRUCTURE	BARORECEPTOR	INFRINGEMENT	SPELLCHECKER
INTERJECTION	SUPERNACULUM	BENEVOLENTLY	INSTRUMENTAL	SPIEGELEISEN
INTERLOCUTOR	SWASHBUCKLER	BENZOPHENONE	INTERPRETING	SPLENOMEGALY
INTERSECTION	SYMBOLICALLY	BETHLEHEMITE	INTERSPERSED	SPOKESPERSON
INTRODUCTION	TERRIFICALLY	BIBLIOPEGIST	INTERSTELLAR	SPRECHGESANG
INTRODUCTORY	TETRACYCLINE	BRACHYCEPHAL	INTRAUTERINE	STERNWHEELER
IRRESPECTIVE	THEATRICALLY	BREATHLESSLY	IRREVERENTLY	STOCKBREEDER
JURISDICTION	THUNDERCLOUD	BRICKFIELDER	LANCASTERIAN	STRANGLEHOLD
KALISTOCRACY	TRALATICIOUS	BUCKLEBEGGAR	LAUREATESHIP	STRANGLEWEED
LAMELLICORNE	TRANSLUCENCE	BUNKOSTEERER	LEPIDOMELANE	SUBSEQUENTLY
LEIOTRICHOUS	UNATTRACTIVE	CALCEAMENTUM	MACABERESQUE	SUFFICIENTLY
LIQUEFACTION	UNPRODUCTIVE	CAMERAPERSON	MARRIAGEABLE	TAPSALTEERIE
LUMINESCENCE	UNSUSPECTING	CANTANKEROUS	METHOTREXATE	TAPSLETEERIE
LUMINISCENCE	VENEPUNCTURE	CARDINDEXING	MICROBREWERY	TERCENTENARY
MAGNETICALLY	ACHLAMYDEOUS	CARDIOMEGALY	MIDDLEWEIGHT	TESTOSTERONE
MAGNIFICENCE	AMBASSADRESS	CHARACTERIZE	MISAPPREHEND	THREADNEEDLE
MAJESTICALLY	BACKWARDNESS	CHASTISEMENT	MISPLACEMENT	TRADESPEOPLE
MECHANICALLY	BACKWOODSMAN	CHEMOTHERAPY	MISREPRESENT	TRANSGRESSOR
MERETRICIOUS	CARBOHYDRATE	COINCIDENTAL	MISSTATEMENT	TRANSOCEANIC
MERITRICIOUS	CONSOLIDATED	COMMENCEMENT	MOSBOLLETJIE	TRICENTENARY
METHODICALLY	CONSOLIDATOR	COMMONWEALTH	MUDDLEHEADED	TURACOVERDIN
MNEMOTECHNIC	DEMIMONDAINE	COMPLACENTLY	NEVERTHELESS	UINTATHERIUM
MOTORCYCLIST	DISCOMEDUSAE	COMPLETENESS	NEWSPAPERMAN	UNAPPARELLED
NEUROTICALLY	EVENHANDEDLY	CONCURRENTLY	OBSOLETENESS	UNCHALLENGED
NONDIRECTIVE	GRASSWIDOWER	CONGLOMERATE	OBSTREPEROUS	UNCHANGEABLE
NONOBJECTIVE	HOBBIDIDANCE	CONSEQUENCES	OMBUDSPERSON	UNFREQUENTED
OBSOLESCENCE	IMPROVIDENCE	CONSEQUENTLY	ORIENTEERING	UNINTERESTED
PANDANACEOUS	INDEBTEDNESS	CONSISTENTLY	ORTHOPAEDICS	UNMANAGEABLE
PANTISOCRACY	INDEPENDENCE	CONVENIENCES	ORTHOPAEDIST	USERFRIENDLY
PATHETICALLY	INFORMIDABLE	CONVENIENTLY	ORTHOPTEROUS	VALENCIENNES
PEDANTICALLY	INTERMEDIARY	CRASSAMENTUM	OUTMANOEUVRE	WELTERWEIGHT
PERIODICALLY	INTERMEDIATE	CREATIVENESS	OVERPOWERING	WHIGMALEERIE
PERTINACIOUS	LAMPADEDROMY	CURMUDGEONLY	PALUDAMENTUM	WICKETKEEPER
PERVICACIOUS	LIVERPUDLIAN	DELICATESSEN	PARANTHELIUM	XIPHISTERNUM
PETRIFACTION	LONGITUDINAL	DEPARTMENTAL	PARENTHESIZE	AFTEREFFECTS
PHONETICALLY	MACROPODIDAE	DISAGREEABLE	PEACEKEEPING	BEACONSFIELD
PREDILECTION	MASSPRODUCED	DISAGREEMENT	PERSISTENTLY	CHESTERFIELD
PRESTRICTION	NEWFOUNDLAND	DISCONCERTED	PERVERSENESS	DISDAINFULLY
PREVARICATOR	NOCONFIDENCE	DISCONNECTED	POPOCATEPETL	MEANINGFULLY
PROLIFICALLY	NONRESIDENCE	DISCONTENTED	POSTPONEMENT	PASSIONFRUIT
PTERODACTYLE	OUTBUILDINGS	DISPLACEMENT	PREPONDERANT	PURPOSEFULLY
PUTREFACTION	PERICARDITIS	DISPOSSESSED	PREPONDERATE	QUARTERFINAL
QUIXOTICALLY	PHYTONADIONE	DONNERWETTER	PREPONDERENT	RESPECTFULLY
RECIPROCALLY	POLYSYNDETON	DOUBLEDECKER	PREPOSSESSED	SUCCESSFULLY
RECOLLECTION	POSTGRADUATE	EFFORTLESSLY	PREPOSTEROUS	THOUGHTFULLY
REMINISCENCE	PREPAREDNESS	EMBEZZLEMENT	PRESBYTERIAN	THUNDERFLASH
REPRODUCTION	RETARDEDNESS	EMBROIDERESS	PROFICIENTLY	UNSATISFYING
REPRODUCTIVE	SURROUNDINGS	ENCIRCLEMENT	PROFITEERING	ADVANTAGEOUS
RESIPISCENCE	TETRAHEDRITE	ENTANGLEMENT	PROGESTERONE	ADVANTAGIOUS
RESURRECTION	UNCONSIDERED	ENTREPRENEUR	PYROCATECHOL	ASTROLOGICAL
RHYTHMICALLY	UNPREJUDICED	ESTRANGEMENT	QUADRAGESIMA	BOONDOGGLING
RHYTIDECTOMY	WRETCHEDNESS	EXCHANGEABLE	RACKETEERING	CARCINOGENIC
ROMANTICALLY	ACCOUCHEMENT	EXPERIMENTAL	RADIOTHERAPY	CLEARSIGHTED
SADISTICALLY	ACCOUTREMENT	FORMALDEHYDE	RECHARGEABLE	CLEISTOGAMIC

DISINTEGRATE	IMPERISHABLE	COMMERCIALLY	INTRANSIGENT	SLOVENLINESS
DRESSINGDOWN	KINAESTHETIC	COMMISSIONED	INTRANSITIVE	SLUBBERINGLY
ETHNOLOGICAL	MOONLIGHTING	COMMISSIONER	INVISIBILITY	SOPHISTICATE
ETYMOLOGICAL	NONALCOHOLIC	COMPROMISING	IRASCIBILITY	SPINECHILLER
ETYMOLOGICON	ONYCHOPHORAN	CONCLUSIVELY	IRRITABILITY	STAGGERINGLY
EXTRAVAGANCE	OREOPITHECUS	CONDUCTIVITY	ISHMAELITISH	STATISTICIAN
EXTRAVAGANZA	OREOPITHEOUS	CONFECTIONER	JENNYSPINNER	STEALTHINESS
FARTHINGLAND	PANAESTHESIA	CONFESSIONAL	JOURNALISTIC	STRONGMINDED
FOOTSLOGGING	PERSULPHURIC	CONTERMINOUS	KLIPSPRINGER	SUBCOMMITTEE
GENEALOGICAL	PHILANTHROPY	CONTRARINESS	LYMANTRIIDAE	SUBCONTINENT
INCORRIGIBLE	POGONOPHORAN	CONVENTIONAL	MALLEABILITY	SUBJECTIVELY
INCORRIGIBLY	PRIGGISHNESS	CONVINCINGLY	MALNUTRITION	SUBJECTIVITY
INTELLIGENCE	PYROTECHNICS	DECORATIVELY	MERCANTILISM	SUBMISSIVELY
INTELLIGIBLE	QUADRAPHONIC	DEHUMIDIFIER	MICROCLIMATE	SUBSERVIENCE
INTERROGATOR	RETRENCHMENT	DERESTRICTED	MILITARISTIC	SUCCESSIVELY
INVESTIGATOR	RHINORRHOEAL	DESIRABILITY	MOISTURIZING	SUGGESTIVELY
KERAUNOGRAPH	ROOMINGHOUSE	DIALECTICIAN	MUCILAGINOUS	SUPERSTITION
MANSLAUGHTER	SCHOPENHAUER	DILATORINESS	MULTIPLICITY	SURPRISINGLY
MARCONIGRAPH	SHEEPISHNESS	DIPRIONIDIAN	NARCISSISTIC	SURREALISTIC
MINDBOGGLING	SHILLYSHALLY	DISAPPOINTED	NATURALISTIC	THANKSGIVING
MYTHOLOGICAL	SITTLICHKEIT	DISCIPLINARY	NAVIGABILITY	THEORETICIAN
NEUROLOGICAL	SIVAPITHECUS	DISCOMFITURE	NEUROSCIENCE	THICKSKINNED
OPISTHOGRAPH	SNOBBISHNESS	DISCRIMINATE	NONCOMMITTAL	TRACTABILITY
ORNITHOGALUM	STEREOPHONIC	DISOBEDIENCE	OBSTETRICIAN	TRANSITIONAL
PATHOLOGICAL	TELEASTHETIC	DISQUISITION	OCCUPATIONAL	UNACQUAINTED
PETTIFOGGERS	THESMOPHORIA	DRINKDRIVING	OLDFASHIONED	UNAPPETIZING
PETTIFOGGERY	THOROUGHBRED	ECCENTRICITY	OPPRESSIVELY	UNCLASSIFIED
PETTIFOGGING	THOROUGHFARE	ENCHEIRIDION	OVERESTIMATE	UNDERSKINKER
PHILOLOGICAL	THOROUGHNESS	ENTERPRISING	PARAMILITARY	UNDERWRITTEN
PRIZEFIGHTER	TRICHOPHYTON	ENTERTAINING	PEDIATRICIAN	UNDIMINISHED
REDINTEGRATE	ULOTRICHALES	ENTREATINGLY	PERCEPTIVELY	UNIDENTIFIED
SACRILEGIOUS	UNDERACHIEVE	EPILEPTIFORM	PERCEPTIVITY	UNOFFICIALLY
SHORTSIGHTED	WOLSTENHOLME	EULENSPIEGEL	PERMEABILITY	UNPRINCIPLED
SOCIOLOGICAL	ACCOMPLISHED	EXCITABILITY	PERMITTIVITY	UNRESTRICTED
STEPDAUGHTER	ADAPTABILITY	EXHAUSTIVELY	PERSUASIVELY	UNSURPRISING
STOCKINGETTE	ADVISABILITY	EXHIBITIONER	PHILISTINISM	VEHMGERICHTE
STUDDINGSAIL	AGGRESSIVELY	EXSUFFLICATE	PINNIEWINKLE	VINDICTIVELY
SUPERHIGHWAY	AGRIBUSINESS	EXTINGUISHER	PLACENTIFORM	WEIGHTLIFTER
TAUTOLOGICAL	ANEMOPHILOUS	FEHMGERICHTE	PLAUSIBILITY	HOMESICKNESS
TRANSMIGRATE	ANTAGONISTIC	FIGURATIVELY	POSSESSIVELY	UNMISTAKABLE
TRANSMOGRIFY	ANTEMERIDIAN	FRAUENDIENST	POSTLIMINARY	ANDOUILLETTE
UNEXPURGATED	ANTHELMINTIC	FRIENDLINESS	POSTPOSITIVE	ARCHIPELAGOS
ADMONISHMENT	ANTONINIANUS	FUSTILLIRIAN	PRACTICIONER	ARTHROPLASTY
ANAMORPHOSIS	ARTIFICIALLY	GENETHLIACON	PRACTITIONER	BERTHOLLETIA
ANTIRACHITIC	ASPARAGINASE	GEOMETRICIAN	PRALLTRILLER	BIPROPELLANT
APPROACHABLE	ATTRACTIVELY	GEOPHYSICIST	PRECONDITION	BREASTPLOUGH
ARISTOPHANES	AUTHENTICATE	GERIATRICIAN	PREDESTINATE	BREATHALYSER
ASTONISHMENT	AUTHENTICITY	HAEMOPHILIAC	PREREQUISITE	CAMPANULARIA
BIOGRAPHICAL	AVAILABILITY	HAIRSPLITTER	PRESENTIMENT	CHEERFULNESS
BLANDISHMENT	AWEINSPIRING	HYDROQUINONE	PROCESSIONAL	CHITTERLINGS
CALLISTHENES	AYUNTAMIENTO	HYPERACIDITY	PRODUCTIVITY	CONTROLLABLE
CHARTERHOUSE	BAMBOCCIADES	IDENTIFIABLE	PROFESSIONAL	COSMOPOLITAN
CHILDISHNESS	BENZOQUINONE	ILLEGIBILITY	PROPORTIONAL	CREMAILLIÈRE
CHURLISHNESS	BESSERWISSER	ILLEGITIMACY	PROTACTINIUM	CUCKOOFLOWER
CLANNISHNESS	BIOCHEMISTRY	ILLEGITIMATE	PROTECTIVELY	CZECHOSLOVAK
CLOTHESHORSE	BLOODTHIRSTY	IMMUTABILITY	PROVERBIALLY	DOUBLEGLAZED
DIENCEPHALON	CAMPODEIFORM	IMPOVERISHED	PUMPERNICKEL	ELECTROLYSIS
ENCROACHMENT	CAPERCAILLIE	IMPRESSIVELY	QUANTIFIABLE	ESPAGNOLETTE
ENTRENCHMENT	CAPERCAILZIE	INCAPABILITY	RECONSTITUTE	ETEPIMELETIC
EPANORTHOSIS	CARTHAGINIAN	INCAPACITATE	RECREATIONAL	FAITHFULNESS
EPENCEPHALON	CEREMONIALLY	INCREASINGLY	REDEMPTIONER	FLORICULTURE
ERATOSTHENES	CHAUVINISTIC	INDEFINITELY	REDISTRIBUTE	FORCEFULNESS
GEOGRAPHICAL	CHLOROPICRIN	INDOCTRINATE	REFLECTIVITY	FREIGHTLINER
HAEMORRHOIDS	CHREMATISTIC	INDUSTRIALLY	REHABILITATE	FRUITFULNESS
HALLANSHAKER	CIRCASSIENNE	INEFFICIENCY	RESPECTIVELY	GRACEFULNESS
HETEROPHORIA	CIRCUMCISION	INEXACTITUDE	SCOPOPHILIAC	GRATEFULNESS
HIERARCHICAL	CLASSIFIABLE	INEXPERIENCE	SEQUENTIALLY	HAPPYGOLUCKY
HISTIOPHORUS	COLLECTIVELY	INFELICITOUS	SHIRTWAISTER	HETEROCLITIC
HOUSETOHOUSE	COLLOQUIALLY	INSOLUBILITY	SINGLEMINDED	HETEROPLASIA

HORTICULTURE	URTRICULARIA	AWARDWINNING	PANTECHNICON	AWAYABSOLUTE
HYDROCHLORIC	VENGEFULNESS	BANDERSNATCH	PAPILIONIDAE	BABINGTONITE
HYPERBOLICAL	VERMICULTURE	BICENTENNIAL	PARAMAGNETIC	BACTERIOLOGY
INCALCULABLE	WATCHFULNESS	BRILLIANTINE	PARSIMONIOUS	BACTERIOSTAT
INCONSOLABLE	YOUTHFULNESS	CARLOVINGIAN	PARTISANSHIP	BARBERMONGER
INDISSOLUBLE	ALPHANUMERIC	CHAIRMANSHIP	PERADVENTURE	BERTILLONAGE
INTERRELATED	ANASTIGMATIC	CHAMPIONSHIP	PERGAMENEOUS	BIOFLAVONOID
LALLAPALOOZA	ANTIMNEMONIC	CHORIZONTIST	PERIODONTICS	BOISTEROUSLY
LILLIBULLERO	ASTRONOMICAL	COLOQUINTIDA	PESTILENTIAL	BRANCHIOPODA
MARSEILLAISE	BLABBERMOUTH	CONFIDENTIAL	PHENOMENALLY	CARDIOLOGIST
MERVEILLEUSE	CABINETMAKER	CONTAMINATED	PHILODENDRON	CATASTROPHIC
MESOTHELIOMA	CATHETOMETER	CONVEYANCING	PHYCOXANTHIN	CHEESEMONGER
METROPOLITAN	CHRESTOMATHY	CRASHLANDING	PHYTOBENTHOS	CHONDRIOSOME
MINDFULLNESS	CLAVICEMBALO	CROSSBENCHER	PLECTOGNATHI	COCCIDIOSTAT
MITRAILLEUSE	COMMANDMENTS	DEUTERANOPIA	POSTPRANDIAL	COLLECTORATE
MONOSYLLABIC	COSCINOMANCY	DIFFERENTIAL	PREDOMINANCE	COMPANIONWAY
MONOSYLLABLE	COUNTERMARCH	DIPLOGENESIS	PREFERENTIAL	CONTEMPORARY
MULTICOLORED	DIAGRAMMATIC	DISADVANTAGE	PRESIDENTIAL	CONTINUOUSLY
OSTEOMALACIA	DIVERTIMENTO	DISINCENTIVE	PRIZEWINNING	COSTERMONGER
OVERWHELMING	ENANTIOMORPH	DISINGENUOUS	PROPAGANDISM	COURAGEOUSLY
PARTICOLORED	EPIGRAMMATIC	DISORGANIZED	PROPAGANDIST	DAGUERROTYPE
PARTICULARLY	ERYTHROMYCIN	DISORIENTATE	PROVIDENTIAL	DEFLATIONARY
PASQUEFLOWER	EXTENSOMETER	DORSIVENTRAL	QUESTIONABLE	DENDROLOGIST
PEACEFULNESS	FLITTERMOUSE	ENTEROPNEUST	QUINQUENNIAL	DISASTROUSLY
PECTORILOQUY	FRANKALMOIGN	FOTHERINGHAY	RELATIONSHIP	DISCONSOLATE
PEDICELLARIA	GALVANOMETER	FRACTIONALLY	RHADAMANTHUS	DYSTELEOLOGY
PERAMBULATOR	GIGANTOMACHY	FUNCTIONALLY	RHODODENDRON	EAVESDROPPER
PERSONALIZED	GOOSEPIMPLES	FUNCTIONLESS	SALESMANSHIP	EDUCATIONIST
PHOSPHOLIPID	HAEMATEMESIS	FUNDAMENTALS	SIMULTANEOUS	EGYPTOLOGIST
PISCICULTURE	HARNESSMAKER	GALLIVANTING	SOUTHERNMOST	ENTEROMORPHA
POINTILLISME	HELLGRAMMITE	GAMESMANSHIP	SOUTHERNWOOD	ENTOMOLOGIST
POLYSYLLABIC	HEPHTHEMIMER	GRANDMONTINE	STREPTONEURA	EPIPHENOMENA
POLYSYLLABLE	HEROICOMICAL	GUARDIANSHIP	STROPHANTHUS	EPISTEMOLOGY
PREMAXILLARY	HOLIDAYMAKER	HALLUCINOGEN	STUBBORNNESS	ESCAPOLOGIST
QUADRIPLEGIA	IRREDEEMABLE	HORSEMANSHIP	SUBCUTANEOUS	ESCHSCHOLZIA
QUARTERLIGHT	LOXODROMICAL	HYPERTENSION	SUPERANNUATE	EVOLUTIONARY
RECORDPLAYER	MELODRAMATIC	HYPOCHONDRIA	TESTAMENTARY	EXTENSIONIST
ROLLERBLADER	MERISTEMATIC	IMPERSONALLY	TOBACCONISTS	EXTORTIONATE
ROLLERBLADES	MILLILAMBERT	IMPERSONATOR	TRANSCENDENT	FASTIDIOUSLY
SCHINDYLESIS	NEPHELOMETER	IMPERTINENCE	TRANSPONTINE	FIRSTFOOTING
SCINTILLATOR	NONFLAMMABLE	IMPRISONMENT	ULTRAMONTANE	FORTUITOUSLY
SELFEMPLOYED	NYCHTHEMERON	INCONTINENCE	UNATTAINABLE	GASTROSOPHER
SESQUIALTERA	PANCHROMATIC	INCONVENIENT	UNCONVINCING	GLADIATORIAL
SHAREHOLDING	PANPHARMACON	INDECLINABLE	UNDERPINNING	GLOBETROTTER
SHIPBUILDING	PHILHARMONIC	INDISTINCTLY	UNIMAGINABLE	GLYCOPROTEIN
SIPUNCULACEA	POTICHOMANIA	INFOTAINMENT	UNOBTAINABLE	GLYNDEBOURNE
SLEEPWALKING	PROGRAMMABLE	INHARMONIOUS	UNPARDONABLE	GRANDISONIAN
SLOCKDOLAGER	PROLEGOMENON	INNATTENTIVE	UNPRETENDING	GRAPHOLOGIST
SLOCKDOLIGER	PYTHONOMORPH	INTERMINABLE	UNREASONABLE	GREENGROCERS
SLOCKDOLOGER	RISORGIMENTO	INTERMINABLY	UNRECOGNISED	GREENGROCERY
SMALLHOLDING	SCAPULIMANCY	INTERVENTION	UNRECOGNIZED	GYNECOLOGIST
SOMATOPLEURE	SCATTERMOUCH	IRRATIONALLY	UNRESPONSIVE	HAMBLETONIAN
SPITEFULNESS	SHORTCOMINGS	KILLIKINNICK	UNRETURNABLE	HAPTOTROPISM
SQUIRRELFISH	SPECTROMETER	LICKTRENCHER	UNSEASONABLE	HARMONIOUSLY
SUPERCILIARY	STREPTOMYCIN	LONGSTANDING	ABOLITIONIST	HARUMFRODITE
SUPERCILIOUS	TRIGONOMETRY	MARKSMANSHIP	ACCORDIONIST	HELIOTROPISM
SURVEILLANCE	TROCHELMINTH	MASSERANDUBA	ACCUSATORIAL	HETEROCONTAE
THANKFULNESS	TROUBLEMAKER	MICHELANGELO	AFFECTIONATE	HETEROSOMATA
THEOPHYLLINE	TURBIDIMETER	MISADVENTURE	AFORETHOUGHT	HYDROGEOLOGY
TORRICELLIAN	UNDETERMINED	NORTHERNMOST	AFTERTHOUGHT	IMMUNOLOGIST
TRABECULATED	UNECONOMICAL	OBSERVANTINE	AGALMATOLITE	INCAUTIOUSLY
TRANQUILIZER	UNFATHOMABLE	OCCASIONALLY	AMPHISTOMOUS	INFLATIONARY
TRANQUILLISE	ACCOMPANYING	ONCORHYNCHUS	ANTHROPOLOGY	INSPECTORATE
TRANQUILLITY	ADDITIONALLY	ORTHODONTICS	ANTILEGOMENA	INTUITIONISM
TRANQUILLIZE	AGAMOGENETIC	ORTHOGENESIS	ANTISTROPHON	ISOLATIONISM
TROPHALLAXIS	APPREHENSION	ORTHOTONESIS	ANTITHROMBIN	ISOLATIONIST
TRUTHFULNESS	APPREHENSIVE	PALINGENESIA	ARFVEDSONITE	LANGUEDOCIAN
TUBERCULOSIS	APPURTENANCE	PALINGENESIS	ARISTOLOCHIA	LASCIVIOUSLY
UNPARALLELED	AUTOHYPNOSIS	PANATHENAEAN	AUSPICIOUSLY	LUGUBRIOUSLY

MACHAIRODONT	STEGOPHOLIST	WEATHERPROOF	INVULNERABLE	WHIPPOORWILL
MERRYTHOUGHT	STORMTROOPER	INCONSEQUENT	LEXICOGRAPHY	WILTSHIREMAN
METICULOUSLY	STRIGIFORMES	MAGNILOQUENT	LILLIBURLERO	YORKSHIREMAN
MINERALOGIST	STRINGCOURSE	APFELSTRUDEL	LONGSHOREMAN	AECIDIOSPORE
MIRACULOUSLY	STROMATOLITE	ARISTOCRATIC	MANOEUVRABLE	AETHRIOSCOPE
MISPRONOUNCE	SUSPICIOUSLY	ARTILLERYMAN	METALLURGIST	BIELORUSSIAN
MONOTONOUSLY	TAGLIACOTIAN	ASYMMETRICAL	METAPHORICAL	BILLINGSGATE
MONTESSORIAN	TAPERECORDER	BARNSTORMING	MISANTHROPIC	BLETHERSKATE
MOUTHBROODER	TECHNOLOGIST	BATTLEGROUND	MISINTERPRET	BRAINWASHING
MUGGLETONIAN	TEETERTOTTER	BELLIGERENCY	MULTIFARIOUS	BROADCASTING
MUSICOLOGIST	THESSALONIAN	BEWILDERMENT	MUTESSARIFAT	BUSINESSLIKE
MYSTERIOUSLY	TOXICOLOGIST	BIBLIOGRAPHY	NEIGHBORHOOD	BYELORUSSIAN
NEOPLATONISM	TREMENDOUSLY	BIODIVERSITY	NIMBOSTRATUS	CARAVANSERAI
NIGHTCLOTHES	TRICHOLOGIST	BLACKCURRANT	OCEANOGRAPHY	CARELESSNESS
NUTRITIONIST	UNCONTROLLED	BLENNORRHOEA	ONEIROCRITIC	CATAPHYSICAL
NYCTITROPISM	UNDERCLOTHES	BOULEVARDIER	OSTEOPOROSIS	CAUTIOUSNESS
OBSEQUIOUSLY	UPROARIOUSLY	BREAKTHROUGH	OSTEOSARCOMA	CONTABESCENT
OCTASTROPHIC	VARICOLOURED	BUREAUCRATIC	OTHERWORLDLY	CONVALESCENT
OPHIOGLOSSUM	VENTRIPOTENT	CASSITERIDES	OVEREXERTION	CONVALESCING
ORTHORHOMBIC	VOCIFEROUSLY	CASTERBRIDGE	PASSEPARTOUT	COVETOUSNESS
OUTRAGEOUSLY	VOLUPTUOUSLY	CHOREOGRAPHY	PERIOSTRACUM	DECONGESTANT
PALEONTOLOGY	WELLINFORMED	COLLABORATOR	PERISTERONIC	DESSERTSPOON
PANDAEMONIUM	WOLLASTONITE	CONCENTRATED	PERSEVERANCE	DEUTEROSCOPY
PARALIPOMENA	ZALAMBDODONT	CONSIDERABLE	PHOSPHORENCE	DISSATISFIED
PARKINSONISM	APOSTROPHISE	CONSIDERABLY	PHOSPHORESCE	EFFERVESCENT
PEREMPTORILY	CATADIOPTRIC	COURTMARTIAL	POLYNEURITIS	EMBARRASSING
PHARMACOLOGY	CLAMJAMPHRIE	CRYPTOGRAPHY	PREDETERMINE	ENTOPLASTRON
PHLEBOTOMIST	CONSCRIPTION	DECIPHERABLE	PROLETARIATE	FEARLESSNESS
PHYSIOLOGIST	CONTRAPPOSTO	DECIPHERMENT	PROTUBERANCE	FRANKENSTEIN
PLAINCLOTHES	COUNTERPOINT	DEMONSTRABLE	REAPPEARANCE	GALLIGASKINS
POLYRIBOSOME	COUNTERPOISE	DEMONSTRABLY	RECEIVERSHIP	GLOCKENSPIEL
POSTHUMOUSLY	ELECTROPLATE	DEMONSTRATOR	REFRIGERATED	GRACIOUSNESS
POTAMOLOGIST	ENANTIOPATHY	DICTATORSHIP	REFRIGERATOR	GUILDENSTERN
PRAISEWORTHY	ENCYCLOPEDIA	DIRECTORSHIP	REMONSTRANCE	HABERDASHERS
PRECARIOUSLY	ENCYCLOPEDIC	DISEMBARRASS	SALTATORIOUS	HABERDASHERY
PRECOCIOUSLY	EVENTEMPERED	DISHONORABLE	SARSAPARILLA	HAIRDRESSERS
PREHISTORIAN	FRONTISPIECE	DISHONORABLY	SCHILLERSPAR	HAIRDRESSING
PROBATIONARY	GYMNOSOPHIST	DRAMATURGIST	SCREENWRITER	HELPLESSNESS
PRODIGIOUSLY	ICHTHYOPSIDA	ELASMOBRANCH	SCRIPTWRITER	HOPELESSNESS
PROFESSORIAL	INTERCEPTION	FRONTIERSMAN	SECRETARIATE	HUDIBRASTICS
PROPITIOUSLY	INTERRUPTION	GAINSBOROUGH	SEPTEMBRISER	INACCESSIBLE
PROTECTORATE	MACROCEPHALY	GLYPTOGRAPHY	SEQUESTRATOR	INADMISSIBLE
PROTHONOTARY	MASTIGOPHORA	GONADOTROPIN	SHORTCIRCUIT	INCANDESCENT
PSEPHOLOGIST	METALLOPHONE	GRANDPARENTS	SINANTHROPUS	INCONSISTENT
PSIPHENOMENA	METAMORPHISM	HAMARTHRITIS	SNOWBOARDING	INDEFENSIBLE
PSYCHOLOGIST	METAMORPHOSE	HEADQUARTERS	SPINSTERHOOD	INTERCESSION
PUGNACIOUSLY	MINICOMPUTER	HEARTSTRINGS	SPORTSGROUND	INTERMISSION
RADIOBIOLOGY	ONOMATOPOEIA	HEARTWARMING	STRUCTURALLY	IRREVERSIBLE
RADIOISOTOPE	ONOMATOPOEIC	HEMICHORDATA	SUPERSTRATUM	KALEIDOSCOPE
RECEPTIONIST	PHILOSOPHIZE	HENCEFORWARD	TERGIVERSATE	KLETTERSCHUE
REFLATIONARY	PRESCRIPTION	HINDQUARTERS	TERRITORIALS	LIFELESSNESS
REINVIGORATE	PRESCRIPTIVE	HOMOTHERMOUS	THIGMOTROPIC	LINCOLNSHIRE
REVERSIONARY	PROSCRIPTION	HOUSEWARMING	THIRDBOROUGH	LISTLESSNESS
RIDICULOUSLY	PROSOPOPOEIA	HYPERPYRETIC	TOGETHERNESS	MADEMOISELLE
SALVATIONIST	PTERIDOPHYTE	HYPERSARCOMA	TRANSFERABLE	MARLINESPIKE
SCANDALOUSLY	RHIPIDOPTERA	IDIOTHERMOUS	TRANSFERENCE	METAPHYSICAL
SCRUPULOUSLY	SARDANAPALUS	IMMEASURABLE	TRANSPARENCY	MYRINGOSCOPE
SCURRILOUSLY	SARRUSOPHONE	IMMEASURABLY	UMBRADARLING	NEOCLASSICAL
SECESSIONIST	SIPHONOPHORA	IMPENETRABLE	UNANSWERABLE	NONRESISTANT
SHARPSHOOTER	STENTORPHONE	INCOMPARABLE	UNAUTHORISED	NORTHEASTERN
SHOSTAKOVICH	STRATOSPHERE	INCOMPARABLY	UNAUTHORIZED	NORTHWESTERN
SOLICITOUSLY	STREPSIPTERA	INCORPORATED	UNCONVERSANT	OSCILLOSCOPE
SPATANGOIDEA	SUBSCRIPTION	INDIFFERENCE	UNDEMOCRATIC	OVERDRESSING
SPECKTIONEER	SYNADELPHITE	INSALUBRIOUS	UNDERCURRENT	PAINLESSNESS
SPELEOLOGIST	TELEGRAPHESE	INSUFFERABLE	UNDERGARMENT	PHRONTISTERY
SPERMATOCYTE	TELEGRAPHIST	INSUFFERABLY	UNFAVOURABLE	PLASTERSTONE
SPERMATOZOID	THYSANOPTERA	INTEMPERANCE	UNILATERALLY	PRAXINOSCOPE
SPERMATOZOON	TROCHOSPHERE	INTERFERENCE	VAINGLORIOUS	PTERIDOSPERM
STAKHANOVITE	UNDEREXPOSED	INTROVERSION	WATERCARRIER	QUARTERSTAFF

QUINTESSENCE	EXTRADITABLE	SURMOUNTABLE	UNSCRUPULOUS	CEREMONIALLY
RECKLESSNESS	FELDSPATHOID	TETRODOTOXIN	VIBRATIUNCLE	CHOREOGRAPHY
RECRUDESCENT	FIDDLESTICKS	THERMOSTATIC	ADJECTIVALLY	CHRESTOMATHY
REPERCUSSION	FULMINATIONS	TIGHTFITTING	BOUGAINVILLE	CIRCUMSTANCE
REPOSSESSION	HAPPENSTANCE	TRALATITIOUS	CANTILEVERED	CLAIRVOYANCE
REPROCESSING	HEADMISTRESS	TRANSACTIONS	IRRESOLVABLE	CLAIRVOYANCY
RESTLESSNESS	HIPPOPOTAMUS	TRANSLATABLE	KATHAREVOUSA	CLASSIFIABLE
RUTHLESSNESS	HORIZONTALLY	UNACCEPTABLE	MISBEHAVIOUR	CLEISTOGAMIC
SIDEWHISKERS	HYMENOPTERAN	UNACCUSTOMED	MISDELIVERED	COLLABORATOR
SIPHONOSTELE	HYPOCRITICAL	UNCHARITABLE	PENNSYLVANIA	COLLOQUIALLY
SOUTHEASTERN	HYPOTHETICAL	UNCHARITABLY	REDISCOVERED	COMMERCIALLY
SOUTHWESTERN	INADVERTENCE	UNDETECTABLE	UNBELIEVABLE	COMMONWEALTH
SPACIOUSNESS	INCIDENTALLY	UNEXPECTEDLY	UNBELIEVABLY	COMMUNICABLE
SPECIOUSNESS	INCOMPATIBLE	UNIMPORTANCE	UNCULTIVATED	CONCENTRATED
SPECTROSCOPE	INCOMPETENCE	UNPROFITABLE	UNDESERVEDLY	CONGENITALLY
SPHAIRISTIKE	INDIGESTIBLE	UNSCIENTIFIC	UNRESERVEDLY	CONQUISTADOR
SPURIOUSNESS	INDISPUTABLE	VERUMONTANUM	ENGLISHWOMAN	CONSIDERABLE
STILBOESTROL	INDISPUTABLY	WASHINGTONIA	ENGLISHWOMEN	CONSIDERABLY
STUDIOUSNESS	INHOSPITABLE	WELLINGTONIA	OVERCROWDING	CONSOLIDATED
SWIZZLESTICK	INSTRUCTIONS	XANTHOPTERIN	SERVICEWOMAN	CONSOLIDATOR
TACTLESSNESS	INSTRUCTRESS	ABSQUATULATE	ARSENOPYRITE	CONTAMINATED
TELEUTOSPORE	INTERMITTENT	ANTEDILUVIAN	ASTROPHYSICS	CONTROLLABLE
THUNDERSTORM	IRRESISTIBLE	BARRANQUILLA	CHALCOPYRITE	COSCINOMANCY
TIMELESSNESS	ISOBILATERAL	BEHAVIOURISM	CIRCUMGYRATE	COUNTERMARCH
TRANSMISSION	LABYRINTHINE	BLEFUSCUDIAN	CLAIRVOYANCE	CRYPTOGRAPHY
TRANSVESTISM	LAMENTATIONS	BREASTSUMMER	CLAIRVOYANCY	DECIPHERABLE
TRANSVESTITE	LATIROSTRATE	CARICATURIST	ELEEMOSYNARY	DEMIMONDAINE
UNCTUOUSNESS	LITHOLATROUS	CHEESEBURGER	GOBBLEDYGOOK	DEMONSTRABLE
UNOPPRESSIVE	LONGDISTANCE	COLDSHOULDER	HIEROGLYPHIC	DEMONSTRABLY
UNSUCCESSFUL	MALACOSTRACA	COMMENSURATE	OXYACETYLENE	DEMONSTRATOR
WAREHOUSEMAN	MALPRACTICES	CONGRATULATE	PHOTOGLYPHIC	DIAGRAMMATIC
ZARATHUSTRIC	MALTREATMENT	CONSTABULARY	POLYETHYLENE	DIENCEPHALON
ACCIDENTALLY	MANUFACTURER	CONSTITUENCY	PRASEODYMIUM	DISAGREEABLE
ACQUAINTANCE	MASTERSTROKE	CONSTITUENTS	PSEUDONYMOUS	DISHONORABLE
ADMINISTRATE	MATHEMATICAL	CONSTITUTION	REDEPLOYMENT	DISHONORABLY
ADSCITITIOUS	METAGNATHOUS	CONTRAPUNTAL	SCHIZOMYCETE	DISREPUTABLE
ADVENTITIOUS	MISTREATMENT	CONTRIBUTION	STEREOTYPING	DOGMATICALLY
AERONAUTICAL	MOUSQUETAIRE	CONTRIBUTORY	UNEMPLOYMENT	DOMESTICATED
AGRICULTURAL	MULLIGATAWNY	CONTRITURATE	WOODBURYTYPE	DOUBLEGLAZED
AIRCRAFTSMAN	MULTILATERAL	CROSSCOUNTRY	RECOGNIZABLE	DRAMATICALLY
ALPHABETICAL	NONEXISTENCE	DISTRIBUTION	RECOGNIZANCE	ECONOMICALLY
AMBIDEXTROUS	OBEDIENTIARY	DISTRIBUTIVE		ECSTATICALLY
ANTINEUTRINO	OSTENTATIOUS	GRISEOFULVIN	**12:9**	ELASMOBRANCH
ANTIPARTICLE	OUTSTRETCHED	HERMENEUTICS	ACADEMICALLY	ELECTRICALLY
ARITHMETICAL	OVERSCUTCHED	HERMENEUTIST	ACCIDENTALLY	EMPHATICALLY
ATTRIBUTABLE	PALPITATIONS	HIGHFALUTING	ACQUAINTANCE	ENANTIOPATHY
BEAUMONTAGUE	PARACENTESIS	INARTICULATE	ADDITIONALLY	ENHYPOSTASIA
BEAUMONTIQUE	PENITENTIARY	INCONCLUSIVE	ADJECTIVALLY	EPENCEPHALON
BENEFACTRESS	POIKILOTHERM	INCUNABULIST	AMPHITHEATER	EPIGRAMMATIC
BLOODLETTING	POLYURETHANE	INDIVIDUALLY	AMPHITHEATRE	ESTHETICALLY
CARRIWITCHET	POSTMISTRESS	IRRESOLUTELY	ANASTIGMATIC	EXCHANGEABLE
CEREBROTONIC	PREMONSTRANT	IRRESOLUTION	ANTIBARBARUS	EXTRADITABLE
CHALICOTHERE	PRESUMPTUOUS	LUXEMBOURGER	ANTONINIANUS	EXTRAVAGANCE
CIRCUMSTANCE	PROPRIETRESS	MANGELWURZEL	APPROACHABLE	EXTRAVAGANZA
CLARINETTIST	PSYCHIATRIST	MARCOBRUNNER	APPURTENANCE	FRACTIONALLY
COMBINATIONS	RAMBUNCTIOUS	MISCALCULATE	ARCHIPELAGOS	FUNCTIONALLY
CONGENITALLY	READJUSTMENT	NEIGHBOURING	ARISTOCRATIC	GENETHLIACON
CONQUISTADOR	RECALCITRANT	PROSTITUTION	ARISTOPHANES	GEOLOGICALLY
CONSPECTUITY	RESUSCITATED	RECAPITULATE	ARTHROPLASTY	GIGANTOMACHY
CONTEMPTIBLE	RHAMPHOTHECA	SKUTTERUDITE	ARTIFICIALLY	GLYPTOGRAPHY
CONTEMPTUOUS	RODOMONTADER	SOMNAMBULISM	ARTISTICALLY	HALLANSHAKER
DARLINGTONIA	SELFPORTRAIT	SOMNAMBULIST	ATTRIBUTABLE	HAMMERHEADED
DISCOURTEOUS	SOUTHCOTTIAN	SUBSTITUTION	BAMBOCCIADES	HAPPENSTANCE
DISREPUTABLE	STEREOPTICON	SUBSTITUTIVE	BANDERSNATCH	HARNESSMAKER
DISTINCTNESS	STRAIGHTAWAY	TELEOSAURIAN	BEAUMONTAGUE	HELIOGABALUS
ELECTROTONUS	STRAIGHTEDGE	THAUMATURGIST	BIBLIOGRAPHY	HERMETICALLY
ENHYPOSTASIA	STRAIGHTNESS	THAUMATURGUS	BUREAUCRATIC	HETEROPLASIA
ENTOMOSTRACA	SUBSTANTIATE	THERAPEUTICS	CABINETMAKER	HIPPOPOTAMUS
EPIDEICTICAL	SUPERNATURAL	UNOBSTRUCTED	CAMPANULARIA	HISTORICALLY

HOBBIDIDANCE	OSTEOMALACIA	TRANSLATABLE	GREENGROCERS	SMALLHOLDING
HOLIDAYMAKER	PANATHENAEAN	TRANSOCEANIC	GREENGROCERY	SNOWBOARDING
HORIZONTALLY	PANCHROMATIC	TROPHALLAXIS	HYPERSARCOMA	TRANSCENDENT
HORRIFICALLY	PANPHARMACON	TROUBLEMAKER	INCANDESCENT	UNPRETENDING
HOUSEBREAKER	PARTICULARLY	ULOTRICHALES	INDISTINCTLY	ZALAMBDODONT
HYGIENICALLY	PATHETICALLY	UNACCEPTABLE	INTERGLACIAL	ACHLAMYDEOUS
HYPNOTICALLY	PEDANTICALLY	UNANSWERABLE	KALEIDOSCOPE	ACQUIESCENCE
HYPOTHECATOR	PEDICELLARIA	UNATTAINABLE	KLETTERSCHUE	ADVANTAGEOUS
HYSTERICALLY	PENNSYLVANIA	UNBELIEVABLE	LANGUEDOCIAN	AFTEREFFECTS
IDENTIFIABLE	PERAMBULATOR	UNBELIEVABLY	LICKTRENCHER	AGAMOGENETIC
IMMEASURABLE	PERIODICALLY	UNCHANGEABLE	MULTIPLICITY	ALPHANUMERIC
IMMEASURABLY	PERIOSTRACUM	UNCHARITABLE	MYRINGOSCOPE	AMBULANCEMAN
IMPENETRABLE	PERSEVERANCE	UNCHARITABLY	NEPENTHACEAE	AMPHISBAENIC
IMPERISHABLE	PHENOMENALLY	UNCULTIVATED	OBSTETRICIAN	ANDOUILLETTE
IMPERSONALLY	PHONETICALLY	UNDEMOCRATIC	ONCORHYNCHUS	ARBORESCENCE
IMPERSONATOR	PLECTOGNATHI	UNDETECTABLE	OSCILLOSCOPE	AYUNTAMIENTO
INAPPLICABLE	POLYSYLLABIC	UNEXPURGATED	OSTEOSARCOMA	BELLIGERENCY
INCALCULABLE	POLYSYLLABLE	UNFATHOMABLE	OUTSTRETCHED	BERTHOLLETIA
INCIDENTALLY	POTICHOMANIA	UNFAVOURABLE	OVERSCUTCHED	BUNKOSTEERER
INCOMPARABLE	PREDOMINANCE	UNILATERALLY	PEDIATRICIAN	CALLISTHENES
INCOMPARABLY	PREVARICATOR	UNIMAGINABLE	PERSPICACITY	CANTILEVERED
INCONSOLABLE	PROGRAMMABLE	UNIMPORTANCE	PRAXINOSCOPE	CARAVANSERAI
INCORPORATED	PROLIFICALLY	UNMANAGEABLE	PROPHYLACTIC	CARCINOGENIC
INDECLINABLE	PROTUBERANCE	UNMISTAKABLE	PUMPERNICKEL	CATHETOMETER
INDISPUTABLE	PROVERBIALLY	UNOBTAINABLE	PYROCATECHOL	CIRCASSIENNE
INDISPUTABLY	QUANTIFIABLE	UNOFFICIALLY	RECRUDESCENT	COMMANDMENTS
INDIVIDUALLY	QUESTIONABLE	UNPARDONABLE	SCHIZOMYCETE	CONSTITUENCY
INDUSTRIALLY	QUIXOTICALLY	UNPROFITABLE	SEMIDETACHED	CONSTITUENTS
INERADICABLE	REAPPEARANCE	UNREASONABLE	SHORTCIRCUIT	DIPLOGENESIS
INEXPLICABLE	RECHARGEABLE	UNRETURNABLE	SINGLEDECKER	DISCOMYCETES
INEXPLICABLY	RECIPROCALLY	UNSEASONABLE	SOPHISTICATE	DISCOURTEOUS
INEXTRICABLE	RECOGNIZABLE	URTRICULARIA	SPECTROSCOPE	DISOBEDIENCE
INEXTRICABLY	RECOGNIZANCE	VERUMONTANUM	SPELLCHECKER	DIVERTIMENTO
INFORMIDABLE	RECORDPLAYER	ANTIMETABOLE	SPERMATOCYTE	ENCYCLOPEDIA
INHOSPITABLE	REFRIGERATED	CLAVICEMBALO	STATISTICIAN	ENCYCLOPEDIC
INSUFFERABLE	REFRIGERATOR	COLLYWOBBLES	STRAITJACKET	ENTEROPNEUST
INSUFFERABLY	REMONSTRANCE	INNOMINABLES	TAMARICACEAE	ERATOSTHENES
INTEMPERANCE	RESUSCITATED	MILLILAMBERT	THEORETICIAN	ESPAGNOLETTE
INTERMINABLE	RHYTHMICALLY	REDISTRIBUTE	UNCONVINCING	ETEPIMELETIC
INTERMINABLY	RODOMONTADER	THOROUGHBRED	UNOBSTRUCTED	EULENSPIEGEL
INTERRELATED	ROLLERBLADER	UNUTTERABLES	UNRESTRICTED	EVENHANDEDLY
INTERROGATOR	ROLLERBLADES	AETHRIOSCOPE	VEHMGERICHTE	EVENTEMPERED
INVESTIGATOR	ROMANTICALLY	AMARANTACEAE	ACKNOWLEDGED	EXSERVICEMAN
INVULNERABLE	SADISTICALLY	ARISTOLOCHIA	ANTEMERIDIAN	EXTENSOMETER
IRRATIONALLY	SARDANAPALUS	AUTHENTICATE	BLEFUSCUDIAN	FLUORESCENCE
IRREDEEMABLE	SARDONICALLY	AUTHENTICITY	BOULEVARDIER	FRANKINCENSE
IRRESOLVABLE	SCAPULIMANCY	CARRIWITCHET	CRASHLANDING	FRAUENDIENST
LEXICOGRAPHY	SCHOPENHAUER	CHIROPRACTIC	DIPRIONIDIAN	GALLINACEOUS
LONGDISTANCE	SCINTILLATOR	CHIROPRACTOR	DRESSINGDOWN	GALVANOMETER
MAGNETICALLY	SEMANTICALLY	CHLOROPICRIN	ENCHEIRIDION	GRANDPARENTS
MAJESTICALLY	SEQUENTIALLY	CONSPIRACIST	GLUBBDUBDRIB	HAEMATEMESIS
MANOEUVRABLE	SEQUESTRATOR	CONTABESCENT	HARUMFRODITE	HYMENOPTERAN
MARRIAGEABLE	SHILLYSHALLY	CONVALESCENT	HEMICHORDATA	HYPERPYRETIC
MARSEILLAISE	SIGNIFICANCE	CONVALESCING	HYPERACIDITY	IMPERTINENCE
MECHANICALLY	SIPUNCULACEA	CONVEYANCING	HYPOCHONDRIA	IMPROVIDENCE
MELODRAMATIC	SLOCKDOLAGER	CROSSBENCHER	LONGSTANDING	INADVERTENCE
MERISTEMATIC	SPECIFICALLY	DERESTRICTED	MACHAIRODONT	INCOMPETENCE
METHODICALLY	SPORADICALLY	DEUTEROSCOPY	MASSERANDUBA	INCONTINENCE
MONOSYLLABIC	STRAIGHTAWAY	DIALECTICIAN	ORTHOPAEDICS	INDEPENDENCE
MONOSYLLABLE	STRUCTURALLY	DISCONNECTED	ORTHOPAEDIST	INDIFFERENCE
MOUSQUETAIRE	SUPERSTRATUM	DOUBLEDECKER	OVERCROWDING	INEFFICIENCY
MUDDLEHEADED	SURMOUNTABLE	ECCENTRICITY	PHILODENDRON	INEXPERIENCE
MULLIGATAWNY	SURVEILLANCE	EFFERVESCENT	POSTPRANDIAL	INTELLIGENCE
NEUROTICALLY	SYMBOLICALLY	EPACRIDACEAE	PROPAGANDISM	INTERFERENCE
NIMBOSTRATUS	TERRIFICALLY	EXSUFFLICATE	PROPAGANDIST	ISOBILATERAL
NONFLAMMABLE	THEATRICALLY	FEHMGERICHTE	RHODODENDRON	KINAESTHETIC
OCCASIONALLY	THERMOSTATIC	GEOMETRICIAN	SHAREHOLDING	LONGSHOREMAN
OCEANOGRAPHY	TRABECULATED	GEOPHYSICIST	SHIPBUILDING	LUMINESCENCE
ORNITHOGALUM	TRANSFERABLE	GERIATRICIAN	SKUTTERUDITE	LUMINISCENCE

MADEMOISELLE	YORKSHIREMAN	FORMALDEHYDE	COSMOPOLITAN	PANTECHNICON
MAGNIFICENCE	CAMPODEIFORM	GESELLSCHAFT	CREMAILLIÈRE	PAPILIONIDAE
MERVEILLEUSE	DEHUMIDIFIER	GYMNOSOPHIST	DISASSOCIATE	PARSIMONIOUS
MISDELIVERED	DISSATISFIED	HABERDASHERS	DISORGANIZED	PATHOLOGICAL
MITRAILLEUSE	EPILEPTIFORM	HABERDASHERY	EPIDEICTICAL	PENITENTIARY
MULTILATERAL	PLACENTIFORM	HANDKERCHIEF	ETHNOLOGICAL	PERICARDITIS
NEPHELOMETER	SHORTSTAFFED	INESCUTCHEON	ETYMOLOGICAL	PERSONALIZED
NEUROSCIENCE	SQUIRRELFISH	LABYRINTHINE	ETYMOLOGICON	PERTINACIOUS
NOCONFIDENCE	THOROUGHFARE	LEIOTRICHOUS	FIDDLESTICKS	PERVICACIOUS
NONEXISTENCE	UNCLASSIFIED	LINCOLNSHIRE	FREIGHTLINER	PHILOLOGICAL
NONRESIDENCE	UNDERSTAFFED	MACROCEPHALY	FRONTISPIECE	PHOSPHOLIPID
NYCHTHEMERON	UNIDENTIFIED	MANSLAUGHTER	FULMINATIONS	PHYTONADIONE
OBSOLESCENCE	WEIGHTLIFTER	MASTIGOPHORA	GASTARBEITER	POINTILLISME
OREOPITHECUS	BIBLIOPEGIST	METAGNATHOUS	GENEALOGICAL	POLYNEURITIS
OREOPITHEOUS	BILLINGSGATE	METALLOPHONE	GEOGRAPHICAL	PROLETARIATE
ORTHOGENESIS	BUCKLEBEGGAR	METAMORPHISM	HAMARTHRITIS	QUARTERFINAL
ORTHOTONESIS	CARDIOLOGIST	METAMORPHOSE	HEARTSTRINGS	QUARTERLIGHT
PALINGENESIA	CARDIOMEGALY	MISAPPREHEND	HEPHTHEMIMER	RAMBUNCTIOUS
PALINGENESIS	CARLOVINGIAN	MNEMOTECHNIC	HEROICOMICAL	SACRILEGIOUS
PANAESTHESIA	CARPETBAGGER	NEIGHBORHOOD	HETEROCLITIC	SALTATORIOUS
PANDANACEOUS	CARPOPHAGOUS	PHILOSOPHIZE	HIERARCHICAL	SARSAPARILLA
PARACENTESIS	DENDROLOGIST	POIKILOTHERM	HYPERBOLICAL	SCREENWRITER
PARAMAGNETIC	DISCOURAGING	POLYURETHANE	HYPOCRITICAL	SCRIPTWRITER
PERGAMENEOUS	DRAMATURGIST	PRIZEFIGHTER	HYPOTHETICAL	SECRETARIATE
PHOSPHORENCE	EGYPTOLOGIST	PTERIDOPHYTE	INACCESSIBLE	SEMIPRECIOUS
PHOSPHORESCE	ENTOMOLOGIST	RHAMPHOTHECA	INADMISSIBLE	SEPTEMBRISER
POLYSYNDETON	ESCAPOLOGIST	SARRUSOPHONE	INAUSPICIOUS	SHORTCOMINGS
PROLEGOMENON	FOOTSLOGGING	SCLERENCHYMA	INCOMPATIBLE	SILVERHAIRED
QUADRIPLEGIA	FOTHERINGHAY	SHORTSIGHTED	INCONVENIENT	SLOCKDOLIGER
QUINTESSENCE	GOBBLEDEGOOK	SIPHONOPHORA	INCORRIGIBLE	SOCIOLOGICAL
REDISCOVERED	GOBBLEDYGOOK	SPINSTERHOOD	INCORRIGIBLY	SPATANGOIDEA
REMINISCENCE	GRAPHOLOGIST	STEEPLECHASE	INDEFENSIBLE	SPIEGELEISEN
RESIPISCENCE	GYNECOLOGIST	STENTORPHONE	INDIGESTIBLE	STEREOPTICON
RISORGIMENTO	IMMUNOLOGIST	STEPDAUGHTER	INHARMONIOUS	SUBCONSCIOUS
SCHINDYLESIS	INTRANSIGENT	STRANGLEHOLD	INSALUBRIOUS	SUBSTANTIATE
SERVICEBERRY	MALLOPHAGOUS	STRATOSPHERE	INSTRUCTIONS	SUPERCILIARY
SHAMEFACEDLY	METALLURGIST	SUPERHIGHWAY	INSUFFICIENT	SUPERCILIOUS
SHIRTSLEEVES	MICHELANGELO	SYNADELPHITE	INTELLIGIBLE	SURROUNDINGS
SHORTSLEEVED	MINERALOGIST	TELEGRAPHESE	INTERMEDIARY	TAUTOLOGICAL
SIMULTANEOUS	MUSICOLOGIST	TELEGRAPHIST	INTERMEDIATE	TERRITORIALS
SIVAPITHECUS	PANTOPHAGOUS	TROCHOSPHERE	IRRESISTIBLE	THEREAGAINST
SOMATOPLEURE	PETTIFOGGERS	ADSCITITIOUS	IRREVERSIBLE	TOBACCONISTS
SPECTROMETER	PETTIFOGGERY	ADVANTAGIOUS	LAMENTATIONS	TRALATICIOUS
STERNWHEELER	PETTIFOGGING	ADVENTITIOUS	LEGIONNAIRES	TRALATITIOUS
STOCKBREEDER	PHYSIOLOGIST	AERONAUTICAL	LONGITUDINAL	TRANQUILIZER
STOCKINGETTE	PHYTOPHAGOUS	AGATHODAIMON	LOXODROMICAL	TRANSACTIONS
STRAIGHTEDGE	POTAMOLOGIST	ALPHABETICAL	LYMANTRIIDAE	TROCHELMINTH
STREPTONEURA	PSEPHOLOGIST	ANTIPARTICLE	MACROPODIDAE	UNAUTHORISED
SUBCUTANEOUS	PSYCHOLOGIST	ANTIRACHITIC	MALPRACTICES	UNAUTHORIZED
SUBSERVIENCE	SPELEOLOGIST	APPENDICITIS	MATHEMATICAL	UNDERACHIEVE
TAPSALTEERIE	SPLENOMEGALY	ARITHMETICAL	MERETRICIOUS	UNDETERMINED
TAPSLETEERIE	SPREADEAGLED	ASTROLOGICAL	MERITRICIOUS	UNECONOMICAL
TELEASTHETIC	TECHNOLOGIST	ASTRONOMICAL	MESOTHELIOMA	UNPREJUDICED
THREADNEEDLE	TOXICOLOGIST	ASYMMETRICAL	METAPHORICAL	UNRECOGNISED
TRANSFERENCE	TRICHOLOGIST	BANTAMWEIGHT	METAPHYSICAL	UNRECOGNIZED
TRANSLUCENCE	ACETALDEHYDE	BARRANQUILLA	METROPOLITAN	UNRESTRAINED
TRANSPARENCY	ANTIBACCHIUS	BEACONSFIELD	MIDDLEWEIGHT	UNSCIENTIFIC
TRIGONOMETRY	APOSTROPHISE	BEAUMONTIQUE	MISBEHAVIOUR	VAINGLORIOUS
TURBIDIMETER	ARCHILOCHIAN	BIOGRAPHICAL	MULTIFARIOUS	WALLYDRAIGLE
UNCONSIDERED	BEAUMARCHAIS	BLOODSTAINED	MUTESSARIFAT	WELTERWEIGHT
UNDESERVEDLY	BIRDWATCHING	BOUGAINVILLE	MYTHOLOGICAL	BACKBREAKING
UNEXPECTEDLY	BLENNORRHOEA	CASSITERIDES	NEOCLASSICAL	BLETHERSKATE
UNPARALLELED	BRAINWASHING	CASTERBRIDGE	NEUROLOGICAL	BLUESTOCKING
UNRESERVEDLY	CHALICOTHERE	CATAPHYSICAL	OBEDIENTIARY	BREATHTAKING
WAREHOUSEMAN	CLAMJAMPHRIE	CHESTERFIELD	ONEIROCRITIC	CAMIKNICKERS
WHIGMALEERIE	CLEARSIGHTED	CHITTERLINGS	OSTENTATIOUS	GALLIGASKINS
WICKETKEEPER	CYMOTRICHOUS	COMBINATIONS	OUTBUILDINGS	POLICYMAKING
WILTSHIREMAN	DISFRANCHISE	CONTEMPTIBLE	OVERSTRAINED	SIDEWHISKERS
XANTHOPTERIN	FELDSPATHOID	CONTUMACIOUS	PALPITATIONS	SITTLICHKEIT

SLEEPWALKING	NEWFOUNDLAND	ENCROACHMENT	BICENTENNIAL	IMPOLITENESS
SWASHBUCKLER	OTHERWORLDLY	ENTANGLEMENT	BIOFLAVONOID	INCOHERENTLY
ABSQUATULATE	OXYACETYLENE	ENTRENCHMENT	CALCEAMENTUM	INCREASINGLY
ADAPTABILITY	PALEONTOLOGY	EPIPHENOMENA	CARELESSNESS	INDEBTEDNESS
ADVISABILITY	PARANTHELIUM	EPITHALAMION	CARTHAGINIAN	INDOCTRINATE
AGALMATOLITE	PERMEABILITY	EPITHALAMIUM	CAUTIOUSNESS	INFLATIONARY
ANEMOPHILOUS	PHARMACOLOGY	ESTRANGEMENT	CHEERFULNESS	INFREQUENTLY
ANTHROPOLOGY	PLAUSIBILITY	GENTLETAMPER	CHEESEMONGER	INSTRUMENTAL
ARISTOTELEAN	POLYETHYLENE	HEARTWARMING	CHILDISHNESS	INTERCHANGED
AVAILABILITY	POLYPETALOUS	HELLGRAMMITE	CHRISTIANITY	INTUITIONISM
AWAYABSOLUTE	POTENTIALITY	HEREDITAMENT	CHURLISHNESS	IRREVERENTLY
BACCHANALIAN	PRACTICALITY	HETEROGAMETE	CLANNISHNESS	ISOLATIONISM
BACTERIOLOGY	PRALLTRILLER	HETEROSOMATA	COINCIDENTAL	ISOLATIONIST
BICAMERALISM	PREMAXILLARY	HIEROGRAMMAT	COMPANIONWAY	JENNYSPINNER
BIPROPELLANT	PRINCIPALITY	HOMOTHERMOUS	COMPLACENTLY	KILLIKINNICK
BOONDOGGLING	RADIOBIOLOGY	HOUSEWARMING	COMPLETENESS	KLEPTOMANIAC
BRICKFIELDER	RECAPITULATE	IDIOTHERMOUS	CONCURRENTLY	KLIPSPRINGER
BUSINESSLIKE	RONCESVALLES	ILLEGITIMACY	CONSEQUENCES	LIFELESSNESS
CAPERCAILLIE	SCOPOPHILIAC	ILLEGITIMATE	CONSEQUENTLY	LISTLESSNESS
CAPERCAILZIE	SOMNAMBULISM	IMPRISONMENT	CONSISTENTLY	LUXULLIANITE
COLDSHOULDER	SOMNAMBULIST	INFOTAINMENT	CONTERMINOUS	MACMILLANITE
CONGRATULATE	SPINECHILLER	INFRINGEMENT	CONTRAPUNTAL	MARCOBRUNNER
CONSTABULARY	SPIRITUALISM	KATZENJAMMER	CONTRARINESS	MINDFULLNESS
CONVIVIALITY	SPIRITUALIST	MALTREATMENT	CONVENIENCES	MISDEMEANOUR
COUNTERBLAST	SPIRITUALITY	MICROCLIMATE	CONVENIENTLY	MUCILAGINOUS
COUNTERCLAIM	SPURTLEBLADE	MISPLACEMENT	CONVINCINGLY	MUGGLETONIAN
CRISTOBALITE	STEGOPHOLIST	MISSTATEMENT	COSTERMONGER	NEOPLATONISM
DECENTRALISE	STROMATOLITE	MISTREATMENT	COVETOUSNESS	NONCHALANTLY
DECENTRALIZE	TARAMASALATA	NORTHERNMOST	CRASSAMENTUM	NUTRITIONIST
DESIRABILITY	TECHNICALITY	ORTHORHOMBIC	CREATIVENESS	NYMPHOMANIAC
DISCONSOLATE	TETRACYCLINE	OVERESTIMATE	CROSSCOUNTRY	OBSOLETENESS
DYSTELEOLOGY	THEOPHYLLINE	OVERWHELMING	DEFLATIONARY	PAINLESSNESS
ELECTROPLATE	THUNDERCLOUD	PARALIPOMENA	DEPARTMENTAL	PALUDAMENTUM
EPISCOPALIAN	THUNDERFLASH	PHLEBOTOMIST	DILATORINESS	PANCHATANTRA
EPISTEMOLOGY	TORRICELLIAN	POSTPONEMENT	DISAPPOINTED	PANDAEMONIUM
ESCHSCHOLZIA	TRACTABILITY	PRASEODYMIUM	DISCIPLINARY	PARKINSONISM
ESSENTIALITY	TRANQUILLISE	PREDETERMINE	DISCONTENTED	PEACEFULNESS
EXCITABILITY	TRANQUILLITY	PRESENTIMENT	DISCRIMINATE	PERMANGANATE
FARTHINGLAND	TRANQUILLIZE	PROTHALAMION	DISENCHANTED	PERSISTENTLY
FUNCTIONLESS	UMBRADARLING	PROTHALAMIUM	DISTINCTNESS	PERVERSENESS
GAMOSEPALOUS	UNAPPARELLED	PSEUDONYMOUS	EDUCATIONIST	PHILISTINISM
GONDWANALAND	UNCONTROLLED	PSIPHENOMENA	ELEEMOSYNARY	PINNIEWINKLE
GRISEOFULVIN	UNIVERSALIST	READJUSTMENT	ENTERTAINING	POSTLIMINARY
HAEMOPHILIAC	UNSCRUPULOUS	REDEPLOYMENT	ENTREATINGLY	PREDESTINATE
HYDROGEOLOGY	WHIMSICALITY	RENOUNCEMENT	ENTREPRENEUR	PREPAREDNESS
ILLEGIBILITY	WINTERHALTER	RESETTLEMENT	ETHEROMANIAC	PRIGGISHNESS
ILLOGICALITY	ACCOUCHEMENT	RETRENCHMENT	EVOLUTIONARY	PRIZEWINNING
IMMUTABILITY	ACCOUTREMENT	SLEDGEHAMMER	EXPERIMENTAL	PROBATIONARY
IMPARTIALITY	ADMONISHMENT	SOUTHERNMOST	EXTENSIONIST	PROFICIENTLY
INARTICULATE	AERODYNAMICS	SULPHONAMIDE	EXTORTIONATE	PROTACTINIUM
INCAPABILITY	AMPHISTOMOUS	UNDERGARMENT	FAITHFULNESS	PYROTECHNICS
INCUNABULIST	ANNOUNCEMENT	UNEMPLOYMENT	FEARLESSNESS	QUINQUENNIAL
INSOLUBILITY	ANTILEGOMENA	YELLOWHAMMER	FLAMBOYANTLY	RECEPTIONIST
INTERSTELLAR	ANTITHROMBIN	ABOLITIONIST	FORCEFULNESS	RECKLESSNESS
INVISIBILITY	APLANOGAMETE	ACCORDIONIST	FRIENDLINESS	REFLATIONARY
IRASCIBILITY	ASTONISHMENT	AFFECTIONATE	FRUITFULNESS	REMEMBRANCER
IRRITABILITY	BARNSTORMING	AGRIBUSINESS	GOVERNMENTAL	RESPONDENTIA
LEPIDOMELANE	BETHLEHEMITE	ANTHELMINTIC	GRACEFULNESS	RESTLESSNESS
LILLIBULLERO	BEWILDERMENT	ARFVEDSONITE	GRACIOUSNESS	RETARDEDNESS
LILLIBURLERO	BLANDISHMENT	ASPARAGINASE	GRANDISONIAN	REVERSIONARY
LIVERPUDLIAN	BREASTSUMMER	AWARDWINNING	GRATEFULNESS	RUTHLESSNESS
MALLEABILITY	CHASTISEMENT	BABINGTONITE	HAMBLETONIAN	SALVATIONIST
MERCANTILISM	COMMENCEMENT	BACKWARDNESS	HELPLESSNESS	SCRIMSHANDER
MINDBOGGLING	CROSSEXAMINE	BANANALANDER	HETEROCONTAE	SCRIMSHANKER
MISCALCULATE	DECIPHERMENT	BARBERMONGER	HIEROPHANTIC	SECESSIONIST
MOTORCYCLIST	DISAGREEMENT	BENEVOLENTLY	HILDEBRANDIC	SECTARIANISM
MUNICIPALITY	DISPLACEMENT	BENZOPHENONE	HOMESICKNESS	SHEEPISHNESS
NAVIGABILITY	EMBEZZLEMENT	BENZOQUINONE	HOPELESSNESS	SINGLEHANDED
NEVERTHELESS	ENCIRCLEMENT	BERTILLONAGE	HYDROQUINONE	SINGLEMINDED

SLOVENLINESS	CZECHOSLOVAK	TRANSITIONAL	CANTANKEROUS	OMBUDSPERSON
SLUBBERINGLY	DARLINGTONIA	TUBERCULOSIS	CARBOHYDRATE	OPISTHOGRAPH
SNOBBISHNESS	DEUTERANOPIA	UNACCUSTOMED	CARICATURIST	ORIENTEERING
SPACIOUSNESS	ELECTROTONUS	UNDEREXPOSED	CHALCOPYRITE	ORTHOPTEROUS
SPECIOUSNESS	ENANTIOMORPH	UNNEIGHBORLY	CHARACTERIZE	OVERPOWERING
SPECKTIONEER	ENGLISHWOMAN	WASHINGTONIA	CHEESEBURGER	PANTISOCRACY
SPITEFULNESS	ENGLISHWOMEN	WELLINGTONIA	CHEESEPARING	PASSIONFRUIT
SPURIOUSNESS	EPANORTHOSIS	WOLSTENHOLME	CHEMOTHERAPY	PEREMPTORILY
STAGGERINGLY	EXHIBITIONER	AECIDIOSPORE	CHILDBEARING	PHILANTHROPY
STEALTHINESS	FLITTERMOUSE	ANTISTROPHON	CHURCHWARDEN	POSTMISTRESS
STRAIGHTNESS	FRANKALMOIGN	BARORECEPTOR	CIRCUMGYRATE	POWERSHARING
STRONGMINDED	GAINSBOROUGH	BOOBYTRAPPED	CIRCUMSCRIBE	PRAISEWORTHY
STRONTIANITE	GONADOTROPIN	BRACHYCEPHAL	COLLECTORATE	PREHISTORIAN
STUBBORNNESS	GRASSWIDOWER	BRANCHIOPODA	COMMENSURATE	PREMONSTRANT
STUDIOUSNESS	HAEMORRHOIDS	CALLIGRAPHIC	COMMISSARIAT	PREPONDERANT
SUBCONTINENT	HALLUCINOGEN	CARTOGRAPHER	CONGLOMERATE	PREPONDERATE
SUBSEQUENTLY	HETEROPHORIA	CARTOGRAPHIC	CONTEMPORARY	PREPONDERENT
SUBTERRANEAN	HISTIOPHORUS	CATASTROPHIC	CONTRITURATE	PREPOSTEROUS
SUFFICIENTLY	HOUSETOHOUSE	DESSERTSPOON	DEMILITARIZE	PRESBYTERIAN
SURPRISINGLY	HYDROCHLORIC	EAVESDROPPER	DISACCHARIDE	PROFESSORIAL
TACTLESSNESS	ICHTHYOCOLLA	GASTROSOPHER	DISAPPEARING	PROFITEERING
TERCENTENARY	KATHAREVOUSA	GLOCKENSPIEL	DISCONCERTED	PROGESTERONE
THANKFULNESS	LALLAPALOOZA	GOOSEPIMPLES	DISEMBARRASS	PROPRIETRESS
THESSALONIAN	LAMELLICORNE	HAPTOTROPISM	DISINTEGRATE	PROTECTORATE
THICKSKINNED	MISANTHROPIC	HELIOTROPISM	DOLPHINARIUM	PSYCHIATRIST
THOROUGHNESS	MOUTHBROODER	HIEROGLYPHIC	EMBROIDERESS	RACKETEERING
TIMELESSNESS	MULTICOLORED	HIPPOCREPIAN	ENTEROMORPHA	RADIOTHERAPY
TOGETHERNESS	NONALCOHOLIC	HOUSEKEEPING	ENTOMOSTRACA	RECALCITRANT
TRADESCANTIA	OCCUPATIONAL	HYDROGRAPHER	FAINTHEARTED	REDINTEGRATE
TRICENTENARY	OLDFASHIONED	HYMNOGRAPHER	FEATHERBRAIN	REINVIGORATE
TRIUMPHANTLY	ONOMATOPOEIA	IAMBOGRAPHER	FLUVIOMARINE	SCATTERBRAIN
TRUTHFULNESS	ONOMATOPOEIC	LITHOGRAPHIC	FUSTILLIRIAN	SCHNEIDERIAN
UNACQUAINTED	ONYCHOPHORAN	MARLINESPIKE	GERONTOCRACY	SCLERODERMIA
UNCHALLENGED	OSTEOPOROSIS	MISINTERPRET	GIBRALTARIAN	SELFCATERING
UNCTUOUSNESS	PARTICOLORED	NYCTITROPISM	GLADIATORIAL	SELFINTEREST
UNDERPINNING	PASQUEFLOWER	OCTASTROPHIC	GROSSULARITE	SELFPORTRAIT
UNDERSKINKER	PECTORILOQUY	PEACEKEEPING	HEADMISTRESS	SERASKIERATE
UNFREQUENTED	PERISTERONIC	PHOTOGLYPHIC	HEREDITARIAN	SESQUITERTIA
USERFRIENDLY	PHILHARMONIC	PHOTOGRAPHER	HUMANITARIAN	SEXAGENARIAN
VALENCIENNES	POGONOPHORAN	PHOTOGRAPHIC	HYDROTHERAPY	SPOKESPERSON
VENGEFULNESS	PRACTICIONER	POPOCATEPETL	HYPNOTHERAPY	STRADIVARIUS
VIBRATIUNCLE	PRACTITIONER	PORNOGRAPHIC	IDIOSYNCRASY	STRIGIFORMES
WATCHFULNESS	PROCESSIONAL	PTERIDOSPERM	INSPECTORATE	SUBLAPSARIAN
WELLBALANCED	PROFESSIONAL	RADIOGRAPHER	INSTRUCTRESS	SUBSIDIARITY
WOLLASTONITE	PROPORTIONAL	STENOGRAPHER	INTERSPERSED	SUPERCHARGED
WRETCHEDNESS	PROSOPOPOEIA	STEREOTYPING	INTRAUTERINE	SUPERCHARGER
YOUTHFULNESS	PYTHONOMORPH	TELEUTOSPORE	INVERTEBRATE	TAPERECORDER
ANAMORPHOSIS	QUADRAPHONIC	UNPRINCIPLED	IRREGULARITY	TELEOSAURIAN
ANTIMNEMONIC	RECREATIONAL	ACCUSATORIAL	KALISTOCRACY	TESTOSTERONE
AUTOHYPNOSIS	REDEMPTIONER	ADMINISTRATE	KERAUNOGRAPH	TETRAHEDRITE
BATTLEGROUND	RHINORRHOEAL	ALEXIPHARMIC	KINDERGARTEN	THAUMATURGIC
BLABBERMOUTH	ROOMINGHOUSE	AMBASSADRESS	LAMPADEDROMY	THAUMATURGUS
BREAKTHROUGH	SCATTERMOUCH	AMBIDEXTROUS	LANCASTERIAN	THREEQUARTER
BREASTPLOUGH	SELFEMPLOYED	ANCHORPERSON	LATIROSTRATE	TOTALITARIAN
BUTTERSCOTCH	SERVICEWOMAN	ANDROSTERONE	LIGHTHEARTED	TRANSMIGRATE
CEREBROTONIC	SHARPSHOOTER	ANECATHARSIS	LITHOLATROUS	TRANSMOGRIFY
CHARTERHOUSE	SHUFFLEBOARD	ANTANANARIVO	LUXEMBOURGER	TURACOVERDIN
CLAPPERBOARD	SINANTHROPUS	ANTIAIRCRAFT	MALACOSTRACA	TURBOCHARGER
CLOTHESHORSE	SLOCKDOLOGER	ANTINEUTRINO	MANGELWURZEL	UINTATHERIUM
COMMISSIONED	SPORTSGROUND	APOLLINARIAN	MARCONIGRAPH	UNDERCURRENT
COMMISSIONER	STELLENBOSCH	AROMATHERAPY	MASTERSTROKE	UNDISCHARGED
CONFECTIONER	STEREOPHONIC	ARSENOPYRITE	MECHITHARIST	UNPOPULARITY
CONFESSIONAL	STEREOSCOPIC	ATMOSPHERICS	MONTESSORIAN	VETERINARIAN
CONTRAPPOSTO	STORMTROOPER	AWEINSPIRING	NEIGHBOURING	WATERCARRIER
CONVENTIONAL	TETRODOTOXIN	BEHAVIOURISM	NEUROFIBROMA	WEATHERPROOF
COUNTERPOINT	THESMOPHORIA	BENEFACTRESS	NEWSPAPERMAN	WELLINFORMED
COUNTERPOISE	THIGMOTROPIC	BLACKCURRANT	NONAGENARIAN	WHOLEHEARTED
CUCKOOFLOWER	THIRDBOROUGH	BLOODTHIRSTY	OBSTREPEROUS	XIPHISTERNUM
CURMUDGEONLY	TRADESPEOPLE	CAMERAPERSON	OCTOGENARIAN	ACCOMPLISHED

AIRCRAFTSMAN	PROGYMNASIUM	CHLORINATION	DILAPIDATION	IMPREGNATION
ANTAGONISTIC	PROTOPLASMAL	CHORIZONTIST	DISADVANTAGE	INACCURATELY
ANTIMACASSAR	PROTOPLASMIC	CIVILISATION	DISCOMFITURE	INADEQUATELY
APPREHENSION	QUADRAGESIMA	CIVILIZATION	DISINCENTIVE	INAUGURATION
APPREHENSIVE	RECEIVERSHIP	CLARINETTIST	DISINFECTANT	INCAPACITATE
ASTROPHYSICS	RELATIONSHIP	CLAUDICATION	DISORIENTATE	INCINERATION
AUSTRALASIAN	RELENTLESSLY	CODIFICATION	DISPENSATION	INCOMPLETELY
AUSTRONESIAN	REPERCUSSION	COHABITATION	DISQUISITION	INCONSISTENT
BACKWOODSMAN	REPOSSESSION	COLLUCTATION	DISREPECTFUL	INCRUSTATION
BACTERIOSTAT	REPROCESSING	COLONIZATION	DISSERTATION	INDEFINITELY
BESSERWISSER	SALESMANSHIP	COLOQUINTIDA	DISSOCIATION	INDISCRETION
BIELORUSSIAN	SCHILLERSPAR	COMMENDATION	DISTILLATION	INEXACTITUDE
BIOCHEMISTRY	SCHOOLMASTER	COMMENDATORY	DISTRIBUTION	INFELICITOUS
BIODIVERSITY	SELFADHESIVE	COMPELLATION	DISTRIBUTIVE	INFILTRATION
BREATHLESSLY	SEPTUAGESIMA	COMPENSATION	DONNERWETTER	INFLAMMATION
BYELORUSSIAN	SHIRTWAISTER	COMPENSATORY	DORSIVENTRAL	INFLAMMATORY
CHAIRMANSHIP	SPRECHGESANG	COMPLICATION	EMANCIPATION	INGRATIATING
CHAMPIONSHIP	STUDDINGSAIL	COMPURGATION	EMASCULATION	INNATTENTIVE
CHAUVINISTIC	SURREALISTIC	CONCILIATION	ENTOPLASTRON	INORDINATELY
CHONDRIOSOME	TERGIVERSATE	CONCILIATORY	EPISTOLATERS	INSEMINATION
CHREMATISTIC	TRANSGRESSOR	CONDEMNATION	EQUIVOCATION	INSTALLATION
CIRCUMCISION	TRANSMISSION	CONDENSATION	EQUIVOCATORY	INSTAURATION
COCCIDIOSTAT	UNCONVERSANT	CONFIDENTIAL	EXACERBATION	INSURRECTION
COMPROMISING	UNDIMINISHED	CONFIRMATION	EXAGGERATION	INTELLECTUAL
DELICATESSEN	UNINTERESTED	CONFIRMATORY	EXASPERATING	INTENERATION
DICTATORSHIP	UNOPPRESSIVE	CONFISCATION	EXASPERATION	INTERCEPTION
DIRECTORSHIP	UNRESPONSIVE	CONGREGATION	EXCRUCIATING	INTERJECTION
DISPOSSESSED	UNSUCCESSFUL	CONSCRIPTION	EXCRUCIATION	INTERMITTENT
DUNNIEWASSAL	UNSURPRISING	CONSECRATION	EXHILARATING	INTERPRETING
ECCLESIASTES	ABBREVIATION	CONSERVATION	EXHILARATION	INTERRUPTION
ECCLESIASTIC	ACCELERATION	CONSERVATISM	EXPLOITATION	INTERSECTION
EFFORTLESSLY	ACCENTUATION	CONSERVATIVE	FERMENTATION	INTERVENTION
EMBARRASSING	ACCUMULATION	CONSERVATORY	FINALIZATION	INTIMIDATING
ENTERPRISING	ADJUDICATION	CONSOCIATION	FIRSTFOOTING	INTIMIDATION
ENTHUSIASTIC	ADULTERATION	CONSTIPATION	FLAGELLATION	INTOXICATING
EXTINGUISHER	ALIMENTATIVE	CONSTITUTION	FLORICULTURE	INTOXICATION
FRONTIERSMAN	ALLITERATION	CONSTRICTION	FLUORIDATION	INTRANSITIVE
GAMESMANSHIP	AMALGAMATION	CONSTRUCTION	FRANKENSTEIN	INTRODUCTION
GUARDIANSHIP	AMELIORATION	CONSTRUCTIVE	FRUMENTATION	INTRODUCTORY
HAIRDRESSERS	ANAESTHETISE	CONSULTATION	FUNDAMENTALS	INVALIDATION
HAIRDRESSING	ANAESTHETIST	CONSULTATIVE	GALLIVANTING	INVIGORATING
HORSEMANSHIP	ANAESTHETIZE	CONSUMMATION	GLOBETROTTER	INVIGORATION
HYPERTENSION	ANNIHILATION	CONTIGNATION	GLYCOPROTEIN	IRRESOLUTELY
ICHTHYOPSIDA	ANNUNCIATION	CONTINUATION	GRANDMONTINE	IRRESOLUTION
ICONOCLASTIC	ANTICIPATION	CONTRIBUTION	GUILDENSTERN	IRRESPECTIVE
IMPOVERISHED	ANTICIPATORY	CONTRIBUTORY	HAIRSPLITTER	ISHMAELITISH
INCONCLUSIVE	APPENDECTOMY	CONVERSATION	HEADQUARTERS	JURISDICTION
INTERCESSION	APPOGGIATURA	COORDINATION	HERMENEUTICS	LABANOTATION
INTERMISSION	APPRECIATION	COURTMARTIAL	HERMENEUTIST	LEGALIZATION
INTROVERSION	APPRECIATIVE	CROSSSECTION	HIGHFALUTING	LEGITIMATELY
JOURNALISTIC	ARCHITECTURE	DAGUERROTYPE	HINDQUARTERS	LIQUEFACTION
KIRSCHWASSER	ARTICULATION	DEAMBULATORY	HIPPOCRATISE	MALFORMATION
LAUREATESHIP	ARTIODACTYLA	DEASPIRATION	HOMOEOPATHIC	MALNUTRITION
MACABERESQUE	ASPHYXIATION	DEBILITATING	HORTICULTURE	MANIPULATION
MARKSMANSHIP	ASSIMILATION	DECAPITATION	HUDIBRASTICS	MANIPULATIVE
MILITARISTIC	ASSUEFACTION	DECELERATION	HUMANIZATION	MASTURBATION
MISREPRESENT	ATHEROMATOUS	DECONGESTANT	HYSTERECTOMY	MENSTRUATION
NARCISSISTIC	AUGMENTATION	DEGENERATION	IDEALIZATION	MINISTRATION
NATURALISTIC	AUGMENTATIVE	DELIBERATELY	ILLUMINATING	MISADVENTURE
OPHIOGLOSSUM	AUSCULTATION	DELIBERATION	ILLUMINATION	MISQUOTATION
OVERDRESSING	BAIRNSFATHER	DENOMINATION	ILLUSTRATION	MOBILIZATION
PARENTHESIZE	BLOODLETTING	DENUNCIATION	ILLUSTRATIVE	MODIFICATION
PARTISANSHIP	BRILLIANTINE	DEPOPULATION	IMMACULATELY	MOONLIGHTING
PASSEMEASURE	BROADCASTING	DEPRECIATION	IMMODERATELY	MOSBOLLETJIE
PERIPHRASTIC	CALUMNIATION	DEPRECIATORY	IMMODERATION	NIGHTCLOTHES
PLEIOCHASIUM	CANCELLATION	DEREGULATION	IMMUNIZATION	NOMENCLATURE
POLYRIBOSOME	CANONIZATION	DESIDERATIVE	IMPERFECTION	NONCOMMITTAL
PREPOSSESSED	CAPITULATION	DICHROMATISM	IMPERFECTIVE	NONDIRECTIVE
PREREQUISITE	CATADIOPTRIC	DIFFERENTIAL	IMPLANTATION	NONOBJECTIVE

NONRESISTANT	RECUPERATIVE	VENTRIPOTENT	STRINGCOURSE	SPERMATOZOID
NORTHEASTERN	REGENERATION	VERIFICATION	SUCCESSFULLY	SPERMATOZOON
NORTHWESTERN	REGISTRATION	VERMICULTURE	SUPERANNUATE	UNAPPETIZING
NOTIFICATION	REHABILITATE	VILIFICATION	SUPERNACULUM	**12:10**
OBLITERATION	REJUVENATION	VILLEGIATURA	SUPERNATURAL	ABSQUATULATE
OBSERVANTINE	REMUNERATION	VITUPERATION	SUSPICIOUSLY	ADMINISTRATE
OPINIONATIVE	REMUNERATIVE	VITUPERATIVE	THOUGHTFULLY	AFFECTIONATE
ORGANISATION	RENUNCIATION	VOCIFERATION	TITANOSAURUS	ANTIAIRCRAFT
ORGANIZATION	REPATRIATION	WOODBURYTYPE	TREMENDOUSLY	AROMATHERAPY
ORTHODONTICS	REPRODUCTION	ZARATHUSTRIC	UPROARIOUSLY	ASPARAGINASE
OSSIFICATION	REPRODUCTIVE	AFORETHOUGHT	VARICOLOURED	AUTHENTICATE
OVEREXERTION	RESTAURATEUR	AFTERTHOUGHT	VOCIFEROUSLY	BEAUMARCHAIS
PACIFICATION	RESURRECTION	AGRICULTURAL	VOLUPTUOUSLY	BERTILLONAGE
PARAMILITARY	RETICULATION	APFELSTRUDEL	WILLIEWAUGHT	BILLINGSGATE
PASSEPARTOUT	RHADAMANTHUS	AUSPICIOUSLY	AGGRESSIVELY	BIPROPELLANT
PASSIONATELY	RHIPIDOPTERA	BOISTEROUSLY	ANTEDILUVIAN	BLACKCURRANT
PENALIZATION	RHYTIDECTOMY	BRONTOSAURUS	ATTRACTIVELY	BLETHERSKATE
PERADVENTURE	SATISFACTION	CONSPECTUITY	COLLECTIVELY	CARBOHYDRATE
PERIODONTICS	SATISFACTORY	CONTEMPTUOUS	CONCLUSIVELY	CARDIOMEGALY
PERNOCTATION	SAUROGNATHAE	CONTINUOUSLY	CONDUCTIVITY	CHEMOTHERAPY
PERPETRATION	SEGMENTATION	COURAGEOUSLY	DECORATIVELY	CIRCUMGYRATE
PERSPIRATION	SESQUIALTERA	DISASTROUSLY	DRINKDRIVING	CLAPPERBOARD
PERTURBATION	SIPHONOSTELE	DISCOMEDUSAE	ENERGYSAVING	CLAVICEMBALO
PESTILENTIAL	SOLICITATION	DISDAINFULLY	EXHAUSTIVELY	COLLECTORATE
PETRIFACTION	SOUTHCOTTIAN	DISINGENUOUS	FIGURATIVELY	COMMENSURATE
PHRONTISTERY	SOUTHEASTERN	DIVERTICULUM	IMPRESSIVELY	CONGLOMERATE
PHYCOXANTHIN	SOUTHWESTERN	FASTIDIOUSLY	LABOURSAVING	CONGRATULATE
PHYTOBENTHOS	SPHACELATION	FORTUITOUSLY	MULTIGRAVIDA	CONSTABULARY
PIGMENTATION	SPHAIRISTIKE	GLYNDEBOURNE	OPPRESSIVELY	CONTEMPORARY
PISCICULTURE	STERNUTATION	HAPPYGOLUCKY	PERCEPTIVELY	CONTRITURATE
PITTERPATTER	STILBOESTROL	HARMONIOUSLY	PERCEPTIVITY	COUNTERBLAST
PLAINCLOTHES	STONECHATTER	INCAUTIOUSLY	PERMITTIVITY	COUNTERCLAIM
PLASTERSTONE	STREPITATION	INCONSEQUENT	PERSUASIVELY	DECONGESTANT
POLARIZATION	STREPSIPTERA	INDISSOLUBLE	PHOTOGRAVURE	DEFLATIONARY
POSTPOSITIVE	STRIDULATION	INTERLOCUTOR	POSSESSIVELY	DISADVANTAGE
PRECONDITION	STROPHANTHUS	LASCIVIOUSLY	PRIMIGRAVIDA	DISASSOCIATE
PREDILECTION	STUPEFACTION	LUGUBRIOUSLY	PRODUCTIVITY	DISCIPLINARY
PREFERENTIAL	SUBARRHATION	MAGNILOQUENT	PROTECTIVELY	DISCONSOLATE
PREGUSTATION	SUBCOMMITTEE	MANUFACTURER	REFLECTIVITY	DISCRIMINATE
PRESCRIPTION	SUBHASTATION	MASSPRODUCED	RESPECTIVELY	DISEMBARRASS
PRESCRIPTIVE	SUBMINIATURE	MEANINGFULLY	SCANDINAVIAN	DISINFECTANT
PRESENTATION	SUBSCRIPTION	MERRYTHOUGHT	SHOSTAKOVICH	DISINTEGRATE
PRESERVATION	SUBSTITUTION	METICULOUSLY	STAKHANOVITE	DISORIENTATE
PRESERVATIVE	SUBSTITUTIVE	MINICOMPUTER	STANISLAVSKI	ELECTROPLATE
PRESIDENTIAL	SUBSTRUCTURE	MIRACULOUSLY	SUBJECTIVELY	ELEEMOSYNARY
PRESTRICTION	SUCCUSSATION	MISPRONOUNCE	SUBJECTIVITY	ENTOMOSTRACA
PREVENTATIVE	SUPERSTITION	MONOTONOUSLY	SUBMISSIVELY	EVOLUTIONARY
PROCLAMATION	SUPPLICATION	MYSTERIOUSLY	SUCCESSIVELY	EXSUFFLICATE
PROLONGATION	SWIZZLESTICK	OBSEQUIOUSLY	SUGGESTIVELY	EXTORTIONATE
PROMULGATION	SYNTAGMATITE	OUTMANOEUVRE	THANKSGIVING	FARTHINGLAND
PROPITIATION	TAGLIACOTIAN	OUTRAGEOUSLY	VINDICTIVELY	FEATHERBRAIN
PROPITIATORY	TEETERTOTTER	PERSULPHURIC	HENCEFORWARD	FUNDAMENTALS
PROSCRIPTION	TESTAMENTARY	POSTGRADUATE	MICROBREWERY	GERONTOCRACY
PROSTITUTION	THERAPEUTICS	POSTHUMOUSLY	SOUTHERNWOOD	GESELLSCHAFT
PROTESTATION	THUNDERSTORM	PRECARIOUSLY	STRANGLEWEED	GONDWANALAND
PROTHONOTARY	THYSANOPTERA	PRECOCIOUSLY	WHIPPOORWILL	HEMICHORDATA
PROVIDENTIAL	TIGHTFITTING	PRESUMPTUOUS	CARDINDEXING	HENCEFORWARD
PSYCHOPATHIC	TRANSPONTINE	PRODIGIOUSLY	HETEROSEXUAL	HETEROSOMATA
PTERODACTYLE	TRANSVESTISM	PROPITIOUSLY	METHOTREXATE	HYDROTHERAPY
PURIFICATION	TRANSVESTITE	PUGNACIOUSLY	ACCOMPANYING	HYPNOTHERAPY
PUTREFACTION	ULTRAMONTANE	PURPOSEBUILT	ARTILLERYMAN	IDIOSYNCRASY
QUANTITATIVE	UNATTRACTIVE	PURPOSEFULLY	BREATHALYSER	ILLEGITIMACY
QUARTERSTAFF	UNDERCLOTHES	RESPECTFULLY	ELECTROLYSIS	ILLEGITIMATE
RADIOISOTOPE	UNDERWRITTEN	RIDICULOUSLY	ERYTHROMYCIN	INARTICULATE
RAMIFICATION	UNPRODUCTIVE	SCANDALOUSLY	STREPTOMYCIN	INCAPACITATE
RATIFICATION	UNSUSPECTING	SCRUPULOUSLY	TRICHOPHYTON	INDOCTRINATE
RECOLLECTION	URBANIZATION	SCURRILOUSLY	UNSATISFYING	INFLATIONARY
RECONSTITUTE	VAPORIZATION	SEMICIRCULAR	MOISTURIZING	INSPECTORATE
RECUPERATION	VENEPUNCTURE	SOLICITOUSLY	SCHEHERAZADE	

INTERMEDIARY	ANTITHROMBIN	SURMOUNTABLE	SIVAPITHECUS	CHASTISEMENT
INTERMEDIATE	APPROACHABLE	TRANSFERABLE	SOCIOLOGICAL	CHEERFULNESS
INVERTEBRATE	ATTRIBUTABLE	TRANSLATABLE	STEREOPTICON	CHESTERFIELD
KALISTOCRACY	CLASSIFIABLE	UNACCEPTABLE	STREPTOMYCIN	CHILDISHNESS
KERAUNOGRAPH	COMMUNICABLE	UNANSWERABLE	TAUTOLOGICAL	CHURLISHNESS
LATIROSTRATE	CONSIDERABLE	UNATTAINABLE	UNECONOMICAL	CLANNISHNESS
LEPIDOMELANE	CONSIDERABLY	UNBELIEVABLE	UNPREJUDICED	COLLECTIVELY
MACROCEPHALY	CONTEMPTIBLE	UNBELIEVABLY	VIBRATIUNCLE	COMMENCEMENT
MALACOSTRACA	CONTROLLABLE	UNCHANGEABLE	WELLBALANCED	COMPLETENESS
MARCONIGRAPH	DECIPHERABLE	UNCHARITABLE	APFELSTRUDEL	CONCLUSIVELY
METHOTREXATE	DEMONSTRABLE	UNCHARITABLY	BAMBOCCIADES	CONTABESCENT
MICROCLIMATE	DEMONSTRABLY	UNDETECTABLE	BANANALANDER	CONTRARINESS
MISCALCULATE	DISAGREEABLE	UNFATHOMABLE	BRICKFIELDER	CONVALESCENT
NEWFOUNDLAND	DISHONORABLE	UNFAVOURABLE	CASSITERIDES	COVETOUSNESS
NONRESISTANT	DISHONORABLY	UNIMAGINABLE	CASTERBRIDGE	CREATIVENESS
OBEDIENTIARY	DISREPUTABLE	UNMANAGEABLE	CHURCHWARDEN	CREMAILLIÈRE
OPISTHOGRAPH	EXCHANGEABLE	UNMISTAKABLE	COLDSHOULDER	DECIPHERMENT
OVERESTIMATE	EXTRADITABLE	UNOBTAINABLE	CONQUISTADOR	DECORATIVELY
PANTISOCRACY	IDENTIFIABLE	UNPARDONABLE	ENCYCLOPEDIA	DELIBERATELY
PARAMILITARY	IMMEASURABLE	UNPROFITABLE	ENCYCLOPEDIC	DILATORINESS
PENITENTIARY	IMMEASURABLY	UNREASONABLE	EVENHANDEDLY	DISAGREEMENT
PERMANGANATE	IMPENETRABLE	UNRETURNABLE	HAMMERHEADED	DISPLACEMENT
POLYURETHANE	IMPERISHABLE	UNSEASONABLE	HILDEBRANDIC	DISTINCTNESS
POSTGRADUATE	INACCESSIBLE	AERONAUTICAL	LYMANTRIIDAE	EFFERVESCENT
POSTLIMINARY	INADMISSIBLE	AFTEREFFECTS	MACROPODIDAE	EMBEZZLEMENT
PREDESTINATE	INAPPLICABLE	ALPHABETICAL	MOUTHBROODER	EMBROIDERESS
PREMAXILLARY	INCALCULABLE	ANTIPARTICLE	MUDDLEHEADED	ENCIRCLEMENT
PREMONSTRANT	INCOMPARABLE	ARITHMETICAL	OTHERWORLDLY	ENCROACHMENT
PREPONDERANT	INCOMPARABLY	ASTROLOGICAL	PAPILIONIDAE	ENTANGLEMENT
PREPONDERATE	INCOMPATIBLE	ASTRONOMICAL	RODOMONTADER	ENTRENCHMENT
PROBATIONARY	INCONSOLABLE	ASYMMETRICAL	ROLLERBLADER	ENTREPRENEUR
PROLETARIATE	INCORRIGIBLE	BIOGRAPHICAL	ROLLERBLADES	EPACRIDACEAE
PROTECTORATE	INCORRIGIBLY	CATAPHYSICAL	SCRIMSHANDER	EPIPHENOMENA
PROTHONOTARY	INDECLINABLE	CONSEQUENCES	SHAMEFACEDLY	EPISTOLATERS
QUARTERSTAFF	INDEFENSIBLE	CONVENIENCES	SINGLEHANDED	ESTRANGEMENT
RADIOTHERAPY	INDIGESTIBLE	EPIDEICTICAL	SINGLEMINDED	EXHAUSTIVELY
RECALCITRANT	INDISPUTABLE	ERYTHROMYCIN	SPATANGOIDEA	FAITHFULNESS
RECAPITULATE	INDISPUTABLY	ETHNOLOGICAL	STOCKBREEDER	FEARLESSNESS
REDINTEGRATE	INDISSOLUBLE	ETYMOLOGICAL	STRAIGHTEDGE	FIGURATIVELY
REFLATIONARY	INERADICABLE	ETYMOLOGICON	STRONGMINDED	FORCEFULNESS
REHABILITATE	INEXPLICABLE	FIDDLESTICKS	TAPERECORDER	FRANKENSTEIN
REINVIGORATE	INEXPLICABLY	GENEALOGICAL	THREADNEEDLE	FRIENDLINESS
REVERSIONARY	INEXTRICABLE	GENETHLIACON	TURACOVERDIN	FRONTISPIECE
SCATTERBRAIN	INEXTRICABLY	GEOGRAPHICAL	UNDESERVEDLY	FRUITFULNESS
SCHEHERAZADE	INFORMIDABLE	GIGANTOMACHY	UNEXPECTEDLY	FUNCTIONLESS
SECRETARIATE	INHOSPITABLE	HAPPYGOLUCKY	UNRESERVEDLY	GLYCOPROTEIN
SELFPORTRAIT	INSUFFERABLE	HEROICOMICAL	USERFRIENDLY	GRACEFULNESS
SERASKIERATE	INSUFFERABLY	HIERARCHICAL	ACCOUCHEMENT	GRACIOUSNESS
SHUFFLEBOARD	INTELLIGIBLE	HYPERBOLICAL	ACCOUTREMENT	GRATEFULNESS
SOPHISTICATE	INTERMINABLE	HYPOCRITICAL	ADMONISHMENT	GREENGROCERS
SPLENOMEGALY	INTERMINABLY	HYPOTHETICAL	AGGRESSIVELY	GREENGROCERY
SPRECHGESANG	INVULNERABLE	LOXODROMICAL	AGRIBUSINESS	GUILDENSTERN
SPURTLEBLADE	IRREDEEMABLE	MALPRACTICES	AMARANTACEAE	HABERDASHERS
STEEPLECHASE	IRRESISTIBLE	MASSPRODUCED	AMBASSADRESS	HABERDASHERY
STUDDINGSAIL	IRRESOLVABLE	MATHEMATICAL	ANNOUNCEMENT	HAIRDRESSERS
SUBSTANTIATE	IRREVERSIBLE	METAPHORICAL	ANTILEGOMENA	HEADMISTRESS
SUPERANNUATE	MANOEUVRABLE	METAPHYSICAL	APLANOGAMETE	HEADQUARTERS
SUPERCILIARY	MARRIAGEABLE	MYTHOLOGICAL	ARISTOTELEAN	HELPLESSNESS
TARAMASALATA	MONOSYLLABIC	NEOCLASSICAL	ASTONISHMENT	HEREDITAMENT
TERCENTENARY	MONOSYLLABLE	NEUROLOGICAL	ATTRACTIVELY	HETEROGAMETE
TERGIVERSATE	NONFLAMMABLE	OREOPITHECUS	BACKWARDNESS	HINDQUARTERS
TERRITORIALS	ORTHORHOMBIC	OSTEOMALACIA	BEACONSFIELD	HOMESICKNESS
TESTAMENTARY	POLYSYLLABIC	PANPHARMACON	BENEFACTRESS	HOPELESSNESS
THOROUGHFARE	POLYSYLLABLE	PANTECHNICON	BEWILDERMENT	IMMACULATELY
THUNDERCLAP	PROGRAMMABLE	PATHOLOGICAL	BLANDISHMENT	IMMODERATELY
TRANSMIGRATE	QUANTIFIABLE	PERIOSTRACUM	CAMIKNICKERS	IMPOLITENESS
TRICENTENARY	QUESTIONABLE	PHILOLOGICAL	CARELESSNESS	IMPRESSIVELY
ULTRAMONTANE	RECHARGEABLE	REMEMBRANCER	CAUTIOUSNESS	IMPRISONMENT
UNCONVERSANT	RECOGNIZABLE	SIPUNCULACEA	CHALICOTHERE	INACCURATELY

799

INADEQUATELY	RECKLESSNESS	UNSCIENTIFIC	IMPOVERISHED	ARFVEDSONITE
INCANDESCENT	RECRUDESCENT	UNSUCCESSFUL	KLETTERSCHUE	ARSENOPYRITE
INCOMPLETELY	REDEPLOYMENT	ACKNOWLEDGED	LAUREATESHIP	ARTICULATION
INCONSEQUENT	RENOUNCEMENT	AFORETHOUGHT	LICKTRENCHER	ASPHYXIATION
INCONSISTENT	RESETTLEMENT	AFTERTHOUGHT	LITHOGRAPHIC	ASSIMILATION
INCONVENIENT	RESPECTIVELY	ARCHIPELAGOS	MARKSMANSHIP	ASSUEFACTION
INDEBTEDNESS	RESTAURATEUR	BANTAMWEIGHT	NIGHTCLOTHES	ASTROPHYSICS
INDEFINITELY	RESTLESSNESS	BARBERMONGER	OCTASTROPHIC	ATMOSPHERICS
INESCUTCHEON	RETARDEDNESS	BEAUMONTAGUE	ONCORHYNCHUS	AUGMENTATION
INFOTAINMENT	RETRENCHMENT	BUCKLEBEGGAR	OUTSTRETCHED	AUGMENTATIVE
INFRINGEMENT	RHAMPHOTHECA	CARPETBAGGER	OVERSCUTCHED	AUSCULTATION
INORDINATELY	RHINORRHOEAL	CHEESEBURGER	PARTISANSHIP	AUSTRALASIAN
INSTRUCTRESS	RHIPIDOPTERA	CHEESEMONGER	PHOTOGLYPHIC	AUSTRONESIAN
INSUFFICIENT	RUTHLESSNESS	CONVINCINGLY	PHOTOGRAPHER	AUTHENTICITY
INTERMITTENT	SCHIZOMYCETE	COSTERMONGER	PHOTOGRAPHIC	AVAILABILITY
INTRANSIGENT	SELFINTEREST	ENTREATINGLY	PHYCOXANTHIN	AWARDWINNING
IRRESOLUTELY	SESQUIALTERA	EULENSPIEGEL	PHYTOBENTHOS	AWEINSPIRING
LEGITIMATELY	SHEEPISHNESS	HALLUCINOGEN	PLAINCLOTHES	BABINGTONITE
LIFELESSNESS	SIDEWHISKERS	INCREASINGLY	PORNOGRAPHIC	BACCHANALIAN
LILLIBULLERO	SIPHONOSTELE	INTERCHANGED	PSYCHOPATHIC	BACKBREAKING
LILLIBURLERO	SITTLICHKEIT	KLIPSPRINGER	PYROCATECHOL	BARNSTORMING
LISTLESSNESS	SLOVENLINESS	LUXEMBOURGER	RADIOGRAPHER	BEHAVIOURISM
MAGNILOQUENT	SNOBBISHNESS	MERRYTHOUGHT	RECEIVERSHIP	BETHLEHEMITE
MALTREATMENT	SOUTHEASTERN	MIDDLEWEIGHT	RELATIONSHIP	BIBLIOPEGIST
MICHELANGELO	SOUTHWESTERN	QUADRIPLEGIA	RHADAMANTHUS	BICAMERALISM
MICROBREWERY	SPACIOUSNESS	QUARTERLIGHT	SALESMANSHIP	BICENTENNIAL
MILLILAMBERT	SPECIOUSNESS	SLOCKDOLAGER	SAUROGNATHAE	BIELORUSSIAN
MINDFULLNESS	SPECKTIONEER	SLOCKDOLIGER	SEMIDETACHED	BIODIVERSITY
MISAPPREHEND	SPITEFULNESS	SLOCKDOLOGER	STENOGRAPHER	BIRDWATCHING
MISPLACEMENT	SPURIOUSNESS	SLUBBERINGLY	STROPHANTHUS	BLEFUSCUDIAN
MISREPRESENT	STEALTHINESS	STAGGERINGLY	UNDERCLOTHES	BLOODLETTING
MISSTATEMENT	STRAIGHTNESS	SUPERCHARGED	UNDIMINISHED	BLUESTOCKING
MISTREATMENT	STRANGLEWEED	SUPERCHARGER	VEHMGERICHTE	BOONDOGGLING
NEPENTHACEAE	STRATOSPHERE	SURPRISINGLY	ABBREVIATION	BOULEVARDIER
NEVERTHELESS	STREPSIPTERA	THAUMATURGIC	ABOLITIONIST	BRAINWASHING
NORTHEASTERN	STUBBORNNESS	THAUMATURGUS	ACCELERATION	BREATHTAKING
NORTHWESTERN	STUDIOUSNESS	TURBOCHARGER	ACCENTUATION	BRILLIANTINE
OBSOLETENESS	SUBCONTINENT	UNCHALLENGED	ACCOMPANYING	BROADCASTING
ONOMATOPOEIA	SUBJECTIVELY	UNDISCHARGED	ACCORDIONIST	BUSINESSLIKE
ONOMATOPOEIC	SUBMISSIVELY	WALLYDRAIGLE	ACCUMULATION	BYELORUSSIAN
OPPRESSIVELY	SUBTERRANEAN	WELTERWEIGHT	ACCUSATORIAL	CALUMNIATION
OXYACETYLENE	SUCCESSIVELY	WILLIEWAUGHT	ADAPTABILITY	CANCELLATION
PAINLESSNESS	SUGGESTIVELY	ACCOMPLISHED	ADJUDICATION	CANONIZATION
PANATHENAEAN	TACTLESSNESS	ANTISTROPHON	ADULTERATION	CAPITULATION
PARALIPOMENA	TAMARICACEAE	ARISTOLOCHIA	ADVISABILITY	CARDINDEXING
PASSIONATELY	TELEGRAPHESE	BAIRNSFATHER	AERODYNAMICS	CARDIOLOGIST
PEACEFULNESS	THANKFULNESS	BRACHYCEPHAL	AGALMATOLITE	CARICATURIST
PERCEPTIVELY	THOROUGHNESS	CALLIGRAPHIC	ALIMENTATIVE	CARLOVINGIAN
PERSUASIVELY	THYSANOPTERA	CARRIWITCHET	ALLITERATION	CARTHAGINIAN
PERVERSENESS	TIMELESSNESS	CARTOGRAPHER	AMALGAMATION	CHALCOPYRITE
PETTIFOGGERS	TOGETHERNESS	CARTOGRAPHIC	AMELIORATION	CHARACTERIZE
PETTIFOGGERY	TRANSCENDENT	CATASTROPHIC	ANAESTHETISE	CHEESEPARING
PHRONTISTERY	TROCHOSPHERE	CHAIRMANSHIP	ANAESTHETIST	CHILDBEARING
POIKILOTHERM	TRUTHFULNESS	CHAMPIONSHIP	ANAESTHETIZE	CHLORINATION
POLYETHYLENE	UNCTUOUSNESS	CROSSBENCHER	ANNIHILATION	CHORIZONTIST
POPOCATEPETL	UNDERACHIEVE	DICTATORSHIP	ANNUNCIATION	CHRISTIANITY
POSSESSIVELY	UNDERCURRENT	DIRECTORSHIP	ANTANANARIVO	CIRCUMCISION
POSTMISTRESS	UNDERGARMENT	EXTINGUISHER	ANTEDILUVIAN	CIRCUMSCRIBE
POSTPONEMENT	UNEMPLOYMENT	FEHMGERICHTE	ANTEMERIDIAN	CIVILISATION
PREPAREDNESS	VENGEFULNESS	FOTHERINGHAY	ANTIBACCHIUS	CIVILIZATION
PREPONDERENT	VENTRIPOTENT	GAMESMANSHIP	ANTICIPATION	CLARINETTIST
PRESENTIMENT	VINDICTIVELY	GASTROSOPHER	ANTINEUTRINO	CLAUDICATION
PRIGGISHNESS	WATCHFULNESS	GUARDIANSHIP	APOLLINARIAN	CODIFICATION
PROPRIETRESS	WRETCHEDNESS	HIEROGLYPHIC	APOSTROPHISE	COHABITATION
PROSOPOPOEIA	YOUTHFULNESS	HOMOEOPATHIC	APPRECIATION	COLLUCTATION
PROTECTIVELY	DISRESPECTFUL	HORSEMANSHIP	APPRECIATIVE	COLONIZATION
PSIPHENOMENA	MUTESSARIFAT	HYDROGRAPHER	APPREHENSION	COLOQUINTIDA
PTERIDOSPERM	SHORTSTAFFED	HYMNOGRAPHER	APPREHENSIVE	COMMENDATION
READJUSTMENT	UNDERSTAFFED	IAMBOGRAPHER	ARCHILOCHIAN	COMMISSARIAT

COMPELLATION	DISAPPEARING	HAEMORRHOIDS	INTRANSITIVE	NYCTITROPISM
COMPENSATION	DISCOURAGING	HAIRDRESSING	INTRAUTERINE	NYMPHOMANIAC
COMPLICATION	DISFRANCHISE	HAMBLETONIAN	INTRODUCTION	OBLITERATION
COMPROMISING	DISINCENTIVE	HANDKERCHIEF	INTROVERSION	OBSERVANTINE
COMPURGATION	DISPENSATION	HAPTOTROPISM	INTUITIONISM	OBSTETRICIAN
CONCILIATION	DISQUISITION	HARUMFRODITE	INVALIDATION	OCTOGENARIAN
CONDEMNATION	DISSATISFIED	HEARTWARMING	INVIGORATING	OPINIONATIVE
CONDENSATION	DISSERTATION	HELIOTROPISM	INVIGORATION	ORGANISATION
CONDUCTIVITY	DISSOCIATION	HELLGRAMMITE	INVISIBILITY	ORGANIZATION
CONFIDENTIAL	DISTILLATION	HEREDITARIAN	IRASCIBILITY	ORIENTEERING
CONFIRMATION	DISTRIBUTION	HERMENEUTICS	IRREGULARITY	ORTHODONTICS
CONFISCATION	DISTRIBUTIVE	HERMENEUTIST	IRRESOLUTION	ORTHOPAEDICS
CONGREGATION	DOLPHINARIUM	HIGHFALUTING	IRRESPECTIVE	ORTHOPAEDIST
CONSCRIPTION	DRAMATURGIST	HIPPOCRATISE	IRRITABILITY	OSSIFICATION
CONSECRATION	DRINKDRIVING	HIPPOCREPIAN	ISHMAELITISH	OVERCROWDING
CONSERVATION	ECCENTRICITY	HOUSEKEEPING	ISOLATIONISM	OVERDRESSING
CONSERVATISM	EDUCATIONIST	HOUSEWARMING	ISOLATIONIST	OVEREXERTION
CONSERVATIVE	EGYPTOLOGIST	HUDIBRASTICS	JURISDICTION	OVERPOWERING
CONSOCIATION	EMANCIPATION	HUMANITARIAN	KILLIKINNICK	OVERWHELMING
CONSPECTUITY	EMASCULATION	HUMANIZATION	KLEPTOMANIAC	PACIFICATION
CONSPIRACIST	EMBARRASSING	HYPERACIDITY	LABANOTATION	PANDAEMONIUM
CONSTIPATION	ENCHEIRIDION	HYPERTENSION	LABOURSAVING	PARANTHELIUM
CONSTITUTION	ENERGYSAVING	ICHTHYOPSIDA	LABYRINTHINE	PARENTHESIZE
CONSTRICTION	ENTERPRISING	IDEALIZATION	LANCASTERIAN	PARKINSONISM
CONSTRUCTION	ENTERTAINING	ILLEGIBILITY	LANGUEDOCIAN	PEACEKEEPING
CONSTRUCTIVE	ENTOMOLOGIST	ILLOGICALITY	LEGALIZATION	PEDIATRICIAN
CONSULTATION	EPISCOPALIAN	ILLUMINATING	LINCOLNSHIRE	PENALIZATION
CONSULTATIVE	EPITHALAMION	ILLUMINATION	LIQUEFACTION	PERCEPTIVITY
CONSUMMATION	EPITHALAMIUM	ILLUSTRATION	LIVERPUDLIAN	PEREMPTORILY
CONTIGNATION	EQUIVOCATION	ILLUSTRATIVE	LONGSTANDING	PERIODONTICS
CONTINUATION	ESCAPOLOGIST	IMMODERATION	LUXULLIANITE	PERMEABILITY
CONTRIBUTION	ESSENTIALITY	IMMUNIZATION	MACMILLANITE	PERMITTIVITY
CONVALESCING	ETHEROMANIAC	IMMUNOLOGIST	MALFORMATION	PERNOCTATION
CONVERSATION	EXACERBATION	IMMUTABILITY	MALLEABILITY	PERPETRATION
CONVEYANCING	EXAGGERATION	IMPARTIALITY	MALNUTRITION	PERSPICACITY
CONVIVIALITY	EXASPERATING	IMPERFECTION	MANIPULATION	PERSPIRATION
COORDINATION	EXASPERATION	IMPERFECTIVE	MANIPULATIVE	PERTURBATION
COUNTERPOINT	EXCITABILITY	IMPLANTATION	MARLINESPIKE	PESTILENTIAL
COUNTERPOISE	EXCRUCIATING	IMPREGNATION	MARSEILLAISE	PETRIFACTION
COURTMARTIAL	EXCRUCIATION	INAUGURATION	MASTURBATION	PETTIFOGGING
CRASHLANDING	EXHILARATING	INCAPABILITY	MECHITHARIST	PHILISTINISM
CRISTOBALITE	EXHILARATION	INCINERATION	MENSTRUATION	PHILOSOPHIZE
CROSSEXAMINE	EXPLOITATION	INCONCLUSIVE	MERCANTILISM	PHLEBOTOMIST
CROSSSECTION	EXTENSIONIST	INCRUSTATION	METALLURGIST	PHYSIOLOGIST
DEASPIRATION	FERMENTATION	INCUNABULIST	METAMORPHISM	PIGMENTATION
DEBILITATING	FINALIZATION	INDISCRETION	MINDBOGGLING	PLAUSIBILITY
DECAPITATION	FIRSTFOOTING	INFILTRATION	MINERALOGIST	PLEIOCHASIUM
DECELERATION	FLAGELLATION	INFLAMMATION	MINISTRATION	POLARIZATION
DECENTRALISE	FLUORIDATION	INGRATIATING	MISQUOTATION	POLICYMAKING
DECENTRALIZE	FLUVIOMARINE	INNATTENTIVE	MOBILIZATION	POSTPOSITIVE
DEGENERATION	FOOTSLOGGING	INSEMINATION	MODIFICATION	POSTPRANDIAL
DEHUMIDIFIER	FRANKALMOIGN	INSOLUBILITY	MOISTURIZING	POTAMOLOGIST
DELIBERATION	FRUMENTATION	INSTALLATION	MONTESSORIAN	POTENTIALITY
DEMILITARIZE	FUSTILLIRIAN	INSTAURATION	MOONLIGHTING	POWERSHARING
DEMIMONDAINE	GALLIGASKINS	INSURRECTION	MOTORCYCLIST	PRACTICALITY
DENDROLOGIST	GALLIVANTING	INTENERATION	MOUSQUETAIRE	PRASEODYMIUM
DENOMINATION	GEOMETRICIAN	INTERCEPTION	MUGGLETONIAN	PRECONDITION
DENUNCIATION	GEOPHYSICIST	INTERCESSION	MULTIGRAVIDA	PREDETERMINE
DEPOPULATION	GERIATRICIAN	INTERGLACIAL	MULTIPLICITY	PREDILECTION
DEPRECIATION	GIBRALTARIAN	INTERJECTION	MUNICIPALITY	PREFERENTIAL
DEREGULATION	GLADIATORIAL	INTERMISSION	MUSICOLOGIST	PREGUSTATION
DESIDERATIVE	GLOCKENSPIEL	INTERPRETING	NAVIGABILITY	PREHISTORIAN
DESIRABILITY	GRANDISONIAN	INTERRUPTION	NEIGHBOURING	PREREQUISITE
DIALECTICIAN	GRANDMONTINE	INTERSECTION	NEOPLATONISM	PRESBYTERIAN
DICHROMATISM	GRAPHOLOGIST	INTERVENTION	NONAGENARIAN	PRESCRIPTION
DIFFERENTIAL	GROSSULARITE	INTIMIDATING	NONDIRECTIVE	PRESCRIPTIVE
DILAPIDATION	GYMNOSOPHIST	INTIMIDATION	NONOBJECTIVE	PRESENTATION
DIPRIONIDIAN	GYNECOLOGIST	INTOXICATING	NOTIFICATION	PRESERVATION
DISACCHARIDE	HAEMOPHILIAC	INTOXICATION	NUTRITIONIST	PRESERVATIVE

PRESIDENTIAL	SHOSTAKOVICH	UMBRADARLING	FRACTIONALLY	UNILATERALLY
PRESTRICTION	SKUTTERUDITE	UNAPPETIZING	FUNCTIONALLY	UNOFFICIALLY
PREVENTATIVE	SLEEPWALKING	UNATTRACTIVE	GEOLOGICALLY	UNPARALLELED
PRIMIGRAVIDA	SMALLHOLDING	UNCLASSIFIED	GOOSEPIMPLES	UNPRINCIPLED
PRINCIPALITY	SNOWBOARDING	UNCONVINCING	HELIOGABALUS	UNUTTERABLES
PRIZEWINNING	SOLICITATION	UNDERPINNING	HERMETICALLY	WOLSTENHOLME
PROCLAMATION	SOMNAMBULISM	UNIDENTIFIED	HISTORICALLY	AGATHODAIMON
PRODUCTIVITY	SOMNAMBULIST	UNIVERSALIST	HORIZONTALLY	AIRCRAFTSMAN
PROFESSORIAL	SOUTHCOTTIAN	UNOPPRESSIVE	HORRIFICALLY	ALEXIPHARMIC
PROFITEERING	SPELEOLOGIST	UNPOPULARITY	HYGIENICALLY	AMBULANCEMAN
PROGYMNASIUM	SPHACELATION	UNPRETENDING	HYPNOTICALLY	ARTILLERYMAN
PROLONGATION	SPHAIRISTIKE	UNPRODUCTIVE	HYSTERICALLY	BACKWOODSMAN
PROMULGATION	SPIRITUALISM	UNRESPONSIVE	ICHTHYOCOLLA	BREASTSUMMER
PROPAGANDISM	SPIRITUALIST	UNSATISFYING	IMPERSONALLY	CLEISTOGAMIC
PROPAGANDIST	SPIRITUALITY	UNSURPRISING	INCIDENTALLY	ENGLISHWOMAN
PROPITIATION	SQUIRRELFISH	UNSUSPECTING	INDIVIDUALLY	ENGLISHWOMEN
PROSCRIPTION	STAKHANOVITE	URBANIZATION	INDUSTRIALLY	EXSERVICEMAN
PROSTITUTION	STATISTICIAN	VAPORIZATION	INNOMINABLES	FRONTIERSMAN
PROTACTINIUM	STEGOPHOLIST	VERIFICATION	INTERSTELLAR	HEPHTHEMIMER
PROTESTATION	STEREOTYPING	VETERINARIAN	IRRATIONALLY	HIEROGRAMMAT
PROTHALAMION	STERNUTATION	VILIFICATION	MADEMOISELLE	HIPPOPOTAMUS
PROTHALAMIUM	STRADIVARIUS	VITUPERATION	MAGNETICALLY	KATZENJAMMER
PROVIDENTIAL	STREPITATION	VITUPERATIVE	MAJESTICALLY	LONGSHOREMAN
PSEPHOLOGIST	STRIDULATION	VOCIFERATION	MEANINGFULLY	NEWSPAPERMAN
PSYCHIATRIST	STROMATOLITE	WATERCARRIER	MECHANICALLY	PROTOPLASMAL
PSYCHOLOGIST	STRONTIANITE	WHIMSICALITY	METHODICALLY	PROTOPLASMIC
PURIFICATION	STUPEFACTION	WHIPPOORWILL	NEUROTICALLY	SCLERODERMIA
PURPOSEBUILT	SUBARRHATION	WOLLASTONITE	NONALCOHOLIC	SERVICEWOMAN
PUTREFACTION	SUBHASTATION	MOSBOLLETJIE	OCCASIONALLY	SLEDGEHAMMER
PYROTECHNICS	SUBJECTIVITY	CABINETMAKER	ORNITHOGALUM	STRIGIFORMES
QUADRAGESIMA	SUBLAPSARIAN	DOUBLEDECKER	PATHETICALLY	UNACCUSTOMED
QUANTITATIVE	SUBSCRIPTION	HALLANSHAKER	PEDANTICALLY	WAREHOUSEMAN
QUINQUENNIAL	SUBSIDIARITY	HARNESSMAKER	PERIODICALLY	WELLINFORMED
RACKETEERING	SUBSTITUTION	HOLIDAYMAKER	PHENOMENALLY	WILTSHIREMAN
RAMIFICATION	SUBSTITUTIVE	HOUSEBREAKER	PHONETICALLY	YELLOWHAMMER
RATIFICATION	SUCCUSSATION	PINNIEWINKLE	PRALLTRILLER	YORKSHIREMAN
RECEPTIONIST	SULPHONAMIDE	PUMPERNICKEL	PROLIFICALLY	ACQUAINTANCE
RECOLLECTION	SUPERSTITION	SCRIMSHANKER	PROVERBIALLY	ACQUIESCENCE
RECUPERATION	SUPPLICATION	SINGLEDECKER	PURPOSEFULLY	AMPHISBAENIC
RECUPERATIVE	SWIZZLESTICK	SPELLCHECKER	QUIXOTICALLY	ANTIMNEMONIC
REFLECTIVITY	SYNADELPHITE	STRAITJACKET	RECIPROCALLY	ANTONINIANUS
REGENERATION	SYNTAGMATITE	TROUBLEMAKER	RESPECTFULLY	APPURTENANCE
REGISTRATION	TAGLIACOTIAN	UNDERSKINKER	RHYTHMICALLY	ARBORESCENCE
REJUVENATION	TECHNICALITY	ACADEMICALLY	ROMANTICALLY	ARISTOPHANES
REMUNERATION	TECHNOLOGIST	ACCIDENTALLY	RONCESVALLES	AYUNTAMIENTO
REMUNERATIVE	TELEGRAPHIST	ADDITIONALLY	SADISTICALLY	BELLIGERENCY
RENUNCIATION	TELEOSAURIAN	ADJECTIVALLY	SARDANAPALUS	BLOODSTAINED
REPATRIATION	TETRACYCLINE	ARTIFICIALLY	SARDONICALLY	CALLISTHENES
REPERCUSSION	TETRAHEDRITE	ARTISTICALLY	SARSAPARILLA	CARCINOGENIC
REPOSSESSION	THANKSGIVING	BARRANQUILLA	SEMANTICALLY	CEREBROTONIC
REPROCESSING	THEOPHYLLINE	BOUGAINVILLE	SEMICIRCULAR	CHITTERLINGS
REPRODUCTION	THEORETICIAN	CAPERCAILLIE	SEQUENTIALLY	CIRCASSIENNE
REPRODUCTIVE	THERAPEUTICS	CEREMONIALLY	SHILLYSHALLY	CIRCUMSTANCE
RESURRECTION	THESSALONIAN	COLLOQUIALLY	SPECIFICALLY	CLAIRVOYANCE
RETICULATION	TIGHTFITTING	COLLYWOBBLES	SPINECHILLER	CLAIRVOYANCY
SALVATIONIST	TORRICELLIAN	COMMERCIALLY	SPORADICALLY	COMMANDMENTS
SATISFACTION	TOTALITARIAN	COMMONWEALTH	SPREADEAGLED	COMMISSIONED
SCANDINAVIAN	TOXICOLOGIST	CONGENITALLY	STERNWHEELER	COMMISSIONER
SCHNEIDERIAN	TRACTABILITY	DIENCEPHALON	STRUCTURALLY	CONFECTIONER
SCOPOPHILIAC	TRANQUILLISE	DISDAINFULLY	SUCCESSFULLY	CONFESSIONAL
SECESSIONIST	TRANQUILLITY	DIVERTICULUM	SUPERNACULUM	CONSTITUENCY
SECTARIANISM	TRANQUILLIZE	DOGMATICALLY	SWASHBUCKLER	CONSTITUENTS
SEGMENTATION	TRANSMISSION	DRAMATICALLY	SYMBOLICALLY	CONVENTIONAL
SELFADHESIVE	TRANSMOGRIFY	ECONOMICALLY	TERRIFICALLY	COSCINOMANCY
SELFCATERING	TRANSPONTINE	ECSTATICALLY	THEATRICALLY	CURMUDGEONLY
SEPTUAGESIMA	TRANSVESTISM	ELECTRICALLY	THOUGHTFULLY	DARLINGTONIA
SEXAGENARIAN	TRANSVESTITE	EMPHATICALLY	ULOTRICHALES	DISOBEDIENCE
SHAREHOLDING	TRICHOLOGIST	EPENCEPHALON	UNAPPARELLED	DIVERTIMENTO
SHIPBUILDING	UINTATHERIUM	ESTHETICALLY	UNCONTROLLED	ELASMOBRANCH

ELECTROTONUS	SHORTCOMINGS	EQUIVOCATORY	PRESUMPTUOUS	CATADIOPTRIC
ERATOSTHENES	SIGNIFICANCE	FELDSPATHOID	PROGESTERONE	CHLOROPICRIN
EXHIBITIONER	STEREOPHONIC	FULMINATIONS	PROPITIATORY	CLAMJAMPHRIE
EXTRAVAGANCE	SUBSERVIENCE	GALLINACEOUS	PSEUDONYMOUS	CLOTHESHORSE
EXTRAVAGANZA	SURROUNDINGS	GAMOSEPALOUS	RADIOBIOLOGY	COUNTERMARCH
FLUORESCENCE	SURVEILLANCE	GOBBLEDEGOOK	RADIOISOTOPE	DORSIVENTRAL
FRANKINCENSE	THEREAGAINST	GOBBLEDYGOOK	RAMBUNCTIOUS	ENANTIOMORPH
FRAUENDIENST	THICKSKINNED	HOMOTHERMOUS	RHYTIDECTOMY	ENTOPLASTRON
FREIGHTLINER	TRANSFERENCE	HYDROGEOLOGY	SACRILEGIOUS	EVENTEMPERED
GRANDPARENTS	TRANSITIONAL	HYDROQUINONE	SALTATORIOUS	GLUBBDUBDRIB
HAPPENSTANCE	TRANSLUCENCE	HYPERSARCOMA	SARRUSOPHONE	GLYNDEBOURNE
HEARTSTRINGS	TRANSOCEANIC	HYSTERECTOMY	SATISFACTORY	HETEROPHORIA
HOBBIDIDANCE	TRANSPARENCY	IDIOTHERMOUS	SEMIPRECIOUS	HISTIOPHORUS
IMPERTINENCE	TROCHELMINTH	INAUSPICIOUS	SIMULTANEOUS	HYDROCHLORIC
IMPROVIDENCE	UNDETERMINED	INFELICITOUS	SIPHONOPHORA	HYMENOPTERAN
INADVERTENCE	UNIMPORTANCE	INFLAMMATORY	SOUTHERNMOST	HYPOCHONDRIA
INCOMPETENCE	UNRESTRAINED	INHARMONIOUS	SOUTHERNWOOD	ISOBILATERAL
INCONTINENCE	VALENCIENNES	INSALUBRIOUS	SPECTROSCOPE	LAMELLICORNE
INDEPENDENCE	VERUMONTANUM	INSTRUCTIONS	SPERMATOZOID	LEGIONNAIRES
INDIFFERENCE	WASHINGTONIA	INTRODUCTORY	SPERMATOZOON	MANUFACTURER
INEFFICIENCY	WELLINGTONIA	KALEIDOSCOPE	SPINSTERHOOD	MISDELIVERED
INEXPERIENCE	XIPHISTERNUM	LALLAPALOOZA	STENTORPHONE	MISINTERPRET
INTELLIGENCE	ACHLAMYDEOUS	LAMENTATIONS	STRANGLEHOLD	MULTICOLORED
INTEMPERANCE	ADSCITITIOUS	LAMPADEDROMY	SUBCONSCIOUS	MULTILATERAL
INTERFERENCE	ADVANTAGEOUS	LEIOTRICHOUS	SUBCUTANEOUS	NYCHTHEMERON
JENNYSPINNER	ADVANTAGIOUS	LITHOLATROUS	SUPERCILIOUS	ONYCHOPHORAN
LONGDISTANCE	ADVENTITIOUS	MACHAIRODONT	TELEUTOSPORE	PARTICOLORED
LONGITUDINAL	AECIDIOSPORE	MALLOPHAGOUS	TESTOSTERONE	PARTICULARLY
LUMINESCENCE	AETHRIOSCOPE	MASTERSTROKE	THUNDERCLOUD	PEDICELLARIA
LUMINISCENCE	AMBIDEXTROUS	MASTIGOPHORA	THUNDERSTORM	PERSULPHURIC
MAGNIFICENCE	AMPHISTOMOUS	MERETRICIOUS	TRALATICIOUS	PHILODENDRON
MARCOBRUNNER	ANDROSTERONE	MERITRICIOUS	TRALATITIOUS	POGONOPHORAN
MISPRONOUNCE	ANEMOPHILOUS	MESOTHELIOMA	TRANSACTIONS	PYTHONOMORPH
MNEMOTECHNIC	ANTHROPOLOGY	METAGNATHOUS	UNSCRUPULOUS	REDISCOVERED
NEUROSCIENCE	ANTICIPATORY	METALLOPHONE	VAINGLORIOUS	RHODODENDRON
NOCONFIDENCE	ANTIMETABOLE	METAMORPHOSE	WEATHERPROOF	SERVICEBERRY
NONEXISTENCE	APPENDECTOMY	MISBEHAVIOUR	ZALAMBDODONT	SILVERHAIRED
NONRESIDENCE	ATHEROMATOUS	MISDEMEANOUR	BIBLIOGRAPHY	STILBOESTROL
OBSOLESCENCE	BACTERIOLOGY	MUCILAGINOUS	BOOBYTRAPPED	STRINGCOURSE
OCCUPATIONAL	BENZOPHENONE	MULTIFARIOUS	CHOREOGRAPHY	SUPERNATURAL
OLDFASHIONED	BENZOQUINONE	MYRINGOSCOPE	CRYPTOGRAPHY	TAPSALTEERIE
OUTBUILDINGS	BIOFLAVONOID	NEIGHBORHOOD	DEUTERANOPIA	TAPSLETEERIE
OVERSTRAINED	BLENNORRHOEA	NEUROFIBROMA	EAVESDROPPER	THESMOPHORIA
PENNSYLVANIA	BRANCHIOPODA	NORTHERNMOST	ENTEROMORPHA	THOROUGHBRED
PERISTERONIC	CAMPODEIFORM	OBSTREPEROUS	GENTLETAMPER	TITANOSAURUS
PERSEVERANCE	CANTANKEROUS	OREOPITHEOUS	GLYPTOGRAPHY	UNCONSIDERED
PHILHARMONIC	CARPOPHAGOUS	ORTHOPTEROUS	GONADOTROPIN	UNNEIGHBORLY
PHOSPHORENCE	CHONDRIOSOME	OSCILLOSCOPE	LEXICOGRAPHY	URTRICULARIA
POTICHOMANIA	COMBINATIONS	OSTENTATIOUS	MISANTHROPIC	VARICOLOURED
PRACTICIONER	COMMENDATORY	OSTEOSARCOMA	OCEANOGRAPHY	WHIGMALEERIE
PRACTITIONER	COMPENSATORY	PALEONTOLOGY	PHOSPHOLIPID	XANTHOPTERIN
PREDOMINANCE	CONCILIATORY	PALPITATIONS	SCHILLERSPAR	ZARATHUSTRIC
PROCESSIONAL	CONFIRMATORY	PANDANACEOUS	SINANTHROPUS	ANAMORPHOSIS
PROFESSIONAL	CONSERVATORY	PANTOPHAGOUS	STEREOSCOPIC	ANCHORPERSON
PROLEGOMENON	CONTEMPTUOUS	PARSIMONIOUS	STORMTROOPER	ANECATHARSIS
PROPORTIONAL	CONTERMINOUS	PASSEPARTOUT	THIGMOTROPIC	ANTIMACASSAR
PROTUBERANCE	CONTRIBUTORY	PERGAMENEOUS	TRADESPEOPLE	ARTHROPLASTY
QUADRAPHONIC	CONTUMACIOUS	PERTINACIOUS	WICKETKEEPER	AUSPICIOUSLY
QUARTERFINAL	CYMOTRICHOUS	PERVICACIOUS	BEAUMONTIQUE	AUTOHYPNOSIS
QUINTESSENCE	DEAMBULATORY	PHARMACOLOGY	MACABERESQUE	BESSERWISSER
REAPPEARANCE	DEPRECIATORY	PHILANTHROPY	PECTORILOQUY	BLOODTHIRSTY
RECOGNIZANCE	DESSERTSPOON	PHYTONADIONE	AGRICULTURAL	BOISTEROUSLY
RECREATIONAL	DEUTEROSCOPY	PHYTOPHAGOUS	ALPHANUMERIC	BREATHALYSER
REDEMPTIONER	DISCOURTEOUS	PLACENTIFORM	ANTIBARBARUS	BREATHLESSLY
REMINISCENCE	DISINGENUOUS	PLASTERSTONE	BRONTOSAURUS	CAMERAPERSON
REMONSTRANCE	DRESSINGDOWN	POLYPETALOUS	BUNKOSTEERER	CONTINUOUSLY
RESIPISCENCE	DYSTELEOLOGY	POLYRIBOSOME	CAMPANULARIA	CONTRAPPOSTO
RISORGIMENTO	EPILEPTIFORM	PRAXINOSCOPE	CANTILEVERED	COURAGEOUSLY
SCAPULIMANCY	EPISTEMOLOGY	PREPOSTEROUS	CARAVANSERAI	DELICATESSEN

DIPLOGENESIS
DISASTROUSLY
DISCOMEDUSAE
DISPOSSESSED
DUNNIEWASSAL
EFFORTLESSLY
ELECTROLYSIS
ENHYPOSTASIA
EPANORTHOSIS
FASTIDIOUSLY
FORTUITOUSLY
HAEMATEMESIS
HARMONIOUSLY
HETEROPLASIA
INCAUTIOUSLY
INTERSPERSED
KIRSCHWASSER
LASCIVIOUSLY
LUGUBRIOUSLY
METICULOUSLY
MIRACULOUSLY
MONOTONOUSLY
MYSTERIOUSLY
OBSEQUIOUSLY
OMBUDSPERSON
OPHIOGLOSSUM
ORTHOGENESIS
ORTHOTONESIS
OSTEOPOROSIS
OUTRAGEOUSLY
PALINGENESIA
PALINGENESIA
PANAESTHESIA
PARACENTESIS
PHOSPHORESCE
POINTILLISME
POSTHUMOUSLY
PRECARIOUSLY
PRECOCIOUSLY
PREPOSSESSED
PRODIGIOUSLY
PROPITIOUSLY
PUGNACIOUSLY
RELENTLESSLY
RIDICULOUSLY
SCANDALOUSLY
SCHINDYLESIS
SCRUPULOUSLY
SCURRILOUSLY
SEPTEMBRISER
SOLICITOUSLY
SPIEGELEISEN
SPOKESPERSON
STANISLAVSKI
STELLENBOSCH
SUSPICIOUSLY
TOBACCONISTS
TRANSGRESSOR
TREMENDOUSLY
TUBERCULOSIS
UNAUTHORISED
UNDEREXPOSED
UNRECOGNISED
UPROARIOUSLY
VOCIFEROUSLY
VOLUPTUOUSLY
AGAMOGENETIC
AMPHITHEATER
AMPHITHEATRE

ANASTIGMATIC
ANDOUILLETTE
ANTAGONISTIC
ANTHELMINTIC
ANTIRACHITIC
APPENDICITIS
ARISTOCRATIC
BACTERIOSTAT
BANDERSNATCH
BARORECEPTOR
BENEVOLENTLY
BERTHOLLETIA
BIOCHEMISTRY
BUREAUCRATIC
BUTTERSCOTCH
CALCEAMENTUM
CATHETOMETER
CHAUVINISTIC
CHIROPRACTIC
CHIROPRACTOR
CHREMATISTIC
CHRESTOMATHY
CLEARSIGHTED
COCCIDIOSTAT
COINCIDENTAL
COLLABORATOR
COMPLACENTLY
CONCENTRATED
CONCURRENTLY
CONSEQUENTLY
CONSISTENTLY
CONSOLIDATED
CONSOLIDATOR
CONTAMINATED
CONTRAPUNTAL
CONVENIENTLY
COSMOPOLITAN
CRASSAMENTUM
CROSSCOUNTRY
DEMONSTRATOR
DEPARTMENTAL
DERESTRICTED
DIAGRAMMATIC
DISAPPOINTED
DISCOMYCETES
DISCONCERTED
DISCONNECTED
DISCONTENTED
DISENCHANTED
DOMESTICATED
DONNERWETTER
ECCLESIASTES
ECCLESIASTIC
ENANTIOPATHY
ENTHUSIASTIC
EPIGRAMMATIC
ESPAGNOLETTE
ETEPIMELETIC
EXPERIMENTAL
EXTENSOMETER
FAINTHEARTED
FLAMBOYANTLY
GALVANOMETER
GASTARBEITER
GLOBETROTTER
GOVERNMENTAL
HAIRSPLITTER
HAMARTHRITIS
HETEROCLITIC

HETEROCONTAE
HIEROPHANTIC
HYPERPYRETIC
HYPOTHECATOR
ICONOCLASTIC
IMPERSONATOR
INCOHERENTLY
INCORPORATED
INDISTINCTLY
INFREQUENTLY
INSTRUMENTAL
INTERLOCUTOR
INTERRELATED
INTERROGATOR
INVESTIGATOR
IRREVERENTLY
JOURNALISTIC
KINAESTHETIC
KINDERGARTEN
LIGHTHEARTED
MANSLAUGHTER
MELODRAMATIC
MERISTEMATIC
METROPOLITAN
MILITARISTIC
MINICOMPUTER
NARCISSISTIC
NATURALISTIC
NEPHELOMETER
NIMBOSTRATUS
NONCHALANTLY
NONCOMMITTAL
ONEIROCRITIC
PALUDAMENTUM
PANCHATANTRA
PANCHROMATIC
PARAMAGNETIC
PERAMBULATOR
PERICARDITIS
PERIPHRASTIC
PERSISTENTLY
PITTERPATTER
PLECTOGNATHI
POLYNEURITIS
POLYSYNDETON
PRAISEWORTHY
PREVARICATOR
PRIZEFIGHTER
PROFICIENTLY
PROPHYLACTIC
REFRIGERATED
REFRIGERATOR
RESPONDENTIA
RESUSCITATED
SCHOOLMASTER
SCINTILLATOR
SCREENWRITER
SCRIPTWRITER
SEQUESTRATOR
SESQUITERTIA
SHARPSHOOTER
SHIRTWAISTER
SHORTSIGHTED
SPECTROMETER
STEPDAUGHTER
STOCKINGETTE
STONECHATTER
SUBCOMMITTEE
SUBSEQUENTLY

SUFFICIENTLY
SUPERSTRATUM
SURREALISTIC
TEETERTOTTER
TELEASTHETIC
THERMOSTATIC
THREEQUARTER
TRABECULATED
TRADESCANTIA
TRICHOPHYTON
TRIGONOMETRY
TRIUMPHANTLY
TURBIDIMETER
UNACQUAINTED
UNCULTIVATED
UNDEMOCRATIC
UNDERWRITTEN
UNEXPURGATED
UNFREQUENTED
UNINTERESTED
UNOBSTRUCTED
UNRESTRICTED
WEIGHTLIFTER
WHOLEHEARTED
WINTERHALTER
APPOGGIATURA
ARCHITECTURE
AWAYABSOLUTE
BATTLEGROUND
BLABBERMOUTH
BREAKTHROUGH
BREASTPLOUGH
CHARTERHOUSE
DISCOMFITURE
ENTEROPNEUST
FLITTERMOUSE
FLORICULTURE
GAINSBOROUGH
HETEROSEXUAL
HORTICULTURE
HOUSETOHOUSE
INEXACTITUDE
INTELLECTUAL
KATHAREVOUSA
MASSERANDUBA
MERVEILLEUSE
MISADVENTURE
MITRAILLEUSE
NOMENCLATURE
PASSEMEASURE
PASSIONFRUIT
PERADVENTURE
PHOTOGRAVURE
PISCICULTURE
RECONSTITUTE
REDISTRIBUTE
ROOMINGHOUSE
SCATTERMOUCH
SCHOPENHAUER
SHORTCIRCUIT
SOMATOPLEURE
SPORTSGROUND
STREPTONEURA
SUBMINIATURE
SUBSTRUCTURE
THIRDBOROUGH
VENEPUNCTURE
VERMICULTURE
VILLEGIATURA

CZECHOSLOVAK
GRISEOFULVIN
OUTMANOEUVRE
SHIRTSLEEVES
SHORTSLEEVED
COMPANIONWAY
CUCKOOFLOWER
GRASSWIDOWER
MULLIGATAWNY
PASQUEFLOWER
STRAIGHTAWAY
SUPERHIGHWAY
TETRODOTOXIN
TROPHALLAXIS
ACETALDEHYDE
ARTIODACTYLA
DAGUERROTYPE
FORMALDEHYDE
PTERIDOPHYTE
PTERODACTYLE
RECORDPLAYER
SCLERENCHYMA
SELFEMPLOYED
SPERMATOCYTE
WOODBURYTYPE
CAPERCAILZIE
DISORGANIZED
DOUBLEGLAZED
ESCHSCHOLZIA
MANGELWURZEL
PERSONALIZED
TRANQUILIZER
UNAUTHORIZED
UNRECOGNIZED

12:11

ACCUSATORIAL
AERONAUTICAL
AGRICULTURAL
AIRCRAFTSMAN
ALPHABETICAL
AMARANTACEAE
AMBULANCEMAN
ANTEDILUVIAN
ANTEMERIDIAN
ANTIMACASSAR
APOLLINARIAN
ARCHILOCHIAN
ARISTOTELEAN
ARITHMETICAL
ARTILLERYMAN
ASTROLOGICAL
ASTRONOMICAL
ASYMMETRICAL
AUSTRALASIAN
AUSTRONESIAN
BACCHANALIAN
BACKWOODSMAN
BACTERIOSTAT
BICENTENNIAL
BIELORUSSIAN
BIOGRAPHICAL
BLEFUSCUDIAN
BRACHYCEPHAL
BUCKLEBEGGAR
BYELORUSSIAN
CARAVANSERAI
CARLOVINGIAN
CARTHAGINIAN

CATAPHYSICAL	METAPHYSICAL	YORKSHIREMAN	REMINISCENCE	CONVENIENCES
COCCIDIOSTAT	METROPOLITAN	CIRCUMSCRIBE	REMONSTRANCE	COSTERMONGER
COINCIDENTAL	MONTESSORIAN	MASSERANDUBA	RESIPISCENCE	CROSSBENCHER
COMMISSARIAT	MUGGLETONIAN	ACQUAINTANCE	RHAMPHOTHECA	CUCKOOFLOWER
COMPANIONWAY	MULTILATERAL	ACQUIESCENCE	SCAPULIMANCY	DEHUMIDIFIER
CONFESSIONAL	MUTESSARIFAT	AERODYNAMICS	SCATTERMOUCH	DELICATESSEN
CONFIDENTIAL	MYTHOLOGICAL	APPURTENANCE	SHOSTAKOVICH	DERESTRICTED
CONTRAPUNTAL	NEOCLASSICAL	ARBORESCENCE	SIGNIFICANCE	DISAPPOINTED
CONVENTIONAL	NEPENTHACEAE	ASTROPHYSICS	STELLENBOSCH	DISCOMYCETES
COSMOPOLITAN	NEUROLOGICAL	ATMOSPHERICS	SUBSERVIENCE	DISCONCERTED
COURTMARTIAL	NEWSPAPERMAN	BANDERSNATCH	SURVEILLANCE	DISCONNECTED
CZECHOSLOVAK	NONAGENARIAN	BELLIGERENCY	SWIZZLESTICK	DISCONTENTED
DEPARTMENTAL	NONCOMMITTAL	BUTTERSCOTCH	THERAPEUTICS	DISENCHANTED
DIALECTICIAN	NYMPHOMANIAC	CIRCUMSTANCE	TRANSFERENCE	DISORGANIZED
DIFFERENTIAL	OBSTETRICIAN	CLAIRVOYANCE	TRANSLUCENCE	DISPOSSESSED
DIPRIONIDIAN	OCCUPATIONAL	CLAIRVOYANCY	TRANSPARENCY	DISSATISFIED
DISCOMEDUSAE	OCTOGENARIAN	CONSTITUENCY	UNIMPORTANCE	DOMESTICATED
DORSIVENTRAL	ONYCHOPHORAN	COSCINOMANCY	ACETALDEHYDE	DONNERWETTER
DUNNIEWASSAL	PANATHENAEAN	COUNTERMARCH	BRANCHIOPODA	DOUBLEDECKER
ENGLISHWOMAN	PAPILIONIDAE	DISOBEDIENCE	COLOQUINTIDA	DOUBLEGLAZED
EPACRIDACEAE	PATHOLOGICAL	ELASMOBRANCH	DISACCHARIDE	EAVESDROPPER
EPIDEICTICAL	PEDIATRICIAN	ENTOMOSTRACA	FORMALDEHYDE	ECCLESIASTES
EPISCOPALIAN	PESTILENTIAL	EXTRAVAGANCE	HAEMORRHOIDS	ENGLISHWOMEN
ETHEROMANIAC	PHILOLOGICAL	FLUORESCENCE	ICHTHYOPSIDA	ERATOSTHENES
ETHNOLOGICAL	POGONOPHORAN	FRONTISPIECE	INEXACTITUDE	EULENSPIEGEL
ETYMOLOGICAL	POSTPRANDIAL	GERONTOCRACY	MULTIGRAVIDA	EVENTEMPERED
EXPERIMENTAL	PREFERENTIAL	HAPPENSTANCE	PRIMIGRAVIDA	EXHIBITIONER
EXSERVICEMAN	PREHISTORIAN	HERMENEUTICS	SCHEHERAZADE	EXTENSOMETER
FOTHERINGHAY	PRESBYTERIAN	HOBBIDIDANCE	SPURTLEBLADE	EXTINGUISHER
FRONTIERSMAN	PRESIDENTIAL	HUDIBRASTICS	SULPHONAMIDE	FAINTHEARTED
FUSTILLIRIAN	PROCESSIONAL	ILLEGITIMACY	ACCOMPLISHED	FREIGHTLINER
GENEALOGICAL	PROFESSIONAL	IMPERTINENCE	ACKNOWLEDGED	GALVANOMETER
GEOGRAPHICAL	PROFESSORIAL	IMPROVIDENCE	AMPHITHEATER	GASTARBEITER
GEOMETRICIAN	PROPORTIONAL	INADVERTENCE	APFELSTRUDEL	GASTROSOPHER
GERIATRICIAN	PROTOPLASMAL	INCOMPETENCE	ARISTOPHANES	GENTLETAMPER
GIBRALTARIAN	PROVIDENTIAL	INCONTINENCE	BAIRNSFATHER	GLOBETROTTER
GLADIATORIAL	QUARTERFINAL	INDEPENDENCE	BAMBOCCIADES	GLOCKENSPIEL
GOVERNMENTAL	QUINQUENNIAL	INDIFFERENCE	BANANALANDER	GOOSEPIMPLES
GRANDISONIAN	RECREATIONAL	INEFFICIENCY	BARBERMONGER	GRASSWIDOWER
HAEMOPHILIAC	RHINORRHOEAL	INEXPERIENCE	BESSERWISSER	HAIRSPLITTER
HAMBLETONIAN	SAUROGNATHAE	INTELLIGENCE	BLENNORRHOEA	HALLANSHAKER
HEREDITARIAN	SCANDINAVIAN	INTEMPERANCE	BLOODSTAINED	HALLUCINOGEN
HEROICOMICAL	SCHILLERSPAR	INTERFERENCE	BOOBYTRAPPED	HAMMERHEADED
HETEROCONTAE	SCHNEIDERIAN	KALISTOCRACY	BOULEVARDIER	HANDKERCHIEF
HETEROSEXUAL	SCOPOPHILIAC	KILLIKINNICK	BREASTSUMMER	HARNESSMAKER
HIERARCHICAL	SEMICIRCULAR	LONGDISTANCE	BREATHALYSER	HEPHTHEMIMER
HIEROGRAMMAT	SERVICEWOMAN	LUMINESCENCE	BRICKFIELDER	HOLIDAYMAKER
HIPPOCREPIAN	SEXAGENARIAN	LUMINISCENCE	BUNKOSTEERER	HOUSEBREAKER
HUMANITARIAN	SOCIOLOGICAL	MAGNIFICENCE	CABINETMAKER	HYDROGRAPHER
HYMENOPTERAN	SOUTHCOTTIAN	MALACOSTRACA	CALLISTHENES	HYMNOGRAPHER
HYPERBOLICAL	STATISTICIAN	MISPRONOUNCE	CANTILEVERED	IAMBOGRAPHER
HYPOCRITICAL	STRAIGHTAWAY	NEUROSCIENCE	CARPETBAGGER	IMPOVERISHED
HYPOTHETICAL	SUBLAPSARIAN	NOCONFIDENCE	CARRIWITCHET	INCORPORATED
INSTRUMENTAL	SUBTERRANEAN	NONEXISTENCE	CARTOGRAPHER	INNOMINABLES
INTELLECTUAL	SUPERHIGHWAY	NONRESIDENCE	CASSITERIDES	INTERCHANGED
INTERGLACIAL	SUPERNATURAL	OBSOLESCENCE	CATHETOMETER	INTERRELATED
INTERSTELLAR	TAGLIACOTIAN	ORTHODONTICS	CHEESEBURGER	INTERSPERSED
ISOBILATERAL	TAMARICACEAE	ORTHOPAEDICS	CHEESEMONGER	JENNYSPINNER
KLEPTOMANIAC	TAUTOLOGICAL	PANTISOCRACY	CHURCHWARDEN	KATZENJAMMER
LANCASTERIAN	TELEOSAURIAN	PERIODONTICS	CLEARSIGHTED	KINDERGARTEN
LANGUEDOCIAN	THEORETICIAN	PERSEVERANCE	COLDSHOULDER	KIRSCHWASSER
LIVERPUDLIAN	THESSALONIAN	PHOSPHORENCE	COLLYWOBBLES	KLIPSPRINGER
LONGITUDINAL	TORRICELLIAN	PHOSPHORESCE	COMMISSIONED	LEGIONNAIRES
LONGSHOREMAN	TOTALITARIAN	PREDOMINANCE	COMMISSIONER	LICKTRENCHER
LOXODROMICAL	TRANSITIONAL	PROTUBERANCE	CONCENTRATED	LIGHTHEARTED
LYMANTRIIDAE	UNECONOMICAL	PYROTECHNICS	CONFECTIONER	LUXEMBOURGER
MACROPODIDAE	VETERINARIAN	QUINTESSENCE	CONSEQUENCES	MALPRACTICES
MATHEMATICAL	WAREHOUSEMAN	REAPPEARANCE	CONSOLIDATED	MANGELWURZEL
METAPHORICAL	WILTSHIREMAN	RECOGNIZANCE	CONTAMINATED	MANSLAUGHTER

MANUFACTURER	STENOGRAPHER	TRANSMOGRIFY	CATADIOPTRIC	ONOMATOPOEIA
MARCOBRUNNER	STEPDAUGHTER	ANTHROPOLOGY	CATASTROPHIC	ONOMATOPOEIC
MASSPRODUCED	STERNWHEELER	BACTERIOLOGY	CEREBROTONIC	ORTHOGENESIS
MINICOMPUTER	STOCKBREEDER	BERTILLONAGE	CHAIRMANSHIP	ORTHORHOMBIC
MISDELIVERED	STONECHATTER	BREAKTHROUGH	CHAMPIONSHIP	ORTHOTONESIS
MISINTERPRET	STORMTROOPER	BREASTPLOUGH	CHAUVINISTIC	OSTEOMALACIA
MOUTHBROODER	STRAITJACKET	CASTERBRIDGE	CHIROPRACTIC	OSTEOPOROSIS
MUDDLEHEADED	STRANGLEWEED	CHITTERLINGS	CHLOROPICRIN	PALINGENESIA
MULTICOLORED	STRIGIFORMES	DISADVANTAGE	CHREMATISTIC	PALINGENESIS
NEPHELOMETER	STRONGMINDED	DYSTELEOLOGY	CLAMJAMPHRIE	PANAESTHESIA
NIGHTCLOTHES	SUBCOMMITTEE	EPISTEMOLOGY	CLEISTOGAMIC	PANCHROMATIC
OLDFASHIONED	SUPERCHARGED	FRANKALMOIGN	COUNTERCLAIM	PARACENTESIS
OUTSTRETCHED	SUPERCHARGER	GAINSBOROUGH	DARLINGTONIA	PARAMAGNETIC
OVERSCUTCHED	SWASHBUCKLER	HEARTSTRINGS	DEUTERANOPIA	PARTISANSHIP
OVERSTRAINED	TAPERECORDER	HYDROGEOLOGY	DIAGRAMMATIC	PASSIONFRUIT
PARTICOLORED	TEETERTOTTER	OUTBUILDINGS	DICTATORSHIP	PEDICELLARIA
PASQUEFLOWER	THICKSKINNED	PALEONTOLOGY	DIPLOGENESIS	PENNSYLVANIA
PERSONALIZED	THOROUGHBRED	PHARMACOLOGY	DIRECTORSHIP	PERICARDITIS
PHOTOGRAPHER	THREEQUARTER	RADIOBIOLOGY	ECCLESIASTIC	PERIPHRASTIC
PITTERPATTER	TRABECULATED	SHORTCOMINGS	ELECTROLYSIS	PERISTERONIC
PLAINCLOTHES	TRANQUILIZER	STRAIGHTEDGE	ENCYCLOPEDIA	PERSULPHURIC
PRACTICIONER	TROUBLEMAKER	SURROUNDINGS	ENCYCLOPEDIC	PHILHARMONIC
PRACTITIONER	TURBIDIMETER	THIRDBOROUGH	ENHYPOSTASIA	PHOSPHOLIPID
PRALLTRILLER	TURBOCHARGER	AFORETHOUGHT	ENTHUSIASTIC	PHOTOGLYPHIC
PREPOSSESSED	ULOTRICHALES	AFTERTHOUGHT	EPANORTHOSIS	PHOTOGRAPHIC
PRIZEFIGHTER	UNACCUSTOMED	BANTAMWEIGHT	EPIGRAMMATIC	PHYCOXANTHIN
PUMPERNICKEL	UNACQUAINTED	BIBLIOGRAPHY	ERYTHROMYCIN	POLYNEURITIS
RADIOGRAPHER	UNAPPARELLED	CHOREOGRAPHY	ESCHSCHOLZIA	POLYSYLLABIC
RECORDPLAYER	UNAUTHORISED	CHRESTOMATHY	ETEPIMELETIC	PORNOGRAPHIC
REDEMPTIONER	UNAUTHORIZED	CRYPTOGRAPHY	FEATHERBRAIN	POTICHOMANIA
REDISCOVERED	UNCHALLENGED	ENANTIOPATHY	FELDSPATHOID	PROPHYLACTIC
REFRIGERATED	UNCLASSIFIED	ENTEROMORPHA	FRANKENSTEIN	PROSOPOPOEIA
REMEMBRANCER	UNCONSIDERED	GIGANTOMACHY	GAMESMANSHIP	PROTOPLASMIC
RESUSCITATED	UNCONTROLLED	GLYPTOGRAPHY	GLUBBDUBDRIB	PSYCHOPATHIC
RODOMONTADER	UNCULTIVATED	LEXICOGRAPHY	GLYCOPROTEIN	QUADRAPHONIC
ROLLERBLADER	UNDERCLOTHES	MERRYTHOUGHT	GONADOTROPIN	QUADRIPLEGIA
ROLLERBLADES	UNDEREXPOSED	MIDDLEWEIGHT	GRISEOFULVIN	RECEIVERSHIP
RONCESVALLES	UNDERSKINKER	OCEANOGRAPHY	GUARDIANSHIP	RELATIONSHIP
SCHOOLMASTER	UNDERSTAFFED	PLECTOGNATHI	HAEMATEMESIS	RESPONDENTIA
SCHOPENHAUER	UNDERWRITTEN	PRAISEWORTHY	HAMARTHRITIS	SALESMANSHIP
SCREENWRITER	UNDETERMINED	QUARTERLIGHT	HETEROCLITIC	SCATTERBRAIN
SCRIMSHANDER	UNDIMINISHED	WELTERWEIGHT	HETEROPHORIA	SCHINDYLESIS
SCRIMSHANKER	UNDISCHARGED	WILLIEWAUGHT	HETEROPLASIA	SCLERODERMIA
SCRIPTWRITER	UNEXPURGATED	AGAMOGENETIC	HIEROGLYPHIC	SELFPORTRAIT
SELFEMPLOYED	UNFREQUENTED	ALEXIPHARMIC	HIEROPHANTIC	SESQUITERTIA
SEMIDETACHED	UNIDENTIFIED	ALPHANUMERIC	HILDEBRANDIC	SHORTCIRCUIT
SEPTEMBRISER	UNINTERESTED	AMPHISBAENIC	HOMOEOPATHIC	SITTLICHKEIT
SHARPSHOOTER	UNOBSTRUCTED	ANAMORPHOSIS	HORSEMANSHIP	SPERMATOZOID
SHIRTSLEEVES	UNPARALLELED	ANASTIGMATIC	HYDROCHLORIC	STEREOPHONIC
SHIRTWAISTER	UNPREJUDICED	ANECATHARSIS	HYPERPYRETIC	STEREOSCOPIC
SHORTSIGHTED	UNPRINCIPLED	ANTAGONISTIC	HYPOCHONDRIA	STREPTOMYCIN
SHORTSLEEVED	UNRECOGNISED	ANTHELMINTIC	ICONOCLASTIC	STUDDINGSAIL
SHORTSTAFFED	UNRECOGNIZED	ANTIMNEMONIC	JOURNALISTIC	SURREALISTIC
SILVERHAIRED	UNRESTRAINED	ANTIRACHITIC	KINAESTHETIC	TAPSALTEERIE
SINGLEDECKER	UNRESTRICTED	ANTITHROMBIN	LAUREATESHIP	TAPSLETEERIE
SINGLEHANDED	UNUTTERABLES	APPENDICITIS	LITHOGRAPHIC	TELEASTHETIC
SINGLEMINDED	VALENCIENNES	ARISTOCRATIC	MARKSMANSHIP	TETRODOTOXIN
SIPUNCULACEA	VARICOLOURED	ARISTOLOCHIA	MELODRAMATIC	THAUMATURGIC
SLEDGEHAMMER	WATERCARRIER	AUTOHYPNOSIS	MERISTEMATIC	THERMOSTATIC
SLOCKDOLAGER	WEIGHTLIFTER	BEAUMARCHAIS	MILITARISTIC	THESMOPHORIA
SLOCKDOLIGER	WELLBALANCED	BERTHOLLETIA	MISANTHROPIC	THIGMOTROPIC
SLOCKDOLIGER	WELLINFORMED	BIOFLAVONOID	MNEMOTECHNIC	TRADESCANTIA
SPATANGOIDEA	WHOLEHEARTED	BUREAUCRATIC	MONOSYLLABIC	TRANSOCEANIC
SPECKTIONEER	WICKETKEEPER	CALLIGRAPHIC	MOSBOLLETJIE	TROPHALLAXIS
SPECTROMETER	WINTERHALTER	CAMPANULARIA	NARCISSISTIC	TUBERCULOSIS
SPELLCHECKER	YELLOWHAMMER	CAPERCAILLIE	NATURALISTIC	TURACOVERDIN
SPIEGELEISEN	ANTIAIRCRAFT	CAPERCAILZIE	NONALCOHOLIC	UNDEMOCRATIC
SPINECHILLER	GESELLSCHAFT	CARCINOGENIC	OCTASTROPHIC	UNSCIENTIFIC
SPREADEAGLED	QUARTERSTAFF	CARTOGRAPHIC	ONEIROCRITIC	URTRICULARIA

WASHINGTONIA	ECONOMICALLY	INFORMIDABLE	PURPOSEBUILT	UNMANAGEABLE
WELLINGTONIA	ECSTATICALLY	INFREQUENTLY	PURPOSEFULLY	UNMISTAKABLE
WHIGMALEERIE	EFFORTLESSLY	INHOSPITABLE	QUANTIFIABLE	UNNEIGHBORLY
XANTHOPTERIN	ELECTRICALLY	INORDINATELY	QUESTIONABLE	UNOBTAINABLE
ZARATHUSTRIC	EMPHATICALLY	INSUFFERABLE	QUIXOTICALLY	UNOFFICIALLY
BUSINESSLIKE	ENTREATINGLY	INSUFFERABLY	RECHARGEABLE	UNPARDONABLE
FIDDLESTICKS	ESTHETICALLY	INTELLIGIBLE	RECIPROCALLY	UNPROFITABLE
HAPPYGOLUCKY	EVENHANDEDLY	INTERMINABLE	RECOGNIZABLE	UNREASONABLE
MARLINESPIKE	EXCHANGEABLE	INTERMINABLY	RELENTLESSLY	UNRESERVEDLY
MASTERSTROKE	EXHAUSTIVELY	INVULNERABLE	RESPECTFULLY	UNRETURNABLE
SPHAIRISTIKE	EXTRADITABLE	IRRATIONALLY	RESPECTIVELY	UNSEASONABLE
STANISLAVSKI	FASTIDIOUSLY	IRREDEEMABLE	RHYTHMICALLY	UPROARIOUSLY
ACADEMICALLY	FIGURATIVELY	IRRESISTIBLE	RIDICULOUSLY	USERFRIENDLY
ACCIDENTALLY	FLAMBOYANTLY	IRRESOLUTELY	ROMANTICALLY	VIBRATIUNCLE
ADDITIONALLY	FORTUITOUSLY	IRRESOLVABLE	SADISTICALLY	VINDICTIVELY
ADJECTIVALLY	FRACTIONALLY	IRREVERENTLY	SARDONICALLY	VOCIFEROUSLY
AGGRESSIVELY	FUNCTIONALLY	IRREVERSIBLE	SARSAPARILLA	VOLUPTUOUSLY
ANTIMETABOLE	FUNDAMENTALS	LASCIVIOUSLY	SCANDALOUSLY	WALLYDRAIGLE
ANTIPARTICLE	GEOLOGICALLY	LEGITIMATELY	SCRUPULOUSLY	WHIPPOORWILL
APPROACHABLE	HARMONIOUSLY	LUGUBRIOUSLY	SCURRILOUSLY	APPENDECTOMY
ARTIFICIALLY	HERMETICALLY	MACROCEPHALY	SEMANTICALLY	CHONDRIOSOME
ARTIODACTYLA	HISTORICALLY	MADEMOISELLE	SEQUENTIALLY	HYPERSARCOMA
ARTISTICALLY	HORIZONTALLY	MAGNETICALLY	SHAMEFACEDLY	HYSTERECTOMY
ATTRACTIVELY	HORRIFICALLY	MAJESTICALLY	SHILLYSHALLY	LAMPADEDROMY
ATTRIBUTABLE	HYGIENICALLY	MANOEUVRABLE	SIPHONOSTELE	MESOTHELIOMA
AUSPICIOUSLY	HYPNOTICALLY	MARRIAGEABLE	SLUBBERINGLY	NEUROFIBROMA
BARRANQUILLA	HYSTERICALLY	MEANINGFULLY	SOLICITOUSLY	OSTEOSARCOMA
BEACONSFIELD	ICHTHYOCOLLA	MECHANICALLY	SPECIFICALLY	POINTILLISME
BENEVOLENTLY	IDENTIFIABLE	METHODICALLY	SPLENOMEGALY	POLYRIBOSOME
BOISTEROUSLY	IMMACULATELY	METICULOUSLY	SPORADICALLY	QUADRAGESIMA
BOUGAINVILLE	IMMEASURABLE	MICHELANGELO	STAGGERINGLY	RHYTIDECTOMY
BREATHLESSLY	IMMEASURABLY	MIRACULOUSLY	STRANGLEHOLD	SCLERENCHYMA
CARDIOMEGALY	IMMODERATELY	MONOSYLLABLE	STRUCTURALLY	SEPTUAGESIMA
CEREMONIALLY	IMPENETRABLE	MONOTONOUSLY	SUBJECTIVELY	WOLSTENHOLME
CHESTERFIELD	IMPERISHABLE	MYSTERIOUSLY	SUBMISSIVELY	ACCOMPANYING
CLASSIFIABLE	IMPERSONALLY	NEUROTICALLY	SUBSEQUENTLY	ACCOUCHEMENT
CLAVICEMBALO	IMPRESSIVELY	NONCHALANTLY	SUCCESSFULLY	ACCOUTREMENT
COLLECTIVELY	INACCESSIBLE	NONFLAMMABLE	SUCCESSIVELY	ADMONISHMENT
COLLOQUIALLY	INACCURATELY	OBSEQUIOUSLY	SUFFICIENTLY	ANDROSTERONE
COMMERCIALLY	INADEQUATELY	OCCASIONALLY	SUGGESTIVELY	ANNOUNCEMENT
COMMUNICABLE	INADMISSIBLE	OPPRESSIVELY	SURMOUNTABLE	ANTILEGOMENA
COMPLACENTLY	INAPPLICABLE	OTHERWORLDLY	SURPRISINGLY	ANTINEUTRINO
CONCLUSIVELY	INCALCULABLE	OUTRAGEOUSLY	SUSPICIOUSLY	ASTONISHMENT
CONCURRENTLY	INCAUTIOUSLY	PARTICULARLY	SYMBOLICALLY	AWARDWINNING
CONGENITALLY	INCIDENTALLY	PASSIONATELY	TERRIFICALLY	AWEINSPIRING
CONSEQUENTLY	INCOHERENTLY	PATHETICALLY	TERRITORIALS	BACKBREAKING
CONSIDERABLE	INCOMPARABLE	PEDANTICALLY	THEATRICALLY	BARNSTORMING
CONSIDERABLY	INCOMPARABLY	PERCEPTIVELY	THOUGHTFULLY	BATTLEGROUND
CONSISTENTLY	INCOMPATIBLE	PEREMPTORILY	THREADNEEDLE	BENZOPHENONE
CONTEMPTIBLE	INCOMPLETELY	PERIODICALLY	TRADESPEOPLE	BENZOQUINONE
CONTINUOUSLY	INCONSOLABLE	PERSISTENTLY	TRANSFERABLE	BEWILDERMENT
CONTROLLABLE	INCORRIGIBLE	PERSUASIVELY	TRANSLATABLE	BIPROPELLANT
CONVENIENTLY	INCORRIGIBLY	PHENOMENALLY	TREMENDOUSLY	BIRDWATCHING
CONVINCINGLY	INCREASINGLY	PHONETICALLY	TRIUMPHANTLY	BLACKCURRANT
COURAGEOUSLY	INDECLINABLE	PINNIEWINKLE	UNACCEPTABLE	BLANDISHMENT
CURMUDGEONLY	INDEFENSIBLE	POLYSYLLABLE	UNANSWERABLE	BLOODLETTING
DECIPHERABLE	INDEFINITELY	POSSESSIVELY	UNATTAINABLE	BLUESTOCKING
DECORATIVELY	INDIGESTIBLE	POSTHUMOUSLY	UNBELIEVABLE	BOONDOGGLING
DELIBERATELY	INDISPUTABLE	PRECARIOUSLY	UNBELIEVABLY	BRAINWASHING
DEMONSTRABLE	INDISPUTABLY	PRECOCIOUSLY	UNCHANGEABLE	BREATHTAKING
DEMONSTRABLY	INDISSOLUBLE	PRODIGIOUSLY	UNCHARITABLE	BRILLIANTINE
DISAGREEABLE	INDISTINCTLY	PROFICIENTLY	UNCHARITABLY	BROADCASTING
DISASTROUSLY	INDIVIDUALLY	PROGRAMMABLE	UNDESERVEDLY	CARDINDEXING
DISDAINFULLY	INDUSTRIALLY	PROLIFICALLY	UNDETECTABLE	CHASTISEMENT
DISHONORABLE	INERADICABLE	PROPITIOUSLY	UNEXPECTEDLY	CHEESEPARING
DISHONORABLY	INEXPLICABLE	PROTECTIVELY	UNFATHOMABLE	CHILDBEARING
DISREPUTABLE	INEXPLICABLY	PROVERBIALLY	UNFAVOURABLE	CIRCASSIENNE
DOGMATICALLY	INEXTRICABLE	PTERODACTYLE	UNILATERALLY	COMBINATIONS
DRAMATICALLY	INEXTRICABLY	PUGNACIOUSLY	UNIMAGINABLE	COMMENCEMENT

COMPROMISING	LABYRINTHINE	TESTOSTERONE	CONCILIATION	IDEALIZATION
CONTABESCENT	LAMELLICORNE	TETRACYCLINE	CONDEMNATION	ILLUMINATION
CONVALESCENT	LAMENTATIONS	THANKSGIVING	CONDENSATION	ILLUSTRATION
CONVALESCING	LEPIDOMELANE	THEOPHYLLINE	CONFIRMATION	IMMODERATION
CONVEYANCING	LONGSTANDING	TIGHTFITTING	CONFISCATION	IMMUNIZATION
COUNTERPOINT	MACHAIRODONT	TRANSACTIONS	CONGREGATION	IMPERFECTION
CRASHLANDING	MAGNILOQUENT	TRANSCENDENT	CONQUISTADOR	IMPERSONATOR
CROSSEXAMINE	MALTREATMENT	TRANSPONTINE	CONSCRIPTION	IMPLANTATION
DEBILITATING	METALLOPHONE	ULTRAMONTANE	CONSECRATION	IMPREGNATION
DECIPHERMENT	MINDBOGGLING	UMBRADARLING	CONSERVATION	INAUGURATION
DECONGESTANT	MISAPPREHEND	UNAPPETIZING	CONSOCIATION	INCINERATION
DEMIMONDAINE	MISPLACEMENT	UNCONVERSANT	CONSOLIDATOR	INCRUSTATION
DISAGREEMENT	MISREPRESENT	UNCONVINCING	CONSTIPATION	INDISCRETION
DISAPPEARING	MISSTATEMENT	UNDERCURRENT	CONSTITUTION	INESCUTCHEON
DISCOURAGING	MISTREATMENT	UNDERGARMENT	CONSTRICTION	INFILTRATION
DISINFECTANT	MOISTURIZING	UNDERPINNING	CONSTRUCTION	INFLAMMATION
DISPLACEMENT	MOONLIGHTING	UNEMPLOYMENT	CONSULTATION	INSEMINATION
DRINKDRIVING	MULLIGATAWNY	UNPRETENDING	CONSUMMATION	INSTALLATION
EFFERVESCENT	NEIGHBOURING	UNSATISFYING	CONTIGNATION	INSTAURATION
EMBARRASSING	NEWFOUNDLAND	UNSURPRISING	CONTINUATION	INSURRECTION
EMBEZZLEMENT	NONRESISTANT	UNSUSPECTING	CONTRIBUTION	INTENERATION
ENCIRCLEMENT	OBSERVANTINE	VENTRIPOTENT	CONVERSATION	INTERCEPTION
ENCROACHMENT	ORIENTEERING	ZALAMBDODONT	COORDINATION	INTERCESSION
ENERGYSAVING	OVERCROWDING	ABBREVIATION	CROSSSECTION	INTERJECTION
ENTANGLEMENT	OVERDRESSING	ACCELERATION	DEASPIRATION	INTERLOCUTOR
ENTERPRISING	OVERPOWERING	ACCENTUATION	DECAPITATION	INTERMISSION
ENTERTAINING	OVERWHELMING	ACCUMULATION	DECELERATION	INTERROGATOR
ENTRENCHMENT	OXYACETYLENE	ADJUDICATION	DEGENERATION	INTERRUPTION
EPIPHENOMENA	PALPITATIONS	ADULTERATION	DELIBERATION	INTERSECTION
ESTRANGEMENT	PARALIPOMENA	AGATHODAIMON	DEMONSTRATOR	INTERVENTION
EXASPERATING	PEACEKEEPING	ALLITERATION	DENOMINATION	INTIMIDATION
EXCRUCIATING	PETTIFOGGING	AMALGAMATION	DENUNCIATION	INTOXICATION
EXHILARATING	PHYTONADIONE	AMELIORATION	DEPOPULATION	INTRODUCTION
FARTHINGLAND	PLASTERSTONE	ANCHORPERSON	DEPRECIATION	INTROVERSION
FIRSTFOOTING	POLICYMAKING	ANNIHILATION	DEREGULATION	INVALIDATION
FLUVIOMARINE	POLYETHYLENE	ANNUNCIATION	DESSERTSPOON	INVESTIGATOR
FOOTSLOGGING	POLYURETHANE	ANTICIPATION	DIENCEPHALON	INVIGORATION
FULMINATIONS	POSTPONEMENT	ANTISTROPHON	DILAPIDATION	IRRESOLUTION
GALLIGASKINS	POWERSHARING	APPRECIATION	DISPENSATION	JURISDICTION
GALLIVANTING	PREDETERMINE	APPREHENSION	DISQUISITION	LABANOTATION
GLYNDEBOURNE	PREMONSTRANT	ARCHIPELAGOS	DISSERTATION	LEGALIZATION
GONDWANALAND	PREPONDERANT	ARTICULATION	DISSOCIATION	LIQUEFACTION
GRANDMONTINE	PREPONDERENT	ASPHYXIATION	DISTILLATION	MALFORMATION
HAIRDRESSING	PRESENTIMENT	ASSIMILATION	DISTRIBUTION	MALNUTRITION
HEARTWARMING	PRIZEWINNING	ASSUEFACTION	EMANCIPATION	MANIPULATION
HEREDITAMENT	PROFITEERING	AUGMENTATION	EMASCULATION	MASTURBATION
HIGHFALUTING	PROGESTERONE	AUSCULTATION	ENCHEIRIDION	MENSTRUATION
HOUSEKEEPING	PSIPHENOMENA	BARORECEPTOR	ENTOPLASTRON	MINISTRATION
HOUSEWARMING	RACKETEERING	CALUMNIATION	EPENCEPHALON	MISQUOTATION
HYDROQUINONE	READJUSTMENT	CAMERAPERSON	EPITHALAMION	MOBILIZATION
ILLUMINATING	RECALCITRANT	CANCELLATION	EQUIVOCATION	MODIFICATION
IMPRISONMENT	RECRUDESCENT	CANONIZATION	ETYMOLOGICON	NEIGHBORHOOD
INCANDESCENT	REDEPLOYMENT	CAPITULATION	EXACERBATION	NOTIFICATION
INCONSEQUENT	RENOUNCEMENT	CHIROPRACTOR	EXAGGERATION	NYCHTHEMERON
INCONSISTENT	REPROCESSING	CHLORINATION	EXASPERATION	OBLITERATION
INCONVENIENT	RESETTLEMENT	CIRCUMCISION	EXCRUCIATION	OMBUDSPERSON
INFOTAINMENT	RETRENCHMENT	CIVILISATION	EXHILARATION	ORGANISATION
INFRINGEMENT	SARRUSOPHONE	CIVILIZATION	EXPLOITATION	ORGANIZATION
INGRATIATING	SELFCATERING	CLAUDICATION	FERMENTATION	OSSIFICATION
INSTRUCTIONS	SHAREHOLDING	CODIFICATION	FINALIZATION	OVEREXERTION
INSUFFICIENT	SHIPBUILDING	COHABITATION	FLAGELLATION	PACIFICATION
INTERMITTENT	SLEEPWALKING	COLLABORATOR	FLUORIDATION	PANPHARMACON
INTERPRETING	SMALLHOLDING	COLLUCTATION	FRUMENTATION	PANTECHNICON
INTIMIDATING	SNOWBOARDING	COLONIZATION	GENETHLIACON	PENALIZATION
INTOXICATING	SPORTSGROUND	COMMENDATION	GOBBLEDEGOOK	PERAMBULATOR
INTRANSIGENT	SPRECHGESANG	COMPELLATION	GOBBLEDYGOOK	PERNOCTATION
INTRAUTERINE	STENTORPHONE	COMPENSATION	HUMANIZATION	PERPETRATION
INVIGORATING	STEREOTYPING	COMPLICATION	HYPERTENSION	PERSPIRATION
LABOURSAVING	SUBCONTINENT	COMPURGATION	HYPOTHECATOR	PERTURBATION

PETRIFACTION	URBANIZATION	INFLAMMATORY	ANAESTHETISE	IDIOSYNCRASY
PHILODENDRON	VAPORIZATION	INFLATIONARY	ANAESTHETIST	IMMUNOLOGIST
PHYTOBENTHOS	VERIFICATION	INTERMEDIARY	APOSTROPHISE	IMPOLITENESS
PIGMENTATION	VILIFICATION	INTRODUCTORY	ASPARAGINASE	INCUNABULIST
POLARIZATION	VITUPERATION	LILLIBULLERO	BACKWARDNESS	INDEBTEDNESS
POLYSYNDETON	VOCIFERATION	LILLIBURLERO	BEHAVIOURISM	INSTRUCTRESS
PRECONDITION	WEATHERPROOF	LINCOLNSHIRE	BENEFACTRESS	INTUITIONISM
PREDILECTION	AETHRIOSCOPE	MASTIGOPHORA	BIBLIOPEGIST	ISHMAELITISH
PREGUSTATION	AROMATHERAPY	MICROBREWERY	BICAMERALISM	ISOLATIONISM
PRESCRIPTION	CHEMOTHERAPY	MILLILAMBERT	CARDIOLOGIST	ISOLATIONIST
PRESENTATION	DAGUERROTYPE	MISADVENTURE	CARELESSNESS	KATHAREVOUSA
PRESERVATION	DEUTEROSCOPY	MOUSQUETAIRE	CARICATURIST	LIFELESSNESS
PRESTRICTION	ENANTIOMORPH	NOMENCLATURE	CAUTIOUSNESS	LISTLESSNESS
PREVARICATOR	HYDROTHERAPY	NORTHEASTERN	CHARTERHOUSE	MARSEILLAISE
PROCLAMATION	HYPNOTHERAPY	NORTHWESTERN	CHEERFULNESS	MECHITHARIST
PROLEGOMENON	KALEIDOSCOPE	OBEDIENTIARY	CHILDISHNESS	MERCANTILISM
PROLONGATION	KERAUNOGRAPH	OUTMANOEUVRE	CHORIZONTIST	MERVEILLEUSE
PROMULGATION	MARCONIGRAPH	PANCHATANTRA	CHURLISHNESS	METALLURGIST
PROPITIATION	MYRINGOSCOPE	PARAMILITARY	CLANNISHNESS	METAMORPHISM
PROSCRIPTION	OPISTHOGRAPH	PASSEMEASURE	CLARINETTIST	METAMORPHOSE
PROSTITUTION	OSCILLOSCOPE	PENITENTIARY	CLOTHESHORSE	MINDFULLNESS
PROTESTATION	PHILANTHROPY	PERADVENTURE	COMPLETENESS	MINERALOGIST
PROTHALAMION	PRAXINOSCOPE	PETTIFOGGERS	CONSERVATISM	MITRAILLEUSE
PURIFICATION	PYTHONOMORPH	PETTIFOGGERY	CONSPIRACIST	MOTORCYCLIST
PUTREFACTION	RADIOISOTOPE	PHOTOGRAVURE	CONTRARINESS	MUSICOLOGIST
PYROCATECHOL	RADIOTHERAPY	PHRONTISTERY	COUNTERBLAST	NEOPLATONISM
RAMIFICATION	SPECTROSCOPE	PISCICULTURE	COUNTERPOISE	NEVERTHELESS
RATIFICATION	WOODBURYTYPE	PLACENTIFORM	COVETOUSNESS	NORTHERNMOST
RECOLLECTION	AECIDIOSPORE	POIKILOTHERM	CREATIVENESS	NUTRITIONIST
RECUPERATION	AMPHITHEATRE	POSTLIMINARY	DECENTRALISE	NYCTITROPISM
REFRIGERATOR	ANTICIPATORY	PREMAXILLARY	DENDROLOGIST	OBSOLETENESS
REGENERATION	APPOGGIATURA	PROBATIONARY	DICHROMATISM	ORTHOPAEDIST
REGISTRATION	ARCHITECTURE	PROPITIATORY	DILATORINESS	PAINLESSNESS
REJUVENATION	BIOCHEMISTRY	PROTHONOTARY	DISEMBARRASS	PARKINSONISM
REMUNERATION	CAMIKNICKERS	PTERIDOSPERM	DISFRANCHISE	PEACEFULNESS
RENUNCIATION	CAMPODEIFORM	REFLATIONARY	DISTINCTNESS	PERVERSENESS
REPATRIATION	CHALICOTHERE	REVERSIONARY	DRAMATURGIST	PHILISTINISM
REPERCUSSION	CLAPPERBOARD	RHIPIDOPTERA	EDUCATIONIST	PHLEBOTOMIST
REPOSSESSION	COMMENDATORY	SATISFACTORY	EGYPTOLOGIST	PHYSIOLOGIST
REPRODUCTION	COMPENSATORY	SERVICEBERRY	EMBROIDERESS	POSTMISTRESS
RESURRECTION	CONCILIATORY	SESQUIALTERA	ENTEROPNEUST	POTAMOLOGIST
RETICULATION	CONFIRMATORY	SHUFFLEBOARD	ENTOMOLOGIST	PREPAREDNESS
RHODODENDRON	CONSERVATORY	SIDEWHISKERS	ESCAPOLOGIST	PRIGGISHNESS
SATISFACTION	CONSTABULARY	SIPHONOPHORA	EXTENSIONIST	PROPAGANDISM
SCINTILLATOR	CONTEMPORARY	SOMATOPLEURE	FAITHFULNESS	PROPAGANDIST
SEGMENTATION	CONTRIBUTORY	SOUTHEASTERN	FEARLESSNESS	PROPRIETRESS
SEQUESTRATOR	CREMAILLIÈRE	SOUTHWESTERN	FLITTERMOUSE	PSEPHOLOGIST
SOLICITATION	CROSSCOUNTRY	STRATOSPHERE	FORCEFULNESS	PSYCHIATRIST
SOUTHERNWOOD	DEAMBULATORY	STREPSIPTERA	FRANKINCENSE	PSYCHOLOGIST
SPERMATOZOON	DEFLATIONARY	STREPTONEURA	FRAUENDIENST	RECEPTIONIST
SPHACELATION	DEPRECIATORY	SUBMINIATURE	FRIENDLINESS	RECKLESSNESS
SPINSTERHOOD	DISCIPLINARY	SUBSTRUCTURE	FRUITFULNESS	RESTLESSNESS
SPOKESPERSON	DISCOMFITURE	SUPERCILIARY	FUNCTIONLESS	RETARDEDNESS
STEREOPTICON	ELEEMOSYNARY	TELEUTOSPORE	GEOPHYSICIST	ROOMINGHOUSE
STERNUTATION	EPILEPTIFORM	TERCENTENARY	GRACEFULNESS	RUTHLESSNESS
STILBOESTROL	EPISTOLATERS	TESTAMENTARY	GRACIOUSNESS	SALVATIONIST
STREPITATION	EQUIVOCATORY	THOROUGHFARE	GRAPHOLOGIST	SECESSIONIST
STRIDULATION	EVOLUTIONARY	THUNDERSTORM	GRATEFULNESS	SECTARIANISM
STUPEFACTION	FLORICULTURE	THYSANOPTERA	GYMNOSOPHIST	SELFINTEREST
SUBARRHATION	GREENGROCERS	TRICENTENARY	GYNECOLOGIST	SHEEPISHNESS
SUBHASTATION	GREENGROCERY	TRIGONOMETRY	HAPTOTROPISM	SLOVENLINESS
SUBSCRIPTION	GUILDENSTERN	TROCHOSPHERE	HEADMISTRESS	SNOBBISHNESS
SUBSTITUTION	HABERDASHERS	VENEPUNCTURE	HELIOTROPISM	SOMNAMBULISM
SUCCUSSATION	HABERDASHERY	VERMICULTURE	HELPLESSNESS	SOMNAMBULIST
SUPERSTITION	HAIRDRESSERS	VILLEGIATURA	HERMENEUTIST	SOUTHERNMOST
SUPPLICATION	HEADQUARTERS	ABOLITIONIST	HIPPOCRATISE	SPACIOUSNESS
TRANSGRESSOR	HENCEFORWARD	ACCORDIONIST	HOMESICKNESS	SPECIOUSNESS
TRANSMISSION	HINDQUARTERS	AGRIBUSINESS	HOPELESSNESS	SPELEOLOGIST
TRICHOPHYTON	HORTICULTURE	AMBASSADRESS	HOUSETOHOUSE	SPIRITUALISM

SPIRITUALIST	CONTRAPPOSTO	PRODUCTIVITY	DIVERTICULUM	STRADIVARIUS
SPITEFULNESS	CONTRITURATE	PROLETARIATE	DOLPHINARIUM	STROPHANTHUS
SPURIOUSNESS	CONVIVIALITY	PROTECTORATE	ELECTROTONUS	SUBCONSCIOUS
SQUIRRELFISH	CRISTOBALITE	PTERIDOPHYTE	ENTREPRENEUR	SUBCUTANEOUS
STEALTHINESS	DESIRABILITY	RECAPITULATE	EPITHALAMIUM	SUPERCILIOUS
STEEPLECHASE	DISASSOCIATE	RECONSTITUTE	GALLINACEOUS	SUPERNACULUM
STEGOPHOLIST	DISCONSOLATE	REDINTEGRATE	GAMOSEPALOUS	SUPERSTRATUM
STRAIGHTNESS	DISCRIMINATE	REDISTRIBUTE	HELIOGABALUS	THAUMATURGUS
STRINGCOURSE	DISINTEGRATE	REFLECTIVITY	HIPPOPOTAMUS	THUNDERCLOUD
STUBBORNNESS	DISORIENTATE	REHABILITATE	HISTIOPHORUS	TITANOSAURUS
STUDIOUSNESS	DIVERTIMENTO	REINVIGORATE	HOMOTHERMOUS	TRALATICIOUS
TACTLESSNESS	ECCENTRICITY	RISORGIMENTO	IDIOTHERMOUS	TRALATITIOUS
TECHNOLOGIST	ELECTROPLATE	SCHIZOMYCETE	INAUSPICIOUS	UINTATHERIUM
TELEGRAPHESE	ESPAGNOLETTE	SECRETARIATE	INFELICITOUS	UNSCRUPULOUS
TELEGRAPHIST	ESSENTIALITY	SERASKIERATE	INHARMONIOUS	UNSUCCESSFUL
THANKFULNESS	EXCITABILITY	SKUTTERUDITE	INSALUBRIOUS	VAINGLORIOUS
THEREAGAINST	EXSUFFLICATE	SOPHISTICATE	KLETTERSCHUE	VERUMONTANUM
THOROUGHNESS	EXTORTIONATE	SPERMATOCYTE	LEIOTRICHOUS	XIPHISTERNUM
THUNDERFLASH	FEHMGERICHTE	SPIRITUALITY	LITHOLATROUS	ALIMENTATIVE
TIMELESSNESS	GRANDPARENTS	STAKHANOVITE	MACABERESQUE	ANTANANARIVO
TOGETHERNESS	GROSSULARITE	STOCKINGETTE	MALLOPHAGOUS	APPRECIATIVE
TOXICOLOGIST	HARUMFRODITE	STROMATOLITE	MERETRICIOUS	APPREHENSIVE
TRANQUILLISE	HELLGRAMMITE	STRONTIANITE	MERITRICIOUS	AUGMENTATIVE
TRANSVESTISM	HEMICHORDATA	SUBJECTIVITY	METAGNATHOUS	CONSERVATIVE
TRICHOLOGIST	HETEROGAMETE	SUBSIDIARITY	MISBEHAVIOUR	CONSTRUCTIVE
TRUTHFULNESS	HETEROSOMATA	SUBSTANTIATE	MISDEMEANOUR	CONSULTATIVE
UNCTUOUSNESS	HYPERACIDITY	SUPERANNUATE	MUCILAGINOUS	DESIDERATIVE
UNIVERSALIST	ILLEGIBILITY	SYNADELPHITE	MULTIFARIOUS	DISINCENTIVE
VENGEFULNESS	ILLEGITIMATE	SYNTAGMATITE	NIMBOSTRATUS	DISTRIBUTIVE
WATCHFULNESS	ILLOGICALITY	TARAMASALATA	OBSTREPEROUS	ILLUSTRATIVE
WRETCHEDNESS	IMMUTABILITY	TECHNICALITY	ONCORHYNCHUS	IMPERFECTIVE
YOUTHFULNESS	IMPARTIALITY	TERGIVERSATE	OPHIOGLOSSUM	INCONCLUSIVE
ABSQUATULATE	INARTICULATE	TETRAHEDRITE	OREOPITHECUS	INNATTENTIVE
ADAPTABILITY	INCAPABILITY	TOBACCONISTS	OREOPITHEOUS	INTRANSITIVE
ADMINISTRATE	INCAPACITATE	TRACTABILITY	ORNITHOGALUM	IRRESPECTIVE
ADVISABILITY	INDOCTRINATE	TRANQUILLITY	ORTHOPTEROUS	MANIPULATIVE
AFFECTIONATE	INSOLUBILITY	TRANSMIGRATE	OSTENTATIOUS	NONDIRECTIVE
AFTEREFFECTS	INSPECTORATE	TRANSVESTITE	PALUDAMENTUM	NONOBJECTIVE
AGALMATOLITE	INTERMEDIATE	TROCHELMINTH	PANDAEMONIUM	OPINIONATIVE
ANDOUILLETTE	INVERTEBRATE	UNPOPULARITY	PANDANACEOUS	POSTPOSITIVE
APLANOGAMETE	INVISIBILITY	VEHMGERICHTE	PANTOPHAGOUS	PRESCRIPTIVE
ARFVEDSONITE	IRASCIBILITY	WHIMSICALITY	PARANTHELIUM	PRESERVATIVE
ARSENOPYRITE	IRREGULARITY	WOLLASTONITE	PARSIMONIOUS	PREVENTATIVE
ARTHROPLASTY	IRRITABILITY	ACHLAMYDEOUS	PASSEPARTOUT	QUANTITATIVE
AUTHENTICATE	LATIROSTRATE	ADSCITITIOUS	PECTORILOQUY	RECUPERATIVE
AUTHENTICITY	LUXULLIANITE	ADVANTAGEOUS	PERGAMENEOUS	REMUNERATIVE
AVAILABILITY	MACMILLANITE	ADVANTAGIOUS	PERIOSTRACUM	REPRODUCTIVE
AWAYABSOLUTE	MALLEABILITY	ADVENTITIOUS	PERTINACIOUS	SELFADHESIVE
AYUNTAMIENTO	METHOTREXATE	AMBIDEXTROUS	PERVICACIOUS	SUBSTITUTIVE
BABINGTONITE	MICROCLIMATE	AMPHISTOMOUS	PHYTOPHAGOUS	UNATTRACTIVE
BETHLEHEMITE	MISCALCULATE	ANEMOPHILOUS	PLEIOCHASIUM	UNDERACHIEVE
BILLINGSGATE	MULTIPLICITY	ANTIBACCHIUS	POLYPETALOUS	UNOPPRESSIVE
BIODIVERSITY	MUNICIPALITY	ANTIBARBARUS	PRASEODYMIUM	UNPRODUCTIVE
BLABBERMOUTH	NAVIGABILITY	ANTONINIANUS	PREPOSTEROUS	UNRESPONSIVE
BLETHERSKATE	OVERESTIMATE	ATHEROMATOUS	PRESUMPTUOUS	VITUPERATIVE
BLOODTHIRSTY	PERCEPTIVITY	BEAUMONTAGUE	PROGYMNASIUM	DRESSINGDOWN
CARBOHYDRATE	PERMANGANATE	BEAUMONTIQUE	PROTACTINIUM	ANAESTHETIZE
CHALCOPYRITE	PERMEABILITY	BRONTOSAURUS	PROTHALAMIUM	CHARACTERIZE
CHRISTIANITY	PERMITTIVITY	CALCEAMENTUM	PSEUDONYMOUS	DECENTRALIZE
CIRCUMGYRATE	PERSPICACITY	CANTANKEROUS	RAMBUNCTIOUS	DEMILITARIZE
COLLECTORATE	PLAUSIBILITY	CARPOPHAGOUS	RESTAURATEUR	EXTRAVAGANZA
COMMANDMENTS	POPOCATEPETL	CONTEMPTUOUS	RHADAMANTHUS	LALLAPALOOZA
COMMENSURATE	POSTGRADUATE	CONTERMINOUS	SACRILEGIOUS	PARENTHESIZE
COMMONWEALTH	POTENTIALITY	CONTUMACIOUS	SALTATORIOUS	PHILOSOPHIZE
CONDUCTIVITY	PRACTICALITY	CRASSAMENTUM	SARDANAPALUS	TRANQUILLIZE
CONGLOMERATE	PREDESTINATE	CYMOTRICHOUS	SEMIPRECIOUS	
CONGRATULATE	PREPONDERATE	DISCOURTEOUS	SIMULTANEOUS	**12:12**
CONSPECTUITY	PREREQUISITE	DISINGENUOUS	SINANTHROPUS	ANTILEGOMENA
CONSTITUENTS	PRINCIPALITY	DISREPECTFUL	SIVAPITHECUS	APPOGGIATURA

ARISTOLOCHIA	WELLINGTONIA	PSYCHOPATHIC	REFRIGERATED	ANDOUILLETTE
ARTIODACTYLA	GLUBBDUBDRIB	QUADRAPHONIC	RESUSCITATED	ANDROSTERONE
BARRANQUILLA	AGAMOGENETIC	SCOPOPHILIAC	SELFEMPLOYED	ANTIMETABOLE
BERTHOLLETIA	ALEXIPHARMIC	STEREOPHONIC	SEMIDETACHED	ANTIPARTICLE
BLENNORRHOEA	ALPHANUMERIC	STEREOSCOPIC	SHORTSIGHTED	APLANOGAMETE
BRANCHIOPODA	AMPHISBAENIC	SURREALISTIC	SHORTSLEEVED	APOSTROPHISE
CAMPANULARIA	ANASTIGMATIC	TELEASTHETIC	SHORTSTAFFED	APPRECIATIVE
COLOQUINTIDA	ANTAGONISTIC	THAUMATURGIC	SHUFFLEBOARD	APPREHENSIVE
DARLINGTONIA	ANTHELMINTIC	THERMOSTATIC	SILVERHAIRED	APPROACHABLE
DEUTERANOPIA	ANTIMNEMONIC	THIGMOTROPIC	SINGLEHANDED	APPURTENANCE
ENCYCLOPEDIA	ANTIRACHITIC	TRANSOCEANIC	SINGLEMINDED	ARBORESCENCE
ENHYPOSTASIA	ARISTOCRATIC	UNDEMOCRATIC	SOUTHERNWOOD	ARCHITECTURE
ENTEROMORPHA	BUREAUCRATIC	UNSCIENTIFIC	SPERMATOZOID	ARFVEDSONITE
ENTOMOSTRACA	CALLIGRAPHIC	ZARATHUSTRIC	SPINSTERHOOD	ARSENOPYRITE
EPIPHENOMENA	CARCINOGENIC	ACCOMPLISHED	SPORTSGROUND	ASPARAGINASE
ESCHSCHOLZIA	CARTOGRAPHIC	ACKNOWLEDGED	SPREADEAGLED	ATTRIBUTABLE
EXTRAVAGANZA	CATADIOPTRIC	BATTLEGROUND	STRANGLEHOLD	AUGMENTATIVE
HEMICHORDATA	CATASTROPHIC	BEACONSFIELD	STRANGLEWEED	AUTHENTICATE
HETEROPHORIA	CEREBROTONIC	BIOFLAVONOID	STRONGMINDED	AWAYABSOLUTE
HETEROPLASIA	CHAUVINISTIC	BLOODSTAINED	SUPERCHARGED	BABINGTONITE
HETEROSOMATA	CHIROPRACTIC	BOOBYTRAPPED	THICKSKINNED	BEAUMONTAGUE
HYPERSARCOMA	CHREMATISTIC	CANTILEVERED	THOROUGHBRED	BEAUMONTIQUE
HYPOCHONDRIA	CLEISTOGAMIC	CHESTERFIELD	THUNDERCLOUD	BENZOPHENONE
ICHTHYOCOLLA	DIAGRAMMATIC	CLAPPERBOARD	TRABECULATED	BENZOQUINONE
ICHTHYOPSIDA	ECCLESIASTIC	CLEARSIGHTED	UNACCUSTOMED	BERTILLONAGE
KATHAREVOUSA	ENCYCLOPEDIC	COMMISSIONED	UNACQUAINTED	BETHLEHEMITE
LALLAPALOOZA	ENTHUSIASTIC	CONCENTRATED	UNAPPARELLED	BILLINGSGATE
MALACOSTRACA	EPIGRAMMATIC	CONSOLIDATED	UNAUTHORISED	BLETHERSKATE
MASSERANDUBA	ETEPIMELETIC	CONTAMINATED	UNAUTHORIZED	BOUGAINVILLE
MASTIGOPHORA	ETHEROMANIAC	DERESTRICTED	UNCHALLENGED	BRILLIANTINE
MESOTHELIOMA	HAEMOPHILIAC	DISAPPOINTED	UNCLASSIFIED	BUSINESSLIKE
MULTIGRAVIDA	HETEROCLITIC	DISCONCERTED	UNCONSIDERED	CAPERCAILLIE
NEUROFIBROMA	HIEROGLYPHIC	DISCONNECTED	UNCONTROLLED	CAPERCAILZIE
ONOMATOPOEIA	HIEROPHANTIC	DISCONTENTED	UNCULTIVATED	CARBOHYDRATE
OSTEOMALACIA	HILDEBRANDIC	DISENCHANTED	UNDEREXPOSED	CASTERBRIDGE
OSTEOSARCOMA	HOMOEOPATHIC	DISORGANIZED	UNDERSTAFFED	CHALCOPYRITE
PALINGENESIA	HYDROCHLORIC	DISPOSSESSED	UNDETERMINED	CHALICOTHERE
PANAESTHESIA	HYPERPYRETIC	DISSATISFIED	UNDIMINISHED	CHARACTERIZE
PANCHATANTRA	ICONOCLASTIC	DOMESTICATED	UNDISCHARGED	CHARTERHOUSE
PARALIPOMENA	JOURNALISTIC	DOUBLEGLAZED	UNEXPURGATED	CHONDRIOSOME
PEDICELLARIA	KINAESTHETIC	EVENTEMPERED	UNFREQUENTED	CIRCASSIENNE
PENNSYLVANIA	KLEPTOMANIAC	FAINTHEARTED	UNIDENTIFIED	CIRCUMGYRATE
POTICHOMANIA	LITHOGRAPHIC	FARTHINGLAND	UNINTERESTED	CIRCUMSCRIBE
PRIMIGRAVIDA	MELODRAMATIC	FELDSPATHOID	UNOBSTRUCTED	CIRCUMSTANCE
PROSOPOPOEIA	MERISTEMATIC	GONDWANALAND	UNPARALLELED	CLAIRVOYANCE
PSIPHENOMENA	MILITARISTIC	HAMMERHEADED	UNPREJUDICED	CLAMJAMPHRIE
QUADRAGESIMA	MISANTHROPIC	HENCEFORWARD	UNPRINCIPLED	CLASSIFIABLE
QUADRIPLEGIA	MNEMOTECHNIC	IMPOVERISHED	UNRECOGNISED	CLOTHESHORSE
RESPONDENTIA	MONOSYLLABIC	INCORPORATED	UNRECOGNIZED	COLLECTORATE
RHAMPHOTHECA	NARCISSISTIC	INTERCHANGED	UNRESTRAINED	COMMENSURATE
RHIPIDOPTERA	NATURALISTIC	INTERRELATED	UNRESTRICTED	COMMUNICABLE
SARSAPARILLA	NONALCOHOLIC	INTERSPERSED	VARICOLOURED	CONGLOMERATE
SCLERENCHYMA	NYMPHOMANIAC	LIGHTHEARTED	WELLBALANCED	CONGRATULATE
SCLERODERMIA	OCTASTROPHIC	MASSPRODUCED	WELLINFORMED	CONSERVATIVE
SEPTUAGESIMA	ONEIROCRITIC	MISAPPREHEND	WHOLEHEARTED	CONSIDERABLE
SESQUIALTERA	ONOMATOPOEIC	MISDELIVERED	ABSQUATULATE	CONSTRUCTIVE
SESQUITERTIA	ORTHORHOMBIC	MUDDLEHEADED	ACETALDEHYDE	CONSULTATIVE
SIPHONOPHORA	PANCHROMATIC	MULTICOLORED	ACQUAINTANCE	CONTEMPTIBLE
SIPUNCULACEA	PARAMAGNETIC	NEIGHBORHOOD	ACQUIESCENCE	CONTRITURATE
SPATANGOIDEA	PERIPHRASTIC	NEWFOUNDLAND	ADMINISTRATE	CONTROLLABLE
STREPSIPTERA	PERISTERONIC	OLDFASHIONED	AECIDIOSPORE	COUNTERPOISE
STREPTONEURA	PERSULPHURIC	OUTSTRETCHED	AETHRIOSCOPE	CREMAILLIÈRE
TARAMASALATA	PHILHARMONIC	OVERSCUTCHED	AFFECTIONATE	CRISTOBALITE
THESMOPHORIA	PHOTOGLYPHIC	OVERSTRAINED	AGALMATOLITE	CROSSEXAMINE
THYSANOPTERA	PHOTOGRAPHIC	PARTICOLORED	ALIMENTATIVE	DAGUERROTYPE
TRADESCANTIA	POLYSYLLABIC	PERSONALIZED	AMARANTACEAE	DECENTRALISE
URTRICULARIA	PORNOGRAPHIC	PHOSPHOLIPID	AMPHITHEATRE	DECENTRALIZE
VILLEGIATURA	PROPHYLACTIC	PREPOSSESSED	ANAESTHETISE	DECIPHERABLE
WASHINGTONIA	PROTOPLASMIC	REDISCOVERED	ANAESTHETIZE	DEMILITARIZE

DEMIMONDAINE	INCONTINENCE	MOUSQUETAIRE	REHABILITATE	UNACCEPTABLE
DEMONSTRABLE	INCORRIGIBLE	MYRINGOSCOPE	REINVIGORATE	UNANSWERABLE
DESIDERATIVE	INDECLINABLE	NEPENTHACEAE	REMINISCENCE	UNATTAINABLE
DISACCHARIDE	INDEFENSIBLE	NEUROSCIENCE	REMONSTRANCE	UNATTRACTIVE
DISADVANTAGE	INDEPENDENCE	NOCONFIDENCE	REMUNERATIVE	UNBELIEVABLE
DISAGREEABLE	INDIFFERENCE	NOMENCLATURE	REPRODUCTIVE	UNCHANGEABLE
DISASSOCIATE	INDIGESTIBLE	NONDIRECTIVE	RESIPISCENCE	UNCHARITABLE
DISCOMEDUSAE	INDISPUTABLE	NONEXISTENCE	ROOMINGHOUSE	UNDERACHIEVE
DISCOMFITURE	INDISSOLUBLE	NONFLAMMABLE	SARRUSOPHONE	UNDETECTABLE
DISCONSOLATE	INDOCTRINATE	NONOBJECTIVE	SAUROGNATHAE	UNFATHOMABLE
DISCRIMINATE	INERADICABLE	NONRESIDENCE	SCHEHERAZADE	UNFAVOURABLE
DISFRANCHISE	INEXACTITUDE	OBSERVANTINE	SCHIZOMYCETE	UNIMAGINABLE
DISHONORABLE	INEXPERIENCE	OBSOLESCENCE	SECRETARIATE	UNIMPORTANCE
DISINCENTIVE	INEXPLICABLE	OPINIONATIVE	SELFADHESIVE	UNMANAGEABLE
DISINTEGRATE	INEXTRICABLE	OSCILLOSCOPE	SERASKIERATE	UNMISTAKABLE
DISOBEDIENCE	INFORMIDABLE	OUTMANOEUVRE	SIGNIFICANCE	UNOBTAINABLE
DISORIENTATE	INHOSPITABLE	OVERESTIMATE	SIPHONOSTELE	UNOPPRESSIVE
DISREPUTABLE	INNATTENTIVE	OXYACETYLENE	SKUTTERUDITE	UNPARDONABLE
DISTRIBUTIVE	INSPECTORATE	PAPILIONIDAE	SOMATOPLEURE	UNPRODUCTIVE
ELECTROPLATE	INSUFFERABLE	PARENTHESIZE	SOPHISTICATE	UNPROFITABLE
EPACRIDACEAE	INTELLIGENCE	PASSEMEASURE	SPECTROSCOPE	UNREASONABLE
ESPAGNOLETTE	INTELLIGIBLE	PERADVENTURE	SPERMATOCYTE	UNRESPONSIVE
EXCHANGEABLE	INTEMPERANCE	PERMANGANATE	SPHAIRISTIKE	UNRETURNABLE
EXSUFFLICATE	INTERFERENCE	PERSEVERANCE	SPURTLEBLADE	UNSEASONABLE
EXTORTIONATE	INTERMEDIATE	PHILOSOPHIZE	STAKHANOVITE	VEHMGERICHTE
EXTRADITABLE	INTERMINABLE	PHOSPHORENCE	STEEPLECHASE	VENEPUNCTURE
EXTRAVAGANCE	INTRANSITIVE	PHOSPHORESCE	STENTORPHONE	VERMICULTURE
FEHMGERICHTE	INTRAUTERINE	PHOTOGRAVURE	STOCKINGETTE	VIBRATIUNCLE
FLITTERMOUSE	INVERTEBRATE	PHYTONADIONE	STRAIGHTEDGE	VITUPERATIVE
FLORICULTURE	INVULNERABLE	PINNIEWINKLE	STRATOSPHERE	WALLYDRAIGLE
FLUORESCENCE	IRREDEEMABLE	PISCICULTURE	STRINGCOURSE	WHIGMALEERIE
FLUVIOMARINE	IRRESISTIBLE	PLASTERSTONE	STROMATOLITE	WOLLASTONITE
FORMALDEHYDE	IRRESOLVABLE	POINTILLISME	STRONTIANITE	WOLSTENHOLME
FRANKINCENSE	IRRESPECTIVE	POLYETHYLENE	SUBCOMMITTEE	WOODBURYTYPE
FRONTISPIECE	IRREVERSIBLE	POLYRIBOSOME	SUBMINIATURE	HANDKERCHIEF
GLYNDEBOURNE	KALEIDOSCOPE	POLYSYLLABLE	SUBSERVIENCE	QUARTERSTAFF
GRANDMONTINE	KLETTERSCHUE	POLYURETHANE	SUBSTANTIATE	WEATHERPROOF
GROSSULARITE	LABYRINTHINE	POSTGRADUATE	SUBSTITUTIVE	ACCOMPANYING
HAPPENSTANCE	LAMELLICORNE	POSTPOSITIVE	SUBSTRUCTURE	AWARDWINNING
HARUMFRODITE	LATIROSTRATE	PRAXINOSCOPE	SULPHONAMIDE	AWEINSPIRING
HELLGRAMMITE	LEPIDOMELANE	PREDESTINATE	SUPERANNUATE	BACKBREAKING
HETEROCONTAE	LINCOLNSHIRE	PREDETERMINE	SURMOUNTABLE	BARNSTORMING
HETEROGAMETE	LONGDISTANCE	PREDOMINANCE	SURVEILLANCE	BIRDWATCHING
HIPPOCRATISE	LUMINESCENCE	PREPONDERATE	SYNADELPHITE	BLOODLETTING
HOBBIDIDANCE	LUMINISCENCE	PREREQUISITE	SYNTAGMATITE	BLUESTOCKING
HORTICULTURE	LUXULLIANITE	PRESCRIPTIVE	TAMARICACEAE	BOONDOGGLING
HOUSETOHOUSE	LYMANTRIIDAE	PRESERVATIVE	TAPSALTEERIE	BRAINWASHING
HYDROQUINONE	MACABERESQUE	PREVENTATIVE	TAPSLETEERIE	BREATHTAKING
IDENTIFIABLE	MACMILLANITE	PROGESTERONE	TELEGRAPHESE	BROADCASTING
ILLEGITIMATE	MACROPODIDAE	PROGRAMMABLE	TELEUTOSPORE	CARDINDEXING
ILLUSTRATIVE	MADEMOISELLE	PROLETARIATE	TERGIVERSATE	CHEESEPARING
IMMEASURABLE	MAGNIFICENCE	PROTECTORATE	TESTOSTERONE	CHILDBEARING
IMPENETRABLE	MANIPULATIVE	PROTUBERANCE	TETRACYCLINE	COMPROMISING
IMPERFECTIVE	MANOEUVRABLE	PTERIDOPHYTE	TETRAHEDRITE	CONVALESCING
IMPERISHABLE	MARLINESPIKE	PTERODACTYLE	THEOPHYLLINE	CONVEYANCING
IMPERTINENCE	MARRIAGEABLE	QUANTIFIABLE	THOROUGHFARE	CRASHLANDING
IMPROVIDENCE	MARSEILLAISE	QUANTITATIVE	THREADNEEDLE	DEBILITATING
INACCESSIBLE	MASTERSTROKE	QUESTIONABLE	TRADESPEOPLE	DISAPPEARING
INADMISSIBLE	MERVEILLEUSE	QUINTESSENCE	TRANQUILLISE	DISCOURAGING
INADVERTENCE	METALLOPHONE	RADIOISOTOPE	TRANQUILLIZE	DRINKDRIVING
INAPPLICABLE	METAMORPHOSE	REAPPEARANCE	TRANSFERABLE	EMBARRASSING
INARTICULATE	METHOTREXATE	RECAPITULATE	TRANSFERENCE	ENERGYSAVING
INCALCULABLE	MICROCLIMATE	RECHARGEABLE	TRANSLATABLE	ENTERPRISING
INCAPACITATE	MISADVENTURE	RECOGNIZABLE	TRANSLUCENCE	ENTERTAINING
INCOMPARABLE	MISCALCULATE	RECOGNIZANCE	TRANSMIGRATE	EXASPERATING
INCOMPATIBLE	MISPRONOUNCE	RECONSTITUTE	TRANSPONTINE	EXCRUCIATING
INCOMPETENCE	MITRAILLEUSE	RECUPERATIVE	TRANSVESTITE	EXHILARATING
INCONCLUSIVE	MONOSYLLABLE	REDINTEGRATE	TROCHOSPHERE	FIRSTFOOTING
INCONSOLABLE	MOSBOLLETJIE	REDISTRIBUTE	ULTRAMONTANE	FOOTSLOGGING

GALLIVANTING	THUNDERFLASH	POPOCATEPETL	UINTATHERIUM	CONFISCATION
HAIRDRESSING	TROCHELMINTH	POSTPRANDIAL	VERUMONTANUM	CONGREGATION
HEARTWARMING	CARAVANSERAI	PREFERENTIAL	XIPHISTERNUM	CONSCRIPTION
HIGHFALUTING	PLECTOGNATHI	PRESIDENTIAL	ABBREVIATION	CONSECRATION
HOUSEKEEPING	STANISLAVSKI	PROCESSIONAL	ACCELERATION	CONSERVATION
HOUSEWARMING	CZECHOSLOVAK	PROFESSIONAL	ACCENTUATION	CONSOCIATION
ILLUMINATING	GOBBLEDEGOOK	PROFESSORIAL	ACCUMULATION	CONSTIPATION
INGRATIATING	GOBBLEDYGOOK	PROPORTIONAL	ADJUDICATION	CONSTITUTION
INTERPRETING	KILLIKINNICK	PROTOPLASMAL	ADULTERATION	CONSTRICTION
INTIMIDATING	SWIZZLESTICK	PROVIDENTIAL	AGATHODAIMON	CONSTRUCTION
INTOXICATING	ACCUSATORIAL	PUMPERNICKEL	AIRCRAFTSMAN	CONSULTATION
INVIGORATING	AERONAUTICAL	PYROCATECHOL	ALLITERATION	CONSUMMATION
LABOURSAVING	AGRICULTURAL	QUARTERFINAL	AMALGAMATION	CONTIGNATION
LONGSTANDING	ALPHABETICAL	QUINQUENNIAL	AMBULANCEMAN	CONTINUATION
MINDBOGGLING	APFELSTRUDEL	RECREATIONAL	AMELIORATION	CONTRIBUTION
MOISTURIZING	ARITHMETICAL	RHINORRHOEAL	ANCHORPERSON	CONVERSATION
MOONLIGHTING	ASTROLOGICAL	SOCIOLOGICAL	ANNIHILATION	COORDINATION
NEIGHBOURING	ASTRONOMICAL	STILBOESTROL	ANNUNCIATION	COSMOPOLITAN
ORIENTEERING	ASYMMETRICAL	STUDDINGSAIL	ANTEDILUVIAN	CROSSSECTION
OVERCROWDING	BICENTENNIAL	SUPERNATURAL	ANTEMERIDIAN	DEASPIRATION
OVERDRESSING	BIOGRAPHICAL	TAUTOLOGICAL	ANTICIPATION	DECAPITATION
OVERPOWERING	BRACHYCEPHAL	TRANSITIONAL	ANTISTROPHON	DECELERATION
OVERWHELMING	CATAPHYSICAL	UNECONOMICAL	ANTITHROMBIN	DEGENERATION
PEACEKEEPING	COINCIDENTAL	UNSUCCESSFUL	APOLLINARIAN	DELIBERATION
PETTIFOGGING	CONFESSIONAL	WHIPPOORWILL	APPRECIATION	DELICATESSEN
POLICYMAKING	CONFIDENTIAL	BEHAVIOURISM	APPREHENSION	DENOMINATION
POWERSHARING	CONTRAPUNTAL	BICAMERALISM	ARCHILOCHIAN	DENUNCIATION
PRIZEWINNING	CONVENTIONAL	CALCEAMENTUM	ARISTOTELEAN	DEPOPULATION
PROFITEERING	COURTMARTIAL	CAMPODEIFORM	ARTICULATION	DEPRECIATION
RACKETEERING	DEPARTMENTAL	CONSERVATISM	ARTILLERYMAN	DEREGULATION
REPROCESSING	DIFFERENTIAL	COUNTERCLAIM	ASPHYXIATION	DESSERTSPOON
SELFCATERING	DISREPECTFUL	CRASSAMENTUM	ASSIMILATION	DIALECTICIAN
SHAREHOLDING	DORSIVENTRAL	DICHROMATISM	ASSUEFACTION	DIENCEPHALON
SHIPBUILDING	DUNNIEWASSAL	DIVERTICULUM	AUGMENTATION	DILAPIDATION
SLEEPWALKING	EPIDEICTICAL	DOLPHINARIUM	AUSCULTATION	DIPRIONIDIAN
SMALLHOLDING	ETHNOLOGICAL	EPILEPTIFORM	AUSTRALASIAN	DISPENSATION
SNOWBOARDING	ETYMOLOGICAL	EPITHALAMIUM	AUSTRONESIAN	DISQUISITION
SPRECHGESANG	EULENSPIEGEL	HAPTOTROPISM	BACCHANALIAN	DISSERTATION
STEREOTYPING	EXPERIMENTAL	HELIOTROPISM	BACKWOODSMAN	DISSOCIATION
THANKSGIVING	GENEALOGICAL	INTUITIONISM	BIELORUSSIAN	DISTILLATION
TIGHTFITTING	GEOGRAPHICAL	ISOLATIONISM	BLEFUSCUDIAN	DISTRIBUTION
UMBRADARLING	GLADIATORIAL	MERCANTILISM	BYELORUSSIAN	DRESSINGDOWN
UNAPPETIZING	GLOCKENSPIEL	METAMORPHISM	CALUMNIATION	EMANCIPATION
UNCONVINCING	GOVERNMENTAL	NEOPLATONISM	CAMERAPERSON	EMASCULATION
UNDERPINNING	HEROICOMICAL	NYCTITROPISM	CANCELLATION	ENCHEIRIDION
UNPRETENDING	HETEROSEXUAL	OPHIOGLOSSUM	CANONIZATION	ENGLISHWOMAN
UNSATISFYING	HIERARCHICAL	ORNITHOGALUM	CAPITULATION	ENGLISHWOMEN
UNSURPRISING	HYPERBOLICAL	PALUDAMENTUM	CARLOVINGIAN	ENTOPLASTRON
UNSUSPECTING	HYPOCRITICAL	PANDAEMONIUM	CARTHAGINIAN	EPENCEPHALON
BANDERSNATCH	HYPOTHETICAL	PARANTHELIUM	CHLORINATION	EPISCOPALIAN
BLABBERMOUTH	INSTRUMENTAL	PARKINSONISM	CHLOROPICRIN	EPITHALAMION
BREAKTHROUGH	INTELLECTUAL	PERIOSTRACUM	CHURCHWARDEN	EQUIVOCATION
BREASTPLOUGH	INTERGLACIAL	PHILISTINISM	CIRCUMCISION	ERYTHROMYCIN
BUTTERSCOTCH	ISOBILATERAL	PLACENTIFORM	CIVILISATION	ETYMOLOGICON
COMMONWEALTH	LONGITUDINAL	PLEIOCHASIUM	CIVILIZATION	EXACERBATION
COUNTERMARCH	LOXODROMICAL	POIKILOTHERM	CLAUDICATION	EXAGGERATION
ELASMOBRANCH	MANGELWURZEL	PRASEODYMIUM	CODIFICATION	EXASPERATION
ENANTIOMORPH	MATHEMATICAL	PROGYMNASIUM	COHABITATION	EXCRUCIATION
GAINSBOROUGH	METAPHORICAL	PROPAGANDISM	COLLUCTATION	EXHILARATION
ISHMAELITISH	METAPHYSICAL	PROTACTINIUM	COLONIZATION	EXPLOITATION
KERAUNOGRAPH	MULTILATERAL	PROTHALAMIUM	COMMENDATION	EXSERVICEMAN
MARCONIGRAPH	MYTHOLOGICAL	PTERIDOSPERM	COMPELLATION	FEATHERBRAIN
OPISTHOGRAPH	NEOCLASSICAL	SECTARIANISM	COMPENSATION	FERMENTATION
PYTHONOMORPH	NEUROLOGICAL	SOMNAMBULISM	COMPLICATION	FINALIZATION
SCATTERMOUCH	NONCOMMITTAL	SPIRITUALISM	COMPURGATION	FLAGELLATION
SHOSTAKOVICH	OCCUPATIONAL	SUPERNACULUM	CONCILIATION	FLUORIDATION
SQUIRRELFISH	PATHOLOGICAL	SUPERSTRATUM	CONDEMNATION	FRANKALMOIGN
STELLENBOSCH	PESTILENTIAL	THUNDERSTORM	CONDENSATION	FRANKENSTEIN
THIRDBOROUGH	PHILOLOGICAL	TRANSVESTISM	CONFIRMATION	FRONTIERSMAN

FRUMENTATION	MISQUOTATION	REPRODUCTION	DICTATORSHIP	INTERSTELLAR
FUSTILLIRIAN	MOBILIZATION	RESURRECTION	DIRECTORSHIP	INVESTIGATOR
GENETHLIACON	MODIFICATION	RETICULATION	GAMESMANSHIP	JENNYSPINNER
GEOMETRICIAN	MONTESSORIAN	RHODODENDRON	GUARDIANSHIP	KATZENJAMMER
GERIATRICIAN	MUGGLETONIAN	SATISFACTION	HORSEMANSHIP	KIRSCHWASSER
GIBRALTARIAN	NEWSPAPERMAN	SCANDINAVIAN	LAUREATESHIP	KLIPSPRINGER
GLYCOPROTEIN	NONAGENARIAN	SCATTERBRAIN	MARKSMANSHIP	LICKTRENCHER
GONADOTROPIN	NORTHEASTERN	SCHNEIDERIAN	PARTISANSHIP	LUXEMBOURGER
GRANDISONIAN	NORTHWESTERN	SEGMENTATION	RECEIVERSHIP	MANSLAUGHTER
GRISEOFULVIN	NOTIFICATION	SERVICEWOMAN	RELATIONSHIP	MANUFACTURER
GUILDENSTERN	NYCHTHEMERON	SEXAGENARIAN	SALESMANSHIP	MARCOBRUNNER
HALLUCINOGEN	OBLITERATION	SOLICITATION	AMPHITHEATER	MINICOMPUTER
HAMBLETONIAN	OBSTETRICIAN	SOUTHCOTTIAN	ANTIMACASSAR	MISBEHAVIOUR
HEREDITARIAN	OCTOGENARIAN	SOUTHEASTERN	BAIRNSHAKER	MISDEMEANOUR
HIPPOCREPIAN	OMBUDSPERSON	SOUTHWESTERN	BANANALANDER	MOUTHBROODER
HUMANITARIAN	ONYCHOPHORAN	SPERMATOZOON	BARBERMONGER	NEPHELOMETER
HUMANIZATION	ORGANISATION	SPHACELATION	BARORECEPTOR	PASQUEFLOWER
HYMENOPTERAN	ORGANIZATION	SPIEGELEISEN	BESSERWISSER	PERAMBULATOR
HYPERTENSION	OSSIFICATION	SPOKESPERSON	BOULEVARDIER	PHOTOGRAPHER
IDEALIZATION	OVEREXERTION	STATISTICIAN	BREASTSUMMER	PITTERPATTER
ILLUMINATION	PACIFICATION	STEREOPTICON	BREATHALYSER	PRACTICIONER
ILLUSTRATION	PANATHENAEAN	STERNUTATION	BRICKFIELDER	PRACTITIONER
IMMODERATION	PANPHARMACON	STREPITATION	BUCKLEBEGGAR	PRALLTRILLER
IMMUNIZATION	PANTECHNICON	STREPTOMYCIN	BUNKOSTEERER	PREVARICATOR
IMPERFECTION	PEDIATRICIAN	STRIDULATION	CABINETMAKER	PRIZEFIGHTER
IMPLANTATION	PENALIZATION	STUPEFACTION	CARPETBAGGER	RADIOGRAPHER
IMPREGNATION	PERNOCTATION	SUBARRHATION	CARTOGRAPHER	RECORDPLAYER
INAUGURATION	PERPETRATION	SUBHASTATION	CATHETOMETER	REDEMPTIONER
INCINERATION	PERSPIRATION	SUBLAPSARIAN	CHEESEBURGER	REFRIGERATOR
INCRUSTATION	PERTURBATION	SUBSCRIPTION	CHEESEMONGER	REMEMBRANCER
INDISCRETION	PETRIFACTION	SUBSTITUTION	CHIROPRACTOR	RESTAURATEUR
INESCUTCHEON	PHILODENDRON	SUBTERRANEAN	COLDSHOULDER	RODOMONTADER
INFILTRATION	PHYCOXANTHIN	SUCCUSSATION	COLLABORATOR	ROLLERBLADER
INFLAMMATION	PIGMENTATION	SUPERSTITION	COMMISSIONER	SCHILLERSPAR
INSEMINATION	POGONOPHORAN	SUPPLICATION	CONFECTIONER	SCHOOLMASTER
INSTALLATION	POLARIZATION	TAGLIACOTIAN	CONQUISTADOR	SCHOPENHAUER
INSTAURATION	POLYSYNDETON	TELEOSAURIAN	CONSOLIDATOR	SCINTILLATOR
INSURRECTION	PRECONDITION	TETRODOTOXIN	COSTERMONGER	SCREENWRITER
INTENERATION	PREDILECTION	THEORETICIAN	CROSSBENCHER	SCRIMSHANDER
INTERCEPTION	PREGUSTATION	THESSALONIAN	CUCKOOFLOWER	SCRIMSHANKER
INTERCESSION	PREHISTORIAN	TORRICELLIAN	DEHUMIDIFIER	SCRIPTWRITER
INTERJECTION	PRESBYTERIAN	TOTALITARIAN	DEMONSTRATOR	SEMICIRCULAR
INTERMISSION	PRESCRIPTION	TRANSMISSION	DONNERWETTER	SEPTEMBRISER
INTERRUPTION	PRESENTATION	TRICHOPHYTON	DOUBLEDECKER	SEQUESTRATOR
INTERSECTION	PRESERVATION	TURACOVERDIN	EAVESDROPPER	SHARPSHOOTER
INTERVENTION	PRESTRICTION	UNDERWRITTEN	ENTREPRENEUR	SHIRTWAISTER
INTIMIDATION	PROCLAMATION	URBANIZATION	EXHIBITIONER	SINGLEDECKER
INTOXICATION	PROLEGOMENON	VAPORIZATION	EXTENSOMETER	SLEDGEHAMMER
INTRODUCTION	PROLONGATION	VERIFICATION	EXTINGUISHER	SLOCKDOLAGER
INTROVERSION	PROMULGATION	VETERINARIAN	FREIGHTLINER	SLOCKDOLIGER
INVALIDATION	PROPITIATION	VILIFICATION	GALVANOMETER	SLOCKDOLOGER
INVIGORATION	PROSCRIPTION	VITUPERATION	GASTARBEITER	SPECKTIONEER
IRRESOLUTION	PROSTITUTION	VOCIFERATION	GASTROSOPHER	SPECTROMETER
JURISDICTION	PROTESTATION	WAREHOUSEMAN	GENTLETAMPER	SPELLCHECKER
KINDERGARTEN	PROTHALAMION	WILTSHIREMAN	GLOBETROTTER	SPINECHILLER
LABANOTATION	PURIFICATION	XANTHOPTERIN	GRASSWIDOWER	STENOGRAPHER
LANCASTERIAN	PUTREFACTION	YORKSHIREMAN	HAIRSPLITTER	STEPDAUGHTER
LANGUEDOCIAN	RAMIFICATION	ANTANANARIVO	HALLANSHAKER	STERNWHEELER
LEGALIZATION	RATIFICATION	ANTINEUTRINO	HARNESSMAKER	STOCKBREEDER
LIQUEFACTION	RECOLLECTION	AYUNTAMIENTO	HEPHTHEMIMER	STONECHATTER
LIVERPUDLIAN	RECUPERATION	CLAVICEMBALO	HOLIDAYMAKER	STORMTROOPER
LONGSHOREMAN	REGENERATION	CONTRAPPOSTO	HOUSEBREAKER	SUPERCHARGER
MALFORMATION	REGISTRATION	DIVERTIMENTO	HYDROGRAPHER	SWASHBUCKLER
MALNUTRITION	REJUVENATION	LILLIBULLERO	HYMNOGRAPHER	TAPERECORDER
MANIPULATION	REMUNERATION	LILLIBURLERO	HYPOTHECATOR	TEETERTOTTER
MASTURBATION	RENUNCIATION	MICHELANGELO	IAMBOGRAPHER	THREEQUARTER
MENSTRUATION	REPATRIATION	RISORGIMENTO	IMPERSONATOR	TRANQUILIZER
METROPOLITAN	REPERCUSSION	CHAIRMANSHIP	INTERLOCUTOR	TRANSGRESSOR
MINISTRATION	REPOSSESSION	CHAMPIONSHIP	INTERROGATOR	TROUBLEMAKER

TURBIDIMETER	DISTINCTNESS	NIGHTCLOTHES	STEALTHINESS	COUNTERPOINT
TURBOCHARGER	ECCLESIASTES	NIMBOSTRATUS	STRADIVARIUS	DECIPHERMENT
UNDERSKINKER	ELECTROLYSIS	OBSOLETENESS	STRAIGHTNESS	DECONGESTANT
WATERCARRIER	ELECTROTONUS	OBSTREPEROUS	STRIGIFORMES	DENDROLOGIST
WEIGHTLIFTER	EMBROIDERESS	ONCORHYNCHUS	STROPHANTHUS	DISAGREEMENT
WICKETKEEPER	EPANORTHOSIS	OREOPITHECUS	STUBBORNNESS	DISINFECTANT
WINTERHALTER	EPISTOLATERS	OREOPITHEOUS	STUDIOUSNESS	DISPLACEMENT
YELLOWHAMMER	ERATOSTHENES	ORTHODONTICS	SUBCONSCIOUS	DRAMATURGIST
ACHLAMYDEOUS	FAITHFULNESS	ORTHOGENESIS	SUBCUTANEOUS	EDUCATIONIST
ADSCITITIOUS	FEARLESSNESS	ORTHOPAEDICS	SUPERCILIOUS	EFFERVESCENT
ADVANTAGEOUS	FIDDLESTICKS	ORTHOPTEROUS	SURROUNDINGS	EGYPTOLOGIST
ADVANTAGIOUS	FORCEFULNESS	ORTHOTONESIS	TACTLESSNESS	EMBEZZLEMENT
ADVENTITIOUS	FRIENDLINESS	OSTENTATIOUS	TERRITORIALS	ENCIRCLEMENT
AERODYNAMICS	FRUITFULNESS	OSTEOPOROSIS	THANKFULNESS	ENCROACHMENT
AFTEREFFECTS	FULMINATIONS	OUTBUILDINGS	THAUMATURGUS	ENTANGLEMENT
AGRIBUSINESS	FUNCTIONLESS	PAINLESSNESS	THERAPEUTICS	ENTEROPNEUST
AMBASSADRESS	FUNDAMENTALS	PALINGENESIS	THOROUGHNESS	ENTOMOLOGIST
AMBIDEXTROUS	GALLIGASKINS	PALPITATIONS	TIMELESSNESS	ENTRENCHMENT
AMPHISTOMOUS	GALLINACEOUS	PANDANACEOUS	TITANOSAURUS	ESCAPOLOGIST
ANAMORPHOSIS	GAMOSEPALOUS	PANTOPHAGOUS	TOBACCONISTS	ESTRANGEMENT
ANECATHARSIS	GOOSEPIMPLES	PARACENTESIS	TOGETHERNESS	EXTENSIONIST
ANEMOPHILOUS	GRACEFULNESS	PARSIMONIOUS	TRALATICIOUS	FRAUENDIENST
ANTIBACCHIUS	GRACIOUSNESS	PEACEFULNESS	TRALATITIOUS	GEOPHYSICIST
ANTIBARBARUS	GRANDPARENTS	PERGAMENEOUS	TRANSACTIONS	GESELLSCHAFT
ANTONINIANUS	GRATEFULNESS	PERICARDITIS	TROPHALLAXIS	GRAPHOLOGIST
APPENDICITIS	GREENGROCERS	PERIODONTICS	TRUTHFULNESS	GYMNOSOPHIST
ARCHIPELAGOS	HABERDASHERS	PERTINACIOUS	TUBERCULOSIS	GYNECOLOGIST
ARISTOPHANES	HAEMATEMESIS	PERVERSENESS	ULOTRICHALES	HEREDITAMENT
ASTROPHYSICS	HAEMORRHOIDS	PERVICACIOUS	UNCTUOUSNESS	HERMENEUTIST
ATHEROMATOUS	HAIRDRESSERS	PETTIFOGGERS	UNDERCLOTHES	HIEROGRAMMAT
ATMOSPHERICS	HAMARTHRITIS	PHYTOBENTHOS	UNSCRUPULOUS	IMMUNOLOGIST
AUTOHYPNOSIS	HEADMISTRESS	PHYTOPHAGOUS	UNUTTERABLES	IMPRISONMENT
BACKWARDNESS	HEADQUARTERS	PLAINCLOTHES	VAINGLORIOUS	INCANDESCENT
BAMBOCCIADES	HEARTSTRINGS	POLYNEURITIS	VALENCIENNES	INCONSEQUENT
BEAUMARCHAIS	HELIOGABALUS	POLYPETALOUS	VENGEFULNESS	INCONSISTENT
BENEFACTRESS	HELPLESSNESS	POSTMISTRESS	WATCHFULNESS	INCONVENIENT
BRONTOSAURUS	HERMENEUTICS	PREPAREDNESS	WRETCHEDNESS	INCUNABULIST
CALLISTHENES	HINDQUARTERS	PREPOSTEROUS	YOUTHFULNESS	INFOTAINMENT
CAMIKNICKERS	HIPPOPOTAMUS	PRESUMPTUOUS	ABOLITIONIST	INFRINGEMENT
CANTANKEROUS	HISTIOPHORUS	PRIGGISHNESS	ACCORDIONIST	INSUFFICIENT
CARELESSNESS	HOMESICKNESS	PROPRIETRESS	ACCOUCHEMENT	INTERMITTENT
CARPOPHAGOUS	HOMOTHERMOUS	PSEUDONYMOUS	ACCOUTREMENT	INTRANSIGENT
CASSITERIDES	HOPELESSNESS	PYROTECHNICS	ADMONISHMENT	ISOLATIONIST
CAUTIOUSNESS	HUDIBRASTICS	RAMBUNCTIOUS	AFORETHOUGHT	MACHAIRODONT
CHEERFULNESS	IDIOTHERMOUS	RECKLESSNESS	AFTERTHOUGHT	MAGNILOQUENT
CHILDISHNESS	IMPOLITENESS	RESTLESSNESS	ANAESTHETIST	MALTREATMENT
CHITTERLINGS	INAUSPICIOUS	RETARDEDNESS	ANNOUNCEMENT	MECHITHARIST
CHURLISHNESS	INDEBTEDNESS	RHADAMANTHUS	ANTIAIRCRAFT	MERRYTHOUGHT
CLANNISHNESS	INFELICITOUS	ROLLERBLADES	ASTONISHMENT	METALLURGIST
COLLYWOBBLES	INHARMONIOUS	RONCESVALLES	BACTERIOSTAT	MIDDLEWEIGHT
COMBINATIONS	INNOMINABLES	RUTHLESSNESS	BANTAMWEIGHT	MILLILAMBERT
COMMANDMENTS	INSALUBRIOUS	SACRILEGIOUS	BEWILDERMENT	MINERALOGIST
COMPLETENESS	INSTRUCTIONS	SALTATORIOUS	BIBLIOPEGIST	MISINTERPRET
CONSEQUENCES	INSTRUCTRESS	SARDANAPALUS	BIPROPELLANT	MISPLACEMENT
CONSTITUENTS	LAMENTATIONS	SCHINDYLESIS	BLACKCURRANT	MISREPRESENT
CONTEMPTUOUS	LEGIONNAIRES	SEMIPRECIOUS	BLANDISHMENT	MISSTATEMENT
CONTERMINOUS	LEIOTRICHOUS	SHEEPISHNESS	CARDIOLOGIST	MISTREATMENT
CONTRARINESS	LIFELESSNESS	SHIRTSLEEVES	CARICATURIST	MOTORCYCLIST
CONTUMACIOUS	LISTLESSNESS	SHORTCOMINGS	CARRIWITCHET	MUSICOLOGIST
CONVENIENCES	LITHOLATROUS	SIDEWHISKERS	CHASTISEMENT	MUTESSARIFAT
COVETOUSNESS	MALLOPHAGOUS	SIMULTANEOUS	CHORIZONTIST	NONRESISTANT
CREATIVENESS	MALPRACTICES	SINANTHROPUS	CLARINETTIST	NORTHERNMOST
CYMOTRICHOUS	MERETRICIOUS	SIVAPITHECUS	COCCIDIOSTAT	NUTRITIONIST
DILATORINESS	MERITRICIOUS	SLOVENLINESS	COMMENCEMENT	ORTHOPAEDIST
DIPLOGENESIS	METAGNATHOUS	SNOBBISHNESS	COMMISSARIAT	PASSEPARTOUT
DISCOMYCETES	MINDFULLNESS	SPACIOUSNESS	CONSPIRACIST	PASSIONFRUIT
DISCOURTEOUS	MUCILAGINOUS	SPECIOUSNESS	CONTABESCENT	PHLEBOTOMIST
DISEMBARRASS	MULTIFARIOUS	SPITEFULNESS	CONVALESCENT	PHYSIOLOGIST
DISINGENUOUS	NEVERTHELESS	SPURIOUSNESS	COUNTERBLAST	POSTPONEMENT

POTAMOLOGIST	BIOCHEMISTRY	ESSENTIALITY	INTERMINABLY	PRACTICALITY
PREMONSTRANT	BIODIVERSITY	ESTHETICALLY	INTRODUCTORY	PRAISEWORTHY
PREPONDERANT	BLOODTHIRSTY	EVENHANDEDLY	INVISIBILITY	PRECARIOUSLY
PREPONDERENT	BOISTEROUSLY	EVOLUTIONARY	IRASCIBILITY	PRECOCIOUSLY
PRESENTIMENT	BREATHLESSLY	EXCITABILITY	IRRATIONALLY	PREMAXILLARY
PROPAGANDIST	CARDIOMEGALY	EXHAUSTIVELY	IRREGULARITY	PRINCIPALITY
PSEPHOLOGIST	CEREMONIALLY	FASTIDIOUSLY	IRRESOLUTELY	PROBATIONARY
PSYCHIATRIST	CHEMOTHERAPY	FIGURATIVELY	IRREVERENTLY	PRODIGIOUSLY
PSYCHOLOGIST	CHOREOGRAPHY	FLAMBOYANTLY	IRRITABILITY	PRODUCTIVITY
PURPOSEBUILT	CHRESTOMATHY	FORTUITOUSLY	KALISTOCRACY	PROFICIENTLY
QUARTERLIGHT	CHRISTIANITY	FOTHERINGHAY	LAMPADEDROMY	PROLIFICALLY
READJUSTMENT	CLAIRVOYANCY	FRACTIONALLY	LASCIVIOUSLY	PROPITIATORY
RECALCITRANT	COLLECTIVELY	FUNCTIONALLY	LEGITIMATELY	PROPITIOUSLY
RECEPTIONIST	COLLOQUIALLY	GEOLOGICALLY	LEXICOGRAPHY	PROTECTIVELY
RECRUDESCENT	COMMENDATORY	GERONTOCRACY	LUGUBRIOUSLY	PROTHONOTARY
REDEPLOYMENT	COMMERCIALLY	GIGANTOMACHY	MACROCEPHALY	PROVERBIALLY
RENOUNCEMENT	COMPANIONWAY	GLYPTOGRAPHY	MAGNETICALLY	PUGNACIOUSLY
RESETTLEMENT	COMPENSATORY	GREENGROCERY	MAJESTICALLY	PURPOSEFULLY
RETRENCHMENT	COMPLACENTLY	HABERDASHERY	MALLEABILITY	QUIXOTICALLY
SALVATIONIST	CONCILIATORY	HAPPYGOLUCKY	MEANINGFULLY	RADIOBIOLOGY
SECESSIONIST	CONCLUSIVELY	HARMONIOUSLY	MECHANICALLY	RADIOTHERAPY
SELFINTEREST	CONCURRENTLY	HERMETICALLY	METHODICALLY	RECIPROCALLY
SELFPORTRAIT	CONDUCTIVITY	HISTORICALLY	METICULOUSLY	REFLATIONARY
SHORTCIRCUIT	CONFIRMATORY	HORIZONTALLY	MICROBREWERY	REFLECTIVITY
SITTLICHKEIT	CONGENITALLY	HORRIFICALLY	MIRACULOUSLY	RELENTLESSLY
SOMNAMBULIST	CONSEQUENTLY	HYDROGEOLOGY	MONOTONOUSLY	RESPECTFULLY
SOUTHERNMOST	CONSERVATORY	HYDROTHERAPY	MULLIGATAWNY	RESPECTIVELY
SPELEOLOGIST	CONSIDERABLY	HYGIENICALLY	MULTIPLICITY	REVERSIONARY
SPIRITUALIST	CONSISTENTLY	HYPERACIDITY	MUNICIPALITY	RHYTHMICALLY
STEGOPHOLIST	CONSPECTUITY	HYPNOTHERAPY	MYSTERIOUSLY	RHYTIDECTOMY
STRAITJACKET	CONSTABULARY	HYPNOTICALLY	NAVIGABILITY	RIDICULOUSLY
SUBCONTINENT	CONSTITUENCY	HYSTERECTOMY	NEUROTICALLY	ROMANTICALLY
TECHNOLOGIST	CONTEMPORARY	HYSTERICALLY	NONCHALANTLY	SADISTICALLY
TELEGRAPHIST	CONTINUOUSLY	IDIOSYNCRASY	OBEDIENTIARY	SARDONICALLY
THEREAGAINST	CONTRIBUTORY	ILLEGIBILITY	OBSEQUIOUSLY	SATISFACTORY
TOXICOLOGIST	CONVENIENTLY	ILLEGITIMACY	OCCASIONALLY	SCANDALOUSLY
TRANSCENDENT	CONVINCINGLY	ILLOGICALITY	OCEANOGRAPHY	SCAPULIMANCY
TRICHOLOGIST	CONVIVIALITY	IMMACULATELY	OPPRESSIVELY	SCRUPULOUSLY
UNCONVERSANT	COSCINOMANCY	IMMEASURABLY	OTHERWORLDLY	SCURRILOUSLY
UNDERCURRENT	COURAGEOUSLY	IMMODERATELY	OUTRAGEOUSLY	SEMANTICALLY
UNDERGARMENT	CROSSCOUNTRY	IMMUTABILITY	PALEONTOLOGY	SEQUENTIALLY
UNEMPLOYMENT	CRYPTOGRAPHY	IMPARTIALITY	PANTISOCRACY	SERVICEBERRY
UNIVERSALIST	CURMUDGEONLY	IMPERSONALLY	PARAMILITARY	SHAMEFACEDLY
VENTRIPOTENT	DEAMBULATORY	IMPRESSIVELY	PARTICULARLY	SHILLYSHALLY
WELTERWEIGHT	DECORATIVELY	INACCURATELY	PASSIONATELY	SLUBBERINGLY
WILLIEWAUGHT	DEFLATIONARY	INADEQUATELY	PATHETICALLY	SOLICITOUSLY
ZALAMBDODONT	DELIBERATELY	INCAPABILITY	PECTORILOQUY	SPECIFICALLY
ACADEMICALLY	DEMONSTRABLY	INCAUTIOUSLY	PEDANTICALLY	SPIRITUALITY
ACCIDENTALLY	DEPRECIATORY	INCIDENTALLY	PENITENTIARY	SPLENOMEGALY
ADAPTABILITY	DESIRABILITY	INCOHERENTLY	PERCEPTIVELY	SPORADICALLY
ADDITIONALLY	DEUTEROSCOPY	INCOMPARABLY	PERCEPTIVITY	STAGGERINGLY
ADJECTIVALLY	DISASTROUSLY	INCOMPLETELY	PEREMPTORILY	STRAIGHTAWAY
ADVISABILITY	DISCIPLINARY	INCORRIGIBLY	PERIODICALLY	STRUCTURALLY
AGGRESSIVELY	DISDAINFULLY	INCREASINGLY	PERMEABILITY	SUBJECTIVELY
ANTHROPOLOGY	DISHONORABLY	INDEFINITELY	PERMITTIVITY	SUBJECTIVITY
ANTICIPATORY	DOGMATICALLY	INDISPUTABLY	PERSISTENTLY	SUBMISSIVELY
APPENDECTOMY	DRAMATICALLY	INDISTINCTLY	PERSPICACITY	SUBSEQUENTLY
AROMATHERAPY	DYSTELEOLOGY	INDIVIDUALLY	PERSUASIVELY	SUBSIDIARITY
ARTHROPLASTY	ECCENTRICITY	INDUSTRIALLY	PETTIFOGGERY	SUCCESSFULLY
ARTIFICIALLY	ECONOMICALLY	INEFFICIENCY	PHARMACOLOGY	SUCCESSIVELY
ARTISTICALLY	ECSTATICALLY	INEXPLICABLY	PHENOMENALLY	SUFFICIENTLY
ATTRACTIVELY	EFFORTLESSLY	INEXTRICABLY	PHILANTHROPY	SUGGESTIVELY
AUSPICIOUSLY	ELECTRICALLY	INFLAMMATORY	PHONETICALLY	SUPERCILIARY
AUTHENTICITY	ELEEMOSYNARY	INFLATIONARY	PHRONTISTERY	SUPERHIGHWAY
AVAILABILITY	EMPHATICALLY	INFREQUENTLY	PLAUSIBILITY	SURPRISINGLY
BACTERIOLOGY	ENANTIOPATHY	INORDINATELY	POSSESSIVELY	SUSPICIOUSLY
BELLIGERENCY	ENTREATINGLY	INSOLUBILITY	POSTHUMOUSLY	SYMBOLICALLY
BENEVOLENTLY	EPISTEMOLOGY	INSUFFERABLY	POSTLIMINARY	TECHNICALITY
BIBLIOGRAPHY	EQUIVOCATORY	INTERMEDIARY	POTENTIALITY	TERCENTENARY

TERRIFICALLY	TRANSMOGRIFY	UNBELIEVABLY	UNOFFICIALLY	VOCIFEROUSLY
TESTAMENTARY	TRANSPARENCY	UNCHARITABLY	UNPOPULARITY	VOLUPTUOUSLY
THEATRICALLY	TREMENDOUSLY	UNDESERVEDLY	UNRESERVEDLY	WHIMSICALITY
THOUGHTFULLY	TRICENTENARY	UNEXPECTEDLY	UPROARIOUSLY	
TRACTABILITY	TRIGONOMETRY	UNILATERALLY	USERFRIENDLY	
TRANQUILLITY	TRIUMPHANTLY	UNNEIGHBORLY	VINDICTIVELY	

13:1

ACCEPTABILITY
ACCEPTILATION
ACCESSIBILITY
ACCOMMODATING
ACCOMMODATION
ACCOMPANIMENT
ACCOUTREMENTS
ACRYLONITRILE
ACUPUNCTURIST
ADMINISTRATOR
ADVENTUROUSLY
ADVERTISEMENT
AESTHETICALLY
AFFENPINSCHER
AFFIRMATIVELY
AFFORESTATION
AFFREIGHTMENT
AGGIORNAMENTO
AGGLOMERATION
AIRCRAFTWOMAN
AIRWORTHINESS
ALLOCHTHONOUS
ALPHABETARIAN
ALTERNATIVELY
ALUMINIFEROUS
ALUMINOTHERMY
AMPHIGASTRIUM
AMPLIFICATION
ANACHRONISTIC
ANIMADVERSION
ANTHELMINTHIC
ANTICLOCKWISE
ANTICOAGULANT
ANTIGROPELOES
ANTIHISTAMINE
ANYTHINGARIAN
APOCATASTASIS
APPORTIONMENT
APPROPINQUATE
APPROPRIATION
APPROXIMATELY
APPROXIMATION
AQUIFOLIACEAE
ARCHAEOLOGIST
ARCHAEOPTERYX
ARCHIMANDRITE
ARCHITECTURAL
ARGUMENTATIVE
ARISTROCRATIC
ARITHMETICIAN
ARMOURPLATING
ARTIFICIALITY
ARUNDINACEOUS
ASCERTAINABLE
ASSASSINATION
ASTONISHINGLY
ATTENTIVENESS
AUTHORISATION
AUTHORITARIAN
AUTHORITATIVE
AUTHORIZATION
AUTOBIOGRAPHY
AUTOCEPHALOUS
AUTOCHTHONOUS
AUTOMATICALLY
BACCALAUREATE
BACTERIOPHAGE

BASIDIOMYCETE
BEATIFICATION
BIBLIOGRAPHER
BIBLIOPHAGIST
BILDUNGSROMAN
BIODEGRADABLE
BIOTECHNOLOGY
BIREFRINGENCE
BLANDISHMENTS
BLOODCURDLING
BOUGAINVILLEA
BOUILLABAISSE
BOUSTROPHEDON
BRACHIOSAURUS
BREASTFEEDING
BROKENHEARTED
BUNGEEJUMPING
BUSINESSWOMAN
BUTTERFINGERS
BUTYRALDEHYDE
CALLISTHENICS
CARBONIFEROUS
CARBONIZATION
CARTILAGINOUS
CATEGORICALLY
CAUTERIZATION
CEPHALOSPORIN
CEREMONIOUSLY
CERTIFICATION
CHANGEABILITY
CHARACTERISED
CHARACTERLESS
CHATEAUBRIAND
CHEESEMONGERS
CHINKERINCHEE
CHOREOGRAPHER
CHRISTMASTIME
CHRONOLOGICAL
CHRYSANTHEMUM
CIRCUMAMBIENT
CIRCUMFERENCE
CIRCUMSTANCES
CIRCUMVENTION
CLAIRAUDIENCE
CLARIFICATION
CLISHMACLAVER
CLOSEDCIRCUIT
COEDUCATIONAL
COLLABORATION
COLLABORATIVE
COLLIESHANGIE
COLLOQUIALISM
COMMEMORATION
COMMEMORATIVE
COMMENSURABLE
COMMERCIALIZE
COMMISERATION
COMMUNICATION
COMMUNICATIVE
COMPANIONABLE
COMPANIONSHIP
COMPARABILITY
COMPARATIVELY
COMPASSIONATE
COMPATIBILITY
COMPLEMENTARY
COMPLIMENTARY
COMPREHENSION
COMPREHENSIVE

COMRADEINARMS
CONCATENATION
CONCENTRATION
CONCEPTIONIST
CONCEPTUALIST
CONCEPTUALIZE
CONCESSIONARY
CONCUPISCENCE
CONDESCENDING
CONDESCENSION
CONDITIONALLY
CONFARREATION
CONFECTIONERS
CONFECTIONERY
CONFEDERATION
CONFIGURATION
CONFLAGRATION
CONFRONTATION
CONGRESSIONAL
CONGRESSWOMAN
CONSANGUINITY
CONSCIENTIOUS
CONSCIOUSNESS
CONSECTANEOUS
CONSECUTIVELY
CONSEQUENTIAL
CONSERVATOIRE
CONSIDERATELY
CONSIDERATION
CONSOLIDATION
CONSPICUOUSLY
CONSPURCATION
CONSTELLATION
CONSTERNATION
CONTAMINATION
CONTEMPLATION
CONTEMPLATIVE
CONTENTEDNESS
CONTINUATIONS
CONTORTIONIST
CONTRABASSOON
CONTRACEPTION
CONTRACEPTIVE
CONTRADICTION
CONTRADICTORY
CONTRAFAGOTTO
CONTRAVENTION
CONTRIBUTIONS
CONTROVERSIAL
CONVALESCENCE
CONVERSAZIONE
CORRESPONDENT
CORRESPONDING
CORROBORATION
CORROBORATORY
COSTEFFECTIVE
COUNTERACTING
COUNTERATTACK
COUNTERCHARGE
COUNTERFEITER
COUNTRYPEOPLE
CRAFTSMANSHIP
CREDULOUSNESS
CRIMINOLOGIST
CROSSQUESTION
CRUISERWEIGHT
CRYPTANALYSIS
DAGUERREOTYPE
DEATHLESSNESS

DECAFFEINATED
DECOMPOSITION
DECOMPRESSION
DECONTAMINATE
DECRIMINALIZE
DEFENSIBILITY
DEFERVESCENCE
DEFIBRILLATOR
DEFORESTATION
DEHYDROGENATE
DEIPNOSOPHIST
DEMILITARIZED
DEMONSTRATION
DEMONSTRATIVE
DENATIONALIZE
DEPENDABILITY
DERMATOLOGIST
DESEGREGATION
DÉSOBLIGEANTE
DETERIORATION
DETERMINATION
DEVELOPMENTAL
DIACATHOLICON
DIAMETRICALLY
DIFFARREATION
DIFFERENTIATE
DISADVANTAGED
DISAPPEARANCE
DISAPPOINTING
DISCOLORATION
DISCONCERTING
DISCONNECTION
DISCONTINUITY
DISCONTINUOUS
DISCREDITABLE
DISCREDITABLY
DISCRETIONARY
DISENGAGEMENT
DISESTIMATION
DISFIGUREMENT
DISGRACEFULLY
DISHEARTENING
DISHONOURABLE
DISHONOURABLY
DISILLUSIONED
DISINTERESTED
DISPARAGEMENT
DISPASSIONATE
DISPROPORTION
DISRESPECTFUL
DISSEMINATION
DISSIMILARITY
DISSIMULATION
DISTINGUISHED
DOCUMENTATION
DOUBLEGLAZING
DRAMATIZATION
DRYOPITHECINE
ECCENTRICALLY
EFFECTIVENESS
EFFERVESCENCE
EFFLORESCENCE
ELECTROCUTION
ELECTROMAGNET
ELECTROMOTIVE
ELEPHANTIASIS
EMBARRASSMENT
EMBELLISHMENT
ENCEPHALOCELE

ENCEPHALOGRAM
ENCOURAGEMENT
ENCULTURATION
ENCYCLOPAEDIA
ENCYCLOPAEDIC
ENERGETICALLY
ENLIGHTENMENT
ENTEROPNEUSTA
ENTERTAINMENT
ENTOMOLOGICAL
ENVIRONMENTAL
EPANADIPLOSIS
EPHEMEROPTERA
EPIPHENOMENON
EPITRACHELION
EQUIPONDERATE
ESCHSCHOLTZIA
ESTABLISHMENT
EXCEPTIONABLE
EXCEPTIONALLY
EXCOMMUNICATE
EXHIBITIONIST
EXPANSIVENESS
EXPEDITIONARY
EXPEDITIOUSLY
EXPOSTULATION
EXPROPRIATION
EXTERMINATION
EXTRAORDINARY
EXTRAPOLATION
EXTRAVAGANTLY
FACETIOUSNESS
FALSIFICATION
FANTASTICALLY
FEATHERWEIGHT
FERROCONCRETE
FERTILISATION
FERTILIZATION
FLABBERGASTED
FONTAINEBLEAU
FOREKNOWLEDGE
FORGETFULNESS
FORMALIZATION
FORTIFICATION
FORTUNETELLER
FOSSILIZATION
FOSTERPARENTS
FRACTIOUSNESS
FRAGMENTATION
FRANKALMOIGNE
FREQUENTATIVE
FRIGHTENINGLY
FRIGHTFULNESS
FRIVOLOUSNESS
FUERTEVENTURA
FUNDAMENTALLY
GALVANIZATION
GARRULOUSNESS
GASTROCNEMIUS
GENERALISSIMO
GENITOURINARY
GEOMETRICALLY
GEOSTATIONARY
GESTICULATION
GLOBETROTTING
GLORIFICATION
GLOSSOGRAPHER
GLUMDALCLITCH
GOODRIGHTEOUS

GRAMMATICALLY	INCONSISTENCY	INVIOLABILITY	METEOROLOGIST	PARANTHROPOUS
GRANDDAUGHTER	INCONSPICUOUS	INVOLUNTARILY	MICROCOMPUTER	PARAPHERNALIA
GRANDILOQUENT	INCONTESTABLE	IRRECOVERABLE	MICROORGANISM	PARENTHETICAL
GRANDPARENTAL	INCONVENIENCE	IRREPLACEABLE	MIDDLEBREAKER	PARLIAMENTARY
GRATIFICATION	INCORPORATION	IRREPRESSIBLE	MISANTHROPIST	PARTHOGENESIS
GRAVITATIONAL	INCORRUPTIBLE	IRRESPONSIBLE	MISCEGENATION	PARTICIPATION
GRIEFSTRICKEN	INCREDULOUSLY	IRRESPONSIBLY	MISCELLANEOUS	PARTICIPATORY
GUILTLESSNESS	INCRIMINATING	IRRETRIEVABLE	MISCHIEVOUSLY	PARTICOLOURED
GYNAECOLOGIST	INCRIMINATORY	IRRETRIEVABLY	MISCONCEPTION	PARTICULARISE
GYNANDROMORPH	INDEFATIGABLE	ISOGEOTHERMAL	MISMANAGEMENT	PARTICULARITY
GYNECOLOGICAL	INDEFATIGABLY	JIGGERYPOKERY	MISSISSIPPIAN	PARTICULARIZE
HALLUCINATION	INDEPENDENTLY	JOLLIFICATION	MISUNDERSTAND	PASSCHENDAELE
HALLUCINATORY	INDESCRIBABLE	JURISPRUDENCE	MISUNDERSTOOD	PASSEMENTERIE
HAMMERKLAVIER	INDESCRIBABLY	JUSTIFICATION	MOCKTECHNICAL	PASSIONFLOWER
HAMMERTHROWER	INDETERMINATE	JUSTIFICATORY	MODERNIZATION	PATERFAMILIAS
HARMONIZATION	INDETERMINISM	JUXTAPOSITION	MOLLIFICATION	PATERNALISTIC
HEARTBREAKING	INDIFFERENTLY	KALEIDOSCOPIC	MONOCOTYLEDON	PATRIOTICALLY
HEMISPHERICAL	INDISPENSABLE	KANGCHENJUNGA	MONONUCLEOSIS	PELOPONNESIAN
HERMAPHRODITE	INDISPOSITION	KAPPELMEISTER	MONOTHALAMOUS	PENETRABILITY
HETERAUXESISM	INDIVIDUALISM	KIDDERMINSTER	MORPHOLOGICAL	PENNSYLVANIAN
HETEROGENEOUS	INDIVIDUALIST	KNICKERBOCKER	MORTIFICATION	PEPTIDOGLYCAN
HIEROGLYPHICS	INDIVIDUALITY	KNICKKNACKERY	MOUTHWATERING	PERAMBULATION
HOMOSEXUALITY	INDUSTRIALIST	KNOWLEDGEABLE	MULTICOLOURED	PEREGRINATION
HORRIPILATION	INDUSTRIALIZE	LACKADAISICAL	MULTINATIONAL	PERFECTIONIST
HORSEFEATHERS	INDUSTRIOUSLY	LAEVOROTATORY	MULTINUCLEATE	PERFUNCTORILY
HORTICULTURAL	INEFFICIENTLY	LAMPADEPHORIA	MULTITUDINOUS	PERPENDICULAR
HOUSEBREAKING	INEVITABILITY	LEATHERJACKET	MYSTIFICATION	PERSONALITIES
HUNDREDWEIGHT	INEXHAUSTIBLE	LECTISTERNIUM	NATIONALISTIC	PERSPICACIOUS
HYALURONIDASE	INEXPERIENCED	LEISURELINESS	NEANDERTHALER	PERVASIVENESS
HYBRIDIZATION	INEXPRESSIBLE	LEPIDOPTERIST	NEIGHBOURHOOD	PETRIFICATION
HYDRAULICALLY	INFALLIBILITY	LEPTOCEPHALUS	NEMATHELMINTH	PETROCHEMICAL
HYDROCEPHALUS	INFINITESIMAL	LEPTOSPIROSIS	NERVELESSNESS	PHARMACOPOEIA
HYDRODYNAMICS	INFLEXIBILITY	LEXICOGRAPHER	NEUROCOMPUTER	PHENCYCLIDINE
HYDROELECTRIC	INFLORESCENCE	LIBRARIANSHIP	NIGHTCLUBBING	PHILADELPHIAN
HYPERCRITICAL	INGENUOUSNESS	LIEBFRAUMILCH	NIGHTWATCHMAN	PHILANTHROPIC
HYPERSTHENITE	INQUISITIVELY	LIECHTENSTEIN	NONCONFORMIST	PHILOSOPHICAL
HYPOCHONDRIAC	INQUISITORIAL	LIGHTFINGERED	NONCONFORMITY	PHOSPHOLIPASE
HYPOVENTILATE	INSECTIVOROUS	LISSOTRICHOUS	NONRESISTANCE	PHOTOCHEMICAL
IDIORRHYTHMIC	INSENSITIVITY	LONGSUFFERING	NONSUFFICIENT	PHOTOELECTRIC
IDIOSYNCRATIC	INSIDIOUSNESS	LUXURIOUSNESS	NORMALIZATION	PHYLLOQUINONE
IGNOMINIOUSLY	INSIGNIFICANT	LYCANTHROPIST	NORTHEASTERLY	PHYSHARMONICA
ILLUMINATIONS	INSPIRATIONAL	MACHIAVELLIAN	NORTHWESTERLY	PHYSIOGNOMIST
IMAGINATIVELY	INSTANTANEOUS	MACHICOLATION	NOSTALGICALLY	PHYSIOLOGICAL
IMPERCEPTIBLE	INSTINCTIVELY	MADETOMEASURE	NUCLEOPROTEIN	PHYSIOTHERAPY
IMPERCEPTIBLY	INSTITUTIONAL	MAGISTERIALLY	NULLIFICATION	PHYSOSTIGMINE
IMPERIALISTIC	INSTRUCTIONAL	MAGNANIMOUSLY	OBJECTIONABLE	PHYTOPLANKTON
IMPERSONATING	INSUBORDINATE	MAGNIFICATION	OBJECTIVENESS	PLATOCEPHALUS
IMPERSONATION	INSUBSTANTIAL	MAGNIFICENTLY	OFFENSIVENESS	PNEUMATICALLY
IMPERTINENTLY	INSUFFICIENCY	MAGNILOQUENCE	OFFICIOUSNESS	PNEUMONECTOMY
IMPERTURBABLE	INSUPPORTABLE	MALADJUSTMENT	OPHTHALMOLOGY	POLIOMYELITIS
IMPERTURBABLY	INTELLIGENTLY	MALLEMAROKING	OPPORTUNISTIC	POLLICITATION
IMPONDERABLES	INTENTIONALLY	MANIFESTATION	OPPORTUNITIES	POLYCHROMATIC
IMPOSSIBILITY	INTERCALATION	MANUFACTURING	ORCHESTRATION	POTENTIOMETER
IMPRACTICABLE	INTERESTINGLY	MASSACHUSETTS	ORNAMENTATION	PRAGMATICALLY
IMPRESSIONISM	INTERMARRIAGE	MASTIGOPHORAN	ORNITHOLOGIST	PRECAUTIONARY
IMPRESSIONIST	INTERMATIONAL	MATERIALISTIC	OUTRECUIDANCE	PRECIPITATELY
IMPROBABILITY	INTERPERSONAL	MATHEMATICIAN	OUTSTANDINGLY	PRECIPITATION
IMPROVIDENTLY	INTERPOLATION	MATRICULATION	OVEREMPHASIZE	PRECONCEPTION
IMPROVISATION	INTERROGATION	MAURIKIGUSARI	OVERSTATEMENT	PREDOMINANTLY
IMPULSIVENESS	INTERROGATIVE	MECHANIZATION	OWNEROCCUPIER	PREFABRICATED
INADVERTENTLY	INTRAMUSCULAR	MEDITERRANEAN	OYSTERCATCHER	PRELIMINARIES
INAPPROPRIATE	INTRANSIGENCE	MEISTERSINGER	PAEDIATRICIAN	PREMEDITATION
INCANDESCENCE	INTRINSICALLY	MERCHANDIZING	PAINSTAKINGLY	PREOCCUPATION
INCARCERATION	INTROSPECTION	MERCILESSNESS	PALAEONTOLOGY	PREPONDERANCE
INCOMBUSTIBLE	INTROSPECTIVE	MESSERSCHMITT	PANDICULATION	PREPOSSESSING
INCOMMUNICADO	INVENTIVENESS	METAGRABOLISE	PANHARMONICON	PREPOSSESSION
INCOMPETENTLY	INVESTIGATION	METAGROBOLISE	PAPAPRELATIST	PREPROGRAMMED
INCONCEIVABLE	INVESTIGATIVE	METAMORPHOSIS	PARADOXICALLY	PRESERVATIVES
INCONSIDERATE	INVINCIBILITY	METAPHYSICIAN	PARALLELOGRAM	PRESSURELOCAL

PRETERNATURAL	REGURGITATION	SIGNIFICATION	SYMPIESOMETER	UNCONQUERABLE
PREVARICATION	REIMBURSEMENT	SIPUNCULOIDEA	SYNTACTICALLY	UNCONSCIOUSLY
PRIMOGENITURE	REINCARNATION	SKATEBOARDING	SYNTHETICALLY	UNCOOPERATIVE
PRIVATIZATION	REINFORCEMENT	SLEEPLESSNESS	TABLESPOONFUL	UNCOORDINATED
PROBLEMATICAL	REINSTATEMENT	SNOWBLINDNESS	TALKATIVENESS	UNDERACHIEVER
PROCLEUSMATIC	REMINISCENCES	SOCIOECONOMIC	TANTALIZINGLY	UNDERCARRIAGE
PROCRASTINATE	REMORSELESSLY	SOLEMNIZATION	TAPERECORDING	UNDERCLOTHING
PROFECTITIOUS	RENSSELAERITE	SOMATOSENSORY	TECHNOLOGICAL	UNDERESTIMATE
PROFESSORSHIP	REPERCUSSIONS	SOMATOTROPHIN	TELEMARKETING	UNDERGRADUATE
PROFITABILITY	REPLENISHMENT	SOPHISTICATED	TEMPERAMENTAL	UNDERSTANDING
PROGNOSTICATE	REPREHENSIBLE	SOUTHEASTERLY	TENDERHEARTED	UNDERSTRAPPER
PROGRESSIVELY	REPREHENSIBLY	SOUTHWESTERLY	TENOSYNOVITIS	UNDISCIPLINED
PROJECTIONIST	REPROACHFULLY	SPASMODICALLY	TETRASYLLABIC	UNEMBARRASSED
PROLIFERATION	REPROGRAPHICS	SPECIFICATION	THANKLESSNESS	UNENLIGHTENED
PROMISCUOUSLY	REPUBLICANISM	SPECTACULARLY	THAUMATURGICS	UNESTABLISHED
PRONOUNCEMENT	RESOURCEFULLY	SPECTROGRAPHY	THAUMATURGIST	UNEXCEPTIONAL
PRONUNCIATION	RESUSCITATION	SPELEOLOGICAL	THEATRICALITY	UNEXPERIENCED
PROPHETICALLY	RETROGRESSION	SPERMATOPHYTE	THEOLOGICALLY	UNFASHIONABLE
PROPORTIONATE	RETROSPECTIVE	SPINDLESHANKS	THEORETICALLY	UNFLINCHINGLY
PROPRIETORIAL	REUNIFICATION	SPINECHILLING	THERMODYNAMIC	UNFORESEEABLE
PROSOPOGRAPHY	REVERBERATION	SPITESPLENDID	THERMONUCLEAR	UNFORGETTABLE
PROTECTIONISM	REVOLUTIONARY	SPONTANEOUSLY	THERMOPLASTIC	UNFORTUNATELY
PROTECTIONIST	REVOLUTIONIZE	SPORTSMANLIKE	THESSALONIANS	UNGENTLEMANLY
PROTESTANTISM	RHADAMANTHINE	SPORTSMANSHIP	THIGMOTROPISM	UNGRAMMATICAL
PROTONOTARIAT	RHYPAROGRAPHY	SPRIGHTLINESS	THORACENTESIS	UNIMAGINATIVE
PROVINCIALISM	RIGHTEOUSNESS	SQUEAMISHNESS	THOROUGHBRACE	UNIMPEACHABLE
PROVISIONALLY	ROLLERBLADING	STABILIZATION	THOROUGHGOING	UNIMPRESSIBLE
PROVOCATIVELY	ROLLERCOASTER	STAPHYLINIDAE	THOUGHTLESSLY	UNINHABITABLE
PSYCHOANALYSE	ROUNDTHEWORLD	STATESMANLIKE	THREATENINGLY	UNINTELLIGENT
PSYCHOANALYST	RUTHERFORDIUM	STATESMANSHIP	THUNDERSTRUCK	UNINTENTIONAL
PSYCHOBIOLOGY	SACCHAROMYCES	STATIONMASTER	THYROIDECTOMY	UNINTERESTING
PSYCHOKINESIS	SALACIOUSNESS	STATISTICALLY	TINTINNABULUM	UNINTERRUPTED
PSYCHOLOGICAL	SANCTIMONIOUS	STEADFASTNESS	TONGUEINCHEEK	UNMENTIONABLE
PSYCHOMETRICS	SARCASTICALLY	STEEPLECHASER	TONGUETWISTER	UNNECESSARILY
PSYCHOSOMATIC	SCANDALMONGER	STEPPINGSTONE	TONSILLECTOMY	UNPARTITIONED
PSYCHOTHERAPY	SCHADENFREUDE	STERCORACEOUS	TOPOGRAPHICAL	UNPRECEDENTED
PULVERIZATION	SCHEMATICALLY	STERILIZATION	TORTOISESHELL	UNPREDICTABLE
PUNCTILIOUSLY	SCHIZOPHRENIA	STOCKBREEDING	TRACTARIANISM	UNPRETENTIOUS
PUSILLANIMITY	SCHIZOPHRENIC	STRANGULATION	TRADITIONALLY	UNPROGRESSIVE
PUSILLANIMOUS	SCHOLARLINESS	STRATEGICALLY	TRANQUILLISER	UNQUESTIONING
PYROTECHNICAL	SCHOOLTEACHER	STRENUOUSNESS	TRANQUILLIZER	UNSERVICEABLE
QUADRAGESIMAL	SCHUTZSTAFFEL	STREPTOCARPUS	TRANSATLANTIC	UNSUBSTANTIAL
QUADRILATERAL	SCINTILLATING	STREPTOCOCCUS	TRANSCRIPTION	UNSYMMETRICAL
QUADRUPLICATE	SCINTILLATION	STRIKEBREAKER	TRANSGRESSION	UNSYMPATHETIC
QUALIFICATION	SCLEROPROTEIN	STYLISTICALLY	TRANSISTORIZE	UNTRUSTWORTHY
QUARTERMASTER	SECRETIVENESS	SUBCONTRACTOR	TRANSLITERATE	UNWILLINGNESS
QUARTODECIMAN	SEDIMENTATION	SUBJECTMATTER	TRANSMUTATION	UPTOTHEMINUTE
QUERULOUSNESS	SEISMOLOGICAL	SUBLIEUTENANT	TRANSPARENTLY	VEGETARIANISM
QUESTIONNAIRE	SELFADDRESSED	SUBMANDIBULAR	TRANSPIRATION	VENTRILOQUISM
QUINQUAGESIMA	SELFCONFESSED	SUBORDINATION	TRANSPORTABLE	VENTRILOQUIST
RADIOACTIVITY	SELFCONFIDENT	SUBSERVIENTLY	TRANSPOSITION	VERCINGETORIX
RAMIFICATIONS	SELFCONSCIOUS	SUBSTANTIALLY	TRAUMATICALLY	VERSIFICATION
RAPPROCHEMENT	SELFCONTAINED	SUOVETAURILIA	TREACHEROUSLY	VICEPRESIDENT
RATIONALALITY	SELFGOVERNING	SUPERABUNDANT	TRIANGULATION	VICTIMIZATION
REALISTICALLY	SEMBLANCECORD	SUPERANNUATED	TRICHOSANTHIN	VIDEOCASSETTE
REARRANGEMENT	SEMIAUTOMATIC	SUPERFICIALLY	TRIPLOBLASTIC	VIDEORECORDER
RECALCITRANCE	SEMICONDUCTOR	SUPERFLUOUSLY	TYPOGRAPHICAL	VITRIFICATION
RECEPTIVENESS	SENSATIONALLY	SUPERLATIVELY	UMBELLIFEROUS	VIVACIOUSNESS
RECITATIONIST	SENSELESSNESS	SUPERNUMERARY	UNACCOMPANIED	VORACIOUSNESS
RECRIMINATION	SENSITIVENESS	SUPERORDINATE	UNACCOUNTABLE	VULCANIZATION
RECRIMINATORY	SENTENTIOUSLY	SUPERSTITIOUS	UNACCOUNTABLY	VULGARIZATION
RECRUDESCENCE	SENTIMENTALLY	SUPPLEMENTARY	UNADULTERATED	VULNERABILITY
RECTIFICATION	SEPTENTRIONES	SUPRANATIONAL	UNANTICIPATED	WEATHERBEATEN
REDEMPTIONIST	SEQUESTRATION	SURREPTITIOUS	UNCEREMONIOUS	WEIGHTLIFTING
REDEVELOPMENT	SERVILEMENTAL	SUSPERCOLLATE	UNCOMFORTABLE	WHOLESOMENESS
REFRIGERATION	SHAPELESSNESS	SWASHBUCKLING	UNCOMFORTABLY	WITWATERSRAND
REFRIGERATORS	SHOULDERBLADE	SWEDENBORGIAN	UNCOMMUNICATE	XIPHIPLASTRON
REFURBISHMENT	SHRINKWRAPPED	SWEETSMELLING	UNCOMPLICATED	**13:2**
REGIMENTATION	SIGNIFICANTLY	SWOLLENHEADED	UNCONDITIONAL	

BACCALAUREATE	PATERNALISTIC	DEVELOPMENTAL	REINCARNATION	CHATEAUBRIAND
BACTERIOPHAGE	PATRIOTICALLY	FEATHERWEIGHT	REINFORCEMENT	CHEESEMONGERS
BASIDIOMYCETE	RADIOACTIVITY	FERROCONCRETE	REINSTATEMENT	CHINKERINCHEE
CALLISTHENICS	RAMIFICATIONS	FERTILISATION	REMINISCENCES	CHOREOGRAPHER
CARBONIFEROUS	RAPPROCHEMENT	FERTILIZATION	REMORSELESSLY	CHRISTMASTIME
CARBONIZATION	RATIONALALITY	GENERALISSIMO	RENSSELAERITE	CHRONOLOGICAL
CARTILAGINOUS	SACCHAROMYCES	GENITOURINARY	REPERCUSSIONS	CHRYSANTHEMUM
CATEGORICALLY	SALACIOUSNESS	GEOMETRICALLY	REPLENISHMENT	PHARMACOPOEIA
CAUTERIZATION	SANCTIMONIOUS	GEOSTATIONARY	REPREHENSIBLE	PHENCYCLIDINE
DAGUERREOTYPE	SARCASTICALLY	GESTICULATION	REPREHENSIBLY	PHILADELPHIAN
FACETIOUSNESS	TABLESPOONFUL	HEARTBREAKING	REPROACHFULLY	PHILANTHROPIC
FALSIFICATION	TALKATIVENESS	HEMISPHERICAL	REPROGRAPHICS	PHILOSOPHICAL
FANTASTICALLY	TANTALIZINGLY	HERMAPHRODITE	REPUBLICANISM	PHOSPHOLIPASE
GALVANIZATION	TAPERECORDING	HETERAUXESISM	RESOURCEFULLY	PHOTOCHEMICAL
GARRULOUSNESS	OBJECTIONABLE	HETEROGENEOUS	RESUSCITATION	PHOTOELECTRIC
GASTROCNEMIUS	OBJECTIVENESS	LEATHERJACKET	RETROGRESSION	PHYLLOQUINONE
HALLUCINATION	ACCEPTABILITY	LECTISTERNIUM	RETROSPECTIVE	PHYSHARMONICA
HALLUCINATORY	ACCEPTILATION	LEISURELINESS	REUNIFICATION	PHYSIOGNOMIST
HAMMERKLAVIER	ACCESSIBILITY	LEPIDOPTERIST	REVERBERATION	PHYSIOLOGICAL
HAMMERTHROWER	ACCOMMODATING	LEPTOCEPHALUS	REVOLUTIONARY	PHYSIOTHERAPY
HARMONIZATION	ACCOMMODATION	LEPTOSPIROSIS	REVOLUTIONIZE	PHYSOSTIGMINE
KALEIDOSCOPIC	ACCOMPANIMENT	LEXICOGRAPHER	SECRETIVENESS	PHYTOPLANKTON
KANGCHENJUNGA	ACCOUTREMENTS	MECHANIZATION	SEDIMENTATION	RHADAMANTHINE
KAPPELMEISTER	ACRYLONITRILE	MEDITERRANEAN	SEISMOLOGICAL	RHYPAROGRAPHY
LACKADAISICAL	ACUPUNCTURIST	MEISTERSINGER	SELFADDRESSED	SHAPELESSNESS
LAEVOROTATORY	ECCENTRICALLY	MERCHANDIZING	SELFCONFESSED	SHOULDERBLADE
LAMPADEPHORIA	SCANDALMONGER	MERCILESSNESS	SELFCONFIDENT	SHRINKWRAPPED
MACHIAVELLIAN	SCHADENFREUDE	MESSERSCHMITT	SELFCONSCIOUS	THANKLESSNESS
MACHICOLATION	SCHEMATICALLY	METAGRABOLISE	SELFCONTAINED	THAUMATURGICS
MADETOMEASURE	SCHIZOPHRENIA	METAGROBOLISE	SELFGOVERNING	THAUMATURGIST
MAGISTERIALLY	SCHIZOPHRENIC	METAMORPHOSIS	SEMBLANCECORD	THEATRICALITY
MAGNANIMOUSLY	SCHOLARLINESS	METAPHYSICIAN	SEMIAUTOMATIC	THEOLOGICALLY
MAGNIFICATION	SCHOOLTEACHER	METEOROLOGIST	SEMICONDUCTOR	THEORETICALLY
MAGNIFICENTLY	SCHUTZSTAFFEL	NEANDERTHALER	SENSATIONALLY	THERMODYNAMIC
MAGNILOQUENCE	SCINTILLATING	NEIGHBOURHOOD	SENSELESSNESS	THERMONUCLEAR
MALADJUSTMENT	SCINTILLATION	NEMATHELMINTH	SENSITIVENESS	THERMOPLASTIC
MALLEMAROKING	SCLEROPROTEIN	NERVELESSNESS	SENTENTIOUSLY	THESSALONIANS
MANIFESTATION	ADMINISTRATOR	NEUROCOMPUTER	SENTIMENTALLY	THIGMOTROPISM
MANUFACTURING	ADVENTUROUSLY	PELOPONNESIAN	SEPTENTRIONES	THORACENTESIS
MASSACHUSETTS	ADVERTISEMENT	PENETRABILITY	SEQUESTRATION	THOROUGHBRACE
MASTIGOPHORAN	IDIORRHYTHMIC	PENNSYLVANIAN	SERVILEMENTAL	THOROUGHGOING
MATERIALISTIC	IDIOSYNCRATIC	PEPTIDOGLYCAN	TECHNOLOGICAL	THOUGHTLESSLY
MATHEMATICIAN	AESTHETICALLY	PERAMBULATION	TELEMARKETING	THREATENINGLY
MATRICULATION	BEATIFICATION	PEREGRINATION	TEMPERAMENTAL	THUNDERSTRUCK
MAURIKIGUSARI	CEPHALOSPORIN	PERFECTIONIST	TENDERHEARTED	THYROIDECTOMY
NATIONALISTIC	CEREMONIOUSLY	PERFUNCTORILY	TENOSYNOVITIS	WHOLESOMENESS
PAEDIATRICIAN	CERTIFICATION	PERPENDICULAR	TETRASYLLABIC	AIRCRAFTWOMAN
PAINSTAKINGLY	DEATHLESSNESS	PERSONALITIES	VEGETARIANISM	AIRWORTHINESS
PALAEONTOLOGY	DECAFFEINATED	PERSPICACIOUS	VENTRILOQUISM	BIBLIOGRAPHER
PANDICULATION	DECOMPOSITION	PERVASIVENESS	VENTRILOQUIST	BIBLIOPHAGIST
PANHARMONICON	DECOMPRESSION	PETRIFICATION	VERCINGETORIX	BILDUNGSROMAN
PAPAPRELATIST	DECONTAMINATE	PETROCHEMICAL	VERSIFICATION	BIODEGRADABLE
PARADOXICALLY	DECRIMINALIZE	REALISTICALLY	WEATHERBEATEN	BIOTECHNOLOGY
PARALLELOGRAM	DEFENSIBILITY	REARRANGEMENT	WEIGHTLIFTING	BIREFRINGENCE
PARANTHROPOUS	DEFERVESCENCE	RECALCITRANCE	AFFENPINSCHER	CIRCUMAMBIENT
PARAPHERNALIA	DEFIBRILLATOR	RECEPTIVENESS	AFFIRMATIVELY	CIRCUMFERENCE
PARENTHETICAL	DEFORESTATION	RECITATIONIST	AFFORESTATION	CIRCUMSTANCES
PARLIAMENTARY	DEHYDROGENATE	RECRIMINATION	AFFREIGHTMENT	CIRCUMVENTION
PARTHOGENESIS	DEIPNOSOPHIST	RECRIMINATORY	EFFECTIVENESS	DIACATHOLICON
PARTICIPATION	DEMILITARIZED	RECRUDESCENCE	EFFERVESCENCE	DIAMETRICALLY
PARTICIPATORY	DEMONSTRATION	RECTIFICATION	EFFLORESCENCE	DIFFARREATION
PARTICOLOURED	DEMONSTRATIVE	REDEMPTIONIST	OFFENSIVENESS	DIFFERENTIATE
PARTICULARISE	DENATIONALIZE	REDEVELOPMENT	OFFICIOUSNESS	DISADVANTAGED
PARTICULARITY	DEPENDABILITY	REFRIGERATION	AGGIORNAMENTO	DISAPPEARANCE
PARTICULARIZE	DERMATOLOGIST	REFRIGERATORS	AGGLOMERATION	DISAPPOINTING
PASSCHENDAELE	DESEGREGATION	REFURBISHMENT	IGNOMINIOUSLY	DISCOLORATION
PASSEMENTERIE	DÉSOBLIGEANTE	REGIMENTATION	CHANGEABILITY	DISCONCERTING
PASSIONFLOWER	DETERIORATION	REGURGITATION	CHARACTERISED	DISCONNECTION
PATERFAMILIAS	DETERMINATION	REIMBURSEMENT	CHARACTERLESS	DISCONTINUITY

DISCONTINUOUS	ELECTROMAGNET	INCREDULOUSLY	PNEUMONECTOMY	COMMENSURABLE
DISCREDITABLE	ELECTROMOTIVE	INCRIMINATING	SNOWBLINDNESS	COMMERCIALIZE
DISCREDITABLY	ELEPHANTIASIS	INCRIMINATORY	UNACCOMPANIED	COMMISERATION
DISCRETIONARY	FLABBERGASTED	INDEFATIGABLE	UNACCOUNTABLE	COMMUNICATION
DISENGAGEMENT	GLOBETROTTING	INDEFATIGABLY	UNACCOUNTABLY	COMMUNICATIVE
DISESTIMATION	GLORIFICATION	INDEPENDENTLY	UNADULTERATED	COMPANIONABLE
DISFIGUREMENT	GLOSSOGRAPHER	INDESCRIBABLE	UNANTICIPATED	COMPANIONSHIP
DISGRACEFULLY	GLUMDALCLITCH	INDESCRIBABLY	UNCEREMONIOUS	COMPARABILITY
DISHEARTENING	ILLUMINATIONS	INDETERMINATE	UNCOMFORTABLE	COMPARATIVELY
DISHONOURABLE	PLATOCEPHALUS	INDETERMINISM	UNCOMFORTABLY	COMPASSIONATE
DISHONOURABLY	SLEEPLESSNESS	INDIFFERENTLY	UNCOMMUNICATE	COMPATIBILITY
DISILLUSIONED	AMPHIGASTRIUM	INDISPENSABLE	UNCOMPLICATED	COMPLEMENTARY
DISINTERESTED	AMPLIFICATION	INDISPOSITION	UNCONDITIONAL	COMPLIMENTARY
DISPARAGEMENT	EMBARRASSMENT	INDIVIDUALISM	UNCONQUERABLE	COMPREHENSION
DISPASSIONATE	EMBELLISHMENT	INDIVIDUALIST	UNCONSCIOUSLY	COMPREHENSIVE
DISPROPORTION	IMAGINATIVELY	INDIVIDUALITY	UNCOOPERATIVE	COMRADEINARMS
DISRESPECTFUL	IMPERCEPTIBLE	INDUSTRIALIST	UNCOORDINATED	CONCATENATION
DISSEMINATION	IMPERCEPTIBLY	INDUSTRIALIZE	UNDERACHIEVER	CONCENTRATION
DISSIMILARITY	IMPERIALISTIC	INDUSTRIOUSLY	UNDERCARRIAGE	CONCEPTIONIST
DISSIMULATION	IMPERSONATING	INEFFICIENTLY	UNDERCLOTHING	CONCEPTUALIST
DISTINGUISHED	IMPERSONATION	INEVITABILITY	UNDERESTIMATE	CONCEPTUALIZE
HIEROGLYPHICS	IMPERTINENTLY	INEXHAUSTIBLE	UNDERGRADUATE	CONCESSIONARY
JIGGERYPOKERY	IMPERTURBABLE	INEXPERIENCED	UNDERSTANDING	CONCUPISCENCE
KIDDERMINSTER	IMPERTURBABLY	INEXPRESSIBLE	UNDERSTRAPPER	CONDESCENDING
LIBRARIANSHIP	IMPONDERABLES	INFALLIBILITY	UNDISCIPLINED	CONDESCENSION
LIEBFRAUMILCH	IMPOSSIBILITY	INFINITESIMAL	UNEMBARRASSED	CONDITIONALLY
LIECHTENSTEIN	IMPRACTICABLE	INFLEXIBILITY	UNENLIGHTENED	CONFARREATION
LIGHTFINGERED	IMPRESSIONISM	INFLORESCENCE	UNESTABLISHED	CONFECTIONERS
LISSOTRICHOUS	IMPRESSIONIST	INGENUOUSNESS	UNEXCEPTIONAL	CONFECTIONERY
MICROCOMPUTER	IMPROBABILITY	INQUISITIVELY	UNEXPERIENCED	CONFEDERATION
MICROORGANISM	IMPROVIDENTLY	INQUISITORIAL	UNFASHIONABLE	CONFIGURATION
MIDDLEBREAKER	IMPROVISATION	INSECTIVOROUS	UNFLINCHINGLY	CONFLAGRATION
MISANTHROPIST	IMPULSIVENESS	INSENSITIVITY	UNFORESEEABLE	CONFRONTATION
MISCEGENATION	UMBELLIFEROUS	INSIDIOUSNESS	UNFORGETTABLE	CONGRESSIONAL
MISCELLANEOUS	ANACHRONISTIC	INSIGNIFICANT	UNFORTUNATELY	CONGRESSWOMAN
MISCHIEVOUSLY	ANIMADVERSION	INSPIRATIONAL	UNGENTLEMANLY	CONSANGUINITY
MISCONCEPTION	ANTHELMINTHIC	INSTANTANEOUS	UNGRAMMATICAL	CONSCIENTIOUS
MISMANAGEMENT	ANTICLOCKWISE	INSTINCTIVELY	UNIMAGINATIVE	CONSCIOUSNESS
MISSISSIPPIAN	ANTICOAGULANT	INSTITUTIONAL	UNIMPEACHABLE	CONSECTANEOUS
MISUNDERSTAND	ANTIGROPELOES	INSTRUCTIONAL	UNIMPRESSIBLE	CONSECUTIVELY
MISUNDERSTOOD	ANTIHISTAMINE	INSUBORDINATE	UNINHABITABLE	CONSEQUENTIAL
NIGHTCLUBBING	ANYTHINGARIAN	INSUBSTANTIAL	UNINTELLIGENT	CONSERVATOIRE
NIGHTWATCHMAN	ENCEPHALOCELE	INSUFFICIENCY	UNINTENTIONAL	CONSIDERATELY
RIGHTEOUSNESS	ENCEPHALOGRAM	INSUPPORTABLE	UNINTERESTING	CONSIDERATION
SIGNIFICANTLY	ENCOURAGEMENT	INTELLIGENTLY	UNINTERRUPTED	CONSOLIDATION
SIGNIFICATION	ENCULTURATION	INTENTIONALLY	UNMENTIONABLE	CONSPICUOUSLY
SIPUNCULOIDEA	ENCYCLOPAEDIA	INTERCALATION	UNNECESSARILY	CONSPURCATION
TINTINNABULUM	ENCYCLOPAEDIC	INTERESTINGLY	UNPARTITIONED	CONSTELLATION
VICEPRESIDENT	ENERGETICALLY	INTERMARRIAGE	UNPRECEDENTED	CONSTERNATION
VICTIMIZATION	ENLIGHTENMENT	INTERNATIONAL	UNPREDICTABLE	CONTAMINATION
VIDEOCASSETTE	ENTEROPNEUSTA	INTERPERSONAL	UNPRETENTIOUS	CONTEMPLATION
VIDEORECORDER	ENTERTAINMENT	INTERPOLATION	UNPROGRESSIVE	CONTEMPLATIVE
VITRIFICATION	ENTOMOLOGICAL	INTERROGATION	UNQUESTIONING	CONTENTEDNESS
VIVACIOUSNESS	ENVIRONMENTAL	INTERROGATIVE	UNSERVICEABLE	CONTINUATIONS
WITWATERSRAND	INADVERTENTLY	INTRAMUSCULAR	UNSUBSTANTIAL	CONTORTIONIST
XIPHIPLASTRON	INAPPROPRIATE	INTRANSIGENCE	UNSYMMETRICAL	CONTRABASSOON
SKATEBOARDING	INCANDESCENCE	INTRINSICALLY	UNSYMPATHETIC	CONTRACEPTION
ALLOCHTHONOUS	INCARCERATION	INTROSPECTION	UNTRUSTWORTHY	CONTRACEPTIVE
ALPHABETARIAN	INCOMBUSTIBLE	INTROSPECTIVE	UNWILLINGNESS	CONTRADICTION
ALTERNATIVELY	INCOMMUNICADO	INVENTIVENESS	BOUGAINVILLEA	CONTRADICTORY
ALUMINIFEROUS	INCOMPETENTLY	INVESTIGATION	BOUILLABAISSE	CONTRAFAGOTTO
ALUMINOTHERMY	INCONCEIVABLE	INVESTIGATIVE	BOUSTROPHEDON	CONTRAVENTION
BLANDISHMENTS	INCONSIDERATE	INVINCIBILITY	COEDUCATIONAL	CONTRIBUTIONS
BLOODCURDLING	INCONSISTENCY	INVIOLABILITY	COLLABORATION	CONTROVERSIAL
CLAIRAUDIENCE	INCONSPICUOUS	INVOLUNTARILY	COLLABORATIVE	CONVALESCENCE
CLARIFICATION	INCONTESTABLE	KNICKERBOCKER	COLLIESHANGIE	CONVERSAZIONE
CLISHMACLAVER	INCONVENIENCE	KNICKKNACKERY	COLLOQUIALISM	CORRESPONDENT
CLOSEDCIRCUIT	INCORPORATION	KNOWLEDGEABLE	COMMEMORATION	CORRESPONDING
ELECTROCUTION	INCORRUPTIBLE	PNEUMATICALLY	COMMEMORATIVE	CORROBORATION

CORROBORATORY	EPHEMEROPTERA	PRECAUTIONARY	PSYCHOANALYST	RUTHERFORDIUM
COSTEFFECTIVE	EPIPHENOMENON	PRECIPITATELY	PSYCHOBIOLOGY	SUBCONTRACTOR
COUNTERACTING	EPITRACHELION	PRECIPITATION	PSYCHOKINESIS	SUBJECTMATTER
COUNTERATTACK	OPHTHALMOLOGY	PRECONCEPTION	PSYCHOLOGICAL	SUBLIEUTENANT
COUNTERCHARGE	OPPORTUNISTIC	PREDOMINANTLY	PSYCHOMETRICS	SUBMANDIBULAR
COUNTERFEITER	OPPORTUNITIES	PREFABRICATED	PSYCHOSOMATIC	SUBORDINATION
COUNTRYPEOPLE	SPASMODICALLY	PRELIMINARIES	PSYCHOTHERAPY	SUBSERVIENTLY
DOCUMENTATION	SPECIFICATION	PREMEDITATION	ATTENTIVENESS	SUBSTANTIALLY
DOUBLEGLAZING	SPECTACULARLY	PREOCCUPATION	STABILIZATION	SUOVETAURILIA
FONTAINEBLEAU	SPECTROGRAPHY	PREPONDERANCE	STAPHYLINIDAE	SUPERABUNDANT
FOREKNOWLEDGE	SPELEOLOGICAL	PREPOSSESSING	STATESMANLIKE	SUPERANNUATED
FORGETFULNESS	SPERMATOPHYTE	PREPOSSESSION	STATESMANSHIP	SUPERFICIALLY
FORMALIZATION	SPINDLESHANKS	PREPROGRAMMED	STATIONMASTER	SUPERFLUOUSLY
FORTIFICATION	SPINECHILLING	PRESERVATIVES	STATISTICALLY	SUPERLATIVELY
FORTUNETELLER	SPITESPLENDID	PRESSURELOCAL	STEADFASTNESS	SUPERNUMERARY
FOSSILIZATION	SPONTANEOUSLY	PRETERNATURAL	STEEPLECHASER	SUPERORDINATE
FOSTERPARENTS	SPORTSMANLIKE	PREVARICATION	STEPPINGSTONE	SUPERSTITIOUS
GOODRIGHTEOUS	SPORTSMANSHIP	PRIMOGENITURE	STERCORACEOUS	SUPPLEMENTARY
HOMOSEXUALITY	SPRIGHTLINESS	PRIVATIZATION	STERILIZATION	SUPRANATIONAL
HORRIPILATION	UPTOTHEMINUTE	PROBLEMATICAL	STOCKBREEDING	SURREPTITIOUS
HORSEFEATHERS	AQUIFOLIACEAE	PROCLEUSMATIC	STRANGULATION	SUSPERCOLLATE
HORTICULTURAL	EQUIPONDERATE	PROCRASTINATE	STRATEGICALLY	VULCANIZATION
HOUSEBREAKING	SQUEAMISHNESS	PROFECTITIOUS	STRENUOUSNESS	VULGARIZATION
JOLLIFICATION	ARCHAEOLOGIST	PROFESSORSHIP	STREPTOCARPUS	VULNERABILITY
LONGSUFFERING	ARCHAEOPTERYX	PROFITABILITY	STREPTOCOCCUS	OVEREMPHASIZE
MOCKTECHNICAL	ARCHIMANDRITE	PROGNOSTICATE	STRIKEBREAKER	OVERSTATEMENT
MODERNIZATION	ARCHITECTURAL	PROGRESSIVELY	STYLISTICALLY	OWNEROCCUPIER
MOLLIFICATION	ARGUMENTATIVE	PROJECTIONIST	AUTHORISATION	SWASHBUCKLING
MONOCOTYLEDON	ARISTROCRATIC	PROLIFERATION	AUTHORITARIAN	SWEDENBORGIAN
MONONUCLEOSIS	ARITHMETICIAN	PROMISCUOUSLY	AUTHORITATIVE	SWEETSMELLING
MONOTHALAMOUS	ARMOURPLATING	PRONOUNCEMENT	AUTHORIZATION	SWOLLENHEADED
MORPHOLOGICAL	ARTIFICIALITY	PRONUNCIATION	AUTOBIOGRAPHY	EXCEPTIONABLE
MORTIFICATION	ARUNDINACEOUS	PROPHETICALLY	AUTOCEPHALOUS	EXCEPTIONALLY
MOUTHWATERING	BRACHIOSAURUS	PROPORTIONATE	AUTOCHTHONOUS	EXCOMMUNICATE
NONCONFORMIST	BREASTFEEDING	PROPRIETORIAL	AUTOMATICALLY	EXHIBITIONIST
NONCONFORMITY	BROKENHEARTED	PROSOPOGRAPHY	BUNGEEJUMPING	EXPANSIVENESS
NONRESISTANCE	CRAFTSMANSHIP	PROTECTIONISM	BUSINESSWOMAN	EXPEDITIONARY
NONSUFFICIENT	CREDULOUSNESS	PROTECTIONIST	BUTTERFINGERS	EXPEDITIOUSLY
NORMALIZATION	CRIMINOLOGIST	PROTESTANTISM	BUTYRALDEHYDE	EXPOSTULATION
NORTHEASTERLY	CROSSQUESTION	PROTONOTARIAT	FUERTEVENTURA	EXPROPRIATION
NORTHWESTERLY	CRUISERWEIGHT	PROVINCIALISM	FUNDAMENTALLY	EXTERMINATION
NOSTALGICALLY	CRYPTANALYSIS	PROVISIONALLY	GUILTLESSNESS	EXTRAORDINARY
POLIOMYELITIS	DRAMATIZATION	PROVOCATIVELY	HUNDREDWEIGHT	EXTRAPOLATION
POLLICITATION	DRYOPITHECINE	TRACTARIANISM	JURISPRUDENCE	EXTRAVAGANTLY
POLYCHROMATIC	FRACTIOUSNESS	TRADITIONALLY	JUSTIFICATION	GYNAECOLOGIST
POTENTIOMETER	FRAGMENTATION	TRANQUILLISER	JUSTIFICATORY	GYNANDROMORPH
ROLLERBLADING	FRANKALMOIGNE	TRANQUILLIZER	JUXTAPOSITION	GYNECOLOGICAL
ROLLERCOASTER	FREQUENTATIVE	TRANSATLANTIC	LUXURIOUSNESS	HYALURONIDASE
ROUNDTHEWORLD	FRIGHTENINGLY	TRANSCRIPTION	MULTICOLOURED	HYBRIDIZATION
SOCIOECONOMIC	FRIGHTFULNESS	TRANSGRESSION	MULTINATIONAL	HYDRAULICALLY
SOLEMNIZATION	FRIVOLOUSNESS	TRANSISTORIZE	MULTINUCLEATE	HYDROCEPHALUS
SOMATOSENSORY	GRAMMATICALLY	TRANSLITERATE	MULTITUDINOUS	HYDRODYNAMICS
SOMATOTROPHIN	GRANDDAUGHTER	TRANSMUTATION	NUCLEOPROTEIN	HYDROELECTRIC
SOPHISTICATED	GRANDILOQUENT	TRANSPARENTLY	NULLIFICATION	HYPERCRITICAL
SOUTHEASTERLY	GRANDPARENTAL	TRANSPIRATION	OUTRECUIDANCE	HYPERSTHENITE
SOUTHWESTERLY	GRATIFICATION	TRANSPORTABLE	OUTSTANDINGLY	HYPOCHONDRIAC
TONGUEINCHEEK	GRAVITATIONAL	TRANSPOSITION	PULVERIZATION	HYPOVENTILATE
TONGUETWISTER	GRIEFSTRICKEN	TRAUMATICALLY	PUNCTILIOUSLY	LYCANTHROPIST
TONSILLECTOMY	IRRECOVERABLE	TREACHEROUSLY	PUSILLANIMITY	MYSTIFICATION
TOPOGRAPHICAL	IRREPLACEABLE	TRIANGULATION	PUSILLANIMOUS	OYSTERCATCHER
TORTOISESHELL	IRREPRESSIBLE	TRICHOSANTHIN	QUADRAGESIMAL	PYROTECHNICAL
VORACIOUSNESS	IRRESPONSIBLE	TRIPLOBLASTIC	QUADRILATERAL	SYMPIESOMETER
APOCATASTASIS	IRRESPONSIBLY	ASCERTAINABLE	QUADRUPLICATE	SYNTACTICALLY
APPORTIONMENT	IRRETRIEVABLE	ASSASSINATION	QUALIFICATION	SYNTHETICALLY
APPROPINQUATE	IRRETRIEVABLY	ASTONISHINGLY	QUARTERMASTER	TYPOGRAPHICAL
APPROPRIATION	ORCHESTRATION	ESCHSCHOLTZIA	QUARTODECIMAN	
APPROXIMATELY	ORNAMENTATION	ESTABLISHMENT	QUERULOUSNESS	**13:3**
APPROXIMATION	ORNITHOLOGIST	ISOGEOTHERMAL	QUESTIONNAIRE	ANACHRONISTIC
EPANADIPLOSIS	PRAGMATICALLY	PSYCHOANALYSE	QUINQUAGESIMA	BEATIFICATION

BLANDISHMENTS	TRANSPIRATION	INCORRUPTIBLE	UNDERCLOTHING	THERMODYNAMIC
BRACHIOSAURUS	TRANSPORTABLE	INCREDULOUSLY	UNDERESTIMATE	THERMONUCLEAR
CHANGEABILITY	TRANSPOSITION	INCRIMINATING	UNDERGRADUATE	THERMOPLASTIC
CHARACTERISED	TRAUMATICALLY	INCRIMINATORY	UNDERSTANDING	THESSALONIANS
CHARACTERLESS	UNACCOMPANIED	LACKADAISICAL	UNDERSTRAPPER	TREACHEROUSLY
CHATEAUBRIAND	UNACCOUNTABLE	LECTISTERNIUM	UNDISCIPLINED	UNEMBARRASSED
CLAIRAUDIENCE	UNACCOUNTABLY	LYCANTHROPIST	VIDEOCASSETTE	UNENLIGHTENED
CLARIFICATION	UNADULTERATED	MACHIAVELLIAN	VIDEORECORDER	UNESTABLISHED
CRAFTSMANSHIP	UNANTICIPATED	MACHICOLATION	BREASTFEEDING	UNEXCEPTIONAL
DEATHLESSNESS	WEATHERBEATEN	MECHANIZATION	CHEESEMONGERS	UNEXPERIENCED
DIACATHOLICON	BIBLIOGRAPHER	MICROCOMPUTER	COEDUCATIONAL	AFFENPINSCHER
DIAMETRICALLY	BIBLIOPHAGIST	MICROORGANISM	CREDULOUSNESS	AFFIRMATIVELY
DRAMATIZATION	EMBARRASSMENT	MOCKTECHNICAL	ELECTROCUTION	AFFORESTATION
EPANADIPLOSIS	EMBELLISHMENT	NUCLEOPROTEIN	ELECTROMAGNET	AFFREIGHTMENT
FEATHERWEIGHT	HYBRIDIZATION	ORCHESTRATION	ELECTROMOTIVE	DEFENSIBILITY
FLABBERGASTED	LIBRARIANSHIP	RECALCITRANCE	ELEPHANTIASIS	DEFERVESCENCE
FRACTIOUSNESS	SUBCONTRACTOR	RECEPTIVENESS	ENERGETICALLY	DEFIBRILLATOR
FRAGMENTATION	SUBJECTMATTER	RECITATIONIST	FREQUENTATIVE	DEFORESTATION
FRANKALMOIGNE	SUBLIEUTENANT	RECRIMINATION	FUERTEVENTURA	DIFFARREATION
GRAMMATICALLY	SUBMANDIBULAR	RECRIMINATORY	HIEROGLYPHICS	DIFFERENTIATE
GRANDDAUGHTER	SUBORDINATION	RECRUDESCENCE	INEFFICIENTLY	EFFECTIVENESS
GRANDILOQUENT	SUBSERVIENTLY	RECTIFICATION	INEVITABILITY	EFFERVESCENCE
GRANDPARENTAL	SUBSTANTIALLY	SACCHAROMYCES	INEXHAUSTIBLE	EFFLORESCENCE
GRATIFICATION	TABLESPOONFUL	SECRETIVENESS	INEXPERIENCED	INFALLIBILITY
GRAVITATIONAL	UMBELLIFEROUS	SOCIOECONOMIC	INEXPRESSIBLE	INFINITESIMAL
HEARTBREAKING	ACCEPTABILITY	TECHNOLOGICAL	LAEVOROTATORY	INFLEXIBILITY
HYALURONIDASE	ACCEPTILATION	UNCEREMONIOUS	LIEBFRAUMILCH	INFLORESCENCE
IMAGINATIVELY	ACCESSIBILITY	UNCOMFORTABLE	LIECHTENSTEIN	OFFENSIVENESS
INADVERTENTLY	ACCOMMODATING	UNCOMFORTABLY	OVEREMPHASIZE	OFFICIOUSNESS
INAPPROPRIATE	ACCOMMODATION	UNCOMMUNICATE	OVERSTATEMENT	REFRIGERATION
LEATHERJACKET	ACCOMPANIMENT	UNCOMPLICATED	PAEDIATRICIAN	REFRIGERATORS
NEANDERTHALER	ACCOUTREMENTS	UNCONDITIONAL	PHENCYCLIDINE	REFURBISHMENT
PHARMACOPOEIA	ARCHAEOLOGIST	UNCONQUERABLE	PNEUMATICALLY	UNFASHIONABLE
PLATOCEPHALUS	ARCHAEOPTERYX	UNCONSCIOUSLY	PNEUMONECTOMY	UNFLINCHINGLY
PRAGMATICALLY	ARCHIMANDRITE	UNCOOPERATIVE	PRECAUTIONARY	UNFORESEEABLE
QUADRAGESIMAL	ARCHITECTURAL	UNCOORDINATED	PRECIPITATELY	UNFORGETTABLE
QUADRILATERAL	ASCERTAINABLE	VICEPRESIDENT	PRECIPITATION	UNFORTUNATELY
QUADRUPLICATE	BACCALAUREATE	VICTIMIZATION	PRECONCEPTION	AGGIORNAMENTO
QUALIFICATION	BACTERIOPHAGE	HYDRAULICALLY	PREDOMINANTLY	AGGLOMERATION
QUARTERMASTER	DECAFFEINATED	HYDROCEPHALUS	PREPONDERANCE	ARGUMENTATIVE
QUARTODECIMAN	DECOMPOSITION	HYDRODYNAMICS	PREPOSSESSING	DAGUERREOTYPE
REALISTICALLY	DECOMPRESSION	HYDROELECTRIC	PREPOSSESSION	INGENUOUSNESS
REARRANGEMENT	DECONTAMINATE	INDEFATIGABLE	PREPROGRAMMED	JIGGERYPOKERY
RHADAMANTHINE	DECRIMINALIZE	INDEFATIGABLY	PRESERVATIVES	LIGHTFINGERED
SCANDALMONGER	DOCUMENTATION	INDEPENDENTLY	PRESSURELOCAL	MAGISTERIALLY
SHAPELESSNESS	ECCENTRICALLY	INDESCRIBABLE	PRETERNATURAL	MAGNANIMOUSLY
SKATEBOARDING	ENCEPHALOCELE	INDESCRIBABLY	PREVARICATION	MAGNIFICATION
SPASMODICALLY	ENCEPHALOGRAM	INDETERMINATE	QUERULOUSNESS	MAGNIFICENTLY
STABILIZATION	ENCOURAGEMENT	INDETERMINISM	QUESTIONNAIRE	MAGNILOQUENCE
STAPHYLINIDAE	ENCULTURATION	INDIFFERENTLY	SLEEPLESSNESS	NIGHTCLUBBING
STATESMANLIKE	ENCYCLOPAEDIA	INDISPENSABLE	SPECIFICATION	NIGHTWATCHMAN
STATESMANSHIP	ENCYCLOPAEDIC	INDISPOSITION	SPECTACULARLY	REGIMENTATION
STATIONMASTER	ESCHSCHOLTZIA	INDIVIDUALISM	SPECTROGRAPHY	REGURGITATION
STATISTICALLY	EXCEPTIONABLE	INDIVIDUALIST	SPELEOLOGICAL	RIGHTEOUSNESS
SWASHBUCKLING	EXCEPTIONALLY	INDIVIDUALITY	SPERMATOPHYTE	SIGNIFICANTLY
THANKLESSNESS	EXCOMMUNICATE	INDUSTRIALIST	STEADFASTNESS	SIGNIFICATION
THAUMATURGICS	FACETIOUSNESS	INDUSTRIALIZE	STEEPLECHASER	UNGENTLEMANLY
THAUMATURGIST	INCANDESCENCE	INDUSTRIOUSLY	STEPPINGSTONE	UNGRAMMATICAL
TRACTARIANISM	INCARCERATION	KIDDERMINSTER	STERCORACEOUS	VEGETARIANISM
TRADITIONALLY	INCOMBUSTIBLE	MADETOMEASURE	STERILIZATION	DEHYDROGENATE
TRANQUILLISER	INCOMMUNICADO	MEDITERRANEAN	SWEDENBORGIAN	EPHEMEROPTERA
TRANQUILLIZER	INCOMPETENTLY	MIDDLEBREAKER	SWEETSMELLING	EXHIBITIONIST
TRANSATLANTIC	INCONCEIVABLE	MODERNIZATION	THEATRICALITY	OPHTHALMOLOGY
TRANSCRIPTION	INCONSIDERATE	RADIOACTIVITY	THEOLOGICALLY	SCHADENFREUDE
TRANSGRESSION	INCONSISTENCY	REDEMPTIONIST	THEORETICALLY	SCHEMATICALLY
TRANSISTORIZE	INCONSPICUOUS	REDEVELOPMENT		SCHIZOPHRENIA
TRANSLITERATE	INCONTESTABLE	SEDIMENTATION		SCHIZOPHRENIC
TRANSMUTATION	INCONVENIENCE	UNDERACHIEVER		SCHOLARLINESS
TRANSPARENTLY	INCORPORATION	UNDERCARRIAGE		SCHOOLTEACHER

SCHUTZSTAFFEL	MALADJUSTMENT	UNMENTIONABLE	MONOTHALAMOUS	PROTECTIONIST
ANIMADVERSION	MALLEMAROKING	BUNGEEJUMPING	NONCONFORMIST	PROTESTANTISM
ARISTROCRATIC	MOLLIFICATION	CONCATENATION	NONCONFORMITY	PROTONOTARIAT
ARITHMETICIAN	MULTICOLOURED	CONCENTRATION	NONRESISTANCE	PROVINCIALISM
CHINKERINCHEE	MULTINATIONAL	CONCEPTIONIST	NONSUFFICIENT	PROVISIONALLY
CLISHMACLAVER	MULTINUCLEATE	CONCEPTUALIST	ORNAMENTATION	PROVOCATIVELY
CRIMINOLOGIST	MULTITUDINOUS	CONCEPTUALIZE	ORNITHOLOGIST	SHOULDERBLADE
DEIPNOSOPHIST	NULLIFICATION	CONCESSIONARY	OWNEROCCUPIER	SNOWBLINDNESS
EPIPHENOMENON	PALAEONTOLOGY	CONCUPISCENCE	PANDICULATION	SPONTANEOUSLY
EPITRACHELION	PELOPONNESIAN	CONDESCENDING	PANHARMONICON	SPORTSMANLIKE
FRIGHTENINGLY	POLIOMYELITIS	CONDESCENSION	PENETRABILITY	SPORTSMANSHIP
FRIGHTFULNESS	POLLICITATION	CONDITIONALLY	PENNSYLVANIAN	STOCKBREEDING
FRIVOLOUSNESS	POLYCHROMATIC	CONFARREATION	PUNCTILIOUSLY	SUOVETAURILIA
GRIEFSTRICKEN	PULVERIZATION	CONFECTIONERS	RENSSELAERITE	SWOLLENHEADED
GUILTLESSNESS	ROLLERBLADING	CONFECTIONERY	SANCTIMONIOUS	THORACENTESIS
IDIORRHYTHMIC	ROLLERCOASTER	CONFEDERATION	SENSATIONALLY	THOROUGHBRACE
IDIOSYNCRATIC	SALACIOUSNESS	CONFIGURATION	SENSELESSNESS	THOROUGHGOING
KNICKERBOCKER	SCLEROPROTEIN	CONFLAGRATION	SENSITIVENESS	THOUGHTLESSLY
KNICKKNACKERY	SELFADDRESSED	CONFRONTATION	SENTENTIOUSLY	WHOLESOMENESS
LEISURELINESS	SELFCONFESSED	CONGRESSIONAL	SENTIMENTALLY	ALPHABETARIAN
MEISTERSINGER	SELFCONFIDENT	CONGRESSWOMAN	SYNTACTICALLY	AMPHIGASTRIUM
NEIGHBOURHOOD	SELFCONSCIOUS	CONSANGUINITY	SYNTHETICALLY	AMPLIFICATION
PAINSTAKINGLY	SELFCONTAINED	CONSCIENTIOUS	TANTALIZINGLY	APPORTIONMENT
PHILADELPHIAN	SELFGOVERNING	CONSCIOUSNESS	TENDERHEARTED	APPROPINQUATE
PHILANTHROPIC	SOLEMNIZATION	CONSECTANEOUS	TENOSYNOVITIS	APPROPRIATION
PHILOSOPHICAL	TALKATIVENESS	CONSECUTIVELY	TINTINNABULUM	APPROXIMATELY
PRIMOGENITURE	TELEMARKETING	CONSEQUENTIAL	TONGUEINCHEEK	APPROXIMATION
PRIVATIZATION	VULCANIZATION	CONSERVATOIRE	TONGUETWISTER	CEPHALOSPORIN
QUINQUAGESIMA	VULGARIZATION	CONSIDERATELY	TONSILLECTOMY	DEPENDABILITY
REIMBURSEMENT	VULNERABILITY	CONSIDERATION	UNNECESSARILY	EXPANSIVENESS
REINCARNATION	ADMINISTRATOR	CONSOLIDATION	VENTRILOQUISM	EXPEDITIONARY
REINFORCEMENT	ARMOURPLATING	CONSPICUOUSLY	VENTRILOQUIST	EXPEDITIOUSLY
REINSTATEMENT	COMMEMORATION	CONSPURCATION	APOCATASTASIS	EXPOSTULATION
SCINTILLATING	COMMEMORATIVE	CONSTELLATION	BIODEGRADABLE	EXPROPRIATION
SCINTILLATION	COMMENSURABLE	CONSTERNATION	BIOTECHNOLOGY	HYPERCRITICAL
SEISMOLOGICAL	COMMERCIALIZE	CONTAMINATION	BLOODCURDLING	HYPERSTHENITE
SPINDLESHANKS	COMMISERATION	CONTEMPLATION	BROKENHEARTED	HYPOCHONDRIAC
SPINECHILLING	COMMUNICATION	CONTEMPLATIVE	CHOREOGRAPHER	HYPOVENTILATE
SPITESPLENDID	COMMUNICATIVE	CONTENTEDNESS	CLOSEDCIRCUIT	IMPERCEPTIBLE
THIGMOTROPISM	COMPANIONABLE	CONTINUATIONS	CROSSQUESTION	IMPERCEPTIBLY
TRIANGULATION	COMPANIONSHIP	CONTORTIONIST	GEOMETRICALLY	IMPERIALISTIC
TRICHOSANTHIN	COMPARABILITY	CONTRABASSOON	GEOSTATIONARY	IMPERSONATING
TRIPLOBLASTIC	COMPARATIVELY	CONTRACEPTION	GLOBETROTTING	IMPERSONATION
UNIMAGINATIVE	COMPASSIONATE	CONTRACEPTIVE	GLORIFICATION	IMPERTINENTLY
UNIMPEACHABLE	COMPATIBILITY	CONTRADICTION	GLOSSOGRAPHER	IMPERTURBABLE
UNIMPRESSIBLE	COMPLEMENTARY	CONTRADICTORY	GOODRIGHTEOUS	IMPERTURBABLY
UNINHABITABLE	COMPLIMENTARY	CONTRAFAGOTTO	ISOGEOTHERMAL	IMPONDERABLES
UNINTELLIGENT	COMPREHENSION	CONTRAVENTION	KNOWLEDGEABLE	IMPOSSIBILITY
UNINTENTIONAL	COMPREHENSIVE	CONTRIBUTIONS	PHOSPHOLIPASE	IMPRACTICABLE
UNINTERESTING	COMRADEINARMS	CONTROVERSIAL	PHOTOCHEMICAL	IMPRESSIONISM
UNINTERRUPTED	DEMILITARIZED	CONVALESCENCE	PHOTOELECTRIC	IMPRESSIONIST
WEIGHTLIFTING	DEMONSTRATION	CONVERSAZIONE	PROBLEMATICAL	IMPROBABILITY
OBJECTIONABLE	DEMONSTRATIVE	DENATIONALIZE	PROCLEUSMATIC	IMPROVIDENTLY
OBJECTIVENESS	HAMMERKLAVIER	FANTASTICALLY	PROCRASTINATE	IMPROVISATION
ALLOCHTHONOUS	HAMMERTHROWER	FONTAINEBLEAU	PROFECTITIOUS	IMPULSIVENESS
BILDUNGSROMAN	HEMISPHERICAL	FUNDAMENTALLY	PROFESSORSHIP	KAPPELMEISTER
CALLISTHENICS	HOMOSEXUALITY	GENERALISSIMO	PROFITABILITY	LEPIDOPTERIST
COLLABORATION	LAMPADEPHORIA	GENITOURINARY	PROGNOSTICATE	LEPTOCEPHALUS
COLLABORATIVE	NEMATHELMINTH	GYNAECOLOGIST	PROGRESSIVELY	LEPTOSPIROSIS
COLLIESHANGIE	RAMIFICATIONS	GYNANDROMORPH	PROJECTIONIST	OPPORTUNISTIC
COLLOQUIALISM	REMINISCENCES	GYNECOLOGICAL	PROLIFERATION	OPPORTUNITIES
ENLIGHTENMENT	REMORSELESSLY	HUNDREDWEIGHT	PROMISCUOUSLY	PAPAPRELATIST
FALSIFICATION	SEMBLANCECORD	IGNOMINIOUSLY	PRONOUNCEMENT	PEPTIDOGLYCAN
GALVANIZATION	SEMIAUTOMATIC	KANGCHENJUNGA	PRONUNCIATION	RAPPROCHEMENT
HALLUCINATION	SEMICONDUCTOR	LONGSUFFERING	PROPHETICALLY	REPERCUSSIONS
HALLUCINATORY	SOMATOSENSORY	MANIFESTATION	PROPORTIONATE	REPLENISHMENT
ILLUMINATIONS	SOMATOTROPHIN	MANUFACTURING	PROPRIETORIAL	REPREHENSIBLE
JOLLIFICATION	SYMPIESOMETER	MONOCOTYLEDON	PROSOPOGRAPHY	REPREHENSIBLY
KALEIDOSCOPIC	TEMPERAMENTAL	MONONUCLEOSIS	PROTECTIONISM	REPROACHFULLY

REPROGRAPHICS	IRRETRIEVABLY	DISGRACEFULLY	ATTENTIVENESS	ARUNDINACEOUS
REPUBLICANISM	JURISPRUDENCE	DISHEARTENING	AUTHORISATION	BOUGAINVILLEA
SEPTENTRIONES	MERCHANDIZING	DISHONOURABLE	AUTHORITARIAN	BOUILLABAISSE
SIPUNCULOIDEA	MERCILESSNESS	DISHONOURABLY	AUTHORITATIVE	BOUSTROPHEDON
SOPHISTICATED	MORPHOLOGICAL	DISILLUSIONED	AUTHORIZATION	CAUTERIZATION
SUPERABUNDANT	MORTIFICATION	DISINTERESTED	AUTOBIOGRAPHY	COUNTERACTING
SUPERANNUATED	NERVELESSNESS	DISPARAGEMENT	AUTOCEPHALOUS	COUNTERATTACK
SUPERFICIALLY	NORMALIZATION	DISPASSIONATE	AUTOCHTHONOUS	COUNTERCHARGE
SUPERFLUOUSLY	NORTHEASTERLY	DISPROPORTION	AUTOMATICALLY	COUNTERFEITER
SUPERLATIVELY	NORTHWESTERLY	DISRESPECTFUL	BUTTERFINGERS	COUNTRYPEOPLE
SUPERNUMERARY	PARADOXICALLY	DISSEMINATION	BUTYRALDEHYDE	CRUISERWEIGHT
SUPERORDINATE	PARALLELOGRAM	DISSIMILARITY	CATEGORICALLY	DOUBLEGLAZING
SUPERSTITIOUS	PARANTHROPOUS	DISSIMULATION	DETERIORATION	EQUIPONDERATE
SUPPLEMENTARY	PARAPHERNALIA	DISTINGUISHED	DETERMINATION	GLUMDALCLITCH
SUPRANATIONAL	PARENTHETICAL	FOSSILIZATION	ENTEROPNEUSTA	HOUSEBREAKING
TAPERECORDING	PARLIAMENTARY	FOSTERPARENTS	ENTERTAINMENT	MAURIKIGUSARI
TOPOGRAPHICAL	PARTHOGENESIS	GASTROCNEMIUS	ENTOMOLOGICAL	MOUTHWATERING
TYPOGRAPHICAL	PARTICIPATION	GESTICULATION	ESTABLISHMENT	NEUROCOMPUTER
UNPARTITIONED	PARTICIPATORY	INSECTIVOROUS	EXTERMINATION	REUNIFICATION
UNPRECEDENTED	PARTICOLOURED	INSENSITIVITY	EXTRAORDINARY	ROUNDTHEWORLD
UNPREDICTABLE	PARTICULARISE	INSIDIOUSNESS	EXTRAPOLATION	SOUTHEASTERLY
UNPRETENTIOUS	PARTICULARITY	INSIGNIFICANT	EXTRAVAGANTLY	SOUTHWESTERLY
UNPROGRESSIVE	PARTICULARIZE	INSPIRATIONAL	HETERAUXESISM	SQUEAMISHNESS
XIPHIPLASTRON	PERAMBULATION	INSTANTANEOUS	HETEROGENEOUS	THUNDERSTRUCK
INQUISITIVELY	PEREGRINATION	INSTINCTIVELY	INTELLIGENTLY	ADVENTUROUSLY
INQUISITORIAL	PERFECTIONIST	INSTITUTIONAL	INTENTIONALLY	ADVERTISEMENT
SEQUESTRATION	PERFUNCTORILY	INSTRUCTIONAL	INTERCALATION	DEVELOPMENTAL
UNQUESTIONING	PERPENDICULAR	INSUBORDINATE	INTERESTINGLY	ENVIRONMENTAL
ACRYLONITRILE	PERSONALITIES	INSUBSTANTIAL	INTERMARRIAGE	INVENTIVENESS
AIRCRAFTWOMAN	PERSPICACIOUS	INSUFFICIENCY	INTERNATIONAL	INVESTIGATION
AIRWORTHINESS	PERVASIVENESS	INSUPPORTABLE	INTERPERSONAL	INVESTIGATIVE
BIREFRINGENCE	PYROTECHNICAL	JUSTIFICATION	INTERPOLATION	INVINCIBILITY
CARBONIFEROUS	SARCASTICALLY	JUSTIFICATORY	INTERROGATION	INVIOLABILITY
CARBONIZATION	SERVILEMENTAL	LISSOTRICHOUS	INTERROGATIVE	INVOLUNTARILY
CARTILAGINOUS	SHRINKWRAPPED	MASSACHUSETTS	INTRAMUSCULAR	REVERBERATION
CEREMONIOUSLY	SPRIGHTLINESS	MASTIGOPHORAN	INTRANSIGENCE	REVOLUTIONARY
CERTIFICATION	STRANGULATION	MESSERSCHMITT	INTRINSICALLY	REVOLUTIONIZE
CHRISTMASTIME	STRATEGICALLY	MISANTHROPIST	INTROSPECTION	VIVACIOUSNESS
CHRONOLOGICAL	STRENUOUSNESS	MISCEGENATION	INTROSPECTIVE	UNWILLINGNESS
CHRYSANTHEMUM	STREPTOCARPUS	MISCELLANEOUS	MATERIALISTIC	JUXTAPOSITION
CIRCUMAMBIENT	STREPTOCOCCUS	MISCHIEVOUSLY	MATHEMATICIAN	LEXICOGRAPHER
CIRCUMFERENCE	STRIKEBREAKER	MISCONCEPTION	MATRICULATION	LUXURIOUSNESS
CIRCUMSTANCES	SURREPTITIOUS	MISMANAGEMENT	METAGRABOLISE	ANYTHINGARIAN
CIRCUMVENTION	THREATENINGLY	MISSISSIPPIAN	METAGROBOLISE	CRYPTANALYSIS
CORRESPONDENT	TORTOISESHELL	MISUNDERSTAND	METAMORPHOSIS	DRYOPITHECINE
CORRESPONDING	VERCINGETORIX	MISUNDERSTOOD	METAPHYSICIAN	PHYLLOQUINONE
CORROBORATION	VERSIFICATION	MYSTIFICATION	METEOROLOGIST	PHYSHARMONICA
CORROBORATORY	VORACIOUSNESS	NOSTALGICALLY	NATIONALISTIC	PHYSIOGNOMIST
DERMATOLOGIST	AESTHETICALLY	OYSTERCATCHER	OUTRECUIDANCE	PHYSIOLOGICAL
FERROCONCRETE	ASSASSINATION	PASSCHENDAELE	OUTSTANDINGLY	PHYSIOTHERAPY
FERTILISATION	BASIDIOMYCETE	PASSEMENTERIE	PATERFAMILIAS	PHYSOSTIGMINE
FERTILIZATION	BUSINESSWOMAN	PASSIONFLOWER	PATERNALISTIC	PHYTOPLANKTON
FOREKNOWLEDGE	COSTEFFECTIVE	PUSILLANIMITY	PATRIOTICALLY	PSYCHOANALYSE
FORGETFULNESS	DESEGREGATION	PUSILLANIMOUS	PETRIFICATION	PSYCHOANALYST
FORMALIZATION	DÉSOBLIGEANTE	RESOURCEFULLY	PETROCHEMICAL	PSYCHOBIOLOGY
FORTIFICATION	DISADVANTAGED	RESUSCITATION	POTENTIOMETER	PSYCHOKINESIS
FORTUNETELLER	DISAPPEARANCE	SUSPERCOLLATE	RATIONALALITY	PSYCHOLOGICAL
GARRULOUSNESS	DISAPPOINTING	UNSERVICEABLE	RETROGRESSION	PSYCHOMETRICS
HARMONIZATION	DISCOLORATION	UNSUBSTANTIAL	RETROSPECTIVE	PSYCHOSOMATIC
HERMAPHRODITE	DISCONCERTING	UNSYMMETRICAL	RUTHERFORDIUM	PSYCHOTHERAPY
HORRIPILATION	DISCONNECTION	UNSYMPATHETIC	TETRASYLLABIC	RHYPAROGRAPHY
HORSEFEATHERS	DISCONTINUITY	ALTERNATIVELY	UNTRUSTWORTHY	STYLISTICALLY
HORTICULTURAL	DISCONTINUOUS	ANTHELMINTHIC	UPTOTHEMINUTE	THYROIDECTOMY
IRRECOVERABLE	DISCREDITABLE	ANTICLOCKWISE	VITRIFICATION	**13:4**
IRREPLACEABLE	DISCREDITABLY	ANTICOAGULANT	WITWATERSRAND	
IRREPRESSIBLE	DISCRETIONARY	ANTIGROPELOES	ACUPUNCTURIST	ASSASSINATION
IRRESPONSIBLE	DISENGAGEMENT	ANTIHISTAMINE	ALUMINIFEROUS	BREASTFEEDING
IRRESPONSIBLY	DISESTIMATION	ARTIFICIALITY	ALUMINOTHERMY	DECAFFEINATED
IRRETRIEVABLE	DISFIGUREMENT	ASTONISHINGLY	AQUIFOLIACEAE	DENATIONALIZE

DISADVANTAGED	DISCONCERTING	QUADRILATERAL	INSENSITIVITY	UNDERSTANDING
DISAPPEARANCE	DISCONNECTION	QUADRUPLICATE	INTELLIGENTLY	UNDERSTRAPPER
DISAPPOINTING	DISCONTINUITY	RHADAMANTHINE	INTENTIONALLY	UNGENTLEMANLY
EMBARRASSMENT	DISCONTINUOUS	SWEDENBORGIAN	INTERCALATION	UNMENTIONABLE
ESTABLISHMENT	DISCREDITABLE	TENDERHEARTED	INTERESTINGLY	UNNECESSARILY
EXPANSIVENESS	DISCREDITABLY	TRADITIONALLY	INTERMARRIAGE	UNSERVICEABLE
GYNAECOLOGIST	DISCRETIONARY	UNADULTERATED	INTERNATIONAL	VEGETARIANISM
GYNANDROMORPH	ELECTROCUTION	ACCEPTABILITY	INTERPERSONAL	VICEPRESIDENT
INCANDESCENCE	ELECTROMAGNET	ACCEPTILATION	INTERPOLATION	VIDEOCASSETTE
INCARCERATION	ELECTROMOTIVE	ACCESSIBILITY	INTERROGATION	VIDEORECORDER
INFALLIBILITY	FRACTIOUSNESS	ADVENTUROUSLY	INTERROGATIVE	CONFARREATION
LYCANTHROPIST	KNICKERBOCKER	ADVERTISEMENT	INVENTIVENESS	CONFECTIONERS
MALADJUSTMENT	KNICKKNACKERY	AFFENPINSCHER	INVESTIGATION	CONFECTIONERY
METAGRABOLISE	LIECHTENSTEIN	ALTERNATIVELY	INVESTIGATIVE	CONFEDERATION
METAGROBOLISE	MERCHANDIZING	ASCERTAINABLE	IRRECOVERABLE	CONFIGURATION
METAMORPHOSIS	MERCILESSNESS	ATTENTIVENESS	IRREPLACEABLE	CONFLAGRATION
METAPHYSICIAN	MISCEGENATION	BIREFRINGENCE	IRREPRESSIBLE	CONFRONTATION
MISANTHROPIST	MISCELLANEOUS	CATEGORICALLY	IRRESPONSIBLE	CRAFTSMANSHIP
NEMATHELMINTH	MISCHIEVOUSLY	CEREMONIOUSLY	IRRESPONSIBLY	DIFFARREATION
ORNAMENTATION	MISCONCEPTION	CHEESEMONGERS	IRRETRIEVABLE	DIFFERENTIATE
PALAEONTOLOGY	NONCONFORMIST	DEFENSIBILITY	IRRETRIEVABLY	DISFIGUREMENT
PAPAPRELATIST	NONCONFORMITY	DEFERVESCENCE	KALEIDOSCOPIC	INEFFICIENTLY
PARADOXICALLY	PRECAUTIONARY	DEPENDABILITY	MADETOMEASURE	PERFECTIONIST
PARALLELOGRAM	PRECIPITATELY	DESEGREGATION	MATERIALISTIC	PERFUNCTORILY
PARANTHROPOUS	PRECIPITATION	DETERIORATION	METEOROLOGIST	PREFABRICATED
PARAPHERNALIA	PRECONCEPTION	DETERMINATION	MODERNIZATION	PROFECTITIOUS
PERAMBULATION	PROCLEUSMATIC	DEVELOPMENTAL	OBJECTIONABLE	PROFESSORSHIP
RECALCITRANCE	PROCRASTINATE	DISENGAGEMENT	OBJECTIVENESS	PROFITABILITY
SALACIOUSNESS	PSYCHOANALYSE	DISESTIMATION	OFFENSIVENESS	SELFADDRESSED
SCHADENFREUDE	PSYCHOANALYST	ECCENTRICALLY	OWNEROCCUPIER	SELFCONFESSED
SOMATOSENSORY	PSYCHOBIOLOGY	EFFECTIVENESS	PARENTHETICAL	SELFCONFIDENT
SOMATOTROPHIN	PSYCHOKINESIS	EFFERVESCENCE	PATERFAMILIAS	SELFCONSCIOUS
STEADFASTNESS	PSYCHOLOGICAL	EMBELLISHMENT	PATERNALISTIC	SELFCONTAINED
STRANGULATION	PSYCHOMETRICS	ENCEPHALOCELE	PENETRABILITY	SELFGOVERNING
STRATEGICALLY	PSYCHOSOMATIC	ENCEPHALOGRAM	PEREGRINATION	BOUGAINVILLEA
THEATRICALITY	PSYCHOTHERAPY	ENTEROPNEUSTA	POTENTIOMETER	BUNGEEJUMPING
TREACHEROUSLY	PUNCTILIOUSLY	ENTERTAINMENT	RECEPTIVENESS	CONGRESSIONAL
TRIANGULATION	SACCHAROMYCES	EPHEMEROPTERA	REDEMPTIONIST	CONGRESSWOMAN
UNFASHIONABLE	SANCTIMONIOUS	EXCEPTIONABLE	REDEVELOPMENT	DISGRACEFULLY
UNPARTITIONED	SARCASTICALLY	EXCEPTIONALLY	REPERCUSSIONS	FORGETFULNESS
VIVACIOUSNESS	SPECIFICATION	EXPEDITIONARY	REVERBERATION	FRAGMENTATION
VORACIOUSNESS	SPECTACULARLY	EXPEDITIOUSLY	SCHEMATICALLY	FRIGHTENINGLY
CARBONIFEROUS	SPECTROGRAPHY	EXTERMINATION	SCLEROPROTEIN	FRIGHTFULNESS
CARBONIZATION	STOCKBREEDING	FACETIOUSNESS	SLEEPLESSNESS	IMAGINATIVELY
DOUBLEGLAZING	SUBCONTRACTOR	FOREKNOWLEDGE	SOLEMNIZATION	ISOGEOTHERMAL
FLABBERGASTED	TRACTARIANISM	GENERALISSIMO	SQUEAMISHNESS	JIGGERYPOKERY
GLOBETROTTING	TRICHOSANTHIN	GRIEFSTRICKEN	STEEPLECHASER	KANGCHENJUNGA
LIEBFRAUMILCH	UNACCOMPANIED	GYNECOLOGICAL	STRENUOUSNESS	LONGSUFFERING
PROBLEMATICAL	UNACCOUNTABLE	HETERAUXESISM	STREPTOCARPUS	NEIGHBOURHOOD
SEMBLANCECORD	UNACCOUNTABLY	HETEROGENEOUS	STREPTOCOCCUS	PRAGMATICALLY
STABILIZATION	VERCINGETORIX	HYPERCRITICAL	SUPERABUNDANT	PROGNOSTICATE
AIRCRAFTWOMAN	VULCANIZATION	HYPERSTHENITE	SUPERANNUATED	PROGRESSIVELY
ANACHRONISTIC	BILDUNGSROMAN	IMPERCEPTIBLE	SUPERFICIALLY	THIGMOTROPISM
APOCATASTASIS	BIODEGRADABLE	IMPERCEPTIBLY	SUPERFLUOUSLY	TONGUEINCHEEK
BACCALAUREATE	COEDUCATIONAL	IMPERIALISTIC	SUPERLATIVELY	TONGUETWISTER
BRACHIOSAURUS	CONDESCENDING	IMPERSONATING	SUPERNUMERARY	VULGARIZATION
CIRCUMAMBIENT	CONDESCENSION	IMPERSONATION	SUPERORDINATE	WEIGHTLIFTING
CIRCUMFERENCE	CONDITIONALLY	IMPERTINENTLY	SUPERSTITIOUS	ALPHABETARIAN
CIRCUMSTANCES	CREDULOUSNESS	IMPERTURBABLE	SWEETSMELLING	AMPHIGASTRIUM
CIRCUMVENTION	FUNDAMENTALLY	IMPERTURBABLY	TAPERECORDING	ANTHELMINTHIC
CONCATENATION	GOODRIGHTEOUS	INDEFATIGABLE	TELEMARKETING	ARCHAEOLOGIST
CONCENTRATION	HUNDREDWEIGHT	INDEFATIGABLY	THREATENINGLY	ARCHAEOPTERYX
CONCEPTIONIST	INADVERTENTLY	INDEPENDENTLY	UMBELLIFEROUS	ARCHIMANDRITE
CONCEPTUALIST	KIDDERMINSTER	INDESCRIBABLE	UNCEREMONIOUS	ARCHITECTURAL
CONCEPTUALIZE	MIDDLEBREAKER	INDESCRIBABLY	UNDERACHIEVER	AUTHORISATION
CONCESSIONARY	PAEDIATRICIAN	INDETERMINATE	UNDERCARRIAGE	AUTHORITARIAN
CONCUPISCENCE	PANDICULATION	INDETERMINISM	UNDERCLOTHING	AUTHORITATIVE
DIACATHOLICON	PREDOMINANTLY	INGENUOUSNESS	UNDERESTIMATE	AUTHORIZATION
DISCOLORATION	QUADRAGESIMAL	INSECTIVOROUS	UNDERGRADUATE	CEPHALOSPORIN

DISHEARTENING	RECITATIONIST	COMMUNICATION	TRANSGRESSION	PREOCCUPATION
DISHONOURABLE	REGIMENTATION	COMMUNICATIVE	TRANSISTORIZE	PYROTECHNICAL
DISHONOURABLY	REMINISCENCES	CRIMINOLOGIST	TRANSLITERATE	REMORSELESSLY
ESCHSCHOLTZIA	SCHIZOPHRENIA	DERMATOLOGIST	TRANSMUTATION	RESOURCEFULLY
LIGHTFINGERED	SCHIZOPHRENIC	DIAMETRICALLY	TRANSPARENTLY	REVOLUTIONARY
MACHIAVELLIAN	SEDIMENTATION	DRAMATIZATION	TRANSPIRATION	REVOLUTIONIZE
MACHICOLATION	SEMIAUTOMATIC	FORMALIZATION	TRANSPORTABLE	SCHOLARLINESS
MATHEMATICIAN	SEMICONDUCTOR	GEOMETRICALLY	TRANSPOSITION	SCHOOLTEACHER
MECHANIZATION	SHRINKWRAPPED	GLUMDALCLITCH	UNANTICIPATED	SUBORDINATION
NIGHTCLUBBING	SOCIOECONOMIC	GRAMMATICALLY	UNENLIGHTENED	TENOSYNOVITIS
NIGHTWATCHMAN	SPRIGHTLINESS	HAMMERKLAVIER	UNINHABITABLE	THEOLOGICALLY
ORCHESTRATION	STRIKEBREAKER	HAMMERTHROWER	UNINTELLIGENT	THEORETICALLY
PANHARMONICON	UNDISCIPLINED	HERMAPHRODITE	UNINTENTIONAL	TOPOGRAPHICAL
RIGHTEOUSNESS	UNWILLINGNESS	MISMANAGEMENT	UNINTERESTING	TYPOGRAPHICAL
RUTHERFORDIUM	PROJECTIONIST	NORMALIZATION	UNINTERRUPTED	UNCOMFORTABLE
SOPHISTICATED	SUBJECTMATTER	PREMEDITATION	VULNERABILITY	UNCOMFORTABLY
TECHNOLOGICAL	BROKENHEARTED	PRIMOGENITURE	ACCOMMODATING	UNCOMMUNICATE
XIPHIPLASTRON	LACKADAISICAL	PROMISCUOUSLY	ACCOMMODATION	UNCOMPLICATED
ADMINISTRATOR	MOCKTECHNICAL	REIMBURSEMENT	ACCOMPANIMENT	UNCONDITIONAL
AFFIRMATIVELY	TALKATIVENESS	SUBMANDIBULAR	ACCOUTREMENTS	UNCONQUERABLE
AGGIORNAMENTO	AGGLOMERATION	UNEMBARRASSED	AFFORESTATION	UNCONSCIOUSLY
ANTICLOCKWISE	AMPLIFICATION	UNIMAGINATIVE	ALLOCHTHONOUS	UNCOOPERATIVE
ANTICOAGULANT	BIBLIOGRAPHER	UNIMPEACHABLE	APPORTIONMENT	UNCOORDINATED
ANTIGROPELOES	BIBLIOPHAGIST	UNIMPRESSIBLE	ARMOURPLATING	UNFORESEEABLE
ANTIHISTAMINE	CALLISTHENICS	ARUNDINACEOUS	ASTONISHINGLY	UNFORGETTABLE
AQUIFOLIACEAE	COLLABORATION	BLANDISHMENTS	AUTOBIOGRAPHY	UNFORTUNATELY
ARTIFICIALITY	COLLABORATIVE	CHANGEABILITY	AUTOCEPHALOUS	UPTOTHEMINUTE
BASIDIOMYCETE	COLLIESHANGIE	CHINKERINCHEE	AUTOCHTHONOUS	ACUPUNCTURIST
BOUILLABAISSE	COLLOQUIALISM	COUNTERACTING	AUTOMATICALLY	COMPANIONABLE
BUSINESSWOMAN	EFFLORESCENCE	COUNTERATTACK	BLOODCURDLING	COMPANIONSHIP
CHRISTMASTIME	GUILTLESSNESS	COUNTERCHARGE	CHRONOLOGICAL	COMPARABILITY
CLAIRAUDIENCE	HALLUCINATION	COUNTERFEITER	DECOMPOSITION	COMPARATIVELY
CRUISERWEIGHT	HALLUCINATORY	COUNTRYPEOPLE	DECOMPRESSION	COMPASSIONATE
DEFIBRILLATOR	HYALURONIDASE	EPANADIPLOSIS	DECONTAMINATE	COMPATIBILITY
DEMILITARIZED	INFLEXIBILITY	FRANKALMOIGNE	DEFORESTATION	COMPLEMENTARY
DISILLUSIONED	INFLORESCENCE	GRANDDAUGHTER	DEMONSTRATION	COMPLIMENTARY
DISINTERESTED	JOLLIFICATION	GRANDILOQUENT	DEMONSTRATIVE	COMPREHENSION
ENLIGHTENMENT	MALLEMAROKING	GRANDPARENTAL	DÉSOBLIGEANTE	COMPREHENSIVE
ENVIRONMENTAL	MOLLIFICATION	MAGNANIMOUSLY	DRYOPITHECINE	CRYPTANALYSIS
EQUIPONDERATE	NUCLEOPROTEIN	MAGNIFICATION	ENCOURAGEMENT	DEIPNOSOPHIST
EXHIBITIONIST	NULLIFICATION	MAGNIFICENTLY	ENTOMOLOGICAL	DISPARAGEMENT
GENITOURINARY	PARLIAMENTARY	MAGNILOQUENCE	EXCOMMUNICATE	DISPASSIONATE
HEMISPHERICAL	PHILADELPHIAN	NEANDERTHALER	EXPOSTULATION	DISPROPORTION
INDIFFERENTLY	PHILANTHROPIC	PAINSTAKINGLY	HOMOSEXUALITY	ELEPHANTIASIS
INDISPENSABLE	PHILOSOPHICAL	PENNSYLVANIAN	HYPOCHONDRIAC	EPIPHENOMENON
INDISPOSITION	PHYLLOQUINONE	PHENCYCLIDINE	HYPOVENTILATE	INAPPROPRIATE
INDIVIDUALISM	POLLICITATION	PRONOUNCEMENT	IDIORRHYTHMIC	INSPIRATIONAL
INDIVIDUALIST	PRELIMINARIES	PRONUNCIATION	IDIOSYNCRATIC	KAPPELMEISTER
INDIVIDUALITY	PROLIFERATION	QUINQUAGESIMA	IGNOMINIOUSLY	LAMPADEPHORIA
INFINITESIMAL	QUALIFICATION	REINCARNATION	IMPONDERABLES	MORPHOLOGICAL
INSIDIOUSNESS	REALISTICALLY	REINFORCEMENT	IMPOSSIBILITY	PERPENDICULAR
INSIGNIFICANT	REPLENISHMENT	REINSTATEMENT	INCOMBUSTIBLE	PREPONDERANCE
INVINCIBILITY	ROLLERBLADING	REUNIFICATION	INCOMMUNICADO	PREPOSSESSING
INVIOLABILITY	ROLLERCOASTER	ROUNDTHEWORLD	INCOMPETENTLY	PREPOSSESSION
JURISPRUDENCE	SPELEOLOGICAL	SCANDALMONGER	INCONCEIVABLE	PREPROGRAMMED
LEPIDOPTERIST	STYLISTICALLY	SCINTILLATING	INCONSIDERATE	PROPHETICALLY
LEXICOGRAPHER	SUBLIEUTENANT	SCINTILLATION	INCONSISTENCY	PROPORTIONATE
MAGISTERIALLY	SWOLLENHEADED	SIGNIFICANTLY	INCONSPICUOUS	PROPRIETORIAL
MANIFESTATION	TABLESPOONFUL	SIGNIFICATION	INCONTESTABLE	RAPPROCHEMENT
MEDITERRANEAN	UNFLINCHINGLY	SPINDLESHANKS	INCONVENIENCE	RHYPAROGRAPHY
NATIONALISTIC	WHOLESOMENESS	SPINECHILLING	INCORPORATION	SHAPELESSNESS
OFFICIOUSNESS	ALUMINIFEROUS	SPONTANEOUSLY	INCORRUPTIBLE	STAPHYLINIDAE
ORNITHOLOGIST	ALUMINOTHERMY	THANKLESSNESS	INVOLUNTARILY	STEPPINGSTONE
POLIOMYELITIS	ANIMADVERSION	THUNDERSTRUCK	MONOCOTYLEDON	SUPPLEMENTARY
PUSILLANIMITY	COMMEMORATION	TRANQUILLISER	MONONUCLEOSIS	SUSPERCOLLATE
PUSILLANIMOUS	COMMEMORATIVE	TRANQUILLIZER	MONOTHALAMOUS	SYMPIESOMETER
RADIOACTIVITY	COMMENSURABLE	TRANSATLANTIC	OPPORTUNISTIC	TEMPERAMENTAL
RAMIFICATIONS	COMMERCIALIZE	TRANSCRIPTION	OPPORTUNITIES	TRIPLOBLASTIC
RATIONALALITY	COMMISERATION		PELOPONNESIAN	FREQUENTATIVE

AFFREIGHTMENT
APPROPINQUATE
APPROPRIATION
APPROXIMATELY
APPROXIMATION
CHARACTERISED
CHARACTERLESS
CHOREOGRAPHER
CLARIFICATION
COMRADEINARMS
CORRESPONDENT
CORRESPONDING
CORROBORATION
CORROBORATORY
DECRIMINALIZE
DISRESPECTFUL
ENERGETICALLY
EXPROPRIATION
EXTRAORDINARY
EXTRAPOLATION
EXTRAVAGANTLY
FERROCONCRETE
FUERTEVENTURA
GARRULOUSNESS
GLORIFICATION
HEARTBREAKING
HIEROGLYPHICS
HORRIPILATION
HYBRIDIZATION
HYDRAULICALLY
HYDROCEPHALUS
HYDRODYNAMICS
HYDROELECTRIC
IMPRACTICABLE
IMPRESSIONISM
IMPRESSIONIST
IMPROBABILITY
IMPROVIDENTLY
IMPROVISATION
INCREDULOUSLY
INCRIMINATING
INCRIMINATORY
INTRAMUSCULAR
INTRANSIGENCE
INTRINSICALLY
INTROSPECTION
INTROSPECTIVE
LIBRARIANSHIP
MATRICULATION
MAURIKIGUSARI
MICROCOMPUTER
MICROORGANISM
NEUROCOMPUTER
NONRESISTANCE
OUTRECUIDANCE
OVEREMPHASIZE
OVERSTATEMENT
PATRIOTICALLY
PETRIFICATION
PETROCHEMICAL
PHARMACOPOEIA
QUARTERMASTER
QUARTODECIMAN
QUERULOUSNESS
REARRANGEMENT
RECRIMINATION
RECRIMINATORY
RECRUDESCENCE
REFRIGERATION

REFRIGERATORS
REPREHENSIBLE
REPREHENSIBLY
REPROACHFULLY
REPROGRAPHICS
RETROGRESSION
RETROSPECTIVE
SECRETIVENESS
SPERMATOPHYTE
SPORTSMANLIKE
SPORTSMANSHIP
STERCORACEOUS
STERILIZATION
SUPRANATIONAL
SURREPTITIOUS
TETRASYLLABIC
THERMODYNAMIC
THERMONUCLEAR
THERMOPLASTIC
THORACENTESIS
THOROUGHBRACE
THOROUGHGOING
THYROIDECTOMY
UNGRAMMATICAL
UNPRECEDENTED
UNPREDICTABLE
UNPRETENTIOUS
UNPROGRESSIVE
UNTRUSTWORTHY
VITRIFICATION
ARISTROCRATIC
BOUSTROPHEDON
CLISHMACLAVER
CLOSEDCIRCUIT
CONSANGUINITY
CONSCIENTIOUS
CONSCIOUSNESS
CONSECTANEOUS
CONSECUTIVELY
CONSEQUENTIAL
CONSERVATOIRE
CONSIDERATELY
CONSIDERATION
CONSOLIDATION
CONSPICUOUSLY
CONSPURCATION
CONSTELLATION
CONSTERNATION
CROSSQUESTION
DISSEMINATION
DISSIMILARITY
DISSIMULATION
FALSIFICATION
FOSSILIZATION
GEOSTATIONARY
GLOSSOGRAPHER
HORSEFEATHERS
HOUSEBREAKING
LEISURELINESS
LISSOTRICHOUS
MASSACHUSETTS
MEISTERSINGER
MESSERSCHMITT
MISSISSIPPIAN
NONSUFFICIENT
OUTSTANDINGLY
PASSCHENDAELE
PASSEMENTERIE
PASSIONFLOWER

PERSONALITIES
PERSPICACIOUS
PHOSPHOLIPASE
PHYSHARMONICA
PHYSIOGNOMIST
PHYSIOLOGICAL
PHYSIOTHERAPY
PHYSOSTIGMINE
PRESERVATIVES
PRESSURELOCAL
PROSOPOGRAPHY
QUESTIONNAIRE
RENSSELAERITE
SEISMOLOGICAL
SENSATIONALLY
SENSELESSNESS
SENSITIVENESS
SPASMODICALLY
SUBSERVIENTLY
SUBSTANTIALLY
SWASHBUCKLING
THESSALONIANS
TONSILLECTOMY
UNESTABLISHED
VERSIFICATION
AESTHETICALLY
ANYTHINGARIAN
ARITHMETICIAN
BACTERIOPHAGE
BEATIFICATION
BIOTECHNOLOGY
BUTTERFINGERS
CARTILAGINOUS
CAUTERIZATION
CERTIFICATION
CHATEAUBRIAND
CONTAMINATION
CONTEMPLATION
CONTEMPLATIVE
CONTENTEDNESS
CONTINUATIONS
CONTORTIONIST
CONTRABASSOON
CONTRACEPTION
CONTRACEPTIVE
CONTRADICTION
CONTRADICTORY
CONTRAFAGOTTO
CONTRAVENTION
CONTRIBUTIONS
CONTROVERSIAL
COSTEFFECTIVE
DEATHLESSNESS
DISTINGUISHED
EPITRACHELION
FANTASTICALLY
FEATHERWEIGHT
FERTILISATION
FERTILIZATION
FONTAINEBLEAU
FORTIFICATION
FORTUNETELLER
FOSTERPARENTS
GASTROCNEMIUS
GESTICULATION
GRATIFICATION
HORTICULTURAL
INSTANTANEOUS
INSTINCTIVELY

INSTITUTIONAL
INSTRUCTIONAL
JUSTIFICATION
JUSTIFICATORY
JUXTAPOSITION
LEATHERJACKET
LECTISTERNIUM
LEPTOCEPHALUS
LEPTOSPIROSIS
MASTIGOPHORAN
MORTIFICATION
MOUTHWATERING
MULTICOLOURED
MULTINATIONAL
MULTINUCLEATE
MULTITUDINOUS
MYSTIFICATION
NORTHEASTERLY
NORTHWESTERLY
NOSTALGICALLY
OPHTHALMOLOGY
OYSTERCATCHER
PARTHOGENESIS
PARTICIPATION
PARTICIPATORY
PARTICOLOURED
PARTICULARISE
PARTICULARITY
PARTICULARIZE
PEPTIDOGLYCAN
PHOTOCHEMICAL
PHOTOELECTRIC
PHYTOPLANKTON
PLATOCEPHALUS
PRETERNATURAL
PROTECTIONISM
PROTECTIONIST
PROTESTANTISM
PROTONOTARIAT
RECTIFICATION
SENTENTIOUSLY
SENTIMENTALLY
SEPTENTRIONES
SKATEBOARDING
SOUTHEASTERLY
SOUTHWESTERLY
SPITESPLENDID
STATESMANLIKE
STATESMANSHIP
STATIONMASTER
STATISTICALLY
SYNTACTICALLY
SYNTHETICALLY
TANTALIZINGLY
TINTINNABULUM
TORTOISESHELL
VENTRILOQUISM
VENTRILOQUIST
VICTIMIZATION
WEATHERBEATEN
ARGUMENTATIVE
DAGUERREOTYPE
DOCUMENTATION
ENCULTURATION
ILLUMINATIONS
IMPULSIVENESS
INDUSTRIALIST
INDUSTRIALIZE
INDUSTRIOUSLY

INQUISITIVELY
INQUISITORIAL
INSUBORDINATE
INSUBSTANTIAL
INSUFFICIENCY
INSUPPORTABLE
LUXURIOUSNESS
MANUFACTURING
MISUNDERSTAND
MISUNDERSTOOD
PNEUMATICALLY
PNEUMONECTOMY
REFURBISHMENT
REGURGITATION
REPUBLICANISM
RESUSCITATION
SCHUTZSTAFFEL
SEQUESTRATION
SHOULDERBLADE
SIPUNCULOIDEA
THAUMATURGICS
THAUMATURGIST
THOUGHTLESSLY
TRAUMATICALLY
UNQUESTIONING
UNSUBSTANTIAL
CONVALESCENCE
CONVERSAZIONE
FRIVOLOUSNESS
GALVANIZATION
GRAVITATIONAL
INEVITABILITY
LAEVOROTATORY
NERVELESSNESS
PERVASIVENESS
PREVARICATION
PRIVATIZATION
PROVINCIALISM
PROVISIONALLY
PROVOCATIVELY
PULVERIZATION
SERVILEMENTAL
SUOVETAURILIA
AIRWORTHINESS
KNOWLEDGEABLE
SNOWBLINDNESS
WITWATERSRAND
INEXHAUSTIBLE
INEXPERIENCED
INEXPRESSIBLE
UNEXCEPTIONAL
UNEXPERIENCED
ACRYLONITRILE
BUTYRALDEHYDE
CHRYSANTHEMUM
DEHYDROGENATE
ENCYCLOPAEDIA
ENCYCLOPAEDIC
POLYCHROMATIC
UNSYMMETRICAL
UNSYMPATHETIC

13:5

ALPHABETARIAN
ANIMADVERSION
APOCATASTASIS
ARCHAEOLOGIST
ARCHAEOPTERYX
BACCALAUREATE

BOUGAINVILLEA	TETRASYLLABIC	GLUMDALCLITCH	INCREDULOUSLY	GRIEFSTRICKEN
CEPHALOSPORIN	THORACENTESIS	GRANDDAUGHTER	INFLEXIBILITY	INDEFATIGABLE
CHARACTERISED	THREATENINGLY	GRANDILOQUENT	ISOGEOTHERMAL	INDEFATIGABLY
CHARACTERLESS	UNGRAMMATICAL	GRANDPARENTAL	JIGGERYPOKERY	INDIFFERENTLY
COLLABORATION	UNIMAGINATIVE	INSIDIOUSNESS	KAPPELMEISTER	INEFFICIENTLY
COLLABORATIVE	VULCANIZATION	LEPIDOPTERIST	KIDDERMINSTER	INSUFFICIENCY
COMPANIONABLE	VULGARIZATION	MALADJUSTMENT	MALLEMAROKING	LIEBFRAUMILCH
COMPANIONSHIP	WITWATERSRAND	NEANDERTHALER	MATHEMATICIAN	MANIFESTATION
COMPARABILITY	AUTOBIOGRAPHY	PARADOXICALLY	MESSERSCHMITT	MANUFACTURING
COMPARATIVELY	DEFIBRILLATOR	ROUNDTHEWORLD	MISCEGENATION	RAMIFICATIONS
COMPASSIONATE	DÉSOBLIGEANTE	SCANDALMONGER	MISCELLANEOUS	REINFORCEMENT
COMPATIBILITY	ESTABLISHMENT	SCHADENFREUDE	NERVELESSNESS	ANTIGROPELOES
COMRADEINARMS	EXHIBITIONIST	SPINDLESHANKS	NONRESISTANCE	CATEGORICALLY
CONCATENATION	FLABBERGASTED	STEADFASTNESS	NUCLEOPROTEIN	CHANGEABILITY
CONFARREATION	INSUBORDINATE	THUNDERSTRUCK	ORCHESTRATION	DESEGREGATION
CONSANGUINITY	INSUBSTANTIAL	AFFREIGHTMENT	OUTRECUIDANCE	ENERGETICALLY
CONTAMINATION	REIMBURSEMENT	ANTHELMINTHIC	OVEREMPHASIZE	ENLIGHTENMENT
CONVALESCENCE	REPUBLICANISM	BACTERIOPHAGE	OYSTERCATCHER	INSIGNIFICANT
DERMATOLOGIST	SNOWBLINDNESS	BIODEGRADABLE	PALAEONTOLOGY	METAGRABOLISE
DIACATHOLICON	UNEMBARRASSED	BIOTECHNOLOGY	PASSEMENTERIE	METAGROBOLISE
DIFFARREATION	UNSUBSTANTIAL	BROKENHEARTED	PERFECTIONIST	PEREGRINATION
DISPARAGEMENT	ALLOCHTHONOUS	BUNGEEJUMPING	PERPENDICULAR	SELFGOVERNING
DISPASSIONATE	ANTICLOCKWISE	BUTTERFINGERS	PREMEDITATION	SPRIGHTLINESS
DRAMATIZATION	ANTICOAGULANT	CAUTERIZATION	PRESERVATIVES	THOUGHTLESSLY
EPANADIPLOSIS	AUTOCEPHALOUS	CHATEAUBRIAND	PRETERNATURAL	TOPOGRAPHICAL
EXTRAORDINARY	AUTOCHTHONOUS	CHOREOGRAPHER	PROFECTITIOUS	TYPOGRAPHICAL
EXTRAPOLATION	CONSCIENTIOUS	CLOSEDCIRCUIT	PROFESSORSHIP	AESTHETICALLY
EXTRAVAGANTLY	CONSCIOUSNESS	COMMEMORATION	PROJECTIONIST	ANACHRONISTIC
FANTASTICALLY	EFFECTIVENESS	COMMEMORATIVE	PROTECTIONISM	ANTIHISTAMINE
FONTAINEBLEAU	ENCYCLOPAEDIA	COMMENSURABLE	PROTECTIONIST	ANYTHINGARIAN
FORMALIZATION	ENCYCLOPAEDIC	COMMERCIALIZE	PROTESTANTISM	ARITHMETICIAN
FUNDAMENTALLY	GYNECOLOGICAL	CONCENTRATION	PULVERIZATION	BRACHIOSAURUS
GALVANIZATION	HYPOCHONDRIAC	CONCEPTIONIST	REPLENISHMENT	CLISHMACLAVER
HERMAPHRODITE	INSECTIVOROUS	CONCEPTUALIST	REPREHENSIBLE	DEATHLESSNESS
HYDRAULICALLY	IRRECOVERABLE	CONCEPTUALIZE	REPREHENSIBLY	ELEPHANTIASIS
IMPRACTICABLE	KANGCHENJUNGA	CONCESSIONARY	ROLLERBLADING	EPIPHENOMENON
INSTANTANEOUS	LEXICOGRAPHER	CONDESCENDING	ROLLERCOASTER	FEATHERWEIGHT
INTRAMUSCULAR	MONOCOTYLEDON	CONDESCENSION	RUTHERFORDIUM	FRIGHTENINGLY
INTRANSIGENCE	OBJECTIONABLE	CONFECTIONERS	SECRETIVENESS	FRIGHTFULNESS
JUXTAPOSITION	OBJECTIVENESS	CONFECTIONERY	SENSELESSNESS	INEXHAUSTIBLE
LACKADAISICAL	OFFICIOUSNESS	CONFEDERATION	SENTENTIOUSLY	LEATHERJACKET
LAMPADEPHORIA	PASSCHENDAELE	CONSECTANEOUS	SEPTENTRIONES	LIECHTENSTEIN
LIBRARIANSHIP	PHENCYCLIDINE	CONSECUTIVELY	SEQUESTRATION	MERCHANDIZING
MAGNANIMOUSLY	POLYCHROMATIC	CONSEQUENTIAL	SHAPELESSNESS	MISCHIEVOUSLY
MASSACHUSETTS	PREOCCUPATION	CONSERVATOIRE	SKATEBOARDING	MORPHOLOGICAL
MECHANIZATION	REINCARNATION	CONTEMPLATION	SPELEOLOGICAL	MOUTHWATERING
MISMANAGEMENT	SALACIOUSNESS	CONTEMPLATIVE	SPINECHILLING	NEIGHBOURHOOD
NORMALIZATION	SELFCONFESSED	CONTENTEDNESS	SPITESPLENDID	NORTHEASTERLY
NOSTALGICALLY	SELFCONFIDENT	CONVERSAZIONE	STATESMANLIKE	NORTHWESTERLY
PANHARMONICON	SELFCONSCIOUS	CORRESPONDENT	STATESMANSHIP	OPHTHALMOLOGY
PERVASIVENESS	SELFCONTAINED	CORRESPONDING	SUBJECTMATTER	PARTHOGENESIS
PHILADELPHIAN	SEMICONDUCTOR	COSTEFFECTIVE	SUBSERVIENTLY	PHYSHARMONICA
PHILANTHROPIC	STERCORACEOUS	DAGUERREOTYPE	SUOVETAURILIA	PROPHETICALLY
PRECAUTIONARY	TREACHEROUSLY	DIAMETRICALLY	SURREPTITIOUS	PSYCHOANALYSE
PREFABRICATED	UNACCOMPANIED	DIFFERENTIATE	SUSPERCOLLATE	PSYCHOANALYST
PREVARICATION	UNACCOUNTABLE	DISHEARTENING	SWEDENBORGIAN	PSYCHOBIOLOGY
PRIVATIZATION	UNACCOUNTABLY	DISRESPECTFUL	TABLESPOONFUL	PSYCHOKINESIS
RHADAMANTHINE	UNEXCEPTIONAL	DISSEMINATION	TEMPERAMENTAL	PSYCHOLOGICAL
RHYPAROGRAPHY	UNNECESSARILY	FORGETFULNESS	TENDERHEARTED	PSYCHOMETRICS
SARCASTICALLY	VIVACIOUSNESS	FOSTERPARENTS	UNPRECEDENTED	PSYCHOSOMATIC
SELFADDRESSED	VORACIOUSNESS	GEOMETRICALLY	UNPREDICTABLE	PSYCHOTHERAPY
SEMIAUTOMATIC	ARUNDINACEOUS	GLOBETROTTING	UNPRETENTIOUS	SACCHAROMYCES
SENSATIONALLY	BASIDIOMYCETE	GYNAECOLOGIST	UNQUESTIONING	SOUTHEASTERLY
SQUEAMISHNESS	BLANDISHMENTS	HAMMERKLAVIER	VULNERABILITY	SOUTHWESTERLY
SUBMANDIBULAR	BLOODCURDLING	HAMMERTHROWER	WHOLESOMENESS	STAPHYLINIDAE
SUPRANATIONAL	DEHYDROGENATE	HORSEFEATHERS	AQUIFOLIACEAE	SWASHBUCKLING
SYNTACTICALLY	DISADVANTAGED	HOUSEBREAKING	ARTIFICIALITY	SYNTHETICALLY
TALKATIVENESS	EXPEDITIONARY	IMPRESSIONISM	BIREFRINGENCE	TRICHOSANTHIN
TANTALIZINGLY	EXPEDITIOUSLY	IMPRESSIONIST	DECAFFEINATED	UNINHABITABLE

WEATHERBEATEN	MULTINUCLEATE	BOUILLABAISSE	TELEMARKETING	AGGLOMERATION
WEIGHTLIFTING	MULTITUDINOUS	COMPLEMENTARY	THAUMATURGICS	AIRWORTHINESS
ALUMINIFEROUS	MYSTIFICATION	COMPLIMENTARY	THAUMATURGIST	APPROPINQUATE
ALUMINOTHERMY	NULLIFICATION	CONFLAGRATION	THERMODYNAMIC	APPROPRIATION
AMPHIGASTRIUM	PAEDIATRICIAN	DEMILITARIZED	THERMONUCLEAR	APPROXIMATELY
AMPLIFICATION	PANDICULATION	DEVELOPMENTAL	THERMOPLASTIC	APPROXIMATION
ARCHIMANDRITE	PARLIAMENTARY	DISILLUSIONED	THIGMOTROPISM	AUTHORISATION
ARCHITECTURAL	PARTICIPATION	DOUBLEGLAZING	TRAUMATICALLY	AUTHORITARIAN
BEATIFICATION	PARTICIPATORY	EMBELLISHMENT	UNCOMFORTABLE	AUTHORITATIVE
BIBLIOGRAPHER	PARTICOLOURED	ENCULTURATION	UNCOMFORTABLY	AUTHORIZATION
BIBLIOPHAGIST	PARTICULARISE	IMPULSIVENESS	UNCOMMUNICATE	CARBONIFEROUS
CALLISTHENICS	PARTICULARITY	INFALLIBILITY	UNCOMPLICATED	CARBONIZATION
CARTILAGINOUS	PARTICULARIZE	INTELLIGENTLY	UNSYMMETRICAL	COLLOQUIALISM
CERTIFICATION	PASSIONFLOWER	INVOLUNTARILY	UNSYMPATHETIC	CONSOLIDATION
CLARIFICATION	PATRIOTICALLY	KNOWLEDGEABLE	ADMINISTRATOR	CONTORTIONIST
COLLIESHANGIE	PEPTIDOGLYCAN	MIDDLEBREAKER	ADVENTUROUSLY	CORROBORATION
COMMISERATION	PETRIFICATION	PARALLELOGRAM	AFFENPINSCHER	CORROBORATORY
CONDITIONALLY	PHYSIOGNOMIST	PHYLLOQUINONE	ASTONISHINGLY	DISCOLORATION
CONFIGURATION	PHYSIOLOGICAL	PROBLEMATICAL	ATTENTIVENESS	DISCONCERTING
CONSIDERATELY	PHYSIOTHERAPY	PROCLEUSMATIC	BUSINESSWOMAN	DISCONNECTION
CONSIDERATION	POLLICITATION	PUSILLANIMITY	CHRONOLOGICAL	DISCONTINUITY
CONTINUATIONS	PRECIPITATELY	PUSILLANIMOUS	DECONTAMINATE	DISCONTINUOUS
CRIMINOLOGIST	PRECIPITATION	RECALCITRANCE	DEFENSIBILITY	DISHONOURABLE
DECRIMINALIZE	PRELIMINARIES	REVOLUTIONARY	DEIPNOSOPHIST	DISHONOURABLY
DISFIGUREMENT	PROFITABILITY	REVOLUTIONIZE	DEMONSTRATION	EFFLORESCENCE
DISSIMILARITY	PROLIFERATION	SCHOLARLINESS	DEMONSTRATIVE	EXPROPRIATION
DISSIMULATION	PROMISCUOUSLY	SEMBLANCECORD	DEPENDABILITY	FERROCONCRETE
DISTINGUISHED	PROVINCIALISM	SHOULDERBLADE	DISENGAGEMENT	FRIVOLOUSNESS
FALSIFICATION	PROVISIONALLY	SUPPLEMENTARY	DISINTERESTED	HARMONIZATION
FERTILISATION	QUALIFICATION	SWOLLENHEADED	ECCENTRICALLY	HIEROGLYPHICS
FERTILIZATION	REALISTICALLY	THEOLOGICALLY	EXPANSIVENESS	HYDROCEPHALUS
FORTIFICATION	RECRIMINATION	TRIPLOBLASTIC	GYNANDROMORPH	HYDRODYNAMICS
FOSSILIZATION	RECRIMINATORY	UMBELLIFEROUS	IMPONDERABLES	HYDROELECTRIC
GESTICULATION	RECTIFICATION	UNENLIGHTENED	INCANDESCENCE	IMPROBABILITY
GLORIFICATION	REFRIGERATION	UNWILLINGNESS	INCONCEIVABLE	IMPROVIDENTLY
GRATIFICATION	REFRIGERATORS	ACCOMMODATING	INCONSIDERATE	IMPROVISATION
GRAVITATIONAL	REUNIFICATION	ACCOMMODATION	INCONSISTENCY	INFLORESCENCE
HORRIPILATION	SENSITIVENESS	ACCOMPANIMENT	INCONSPICUOUS	INTROSPECTION
HORTICULTURAL	SENTIMENTALLY	ARGUMENTATIVE	INCONTESTABLE	INTROSPECTIVE
HYBRIDIZATION	SERVILEMENTAL	AUTOMATICALLY	INCONVENIENCE	INVIOLABILITY
IMAGINATIVELY	SIGNIFICANTLY	CEREMONIOUSLY	INFINITESIMAL	LAEVOROTATORY
INCRIMINATING	SIGNIFICATION	DECOMPOSITION	INGENUOUSNESS	LEPTOCEPHALUS
INCRIMINATORY	SOPHISTICATED	DECOMPRESSION	INSENSITIVITY	LEPTOSPIROSIS
INEVITABILITY	SPECIFICATION	DOCUMENTATION	INTENTIONALLY	LISSOTRICHOUS
INQUISITIVELY	STABILIZATION	ENTOMOLOGICAL	INVENTIVENESS	METEOROLOGIST
INQUISITORIAL	STATIONMASTER	EPHEMEROPTERA	INVINCIBILITY	MICROCOMPUTER
INSPIRATIONAL	STATISTICALLY	EXCOMMUNICATE	INVIOLABILITY	MICROORGANISM
INSTINCTIVELY	STERILIZATION	FRAGMENTATION	LYCANTHROPIST	MISCONCEPTION
INSTITUTIONAL	STYLISTICALLY	GRAMMATICALLY	MISANTHROPIST	NATIONALISTIC
INTRINSICALLY	SUBLIEUTENANT	IGNOMINIOUSLY	MISUNDERSTAND	NEUROCOMPUTER
JOLLIFICATION	SYMPIESOMETER	ILLUMINATIONS	MISUNDERSTOOD	NONCONFORMIST
JUSTIFICATION	TINTINNABULUM	INCOMBUSTIBLE	MONONUCLEOSIS	NONCONFORMITY
JUSTIFICATORY	TONSILLECTOMY	INCOMMUNICADO	OFFENSIVENESS	PERSONALITIES
KALEIDOSCOPIC	TRADITIONALLY	INCOMPETENTLY	PARANTHROPOUS	PETROCHEMICAL
LECTISTERNIUM	UNFLINCHINGLY	METAMORPHOSIS	PARENTHETICAL	PHILOSOPHICAL
MACHIAVELLIAN	VERCINGETORIX	ORNAMENTATION	POTENTIOMETER	PHOTOCHEMICAL
MACHICOLATION	VERSIFICATION	PERAMBULATION	PROGNOSTICATE	PHOTOELECTRIC
MAGNIFICATION	VICTIMIZATION	PHARMACOPOEIA	REMINISCENCES	PHYSOSTIGMINE
MAGNIFICENTLY	VITRIFICATION	PNEUMATICALLY	SHRINKWRAPPED	PHYTOPLANKTON
MAGNILOQUENCE	XIPHIPLASTRON	PNEUMONECTOMY	SIPUNCULOIDEA	PLATOCEPHALUS
MASTIGOPHORAN	CHINKERINCHEE	PRAGMATICALLY	STRANGULATION	POLIOMYELITIS
MATRICULATION	FOREKNOWLEDGE	REDEMPTIONIST	STRENUOUSNESS	PRECONCEPTION
MAURIKIGUSARI	FRANKALMOIGNE	REGIMENTATION	TECHNOLOGICAL	PREDOMINANTLY
MERCILESSNESS	KNICKERBOCKER	SCHEMATICALLY	TRIANGULATION	PREPONDERANCE
MISSISSIPPIAN	KNICKKNACKERY	SEDIMENTATION	UNCONDITIONAL	PREPOSSESSING
MOLLIFICATION	STOCKBREEDING	SEISMOLOGICAL	UNCONQUERABLE	PREPOSSESSION
MORTIFICATION	STRIKEBREAKER	SOLEMNIZATION	UNCONSCIOUSLY	PRIMOGENITURE
MULTICOLOURED	THANKLESSNESS	SPASMODICALLY	UNGENTLEMANLY	PRONOUNCEMENT
MULTINATIONAL	ACRYLONITRILE	SPERMATOPHYTE	UNMENTIONABLE	PROPORTIONATE
			AGGIORNAMENTO	

PROSOPOGRAPHY	COMPREHENSIVE	PROPRIETORIAL	PAINSTAKINGLY	SOMATOSENSORY
PROTONOTARIAT	CONFRONTATION	QUADRAGESIMAL	PENNSYLVANIAN	SOMATOTROPHIN
PROVOCATIVELY	CONGRESSIONAL	QUADRILATERAL	PRESSURELOCAL	SPECTACULARLY
RADIOACTIVITY	CONGRESSWOMAN	QUADRUPLICATE	REINSTATEMENT	SPECTROGRAPHY
RATIONALALITY	CONTRABASSOON	RAPPROCHEMENT	RENSSELAERITE	SPONTANEOUSLY
REPROACHFULLY	CONTRACEPTION	REARRANGEMENT	RESUSCITATION	SPORTSMANLIKE
REPROGRAPHICS	CONTRACEPTIVE	REFURBISHMENT	TENOSYNOVITIS	SPORTSMANSHIP
RETROGRESSION	CONTRADICTION	REGURGITATION	THESSALONIANS	STRATEGICALLY
RETROSPECTIVE	CONTRADICTORY	REMORSELESSLY	TRANSATLANTIC	SUBSTANTIALLY
SCHOOLTEACHER	CONTRAFAGOTTO	REPERCUSSIONS	TRANSCRIPTION	SWEETSMELLING
SOCIOECONOMIC	CONTRAVENTION	REVERBERATION	TRANSGRESSION	THEATRICALITY
SUBCONTRACTOR	CONTRIBUTIONS	SCLEROPROTEIN	TRANSISTORIZE	TRACTARIANISM
THOROUGHBRACE	CONTROVERSIAL	SUBORDINATION	TRANSLITERATE	UNANTICIPATED
THOROUGHGOING	DEFERVESCENCE	SUPERABUNDANT	TRANSMUTATION	UNESTABLISHED
THYROIDECTOMY	DEFORESTATION	SUPERANNUATED	TRANSPARENTLY	UNINTELLIGENT
TORTOISESHELL	DETERIORATION	SUPERFICIALLY	TRANSPIRATION	UNINTENTIONAL
UNCOOPERATIVE	DETERMINATION	SUPERFLUOUSLY	TRANSPORTABLE	UNINTERESTING
UNCOORDINATED	DISCREDITABLE	SUPERLATIVELY	TRANSPOSITION	UNINTERRUPTED
UNPROGRESSIVE	DISCREDITABLY	SUPERNUMERARY	UNDISCIPLINED	UPTOTHEMINUTE
VIDEOCASSETTE	DISCRETIONARY	SUPERORDINATE	UNFASHIONABLE	VEGETARIANISM
VIDEORECORDER	DISGRACEFULLY	SUPERSTITIOUS	ARISTROCRATIC	ACCOUTREMENTS
ACCEPTABILITY	DISPROPORTION	TAPERECORDING	BOUSTROPHEDON	ACUPUNCTURIST
ACCEPTILATION	EFFERVESCENCE	THEORETICALLY	CONSTELLATION	ARMOURPLATING
CONSPICUOUSLY	EMBARRASSMENT	UNCEREMONIOUS	CONSTERNATION	BILDUNGSROMAN
CONSPURCATION	ENTEROPNEUSTA	UNDERACHIEVER	COUNTERACTING	CIRCUMAMBIENT
DISAPPEARANCE	ENTERTAINMENT	UNDERCARRIAGE	COUNTERATTACK	CIRCUMFERENCE
DISAPPOINTING	ENVIRONMENTAL	UNDERCLOTHING	COUNTERCHARGE	CIRCUMSTANCES
DRYOPITHECINE	EPITRACHELION	UNDERESTIMATE	COUNTERFEITER	CIRCUMVENTION
ENCEPHALOCELE	EXTERMINATION	UNDERGRADUATE	COUNTRYPEOPLE	COEDUCATIONAL
ENCEPHALOGRAM	GASTROCNEMIUS	UNDERSTANDING	CRAFTSMANSHIP	COMMUNICATION
EQUIPONDERATE	GENERALISSIMO	UNDERSTRAPPER	CRYPTANALYSIS	COMMUNICATIVE
EXCEPTIONABLE	GOODRIGHTEOUS	UNFORESEEABLE	DENATIONALIZE	CONCUPISCENCE
EXCEPTIONALLY	HETERAUXESISM	UNFORGETTABLE	ELECTROCUTION	CREDULOUSNESS
INAPPROPRIATE	HETEROGENEOUS	UNFORTUNATELY	ELECTROMAGNET	ENCOURAGEMENT
INDEPENDENTLY	HUNDREDWEIGHT	UNPARTITIONED	ELECTROMOTIVE	FORTUNETELLER
INEXPERIENCED	HYPERCRITICAL	UNSERVICEABLE	FACETIOUSNESS	FREQUENTATIVE
INEXPRESSIBLE	HYPERSTHENITE	VENTRILOQUISM	FRACTIOUSNESS	GARRULOUSNESS
INSUPPORTABLE	IDIORRHYTHMIC	VENTRILOQUIST	FUERTEVENTURA	HALLUCINATION
IRREPLACEABLE	IMPERCEPTIBLE	ACCESSIBILITY	GENITOURINARY	HALLUCINATORY
IRREPRESSIBLE	IMPERCEPTIBLY	ASSASSINATION	GEOSTATIONARY	HYALURONIDASE
METAPHYSICIAN	IMPERIALISTIC	BREASTFEEDING	GUILTLESSNESS	LEISURELINESS
PAPAPRELATIST	IMPERSONATING	CHEESEMONGERS	HEARTBREAKING	NONSUFFICIENT
PARAPHERNALIA	IMPERSONATION	CHRISTMASTIME	INDETERMINATE	PERFUNCTORILY
PELOPONNESIAN	IMPERTINENTLY	CHRYSANTHEMUM	INDETERMINISM	PRONUNCIATION
PERSPICACIOUS	IMPERTURBABLE	CROSSQUESTION	IRRETRIEVABLE	QUERULOUSNESS
PHOSPHOLIPASE	IMPERTURBABLY	CRUISERWEIGHT	IRRETRIEVABLY	RECRUDESCENCE
RECEPTIVENESS	INCARCERATION	DISESTIMATION	LIGHTFINGERED	RESOURCEFULLY
SLEEPLESSNESS	INCORPORATION	ESCHSCHOLTZIA	MADETOMEASURE	TONGUEINCHEEK
STEEPLECHASER	INCORRUPTIBLE	EXPOSTULATION	MEDITERRANEAN	TONGUETWISTER
STEPPINGSTONE	INSTRUCTIONAL	GLOSSOGRAPHER	MEISTERSINGER	UNADULTERATED
STREPTOCARPUS	INTERCALATION	HEMISPHERICAL	MOCKTECHNICAL	UNTRUSTWORTHY
STREPTOCOCCUS	INTERESTINGLY	HOMOSEXUALITY	MONOTHALAMOUS	HYPOVENTILATE
UNEXPERIENCED	INTERMARRIAGE	IDIOSYNCRATIC	NEMATHELMINTH	INADVERTENTLY
UNIMPEACHABLE	INTERNATIONAL	IMPOSSIBILITY	NIGHTCLUBBING	INDIVIDUALISM
UNIMPRESSIBLE	INTERPERSONAL	INDESCRIBABLE	NIGHTWATCHMAN	INDIVIDUALIST
VICEPRESIDENT	INTERPOLATION	INDESCRIBABLY	ORNITHOLOGIST	INDIVIDUALITY
QUINQUAGESIMA	INTERROGATION	INDISPENSABLE	OUTSTANDINGLY	REDEVELOPMENT
TRANQUILLISER	INTERROGATIVE	INDISPOSITION	PENETRABILITY	SCHIZOPHRENIA
TRANQUILLIZER	LUXURIOUSNESS	INDUSTRIALIST	PUNCTILIOUSLY	SCHIZOPHRENIC
ADVERTISEMENT	MATERIALISTIC	INDUSTRIALIZE	PYROTECHNICAL	**13:6**
AFFIRMATIVELY	MODERNIZATION	INDUSTRIOUSLY	QUARTERMASTER	AIRCRAFTWOMAN
AFFORESTATION	OPPORTUNISTIC	INVESTIGATION	QUARTODECIMAN	AUTOMATICALLY
AIRCRAFTWOMAN	OPPORTUNITIES	INVESTIGATIVE	QUESTIONNAIRE	BUTYRALDEHYDE
ALTERNATIVELY	OWNEROCCUPIER	IRRESPONSIBLE	RECITATIONIST	CHATEAUBRIAND
APPORTIONMENT	PATERFAMILIAS	IRRESPONSIBLY	RIGHTEOUSNESS	CHRYSANTHEMUM
ASCERTAINABLE	PATERNALISTIC	JURISPRUDENCE	SANCTIMONIOUS	CLAIRAUDIENCE
BUTYRALDEHYDE	PREPROGRAMMED	LONGSUFFERING	SCHUTZSTAFFEL	CONFLAGRATION
CLAIRAUDIENCE	PROCRASTINATE	MAGISTERIALLY	SCINTILLATING	CONTRABASSOON
COMPREHENSION	PROGRESSIVELY	OVERSTATEMENT	SCINTILLATION	

CONTRACEPTION
CONTRACEPTIVE
CONTRADICTION
CONTRADICTORY
CONTRAFAGOTTO
CONTRAVENTION
CRYPTANALYSIS
DISGRACEFULLY
DISHEARTENING
ELEPHANTIASIS
EPITRACHELION
FRANKALMOIGNE
GENERALISSIMO
GEOSTATIONARY
GLUMDALCLITCH
GRAMMATICALLY
HETERAUXESISM
INDEFATIGABLE
INDEFATIGABLY
INEXHAUSTIBLE
MACHIAVELLIAN
MANUFACTURING
MERCHANDIZING
OPHTHALMOLOGY
OUTSTANDINGLY
PAEDIATRICIAN
PARLIAMENTARY
PHARMACOPOEIA
PHYSHARMONICA
PNEUMATICALLY
PRAGMATICALLY
PROCRASTINATE
QUADRAGESIMAL
RADIOACTIVITY
REARRANGEMENT
RECITATIONIST
REINCARNATION
REPROACHFULLY
SACCHAROMYCES
SCANDALMONGER
SCHEMATICALLY
SCHOLARLINESS
SEMBLANCECORD
SPECTACULARLY
SPERMATOPHYTE
SPONTANEOUSLY
SUBSTANTIALLY
SUPERABUNDANT
SUPERANNUATED
TELEMARKETING
THAUMATURGICS
THAUMATURGIST
THESSALONIANS
TRACTARIANISM
TRANSATLANTIC
TRAUMATICALLY
UNDERACHIEVER
UNEMBARRASSED
UNESTABLISHED
UNINHABITABLE
VEGETARIANISM
ALPHABETARIAN
COLLABORATION
COLLABORATIVE
CORROBORATION
CORROBORATORY
HEARTBREAKING
HOUSEBREAKING
IMPROBABILITY

INCOMBUSTIBLE
NEIGHBOURHOOD
PERAMBULATION
PREFABRICATED
REFURBISHMENT
REVERBERATION
SKATEBOARDING
STOCKBREEDING
SWASHBUCKLING
BIOTECHNOLOGY
BLOODCURDLING
CHARACTERISED
CHARACTERLESS
COEDUCATIONAL
CONFECTIONERS
CONFECTIONERY
CONSECTANEOUS
CONSECUTIVELY
ESCHSCHOLTZIA
FERROCONCRETE
GESTICULATION
GYNAECOLOGIST
HALLUCINATION
HALLUCINATORY
HORTICULTURAL
HYDROCEPHALUS
HYPERCRITICAL
IMPERCEPTIBLE
IMPERCEPTIBLY
IMPRACTICABLE
INCARCERATION
INCONCEIVABLE
INDESCRIBABLE
INDESCRIBABLY
INTERCALATION
INVINCIBILITY
LEPTOCEPHALUS
MACHICOLATION
MASSACHUSETTS
MATRICULATION
MICROCOMPUTER
MULTICOLOURED
NEUROCOMPUTER
NIGHTCLUBBING
OUTRECUIDANCE
PANDICULATION
PARTICIPATION
PARTICIPATORY
PARTICOLOURED
PARTICULARISE
PARTICULARITY
PARTICULARIZE
PERFECTIONIST
PETROCHEMICAL
PHOTOCHEMICAL
PLATOCEPHALUS
POLLICITATION
PREOCCUPATION
PROFECTITIOUS
PROJECTIONIST
PROTECTIONISM
PROTECTIONIST
PROVOCATIVELY
RECALCITRANCE
REPERCUSSIONS
RESUSCITATION
SIPUNCULOIDEA
SPINECHILLING
SUBJECTMATTER

SYNTACTICALLY
THORACENTESIS
TRANSCRIPTION
UNDERCARRIAGE
UNDERCLOTHING
UNDISCIPLINED
UNPRECEDENTED
VIDEOCASSETTE
ANIMADVERSION
CLOSEDCIRCUIT
COMRADEINARMS
CONFEDERATION
CONSIDERATELY
CONSIDERATION
DEPENDABILITY
EPANADIPLOSIS
GRANDDAUGHTER
GYNANDROMORPH
HYBRIDIZATION
HYDRODYNAMICS
IMPONDERABLES
INCANDESCENCE
INCREDULOUSLY
KALEIDOSCOPIC
LACKADAISICAL
LAMPADEPHORIA
MISUNDERSTAND
MISUNDERSTOOD
PEPTIDOGLYCAN
PHILADELPHIAN
PREMEDITATION
RECRUDESCENCE
SELFADDRESSED
SHOULDERBLADE
SUBORDINATION
UNCONDITIONAL
UNPREDICTABLE
AESTHETICALLY
AFFORESTATION
ARCHAEOLOGIST
ARCHAEOPTERYX
ARGUMENTATIVE
AUTOCEPHALOUS
BUNGEEJUMPING
BUSINESSWOMAN
CHANGEABILITY
CHEESEMONGERS
CHINKERINCHEE
COLLIESHANGIE
COMPLEMENTARY
COMPREHENSION
COMPREHENSIVE
CONGRESSIONAL
CONGRESSWOMAN
CONSTELLATION
CONSTERNATION
COUNTERACTING
COUNTERATTACK
COUNTERCHARGE
COUNTERFEITER
CRUISERWEIGHT
DEFORESTATION
DISCREDITABLE
DISCREDITABLY
DISCRETIONARY
DOCUMENTATION
DOUBLEGLAZING
ENERGETICALLY
EPHEMEROPTERA

EPIPHENOMENON
FEATHERWEIGHT
FLABBERGASTED
FRAGMENTATION
FREQUENTATIVE
FUERTEVENTURA
HOMOSEXUALITY
HUNDREDWEIGHT
HYDROELECTRIC
HYPOVENTILATE
INADVERTENTLY
INDEPENDENTLY
INDETERMINATE
INDETERMINISM
INEXPERIENCED
INTERESTINGLY
KNICKERBOCKER
KNOWLEDGEABLE
LEATHERJACKET
MANIFESTATION
MEDITERRANEAN
MEISTERSINGER
MIDDLEBREAKER
MOCKTECHNICAL
NEANDERTHALER
NORTHEASTERLY
ORNAMENTATION
PHOTOELECTRIC
PROBLEMATICAL
PROCLEUSMATIC
PROGRESSIVELY
PROPHETICALLY
PYROTECHNICAL
QUARTERMASTER
REDEVELOPMENT
REGIMENTATION
RENSSELAERITE
RIGHTEOUSNESS
SCHADENFREUDE
SEDIMENTATION
SOCIOECONOMIC
SOUTHEASTERLY
STRATEGICALLY
STRIKEBREAKER
SUBLIEUTENANT
SUPPLEMENTARY
SWOLLENHEADED
SYMPIESOMETER
SYNTHETICALLY
TAPERECORDING
THEORETICALLY
THUNDERSTRUCK
TONGUEINCHEEK
TONGUETWISTER
UNCEREMONIOUS
UNDERESTIMATE
UNEXCEPTIONAL
UNEXPERIENCED
UNFORESEEABLE
UNIMPEACHABLE
UNINTELLIGENT
UNINTENTIONAL
UNINTERESTING
UNINTERRUPTED
UNNECESSARILY
WEATHERBEATEN
AMPLIFICATION
BEATIFICATION
CERTIFICATION

CLARIFICATION
COSTEFFECTIVE
DECAFFEINATED
FALSIFICATION
FORTIFICATION
GLORIFICATION
GRATIFICATION
HORSEFEATHERS
INDIFFERENTLY
INSUFFICIENCY
JOLLIFICATION
JUSTIFICATION
JUSTIFICATORY
LIGHTFINGERED
MAGNIFICATION
MAGNIFICENTLY
MOLLIFICATION
MORTIFICATION
MYSTIFICATION
NONSUFFICIENT
NULLIFICATION
PATERFAMILIAS
PETRIFICATION
PROLIFERATION
QUALIFICATION
RECTIFICATION
REUNIFICATION
SIGNIFICANTLY
SIGNIFICATION
SPECIFICATION
STEADFASTNESS
SUPERFICIALLY
SUPERFLUOUSLY
UNCOMFORTABLE
UNCOMFORTABLY
VERSIFICATION
VITRIFICATION
AMPHIGASTRIUM
BIODEGRADABLE
CONFIGURATION
DISENGAGEMENT
DISFIGUREMENT
HIEROGLYPHICS
MASTIGOPHORAN
MISCEGENATION
PRIMOGENITURE
REFRIGERATION
REFRIGERATORS
REGURGITATION
REPROGRAPHICS
RETROGRESSION
STRANGULATION
TRANSGRESSION
TRIANGULATION
UNDERGRADUATE
UNFORGETTABLE
UNIMAGINATIVE
UNPROGRESSIVE
ALLOCHTHONOUS
AUTOCHTHONOUS
ENCEPHALOCELE
ENCEPHALOGRAM
ENLIGHTENMENT
HYPOCHONDRIAC
KANGCHENJUNGA
METAPHYSICIAN
MONOTHALAMOUS
NEMATHELMINTH
ORNITHOLOGIST

PARAPHERNALIA	UNENLIGHTENED	AFFIRMATIVELY	FOREKNOWLEDGE	INSUBORDINATE
PASSCHENDAELE	VENTRILOQUISM	AGGLOMERATION	FORTUNETELLER	IRRECOVERABLE
PHOSPHOLIPASE	VENTRILOQUIST	ARCHIMANDRITE	GALVANIZATION	ISOGEOTHERMAL
POLYCHROMATIC	VIVACIOUSNESS	ARITHMETICIAN	HARMONIZATION	LEPIDOPTERIST
REPREHENSIBLE	VORACIOUSNESS	CIRCUMAMBIENT	IMAGINATIVELY	LEXICOGRAPHER
REPREHENSIBLY	MALADJUSTMENT	CIRCUMFERENCE	INSIGNIFICANT	MADETOMEASURE
SPRIGHTLINESS	KNICKKNACKERY	CIRCUMSTANCES	INSTANTANEOUS	METAMORPHOSIS
THOUGHTLESSLY	MAURIKIGUSARI	CIRCUMVENTION	INSTINCTIVELY	MICROORGANISM
TREACHEROUSLY	SHRINKWRAPPED	CLISHMACLAVER	INTERNATIONAL	MONOCOTYLEDON
UNFASHIONABLE	ANTHELMINTHIC	COMMEMORATION	INTRANSIGENCE	MORPHOLOGICAL
UPTOTHEMINUTE	ANTICLOCKWISE	COMMEMORATIVE	INTRINSICALLY	NUCLEOPROTEIN
ADMINISTRATOR	BACCALAUREATE	CONTAMINATION	MAGNANIMOUSLY	OWNEROCCUPIER
AFFREIGHTMENT	BOUILLABAISSE	CONTEMPLATION	MECHANIZATION	PALAEONTOLOGY
ANTIHISTAMINE	CARTILAGINOUS	CONTEMPLATIVE	MISCONCEPTION	PARADOXICALLY
ANYTHINGARIAN	CEPHALOSPORIN	DECRIMINALIZE	MISMANAGEMENT	PARTHOGENESIS
ARTIFICIALITY	CONSOLIDATION	DETERMINATION	MODERNIZATION	PASSIONFLOWER
ARUNDINACEOUS	CONVALESCENCE	DISSEMINATION	MULTINATIONAL	PATRIOTICALLY
ASTONISHINGLY	CREDULOUSNESS	DISSIMILARITY	MULTINUCLEATE	PELOPONNESIAN
AUTOBIOGRAPHY	DEATHLESSNESS	DISSIMULATION	NATIONALISTIC	PHYLLOQUINONE
BASIDIOMYCETE	DÉSOBLIGEANTE	EXCOMMUNICATE	NONCONFORMIST	PHYSIOGNOMIST
BLANDISHMENTS	DISCOLORATION	EXTERMINATION	NONCONFORMITY	PHYSIOLOGICAL
BOUGAINVILLEA	DISILLUSIONED	FUNDAMENTALLY	PATERNALISTIC	PHYSIOTHERAPY
BRACHIOSAURUS	EMBELLISHMENT	INCOMMUNICADO	PERFUNCTORILY	PNEUMONECTOMY
COMPLIMENTARY	ENCYCLOPAEDIA	INCRIMINATING	PERPENDICULAR	PREPROGRAMMED
CONSCIENTIOUS	ENCYCLOPAEDIC	INCRIMINATORY	PERSONALITIES	PROGNOSTICATE
CONSCIOUSNESS	ESTABLISHMENT	INTERMARRIAGE	PHILANTHROPIC	PSYCHOANALYSE
CONSPICUOUSLY	FERTILISATION	INTRAMUSCULAR	PRECONCEPTION	PSYCHOANALYST
CONTRIBUTIONS	FERTILIZATION	MALLEMAROKING	PREPONDERANCE	PSYCHOBIOLOGY
DEMILITARIZED	FORMALIZATION	MATHEMATICIAN	PRONUNCIATION	PSYCHOKINESIS
DENATIONALIZE	FOSSILIZATION	OVEREMPHASIZE	PROTONOTARIAT	PSYCHOLOGICAL
DETERIORATION	FRIVOLOUSNESS	PASSEMENTERIE	PROVINCIALISM	PSYCHOMETRICS
DRYOPITHECINE	GARRULOUSNESS	POLIOMYELITIS	RATIONALALITY	PSYCHOSOMATIC
EXHIBITIONIST	GUILTLESSNESS	PREDOMINANTLY	REPLENISHMENT	PSYCHOTHERAPY
EXPEDITIONARY	INFALLIBILITY	PRELIMINARIES	SENTENTIOUSLY	QUARTODECIMAN
EXPEDITIOUSLY	INTELLIGENTLY	RECRIMINATION	SEPTENTRIONES	RAPPROCHEMENT
FACETIOUSNESS	INVIOLABILITY	RECRIMINATORY	SOLEMNIZATION	REINFORCEMENT
FONTAINEBLEAU	IRREPLACEABLE	RHADAMANTHINE	SUBCONTRACTOR	SCHIZOPHRENIA
FRACTIOUSNESS	KAPPELMEISTER	SENTIMENTALLY	SUBMANDIBULAR	SCHIZOPHRENIC
GOODRIGHTEOUS	MAGNILOQUENCE	SQUEAMISHNESS	SUPERNUMERARY	SCLEROPROTEIN
GRANDILOQUENT	MERCILESSNESS	TRANSMUTATION	SUPRANATIONAL	SEISMOLOGICAL
IGNOMINIOUSLY	MISCELLANEOUS	UNCOMMUNICATE	SWEDENBORGIAN	SELFCONFESSED
ILLUMINATIONS	NERVELESSNESS	UNGRAMMATICAL	TINTINNABULUM	SELFCONFIDENT
IMPERIALISTIC	NORMALIZATION	UNSYMMETRICAL	UNFLINCHINGLY	SELFCONSCIOUS
INDIVIDUALISM	NOSTALGICALLY	VICTIMIZATION	VERCINGETORIX	SELFCONTAINED
INDIVIDUALIST	PARALLELOGRAM	ACUPUNCTURIST	VULCANIZATION	SELFGOVERNING
INDIVIDUALITY	PUSILLANIMITY	ALTERNATIVELY	ACRYLONITRILE	SEMICONDUCTOR
INEFFICIENTLY	PUSILLANIMOUS	ALUMINIFEROUS	ANTICOAGULANT	SOMATOSENSORY
INFINITESIMAL	QUERULOUSNESS	ALUMINOTHERMY	AQUIFOLIACEAE	SOMATOTROPHIN
INSIDIOUSNESS	REPUBLICANISM	BILDUNGSROMAN	BIBLIOGRAPHER	SPASMODICALLY
LUXURIOUSNESS	SCHOOLTEACHER	BROKENHEARTED	BIBLIOPHAGIST	SPELEOLOGICAL
MATERIALISTIC	SENSELESSNESS	CARBONIFEROUS	CATEGORICALLY	STATIONMASTER
MISCHIEVOUSLY	SERVILEMENTAL	CARBONIZATION	CEREMONIOUSLY	STERCORACEOUS
OFFICIOUSNESS	SHAPELESSNESS	COMMENSURABLE	CHOREOGRAPHER	SUPERORDINATE
PERSPICACIOUS	SLEEPLESSNESS	COMMUNICATION	CHRONOLOGICAL	TECHNOLOGICAL
PROPRIETORIAL	SNOWBLINDNESS	COMMUNICATIVE	CONFRONTATION	THEOLOGICALLY
PUNCTILIOUSLY	SPINDLESHANKS	COMPANIONABLE	CONTROVERSIAL	THERMODYNAMIC
QUADRILATERAL	STABILIZATION	COMPANIONSHIP	DEIPNOSOPHIST	THERMONUCLEAR
QUESTIONNAIRE	STEEPLECHASER	CONCENTRATION	DEVELOPMENTAL	THERMOPLASTIC
RAMIFICATIONS	STERILIZATION	CONSANGUINITY	DISPROPORTION	THIGMOTROPISM
REMINISCENCES	SUPERLATIVELY	CONTENTEDNESS	ENTEROPNEUSTA	TRICHOSANTHIN
SALACIOUSNESS	TANTALIZINGLY	CONTINUATIONS	ENTOMOLOGICAL	TRIPLOBLASTIC
SANCTIMONIOUS	THANKLESSNESS	CRIMINOLOGIST	ENVIRONMENTAL	UNACCOMPANIED
SCINTILLATING	TONSILLECTOMY	DISCONCERTING	EQUIPONDERATE	UNACCOUNTABLE
SCINTILLATION	TRANSLITERATE	DISCONNECTION	EXTRAORDINARY	UNACCOUNTABLY
STEPPINGSTONE	UMBELLIFEROUS	DISCONTINUITY	GASTROCNEMIUS	ACCOMPANIMENT
THYROIDECTOMY	UNADULTERATED	DISCONTINUOUS	GENITOURINARY	AFFENPINSCHER
TORTOISESHELL	UNWILLINGNESS	DISHONOURABLE	GLOSSOGRAPHER	APPROPINQUATE
TRANSISTORIZE	ACCOMMODATING	DISHONOURABLY	GYNECOLOGICAL	APPROPRIATION
UNANTICIPATED	ACCOMMODATION	DISTINGUISHED	HETEROGENEOUS	CONCEPTIONIST

CONCEPTUALIST
CONCEPTUALIZE
CONCUPISCENCE
DECOMPOSITION
DECOMPRESSION
DISAPPEARANCE
DISAPPOINTING
EXPROPRIATION
EXTRAPOLATION
GRANDPARENTAL
HEMISPHERICAL
HERMAPHRODITE
HORRIPILATION
INCOMPETENTLY
INCORPORATION
INDISPENSABLE
INDISPOSITION
INSUPPORTABLE
INTERPERSONAL
INTERPOLATION
IRRESPONSIBLE
IRRESPONSIBLY
JURISPRUDENCE
JUXTAPOSITION
PHYTOPLANKTON
PRECIPITATELY
PRECIPITATION
PROSOPOGRAPHY
REDEMPTIONIST
SURREPTITIOUS
TRANSPARENTLY
TRANSPIRATION
TRANSPORTABLE
TRANSPOSITION
UNCOMPLICATED
UNCOOPERATIVE
UNSYMPATHETIC
XIPHIPLASTRON
COLLOQUIALISM
CONSEQUENTIAL
CROSSQUESTION
UNCONQUERABLE
AGGIORNAMENTO
AIRWORTHINESS
ANACHRONISTIC
ANTIGROPELOES
ARISTROCRATIC
ARMOURPLATING
AUTHORISATION
AUTHORITARIAN
AUTHORITATIVE
AUTHORIZATION
BACTERIOPHAGE
BIREFRINGENCE
BOUSTROPHEDON
BUTTERFINGERS
CAUTERIZATION
COMMERCIALIZE
COMPARABILITY
COMPARATIVELY
CONFARREATION
CONSERVATOIRE
CONTORTIONIST
CONVERSAZIONE
COUNTRYPEOPLE
DAGUERREOTYPE
DEFIBRILLATOR
DEHYDROGENATE
DESEGREGATION

DIFFARREATION
DIFFERENTIATE
DISPARAGEMENT
EFFLORESCENCE
ELECTROCUTION
ELECTROMAGNET
ELECTROMOTIVE
EMBARRASSMENT
ENCOURAGEMENT
FOSTERPARENTS
HAMMERKLAVIER
HAMMERTHROWER
HYALURONIDASE
IDIORRHYTHMIC
INAPPROPRIATE
INCORRUPTIBLE
INEXPRESSIBLE
INFLORESCENCE
INSPIRATIONAL
INTERROGATION
INTERROGATIVE
IRREPRESSIBLE
IRRETRIEVABLE
IRRETRIEVABLY
JIGGERYPOKERY
KIDDERMINSTER
LAEVOROTATORY
LEISURELINESS
LIBRARIANSHIP
LIEBFRAUMILCH
MESSERSCHMITT
METAGRABOLISE
METAGROBOLISE
METEOROLOGIST
OYSTERCATCHER
PANHARMONICON
PAPAPRELATIST
PENETRABILITY
PEREGRINATION
PRESERVATIVES
PRETERNATURAL
PREVARICATION
PROPORTIONATE
PULVERIZATION
RESOURCEFULLY
RHYPAROGRAPHY
ROLLERBLADING
ROLLERCOASTER
RUTHERFORDIUM
SPECTROGRAPHY
SUBSERVIENTLY
SUSPERCOLLATE
TEMPERAMENTAL
TENDERHEARTED
THEATRICALITY
TOPOGRAPHICAL
TYPOGRAPHICAL
UNCOORDINATED
UNIMPRESSIBLE
VICEPRESIDENT
VIDEORECORDER
VULGARIZATION
VULNERABILITY
ACCESSIBILITY
ASSASSINATION
CALLISTHENICS
COMMISERATION
COMPASSIONATE
CONCESSIONARY

CONDESCENDING
CONDESCENSION
CORRESPONDENT
CORRESPONDING
CRAFTSMANSHIP
DEFENSIBILITY
DEMONSTRATION
DEMONSTRATIVE
DISPASSIONATE
DISRESPECTFUL
EXPANSIVENESS
FANTASTICALLY
GRIEFSTRICKEN
HYPERSTHENITE
IMPERSONATING
IMPERSONATION
IMPOSSIBILITY
IMPRESSIONISM
IMPRESSIONIST
IMPULSIVENESS
INCONSIDERATE
INCONSISTENCY
INCONSPICUOUS
INQUISITIVELY
INQUISITORIAL
INSENSITIVITY
INSUBSTANTIAL
INTROSPECTION
INTROSPECTIVE
LECTISTERNIUM
LEPTOSPIROSIS
MISSISSIPPIAN
NONRESISTANCE
OFFENSIVENESS
ORCHESTRATION
PERVASIVENESS
PHILOSOPHICAL
PHYSOSTIGMINE
PREPOSSESSING
PREPOSSESSION
PROFESSORSHIP
PROMISCUOUSLY
PROTESTANTISM
PROVISIONALLY
REALISTICALLY
REMORSELESSLY
RETROSPECTIVE
SARCASTICALLY
SEQUESTRATION
SOPHISTICATED
SPITESPLENDID
SPORTSMANLIKE
SPORTSMANSHIP
STATESMANLIKE
STATESMANSHIP
STATISTICALLY
STYLISTICALLY
SUPERSTITIOUS
SWEETSMELLING
TABLESPOONFUL
TETRASYLLABIC
UNCONSCIOUSLY
UNDERSTANDING
UNDERSTRAPPER
UNQUESTIONING
UNSUBSTANTIAL
UNTRUSTWORTHY
WHOLESOMENESS
ACCEPTABILITY

ACCEPTILATION
ACCOUTREMENTS
ADVENTUROUSLY
ADVERTISEMENT
APOCATASTASIS
APPORTIONMENT
ARCHITECTURAL
ASCERTAINABLE
ATTENTIVENESS
BREASTFEEDING
CHRISTMASTIME
COMPATIBILITY
CONCATENATION
CONDITIONALLY
DECONTAMINATE
DERMATOLOGIST
DIACATHOLICON
DIAMETRICALLY
DISESTIMATION
DISINTERESTED
DRAMATIZATION
ECCENTRICALLY
EFFECTIVENESS
ENCULTURATION
ENTERTAINMENT
EXCEPTIONABLE
EXCEPTIONALLY
EXPOSTULATION
FORGETFULNESS
FRIGHTENINGLY
FRIGHTFULNESS
GEOMETRICALLY
GLOBETROTTING
GRAVITATIONAL
IMPERTINENTLY
IMPERTURBABLE
IMPERTURBABLY
INCONTESTABLE
INDUSTRIALIST
INDUSTRIALIZE
INDUSTRIOUSLY
INEVITABILITY
INSECTIVOROUS
INSTITUTIONAL
INTENTIONALLY
INVENTIVENESS
INVESTIGATION
INVESTIGATIVE
LIECHTENSTEIN
LISSOTRICHOUS
LYCANTHROPIST
MAGISTERIALLY
MISANTHROPIST
MULTITUDINOUS
OBJECTIONABLE
OBJECTIVENESS
OPPORTUNISTIC
OPPORTUNITIES
OVERSTATEMENT
PAINSTAKINGLY
PARANTHROPOUS
PARENTHETICAL
POTENTIOMETER
PRIVATIZATION
PROFITABILITY
RECEPTIVENESS
REINSTATEMENT
ROUNDTHEWORLD
SECRETIVENESS

SENSATIONALLY
SENSITIVENESS
STREPTOCARPUS
STREPTOCOCCUS
SUOVETAURILIA
TALKATIVENESS
THREATENINGLY
TRADITIONALLY
UNFORTUNATELY
UNGENTLEMANLY
UNMENTIONABLE
UNPARTITIONED
UNPRETENTIOUS
WEIGHTLIFTING
WITWATERSRAND
CONSPURCATION
HYDRAULICALLY
INGENUOUSNESS
INSTRUCTIONAL
INVOLUNTARILY
LONGSUFFERING
MONONUCLEOSIS
PRECAUTIONARY
PRESSURELOCAL
PRONOUNCEMENT
QUADRUPLICATE
QUINQUAGESIMA
REIMBURSEMENT
REVOLUTIONARY
REVOLUTIONIZE
SEMIAUTOMATIC
STRENUOUSNESS
THOROUGHBRACE
THOROUGHGOING
TRANQUILLISER
TRANQUILLIZER
DEFERVESCENCE
DISADVANTAGED
EFFERVESCENCE
EXTRAVAGANTLY
IMPROVIDENTLY
IMPROVISATION
INCONVENIENCE
UNSERVICEABLE
MOUTHWATERING
NIGHTWATCHMAN
NORTHWESTERLY
SOUTHWESTERLY
APPROXIMATELY
APPROXIMATION
INFLEXIBILITY
IDIOSYNCRATIC
PENNSYLVANIAN
PHENCYCLIDINE
STAPHYLINIDAE
TENOSYNOVITIS
SCHUTZSTAFFEL

13:7

ACCEPTABILITY
ACCOMPANIMENT
AFFIRMATIVELY
ALTERNATIVELY
AMPHIGASTRIUM
ANTICOAGULANT
APOCATASTASIS
ARCHIMANDRITE
ASCERTAINABLE
BACCALAUREATE

BOUILLABAISSE	TYPOGRAPHICAL	INDIVIDUALITY	PARAPHERNALIA	THEOLOGICALLY
CARTILAGINOUS	UNDERCARRIAGE	KNOWLEDGEABLE	PASSCHENDAELE	THOROUGHBRACE
CHANGEABILITY	UNIMPEACHABLE	PERPENDICULAR	PASSEMENTERIE	THOROUGHGOING
CIRCUMAMBIENT	UNSYMPATHETIC	PREPONDERANCE	PHILADELPHIAN	UNENLIGHTENED
CLISHMACLAVER	VIDEOCASSETTE	QUARTODECIMAN	PLATOCEPHALUS	VERCINGETORIX
COEDUCATIONAL	VULNERABILITY	SELFADDRESSED	PRIMOGENITURE	BIOTECHNOLOGY
COMPARABILITY	CONTRABASSOON	SPASMODICALLY	PROLIFERATION	BROKENHEARTED
COMPARATIVELY	CONTRIBUTIONS	SUBMANDIBULAR	PROPRIETORIAL	COMPREHENSION
DECONTAMINATE	MIDDLEBREAKER	THERMODYNAMIC	RECRUDESCENCE	COMPREHENSIVE
DEPENDABILITY	PSYCHOBIOLOGY	THYROIDECTOMY	REFRIGERATION	DIACATHOLICON
DISADVANTAGED	ROLLERBLADING	UNCOORDINATED	REFRIGERATORS	ESCHSCHOLTZIA
DISENGAGEMENT	STRIKEBREAKER	AGGLOMERATION	REMORSELESSLY	HEMISPHERICAL
DISPARAGEMENT	SUPERABUNDANT	ALPHABETARIAN	REPREHENSIBLE	HERMAPHRODITE
EMBARRASSMENT	SWEDENBORGIAN	ARCHITECTURAL	REPREHENSIBLY	IDIORRHYTHMIC
ENCEPHALOCELE	TRIPLOBLASTIC	ARITHMETICIAN	REVERBERATION	LYCANTHROPIST
ENCEPHALOGRAM	UNESTABLISHED	COMMISERATION	SENSELESSNESS	MASSACHUSETTS
ENCOURAGEMENT	UNINHABITABLE	COMRADEINARMS	SENTIMENTALLY	MISANTHROPIST
ENTERTAINMENT	ACUPUNCTURIST	CONCATENATION	SERVILEMENTAL	PARANTHROPOUS
EXTRAVAGANTLY	ARTIFICIALITY	CONFEDERATION	SHAPELESSNESS	PARENTHETICAL
GRANDDAUGHTER	CLOSEDCIRCUIT	CONSCIENTIOUS	SHOULDERBLADE	PETROCHEMICAL
GRANDPARENTAL	COMMERCIALIZE	CONSIDERATELY	SLEEPLESSNESS	PHOTOCHEMICAL
GRAVITATIONAL	CONDESCENDING	CONSIDERATION	SOUTHWESTERLY	ROUNDTHEWORLD
IMAGINATIVELY	CONDESCENSION	CONVALESCENCE	SPINDLESHANKS	SPINECHILLING
IMPERIALISTIC	CONSPICUOUSLY	DEATHLESSNESS	STEEPLECHASER	TENDERHEARTED
IMPROBABILITY	CONTRACEPTION	DECAFFEINATED	THANKLESSNESS	ACCEPTILATION
INEVITABILITY	CONTRACEPTIVE	DEFERVESCENCE	THORACENTESIS	ACCESSIBILITY
INSPIRATIONAL	DISCONCERTING	DESEGREGATION	THREATENINGLY	ADVERTISEMENT
INTERCALATION	DISGRACEFULLY	DIFFERENTIATE	TREACHEROUSLY	AFFENPINSCHER
INTERMARRIAGE	EPITRACHELION	DISAPPEARANCE	UNCOOPERATIVE	ALUMINIFEROUS
INTERNATIONAL	GASTROCNEMIUS	DISINTERESTED	UNFORGETTABLE	AMPLIFICATION
INVIOLABILITY	INEFFICIENTLY	EFFERVESCENCE	UNIMPRESSIBLE	APPORTIONMENT
IRREPLACEABLE	INSTINCTIVELY	EFFLORESCENCE	UNPRECEDENTED	APPROPINQUATE
LACKADAISICAL	INSTRUCTIONAL	FORTUNETELLER	UNPRETENTIOUS	APPROXIMATELY
LIEBFRAUMILCH	MANUFACTURING	FRIGHTENINGLY	UNSYMMETRICAL	APPROXIMATION
MALLEMAROKING	MISCONCEPTION	FUNDAMENTALLY	UPTOTHEMINUTE	ASSASSINATION
MATERIALISTIC	MOCKTECHNICAL	GUILTLESSNESS	VICEPRESIDENT	ATTENTIVENESS
MATHEMATICIAN	MONONUCLEOSIS	HORSEFEATHERS	VIDEORECORDER	AUTHORISATION
METAGRABOLISE	OWNEROCCUPIER	HYDROCEPHALUS	WITWATERSRAND	AUTHORITARIAN
MISMANAGEMENT	OYSTERCATCHER	IMPERCEPTIBLE	AIRCRAFTWOMAN	AUTHORITATIVE
MONOTHALAMOUS	PERFUNCTORILY	IMPERCEPTIBLY	BREASTFEEDING	AUTHORIZATION
MOUTHWATERING	PERSPICACIOUS	IMPONDERABLES	BUTTERFINGERS	BACTERIOPHAGE
MULTINATIONAL	PHARMACOPOEIA	INCANDESCENCE	CIRCUMFERENCE	BEATIFICATION
NATIONALISTIC	PHENCYCLIDINE	INCARCERATION	CONTRAFAGOTTO	BIREFRINGENCE
NIGHTWATCHMAN	PRECONCEPTION	INCOMPETENTLY	COSTEFFECTIVE	CARBONIFEROUS
NORTHEASTERLY	PROMISCUOUSLY	INCONCEIVABLE	FORGETFULNESS	CARBONIZATION
OVERSTATEMENT	PRONUNCIATION	INCONTESTABLE	FRIGHTFULNESS	CAUTERIZATION
PAINSTAKINGLY	PROVINCIALISM	INCONVENIENCE	LONGSUFFERING	CERTIFICATION
PATERFAMILIAS	PYROTECHNICAL	INDIFFERENTLY	NONCONFORMIST	CLARIFICATION
PATERNALISTIC	RADIOACTIVITY	INDISPENSABLE	NONCONFORMITY	COMMUNICATION
PENETRABILITY	RAMIFICATIONS	INEXPRESSIBLE	NONSUFFICIENT	COMMUNICATIVE
PERSONALITIES	RAPPROCHEMENT	INFLORESCENCE	RUTHERFORDIUM	COMPANIONABLE
PROFITABILITY	REPROACHFULLY	INTERPERSONAL	AFFREIGHTMENT	COMPANIONSHIP
PROVOCATIVELY	RESOURCEFULLY	IRREPRESSIBLE	BIBLIOGRAPHER	COMPATIBILITY
PSYCHOANALYSE	ROLLERCOASTER	KANGCHENJUNGA	BILDUNGSROMAN	CONCUPISCENCE
PSYCHOANALYST	SOCIOECONOMIC	LAMPADEPHORIA	CHOREOGRAPHER	CONDITIONALLY
PUSILLANIMITY	SPECTACULARLY	LEISURELINESS	CONFLAGRATION	CONSOLIDATION
PUSILLANIMOUS	SUSPERCOLLATE	LEPTOCEPHALUS	CONSANGUINITY	CONTAMINATION
QUINQUAGESIMA	TAPERECORDING	LIECHTENSTEIN	DISTINGUISHED	DECRIMINALIZE
RATIONALALITY	UNANTICIPATED	MAGISTERIALLY	DOUBLEGLAZING	DEFENSIBILITY
REINSTATEMENT	UNCONSCIOUSLY	MERCILESSNESS	GLOSSOGRAPHER	DEFIBRILLATOR
RHADAMANTHINE	UNDERACHIEVER	MISCEGENATION	GOODRIGHTEOUS	DÉSOBLIGEANTE
SOUTHEASTERLY	UNFLINCHINGLY	MISCHIEVOUSLY	HETEROGENEOUS	DETERMINATION
STEADFASTNESS	CONTRADICTION	MISUNDERSTAND	LEXICOGRAPHER	DISESTIMATION
SUOVETAURILIA	CONTRADICTORY	MISUNDERSTOOD	NOSTALGICALLY	DISSEMINATION
SUPERLATIVELY	DISCREDITABLE	NEMATHELMINTH	PARTHOGENESIS	DISSIMILARITY
SUPRANATIONAL	DISCREDITABLY	NERVELESSNESS	PHYSIOGNOMIST	DRAMATIZATION
TEMPERAMENTAL	HUNDREDWEIGHT	NORTHWESTERLY	PREPROGRAMMED	EFFECTIVENESS
TOPOGRAPHICAL	INDIVIDUALISM	PAPAPRELATIST	QUADRAGESIMAL	EMBELLISHMENT
TRANSPARENTLY	INDIVIDUALIST	PARALLELOGRAM	STRATEGICALLY	EPANADIPLOSIS

ESTABLISHMENT	POLLICITATION	GENERALISSIMO	CONFRONTATION	CRIMINOLOGIST
EXCEPTIONABLE	POTENTIOMETER	GLUMDALCLITCH	CRYPTANALYSIS	DECOMPOSITION
EXCEPTIONALLY	PRECIPITATELY	GRANDILOQUENT	DISCONNECTION	DEHYDROGENATE
EXPANSIVENESS	PRECIPITATION	GYNECOLOGICAL	DOCUMENTATION	DENATIONALIZE
EXTERMINATION	PREDOMINANTLY	HIEROGLYPHICS	ELEPHANTIASIS	DERMATOLOGIST
FALSIFICATION	PRELIMINARIES	HYDRAULICALLY	ENVIRONMENTAL	DETERIORATION
FERTILISATION	PREMEDITATION	HYDROELECTRIC	EPIPHENOMENON	DISAPPOINTING
FERTILIZATION	PREVARICATION	MISCELLANEOUS	EQUIPONDERATE	DISCOLORATION
FORMALIZATION	PRIVATIZATION	MORPHOLOGICAL	FONTAINEBLEAU	DISHONOURABLE
FORTIFICATION	PROVISIONALLY	NIGHTCLUBBING	FRAGMENTATION	DISHONOURABLY
FOSSILIZATION	PULVERIZATION	OPHTHALMOLOGY	FREQUENTATIVE	ELECTROCUTION
GALVANIZATION	QUALIFICATION	PENNSYLVANIAN	HYPOVENTILATE	ELECTROMAGNET
GLORIFICATION	RECALCITRANCE	PHOTOELECTRIC	IDIOSYNCRATIC	ELECTROMOTIVE
GRATIFICATION	RECEPTIVENESS	PHYSIOLOGICAL	IGNOMINIOUSLY	ENCYCLOPAEDIA
HALLUCINATION	RECRIMINATION	PHYTOPLANKTON	ILLUMINATIONS	ENCYCLOPAEDIC
HALLUCINATORY	RECRIMINATORY	PSYCHOLOGICAL	INDEPENDENTLY	EXTRAPOLATION
HARMONIZATION	RECTIFICATION	PUNCTILIOUSLY	INVOLUNTARILY	FACETIOUSNESS
HORRIPILATION	REFURBISHMENT	QUADRILATERAL	KNICKKNACKERY	FERROCONCRETE
HYBRIDIZATION	REGURGITATION	REDEVELOPMENT	MERCHANDIZING	FOREKNOWLEDGE
IMPERTINENTLY	REPLENISHMENT	RENSSELAERITE	ORNAMENTATION	FRACTIOUSNESS
IMPOSSIBILITY	REPUBLICANISM	SCANDALMONGER	OUTSTANDINGLY	FRIVOLOUSNESS
IMPROVIDENTLY	RESUSCITATION	SCINTILLATING	PALAEONTOLOGY	GARRULOUSNESS
IMPROVISATION	REUNIFICATION	SCINTILLATION	PASSIONFLOWER	GYNAECOLOGIST
IMPULSIVENESS	SECRETIVENESS	SEISMOLOGICAL	PELOPONNESIAN	HYALURONIDASE
INCONSIDERATE	SENSATIONALLY	SPELEOLOGICAL	PNEUMONECTOMY	HYPOCHONDRIAC
INCONSISTENCY	SENSITIVENESS	STAPHYLINIDAE	PRETERNATURAL	IMPERSONATING
INCRIMINATING	SIGNIFICANTLY	SUPERFLUOUSLY	PRONOUNCEMENT	IMPERSONATION
INCRIMINATORY	SIGNIFICATION	TECHNOLOGICAL	REARRANGEMENT	INAPPROPRIATE
INFALLIBILITY	SNOWBLINDNESS	THESSALONIANS	REGIMENTATION	INCORPORATION
INFLEXIBILITY	SOLEMNIZATION	TONSILLECTOMY	SCHADENFREUDE	INDISPOSITION
INQUISITIVELY	SPECIFICATION	UNCOMPLICATED	SEDIMENTATION	INGENUOUSNESS
INQUISITORIAL	SQUEAMISHNESS	UNDERCLOTHING	SELFCONFESSED	INSIDIOUSNESS
INSECTIVOROUS	STABILIZATION	UNGENTLEMANLY	SELFCONFIDENT	INSUPPORTABLE
INSENSITIVITY	STERILIZATION	UNINTELLIGENT	SELFCONSCIOUS	INTERPOLATION
INSIGNIFICANT	SUBORDINATION	VENTRILOQUISM	SELFCONTAINED	INTERROGATION
INSUFFICIENCY	SUPERFICIALLY	VENTRILOQUIST	SEMBLANCECORD	INTERROGATIVE
INTELLIGENTLY	TALKATIVENESS	WEIGHTLIFTING	SEMICONDUCTOR	IRRESPONSIBLE
INTENTIONALLY	TANTALIZINGLY	XIPHIPLASTRON	SPONTANEOUSLY	IRRESPONSIBLY
INVENTIVENESS	THEATRICALITY	ANTHELMINTHIC	STATIONMASTER	JUXTAPOSITION
INVESTIGATION	TONGUEINCHEEK	CHEESEMONGERS	STEPPINGSTONE	KALEIDOSCOPIC
INVESTIGATIVE	TRADITIONALLY	CHRISTMASTIME	SUBSTANTIALLY	LAEVOROTATORY
INVINCIBILITY	TRANQUILLISER	COMPLEMENTARY	SUPERANNUATED	LUXURIOUSNESS
IRRETRIEVABLE	TRANQUILLIZER	COMPLIMENTARY	SWOLLENHEADED	MACHICOLATION
IRRETRIEVABLY	TRANSLITERATE	CRAFTSMANSHIP	TENOSYNOVITIS	MAGNILOQUENCE
JOLLIFICATION	TRANSPIRATION	KAPPELMEISTER	THERMONUCLEAR	MASTIGOPHORAN
JUSTIFICATION	UMBELLIFEROUS	KIDDERMINSTER	TINTINNABULUM	METAGROBOLISE
JUSTIFICATORY	UNCONDITIONAL	MADETOMEASURE	UNINTENTIONAL	METEOROLOGIST
LIBRARIANSHIP	UNDISCIPLINED	PANHARMONICON	ACCOMMODATING	MICROCOMPUTER
LIGHTFINGERED	UNFASHIONABLE	PARLIAMENTARY	ACCOMMODATION	MULTICOLOURED
MAGNANIMOUSLY	UNIMAGINATIVE	PROBLEMATICAL	ALUMINOTHERMY	NEIGHBOURHOOD
MAGNIFICATION	UNMENTIONABLE	PSYCHOMETRICS	ANACHRONISTIC	NEUROCOMPUTER
MAGNIFICENTLY	UNPARTITIONED	SANCTIMONIOUS	ANTICLOCKWISE	OFFICIOUSNESS
MAURIKIGUSARI	UNPREDICTABLE	SPORTSMANLIKE	ANTIGROPELOES	ORNITHOLOGIST
MECHANIZATION	UNSERVICEABLE	SPORTSMANSHIP	ARCHAEOLOGIST	PARTICOLOURED
MODERNIZATION	UNWILLINGNESS	STATESMANLIKE	ARCHAEOPTERYX	PEPTIDOGLYCAN
MOLLIFICATION	VERSIFICATION	STATESMANSHIP	ARISTOCRATIC	PHILOSOPHICAL
MORTIFICATION	VICTIMIZATION	SUPPLEMENTARY	AUTOBIOGRAPHY	PHOSPHOLIPASE
MYSTIFICATION	VITRIFICATION	SWEETSMELLING	BASIDIOMYCETE	PROSOPOGRAPHY
NONRESISTANCE	VULCANIZATION	UNACCOMPANIED	BOUSTROPHEDON	PROTONOTARIAT
NORMALIZATION	VULGARIZATION	UNCEREMONIOUS	BRACHIOSAURUS	QUERULOUSNESS
NULLIFICATION	BUNGEEJUMPING	UNGRAMMATICAL	CEPHALOSPORIN	QUESTIONNAIRE
OBJECTIONABLE	HAMMERKLAVIER	ACRYLONITRILE	COLLABORATION	RHYPAROGRAPHY
OBJECTIVENESS	PSYCHOKINESIS	AGGIORNAMENTO	COLLABORATIVE	RIGHTEOUSNESS
OFFENSIVENESS	AQUIFOLIACEAE	ANYTHINGARIAN	COMMEMORATION	SALACIOUSNESS
PARTICIPATION	BUTYRALDEHYDE	ARGUMENTATIVE	COMMEMORATIVE	SKATEBOARDING
PARTICIPATORY	CHRONOLOGICAL	ARUNDINACEOUS	CONSCIOUSNESS	SPECTROGRAPHY
PEREGRINATION	CONSTELLATION	BOUGAINVILLEA	CORROBORATION	STRENUOUSNESS
PERVASIVENESS	ENTOMOLOGICAL	CEREMONIOUSLY	CORROBORATORY	STREPTOCARPUS
PETRIFICATION	FRANKALMOIGNE	CHRYSANTHEMUM	CREDULOUSNESS	STREPTOCOCCUS

TRANSPORTABLE	INDETERMINATE	PREPOSSESSING	PRAGMATICALLY	IMPERTURBABLY
TRANSPOSITION	INDETERMINISM	PREPOSSESSION	PRECAUTIONARY	INCOMBUSTIBLE
UNCOMFORTABLE	INDUSTRIALIST	PROCRASTINATE	PROFECTITIOUS	INCOMMUNICADO
UNCOMFORTABLY	INDUSTRIALIZE	PROFESSORSHIP	PROJECTIONIST	INCORRUPTIBLE
VIVACIOUSNESS	INDUSTRIOUSLY	PROGNOSTICATE	PROPHETICALLY	INCREDULOUSLY
VORACIOUSNESS	INEXPERIENCED	PROGRESSIVELY	PROPORTIONATE	INEXHAUSTIBLE
WHOLESOMENESS	INSUBORDINATE	PSYCHOSOMATIC	PROTECTIONISM	INSTITUTIONAL
ARMOURPLATING	JURISPRUDENCE	REMINISCENCES	PROTECTIONIST	INTRAMUSCULAR
AUTOCEPHALOUS	KNICKERBOCKER	SCHUTZSTAFFEL	PROTESTANTISM	MALADJUSTMENT
BIBLIOPHAGIST	LEATHERJACKET	SOMATOSENSORY	PSYCHOTHERAPY	MATRICULATION
CONTEMPLATION	LISSOTRICHOUS	SYMPIESOMETER	REALISTICALLY	MULTINUCLEATE
CONTEMPLATIVE	MEDITERRANEAN	TORTOISESHELL	RECITATIONIST	MULTITUDINOUS
CORRESPONDENT	MEISTERSINGER	TRANSISTORIZE	REDEMPTIONIST	OPPORTUNISTIC
CORRESPONDING	METAMORPHOSIS	TRICHOSANTHIN	REVOLUTIONARY	OPPORTUNITIES
DEVELOPMENTAL	MICROORGANISM	UNDERESTIMATE	REVOLUTIONIZE	OUTRECUIDANCE
DISPROPORTION	NEANDERTHALER	UNFORESEEABLE	SARCASTICALLY	PANDICULATION
DISRESPECTFUL	PHYSHARMONICA	UNNECESSARILY	SCHEMATICALLY	PARTICULARISE
ENTEROPNEUSTA	POLYCHROMATIC	AESTHETICALLY	SCHOOLTEACHER	PARTICULARITY
FOSTERPARENTS	PREFABRICATED	AIRWORTHINESS	SEMIAUTOMATIC	PARTICULARIZE
INCONSPICUOUS	PRESSURELOCAL	ALLOCHTHONOUS	SENTENTIOUSLY	PERAMBULATION
INTROSPECTION	QUARTERMASTER	AUTOCHTHONOUS	SEPTENTRIONES	PREOCCUPATION
INTROSPECTIVE	REIMBURSEMENT	AUTOMATICALLY	SEQUESTRATION	PROCLEUSMATIC
LEPIDOPTERIST	REINCARNATION	CALLISTHENICS	SOMATOTROPHIN	REPERCUSSIONS
LEPTOSPIROSIS	REINFORCEMENT	CHARACTERISED	SOPHISTICATED	SIPUNCULOIDEA
NUCLEOPROTEIN	REPROGRAPHICS	CHARACTERLESS	SPERMATOPHYTE	STRANGULATION
OVEREMPHASIZE	RETROGRESSION	CONCENTRATION	SPRIGHTLINESS	SUBLIEUTENANT
QUADRUPLICATE	SACCHAROMYCES	CONCEPTIONIST	STATISTICALLY	SUPERNUMERARY
RETROSPECTIVE	SCHOLARLINESS	CONCEPTUALIST	STYLISTICALLY	SWASHBUCKLING
SCHIZOPHRENIA	STERCORACEOUS	CONCEPTUALIZE	SUBCONTRACTOR	TRANSMUTATION
SCHIZOPHRENIC	STOCKBREEDING	CONFECTIONERS	SUBJECTMATTER	TRIANGULATION
SCLEROPROTEIN	SUPERORDINATE	CONFECTIONERY	SUPERSTITIOUS	UNACCOUNTABLE
SPITESPLENDID	TELEMARKETING	CONSECTANEOUS	SURREPTITIOUS	UNACCOUNTABLY
TABLESPOONFUL	THUNDERSTRUCK	CONTENTEDNESS	SYNTACTICALLY	UNCOMMUNICATE
THERMOPLASTIC	TRACTARIANISM	CONTORTIONIST	SYNTHETICALLY	UNCONQUERABLE
UNEXCEPTIONAL	TRANSCRIPTION	DEMILITARIZED	THAUMATURGICS	UNFORTUNATELY
PHYLLOQUINONE	TRANSGRESSION	DEMONSTRATION	THAUMATURGIST	ANIMADVERSION
ACCOUTREMENTS	UNDERGRADUATE	DEMONSTRATIVE	THEORETICALLY	CIRCUMVENTION
APPROPRIATION	UNEMBARRASSED	DISCONTINUITY	THIGMOTROPISM	CONSERVATOIRE
BIODEGRADABLE	UNEXPERIENCED	DISCONTINUOUS	THOUGHTLESSLY	CONTRAVENTION
CATEGORICALLY	UNINTERESTING	DISCRETIONARY	TONGUETWISTER	CONTROVERSIAL
CHINKERINCHEE	UNINTERRUPTED	DRYOPITHECINE	TRANSATLANTIC	FUERTEVENTURA
CONFARREATION	UNPROGRESSIVE	ENERGETICALLY	TRAUMATICALLY	IRRECOVERABLE
CONSPURCATION	VEGETARIANISM	ENLIGHTENMENT	UNADULTERATED	MACHIAVELLIAN
CONSTERNATION	WEATHERBEATEN	EXHIBITIONIST	UNDERSTANDING	PRESERVATIVES
COUNTERACTING	ADMINISTRATOR	EXPEDITIONARY	UNDERSTRAPPER	SELFGOVERNING
COUNTERATTACK	AFFORESTATION	EXPEDITIOUSLY	UNQUESTIONING	SUBSERVIENTLY
COUNTERCHARGE	ANTIHISTAMINE	FANTASTICALLY	UNSUBSTANTIAL	SHRINKWRAPPED
COUNTERFEITER	ASTONISHINGLY	GEOSTATIONARY	UNTRUSTWORTHY	HOMOSEXUALITY
CRUISERWEIGHT	BLANDISHMENTS	GRAMMATICALLY	ADVENTUROUSLY	PARADOXICALLY
DAGUERREOTYPE	BUSINESSWOMAN	GRIEFSTRICKEN	BLOODCURDLING	COUNTRYPEOPLE
DECOMPRESSION	CIRCUMSTANCES	HAMMERTHROWER	CHATEAUBRIAND	HYDRODYNAMICS
DIAMETRICALLY	COLLIESHANGIE	HYPERSTHENITE	CLAIRAUDIENCE	JIGGERYPOKERY
DIFFARREATION	COMMENSURABLE	IMPRACTICABLE	COLLOQUIALISM	METAPHYSICIAN
DISHEARTENING	COMPASSIONATE	INDEFATIGABLE	CONFIGURATION	POLIOMYELITIS
ECCENTRICALLY	CONCESSIONARY	INDEFATIGABLY	CONSECUTIVELY	TETRASYLLABIC
EPHEMEROPTERA	CONGRESSIONAL	INFINITESIMAL	CONSEQUENTIAL	
EXPROPRIATION	CONGRESSWOMAN	INSTANTANEOUS	CONTINUATIONS	**13:8**
EXTRAORDINARY	CONVERSAZIONE	INSUBSTANTIAL	CROSSQUESTION	
FEATHERWEIGHT	DEFORESTATION	ISOGEOTHERMAL	DISFIGUREMENT	AGGIORNAMENTO
FLABBERGASTED	DEIPNOSOPHIST	LECTISTERNIUM	DISILLUSIONED	ARUNDINACEOUS
GEOMETRICALLY	DISPASSIONATE	MONOCOTYLEDON	DISSIMULATION	BIODEGRADABLE
GLOBETROTTING	IMPRESSIONISM	ORCHESTRATION	ENCULTURATION	CHRISTMASTIME
GYNANDROMORPH	IMPRESSIONIST	PAEDIATRICIAN	EXCOMMUNICATE	CONSECTANEOUS
HEARTBREAKING	INTERESTINGLY	PATRIOTICALLY	EXPOSTULATION	CONSERVATOIRE
HOUSEBREAKING	INTRANSIGENCE	PERFECTIONIST	GENITOURINARY	CONTINUATIONS
HYPERCRITICAL	INTRINSICALLY	PHILANTHROPIC	GESTICULATION	CONTRABASSOON
INADVERTENTLY	MANIFESTATION	PHYSIOTHERAPY	HETERAUXESISM	CONTRAFAGOTTO
INDESCRIBABLE	MESSERSCHMITT	PHYSOSTIGMINE	HORTICULTURAL	CONVERSAZIONE
INDESCRIBABLY	MISSISSIPPIAN	PNEUMATICALLY	IMPERTURBABLE	COUNTERACTING
				COUNTERATTACK

CRAFTSMANSHIP	CONSPURCATION	CHARACTERISED	STOCKBREEDING	MOCKTECHNICAL
CRYPTANALYSIS	COUNTERCHARGE	CHARACTERLESS	SUPPLEMENTARY	OVEREMPHASIZE
DEMILITARIZED	ELECTROCUTION	CIRCUMFERENCE	SWEETSMELLING	PHILANTHROPIC
DISAPPEARANCE	FALSIFICATION	CIRCUMVENTION	TENDERHEARTED	PHYSIOTHERAPY
FOSTERPARENTS	FORTIFICATION	COMPLEMENTARY	THYROIDECTOMY	PSYCHOTHERAPY
HORSEFEATHERS	GLORIFICATION	COMPLIMENTARY	TONSILLECTOMY	PYROTECHNICAL
ILLUMINATIONS	GLUMDALCLITCH	COMPREHENSION	TORTOISESHELL	RAPPROCHEMENT
INSTANTANEOUS	GRATIFICATION	COMPREHENSIVE	TRANSGRESSION	REPROACHFULLY
INSUBSTANTIAL	IDIOSYNCRATIC	CONDESCENDING	UNADULTERATED	SCHIZOPHRENIA
KNICKKNACKERY	INSUFFICIENCY	CONDESCENSION	UNCONQUERABLE	SCHIZOPHRENIC
LIBRARIANSHIP	IRREPLACEABLE	CONFARREATION	UNFORESEEABLE	SWOLLENHEADED
MISCELLANEOUS	JOLLIFICATION	CONSEQUENTIAL	UNGENTLEMANLY	THOROUGHBRACE
OYSTERCATCHER	JUSTIFICATION	CONTENTEDNESS	UNINTERESTING	THOROUGHGOING
PERSPICACIOUS	JUSTIFICATORY	CONTRACEPTION	UNPROGRESSIVE	UNDERACHIEVER
PHYTOPLANKTON	MAGNIFICATION	CONTRACEPTIVE	VERCINGETORIX	UNENLIGHTENED
PRESERVATIVES	MAGNIFICENTLY	CONTRAVENTION	ALUMINIFEROUS	UNFLINCHINGLY
PRETERNATURAL	MESSERSCHMITT	CONTROVERSIAL	CARBONIFEROUS	ACRYLONITRILE
PROBLEMATICAL	MOLLIFICATION	COSTEFFECTIVE	COUNTERFEITER	AESTHETICALLY
PROTESTANTISM	MORTIFICATION	CROSSQUESTION	INSIGNIFICANT	ANTHELMINTHIC
QUADRILATERAL	MULTINUCLEATE	DAGUERREOTYPE	LONGSUFFERING	APPROPRIATION
RAMIFICATIONS	MYSTIFICATION	DECOMPRESSION	PASSIONFLOWER	AQUIFOLIACEAE
RENSSELAERITE	NULLIFICATION	DIFFARREATION	SCHADENFREUDE	ARTIFICIALITY
REPROGRAPHICS	OWNEROCCUPIER	DISCONCERTING	SELFCONFESSED	ASCERTAINABLE
SKATEBOARDING	PETRIFICATION	DISCONNECTION	SELFCONFIDENT	AUTOMATICALLY
SPORTSMANLIKE	PREVARICATION	DISGRACEFULLY	UMBELLIFEROUS	BUTTERFINGERS
SPORTSMANSHIP	PRONOUNCEMENT	DISRESPECTFUL	ANTICOAGULANT	CATEGORICALLY
STATESMANLIKE	QUALIFICATION	ENLIGHTENMENT	ANYTHINGARIAN	CEREMONIOUSLY
STATESMANSHIP	RECTIFICATION	FONTAINEBLEAU	AUTOBIOGRAPHY	CHINKERINCHEE
STERCORACEOUS	REINFORCEMENT	FUERTEVENTURA	CARTILAGINOUS	CLOSEDCIRCUIT
TINTINNABULUM	REMINISCENCES	HEARTBREAKING	DEHYDROGENATE	COLLOQUIALISM
TRICHOSANTHIN	REPUBLICANISM	HEMISPHERICAL	DESEGREGATION	COMMERCIALIZE
UNDERGRADUATE	REUNIFICATION	HETEROGENEOUS	DÉSOBLIGEANTE	COMPASSIONATE
UNDERSTANDING	SEMBLANCECORD	HOUSEBREAKING	DISENGAGEMENT	COMRADEINARMS
UNGRAMMATICAL	SIGNIFICANTLY	HYDROELECTRIC	DISPARAGEMENT	CONCEPTIONIST
UNSUBSTANTIAL	SIGNIFICATION	INFINITESIMAL	ENCOURAGEMENT	CONCESSIONARY
XIPHIPLASTRON	SPECIFICATION	INTROSPECTION	EXTRAVAGANTLY	CONFECTIONERS
ACCEPTABILITY	STEEPLECHASER	INTROSPECTIVE	FLABBERGASTED	CONFECTIONERY
ACCESSIBILITY	STREPTOCARPUS	IRRECOVERABLE	INTELLIGENTLY	CONTORTIONIST
BOUILLABAISSE	STREPTOCOCCUS	IRRETRIEVABLE	INTERROGATION	CONTRADICTION
CHANGEABILITY	SUPERFICIALLY	IRRETRIEVABLY	INTERROGATIVE	CONTRADICTORY
CHATEAUBRIAND	SWASHBUCKLING	KAPPELMEISTER	INVESTIGATION	DECAFFEINATED
COMPARABILITY	THEATRICALITY	LECTISTERNIUM	INVESTIGATIVE	DIAMETRICALLY
COMPATIBILITY	UNIMPEACHABLE	MACHIAVELLIAN	KNOWLEDGEABLE	DISAPPOINTING
DEFENSIBILITY	UNPREDICTABLE	MADETOMEASURE	MAURIKIGUSARI	DISCONTINUITY
DEPENDABILITY	UNSERVICEABLE	MISCONCEPTION	MICROORGANISM	DISCONTINUOUS
IMPOSSIBILITY	VERSIFICATION	PARENTHETICAL	MISMANAGEMENT	DISCREDITABLE
IMPROBABILITY	VIDEORECORDER	PARLIAMENTARY	PEPTIDOGLYCAN	DISCREDITABLY
INEVITABILITY	VITRIFICATION	PARTHOGENESIS	PROSOPOGRAPHY	DISCRETIONARY
INFALLIBILITY	ACCOMMODATING	PETROCHEMICAL	QUINQUAGESIMA	DISPASSIONATE
INFLEXIBILITY	ACCOMMODATION	PHOTOCHEMICAL	REARRANGEMENT	ECCENTRICALLY
INVINCIBILITY	BUTYRALDEHYDE	PHOTOELECTRIC	RHYPAROGRAPHY	ENERGETICALLY
INVIOLABILITY	CLAIRAUDIENCE	PNEUMONECTOMY	SPECTROGRAPHY	ENTERTAINMENT
KNICKERBOCKER	CONSOLIDATION	POLIOMYELITIS	STEPPINGSTONE	EXHIBITIONIST
METAGRABOLISE	EQUIPONDERATE	PRECONCEPTION	AFFREIGHTMENT	EXPEDITIONARY
METAGROBOLISE	EXTRAORDINARY	PREPONDERANCE	AIRWORTHINESS	EXPEDITIOUSLY
PENETRABILITY	IMPROVIDENTLY	PREPOSSESSING	ALLOCHTHONOUS	EXPROPRIATION
PROFITABILITY	INCONSIDERATE	PREPOSSESSION	ASTONISHINGLY	FANTASTICALLY
VULNERABILITY	INDEPENDENTLY	PRESSURELOCAL	AUTOCEPHALOUS	GENERALISSIMO
WEATHERBEATEN	INSUBORDINATE	PSYCHOMETRICS	AUTOCHTHONOUS	GEOMETRICALLY
AMPLIFICATION	MERCHANDIZING	QUADRAGESIMAL	BIBLIOPHAGIST	GEOSTATIONARY
ANTICLOCKWISE	MULTITUDINOUS	QUARTODECIMAN	BLANDISHMENTS	GRAMMATICALLY
ARCHITECTURAL	OUTSTANDINGLY	RESOURCEFULLY	CALLISTHENICS	HYDRAULICALLY
ARISTROCRATIC	SEMICONDUCTOR	RETROGRESSION	COLLIESHANGIE	HYPERCRITICAL
BEATIFICATION	SUPERORDINATE	RETROSPECTIVE	DRYOPITHECINE	IGNOMINIOUSLY
CERTIFICATION	UNPRECEDENTED	ROUNDTHEWORLD	EPITRACHELION	IMPRACTICABLE
CLARIFICATION	ACCOUTREMENTS	SCHOOLTEACHER	GOODRIGHTEOUS	IMPRESSIONISM
CLISHMACLAVER	ANIMADVERSION	SELFGOVERNING	HAMMERTHROWER	IMPRESSIONIST
COMMUNICATION	BREASTFEEDING	SOMATOSENSORY	HYPERSTHENITE	INCONCEIVABLE
COMMUNICATIVE	BROKENHEARTED	SPONTANEOUSLY	ISOGEOTHERMAL	INCONSPICUOUS

INDEFATIGABLE	UNEXPERIENCED	THERMOPLASTIC	IMPERTINENTLY	INTENTIONALLY
INDEFATIGABLY	UNINHABITABLE	THOUGHTLESSLY	INCOMMUNICADO	MORPHOLOGICAL
INDESCRIBABLE	UNQUESTIONING	TRANQUILLISER	INCONVENIENCE	NONCONFORMIST
INDESCRIBABLY	VEGETARIANISM	TRANQUILLIZER	INCRIMINATING	NONCONFORMITY
INDUSTRIALIST	WEIGHTLIFTING	TRANSATLANTIC	INCRIMINATORY	OBJECTIONABLE
INDUSTRIALIZE	LEATHERJACKET	TRIANGULATION	INDISPENSABLE	PANHARMONICON
INDUSTRIOUSLY	PAINSTAKINGLY	TRIPLOBLASTIC	IRRESPONSIBLE	PHARMACOPOEIA
INEFFICIENTLY	TELEMARKETING	UNESTABLISHED	IRRESPONSIBLY	PHYSIOLOGICAL
INEXPERIENCED	ACCEPTILATION	UNINTELLIGENT	KANGCHENJUNGA	POLYCHROMATIC
INTRANSIGENCE	ARCHAEOLOGIST	APPROXIMATELY	LIECHTENSTEIN	POTENTIOMETER
INTRINSICALLY	ARMOURPLATING	APPROXIMATION	LIGHTFINGERED	PROFESSORSHIP
KIDDERMINSTER	CONSTELLATION	BASIDIOMYCETE	MISCEGENATION	PROVISIONALLY
LACKADAISICAL	CONTEMPLATION	CIRCUMAMBIENT	OPPORTUNISTIC	PSYCHOLOGICAL
LEPTOSPIROSIS	CONTEMPLATIVE	DECONTAMINATE	OPPORTUNITIES	PSYCHOSOMATIC
LISSOTRICHOUS	CRIMINOLOGIST	DEVELOPMENTAL	PASSCHENDAELE	REDEVELOPMENT
MISSISSIPPIAN	DEFIBRILLATOR	DISESTIMATION	PASSEMENTERIE	ROLLERCOASTER
NONSUFFICIENT	DERMATOLOGIST	ELECTROMAGNET	PELOPONNESIAN	RUTHERFORDIUM
NOSTALGICALLY	DISSIMILARITY	ELECTROMOTIVE	PEREGRINATION	SACCHAROMYCES
OUTRECUIDANCE	DISSIMULATION	ENVIRONMENTAL	PHYSIOGNOMIST	SANCTIMONIOUS
PARADOXICALLY	DOUBLEGLAZING	FRANKALMOIGNE	PREDOMINANTLY	SEISMOLOGICAL
PATRIOTICALLY	ENCEPHALOCELE	INDETERMINATE	PRELIMINARIES	SEMIAUTOMATIC
PERFECTIONIST	ENCEPHALOGRAM	INDETERMINISM	PRIMOGENITURE	SENSATIONALLY
PERPENDICULAR	EXPOSTULATION	MAGNANIMOUSLY	PSYCHOANALYSE	SOCIOECONOMIC
PHYSOSTIGMINE	EXTRAPOLATION	MICROCOMPUTER	PSYCHOANALYST	SPELEOLOGICAL
PNEUMATICALLY	GESTICULATION	NEUROCOMPUTER	PUSILLANIMITY	SPERMATOPHYTE
PRAGMATICALLY	GYNAECOLOGIST	OPHTHALMOLOGY	PUSILLANIMOUS	SUSPERCOLLATE
PRECAUTIONARY	HAMMERKLAVIER	PATERFAMILIAS	QUESTIONNAIRE	SWEDENBORGIAN
PREFABRICATED	HORRIPILATION	PHYSHARMONICA	RECRIMINATION	SYMPIESOMETER
PROFECTITIOUS	HORTICULTURAL	QUARTERMASTER	RECRIMINATORY	TABLESPOONFUL
PROJECTIONIST	IMPERIALISTIC	SCANDALMONGER	REINCARNATION	TAPERECORDING
PRONUNCIATION	INCREDULOUSLY	SERVILEMENTAL	REPREHENSIBLE	TECHNOLOGICAL
PROPHETICALLY	INTERCALATION	STATIONMASTER	REPREHENSIBLY	TENOSYNOVITIS
PROPORTIONATE	INTERPOLATION	SUBJECTMATTER	RHADAMANTHINE	THESSALONIANS
PROTECTIONISM	LEISURELINESS	SUPERNUMERARY	SENTIMENTALLY	TRADITIONALLY
PROTECTIONIST	MACHICOLATION	TEMPERAMENTAL	SNOWBLINDNESS	UNCEREMONIOUS
PROVINCIALISM	MATERIALISTIC	UPTOTHEMINUTE	SUBORDINATION	UNDERCLOTHING
PSYCHOBIOLOGY	MATRICULATION	WHOLESOMENESS	SUPERANNUATED	UNFASHIONABLE
PSYCHOKINESIS	METEOROLOGIST	ACCOMPANIMENT	THORACENTESIS	UNMENTIONABLE
PUNCTILIOUSLY	MONONUCLEOSIS	AFFENPINSCHER	THREATENINGLY	VENTRILOQUISM
REALISTICALLY	MONOTHALAMOUS	ANACHRONISTIC	TONGUEINCHEEK	VENTRILOQUIST
RECITATIONIST	MULTICOLOURED	APPROPINQUATE	UNACCOUNTABLE	ANTIGROPELOES
REDEMPTIONIST	NATIONALISTIC	ARCHIMANDRITE	UNACCOUNTABLY	ARCHAEOPTERYX
REVOLUTIONARY	NEMATHELMINTH	ASSASSINATION	UNCOMMUNICATE	BOUSTROPHEDON
REVOLUTIONIZE	ORNITHOLOGIST	BIOTECHNOLOGY	UNFORTUNATELY	COUNTRYPEOPLE
SARCASTICALLY	PANDICULATION	BIREFRINGENCE	UNIMAGINATIVE	ENCYCLOPAEDIA
SCHEMATICALLY	PAPAPRELATIST	CONCATENATION	UNPRETENTIOUS	ENCYCLOPAEDIC
SENTENTIOUSLY	PARALLELOGRAM	CONSCIENTIOUS	UNWILLINGNESS	EPANADIPLOSIS
SOPHISTICATED	PARTICOLOURED	CONSTERNATION	APPORTIONMENT	HYDROCEPHALUS
SPASMODICALLY	PARTICULARISE	CONTAMINATION	BACTERIOPHAGE	IMPERCEPTIBLE
SPINECHILLING	PARTICULARITY	DECRIMINALIZE	CHEESEMONGERS	IMPERCEPTIBLY
STAPHYLINIDAE	PARTICULARIZE	DENATIONALIZE	CHRONOLOGICAL	INAPPROPRIATE
STATISTICALLY	PATERNALISTIC	DETERMINATION	COMPANIONABLE	INCORRUPTIBLE
STRATEGICALLY	PERAMBULATION	DIFFERENTIATE	COMPANIONSHIP	JIGGERYPOKERY
STYLISTICALLY	PERSONALITIES	DISADVANTAGED	CONDITIONALLY	LAMPADEPHORIA
SUBMANDIBULAR	PHENCYCLIDINE	DISSEMINATION	CORRESPONDENT	LEPTOCEPHALUS
SUBSERVIENTLY	PHILADELPHIAN	ENTEROPNEUSTA	CORRESPONDING	MASTIGOPHORAN
SUPERSTITIOUS	PHOSPHOLIPASE	EXCOMMUNICATE	DEIPNOSOPHIST	METAMORPHOSIS
SURREPTITIOUS	QUADRUPLICATE	EXTERMINATION	DIACATHOLICON	PARTICIPATION
SYNTACTICALLY	RATIONALALITY	FERROCONCRETE	DISPROPORTION	PARTICIPATORY
SYNTHETICALLY	REMORSELESSLY	FRIGHTENINGLY	ENTOMOLOGICAL	PHILOSOPHICAL
THEOLOGICALLY	ROLLERBLADING	FUNDAMENTALLY	EPHEMEROPTERA	PLATOCEPHALUS
THEORETICALLY	SCHOLARLINESS	GASTROCNEMIUS	EPIPHENOMENON	PREOCCUPATION
TRACTARIANISM	SCINTILLATING	HALLUCINATION	ESCHSCHOLTZIA	TOPOGRAPHICAL
TRANSCRIPTION	SCINTILLATION	HALLUCINATORY	EXCEPTIONABLE	TYPOGRAPHICAL
TRAUMATICALLY	SIPUNCULOIDEA	HYALURONIDASE	EXCEPTIONALLY	UNACCOMPANIED
UNANTICIPATED	SPITESPLENDID	HYDRODYNAMICS	GLOBETROTTING	UNDISCIPLINED
UNCOMPLICATED	SPRIGHTLINESS	HYPOCHONDRIAC	GRANDILOQUENT	MAGNILOQUENCE
UNCONSCIOUSLY	STRANGULATION	IMPERSONATING	GYNANDROMORPH	ADVENTUROUSLY
UNCOORDINATED	TETRASYLLABIC	IMPERSONATION	GYNECOLOGICAL	AGGLOMERATION

BIBLIOGRAPHER
BLOODCURDLING
CHOREOGRAPHER
COLLABORATION
COLLABORATIVE
COMMEMORATION
COMMEMORATIVE
COMMISERATION
CONCENTRATION
CONFEDERATION
CONFIGURATION
CONFLAGRATION
CONSIDERATELY
CONSIDERATION
CORROBORATION
CORROBORATORY
DEMONSTRATION
DEMONSTRATIVE
DETERIORATION
DISCOLORATION
DISFIGUREMENT
DISINTERESTED
ENCULTURATION
GENITOURINARY
GLOSSOGRAPHER
GRANDPARENTAL
GRIEFSTRICKEN
HERMAPHRODITE
IMPERTURBABLE
IMPERTURBABLY
IMPONDERABLES
INCARCERATION
INCORPORATION
INDIFFERENTLY
INSUPPORTABLE
INTERMARRIAGE
INTERPERSONAL
LEXICOGRAPHER
LYCANTHROPIST
MAGISTERIALLY
MALLEMAROKING
MEDITERRANEAN
MIDDLEBREAKER
MISANTHROPIST
MISUNDERSTAND
MISUNDERSTOOD
NUCLEOPROTEIN
ORCHESTRATION
PAEDIATRICIAN
PARANTHROPOUS
PARAPHERNALIA
PREPROGRAMMED
PROLIFERATION
REFRIGERATION
REFRIGERATORS
REVERBERATION
SCLEROPROTEIN
SELFADDRESSED
SEPTENTRIONES
SEQUESTRATION
SHOULDERBLADE
SHRINKWRAPPED
SOMATOTROPHIN
STRIKEBREAKER
SUBCONTRACTOR
THIGMOTROPISM
TRANSPARENTLY
TRANSPIRATION
TRANSPORTABLE

TREACHEROUSLY
UNCOMFORTABLE
UNCOMFORTABLY
UNCOOPERATIVE
UNDERCARRIAGE
UNDERSTRAPPER
UNEMBARRASSED
UNINTERRUPTED
WITWATERSRAND
ADVERTISEMENT
AMPHIGASTRIUM
APOCATASTASIS
AUTHORISATION
BILDUNGSROMAN
BRACHIOSAURUS
BUSINESSWOMAN
CEPHALOSPORIN
CONCUPISCENCE
CONGRESSIONAL
CONGRESSWOMAN
CONVALESCENCE
DEATHLESSNESS
DECOMPOSITION
DEFERVESCENCE
DISILLUSIONED
EFFERVESCENCE
EFFLORESCENCE
EMBARRASSMENT
EMBELLISHMENT
ESTABLISHMENT
FERTILISATION
GUILTLESSNESS
IMPROVISATION
INCANDESCENCE
INCOMBUSTIBLE
INCONSISTENCY
INCONTESTABLE
INDISPOSITION
INEXHAUSTIBLE
INEXPRESSIBLE
INFLORESCENCE
INTRAMUSCULAR
IRREPRESSIBLE
JUXTAPOSITION
KALEIDOSCOPIC
MALADJUSTMENT
MEISTERSINGER
MERCILESSNESS
METAPHYSICIAN
NERVELESSNESS
NONRESISTANCE
NORTHEASTERLY
NORTHWESTERLY
PROCLEUSMATIC
PROGRESSIVELY
RECRUDESCENCE
REFURBISHMENT
REIMBURSEMENT
REPERCUSSIONS
REPLENISHMENT
SELFCONSCIOUS
SENSELESSNESS
SHAPELESSNESS
SLEEPLESSNESS
SOUTHEASTERLY
SOUTHWESTERLY
SPINDLESHANKS
SQUEAMISHNESS
STEADFASTNESS

THANKLESSNESS
THUNDERSTRUCK
TRANSPOSITION
UNIMPRESSIBLE
UNNECESSARILY
VICEPRESIDENT
VIDEOCASSETTE
ACUPUNCTURIST
ADMINISTRATOR
AFFIRMATIVELY
AFFORESTATION
AIRCRAFTWOMAN
ALPHABETARIAN
ALTERNATIVELY
ALUMINOTHERMY
ANTIHISTAMINE
ARGUMENTATIVE
ARITHMETICIAN
AUTHORITARIAN
AUTHORITATIVE
CHRYSANTHEMUM
CIRCUMSTANCES
COEDUCATIONAL
COMPARATIVELY
CONFRONTATION
CONSECUTIVELY
DEFORESTATION
DISHEARTENING
DOCUMENTATION
ELEPHANTIASIS
FORTUNETELLER
FRAGMENTATION
FREQUENTATIVE
GRAVITATIONAL
HYPOVENTILATE
IMAGINATIVELY
INADVERTENTLY
INCOMPETENTLY
INQUISITIVELY
INQUISITORIAL
INSENSITIVITY
INSPIRATIONAL
INSTINCTIVELY
INSTITUTIONAL
INSTRUCTIONAL
INTERESTINGLY
INTERNATIONAL
INVOLUNTARILY
LAEVOROTATORY
LEPIDOPTERIST
MANIFESTATION
MANUFACTURING
MATHEMATICIAN
MOUTHWATERING
MULTINATIONAL
NEANDERTHALER
NIGHTWATCHMAN
ORNAMENTATION
OVERSTATEMENT
PALAEONTOLOGY
PERFUNCTORILY
POLLICITATION
PRECIPITATELY
PRECIPITATION
PREMEDITATION
PROCRASTINATE
PROGNOSTICATE
PROPRIETORIAL
PROTONOTARIAT

PROVOCATIVELY
RADIOACTIVITY
RECALCITRANCE
REGIMENTATION
REGURGITATION
REINSTATEMENT
RESUSCITATION
SCHUTZSTAFFEL
SEDIMENTATION
SELFCONTAINED
SUBLIEUTENANT
SUBSTANTIALLY
SUPERLATIVELY
SUPRANATIONAL
TRANSISTORIZE
TRANSLITERATE
TRANSMUTATION
UNCONDITIONAL
UNDERESTIMATE
UNEXCEPTIONAL
UNFORGETTABLE
UNINTENTIONAL
UNPARTITIONED
UNSYMMETRICAL
UNSYMPATHETIC
BACCALAUREATE
BUNGEEJUMPING
COMMENSURABLE
CONCEPTUALIST
CONCEPTUALIZE
CONSANGUINITY
CONSCIOUSNESS
CONSPICUOUSLY
CONTRIBUTIONS
CREDULOUSNESS
DISHONOURABLE
DISHONOURABLY
DISTINGUISHED
FACETIOUSNESS
FORGETFULNESS
FRACTIOUSNESS
FRIGHTFULNESS
FRIVOLOUSNESS
GARRULOUSNESS
GRANDDAUGHTER
HOMOSEXUALITY
INDIVIDUALISM
INDIVIDUALIST
INDIVIDUALITY
INGENUOUSNESS
INSIDIOUSNESS
JURISPRUDENCE
LIEBFRAUMILCH
LUXURIOUSNESS
MASSACHUSETTS
NEIGHBOURHOOD
NIGHTCLUBBING
OFFICIOUSNESS
PHYLLOQUINONE
PROMISCUOUSLY
QUERULOUSNESS
RIGHTEOUSNESS
SALACIOUSNESS
SPECTACULARLY
STRENUOUSNESS
SUOVETAURILIA
SUPERABUNDANT
SUPERFLUOUSLY
THAUMATURGICS

THAUMATURGIST
THERMONUCLEAR
VIVACIOUSNESS
VORACIOUSNESS
ATTENTIVENESS
BOUGAINVILLEA
EFFECTIVENESS
EXPANSIVENESS
IMPULSIVENESS
INSECTIVOROUS
INVENTIVENESS
MISCHIEVOUSLY
OBJECTIVENESS
OFFENSIVENESS
PENNSYLVANIAN
PERVASIVENESS
RECEPTIVENESS
SECRETIVENESS
SENSITIVENESS
TALKATIVENESS
CRUISERWEIGHT
FEATHERWEIGHT
FOREKNOWLEDGE
HUNDREDWEIGHT
TONGUETWISTER
UNTRUSTWORTHY
HETERAUXESISM
HIEROGLYPHICS
IDIORRHYTHMIC
MONOCOTYLEDON
THERMODYNAMIC
AUTHORIZATION
CARBONIZATION
CAUTERIZATION
DRAMATIZATION
FERTILIZATION
FORMALIZATION
FOSSILIZATION
GALVANIZATION
HARMONIZATION
HYBRIDIZATION
MECHANIZATION
MODERNIZATION
NORMALIZATION
PRIVATIZATION
PULVERIZATION
SOLEMNIZATION
STABILIZATION
STERILIZATION
TANTALIZINGLY
VICTIMIZATION
VULCANIZATION
VULGARIZATION

13:9

ACCEPTILATION
ACCOMMODATING
ACCOMMODATION
AFFORESTATION
AGGLOMERATION
ALPHABETARIAN
AMPLIFICATION
ANTIHISTAMINE
ANYTHINGARIAN
APPROPRIATION
APPROXIMATELY
APPROXIMATION
AQUIFOLIACEAE
ARGUMENTATIVE

ARMOURPLATING
ARTIFICIALITY
ASSASSINATION
AUTHORISATION
AUTHORITARIAN
AUTHORITATIVE
AUTHORIZATION
AUTOCEPHALOUS
BEATIFICATION
BIBLIOGRAPHER
BIBLIOPHAGIST
BOUILLABAISSE
BRACHIOSAURUS
BROKENHEARTED
CARBONIZATION
CAUTERIZATION
CERTIFICATION
CHOREOGRAPHER
CIRCUMSTANCES
CLARIFICATION
COLLABORATION
COLLABORATIVE
COLLIESHANGIE
COLLOQUIALISM
COMMEMORATION
COMMEMORATIVE
COMMERCIALIZE
COMMISERATION
COMMUNICATION
COMMUNICATIVE
CONCATENATION
CONCENTRATION
CONCEPTUALIST
CONCEPTUALIZE
CONFARREATION
CONFEDERATION
CONFIGURATION
CONFLAGRATION
CONFRONTATION
CONSIDERATELY
CONSIDERATION
CONSOLIDATION
CONSPURCATION
CONSTELLATION
CONSTERNATION
CONTAMINATION
CONTEMPLATION
CONTEMPLATIVE
CORROBORATION
CORROBORATORY
DECRIMINALIZE
DEFORESTATION
DEMONSTRATION
DEMONSTRATIVE
DENATIONALIZE
DESEGREGATION
DETERIORATION
DETERMINATION
DIFFARREATION
DISCOLORATION
DISESTIMATION
DISSEMINATION
DISSIMILARITY
DISSIMULATION
DOCUMENTATION
DOUBLEGLAZING
DRAMATIZATION
ELECTROMAGNET
ENCULTURATION

ENCYCLOPAEDIA
ENCYCLOPAEDIC
EXPOSTULATION
EXPROPRIATION
EXTERMINATION
EXTRAPOLATION
EXTRAVAGANTLY
FALSIFICATION
FERTILISATION
FERTILIZATION
FLABBERGASTED
FORMALIZATION
FORTIFICATION
FOSSILIZATION
FRAGMENTATION
FREQUENTATIVE
GALVANIZATION
GESTICULATION
GLORIFICATION
GLOSSOGRAPHER
GRATIFICATION
HALLUCINATION
HALLUCINATORY
HAMMERKLAVIER
HARMONIZATION
HEARTBREAKING
HOMOSEXUALITY
HORRIPILATION
HOUSEBREAKING
HYBRIDIZATION
HYDRODYNAMICS
IMPERSONATING
IMPERSONATION
IMPONDERABLES
IMPROVISATION
INCARCERATION
INCORPORATION
INCRIMINATING
INCRIMINATORY
INDIVIDUALISM
INDIVIDUALIST
INDIVIDUALITY
INDUSTRIALIST
INDUSTRIALIZE
INTERCALATION
INTERPOLATION
INTERROGATION
INTERROGATIVE
INVESTIGATION
INVESTIGATIVE
INVOLUNTARILY
JOLLIFICATION
JUSTIFICATION
JUSTIFICATORY
LAEVOROTATORY
LEATHERJACKET
LEXICOGRAPHER
MACHICOLATION
MADETOMEASURE
MAGNIFICATION
MANIFESTATION
MATRICULATION
MECHANIZATION
MEDITERRANEAN
MICROORGANISM
MISCEGENATION
MODERNIZATION
MOLLIFICATION
MONOTHALAMOUS

MORTIFICATION
MYSTIFICATION
NORMALIZATION
NULLIFICATION
ORCHESTRATION
ORNAMENTATION
OVEREMPHASIZE
PANDICULATION
PAPAPRELATIST
PARTICIPATION
PARTICIPATORY
PARTICULARISE
PARTICULARITY
PARTICULARIZE
PENNSYLVANIAN
PERAMBULATION
PEREGRINATION
PETRIFICATION
POLLICITATION
PRECIPITATELY
PRECIPITATION
PREDOMINANTLY
PRELIMINARIES
PREMEDITATION
PREOCCUPATION
PREPROGRAMMED
PREVARICATION
PRIVATIZATION
PROLIFERATION
PRONUNCIATION
PROTONOTARIAT
PROVINCIALISM
PSYCHOANALYSE
PSYCHOANALYST
PULVERIZATION
QUALIFICATION
QUARTERMASTER
RATIONALALITY
RECRIMINATION
RECRIMINATORY
RECTIFICATION
REFRIGERATION
REFRIGERATORS
REGIMENTATION
REGURGITATION
REINCARNATION
REPUBLICANISM
RESUSCITATION
REUNIFICATION
REVERBERATION
ROLLERBLADING
ROLLERCOASTER
SCHOOLTEACHER
SCHUTZSTAFFEL
SCINTILLATING
SCINTILLATION
SEDIMENTATION
SELFCONTAINED
SEQUESTRATION
SHRINKWRAPPED
SIGNIFICANTLY
SIGNIFICATION
SOLEMNIZATION
SPECIFICATION
STABILIZATION
STATIONMASTER
STERILIZATION
STRANGULATION
STREPTOCARPUS

SUBCONTRACTOR
SUBJECTMATTER
SUBORDINATION
TENDERHEARTED
THEATRICALLY
THERMOPLASTIC
TRACTARIANISM
TRANSATLANTIC
TRANSMUTATION
TRANSPIRATION
TRIANGULATION
TRIPLOBLASTIC
UNACCOMPANIED
UNCOOPERATIVE
UNDERSTRAPPER
UNEMBARRASSED
UNFORTUNATELY
UNIMAGINATIVE
UNNECESSARILY
VEGETARIANISM
VERSIFICATION
VICTIMIZATION
VITRIFICATION
VULCANIZATION
VULGARIZATION
CIRCUMAMBIENT
FONTAINEBLEAU
IMPERTURBABLE
IMPERTURBABLY
INDESCRIBABLE
INDESCRIBABLY
NIGHTCLUBBING
SHOULDERBLADE
SUBMANDIBULAR
THOROUGHBRACE
TINTINNABULUM
AESTHETICALLY
ARUNDINACEOUS
AUTOMATICALLY
CATEGORICALLY
CONCUPISCENCE
CONTRADICTION
CONTRADICTORY
CONVALESCENCE
COSTEFFECTIVE
COUNTERACTING
DEFERVESCENCE
DIAMETRICALLY
DISCONNECTION
DISRESPECTFUL
ECCENTRICALLY
EFFERVESCENCE
EFFLORESCENCE
ENERGETICALLY
FANTASTICALLY
FERROCONCRETE
GEOMETRICALLY
GRAMMATICALLY
HYDRAULICALLY
HYDROELECTRIC
IMPRACTICABLE
INCANDESCENCE
INCONSPICUOUS
INFLORESCENCE
INTRAMUSCULAR
INTRINSICALLY
INTROSPECTION
INTROSPECTIVE
KALEIDOSCOPIC

KNICKKNACKERY
LISSOTRICHOUS
NIGHTWATCHMAN
NONSUFFICIENT
NOSTALGICALLY
PARADOXICALLY
PATRIOTICALLY
PERPENDICULAR
PERSPICACIOUS
PHOTOELECTRIC
PNEUMATICALLY
PNEUMONECTOMY
PRAGMATICALLY
PREFABRICATED
PROPHETICALLY
QUARTODECIMAN
REALISTICALLY
RECRUDESCENCE
RETROSPECTIVE
SARCASTICALLY
SCHEMATICALLY
SELFCONSCIOUS
SOPHISTICATED
SPASMODICALLY
STATISTICALLY
STERCORACEOUS
STRATEGICALLY
STYLISTICALLY
SYNTACTICALLY
SYNTHETICALLY
THEOLOGICALLY
THEORETICALLY
THERMONUCLEAR
THYROIDECTOMY
TONGUEINCHEEK
TONSILLECTOMY
TRAUMATICALLY
UNCOMPLICATED
ARCHIMANDRITE
BIODEGRADABLE
BLOODCURDLING
CONTENTEDNESS
HYPOCHONDRIAC
JURISPRUDENCE
OUTRECUIDANCE
PASSCHENDAELE
SNOWBLINDNESS
UNDERGRADUATE
ADVERTISEMENT
ALUMINIFEROUS
ANTIGROPELOES
ATTENTIVENESS
BREASTFEEDING
BUTYRALDEHYDE
CALLISTHENICS
CARBONIFEROUS
COUNTERFEITER
COUNTRYPEOPLE
CRUISERWEIGHT
DEHYDROGENATE
DÉSOBLIGEANTE
DEVELOPMENTAL
DISENGAGEMENT
DISFIGUREMENT
DISHEARTENING
DISINTERESTED
DISPARAGEMENT
DRYOPITHECINE
EFFECTIVENESS

ENCOURAGEMENT	THOUGHTLESSLY	CLAIRAUDIENCE	PHENCYCLIDINE	BLANDISHMENTS
ENTEROPNEUSTA	TRANSLITERATE	COEDUCATIONAL	PHOSPHOLIPASE	BUNGEEJUMPING
ENVIRONMENTAL	TRANSPARENTLY	COMPARABILITY	PHYLLOQUINONE	EPIPHENOMENON
EPITRACHELION	UMBELLIFEROUS	COMPARATIVELY	PRIMOGENITURE	GYNANDROMORPH
EQUIPONDERATE	UNEXPERIENCED	COMPATIBILITY	PROCRASTINATE	LIEBFRAUMILCH
EXPANSIVENESS	UNFORESEEABLE	CONGRESSIONAL	PROFITABILITY	NEMATHELMINTH
FEATHERWEIGHT	UNPRECEDENTED	CONSANGUINITY	PROGNOSTICATE	PETROCHEMICAL
FORTUNETELLER	UNSERVICEABLE	CONSECUTIVELY	PROGRESSIVELY	PHOTOCHEMICAL
GASTROCNEMIUS	WEATHERBEATEN	DECOMPOSITION	PROVOCATIVELY	POLYCHROMATIC
GRANDPARENTAL	WHOLESOMENESS	DECONTAMINATE	PUSILLANIMITY	POTENTIOMETER
HETERAUXESISM	DISGRACEFULLY	DEFENSIBILITY	PUSILLANIMOUS	PROCLEUSMATIC
HUNDREDWEIGHT	REPROACHFULLY	DEPENDABILITY	QUADRUPLICATE	PSYCHOSOMATIC
HYPERSTHENITE	RESOURCEFULLY	DISILLUSIONED	RADIOACTIVITY	SACCHAROMYCES
IMPERTINENTLY	WEIGHTLIFTING	DISTINGUISHED	SCHOLARLINESS	SEMIAUTOMATIC
IMPROVIDENTLY	BIREFRINGENCE	ELEPHANTIASIS	SELFCONFIDENT	SYMPIESOMETER
IMPULSIVENESS	CHRONOLOGICAL	EXCOMMUNICATE	SEPTENTRIONES	UNGENTLEMANLY
INADVERTENTLY	CONTRAFAGOTTO	EXTRAORDINARY	SPRIGHTLINESS	ANTHELMINTHIC
INCOMPETENTLY	ENTOMOLOGICAL	FRIGHTENINGLY	SUBSTANTIALLY	APPORTIONMENT
INCONSIDERATE	GRANDDAUGHTER	GENITOURINARY	SUPERFICIALLY	ASCERTAINABLE
INDEPENDENTLY	GYNECOLOGICAL	GRAVITATIONAL	SUPERLATIVELY	BUTTERFINGERS
INDIFFERENTLY	INDEFATIGABLE	GRIEFSTRICKEN	SUPERORDINATE	CHEESEMONGERS
INEFFICIENTLY	INDEFATIGABLY	HYALURONIDASE	SUPRANATIONAL	CHINKERINCHEE
INEXPERIENCED	INTRANSIGENCE	HYPOVENTILATE	TANTALIZINGLY	CIRCUMVENTION
INTELLIGENTLY	LIGHTFINGERED	IMAGINATIVELY	THREATENINGLY	COMPANIONABLE
INVENTIVENESS	MORPHOLOGICAL	IMPERIALISTIC	TONGUETWISTER	COMPANIONSHIP
IRREPLACEABLE	PHYSIOLOGICAL	IMPOSSIBILITY	TRANSPOSITION	COMPLEMENTARY
ISOGEOTHERMAL	PHYSOSTIGMINE	IMPROBABILITY	UNCOMMUNICATE	COMPLIMENTARY
KNOWLEDGEABLE	PSYCHOLOGICAL	INCOMMUNICADO	UNCONDITIONAL	COMPREHENSION
LEPIDOPTERIST	SEISMOLOGICAL	INCONVENIENCE	UNDERACHIEVER	COMPREHENSIVE
LONGSUFFERING	SPELEOLOGICAL	INDETERMINATE	UNDERESTIMATE	COMRADEINARMS
MAGNIFICENTLY	TECHNOLOGICAL	INDETERMINISM	UNESTABLISHED	CONDESCENDING
MIDDLEBREAKER	THOROUGHGOING	INDISPOSITION	UNEXCEPTIONAL	CONDESCENSION
MISMANAGEMENT	UNWILLINGNESS	INEVITABILITY	UNFLINCHINGLY	CONDITIONALLY
MONONUCLEOSIS	ALUMINOTHERMY	INFALLIBILITY	UNINTELLIGENT	CONSECTANEOUS
MOUTHWATERING	BOUSTROPHEDON	INFLEXIBILITY	UNINTENTIONAL	CONSEQUENTIAL
OBJECTIVENESS	CHRYSANTHEMUM	INQUISITIVELY	UNPARTITIONED	CONTRAVENTION
OFFENSIVENESS	COUNTERCHARGE	INSENSITIVITY	UPTOTHEMINUTE	CORRESPONDENT
OVERSTATEMENT	EMBELLISHMENT	INSIGNIFICANT	VICEPRESIDENT	CORRESPONDING
PELOPONNESIAN	ESTABLISHMENT	INSPIRATIONAL	VULNERABILITY	CRAFTSMANSHIP
PERVASIVENESS	HYDROCEPHALUS	INSTINCTIVELY	KANGCHENJUNGA	DECAFFEINATED
PHYSIOTHERAPY	LAMPADEPHORIA	INSTITUTIONAL	ANTICLOCKWISE	DISAPPOINTING
PRONOUNCEMENT	LEPTOCEPHALUS	INSTRUCTIONAL	SWASHBUCKLING	DISCONTINUITY
PSYCHOTHERAPY	MASTIGOPHORAN	INSUBORDINATE	CLISHMACLAVER	DISCONTINUOUS
QUINQUAGESIMA	MESSERSCHMITT	INSUFFICIENCY	CRYPTANALYSIS	ENLIGHTENMENT
RAPPROCHEMENT	METAMORPHOSIS	INTERESTINGLY	DEFIBRILLATOR	ENTERTAINMENT
REARRANGEMENT	NEANDERTHALER	INTERNATIONAL	DIACATHOLICON	EXCEPTIONABLE
RECEPTIVENESS	PHILOSOPHICAL	INVINCIBILITY	EPANADIPLOSIS	EXCEPTIONALLY
REIMBURSEMENT	PLATOCEPHALUS	INVIOLABILITY	ESCHSCHOLTZIA	FUERTEVENTURA
REINFORCEMENT	REFURBISHMENT	JUXTAPOSITION	FOREKNOWLEDGE	HETEROGENEOUS
REINSTATEMENT	REPLENISHMENT	KAPPELMEISTER	FORGETFULNESS	INSTANTANEOUS
REMINISCENCES	SPINDLESHANKS	LEISURELINESS	FRIGHTFULNESS	INSUBSTANTIAL
REMORSELESSLY	SQUEAMISHNESS	MAGISTERIALLY	GLUMDALCLITCH	INTENTIONALLY
RENSSELAERITE	STEEPLECHASER	MATERIALISTIC	MACHIAVELLIAN	KIDDERMINSTER
SECRETIVENESS	TOPOGRAPHICAL	MATHEMATICIAN	MONOCOTYLEDON	LIBRARIANSHIP
SELFADDRESSED	TYPOGRAPHICAL	MEISTERSINGER	MULTINUCLEATE	MISCELLANEOUS
SELFCONFESSED	UNIMPEACHABLE	MERCHANDIZING	PASSIONFLOWER	MOCKTECHNICAL
SEMBLANCECORD	UNSYMPATHETIC	METAPHYSICIAN	PEPTIDOGLYCAN	OBJECTIONABLE
SENSITIVENESS	ACCEPTABILITY	MULTINATIONAL	POLIOMYELITIS	PANHARMONICON
SERVILEMENTAL	ACCESSIBILITY	MULTITUDINOUS	PRESSURELOCAL	PARAPHERNALIA
SPITESPLENDID	ACCOMPANIMENT	NATIONALISTIC	SPECTACULARLY	PARLIAMENTARY
STOCKBREEDING	AFFIRMATIVELY	OPPORTUNISTIC	SPINECHILLING	PARTHOGENESIS
STRIKEBREAKER	AIRWORTHINESS	OPPORTUNITIES	SUSPERCOLLATE	PHYTOPLANKTON
SUBLIEUTENANT	ALTERNATIVELY	OUTSTANDINGLY	SWEETSMELLING	PROTESTANTISM
SUBSERVIENTLY	ANACHRONISTIC	PAEDIATRICIAN	TETRASYLLABIC	PROVISIONALLY
SUPERNUMERARY	ARITHMETICIAN	PAINSTAKINGLY	TRANQUILLISER	PSYCHOKINESIS
SWOLLENHEADED	ASTONISHINGLY	PATERFAMILIAS	TRANQUILLIZER	PYROTECHNICAL
TALKATIVENESS	BOUGAINVILLEA	PATERNALISTIC	UNDISCIPLINED	QUESTIONNAIRE
TELEMARKETING	CARTILAGINOUS	PENETRABILITY	ACCOUTREMENTS	SANCTIMONIOUS
TEMPERAMENTAL	CHANGEABILITY	PERSONALITIES	AGGIORNAMENTO	SENSATIONALLY

843

SOCIOECONOMIC	PARALLELOGRAM	CLOSEDCIRCUIT	LUXURIOUSNESS	PARENTHETICAL
SOMATOSENSORY	PARANTHROPOUS	COMMENSURABLE	MASSACHUSETTS	PASSEMENTERIE
SPORTSMANLIKE	PARTICOLOURED	CONTROVERSIAL	MERCILESSNESS	PRESERVATIVES
SPORTSMANSHIP	PERFECTIONIST	DEMILITARIZED	MISUNDERSTAND	PRETERNATURAL
STAPHYLINIDAE	PERFUNCTORILY	DISAPPEARANCE	MISUNDERSTOOD	PROBLEMATICAL
STATESMANLIKE	PHYSHARMONICA	DISCONCERTING	NERVELESSNESS	PROFECTITIOUS
STATESMANSHIP	PHYSIOGNOMIST	DISHONOURABLE	OFFICIOUSNESS	PSYCHOMETRICS
SUPERABUNDANT	PRECAUTIONARY	DISHONOURABLY	PREPOSSESSING	QUADRILATERAL
SUPPLEMENTARY	PROJECTIONIST	DISPROPORTION	PREPOSSESSION	RAMIFICATIONS
THERMODYNAMIC	PROMISCUOUSLY	FOSTERPARENTS	QUADRAGESIMAL	RHADAMANTHINE
THESSALONIANS	PROPORTIONATE	HAMMERTHROWER	QUERULOUSNESS	SENTIMENTALLY
TRADITIONALLY	PROPRIETORIAL	HEMISPHERICAL	REPERCUSSIONS	SOUTHEASTERLY
TRICHOSANTHIN	PROTECTIONISM	IDIOSYNCRATIC	REPREHENSIBLE	SOUTHWESTERLY
UNCEREMONIOUS	PROTECTIONIST	INAPPROPRIATE	REPREHENSIBLY	STEADFASTNESS
UNCOORDINATED	PSYCHOBIOLOGY	INTERMARRIAGE	RETROGRESSION	SUPERSTITIOUS
UNDERSTANDING	PUNCTILIOUSLY	IRRECOVERABLE	RIGHTEOUSNESS	SURREPTITIOUS
UNFASHIONABLE	RECITATIONIST	LECTISTERNIUM	SALACIOUSNESS	THORACENTESIS
UNMENTIONABLE	REDEMPTIONIST	LEPTOSPIROSIS	SENSELESSNESS	THUNDERSTRUCK
UNSUBSTANTIAL	REVOLUTIONARY	NEIGHBOURHOOD	SHAPELESSNESS	TRANSPORTABLE
ADVENTUROUSLY	REVOLUTIONIZE	NONCONFORMIST	SLEEPLESSNESS	UNACCOUNTABLE
ALLOCHTHONOUS	SCANDALMONGER	NONCONFORMITY	STEPPINGSTONE	UNACCOUNTABLY
ARCHAEOLOGIST	SCLEROPROTEIN	PHILANTHROPIC	STRENUOUSNESS	UNCOMFORTABLE
AUTOCHTHONOUS	SENTENTIOUSLY	PREPONDERANCE	THANKLESSNESS	UNCOMFORTABLY
BIOTECHNOLOGY	SIPUNCULOIDEA	PROFESSORSHIP	TORTOISESHELL	UNDERCLOTHING
CEREMONIOUSLY	SOMATOTROPHIN	PROSOPOGRAPHY	TRANSGRESSION	UNENLIGHTENED
COMPASSIONATE	SPONTANEOUSLY	RECALCITRANCE	UNIMPRESSIBLE	UNFORGETTABLE
CONCEPTIONIST	STREPTOCOCCUS	RHYPAROGRAPHY	UNINTERESTING	UNGRAMMATICAL
CONCESSIONARY	SUPERFLUOUSLY	RUTHERFORDIUM	UNPROGRESSIVE	UNINHABITABLE
CONFECTIONERS	TABLESPOONFUL	SCHADENFREUDE	VIDEOCASSETTE	UNPREDICTABLE
CONFECTIONERY	THIGMOTROPISM	SCHIZOPHRENIA	VIVACIOUSNESS	UNPRETENTIOUS
CONSPICUOUSLY	TRANSISTORIZE	SCHIZOPHRENIC	VORACIOUSNESS	VERCINGETORIX
CONTORTIONIST	TREACHEROUSLY	SELFGOVERNING	WITWATERSRAND	ACUPUNCTURIST
CRIMINOLOGIST	UNCONSCIOUSLY	SKATEBOARDING	XIPHIPLASTRON	ANTICOAGULANT
DAGUERREOTYPE	UNQUESTIONING	SPECTROGRAPHY	ACRYLONITRILE	ELECTROCUTION
DERMATOLOGIST	UNTRUSTWORTHY	SUOVETAURILIA	AFFREIGHTMENT	MAGNILOQUENCE
DISCRETIONARY	VIDEORECORDER	SWEDENBORGIAN	AMPHIGASTRIUM	MANUFACTURING
DISPASSIONATE	BACTERIOPHAGE	TAPERECORDING	APOCATASTASIS	MAURIKIGUSARI
ELECTROMOTIVE	CEPHALOSPORIN	THAUMATURGICS	ARCHAEOPTERYX	OWNEROCCUPIER
ENCEPHALOCELE	CONTRACEPTION	THAUMATURGIST	ARCHITECTURAL	SEMICONDUCTOR
ENCEPHALOGRAM	CONTRACEPTIVE	UNADULTERATED	CONSCIENTIOUS	SUPERANNUATED
EXHIBITIONIST	DEIPNOSOPHIST	UNCONQUERABLE	CONSERVATOIRE	UNINTERRUPTED
EXPEDITIONARY	EPHEMEROPTERA	UNDERCARRIAGE	CONTINUATIONS	INCONCEIVABLE
EXPEDITIOUSLY	HIEROGLYPHICS	UNSYMMETRICAL	CONTRIBUTIONS	IRRETRIEVABLE
FRANKALMOIGNE	MICROCOMPUTER	AFFENPINSCHER	COUNTERATTACK	IRRETRIEVABLY
GEOSTATIONARY	MISCONCEPTION	CHRISTMASTIME	DIFFERENTIATE	TENOSYNOVITIS
GYNAECOLOGIST	MISSISSIPPIAN	CONSCIOUSNESS	DISADVANTAGED	AIRCRAFTWOMAN
HERMAPHRODITE	NEUROCOMPUTER	CONTRABASSOON	DISCREDITABLE	BUSINESSWOMAN
IGNOMINIOUSLY	PHARMACOPOEIA	CREDULOUSNESS	DISCREDITABLY	CONGRESSWOMAN
IMPRESSIONISM	PHILADELPHIAN	CROSSQUESTION	FUNDAMENTALLY	ROUNDTHEWORLD
IMPRESSIONIST	PRECONCEPTION	DEATHLESSNESS	GLOBETROTTING	BASIDIOMYCETE
INCREDULOUSLY	REDEVELOPMENT	DECOMPRESSION	GOODRIGHTEOUS	CONVERSAZIONE
INDUSTRIOUSLY	REPROGRAPHICS	EMBARRASSMENT	HORSEFEATHERS	
INQUISITORIAL	SPERMATOPHYTE	FACETIOUSNESS	HORTICULTURAL	**13:10**
INSECTIVOROUS	TRANSCRIPTION	FRACTIOUSNESS	HYPERCRITICAL	
JIGGERYPOKERY	UNANTICIPATED	FRIVOLOUSNESS	IDIORRHYTHMIC	ADMINISTRATOR
KNICKERBOCKER	APPROPINQUATE	GARRULOUSNESS	ILLUMINATIONS	AESTHETICALLY
LYCANTHROPIST	GRANDILOQUENT	GENERALISSIMO	IMPERCEPTIBLE	APOCATASTASIS
MAGNANIMOUSLY	VENTRILOQUISM	GUILTLESSNESS	IMPERCEPTIBLY	ARISTROCRATIC
MALLEMAROKING	VENTRILOQUIST	INDISPENSABLE	INCOMBUSTIBLE	ASCERTAINABLE
METAGRABOLISE	ADMINISTRATOR	INEXPRESSIBLE	INCONSISTENCY	AUTOBIOGRAPHY
METAGROBOLISE	ANIMADVERSION	INFINITESIMAL	INCONTESTABLE	AUTOMATICALLY
METEOROLOGIST	ARISTROCRATIC	INGENUOUSNESS	INCORRUPTIBLE	BIODEGRADABLE
MISANTHROPIST	AUTOBIOGRAPHY	INSIDIOUSNESS	INEXHAUSTIBLE	CATEGORICALLY
MISCHIEVOUSLY	BACCALAUREATE	INTERPERSONAL	INSUPPORTABLE	CLISHMACLAVER
MULTICOLOURED	BILDUNGSROMAN	IRREPRESSIBLE	MALADJUSTMENT	COMMENSURABLE
NUCLEOPROTEIN	CHARACTERISED	IRRESPONSIBLE	NONRESISTANCE	COMPANIONABLE
OPHTHALMOLOGY	CHARACTERLESS	IRRESPONSIBLY	NORTHEASTERLY	COMRADEINARMS
ORNITHOLOGIST	CHATEAUBRIAND	LACKADAISICAL	NORTHWESTERLY	CONDITIONALLY
PALAEONTOLOGY	CIRCUMFERENCE	LIECHTENSTEIN	OYSTERCATCHER	COUNTERCHARGE
				DECAFFEINATED

DEFIBRILLATOR	SENSATIONALLY	STREPTOCOCCUS	SOUTHEASTERLY	INCOMBUSTIBLE
DÉSOBLIGEANTE	SENTIMENTALLY	SUBCONTRACTOR	SOUTHWESTERLY	INCORRUPTIBLE
DIAMETRICALLY	SOPHISTICATED	UNCOMMUNICATE	STERCORACEOUS	INEXHAUSTIBLE
DISADVANTAGED	SPASMODICALLY	BREASTFEEDING	SYMPIESOMETER	INEXPRESSIBLE
DISAPPEARANCE	SPECTACULARLY	CONDESCENDING	THORACENTESIS	INFINITESIMAL
DISCREDITABLE	SPECTROGRAPHY	CORRESPONDENT	UNDERACHIEVER	INTERMARRIAGE
DISCREDITABLY	SPINDLESHANKS	CORRESPONDING	UNENLIGHTENED	IRREPRESSIBLE
DISHONOURABLE	STATISTICALLY	HERMAPHRODITE	UNSYMPATHETIC	IRRESPONSIBLE
DISHONOURABLY	STEEPLECHASER	HYALURONIDASE	VIDEOCASSETTE	IRRESPONSIBLY
ECCENTRICALLY	STRATEGICALLY	PHENCYCLIDINE	SCHUTZSTAFFEL	LACKADAISICAL
ELEPHANTIASIS	STRIKEBREAKER	ROLLERBLADING	ARCHAEOLOGIST	LIEBFRAUMILCH
ENERGETICALLY	STYLISTICALLY	RUTHERFORDIUM	BIBLIOPHAGIST	MOCKTECHNICAL
EXCEPTIONABLE	SUBSTANTIALLY	SELFCONFIDENT	BUTTERFINGERS	MORPHOLOGICAL
EXCEPTIONALLY	SUPERANNUATED	SKATEBOARDING	CHEESEMONGERS	NEMATHELMINTH
FANTASTICALLY	SUPERFICIALLY	STOCKBREEDING	CRIMINOLOGIST	NONSUFFICIENT
FUNDAMENTALLY	SWOLLENHEADED	SUPERABUNDANT	DERMATOLOGIST	PANHARMONICON
GEOMETRICALLY	SYNTACTICALLY	TAPERECORDING	ELECTROMAGNET	PARENTHETICAL
GRAMMATICALLY	SYNTHETICALLY	UNDERSTANDING	ENCEPHALOGRAM	PERSPICACIOUS
HYDRAULICALLY	TETRASYLLABIC	VICEPRESIDENT	GYNAECOLOGIST	PETROCHEMICAL
HYDROCEPHALUS	THEOLOGICALLY	ACCOUTREMENTS	METEOROLOGIST	PHILOSOPHICAL
IDIOSYNCRATIC	THEORETICALLY	AGGIORNAMENTO	ORNITHOLOGIST	PHOTOCHEMICAL
IMPERTURBABLE	THERMODYNAMIC	ALUMINOTHERMY	PARALLELOGRAM	PHYSIOLOGICAL
IMPERTURBABLY	TRADITIONALLY	ARCHAEOPTERYX	SWEDENBORGIAN	POLIOMYELITIS
IMPRACTICABLE	TRANSPORTABLE	ARUNDINACEOUS	THAUMATURGICS	PRESERVATIVES
INCONCEIVABLE	TRAUMATICALLY	BACCALAUREATE	THAUMATURGIST	PROBLEMATICAL
INCONTESTABLE	UNACCOUNTABLE	BIREFRINGENCE	UNINTELLIGENT	PROFECTITIOUS
INDEFATIGABLE	UNACCOUNTABLY	BLANDISHMENTS	BACTERIOPHAGE	PSYCHOLOGICAL
INDEFATIGABLY	UNADULTERATED	BOUSTROPHEDON	BUTYRALDEHYDE	PYROTECHNICAL
INDESCRIBABLE	UNANTICIPATED	CHRYSANTHEMUM	DEIPNOSOPHIST	QUADRAGESIMAL
INDESCRIBABLY	UNCOMFORTABLE	CIRCUMFERENCE	GRANDDAUGHTER	QUARTODECIMAN
INDISPENSABLE	UNCOMFORTABLY	CLAIRAUDIENCE	HIEROGLYPHICS	RAMIFICATIONS
INSUPPORTABLE	UNCOMPLICATED	CONCUPISCENCE	HORSEFEATHERS	REPERCUSSIONS
INTENTIONALLY	UNCONQUERABLE	CONSECTANEOUS	IDIORRHYTHMIC	REPREHENSIBLE
INTRINSICALLY	UNCOORDINATED	CONVALESCENCE	LISSOTRICHOUS	REPREHENSIBLY
IRRECOVERABLE	UNFASHIONABLE	DEFERVESCENCE	NEIGHBOURHOOD	SANCTIMONIOUS
IRREPLACEABLE	UNFORESEEABLE	EFFERVESCENCE	NIGHTWATCHMAN	SEISMOLOGICAL
IRRETRIEVABLE	UNFORGETTABLE	EFFLORESCENCE	PHILADELPHIAN	SELFCONSCIOUS
IRRETRIEVABLY	UNGENTLEMANLY	ENCYCLOPAEDIA	REPROGRAPHICS	SELFCONTAINED
KNOWLEDGEABLE	UNIMPEACHABLE	ENCYCLOPAEDIC	RHADAMANTHINE	SIPUNCULOIDEA
LEPTOCEPHALUS	UNINHABITABLE	EPIPHENOMENON	SPERMATOPHYTE	SPELEOLOGICAL
MAGISTERIALLY	UNMENTIONABLE	FOREKNOWLEDGE	TONGUEINCHEEK	STAPHYLINIDAE
MIDDLEBREAKER	UNPREDICTABLE	FOSTERPARENTS	TORTOISESHELL	SUOVETAURILIA
NEANDERTHALER	UNSERVICEABLE	GOODRIGHTEOUS	UNDERCLOTHING	SUPERSTITIOUS
NONRESISTANCE	WEATHERBEATEN	HETEROGENEOUS	BOUILLABAISSE	SURREPTITIOUS
NOSTALGICALLY	IMPONDERABLES	INCANDESCENCE	CHARACTERISED	TECHNOLOGICAL
OBJECTIONABLE	NIGHTCLUBBING	INCONSISTENCY	CHATEAUBRIAND	TENOSYNOVITIS
OUTRECUIDANCE	AFFENPINSCHER	INCONVENIENCE	CHRONOLOGICAL	THESSALONIANS
PARADOXICALLY	AQUIFOLIACEAE	INFLORESCENCE	CIRCUMAMBIENT	TOPOGRAPHICAL
PARAPHERNALIA	ARITHMETICIAN	INSTANTANEOUS	CONSCIENTIOUS	TRANQUILLISER
PASSCHENDAELE	BASIDIOMYCETE	INSUFFICIENCY	CONTINUATIONS	TRANQUILLIZER
PATRIOTICALLY	CHINKERINCHEE	INTRANSIGENCE	CONTRIBUTIONS	TYPOGRAPHICAL
PLATOCEPHALUS	CLOSEDCIRCUIT	JURISPRUDENCE	CONVERSAZIONE	UNCEREMONIOUS
PNEUMATICALLY	DRYOPITHECINE	LIGHTFINGERED	COUNTERFEITER	UNDERCARRIAGE
POLYCHROMATIC	ENCEPHALOCELE	MAGNILOQUENCE	CRUISERWEIGHT	UNDISCIPLINED
PRAGMATICALLY	EXCOMMUNICATE	MASSACHUSETTS	DEMILITARIZED	UNGRAMMATICAL
PREFABRICATED	GRIEFSTRICKEN	MISCELLANEOUS	DIACATHOLICON	UNIMPRESSIBLE
PREPONDERANCE	INCOMMUNICADO	MONOCOTYLEDON	DIFFERENTIATE	UNPRETENTIOUS
PROCLEUSMATIC	INSIGNIFICANT	MULTINUCLEATE	ENTOMOLOGICAL	UNSYMMETRICAL
PROPHETICALLY	KNICKERBOCKER	NORTHEASTERLY	FEATHERWEIGHT	HEARTBREAKING
PROSOPOGRAPHY	LEATHERJACKET	NORTHWESTERLY	FRANKALMOIGNE	HOUSEBREAKING
PROVISIONALLY	MATHEMATICIAN	PARTHOGENESIS	GLUMDALCLITCH	JIGGERYPOKERY
PSYCHOSOMATIC	METAPHYSICIAN	PASSEMENTERIE	GYNECOLOGICAL	KNICKKNACKERY
QUESTIONNAIRE	OYSTERCATCHER	POTENTIOMETER	HEMISPHERICAL	MALLEMAROKING
REALISTICALLY	PAEDIATRICIAN	PSYCHOKINESIS	HUNDREDWEIGHT	PHYTOPLANKTON
RECALCITRANCE	PROGNOSTICATE	QUADRILATERAL	HYPERCRITICAL	ACCEPTABILITY
RHYPAROGRAPHY	QUADRUPLICATE	RECRUDESCENCE	ILLUMINATIONS	ACCESSIBILITY
SARCASTICALLY	SCHOOLTEACHER	SCHADENFREUDE	IMPERCEPTIBLE	ANTICOAGULANT
SCHEMATICALLY	SEMBLANCECORD	SCHIZOPHRENIA	IMPERCEPTIBLY	ANTIGROPELOES
SEMIAUTOMATIC	SEMICONDUCTOR	SCHIZOPHRENIC	INAPPROPRIATE	ARTIFICIALITY

AUTOCEPHALOUS	ESTABLISHMENT	HYPERSTHENITE	SPRIGHTLINESS	BUNGEEJUMPING
BIOTECHNOLOGY	GASTROCNEMIUS	IMPERTINENTLY	SQUEAMISHNESS	CHOREOGRAPHER
BLOODCURDLING	HYDRODYNAMICS	IMPRESSIONISM	STEADFASTNESS	GLOSSOGRAPHER
BOUGAINVILLEA	MALADJUSTMENT	IMPRESSIONIST	STRENUOUSNESS	LEXICOGRAPHER
CHANGEABILITY	MESSERSCHMITT	IMPROVIDENTLY	SUBLIEUTENANT	LYCANTHROPIST
CHARACTERLESS	MISMANAGEMENT	IMPULSIVENESS	SUBSERVIENTLY	MISANTHROPIST
COLLOQUIALISM	MONOTHALAMOUS	INADVERTENTLY	SUPERORDINATE	MISSISSIPPIAN
COMMERCIALIZE	NONCONFORMIST	INCOMPETENTLY	TABLESPOONFUL	OWNEROCCUPIER
COMPARABILITY	NONCONFORMITY	INDEPENDENTLY	TALKATIVENESS	PARANTHROPOUS
COMPATIBILITY	OVERSTATEMENT	INDETERMINATE	TANTALIZINGLY	PHOSPHOLIPASE
CONCEPTUALIST	PHYSIOGNOMIST	INDETERMINISM	TEMPERAMENTAL	SHRINKWRAPPED
CONCEPTUALIZE	PHYSOSTIGMINE	INDIFFERENTLY	THANKLESSNESS	SOMATOTROPHIN
DECRIMINALIZE	PREPROGRAMMED	INEFFICIENTLY	THREATENINGLY	THIGMOTROPISM
DEFENSIBILITY	PRONOUNCEMENT	INEXPERIENCED	TRACTARIANISM	UNDERSTRAPPER
DENATIONALIZE	PUSILLANIMITY	INGENUOUSNESS	TRANSATLANTIC	UNINTERRUPTED
DEPENDABILITY	PUSILLANIMOUS	INSIDIOUSNESS	TRANSPARENTLY	ACRYLONITRILE
EPITRACHELION	RAPPROCHEMENT	INSUBORDINATE	UNACCOMPANIED	ACUPUNCTURIST
FONTAINEBLEAU	REARRANGEMENT	INTELLIGENTLY	UNEXPERIENCED	ALPHABETARIAN
FORTUNETELLER	REDEVELOPMENT	INTERESTINGLY	UNFLINCHINGLY	ALUMINIFEROUS
HOMOSEXUALITY	REFURBISHMENT	INVENTIVENESS	UNPRECEDENTED	AMPHIGASTRIUM
HYPOVENTILATE	REIMBURSEMENT	LECTISTERNIUM	UNQUESTIONING	ANYTHINGARIAN
IMPOSSIBILITY	REINFORCEMENT	LEISURELINESS	UNWILLINGNESS	ARCHIMANDRITE
IMPROBABILITY	REINSTATEMENT	LUXURIOUSNESS	UPTOTHEMINUTE	AUTHORITARIAN
INDIVIDUALISM	REPLENISHMENT	MAGNIFICENTLY	VEGETARIANISM	BROKENHEARTED
INDIVIDUALIST	UNDERESTIMATE	MEDITERRANEAN	VIVACIOUSNESS	CARBONIFEROUS
INDIVIDUALITY	AIRWORTHINESS	MEISTERSINGER	VORACIOUSNESS	DISSIMILARITY
INDUSTRIALIST	ALLOCHTHONOUS	MERCILESSNESS	WHOLESOMENESS	EQUIPONDERATE
INDUSTRIALIZE	ASTONISHINGLY	MICROORGANISM	AIRCRAFTWOMAN	FERROCONCRETE
INEVITABILITY	ATTENTIVENESS	MULTITUDINOUS	BILDUNGSROMAN	HYPOCHONDRIAC
INFALLIBILITY	AUTOCHTHONOUS	NERVELESSNESS	BUSINESSWOMAN	INCONSIDERATE
INFLEXIBILITY	CALLISTHENICS	OBJECTIVENESS	CEPHALOSPORIN	INQUISITORIAL
INVINCIBILITY	CARTILAGINOUS	OFFENSIVENESS	COEDUCATIONAL	INSECTIVOROUS
INVIOLABILITY	CIRCUMSTANCES	OFFICIOUSNESS	CONGRESSIONAL	INVOLUNTARILY
MACHIAVELLIAN	COLLIESHANGIE	OUTSTANDINGLY	CONGRESSWOMAN	ISOGEOTHERMAL
METAGRABOLISE	COMPASSIONATE	PAINSTAKINGLY	CONSERVATOIRE	LEPIDOPTERIST
METAGROBOLISE	CONCEPTIONIST	PENNSYLVANIAN	CONTRAFAGOTTO	LONGSUFFERING
OPHTHALMOLOGY	CONCESSIONARY	PERFECTIONIST	COUNTRYPEOPLE	MANUFACTURING
PALAEONTOLOGY	CONFECTIONERS	PERVASIVENESS	DISILLUSIONED	MOUTHWATERING
PATERFAMILIAS	CONFECTIONERY	PHYLLOQUINONE	EPANADIPLOSIS	PARTICULARISE
PENETRABILITY	CONSANGUINITY	PHYSHARMONICA	GRAVITATIONAL	PARTICULARITY
PROFITABILITY	CONSCIOUSNESS	PRECAUTIONARY	GYNANDROMORPH	PARTICULARIZE
PROVINCIALISM	CONTENTEDNESS	PREDOMINANTLY	HAMMERTHROWER	PERFUNCTORILY
PSYCHOANALYSE	CONTORTIONIST	PROCRASTINATE	INSPIRATIONAL	PHYSIOTHERAPY
PSYCHOANALYST	CREDULOUSNESS	PROJECTIONIST	INSTITUTIONAL	PRELIMINARIES
PSYCHOBIOLOGY	DEATHLESSNESS	PROPORTIONATE	INSTRUCTIONAL	PROPRIETORIAL
RATIONALALITY	DECONTAMINATE	PROTECTIONISM	INTERNATIONAL	PROTONOTARIAT
SHOULDERBLADE	DEHYDROGENATE	PROTECTIONIST	INTERPERSONAL	PSYCHOMETRICS
SPINECHILLING	DEVELOPMENTAL	QUERULOUSNESS	KALEIDOSCOPIC	PSYCHOTHERAPY
SPORTSMANLIKE	DISCRETIONARY	RECEPTIVENESS	LAMPADEPHORIA	RENSSELAERITE
STATESMANLIKE	DISHEARTENING	RECITATIONIST	LEPTOSPIROSIS	STREPTOCARPUS
SUSPERCOLLATE	DISPASSIONATE	REDEMPTIONIST	MASTIGOPHORAN	SUPERNUMERARY
SWASHBUCKLING	EFFECTIVENESS	REMINISCENCES	METAMORPHOSIS	TENDERHEARTED
SWEETSMELLING	ENVIRONMENTAL	REPUBLICANISM	MONONUCLEOSIS	THOROUGHBRACE
THEATRICALITY	EXHIBITIONIST	REVOLUTIONARY	MULTINATIONAL	THUNDERSTRUCK
THERMONUCLEAR	EXPANSIVENESS	REVOLUTIONIZE	PASSIONFLOWER	TRANSISTORIZE
VULNERABILITY	EXPEDITIONARY	RIGHTEOUSNESS	PHARMACOPOEIA	TRANSLITERATE
ACCOMPANIMENT	EXTRAORDINARY	SALACIOUSNESS	PHILANTHROPIC	UMBELLIFEROUS
ADVERTISEMENT	EXTRAVAGANTLY	SCANDALMONGER	PRESSURELOCAL	UNNECESSARILY
AFFREIGHTMENT	FACETIOUSNESS	SCHOLARLINESS	ROUNDTHEWORLD	UNTRUSTWORTHY
ANTIHISTAMINE	FORGETFULNESS	SECRETIVENESS	SEPTENTRIONES	VIDEORECORDER
APPORTIONMENT	FRACTIOUSNESS	SELFGOVERNING	SOCIOECONOMIC	WITWATERSRAND
DISENGAGEMENT	FRIGHTENINGLY	SENSELESSNESS	SUPRANATIONAL	ANACHRONISTIC
DISFIGUREMENT	FRIGHTFULNESS	SENSITIVENESS	THOROUGHGOING	ANIMADVERSION
DISPARAGEMENT	FRIVOLOUSNESS	SERVILEMENTAL	UNCONDITIONAL	COMPANIONSHIP
EMBARRASSMENT	GARRULOUSNESS	SHAPELESSNESS	UNEXCEPTIONAL	COMPREHENSION
EMBELLISHMENT	GENITOURINARY	SIGNIFICANTLY	UNINTENTIONAL	COMPREHENSIVE
ENCOURAGEMENT	GEOSTATIONARY	SLEEPLESSNESS	UNPARTITIONED	CONDESCENSION
ENLIGHTENMENT	GRANDPARENTAL	SNOWBLINDNESS	VERCINGETORIX	CONTRABASSOON
ENTERTAINMENT	GUILTLESSNESS	SPITESPLENDID	BIBLIOGRAPHER	CONTROVERSIAL

CRAFTSMANSHIP	COMMUNICATION	FUERTEVENTURA	PREMEDITATION	GRANDILOQUENT
DECOMPRESSION	COMMUNICATIVE	GALVANIZATION	PREOCCUPATION	HORTICULTURAL
DISINTERESTED	COMPLEMENTARY	GESTICULATION	PREVARICATION	IGNOMINIOUSLY
DISTINGUISHED	COMPLIMENTARY	GLOBETROTTING	PRIMOGENITURE	INCONSPICUOUS
FLABBERGASTED	CONCATENATION	GLORIFICATION	PRIVATIZATION	INCREDULOUSLY
GENERALISSIMO	CONCENTRATION	GRATIFICATION	PROLIFERATION	INDUSTRIOUSLY
HETERAUXESISM	CONFARREATION	HALLUCINATION	PRONUNCIATION	INTRAMUSCULAR
IMPERIALISTIC	CONFEDERATION	HALLUCINATORY	PROTESTANTISM	KANGCHENJUNGA
KAPPELMEISTER	CONFIGURATION	HARMONIZATION	PULVERIZATION	MAGNANIMOUSLY
KIDDERMINSTER	CONFLAGRATION	HORRIPILATION	QUALIFICATION	MICROCOMPUTER
LIBRARIANSHIP	CONFRONTATION	HYBRIDIZATION	RECRIMINATION	MISCHIEVOUSLY
MADETOMEASURE	CONSEQUENTIAL	HYDROELECTRIC	RECRIMINATORY	MULTICOLOURED
MATERIALISTIC	CONSIDERATELY	IMPERSONATING	RECTIFICATION	NEUROCOMPUTER
MAURIKIGUSARI	CONSIDERATION	IMPERSONATION	REFRIGERATION	PARTICOLOURED
NATIONALISTIC	CONSOLIDATION	IMPROVISATION	REFRIGERATORS	PERPENDICULAR
OPPORTUNISTIC	CONSPURCATION	INCARCERATION	REGIMENTATION	PRETERNATURAL
OVEREMPHASIZE	CONSTELLATION	INCORPORATION	REGURGITATION	PROMISCUOUSLY
PATERNALISTIC	CONSTERNATION	INCRIMINATING	REINCARNATION	PUNCTILIOUSLY
PELOPONNESIAN	CONTAMINATION	INCRIMINATORY	RESUSCITATION	REPROACHFULLY
PREPOSSESSING	CONTEMPLATION	INDISPOSITION	RETROSPECTIVE	RESOURCEFULLY
PREPOSSESSION	CONTEMPLATIVE	INSUBSTANTIAL	REUNIFICATION	SENTENTIOUSLY
PROFESSORSHIP	CONTRACEPTION	INTERCALATION	REVERBERATION	SPONTANEOUSLY
QUARTERMASTER	CONTRACEPTIVE	INTERPOLATION	SCINTILLATING	SUBMANDIBULAR
QUINQUAGESIMA	CONTRADICTION	INTERROGATION	SCINTILLATION	SUPERFLUOUSLY
REMORSELESSLY	CONTRADICTORY	INTERROGATIVE	SCLEROPROTEIN	TINTINNABULUM
RETROGRESSION	CONTRAVENTION	INTROSPECTION	SEDIMENTATION	TREACHEROUSLY
ROLLERCOASTER	CORROBORATION	INTROSPECTIVE	SEQUESTRATION	UNCONSCIOUSLY
SELFADDRESSED	CORROBORATORY	INVESTIGATION	SIGNIFICATION	UNDERGRADUATE
SELFCONFESSED	COSTEFFECTIVE	INVESTIGATIVE	SOLEMNIZATION	VENTRILOQUISM
SOMATOSENSORY	COUNTERACTING	JOLLIFICATION	SPECIFICATION	VENTRILOQUIST
SPORTSMANSHIP	COUNTERATTACK	JUSTIFICATION	STABILIZATION	AFFIRMATIVELY
STATESMANSHIP	CROSSQUESTION	JUSTIFICATORY	STEPPINGSTONE	ALTERNATIVELY
STATIONMASTER	DAGUERREOTYPE	JUXTAPOSITION	STERILIZATION	COMPARATIVELY
THERMOPLASTIC	DECOMPOSITION	LAEVOROTATORY	STRANGULATION	CONSECUTIVELY
THOUGHTLESSLY	DEFORESTATION	LIECHTENSTEIN	SUBJECTMATTER	HAMMERKLAVIER
TONGUETWISTER	DEMONSTRATION	MACHICOLATION	SUBORDINATION	IMAGINATIVELY
TRANSGRESSION	DEMONSTRATIVE	MAGNIFICATION	SUPPLEMENTARY	INQUISITIVELY
TRIPLOBLASTIC	DESEGREGATION	MANIFESTATION	TELEMARKETING	INSENSITIVITY
UNEMBARRASSED	DETERIORATION	MATRICULATION	THYROIDECTOMY	INSTINCTIVELY
UNESTABLISHED	DETERMINATION	MECHANIZATION	TONSILLECTOMY	PROGRESSIVELY
UNPROGRESSIVE	DIFFARREATION	MISCEGENATION	TRANSCRIPTION	PROVOCATIVELY
ACCEPTILATION	DISAPPOINTING	MISCONCEPTION	TRANSMUTATION	RADIOACTIVITY
ACCOMMODATING	DISCOLORATION	MISUNDERSTAND	TRANSPIRATION	SUPERLATIVELY
ACCOMMODATION	DISCONCERTING	MISUNDERSTOOD	TRANSPOSITION	ANTICLOCKWISE
AFFORESTATION	DISCONNECTION	MODERNIZATION	TRIANGULATION	CRYPTANALYSIS
AGGLOMERATION	DISESTIMATION	MOLLIFICATION	TRICHOSANTHIN	PEPTIDOGLYCAN
AMPLIFICATION	DISPROPORTION	MORTIFICATION	UNCOOPERATIVE	SACCHAROMYCES
ANTHELMINTHIC	DISRESPECTFUL	MYSTIFICATION	UNFORTUNATELY	DOUBLEGLAZING
APPROPRIATION	DISSEMINATION	NORMALIZATION	UNIMAGINATIVE	MERCHANDIZING
APPROXIMATELY	DISSIMULATION	NUCLEOPROTEIN	UNINTERESTING	**13:11**
APPROXIMATION	DOCUMENTATION	NULLIFICATION	UNSUBSTANTIAL	
ARGUMENTATIVE	DRAMATIZATION	OPPORTUNITIES	VERSIFICATION	ANTICOAGULANT
ARMOURPLATING	ELECTROCUTION	ORCHESTRATION	VICTIMIZATION	APPROPINQUATE
ASSASSINATION	ELECTROMOTIVE	ORNAMENTATION	VITRIFICATION	BACCALAUREATE
AUTHORISATION	ENCULTURATION	PANDICULATION	VULCANIZATION	BACTERIOPHAGE
AUTHORITATIVE	EPHEMEROPTERA	PAPAPRELATIST	VULGARIZATION	CHATEAUBRIAND
AUTHORIZATION	ESCHSCHOLTZIA	PARLIAMENTARY	WEIGHTLIFTING	COMPASSIONATE
BEATIFICATION	EXPOSTULATION	PARTICIPATION	XIPHIPLASTRON	COMPLEMENTARY
CARBONIZATION	EXPROPRIATION	PARTICIPATORY	ADVENTUROUSLY	COMPLIMENTARY
CAUTERIZATION	EXTERMINATION	PERAMBULATION	APPROPINQUATE	CONCESSIONARY
CERTIFICATION	EXTRAPOLATION	PEREGRINATION	ARCHITECTURAL	COUNTERATTACK
CHRISTMASTIME	FALSIFICATION	PERSONALITIES	BRACHIOSAURUS	DECONTAMINATE
CIRCUMVENTION	FERTILISATION	PETRIFICATION	CEREMONIOUSLY	DEHYDROGENATE
CLARIFICATION	FERTILIZATION	PHOTOELECTRIC	CONSPICUOUSLY	DIFFERENTIATE
COLLABORATION	FORMALIZATION	PNEUMONECTOMY	DISCONTINUITY	DISCRETIONARY
COLLABORATIVE	FORTIFICATION	POLLICITATION	DISCONTINUOUS	DISPASSIONATE
COMMEMORATION	FOSSILIZATION	PRECIPITATELY	DISGRACEFULLY	EQUIPONDERATE
COMMEMORATIVE	FRAGMENTATION	PRECIPITATION	ENTEROPNEUSTA	EXCOMMUNICATE
COMMISERATION	FREQUENTATIVE	PRECONCEPTION	EXPEDITIOUSLY	EXPEDITIONARY

EXTRAORDINARY	IRRESPONSIBLE	AFFIRMATIVELY	OVERSTATEMENT	CHOREOGRAPHER
GENITOURINARY	IRRESPONSIBLY	AFFREIGHTMENT	PASSCHENDAELE	COMPANIONSHIP
GEOSTATIONARY	IRRETRIEVABLE	AIRWORTHINESS	PERVASIVENESS	CRAFTSMANSHIP
HYALURONIDASE	IRRETRIEVABLY	ALTERNATIVELY	PHARMACOPOEIA	DISTINGUISHED
HYPOVENTILATE	KNOWLEDGEABLE	APPORTIONMENT	PRECIPITATELY	GLOSSOGRAPHER
INAPPROPRIATE	OBJECTIONABLE	APPROXIMATELY	PROGRESSIVELY	LEXICOGRAPHER
INCOMMUNICADO	REPREHENSIBLE	AQUIFOLIACEAE	PRONOUNCEMENT	LIBRARIANSHIP
INCONSIDERATE	REPREHENSIBLY	ATTENTIVENESS	PROVOCATIVELY	OYSTERCATCHER
INDETERMINATE	TETRASYLLABIC	BASIDIOMYCETE	QUERULOUSNESS	PROFESSORSHIP
INSIGNIFICANT	TRANSPORTABLE	BUTTERFINGERS	RAPPROCHEMENT	SCHOOLTEACHER
INSUBORDINATE	UNACCOUNTABLE	CHARACTERLESS	REARRANGEMENT	SOMATOTROPHIN
INTERMARRIAGE	UNACCOUNTABLY	CHEESEMONGERS	RECEPTIVENESS	SPORTSMANSHIP
MAURIKIGUSARI	UNCOMFORTABLE	CIRCUMAMBIENT	REDEVELOPMENT	STATESMANSHIP
MISUNDERSTAND	UNCOMFORTABLY	COMPARATIVELY	REFURBISHMENT	TRICHOSANTHIN
MULTINUCLEATE	UNCONQUERABLE	CONFECTIONERS	REIMBURSEMENT	UNESTABLISHED
PARLIAMENTARY	UNFASHIONABLE	CONFECTIONERY	REINFORCEMENT	ACCEPTABILITY
PHOSPHOLIPASE	UNFORESEEABLE	CONSCIOUSNESS	REINSTATEMENT	ACCEPTILATION
PHYSIOTHERAPY	UNFORGETTABLE	CONSECUTIVELY	REPLENISHMENT	ACCESSIBILITY
PRECAUTIONARY	UNIMPEACHABLE	CONSIDERATELY	RIGHTEOUSNESS	ACCOMMODATING
PROCRASTINATE	UNIMPRESSIBLE	CONTENTEDNESS	SALACIOUSNESS	ACCOMMODATION
PROGNOSTICATE	UNINHABITABLE	CORRESPONDENT	SCHOLARLINESS	ACRYLONITRILE
PROPORTIONATE	UNMENTIONABLE	CREDULOUSNESS	SCLEROPROTEIN	ACUPUNCTURIST
PSYCHOTHERAPY	UNPREDICTABLE	DEATHLESSNESS	SECRETIVENESS	AFFORESTATION
QUADRUPLICATE	UNSERVICEABLE	DISENGAGEMENT	SELFCONFIDENT	AGGLOMERATION
REVOLUTIONARY	CHRONOLOGICAL	DISFIGUREMENT	SENSELESSNESS	ALPHABETARIAN
SHOULDERBLADE	CIRCUMSTANCES	DISPARAGEMENT	SENSITIVENESS	AMPHIGASTRIUM
SUBLIEUTENANT	DIACATHOLICON	EFFECTIVENESS	SHAPELESSNESS	AMPLIFICATION
SUPERABUNDANT	ENTOMOLOGICAL	EMBARRASSMENT	SLEEPLESSNESS	ANIMADVERSION
SUPERNUMERARY	GYNECOLOGICAL	EMBELLISHMENT	SNOWBLINDNESS	ANTICLOCKWISE
SUPERORDINATE	HEMISPHERICAL	ENCEPHALOCELE	SPRIGHTLINESS	ANTIHISTAMINE
SUPPLEMENTARY	HYPERCRITICAL	ENCOURAGEMENT	SQUEAMISHNESS	ANYTHINGARIAN
SUSPERCOLLATE	INEXPERIENCED	ENLIGHTENMENT	STEADFASTNESS	APPROPRIATION
THESSALONIANS	LACKADAISICAL	ENTERTAINMENT	STRENUOUSNESS	APPROXIMATION
THOROUGHBRACE	MOCKTECHNICAL	EPHEMEROPTERA	SUPERLATIVELY	ARCHAEOLOGIST
TRANSLITERATE	MORPHOLOGICAL	ESTABLISHMENT	TALKATIVENESS	ARCHIMANDRITE
UNCOMMUNICATE	PANHARMONICON	EXPANSIVENESS	THANKLESSNESS	ARGUMENTATIVE
UNDERCARRIAGE	PARENTHETICAL	FACETIOUSNESS	THERMONUCLEAR	ARITHMETICIAN
UNDERESTIMATE	PEPTIDOGLYCAN	FERROCONCRETE	TONGUEINCHEEK	ARMOURPLATING
UNDERGRADUATE	PETROCHEMICAL	FONTAINEBLEAU	TORTOISESHELL	ARTIFICIALITY
WITWATERSRAND	PHILOSOPHICAL	FORGETFULNESS	UNFORTUNATELY	ASSASSINATION
ASCERTAINABLE	PHOTOCHEMICAL	FRACTIOUSNESS	UNINTELLIGENT	AUTHORISATION
BIODEGRADABLE	PHYSIOLOGICAL	FRIGHTFULNESS	UNWILLINGNESS	AUTHORITARIAN
COMMENSURABLE	PRESSURELOCAL	FRIVOLOUSNESS	VICEPRESIDENT	AUTHORITATIVE
COMPANIONABLE	PROBLEMATICAL	GARRULOUSNESS	VIVACIOUSNESS	AUTHORIZATION
DISCREDITABLE	PSYCHOLOGICAL	GRANDILOQUENT	VORACIOUSNESS	BEATIFICATION
DISCREDITABLY	PYROTECHNICAL	GUILTLESSNESS	WHOLESOMENESS	BIBLIOPHAGIST
DISHONOURABLE	REMINISCENCES	HORSEFEATHERS	DISRESPECTFUL	BLOODCURDLING
DISHONOURABLY	SACCHAROMYCES	IMAGINATIVELY	SCHUTZSTAFFEL	BREASTFEEDING
EXCEPTIONABLE	SEISMOLOGICAL	IMPULSIVENESS	TABLESPOONFUL	BUNGEEJUMPING
IMPERCEPTIBLE	SPELEOLOGICAL	INGENUOUSNESS	ASTONISHINGLY	CALLISTHENICS
IMPERCEPTIBLY	STREPTOCOCCUS	INQUISITIVELY	COLLIESHANGIE	CARBONIZATION
IMPERTURBABLE	TECHNOLOGICAL	INSIDIOUSNESS	CRUISERWEIGHT	CAUTERIZATION
IMPERTURBABLY	TOPOGRAPHICAL	INSTINCTIVELY	DISADVANTAGED	CERTIFICATION
IMPRACTICABLE	TYPOGRAPHICAL	INVENTIVENESS	FEATHERWEIGHT	CHANGEABILITY
INCOMBUSTIBLE	UNEXPERIENCED	JIGGERYPOKERY	FRANKALMOIGNE	CHRISTMASTIME
INCONCEIVABLE	UNGRAMMATICAL	KNICKKNACKERY	FRIGHTENINGLY	CIRCUMVENTION
INCONTESTABLE	UNSYMMETRICAL	LEISURELINESS	HUNDREDWEIGHT	CLARIFICATION
INCORRUPTIBLE	BOUSTROPHEDON	LIECHTENSTEIN	INTERESTINGLY	COLLABORATION
INDEFATIGABLE	ENCYCLOPAEDIA	LUXURIOUSNESS	MEISTERSINGER	COLLABORATIVE
INDEFATIGABLY	ENCYCLOPAEDIC	MALADJUSTMENT	OUTSTANDINGLY	COLLOQUIALISM
INDESCRIBABLE	FOREKNOWLEDGE	MEDITERRANEAN	PAINSTAKINGLY	COMMEMORATION
INDESCRIBABLY	MONOCOTYLEDON	MERCILESSNESS	SCANDALMONGER	COMMEMORATIVE
INDISPENSABLE	SIPUNCULOIDEA	MISMANAGEMENT	TANTALIZINGLY	COMMERCIALIZE
INEXHAUSTIBLE	SPITESPLENDID	NERVELESSNESS	THREATENINGLY	COMMISERATION
INEXPRESSIBLE	STAPHYLINIDAE	NONSUFFICIENT	UNFLINCHINGLY	COMMUNICATION
INSUPPORTABLE	SWOLLENHEADED	NUCLEOPROTEIN	AFFENPINSCHER	COMMUNICATIVE
IRRECOVERABLE	VIDEORECORDER	OBJECTIVENESS	ANTHELMINTHIC	COMPARABILITY
IRREPLACEABLE	ACCOMPANIMENT	OFFENSIVENESS	BIBLIOGRAPHER	COMPATIBILITY
IRREPRESSIBLE	ADVERTISEMENT	OFFICIOUSNESS	CHINKERINCHEE	COMPREHENSION

COMPREHENSIVE	EPITRACHELION	INVOLUNTARILY	PRELIMINARIES	THEATRICALITY
CONCATENATION	EXHIBITIONIST	JOLLIFICATION	PREMEDITATION	THIGMOTROPISM
CONCENTRATION	EXPOSTULATION	JUSTIFICATION	PREOCCUPATION	THOROUGHGOING
CONCEPTIONIST	EXPROPRIATION	JUXTAPOSITION	PREPOSSESSING	TRACTARIANISM
CONCEPTUALIST	EXTERMINATION	LECTISTERNIUM	PREPOSSESSION	TRANSCRIPTION
CONCEPTUALIZE	EXTRAPOLATION	LEPIDOPTERIST	PREVARICATION	TRANSGRESSION
CONDESCENDING	FALSIFICATION	LONGSUFFERING	PRIVATIZATION	TRANSISTORIZE
CONDESCENSION	FERTILISATION	LYCANTHROPIST	PROFITABILITY	TRANSMUTATION
CONFARREATION	FERTILIZATION	MACHIAVELLIAN	PROJECTIONIST	TRANSPIRATION
CONFEDERATION	FORMALIZATION	MACHICOLATION	PROLIFERATION	TRANSPOSITION
CONFIGURATION	FORTIFICATION	MAGNIFICATION	PRONUNCIATION	TRIANGULATION
CONFLAGRATION	FOSSILIZATION	MALLEMAROKING	PROPRIETORIAL	UNACCOMPANIED
CONFRONTATION	FRAGMENTATION	MANIFESTATION	PROTECTIONISM	UNCOOPERATIVE
CONSANGUINITY	FREQUENTATIVE	MANUFACTURING	PROTECTIONIST	UNDERCLOTHING
CONSEQUENTIAL	GALVANIZATION	MATHEMATICIAN	PROTESTANTISM	UNDERSTANDING
CONSERVATOIRE	GASTROCNEMIUS	MATRICULATION	PROTONOTARIAT	UNIMAGINATIVE
CONSIDERATION	GENERALISSIMO	MECHANIZATION	PROVINCIALISM	UNINTERESTING
CONSOLIDATION	GESTICULATION	MERCHANDIZING	PSYCHOMETRICS	UNNECESSARILY
CONSPURCATION	GLOBETROTTING	MESSERSCHMITT	PULVERIZATION	UNPROGRESSIVE
CONSTELLATION	GLORIFICATION	METAGRABOLISE	PUSILLANIMITY	UNQUESTIONING
CONSTERNATION	GRATIFICATION	METAGROBOLISE	QUALIFICATION	UNSUBSTANTIAL
CONTAMINATION	GYNAECOLOGIST	METAPHYSICIAN	QUESTIONNAIRE	VEGETARIANISM
CONTEMPLATION	HALLUCINATION	METEOROLOGIST	QUINQUAGESIMA	VENTRILOQUISM
CONTEMPLATIVE	HAMMERKLAVIER	MICROORGANISM	RADIOACTIVITY	VENTRILOQUIST
CONTORTIONIST	HARMONIZATION	MISANTHROPIST	RATIONALALITY	VERSIFICATION
CONTRACEPTION	HEARTBREAKING	MISCEGENATION	RECITATIONIST	VICTIMIZATION
CONTRACEPTIVE	HERMAPHRODITE	MISCONCEPTION	RECRIMINATION	VITRIFICATION
CONTRADICTION	HETERAUXESISM	MISSISSIPPIAN	RECTIFICATION	VULCANIZATION
CONTRAVENTION	HIEROGLYPHICS	MODERNIZATION	REDEMPTIONIST	VULGARIZATION
CONTROVERSIAL	HOMOSEXUALITY	MOLLIFICATION	REFRIGERATION	VULNERABILITY
CORRESPONDING	HORRIPILATION	MORTIFICATION	REGIMENTATION	WEIGHTLIFTING
CORROBORATION	HOUSEBREAKING	MOUTHWATERING	REGURGITATION	GRIEFSTRICKEN
COSTEFFECTIVE	HYBRIDIZATION	MYSTIFICATION	REINCARNATION	KNICKERBOCKER
COUNTERACTING	HYDRODYNAMICS	NIGHTCLUBBING	RENSSELAERITE	LEATHERJACKET
CRIMINOLOGIST	HYPERSTHENITE	NONCONFORMIST	REPROGRAPHICS	MIDDLEBREAKER
CROSSQUESTION	HYPOCHONDRIAC	NONCONFORMITY	REPUBLICANISM	STRIKEBREAKER
DECOMPOSITION	IMPERSONALITY	NORMALIZATION	RESUSCITATION	AESTHETICALLY
DECOMPRESSION	IMPERSONATION	NULLIFICATION	RETROGRESSION	AUTOMATICALLY
DECRIMINALIZE	IMPOSSIBILITY	OPPORTUNITIES	RETROSPECTIVE	BOUGAINVILLEA
DEFENSIBILITY	IMPRESSIONISM	ORCHESTRATION	REUNIFICATION	CATEGORICALLY
DEFORESTATION	IMPRESSIONIST	ORNAMENTATION	REVERBERATION	CONDITIONALLY
DEIPNOSOPHIST	IMPROBABILITY	ORNITHOLOGIST	REVOLUTIONIZE	DIAMETRICALLY
DEMONSTRATION	IMPROVISATION	OVEREMPHASIZE	RHADAMANTHINE	DISGRACEFULLY
DEMONSTRATIVE	INCARCERATION	OWNEROCCUPIER	ROLLERBLADING	ECCENTRICALLY
DENATIONALIZE	INCORPORATION	PAEDIATRICIAN	RUTHERFORDIUM	ENERGETICALLY
DEPENDABILITY	INCRIMINATING	PANDICULATION	SCINTILLATING	EXCEPTIONALLY
DERMATOLOGIST	INDETERMINISM	PAPAPRELATIST	SCINTILLATION	FANTASTICALLY
DESEGREGATION	INDISPOSITION	PARTICIPATION	SEDIMENTATION	FORTUNETELLER
DETERIORATION	INDIVIDUALISM	PARTICULARISE	SELFGOVERNING	FUNDAMENTALLY
DETERMINATION	INDIVIDUALIST	PARTICULARITY	SEQUESTRATION	GEOMETRICALLY
DIFFARREATION	INDIVIDUALITY	PARTICULARIZE	SIGNIFICATION	GRAMMATICALLY
DISAPPOINTING	INDUSTRIALIST	PATERFAMILIAS	SKATEBOARDING	HYDRAULICALLY
DISCOLORATION	INDUSTRIALIZE	PELOPONNESIAN	SOLEMNIZATION	HYDROCEPHALUS
DISCONCERTING	INEVITABILITY	PENETRABILITY	SPECIFICATION	IMPONDERABLES
DISCONNECTION	INFALLIBILITY	PENNSYLVANIAN	SPINECHILLING	INTENTIONALLY
DISCONTINUITY	INFLEXIBILITY	PERAMBULATION	SPORTSMANLIKE	INTRAMUSCULAR
DISESTIMATION	INQUISITORIAL	PEREGRINATION	STABILIZATION	INTRINSICALLY
DISHEARTENING	INSENSITIVITY	PERFECTIONIST	STATESMANLIKE	LEPTOCEPHALUS
DISPROPORTION	INSUBSTANTIAL	PERFUNCTORILY	STERILIZATION	LIEBFRAUMILCH
DISSEMINATION	INTERCALATION	PERSONALITIES	STOCKBREEDING	MAGISTERIALLY
DISSIMILARITY	INTERPOLATION	PETRIFICATION	STRANGULATION	NEANDERTHALER
DISSIMULATION	INTERROGATION	PHENCYCLIDINE	SUBORDINATION	NOSTALGICALLY
DOCUMENTATION	INTERROGATIVE	PHILADELPHIAN	SWASHBUCKLING	PARADOXICALLY
DOUBLEGLAZING	INTROSPECTION	PHYSHARMONICA	SWEDENBORGIAN	PARAPHERNALIA
DRAMATIZATION	INTROSPECTIVE	PHYSIOGNOMIST	SWEETSMELLING	PATRIOTICALLY
DRYOPITHECINE	INVESTIGATION	PHYSOSTIGMINE	TAPERECORDING	PERPENDICULAR
ELECTROCUTION	INVESTIGATIVE	POLLICITATION	TELEMARKETING	PLATOCEPHALUS
ELECTROMOTIVE	INVINCIBILITY	PRECIPITATION	THAUMATURGICS	PNEUMATICALLY
ENCULTURATION	INVIOLABILITY	PRECONCEPTION	THAUMATURGIST	PRAGMATICALLY

PROPHETICALLY
PROVISIONALLY
REALISTICALLY
REPROACHFULLY
RESOURCEFULLY
SARCASTICALLY
SCHEMATICALLY
SENSATIONALLY
SENTIMENTALLY
SPASMODICALLY
STATISTICALLY
STRATEGICALLY
STYLISTICALLY
SUBMANDIBULAR
SUBSTANTIALLY
SUOVETAURILIA
SUPERFICIALLY
SYNTACTICALLY
SYNTHETICALLY
THEOLOGICALLY
THEORETICALLY
TINTINNABULUM
TRADITIONALLY
TRAUMATICALLY
AIRCRAFTWOMAN
BILDUNGSROMAN
BUSINESSWOMAN
CHRYSANTHEMUM
CONGRESSWOMAN
IDIORRHYTHMIC
INFINITESIMAL
ISOGEOTHERMAL
NIGHTWATCHMAN
PREPROGRAMMED
QUADRAGESIMAL
QUARTODECIMAN
SOCIOECONOMIC
THERMODYNAMIC
ACCOUTREMENTS
AGGIORNAMENTO
BIREFRINGENCE
BLANDISHMENTS
CIRCUMFERENCE
CLAIRAUDIENCE
COEDUCATIONAL
CONCUPISCENCE
CONGRESSIONAL
CONVALESCENCE
DEFERVESCENCE
DÉSOBLIGEANTE
DISAPPEARANCE
DISILLUSIONED
EFFERVESCENCE
EFFLORESCENCE
ELECTROMAGNET
EPIPHENOMENON
FOSTERPARENTS
GRAVITATIONAL
INCANDESCENCE
INCONSISTENCY
INCONVENIENCE
INFLORESCENCE
INSPIRATIONAL
INSTITUTIONAL
INSTRUCTIONAL
INSUFFICIENCY
INTERNATIONAL
INTERPERSONAL
INTRANSIGENCE

JURISPRUDENCE
KANGCHENJUNGA
MAGNILOQUENCE
MULTINATIONAL
NEMATHELMINTH
NONRESISTANCE
OUTRECUIDANCE
PREPONDERANCE
RECALCITRANCE
RECRUDESCENCE
SCHIZOPHRENIA
SCHIZOPHRENIC
SELFCONTAINED
SEPTENTRIONES
SPINDLESHANKS
SUPRANATIONAL
UNCONDITIONAL
UNDISCIPLINED
UNENLIGHTENED
UNEXCEPTIONAL
UNGENTLEMANLY
UNINTENTIONAL
UNPARTITIONED
ALLOCHTHONOUS
ALUMINIFEROUS
ANTIGROPELOES
ARUNDINACEOUS
AUTOCEPHALOUS
AUTOCHTHONOUS
BIOTECHNOLOGY
CARBONIFEROUS
CARTILAGINOUS
CONSCIENTIOUS
CONSECTANEOUS
CONTINUATIONS
CONTRABASSOON
CONTRADICTORY
CONTRIBUTIONS
CONVERSAZIONE
CORROBORATORY
DISCONTINUOUS
GOODRIGHTEOUS
HALLUCINATORY
HETEROGENEOUS
ILLUMINATIONS
INCONSPICUOUS
INCRIMINATORY
INSECTIVOROUS
INSTANTANEOUS
JUSTIFICATORY
LAEVOROTATORY
LISSOTRICHOUS
MISCELLANEOUS
MISUNDERSTOOD
MONOTHALAMOUS
MULTITUDINOUS
NEIGHBOURHOOD
OPHTHALMOLOGY
PALAEONTOLOGY
PARANTHROPOUS
PARTICIPATORY
PERSPICACIOUS
PHYLLOQUINONE
PNEUMONECTOMY
PROFECTITIOUS
PSYCHOBIOLOGY
PUSILLANIMOUS
RAMIFICATIONS
RECRIMINATORY

REFRIGERATORS
REPERCUSSIONS
SANCTIMONIOUS
SELFCONSCIOUS
SEMBLANCECORD
SOMATOSENSORY
STEPPINGSTONE
STERCORACEOUS
SUPERSTITIOUS
SURREPTITIOUS
THYROIDECTOMY
TONSILLECTOMY
UMBELLIFEROUS
UNCEREMONIOUS
UNPRETENTIOUS
AUTOBIOGRAPHY
COUNTRYPEOPLE
KALEIDOSCOPIC
PHILANTHROPIC
PROSOPOGRAPHY
RHYPAROGRAPHY
SHRINKWRAPPED
SPECTROGRAPHY
STREPTOCARPUS
UNDERSTRAPPER
ALUMINOTHERMY
ARCHAEOPTERYX
ARCHITECTURAL
BRACHIOSAURUS
CEPHALOSPORIN
COMRADEINARMS
COUNTERCHARGE
ENCEPHALOGRAM
GYNANDROMORPH
HORTICULTURAL
HYDROELECTRIC
LAMPADEPHORIA
LIGHTFINGERED
MASTIGOPHORAN
MULTICOLOURED
NORTHEASTERLY
NORTHWESTERLY
PARALLELOGRAM
PARTICOLOURED
PASSEMENTERIE
PHOTOELECTRIC
PRETERNATURAL
QUADRILATERAL
ROUNDTHEWORLD
SOUTHEASTERLY
SOUTHWESTERLY
SPECTACULARLY
VERCINGETORIX
XIPHIPLASTRON
ADVENTUROUSLY
APOCATASTASIS
BOUILLABAISSE
CEREMONIOUSLY
CHARACTERISED
CONSPICUOUSLY
CRYPTANALYSIS
ELEPHANTIASIS
ENTEROPNEUSTA
EPANADIPLOSIS
EXPEDITIOUSLY
IGNOMINIOUSLY
INCREDULOUSLY
INDUSTRIOUSLY
LEPTOSPIROSIS

MAGNANIMOUSLY
METAMORPHOSIS
MISCHIEVOUSLY
MONONUCLEOSIS
PARTHOGENESIS
PROMISCUOUSLY
PSYCHOKINESIS
PUNCTILIOUSLY
REMORSELESSLY
SELFADDRESSED
SELFCONFESSED
SENTENTIOUSLY
SPONTANEOUSLY
STEEPLECHASER
SUPERFLUOUSLY
THORACENTESIS
THOUGHTLESSLY
TRANQUILLISER
TREACHEROUSLY
UNCONSCIOUSLY
UNEMBARRASSED
ADMINISTRATOR
ANACHRONISTIC
ARISTROCRATIC
BROKENHEARTED
CONTRAFAGOTTO
COUNTERFEITER
DECAFFEINATED
DEFIBRILLATOR
DEVELOPMENTAL
DISINTERESTED
ENVIRONMENTAL
EXTRAVAGANTLY
FLABBERGASTED
GLUMDALCLITCH
GRANDDAUGHTER
GRANDPARENTAL
IDIOSYNCRATIC
IMPERIALISTIC
IMPERTINENTLY
IMPROVIDENTLY
INADVERTENTLY
INCOMPETENTLY
INDEPENDENTLY
INDIFFERENTLY
INEFFICIENTLY
INTELLIGENTLY
KAPPELMEISTER
KIDDERMINSTER
MAGNIFICENTLY
MASSACHUSETTS
MATERIALISTIC
MICROCOMPUTER
NATIONALISTIC
NEUROCOMPUTER
OPPORTUNISTIC
PATERNALISTIC
PHYTOPLANKTON
POLIOMYELITIS
POLYCHROMATIC
POTENTIOMETER
PREDOMINANTLY
PREFABRICATED
PROCLEUSMATIC
PSYCHOSOMATIC
QUARTERMASTER
ROLLERCOASTER
SEMIAUTOMATIC
SEMICONDUCTOR

SERVILEMENTAL
SIGNIFICANTLY
SOPHISTICATED
STATIONMASTER
SUBCONTRACTOR
SUBJECTMATTER
SUBSERVIENTLY
SUPERANNUATED
SYMPIESOMETER
TEMPERAMENTAL
TENDERHEARTED
TENOSYNOVITIS
THERMOPLASTIC
TONGUETWISTER
TRANSATLANTIC
TRANSPARENTLY
TRIPLOBLASTIC
UNADULTERATED
UNANTICIPATED
UNCOMPLICATED
UNCOORDINATED
UNINTERRUPTED
UNPRECEDENTED
UNSYMPATHETIC
UNTRUSTWORTHY
VIDEOCASSETTE
WEATHERBEATEN
CLOSEDCIRCUIT
FUERTEVENTURA
MADETOMEASURE
PRIMOGENITURE
SCHADENFREUDE
THUNDERSTRUCK
UPTOTHEMINUTE
CLISHMACLAVER
PRESERVATIVES
UNDERACHIEVER
HAMMERTHROWER
PASSIONFLOWER
BUTYRALDEHYDE
DAGUERREOTYPE
PSYCHOANALYSE
PSYCHOANALYST
SPERMATOPHYTE
DEMILITARIZED
ESCHSCHOLTZIA
TRANQUILLIZER

13:12

AIRCRAFTWOMAN
ALPHABETARIAN
ANYTHINGARIAN
AQUIFOLIACEAE
ARCHITECTURAL
ARITHMETICIAN
AUTHORITARIAN
BILDUNGSROMAN
BUSINESSWOMAN
CHRONOLOGICAL
COEDUCATIONAL
CONGRESSIONAL
CONGRESSWOMAN
CONSEQUENTIAL
CONTROVERSIAL
DEVELOPMENTAL
ENCEPHALOGRAM
ENTOMOLOGICAL
ENVIRONMENTAL
FONTAINEBLEAU

GRANDPARENTAL	BIREFRINGENCE	LEXICOGRAPHER	PALAEONTOLOGY	TRANSATLANTIC
GRAVITATIONAL	CALLISTHENICS	LIGHTFINGERED	PSYCHOBIOLOGY	TRICHOSANTHIN
GYNECOLOGICAL	CIRCUMFERENCE	MEISTERSINGER	UNDERCARRIAGE	TRIPLOBLASTIC
HEMISPHERICAL	CLAIRAUDIENCE	MICROCOMPUTER	AUTOBIOGRAPHY	UNSYMPATHETIC
HORTICULTURAL	CONCUPISCENCE	MIDDLEBREAKER	CRUISERWEIGHT	VERCINGETORIX
HYPERCRITICAL	CONVALESCENCE	MULTICOLOURED	FEATHERWEIGHT	SPINDLESHANKS
HYPOCHONDRIAC	COUNTERATTACK	NEANDERTHALER	HUNDREDWEIGHT	SPORTSMANLIKE
INFINITESIMAL	DEFERVESCENCE	NEUROCOMPUTER	PROSOPOGRAPHY	STATESMANLIKE
INQUISITORIAL	DISAPPEARANCE	OPPORTUNITIES	RHYPAROGRAPHY	ACRYLONITRILE
INSPIRATIONAL	EFFERVESCENCE	OWNEROCCUPIER	SPECTROGRAPHY	ADVENTUROUSLY
INSTITUTIONAL	EFFLORESCENCE	OYSTERCATCHER	UNTRUSTWORTHY	AESTHETICALLY
INSTRUCTIONAL	GLUMDALCLITCH	PARTICOLOURED	ANACHRONISTIC	AFFIRMATIVELY
INSUBSTANTIAL	HIEROGLYPHICS	PASSIONFLOWER	ANTHELMINTHIC	ALTERNATIVELY
INTERNATIONAL	HYDRODYNAMICS	PERSONALITIES	APOCATASTASIS	APPROXIMATELY
INTERPERSONAL	INCANDESCENCE	POTENTIOMETER	ARISTOCRATIC	ASCERTAINABLE
INTRAMUSCULAR	INCONSISTENCY	PREFABRICATED	CEPHALOSPORIN	ASTONISHINGLY
ISOGEOTHERMAL	INCONVENIENCE	PRELIMINARIES	CLOSEDCIRCUIT	AUTOMATICALLY
LACKADAISICAL	INFLORESCENCE	PREPROGRAMMED	COLLIESHANGIE	BIODEGRADABLE
MACHIAVELLIAN	INSUFFICIENCY	PRESERVATIVES	COMPANIONSHIP	CATEGORICALLY
MASTIGOPHORAN	INTRANSIGENCE	QUARTERMASTER	CRAFTSMANSHIP	CEREMONIOUSLY
MATHEMATICIAN	JURISPRUDENCE	REMINISCENCES	CRYPTANALYSIS	COMMENSURABLE
MEDITERRANEAN	LIEBFRAUMILCH	ROLLERCOASTER	ELEPHANTIASIS	COMPANIONABLE
METAPHYSICIAN	MAGNILOQUENCE	SACCHAROMYCES	ENCYCLOPAEDIA	COMPARATIVELY
MISSISSIPPIAN	NONRESISTANCE	SCANDALMONGER	ENCYCLOPAEDIC	CONDITIONALLY
MOCKTECHNICAL	OUTRECUIDANCE	SCHOOLTEACHER	EPANADIPLOSIS	CONSECUTIVELY
MORPHOLOGICAL	PHYSHARMONICA	SCHUTZSTAFFEL	ESCHSCHOLTZIA	CONSIDERATELY
MULTINATIONAL	PREPONDERANCE	SELFADDRESSED	HYDROELECTRIC	CONSPICUOUSLY
NIGHTWATCHMAN	PSYCHOMETRICS	SELFCONFESSED	IDIORRHYTHMIC	COUNTRYPEOPLE
PAEDIATRICIAN	RECALCITRANCE	SELFCONTAINED	IDIOSYNCRATIC	DIAMETRICALLY
PARALLELOGRAM	RECRUDESCENCE	SEPTENTRIONES	IMPERIALISTIC	DISCREDITABLE
PARENTHETICAL	REPROGRAPHICS	SHRINKWRAPPED	KALEIDOSCOPIC	DISCREDITABLY
PATERFAMILIAS	THAUMATURGICS	SIPUNCULOIDEA	LAMPADEPHORIA	DISGRACEFULLY
PELOPONNESIAN	THOROUGHBRACE	SOPHISTICATED	LEPTOSPIROSIS	DISHONOURABLE
PENNSYLVANIAN	THUNDERSTRUCK	STATIONMASTER	LIBRARIANSHIP	DISHONOURABLY
PEPTIDOGLYCAN	BUTYRALDEHYDE	STEEPLECHASER	LIECHTENSTEIN	ECCENTRICALLY
PERPENDICULAR	INCOMMUNICADO	STRIKEBREAKER	MATERIALISTIC	ENCEPHALOCELE
PETROCHEMICAL	SCHADENFREUDE	SUBJECTMATTER	METAMORPHOSIS	ENERGETICALLY
PHILADELPHIAN	SHOULDERBLADE	SUPERANNUATED	MONONUCLEOSIS	EXCEPTIONABLE
PHILOSOPHICAL	AFFENPINSCHER	SWOLLENHEADED	NATIONALISTIC	EXCEPTIONALLY
PHOTOCHEMICAL	ANTIGROPELOES	SYMPIESOMETER	NUCLEOPROTEIN	EXPEDITIOUSLY
PHYSIOLOGICAL	BIBLIOGRAPHER	TENDERHEARTED	OPPORTUNISTIC	EXTRAVAGANTLY
PRESSURELOCAL	BOUGAINVILLEA	TONGUEINCHEEK	PARAPHERNALIA	FANTASTICALLY
PRETERNATURAL	BROKENHEARTED	TONGUETWISTER	PARTHOGENESIS	FRIGHTENINGLY
PROBLEMATICAL	CHARACTERISED	TRANQUILLISER	PASSEMENTERIE	FUNDAMENTALLY
PROPRIETORIAL	CHINKERINCHEE	TRANQUILLIZER	PATERNALISTIC	GEOMETRICALLY
PROTONOTARIAT	CHOREOGRAPHER	UNACCOMPANIED	PHARMACOPOEIA	GRAMMATICALLY
PSYCHOLOGICAL	CIRCUMSTANCES	UNADULTERATED	PHILANTHROPIC	HYDRAULICALLY
PYROTECHNICAL	CLISHMACLAVER	UNANTICIPATED	PHOTOELECTRIC	IGNOMINIOUSLY
QUADRAGESIMAL	COUNTERFEITER	UNCOMPLICATED	POLIOMYELITIS	IMAGINATIVELY
QUADRILATERAL	DECAFFEINATED	UNCOORDINATED	POLYCHROMATIC	IMPERCEPTIBLE
QUARTODECIMAN	DEMILITARIZED	UNDERACHIEVER	PROCLEUSMATIC	IMPERCEPTIBLY
SEISMOLOGICAL	DISADVANTAGED	UNDERSTRAPPER	PROFESSORSHIP	IMPERTINENTLY
SERVILEMENTAL	DISILLUSIONED	UNDISCIPLINED	PSYCHOKINESIS	IMPERTURBABLE
SPELEOLOGICAL	DISINTERESTED	UNEMBARRASSED	PSYCHOSOMATIC	IMPERTURBABLY
STAPHYLINIDAE	DISTINGUISHED	UNENLIGHTENED	SCHIZOPHRENIA	IMPRACTICABLE
SUBMANDIBULAR	ELECTROMAGNET	UNESTABLISHED	SCHIZOPHRENIC	IMPROVIDENTLY
SUPRANATIONAL	FLABBERGASTED	UNEXPERIENCED	SCLEROPROTEIN	INADVERTENTLY
SWEDENBORGIAN	FORTUNETELLER	UNINTERRUPTED	SEMIAUTOMATIC	INCOMBUSTIBLE
TECHNOLOGICAL	GLOSSOGRAPHER	UNPARTITIONED	SOCIOECONOMIC	INCOMPETENTLY
TEMPERAMENTAL	GRANDDAUGHTER	UNPRECEDENTED	SOMATOTROPHIN	INCONCEIVABLE
THERMONUCLEAR	GRIEFSTRICKEN	VIDEORECORDER	SPITESPLENDID	INCONTESTABLE
TOPOGRAPHICAL	HAMMERKLAVIER	WEATHERBEATEN	SPORTSMANSHIP	INCORRUPTIBLE
TYPOGRAPHICAL	HAMMERTHROWER	BACTERIOPHAGE	STATESMANSHIP	INCREDULOUSLY
UNCONDITIONAL	IMPONDERABLES	BIOTECHNOLOGY	SUOVETAURILIA	INDEFATIGABLE
UNEXCEPTIONAL	INEXPERIENCED	COUNTERCHARGE	TENOSYNOVITIS	INDEFATIGABLY
UNGRAMMATICAL	KAPPELMEISTER	FOREKNOWLEDGE	TETRASYLLABIC	INDEPENDENTLY
UNINTENTIONAL	KIDDERMINSTER	INTERMARRIAGE	THERMODYNAMIC	INDESCRIBABLE
UNSUBSTANTIAL	KNICKERBOCKER	KANGCHENJUNGA	THERMOPLASTIC	INDESCRIBABLY
UNSYMMETRICAL	LEATHERJACKET	OPHTHALMOLOGY	THORACENTESIS	INDIFFERENTLY

INDISPENSABLE	SUPERFLUOUSLY	DRYOPITHECINE	ADMINISTRATOR	FALSIFICATION
INDUSTRIOUSLY	SUPERLATIVELY	EMBARRASSMENT	AFFORESTATION	FERTILISATION
INEFFICIENTLY	SYNTACTICALLY	EMBELLISHMENT	AGGLOMERATION	FERTILIZATION
INEXHAUSTIBLE	SYNTHETICALLY	ENCOURAGEMENT	AMPLIFICATION	FORMALIZATION
INEXPRESSIBLE	TANTALIZINGLY	ENLIGHTENMENT	ANIMADVERSION	FORTIFICATION
INQUISITIVELY	THEOLOGICALLY	ENTERTAINMENT	APPROPRIATION	FOSSILIZATION
INSTINCTIVELY	THEORETICALLY	ESTABLISHMENT	APPROXIMATION	FRAGMENTATION
INSUPPORTABLE	THOUGHTLESSLY	FRANKALMOIGNE	ASSASSINATION	GALVANIZATION
INTELLIGENTLY	THREATENINGLY	GLOBETROTTING	AUTHORISATION	GESTICULATION
INTENTIONALLY	TORTOISESHELL	GRANDILOQUENT	AUTHORIZATION	GLORIFICATION
INTERESTINGLY	TRADITIONALLY	HEARTBREAKING	BEATIFICATION	GRATIFICATION
INTRINSICALLY	TRANSPARENTLY	HOUSEBREAKING	BOUSTROPHEDON	HALLUCINATION
INVOLUNTARILY	TRANSPORTABLE	ILLUMINATIONS	CARBONIZATION	HARMONIZATION
IRRECOVERABLE	TRAUMATICALLY	IMPERSONATING	CAUTERIZATION	HORRIPILATION
IRREPLACEABLE	TREACHEROUSLY	INCRIMINATING	CERTIFICATION	HYBRIDIZATION
IRREPRESSIBLE	UNACCOUNTABLE	INSIGNIFICANT	CIRCUMVENTION	IMPERSONATION
IRRESPONSIBLE	UNACCOUNTABLY	LONGSUFFERING	CLARIFICATION	IMPROVISATION
IRRESPONSIBLY	UNCOMFORTABLE	MALADJUSTMENT	COLLABORATION	INCARCERATION
IRRETRIEVABLE	UNCOMFORTABLY	MALLEMAROKING	COMMEMORATION	INCORPORATION
IRRETRIEVABLY	UNCONQUERABLE	MANUFACTURING	COMMISERATION	INDISPOSITION
KNOWLEDGEABLE	UNCONSCIOUSLY	MERCHANDIZING	COMMUNICATION	INTERCALATION
MAGISTERIALLY	UNFASHIONABLE	MISMANAGEMENT	COMPREHENSION	INTERPOLATION
MAGNANIMOUSLY	UNFLINCHINGLY	MISUNDERSTAND	CONCATENATION	INTERROGATION
MAGNIFICENTLY	UNFORESEEABLE	MOUTHWATERING	CONCENTRATION	INTROSPECTION
MISCHIEVOUSLY	UNFORGETTABLE	NIGHTCLUBBING	CONDESCENSION	INVESTIGATION
NORTHEASTERLY	UNFORTUNATELY	NONSUFFICIENT	CONFARREATION	JOLLIFICATION
NORTHWESTERLY	UNGENTLEMANLY	OVERSTATEMENT	CONFEDERATION	JUSTIFICATION
NOSTALGICALLY	UNIMPEACHABLE	PHENCYCLIDINE	CONFIGURATION	JUXTAPOSITION
OBJECTIONABLE	UNIMPRESSIBLE	PHYLLOQUINONE	CONFLAGRATION	MACHICOLATION
OUTSTANDINGLY	UNINHABITABLE	PHYSOSTIGMINE	CONFRONTATION	MAGNIFICATION
PAINSTAKINGLY	UNMENTIONABLE	PREPOSSESSING	CONSIDERATION	MANIFESTATION
PARADOXICALLY	UNNECESSARILY	PRONOUNCEMENT	CONSOLIDATION	MATRICULATION
PASSCHENDAELE	UNPREDICTABLE	RAMIFICATIONS	CONSPURCATION	MECHANIZATION
PATRIOTICALLY	UNSERVICEABLE	RAPPROCHEMENT	CONSTELLATION	MISCEGENATION
PERFUNCTORILY	ALUMINOTHERMY	REARRANGEMENT	CONSTERNATION	MISCONCEPTION
PNEUMATICALLY	CHRISTMASTIME	REDEVELOPMENT	CONTAMINATION	MISUNDERSTOOD
PRAGMATICALLY	COMRADEINARMS	REFURBISHMENT	CONTEMPLATION	MODERNIZATION
PRECIPITATELY	GENERALISSIMO	REIMBURSEMENT	CONTRABASSOON	MOLLIFICATION
PREDOMINANTLY	PNEUMONECTOMY	REINFORCEMENT	CONTRACEPTION	MONOCOTYLEDON
PROGRESSIVELY	QUINQUAGESIMA	REINSTATEMENT	CONTRADICTION	MORTIFICATION
PROMISCUOUSLY	THYROIDECTOMY	REPERCUSSIONS	CONTRAVENTION	MYSTIFICATION
PROPHETICALLY	TONSILLECTOMY	REPLENISHMENT	CORROBORATION	NEIGHBOURHOOD
PROVISIONALLY	ACCOMMODATING	RHADAMANTHINE	CROSSQUESTION	NORMALIZATION
PROVOCATIVELY	ACCOMPANIMENT	ROLLERBLADING	DECOMPOSITION	NULLIFICATION
PUNCTILIOUSLY	ADVERTISEMENT	SCINTILLATING	DECOMPRESSION	ORCHESTRATION
REALISTICALLY	AFFREIGHTMENT	SELFCONFIDENT	DEFIBRILLATOR	ORNAMENTATION
REMORSELESSLY	ANTICOAGULANT	SELFGOVERNING	DEFORESTATION	PANDICULATION
REPREHENSIBLE	ANTIHISTAMINE	SKATEBOARDING	DEMONSTRATION	PANHARMONICON
REPREHENSIBLY	APPORTIONMENT	SPINECHILLING	DESEGREGATION	PARTICIPATION
REPROACHFULLY	ARMOURPLATING	STEPPINGSTONE	DETERIORATION	PERAMBULATION
RESOURCEFULLY	BLOODCURDLING	STOCKBREEDING	DETERMINATION	PEREGRINATION
ROUNDTHEWORLD	BREASTFEEDING	SUBLIEUTENANT	DIACATHOLICON	PETRIFICATION
SARCASTICALLY	BUNGEEJUMPING	SUPERABUNDANT	DIFFARREATION	PHYTOPLANKTON
SCHEMATICALLY	CHATEAUBRIAND	SWASHBUCKLING	DISCOLORATION	POLLICITATION
SENSATIONALLY	CIRCUMAMBIENT	SWEETSMELLING	DISCONNECTION	PRECIPITATION
SENTENTIOUSLY	CONDESCENDING	TAPERECORDING	DISESTIMATION	PRECONCEPTION
SENTIMENTALLY	CONTINUATIONS	TELEMARKETING	DISPROPORTION	PREMEDITATION
SIGNIFICANTLY	CONTRIBUTIONS	THESSALONIANS	DISSEMINATION	PREOCCUPATION
SOUTHEASTERLY	CONVERSAZIONE	THOROUGHGOING	DISSIMULATION	PREPOSSESSION
SOUTHWESTERLY	CORRESPONDENT	UNDERCLOTHING	DOCUMENTATION	PREVARICATION
SPASMODICALLY	CORRESPONDING	UNDERSTANDING	DRAMATIZATION	PRIVATIZATION
SPECTACULARLY	COUNTERACTING	UNINTELLIGENT	ELECTROCUTION	PROLIFERATION
SPONTANEOUSLY	DISAPPOINTING	UNINTERESTING	ENCULTURATION	PRONUNCIATION
STATISTICALLY	DISCONCERTING	UNQUESTIONING	EPIPHENOMENON	PULVERIZATION
STRATEGICALLY	DISENGAGEMENT	VICEPRESIDENT	EPITRACHELION	QUALIFICATION
STYLISTICALLY	DISFIGUREMENT	WEIGHTLIFTING	EXPOSTULATION	RECRIMINATION
SUBSERVIENTLY	DISHEARTENING	WITWATERSRAND	EXPROPRIATION	RECTIFICATION
SUBSTANTIALLY	DISPARAGEMENT	ACCEPTILATION	EXTERMINATION	REFRIGERATION
SUPERFICIALLY	DOUBLEGLAZING	ACCOMMODATION	EXTRAPOLATION	REGIMENTATION

REGURGITATION	SOMATOSENSORY	PROTECTIONIST	IMPOSSIBILITY	PLATOCEPHALUS
REINCARNATION	SUPERNUMERARY	PROTESTANTISM	IMPROBABILITY	PROFECTITIOUS
RESUSCITATION	SUPPLEMENTARY	PROVINCIALISM	INAPPROPRIATE	PUSILLANIMOUS
RETROGRESSION	ACUPUNCTURIST	PSYCHOANALYSE	INCONSIDERATE	RUTHERFORDIUM
REUNIFICATION	AIRWORTHINESS	PSYCHOANALYST	INDETERMINATE	SANCTIMONIOUS
REVERBERATION	ANTICLOCKWISE	QUERULOUSNESS	INDIVIDUALITY	SELFCONSCIOUS
SCINTILLATION	ARCHAEOLOGIST	RECEPTIVENESS	INEVITABILITY	STERCORACEOUS
SEDIMENTATION	ATTENTIVENESS	RECITATIONIST	INFALLIBILITY	STREPTOCARPUS
SEMICONDUCTOR	BIBLIOPHAGIST	REDEMPTIONIST	INFLEXIBILITY	STREPTOCOCCUS
SEQUESTRATION	BOUILLABAISSE	REPUBLICANISM	INSENSITIVITY	SUPERSTITIOUS
SIGNIFICATION	CHARACTERLESS	RIGHTEOUSNESS	INSUBORDINATE	SURREPTITIOUS
SOLEMNIZATION	COLLOQUIALISM	SALACIOUSNESS	INVINCIBILITY	TABLESPOONFUL
SPECIFICATION	CONCEPTIONIST	SCHOLARLINESS	INVIOLABILITY	TINTINNABULUM
STABILIZATION	CONCEPTUALIST	SECRETIVENESS	MASSACHUSETTS	UMBELLIFEROUS
STERILIZATION	CONSCIOUSNESS	SENSELESSNESS	MESSERSCHMITT	UNCEREMONIOUS
STRANGULATION	CONTENTEDNESS	SENSITIVENESS	MULTINUCLEATE	UNPRETENTIOUS
SUBCONTRACTOR	CONTORTIONIST	SHAPELESSNESS	NEMATHELMINTH	ARGUMENTATIVE
SUBORDINATION	CREDULOUSNESS	SLEEPLESSNESS	NONCONFORMITY	AUTHORITATIVE
TRANSCRIPTION	CRIMINOLOGIST	SNOWBLINDNESS	PARTICULARITY	COLLABORATIVE
TRANSGRESSION	DEATHLESSNESS	SPRIGHTLINESS	PENETRABILITY	COMMEMORATIVE
TRANSMUTATION	DEIPNOSOPHIST	SQUEAMISHNESS	PROCRASTINATE	COMMUNICATIVE
TRANSPIRATION	DERMATOLOGIST	STEADFASTNESS	PROFITABILITY	COMPREHENSIVE
TRANSPOSITION	EFFECTIVENESS	STRENUOUSNESS	PROGNOSTICATE	CONTEMPLATIVE
TRIANGULATION	EXHIBITIONIST	TALKATIVENESS	PROPORTIONATE	CONTRACEPTIVE
VERSIFICATION	EXPANSIVENESS	THANKLESSNESS	PUSILLANIMITY	COSTEFFECTIVE
VICTIMIZATION	FACETIOUSNESS	THAUMATURGIST	QUADRUPLICATE	DEMONSTRATIVE
VITRIFICATION	FORGETFULNESS	THIGMOTROPISM	RADIOACTIVITY	ELECTROMOTIVE
VULCANIZATION	FRACTIOUSNESS	TRACTARIANISM	RATIONALALITY	FREQUENTATIVE
VULGARIZATION	FRIGHTFULNESS	UNWILLINGNESS	RENSSELAERITE	INTERROGATIVE
XIPHIPLASTRON	FRIVOLOUSNESS	VEGETARIANISM	SPERMATOPHYTE	INTROSPECTIVE
DAGUERREOTYPE	GARRULOUSNESS	VENTRILOQUISM	SUPERORDINATE	INVESTIGATIVE
GYNANDROMORPH	GUILTLESSNESS	VENTRILOQUIST	SUSPERCOLLATE	RETROSPECTIVE
PHYSIOTHERAPY	GYNAECOLOGIST	VIVACIOUSNESS	THEATRICALITY	UNCOOPERATIVE
PSYCHOTHERAPY	HETERAUXESISM	VORACIOUSNESS	TRANSLITERATE	UNIMAGINATIVE
BUTTERFINGERS	HYALURONIDASE	WHOLESOMENESS	UNCOMMUNICATE	UNPROGRESSIVE
CHEESEMONGERS	IMPRESSIONISM	ACCEPTABILITY	UNDERESTIMATE	ARCHAEOPTERYX
COMPLEMENTARY	IMPRESSIONIST	ACCESSIBILITY	UNDERGRADUATE	COMMERCIALIZE
COMPLIMENTARY	IMPULSIVENESS	ACCOUTREMENTS	UPTOTHEMINUTE	CONCEPTUALIZE
CONCESSIONARY	INDETERMINISM	AGGIORNAMENTO	VIDEOCASSETTE	DECRIMINALIZE
CONFECTIONERS	INDIVIDUALISM	APPROPINQUATE	VULNERABILITY	DENATIONALIZE
CONFECTIONERY	INDIVIDUALIST	ARCHIMANDRITE	ALLOCHTHONOUS	INDUSTRIALIZE
CONSERVATOIRE	INDUSTRIALIST	ARTIFICIALITY	ALUMINIFEROUS	OVEREMPHASIZE
CONTRADICTORY	INGENUOUSNESS	BACCALAUREATE	AMPHIGASTRIUM	PARTICULARIZE
CORROBORATORY	INSIDIOUSNESS	BASIDIOMYCETE	ARUNDINACEOUS	REVOLUTIONIZE
DISCRETIONARY	INVENTIVENESS	BLANDISHMENTS	AUTOCEPHALOUS	TRANSISTORIZE
EPHEMEROPTERA	LEISURELINESS	CHANGEABILITY	AUTOCHTHONOUS	
EXPEDITIONARY	LEPIDOPTERIST	COMPARABILITY	BRACHIOSAURUS	**13:13**
EXTRAORDINARY	LUXURIOUSNESS	COMPASSIONATE	CARBONIFEROUS	
FUERTEVENTURA	LYCANTHROPIST	COMPATIBILITY	CARTILAGINOUS	BOUGAINVILLEA
GENITOURINARY	MERCILESSNESS	CONSANGUINITY	CHRYSANTHEMUM	ENCYCLOPAEDIA
GEOSTATIONARY	METAGRABOLISE	CONTRAFAGOTTO	CONSCIENTIOUS	ENTEROPNEUSTA
HALLUCINATORY	METAGRABOLISE	DECONTAMINATE	CONSECTANEOUS	EPHEMEROPTERA
HORSEFEATHERS	METEOROLOGIST	DEFENSIBILITY	DISCONTINUOUS	ESCHSCHOLTZIA
INCRIMINATORY	MICROORGANISM	DEHYDROGENATE	DISRESPECTFUL	FUERTEVENTURA
JIGGERYPOKERY	MISANTHROPIST	DEPENDABILITY	GASTROCNEMIUS	KANGCHENJUNGA
JUSTIFICATORY	NERVELESSNESS	DÉSOBLIGEANTE	GOODRIDDANCE	LAMPADEPHORIA
KNICKKNACKERY	NONCONFORMIST	DIFFERENTIATE	HETEROGENEOUS	PARAPHERNALIA
LAEVOROTATORY	OBJECTIVENESS	DISCONTINUITY	HYDROCEPHALUS	PHARMACOPOEIA
MADETOMEASURE	OFFENSIVENESS	DISPASSIONATE	INCONSPICUOUS	PHYSHARMONICA
MAURIKIGUSARI	OFFICIOUSNESS	DISSIMILARITY	INSECTIVOROUS	QUINQUAGESIMA
PARLIAMENTARY	ORNITHOLOGIST	ENTEROPNEUSTA	INSTANTANEOUS	SCHIZOPHRENIA
PARTICIPATORY	PAPAPRELATIST	EQUIPONDERATE	LECTISTERNIUM	SIPUNCULOIDEA
PRECAUTIONARY	PARTICULARISE	EXCOMMUNICATE	LEPTOCEPHALUS	SUOVETAURILIA
PRIMOGENITURE	PERFECTIONIST	FERROCONCRETE	LISSOTRICHOUS	ANACHRONISTIC
QUESTIONNAIRE	PERVASIVENESS	FOSTERPARENTS	MISCELLANEOUS	ANTHELMINTHIC
RECRIMINATORY	PHOSPHOLIPASE	HERMAPHRODITE	MONOTHALAMOUS	ARISTROCRATIC
REFRIGERATORS	PHYSIOGNOMIST	HOMOSEXUALITY	MULTITUDINOUS	ENCYCLOPAEDIC
REVOLUTIONARY	PROJECTIONIST	HYPERSTHENITE	PARANTHROPOUS	HYDROELECTRIC
SEMBLANCECORD	PROTECTIONISM	HYPOVENTILATE	PERSPICACIOUS	HYPOCHONDRIAC
				IDIORRHYTHMIC

IDIOSYNCRATIC	AQUIFOLIACEAE	INCOMBUSTIBLE	THOROUGHBRACE	MAURIKIGUSARI
IMPERIALISTIC	ARCHIMANDRITE	INCONCEIVABLE	TRANSISTORIZE	COUNTERATTACK
KALEIDOSCOPIC	ARGUMENTATIVE	INCONSIDERATE	TRANSLITERATE	THUNDERSTRUCK
MATERIALISTIC	ASCERTAINABLE	INCONTESTABLE	TRANSPORTABLE	TONGUEINCHEEK
NATIONALISTIC	AUTHORITATIVE	INCONVENIENCE	UNACCOUNTABLE	ARCHITECTURAL
OPPORTUNISTIC	BACCALAUREATE	INCORRUPTIBLE	UNCOMFORTABLE	CHRONOLOGICAL
PATERNALISTIC	BACTERIOPHAGE	INDEFATIGABLE	UNCOMMUNICATE	COEDUCATIONAL
PHILANTHROPIC	BASIDIOMYCETE	INDESCRIBABLE	UNCONQUERABLE	CONGRESSIONAL
PHOTOELECTRIC	BIODEGRADABLE	INDETERMINATE	UNCOOPERATIVE	CONSEQUENTIAL
POLYCHROMATIC	BIREFRINGENCE	INDISPENSABLE	UNDERCARRIAGE	CONTROVERSIAL
PROCLEUSMATIC	BOUILLABAISSE	INDUSTRIALIZE	UNDERESTIMATE	DEVELOPMENTAL
PSYCHOSOMATIC	BUTYRALDEHYDE	INEXHAUSTIBLE	UNDERGRADUATE	DISRESPECTFUL
SCHIZOPHRENIC	CHINKERINCHEE	INEXPRESSIBLE	UNFASHIONABLE	ENTOMOLOGICAL
SEMIAUTOMATIC	CHRISTMASTIME	INFLORESCENCE	UNFORESEEABLE	ENVIRONMENTAL
SOCIOECONOMIC	CIRCUMFERENCE	INSUBORDINATE	UNFORGETTABLE	GRANDPARENTAL
TETRASYLLABIC	CLAIRAUDIENCE	INSUPPORTABLE	UNIMAGINATIVE	GRAVITATIONAL
THERMODYNAMIC	COLLABORATIVE	INTERMARRIAGE	UNIMPEACHABLE	GYNECOLOGICAL
THERMOPLASTIC	COLLIESHANGIE	INTERROGATIVE	UNIMPRESSIBLE	HEMISPHERICAL
TRANSATLANTIC	COMMEMORATIVE	INTRANSIGENCE	UNINHABITABLE	HORTICULTURAL
TRIPLOBLASTIC	COMMENSURABLE	INTROSPECTIVE	UNMENTIONABLE	HYPERCRITICAL
UNSYMPATHETIC	COMMERCIALIZE	INVESTIGATIVE	UNPREDICTABLE	INFINITESIMAL
BROKENHEARTED	COMMUNICATIVE	IRRECOVERABLE	UNPROGRESSIVE	INQUISITORIAL
CHARACTERISED	COMPANIONABLE	IRREPLACEABLE	UNSERVICEABLE	INSPIRATIONAL
CHATEAUBRIAND	COMPASSIONATE	IRREPRESSIBLE	UPTOTHEMINUTE	INSTITUTIONAL
DECAFFEINATED	COMPREHENSIVE	IRRESPONSIBLE	VIDEOCASSETTE	INSTRUCTIONAL
DEMILITARIZED	CONCEPTUALIZE	IRRETRIEVABLE	ACCOMMODATING	INSUBSTANTIAL
DISADVANTAGED	CONCUPISCENCE	JURISPRUDENCE	ARMOURPLATING	INTERNATIONAL
DISILLUSIONED	CONSERVATOIRE	KNOWLEDGEABLE	BLOODCURDLING	INTERPERSONAL
DISINTERESTED	CONTEMPLATIVE	MADETOMEASURE	BREASTFEEDING	ISOGEOTHERMAL
DISTINGUISHED	CONTRACEPTIVE	MAGNILOQUENCE	BUNGEEJUMPING	LACKADAISICAL
FLABBERGASTED	CONVALESCENCE	METAGRABOLISE	CONDESCENDING	MOCKTECHNICAL
INEXPERIENCED	CONVERSAZIONE	METAGROBOLISE	CORRESPONDING	MORPHOLOGICAL
LIGHTFINGERED	COSTEFFECTIVE	MULTINUCLEATE	COUNTERACTING	MULTINATIONAL
MISUNDERSTAND	COUNTERCHARGE	NONRESISTANCE	DISAPPOINTING	PARENTHETICAL
MISUNDERSTOOD	COUNTRYPEOPLE	OBJECTIONABLE	DISCONCERTING	PETROCHEMICAL
MULTICOLOURED	DAGUERREOTYPE	OUTRECUIDANCE	DISHEARTENING	PHILOSOPHICAL
NEIGHBOURHOOD	DECONTAMINATE	OVEREMPHASIZE	DOUBLEGLAZING	PHOTOCHEMICAL
PARTICOLOURED	DECRIMINALIZE	PARTICULARISE	GLOBETROTTING	PHYSIOLOGICAL
PREFABRICATED	DEFERVESCENCE	PARTICULARIZE	HEARTBREAKING	PRESSURELOCAL
PREPROGRAMMED	DEHYDROGENATE	PASSCHENDAELE	HOUSEBREAKING	PRETERNATURAL
ROUNDTHEWORLD	DEMONSTRATIVE	PASSEMENTERIE	IMPERSONATING	PROBLEMATICAL
SELFADDRESSED	DENATIONALIZE	PHENCYCLIDINE	INCRIMINATING	PROPRIETORIAL
SELFCONFESSED	DÉSOBLIGEANTE	PHOSPHOLIPASE	LONGSUFFERING	PSYCHOLOGICAL
SELFCONTAINED	DIFFERENTIATE	PHYLLOQUINONE	MALLEMAROKING	PYROTECHNICAL
SEMBLANCECORD	DISAPPEARANCE	PHYSOSTIGMINE	MANUFACTURING	QUADRAGESIMAL
SHRINKWRAPPED	DISCREDITABLE	PREPONDERANCE	MERCHANDIZING	QUADRILATERAL
SOPHISTICATED	DISHONOURABLE	PRIMOGENITURE	MOUTHWATERING	SCHUTZSTAFFEL
SPITESPLENDID	DISPASSIONATE	PROCRASTINATE	NIGHTCLUBBING	SEISMOLOGICAL
SUPERANNUATED	DRYOPITHECINE	PROGNOSTICATE	PREPOSSESSING	SERVILEMENTAL
SWOLLENHEADED	EFFERVESCENCE	PROPORTIONATE	ROLLERBLADING	SPELEOLOGICAL
TENDERHEARTED	EFFLORESCENCE	PSYCHOANALYSE	SCINTILLATING	SUPRANATIONAL
UNACCOMPANIED	ELECTROMOTIVE	QUADRUPLICATE	SELFGOVERNING	TABLESPOONFUL
UNADULTERATED	ENCEPHALOCELE	QUESTIONNAIRE	SKATEBOARDING	TECHNOLOGICAL
UNANTICIPATED	EQUIPONDERATE	RECALCITRANCE	SPINECHILLING	TEMPERAMENTAL
UNCOMPLICATED	EXCEPTIONABLE	RECRUDESCENCE	STOCKBREEDING	TOPOGRAPHICAL
UNCOORDINATED	EXCOMMUNICATE	RENSSELAERITE	SWASHBUCKLING	TORTOISESHELL
UNDISCIPLINED	FERROCONCRETE	REPREHENSIBLE	SWEETSMELLING	TYPOGRAPHICAL
UNEMBARRASSED	FOREKNOWLEDGE	RETROSPECTIVE	TAPERECORDING	UNCONDITIONAL
UNENLIGHTENED	FRANKALMOIGNE	REVOLUTIONIZE	TELEMARKETING	UNEXCEPTIONAL
UNESTABLISHED	FREQUENTATIVE	RHADAMANTHINE	THOROUGHGOING	UNGRAMMATICAL
UNEXPERIENCED	HERMAPHRODITE	SCHADENFREUDE	UNDERCLOTHING	UNINTENTIONAL
UNINTERRUPTED	HYALURONIDASE	SHOULDERBLADE	UNDERSTANDING	UNSUBSTANTIAL
UNPARTITIONED	HYPERSTHENITE	SPERMATOPHYTE	UNINTERESTING	UNSYMMETRICAL
UNPRECEDENTED	HYPOVENTILATE	SPORTSMANLIKE	UNQUESTIONING	AMPHIGASTRIUM
WITWATERSRAND	IMPERCEPTIBLE	STAPHYLINIDAE	WEIGHTLIFTING	CHRYSANTHEMUM
ACRYLONITRILE	IMPERTURBABLE	STATESMANLIKE	GLUMDALCLITCH	COLLOQUIALISM
ANTICLOCKWISE	IMPRACTICABLE	STEPPINGSTONE	GYNANDROMORPH	ENCEPHALOGRAM
ANTIHISTAMINE	INAPPROPRIATE	SUPERORDINATE	LIEBFRAUMILCH	HETERAUXESISM
APPROPINQUATE	INCANDESCENCE	SUSPERCOLLATE	NEMATHELMINTH	IMPRESSIONISM

INDETERMINISM	DECOMPRESSION	MONOCOTYLEDON	WEATHERBEATEN	BRACHIOSAURUS
INDIVIDUALISM	DEFORESTATION	MORTIFICATION	XIPHIPLASTRON	BUTTERFINGERS
LECTISTERNIUM	DEMONSTRATION	MYSTIFICATION	AGGIORNAMENTO	CALLISTHENICS
MICROORGANISM	DESEGREGATION	NIGHTWATCHMAN	CONTRAFAGOTTO	CARBONIFEROUS
PARALLELOGRAM	DETERIORATION	NORMALIZATION	GENERALISSIMO	CARTILAGINOUS
PROTECTIONISM	DETERMINATION	NUCLEOPROTEIN	INCOMMUNICADO	CHARACTERLESS
PROTESTANTISM	DIACATHOLICON	NULLIFICATION	COMPANIONSHIP	CHEESEMONGERS
PROVINCIALISM	DIFFARREATION	ORCHESTRATION	CRAFTSMANSHIP	CIRCUMSTANCES
REPUBLICANISM	DISCOLORATION	ORNAMENTATION	LIBRARIANSHIP	COMRADEINARMS
RUTHERFORDIUM	DISCONNECTION	PAEDIATRICIAN	PROFESSORSHIP	CONFECTIONERS
THIGMOTROPISM	DISESTIMATION	PANDICULATION	SPORTSMANSHIP	CONSCIENTIOUS
TINTINNABULUM	DISPROPORTION	PANHARMONICON	STATESMANSHIP	CONSCIOUSNESS
TRACTARIANISM	DISSEMINATION	PARTICIPATION	ADMINISTRATOR	CONSECTANEOUS
VEGETARIANISM	DISSIMULATION	PELOPONNESIAN	AFFENPINSCHER	CONTENTEDNESS
VENTRILOQUISM	DOCUMENTATION	PENNSYLVANIAN	BIBLIOGRAPHER	CONTINUATIONS
ACCEPTILATION	DRAMATIZATION	PEPTIDOGLYCAN	CHOREOGRAPHER	CONTRIBUTIONS
ACCOMMODATION	ELECTROCUTION	PERAMBULATION	CLISHMACLAVER	CREDULOUSNESS
AFFORESTATION	ENCULTURATION	PEREGRINATION	COUNTERFEITER	CRYPTANALYSIS
AGGLOMERATION	EPIPHENOMENON	PETRIFICATION	DEFIBRILLATOR	DEATHLESSNESS
AIRCRAFTWOMAN	EPITRACHELION	PHILADELPHIAN	FORTUNETELLER	DISCONTINUOUS
ALPHABETARIAN	EXPOSTULATION	PHYTOPLANKTON	GLOSSOGRAPHER	EFFECTIVENESS
AMPLIFICATION	EXPROPRIATION	POLLICITATION	GRANDDAUGHTER	ELEPHANTIASIS
ANIMADVERSION	EXTERMINATION	PRECIPITATION	HAMMERKLAVIER	EPANADIPLOSIS
ANYTHINGARIAN	EXTRAPOLATION	PRECONCEPTION	HAMMERTHROWER	EXPANSIVENESS
APPROPRIATION	FALSIFICATION	PREMEDITATION	INTRAMUSCULAR	FACETIOUSNESS
APPROXIMATION	FERTILISATION	PREOCCUPATION	KAPPELMEISTER	FORGETFULNESS
ARITHMETICIAN	FERTILIZATION	PREPOSSESSION	KIDDERMINSTER	FOSTERPARENTS
ASSASSINATION	FORMALIZATION	PREVARICATION	KNICKERBOCKER	FRACTIOUSNESS
AUTHORISATION	FORTIFICATION	PRIVATIZATION	LEXICOGRAPHER	FRIGHTFULNESS
AUTHORITARIAN	FOSSILIZATION	PROLIFERATION	MEISTERSINGER	FRIVOLOUSNESS
AUTHORIZATION	FRAGMENTATION	PRONUNCIATION	MICROCOMPUTER	GARRULOUSNESS
BEATIFICATION	GALVANIZATION	PULVERIZATION	MIDDLEBREAKER	GASTROCNEMIUS
BILDUNGSROMAN	GESTICULATION	QUALIFICATION	NEANDERTHALER	GOODRIGHTEOUS
BOUSTROPHEDON	GLORIFICATION	QUARTODECIMAN	NEUROCOMPUTER	GUILTLESSNESS
BUSINESSWOMAN	GRATIFICATION	RECRIMINATION	OWNEROCCUPIER	HETEROGENEOUS
CARBONIZATION	GRIEFSTRICKEN	RECTIFICATION	OYSTERCATCHER	HIEROGLYPHICS
CAUTERIZATION	HALLUCINATION	REFRIGERATION	PASSIONFLOWER	HORSEFEATHERS
CEPHALOSPORIN	HARMONIZATION	REGIMENTATION	PERPENDICULAR	HYDROCEPHALUS
CERTIFICATION	HORRIPILATION	REGURGITATION	POTENTIOMETER	HYDRODYNAMICS
CIRCUMVENTION	HYBRIDIZATION	REINCARNATION	QUARTERMASTER	ILLUMINATIONS
CLARIFICATION	IMPERSONATION	RESUSCITATION	ROLLERCOASTER	IMPONDERABLES
COLLABORATION	IMPROVISATION	RETROGRESSION	SCANDALMONGER	IMPULSIVENESS
COMMEMORATION	INCARCERATION	REUNIFICATION	SCHOOLTEACHER	INCONSPICUOUS
COMMISERATION	INCORPORATION	REVERBERATION	SEMICONDUCTOR	INGENUOUSNESS
COMMUNICATION	INDISPOSITION	SCINTILLATION	STATIONMASTER	INSECTIVOROUS
COMPREHENSION	INTERCALATION	SCLEROPROTEIN	STEEPLECHASER	INSIDIOUSNESS
CONCATENATION	INTERPOLATION	SEDIMENTATION	STRIKEBREAKER	INSTANTANEOUS
CONCENTRATION	INTERROGATION	SEQUESTRATION	SUBCONTRACTOR	INVENTIVENESS
CONDESCENSION	INTROSPECTION	SIGNIFICATION	SUBJECTMATTER	LEISURELINESS
CONFARREATION	INVESTIGATION	SOLEMNIZATION	SUBMANDIBULAR	LEPTOCEPHALUS
CONFEDERATION	JOLLIFICATION	SOMATOTROPHIN	SYMPIESOMETER	LEPTOSPIROSIS
CONFIGURATION	JUSTIFICATION	SPECIFICATION	THERMONUCLEAR	LISSOTRICHOUS
CONFLAGRATION	JUXTAPOSITION	STABILIZATION	TONGUETWISTER	LUXURIOUSNESS
CONFRONTATION	LIECHTENSTEIN	STERILIZATION	TRANQUILLISER	MASSACHUSETTS
CONGRESSWOMAN	MACHIAVELLIAN	STRANGULATION	TRANQUILLIZER	MERCILESSNESS
CONSIDERATION	MACHICOLATION	SUBORDINATION	UNDERACHIEVER	METAMORPHOSIS
CONSOLIDATION	MAGNIFICATION	SWEDENBORGIAN	UNDERSTRAPPER	MISCELLANEOUS
CONSPURCATION	MANIFESTATION	TRANSCRIPTION	VIDEORECORDER	MONONUCLEOSIS
CONSTELLATION	MASTIGOPHORAN	TRANSGRESSION	ACCOUTREMENTS	MONOTHALAMOUS
CONSTERNATION	MATHEMATICIAN	TRANSMUTATION	AIRWORTHINESS	MULTITUDINOUS
CONTAMINATION	MATRICULATION	TRANSPIRATION	ALLOCHTHONOUS	NERVELESSNESS
CONTEMPLATION	MECHANIZATION	TRANSPOSITION	ALUMINIFEROUS	OBJECTIVENESS
CONTRABASSOON	MEDITERRANEAN	TRIANGULATION	ANTIGROPELOES	OFFENSIVENESS
CONTRACEPTION	METAPHYSICIAN	TRICHOSANTHIN	APOCATASTASIS	OFFICIOUSNESS
CONTRADICTION	MISCEGENATION	VERSIFICATION	ARUNDINACEOUS	OPPORTUNITIES
CONTRAVENTION	MISCONCEPTION	VICTIMIZATION	ATTENTIVENESS	PARANTHROPOUS
CORROBORATION	MISSISSIPPIAN	VITRIFICATION	AUTOCEPHALOUS	PARTHOGENESIS
CROSSQUESTION	MODERNIZATION	VULCANIZATION	AUTOCHTHONOUS	PATERFAMILIAS
DECOMPOSITION	MOLLIFICATION	VULGARIZATION	BLANDISHMENTS	PERSONALITIES

PERSPICACIOUS	CONTORTIONIST	ACCEPTABILITY	INCOMPETENTLY	PSYCHOTHERAPY
PERVASIVENESS	CORRESPONDENT	ACCESSIBILITY	INCONSISTENCY	PUNCTILIOUSLY
PLATOCEPHALUS	CRIMINOLOGIST	ADVENTUROUSLY	INCREDULOUSLY	PUSILLANIMITY
POLIOMYELITIS	CRUISERWEIGHT	AESTHETICALLY	INCRIMINATORY	RADIOACTIVITY
PRELIMINARIES	DEIPNOSOPHIST	AFFIRMATIVELY	INDEFATIGABLY	RATIONALALITY
PRESERVATIVES	DERMATOLOGIST	ALTERNATIVELY	INDEPENDENTLY	REALISTICALLY
PROFECTITIOUS	DISENGAGEMENT	ALUMINOTHERMY	INDESCRIBABLY	RECRIMINATORY
PSYCHOKINESIS	DISFIGUREMENT	APPROXIMATELY	INDIFFERENTLY	REMORSELESSLY
PSYCHOMETRICS	DISPARAGEMENT	ARTIFICIALITY	INDIVIDUALITY	REPREHENSIBLY
PUSILLANIMOUS	ELECTROMAGNET	ASTONISHINGLY	INDUSTRIOUSLY	REPROACHFULLY
QUERULOUSNESS	EMBARRASSMENT	AUTOBIOGRAPHY	INEFFICIENTLY	RESOURCEFULLY
RAMIFICATIONS	EMBELLISHMENT	AUTOMATICALLY	INEVITABILITY	REVOLUTIONARY
RECEPTIVENESS	ENCOURAGEMENT	BIOTECHNOLOGY	INFALLIBILITY	RHYPAROGRAPHY
REFRIGERATORS	ENLIGHTENMENT	CATEGORICALLY	INFLEXIBILITY	SARCASTICALLY
REMINISCENCES	ENTERTAINMENT	CEREMONIOUSLY	INQUISITIVELY	SCHEMATICALLY
REPERCUSSIONS	ESTABLISHMENT	CHANGEABILITY	INSENSITIVITY	SENSATIONALLY
REPROGRAPHICS	EXHIBITIONIST	COMPARABILITY	INSTINCTIVELY	SENTENTIOUSLY
RIGHTEOUSNESS	FEATHERWEIGHT	COMPARATIVELY	INSUFFICIENCY	SENTIMENTALLY
SACCHAROMYCES	GRANDILOQUENT	COMPATIBILITY	INTELLIGENTLY	SIGNIFICANTLY
SALACIOUSNESS	GYNAECOLOGIST	COMPLEMENTARY	INTENTIONALLY	SOMATOSENSORY
SANCTIMONIOUS	HUNDREDWEIGHT	COMPLIMENTARY	INTERESTINGLY	SOUTHEASTERLY
SCHOLARLINESS	IMPRESSIONIST	CONCESSIONARY	INTRINSICALLY	SOUTHWESTERLY
SECRETIVENESS	INDIVIDUALIST	CONDITIONALLY	INVINCIBILITY	SPASMODICALLY
SELFCONSCIOUS	INDUSTRIALIST	CONFECTIONERY	INVIOLABILITY	SPECTACULARLY
SENSELESSNESS	INSIGNIFICANT	CONSANGUINITY	INVOLUNTARILY	SPECTROGRAPHY
SENSITIVENESS	LEATHERJACKET	CONSECUTIVELY	IRRESPONSIBLY	SPONTANEOUSLY
SEPTENTRIONES	LEPIDOPTERIST	CONSIDERATELY	IRRETRIEVABLY	STATISTICALLY
SHAPELESSNESS	LYCANTHROPIST	CONSPICUOUSLY	JIGGERYPOKERY	STRATEGICALLY
SLEEPLESSNESS	MALADJUSTMENT	CONTRADICTORY	JUSTIFICATORY	STYLISTICALLY
SNOWBLINDNESS	MESSERSCHMITT	CORROBORATORY	KNICKKNACKERY	SUBSERVIENTLY
SPINDLESHANKS	METEOROLOGIST	DEFENSIBILITY	LAEVOROTATORY	SUBSTANTIALLY
SPRIGHTLINESS	MISANTHROPIST	DEPENDABILITY	MAGISTERIALLY	SUPERFICIALLY
SQUEAMISHNESS	MISMANAGEMENT	DIAMETRICALLY	MAGNANIMOUSLY	SUPERFLUOUSLY
STEADFASTNESS	NONCONFORMIST	DISCONTINUITY	MAGNIFICENTLY	SUPERLATIVELY
STERCORACEOUS	NONSUFFICIENT	DISCREDITABLY	MISCHIEVOUSLY	SUPERNUMERARY
STRENUOUSNESS	ORNITHOLOGIST	DISCRETIONARY	NONCONFORMITY	SUPPLEMENTARY
STREPTOCARPUS	OVERSTATEMENT	DISGRACEFULLY	NORTHEASTERLY	SYNTACTICALLY
STREPTOCOCCUS	PAPAPRELATIST	DISHONOURABLY	NORTHWESTERLY	SYNTHETICALLY
SUPERSTITIOUS	PERFECTIONIST	DISSIMILARITY	NOSTALGICALLY	TANTALIZINGLY
SURREPTITIOUS	PHYSIOGNOMIST	ECCENTRICALLY	OPHTHALMOLOGY	THEATRICALITY
TALKATIVENESS	PROJECTIONIST	ENERGETICALLY	OUTSTANDINGLY	THEOLOGICALLY
TENOSYNOVITIS	PRONOUNCEMENT	EXCEPTIONALLY	PAINSTAKINGLY	THEORETICALLY
THANKLESSNESS	PROTECTIONIST	EXPEDITIONARY	PALAEONTOLOGY	THOUGHTLESSLY
THAUMATURGICS	PROTONOTARIAT	EXPEDITIOUSLY	PARADOXICALLY	THREATENINGLY
THESSALONIANS	PSYCHOANALYST	EXTRAORDINARY	PARLIAMENTARY	THYROIDECTOMY
THORACENTESIS	RAPPROCHEMENT	EXTRAVAGANTLY	PARTICIPATORY	TONSILLECTOMY
UMBELLIFEROUS	REARRANGEMENT	FANTASTICALLY	PARTICULARITY	TRADITIONALLY
UNCEREMONIOUS	RECITATIONIST	FRIGHTENINGLY	PATRIOTICALLY	TRANSPARENTLY
UNPRETENTIOUS	REDEMPTIONIST	FUNDAMENTALLY	PENETRABILITY	TRAUMATICALLY
UNWILLINGNESS	REDEVELOPMENT	GENITOURINARY	PERFUNCTORILY	TREACHEROUSLY
VIVACIOUSNESS	REFURBISHMENT	GEOMETRICALLY	PHYSIOTHERAPY	UNACCOUNTABLY
VORACIOUSNESS	REIMBURSEMENT	GEOSTATIONARY	PNEUMATICALLY	UNCOMFORTABLY
WHOLESOMENESS	REINFORCEMENT	GRAMMATICALLY	PNEUMONECTOMY	UNCONSCIOUSLY
ACCOMPANIMENT	REINSTATEMENT	HALLUCINATORY	PRAGMATICALLY	UNFLINCHINGLY
ACUPUNCTURIST	REPLENISHMENT	HOMOSEXUALITY	PRECAUTIONARY	UNFORTUNATELY
ADVERTISEMENT	SELFCONFIDENT	HYDRAULICALLY	PRECIPITATELY	UNGENTLEMANLY
AFFREIGHTMENT	SUBLIEUTENANT	IGNOMINIOUSLY	PREDOMINANTLY	UNNECESSARILY
ANTICOAGULANT	SUPERABUNDANT	IMAGINATIVELY	PROFITABILITY	UNTRUSTWORTHY
APPORTIONMENT	THAUMATURGIST	IMPERCEPTIBLY	PROGRESSIVELY	VULNERABILITY
ARCHAEOLOGIST	UNINTELLIGENT	IMPERTINENTLY	PROMISCUOUSLY	
BIBLIOPHAGIST	VENTRILOQUIST	IMPERTURBABLY	PROPHETICALLY	
CIRCUMAMBIENT	VICEPRESIDENT	IMPOSSIBILITY	PROSOPOGRAPHY	
CLOSEDCIRCUIT	FONTAINEBLEAU	IMPROBABILITY	PROVISIONALLY	
CONCEPTIONIST	ARCHAEOPTERYX	IMPROVIDENTLY	PROVOCATIVELY	
CONCEPTUALIST	VERCINGETORIX	INADVERTENTLY	PSYCHOBIOLOGY	

14:1

ABSTEMIOUSNESS
ACCOMPLISHMENT
ACCOUNTABILITY
ACHONDROPLASIA
ACKNOWLEDGMENT
ADMINISTRATION
ADMINISTRATIVE
AFFECTIONATELY
AFOREMENTIONED
AGGRANDISEMENT
AGGRESSIVENESS
AIRCONDITIONED
AIRCONDITIONER
AIRCRAFTSWOMAN
ALLELOCHEMICAL
ALLOIOSTROPHUS
ALPHABETICALLY
ANTHROPOLOGIST
ANTHROPOPHAGUS
ANTIDEPRESSANT
ANTIFEDERALIST
ANTILYMPHOCYTE
ANTIMETATHESIS
ANTIMONARCHIST
ANTIODONTALGIC
ANTIPERSPIRANT
APOLOGETICALLY
APPREHENSIVELY
APPRENTICESHIP
APPROVECOMMENT
ARCHAEBACTERIA
ARCHAEOLOGICAL
ARCHGENETHLIAC
ARRONDISSEMENT
ASTROGEOLOGIST
ASTRONOMICALLY
AUTHENTICATION
AUTOCRATICALLY
AUTORADIOGRAPH
AUTOSUGGESTION
AUTOTRANSPLANT
BACTERIOLOGIST
BALUCHITHERIUM
BATTERYPOWERED
BIOENGINEERING
BOISTEROUSNESS
BREATHLESSNESS
BROBDINGNAGIAN
CAMELOPARDALIS
CAPITALIZATION
CAPRICIOUSNESS
CARCINOMATOSIS
CARDIOVASCULAR
CASTRAMETATION
CENTRALIZATION
CENTROLECITHAL
CHARACTERISTIC
CHINCHERINCHEE
CINEMATOGRAPHY
CIRCUMLOCUTION
CIRCUMNAVIGATE
CIRCUMSCISSILE
CIRCUMSTANTIAL
CLASSIFICATION
CLAUSTROPHOBIA
CLAUSTROPHOBIC
COINCIDENTALLY

COMMISSIONAIRE
COMPREHENSIBLE
CONFIDENTIALLY
CONGLOMERATION
CONGRATULATION
CONGRATULATORY
CONGREGATIONAL
CONJUNCTIVITIS
CONSERVATIVELY
CONSPIRATORIAL
CONSTANTINOPLE
CONSTITUTIONAL
CONSTRUCTIVELY
CONSTRUCTIVISM
CONTESSERATION
CONTROVERTIBLE
CONVENTIONALLY
CONVERSATIONAL
CONVERTIBILITY
CORRESPONDENCE
CORRUPTIBILITY
COUNTERBALANCE
COUNTERMEASURE
CREEPYCRAWLIES
CROSSREFERENCE
CRYPTAESTHETIC
CRYSTALLOMANCY
CZECHOSLOVAKIA
DECISIONMAKING
DEMOBILIZATION
DEMOCRATICALLY
DEMORALIZATION
DENOMINATIONAL
DERMATOLOGICAL
DESISTABSTRACT
DEXTROROTATORY
DIPLOMATICALLY
DISAPPOINTMENT
DISAPPROBATION
DISAPPROVINGLY
DISASSOCIATION
DISCIPLINARIAN
DISCOLOURATION
DISCOMBOBERATE
DISCOMBOBULATE
DISCONSOLATELY
DISCONTENTMENT
DISCOUNTENANCE
DISCOURAGEMENT
DISCOURTEOUSLY
DISCRIMINATING
DISCRIMINATION
DISCRIMINATORY
DISEMBARKATION
DISENCHANTMENT
DISENFRANCHISE
DISINCLINATION
DISINFORMATION
DISINTEGRATION
DISORIENTATION
DISTINGUISHING
DIVERTISSEMENT
ECCLESIASTICAL
ECCLESIASTICUS
EDUCATIONALIST
EGALITARIANISM
ELECTIONEERING
ELECTROMYOGRAM
ELECTRONICALLY

EMBELLISHMENTS
ENCEPHALOPATHY
ESTABLISHVERSE
EXISTENTIALISM
EXISTENTIALIST
EXPERIMENTALLY
EXPRESSIONLESS
FASTIDIOUSNESS
FERRIMAGNETISM
FORTUNETELLING
FRATERNIZATION
FRUCTIFICATION
FUNDAMENTALISM
FUNDAMENTALIST
GENERALIZATION
GENTRIFICATION
GEOGRAPHICALLY
GEWÜRZTRAMINER
GRANDILOQUENCE
GYNAECOLOGICAL
HALLUCINATIONS
HALLUCINOGENIC
HEARTSEARCHING
HEMIMETABOLOUS
HIEROSOLYMITAN
HOMOGENIZATION
HORTICULTURIST
HYDROCORTISONE
HYPERSENSITIVE
HYPOTHETICALLY
IDENTIFICATION
ILLEGITIMATELY
IMMOBILIZATION
IMMUNOGLOBULIN
IMPERMEABILITY
IMPLEMENTATION
IMPOVERISHMENT
IMPREGNABILITY
IMPRESSIONABLE
INCONCLUSIVELY
INCONSIDERABLE
INCONVENIENTLY
INDECIPHERABLE
INDESTRUCTIBLE
INDETERMINABLE
INDISCRIMINATE
INDOCTRINATION
INEXPRESSIBLES
INFRALAPSARIAN
INFRASTRUCTURE
INSIGNIFICANCE
INSUFFICIENTLY
INSURMOUNTABLE
INTELLECTUALLY
INTELLIGENTSIA
INTERCONNECTED
INTERFEROMETER
INTERMITTENTLY
INTERNATIONALE
INTERPELLATION
INTERPLANETARY
INTERPRETATION
INTERPRETATIVE
IRRECONCILABLE
IRREPROACHABLE
JOHANNISBERGER
KNICKERBOCKERS
KNIPPERDOLLING
KNOTENSCHIEFER

LASCIVIOUSNESS
LIBERALIZATION
LICENTIOUSNESS
LIGHTSENSITIVE
LONGITUDINALLY
LOQUACIOUSNESS
MACROECONOMICS
MALAPPROPRIATE
MATHEMATICALLY
MEGASPORANGIUM
MEPHISTOPHELES
METAMORPHOSING
METAPHORICALLY
METEMPSYCHOSIS
METEOROLOGICAL
METICULOUSNESS
MICROPROCESSOR
MICROSPOROCYTE
MILLENARIANISM
MISAPPLICATION
MISAPPROPRIATE
MISCALCULATION
MONOCARPELLARY
MONOCHROMATISM
MONOPOLIZATION
MONOSACCHARIDE
MOUNTAINEERING
MULTIFACTORIAL
MULTIPLICATION
NATURALIZATION
NEBUCHADNEZZAR
NETHERSTOCKING
NEUTRALIZATION
NIBELUNGENLIED
NITROBACTERIUM
NITROCELLULOSE
NITROGLYCERINE
OBSEQUIOUSNESS
ONCHOCERCIASIS
OPPRESSIVENESS
OPTIMISTICALLY
ORGANIZATIONAL
ORNITHOLOGICAL
ORTHOCHROMATIC
ORTHOGRAPHICAL
OSTENTATIOUSLY
OSTEOARTHRITIS
OTOLARYNGOLOGY
OVERPRODUCTION
OVERSUBSCRIBED
PARALEIPOMENON
PARAPSYCHOLOGY
PARSIMONIOUSLY
PARTRIDGEBERRY
PASTEURIZATION
PERCEPTIVENESS
PEREGRINATIONS
PERMISSIVENESS
PERSUASIVENESS
PHANTASMAGORIA
PHARMACEUTICAL
PHARMACOLOGIST
PHENOBARBITONE
PHILANTHROPIST
PHLEGMATICALLY
PHOSPHORESCENT
PHOTOSYNTHESIS
PHYTOGEOGRAPHY
POIKILOTHERMIC

POLYMERIZATION
POPULARIZATION
PORPHYROGENITE
POSSESSINHUMAN
PRACTICABILITY
PRECOCIOUSNESS
PREDESTINATION
PREDISPOSITION
PREFABRICATION
PRESSURIZATION
PRESUMPTUOUSLY
PRESUPPOSITION
PRODUCTIVENESS
PROFESSIONALLY
PROHIBITIONIST
PRONUNCIAMENTO
PROPORTIONALLY
PROTOCONTINENT
PROVIDENTIALLY
PSYCHOANALYSIS
PURPOSEFULNESS
QUALIFICATIONS
QUINTESSENTIAL
RADIOTELEPHONE
RECAPITULATION
RECOMMENDATION
RECONCILIATION
RECONNAISSANCE
RECONSTITUTION
RECONSTRUCTION
RECORDBREAKING
REGULARIZATION
REHABILITATION
RELINQUISHMENT
REORGANIZATION
REPRESENTATION
REPRESENTATIVE
RESPECTABILITY
RESPONSIBILITY
RESPONSIVENESS
RIDICULOUSNESS
ROADWORTHINESS
SANCTIFICATION
SANSCULOTTERIE
SATISFACTORILY
SCAREMONGERING
SCATTERBRAINED
SCHOOLCHILDREN
SCHOOLMISTRESS
SCIENTIFICALLY
SCRUPULOUSNESS
SCURRILOUSNESS
SELFASSESSMENT
SELFCONFIDENCE
SELFGOVERNMENT
SELFRESPECTING
SELFSUFFICIENT
SENSATIONALISM
SENTIMENTALITY
SEPTUAGENARIAN
SERVOMECHANISM
SESQUIPEDALIAN
SESQUIPEDALION
SEXCENTENARIAN
SHRINKWRAPPING
SIMPLIFICATION
SIMULTANEOUSLY
SINGLEBREASTED
SINGLEMINDEDLY

SLAUGHTERHOUSE
SOLIDIFICATION
SOPHISTICATION
SPECIALIZATION
STAPHYLOCOCCUS
STEGANOGRAPHIC
STRAIGHTFOWARD
STRATIFICATION
STULTIFICATION
SUBCONSCIOUSLY
SUBMICROSCOPIC
SUBMISSIVENESS
SUBSTANTIATION
SULPHANILAMIDE
SUPERABUNDANCE
SUPERANNUATION
SUPERCILIOUSLY
SUPERCONTINENT
SUPEREROGATION
SUPERFICIALITY
SUPERINTENDENT
SUPERNATURALLY
SUPERPHOSPHATE
SUPERSCRIPTION
SUPERSTRUCTURE
SUSCEPTIBILITY
SYSTEMATICALLY
TATTERDEMALION
TELETYPEWRITER
TERMINOLOGICAL
THERMODYNAMICS
THOUGHTFULNESS
THREEHALFPENCE
THROMBOPLASTIN
TINTINNABULATE
TRADITIONALIST
TRANSCENDENTAL
TRANSFORMATION
TRANSMIGRATION
TRANSPORTATION
TRICHOPHYTOSIS
TROUBLESHOOTER
ULTRACREPIDATE
UNAPPROACHABLE
UNATTRIBUTABLE
UNCOMPROMISING
UNCONSCIONABLE
UNCONTROLLABLE
UNCONVENTIONAL
UNCORROBORATED
UNDERDEVELOPED
UNDERMENTIONED
UNDERNOURISHED
UNDERSECRETARY
UNDERSTANDABLE
UNDERSTANDABLY
UNDERSTATEMENT
UNDESIRABILITY
UNENTHUSIASTIC
UNINTELLIGIBLE
UNMENTIONABLES
UNPLEASANTNESS
UNPREMEDITATED
UNPREPAREDNESS
UNPROFESSIONAL
UNQUESTIONABLE
UNQUESTIONABLY
UNRECOGNIZABLE
UNSATISFACTORY

UNSKILLFULNESS
VALETUDINARIAN
VERISIMILITUDE
VERTICILLASTER
VESPERTILIONID
VINDICTIVENESS
WEIGHTLESSNESS
WELTANSCHAUUNG
WESTERNIZATION
WHIPPERSNAPPER
WHOLEHEARTEDLY
ZOROASTRIANISM

14:2

BACTERIOLOGIST
BALUCHITHERIUM
BATTERYPOWERED
CAMELOPARDALIS
CAPITALIZATION
CAPRICIOUSNESS
CARCINOMATOSIS
CARDIOVASCULAR
CASTRAMETATION
FASTIDIOUSNESS
HALLUCINATIONS
HALLUCINOGENIC
LASCIVIOUSNESS
MACROECONOMICS
MALAPPROPRIATE
MATHEMATICALLY
NATURALIZATION
PARALEIPOMENON
PARAPSYCHOLOGY
PARSIMONIOUSLY
PARTRIDGEBERRY
PASTEURIZATION
RADIOTELEPHONE
SANCTIFICATION
SANSCULOTTERIE
SATISFACTORILY
TATTERDEMALION
VALETUDINARIAN
ABSTEMIOUSNESS
OBSEQUIOUSNESS
ACCOMPLISHMENT
ACCOUNTABILITY
ACHONDROPLASIA
ACKNOWLEDGMENT
ECCLESIASTICAL
ECCLESIASTICUS
SCAREMONGERING
SCATTERBRAINED
SCHOOLCHILDREN
SCHOOLMISTRESS
SCIENTIFICALLY
SCRUPULOUSNESS
SCURRILOUSNESS
ADMINISTRATION
ADMINISTRATIVE
EDUCATIONALIST
IDENTIFICATION
CENTRALIZATION
CENTROLECITHAL
DECISIONMAKING
DEMOBILIZATION
DEMOCRATICALLY
DEMORALIZATION
DENOMINATIONAL
DERMATOLOGICAL

DESISTABSTRACT
DEXTROROTATORY
FERRIMAGNETISM
GENERALIZATION
GENTRIFICATION
GEOGRAPHICALLY
GEWÜRZTRAMINER
HEARTSEARCHING
HEMIMETABOLOUS
MEGASPORANGIUM
MEPHISTOPHELES
METAMORPHOSING
METAPHORICALLY
METEMPSYCHOSIS
METEOROLOGICAL
METICULOUSNESS
NEBUCHADNEZZAR
NETHERSTOCKING
NEUTRALIZATION
PERCEPTIVENESS
PEREGRINATIONS
PERMISSIVENESS
PERSUASIVENESS
RECAPITULATION
RECOMMENDATION
RECONCILIATION
RECONNAISSANCE
RECONSTITUTION
RECONSTRUCTION
RECORDBREAKING
REGULARIZATION
REHABILITATION
RELINQUISHMENT
REORGANIZATION
REPRESENTATION
REPRESENTATIVE
RESPECTABILITY
RESPONSIBILITY
RESPONSIVENESS
SELFASSESSMENT
SELFCONFIDENCE
SELFGOVERNMENT
SELFRESPECTING
SELFSUFFICIENT
SENSATIONALISM
SENTIMENTALITY
SEPTUAGENARIAN
SERVOMECHANISM
SESQUIPEDALIAN
SESQUIPEDALION
SEXCENTENARIAN
TELETYPEWRITER
TERMINOLOGICAL
VERISIMILITUDE
VERTICILLASTER
VESPERTILIONID
WEIGHTLESSNESS
WELTANSCHAUUNG
WESTERNIZATION
AFFECTIONATELY
AFOREMENTIONED
AGGRANDISEMENT
AGGRESSIVENESS
EGALITARIANISM
CHARACTERISTIC
CHINCHERINCHEE
PHANTASMAGORIA
PHARMACEUTICAL
PHARMACOLOGIST

PHENOBARBITONE	ALLELOCHEMICAL	UNDERSTANDABLE	ARCHAEOLOGICAL
PHILANTHROPIST	ALLOIOSTROPHUS	UNDERSTANDABLY	ARCHGENETHLIAC
PHLEGMATICALLY	ALPHABETICALLY	UNDERSTATEMENT	ARRONDISSEMENT
PHOSPHORESCENT	CLASSIFICATION	UNDESIRABILITY	BREATHLESSNESS
PHOTOSYNTHESIS	CLAUSTROPHOBIA	UNENTHUSIASTIC	BROBDINGNAGIAN
PHYTOGEOGRAPHY	CLAUSTROPHOBIC	UNINTELLIGIBLE	CREEPYCRAWLIES
SHRINKWRAPPING	ELECTIONEERING	UNMENTIONABLES	CROSSREFERENCE
THERMODYNAMICS	ELECTROMYOGRAM	UNPLEASANTNESS	CRYPTAESTHETIC
THOUGHTFULNESS	ELECTRONICALLY	UNPREMEDITATED	CRYSTALLOMANCY
THREEHALFPENCE	ILLEGITIMATELY	UNPREPAREDNESS	FRATERNIZATION
THROMBOPLASTIN	SLAUGHTERHOUSE	UNPROFESSIONAL	FRUCTIFICATION
WHIPPERSNAPPER	ULTRACREPIDATE	UNQUESTIONABLE	GRANDILOQUENCE
WHOLEHEARTEDLY	EMBELLISHMENTS	UNQUESTIONABLY	IRRECONCILABLE
AIRCONDITIONED	IMMOBILIZATION	UNRECOGNIZABLE	IRREPROACHABLE
AIRCONDITIONER	IMMUNOGLOBULIN	UNSATISFACTORY	ORGANIZATIONAL
AIRCRAFTSWOMAN	IMPERMEABILITY	UNSKILLFULNESS	ORNITHOLOGICAL
BIOENGINEERING	IMPLEMENTATION	BOISTEROUSNESS	ORTHOCHROMATIC
CINEMATOGRAPHY	IMPOVERISHMENT	COINCIDENTALLY	ORTHOGRAPHICAL
CIRCUMLOCUTION	IMPREGNABILITY	COMMISSIONAIRE	PRACTICABILITY
CIRCUMNAVIGATE	IMPRESSIONABLE	COMPREHENSIBLE	PRECOCIOUSNESS
CIRCUMSCISSILE	ANTHROPOLOGIST	CONFIDENTIALLY	PREDESTINATION
CIRCUMSTANTIAL	ANTHROPOPHAGUS	CONGLOMERATION	PREDISPOSITION
DIPLOMATICALLY	ANTIDEPRESSANT	CONGRATULATION	PREFABRICATION
DISAPPOINTMENT	ANTIFEDERALIST	CONGRATULATORY	PRESSURIZATION
DISAPPROBATION	ANTILYMPHOCYTE	CONGREGATIONAL	PRESUMPTUOUSLY
DISAPPROVINGLY	ANTIMETATHESIS	CONJUNCTIVITIS	PRESUPPOSITION
DISASSOCIATION	ANTIMONARCHIST	CONSERVATIVELY	PRODUCTIVENESS
DISCIPLINARIAN	ANTIODONTALGIC	CONSPIRATORIAL	PROFESSIONALLY
DISCOLOURATION	ANTIPERSPIRANT	CONSTANTINOPLE	PROHIBITIONIST
DISCOMBOBERATE	ENCEPHALOPATHY	CONSTITUTIONAL	PRONUNCIAMENTO
DISCOMBOBULATE	INCONCLUSIVELY	CONSTRUCTIVELY	PROPORTIONALLY
DISCONSOLATELY	INCONSIDERABLE	CONSTRUCTIVISM	PROTOCONTINENT
DISCONTENTMENT	INCONVENIENTLY	CONTESSERATION	PROVIDENTIALLY
DISCOUNTENANCE	INDECIPHERABLE	CONTROVERTIBLE	TRADITIONALIST
DISCOURAGEMENT	INDESTRUCTIBLE	CONVENTIONALLY	TRANSCENDENTAL
DISCOURTEOUSLY	INDETERMINABLE	CONVERSATIONAL	TRANSFORMATION
DISCRIMINATING	INDISCRIMINATE	CONVERTIBILITY	TRANSMIGRATION
DISCRIMINATION	INDOCTRINATION	CORRESPONDENCE	TRANSPORTATION
DISCRIMINATORY	INEXPRESSIBLES	CORRUPTIBILITY	TRICHOPHYTOSIS
DISEMBARKATION	INFRALAPSARIAN	COUNTERBALANCE	TROUBLESHOOTER
DISENCHANTMENT	INFRASTRUCTURE	COUNTERMEASURE	ASTROGEOLOGIST
DISENFRANCHISE	INSIGNIFICANCE	FORTUNETELLING	ASTRONOMICALLY
DISINCLINATION	INSUFFICIENTLY	HOMOGENIZATION	ESTABLISHVERSE
DISINFORMATION	INSURMOUNTABLE	HORTICULTURIST	OSTENTATIOUSLY
DISINTEGRATION	INTELLECTUALLY	JOHANNISBERGER	OSTEOARTHRITIS
DISORIENTATION	INTELLIGENTSIA	LONGITUDINALLY	PSYCHOANALYSIS
DISTINGUISHING	INTERCONNECTED	LOQUACIOUSNESS	OTOLARYNGOLOGY
DIVERTISSEMENT	INTERFEROMETER	MONOCARPELLARY	STAPHYLOCOCCUS
HIEROSOLYMITAN	INTERMITTENTLY	MONOCHROMATISM	STEGANOGRAPHIC
LIBERALIZATION	INTERNATIONALE	MONOPOLIZATION	STRAIGHTFOWARD
LICENTIOUSNESS	INTERPELLATION	MONOSACCHARIDE	STRATIFICATION
LIGHTSENSITIVE	INTERPLANETARY	MOUNTAINEERING	STULTIFICATION
MICROPROCESSOR	INTERPRETATION	POIKILOTHERMIC	AUTHENTICATION
MICROSPOROCYTE	INTERPRETATIVE	POLYMERIZATION	AUTOCRATICALLY
MILLENARIANISM	KNICKERBOCKERS	POPULARIZATION	AUTORADIOGRAPH
MISAPPLICATION	KNIPPERDOLLING	PORPHYROGENITE	AUTOSUGGESTION
MISAPPROPRIATE	KNOTENSCHIEFER	POSSESSINHUMAN	AUTOTRANSPLANT
MISCALCULATION	ONCHOCERCIASIS	ROADWORTHINESS	FUNDAMENTALISM
NIBELUNGENLIED	UNAPPROACHABLE	SOLIDIFICATION	FUNDAMENTALIST
NITROBACTERIUM	UNATTRIBUTABLE	SOPHISTICATION	MULTIFACTORIAL
NITROCELLULOSE	UNCOMPROMISING	ZOROASTRIANISM	MULTIPLICATION
NITROGLYCERINE	UNCONSCIONABLE	APOLOGETICALLY	PURPOSEFULNESS
RIDICULOUSNESS	UNCONTROLLABLE	APPREHENSIVELY	QUALIFICATIONS
SIMPLIFICATION	UNCONVENTIONAL	APPRENTICESHIP	QUINTESSENTIAL
SIMULTANEOUSLY	UNCORROBORATED	APPROVECOMMENT	SUBCONSCIOUSLY
SINGLEBREASTED	UNDERDEVELOPED	OPPRESSIVENESS	SUBMICROSCOPIC
SINGLEMINDEDLY	UNDERMENTIONED	OPTIMISTICALLY	SUBMISSIVENESS
TINTINNABULATE	UNDERNOURISHED	SPECIALIZATION	SUBSTANTIATION
VINDICTIVENESS	UNDERSECRETARY	ARCHAEBACTERIA	SULPHANILAMIDE

859

SUPERABUNDANCE
SUPERANNUATION
SUPERCILIOUSLY
SUPERCONTINENT
SUPEREROGATION
SUPERFICIALITY
SUPERINTENDENT
SUPERNATURALLY
SUPERPHOSPHATE
SUPERSCRIPTION
SUPERSTRUCTURE
SUSCEPTIBILITY
OVERPRODUCTION
OVERSUBSCRIBED
EXISTENTIALISM
EXISTENTIALIST
EXPERIMENTALLY
EXPRESSIONLESS
GYNAECOLOGICAL
HYDROCORTISONE
HYPERSENSITIVE
HYPOTHETICALLY
SYSTEMATICALLY
CZECHOSLOVAKIA

14:3

CHARACTERISTIC
CLASSIFICATION
CLAUSTROPHOBIA
CLAUSTROPHOBIC
EGALITARIANISM
FRATERNIZATION
GRANDILOQUENCE
HEARTSEARCHING
PHANTASMAGORIA
PHARMACEUTICAL
PHARMACOLOGIST
PRACTICABILITY
QUALIFICATIONS
ROADWORTHINESS
SCAREMONGERING
SCATTERBRAINED
SLAUGHTERHOUSE
STAPHYLOCOCCUS
TRADITIONALIST
TRANSCENDENTAL
TRANSFORMATION
TRANSMIGRATION
TRANSPORTATION
UNAPPROACHABLE
UNATTRIBUTABLE
EMBELLISHMENTS
LIBERALIZATION
NEBUCHADNEZZAR
NIBELUNGENLIED
SUBCONSCIOUSLY
SUBMICROSCOPIC
SUBMISSIVENESS
SUBSTANTIATION
ACCOMPLISHMENT
ACCOUNTABILITY
ARCHAEBACTERIA
ARCHAEOLOGICAL
ARCHGENETHLIAC
BACTERIOLOGIST
DECISIONMAKING
ECCLESIASTICAL
ECCLESIASTICUS
ENCEPHALOPATHY

INCONCLUSIVELY
INCONSIDERABLE
INCONVENIENTLY
LICENTIOUSNESS
MACROECONOMICS
MICROPROCESSOR
MICROSPOROCYTE
ONCHOCERCIASIS
RECAPITULATION
RECOMMENDATION
RECONCILIATION
RECONNAISSANCE
RECONSTITUTION
RECONSTRUCTION
RECORDBREAKING
UNCOMPROMISING
UNCONSCIONABLE
UNCONTROLLABLE
UNCONVENTIONAL
UNCORROBORATED
HYDROCORTISONE
INDECIPHERABLE
INDESTRUCTIBLE
INDETERMINABLE
INDISCRIMINATE
INDOCTRINATION
RADIOTELEPHONE
RIDICULOUSNESS
UNDERDEVELOPED
UNDERMENTIONED
UNDERNOURISHED
UNDERSECRETARY
UNDERSTANDABLE
UNDERSTANDABLY
UNDERSTATEMENT
UNDESIRABILITY
BREATHLESSNESS
CREEPYCRAWLIES
CZECHOSLOVAKIA
ELECTIONEERING
ELECTROMYOGRAM
ELECTRONICALLY
HIEROSOLYMITAN
IDENTIFICATION
INEXPRESSIBLES
OVERPRODUCTION
OVERSUBSCRIBED
PHENOBARBITONE
PRECOCIOUSNESS
PREDESTINATION
PREDISPOSITION
PREFABRICATION
PRESSURIZATION
PRESUMPTUOUSLY
PRESUPPOSITION
SPECIALIZATION
STEGANOGRAPHIC
THERMODYNAMICS
UNENTHUSIASTIC
AFFECTIONATELY
INFRALAPSARIAN
INFRASTRUCTURE
AGGRANDISEMENT
AGGRESSIVENESS
LIGHTSENSITIVE
MEGASPORANGIUM
ORGANIZATIONAL
REGULARIZATION
ACHONDROPLASIA

JOHANNISBERGER
REHABILITATION
SCHOOLCHILDREN
SCHOOLMISTRESS
BOISTEROUSNESS
CHINCHERINCHEE
COINCIDENTALLY
EXISTENTIALISM
EXISTENTIALIST
KNICKERBOCKERS
KNIPPERDOLLING
PHILANTHROPIST
POIKILOTHERMIC
QUINTESSENTIAL
SCIENTIFICALLY
TRICHOPHYTOSIS
UNINTELLIGIBLE
WEIGHTLESSNESS
WHIPPERSNAPPER
ACKNOWLEDGMENT
ALLELOCHEMICAL
ALLOIOSTROPHUS
BALUCHITHERIUM
HALLUCINATIONS
HALLUCINOGENIC
ILLEGITIMATELY
MALAPPROPRIATE
MILLENARIANISM
MULTIFACTORIAL
MULTIPLICATION
PHLEGMATICALLY
POLYMERIZATION
RELINQUISHMENT
SELFASSESSMENT
SELFCONFIDENCE
SELFGOVERNMENT
SELFRESPECTING
SELFSUFFICIENT
SOLIDIFICATION
SULPHANILAMIDE
TELETYPEWRITER
VALETUDINARIAN
WELTANSCHAUUNG
ADMINISTRATION
ADMINISTRATIVE
CAMELOPARDALIS
COMMISSIONAIRE
COMPREHENSIBLE
DEMOBILIZATION
DEMOCRATICALLY
DEMORALIZATION
HEMIMETABOLOUS
HOMOGENIZATION
IMMOBILIZATION
IMMUNOGLOBULIN
SIMPLIFICATION
SIMULTANEOUSLY
UNMENTIONABLES
CENTRALIZATION
CENTROLECITHAL
CINEMATOGRAPHY
CONFIDENTIALLY
CONGLOMERATION
CONGRATULATION
CONGRATULATORY
CONGREGATIONAL
CONJUNCTIVITIS
CONSERVATIVELY
CONSPIRATORIAL

CONSTANTINOPLE
CONSTITUTIONAL
CONSTRUCTIVELY
CONSTRUCTIVISM
CONTESSERATION
CONTROVERTIBLE
CONVENTIONALLY
CONVERSATIONAL
CONVERTIBILITY
DENOMINATIONAL
FUNDAMENTALISM
FUNDAMENTALIST
GENERALIZATION
GENTRIFICATION
GYNAECOLOGICAL
LONGITUDINALLY
MONOCARPELLARY
MONOCHROMATISM
MONOPOLIZATION
MONOSACCHARIDE
ORNITHOLOGICAL
SANCTIFICATION
SANSCULOTTERIE
SENSATIONALISM
SENTIMENTALITY
SINGLEBREASTED
SINGLEMINDEDLY
TINTINNABULATE
VINDICTIVENESS
AFOREMENTIONED
APOLOGETICALLY
BIOENGINEERING
BROBDINGNAGIAN
CROSSREFERENCE
GEOGRAPHICALLY
KNOTENSCHIEFER
OTOLARYNGOLOGY
PHOSPHORESCENT
PHOTOSYNTHESIS
PRODUCTIVENESS
PROFESSIONALLY
PROHIBITIONIST
PRONUNCIAMENTO
PROPORTIONALLY
PROTOCONTINENT
PROVIDENTIALLY
REORGANIZATION
THOUGHTFULNESS
TROUBLESHOOTER
WHOLEHEARTEDLY
ALPHABETICALLY
APPREHENSIVELY
APPRENTICESHIP
APPROVECOMMENT
CAPITALIZATION
CAPRICIOUSNESS
DIPLOMATICALLY
EXPERIMENTALLY
EXPRESSIONLESS
HYPERSENSITIVE
HYPOTHETICALLY
IMPERMEABILITY
IMPLEMENTATION
IMPOVERISHMENT
IMPREGNABILITY
IMPRESSIONABLE
IMPRESSIONISTE
MEPHISTOPHELES
OPPRESSIVENESS
POPULARIZATION

REPRESENTATION	DISCIPLINARIAN	INTERPRETATIVE	CZECHOSLOVAKIA
REPRESENTATIVE	DISCOLOURATION	MATHEMATICALLY	DISCIPLINARIAN
SEPTUAGENARIAN	DISCOMBOBERATE	METAMORPHOSING	DISCOLOURATION
SOPHISTICATION	DISCOMBOBULATE	METAPHORICALLY	DISCOMBOBERATE
SUPERABUNDANCE	DISCONSOLATELY	METEMPSYCHOSIS	DISCOMBOBULATE
SUPERANNUATION	DISCONTENTMENT	METEOROLOGICAL	DISCONSOLATELY
SUPERCILIOUSLY	DISCOUNTENANCE	METICULOUSNESS	DISCONTENTMENT
SUPERCONTINENT	DISCOURAGEMENT	NATURALIZATION	DISCOUNTENANCE
SUPEREROGATION	DISCOURTEOUSLY	NETHERSTOCKING	DISCOURAGEMENT
SUPERFICIALITY	DISCRIMINATING	NITROBACTERIUM	DISCOURTEOUSLY
SUPERINTENDENT	DISCRIMINATION	NITROCELLULOSE	DISCRIMINATING
SUPERNATURALLY	DISCRIMINATORY	NITROGLYCERINE	DISCRIMINATION
SUPERPHOSPHATE	DISEMBARKATION	OPTIMISTICALLY	DISCRIMINATORY
SUPERSCRIPTION	DISENCHANTMENT	ORTHOCHROMATIC	EDUCATIONALIST
SUPERSTRUCTURE	DISENFRANCHISE	ORTHOGRAPHICAL	ELECTIONEERING
UNPLEASANTNESS	DISINCLINATION	OSTENTATIOUSLY	ELECTROMYOGRAM
UNPREMEDITATED	DISINFORMATION	OSTEOARTHRITIS	ELECTRONICALLY
UNPREPAREDNESS	DISINTEGRATION	SATISFACTORILY	FRUCTIFICATION
UNPROFESSIONAL	DISORIENTATION	TATTERDEMALION	KNICKERBOCKERS
LOQUACIOUSNESS	DISTINGUISHING	ULTRACREPIDATE	LASCIVIOUSNESS
UNQUESTIONABLE	FASTIDIOUSNESS	COUNTERBALANCE	MISCALCULATION
UNQUESTIONABLY	INSIGNIFICANCE	COUNTERMEASURE	PERCEPTIVENESS
AIRCONDITIONED	INSUFFICIENTLY	EDUCATIONALIST	PRACTICABILITY
AIRCONDITIONER	INSURMOUNTABLE	FRUCTIFICATION	PRECOCIOUSNESS
AIRCRAFTSWOMAN	LASCIVIOUSNESS	MOUNTAINEERING	PSYCHOANALYSIS
ARRONDISSEMENT	MISAPPLICATION	NEUTRALIZATION	SANCTIFICATION
CARCINOMATOSIS	MISAPPROPRIATE	SCURRILOUSNESS	SEXCENTENARIAN
CARDIOVASCULAR	MISCALCULATION	STULTIFICATION	SPECIALIZATION
CIRCUMLOCUTION	OBSEQUIOUSNESS	DIVERTISSEMENT	SUBCONSCIOUSLY
CIRCUMNAVIGATE	PASTEURIZATION	GEWÜRZTRAMINER	SUSCEPTIBILITY
CIRCUMSCISSILE	POSSESSINHUMAN	DEXTROROTATORY	TRICHOPHYTOSIS
CIRCUMSTANTIAL	RESPECTABILITY	SEXCENTENARIAN	CARDIOVASCULAR
CORRESPONDENCE	RESPONSIBILITY	CRYPTAESTHETIC	FUNDAMENTALISM
CORRUPTIBILITY	RESPONSIVENESS	CRYSTALLOMANCY	FUNDAMENTALIST
DERMATOLOGICAL	SESQUIPEDALIAN	PHYTOGEOGRAPHY	PREDESTINATION
FERRIMAGNETISM	SESQUIPEDALION	PSYCHOANALYSIS	PREDISPOSITION
FORTUNETELLING	SUSCEPTIBILITY		PRODUCTIVENESS
HORTICULTURIST	SYSTEMATICALLY	**14:4**	ROADWORTHINESS
IRRECONCILABLE	UNSATISFACTORY		TRADITIONALIST
IRREPROACHABLE	UNSKILLFULNESS	BREATHLESSNESS	VINDICTIVENESS
PARALEIPOMENON	VESPERTILIONID	DISAPPOINTMENT	AFFECTIONATELY
PARAPSYCHOLOGY	WESTERNIZATION	DISAPPROBATION	ALLELOCHEMICAL
PARSIMONIOUSLY	ANTHROPOLOGIST	DISAPPROVINGLY	BIOENGINEERING
PARTRIDGEBERRY	ANTHROPOPHAGUS	DISASSOCIATION	CAMELOPARDALIS
PERCEPTIVENESS	ANTIDEPRESSANT	ESTABLISHVERSE	CINEMATOGRAPHY
PEREGRINATIONS	ANTIFEDERALIST	GYNAECOLOGICAL	CREEPYCRAWLIES
PERMISSIVENESS	ANTILYMPHOCYTE	JOHANNISBERGER	DISEMBARKATION
PERSUASIVENESS	ANTIMETATHESIS	MALAPPROPRIATE	DISENCHANTMENT
PORPHYROGENITE	ANTIMONARCHIST	MEGASPORANGIUM	DISENFRANCHISE
PURPOSEFULNESS	ANTIODONTALGIC	METAMORPHOSING	DIVERTISSEMENT
SCRUPULOUSNESS	ANTIPERSPIRANT	METAPHORICALLY	EMBELLISHMENTS
SERVOMECHANISM	ASTROGEOLOGIST	MISAPPLICATION	ENCEPHALOPATHY
SHRINKWRAPPING	ASTRONOMICALLY	MISAPPROPRIATE	EXPERIMENTALLY
STRAIGHTFOWARD	AUTHENTICATION	ORGANIZATIONAL	GENERALIZATION
STRATIFICATION	AUTOCRATICALLY	PARALEIPOMENON	HYPERSENSITIVE
TERMINOLOGICAL	AUTORADIOGRAPH	PARAPSYCHOLOGY	ILLEGITIMATELY
THREEHALFPENCE	AUTOSUGGESTION	RECAPITULATION	IMPERMEABILITY
THROMBOPLASTIN	AUTOTRANSPLANT	REHABILITATION	INDECIPHERABLE
UNRECOGNIZABLE	BATTERYPOWERED	STRAIGHTFOWARD	INDESTRUCTIBLE
VERISIMILITUDE	ESTABLISHVERSE	STRATIFICATION	INDETERMINABLE
VERTICILLASTER	INTELLECTUALLY	UNSATISFACTORY	INTELLECTUALLY
ZOROASTRIANISM	INTELLIGENTSIA	BRODBINGNAGIAN	INTELLIGENTSIA
ABSTEMIOUSNESS	INTERCONNECTED	AIRCONDITIONED	INTERCONNECTED
CASTRAMETATION	INTERFEROMETER	AIRCONDITIONER	INTERFEROMETER
DESISTABSTRACT	INTERMITTENTLY	AIRCRAFTSWOMAN	INTERMITTENTLY
DISAPPOINTMENT	INTERNATIONALE	CARCINOMATOSIS	INTERNATIONALE
DISAPPROBATION	INTERPELLATION	CIRCUMLOCUTION	INTERPELLATION
DISAPPROVINGLY	INTERPLANETARY	CIRCUMNAVIGATE	INTERPLANETARY
DISASSOCIATION	INTERPRETATION	CIRCUMSCISSILE	INTERPRETATION
		CIRCUMSTANTIAL	

INTERPRETATIVE
IRRECONCILABLE
IRREPROACHABLE
LIBERALIZATION
LICENTIOUSNESS
METEMPSYCHOSIS
METEOROLOGICAL
NIBELUNGENLIED
OBSEQUIOUSNESS
OSTENTATIOUSLY
OSTEOARTHRITIS
PEREGRINATIONS
PHLEGMATICALLY
SCIENTIFICALLY
SUPERABUNDANCE
SUPERANNUATION
SUPERCILIOUSLY
SUPERCONTINENT
SUPEREROGATION
SUPERFICIALITY
SUPERINTENDENT
SUPERNATURALLY
SUPERPHOSPHATE
SUPERSCRIPTION
SUPERSTRUCTURE
TELETYPEWRITER
THREEHALFPENCE
UNDERDEVELOPED
UNDERMENTIONED
UNDERNOURISHED
UNDERSECRETARY
UNDERSTANDABLE
UNDERSTANDABLY
UNDERSTATEMENT
UNDESIRABILITY
UNMENTIONABLES
UNRECOGNIZABLE
VALETUDINARIAN
CONFIDENTIALLY
PREFABRICATION
PROFESSIONALLY
SELFASSESSMENT
SELFCONFIDENCE
SELFGOVERNMENT
SELFRESPECTING
SELFSUFFICIENT
CONGLOMERATION
CONGRATULATION
CONGRATULATORY
CONGREGATIONAL
GEOGRAPHICALLY
LONGITUDINALLY
SINGLEBREASTED
SINGLEMINDEDLY
STEGANOGRAPHIC
WEIGHTLESSNESS
ALPHABETICALLY
ANTHROPOLOGIST
ANTHROPOPHAGUS
ARCHAEBACTERIA
ARCHAEOLOGICAL
ARCHGENETHLIAC
AUTHENTICATION
LIGHTSENSITIVE
MATHEMATICALLY
MEPHISTOPHELES
NETHERSTOCKING
ONCHOCERCIASIS
ORTHOCHROMATIC

ORTHOGRAPHICAL
PROHIBITIONIST
SOPHISTICATION
ADMINISTRATION
ADMINISTRATIVE
ANTIDEPRESSANT
ANTIFEDERALIST
ANTILYMPHOCYTE
ANTIMETATHESIS
ANTIMONARCHIST
ANTIODONTALGIC
ANTIPERSPIRANT
CAPITALIZATION
DECISIONMAKING
DESISTABSTRACT
DISINCLINATION
DISINFORMATION
DISINTEGRATION
HEMIMETABOLOUS
INDISCRIMINATE
INSIGNIFICANCE
METICULOUSNESS
OPTIMISTICALLY
ORNITHOLOGICAL
RADIOTELEPHONE
RELINQUISHMENT
RIDICULOUSNESS
SATISFACTORILY
SHRINKWRAPPING
SOLIDIFICATION
VERISIMILITUDE
CONJUNCTIVITIS
POIKILOTHERMIC
UNSKILLFULNESS
APOLOGETICALLY
DIPLOMATICALLY
ECCLESIASTICAL
ECCLESIASTICUS
EGALITARIANISM
HALLUCINATIONS
HALLUCINOGENIC
IMPLEMENTATION
MILLENARIANISM
OTOLARYNGOLOGY
PHILANTHROPIST
QUALIFICATIONS
STULTIFICATION
UNPLEASANTNESS
WHOLEHEARTEDLY
COMMISSIONAIRE
DERMATOLOGICAL
PERMISSIVENESS
SUBMICROSCOPIC
SUBMISSIVENESS
TERMINOLOGICAL
ACKNOWLEDGMENT
CHINCHERINCHEE
COINCIDENTALLY
COUNTERBALANCE
COUNTERMEASURE
GRANDILOQUENCE
IDENTIFICATION
MOUNTAINEERING
PHANTASMAGORIA
PHENOBARBITONE
PRONUNCIAMENTO
QUINTESSENTIAL
TRANSCENDENTAL
TRANSFORMATION

TRANSMIGRATION
TRANSPORTATION
UNENTHUSIASTIC
UNINTELLIGIBLE
ACCOMPLISHMENT
ACCOUNTABILITY
ACHONDROPLASIA
ALLOIOSTROPHUS
ARRONDISSEMENT
AUTOCRATICALLY
AUTORADIOGRAPH
AUTOSUGGESTION
AUTOTRANSPLANT
DEMOBILIZATION
DEMOCRATICALLY
DEMORALIZATION
DENOMINATIONAL
DISORIENTATION
HOMOGENIZATION
HYPOTHETICALLY
IMMOBILIZATION
IMPOVERISHMENT
INCONCLUSIVELY
INCONSIDERABLE
INCONVENIENTLY
INDOCTRINATION
MONOCARPELLARY
MONOCHROMATISM
MONOPOLIZATION
MONOSACCHARIDE
RECOMMENDATION
RECONCILIATION
RECONNAISSANCE
RECONSTITUTION
RECONSTRUCTION
RECORDBREAKING
SCHOOLCHILDREN
SCHOOLMISTRESS
THROMBOPLASTIN
UNCOMPROMISING
UNCONSCIONABLE
UNCONTROLLABLE
UNCONVENTIONAL
UNCORROBORATED
ZOROASTRIANISM
COMPREHENSIBLE
CRYPTAESTHETIC
KNIPPERDOLLING
PORPHYROGENITE
PROPORTIONALLY
PURPOSEFULNESS
RESPECTABILITY
RESPONSIBILITY
RESPONSIVENESS
SIMPLIFICATION
STAPHYLOCOCCUS
SULPHANILAMIDE
UNAPPROACHABLE
VESPERTILIONID
WHIPPERSNAPPER
SESQUIPEDALIAN
SESQUIPEDALION
AFOREMENTIONED
AGGRANDISEMENT
AGGRESSIVENESS
APPREHENSIVELY
APPRENTICESHIP
APPROVECOMMENT
ASTROGEOLOGIST

ASTRONOMICALLY
CAPRICIOUSNESS
CHARACTERISTIC
CORRESPONDENCE
CORRUPTIBILITY
EXPRESSIONLESS
FERRIMAGNETISM
HEARTSEARCHING
HIEROSOLYMITAN
HYDROCORTISONE
IMPREGNABILITY
IMPRESSIONABLE
INFRALAPSARIAN
INFRASTRUCTURE
MACROECONOMICS
MICROPROCESSOR
MICROSPOROCYTE
NITROBACTERIUM
NITROCELLULOSE
NITROGLYCERINE
OPPRESSIVENESS
OVERPRODUCTION
OVERSUBSCRIBED
PHARMACEUTICAL
PHARMACOLOGIST
REORGANIZATION
REPRESENTATION
REPRESENTATIVE
SCAREMONGERING
SCURRILOUSNESS
THERMODYNAMICS
ULTRACREPIDATE
UNPREMEDITATED
UNPREPAREDNESS
UNPROFESSIONAL
BOISTEROUSNESS
CLASSIFICATION
CONSERVATIVELY
CONSPIRATORIAL
CONSTANTINOPLE
CONSTITUTIONAL
CONSTRUCTIVELY
CONSTRUCTIVISM
CROSSREFERENCE
CRYSTALLOMANCY
EXISTENTIALISM
EXISTENTIALIST
PARSIMONIOUSLY
PERSUASIVENESS
PHOSPHORESCENT
POSSESSINHUMAN
PRESSURIZATION
PRESUMPTUOUSLY
PRESUPPOSITION
SANSCULOTTERIE
SENSATIONALISM
SUBSTANTIATION
ABSTEMIOUSNESS
BACTERIOLOGIST
BATTERYPOWERED
CASTRAMETATION
CENTRALIZATION
CENTROLECITHAL
CONTESSERATION
CONTROVERTIBLE
DEXTROROTATORY
DISTINGUISHING
FASTIDIOUSNESS
FORTUNETELLING

FRATERNIZATION
GENTRIFICATION
HORTICULTURIST
KNOTENSCHIEFER
MULTIFACTORIAL
MULTIPLICATION
NEUTRALIZATION
PARTRIDGEBERRY
PASTEURIZATION
PHOTOSYNTHESIS
PHYTOGEOGRAPHY
PROTOCONTINENT
SCATTERBRAINED
SENTIMENTALITY
SEPTUAGENARIAN
SYSTEMATICALLY
TATTERDEMALION
TINTINNABULATE
UNATTRIBUTABLE
VERTICILLASTER
WELTANSCHAUUNG
WESTERNIZATION
BALUCHITHERIUM
CLAUSTROPHOBIA
CLAUSTROPHOBIC
GEWÜRZTRAMINER
IMMUNOGLOBULIN
INSUFFICIENTLY
INSURMOUNTABLE
LOQUACIOUSNESS
NATURALIZATION
NEBUCHADNEZZAR
POPULARIZATION
REGULARIZATION
SCRUPULOUSNESS
SIMULTANEOUSLY
SLAUGHTERHOUSE
THOUGHTFULNESS
TROUBLESHOOTER
UNQUESTIONABLE
UNQUESTIONABLY
CONVENTIONALLY
CONVERSATIONAL
CONVERTIBILITY
PROVIDENTIALLY
SERVOMECHANISM
INEXPRESSIBLES
POLYMERIZATION

14:5

AGGRANDISEMENT
ALPHABETICALLY
ARCHAEBACTERIA
ARCHAEOLOGICAL
CHARACTERISTIC
DERMATOLOGICAL
EDUCATIONALIST
FUNDAMENTALISM
FUNDAMENTALIST
INFRALAPSARIAN
INFRASTRUCTURE
LOQUACIOUSNESS
MISCALCULATION
OTOLARYNGOLOGY
PHILANTHROPIST
PREFABRICATION
SELFASSESSMENT
SENSATIONALISM
STEGANOGRAPHIC

ULTRACREPIDATE
WELTANSCHAUUNG
ZOROASTRIANISM
DEMOBILIZATION
ESTABLISHVERSE
IMMOBILIZATION
REHABILITATION
TROUBLESHOOTER
AFFECTIONATELY
AUTOCRATICALLY
BALUCHITHERIUM
CHINCHERINCHEE
COINCIDENTALLY
DEMOCRATICALLY
INDECIPHERABLE
INDOCTRINATION
IRRECONCILABLE
METICULOUSNESS
MONOCARPELLARY
MONOCHROMATISM
NEBUCHADNEZZAR
RIDICULOUSNESS
SANSCULOTTERIE
SELFCONFIDENCE
UNRECOGNIZABLE
ANTIDEPRESSANT
BROBDINGNAGIAN
GRANDILOQUENCE
SOLIDIFICATION
ABSTEMIOUSNESS
AFOREMENTIONED
AGGRESSIVENESS
APPREHENSIVELY
APPRENTICESHIP
AUTHENTICATION
BACTERIOLOGIST
BATTERYPOWERED
CONSERVATIVELY
CONTESSERATION
CONVENTIONALLY
CONVERSATIONAL
CONVERTIBILITY
CORRESPONDENCE
ECCLESIASTICAL
ECCLESIASTICUS
EXPRESSIONLESS
FRATERNIZATION
GYNAECOLOGICAL
IMPLEMENTATION
IMPREGNABILITY
IMPRESSIONABLE
KNOTENSCHIEFER
MATHEMATICALLY
MILLENARIANISM
NETHERSTOCKING
OPPRESSIVENESS
PASTEURIZATION
PERCEPTIVENESS
POSSESSINHUMAN
PREDESTINATION
PROFESSIONALLY
REPRESENTATION
REPRESENTATIVE
RESPECTABILITY
SCAREMONGERING
SEXCENTENARIAN
SUSCEPTIBILITY
SYSTEMATICALLY
TATTERDEMALION

THREEHALFPENCE
UNPLEASANTNESS
UNPREMEDITATED
UNPREPAREDNESS
UNQUESTIONABLE
UNQUESTIONABLY
VESPERTILIONID
WESTERNIZATION
WHOLEHEARTEDLY
ANTIFEDERALIST
INSUFFICIENTLY
ARCHGENETHLIAC
HOMOGENIZATION
ILLEGITIMATELY
INSIGNIFICANCE
PEREGRINATIONS
PHLEGMATICALLY
REORGANIZATION
SELFGOVERNMENT
SLAUGHTERHOUSE
THOUGHTFULNESS
CZECHOSLOVAKIA
PORPHYROGENITE
PSYCHOANALYSIS
STAPHYLOCOCCUS
SULPHANILAMIDE
TRICHOPHYTOSIS
WEIGHTLESSNESS
ALLOIOSTROPHUS
CAPRICIOUSNESS
CARCINOMATOSIS
CARDIOVASCULAR
COMMISSIONAIRE
CONFIDENTIALLY
DISCIPLINARIAN
DISTINGUISHING
EGALITARIANISM
FASTIDIOUSNESS
FERRIMAGNETISM
HORTICULTURIST
LASCIVIOUSNESS
LONGITUDINALLY
MEPHISTOPHELES
MULTIFACTORIAL
MULTIPLICATION
PARSIMONIOUSLY
PERMISSIVENESS
POIKILOTHERMIC
PREDISPOSITION
PROHIBITIONIST
PROVIDENTIALLY
QUALIFICATIONS
SENTIMENTALITY
SOPHISTICATION
SPECIALIZATION
STRAIGHTFOWARD
SUBMICROSCOPIC
SUBMISSIVENESS
TERMINOLOGICAL
TINTINNABULATE
TRADITIONALIST
UNSKILLFULNESS
VERTICILLASTER
VINDICTIVENESS
KNICKERBOCKERS
ALLELOCHEMICAL
ANTILYMPHOCYTE
CAMELOPARDALIS
CONGLOMERATION

EMBELLISHMENTS
INTELLECTUALLY
INTELLIGENTSIA
NIBELUNGENLIED
PARALEIPOMENON
POPULARIZATION
REGULARIZATION
SIMPLIFICATION
SIMULTANEOUSLY
SINGLEBREASTED
SINGLEMINDEDLY
ACCOMPLISHMENT
ANTIMETATHESIS
ANTIMONARCHIST
CINEMATOGRAPHY
DENOMINATIONAL
DISEMBARKATION
HEMIMETABOLOUS
METAMORPHOSING
METEMPSYCHOSIS
OPTIMISTICALLY
PHARMACEUTICAL
PHARMACOLOGIST
POLYMERIZATION
RECOMMENDATION
THERMODYNAMICS
THROMBOPLASTIN
UNCOMPROMISING
ACHONDROPLASIA
ADMINISTRATION
ADMINISTRATIVE
ARRONDISSEMENT
BIOENGINEERING
DISENCHANTMENT
DISENFRANCHISE
DISINCLINATION
DISINFORMATION
DISINTEGRATION
IMMUNOGLOBULIN
INCONCLUSIVELY
INCONSIDERABLE
INCONVENIENTLY
JOHANNISBERGER
LICENTIOUSNESS
ORGANIZATIONAL
OSTENTATIOUSLY
RECONCILIATION
RECONNAISSANCE
RECONSTITUTION
RECONSTRUCTION
RELINQUISHMENT
SCIENTIFICALLY
SHRINKWRAPPING
UNCONSCIONABLE
UNCONTROLLABLE
UNCONVENTIONAL
UNMENTIONABLES
ACKNOWLEDGMENT
AIRCONDITIONED
AIRCONDITIONER
ANTIODONTALGIC
APOLOGETICALLY
APPROVECOMMENT
ASTROGEOLOGIST
ASTRONOMICALLY
DIPLOMATICALLY
DISCOLOURATION
DISCOMBOBERATE
DISCOMBOBULATE

DISCONSOLATELY	DEXTROROTATORY	VERISIMILITUDE	CONGRATULATORY
DISCONTENTMENT	DISCRIMINATING	AUTOTRANSPLANT	CONSTANTINOPLE
DISCOUNTENANCE	DISCRIMINATION	BOISTEROUSNESS	CRYPTAESTHETIC
DISCOURAGEMENT	DISCRIMINATORY	BREATHLESSNESS	CRYSTALLOMANCY
DISCOURTEOUSLY	DISORIENTATION	CAPITALIZATION	DEMORALIZATION
HIEROSOLYMITAN	DIVERTISSEMENT	CONSTANTINOPLE	GENERALIZATION
HYDROCORTISONE	EXPERIMENTALLY	CONSTITUTIONAL	GEOGRAPHICALLY
MACROECONOMICS	GENERALIZATION	CONSTRUCTIVELY	LIBERALIZATION
METEOROLOGICAL	GENTRIFICATION	CONSTRUCTIVISM	MONOCARPELLARY
MICROPROCESSOR	GEOGRAPHICALLY	COUNTERBALANCE	MONOSACCHARIDE
MICROSPOROCYTE	GEWÜRZTRAMINER	COUNTERMEASURE	MOUNTAINEERING
NITROBACTERIUM	HYPERSENSITIVE	CRYPTAESTHETIC	NATURALIZATION
NITROCELLULOSE	IMPERMEABILITY	CRYSTALLOMANCY	NEUTRALIZATION
NITROGLYCERINE	INSURMOUNTABLE	ELECTIONEERING	OSTEOARTHRITIS
ONCHOCERCIASIS	INTERCONNECTED	ELECTROMYOGRAM	PERSUASIVENESS
ORTHOCHROMATIC	INTERFEROMETER	ELECTRONICALLY	PHANTASMAGORIA
ORTHOGRAPHICAL	INTERMITTENTLY	EXISTENTIALISM	PHARMACEUTICAL
OSTEOARTHRITIS	INTERNATIONALE	EXISTENTIALIST	PHARMACOLOGIST
PHENOBARBITONE	INTERPELLATION	FRUCTIFICATION	POPULARIZATION
PHOTOSYNTHESIS	INTERPLANETARY	HEARTSEARCHING	REGULARIZATION
PHYTOGEOGRAPHY	INTERPRETATION	HYPOTHETICALLY	REORGANIZATION
PRECOCIOUSNESS	INTERPRETATIVE	IDENTIFICATION	SEPTUAGENARIAN
PROPORTIONALLY	LIBERALIZATION	INDETERMINABLE	SPECIALIZATION
PROTOCONTINENT	NATURALIZATION	LIGHTSENSITIVE	SUBSTANTIATION
PURPOSEFULNESS	NEUTRALIZATION	MOUNTAINEERING	SULPHANILAMIDE
RADIOTELEPHONE	PARTRIDGEBERRY	ORNITHOLOGICAL	SUPERABUNDANCE
RESPONSIBILITY	RECORDBREAKING	PHANTASMAGORIA	SUPERANNUATION
RESPONSIVENESS	SCURRILOUSNESS	PRACTICABILITY	UNPLEASANTNESS
SCHOOLCHILDREN	SELFRESPECTING	QUINTESSENTIAL	ALPHABETICALLY
SCHOOLMISTRESS	SUPERABUNDANCE	SANCTIFICATION	DISEMBARKATION
SERVOMECHANISM	SUPERANNUATION	SCATTERBRAINED	NITROBACTERIUM
SUBCONSCIOUSLY	SUPERCILIOUSLY	STRATIFICATION	PHENOBARBITONE
UNPROFESSIONAL	SUPERCONTINENT	STULTIFICATION	PREFABRICATION
ANTIPERSPIRANT	SUPEREROGATION	SUBSTANTIATION	PROHIBITIONIST
CONSPIRATORIAL	SUPERFICIALITY	TELETYPEWRITER	THROMBOPLASTIN
CREEPYCRAWLIES	SUPERINTENDENT	UNATTRIBUTABLE	CAPRICIOUSNESS
DISAPPOINTMENT	SUPERNATURALLY	UNENTHUSIASTIC	CHARACTERISTIC
DISAPPROBATION	SUPERPHOSPHATE	UNINTELLIGIBLE	DISENCHANTMENT
DISAPPROVINGLY	SUPERSCRIPTION	UNSATISFACTORY	DISINCLINATION
ENCEPHALOPATHY	SUPERSTRUCTURE	VALETUDINARIAN	GYNAECOLOGICAL
INEXPRESSIBLES	UNCORROBORATED	ACCOUNTABILITY	HALLUCINATIONS
IRREPROACHABLE	UNDERDEVELOPED	CIRCUMLOCUTION	HALLUCINOGENIC
KNIPPERDOLLING	UNDERMENTIONED	CIRCUMNAVIGATE	HORTICULTURIST
MALAPPROPRIATE	UNDERNOURISHED	CIRCUMSCISSILE	HYDROCORTISONE
METAPHORICALLY	UNDERSECRETARY	CIRCUMSTANTIAL	INCONCLUSIVELY
MISAPPLICATION	UNDERSTANDABLE	CONJUNCTIVITIS	INDISCRIMINATE
MISAPPROPRIATE	UNDERSTANDABLY	CORRUPTIBILITY	INTERCONNECTED
MONOPOLIZATION	UNDERSTATEMENT	FORTUNETELLING	LOQUACIOUSNESS
OVERPRODUCTION	AUTOSUGGESTION	HALLUCINATIONS	NITROCELLULOSE
PARAPSYCHOLOGY	CLASSIFICATION	HALLUCINOGENIC	ONCHOCERCIASIS
PHOSPHORESCENT	CLAUSTROPHOBIA	PERSUASIVENESS	ORTHOCHROMATIC
RECAPITULATION	CLAUSTROPHOBIC	PRESUMPTUOUSLY	PRECOCIOUSNESS
SCRUPULOUSNESS	CROSSREFERENCE	PRESUPPOSITION	PRODUCTIVENESS
UNAPPROACHABLE	DECISIONMAKING	PRODUCTIVENESS	PROTOCONTINENT
WHIPPERSNAPPER	DESISTABSTRACT	PRONUNCIAMENTO	RECONCILIATION
OBSEQUIOUSNESS	DISASSOCIATION	SEPTUAGENARIAN	RESPECTABILITY
AIRCRAFTSWOMAN	INDESTRUCTIBLE	SESQUIPEDALIAN	SUBMICROSCOPIC
ANTHROPOLOGIST	INDISCRIMINATE	SESQUIPEDALION	SUPERCILIOUSLY
ANTHROPOPHAGUS	MEGASPORANGIUM	IMPOVERISHMENT	SUPERCONTINENT
AUTORADIOGRAPH	MONOSACCHARIDE	ROADWORTHINESS	TRANSCENDENTAL
CASTRAMETATION	OVERSUBSCRIBED		ULTRACREPIDATE
CENTRALIZATION	PRESSURIZATION	**14:6**	VERTICILLASTER
CENTROLECITHAL	SATISFACTORILY		VINDICTIVENESS
COMPREHENSIBLE	SELFSUFFICIENT	AIRCRAFTSWOMAN	ACHONDROPLASIA
CONGRATULATION	TRANSCENDENTAL	AUTORADIOGRAPH	ANTIODONTALGIC
CONGRATULATORY	TRANSFORMATION	CAPITALIZATION	ARRONDISSEMENT
CONGREGATIONAL	TRANSMIGRATION	CASTRAMETATION	CONFIDENTIALLY
CONTROVERTIBLE	TRANSPORTATION	CENTRALIZATION	FASTIDIOUSNESS
DEMORALIZATION	UNDESIRABILITY	CINEMATOGRAPHY	PROVIDENTIALLY
		CONGRATULATION	

RECORDBREAKING	BROBDINGNAGIAN	PARSIMONIOUSLY	DISAPPROBATION
UNDERDEVELOPED	CLASSIFICATION	PHLEGMATICALLY	DISAPPROVINGLY
ANTIDEPRESSANT	COINCIDENTALLY	PRESUMPTUOUSLY	DISCIPLINARIAN
ANTIFEDERALIST	CONSPIRATORIAL	RECOMMENDATION	INTERPELLATION
ANTIMETATHESIS	CONSTITUTIONAL	SCAREMONGERING	INTERPLANETARY
ANTIPERSPIRANT	DECISIONMAKING	SENTIMENTALITY	INTERPRETATION
ARCHAEBACTERIA	DEMOBILIZATION	SERVOMECHANISM	INTERPRETATIVE
ARCHAEOLOGICAL	DENOMINATIONAL	SYSTEMATICALLY	MALAPPROPRIATE
ARCHGENETHLIAC	DISCRIMINATING	TRANSMIGRATION	MEGASPORANGIUM
BOISTEROUSNESS	DISCRIMINATION	UNDERMENTIONED	METEMPSYCHOSIS
COMPREHENSIBLE	DISCRIMINATORY	UNPREMEDITATED	MICROPROCESSOR
CONGREGATIONAL	DISORIENTATION	ACCOUNTABILITY	MISAPPLICATION
COUNTERBALANCE	ELECTIONEERING	AGGRANDISEMENT	MISAPPROPRIATE
COUNTERMEASURE	EXPERIMENTALLY	AIRCONDITIONED	MULTIPLICATION
EXISTENTIALISM	FRUCTIFICATION	AIRCONDITIONER	PERCEPTIVENESS
EXISTENTIALIST	GENTRIFICATION	APPRENTICESHIP	PRESUPPOSITION
HEMIMETABOLOUS	GRANDILOQUENCE	ASTRONOMICALLY	SUPERPHOSPHATE
HOMOGENIZATION	IDENTIFICATION	AUTHENTICATION	SUSCEPTIBILITY
IMPOVERISHMENT	ILLEGITIMATELY	CARCINOMATOSIS	TRANSPORTATION
INDETERMINABLE	IMMOBILIZATION	CONJUNCTIVITIS	UNCOMPROMISING
KNICKERBOCKERS	INDECIPHERABLE	CONVENTIONALLY	UNPREPAREDNESS
KNIPPERDOLLING	OPTIMISTICALLY	DISCONSOLATELY	RELINQUISHMENT
MACROECONOMICS	ORGANIZATIONAL	DISCONTENTMENT	AUTOCRATICALLY
PARALEIPOMENON	PARTRIDGEBERRY	DISTINGUISHING	AUTOTRANSPLANT
POLYMERIZATION	PRACTICABILITY	FORTUNETELLING	BACTERIOLOGIST
QUINTESSENTIAL	RECAPITULATION	INSIGNIFICANCE	BATTERYPOWERED
SCATTERBRAINED	REHABILITATION	INTERNATIONALE	CONSERVATIVELY
SELFRESPECTING	SANCTIFICATION	JOHANNISBERGER	CONSTRUCTIVELY
SINGLEBREASTED	SCURRILOUSNESS	KNOTENSCHIEFER	CONSTRUCTIVISM
SINGLEMINDEDLY	SESQUIPEDALIAN	MILLENARIANISM	CONVERSATIONAL
SUPEREROGATION	SESQUIPEDALION	PHILANTHROPIST	CONVERTIBILITY
UNINTELLIGIBLE	SIMPLIFICATION	PRONUNCIAMENTO	CROSSREFERENCE
WHIPPERSNAPPER	SOLIDIFICATION	RECONNAISSANCE	DEMOCRATICALLY
DISENFRANCHISE	STRATIFICATION	RESPONSIBILITY	ELECTROMYOGRAM
DISINFORMATION	STULTIFICATION	RESPONSIVENESS	ELECTRONICALLY
INSUFFICIENTLY	SUPERINTENDENT	SEXCENTENARIAN	FRATERNIZATION
INTERFEROMETER	UNDESIRABILITY	STEGANOGRAPHIC	INEXPRESSIBLES
MULTIFACTORIAL	UNSATISFACTORY	SUBCONSCIOUSLY	IRREPROACHABLE
QUALIFICATIONS	VERISIMILITUDE	SUPERNATURALLY	METEOROLOGICAL
SATISFACTORILY	SHRINKWRAPPING	TERMINOLOGICAL	NETHERSTOCKING
SUPERFICIALITY	DISCOLOURATION	TINTINNABULATE	OTOLARYNGOLOGY
TRANSFORMATION	EMBELLISHMENTS	UNDERNOURISHED	OVERPRODUCTION
UNPROFESSIONAL	ESTABLISHVERSE	WELTANSCHAUUNG	PEREGRINATIONS
APOLOGETICALLY	INFRALAPSARIAN	ALLELOCHEMICAL	PROPORTIONALLY
ASTROGEOLOGIST	INTELLECTUALLY	ALLOIOSTROPHUS	TATTERDEMALION
BIOENGINEERING	INTELLIGENTSIA	ANTHROPOLOGIST	UNAPPROACHABLE
IMPREGNABILITY	MISCALCULATION	ANTHROPOPHAGUS	UNATTRIBUTABLE
NITROGLYCERINE	POIKILOTHERMIC	ANTIMONARCHIST	UNCORROBORATED
ORTHOGRAPHICAL	SCHOOLCHILDREN	CAMELOPARDALIS	VESPERTILIONID
PHYTOGEOGRAPHY	SCHOOLMISTRESS	CARDIOVASCULAR	WESTERNIZATION
STRAIGHTFOWARD	TROUBLESHOOTER	CENTROLECITHAL	AGGRESSIVENESS
APPREHENSIVELY	UNSKILLFULNESS	CONGLOMERATION	COMMISSIONAIRE
BALUCHITHERIUM	ABSTEMIOUSNESS	CONTROVERTIBLE	CONTESSERATION
BREATHLESSNESS	AFOREMENTIONED	CZECHOSLOVAKIA	CORRESPONDENCE
CHINCHERINCHEE	CIRCUMLOCUTION	DEXTROROTATORY	DISASSOCIATION
ENCEPHALOPATHY	CIRCUMNAVIGATE	IMMUNOGLOBULIN	ECCLESIASTICAL
HYPOTHETICALLY	CIRCUMSCISSILE	IRRECONCILABLE	ECCLESIASTICUS
METAPHORICALLY	CIRCUMSTANTIAL	METAMORPHOSING	EXPRESSIONLESS
MONOCHROMATISM	DIPLOMATICALLY	MONOPOLIZATION	HEARTSEARCHING
NEBUCHADNEZZAR	DISCOMBOBERATE	PSYCHOANALYSIS	HIEROSOLYMITAN
ORNITHOLOGICAL	DISCOMBOBULATE	ROADWORTHINESS	HYPERSENSITIVE
PHOSPHORESCENT	FERRIMAGNETISM	SELFCONFIDENCE	IMPRESSIONABLE
SLAUGHTERHOUSE	FUNDAMENTALISM	SELFGOVERNMENT	INCONSIDERABLE
THOUGHTFULNESS	FUNDAMENTALIST	THERMODYNAMICS	INFRASTRUCTURE
THREEHALFPENCE	IMPERMEABILITY	TRICHOPHYTOSIS	LIGHTSENSITIVE
UNENTHUSIASTIC	IMPLEMENTATION	UNRECOGNIZABLE	MEPHISTOPHELES
WHOLEHEARTEDLY	INSURMOUNTABLE	ACCOMPLISHMENT	MICROSPOROCYTE
ADMINISTRATION	INTERMITTENTLY	CORRUPTIBILITY	OPPRESSIVENESS
ADMINISTRATIVE	MATHEMATICALLY	DISAPPOINTMENT	PARAPSYCHOLOGY

PERMISSIVENESS
PHOTOSYNTHESIS
POSSESSINHUMAN
PREDESTINATION
PREDISPOSITION
PROFESSIONALLY
PURPOSEFULNESS
RECONSTITUTION
RECONSTRUCTION
REPRESENTATION
REPRESENTATIVE
SELFASSESSMENT
SOPHISTICATION
SUBMISSIVENESS
SUPERSCRIPTION
SUPERSTRUCTURE
UNCONSCIONABLE
UNDERSECRETARY
UNDERSTANDABLE
UNDERSTANDABLY
UNDERSTATEMENT
UNQUESTIONABLE
UNQUESTIONABLY
ZOROASTRIANISM
AFFECTIONATELY
CLAUSTROPHOBIA
CLAUSTROPHOBIC
DERMATOLOGICAL
DESISTABSTRACT
DISINTEGRATION
DIVERTISSEMENT
EDUCATIONALIST
EGALITARIANISM
INDESTRUCTIBLE
INDOCTRINATION
LICENTIOUSNESS
LONGITUDINALLY
OSTENTATIOUSLY
RADIOTELEPHONE
SCIENTIFICALLY
SENSATIONALISM
SIMULTANEOUSLY
TRADITIONALIST
UNCONTROLLABLE
UNMENTIONABLES
WEIGHTLESSNESS
AUTOSUGGESTION
DISCOUNTENANCE
DISCOURAGEMENT
DISCOURTEOUSLY
METICULOUSNESS
NIBELUNGENLIED
OBSEQUIOUSNESS
OVERSUBSCRIBED
PASTEURIZATION
PRESSURIZATION
RIDICULOUSNESS
SANSCULOTTERIE
SCRUPULOUSNESS
SELFSUFFICIENT
VALETUDINARIAN
APPROVECOMMENT
INCONVENIENTLY
LASCIVIOUSNESS
UNCONVENTIONAL
ACKNOWLEDGMENT
ANTILYMPHOCYTE
CREEPYCRAWLIES
PORPHYROGENITE

STAPHYLOCOCCUS
TELETYPEWRITER
GEWÜRZTRAMINER

14:7

AUTOCRATICALLY
AUTOTRANSPLANT
DEMOCRATICALLY
DESISTABSTRACT
DIPLOMATICALLY
DISEMBARKATION
EGALITARIANISM
ENCEPHALOPATHY
FERRIMAGNETISM
INFRALAPSARIAN
INTERNATIONALE
MATHEMATICALLY
MILLENARIANISM
MULTIFACTORIAL
NEBUCHADNEZZAR
NITROBACTERIUM
OSTENTATIOUSLY
PHENOBARBITONE
PHLEGMATICALLY
PSYCHOANALYSIS
RECONNAISSANCE
SATISFACTORILY
SIMULTANEOUSLY
SUPERNATURALLY
SYSTEMATICALLY
THREEHALFPENCE
UNPREPAREDNESS
ARCHAEBACTERIA
DISCOMBOBERATE
DISCOMBOBULATE
OVERSUBSCRIBED
RECORDBREAKING
SINGLEBREASTED
SUPERABUNDANCE
ALLELOCHEMICAL
CONJUNCTIVITIS
CREEPYCRAWLIES
MACROECONOMICS
MISCALCULATION
MONOSACCHARIDE
PHARMACEUTICAL
PHARMACOLOGIST
PRACTICABILITY
PRONUNCIAMENTO
SCHOOLCHILDREN
SUPERSCRIPTION
UNCONSCIONABLE
AGGRANDISEMENT
AIRCONDITIONED
AIRCONDITIONER
ANTIFEDERALIST
AUTORADIOGRAPH
COINCIDENTALLY
PARTRIDGEBERRY
TATTERDEMALION
THERMODYNAMICS
VALETUDINARIAN
AFOREMENTIONED
ALPHABETICALLY
APOLOGETICALLY
APPREHENSIVELY
APPROVECOMMENT
ASTROGEOLOGIST
CHINCHERINCHEE

CONFIDENTIALLY
CROSSREFERENCE
CRYPTAESTHETIC
DISINTEGRATION
DISORIENTATION
FORTUNETELLING
FUNDAMENTALISM
FUNDAMENTALIST
HEARTSEARCHING
HYPERSENSITIVE
HYPOTHETICALLY
IMPERMEABILITY
IMPLEMENTATION
INCONVENIENTLY
INEXPRESSIBLES
INTELLECTUALLY
INTERFEROMETER
INTERPELLATION
LIGHTSENSITIVE
NITROCELLULOSE
ONCHOCERCIASIS
PHYTOGEOGRAPHY
PROVIDENTIALLY
PURPOSEFULNESS
RADIOTELEPHONE
RECOMMENDATION
REPRESENTATION
REPRESENTATIVE
SENTIMENTALITY
SERVOMECHANISM
TRANSCENDENTAL
TROUBLESHOOTER
UNCONVENTIONAL
UNDERDEVELOPED
UNDERMENTIONED
UNDERSECRETARY
UNPREMEDITATED
UNPROFESSIONAL
WHOLEHEARTEDLY
AIRCRAFTSWOMAN
CLASSIFICATION
FRUCTIFICATION
GENTRIFICATION
IDENTIFICATION
SANCTIFICATION
SELFSUFFICIENT
SIMPLIFICATION
SOLIDIFICATION
STRATIFICATION
STULTIFICATION
AUTOSUGGESTION
CONGREGATIONAL
DISTINGUISHING
IMMUNOGLOBULIN
SEPTUAGENARIAN
UNRECOGNIZABLE
COMPREHENSIBLE
DISENCHANTMENT
ORTHOCHROMATIC
STRAIGHTFOWARD
SUPERPHOSPHATE
ABSTEMIOUSNESS
AFFECTIONATELY
ARRONDISSEMENT
BACTERIOLOGIST
BALUCHITHERIUM
BIOENGINEERING
CAPRICIOUSNESS
DIVERTISSEMENT

ECCLESIASTICAL
ECCLESIASTICUS
EDUCATIONALIST
EMBELLISHMENTS
ESTABLISHVERSE
FASTIDIOUSNESS
HALLUCINATIONS
HALLUCINOGENIC
INCONSIDERABLE
INSIGNIFICANCE
INSUFFICIENTLY
INTELLIGENTSIA
INTERMITTENTLY
JOHANNISBERGER
LASCIVIOUSNESS
LICENTIOUSNESS
LOQUACIOUSNESS
MOUNTAINEERING
OBSEQUIOUSNESS
PARALEIPOMENON
PEREGRINATIONS
PRECOCIOUSNESS
PROHIBITIONIST
QUALIFICATIONS
RECONCILIATION
SCIENTIFICALLY
SENSATIONALISM
SUPERCILIOUSLY
SUPERFICIALITY
TRADITIONALIST
TRANSMIGRATION
UNATTRIBUTABLE
UNMENTIONABLES
VERTICILLASTER
ACCOMPLISHMENT
ACKNOWLEDGMENT
BREATHLESSNESS
CAPITALIZATION
CENTRALIZATION
CENTROLECITHAL
CIRCUMLOCUTION
CRYSTALLOMANCY
DEMOBILIZATION
DEMORALIZATION
DISCIPLINARIAN
DISINCLINATION
GENERALIZATION
GRANDILOQUENCE
IMMOBILIZATION
INCONCLUSIVELY
INTERPLANETARY
LIBERALIZATION
METICULOUSNESS
MISAPPLICATION
MONOPOLIZATION
MULTIPLICATION
NATURALIZATION
NEUTRALIZATION
NITROGLYCERINE
REHABILITATION
RIDICULOUSNESS
SANSCULOTTERIE
SCRUPULOUSNESS
SCURRILOUSNESS
SPECIALIZATION
STAPHYLOCOCCUS
UNINTELLIGIBLE
UNSKILLFULNESS
WEIGHTLESSNESS

ANTILYMPHOCYTE	UNDERNOURISHED	COMMISSIONAIRE	CONSTRUCTIVISM
CASTRAMETATION	ANTHROPOLOGIST	CONTESSERATION	HORTICULTURIST
CONGLOMERATION	ANTHROPOPHAGUS	CONVERSATIONAL	LONGITUDINALLY
DISCRIMINATING	ANTIDEPRESSANT	CZECHOSLOVAKIA	RELINQUISHMENT
DISCRIMINATION	CAMELOPARDALIS	DISCONSOLATELY	UNENTHUSIASTIC
DISCRIMINATORY	CORRESPONDENCE	EXPRESSIONLESS	CARDIOVASCULAR
EXPERIMENTALLY	GEOGRAPHICALLY	IMPRESSIONABLE	CONSERVATIVELY
SCHOOLMISTRESS	INDECIPHERABLE	KNOTENSCHIEFER	CONTROVERTIBLE
SINGLEMINDEDLY	MICROSPOROCYTE	METEMPSYCHOSIS	SELFGOVERNMENT
VERISIMILITUDE	PREDISPOSITION	NETHERSTOCKING	SHRINKWRAPPING
ANTIMONARCHIST	PRESUMPTUOUSLY	OPPRESSIVENESS	BATTERYPOWERED
ARCHGENETHLIAC	PRESUPPOSITION	OPTIMISTICALLY	OTOLARYNGOLOGY
BROBDINGNAGIAN	SESQUIPEDALIAN	PERMISSIVENESS	PARAPSYCHOLOGY
CIRCUMNAVIGATE	SESQUIPEDALION	PERSUASIVENESS	PHOTOSYNTHESIS
CONSTANTINOPLE	TELETYPEWRITER	PHANTASMAGORIA	ORGANIZATIONAL
DENOMINATIONAL	TRICHOPHYTOSIS	POSSESSINHUMAN	
DISCOUNTENANCE	ACHONDROPLASIA	PROFESSIONALLY	**14:8**
EXISTENTIALISM	ANTIPERSPIRANT	QUINTESSENTIAL	ACCOUNTABILITY
EXISTENTIALIST	BOISTEROUSNESS	RESPONSIBILITY	ANTIMETATHESIS
FRATERNIZATION	CLAUSTROPHOBIA	RESPONSIVENESS	ANTIMONARCHIST
HOMOGENIZATION	CLAUSTROPHOBIC	SELFASSESSMENT	ARCHAEBACTERIA
IMPREGNABILITY	CONSPIRATORIAL	SELFRESPECTING	CAMELOPARDALIS
IRRECONCILABLE	COUNTERBALANCE	SUBCONSCIOUSLY	CARDIOVASCULAR
NIBELUNGENLIED	COUNTERMEASURE	SUBMISSIVENESS	CIRCUMNAVIGATE
REORGANIZATION	DEXTROROTATORY	UNPLEASANTNESS	CONGREGATIONAL
SELFCONFIDENCE	DISAPPROBATION	UNSATISFACTORY	CONSERVATIVELY
SUBSTANTIATION	DISAPPROVINGLY	WELTANSCHAUUNG	CONSPIRATORIAL
SULPHANILAMIDE	DISCOURAGEMENT	ACCOUNTABILITY	CONVERSATIONAL
SUPERANNUATION	DISCOURTEOUSLY	ANTIMETATHESIS	DENOMINATIONAL
SUPERINTENDENT	DISENFRANCHISE	APPRENTICESHIP	DISCOURAGEMENT
TINTINNABULATE	IMPOVERISHMENT	AUTHENTICATION	DISENCHANTMENT
WESTERNIZATION	INDESTRUCTIBLE	CHARACTERISTIC	DISENFRANCHISE
ANTIODONTALGIC	INDETERMINABLE	CINEMATOGRAPHY	ECCLESIASTICAL
ARCHAEOLOGICAL	INDISCRIMINATE	CONGRATULATION	ECCLESIASTICUS
ASTRONOMICALLY	INDOCTRINATION	CONGRATULATORY	HEARTSEARCHING
CARCINOMATOSIS	INTERPRETATION	CONSTITUTIONAL	HEMIMETABOLOUS
DECISIONMAKING	INTERPRETATIVE	CONVENTIONALLY	IMPERMEABILITY
DERMATOLOGICAL	KNICKERBOCKERS	CONVERTIBILITY	IMPREGNABILITY
DISAPPOINTMENT	KNIPPERDOLLING	CORRUPTIBILITY	INTERPLANETARY
DISASSOCIATION	MALAPPROPRIATE	DISCONTENTMENT	IRREPROACHABLE
DISCOLOURATION	METAMORPHOSING	GEWÜRZTRAMINER	ORGANIZATIONAL
DISINFORMATION	MICROPROCESSOR	HEMIMETABOLOUS	ORTHOGRAPHICAL
ELECTIONEERING	MISAPPROPRIATE	ILLEGITIMATELY	PRACTICABILITY
ELECTROMYOGRAM	MONOCARPELLARY	INFRASTRUCTURE	RESPECTABILITY
ELECTRONICALLY	MONOCHROMATISM	MEPHISTOPHELES	TINTINNABULATE
GYNAECOLOGICAL	ORTHOGRAPHICAL	PERCEPTIVENESS	UNAPPROACHABLE
HIEROSOLYMITAN	OSTEOARTHRITIS	PHILANTHROPIST	UNDERSTANDABLE
HYDROCORTISONE	PASTEURIZATION	PREDESTINATION	UNDERSTANDABLY
INSURMOUNTABLE	POLYMERIZATION	PRODUCTIVENESS	UNDERSTATEMENT
INTERCONNECTED	POPULARIZATION	PROPORTIONALLY	UNDESIRABILITY
IRREPROACHABLE	PORPHYROGENITE	RECAPITULATION	UNPLEASANTNESS
MEGASPORANGIUM	PREFABRICATION	RECONSTITUTION	WHOLEHEARTEDLY
METAPHORICALLY	PRESSURIZATION	RECONSTRUCTION	COUNTERBALANCE
METEOROLOGICAL	REGULARIZATION	RESPECTABILITY	DESISTABSTRACT
ORNITHOLOGICAL	ROADWORTHINESS	SEXCENTENARIAN	KNICKERBOCKERS
OVERPRODUCTION	SCATTERBRAINED	SLAUGHTERHOUSE	SCATTERBRAINED
PARSIMONIOUSLY	SUBMICROSCOPIC	SOPHISTICATION	UNATTRIBUTABLE
PHOSPHORESCENT	SUPEREROGATION	SUPERSTRUCTURE	UNCORROBORATED
POIKILOTHERMIC	ULTRACREPIDATE	SUSCEPTIBILITY	APPROVECOMMENT
PROTOCONTINENT	UNCOMPROMISING	THOUGHTFULNESS	CIRCUMSCISSILE
SCAREMONGERING	UNCONTROLLABLE	UNDERSTANDABLE	CONSTRUCTIVELY
STEGANOGRAPHIC	UNDESIRABILITY	UNDERSTANDABLY	CONSTRUCTIVISM
SUPERCONTINENT	WHIPPERSNAPPER	UNDERSTATEMENT	DISASSOCIATION
TERMINOLOGICAL	ADMINISTRATION	UNQUESTIONABLE	INSUFFICIENTLY
THROMBOPLASTIN	ADMINISTRATIVE	UNQUESTIONABLY	INTELLECTUALLY
TRANSFORMATION	AGGRESSIVENESS	VESPERTILIONID	IRRECONCILABLE
TRANSPORTATION	ALLOIOSTROPHUS	VINDICTIVENESS	KNOTENSCHIEFER
UNAPPROACHABLE	CIRCUMSCISSILE	ZOROASTRIANISM	MONOSACCHARIDE
UNCORROBORATED	CIRCUMSTANTIAL	CONSTRUCTIVELY	MULTIFACTORIAL

NITROBACTERIUM	AGGRESSIVENESS	SPECIALIZATION	REPRESENTATIVE
PARAPSYCHOLOGY	AIRCONDITIONED	STRATIFICATION	SCAREMONGERING
QUALIFICATIONS	AIRCONDITIONER	STULTIFICATION	SENTIMENTALITY
SATISFACTORILY	APPRENTICESHIP	SUBMISSIVENESS	SIMULTANEOUSLY
SERVOMECHANISM	AUTHENTICATION	SULPHANILAMIDE	SUPERANNUATION
SUBCONSCIOUSLY	AUTORADIOGRAPH	SUSCEPTIBILITY	SUPERCONTINENT
SUPERFICIALITY	CAPITALIZATION	UNCONSCIONABLE	TRANSCENDENTAL
UNDERSECRETARY	CENTRALIZATION	UNQUESTIONABLE	UNCONVENTIONAL
WELTANSCHAUUNG	CLASSIFICATION	UNQUESTIONABLY	UNDERMENTIONED
INCONSIDERABLE	COMMISSIONAIRE	VALETUDINARIAN	UNRECOGNIZABLE
KNIPPERDOLLING	CONVENTIONALLY	VERISIMILITUDE	ABSTEMIOUSNESS
LONGITUDINALLY	CONVERTIBILITY	VESPERTILIONID	ACHONDROPLASIA
NEBUCHADNEZZAR	CORRUPTIBILITY	VINDICTIVENESS	AFFECTIONATELY
OVERPRODUCTION	DEMOBILIZATION	WESTERNIZATION	ANTHROPOLOGIST
UNPREMEDITATED	DEMORALIZATION	ARCHAEOLOGICAL	ANTHROPOPHAGUS
ACKNOWLEDGMENT	DISAPPOINTMENT	CRYSTALLOMANCY	ASTROGEOLOGIST
ANTIFEDERALIST	DISCIPLINARIAN	CZECHOSLOVAKIA	BACTERIOLOGIST
ARCHGENETHLIAC	DISCRIMINATING	DERMATOLOGICAL	BOISTEROUSNESS
BREATHLESSNESS	DISCRIMINATION	ENCEPHALOPATHY	CAPRICIOUSNESS
CASTRAMETATION	DISCRIMINATORY	GYNAECOLOGICAL	CINEMATOGRAPHY
CENTROLECITHAL	DISINCLINATION	HIEROSOLYMITAN	CIRCUMLOCUTION
CHARACTERISTIC	EXPRESSIONLESS	HORTICULTURIST	CLAUSTROPHOBIA
COINCIDENTALLY	FRATERNIZATION	IMMUNOGLOBULIN	CLAUSTROPHOBIC
COMPREHENSIBLE	FRUCTIFICATION	INTERPELLATION	CORRESPONDENCE
CONGLOMERATION	GENERALIZATION	METEOROLOGICAL	DEXTROROTATORY
CONTESSERATION	GENTRIFICATION	NITROCELLULOSE	DISAPPROBATION
CONTROVERTIBLE	HOMOGENIZATION	ORNITHOLOGICAL	DISAPPROVINGLY
DISCONTENTMENT	IDENTIFICATION	RADIOTELEPHONE	DISCOMBOBERATE
EXPERIMENTALLY	ILLEGITIMATELY	RECONCILIATION	DISCOMBOBULATE
INTERPRETATION	IMMOBILIZATION	SUPERCILIOUSLY	DISCONSOLATELY
INTERPRETATIVE	IMPOVERISHMENT	TERMINOLOGICAL	EDUCATIONALIST
PHARMACEUTICAL	IMPRESSIONABLE	THREEHALFPENCE	FASTIDIOUSNESS
SELFASSESSMENT	INDISCRIMINATE	UNINTELLIGIBLE	GRANDILOQUENCE
SELFGOVERNMENT	INDOCTRINATION	VERTICILLASTER	LASCIVIOUSNESS
SEPTUAGENARIAN	LIBERALIZATION	ASTRONOMICALLY	LICENTIOUSNESS
SESQUIPEDALIAN	MISAPPLICATION	CARCINOMATOSIS	LOQUACIOUSNESS
SESQUIPEDALION	MONOPOLIZATION	COUNTERMEASURE	MACROECONOMICS
SEXCENTENARIAN	MULTIPLICATION	ELECTROMYOGRAM	MALAPPROPRIATE
SLAUGHTERHOUSE	NATURALIZATION	INDETERMINABLE	MEPHISTOPHELES
TATTERDEMALION	NEUTRALIZATION	PHANTASMAGORIA	METICULOUSNESS
TELETYPEWRITER	OPPRESSIVENESS	AFOREMENTIONED	MICROPROCESSOR
ULTRACREPIDATE	PASTEURIZATION	ANTIODONTALGIC	MICROSPOROCYTE
WEIGHTLESSNESS	PERCEPTIVENESS	APPREHENSIVELY	MISAPPROPRIATE
CROSSREFERENCE	PERMISSIVENESS	AUTOTRANSPLANT	MONOCHROMATISM
INSIGNIFICANCE	PERSUASIVENESS	BIOENGINEERING	OBSEQUIOUSNESS
PURPOSEFULNESS	POLYMERIZATION	CONFIDENTIALLY	PHARMACOLOGIST
SCIENTIFICALLY	POPULARIZATION	DECISIONMAKING	PHYTOGEOGRAPHY
SELFCONFIDENCE	POSSESSINHUMAN	DISORIENTATION	PORPHYROGENITE
SELFSUFFICIENT	PREDESTINATION	ELECTIONEERING	PRECOCIOUSNESS
THOUGHTFULNESS	PREFABRICATION	ELECTRONICALLY	PREDISPOSITION
UNSATISFACTORY	PRESSURIZATION	FUNDAMENTALISM	PRESUPPOSITION
UNSKILLFULNESS	PRODUCTIVENESS	FUNDAMENTALIST	RIDICULOUSNESS
AUTOSUGGESTION	PROFESSIONALLY	HALLUCINATIONS	SANSCULOTTERIE
BROBDINGNAGIAN	PRONUNCIAMENTO	HALLUCINOGENIC	SCRUPULOUSNESS
DISINTEGRATION	PROPORTIONALLY	HYPERSENSITIVE	SCURRILOUSNESS
FERRIMAGNETISM	RECONNAISSANCE	IMPLEMENTATION	SENSATIONALISM
INTELLIGENTSIA	RECONSTITUTION	INCONVENIENTLY	STAPHYLOCOCCUS
NIBELUNGENLIED	REGULARIZATION	INTERCONNECTED	SUBMICROSCOPIC
PARTRIDGEBERRY	REHABILITATION	LIGHTSENSITIVE	SUPEREROGATION
STEGANOGRAPHIC	RELINQUISHMENT	MOUNTAINEERING	SUPERPHOSPHATE
TRANSMIGRATION	REORGANIZATION	OTOLARYNGOLOGY	TRADITIONALIST
ALLELOCHEMICAL	RESPONSIBILITY	PARSIMONIOUSLY	UNCOMPROMISING
GEOGRAPHICALLY	RESPONSIVENESS	PEREGRINATIONS	UNCONTROLLABLE
INDECIPHERABLE	SANCTIFICATION	PHOTOSYNTHESIS	UNMENTIONABLES
PHILANTHROPIST	SCHOOLMISTRESS	PROTOCONTINENT	ANTILYMPHOCYTE
SCHOOLCHILDREN	SIMPLIFICATION	PROVIDENTIALLY	BATTERYPOWERED
TRICHOPHYTOSIS	SINGLEMINDEDLY	PSYCHOANALYSIS	INFRALAPSARIAN
ACCOMPLISHMENT	SOLIDIFICATION	RECOMMENDATION	METAMORPHOSING
AGGRANDISEMENT	SOPHISTICATION	REPRESENTATION	MONOCARPELLARY

PARALEIPOMENON
SELFRESPECTING
THROMBOPLASTIN
ANTIDEPRESSANT
CHINCHERINCHEE
CREEPYCRAWLIES
DISEMBARKATION
DISINFORMATION
EGALITARIANISM
GEWÜRZTRAMINER
HYDROCORTISONE
INFRASTRUCTURE
INTERFEROMETER
MEGASPORANGIUM
METAPHORICALLY
MILLENARIANISM
ONCHOCERCIASIS
ORTHOCHROMATIC
PHENOBARBITONE
PHOSPHORESCENT
RECONSTRUCTION
RECORDBREAKING
SHRINKWRAPPING
SINGLEBREASTED
SUPERSCRIPTION
SUPERSTRUCTURE
TRANSFORMATION
TRANSPORTATION
UNPREPAREDNESS
ZOROASTRIANISM
ANTIPERSPIRANT
ARRONDISSEMENT
CRYPTAESTHETIC
DIVERTISSEMENT
EMBELLISHMENTS
ESTABLISHVERSE
INEXPRESSIBLES
JOHANNISBERGER
OVERSUBSCRIBED
QUINTESSENTIAL
TROUBLESHOOTER
UNENTHUSIASTIC
UNPROFESSIONAL
WHIPPERSNAPPER
ADMINISTRATION
ADMINISTRATIVE
AIRCRAFTSWOMAN
ALLOIOSTROPHUS
ALPHABETICALLY
APOLOGETICALLY
AUTOCRATICALLY
BALUCHITHERIUM
CIRCUMSTANTIAL
CONJUNCTIVITIS
CONSTANTINOPLE
DEMOCRATICALLY
DIPLOMATICALLY
DISCOUNTENANCE
DISCOURTEOUSLY
EXISTENTIALISM
EXISTENTIALIST
FORTUNETELLING
HYPOTHETICALLY
INTERMITTENTLY
INTERNATIONALE
MATHEMATICALLY
NETHERSTOCKING
OPTIMISTICALLY
OSTENTATIOUSLY

OSTEOARTHRITIS
PHLEGMATICALLY
POIKILOTHERMIC
PRESUMPTUOUSLY
PROHIBITIONIST
ROADWORTHINESS
STRAIGHTFOWARD
SUBSTANTIATION
SUPERINTENDENT
SUPERNATURALLY
SYSTEMATICALLY
CONGRATULATION
CONGRATULATORY
CONSTITUTIONAL
DISCOLOURATION
DISTINGUISHING
INCONCLUSIVELY
INDESTRUCTIBLE
INSURMOUNTABLE
MISCALCULATION
RECAPITULATION
SUPERABUNDANCE
UNDERNOURISHED
UNDERDEVELOPED
METEMPSYCHOSIS
NITROGLYCERINE
THERMODYNAMICS

14:9

CARCINOMATOSIS
CIRCUMSTANTIAL
COUNTERBALANCE
CREEPYCRAWLIES
GEWÜRZTRAMINER
HALLUCINATIONS
MEGASPORANGIUM
PEREGRINATIONS
PHANTASMAGORIA
PRONUNCIAMENTO
PSYCHOANALYSIS
QUALIFICATIONS
SHRINKWRAPPING
UNSATISFACTORY
ACCOUNTABILITY
CONVERTIBILITY
CORRUPTIBILITY
DISAPPROBATION
DISCOMBOBERATE
DISCOMBOBULATE
HEMIMETABOLOUS
IMPERMEABILITY
IMPREGNABILITY
JOHANNISBERGER
PHENOBARBITONE
PRACTICABILITY
RESPECTABILITY
RESPONSIBILITY
SUSCEPTIBILITY
TINTINNABULATE
UNDESIRABILITY
APPRENTICESHIP
ARCHAEBACTERIA
AUTHENTICATION
CENTROLECITHAL
CIRCUMLOCUTION
CLASSIFICATION
FRUCTIFICATION
GENTRIFICATION
IDENTIFICATION

INDESTRUCTIBLE
IRREPROACHABLE
METEMPSYCHOSIS
MICROPROCESSOR
MISAPPLICATION
MULTIPLICATION
NITROGLYCERINE
ONCHOCERCIASIS
OVERSUBSCRIBED
PREFABRICATION
SANCTIFICATION
SIMPLIFICATION
SOLIDIFICATION
SOPHISTICATION
STAPHYLOCOCCUS
STRATIFICATION
STULTIFICATION
UNAPPROACHABLE
ACKNOWLEDGMENT
RECOMMENDATION
SESQUIPEDALIAN
SESQUIPEDALIAN
TRANSCENDENTAL
ALLELOCHEMICAL
ANTIDEPRESSANT
AUTOSUGGESTION
BIOENGINEERING
COUNTERMEASURE
CROSSREFERENCE
DISCOUNTENANCE
DISCOURTEOUSLY
ELECTIONEERING
FORTUNETELLING
INCONSIDERABLE
INDECIPHERABLE
INTELLIGENTSIA
MONOCARPELLARY
MOUNTAINEERING
NIBELUNGENLIED
PARTRIDGEBERRY
PHOSPHORESCENT
QUINTESSENTIAL
RADIOTELEPHONE
RECORDBREAKING
SELFRESPECTING
SIMULTANEOUSLY
SINGLEBREASTED
SUPERINTENDENT
UNDERDEVELOPED
UNPREPAREDNESS
STRAIGHTFOWARD
THREEHALFPENCE
CINEMATOGRAPHY
DISCOURAGEMENT
OTOLARYNGOLOGY
PHYTOGEOGRAPHY
PORPHYROGENITE
SCAREMONGERING
SUPEREROGATION
ANTILYMPHOCYTE
BALUCHITHERIUM
EMBELLISHMENTS
ESTABLISHVERSE
KNOTENSCHIEFER
METAMORPHOSING
MONOSACCHARIDE
OSTEOARTHRITIS
PARAPSYCHOLOGY
POIKILOTHERMIC

ROADWORTHINESS
SERVOMECHANISM
TROUBLESHOOTER
WELTANSCHAUUNG
ALPHABETICALLY
APOLOGETICALLY
ASTRONOMICALLY
AUTOCRATICALLY
CHINCHERINCHEE
CIRCUMSCISSILE
CONJUNCTIVITIS
CONSTANTINOPLE
DEMOCRATICALLY
DIPLOMATICALLY
DISASSOCIATION
DISTINGUISHING
EGALITARIANISM
ELECTRONICALLY
EXISTENTIALISM
EXISTENTIALIST
GEOGRAPHICALLY
HYPOTHETICALLY
INCONVENIENTLY
INDETERMINABLE
INSIGNIFICANCE
INSUFFICIENTLY
INTERNATIONALE
IRRECONCILABLE
LONGITUDINALLY
MATHEMATICALLY
METAPHORICALLY
MILLENARIANISM
OPTIMISTICALLY
OSTENTATIOUSLY
PARSIMONIOUSLY
PHLEGMATICALLY
PROHIBITIONIST
RECONCILIATION
SCHOOLCHILDREN
SCIENTIFICALLY
SELFCONFIDENCE
SELFSUFFICIENT
SUBCONSCIOUSLY
SUBSTANTIATION
SUPERCILIOUSLY
SUPERFICIALITY
SUPERSCRIPTION
SYSTEMATICALLY
UNENTHUSIASTIC
UNINTELLIGIBLE
UNPREMEDITATED
UNRECOGNIZABLE
ZOROASTRIANISM
DISEMBARKATION
ANTHROPOLOGIST
ASTROGEOLOGIST
BACTERIOLOGIST
CONGRATULATION
CONGRATULATORY
DISCONSOLATELY
INTERPELLATION
MISCALCULATION
NITROCELLULOSE
PHARMACOLOGIST
RECAPITULATION
SULPHANILAMIDE
THROMBOPLASTIN
UNCONTROLLABLE
VERISIMILITUDE

VERTICILLASTER
VESPERTILIONID
DECISIONMAKING
DISINFORMATION
ILLEGITIMATELY
INDISCRIMINATE
MONOCHROMATISM
TATTERDEMALION
TRANSFORMATION
UNCOMPROMISING
AFFECTIONATELY
BROBDINGNAGIAN
COINCIDENTALLY
COMPREHENSIBLE
CORRESPONDENCE
DISAPPOINTMENT
DISCIPLINARIAN
DISCONTENTMENT
DISCRIMINATING
DISCRIMINATION
DISCRIMINATORY
DISENCHANTMENT
DISENFRANCHISE
DISINCLINATION
EDUCATIONALIST
EXPERIMENTALLY
FERRIMAGNETISM
INDOCTRINATION
INSURMOUNTABLE
INTERCONNECTED
INTERPLANETARY
MACROECONOMICS
NEBUCHADNEZZAR
POSSESSINHUMAN
PREDESTINATION
SENSATIONALISM
SEPTUAGENARIAN
SEXCENTENARIAN
SINGLEMINDEDLY
SUPERABUNDANCE
THERMODYNAMICS
TRADITIONALIST
UNDERSTANDABLE
UNDERSTANDABLY
UNMENTIONABLES
UNPLEASANTNESS
VALETUDINARIAN
WHIPPERSNAPPER
APPROVECOMMENT
ARCHAEOLOGICAL
AUTORADIOGRAPH
BATTERYPOWERED
COMMISSIONAIRE
CONVENTIONALLY
CRYSTALLOMANCY
CZECHOSLOVAKIA
DERMATOLOGICAL
ENCEPHALOPATHY
EXPRESSIONLESS
GYNAECOLOGICAL
HALLUCINOGENIC
IMMUNOGLOBULIN
IMPRESSIONABLE
INTERFEROMETER
KNICKERBOCKERS
KNIPPERDOLLING
METEOROLOGICAL
NETHERSTOCKING
ORNITHOLOGICAL

ORTHOCHROMATIC
PARALEIPOMENON
PROFESSIONALLY
PROPORTIONALLY
TERMINOLOGICAL
UNCONSCIONABLE
UNCORROBORATED
UNQUESTIONABLE
UNQUESTIONABLY
ACHONDROPLASIA
ANTHROPOPHAGUS
ANTIPERSPIRANT
CLAUSTROPHOBIA
CLAUSTROPHOBIC
MALAPPROPRIATE
MEPHISTOPHELES
MISAPPROPRIATE
ORTHOGRAPHICAL
ULTRACREPIDATE
GRANDILOQUENCE
ADMINISTRATION
ADMINISTRATIVE
ALLOIOSTROPHUS
ANTIFEDERALIST
ANTIMONARCHIST
CAMELOPARDALIS
CHARACTERISTIC
CONGLOMERATION
CONTESSERATION
CONTROVERTIBLE
DISCOLOURATION
DISINTEGRATION
HEARTSEARCHING
MICROSPOROCYTE
PHILANTHROPIST
SCATTERBRAINED
SELFGOVERNMENT
SLAUGHTERHOUSE
STEGANOGRAPHIC
TRANSMIGRATION
UNDERNOURISHED
UNDERSECRETARY
WHOLEHEARTEDLY
ACCOMPLISHMENT
AGGRANDISEMENT
AIRCRAFTSWOMAN
APPREHENSIVELY
ARRONDISSEMENT
AUTOTRANSPLANT
BREATHLESSNESS
CARDIOVASCULAR
DESISTABSTRACT
DIVERTISSEMENT
ECCLESIASTICAL
ECCLESIASTICUS
HYPERSENSITIVE
IMPOVERISHMENT
INCONCLUSIVELY
INEXPRESSIBLES
INFRALAPSARIAN
LIGHTSENSITIVE
PREDISPOSITION
PRESUPPOSITION
RECONNAISSANCE
RELINQUISHMENT
SCHOOLMISTRESS
SELFASSESSMENT
SUBMICROSCOPIC
SUPERPHOSPHATE

UNPROFESSIONAL
WEIGHTLESSNESS
AFOREMENTIONED
AIRCONDITIONED
AIRCONDITIONER
ANTIMETATHESIS
ANTIODONTALGIC
ARCHGENETHLIAC
CASTRAMETATION
CONFIDENTIALLY
CONGREGATIONAL
CONSERVATIVELY
CONSPIRATORIAL
CONSTITUTIONAL
CONSTRUCTIVELY
CONSTRUCTIVISM
CONVERSATIONAL
CRYPTAESTHETIC
DENOMINATIONAL
DEXTROROTATORY
DISORIENTATION
FUNDAMENTALISM
FUNDAMENTALIST
HORTICULTURIST
HYDROCORTISONE
IMPLEMENTATION
INTELLECTUALLY
INTERMITTENTLY
INTERPRETATION
INTERPRETATIVE
MULTIFACTORIAL
NITROBACTERIUM
ORGANIZATIONAL
PHOTOSYNTHESIS
PROTOCONTINENT
PROVIDENTIALLY
RECONSTITUTION
REHABILITATION
REPRESENTATION
REPRESENTATIVE
SANSCULOTTERIE
SATISFACTORILY
SENTIMENTALITY
SUPERCONTINENT
TRANSPORTATION
UNCONVENTIONAL
UNDERMENTIONED
UNDERSTATEMENT
ABSTEMIOUSNESS
BOISTEROUSNESS
CAPRICIOUSNESS
FASTIDIOUSNESS
INFRASTRUCTURE
LASCIVIOUSNESS
LICENTIOUSNESS
LOQUACIOUSNESS
METICULOUSNESS
OBSEQUIOUSNESS
OVERPRODUCTION
PHARMACEUTICAL
PRECOCIOUSNESS
PRESUMPTUOUSLY
PURPOSEFULNESS
RECONSTRUCTION
RIDICULOUSNESS
SCRUPULOUSNESS
SCURRILOUSNESS
SUPERANNUATION
SUPERNATURALLY

SUPERSTRUCTURE
THOUGHTFULNESS
UNATTRIBUTABLE
UNSKILLFULNESS
AGGRESSIVENESS
CIRCUMNAVIGATE
DISAPPROVINGLY
OPPRESSIVENESS
PERCEPTIVENESS
PERMISSIVENESS
PERSUASIVENESS
PRODUCTIVENESS
RESPONSIVENESS
SUBMISSIVENESS
VINDICTIVENESS
TELETYPEWRITER
ELECTROMYOGRAM
HIEROSOLYMITAN
TRICHOPHYTOSIS
CAPITALIZATION
CENTRALIZATION
DEMOBILIZATION
DEMORALIZATION
FRATERNIZATION
GENERALIZATION
HOMOGENIZATION
IMMOBILIZATION
LIBERALIZATION
MONOPOLIZATION
NATURALIZATION
NEUTRALIZATION
PASTEURIZATION
POLYMERIZATION
POPULARIZATION
PRESSURIZATION
REGULARIZATION
REORGANIZATION
SPECIALIZATION
WESTERNIZATION

14:10

ADMINISTRATION
ADMINISTRATIVE
AFFECTIONATELY
ANTIFEDERALIST
ANTIODONTALGIC
AUTHENTICATION
BROBDINGNAGIAN
CAPITALIZATION
CASTRAMETATION
CENTRALIZATION
CLASSIFICATION
CONGLOMERATION
CONGRATULATION
CONGRATULATORY
CONTESSERATION
COUNTERMEASURE
DECISIONMAKING
DEMOBILIZATION
DEMORALIZATION
DEXTROROTATORY
DISAPPROBATION
DISASSOCIATION
DISCIPLINARIAN
DISCOLOURATION
DISCONSOLATELY
DISCRIMINATING
DISCRIMINATION
DISCRIMINATORY

DISEMBARKATION	SUPERANNUATION	INCONVENIENTLY	CONVERTIBILITY
DISINCLINATION	SUPEREROGATION	INSUFFICIENTLY	CORRUPTIBILITY
DISINFORMATION	SUPERFICIALITY	INTERCONNECTED	DENOMINATIONAL
DISINTEGRATION	TATTERDEMALION	INTERMITTENTLY	DISAPPROVINGLY
DISORIENTATION	THERMODYNAMICS	INTERPLANETARY	HYDROCORTISONE
EDUCATIONALIST	THROMBOPLASTIN	JOHANNISBERGER	HYPERSENSITIVE
EGALITARIANISM	TRADITIONALIST	MICROPROCESSOR	IMPERMEABILITY
EXISTENTIALISM	TRANSFORMATION	MOUNTAINEERING	IMPREGNABILITY
EXISTENTIALIST	TRANSMIGRATION	NEBUCHADNEZZAR	INCONCLUSIVELY
FRATERNIZATION	TRANSPORTATION	NITROBACTERIUM	INDISCRIMINATE
FRUCTIFICATION	UNENTHUSIASTIC	NITROGLYCERINE	INEXPRESSIBLES
FUNDAMENTALISM	UNMENTIONABLES	OPPRESSIVENESS	KNOTENSCHIEFER
FUNDAMENTALIST	VALETUDINARIAN	PERCEPTIVENESS	LIGHTSENSITIVE
GENERALIZATION	VERTICILLASTER	PERMISSIVENESS	ONCHOCERCIASIS
GENTRIFICATION	WELTANSCHAUUNG	PERSUASIVENESS	ORGANIZATIONAL
HOMOGENIZATION	WESTERNIZATION	POIKILOTHERMIC	PHENOBARBITONE
IDENTIFICATION	WHIPPERSNAPPER	PORPHYROGENITE	PRACTICABILITY
ILLEGITIMATELY	ZOROASTRIANISM	PRODUCTIVENESS	PREDISPOSITION
IMMOBILIZATION	IMMUNOGLOBULIN	RESPONSIVENESS	PRESUPPOSITION
IMPLEMENTATION	PARTRIDGEBERRY	SCAREMONGERING	PROTOCONTINENT
INDOCTRINATION	ALPHABETICALLY	SUBMISSIVENESS	PROVIDENTIALLY
INFRALAPSARIAN	ANTIMONARCHIST	TRANSCENDENTAL	RESPECTABILITY
INTERPELLATION	APOLOGETICALLY	UNDERSECRETARY	RESPONSIBILITY
INTERPRETATION	ASTRONOMICALLY	UNDERSTATEMENT	ROADWORTHINESS
INTERPRETATIVE	AUTOCRATICALLY	VINDICTIVENESS	SUPERCONTINENT
LIBERALIZATION	CARDIOVASCULAR	ACKNOWLEDGMENT	SUSCEPTIBILITY
MILLENARIANISM	DEMOCRATICALLY	ARCHAEOLOGICAL	ULTRACREPIDATE
MISAPPLICATION	DIPLOMATICALLY	AUTORADIOGRAPH	UNCOMPROMISING
MISCALCULATION	DISENFRANCHISE	DERMATOLOGICAL	UNCONVENTIONAL
MONOCHROMATISM	ELECTRONICALLY	GYNAECOLOGICAL	UNDERMENTIONED
MONOPOLIZATION	GEOGRAPHICALLY	HALLUCINOGENIC	UNDERNOURISHED
MONOSACCHARIDE	HEARTSEARCHING	METEOROLOGICAL	UNDESIRABILITY
MULTIPLICATION	HYPOTHETICALLY	ORNITHOLOGICAL	UNPROFESSIONAL
NATURALIZATION	INFRASTRUCTURE	PHANTASMAGORIA	VERISIMILITUDE
NEUTRALIZATION	INSIGNIFICANCE	TERMINOLOGICAL	VESPERTILIONID
PASTEURIZATION	KNICKERBOCKERS	UNINTELLIGIBLE	ACHONDROPLASIA
POLYMERIZATION	MATHEMATICALLY	ACCOMPLISHMENT	COUNTERBALANCE
POPULARIZATION	METAPHORICALLY	ANTHROPOPHAGUS	FORTUNETELLING
PREDESTINATION	NETHERSTOCKING	ANTIMETATHESIS	IRRECONCILABLE
PREFABRICATION	OPTIMISTICALLY	ARCHGENETHLIAC	KNIPPERDOLLING
PRESSURIZATION	OVERPRODUCTION	CLAUSTROPHOBIA	MONOCARPELLARY
RECAPITULATION	PHLEGMATICALLY	CLAUSTROPHOBIC	PSYCHOANALYSIS
RECOMMENDATION	RECONSTRUCTION	CRYPTAESTHETIC	PURPOSEFULNESS
RECONCILIATION	SCIENTIFICALLY	IMPOVERISHMENT	SCHOOLCHILDREN
RECORDBREAKING	SELFRESPECTING	IRREPROACHABLE	THOUGHTFULNESS
REGULARIZATION	SELFSUFFICIENT	MEPHISTOPHELES	UNCONTROLLABLE
REHABILITATION	SUBMICROSCOPIC	METEMPSYCHOSIS	UNDERDEVELOPED
REORGANIZATION	SUPERSTRUCTURE	ORTHOGRAPHICAL	UNSKILLFULNESS
REPRESENTATION	SYSTEMATICALLY	PHOTOSYNTHESIS	ALLELOCHEMICAL
REPRESENTATIVE	UNSATISFACTORY	POSSESSINHUMAN	APPROVECOMMENT
SANCTIFICATION	CAMELOPARDALIS	RELINQUISHMENT	CRYSTALLOMANCY
SCATTERBRAINED	CORRESPONDENCE	SLAUGHTERHOUSE	EMBELLISHMENTS
SENSATIONALISM	SELFCONFIDENCE	UNAPPROACHABLE	GEWÜRZTRAMINER
SENTIMENTALITY	SINGLEMINDEDLY	ACCOUNTABILITY	HIEROSOLYMITAN
SEPTUAGENARIAN	SUPERABUNDANCE	AFOREMENTIONED	INTERFEROMETER
SERVOMECHANISM	UNDERSTANDABLE	AIRCONDITIONED	ORTHOCHROMATIC
SESQUIPEDALIAN	UNDERSTANDABLY	AIRCONDITIONER	PARALEIPOMENON
SESQUIPEDALION	UNPREPAREDNESS	ANTIPERSPIRANT	PRONUNCIAMENTO
SEXCENTENARIAN	AGGRANDISEMENT	APPREHENSIVELY	CHINCHERINCHEE
SIMPLIFICATION	AGGRESSIVENESS	CENTROLECITHAL	CIRCUMSTANTIAL
SINGLEBREASTED	APPRENTICESHIP	CHARACTERISTIC	COMMISSIONAIRE
SOLIDIFICATION	ARRONDISSEMENT	CIRCUMNAVIGATE	CONSTANTINOPLE
SOPHISTICATION	BALUCHITHERIUM	CONFIDENTIALLY	CONVENTIONALLY
SPECIALIZATION	BIOENGINEERING	CONGREGATIONAL	DISCOUNTENANCE
STEGANOGRAPHIC	DISCOMBOBERATE	CONSERVATIVELY	EXPRESSIONLESS
STRATIFICATION	DISCOURAGEMENT	CONSTITUTIONAL	IMPRESSIONABLE
STULTIFICATION	DIVERTISSEMENT	CONSTRUCTIVELY	INDETERMINABLE
SUBSTANTIATION	ELECTIONEERING	CONSTRUCTIVISM	INTELLIGENTSIA
SULPHANILAMIDE	FERRIMAGNETISM	CONVERSATIONAL	LONGITUDINALLY

MEGASPORANGIUM	LICENTIOUSNESS	DIPLOMATICALLY	PHOTOSYNTHESIS
NIBELUNGENLIED	LOQUACIOUSNESS	DISCOUNTENANCE	PRONUNCIAMENTO
PROFESSIONALLY	METICULOUSNESS	ELECTRONICALLY	SANSCULOTTERIE
PROPORTIONALLY	OBSEQUIOUSNESS	ENCEPHALOPATHY	SELFCONFIDENCE
QUINTESSENTIAL	PHOSPHORESCENT	EXPERIMENTALLY	SINGLEMINDEDLY
SELFGOVERNMENT	PRECOCIOUSNESS	GEOGRAPHICALLY	THREEHALFPENCE
SUPERINTENDENT	RECONNAISSANCE	HYPOTHETICALLY	WHOLEHEARTEDLY
UNCONSCIONABLE	RIDICULOUSNESS	IMPRESSIONABLE	ANTHROPOLOGIST
UNQUESTIONABLE	SCRUPULOUSNESS	INCONSIDERABLE	ASTROGEOLOGIST
UNQUESTIONABLY	SCURRILOUSNESS	INDECIPHERABLE	BACTERIOLOGIST
ALLOIOSTROPHUS	SELFASSESSMENT	INDETERMINABLE	BROBDINGNAGIAN
ANTHROPOLOGIST	WEIGHTLESSNESS	INSIGNIFICANCE	CIRCUMNAVIGATE
ANTILYMPHOCYTE	ARCHAEBACTERIA	INSURMOUNTABLE	ELECTROMYOGRAM
ASTROGEOLOGIST	CARCINOMATOSIS	INTELLECTUALLY	MEGASPORANGIUM
BACTERIOLOGIST	COINCIDENTALLY	IRRECONCILABLE	PHARMACOLOGIST
CONSPIRATORIAL	CONTROVERTIBLE	IRREPROACHABLE	ANTIMONARCHIST
DISCOURTEOUSLY	DESISTABSTRACT	LONGITUDINALLY	DISENFRANCHISE
ELECTROMYOGRAM	DISAPPOINTMENT	MATHEMATICALLY	DISTINGUISHING
HEMIMETABOLOUS	DISCONTENTMENT	METAPHORICALLY	HEARTSEARCHING
INTERNATIONALE	DISENCHANTMENT	ONCHOCERCIASIS	RADIOTELEPHONE
MACROECONOMICS	ECCLESIASTICAL	OPTIMISTICALLY	SUPERPHOSPHATE
METAMORPHOSING	ECCLESIASTICUS	ORTHOCHROMATIC	ALLELOCHEMICAL
MICROSPOROCYTE	EXPERIMENTALLY	PHLEGMATICALLY	ARCHAEOLOGICAL
MULTIFACTORIAL	HALLUCINATIONS	PHYTOGEOGRAPHY	COMPREHENSIBLE
OSTENTATIOUSLY	INDESTRUCTIBLE	PROFESSIONALLY	CONJUNCTIVITIS
OTOLARYNGOLOGY	INSURMOUNTABLE	PROPORTIONALLY	CONTROVERTIBLE
PARAPSYCHOLOGY	PEREGRINATIONS	PROVIDENTIALLY	DERMATOLOGICAL
PARSIMONIOUSLY	PHARMACEUTICAL	RECONNAISSANCE	ECCLESIASTICAL
PHARMACOLOGIST	QUALIFICATIONS	SCIENTIFICALLY	ECCLESIASTICUS
PHILANTHROPIST	SANSCULOTTERIE	SUPERABUNDANCE	GEWÜRZTRAMINER
PRESUMPTUOUSLY	SCHOOLMISTRESS	SUPERNATURALLY	GYNAECOLOGICAL
PROHIBITIONIST	TRICHOPHYTOSIS	SYSTEMATICALLY	HALLUCINATIONS
SATISFACTORILY	UNATTRIBUTABLE	UNAPPROACHABLE	HIEROSOLYMITAN
SIMULTANEOUSLY	UNPLEASANTNESS	UNATTRIBUTABLE	INDESTRUCTIBLE
STAPHYLOCOCCUS	UNPREMEDITATED	UNCONSCIONABLE	MALAPPROPRIATE
STRAIGHTFOWARD	WHOLEHEARTEDLY	UNCONTROLLABLE	METEOROLOGICAL
SUBCONSCIOUSLY	CIRCUMLOCUTION	UNCORROBORATED	MISAPPROPRIATE
SUPERCILIOUSLY	DISCOMBOBULATE	UNDERSTANDABLE	ORNITHOLOGICAL
TROUBLESHOOTER	GRANDILOQUENCE	UNDERSTANDABLY	ORTHOGRAPHICAL
AUTOTRANSPLANT	HORTICULTURIST	UNPREMEDITATED	OSTEOARTHRITIS
ENCEPHALOPATHY	INTELLECTUALLY	UNQUESTIONABLE	OVERSUBSCRIBED
RADIOTELEPHONE	NITROCELLULOSE	UNQUESTIONABLY	PEREGRINATIONS
SHRINKWRAPPING	RECONSTITUTION	UNRECOGNIZABLE	PHARMACEUTICAL
SUPERPHOSPHATE	TINTINNABULATE	INEXPRESSIBLES	QUALIFICATIONS
SUPERSCRIPTION	CONJUNCTIVITIS	UNMENTIONABLES	SCATTERBRAINED
THREEHALFPENCE	CZECHOSLOVAKIA	ANTILYMPHOCYTE	SELFSUFFICIENT
CINEMATOGRAPHY	ESTABLISHVERSE	CHINCHERINCHEE	TELETYPEWRITER
CROSSREFERENCE	AIRCRAFTSWOMAN	INTERCONNECTED	TERMINOLOGICAL
INCONSIDERABLE	BATTERYPOWERED	MICROSPOROCYTE	UNINTELLIGIBLE
INDECIPHERABLE	CREEPYCRAWLIES	PHOSPHORESCENT	DECISIONMAKING
MALAPPROPRIATE	UNRECOGNIZABLE	STAPHYLOCOCCUS	KNICKERBOCKERS
MISAPPROPRIATE		SCHOOLCHILDREN	NETHERSTOCKING
OSTEOARTHRITIS	**14:11**	SUPERINTENDENT	RECORDBREAKING
OVERSUBSCRIBED	ACHONDROPLASIA	ULTRACREPIDATE	ACCOUNTABILITY
PHYTOGEOGRAPHY	ALPHABETICALLY	ANTIMETATHESIS	ANTIFEDERALIST
SUPERNATURALLY	ANTHROPOPHAGUS	ARCHAEBACTERIA	ANTIODONTALGIC
TELETYPEWRITER	APOLOGETICALLY	BATTERYPOWERED	ARCHGENETHLIAC
UNCORROBORATED	ASTRONOMICALLY	CORRESPONDENCE	AUTOTRANSPLANT
ABSTEMIOUSNESS	AUTOCRATICALLY	CROSSREFERENCE	CONVERTIBILITY
ANTIDEPRESSANT	CAMELOPARDALIS	CRYPTAESTHETIC	CORRUPTIBILITY
AUTOSUGGESTION	CINEMATOGRAPHY	EMBELLISHMENTS	CREEPYCRAWLIES
BOISTEROUSNESS	COINCIDENTALLY	ESTABLISHVERSE	DISCOMBOBULATE
BREATHLESSNESS	COMMISSIONAIRE	GRANDILOQUENCE	EDUCATIONALIST
CAPRICIOUSNESS	CONFIDENTIALLY	HALLUCINOGENIC	EXISTENTIALISM
CIRCUMSCISSILE	CONVENTIONALLY	INTERFEROMETER	EXISTENTIALIST
COMPREHENSIBLE	COUNTERBALANCE	KNOTENSCHIEFER	EXPRESSIONLESS
DISTINGUISHING	CRYSTALLOMANCY	MEPHISTOPHELES	FORTUNETELLING
FASTIDIOUSNESS	CZECHOSLOVAKIA	PARALEIPOMENON	FUNDAMENTALISM
LASCIVIOUSNESS	DEMOCRATICALLY	PARTRIDGEBERRY	FUNDAMENTALIST

HEMIMETABOLOUS
IMPERMEABILITY
IMPREGNABILITY
KNIPPERDOLLING
MONOCARPELLARY
NIBELUNGENLIED
NITROCELLULOSE
OTOLARYNGOLOGY
PARAPSYCHOLOGY
PRACTICABILITY
RESPECTABILITY
RESPONSIBILITY
SENSATIONALISM
SENTIMENTALITY
SESQUIPEDALIAN
SESQUIPEDALION
SUPERFICIALITY
SUSCEPTIBILITY
TATTERDEMALION
TINTINNABULATE
TRADITIONALIST
UNDESIRABILITY
ACCOMPLISHMENT
ACKNOWLEDGMENT
AGGRANDISEMENT
APPROVECOMMENT
ARRONDISSEMENT
DISAPPOINTMENT
DISCONTENTMENT
DISCOURAGEMENT
DISENCHANTMENT
DIVERTISSEMENT
IMPOVERISHMENT
MACROECONOMICS
RELINQUISHMENT
SELFASSESSMENT
SELFGOVERNMENT
SULPHANILAMIDE
THERMODYNAMICS
UNDERSTATEMENT
ABSTEMIOUSNESS
AGGRESSIVENESS
BOISTEROUSNESS
BREATHLESSNESS
CAPRICIOUSNESS
DISAPPROVINGLY
EGALITARIANISM
FASTIDIOUSNESS
INCONVENIENTLY
INDISCRIMINATE
INSUFFICIENTLY
INTERMITTENTLY
INTERNATIONALE
LASCIVIOUSNESS
LICENTIOUSNESS
LOQUACIOUSNESS
METICULOUSNESS
MILLENARIANISM
OBSEQUIOUSNESS
OPPRESSIVENESS
PERCEPTIVENESS
PERMISSIVENESS
PERSUASIVENESS
PORPHYROGENITE
PRECOCIOUSNESS
PRODUCTIVENESS
PROHIBITIONIST
PROTOCONTINENT
PURPOSEFULNESS

RESPONSIVENESS
RIDICULOUSNESS
ROADWORTHINESS
SCRUPULOUSNESS
SCURRILOUSNESS
SERVOMECHANISM
SUBMISSIVENESS
SUPERCONTINENT
THOUGHTFULNESS
TRANSCENDENTAL
UNPLEASANTNESS
UNPREPAREDNESS
UNSKILLFULNESS
VINDICTIVENESS
WEIGHTLESSNESS
ZOROASTRIANISM
AFOREMENTIONED
AIRCONDITIONED
AIRCONDITIONER
AIRCRAFTSWOMAN
CARCINOMATOSIS
CLAUSTROPHOBIA
CLAUSTROPHOBIC
CONGREGATIONAL
CONSTANTINOPLE
CONSTITUTIONAL
CONVERSATIONAL
DENOMINATIONAL
METEMPSYCHOSIS
ORGANIZATIONAL
PHANTASMAGORIA
SLAUGHTERHOUSE
SUBMICROSCOPIC
TRICHOPHYTOSIS
TROUBLESHOOTER
UNCONVENTIONAL
UNDERDEVELOPED
UNDERMENTIONED
UNPROFESSIONAL
VESPERTILIONID
ALLOIOSTROPHUS
PHILANTHROPIST
SHRINKWRAPPING
STEGANOGRAPHIC
WHIPPERSNAPPER
ANTIPERSPIRANT
AUTORADIOGRAPH
BALUCHITHERIUM
BIOENGINEERING
CONSPIRATORIAL
DESISTABSTRACT
DISCIPLINARIAN
DISCOMBOBERATE
ELECTIONEERING
HORTICULTURIST
INFRALAPSARIAN
JOHANNISBERGER
MONOSACCHARIDE
MOUNTAINEERING
MULTIFACTORIAL
NITROBACTERIUM
NITROGLYCERINE
POIKILOTHERMIC
SATISFACTORILY
SCAREMONGERING
SCHOOLMISTRESS
SEPTUAGENARIAN
SEXCENTENARIAN
VALETUDINARIAN

ANTIDEPRESSANT
APPRENTICESHIP
CHARACTERISTIC
CIRCUMSCISSILE
COUNTERMEASURE
HYDROCORTISONE
METAMORPHOSING
MICROPROCESSOR
SINGLEBREASTED
THROMBOPLASTIN
UNCOMPROMISING
UNDERNOURISHED
UNENTHUSIASTIC
VERTICILLASTER
ADMINISTRATION
ADMINISTRATIVE
AFFECTIONATELY
AUTHENTICATION
AUTOSUGGESTION
CAPITALIZATION
CASTRAMETATION
CENTRALIZATION
CENTROLECITHAL
CIRCUMLOCUTION
CIRCUMSTANTIAL
CLASSIFICATION
CONGLOMERATION
CONGRATULATION
CONGRATULATORY
CONTESSERATION
DEMOBILIZATION
DEMORALIZATION
DEXTROROTATORY
DISAPPROBATION
DISASSOCIATION
DISCOLOURATION
DISCONSOLATELY
DISCRIMINATING
DISCRIMINATION
DISCRIMINATORY
DISEMBARKATION
DISINCLINATION
DISINFORMATION
DISINTEGRATION
DISORIENTATION
FERRIMAGNETISM
FRATERNIZATION
FRUCTIFICATION
GENERALIZATION
GENTRIFICATION
HOMOGENIZATION
HYPERSENSITIVE
IDENTIFICATION
ILLEGITIMATELY
IMMOBILIZATION
IMPLEMENTATION
INDOCTRINATION
INFRASTRUCTURE
INTELLIGENTSIA
INTERPELLATION
INTERPLANETARY
INTERPRETATION
INTERPRETATIVE
LIBERALIZATION
LIGHTSENSITIVE
MISAPPLICATION
MISCALCULATION
MONOCHROMATISM
MONOPOLIZATION

MULTIPLICATION
NATURALIZATION
NEUTRALIZATION
OVERPRODUCTION
PASTEURIZATION
PHENOBARBITONE
POLYMERIZATION
POPULARIZATION
PREDESTINATION
PREDISPOSITION
PREFABRICATION
PRESSURIZATION
PRESUPPOSITION
QUINTESSENTIAL
RECAPITULATION
RECOMMENDATION
RECONCILIATION
RECONSTITUTION
RECONSTRUCTION
REGULARIZATION
REHABILITATION
REORGANIZATION
REPRESENTATION
REPRESENTATIVE
SANCTIFICATION
SELFRESPECTING
SIMPLIFICATION
SOLIDIFICATION
SOPHISTICATION
SPECIALIZATION
STRATIFICATION
STULTIFICATION
SUBSTANTIATION
SUPERANNUATION
SUPEREROGATION
SUPERSCRIPTION
SUPERSTRUCTURE
TRANSFORMATION
TRANSMIGRATION
TRANSPORTATION
UNDERSECRETARY
UNSATISFACTORY
VERISIMILITUDE
WESTERNIZATION
CARDIOVASCULAR
DISCOURTEOUSLY
IMMUNOGLOBULIN
OSTENTATIOUSLY
PARSIMONIOUSLY
POSSESSINHUMAN
PRESUMPTUOUSLY
SIMULTANEOUSLY
SUBCONSCIOUSLY
SUPERCILIOUSLY
WELTANSCHAUUNG
APPREHENSIVELY
CONSERVATIVELY
CONSTRUCTIVELY
CONSTRUCTIVISM
INCONCLUSIVELY
STRAIGHTFOWARD
PSYCHOANALYSIS
NEBUCHADNEZZAR

14:12

ANTIDEPRESSANT
ANTIPERSPIRANT
AUTORADIOGRAPH
AUTOTRANSPLANT

CIRCUMNAVIGATE
DESISTABSTRACT
DISCOMBOBERATE
DISCOMBOBULATE
INDISCRIMINATE
INTERNATIONALE
INTERPLANETARY
MALAPPROPRIATE
MISAPPROPRIATE
MONOCARPELLARY
STRAIGHTFOWARD
SUPERPHOSPHATE
TINTINNABULATE
ULTRACREPIDATE
UNDERSECRETARY
CLAUSTROPHOBIA
CLAUSTROPHOBIC
COMPREHENSIBLE
CONTROVERTIBLE
IMPRESSIONABLE
INCONSIDERABLE
INDECIPHERABLE
INDESTRUCTIBLE
INDETERMINABLE
INSURMOUNTABLE
IRRECONCILABLE
IRREPROACHABLE
OVERSUBSCRIBED
UNAPPROACHABLE
UNATTRIBUTABLE
UNCONSCIONABLE
UNCONTROLLABLE
UNDERSTANDABLE
UNDERSTANDABLY
UNINTELLIGIBLE
UNQUESTIONABLE
UNQUESTIONABLY
UNRECOGNIZABLE
ALLELOCHEMICAL
ARCHAEOLOGICAL
DERMATOLOGICAL
ECCLESIASTICAL
ECCLESIASTICUS
GYNAECOLOGICAL
METEOROLOGICAL
ORNITHOLOGICAL
ORTHOGRAPHICAL
PHARMACEUTICAL
STAPHYLOCOCCUS
TERMINOLOGICAL
SINGLEMINDEDLY
WHOLEHEARTEDLY
ABSTEMIOUSNESS
ACCOMPLISHMENT
ACKNOWLEDGMENT
AFFECTIONATELY
AGGRANDISEMENT
AGGRESSIVENESS
APPREHENSIVELY
APPROVECOMMENT
ARRONDISSEMENT
BOISTEROUSNESS
BREATHLESSNESS
CAPRICIOUSNESS
CONSERVATIVELY
CONSTRUCTIVELY
DISAPPOINTMENT
DISCONSOLATELY
DISCONTENTMENT

DISCOURAGEMENT
DISENCHANTMENT
DIVERTISSEMENT
EXPRESSIONLESS
FASTIDIOUSNESS
ILLEGITIMATELY
IMPOVERISHMENT
INCONCLUSIVELY
KNICKERBOCKERS
LASCIVIOUSNESS
LICENTIOUSNESS
LOQUACIOUSNESS
METICULOUSNESS
OBSEQUIOUSNESS
OPPRESSIVENESS
PERCEPTIVENESS
PERMISSIVENESS
PERSUASIVENESS
PHOSPHORESCENT
PRECOCIOUSNESS
PRODUCTIVENESS
PROTOCONTINENT
PURPOSEFULNESS
RELINQUISHMENT
RESPONSIVENESS
RIDICULOUSNESS
ROADWORTHINESS
SCHOOLMISTRESS
SCRUPULOUSNESS
SCURRILOUSNESS
SELFASSESSMENT
SELFGOVERNMENT
SELFSUFFICIENT
SUBMISSIVENESS
SUPERCONTINENT
SUPERINTENDENT
THOUGHTFULNESS
UNDERSTATEMENT
UNPLEASANTNESS
UNPREPAREDNESS
UNSKILLFULNESS
VINDICTIVENESS
WEIGHTLESSNESS
KNOTENSCHIEFER
ANTHROPOPHAGUS
ANTIODONTALGIC
DISAPPROVINGLY
JOHANNISBERGER
ALLOIOSTROPHUS
APPRENTICESHIP
CENTROLECITHAL
CHINCHERINCHEE
STEGANOGRAPHIC
UNDERNOURISHED
ACCOUNTABILITY
ADMINISTRATION
ADMINISTRATIVE
ANTHROPOLOGIST
ANTIFEDERALIST
ANTIMONARCHIST
ARCHGENETHLIAC
ASTROGEOLOGIST
AUTHENTICATION
AUTOSUGGESTION
BACTERIOLOGIST
BALUCHITHERIUM
BIOENGINEERING
BROBDINGNAGIAN
CAPITALIZATION

CASTRAMETATION
CENTRALIZATION
CIRCUMLOCUTION
CIRCUMSCISSILE
CIRCUMSTANTIAL
CLASSIFICATION
COMMISSIONAIRE
CONGLOMERATION
CONGRATULATION
CONSPIRATORIAL
CONSTRUCTIVISM
CONTESSERATION
CONVERTIBILITY
CORRUPTIBILITY
CREEPYCRAWLIES
DECISIONMAKING
DEMOBILIZATION
DEMORALIZATION
DISAPPROBATION
DISASSOCIATION
DISCIPLINARIAN
DISCOLOURATION
DISCRIMINATING
DISCRIMINATION
DISEMBARKATION
DISENFRANCHISE
DISINCLINATION
DISINFORMATION
DISINTEGRATION
DISORIENTATION
DISTINGUISHING
EDUCATIONALIST
EGALITARIANISM
ELECTIONEERING
EXISTENTIALISM
EXISTENTIALIST
FERRIMAGNETISM
FORTUNETELLING
FRATERNIZATION
FRUCTIFICATION
FUNDAMENTALISM
FUNDAMENTALIST
GENERALIZATION
GENTRIFICATION
HEARTSEARCHING
HOMOGENIZATION
HORTICULTURIST
HYPERSENSITIVE
IDENTIFICATION
IMMOBILIZATION
IMPERMEABILITY
IMPLEMENTATION
IMPREGNABILITY
INDOCTRINATION
INFRALAPSARIAN
INTERPELLATION
INTERPRETATION
INTERPRETATIVE
KNIPPERDOLLING
LIBERALIZATION
LIGHTSENSITIVE
MACROECONOMICS
MEGASPORANGIUM
METAMORPHOSING
MILLENARIANISM
MISAPPLICATION
MISCALCULATION
MONOCHROMATISM
MONOPOLIZATION

MONOSACCHARIDE
MOUNTAINEERING
MULTIFACTORIAL
MULTIPLICATION
NATURALIZATION
NETHERSTOCKING
NEUTRALIZATION
NIBELUNGENLIED
NITROBACTERIUM
NITROGLYCERINE
OVERPRODUCTION
PASTEURIZATION
PHARMACOLOGIST
PHILANTHROPIST
POLYMERIZATION
POPULARIZATION
PORPHYROGENITE
PRACTICABILITY
PREDESTINATION
PREDISPOSITION
PREFABRICATION
PRESSURIZATION
PRESUPPOSITION
PROHIBITIONIST
QUINTESSENTIAL
RECAPITULATION
RECOMMENDATION
RECONCILIATION
RECONSTITUTION
RECONSTRUCTION
RECORDBREAKING
REGULARIZATION
REHABILITATION
REORGANIZATION
REPRESENTATION
REPRESENTATIVE
RESPECTABILITY
RESPONSIBILITY
SANCTIFICATION
SATISFACTORILY
SCAREMONGERING
SELFRESPECTING
SENSATIONALISM
SENTIMENTALITY
SEPTUAGENARIAN
SERVOMECHANISM
SESQUIPEDALIAN
SESQUIPEDALION
SEXCENTENARIAN
SHRINKWRAPPING
SIMPLIFICATION
SOLIDIFICATION
SOPHISTICATION
SPECIALIZATION
STRATIFICATION
STULTIFICATION
SUBSTANTIATION
SULPHANILAMIDE
SUPERANNUATION
SUPEREROGATION
SUPERFICIALITY
SUPERSCRIPTION
SUSCEPTIBILITY
TATTERDEMALION
THERMODYNAMICS
TRADITIONALIST
TRANSFORMATION
TRANSMIGRATION
TRANSPORTATION

UNCOMPROMISING	CONGRATULATORY	SUPERSTRUCTURE	INEXPRESSIBLES
UNDESIRABILITY	DEXTROROTATORY	VERISIMILITUDE	INTERCONNECTED
VALETUDINARIAN	DISCRIMINATORY	WELTANSCHAUUNG	INTERFEROMETER
WESTERNIZATION	HALLUCINATIONS	ANTILYMPHOCYTE	JOHANNISBERGER
ZOROASTRIANISM	HEMIMETABOLOUS	MICROSPOROCYTE	KNOTENSCHIEFER
CZECHOSLOVAKIA	HYDROCORTISONE	NEBUCHADNEZZAR	MEPHISTOPHELES
ALPHABETICALLY	NITROCELLULOSE		NIBELUNGENLIED
APOLOGETICALLY	OTOLARYNGOLOGY	**14:13**	OVERSUBSCRIBED
ASTRONOMICALLY	PARAPSYCHOLOGY	AIRCRAFTSWOMAN	SCATTERBRAINED
AUTOCRATICALLY	PEREGRINATIONS	ALLELOCHEMICAL	SCHOOLCHILDREN
CAMELOPARDALIS	PHENOBARBITONE	ARCHAEOLOGICAL	SINGLEBREASTED
CARDIOVASCULAR	QUALIFICATIONS	ARCHGENETHLIAC	TELETYPEWRITER
COINCIDENTALLY	RADIOTELEPHONE	BROBDINGNAGIAN	TROUBLESHOOTER
CONFIDENTIALLY	UNSATISFACTORY	CARDIOVASCULAR	UNCORROBORATED
CONVENTIONALLY	CINEMATOGRAPHY	CENTROLECITHAL	UNDERDEVELOPED
DEMOCRATICALLY	CONSTANTINOPLE	CIRCUMSTANTIAL	UNDERMENTIONED
DIPLOMATICALLY	PHYTOGEOGRAPHY	CONGREGATIONAL	UNDERNOURISHED
ELECTRONICALLY	SUBMICROSCOPIC	CONSPIRATORIAL	UNMENTIONABLES
EXPERIMENTALLY	UNDERDEVELOPED	CONSTITUTIONAL	UNPREMEDITATED
GEOGRAPHICALLY	WHIPPERSNAPPER	CONVERSATIONAL	VERTICILLASTER
HYPOTHETICALLY	ARCHAEBACTERIA	DENOMINATIONAL	WHIPPERSNAPPER
IMMUNOGLOBULIN	BATTERYPOWERED	DERMATOLOGICAL	OTOLARYNGOLOGY
INEXPRESSIBLES	ELECTROMYOGRAM	DISCIPLINARIAN	PARAPSYCHOLOGY
INTELLECTUALLY	ESTABLISHVERSE	ECCLESIASTICAL	CINEMATOGRAPHY
LONGITUDINALLY	PARTRIDGEBERRY	ELECTROMYOGRAM	ENCEPHALOPATHY
MATHEMATICALLY	PHANTASMAGORIA	GYNAECOLOGICAL	PHYTOGEOGRAPHY
MEPHISTOPHELES	SANSCULOTTERIE	HIEROSOLYMITAN	ACHONDROPLASIA
METAPHORICALLY	SCHOOLCHILDREN	INFRALAPSARIAN	ANTIMETATHESIS
OPTIMISTICALLY	ACHONDROPLASIA	METEOROLOGICAL	ANTIODONTALGIC
PHLEGMATICALLY	ANTIMETATHESIS	MULTIFACTORIAL	APPRENTICESHIP
PROFESSIONALLY	CARCINOMATOSIS	NEBUCHADNEZZAR	ARCHAEBACTERIA
PROPORTIONALLY	DISCOURTEOUSLY	ORGANIZATIONAL	CAMELOPARDALIS
PROVIDENTIALLY	INTELLIGENTSIA	ORNITHOLOGICAL	CARCINOMATOSIS
SCIENTIFICALLY	METEMPSYCHOSIS	ORTHOGRAPHICAL	CHARACTERISTIC
SUPERNATURALLY	MICROPROCESSOR	PHARMACEUTICAL	CLAUSTROPHOBIA
SYSTEMATICALLY	ONCHOCERCIASIS	POSSESSINHUMAN	CLAUSTROPHOBIC
UNMENTIONABLES	OSTENTATIOUSLY	QUINTESSENTIAL	CONJUNCTIVITIS
AIRCRAFTSWOMAN	PARSIMONIOUSLY	SEPTUAGENARIAN	CRYPTAESTHETIC
POIKILOTHERMIC	PHOTOSYNTHESIS	SESQUIPEDALIAN	CZECHOSLOVAKIA
POSSESSINHUMAN	PRESUMPTUOUSLY	SEXCENTENARIAN	HALLUCINOGENIC
AFOREMENTIONED	PSYCHOANALYSIS	TERMINOLOGICAL	IMMUNOGLOBULIN
AIRCONDITIONED	SIMULTANEOUSLY	TRANSCENDENTAL	INTELLIGENTSIA
AIRCONDITIONER	SUBCONSCIOUSLY	UNCONVENTIONAL	METEMPSYCHOSIS
CONGREGATIONAL	SUPERCILIOUSLY	UNPROFESSIONAL	ONCHOCERCIASIS
CONSTITUTIONAL	TRICHOPHYTOSIS	VALETUDINARIAN	ORTHOCHROMATIC
CONVERSATIONAL	CHARACTERISTIC	CORRESPONDENCE	OSTEOARTHRITIS
CORRESPONDENCE	CONJUNCTIVITIS	COUNTERBALANCE	PHANTASMAGORIA
COUNTERBALANCE	CRYPTAESTHETIC	CROSSREFERENCE	PHOTOSYNTHESIS
CROSSREFERENCE	ENCEPHALOPATHY	CRYSTALLOMANCY	POIKILOTHERMIC
CRYSTALLOMANCY	HIEROSOLYMITAN	DESISTABSTRACT	PSYCHOANALYSIS
DENOMINATIONAL	INCONVENIENTLY	DISCOUNTENANCE	SANSCULOTTERIE
DISCOUNTENANCE	INSUFFICIENTLY	GRANDILOQUENCE	STEGANOGRAPHIC
EMBELLISHMENTS	INTERCONNECTED	INSIGNIFICANCE	SUBMICROSCOPIC
GEWÜRZTRAMINER	INTERFEROMETER	MACROECONOMICS	THROMBOPLASTIN
GRANDILOQUENCE	INTERMITTENTLY	RECONNAISSANCE	TRICHOPHYTOSIS
HALLUCINOGENIC	ORTHOCHROMATIC	SELFCONFIDENCE	UNENTHUSIASTIC
INSIGNIFICANCE	OSTEOARTHRITIS	SUPERABUNDANCE	VESPERTILIONID
ORGANIZATIONAL	SINGLEBREASTED	THERMODYNAMICS	AFFECTIONATELY
PARALEIPOMENON	TELETYPEWRITER	THREEHALFPENCE	ALPHABETICALLY
PRONUNCIAMENTO	THROMBOPLASTIN	MONOSACCHARIDE	APOLOGETICALLY
RECONNAISSANCE	TRANSCENDENTAL	SULPHANILAMIDE	APPREHENSIVELY
SCATTERBRAINED	TROUBLESHOOTER	VERISIMILITUDE	ASTRONOMICALLY
SELFCONFIDENCE	UNCORROBORATED	AFOREMENTIONED	AUTOCRATICALLY
SUPERABUNDANCE	UNENTHUSIASTIC	AIRCONDITIONED	CIRCUMSCISSILE
THREEHALFPENCE	UNPREMEDITATED	AIRCONDITIONER	COINCIDENTALLY
UNCONVENTIONAL	VERTICILLASTER	BATTERYPOWERED	COMPREHENSIBLE
UNDERMENTIONED	COUNTERMEASURE	CHINCHERINCHEE	CONFIDENTIALLY
UNPROFESSIONAL	INFRASTRUCTURE	CREEPYCRAWLIES	CONSERVATIVELY
VESPERTILIONID	SLAUGHTERHOUSE	GEWÜRZTRAMINER	CONSTANTINOPLE

CONSTRUCTIVELY	DISCOURAGEMENT	MICROPROCESSOR	DISENFRANCHISE
CONTROVERTIBLE	DISCRIMINATING	MISAPPLICATION	EDUCATIONALIST
CONVENTIONALLY	DISENCHANTMENT	MISCALCULATION	EGALITARIANISM
DEMOCRATICALLY	DISTINGUISHING	MONOPOLIZATION	ESTABLISHVERSE
DIPLOMATICALLY	DIVERTISSEMENT	MULTIPLICATION	EXISTENTIALISM
DISAPPROVINGLY	ELECTIONEERING	NATURALIZATION	EXISTENTIALIST
DISCONSOLATELY	FORTUNETELLING	NEUTRALIZATION	EXPRESSIONLESS
DISCOURTEOUSLY	HALLUCINATIONS	OVERPRODUCTION	FASTIDIOUSNESS
ELECTRONICALLY	HEARTSEARCHING	PARALEIPOMENON	FERRIMAGNETISM
EXPERIMENTALLY	HYDROCORTISONE	PASTEURIZATION	FUNDAMENTALISM
GEOGRAPHICALLY	IMPOVERISHMENT	POLYMERIZATION	FUNDAMENTALIST
HYPOTHETICALLY	KNIPPERDOLLING	POPULARIZATION	HORTICULTURIST
ILLEGITIMATELY	METAMORPHOSING	PREDESTINATION	LASCIVIOUSNESS
IMPRESSIONABLE	MOUNTAINEERING	PREDISPOSITION	LICENTIOUSNESS
INCONCLUSIVELY	NETHERSTOCKING	PREFABRICATION	LOQUACIOUSNESS
INCONSIDERABLE	NITROGLYCERINE	PRESSURIZATION	METICULOUSNESS
INCONVENIENTLY	PEREGRINATIONS	PRESUPPOSITION	MILLENARIANISM
INDECIPHERABLE	PHENOBARBITONE	RECAPITULATION	MONOCHROMATISM
INDESTRUCTIBLE	PHOSPHORESCENT	RECOMMENDATION	NITROCELLULOSE
INDETERMINABLE	PROTOCONTINENT	RECONCILIATION	OBSEQUIOUSNESS
INSUFFICIENTLY	QUALIFICATIONS	RECONSTITUTION	OPPRESSIVENESS
INSURMOUNTABLE	RADIOTELEPHONE	RECONSTRUCTION	PERCEPTIVENESS
INTELLECTUALLY	RECORDBREAKING	REGULARIZATION	PERMISSIVENESS
INTERMITTENTLY	RELINQUISHMENT	REHABILITATION	PERSUASIVENESS
INTERNATIONALE	SCAREMONGERING	REORGANIZATION	PHARMACOLOGIST
IRRECONCILABLE	SELFASSESSMENT	REPRESENTATION	PHILANTHROPIST
IRREPROACHABLE	SELFGOVERNMENT	SANCTIFICATION	PRECOCIOUSNESS
LONGITUDINALLY	SELFRESPECTING	SESQUIPEDALION	PRODUCTIVENESS
MATHEMATICALLY	SELFSUFFICIENT	SIMPLIFICATION	PROHIBITIONIST
METAPHORICALLY	SHRINKWRAPPING	SOLIDIFICATION	PURPOSEFULNESS
OPTIMISTICALLY	SUPERCONTINENT	SOPHISTICATION	RESPONSIVENESS
OSTENTATIOUSLY	SUPERINTENDENT	SPECIALIZATION	RIDICULOUSNESS
PARSIMONIOUSLY	UNCOMPROMISING	STRATIFICATION	ROADWORTHINESS
PHLEGMATICALLY	UNDERSTATEMENT	STULTIFICATION	SCHOOLMISTRESS
PRESUMPTUOUSLY	WELTANSCHAUUNG	SUBSTANTIATION	SCRUPULOUSNESS
PROFESSIONALLY	ADMINISTRATION	SUPERANNUATION	SCURRILOUSNESS
PROPORTIONALLY	AUTHENTICATION	SUPEREROGATION	SENSATIONALISM
PROVIDENTIALLY	AUTOSUGGESTION	SUPERSCRIPTION	SERVOMECHANISM
SATISFACTORILY	CAPITALIZATION	TATTERDEMALION	SLAUGHTERHOUSE
SCIENTIFICALLY	CASTRAMETATION	TRANSFORMATION	SUBMISSIVENESS
SIMULTANEOUSLY	CENTRALIZATION	TRANSMIGRATION	THOUGHTFULNESS
SINGLEMINDEDLY	CIRCUMLOCUTION	TRANSPORTATION	TRADITIONALIST
SUBCONSCIOUSLY	CLASSIFICATION	WESTERNIZATION	UNPLEASANTNESS
SUPERCILIOUSLY	CONGLOMERATION	AUTORADIOGRAPH	UNPREPAREDNESS
SUPERNATURALLY	CONGRATULATION	COMMISSIONAIRE	UNSKILLFULNESS
SYSTEMATICALLY	CONTESSERATION	CONGRATULATORY	VINDICTIVENESS
UNAPPROACHABLE	DEMOBILIZATION	COUNTERMEASURE	WEIGHTLESSNESS
UNATTRIBUTABLE	DEMORALIZATION	DEXTROROTATORY	ZOROASTRIANISM
UNCONSCIONABLE	DISAPPROBATION	DISCRIMINATORY	ACCOUNTABILITY
UNCONTROLLABLE	DISASSOCIATION	INFRASTRUCTURE	ANTILYMPHOCYTE
UNDERSTANDABLE	DISCOLOURATION	INTERPLANETARY	CIRCUMNAVIGATE
UNDERSTANDABLY	DISCRIMINATION	KNICKERBOCKERS	CONVERTIBILITY
UNINTELLIGIBLE	DISEMBARKATION	MONOCARPELLARY	CORRUPTIBILITY
UNQUESTIONABLE	DISINCLINATION	PARTRIDGEBERRY	DISCOMBOBERATE
UNQUESTIONABLY	DISINFORMATION	STRAIGHTFOWARD	DISCOMBOBULATE
UNRECOGNIZABLE	DISINTEGRATION	SUPERSTRUCTURE	EMBELLISHMENTS
WHOLEHEARTEDLY	DISORIENTATION	UNDERSECRETARY	IMPERMEABILITY
ACCOMPLISHMENT	FRATERNIZATION	UNSATISFACTORY	IMPREGNABILITY
ACKNOWLEDGMENT	FRUCTIFICATION	ABSTEMIOUSNESS	INDISCRIMINATE
AGGRANDISEMENT	GENERALIZATION	AGGRESSIVENESS	MALAPPROPRIATE
ANTIDEPRESSANT	GENTRIFICATION	ANTHROPOLOGIST	MICROSPOROCYTE
ANTIPERSPIRANT	HOMOGENIZATION	ANTIFEDERALIST	MISAPPROPRIATE
APPROVECOMMENT	IDENTIFICATION	ANTIMONARCHIST	PORPHYROGENITE
ARRONDISSEMENT	IMMOBILIZATION	ASTROGEOLOGIST	PRACTICABILITY
AUTOTRANSPLANT	IMPLEMENTATION	BACTERIOLOGIST	PRONUNCIAMENTO
BIOENGINEERING	INDOCTRINATION	BOISTEROUSNESS	RESPECTABILITY
DECISIONMAKING	INTERPELLATION	BREATHLESSNESS	RESPONSIBILITY
DISAPPOINTMENT	INTERPRETATION	CAPRICIOUSNESS	SENTIMENTALITY
DISCONTENTMENT	LIBERALIZATION	CONSTRUCTIVISM	SUPERFICIALITY

SUPERPHOSPHATE	ESTABLISHVERSE	CIRCUMSTANTIAL	INDOCTRINATION
SUSCEPTIBILITY	GRANDILOQUENCE	CONGREGATIONAL	INFRALAPSARIAN
TINTINNABULATE	HYDROCORTISONE	CONSPIRATORIAL	INTERPELLATION
ULTRACREPIDATE	HYPERSENSITIVE	CONSTITUTIONAL	INTERPRETATION
UNDESIRABILITY	IMPRESSIONABLE	CONVERSATIONAL	LIBERALIZATION
ALLOIOSTROPHUS	INCONSIDERABLE	DENOMINATIONAL	MISAPPLICATION
ANTHROPOPHAGUS	INDECIPHERABLE	DERMATOLOGICAL	MISCALCULATION
BALUCHITHERIUM	INDESTRUCTIBLE	ECCLESIASTICAL	MONOPOLIZATION
ECCLESIASTICUS	INDETERMINABLE	GYNAECOLOGICAL	MULTIPLICATION
HEMIMETABOLOUS	INDISCRIMINATE	METEOROLOGICAL	NATURALIZATION
MEGASPORANGIUM	INFRASTRUCTURE	MULTIFACTORIAL	NEUTRALIZATION
NITROBACTERIUM	INSIGNIFICANCE	ORGANIZATIONAL	OVERPRODUCTION
STAPHYLOCOCCUS	INSURMOUNTABLE	ORNITHOLOGICAL	PARALEIPOMENON
ADMINISTRATIVE	INTERNATIONALE	ORTHOGRAPHICAL	PASTEURIZATION
HYPERSENSITIVE	INTERPRETATIVE	PHARMACEUTICAL	POLYMERIZATION
INTERPRETATIVE	IRRECONCILABLE	QUINTESSENTIAL	POPULARIZATION
LIGHTSENSITIVE	IRREPROACHABLE	TERMINOLOGICAL	POSSESSINHUMAN
REPRESENTATIVE	LIGHTSENSITIVE	TRANSCENDENTAL	PREDESTINATION
	MALAPPROPRIATE	UNCONVENTIONAL	PREDISPOSITION
14:14	MICROSPOROCYTE	UNPROFESSIONAL	PREFABRICATION
ACHONDROPLASIA	MISAPPROPRIATE	BALUCHITHERIUM	PRESSURIZATION
ARCHAEBACTERIA	MONOSACCHARIDE	CONSTRUCTIVISM	PRESUPPOSITION
CLAUSTROPHOBIA	NITROCELLULOSE	EGALITARIANISM	RECAPITULATION
CZECHOSLOVAKIA	NITROGLYCERINE	ELECTROMYOGRAM	RECOMMENDATION
INTELLIGENTSIA	PHENOBARBITONE	EXISTENTIALISM	RECONCILIATION
PHANTASMAGORIA	PORPHYROGENITE	FERRIMAGNETISM	RECONSTITUTION
ANTIODONTALGIC	RADIOTELEPHONE	FUNDAMENTALISM	RECONSTRUCTION
ARCHGENETHLIAC	RECONNAISSANCE	MEGASPORANGIUM	REGULARIZATION
CHARACTERISTIC	REPRESENTATIVE	MILLENARIANISM	REHABILITATION
CLAUSTROPHOBIC	SANSCULOTTERIE	MONOCHROMATISM	REORGANIZATION
CRYPTAESTHETIC	SELFCONFIDENCE	NITROBACTERIUM	REPRESENTATION
HALLUCINOGENIC	SLAUGHTERHOUSE	SENSATIONALISM	SANCTIFICATION
ORTHOCHROMATIC	SULPHANILAMIDE	SERVOMECHANISM	SCHOOLCHILDREN
POIKILOTHERMIC	SUPERABUNDANCE	ZOROASTRIANISM	SEPTUAGENARIAN
STEGANOGRAPHIC	SUPERPHOSPHATE	ADMINISTRATION	SESQUIPEDALIAN
SUBMICROSCOPIC	SUPERSTRUCTURE	AIRCRAFTSWOMAN	SESQUIPEDALION
UNENTHUSIASTIC	THREEHALFPENCE	AUTHENTICATION	SEXCENTENARIAN
AFOREMENTIONED	TINTINNABULATE	AUTOSUGGESTION	SIMPLIFICATION
AIRCONDITIONED	ULTRACREPIDATE	BROBDINGNAGIAN	SOLIDIFICATION
BATTERYPOWERED	UNAPPROACHABLE	CAPITALIZATION	SOPHISTICATION
INTERCONNECTED	UNATTRIBUTABLE	CASTRAMETATION	SPECIALIZATION
NIBELUNGENLIED	UNCONSCIONABLE	CENTRALIZATION	STRATIFICATION
OVERSUBSCRIBED	UNCONTROLLABLE	CIRCUMLOCUTION	STULTIFICATION
SCATTERBRAINED	UNDERSTANDABLE	CLASSIFICATION	SUBSTANTIATION
SINGLEBREASTED	UNINTELLIGIBLE	CONGLOMERATION	SUPERANNUATION
STRAIGHTFOWARD	UNQUESTIONABLE	CONGRATULATION	SUPEREROGATION
UNCORROBORATED	UNRECOGNIZABLE	CONTESSERATION	SUPERSCRIPTION
UNDERDEVELOPED	VERISIMILITUDE	DEMOBILIZATION	TATTERDEMALION
UNDERMENTIONED	BIOENGINEERING	DEMORALIZATION	THROMBOPLASTIN
UNDERNOURISHED	DECISIONMAKING	DISAPPROBATION	TRANSFORMATION
UNPREMEDITATED	DISCRIMINATING	DISASSOCIATION	TRANSMIGRATION
VESPERTILIONID	DISTINGUISHING	DISCIPLINARIAN	TRANSPORTATION
ADMINISTRATIVE	ELECTIONEERING	DISCOLOURATION	VALETUDINARIAN
ANTILYMPHOCYTE	FORTUNETELLING	DISCRIMINATION	WESTERNIZATION
CHINCHERINCHEE	HEARTSEARCHING	DISEMBARKATION	PRONUNCIAMENTO
CIRCUMNAVIGATE	KNIPPERDOLLING	DISINCLINATION	APPRENTICESHIP
CIRCUMSCISSILE	METAMORPHOSING	DISINFORMATION	AIRCONDITIONER
COMMISSIONAIRE	MOUNTAINEERING	DISINTEGRATION	CARDIOVASCULAR
COMPREHENSIBLE	NETHERSTOCKING	DISORIENTATION	GEWÜRZTRAMINER
CONSTANTINOPLE	RECORDBREAKING	FRATERNIZATION	INTERFEROMETER
CONTROVERTIBLE	SCAREMONGERING	FRUCTIFICATION	JOHANNISBERGER
CORRESPONDENCE	SELFRESPECTING	GENERALIZATION	KNOTENSCHIEFER
COUNTERBALANCE	SHRINKWRAPPING	GENTRIFICATION	MICROPROCESSOR
COUNTERMEASURE	UNCOMPROMISING	HIEROSOLYMITAN	NEBUCHADNEZZAR
CROSSREFERENCE	WELTANSCHAUUNG	HOMOGENIZATION	TELETYPEWRITER
DISCOMBOBERATE	AUTORADIOGRAPH	IDENTIFICATION	TROUBLESHOOTER
DISCOMBOBULATE	ALLELOCHEMICAL	IMMOBILIZATION	VERTICILLASTER
DISCOUNTENANCE	ARCHAEOLOGICAL	IMMUNOGLOBULIN	WHIPPERSNAPPER
DISENFRANCHISE	CENTROLECITHAL	IMPLEMENTATION	ABSTEMIOUSNESS

AGGRESSIVENESS	SCHOOLMISTRESS	RELINQUISHMENT	INTELLECTUALLY
ALLOIOSTROPHUS	SCRUPULOUSNESS	SELFASSESSMENT	INTERMITTENTLY
ANTHROPOPHAGUS	SCURRILOUSNESS	SELFGOVERNMENT	INTERPLANETARY
ANTIMETATHESIS	STAPHYLOCOCCUS	SELFSUFFICIENT	LONGITUDINALLY
BOISTEROUSNESS	SUBMISSIVENESS	SUPERCONTINENT	MATHEMATICALLY
BREATHLESSNESS	THERMODYNAMICS	SUPERINTENDENT	METAPHORICALLY
CAMELOPARDALIS	THOUGHTFULNESS	TRADITIONALIST	MONOCARPELLARY
CAPRICIOUSNESS	TRICHOPHYTOSIS	UNDERSTATEMENT	OPTIMISTICALLY
CARCINOMATOSIS	UNMENTIONABLES	ACCOUNTABILITY	OSTENTATIOUSLY
CONJUNCTIVITIS	UNPLEASANTNESS	AFFECTIONATELY	OTOLARYNGOLOGY
CREEPYCRAWLIES	UNPREPAREDNESS	ALPHABETICALLY	PARAPSYCHOLOGY
ECCLESIASTICUS	UNSKILLFULNESS	APOLOGETICALLY	PARSIMONIOUSLY
EMBELLISHMENTS	VINDICTIVENESS	APPREHENSIVELY	PARTRIDGEBERRY
EXPRESSIONLESS	WEIGHTLESSNESS	ASTRONOMICALLY	PHLEGMATICALLY
FASTIDIOUSNESS	ACCOMPLISHMENT	AUTOCRATICALLY	PHYTOGEOGRAPHY
HALLUCINATIONS	ACKNOWLEDGMENT	CINEMATOGRAPHY	PRACTICABILITY
HEMIMETABOLOUS	AGGRANDISEMENT	COINCIDENTALLY	PRESUMPTUOUSLY
INEXPRESSIBLES	ANTHROPOLOGIST	CONFIDENTIALLY	PROFESSIONALLY
KNICKERBOCKERS	ANTIDEPRESSANT	CONGRATULATORY	PROPORTIONALLY
LASCIVIOUSNESS	ANTIFEDERALIST	CONSERVATIVELY	PROVIDENTIALLY
LICENTIOUSNESS	ANTIMONARCHIST	CONSTRUCTIVELY	RESPECTABILITY
LOQUACIOUSNESS	ANTIPERSPIRANT	CONVENTIONALLY	RESPONSIBILITY
MACROECONOMICS	APPROVECOMMENT	CONVERTIBILITY	SATISFACTORILY
MEPHISTOPHELES	ARRONDISSEMENT	CORRUPTIBILITY	SCIENTIFICALLY
METEMPSYCHOSIS	ASTROGEOLOGIST	CRYSTALLOMANCY	SENTIMENTALITY
METICULOUSNESS	AUTOTRANSPLANT	DEMOCRATICALLY	SIMULTANEOUSLY
OBSEQUIOUSNESS	BACTERIOLOGIST	DEXTROROTATORY	SINGLEMINDEDLY
ONCHOCERCIASIS	DESISTABSTRACT	DIPLOMATICALLY	SUBCONSCIOUSLY
OPPRESSIVENESS	DISAPPOINTMENT	DISAPPROVINGLY	SUPERCILIOUSLY
OSTEOARTHRITIS	DISCONTENTMENT	DISCONSOLATELY	SUPERFICIALITY
PERCEPTIVENESS	DISCOURAGEMENT	DISCOURTEOUSLY	SUPERNATURALLY
PEREGRINATIONS	DISENCHANTMENT	DISCRIMINATORY	SUSCEPTIBILITY
PERMISSIVENESS	DIVERTISSEMENT	ELECTRONICALLY	SYSTEMATICALLY
PERSUASIVENESS	EDUCATIONALIST	ENCEPHALOPATHY	UNDERSECRETARY
PHOTOSYNTHESIS	EXISTENTIALIST	EXPERIMENTALLY	UNDERSTANDABLY
PRECOCIOUSNESS	FUNDAMENTALIST	GEOGRAPHICALLY	UNDESIRABILITY
PRODUCTIVENESS	HORTICULTURIST	HYPOTHETICALLY	UNQUESTIONABLY
PSYCHOANALYSIS	IMPOVERISHMENT	ILLEGITIMATELY	UNSATISFACTORY
PURPOSEFULNESS	PHARMACOLOGIST	IMPERMEABILITY	WHOLEHEARTEDLY
QUALIFICATIONS	PHILANTHROPIST	IMPREGNABILITY	
RESPONSIVENESS	PHOSPHORESCENT	INCONCLUSIVELY	
RIDICULOUSNESS	PROHIBITIONIST	INCONVENIENTLY	
ROADWORTHINESS	PROTOCONTINENT	INSUFFICIENTLY	

15:1

ACCLIMATIZATION
ACKNOWLEDGEMENT
ACQUISITIVENESS
ADVENTUROUSNESS
AGRICULTURALIST
AIRCONDITIONING
ALLOTRIOMORPHIC
ANCYLOSTOMIASIS
ANTHROPOLOGICAL
ANTHROPOMORPHIC
ATTORNEYGENERAL
AUTHORITATIVELY
BACKWARDLOOKING
BACTERIOLOGICAL
BATTERYOPERATED
BIBLIOGRAPHICAL
BIOACCUMULATION
CHARACTERISTICS
CHOLECYSTOKININ
CHRISTADELPHIAN
CHRONOLOGICALLY
CHURRIGUERESQUE
CINEMATOGRAPHIC
CIRCUMSCRIPTION
CIRCUMSTANTIATE
COINSTANTANEOUS
COMPASSIONATELY
COMPUTERIZATION
CONFIDENTIALITY
CONFRONTATIONAL
CONGRATULATIONS
CONSCIENTIOUSLY
CONSERVATIONIST
CONTEMPORANEOUS
CONTRAVALLATION
CORRESPONDINGLY
CROSSOPTERYGIAN
CRYSTALLIZATION
CRYSTALLOGRAPHY
DECONTAMINATION
DESERTIFICATION
DESTRUCTIVENESS
DIFFERENTIATION
DISADVANTAGEOUS
DISILLUSIONMENT
DISPASSIONATELY
DISSATISFACTION
DISTINGUISHABLE
DIVERSIFICATION
DOLICHOCEPHALIC
DRAUGHTSMANSHIP
ECHOCARDIOGRAPH
ELECTRIFICATION
ELECTROACOUSTIC
ELECTROMAGNETIC
ELECTROMYOGRAPH
ELECTRONEGATIVE
ELECTROPHORESIS
ELECTROPOSITIVE
ENTREPRENEURIAL
EUPHEMISTICALLY
EXCOMMUNICATION
EXPERIMENTATION
EXTRAORDINARILY
FAMILIARIZATION
FLIBBERTIGIBBET
GASTROENTERITIS

GLEICHSCHALTUNG
GOTTERDAMMERUNG
GOVERNORGENERAL
HETEROCHROMATIN
HETERODACTYLOUS
HOSPITALIZATION
HYPERCORRECTION
HYPERTHYROIDISM
ICHTHYODUROLITE
IMPENETRABILITY
IMPRESSIONISTIC
INCOMMENSURABLE
INCOMPATIBILITY
INCOMPHEHENSION
INCONSEQUENTIAL
INCONSIDERATELY
INCONSPICUOUSLY
INDEMNIFICATION
INDIVIDUALISTIC
INQUISITIVENESS
INSTANTANEOUSLY
INSTRUMENTALIST
INSTRUMENTATION
INSUBORDINATION
INTELLIGIBILITY
INTENSIFICATION
INTERCHANGEABLE
INTERNATIONALLY
INTERVENTIONIST
LEATHERSTOCKING
LIFETHREATENING
LONGSIGHTEDNESS
LOPHOBRANCHIATE
MALPRACTITIONER
MANOEUVRABILITY
MICROSPORANGIUM
MICROSPOROPHYLL
MISAPPREHENSION
MISCHIEVOUSNESS
MISCONSTRUCTION
MISINTELLIGENCE
NATIONALIZATION
NONCOMMISSIONED
NONGOVERNMENTAL
NONPROFESSIONAL
NONPROFITMAKING
NOTHINGARIANISM
NOTWITHSTANDING
OLIGOSACCHARIDE
OMNIDIRECTIONAL
ONYCHOCRYPTOSIS
OPHTHALMOLOGIST
ORNITHORHYNCHUS
OVERSENTIMENTAL
PALAEONTOLOGIST
PARASYMPATHETIC
PARLIAMENTARIAN
PERPENDICULARLY
PERSONIFICATION
PESSIMISTICALLY
PHARMACOLOGICAL
PHILOSOPHICALLY
PHOSPHOCREATINE
PHOSPHORESCENCE
PHOTOMULTIPLIER
PHYSIOTHERAPIST
PLENIPOTENTIARY
POLYUNSATURATED
PRESTIDIGITATOR

PRETENTIOUSNESS
PROCRASTINATING
PROCRASTINATION
PROFESSIONALISM
PROGNOSTICATION
PROPORTIONATELY
PROSELYTIZATION
PSYCHOLOGICALLY
PSYCHOTHERAPIST
PUNCTILIOUSNESS
RADIOPHOTOGRAPH
RATIONALIZATION
REPRESENTATIVES
RESOURCEFULNESS
RHYNCHOBDELLIDA
RUMPELSTILTSKIN
SACRAMENTMYSTIC
SANCTIMONIOUSLY
SCAPHOCEPHALATE
SCHISTOSOMIASIS
SCHOOLMASTERING
SELFEXPLANATORY
SELFSUFFICIENCY
STANDARDIZATION
STANDOFFISHNESS
STILPNOSIDERITE
STRAIGHTFORWARD
STREPHOSYMBOLIA
SUBLAPSARIANISM
SURREPTITIOUSLY
SYMPATHETICALLY
SYNCHRONIZATION
TARSOMETATARSUS
TECHNOLOGICALLY
TEMPERAMENTALLY
THERAPEUTICALLY
THOUGHTLESSNESS
THUNDERSTRICKEN
TOTALITARIANISM
TRANSFIGURATION
TRANSLITERATION
TRIGONOMETRICAL
TRINITROTOLUENE
TRUSTWORTHINESS
UNCEREMONIOUSLY
UNCOMMUNICATIVE
UNCOMPANIONABLE
UNCOMPLIMENTARY
UNCOMPREHENDING
UNCONDITIONALLY
UNCONSCIOUSNESS
UNDEMONSTRATIVE
UNDERPRIVILEGED
UNDISTINGUISHED
UNEXCEPTIONABLE
UNPARLIAMENTARY
UNPREPOSSESSING
UNPRONOUNCEABLE
UNRIGHTEOUSNESS
UNSOPHISTICATED
UNSPORTSMANLIKE
WEATHERBOARDING
WELLESTABLISHED

15:2

BACKWARDLOOKING
BACTERIOLOGICAL
BATTERYOPERATED
FAMILIARIZATION

GASTROENTERITIS
MALPRACTITIONER
MANOEUVRABILITY
NATIONALIZATION
PALAEONTOLOGIST
PARASYMPATHETIC
PARLIAMENTARIAN
RADIOPHOTOGRAPH
RATIONALIZATION
SACRAMENTMYSTIC
SANCTIMONIOUSLY
TARSOMETATARSUS
ACCLIMATIZATION
ACKNOWLEDGEMENT
ACQUISITIVENESS
ECHOCARDIOGRAPH
ICHTHYODUROLITE
SCAPHOCEPHALATE
SCHISTOSOMIASIS
SCHOOLMASTERING
ADVENTUROUSNESS
DECONTAMINATION
DESERTIFICATION
DESTRUCTIVENESS
HETEROCHROMATIN
HETERODACTYLOUS
LEATHERSTOCKING
PERPENDICULARLY
PERSONIFICATION
PESSIMISTICALLY
REPRESENTATIVES
RESOURCEFULNESS
SELFEXPLANATORY
SELFSUFFICIENCY
TECHNOLOGICALLY
TEMPERAMENTALLY
WEATHERBOARDING
WELLESTABLISHED
AGRICULTURALIST
CHARACTERISTICS
CHOLECYSTOKININ
CHRISTADELPHIAN
CHRONOLOGICALLY
CHURRIGUERESQUE
PHARMACOLOGICAL
PHILOSOPHICALLY
PHOSPHOCREATINE
PHOSPHORESCENCE
PHOTOMULTIPLIER
PHYSIOTHERAPIST
RHYNCHOBDELLIDA
THERAPEUTICALLY
THOUGHTLESSNESS
THUNDERSTRICKEN
AIRCONDITIONING
BIBLIOGRAPHICAL
BIOACCUMULATION
CINEMATOGRAPHIC
CIRCUMSCRIPTION
CIRCUMSTANTIATE
DIFFERENTIATION
DISADVANTAGEOUS
DISILLUSIONMENT
DISPASSIONATELY
DISSATISFACTION
DISTINGUISHABLE
DIVERSIFICATION
LIFETHREATENING
MICROSPORANGIUM

MICROSPOROPHYLL	CONTRAVALLATION	BIBLIOGRAPHICAL	COMPUTERIZATION
MISAPPREHENSION	CORRESPONDINGLY	SUBLAPSARIANISM	FAMILIARIZATION
MISCHIEVOUSNESS	DOLICHOCEPHALIC	ACCLIMATIZATION	RUMPELSTILTSKIN
MISCONSTRUCTION	GOTTERDAMMERUNG	ANCYLOSTOMIASIS	SYMPATHETICALLY
MISINTELLIGENCE	GOVERNORGENERAL	BACKWARDLOOKING	TEMPERAMENTALLY
ALLOTRIOMORPHIC	HOSPITALIZATION	BACTERIOLOGICAL	CINEMATOGRAPHIC
ELECTRIFICATION	LONGSIGHTEDNESS	DECONTAMINATION	CONFIDENTIALITY
ELECTROACOUSTIC	LOPHOBRANCHIATE	EXCOMMUNICATION	CONFRONTATIONAL
ELECTROMAGNETIC	NONCOMMISSIONED	INCOMMENSURABLE	CONGRATULATIONS
ELECTROMYOGRAPH	NONGOVERNMENTAL	INCOMPATIBILITY	CONSCIENTIOUSLY
ELECTRONEGATIVE	NONPROFESSIONAL	INCOMPHEHENSION	CONSERVATIONIST
ELECTROPHORESIS	NONPROFITMAKING	INCONSEQUENTIAL	CONTEMPORANEOUS
ELECTROPOSITIVE	NOTHINGARIANISM	INCONSIDERATELY	CONTRAVALLATION
FLIBBERTIGIBBET	NOTWITHSTANDING	INCONSPICUOUSLY	LONGSIGHTEDNESS
GLEICHSCHALTUNG	POLYUNSATURATED	MICROSPORANGIUM	MANOEUVRABILITY
OLIGOSACCHARIDE	TOTALITARIANISM	MICROSPOROPHYLL	NONCOMMISSIONED
PLENIPOTENTIARY	OPHTHALMOLOGIST	SACRAMENTMYSTIC	NONGOVERNMENTAL
IMPENETRABILITY	CROSSOPTERYGIAN	TECHNOLOGICALLY	NONPROFESSIONAL
IMPRESSIONISTIC	CRYSTALLIZATION	UNCEREMONIOUSLY	NONPROFITMAKING
OMNIDIRECTIONAL	CRYSTALLOGRAPHY	UNCOMMUNICATIVE	OMNIDIRECTIONAL
ANCYLOSTOMIASIS	DRAUGHTSMANSHIP	UNCOMPANIONABLE	ORNITHORHYNCHUS
ANTHROPOLOGICAL	ORNITHORHYNCHUS	UNCOMPLIMENTARY	PUNCTILIOUSNESS
ANTHROPOMORPHIC	PRESTIDIGITATOR	UNCOMPREHENDING	SANCTIMONIOUSLY
ENTREPRENEURIAL	PRETENTIOUSNESS	UNCONDITIONALLY	SYNCHRONIZATION
INCOMMENSURABLE	PROCRASTINATING	UNCONSCIOUSNESS	BIOACCUMULATION
INCOMPATIBILITY	PROCRASTINATION	INDEMNIFICATION	CHOLECYSTOKININ
INCOMPHEHENSION	PROFESSIONALISM	INDIVIDUALISTIC	CROSSOPTERYGIAN
INCONSEQUENTIAL	PROGNOSTICATION	RADIOPHOTOGRAPH	PHOSPHOCREATINE
INCONSIDERATELY	PROPORTIONATELY	UNDEMONSTRATIVE	PHOSPHORESCENCE
INCONSPICUOUSLY	PROSELYTIZATION	UNDERPRIVILEGED	PHOTOMULTIPLIER
INDEMNIFICATION	TRANSFIGURATION	UNDISTINGUISHED	PROCRASTINATING
INDIVIDUALISTIC	TRANSLITERATION	ELECTRIFICATION	PROCRASTINATION
INQUISITIVENESS	TRIGONOMETRICAL	ELECTROACOUSTIC	PROFESSIONALISM
INSTANTANEOUSLY	TRINITROTOLUENE	ELECTROMAGNETIC	PROGNOSTICATION
INSTRUMENTALIST	TRUSTWORTHINESS	ELECTROMYOGRAPH	PROPORTIONATELY
INSTRUMENTATION	PSYCHOLOGICALLY	ELECTRONEGATIVE	PROSELYTIZATION
INSUBORDINATION	PSYCHOTHERAPIST	ELECTROPHORESIS	THOUGHTLESSNESS
INTELLIGIBILITY	ATTORNEYGENERAL	ELECTROPOSITIVE	EUPHEMISTICALLY
INTENSIFICATION	STANDARDIZATION	GLEICHSCHALTUNG	EXPERIMENTATION
INTERCHANGEABLE	STANDOFFISHNESS	OVERSENTIMENTAL	HYPERCORRECTION
INTERNATIONALLY	STILPNOSIDERITE	PLENIPOTENTIARY	HYPERTHYROIDISM
INTERVENTIONIST	STRAIGHTFORWARD	PRESTIDIGITATOR	IMPENETRABILITY
ONYCHOCRYPTOSIS	STREPHOSYMBOLIA	PRETENTIOUSNESS	IMPRESSIONISTIC
UNCEREMONIOUSLY	AUTHORITATIVELY	THERAPEUTICALLY	LOPHOBRANCHIATE
UNCOMMUNICATIVE	EUPHEMISTICALLY	UNEXCEPTIONABLE	REPRESENTATIVES
UNCOMPANIONABLE	PUNCTILIOUSNESS	DIFFERENTIATION	UNPARLIAMENTARY
UNCOMPLIMENTARY	RUMPELSTILTSKIN	LIFETHREATENING	UNPREPOSSESSING
UNCOMPREHENDING	SUBLAPSARIANISM	ECHOCARDIOGRAPH	UNPRONOUNCEABLE
UNCONDITIONALLY	SURREPTITIOUSLY	ICHTHYODUROLITE	ACQUISITIVENESS
UNCONSCIOUSNESS	OVERSENTIMENTAL	OPHTHALMOLOGIST	INQUISITIVENESS
UNDEMONSTRATIVE	EXCOMMUNICATION	SCHISTOSOMIASIS	AGRICULTURALIST
UNDERPRIVILEGED	EXPERIMENTATION	SCHOOLMASTERING	AIRCONDITIONING
UNDISTINGUISHED	EXTRAORDINARILY	COINSTANTANEOUS	CHRISTADELPHIAN
UNEXCEPTIONABLE	HYPERCORRECTION	FLIBBERTIGIBBET	CHRONOLOGICALLY
UNPARLIAMENTARY	HYPERTHYROIDISM	OLIGOSACCHARIDE	CIRCUMSCRIPTION
UNPREPOSSESSING	SYMPATHETICALLY	PHILOSOPHICALLY	CIRCUMSTANTIATE
UNPRONOUNCEABLE	SYNCHRONIZATION	STILPNOSIDERITE	CORRESPONDINGLY
UNRIGHTEOUSNESS		TRIGONOMETRICAL	PARASYMPATHETIC
UNSOPHISTICATED	**15:3**	TRINITROTOLUENE	PARLIAMENTARIAN
UNSPORTSMANLIKE	CHARACTERISTICS	ACKNOWLEDGEMENT	PERPENDICULARLY
COINSTANTANEOUS	DRAUGHTSMANSHIP	ALLOTRIOMORPHIC	PERSONIFICATION
COMPASSIONATELY	LEATHERSTOCKING	DOLICHOCEPHALIC	STRAIGHTFORWARD
COMPUTERIZATION	PHARMACOLOGICAL	MALPRACTITIONER	STREPHOSYMBOLIA
CONFIDENTIALITY	SCAPHOCEPHALATE	PALAEONTOLOGIST	SURREPTITIOUSLY
CONFRONTATIONAL	STANDARDIZATION	POLYUNSATURATED	TARSOMETATARSUS
CONGRATULATIONS	STANDOFFISHNESS	SELFEXPLANATORY	UNRIGHTEOUSNESS
CONSCIENTIOUSLY	TRANSFIGURATION	SELFSUFFICIENCY	DESERTIFICATION
CONSERVATIONIST	TRANSLITERATION	WELLESTABLISHED	DESTRUCTIVENESS
CONTEMPORANEOUS	WEATHERBOARDING	COMPASSIONATELY	DISADVANTAGEOUS

DISILLUSIONMENT
DISPASSIONATELY
DISSATISFACTION
DISTINGUISHABLE
GASTROENTERITIS
HOSPITALIZATION
INSTANTANEOUSLY
INSTRUMENTALIST
INSTRUMENTATION
INSUBORDINATION
MISAPPREHENSION
MISCHIEVOUSNESS
MISCONSTRUCTION
MISINTELLIGENCE
PESSIMISTICALLY
RESOURCEFULNESS
UNSOPHISTICATED
UNSPORTSMANLIKE
ANTHROPOLOGICAL
ANTHROPOMORPHIC
ATTORNEYGENERAL
AUTHORITATIVELY
BATTERYOPERATED
ENTREPRENEURIAL
EXTRAORDINARILY
GOTTERDAMMERUNG
HETEROCHROMATIN
HETERODACTYLOUS
INTELLIGIBILITY
INTENSIFICATION
INTERCHANGEABLE
INTERNATIONALLY
INTERVENTIONIST
NATIONALIZATION
NOTHINGARIANISM
NOTWITHSTANDING
RATIONALIZATION
TOTALITARIANISM
CHURRIGUERESQUE
THUNDERSTRICKEN
TRUSTWORTHINESS
ADVENTUROUSNESS
DIVERSIFICATION
GOVERNORGENERAL
CRYSTALLIZATION
CRYSTALLOGRAPHY
ONYCHOCRYPTOSIS
PHYSIOTHERAPIST
PSYCHOLOGICALLY
PSYCHOTHERAPIST
RHYNCHOBDELLIDA

15:4

BIOACCUMULATION
DISADVANTAGEOUS
MISAPPREHENSION
PALAEONTOLOGIST
PARASYMPATHETIC
STRAIGHTFORWARD
TOTALITARIANISM
UNPARLIAMENTARY
FLIBBERTIGIBBET
AIRCONDITIONING
CIRCUMSCRIPTION
CIRCUMSTANTIATE
ELECTRIFICATION
ELECTROACOUSTIC
ELECTROMAGNETIC
ELECTROMYOGRAPH

ELECTRONEGATIVE
ELECTROPHORESIS
ELECTROPOSITIVE
MISCHIEVOUSNESS
MISCONSTRUCTION
NONCOMMISSIONED
ONYCHOCRYPTOSIS
PROCRASTINATING
PROCRASTINATION
PSYCHOLOGICALLY
PSYCHOTHERAPIST
PUNCTILIOUSNESS
SANCTIMONIOUSLY
SYNCHRONIZATION
ADVENTUROUSNESS
CINEMATOGRAPHIC
DESERTIFICATION
DIVERSIFICATION
EXPERIMENTATION
GOVERNORGENERAL
HETEROCHROMATIN
HETERODACTYLOUS
HYPERCORRECTION
HYPERTHYROIDISM
IMPENETRABILITY
INDEMNIFICATION
INTELLIGIBILITY
INTENSIFICATION
INTERCHANGEABLE
INTERNATIONALLY
INTERVENTIONIST
LIFETHREATENING
STREPHOSYMBOLIA
UNCEREMONIOUSLY
UNDEMONSTRATIVE
UNDERPRIVILEGED
CONFIDENTIALITY
CONFRONTATIONAL
DIFFERENTIATION
PROFESSIONALISM
SELFEXPLANATORY
SELFSUFFICIENCY
CONGRATULATIONS
LONGSIGHTEDNESS
NONGOVERNMENTAL
OLIGOSACCHARIDE
PROGNOSTICATION
TRIGONOMETRICAL
ANTHROPOLOGICAL
ANTHROPOMORPHIC
AUTHORITATIVELY
EUPHEMISTICALLY
LOPHOBRANCHIATE
NOTHINGARIANISM
TECHNOLOGICALLY
AGRICULTURALIST
CHRISTADELPHIAN
DISILLUSIONMENT
DOLICHOCEPHALIC
FAMILIARIZATION
GLEICHSCHALTUNG
INDIVIDUALISTIC
MISINTELLIGENCE
NATIONALIZATION
OMNIDIRECTIONAL
ORNITHORHYNCHUS
RADIOPHOTOGRAPH
RATIONALIZATION
SCHISTOSOMIASIS

UNDISTINGUISHED
UNRIGHTEOUSNESS
BACKWARDLOOKING
ACCLIMATIZATION
BIBLIOGRAPHICAL
CHOLECYSTOKININ
PARLIAMENTARIAN
PHILOSOPHICALLY
STILPNOSIDERITE
SUBLAPSARIANISM
WELLESTABLISHED
ACKNOWLEDGEMENT
COINSTANTANEOUS
PLENIPOTENTIARY
RHYNCHOBDELLIDA
STANDARDIZATION
STANDOFFISHNESS
THUNDERSTRICKEN
TRANSFIGURATION
TRANSLITERATION
TRINITROTOLUENE
ALLOTRIOMORPHIC
ATTORNEYGENERAL
CHRONOLOGICALLY
DECONTAMINATION
ECHOCARDIOGRAPH
EXCOMMUNICATION
INCOMMENSURABLE
INCOMPATIBILITY
INCOMPHEHENSION
INCONSEQUENTIAL
INCONSIDERATELY
INCONSPICUOUSLY
MANOEUVRABILITY
RESOURCEFULNESS
SCHOOLMASTERING
UNCOMMUNICATIVE
UNCOMPANIONABLE
UNCOMPLIMENTARY
UNCOMPREHENDING
UNCONDITIONALLY
UNCONSCIOUSNESS
UNSOPHISTICATED
COMPASSIONATELY
COMPUTERIZATION
DISPASSIONATELY
HOSPITALIZATION
MALPRACTITIONER
NONPROFESSIONAL
NONPROFITMAKING
PERPENDICULARLY
PROPORTIONATELY
RUMPELSTILTSKIN
SCAPHOCEPHALATE
SYMPATHETICALLY
TEMPERAMENTALLY
UNSPORTSMANLIKE
CHARACTERISTICS
CHURRIGUERESQUE
CORRESPONDINGLY
ENTREPRENEURIAL
EXTRAORDINARILY
IMPRESSIONISTIC
MICROSPORANGIUM
MICROSPOROPHYLL
OVERSENTIMENTAL
PHARMACOLOGICAL
REPRESENTATIVES
SACRAMENTMYSTIC

SURREPTITIOUSLY
THERAPEUTICALLY
UNPREPOSSESSING
UNPRONOUNCEABLE
CONSCIENTIOUSLY
CONSERVATIONIST
CROSSOPTERYGIAN
CRYSTALLIZATION
CRYSTALLOGRAPHY
DISSATISFACTION
PERSONIFICATION
PESSIMISTICALLY
PHOSPHOCREATINE
PHOSPHORESCENCE
PHYSIOTHERAPIST
PRESTIDIGITATOR
PROSELYTIZATION
TARSOMETATARSUS
TRUSTWORTHINESS
BACTERIOLOGICAL
BATTERYOPERATED
CONTEMPORANEOUS
CONTRAVALLATION
DESTRUCTIVENESS
DISTINGUISHABLE
GASTROENTERITIS
GOTTERDAMMERUNG
ICHTHYODUROLITE
INSTANTANEOUSLY
INSTRUMENTALIST
INSTRUMENTATION
LEATHERSTOCKING
OPHTHALMOLOGIST
PHOTOMULTIPLIER
PRETENTIOUSNESS
WEATHERBOARDING
ACQUISITIVENESS
DRAUGHTSMANSHIP
INQUISITIVENESS
INSUBORDINATION
THOUGHTLESSNESS
NOTWITHSTANDING
UNEXCEPTIONABLE
ANCYLOSTOMIASIS
POLYUNSATURATED

15:5

CHARACTERISTICS
COMPASSIONATELY
DISPASSIONATELY
DISSATISFACTION
EXTRAORDINARILY
INSTANTANEOUSLY
SACRAMENTMYSTIC
SUBLAPSARIANISM
SYMPATHETICALLY
THERAPEUTICALLY
FLIBBERTIGIBBET
INSUBORDINATION
AGRICULTURALIST
BIOACCUMULATION
CONSCIENTIOUSLY
DOLICHOCEPHALIC
ECHOCARDIOGRAPH
GLEICHSCHALTUNG
RHYNCHOBDELLIDA
UNEXCEPTIONABLE
DISADVANTAGEOUS
OMNIDIRECTIONAL

STANDARDIZATION	UNCOMPLIMENTARY	PROCRASTINATING	UNEXCEPTIONABLE
STANDOFFISHNESS	UNCOMPREHENDING	PROCRASTINATION	WEATHERBOARDING
THUNDERSTRICKEN	UNDEMONSTRATIVE	UNCEREMONIOUSLY	TRANSFIGURATION
BACTERIOLOGICAL	ADVENTUROUSNESS	UNDERPRIVILEGED	STRAIGHTFORWARD
BATTERYOPERATED	CHRONOLOGICALLY	UNPARLIAMENTARY	DOLICHOCEPHALIC
CHOLECYSTOKININ	DECONTAMINATION	CHRISTADELPHIAN	DRAUGHTSMANSHIP
CONSERVATIONIST	IMPENETRABILITY	COINSTANTANEOUS	GLEICHSCHALTUNG
CONTEMPORANEOUS	INCONSEQUENTIAL	CROSSOPTERYGIAN	LIFETHREATENING
CORRESPONDINGLY	INCONSIDERATELY	LONGSIGHTEDNESS	ORNITHORHYNCHUS
DIFFERENTIATION	INCONSPICUOUSLY	OVERSENTIMENTAL	PHOSPHOCREATINE
ENTREPRENEURIAL	INTENSIFICATION	PARASYMPATHETIC	PHOSPHORESCENCE
EUPHEMISTICALLY	MISINTELLIGENCE	SCHISTOSOMIASIS	RHYNCHOBDELLIDA
GOTTERDAMMERUNG	PROGNOSTICATION	SELFSUFFICIENCY	STREPHOSYMBOLIA
IMPRESSIONISTIC	TECHNOLOGICALLY	TRANSFIGURATION	THOUGHTLESSNESS
MANOEUVRABILITY	UNCONDITIONALLY	TRANSLITERATION	UNRIGHTEOUSNESS
PALAEONTOLOGIST	UNCONSCIOUSNESS	UNDISTINGUISHED	UNSOPHISTICATED
PERPENDICULARLY	ACKNOWLEDGEMENT	ALLOTRIOMORPHIC	CHURRIGUERESQUE
PRETENTIOUSNESS	AIRCONDITIONING	CRYSTALLIZATION	CONSCIENTIOUSLY
PROFESSIONALISM	AUTHORITATIVELY	CRYSTALLOGRAPHY	EXPERIMENTATION
PROSELYTIZATION	LOPHOBRANCHIATE	ELECTRIFICATION	FAMILIARIZATION
REPRESENTATIVES	MICROSPORANGIUM	ELECTROACOUSTIC	INDIVIDUALISTIC
RUMPELSTILTSKIN	MICROSPOROPHYLL	ELECTROMAGNETIC	LONGSIGHTEDNESS
SELFEXPLANATORY	MISCONSTRUCTION	ELECTROMYOGRAPH	MISCHIEVOUSNESS
SURREPTITIOUSLY	NATIONALIZATION	ELECTRONEGATIVE	OMNIDIRECTIONAL
TEMPERAMENTALLY	NONCOMMISSIONED	ELECTROPHORESIS	PRESTIDIGITATOR
UNPREPOSSESSING	NONGOVERNMENTAL	ELECTROPOSITIVE	PUNCTILIOUSNESS
WELLESTABLISHED	OLIGOSACCHARIDE	LIFETHREATENING	SANCTIMONIOUSLY
DRAUGHTSMANSHIP	PERSONIFICATION	ORNITHORHYNCHUS	TOTALITARIANISM
THOUGHTLESSNESS	PHILOSOPHICALLY	PRESTIDIGITATOR	DISILLUSIONMENT
UNRIGHTEOUSNESS	PHOTOMULTIPLIER	PUNCTILIOUSNESS	INTELLIGIBILITY
ICHTHYODUROLITE	PROPORTIONATELY	SANCTIMONIOUSLY	PROSELYTIZATION
LEATHERSTOCKING	RADIOPHOTOGRAPH	TRUSTWORTHINESS	RUMPELSTILTSKIN
MISCHIEVOUSNESS	RATIONALIZATION	CIRCUMSCRIPTION	SCHOOLMASTERING
ONYCHOCRYPTOSIS	SCHOOLMASTERING	CIRCUMSTANTIATE	TRANSLITERATION
OPHTHALMOLOGIST	TARSOMETATARSUS	COMPUTERIZATION	UNPARLIAMENTARY
PSYCHOLOGICALLY	TRIGONOMETRICAL	POLYUNSATURATED	ACCLIMATIZATION
PSYCHOTHERAPIST	UNPRONOUNCEABLE	RESOURCEFULNESS	CIRCUMSCRIPTION
SCAPHOCEPHALATE	UNSPORTSMANLIKE	INDIVIDUALISTIC	CIRCUMSTANTIATE
SYNCHRONIZATION	MISAPPREHENSION	BACKWARDLOOKING	CONTEMPORANEOUS
WEATHERBOARDING	PHOSPHOCREATINE		EUPHEMISTICALLY
ACCLIMATIZATION	PHOSPHORESCENCE	**15:6**	EXCOMMUNICATION
ACQUISITIVENESS	STILPNOSIDERITE		INCOMMENSURABLE
BIBLIOGRAPHICAL	STREPHOSYMBOLIA	BACKWARDLOOKING	NONCOMMISSIONED
CONFIDENTIALITY	UNSOPHISTICATED	CINEMATOGRAPHIC	PESSIMISTICALLY
DISTINGUISHABLE	ANTHROPOLOGICAL	CONGRATULATIONS	PHOTOMULTIPLIER
HOSPITALIZATION	ANTHROPOMORPHIC	CONTRAVALLATION	SACRAMENTMYSTIC
INQUISITIVENESS	ATTORNEYGENERAL	CRYSTALLIZATION	TARSOMETATARSUS
NOTHINGARIANISM	CHURRIGUERESQUE	CRYSTALLOGRAPHY	UNCOMMUNICATIVE
NOTWITHSTANDING	CONFRONTATIONAL	ECHOCARDIOGRAPH	AIRCONDITIONING
PARLIAMENTARIAN	CONGRATULATIONS	MALPRACTITIONER	ATTORNEYGENERAL
PESSIMISTICALLY	CONTRAVALLATION	OPHTHALMOLOGIST	DISTINGUISHABLE
PHYSIOTHERAPIST	DESERTIFICATION	PARLIAMENTARIAN	GOVERNORGENERAL
PLENIPOTENTIARY	DESTRUCTIVENESS	PHARMACOLOGICAL	INDEMNIFICATION
STRAIGHTFORWARD	DIVERSIFICATION	PROCRASTINATING	INSTANTANEOUSLY
TRINITROTOLUENE	EXPERIMENTATION	PROCRASTINATION	INTERNATIONALLY
ANCYLOSTOMIASIS	GASTROENTERITIS	STANDARDIZATION	MISCONSTRUCTION
DISILLUSIONMENT	GOVERNORGENERAL	LOPHOBRANCHIATE	NATIONALIZATION
FAMILIARIZATION	HETEROCHROMATIN	BIOACCUMULATION	NOTHINGARIANISM
INTELLIGIBILITY	HETERODACTYLOUS	CHARACTERISTICS	PERPENDICULARLY
TOTALITARIANISM	HYPERCORRECTION	CHOLECYSTOKININ	PERSONIFICATION
CINEMATOGRAPHIC	HYPERTHYROIDISM	HYPERCORRECTION	POLYUNSATURATED
EXCOMMUNICATION	INSTRUMENTALIST	INTERCHANGEABLE	PRETENTIOUSNESS
INCOMMENSURABLE	INSTRUMENTATION	CONFIDENTIALITY	RATIONALIZATION
INCOMPATIBILITY	INTERCHANGEABLE	UNCONDITIONALLY	STILPNOSIDERITE
INCOMPHEHENSION	INTERNATIONALLY	FLIBBERTIGIBBET	TRIGONOMETRICAL
INDEMNIFICATION	INTERVENTIONIST	IMPENETRABILITY	UNPRONOUNCEABLE
PHARMACOLOGICAL	MALPRACTITIONER	LEATHERSTOCKING	ANCYLOSTOMIASIS
UNCOMMUNICATIVE	NONPROFESSIONAL	OVERSENTIMENTAL	ANTHROPOLOGICAL
UNCOMPANIONABLE	NONPROFITMAKING	THUNDERSTRICKEN	ANTHROPOMORPHIC
		UNCEREMONIOUSLY	

BIBLIOGRAPHICAL
CHRONOLOGICALLY
CONFRONTATIONAL
CROSSOPTERYGIAN
EXTRAORDINARILY
GASTROENTERITIS
HETEROCHROMATIN
HETERODACTYLOUS
INSUBORDINATION
NONPROFESSIONAL
NONPROFITMAKING
ONYCHOCRYPTOSIS
PALAEONTOLOGIST
PHYSIOTHERAPIST
PROGNOSTICATION
PSYCHOLOGICALLY
PSYCHOTHERAPIST
SCAPHOCEPHALATE
STANDOFFISHNESS
TECHNOLOGICALLY
UNDEMONSTRATIVE
ENTREPRENEURIAL
INCOMPATIBILITY
INCOMPHEHENSION
MISAPPREHENSION
PLENIPOTENTIARY
RADIOPHOTOGRAPH
SUBLAPSARIANISM
SURREPTITIOUSLY
THERAPEUTICALLY
UNCOMPANIONABLE
UNCOMPLIMENTARY
UNCOMPREHENDING
UNDERPRIVILEGED
UNPREPOSSESSING
ALLOTRIOMORPHIC
AUTHORITATIVELY
BACTERIOLOGICAL
BATTERYOPERATED
CONSERVATIONIST
DIFFERENTIATION
ELECTRIFICATION
ELECTROACOUSTIC
ELECTROMAGNETIC
ELECTROMYOGRAPH
ELECTRONEGATIVE
ELECTROPHORESIS
ELECTROPOSITIVE
GOTTERDAMMERUNG
PROPORTIONATELY
RESOURCEFULNESS
SYNCHRONIZATION
TEMPERAMENTALLY
UNSPORTSMANLIKE
ACQUISITIVENESS
COMPASSIONATELY
CORRESPONDINGLY
DISPASSIONATELY
DIVERSIFICATION
IMPRESSIONISTIC
INCONSEQUENTIAL
INCONSIDERATELY
INCONSPICUOUSLY
INQUISITIVENESS
INTENSIFICATION
MICROSPORANGIUM
MICROSPOROPHYLL
OLIGOSACCHARIDE
PHILOSOPHICALLY

PROFESSIONALISM
REPRESENTATIVES
UNCONSCIOUSNESS
WELLESTABLISHED
ADVENTUROUSNESS
CHRISTADELPHIAN
COINSTANTANEOUS
COMPUTERIZATION
DECONTAMINATION
DESERTIFICATION
DISSATISFACTION
HOSPITALIZATION
HYPERTHYROIDISM
MISINTELLIGENCE
NOTWITHSTANDING
SCHISTOSOMIASIS
SYMPATHETICALLY
TRINITROTOLUENE
UNDISTINGUISHED
AGRICULTURALIST
DESTRUCTIVENESS
INSTRUMENTALIST
INSTRUMENTATION
MANOEUVRABILITY
SELFSUFFICIENCY
DISADVANTAGEOUS
INTERVENTIONIST
NONGOVERNMENTAL
ACKNOWLEDGEMENT
TRUSTWORTHINESS
SELFEXPLANATORY
ICHTHYODUROLITE
PARASYMPATHETIC

15:7

ACCLIMATIZATION
CHRISTADELPHIAN
COINSTANTANEOUS
DECONTAMINATION
DISADVANTAGEOUS
FAMILIARIZATION
HOSPITALIZATION
INCOMPATIBILITY
INTERNATIONALLY
NATIONALIZATION
OLIGOSACCHARIDE
RATIONALIZATION
TEMPERAMENTALLY
UNCOMPANIONABLE
DESTRUCTIVENESS
HETEROCHROMATIN
MALPRACTITIONER
ONYCHOCRYPTOSIS
PHARMACOLOGICAL
RESOURCEFULNESS
SCAPHOCEPHALATE
UNCONSCIOUSNESS
AIRCONDITIONING
GOTTERDAMMERUNG
HETERODACTYLOUS
INDIVIDUALISTIC
PERPENDICULARLY
PRESTIDIGITATOR
ATTORNEYGENERAL
COMPUTERIZATION
CONFIDENTIALITY
CONSCIENTIOUSLY
DIFFERENTIATION
GASTROENTERITIS

INCOMMENSURABLE
INCONSEQUENTIAL
INTERVENTIONIST
MISCHIEVOUSNESS
MISINTELLIGENCE
NONGOVERNMENTAL
REPRESENTATIVES
SACRAMENTMYSTIC
TARSOMETATARSUS
THERAPEUTICALLY
NONPROFESSIONAL
NONPROFITMAKING
SELFSUFFICIENCY
STANDOFFISHNESS
BIBLIOGRAPHICAL
CHURRIGUERESQUE
DISTINGUISHABLE
LONGSIGHTEDNESS
NOTHINGARIANISM
HYPERTHYROIDISM
INCOMPHEHENSION
INTERCHANGEABLE
NOTWITHSTANDING
RADIOPHOTOGRAPH
STRAIGHTFORWARD
SYMPATHETICALLY
ACQUISITIVENESS
ALLOTRIOMORPHIC
AUTHORITATIVELY
BACTERIOLOGICAL
DESERTIFICATION
DISSATISFACTION
DIVERSIFICATION
ELECTRIFICATION
EUPHEMISTICALLY
INCONSIDERATELY
INDEMNIFICATION
INQUISITIVENESS
INTELLIGIBILITY
INTENSIFICATION
PERSONIFICATION
PESSIMISTICALLY
TRANSFIGURATION
TRANSLITERATION
UNCONDITIONALLY
UNDISTINGUISHED
UNPARLIAMENTARY
UNSOPHISTICATED
ACKNOWLEDGEMENT
AGRICULTURALIST
CHRONOLOGICALLY
CRYSTALLIZATION
CRYSTALLOGRAPHY
OPHTHALMOLOGIST
PSYCHOLOGICALLY
PUNCTILIOUSNESS
TECHNOLOGICALLY
UNCOMPLIMENTARY
EXPERIMENTATION
INSTRUMENTALIST
INSTRUMENTATION
NONCOMMISSIONED
PARASYMPATHETIC
PARLIAMENTARIAN
SANCTIMONIOUSLY
SCHOOLMASTERING
UNCEREMONIOUSLY
CONFRONTATIONAL
OVERSENTIMENTAL

PALAEONTOLOGIST
UNDEMONSTRATIVE
DOLICHOCEPHALIC
ELECTROACOUSTIC
ELECTROMAGNETIC
ELECTROMYOGRAPH
ELECTRONEGATIVE
ELECTROPHORESIS
ELECTROPOSITIVE
GOVERNORGENERAL
HYPERCORRECTION
ICHTHYODUROLITE
ORNITHORHYNCHUS
PHILOSOPHICALLY
PHOSPHOCREATINE
PHOSPHORESCENCE
PLENIPOTENTIARY
RHYNCHOBDELLIDA
SCHISTOSOMIASIS
STILPNOSIDERITE
STREPHOSYMBOLIA
SYNCHRONIZATION
TRIGONOMETRICAL
TRUSTWORTHINESS
UNPREPOSSESSING
UNPRONOUNCEABLE
ANTHROPOLOGICAL
ANTHROPOMORPHIC
CONTEMPORANEOUS
CORRESPONDINGLY
CROSSOPTERYGIAN
INCONSPICUOUSLY
MICROSPORANGIUM
MICROSPOROPHYLL
SELFEXPLANATORY
UNEXCEPTIONABLE
BACKWARDLOOKING
ECHOCARDIOGRAPH
ENTREPRENEURIAL
EXTRAORDINARILY
FLIBBERTIGIBBET
INSUBORDINATION
LEATHERSTOCKING
LIFETHREATENING
LOPHOBRANCHIATE
MISAPPREHENSION
OMNIDIRECTIONAL
STANDARDIZATION
THUNDERSTRICKEN
TRINITROTOLUENE
UNCOMPREHENDING
UNDERPRIVILEGED
WEATHERBOARDING
ANCYLOSTOMIASIS
CIRCUMSCRIPTION
CIRCUMSTANTIATE
COMPASSIONATELY
DISPASSIONATELY
GLEICHSCHALTUNG
IMPRESSIONISTIC
MISCONSTRUCTION
POLYUNSATURATED
PROCRASTINATING
PROCRASTINATION
PROFESSIONALISM
PROGNOSTICATION
RUMPELSTILTSKIN
SUBLAPSARIANISM
CHARACTERISTICS

CINEMATOGRAPHIC
CONGRATULATIONS
DRAUGHTSMANSHIP
IMPENETRABILITY
INSTANTANEOUSLY
PHYSIOTHERAPIST
PRETENTIOUSNESS
PROPORTIONATELY
PSYCHOTHERAPIST
SURREPTITIOUSLY
THOUGHTLESSNESS
TOTALITARIANISM
UNRIGHTEOUSNESS
UNSPORTSMANLIKE
WELLESTABLISHED
ADVENTUROUSNESS
BIOACCUMULATION
DISILLUSIONMENT
EXCOMMUNICATION
PHOTOMULTIPLIER
UNCOMMUNICATIVE
CONSERVATIONIST
CONTRAVALLATION
MANOEUVRABILITY
BATTERYOPERATED
CHOLECYSTOKININ
PROSELYTIZATION

15:8

CONSERVATIONIST
CONTRAVALLATION
ELECTROACOUSTIC
GOTTERDAMMERUNG
HETERODACTYLOUS
INSTANTANEOUSLY
INTERCHANGEABLE
LOPHOBRANCHIATE
NOTHINGARIANISM
POLYUNSATURATED
SCHOOLMASTERING
SUBLAPSARIANISM
TOTALITARIANISM
UNPARLIAMENTARY
WELLESTABLISHED
RHYNCHOBDELLIDA
WEATHERBOARDING
CIRCUMSCRIPTION
DOLICHOCEPHALIC
GLEICHSCHALTUNG
OLIGOSACCHARIDE
PHOSPHOCREATINE
BACKWARDLOOKING
CHRISTADELPHIAN
ECHOCARDIOGRAPH
EXTRAORDINARILY
ICHTHYODUROLITE
INCONSIDERATELY
INSUBORDINATION
STANDARDIZATION
ACKNOWLEDGEMENT
CHARACTERISTICS
ENTREPRENEURIAL
EXPERIMENTATION
INCOMPHEHENSION
INSTRUMENTALIST
INSTRUMENTATION
LIFETHREATENING
MISAPPREHENSION
NONPROFESSIONAL

OMNIDIRECTIONAL
PARLIAMENTARIAN
RESOURCEFULNESS
SCAPHOCEPHALATE
SYMPATHETICALLY
UNCOMPREHENDING
UNRIGHTEOUSNESS
DESERTIFICATION
DIVERSIFICATION
ELECTRIFICATION
INDEMNIFICATION
INTENSIFICATION
PERSONIFICATION
SELFSUFFICIENCY
STANDOFFISHNESS
INTELLIGIBILITY
TRANSFIGURATION
HETEROCHROMATIN
LONGSIGHTEDNESS
PHYSIOTHERAPIST
PSYCHOTHERAPIST
AIRCONDITIONING
COMPASSIONATELY
DISPASSIONATELY
IMPRESSIONISTIC
INCONSPICUOUSLY
NONCOMMISSIONED
NONPROFITMAKING
PERPENDICULARLY
PRESTIDIGITATOR
PRETENTIOUSNESS
PROFESSIONALISM
PROPORTIONATELY
PUNCTILIOUSNESS
SURREPTITIOUSLY
UNCOMPLIMENTARY
UNCONSCIOUSNESS
UNDERPRIVILEGED
CRYSTALLIZATION
CRYSTALLOGRAPHY
HOSPITALIZATION
MISINTELLIGENCE
NATIONALIZATION
PHOTOMULTIPLIER
RATIONALIZATION
SELFEXPLANATORY
THOUGHTLESSNESS
BIOACCUMULATION
DECONTAMINATION
ELECTROMAGNETIC
ELECTROMYOGRAPH
OPHTHALMOLOGIST
TEMPERAMENTALLY
TRIGONOMETRICAL
COINSTANTANEOUS
CONFIDENTIALITY
CONSCIENTIOUSLY
DIFFERENTIATION
DISADVANTAGEOUS
ELECTRONEGATIVE
EXCOMMUNICATION
GASTROENTERITIS
INCOMMENSURABLE
INTERVENTIONIST
REPRESENTATIVES
SACRAMENTMYSTIC
SYNCHRONIZATION
UNCOMMUNICATIVE
UNCOMPANIONABLE

UNDISTINGUISHED
ALLOTRIOMORPHIC
ANTHROPOLOGICAL
ANTHROPOMORPHIC
BACTERIOLOGICAL
BATTERYOPERATED
CHRONOLOGICALLY
CINEMATOGRAPHIC
CONTEMPORANEOUS
CORRESPONDINGLY
MICROSPORANGIUM
MICROSPOROPHYLL
PHARMACOLOGICAL
PSYCHOLOGICALLY
RADIOPHOTOGRAPH
SANCTIMONIOUSLY
TECHNOLOGICALLY
TRINITROTOLUENE
UNCEREMONIOUSLY
ELECTROPHORESIS
ELECTROPOSITIVE
PARASYMPATHETIC
PHILOSOPHICALLY
INCONSEQUENTIAL
ADVENTUROUSNESS
BIBLIOGRAPHICAL
COMPUTERIZATION
FAMILIARIZATION
GOVERNORGENERAL
HYPERCORRECTION
IMPENETRABILITY
MANOEUVRABILITY
NONGOVERNMENTAL
ONYCHOCRYPTOSIS
ORNITHORHYNCHUS
PHOSPHORESCENCE
TRUSTWORTHINESS
CHOLECYSTOKININ
DISILLUSIONMENT
DISSATISFACTION
DRAUGHTSMANSHIP
EUPHEMISTICALLY
LEATHERSTOCKING
NOTWITHSTANDING
PESSIMISTICALLY
SCHISTOSOMIASIS
STILPNOSIDERITE
STREPHOSYMBOLIA
THUNDERSTRICKEN
UNDEMONSTRATIVE
UNREPOSSESSING
UNSOPHISTICATED
UNSPORTSMANLIKE
ACCLIMATIZATION
ACQUISITIVENESS
AGRICULTURALIST
ANCYLOSTOMIASIS
AUTHORITATIVELY
CIRCUMSTANTIATE
CONFRONTATIONAL
CROSSOPTERYGIAN
DESTRUCTIVENESS
FLIBBERTIGIBBET
INCOMPATIBILITY
INQUISITIVENESS
INTERNATIONALLY
MALPRACTITIONER
MISCONSTRUCTION
OVERSENTIMENTAL

PALAEONTOLOGIST
PLENIPOTENTIARY
PROCRASTINATING
PROCRASTINATION
PROGNOSTICATION
PROSELYTIZATION
RUMPELSTILTSKIN
STRAIGHTFORWARD
TARSOMETATARSUS
TRANSLITERATION
UNCONDITIONALLY
UNEXCEPTIONABLE
CHURRIGUERESQUE
CONGRATULATIONS
DISTINGUISHABLE
INDIVIDUALISTIC
THERAPEUTICALLY
UNPRONOUNCEABLE
MISCHIEVOUSNESS
ATTORNEYGENERAL
HYPERTHYROIDISM

15:9

AUTHORITATIVELY
BIBLIOGRAPHICAL
CIRCUMSTANTIATE
CONFRONTATIONAL
ELECTROMAGNETIC
IMPENETRABILITY
INDIVIDUALISTIC
LIFETHREATENING
MANOEUVRABILITY
PARASYMPATHETIC
SELFEXPLANATORY
TARSOMETATARSUS
WELLESTABLISHED
ELECTROACOUSTIC
HETERODACTYLOUS
INCONSPICUOUSLY
OLIGOSACCHARIDE
OMNIDIRECTIONAL
PERPENDICULARLY
ACKNOWLEDGEMENT
RHYNCHOBDELLIDA
CHRISTADELPHIAN
CHURRIGUERESQUE
CROSSOPTERYGIAN
DOLICHOCEPHALIC
ELECTRONEGATIVE
INCONSIDERATELY
PHOSPHORESCENCE
PHYSIOTHERAPIST
PLENIPOTENTIARY
PSYCHOTHERAPIST
TEMPERAMENTALLY
THOUGHTLESSNESS
TRANSLITERATION
TRIGONOMETRICAL
DISSATISFACTION
RESOURCEFULNESS
STRAIGHTFORWARD
ATTORNEYGENERAL
CHRONOLOGICALLY
CINEMATOGRAPHIC
GOVERNORGENERAL
PRESTIDIGITATOR
PSYCHOLOGICALLY
TECHNOLOGICALLY
UNDISTINGUISHED

ELECTROPHORESIS
GLEICHSCHALTUNG
INCOMPHEHENSION
MISAPPREHENSION
ORNITHORHYNCHUS
PHILOSOPHICALLY
UNCOMPREHENDING
ACCLIMATIZATION
ACQUISITIVENESS
COMPUTERIZATION
CRYSTALLIZATION
DECONTAMINATION
DESERTIFICATION
DESTRUCTIVENESS
DISILLUSIONMENT
DISTINGUISHABLE
DIVERSIFICATION
ECHOCARDIOGRAPH
ELECTRIFICATION
EXCOMMUNICATION
EXTRAORDINARILY
FAMILIARIZATION
FLIBBERTIGIBBET
HOSPITALIZATION
INCOMPATIBILITY
INDEMNIFICATION
INQUISITIVENESS
INSUBORDINATION
INTELLIGIBILITY
INTENSIFICATION
INTERNATIONALLY
MALPRACTITIONER
NATIONALIZATION
OVERSENTIMENTAL
PERSONIFICATION
PROCRASTINATING
PROCRASTINATION
PROGNOSTICATION
PROSELYTIZATION
RATIONALIZATION
RUMPELSTILTSKIN
SELFSUFFICIENCY
STANDARDIZATION
STANDOFFISHNESS
STILPNOSIDERITE
SYNCHRONIZATION
UNCOMMUNICATIVE
UNCOMPANIONABLE
UNCONDITIONALLY
UNEXCEPTIONABLE
ANTHROPOLOGICAL
BACKWARDLOOKING
BACTERIOLOGICAL
CONGRATULATIONS
CONTRAVALLATION
MISINTELLIGENCE
PHARMACOLOGICAL
ALLOTRIOMORPHIC
ANTHROPOMORPHIC
DRAUGHTSMANSHIP
GOTTERDAMMERUNG
UNCOMPLIMENTARY
UNPARLIAMENTARY
UNSPORTSMANLIKE
CORRESPONDINGLY
ENTREPRENEURIAL
EXPERIMENTATION
INSTANTANEOUSLY
INSTRUMENTALIST

INSTRUMENTATION
INTERCHANGEABLE
LOPHOBRANCHIATE
NONGOVERNMENTAL
PARLIAMENTARIAN
SANCTIMONIOUSLY
UNCEREMONIOUSLY
UNPRONOUNCEABLE
ADVENTUROUSNESS
ANCYLOSTOMIASIS
COMPASSIONATELY
CRYSTALLOGRAPHY
DISPASSIONATELY
ELECTROPOSITIVE
IMPRESSIONISTIC
MISCHIEVOUSNESS
OPHTHALMOLOGIST
PALAEONTOLOGIST
PRETENTIOUSNESS
PROFESSIONALISM
PROPORTIONATELY
PUNCTILIOUSNESS
SCHISTOSOMIASIS
UNCONSCIOUSNESS
UNRIGHTEOUSNESS
WEATHERBOARDING
BATTERYOPERATED
SCAPHOCEPHALATE
CHARACTERISTICS
CIRCUMSCRIPTION
CONTEMPORANEOUS
HETEROCHROMATIN
HYPERCORRECTION
HYPERTHYROIDISM
MICROSPORANGIUM
MICROSPOROPHYLL
MISCONSTRUCTION
NOTHINGARIANISM
PHOSPHOCREATINE
SUBLAPSARIANISM
TOTALITARIANISM
INCOMMENSURABLE
NONCOMMISSIONED
NONPROFESSIONAL
SCHOOLMASTERING
UNPREPOSSESSING
AIRCONDITIONING
CHOLECYSTOKININ
COINSTANTANEOUS
CONFIDENTIALITY
CONSCIENTIOUSLY
CONSERVATIONIST
DIFFERENTIATION
DISADVANTAGEOUS
EUPHEMISTICALLY
GASTROENTERITIS
INTERVENTIONIST
LEATHERSTOCKING
LONGSIGHTEDNESS
NONPROFITMAKING
NOTWITHSTANDING
PESSIMISTICALLY
PHOTOMULTIPLIER
POLYUNSATURATED
RADIOPHOTOGRAPH
REPRESENTATIVES
SACRAMENTMYSTIC
SURREPTITIOUSLY
SYMPATHETICALLY

THERAPEUTICALLY
THUNDERSTRICKEN
TRINITROTOLUENE
TRUSTWORTHINESS
UNDEMONSTRATIVE
UNSOPHISTICATED
AGRICULTURALIST
BIOACCUMULATION
ICHTHYODUROLITE
INCONSEQUENTIAL
TRANSFIGURATION
UNDERPRIVILEGED
ELECTROMYOGRAPH
ONYCHOCRYPTOSIS
STREPHOSYMBOLIA

15:10

COINSTANTANEOUS
CONGRATULATIONS
CONTEMPORANEOUS
DISADVANTAGEOUS
DISSATISFACTION
DRAUGHTSMANSHIP
GLEICHSCHALTUNG
MICROSPORANGIUM
NOTWITHSTANDING
REPRESENTATIVES
UNSPORTSMANLIKE
WEATHERBOARDING
IMPENETRABILITY
INCOMPATIBILITY
INTELLIGIBILITY
MANOEUVRABILITY
DESERTIFICATION
DIVERSIFICATION
ELECTRIFICATION
EXCOMMUNICATION
INDEMNIFICATION
INTENSIFICATION
LOPHOBRANCHIATE
PERSONIFICATION
PROGNOSTICATION
SELFSUFFICIENCY
UNCOMMUNICATIVE
UNPRONOUNCEABLE
CORRESPONDINGLY
STILPNOSIDERITE
ATTORNEYGENERAL
BATTERYOPERATED
ENTREPRENEURIAL
GASTROENTERITIS
GOVERNORGENERAL
HYPERCORRECTION
INCOMPHEHENSION
INCONSEQUENTIAL
INSTANTANEOUSLY
LONGSIGHTEDNESS
MISAPPREHENSION
PHOSPHOCREATINE
RHYNCHOBDELLIDA
UNCOMPLIMENTARY
UNCOMPREHENDING
UNPARLIAMENTARY
UNPREPOSSESSING
ACKNOWLEDGEMENT
CRYSTALLOGRAPHY
ELECTROMAGNETIC
ELECTRONEGATIVE
FLIBBERTIGIBBET

INTERCHANGEABLE
OLIGOSACCHARIDE
SCAPHOCEPHALATE
TRUSTWORTHINESS
AIRCONDITIONING
CHARACTERISTICS
CHRONOLOGICALLY
CIRCUMSCRIPTION
CONFIDENTIALITY
CONSCIENTIOUSLY
CONSERVATIONIST
DIFFERENTIATION
EUPHEMISTICALLY
INTERVENTIONIST
MISINTELLIGENCE
NOTHINGARIANISM
PESSIMISTICALLY
PHILOSOPHICALLY
PHOTOMULTIPLIER
PRESTIDIGITATOR
PSYCHOLOGICALLY
SANCTIMONIOUSLY
SUBLAPSARIANISM
SURREPTITIOUSLY
SYMPATHETICALLY
TECHNOLOGICALLY
THERAPEUTICALLY
TOTALITARIANISM
UNCEREMONIOUSLY
UNDERPRIVILEGED
UNSOPHISTICATED
BIOACCUMULATION
CHRISTADELPHIAN
CONTRAVALLATION
INDIVIDUALISTIC
OPHTHALMOLOGIST
PALAEONTOLOGIST
RUMPELSTILTSKIN
WELLESTABLISHED
ANCYLOSTOMIASIS
GOTTERDAMMERUNG
NONGOVERNMENTAL
NONPROFITMAKING
OVERSENTIMENTAL
SACRAMENTMYSTIC
SCHISTOSOMIASIS
STREPHOSYMBOLIA
CIRCUMSTANTIATE
COMPASSIONATELY
DECONTAMINATION
DISPASSIONATELY
EXTRAORDINARILY
IMPRESSIONISTIC
INSUBORDINATION
PLENIPOTENTIARY
PROCRASTINATING
PROCRASTINATION
PROFESSIONALISM
PROPORTIONATELY
SELFEXPLANATORY
TEMPERAMENTALLY
ALLOTRIOMORPHIC
ANTHROPOLOGICAL
ANTHROPOMORPHIC
BACKWARDLOOKING
BACTERIOLOGICAL
CHOLECYSTOKININ
DISILLUSIONMENT
ECHOCARDIOGRAPH

ELECTROACOUSTIC
ELECTROMYOGRAPH
ELECTROPHORESIS
HETEROCHROMATIN
HYPERTHYROIDISM
INTERNATIONALLY
LEATHERSTOCKING
MICROSPOROPHYLL
PHARMACOLOGICAL
RADIOPHOTOGRAPH
STRAIGHTFORWARD
TRINITROTOLUENE
UNCOMPANIONABLE
UNCONDITIONALLY
UNEXCEPTIONABLE
BIBLIOGRAPHICAL
DOLICHOCEPHALIC
ONYCHOCRYPTOSIS
AGRICULTURALIST
CHURRIGUERESQUE
CINEMATOGRAPHIC
CROSSOPTERYGIAN
ICHTHYODUROLITE
INCONSIDERATELY
PHYSIOTHERAPIST
PSYCHOTHERAPIST
THUNDERSTRICKEN
TRANSFIGURATION
TRANSLITERATION
UNDEMONSTRATIVE
DISTINGUISHABLE
ELECTROPOSITIVE
NONCOMMISSIONED
NONPROFESSIONAL
PHOSPHORESCENCE
STANDOFFISHNESS
THOUGHTLESSNESS
AUTHORITATIVELY
CONFRONTATIONAL
EXPERIMENTATION
HETERODACTYLOUS
INSTRUMENTALIST
INSTRUMENTATION
LIFETHREATENING
MALPRACTITIONER
OMNIDIRECTIONAL
PARASYMPATHETIC
PARLIAMENTARIAN
SCHOOLMASTERING
TARSOMETATARSUS
TRIGONOMETRICAL
ADVENTUROUSNESS
INCOMMENSURABLE
INCONSPICUOUSLY
MISCHIEVOUSNESS
MISCONSTRUCTION
PERPENDICULARLY
POLYUNSATURATED
PRETENTIOUSNESS
PUNCTILIOUSNESS
RESOURCEFULNESS
UNCONSCIOUSNESS
UNDISTINGUISHED
UNRIGHTEOUSNESS
ACQUISITIVENESS
DESTRUCTIVENESS
INQUISITIVENESS
ORNITHORHYNCHUS
ACCLIMATIZATION

COMPUTERIZATION
CRYSTALLIZATION
FAMILIARIZATION
HOSPITALIZATION
NATIONALIZATION
PROSELYTIZATION
RATIONALIZATION
STANDARDIZATION
SYNCHRONIZATION

15:11

ACCLIMATIZATION
AGRICULTURALIST
BIOACCUMULATION
CINEMATOGRAPHIC
COMPASSIONATELY
COMPUTERIZATION
CONFIDENTIALITY
CONTRAVALLATION
CRYSTALLIZATION
DECONTAMINATION
DESERTIFICATION
DIFFERENTIATION
DISPASSIONATELY
DIVERSIFICATION
ELECTRIFICATION
ELECTRONEGATIVE
EXCOMMUNICATION
EXPERIMENTATION
EXTRAORDINARILY
FAMILIARIZATION
HOSPITALIZATION
INCONSIDERATELY
INDEMNIFICATION
INSTRUMENTALIST
INSTRUMENTATION
INSUBORDINATION
INTENSIFICATION
NATIONALIZATION
NONPROFITMAKING
NOTHINGARIANISM
OLIGOSACCHARIDE
PARLIAMENTARIAN
PERSONIFICATION
PHOSPHOCREATINE
PHYSIOTHERAPIST
PROCRASTINATING
PROCRASTINATION
PROFESSIONALISM
PROGNOSTICATION
PROPORTIONATELY
PROSELYTIZATION
PSYCHOTHERAPIST
RATIONALIZATION
SCAPHOCEPHALATE
SELFEXPLANATORY
STANDARDIZATION
SUBLAPSARIANISM
SYNCHRONIZATION
TARSOMETATARSUS
TOTALITARIANISM
TRANSFIGURATION
TRANSLITERATION
UNCOMMUNICATIVE
UNDEMONSTRATIVE
STREPHOSYMBOLIA
CHRONOLOGICALLY
DISSATISFACTION
EUPHEMISTICALLY

HYPERCORRECTION
LEATHERSTOCKING
MISCONSTRUCTION
PESSIMISTICALLY
PHILOSOPHICALLY
PHOSPHORESCENCE
PSYCHOLOGICALLY
SYMPATHETICALLY
TECHNOLOGICALLY
THERAPEUTICALLY
UNSOPHISTICATED
LONGSIGHTEDNESS
ACKNOWLEDGEMENT
ACQUISITIVENESS
CHURRIGUERESQUE
DESTRUCTIVENESS
GOTTERDAMMERUNG
INQUISITIVENESS
INTERCHANGEABLE
LIFETHREATENING
NONGOVERNMENTAL
OVERSENTIMENTAL
SCHOOLMASTERING
STILPNOSIDERITE
UNPRONOUNCEABLE
ANTHROPOLOGICAL
BACTERIOLOGICAL
DISADVANTAGEOUS
ECHOCARDIOGRAPH
ELECTROMYOGRAPH
MISINTELLIGENCE
PHARMACOLOGICAL
RADIOPHOTOGRAPH
BIBLIOGRAPHICAL
DISTINGUISHABLE
DOLICHOCEPHALIC
LOPHOBRANCHIATE
PARASYMPATHETIC
STANDOFFISHNESS
ANCYLOSTOMIASIS
AUTHORITATIVELY
CONFRONTATIONAL
CORRESPONDINGLY
ELECTROPOSITIVE
FLIBBERTIGIBBET
HYPERTHYROIDISM
IMPENETRABILITY
IMPRESSIONISTIC
INCOMPATIBILITY
INDIVIDUALISTIC
INTELLIGIBILITY
MALPRACTITIONER
MANOEUVRABILITY
NONCOMMISSIONED
NONPROFESSIONAL
OMNIDIRECTIONAL
SCHISTOSOMIASIS
SELFSUFFICIENCY
THUNDERSTRICKEN
TRUSTWORTHINESS
UNDISTINGUISHED
WELLESTABLISHED
CHOLECYSTOKININ
GLEICHSCHALTUNG
PERPENDICULARLY
RESOURCEFULNESS
RHYNCHOBDELLIDA
TRINITROTOLUENE
UNDERPRIVILEGED

HETEROCHROMATIN
ATTORNEYGENERAL
COINSTANTANEOUS
CONTEMPORANEOUS
DISILLUSIONMENT
DRAUGHTSMANSHIP
ELECTROMAGNETIC
GOVERNORGENERAL
INCOMPHEHENSION
INCONSEQUENTIAL
INTERNATIONALLY
MICROSPORANGIUM
MISAPPREHENSION
NOTWITHSTANDING
ORNITHORHYNCHUS
UNCOMPANIONABLE
UNCOMPLIMENTARY
UNCOMPREHENDING
UNCONDITIONALLY
UNEXCEPTIONABLE
UNPARLIAMENTARY
UNSPORTSMANLIKE
AIRCONDITIONING
BACKWARDLOOKING
CONSCIENTIOUSLY
CONSERVATIONIST
ICHTHYODUROLITE
INCONSPICUOUSLY
INSTANTANEOUSLY
INTERVENTIONIST
OPHTHALMOLOGIST
PALAEONTOLOGIST
SANCTIMONIOUSLY
SURREPTITIOUSLY
UNCEREMONIOUSLY
CHRISTADELPHIAN
CIRCUMSCRIPTION
MICROSPOROPHYLL
PHOTOMULTIPLIER
ALLOTRIOMORPHIC
ANTHROPOMORPHIC
BATTERYOPERATED
CRYSTALLOGRAPHY
ELECTROPHORESIS
GASTROENTERITIS
INCOMMENSURABLE
POLYUNSATURATED
STRAIGHTFORWARD
TRIGONOMETRICAL
WEATHERBOARDING
ADVENTUROUSNESS
CHARACTERISTICS
MISCHIEVOUSNESS
PRETENTIOUSNESS
PUNCTILIOUSNESS
THOUGHTLESSNESS
UNCONSCIOUSNESS
UNPREPOSSESSING
UNRIGHTEOUSNESS
CIRCUMSTANTIATE
CONGRATULATIONS
ONYCHOCRYPTOSIS
PLENIPOTENTIARY
PRESTIDIGITATOR
REPRESENTATIVES
RUMPELSTILTSKIN
TEMPERAMENTALLY
ELECTROACOUSTIC
ENTREPRENEURIAL

CROSSOPTERYGIAN
HETERODACTYLOUS
SACRAMENTMYSTIC

15:12

ANCYLOSTOMIASIS
BATTERYOPERATED
CHRONOLOGICALLY
CRYSTALLOGRAPHY
DISTINGUISHABLE
DOLICHOCEPHALIC
EUPHEMISTICALLY
HETEROCHROMATIN
INCOMMENSURABLE
INTERCHANGEABLE
INTERNATIONALLY
PERPENDICULARLY
PESSIMISTICALLY
PHILOSOPHICALLY
POLYUNSATURATED
PRESTIDIGITATOR
PSYCHOLOGICALLY
SCHISTOSOMIASIS
SYMPATHETICALLY
TECHNOLOGICALLY
TEMPERAMENTALLY
THERAPEUTICALLY
UNCOMPANIONABLE
UNCONDITIONALLY
UNEXCEPTIONABLE
UNPRONOUNCEABLE
UNSOPHISTICATED
FLIBBERTIGIBBET
ORNITHORHYNCHUS
THUNDERSTRICKEN
HYPERTHYROIDISM
NOTWITHSTANDING
UNCOMPREHENDING
WEATHERBOARDING
ATTORNEYGENERAL
COINSTANTANEOUS
CONTEMPORANEOUS
DISADVANTAGEOUS
ELECTROMAGNETIC
ELECTROPHORESIS
GOVERNORGENERAL
MISINTELLIGENCE
PARASYMPATHETIC
PHOSPHORESCENCE
SELFSUFFICIENCY
UNDERPRIVILEGED
CROSSOPTERYGIAN
MICROSPORANGIUM
OPHTHALMOLOGIST
PALAEONTOLOGIST
CHRISTADELPHIAN
MICROSPOROPHYLL
ANTHROPOLOGICAL
BACTERIOLOGICAL
BIBLIOGRAPHICAL
CHOLECYSTOKININ
CIRCUMSTANTIATE
CONGRATULATIONS
GASTROENTERITIS
LOPHOBRANCHIATE
PHARMACOLOGICAL
PLENIPOTENTIARY
REPRESENTATIVES
TRIGONOMETRICAL

BACKWARDLOOKING
LEATHERSTOCKING
NONPROFITMAKING
AGRICULTURALIST
CONFIDENTIALITY
HETERODACTYLOUS
ICHTHYODUROLITE
IMPENETRABILITY
INCOMPATIBILITY
INSTRUMENTALIST
INTELLIGIBILITY
MANOEUVRABILITY
PHOTOMULTIPLIER
PROFESSIONALISM
RHYNCHOBDELLIDA
SCAPHOCEPHALATE
UNSPORTSMANLIKE
ACKNOWLEDGEMENT
DISILLUSIONMENT
ACQUISITIVENESS
ADVENTUROUSNESS
AIRCONDITIONING
CONSERVATIONIST
CORRESPONDINGLY
DESTRUCTIVENESS
INQUISITIVENESS
INTERVENTIONIST
LIFETHREATENING
LONGSIGHTEDNESS
MISCHIEVOUSNESS
NONGOVERNMENTAL
NOTHINGARIANISM
OVERSENTIMENTAL
PRETENTIOUSNESS
PUNCTILIOUSNESS
RESOURCEFULNESS
STANDOFFISHNESS
SUBLAPSARIANISM
THOUGHTLESSNESS
TOTALITARIANISM
TRUSTWORTHINESS
UNCONSCIOUSNESS
UNRIGHTEOUSNESS
CONFRONTATIONAL
MALPRACTITIONER
NONCOMMISSIONED
NONPROFESSIONAL
OMNIDIRECTIONAL
ONYCHOCRYPTOSIS
STREPHOSYMBOLIA
ALLOTRIOMORPHIC
ANTHROPOMORPHIC
CINEMATOGRAPHIC
PHYSIOTHERAPIST
PSYCHOTHERAPIST
ECHOCARDIOGRAPH
ELECTROMYOGRAPH
ENTREPRENEURIAL
EXTRAORDINARILY
GOTTERDAMMERUNG
OLIGOSACCHARIDE
PARLIAMENTARIAN
RADIOPHOTOGRAPH
SCHOOLMASTERING
STILPNOSIDERITE
TARSOMETATARSUS
CHURRIGUERESQUE
DRAUGHTSMANSHIP
ELECTROACOUSTIC

IMPRESSIONISTIC
INCOMPHEHENSION
INDIVIDUALISTIC
MISAPPREHENSION
RUMPELSTILTSKIN
SACRAMENTMYSTIC
UNDISTINGUISHED
UNPREPOSSESSING
WELLESTABLISHED
ACCLIMATIZATION
BIOACCUMULATION
CHARACTERISTICS
CIRCUMSCRIPTION
COMPASSIONATELY
COMPUTERIZATION
CONTRAVALLATION
CRYSTALLIZATION
DECONTAMINATION
DESERTIFICATION
DIFFERENTIATION
DISPASSIONATELY
DISSATISFACTION
DIVERSIFICATION
ELECTRIFICATION
ELECTRONEGATIVE
ELECTROPOSITIVE
EXCOMMUNICATION
EXPERIMENTATION
FAMILIARIZATION
GLEICHSCHALTUNG
HOSPITALIZATION
HYPERCORRECTION
INCONSEQUENTIAL
INCONSIDERATELY
INDEMNIFICATION
INSTRUMENTATION
INSUBORDINATION
INTENSIFICATION
MISCONSTRUCTION
NATIONALIZATION
PERSONIFICATION
PHOSPHOCREATINE
PROCRASTINATING
PROCRASTINATION
PROGNOSTICATION
PROPORTIONATELY
PROSELYTIZATION
RATIONALIZATION
SELFEXPLANATORY
STANDARDIZATION
SYNCHRONIZATION
TRANSFIGURATION
TRANSLITERATION
UNCOMMUNICATIVE
UNCOMPLIMENTARY
UNDEMONSTRATIVE
UNPARLIAMENTARY
CONSCIENTIOUSLY
INCONSPICUOUSLY
INSTANTANEOUSLY
SANCTIMONIOUSLY
SURREPTITIOUSLY
TRINITROTOLUENE
UNCEREMONIOUSLY
AUTHORITATIVELY
STRAIGHTFORWARD

15:13

CIRCUMSTANTIATE

ECHOCARDIOGRAPH
ELECTROMYOGRAPH
LOPHOBRANCHIATE
PLENIPOTENTIARY
RADIOPHOTOGRAPH
SCAPHOCEPHALATE
STRAIGHTFORWARD
UNCOMPLIMENTARY
UNPARLIAMENTARY
DISTINGUISHABLE
FLIBBERTIGIBBET
INCOMMENSURABLE
INTERCHANGEABLE
UNCOMPANIONABLE
UNEXCEPTIONABLE
UNPRONOUNCEABLE
ANTHROPOLOGICAL
BACTERIOLOGICAL
BIBLIOGRAPHICAL
PHARMACOLOGICAL
TRIGONOMETRICAL
ACKNOWLEDGEMENT
ACQUISITIVENESS
ADVENTUROUSNESS
AUTHORITATIVELY
COMPASSIONATELY
DESTRUCTIVENESS
DISILLUSIONMENT
DISPASSIONATELY
INCONSIDERATELY
INQUISITIVENESS
LONGSIGHTEDNESS
MISCHIEVOUSNESS
PRETENTIOUSNESS
PROPORTIONATELY
PUNCTILIOUSNESS
RESOURCEFULNESS
STANDOFFISHNESS
THOUGHTLESSNESS
TRINITROTOLUENE
TRUSTWORTHINESS
UNCONSCIOUSNESS
UNRIGHTEOUSNESS
CORRESPONDINGLY
UNDERPRIVILEGED
ALLOTRIOMORPHIC
ANTHROPOMORPHIC
CINEMATOGRAPHIC
DRAUGHTSMANSHIP
ORNITHORHYNCHUS
UNDISTINGUISHED
WELLESTABLISHED
ACCLIMATIZATION
AGRICULTURALIST
AIRCONDITIONING
BACKWARDLOOKING
BIOACCUMULATION
CHARACTERISTICS
CHRISTADELPHIAN
CIRCUMSCRIPTION
COMPUTERIZATION
CONFIDENTIALITY
CONSERVATIONIST
CONTRAVALLATION
CROSSOPTERYGIAN
CRYSTALLIZATION
DECONTAMINATION
DESERTIFICATION
DIFFERENTIATION

DISSATISFACTION
DIVERSIFICATION
ELECTRIFICATION
ELECTRONEGATIVE
ELECTROPOSITIVE
ENTREPRENEURIAL
EXCOMMUNICATION
EXPERIMENTATION
EXTRAORDINARILY
FAMILIARIZATION
HOSPITALIZATION
HYPERCORRECTION
HYPERTHYROIDISM
ICHTHYODUROLITE
IMPENETRABILITY
INCOMPATIBILITY
INCOMPHEHENSION
INCONSEQUENTIAL
INDEMNIFICATION
INSTRUMENTALIST
INSTRUMENTATION
INSUBORDINATION
INTELLIGIBILITY
INTENSIFICATION
INTERVENTIONIST
LEATHERSTOCKING
LIFETHREATENING
MANOEUVRABILITY
MICROSPORANGIUM
MISAPPREHENSION
MISCONSTRUCTION
NATIONALIZATION
NONPROFITMAKING
NOTHINGARIANISM
NOTWITHSTANDING
OLIGOSACCHARIDE
OPHTHALMOLOGIST
PALAEONTOLOGIST
PARLIAMENTARIAN
PERSONIFICATION
PHOSPHOCREATINE
PHOTOMULTIPLIER
PHYSIOTHERAPIST
PROCRASTINATING
PROCRASTINATION
PROFESSIONALISM
PROGNOSTICATION
PROSELYTIZATION
PSYCHOTHERAPIST
RATIONALIZATION
RHYNCHOBDELLIDA
SCHOOLMASTERING
STANDARDIZATION
STILPNOSIDERITE
SUBLAPSARIANISM
SYNCHRONIZATION
TOTALITARIANISM
TRANSFIGURATION
TRANSLITERATION
UNCOMMUNICATIVE
UNCOMPREHENDING
UNDEMONSTRATIVE
UNPREPOSSESSING
UNSPORTSMANLIKE
WEATHERBOARDING
RUMPELSTILTSKIN
THUNDERSTRICKEN
CHRONOLOGICALLY
DOLICHOCEPHALIC

EUPHEMISTICALLY
INTERNATIONALLY
PESSIMISTICALLY
PHILOSOPHICALLY
PSYCHOLOGICALLY
STREPHOSYMBOLIA
SYMPATHETICALLY
TECHNOLOGICALLY
TEMPERAMENTALLY
THERAPEUTICALLY
UNCONDITIONALLY
CHOLECYSTOKININ
CONFRONTATIONAL
MALPRACTITIONER
MISINTELLIGENCE
NONCOMMISSIONED
NONPROFESSIONAL
OMNIDIRECTIONAL
PHOSPHORESCENCE
SELFSUFFICIENCY
COINSTANTANEOUS
CONGRATULATIONS
CONTEMPORANEOUS
DISADVANTAGEOUS
HETERODACTYLOUS
SELFEXPLANATORY
CRYSTALLOGRAPHY
CHURRIGUERESQUE
ATTORNEYGENERAL
GOVERNORGENERAL
PERPENDICULARLY
ANCYLOSTOMIASIS
CONSCIENTIOUSLY
ELECTROPHORESIS
INCONSPICUOUSLY
INSTANTANEOUSLY
ONYCHOCRYPTOSIS
SANCTIMONIOUSLY
SCHISTOSOMIASIS
SURREPTITIOUSLY
TARSOMETATARSUS
UNCEREMONIOUSLY
BATTERYOPERATED
ELECTROACOUSTIC
ELECTROMAGNETIC
GASTROENTERITIS
HETEROCHROMATIN
IMPRESSIONISTIC
INDIVIDUALISTIC
NONGOVERNMENTAL
OVERSENTIMENTAL
PARASYMPATHETIC
POLYUNSATURATED
PRESTIDIGITATOR
SACRAMENTMYSTIC
UNSOPHISTICATED
GLEICHSCHALTUNG
GOTTERDAMMERUNG
REPRESENTATIVES
MICROSPOROPHYLL

15:14

ANTHROPOLOGICAL
ATTORNEYGENERAL
BACTERIOLOGICAL
BIBLIOGRAPHICAL
CHRISTADELPHIAN
CONFRONTATIONAL
CROSSOPTERYGIAN

ENTREPRENEURIAL
GOVERNORGENERAL
INCONSEQUENTIAL
NONGOVERNMENTAL
NONPROFESSIONAL
OMNIDIRECTIONAL
OVERSENTIMENTAL
PARLIAMENTARIAN
PHARMACOLOGICAL
TRIGONOMETRICAL
CHARACTERISTICS
MISINTELLIGENCE
PHOSPHORESCENCE
SELFSUFFICIENCY
OLIGOSACCHARIDE
RHYNCHOBDELLIDA
BATTERYOPERATED
FLIBBERTIGIBBET
MALPRACTITIONER
NONCOMMISSIONED
PHOTOMULTIPLIER
POLYUNSATURATED
REPRESENTATIVES
THUNDERSTRICKEN
UNDERPRIVILEGED
UNDISTINGUISHED
UNSOPHISTICATED
WELLESTABLISHED
CRYSTALLOGRAPHY
ALLOTRIOMORPHIC
ANCYLOSTOMIASIS
ANTHROPOMORPHIC
CHOLECYSTOKININ
CINEMATOGRAPHIC
DOLICHOCEPHALIC
DRAUGHTSMANSHIP
ELECTROACOUSTIC
ELECTROMAGNETIC
ELECTROPHORESIS
GASTROENTERITIS
HETEROCHROMATIN
IMPRESSIONISTIC
INDIVIDUALISTIC
ONYCHOCRYPTOSIS
PARASYMPATHETIC
RUMPELSTILTSKIN
SACRAMENTMYSTIC
SCHISTOSOMIASIS
STREPHOSYMBOLIA
UNSPORTSMANLIKE
AUTHORITATIVELY
CHRONOLOGICALLY
COMPASSIONATELY
CONSCIENTIOUSLY
CORRESPONDINGLY
DISPASSIONATELY
DISTINGUISHABLE
EUPHEMISTICALLY
EXTRAORDINARILY
INCOMMENSURABLE
INCONSIDERATELY
INCONSPICUOUSLY
INSTANTANEOUSLY
INTERCHANGEABLE
INTERNATIONALLY
MICROSPOROPHYLL
PERPENDICULARLY
PESSIMISTICALLY
PHILOSOPHICALLY

PROPORTIONATELY
PSYCHOLOGICALLY
SANCTIMONIOUSLY
SURREPTITIOUSLY
SYMPATHETICALLY
TECHNOLOGICALLY
TEMPERAMENTALLY
THERAPEUTICALLY
UNCEREMONIOUSLY
UNCOMPANIONABLE
UNCONDITIONALLY
UNEXCEPTIONABLE
UNPRONOUNCEABLE
ACKNOWLEDGEMENT
AIRCONDITIONING
BACKWARDLOOKING
CONGRATULATIONS
DISILLUSIONMENT
GLEICHSCHALTUNG
GOTTERDAMMERUNG
LEATHERSTOCKING
LIFETHREATENING
NONPROFITMAKING
NOTWITHSTANDING
PHOSPHOCREATINE
PROCRASTINATION
SCHOOLMASTERING
TRINITROTOLUENE
UNCOMPREHENDING
UNPREPOSSESSING
WEATHERBOARDING
ACCLIMATIZATION
BIOACCUMULATION
CIRCUMSCRIPTION
COMPUTERIZATION
CONTRAVALLATION
CRYSTALLIZATION
DECONTAMINATION
DESERTIFICATION
DIFFERENTIATION
DISSATISFACTION
DIVERSIFICATION
ELECTRIFICATION
EXCOMMUNICATION
EXPERIMENTATION
FAMILIARIZATION
HOSPITALIZATION
HYPERCORRECTION
INCOMPHEHENSION
INDEMNIFICATION
INSTRUMENTATION
INSUBORDINATION
INTENSIFICATION
MISAPPREHENSION
MISCONSTRUCTION
NATIONALIZATION
PERSONIFICATION
PRESTIDIGITATOR
PROCRASTINATION
PROGNOSTICATION
PROSELYTIZATION
RATIONALIZATION
STANDARDIZATION
SYNCHRONIZATION
TRANSFIGURATION
TRANSLITERATION
ECHOCARDIOGRAPH
ELECTROMYOGRAPH
RADIOPHOTOGRAPH

◻◻◻◻◻◻◻◻◻◻◻◻◻◻■

PLENIPOTENTIARY
SELFEXPLANATORY
STRAIGHTFORWARD
UNCOMPLIMENTARY
UNPARLIAMENTARY
ACQUISITIVENESS
ADVENTUROUSNESS
AGRICULTURALIST
CONSERVATIONIST
DESTRUCTIVENESS
HYPERTHYROIDISM
INQUISITIVENESS
INSTRUMENTALIST
INTERVENTIONIST
LONGSIGHTEDNESS
MISCHIEVOUSNESS
NOTHINGARIANISM
OPHTHALMOLOGIST
PALAEONTOLOGIST
PHYSIOTHERAPIST
PRETENTIOUSNESS
PROFESSIONALISM
PSYCHOTHERAPIST
PUNCTILIOUSNESS
RESOURCEFULNESS
STANDOFFISHNESS
SUBLAPSARIANISM
THOUGHTLESSNESS
TOTALITARIANISM
TRUSTWORTHINESS
UNCONSCIOUSNESS
UNRIGHTEOUSNESS
CIRCUMSTANTIATE
CONFIDENTIALITY
ICHTHYODUROLITE
IMPENETRABILITY
INCOMPATIBILITY
INTELLIGIBILITY
LOPHOBRANCHIATE
MANOEUVRABILITY
SCAPHOCEPHALATE
STILPNOSIDERITE
CHURRIGUERESQUE
COINSTANTANEOUS
CONTEMPORANEOUS
DISADVANTAGEOUS
HETERODACTYLOUS
MICROSPORANGIUM
ORNITHORHYNCHUS
TARSOMETATARSUS
ELECTRONEGATIVE
ELECTROPOSITIVE
UNCOMMUNICATIVE
UNDEMONSTRATIVE

15:15

RHYNCHOBDELLIDA
STREPHOSYMBOLIA
ALLOTRIOMORPHIC
ANTHROPOMORPHIC
CINEMATOGRAPHIC
DOLICHOCEPHALIC
ELECTROACOUSTIC
ELECTROMAGNETIC
IMPRESSIONISTIC
INDIVIDUALISTIC

PARASYMPATHETIC
SACRAMENTMYSTIC
BATTERYOPERATED
NONCOMMISSIONED
POLYUNSATURATED
STRAIGHTFORWARD
UNDERPRIVILEGED
UNDISTINGUISHED
UNSOPHISTICATED
WELLESTABLISHED
CHURRIGUERESQUE
CIRCUMSTANTIATE
DISTINGUISHABLE
ELECTRONEGATIVE
ELECTROPOSITIVE
ICHTHYODUROLITE
INCOMMENSURABLE
INTERCHANGEABLE
LOPHOBRANCHIATE
MISINTELLIGENCE
OLIGOSACCHARIDE
PHOSPHOCREATINE
PHOSPHORESCENCE
SCAPHOCEPHALATE
STILPNOSIDERITE
TRINITROTOLUENE
UNCOMMUNICATIVE
UNCOMPANIONABLE
UNDEMONSTRATIVE
UNEXCEPTIONABLE
UNPRONOUNCEABLE
UNSPORTSMANLIKE
AIRCONDITIONING
BACKWARDLOOKING
GLEICHSCHALTUNG
GOTTERDAMMERUNG
LEATHERSTOCKING
LIFETHREATENING
NONPROFITMAKING
NOTWITHSTANDING
PROCRASTINATING
SCHOOLMASTERING
UNCOMPREHENDING
UNPREPOSSESSING
WEATHERBOARDING
ECHOCARDIOGRAPH
ELECTROMYOGRAPH
RADIOPHOTOGRAPH
ANTHROPOLOGICAL
ATTORNEYGENERAL
BACTERIOLOGICAL
BIBLIOGRAPHICAL
CONFRONTATIONAL
ENTREPRENEURIAL
GOVERNORGENERAL
INCONSEQUENTIAL
MICROSPOROPHYLL
NONGOVERNMENTAL
NONPROFESSIONAL
OMNIDIRECTIONAL
OVERSENTIMENTAL
PHARMACOLOGICAL
TRIGONOMETRICAL
HYPERTHYROIDISM
MICROSPORANGIUM

NOTHINGARIANISM
PROFESSIONALISM
SUBLAPSARIANISM
TOTALITARIANISM
ACCLIMATIZATION
BIOACCUMULATION
CHOLECYSTOKININ
CHRISTADELPHIAN
CIRCUMSCRIPTION
COMPUTERIZATION
CONTRAVALLATION
CROSSOPTERYGIAN
CRYSTALLIZATION
DECONTAMINATION
DESERTIFICATION
DIFFERENTIATION
DISSATISFACTION
DIVERSIFICATION
ELECTRIFICATION
EXCOMMUNICATION
EXPERIMENTATION
FAMILIARIZATION
HETEROCHROMATIN
HOSPITALIZATION
HYPERCORRECTION
INCOMPHEHENSION
INDEMNIFICATION
INSTRUMENTATION
INSUBORDINATION
INTENSIFICATION
MISAPPREHENSION
MISCONSTRUCTION
NATIONALIZATION
PARLIAMENTARIAN
PERSONIFICATION
PROCRASTINATION
PROGNOSTICATION
PROSELYTIZATION
RATIONALIZATION
RUMPELSTILTSKIN
STANDARDIZATION
SYNCHRONIZATION
THUNDERSTRICKEN
TRANSFIGURATION
TRANSLITERATION
DRAUGHTSMANSHIP
MALPRACTITIONER
PHOTOMULTIPLIER
PRESTIDIGITATOR
ACQUISITIVENESS
ADVENTUROUSNESS
ANCYLOSTOMIASIS
CHARACTERISTICS
COINSTANTANEOUS
CONGRATULATIONS
CONTEMPORANEOUS
DESTRUCTIVENESS
DISADVANTAGEOUS
ELECTROPHORESIS
GASTROENTERITIS
HETERODACTYLOUS
INQUISITIVENESS
LONGSIGHTEDNESS
MISCHIEVOUSNESS
ONYCHOCRYPTOSIS

ORNITHORHYNCHUS
PRETENTIOUSNESS
PUNCTILIOUSNESS
REPRESENTATIVES
RESOURCEFULNESS
SCHISTOSOMIASIS
STANDOFFISHNESS
TARSOMETATARSUS
THOUGHTLESSNESS
TRUSTWORTHINESS
UNCONSCIOUSNESS
UNRIGHTEOUSNESS
ACKNOWLEDGEMENT
AGRICULTURALIST
CONSERVATIONIST
DISILLUSIONMENT
FLIBBERTIGIBBET
INSTRUMENTALIST
INTERVENTIONIST
OPHTHALMOLOGIST
PALAEONTOLOGIST
PHYSIOTHERAPIST
PSYCHOTHERAPIST
AUTHORITATIVELY
CHRONOLOGICALLY
COMPASSIONATELY
CONFIDENTIALITY
CONSCIENTIOUSLY
CORRESPONDINGLY
CRYSTALLOGRAPHY
DISPASSIONATELY
EUPHEMISTICALLY
EXTRAORDINARILY
IMPENETRABILITY
INCOMPATIBILITY
INCONSIDERATELY
INCONSPICUOUSLY
INSTANTANEOUSLY
INTELLIGIBILITY
INTERNATIONALLY
MANOEUVRABILITY
PERPENDICULARLY
PESSIMISTICALLY
PHILOSOPHICALLY
PLENIPOTENTIARY
PROPORTIONATELY
PSYCHOLOGICALLY
SANCTIMONIOUSLY
SELFEXPLANATORY
SELFSUFFICIENCY
SURREPTITIOUSLY
SYMPATHETICALLY
TECHNOLOGICALLY
TEMPERAMENTALLY
THERAPEUTICALLY
UNCEREMONIOUSLY
UNCOMPLIMENTARY
UNCONDITIONALLY
UNPARLIAMENTARY